VARIETY MOVIE GUIDE

Variety Staff Writers
with consulting editor
DEREK ELLEY

Foreword by
Sir Richard Attenborough

PRENTICE HALL GENERAL REFERENCE

New York London Toronto Sydney Tokyo Singapore

ACKNOWLEDGMENTS

This guide has been the work of many hands, often labouring well
beyond the call of duty. For their help with editing the enormous
manuscript and compiling credits, I would like to thank (in order of
workload) Alan Stanbrook, Miles Smith-Morris, Allen Eyles, Sally
Hibbin, Ingrid Aaroe, David Pilling, and David McGillivray. Graham
Berry provided valuable help at a late stage with extra credits, and Jack
Pitman of *Variety's* London bureau kindly cast a veteran's eye over the
Glossary. Last but not least, I would like to thank Peter Cowie,
European Publishing Director of *Variety*, for his overall support, and
Julian Brown, Managing Editor at Octopus, for all his understanding
and calmness under fire.

PRENTICE HALL GENERAL REFERENCE
15 Columbus Circle
New York, New York, 10023

Copyright © 1992 Variety Inc.

Library of Congress Cataloging-in-Publication Data

Variety movie guide
                p. cm.
    Includes indexes
    ISBN 0-13-928359-5
    1. Motion pictures — Reviews. I. Variety (New York, N.Y.)
PN1995.V345 1991
791.43'75—dc20   91-2164
                            CIP

Designed by The Image

Manufactured in the United States

10 9 8 7 6 5 4 3 2 1

First Prentice Hall Edition

CONTENTS

VII   Foreword
by Richard Attenborough

IX   Introduction

XI   Glossary

XIII   **THE MOVIE GUIDE A-Z**

Index to Directors and their Movies
page 693

FOREWORD

As any moviemaker like myself knows, critical fashions wax and wane but *Variety* never changes – hard-nosed, dedicated to the business (as well as the art) of cinema and unsparing in both its brickbats and bouquets. That is why we treasure it, even though – when directed at our own performances or productions – its wrath may distress us profoundly.

As the world's longest-running newspaper dedicated to the entertainment industry, *Variety* is itself a crucial part of the history it has charted. The 5000 plus reviews extracted here from the past 80 years do not reflect the opinions of critics looking back from the present but, far more revealing, reflect the views of reporters who were there at the time. Some of them may surprise now; but they never fail to give a valuable insight into how these movies were regarded during their age.

And one of the great pleasures of reading *Variety* is, of course, its language. Trade paper it may be, but dry it never is. Colourful jargon like 'oater', 'helmer', 'lensing', 'pic' and 'thesping' makes its prose leap off the page with an immediacy that remains unequalled by any other movie publication. Indeed, many of these expressions have passed into the language without people being aware of their origin.

Reading this new guide, I am reminded of my own first notice in *Variety* which appeared in 1947. The film, adapted from a Graham Greene novel and my seventh as a screen actor, was called *The Man Within*. It was the first Technicolor movie to be made at Shepherd's Bush studios and I, still a rookie in my mid-20s, was fourth-billed. I opened the paper and there, way down in the fifth paragraph of the review, were the words: 'Attenborough, as the coward who finds courage, has his moments'. Rightly or wrongly, I felt that Hollywood must surely be just around the corner!

Richard Attenborough

INTRODUCTION

So what's so different about *this* movie guide from the heap of others?

Three things, mainly. For a start, it includes fuller reviews and credits than any other publication of its kind, making it an unrivalled reference work within a single volume. Two, it's a concise crib for those who can't afford $3,000 for the 21-volume *Variety Film Reviews (1907–90)*. And three, it's the only movie guide to escape that bane of film writing, received opinion. All the reviews here are by critics who actually saw the movies at the time and, thanks to *Variety's* trade orientation, with a critically clear eye.

This book contains more than 5,000 reviews selected from the 50,000 or so published over the past 84 years, between 1907 and 1991. The earliest review included is of D.W. Griffith's *Judith of Bethulia* (1914); the most recent, the Kevin Costner version of Robin Hood. Although *Variety* stopped publishing film reviews for a short spell (between March 1911 and January 1913), the paper is the longest unbroken source of film criticism still in existence. It's thus an invaluable guide to how movies were perceived on first release, as well as a mine of trade information.

Because of space, the selection has been limited to movies made in the English language. In editing the reviews down (often from many times their original length) much detail has unavoidably been lost. But we have tried to preserve the useful basics – a snappy intro, plot essentials, assessments of the main performances and technical merits, and any interesting background.

Reviewers' box-office predictions ('Fort Knox, move over' – *A Star Is Born*) have been cut out, as well as plot revelations. Minor changes have been made so that the reviews 'read' from a modern viewpoint, and any now-meaningless contemporary references and prejudices (especially during the two world wars and the McCarthy period) have been toned down or deleted.

Any rewriting has been kept to the absolute minimum to preserve the flavour and opinions of the originals, although until the mid-1930s, when *Variety* reviews began to take on their current shape, editing has had to be considerably heavier. (Early reviews were more like scattergun essays; 'film criticism' as we now know it did not arrive until the 1930s.)

American spellings and *Variety* 'slanguage' have been retained (see Glossary); any annotations to the reviews have been put in square brackets. Although *Variety* recently began to include accents on foreign names, this book adheres to tradition by omitting them.

Assembling credits for each film has often involved extra research, and this in turn has been limited by the usual constraints of time and money. *Variety* only started regularly to publish cast lists and limited technical credits in the mid-1920s; fuller credits began from the late 1930s. Mistakes and misprints have been corrected where possible; real names put in square brackets after pseudonyms; and the latest version of people's names used throughout for consistency in the present format. The following are the main criteria used:

■ **Film title.** The original title in country of origin (or 'majority' country, in the case of co-productions). The form of the title is that used on the print itself, not that on secondary material like posters or press handouts. Subsidiary titles (a growing trend since the 1980s) are put on a separate line. Films are listed in strict A–Z order; those starting with numerals are positioned as if the figures were spelt out. All films included have received a theatrical showing at some time in their life.

■ **Year.** The year of first public release in its country of origin (or, with co-productions, 'majority' country). Sneaks, out-of-town tryouts and festival screenings don't count; end-of-year Oscar-qualifying runs do. Establishing some films' opening dates is still problematical.

■ **Running time.** The hardest nut to crack. Except when it's obvious the reviewer has been shown a rough-cut, *Variety's* original running times are used. For silent films a *very* approximate conversion has been made, based on the number of reels or on information contained in the review. Films tend to get shorter over the years as they're trimmed, cut for TV and generally mangled; more recently there has been a trend towards issuing longer versions for TV or video. No running time should be taken as gospel.

■ **Country of origin.** The second hardest nut. The rule here has been where the money actually came from, rather than where a film was shot, what passport the director had, or what language the cast spoke in. With co-productions, the first country listed is the 'majority' one (which decides its official title – see above). In the case of many British and American movies, especially since the 1950s, deciding whether some are UK/US, US/UK, or even UK or US is virtually impossible.

■ **Colour.** All films in colour, partly in colour, or tinted carry the symbol ◇. Some in the last two categories are now only shown in black-and-white (e.g. *Spellbound*, *Portrait of Jennie*) but still carry the colour symbol as this denotes their original form.

■ **Silent.** Films originally shown without a synchronised soundtrack are indicated with the symbol ⊗.

■ **Video.** A nightmare. Films which have been released on video (at one time or another) carry the following symbols:
ⓥ = available in both the US and UK;
ⓥ = available in the US only; and
ⓥ = available in the UK only.
But given the difference from country to country, and the rapid pace of deletions, don't necessarily expect to find a copy in your local store. Catalogue numbers are of little practical use, so have not been included.

■ **Director.** The film's officially credited director or co-directors. Some productions are in fact the work of several hands (especially during Hollywood's studio era); only well-known uncredited contributions are noted in square brackets. Second unit or dance-number directors are occasionally included if their contribution merits it.

■ **Producer.** This includes co-producers but not associate, executive or line producers.

■ **Script.** The official scriptwriters or dialogue writers; not adaptors, story writers or authors of the original novel, play or musical (their names generally appear in the review, or have been added in square brackets). Because of changes in terminology over the years, deciding the scriptwriter credit for films up to the early 1930s is especially difficult; when in doubt, a name has been included.

■ **Photography.** The director of photography, also known as 'lighting cameraman'. Generally includes those credited with 'additional photography'

but not camera operators or (apart from rare instances) second-unit directors of photography.

■ **Editor.** Includes supervising editor, if there is one, but not assistants.

■ **Music.** A thorny problem. The general rule has been to include composers who actually contributed a dramatic score to the movie. With musicals/song movies, the musical director/arranger/adapter is listed rather than those who wrote the original musical or songs (their names generally appear in the review, or have been added in square brackets). Dates against names of musicals in the text are those of their first production.

■ **Art director.** When a film carries a production designer as well as an art director credit, the former is chosen. Does not include set decorators, costume designers or any other artistic types. *Variety* only began regularly to credit art directors from the late 1960s; prior to that they were sometimes mentioned in the reviews themselves, if notable.

■ **Cast lists.** For space reasons, these have been limited to a maximum of six, not necessarily in their original order of billing. Early appearances by later stars are often included for interest's sake, even though they may only be bit-parts. For consistency, actors who later changed names are listed by their latest moniker.

■ **Production company.** More and more difficult thanks to the growing complexity of production credits. The general rule, as in deciding the country of origin, has been to list those companies which actually stumped up the cash, but that too is often difficult to decipher. For space reasons, the shortest forms possible are used. Companies that simply distributed the finished product are not included; nor are those credited as 'in association with'.

■ **Academy awards/nominations.** The date is that of the Oscar award not of the ceremony (generally held the following spring).

Any corrections from readers will be more than welcome for future editions. Next time, we'll be back even bigger and better.

DEREK ELLEY London, 1991

GLOSSARY

The following is a guide to 80 years of *Variety* 'slanguage' as occurs in the reviews selected; it is not exhaustive and is intended especially for non-American and more general readers.

Variety's snazzy coinages are a goulash of publishing and showbiz/movie jargon, foreign words, Yiddish, street slang, contractions and acronyms that since the mid-1930s (when the reviews took on a recognisable style) have since acquired a reputation and life of their own.

Many of the words have long vanished from use in the paper (along with the slang that inspired them); new ones are still being invented by writers. The only rule is that they sound 'right' and carry on the tradition of sharp, tabloid, flavourful prose. As a further aid for general readers we have also included some words that are simple movie jargon or archaic slang rather than pure *Variety* slanguage.

a.k.	ass-kisser
a.k.a.	also known as
alky	alcoholic
ankle	leave, quit
anent	regarding
avoirdupois	weight
back-to-back	(two or more films shot) at the same time or without a break between
b.b.	big business
beer stube	bar
belter	boxer
b.f.	boyfriend
Big Apple	New York
burley	burlesque, music hall
bow	debut; praise
b.r.	bankroll; sum of money
cannon	gun
carny	carnival
Chi	Chicago
chick	girl
chili	Mexican
chirp(er)	sing(er)
chopsocky	martial arts (film)
chore	job; routine assignment
chump	crazy (in love)
cleff(er)	compose(r)
click	hit; success
coin	money; finance
contempo	contemporary
d.a.	district attorney
dick	detective
doughboy	infantry soldier
dualer	double-billed feature film
femme	female; woman
flap	flapper
flivver	car
G	$1,000
gat	gun
g.f.	girlfriend
gob	sailor
Gotham	New York
gyp	swindler; cheat
habiliments	clothing
helm(er)	direct(or)
histrionics	performance(s)
histrionically	performance-wise
hoke	hokum
hoke up	over-act
hoofology	dancing
hotcha	excellent
hoyden(ish)	tomboy(ish)
indie	independent (production or company), i.e. not by an established major studio
ink	sign
i.r.	inquiring reporter; investigative reporter
jitterbug	(1940s) jazz dance(r); nervous person
kayo	knockout
legit(imate)	theatrical, theatre, stage
legiter	stage play
legituner	stage musical
lense(r)	photograph(er)
limn	portray
lingo	dialogue
longhair	intellectual; highbrow
lower case	minor (quality)
LST	landing ship tank (a WWII landing craft)
manse	mansion
medico	doctor
meg(aphoner)	direct(or)
megger	director
meller	melodrama(tic)
milquetoast	meek man
moppet	child
nabes	suburbs
negative cost	production cost
nitery	nightclub
oater	Western
ofay	white man
oke	okay
one-shot	one-off
o.o.	once-over
opp	opposite
org	organization
ozoner	drive-in theatre
p.a.	press agent
pactee	contract player
Par	Paramount
pen	penitentiary; prison
Pennsy	Pennsylvania
photog	photographer

pic	picture; movie	slugfest	fight	topline(r)	star
plat	platinum blonde	smokeater	fireman	trick work	special effects
p.m.	professional model	sock(eroo)	excellent; powerful	troubadour	singer
p.o.v.	point of view	solon	lawmaker	trouping	acting
p.r.	public relations (company)	speak	speakeasy	tube	TV
prexy	president	spec	spectacle	20th	20th Century-Fox
profesh	profession	stepping	dancing		
programmer	B-movie fodder	stew	drinking bout	U	Universal
pug	boxer	stock	repertory	unreel	play
		sudser	soap opera	unspool	play
quondam	one time	super	super-production	upper case	major (quality)
		switcheroo	(plot) twist		
ridic	ridiculous			vaude	vaudeville
rod-man	gunman	tab	tabloid	vet	veteran
RR	railroad; railway	tapster	tap-dancer	vignetting	describing
		ten-twent-thirt/10-20-30	amateurish (acting)	vis-a-vis	(romantic/ sexual/billing) partner
		terp(ing)	danc(ing)		
s.a.	sex appeal	terpsichore	dancing		
sagebrush saga	Western	thesp(ing)	actor, act(ing)		
sauce	alcohol	thespically	performance-wise	warbling	singing
schtick	comic routine(s)			WB	Warner Bros.
		thespics	acting	w.k.	well-known
scripter	scriptwriter	tint(ed)	colour(ed)		
sec	secretary	tintuner	showbiz musical	yahoo	redneck
sheet	screen; newspaper			yak	joke
		topkick	boss	yclept	played by
shutterbug	photographer	topper	boss	yock	joke

THE MOVIE GUIDE A-Z

ABBA – THE MOVIE

1977, 94 MINS, SWEDEN/AUSTRALIA ◇ ▽
Dir Lasse Hallstrom   *Prod* Stig Andersson, Reg
Grundy   *Scr* Lasse Hallstrom, Bob Caswell   *Ph* Jack
Churchill   *Ed* Lasse Hallstrom, Malou Hallstrom, Ulf
Neidemar   *Mus* Benny Andersson, Bjorn Ulvaeus, Stig
Andersson
● Anni-Frid Lyngstad, Agneta Faltskog, Benny
Andersson, Bjorn Ulvaeus, Bruce Barry, Robert Hughes
(Polar/Grundy)

ABBA – The Movie is a handsomely-produced,
smooth, fast and wittily-edited musical entertainment that, in Lasse Hallstrom's script
and direction, is both a bit of a documentary
of Swedish group ABBA's Australian tour
and of its four personable performers' background and work methods. There's also a
slight but funny story about an Aussie disk-
jockey's chasing of the group and being most
of the way thwarted in his attempts to do a
taped in-depth interview with the Swedes.

The Australian actors perform with
obvious gusto. So does ABBA as a group
whereas they have not wished to attempt any
acting.

Apart from glimpses of them receiving
adoring crowds of fans, they are seen mostly
doing their stage work.

ABDICATION, THE

1974, 103 MINS, UK ◇
Dir Anthony Harvey   *Prod* Robert Fryer, James
Cresson   *Scr* Ruth Wolff   *Ph* Geoffrey Unsworth
Ed John Bloom   *Mus* Nino Rota   *Art Dir* Alan Tomkins
● Liv Ullmann, Peter Finch, Cyril Cusack, Graham
Crowden, Michael Dunn (Warner)

The Abdication is a period film in more ways
than one. The Ruth Wolff script from her
play, based on the 17th-century abdication of
Queen Christina of Sweden, has been
directed by Anthony Harvey, like a trite
1930s sob-sister meller, with dainty
debauchery and titillating tease straight
from 1920s women's pulp magazines.

Peter Finch plays a Vatican-based Cardinal assigned to investigate the background
and the motivations of Liv Ullmann, who has
quit her throne after converting to Roman
Catholicism late in 1655.

Ullmann's early life was a mess: her kindly
father (Edward Underdown) died when she
was six: her mother (Kathleen Byron) was a
horror; she was reared as a boy; and
chancellor Cyril Cusack keeps chiding her
on her queenly duties.

Michael Dunn, engaged as queen
Ullmann's dwarf companion, died
during Pinewood Studios shooting, and the
covering substitute is too different to
escape casual notice.

ABIE'S IRISH ROSE

1946, 96 MINS, US
Dir A. Edward Sutherland   *Prod* Bing Crosby
Scr Anne Nichols   *Ph* William Mellor   *Mus* John Scott
Trotter   *Art Dir* William Flannery
● Joanne Dru, Richard Norris, Michael Chekhov, J.M.
Kerrigan (United Artists/Crosby)

The essence of film fare is obviously to entertain. This one doesn't. It can't, when the fundamentals are as meretricious as unwind in
these hokey 96 minutes.

Fundamentally the story is a topical misfit.

It opens with ultra-modern young Abie Levy
meeting USO-Camp Shows entertainer
Rosemary Murphy in a V-E Day London
mixup, resulting in their marriage by an
army chaplain (incidentally Protestant, so as
to get in all the three faiths, which didn't exist
in the original play by Anne Nichols). Papa
Levy is patently a prosperous Bronx department store owner; his place of business, his
household and his friends bespeak prosperity.
But thereafter this premise falls apart for he
has the prejudices of a pushcart peddler, and
barrister Isaac Cohen (George E. Stone) and
Mrs Levy (Vera Gordon who, somehow,
manages a slightly more restrained characterization) are depicted as narrowminded
nitwits.

ABOMINABLE DOCTOR PHIBES, THE

1971, 94 MINS, UK ◇ ▽
Dir Robert Fuest   *Prod* Louis M. Heyward, Ronald S.
Dunas   *Scr* James Whiton, William Goldstein
Ph Norman Warwick   *Ed* Tristam Cones   *Mus* Basil
Kirchen, Jack Nathan   *Art Dir* Brian Eatwell
● Vincent Price, Joseph Cotten, Virginia North,
Terry-Thomas, Hugh Griffith, Peter Jeffrey
(American International)

The Abominable Doctor Phibes stars Vincent
Price as a living corpse, out for revenge on the
nine medics in attendance when his wife died
in surgery. Anachronistic period horror musical camp fantasy is a fair description, loaded
with comedic gore of the type that packs
theatres and drives child psychologists up the
walls. Joseph Cotten also stars as an intended
victim who foils the plot.

James Whiton and William Goldstein
wrote a well-structured screenplay which
starts in motion a series of inventive murders,
and later drops the requisite expository clues.
Price, presumed dead until Cotten and gumshoe Peter Jeffrey discover his and the wife's
coffins bare, concocts revenge on nine doctors
according to the pattern of 10 curses upon the
Pharaoh, from the Old Testament.

Terry-Thomas is one of the victims, all of
whom die from some bizarre use of rats, bees,
bats, boils, etc. Assisting Price is the silent
Virginia North. Price's makeup, by Trevor
Crole-Rees, is outstanding in depicting
without revulsion the look of a living corpse
covered with scars.

'ABOUT LAST NIGHT . . .'

1986, 113 MINS, US ◇ ▽
Dir Edward Zwick   *Prod* Jason Brett, Stuart Oken
Scr Tim Kazurinsky, Denise DeClue   *Ph* Andrew
Dintenfass   *Ed* Harry Keramidas   *Mus* Miles
Goodman   *Art Dir* Ida Random
● Rob Lowe, Demi Moore, Jim Belushi, Elizabeth
Perkins (TriStar-Delphi IV & V)

'About Last Night . . .' has little to do with perversity, let alone *Sexual Perversity in Chicago*,
the David Mamet play on which it ostensibly
is based. Film lacks much of Mamet's gritti-
ness, but is likable in its own right.

Film presents a look at the mating habits of
young Americans, the ones who frequent
singles bars and regard commitment as a lifelong disease.

Focus of the story is on Danny (Rob Lowe)
and Debbie (Demi Moore) who meet, move
in together, separate and get back together
with an ease and casualness that makes it
both appealing and disturbing. Ups and
downs of the relationship are delivered in a
series of montages that look like soft-drink
commercials for the now generation.

As the sour note, Jim Belushi is probably
the high point of the film. Performance borrows much from his late brother (John) in its
outrageousness and unpredictability.

ABOVE SUSPICION

1943, 90 MINS, US
Dir Richard Thorpe   *Prod* Victor Saville   *Scr* Keith
Winter, Melville Baker, Patricia Coleman   *Ph* Robert
Planck   *Ed* George Hively   *Mus* Bronislau Kaper
● Joan Crawford, Fred MacMurray, Conrad Veidt,
Basil Rathbone, Reginald Owen (M-G-M)

After establishing Fred MacMurray and
Joan Crawford as newlywed Americans in
England, planning honeymoon in south of
Germany just prior to outbreak of the war,
yarn has British secret service drafting them
for mission to secure vital confidential plans
for the secret weapon – a magnetic mine. Pair
pick up the trail in Paris and then hop to
Salzburg, where it becomes a mysterious
chase with various and sundry characters
peering out of shadows and suddenly turning
up in the most approved spy fashion.

Picture is filled with various incidents that
crop up and then vanish, with no reason for
their inclusion except to confuse the audience
and by-pass straight-line exposition of the
tale.

Both MacMurray and Crawford competently handle their roles, despite drawbacks
of script material. Conrad Veidt clicks solidly
in major supporting spot, along with brief
appearances of Basil Rathbone as a Gestapo
leader.

ABSENCE OF MALICE

1981, 116 MINS, US ◇
Dir Sydney Pollack   *Prod* Sydney Pollack   *Scr* Kurt
Luedtke   *Ph* Owen Roizman   *Ed* Sheldon Kahn
Mus Dave Grusin   *Art Dir* Terence Marsh
● Paul Newman, Sally Field, Bob Balaban, Melinda
Dillon, Luther Adler (Columbia)

Absence of Malice is the flipside of *All The President's Men*, a splendidly disturbing look at the
power of sloppy reporting to inflict harm on
the innocent.

Tackling a long-standing public issue that
has no resolution, producer-director Sydney
Pollack neatly keeps all the points in focus
while sustaining traditional entertainment
values. This is, quite simply, a whale of a
good story with something important to say.
For that, much of the credit undoubtedly
should go to writer Kurt Luedtke, a veteran
newsman himself.

More typical of her trade than a Woodward
or Bernstein, Sally Field is a workaday reporter on a Miami paper, trying to stay on
top of a breaking story about the mysterious
disappearance of a local longshore labor
leader.

Paul Newman is the son of a mobster whose
late father kept him straight and out of the
rackets, running a legitimate business. But he
still has unsavory family ties, particularly
uncle Luther Adler, and Bob Balaban the
head of a federal task force investigating the
case, believes a little pressure on Newman
might force his help in solving the
disappearance.

Though Newman has no connection with a
crime, Balaban suckers Field into printing a
story identifying him – with editor Josef Sommer's zealous encouragement – as a prime
suspect.

Not surprisingly, the story produces tragedy, finally shaking Field's faith in her calling. It also outrages Newman and his
grievous, angry confrontation with Field may
be the best single scene the actor has ever
performed.

ABSENT MINDED PROFESSOR, THE

1961, 90 MINS, US
Dir Robert Stevenson   *Prod* Walt Disney   *Scr* Bill
Walsh   *Ph* Edward Colman   *Ed* Cotton Warburton
Mus George Bruns   *Art Dir* Carroll Clark

● Fred MacMurray, Nancy Olson, Keenan Wynn, Tommy Kirk, Leon Ames, Ed Wynn (Walt Disney)

On the surface, Walt Disney's *The Absent Minded Professor* is a a comedy-fantasy of infectious absurdity, a natural follow-up to the studio's *Shaggy Dog*. But deeply rooted within the screenplay is a subtle protest against the detached, impersonal machinery of modern progress.

The Professor (Fred MacMurray) is an easygoing, likeable smalltown practical chemist who comes up with a practical discovery – a gooey substance endowed with the elusive quality of anti-gravity. He dubs it 'flubber' (flying rubber) and proceeds to put it to use in incongruous ways.

In the film's most hilarious passage, he applies it at half time to the gym shoes of a basketball team hopelessly outclassed by its opponents' height, whereupon the beaten boys promptly stage a bouncy aerial second half ballet.

MacMurray is ideally cast as the car-hopping prof, and plays the role with warmth and gusto. Nancy Olson attractively supplies romantic interest. Keenan Wynn is a delight in a delicious satirical role – that of a moneyman loan tycoon who would sell his own alma mater for a buck.

■ ABSOLUTE BEGINNERS

1986, 107 MINS, UK ◇ Ⓥ
Dir Julien Temple   *Prod* Stephen Woolley, Chris Brown   *Scr* Richard Burridge, Christopher Wicking, Don MacPherson   *Ph* Oliver Stapleton   *Ed* Michael Bradsell, Gerry Hambling, Richard Bedford, Russell Lloyd   *Mus* Gil Evans (arr.)   *Art Dir* John Beard
● Eddie O'Connell, Patsy Kensit, David Bowie, James Fox, Ray Davies, Steven Berkoff (Virgin/Goldcrest/Palace)

Absolute Beginners is a terrifically inventive original musical for the screen. Daring attempt to portray the birth of teenagedom in London, 1958, almost exclusively through song is based upon Colin MacInnes' cult novel about teen life and pop fashion in the percolating moments just before the youth cultural explosion in the early 1960s.

Tenuous storyline is a typical one of teen love achieved, lost and regained, and is used as a mere string to which a constant parade of musical numbers and flights of fancy are attached.

Aspiring photographer Colin (Eddie O'Connell) and tyro fashon designer Suzette (Patsy Kensit) seem a perfect match, but when the latter begins getting ahead and becomes engaged to a snooty couturier played by James Fox, Colin decides to sell out and make the most of his connections in a lastditch effort to win back his lady love.

In creating a stylized view of 1950s culture, director Julien Temple and lenser Oliver Stapleton have made great use of fabulous sets fashioned by production designer John Beard. An astonishing moving camera take throughout the Soho set in the early going represents a fully worthy homage to the opening shot of Orson Welles' *Touch of Evil*.

■ ABSOLUTION

1981, 95 MINS, UK ◇
Dir Anthony Page   *Prod* Elliott Kastner, Danny O'Donovan   *Scr* Anthony Shaffer   *Ph* John Coquillon   *Ed* John Victor Smith   *Mus* Stanley Myers   *Art Dir* Natasha Kroll
● Richard Burton, Dominic Guard, Billy Connolly, Dai Bradley, Andrew Keir (Kastner-O'Donovan)

Absolution is a dull, gloomy, nasty, contrived marketplace misfit, apparently designed to ride on Richard Burton's shirttails.

Or in this case his cassock since the actor portrays a stern, super devout priest-teacher in a Catholic boarding school for boys. Gist of Anthony Shaffer's melodramatic plot has to do with a catch-22 test of Burton's faith as two embittered students, taking advantage of the secrecy of the confessional box, conspire to drive him round the bend and to an unwitting killing.

It's heavy, artless going, with an abrupt, embarrassing (for Burton) conclusion. Anthony Page's direction is routine, perhaps unavoidably.

■ ABYSS, THE

1989, 140 MINS, US ◇ Ⓥ
Dir James Cameron   *Prod* Gale Anne Hord
Scr James Cameron   *Ph* Mikael Salomon   *Ed* Joel Goodman   *Mus* Alan Silvestri   *Art Dir* Leslie Dilley
● Ed Harris, Mary Elizabeth Mastrantonio, Michael Biehn, Leo Burmester, Todd Graff, Kimberley Scott (20th Century-Fox)

A firstrate underwater suspenser with an otherworldly twist, *The Abyss* suffers from a payoff unworthy of its buildup. Same sensibilities that enable writer-director James Cameron to deliver riveting, supercharged action segments get soggy when the 'aliens' turn out to be friendly.

Action is launched when a navy nuclear sub suffers a mysterious power failure and crashes into a rock wall. Bud Brigman (Ed Harris) and his gamy crew of undersea oil-rig workers are hired to dive for survivors.

At the last minute Brigman's flinty estranged wife, Lindsey (Mary Elizabeth Mastrantonio), who designed their submersible oil rig, insists on coming aboard to lend an uninvited hand.

Crew finds nothing but a lot of corpses floating eerily in the water-filled sub, but meanwhile, Lindsey has a close encounter with a kind of swift-moving neon-lit jellyfish she's convinced is a friendly alien.

When turbulence from a hurricane rocking the surface cuts off the crew's ties to their command ship, their underwater stay is perilously extended.

The Abyss has plenty of elements in its favor, not least the performances by Harris as the compassionate crewleader and Mastrantonio as his steel-willed counterpart. Not even the $50 million-plus pic's elaborate technical achievements can overshadow these two.

■ ACCIDENT

1967, 105 MINS, UK ◇ Ⓥ
Dir Joseph Losey   *Prod* Joseph Losey, Norman Priggen   *Scr* Harold Pinter   *Ph* Gerry Fisher
Ed Reginald Beck   *Mus* John Dankworth   *Art Dir* Carmen Dillon
● Dirk Bogarde, Stanley Baker, Jacqueline Sassard, Michael York, Vivien Merchant, Harold Pinter (London)

The team that turned *The Servant* into a success took another novel as their plot material – Nicholas Mosley's *Accident* – and jacked it into a haunting study in relationships, with Harold Pinter's flair for spare, suggestive dialog getting full scope in an adaptation which stays remarkably faithful to the book.

It starts with a car crash splitting that night air of the quiet countryside outside Oxford. A male student has been killed, and his female companion, a campus gal, is taken into the neighboring mansion, occupied by the university teacher (Dirk Bogarde) who has been instructing them both in philosophy.

The accident sparks the prolonged flashback that explores the tight-knit relationship of this enclosed community.

A firstrate cast is headed by Bogarde, who wins sympathy for his superficially cold character, and his contained way with emotion is superbly right. But the main acting surprise is contributed by Stanley Baker, unusually bespectacled as the amorous Charlie, and wittily suggesting the man's self-esteem and his lonely search for horizontal satisfaction.

■ ACCIDENTAL TOURIST, THE

1988, 121 MINS, US ◇ Ⓥ
Dir Lawrence Kasdan   *Prod* Lawrence Kasdan, Charles Okun, Michael Grillo   *Scr* Frank Galati, Lawrence Kasdan   *Ph* John Bailey   *Ed* Carol Littleton
Mus John Williams   *Art Dir* Bo Welch
● William Hurt, Kathleen Turner, Geena Davis, Amy Wright, Bill Pullman, Ed Begley Jr (Warner)

The Accidental Tourist is a slow, sonorous and largely satisfying adaptation of Anne Tyler's bestseller of one man's intensely self-contained passage from a state of grief to one of newfound love.

William Hurt is an uptight, travel book writer from the slightly eccentric, financially comfortable Leary family of unmarried middle-aged siblings in this essentially simple narrative story awash in warmth and wisdom about the emotional human animal.

Weighty tone is set from the opening scene where Kathleen Turner, having just made tea for Hurt upon his return from a travel-writing excursion, calmly informs she's moving out.

Then, in a series of strange, unpredictable and out-of-character encounters with his unruly dog's trainer (Geena Davis), Hurt finds himself in another, vastly different, relationship.

Davis is unabashedly forward, poor, openly vulnerable, a flamboyant dresser and most importantly, has a sickly son (Robert Gorman) who fills the parental void in Hurt's life.

That Hurt remains expressionless and speaks in a monotone, except at the very end, puts a damper on the hopefulness of his changing situation. Davis is the constant, upbeat force in the proceedings. Turner is equally compelling and sympathetic throughout.
□ 1988: Best Picture (Nomination)

■ ACCUSED, THE

1988, 110 MINS, US ◇ Ⓥ
Dir Jonathan Kaplan   *Prod* Stanley R. Jaffe, Sherry Lansing   *Scr* Tom Topor   *Ph* Ralf Bode   *Ed* Jerry Greenberg, O. Nicholas Brown   *Mus* Brad Fiedel
Art Dir Richard Kent Wilcox
● Kelly McGillis, Jodie Foster, Bernie Coulson, Leo Rossi, Ann Hearn (Paramount)

The Accused is a dry case study of a rape incident whose only impact comes from the sobering crime itself, not the dramatic treatment.

Inspired by, but not based upon the 1983 barroom pooltable gang rape in New Bedford, Mass, screenplay is designed to pose questions about the thin line between sexual provocation and assault, seduction and force, and observation of and participation in a crime.

Pic begins with a bloodied, dishevelled Jodie Foster stumbling out of a roadhouse. A young patron calls the police to report an incident, and in short order three men plead guilty to the reduced charge of 'reckless endangerment' (the film's original title) rather than rape.

All this takes place without the participation of the victim, who becomes furious with her lawyer (Kelly McGillis) when she learns via television of the legal deal. McGillis abruptly decides to pursue the matter much further by prosecuting some of the onlookers in the bar for criminal solicitation.

Foster is edgy and spunky but McGillis' role, as conceived, is a joke, since she exists only as a stick figure with no psychology or background offered up over the course of nearly two hours.

With British Columbia standing in for Washington State, pic looks only okay.

. . . .

■ ACE IN THE HOLE

1951, 111 MINS, US ▽
Dir Billy Wilder *Prod* Billy Wilder *Scr* Billy Wilder, Lesser Samuels, Walter Newman *Ph* Charles B. Lang *Ed* Arthur Schmidt *Mus* Hugo Friedhofer *Art Dir* Hal Pereira, Earl Hedrick
● Kirk Douglas, Jan Sterling, Bob Arthur, Porter Hall, Frank Cady, Richard Benedict (Paramount)

The grim story of an unscrupulous reporter who wins brief fame at the expense of a cave-in victim is rather graphically unfolded in *Ace in the Hole*.

Kirk Douglas is the reportorial opportunist. He has been exiled to a small New Mexico daily after being kicked off top eastern sheets for dishonesty, drinking and a variety of insubordination. One day he accidentally stumbles on a story that he believes can get him back in the big leagues, if he plays the yarn long enough and can keep it to himself.

A dealer in Indian curios has become trapped by a cave-in in an ancient cliff dwelling. Douglas is the first to reach the victim (Richard Benedict), sees the story possibilities and makes a deal with a crooked sheriff and a contractor to delay the rescue as long as possible while he arranges exclusive coverage.

The performances are fine. Douglas enacts the heel reporter ably, giving it color to balance its unsympathetic character. Jan Sterling also is good in a role that has no softening touches, and Benedict's victim portrayal is first-rate. Billy Wilder's direction captures the feel of morbid expectancy that always comes out in the curious that flock to scenes of tragedy.

. . . .

■ ACES HIGH

1976, 114 MINS, UK/FRANCE ◇ ▽
Dir Jack Gold *Prod* S. Benjamin Fisz *Scr* Howard Barker *Ph* Gerry Fisher *Ed* Anne V. Coates *Mus* Richard Hartley *Art Dir* Syd Cain
● Malcolm McDowell, Christopher Plummer, Simon Ward, Peter Firth, John Gielgud, Trevor Howard (EMI/Fisz)

Pic is based on R. C. Sheriff's 1929 London and Broadway stageplay, *Journey's End*, a classic on the theme of the futility and boredom of trench warfare in which some men cracked up while others found ways – like the bottle – of averting crackup. *Aces High* packs little of the involving emotional credibility and impact of the play.

Characterization in the film is without sufficient ambiguity and dimension. Thus, the young British airmen of 76 Squadron are either bushy-tailed rookies (Peter Firth), disciplined but emotionally soft (Christopher Plummer), or scared stiff and bucking for medical discharge (Simon Ward). As their squadron leader, Malcolm McDowell is both brave and scared – and dependent on whisky to sustain him as a credible leader of machine-gun fodder.

. . . .

■ ACROSS 110TH STREET

1972, 102 MINS, US ◇ ▽
Dir Barry Shear *Prod* Ralph Serpe, Fouad Said *Scr* Luther Davis *Ph* Jack Priestley *Ed* Byron Brandt *Mus* J.J. Johnson *Art Dir* Perry Watkins
● Anthony Quinn, Yaphet Kotto, Anthony Franciosa, Paul Benjamin, Ed Bernard, Richard Ward (Film Guarantors/United Artists)

Across 110th Street is not for the squeamish. From the beginning it is a virtual bloodbath. Those portions of it which aren't bloody violent are filled in by the squalid location sites in New York's Harlem or equally unappealing ghetto areas leaving no relief from depression

and oppression. Based upon the novel *Across 110th* by Wally Ferris, it is strong and relentless in its pursuit of violence.

With the knock-over by three Harlem blacks (Paul Benjamin, Ed Bernard, Antonio Fargas) of 'the family's' $300,000 take from the streets, Anthony Franciosa, uncool son-in-law of org's head, goes out to 'teach them a lesson'.

Quinn's performance is controlled, but the character is not clearly defined.

. . . .

■ ACROSS THE BRIDGE

1957, 103 MINS, UK
Dir Ken Annakin *Prod* John Stafford *Scr* Guy Elmes, Denis Freeman *Ph* Reginald Wyer *Ed* Alfred Roome *Mus* James Bernard *Art Dir* Cedric Dawe
● Rod Steiger, David Knight, Marla Landi, Noel Willman, Bernard Lee (Rank)

Across the Bridge, based on Graham Greene's story, unfolds slowly. But this is strong on situation and acting stints and winds up with a sure-fire climax. In essence, it is a gripping character study of an arrogant man who, through his own crooked folly and greed, topples from power to degrading death as a gutter outcast.

Rod Steiger is a shady international financier who is on the lam from Scotland Yard and the FBI. On the train he meets up with a gabby Mexican stranger and, by skullduggery, assumes the stranger's identity and acquires his passport. In Mexico, he is caught between the Scotland Yard man, trying to lure him into American territory, and the Mexican police chief, who withholds Steiger's own passport in order to indulge in a spot of astute blackmail.

These complicated goings-on are background to a remarkable study of mental and physical decay by Steiger. At times it is irritatingly over-fussy and mannered, but he dominates the screen.

Aided by skillful lensing, director Ken Annakin has excellently built up the atmosphere of a sleepy, brooding Mexican bordertown. Exteriors were shot in Spain.

As the Mexican police chief, Noel Willman gives a wily, subtle performance which, because of its very restraint, contrasts admirably with the Steiger technique. The scenes between the two are filmic highlights.

. . . .

■ ACROSS THE PACIFIC

1942, 86 MINS, US
Dir John Huston *Prod* Jerry Wald, Jack Saper *Scr* Richard Macauley *Ph* Arthur Edeson *Ed* Frank Magee *Mus* Adolph Deutsch
● Humphrey Bogart, Sydney Greenstreet, Mary Astor (Warner)

Warners had a problem in transferring the Robert Carson *Sat Eve Post* serial to the screen. Original, under title of *Aloha Means Goodbye*, depicted a spy melodrama on ship that finally reached Hawaii – but after the war's start and studio purchase scripter Richard Macauley had to change things around.

Result is switch of locale from the west to east coast – and the yarn never gets into the Pacific Ocean, despite the title.

After Humphrey Bogart is court-martialed out of the army coast artillery, he shifts to Canada in attempt to enlist in the Dominion artillery. Turned down, he gets passage on a Jap freighter bound for Panama and the Orient.

Although picture does not quite hit the edge-of-seat tension engendered by *Maltese Falcon*, it's a breezy and fast-paced melodrama. Huston directs deftly from thrill-packed script by Macauley.

. . . .

■ ACROSS THE WIDE MISSOURI

1951, 78 MINS, US ◇
Dir William A. Wellman *Prod* Robert Sisk *Scr* Talbot Jennings *Ph* William C. Mellor *Ed* John Dunning *Mus* David Raksin *Art Dir* Cedric Gibbons, James Basevi
● Clark Gable, Ricardo Montalban, John Hodiak, Adolphe Menjou, Maria Elena Marques, J. Carrol Naish (M-G-M)

There's much that will seize audience attention in *Missouri*. The color lensing of the rugged outdoor locations backgrounding the story of beaver trappers and Indians in the early west brings the sites to the screen with breathtaking beauty. Critically, though, the presentation is choppy and episodic, and the device of having the Indian dialog lengthily translated, is dull and boring.

Story is narrated by an unseen voice (Howard Keel) identified as the son of Clark Gable and his Indian wife, played by Mexican film star Maria Elena Marques.

Plot finds Gable, a rough and ready trapper, taking Marques as a bride because he believes it will help him get into some untouched beaver country controlled by an Indian tribe led by the bride's grandfather (Jack Holt). Gable, the wife and other trappers make the long trek and, upon arrival, are temporarily repulsed by young Indians led by Ricardo Montalban.

Wellman's direction clicks when he has the story on the move in the battle and trekking sequences. He's not able to do much when the script requires the actors to sit down and talk out the long translations.

. . . .

■ ADAM'S RIB

1949, 103 MINS, US ▽
Dir George Cukor *Prod* Lawrence Weingarten *Scr* Ruth Gordon, Garson Kanin *Ph* George J. Folsey *Ed* George Boemler *Mus* Miklos Rozsa
● Spencer Tracy, Katharine Hepburn, Judy Holliday, Tom Ewell, David Wayne, Jean Hagen (M-G-M)

Adam's Rib is a bright comedy success, belting over a succession of sophisticated laughs. Ruth Gordon and Garson Kanin have fashioned their amusing screenplay around the age-old battle of the sexes.

Setup has Spencer Tracy as an assistant d.a., married to femme attorney Katharine Hepburn. He believes no woman has the right to take shots at another femme. Hepburn believes a woman has the same right to invole the unwritten law as a man. They do courtroom battle over their theories when Tracy is assigned to prosecute Judy Holliday.

This is the sixth Metro teaming of Tracy and Hepburn, and their approach to marital relations around their own hearth is delightfully saucy. A better realization on type than Holliday's portrayal of a dumb Brooklyn femme doesn't seem possible.

. . . .

■ ADMIRABLE CRICHTON, THE

1957, 93 MINS, UK ◇
Dir Lewis Gilbert *Prod* Ian Dalrymple *Scr* Vernon Harris, Lewis Gilbert *Ph* Wilkie Cooper *Ed* Peter Hunt *Mus* Douglas Gamley *Art Dir* William Kellro
● Kenneth More, Diane Cilento, Cecil Parker, Sally Ann Howes, Martita Hunt, Jack Watling (Modern Screen Play)

Staged many times since its original production in London in 1902, and filmed in the silent days [1919] as *Male and Female*, this story of a butler who becomes master on a desert island is a sound starrer for Kenneth More.

A peer of one of England's stately homes takes his three daughters off on a yachting cruise with a few friends and domestic staff. They are shipwrecked and marooned on an uncharted island, and dig themselves in

3

awaiting rescue. Crichton (More), the impeccable butler, is obliged to take complete control, because of the inefficiency of the other castaways. He now gives, not takes orders, and establishes himself as benevolent dictator.

Although More lacks the accepted stature of an English butler, his personality makes a more human and sympathetic figure of the servant who has a firmer sense of snob values than his master. Cecil Parker, alternately genial and pompous as the father, is perhaps more in keeping with the period.

· ·

■ ADVENTURE OF SHERLOCK HOLMES' SMARTER BROTHER, THE

1975, 91 MINS, UK ◇

Dir Gene Wilder   *Prod* Richard A. Roth   *Scr* Gene Wilder   *Ph* Gerry Fisher   *Ed* Jim Clark   *Mus* John Morris   *Art Dir* Terence Marsh
● Gene Wilder, Madeline Kahn, Marty Feldman, Dom DeLuise, Leo McKern, Roy Kinnear (20th-Century Fox)

Gene Wilder joins Mel Brooks in that elusive pantheon of madcap humor, by virtue of Wilder's script, title characterization and directorial debut, all of which are outstanding.

Wilder's script sends the famous Holmes (played by Douglas Wilmer) and Dr Watson (Thorley Walters) ostensibly out of England, in order to fool Prof Moriarty (Leo McKern). Latter has a plot going with Dom DeLuise, the most unlikely blackmailing opera freak of the season, to obtain some official state papers stolen from nobleman John Le Mesurier.

Holmes' strategy is to use his younger brother, played by Wilder, as a decoy, backstopped by Feldman, a policeman blessed with a photographic memory. Together, this fearless duo fumbles its way to ultimate success.

· ·

■ ADVENTURERS, THE

1970, 171 MINS, US ◇ ▼

Dir Lewis Gilbert   *Prod* Lewis Gilbert   *Scr* Michael Hastings, Lewis Gilbert   *Ph* Claude Renoir   *Ed* Anne Coates   *Mus* Antonio Carlos Jobim   *Art Dir* Tony Masters
● Bekim Fehmiu, Charles Aznavour, Alan Badel, Candice Bergen, Thommy Berggren, Ernest Borgnine (Paramount)

The Adventurers is a classic monument to bad taste. Film is marked by profligate and squandered production opulence; inferior, imitative and curiously old-hat direction; banal, ludicrous dialog; sub-standard, lifeless and embarrassing acting; cornball music; indulgent, gratuitous and boring violence; and luridly non-erotic sex.

Harold Robbins' guess-who novel about the jet set and South American politics was as commercial as it was trashy; film version may be fairly said to make the novel look better.

Story depicts the life of a South American playboy who, if one were to swallow the specious sociology, was a victim of childhood traumas which crystalized revolutionary violence and brutal rape.

On the romantic front there is Candice Bergen, about the only principal to salvage anything from the film, playing a fabulously wealthy girl who marries the hero, but loses their baby in a swing accident, becomes barren, and eventually turns lesbian.

· ·

■ ADVENTURES OF BARON MUNCHAUSEN, THE

1989, 125 MINS, UK/W. GERMANY ◇ ▼

Dir Terry Gilliam   *Prod* Thomas Schuhly   *Scr* Charles McKeown, Terry Gilliam   *Ph* Giuseppe Rotunno   *Ed* Peter Hollywood   *Mus* Michael Kamen   *Art Dir* Dante Ferretti

● John Neville, Eric Idle, Sarah Polley, Oliver Reed, Charles McKeown (Prominent/Laura/Allied)

A fitting final installment in Terry Gilliam's trilogy begun with *Time Bandits* and continued with *Brazil*, *The Adventures of Baron Munchausen* shares many of those films' strengths and weaknesses, but doesn't possess the visionary qualities of the latter.

The film offers a continual feast for the eyes, and not enough for the funnybone or the heart. Set in Europe in the 18th century, tale begins with a city under intense siege by the Turks. An elderly gent who purports to be the Baron begins relating the true story of how he caused his war.

With this, Gilliam takes the viewer into the exquisite palace of the sultan, whose ferocity is aroused when he loses a bet to the visiting baron (John Neville). With the help of his variously and superhumanly gifted gang of four, which consists of the fastest runner in the world, a dwarf who can exhale with hurricane force, an expert sharpshooter and an immeasurably strong black man, the Baron makes off with the sultan's entire treasure, but his city is left to suffer the consequences.

Promising to save the city from the renewed attack, the Baron escapes in a gigantic hot-air balloon fashioned out of ladies' underwear, and goes in search of his four comrades. This journey takes the unlikely pair to some unlikely places where they meet some unlikely people.

· ·

■ ADVENTURES OF BARRY MCKENZIE, THE

1972, 117 MINS, AUSTRALIA ◇

Dir Bruce Beresford   *Prod* Phillip Adams   *Scr* Bruce Beresford, Barry Humphries   *Ph* Don McAlpine   *Ed* John Scott   *Mus* Peter Best   *Art Dir* John Stoddart
● Barry Crocker, Barry Humphries, Paul Bertram, Dennis Price, Avice Landon, Peter Cook (Longford)

Satirist Barry Humphries has put his talents to a film, as coauthor and costar. The result is what one would expect if the Marx Brothers were put into an Aussie-brand *Carry On* pic. It's based on a comic strip [*The Wonderful World of Barry McKenzie*], written by Humphries, around a very Aussie character in London known as Bazza.

Barry Crocker plays title role of the gauche young Aussie visiting Britain for the first time. His turns of phrases are witty and original, often with a bawdy twinge, and although much is in the Australian vernacular (frequently invented by Humphries), few are likely to miss the drift of the remarks.

· ·

■ ADVENTURES OF BUCKAROO BANZAI, ACROSS THE 8TH DIMENSION, THE

1984, 103 MINS, US ◇

Dir W.D. Richter   *Prod* Neil Canton, W.D. Richter   *Scr* Earl MayRauch   *Ph* Fred J. Koenekamp   *Ed* Richard Marks, George Bowers   *Mus* Michael Boddicker   *Art Dir* J. Michael Riva
● Peter Weller, John Lithgow, Ellen Barkin, Jeff Goldblum, Christopher Lloyd, Rosalind Cash (Sherwood)

The Adventures of Buckaroo Banzai plays more like an experimental film than a Hollywood production aimed at a mass audience. It violates every rule of storytelling and narrative structure in creating a self-contained world of its own.

First-time director W.D. Richter and writer Earl Mac Rauch have created a comic book world chock full of references, images, pseudo scientific ideas and plain mumbo jumbo.

Buried within all this Banzai trivia is an indecipherable plot involving a modern band of Robin Hoods who go to battle with enemy aliens released accidentally from the eighth dimension as a result of Buckaroo's experiments with particle physics.

Buckaroo is a world-class neurosurgeon,

physicist, race car driver and, with his band of merry pranksters, the Hong Kong Cavaliers, a rock 'n' roll star.

As the great one (Buckaroo), Peter Weller presents a moving target that is tough to hit. Also very funny is Jeff Goldblum, coming as if from another dimension as every mother's Jewish son. Ellen Barkin does a turn as Buckaroo's mysterious girlfriend and looks great but is another emotionless character.

· ·

■ ADVENTURES OF DON JUAN

1948, 110 MINS, US ◇ ▼

Dir Vincent Sherman   *Prod* Jerry Wald   *Scr* George Oppenheimer, Harry Kurnitz   *Ph* Elwood Bredell   *Ed* Alan Crosland Jr   *Mus* Max Steiner   *Art Dir* Edward Carrere
● Errol Flynn, Viveca Lindfors, Robert Douglas, Raymond Burr (Warner)

The loves and escapades of the fabulous Don Juan are particularly adapted to the screen abilities of Errol Flynn and he gives them a flair that pays off strongly.

Plot depicts Don Juan adventuring in England. Opening has him escaping an angry husband, only to become immediately involved again with another femme. This time his wooing ruins a state-arranged wedding and he's shipped off to Spain to face his angry monarch. The queen assigns him to post of instructor in the royal fencing academy, he discovers a plot against her majesty, instigated by a conniving prime minister. Viveca Lindfors co-stars as the queen and she brings a compelling beauty to the role.

Top action is reached in the deadly duel between Flynn and Robert Douglas, the crooked prime minister, climaxing with a long leap down a huge flight of castle stairs.

· ·

■ ADVENTURES OF FORD FAIRLANE, THE

1990, 104 MINS, US ◇ ▼

Dir Renny Harlin   *Prod* Joel Silver, Steve Perry   *Scr* Daniel Waters, James Cappe, David Arnott   *Ph* Oliver Wood   *Ed* Michael Tronick   *Mus* Yello   *Art Dir* John Vallone
● Andrew Dice Clay, Wayne Newton, Priscilla Presley, Morris Day, Lauren Holly, Robert Englund (20th Century-Fox/Silver)

Surprisingly funny and expectedly rude, this first starring vehicle by vilified standup comic Andrew Dice Clay has a decidedly lowbrow humor that is a sort of modern equivalent of that of the Three Stooges.

Clay plays Ford Fairlane, a private eye specializing in cases involving rock acts (hence his overused nickname, 'the rock & roll detective'). He gets drawn into a murder mystery linked to a shock-radio deejay (Gilbert Gottfried, in a hilarious cameo), and a sleazy record executive (Wayne Newton) and his ex-wife (Priscilla Presley).

With its heavy rock bent and the direction of Renny Harlin (*Die Hard 2*), much of the film resembles a musicvideo.

Aside from his appeal to rednecks and high-school boys overly impressed by certain four-letter words, Clay's chain-smoking goombah in many ways self-parodies the macho ethic that prize rock 'n' roll, fast cars and cheap bimbos above all else.

The film's most significant find, undoubtedly, is Lauren Holly who brings a lot of flash and charisma to a difficult role as Fairlane's longing girl Friday. Also, Robert Englund (aka Freddy Krueger) plays a sadistic killer, sans makeup.

· ·

■ ADVENTURES OF HUCKLEBERRY FINN, THE

1960, 90 MINS, US ◇

Dir Michael Curtiz   *Prod* Samuel Goldwyn Jr   *Scr* James Lee   *Ph* Ted McCord   *Ed* Freeric

Steinkamp   *Mus* Jerome Moross   *Art Dir* George W. Davis, McClure Capps
● Tony Randall, Eddie Hodges, Archie Moore, Patty McCormack, Neville Brand, Mickey Shaughnessy (M-G-M)

Mark Twain's Huckleberry Finn is all boy. Eddie Hodges' Huck isn't. Therein lurks the basic reason this production of the Twain classic is not all it could, and should, be.

There is something artificial and self-conscious about young Hodges' all-important portrayal of Huck, a lack of actor-character chemistry for which he's certainly not wholly responsible. An equal share of the rap must be shouldered by director Michael Curtiz, not only for the youthful star's shortcomings in the role, but for a general slack, a disturbing shortage of vitality noticeable at several key junctures.

James Lee's screenplay simplifies Twain's episodic tale, erasing some of the more complex developments and relationships, presumably for the benefit of the young audience. Some of the more sinister, frightening aspects of the story have been forgotten.

On the brighter side of the ledger, there are some stimulating performances and the handsome physical production itself. An extremely colorful and experienced cast has been assembled. There is Tony Randall, whose work as the roguish 'King' is a delightful balance of whimsy and threat. There is Archie Moore, the light heavyweight champion of the world, who brings the story its only moments of real warmth and tenderness.

And there is the solid supporting work of Neville Brand (as Huck's father), Mickey Shaughnessy (the 'Duke'), Andy Devine (the circus owner), Buster Keaton (the lion tamer), Finlay Currie (the steamboat captain), Royal Dano (the sheriff), Sterling Holloway (the barber) and Josephine Hutchinson (the widow).

● ●

■ ADVENTURES OF MARCO POLO, THE

1938, 100 MINS, US
Dir Archie Mayo   *Prod* Samuel Goldwyn   *Scr* Robert E. Sherwood   *Ph* Rudolph Mate   *Ed* Fred Allen   *Mus* Hugo Friedhofer   *Art Dir* Richard Day
● Gary Cooper, Sigrid Gurie, Basil Rathbone, George Barbier, Binnie Barnes, Ernest Truex (Goldwyn/United Artists)

A glamorous figure in history, which places him in the 13th century as the first European to visit the Orient, Marco Polo has been portrayed in as many different guises as imagination permits; as traveler, adventurer, merchant, diplomat. He probably was all of these and a first-class liar besides. Robert E. Sherwood, who penned the screenscript [from a story by N.A. Pogson], conceives him also as an ardent lover and politician. Gary Cooper fits the character to the apex of his six feet two.

The plot is strictly meller, starting with Ahmed (Basil Rathbone) as a conniving prime minister to the Chinese ruler, Kublai Kahn (George Barbier). Schemer has his eye on the throne and a desire for the dynastic princess for his queen. Into such a vortex of beauty and villainy come Marco Polo and his business agent.

Marco Polo is admitted to the court and there glimpses the beautiful princess, who is much taken with his six feet two and easy manner of love-making behind the Chinese fountain.

It is all played on the dead level by a fine cast. Rathbone is an excellent plotter, and Sigrid Gurie, a Norwegian actress who makes her American film debut in the picture, possesses beauty of a kind to start civil war in any country.

● ●

■ ADVENTURES OF MARK TWAIN, THE

1944, 130 MINS, US
Dir Irving Rapper   *Prod* Jesse L. Lasky   *Scr* Alan LeMay, Harold M. Sherman, Harry Chandlee   *Ph* Sol Polito   *Ed* Ralph Dawson   *Mus* Max Steiner   *Art Dir* John Hughes
● Fredric March, Alexis Smith, Donald Crisp, C. Aubrey Smith, John Carradine (Warner)

So rich and full was the life of Mark Twain, born Sam Clemens, that it requires two hours-plus to tell the full tale. It is a film that has its measure of symbolism: linking the humorist's lifetime of 75 years to appearances of Halley's Comet. The astronomical display was visible when Sam Clemens was born in Hannibal, Mo, on the banks of the Mississippi, and, 75 years later, when the Chancellor of Oxford extols the great American writer, at a time when the famed university is also paying honor to Rudyard Kipling with an honorary doctorate of literature, it again makes its astral appearance.

In between Clemens has adventured as a river boatman, journeyman reporter, and western goldrusher, only to find sudden fame with his saga of the jumping frogs. Soon follow renown and fortune as Tom Sawyer, Huck Finn and the rest of his 'funny books' capture the hearts and the minds of all America, only to be dissipated in abortive attempts with an automatic printing press, extravagant publishing ventures and the like.

● ●

■ ADVENTURES OF ROBIN HOOD, THE

1938, 104 MINS, US ◇ ⓥ
Dir Michael Curtiz, William Keighley   *Scr* Norman Reilly Raine, Seton I. Miller   *Ph* Tony Gaudio, Sol Polito, W. Howard Greene   *Ed* Ralph Dawson   *Mus* Erich Wolfgang Korngold   *Art Dir* Carl Jules Weyl
● Errol Flynn, Olivia de Havilland, Basil Rathbone, Claude Rains, Patric Knowles, Eugene Pallette (Warner)

Warners revives the legend with Errol Flynn in the role in which Douglas Fairbanks Sr scored his first big success in 1922. It is cinematic pageantry at its best, a highly imaginative telling of folklore in all the hues of Technicolor.

Film is done in the grand manner of silent-day spectacles with sweep and breadth of action, swordplay and hand-to-hand battles between Norman and Saxon barons. Superlative on the production side.

Played with intensity by an excellent company of actors, an illusion of fairy-story quality is retained throughout. Michael Curtiz and William Keighley are credited as co-directors, the former having picked up the story soon after its filming started when Keighley was incapacitated by illness. There is skillful blending of their joint work.

Flynn makes the heroic Robin a somewhat less agile savior of the poor than Fairbanks portrayed him, but the Warner version emphasizes the romance. Teamed with Olivia de Havilland as Marian, Flynn is an ardent suitor and a gallant courtier. There are some convincing histrionics by Basil Rathbone, Claude Rains, Patric Knowles, Eugene Pallette, Alan Hale and Melville Cooper. Lighter moments are furnished by Una O'Connor and Herbert Mundin.
□ 1938: Best Picture (Nomination)

● ●

■ ADVENTURES OF SHERLOCK HOLMES, THE

1939, 71 MINS, US ⓥ
Dir Alfred Werker   *Prod* Gene Markey   *Scr* Edwin Blum, William Drake   *Ph* Leon Shamroy   *Ed* Robert Bischoff   *Mus* Cyril J. Mockridge (dir.)   *Art Dir* Richard Day, Hans Peters
● Basil Rathbone, Nigel Bruce, Ida Lupino, Alan Marshal, E.E. Clive (20th Century-Fox)

Choice of Basil Rathbone as Sherlock was a

wise one. Nigel Bruce as Doctor Watson is equally expert. With the two key characters thus capably handled, the film has the additional asset of being well conceived and grippingly presented.

Plenty of ingenuity is concentrated into two concurrent mysteries with the impossible clues not made too absurd or too obvious for mystery devotees. The 'elementary, my dear Watson' type of dialog is soft-pedalled for more modern phrases or understandable patter.

George Zucco offers a splendid characterization as the arch-criminal and Ida Lupino is highly competent as the sole romantic figure in the mystery fable.

● ●

■ ADVENTURES OF TOM SAWYER, THE

1938, 93 MINS, US ◇ ⓥ
Dir Norman Taurog   *Prod* David O. Selznick   *Scr* John V.A. Weaver   *Ph* James Wong Howe, Wilfrid M. Cline   *Ed* Hal C. Kern, Margaret Clancey   *Mus* Lou Forbes   *Art Dir* Lyle Wheeler, William Cameron Menzies, Casey Roberts
● Tommy Kelly, Jackie Moran, Ann Gillis, May Robson, Walter Brennan, Victor Jory (Selznick/United Artists)

Adventures of Tom Sawyer is in Technicolor and contains visual beauty and appeal in addition to a faithful and nearly literal adaptation of the Mark Twain story.

The story of the boy in an isolated Missouri community of the 1880s, who made fence-painting an enviable art, who attended his own funeral services, who was the cynosure of all eyes in the witness chair at an exciting murder trial, who teased and plagued his elders and melted in tears at the slightest kindness, is imperishable.

Casting of the picture was reported a laborious job, in the course of which hundreds of boys were tested before Tommy Kelly, from the Bronx, NY, was selected for the role of Tom. His early scenes show self-consciousness but in the final sequences when he is being pursued by Injun Joe, Kelly performs like a veteran.

Walter Brennan is a standout among the adult players. He is the village drunkard, Muff Potter, accused of the graveyard murder.

May Robson loses no opportunities as Aunt Polly, whose life by turn is celestial and hellish depending upon the vagaries of Tom's vivid imagination.

Injun Joe is played by Victor Jory with all the fiendish villainy in the part.

● ●

■ ADVISE AND CONSENT

1962, 140 MINS, US ⓥ
Dir Otto Preminger   *Prod* Otto Preminger   *Scr* Wendell Mayes   *Ph* Sam Leavitt   *Ed* Louis Loeffler   *Mus* Jerry Fielding   *Art Dir* Lyle R. Wheeler
● Henry Fonda, Charles Laughton, Don Murray, Walter Pidgeon, Gene Tierney, Peter Lawford (Columbia)

Allen Drury's big-selling novel has also served as a stage play. There are recognizable projections of character assassination, McCarthy-like demagoguery and use of the two hard-to-answer smears of this ill-natured generation: 'Are you now or were you once a homosexual and/or a communist?'

As interpreted by producer-director Otto Preminger and scripter Wendell Mayes, *Advise and Consent* is intermittently well dialogued and too talky, and, strangely, arrested in its development and illogical.

Preminger has endowed his production with wholly capable performers. Henry Fonda as the Secretary of State nominee, Charles Laughton as a Southern-smooth rebellious Solon, Don Murray as the focal point of the homo-suicidal scandal and Walter Pidgeon as a Majority leader fighting in best stentorian tradion in Fonda's behalf all register firmly. The characterizations come through with fine clarity.

Disturbing is lack of sufficiently clear motivation for the nub of the action. Why are Pidgeon and Laughton so pro and con about confirmation of the Presidential appointee? And isn't the Murray character too strong to kill himself?

The settings are powerfully like real. A Senate hearing room, the Senate itself, a party home in immediate Washington and varying apartments plus a place in DC suburbia all have the look of genuineness.

● ●

■ **AFFAIR TO REMEMBER, AN**

1957, 115 MINS, US ◇

Dir Leo McCarey   *Prod* Jerry Wald   *Scr* Delmer Daves, Leo McCarey   *Ph* Milton Krasner   *Ed* James B. Clark   *Mus* Hugo Friedhofer, Harry Warren   *Art Dir* Lyle R. Wheeler, Jack Martin Smith
● Cary Grant, Deborah Kerr, Richard Denning, Neva Patterson, Cathleen Nesbitt (20th Century-Fox)

Adding comedy lines, music, color and CinemaScope, Jerry Wald and Leo McCarey turn this remake of the 1939 *Love Affair* into a winning film that is alternately funny and tenderly sentimental. *An Affair to Remember*, using plenty of attractive settings (on and off the USS *Constitution*), is still primarily a film about two people; and since those two happen to be Cary Grant and Deborah Kerr the bitter-sweet romance sparkles and crackles with high spirits.

Story has Grant and Kerr fall in love aboard ship, though both are engaged to other people. They decide to meet in six months atop the Empire State Building. Meanwhile, Grant, a faintly notorious bachelor, is to change his life in a more useful direction. He shows up for the rendezvous, but she is struck by a car on her way to the meeting and may never walk again.

McCarey, who with Delmer Daves wrote the screenplay, has done a fine job, and has gotten the most out of his players' talents. Both are experts in restrained, sophisticated comedy. Both are able to get a laugh by waving a hand or raising an eyebrow. The Grant-Kerr romance is never maudlin, not even at the end.

● ●

■ **AFFAIRS OF SUSAN, THE**

1945, 110 MINS, US

Dir William A. Seiter   *Prod* Hal B. Wallis   *Scr* Thomas Monroe, Laszlo Gorog, Richard Flournoy   *Ph* David Abel   *Ed* Eda Warren   *Mus* Frederick Hollander   *Art Dir* Hans Dreier, Franz Bachelin
● Joan Fontaine, George Brent, Dennis O'Keefe, Don DeFore, Walter Abel (Paramount)

In this tale [from an original story by Thomas Monroe and Laszlo Gorog] about the four loves of Susan Darell (Joan Fontaine), producer Hal B. Wallis has invested the picture with considerable production values, but making the story and action the thing.

Fontaine, as Susan, legit actress just back from a USO Camp tour, accepts Walter Abel's proposal of marriage. He soon learns that there have been three men in her life previously.

Abel tosses a bachelor dinner party for the three, her ex-husband and stage producer, a young lumber millionaire, and the ardent author. They recite how they figured in Susan's life, with most of flashback sequences devoted to her contact with producer George Brent, her lone marriage.

Fontaine's sparkle in this first comedienne role is impressive. She swings easily from plain Jane to the seasoned actress type, then to the glamorous, and finally to the intellectual. Top male contribution is Brent, as the

producer. He's a fine combination of the hardboiled showman and admiring husband.

● ●

■ **AFRICAN QUEEN, THE**

1951, 104 MINS, UK ◇ Ⓥ

Dir John Huston   *Prod* S.P. Eagle [=Sam Spiegel]   *Scr* James Agee, John Huston   *Ph* Jack Cardiff   *Ed* Ralph Kemplen   *Mus* Allan Gray   *Art Dir* Wilfrid Shingleton
● Humphrey Bogart, Katharine Hepburn, Robert Morley, Peter Bull, Theodore Bikel, Walter Gotell (Horizon/Romulus)

This story of adventure and romance, experienced by a couple in Africa just as World War I got underway, is an engrossing motion picture. Just offbeat enough in story, locale and star teaming of Humphrey Bogart and Katharine Hepburn to stimulate the imagination. It is a picture with an unassuming warmth and naturalness.

The independent production unit took stars and cameras to Africa to film C.S. Forester's novel, *African Queen*, against its actual background. Performance-wise, Bogart has never been seen to better advantage. Nor has he ever had a more knowing, talented film partner than Hepburn.

The plot concerns a man and woman, completely incongruous as to coupling, who are thrown together when the war news comes to German East Africa in 1914. The man, a sloven gin-swilling, ne'er-do-well pilot of a steam-driven river launch, teams with the angular, old-maid sister of a dead English missionary to contribute a little to the cause of the Empire.

The impossible deed they plan is taking the little, decrepit 30-foot launch known as *African Queen* down uncharted rivers to a large Central Africa lake and then use the small boat as a torpedo to sink a German gunboat that is preventing invasion by British forces.

John Huston's scripting and direction, and the playing, leaven the story telling with a lot of good humor. Unfoldment has a leisureness that goes with the characters and situations.

● ●

■ **AFRICA – TEXAS STYLE**

1967, 110 MINS, US ◇ Ⓥ

Dir Andrew Marton   *Prod* Andrew Marton   *Scr* Andy White   *Ph* Paul Beeson   *Ed* Henry Richardson   *Mus* Malcolm Arnold   *Art Dir* Maurice Fowler
● Hugh O'Brian, John Mills, Nigel Green, Tom Nardini, Adrienne Corri (Paramount/Ivan Tors)

Africa – Texas Style is a slick and exceptionally well-turned-out piece of adventure picture-making, its title the only weight of heaviness about it.

Shot entirely in Kenya, director Andrew Marton, scripter Andy White and cameraman Paul Beeson have thoroughly caught feeling of Africa. They make effective use of the terrain as an atmospheric setting and thousands of animals of all descriptions to lend authenticity.

Story twirls about the subject of game ranching, the domestication and breeding of wild animal life as a potentially huge source of meat and as a means of preserving many of Africa's rapidly vanishing species of wild beasts.

Premise is given punch via its human story of rancher John Mills importing Texas cowboys Hugh O'Brian and his Navajo pal Tom Nardini to rope and corral as many animals as they can ride down.

● ●

■ **AFTER HOURS**

1985, 97 MINS, US ◇ Ⓥ

Dir Martin Scorsese   *Prod* Amy Robinson, Griffin Dunne, Robert F. Colesberry   *Scr* Joseph Minton   *Ph* Michael Ballhaus   *Ed* Thelma Schoonmaker   *Mus* Howard Shore   *Art Dir* Jeffrey Townsend

● Griffin Dunne, Rosanna Arquette, Verna Bloom, Thomas Chong, Linda Fiorentino, Teri Garr (Geffen/Double Play)

The cinema of paranoia and persecution reaches an apogee in *After Hours*, a nightmarish black comedy from Martin Scorsese. Anxiety-ridden picture would have been pretty funny if it didn't play like a confirmation of everyone's worst fears about contemporary urban life.

A description of one rough night in the life of a mild-mannered New York computer programmer, film is structured like a 'Pilgrim's Progress' through the anarchic, evertreachous streets of SoHo. Every corner represents a turn for the worse, and by the end of the night, he's got to wonder, like Kafka's K, if he might not actually be guilty of something.

It all starts innocently enough, as Griffin Dunne gets a come-on from Rosanna Arquette and ends up visiting her in the loft of avant-garde sculptress Linda Fiorentino. Both girls turn out to be too weird for Dunne, but he can't get home for lack of cash, so he veers from one stranger to another in search of the most mundane salvation and finds nothing but trouble.

This was Scorsese's first fictional film in a decade without Robert De Niro in the leading part, and Dunne, who doubled as co-producer, plays a mostly reactive role, permitting easy identification of oneself in his place. Supporting roles are filled by uniformly vibrant and interesting thesps.

● ●

■ **AFTER THE FOX**

1966, 102 MINS, UK/ITALY ◇ Ⓥ

Dir Vittorio De Sica   *Prod* John Bryan   *Scr* Neil Simon, Cesare Zavattini   *Ph* Leonida Barboni   *Ed* Russell Lloyd   *Mus* Burt Bacharach   *Art Dir* Mario Garbugha
● Peter Sellers, Britt Ekland, Lidia Brazzi, Paola Stoppa, Victor Mature, Martin Balsam (Delagate/Nancy)

Peter Sellers is in nimble, lively form in this whacky comedy which, though sometimes strained, has a good comic idea and gives the star plenty of scope for his usual range of impersonations.

Neil Simon's screenplay is uneven but naturally has a good quota of wit, and Vittorio De Sica's direction plays throughout for laughs. The Fox is a quickwitted crook who nevertheless manages to find himself in the cooler seven times in nine years. But he's equally adroit at getting out. This time he makes the break (a) because he's worried about his sister who, he has a hunch, is getting into bad habits as a film starlet, and (b) to arrange for the smuggling into Rome of the loot from a $3 million Cairo bullion robbery. He hits on the idea of pretending to make a film on an Italian beach and conning the local villagers and the police into landing the gold ashore as part of the 'film script'.

The filming parody is better in promise than when start of shooting is actually being made, but even these sequences are good for plenty of yocks. Much of this is created by Victor Mature, roped into the film within the film as an aging, corseted film star fighting the wrinkles and still living in the past.

● ●

■ **AFTER THE THIN MAN**

1936, 107 MINS, US Ⓥ

Dir W.S. Van Dyke   *Prod* Hunt Stromberg   *Scr* Frances Goodrich, Albert Hackett   *Ph* Oliver T. Marsh   *Ed* Robert J. Kern   *Mus* Herbert Stothart, Edward Ward   *Art Dir* Cedric Gibbons, Harry McAfee
● William Powell, Myrna Loy, James Stewart, Elissa Landi, Joseph Calleia, Jessie Ralph (M-G-M)

First thing everyone will want to know about this one is whether it is as good as *The Thin Man*, and the answer is that it is – and it isn't. It has the same stars, William Powell and

Myrna Loy; the same style of breezy direction by W.S. Van Dyke; almost as many sparkling lines of dialog and amusing situations; but it hasn't, and probably couldn't have, the same freshness and originality of its predecessor.

The same author, Dashiell Hammett, wrote it, and the same screen writers, Frances Goodrich and Albert Hackett, did the adaptation. It's the 'same' all the way through, and while that's a guarantee of a certain general excellence, it's the reason why it does not shine so brightly.

Powell as the amateur detective, with Loy tagging along and getting herself tangled up in the plot, eventually gets his man. The two leading players seem to have a swell time throughout. They do a bedroom scene which is packed with laughs, but which is topped by a subsequent sequence when, having slept through an entire day, they have their breakfast in the evening and appear unable, or unwilling, to adjust themselves to the passing of time.

● ●

■ AGATHA

1979, 98 MINS, UK ◇ Ⓥ
Dir Michael Apted   *Prod* Jarvis Astaire, Gavrik Losey
Scr Kathleen Tynan, Arthur Hopcraft   *Ph* Vittorio Storaro   *Ed* Jim Clark   *Mus* Johnny Mandel
Art Dir Shirley Russell
● Dustin Hoffman, Vanessa Redgrave, Timothy Dalton, Helen Morse, Celia Gregory, Paul Brooke
(Warner/First Artists/Sweetwal/Casablanca)

Billed as 'an imaginary solution to an authentic mystery', Kathleen Tynan's original story fills in the gaps of Agatha Christie's well-publicized disappearance in 1926.

Christie, portrayed by Vanessa Redgrave in superlative fashion, is confronted with the breakdown of her marriage to war hero Timothy Dalton, who is prepared to marry his secretary (Celia Gregory). She flees to a remote health spa, where she sets in motion a unique form of revenge, while thousands scour the British countryside for some sign of her.

Enter Dustin Hoffman as a celebrated American journalist. He, too, joins the search, at first with the idea of a story, and then pursuing more romantic notions.

Director Michael Apted has perfectly recaptured the mood of post-World War I Britain, and the film is gorgeously photographed by Italian cinematographer Vittorio Storaro.

Agatha packs a surprise twist that the real Agatha Christie might have envied.

● ●

■ AGE OF CONSENT

1932, 80 MINS, US
Dir Gregory La Cava   *Scr* Sarah Y. Mason, Francis Cockrell   *Ph* J. Roy Hunt   *Ed* Jack Kitchin
● Dorothy Wilson, Richard Cromwell, Eric Linden, Arline Judge, John Halliday (Radio)

Picture marks the first release of Dorothy Wilson, the stenographer in the Radio coast studio offices who was skyrocketed from her typewriter into semi-stardom.

Wilson turns out to be a highly interesting young type, suggesting in appearance a flapper Norma Shearer. The part of a college co-ed does not call for any histrionic fireworks, but the newcomer reveals a remarkable aptitude for natural acting.

Story is a sexy tale [based on the play *Cross Roads* by Martin Flavin, adapted by H. N. Swanson], dealing in often sprightly manner with the adolescent amours of a co-ed campus and its environs, this angle being insidiously exploited under cover of being a sympathetic study of the love problems of the young.

Cast is made up of young people, with just

the leavening in the professor character, deftly handled as usual by John Halliday. Central male characters are played by Richard Cromwell, an excellent choice as the young hero, and Eric Linden, once more a philandering student high-flyer.

● ●

■ AGE OF CONSENT

1969, 103 MINS, AUSTRALIA ◇ Ⓥ
Dir Michael Powell   *Prod* Michael Powell, James Mason   *Scr* Peter Yeldham   *Ph* Hannes Staudinger
Ed Anthony Buckley   *Mus* Stanley Myers   *Art Dir* Dennis Gentle
● James Mason, Helen Mirren, Jack MacGowran, Neva Carr-Glyn, Antonia Katsaros (Nautilus)

Bradley Morahan (James Mason) is a famous Australian painter, paying a lot of alimony and about to return to his homeland.

He proceeds to the Great Barrier Reef to settle in a broken-down shack on a dream island, close to the mainland. The only other inhabitants are a gin-sodden old hag, her granddaughter Cora (Helen Mirren) and Isabel Marley, (Antonia Katsaros), a man-hungry spinster living on annuity, but also rearing chickens and growing vegetables.

The film [from a novel by Norman Lindsay] has plenty of corn, is sometimes too slow, repetitious and badly edited, almost as if scenes had been deleted. Yet the picture has immense charm and the actual photography (particularly underwater scenes) and superb scenery make it a good travelog ad for the Great Barrier Reef area where most of it was filmed.

● ●

■ AGNES OF GOD

1985, 98 MINS, US ◇ Ⓥ
Dir Norman Jewison   *Prod* Patrick Palmer, Norman Jewison   *Scr* John Pielmeier   *Ph* Sven Nykvist
Ed Antony Gibbs   *Mus* Georges Delerue   *Art Dir* Ken Adam
● Jane Fonda, Anne Bancroft, Meg Tilly, Anne Pitoniak, Winston Rekert, Gratien Gelinas (Columbia-Delphi IV)

John Pielmeier penned the screenplay from his own 1982 play about a young nun who is found to have given birth and then strangled the baby at an isolated convent. A psychiatrist, played by Jane Fonda, is appointed by the court to determine whether or not the young woman (Meg Tilly) is fit to stand trial, and is assured that the seemingly innocent, naive girl has no recollection of the child or conception.

In her aggressive quest for the facts in the case, Fonda goes head to head with Mother Superior Anne Bancroft, a cagey, very hip woman of God whose past as a wife and mother gives her a strong knowledge of the real world values represented by Fonda.

Fonda's relentless interrogating, mannered chain-smoking and enforced two dimensionality cause her to become tiresome very early on. She remains a brittle cliche of a modern professional woman.

Bancroft gives a generally highly engaging performance as a religious woman too knowledgeable to be one-upped by even the craftiest layman.

Tilly is angelically beautiful as the troubled youngster and brings a convincing innocence and sincerity to the role that would be hard to match.

● ●

■ AGONY AND THE ECSTASY, THE

1965, 136 MINS, US ◇ Ⓥ
Dir Carol Reed   *Prod* Carol Reed   *Scr* Philip Dunne   *Ph* Leon Shamroy   *Ed* Samuel E. Beetley   *Mus* Alex North, Franco Potenza   *Art Dir* Jack Martin Smith
● Charlton Heston, Rex Harrison, Diane Cilento, Harry Andrews, Alberto Lupo, Adolfo Celi (International Classics/20th Century-Fox

Against a backdrop of political-religious upheaval during the Italian Renaissance, *The Agony and the Ecstasy* focuses on the personal conflict between sculptor-painter Michelangelo and his patron, Pope Julius II.

Scripter Philip Dunne zeroed in on a four-year span during which the painter labored on the ceiling frescoes for the Sistine Chapel. The potent seeds in Dunne's excellent treatment are the artistic arrogance of Michelangelo and equally stubborn mind of the soldier Pontiff Julius.

Rex Harrison is outstanding as the Pope, from the moment of his striking entrance as a hooded soldier leading the suppression of a pocket of revolt, to his later scenes as an urbane, yet sensitive, pragmatic ruler of a worldly kingdom.

Charlton Heston's Michelangelo is, in its own way, also outstanding. Combination of austere garb, thinned face, short hair and beard, plus underplaying in early scenes, effectively submerge the Heston image fostered by his earlier epix.

Assisting Harrison's verbal whiplashes are the grandiose engineering plans of the architect Bramante, then engaged in building the new basilica of St Peter. Harry Andrews excels in the role, while his protege, the painter Raphael, played by Thomas Milian, projects very well as Heston's possible replacement.

● ●

■ AIR AMERICA

1990, 112 MINS, US ◇ Ⓥ
Dir Roger Spottiswoode   *Prod* Daniel Melnick
Scr John Eskow, Richard Rush   *Ph* Roger Deakins
Ed John Bloom, Lois Freeman-Fox   *Mus* Charles Gross   *Art Dir* Allan Cameron
● Mel Gibson, Robert Downey Jr, Nancy Travis, Ken Jenkins, David Marshall Grant, Lane Smith (Carolco)

Spectacular action sequences and engaging perfs by Mel Gibson and Robert Downey Jr make this big-budgeter entertaining and provocative.

It's probably news to most even at this late date that the CIA, through its proprietary Air America, was using drug money to finance the war in Southeast Asia and condoning the refining and exportation of heroin both to GIs in that part of the world and to the American public. Air America became known as 'a dope airline', as Christopher Robbins' 1979 source book puts it, and the filmmakers don't shrink from showing Gibson knowingly flying opium and cynically justifying it as essential to the US war effort.

Starting off as a reckless radio station helicopter pilot in a wild stunt sequence on an LA freeway in 1969, Downey is recruited by the CIA to perform his hair-raising flying feats for Uncle Sam in Laos, where oxymoronic military intelligence officer David Marshall Grant insists, 'We're not actually here.'

With his reported $35 million budget and a vast army of tech assistants to help carry out the stunt flying and crashes on the atmospheric Thailand locations, director Roger Spottiswoode does an efficient job in marshaling his forces and walking the thin line required to keep a black comedy from becoming gruesome or flippant.

● ●

■ AIRPLANE!

1980, 88 MINS, US ◇ Ⓥ
Dir Jim Abrahams, David Zucker, Jerry Zucker
Prod Jon Davison   *Scr* Jim Abrahams, David Zucker, Jerry Zucker   *Ph* Joseph Biroc   *Ed* Patrick Kennedy
Mus Elmer Bernstein   *Art Dir* Ward Preston
● Robert Hays, Julie Hagerty, Lloyd Bridges, Peter Graves, Leslie Nielsen, Robert Stack (Paramount)

Airplane! is what they used to call a laff-riot. Made by team which turned out *Kentucky*

Fried Movie, this spoof of disaster features beats any other film for sheer number of comic gags.

Writer-directors leave no cliche unturned as they lay waste to the *Airport*-style disaster cycle, among other targets. From the clever *Jaws* take-off opening to the final, irreverent title card, laughs come thick and fast.

Plot has former pilot Robert Hays, now terrified of flying due to wartime malfeasance, boarding an LA-to-Chicago flight in pursuit of ex-girlfriend stewardess Julie Hagerty.

When flight personnel, including sexually-deviant pilot Peter Graves and co-pilot Kareem Abdul-Jabbar, contract food poisoning on board, Hays is called upon to land the craft safely, an effort not made easier by fact that air controller Lloyd Bridges is completely crazed.

● ●

■ AIRPLANE II THE SEQUEL

1982, 85 MINS, US ◇ ⓥ

Dir Ken Finkleman *Prod* Howard W. Koch *Scr* Ken Finkleman *Ph* Joseph Biroc *Ed* Dennis Virkler *Mus* Elmer Bernstein *Art Dir* William Sandell
● Robert Hays, Julie Hagerty, Lloyd Bridges, Peter Graves, William Shatner, Chad Everett (Paramount)

It can't be said that *Airplane II* is no better or worse than its predecessor. It is far worse, but might seem funnier had there been no original.

In the first *Airplane*, Jim Abrahams, David Zucker and Jerry Zucker had a fresh satirical crack at that hoary old genre, the airborne disaster film. But they wisely chose not to tackle a sequel, leaving incoming writer-director Ken Finkleman a tough task for his feature debut.

Robert Hays is still solid as the fearful pilot destined to take the controls. Ditto his daffy girlfriend Julie Hagerty. But instead of their hilariously earnest efforts the first time around, they seem (perhaps subconsciously) too aware what they're doing is supposed to be funny.

Peter Graves remains amusing as the captain with a fondness for naughty talk with young boys. Among those with nothing much to do are Raymond Burr, Sonny Bono, Chuck Connors, John Dehner, Rip Torn and Chad Everett. Among those with too much to do is William Shatner.

● ●

■ AIRPORT

1970, 137 MINS, US ◇ ⓥ

Dir George Seaton *Prod* Ross Hunter *Scr* George Seaton *Ph* Ernest Laszlo *Ed* Stuart Gilmore *Mus* Alfred Newman *Art Dir* Alexander Golitzen, E. Preston Ames
● Burt Lancaster, Dean Martin, Jean Seberg, Jacqueline Bisset, George Kennedy, Helen Hayes (Universal)

Based on the novel by Arthur Hailey, over-produced by Ross Hunter with a cast of stars as long as a jet runway, and adapted and directed by George Seaton in a glossy, slick style, *Airport* is a handsome, often dramatically involving $10 million epitaph to a bygone brand of filmmaking.

However, the ultimate dramatic situation of a passenger-loaded jet liner with a psychopathic bomber aboard that has to be brought into a blizzard-swept airport with runway blocked by a snow-stalled plane actually does not create suspense because the audience knows how it's going to end.

As the cigar chomping, bull boss of the maintenance men, George Kennedy gives a strong portrayal. But here again there's not a moment of plot doubt that he is going to get that stuck plane cleared off the runway in time for the emergency landing.

□ 1970: Best Picture (Nomination)

● ●

■ AIRPORT 1975

1974, 106 MINS, US ◇ ⓥ

Dir Jack Smight *Prod* William Frye *Scr* Don Ingalls *Ph* Philip Lathrop *Ed* J. Terry Williams *Mus* John Cacavas *Art Dir* George C. Webb
● Charlton Heston, Karen Black, George Kennedy, Efrem Zimbalist Jr, Susan Clark, Gloria Swanson (Universal)

Airport 1975 gathers its specimens into a 747 jetliner which collides mid-air with a private plane, precipitating a complicated rescue effort. Charlton Heston's formula characterization is, quite literally, Messiah-exmachina.

Don Ingalls is credited with the scripture, 'inspired' (as the crawl says) by Ross Hunter's 1970 pic which, in turn, came from Arthur Hailey's novel. Jack Smight's direction has the refreshing pace of a filmmaker who knows his plot can crash unless he hurries.

The redundant script massaging of the 747's elaborate backup controls, safety features and all those other yum-yum goodies that airlines keep yacking about would suggest that some of the dialog was written by Boeing.

● ●

■ AIRPORT '77

1977, 113 MINS, US ◇ ⓥ

Dir Jerry Jameson *Prod* William Frye *Scr* Michael Scheff, David Spector *Ph* Philip Lathrop *Ed* J. Terry Williams, Robert Watts *Mus* John Cacavas *Art Dir* George C. Webb
● Jack Lemmon, Lee Grant, Brenda Vaccaro, Joseph Cotten, Olivia de Havilland, Darren McGavin (Universal)

Charlton Heston either busy elsewhere or exhausted from earthquakes, World War II and previous aerial disasters, Jack Lemmon assumed the Noah lead in *Airport '77*. This time around, a giant private jet gets hijacked and crashes off the Florida coast.

The story's formula banality is credible most of the time and there's some good actual US Navy search and rescue procedure interjected in the plot.

The story peg here has James Stewart, billionaire who has converted his home to museum status, loading his private plane with priceless paintings and a broader quality of people for a junket to the estate. However, Lemmon's copilot Robert Foxworth has joined with Monte Markham and Michael Pataki to hijack the plane for the art work.

● ●

■ AKENFIELD

1975, 95 MINS, UK ◇

Dir Peter Hall *Prod* Peter Hall, Rex Pyke *Scr* Ronald Blythe *Ph* Ivan Strasberg *Mus* Michael Tippett *Art Dir* Ian Whittaker, Roger Christian
● Garrow Shand, Peggy Cole, Barbara Tilney, Lyn Brooks, Ida Page, Ted Dedman (Angle Films)

Adapted from Ronald Blythe's social study of a Suffolk village, this is the story of three generations of farm laboring, intercutting flashbacks with present day to demonstrate that the more things change, the more they remain the same. It is funny and touching and seldom less than engrossing.

A virtue is that Hall has not idealized the subject. Throughout there's a strong current of melancholy, of dreams crushed and human potential stunted. Though it's not a despairing film, one is apt to feel that Suffolk's a lovely place to visit – only.

Ivan Strasberg's color photography, using only natural light (even indoors), is one of the conspicuous delights. His composition of the rolling English countryside is often lyrical, sometimes magical.

■ ALAMO, THE

1960, 192 MINS, US ◇ ⓥ

Dir John Wayne *Prod* John Wayne *Scr* James Edward Grant *Ph* William H. Clothier *Ed* Stuart Gilmore *Mus* Dimitri Tiomkin *Art Dir* Alfred Ybarra
● John Wayne, Richard Widmark, Laurence Harvey, Frankie Avalon, Patrick Wayne, Linda Cristal (United Artists)

The Alamo, which was shot in 91 days at a stated cost of $12 million, has a good measure of mass appeal in its 192 minutes. But to get it, producer-director-star John Wayne has loaded the telling of the tale with happy homilies on American virtues and patriotic platitudes under life-and-death fire which smack of yesteryear theatricalism rather than the realism of modern battle drama.

Obviously Wayne and James Edward Grant, who penned the original screenplay, had an entertainment, not a history lesson, in mind. But in their zeal to reproduce a colorful, homespun account of what went on in the course of those 13 remarkable days in 1836, they have somehow shrouded some of the fantastic facts of the original with some of the frivolous fancies of their re-creation.

In spite of the painstaking attempts to explore the characters of the picture's three principal heroes (Bowie, Crockett, Travis), there is an absence of emotional feeling, of a sense of participation. It is almost as if the writer is willing to settle for the popular conception of familiar heroes such as Davy Crockett and Jim Bowie as sufficient explanation of their presence and activities.

With the rousing battle sequence at the climax (for which a goodly share of credit must go to second unit director Cliff Lyons) the picture really commands rapt attention.

It is as actor that Wayne functions under his own direction in his least successful capacity. Generally playing with one expression on his face, he seems at times to be acting like a man with $12 million on his conscience. Both Widmark and Harvey suffer minor lapses in their performances but there is vigor and color in them. Younger players Frankie Avalon and Patrick Wayne show spirit.

□ 1960: Best Picture (Nomination)

● ●

■ ALAMO BAY

1985, 98 MINS, US ◇ ⓥ

Dir Louis Malle *Prod* Louis Malle, Vincent Malle *Scr* Alice Arlen *Ph* Curtis Clark *Ed* James Bruce *Mus* Ry Cooder *Art Dir* Trevor Williams
● Amy Madigan, Ed Harris, Ho Nguyen, Donald Moffat, Truyen V. Tran, Rudy Young (Tri-Star/Delphi III)

Alamo Bay is a failed piece of social consciousness. The peripatetic Louis Malle hasn't managed to shed any meaningful light on his current subject, that of the conflict between refugee Vietnamese and local fisherfolk around Galveston Bay, Texas, circa 1979–81.

Malle dared to place an exceedingly unsympathetic character at the center of his drama. Here it is Ed Harris, a bruising, philandering, unreflective lout who resents the intrusion of Vietnamese into his community and finally resorts to the easiest method of dealing with them, i.e. brutal, illegal violence.

Scene-setting is devoted to the native whites and newcomer Asians trying to fish the same waters, with the whites becoming increasingly irritated as the Vietnamese, in their view, horn in on their traditional territory, and work for lower wages to boot.

Mixed in with this is a re-ignition of a romance between Harris and Amy Madigan, latter being the daughter of controversial fish factory operator Donald Moffat and now at odds politically with her former boy friend. On the other side of the fence is new arrival

Ho Nguyen, who at first wears a permanent, subservient smile in hopes of ingratiating himself, but later refuses to be intimidated along with the rest of his people.

....

■ **ALBERT, R.N.**

1953, 88 MINS, UK

Dir Lewis Gilbert   *Prod* Daniel M. Angel   *Scr* Vernon Harris, Guy Morgan   *Ph* Jack Asher   *Ed* Charles Hasse   *Mus* Malcolm Arnold   *Art Dir* Bernard Robinson
● Anthony Steel, Jack Warner, Robert Beatty, William Sylvester, Guy Middleton, Anton Diffring (Eros)

The setting is a German camp for Allied naval officers, the action taking place late in 1944. The camp is regarded by its German masters as escape-proof and admittedly various attempts to breakout have been frustrated by alert prison guards. That is, until one of the internees hits on the idea of making a dummy to cover up for an absentee. The result is 'Albert, R.N.' with a papier mache head and a wire-framed body.

Camp atmosphere is effective. There is plenty of talk about women but it is an all-male cast. The main problem is the battle against monotony and for liberty.

A solid all-round cast admirably fits into the plot [from the play by Guy Morgan and Edward Sammis]. Anthony Steel handsomely suggests the young artist responsible for the creation of 'Albert' and Jack Warner is reliably cast as the senior British officer who maintains discipline with understanding in the camp. Frederick Valk is a sympathetic camp commandant, but Anton Diffring suggests the typical ruthless Nazi type.

....

■ **AL CAPONE**

1959, 105 MINS, US ▼

Dir Richard Wilson   *Prod* John H. Burrows, Leonard J. Ackerman   *Scr* Malvin Wald, Henry F. Greenberg   *Ph* Lucien Ballard   *Ed* Walter Hannemann   *Mus* David Raksin   *Art Dir* Hilyard Brown
● Rod Steiger, Fay Spain, James Gregory, Martin Balsam, Nehemiah Persoff (Allied Artists)

A tough, ruthless and generally unsentimental account of the most notorious gangster of the prohibition-repeal era, *Al Capone* is also a very well-made picture. There isn't much 'motivation' given for Capone, at least not in the usual sense. But the screenplay does supply reasons and they are more logical than the usual once-over-lightly on the warped youth bit.

Capone, played by Rod Steiger, is shown as an amoral personality with a native genius for leadership and organization. He became rich and famous in a way that seemed to him dandy. Nobody was more genuinely surprised than Capone when the revulsion his acts caused finally overwhelmed him.

The story picks up when Steiger is brought to Chicago as a low-grade torpedo by a fellow countryman (Nehemiah Persoff) to act as bouncer in his gambling establishment. Capone begins his rise when he murders the local political boss (Joe DeSantis), and eventually takes over Persoff's territory, on the latter's retirement. He teams with Bugs Moran and Dion O'Banion, to divide Chicago into territories.

Steiger's performance is mostly free of obvious technique, getting inside the character both physically and emotionally. Fay Spain has a role, that of the romantic attachment of Capone's life, that is probably more distracting than helpful. But she plays well. James Gregory as the honest cop, Martin Balsam as the dishonest reporter and Persoff as Capone's mentor, give skillful performances.

....

■ **ALEXANDER'S RAGTIME BAND**

1938, 105 MINS, US

Dir Henry King   *Prod* Harry Joe Brown   *Scr* Kathryn Scola, Lamar Trotti, Richard Sherman   *Ph* Peverell Marley   *Ed* Barbara McLean   *Mus* Alfred Newman (dir.)
● Tyrone Power, Alice Faye, Don Ameche, Ethel Merman, Jack Haley, Jean Hersholt (20th Century-Fox)

Irving Berlin's *Alexander's Ragtime Band* is a grand filmusical which stirs and thrills, a medley of more than 30 pieces, selected from some 600 which Berlin has composed.

Although the story opens back in 1911, the narrative moves swiftly through the years. None of the characters ages a single grey hair in 25 years.

Richard Sherman conceived the story idea with a central figure, a San Francisco bandmaster who adopts the name of Alexander. It is strictly fiction with only slight similarity to the Berlin biog. The screenplay is a fine piece of work in its subtle and logical inclusions of the Berlin ballads. Henry King directs with humor and sentiment, letting loose with an occasional broadside of mass movement.

Berlin supervised the musical angles and, in addition, tossed off three new numbers, 'Now I Can Be told', 'My Walking Stick' and 'Marching Along with Time'.

In the foreground are Tyrone Power, as Alexander; Alice Faye; and Don Ameche, who carries most of the story with an occasional song number of his own. Cast is heavy with featured names. Although Ethel Merman is a late entry into the proceedings, she sings and acts excellently. Jack Haley shows advantageously in comedy.

□ 1938: Best Picture (Nomination)

....

■ **ALEXANDER THE GREAT**

1956, 143 MINS, US ◇ ▼

Dir Robert Rossen   *Prod* Robert Rossen   *Scr* Robert Rossen   *Ph* Robert Krasker   *Ed* Ralph Kemplen   *Mus* Mario Nascimbene   *Art Dir* Andre Andrejew
● Richard Burton, Fredric March, Claire Bloom, Danielle Darrieux, Harry Andrews, Stanley Baker (Rossen/United Artists)

It took Alexander the Great some 10 years to conquer the known world back in the fourth century B.C. It seems to take Robert Rossen almost as long to recreate on film this slice of history. Despite the length, however, he has fashioned a spectacle of tremendous size.

Written, produced and directed by Rossen, the presentation is neither niggardly in the coin lavished on its physical makeup nor in the outlay for the talented international cast that enacts the historical saga of a man who believed both that he was a god and in his destiny to unite the world.

Rossen is not always able to hold interest in his story and action, resulting in some long, dull stretches.

Nor do the players have much chance to be more than puppets against the giant sweep of the spectacle. There are a number of single scenes that give the individual characters a chance to grow.

Alexander's romance with Barsine (Claire Bloom) is more implied than realized, but she does have some fine, expressive moments.

....

■ **ALEX AND THE GYPSY**

1976, 99 MINS, US ◇

Dir John Korty   *Prod* Richard Shepherd   *Scr* Lawrence B. Marcus   *Ph* Bill Butler   *Ed* Donn Cambern   *Mus* Henry Mancini
● Jack Lemmon, Genevieve Bujold, James Woods, Gino Ardito, Robert Emhardt, Joseph X. Flaherty ((20th Century-Fox)

Alex and the Gypsy is a cynical, distasteful film, full of grubby characters and situations.

Jack Lemmon stars as a burned-out tank-town bailbondsman still hung up on the gypsy girl (Genevieve Bujold) who long ago jilted him, but now needs his professional help. John Korty's direction brings out the pervasive and repulsive nihilism in the story and its people.

Lawrence B. Marcus has adapted Stanley Elkin's novella, *The Bailbondsman*, into a caterwauling and strident script lacking empathy, interest, humanity and punch. When Bujold is arrested for assault on her lover, Lemmon grudgingly (and partly sadistically) bails her out, knowing that they must be in close contact if he is to get his money back. They scream a lot, reminisce a lot, cavort about the countryside a lot.

....

■ **ALEX IN WONDERLAND**

1970, 110 MINS, US ◇

Dir Paul Mazursky   *Prod* Larry Tucker   *Scr* Paul Mazursky   *Ph* Laszlo Kovacs   *Ed* Stuart H. Pappe   *Mus* Tom O'Horgan   *Art Dir* Pato Guzman
● Donald Sutherland, Ellen Burstyn, Meg Mazursky, Glenna Sergent, Viola Spolin, Federico Fellini (M-G-M)

This fictional account of the personal and professional travails of a hotshot film director, played by Donald Sutherland, is partly admirable, partly realized, but also partly dull and somewhat deja vu to boot.

Sutherland is brought to a big studio after what must be presumed to be the sort of flop d'estime that has 'uncovered' many a real-life counterpart. With wife, played superbly by Ellen Burstyn, and children, Meg Mazursky and Glenna Sergent, Sutherland attempts to retain his integrity amid the trappings of fame and too-expensive Beverly Hills living accommodations.

Shortly into the film, however, Sutherland's character becomes as secondary as the various vignettes become all-too-overpowering. Perhaps Sutherland's man never had much to begin with.

....

■ **ALFIE**

1966, 114 MINS, UK ◇ ▼

Dir Lewis Gilbert   *Prod* Lewis Gilbert   *Scr* Bill Naughton   *Ph* Otto Heller   *Ed* Thelma Connell   *Mus* Sonny Rollins   *Art Dir* Peter Mullins
● Michael Caine, Shelley Winters, Millicent Martin, Julia Foster, Jane Asher, Shirley Anne Field (Paramount)

Alfie pulls few punches. With Michael Caine giving a powerfully strong performance as the woman-mad anti-hero, and with dialog and situations that are humorous, tangy, raw and, ultimately, often moving, the film may well shock. But behind its alley-cat philosophy, there's some shrewd sense, some pointed barbs and a sharp moral.

One of the biggest chances that the film takes is in its frequent use of the direct speech approach to the audience. This does not always come off in the picture as well as it used to do with Groucho in the old Marx Bros films. But the device served well enough in Bill Naughton's play, and does here.

Story concerns a glib, cynical young Cockney whose passion in life is chasing dames of all shapes, sizes, and dispositions, providing they are accommodating. The film traces the promiscuous path of this energetic young amoralist as he flits from one to the other without finding much lasting pleasure. In fact, he finishes up as a somewhat jaded, cutprice Lothario, disillusioned but still on the chase.

Caine brings persuasiveness, and a sardonic, thoroughly shabby and humorous charm to the role. The two best performances among the women come from Julia Foster, becomingly wistful throughout, and Vivien Merchant as the married woman who suffers an abortion.

□ 1966: Best Picture (Nomination)

....

ALFRED THE GREAT

1969, 122 MINS, UK ◇

Dir Clive Donner   *Prod* Bernard Smith, James R. Webb   *Scr* Ken Taylor, James R. Webb   *Ph* Alex Thomson   *Ed* Fergus McDonell   *Mus* Raymond Leppard   *Art Dir* Michael Stringer

● David Hemmings, Michael York, Prunella Ransome, Colin Blakely, Julian Glover, Ian McKellen (M-G-M)

Idea was to show that Alfred, Prince of Wessex, who became the first and only British King to be called 'Great', was not just a guy who burned the cakes.

He was the man who wanted to be a priest and only became a warrior against his will. He 'invented' the British Navy. He raised the standards of education and brought new laws to his subjects. But most of these facts have got lost in heavy-handed script.

Result is a film which hasn't the power or the passion to be a lavish historical film saga. Hints of the man's personality are given but they are sandwiched between two or three well staged hand-to-hand battles between Alfred's troops and the marauding Danes.

David Hemmings plays the title role with intelligence, and does his best to suggest the inner complexities of the man, but he is under age for the role and rarely matches the stature of the man he is portraying.

ALGIERS

1938, 93 MINS, US Ⓥ

Dir John Cromwell   *Prod* Walter Wanger   *Scr* John Howard Lawson, James M. Cain   *Ph* James Wong Howe   *Ed* Otho Lovering, William Reynolds   *Mus* Vincent Scott, Mohammed Igorbouchen   *Art Dir* Alexander Toluboff

● Charles Boyer, Hedy Lamarr, Sigrid Gurie, Joseph Calleia, Gene Lockhart, Alan Haleei (Wanger/United Artists)

Charles Boyer creates an interesting portrait of a continental gangster, jewel thief and tough guy in *Algiers*. Other meritorious aspects include John Cromwell's direction and the first appearance in an American-made film of Hedy Lamarr, the alluring natatorial star of the much-censored *Ecstasy*.

Film is a remake of *Pepe le Moko* (1937), a French picture directed by Julien Duvivier in which Jean Gabin starred. Wanger purchased the world rights, retired the prints from the domestic field, and assigned John Howard Lawson to write the English adaptation.

Boyer is a Parisian youth who is hunted by police and finally located in the native section of Algiers. So long as he stays within the prescribed area and lives and moves among the natives, without attempting escape to the European section, he is allowed his liberty. Police informants report his whereabouts; an inspector of detectives is his confidante; yet he dares not show himself outside.

At this juncture Boyer meets Lamarr, a beautiful Parisian girl who falls madly in love with him. She cannot remain in the restricted section; to possess her he must escape and return to Paris.

In performances by a fine cast, Lamarr comes next to Boyer in a photo finish. On the side of the unrelenting police is Joseph Calleia, as the inspector. Gene Lockhart is a stand-out as one of the informers.

ALIBI

1929, 90 MINS, US

Dir Roland West   *Prod* Roland West   *Scr* Roland West, C. Gardner Sullivan   *Ph* Ray June   *Mus* Hugo Riesenfeld

● Chester Morris, Harry Stubbs, Mae Busch, Eleanor Griffith, Irma Harrison, Regis Toomey (United Artists/Roland West

Jolt-packed crook melodrama in dialog. Lots of reliable excitement, de luxe production values and general audience satisfaction.

From the human interest standpoint picture belongs to Chester Morris, virile stage juvenile. In this picture he is a cruel, cold-blooded gangster.

Alibi starts out to give the cops the losing end of an expository tract on brutality. It winds up by hinting that the gendarmes have to be tough. Morris impersonates a clever young rodent with the instincts of a Chinese brigand. Picture is dedicated to the proposition that the man with a gun is a dirty name to start with.

There are loose ends and desultory passages in *Alibi*, but in general it has tempo and is punched with some gripping sequences. Police atmosphere and detail have realism and the ring of authenticity.

Roland West is the only entirely independent producer releasing through United Artists. He can sleep in peace in the security that his investment is safe and his picture there.

☐ 1928/29: Best Picture (Nomination)

ALICE

1990, 106 MINS, US ◇

Dir Woody Allen   *Prod* Robert Greenhut   *Scr* Woody Allen   *Ph* Carlo Di Palma   *Ed* Susan E. Morse   *Art Dir* Santo Loquasto

● Mia Farrow, Joe Mantegna, Alec Baldwin, Blythe Danner, Judy Davis, William Hurt (Orion)

If *Stardust Memories* was Woody Allen's *8¹/₂* and *Radio Days* his *Amarcord*, then *Alice* is his *Juliet of the Spirits*. It's a subtler, gentler retelling of Federico Fellini's tale of a pampered but unappreciated housewife who learns to shed her illusions by giving in to her fantasies.

In quick, hilarious strokes, Allen introduces Alice (Mia Farrow), who's been married 16 years to ultra-successful businessman William Hurt. Though her deepest daily concerns are gossip, decorators, fitness trainers, Bergdorf Goodman and pedicures, she feels a kinship with Mother Theresa.

But sudden fantasies about a divorced father (Joe Mantegna) at her kids' school and a trip to an unorthodox herbalist-acupuncturist (Keye Luke) set off a chain of sexual, mystical, frequently comic events.

Performances are strong all around, with a succession of top actors making the most of their brief turns. Alec Baldwin is Farrow's first love, who turns up in a surprising way; Bernadette Peters does some of her best film work in about two minutes on screen; Luke is the gruff-voiced, chain-smoking healer; and Gwen Verdon and Blythe Danner are Farrow's mom and sister, respectively. But the center of the pic is Farrow, who's funny and touching.

ALICE ADAMS

1935, 95 MINS, US Ⓥ

Dir George Stevens   *Prod* Pandro S. Berman   *Scr* Dorothy Yost, Mortimer Offner, Jane Murfin   *Ph* Robert De Grasse   *Ed* Jane Loring   *Mus* Max Steiner

● Katharine Hepburn, Fred MacMurray, Fred Stone, Evelyn Venable, Frank Albertson, Ann Shoemaker (RKO)

Translating Booth Tarkington's sometimes poignant and pathetic 1921 novel of the pretending, wistful Alice, whose economic background almost proves too much of a hurdle to surmount, must have been a yeoman task. That George Stevens' direction captures the wistfulness of Katharine Hepburn's superb histrionism, and yet has not sacrificed audience values at the altar of too much drabness and prosaic realism, is an achievement of no small order.

The star's own performance in uncompromising and unvacillating. If she's a silly little ninny in her pretenses and simple pretexts, she is permitted to run almost berserk on the petty inanities of small-town aspirations.

Ann Shoemaker, as the ambitious but firm and understanding mother, is effective contrast to Fred Stone's cinematic debut performance as the thankful-for-small-favors head of the Adams household.

Likewise, good taste in Evelyn Venable's rich girl's aspirant for Fred MacMurray, principal juve, is shown in not toughening up the role unnecessarily.

☐ 1935: Best Picture (Nomination)

ALICE DOESN'T LIVE HERE ANYMORE

1974, 112 MINS, US ◇ Ⓥ

Dir Martin Scorsese   *Prod* David Susskind, Audrey Maas   *Scr* Robert Getchell   *Ph* Kent L. Wakeford   *Ed* Marcia Lucas   *Mus* Richard LaSalle   *Art Dir* Toby Carr Rafelson

● Ellen Burstyn, Kris Kristofferson, Billy Green Bush, Diane Ladd, Lelia Goldoni, Harvey Keitel (Warner)

Alice Doesn't Live Here Anymore takes a group of wellcast film players and largely wastes them on a smaller-than-life film – one of those 'little people' dramas that make one despise little people.

Script establishes Ellen Burstyn as the lovingly slovenly wife of Billy Green Bush, who gets killed near their New Mexico tract home. Burstyn decides to return to her long-ago Monterey origins.

Burstyn's young fatherless child is played to excruciating repulsiveness by Alfred Lutter. The pair wander westward through the story. Burstyn resumes her singing career as a saloon entertainer, then a waitress, as assorted minor characters come and go.

Eventually, just over an hour into the proceedings enter Kris Kristofferson. The last half of the film is, indeed, a picture; but as a whole it's a distended bore.

ALICE'S ADVENTURES IN WONDERLAND

1972, 96 MINS, UK ◇ Ⓥ

Dir William Sterling   *Prod* Derek Horne   *Scr* William Sterling   *Ph* Geoffrey Unsworth   *Ed* Peter Weatherley   *Mus* John Barry   *Art Dir* Michael Stringer

● Fiona Fullerton, Michael Crawford, Ralph Richardson, Flora Robson, Peter Sellers, Robert Helpmann (Fox-Rank)

Alice's Adventures in Wonderland, from the Lewis Carroll classic, is a major disappointment. Superior stylistic settings and often terrific process effects are largely wasted by the limp, lifeless pacing of adapter-director William Sterling.

The secret of family-film conception is providing interest to all age groups. Some such films forget teenagers and adults in favor of catering strictly to moppets. This film largely forgets all audience segments in favor of static tableaux and one-two-three-kick direction, and even the John Barry-Don Black score of 16 tunes is confined to key largo.

Fiona Fullerton is a pleasantly bland Alice as are all other players. The film just lies there, and dies there, for 96 minutes.

ALICE'S RESTAURANT

1969, 111 MINS, US ◇ Ⓥ

Dir Arthur Penn   *Prod* Hillard Elkins, Joe Manduke   *Scr* Venable Herndon, Arthur Penn   *Ph* Michael Nebbia   *Ed* Dede Allen   *Mus* Arlo Guthrie   *Art Dir* Warren Clymer

● Arlo Guthrie, Pat Quinn, James Broderick, Michael McClanathan, Geoff Outlaw, Tina Chen (United Artists/Florin)

Alice's Restaurant is the phantasmagorial account of the misadventures of a young folk singer in his brushes with the law and his draft board. Based on folk singer Arlo Guthrie's 18 minute, 20 second hit recording, 'Alice's Restaurant Massacree', in which he limned some of his real-life experiences, the whole is a rather weird collection of episodes losely strung together.

There are occasional flashes of wry humor and some rib-tickling sequences. But they are all too few.

The opening sequences particularly are too wispily-contrived to rivet full attention, their sole purpose seemingly to introduce Arlo as a very odd fellow indeed. Plotline is virtually nil.

Some of the acting is very good, but Arlo's performance is of the uncertain type and he appears to be living in a world of his own.

· ·

■ **ALIEN**

1979, 124 MINS, US ◇ ▼
Dir Ridley Scott   *Prod* Gordon Carroll, David Giler, Walter Hill   *Scr* Dan O'Bannon   *Ph* Derek Vanlint   *Ed* Terry Rawlings   *Mus* Jerry Goldsmith   *Art Dir* Michael Seymour
● Tom Skerritt, Sigourney Weaver, Veronica Cartwright, Harry Dean Stanton, John Hurt, Ian Holm (20th Century-Fox/Brandywine)

Plainly put, *Alien* is an old-fashioned scary movie set in a highly realistic sci-fi future, made all the more believable by expert technical craftmanship.

Director Ridley Scott, cameraman Derek Vanlint and composer Jerry Goldsmith propel the emotions relentlessly from one visual surprise – and horror – to the next.

There is very little involvement with the characters themselves.

Alien initially presents a mundane commercial spacecraft with crew members bitching and moaning about wages and conditions.

The tedium is shared by captain Tom Skerritt, his aide Sigourney Weaver and the rest of the crew, played by a generally good cast in cardboard roles.

Eventually, it is Weaver who gets the biggest chance and she carries it off well.

· ·

■ **ALIENS**

1986, 137 MINS, US ◇ ▼
Dir James Cameron   *Prod* Gale Anne Hurd
Scr James Cameron   *Ph* Adrian Biddle   *Ed* Ray Lovejoy   *Mus* James Horner   *Art Dir* Peter Lamont
● Sigourney Weaver, Carrie Henn, Michael Biehn, Lance Henriksen, Paul Reiser, Jenette Goldstein (20th Century-Fox/Brandywine)

Aliens proves a very worthy followup to Ridley Scott's 1979 sci-fi shocker, *Alien*. James Cameron's vault into the big time after scoring with the exploitation actioner *The Terminator* makes up for lack of surprise with sheer volume of thrills and chills – emphasis is decidedly on the plural aspect of the title.

Cameron [working from a story by him, David Giler and Walter Hill] picks up the thread 57 years later, when Sigourney Weaver and her cat (who have been in hibernation) are rescued by a deep space salvage team. The authorities ask her to accompany a team of marines back to the planet to investigate why all contact with the colony has suddenly been lost. Group sent this time consists of a bunch of tough grunts with a sour attitude about having been sent on such a dippy mission.

Weaver finds one human survivor – a cute, tough, terrified little girl played by Carrie Henn – on the planet.

The odds against the crew are, in a word, monstrous, and unsurprisingly, its members are dispatched one by one until it once again

comes down to a battle royal between Weaver and one last monster.

Although film accomplishes everything it aims to do, overall impression is of a film made by an expert craftsman, while Scott clearly had something of an artist in him.

Weaver does a smashing job as Ripley. Carrie Henn is very appealing as the little girl and Jenette Goldstein makes a striking impression as a body-building recruit who is tougher than any of the guys in the outfit.

· ·

■ **ALL ABOUT EVE**

1950, 138 MINS, US ▼
Dir Joseph L. Mankiewicz   *Prod* Darryl F. Zanuck   *Scr* Joseph L. Mankiewicz   *Ph* Milton Krasner   *Ed* Barbara McLean   *Mus* Alfred Newman
● Bette Davis, Anne Baxter, George Sanders, Celeste Holm, Gary Merrill, Thelma Ritter (20th Century-Fox)

Anne Baxter, in the title role, is the radiant newcomer who has attained the thespic heights. And as she mounts the podium to receive the supreme accolade, the intimates who figured in her breathless success story project their own vignettes on what made this hammy glammy run.

Baxter plays a starry-eyed wouldbe actress who, by extraordinary design, finally meets Bette Davis, her histrionic idol (through the kind offices of Celeste Holm). She is taken into the household, machinates an understudy chore – and in return is ruthless in her pitch for both the beau and the husband of the two women who most befriended her.

The basic story is garnished with exceedingly well-cast performances wherein Davis does not spare herself, makeup-wise, in the aging star assignment. Baxter gives the proper shading to her cool and calculating approach in the process of ingratiation and ultimate opportunities.

Backgrounding are Gregory Ratoff, as the producer, and George Sanders as the debonair, machiavellian dramatic critic who knows the angles – plus.

It is obvious author-director Joe Mankiewicz knew what and how he wanted his cast to say and interpret.
□ 1950: Best Picture

· ·

■ **ALLAN QUATERMAIN AND THE CITY OF GOLD**

1987, 99 MINS, US ◇ ▼
Dir Gary Nelsen   *Prod* Menahem Golan, Yoram Globus   *Scr* Gene Quintano   *Ph* Alex Phillips, Frederick Elmes   *Ed* Alain Jakobowicz   *Mus* Michael Linn, Jerry Goldsmith   *Art Dir* Trevor Williams, Leslie Dilley
● Richard Chamberlain, Sharon Stone, James Earl Jones, Henry Silva, Robert Donner (Cannon)

Pic is a remake of Harry Alan Towers' 1977 film *King Solomon's Treasure*, which starred John Colicos as H. Rider Haggard's adventure hero Allan Quatermain (from the book by that name).

Embarrassing screenplay jettisons Haggard's enduring fantasy and myth-making in favor of a back-of-the-envelope plotline and anachronistic jokes about Cleveland. Quatermain (Richard Chamberlain) receives a gold piece from a dying man that inspires him to trek to East Africa in search of his brother Robeson (Martin Rabbett). Joining him are his archeologist girlfriend (Sharon Stone) and African warrior (James Earl Jones), a comic relief mystic (Robert Donner camping it up) and five expendable bearers.

After considerable filler, they find the lost race of Phoenicians, ruled by bland beauty contest queen Nyleptha (Aileen Marson).

A poor followup to the same producers' 1985 *King Solomon's Mines*, film relies frequently on a very phony gimmick of a spear-proof tunic and story completely runs out of

gas once the heroes arrive at their destination.

· ·

■ **ALL FALL DOWN**

1962, 111 MINS, US
Dir John Frankenheimer   *Prod* John Houseman   *Scr* William Inge   *Ph* Lionel Lindon   *Ed* Fredric Steinkamp   *Mus* Alex North   *Art Dir* George W. Davis, Preston Ames
● Eva Marie Saint, Warren Beatty, Karl Malden, Angela Lansbury, Brandon de Wilde (M-G-M)

Within John Houseman's production of *All Fall Down* there are some truly memorable passages – moments and scenes of great pith, poignance, truth and sensitivity. How disheartening it is, then, that the sum total is an artfully produced, cinematically rich, historically noteworthy, dramatically uneven near-miss.

A 16-year-old boy (Brandon de Wilde) who idolizes his emotionally unstable older brother (Beatty) is the pivotal figure in William Inge's screenplay based on James Leo Herlihy's novel. The important issue is that the adolescent matures into a decent young man. But his path to maturity is threatened by his adulation for this brother, a selfish, irrational free spirit who survives on odd jobs and loose women. When the older boy proceeds to destroy a young spinster (Eva Marie Saint) whom de Wilde adores in a hopeless, adolescent fashion, the latter has his moment of reckoning.

Angela Lansbury and Karl Malden, as the tragicomic elders, create indelible, dimensional and deeply affecting people.

· ·

■ **ALL I DESIRE**

1953, 79 MINS, US
Dir Douglas Sirk   *Prod* Ross Hunter   *Scr* James Gunn, Robert Blees   *Ph* Carl Guthrie   *Ed* Milton Carruth   *Mus* Joseph Gershenson   *Art Dir* Bernard Herzbrun, Alexander Golitzen
● Barbara Stanwyck, Richard Carlson, Lyle Bettger, Marcia Henderson, Maureen O'Sullivan, Lori Nelson (Universal)

Plot [from the novel *Stopover* by Carol Brink, adapted by Gina Kaus] concerns the return of a mother to the family she ran away from 10 years previously for a fling at the stage. Homecoming is to see her daughter in the high school graduation play, but, secretly, the mother hopes for a reconciliation. Things are moving to this end, until the smalltown lothario, who had figured in her previous flight, tries to renew the affair.

The Ross Hunter production and Douglas Sirk's direction pull all stops to make the picture a 79-minute excursion into sentimentality. With help of Barbara Stanwyck's performance, the soap-operish tear-jerking is palatable. Richard Carlson plays the stiff-necked husband character straight to make it acceptable. Lyle Bettger is sadly misused as the former lover. Maureen O'Sullivan does what she can with the role of a school teacher hopelessly in love with Carlson.

· ·

■ **ALLIGATOR EYES**

1990, 101 MINS, US ◇ ▼
Dir John Feldman   *Prod* John Feldman, Ken Schwenker   *Scr* John Feldman   *Ph* Todd Crockett   *Ed* Cynthia Rogers   *Mus* Sheila Silver
● Annabelle Larsen, Roger Kabler, Allen McCullough, Mary McLain, John Mackay (Laughing Man)

With this low-budget feature, first-time writer-director John Feldman creates some unusually strong characters and situations out of what could have been a routine road movie.

Pauline (Annabelle Larsen) is hitchhiking alone when picked up by a trio of friends from

New York who take her along for the ride, not knowing at first that she's blind. Robbie (Roger Kabler) is a wise-cracking type on the rebound after a failed relationship. He immediately latches on to the pretty Pauline, and sleeps with her. Marjorie (Mary McLain) is recently divorced and trying to renew a relationship with former boyfriend Lance (Allen McCullough). The trio originally planned a vacation in North Carolina, but find that Pauline is directing their movements.

It's only when it attempts to become a thriller in the final reel that *Alligator Eyes* starts to falter; all the mythic details brought into the film prepare the way for something more intriguing as a resolution.

....

■ ALL MY SONS

1948, 98 MINS, US

Dir Irving Reis   *Prod* Chester Erskine   *Scr* Chester Erskine   *Ph* Russell Metty   *Ed* Ralph Dawson   *Mus* Leith Stevens   *Art Dir* Bernard Herzbrun, Hilyard Brown

● Edward G. Robinson, Burt Lancaster, Mady Christians, Howard Duff (Universal)

All My Sons comes to the screen with a potent impact. Whatever message may have been in the stage presentation has been resolved to the more fundamental one of man's duty to man, and gains strength by that switch. It's a serious, thoughtful study, loaded with dramatic dynamite.

Chester Erskine's approach to the Arthur Miller play benefits from the broader movement permitted by the screen. It's an ace scripting and production job that carefully measures every value to be found in the plot.

Script makes the point that we all are our brothers' keepers with a responsibility that can't be shunted aside for purely personal desires. Rather than hammering point over, it is gradually brought out in telling of a man who, in a desire for success, becomes responsible for the death of 21 fliers during the war.

Edward G. Robinson gives an effective performance as the small-town manufacturer who sends defective parts to the Army Air Forces. It's a humanized study that rates among his best and lends the thought behind the film much strength. Burt Lancaster, as his war-embittered son, shades the assignment with just the right amount of intensity. His love and belief in his dad, whom he must betray to right the wrong done, cloaks the role with that human touch that marks all of the characters.

....

■ ALL NEAT IN BLACK STOCKINGS

1969, 106 MINS, UK

Dir Christopher Morahan   *Prod* Leon Clore   *Scr* Jane Gaskell, Hugh Whitemore   *Ph* Larry Pizer   *Ed* Misha Norland   *Mus* Robert Cornford   *Art Dir* David Brockhurst

● Victor Henry, Susan George, Jack Shepherd, Clare Kelly, Anna Cropper (Warner)

A trite story taken from a Jane Gaskell novel, it suggests that it was aimed directly at the socalled woman's market.

Victor Henry plays an exuberant young window-cleaner with a lack of responsibility and a roving eye for the birds. Falling for a suburban chick that he picks up in a local tavern, he realizes that this is 'the real thing'. But he's thwarted by her over-possessive widowed mother.

Eventually his buddy, a young layabout with whom Henry shares everything, good chicks, gets the girl pregnant at a wild party, but is unaware of it.

There's not much to be done with such an anecdote, but brighten it up with smart dialog and standout performances. This one gets neither. Aforementioned Henry brings some humor and guts to the anti-hero's role and

Jack Shepherd, as his mate, is laconic and personable.

....

■ ALL NIGHT LONG

1981, 88 MINS, US

Dir Jean-Claude Tramont   *Prod* Leonard Goldberg, Jerry Weintraub   *Scr* W.D. Richter   *Ph* Philip Lathrop   *Ed* Marion Rothman   *Mus* Ira Newborn   *Art Dir* Peter Jamison

● Gene Hackman, Barbra Streisand, Diane Ladd, Dennis Quaid, Annie Girardot (Universal)

A weary premise and a hackeneyed theme are given some wry, offbeat twists in *All Night Long*. Film has the distinction of being one of the few – if not the only – Barbra Streisand starrers which was not designed as a vehicle for her.

Plot is the same old middle-age-blues song, with Hackman chucking his dreary job, wife and lifestyle in favor of a younger woman and new reputation as a goofy carefree iconoclast. Familiar targets, such as uptight career businessmen, frivolous middle-class society ladies and sterile suburbia are knocked with easy precision.

With just one French feature, *Focal Point*, behind him, director Jean-Claude Tramont makes a good American debut here. Even though he has lived off-and-on in the US for years, he lends an appealingly different eye to the Southern California lifestyle.

Hackman brings even more to his role than might have been apparent in the script. Playing a clearly subordinate role which she took over from Lisa Eichhorn shortly after lensing began, Streisand is more subdued than usual and effective as such.

....

■ ALL QUIET ON THE WESTERN FRONT

1930, 152 MINS, US

Dir Lewis Milestone   *Prod* Carl Laemmle Jr   *Scr* Maxwell Anderson, Del Andrews, George Abbott   *Ph* Arthur Edeson, Karl Freund, Tony Gaudio   *Ed* Edgar Adams, Milton Carruth   *Mus* David Broekman   *Art Dir* Charles D. Hall, William R. Schmidt

● Lew Ayres, Louis Wolheim, John Wray, Raymond Griffith (Universal)

A harrowing, gruesome, morbid tale of war, compelling in its realism, bigness and repulsiveness.

Driving men and boys to their certain finish before murderous machine guns, dodging all kinds of missiles from the air, living with rats, starving while fighting, forgetting country and home, just becoming a fighting machine – that's the story and picture.

The story carries a group of German school boys, enthused by their professor's plea for fealty to country, from their training days through warfare to their deaths. In performance one might say it's due to Lewis Milestone's direction and let it go at that. But there are standout performances, even in bits. *All Quiet on the Western Front* [from the novel by Erich Maria Remarque] cost Universal $1.2 million.

□ 1929/30: Best Picture

....

■ ALL THAT HEAVEN ALLOWS

1955, 89 MINS, US

Dir Douglas Sirk   *Prod* Ross Hunter   *Scr* Peg Fenwick   *Ph* Russell Metty   *Ed* Frank Gross   *Mus* Frank Skinner   *Art Dir* Alexander Golitzen, Eric Orbom

● Jane Wyman, Rock Hudson, Agnes Moorehead, Conrad Nagel, Virginia Grey, Gloria Talbott (Universal)

Although this story of a long-suffering woman who, at 40 or so, finds romance with a man between 10 and 15 years her junior, is hardly designed to ignite prairie fires, scripter Peg Fenwick nevertheless has managed to turn the Edna L. and Harry Lee story into a slightly offbeat yarn with some interesting

overtones that accent the social prejudices of a small town.

Jane Wyman is appealing and properly long-suffering. The script makes her into a rather weak character and it's difficult, after a while, to rouse much sympathy for her plight.

Hudson is handsome and somewhat wooden. Laconic of speech, and imbued with an angel's patience and understanding, it's at times hard to understand his passion for the widow, what with pretty girls just spoiling for his attention.

Standout performance is delivered by a young newcomer, Gloria Talbott, playing Wyman's teenage daughter.

....

■ ALL THAT JAZZ

1979, 123 MINS, US

Dir Bob Fosse   *Prod* Robert Alan Aurthur   *Scr* Bob Fosse, Robert Alan Aurthur   *Ph* Giuseppe Rotunno   *Ed* Alan Heim   *Mus* Ralph Burns   *Art Dir* Philip Rosenberg

● Roy Scheider, Jessica Lange, Ann Reinking, Cliff Gorman, John Lithgow, Erzebet Foldi (20th Century-Fox/ Columbia)

All That Jazz is a self-important, egomaniacal, wonderfully choreographed, often compelling film which portrays the energetic life, and preoccupation with death, of a director-choreographer who ultimately suffers a heart attack.

The picture, reportedly based heavily on aspects of the real life of its director, Bob Fosse, deals with the director-choreographer Joe Gideon's career and his involvements with women.

Roy Scheider gives a superb performance as Gideon, creating a character filled with nervous energy. Running from project to project, the film portrays Gideon completing work on one film while working simultaneously on another project.

The film's major flaw lies in its lack of real explanation of what, beyond ego, really motivates Gideon.

□ 1979: Best Picture (Nomination)

....

■ ALL THE BROTHERS WERE VALIANT

1953, 94 MINS, US

Dir Richard Thorpe   *Prod* Pandro S. Berman   *Scr* Harry Brown   *Ph* George Folsey   *Ed* Ferris Webster   *Mus* Miklos Rozsa   *Art Dir* Cedric Gibbons, Randall Duell

● Robert Taylor, Stewart Granger, Ann Blyth, Betta St John, Keenan Wynn, James Whitmore (M-G-M)

Special effects are used to advantage to spotlight the high romance of adventuring on the bounding main. Film's big moments include the excitement stirred up by the dangers of 19th century whaling and the climactic mass battle with mutineers aboard a sailing vessel.

Directorial vigor of Richard Thorpe helps picture through its faltering spots. The latter come from shallow character development in the script [from a novel by Ben Ames Williams] and a rambling story line. Stars Robert Taylor, Stewart Granger and Ann Blyth are competent but the people they portray haven't enough depth or reality to come robustly alive.

Taylor and Granger are brothers in a seafaring family. When Granger, the elder, disappears on a whaling voyage, Taylor takes over his ship and, with his bride (Blyth) sails off to find him. At a South Seas stopover he finds Granger who goes for his brother's bride and incites a mutiny aboard ship, which he wants to use to recover a fortune in pearls he had found during his disappearance.

....

A

■ ALL THE FINE YOUNG CANNIBALS

1960, 112 MINS, US ◇

Dir Michael Anderson *Prod* Pandro S. Berman
Scr Robert Thom *Ph* William H. Daniels *Ed* John
McSweeney *Mus* Jeff Alexander *Art Dir* George W.
Davis, Edward Carfagno
● Robert Wagner, Natalie Wood, Susan Kohner,
George Hamilton, Pearl Bailey (M-G-M)

The handsome production surrounds a ludicrous *Modern Romances* sort of screenplay which was suggested by Rosamond Marshall's novel *The Bixby Girls*. Under scrutiny is the accelerated world of troubled youth where a one-night stand invariably results in pregnancy, fame or attempted suicide.

More specifically, the scenario explores the affairs of two young couples, (Natalie Wood-George Hamilton and Robert Wagner-Susan Kohner) who eventually learn to live with the fact they share a mutual tax-deduction in the form of a bouncing babe who bounced out of the pre-marital union of one-half of each partnership (Wagner and Wood).

Director Michael Anderson attempts to establish and link the individual personalities of the central foursome by flashing rapidly to and fro from family to family. The technique backfires in that, by attempting to take in too much too swiftly, it leaves the audience out of focus on all four individual sets of motivations.

Wood is very pleasant to behold, even though a pained expression is about all she is required to project here. Kohner is not very convincing in her efforts to appear alternately gay, bored and distressed. Even less at ease are Wagner and Hamilton in a pair of incredibly unmasculine roles. Best emoting is done by Pearl Bailey, but even she can barely cope with a preposterous role of a celebrated blues singer who dies of a broken heart when jilted by 'that man who played horn for her.'

■ ALL THE KING'S MEN

1949, 109 MINS, US ⓥ

Dir Robert Rossen *Prod* Robert Rossen *Scr* Robert
Rossen *Ph* Burnett Guffey *Ed* Al Clark *Mus* Louis
Gruenberg
● Broderick Crawford, John Derek, Joanne Dru, John
Ireland, Mercedes McCambridge (Columbia)

The rise and fall of a backwoods political messiah, and the mark he left on the American scene, is given graphic celluloid treatment in *All the King's Men*.

Robert Rossen has produced and directed from his own script, based upon the Pulitzer Prize novel by Robert Penn Warren.

As a great man using the opinionless, follow-the-leader instinct of the more common voter, Broderick Crawford does a standout performance.

The story is told through the eyes of John Ireland, newspaperman. He becomes a devotee pursuing the Crawford career from small-time into bigtime.

Joanne Dru appears to advantage as a friend of Ireland's, but the most compelling of the femme players is Mercedes McCambridge, the mistress to the great man.
□ 1949: Best Picture

■ ...ALL THE MARBLES

1981, 113 MINS, US ◇

Dir Robert Aldrich *Prod* William Aldrich *Scr* Mel
Frohman *Ph* Joseph Biroc *Ed* Irving C. Rosenblum,
Richard Lane *Mus* Frank De Vol *Art Dir* Carl
Anderson
● Peter Falk, Vicki Frederick, Laurene Landon, Burt
Young, Tracy Reed, Richard Jaeckel (M-G-M/United
Artists)

By any measure *Marbles* is a major disappointment, given the deft casting of Peter Falk as a seedy, selfish and demanding manager of a couple of tag-team women wrestlers

(Vicki Frederick and Laurene Landon).

The lead trio does get solid help from Burt Young as a crooked promoter and John Hancock as the decent manager of the opposing team consisting of Tracy Reed and Ursaline Bryant-Young.

For some odd reason, however, director Robert Aldrich and writer Mel Frohman have chosen to portray women's wrestling as a serious sport, aiming for another *Rocky*-like climb from obscurity to triumph. It never works for a minute. Except for a busted lip occasionally and a bruise or two, Frederick and Landon are always sprightly, pretty and ready for the road again after each bout.

Though Aldrich sometimes hints of hanky-panky and collusion among the teams, he generally insists that each match is won or lost on ability alone, building the 'California Dolls' up to a legitimate contest for the championship in Reno.

■ ALL THE PRESIDENT'S MEN

1976, 138 MINS, US ◇ ⓥ

Dir Alan J. Pakula *Prod* Walter Coblenz *Scr* William
Goldman *Ph* Gordon Willis *Ed* Robert L. Wolfe
Mus David Shire *Art Dir* George Jenkins
● Dustin Hoffman, Robert Redford, Jack Warden,
Martin Balsam, Hal Holbrook, Jason Robards (Warner)

Some ingenious direction by Alan J. Pakula and scripting by William Goldman remove much of the inherent dramatic lethargy in any story of reporters running down a story.

Thus, *All the President's Men*, from the Bob Woodward-Carl Bernstein book about their experiences uncovering the Watergate coverup for *The Washington Post*, emerges close to being an American *Z*. Robert Redford and especially Dustin Hoffman excel in their starring roles.

As Deep Throat, the official who assisted the reporters in filtering out the facts, Hal Holbrook is outstanding; this actor is as compelling as he is in virtually every role played.

Jason Robards as *Post* exec editor Ben Bradlee, provides an excellent characterization.
□ 1976: Best Picture (Nomination)

■ ALL THE RIGHT MOVES

1983, 91 MINS, US ◇ ⓥ

Dir Michael Chapman *Prod* Stephen Deutsch, Phillip
Goldfarb *Scr* Michael Kane *Ph* Jan De Bont
Ed David Garfield *Mus* David Campbell
Art Dir Mary Ann Biddle
● Tom Cruise, Craig T. Nelson, Lea Thompson, Charles
Cioffi, Paul Carafotes, Christopher Penn (20th Century-
Fox)

A smash directorial debut by well-known cinematographer Michael Chapman, *All the Right Moves* crackles with authenticity. The story is centered on characters fighting to get out of a dying Pennsylvania mill town to make a better life for themselves.

In a nice twist on expectations, the driven include Tom Cruise's girlfriend, sharply played by newcomer Lea Thompson, whose own aspirations take the frill out of the coed image, and the hard-nosed high school coach, superbly portrayed by Craig T. Nelson, who wants the big time as much as Cruise, his star safety.

Another welcome surprise is the touching relationship between high school senior Cruise and his father. For once, here's a pop in a redneck town who treats his son like a human being, and Charles Cioffi, however brief his screentime, conveys a durable dignity.

■ ALL THIS AND HEAVEN TOO

1940, 140 MINS, US ⓥ

Dir Anatole Litvak *Prod* Hal B. Wallis, David Lewis
Scr Casey Robinson *Ph* Ernest Haller *Ed* Warren
Low *Mus* Max Steiner *Art Dir* Carl Jules Weyl

● Bette Davis, Charles Boyer, Jeffrey Lynn, Barbara
O'Neil, Virginia Weidler, Helen Westley (Warner)

Heaven is film theatre at its best. In the two starring roles are Bette Davis, as the young French governess, Henriette Deluzy-Desportes, and Charles Boyer, projecting one of his best performances as Duc de Praslin. The tragedy of their love affair, which resulted in the murder of the Duchesse de Praslin (Barbara O'Neil), the suicide of the Duc and the subsequent glimpse of some happiness for Henriette in her marriage to the American theological student, Henry Martyn Field (Jeffrey Lynn), is strong fare, involving delicate psychological shadings and understandings.

Casey Robinson in the scripting captures the quaintness of the manners and customs of Paris in 1848, and succeeds admirably in retaining both spirit and characters of Rachel Field's novel, despite much deletion of material. Anatole Litvak's direction is outstanding. Film throughout bears the mark of earnest and expert workmanship in all departments.

There are unusually effective performances of four youthful players as the de Praslin children. Every progressive step in the story is built around these youngsters, a bit of plot unfolding that takes the film far from conventional grooves. The children' roles are played with fine emotional results by Virginia Weidler, June Lockhart, Ann Todd and Richard Nichols.

As for Davis, she is off the screen during the briefest interludes. In her scenes with Boyer, she retains an outward composure which only intensifies her real feelings, never completely expressed. It is acting so restrained that a single overdrawn passage or expression would shatter the illusion.
□ 1940: Best Picture (Nomination)

■ ALMOST AN ANGEL

1990, 95 MINS, US ◇ ⓥ

Dir John Cornell *Prod* John Cornell *Scr* Paul
Hogan *Ph* Russell Boyd *Ed* David Stiven
Mus Maurice Jarre *Art Dir* Henry Bumstead
● Paul Hogan, Elias Koteas, Linda Kozlowski, Charlton
Heston, Doreen Lang, Joe Dallesandro
(Paramount/Ironbark)

Almost an Angel is simply a no-effort vanity project with only Paul Hogan's easygoing charm to fill the space between the sprocket holes.

Instead of stretching his acting muscles, Hogan assigns himself the comfortable role of an electronics expert/cracksman just released from prison who turns into an inveterate do-gooder. In between bank heists, he instinctively saves a guy from a traffic accident and is himself run down.

Hospital scene has him dreaming of (or actually) floating to the clouds where uncredited guest star Charlton Heston as God reads him the riot act. He sends Hogan back to Earth for a second chance as an angel of mercy on probation.

Trekking to the small town of Fillmore, California, he sets about being kind to people. Chief recipients of his largesse are Elias Koteas, a bitter young man suffering from a terminal illness confining him to a wheelchair, and his self-sacrificing sister, Hogan's real-life wife and inevitable co-star Linda Kozlowski.

Koteas is affecting as the cripple with a chip on his shoulder. Kozlowski, styled plain with dark hair, is wasted as the mildest of romantic interests.

■ ALMOST PERFECT AFFAIR, AN

1979, 93 MINS, US ◇ ▼
Dir Michael Ritchie   *Prod* Terry Carr   *Scr* Walter Bernstein, Don Peterson   *Ph* Henri Decae   *Ed* Richard A. Harris   *Mus* Georges Delerue   *Art Dir* Willy Holt
● Keith Carradine, Monica Vitti, Raf Vallone, Christian De Sica (Paramount)

The emotions director Michael Ritchie is parlaying in this slim fable, which revolve around tender egos and unlimited ambition, are universal. But the details are so specific, and so grounded in film industry reality, that the larger implications may be lost.

Keith Carradine is a young filmmaker, who wraps up two years of devotion to a film about executed murderer Gary Gilmore, *Choice of Ending*, by sinking all his remaining funds into a trip to Cannes. His film is seized at French customs until the censor can see it, an unlikely possibility until Monica Vitti intercedes on his behalf.

Carradine mirrors lotsa nouveau helmers adrift in their initial dealings with industry salesmanship.

Focus is the intriguing relationship between Vitti and Carradine, which starts out as a one-nighter, and turns into a brief, but ill-fated romance.

■ ALONG CAME JONES

1945, 90 MINS, US
Dir Stuart Heisler   *Prod* Gary Cooper   *Scr* Nunnally Johnson   *Ph* Milton Krasner   *Ed* Thomas Neff   *Mus* Arthur Lange   *Art Dir* Wiard B. Ihnen
● Gary Cooper, Loretta Young, William Demarest, Dan Duryea (RICO/International)

For his first independent production, Gary Cooper turned out a better-than-average western [from an original story by Alan Le May]. Cooper is not only the producer but also the star, along with Loretta Young. Without Cooper and Young *Jones* would be just another horse opera.

Cooper plays a mild-mannered cowpoke who drifts into a small town with his sidekick (William Demarest), thus precipitating a situation in which he's mistaken for a notorious road agent. Cooper, actually, can't even handle a gun, but the inevitable result finds him the unwitting and indirect cause of the holdupman's slaying. And, of course, he gets the latter's girl (Young).

Cooper plays his usually languid self impressively, while Young is decorative and photographed well. Demarest is in for some comedy relief, of which there is too little, while Dan Duryea is properly menacing as the killer.

■ ALTERED STATES

1980, 102 MINS, US ◇ ▼
Dir Ken Russell   *Prod* Howard Gottfried   *Scr* Sidney Aaron [= Paddy Chayefsky]   *Ph* Jordan Cronenweth   *Ed* Eric Jenkins   *Mus* John Corigliano   *Art Dir* Richard McDonald
● William Hurt, Blair Brown, Bob Balaban, Charles Haid (Warner)

Altered States is an exciting combo science fiction-horror film. Direction by Ken Russell has energy to spare, with appropriate match-up of his baroque visual style to special effects intensive material.

Producers weathered stormy pre-production problems, including the ankling of director Arthur Penn late in 1978, departure soon after of special effects wiz John Dykstra, and transfer of project from Columbia to Warners as proposed budget grew to $15 million.

Tall tale concerns a young psychophysiologist, Edward Jessup (William Hurt), working in New York and later at Harvard on dangerous experiments involving human consciousness.

Using himself as the subject, Jessup makes use of a sensory deprivation tank to hallucinate back to the event of his birth and beyond, regressing into primitive stages of human evolution.

Shattering use of Dolby stereo effects conspires with the images to give the viewer a vicarious LSD-type experience sans drugs. Hurt's feature film debut is arresting, especially during the grueling climactic sequence.

■ ALVAREZ KELLY

1966, 110 MINS, US ◇ ▼
Dir Edward Dmytryk   *Prod* Sol C. Siegel   *Scr* Franklin Coen, Elliott Arnold   *Ph* Joseph MacDonald   *Ed* Harold F. Kress   *Mus* John Green   *Art Dir* Walter M. Simonds
● William Holden, Richard Widmark, Janice Rule, Patrick O'Neal, Victoria Shaw, Roger C. Carmel (Columbia)

Based on a true US Civil War incident, *Alvarez Kelly* concerns successful cattle grab engineered by Southern forces and executed under the noses of Northern troops. Outdoor action sequences, including an exciting stampede, enliven a tame script, routinely directed and performed erratically.

Franklin Coen and Elliott Arnold scripted Coen's story, which pits Mexican-Irish William Holden (hence, the title) against Confederate officer Richard Widmark, eyeing Holden's cattle as food for a starving South.

A lot of double-crossing takes place, with Victoria Shaw, mistress of a captured mansion, causing Holden's kidnapping by Widmark, who forces the former to teach his troops how to handle cattle. Janice Rule, Widmark's faithful sweetie, gives up her marriage hopes, and Holden helps her escape to NY with Scottish sea captain Roger C. Carmel. Patrick O'Neal is the Northern officer who is depicted in unsympathetic hues.

Director Edward Dmytryk has achieved uneven response from his players, in part due to scripting which overdevelops some characters and situations, and underdevelops others.

■ ALVIN PURPLE

1973, 97 MINS, AUSTRALIA ◇ ▼
Dir Tim Burstall   *Prod* Tim Burstall   *Scr* Alan Hopgood   *Ph* John Seale   *Mus* Brian Cadd
● Graeme Blundell, George Whaley, Penne Hackforth-Jones, Elli Maclure, Jacki Weaver, Lynette Curran (Hexagon)

Alvin Purple is a young man whom women find irresistible. At 16 he flees from schoolgirls right into the clutches of his school teacher's wife. At 21, still running from the opposite sex, Alvin becomes a waterbed salesman and discovers it isn't only the water-bed a bored housewife, body-painting fanatic, kinky woman, and a drag queen are after. Exhausted and bewildered by these multiple activities Alvin confesses to his girl friend Tina (with whom his relationship is utterly platonic) he is unable to resist sex.

This comedy, made in Melbourne with local actors, is beautifully scripted by Aussie playwright Alan Hopgood with double entendres and situations abounding. Pace is slick and the pic never sags.

In the title role Graeme Blundell gives a thoroughly convincing performance.

■ ALWAYS

1985, 105 MINS, US ◇ ▼
Dir Henry Jaglom   *Prod* Henry Jaglom   *Scr* Henry Jaglom   *Ph* Hanania Baer   *Mus* Miles Kreuger (consult.)
● Patrice Townsend, Henry Jaglom, Joanna Frank, Alan Rachins, Melissa Leo, Jonathan Kaufer (Jagtown

Always is writer-director-producer Henry Jaglom's confessional comedy about his divorce from actress Patrice Townsend. The two star, more or less, as themselves, and are joined by two other couples who are, respectively, near the beginning and toward the middle of the marriage process for an alternately awkward, painful, loving and farcical July Fourth weekend. Pic's subject matter is at once highly personal and utterly universal.

Jaglom frames the proceedings with ruminations directed straight at the viewer, then jumps into a telling of how Townsend showed up one night at Jaglom's home to sign the divorce papers and ended up staying on for a weekend of emotional confrontations, recriminations, joyful reminiscences and partial reconciliation.

In French farce style, two unexpected flings take place, but mainly, picture is wall-to-wall talk about what went wrong between Jaglom and Townsend, about emotional happiness and lack of same, about sexual matters, and many related topics.

■ ALWAYS

1989, 121 MINS, US ◇ ▼
Dir Steven Spielberg   *Prod* Steven Spielberg, Frank Marshall, Kathleen Kennedy, Richard Vane   *Scr* Jerry Belson   *Ph* Mikael Salomon   *Ed* Michael Kahn   *Mus* John Williams   *Art Dir* James Bissell
● Richard Dreyfuss, Holly Hunter, Brad Johnson, John Goodman, Audrey Hepburn (Universal/United Artists/Amblin)

Always is a relatively small scale, engagingly casual, somewhat silly, but always entertaining fantasy.

Richard Dreyfuss charmingly inherits the lead role of a pilot returned from the dead in this remake of the 1943 Spencer Tracy pic *A Guy Named Joe* set among fire-fighters in national parks.

Steven Spielberg's transposition of the fondly remembered original to the spectacularly burning Montana forests – incorporating footage shot during the devastating 1988 fires at Yellowstone National Park – is a valid equivalent, for the most part, especially since his action sequences using old World War II-era planes are far more thrilling than those of *A Guy Named Joe*.

Holly Hunter's dispatcher and semi-skilled aspiring pilot, lacking the womanly grace Irene Dunne brought to the part, comes off as gawky and ditzy in the early parts of *Always*. Bereavement seems to visibly mature the actress, whose emotional struggle between the memory of Dreyfuss and new love Brad Johnson becomes spirited and gripping.

■ AMADEUS

1984, 158 MINS, US ◇ ▼
Dir Milos Forman   *Prod* Saul Zaentz   *Scr* Peter Shaffer   *Ph* Miroslav Ondricek   *Ed* Nena Danevic, Michael Chandler   *Mus* John Strauss   *Art Dir* Patrizia Von Brandenstein
● F. Murray Abraham, Tom Hulce, Elizabeth Berridge, Simon Callow, Roy Dotrice, Christine Ebersole (Zaentz)

On a production level and as an evocation of a time and place, *Amadeus* is loaded with pleasures, the greatest of which derive from the on-location filming in Prague, the most 18th-century of all European cities.

With great material and themes to work with, and such top talent involved, film nevertheless arrives as a disappointment. Although Peter Shaffer adapted his own outstanding play for the screen, the stature and power the work possessed onstage have been noticeably diminished, and Milos Forman's handling is perhaps too naturalistic for what was conceived as a highly stylized piece.

Amadeus is Shaffer's fictionalized account, based on well-informed speculation, of the relationship between Viennese court composer

Antonio Salieri and Wolfgang Amadeus Mozart, during the 10 final years of the latter's life. It is a caustic study of the collision between mediocrity and genius, it is based on the provocative premise that the manipulative Salieri may have intentionally caused Mozart's death in 1791.

Shaffer has drawn Salieri as a character of Mephistophelian proportions, a man who needs to drag Mozart down in order to cope with his awareness of his own shortcomings.

Fueling the fire of Salieri's fury is Mozart's offensive personality. In opposition to the idealized, romanticized 19th-century view of the composer, the character is an outlandish vulgarian. As played by Tom Hulce, Mozart emerges as the John McEnroe of classical music.

□ 1984: Best Picture

■ AMAZING DR. CLITTERHOUSE, THE

1938, 87 MINS, US

Dir Anatole Litvak *Prod* Robert Lord *Scr* John Wexley, John Huston *Ph* Tony Gaudio *Ed* Warren Low *Mus* Max Steiner *Art Dir* Carl Jules Weyl
● Edward G. Robinson, Claire Trevor, Humphrey Bogart, Allen Jenkins, Donald Crisp, Gale Page (Warner)

The Amazing Dr Clitterhouse was successful on the London stage and mildly so in New York.

The producers have retained the basic idea from the play [by Barre Lyndon] – that of a veteran physician whose study of the physiological effects of crime on its habitues takes him on a series of ventures with a skilled gang of crooks. This thread has been followed even to the deliberate poisoning of the gangster chief by the doctor when he learns of a hoodlum's blackmailing scheme.

But in many respects it is an outright gangster film with the medico's study of criminals as the excuse for carefully diagraming the gang's operations. In addition, the feature inculcates a bit of the sherlocking theme and modified romance. Claire Trevor, the ace fence for the thieves, is the sole romance that enters the doctor's life.

Edward G. Robinson, in the role of the criminal medico, is at his best. Humphrey Bogart's interpretation of the gangster chief, whose jealousy of Clitterhouse eventually builds to the blackmail scheme, is topflight.

■ AMAZING GRACE AND CHUCK

1987, 115 MINS, US

Dir Mike Newell *Prod* David Field *Scr* David Field *Ph* Robert Elswit *Ed* Peter Hollywood *Mus* Elmer Bernstein *Art Dir* Dena Roth
● Jamie Lee Curtis, Alex English, Gregory Peck, William L. Peterson, Joshua Zuehlke (Tri-Star/Rastar/Turnstar)

Amazing Grace and Chuck is destined to go down in history as the camp classic of the anti-nuke genre. As amazingly bad as it is audacious, film will live forever in the hearts of connoisseurs of Hollywood's most memorably outrageous moments.

Little League baseball pitcher Chuck Murdock, having been shown a Minuteman missile under the Montana prairie, announces, 'I can't play because of nuclear weapons.' Who should read a news report of the incident but Boston Celtics star Amazing Grace Smith (played by Denver Nuggets great Alex English), who promptly gives up his $1 million-per-year salary to join Chuck in protest of nukes. In no time, hundreds of athletes on both sides of the Iron Curtain are refusing to play until the ultimate weapon is eliminated.

When it looks as though the upcoming baseball season will have to be cancelled the President of the United States (an impressive Gregory Peck) summons young Chuck to the White House to drum some sense into him.

■ AMAZON WOMEN ON THE MOON

1987, 85 MINS, US

Dir Joe Dante, Carl Gottlieb, Peter Horton, John Landis, Robert K. Weiss *Prod* Robert K. Weiss *Scr* Michael Barrie, Jim Malholland *Ph* Daniel Pearl *Ed* Bert Lovitt, Marshall Harvey, Malcolm Campbell *Art Dir* Alex Hajdu
● Rosanna Arquette, Ralph Bellamy, Carrie Fisher, Griffin Dunne, Steve Guttenberg, Russ Meyer (Universal)

Amazon Women on the Moon is irreverent, vulgar and silly and has some hilarious moments and some real groaners too. John Landis & Co have found some 1980s things to satirize – like yuppies, the vidcassette biz, dating, condoms – done up in a way that's not particularly shocking anymore.

Besides Landis, directors Joe Dante, Carl Gottlieb, Peter Horton and Robert K. Weiss take turns doing sketches – Weiss' *Amazon Women on the Moon* 1950s parody of bad sci-fi pics being the one that was stretched piecemeal throughout the film in a semi-successful attempt to hold this anthology together as one comedic work.

Eighteen other segs fill up the pic's 85 minutes, some mercifully short like Weiss' *Silly Pate* while Landis' *Hospital* is one of those slow-building, totally zany bits where the chuckles grow as the situation gets more ridiculous and you wish there was more.

■ AMBUSHERS, THE

1968, 101 MINS, US

Dir Henry Levin *Prod* Irving Allen *Scr* Herbert Baker *Ph* Burnett Guffey *Ed* Harold F. Kress *Mus* Hugo Montenegro
● Dean Martin, Senta Berger, Janice Rule, James Gregory, Albert Salmi, Kurt Kasznar (Columbia/Meadway-Claude)

This third Matt Helm pic starts out with silly double entendre, then shifts for last half to tedious plot resolution. While production values remain strong, acting, writing and direction are pedestrian.

Plot is simple: US flying sauceress Janice Rule is kidnapped by despicable beast Albert Salmi; James Gregory sends Dean Martin to find out why; Senta Berger reps another foreign government (lucky place, too); Kurt Kasznar is a funny bad guy – a Mexican beer baron; assorted heavies get their desserts.

Although visual aspects – the Oleg Cassini wardrobe and overall fashion supervision – are very good, pic at same time has that slapdash quickie look.

■ AMERICA AMERICA

1963, 177 MINS, US

Dir Elia Kazan *Prod* Elia Kazan *Scr* Elia Kazan *Ph* Haskell Wexler *Ed* Dede Allen *Mus* Manos Hadjidakis *Art Dir* Gene Callahan
● Stathis Giallelis, Frank Wolf, Harry Davis, Linda Marsh, Paul Mann, Lou Antonio (Warner)

Elia Kazan gives a penetrating, thorough and profoundly affecting account of the hardships endured and surmounted at the turn of the century by a young Greek lad in attempting to fulfill his cherished dream – getting to America from the old country.

Kazan's film stems from his book of the same title which evidently was inspired by tales of the experiences of his own ancestors that sifted down through the family grapevine. The picture begins with the young Greek hero witnessing Turkish oppression of Greek and Armenian minorities, circa 1896. It follows him to Constantinople, to which he has been sent by his family with its entire fortune to pave their way. He finally arrives in the promised land – America – where, as a lowly shoeshine boy, he painstakingly earns and saves the money that will bring the other members of his large family across the sea.

The acting is incredibly good. In the all-important focal role of the young man with the dream, Stathis Giallelis, an unknown, makes a striking screen debut. Virtually everyone is memorable, perhaps the three most vivid are Linda Marsh as the plain and unassuming maiden to whom the hero is treacherously betrothed, Paul Mann as her sybaritic, self-indulgent father and Lou Antonio as a thoroughly detestable crook.

□ 1963: Best Picture (Nomination)

■ AMERICAN FLYERS

1985, 114 MINS, US

Dir John Badham *Prod* Gareth Wigan, Paula Weinstein *Scr* Steve Tesich *Ph* Don Peterman *Ed* Frank Morriss *Mus* Lee Ritenour, Greg Mathieson *Art Dir* Lawrence G. Paull
● Kevin Costner, David Grant, Rae Dawn Chong, Alexandra Paul, Janice Rule, Luca Bercovici (Warner)

Story of two brothers who untangle their mixed emotions as they compete in a grueling bicycle race, *American Flyers* is most entertaining when it rolls along unencumbered by big statements. Unfortunately, overblown production just pumps hot air in too many directions and comes up limp.

Basic conflict between under-achiever David (David Grant) and older brother Marcus (Kevin Costner), a fierce competitor and no-nonsense sports doctor, is crammed into a hotbed of family problems including a career-woman mother (Janice Rule) who emotionally abandoned her dying husband.

If this isn't enough, one of the boys is destined for the same fate as the father. So, with the shadow of death hanging over them, the brothers set off for Colorado for 'the toughest bicycle race in America.'

Combativeness between brothers yields to comaraderie, but true nature of their conflict is difficult to get a handle on.

Performances are adequate considering that over-production makes the characters seem larger than life without being lifelike.

■ AMERICAN FRIENDS

1991, 95 MINS, UK

Dir Tristram Powell *Prod* Patrick Cassavetti, Steve Abbott *Scr* Michael Palin, Tristram Powell *Ph* Philip Bonham-Carter *Ed* George Akers *Mus* Georges Delerue *Art Dir* Andrew McAlpine
● Michael Palin, Connie Booth, Trini Alvarado, Alfred Molina, David Calder (Millenium/Mayday/Prominent/British Screen/BBC)

Easy on the eyes and on the emotions, *American Friends* is a slim vignete about two Yank women who fall for a reserved Oxford don.

Pic opens in the 1860s at a stuffy Oxford college where bachelor classics don Francis Ashby (Michael Palin) is setting off for a walking vacation in Switzerland. Atop the Alps, he meets two Americans, Caroline (Connie Booth) and her doe-eyed ward, Elinor (Trini Alvarado). Emotions are stirred, and Elinor gets the first kiss.

Back in Oxford, Ashby is one of two candidates lined up to take over as college president when the current one dies. Ashby rival Oliver Syme (Alfred Molina) has hyperactive hormones, so if Ashby can stay respectably celibate, the job's virtually his. Enter, en route to Philadelphia, the two Yanks – and much trouble for Ashby.

There's a lot going on beneath the surface, but not much of it reaches the screen. Lack of dramatic tension can be blamed, in part, on the ex-Monty Python trouper's performance. Although yarn is based on an actual event discovered in his great-grandfather Edward's travel diaries, Palin is too lightweight for such a key role. His crusty, middle-aged bachelor doesn't ring true. Thesping otherwise is crisp and reliable.

■ AMERICAN GIGOLO

1980, 117 MINS, US ◇ ⓥ

Dir Paul Schrader   *Prod* Jerry Bruckheimer   *Scr* Paul
Schrader   *Ph* John Bailey   *Ed* Richard Halsey
Mus Giorgio Moroder   *Art Dir* Fernando Scarfiotti
● Richard Gere, Lauren Hutton, Hector Elizondo, Nina
Van Pallandt, Bill Duke, Brian Davies (Paramount)

A hot subject, cool style and overly contrived
plotting don't all mesh in *American Gigolo*.
Paul Schrader's third outing as a director is
betrayed by a curious, uncharacteristic
evasiveness at its core.

Things begin to go awry, both for Richard
Gere and the picture, when senator's wife
Lauren Hutton begins taking more than a
passing interest in her man-for-hire and when
a kinky sex murder is laid at his door. Gere's
character has been portrayed with such
moral and emotional ambivalence, which
makes caring about his predicament and
ultimate fate difficult.

As with several of Schrader's other scripts,
this one charts the course of a loner, a solo
driver navigating in a sea of sharks ready to
eat him alive. Rarely offscreen, Gere is
notably convincing in look and manner. Very
lowkeyed, Hutton is not quite up to the difficult part of a woman-with-everything who
throws it all over for her questionable lover.

■ AMERICAN GRAFFITI

1973, 109 MINS, US ◇ ⓥ

Dir George Lucas   *Prod* Francis Coppola, Gary Kurtz
Scr George Lucas, Gloria Katz, Willard Huyck
Ph Haskell Wexler   *Ed* Verna Fields, Marcia Lucas
Mus Karin Green (sup.)   *Art Dir* Dennis Clark
● Richard Dreyfuss, Ron Howard, Paul Le Mat, Charles
Martin Smith, Cindy Williams, Candy Clark (Universal)

Set in 1962 but reflecting the culmination of
the 1950s, the film is a most vivid recall of
teenage attitudes and mores, told with outstanding empathy and compassion through
an exceptionally talented cast.

Design consultant Al Locatelli, art director
Dennis Clark and set director Douglas Freeman have brilliantly reconstructed the fabric
and texture of the time, while Walter
Murch's outstanding sound collage – an unending stream of early rock platter hits –
complements in the aural department.

Against this chrome and neon backdrop is
told the story of one long summer night in the
lives of four school chums: Richard Dreyfuss,
on his last night before leaving for an eastern
college; Ron Howard, less willing to depart
the presence of Cindy Williams; Charles
Martin Smith, a bespectacled fumbler whose
misadventures with pubescent swinger
Candy Clark are as touching as they are hilarious; and Paul Le Mat, 22 years old on a
birth certificate but still strutting as he did
four years earlier.

□ 1973: Best Picture (Nomination)

**■ AMERICAN GUERRILLA IN THE
PHILIPPINES, AN**

1950, 104 MINS, US ◇

Dir Fritz Lang   *Prod* Lamar Trotti   *Scr* Lamar Trotti
Ph Harry Jackson   *Ed* Robert Simpson   *Mus* Cyril J.
Mockridge   *Art Dir* Lyle Wheeler, J. Russell Spencer
● Tyrone Power, Micheline Presle, Tom Ewell, Bob
Patton, Jack Elam, Robert Barrat (20th Century-Fox)

20th-Fox has made an interesting, if somewhat long, film version of Ira Wolfert's *American Guerrilla in the Philippines*. A story of the
Second World War in the Pacific, from the
spring of 1942 up to General MacArthur's
return to the islands, it is neatly staged.

The Philippine locales supply a lush tropical dressing to brighten the heroics of a small
band of Americans and natives who fight the
US cause against the invading Japs. Tyrone

Power and Tom Ewell, escape into the jungle
after the sinking of their P-T boat. They join
the natives to fight guerrilla fashion against
the Japs.

Footage has some good, male humor mixed
in with the derrin-do, and Fritz Lang's direction develops a strong sense of expectancy
and suspense in the story-telling.

■ AMERICAN IN PARIS, AN

1951, 113 MINS, US ◇ ⓥ

Dir Vincente Minnelli   *Prod* Arthur Freed   *Scr* Alan
Jay Lerner   *Ph* Alfred Gilks, John Alton   *Ed* Adrienne
Fazan   *Mus* Johnny Green (dir.)   *Art Dir* Cedric
Gibbons, Preston Ames
● Gene Kelly, Leslie Caron, Oscar Levant, Georges
Guetary, Nina Foch, Eugene Borden (M-G-M)

An American in Paris is one of the most
imaginative musical confections turned
out by Hollywood, spotlighting Gene Kelly,
Oscar Levant, Nina Foch, and a pair
of bright newcomers (Leslie Caron and
Georges Guetary) against a cavalcade of
George and Ira Gershwin's music.

Kelly is the picture's top star and rates
every inch of his billing. His diversified
dancing is great as ever and his thesping is
standout. But he reveals new talents in this
one with his choreography. There's a lengthy
ballet to the film's title song for the finale,
which is a masterpiece of design, lighting,
costumes and color photography. It's a
unique blending of classical and modern
dance with vaude-style tapping.

Caron is a beauteous, lissome number with
an attractively pert personality and plenty of
s.a. She scores neatly with her thesping,
particularly in the appealing love scenes with
Kelly, and displays standout dancing ability.
Guetary demonstrates a socko musicomedy
tenor and okay acting talents. He's cast
neatly as the older man whom Caron almost
marries out of gratitude.

Story is a sprightly yarn about an American
GI (Kelly) who stayed on in Paris after the
war to further his art study. Foch, as a
wealthy American playgal, 'discovers' his art
talents and takes him on as her protege to
add him to her retinue of lovers. Kelly
accepts the idea warily but then meets and
falls for Caron.

Gershwin's music gets boffo treatment
throughout. While some 10 songs get special
handling, true Gershwin fans will recognize
strains of most of his other tunes in the
background score.

□ 1951: Best Picture

■ AMERICANIZATION OF EMILY, THE

1964, 115 MINS, US

Dir Arthur Hiller   *Prod* Martin Ransohoff   *Scr* Paddy
Chayefsky   *Ph* Philip Lathrop   *Ed* Tom McAdoo
Mus Johnny Mandel   *Art Dir* George W. Davis, Hans
Peters, Elliot Scott
● James Garner, Julie Andrews, Melvyn Douglas,
James Coburn, Joyce Grenfell, Edward Binns (M-G-M)

Emily, with Julie Andrews in title role as an
English motor pool driver in World War II,
takes place immediately before the Normandy invasion. Most of the action unspools
in London where Garner, a lieutenant commander who makes avowed cowardice his
career, is 'dog robber' to Melvyn Douglas, an
erratic admiral and one of the heads of the
oncoming onslaught on the French coast.

Most of Garner's duties consist of rounding up delicacies and services, impossible to get,
for his boss, until the admiral, a navy traditionalist who believes his branch of the service is being overshadowed by the army,
orders him to make a film showing activities
of navy demolition on their landing at
Omaha Beach.

Basic idea builds around the admiral being

beset with an obsession to have the first man
killed on Omaha Beach a sailor, to show the
navy can have no peer in the service, and the
script takes it from there.

Pic [based on the novel by William Bradford Huie] is primarily interesting for the
romance between Andrews and Garner, the
former struggling against being Americanized through her contact with the outgoing
and freewheeling Garner.

Garner sometimes forces his comedy scenes
but generally delivers a satisfactory performance. Douglas plays the admiral strictly for
laughs. James Coburn as a navy officer is outstanding particularly for his comedy scenes.
Joyce Grenfell as femme star's mother and
Keenan Wynn, a salty old salt, likewise handle their roles well.

■ AMERICAN NINJA

1985, 95 MINS, US ◇ ⓥ

Dir Sam Firstenberg   *Prod* Menahem Golan, Yoram
Globus   *Scr* Paul de Mielche   *Ph* Hanania Baer
Ed Michael J. Duthie   *Mus* Michael Linn
Art Dir Adrian Gorton
● Michael Dudikoff, Steve James, Judie Aronson,
Guich Koock, John Fujioka, Don Stewart (Cannon)

Michael Dudikoff is the titular hero, a sullen
GI named Joe who arrives at US Army base
Fort Sonora with a chip on his shoulder. He
quickly alienates everyone except the pretty
daughter of the commanding officer, Patricia
Hickock (Judie Aronson), by singlehandedly
saving her from the deadly ninjas working for
corrupt arms dealer Ortega (Don Stewart).

Director Sam Firstenberg stages the numerous action scenes well, but engenders little
interest in the non-story [by Avi Kleinberger
and Gideon Amir].

Dudikoff comes off awkwardly as a new
James Dean clone who's been pumping iron.
Most winning performance is turned in by
Steve James, Joe's sole pal on the base.

**■ AMERICAN NINJA 2
THE CONFRONTATION**

1987, 89 MINS, US ◇ ⓥ

Dir Sam Firstenberg   *Prod* Menahem Golan, Yoram
Globus   *Scr* Gary Conway, James Booth   *Ph* Gideon
Porath   *Ed* Michael J. Duthie   *Mus* George S.
Clinton   *Art Dir* Holger Gross
● Michael Dudikoff, Steve James, Larry Poindexter,
Gary Conway, Jeff Weston, Michelle Botes
(Golan-Globus)

This time out, after *American Ninja* (1985) and
Avenging Force (1986), globetrotting army
hardbodies Michael Dudikoff and Steve
James arrive on a small Caribbean island to
investigate the disappearance of four US
Marines. It turns out that a local drug kingpin is kidnaping soldiers and others to turn
them into genetically reengineered ninja
assassins who will do his bidding worldwide.

All this merely provides an excuse for an
ample number of martial arts showdowns between the heroes and the black-robed baddies
who swarm from all directions only to be dispatched in tidy fashion by the good guys.

Script by actors Gary Conway (who plays
the narcotics overlord) and James Booth
trades heavily upon the notion of Americans'
inherent mental and physical superiority to
native warriors, who are a dime a dozen, but
in such a comic way that the viewer can
laugh with it rather than at it.

Pic was lensed in South Africa, and is
extremely picturesque despite the modest
means.

■ AMERICAN ROMANCE, AN

1944, 151 MINS, US ◇

Dir King Vidor   *Prod* King Vidor   *Scr* Herbert Delmas,
William Ludwig   *Ph* Harold Rosson   *Ed* Conrad A.
Nervig   *Mus* Louis Gruenberg   *Art Dir* Cedric
Gibbons, Urie McCleary

● Brian Donlevy, Ann Richards, Walter Abel, John Qualen, Horace McNally (M-G-M)

One of Metro's greatest efforts (claimed to be two years in the making and cost over $3 million), this film is Brian Donlevy's baby from opening to closing, as the Czech immigrant who runs the gamut from poverty to become a wealthy industrialist.

King Vidor's story, coupled with his forthright direction and the excellent acting, are assets that add up to a winning total. The one fault with *Romance* is that it is much too long in the telling.

Yarn takes more than an hour to get down to business. During that hour, true, Vidor lays the setting for the rest of the film, showing how Donlevy, who is held up at Ellis Island on landing in America because he did not own the equivalent of $25 in US money, overcomes this proverty by hard work in the Mesabi iron ore pits of Minnesota, and meets the girl whom he is to marry (Ann Richards).

Photographed in beautiful Technicolor, this romantic drama is notable for the documented montage shots of the intricate mining and shipping of iron ore; the making of steel in the huge mills of the midwest; films showing the way autos are made; and the excellent details of airplane-making.

■ **AMERICAN SUCCESS COMPANY, THE**

1979, 94 MINS, US/W. GERMANY ◇

Dir William Richert   *Prod* Daniel H. Blatt, Edgar J. Scherrick   *Scr* William Richert, Larry Cohen   *Ph* Anthony Richmond   *Ed* Ralph E. Winters   *Mus* Maurice Jarre   *Art Dir* Rolf Zehetbauer
● Jeff Bridges, Belinda Bauer, Ned Beatty, Bianca Jagger, Steven Keats, John Glover (Columbia/Geria)

Although almost everything that happens on screen is done with considerable style and a morbid sense of humor, lack of overall point to the proceedings ultimately sinks the picture.

Jeff Bridges here plays the mild-mannered son-in-law of international credit card tycoon Ned Beatty. Called a loser by his boss and under the thumb of gorgeous wife Belinda Bauer, youth decides to turn the tables on them by assuming the guise of a gangsterish tough-guy, then commencing to push them around to get his way in both professional and private life.

Undeniable is William Richert's visual flair and sometimes startling sense of the absurd. Billed as 'A William Richert-Larry Cohen Film', pic was to have been helmed by Cohen, writer of the original story, and was known during production as *The Ringer*.

■ **AMERICAN TAIL, AN**

1986, 80 MINS, US Ⓥ

Dir Don Bluth   *Prod* Don Bluth, John Pomeroy, Gary Goldman   *Scr* Judy Freudberg, Tony Geiss   *Mus* James Horner
● (Amblin)

The film endeavors to tell the story of Russian immigrants, who happen in this case to be mice of the Mousekewitz clan, and their flight in the late 1800s to the United States, where, Papa Mousekewitz insists, 'There are no cats.'

Cartoons with ambitions even this noble are as rare as Steven Spielberg films that lose money, but every character and every situation presented herein have been seen a thousand times before.

The mouse-vs-cat stand-off is as old as animation itself, Dom DeLuise's friendly feline is uncomfortably close to the Cowardly Lion in concept, a little bug smacks directly of Jiminy Cricket, and assorted villains are straight out of Dickens by way of Damon Runyon.

■ **AMERICAN TRAGEDY, AN**

1931, 96 MINS, US

Dir Josef von Sternberg   *Scr* Samuel Hoffenstein   *Ph* Lee Garmes   *Art Dir* Hans Dreier
● Phillips Holmes, Sylvia Sidney, Francis Dee, Irving Pichel, Frederick Burton, Claire McDowell (Paramount)

An American Tragedy unreels as an ordinary program effort with an unhappy ending. Its relations to the book [by Theodore Dreiser] upon which it is based are decidedly strained. As Von Sternberg has seen fit to present it this celluloid structure is slow, heavy and not always interesting drama.

There is not a performance in the cast of any real interest. Histrionic honors belong to the elegantly voiced Irving Pichel, a veteran of the legit stage and one of the original founders of the Theatre Guild, as the district attorney.

The film spends a third or more of its 96 minutes on the trial. It's a big and theatrically good atmospheric scene, but has the handicap of involving neither of the girls as Roberta (for whose murder Clyde is convicted) is already dead, with Sondra escaping through the influence of a wealthy father. So the entire burden is on Phillips Holmes, as the floundering victim, which he is incapable of upholding for the camera.

On the sympathetic end Sylvia Sidney as the trusting Roberta, which she mainly accomplishes by means of a wistful smile. Frances Dee, as Sondra, merely registers as the Hollywood conception of a debutante and is not important, except as the brusque motivation for Clyde's reversal of his relations with Roberta and his longing to become of the younger social set of the small town.

It's questionable if even the admirers of this author's work condone the evident publicity complex he had developed, so it shouldn't be a matter of inflamed indignation by the minority in defense of the writer over the picture as an illustrated interpretation of the novel. Dreiser complained that the script first prepared by Sergei Eisenstein, to have directed, was entirely satisfactory. This, however was not the treatment finally used, with Von Sternberg replacing the Russian in the directorial chair.

■ **AMERICAN WEREWOLF IN LONDON, AN**

1981, 97 MINS, US ◇

Dir John Landis   *Prod* George Folsey Jr   *Scr* John Landis   *Ph* Robert Paynter   *Ed* Malcolm Campbell   *Mus* Elmer Bernstein   *Art Dir* Leslie Dilley
● David Naughton, Jenny Agutter, Griffin Dunne, John Woodvine, Brian Glover, Frank Oz (Universal/Lycanthrope)

A clever mixture of comedy and horror which succeeds in being both funny and scary, *An American Werewolf in London* possesses an overriding eagerness to please that prevents it from becoming off-putting, and special effects freaks get more than their money's worth.

Bumming around Europe, two American students (David Naughton and Griffin Dunne) seek refuge from the nasty North England elements in the Slaughtered Lamb pub. Natives there are uncommonly hostile, to the point of forcing the lads out into the night despite indications that there's trouble in these parts.

In short order, they're attacked by a fierce beast and, after the good-natured humor of this prelude, audience is instantly sobered up when Dunne is killed and Naughton is heavily gashed and gored.

Recovering in a London Hospital and, later, in the flat of amorous nurse Jenny Agutter, Naughton experiences some disturbing and visually outrageous nightmares and is visited by the 'Undead' Dunne, who urges his friend to commit suicide or turn into a werewolf with the next full moon.

Naughton ignores the advice and, sure enough, undergoes a complete transformation on camera, a highlight in which talents of special make-up effects designer Rick Baker are shown in full flower.

■ **AMITYVILLE HORROR, THE**

1979, 117 MINS, US ◇ Ⓥ

Dir Stuart Rosenberg   *Prod* Ronald Saland, Elliot Geisinger   *Scr* Sandor Stern   *Ph* Fred J. Koenekamp   *Ed* Robert Brown   *Mus* Lalo Schifrin   *Art Dir* Kim Swados
● James Brolin, Margot Kidder, Rod Steiger, Don Stroud, Natasha Ryan (American International)

Taken from the Jay Anson tome, Sandor Stern's script deals faithfully with the supposedly true (but since challenged) story of the Lutz family who move into a home in Amityville, NY, at a knocked-down price because of its bloody history. The Lutz' fled 28 days later in terror.

Stepfather James Brolin, mother Margot Kidder and moppets Natasha Ryan, Meeno Peluce and K.C. Martel sympathetically play the happy innocent family and director Stuart Rosenberg – ably aided by efex specialists William Cruse and Delwyn Rheaume – have the house all ready for them.

Flies swarm where they shouldn't; pipes and walls ooze ick; doors fly open; and priests and psychic sensitives cringe and flee in panic. It's definitely a house that audiences will enjoy visiting, especially if unfamiliar with the ending.

■ **AMITYVILLE II**
THE POSSESSION

1982, 104 MINS, US ◇ Ⓥ

Dir Damiano Damiani   *Prod* Ira N. Smith, Stephen R. Greenwald   *Scr* Tommy Lee Wallace   *Ph* Franco DiGiacomo   *Ed* Sam O'Steen   *Mus* Lalo Schifrin   *Art Dir* Pierluigi Basile
● Burt Young, Rutanya Alda, James Olson, Jack Magner, Diane Franklin, Andrew Prine (Orion/De Laurentiis)

It is never quite explained in the context of the film whether this is a prequel, sequel or entirely new version of the Amityville story. No matter. We still have the same house of horrors about to be occupied by a family who, as usual, never think to leave the house once it starts taking on a personality of its own.

Of course, this is not the typical American family. Burt Young, who gives new meaning to the word one-dimensional in his portrait of the father, loves beating the daylights out of his wife and kids. Jack Magner, a screen newcomer saddled with the plum (?) role of the troubled oldest son, begins finding his sister sexually attractive. And Rutanya Alda, who does a lot of screaming as the spineless mother, spends a lot of time praying her problem will go away.

There are actually two films meandering in this mess – one a second-rate horror flick about a family in peril, and another that is a slight variation on the demon-possessed *Exorcist* theme.

■ **AMOROUS ADVENTURES OF MOLL FLANDERS, THE**

1965, 123 MINS, UK ◇

Dir Terence Young   *Prod* Marcel Hellman   *Scr* Denis Cannan, Roland Kibbee   *Ph* Ted Moore   *Ed* Frederick Wilson   *Mus* John Addison   *Art Dir* Syd Cain
● Kim Novak, Richard Johnson, Angela Lansbury, George Sanders, Leo McKern, Vittorio De Sica (Paramount)

Moll Flanders – the amorous adventures of – is a sprawling, brawling, gaudy, bawdy, tongue-in-cheek comedy that seeks to caricaturize an 18th-century London wench's desire to be a gentlewoman and her varying exploits thereof. Starring Kim Novak in title role, it has sex and color, slapstick and lusty, busty characterization, action which is sometimes very funny and, again, equally unfunny.

The foreword slyly states: 'Any similarity between this film and any other film is purely coincidental.' However that may be, it was a natural that the success scored by *Tom Jones* should be followed by a femme counterpart in this adaptation of Daniel Defoe's novel.

Director Terence Young seems constantly to keep in mind the comic potentialities of his subject and his helming is always broad, leavened with old-fashioned sight gags. The screenplay follows Moll as she goes to London, to seek her goal through a variety of affairs and marriages which culminate in a ceremony with a highwayman whom she mistook to be a wealthy landowner.

Richard Johnson (whom Novak wed after pic ended) gives colorful and romantic enactment to the highwayman character. George Sanders' portrayal of a rich banker wed to Moll is robust and comical. Leo McKern, as Johnson's outlaw henchman, also scores a comedy hit.

■ ANASTASIA

1956, 105 MINS, US ◇ ▽
Dir Anatole Litvak *Prod* Buddy Adler *Scr* Arthur Laurents *Ph* Jack Hildyard *Ed* Bert Bates *Mus* Alfred Newman *Art Dir* Andrei Andrejew, Bill Andrews
● Ingrid Bergman, Yul Brynner, Helen Hayes, Akim Tamiroff, Martita Hunt, Felix Aylmer (20th Century-Fox)

The legit hit *Anastasia* has been made into a wonderfully moving and entertaining motion picture from start to finish, and the major credit inevitably must go to Ingrid Bergman who turns in a great performance.

Yet the picture is by no means all Bergman. Yul Brynner as General Bounine, the tough Russian exile, etches a strong and convincing portrait that stands up perfectly to Bergman's Anastasia, and Helen Hayes has great dignity as the Empress.

Story basically is the one from the French play of Marcelle Maurette adapted by Guy Bolton. Brynner and a group of conspirators are working in Paris to produce an Anastasia who might help them collect the £10 million deposited in England by the Czar's family. Brynner keeps the destitute Bergman from suicide, then grooms her to play Anastasia's part.

Bergman bears an amazing resemblance to the Czar's youngest daughter who was supposed to have been killed by the Reds in 1918. Desperate to forget the past, Bergman first resists, then begins to recover her regal bearing – and her memories.

Director Anatole Litvak and producer Buddy Adler imbue the story with realistic settings.

■ ANATOMY OF A MURDER

1959, 160 MINS, US ▽
Dir Otto Preminger *Prod* Otto Preminger *Scr* Wendell Mayes *Ph* Sam Leavitt *Ed* Louis R. Loeffler *Mus* Boris Leven *Art Dir* Duke Ellington
● James Stewart, Lee Remick, Ben Gazzara, Arthur O'Connell, Eve Arden, Kathryn Grant (Columbia/Carlyle)

Director Otto Preminger got his film on the screen for preview only 21 days after the final shooting on Michigan location. This dispatch may be one reason why *Anatomy* is over-long.

Wendell Mayes' screenplay otherwise is a large reason for the film's general excellence. In swift, brief strokes it introduces a large number of diverse characters and sets them in motion. An army lieutenant (Ben Gazzara) has killed a tavern operator whom he suspects of attempting to rape his wife (Lee

Remick). James Stewart, former district attorney and now a privately-practicing attorney in a small Michigan city, is engaged for the defense.

Mayes' screenplay, from the book by the Michigan judge who uses the nom de plume Robert Traver, differs in some respects from the novel. Partly through casting, there is considerable doubt about the real innocence of Gazzara and Remick. This handsome young couple astray of the law are far from admirable.

Preminger purposely creates situations that flicker with uncertainty, that may be evaluated in different ways. Motives are mixed and dubious, and, therefore, sustain interest.

Balancing the fascinating nastiness of the younger players, there is the warmth and intelligence of Stewart and Arthur O'Connell. O'Connell, a bright, but booze-prone Irishman of great charm, is his ally. Joseph N. Welch, Boston attorney, is tremendous as the trial judge. George C. Scott, as the prosecution attorney, has the suave menace of a small-time Torquemada.

□ 1959: Best Picture (Nomination)

■ ANCHORS AWEIGH

1945, 138 MINS, US ◇ ▽
Dir George Sidney *Prod* Joe Pasternak *Scr* Isabel Lennart *Ph* Robert Planck, Charles Boyle *Ed* Adrienne Fazan *Mus* George Stoll *Art Dir* Cedric Gibbons, Randall Duell
● Frank Sinatra, Kathryn Grayson, Gene Kelly, Jose Iturbi, Dean Stockwell, Sharon McManus (M-G-M)

Anchors Aweigh is solid musical fare. The production numbers are zingy; the songs are extremely listenable; the color treatment outstanding.

Two of the potent entertainment factors are the tunes and Gene Kelly's hoofing. Jule Styne and Sammy Cahn cleffed five new numbers, three of which are given the Frank Sinatra treatment for boff results.

In the dance department Kelly sells top terping. There is a clever Tom and Jerry sequence combining Kelly's live action with a cartoon fairy story. Kelly also combines three Spanish tunes into another sock number executed with little Sharon McManus. His third is a class tango.

Kathryn Grayson, one of the three co-stars, figures importantly in the score with her vocaling. Jose Iturbi plays and conducts *Donkey Serenade*, Piano Concerto and *Hungarian Rhapsody No. 2* for additional potent musical factor.

Sinatra and Kelly are sailors on liberty. They come to Hollywood. Sinatra is a shy Brooklynite who's being instructed in the art of pickups by Kelly, the traditional gob with a gal in every port.

□ 1945: Best Picture (Nomination)

■ AND BABY MAKES THREE

1949, 83 MINS, US
Dir Henry Levin *Prod* Robert Lord *Scr* Lou Breslow, Joseph Hoffman *Ph* Burnett Guffey *Ed* Viola Lawrence *Mus* George Duning
● Robert Young, Barbara Hale, Robert Hutton, Janis Carter, Billie Burke (Columbia/Santana)

Fun starts confusingly but mood warms up as footage unfolds and plot line becomes clear. Robert Young has been divorced by Barbara Hale after being caught in a compromising spot. It's a hurry-up Reno untying and Hale is ready to do a quick re-bound marriage when she faints on the way to the altar. Pregnancy is the diagnosis. This upsets wedding plans with Robert Hutton and complications also develop when Young announces he'll fight for partial custody.

Young is his usual able self in taking care of

his part of the footage. Hale delights as the wouldbe mother. Henry Levin's direction gets good movement into the script and comedy touches are neatly devised.

■ AND GOD CREATED WOMAN

1988, 94 MINS, US ◇ ▽
Dir Roger Vadim *Prod* George C. Braunstein, Ron Hamady *Scr* R.J. Stewart *Ph* Stephen M. Katz *Ed* Suzanne Petit *Mus* Thomas Chase, Steve Rucker *Art Dir* Victor Kempster
● Rebecca DeMornay, Vincent Spano, Frank Langella, Donovan Leitch, Judith Chapman (Crow/Vestron)

A remake in name only of his first feature, made 32 years earlier, Roger Vadim's new film is considerably more legitimate dramatically than one might expect.

Vadim tells a modestly involving tale about how a woman with two strikes against her gives herself a shot at life through a combination of sex, imagination, energy and plenty of scheming.

Attention-grabbing opening has inmate Rebecca DeMornay escaping from prison and hitching a ride in a limo belonging to New Mexico gubernatorial candidate Frank Langella, only to be deposited right back where she came from.

In the picture's hottest scene, she then gets it on with carpenter Vincent Spano and wins early parole by convincing this earnest young single father to marry her. DeMornay lays a major surprise on her husband when she announces that their marriage contract does not include sex.

DeMornay throws herself deeply into the part as a life-long loser determined to win at all costs. Spano's macho exterior is nicely modified as the story progresses with considerable emotional shading, and Langella is just right as the politico who is most intrigued by DeMornay but knows he could get burned by her.

■ ANDERSON TAPES, THE

1971, 98 MINS, US ◇ ▽
Dir Sidney Lumet *Prod* Robert M. Weitman *Scr* Frank Pierson *Ph* Arthur Ornitz *Ed* Joanne Burke *Mus* Quincy Jones *Art Dir* Philip Rosenberg
● Sean Connery, Dyan Cannon, Martin Balsam, Alan King, Ralph Meeker, Christopher Walken (Columbia)

Sean Connery plays an ex-con who schemes to burglarize an entire apartment house on Manhattan's plush upper East Side. With backing from a new breed of organized mobster, led by Alan King, Connery recruits a band of diverse helpmates ranging from a homosexual antique dealer (Martin Balsam) to a fellow ex-con just released after 40 years in prison (Stan Gottlieb).

Overriding the machinations of the plot are the Anderson tapes themselves. Lawrence Sanders' novel was composed of snippets of surreptitious recordings compiled by local police, FBI agents, private investigators, treasury spies, etc., all snooping on the activities for various reasons, and all unable to piece together what they're overhearing.

Scripter Frank Pierson with director Sidney Lumet has injected broadly comic aspects and the laughs work without reducing suspense.

Essentially miscast but trying mightily to keep his accent under control, Connery's presence is strong. As a high priced mistress, frigid until Connery melts her, Dyan Cannon has little to do but look appetizing.

With the flashiest role, Martin Balsam swishes off with the honors, although gay activists will take umbrage at the abundance of conventional fag jokes.

...AND JUSTICE FOR ALL

1979, 120 MINS, US ◇ Ⓥ

Dir Norman Jewison *Prod* Norman Jewison, Patrick Palmer *Scr* Valerie Curtin, Barry Levinson *Ph* Victor J. Kemper *Ed* John F. Burnett *Mus* Dave Grusin *Art Dir* Richard MacDonald

● Al Pacino, Jack Warden, John Forsythe, Lee Strasberg, Christine Lahti (Columbia)

...And Justice for All is a film that attempts to alternate between comedy and drama, handling neither one incompetently, but also not excelling at either task.

Centering on the impossible circumstances a sensitive lawyer encounters when dealing with the complexities and corruption of the American judicial system, pic is another good vehicle for Al Pacino.

Pic begins on a serious note with Pacino, jailed for contempt of court, witnessing jailers and inmates terrify a transvestite being locked up for robbery.

Mood quickly changes to comedy with Pacino going off to the scene of a car accident to aid an overemotional client.

The story most explored, that of John Forsythe's judge accused of brutally raping a young girl, is compelling but never fully fleshed out to satisfaction.

AND SOON THE DARKNESS

1970, 100 MINS, UK ◇ Ⓥ

Dir Robert Fuest *Prod* Albert Fennell, Brian Clemens *Scr* Brian Clemens, Terry Nation *Ph* Ian Wilson *Ed* Ann Chegwidden *Mus* Laurie Johnson

● Pamela Franklin, Michele Dotrice, Sandor Eles, John Nettleton, Clare Kelly, Hanna-Maria Pravda (Associated British)

Story concerns two young British girls pedalling through a dull, flat, deserted part of France on vacation. One's a pert miss (Michele Dotrice), her chum is a more down-to-earth girl (Pamela Franklin), worried by her chum's desire to sunbathe, ogle the local lads and generally throw a spanner wrench into the timetable of the holiday.

After a tiff the two separate. Franklin, lonely and remorseful, returns to find Dotrice. But she is missing. The film mainly concerns the trouble Franklin gets into while trying to solve the problem of what happened to her friend.

French atmosphere is conveyed excellently and helps reward the doom-laden gloom but overall there's a leering, sinister feeling about this piece which is repellent.

ANDROCLES AND THE LION

1952, 98 MINS, US Ⓥ

Dir Chester Erskine *Prod* Gabriel Pascal *Scr* Chester Erskine, Ken Englund *Ph* Harry Stradling *Ed* Roland Cross *Mus* Frederick Hollander

● Jean Simmons, Alan Young, Victor Mature, Robert Newton, Maurice Evans, Elsa Lanchester (RKO)

Bernard Shaw's satirical comedy on Romans and Christians provides the basis for a fair film offering. Picture is a curious mixture of basic comedy and Shavian wit. The romance between the Christian girl and the Roman captain is the most effective part of the film, differing from the original play.

The first filming of a Shaw play in Hollywood, the presentation has the confined feeling of having been made indoors. There's an amusing superficiality to some of the sequences involving the decadent Roman court, its customs and reactions, with real wit in the Shaw dialog.

Director Chester Erskine's strongest guidance is evidenced in the scenes with Jean Simmons and Victor Mature as the Christian girl and the Roman captain.

The familiar story deals with Androcles' love of animals, a feeling that saves the Greek tailor when he frees a lion from a thorn and later meets that lion in the Roman arena.

ANDROID

1982, 80 MINS, US ◇ Ⓥ

Dir Aaron Lipstadt *Prod* Mary Ann Fisher *Scr* James Reigle, Don Opper *Ph* Tim Suhrstedt *Ed* R.J. Kizor, Andy Horvitch *Mus* Don Preston *Art Dir* K.C. Sheibel, Wayne Springfield

● Klaus Kinski, Brie Howard, Norbert Weisser, Crofton Hardester, Kendra Kirchner, Don Opper (New World)

Obsessed researcher Klaus Kinski inhabits a remote space station in the year 2036 with his android assistant, Max 404, played by co-writer Don Opper. Doctor is on the verge of perfecting his masterpiece, a perfect robot who happens to be a beautiful blonde, and who will render Max obsolete.

Onto the craft from a prison ship come three escaped convicts with no precise plans but with dangerous personalities. One way or another, they intend to make their way back to Earth, where a revolt by androids proved of sufficient magnitude to make them illegal.

Although there are the obligatory fight scenes and nudity, film works mainly due to the unusual interaction between the all-too-human Max robot and those around him.

Most pics of this ilk offer nothing but cardboard characters, so it's commendable that not only Max but the three fugitives come across with strong personalities. Kinski has relatively little to do, but is nevertheless plausible as a Dr Frankenstein type.

ANDROMEDA STRAIN, THE

1971, 127 MINS, US ◇ Ⓥ

Dir Robert Wise *Prod* Robert Wise *Scr* Nelson Gidding *Ph* Richard H. Kline *Ed* Stuart Gilmore, John W. Holmes *Mus* Gil Melle *Art Dir* Boris Leven

● Arthur Hill, David Wayne, James Olson, Kate Reid, Paula Kelly, George Mitchell (Universal)

The Andromeda Strain is a high-budget 'science-fact' melodrama, marked by superb production, an excellent score, an intriguing story premise and an exciting conclusion. But Nelson Gidding's adaptation of the Michael Crichton novel is too literal and talky.

In four acts representing days, a team of civilian medics attempt to find and isolate an unknown phenomenon which has killed most of a desert town near the place where a space satellite has fallen to earth. Arthur Hill, David Wayne, James Olson and Kate Reid are the specialists racing against time.

In the first half hour, the plot puzzle and eerie mood are well established, and in the final half hour there is a dramatically exciting climax with massive self-destruction machinery. The middle hour, however, drags proceedings numbingly. The four scientists repeatedly get into long-winded discussions. There are times when one wants to shout at the players to get on with it.

The glacial internal plot evolution is not at all relieved by the performances. Hill is dull; Wayne is dull; Olson caroms from another dull character to a petulant kid; and Reid's unexplained-until-later epilepsy condition does not generate much interest. Mitchell and nurse Paula Kelly are most refreshing changes of pace.

ANGEL

1982, 90 MINS, IRELAND ◇ ⑰

Dir Neil Jordan *Prod* Barry Blackmore *Scr* Neil Jordan *Ph* Chris Menges *Ed* Pat Duffner *Mus* Paddy Meegan *Art Dir* John Lucas

● Stephen Rea, Alan Devlin, Veronica Quilligan, Peter Caffrey, Honor Heffernan, Ray McAnally (MPCI)

Angel carries knockout power. A story of retribution set against the troubles in Northern Ireland which are kept way in the background, it's an impressive pic debut for director-scripter Neil Jordan.

A saxophonist with a traveling band unwittingly observes the murder of the band's manager (involved in extortion payoffs) and that of a deaf and dumb girl witness. The musician, vigorously played by Stephen Rea, is obsessed to hunt down the murderers and does so, becoming a murderer himself several times over.

Played out with a minimum of violence, despite its theme, *Angel* contrasts the sweetness of dance music and the dark side of daily life. The acting is strong.

Camerawork by Chris Menges (the only non-Irish native involved in the production) is striking as are other credits.

ANGEL FACE

1952, 91 MINS, US

Dir Otto Preminger *Prod* Otto Preminger *Scr* Frank Nugent, Oscar Millard *Ph* Harry Stradling *Ed* Frederic Knudson *Mus* Dimitri Tiomkin *Art Dir* Albert S. D'Agostino, Carroll Clark

● Robert Mitchum, Jean Simmons, Mona Freeman, Herbert Marshall, Leon Ames, Barbara O'Neil (RKO)

Jean Simmons portrays the title role of a young lady behind whose beautiful face is a diseased mind that plots to murder her wealthy stepmother (Barbara O'Neil). Drawn into this scheme, although innocently, is Robert Mitchum, an ambulance driver who attends the stepmother when Simmons' first murder attempt backfires. Attracted to Mitchum, she gets him a chauffeur job with the family.

Mitchum and Simmons make a good team, both delivering the demands of the script [from a story by Chester Erskine] and Preminger's direction ably. Co-starred are Mona Freeman, the girl Mitchum casts off for Simmons, and Herbert Marshall, but neither has much to do in the footage.

ANGEL HEART

1987, 113 MINS, US ◇ Ⓥ

Dir Alan Parker *Prod* Alan Marshall, Elliott Kastner *Scr* Alan Parker *Ph* Michael Seresin *Ed* Gerry Hambling *Mus* Trevor Jones *Art Dir* Brian Morris

● Mickey Rourke, Robert De Niro, Lisa Bonet, Charlotte Rampling (Carolco/Winkast-Union)

Even if it may be a specious work at its core, *Angel Heart* still proves a mightily absorbing mystery, a highly exotic telling of a small-time detective's descent into hell, with Faustian theme, heavy bloodletting and pervasive grimness.

Based on William Hjortsberg's novel *Falling Angel*, Alan Parker's screenplay, set in 1955, has seedy Gotham gumshoe Mickey Rourke engaged by mysterious businessman Robert De Niro to locate a certain Johnny Favorite, a big band singer from the pre-war days who, De Niro says, failed to live up to the terms of a contract.

Rourke as Harry Angel, quickly discovers that Favorite, a war casualty and reportedly a vegetable, was removed years earlier from the nursing home where he was supposedly under care, and follows his leads to New Orleans, and particularly the jazz and voodoo elements within its black community.

Rourke is a commanding lead, putting everyone around him (except De Niro) on edge. Charlotte Rampling is very briefly as an elegant fortune teller, while Lisa Bonet's striking looks are rather undercut by her Valley Girl accent, not terribly convincing for a poor black girl from bayou country.

Controversial lovemaking scene between Rourke and Bonet becomes rather rough but, probably more to the point, involves torrents of blood leaking down on them from the ceiling, all of this being intercut with glimpses of voodoo rituals.

•••••••••••••••••••••••••••••••

■ ANGELS ONE FIVE

1952, 97 MINS, UK

Dir George More O'Ferrall   *Prod* John W. Gossage, Derek Twist   *Scr* Derek Twist   *Ph* Christopher Challis, Stanley Grant   *Ed* Daniel Birt   *Mus* John Woodridge   *Art Dir* Fred Pusey

● Jack Hawkins, Michael Denison, Andrew Osborn, Cyril Raymond, Humphrey Lestocq, John Gregson (Templar/Associated British)

Action of *Angels One Five* takes place during the period described by Winston Churchill as 'Britain's finest hour', when a handful of fighter pilots (the few against the many) stemmed the air invasion by Nazi war planes.

Breaking away from the more conventional treatment, the script watches the progress of the battle, not from the actual combats, but from the messages received by and emanating from the operational control room.

Competent acting is followed by whole cast. Jack Hawkins and Michael Denison are the two big shots of the base and their sharp discipline is tempered by a generous measure of understanding. Dulcie Gray has little more to do than appear sympathetic as the wife of the harassed control room chief.

•••••••••••••••••••••••••••••••

■ ANGELS OVER BROADWAY

1940, 78 MINS, US

Dir Ben Hecht, Lee Garmes   *Prod* Ben Hecht, Douglas Fairbanks Jr   *Scr* Ben Hecht   *Ph* Lee Garmes   *Ed* Gene Havlick   *Mus* George Antheil   *Art Dir* Lionel Banks

● Douglas Fairbanks Jr, Rita Hayworth, Thomas Mitchell, John Qualen (Columbia)

Angels over Broadway is a synthetic tale of Broadway nightlife and the characters that roam around Times Square. Aside from Thomas Mitchell, as a screwball playwright who sees a story in every individual, and who delights in plotting a finish, there's nothing much in the Hechtian tale. Picture stutters and sputters too often to carefully etch human beings, with result that it develops into an over-dramatic stage play transformed to celluloid.

Writer-director-producer Ben Hecht gets little movement in the unwinding, and depends too much on stage technique in trying to put over his points. An embezzler (John Qualen) is saved from committing suicide by the zany playwright (Mitchell) who proceeds to try and help the former out of his jam and give him a new lease on life. Douglas Fairbanks Jr is a slick youth who shills for a big poker game, and sets his sights for Qualen who he assumes is a rural hick. There's much byplay between the trio and a girl who moves in (Rita Hayworth) before plan is worked out to recoup the coin in the come-on game.

Characters are all over-drawn, with Mitchell providing many sharp cracks on the philosophy of life and living. Mitchell does much to hold together the minor interest retained in the running. Fairbanks fails to get much sympathy or attention as the wise young Broadwayite who knows all the angles. Hayworth is passable as the girl, while Qualen is bewildered enough as the prospective suicide.

•••••••••••••••••••••••••••••••

■ ANGELS WITH DIRTY FACES

1938, 97 MINS, US

Dir Michael Curtiz   *Prod* Sam Bischoff   *Scr* John Wexley, Warren Duff   *Ph* Sol Polito   *Ed* Owen Marks   *Mus* Max Steiner   *Art Dir* Robert Haas

● James Cagney, Pat O'Brien, Humphrey Bogart, Ann Sheridan, George Bancroft, Billy Halop (Warner)

Another typical *Dead End* kids picture, but with the single exception that it has James Cagney and Pat O'Brien to bolster the dramatic interest.

Cagney is the tenderloin toughie who's the idol of the gutter-bred youngsters because of his criminal exploits and cocky belligerence. O'Brien is the priest who was a boyhood chum of Cagney's and who seeks to retrieve the neighborhood kids from trying to emulate their gangster hero. There's a singular ending for the story which has Cagney pretending to turn yellow as he goes to the electric chair so he'll kill the kids' unhealthy adoration. It is a novel twist to a commonplace story [by Rowland Brown], but it's thoroughly hokey.

The screenplay contains many effective cinematic touches. However, in at least one instance the same set is used for two supposedly different locales.

Cagney and O'Brien form an irresistible team. Their personalities and acting styles offer both a blend and an eloquent contrast. Cagney has a swagger and an aw-go-to-hell pugnacity. O'Brien gives an eminently credible performance of the mild-mannered, twofisted, compassionate priest. The *Dead End* kids are as rambunctious as usual.

•••••••••••••••••••••••••••••••

■ ANGRY HILLS, THE

1959, 105 MINS, UK

Dir Robert Aldrich   *Prod* Raymond Stross   *Scr* A.I. Bezzerides   *Ph* Stephen Dade   *Ed* Peter Tanner   *Mus* Richard Rodney Bennett

● Robert Mitchum, Elisabeth Mueller, Stanley Baker, Gia Scala, Theodore Bikel, Donald Wolfit (M-G-M)

The Angry Hills, set in Greece, is a rather confused yarn but has the merit of good direction by Robert Aldrich and some very competent performances.

Robert Mitchum plays an American war correspondent who is hunted by Gestapo chief Stanley Baker and fifth columnist Theodore Bikel when he arrives in Athens as Greece is about to fall to the Nazis. Baker and Bikel want Mitchum because he has a list of 16 Greek underground leaders which he is conveying to British intelligence in London. He is helped by Gia Scala and also by Elisabeth Mueller, both of whom fall in love with Mitchum.

Both Baker and Mitchum give very sound performances. Mueller brings a radiant charm to the part of the widow. A. I. Bezzerides' screenplay [from Leon Uris' book] falters towards the end when the love complications arise but he tells the story briskly and well.

•••••••••••••••••••••••••••••••

■ ANGRY SILENCE, THE

1960, 95 MINS, UK

Dir Guy Green   *Prod* Richard Attenborough, Bryan Forbes   *Scr* Bryan Forbes   *Ph* Arthur Ibbetson   *Ed* Anthony Harvey   *Mus* Malcolm Arnold

● Richard Attenborough, Pier Angeli, Michael Craig, Bernard Lee, Alfred Burke, Penelope Horner (Beaver)

The Angry Silence details the impact of industrial unrest on individuals, told with passion, integrity and guts, but without false theatrical gimmicks. Apart from the message, there is a solid core of entertainment produced by taut writing, deft direction and topnotch acting.

Plot concerns a worker in a factory where there has been no trouble until a political troublemaker moves in. Insidiously he stirs up unrest, makes one of the workers his catspaw, creates a wildcat strike and then quietly moves on to spread his poison in other factories. The main victim of the strike is played by Richard Attenborough who, because he refuses to be pushed around, is sent to Coventry (shunned by his workmates) and is beaten up, and his family intimidated.

Original story by Richard Gregson and

Michael Craig has been skilfully written for the screen by Bryan Forbes. Perhaps the end is slightly contrived, but Guy Green has directed with quiet skill, leaving the film to speak for itself.

Attenborough, as the quiet little man who just wants to be left alone to grapple with his home problems, has done nothing better on the screen for a long time. That goes, too, for Pier Angeli as his wife. Here she is a creature of flesh and blood, unhappily involved in a problem that she cannot understand. Michael Craig, as Attenborough's best friend, is also in his best form.

•••••••••••••••••••••••••••••••

■ ANIMAL CRACKERS

1930, 97 MINS, US

Dir Victor Heerman   *Scr* Morrie Ryskind   *Ph* George Folsey

● Groucho Marx, Harpo Marx, Chico Marx, Zeppo Marx, Lillian Roth, Margaret Dumont (Paramount)

First give Paramount extreme credit for reproducing *Animal Crackers* intact from the stage [musical written by George S. Kaufman, Morrie Ryskind, Harry Ruby and Bert Kalmar], without too much of the songs and musical numbers.

Among the Marx boys there is no preference. Groucho shines; Harpo remains a pantomimic clown who ranks with the highest; Chico adds an unusual comedy sense to his dialog as well as business and piano playing; and Zeppo, if in on a split, is lucky.

Lillian Roth may have been cast here to work out a contract. She can't hurt because the Marxes are there, but if Roth is in for any other reason it doesn't appear. She sings one song in the ingenue role. That song is useless. Opposite is Hal Thompson, a juve who doesn't prove it here.

•••••••••••••••••••••••••••••••

■ ANIMAL FARM

1954, 72 MINS, UK ◇ ⊽

Dir John Halas, Joy Batchelor, (animation) John Reed   *Prod* John Halas, Joy Batchelor   *Scr* John Halas, Joy Batchelor, Lothar Wolff, Borden Mace, Philip Stapp   *Ph* S.G. Griffiths   *Mus* Matyas Seiber

● (Halas & Batchelor)

Human greed, selfishness and conniving are lampooned in *Animal Farm* with the pigs behaving in a pig-like manner and the head pig, named Napoleon, corrupting and perverting an honest revolt against evil social conditions into a new tyranny as bad as, and remarkably similar to, the old regime. In short, this cartoon feature [from the novel by George Orwell] is a sermon against all that is bestial in politics and rotten in the human will to live in luxury at the expense of slaves.

Made in Britain, the cartoon is vividly realized pictorially. The musical score, the narration, the sound effects and the editing all are of impressive imaginative quality.

•••••••••••••••••••••••••••••••

■ ANNA AND THE KING OF SIAM

1946, 128 MINS, US

Dir John Cromwell   *Prod* Louis D. Lighton   *Scr* Talbot Jennings, Sally Benson   *Ph* Arthur Miller   *Ed* Harmon Jones   *Mus* Bernard Herrmann   *Art Dir* Lyle R. Wheeler, William Darling

● Irene Dunne, Rex Harrison, Linda Darnell, Lee J. Cobb, Gale Sondergaard (20th Century-Fox)

Socko adult drama. *Anna and the King of Siam* is a rather faithful screen adaptation of Margaret Landon's biography, intelligently handled to spellbind despite its long footage.

Anna tells a straightforward narrative, bringing in the natural humor, suspense and other dramatic values of the story of an English widow who finds herself confronted with the many problems of educating the children and some of the wives of the King of

Siam. The monarch, himself, needs some education, and Anna sees that he gets it.

Script builds fascinating adult interest without ever implying that relationship between teacher and pupil goes beyond the friendship stage.

Irene Dunne does a superb enactment of Anna, the woman who influenced Siamese history by being teacher and confidante to a kingly barbarian. Rex Harrison shines particularly in his American film debut. It's a sustained characterization of the King of Siam that makes the role real. Linda Darnell, third star, has little more than a bit as one of the king's wives, who incurs his displeasure and is burned at the stake. She does well.

ANNA CHRISTIE

1923, 87 MINS, US ⊗
Dir John Griffith Wray   *Prod* Thomas H. Ince
Scr Bradley King   *Ph* Henry Sharp
● Blanche Sweet, William Russell, George F. Marion, Eugenie Besserer (Ince/Associated First National)

Anna Christie is a picture that is as different to the regular runs of screen productions as the Eugene O'Neill plays are to the majority of hits and near-hits that come to the spoken stage.

There is one mistake John Griffith Wray makes in the direction. In the usual picture fashion he tries to force his leading woman to overshadow the character role. Blanche Sweet isn't the Anna Christie Pauline Lord was on the stage, but George Marion is Chris and as such he so far overshadows the leading woman that the director is undoubtedly forced to take the extremes he does to keep her in the eye of the audience. But that is not good direction.

William Russell makes Matt Burke a convincing sort of a brute Irish coal passer on a steam tramp and puts over his role with a wallop, and likewise Eugenie Besserer handles Marthy, so that in all Sweet is the only weak spot of the cast of four.

ANNA CHRISTIE

1930, 86 MINS, US Ⓥ
Dir Clarence Brown   *Scr* Frances Marion   *Ph* William Daniels   *Ed* Hugh Wynn   *Art Dir* Cedric Gibbons
● Greta Garbo, George F. Marion, Marie Dressler, Charles Bickford (M-G-M)

In all departments a wow picture. Comparison is inevitable with the silent version made by Thomas Ince eight years earlier with Blanche Sweet and William Russell. In both instances Hollywood closely follows the Eugene O'Neill play.

Infinite care in developing each sequence, just the proper emphasis on characterizations and a part that exactly fits Greta Garbo put *Anna Christie* safely in the realm of the superlative.

'Garbo talks' is, beyond quarrel, an event. La Garbo's accent is nicely edged with a Norse 'yah', but once the ear gets the pitch it's okay.

George Marion, in the original Ince production, again plays the old sentiment-hungry seagoing father. Charles Bickford as the Irish sailor of massive muscles and primitive ideals is magnificent. Perhaps the greatest surprise is Marie Dressler, who steps out of her usual straight slapstick to stamp herself an actress.

ANNA KARENINA

1935, 95 MINS, US Ⓥ
Dir Clarence Brown   *Prod* David O. Selznick
Scr Clemence Dane, Salka Viertel, S.N. Behrman
Ph William Daniels   *Ed* Robert J. Kern   *Mus* Herbert Stothart

● Greta Garbo, Fredric March, Freddie Bartholomew, Basil Rathbone, Maureen O'Sullivan, May Robson (M-G-M)

Greta Garbo starred in this story once before in 1927. Silent film was titled *Love* and John Gilbert had the role now handled by Fredric March. March handles his assignment firmly and with understanding and the film in toto is a more honest and sincere rendition of the Tolstoy classic than the silent.

Garbo, too, seems to have grown since 1927. There is no flaw to be found in her rendition of the love-wracked Russian girl, Anna.

Trimmed to its essentials the story is an extremely simple one: a married woman, hating her cold, unloving, hypocritical husband, falls in love with a young officer of the guards. Love sweeps everything from under her. Her husband won't give her a divorce. She gives up everything she has in life, including her baby, to go to her lover.

Casting throughout is excellent, although just a trifle annoying. There is a distinct clash of accents which might have been avoided. Reginald Denny, Basil Rathbone and Reginald Owen speak Oxfordese English, as opposed to Garbo's Stockholmese.

ANNA KARENINA

1948, 139 MINS, UK Ⓥ
Dir Julien Duvivier   *Prod* Alexander Korda   *Scr* Jean Anouilh, Guy Morgan, Julien Duvivier   *Ph* Henri Alekan   *Ed* Russell Lloyd   *Mus* Constant Lambert   *Art Dir* Andre Andrejeff
● Vivien Leigh, Ralph Richardson, Kieron Moore (London)

Fine as this fourth production of Tolstoy's novel is (Fox 1915, Metro 1927 and 1935), it misses greatness and has tedious stretches.

It would appear that far too much attention was paid to the sets and the artistic structure at the expense of the players. It would have been wise for Korda and Duvivier to realize that the story, for screen purposes, is frankly Victorian melodrama, and that there was always the danger of reducing the characters to puppets.

It speaks volumes for Leigh and Richardson that they are able to disentangle themselves from their overwhelming surroundings and become credibly human. Leigh dominates the picture, as she rightly should with her beauty, charm and skill. It isn't her fault that eyes remain dry and hearts unwrung when she moves to inevitable tragedy, as the neglected wife and discarded lover.

Richardson's portrayal of the priggish, unlikeable husband is masterly yet uneven. Sometimes he gives the impression of a Chinese philosopher with accent and staccato phrase. Incidentally, the multiplicity of pronunciations of 'Karenina' by various people is a trifle distracting.

ANNE OF THE THOUSAND DAYS

1970, 145 MINS, UK ◇ Ⓥ
Dir Charles Jarrott   *Prod* Hal B. Wallis   *Scr* Bridget Boland, John Hale   *Ph* Arthur Ibbetson   *Ed* Richard Marden   *Mus* Georges Delerue   *Art Dir* Maurice Carter
● Richard Burton, Genevieve Bujold, Irene Papas, Anthony Quayle, John Colicos, Michael Horden (Universal)

With Richard Burton as Henry VIII and Genevieve Bujold in the title role of Anne Boleyn, *Anne of the Thousand Days* is a stunning-acted, sumptuous, grand-scale widescreen drama of the royal bed chamber and political intrigues that created the Church of England.

Although Burton's portrayal is sensitive, vivid and arresting, it is still basically an unsympathetic role.

The screenplay, as adapted by Richard Sokolove, based on Maxwell Anderson's stage play, bristles with sharp epigrammatic dialog.

In his first feature film, TV director Charles Jarrot frames his Renaissance pageant handsomely and handles the skilled cast to achieve an effective uniform period style. However, there is a basically stagey pace to the drama that makes it more static and less cinematic than it might have been.
□ 1969: Best Picture (Nomination)

ANNIE

1982, 128 MINS, US ◇ Ⓥ
Dir John Huston   *Prod* Ray Stark   *Scr* Carol Sobelski   *Ph* Richard Moore   *Ed* Michael A. Stevenson   *Mus* Charles Strouse   *Art Dir* Dale Hennesy
● Albert Finney, Carol Burnett, Aileen Quinn, Ann Reinking, Bernadette Peters, Tim Curry (Columbia)

Many people said John Huston was an odd choice to direct *Annie* and he proves them right. In an effort to be more 'realistic' *Annie* winds up exposing just how weak a story it had to start with [stage play book by Thomas Meehan], not helped here by the music. Aside from the memorable 'Tomorrow' the show's songs weren't all that much in the first place and four new tunes penned for the $35 million film aren't any better.

In the title role, little Aileen Quinn acquits herself quite well. Carol Burnett gets most of what chuckles there are as the drunken Miss Hannigan who runs the orphanage.

Albert Finney is best of the bunch as Daddy Warbucks, but it's really not a test for his talents. Edward Herrman is acceptable as FDR, a part he has down pat. As the villainous phony parents, Bernadette Peters and Tim Curry, add little.

ANNIE GET YOUR GUN

1950, 107 MINS, US ◇
Dir George Sidney   *Prod* Arthur Freed   *Scr* Sidney Sheldon   *Ph* Charles Rosher   *Ed* James E. Newcom   *Mus* Irving Berlin
● Betty Hutton, Howard Keel, Louis Calhern, J. Carrol Naish, Edward Arnold, Keenan Wynn (M-G-M)

Annie Get Your Gun is socko musical entertainment on film, just as it was on the Broadway stage [in 1946]. In many respects, the film version gets the nod over the legit piece; at least there is enough pro and con to reprise that great novelty number, 'Anything You Can Do'.

Ten of the *Annie* Irving Berlin hits are used and two are reprised.

Briefly, Annie is a backwoods gal, a deadshot who is taken into a wildwest show, soon supplants the show's male marksman, goes on to become a star and then wins her man by losing a shooting match.

Annie is Wild West, shooting, Indians, daredevil-riding and action, never slowing a minute as put together for the screen by producer Arthur Freed and director George Sidney. They will find it hard to top.

ANNIE HALL

1977, 93 MINS, US ◇ Ⓥ
Dir Woody Allen   *Prod* Charles H. Joffe   *Scr* Woody Allen   *Ph* Gordon Willis   *Ed* Ralph Rosenblum   *Art Dir* Mel Bourne
● Woody Allen, Diane Keaton, Tony Roberts, Carol Kane, Paul Simon, Colleen Dewhurst (United Artists)

Woody Allen's four romantic comedies with Diane Keaton strike a chord of believability that makes them nearly the 1970s equivalent of the Tracy-Hepburn films. *Annie Hall*, is by far the best, a touching and hilarious three-dimensional love story.

The gags fly by in almost non-stop

profusion, but there is an undercurrent of sadness and pain reflecting a maturation of style. Allen tells Keaton in the film that he has 'a very pessimistic view of life,'' and it's true.

The script is loosely structured, virtually a two-character running conversation between Allen and Keaton as they meet, fall in love, quarrel, and break up. Meanwhile, he continues his career as a moderately successful TV-nightclub comic and she develops a budding career as a singer.
□ 1977: Best Picture

....

■ ANNIVERSARY, THE

1968, 95 MINS, UK ◇ ⊛
Dir Roy Ward Baker *Prod* Jimmy Sangster *Scr* Jimmy Sangster *Ph* Harry Waxman *Ed* Peter Wetherley *Mus* Philip Martell
● Bette Davis, Sheila Hancock, Jack Hedley, James Cossins, Elaine Taylor, Christian Roberts (Hammer)

Derived from Bill McIllwraith's legit original, this was turned into a vehicle for the extravagant tantrums of Bette Davis, in her most ghoulish mood. This, together with its modish black-comedy lines and bold situation, is its chief asset.

Because it skates near the bone of family relationships, it rouses plenty of understanding yocks, but the exaggeration of the concept doesn't wear as well on film as it did on stage. It is a highly theatrical piece, and needs remoteness, rather than closeups, for its bitter characterizations not to come across as caricature.

Davis gets her teeth into the role of the ultra-possessive ma and hurls it out with splendid panache and flamboyance, but some might find her outsize portrayal too stark to carry the conviction. She bosses it over a family of three sons, all of whom are in an advanced stage of spinelessness.

The action, which little attempt has been made to transfer into the wider visual terms of a feature pic, takes place on the anniversary of Davis' husband's death, and the family gathers to do him honor.

....

■ ANOTHER COUNTRY

1984, 90 MINS, UK ◇ ⊛
Dir Marek Kanievska *Prod* Alan Marshall *Scr* Julian Mitchell *Ph* Peter Biziou *Ed* Gerry Hambling *Mus* Michael Storey *Art Dir* Brian Morris
● Rupert Everett, Colin Firth, Michael Jenn, Robert Addie, Rupert Wainwright, Anna Massey (Goldcrest)

Julian Mitchell's adaptation of his successful West End play *Another Country* is an absorbing tale about life in a British public (i.e. private) boarding school in the 1930s. Story is supposedly based on the early friendship of Guy Burgess and Donald MacLean who, in the 1950s, spied for the USSR while working for the British government but defected to Moscow before they could be arrested.

Mitchell's contention is that the homosexuality of Burgess, called Bennett here, made him as much an outsider in the claustrophobic atmosphere of the British uppercrust as did MacLean's (Judd's) Marxism.

Film is marvelously acted down the line, with Rupert Everett a standout as the tormented Bennett.

....

■ ANOTHER 48 HRS.

1990, 95 MINS, US ◇ ⊛
Dir Walter Hill *Prod* Lawrence Gordon *Scr* John Fasano, Jeb Stuart, Larry Gross *Ph* Matthew F. Leonetti *Ed* Freeman Davies, Carmel Davies, Donn Aron *Mus* James Horner *Art Dir* Joseph C. Nemec III
● Eddie Murphy, Nick Nolte, Brion James, Kevin Tighe, Ed O'Ross (Paramount/Eddie Murphy)

Pic's really misnamed, since it's not *Another*

48HRS. but the same *48HRS*., the 1982 mismatched buddy action pic.

Director Walter Hill, reprising those chores, knows the terrain and tills it with all the familiar elements: bawdy humor, cannonloud gunplay, hissable bad guys and plenty of action.

Eddie Murphy and Nick Nolte manage to recapture some of their initial chemistry, but for the most part the film is curiously flat – in part due to a jumped plot that's so quickly tied up at the end it seems everyone was in a hurry to get their checks and get out of town.

The plot even hinges on the first film, as two hit men are dispatched to kill Murphy, one the brother of the lead baddie offed in *48HRS*. Nolte, meanwhile, has spent the past four years chasing a faceless drug kingpin called the Iceman, who paid for the hit on Murphy. He's been thwarted at every turn, however, leading Murphy to suspect corruption within the police department.

Hill and his trio of screenwriters choose the stale and predictable route at almost every turn, the plot being strictly a slender means of allowing Murphy and Nolte to strut their stuff.

....

■ ANOTHER MAN ANOTHER CHANCE

1977, 132 MINS, FRANCE ◇ ⊛
Dir Claude Lelouch *Prod* Alexandre Mnouchkine *Scr* Claude Lelouch *Ph* Jacques Lefrancois, Stanley Cortez *Ed* Georges Klotz *Mus* Francis Lai *Art Dir* Robert Clatworthy
● James Caan, Genevieve Bujold, Francis Huster, Susan Tyrrell, Jennifer Warren (Films 13/Ariane/Artistes Associes)

A sort of valentine to the American western film with James Caan and Genevieve Bujold for the he-she interest. It's a Frenchman's perspective on the US.

It begins with a passage in steerage to America by Bujold and her boyfriend (Francis Huster), a photographer, in the 1870s.

James Caan meanwhile has been paralleled to Bujold's life and out west they pass each other often and finally meet. He is a Yank veterinarian, happy in his work.

Caan and Bujold finally fall in love. There are some simple observations of life in the west but not imitative of the general oater. They are at ease and inventive in their roles of headstrong, piquant woman settler and he as a relaxed charmer. Caan has warm failings as when he emerges a worse shot than his eight-year-old son.

It has good production dress and is spoken in French, when the French are on, and English in America when the Yanks are on.

....

■ ANOTHER TIME, ANOTHER PLACE

1983, 101 MINS, UK ◇ ⊛
Dir Michael Radford *Prod* Simon Perry *Scr* Michael Radford *Ph* Roger Deakins *Ed* Tom Priestley *Mus* John McLeod *Art Dir* Hayden Pearce
● Phyllis Logan, Giovanni Mauriello, Gian Luca Favilla, Claudio Rosini, Paul Young, Gregor Fisher (Umbrella)

It's not often that a British film is realized with as much creative integrity as *Another Time, Another Place*. The plot springs from the cultural difference between the inhabitants of a bleak Scottish agricultural village and a trio of Italians confined to the community during the Second World War. One Italian in particular, the passionate Neopolitan Luigi (Giovanni Mauriello) mesmerizes Janie (Phyllis Logan) by seeming to offer an alternative to an emotionally cold marriage and a laborious penny-pinching life. The rest of the Scottish community remain suspicious of the strangers in their midst.

The developing relationship is narrated with a light and humorous touch, even

though both parties are drawn to each other out of desperation.

Central to the film's effectiveness is the performance of Logan as the girl entranced. Eyes and gestures capture the initial longing followed by the remorse that follows surrender.

The film's impact derives also from representations of daily life and a landscape that changes with the seasons.

....

■ ANOTHER WOMAN

1988, 84 MINS, US ◇ ⊛
Dir Woody Allen *Prod* Robert Greenhut *Scr* Woody Allen *Ph* Sven Nykvist *Ed* Susan E. Morse *Art Dir* Santo Loquasto
● Gena Rowlands, Mia Farrow, Ian Holm, Blythe Danner, Gene Hackman, Martha Plimpton (Rollins/Joffe)

Woody Allen once again explores the human condition via the inner turmoil of gifted New Yorkers.

Story deals with a very successful, often idolized character who discovers around the time of her 50th birthday that she has made many mistakes, but people have been more or less too deferential to confront her.

Gena Rowlands plays Marion Post, head of a graduate philosophy department, married to a doctor. She takes an apartment downtown in which to write a book, and begins overhearing analysis sessions from the psychiatrist's office next door. At first she's annoyed, then gets hooked as a patient (Mia Farrow) tells of her unsettling conviction that her marriage has begun to disintegrate.

Soon, she's reliving some of the turning points in her life, through dreams, flashbacks and chance encounters with family and friends. Throughout, she's haunted by the memory of a man (Gene Hackman) who once loved her passionately.

Film that emerges is brave, in many ways fascinating, and in all respects of a caliber rarely seen.

....

■ ANTHONY ADVERSE

1936, 139 MINS, US ⊛
Dir Mervyn LeRoy *Prod* Henry Blanke *Scr* Sheridan Gibney *Ph* Tony Gaudio *Ed* Ralph Dawson *Mus* Erich Wolfgang Korngold *Art Dir* Anton Grot
● Fredric March, Olivia de Havilland, Edmund Gwenn, Claude Rains, Anita Louise (Warner)

In transmuting the Hervey Allen bestseller to the screen the producers were faced with the unusual problem of too much material. They have maneuvered a straightforward and comparatively logical story. It's a bit choppy and it's a bit long-winded, but it is a direct line and easy to follow.

Writer Sheridan Gibney managed to hew a straight course through the 1,200 pages of Allen's writing by concentrating on his titular character and avoiding the danger of skirting off and away. Thus he clips off the entire last portion of the book, for instance, and plenty of juicy matter in between.

Fredric March as Adverse is an ace choice, playing the role to the hilt. Much less theatrical than he occasionally becomes, March is convincing through a varied series of moods and portrayals.

Olivia de Havilland has, perhaps, the next important role as Adverse's wife, Angela. She handles it acceptably, especially in the emotional scenes. In the opera sequences she uncovers a lovely singing voice. In the supporting cast, Edmund Gwenn makes the past of John Bonyweather stand out. Claude Rains does a splendid job as Don Luis.

Pleasant rather than exciting, is Eric Wolfang Korngold's musical accompaniment.
□ 1936: Best Picture (Nomination)

....

A

■ ANTONY AND CLEOPATRA

1972, 160 MINS, UK ◇ ⓥ

Dir Charlton Heston *Prod* Peter Snell *Scr* Charlton
Heston *Ph* Rafael Pacheco *Ed* Eric Boyd-Perkins
Mus John Scott *Art Dir* Maurice Pelling
● Charlton Heston, Hildegard Neil, Eric Porter, John
Castle, Fernando Rey, Freddie Jones (Snell)

Charlton Heston, whose ardor for Shakespeare goes back to his 16mm film college days in Chicago, has herein come up with a very creditable retelling of the Bard's Antony & Cleopatra passion. It is impressively mounted and well played, and though lengthy it sustains well.

The finished film is a neat balance of close-up portraiture and panoramic action; the big battle sequences on land and sea are impressive achievements, and the Spanish location landscape provides a stunning backdrop.

Heston's adaptation, for the most part, succeeds in avoiding the sort of character simplification that would have produced a picture simply for the eye. Hildegard Neil proves one of Cleo's more convincing screen incarnations.

Heston himself as Antony very often succeeds in capturing the nobility of the character. The real handicap is borne by John Castle as Octavius Caesar. It's one of those monochromatic, steadily dour parts that doesn't leave the actor much room.

■ ANY WEDNESDAY

1966, 109 MINS, US ◇ ⓥ

Dir Robert Ellis Miller *Prod* Julius J. Epstein *Scr* Julius
J. Epstein *Ph* Harold Lipstein *Ed* Stefan Arnsten
Mus George Duning *Art Dir* Al Sweeney
● Jane Fonda, Jason Robards, Dean Jones, Rosemary
Murphy, Ann Prentiss, Jack Fletcher (Warner)

Based on Muriel Resnik's popular legiter, *Any Wednesday* emerges in screen translation as an outstanding sophisticated comedy about marital infidelity. Adaptation and production by Julius J. Epstein is very strong, enhanced by solid direction and excellent performances.

Epstein's zesty adaptation wisely distributes the comedy emphasis among all four principals – Jason Robards, the once-a-week philanderer; Jane Fonda, his two-year Wednesday date; Dean Jones, whose arrival rocks Robards' dreamboat; and Rosemary Murphy, recreating in superior fashion her original Broadway role as Robards' wife.

Interactions between principals are uniformly strong, both in dialog and acting as well as in very effective use of split-screen effects.

Fonda comes across quite well as the girl who can't make up her mind, although she has a tendency to overplay certain bits in what might be called an exaggerated Doris Day manner. Jones impresses as a likeable comedy performer whose underlying dramatic ability gets a good showcasing here. Robards is outstanding as the likeable lecher who winds up losing both his mistress and his wife.

■ ANYTHING CAN HAPPEN

1952, 107 MINS, US

Dir George Seaton *Prod* William Perlberg
Scr George Seaton, George Oppenheimer *Ph* Daniel
L. Fapp *Ed* Alma Macrorie *Mus* Victor Young
● Jose Ferrer, Kim Hunter, Kurt Kasznar, Eugenie
Leontovich, Oscar Karlweis, Nick Dennis (Paramount)

Anything Can Happen, based on the bestselling book by George and Helen Papashvily detailing their own real-life adventures, is a heartwarming comedy, engagingly acted, slickly produced and directed.

Film concerns a loveable group of Near Eastern immigrants and their devotion for the new homeland in America. It shows Jose Ferrer's arrival in the new, strange country, his struggles with the English language, his shy courting of an American (Kim Hunter), and his eventual ownership of a California orange grove on which he is privileged to pay US taxes.

Ferrer proves his versatility with a restrained, believable performance. Hunter is always convincing as the seemingly unattainable American whose friendliness and interest in the 'foreigner' turn to real love.

■ ANYTHING GOES

1935, 90 MINS, US

Dir Lewis Milestone *Prod* Benjamin Glazer
Scr [uncredited] *Ph* Karl Struss *Ed* Eda Warren
● Bing Crosby, Ethel Merman, Charlie Ruggles, Ida
Lupino, Grace Bradley, Arthur Treacher (Paramount)

Cole Porter's lyrics, which were the essence and chief asset of the original [1934] stage *Anything Goes*, have been replaced by plot motion in this adaptation. Of the Porter poetical sleight-of-hand which listened so well on Broadway for a couple of seasons, only 'I Get a Kick Out of You' and 'You're the Top' are used. The title song is in also, but just for thematic and strictly instrumental use. There are four new numbers, of which 'My Heart and I,' 'Sailor Beware' and 'Moonburn' are the most likely.

Ethel Merman comes from the original cast and her job in the picture equals her job in the stage version, which means aces. But Charlie Ruggles as the gag gangster is miscast. His delivery is too vigorous for the sap character, and the role calls for low comeding, which is out of Ruggles' line.

With the story opening in a cabaret and finishing in a production scene, with most of the bulk in between taking place on a big ocean liner, the production is lavish, and logical most of the time. Only in the closing flash does it go beyond credibility. This occurs on the 'dock' at Southampton, upon the boat landing on the other side.

Crosby is fine singing 'Sailor Beware' alone. And he's also there when it comes to getting his quota of laughs.

■ ANYTHING GOES

1956, 106 MINS, US ◇

Dir Robert Lewis *Prod* Robert Emmett Dolan
Scr Sidney Sheldon *Ph* John F. Warren *Ed* Frank
Bracht *Mus* Cole Porter
● Bing Crosby, Donald O'Connor, Zizi Jeanmaire,
Mitzi Gaynor, Phil Harris, Kurt Kasznar (Paramount)

Paramount's sock musical package borrows the title and songs from that yesteryear stage hit, *Anything Goes*. Male topliners Bing Crosby and Donald O'Connor go together as though born to give the zip to what scripter Sidney Sheldon has concocted.

While there are Cole Porter songs and the legit handle is still carried, that's about all that remains of what went on behind the footlights, and there's scant resemblance to Paramount's 1936 film version, in which Crosby also starred with Ethel Merman.

Choice of the two femme stars, Zizi Jeanmaire and Mitzi Gaynor, both leggy and appealing, is a click factor.

Script provides Crosby with plenty of those sotto voce, throwaway cracks he and his fans dote on. Plot, simply, has Crosby and O'Connor agreeing to do a B'way musical together after European vacations. Abroad, each signs a femme star and the remainder concerns fitting the gals in with previous plans.

Jeanmaire has two ballets that are clicks. Gaynor belts the title tune staged by Ernie Platt to score solidly in her solo showcasing.

■ ANY WHICH WAY YOU CAN

1980, 116 MINS, US ◇ ⓥ

Dir Buddy Van Horn *Prod* Fritz Manes *Scr* Stanford
Sherman *Ph* David Worth *Ed* Ferris Webster, Ron
Spang *Mus* Snuff Garrett (sup.) *Art Dir* William J.
Creber
● Clint Eastwood, Sondra Locke, Ruth Gordon, William
Smith, Harry Guardino, Geoffrey Lewis (Warner)

Any Which Way You Can is a benign continuation of *Every Which Way But Loose*.

Clint Eastwood, Sondra Locke, Geoffrey Lewis, Ruth Gordon and numerous supporting players all repeat their characterizations from the first outing to similar effect. Main difference is that individuals this time seem almost forgiving, loving and considerate.

Eastwood's Philo Beddoe swears off his lucrative sideline career, better to settle down with Ma Gordon, a significantly tamed Locke and orangutan chum Clyde. However, the mob makes him an offer he can't refuse to battle he-man William Smith, and the two, despite having become good pals, end up in an epic brawl.

Original ape from *Loose* was not available to Eastwood here, but substitute performs heroically.

■ ANZIO

1968, 117 MINS, ITALY ◇ ⓥ

Dir Edward Dmytryk *Prod* Dino De Laurentiis
Scr Harry A.L. Craig *Ph* Giuseppe Rotunno
Ed Alberto Gallitti, Peter Taylor *Mus* Riz Ortolani *Art
Dir* Luigi Scaccianoce
● Robert Mitchum, Peter Falk, Robert Ryan, Arthur
Kennedy, Earl Holliman, Mark Damon (Columbia)

Anzio, based on the World War II campaign in Italy, suffers from flat writing, stock performances, uninspired direction and dull pacing. Produced by Dino De Laurentiis, film would seem to be a largescale war epic, but it really is a pale tale of a small group of men trapped behind German lines. Robert Mitchum stars in a cast that is far better in potential than in reality.

Two US generals, (Arthur Kennedy and Robert Ryan) play a cautious and a headline-hungry type, respectively. But from the moment the film begins, it is apparent that the overall pace is going to limp.

Mitchum's character, a wiseguy newspaper reporter, plays off against the brass, whom he puts down, and his seven army cohorts, who put him down for not getting involved. Only Earl Holliman has any significant life.

Peter Falk overacts an overwritten part of a rough-guy-with-heart-of-tin. He and Mitchum discuss some basic philosophical points, one of several forced injections of 'meaning' which not only fail to elevate the story, but actually depress it further into banality.

■ APACHE

1954, 86 MINS, US ◇

Dir Robert Aldrich *Prod* Harold Hecht *Scr* James R.
Webb *Ph* Leonard Doss *Ed* Alan Crosland Jr
Mus David Raksin
● Burt Lancaster, Jean Peters, John McIntyre, Charles
Bronson, John Dehner, Paul Guilfoyle (United Artists)

This initial Hecht–Lancaster release through United Artists is a rugged action saga in best Burt Lancaster style of muscle-flexing. Production is based on history, re-telling story of a diehard Apache who waged one-man war against United States and thereafter became a tribal legend. While its roots are historic, the James R. Webb screenplay from Paul I. Wellman novel, *Bronco Apache* gives it good old outdoor action punch true to western film tradition.

Main plot switch is viewing Indian from sympathetic angle, even though his knife, arrows, bullets often find their marks among white soldiers.

Lancaster and Jean Peters play their Indian roles understandingly without usual screen stereotyping.

Robert Aldrich, making second start as feature film director, handles cast and action well, waste movement being eliminated and only essentials to best storytelling retained, as attested by comparatively short running time.

●●●●●●●●●●●●●●●●●●●●●●●●●●●●

■ APARTMENT, THE

1960, 124 MINS, US ◇ ⓥ

Dir Billy Wilder   *Prod* Billy Wilder   *Scr* Billy Wilder, I.A.L. Diamond   *Ph* Joseph LaShelle   *Ed* Daniel Mandell   *Mus* Adolph Deutsch   *Art Dir* Alexander Trauner

● Jack Lemmon, Shirley MacLaine, Fred MacMurray, Ray Walston, Edie Adams, Jack Kruschen (Mirisch/United Artists)

Billy Wilder furnishes *The Apartment* with a one-hook plot that comes out high in comedy, wide in warmth and long in running time. As with *Some Like It Hot*, the broad handling is of more consequence than the package.

The story is simple. Lemmon is a lonely insurance clerk with a convenient, if somewhat antiquated, apartment which has become the rendezvous point for five of his bosses and their amours. In return, he's promoted from the 19th floor office pool to a 27th floor wood-paneled office complete with key to the executive washroom. When he falls in love with Shirley MacLaine, an elevator girl who's playing Juliet to top executive Fred MacMurray's Romeo, he turns in his washroom key.

The screenplay fills every scene with touches that spring only from talented, imaginative filmmakers. But where their *Some Like It Hot* kept you guessing right up to fadeout, *Apartment* reveals its hand early in the game. Second half of the picture is loosely constructed and tends to lag.

Apartment is all Lemmon, with a strong twist of MacLaine. The actor uses comedy as it should be used, to evoke a rainbow of emotions. He's lost in a cool world, this lonely bachelor, and he is not so much the shnook as the well-meaning, ambitious young man who lets good be the ultimate victor. MacLaine, in pixie hairdo, is a prize that's consistent with the fight being waged for her affections. Her ability to play it broad where it should be broad, subtle where it must be subtle, enables the actress to effect reality and yet do much more.

□ 1960: Best Picture

●●●●●●●●●●●●●●●●●●●●●●●●●●●●

■ APARTMENT ZERO

1989, 124 MINS, UK ◇ ⓥ

Dir Martin Donovan   *Prod* Martin Donovan, David Koepp   *Scr* Martin Donovan, David Koepp   *Ph* Miguel Rodriguez   *Ed* Conrad M. Gonzalez   *Mus* Elia Cmiral   *Art Dir* Miguel Angel Lumaldo

● Colin Firth, Hart Bochner, Dora Bryan, Liz Smith, Fabrizio Bentivoglio (Summit)

Apartment Zero emerges as a genuinely creepy, disturbing and gripping psychological piece.

Story's fundamental opposition is between Colin Firth, the nervously repressed, emotionally constipated British cinephile, and Hart Bochner, a charming, loose, Yankee rascal whom Firth takes into his lovely flat as a boarder when finances demand it.

Periodically, there are reports of serial murders taking place throughout Buenos Aires, and suggestions that mercenary foreigners who came to Argentina in the employ of the Death Squads may still be active. Suspicion grows that the enigmatic Bochner may not be what he claims.

Both actors are excellent, with Firth

expressing and transcending the irritating emotional constriction of a non-participant in life, and Bochner displaying hitherto unrevealed talent portraying a profoundly split personality.

●●●●●●●●●●●●●●●●●●●●●●●●●●●●

■ APOCALYPSE NOW

1979, 139 MINS, US ◇ ⓥ

Dir Francis Coppola   *Prod* Francis Coppola   *Scr* John Milius, Francis Coppola   *Ph* Vittorio Storaro   *Ed* Barry Malkin   *Mus* Carmine Coppola   *Art Dir* Dean Tavoularis

● Marlon Brando, Martin Sheen, Robert Duvall, Frederic Forrest, Dennis Hopper, Harrison Ford (United Artists)

Apocalypse Now, alternately a brilliant and bizarre $40 million war epic, Coppola's vision of Hell-on-Earth hews closely to Joseph Conrad's novella, *Heart of Darkness* and therein lies the film's principal commercial defect.

It's the first film to directly excoriate US involvement in the Indochina war. Coppola virtually creates World War III onscreen. There are no models or miniatures, no tank work, nor process screens for the airborne sequences.

Coppola narrows his focus on the members of a patrol boat crew entrusted with taking Intelligence assassin Martin Sheen on a hazardous mission upriver into Cambodia to track down Marlon Brando, an officer whose methods and motives have become 'unsound', as he leads an army of tribesmen on random genocide missions.

Apocalypse Now is emblazoned with firsts: a 70mm version without credits, a director putting himself personally on the hook for the film's $18 million cost overrun, and then obtaining rights to the pic in perpetuity, and a revolutionary sound system that adds immeasurably to the film's impact.

□ 1979: Best Picture (Nomination)

●●●●●●●●●●●●●●●●●●●●●●●●●●●●

■ APPLAUSE

1929, 80 MINS, US ⓥ

Dir Rouben Mamoulian   *Prod* Monta Bell   *Scr* Garret Fort   *Ph* George Folsey

● Helen Morgan, Joan Peers, Fuller Mellish Jr, Jack Cameron, Henry Wadsworth, Dorothy Cumming (Paramount)

This is the real old burlesque, in its background, people and atmosphere. So was Beth Brown's book, and Garret Fort has adapted with sufficient fidelity to hold together the odd story that makes an odd picture.

Helen Morgan is Kitty Darling, a fading star of burlesque, aging on the stage as her daughter, born in a dressing room, grows up.

Joan Peers comes to the front toward the finish as the daughter, April. Earlier in the convent scenes she doesn't convince.

Hitch Nelson as done by Fuller Mellish Jr is the pi, Kitty's husband who tries to make the daughter. A turkey burlesque chiseler with the women stuff on the side, and always bullyragging his woman. A good performance every minute by Mellish. Henry Wadsworth is the juve, opposite Peers.

The picture was made at Paramount's Long Island studio.

●●●●●●●●●●●●●●●●●●●●●●●●●●●●

■ APPOINTMENT, THE

1969, 100 MINS, US ◇ ⓥ

Dir Sidney Lumet   *Prod* Martin Poll   *Scr* James Salter   *Ph* Carlo Di Palma   *Ed* Thelma Connell   *Mus* John Barry, Don Walker   *Art Dir* Piero Gherardi

● Omar Sharif, Anouk Aimee, Lotte Lenya, Fausto Tozzi, Ennio Balbo (M-G-M/Marpol)

A flimsy love story which never really catches fire emerges from an Antonio Leonviola original which James Salter has shaped for the

screen in this disappointing Sidney Lumet effort.

Omar Sharif plays a Roman lawyer who falls for a colleague's fiancee, a mannequin played by Anouk Aimee, and eventually marries her, undeterred by his pal's fear that she's secretly a high-priced call girl. Soon, however, suspicion begins to gnaw and he begins to tail his spouse.

Flat writing and an over-rigid performance by Sharif in a crucial role, which at times skirts the laughable, seriously flaw what might otherwise have been an intriguing love tale cum suspenser.

Instead, the love affair is never convincingly established from the start, and with the exception of a largely wasted contribution by Aimee the film drags along to its mellerish windup.

●●●●●●●●●●●●●●●●●●●●●●●●●●●●

■ APPOINTMENT FOR LOVE

1941, 88 MINS, US

Dir William A. Seiter   *Prod* Bruce Manning   *Scr* Bruce Manning, Felix Jackson   *Ph* Joseph Valentine   *Ed* Ted Kent   *Mus* Frank Skinner

● Charles Boyer, Margaret Sullavan, Rita Johnson, Eugene Pallette, Ruth Terry, Cecil Kellaway (Universal)

Appointment for Love is a neatly constructed piece of bright entertainment. Producer Bruce Manning, who also collaborated on the script with Felix Jackson [from an original by Ladislas Bus-Fekete], points up the romantic adventure while injecting numerous refreshing episodes to the oft-told tale of newlywed problems.

Charles Boyer, a successful playwright, suave with the femmes, falls in love with Margaret Sullavan, seriously immersed in the practice of medicine and with very novel and unusual ideas about marriage and continuance of separate careers. Sullavan takes a separate apartment in the same building with Boyer, explaining this unusual procedure in difference in time schedules of their work.

Situation created upsets Boyer, with conflict between the pair raging in merriest mood, including setups for jealousies on both sides.

William Seiter paces the direction with an expert hand, deftly timing the smacko laugh lines and situations for brightest effect. Boyer handles his assignment with utmost assurance. Sullavan provides both charm and ability to her role of the serious medic who finally turns romantic.

●●●●●●●●●●●●●●●●●●●●●●●●●●●●

■ APPOINTMENT WITH DANGER

1951, 90 MINS, US

Dir Lewis Allen   *Prod* Robert Fellows   *Scr* Richard Breen, Warren Duff   *Ph* John F. Seitz   *Ed* LeRoy Stone   *Art Dir* Victor Young

● Alan Ladd, Phyllis Calvert, Paul Stewart, Jan Sterling, Jack Webb, Henry Morgan (Paramount)

Exploits of the Postal Inspection Service furnish Alan Ladd with a good cops-and-robbers actioner. Film deals with government detectives tracking down the killers of a fellow postal inspector and preventing a million-dollar mail robbery. Ladd is right at home as the tightlipped, tough inspector assigned to the case. There is a neat contrasting byplay in the nun character done by Phyllis Calvert as co-star, which adds an offbeat note to the meller plot.

While investigating the murder of an inspector, Ladd comes across a plot to loot the mails of a large cash shipment during transfer from one railway station to another. He sets himself up as a cop who can be bribed by demanding money from the gang on threat of spilling the robbery plans.

Calvert's character figures importantly as she is the only witness who can tie the gang to the original murder. Paul Stewart dominates

A

the crooks, with capable assists on menace from Jack Webb, Stacy Harris and Henry Morgan. Jan Sterling supplies the s.a. on the wrong side of the law as Stewart's moll.

••••••••••••••••••••••••••

■ APPRENTICESHIP OF DUDDY KRAVITZ, THE

1974, 120 MINS, CANADA ◇ Ⓥ

Dir Ted Kotcheff   *Prod* John Kemeny   *Scr* Mordecai Richler   *Ph* Brian West   *Ed* Thom Noble   *Mus* Stanley Myers   *Art Dir* Anne Pritchard
● Richard Dreyfuss, Micheline Lanctot, Jack Warden, Randy Quaid, Joseph Wiseman, Denholm Elliott (International Cinemedia/CFDC)

Director Ted Kotcheff has taken Mordecai Richler's novel by the scruff of the neck and worked a zesty but somewhat muted nostalgic look at a nervy Jewish kid on the make in the 1940s.

On screen, *Duddy Kravitz* remains as it was when first published in 1959 to outraged cries from Jewish groups across North America and more particularly from Montreal where it is authentically set. That is an at-times bitter, satiric portrayal of a 19-year-old who gets his money, women and power by emulating the richest of those around him, selling everyone, closest friends included, out.

Kravitz, played by a continually-grinning, scratching, nervous-making yet vulnerable Richard Dreyfuss, comes across effectively and with force.

••••••••••••••••••••••••••

■ APRIL FOOLS, THE

1969, 95 MINS, US ◇ Ⓥ

Dir Stuart Rosenberg   *Prod* Gordon Carroll   *Scr* Hal Dresner   *Ph* Michel Hugo   *Ed* Bob Wyman   *Mus* Marvin Hamlisch   *Art Dir* Richard Sylbert
● Jack Lemmon, Catherine Deneuve, Peter Lawford, Jack Weston, Myrna Loy, Charles Boyer (Cinema Center/Jalem)

Jack Lemmon is both funny and touching as the mild-mannered stockbroker, tied to a nothing of a wife. Given a big promotion by his boss (Peter Lawford), he meets the latter's wife (Catherine Deneuve) at a stultifying cocktail party. She's bored and he doesn't know her real identity but they depart for a night of self-discovery.

In addition to Lemmon, comedians Jack Weston (as his lawyer) and Harvey Korman (as a drinking companion they encounter in the commuter train's drinking car) provide their own brand of laughs and the contrasting styles of the three actors gives the plot most of its action.

Things slow down to a mere simmer, by contrast, in the romantic segments although Deneuve, in her first American film, is worth just looking at.

••••••••••••••••••••••••••

■ ARABELLA

1969, 88 MINS, ITALY ◇

Dir Mauro Bolognini   *Prod* Maleno Malenotti   *Scr* Adriano Baracco   *Ph* Ennio Guarnieri   *Ed* Eraldo Da Roma   *Mus* Ennio Morricone   *Art Dir* Alberto Boccianti
● Virna Lisi, James Fox, Margaret Rutherford, Terry-Thomas, Paola Borboni, Giancarlo Giannini (Universal/Malenotti)

Arabella, Italian-produced with an English and Italian cast, is a series of episodes none too adroitly woven together which focus on the larcenous activities of Virna Lisi as she tries to help her Italian princess-grandma (Margaret Rutherford) pay taxes dating back to 1895. There are bright flashes of comedy, and as many long sequences of contrived and amateurish action, which add up to a mildly amusing film.

One of the more humorous aspects of feature is Terry-Thomas, portraying three dif-

ferent characters in as many sequences, involving Lisi in her scramble to latch onto a bundle.

The production, benefitting by lush sets and costumes of the Italian 1928 period, is overly-burdened with a script not sufficiently developed and attempting comedy that frequently does not jell.

••••••••••••••••••••••••••

■ ARABESQUE

1966, 107 MINS, US ◇ Ⓥ

Dir Stanley Donen   *Prod* Stanley Donen   *Scr* Julian Mitchell, Stanley Price, Pierre Marton [= Peter Stone]   *Ph* Christopher Challis   *Ed* Frederick Wilson   *Mus* Henry Mancini   *Art Dir* Reece Pemberton
● Gregory Peck, Sophia Loren, Alan Badel, Kieron Moore, Carl Duering, John Merivale (Universal)

Arabesque packs the names of Gregory Peck and Sophia Loren and a foreign intrigue theme, but doesn't always progress on a true entertainment course. Fault lies in a shadowy plotline and confusing characters, particularly in the miscasting of Peck in a cute role.

Based on the Gordon Cotler novel, *The Cipher*, script projects Peck as an American exchange professor of ancient languages at Oxford drawn into a vortex of hazardous endeavor. He is called upon to decipher a secret message written in hieroglyphics, a document and its translation sought by several different factions from the Middle East. He is assisted by the paradoxical character played by Loren, as an Arab sexpot who seems to be on everyone's side. There are chases, murders and attempted assassinations to whet the appetite, as well as misuses of comedy.

Peck tries valiantly with a role unsuited to him and Loren displays her usual lush and plush presence. If her part is an enigma to Peck, it is to the spectator, too.

Menace is provided by Alan Badel and Kieron Moore, both trying to latch onto contents of the cipher and out to dispose of Peck.

••••••••••••••••••••••••••

■ ARACHNOPHOBIA

1990, 109 MINS, US ◇ Ⓥ

Dir Frank Marshall   *Prod* Kathleen Kennedy, Richard Vane   *Scr* Don Jakoby, Wesley Strick   *Ph* Mikael Salomon   *Ed* Michael Kahn   *Mus* Trevor Jones   *Art Dir* James Bissell
● Jeff Daniels, Harley Jane Kozak, John Goodman, Julian Sands, Stuart Pankin, Brian McNamara (Tangled Web/Amblin)

Arachnophobia expertly blends horror and tongue-in cheek comedy in the tale of a small California coastal town overrun by Venezuelan killer spiders. Frank Marshall's sophisticated feature directing debut never indulges in ultimate gross-out effects and carefully chooses both its victims and its means of depicting their dispatch.

Beginning like an *Indiana Jones* film with an 18-minute prolog of British entomologist Julian Sands' expedition in the Venezuelan jungle, *Arachnophobia* cleverly follows the route of a prehistoric male spider hitching a ride to California and escaping to the farm of newly arrived town doctor Jeff Daniels.

The droll John Goodman has a relatively small part as the town's magnificently slobby and incompetent exterminator. Daniels is the one with the arachnophobia, which, like James Stewart's trauma in Hitchcock's *Vertigo*, must be agonizingly overcome in the spectacular climax.

Marshall has the directorial confidence to allow scripters (working from a story by Don Jakoby and Al Williams) plenty of screen time to develop characters more fully than usual in a horror film. With a variety of versatile spider performers including live South American tarantulas and more than 40 mechanical creatures devised by Chris Walas,

Marshall is able to do just about anything he wants in terms of creepy-crawly effects.

••••••••••••••••••••••••••

■ ARCH OF TRIUMPH

1948, 120 MINS, US

Dir Lewis Milestone   *Prod* David Lewis   *Scr* Lewis Milestone, Harry Brown   *Ph* Russell Metty   *Ed* Duncan Mansfield   *Mus* Louis Gruenberg   *Art Dir* William Cameron Menzies
● Charles Boyer, Ingrid Bergman, Charles Laughton, Louis Calhern, Michael Romanoff, Ruth Warrick (United Artists)

The Remarque novel, by very suggestion of authorship and the Lewis Milestone association, conjures up analogy to the now classic *All Quiet*, the post-First World War film, also from a Remarque work. The analogy ends there because the character of both differs strikingly. Current entry is a frank romantic item, laid in a setting of Paris intrigue just before open war with the western allies broke out.

The surcharged atmosphere of pre-Polish aggression and its repercussions in the City of Light that suddenly grows into blackout is a dramatic background for the Boyer-Bergman romance. The very atmosphere of the boulevards, from the Eternal Light underneath the Arc de Triomphe to the gaiety of the Sheherezade and kindred boites 'on the hill' (Montmartre) make for surefire appeal.

Charles Laughton is rather wasted as a Nazi menace, obviously the victim of the cutting room shears, as was Ruth Warrick, the American dilettante. There is no question but that over $1 million of this film's cost never shows on the screen. It's reported to have hit near the $4 million negative cost.

••••••••••••••••••••••••••

■ ARIA

1987, 98 MINS, US/UK ◇ Ⓥ

Dir Nicolas Roeg, Charles Sturridge, Jean-Luc Godard, Julien Temple, Bruce Beresford, Robert Altman, Franc Roddam, Ken Russell, Derek Jarman, Bill Bryden   *Prod* Don Boyd   *Ph* Harvey Harrison, Gale Tattersall, Carolyn Champetier, Oliver Stapleton, Dante Spinotti, Pierre Mignot, Frederick Elmes, Mike Southon, Gabriel Beristain   *Ed* Tony Lawson, Matthew Longfellow, Jean-Luc Godard, Neil Abrahamson, Marie-Therese Boiche, Robert Altman, Rick Elgood, Michael Bradsell, Peter Cartwright, Mike Cragg
● Theresa Russell, Nicola Swain, Buck Henry, Julie Hagerty, Tilda Swinton, John Hurt (RVP/Virgin)

Aria, a string of selections from 10 operas illustrated by 10 directors, is a film that could not have happened without the advent of music videos.

Producer Don Boyd, who orchestrated the project, instructed the directors not to depict what was happening to the characters in the operas but to create something new out of the emotion and content expressed in the music. The arias were the starting point.

Result is both exhilaratingly successful and distractingly fragmented. Individual segments are stunning but they come in such speedy succession that overall it is not a fully satisfying film experience.

Selections also represent a variety of film-making styles from Bruce Beresford's rather pedestrian working of a love theme from Korngold's *Die tote Stadt* to Ken Russell's characteristically excessive treatment of an idea distilled from Puccini's *Turandot*.

Structurally, the most ambitious of the selections is Jean-Luc Godard's working of Lully's *Armide* which he transposes to a body building gym where two naked women try to attract the attention of the men.

The most striking clash of images is achieved by Franc Roddam who moves Wagner's *Tristan und Isolde* to Las Vegas. As the lush strains of the music blare, the neon sea of the casinos has never looked more strange.

••••••••••••••••••••••••••••••••••

■ ARISTOCATS, THE

1970, 78 MINS, US ◇

Dir Wolfgang Reitherman   *Prod* Walt Disney, Wolfgang Reitherman, Winston Hibler   *Scr* Larry Clemmons   *Ed* Tom Acosta   *Mus* George Bruns
● (Walt Disney)

The Aristocats is a good animated feature from Walt Disney Studios, an original period comedy with drama about a feline family rescued from the plans of an evil butler who would prefer his mistress not to leave her fortune to the cats.

Helped immeasurably by the voices of Phil Harris, Eva Gabor, Sterling Holloway, Scatman Crothers and others, plus some outstanding animation, songs, sentiment, some excellent dialog and even a touch of psychedelia.

Harris, who gave *Jungle Book* a lot of its punch, is even more prominent here as the voice of an alley cat who rescues Gabor and her three kittens. Gabor's voice and related animation are excellent, ditto that for two hound dogs, Pat Buttram and George Lindsey.

The technical details of the $4 million cartoon are marvelous to behold.

••••••••••••••••••••••••••••••••••

■ ARMED AND DANGEROUS

1986, 88 MINS, US ◇ ⓥ

Dir Mark L. Lester   *Prod* Brian Grazer, James Keach   *Scr* Harold Ramis, Peter Torokvei   *Ph* Fred Schuler   *Ed* Michael Hill, Daniel Hanley, George Pedugo   *Mus* Bill Meyers   *Art Dir* David L. Snyder
● John Candy, Eugene Levy, Robert Loggia, Kenneth McMillan, Meg Ryan, Brion James (Columbia)

Armed and Dangerous is a broad farce slightly elevated by the presence of John Candy and Eugene Levy.

Story [by Brian Grazer, Harold Ramis and James Keach] functions as little more than a fashion show for Candy. The piece de resistance is Candy in a blue tuxedo with a ruffled shirt that makes his enormous bulk look like a wrapped Christmas present.

Candy plays one of LA's finest until he's wrongfully kicked off the force for corruption. He winds up at Guard Dog Security where he teams with shyster lawyer Levy on a new career. Company, it turns out, is under the thumb of the mob headed by union honcho Robert Loggia.

It's all pretty basic stuff delivered with a minimum of imagination.

••••••••••••••••••••••••••••••••••

■ AROUND THE WORLD IN 80 DAYS

1956, 175 MINS, US ◇ ⓥ

Dir Michael Anderson   *Prod* Michael Todd   *Scr* S.J. Perelman, John Farrow, James Poe   *Ph* Lionel Lindon   *Ed* Gene Ruggiero, Paul Weatherwax   *Mus* Victor Young   *Art Dir* James Sullivan
● David Niven, Cantinflas, Robert Newton, Shirley MacLaine, Charles Boyer, Ronald Colman (Todd/United Artists)

This is a long picture – two hours and 55 minutes plus intermission. Little time has been wasted and the story races on as Phileas Fogg and company proceed from London to Paris, thence via balloon to Spain and the bullfights; from there to Marseilles and India, where Fogg and Passepartout rescue beautiful Shirley MacLaine from death on a funeral pyre; to Hong Kong, Japan, San Francisco, across the country by train to New York (notwithstanding an Indian attack) and thence back to England.

Todd-AO system here, for the first time, is properly used and fills the screen with wondrous effects. Images are extraordinarily sharp and depth of focus is striking in many scenes.

David Niven, as Fogg, is the perfect stereotype of the unruffled English gentleman and quite intentionally, a caricature of 19th-century British propriety. Matching him is Mexican star Cantinflas (Mario Moreno) as Passepartout. Robert Newton in the role of Mr Fix, the detective who trails Fogg whom he suspects of having robbed the Bank of London, is broad comic all the way through, and MacLaine is appealing as the princess.

There's rarely been a picture that can boast of so many star names in bit parts. Just to name a few in the more important roles: John Carradine as the pompous Col. Proctor; Finlay Currie, Ronald Squires, Basil Sydney, A.E. Matthews and Trevor Howard as members of the Reform Club who bet against Fogg; Robert Morley as the stodgy governor of the Bank of England; Cedric Hardwicke as a colonial militarist; Red Skelton, as a drunk; Marlene Dietrich and George Raft. There are many others, including Frank Sinatra in a flash shot as a piano player. Jose Greco, early in the footage, wows with a heel fandango.

Pic's sound is extraordinarily vivid and effective and a major asset. Saul Bass' final titles are a tribute to the kind of taste and imagination, the ingenuity and the splendor that mark this entire Todd production. It's all on the screen, every penny of the $5–6 million that went into the making.

□ 1956: Best Picture

••••••••••••••••••••••••••••••••••

■ ARRANGEMENT, THE

1969, 125 MINS, US ◇ ⓥ

Dir Elia Kazan   *Prod* Elia Kazan   *Scr* Elia Kazan   *Ph* Robert Surtees   *Ed* Stefan Arnsten   *Mus* David Amram   *Art Dir* Gene Callahan
● Kirk Douglas, Faye Dunaway, Deborah Kerr, Richard Boone, Hume Cronyn (Warner)

The Arrangement is a one-man production show; consequently, one man is responsible for a confused, overly-contrived and over-length film peopled with a set of characters about whom the spectator couldn't care less. In a four-way plunge, Elia Kazan produced and directed from his own screenplay based upon his own 1967 novel.

Three principals in a story focusing on a man's problems and bafflements are Kirk Douglas, Deborah Kerr and Faye Dunaway.

The talents of cast are taxed but they almost rise above their assignments. Douglas plays a successful Los Angeles advertising man, apparently a wizard account exec, wed to Kerr, a long-suffering wife who tries to understand her husband's obsession for Dunaway, with whom he's been carrying on a tumultous affair.

••••••••••••••••••••••••••••••••••

■ ARSENE LUPIN

1932, 64 MINS, US

Dir Jack Conway   *Scr* Carey Wilson, Bayard Veiller, Lenore Coffee   *Ph* Oliver T. Marsh   *Ed* Hugh Wynn
● John Barrymore, Lionel Barrymore, Karen Morley, John Miljan, Tully Marshall, Henry Armetta (M-G-M)

First screen appearance of John and Lionel Barrymore together and their fine acting lifts the production to a high artistic level.

But the action often is allowed to lapse for dangerously long intervals while the two Barrymores elaborate their interpretation of the super-thief (John) and the dogged detective (Lionel).

A neat angle of this film version [of the French play by Maurice LeBlanc and Francis de Croisset] is the fact that the audience never sees Lupin in the act of larceny itself. This literary scheme is maintained until the last episode, when the elaborate plot to steal the Mona Lisa from the Louvre is worked out in detail and in sight, a fitting climax and a well-paced and balanced sequence.

Story has a touch of discreet but sophisticated spice in the love affair between Lupin and Sonia, the girl released from prison on parole and forced to aid the police in the pursuit. Femme lead is played by Karen Morley with a beautiful balance of reticence and occasional emphasis.

••••••••••••••••••••••••••••••••••

■ ARSENIC AND OLD LACE

1944, 118 MINS, US ⓥ

Dir Frank Capra   *Prod* Frank Capra   *Scr* Julius J. Epstein, Philip G. Epstein   *Ph* Sol Polito   *Ed* Daniel Mandell   *Mus* Max Steiner   *Art Dir* Max Parker
● Cary Grant, Priscilla Lane, Raymond Massey, Jack Carson, Peter Lorre, Edward Everett Horton (Warner)

Despite the fact that picture runs 118 minutes, Frank Capra has expanded on the original play [by Joseph Kesselring] to a sufficient extent to maintain a steady, consistent pace. With what he has crammed into the running time, film doesn't seem that long. The majority of the action is confined to one set, that of the home of the two amiably nutty aunts who believe it's kind to poison people they come in contact with and their non-violently insane brother who thinks he's Teddy Roosevelt.

Cary Grant and Priscilla Lane are paired romantically. They open the picture getting married but are delayed in their honeymoon when Grant finds his two screwy aunts have been bumping off people in their house, burying them in the cellar and even holding thoughtful funeral ceremonies for them. The laughs that surround his efforts to get John Alexander, the 'Teddy Roosevelt' of the picture, committed to an institution; troubles that come up when a maniacal long-lost brother shows up after a world tour of various murders with a phoney doctor, and other plot elements make for diversion of a very agreeable character.

••••••••••••••••••••••••••••••••••

■ ARTHUR

1981, 117 MINS, US ◇

Dir Steve Gordon   *Prod* Robert Greenhut   *Scr* Steve Gordon   *Ph* Fred Schules   *Ed* Susan E. Morse   *Mus* Burt Bacharach   *Art Dir* Stephen Hendrickson
● Dudley Moore, Liza Minnelli, John Gielgud, Geraldine Fitzgerald, Jill Eikenberry (Orion)

Arthur is a sparkling entertainment which attempts, with a large measure of success, to resurrect the amusingly artificial conventions of 1930s screwball romantic comedies. Dudley Moore is back in top-'*10*' form as a layabout drunken playboy who finds himself falling in love with working-class girl Liza Minnelli just as he's being forced into an arranged marriage with a society WASP.

Central dilemma, which dates back to Buster Keaton at least, has wastrel Moore faced with the choice of marrying white bread heiress Jill Eikenberry or being cut off by his father from $750 million. After much procrastination, he finally agrees to the union, but situation is complicated when, in a vintage (meet cute), he protects shoplifter Minnelli from the authorities and finds himself genuinely falling for someone for the first time in his padded life.

As Moore's eternally supportive but irrepressibly sarcastic valet, John Gielgud gives a priceless performance. Minnelli fills the bill in a less showbizzy and smaller part than usual, but pic's core is really the wonderful relationship between Moore and Gielgud.

••••••••••••••••••••••••••••••••••

■ ARTHUR 2 ON THE ROCKS

1988, 113 MINS, US ◇ ⓥ

Dir Bud Yorkin   *Prod* Robert Shapiro   *Scr* Andy Breckman   *Ph* Stephen H. Burum   *Ed* Michael Kahn   *Mus* Burt Bacharach   *Art Dir* Gene Callahan

A

● Dudley Moore, Liza Minelli, Geraldine Fitzgerald, Paul Benedict, John Gielgud, Cynthia Sikes (Warner)

Arthur 2 is not as classy a farce as the original, but still manages to be an amusing romp.

Five years into their marriage and living the enviable Park Avenue lifestyle with the kind of digs photographed by Architectural Digest wife Linda (Liza Minnelli) finds she's unable to conceive and goes about adopting a baby.

While Minnelli is gung ho to expand the fold, Arthur's ex-girlfriend's father (Stephen Elliott) seeks to break it apart. Vindictive over having his love-struck daughter stood up at the altar by Arthur last time around, he works up a legal trick to take away the wastrel's $750 million fortune and force him to marry his daughter after all.

Though not critical to the pleasures of watching Moore in one of his best screen roles, it does undermine his performance when he has lesser personalities to tease. Minnelli loses some of her working class sassiness as the downtown-gone-uptown-gone-downtown wife trying to put her house in order, though credit is due her for carrying plot's best scenes.

. . . .

■ ARTISTS AND MODELS

1955, 108 MINS, US ◇

Dir Frank Tashlin   *Prod* Hal Wallis   *Scr* Frank Tashlin, Hal Kanter, Herbert Baker   *Ph* Daniel L. Fapp   *Ed* Warren Low   *Mus* Walter Scharf
● Dean Martin, Jerry Lewis, Shirley MacLaine, Dorothy Malone, Eddie Mayehoff, Anita Ekberg (Paramount)

Comedic diversion in the Martin and Lewis manner has been put together in this overdone, slaphappy melange of gags and gals. Six writers [three scripters, plus adaptation by Don McGuire from a play by Michael Davidson and Norman Lessing] figure in the production and, while giving the comics a story line to follow, also worked in everything but the proverbial kitchen sink.

Co-starring with the comedy team are Shirley MacLaine and Dorothy Malone. The former tackles her role of model with a bridling cuteness but has a figure to take the viewer's mind off her facial expression. Ditto Dorothy Malone, her artist roommate.

Dean Martin is an artist and Jerry Lewis is a would-be writer of kiddie stories, both starving in NY.

. . . .

■ ASH WEDNESDAY

1973, 99 MINS, US ◇ Ⓥ

Dir Larry Peerce   *Prod* Dominick Dunne   *Scr* Jean-Claude Tramont   *Ph* Ennio Guarnieri   *Ed* Marion Rothman   *Mus* Maurice Jarre   *Art Dir* Philip Abramson
● Elizabeth Taylor, Henry Fonda, Helmut Berger, Keith Baxter, Maurice Teynac, Margaret Blye (Sagittarius/Paramount)

Ash Wednesday is a jolting tearjerker about middle-age marital trauma, compounded by the superficial and spiritual uplift of cosmetic surgery. Elizabeth Taylor stars as the fiftyish wife of Henry Fonda, and Helmut Berger is featured as her brief Italian resort affair after the beautification process has restored her surface charm.

Script is essentially a three-act play, about evenly divided over the film's 99 minutes. Act 1 is a gruesome, overdone series of ugly surgical scenes. Act 2 introduces Taylor to a new world of uncertain poise, while Act 3 precipitates the powerful, neatly restrained dissolution of her marriage to Fonda.

Taylor, fashionably gowned and bejewelled carries the film almost single-handedly. Fonda is excellent in his climatic appearance, an usually superb casting idea.

. . . .

■ ASHANTI

1979, 117 MINS, SWITZERLAND ◇ Ⓥ

Dir Richard Fleischer   *Prod* Georges-Alain Vuille   *Scr* Stephen Geller   *Ph* Aldo Tonti   *Mus* Michael Melvoin   *Art Dir* Aurelio Crugnola
● Michael Caine, Peter Ustinov, Beverly Johnson, Omar Sharif, Rex Harrison, Willliam Holden (Columbia)

A polished but lacklustre adventure entertainment.

Michael Caine and Beverly Johnson are World Health Organization medics on a visit to an African tribe when the lady becomes a prize catch of Arabian slave trader Peter Ustinov. Caine's retrieval odyssey thereafter is variously aided by Rex Harrison as an ambiguous go-between, William Holden as a mercenary helicopter pilot, and Indian actor Kabir Bedi as a Bedouin with his own score to settle with Ustinov. All acquit with professional grace but unremarkable impact.

No help to the film's grip on interest is director Richard Fleischer's minuet pacing. He seems to have come under the spell of those Saharan sand dunes lavishly and lengthily dwelled on as Caine and Bedi pick up Ustinov's trail.

. . . .

■ ASK A POLICEMAN

1939, 83 MINS, UK

Dir Marcel Varnel   *Scr* Marriott Edgar, Val Guest   *Ph* Derick Williams
● Will Hay, Graham Moffatt, Moore Marriott, Glennis Lorimer, Peter Gawthorne, Charles Oliver (Gainsborough)

Bits of *Dr Syn* (1937), with George Arliss, and *The Ghost Train* (1931) blend happily with amusing dialog and situations [story by Sidney Gilliatt] usually associated with Will Hay and his two stooges, the fat boy and old man.

A village police station becomes the center of interest when it's discovered there's been no crime there for over 10 years. The sergeant (Hay) in command of two subordinates (Graham Moffatt, Moore Marriott), hearing they're likely to be transferred or fired because of lack of 'business', plans to frame one or two cases.

Planting a keg of brandy on the beach, to stage a smuggler's racket, they discover another, real contraband keg. From then on it's a wild chase between the three witnits and a band headed by the local squire (Charles Oliver) which is carrying on a lucrative haul.

. . . .

■ ASPHALT JUNGLE, THE

1950, 112 MINS, US Ⓥ

Dir John Huston   *Prod* Arthur Hornblow Jr   *Scr* Ben Maddow, John Huston   *Ph* Harold Rosson   *Ed* George Boemler   *Mus* Miklos Rozsa
● Sterling Hayden, Louis Calhern, Sam Jaffe, James Whitmore, Jean Hagen, Marilyn Monroe (M-G-M)

The Asphalt Jungle is a study in crime, hard-hitting in its expose of the underworld. Ironic realism is striven for and achieved in the writing, production and direction. An audience will quite easily pull for the crooks in their execution of the million-dollar jewelry theft around which the plot is built.

W.R. Burnett's lusty novel about criminal types, from the cheap hood to the mastermind, provided the punchy basis for the script. The actual heist is a suspenseful piece of filming, as is the following police chase and gradual disintegration of the gang.

Sterling Hayden and Louis Calhern star as contrasting criminals, the former a mean, bitter hood who dreams of restoring an old Kentucky horse farm, and Calhern a crooked attorney who needs money to continue sating his desire for curvy blondes and high living.

. . . .

■ ASSASSINATION OF TROTSKY, THE

1972, 105 MINS, FRANCE/ITALY ◇ Ⓥ

Dir Joseph Losey   *Prod* Norman Priggen, Joseph Losey   *Scr* Nicholas Mosley   *Ph* Pasqualino De Santis   *Ed* Roberto Siti   *Mus* Egisto Macchi   *Art Dir* Richard Macdonald
● Richard Burton, Alain Delon, Romy Schneider, Valentina Cortese, Luigi Vanucchi, Giorgio Albertazzi (Cinettel/CIAC/De Laurentiis)

The last days (1940) in the life of the Russian revolutionary figure, Leon Trotsky, are traced in this fairly cryptic film.

Intended as a sort of political thriller, the film remains cloudy vis-a-vis the Stalin menace though it works up dread, and the foreshadowed (pickaxe, skull-shattering) death. But there is too much forced symbolism, diffuse characterization and a sort of schematic feel sans enough interplay of people, historical perspective, or new insights into this political or psychological murder.

Richard Burton sometimes catches a cantankerous and surface aspect of the aging revolutionary, once almost as popular as Lenin in Russia.

The film rarely transcends a sort of banal look at the murder. It has little to say about political hatred and fanaticism.

. . . .

■ ASSASSIN OF THE TSAR

1991, 104 MINS, UK/USSR ◇ Ⓥ

Dir Karen Shakhnazarov   *Prod* Christopher Gawor, Erik Vaisberg, Anthony Sloman   *Scr* Alexander Borodyansky, Karen Shakhnazarov   *Ph* Nikolai Nemolyaev   *Ed* Anthony Sloman, Lidia Milioti   *Mus* John Altman, Vladimir Shut   *Art Dir* Ludmila Kusakova
● Malcolm McDowell, Oleg Yankovsky, Armen Dzhigarkhanian, Yuri Sherstnyov (Spectator/Mosfilm/Courier)

Part historical drama, part psycho suspenser, *Assassin of the Tsar* doesn't score clean hits on all its targets, but has powerful playing by topper Malcolm McDowell and excellent all-round production values.

Pic kicks off with a tinted re-creation of Tsar Alexander II's assassination in 1881. It's the first of a series of delusions told to doctors by Timofeyev (Malcolm McDowell), a schizo in a present-day Moscow hospital who thinks he singlehandedly wiped out the Russian royals.

Timofeyev thinks he was Yakov Yurovsky, in charge of icing Tsar Nicholas II and his family in 1918. Despite Timofeyev's claim that he's cured, new medico Smirnov (Oleg Yankovsky) reckons there's still a ghost to be exorcised. Smirnov becomes obsessed with discovering the truth of the assassination and even taking on the role of Nicholas II in Timofeyev's fantasies.

Climax comes when the haggard Smirnov visits Sverdlovsk (site of the 1918 slayings) and joins minds with Timofeyev to relive the actual assassination.

White-haired and craggy-faced as the wily loony, and dead-eyed as the secret police nobody, McDowell's totally believable in both roles. Soviet superstar Yankovsky is restricted in an underwritten part as the medico/tsar, but gives solid support. Other roles are mainly bits.

Pic was lensed in Moscow and Leningrad in two language versions, virtually identical shot-for-shot.

. . . .

■ ASSAULT ON A QUEEN

1966, 106 MINS, US ◇

Dir Jack Donohue   *Prod* William Goetz   *Scr* Rod Serling   *Ph* William H. Daniels   *Ed* Archie Marshek   *Mus* Duke Ellington   *Art Dir* Paul Groesse
● Frank Sinatra, Virna Lisi, Anthony Franciosa, Richard Conte, Alf Kjellin, Errol John (Seven Arts/Sinatra)

Producer William Goetz has supervised a remarkable job of making plausible the admittedly wild-eyed adventures of an odd assortment of moral derelicts who salvage a submarine with the intent of robbing the *Queen Mary* (hence the title) [based on the novel by Jack Finney].

Virna Lisi, Anthony Franciosa and Alf Kjellin, on the hunt for a sunken treasure ship off the Bahamas, hire Frank Sinatra and his partner, Errol John, who run a fishing boat business, to help them find the treasure. Sinatra, instead, finds a small sunken German submarine. Kjellin, a former German U-boat commander, talks the group into salvaging it and holding up the *Queen Mary*.

Only Kjellin is able to create a well-rounded character and is outstanding as the apparently bland German, holding in control his diabolic intent. Sinatra and Lisi are very good in roles that make few demands on their acting ability. John, while efficient in the tenser moments, seems inhibited in scenes where he must wax sentimental over his rehabilitation by Sinatra.

● ●

■ ASSAULT ON PRECINCT 13

1976, 91 MINS, US ◇ Ⓥ

Dir John Carpenter *Prod* J.S. Kaplan *Scr* John Carpenter *Ph* Douglas Knapp *Ed* John T. Chance *Mus* John Carpenter *Art Dir* Tommy Wallace
● Austin Stoker, Darwin Joston, Laurie Zimmer, Martin West, Tony Burton, Charles Cyphers (CKK)

Novelty of a gang swearing a blood oath to destroy a precinct station and all inside is sufficiently compelling for the gory-minded to assure acceptance.

Gang is motivated by a man who kills one of their members for the murder of his small daughter and takes refuge in the Los Angeles station so distraught he cannot explain. Assault closely follows his arrival, and it's a war.

Precinct station is within hours of closing to move to new quarters, which explains why only a single cop and a policewoman remains to hold down the fort, abetted by two prisoners who are temporarily incarcerated on their way to Death Row in Salinas.

John Carpenter's direction of his screenplay, after a pokey opening half, is responsible for realistic movement.

● ●

■ ASSIGNMENT, THE

1977, 97 MINS, SWEDEN ◇ Ⓥ

Dir Mats Arehn *Prod* Ingemar Ejve *Scr* Lars Magnus Jansson, Ingemar Ejve, Mats Arehn *Ph* Lennart Carlsson *Ed* Ingemar Ejve
● Thomas Hellberg, Christopher Plummer, Carolyn Seymour, Fernando Rey, Per Oscarsson (Nordisk/Svensk/SFI)

Story based on an early novel by Per Wahloo about a young Swedish diplomat sent to a violence-torn Latin American state as mediator. From the moment of his arrival, it is clear that everybody distrusts him and most want him killed.

The mediator, played as a man of civil courage in spite of obvious fear by Thomas Hellberg, asserts his authority, what little he has, over such warring parties as a police captain, the local Mr Big and the Liberation Front leader, a village doctor and others. Carolyn Seymour as the mediator's secretary supplies a coolly sensual presence.

Film, fortunately, preaches no moral, but in its mix of solid little chills and thrills, it features both tender compassion, rage against injustice and a lot of subdued humor.

● ●

■ ASYLUM

1972, 88 MINS, UK ◇ Ⓥ

Dir Roy Ward Baker *Prod* Max J. Rosenberg, Milton Subotsky *Scr* Robert Bloch *Ph* Denys Coop *Ed* Peter Tanner *Mus* Douglas Gamley *Art Dir* Tony Curtis

● Peter Cushing, Britt Ekland, Herbert Lom, Patrick Magee, Sylvia Syms, Barbara Parkins (Amicus)

Herewith a dependable programmer off the Amicus belt line. It's a trim little chiller, with a moderate quota of blood and mayhem, polished performances and smooth direction. It also boasts some imaginative props – like the decapitated limbs, etc., of Sylvia Syms metaphysically killing her murderer and errant husband, Richard Todd, and his sweetie Barbara Parkins.

The plot is essentially about a young shrink's (Robert Powell) voyage of discovery in an insane asylum where he hopes to become a staffer. He arrives to find that the bossman has himself become confined as a homicidal nut case. His successor (Patrick Magee), by way of putting the young doc to the test, has him interview several psychos.

Very few of the key thesps remain robust and vertical by the windup, for which scripter Robert Bloch comes up with an effective trick ending.

● ●

■ AS YOU DESIRE ME

1932, 70 MINS, US

Dir George Fitzmaurice *Scr* Gene Markey *Ph* William Daniels *Ed* George Hiveley
● Greta Garbo, Melvyn Douglas, Erich von Stroheim, Owen Moore, Hedda Hopper, Rafaela Ottiano (M-G-M)

A romantic problem play interestingly played by the fascinating Greta Garbo, treated in a manner of high drama. The original [play by Luigi Pirandello] hasn't been broadly hoked in the manner that Metro has so often followed.

Story has to do with an Italian countess, victim of the Austrian invasion and violence from drunken soldiers and driven into a mental fog which has blotted out her past. She is recognized 10 years later in her wanderings as a music-hall singer by the painter who had done her portrait as a bride, and by him brought back to her grief-stricken husband.

But she cannot recall the past and is never entirely received by the people of her former life, with the exception of the portrait painter, who sees with the eyes of faith.

Garbo's performance is always absorbing, vivid in its acting and compelling in appeal. Melvyn Douglas is a rather lukewarm actor in a stencil husband role, impeccably played but unexciting. Owen Moore grabs the acting honors among the men with his jaunty handling of a minor part, while Erich von Stroheim fails signally to make himself the man you love to hate by revealing an accent of blended Yorkville and Ninth Avenue.

● ●

■ AT CLOSE RANGE

1986, 111 MINS, US ◇ Ⓥ

Dir James Foley *Prod* Elliott Lewitt, Don Guest *Scr* Nicholas Kazan *Ph* Juan Ruiz-Anchia *Ed* Howard Smith *Mus* Patrick Leonard *Art Dir* Peter Jamison
● Sean Penn, Christopher Walken, Mary Stuart Masterson, Christopher Penn, Millie Perkins (Hemdale)

A downbeat tale of brutal family relations, James Foley's *At Close Range* is a very tough picture. Violent without being vicarious, this true story is set in a small Pennsylvania town in 1978. Story introduces young Brad (Sean Penn) as just another rather tough kid with an eye for a new girl (the charming Mary Stuart Masterson) and fiercely protective of his brother (Christopher Penn).

Along comes Brad's father (Christopher Walken) who has a reputation as a criminal. Intrigued by his seemingly exciting parent, Brad Jr is encouraged to form his own gang to carry out more modest heists.

General audiences will respond to the very strong performances of the two leads, especially Walken in one of his best roles.

● ●

■ AT LONG LAST LOVE

1975, 118 MINS, US ◇

Dir Peter Bogdanovich *Prod* Peter Bogdanovich *Scr* Peter Bogdanovich *Ph* Laszlo Kovacs *Mus* Artie Butler *Art Dir* Gene Allen
● Burt Reynolds, Cybill Shepherd, Madeline Kahn, Duilio Del Prete, Eileen Brennan, John Hillerman (20th Century-Fox)

At Long Last Love, Peter Bogdanovich's experiment with a mostly-singing 1930s upper-class romance, is a disappointing and embarrassing waste of talent.

Utilizing 16 Cole Porter songs, many of them not heard for years and all of them replete with additional lyrics hardly ever used, writer-producer-director Bogdanovich tries to float a bubble of gaiety involving three couples: bored playboy Reynolds with rent-hungry Deb Cybill Shepherd; Broadway star Madeline Kahn and immigrant gambler Duilio Del Prete; and Eileen Brennan (Shepherd's maid) and John Hillerman (Reynold's urbane valet). The customary plot crises and romantic complications, recognized and adored by vintage film buffs, eventually resolve themselves.

The principals sang their numbers while being filmed, with orchestrations dubbed in later, in an attempt to eliminate the lifelessness of post-sync when it is done poorly. On the basis of this experiment, pre-recording can rest its case.

● ●

■ AT THE CIRCUS

1939, 86 MINS, US Ⓥ

Dir Edward Buzzell *Prod* Mervyn LeRoy *Scr* Irving Brecher *Ph* Leonard M. Smith *Ed* William H. Terhune *Mus* Franz Waxman (dir.) *Art Dir* Cedric Gibbons, Stan Rogers
● Groucho Marx, Chico Marx, Harpo Marx, Margaret Dumont, Florence Rice, Eve Arden (M-G-M)

The Marx Bros. revert to the rousing physical comedy and staccato gag dialog of their earlier pictures in *At the Circus*.

Story is slight but unimportant. Kenny Baker, owner of a circus, is harrassed by pursuing James Burke, who wants to foreclose the mortgage he holds on the outfit. When Baker's bankroll is stolen, Chico and Harpo call in Groucho to straighten out the difficulties. Groucho winds up by selling the circus for one performance to Margaret Dumont, Baker's rich aunt and Newport social leader.

Chico does his pianolog in circus car, while Harpo's turn for a harp solo is set up in the menagerie with a production and choral background. A colored kid band and adult chorus (from Hollywood company of *Swing Mikado*) are used here.

● ●

■ ATLANTIC CITY

1980, 104 MINS, CANADA/FRANCE/US ◇ Ⓥ

Dir Louis Malle *Prod* Denis Heroux, Gabriel Boustani *Scr* John Guare *Ph* Richard Ciupka *Ed* Suzanne Baron *Mus* Michel Legrand
● Burt Lancaster, Susan Sarandon, Michel Piccoli, Kate Reid, Robert Joy, Hollis MacLaren (Selta/Kfouri/Cine Neighbor/FR3/SDICC)

Film is blessed with a spare, intriguing script by Yank John Guare, which always skirts impending cliches and predictability by finding unusual facets in his characters and their actions.

The film is well limned by Burt Lancaster as a smalltime, mythomaniacal, aging mafia hood, Susan Sarandon as an ambitious young woman, Kate Reid as a fading moll and Robert Joy and Hollis MacLaren as

A

Sarandon's husband and young sister.

Atlantic City is also a character as director Louis Malle adroitly uses decrepit old and new facades; New Jersey voted to allow gambling at this resort which had boasted gangsters, prohibition capers and big show attractions.

☐ 1981: Best Picture (Nomination)

. . . .

■ ATLANTIS, THE LOST CONTINENT

1961, 91 MINS, US ◇

Dir George Pal   *Prod* George Pal   *Scr* Daniel Mainwaring   *Ph* Harold E. Wellman   *Ed* Ben Lewis   *Mus* Russell Garcia   *Art Dir* George W. Davis, William Ferrari

● Anthony Hall, Joyce Taylor, Frank De Kova, John Dall (M-G-M)

After establishing legendary significance via an arresting prolog in which the basis for age-old suspicion of the existence of a lost continental cultural link in the middle of the Atlantic is discussed, scenarist Daniel Mainwaring promptly proceeds to ignore the more compelling possibilities of the hypothesis in favor of erecting a tired, shopworn melodrama out of Gerald Hargreaves' play.

There is an astonishing similarity to the stevereevesian spectacles. An 'ordeal by fire and water' ritual conducted in a great, crowded stadium seems almost a replica of gladiatorial combat in the Colosseum. When Atlantis is burning to a cinder at the climax, one can almost hear Nero fiddling. Even Russ Garcia's score has that pompous, martial Roman air about it. And at least several of the mob spectacle scenes have been lifted from Roman screen spectacles of the past (the 1951 version of *Quo Vadis* looks like the source). The acting is routine.

. . . .

■ ATTACK OF THE 50 FT. WOMAN

1958, 65 MINS, US

Dir Nathan Hertz   *Prod* Bernard Woolner   *Scr* Mark Hanna   *Ph* Jacques R. Marquette   *Ed* Edward Mann   *Mus* Ronald Stein

● Allison Hayes, William Hudson, Yvette Vickers, Roy Gordon, George Douglas, Ken Terrell (Allied Artists)

Attack of the 50 Ft. Woman shapes up as a minor offering for the scifi trade where demands aren't too great.

The production is the story of a femme who overnight grows into a murderous giantess, out to get husband who's cheating with another woman. Growth was caused by ray burns suffered when she's seized by huge monster, who lands in the desert near home in a satellite from outer space. Breaking the chains used to restrain her in her luxurious mansion, she makes her way to a tavern where spouse is with his lady love and literally squeezes him to death before the sheriff kills her with a riot gun.

Allison Hayes takes title role as a mentally-disturbed woman who has been in a sanitarium, William Hudson is the husband and Yvette Vickers his girl friend, all good enough in their respective characters.

. . . .

■ ATTACK OF THE KILLER TOMATOES

1979, 87 MINS, US ◇

Dir John De Bello   *Prod* Steve Peace, John De Bello   *Scr* Costa Dillon, Steve Peace, John De Bello   *Ph* John K. Culley   *Ed* John De Bello   *Mus* Gordon Goodwin, Paul Sundfor

● David Miller, George Wilson, Sharon Taylor, Jack Riley (Four Square)

Attack of the Killer Tomatoes, a low-budget indie production made by a group of young San Diego filmmakers, isn't even worthy of sarcasm. Plot, if it can be called that, concerns sudden growth spurt of tomatoes and their rampage.

Only saving grace is the satire pic's opening titles, a clever lampoon of theatre trailers and advertising pitches, including a mid-credit title card that boasts, 'This space for rent'. There's also a tongue-in-cheek parody of disaster pic music, sung in a deep basso voice, but that's over in about two minutes. Thereafter it's all downhill, rapidly.

. . . .

■ AUDREY ROSE

1977, 112 MINS, US ◇

Dir Robert Wise   *Prod* Joe Wizan, Frank De Felitta   *Scr* Frank De Felitta   *Ph* Victor J. Kemper   *Ed* Carl Kress   *Mus* Michael Small   *Art Dir* Harry Horner

● Marsha Mason, Anthony Hopkins, John Beck, Susan Swift, Norman Lloyd, John Hillerman (United Artists)

Frank De Felitta's novel and screenplay of reincarnation comes to the screen fully realized in all creative aspects.

Film takes upper middle-class couple Marsha Mason and John Beck into a nightmare of torment when daughter Susan Swift begins acting strangely. Anthony Hopkins simultaneously menaces as the outsider who has a mysterious influence on the child.

The script does a good job in interpolating the necessary philosophical and metaphysical explanations of reincarnation without being overly didactic or tediously expository.

Herein, city streets, courtrooms, schools and other mundane locations familiar to audiences are the setting for the plot making the ethereal aspects even more subtly powerful.

. . . .

■ AUNTIE MAME

1958, 143 MINS, US ◇

Dir Morton DaCosta   *Scr* Betty Comden, Adolph Green   *Ph* Harry Stradling Sr   *Ed* William Ziegler   *Mus* Bronislau Kaper   *Art Dir* Malcolm Bert

● Rosalind Russell, Forrest Tucker, Coral Browne, Fred Clark, Roger Smith, Joanna Barnes (Warner)

Auntie Mame is a faithfully funny recording of the hit play, changed only in some small details. Rosalind Russell recreates the title role for the film. Betty Comden and Adolph Green did the screenplay, based on the play by Jerome Lawrence and Robert E. Lee, which in turn was taken from the novel of Patrick Dennis.

Russell plays the character described in the dialog as 'a loving woman – odd, but loving'. She is a high-class – or, at least, rich – Bohemian. She mixes Greek Orthodox bishops with Gertrude Stein-type females, for her own amusement, directing this chorus of mixed voices with a cigarette holder loaded with gems as phony as most of her guests. 'Life is a banquet' is her philosophy. Even when the stock market crash wipes her out, the depression that follows fails to depress her for long.

Russell scores because her native intelligence augments her sharp comedy sense. She can spike a line and drive it in, but she can also carry off the scenes of mother love and romance with her nephew and her husband.

As in the legit version, Peggy Cass is a comedy standout as the helpless Agnes Gooch. Coral Browne, as the alcoholic actress who is Mame's best friend, and Fred Clark, as the baffled banker assigned to trustee Mame's nephew, are also strong comedy supports. Forrest Tucker, playing somewhat straighter, makes a human figure of his Southern millionaire but gets a great deal of fun out of it, too.

☐ 1958: Best Picture (Nomination)

. . . .

■ AUTHOR! AUTHOR!

1982, 110 MINS, US ◇

Dir Arthur Hiller   *Prod* Irwin Winkler   *Scr* Israel Horovitz   *Ph* Victor J. Kemper   *Ed* William Reynolds   *Mus* Dave Grusin   *Art Dir* Gene Rudolf

● Al Pacino, Dyan Cannon, Tuesday Weld, Alan King, Bob Dishy, Bob Elliott (20th Century-Fox)

Author! Author! is rather a mess, but a quite amiable one. This *Kramer vs Kramer* multiplied by five kids by no means approaches its full comic or emotional potential, but Israel Horovitz's marvelous screenplay and Al Pacino's warm performance provide constant pleasure.

Pacino plays a New York playwright who's attempting to get his first play in two years off the ground. Tale runs the course of the comedy's preparation, from initial director change to casting, rehearsals, rewrites and, finally, opening night.

Heart of the film, however, lies in Pacino's domestic life. His wife (Tuesday Weld) leaves him for another man, stranding kids of their own as well as from her previous three marriages.

Pacino takes it hard, but is momentarily soothed by the friendly attentions of Hollywood star Dyan Cannon, making the Broadway plunge for the first time in the leading role of the play.

. . . .

■ AVALANCHE

1978, 91 MINS, US ◇

Dir Corey Allen   *Prod* Roger Corman   *Scr* Claude Pola, Corey Allen   *Ph* Pierre-William Glenn   *Ed* Stuart Schoolnik, Larry Bock   *Mus* William Kraft   *Art Dir* Phillip Thomas

● Rock Hudson, Mia Farrow, Robert Forster, Jeanette Nolan, Rick Moses, Steve Franken (New World)

Rock Hudson and Mia Farrow head the cast of characters gathered at a ski lodge beneath an uneasy cornice of snow. They warned Hudson not to build the lodge on this particular spot, but he went ahead with the same stubbornness that cost him the wife he still loves.

Farrow, that's the ex-wife, is on hand for the grand opening and quickly beds down with Robert Forster, the naturalist photographer who keeps complaining about the trees Hudson is cutting down. Hudson, in turn, is having a steam-room fling with his secretary.

Eventually, the whole mountain top comes down on the crowd of skaters, skiers and sledders. Using a lot of archive footage of an actual massive avalanche, director Corey Allen and crew have done a very good job of creating realistic scenes. Unfortunately, much of the archive footage is badly scratched so some of the big boulders look like they're sliding down on wires.

Overall, the performances are fine.

. . . .

■ AVALON

1990, 126 MINS, US ◇

Dir Barry Levinson   *Prod* Mark Johnson, Barry Levinson   *Scr* Barry Levinson   *Ph* Allen Daviau   *Ed* Stu Linder   *Mus* Randy Newman   *Art Dir* Norman Reynolds

● Leo Fuchs, Eve Gordon, Lou Jacobi, Armin Mueller-Stahl, Elizabeth Perkins, Joan Plowright (Tri-Star/Baltimore)

Dealing with an extended Jewish family headed by brothers who left Europe in the early 20th century, *Avalon* seeks to recapture both a period (the post-Second World War era, as television became king) and the essence of family life, with all its feuding, pettiness and tumult.

Still, beyond the beautiful photography, spotless classic cars and slavishly detailed sets, the film lacks focus or a real reason for being. The patriarch of the central nuclear family is Sam Krichinsky (Armin Mueller-Stahl), who arrives wide-eyed in the US on the Fourth of July. His reminiscences to his grandchildren introduce us to the extended clan.

Son Jules (Aidan Quinn) changes his name

B

and goes into business selling TV sets. Jules marries and has his own son (Elijah Wood), who becomes close to Sam, while Jules' wife (Elizabeth Perkins) chafes under the intrusiveness of his mother (Joan Plowright).

After meandering through the family life for nearly two hours, Levinson rushes to what proves a moving conclusion, one that seeks to connect all that proceeded it on some higher level.

••••••••••••••••••••••••••••••••••••••

■ AVANTI!

1972, 143 MINS, US ◇ Ⓥ
Dir Billy Wilder   *Prod* Billy Wilder   *Scr* Billy Wilder, I.A.L. Diamond   *Ph* Luigi Kuveiller   *Ed* Ralph E. Winters   *Mus* Carlo Rustichelli (arr.)   *Art Dir* Ferdinando Scarfiotti
● Jack Lemmon, Juliet Mills, Clive Revill, Edward Andrews, Gianfranco Barra, Franco Angrisano (Phalanx/Jalem/United Artists)

Billy Wilder has taken the Samuel Taylor Broadway play and given it his own peculiar treatment. In casting Jack Lemmon as an American corporation executive come to Italy to claim the body of his father, killed when he drove his car off a high cliff, he has the perfect foil for the building situations, marking the fifth time pair have teamed up in a picture.

Scripted by Wilder and I.A.L. Diamond, two basic themes are nicely blended to lend motivation. There is the sort-of romance between Lemmon and Juliet Mills and the endless Italian governmental red tape which cues all the action.

Basic situation takes form as Lemmon discovers another person also met her death in the tragic accident, his father's longtime English mistress with whom he's been carrying on a clandestine love affair for past 12 years. He meets a chubby English dumpling (Mills) whom he learns is the daughter of the lady in question also heading to claim her mother's body.

Lemmon displays his usual aptitude in a frantic role, here a hardboiled American exec who is gradually drawn into the aura in which his father had found himself. Mills, who is said to have put on 25 pounds for character, which demands chubbiness, is a happy choice, endowing part with warmth and understanding.

••••••••••••••••••••••••••••••••••••••

■ AWAKENING, THE

1980, 102 MINS, UK ◇ Ⓥ
Dir Mike Newell   *Prod* Robert Solo, Andrew Scheinman   *Scr* Allan Scott, Chris Bryant, Clive Exton   *Ph* Jack Cardiff   *Ed* Terry Rawlings   *Mus* Claude Bolling   *Art Dir* Michael Stringer
● Charlton Heston, Susannah York, Jill Townsend, Stephanie Zimbalist, Patrick Drury (Orion)

It seems that there was once a certain Egyptian Queen Kara whose father, following the custom of the day, induced her into an incestuous relationship. In revenge, Kara killed him and proceeded to have slaughtered everyone in the land who had even spoken with the late pharaoh. Dead at 18, the evil queen was buried, amidst the usual riches, in an isolated tomb bearing a 'do not disturb' sign.

Story [based on the novel *The Jewel of the Seven Stars* by Bram Stoker] possesses a strange fascination for archeologist Charlton Heston, who finally penetrates the chamber centuries later. Kara's nasty spirit transforms neatly to Heston's baby daughter.

It's hokum through and through. Veteran lenser Jack Cardiff contributes a highly professional sheen but first-time feature director Mike Newell exhibits a jumpy, disjointed style.

••••••••••••••••••••••••••••••••••••••

■ AWAKENINGS

1990, 121 MINS, US ◇ Ⓥ
Dir Penny Marshall   *Prod* Walter F. Parkes, Lawrence Lasker   *Scr* Steven Zillian   *Ph* Miroslav Ondricek   *Ed* Jerry Greenberg, Battle Davis   *Mus* Randy Newman   *Art Dir* Anton Furst
● Robin Williams, Robert De Niro, Julie Kavner, Ruth Nelson, John Heard, Penelope Ann Miller (Columbia)

Robin Williams joins Robert De Niro in enacting the story of neurologist Oliver Sacks, who in 1966 encountered a group of statue-like paralytics in a Bronx hospital and insisted something could be done for them. Sacks/Sayer (Williams) discovers they were stricken with encephalitis, which claimed many victims in the 1920s.

Sayer wins permission to test L-DOPA, a new drug then being used to combat Parkinson's disease, and is able to 'awaken' Leonard Lowe (De Niro), frozen since contracting the sleeping sickness 30 years before. But the miracle cure proves temporary.

Rendered broadly and brightly accessible in the hands of director Penny Marshall and screenwriter Steven Zillian, who adapted Sacks' book, *Awakenings* dwells predictably on the picture's upbeat themes: the miracle of health taken for granted, and the joy and meaning in life's simple things.

Enacting the shy, fidgety doctor, Williams extends the extraordinary dramatic gifts he displayed in *Dead Poets Society*. Sympathy and tenderness shine from his bright blue eyes. De Niro, far more effective here than in his portrayal of an illiterate man in *Stanley & Iris*, has this visceral, demanding role by the tail.
☐ 1990: Best Film (Nomination)

••••••••••••••••••••••••••••••••••••••

■ BABES IN ARMS

1939, 93 MINS, US Ⓥ
Dir Busby Berkeley   *Prod* Arthur Freed   *Scr* Jack MacGowan, Kay Van Riper   *Ph* Ray June   *Ed* Frank Sullivan   *Mus* Georgie Stoll (dir.)   *Art Dir* Cedric Gibbons, Merrill Pye
● Mickey Rooney, Judy Garland, Charles Winninger, Guy Kibbee, June Preisser (M-G-M)

Film version of the Rodgers and Hart [1937] musical has been considerably embellished in its transfer to the screen. Basic idea is there, and two songs are retained. Otherwise, it's a greatly enhanced piece of entertainment, with Mickey Rooney having a field day parading his versatile talents.

He sings, dances, gives out with a series of imitations including Eddie Leonard, Clark Gable, Lionel Barrymore, President Roosevelt.

With Judy Garland he sings 'Good Morning', a new tune by Nacio Herb Brown and producer Arthur Freed; he pounds the ivories; he directs a kid show to provide impersonations, and a dinner table sequence, with mixup of decision on the silverware, is an old routine but his technique and timing make for grand fun.

Direction by Busby Berkeley is enthusiastic and at a fast clip throughout.

••••••••••••••••••••••••••••••••••••••

■ BABES ON BROADWAY

1941, 121 MINS, US Ⓥ
Dir Busby Berkeley   *Prod* Arthur Freed   *Scr* Fred Finklehoffe, Elaine Ryan   *Ph* Lester White   *Ed* Frederick Y. Smith

● Mickey Rooney, Judy Garland, Richard Quine, Fay Bainter (M-G-M)

If all the energy used by Mickey Rooney in making *Babes on Broadway* could be assembled in one place, there would be enough to sustain a flying fortress in the stratosphere from Hollywood to New York and return, nonstop. And there might be some left over. Teamed with Judy Garland in a filmusical which is very similar to their previous efforts, Rooney is as fresh as the proverbial daisy at the end of two hours of strenuous theatrical calisthenics. He dances, sings, acts and does imitations – dozens of them.

There isn't time to catch one's breath from the opening moment to the closing fadeout of Rooney and Garland giving their all in one of those Metro production numbers, where the stage, the scenery, the actors and some of the audience are doing a gigantic revolution around the camera. In between, there is related a story about young performers battling for their 'chance' on Broadway.

Busby Berkeley directs this sort of thing about as well as anybody. But both Rooney and Garland are fast outgrowing this type of presentation, which depends entirely on the ah's and oh's that spring from watching precocious children.

••••••••••••••••••••••••••••••••••••••

■ BABY

1985, 95 MINS, US ◇
Dir B.W.L. Norton   *Prod* Jonathan T. Taplin   *Scr* Clifford Green, Ellen Green   *Ph* John Alcott   *Ed* Howard Smith, David Bretherton   *Mus* Jerry Goldsmith   *Art Dir* Raymond G. Storey
● William Katt, Sean Young, Patrick McGoohan, Julian Fellowes, Kyalo Mativo, Hugh Quarshie (Touchstone)

A huggable prehistoric hatchling is discovered by a young American couple in an African rain forest. Story has an engaging performance from William Katt, who plays the sportswriter husband of paleontologist Sean Young. Latter, whose maternal and scientific instincts propel events, is rather bland.

Evil foil is Patrick McGoohan as a rival, ruthless paleontologist who enlists the aid of a rapacious revolutionary army to capture Baby's towering brontosaurus mama, after overzealous soldiers gun down the 70-or-so-foot tall papa.

Katt and Young risk their lives to save the baby, who stretches 10 feet, has a kind of *E.T.* winsomeness, and once even hops like a shaggy family pooch in between the covers of Katt and Young.

Dinosaur movements derive from both cable and from operators who were inside the gargantuan structures.

••••••••••••••••••••••••••••••••••••••

■ BABY BOOM

1987, 103 MINS, US ◇ Ⓥ
Dir Charles Shyer   *Prod* Nancy Meyers   *Scr* Nancy Meyers, Charles Shyer   *Ph* William A. Fraker   *Ed* Lynzee Klingman   *Mus* Bill Conti   *Art Dir* Jeffrey Howard
● Diane Keaton, Harold Ramis, Sam Wanamaker, James Spader, Pat Hingle, Sam Shepard (United Artists)

A transparent and one-dimensional parable about a power-devouring female careerist and the unwanted bundle of joy that turns her obsessive fast-track life in Gotham upside down. Constructed almost entirely upon facile and familiar media cliches about 'parenting' and the super-yuppie set, *Baby Boom* has the superficiality of a project inspired by a lame New York magazine cover story and sketched out on a cocktail napkin at Spago's.

J.C. Wiatt (Diane Keaton) is a dressed-for-success management consultant whose steamroller ambition has earned this workaholic the proudly flaunted nickname, 'Tiger

Lady'. She lives in trendy high-rise splendor with bland investment banker Steven Buchner (Harold Ramis), to whom she reluctantly allots a four-minute slot for lovemaking before returning to late-night paperwork.

Suddenly, J.C. learns that a cousin has died together with her husband in an accident in England. J.C. is intrigued to learn that she's inherited something from this misfortune but, to her considerable shock, this turns out to be a precious apple-cheeked 12-month old girl, Elizabeth (Kristina and Michelle Kennedy).

Baby Boom tries to be a lot funnier than it actually is, and handsome production design and cinematography do little to compensate for its annoying over-reliance on cornball action montages and a dreadfully saccharine soudtrack score.

• •

■ BABY DOLL

1956, 114 MINS, US ⓥ

Dir Elia Kazan   *Prod* Elia Kazan   *Scr* Tennessee Williams   *Ph* Boris Kaufman   *Ed* Gene Milford   *Mus* Kenyon Hopkins   *Art Dir* Richard Sylbert
● Karl Malden, Carroll Baker, Eli Wallach, Mildred Dunnock (Newtown/Warner)

Except for moments of humor that are strictly inherent in the character of the principals, *Baby Doll* plays off against a sleazy, dirty, depressing Southern background. Over it hangs a feeling of decay, expertly nurtured by director Elia Kazan.

Baby Doll is based on a 1941 Tennessee Williams vignette, dramatized on Broadway in 1955 as *27 Wagons Full of Cotton*.

Story briefly has Carroll Baker, an immature teenager, married to middle-aged Karl Malden who runs a cotton gin. When their on-credit furniture is carted away, Malden sets fire to the Syndicate cotton gin in town. Suspecting Malden, Eli Wallach – owner of the gin – carts his cotton to Malden's gin for processing but then proceeds to seduce Baker who signs a note confessing that Malden committed the arson. Malden, who has promised not to touch his young wife until one year after their marriage finds Baker and Wallach together in the house and goes berserk with jealousy.

Baker's performance captures all the animal charm, the naivete, the vanity, contempt and rising passion of Baby Doll.

Wallach as the vengeful Vacarro plays it to the hilt. Malden is cast to perfection and turns in a sock performance.

• •

■ BABY FACE NELSON

1957, 85 MINS, US ⓥ

Dir Don Siegel   *Prod* Al Zimbalist   *Scr* Irving Shulman, Daniel Mainwaring   *Ph* Hal Mohr   *Ed* Leon Barsha   *Mus* Van Alexander
● Mickey Rooney, Carolyn Jones, Cedric Hardwicke, Leo Gordon, Anthony Caruso, Jack Elam (Fryman-ZS/United Artists)

Nelson was a member of the notorious Dillinger gang that scourged the midwest circa 1933. The script makes him a ruthless, trigger-happy, coldblooded killer.

The versatile Mickey Rooney is not particularly convincing as the pint-sized Nelson. He snarls, boils with hatred and is unrepentant. But he merely seems to be going through the motions and his performance never matches the acting found in gangster classics.

More impressive is Carolyn Jones' portrayal of Rooney's loyal moll. She's a plain jane who's attracted to him by some strange affection. But with the FBI closing in on the wounded Rooney, it is she who kills him when he admits he would even shoot down small boys.

• •

■ BABY MAKER, THE

1970, 109 MINS, US ◇ ⓥ

Dir James Bridges   *Prod* Richard Goldstone   *Scr* James Bridges   *Ph* Charles Rosher Jr   *Ed* Walter Thompson   *Mus* Fred Karlin   *Art Dir* Mort Rabinowitz
● Barbara Hershey, Collin Wilcox-Horne, Sam Groom, Scott Glenn, Jeannie Berlin, Lili Valenty (National General/Wise)

The Baby Maker is an offbeat story of a childless couple who hire a young girl to conceive by the husband.

Director James Bridges' story is stronger than his direction of players, though the physical staging is admirable.

Collin Wilcox-Horne and Sam Groom are a barren couple, who hire Barbara Hershey to bear his child. This in turn shatters the girl's relationship with Scott Glenn, both of whom are from the love generation. Development of an emotional relationship between Hershey and Groom is more than implicit.

Wilcox-Horne is excellent in a multi-faceted performance: sometimes warm and loving, occasionally on the verge of jealousy, but always sincere in her character's motivations and reactions. Hers is the film's best performance.

Glenn comes over well as the frustrated but likeable lover. His role is important if subsidiary, and he handles it very well.

• •

■ BABY, THE RAIN MUST FALL

1965, 93 MINS, US ⓥ

Dir Robert Mulligan   *Prod* Alan J. Pakula   *Scr* Horton Foote   *Ph* Ernest Laszlo   *Ed* Aaron Stell   *Mus* Elmer Bernstein   *Art Dir* Roland Anderson
● Lee Remick, Steve McQueen, Don Murray, Paul Fix, Josephine Hutchinson, Ruth White (Columbia)

Chief assets of Pakula-Mulligan's *Baby, The Rain Must Fall* [from Horton Foote's play *The Traveling Lady*] are outstanding performances by its stars and an emotional punch that lingers. Steve McQueen is exactly right as irresponsible rockabilly singer, Lee Remick portrays his wife sensitively, and newcomer Kimberly Block is charming and unaffected as their six-year-old daughter.

McQueen, raised by dictatorial spinster (Georgia Simmons) who disapproves of his singing in road-houses, is troubleprone rebel. When story opens he is free on parole for a stabbing, and is joined by Remick and Block, wife and daughter he had kept secret.

Remick is vividly alive in spontaneous-appearing scenes with daughter. But director Robert Mulligan apparently was so determined to avoid soap-opera cliches that he did not permit actress to register negative emotion beyond look of distraught unhappiness even though sad events should have allowed room for tears.

Other cast members are adequate, but roles suffer from editorial cuts (confirmed by director) that leave sub-plots dangling.

• •

■ BABYLON

1980, 95 MINS, UK ◇

Dir Franco Rosso   *Prod* Gavrik Losey   *Scr* Martin Stellman, Franco Rosso   *Ph* Chris Menges   *Ed* Thomas Schwalm   *Mus* Denis Bovell, Aswad   *Art Dir* Brian Savegar
● Brinsley Forde, Karl Howman, Trevor Laird (Diversity Music/NFFC/Chrysalis/Lee Electric)

Like the reggae music that pulses through it, *Babylon* is rich, rough and real. And like the streetlife of the young black Londoners it portrays, it's threatening, touching, violent and funny. This one seems to explode in the gut with a powerful mix of pain and pleasure.

The screenplay was originally commissioned as a BBC-TV play. Subsequent rewrites, while triumphantly upgrading it to the level of big-screen fare, have at the same time sharpened rather than softened that controversial angle.

Brinsley Forde plays the dreadlocked fellow whose problems at the outset are no more than everyday irritants.

By the end, however, he's lost his job; been chased; beaten by police; discovered his precious sound equipment has been ripped to pieces at the group's backstreet base by nearby white residents; and he's plunged a screwdriver into the stomach of the man he knows is responsible.

• •

■ BACHELOR MOTHER

1939, 80 MINS, US ⓥ

Dir Garson Kanin   *Prod* Buddy De Sylva   *Scr* Norman Krasna   *Ph* Robert de Grasse   *Ed* Henry Berman, Robert Wise   *Mus* Roy Webb   *Art Dir* Van Nest Polglase, Carroll Clark
● Ginger Rogers, David Niven, Charles Coburn, Frank Albertson, E.E. Clive (RKO)

Story itself is a rather ordinary Cinderella yarn, gaining substance and strength through adroit direction, excellently tempoed lines and situations, and topnotch cast performances.

Ginger Rogers blossoms forth as a most competent comedienne. David Niven delivers strongly as the romantic interest.

Picking up a baby on the steps of a foundling home, Rogers finds her excuses inadequate and she's tabbed as the unwed mother of the child. Girl easily adopts maternal love for the baby, finding the home's intervention with her boss saves her job in the department store.

Niven, playboy son of the department store owner, becomes curiously interested in the foundling, and gradually generates romantic inclinations toward Rogers.

Garson Kanin's direction keeps up a breezy and steady pace.

• •

■ BACHELOR OF HEARTS

1958, 94 MINS, UK ◇

Dir Wolf Rilla   *Prod* Vivian A. Cox   *Scr* Leslie Bricusse, Frederic Raphael   *Ph* Geoffrey Unsworth   *Ed* Eric Boyd-Perkins   *Mus* Hubert Clifford   *Art Dir* Edward Carrick
● Hardy Kruger, Sylvia Syms, Ronald Lewis, Jeremy Burnham, Miles Malleson, Eric Barker (Rank)

Bachelor of Hearts is a switch on *A Yank at Oxford*, and might have been more simply titled *A German at Cambridge*. It is a facetious, rather embarrassing glimpse of life at Cambridge University. Since the screenplay was written by two ex-Cambridge students it must be assumed to be authentic. In which case, some rather adolescent malarkey appears to go on at the university.

The thin yarn has Hardy Kruger as a German student on an exchange scholarship system. At first treated with suspicion, he proves himself a good fellow, passes his exams and falls in love. But the story is only an excuse for some predictable situations and jokes. This might have been acceptable had there been more wit, but the wisecracks mostly depend on the young German's inability to understand the English idiom or the traditional behaviour at the university.

Kruger, who made a big impression with his first British pic, *The One That Got Away*, is less happy in this comedy. But he has a pleasant personality to make his slight love affair with Sylvia Syms acceptable.

• •

■ BACHELOR PARTY, THE

1957, 92 MINS, US ⓥ

Dir Delbert Mann   *Prod* Harold Hecht   *Scr* Paddy Chayefsky   *Ph* Joseph LaShelle   *Ed* William B. Murphy   *Mus* Paul Madeira   *Art Dir* Edward Haworth

● Don Murray, E.G. Marshall, Jack Warden, Philip Abbott, Carolyn Jones, Patricia Smith (United Artists/Norma)

The title tips that the comedy will come from the international institution of giving the groom-to-be his last fling as a single man. The script [from Paddy Chayefsky's own TV play] gets it all in – the drinking dinner, the stag movies, the pub-crawling, the visit to a strip show, and finally, the calling on a professional lady. Each sequence is vividly etched.

Cast, mostly from television and stage, is headed by Don Murray. He's good as the bookkeeper husband of Patricia Smith, who is expecting a child. As he becomes a reluctant member of the bachelor party, the round of tawdry revelry is seen through his eyes, and revealing viewing it is, even involving him temporarily with a sexpot Greenwich Village character, played with great vitality by Carolyn Jones.

Philip Abbott scores as the frightened groom-to-be, his manly abilities as yet untried. The sequences wherein he makes an abortive attempt to go through with the introduction to sex arranged by the boys with Barbara Ames is a standout. Jack Warden shows up well as the office bachelor who masterminds the party for Abbott, as does Larry Blyden, married man who early departs the festivities.

■ **BACKDRAFT**

1991, 135 MINS, US ◇ ▼
Dir Ron Howard   *Prod* Richard B. Lewis, Pen Densham, John Watson   *Scr* Gregory Widen   *Ph* Michael Salomon   *Ed* Daniel Hanley, Michael Hill   *Mus* Hans Zimmer   *Art Dir* Albert Brenner
● Kurt Russell, William Baldwin, Robert De Niro, Donald Sutherland, Jennifer Jason Leigh, Scott Glenn (Universal/Imagine/Trilogy)

Director Ron Howard torches off more thrilling scenes in *Backdraft* than any Saturday matinee serial ever dared. Visually, pic often is exhilarating, but it's shapeless and dragged down by corny, melodramatic characters and situations.

Ex-fireman Gregory Widen's script about Chicago smokeaters begins with a scene of the two central characters as boys in 1971. This provides shorthand for later formulaic conflicts between fire-fighting brothers Kurt Russell and William Baldwin.

Baldwin is ambivalent about fire-fighting as a result of a childhood experience. His older brother, the charismatic Russell, is a hardboiled sort, even more recklessly heroic than the father.

Widen uncertainly blends these tiresome family quarrels with a suspense plot involving fire department investigator Robert De Niro's search for a mysterious arsonist. His intense obsessive characterization is a major plus for the film but isn't given enough screen time.

Though De Niro is portrayed as the Sherlock Holmes of arson investigators, script has him and Baldwin led to the truth by the airheaded assistant (Jennifer Jason Leigh) of a corrupt local alderman (J.T. Walsh) and by an institutionalized pyromaniac played by Donald Sutherland with his customary glee.

The spectacular fire scenes are done with terrifying believability (usually with the actors in the same shot as the fire effects) and a kind of sci-fi grandeur.

■ **BACK ROADS**

1981, 94 MINS, US ◇
Dir Martin Ritt   *Prod* Ronald Shedlo   *Scr* Gary DeVore   *Ph* John A. Alonzo   *Ed* Sidney Levin   *Mus* Henry Mancini   *Art Dir* Walter Scott Herndon
● Sally Field, Tommy Lee Jones, Michael Gazzo, M. Emmet Walsh (Warner

Plot focuses on Southern hooker Sally Field who meets down-on-his-luck-boxer Tommy Lee Jones in the course of a working night. Jones can't pay for his fun but is intrigued by the spunky Field – so much so that he punches out a policeman about to bust her.

Forced to move out of her temporary abode, Field spends the night at Jones' meager surroundings and sneaks out the next morning to take a look at the little boy she gave up for adoption some years ago. After the adoptive mother threatens to call the police if she persists trying to make contact. Field returns to Jones (who just lost his car-washing job) and the pair decide to leave Alabama for the promising California shores. Thrust of the film is their adventures hitch-hiking along the road.

Although both stars rise above script contrivances, they are somehow never an affecting romantic pair. All of their shared troubles would seem to make a great love story but they never share enough really intimate moments to carry it off.

■ **BACK STREET**

1932, 86 MINS, US
Dir John M. Stahl   *Prod* Carl Laemmle Jr.   *Scr* Gladys Lehman, Lynn Starling   *Ph* Karl Freund   *Ed* Milton Carruth   *Art Dir* Charles D. Hall
● Irene Dunne, John Boles, June Clyde, George Meeker, ZaSu Pitts, Shirley Grey (Universal)

Just as Fannie Hurst's bestseller must have fired the imagination of readers, this saga of Ray Schmidt who lives in a shadowy 'back street', and technically meretricious relationship with Walter Saxel, leaps off the screen and smacks the viewer above the gray matter and under the heart.

The sympathy for Schmidt is naturally, humanly and wallopingly developed, even unto Irene Dunne's superb characterization winning her audience away from a slightly unconventional start where she is shown hob-nobbing gaily, but harmlessly, with the travelling salesmen in the Over-the-Rhine beer gardens of Cincinnati.

Her ready acquiescence to every demand of her lover (John Boles) despite his own imminent marriage, 'for family reasons', is as natural in its artlessness as having a cup of coffee, and yet it is packed with human interest.

Dunne is excellent as Schmidt. She is the personification of 'a real woman'. Boles, too, is very effective, deftly highlighting the somewhat selfish man who makes heavy demands of his mistress, and yet withal genuinely in love with the No. 2 woman in his life.

■ **BACK TO BATAAN**

1945, 95 MINS, US ▼
Dir Edward Dmytryk   *Prod* Robert Fellows   *Scr* Ben Barzman, Richard H. Landau   *Ph* Nicholas Musuraca   *Ed* Marston Fay   *Mus* Roy Webb   *Art Dir* Albert S. D'Agostino, Ralph Berges
● John Wayne, Anthony Quinn, Beulah Bondi, Fely Franquelli, Richard Loo, Philip Ahn (RKO)

Events are based on fact, according to foreword, and clips of several US fighting men released from Jap prison camps with the return of MacArthur's army are used both at beginning and end. Plot [from a story by Aeneas Mackenzie and William Gordon] spans time from fall of Bataan and Corregidor to the Yank landings on Leyte, and depicts adventures of John Wayne as a colonel leading Filipino patriots in undercover sabotage against the 'islands' temporary conquerors.

Love interest is given over to Anthony Quinn, portraying the descendant of the Filipino hero, Bonifacio, and Fely Franquelli, Manila contact for the band of heroes. Quinn

does a particularly outstanding job, as does Franquelli. Wayne makes a stalwart leader for the guerrillas, commendably underplaying the role for best results.

■ **BACK TO THE FUTURE**

1985, 116 MINS, US ◇ ▼
Dir Robert Zemeckis   *Prod* Bob Gale, Neil Canton   *Scr* Robert Zemeckis, Bob Gale   *Ph* Dean Cundey   *Ed* Arthur Schmidt, Harry Keramidas   *Mus* Alan Silvestri   *Art Dir* Lawrence G. Paull
● Michael J. Fox, Christopher Lloyd, Crispin Glover, Lea Thompson, Claudia Wells, Thomas F. Wilson (Amblin)

The central winning elements in the scenario are twofold; hurtling the audience back to 1955, which allows for lots of comparative, pop culture humor, and delivering a 1985 teenager (Michael J. Fox) at the doorstep of his future parents when they were 17-year-old kids. That encounter is a delicious premise, especially when the young hero's mother-to-be develops the hots for her future son and his future father is a bumbling wimp.

Film is also sharply anchored by zestful byplay between Fox's Arthurian knight figure and Christopher Lloyd's Merlin-like, crazed scientist. The latter has mounted a nuclear-powered time machine in a spaced-out DeLorean car, which spirits the bedazed Fox 30 years back in time to the same little town in which he grew up.

In the film's opening sequences, the father (wonderfully played by Crispin Glover) is an unctuous nitwit, and the mother (Lea Thompson) a plump, boozey, turtle-necked frau.

Performances by the earnest Fox, the lunatic Lloyd, the deceptively passionate Lea Thompson, and, particularly, the bumbling-to-confident Glover, who runs away with the picture, merrily keep the ship sailing.

■ **BACK TO THE FUTURE PART II**

1989, 107 MINS, US ◇ ▼
Dir Robert Zemeckis   *Prod* Bob Gale, Neil Canton   *Scr* Bob Gale   *Ph* Dean Cundey   *Ed* Arthur Schmidt, Harry Keramidas   *Mus* Alan Silvestri   *Art Dir* Rick Carter
● Michael J. Fox, Christopher Lloyd, Lea Thompson, Thomas F. Wilson, Harry Waters Jr, Elizabeth Shue (Amblin/Universal)

The energy and heart which Robert Zemeckis and strong-writing partner Bob Gale (who takes solo screenplay credit this time) poured into the ingenious story of part one is diverted into narrative mechanics and camera wizardry in *Future II*.

The story starts exactly where the original left off, with Michael J. Fox's Marty McFly and Christopher Lloyd's visionary inventor Dr Emmett Brown taking off in their flying DeLorean time machine for 2015 on an urgent mission to save Fox's children from a terrible fate.

Future II finds the McFly family living in shabby lower-middle class digs in a world that isn't so much Orwellian as a gaudier and tackier projection of the present day.

What matters to Fox is that his son has become a wimp, just like his father was in the 1955 segment of the original film.

Then, in a curious narrative lapse, Fox picks up a sports almanac which, if taken back to the past, will enable him to get rich by gambling on future events. But villainous Biff (Thomas F. Wilson) absconds with it in the time machine to give it to his 1955 self, and the chase begins.

Zemeckis' fascination with having characters interact at different ages of their lives hurts the film visually, and strains credibility past the breaking point, by forcing him to rely on some very cheesy makeup designs.

■ **BACK TO THE FUTURE PART III**

1990, 118 MINS, US ◇ ⓥ

Dir Robert Zemeckis *Prod* Bob Gale, Neil Canton
Scr Bob Gale *Ph* Dean Cundey *Ed* Arthur Schmidt,
Harry Keramidas *Mus* Alan Silvestri *Art Dir* Rick
Carter

● Michael J. Fox, Christopher Lloyd, Mary
Steenburgen, Thomas F. Wilson, Lea Thompson,
Elisabeth Shue (Amblin)

Back to the Future Part III recovers the style
and wit and grandiose fantasy elements in the
original. The simplicity of plot, and the wide
expansiveness of its use of space, are a
refreshing change from the convoluted, visually cramped and cluttered second part.

Michael J. Fox's Marty McFly in his time-
travelling DeLorean finds himself in the
midst of a band of charging Indians in John
Ford country, Monument Valley 1885. His
mission is to bring back Doc (Christopher
Lloyd) before he is shot in the back by Thomas F. Wilson's hilariously unhinged Buford
'Mad Dog' Tannen, an ancestor of McFly's
20th century nemesis Biff Tannen.

Fox steps into the background of the story
and lets Lloyd have the chance to play the
romantic lead for a change. Doc's offbeat
romance with Mary Steenburgen's Clara
Clayton, a spinster schoolmarm who shares
his passion for Jules Verne, is funny, touching and exhilarating. Their ultimate journey
through time gives the plot trajectory an
unexpected and entirely satisfying resolution.

The fun of this meta-Western is partly the
recognition of elements familiar from genre
classics: the dance from *My Darling Clementine*, the sobering-up concoction from *El
Dorado*, the costume from *Fistful of Dollars*.
Fox reexperiences all this, literally flying
through the screen (at an incongruous Monument Valley drive-in) into every Western
fan's dream of being a character in a 'real'
Western.

....

■ **BAD**

1977, 105 MINS, US ◇ ⓥ

Dir Jed Johnson *Prod* Jeff Tornberg *Scr* Pat Hackett,
George Abagnalo *Ph* Allan Metzger *Ed* Franca Silvi,
David McKenna *Mus* Mike Bloomfield
Art Dir Eugene Rudolph

● Carroll Baker, Perry King, Susan Tyrrell, Stefania
Cassini, Cyrinda Foxe, Mary Boylan (New World)

Watching Andy Warhol's *Bad*, is a compellingly revolting experience. This is among the
blackest of black comedies, featuring Carroll
Baker as a Queens housewife who sup-
plements her home electrolysis business by
arranging for young girls to do repulsive
errands for clients – killing dogs, retarded
babies, etc. Don't see it after eating.

Pat Hackett and George Abagnalo wrote
the script which, on a professional level, is a
good piece of craftsmanship. Jed Johnson,
who has edited prior Warhol pix, handles the
direction in top fashion.

Baker plays a suburban Ma Barker,
cherishing her TV commercial middle-class
materialistic standards, while thinking
nothing about her gruesome sideline.
Susan Tyrrell is Baker's slovenly and
abandoned daughter-in-law, complete with
sniveling infant. Baker's crew of hit-persons
is mainly a gaggle of slatternly young street
maidens who carry out their assignments
with a truly frightening aplomb.

....

■ **BAD AND THE BEAUTIFUL, THE**

1952, 116 MINS, US ⓥ

Dir Vincente Minnelli *Prod* John Houseman
Scr Charles Schnee *Ph* Robert Surtees *Ed* Conrad A.
Nervig *Mus* David Raksin

● Kirk Douglas, Lana Turner, Walter Pidgeon, Dick
Powell, Barry Sullivan, Gloria Grahame (M-G-M)

Contemporary Hollywood, including composites of the characters that make the town the
glamour capital it is, is the setting for *The Bad
and the Beautiful*.

It is the story of a first-class heel, a ruthless,
driving individual whose insistent push
changes a number of lives to the end that all
have benefited in some way from his multiple
double-crosses, despite the personal sorrow
or loss experienced. The screenplay of the
George Bradshaw story is exceptionally
well-written.

Kirk Douglas scores as the ruthless individual out to prove he is the best when it comes
to making pictures. Swung along with him is
Lana Turner, the drunken, inferiority-com-
plexed daughter of a former screen great;
Dick Powell, the self-satisfied southern pro-
fessor-writer who is pulled into the Hollywood mill; and Barry Sullivan, who, as an
embryo director, gets Douglas his first chance
and is double-crossed for the helping hand.

....

■ **BAD BLOOD**

1982, 105 MINS, UK/NEW ZEALAND ◇ ⓥ

Dir Mike Newell *Prod* Andrew Brown *Scr* Andrew
Brown *Ph* Gary Hansen *Ed* Peter Hollywood
Mus Richard Hartley *Art Dir* Kai Hawkins

● Jack Thompson, Carol Burns, Dennis Lill, Donna
Akersten, Martyn Sanderson, Marshall Napier
(Southern)

Story revolves around Stan (Jack Thompson)
and Dorothy Graham (Carol Burns), gunhappy dairy farmers who by 1941 have
become ostracized from their neighbors in the
isolated, close-knit New Zealand town of
Kowhiterangi, mainly due to their own
paranoia.

A gunpoint confrontation with two neighbors forces until now patient constable Ted
Best (Dennis Lill) to confiscate Thompson's
rifle, backed by a trio of fellow officers. When
the gendarmes invade Thompson's
farmhouse, his last refuge from a world of his
own making, the inevitable violence ensues.
Thompson then flees into the bush, and more
will die before an amateurish manhunt
reaches its inevitable conclusion.

Direction by Mike Newell stands out for
conveying more meaning with pictures than
words, though the film [from the book
Manhunt: The Story of Stanley Graham by
Howard Willis] stumbles somewhat through
the narrative until the carnage begins.

Thompson turns in an okay performance,
and he's clearly better in the early scenes
when his character is still a semi-rational
being. The actor seems stretched thin once
his mainspring snaps.

....

■ **BAD BOYS**

1983, 123 MINS, US ◇ ⓥ

Dir Richard Rosenthal *Prod* Robert Solo *Scr* Richard
Dilello *Ph* Bruce Surtees, Donald Thorin *Ed* Antony
Gibbs *Mus* Bill Conti *Art Dir* J. Michael Riva

● Sean Penn, Reni Santoni, Esai Morales, Eric Gurry,
Jim Moody, Ally Sheedy (EMI)

Bad Boys is a troubling and often riveting
drama about juvenile delinquency. Director
Richard Rosenthal does a topnotch job of
bringing to life the seedy, hopeless
environment of a jail for juvenile offenders
and has gotten some terribly convincing
performances from his young cast,
notably topliner Sean Penn.

From the first scene where 16-year-old
tough guy Penn breaks the window of a car
and steals a woman's purse, it's clear this is
not going to be the picture of youth most
people are used to.

Penn's only safety is in the love of girlfriend
Ally Sheedy, the one person who has ever

seemingly seen the softer side of his nature.
It is in jail that the film really takes off,
pitting Penn against the abuses of his fellow
inmates and the inherent hopelessness of his
situation.

Penn is nothing short of terrific in the key
role, which, given a minimal amount of
dialog, calls for him to rely primarily on his
emotional and physical abilities.

....

■ **BAD COMPANY**

1972, 91 MINS, US ◇ ⓥ

Dir Robert Benton *Prod* Stanley R. Jaffe *Scr* David
Newman, Robert Benton *Ph* Gordon Willis *Ed* Ralph
Rosenblum, Ron Kalish *Mus* Harvey Schmidt *Art
Dir* Paul Sylbert

● Jeff Bridges, Barry Brown, Jim Davis, David
Huddleston, John Savage, Jerry Houser (Jaffilms/
Paramount)

Bad Company is an excellent film which combines wry humor and gritty action with in-
depth characterizations of two youths on the
lam in the Civil War west. The production is
generally sensitive in its treatment, though
pockmarked with some incongruous 'fun-
and-poetic' type violence unworthy of the
otherwise quality story-telling. Robert Benton, who co-wrote the fine original script,
makes a noteworthy directorial debut.

It's an intriguing story of the maturing-
under-fire of Barry Brown, a midwest draft
dodger but otherwise of 'good' stock, who
gradually develops the educated, pragmatic
survival instinct necessary in the old west. In
this he is influenced primarily by Jeff Bridges,
a more primitive con-artist character who
knows the ropes of street-fighting and
finagling.

Among the many highlights of the film is an
outstanding performance by Brown.

....

■ **BAD DAY AT BLACK ROCK**

1954, 81 MINS, US ◇ ⓥ

Dir John Sturges *Prod* Dore Schary *Scr* Millard
Kaufman, Don McGuire *Ph* William C. Mellor
Ed Newell P. Kimlin *Mus* Andre Previn

● Spencer Tracy, Robert Ryan, Anne Francis, Dean
Jagger, Walter Brennan, John Ericson (M-G-M)

Considerable excitement is whipped up in
this suspense drama, and fans who go for
tight action will find it entirely satisfactory.
Besides telling a yarn of tense suspense, the
picture is concerned with a social message on
civic complacency.

Basis for the smoothly valued production is
a story by Howard Breslin, adapted by Don
McGuire. To the tiny town of Black Rock,
one hot summer day in 1945, comes Spencer
Tracy, war veteran with a crippled left arm.
He wants to find a Japanese farmer and give
to him the medal won by his son in an action
that left the latter dead and Tracy crippled.
Tracy is greeted with an odd hostility and his
own life is endangered when he puts together
the reason for the cold, menacing treatment.

Film is paced to draw suspense tight and
keep expectancy mounting as the plot crosses
the point where Tracy could have left without
personal danger and plunges him into deadly
menace when he becomes the hunted.

There's not a bad performance from any
member of the cast, each socking their characters for full value.

....

■ **BAD GIRL**

1931, 90 MINS, US

Dir Frank Borzage *Scr* Edwin Burke *Ph* Chester
Lyons *Ed* Margaret Clancy

● Sally Eilers, James Dunn, Minna Gombell, William
Pawley, Frank Darien (Fox)

Story tells of two kids (Sally Eilers and James
Dunn) who meet on a Coney Island boat,

delve into marriage after a night in his boarding house room and Dorothy (Eilers) is consequently kicked out of a parentless home by her brother. Then Eddie (Dunn) gives up his dream of a radio shop of his own to furnish a new flat for his wife with the added complication of the baby which she has kept a secret from her inarticulate husband.

After which there is the misunderstanding of both thinking the other doesn't want the child, which is not brought out as strongly here as in the stage version [based on the novel by Vina Delmar]. Minna Gombell figures as the widowed girl friend of Dorothy and a constant source of annoyance to Eddie as his wife's advisor.

As a whole *Bad Girl* classes as a workmanlike job, with Dunn's scene with the doctor as its strong point.

□ 1931/32: Best Picture (Nomination)

■ **BAD INFLUENCE**

1990, 99 MINS, US ◇ ⓥ

Dir Curtis Hanson   *Prod* Steve Tisch   *Scr* David Koepp   *Ph* Robert Elswitt   *Ed* Bonnie Koehler   *Mus* Trevor Jones   *Art Dir* Ron Foreman
● Rob Lowe, James Spader, Lisa Zane, Christian Clemenson, Kathlene Wilhoite, Tony Maggio (Epic/Sarlui-Diamant/PRO)

Bad Influence proves a reasonably taut, suspenseful thriller that provides its share of twists before straying into silliness. Rob Lowe doesn't really project enough menace or charisma to pull off his role as Alex, a babyfaced psycho who slowly leads Michael (James Spader) through a liberating fantasy that ultimately turns into a yuppie nightmare.

Director and writer seem to draw their inspiration most closely from Alfred Hitchcock's *Strangers on a Train* – a chance meeting between a regular guy and an outwardly normal stranger whose hidden darkness ultimately leads to fatal complications.

Foremost, however, the film is about Michael's seduction by Alex's free-wheeling attitude, only to find that the rewards don't come cheap.

Spader delivers a terrific performance, and some of the scenes have tremendous impact, especially when – via video – he discovers the depth of Alex's depravity, as fantasy turns into fatal distraction.

Director Curtis Hanson and writer David Koepp create a continued sense of tension and invest many scenes with much-needed humor.

■ **BADLANDERS, THE**

1958, 85 MINS, US ◇

Dir Delmer Daves   *Prod* Aaron Rosenberg   *Scr* Richard Collins   *Ph* John F. Seitz   *Ed* William H. Webb, James Baiotto   *Art Dir* William A. Horning, Daniel B. Cathcart
● Alan Ladd, Ernest Borgnine, Katy Jurado, Claire Kelly, Nehemiah Persoff, Kent Smith (M-G-M)

It is possible to make an adult western without making it a psychological western. Aaron Rosenberg proves the point with his production of *The Badlanders*, a truly original frontier drama, a suspense melodrama on one level and a huge horselaugh on another, with each element playing off on the other.

The heroes of the screenplay, based on a novel by W.R. Burnett [*The Asphalt Jungle*], are two ex-cons, released from the Nevada Territorial Prison, circa 1900, with little but revenge and larceny in their hearts. It is the plan of one of them (Alan Ladd) to do nothing less than rob a gold mine, and he enlists the other (Ernest Borgnine) in support. The problem, of course, is formidable. They must blast the ore – half a ton of it – from a spot right next to a mine full of workmen, then get the huge load away from under the noses

(and shotguns) of the legal owners.

Delmer Daves' direction has a facility of throwing a laugh into the midst of a suspense buildup, relieving and heightening it with flashes of humor.

Ladd is not required over-heroic, physically. His strength is emotional, and with casual grace and a way with an ironic line, he creates an effective contrast to Borgnine. Katy Jurado is handsomely colorful and alternatively touching as a Mexican girl. Claire Kelly, who makes her major bow in this picture, is a stunning redhead but she is not yet a strong enough actress to hold her own with this trio.

■ **BADLANDS**

1973, 95 MINS, US ◇ ⓥ

Dir Terrence Malick   *Prod* Terrence Malick   *Scr* Terrence Malick   *Ph* Brian Probyn, Tak Fujimoto, Stevan Larner   *Ed* Robert Estrin   *Mus* George Tipton   *Art Dir* Jack Fisk
● Martin Sheen, Sissy Spacek, Warren Oates, Alan Vint, Ramon Bieri (Pressman Williams)

Badlands is a uniquely American fairy tale, a romantic account set in the late 1950s of a 15-year-old girl's journey into violence and out of love with a 25-year-old South Dakota garbageman turned thrill killer. Pic is told through the girl's eyes as she narrates in dumb *Teen Romance* style the saga of her hero, a James Dean carbon, who kills her father and whisks her away on a flight into myth that ends in the badlands of Montana.

Written, produced and directed by Terrence Malick, pic is his first feature and it's an impressive debut.

The killer-lead, played with cunning and charm by Martin Sheen, is a perverse Horatio Alger, a culturally-deprived American boy weaned on James Dean pix who works at his rebel image and achieves success, i.e. notoriety, capture, fame and death.

His girl (Sissy Spacek) is one of those mid-teen catatonics whose life is defined in terms of Hollywood gossip and visions of white knights. Together they litter their escape route with the dead.

■ **BAD NEWS BEARS, THE**

1976, 102 MINS, US ◇ ⓥ

Dir Michael Ritchie   *Prod* Stanley R. Jaffe   *Scr* Bill Lancaster   *Ph* John A. Alonzo   *Ed* Richard A. Harris   *Mus* Jerry Fielding   *Art Dir* Polly Platt
● Walter Matthau, Tatum O'Neal, Vic Morrow, Joyce Van Patten, Ben Piazza, Jackie Earle Haley (Paramount)

The Bad News Bears is an extremely funny adult-child comedy film. Walter Matthau stars to perfection as a bumbling baseball coach in the sharp production about the foibles and follies of little-league athletics. Tatum O'Neal also stars as Matthau's ace pitcher.

Michael Ritchie's film has the correct balance of warmth and empathy to make the gentle social commentary very effective.

Premise finds activist politico Ben Piazza having won a class action suit to admit some underprivileged kids to an otherwise upwardly-mobile WASP suburban little league schedule.

Piazza recruits Matthau, a one-time minor leaguer now cleaning swimming pools to coach the slapdash outfit. O'Neal and Jackie Earle Haley reluctantly join their juvenile peers to spark the team to a second place win.

■ **BAD NEWS BEARS GO TO JAPAN, THE**

1978, 91 MINS, US ◇ ⓥ

Dir John Berry   *Prod* Michael Ritchie   *Scr* Bill Lancaster   *Ph* Gene Polito, Kozo Okazaki   *Ed* Richard A. Harris   *Mus* Paul Chihara   *Art Dir* Walter Scott Herndon

● Tony Curtis, Jackie Earle Haley, Tomisaburo Wakayama, Hatsune Ishihara, George Wyner, Lonny Chapman (Paramount)

The dangers inherent in sequel-making are clearly apparent in *The Bad News Bears Go to Japan*, third in the series of junior baseball antics that began with the smash *Bad News Bears* in 1976. Producer Michael Ritchie (who directed the first installment) and writer-creator Bill Lancaster encore with *Japan* resulting in a more vigorous film than the sodden *Bad News Bears in Breaking Training* [1977].

In keeping with tradition, the boys are taken in by yet another hustler (following in the steps of Walter Matthau and William Devane), this time Tony Curtis as a Hollywood agent out for big bucks via promoting a game between the Bears and the Japanese all-star Little Leaguers.

Formula is strictly standard, with Curtis inviting the enmity of the kids, with exception of moppet Scoody Thornton, only to be reformed before the final game which, of course, the Bears win. Japanese locations at least add a different look, and there is much joking about language and cultural customs, humor that went out of style with *Sayonara*.

■ **BAD SEED, THE**

1956, 127 MINS, US ⓥ

Dir Mervyn LeRoy   *Prod* Mervyn LeRoy   *Scr* John Lee Mahin   *Ph* Hal Rosson   *Ed* Warren Low   *Mus* Alex North
● Nancy Kelly, Patty McCormack, Henry Jones, Eileen Heckart, Evelyn Varden, William Hopper (Warner)

This melodrama about a child with an inbred talent for homicide is pretty unpleasant stuff on its own. Taken from Maxwell Anderson's stage play, adapted from William March's novel, the film remains more of the theatre than of the motion picture field. Nonetheless, it is well done within that qualification.

With the possible exception of the Production Code-conscious ending, the screenplay varies little from the Anderson legit piece. Some of the casting is from the stage success, too, with young Patty McCormack as the innocent-looking murderess, and Nancy Kelly as her distraught mother. Both are outstanding.

Scoring also is William Hopper, the father who never sees through the evil of his little girl.

It is the story of a woman who discovers that her daughter, a sweet, innocent-faced child, is a killer. Director Mervyn LeRoy mounts sequences with shocking horror as it is brought out the girl deliberately murdered a schoolmate because she wanted the penmanship medal he had won.

■ **BAD TIMING**

1980, 123 MINS, UK ◇ ⓥ

Dir Nicolas Roeg   *Prod* Jeremy Thomas   *Scr* Yale Udoff   *Ph* Anthony Richmond   *Ed* Tony Lawson   *Mus* Richard Hartley   *Art Dir* David Brockhurst
● Art Garfunkel, Theresa Russell, Harvey Keitel, Denholm Elliott, Daniel Massey, Dana Gillespie (Recorded Picture)

Technically flashy, and teeming with degenerate chic, this downbeat tale of two destructively selfish lovers is unrelieved by its tacked-on thriller ending, and deals purely in despair.

Every scene is shot with at least one eye and one ear to the editing table: results are generally masterful but at times obtrusively pretentious. Director Nicolas Roeg's visual sense remains a peculiar talent.

Yale Udoff's screenplay plots the often

brutal love affair exhaustively in terms of what the parties do to each other, but seldom why – beyond the fact that he is the possessive type and she isn't.

Most milestones are missing along the presumably tortuous psychological route by which Art Garfunkel's jealousy reaches such a pitch of hatred that he ravishes the girl's (Theresa Russell) drugged and senseless body instead of calling an ambulance. Alienation sets in early.

• •

■ BALCONY, THE

1963, 84 MINS, US Ⓥ

Dir Joseph Strick   *Prod* Ben Maddow, Joseph Strick
Scr Ben Maddow   *Ph* George Folsey   *Ed* Chester W. Schaeffer
● Shelley Winters, Peter Falk, Lee Grant, Peter Brocco, Jeff Corey, Ruby Dee
(Walter Reade-Sterling/Allen Hodgdon/City Film)

With Jean Genet's apparent approval, Joe Strick and Ben Maddow have eliminated the play's obscene language (though it's still plenty rough) and clarified some of its obscurations. The result is a tough, vivid and dispassionate fantasy.

This is never an easy film to watch, but also it is never boring or pretentious, and often it is acidly funny. Most of the action of the film, located in an unnamed city in the throes of a bloody revolution, takes place in a highly special kind of brothel, equipped like a movie studio with sets, costumes, rear projection devices etc, which permit the patrons to enact their darkest fantasies (they can also pay with credit cards).

Presiding over the macabre revels is Shelley Winters, the madame who designs the illusions and is all the more ominous for her complete, almost tender detachment. The peace of the brothel is shattered with the arrival of the police chief, Peter Falk, the madame's occasional lover who is fighting a last ditch stand outside to destroy the revolution.

Strick and Maddow have provided this fantastic film with its own reality. It is never capricious nor purposefully obscure, proceeding always with a recognizable logic. It is full of chilling detail and knife-sharp scenes, as when the police chief harangues the populace via radio from the brothel, speaking a furious jargon of nonsensical political and TV commercial cliches.

The performances are excellent, beginning with those of Winters, Falk and Lee Grant, and including the entire supporting cast.

• •

■ BALLAD OF CABLE HOGUE, THE

1970, 121 MINS, US ◇ Ⓥ

Dir Sam Peckinpah   *Prod* Sam Peckinpah   *Scr* John Crawford, Edmund Penney   *Ph* Lucien Ballard
Ed Frank Santillo, Lou Lombardo   *Mus* Jerry Goldsmith   *Art Dir* Leroy Coleman
● Jason Robards, Stella Stevens, David Warner, Strother Martin, Slim Pickens, L.Q. Jones (Warner)

The Ballad of Cable Hogue is a Damon Runyon-esque oater comedy from Sam Peckinpah. Jason Robards is the title character, a charming desert rat; Stella Stevens is the cow-town harlot with the heart of gold; and David Warner is a preacher of sorts.

Robards is a grizzled prospector left to die in the desert wastes by Strother Martin and L. Q. Jones, two bumbling villains. Robards instead finds water where nobody ever had, and prospers as a rest-stop owner on a stage route owned by R. G. Armstrong, where Slim Pickens and Max Evans are the carriage drivers. Stevens becomes Robards' big romance, but exits for Frisco on her gold-digging hunt.

Characterizations are fully-developed.

• • • • • • • • • • • • • • • • • • •

■ BALLAD OF THE SAD CAFE, THE

1991, 100 MINS, US/UK ◇ Ⓥ

Dir Simon Callow   *Prod* Ismail Merchant   *Scr* Michael Hirst   *Ph* Walter Lassally   *Ed* Andrew Marcus
Mus Richard Robbins   *Art Dir* Bruno Santini
● Vanessa Redgrave, Keith Carradine, Cork Hubbert, Rod Steiger, Austin Pendleton, Beth Dixon (Merchant Ivory/Film Four)

Simon Callow makes an assured feature directing debut adapting Carson McCullers' novella *The Ballad of the Sad Cafe*, a demanding, abstract fable.

Amelia (Vanessa Redgrave) is a violent, mannishly styled woman who threw out her husband (Keith Carradine) on their wedding night and has become a legendary figure in her little Southern town in the 1930s. With cropped hair and unglamorous makeup, Redgrave throws herself into the role with uncensored force.

Carradine, who replaced Sam Shepard, brings a naturalism to his embittered role as the ex-con and spurned spouse.

Catalyst in the piece is the fantasy character of Cousin Lymon (Cork Hubbert), a hunchbacked dwarf who pops up out of nowhere claiming to be Redgrave's cousin. He gets Redgrave to convert her general store into a cafe, serving the moonshine she prepares at her still. Carradine shows up midway through the pic fresh out of the state pen. He's out to avenge himself against Redgrave.

Film climaxes memorably in a bare-knuckles boxing match staged at the cafe between Carradine and Redgrave to settle their differences once and for all.

Redgrave's body English, strange accent and physical outbursts are a triumph of pure acting. Carradine's more natural approach helps bring pic closer to reality. An intense supporting performance by Rod Steiger also provides exposition as the town preacher.

• •

■ BALL OF FIRE

1941, 110 MINS, US Ⓥ

Dir Howard Hawks   *Prod* Samuel Goldwyn
Scr Charles Brackett, Billy Wilder   *Ph* Gregg Toland
Ed Daniel Mandell   *Mus* Alfred Newman
● Gary Cooper, Barbara Stanwyck, Oscar Homolka, Dana Andrews, Dan Duryea (RKO/Samuel Goldwyn)

A simple gag is hardly enough on which to string 110 minutes of film. And that's all – one funny situation – that Samuel Goldwyn's director and writers have to support *Ball of Fire*. It's sufficient, however, to provide quite a few chuckles.

Gag on which the whole thing is based is Gary Cooper's professorial efforts to write a learned piece on slang for an encyclopedia. He needs, for research purposes, someone who's hep to the last syllable of the lingo and brings into a sanctum, where he and seven colleagues are working on the encyclopedia, a burlesque stripper (Barbara Stanwyck). She upsets and excites the eight old men in the expected manner. Much of the dialog is rapid-fire slang, plenty labored, but frequently good for laughs.

Casting is meticulously perfect to make every character a caricature of itself. Cooper is in the familiar 'Mr Smith-John Doe' role of the brainy guy who's not quite hep to his surroundings until near the end, when he wises up in time to snatch victory from the smart boys. Stanwyck is likewise in a familiar part that she can play for maximum results.

• •

■ BALTIMORE BULLET, THE

1980, 103 MINS, US ◇ Ⓥ

Dir Robert Ellis Miller   *Prod* John F. Brascia   *Scr* John F. Brascia, Vincent O'Neill   *Ph* James A. Crabe
Ed Jerry Brady   *Mus* Johnny Mandel   *Art Dir* Herman Blumenthal
● James Coburn, Omar Sharif, Bruce Boxleitner, Ronee Blakely (Avco Embassy)

James Coburn and Bruce Boxleitner limn a kind of father-son pool hustling team who make their living traveling through the country taking advantage of local would-be billiard sharks. They do occasionally enter tournaments, one of which will enable Coburn to reunite with his arch nemesis Omar Sharif.

Coburn and Boxleitner work well together although the former looks and speaks more like someone sipping champagne aboard a yacht than a journeyman dashing through an endlessly array of hick towns. Ronee Blakely is picked up by the pair along the way for moral support and fulfills the limited duties asked of her.

Problem here is script. Situations are just too inane to take seriously and not funny enough to be laughed at.

• •

■ BAMBI

1942, 70 MINS, US ◇ Ⓥ

Dir David D. Hand   *Prod* Walt Disney   *Scr* Larry Morey   *Mus* Frank Churchill, Edward Plumb
● (Walt Disney)

Bambi is gem-like in its reflection of the color and movement of sylvan plant and animal life. The transcription of nature in its moments of turbulence and peace heightens the brilliance of the canvas. The story is full of tenderness and the characters tickle the heart.

Thumper, the rabbit, steals the picture. His human attributes are amazing and the voice that is attached to him in the earlier sequences proves an admirable piece of casting. It's a regret that there wasn't much more of him in the picture.

In this story of Bambi, and his friends of the forest, the span of the central character is from birth to the period in which he reaches bull buckhood. The episodes in between show him learning to adapt himself to his surroundings and to outwit the biped with the gun, falling in love, entering parenthood and finally taking his place beside his proud and hoary father, prince of the forest. The dramatic highlights of Bambi's career include the death of his mother by gunshot (a scene of deep pathos), and his fight to the death with another buck over the doe, Phylline.

The interplay of color and movement makes their sharpest impress on the sensibilities during the sequences depicting the advent and passing of the various seasons. The glow and texture of the Disney brush reach new heights, especially in the treatment of a summer thunderstorm and a raging snowstorm.

• •

■ BANANAS

1971, 82 MINS, US ◇ Ⓥ

Dir Woody Allen   *Prod* Jack Rollins, Charles H. Joffe
Scr Woody Allen, Mickey Rose   *Ph* Andrew M. Costikyan   *Ed* Ron Kalish   *Mus* Marvin Hamlisch
● Woody Allen, Louise Lasser, Carlos Montalban, Natividad Abascal, Jacobo Morales, Miguel Suarez (United Artists)

Bananas is chockfull of sight gags, one-liners and swiftly executed unnecessary excursions into vulgarity whose humor for the most part can't make up for content.

Woody Allen, as bumbling New Yorker working for an automation film, is rejected by his activist sweetheart Louise Lasser who is involved in revolutions, particularly in fictional San Marcos where dictator Carlos Montalban has seized control. Allen, disconsolate, bids farewell to parents Charlotte Rae and Stanley Ackerman while they are performing medical operation. Landing in San Marcos, he is feted by Montalban, who is setting him up as pigeon to be erased supposedly by revolutionary Jacobo Morales' men. Allen and Mickey Rose have written some funny stuff, and Allen, both as director and actor, knows what to do with it. Scenes between Lasser and comedian have wonderfully fresh, incisive touch. Montalban's dictator is properly arrogant. Morales performs with assurance right up to the point when, drunk with power, he proclaims Swedish the national language.

■ BANDIT OF SHERWOOD FOREST, THE

1946, 85 MINS, US ◇

Dir George Sherman, Henry Levin *Prod* Leonard S. Picker, Clifford Sanforth *Scr* Wilfrid H. Pettitt, Melvin Levy *Ph* Tony Gaudio, William Snyder, George B. Meehan Jr *Ed* Richard Fanti *Mus* Hugo Friedhofer *Art Dir* Stephen Goosson, Rudolph Sternad
● Cornel Wilde, Anita Louise, Henry Daniell, George Macready, Jill Esmond (Columbia)

Technicolor spectacle of high adventure in Sherwood Forest. It's a costume western, in effect, offering the fictional escapades of the son of Robin Hood, a hard-riding, hard-loving hombre who uses his trusty bow and arrow to right injustice and tyranny back in the days of feudal England.

There is considerable ineptness in writing, production and direction but it still stands up as okay escapist film fare for the not-too-critical.

There is a concentration of chases and 'they-went-thata-way' flavor about the doings that hints at the western feature training of producers and directors.

Plot has the son of Robin Hood coming back to Sherwood Forest to save England's Magna Carta and young king from the cruel plotting of a wicked regent. With his long bow, sword and trusty horse, Wilde proves himself more than a match for the villain, saves the young king's life, the Magna Carta and wins true love and knighthood. Concocting the script, full of dialog cliches and ten-twent-thirt dramatics, were Wilfrid H. Pettitt and Melvin Levy, working from a story by Paul A. Castleton and Pettitt, based on the novel *Son of Robin Hood* by Castleton.

Wilde is properly swashbuckling as the hero, and probably had himself a time enacting the dare-and-do.

■ BANDOLERO!

1968, 107 MINS, US ◇ ⓥ

Dir Andrew V. McLaglen *Prod* Robert L. Jacks *Scr* James Lee Barrett *Ph* William H. Clothier *Ed* Folmar Blangsted *Mus* Jerry Goldsmith *Art Dir* Jack Martin Smith, Alfred Sweeney Jr
● James Stewart, Dean Martin, Raquel Welch, George Kennedy, Andrew Prine, Will Geer (20th Century-Fox)

Bandolero! is a dull western meller. Though competently produced, film suffers from distended scripting, routine direction and overlength.

Basic story is the escape and capture of a gang of post-Civil War vagabonds. Dean Martin heads an outlaw group which includes Will Geer, Tom Heaton, Sean McClory and Clint Ritchie.

Pre-title bank heist, in which Raquel Welch's husband is killed, lands the group in George Kennedy's jail, awaiting hanging by itinerant executioner Guy Raymond. Stewart, Martin's older brother who always has rescued him from mistakes, takes Raymond's place in order to effect gang's escape. Having accomplished this, the upright Stewart then robs a bank. This opening action, well developed, takes 40 minutes.

Welch is got up to look like a Mexican Sophia Loren. Her makeup is distressingly false-looking, her accent moreso. Of Kennedy, she says at one point, 'hee ees a good mahn.'

■ BAND OF ANGELS

1957, 125 MINS, US ◇

Dir Raoul Walsh *Prod* Jerry Wald *Scr* John Twist, Ivan Goff, Ben Roberts *Ph* Lucien Ballard *Ed* Folmar Blangsted *Mus* Max Steiner *Art Dir* Franz Bachelin
● Clark Gable, Yvonne De Carlo, Sidney Poitier, Efrem Zimbalist Jr, Patric Knowles, Carolle Drake (Warner)

Subject of miscegenation is explored and developed in this colorful production of the Old South. Raoul Walsh is in top form in direction of the screenplay derived from a Robert Penn Warren novel. Screenwriters have captured the mood and spirit of the Deep South narrative which deals with a young woman of quality discovering that her mother was a slave.

Sold on the auction block to a former slave-trader, unfoldment dwells on the pair's relations, both in New Orleans and later on a plantation up-river. Beautiful and realistic backgrounds are achieved through locationing in Louisiana.

Clark Gable's characterization is reminiscent of his Rhett Butler in *Gone with the Wind*, although there is obviously no paralleling of plot. As former slave-runner turned New Orleans gentleman, with bitter memories of his earlier days, he contributes a warm, decisive portrayal that carries tremendous authority.

Yvonne De Carlo is beautiful as the mulatto, who learns of her true status when she returns from a Cincinnati finishing school to attend her father's funeral. Sidney Poitier impresses as Gable's educated protege, whom slaver picked up as an infant in Africa and reared as his son.

■ BAND WAGON, THE

1953, 111 MINS, US ◇ ⓥ

Dir Vincente Minnelli *Prod* Arthur Freed *Scr* Betty Comden, Adolph Green *Ph* Harry Jackson *Ed* Albert Akst *Mus* Adolph Deutsch (dir.) *Art Dir* Cedric Gibbons, Preston Ames
● Fred Astaire, Cyd Charisse, Oscar Levant, Nanette Fabray, Jack Buchanan, James Mitchell (M-G-M)

Plot is the one about a dancing film star whose pictures aren't selling. A couple of writing pals conceive a stage musical for him and the rest of the story is concerned with making the show a success after a flop tryout and weeks of rewriting and new starts.

Twelve songs from various Broadway musicals are either chirped or terped. Showing up as an imaginative highlight is 'Girl Hunt', the modern jazz ballet finale done to a turn by Fred Astaire and Cyd Charisse. A takeoff in dance on the Mickey Spillane type of private eye, number is a new cleffing for the picture by Howard Dietz and Arthur Schwartz, credited with all of the songs.

Astaire, as the film star, shows his ability with a song and dance character. Oscar Levant and Nanette Fabray make up the writing team. Fabray is given enough chance to display her talent from legit musicals, and her personality is caught by the cameras. Charisse is an eye-filling filly, especially when dancing. Levant is his usual phlegmatic self. Buchanan enacts the show's director and costar and is one of the picture's strong-points with his comedy moments.

■ BANK DICK, THE

1940, 69 MINS, US ⓥ

Dir Edward Cline *Scr* Mahatma Kane Jeeves [= W.C. Fields] *Ph* Milton Krasner *Ed* Arthur Hilton *Art Dir* Jack Otterson
● W.C. Fields, Cora Witherspoon, Una Merkel, Jessie Ralph, Franklin Pangborn, Grady Sutton (Universal)

Story is credited to Mahatma Kane Jeeves, Fields' own humorous nom de plume. It's a deliberate rack on which to hang the varied

Fieldsian comedic routines, many of them repeats from previous pictures but with enough new material inserted to overcome the antique gags. A wild auto ride down the mountainside for the climax is an old formula dating back to the Mack Sennett days, but director Edward Cline has refurbished the episode with new twists that make it a thrill-laugh dash of top proportions.

Fields is the town's foremost elbow bender who injects himself into any situation without invitation. The unexpected hero of a bank robbery, he is rewarded with the job of detective to guard against future holdups. He involves his prospective son-in-law as a temporary embezzler to buy wildcat mining stock, and then holds off the bank examiner via the Mickey Finn route. Repeat bank robbery again results in Fields' accepting hero honors, the reward and sudden riches from a film directing contract.

Several times, Fields reaches into satirical pantomime reminiscent of Charlie Chaplin's best efforts during his Mutual and Essanay days. Directorial guidance by Edward Cline (graduate of the Keystone Kop school) smacks over every gag line and situation to the fullest extent.

Fields has a field day in tabbing the various characters. His own screen name, he is careful to explain, is pronounced Soo-zay, and not Souse, as it appears from English pronunciation.

■ BANK HOLIDAY

1938, 86 MINS, UK

Dir Carol Reed *Scr* Rodney Ackland, Roger Burford *Ph* Arthur Crabtree *Ed* R.E. Dearing
● John Lodge, Margaret Lockwood, Hugh Williams, Rene Ray, Kathleen Harrison, Felix Aylmer (Gainsborough)

This is good entertainment. A young nurse, Catherine (Margaret Lockwood), has planned to spend an illicit weekend with a man to whom she cannot be married until their financial position improves. Her patient dies in childbirth and her pity for the forlorn husband changes her whole life.

In the hectic rush of London's termini, she joins her waiting lover. They reach the coast, only to find no rooms available; they spend the night on the beach, duly chaperoned by hundreds of others. The tragedy she has left behind mars her pleasure; she flees her lover and with the aid of the police saves the widower from suicide.

Interspersed are many rich characters: a cockney family with squabbling kids, two young soldiers on leave, entrants for a beauty prize – one trying to get over a jilt, another aping society and making all the judges. None is overdrawn and all are depicted with human interest.

■ BARABBAS

1962, 144 MINS, ITALY ◇ ⓥ

Dir Richard Fleischer *Prod* Dino De Laurentiis *Scr* Christopher Fry, Diego Fabbri, Ivo Perilli, Nigel Balchin *Ph* Aldo Tonti *Ed* Raymond Poulton *Mus* Mario Nascimbene *Art Dir* Mario Chiari
● Anthony Quinn, Silvana Mangano, Arthur Kennedy, Jack Palance, Vittorio Gassmann, Ernest Borgnine (Columbia)

Barabbas is technically a fine job of work, reflecting big thinking and infinite patience on the parts of producer Dino De Laurentiis and director Richard Fleischer. In Technirama 70 and shot in Technicolor it has one or two sequences which stand up to the chariot race highlight in *Ben-Hur*.

Set in Jerusalem 2,000 years ago, the film [based on the novel by Par Lagerkvist] tells the story of Barabbas, thief and murderer, who was released from prison by the will of the people and replaced, in jail and on the Cross, by Jesus Christ. Barabbas' conscience plagues him. In a struggling, almost bovine manner he tries to find the truth about the new wave of faith that is sweeping the country.

Where the film hits the bell is in Fleischer's bold, dramatic handling of certain scenes, allied to some slick lensing by Aldo Tonti. The scenes in the Rome gladiatorial pit, sharply etched by Jack Palance as the top boy, have an urgent excitement, with Palance's sadism matched only by Quinn's bewildered concentration.

Individually, the performances are uneven. Quinn is firstclass in a role which could have become monotonous after his beefy approach to his scenes with a vital Katy Jurado following his release from jail. Palance plays the sadistic gladiator with a liplicking panache that tends to pinpoint the fact that the whole pic is a shade too violent, but certainly the thesp makes Torvald a vivid and urgent figure in the setup.

Silvana Mangano does an adequate job of work as Rachel, but the part never comes to life, nor does that of Ernest Borgnine as a Christian doing undercover work among the Romans.

■ **BARBARELLA**

1968, 98 MINS, FRANCE/ITALY ◇ ⓥ

Dir Roger Vadim *Prod* Dino De Laurentiis *Scr* Terry Southern, Roger Vadim, Claude Brule, Vittorio Bonicelli, Clement Biddle Wood, Brian Degas, Tudor Gates, Jean Claude Forest *Ph* Claude Renoir *Ed* Victoria Mercanton *Mus* Michel Magne, Charles Fox *Art Dir* Mario Garbuglia

● Jane Fonda, John Phillip Law, Anita Pallenberg, Milo O'Shea, David Hemmings, Marcel Marceau (Marianne/De Laurentiis)

Despite a certain amount of production dash and polish and a few silly-funny lines of dialog, *Barbarella* isn't very much of a film. Based on what has been called an adult comic strip [by Jean Claude Forest], the Dino De Laurentiis production is flawed with a cast that is not particularly adept at comedy, a flat script, and direction which can't get this beached whale afloat.

Jane Fonda stars in the title role, and comes across as an ice-cold, antiseptic, wide-eyed girl who just can't say no. Fonda's abilities are stretched to the breaking point along with her clothes.

In key supporting roles, John Phillip Law is inept as a simp angel while Anita Pallenberg, as the lesbian queen, fares better because of a well defined character.

Made at De Laurentiis' Rome studios, film can't really be called overproduced, considering the slapdash special effects, grainy process and poor calibre of the props, though put together on a massive scale so as to appear of spectacle proportions.

■ **BARBARIAN AND THE GEISHA, THE**

1958, 105 MINS, US ◇ ⓥ

Dir John Huston *Prod* Eugene Frenke *Scr* Charles Grayson *Ph* Charles G. Clarke *Ed* Stuart Gilmore *Mus* Hugo Friedhofer *Art Dir* Lyle R. Wheeler, Jack Martin Smith

● John Wayne, Eiko Ando, Sam Jaffe, So Yamamura, Morita, Hiroshi Yamato (20th Century-Fox)

The Barbarian and the Geisha is an Oriental pageant of primitive beauty based on the 'true' story of the exploits of the first US consul to establish headquarters in Japan. The production is lavish but it is light in other departments.

Once opened to Christian missionaries, then closed, Japan was a Forbidden Kingdom to outsiders in 1856 when US Consul-General Townsend Harris (John Wayne)

arrives off the port of Shimoda, where the screenplay, based on Ellis St Joseph's story, begins. Harris is under orders to open the door on the hermetically-sealed country, and, armed only with his own personality and accompanied only by his European translator (Sam Jaffe) he prepares to do so.

After initial harassing and setbacks, Wayne gains the confidence of the local noble (So Yamamura) who agrees to take him to the court of the Shogun to plead his case. Meantime, to make Wayne's isolation easier, Yamamura delivers a geisha (Eiko Ando) to the non-Nipponese barbarian.

The Barbarian and the Geisha (originally titled *The Townsend Harris Story*) is rich in atmosphere and in some stirringly-staged scenes, such as Wayne's arrival by ship at Shimoda, his presentation to the Shogun's court and an archery meet of medieval pomp. It is less exciting in its personal delineations. Huston uses a technique of having the Japanese speak Japanese throughout. The character played by Ando acts as the narrator behind some of this action, but this device is only partially successful.

■ **BARBAROSA**

1982, 90 MINS, US ◇ ⓥ

Dir Fred Schepisi *Prod* Paul N. Lazarus III, William D. Wittliff *Scr* William D. Wittliff *Ph* Ian Baker *Ed* Don Zimmerman, David Ramirez *Mus* Bruce Smeaton *Art Dir* Michael Levesque

● Willie Nelson, Gary Busey, Isela Vega, Gilbert Roland, Danny De La Paz, Alma Martinez (Universal/Associated/ITC)

Australian director Fred Schepisi does a careful job of bringing the western legend to light with endearing performances from actors Willie Nelson and Gary Busey.

Nelson limns the renowned title character, who in essence is nothing more than a 'sensitive' outlaw forever eluding the assassination attempts of his wife's over-protective family. Nelson visits his spouse and daughter (who live with the family) several times a year, but past events coupled with his yearning for freedom make it impossible to live a normal life.

Busey turns in a natural portrayal of the poor, goofy farm boy the outlaw takes under his wing. While it's an honorable performance, the Busey character and his growth into a soulful human being primarily serves to point up what a nice guy Nelson is.

■ **BARBARY COAST**

1935, 97 MINS, US ⓥ

Dir Howard Hawks *Prod* Samuel Goldwyn *Scr* Ben Hecht, Charles MacArthur *Ph* Ray June *Ed* Edward Curtiss *Mus* Alfred Newman *Art Dir* Richard Day

● Miriam Hopkins, Edward G. Robinson, Joel McCrea, Walter Brennan, Frank Craven, Brian Donlevy (Goldwyn/United Artists)

Sam Goldwyn picked *Barbary Coast* as a title and called in Ben Hecht and Charles MacArthur to write a story to fit. Result is a picture that has all it takes to get along in thoroughbred company.

Atmosphere of the period has been richly caught, even if the girl's efforts to free herself from the gambling hall proprietor aren't so sincere.

Miriam Hopkins is introduced when she arrives in Frisco to meet the man she is going to marry, admittedly because he has struck it rich. When learning he has been killed over a gambling loss, she throws herself toward Edward G. Robinson, town's underworld leader. Story makes Hopkins a partially unsympathetic character until she falls in love with a young prospector and finds herself tangled up through prior associations. It is mostly Hopkins' picture but Robinson and Joel McCrea are also strong.

Harry Carey plays the organizer of vigilantes and gives a good performance. Other standout small parts are by Walter Brennan and Frank Craven.

■ **BAREFOOT CONTESSA, THE**

1954, 128 MINS, US ◇

Dir Joseph L. Mankiewicz *Prod* Forrest E. Johnston *Scr* Joseph L. Mankiewicz *Ph* Jack Cardiff *Ed* William Hornbeck *Mus* Mario Nascimbene

● Humphrey Bogart, Ava Gardner, Edmond O'Brien, Marius Goring, Valentina Cortese, Rossano Brazzi (United Artists/Figaro)

Sharpness of the characters, the high-voltage dialog, the cynicism and wit and wisdom of the story, the spectacular combination of the immorally rich and the immorally sycophantic – these add up to a click feature from writer-director Joseph L. Mankiewicz.

Ava Gardner is the contessa of the title, 'discovered' in a second-rate flamenco nitery in Madrid. The trio of discoverers: Humphrey Bogart as a writer-director and determined member of Alcoholics' Anonymous; Edmond O'Brien, as a glib, nervous, perspiring combination of pressagent and (apparent) procurer; and Warren Stevens, the rich producer.

Gardner is ideal in her spot, looking every inch the femme magnetism around which all the action revolves. Bogart is splendid throughout, taking part quietly and with maximum effectiveness in the twists and turns of the intriguing story.

At times, Mankiewicz, the writer, seems over-generous in providing his characters with words.

Mankiewicz has been quoted as saying none of his characters is for real. This was in answer to suspicion that the moneybags producer might be an only slightly distorted mirroring of Howard Hughes.

■ **BAREFOOT IN THE PARK**

1967, 104 MINS, US ◇ ⓥ

Dir Gene Saks *Prod* Hal B. Wallis *Scr* Neil Simon *Ph* Joseph LaShelle *Ed* William A. Lyon *Mus* Neal Hefti *Art Dir* Hal Pereira, Walter Tyler

● Robert Redford, Jane Fonda, Charles Boyer, Mildred Natwick, Herbert Edelman, Mabel Albertson (Paramount)

Barefoot in the Park is one howl of a picture. Adapted by Neil Simon from his legit smash, retaining Robert Redford and Mildred Natwick from the original cast, and adding Jane Fonda and Charles Boyer to round out the principals, this is a thoroughly entertaining comedy delight about young marriage. Director Gene Saks makes a sock debut.

Redford is outstanding, particularly adept in light comedy. Fonda is excellent, ditto Natwick, her mother. A genuine surprise casting is Boyer, as the Bohemian who lives in the attic above the newlyweds' top-floor flat. With only one slight flagging pace – about 30 minutes from the end, when Redford and Fonda have their late-night squabble – pic moves along smartly.

■ **BARFLY**

1987, 99 MINS, US ◇ ⓥ

Dir Barbet Schroeder *Prod* Barbet Schroeder *Scr* Charles Bukowski *Ph* Robby Muller *Ed* Eva Gardos *Art Dir* Bob Ziembicki

● Mickey Rourke, Faye Dunaway, Alice Krige, Jack Nance, J.C. Quinn, Frank Stallone (Coppola/Cannon)

Barfly is a lowlife fairytale, an ethereal serio-comedy about gutter existence from the pen of one who's been there, Charles Bukowski. First American fictional feature from Swiss-French director Barbet Schroeder is spiked with unexpected doses of humor, much of it due to Mickey Rourke' quirky, unpredictable, most engaging performance as the boozy hero.

Much as in a Bukowski short story, a bar is the center of the universe here. Populating the dive in a seedy section of Los Angeles are a floating assortment of winos and derelicts, of which one of the youngest and most volatile is Henry (Rourke), a self-styled poet of the bottle.

He meets a terribly attractive fellow alcoholic, Wanda (Faye Dunaway), who immediately takes him in and keeps him well plied with drink and sex, to the extent they are both interested in and capable of the latter.

Rourke's performance is the centerpiece of the film, and keeps it buoyantly alive throughout. Dunaway also is on the right wavelength as the 'distressed goddess' who grows dependent upon and loyal to the wildly unreliable Rourke.

. . . .

■ BARKLEYS OF BROADWAY, THE

1949, 102 MINS, US ◇ ⓥ
Dir Charles Walters *Prod* Arthur Freed *Scr* Betty Comden, Adolph Green *Ph* Harry Stradling *Ed* Albert Akst *Mus* Lenny Hayton
● Fred Astaire, Ginger Rogers, Oscar Levant, Billie Burke, Gale Robbins (M-G-M)

With Fred Astaire and Ginger Rogers *The Barkleys of Broadway* is an ace dance fest, presenting them at their terpsichorean best against a production background that is Metro at its lushest. However, the songs are ordinary.

The screen's most complementary dance team glides through five dance numbers with the grace and apparent spontaneity that is their trademark when appearing together.

Sixth dance number is done solo by Astaire. It is the combination of special effects and Astaire hoofing in a dance with shoes that spellbinds into standout terping.

Plot is light, but ties together neatly in depicting a more or less standard story of a Broadway star team of man and wife who have a misunderstanding, separate and then get back together for the finale. Dialog is good and the cast is very competent.

. . . .

■ BARRETTS OF WIMPOLE STREET, THE

1934, 110 MINS, US
Dir Sidney Franklin *Prod* Irving G. Thalberg *Scr* Claudine West, Ernest Vajda, Donald Ogden Stewart *Ph* William Daniels *Ed* Margaret Booth *Mus* Herbert Stothart
● Norma Shearer, Fredric March, Charles Laughton, Maureen O'Sullivan, Katharine Alexander, Una O'Connor (M-G-M)

The Barretts of Wimpole Street is an artistic cinematic translation of the Katherine Cornell stage success [by Rudolph Besier].

As a film it's slow. Very. The first hour is wandering, planting-the-plot stuff that has some difficulty cementing the interest, but in the final stretch it grips and holds. It's talky throughout – truly an actor's picture, with long speeches, verbose philosophical observations.

The romance between Elizabeth Barrett (Norma Shearer) and Robert Browning (Fredric March) is a beautiful exposition in its ethereal and physically rehabilitating effect on the ailing Barrett. The unnatural love of Papa Barrett is graphically depicted by Charles Laughton, as the psychopathic, hateful character whose twisted affections for his children especially daughter Elizabeth, almost proves her physical and spiritual undoing.

Not the least of the many good performances is the nifty chore turned in by Marion Clayton as the lisping Bella Hadley.

Maureen O'Sullivan, Katharine Alexander, Una O'Connor (exceptional as the mincing Wilson, the maid) and Ralph Forbes all register in a long but not too involved cast which director Sidney Franklin has at all times kept well in hand and never permitted to become confusing.

The confining locale of London's Wimpole Street in 1845 limits the action to the interior of the Barretts' home, but the general persuasiveness of all the histrionics achieves much in offsetting the lack of physical action.

March's bravado style is well suited to the role of the ardent Browning, the poet. Shearer is at all times sincerely compelling in her role, even in the bedridden portions.
□ 1934: Best Picture (Nomination)

. . . .

■ BARRETTS OF WIMPOLE STREET, THE

1957, 104 MINS, US/UK ◇
Dir Sidney Franklin *Prod* Sam Zimbalist *Scr* John Dighton *Ph* F.A. Young *Ed* Frank Clarke *Mus* Bronislau Kaper *Art Dir* Alfred Junge
● Jennifer Jones, John Gielgud, Bill Travers, Virginia McKenna, Jean Anderson, Vernon Gray (M-G-M)

Lovers of the classics will find *The Barretts of Wimpole Street* a reliving of the romance between Elizabeth Barrett and Robert Browning as originally plotted in Rudolf Besier's play and in a 1934 screen version, also made by Metro.

Sidney Franklin, who directed the original film version starring Norma Shearer and Fredric March, helms this production.

Jennifer Jones, while a surprisingly healthy-looking Elizabeth, plays the invalid literary figure with great skill. Bill Travers' Browning, the vigorous, colorful poet who managed to court and win the delicate Elizabeth under the nose of her despotic father, is personable and competent enough.

John Gielgud, the father with an almost incestuous attachment for his daughter, repeats the role originally done by Charles Laughton with all the stern menace it requires. Virginia McKenna is lively and appealing as the younger sister, Henrietta, secretly in love with Vernon Gray, good as Captain Surtees Cook.

. . . .

■ BARRY LYNDON

1975, 184 MINS, UK ◇
Dir Stanley Kubrick *Prod* Stanley Kubrick *Scr* Stanley Kubrick *Ph* John Alcott *Ed* Tony Lawson *Mus* Leonard Rosenman (sup.) *Art Dir* Ken Adam
● Ryan O'Neal, Marisa Berenson, Patrick Magee, Hardy Kruger, Gay Hamilton, Leonard Rossiter (Warner)

Stanley Kubrick scripts and directs a most elegant and handsome adaptation of William Makepeace Thackeray's early 19th-century novel.

Ryan O'Neal's character evolves from a passive, likable Irish lad, enamored of cousin Gay Hamilton whose eyes are fixed on the pocketbook of British officer Leonard Rossiter. Conned into fleeing his home after a fake duel, O'Neal learns about life from a highwayman, a Prussian captor-benefactor and a spy. O'Neal emerges from these trials as a cynical manipulator of people.

The pile of victims eventually includes Marisa Berenson, whose means provide a possible avenue to O'Neal's security in a peerage.

But up from the ashes comes a discarded stepson who brings down O'Neal.

. . . .

■ BARTLEBY

1971, 78 MINS, UK ◇
Dir Anthony Friedmann *Prod* Rodney Carr-Smith *Scr* Rodney Carr-Smith, Anthony Friedmann *Ph* Ian Wilson *Ed* John S. Smith *Mus* Roger Webb *Art Dir* Simon Holland

● Paul Scofield, John McEnery, Thorley Walters, Colin Jeavons, Raymond Mason, Charles Kinross (Pantheon)

It's understandable that Paul Scofield, an intelligent, choosey actor, should have been intrigued by this enigmatic, short film.

Bartleby is virtually a duel between Scofield and John McEnery, who plays a young audit clerk, a fallout from society. He is no rebel or rabble-raiser; just a guy who can't adjust himself to the demands of these times. He gets a job with Scofield who patiently employs him but is astounded at the young man's attitude. Very politely he insists that 'he prefers not do this or that'. Baffled, Scofield does everything possible to get through to the young man but is thwarted and eventually, irritated, fires him. But Bartleby prefers not to go.

This modestly-budgeted picture, from Herman Melville's story, is downbeat. But it is intriguing because of the two main performances. Scofield, who radiates thought and integrity in every speech movement and gesture is fine. McEnery underplays the incomprehensible, pitiful Bartleby with just the right note to engender sympathy but not ridicule.

The film is a riddle but it should intrigue any thoughtful filmgoer.

. . . .

■ BARTON FINK

1991, 116 MINS, US ◇ ⓥ
Dir Joel Coen *Prod* Ethan Coen *Scr* Ethan Coen, Joel Coen *Ph* Roger Deakins *Ed* Roderick Jaynes *Mus* Carter Burwell *Art Dir* Dennis Gassner
● John Turturro, John Goodman, Judy Davis, Michael Lerner, John Mahoney (20th Century-Fox/Circle)

Joel and Ethan Coen's hermetic tale of a 'genius' playwright's brief stint as a studio contract writer is a painstakingly miniaturist work that can be read any number of ways. This film will appeal to buffs at least as much as the brothers' last, *Miller's Crossing*.

Title character, played with a creepily growing sense of dread by John Turturro, is a gravely serious New York dramatist who scores a soaring triumph on Broadway in 1941 with a deep-dish think piece about the working class. In Hollywood he is assigned a Wallace Beery wrestling programmer and told to come up with something by the end of the week.

Checking into a huge, slightly frayed and weirdly underpopulated hotel, he becomes friendly with the hulking fellow bachelor next door, Charlie Meadows (John Goodman), an insurance salesman with a gift for gab. Working at home, Fink suffers from intense writer's block.

After a little more than an hour, the pic is thrown in a wholly unexpected direction. There is a shocking murder, the presence of a mysterious box in Fink's room, the revelation of another's character's sinister true identity, three more killings, a truly weird hotel fire and the humiliation of the writer after he believes he's finally turned out a fine scrfipt.

Scene after scene is filled with a ferocious strength and humor. Michael Lerner's performance as a Mayer-like studio overlord is sensational. Goodman is marvelous as the folksy neighbor, rolling his tongue around pages of wonderful dialog. Judy Davis nicely etches a woman who has a way with difficult writers, and John Mahoney turns up as a near dead ringer for William Faulkner in his Hollywood period.

. . . .

■ BASKET CASE 2

1990, 89 MINS, US ◇ ⓥ
Dir Frank Henenlotter *Prod* Edgar Ievens *Scr* Frank Henenlotter *Ph* Robert M. Baldwin *Ed* Kevin Tent *Mus* Joe Renzetti *Art Dir* Michael Moran

● Kevin Van Hentenryck, Annie Ross, Kathryn Meisle, Heather Rattray, Matt Mitler, Ted Sorel (Shapiro-Glickenhaus)

Belated sequel to the 1982 cult horror film, *Basket Case 2* is a hilarious genre spoof. Here Frank Henenlotter's paying homage to Tod Browning's 1932 classic *Freaks*.

Annie Ross as Granny Ruth is a crusader for the rights of 'unique individuals' (i.e. freaks) and welcomes the Siamese twin brothers Kevin and Belial to her home in Staten Island. Weird menagerie of youngsters, mostly crazy variations on the Elephant Man by makeup whiz Gabe Bartalos, are treated very sympathetically at first, but as in Browning's film their potential for scaring the audience also is exploited.

Pic climaxes with Belial's ultraviolent attacks on foes of freaks, namely tabloid reporter Kathryn Meisle, her shutterbug assistant Matt Mitler and cop Ted Sorel. En route is one of the oddest scenes in recent horror pics, Belial making love to Eve, a similarly grotesque Siamese twin.

Casting coup is Annie Ross, the legendary jazz singer, who is a lot of fun as the demented granny who goads her freakish charges to fight back.

■ BAT WHISPERS, THE

1931, 82 MINS, US ⓥ
Dir Roland West *Prod* Roland West *Ph* Ray June (standard version), Robert H. Planck (65mm version) *Ed* James Smith *Art Dir* Paul Roe Crawley
● Chester Morris, Una Merkel, Chance Ward, Richard Tucker, Wilson Benge, DeWitt Jennings (Art Cinema/United Artists)

Of the clutching hand school that the stage smash, *The Bat* [by Mary Roberts Rinehart and Avery Hopwood], was probably the real parent of, *The Bat Whispers*, in its talking version.

The wide-screen film, United Artists' first, is somewhat grandiloquent. Bits of direction with the camera, particularly early on, are very engaging. The same effects will come over in a lesser way on the standard size screen.

Most of the comedy is by Maude Eburne, as the lady's maid. Some more is quietly injected by Spencer Chartres. It's not the noisy kind of ghostly slapstick so long associated with haunted house stories.

Chester Morris [as Detective Anderson] has little to do. It's some time before his appearance and shortly after that he's knocked out for another lapse. At the finale the audience is halted by a cry from the screen not to leave, and, as a sort of epilog, Morris reappears to request the audience not to divulge the identity of the Bat in the picture. Other cast players take care of their portions without distinction either way. Una Merkel is the girl, with William Bakewell opposite.

■ BATAAN

1943, 113 MINS, US ⓥ
Dir Tay Garnett *Prod* Irving Starr *Scr* Robert D. Andrews *Ph* Sidney Wagner *Ed* George White *Mus* Bronislau Kaper
● Robert Taylor, George Murphy, Thomas Mitchell, Lloyd Nolan, Robert Walker, Desi Arnaz (M-G-M)

Bataan is a melodramatic re-enactment of the last ditch stand of an American patrol detailed to guard a road in the Philippines following the evacuation of Manila. Picture pulls no punches in displaying the realistically grim warfare.

There's a sufficient amount of jungle battle action and a couple of hand-to-hand skirmishes where bayonets are brought into play, but major portion of the extended running time is devoted to dramatic incidents revolving around the hastily-recruited patrol unit and their efforts to stave off the Jap's advance into the Bataan peninsula so that the main American and Philippine forces could dig in.

Robert Taylor gives a strong performance as the commanding sergeant, but picture focuses attention on screen debut of Robert Walker, who smacks over an arresting portrayal as the sensitive and sympathetic young sailor who attaches himself to the outfit to get a crack at the Japs.

■ BATMAN

1966, 105 MINS, US ◇ ⓥ
Dir Leslie H. Martinson *Prod* William Dozier *Scr* Lorenzo Semple Jr *Ph* Howard Schwartz *Ed* Harry Gerstad *Mus* Nelson Riddle *Art Dir* Jack Martin Smith, Serge Krizman
● Adam West, Burt Ward, Lee Merriwether, Cesar Romero, Burgess Meredith, Frank Gorshin (20th Century-Fox)

Batman is packed with action, clever sight gags, interesting complications and goes all out on bat with batmania: batplane, batboat, batcycle, etc. etc. Humor is stretched to the limit, color is comic-strip sharp and script retrieves every trick from the highly popular teleseries' oatbag, adding a few more sophisticated touches.

It's nearly impossible to attempt to relate plot. Suffice to say that it's Batman and Robin against his four arch-enemies, Catwoman, The Joker, The Penguin and The Riddler. Quartet have united and are out to take over the world. They elaborately plot the dynamic duo's death again and again but in every instance duo escape by the skin of their tights.

The acting is uniformly impressively improbable. The intense innocent enthusiasm of Cesar Romero, Burgess Meredith and Frank Gorshin as the three criminals is balanced against the innocent calm of Adam West and Burt Ward, Batman and Robin respectively.

■ BATMAN

1989, 126 MINS, US ◇ ⓥ
Dir Tim Burton *Prod* Jon Peters, Peter Guber *Scr* Sam Hamm, Warran Skaaren *Ph* Roger Pratt *Ed* Ray Lovejoy *Mus* Danny Elfman, Prince *Art Dir* Anton Furst
● Michael Keaton, Jack Nicholson, Kim Basinger, Robert Wohl, Pat Hingle, Billy Dee Williams (Guber-Peters/Warner)

Director Tim Burton effectively echoes the visual style of the original Bob Kane comics while conjuring up a nightmarish world of his own.

Going back to the source elements of the cartoon figure, who made his debut in 1939 for Detective (now DC) Comics, the Jon Peters-Peter Guber production will appeal to purists who prefer their heroes as straight as Clint Eastwood.

In a striking departure from his usual amiable comic-style, Michael Keaton captures the haunted intensity of the character, and seems particularly lonely and obsessive without Robin around to share his exploits.

The gorgeous Kim Basinger takes the sidekick's place, in a determined bow to heterosexuality which nonetheless leaves Batman something less than enthusiastic.

It comes as no surprise that Jack Nicholson steals every scene in a sizable role as the hideously disfigured Joker. Nicholson embellishes fascinatingly baroque designs with his twisted features, lavish verbal pirouettes and inspired excursions into the outer limits of psychosis. It's a masterpiece of sinister comic acting.

What keeps the film arresting is the visual stylization. It was a shrewd choice for Burton to emulate the jarring angles and creepy lighting of film noir.

■ BATTLE BEYOND THE STARS

1980, 104 MINS, US ◇ ⓥ
Dir Jimmy T. Murakami *Prod* Ed Carlin *Scr* John Sayles *Ph* Daniel Lacambre *Mus* James Horner *Art Dir* John Zabrucky
● Richard Thomas, Robert Vaughn, George Peppard, John Saxon, Darlanne Fleugel, Sybil Danning (New World)

The fascination of watching how the defenseless cope with marauding barbarians is put to the test with New World's production of *Battle beyond the Stars*.

In unfolding its saga of how the peace-loving bunch on a small planet rebuffs a genetically deficient but vicious band of bad guys, *Battle* incorporates touches of an old-fashioned western, horror pics and even a touch of softcore.

Despite the expense involved, the pic appears not to take itself too seriously. Principal characterizations are skin deep. Dialog takes the form of relaxed banter with a minimum of homilies.

George Peppard has fun as a Scotch-tippling cowboy from earth who turns up as one of the mercenaries hired by the planet's earnest young soldier (Richard Thomas). John Saxon is hilarious as the chief bad guy.

■ BATTLE FOR RUSSIA, THE

1943, 80 MINS, US
Dir Frank Capra *Prod* Anatole Litvak *Ed* William C. Hornbeck, William A. Lyon *Mus* Dimitri Tiomkin
● (US War Department)

In *The Battle for Russia*, Lt Col Frank Capra, of the Special Service Division, Army Service Forces, turns out by far the most notable in the series of *Why We Fight* army orientation pictures. Fifth of the series of seven documentaries, *Battle for Russia* is a powerful, yet simple, drama vividly depicting the greatest military achievement of all time.

As in the case of its predecessors, *Prelude to War*, *The Nazis Strike*, *Divide and Conquer* and *Battle of Britain*, *Russia* is a brilliant compilation of carefully edited footage culled, in the latter instance, from official Soviet sources and from newsreel and Signal Corps film, with a good part of the Russian material made available to the War Dept exclusively for this production.

Portraying the historical background of Russia from the time of Alexander Nevsky to the present, the film explains the reasons motivating the various conquests over Russia. Effective use of animated maps helps detail its enormous resources, raw materials, manpower, etc.

Keyed to Gen Douglas MacArthur's statement that: 'The scale and grandeur of the (Russian) effort mark it as the greatest military achievement in all history', this Capra-Litvak documentary is primarily the story of the titanic struggle up to the successful defense of Stalingrad.

■ BATTLE FOR THE PLANET OF THE APES

1973, 88 MINS, US ◇ ⓥ
Dir J. Lee Thompson *Prod* Arthur P. Jacobs *Scr* John William Corrington, Joyce Hooper Corrington *Ph* Richard H. Kline *Ed* Alan L. Jaggs, John C. Horger *Mus* Leonard Rosenman *Art Dir* Dale Hennesy
● Roddy McDowall, Claude Akins, Natalie Trundy, Severn Darden, Lew Ayres, John Huston (20th Century-Fox)

The fifth and last film of the series depicts the confrontation between the apes and the nuclear mutated humans inhabiting a large city destroyed in previous episode. Roddy McDowall encores as the ape's leader, having his own tribal strife with Claude Akins, a militant trouble-maker.

Considering the usual fate of sequels, it's not so much that this final effort [from a story by Paul Dehn] is limp, but that the previous four pix maintained for so long a good quality level.

McDowell and Natalie Trundy head the cast, in which Paul Williams plays a philosopher-type, and Austin Soker is a black counselor, most respected of the humans who are more or less captives of the apes. Severn Darden is leader of the mutated humans. Lew Ayres has a good bit, and John Huston appears in another pompous cameo as an aged philosopher of future generations who sets the flashback motif for the story.

■ **BATTLE OF BRITAIN**

1969, 133 MINS, UK ◇ ⓥ

Dir Guy Hamilton   *Prod* Harry Saltzman, S. Benjamin Fisz   *Scr* James Kennaway, Wilfred Greatorex   *Ph* Freddie Young   *Mus* Ron Goodwin, William Walton   *Art Dir* Maurice Carter

● Laurence Olivier, Trevor Howard, Michael Caine, Ralph Richardson, Susannah York, Michael Redgrave (United Artists)

Battle sequences in the air are splendidly conceived and sweepingly dramatic, though sometimes repetitious.

The $12 million-plus film strikes a happy medium between action and human interest. Stressed admirably are the strained headaches of the RAF top brass as they tackled the perilous problems. The battle fatigue, the difference of opinion on tactics, the shortage of planes and pilots, and the dreadful anxiety of time running out are all revealed.

Standouts among the stars are Laurence Olivier as Sir Hugh Dowding, Fighter Command's supremo, and Trevor Howard as the tight-lipped, dedicated Air Vice-Marshall Keith Park.

Some of the star names are woefully wasted, notably Michael Caine, Patrick Wymark and Kenneth More, all playing routine parts.

■ **BATTLE OF THE BULGE**

1965, 167 MINS, US ⓥ

Dir Ken Annakin   *Prod* Milton Sperling, Philip Yordan   *Scr* Milton Sperling, Philip Yordan, John Nelson   *Ph* Jack Hildyard   *Ed* Derek Parsons   *Mus* Benjamin Frankel   *Art Dir* Eugene Lourie

● Henry Fonda, Robert Shaw, Robert Ryan, Dana Andrews, George Montgomery, Ty Hardin (Cinerama)

Based on the pivotal action which precipitated the end of the Second World War in Europe, but otherwise fictionalized, *Battle of the Bulge* is a rousing, commercial battlefield action-drama of the emotions and activities of US and German forces.

Script pits hard-charging German tank commander Robert Shaw against a US military hierarchy topped by Robert Ryan, intelligence chief Dana Andrews, and latter's assistant (Henry Fonda) who is initially unpopular with the higher brass because he insists that the Germans are building towards a winter offensive.

Shaw is outstanding in a multifaceted role which demands he be a true war-lover, coolly rational under battle pressure and somewhat contemptuous of rear echelon chief Werner Peters.

On the US side script is flawed in the introduction of stock military types. Ken Annakin's direction and the adroit spacing of skirmishes minimize the script softness, exemplified by Fonda's character, whose solo sleuthing and tactical analysis strains credulity. Withal, Fonda is excellent.

■ **BATTLE OF THE VILLA FIORITA, THE**

1965, 111 MINS, US ◇

Dir Delmer Daves   *Prod* Delmer Daves   *Scr* Delmer Daves   *Ph* Oswald Morris   *Ed* Bert Bates   *Mus* Mischa Spoliansky   *Art Dir* Carmen Dillon

● Maureen O'Hara, Rossano Brazzi, Richard Todd, Phyllis Calvert, Olivia Hussey, Maxine Audley (Warner)

The Battle of the Villa Fiorita is a beautifully-photographed and well-mounted Delmer Daves production which falls short artistically by switching gears.

Daves' script (from Rumer Godden's novel) propels Maureen O'Hara into affair with Italian composer Rossano Brazzi when latter attends English tunefest during one of hubby Richard Todd's frequent absences from home. The lovers hie to Italian villa and set up housekeeping before her divorce action jells.

At this point concept shifts to attempts by her kids (Martin Stephens and Elizabeth Dear) to break it up, joined later by Brazzi's moppet, Olivia Hussey. Idea is played for laffs, from juves' trek from England through hunger strikes, faked illness and other gambits.

O'Hara looks appropriately shook up but script does not permit much acting. Brazzi projects very well as lover, father and foil. Phyllis Calvert is on for seconds as gossipy English lady.

■ **BATTLETRUCK**

1982, 91 MINS, US ◇ ⓥ

Dir Harley Cokliss   *Prod* Lloyd Philips, Rob Whitehouse   *Scr* Irving Austin, Harley Cokliss, John Beech   *Ph* Chris Menges   *Ed* Michael Horton   *Mus* Kevin Peck   *Art Dir* Gary Hansen

● Michael Beck, Annie McEnroe, James Wainwright, John Ratzenberger, Randolph Powell, Bruno Lawrence (New World)

Battletruck is a well-made and engaging action picture. This is a feature debut for director Harley Cokliss, who was second-unit director of *The Empire Strikes Back*. Working on a limited budget in New Zealand, Cokliss gets more performing subtleties from his characters than these films usually have.

Pic takes place after civilization has nearly collapsed after the 'oil wars' depletes most of the world's petroleum supplies. The big truck is the main weapon for an outlaw army commandered by Straker (James Wainwright), excellent as a cold-blooded killer. However, his daughter Corlie (Annie McEnroe), doesn't share his ideas of a great career.

She flees and is befriended by reclusive biker Hunter (Michael Beck) and a peaceful community headed by Rusty (John Ratzenberger). From then on, it's a matter of counting the battles between Straker's band and Hunter's troops.

■ **BAXTER!**

1973, 105 MINS, UK ◇

Dir Lionel Jeffries   *Prod* Arthur Lewis   *Scr* Reginald Rose   *Ph* Geoffrey Unsworth   *Ed* Teddy Darvas   *Mus* Michael J. Lewis   *Art Dir* Anthony Pratt

● Patricia Neal, Jean-Pierre Cassel, Britt Ekland, Lynn Carlin, Scott Jacoby, Sally Thomsett (Anglo-EMI/Group W/Hanna-Barbera)

Baxter! is a good tearjerker about a young boy with a psychosomatic speech defect plus a bad family problem. Well directed by Lionel Jeffries, the British-lensed drama [from the novel *The Boy Who Could Make Himself Disappear* by Kin Platt] stars Patricia Neal as a speech therapist, Britt Ekland and Jean-Pierre Cassel as lovers who help Scott Jacoby in the title character role, and Lynn Carlin, as the boy's mother.

This is Jeffries' second feature directorial work (*The Railway Children* marked his bow),

and he does a very fine job, aided by Geoffrey Unsworth's strong camerawork.

Neal's dancing voice and eyes are as magnificent as ever. Carlin is particularly excellent as the mother.

■ **BAY BOY**

1984, 104 MINS, CANADA ◇ ⓥ

Dir Daniel Petrie   *Prod* John Kemeny, Denis Heroux, Rene Cleitman   *Scr* Daniel Petrie   *Ph* Claude Agostini   *Ed* Susan Shanks   *Mus* Claude Bolling   *Art Dir* Wolf Kroeger

● Liv Ullmann, Kiefer Sutherland, Alan Scarfe, Mathieu Carriere, Peter Donat, Isabelle Mejias (ICC)

Canadian-born director Daniel Petrie had long cherished making a film about his early days in Nova Scotia. *Bay Boy* is the realization of that dream, but it's far from the pot of gold at the end of his rainbow.

Setting is a coastal mining community circa 1937. Principals are a family of non-miners barely eking out an existence during the Depression. Kiefer Sutherland has the pivotal part of Donald Campbell, a teenager whose family envision his future with the clergy. He's more dubious about this path.

The family travails – father's precarious fortunes, brother's debilitating disease, mother's profound religious guilt, etc – are cut with humorous vignettes and insights. However, Donald witnesses the murder of an old Jewish couple by a local policeman.

■ **BEACH PARTY**

1963, 104 MINS, US ◇ ⓥ

Dir William Asher   *Prod* James H. Nicholson, Lou Rusoff   *Scr* Lou Rusoff   *Ph* Kay Norton   *Ed* Homer Powell   *Mus* Les Baxter

● Robert Cummings, Dorothy Malone, Frankie Avalon, Annette Funicello, Harvey Lembeck, Jody McCrea (American International)

Beach Party is a bouncy bit of lightweight fluff, attractively cast, beautifully set (Malibu Beach), and scored throughout with a big twist beat. It has a kind of direct, simple-minded cheeriness.

The comparatively elderly Robert Cummings toplines the cast (with Dorothy Malone) and provides the picture with what real comic substance it has. Plot is pegged on a study of teenage sex habits undertaken by anthropologist Cummings on the beach at Malibu.

As the square professor, Cummings shows himself to be an able farceur and notably at ease in surroundings which might embarrass a less professional star. Malone is along just for the ride in a small role as the prof's long-suffering secretary. It's a waste of her talent.

What plot complications there are centre around the romantic problems of a group of young surfers, principally Frankie Avalon and Annette Funicello, each of whom undertakes a campaign to make the other jealous – he with buxom Eva Six, she with the erudite professor. Story is padded out with some lovely surf-riding sequences and a whole string of Les Baxter songs.

■ **BEACHES**

1988, 123 MINS, US ◇ ⓥ

Dir Garry Marshall   *Prod* Bonnie Bruckheimer-Martell, Bettle Midler, Margaret Jennings South, Nick Abdo   *Scr* Mary Agnes Donoghue   *Ph* Dante Spinotti   *Ed* Richard Halsey   *Mus* Georges Delerue   *Art Dir* Albert Brenner

● Bette Midler, Barbara Hershey, John Heard, Spalding Gray, Lainie Kazan (Touchstone/Silver Screen Partners IV/South-All Girl)

Story of this engaging tearjerker [from the novel by Iris Rainer Dart] is one of a profound friendship, from childhood to beyond the grave, between two wildly mismatched women, a lower-class Jew (Bette Midler) from the Bronx whose every breath is show-biz, and a San Francisco blueblood (Barbara Hershey) destined for a pampered but troubled life. Men, marriages and career vicissitudes come and go, but their bond ultimately cuts through it all.

Midler's strutting, egotistical, self-aware character gets off any number of zingers, but all in the context of a vulnerable woman who seems to accept, finally, that certain things in life, notably happiness in romance and family, are probably unreachable for her.

By way of contrast, Hershey plays her more emotionally untouchable part with an almost severe gravity. Hillary seems to have no real center, which in Hershey's interpretation could be part of the point, as nothing really works out for this woman who has everything, looks, intelligence, money – going for her.

．．．．．．．．．．．．．．．．．．．．．．．．．．

■ BEACH RED

1967, 105 MINS, US ◇
Dir Cornel Wilde   *Prod* Cornel Wilde   *Scr* Clint Johnston, Donald A. Peters, Jefferson Pascal   *Ph* Cecil R. Cooney   *Ed* Frank P. Keller   *Mus* Elbey Vid, Antonio Buenaventura   *Art Dir* Francisco Balangue
● Cornel Wilde, Rip Torn, Burr DeBenning, Patrick Wolfe, Jean Wallace, Jaime Sanchez (United Artists)

In contrast to many professedly anti-war films, *Beach Red* is indisputably sincere in its war is hell message. Except for brief reveries of civilian life, the film focuses entirely on a single dreary campaign by an American unit out to take a Japanese-held island in the Pacific.

Notably absent are the usual stereotypes: the tough-talking sarge with the heart of gold, the frightened kid who becomes a man in combat, etc. The trouble with the screenplay, adapted from Peter Bowman's 1945 novel, is that little is substituted for these wisely-avoided cliches. The central characters are spokesmen for differing points of view, not real, full-bodied people. The acting quality suffers as a result.

The captain (Cornel Wilde) loves his wife and hates war. The sergeant (Rip Torn) derives sadistic pleasure from the war. An 18-year-old minister's son (Patrick Wolfe) remembers his girl back home and inarticulately echoes the captain's pacificism. His Southern sidekick (Burr DeBenning) is a hearty illiterate for whom the armed forces is a haven.

．．．．．．．．．．．．．．．．．．．．．．．．．．

■ BEAST FROM 20,000 FATHOMS, THE

1953, 80 MINS, US ⊙
Dir Eugene Lourie   *Prod* Hal Chester, Jack Dietz   *Scr* Lou Morheim, Fred Freiberger   *Ph* Jack Russell   *Ed* Bernard W. Burton   *Mus* David Buttolph   *Art Dir* Eugene Lourie
● Paul Christian, Paula Raymond, Cecil Kellaway, Kenneth Tobey, Donald Woods, Lee Van Cleef (Warner)

Producers have created a prehistoric monster that makes Kong seem like a chimpanzee. It's a gigantic amphibious beast that towers above some of New York's highest buildings. The sight of the beast stalking through Gotham's downtown streets is awesome. Special credit should go to Ray Harryhausen for the socko technical effects.

An experimental atomic blast in the Arctic region results in the 'unfreezing' of the strange prehistoric reptile of the dinosaur family. Scientist Tom Nesbitt's (Paul Christian) report of the beast is attributed to hallucination resulting from Arctic exposure.

After several unsuccessful attempts, Nesbitt enlists the aid of Prof Thurgood Elson (Cecil Kellaway) and his pretty assistant Lee Hun-

ter (Paula Raymond). Elson is killed by the monster while exploring an undersea canyon in a diving bell 150 miles from New York. The beast finally turns up in Manhattan.

Christian is firstrate as the determined scientist and Kellaway scores as the doubting professor. Raymond appears too stiff and unconvincing as the professor's assistant and Christian's romantic vis-a-vis. Screenplay [suggested by the *Saturday Evening Post* story *The Fog Horn* by Ray Bradbury] has a documentary flavor, which Jack Russell's camera captures expertly.

．．．．．．．．．．．．．．．．．．．．．．．．．．

■ BEAST WITH FIVE FINGERS, THE

1946, 90 MINS, US ⊙
Dir Robert Florey   *Prod* William Jacobs   *Scr* Curt Siodmak   *Ph* Wesley Anderson   *Ed* Frank Magee   *Mus* Max Steiner   *Art Dir* Stanley Fleischer
● Robert Alda, Andrea King, Peter Lorre, Victor Francen (Warner)

The Beast with Five Fingers is a weird, Grand Guignol-ish conconction that puts the customers strictly on their own. Till the last gasp, when J. Carrol Naish winks into the lens and gives out with a crack that 'it could happen', it gives more credit for intelligence than the average thriller.

Victor Francen, as a semi-invalid concert pianist, lives in a gloomy villa in northern Italy. His companions are his secretary, Peter Lorre; his nurse, Andrea King; a composer friend, Robert Alda, and his attorney, David Hoffman.

A good deal of the plot is projected through Lorre's eyes, without any explanation of the switches from straight narration to scenes registered by Lorre's deranged mind. Best and most gruesome parts of the picture are when Lorre is alone with his vivid imagination. He chases a ghoulish hand around the library several times, catching it finally and hammering it down in a bloodcurdling scene reminiscent in mood of *The Cabinet of Dr Caligari*. Still it pursues him, escaping at last from the burning coals into which he has thrown it.

．．．．．．．．．．．．．．．．．．．．．．．．．．

■ BEAST WITHIN, THE

1982, 90 MINS, US ◇ ⊙
Dir Philippe Mora   *Prod* Harvey Bernhard, Gabriel Katzka   *Scr* Tom Holland   *Ph* Jack L. Richards   *Ed* Robert Brown, Bert Lovitt   *Mus* Les Baxter   *Art Dir* David M. Haber
● Ronny Cox, Bibi Besch, Paul Clemens, Don Gordon, R.G. Armstrong, Kitty Moffat (M-G-M/United Artists)

Honeymooning, Ronny Cox and Bibi Besch get their car stuck in the woods and while he goes for help, she gets raped by something with hairy legs. Fastforward 17 years to find them parents of that most dreaded of monsters – a teenager. [Film is based on the novel by Edward Levy.]

The teenager (Paul Clemens) is bad sick, and reluctantly Mom and Dad go back to the Mississippi town where he was raped to see if there could be any connection between his illness and the hairy legs.

Feeling better, young Clemens follows and starts to chomp people.

There does come a time when Clemens has to get out of his body and get on with being a bigtime monster. Thanks to Thomas R. Burman's make-up effects, this sequence actually creates chills as the boy's head bubbles and bursts and his skin pops and stretches.

．．．．．．．．．．．．．．．．．．．．．．．．．．

■ BEASTMASTER, THE

1982, 118 MINS, US ◇ ⊙
Dir Don Coscarelli   *Prod* Paul Pepperman, Sylvio Tabet   *Scr* Don Coscarelli, Paul Pepperman   *Ph* John Alcott   *Ed* Roy Watts   *Mus* Lee Holdridge   *Art Dir* Conrad E. Angone

● Marc Singer, Tanya Roberts, Rip Torn, John Amos, Josh Milrad, Rod Loomis (M-G-M/United Artists)

When *The Beastmaster* begins, it is very hard to tell what it is all about. An hour later, it is very hard to care what it is all about. Another hour later, it is very hard to remember what it was all about. From the early confusion, in which it seems that a cow gives birth to a baby boy, Marc Singer emerges as Dar.

Singer's destiny is to go after the villains led by Rip Torn to revenge the destruction of the village. Along the way he teams up with two ferrets, an eagle, a panther, Tanya Roberts and John Amos and other assorted creatures of equal acting ability. Much of the time they are involved in rescuing each other from rather noninteresting situations.

．．．．．．．．．．．．．．．．．．．．．．．．．．

■ BEAT THE DEVIL

1953, 100 MINS, UK/ITALY ⊙
Dir John Huston   *Scr* John Huston, Anthony Veiller, Peter Viertel, Truman Capote   *Ph* Oswald Morris   *Ed* Ralph Kemplen   *Mus* Franco Mannino   *Art Dir* Wilfrid Shingleton
● Humphrey Bogart, Jennifer Jones, Gina Lollobrigida, Robert Morley, Peter Lorre, Edward Underdown (Romulus/Santana)

In an easy sort of way, the story [from a novel by James Helvick] describes the adventures of a bunch of uranium exploiteers who want to get hold of some valuable land in Africa. While they're waiting for a passage from Italy, their go-between (Humphrey Bogart) becomes involved with a young couple, played by Jennifer Jones and Edward Underdown. The way in which they get done out of their property, and the potential millions that go with it, provides the background for all the action.

All the exteriors were lensed on location in Italy, with fine matching work at Shepperton Studios. There are carefully timed laughs in the script as well as intended comedy situations that misfire. The best gag is derived from Bogart's interview with an Arab bigwig who provides a slow boat to Africa in exchange for a promised introduction to Rita Hayworth.

Under John Huston's stylish direction a fine acting standard is maintained by a front-ranking cast. Bogart's virile performance is handsomely matched by Jones' pert and vivacious study of the wife of the Englishman who pretends to status and riches which neither has enjoyed.

Gina Lollobrigida gives a provocative portrayal as Bogart's wife while Edward Underdown stands out as the Englishman.

．．．．．．．．．．．．．．．．．．．．．．．．．．

■ BEAU BRUMMELL

1924, 120 MINS, US ⊗ ⊙
Dir Harry Beaumont   *Scr* Dorothy Farnum   *Ph* David Abel
● John Barrymore, Mary Astor, Willard Louis, Irene Rich, Alec B. Francis, Carmel Myers (Warner)

This has John Barrymore at the head of a cast that holds some strong picture names. The direction is not what it might have been, and the casting is also somewhat faulty. Irene Rich as the Duchess of York would have undoubtedly made a much better Lady Margery than Mary Astor, who played it. Although Astor is seen to advantage from the standpoint of beauty, she does not display any great histrionic ability.

Willard Louis as George, Prince of Wales, is one of the real outstanding figures. He walks away with practically every scene in which he appears.

Carmel Myers as a vamp is a modern vamp rather than one of the period in which the action is laid. Alec B. Francis as the servant to Beau Brummell makes a work of art of his role.

As to Barrymore, there are flashes in his characterization of the London dandy that are inspired, and there are other moments when he does not seem to get over at all.

• •

■ BEAU GESTE

1926, 129 MINS, US ⊗

Dir Herbert Brenon   *Scr* Paul Schofield, John Russell, Herbert Brenon   *Ph* J. Roy Hunt   *Art Dir* Julian Boone Fleming

● Ronald Colman, Neil Hamilton, Ralph Forbes, Alice Joyce, Mary Brian, Noah Beery (Paramount)

Beau Geste is a 'man's' picture. The story revolves around three brothers and their love for each other. And a great looking trio – Ronald Colman, Neil Hamilton and Ralph Forbes. Beyond that the love interest is strictly secondary, practically nil.

The picture is all story. In fact, only one cast member seems to get above the scenario. This is Noah Beery as the bestial sergeant-major. A part that only comes along every so often, and Beery gives it the same prominence in which P.C. Wren, the author, conceived it. It's undoubtedly one of his best portrayals.

When all is said and done, Colman, in the title role, hasn't so very much to do. Hamilton equals him for footage and Forbes exceeds him. Forbes, in his first picture, impresses all the way. Hamilton also gives a sincere performance. But there can be no question that Beery is the outstanding figure of the picture.

• •

■ BEAU GESTE

1939, 114 MINS, US ▼

Dir William A. Wellman   *Prod* William A. Wellman   *Scr* Robert Carson   *Ph* Theodor Sparkuhl   *Ed* Thomas Scott   *Mus* Alfred Newman   *Art Dir* Hans Dreier, Robert Odell

● Gary Cooper, Ray Milland, Robert Preston, Brian Donlevy, Susan Hayward, Broderick Crawford (Paramount)

Beau Geste has been produced with vigorous realism and spectacular sweep. Director William Wellman has focused attention on the melodramatic and vividly gruesome aspects of the story, and skimmed lightly over the episodes and motivation which highlighted Percival Christopher Wren's original novel.

Beau employs the flashback method in unfolding the adventures of three Geste brothers in the Foreign Legion. Audience interest is gained at the start with presentation of the mystery of the desert fort with relief patrol finding the entire garrison dead and dead soldiers propped up for battle in the parapets. Confused by the weirdness of the situation, the head of the patrol pitches camp in the nearby oasis. Suddenly the fort is enveloped in flames and destroyed.

Gary Cooper is okay in the title spot. Ray Milland and Robert Preston work hard and competently to get over their respective characterizations. Trio are overshadowed, however, by the vivid Brian Donlevy as the savagely brutal sergeant of the Legion.

• •

■ BEAUTIFUL BLONDE FROM BASHFUL BEND, THE

1949, 76 MINS, US ◇ ▼

Dir Preston Sturges   *Proa* Preston Sturges   *Scr* Preston Sturges   *Ph* Harry Jackson   *Ed* Robert Fritch   *Mus* Cyril Mockridge

● Betty Grable, Cesar Romero, Rudy Vallee, Olga San Juan (20th Century-Fox)

Blonde is basically a rather silly western farce, loosely concocted. Producer-director-writer Preston Sturges plays his script [based on a story by Earl Felton] with frantic slapstick, stressing raw, bawdy comedy rather than genuine humor, to get the laughs. The pacing is erratic, as is the film editing.

Betty Grable is the chief asset as a western dancehall gal who knows how to handle a gun—and gets into trouble because of it. The boy friend is Cesar Romero. It's the latter that starts the trouble. Grable is out to kill him for two-timing but, in a dark room, shoots a judge in the posterior by mistake.

Cast goes about its business okay in answering Sturges's demands for burlesquing of the characters and occasionally makes the coarse humor pay off.

• •

■ BEAUTIFUL DREAMERS

1990, 105 MINS, CANADA ◇

Dir John Kent Harrison   *Prod* Michael Maclear, Martin Walters   *Scr* John Kent Harrison   *Ph* Francois Protat   *Ed* Ron Wisman   *Mus* Laurence Shragge   *Art Dir* Seamus Flannery

● Colm Feore, Rip Torn, Wendel Meldrum, Sheila McCarthy, Colin Fox (Cinexus/Famous Players)

A first pic by John Dent Harrison, *Beautiful Dreamers* is full of good intentions, but only some of them are realized. Pic centers on free-thinker Walt Whitman's actual visit to London, Ontario, in 1880, bringing fresh winds to the city's mental asylum and churning up most of the church and civic elite.

Much is made of the friendship between the older, white-bearded Whitman and the asylum's young superintendent, forcefully played by Canadian actor Colm Feore, who resists then traditionally harsh methods of treating the mentally ill.

Rip Torn plays Whitman large as a legend rather than on a human scale, but his grand actorly characterization bores quickly. Standout is Wendel Meldrum, a radiant beauty with classy acting skills to boot, who as the superintendent's wife is jealous of the time her husband spends with Whitman. Sheila McCarthy makes a powerful wordless cameo appearance as a married patient driven to the point of mad despair by overwork.

• •

■ BEAUTY JUNGLE, THE

1964, 114 MINS, UK ◇

Dir Val Guest   *Prod* Val Guest   *Scr* Robert Muller, Val Guest   *Ph* Arthur Grant   *Ed* Bill Lenny   *Mus* Laurie Johnson   *Art Dir* Maurice Carter

● Ian Hendry, Janette Scott, Ronald Fraser, Edmund Purdom, Tommy Trinder, Francis Matthews (Rank)

There's some lively, if not over subtle, comedy in this yarn of a girl who gains quick rewards as a beauty queen, but finds the going full of disillusionment and pitfalls.

Screenplay tends to soft pedal the problems involved and the writers (Val Guest and an observant journalist-author Robert Muller, who studied the beauty queen scene) seem reluctant to come out with their views on whether such contests are degrading or even dangerous to comely damsels who take them too seriously, or whether they are just a harmless giggle.

Story concerns a pretty stenographer (Janette Scott) who is joshed by a local newspaper columnist into entering a seaside pier contest. She wins and he takes over and builds her up into a regular contestant at such junkets who progresses steadily around the familiar circuit and gets into the big time league of big money, overblown publicity, commercialism and spurious glitter that's the magnet.

Ian Hendry, as the poor man's Svengali, is brisk and credible while Ronald Fraser, as his lenser buddy, also turns in a ripe performance.

• •

■ BECKET

1964, 148 MINS, US ▼

Dir Peter Glenville   *Prod* Hal Wallis   *Scr* Edward Anhalt   *Ph* Geoffrey Unsworth   *Ed* Anne V. Coates   *Mus* Laurence Rosenthal   *Prod Des* John Bryan

● Richard Burton, Peter O'Toole, John Gielgud, Donald Wolfit, Martita Hunt, Pamela Brown (Paramount)

Made in Shepperton Studios in the UK, this is a very fine, perhaps great, motion picture. It is costume drama but not routine, invigorated by story substance, personality clash, bright dialog and religious interest. Not least among its virtues is the pace of the narrative in the astute handing of Peter Glenville, with his advantage of having also mounted the stage play from which the film is derived.

The screenplay owes much to Jean Anouilh's orginal stage script. The modern psychology of Anouilh lends fascination to these 12th century shenanigans by investing them with special motivational insights rare in costume drama. The basic story is, of course, historic, the murder on 29 December 1170 in the cathedral of Canterbury of its archbishop, Becket, by barons from the entourage of Henry II, greatgrandson of William the Conqueror. For fictional purposes, Becket and the King had been old roustabouts together, much as, later in English history, Henry V and Falstaff were.

In the title role, Richard Burton gives a generally convincing and resourceful performance. The transition from the cold, calculating Saxon courtier of a Norman king into a duty-obsessed sincere churchman is not easily managed. Burton does manage.

As Henry II, Peter O'Toole emerges as the fatter role, and the more colorful. The king is an unhappy monarch who has known little affection in life. His only satisfying companionship has been provided by the Saxon Becket. Hating-loving, miserably lonely when deserted by his friend, O'Toole makes of the king a tormented, many-sided baffled, believable human being.

☐ 1964: Best Picture (Nomination)

• •

■ BECKY SHARP

1935, 84 MINS, US ◇ ▼

Dir Rouben Mamoulian   *Prod* Kenneth Macgowan   *Scr* Francis Edward Faragoh   *Ph* Ray Rennahan   *Ed* Archie Marshek   *Mus* Roy Webb   *Art Dir* Robert Edmond Jones, Wiard B. Ihnen

● Miriam Hopkins, Cedric Hardwicke, Nigel Bruce, Frances Dee, Alan Mowbray, G.P. Huntley Jr (Pioneer/RKO)

The first full-length talker in highly improved Technicolor, cinematographically it's a tribute to the new process and to Robert Edmond Jones' beautiful splashes of multitone visual values. The pastel shades of the interior properties, the faithful reproduction even of the femmes' makeup, the gay carnival splashes of color such as that in the Brussels waltz-quadrille scene (climaxed by Napoleon's Waterloo return) impress optically, but the story falls flat dramatically and the dialog is likewise fraught with too much discordant stridency of tone.

Miriam Hopkins at times fairly shrieks her way through the footage [based on Thackeray's *Vanity Fair* and the play by Langdon Mitchell]. She's basically handicapped by a negative characterization. As the calculating Becky, her role of a temptress is neither lurid nor winsome. It's a wishy-washy compromise of a gamin who annexes a sextet of masculine conquests, with the character not sufficiently definite to impress her as a great siren.

With the exceptions of G.P. Huntley Jr, Nigel Bruce and Cedric Hardwicke, none of the support is particularly distinguished nor has it much opportunity for distinction.

• •

BEDAZZLED

1967, 104 MINS, UK ◇ Ⓥ

Dir Stanley Donen *Prod* Stanley Donen *Scr* Peter
Cook, Dudley Moore *Ph* Austin Dempster
Ed Richard Marden *Mus* Dudley Moore
Art Dir Terence Knight

● Peter Cook, Dudley Moore, Eleanor Bron, Raquel
Welch, Robert Russell, Barry Humphries (20th Century-
Fox)

Bedazzled is smartly-styled and typical of certain types of high British comedy. It's a fantasy of a London short-order cook madly in love with a waitress, who is offered seven wishes by the Devil in return for his soul.

Stanley Donen production is pretty much the work of two of its three stars, Peter Cook and Dudley Moore. Pair scripted from Cook's original story, and Moore also composed music score. Eleanor Bron is third star, plus Raquel Welch, whose brief appearance is equalled only by her scant attire.

Mephistophelean overtones are inserted in this modern-day Faust legend tacked onto Moore, who would give his soul to possess Margaret, the waitress (Bron). Cook (Mephistopheles), parading under the mundane name of George Spiggot, appears mysteriously in Moore's flat as he flubs a suicide attempt and grants all of the cook's wishes.

BEDFORD INCIDENT, THE

1965, 102 MINS, US Ⓥ

Dir James B. Harris *Prod* James B. Harris, Richard
Widmark *Scr* James Poe *Ph* Gilbert Taylor *Ed* John
Jympson *Mus* Gerard Schurmann *Art Dir* Arthur
Lawson

● Richard Widmark, Sidney Poitier, James MacArthur,
Martin Balsam, Wally Cox, Eric Portman (Bedford/
Columbia)

The Bedford Incident is an excellent contemporary sea drama based on a little-known but day-to-day reality of the Cold War, the monitoring of Russian submarine activity by US Navy destroyers. The production, made at England's Shepperton Studios, has salty scripting and solid performances, including one of the finest in Widmark's career.

James Poe's adaptation of the Mark Rascovich novel depicts the 'hunt-to-exhaustion' tactic in anti-submarine warfare, whereby a sub contact is pursued until one side or the other either gives up or eludes.

Widmark stars as the skipper of the USS *Bedford*, a modern destroyer, equipped with tactical nuclear weapons, on patrol in the North Atlantic. Widmark's skipper is that rare breed whom the crew not only follows, but worships. The character of this sea dog is drawn out by the helicopter arrival of Sidney Poitier, as a wise-guy magazine writer, and Martin Balsam, a Reserve medic back on active duty.

Poitier does an excellent job in both the light and serious aspects of his role, and manages to leave a personal stamp on his scenes.

BEDKNOBS & BROOMSTICKS

1971, 117 MINS, US ◇ Ⓥ

Dir Robert Stevenson *Prod* Bill Walsh *Scr* Bill Walsh,
Don DaGradi *Ph* Frank Philips *Ed* Cotton
Warburton *Mus* Richard M. Sherman, Robert B.
Sherman

● Angela Lansbury, David Tomlinson, Roddy
McDowall, Sam Jaffe, John Ericson, Bruce Forsyth
(Walt Disney)

The magic of Walt Disney lingers magnificently on in *Bedknobs & Broomsticks*.

The setting is a quaint olde-worlde English seaside village during the earlier days of World War II. Three Cockney kids, Roy Smart, Ian Weighall and Cindy O'Callaghan, are evacuated there and are as appalled by the dullness of it all as they are with

the eccentricities and rules of Angela Lansbury with whom they are billetted. Then they discover she is studying witchcraft by correspondence course with the idea of using it against the Germans should they invade. Life takes on a rosier hue. They learn to perform all sorts of magic, fly to London on a bedstead and spend a joyous time in the never-never lands.

It is when the film dives deeply into the realms of fantasy that it is most enjoyable. The trip with the principals on the bedstead through the underwater kingdom of the fishes and animated football match between jungle animals with a superimposed David Tomlinson refereeing are not only sheer delights but technic masterpieces.

BEDROOM WINDOW, THE

1986, 112 MINS, US ◇ Ⓥ

Dir Curtis Hanson *Prod* Martha Schumacher
Scr Curtis Hanson *Ph* Gil Taylor *Ed* Scott Conrad
Mus Michael Shrieve, Patrick Gleeson *Art Dir* Rafael
Caro

● Steve Guttenberg, Elizabeth McGovern, Isabelle
Huppert, Paul Shenar, Wallace Shawn (De Laurentiis)

Cast against type, Steve Guttenberg plays a malleable young executive carrying on an affair with his boss' wife, the sexy Sylvia (Isabelle Huppert). During a tryst at Guttenberg's apartment one night after a party, Huppert, looking out his bedroom window, sees a girl (Elizabeth McGovern) being assaulted outside.

Guttenberg ultimately becomes a suspect in the rash of rape and murder cases, forcing him in the Hitchcock tradition to begin his own investigation in trying to prove who the real killer is.

Hanson's screenplay involves several ingenious plot twists. Huppert carries the first half of the film, replaced by McGovern in importance in the final reels and both actresses are alluring and mysterious in keeping the piece suspenseful. Unfortunately, a lot of coincidences and just plain stupid actions by Guttenberg are relied upon to keep the pot boiling.

BED SITTING ROOM, THE

1970, 90 MINS, UK ◇ Ⓥ

Dir Richard Lester *Prod* Oscar Lewenstein, Richard
Lester *Scr* John Antrobus, Charles Wood *Ph* David
Watkin *Ed* John Victor Smith *Mus* Ken Thorne
Art Dir Assheton Gordon

● Rita Tushingham, Ralph Richardson, Peter Cook,
Dudley Moore, Spike Milligan, Michael Hordern (United
Artists)

A play by Spike Milligan and John Antrobus serves as an ideal springboard for an offbeat anti-war film by Richard Lester which, miraculously, manages to convey its grim message with humor.

Sketch-like pic catches glimpses and comments of the 20-odd survivors of a London shredded by an A-bomb as they dig out of their holes to try and cope with the grey new world before they, too, become animals.

In the manner of vaude blackouts, they soon meld into a general mosaic of stiff-upper-lip acceptance of new conditions, some fizzlers but others very amusing.

Ralph Richardson is superb in a relatively brief stint as the diehard traditionalist who eventually 'becomes' the title's bed-sitting room, but all in a carefully-chosen roster of British character thesps who contribute stellar bits in almost impossibly difficult roles.

BEDTIME STORY

1941, 83 MINS, US

Dir Alexander Hall *Prod* B.P. Schulberg *Scr* Richard
Flournoy *Ph* Joseph Walker *Ed* Viola Lawrence

● Fredric March, Loretta Young, Robert Benchley,
Allyn Joslyn, Eve Arden, Helen Westley (Columbia

Picture is a combo of slick scripting, fast-paced direction and excellent performances. Richard Flournoy to laugh embellishment to the original story by Horace Jackson and Grant Garrett; director Alexander Hall keeps his foot on the speed throttle from start to finish; and Fredric March teams with Loretta Young for a pair of topnotch performances in the starring spots.

Despite the light and fluffy tale unreeled, maximum entertainment is provided in the breezy exposition of the marital problems of producer-playwright March and his star-wife Young. After seven years of marriage and struggle, pair are top successes in their respective endeavors.

The wife desires to retire to their farm in Connecticut, while the energetic March hatches a new play in which he wants Young to star. Both Young and the audience keep intrigued by the inventive devices concocted by the playwright in trying to swing his wife into the new play.

BEDTIME STORY

1964, 99 MINS, US ◇ Ⓥ

Dir Ralph Levy *Prod* Stanley Shapiro *Scr* Stanley
Shapiro, Paul Henning *Ph* Clifford Stine *Ed* Milton
Garruth *Mus* Hans J. Salter *Art Dir* Alexander
Golitzen, Robert Clatworthy

● Marlon Brando, David Niven, Shirley Jones, Dody
Goodman, Aram Stephan, Marie Windsor (Universal)

Bedtime Story will divert the less discriminating, although there are times when even such major league performers as Marlon Brando and David Niven have to strain to sustain the overall meager romantic comedy material.

Some of the lines snap and crackle, and several of the situations (done with slapstick overtones) in which Brando and Niven find themselves involved as conmen in competition on the French Riviera are broadly funny.

The screenplay has Niven as a bigtime operator and Brando a relatively petty practitioner of the confidence art who comes to challenge the 'king of the mountain' in his own background. The mercenary contest centers around 'American soap queen' Shirley Jones, who turns out to be merely the penniless winner of a soap queen contest.

Brando wins the girl, but he loses the histrionic contest to Niven, whose effortless flair for sophisticated comedy is not matched by his co-star.

BEETLEJUICE

1988, 92 MINS, US ◇ Ⓥ

Dir Tim Burton *Prod* Michael Bender, Larry Wilson,
Richard Hashimoto *Scr* Michael McDowell, Warren
Skaaren *Ph* Thomas Ackerman *Ed* Jane Kurson
Mus Danny Elfman *Art Dir* Bo Welch

● Alec Baldwin, Geena Davis, Michael Keaton,
Catherine O'Hara, Glenn Shadix (Geffen)

Beetlejuice springs to life when the raucous and repulsive Betelgeuse (Michael Keaton) rises from his moribund state to wreak havoc on fellow spooks and mortal enemies.

Geena Davis and Alec Baldwin are a couple of affectionate New Englanders who live in a big barn of a house that they lovingly are restoring. But they crash over a covered bridge and drown – consigned to an afterlife that keeps them stuck at home forever invisible to anyone not similarly situated.

No sooner is their funeral over when their beloved house is sold to a rich New York financier (Jeffrey Jones) and his wife, the affected artiste (Catherine O'Hara).

Help comes via a cryptically written book for the newly deceased that takes Davis and Baldwin into the afterlife – kind of a comical holding cell for people who died of unnatural causes like themselves – but better yet, from this freak of a character named Betelgeuse that lives in the graveyard that's part of the miniature table-top town that Baldwin built.

In the script [from a story by Michael McDowell and Larry Wilson], things above ground aren't nearly as inventive as they are below. Luckily, Keaton pops up from his grave to liven things up when the antics pitting the good ghosts against the intruders become a trite cat & mouse game.

••••••••••••••••••••••••••••••••••

■ BEFORE WINTER COMES

1969, 107 MINS, UK ◇
Dir J. Lee Thompson   *Prod* Robert Emmett Ginns   *Scr* Andrew Sinclair   *Ph* Gil Taylor   *Ed* Willy Kemplen   *Mus* Ron Grainer   *Art Dir* John Blezard
● David Niven, Topol, Anna Karina, John Hurt, Anthony Quayle, Ori Levy (Columbia/Windward)

An unevenly-scripted, confusingly-directed drama about the treatment of displaced persons in Austria immediately following VE Day.

Before Winter Comes is a modestly-budgeted British drama about conflict between military authority and humanistic concepts in the peacetime army.

David Niven turns in his usual competent professional job as a major assigned to run a camp for displaced persons during the spring of 1945. Topol is the multilingual magician from among the DPs whom Niven chooses to assist him in deciding who should be turned over to American and who to Russian authorities.

To its basic military story [from the short story *The Interpreter* by Frederick L. Keefe] film tries to add a *Zorba the Greek* aspect, with Topol representing an earthy life-force counter to Niven's harsh rigidity.

Nothing dims Topol's impact. He exudes a romantic masculinity not without sexual charm at the same time that he shows a formidable comedic timing and grace.

••••••••••••••••••••••••••••••••••

■ BEGGAR'S OPERA, THE

1953, 94 MINS, UK ◇ Ⓥ
Dir Peter Brook   *Prod* Herbert Wilcox, Laurence Olivier   *Scr* Dennis Cannan, Christopher Fry   *Ph* Guy Green   *Ed* Reginald Beck   *Mus* Arthur Bliss   *Art Dir* William C. Andrews
● Laurence Olivier, Stanley Holloway, George Devine, Hugh Griffith, Athene Syler, Dorothy Tutin (British Lion)

A bold experiment which does not come off, *The Beggar's Opera* is an example of the uneasy partnership between screen and opera.

Herbert Wilcox, who promoted the production, cast his net over a wide field for new and promising talent. Peter Brook was recruited from legit to direct his first motion picture. Denis Cannan, the noted playwright, authored the screenplay and additional dialog and lyrics were penned by Christopher Fry. Most important of all was the casting of Laurence Olivier in his first singing role.

At constant intervals events are brought to a standstill by the John Gay lyrics and, attractive though they are in their own right, they do not merge too happily in the film.

Brook brings an obviously arty approach to his direction, resorting to a surplus of subdued lights. He is at his best in handling the big crowd scenes. The sequence in which Macheath is being driven from Newgate Gaol to the gallows is boldly and imaginatively presented.

Apart from Olivier and Stanley Holloway, the singing voices of the cast are dubbed by leading British vocalists and the contrast is clear and distinct. Olivier's light baritone, pleasant enough in its own way, is no match for the other voices. This apart, his performance is as robust and as lively as could be expected.

Holloway as Lockit, the jailer, is a polished singer as well as being a first-class thesper and his is one of the best individual contributions to the pic. Arthur Bliss' score is outstanding.

••••••••••••••••••••••••••••••••••

■ BEGUILED, THE

1971, 105 MINS, US ◇ Ⓥ
Dir Don Siegel   *Prod* Don Siegel   *Scr* John B. Sherry, Grimes Grice   *Ph* Bruce Surtees   *Ed* Carl Pingitore   *Mus* Lalo Schifrin   *Art Dir* Ted Haworth
● Clint Eastwood, Geraldine Page, Elizabeth Hartman, Jo Ann Harris, Darleen Carr, Mae Mercer (Malpaso/Universal)

Marking a distinct change of pace for both director Don Siegel and star Clint Eastwood, *The Beguiled* doesn't come off, and cues laughter in all the wrong places.

Eastwood eschews his usual action character to portray a wounded Union soldier recuperating within the confines of a small school for southern girls run by Geraldine Page. His presence cues a series of diverse sexual frustrations, and his wily handling of the ladies, spark jealousies of meller proportions.

Pic is essentially black comedy, but treatment is consistently heavy-handed. Script [from novel by Thomas Cullinan] resorts to tired symbolism, including that chestnut that equates southern womanhood with incestuous dreams under the Spanish moss.

Eastwood is not called upon to do much emoting; that is left in spades to the ladies. Page, per usual, runs away with the honors, whether girlishly remembering her erotic relationship with her brother or grimly sawing off Eastwood's leg in a sequence that would be nauseating if it weren't so funny.

••••••••••••••••••••••••••••••••••

■ BEHIND THE GREEN DOOR

1972, 72 MINS, US ◇
Dir Jim Mitchell, Art Mitchell   *Prod* Jim Mitchell, Art Mitchell   *Scr* Jim Mitchell   *Ph* Jon Fontana   *Ed* Jon Fontana
● Marilyn Chambers, George S. McDonald, Johnny Keyes, Ben Davidson (Mitchell Brothers)

Football fans attracted to the hardcore debut of Oakland Raider pro Ben Davidson should flag him for boxoffice clipping. His fully-clothed cameo appearance is hardly worth the time. But sports fans won't go away entirely disappointed, since ex-middleweight boxing champ Johnny Keyes is also featured – and he goes all the way.

Marilyn Chambers makes her hardcore debut in *Behind the Green Door*. Unlike the crones who used to populate pornos, Chambers may be remembered as the fresh-faced 'innocent' in *Together* [1971, directed by Sean S. Cunningham]. In that one, she was bare a lot, but never went all the way. In this, she does everything, quite realistically. Unfortunately, she never has enough to say to judge whether she qualifies as an actress.

Filmmakers lavished $50,000 on this feature, their biggest budget to date.

••••••••••••••••••••••••••••••••••

■ BEHOLD A PALE HORSE

1964, 119 MINS, US Ⓥ
Dir Fred Zinnemann   *Prod* Fred Zinnemann   *Scr* J.P. Miller   *Ph* Jean Badal   *Ed* Walter Thompson   *Mus* Maurice Jarre   *Art Dir* Alexandre Trauner
● Gregory Peck, Anthony Quinn, Omar Sharif, Raymond Pellegrin, Paola Stoppa, Mildred Dunnock (Columbia)

Pale Horse [from the novel *Killing a Mouse on Sunday* by Emeric Pressburger] is rooted in the Spanish Civil War, using introductory newsreel footage and the fighting to set the background for a story that happens 20 years

later and essentially concerns a Spanish guerrilla (Gregory Peck) who continues to live the war alone. He is thrown again into the fray in a personal attack against a vain and arrogant police captain (Anthony Quinn) who has vowed his death.

The one-man fight against a corrupt and powerful adversary is an obvious losing battle, but the guerrilla's last stand, he knows, can be his most effective.

Peck is a worn-out, untidy broken man who once again surges with force and energy in a characterization that ranks among the better in his long career. There also is an excellent performance from Quinn, who is coarse, crude and worldly as the arrogant police chief but shows his own insecurity beneath a physically courageous false front. Omar Sharif shows a warm, sensitive side in this film, playing the role of a young priest torn between obligations of personal morality and the official laws of government.

••••••••••••••••••••••••••••••••••

■ BEING THERE

1979, 130 MINS, US ◇
Dir Hal Ashby   *Prod* Andrew Braunsberg   *Scr* Jerzy Kosinski   *Ph* Caleb Deschanel   *Ed* Don Zimmerman   *Mus* John Mandel   *Art Dir* Michael Haller
● Peter Sellers, Shirley MacLaine, Melvyn Douglas, Jack Warden, Richard Basehart (United Artists/Lorimar)

Being There is a highly unusual and an unusually fine film. A faithful but nonetheless imaginative adaptation of Jerzy Kosinski's quirky comic novel, pic marks a significant achievement for director Hal Ashby and represents Peter Sellers' most smashing work since the mid-1960s.

Kosinski's story is a quietly outrageous fable which takes Sellers from his position as a childlike, unblinking naif who can't read or write to that of a valued advisor to an industrial giant and ultimately to the brink of a presidential nomination.

Tale possesses political, religious and consumer society undertones, but by no means is an overly symbolic affair trying to impress with its deep meanings.

Sellers' performance stands as the centerpiece of the film, and it's a beauty.

Shirley MacLaine is subtle and winning, retaining her dignity despite several precarious opportunities to lose it. If such is possible in a picture dominated by Sellers, Melvyn Douglas almost steals the film with his spectacular performance as the dying financial titan.

••••••••••••••••••••••••••••••••••

■ BELL, BOOK AND CANDLE

1958, 106 MINS, US ◇ Ⓥ
Dir Richard Quine   *Prod* Julian Blaustein   *Scr* Daniel Taradash   *Ph* James Wong Howe   *Ed* Charles Nelson   *Mus* George Duning   *Art Dir* Cary Odell
● James Stewart, Kim Novak, Jack Lemmon, Ernie Kovacs, Hermione Gingold, Elsa Lanchester (Phoenix/Columbia)

Richard Quine's direction gets everything possible out of the screenplay and the cast. But with Kim Novak the central figure, the picture lacks the spontaneity and sparkle written in by playwright John Van Druten.

The offbeat story is concerned with witches and warlocks (male gender of the broomstick set) operating against today's world of skepticism and realism. James Stewart is the straight man thrust by chance into a group of people, headed by Novak, where incantations, spells and sorcery are accepted as realities as commonplace as processed foods. Novak literally weaves a spell on Stewart to make him fall in love with her.

There are some wonderfully weird proceedings here, including Elsa Lanchester and Hermione Gingold as rival witches, and Jack

Lemmon as a clean-cut, bongo-beating warlock.

The hazard of the story is that there is really only one joke. This was sustained in the play by Van Druten's witty dialog. It is undercut in the picture by the fact that the backgrounds are too often as weird as the situations.

■ **BELLE OF NEW YORK, THE**

1952, 82 MINS, US ◇ ⊗

Dir Charles Walters *Prod* Arthur Freed *Scr* Robert O'Brien, Irving Elinson *Ph* Robert Planck *Ed* Albert Akst *Mus* Harry Warren *Art Dir* Cedric Gibbons, Jack Martin Smith

● Fred Astaire, Vera-Ellen, Marjorie Main, Keenan Wynn, Alice Pearce, Clinton Sundberg (M-G-M)

A film musical usually can get by with the lightest plot if the dance numbers and tunes are sock, but *Belle* has an even lighter plot than usual, and the numbers are just ordinary. It's all done pleasantly but not of a quality that rates more than passing interest.

Score contains nine songs, most of which are given some eye appeal in production staging, although not elaborately. Most pleasing is Vera-Ellen's 'Naughty But Nice', which she sings and dances to fit a story situation.

Script has Astaire as an early-New York playboy who falls for a Bowery mission worker (Vera-Ellen) and changes his ways, even getting employment to prove he is worthy of her pure, honest affection. Tunes and production numbers are hung on that framework.

■ **BELLE OF THE NINETIES**

1934, 75 MINS, US

Dir Leo McCarey *Prod* William LeBaron *Scr* Mae West *Ph* Karl Struss *Ed* LeRoy Stone *Art Dir* Hans Dreier, Bernard Herzbrun

● Mae West, Roger Pryor, John Mack Brown, Katherine DeMille, John Miljan (Paramount)

Mae West's opera, *Belle of the Nineties*, is as ten-twent-thirt as its mauve decade time and locale. The melodramatics are put on a bit thick, including the arch-villain who is an arch-renegade, a would-be murderer, a welcher, an arsonist and everything else in the book of ye good old-time mellers.

The original songs by Sam Coslow and Arthur Johnston are 'My Old Flame', 'American Beauty' and 'Troubled Waters'. Duke Ellington's nifty jazzique is a natural for the Westian song delivery.

Just like she makes stooges of almost anybody assigned to bandy talk with her, West dittoes with her principal support, including Roger Pryor, the fave vis-a-vis, John Mack Brown as the good time Charlie, and John Miljan, a villyun of darkest mien. Katherine DeMille as the spurned gambler's sweetheart looks better and suggests better opportunities than the prima facie script accords her.

■ **BELLES OF ST. TRINIAN'S, THE**

1954, 91 MINS, UK ⊗

Dir Frank Launder *Prod* Frank Launder, Sidney Gilliat *Scr* Frank Launder, Sidney Gilliat, Val Valentine *Ph* Stanley Pavey *Ed* Thelma Connell *Mus* Malcolm Arnold

● Alastair Sim, Joyce Grenfell, George Cole, Hermione Baddeley, Betty Ann Davies, Renee Houston (British Lion/London)

Inspired by Ronald Searle's British cartoons about the little horrors of a girls' school, *The Belles of St. Trinian's* makes an excellent start but never lives up to the promise of the opening reel.

By way of a story, Frank Launder and Sidney Gilliat have concocted an involved yarn about a plot to steal the favorite horse in a big race which is foiled by the girls in the fourth form after a battle royal with the sixth form.

Unrestrained direction by Launder is matched by the lively and energetic performances by most of the cast. As both the headmistress and her bookmaker brother, Alastair Sim rarely reaches comedy heights. Joyce Grenfell, however, as a police spy posing as a games teacher, is good for plenty of laughs. Best individual contribution is by George Cole, playing a wide-shouldered wiseguy, who acts as selling agent for the homemade gin brewed in the school lab, and also as go-between for the girls and the local bookie.

■ **BELL FOR ADANO, A**

1945, 103 MINS, US

Dir Henry King *Prod* Louis D. Lighton, Lamar Trotti *Scr* Lamar Trotti, Norman Reilly Raine *Ph* Joseph La Shelle *Ed* Barbara McLean *Mus* Alfred Newman *Art Dir* Lyle R. Wheeler, Mark-Lee Kirk

● Gene Tierney, John Hodiak, William Bendix, Richard Conte (20th Century-Fox)

John Hersey's story of an American major's administration of a town in Sicily, and his attempts to return it to its peaceful prewar status, has not been tampered with or elaborated upon. The film begins quietly to set the simple keynote, has some very beautiful, inspired moments, and finishes off with several scenes of emotional brilliance.

John Hodiak, in the difficult role of Major Joppolo, presents the right hardboiled type of civil affairs officer, determined to bring spiritual rebirth (through the return of its city-hall bell) to the community. Gene Tierney, too, as the blonde fisherman's daughter, has a certain quiet grace without always bringing sufficient poignancy to the role.

William Bendix, as the major's orderly, plays the part in subdued fashion for the most convincing portrayal of the three leads, rising superbly to his one big scene at the end. Here Bendix goes roaring drunk at learning that the major is to be displaced.

Henry King's direction caps the story's mood superbly, because of his ability to instill the thought of movement frequently where no action actually exists.

■ **BELL JAR, THE**

1979, 107 MINS, US ◇ ⊗

Dir Larry Peerce *Prod* Jerrold Brandt Jr *Scr* Marjorie Kellogg *Ph* Gerald Hirschfeld *Ed* Marvin Wallowitz *Mus* Gerald Fried *Art Dir* John Robert Lloyd

● Marilyn Hassett, Julie Harris, Anne Jackson, Barbara Barrie, Donna Mitchell, Robert Klein (Avco Embassy)

The Bell Jar, based on the late poet Sylvia Plath's autobiographical novel, evokes neither understanding nor sympathy for the plight of its heroine, Esther Greenwood, the epitome of a straight-A, golden-girl-over-achiever, who is mentally 'coming apart at the seams.'

As played by Marilyn Hassett, Esther emerges as a selfish, morbid little prig. She eventually confesses to hating her mother, admirably played by Julie Harris, presumably because he mother refuses to wallow in the details of her father's death with her.

Marjorie Kellogg's screenplay seems fairly faithful to the novel's spirit.

Larry Peerce's direction provides a sense of headachey dullness 15 minutes into the film.

Donald Brooks' costumes are the perfect evocation of 1950s style, the film's time period, and the color of Gerald Hirschfeld's camera is almost too pretty.

■ **BELLS ARE RINGING**

1960, 126 MINS, US ◇ ⊗

Dir Vincente Minnelli *Prod* Arthur Freed *Scr* Betty Comden, Adolph Green *Ph* Milton Krasner *Ed* Adrienne Fazan *Mus* Andre Previn (adapt.) *Art Dir* George W. Davis, Preston Ames

● Judy Holliday, Dean Martin, Fred Clark, Eddie Foy, Jean Stapleton, Frank Gorshin (M-G-M)

Better Broadway musicals than *Bells Are Ringing* have come to Hollywood, but few have been translated to the screen so effectively. *Bells* is ideally suited to the intimacy of the film medium. Where it might have a tendency in several passages to become dwarfed on a big stage, it's always bigger than life onscreen, which actually is a desirable factor in broad, free-wheeling comedy such as this.

The Betty Comden-Adolph Green screenplay, based on their book musical, is not by any means the sturdiest facet of the picture, but it's a pleasant yarn from which several rather inspired musical numbers spring. 'Just in Time' and 'The Party's Over' are delivered smoothly by Dean Martin and Judy Holliday. The latter's outstanding turn, however, occurs near the end of the picture, when she demonstrates her verve and versatility on the amusing 'I'm Goin' Back' (Where I Can Be Me, at the Bonjour Tristesse Brassiere Factory).

Martin has a chance to get in some solid licks on the alcoholically-inspired 'Do It Yourself' and in a traffic-stopping, crowd elbowing street sequence labelled 'Hello'. A real show-stopper is a production number with symphonic overtones presided over dynamically by Eddie Foy.

Vincente Minnelli's graceful, imaginative direction puts spirit and snap into the musical sequences, warmth and humor into the straight passages, and manages to knit it all together without any traces of awkwardness in transition, a frequent stumbling block in filmusicals. Jule Styne's bright score has been vibrantly adapted and conducted by Andre Previn.

Holliday, as might be expected, steals show with a performance of remarkable variety and gusto as a girl who takes her switchboard and humanity seriously, Martin is excellent as her writer friend, displaying more animation than customary.

■ **BELLS GO DOWN, THE**

1943, 86 MINS, UK

Dir Basil Dearden *Prod* Michael Balcon *Scr* Roger MacDougall *Ph* Ernest Palmer, G. Gibbs *Ed* Mary Habberfield *Mus* Roy Douglas

● Tommy Trinder, James Mason, Philip Friend, Mervyn Johns (Ealing)

Like *Fires Were Started* this film depicts the activities of life in the London Auxiliary Fire Service. But the first one out was more legitimate in that it was portrayed by actual members of the service.

Viewed as a mere low comedy, *The Bells Go Down* ambles along amiably. There is a running commentary patterned on the lines of those made familiar by Quentin Reynolds, and the fire scenes alternate with the wisecracking of Tommy Trinder, which are often without provocation. Thrillingly effective conflagration scenes deserve a large share of the honors.

Trinder enacts a lovable East Side young man whose mother runs a fish-and-chip shop, and who owns a racing greyhound that never wins until his comrades have gone broke backing the pooch.

The supporting cast is very well chosen, with Mervyn Johns ofering a scintillating portrayal. James Mason, as a fireman, scores as usual; Beatrice Varley, as Trinder's mother, and fully a score of others can be set down as efficient support. Direction, production and photography are praiseworthy.

....

■ **BELLS OF ST. MARY'S, THE**

1945, 126 MINS, US ⑰

Dir Leo McCarey *Prod* Leo McCarey *Scr* Dudley Nichols *Ph* George Barnes *Ed* Henry Marker *Mus* Robert Emmett Dolan *Art Dir* William Flannery

● Bing Crosby, Ingrid Bergman, Henry Travers, Ruth Donnelly, Rhys Williams, Una O'Connor (RKO/Rainbow)

The Bells of St. Mary's is warmly sentimental, has a simple story leavened with many laughs and bears comparison with *Going My Way*. Leo McCarey, who demonstrated his ability to combine wholesome sentiment into a potent attraction with *Going My Way*, duplicates that ability as producer-director on this one.

Bing Crosby's Father O'Malley is the same priest character seen in *Way*, and *Bells* tells of his new assignment as parish priest at the parochial school, St. Mary's.

Story tells of how he aids the nuns' prayers for a new school building with a more practical application of guidance; steers a young girl through an unhappy domestic situation, and brings the parents together again. It's all done with the natural ease that is Crosby's trademark.

Ingrid Bergman again demonstrates her versatility as the sister in charge. Her clashes with Crosby – all good-mannered – over proper methods of educating children, her venture into athletics, and coaching of a youngster to return a good left hook instead of the other cheek, are moments that will have an audience alternately laughing and sniffling.

☐ 1945: Best Picture (Nomination)

....

■ **BELLY OF AN ARCHITECT, THE**

1987, 118 MINS, UK ◇ ⑰

Dir Peter Greenaway *Prod* Colin Callender, Walter Donohue *Scr* Peter Greenaway *Ph* Sacha Vierny *Ed* John Wilson *Mus* Wim Mertens, Glenn Branca *Art Dir* Luciana Vedovelli

● Brian Dennehy, Chloe Webb, Lambert Wilson, Vanni Corbellini, Sergio Fantoni (Callender)

The Belly of an Architect is a visual treat, almost an homage to the style of Rome's architecture, lensed with skill and packed with esoteric nuances, but doubts about the story and the skill of the acting linger.

The belly in question is the stomach of a US architect, played by a suitably paunchy Brian Dennehy, who arrives in Rome with his fickle wife to set up an exhibition celebrating French architect Boullee. He becomes convinced he is being slowly poisoned by his wife (Chloe Webb) who is having an affair with a rival Italian architect (Lambert Wilson).

Dennehy, usually spotted in Yank actioners, makes an admirable effort as the troubled architect, but the rest of the cast – mostly European – turn in generally poor efforts. Webb as his wife looks okay, but her voice (apt in *Sid and Nancy*) just seems irritating, while Wilson as the rival architect/lover is little more than a clotheshorse.

....

■ **BEN**

1972, 83 MINS, US ◇ ⑰

Dir Phil Karlson *Prod* Mort Briskin *Scr* Gilbert A. Ralston *Ph* Russell Metty *Ed* Harry Gerstad *Mus* Walter Scharf *Art Dir* Rolland M. Brooks

● Lee Harcourt Montgomery, Joseph Campanella, Arthur O'Connell, Rosemary Murphy, Meredith Baxter, Kaz Garas (Cinerama/Crosby)

Willard has a tension-packed sequel in *Ben*, which takes up minutes after Willard, the man who trained rats, was killed off by his rodents in original entry. Ben, the rat heavy

of the other, plays title role here.

Chief protagonist is a young boy played by Lee Harcourt Montgomery, who befriends Ben. Latter's army of rats obey his orders, and they create a reign of terror as they indulge in a wave of killing.

Moppet plays his part to perfection and Phil Karlson's direction is responsible for mounting moments of excitement, well handled by cast headed by Joseph Campanella as a police lieutenant in charge of crisis and Meredith Baxter, Ben's sister.

....

■ **BEND OF THE RIVER**

1952, 91 MINS, US ◇ ⑰

Dir Anthony Mann *Prod* Aaron Rosenberg *Scr* Borden Chase *Ph* Irving Glassberg *Ed* Russell Schoengarth *Mus* Hans J. Salter *Art Dir* Bernard Herzbrun, Nathan Juran

● James Stewart, Arthur Kennedy, Julie Adams, Rock Hudson, Lori Nelson, Jay C. Flippen (Universal)

Basic plot line is a simple affair, as lifted from Bill Gulick's novel, *Bend of the Snake*. It deals with a band of settlers who make a long, wagon train trek into Oregon to claim the country from the wilderness and the hardships of such pioneering.

James Stewart is the wagon train guide, leading the settlers into Oregon. He rescues Arthur Kennedy, a former Missouri raider, from a hanging and the latter joins the party for the trek to Portland, where group boards a river steamer for a journey into the back country. The summer passes and promised supplies that are to carry the settlers through the winter do not arrive. Stewart returns to Portland, finds the town gold-mad and the supplies held up for more money.

Stewart's handling of his role has punch. Kennedy socks his likeable heavy role. Julie Adams fulfills romantic demands of her top femme role, and Rock Hudson pleasantly projects the part of a young gambler who joins the settlers.

....

■ **BENEATH THE PLANET OF THE APES**

1970, 95 MINS, US ◇ ⑰

Dir Ted Post *Prod* Arthur P. Jacobs *Scr* Paul Dehn *Ph* Milton Krasner *Ed* Marion Rothman *Mus* Leonard Rosenman *Art Dir* Jack Martin

● James Franciscus, Kim Hunter, Maurice Evans, Linda Harrison, Charlton Heston, Victor Buono (20th Century-Fox)

This sequel to the 1968 smash, *Planet of the Apes*, is hokey and slapdash. The story and Ted Post's direction fall far short of the original.

Film utilizes closing sequence of the original – where Charlton Heston and the silent Linda Harrison ride into an unknown country on the supposedly unknown planet, only to find the head of the Statue of Liberty buried in the sand. Heston's curtain cry of anguish now is followed by new footage, as he and Harrison wander the vast wasteland, in which Heston suddenly disappears.

James Franciscus is yet another space explorer who crash-lands, centuries out of time. Dialog, acting and direction are substandard.

Heston appears in some new footage, and Franciscus looks just like a twin brother by this time, in face and in voice.

....

■ **BENEATH THE 12-MILE REEF**

1953, 102 MINS, US ◇ ⑰

Dir Robert D. Webb *Prod* Robert Bassler *Scr* A.I. Bezzerides *Ph* Edward Cronjager *Ed* William Reynolds *Mus* Bernard Herrmann *Art Dir* Lyle R. Wheeler, George Patrick

● Robert Wagner, Terry Moore, Gilbert Roland, J. Carrol Naish, Richard Boone, Peter Graves (20th Century-Fox)

Set among the sponge-diving Greek colony at Tarpon Springs, Fla, the squeeze-lensing gives punch in the display of underwater wonders, the seascapes and the brilliant, beautiful sunrises and sunsets of the Florida Gulf coast.

In handling the young cast, Robert D. Webb's direction is less effective, particularly in the case of Robert Wagner and Terry Moore. Both are likable, so the shallowness of their performances is no serious handicap to the entertainment. Thesping quality is maintained by the more experienced casters. Scoring resoundingly is Gilbert Roland, colorful Greek diver and father of Wagner. Angela Clarke also clicks as the wife and mother.

The plot takes on two lines of conflict – the age-old battle between man and the sea, the more personal rivalry between the diving Greeks of Tarpon Springs and the hook-spongers of the shallow Key West waters.

Romance gets in its licks when the daring Gilbert ventures into Key West waters controlled by Boone and the young Wagner meets conch-girl Moore. It's an instant attraction between the pair and their romance builds to a runaway marriage after Gilbert is killed diving at the dangerous 12-mile reef. Wagner then becomes the man of the family, proving his right to the title by diving where his father met death, fighting off an octopus and beating Graves in an underwater battle.

....

■ **BENEATH THE VALLEY OF THE ULTRA VIXENS**

1979, 93 MINS, US ◇

Dir Russ Meyer *Prod* Russ Meyer *Scr* R. Hyde [= Roger Ebert], B. Callum [= Russ Meyer] *Ph* Russ Meyer *Ed* Russ Meyer *Mus* William Tasker *Art Dir* Michele Levesque

● Francesca 'Kitten' Natividad, Anne Marie, Ken Kerr, June Mack, Lola Langusta (RM International)

For the fanciers of pneumatic pulchritude, Russ Meyer is back with *Beneath the Valley of the Ultra Vixens* which as the onscreen narrator says 'is a very simple story', presumably for very simple people.

Briefly, the strand of plot concerns Lavonia (Francesca 'Kitten' Natividad), whose only fault is 'enthusiasm' and her unsatisfactory sex relationship with her man Lamar (Ken Kerr). In the course of curing Lamar so that he will straighten up and satisfy, Lavonia has a hot time with everybody in town.

This is the umpteenth in Meyer's vixen series. But are they satire, as Meyer would have one believe, or fantasy, or both? If anything, they are funny and though a bit too long, Meyer, who does everything (directs, edits, photographs and produces), keeps the action fast and furious.

....

■ **BEN-HUR**

1959, 212 MINS, US ◇ ⑰

Dir William Wyler *Prod* Sam Zimbalist *Scr* Karl Tunberg *Ph* Robert L. Surtees *Ed* Ralph E. Winters, John D. Dunning *Mus* Miklos Rozsa *Art Dir* William Horning, Edward Carfagno

● Charlton Heston, Jack Hawkins, Stephen Boyd, Haya Harareet, Hugh Griffith, Sam Jaffe (M-G-M)

The $15 million *Ben-Hur* is a majestic achievement, representing a superb blending of the motion picture arts by master craftsmen.

The big difference between *Ben-Hur* and other spectacles, biblical or otherwise, is its sincere concern for human beings. They're not just pawns reciting flowery dialog to fill gaps between the action. This has been accomplished without sacrificing the impact of the spectacle elements.

The famous chariot race between Ben-Hur,

B

the Prince of Judea, and Messala, the Roman tribune – directed by Andrew Marton and Yakima Canutt – represents some 40 minutes of the most hair-raising excitement ever witnessed.

Wisely, however, the film does not depend wholly on sheer spectacle. The family relationship between Ben-Hur and his mother Miriam and his sister Tirzah; his touching romance with Esther; his admiration of the Roman consul, Quintus Arrius, whom he rescues after a sea battle; his association with the Arab horseowner, Sheik Ilderim; and his struggle with Messala, the boyhood friend who becomes his mortal enemy, make moving scenes. And overshadowing these personal conflicts is the deeply religious theme involving the birth and crucifixion of Christ.

Karl Tunberg receives sole screen credit, although such heavyweight writers as Maxwell Anderson, S.N. Behrman, Gore Vidal and Christopher Fry also worked on the film. Fry, a respected British poet-playwright, was present on the set throughout the production in Rome.

Charlton Heston is excellent as the brawny yet kindly Ben-Hur who survives the life of a galley slave to seek revenge of his enemy Messala. Haya Harareet, an Israeli actress making her first appearance in an American film is sensitive and revealing as Esther. Jack Hawkins, as Quintus Arrius, the Roman consul who adopts Ben-Hur, adds another fine depiction to his career. Stephen Boyd, as Ben-Hur's enemy Messala, is not the standard villain, but succeeds in giving understanding to this position in his dedication to the Roman Empire.

The film took 10 months to complete at Rome's Cinecittà Studios. The 300 sets are one of the highlights of the film, particularly the massive arena for the chariot sequence. The musical score by Miklos Rozsa also contributes to the overall excellence of the giant project.

Ben-Hur is a fitting climax to Zimbalist's career as a producer. He died of a heart attack in Rome when the film was near completion.

☐ 1959: Best Picture

....

■ **BEN-HUR
A TALE OF THE CHRIST**

1925, 128 MINS, US ◇ ⊗ ⒱

Dir Fred Niblo   *Prod* Louis B. Mayer, Irving Thalberg
Scr Bess Meredyth, Carey Wilson, June Mathis, Katherine Hilliker, H.H. Caldwell   *Ph* Rene Guissart, Percy Hilburn, Karl Struss, Clyde De Vinna   *Ed* Lloyd Nosler   *Art Dir* Cedric Gibbons, Horace Jackson, Arnold Gillespie
● Ramon Novarro, Francis X. Bushman, May McAvoy, Betty Bronson, Carmel Myers (M-G-M)

Ben Hur is a picture that rises above spectacle, even though it is spectacle. On the sceeen it isn't the chariot race or the great battle scenes between the fleet of Rome and the pirate galleys of Golthar. It is the tremendous heart throbs that one experiences leading to those scenes that make them great.

It is the story of the oppression of the Jews, the birth of the Saviour, the progression of the Christus to the time of his crucifixion, the enslavement of the race from which Jesus himself sprang, and the tremendous love tale of the bond slave and a prince of Jerusalem that holds an audience spell bound.

As to individual performance: first the Mary of Betty Bronson. It is without doubt the most tremendous individual score that any actress has ever made, with but a single scene with a couple of close-ups. And in the color scenes she appears simply superb.

Then as to Ramon Novarro: anyone who sees him in this picture will have to admit that he is without doubt a man's man and 100 per cent of that. Francis X. Bushman

does a comeback in the role of the heavy (Messala) that makes him stand alone.

As to the women, following Bronson, May McAvoy in blonde tresses as Esther deserves a full measure of credit for her performance. While Claire McDowell, as the mother of Hur, and Kathleen Key, as his sister, both score tremendously. Carmel Myers, as the vamp Iras, looks a million dollars' worth of woman and it is hard to understand how Ben-Hur could finally resist her.

....

■ **BENJI**

1974, 85 MINS, US ◇ ⒱

Dir Joe Camp   *Prod* Joe Camp   *Scr* Joe Camp
Ph Don Reddy   *Ed* Leon Smith   *Mus* Euel Box
Art Dir Harland Wright
● Patsy Garrett, Allen Fiuzat, Cynthia Smith, Peter Breck, Edgar Buchanan (Mulberry Square)

Benji is a dog's picture from first to last. From the moment he pokes his head through a broken door in a deserted house where he has his pad until he's adopted by the family whose two children he saves from kidnappers, interest rests squarely on the head of this pooch, of uncertain parentage.

One of the wonders of the production, told simply and with no pretense of grandiose style, is the manner in which Benji – real name Higgins – performs. In this case, it isn't a dog performing, but a dog acting, just as humans act.

Much of the footage is shot from about 18 inches above the ground, upward from Benji's point of view, and innovation is fascinating.

....

■ **BENNY GOODMAN STORY, THE**

1955, 116 MINS, US ◇ ⒱

Dir Valentine Davies   *Prod* Aaron Rosenberg
Scr Valentine Davies   *Ph* William Daniels   *Ed* Russell Schoengarth   *Mus* Henry Mancini
● Steve Allen, Donna Reed, Berta Gersten, Herbert Anderson, Robert F. Simon (Universal)

The Benny Goodman Story is of the same stripe as Universal's previously socko bandleader saga, *The Glenn Miller Story*. Both have bespectacled bandleaders with titles, both are Aaron Rosenberg productions.

If the romantics of the script and Steve Allen and Donna Reed's interpretations lack a bit, they are sufficiently glossed over because the major canvas is the saga of the Chicago youth with the licorice stick and his dedication to the cause of a new exciting tempo, later interpreted as 'swing'.

The unfolding is uncompromising on several fronts. The closeups on the very poor Jewish family and Goodman's humble environments are not glossed over. In the same idiom there is no fanfare about the interracial mixing, socially or professionally.

....

■ **BEQUEST TO THE NATION**

1973, 115 MINS, UK ◇

Dir James Cellan Jones   *Prod* Hal B. Wallis
Scr Terence Rattigan   *Ph* Gerry Fisher   *Ed* Anne V. Coates   *Mus* Michel Legrand   *Art Dir* Carmen Dillon
● Glenda Jackson, Peter Finch, Michael Jayston, Anthony Quayle, Margaret Leighton, Dominic Guard (Universal)

This is a deliberate, though stylish and genteel, de-glamorizing of the affair between Lord Nelson and Lady Hamilton which scandalized England. Production is based on Terence Rattigan's adaptation of his own play, and never completely escapes its legit origins.

The plot introduces Peter Finch's Nelson just returned from a successful thwarting of Napoleon's maritime maneuvers, as executed by Andre Maranne as French Admiral Ville-

neuve. Begging several months' leave, Nelson repairs to his adored mistress (Glenda Jackson), who like him, is showing signs of less-than-graceful aging. Increasingly embittered by their status as social pariahs and pressed by his superiors to return to sea, Nelson engages in a series of harangues with his love, who finally urges his return to sea.

The story-as-is permits Jackson to display a variety of her dramatic abilities. Finch is slightly less effective as Nelson, though he manages to project the complex facets of character.

....

■ **BERKELEY SQUARE**

1933, 87 MINS, US

Dir Frank Lloyd   *Prod* Jesse L. Lasky   *Scr* Sonya Levien, John L. Balderston   *Ph* Ernest Palmer
Mus Louis De Francesco (dir.)   *Art Dir* William Darling
● Leslie Howard, Heather Angel, Valerie Taylor, Irene Browne, Alan Mowbray, Juliette Compton (Fox)

Berkeley Square is an imaginative, beautiful and well-handled production.

The atmosphere of Berkeley Square, London, is resurrected almost perfectly, as it is today, and presumably as it was in the 18th century. There's a devotion to detail and atmospherics that is almost painfully exacting.

Leslie Howard in the same role he played on the stage he produced the stage play [by John L. Balderston] himself) is as near perfection as can be hoped for in screen characterization. The rest of the cast is more than adequate.

Story of *Berkeley Square* is still another variation on Mark Twain's *A Connecticut Yankee in King Arthur's Court*. Where Twain used the idea of flashing a character into another century for fun. However, Balderston takes the thing very seriously. Balderston's character, Peter Standish (Howard) moves back into a spot used by one of his forefathers and falls in love with a gal of that period. It's a new kind of love story.

Heather Angel, as the girl, turns in a splendid performance.

....

■ **BERLIN EXPRESS**

1948, 86 MINS, US ⒱

Dir Jacques Tourneur   *Prod* Bert Granet   *Scr* Harold Medford   *Ph* Lucien Ballard   *Ed* Sherman Todd
Mus Frederick Hollander   *Art Dir* Albert S. D'Agostino, Alfred Herman
● Merle Oberon, Robert Ryan, Charles Korvin, Paul Lukas (RKO)

Most striking feature of this production is its extraordinary background of war-ravaged Germany. With a documentary eye, this film etches a powerfully grim picture of life amidst the shambles. It makes awesome and exciting cinema.

Chief defect of the screenplay [based on a story by Curt Siodmak] is its failure to break away from the formula of anti-Nazi films. The Nazis, now underground, are still the heavies but it's difficult to get excited about such a group of ragged hoodlums. Their motivation in the pic, moreover, is never explained satisfactorily as they set about kidnapping a prominent German democrat, played by Paul Lukas.

Starting out on the Paris-to-Berlin express to an Allied conference on the unification of Germany, Lukas gets waylaid in Frankfurt despite an over-elaborate scheme of guarding him. Symbolizing the Big Four powers, other passengers on the train include an American (Robert Ryan), a Frenchwoman (Merle Oberon), an Englishman (Robert Coote), and a Russian (Roman Toporow) plus a dubious character of unknown nationality (Charles Korvin).

Ryan establishes himself as a firstrate actor

in this film, demonstrating conclusively that his brilliant performance in *Crossfire* was no one-shot affair.

....

■ BEST FRIENDS

1982, 116 MINS, US ◇ Ⓥ

Dir Norman Jewison *Prod* Norman Jewison
Scr Valerie Curtin, Barry Levinson *Ph* Jordan Cronenweth *Ed* Don Zimmerman *Mus* Michel Legrand *Art Dir* Joe Russo
● Burt Reynolds, Goldie Hawn, Jessica Tandy, Barnard Hughes, Audra Lindley, Keenan Wynn (Warner)

Best Friends is probably not the light romantic comedy audiences expect from a Burt Reynolds-Goldie Hawn screen pairing but is nevertheless a very engaging film. Addressing the problems two writers in a professional and personal relationship encounter when they decide to get married, almost all of the picture's funny moments are underscored by the more serious issues they face from themselves, their families and society as a 'married couple'.

Both stars are tremendously aided by an intelligent screenplay from Valerie Curtin and Barry Levinson, who are said to have based at least part of this work on their own relationship. They leave Hawn and Reynolds more than enough room to inject their own nuances.

Director Norman Jewison does a capable job of moving things along and a nice balance between comedy and drama.

....

■ BEST LITTLE WHOREHOUSE IN TEXAS, THE

1982, 114 MINS, US ◇ Ⓥ

Dir Colin Higgins *Prod* Thomas L. Miller, Edward K. Milkis, Robert L. Boyett *Scr* Larry L. King, Peter Masterson, Colin Higgins *Ph* William A. Fraker *Ed* Pembroke J. Herring, David Bretherton, Jack Hofstra, Nicholas Eliopoulos *Mus* Patrick Williams *Art Dir* Robert F. Boyle
● Burt Reynolds, Dolly Parton, Dom DeLuise, Charles Durning, Jim Nabors, Robert Mandan (Universal-RKO)

The Best Little Whorehouse in Texas is just about everything it's meant to be – a couple of diverting hours in the dark. Rollicking, good-natured, a bit spicy and with just enough heart to avoid seeming totally synthetic, the $26 million adaptation of the 1978 Broadway hit [by Larry L. King and Peter Masterson] ideally teams powerhouse stars Burt Reynolds and Dolly Parton.

Nifty prolog sketches how the title establishment is a regular Texas institution. Modest abode is currently under the proprietorship of Miss Mona, a super lady played by Parton with all her accustomed humor, warmth and knockout charm. Local Sheriff Reynolds is her b.f. of long standing, a down-home boy technically corrupt because he protects the illegal goings-on.

But nothing is sacred to media crusader Dom DeLuise, an outrageously self-serving muckraker who 'exposes' the bawdyhouse on his glitzy, song-and-dance TV news show and will stop at nothing to shut the place down.

....

■ BEST MAN, THE

1964, 102 MINS, US Ⓥ

Dir Franklin J. Schaffner *Prod* Stuart Millar, Lawrence Turman *Scr* Gore Vidal *Ph* Haskell Wexler *Ed* Robert E. Swink *Mus* Mort Lindsey *Art Dir* Lyle R. Wheeler
● Henry Fonda, Cliff Robertson, Edie Adams, Margaret Leighton, Shelley Berman, Lee Tracy (United Artists)

Gore Vidal's provocative drama of political infighting on the national level has been skillfully converted to film. Although not an es-

pecially fresh or profound piece of work, it is certainly a worthwhile, lucid and engaging dramatization of a behind-the-scenes party power struggle that accompanies a contest for presidential nomination.

Vidal's straightforward, sharply-drawn scenario describes the bitter struggle for a party's presidential nomination between an ambitious self-righteous character assassin (many will see him as a Nixon-McCarthy composite) and a scrupulous intellectual (of Stevensonian essence) who, ultimately faced with a choice of resorting to his opponent's smear tactics or bowing out of the race gracefully, decides he'd rather be right than president – leading to a somewhat pat and convenient conclusive development.

Between these two antagonists, portrayed with conviction and sensitivity by Cliff Robertson and Henry Fonda respectively, stands the imposing figure of the mortally ill but still politically virile expresident, a character likely to be associated with Harry S. Truman. Lee Tracy repeats his Broadway characterization in the role and just about steals the show with his expressive, colorful portrayal.

....

■ BEST OF ENEMIES, THE

1961, 104 MINS, UK/ITALY ◇

Dir Guy Hamilton *Prod* Dino De Laurentiis *Scr* Jack Pulman, Incrocci Agenore, Furio Scaroelli, Suso Cecchi D'Amico *Ph* Giuseppe Rotunno *Ed* Bert Bates *Mus* Nino Rota
● David Niven, Alberto Sordi, Michael Wilding, Amedeo Nazzari, Harry Andrews, David Opatoshu (Columbia)

The Best of Enemies produced by Italy's Dino De Laurentiis for Columbia, is a splendidly warm, wryly witty and amusing hybrid. Written by one Englishman and two Italians, it is directed by an Englishman (Guy Hamilton), has an Anglo-Italian star cast, with a few exceptions (one being American David Opatoshu), and an Anglo-Italian crew. It was shot mainly in Israel, with some location and studio work in Italy. Israelites were used as extras. Some Abyssinians were imported to play Abyssinians, and two trained gazelles were recruited in Frankfurt, Germany.

It's a wartime comedy, with a gently serious undertone for those who seek it. Locale is the Ethiopian desert in 1941. David Niven, a British major, and his pilot RAF officer Michael Wilding, crash on a reconnaissance trip. They are captured by an Italian patrol, led by an Italian officer (Alberto Sordi). He releases them on condition that they let his patrol move freely to a nearby fort. Back in base, Niven is ordered to attack the fort and does so reluctantly. From then on it's an hilarious, cat-and-mouse game, with captor and captive alternating as the fortunes of war sway. The serious undertone? That war is crazy.

The screenplay is peppered with brisk jokes and unexpected offbeat situations which keep the proceedings light and easy. Hamilton has directed with a sure touch which brings out the characteristics of the two opposed nations admirably. Niven, debonair, nonchalant and skilfully underplaying, is matched excellently by Sordi, playing his first English-speaking role.

....

■ BEST THINGS IN LIFE ARE FREE, THE

1956, 104 MINS, US ◇

Dir Michael Curtiz *Prod* Henry Ephron *Scr* William Bowers, Phoebe Ephron *Ph* Leon Shamroy *Ed* Dorothy Spencer *Mus* Lionel Newman
● Gordon MacRae, Dan Dailey, Sheree North, Ernest Borgnine, Tommy Noonan, Murvyn Vye (20th Century-Fox)

In *The Best Things in Life Are Free*, producer

Henry Ephron and director Michael Curtiz went on the reasonably sound theory that, in telling the story of Tin Pan Alley's fabulous team of Buddy DeSylva, Lew Brown and Ray Henderson, all that was necessary was to fill the widescreen with a huge potpourri of their works.

Considering that John O'Hara wrote the story, this CinemaScope tinter leaves a few things to wish for in that department. It catches little of the Jazz Age feeling, except in its costumes and the frantic shimmy and Black Bottom numbers, and the songwriting trio barely come to life as real people.

It's a sparkling string of hits that's presented with all the nostalgic attention they deserve. Performances are top calibre, from Gordon MacRae's and Dan Dailey's pleasant crooning, to Ernest Borgnine's clowning and Sheree North's agile terp routines.

There are no fewer than 20 numbers in this opus. Outstanding are the big production numbers – 'Birth of the Blues' and 'Black Bottom' – choreographed by Rod Alexander. North, who has trouble with her diction in the speaking parts, is standout in the dance numbers.

....

■ BEST YEARS OF OUR LIVES, THE

1946, 163 MINS, US Ⓥ

Dir William Wyler *Prod* Samuel Goldwyn *Scr* Robert E. Sherwood *Ph* Gregg Toland *Ed* Daniel Mandell *Mus* Hugo Friedhofer *Art Dir* Perry Ferguson, George Jenkins
● Fredric March, Myrna Loy, Dana Andrews, Teresa Wright, Harold Russell, Cathy O'Donnell (RKO/Goldwyn)

The postwar saga [based on a book by MacKinlay Kantor] of the soda jerk who became an army officer; the banker who was mustered out as the sergeant; and a seaman who came back to glory minus both his hands.

Inspired casting has newcomer Harold Russell, a real-life amputee, pacing the seasoned trouper, Fredric March, for personal histrionic triumphs. But all the other performances are equally good. Myrna Loy is the smalltown bank veepee's beauteous wife. Teresa Wright plays their daughter, who goes for the already-married Dana Andrews with full knowledge of his wife (Virginia Mayo, who does a capital job as the cheating looker). Both femmes in this triangle, along with Andrews, do their stuff convincingly.

Cathy O'Donnell does her sincerely-in-love chore with the same simplicity as Harold Russell, the $200-a-month war-pensioned hero, who, since he has lost his hands in combat, spurns O'Donnell because he never wants to be a burden. That scene, as he skilfully manages the wedding ring, is but one of several memorable high spots.

The pace of the picture is a bit leisurely. Almost a full hour is required to set the mood and the motivation, but never does it pall. Not a line or scene is spurious. The people live; they are not mere shadow etchings on a silver sheet.

☐ 1946: Best Picture

....

■ BETHUNE
THE MAKING OF A HERO

1990, 115 MINS, CANADA/CHINA/FRANCE ◇

Dir Phillip Borsos *Prod* Pieter Kroonenburg, Nicolas Clermont *Scr* Ted Allan *Ph* Mike Molloy, Raoul Coutard *Ed* Yves Langlois, Angelo Corrao *Mus* Alan Reeves
● Donald Sutherland, Helen Mirren, Helen Shaver, Harrison Liu, Anouk Aimee, Ronald Pickup (Filmline/August 1st/Parmentier/Belstar)

This C$18 million political saga is a thorough documenting of the life of Canadian doctor Norman Bethune, a hero in China for his medical input during the long march in Mao Tse-tung's revolution.

The film belongs to Donald Sutherland, who delivers a stunning performance as the complex and controversial surgeon. Harrison Liu delivers a fine performance as Bethune's protégé, Dr Fong, but Helen Shaver (as a missionary in China) and Helen Mirren (as Bethune's wife) pale beside Sutherland.

Bethune was at once a boozing womanizer, a loving husband, a revolutionary surgeon and an ardently committed anti-fascist. He made a slew of enemies among colleagues and government officials before he declared himself a 'red' and headed first to Spain and then to China (the latter of which provides magnificent scenery in the film).

After several years of financial problems from both coprod partners (China and Canada), it's a relief that the film is better than expected and a disappointment that it is not as good as hoped.

. . . .

■ **BETRAYAL**

1983, 95 MINS, UK ◇ ⊛

Dir David Jones   *Prod* Sam Spiegel   *Scr* Harold Pinter   *Ph* Mike Fash   *Ed* John Bloom   *Mus* Dominic Muldowney   *Art Dir* Eileen Diss

● Jeremy Irons, Ben Kingsley, Patricia Hodge (Horizon)

As it was onstage in 1978, *Betrayal* is an absorbing, quietly amusing chamber drama for those attuned to Harold Pinter's way with words.

In laying out his study of a rather conventional menage-a-trois among two male best friends and the wife of one of them, Pinter's gambit was to present it in reverse chronological order. Tale thus starts in the present and gradually steps backwards over the course of nine years.

Kingsley comes across best, as the film only springs fully to life when he's onscreen. Irons also seems very much at home with the required style. As the fulcrum of the tale, Patricia Hodge knows her way around dialog but pales somewhat in the presence of the two men and lacks allure.

. . . .

■ **BETRAYED**

1988, 127 MINS, US ◇ ⊛

Dir Constantin Costa-Gavras   *Prod* Irwin Winkler   *Scr* Joe Eszterhas   *Ph* Patrick Blossier   *Ed* Joele Van Effenterre   *Mus* Bill Conti   *Art Dir* Patrizia Von Brandenstein

● Debra Winger, Tom Berenger, John Heard, Betsy Blair, John Mahoney (United Artists)

Betrayed is a political thriller that is more political than thrilling but never less than absorbing due to the combustible subject matter, that of the white supremacist movement.

Clearly inspired by the murder of Denver radio talk show host Alan Berg, opening scene has abrasive Chicago broadcaster Richard Libertini followed home and gunned down by assailants who identify themselves only by spraying the letters 'ZOG' on the victim's car.

Cut to the endless wheat fields of the rural Midwest, where Debra Winger has come up from Texas as a 'combine girl'. Local farmer Tom Berenger quickly takes a shine to the new gal in town, while she responds to the warmth of his family life. Winger soon hops back to Chicago to brief her superiors at the FBI on her progress in infiltrating the group suspected of perpetrating Libertini's murder.

Like Ingrid Bergman in *Notorious*, Winger is pushed even further in her masquerade by her chief government contact (John Heard) who from all appearances is in love with her himself.

Berenger proves forceful and properly

unpredictable in his vulnerable macho role, and entire cast is nicely low-keyed.

. . . .

■ **BETSY, THE**

1978, 125 MINS, US ◇ ⊛

Dir Daniel Petrie   *Prod* Robert R. Weston   *Scr* William Bast, Walter Bernstein   *Ph* Mario Tosi   *Ed* Rita Roland   *Mus* John Barry   *Art Dir* Herman A. Blumenthal

● Laurence Olivier, Robert Duvall, Katharine Ross, Tommy Lee Jones, Jane Alexander, Lesley-Ann Down (Allied Artists/Robbins)

It's a backhanded criticism, but there's something too classy about this version of the Harold Robbins novel. It's too tame. And too solemn.

To be blunt, where's the raunch? This should be *Peyton Place* with plenty of flesh. Don't entice audiences with the name of an author associated with a long list of best-selling seamy novels and then deliver a 125-minute film you wouldn't be embarrassed to bring your mother to.

The script has four main interests: cars, sex, money and power. It's an American movie. Laurence Olivier is retired auto tycoon Loren Hardeman Sr, founder of Bethlehem Motor Co, now interested in manufacturing a revolutionary car – one too efficient, too practical and too benevolent for American industry. It is to be called the Betsy, after his great-granddaughter.

Through a series of flashbacks, Olivier ages from 40 to 90. Complete with midwest accent, he's on target, maybe too much so. Ditto for Robert Duvall as his grandson and current president of the auto company, Jane Alexander as Duvall's wife and Katharine Ross as Olivier's daughter-in-law and lover.

Tommy Lee Jones as a dare-devil race driver hired by Olivier to build the dream car plays his role with a mixture of edginess and off-handedness – a combination of Burt Reynolds and Harvey Keitel. His style – it's got a sense of humor and a campy quality to it – seems more to the point. It's almost trashy. (Now that's Harold Robbins.)

Lesley-Ann Down, as a jetsetting designer who becomes involved with both Jones and Duvall, adopts the same tone, as does Edward Herrmann, Duvall's right-hand man.

. . . .

■ **BETSY'S WEDDING**

1990, 98 MINS, US ◇ ⊛

Dir Alan Alda   *Prod* Martin Bregman, Louis A. Stroller   *Scr* Alan Alda   *Ph* Kelvin Pike   *Ed* Michael Polakow   *Mus* Bruce Broughton   *Art Dir* John Jay Moore

● Alan Alda, Madeline Kahn, Molly Ringwald, Ally Sheedy, Anthony LaPaglia, Joe Pesci (Touchstone/Silver Screen Partners IV)

From a bolt of ordinary cloth Alan Alda fashions a thoroughly engaging matrimonial romp in *Betsy's Wedding*. Most of the action comes from the clash of personalities and wills as unconventional daughter Betsy (Molly Ringwald) announces her plans to wed boyfriend Jake (Dylan Walsh), and everyone jumps into the act.

Overreaching dad (Alda) wants a big, wonderful Italian Jewish wedding, and plans accelerate into a one-upmanship contest when Jake's wealthy WASP parents try to take the reins. To finance the bash, Alda, a contractor, unwittingly throws in with some funny-money Italian business partners, as arranged by his double-dealing brother-in-law (Joe Pesci).

Setting a buoyant, anything-could-happen tone from the outset, Alda as director creates what he's striving for: a feeling of being caught up in the warm craziness of this family, as all its vivid characters push and

tug to impose their will on the proceedings. His punchy, inpertinent script is equally good.

. . . .

■ **BETWEEN THE LINES**

1977, 101 MINS, US ◇ ⊛

Dir Joan Micklin Silver   *Prod* Raphael D. Silver   *Scr* Fred Barron   *Ph* Kenneth Van Sickle   *Ed* John Carter   *Mus* Southside Johnny and the Asbury Jukes   *Art Dir* Stuart Wurtzel

● John Heard, Lindsay Crouse, Jeff Goldblum, Jill Eikenberry, Bruno Kirby, Gwen Welles (Midwest/Silver)

A fresh and uncluttered look at what goes on behind the scenes at a grubby, underpaid but undaunted little newspaper.

Where it is strong is partially due to the excellently-written script, partially due to the overall firstrate acting by the entire cast.

It's a series of inter-relationships, professionally and romantically, between staff photographer Lindsay Crouse and top investigative reporter John Heard; reporter-cum-bookwriter Stephen Collins and staffer Gwen Welles; plus the story of underpaid and overworked rock music critic Jeff Goldblum, copyboy and would-be reporter Bruno Kirby and the other oddballs who work for the newspaper, due to be taken over any day by a communications conglomerate.

. . . .

■ **BETWEEN TWO WORLDS**

1944, 112 MINS, US

Dir Edward A. Blatt   *Prod* Mark Hellinger   *Scr* Daniel Fuchs   *Ph* Carl Guthrie   *Ed* Rudi Fehr   *Mus* Erich Wolfgang Korngold   *Art Dir* Hugh Reticker

● John Garfield, Paul Henreid, Sydney Greenstreet, Eleanor Parker, Edmund Gwenn (Warner)

An artistic transcription of [Sutton Vane's] *Outward Bound*, the Broadway stage hit of 1925, this film was earlier brought to the screen by Warner Bros in 1930.

A 1944 opening has been provided here, the locale being an unidentified port in England from which a small assorted group of persons is preparing to sail for America. Unable to leave because his papers aren't in order is Paul Henreid, former pianist, who recently had fought with the Free French. As result he and his wife, played with much feeling by Eleanor Parker, take to the gaspipe, both wanting to die together. Meantime, in an air raid the bus carrying others to the evacuation ship are killed.

From here the action shifts to a mystery ship which, it finally becomes evident, is bound for the Great Beyond, with Henreid, Parker and the group which had been killed in the bomb raid. Brilliant dialog and excellent performances, as well as thoughtful, imaginative direction by Edward A. Blatt, neatly sustain the interest aboard ship on the long voyage. There is no place in the story for comedy relief.

On reaching High Olympus and judgement day, Sydney Greenstreet enters the scene as the examiner, taking his new arrivals one by one. His performance is outstanding, and the sequence, though quite lengthy, represents a productional, directional and acting triumph.

. . . .

■ **BEVERLY HILLS COP**

1984, 105 MINS, US ◇ ⊛

Dir Martin Brest   *Prod* Don Simpson, Jerry Bruckheimer   *Scr* Daniel Petrie Jr.   *Ph* Bruce Surtees   *Ed* Billy Weber, Arthur Coburn   *Mus* Harold Faltermeyer   *Art Dir* Angelo Graham

● Eddie Murphy, Judge Reinhold, Lisa Eilbacher, John Ashton, Ronny Cox, Steven Berkoff (Paramount)

Beverly Hills Cop is more cop show than comedy riot. Expectations that Eddie Murphy's street brand of rebelliousness would devastate staid and glittery Beverly Hills are not entirely met in a film that grows increasingly dramatic as Murphy's recalcitrant cop from Detroit runs down the killers of his best friend.

Film was originally tagged for Sylvester Stallone and the finished product still carries the melodramatic residue of a hard, violent property, pre-Murphy.

Strong assists come from a deceptively likable performance from Judge Reinhold as a naive Beverly Hills detective, from by-the-book chief Ronny Cox, and from the serpentine villainy of Steven Berkoff, who plays an art dealer involved in nefarious endeavors.

Best moments arrive early when Murphy, bouncy, determined and vengeful, arrives in Beverly Hills in what old Detroit friend turned Beverly Hills art dealer Lisa Eilbacher correctly calls his 'crappy blue Chevy Nova'.

● ●

■ BEVERLY HILLS COP II

1987, 102 MINS, US ◇ ⓥ
Dir Tony Scott *Prod* Don Simpson, Jerry Bruckheimer
Scr Larry Ferguson, Warren Skaaren *Ph* Jeffrey L. Kimball *Ed* Billy Weber, Chris Lebenson, Michael Tronick *Mus* Harold Faltermeyer *Art Dir* Ken Davis
● Eddie Murphy, Judge Reinhold, Jurgen Prochnow, Ronny Cox, John Ashton, Brigitte Nielsen (Paramount/Murphy)

Beverly Hills Cop II is a noisy, numbing, unimaginative, heartless remake of the original film.

Getting Eddie Murphy back to Beverly Hills from his native Detroit turf is the critical wounding of police captain Ronny Cox by a group of rich baddies committing the 'Alphabet Crimes', a series of violent robberies at heavily guarded locations. Once again he goads reluctant cops Judge Reinhold and John Ashton into straying from the straight and narrow, once again the group visits a strip joint that looks like a *Flashdance* spinoff, and finally shoot it out with the villains.

Criminal element is represented by enforcer Dean Stockwell, towering hitwoman Brigitte Nielsen, who looks like Max Headroom's sister, and kingpin Jurgen Prochnow.

Murphy keeps things entertainingly afloat with his sassiness, raunchy one-liners, take-charge brazenness and innate irreverence. Murphy's a hoot in numerous scenes, but less so than on other occasions because of the frosty context for his shenanigans.

● ●

■ BEYOND THE FOREST

1949, 95 MINS, US ⓥ
Dir King Vidor *Prod* Henry Blanke *Scr* Lenore Coffee *Ph* Robert Burks *Ed* Rudi Fehr *Mus* Max Steiner
● Bette Davis, Joseph Cotten, David Brian, Ruth Roman, Regis Toomey (Warner)

Beyond the Forest gives Bette Davis a chance to portray the neurotic femme she does so well. The character of Rosa Moline, a woman who yearns for broader vistas than those supplied by the Wisconsin mill town to which she is tied, furnishes plenty of bite for the Davis technique and she belts it across.

Character is a modern-day Madame Bovary, a woman who sets her traps for a rich man. Davis gets over the character of the black-hearted Rosa, expressing the part with a vitality and earnestness that gives it a stylized vividness.

Joseph Cotten is the small-town minded doctor married to Rosa. His chore as the doctor is quiet and effective and David Brian is colorful as the man on whom Rosa has set her sights. He and Davis make their scenes particularly red-blooded playing of illicit love.

King Vidor seldom falters in his direction.

● ●

■ BEYOND THE POSEIDON ADVENTURE

1979, 122 MINS, US ◇ ⓥ
Dir Irwin Allen *Prod* Irwin Allen *Scr* Nelson Gidding *Ph* Joseph Biroc *Ed* Bill Brame *Mus* Jerry Fielding *Art Dir* Preston Ames
● Michael Caine, Sally Field, Telly Savalas, Peter Boyle, Jack Warden, Karl Malden (Warner)

Beyond the Poseidon Adventure comes off as a virtual remake of the 1972 original, without that film's mounting suspense and excitement. Recap of original premise, a luxury liner turned upside down by gigantic tidal wave, is accomplished in a few seconds.

New plot turn pits salvage tug operators Michael Caine, Karl Malden and Sally Field against evildoer Telly Savalas for looting rights to the big boat. Caine and company are after hard cash, while Savalas, posing as a medico, is searching out a cargo of valuable plutonium.

The only change in this group's struggle to reach the top (really, the bottom) of the boat is a set of different faces.

Because the outcome is so predictable, the defects in the script take on greater magnitude.

● ●

■ BEYOND THE VALLEY OF THE DOLLS

1970, 109 MINS, US ◇ ⓥ
Dir Russ Meyer *Prod* Russ Meyer *Scr* Roger Ebert *Ph* Fred J. Koenekamp *Ed* Dann Cahn, Dick Wormel *Mus* Stu Phillips *Art Dir* Jack Martin Smith
● Dolly Read, Cynthia Myers, Marcia McBroom, John La Zar, Michael Blodgett, David Gurian (20th Century-Fox)

This trashy, gaudy, sound-stage vulgarity about low life among the high life is as funny as a burning orphanage.

Dolly Read, Cynthia Myers and Marcia McBroom head a busty cast as three pop singers who come to swinging Hollywood with manager David Gurian. Read has determined to pry some inheritance money from aunt Phyllis Davis, who runs with a super-groovy set, shepherded by John LaZar, a Shakespeare-spouting effete.

Michael Blodgett plays a film hero louse, Edy Williams a sex goddess, Erica Gavin the obligatory lesbian, and Duncan McLeod an unscrupulous lawyer. The sole good running gag involves Williams and Gurian; she's ready for sex any place except in bed.

● ●

■ BHOWANI JUNCTION

1956, 110 MINS, US ◇
Dir George Cukor *Prod* Pandro S. Berman *Scr* Sonya Levien, Ivan Moffat *Ph* Freddie Young *Ed* Frank Clarke, George Boemler *Mus* Miklos Rozsa *Art Dir* Gene Allen, John Howell
● Ava Gardner, Stewart Granger, Bill Travers, Abraham Sofaer, Francis Matthews (M-G-M)

To make *Bhowani Junction*, based on the John Masters novel, Metro went to Pakistan to shoot a film about India. The journey paid rich dividends, for the sense of realism in the film is one of the best things about it.

Bhowani Junction, starring Ava Gardner as an Anglo-Indian, and Stewart Granger as a British colonel who falls in love with her, is a horse of many colors. Picture goes off in quite a few directions, ranging from romance and action to a half-hearted attempt to explain the Indians and a more serious effort to dramatize the social twilight into which the British withdrawal from India tossed a small group of people who were of mixed Indian and British blood.

Story has Gardner as the half-caste returning home to an India seething with discontent and boiling with riots prior to the departure of the British. At Bhowani Junction, a railroad center, she meets Granger who's been sent to command a security detail

to guard the rail line against Communist saboteurs.

Gardner thinks she loves Bill Travers, the local rail superintendent, also an Anglo-Indian. She's soon torn between being European and Indian, kills a British lieutenant who's trying to rape her and is temporarily saved by the Communist boss (Peter Illing).

Director George Cukor, in staging his crowd scenes, achieves some magnificent effects and Freddie Young's lensing is first-strate. The milling, sweating, shouting crowds, egged on by Red agents, are almost frighteningly real and the screen comes alive with an abundance of movement.

● ●

■ BIBLE, THE
IN THE BEGINNING ...

1966, 174 MINS, US ◇ ⓥ
Dir John Huston *Prod* Dino De Laurentiis *Scr* Christopher Fry *Ph* Giuseppe Rotunno *Ed* Ralph Kemplen *Mus* Toshiro Mayuzumi *Art Dir* Mario Chiari
● Michael Parks, Ulla Bergryd, Richard Harris, John Huston, Stephen Boyd, George C. Scott (De Laurentiis/20th Century-Fox/Seven Arts)

The world's oldest story – the origins of Mankind, as told in the Book of Genesis – is put upon the screen by director John Huston and producer Dino De Laurentiis with consummate skill, taste and reverence.

Christopher Fry, who wrote the screenplay with the assistance of Biblical scholars and religious consultants, has fashioned a straightforward, sensitive and dramatic telling, through dialog and narration, of the first 22 chapters of Genesis.

A lavish, but always tasteful production – assaults and rewards the eye and ear with awe-inspiring realism.

Huston's rich voice functions in narration, and he also plays Noah with heart-warming humility, compassion and humor.

The seduction of Eve by the serpent, the latter well represented by a man reclining in a tree, cues a sudden shift of mood and pace. Richard Harris plays the jealous and remorseful Cain with a sure feeling, while Franco Nero's Abel conveys in very brief footage the image of a sensitive, obedient young man whose murder provoked a supreme outrage.

The 45-minute sequence devoted to Noah and the Flood is, in itself, a triumph in filmmaking. It plays dramatically and fluidly, and belies monumental logistics of production. Huston's Noah is, again, perfect casting.

Stephen Boyd then emerges as Nimrod, the proud king, whose egocentric monument became the Tower of Babel where the languages of his people suddenly were changed. The remainder of the film is devoted to Abraham, played with depth by George C. Scott. Ava Gardner is very good as the barren Sarah who, to give her husband a male heir, urges him to conceive with her servant, Zoe Sallis.

● ●

■ BIG

1988, 102 MINS, US ◇ ⓥ
Dir Penny Marshall *Prod* James L. Brooks, Robert Greenhut *Scr* Gary Ross, Anne Spielberg *Ph* Barry Sonnenfeld *Ed* Barry Malkin *Mus* Howard Shore *Art Dir* Santo Loquasto
● Tom Hanks, Elizabeth Perkins, John Heard, Jared Rushton, Robert Loggia, David Moscow (20th Century-Fox)

A 13-year-old junior high kid Josh (David Moscow) is transformed into a 35-year-old's body (Tom Hanks) by a carnival wishing machine in this pic which unspools with enjoyable genuineness and ingenuity.

Immediate dilemma, since going back to school is not an option and his mom thinks he's an intruder and doesn't buy into the

B

explanation that he's changed into a man, is to escape to anonymous New York City and hide out in a seedy hotel.

Pretty soon, the viewer forgets that what's happening on screen has no basis in reality. The characters are having too much fun enjoying life away from responsibility, which begs the question why adults get so serious when there is fun to be had in almost any situation.

Hanks plays chopsticks on a walking piano at F.A.O. Schwarz with a man who turns out to be his boss (Robert Loggia) and as a result of this freespirited behavior is promoted way beyond his expectations, but it's what he does with all his newfound self-worth that propels this 'dramedy'.

Greatest growth comes from his involvement with coworker Elizabeth Perkins, though by no means is he the only one getting an education.

● ●

■ BIG BAD MAMA

1974, 83 MINS, US ◇ Ⓥ

Dir Steve Carver *Prod* Roger Corman *Scr* William Norton, Frances Doel *Ph* Bruce Logan *Ed* Tina Hirsch *Mus* David Grisman *Art Dir* Peter Jamison
● Angie Dickinson, William Shatner, Tom Skerritt, Susan Sennett, Robbie Lee, Noble Willingham (New World)

The plotline is flimsy at best, opening circa 1932 with Angie Dickinson posturing as a hard-bitten mother, rum runner, bank robber, jewel thief, kidnapper and queen bee in the sack. Both producer Roger Corman and director Steve Carver make a feeble attempt at social import by having Mama and true-blue lover Tom Skerritt martyr themselves so that the children may live and spend their ill-got gains.

Carver's direction mostly consists of winks at the film buffs in the crowd, as he apes the wedding scene from *The Graduate* and swipes bank robbery and shootout scenes, as well as the bluegrass tempo from *Bonnie and Clyde*.

Big Bad Mama is mostly rehashed *Bonnie and Clyde*, with a bit more blood and Angie Dickinson taking off her clothes for sex scenes with the crooks in her life.

● ●

■ BIG BRAWL, THE

1980, 95 MINS, US/HONG KONG ◇ Ⓥ

Dir Robert Clouse *Prod* Fred Weintraub, Terry Morse Jr *Scr* Robert Clouse *Ph* Robert Jessup *Ed* George Grenville *Mus* Lalo Schifrin *Art Dir* Joe Altadonna
● Jackie Chan, Jose Ferrer, Kristine De Bell, Mako, Rosalind Chao, Mary Ellen O'Neill (Warner/Golden Harvest)

Hong Kong martial arts star Jackie Chan makes an amiable American film debut in *The Big Brawl*, an amusing chopsocky actioner whose appeal is not limited to the usual audience for this genre. Key ingredient here is humor.

Story is set in Chicago, 1938, and filmed with engagingly artificial style that resembles vintage gangster pix. Epicene gangster lord Jose Ferrer runs his terrain with the aid of his foul-mouthed, cigar-chomping mother (Mary Ellen O'Neill).

Attempts to strong-arm a Chinese restaurateur run afoul when his son (Chan) gets into the act with chopsocky skills. Chan eventually is recruited by Ferrer to be his entrant into a Texas free for all (the 'big brawl' of the title).

Chan's physical prowess grows, leaving the flashiest stuff for the finale.

● ●

■ BIG BROADCAST, THE

1932, 80 MINS, US

Dir Frank Tuttle *Scr* George Marion Jr *Ph* George Folsey
● Stuart Erwin, Bing Crosby, George Burns, Gracie Allen, Leila Hyams (Paramount

It's an all-star show with a flock of the biggest air favorites. Bing Crosby, Burns and Allen, Kate Smith, Boswell Sisters, Arthur Tracy (The Street Singer), Donald Novis, and the Vincent Lopez and Cab Calloway orchestras are as varied a galaxy of radio favorites as they are ether-renowned.

Crosby and Burns and Allen alone went to the Coast to participate in the actual production, having lines and parts, with the rest shot in the east and cut in for their specialties. While disjointed in action, the cutting in of the variety interludes is skillfully accomplished.

The film is a credit to Crosby as a screen juve possibility, although he has a decidedly dizzy and uncertain role which makes him misbehave as no human being does. George Burns with his serious-miened straighting for the dumbdora-ish Gracie Allen are a sock interlude in themselves as the station manager and dumb stenog, although it evolves into more or less a specialty routine.

The chief fault with *Broadcast* is that it's not a feature film but a succession of talking shorts. The story is rather childish.

● ●

■ BIG BROADCAST OF 1936, THE

1935, 97 MINS, US

Dir Norman Taurog *Prod* Benjamin Glazer *Scr* Walter DeLeon, Francis Martin, Ralph Spence *Ph* Leo Tover
● Jack Oakie, George Burns, Gracie Allen, Lyda Roberti, Bing Crosby, Ethel Merman (Paramount)

Big Broadcast of 1936 is a film broadcaster of plenty of names and considerable entertainment. It hasn't much story, but the lack won't bother much.

Names are in and out as fast and as often as a firefly's tail light. There just isn't time for a 'plot', and probably best that none was attempted. Jack Oakie, Burns and Allen, Lyda Roberti, Wendy Barrie, Henry Wadsworth, C. Henry Gordon and a few others carry on whatever yarn there is and they play it lightly, as required.

You have to look quickly to see such names as Bing Crosby, Ethel Merman, Ray Noble's band, Amos 'n' Andy, Boland and Ruggles and Bill Robinson. These and other specialty turns are worked into the continuity via a crazy television gag.

Oakie is the slightly bankrupt operator of a small time station and doubles as the outlet's 'great lover'. Oakie does the spieling and his partner (Henry Wadsworth) the crooning. Burns and Allen come in with an ingenious and also nutty television contraption, invented by Gracie's uncle, which can pick up any event and also send. The plot flows in between frequent 'television' specialties, with the telebox the vital prop of the picture.

● ●

■ BIG BROADCAST OF 1937, THE

1936, 100 MINS, US

Dir Mitchell Leisen *Prod* Lewis E. Gensler *Scr* Edwin Gelsey, Arthur Kober, Barry Trivers, Walter DeLeon, Francis Martin *Ph* Theodor Sparkuhl *Ed* Stuart Heisler *Art Dir* Hans Dreier, Robert Usher
● Jack Benny, George Burns, Gracie Allen, Martha Raye, Shirley Ross, Ray Milland (Paramount)

The third in the *Big Broadcast* series from Paramount, this one, with its large cast of radio, stage and screen talent, far outdistances the two that preceded it.

There are enough comedians of one form or another in *Broadcast* to make it a hit solely on the strength of the laughs: Jack Benny, Martha Raye, Bob Burns and Burns & Allen are the prominents poking at audience ribs.

Burns' best scenes are those in which he busts in on radio programs which are on the air, while looking for conductor Leopold Sto-

kowski. Raye is slow to get started but finishes strong. Toward the end she socks through with the 'Vote for Mr Rhythm' number.

Benny plays the manager of the radio studios. He is mostly having his troubles with everyone from Gracie Allen down. The latter clicks from the outset, getting in for the earlier laughs built around the rehearsal of a skit under cute circumstances.

Several well known New York niteries get their names into the footage through the director's manner of suggesting how Ray Milland and Shirley Ross make the town one night.

● ●

■ BIG BROADCAST OF 1938, THE

1938, 88 MINS, US

Dir Mitchell Leisen *Prod* Harlan Thompson *Scr* Walter DeLeon, Francis Martin, Ken Englund, Howard Lindsay, Russell Crouse *Ph* Harry Fischbeck *Ed* Eda Warren, Chandler House *Mus* Boris Morros *Art Dir* Hans Dreier, Ernst Fegte
● W.C. Fields, Martha Raye, Dorothy Lamour, Shirley Ross, Lynne Overman, Bob Hope (Paramount)

With the rejuvenated W.C. Fields at his inimitable best in a streamlined production which combines spectacle, melody and dance, *Big Broadcast of 1938* is pictorially original and alluring.

The outstanding moment of the film, however, is a contribution by Kirsten Flagstad, of the Metropolitan opera company, singing an aria from *Die Walkure*.

Surrounding Fields and the diva is a company of players who keep alive interest in a better than usual libretto and, at the same time, turn in a full quota of laughs and musical numbers. Martha Raye, Dorothy Lamour, Shirley Ross, Lynne Overman, Bob Hope, Ben Blue, Leif Erikson, Rufe Davis and Grace Bradley are clicks. Specialties also come from Tito Guizar and Patricia Wilder. Shep Fields and his orchestra appear in a cartoon novelty.

There are half a dozen good musical numbers by Ralph Rainger and Leo Robin. The smash production number is 'The Waltz Lives On', which is a fanciful bit of terp and song that carries the waltz strain through the past 100 years. Staged by LeRoy Prinz and featuring Shirley Ross and Bob Hope it is the high spot of Mitchell Leisen's direction.

Screenplay starting with Frederick Hazlitt Brennan's original story, has something to do with a transatlantic steamship race between two greyhounds of the deep, one of which is owned by Fields. Specialties are introduced as the entertainment supplied to the passengers.

● ●

■ BIG BUS, THE

1976, 88 MINS, US ◇ Ⓥ

Dir James Frawley *Prod* Fred Freeman, Lawrence J. Cohen *Scr* Fred Freeman, Lawrence J. Cohen *Ph* Harry Stradling Jr *Ed* Edward Warschilka *Mus* David Shire *Art Dir* Joel Schiller
● Joseph Bologna, Stockard Channing, John Beck, Rene Auberjonois, Ned Beatty, Bob Dishy (Paramount)

Heading the cast of this overkill spoof is Joseph Bologna, good as a down-and-out bus driver whose chance to make a comeback is the nuclear-powered behemoth designed by Stockard Channing and father Harold Gould.

The first half hour or so is devoted to preparations for boarding. Herein is presented also John Beck, assistant driver with only one hangup (he blacks out on the road); computerized control center; Larry Hagman, malpractice-wary doctor treating Gould for injuries from industrial sabotage efforts led by iron-lung-bound Jose Ferrer.

Next comes the parade of passengers, each

with their own formula destiny.

Finally come the complications, too numerous to mention. Suffice it to say that no cliche is left unattached.

．．．．．．．．．．．．．．．．．．．．．．．．．．．．

■ **BIG BUSINESS**

1988, 97 MINS, US ◇ Ⓥ
Dir Jim Abrahams *Prod* Steve Tisch, Michael Peyser
Scr Dori Pierson, Marc Rubel *Ph* Dean Cundey
Ed Harry Keramidas *Mus* Lee Holdridge
Art Dir William Sandell
● Bette Midler, Lily Tomlin, Fred Ward, Edward Herrmann, Michele Placido (Touchstone/Silver Screen Partners III)

Big Business is a shrill, unattractive comedy which stars Bette Midler and Lily Tomlin, who play two sets of twins mixed up at birth. They have distinctly different comic styles, with the former's loud brashness generally dominating the latter's sly skittishness.

A mishap at a rural hospital pairs off the daughters of a hick couple with the sprigs of a major industrialist and his society wife. Jump to New York today, where dynamic Mora-max Corp board chairman Sadie Shelton (Midler) is forced to tolerate her scatterbrained, sentimental sister Rose (Tomlin) while trying to push through the sale of a subsidiary firm in their birthplace of Jupiter Hollow.

To try to thwart the sale at a stockholders' meeting, another Sadie and Rose, of the Ratcliff clan, leave Jupiter Hollow for the big city. As soon as they arrive at the airport, the complications begin.

Of the four performances by the two leads, the one easiest to enjoy is Midler's as venal corporate boss. Dressed to the nines and sporting a mincing but utterly determined walk, Midler tosses off her waspish one-liners with malevolent glee, stomping on everyone in her path.

There are moments of delight as well in her other characterization as a country bumpkin who has always yearned for the material pleasures of Babylon.

Tomlin has her moments, too, but her two sweetly flakey, nay-saying characters for a while seem so similar.

．．．．．．．．．．．．．．．．．．．．．．．．．．．．

■ **BIG CHILL, THE**

1983, 103 MINS, US ◇ Ⓥ
Dir Lawrence Kasdan *Prod* Michael Shamberg
Scr Lawrence Kasdan, Barbara Benedek *Ph* John Bailey *Ed* Carol Littleton *Mus* John Williams
Art Dir Ida Random
● Tom Berenger, Glenn Close, Jeff Goldblum, William Hurt, Kevin Kline, JoBeth Williams (Carson/ Columbia Delphi)

The Bill Chill is an amusing, splendidly-acted but rather shallow look at what's happened to the generation formed by the 1960s.

Framework has seven old college friends gathering on the Southeastern seaboard for the funeral of another old pal, who has committed suicide in the home of happily-married Glenn Close and Kevin Kline.

Others in attendance are: sharp-looking Tom Berenger, who has gained nationwide fame as a Tom Selleck-type private eye on TV; Jeff Goldblum, horny wiseacre who writes for People magazine; William Hurt, the Jake Barnes of the piece by virtue of having been strategically injured in Vietnam; Mary Kay Place, a successful career woman who just hasn't met the right man; and JoBeth Williams, whose older husband returns home to the two kids before the weekend has barely begun.

Also provocatively on hand is Meg Tilly, much younger girlfriend of the deceased who doesn't react with sufficient depth to the tragedy in the eyes of the older folk.

Except perhaps for Hurt, who still takes

drugs heavily and is closest in personality to the dead man [played by Kevin Costner, but edited out of the finished film], characters are generally middle-of-the-roaders, and pic lacks a tough-minded spokesman who might bring them all up short for a moment.
□ 1983: Best Picture (Nomination)

．．．．．．．．．．．．．．．．．．．．．．．．．．．．

■ **BIG CLOCK, THE**

1948, 95 MINS, US
Dir John Farrow *Prod* Richard Maibaum
Scr Jonathan Latimer *Ph* John F. Seitz *Ed* Eda Warren *Mus* Victor Young *Art Dir* Hans Dreier, Roland Anderson, Albert Nozaki
● Ray Milland, Charles Laughton, Maureen O'Sullivan, George Macready, Elsa Lanchester (Paramount)

There are weaknesses lurking in this pic [based on the novel by Kenneth Fearing], namely a too-patly tailored yarn and some spotty acting, but these matter little. The pace is so red-hot that there's no time or inclination, during the unfolding, to question coincident or misplaced mugging.

Laughton, in this instance, is cracking the whip as the topkick in a gigantic publishing house. Toiling under him is Ray Milland, editor of a crime mag, whose peculiar value is his ability to run down concealed felons and expose them in his sheet. Goaded by insane jealousy, Laughton kills his mistress and scurries for cover. It's at this point that story's peculiar twist shoves it into high.

Laughton is aware that he's been sighted by his unknown rival. As he sees it, there's only one way out, and that's to locate the sole witness and either buy him off or cancel him in some other way. Milland, of course, is hired for that job, and his desperate efforts are directed towards covering his own tracks while pinning the goods on the real murderer.

Milland turns in a workmanlike job, polished to groove to the unrelenting speed of the plot. Laughton, unfortunately, overplays his hand so that his tycoon-sans-heart takes on the quality of parodying the real article.

．．．．．．．．．．．．．．．．．．．．．．．．．．．．

■ **BIG COUNTRY, THE**

1958, 166 MINS, US Ⓥ
Dir William Wyler *Prod* William Wyler, Gregory Peck *Scr* James R. Webb, Sy Bartlett, Robert Wilder *Ph* Franz F. Planer *Ed* Robert Belcher, John Faure *Mus* Jerome Moross *Art Dir* Frank Hotaling
● Gregory Peck, Jean Simmons, Carroll Baker, Charlton Heston, Burl Ives, Charles Bickford (United Artists/Anthony-Worldwide)

The Big Country lives up to its title. The camera has captured a vast section of the southwest with such fidelity that the long stretches of dry country, in juxtaposition to tiny western settlements, and the giant canyon country in the arid area, have been recorded with almost three-dimensional effect.

Although the story – based on Donald Hamilton's novel, with Jessamyn West and Robert Wyler credited with the screen adaptation – is dwarfed by the scenic outpourings, *The Big Country* is nonetheless armed with a serviceable, adult western yarn.

Basically it concerns the feud between Major Henry Terrill (Charles Bickford) and Rufus Hannassey (Burl Ives), rugged individualists who covet the same watering area for their cattle. The water spot is open to both camps since it is the property of Julie Maragon (Jean Simmons) who has been willed the property by her grandfather.

Bickford is the 'have' rancher of the area, with a fine home, a large head of cattle, a beautiful daughter (Carroll Baker), and a full crew of ranch hands. Ives is the 'have not', with a brood of unruly and uncouth sons, a bunch of shacks, and an army of 'white trash' relatives. Into the atmosphere of hate and vengeance comes Gregory Peck, a genteel

eastern dude, to marry Baker. Peck arouses Baker's displeasure when he refuses to ride a wild horse and backs away from a fight with Charlton Heston, Bickford's truculent foreman who's after Baker himself.

As the peace-loving easterner, Peck gives one of his better performances. Ives is topnotch as the rough but fair-minded Hannassey; Bickford is fine as the ruthless, unforgiving rancher. Chuck Connors, a former professional baseball player, is especially convincing as Ives' uncouth son who attempts to rape Simmons. Jerome Moross' musical score is also on the plus side.

．．．．．．．．．．．．．．．．．．．．．．．．．．．．

■ **BIG EASY, THE**

1986, 108 MINS, US ◇ Ⓥ
Dir Jim McBride *Prod* Stephen Friedman *Scr* Dan Petrie Jr. *Ph* Afonso Beato *Ed* Mia Goldman
Mus Brad Feidel *Art Dir* Jeannine Claudia Oppewall
● Dennis Quaid, Ellen Barkin, Ned Beatty, John Goodman (Kings Road)

Until conventional plot contrivances begin to spoil the fun, *The Big Easy* is a snappy, sassy battle of the sexes in the guise of a melodrama about police corruption.

Buildup is quite engaging. In the classic screwball comedy tradition of opposites irresistibly attracting, brash New Orleans homicide detective Dennis Quaid puts the make on Ellen Barkin, a northern import assigned by the d.a.'s office to investigate possible illegal activities in the department.

Not necessarily the likeliest of couples, Quaid and Barkin bring great energy and an offbeat wired quality to their roles. Quaid's character is always 'on', always performing for effect, during most of the action, and actor's natural charm easily counterbalances character's overbearing tendencies. Barkin is sexy and convincing as the initially uptight target of Quaid's attentions.

Ned Beatty projects an appealing paternalism as the homicide chief, while top supporting turn comes from the Ridiculous Theater Co.'s Charles Ludlam as a very Tennessee Williams-ish defense attorney.

．．．．．．．．．．．．．．．．．．．．．．．．．．．．

■ **BIG FISHERMAN, THE**

1959, 180 MINS, US ◇
Dir Frank Borzage *Prod* Rowland V. Lee
Scr Howard Estabrook, Rowland V. Lee *Ph* Lee Garmes *Ed* Paul Weatherwax *Mus* Albert Hay Malotte *Art Dir* John De Cuir
● Howard Keel, Susan Kohner, John Saxon, Martha Hyer, Herbert Lom, Ray Stricklyn (Buena Vista)

The Big Fisherman is a pious but plodding account of the conversion to Christianity of Simon-Peter, the apostle called 'the fisher of men'. Its treatment is reverent but far from rousing.

There is plenty of opportunity for both spectacle and sex, and it is all the more curious, considering its big budget and leisurely production schedule, that both are almost absent. Although the climax of the film is in Herod's palace where Salome served the head of John the Baptist to the tyrant, this scene, laid in a sumptuous and impressively lavish banquet hall, is done almost entirely by shadows and is swiftly over. Salome, in fact, is not only never shown, she is never mentioned.

Although the title seems to make Simon-Peter the central character, the film [from the novel by Lloyd C. Douglas] is only incidentally about him. His part in the story is his influence on two young lovers, John Saxon as an Arab prince and Susan Kohner as the daughter of Herod by an Arab princess. Saxon wants to succeed his father as chieftan of an Arab tribe and Kohner wants to kill her father for the unhappiness he has inflicted on her mother.

Kohnner and Saxon make a handsome young couple. But their problems seem trivial against the turbulent era. Howard Keel is handsomely picturesque as Simon-Peter, and shows he can hold his own as a straight actor. It is not his fault that there is no suggestion of the doughty strength identified with the chief apostle.

The 'Palestine' that is the film's setting was shot entirely on locations in the San Fernando Valley and the California desert. It seems entirely authentic.

....

■ **BIG FIX, THE**

1978, 108 MINS, US ◇ ⊙

Dir Jeremy Paul Kagan   *Prod* Carl Borack, Richard Dreyfuss   *Scr* Roger L. Simon   *Ph* Frank Stanley   *Ed* Patrick Kennedy   *Mus* Bill Conti   *Art Dir* Robert F. Boyle

● Richard Dreyfuss, Susan Anspach, Bonnie Bedelia, John Lithgow, Ofelia Medina, F. Murray Abraham (Universal)

In *The Big Fix* Richard Dreyfuss delivers what is for him a particularly relaxed and confident performance as Moses Wine, the 1970s answer to Philip Marlowe, Lew Archer and Sam Spade.

Simply as a detective thriller, *The Bix Fix* has strong appeal. As a centerpiece it has a tough, cynical, intelligent detective – an independent man with a rathole for an apartment, a personal life in need of some investigating and a full supply of wisecracks.

Briefly, the film finds Dreyfuss employed by Susan Anspach, like Dreyfuss a former campus activist, gone straight as a campaign worker for a gubernatorial candidate. Someone is trying to sabotage the election by distributing leaflets linking the middle-of-the-road candidate with radical elements. Dreyfuss is a natural for the case because he knew people in the radical movement.

The trail leads through Los Angeles – from the Beverly Hills mansions and social clubs to the Mexican barrios. Jeremy Paul Kagan's direction is nicely paced, starting off slow with the development of Dreyfuss' character and then speeding up as the plot complications mount.

....

■ **BIG HEAT, THE**

1953, 89 MINS, US ⊙

Dir Fritz Lang   *Prod* Robert Arthur   *Scr* Sydney Boehm   *Ph* Charles Lang   *Ed* Charles Nelson   *Mus* Daniele Amfitheatrof   *Art Dir* Robert Peterson

● Glenn Ford, Gloria Grahame, Jocelyn Brando, Alexander Scourby, Lee Marvin, Jeanette Nolan (Columbia)

The picture starts with a tight, believable screenplay by Sydney Boehm, based on the William P. McGivern *SatEvePost* serial, and goes on from there through tense, forceful direction by Fritz Lang and topnotch trouping led by Glenn Ford.

It's the story of a cop, a homicide sergeant, who busts up the crime syndicate strangling his city and its administration. Because he prefers to do his job and collect his pay honestly, he finds the going tough. So tough that his wife is murdered by an auto bomb intended for him, his child is threatened with kidnapping, and he loses his police job because of pressure from higher ups.

Ford's portrayal of the homicide sergeant is honest and packs much wallop. Lang's direction builds taut suspense, throwing unexpected, and believable, thrills at the audience.

Gloria Grahame's character, that of a gangster's sweetie, is choice and she makes it a colorful, important part of the picture.

Alexander Scourby, the man who heads the corrupt syndicate; Lee Marvin, his chief lieutenant; and Jeanette Nolan, the widow of a crooked cop who blackmails the syndicate, turn in strong individual performances.

....

■ **BIG JAKE**

1971, 109 MINS, US ◇ ⊙

Dir George Sherman   *Prod* Michael Wayne   *Scr* Harry Julian Fink, R.M. Fink   *Ph* William Clothier   *Ed* Harry Gerstad   *Mus* Elmer Bernstein   *Art Dir* Carl Anderson

● John Wayne, Richard Boone, Maureen O'Hara, Patrick Wayne, Chris Mitchum, Bobby Vinton (Batjac)

Big Jake is an extremely slick and commercial John Wayne starrer, this time as a long-gone husband out to rescue a grandson from kidnapper Richard Boone.

Harry Julian Fink and R.M. Fink's original story and script is well-structured and fleshed with solid dialog. It opens with a 10-person slaughter 13 minutes into the film. Maureen O'Hara, as a strong-willed woman whose husband (Wayne) has long since departed, sends for him to track down Boone's gang which has kidnapped grandson John Ethan Wayne (the star's own eight-year-old son). Sons Patrick Wayne and Christopher Mitchum mature, in a manner of speaking, when they team up with their father. Bruce Cabot's performance as an Indian scout is excellent.

There is gore spattered all over the screen. A Wayne film doesn't have to resort to such excess. Performances are totally professional. Wayne and Boone snarl extremely well at each other. Patrick Wayne handles his role with a fine cockiness. Mitchum is very good. Bobby Vinton plays another son who has little footage.

....

■ **BIG JIM MCLAIN**

1952, 90 MINS, US ◇

Dir Edward Ludwig   *Prod* Robert Fellows   *Scr* James Edward Grant, Richard English, Eric Taylor   *Ph* Archie Stout   *Ed* Jack Murray   *Mus* Emil Newman   *Art Dir* Alfred Ybarra

● John Wayne, Nancy Olson, James Arness, Alan Napier, Veda Ann Borg, Hans Conried (Wayne-Fellows/Warner)

Honolulu forms the setting for a story of the work to expose Communist activities. The picture was rushed into the market and bears evidence of that haste. Continuity is choppy, the script sketchy and lacking in clarity.

John Wayne and James Arness are crack investigators for the House Committee on Un-American Activities. When it is learned the Communists are threatening in the islands, the pair is dispatched there to get evidence against the Red cells that can be used for a documented public hearing.

The investigation is tedious and not too fruitful. During its course Wayne meets and falls for Nancy Olson, a secretary working for a suspected doctor (Gayne Whitman). He pursues Olson and the Commies, gradually making time on both counts.

....

■ **BIG KNIFE, THE**

1955, 111 MINS, US

Dir Robert Aldrich   *Prod* Robert Aldrich   *Scr* James Poe   *Ph* Ernest Laszlo   *Ed* Michael Luciano   *Mus* Frank DeVol

● Jack Palance, Ida Lupino, Wendell Corey, Shelley Winters, Jean Hagen, Rod Steiger (United Artists)

Film is of the *Sunset Boulevard* and *Star Is Born* genre, an inside Hollywood story. It's sometimes so brittle and brutal as to prove disturbing. It differs from the Clifford Odets stage play of 1949, when John Garfield starred.

Rod Steiger vividly interprets the Janus aspects of the studio head who knows when to con and cajole Jack Palance into a 14-year deal. He has no compunction about staging an 'accidental death' of one of those 'casting couch contractees' (Shelley Winters), foiled by his laconic and resourceful publicity director.

Wendell Corey is properly 'the cynical Celt', Steiger's resourceful hatchet-man in the clinches. Ida Lupino scores as the realistic wife who wants Palance to forget the Hollywood loot and return to his 'ideals'.

....

■ **BIG MAN, THE**

1990, 115 MINS, UK ◇ ⊙

Dir David Leland   *Prod* Stephen Wooley   *Scr* Don MacPherson   *Ph* Ian Wilson   *Ed* George Akers   *Mus* Ennio Morricone   *Art Dir* Caroline Amies

● Liam Neeson, Joanne Whalley-Kilmer, Ian Bannen, Billy Connolly, Maurice Roeves, Hugh Grant (Palace/Miramax/BSB/British Screen)

Though unquestionably well-intentioned and determined not to pull any punches, *The Big Man* [from the book by William McIlvanney] has a depressing theme and ultra-violent conclusion.

The early scenes, set in a depressed Scottish village where an abandoned coal mine and mass unemployment reflect the aftermath of Britain's crippling miners' strike, look promising. Liam Neeson comes on strong as the unemployed Danny, who was imprisoned during the strike for hitting a policeman and now has a middle-class wife (Joanne Whalley-Kilmer) and two bright children to support.

His best friend, Frankie (an engaging 'straight' turn from Scottish comedian Billy Connolly), acts as a runner for Mason (Ian Bannen), a corrupt businessman who needs Danny to fight for him. Motives for the fight, a bare-knuckle affair with no rules, are obscure.

The fight, when it comes, is one of the most grueling ever caught on film. Top marks go to the makeup team, which provided the battered and bloodied faces for the actors.

....

■ **BIG MEAT EATER**

1982, 77 MINS, CANADA ◇ ⊙

Dir Chris Windsor   *Prod* Laurence Keane   *Scr* Phil Sarath, Laurence Keane   *Ph* Doug MacKay   *Ed* Laurence Keane, Chris Windsor, Lilla Pederson   *Mus* J. Douglas Dodd

● George Dawson, Andrew Gillies, Big Miller, Stephen Dimopoulos, Georgina Hegedos (BDC Entertainment)

A delightfully unpretentious musical comedy which defies classification, although billed as a 'bizarre new wave comedy'.

The small town parable about progress owes something to both Canadian humorist Stephen Leacock and to Harold Lloyd. The principal figure is a cheery family butcher who has invented a new universal language and is a great booster for his hometown of Burquitlam.

From the massive, murderous heating engineer Abdulla, played effortlessly by an Albertan jazz singer, Big Miller, to the highly strung teenage whiz-kid Jan Wczinski, beautifully rendered by Christopher Reeve look-alike Andrew Gillies, the cast is put through its paces with great style by debuting director Chris Windsor. Modest budget was $150,000.

....

■ **BIG PARADE, THE**

1925, 150 MINS, US ⊗ ⊙

Dir King Vidor   *Scr* Laurence Stallings, Harry Behn, Joseph W. Farnham   *Ph* John Arnold   *Ed* Hugh Wynn   *Mus* David Mendoza, William Axt   *Art Dir* Cedric Gibbons, James Basevi

● John Gilbert, Renee Adoree, Hobart Bosworth, Claire McDowell, Claire Adams, Karl Dane (M-G-M)

King Vidor had a tough subject to deal with.

He knew that he would have to show the horrors of war, and therefore worked his story out in such a manner that it has plenty of comedy relief and a love sequence.

John Gilbert's performance is a superb thing, while Renee Adoree, as the little French peasant, figuratively lives the role. The same may as well be said for Karl Dane and Tom O'Brien, for it is the excellent work of all these players and the manner in which Vidor has handled them that lift this production far above the ordinary.

Teamwork has made this picture. It makes 'em laugh, cry, and it thrills – plenty. Besides which the captions are an example and a lesson of how it should be done.

The continuity is replete with little things that ordinarily wouldn't draw attention. For example, while a company of infantry is advancing a German machine gun opens up and sprays the line. Four or five men drop and the middle private of the group becomes rooted to the ground in terror, with his knees trembling.

■ **BIG RED ONE, THE**

1980, 111 MINS, US ◇ ⓥ

Dir Samuel Fuller *Prod* Gene Corman *Scr* Samuel Fuller *Ph* Adam Greenberg *Ed* David Bretherton, Morton Tubor *Mus* Dana Kaproff *Art Dir* Peter Jamison
● Lee Marvin, Mark Hamill, Robert Carradine, Bobby DiCicco, Stephane Audran, Kelly Ward (Lorimar)

The Big Red One was two years in the making and 35 years in Samuel Fuller's head. It's a terrific war yarn, a picture of palpable raw power which manages both intense intimacy and great scope at the same time.

The story of the First Infantry Division's exploits in North Africa and Europe between 1942–45, fast-paced pic attempts to tell entire story of the European land war through the eyes of five foot soldiers and pulls it off to a great degree.

Based on writer-director's own experiences as a GI, pic was announced as a John Wayne-starrer in the late 1950s and came close to realization on many other occasions, but only came together when producer Gene Corman found means to make it almost entirely in Israel.

Approach eschews usual sociological analysis used in many war pix. These men are there for one reason only, to survive the war.

■ **BIG SKY, THE**

1952, 140 MINS, US ⓥ

Dir Howard Hawks *Prod* Howard Hawks *Scr* Dudley Nichols *Ph* Russell Harlan *Ed* Christian Nyby *Mus* Dimitri Tiomkin *Art Dir* Albert S. D'Agostino, Perry Ferguson
● Kirk Douglas, Dewey Martin, Elizabeth Threatt, Arthur Hunnicutt, Hank Worden, Jim Davis (Winchester/RKO)

Howard Hawks has spared nothing in the filming of A.B. Guthrie Jr's novel, *The Big Sky*, except the cutting shears. Pic is a gigantic outdoor epic, but its impact is dissipated by the marathon running time.

Kirk Douglas is cast as a Kentucky mountaineer. Story involves his joining a keelboat expedition up the Missouri river in the 1830s.

Story line centers on the 1,200-mile trek up the Missouri from St. Louis to the Blackfoot Indian tribe in the northwest. Expedition is headed by French fur trader, Jourdonnais, excellently played by Steven Geray. The long trip is filled with the usual obstacles, warring Indians, treacherous white men, nature's forces, etc.

Femme interest is supplied by newcomer Elizabeth Threatt, who plays the daughter of a Blackfoot chief being returned to her tribe by Geray.

■ **BIG SLEEP, THE**

1946, 113 MINS, US ⓥ

Dir Howard Hawks *Prod* Howard Hawks *Scr* William Faulkner, Leigh Brackett, Jules Furthman *Ph* Sid Hickox *Ed* Christian Nyby *Mus* Max Steiner *Art Dir* Carl Jules Weyl
● Humphrey Bogart, Lauren Bacall, Martha Vickers, Dorothy Malone, Elisha Cook Jr (Warner)

Brittle Chandler characters have been transferred to the screen with punch by Howard Hawks' production and direction, providing full load of rough, tense action most of the way.

Humphrey Bogart as Philip Marlowe and Lauren Bacall as Vivian, Marlowe's chief romantic interest, make a smooth team to get over the amatory play and action in the script. Hawks has given story a staccato pace in the development, using long stretches of dialogless action and then whipping in fast talk between characters. This helps to punch home high spots of suspense, particularly in latter half of picture.

Chandler plot, deals with adventures of Bogart when he takes on a case for the eccentric Sternwood family. There are six deaths to please whodunit fans, plenty of lusty action, both romantic and physical, as Bogart matches wits with dealers in sex literature, blackmail, gambling and murder. Before he closes his case he has dodged sudden death, been unmercifully beaten, threatened, fought off mad advances of one of the Sternwood females, and fallen in love with another.

Some good scenes are tossed to others in the cast. Dorothy Malone, a bookshop proprietress, has her big moment in a sequence shot with sex implications as she goes on the make for Bogart.

■ **BIG SLEEP, THE**

1978, 99 MINS, UK ◇ ⓥ

Dir Michael Winner *Prod* Elliott Kastner, Michael Winner *Scr* Michael Winner *Ph* Robert Paynter *Ed* Freddie Wilson *Mus* Jerry Fielding *Art Dir* Harry Pottle
● Robert Mitchum, Sarah Miles, Richard Boone, Candy Clark, Joan Collins, Edward Fox (United Artists)

Howard Hawks' lusty, if confusing, 1946 filming of Raymond Chandler's *The Big Sleep* takes on even more filmic history in light of this remake which transplants from 1940-California to 1970-London. The move denatures the Chandler environment. Robert Mitchum encores as he did in the 1975 *Farewell My Lovely* remake.

Mitchum is hired by wealthy cripple James Stewart to probe possible blackmail. This leads him into the tangled lives of the client's daughters – semi-nympho Candy Clark and the more mature Sarah Miles. Latter has a relationship with gambler Oliver Reed whose wife Diana Quick has disappeared. Edward Fox was once in love with Clark; he is killed by Simon Turner. Bookstore staff includes Joan Collins. Weak-willed Colin Blakely is no match for hitman Richard Boone.

As for the police, the shift to London introduces John Mills, Richard Todd and James Donald. Back at the mansion, butler Harry Andrews acts officiously, while chauffeur Martin Potter dies in attempt to help Clark avoid implication in pornographer John Justin's murder; she has been posing for nude pix.

The production is handsome, but in the updating and relocation a lot has been lost. In particular, gone is the 1940s LA feel. Only Clark seems to project the requisite spoiled-rotten youthful spark. Nearly every other principal seems beyond the point of really caring.

■ **BIG STEAL, THE**

1949, 78 MINS, US ⓥ

Dir Don Siegel *Prod* Jack J. Gross *Scr* Geoffrey Homes, Gerald Drayson Adams *Ph* Harry J. Wild *Ed* Samuel F. Beetley *Mus* Leigh Harline
● Robert Mitchum, Jane Greer, William Bendix, Patric Knowles, Ramon Novarro (RKO)

Steal was lensed on location in and around Mexico City. It gains added sight interest from this, as well as strengthened melodramatics. It takes a little time for an audience to sort out what all the shootin's about since the script dives immediately into its story without explanatory footage.

When it does become clear the interest is strong as director Don Siegel unfolds a good chase yarn. Dialog is often racy and saucy, sharpening Jane Greer's s.a. factors.

Footage is one long chase through Mexico. Robert Mitchum is chasing Patric Knowles and, in turn, is being chased by William Bendix. All are interested in a $300,000 army payroll, stolen from Mitchum by Knowles.

There's a nifty performance by Ramon Novarro as the hep Mexican police officer.

■ **BIG STEAL, THE**

1990, 100 MINS, AUSTRALIA ◇

Dir Nadia Tass *Prod* Nadia Tass, David Parker *Scr* David Parker *Ph* David Parker *Ed* Peter Carrodus *Art Dir* Paddy Reardon
● Ben Mendelsohn, Claudia Karvan, Steve Bisley, Marshall Napier, Tim Robertson (Cascade)

The third feature from husband-and-wife team Nadia Tass and David Parker has a low-key charm that's appealing, and a couple of riotously funny scenes.

Ben Mendelsohn is Danny, a shy 18-year-old who wants two things: to own a Jaguar and to date Joanna (Claudia Karvan). Danny's father (Marshall Napier in a rich comic performance) gives him a car for his birthday, but it's a 1963 Nissan Cedric the family has owned for years. Danny decides to trade this in for a 1973 Jag in time for his first date.

Trouble is that car dealer Gordon Farkas (Steve Bisley giving a splendidly sleazy performance) is a crook who's switched engines on Danny. He and his mates decide to hit back by lifting the engine from Farkas' Jag while he's having a drunken time at a sex club.

Teens here are incredibly unsophisticated compared to 18-year-olds in Hollywood teen comedies, and that's part of the film's charm. Mendelsohn and Karvan are quite sweet in their roles.

■ **BIG STREET, THE**

1942, 88 MINS, US ⓥ

Dir Irving Reis *Prod* Damon Runyon *Scr* Leonard Spigelgass *Ph* Russell Metty *Ed* William Hamilton *Mus* Roy Webb
● Henry Fonda, Lucille Ball, Agnes Moorehead, Barton MacLane, Eugene Pallette, Sam Levene (RKO)

Taken from a *Collier* mag story [*Little Pinks*] by Damon Runyon, this is a Cinderella-like fable of a Broadway cafe-singing golddigger who becomes more human long after a fall cripples her for life. Scripter Leonard Spigelgass makes the transition from the grasping, selfish little beauty to a bitter disillusioned girl entirely life-like albeit a prolonged affair. He's done a neat job of transferring the spirit of the piece to the screen, studding it with typical Runyon humor.

Lucille Ball, cast at first in an unsympathetic role, comes through with high laurels. Henry Fonda, as the mooning but intensely loyal Little Pinks, is at his best. Eugene Pallette is well teamed with Agnes Moorehead, the food-loving but realistic Violette whom he weds.

BIG TOP PEE-WEE

1988, 86 MINS, US ◇ ▣

Dir Randal Kleiser *Prod* Paul Reubens, Debra Hill
Scr Paul Reubens, George McGrath *Ph* Steven
Poster *Ed* Jeff Gourson *Mus* Danny Elfman
Art Dir Stephen Marsh
● Paul Reubens, Kris Kristofferson, Valeria Golino,
Penelope Ann Miller, Susan Tyrrell, Albert Henderson
(Paramount)

Big Top Pee-wee again demonstrates that Pee-wee Herman is one very strange screen personality; he previously scored with his 1985 feature debut, *Pee-wee's Big Adventure*.

Surrounded by animals as strange as himself, Herman pursues a career in agricultural extravagance with the help of his goggled talking pig Vincent (amusingly voiced by Wayne White). Together, they grow outsized vegetables and a hot dog tree while wanly romancing pretty Penelope Ann Miller.

A storm brings a broken-down circus to Herman's farm, adding a menagerie of freakish animals and people to his already curious collection. Kris Kristofferson oversees the visitors and keeps them rallied with hearty circus sayings, along with explanations of how he came to marry his miniature wife (Susan Tyrrell) whom he carries around in his pocket.

Very little of this is interesting or amusing on paper, which must have been a real challenge to director Randal Kleiser, who ably keeps all the surrounding players in tune to whatever it is that Herman's up to at any given moment.

BIG TROUBLE IN LITTLE CHINA

1986, 99 MINS, US ◇ ▣

Dir John Carpenter *Prod* Larry J. Franco *Scr* Gary
Goldman, David Z. Weinstein, [W.D. Richter] *Ph* Dean
Cundey *Ed* Mark Warner, Steve Mirkovitch, Edward A
Warschilka *Mus* John Carpenter *Art Dir* John J.
Lloyd
● Kurt Russell, Kim Cattrall, Dennis Dun, James Hong,
Victor Wong, Kate Burton (20th Century-Fox)

Story is promising, involving an ancient Chinese magician Lo Pan (James Hong) who controls an evil empire beneath San Francisco's Chinatown while he searches to find a green-eyed Chinese beauty to mate with and make him mortal.

Director John Carpenter seems to be trying to make an action-adventure along the lines of *Indiana Jones and the Temple of Doom*. The effect goes horribly awry.

Leading the cast is Kurt Russell who looks embarrassed, and should be, playing his CB philosophizing truck driver character as a cross between a swaggering John Wayne, adventurous Harrison Ford and wacky Bill Murray.

He's caught in Hong's supposedly ghostly underworld with restaurateur friend Wang Chi (Dennis Dun) while trying to rescue Wang's green-eyed Chinese fiancee, Miao Yin (Suzee Pai), from Hong's lascivious clutches.

BIG WEDNESDAY

1978, 126 MINS, US ◇ ▣

Dir John Milius *Prod* Buzz Feitshans *Scr* John Milius,
Dennis Aaberg *Ph* Bruce Surtees *Ed* Robert L. Wolfe,
Tim O'Meara *Mus* Basil Poledouris *Art Dir* Charles
Rosen
● Jan-Michael Vincent, William Katt, Gary Busey, Patti
D'Arbanville, Lee Purcell, Robert Englund
(A-Team/Warner)

A rubber stamp wouldn't do for John Milius. So he took a sledgehammer and pounded Important all over *Big Wednesday*. This film about three Malibu surfers in the 1960s has been branded major statement and it's got Big Ideas about adolescence, friendship and the 1960s.

Big Wednesday has a character named Bear, a combination John Milius-Ernest Hemingway, played by Sam Melville. He is described this way: 'He knew where the waves came from and why'. Really.

But Melville is a secondary character. The film revolves around three friends, Jan-Michael Vincent, William Katt and Gary Busey. Each is a noted surfer with Vincent something of a legend. Their life is surfing, but man – not even boy – can not live by salt water alone. So they grow up, awkwardly.

The movie is divided into four movements with each section moving ahead a few years. It climaxes at the final segment, Big Wednesday, when the surf has swelled to unknown proportions and the three reunite as men to again conquer the ocean.

BIGGER SPLASH, A

1975, 105 MINS, UK ◇

Dir Jack Hazan *Scr* Jack Hazan, David Mingay
Ph Jack Hazan *Ed* David Mingay *Mus* Patrick
Gowers
● David Hockney, Peter Schlesinger, Celia Birtwell, Mo
McDermott, Henry Geldzahler, Kasmin (Buzzy)

A Bigger Splash is a revealing last ripple of the so-called life style of 'Swinging London' invented mainly by journalists.

Jack Hazan uses painter David Hockney, his art dealer in the US and his fashion creator friend and the latter's wife. It has Hockney breaking with a boyfriend and not being able to work as his friends worry and his American dealer exhorts him. He finally does begin one on a swimming pool, which eventually has a man floating in it and the one who left him standing outside and staring.

Real people play themselves around a partly-fictionalized tale. Hockney was noted for his color and specialization in California subjects. The gay life around him is indicated with style and taste.

BIGGER THAN LIFE

1956, 95 MINS, US ◇

Dir Nicholas Ray *Prod* James Mason *Scr* Cyril Hume,
Richard Maibaum *Ph* Joe MacDonald *Ed* Louis
Loeffler *Mus* David Raksin
● James Mason, Barbara Rush, Walter Matthau,
Robert Simon, Christopher Olsen, Roland Winters (20th
Century-Fox)

James Mason has picked a powerful subject for his first 20th-Fox production and delivers it with quite a bit of dramatic distinction in carrying out the supervisory duties and as the male lead. *Bigger Than Life* exposes the good and bad in cortisone.

A great deal of care is taken in the forceful, realistically drafted screenplay [based on a *New Yorker* article by Berton Rouche] to give both sides of the case, while at the same time telling a gripping, dramatic story of people that become very real under Nicholas Ray's wonder-working direction. The performances are standout, with Barbara Rush earning particular praise as Mason's wife.

Mason is exceptionally fine as the modestly-circumstanced grade school teacher who undergoes a series of experiments with cortisone in the hope he can be cured of a usually fatal disease. At first the experiments progress promisingly, but he begins to overdose himself and some startling personality changes occur.

Christopher Olsen scores with his tremendously effective study of Mason's young son.

BIGGEST BUNDLE OF THEM ALL, THE

1968, 105 MINS, US ◇

Dir Ken Annakin *Prod* Josef Shaftel *Scr* Sy
Salkowitz *Ph* Piero Portalupi *Ed* Ralph Sheldon
Mus Riz Ortolani *Art Dir* Arrigo Equini
● Vittorio De Sica, Raquel Welch, Robert Wagner,
Godfrey Cambridge, Francesco Mule, Edward G.
Robinson (M-G-M)

Title refers to the theft of $5 million in platinum ingots – by a gang composed of a deported Italian mobster and four amateurs.

Screenplay by Sy Salkowitz, from an original by the producer, is amusing, although never of the belly-laugh genre, and Ken Annakin's direction is imaginative enough to maintain a light mood. Yarn has a set of characters which fit nicely into the action.

What appeals most is the general ineptitude of the would-be criminals as they seek to rob the train bearing the ingots. In need of $3,000 to buy proper equipment for the caper, all their plans go wrong.

Vittorio De Sica pumps plenty of heart and humor into his role of the erstwhile Chicago mobster who attends the funeral in Naples of a Chi comrade-in-arms and finds himself kidnapped by four strangers, headed by American Robert Wagner.

Wagner handles himself satisfactorily, and Raquel Welch is his voluptuous girl-friend, still playing bikini queen.

BILL & TED'S EXCELLENT ADVENTURE

1989, 90 MINS, US ◇ ▣

Dir Stephen Herek *Prod* Scott Kroopf, Michael S.
Murphey, Joel Soisson *Scr* Chris Matheson, Ed
Solomon *Ph* Timothy Suhrsedt *Ed* Larry Bock, Patrick
Rand *Mus* David Newman *Art Dir* Ray Forge Smith
● Keanu Reeves, Alex Winter, George Carlin, Terry
Camilleri, Dan Shor (Nelson/Interscope/Soisson-
Murphey)

Keanu Reeves (Ted) and Alex Winter (Bill) play San Dimas 'dudes' so close they seem wired together.

Preoccupied with plans for 'a most triumphant video' to launch their two-man rock band, The Wyld Stallyns, they're suddenly, as Bill put it, 'in danger of flunking most heinously' out of history.

George Carlin appears as a cosmic benefactor who offers them a chance to travel back through history and gather up the speakers they need for an awesome presentation.

Through brief, perilous stops here and there, they end up jamming Napoleon, Billy The Kid, Sigmund Freud, Socrates, Joan of Arc, Genghis Khan, Abraham Lincoln and Mozart into their time-traveling phone booth.

Each encounter is so brief and utterly cliched that history has little chance to contribute anything to this pic's two dimensions.

Reeves, with his beguilingly blank face and loose-limbed, happy-go-lucky physical vocabulary, and Winter, with his golden curls, gleefully good vibes and 'bodacious' vocabulary, propel this adventure as long as they can.

BILLIE

1965, 86 MINS, US ◇

Dir Don Weis *Prod* Don Weis *Scr* Ronald
Alexander *Ph* John Russell *Ed* Adrienne Fazan
Mus Dominic Frontiere *Art Dir* Arthur Lonergan
● Patty Duke, Jim Backus, Jane Greer, Warren
Berlinger, Billy De Wolfe, Charles Lane (Chrislaw/
United Artists)

Patty Duke stars as *Billie*, the tomboy who complicates her family life before shedding athletic gear for maiden attire.

Ronald Alexander adapted his *Time Out for Ginger* legiter of the early 1950s, cutting some characters to focus on Duke, the younger daughter of understanding Jane Greer and bumbling Jim Backus who shines in field meets via a mental gimmick. Coach Charles Lane uses her to goad his less proficient males, including Warren Berlinger to whom the gal eventually reveals her secret and gives her heart.

Complications, pat and unreal, include a mayoralty battle between Backus and Billy De Wolfe, wasted herein as a heavy who exploits pop's platform in terms of barbs at Billie and older sister Susan Seaforth. Latter pair stand out, as does Berlinger.

Backus is good in his now-standard characterization, while Greer is radiant and charming. Duke has an infectious personality which comes across.

●●●●●●●●●●●●●●●●●●●●●●●●●●●●●●●●●●●

■ **BILLION DOLLAR BRAIN**

1967, 111 MINS, UK ◇ ▽

Dir Ken Russell *Prod* Harry Saltzman *Scr* John McGrath *Ph* Billy Williams *Ed* Alan Osbiston *Mus* Richard Rodney Bennett *Art Dir* Bert Davey
● Michael Caine, Karl Malden, Francoise Dorleac, Oscar Homolka, Ed Begley (United Artists)

Plot takes too long to get moving, and when it does it is quite incredible and hard to follow. Harry Palmer (Michael Caine) is instructed by an electronic voice over the phone to take a package containing mysterious eggs to Finland, and meets up with a former American CIA man, Ed Newbigin (Karl Malden), whose life he has saved in the past.

Palmer, whose mission is known to his previous MI5 employers, pretends to join the organization, which turns out to be controlled by a crazy American General (Ed Begley) with a Senator McCarthy attitude re Commies and a determination to defeat them by fomenting revolution in satellite countries and attacking with his own private army.

It doesn't matter so much that the storyline offends belief – so do the Bond gambols – but it is deployed by director Ken Russell with such abrupt speed that it doesn't make immediate sense in its own frivolous terms.

Malden and Begley, always reliable, do what they can with roles conceived as stereotypes of greed and fanaticism respectively, and Francoise Dorleac introduces a touch of glamor as an agent who might be working for anybody.

●●●●●●●●●●●●●●●●●●●●●●●●●●●●●●●●●●●

■ **BILL OF DIVORCEMENT, A**

1932, 75 MINS, US

Dir George Cukor *Scr* Howard Estabrook, Harry Wagstaff Gribble *Ph* Sid Hickox *Ed* Arthur Roberts *Mus* Max Steiner *Art Dir* Carroll Clark
● John Barrymore, Billie Burke, Katharine Hepburn, David Manners, Bramwell Fletcher (Radio)

Standout here is the smash impression made by Katharine Hepburn in her first picture assignment. She has a vital something that sets her apart from the picture galaxy.

The play [of the same name by Clemence Dane] has lost none of its tremendous grip in translation to celluloid. Ten years after its stage success, this peculiarly British version of the Ibsen *Ghosts* theme still has power to grip and hold.

John Barrymore distinguishes himself anew in the role of the unhappy Hilary, a part far from his accustomed range. For Billie Burke, the role of the distracted wife holds out small promise of flourish and histrionic parade, but she looks miraculously fresh and young, giving much charm to the character of the secondary femme character. David Manners as the heroine's young sweetheart is another happy choice.

●●●●●●●●●●●●●●●●●●●●●●●●●●●●●●●●●●●

■ **BILL OF DIVORCEMENT, A**

1940, 70 MINS, US

Dir John Farrow *Prod* Lee Marcus *Scr* Dalton Trumbo *Ph* Nicholas Musuraca *Ed* Harry Marker
● Maureen O'Hara, Adolphe Menjou, Fay Bainter, Herbert Marshall, May Whitty, C. Aubrey Smith (RKO)

Clemence Dane's play, originally turned out

by RKO [in 1932], skyrocketed Katharine Hepburn into prominence and marquee lights. Maureen O'Hara, a capable Irish actress imported by Erich Pommer and Charles Laughton, essays the Hepburn role in this remake with utmost confidence and ability.

Story is of a woman's sacrifice of love, marriage, and an anticipated family in order to care for her demented father. Adolphe Menjou, escaping from an institution for the insane, returns to his English manor home on Xmas to find his wife has divorced him and is ready to remarry. His appearance upsets plans, including those of his young daughter (O'Hara) who is engaged to a young Australian.

O'Hara takes fullest advantage of a meaty role which is attention-arresting and rich in acting opportunity. Menjou provides an excellent characterization of the father (previously handled by John Barrymore). Fay Bainter delivers her usual warmful and sincere performance as the wife who falls in love with Herbert Marshall and gets a new start for happiness. May Whitty commands attention as the elderly Victorian aunt of the household.

Direction by John Farrow provides dramatic power in his handling of a delicate subject. Script by Dalton Trumbo is workmanlike, although here and there are found long dialog stretches that carry over from the stage technique of the original play.

●●●●●●●●●●●●●●●●●●●●●●●●●●●●●●●●●●●

■ **BILLY BUDD**

1962, 123 MINS, US/UK ▽

Dir Peter Ustinov *Prod* Peter Ustinov *Scr* Peter Ustinov, Robert Rossen *Ph* Robert Krasker *Ed* Jack Harris *Mus* Anthony Hopkins *Art Dir* Don Ashton
● Robert Ryan, Peter Ustinov, Melvyn Douglas, Terence Stamp, Ronald Lewis, David McCallum (Allied Artists)

Peter Ustinov's production of *Billy Budd* is a near miss, and Ustinov, alas, is the culprit. The ubiquitous Mr U is to be commended for spearheading the noble effort to translate Herman Melville's highly-regarded, thought-provoking last story to the screen – a difficult task. But as director he is guilty of at least one major flaw of execution in which Ustinov, the actor is most prominently implicated.

Billy Budd is the allegorical tale of the clash of an incredibly good-hearted young foretopman and an inhumanly sadistic master-at-arms aboard a British fighting vessel in 1797, and the issue of moral justice vs. the wartime military code that arises when the former is condemned to hang for killing the latter, though recognized even by those who sit in judgment upon him as being spirituallly innocent.

The clash between Budd and his tormentor, Claggart – archtypes of good and evil – has been carried off well by Terence Stamp and Robert Ryan under Ustinov's guidance. Where Ustinov has slipped is in the development and delineation of the character he himself plays – the overly conscientious Captain Vere, whose judgment in favor of military over moral ramifications of the issue sends Budd to his death.

●●●●●●●●●●●●●●●●●●●●●●●●●●●●●●●●●●●

■ **BILLY JACK**

1971, 115 MINS, US ◇ ▽

Dir T.C. Frank [= Tom Laughlin] *Prod* Mary Rose Solti *Scr* T.C Frank, Teresa Cristina [= Delores Taylor] *Ph* Fred Koenekamp, John Stephens *Ed* Larry Heath, Marion Rothman *Mus* Mundell Lowe
● Tom Laughlin, Delores Taylor, Clark Howat, Bert Freed, Julie Webb, Ken Tobey (National Student)

Billy Jack appears to be a labor of love in which the plight of the American Indian, are pinpointed.

Produced by National Student Film Corp,

Warners bought picture outright. Leading character is a half-breed named Billy Jack, guardian of the Redman's rights and nemesis of any white who may intrude on these rights. He finds plenty of opportunity to assert himself, what with defending wild horses on the Arizona reservation, wild kids, a school on the reservation, and the actions of residents of a neighboring town violently opposed both to the school and Billy himself.

Screenplay attempts to encompass too many story facets. Result is that the action frequently drags and interest palls as some of the young people in the school, many of them white, spout their philosophy and question the behavior of the whites.

Tom Laughlin, as the invincible defender, is firstrate, handling himself effectively. So, too, does Delores Taylor, a white woman who runs the school. Clark Howat, as the sheriff who understands the Indians' problems, is convincing.

●●●●●●●●●●●●●●●●●●●●●●●●●●●●●●●●●●●

■ **BILLY JACK GOES TO WASHINGTON**

1977, 155 MINS, US ◇

Dir T.C. Frank [=Tom Laughlin] *Prod* Frank Capra Jr *Scr* T.C. Frank, Teresa Cristina [=Delores Taylor] *Ph* Jack Merta *Mus* Elmer Bernstein *Art Dir* Hilyard Brown
● Tom Laughlin, Delores Taylor, E.G. Marshall, Teresa Laughlin, Sam Wanamaker, Lucie Arnaz (Taylor-Laughlin)

Billy Jack Goes to Washington, a remake of the 1939 Frank Capra classic *Mr Smith Goes to Washington*, compensates for its lack of subtlety with an angry, attack on governmental corruption.

The corruption of the Senate in the Capra film is changed here to the issue of nuclear plants.

In the old James Stewart role of the innocent-turned-Senator, Tom Laughlin is fighting against the scheme of political boss Sam Wanamaker and corrupt fellow Senator E.G. Marshall to exploit a planned nuclear plant for their financial gain.

Laughlin, identified with activist groups, takes the same stand against the establishment Stewart did in the original.

By comparison with the brilliance of the Capra version, the pic is much flatter and largely devoid of performing or visual nuances.

●●●●●●●●●●●●●●●●●●●●●●●●●●●●●●●●●●●

■ **BILLY LIAR**

1963, 98 MINS, UK ▽

Dir John Schlesinger *Prod* Joseph Janni *Scr* Keith Waterhouse, Willis Hall *Ph* Denys Coop *Ed* Roger Cherrill *Mus* Richard Rodney Bennett
● Tom Courtenay, Julie Christie, Wilfred Pickles, Mona Washbourne, Finlay Currie, Rodney Bewes (Vic/Anglo-Amalgamated)

Based on a West End hit play by Keith Waterhouse (who wrote the novel) and Willis Hall, *Billy Liar* is an imaginative, fascinating film. It is perhaps unfair to label the film as entirely realistic, since it moves into a world of Walter Mitty-like fantasy, and that is its only weakness. These scenes lack impact.

Billy Liar (Tom Courtenay) is a day-dreaming young man who leads an irresponsible life as a funeral director's clerk. He fiddles the petty cash, he is at war with his parents, he has become involved with two young women who share an engagement ring. Above all, he is an incorrigible liar, dreaming dreams and, whenever possible, retreating into an invented world where he is the dictator of an imagined slice of Ruritania.

Courtenay who took over from Albert Finney in the legit version of *Billy Liar*, has a hefty part and is rarely off the screen. Of the three girls with whom he is involved, Julie Christie is the only one who really understands him. Christie turns in a glowing performance. Helen Fraser and Gwendolyn Watts provide sharply contrasting performances as the other young women in Billy Liar's complicated, muddled existence.

Mona Washbourne, as his dim mother, Wilfred Pickles, playing a hectoring, stupid father, and grandmother Ethel Griffies also lend considerable color.

■ **BILLY ROSE'S JUMBO**

1962, 123 MINS, US ◇ ⊛
Dir Charles Walters *Prod* Joe Pasternak, Martin Melcher *Scr* Sidney Sheldon *Ph* William H. Daniels *Ed* Richard W. Farrell *Art Dir* George W. Davis, Preston Ames
● Doris Day, Stephen Boyd, Jimmy Durante, Martha Raye, Dean Jagger (M-G-M)

One of the final productions ever seen in the old N.Y. Hippodrome, *Jumbo* was a dull book musical of the 1935 season, with a curious mid-Depression tie-in with Texaco Gas. The showmanship of Metro has turned the combo musical and circus into a great film entertainment.

Much of the Rodgers and Hart score for the 1935 legit version has been retained, some of it necessarily being used only as background. The big hits, however – 'Little Girl Blue', 'My Romance', and 'Most Beautiful Girl in the World' – are given fullscale production. 'This Can't Be Love', from Rodgers and Hart's 1938 *Boys From Syracuse* and 'Why Can't I?' from their 1929 *Spring Is Here*, have been added to the score, the latter as a delightful duet by the two femme leads.

In the legit version Durante was Claudius B. Bowers, a circus press agent. He is now the circus-owner, with Doris Day as his daughter, and Martha Raye as his 14-year-awaiting fiancee. Durante plays the role as Durante.

Stephen Boyd, handsome, virile, excellent within the limits of his role, has star billing but his part is strictly in support of his leading lady. It's doubtful that singing is his own, but he handles his musical sequences well, especially the 'What Is a Circus' number where he can do his own lines as a diseur, rather than trying to sing.

Sidney Sheldon's screenplay (he receives full credit although report has it that several scripters have had a go at it) retains only the basic circus-boy-meets-circus-girl format of Ben Hecht and Charles MacArthur's original book, with the ending the most important switch. Instead of the originally-conceived merger of the two circuses then the wedding of the boy and girl, Dean Jagger's villainy drives Boyd into leaving, with Jumbo rejoining Day, Durante and Martha Raye.

■ **BILLY TWO HATS**

1973, 80 MINS, US ◇ ⊛
Dir Ted Kotcheff *Prod* Norman Jewison, Patrick Palmer *Scr* Alan Sharp *Ph* Brian West *Mus* John Scott *Art Dir* Tony Pratt
● Gregory Peck, Desi Arnaz Jr, Jack Warden, Sian Barbara Allen, David Huddleston, John Pearce (Algonquin)

This is a fresh, different oater (the first filmed in Israel) that opens with violence and contains some throughout but never lingers lovingly on mayhem and gore.

A Scot and a young half-Indian (Billy Two Hats, because his white father was an important man) commit a robbery with an unintended murder that nets them only $420. They get away, but the far-off Scot is shot in the leg with a buffalo gun. The lad makes a rough stretcher and hauls him behind his horse. They stop at the home of an old rancher with a young wife he'd bought for $100 in St. Louis.

Gregory Peck, almost unrecognizable

behind a broad Highland brogue and a bushy beard, is splendid. Desi Arnaz Jr as the 'breed' treated with contempt by almost everyone, is okay and shows promise.

■ **BILOXI BLUES**

1988, 106 MINS, US ◇ ⊛
Dir Mike Nichols *Prod* Ray Stark *Scr* Neil Simon *Ph* Bill Butler *Ed* Sam O'Steen *Mus* Georges Delerue *Art Dir* Paul Sylbert
● Matthew Broderick, Christopher Walken, Matt Mulhern, Corey Parker, Markus Flanagan (Rastar/Universal)

Biloxi Blues is an agreeable but hardly inspired film version of Neil Simon's second installment of his autobiographical trilogy, which bowed during the 1984–85 season. Even with high-powered talents Mike Nichols and Matthew Broderick aboard, World War II barracks comedy provokes just mild laughs and smiles rather than the guffaws Simon's work often elicits in the theater.

Film is narrated from an adult perspective by Simon's alter ego, Eugene Morris Jerome (Broderick), an aspiring writer called up for service in the waning months of the war.

With 10 weeks of boot camp ahead of them, it's not at all sure that Eugene and his cohorts will ever see action, but that doesn't prevent basic training from being a living hell relieved only by an excursion into town to party and look for ladies.

Playing a character perched precisely on the point between adolescence and manhood, Broderick is enjoyable all the way.

Penelope Ann Miller is adorable as the girl who inspires love at first sight in Eugene at a dance, while the most intriguing performance comes from Christopher Walken as the weird sergeant.

■ **BINGO LONG TRAVELING ALL-STARS AND MOTOR KINGS, THE**

1976, 110 MINS, US ◇
Dir John Badham *Prod* Rob Cohen *Scr* Hal Barwood, Matthew Robbins *Ph* Bill Butler *Ed* David Rawlins *Mus* William Goldstein *Art Dir* Lawrence G. Paull
● Billy Dee Williams, James Earl Jones, Richard Pryor, Rico Dawson, Sam 'Birmingham' Brison, Jophery Brown (Motown/Pan-Arts)

Billy Dee Williams and James Earl Jones are superb as leaders of a barnstorming black baseball team circa 1939. Based on a William Brashler novel, the script is an adroit mix of broad comedy and credible dramatic conflict.

Fed up with the hard-nosed ways of team owner Ted Ross, Williams quits a team in the old Negro (remember the film's period) baseball league. Shut out of the league, and not yet admitted to mainstream sports, the slap-happy crew discovers success by combining top performance with farce.

But Ross's goons (Ken Force and Carl Gordon) eventually get the upper hand.

Among the standout featured players is Richard Pryor, shifting amusingly from Cuban to Indian heritages as a way to break the black barrier.

■ **BIRD**

1988, 161 MINS, US ◇ ⊛
Dir Clint Eastwood *Prod* Clint Eastwood *Scr* Joel Oliansky *Ph* Jack N. Green *Ed* Joel Cox *Mus* Lennie Niehaus *Art Dir* Edward C. Carfagno
● Forest Whitaker, Diane Venora, Michael Zelniker, Samuel E. Wright, Keith David (Malpaso/Warner)

In taking on a biopic of late jazz great Charlie Parker, Clint Eastwood has had to chart bold new territory for himself as a director, and he has pulled it off in most impressive fashion.

Sensitively acted, beautifully planned visu-

ally and dynamite musically, this is a dramatic telling of the troubled life of a revolutionary artist.

That Parker (Forest Whitaker), who died in 1955 at 34, was the greatest sax man of them all is virtually undisputed, but he also lived a messy, complicated life, mixing drug addiction and a multitude of women with an ongoing attempt at a home life with his wife Chan (Diane Venora) and their two children.

Joel Oliansky's big-framed script, originally written for Richard Pryor at Columbia some years earlier jumps around considerably at the beginning, skipping strikingly from Parker's childhood to a suicide attempt in 1954, then to some other key incidents.

Naturally, the prolific artist's music provides the continuing thread for the film, and jazzman Lennie Niehaus does a sensational job in blending Bird's actual sax solos with fresh backups by contemporary musicians.

Whitaker makes an imposing, likable, very hip genius, with an especially memorable death scene. Venora is so riveting that her occasional long absences from the story are sorely missed. The one person who could really understand Bird is presented as a feisty woman of great character, awareness and strength.

■ **BIRD ON A WIRE**

1990, 110 MINS, US ◇ ⊛
Dir John Badham *Prod* Rob Cohen *Scr* David Seltzer, Louis Venosta, Eric Lerner *Ph* Robert Primes *Ed* Frank Morriss, Dallas Puett *Mus* Hans Zimmer *Art Dir* Philip Harrison
● Mel Gibson, Goldie Hawn, David Carradine, Bill Duke, Joan Severance, Stephen Tobolowsky (Badham-Cohen/Interscope)

Frank Capra's *It Happened One Night* established the format, but John Badham is stuck with a terrible script on this 1990s version. Only the chemistry of Goldie Hawn and Mel Gibson makes the film watchable.

Gibson plays a shnook who's been hiding out for 15 years under an FBI witness relocation program. He gave testimony on a drug deal and the man he fingered (David Carradine) is just out of prison. Contrived and thoroughly unconvincing plot cog has Gibson discovered incognito by old flame Hawn at the Detroit gas station where he works just as Carradine and partner Duke catch up with him. Resulting shootout throws Hawn and Gibson together on the lam for the rest of the pic.

Rekindling of duo's romance is best thing about the repetitive chase format, set in numerous US locations but shot almost entirely in British Columbia. Main kudos goes to British designer Philip Harrison, who's allowed to run hog wild in a largescale climax set at a zoo exhibit depicting a Brazilian rain forest.

■ **BIRDMAN OF ALCATRAZ**

1962, 147 MINS, US
Dir John Frankenheimer *Prod* Stuart Millar, Guy Trosper *Scr* Guy Trosper *Ph* Burnett Guffey *Ed* Edward Mann *Mus* Elmer Bernstein *Art Dir* Ferdie Carrere
● Burt Lancaster, Karl Malden, Thelma Ritter, Neville Brand, Telly Savalas, Edmond O'Brien (United Artists/Harold Hecht)

Birdman of Alcatraz is not really a prison picture in the traditional and accepted sense of the term. *Birdman* reverses the formula and brings a new breadth and depth to the form. In telling, with reasonable objectivity but understandably deep compassion the true story of Robert Stroud, it achieves a human dimension way beyond its predecessors.

Trosper's penetrating and affecting screenplay, based on the book by Thomas E. Gad-

57

dis, delicately and artfully sketches the 53-year imprisonment of the 72-year-old 'Birdman', Stroud, illustrating the highlights and lowlights of that terrible, yet miraculously ennobling span. The screenplay's, and the film's only real flaw is its dismissal of Stroud's background, leaving the audience to mull over psychological ramifications and expositional data by and large denied it.

Lancaster gives a superbly natural, unaffected performance – one in which nobility and indestrucibility can be seen cumulatively developing and shining from within through a weary exterior eroded by the deep scars of time and enforced privacy in a 'prison within a prison'. His running clash with the narrow-minded and vengeful warden Shoemaker is a highlight of the film, consummating in a powerful scene depicting their opposing views on penology. Karl Malden is excellent as the warden.

Four distinguished top supporting performances light up the picture. They are those of Telly Savalas as a fellow inmate and bird-keeper, Thelma Ritter (in a change of pace from her customary characterization) as Stroud's mother (whose seemingly unselfish devotion to the cause of her son ultimately grows suspect), Neville Brand as an understanding guard, and Betty Field as the woman who married Stroud in prison, then reluctantly drifts away at his realistic request. Edmond O'Brien narrates and plays the author.

....

■ **BIRDS, THE**

1963, 120 MINS, US ◇ ⓥ

Dir Alfred Hitchcock *Prod* Alfred Hitchcock *Scr* Evan Hunter *Ph* Robert Burks *Ed* George Tomasini *Art Dir* Robert Boyle

● Rod Taylor, Tippi Hedren, Jessica Tandy, Suzanne Pleshette, Veronica Cartwright (Universal)

Beneath all of this elaborate featherbedlam lies a Hitch cock-and-bull story that's essentially a fowl ball.

The premise is fascinating. The idea of billions of bird-brains refusing to eat crow any longer and adopting the hunt-and-peck system, with homo sapiens as their ornithological target, is fraught with potential. Cinematically, Hitchcock & Co have done a masterful job of meeting this formidable challenge. But dramatically, *The Birds* is little more than a shocker-for shock's-sake. It is a parody of Hitchcock by Hitchcock.

Evan Hunter's screenplay, from Daphne du Maurier's story, has it that a colony of our feathered 'friends' over California's Bodega Bay (it's never clear how far-reaching this avian mafia extends) suddenly decides, for no apparent reason other than just plain orneriness, to swoop down en masse on the human population, beaks first. These bird raids are captivatingly bizarre and terrifying.

Where the scenario and picture slip is in the sphere of the human element. An unnecessary elaborate romantic plot has been cooked up and then left suspended. It involves a young bachelor attorney (Rod Taylor), his sister (Veronica Cartwright), their mother (Jessica Tandy) whose dread of loneliness manifests itself in possessiveness, and a plucky, mysterious playgirl (Tippi Hedren) whose arrival from San Francisco with a pair of caged lovebirds for Taylor coincides with the outbreak of avian hostility.

Aside from the birds, the film belongs to Hedren, who makes an auspicious screen bow. She virtually has to carry the picture alone for the first 45-minute stretch, prior to the advent of the first wave of organized attackers from the sky.

Of the others, Tandy, a first-class actress, makes the most vivid impression. Taylor emotes with strength and attractiveness.

Suzanne Pleshette is stuck with a character that is poorly defined.

....

■ **BIRDY**

1984, 120 MINS, US ◇ ⓥ

Dir Alan Parker *Prod* Alan Marshall *Scr* Sandy Kroopf, Jack Behr *Ph* Michael Seresin *Ed* Gerry Hambling *Mus* Peter Gabriel *Art Dir* Geoffrey Kirkland

● Matthew Modine, Nicolas Cage, John Harkins, Sandy Baron, Karen Young, George Buck (Tri-Star)

Belying the lightheartedness of its title, *Birdy* is a heavy adult drama about best friends and the after-effects of war, but it takes too long to live up to its ambitious premise.

Matthew Modine stars in the adaptation of William Wharton's novel as the title character who had been missing in action and now, psychologically ill and institutionalized, spends much of his time naked, curled up in bird-like positions and speaking to no one.

These posturings stem from a childhood affinity to birds which he shared to a significant degree with Nicolas Cage, who himself is banged up from the fighting, but is brought in to try to communicate with his boyhood pal.

Alan Parker's flashback direction ultimately serves to disjoint *Birdy*.

....

■ **BIRTH OF A NATION, THE**

1915, 187 MINS, US ⊗

Dir D.W. Griffith *Prod* D.W. Griffith, Harry E. Aitken *Scr* D.W.Griffith, Frank E. Woods *Ph* Billy Bitzer *Ed* James E. Smith *Mus* Joseph Carl Breil

● Henry B. Walthall, Miriam Cooper, Mae Marsh, Lillian Gish, Donald Crisp, Raoul Walsh (Epoch)

The Birth of a Nation is the main title David Wark Griffith gave to his version of Thomas Dixon's story of the South, *The Clansman*.It received its first New York public presentation in the Liberty theatre, New York, 3 March. The daily newspaper reviewers pronounced it as the last word in picture making.

The story involves: the Camerons of the south and the Stonemans of the north and Silas Lynch, the mulatto Lieutenant-Governor; the opening and finish of the Civil War; the scenes attendant upon the assassination of Abraham Lincoln; the period of carpet-bagging days and union reconstruction following Lee's surrender; and the terrorizing of the southern whites by the newly freed blacks and the rise of the Ku Klux Klan. All these including some wonderfully well staged battle scenes taken at night are realistically, graphically and most superbly depicted by the camera.

Griffith took his time. Thousands of feet of celluloid were used and for some six months or so he and his co-directors worked day and night to shape the story into a thrilling, dramatic wordless play. The battle scenes are wonderfully conceived, the departure of the soldiers splendidly arranged, and the death of the famous martyred president deftly and ably handled. Henry Walthall makes a manly, straightforward character of the 'Little Colonel' and handles his big scenes most effectively. Mae Marsh as the pet sister does some remarkable work as the little girl who loves the south and loves her brother. Ralph Lewis is splendid as the leader of the House who helps Silas Lynch rise to power. George Siegmann gets all there can be gotten out of the despicable character of Lynch. Walter Long makes Gus, the renegade negro, a hated, much despised type, his acting and makeup being complete.

The Birth of a Nation is said to have cost $300,000.

....

■ **BIRTHDAY PARTY, THE**

1968, 123 MINS, UK ◇

Dir William Friedkin *Prod* Max Rosenberg, Milton Subotsky *Scr* Harold Pinter *Ph* Denys Coop *Ed* Tony Gibbs

● Robert Shaw, Patrick McGee, Dandy Nichols, Sydney Tafler (Continental/Palomar)

Harold Pinter's comedy of menace has been transfered to the screen as an intellectual exercise in verbal gymnastics. Its study of unreality at a dingy British seaside resort is geared for thoughtful interpretation by alert audiences.

Robert Shaw is the pivotal force in *The Birthday Party*. He is the frightened lost soul, put upon as humanity's non-conformist. It appears, and Shaw is least sure of all, that prior to vegetating the past year at Dandy Nichols' boarding-house he may have been a piano player and a deserting member of a criminal organization.

Sydney Tafler and cohort Patrick McGee are the organization men sent to get Shaw.

On these bones, Pinter fleshes out his philosophy of the complex fictions people employ. The completed film is thus an elaboration of the images of reality.

Tafler milks the role for laughs on whatever intellectual level, and comes off quite well.

Director William Friedkin has obvious respect for Pinter's written word and left the film an observation on abstract ideas.

....

■ **BISHOP'S WIFE, THE**

1947, 106 MINS, US ⓥ

Dir Henry Koster *Prod* Samuel Goldwyn *Scr* Robert E. Sherwood, Leonard Bercovici *Ph* Gregg Toland *Ed* Monica Collingwood *Mus* Hugo Friedhofer *Art Dir* George Jenkins, Perry Ferguson

● Cary Grant, Loretta Young, David Niven, Gladys Cooper, Elsa Lanchester (RKO)

While a fantasy, there are no fantastic heavenly manifestations. There's a humanness about the characters, even the angel, that beguiles full attention. Henry Koster's sympathetic direction deftly gets over the warm humor supplied by the script, taken from Robert Nathan's novel of the same title.

Cary Grant is the angel of the piece and has never appeared to greater advantage. Role, with the exception of a minor miracle or two, is potently pointed to indicate character could have been a flesh-and-blood person, a factor that embellishes sense of reality as the angel sets about answering the troubled prayers of Episcopalian bishop (David Niven).

Plot, essentially, deals with Grant's assignment to make people act like human beings. In great need of his help is Niven, a young bishop who has lost the common touch and marital happiness because of his dream of erecting a massive cathedral.

Loretta Young gives a moving performance as the wife whose life is touched by an angel without her knowledge of his heavenly origin. Niven's cleric character is played straight but his anxieties and jealousy loosen much of the warm humor gracing the plot.

Gregg Toland's camera work and the music score by Hugo Friedhofer, directed by Emil Newman, are ace credits among the many expert contributions.

☐ 1947: Best Picture (Nomination)

....

■ **BITCH, THE**

1979, 90 MINS, UK ◇ ⓥ

Dir Gerry O'Hara *Prod* John Quested *Scr* Gerry O'Hara *Ph* Denis Lewiston *Art Dir* Malcolm Middleton

● Joan Collins, Michael Coby, Kenneth Haigh, Ian Hendry, Carolyn Seymour, Sue Lloyd (Brent Walker)

The Bitch offers more mock orgasm than plot

B

as it oscillates between the disco floor and the sack – or the pool, shower, or wherever a couple can couple. Two lesbos, at one point, are glimpsed pawing each other in a sauna.

Not to mince about, the production, scripted and feverishly directed by Gerry O'Hara, is corny and coarse, but at least mercifully brief at 90 minutes.

Between all the sex and sybaritic palaver, there's some nuisance plotting involving Michael Coby as a debonair hustler in trouble with the mob.

Pic's ending, ostensibly ironic, only seems confusing as to who done what to whom. But for disco freaks, there's plenty of their kind of action. Joan Collins does her spoiled nympho rich girl turn with assurance.

••••••••••••••••••••••••••••••

■ **BITE THE BULLET**

1975, 131 MINS, US ◇

Dir Richard Brooks *Prod* Richard Brooks *Scr* Richard Brooks *Ph* Harry Stradling Jr *Ed* George Granville *Mus* Alex North *Art Dir* Robert Boyle

● Gene Hackman, Candice Bergen, James Coburn, Ben Johnson, Ian Bannen, Jan-Michael Vincent (Columbia)

Bite the Bullet is an excellent, literate action drama probing the diverse motivations of participants in an endurance horse race. The contestants include Gene Hackman and James Coburn as ex-San Juan Hill Rough Riders; Candice Bergen as a former resident of Jean Willes frontier pleasure shanty, seeking money to help her imprisoned lover; vagabond Ben Johnson desperately wanting to 'be somebody' for a brief moment in life.

After a leisurely though intriguing buildup, the race begins, and during the daily ordeals of mountain, desert, rain, sun, cold and heat, the pressures and the secrets of the characters emerge plausibly and rationally.

Bergen's ulterior motivation in particular triggers a surprise, pre-climactic turn. Effective use of slow-motion in the final scene lends suspense to the outcome as the two surviving riders inch towards the ribbon.

••••••••••••••••••••••••••••••

■ **BITTER HARVEST**

1963, 96 MINS, UK ◇

Dir Peter Graham Scott *Prod* Albert Fennell *Scr* Ted Willis *Ph* Ernest Steward *Ed* Russell Lloyd *Mus* Laurie Johnson *Art Dir* Alex Vetchinsky

● Janet Munro, John Stride, Anne Cunningham, Alan Badel, Barbara Ferris (Wintle-Parkyn)

The story of the country innocent who gets caught up in the dizzy pitfalls of London nightlife is taken from a Patrick Hamilton novel, *The Street Has a Thousand Skies*. Surprising thing is that scripter Ted Willis has not come up with any surprises or twist, and director Peter Graham Scott has been no help in this matter, either. Result is a conventional yarn. Munro is given opportunities to portray innocence, gaiety, cupidity, depression, vanity, fear, cunning, tenderness, harshness, wonder and anger. All the emotions are fleeting but the star helps to mould them into a well-drawn picture of an innocent who learns quickly.

John Stride is solid, charming and resourceful as the infatuated bartender. Alan Badel makes a brief but telling contribution as a steely, unscrupulous theatre boss. There is also a beautifully underplayed performance by Anne Cunningham as a barmaid who has long been secretly in love with Stride.

••••••••••••••••••••••••••••••

■ **BITTER SWEET**

1933, 76 MINS, UK

Dir Herbert Wilcox *Prod* Herbert Wilcox *Scr* Herbert Wilcox, Lydia Hayward, Monckton Hoffe *Ph* F. A. Young *Mus* Noel Coward *Art Dir* L. P. Williams

● Anna Neagle, Fernand Gravet, Esme Percy, Clifford Heatherly, Ivy St Helier, Miles Mander (British & Dominions/United Artists)

Direction hampers Anna Neagle, a stunning blonde of compelling grace, but here restricted to an acting style. She is permitted no emotional range and her performance is flavorless except that she does manage to suggest that if she broke loose she might start something.

Fernand Gravet is young, dark and a vital type, a vigorous personality. Chief support role here doesn't bring out his engaging personality in full.

Clifford Heatherly does the Vienna cafe proprietor, Herr Schlick, contributing a splendidly flexible performance with a capital knack of legitimate comedy. Suggests something of the Charles Laughton technique in subtle villainy. Last of the quartet is Ivy St Helier, obviously French, who plays the soubrette role to the hilt.

Continuity takes many liberties with the operetta script [by Noel Coward], usually without improving it. Story progress is jerky. Whole episode of the singer's second marriage is omitted, which is all right for economy of narrative though it does fog up the finish, which leaves the heroine rather indefinite. Love scenes are stretched out to great lengths.

Coward's score, hailed at the time of the stage presentation as brilliant, is a part of the picture and helps its class tone. The leads handle several numbers agreeably.

••••••••••••••••••••••••••••••

■ **BITTER TEA OF GENERAL YEN, THE**

1933, 87 MINS, US

Dir Frank Capra *Prod* Frank Capra *Scr* Edward Paramore *Ph* Joseph Walker *Ed* Edward Curtis *Mus* W. Frank Harling

● Barbara Stanwyck, Nils Asther, Gavin Gordon, Toshia Mori, Walter Connolly (Columbia)

This picture is a queer story [from a novel by Grace Zaring Stone] of a romance in China between a Chinese and a white woman. A young New England girl arrives in Shanghai to join her sweetheart missionary. They are to be married. China's unceasing civil wars are made the background of the girl's experiences from that point.

The Chinese war lord around whom the plot is built is a curious and rather questionable human composition of a poet, philosopher and bandit. He speaks rather fluent English and essays somewhat dainty American mannerisms, especially in manipulating a handkerchief. Nils Asther plays the role.

After the Chinese general goes on the make for the white girl the picture goes blah. That's before the film is even half way.

Barbara Stanwyck is the white girl. Pleasant enough and for the first half where she repulses the Chinaman gathers some audience sympathy. Subsequently, where the photography attempts to simulate that the girl, in her dreams, loves the Chinese, the role fails her. Besides which, as a New England missionary type, Stanwyck does not fit.

A fine actor from the legit, Walter Connolly takes the acting honors as the adventurous American financial advisor of General Yen. A kind of a tramp philosopher which Connolly does admirably.

••••••••••••••••••••••••••••••

■ **BITTER VICTORY**

1958, 97 MINS, FRANCE/US

Dir Nicholas Ray *Prod* Paul Graetz *Scr* Nicholas Ray, Gavin Lambert, Rene Hardy *Ph* Michel Kelber *Ed* Leonide Azar *Mus* Maurice Le Roux *Art Dir* Jean d'Eaubonne

● Curt Jurgens, Richard Burton, Ruth Roman, Raymond Pellegrin (Transcontinental)

Rene Hardy's novel has been translated for the screen into a literary, hard-hitting screenplay which almost always manages to overcome some of the incongruities of the original story line. This sets up a deadly struggle between two British Army officers during the Second World War African campaign.

Conflict between Capt Leith and Major Brand derives from fact that Leith knows of Brand's basic cowardice in action, and also from jealousy over Brand's wife, with whom Leith has had an affair. Returning from a dangerous mission in German-held Benghazi, Brand tries twice indirectly to bring about Leith's death, once by leaving him behind to guard two wounded Germans, again by deliberately letting a scorpion bite his rival.

Script is basically flawed by the unclearly delineated key character of the major – and Curt Jurgens' competent, straightforward performance is less successful because of it. Fine thesping by Richard Burton leads a series of top performances by other members of large cast.

••••••••••••••••••••••••••••••

■ **BLACK ARROW, THE**

1948, 76 MINS, US ⓥ

Dir Gordon M. Douglas *Prod* Edward Small *Scr* Richard Schayer, David P. Sheppard, Thomas Seller *Ph* Charles Lawton *Ed* Jerome Thoms *Mus* Paul Sawtell *Art Dir* Stephen Goosson; A. Leslie Thomas

● Louis Hayward, Janet Blair, George Macready, Edgar Buchanan (Columbia)

Using Robert Louis Stevenson's *The Black Arrow* for the takeoff, Columbia has made an action-filled cloak-and-dagger romance. The picture is virtually a western of lethal combat, hard riding, intrigue and deep-dyed villainy – all in when-knighthood-was-in-flower terms. Maybe it isn't exactly art, but it is good entertainment.

The romantic angle has been accented heavily in the translation from Stevenson's dispassionate narrative. The red-blooded hero returns from the 30 Years War to learn that his uncle has murdered his father to seize the House of York and has had the neighboring Lord of the House of Lancaster executed for the crime. And he understandably tumbles hard for the nifty Lancaster daughter.

••••••••••••••••••••••••••••••

■ **BLACK BELT JONES**

1974, 85 MINS, US ◇ ⓥ

Dir Robert Clouse *Prod* Fred Weintraub, Paul Heller *Scr* Oscar Williams *Ph* Kent Wakeford *Ed* Michael Kahn *Mus* Luchi De Jesus, Dennis Coffy

● Jim Kelly, Gloria Hendry, Scatman Crothers, Alan Weeks, Eric Laneuville, Andre Phillipe (Warner)

Black Belt Jones reteams the *Enter the Dragon* producing team and director Robert Clouse, also Jim Kelly, this time heading the cast. The story strand pits a group of graceful black martial arts students against some cliche white gangsters, neither side taking things seriously.

Kelly, between the thousands of body blows given and taken, has time for Gloria Hendry, equally adept at physical jousting as providing a good romantic interest. She's the daughter of Scatman Crothers, whose karate studio is on land eyed for a building project by Malik Carter and his own crime superior (Andre Phillipe), a clumsy godfather-type.

The action sequences, coordinated by Robert Wall, are standard steps in the choreography of martial arts.

••••••••••••••••••••••••••••••

■ **BLACK BIRD, THE**

1926, 76 MINS, US ⊗

Dir Tod Browning *Scr* Tod Browning, Waldemar Young *Ph* Percy Hilburn *Ed* Errol Taggart *Art Dir* Cedric Gibbons, Arnold Gillespie

59

● Lon Chaney, Renee Adoree, Owen Moore, Doris Lloyd (MGM)

In *The Black Bird* Lon Chaney plays a dual role, that of a crook and of his brother, a Limehouse missionary. Although the reverend fellow is crippled up plenty, the curse is taken off by one shot showing the crook throwing his arm and leg out of joint and then assuming the role of the man whom the world thought to be his brother. That's the basis of the story, for the crook falls in love with a music hall performer, while a flashier crook from the West End also goes for the same girl.

It's a good melodrama, excellently produced. Chaney handles his two parts well and Waldemar Young's scenario has been so constructed that the rather unique dual role is plausible at all times.

■ BLACK BIRD, THE

1975, 98 MINS, US ◇
Dir David Giler *Prod* Michael Levee *Scr* David Giler *Ph* Phil Lathrop *Ed* Margaret Booth, Walter Thompson, Lou Lombardo *Mus* Jerry Fielding *Art Dir* Harry Horner
● George Segal, Stephane Andran, Lionel Stander, Lee Patrick, Elisha Cook Jr, Felix Silla (Columbia/Rastar)

This satirical contemporary update of Dashiell Hammett's novel *The Maltese Falcon* emerges as fair whimsy.

Basis of the plot [from a story by Don M. Mankiewitz and Gordon Cotler] is that George Segal, as Sam Spade's son, has inherited the detective agency, still in its old location, but now a rundown black neighborhood. Lee Patrick, in a delightful recasting as Effie, the secretary, hangs in there, partly because she hasn't been paid in years, and despite an animosity towards Segal. The search for the elusive Maltese Falcon is reinstated, bringing in all sorts of mysterious characters.

The general tenor of the film shows a sentimental empathy for the original material with no heartless put-downs marring the work. There are lots of smiles, many chuckles, and a few strong laughs.

■ BLACKBOARD JUNGLE, THE

1955, 100 MINS, US ▼
Dir Richard Brooks *Prod* Pandro S. Berman *Scr* Richard Brooks *Ph* Russell Harlan *Ed* Ferris Webster *Mus* Charles Wolcott
● Glenn Ford, Anne Francis, Louis Calhern, Vic Morrow, Sidney Poitier, Margaret Hayes (M-G-M)

Director-scripter Richard Brooks, working from novel by Evan Hunter, has fashioned an angry picture that flares out in moral and physical rage at mental slovenliness, be it juvenile, mature, or in the pattern of society acceptance of things as they are because no one troubles to devise a better way.

The main issue is the juvenile bum who terrorizes schoolrooms and teachers.

The strong among the evil element, here represented by Vic Morrow, is already beyond any reform. The good, represented by Sidney Poitier, has had no stimulus to awaken his leadership abilities because he is a Negro. Glenn Ford, Morrow and Poitier are so real in their performances under the probing direction by Brooks that the picture alternatingly has the viewer pleading, indignant and frightened before the conclusion.

■ BLACK CAT, THE

1934, 65 MINS, US
Dir Edgar G. Ulmer *Prod* Carl Laemmle Jr *Scr* Peter Ruric *Ph* Jack Mescal *Mus* Heinz Roemheld *Art Dir* Charles D. Hall
● Boris Karloff, Bela Lugosi, David Manners, Julie Bishop, Andy Devine, John Carradine (Universal)

Story is confused and confusing, and while with the aid of heavily-shadowed lighting and mausoleum-like architecture, a certain eeriness has been achieved, it's all a poor imitation of things seen before.

Boris Karloff occupies a spooky manor built over the ruins of a world war fort where 10,000 soldiers drenched the valley in blood in a terrible military defeat caused by Karloff's treachery. That is told but not shown. Bela Lugosi is a batty doctor just out of a cruel jail in which he spent 15 years. Also due to Karloff's unworthy character.

Clash of the two eyebrow-squinting nuts involves an American bridal couple temporarily caught in the manor. It is the playful notion of nasty Karloff to make the bride Exhibit A in a devil cult of which he is the head, and it is the revenge of Lugosi to torture his enemy by skinning him alive.

Corpses standing upright in glass cases and operating table murders are other tricks which the story uses. Edgar Allan Poe's name is used for publicity purposes. All that is used is the title which belongs to a Poe short story.

Karloff and Lugosi are sufficiently sinister and convincingly demented.

■ BLACK CAULDRON, THE

1985, 80 MINS, US ◇ ▼
Dir Ted Berman, Richard Rich *Prod* Joe Hale *Scr* David Jonas, Vance Gerry, Ted Berman, Richard Rich, Al Wilson, Roy Morita, Peter Young, Art Stevens, Joe Hale, Rosemary Anne Sisson, Roy Edward Disney *Ed* James Melton, Kim Koford, Armetta Jackson *Mus* Elmer Bernstein
● (Walt Disney)

By any hard measure, the $25 million animated *Cauldron* is not very original. The characters, though cute and cuddly and sweet and mean and ugly and simply awful, don't really have much to do that would remain of interest to any but the youngest minds.

Storyline [based on *The Chronicles of Prydain* series by Lloyd Alexander] is fairly stock sword-and-sorcery, with a band of likable youngsters, animals and creatures forced to tackle an evil mob of monsters to keep them from using a magic cauldron to raise an army of the dead. No need to guess who wins. [Prolog is narrated by John Huston.]

■ BLACK CHRISTMAS

1974, 93 MINS, CANADA ◇ ▼
Dir Bob Clark *Prod* Bob Clark, Gerry Arbeid *Scr* Roy Moore *Ph* Reg Morris *Ed* Stan Cole *Mus* Carl Zittrer *Art Dir* Karen Bromley
● Olivia Hussey, Keir Dullea, Margot Kidder, Andrea Martin, John Saxon, Marian Waldman (August)

Black Christmas, a bloody, senseless kill-for-kicks feature, exploits unnecessary violence in a university sorority house operated by an implausibly alcoholic ex-hoofer. Its slow-paced, murky tale involves an obscene telephone caller who apparently delights in killing the girls off one by one, even the hapless house-mother.

The plot has the usual abundant cliches: a drunken girl student, played by Margot Kidder, who goes to her death much too late in the film; a house-mother, who finds her hidden whiskey bottles after much swearing; a 'nice' girl, who finds herself pregnant much to the horror of her psycho piano student boy friend; and stock dumb policemen.

Only Marian Waldman as the house-mother comes across with any life.

■ BLACK HOLE, THE

1979, 97 MINS, US ◇
Dir Gary Nelson *Prod* Ron Miller *Scr* Jeb Rosebrook, Gerry Day *Ph* Frank Phillips *Ed* Gregg McLaughlin *Mus* John Barry *Art Dir* Peter Ellenshaw

● Maximilian Schell, Anthony Perkins, Robert Forster, Joseph Bottoms, Yvette Mimieux, Ernest Borgnine (Walt Disney)

The black hole itself gets short shrift in the screenplay, based on a story by Jeb Rosebrook, Bob Barbash and Richard Landau. Most of the pic is devoted to setting up the story of mad scientist Maximilian Schell, poised on the brink of his voyage to the unknown. An exploration ship staffed by Robert Forster, Anthony Perkins, Joseph Bottoms, Yvette Mimieux and Ernest Borgnine, stumbles on both Schell and the nearby black hole, with unpredictable results.

What ensues is sometimes talky but never dull. Director Gary Nelson's pacing and visual sense are right on target.

In typical Disney fashion, the most attractive and sympathetic characters are not human at all. George F. McGinnis has constructed a bevy of robots that establish a mechanical world all their own.

■ BLACK JACK

1979, 106 MINS, UK ◇
Dir Kenneth Loach *Prod* Tony Garnett *Scr* Kenneth Loach *Ph* Chris Menges *Ed* Bill Shapter *Mus* Bob Pegg *Art Dir* Martin Johnson
● Jean Franval, Stephen Hirst, Louise Cooper, Andrew Bennett (Kestrel Films)

Basically an adventure yarn set in northern England in 1750, this collaboration of writer-director Kenneth Loach and producer Tony Garnett add first rate period recreation (more than could have been expected from the $1 million budget) to their already-established talents for sharp, telling realism.

Loach's screenplay, adapted from Leon Garfield's same-title novel, suffers from a meandering plotline, but that hardly matters as it is continuously engrossing, and enlivened with a wry wit.

After miraculously surviving a hanging, Black Jack, a gigantic Frenchman with few words of English, endearingly played by Jean Franval, takes along a young boy (Stephen Hirst) with him on his escape, to 'speak for him.' The main plot concerns a girl (Louise Cooper) they encounter by chance, whose irrational behavior has caused her wealthy parents to commit her to a privately run madhouse for fear of possible scandal.

■ BLACKMAIL

1929, 88 MINS, UK ▼
Dir Alfred Hitchcock *Prod* John Maxwell *Scr* Alfred Hitchcock, Ben W. Levy, Charles Bennett *Ph* Jack Cox *Ed* Emile de Ruelle *Mus* Hubert Bath, Henry Stafford (arr) *Art Dir* Wilfred C. Arnold, Norman Arnold
● Anny Ondra, Sara Allgood, Charles Paton, Donald Calthrop, John Longden, Cyril Ritchard (British International)

Blackmail is most draggy. It has no speed or pace and very little suspense. Everything's open-face. It's a story [from the play by Charles Bennett] that has been told in different disguises – the story of a girl who kills a man trying to assault her.

The girl, Anny Ondra, leaves a very lively scene in one of the Lyons feederies after flirting with a stranger and airing her steady, a regular Scotland Yard dick, to join the other half of the flirtation. The other half lives near the cigar store of her father, and asks the girl upstairs to see his studio, he being an artist. She foolishly assents, and then follows the jam.

In performance the standout is Donald Calthrop as the rat crook. He looks it. Ondra is excellent as the girl.

Dialog is ordinary but sufficient. Camerawork rather well, especially on the British Museum [in the chase finale] and the eating house scenes. A bit of comedy here and there, but not enough to be called relief.

．．．．．．．．．．．．．．．．．．．．．．．．．

■ BLACK MARBLE, THE

1980, 112 MINS, US ◇ Ⓥ

Dir Harold Becker *Prod* Frank Capra Jr *Scr* Joseph Wambaugh *Ph* Owen Roizman *Ed* Maury Winetrobe *Mus* Maurice Jarre *Art Dir* Alfred Sweeney

● Robert Foxworth, Paula Prentiss, Harry Dean Stanton, Barbara Babcock, James Woods (Avco Embassy)

With *The Black Marble*, Joseph Wambaugh [adapting his own novel] at last comes close to presenting police as human, even humorous, beings, capable of balancing remorse, regret and romance without becoming total psychotics.

Transferred out of homicide after too much exposure to a string of child murders, Robert Foxworth is teamed on a burglary detail with Paula Prentiss.

The crime is either terribly serious or impossibly trivial, depending on your love of animals. Barbara Babcock's showdog is kidnapped and she proves superb in the role of a lonely, sex-starved woman with her whole life wrapped up in her schnauzer.

Director Harold Becker is at his best in maneuvering carefully through the minefields of animal worship.

Much of the credit for making the picture work goes to Harry Dean Stanton as the dognapper, driven to his dirty deed by debt.

．．．．．．．．．．．．．．．．．．．．．．．．．

■ BLACK NARCISSUS

1947, 100 MINS, UK ◇ Ⓥ

Dir Michael Powell, Emeric Pressburger *Prod* Michael Powell, Emeric Pressburger *Scr* Michael Powell, Emeric Pressburger *Ph* Jack Cardiff *Ed* Reginald Mills *Mus* Brian Easdale *Art Dir* Alfred Junge

● Deborah Kerr, Sabu, David Farrar, Kathleen Byron, Flora Robson, Jean Simmons (Archers)

Cynics may dub this lavish production *Brief Encounter in the Himalayas* and not without reason. Stripped of most of its finery, the picture [based on the novel by Rumer Godden] resolves itself into the story of two sex-starved women and a man. And since the women are nuns, there can be no happy ending except perhaps in the spiritual sense.

At the invitation of an Indian ruler, five sisters of an Anglo-Catholic order open a school and hospital in a remote Himalayan village. They occupy an ancient palace, once known as 'The House of Women,' built on a ledge 6,000 feet in the air. The nuns find their task overwhelming and Deborah Kerr, as the sister in charge, has to call for help on the cynical British agent, David Farrar, in spite of her instinctive antagonism.

To add to their worries, a native girl in need of a few months cloistering is boarded with the nuns by Farrar. The peace of the convent is further disturbed when the young general heir to the ruler enrolls as a pupil. Materially the work of the convent prospers, but Sister Kerr feels that spiritually most of the nuns are out of harmony. Her thoughts stray back to her girlhood sweetheart in Ireland. Another Sister is obviously thinking too much of Farrar and is taken to task.

Production has gained much through being in color. The production and camerawork atone for minor lapses in the story, Jack Cardiff's photography being outstanding.

The cast has been well chosen, but Kerr gets only occasional opportunities to reveal her talents.

Most effective acting comes from Kathleen Byron who has the picture's plum as the neurotic half-crazed Sister Ruth.

．．．．．．．．．．．．．．．．．．．．．．．．．

■ BLACK ORCHID, THE

1959, 94 MINS, US Ⓥ

Dir Martin Ritt *Prod* Carlo Ponti, Marcello Girosi *Scr* Joseph Stefano *Ph* Robert Burks *Ed* Howard Smith *Mus* Alessandro Cicognini *Art Dir* Hal Pereira, Roland Anderson

● Sophia Loren, Anthony Quinn, Mark Richman (Paramount)

Orchid has a flavor of *Marty*, a touch of *Wild Is the Wind*. The story threads and changing emotions are securely locked in through Martin Ritt's honest direction. Without pushing, he tells an intricately drawn story with a smooth, authoritative hand.

As the widower who falls in love with the pretty widow, Anthony Quinn is excellent, uniting charm with strength. Sophia Loren plays with notable feeling, convincingly portraying the mother, the widow and the bride.

The black orchid literally is a white rose – Rose Bianco – who is the late widow of a man she helped turn to crime to satisfy her own desires. Played by Loren, she mourns her husband and mourns what she has done when a widower (Quinn), with a daughter about to be married, comes along with a joyous manner and serious intentions.

The film technically is excellent, Robert Burks' photography standing out adeptly in black-and-white VistaVision. The musical score by Alessandro Cicognini aptly points up contrasts in the story.

．．．．．．．．．．．．．．．．．．．．．．．．．

■ BLACK RAIN

1989, 126 MINS, US ◇ Ⓥ

Dir Ridley Scott *Prod* Stanley R. Jaffe, Sherry Lansing *Scr* Craig Bolotin, Warren Lewis *Ph* Jan DeBont *Ed* Tom Rolf *Mus* Hans Zimmer *Art Dir* Norris Spencer

● Michael Douglas, Andy Garcia, Ken Takakura, Kate Capshaw, Yusaku Matsuda, John Spencer (Paramount)

Since this is a Ridley Scott film, *Black Rain* is about 90% atmosphere and 10% story. But what atmosphere! This gripping crime thriller about hardboiled NY cop Michael Douglas tracking a yakuza hood in Osaka, Japan, boasts magnificent lensing and powerfully baroque production design.

Douglas is utterly believable as a reckless and scummy homicide detective who takes kickbacks from drug dealers and resorts to the most brutal methods to capture escaped counterfeiter Yusaka Matsuda.

First collaring Matsuda after a shocking outbreak of violence in a NY restaurant, Douglas is sent with him to Osaka, where he promptly loses him to the yakuza and watches helplessly as his partner Andy Garcia is murdered. Coming into conflict with the Japanese police, Douglas turns to the criminal underground to help bring in his prey.

Script fascinatingly depicts the growing influence of Takakura's higher concepts of honour and loyalty on Douglas, who in turn causes some of his expedient lack of morality to rub off on the Japanese police inspector.

．．．．．．．．．．．．．．．．．．．．．．．．．

■ BLACK RAINBOW

1990, 113 MINS, UK ◇ Ⓥ

Dir Mike Hodges *Prod* John Quested, Geoffrey Helman *Scr* Mike Hodges *Ph* Gerry Fisher *Ed* Malcolm Cooke *Mus* John Scott *Art Dir* Voytek

● Rosanna Arquette, Jason Robards, Tom Hulce, Mark Joy, Ron Rosenthal, John Bennes (Goldcrest)

This enjoyable supernatural thriller is set in the fundamentalist society of crumbling industrial towns where folks have a deep-rooted faith in the spiritualist movement. Pic opens with journalist Tom Hulce tracking down traveling clairvoyant Rosanna Arquette to fill in the background to a story he himself was involved in some years before.

During one act Arquette receives a message from a murdered man to pass on to his wife in the audience. Unfortunately he is not dead and his wife gets rather upset. Later that night the man is killed in his home.

Small-town reporter Hulce sets about uncovering the scoop, and follows Arquette and Jason Robards to their next town. There he gets drunk with Robards and sleeps with Arquette, but still doesn't believe her 'gift.' That night she predicts even more deaths, and again her vision comes true.

Arquette is excellent as the strange but seductive Martha. She has an ethereal quality combined with innate sexuality. Robards is in his element as the drunkard father. Hulce is intelligently restrained.

．．．．．．．．．．．．．．．．．．．．．．．．．

■ BLACK ROSE, THE

1950, 120 MINS, US ◇ Ⓥ

Dir Henry Hathaway *Prod* Louis D. Lighton *Scr* Talbot Jennings *Ph* Jack Cardiff *Ed* Manuel Del Campo *Mus* Richard Addinsell

● Tyrone Power, Orson Welles, Cecile Aubry, Jack Hawkins, Michael Rennie, Herbert Lom (20th Century-Fox)

Produced in England and North Africa with frozen currency, and with a supporting British cast, *Rose* is an adaptation of the Thomas Costain bestseller. It is 13th-century drama that seems hardly to have ignored a thing in its plotting.

Black Rose is the story of Saxon revolt against Norman domination, 200 years after the conquest. The central figure in the Saxon fight is Walter of Gurnie (Tyrone Power), the illegitimate son of a Saxon peer.

In a picture of warring, there is only the suggestion of battle. Perhaps one good scene, with some honest-to-goodness cinematic blood-letting, might have done something to increase the tempo of the picture.

Power is credible in the lead role, while Welles underplays effectively the part of Bayan.

．．．．．．．．．．．．．．．．．．．．．．．．．

■ BLACK STALLION, THE

1979, 118 MINS, US ◇ Ⓥ

Dir Carroll Ballard *Prod* Fred Roos, Tom Sternberg *Scr* Melissa Mathison, Jeanne Rosenberg, William D. Wittliff *Ph* Caleb Deschanel *Ed* Robert Dalva *Mus* Carmine Coppola *Art Dir* Aurelio Crugnola, Earl Preston

● Kelly Reno, Mickey Rooney, Teri Garr (United Artists)

The Black Stallion is a perfect gem. Based on Walter Farley's 1941 novel, Carroll Ballard's feature debut is rich in adventure, suspense and mythical elements and marks the prize-winning short-subjects director as a major talent. Ballard's camera eye and powers of sequence conceptualization are manifestly extraordinary.

Opening sees the American boy Alec on a ship with his amiable father. Also on board is 'the Black,' stallion.

After both end up overboard, Alec and the horse find sanctuary on a deserted Mediterranean island, filmed on unusual Sardinian locations. Ensuing half hour, in which the two gradually make contact and establish rapport is pulled off completely without dialog, backed instead by Carmine Coppola's richly complementary score.

．．．．．．．．．．．．．．．．．．．．．．．．．

■ BLACK STALLION RETURNS, THE

1983, 93 MINS, US ◇ Ⓥ

Dir Robert Dalva *Prod* Tom Sternberg, Fred Roos, Doug Claybourne *Scr* Richard Kletter, Jerome Kass *Ph* Carlo Di Palma, Caleb Deschanel *Ed* Paul Hirsch *Mus* Georges Delerue *Art Dir* Aurelio Crugnola

● Kelly Reno, Vincent Spano, Allen Garfield, Woody Strode, Ferdy Mayne, Teri Garr (Zoetrope)

The Black Stallion Returns is little more than a contrived, cornball story that most audiences will find to be an interminable bore. Much of the charm and innocence of the original are absent here as now young teen-hero Kelly Reno follows the unlikeliest of searches through the Sahara Desert for his devoted horse.

A band of supposed 'good guy' Moroccans steal the horse in order to bring him back to his real home in the deserts of nothern Africa (where he will run in a once-every-five-years horse race) much to the chagrin of the 'bad guy' Moroccans who represent a supposedly evil tribe.

Robert Dalva, who edited *The Black Stallion* serves as director here but doesn't manage to convincingly merge the feelings of fantasy and reality that made the first film so charming.

....

■ **BLACK SUNDAY**

1977, 143 MINS, US ◇ ⓥ

Dir John Frankenheimer   *Prod* Robert Evans
Scr Ernest Lehman, Kenneth Ross, Ivan Moffat   *Ph* John A. Alonzo   *Ed* Tom Rolf   *Mus* John Williams
Art Dir Walter Tyler
● Robert Shaw, Bruce Dern, Marthe Keller, Fritz Weaver, Steven Keats, Bekim Fehmiu (Paramount)

John Frankenheimer's film of *Black Sunday* is an intelligent and meticulous depiction of an act of outlandish terrorism – the planned slaughter of the Super Bowl stadium audience.

Strong scripting and performances elevate Robert Evans' handsome production far above the crass exploitation level, which at least mitigates subject matter that can never be completely comfortable on the minds of an audience.

Thomas Harris' novel has been adapted into a well-plotted, well-executed countdown to potential mass disaster. The motivations of stars Robert Shaw, as an Israeli guerrilla, Black September activist Marthe Keller and mentally unbalanced pilot Bruce Dern are handled with unusual dramatic depth which displays the gray areas of real life.

....

■ **BLACK WIDOW**

1987, 103 MINS, US ◇ ⓥ

Dir Bob Rafelson   *Prod* Harold Schneider   *Scr* Ronald Bass   *Ph* Conrad L. Hall   *Ed* John Bloom   *Mus* Peter Rafelson   *Art Dir* Gene Callahan
● Debra Winger, Theresa Russell, Sami Frey, Dennis Hopper, Nicol Williamson (Laurence Mark/Americent/American Entertainment)

Lacking the snap and sharpness that might have made it a firstrate thriller, *Black Widow* instead plays as a moderately interesting tale of one woman's obsession for another's glamorous and criminal lifestyle.

Theresa Russell portrays an icy-hard, beautiful woman who, it quickly becomes clear, makes an exceptionally handsome living by marrying wealthy men, murdering them, then collecting the settlements from the wills.

Pattern would go unnoticed were it not for conscientious, disheveled Justice Dept agent Debra Winger, who thinks she smells a rat and begs permission to pursue the case.

Winger first takes off after her prey for purely professional reasons, but the most intriguing aspect of screenplay is the barely submerged sexual jealousy the overworked government employee feels for the sexy, utterly confident manipulator of sex and lives.

Winger and Russell are both talented and watchable young actresses, so the picture has a lot going for it thanks to their casting alone. At the same time, both play very tense, brittle women rather near the breaking point, so

there is a nervousness and restraint in both performances that harnesses them slightly.

....

■ **BLACK WINDMILL, THE**

1974, 106 MINS, UK ◇ ⓥ

Dir Don Siegel   *Prod* Don Siegel   *Scr* Leigh Vance   *Ph* Ousama Rawi   *Ed* Antony Gibbs   *Mus* Roy Budd   *Art Dir* Peter Murton
● Michael Caine, Donald Pleasence, Delphine Seyrig, Clive Revill, John Vernon, Joss Ackland (Universal)

Don Siegel's filmmaking takes a dip in *The Black Windmill*, a British espionage drama with Michael Caine as an agent whose son has been kidnapped by one of his own spy colleagues. All principal players are well cast, but the production fizzles in its final half-hour because the story premise gets clobbered by clumsy and ineffective resolution and execution.

Clive Egleton's novel, *Seven Days to a Killing*, has been adapted by Leigh Vance. Script sets Caine up well: his superior (Donald Pleasence) hates him anyway, so the kidnapping and later circumstantial evidence suggests Caine himself has arranged the snatch. Janet Suzman, estranged from Caine because of his work, returns to his side. John Vernon and Delphine Seyrig are key figures in the kidnap and concurrent entrapment of Caine.

....

■ **BLACULA**

1972, 92 MINS, US ◇ ⓥ

Dir William Crain   *Prod* Joseph T. Naar   *Scr* Joan Torres, Raymond Koenig   *Ph* John Stevens   *Ed* Allan Jacobs   *Mus* Gene Page   *Art Dir* Walter Herndon
● William Marshall, Vonetta McGee, Denise Nicholas, Thalmus Rasulala, Gordon Pinsent, Charles McCauley (American International)

Count Dracula has a black counterpart. Following a prolog located in Transylvania (where else?), when Count Dracula places the vampire curse upon an African prince and condemns him to the realm of the undead, plot picks up in Los Angeles nearly two centuries later. A pair of interior decorators have purchased all the furnishings of Castle Dracula and shipped them to America, including the locked coffin in which Blacula is resting.

William Marshall portrays title role with a flourish and gets first rate support right down the line: Vonetta McGee, whom he believes to be his reincarnated wife; Thalmus Rasulala, a black doctor who hits upon mystery of the rash of murders in LA; and Gordon Pinsent, homicide lieutenant who learns the hard way that murders are the work of vampires.

....

■ **BLADE RUNNER**

1982, 114 MINS, US ◇ ⓥ

Dir Ridley Scott   *Prod* Michael Deeley   *Scr* Hampton Fancher, David Peoples   *Ph* Jordan Cronenweth   *Ed* Marsha Nakashima   *Mus* Vangelis   *Art Dir* Lawrence G. Paull
● Harrison Ford, Rutger Hauer, Sean Young, Edward James Olmos, M. Emmet Walsh, Daryl Hannah (Warner/Ladd)

Ridley Scott's reported $30 million picture is a stylistically dazzling film noir set 37 years hence in a brilliantly imagined Los Angeles marked by both technological wonders and horrendous squalor.

Basic premise taken from a novel [*Do Androids Dream of Electric Sheep*] by Philip K. Dick provides a strong dramatic hook – replicants, robots designed to supply 'Off World' slave labor, are outlawed on earth. But a few of them have infiltrated LA, and retired enforcer Harrison Ford is recruited to eliminate them before they can do any damage.

One of them, beautiful Sean Young, is an advanced model with implanted memories so

'real' that even she doesn't know she's a replicant until she's tested by Ford.

Unfortunately, Young disappears for long stretches at a time, and at others Ford merely sits morosely around his apartment staring at photographs, which slows up the action.

Dramatically, film is virtually taken over at the midway point by top replicant Rutger Hauer. After destroying his creator, the massive, albino-looking Hauer takes off after Ford, and the villain here is so intriguing and charismatic that one almost comes to prefer him to the more stolid hero.

....

■ **BLAME IT ON RIO**

1984, 110 MINS, US ◇ ⓥ

Dir Stanley Donen   *Prod* Stanley Donen   *Scr* Charlie Peters, Larry Gelbart   *Ph* Reynaldo Villalobos   *Ed* George Hively, Richard Marden   *Mus* Ken Wannberg, Oscar Castro Neves   *Art Dir* Marcos Flaksman
● Michael Caine, Joseph Bologna, Valerie Harper, Michelle Johnson, Jose Lewgoy, Demi Moore (Sherwood/20th Century-Fox)

Central premise of a secret romance between Michael Caine and the love-smitten daughter of his best friend (Joe Bologna) while the trio vacations together in torrid Rio may be adventurous comedy. Zany comedic conflict, however, is offputting, even at times nasty, in this essentially dead-ahead comedy that sacrifices charm and a light touch for too much realism.

Newcomer Michelle Johnson comes off as callow and disagreeably spoiled in key role of buxom daughter lusting after dad's best buddy.

Caine and Bologna play colleagues in a Sao Paulo coffee company whose marriages are toppling – Bologna is getting a divorce and Caine's wife (Valerie Harper) tells Caine while couple is packing for Rio that she's splitting for Bahia in a separate vacation.

Director Stanley Donen gets sharp, comic performances from Caine and Bologna.

....

■ **BLAZE**

1989, 108 MINS, US ◇ ⓥ

Dir Ron Shelton   *Prod* Gil Friesen, Dale Pollock   *Scr* Ron Shelton   *Ph* Haskell Wexler   *Ed* Robert Leighton   *Mus* Bennie Wallace   *Art Dir* Armin Ganz
● Paul Newman, Lolita Davidovich, Jerry Hardin, Gailard Sartain, Jeffrey DeMunn (Touchstone/Silver Screen Partners IV)

A bawdy and audacious tale of politics and scandal, *Blaze* delivers a good love story and a brave and marvelous character turn by Paul Newman.

Newman plays Louisiana governor Earl K. Long in 1959-60 during his May-December romance with famed New Orleans stripper Blaze Starr (Lolita Davidovich).

'Ol' Earl', a self-described 'pro-gressive thinker', was a stump speaker extraordinaire, an advocate of black voting rights and a friend of the poor man. He was also, many believed, a tax evader, a drunk and a madman. Starr was a queen of tawdry New Orleans showbiz who'd come up from poverty in the Tennessee hills.

In Shelton's hands, their relationship, which churned up newspaper headlines and plagued Long's teetering career, is a great and comic love story.

Davidovich is impressive, taking the character from a clunky, overripe hillbilly teenager to a woman with her powers fully focused.

....

■ **BLAZING SADDLES**

1974, 93 MINS, US ◇ ⓥ

Dir Mel Brooks   *Prod* Michael Hertzberg   *Scr* Mel Brooks, Norman Steinberg, Andrew Bergman Richard Pryor, Alan Uger   *Ph* Joseph Biroc   *Ed* John C.

Howard, Danford Greene *Mus* John Morris
Art Dir Peter Wooley
● Cleavon Little, Gene Wilder, Slim Pickens, David Huddleston, Mel Brooks, Madeline Kahn (Warner)

Blazing Saddles spoofs oldtime westerns with an avalanche of one-liners, vaudeville routines, campy shticks, sight gags, satiric imitations and comic anachronisms. Pic is essentially a raunchy, protracted version of a television comedy skit.

Although Cleavon Little and Gene Wilder head a uniformly competent cast, pic is handily stolen by Harvey Korman and Madeline Kahn. Kahn is simply terrific doing a Marlene Dietrich lampoon.

Rest of cast is fine, although Little's black sheriff doesn't blend too well with Brooks' Jewish-flavored comic style. Wilder is amusingly low-key in a relatively small role.

．．．．．．．．．．．．．．．．．．．．．．．．．．

■ BLEAK MOMENTS

1972, 110 MINS, UK ◇
Dir Mike Leigh *Prod* Les Blair *Scr* Mike Leigh
Ph Bahram Manoochehri *Ed* Les Blair *Mus* Mike Bardwell *Art Dir* Richard Rambant
● Anne Raitt, Sarah Stephenson, Eric Allan, Joolia Cappleman, Mike Bradwell, Liz Smith (Autumn/Memorial/BFI)

A film with downbeat themes of solitude, difficulties of communication, coping with a retarded 29-year-old sister, it has enough human insight sans mawkishness or undue sentimentality to make it wryly funny, with its recognition of human foibles that gives it an edge, charm and warmth, tempered with compassion.

Anne Raitt, a handsome, heavyset woman, works in an office with a candy-eating friend who dreams of a possible, but not probable, marriage. Raitt has a quiet suitor who turns out to be impotent. Their night out in a Chinese restaurant is a revealing setpiece. Raitt has rented her garage to a hippie who publishes an underground newspaper. As the hippie leaves, all revert to their original bleak but never depressing lives, which will go on unless something good or better comes along or they take a more affirmative stand.

．．．．．．．．．．．．．．．．．．．．．．．．．．

■ BLIND DATE

1987, 93 MINS, US ◇ Ⓥ
Dir Blake Edwards *Prod* Tony Adams *Scr* Dale Launer *Ph* Harry Stradling *Ed* Robert Pergament *Mus* Henry Mancini *Art Dir* Rodger Maus
● Kim Basinger, Bruce Willis, John Larroquette, William Daniels (Tri-Star)

Bruce Willis abandons his mugging TV personality in favor of playing an animated, amiable, hard-working, ambitious financial analyst in LA.

Stuck without a date for a company function, he reluctantly agrees to ask his brother's wife's cousin (Kim Basinger) to accompany him. His first impression: she's darling. His first mistake: he's not supposed to let her drink and ignores the advice. Two sips of champagne later, she's out of control.

Theme of pure mayhem works well because of chemistry between the main trio of actors, Willis, Basinger and her spurned ex-beau (John Larroquette).

Basinger is cool when sober and wacky when drunk. Her part is really secondary to Willis', who starts out a befuddled date with the manners of a gentleman and ends up not only befuddled, but crazy for the woman.

It's really the psychotic Larroquette who drives this romp. While Willis tries to control his date (or at least figure her out), Larroquette is hot on his tail trying to get her back. Their skirmishes are hilarious.

Pic is essentially a running string of gags with snippets of catchy dialog in-between.

．．．．．．．．．．．．．．．．．．．．．．．．．．

■ BLINDFOLD

1966, 102 MINS, US ◇
Dir Philip Dunne *Prod* Marvin Schwartz *Scr* Philip Dunne, W.H. Menger *Ph* Joseph MacDonald *Ed* Ted J. Kent *Mus* Lalo Schifrin *Art Dir* Alexander Golitzen, Henry Bumstead
● Rock Hudson, Claudia Cardinale, Jack Warden, Guy Stockwell, Brad Dexter, Alejandro Rey (Universal)

In their adaptation of Lucille Fletcher's novel, scripters have approached their task with sights set on combining romantic comedy with tome's adventurous elements. Director Philip Dunne follows through with this tenor in his visual exposition.

Hudson plays part of a famed NY psychologist treating a mentally-disturbed scientist sought by an international ring, who becomes involved in a plot to kidnap scientist from a top-secret hideout. Film takes its title from his being blindfolded whenever he is to visit his patient, held for self-protection by the government in a secluded spot in the swamp country of the South, where doctor is flown every night from NY.

Hudson offers one of his customary light portrayals, sometimes on the cloyingly coy side, and is in for more physical action than usual. Claudia Cardinale, as the chorus-girl sister of the scientist, displays plenty of appeal. Jack Warden, as an American general in charge of protecting the scientist and who hires Hudson to bring him out of his despondency, knows his way through a line and Guy Stockwell heads the ring.

．．．．．．．．．．．．．．．．．．．．．．．．．．

■ BLIND FURY

1989, 85 MINS, US ◇ Ⓥ
Dir Phillip Noyce *Prod* Daniel Grodnik, Tim Matheson *Scr* Charles Robert Carner *Ph* Don Burgess *Ed* David Simmons *Mus* J. Peter Robinson *Art Dir* Peter Murton
● Rutger Hauer, Brandon Call, Terrance O'Quinn, Lisa Blount, Meg Foster, Sho Kosugi (Tri-Star/Interscope)

Blind Fury is an action film with an amusing gimmick, toplining Rutger Hauer, as an apparently invincible blind Vietnam vet who wields a samurai sword with consummate skill.

Nick Parker (Hauer) is actually based on Zatoichi, the heroic blind samurai who starred in a couple of dozen popular actions films for Japanese company Daiei in the 1960s and early 1970s.

First problem for writer Charles Robert Carner [adapting a screen play by Ryozo Kasahara] is to find a way to Americanize such a character. This is solved by having Parker blinded and lost in action in Vietnam and then trained by friendly Vietnamese to use his other senses to survive.

Twenty years later, Parker is back in Miami to look up an old army buddy, Frank Deveraux (Terrance O'Quinn) who's in trouble with the mob in Reno. Parker's in time to prevent the kidnapping of Billy (Brandon Call), Frank's son, but not to stop the murder of Frank's ex-wife, Lynn (Meg Foster, in for only one scene) by the vicious Slag, played by Randall 'Tex' Cobb.

The rest of the film is simply a series of fights and chases as Parker heads for Reno to reunite Billy with his father.

．．．．．．．．．．．．．．．．．．．．．．．．．．

■ BLISS

1985, 135 MINS, AUSTRALIA ◇ Ⓥ
Dir Ray Lawrence *Prod* Anthony Buckley *Scr* Ray Lawrence, Peter Carey *Ph* Paul Murphy *Ed* Wayne Le Clos *Mus* Peter Best *Art Dir* Owen Paterson
● Barry Otto, Lynette Curran, Helen Jones, Miles Buchanan, Gia Carides, Tim Robertson (Window III/NSW Film Corp.)

Pic opens with the death of Harry Joy (Barry Otto), its central character. He runs an ad

agency and leads an apparently happy life with wife and two children. A heart attack fells him during a family gathering, and he's dead for four minutes. When he recovers, he believes he has entered Hell.

That's because everything seems to have changed. His loving wife (Lynette Curran) is having an open affair with his sleazy business partner (Jeff Truman); his son (Miles Buchanan) is a drug runner with ambitions to join the mafia; his daughter (Gia Carides) is an addict who gives her brother sexual favors to get free dope; and Harry discovers, too, that his biggest client manufacturers products known to cause cancer.

Faced with these unexpected upheavals, Harry goes a little mad.

The biggest flaw in *Bliss* is the way the novel has been adapted by its author, Peter Carey, and director Ray Lawrence. The best films of difficult books (and *Bliss* was a difficult book) have pared down the source material while keeping the spirit and intention of the original. Carey and Lawrence have left nothing out; the film teems with characters.

．．．．．．．．．．．．．．．．．．．．．．．．．．

■ BLISS OF MRS. BLOSSOM, THE

1968, 93 MINS, UK ◇
Dir Joseph MacGrath *Prod* Josef Shaftel *Scr* Alec Coppel, Denis Norden *Ph* Geoffrey Unsworth *Ed* Ralph Sheldon *Mus* Riz Ortolani *Art Dir* Assheton Gorton
● Shirley MacLaine, Richard Attenborough, James Booth, Freddie Jones, William Rushton, Bob Monkhouse (Paramount)

The Bliss of Mrs Blossom is a silly, campy and sophisticated marital comedy, always amusing and often hilarious in impact. Shirley MacLaine stars as a wife with two husbands – Richard Attenborough, the legal and nighttime spouse, and James Booth, who lives in the attic. Script covers the laugh spectrum from throwaway verbal and sight gags through broad comedy to satirical pokes at old-fashioned film romances.

MacLaine, bored but adoring wife, calls Attenborough, a noted brassiere manufacturer, for help when her sewing machine breaks down. Only plant worker available is the bumbling Booth, who is seduced by MacLaine. He refuses to leave the attic, and MacLaine gets to liking the cozy arrangement. Gumshoes Freddie Jones and William Rushton pursue Booth's 'disappearance' over the course of many years.

Although basically a one-joke story, idea is fleshed out most satisfactorily so as to take undue attention away from the premise.

Performances are all very good, Attenborough's in particular.

．．．．．．．．．．．．．．．．．．．．．．．．．．

■ BLITHE SPIRIT

1945, 96 MINS, UK ◇
Dir David Lean *Prod* Noel Coward *Scr* Anthony Havelock-Allan, David Lean, Ronald Neame *Ph* Ronald Neame *Ed* Jack Harris *Mus* Richard Addinsell *Art Dir* C.P. Norman
● Rex Harrison, Constance Cummings, Kay Hammond, Margaret Rutherford, Hugh Wakefield, Joyce Carey (Two Cities/Cineguild)

Inasmuch as this is largely a photographed copy of the stage play [by Noel Coward], the camerawork is outstandingly good and helps to put across the credibility of the ghost story more effectively than the flesh and blood performance does.

Acting honors go to Margaret Rutherford as Mme Arcati, a trance medium who makes you believe she's on the level. There is nothing ethereal about this 200-pounder. Her dynamic personality has all the slapdash of Fairbanks Sr in his prime.

Kay Hammond, as dead Wife No 1, brings to the screen a faithful repetition of the performance she has been giving in the flesh for nearly four years. As a spoiled darling with murder in her heart for Wife No 2, she is as much a smiling menace as she is wistfully wraithlike.

As Ruth, the very much alive Wife No 2, Constance Cummings more than holds her own in an altogether capable cast – until her death in the automobile accident engineered by Elvira. As a ghost, Cummings is not at all convincing. As Charles Condomine, twice married novelist, Rex Harrison repeats his stage performance, which is so flawless as to merit some critics' charge of under-acting.

• •

■ BLOB, THE

1958, 85 MINS, US ◇ ⓥ

Dir Irvin S. Yeaworth Jr   *Prod* Jack H. Harris
Scr Theodore Simonson, Kate Phillips   *Ph* Thomas Spalding   *Ed* Alfred Hillman   *Mus* Jean Yeaworth
Art Dir William Jersey, Karl Karlson
● Steve McQueen, Aneta Corseaut, Earl Rowe, Olin Howlin (Paramount/Tonylyn)

The initial production of Jack H. Harris, a regional distrib in the Philadelphia area, *The Blob* had a reported budget of $240,000. Story, from an idea by Irvine H. Millgate, will tax the imagination of adult patrons.

A small Pennsylvania town has been plagued by teenage pranks. Hence, when highschoolers Steve McQueen and Aneta Corseaut report that a parasitic substance from outer space has eaten the local doctor and his nurse, no one will believe them. Especially when no bodies can be found.

Neither the acting nor direction is particularly creditable. McQueen, who's handed star billing, makes with the old college try while Corseaut also struggles valiantly as his girlfriend.

Star performers, however, are the camerawork of Thomas Spalding and Barton Sloane's special effects. Production values otherwise are geared to economy. Intriguing is the title number, written by Burt Bacharach and Mack David. It's sung offscreen by a harmony group as the credits unreel. Picture was lensed at the Valley Forge, Pa, studios.

• •

■ BLONDE VENUS

1932, 93 MINS, US ⓥ

Dir Josef von Sternberg   *Scr* S. K. Lauren, Jules Furthman   *Ph* Bert Glennon   *Art Dir* Wiard Ihnen
● Marlene Dietrich, Herbert Marshall, Cary Grant, Dickie Moore, Francis Sayles, Robert Emmett O'Connor (Paramount)

A disappointer. Much of the blame is to be laid at director Josef von Sternberg's doorstep. In a desire to glamorously built up Marlene Dietrich he sloughs almost every other element that goes to round out a box office production. He devotes two reels to her flight from her husband and all the drab details that went with it, as she scrams from Baltimore to Washington to Nashville to Chattanooga to Savannah to New Orleans, etc, etc. The police reports of her hunt sound like a railroad timetable.

Then in a meteoric rise, with no details whatsoever, she's suddenly again the queen of the nite clubs, this time in Paris, where Cary Grant (who had formerly maintained her) once again meets up with her. In this and previous nite club scenes, Dietrich sings two numbers in that deep, throaty manner of hers, one chorus being in French.

Herbert Marshall is sadly miscast as the radium-poisoned husband who needs funds so badly for a European cure that his devoted wife takes resource to financial succor from such a remote source as influential politician (Grant).

The 93 minutes, despite their episodic and

ofttimes ragged sequences, are much too much considering the triteness of the basic story, a theme of mother love of the German-American cafe songstress whose child (well played by Dickie Moore, in perhaps the only convincing casting) is the sympathetic basis of it all. Otherwise there's little sympathy for any of the characters; neither the hapless husband, the faithless wife nor the other man.

• •

■ BLONDIE OF THE FOLLIES

1932, 91 MINS, US

Dir Edmund Goulding   *Scr* Frances Marion, Anita Loos   *Ph* George Barnes
● Marion Davies, Robert Montgomery, Billie Dove, Jimmy Durante, James Gleason, ZaSu Pitts (M-G-M)

Jimmy Durante is rushed into a house party scene for his first and only appearance after the picture has gone 70 minutes. That's the best evidence that this picture's big weakness was analyzed by the producers. In the five minutes that Durante is on, his Barrymore-Garbo takeoff with Marion Davies easily becomes the bright spot on the picture.

The story is simply the rise of two New York girls of the poor class to *Follies* girl status, their temporary enjoyment of the luxurious fancy living and then their return to normalcy.

Chief situation is love rivalry between the two girl pals, with Blondie (Davies) finally winning out.

Davies and Billie Dove are both real life Follies grads, so their backstage conduct in this picture probably is authentic. Of the two Dove is more the showgirl type in looks and manner. As usual, Davies is best in her few comedy chances, but on the whole this try is under par for her.

• •

■ BLOOD AND SAND

1922, 110 MINS, US ⊗ ⓥ

Dir Fred Niblo   *Prod* Jesse L. Lasky   *Scr* June Mathis   *Ph* Alvin Wyckoff
● Rudolph Valentino, Lila Lee, Nita Naldi, George Field, Walter Long (Paramount)

Rudolph Valentino's switch to a St Anthony type comes as a shock. The essential moral conflict of the bullfighter never gets to the surface. He is just a bewildered simpleton, which makes his gaudy clothes ridiculous.

The story [from the novel by Vicente Blasco Ibanez and the play by Tom Cushing] has many picturesque elements but it is episodic and scattered. It starts with the theme of a humble shoemaker raised to eminence as a national hero of the bull ring and an idol of the people

Soon the problem is changed to 'What will be the fate of a man who lives by blood and cruelty?' Then the conflict appears to be an attack on the institution of the bull fight.

'Poor matador; poor beast,' says the benign philosopher, 'But the real bull is out there (the crowd around the arena). There is the beast with 10,000 heads'.

• •

■ BLOOD AND SAND

1941, 123 MINS, US ◇ ⓥ

Dir Rouben Mamoulian   *Prod* Darryl F. Zanuck   *Scr* Jo Swerling   *Ph* Ernest Palmer, Ray Rennahan   *Ed* Robert Bischoff   *Mus* Alfred Newman
● Tyrone Power, Linda Darnell, Rita Hayworth, Nazimova, Anthony Quinn, John Carradine (20th Century-Fox)

Blood and Sand [from the novel by Blasco Vicente Ibanez] is associated in the memories of theatre-goers as a hot and decidedly sexy piece of merchandise, chiefly because of Valentino's silent version two decades ago. The revival follows the original as a straight drama of the bullfight ring.

Especially effective are the bullfight arena sequences, which disclose exceptional camera angles and intercutting of shots of crowds at arena in Mexico City with studio shots.

Tyrone Power is a peon kid in Seville, son of a bullfighter killed in the ring, decidedly illiterate, and with a passion for bullfighting. He has an adolescent love for Linda Darnell, and finally runs off to Madrid with a bunch of his pals. Ten years later, as a minor league matador, he returns to Seville, marries Darnell and goes on to become the most famous and widely acclaimed matador of the time. Surrounded by leeches, Power is continually in debt, but happy with his wife until fascinated by sexy Rita Hayworth, socialite flame.

Power delivers a persuasive performance as Ibanez's hero while Darnell is pretty and naive as the young wife. Hayworth is excellent as the vamp and catches major attention on a par with Nazimova, who gives a corking performance as Power's mother.

• •

■ BLOODBROTHERS

1978, 116 MINS, US ◇ ⓥ

Dir Robert Mulligan   *Prod* Stephen Friedman   *Scr* Walter Newman   *Ph* Robert Surtees   *Ed* Shelly Kahn   *Mus* Elmer Bernstein   *Art Dir* Gene Callahan
● Paul Sorvino, Tony Lo Bianco, Richard Gere, Lelia Goldoni, Yvonne Wilder, Kenneth McMillan (Warner)

Bloodbrothers is an ambitious, if uneven probe into the disintegration of an Italian-American family [from the novel by Richard Price]. Under Robert Mulligan's forceful direction, sharply-drawn characters clash, scream and argue, but fail to resolve any of their or the film's conflicts.

Bloodbrothers delves into the steamy emotional mess known as the De Coco clan, headed by construction worker father Tony Lo Bianco, his brother Paul Sorvino, wife Lelia Goldoni, and sons Richard Gere and Michael Hershewe.

Although the focus of the film isn't clear until about half-way through, *Bloodbrothers* is concerned primarily with the plight of Gere, who is trying to make one of those crucial life decisions about whether he wants to join the men on the construction girders or opt for the job that gives him real pleasure, working with small children.

This pedestrian tale is placed against a background of vibrant machoism, with numerous scenes of boozing, whoring and fighting set in the Bronx.

• •

■ BLOOD FOR DRACULA

1974, 90 MINS, FRANCE/ITALY ◇ ⓥ

Dir Paul Morrissey   *Prod* Andrew Braunsberg   *Scr* Paul Morrissey   *Ph* Luigi Kueveillier   *Ed* Ted Johnson   *Mus* Claudio Gizzi
● Joe Dallesandro, Udo Kier, Vittorio De Sica, Maxime McKendry, Arno Juerging, Milena Vukotic (CC-Champion & 1/Ponti/Yanne/Rassam)

Dracula has about been Hammered to bits in his many British incarnations. Now Paul Morrissey takes a turn at the old bloodsucker, made in Italy in English [back-to-back with *Flesh for Frankenstein*] with a mixture of nationalities acting in it.

Morrissey long showed that his films, although more implicit in sex, drugs and characterizations, were really Hollywood films at the core.

Udo Kier is a youngish Dracula, in the 1930s. It seems he will die unless he getsvirgin blood. So he has to leave his Transylvanian lair to go to Italy for that, since a Catholic country should have some.

Accepted by a supposedly rich family, who have four pretty daughters, Dracula gets his come-uppance.

• •

B

BLOOD FROM THE MUMMY'S TOMB

1971, 94 MINS, UK ◇
Dir Seth Holt, [Michael Carreras] *Prod* Howard Brandy *Scr* Christopher Wicking *Ph* Arthur Grant *Ed* Peter Weatherley *Mus* Tristram Cary *Art Dir* Scott MacGregor
● Andrew Keir, Valerie Leon, James Villiers, Hugh Burden, George Coulouris, Mark Edwards (Hammer)

This polished and well-acted but rather tame Hammer horror entry revolves around an exploration group who discovered an ancient Egyptian tomb and brought relics, including the Princess Tera's mummy; home to England. The sacrilege is savagely avenged by Tera being reincarnated in the leader's beautiful daughter.

Valerie Leon has the dual role of the princess and the modern miss who brings a reign of terror to a quiet London suburb. Solid support comes from Andrew Keir, James Villiers, Hugh Burden, George Coulouris, Rosalie Crutchley and James Cossins who bring credence to the proceedings.

Director Seth Holt died suddenly a few days before shooting was completed and the lack of his guiding hand through post-production could explain, without justifying, certain vagaries and roughness.

BLOODHOUNDS OF BROADWAY

1989, 101 MINS, US ◇ Ⓥ
Dir Howard Brookner *Prod* Howard Brookner *Scr* Howard Brookner, Colman DeKay *Ph* Elliot Davis *Ed* Camilla Toniolo *Mus* Jonathan Sheffner, Roma Baran *Art Dir* Linda Conaway-Parsloe
● Julie Hagerty, Randy Quaid, Madonna, Jennifer Grey, Rutger Hauer, Matt Dillon (American Playhouse)

Howard Brookner (who died after completing this first feature) and Colman DeKay interweave four of Damon Runyon's famous *Broadway* short stories [*The Bloodhound of Broadway, A Very Honorable Guy, Social Error* and *The Brain Goes Home*] about New Year's Eve on Broadway in 1928. It's a gangster's farce that falls somewhat short of true comic inspiration.

Strong character acting by an all-star cast enlivens this fluffy little piece about romance and gangsters during Prohibition.

There's Harriet Mackyle (Julie Hagerty), who delivered a fine performance as a rich society babe who's throwing the party and invites some local mobsters for added color.

Randy Quaid as Feet Samuels does a satisfying job as an honorable dimwit who's madly in love with a beautiful, diamond-hungry showgirl, Hortense Hathaway, very adeptly played by Madonna.

Matt Dillon gives a rather tepid performance as Regret, Broadway's lousiest horse player, especially in comparison with Jennifer Grey, who does a good job as Lovey Lou, an angel-faced showgirl in love with Regret.

BLOODLINE

1979, 116 MINS, US ◇ Ⓥ
Dir Terence Young *Prod* David V. Picker, Sidney Beckerman *Scr* Laird Koenig *Ph* Freddie Young *Ed* Bud Molin *Mus* Ennio Morricone *Art Dir* Ted Haworth
● Audrey Hepburn, Ben Gazzara, James Mason, Irene Papas, Romy Schneider, Omar Sharif (Paramount/Geria)

Even for the never-never land of high chic melodrama the film inhabits, the tale of a woman who, unprepared, inherits control of her father's vast pharmaceutical empire contains wild implausibilities.

Flashback reveal papa's medical genius in a Jewish Polish slum. Audience is then asked to swallow premise that, 40-odd years later, his family, making up the company's scheming

board of directors, contains Italian and French upper-crusters as well as a member of the British Parliament.

This is Terence Young's first completed film since *The Klansman* five years earlier and he's clearly out of practice, as his performers range unevenly in tone from the comic (Omar Sharif, Irene Papas, Gert Frobe) to the merely drab (James Mason, Michelle Phillips, Maurice Ronet).

BLOOD MONEY

1988, 90 MINS, UK/US ◇ Ⓥ
Dir Jerry Schatzberg *Prod* Donald March *Scr* Robert Foster *Ph* Isidore Mankovsky *Ed* David Ray *Mus* Jan Hammer *Art Dir* Howard Barker
● Andy Garcia, Ellen Barkin, Morgan Freeman, Michael Lombard, Brad Sullivan (ITC)

Clinton and Nadine are the lead couple who muddle through a murder mystery tale linked to illicit Contra fundraising.

Andy Garcia is Clinton, a parrot smuggler who stumbles onto his brother's slaying and foils murderers' attempts to escape with a backpack containing some audiocassettes.

Clinton also came away from the crime scene with a purse belonging to Nadine Powers (Ellen Barkin), a hooker on the run from the refuge of his brother's home. Lonely and confused, she is drawn reluctantly into Clinton's attempt to track down those responsible for the murders.

By the time the pair become lovers, one hardly cares and problem is compounded when the story becomes bewildering as everyone is transposed suddenly to Costa Rica for the denouement.

BLOOD OATH

1990, 105 MINS, AUSTRALIA ◇ Ⓥ
Dir Stephen Wallace *Prod* Charles Waterstreet, Denis Whitburn, Brian Williams *Scr* Denis Whitburn, Brian Williams *Ph* Russell Boyd *Ed* Nicholas Beauman *Mus* David McHugh, Stewart D'Arrietta, Don Miller-Robinson *Art Dir* Bernard Hides
● Bryan Brown, George Takei, Terry O'Quinn, Toshi Shioya, John Bach, Deborah Unger (Village Roadshow/Blood Oath)

Blood Oath is a courtroom drama that raises questions about wartime crime and punishment. The drama, based on actual incidents, takes place on the Indonesian island of Ambon in late 1945.

Ambon, site of a Japanese POW camp for Australian prisoners, was under the command of aristocratic, Oxford-educated Vice-Admiral Baron Takahashi (George Takei). Bryan Brown plays Capt. Cooper, Aussie officer assigned to prosecute Takashahi and his men for war crimes. He finds his hands tied at every turn, mainly because an American 'observer' at the trial, Major Beckett (Terry O'Quinn), doesn't want Takahashi found guilty, figuring he'll be more useful in reconstructed postwar Japan.

At least half the film takes place in the courtroom, and director Stephen Wallace stages these surefire scenes with maximum tension. Brown brings sardonic humor and a wholly convincing feeling of frustration to the tenacious character of Cooper (based on the father of coscripter/coproducer Brian A. Williams).

BLOOD ON THE SUN

1945, 98 MINS, US Ⓥ
Dir Frank Lloyd *Prod* William Cagney *Scr* Lester Cole *Ph* Theodor Sparkuhl *Ed* Truman K. Wood, Walter Hanneman *Mus* Miklos Rozsa *Art Dir* Wiard B. Ihnen
● James Cagney, Sylvia Sidney, Wallace Ford, Robert Armstrong, John Emery, Rosemary De Camp (United Artists)

Cagney portrays an American editor of a Tokyo newspaper who dares to print the story of the world-conquest plan formulated by Jap militarists. Naturally, the fur flies when the sheet hits the street – the police confiscating the papers, the Jap secret police demanding a retraction from the publisher, and the editor threatening to walk out if the latter does so. Quickly, Cagney finds himself in the midst of a dual murder committed by the Japs upon a US newspaper pal and his wife, who were leaving Japan to bring to America the document describing the world-conquest plot in detail.

The stars of this picture are given plenty of opportunity to display their histrionics. Cagney is the same rough and tumble character he's always been, ready to tell the Jap bigshots off at the drop of a hat.

There are a couple of over-dramatic sequences, but they just add to the tension of whether they're going to get the envelope with the plot out of the country, or not.

BLOOD RED

1989, 91 MINS, US ◇ Ⓥ
Dir Peter Masterson *Prod* Judd Bernard, Patricia Casey *Scr* Ron Cutler *Ph* Toyomichi Kurita *Ed* Randy Thornton *Mus* Carmine Coppola *Art Dir* Bruno Rubeo
● Eric Roberts, Giancarlo Giannini, Dennis Hopper, Burt Young, Carlin Glynn, Julia Roberts (Kettledrum)

Blood Red, a saga of oppressed Sicilian winegrowers in 19th century California, is an unsuccessful throwback to earlier forms of filmmaking. Project was announced in 1976 by producer Judd Bernard, filmed in 1986 and given a perfunctory regional release in summer 1989. It was the first-time screen teaming of siblings Eric and Julia Roberts.

A robust Giannini is patriarch of one of two families in Brandon, Calif., and soon is warring with robber baron railroad magnate Dennis Hopper (fitted with an unconvincing Scottish brogue here) determined to get his land for his railroad's right of way. Giannini's rebellious son (Roberts), is in love with the beautiful daughter (Lara Harris) of another winegrowing clan.

Roberts is more subdued than usual as the script fails to develop a three-dimensional character for him. His scenes with real-life sister Julia, cast as his sister, are intriguing because of the visual match. She doesn't get much chance to emote, but that nascent star quality already is evident.

BLOOD SIMPLE

1984, 97 MINS, US ◇ Ⓥ
Dir Joel Coen *Prod* Ethan Coen *Scr* Joel Coen, Ethan Coen *Ph* Barry Sonnenfeld *Ed* Roderick Jaynes, Don Wiegmann *Mus* Carter Burwell *Art Dir* Jane Musky
● John Getz, Frances McDormand, Dan Hedaya, Samm-Art Williams, M. Emmet Walsh (River Road)

An inordinately good low-budget film noir thriller, *Blood Simple* is written, directed and produced by brothers Joel and Ethan Coen.

Aside from the subtle performances, usually lacking in a film of this size (around $1.5 million), the observant viewer will find a cornucopia of detail.

Dan Hedaya plays Marty, a brooding owner of a Texas bar. Hedaya hires a sleazy, onerous malcreant named Visser (played with appropriate malice by M. Emmet Walsh) to kill his wayward wife and her boyfriend Ray (John Getz).

Walsh takes a snapshot of the lovers asleep in bed, doctors the photo to make it appear he's fulfilled the contract, and meets Hedaya at the bar after hours to collect. Upon payment, Walsh pulls out the wife's gun and shoots Marty dead in the chest. But the victim has swapped the photo and put it in the office safe before his demise, making Walsh's perfect crime not so.

Final confrontation between Walsh and the lovers is outright horrific.

Performances are top-notch all around, Walsh in particular conveying the villainy and scummy aspects of his character with convincing glee.

. . . .

■ BLOODY MAMA

1970, 90 MINS, US ◇ ⓥ

Dir Roger Corman *Prod* Roger Corman *Scr* Robert Thorn *Ph* John Alonzo *Ed* Eve Newman *Mus* Don Randi

● Shelley Winters, Pat Hingle, Don Stroud, Diane Varsi, Bruce Dern, Robert De Niro (American International)

The story of Kate (Ma) Barker, who with her four killer sons terrorized mountain country in the Depression era, *Bloody Mama* is a pseudo-biopic starring Shelley Winters in one of those all-over-the-screen performances which sometimes are labelled as bravura acting.

Film was made entirely on location in Arkansas, and manifests an apparently deliberate attempt at naturalistic filming.

Story is a loosely-connected string of macabre vignettes, with an emphasis on dramatic peaks but very little character development or motivation. Cast as ma's brood are Don Stroud as the psychotic, Robert Walden as the masochistic homosexual, Robert De Niro as the drug addict, and Clint Kimbrough as the quiet boy. Bruce Dern plays a sadistic homosexual, mated with Walden, and Diane Varsi is Stroud's girl, a stray hooker.

The best performance in the film, and one of the most outstanding screen portrayals in many moons, is that of Pat Hingle, playing a wealthy businessman kidnapped for high ransom.

. . . .

■ BLOSSOMS IN THE DUST

1941, 98 MINS, US ◇

Dir Mervyn LeRoy *Prod* Mervyn LeRoy *Scr* Anita Loos *Ph* Karl Freund, M. Howard Green *Ed* George Boemler *Mus* Herbert Stothart

● Greer Garson, Walter Pidgeon, Felix Bressart, Marsha Hunt (M-G-M)

What Father Flanagan is to Boys Town in Nebraska, Edna Gladney is to an orphans' home in Texas operated entirely on a strong mother love instinct and the gracious donations of Texans. The home is the Texas Children's Home and Aid Society of Ft Worth. *Blossoms in the Dust* is a worthy production on which much care has been showered by Mervyn LeRoy and others, but the picture fails to impress as being big.

There are almost too many kids, with much attention paid to them. Result is a sentimentally sugary flavor which also extends over the romantic portions of the film. There is no comedy relief.

Pidgeon is the Texan who marries Edna Gladney of Wisconsin and worships her. The baby born to them dies and subsequently Pidgeon passes away suddenly after they have done some charity work for poor kids and foundlings. From there on Garson takes up the placement of unfortunate children as a lifetime work and ultimately is instrumental in passing a law which eliminates from public record whether orphans were born illegitimately or not.

Playing Edna Gladney, Garson spans many years but does not appreciably age.

□ 1941: Best Picture (Nomination)

. . . .

■ BLOW OUT

1981, 107 MINS, US ◇

Dir Brian De Palma *Prod* George Litto *Scr* Brian De Palma *Ph* Vilmos Zsigmond *Ed* Paul Hirsch *Mus* Pino Donaggio *Art Dir* Paul Sylbert

● John Travolta, Nancy Allen, John Lithgow, Dennis Franz, Peter Boyden (Filmways/Litto)

Writer-director Brian De Palma's *Blow Out* is a frequently exciting $18 million suspense thriller which suffers from a distracting emphasis upon homages to other motion pictures.

Travolta appears as a Philadelphia-based sound man working out of his studio on low-budget horror films. Film turns serious with plot of Travolta caught up in a murder and coverup scheme when the tire of a politician's car is blown out by a rifle shot at a bridge where he is recording sounds.

Saving a young woman (Nancy Allen) from drowning in the car, Travolta's fate becomes entwined with hers as he uses his professional expertise to unravel the murder mystery while both of them dodge the assassin (John Lithgow).

With attractive leads and a stylish flair for suspense, De Palma misses sustaining involvement by his distracting allusions to prior films (ranging broadly from *Blowup* to *Touch of Evil*).

Travolta scores with a combo of intensity and naturalism in the sympathetic lead role, but co-star Nancy Allen is stuck essaying a helpless loser instead of the romantic teammate favored by De Palma's avowed mentor, Alfred Hitchcock.

. . . .

■ BLOWUP

1967, 110 MINS, UK ◇ ⓥ

Dir Michelangelo Antonioni *Prod* Carlo Ponti *Scr* Michelangelo Antonioni, Tonino Guerra, Edward Bond *Ph* Carlo Di Palma *Ed* Frank Clarke *Mus* Herbie Hancock *Art Dir* Assheton Gorton

● David Hemmings, Vanessa Redgrave, Sarah Miles, Peter Bowles, Verushka, Jane Birkin (Bridge/M-G-M)

There may be some meaning, some commentary about life being a game, beyond what remains locked in the mind of film's creator, Italian director-writer Michelangelo Antonioni. But it is doubtful that the general public will get the 'message' of this film, [from a short story by Julio Cortazar]. As a commentary on a sordid, confused side of humanity in this modern age it's a bust.

Filmed in England and Antonioni's first English-speaking production, interesting use is made of London backgrounds. There also is certain sustained interest at times as the audience presses hopefully to piece together the significance of the story (?).

Footage centers on a topflight London fashion photographer who learns of a murder through his secret lensing of a couple he sees embracing in a park. Through a series of blow-ups of the many exposures he snapped he finds indications of a murder, and visiting the park again discovers the body of the man whom he had been photographing.

David Hemmings makes an interesting impression as the bulber whose studio is invaded by various femmes, and Vanessa Redgrave, as the woman involved in the park, projects another vivid impression.

. . . .

■ BLUE

1968, 113 MINS, US ◇

Dir Silvio Narizzano *Prod* Judd Bernard, Irwin Winkler *Scr* Meade Roberts *Ph* Stanley Cortez *Ed* Stewart Linder *Mus* Manos Hadjidakis *Art Dir* Hal Pereira

● Terence Stamp, Joanna Pettet, Karl Malden, Ricardo Montalban, Anthony Costello, Joe De Santis (Paramount/Kettledrum)

Poor writing, dull performances and preten-

tious direction waste the rugged physical beauty of the location area. The $5 million-plus film is neither the intellectual drama it apparently was meant to be, nor even a reasonably satisfying programmer.

Terence Stamp stars in a title role which can't amount to more than 200 words, many of them dubbed, the rest in his British accent, incongruous to plot. Basic trouble with *Blue* is that there seems to have been an attempt to make a 'great' or 'definitive' film.

Setting is the uneasy border between Mexico and Texas, across which bandits Ricardo Montalban, and older brother Joe de Santis come for looting raids. Stamp, raised by Montalban is supposedly torn between loyalty to Montalban and his own (undefined) kin.

Allowing for the last-minute casting of Stamp, his performance is dull. He does not speak a word for 50 minutes (though he grunts a bit), and the first sentence is 'I'll do it,' betraying therein his native accent.

. . . .

■ BLUE ANGEL, THE

1930, 99 MINS, GERMANY ⓥ

Dir Josef von Sternberg *Prod* Erich Pommer *Scr* Robert Liebmann, Carl Zuckmayer, Karl Vollmoller *Ph* Gunther Rittau, Hans Schneeberger *Mus* Frederick Hollander *Art Dir* Otto Hunte, Emil Hasler

● Emil Jannings, Marlene Dietrich, Kurt Gerron, Rosa Valetti, Hans Albers (UFA)

Splendid English version of a German original [released earlier the same year]. It's Emil Jannings' first talker with his name over the title and Marlene Dietrich's underneath.

It's a standout picture along typical UFA lines – meaning that the story [from the novel *Professor Unrath* by Heinrich Mann] is heavy, tends to drag and holds up more on the strength of the two principals than anything else.

Dietrich, as a cabaret girl of liberal morals with those Continental soubret costumes of much stocking, bare limb and garters, is an eyeful. She seems a bit timid as regard the dialog. This is not so when she sings. One tune carries a plaintive melody which has a tendency to linger, and Dietrich sings it better in English than in German.

Dietrich's final rendition of the main song astride a chair, as she tosses it with almost a sneer on her face at the low-brow mob in the sailors' dive, is something of a classic.

Emil Jannings gives a fine characterization of the circumspect school teacher who falls completely for the cabaret singer whom his students have been nightly sneaking away to see. He descends to become the pantomimic clown assistant of the magician-manager of the show, with the mimicking of a rooster as his comedy punch.

Josef von Sternberg, directing, stretches the picture beyond its limit but shows high judgment in handling the dialog.

. . . .

■ BLUE ANGEL, THE

1959, 107 MINS, US ◇

Dir Edward Dmytryk *Prod* Jack Cummings *Scr* Nigel Balchin *Ph* Leon Shamroy *Ed* Jack W. Holmes *Mus* Hugo Friedhofer *Art Dir* Lyle R. Wheeler, Maurice Ransford

● Curt Jurgens, May Britt, Theodore Bikel, John Banner, Fabrizio Mioni (20th Century-Fox)

When UFA made *Der blaue Engel* it catapulted Emil Jannings, Marlene Dietrich, producer Erich Pommer and director Josef von Sternberg into international repute. Later that year (1930), Paramount dubbed an English version and 'Legs' Dietrich was on the road to Hollywood renown. This remake is not the rocker that the Jannings-Dietrich impact made but neither Germany's Curt Jurgens nor Sweden's May Britt need be ashamed of their performances.

Perhaps counting the most against them is the somewhat familiar plot motivationn – the femme fatale and the destruction of the German professor who succumbs to her wiles – plus the indelible impact Jannings and Dietrich made in their earlier approach to the same plot. But the prime shortcoming is the decision to give this saga a post-midcentury topicality in present-day West Germany.

Britt is an eyeful as the seductress. Her shoulder-length blonde hair; her saucy mien and manner; the Dietrichesque style of straddling the chairs, which she utilizes as props, showing off her saucy gams, are eyefuls in every department. She handles two vocal reprises of Frederick Hollander's 'Falling in Love Again' and also projects the new thematic, 'Lola Lola' which Jay Livingston and Ray Evans fashioned for her.

Jurgens proves a flexible performer. He disguises his masculine attractiveness under an authentic German academician's mien, impersonating the unworldly schoolmaster with conviction.

Film was part-shot in Bavaria and the interiors in Hollywood. Support is authentic from the rowdiest students to Theodore Bikel as the machiavellian impresario-magician of this itinerant troupe.

■ BLUEBEARD

1972, 123 MINS, US ◇ Ⓥ
Dir Edward Dmytryk *Prod* Alexander Salkind *Scr* Ennio De Concini, Edward Dmytryk, Maria Pia Fusco *Ph* Gabor Pogany *Ed* Jean Ravel *Mus* Ennio Morricone *Art Dir* Tomas Vayer
● Richard Burton, Raquel Welch, Joey Heatherton, Virna Lisi, Nathalie Delon, Sybil Danning (Vulcano)

Bluebeard is high camp. Richard Burton portrays title role in a modernized version of the legendary character who had a way with women – doing them in – and in dignified tread saunters through a whole phantasmagoria of murders and a veritable shower of bare bosoms to a finale which shows why he was that way, poor guy.

Joey Heatherton is the principal protagonist, who discovers all his victims in a huge refrigerator-room and who, as a result of her discovery, is to be his next victim. To her, he relates in flashback form the fate of his other wives.

One of the most entertaining sequences focuses on Nathalie Delon, who after getting nowhere with Burton in bed prevails upon a prostitute (Sybil Danning) to instruct her in the art of seduction. Lesson ends with her learning the total ways of lesbianism and Burton drops a pointed chandelier on them.

■ BLUE BIRD, THE

1976, 100 MINS, US/USSR ◇ Ⓥ
Dir George Cukor *Prod* Paul Maslansky, Lee Savin, Paul Radnia *Scr* Hugh Whitemore, Alfred Hayes, Alexei Kapler *Ph* Freddie Young, Ionas Gritzus *Ed* Ernest Walter, Tatyana Shaprio, Stanford C. Allen *Mus* Irwin Kostal *Art Dir* Brian Wildsmith
● Elizabeth Taylor, Jane Fonda, Ava Gardner, Cicely Tyson, Robert Morley, Harry Andrews (20th Century-Fox)

Third film version of the Maurice Maeterlinck novel (after 1918 and 1939) takes spoiled peasant children Todd Lookinland (excellent, by the way) and Patsy Kensit on a dream trip from their humble abode through a fantasy world in search of the bluebird of happiness.

Elizabeth Taylor's four roles include the dominant (and dazzling) one as (a) Light; as mother (b) she's uncomfortable; as witch (c) she's fun to guess at; as maternal love (d) she's elegantly simple and believable.

Jane Fonda does Night, the princess of

darkness, with a flair, while Ava Gardner is extremely effective as Luxury.

Nobody's going to laugh in ridicule at any of it (it's that good) but nobody's going to be strongly moved (it's that bad).

■ BLUE COLLAR

1978, 110 MINS, US ◇ Ⓥ
Dir Paul Schrader *Prod* Don Guest *Scr* Paul Schrader, Leonard Schrader *Ph* Bobby Byrne *Ed* Tom Rolf *Mus* Jack Nitzsche *Art Dir* Lawrence G. Paull
● Richard Pryor, Harvey Keitel, Yaphet Kotto, Ed Begley Jr, Harry Bellaver, George Memmoli (TAT)

Paul Schrader's directorial debut is an artistic triumph. Schrader has transformed a carefully researched original screenplay penned by him and his brother Leonard into a powerful, gritty, seamless profile of three automobile assembly line workers banging their heads against the monotony and corruption that is the factory system.

It is a picture about the monotony and routine of factory life that isn't monotonous, but *is* realistic. Regardless of where individual scenes are set – at the after-work tavern, at a bowling alley, at a worker's home, in the union headquarters, or in a Detroit street – the factory dominates every frame of this film.

The film's three stars – Richard Pryor, Harvey Keitel and Yaphet Kotto – all turn in outstanding and disciplined performances.

Plot centers around the three workers' attempts to confront and battle the reality of this system as Schrader views it. The three devise a plan to rob the union, which in the end turns into another helpless action.

■ BLUE DAHLIA, THE

1946, 96 MINS, US
Dir George Marshall *Prod* John Houseman *Scr* Raymond Chandler *Ph* Lionel Lindon *Ed* Arthur Schmidt *Mus* Victor Young *Art Dir* Hans Dreier, Walter Tyler
● Alan Ladd, Veronica Lake, William Bendix, Howard da Silva, Doris Dowling (Paramount)

Playing a discharged naval flier returning home from the Pacific first to find his wife unfaithful, then to find her murdered and himself in hiding as the suspect, Alan Ladd does a bangup job. Performance has a warm appeal, while in his relentless track down of the real criminal, Ladd has a cold, steel-like quality that is potent. Fight scenes are stark and brutal, and tremendously effective.

Story gets off to a slow start, but settles to an even pace that never lets down in interest. Audience may guess the killer, as the story follows several alleys of suspects, but pic always has suspense, with sufficient variations in mood. Ladd is one of trio to return from the wars, others being William Bendix and Hugh Beaumont. Ladd's path crosses Veronica Lake's, latter being separated wife of a nightclub owner who is one of the killer-suspects. Scenes between Ladd and Lake are surprisingly sensitive, with an economy of dialog and emotion doubly appealing.

■ BLUE DENIM

1959, 89 MINS, US ◇
Dir Philip Dunne *Prod* Charles Brackett *Scr* Philip Dunne, Edith Sommer *Ph* Leo Tover *Ed* William Reynolds *Mus* Bernard Herrmann *Art Dir* Lyle R. Wheeler, Leland Fuller
● Carol Lynley, Brandon de Wilde, Macdonald Carey, Marsha Hunt, Warren Berlinger, Vaughn Taylor (20th Century-Fox)

Based on the Broadway stage play by James Leo Herlihy and William Noble, *Blue Denim* recounts, often movingly and intelligently,

the torments of a pair of high school lovers who are about to become unwed parents. The desperation of these babes in the basement – a 15-year-old girl and a 16-year-old boy – is further highlighted by their inability to communicate with their parents.

The girl's father is a college professor determined to raise his only daughter to emulate his dead wife. The boy's father is a retired army officer given to reciting platitudes about the value of service life and unable to forget his moments of past glory.

The screenplay has been considerably watered down. The word 'abortion' is never mentioned although it is obvious what is taking place. Moreover, the ending deteriorates to cliche melodrama.

Carol Lynley repeats her stage role with the same eclat and sensitivity. As her young lover, Brandon de Wilde gives a moving performance as the confused 16-year-old learning the realities of sex. Warren Berliner, also from the stage play, is fine as his wise-cracking buddy and confidante.

■ BLUE GARDENIA, THE

1953, 90 MINS, US
Dir Fritz Lang *Prod* Alex Gottlieb *Scr* Charles Hoffman *Ph* Nicholas Musuraca *Ed* Edward Mann *Mus* Raoul Kraushaar *Art Dir* Daniel Hall
● Anne Baxter, Richard Conte, Ann Sothern, Raymond Burr, Jeff Donnell, Nat 'King' Cole (Warner)

A stock story and handling keep *The Blue Gardenia* from being anything more than a regulation mystery melodrama, from a yarn by Vera Caspary. Formula development has an occasional bright spot, mostly because Ann Sothern breathes some life into a stock character and quips.

Anne Baxter is a telephone operator who believes she committed murder when she was drinking away the tears of a broken romance. Too much rum with Raymond Burr, a licentious artist, has blacked out her memory and when she reads a newspaper account of his violent death, she naturally thinks she did it while fighting for her honor. Richard Conte, all-powerful newspaper columnist, masterminds the disclosure of her identity strictly to get an exclusive, but falls in love with her and has to uncover the real killer.

Baxter and Conte do what they can but fight a losing battle with the script while Burr is a rather obvious wolf. Nat 'King' Cole is spotted to sing the title tune, written by Bob Russell and Lester Lee.

■ BLUE HAWAII

1961, 103 MINS, US ◇ Ⓥ
Dir Norman Taurog *Prod* Hal Wallis *Scr* Hal Kanter *Ph* Charles Lang Jr *Ed* Warren Low, Terry Morse *Mus* Joseph J. Lilley *Art Dir* Hal Pereira, Walter Tyler
● Elvis Presley, Joan Blackman, Nancy Walters, Roland Winters, Angela Lansbury, Howard McNear (Paramount)

Hal Kanter's breezy screenplay, from a story by Allan Weiss, is the slim, but convenient, foundation for a handsome, picture-postcard production crammed with typical South Seas musical hullaballoo. Plot casts Elvis Presley as the rebellious son of a pineapple tycoon who wants to make his own way in life, a project in which he succeeds after numerous romantic entanglements and misunderstandings.

Under Norman Taurog's broad direction, Presley, in essence, is playing himself. Romantic support is attractively dispatched by Joan Blackman and Nancy Walters. In a somewhat over-emphasized and incompletely-motivated role of an unhappy young tourist, pretty Jenny Maxwell emotes with youthful relish and spirit.

Musical numbers, about a dozen of them, are effectively staged by Charles O'Curran.

....

■ BLUE LAGOON, THE

1949, 103 MINS, UK ◇

Dir Frank Launder, Sidney Gilliat   *Prod* Frank Launder, Sidney Gilliat   *Scr* Frank Launder, John Baines, Michael Hogan   *Ph* Geoffrey Unsworth, Arthur Ibbetson   *Ed* Thelma Myers   *Mus* Clifton Parker
● Jean Simmons, Donald Houston, Noel Purcell, James Hayter, Cyril Cusack (Individual)

Technicolor photography of a glorious South Sea setting provides appropriate romantic background for this picturization of H. de Vere Stacpoole's novel.

There is very little plot to the film and the story of the two children, who are shipwrecked on a South Sea Island, is developed by a series of incidents rather than by a woven theme.

As the production relies for its appeal mainly on its eye-filling virtues, little demand has been made on the cast. Jean Simmons displays a sarong to advantage and Donald Houston has little more to do than show off his manly torso. Noel Purcell gives a warm study as the irascible old sailor shipwrecked with them.

....

■ BLUE LAGOON, THE

1980, 102 MINS, US ◇ Ⓥ

Dir Randal Kleiser   *Prod* Randal Kleiser   *Scr* Douglas Day Stewart   *Ph* Nestor Almendros   *Ed* Robert Gordon   *Mus* Basil Poledouris   *Art Dir* Jon Dowding
● Brooke Shields, Christopher Atkins, Leo McKern, William Daniels, Elva Josephson, Glenn Kohan (Columbia)

The Blue Lagoon is a beautifully mounted production, a low-keyed love story stressing the innocent eroticism of Brooke Shields and newcomer Christopher Atkins. This is the second adaptation of the 1903 novel by Henry DeVere Stacpoole about two shipwrecked children who grow from childhood in an isolated South Seas paradise.

Producer-director Randal Kleiser takes the pair through puberty and into parenthood with a charming candor that stresses natural, instinctive sexual development without leering at it.

Their romance is enhanced by Nestor Almendros' exquisite photography (and Basil Poledouris' score), as is the stunning beauty of the Fiji island where it was filmed.

....

■ BLUE LAMP, THE

1950, 82 MINS, UK

Dir Basil Dearden   *Prod* Michael Balcon   *Scr* T.E.B. Clarke   *Ph* Gordon Dines   *Ed* Peter Tanner   *Mus* Ernest Irving   *Art Dir* Jim Morahan
● Jack Warner, Jimmy Hanley, Dirk Bogarde, Patric Doonan, Bernard Lee, Dora Bryan (Ealing)

Dedicated to the British police force, the story describes the post-war crime wave as seen through the eyes of the man on the beat. Clear-cut direction and interesting location shots of London's back streets help the story along.

The crime-wave is spotlighted on two characters. At first they are smalltime crooks, but gradually become ambitious and go for the bigger stuff.

The all-round cast is topped by Jack Warner, who as always turns in a human, workmanlike performance. He takes the part of the constable and brings to that role the typical humor associated with the London copper. Jimmy Hanley plays a raw recruit to the police force with feeling, but the best performance comes from Dirk Bogarde who, with Patric Doonan, are the criminals.

....

■ BLUE MAX, THE

1966, 154 MINS, UK ◇ Ⓥ

Dir John Guillermin   *Prod* Christian Ferry   *Scr* David Pursall, Jack Seddon, Gerald Hanley   *Ph* Douglas Slocombe   *Ed* Max Benedict   *Mus* Jerry Goldsmith   *Art Dir* Wilfrid Shingleton
● George Peppard, James Mason, Ursula Andress, Jeremy Kemp, Karl Michael Vogler, Anton Diffring (20th Century-Fox)

The Blue Max is a World War I drama [from a novel by Jack D. Hunter] with some exciting aerial combat sequences helping to enliven a somewhat grounded, meller script in which no principal character engenders much sympathy.

A downbeat air prevails in the drama. The hero, a lowerclass climber played by George Peppard, is a heel; his adversary in the ranks of an air squadron, also for the free affections of Ursula Andress, is also a negative character, played by Jeremy Kemp. James Mason, husband of Andress, is looking for a propaganda symbol, finds it in Peppard, and eventually causes the latter's death. Only Karl Michael Vogler, the squadron commander, evokes any sympathy as a gentleman.

Director John Guillermin, who derived the uniformly fine performances within the given plot frame, has at times an exciting visual sense. On the other hand, his technique in more intimate sequences becomes obvious and mechanical.

....

■ BLUES BROTHERS, THE

1980, 133 MINS, US ◇ Ⓥ

Dir John Landis   *Prod* Robert K. Weiss   *Scr* Dan Aykroyd, John Landis   *Ph* Stephen M. Katz   *Ed* George Folsey Jr   *Mus* Ira Newborn   *Art Dir* John J. Lloyd
● John Belushi, Dan Aykroyd, James Brown, Ray Charles, Carrie Fisher, Aretha Franklin (Universal)

If Universal had made it 35 years earlier, *The Blues Brothers* might have been called *Abbott & Costello in Soul Town*. Level of inspiration is about the same now as then, the humor as basic, the enjoyment as fleeting. But at $30 million, this is a whole new ball-game.

Enacting Jake and Elwood Blues roles created for their popular concert and recording act, John Belushi and Dan Aykroyd use the slenderest of stories – attempt to raise $5,000 for their childhood parish by putting their old band back together – as an excuse to wreak havoc on the entire city of Chicago and much of the Midwest.

Film's greatest pleasure comes from watching the likes of James Brown, Cab Calloway, Ray Charles and especially Aretha Franklin do their musical things.

Given all the chaos, director and, with Aykroyd, cowriter, John Landis manages to keep things reasonably controlled and in a straight line. Pic plays as a spirited tribute by white boys to black musical culture, which was inspiration for the Blues Brothers act in the first place.

....

■ BLUE SKIES

1946, 104 MINS, US ◇

Dir Stuart Heisler   *Prod* Sol C. Siegel   *Scr* Arthur Sheekman   *Ph* Charles Lang   *Ed* LeRoy Stone   *Mus* Robert Emmett Dolan   *Art Dir* Hans Dreier, Hal Pereira
● Bing Crosby, Fred Astaire, Joan Caulfield (Paramount)

The cue sheet on *Blue Skies* lists 42 different Irving Berlin song items but some of it has been excised and the rest so skillfully arranged, orchestrated and presented that the nostalgic musical cavalcade doesn't pall. Fred Astaire's 'Puttin' on the Ritz' (originally written for Harry Richman) is the musical standout of the more than 30 items which

have been retained.

The story of *Blue Skies* is of familiar pattern and rather sketchily hung together by Astaire. He's cast as a disk jockey stringing the cavalcade of Berliniana together by recounting the nostalgic episodes behind the success of the platters as they are miked.

Bing Crosby is the romantic winnah throughout. Joan Caulfield is partial to the nitery troubadour (Crosby) whose unusual flair for opening and closing niteries is a plot keynote. Astaire is the suave dancing star and she's in the line of one of his shows. Astaire's romantic interest carries her along but Crosby's crooning charms her.

Mark Sandrich, who with Berlin, Crosby and Astaire whipped up *Holiday Inn* was the key man in *Blue Skies* until his sudden death interrupted production plans for the pic. Then, too, there was the emergency substitution of Astaire for Paul Draper, but with it all this film emerges a winner in every respect.

....

■ BLUE STEEL

1990, 102 MINS, US ◇ Ⓥ

Dir Kathryn Bigelow   *Prod* Edward R. Pressman, Oliver Stone, Michael Rausch   *Scr* Kathryn Bigelow, Eric Red   *Ph* Amir Mokri   *Ed* Lee Percy   *Mus* Brad Fiedel   *Art Dir* Tony Corbett
● Jamie Lee Curtis, Ron Silver, Clancy Brown, Elizabeth Pena, Louise Fletcher, Philip Bosco (United Artists/ Vestron/Lightning)

A taut, relentless thriller that hums with an electric current of outrage. Director and co-writer Kathryn Bigelow makes the most of her hook – the use of a female star (Jamie Lee Curtis) in a tough action pic – by stressing the character's vulnerability in remarkable early scenes.

As rookie cop Megan Turner, Curtis is hit with doubts and resistance from all corners, then suspended after she kills an armed robber (Tom Sizemore) her first night out and no gun is found at the scene. The psycho bystander who picked the gun up (Ron Silver) starts commiting serial murders with bullets he's carved his name onto, and Curtis, under deep suspicion, gets dragged back onto the force to help find him.

Curtis gives an eerily effective performance as Turner, getting across in palpable waves her shaky determination and inner steeliness. Script is at its weakest where the villain (Silver) is concerned – his characterization as a schizophrenic nutso with violent religious hallucinations is a writeoff. Even so, pic lacks nothing for menace and suspense, and has a frightening, explosively violent second half.

....

■ BLUE THUNDER

1983, 108 MINS, US ◇ Ⓥ

Dir John Badham   *Prod* Gordon Carroll   *Scr* Dan O'Bannan, Don Jakoby   *Ph* John A. Alonzo   *Ed* Frank Morriss, Edward Abroms   *Mus* Arthur B. Rubinstein   *Art Dir* Sidney Z. Litwack
● Roy Scheider, Malcolm McDowell, Warren Oates, Candy Clark, Daniel Stern, Paul Roebling (Rastar/Columbia)

Blue Thunder is a ripsnorting live-action cartoon, utterly implausible but no less enjoyable for that.

Opening 15 minutes take vet LA police helicopter pilot Roy Scheider and rookie Daniel Stern on nocturnal rounds, which encompass apprehension of some liquor store hold-up men, a little voyeurism outside the window of a sexy babe and, more seriously, trying to help stem an assault on a female city councilwoman at her home.

Reprimanded by boss Warren Oates for the sex-show detour, Scheider is nevertheless invited to a demonstration of the Feds' latest creation, Blue Thunder, a top-secret anti-terrorist chopper loaded with artillery and all manner of privacy invasion technology.

Craft has been brought to LA for possible use against subversives during the 1984 Olympic Games, and among those in charge of the program is cardboard villain Malcolm McDowell, with whom Scheider served in Vietnam. For sketchy reasons, they hated each other then and they hate each other now.

Although brief Vietnam flashbacks punctuate the film to 'explain' animosity between Scheider and McDowell, streamlined script has been shorn of almost all psychology and complexity, and it hardly matters.

● ●

■ **BLUE VEIL, THE**

1951, 113 MINS, US

Dir Curtis Bernhardt *Prod* Jerry Wald, Norman Krasna *Scr* Norman Corwin *Ph* Franz Planer *Ed* George J. Amy *Mus* Franz Waxman *Art Dir* Albert S. D'Agostino, Carroll Clark
● Jane Wyman, Charles Laughton, Joan Blondell, Richard Carlson, Agnes Moorehead, Don Taylor (Wald-Krasna/RKO)

Story [by Francois Campaux] is nothing more than a series of episodes strung together by the central character of a First World War war-widow who devotes her life to children after losing her only child. Footage opens with the child's death, a moving sequence, and carries Jane Wyman through a succession of jobs as a baby nurse until, old and wornout physically, she is given the lifetime job of caring for the offspring of one of her former charges.

Charles Laughton, as a portly, kindly corset manufacturer, is Wyman's first costar, in the initial episode.

Romance makes a bid for Wyman in her new job in the home of wealthy Agnes Moorehead, but she is unable to leave her charge to go off to foreign lands with Richard Carlson, a tutor who courts her.

Next is the episode in which she cares for Natalie Wood, daughter of fading musical actress Joan Blondell. This sequence is considerably enlivened by the pert vivacity of Blondell and her singing of two old tunes.

Wyman experiences real heartbreak at the end of eight years of caring for the abandoned son of Audrey Totter when the latter returns from England after the Second World War, with a stepfather, and claims the boy.

Curtis Bernhardt's direction handles the drama surely, if at times a bit measured, and never strives for dramatic tricks beyond the level of the simple, warm story being told.

● ●

■ **BLUE VELVET**

1986, 120 MINS, US ◇ Ⓥ

Dir David Lynch *Prod* Fred Caruso *Scr* David Lynch *Ph* Frederick Elmes *Ed* Duwayne Dunham *Mus* Angelo Badalamenti *Art Dir* Patricia Norris
● Kyle MacLachlan, Isabella Rossellini, Dennis Hopper, Laura Dern, Hope Lange, Dean Stockwell (De Laurentiis)

Blue Velvet finds David Lynch back on familiar, strange, territory. Picture takes a disturbing and at times devastating look at the ugly underside of Middle American life.

The modest proportions of the film are just right for the writer-director's desire to investigate the inexplicable demons that drive people to deviate from expected norms of behavior and thought.

The setting, a small town called Lumberton, seems on the surface to be utterly conventional, placid, comforting and serene. The bland perfection is disrupted when a man collapses in Kyle MacLachlan's yard and is further upset when he discovers a disembodied human ear in an empty lot.

He begins investigating whose ear he might

have found, and ends up spying on local roadhouse chanteuse and prostie Isabella Rossellini. Peeping through a closet keyhole, what he sees violent client Dennis Hopper do to sweet Laura Dern launches MacLachlan into another world, into an unfamiliar, dangerously provocative state of mind.

Rossellini, dressed in lingerie or less much of the time, throws herself into this mad role with complete abandon. Hopper creates a flabbergasting portrait of unrepentent, irredeemable evil.

● ●

■ **BLUME IN LOVE**

1973, 115 MINS, US

Dir Paul Mazursky *Prod* Paul Mazursky *Scr* Paul Mazursky *Ph* Bruce Surtees *Ed* Donn Cambern *Mus* Bill Conti *Art Dir* Pato Guzman
● George Segal, Susan Anspach, Kris Kristofferson, Marsha Mason, Shelley Winters, Paul Mazursky (Warner)

Blume in Love is a technically well made, but dramatically distended comedy-drama starring George Segal as a man determined to win back the affections of Susan Anspach, the wife who divorced him for infidelity. Needless time-juggling flashback, indulgent writing, lazy structure, and pretentious social commentary blunt some fine performances which occasionally inject life into the plot.

It takes Segal 115 minutes to win back Anspach's affections, the road being littered with relentless footage from Venice, Italy, and lots of cutesy sidebar micro-vignette which is lingeringly set up only for a fast cut from some limp gag line. There are a few good laughs, a handful of chuckles, several smiles, and a ton of songs, some by Kris Kristofferson who is starred as Anspach's dropout lover.

● ●

■ **BOARDWALK**

1979, 98 MINS, US ◇ Ⓥ

Dir Stephen Verona *Prod* George Willoughby *Scr* Stephen Verona, Leigh Chapman *Ph* Billy Williams
● Ruth Gordon, Lee Strasberg, Janet Leigh, Joe Silver, Eddie Barth, Kim Delgado (Atlantic Releasing)

At times genuinely affecting, at others patently manipulative, *Boardwalk* is a small, well-wrought feature that centers on the efforts of an elderly Jewish couple to survive the barrenness and dangers of their decaying Brooklyn neighborhood.

But although there's a strong emotional core (and ample talent) to its portrait of the stubbornly 'youthful' eldsters (Lee Strasberg and Ruth Gordon), it's the film's chronicle of their mounting terrorization at the hands of a black youth gang that overrides its tone, shading the pic into a *Death Wish* finale.

Director and co-scripter Stephen Verona quickly establishes his focal family as a tight-knit, mostly loving unit.

● ●

■ **BOB & CAROL & TED & ALICE**

1969, 104 MINS, US ◇ Ⓥ

Dir Paul Mazursky *Prod* Larry Tucker *Scr* Paul Mazursky, Larry Tucker *Ph* Charles E. Lang *Ed* Stuart Pappe *Mus* Quincy Jones *Art Dir* Pato Guzman
● Natalie Wood, Robert Culp, Elliott Gould, Dyan Cannon, Horst Ebersberg, Lee Bergere (Columbia/Frankovich)

The story concerns a young documentary filmmaker (Robert Culp) and his wife (Natalie Wood) who visit an institute in Southern California which supposedly helps people expand their capacities for love and understanding. When our friends are back in their swank surroundings, chatting with friends, Elliott Gould and wife Dyan Cannon, the comedy begins and never lets up until the

final scenes when the sociological effects of this pseudo-liberal thinking come into play.

The acting is superb. Cannon proves an expert comedienne. She and Gould practically steal the film, although admittedly they have the best lines. Wood and Culp give equally fine performances.

The film is almost flawless, presenting the issues in a pleasing, entertaining and thought-provoking manner.

● ●

■ **BOBBY DEERFIELD**

1977, 124 MINS, US ◇ Ⓥ

Dir Sydney Pollack *Prod* Sydney Pollarck *Scr* Alvin Sargent *Ph* Henri Decae *Ed* Fredric Steinkamp *Mus* Dave Grusin *Art Dir* Stephen Grimes
● Al Pacino, Marthe Keller, Anny Duperey, Walter McGinn, Romolo Valli, Stephan Meldegg (Columbia)

Bobby Deerfield is a brilliantly unusual love story, told in a European fashion which makes the Sydney Pollack film at first irritating, then intriguing, finally most rewarding and emotionally satisfying.

Stars Al Pacino and Marthe Keller are both excellent as shallow jet-set floaters who become whole persons in their romance. Foreign location footage is lavish.

Erich Maria Remarque's novel, *Heaven Has No Favorites*, served as the basis for screenplay. Pacino plays the title character, a Newark boy whose interest in car racing has propelled him into international celeb status where he'd rather forget his origins. Keller is a wealthy and elusive character, manic in her life style because of terminal illness.

● ●

■ **BODY AND SOUL**

1947, 101 MINS, US Ⓥ

Dir Robert Rossen *Prod* Bob Roberts *Scr* Abraham Polonsky *Ph* James Wong Howe *Ed* Francis Lyon, Robert Parrish *Mus* Hugo Friedhofer *Art Dir* Nathan Juran
● John Garfield, Lilli Palmer, Anne Revere, Canada Lee (United Artists/Enterprise)

Body and Soul has a somewhat familiar title and a likewise familiar narrative. It's the telling, however, that's different.

The story concerns a youngster with a punching flair who emerges from the amateurs to ride along the knockout trail to the middleweight championship. But to get himself a crack at the title he has to sell 50 per cent of himself to a bigtime gambler with a penchant for making and breaking champs at will.

There are a flock of loopholes in this story, but interest seldom lags. Some of the 'inside boxing' is authentic, but the 'inside gambling' is another story in itself, which this pic doesn't tell. John Garfield is convincing in the lead part, and the boxing scenes look the McCoy.

Poolhall and beer stube environments are effectively captured to indicate the sordidness that backgrounds the early careers of most boxers, who turn to the ring because of a proficiency with their fists on the streetcorner. Lilli Palmer is miscast as Garfield's sweetheart and inspiration, especially with a continental accent that even the dialog can't properly clarify.

● ●

■ **BODY DOUBLE**

1984, 109 MINS, US ◇ Ⓥ

Dir Brian De Palma *Prod* Brian De Palma *Scr* Robert J. Avrech, Brian De Palma *Ph* Stephen H. Burum *Ed* Jerry Greenberg, Bill Pankow *Mus* Pino Donaggio *Art Dir* Ida Random
● Craig Wasson, Gregg Henry, Melanie Griffith, Deborah Shelton, Guy Boyd, Dennis Franz (Columbia/Delphi Prods II)

Brian De Palma lets all his obsessions hang

out in *Body Double*. A voyeur's delight and a feminist's nightmare, sexpenser features an outrageously far-fetched and flimsy plot.

The first half offers up virtually no storyline. Down-on-his-luck Hollywood actor Craig Wasson is befriended by fellow actor Gregg Henry, who invites him to housesit for him at a rich man's hilltop pad.

In a house across the way a beautiful woman enacts an elaborate striptease dance at the same hour every evening. Wasson digs the lady's act so much that he follows her the next day, when she is also pursued by a hideous-looking Indian.

Pivotal murder scene occurs at about the midpoint, and it's an offensive lulu, being performed with an enormous power drill.

Remainder of the film sees Wasson getting involved in the porno film world as a way of solving the murder.

Thesping by Wasson, Henry and former Miss USA Deborah Shelton, as the lady across the hill, is serviceable, while Melanie Griffith, with punky dyed hair and teensy voice, is just right as a porno queen.

●●●●●●●●●●●●●●●●●●●●●●●●●●●●●●●●

■ **BODY HEAT**

1981, 113 MINS, US ◇
Dir Lawrence Kasdan   *Prod* Fred T. Gallo
Scr Lawrence Kasdan   *Ph* Richard H. Cline   *Ed* Carol Littleton   *Mus* John Barry   *Art Dir* Bill Kenney
● William Hurt, Kathleen Turner, Richard Crenna, Ted Danson, Mickey Rourke, J.A. Preston (Warner/Ladd)

Body Heat is an engrossing, mightily stylish meller in which sex and crime walk hand in hand down the path to tragedy, just like in the old days. Working in the imposing shadow of the late James M. Cain screenwriter Lawrence Kasdan makes an impressively confident directorial debut.

William Hurt is a spirited but struggling lawyer just getting by in a marginal Florida coast town whose persistent pursuit of sultry Kathleen Turner pays off in the way of a torrid affair, highly satisfying for both parties.

She's the young wife of loaded middle-aged businessman Richard Crenna, and it isn't long before the passion can't tolerate the limitations imposed. Just as in *Double Indemnity* it's the dame who hatches the murder plot, with the guy finally falling into line and coming up with the ingenious way to pull it off.

However familiar the elements, Kasdan has brought the drama alive by steeping it in humid, virtually oozing atmosphere. The heat of the title is palpably evident, both mundanely in the weather and in the irresistible attraction of the sexy leads.

Hurt successfully mixes both laconicism and innocence. In her film debut, Turner registers strongly as a hard gal with a past. Her deep-voiced delivery instantly recalls that of young Lauren Bacall without seeming like an imitation.

●●●●●●●●●●●●●●●●●●●●●●●●●●●●●●●●

■ **BOEING BOEING**

1965, 102 MINS, US ◇
Dir John Rich   *Prod* Hal Wallis   *Scr* Edward Anhalt
Ph Lucien Ballard   *Ed* Warren Low, Archie Marshek
Mus Neal Hefti   *Art Dir* Hal Pereira, Walter Tyler
● Tony Curtis, Jerry Lewis, Dany Saral, Christine Schmidtmer, Suzanna Leigh, Thelma Ritter (Paramount)

Boeing Boeing is an excellent modern comedy about two newshawks with a yen for airline hostesses. Firstrate performances and direction make the most of a very good script.

The fanciful dream of a dedicated bachelor is realized in this adaptation of a Marc Camoletti play in which Paris-based US newsman Tony Curtis has three airline gals on a string.

Director John Rich has done a topnotch job in overcoming what is essentially (except for a few Paris exteriors) a one-set, one-joke

comedy. Curtis is excellent and neatly restrained as the harem keeper whose cozy scheme approaches collapse when advanced design Boeing aircraft (hence, the title) augur a disastrous overlap in femme availability.

Rich has also brought out a new dimension in Lewis, herein excellent in a solid comedy role as Curtis' professional rival who threatens to explode the plan.

The outstanding performance is delivered by Thelma Ritter, Curtis' harried housekeeper who makes the necessary domestic changes in photos, clothing and menu so that the next looker will continue to believe that she, alone, is mistress of the flat.

●●●●●●●●●●●●●●●●●●●●●●●●●●●●●●●●

■ **BOFORS GUN, THE**

1968, 105 MINS, UK ◇
Dir James Gold   *Prod* Robert A. Goldston   *Scr* John McGrath   *Ph* Alan Hume   *Ed* Anne V. Coates
Mus Carl Davis   *Art Dir* Terence Knight
● Nicol Williamson, Ian Holm, David Warner, Peter Vaughan, Richard O'Callaghan, Barry Jackson (Universal)

No question of the quality of this absorbing, though downbeat military pic set in a British barracks in Germany in the mid-1950s.

It has all the gripping fascination of a tussle between two wily, desperate young animals. Taut, icy direction and acting flawlessly tuned to what the writer has in mind bring a faultless realism.

Clash is between David Warner as an immature, indecisive one-striper and Nicol Williamson as a half-crazy, embittered Irish rebel, alcoholic and self-tortured. Events sizzle powerfully on the night before Warner is due to go to England for an officers' course. Williamson is attached to Warner's guard and, with rebellion and anger rankling inside him, sets out to humiliate the NCO and wreck his prospects of promotion.

Williamson brings out the rebel's mood brilliantly, his features, speech and behavior veering alarmingly from good-humored cynicism to anger and viciousness. Warner is just as good as the weak young man.

●●●●●●●●●●●●●●●●●●●●●●●●●●●●●●●●

■ **BOHEMIAN GIRL, THE**

1936, 80 MINS, US ▽
Dir James W. Horne, Charles Rogers   *Prod* Hal Roach   *Scr* [uncredited]   *Ph* Art Lloyd, Francis Corby
Ed Bert Jordan, Louis McManus   *Art Dir* Arthur I. Royce, William L. Stevens
● Stan Laurel, Oliver Hardy, Thelma Todd, Antonio Moreno, Jacqueline Wells, James Finlayson (M-G-M)

A comedy with little or no comedy. Laurel and Hardy are snatch-purses with an 18th-century band of roving gypsies. In retaliation for the flogging of a fellow-member (Antonio Moreno), caught red-handed in an attempted burglary, the gypsies steal the child of a nobleman and bring her up as one of their own. In the end the customary tell-tale medallion saves the peeress and restores her to her daddy.

There are no credits for screen adaptation. Responsibility is thrown back upon Michael Balfe who wrote the original opera in 1843 and should be permitted to rest in peace. He composed the score; original librettists also not credited – or blamed.

Chained to such a scenario, the picture has the additional liability of inept direction. Thelma Todd who goes through the motions of singing (a mere bit) with the voice track poorly synchronized to her lips, seems strangely unlike herself. (A good deal of her footage, fortunately for her rep, was cut out just prior to release).

●●●●●●●●●●●●●●●●●●●●●●●●●●●●●●●●

■ **BOLERO**

1984, 104 MINS, US ◇ ▽
Dir John Derek   *Prod* Bo Derek   *Scr* John Derek
Ph John Derek   *Ed* John Derek   *Mus* Peter Bernstein, Elmer Bernstein   *Art Dir* Alan Roderick-Jones
● Bo Derek, George Kennedy, Andrea Occhipinti, Ana Obregon, Olivia D'Abo, Greg Bensen (Cannon/City)

Bolero is all about Bo Derek's determination to lose her virginity after graduating from an English boarding school. Accompanied by friend Ana Obregon and family retainer George Kennedy, Bo ventures first to Arabia where a sheik falls asleep in her arms.

Still unviolated, Bo moves on to Spain where she meets handsome bullfighter Andrea Occhipinti. Ready for womanhood, Bo utters the immortal lines: 'Do everything to me. Show me how I can do everything to you. Is there enough I can do for you so you can give ecstasy to me?'

Then the dog barks and the deed is done. But poor Bo no sooner has her initial introduction to amour than the new lover gets gored in a sensitive location, putting him out of commission.

●●●●●●●●●●●●●●●●●●●●●●●●●●●●●●●●

■ **BONFIRE OF THE VANITIES, THE**

1990, 125 MINS, US ◇ ▽
Dir Brian De Palma   *Prod* Brian De Palma
Scr Michael Cristofer   *Ph* Vilmos Zsigmond   *Ed* David Ray, Bill Pankow   *Mus* Dave Grusin   *Art Dir* Richard Sylbert
● Tom Hanks, Bruce Willis, Melanie Griffith, Kim Cattrall, Morgan Freeman, F. Murray Abraham (Warner)

Brian de Palma's take on Tom Wolfe's *The Bonfire of the Vanities* is a misfire of inanities. Wolfe's first novel boasted rich characters and teeming incident that proved highly alluring to filmmakers. Unfortunately, De Palma was not the man for the job. It doesn't take long to turn off and tune out on this glitzy $45 million-plus dud.

Early sequences of marital discord between Wall Street maestro Sherman McCoy (Tom Hanks) and wife Judy (Kim Cattrall) possess a grating, uncertain quality, and film never manages to locate a consistent tone. McCoy is having an affair with Southern bombshell Maria Ruskin (Melanie Griffith), and clearly stands as a symbol for Success, 1980s style. Monkeywrench arrives in the form of an automobile mishap one night in deepest Bronx.

Seemingly threatened by two black youths, Maria backs Sherman's Mercedes into one of them, slightly injuring him. When the kid falls into a coma, the machinery of law, politics and journalism begins grinding. The rich man's status makes him an ideal scapegoat for multifarious social ills, as well for as the personal agendas of the city's most shameless operators, most prominently, Peter Fallow (Bruce Willis), a down-and-out alcoholic reporter who parlays the McCoy story into fame and fortune.

Unfortunately, the caricatures are so crude and the 'revelations' so unenlightening of the human condition, that the satire is about as socially incisive as a *Police Academy* entry.

●●●●●●●●●●●●●●●●●●●●●●●●●●●●●●●●

■ **BONJOUR TRISTESSE**

1958, 94 MINS, US ◇ ▽
Dir Otto Preminger   *Prod* Otto Preminger   *Scr* Arthur Laurents   *Ph* Georges Perinal   *Ed* Helga Cranston
Mus Georges Auric   *Art Dir* Roger Furse
● Deborah Kerr, David Niven, Jean Seberg, Mylene Demongeot, Geoffrey Horne, Juliette Greco (Columbia)

In transplanting Francoise Sagan's thin book to the screen, producer-director Otto Preminger basically has stayed with her first-person tale of the amours of a middle-aged, charming and wealthy Frenchman within both view and earshot of his daughter who, like the author at the time, is 17. It's hardly a matter of wonder that pere's free-living escapades should prove contagious, that the girl, too, should take a fling at same.

But it is not a Class A effort. Script deficiencies and awkward reading – some lines are spoken as though just that – have static results.

Detracting from the make-believe also is Jean Seberg's deportment. In her second cinematic try (her first was in Preminger's unfortunate *Saint Joan*), Seberg's Cecile is more suggestive of a high school senior back home than the frisky, knowing, close friend and daughter of a roue living it up in the sumptuous French setting. She is, of course, a selfish and malicious character to start with.

David Niven is properly affable as the father who travels with a mistress and makes no attempt to disguise his pursuits. Deborah Kerr is a standout talent as the artist whom Niven proposes to marry and who speeds away to apparent suicide upon finding him in another illicit situation, but there are instances where she, too, has difficulty with the stiltedness of the dialog.

Mylene Demongeot fits in well as a silly, sunburned blonde; Geoffrey Horne rates adequate as playmate for Cecile; and Walter Chiari comes off as something of a cariacature of a rich South American.

● ●

■ **BONNIE AND CLYDE**

1967, 111 MINS, US ◇ ▼

Dir Arthur Penn   *Prod* Warren Beatty   *Scr* David Newman, Robert Benton   *Ph* Burnett Guffey   *Ed* Dede Allen   *Mus* Charles Strouse   *Art Dir* Dean Tavoularis
● Warren Beatty, Faye Dunaway, Michael J. Pollard, Gene Hackman, Estelle Parsons, Denver Pyle (Warner/ Seven Arts/Tatira-Hiller)

Warren Beatty's *Bonnie and Clyde* incongruously couples comedy with crime, in this biopic of Bonnie Parker and Clyde Barrow, a pair of Texas desperadoes who roamed and robbed the southwest and midwest during the bleak Depression days of the early 1930s.

Conceptually, the film leaves much to be desired, because killings and the backdrop of the Depression are scarcely material for a bundle of laughs. However, the film does have some standout interludes.

Scripters Newman and Benton have depicted these real-life characters as inept, bumbling, moronic types, and if this had been true they would have been erased in their first try. It's a picture with conflicting moods, racing from crime to comedy, and intermingling genuinely moving love scenes between Faye Dunaway as Bonnie and Beatty as Clyde.

This inconsistency of direction is the most obvious fault of *Bonnie and Clyde*, which has some good ingredients, although they are not meshed together well. Like the film itself, the performances are mostly erratic. Beatty is believable at times, but his characterization lacks any consistency. Dunaway is a knockout as Bonnie Parker, registers with deep sensitivity in the love scenes, and conveys believability to her role. Michael J. Pollard and Gene Hackman are more clowns than baddies as gang members; Estelle Parsons is good.

□ 1967: Best Picture (Nomination)

● ●

■ **BOOM**

1968, 112 MINS, US/UK ◇

Dir Joseph Losey   *Prod* John Heyman   *Scr* Tennessee Williams   *Ph* Douglas Slocombe   *Ed* Reginald Beck   *Mus* John Barry   *Art Dir* Richard MacDonald
● Elizabeth Taylor, Richard Burton, Noel Coward, Joanna Shimkus, Michael Dunn, Romolo Valli (Universal)

The translation to film of Tennessee Wil-

liams' much-revised play, *The Milk Train Doesn't Stop Here Anymore*, has at least given more physical movement to the symbolic drama of not-so-dolce vita among the jaded rich. Joseph Losey directs stars Elizabeth Taylor, Richard Burton and Noel Coward in John Heyman's plush production.

Film is the uninteresting tale of a multi-married, aging shrew, played by Taylor.

Coward, a neighboring swish from Capri, adds a good shot of life, unfortunately too early and too little.

Taylor's delineation of the lead role is off the mark; instead of an earthy dame, hypochondriac and hyperemotional, who has survived six wealthy husbands, she plays it like she has just lost the first, who would appear to have taken her away from a roadside truck stop job. The wealth is shown in too nouveau riche a manner. The gowns, jewels and sets only emphasize the point. Burton is far more believable as a freeloading poet working the Mediterranean circuit.

● ●

■ **BOOMERANG!**

1947, 87 MINS, US

Dir Elia Kazan   *Prod* Louis de Rochemont   *Scr* Richard Murphy   *Ph* Norbert Brodine   *Ed* Harmon Jones   *Mus* David Buttolph   *Art Dir* Richard Day, Chester Gore
● Dana Andrews, Jane Wyatt, Lee J. Cobb, Arthur Kennedy, Karl Malden, Sam Levene   (20th Century-Fox)

Boomerang! is gripping, real-life melodrama, told in semi-documentary style. Lensing was done on location at Stamford, Conn, the locale adding to realism. Based on a still unsolved murder case in Bridgeport, Conn, plot is backed up with strong cast.

Dana Andrews heads the convincing cast. His role is realistic and a top performance job. While carrying a fictional name as state's attorney, the role, in real life, has its counterpart in Homer Cummings, who went on from the state post to become Attorney-General of the United States. Case on which plot is based deals with murder of a Bridgeport priest and how the prosecuting attorney establishes the innocence of the law's only suspect.

All the leads have the stamp of authenticities. The dialog and situations further the factual technique. Lee J. Cobb shows up strongly as chief detective, harassed by press and politicians alike while trying to carry out his duties. Arthur Kennedy is great as the law's suspect.

● ●

■ **BOOST, THE**

1988, 95 MINS, US ◇ ▼

Dir Harold Becker   *Prod* Daniel H. Blatt, Mel Howard   *Scr* Darryl Ponicsan   *Ph* Howard Atherton   *Ed* Maury Winetrobe   *Mus* Stanley Myers   *Art Dir* Waldemar Kalinowski
● James Woods, Sean Young, John Kapelos, Steven Hill, Kelle Kerr, Amanda Blake (Hemdale)

Based on Benjamin Stein's book *Ludes*, well-wrought screenplay is a cautionary tale about a couple involved in a mutually destructive, coke-dominated lifestyle.

Young and very much in love, Lenny and Linda Brown (James Woods and Sean Young) are still struggling to make ends meet in New York City when Lenny, a born hustler with financial smarts, receives an extraordinary opportunity from businessman Steven Hill to make his fortune by moving to Los Angeles and selling tax shelters.

His expanding balloon is popped by word that Congress proposed to close the tax loopholes through which he and his clients are benefiting. Lenny suddenly finds himself deep in the hole financially, as well as hooked on the cocaine he started taking only as a 'boost' to get him through rough times.

For the film to work at all, the love story be-

tween Lenny and Linda must feel as overpowering as it is meant to, and Woods and Young put this over with miles to spare. Both actors are live wires, so the passion, care and commitment the characters have for one another is palpable at all times.

● ●

■ **BORDER, THE**

1982, 107 MINS, US ◇ ▼

Dir Tony Richardson   *Prod* Edgar Bronfman Jr   *Scr* Deric Washburn, Walon Green, David Freeman   *Ph* Ric Waite, Vilmos Zsigmond   *Ed* Robert K. Lambert   *Mus* Ry Cooder   *Art Dir* Toby Rafelson
● Jack Nicholson, Harvey Keitel, Valerie Perrine, Warren Oates, Elpidia Carrillo, Shannon Wilcox (Universal/RKO/Efer)

Despite Jack Nicholson's multi-leveled performance, *The Border* is a surprisingly uninvolving film. Story of the personal and professional pressures on border patrol guard Nicholson, caught between right and wrong on both fronts, becomes murky and disjointed under Tony Richardson's uninspired direction.

Nicholson etches a nice guy victimized by his surroundings instead of an eccentric. Living in depressed circumstances with whiney, materialistic wife Valerie Perrine, he is the quintessential poor working stiff.

Nicholson is then befriended by Harvey Keitel, husband of Perrine's bimbo girlfriend and a fellow guard. It is their job to make sure none of the Mexicans over the border get into the US a task to which the humane Nicholson is ill-suited.

This is particularly the case once Nicholson views the rampant corruption of his fellow workers. The situation escalates as the baby of a poor, beautiful Mexican girl is kidnapped for adoption and Nicholson has to decide whether to stand by or take action.

The picture was already in the can when Universal decided to go back and shoot a much more upbeat ending where Nicholson emerges as hero.

● ●

■ **BORDERLINE**

1980, 97 MINS, US ◇ ▼

Dir Gerrold Freedman   *Prod* Martin Starger   *Scr* Steve Kline, Gerrold Freedman   *Ph* Tak Fujimoto   *Ed* John Link   *Mus* Gil Melle   *Art Dir* Michael Levesque
● Charles Bronson, Bruno Kirby, Ed Harris, Karmin Murcelo, Michael Lerner (ITC)

This Charles Bronson vehicle tackles a serious subject – the profiteering in illicit Mexican immigration – with workmanlike dramatic skill and a notable preference for realism over hokum.

The film's big name is self-effacing almost to the point of elusiveness. As a long-serving, compassionate border patrolman, Bronson is hunched and hated virtually throughout; his face is mostly masked by heavy shadow.

The professionally-honed, conventional plot pits him against a younger, ruthless racketeer who runs wetbacks across the border at an exploitative price on behalf of a US business corporation.

Newcomer Ed Harris is memorable as the frontline villain, displaying screen presence to match the star's and thus injecting a powerful sense of danger.

● ●

■ **BORN FREE**

1966, 95 MINS, UK ◇ ▼

Dir James Hill   *Prod* Sam Jaffe, Paul Radin   *Scr* Gerald L.C. Copley   *Ph* Kenneth Talbot   *Ed* Don Deacon   *Mus* John Barry
● Virginia McKenna, Bill Travers, Geoffrey Keen, Peter Lukoye, Omar Chambati, Bill Godden (Open Road/ High Road)

Born Free is a heart-warming story of a British couple in Africa who, at the maturity of their pet lioness, educate the beast to survive in the bush.

It's an excellent adaptation of Joy Adamson's books (which were as much photos as text) with restraint, loving care, and solid emotional appeal that seldom becomes banal.

Gerald L. C. Copley has done a first rate adaptation of the true story of Joy Adamson, who with hubby George involuntarily domesticated several pet lions. They kept one, Elsa, until she was fully grown and then, to save her from government-ordered zoo captivity, trained her to survive as a wild animal. The apparently childless couple are portrayed in top form by real-life married couple Virginia McKenna and Bill Travers.

Geoffrey Keen is excellent as the friendly government commissioner who finally convinces them the lioness should be sent to a zoo or set free. Keen gives the role much depth via the humor engendered from his natural aversion to the lioness, balanced by his British reserve.

■ BORN IN FLAMES

1983, 90 MINS, US ◇

Dir Lizzie Borden   *Prod* Lizzie Borden   *Scr* Lizzie Borden   *Ph* Ed Bowes, Al Santana, Phil O'Reilly   *Ed* Lizzie Borden   *Mus* The Bloods, The Red Crayolas, Ibis

● Honey, Jeanne Satterfield, Adele Bertei, Becky Johnson, Pat Murphy, Kathy Bigelow (Jerome Foundation)

Lizzie Borden's 16mm independent production, which took some two years to complete, appears to have all the advantages and the disadvantages of a home movie. It is impertinent, audacious, abounding in fresh ideas, considerably untraditional ideas. On the other hand, it is disjointed, with no real characters, preachy, the script unsufficiently developed and the acting often amateurish.

Situated in the near future after America has gone through a socialist revolution which has turned it into a sort of one-party progressive democracy, the story deals with the condition of women in that new society, conditions that, in Borden's opinion, changed very little from those prevalent today.

Borden shows how the extremists are proven right, and how such a revolution should be prepared in future.

The film's main grace is its sense of humor, a rare quality indeed in a militant film. Nervously edited, it has an almost documentary touch in the use of the camera on real New York locations, and a powerful beat soundtrack.

■ BORN ON THE FOURTH OF JULY

1989, 144 MINS, US ◇ ▼

Dir Oliver Stone   *Prod* A. Kitman Ho   *Scr* Ron Kovic, Oliver Stone   *Ph* Robert Richardson   *Ed* David Brenner   *Mus* John Williams   *Art Dir* Bruno Rubeo

● Tom Cruise, Raymond J. Barry, Caroline Kava, Kyra Sedgwick, Willem Dafoe, Jerry Levine (Ixtlan/Universal)

Oliver Stone again shows America to itself in a way it won't forget. His collaboration with Vietnam veteran Ron Kovic to depict Kovic's odyssey from teenage true believer to wheelchair-bound soldier in a very different war results in a gripping, devastating and telling film about the Vietnam era.

Stone creates a portrait of a fiercely pure-hearted boy who loved his country and believed that to serve it and to be a man was to fight a war. It turned out to be Vietnam, and that's where the belief was shattered.

In 'Nam, things go terribly wrong – young Sgt Kovic accidentally kills a fellow marine in battle. His attempted confession is harshly denied him by a c.o. Later, he's shot in the foot, gets up for a gritty round of Sgt Rock grandstanding, and is hit again and paralyzed.

Stone drenches the picture in visceral reality, from the agonizing chaos of a field hospital to the dead stalemate of a Bronx veteran's hospital infested with rats, drugs and the humiliation of lying helplessly in one's own excrement.

The US Kovic left behind is unrecognizable, yet as he struggles uselessly to regain control of his body he remains steadfast in his ideas, shouting 'Love it or leave it!' at his peacenik brother (Josh Evans).

Tom Cruise, who takes Kovic from clean-cut eager teen to impassioned long-haired activist, is stunning. Dafoe, as a disabled vet hiding out in a Mexican beach town in a haze of mescal, whores and poker, gives a startling, razor-sharp performance.

□ 1989: Best Picture (Nomination)

■ BORN TO DANCE

1936, 105 MINS, US

Dir Roy Del Ruth   *Prod* Jack Cummings   *Scr* Jack McGowan, Sid Silvers, B.G. DeSylva   *Ph* Ray June   *Ed* Blanche Sewell   *Mus* Alfred Newman (dir.)

● Eleanor Powell, James Stewart, Virginia Bruce, Una Merkel, Sid Silvers, Frances Langford (M-G-M)

Born to Dance is corking entertainment, more nearly approaching the revue type than most musical films, despite the presence of a 'book'. Cast is youthful, sight stuff is lavish, the specialties are meritorious, and as for songs, the picture is positively filthy with them. Cole Porter included at least two hits among the seven numbers delivered.

Eleanor Powell becomes a star in her second picture. She is given an opportunity to show that she's not just a good buck dancer, but an exceptionally versatile girl. As an actress she still has not arrived, as indicated in the few occasions when this plot calls for acting.

James Stewart's assignment calls for a shy youth. His singing and dancing are rather painful on their own, but he's surrounded by good people, and it's all done in a spirit of fun. Frances Langford has a running part, but her big responsibility is the singing build-up to Powell's finale dance and the pretentious production topper of the picture.

Buddy Ebsen has a couple of spots for his eccentric dancing and tackles the comedy, along with Sid Silvers, Una Merkel and Raymond Walburn.

It's a combination navy-backstage story, with the sailors, as usual, looking for their old girlfriends while on leave in the big town, and the understudy follows the rules by stepping into the indisposed star's part at the last moment.

■ BORN YESTERDAY

1950, 102 MINS, US ▼

Dir George Cukor   *Prod* S. Sylvan Simon   *Scr* Albert Mannheimer   *Ph* Joseph Walker   *Ed* Charles Nelson   *Mus* Frederick Hollander

● Broderick Crawford, Judy Holliday, William Holden, Howard St John, Frank Otto, Larry Oliver (Columbia)

The bright, biting comedy of the Garson Kanin legit hit adapts easily to film.

Judy Holliday repeats her legit success here as femme star of the film version. Almost alone, she makes *Born Yesterday*.

Holliday delights as she tosses off the mala-props that so aptly fit the character. Even though considerable amount of the dialog is unintelligible, its sound and her artful delivery smite the risibilities. William Holden is quietly effective as the newspaperman hired to coach her in social graces so she will better fit in with her junkman's ambitious plans.

Broderick Crawford, as the selfmade dealer in junk, comes off much less successfully. The actual and implied sympathy is missing, leaving it just a loud-shouting, boorish person.

□ 1950: Best Picture (Nomination)

■ BOSTONIANS, THE

1984, 120 MINS, UK ◇ ▼

Dir James Ivory   *Prod* Ismail Merchant   *Scr* Ruth Prawer Jhabvala   *Ph* Walter Lassally   *Ed* Katherine Wenning, Mark Potter   *Mus* Richard Robbins   *Art Dir* Leo Austin

● Christopher Reeve, Vanessa Redgrave, Madeleine Potter, Jessica Tandy, Nancy Marchand, Wesley Addy (Merchant-Ivory/Rank/Rediffusion)

Like the Merchant-Ivory-Jhabvala team's 1979 *The Europeans*, this is a classy adaptation of a Henry James novel.

From the film's opening sequence at a women's meeting in late 19th-century Boston, the dice are loaded against the feminist cause. The young Verena Tarrant offers an impassioned exposition of woman's sufferings only after being 'touched' by the hands of her faith-healer father.

The emotional weight of the pic is carried by the relationship that evolves between Verena (Madeleine Potter) and Olive Chancellor (Vanessa Redgrave). Latter is a mature spinster who attempts to secure her charge to the cause with a promise that she will never marry.

Central obstacle to Olive's ambition is Basil Ransome, a persuasive lawyer from the south.

The film is ultimately convincing because of the central performance by newcomer Madeleine Potter as Verena who conveys all the dilemmas of a naive but strong-minded girl caught between her attachment to the cause and her longing for love.

■ BOSTON STRANGLER, THE

1968, 116 MINS, US ◇ ▼

Dir Richard Fleischer   *Prod* Robert Fryer   *Scr* Edward Anhalt   *Ph* Richard H. Kline   *Ed* Marion Rothman   *Mus* [none]   *Art Dir* Jack Martin Smith, Richard Day

● Tony Curtis, Henry Fonda, George Kennedy, Mike Kellin, Murray Hamilton (20th Century-Fox)

The Boston Strangler, based on Gerold Frank's book, emerges as a triumph of taste and restraint with a telling, low-key semi-documentary style. Adaptation is topnotch not only in structure but also in the incisive, spare dialog which defines neatly over 100 speaking parts.

Among other things it makes a very strong, but implicit, comment on police sleuthing. The screenplay suggests the irony that instinctive police methods remain the rounding up of pitiable segments of society which do harm only to themselves. As told here, police got onto the prime suspect only via the fluke of an elevator ride.

Action cross-cuts between police work and off-screen depictions of the earlier murders.

Henry Fonda's performance as rep of Massachusetts Attorney-General is excellent, from his initial dislike of the task assigned through a quiet, dogged determination to break down Tony Curtis' mental barriers.

■ BOULEVARD NIGHTS

1979, 102 MINS, US ◇ ▼

Dir Michael Pressman   *Prod* Bill Benenson   *Scr* Desmond Nakano   *Ph* John Bailey   *Ed* Richard Halsey   *Mus* Lalo Schifrin   *Art Dir* Jackson DeGovia

● Richard Yniguez, Danny De La Paz, Marta du Bois, James Victor (Warner)

The film fails to carve out a separate identity of its own, rehashing a familiar story about inter-family conflicts.

The decision to film *Boulevard Nights* on location in the barrios, using a largely Hispanic

B

cast, is admirable, but does not automatically provide a raison d'etre for the pic.

Authenticity is the key here, and director Michael Pressman has accurately captured the sense of despair in this community.

Richard Yniguez plays a graduate of the VGV gang, who still maintains his ties with the group. Yniguez' g.f. (Marta du Bois) has dreams of upward social mobility, but is unable to shake him loose from his ties to the machismo competition of 'hopping' hydraulic car lifts. Meanwhile his brother, Danny De La Paz, becomes heavily involved in a gang war, until a pat dramatic crisis wraps up the film in a depressing and inconclusive fashion.

....

■ BOUND FOR GLORY

1976, 147 MINS, US ◇

Dir Hal Ashby   *Prod* Robert F. Blumofe, Harold Leventhal   *Scr* Robert Getchell   *Ph* Haskell Wexler   *Ed* Robert Jones, Pembroke J. Herring   *Mus* Leonard Rosenman   *Art Dir* Michael Haller
● David Carradine, Ronny Cox, Melinda Dillon, Gail Strickland, John Lehne, Ji-Tu Cumbuka (United Artists)

Bound for Glory is outstanding biographical cinema, not only of the late Woody Guthrie but also of the 1930s Depression era which served to disillusion, inspire and radicalize him and millions of other Americans.

The plot [based on Guthrie's autobiography] advances smoothly and sensitively through about six major phases of Guthrie's earlier life: the natural tragedy of the southwest dust bowl; Guthrie's transit to California; his exposure to the horrors in the migrant worker valleys; his initial radio career; his political activism, finally his decision to strike out for large urban areas where his songs and experience might add some momentum to change.

Leonard Rosenman's selection of many Guthrie songs makes for discreet but effective underscoring.

□ 1976: Best Picture (Nomination)

....

■ BOUNTY, THE

1984, 130 MINS, US ◇ Ⓥ

Dir Roger Donaldson   *Prod* Bernard Williams   *Scr* Robert Bolt   *Ph* Arthur Ibbetson   *Ed* Tony Lawson   *Mus* Vangelis   *Art Dir* John Graysmark
● Mel Gibson, Anthony Hopkins, Laurence Olivier, Edward Fox, Daniel Day-Lewis, Bernard Hill (De Laurentiis)

The Bounty is an intelligent, firstrate, revisionist telling of the famous tale of Fletcher Christian's mutiny against Captain Bligh. The $20 million-plus film is particularly distinguished by a sensational, and startlingly human, performance by Anthony Hopkins as Bligh, heretofore one of history's most one-dimensional villains.

Present third version of the yarn was initiated by director David Lean, who brought Robert Bolt aboard to write the entire *Bounty* saga. Lean eventually moved on, and Dino De Laurentiis, paid for the construction of a replica ship.

This is a remake with a reason, that being the exoneration and rehabilitation of the reputation of William Bligh. A British Naval court-martial, which serves to frame Bolt's dramatization, ultimately absolved Bligh of blame for the mutiny, and he went on to enjoy a distinguished career.

The mutiny itself is here presented as a chaotic mess, with Christian nearly delirious. Bligh's subsequent 4,000-mile voyage to safety in an open boat is depicted as the amazing, arduous achievement that it was.

Tailor-made physically to fit the mold of old-style heroes, Mel Gibson gets across Christian's melancholy and torn motivations in excellent fashion.

....

■ BOWERY, THE

1933, 92 MINS, US

Dir Raoul Walsh   *Prod* Darryl F. Zanuck, William Goetz, Raymond Griffith   *Scr* Howard Estabrook, James Gleason   *Ph* Barney McGill   *Ed* Allen McNeil   *Mus* Alfred Newman (dir.)   *Art Dir* Richard Day
● Wallace Beery, George Raft, Jackie Cooper, Fay Wray, Pert Kelton, George Walsh (20th Century/United Artists)

Two old Bowery characters, Steve Brodie and Chuck Connors, have been dramatized to a point where the only thing that's recognizable from the record books about them are the jump from Brooklyn Bridge and Bowery lingo respectively.

This script [from the novel by Raymond Griffith and Michael Simmons] makes them rivals for mass leadership on the old street, but the important point is that as rewritten the two practically legendary characters make good entertainment.

The Connors-Brodie honest rivalry over everything, from gals to fighting ability, giving the tale a Flagg-Quirt glow, is the story. Brodie (George Raft) gets the girl. But he takes a licking from Connors (Wallace Beery) in their private finish fight on a river barge. The fight is an exciting interlude, and it comes in handy where it's placed – under the finale. Previously, in the extremely well-staged Brodie bridge leap, the picture has reached its peak. It then stumbles until the fight arrives, but the latter brings home the bacon.

Beery is doing *The Champ* all over again to a great extent, with Jackie Cooper again as his foil. The Cooper kid, obviously outgrowing the baby type, is still a trouper and sends in another gem performance. Raft, much improved, is an okay choice as Brodie. The other meat parts are carried by Fay Wray, who plays straight to the boys, and Pert Kelton, who sings and dances as a Bowery soubrette in Connors' joint.

....

■ BOXCAR BERTHA

1972, 88 MINS, US ◇ Ⓥ

Dir Martin Scorsese   *Prod* Roger Corman   *Scr* Joyce H. Corrington, John William Corrington   *Ph* John Stephens   *Ed* Buzz Feitshans   *Mus* Gib Guilbeau, Thad Maxwell
● Barbara Hershey, David Carradine, Barry Primus, Bernie Casey, John Carradine (American International)

Whatever its intentions, *Boxcar Bertha* is not much more than an excuse to slaughter a lot of people. Barbara Hershey stars in title role as a Depression wanderer. The Roger Corman production, shot on an austere budget in Arkansas area, is routinely directed by Martin Scorsese.

Joyce H. Corrington and John William Corrington adapted *Sister of the Road*, an autobiog by Boxcar Bertha Thompson. Hershey is introduced as a rural girl whose father dies in an unsafe airplane. She is upset, naturally, and suddenly begins a life of vagrancy.

Performances are dull. Whatever sociological, political or dramatic motivations may once have existed in the story have been ruthlessly stripped from the plot, leaving all characters bereft of empathy or sympathy. There's hardly a pretense toward justifying the carnage.

....

■ BOY, DID I GET A WRONG NUMBER!

1966, 98 MINS, US ◇ Ⓥ

Dir George Marshall   *Prod* Edward Small   *Scr* Burt Styler, Albert E. Lewin, George Kennett   *Ph* Lionel Lindon   *Ed* Grant Whytlock   *Mus* Richard LaSalle, 'By' Dunham   *Art Dir* Frank Sylos
● Bob Hope, Elke Sommer, Phyllis Diller, Cesare Danova, Marjorie Lord, Kelly Thordsen (United Artists)

Bob Hope enters the realm of near-bedroom

farce as he finds a near-unclad film star on his hands in a lake cottage and his ever-loving spouse continually appearing on the scene. If the action sometimes seems to get out of hand it really doesn't matter, for Phyllis Diller is there too, to help him hide the delectable Elke Sommer from the missus.

Hope plays his role straight for the most part, making the most of the situation. George Marshall's direction sparks events in proper perspective, wisely allowing his characters to go their separate ways in their own particular styles. Sommer, who knows her way through a comedy scene either with or without clothes, elects the latter state for most of her thesping, raimented mostly in a shirt. Diller is immense as the nosy domestic responsible for the majority of the funny lines that abound throughout the fast unfoldment.

....

■ BOY FRIEND, THE

1972, 108 MINS, UK ◇ Ⓥ

Dir Ken Russell   *Prod* Ken Russell   *Scr* Ken Russell   *Ph* David Watkin   *Ed* Michael Bradsell   *Mus* Peter Maxwell Davies (arr.)   *Art Dir* Tony Walton
● Twiggy, Christopher Gable, Max Adrian, Bryan Pringle, Murray Melvin, Glenda Jackson (M-G-M)

If for nothing else – but film has more – Ken Russell's screen translation of *The Boy Friend* is a beautiful vehicle for Twiggy, a clever young performer. It is delightful entertainment, novel and engaging.

Russell, who also directed and scripted the Sandy Wilson musical, has adopted a play within a play concept for the telling. Film might be a glorification of the Busby Berkeley manner of production. Russell has expanded the play into a kaleidoscope of the dance director's techniques during his heyday.

Narrative revolves around the personal lives of a group of repertory players who stage an English provincial production of *The Boy Friend*, and a film director strives to catch the performance.

Twiggy plays the unsophisticated young assistant stage manager – also errand and jack-of-all-trades girl – suddenly thrust into top role when the star injures her ankle. (Glenda Jackson unbilled, cameos as the injured 'star'.)

Twiggy acquits herself charmingly and professionally. There's an unspoiled charm about her, and she weaves a spell of her own both with her singing and dancing.

....

■ BOY ON A DOLPHIN

1957, 103 MINS, US ◇

Dir Jean Negulesco   *Prod* Samuel G. Engel   *Scr* Ivan Moffat, Dwight Taylor   *Ph* Milton Krasner   *Ed* William Mace   *Mus* Hugo Friedhofer   *Art Dir* Lyle R. Wheeler, Jack Martin Smith
● Alan Ladd, Sophia Loren, Clifton Webb, Jorge Mistral, Laurence Naismith, Alexis Minotis (20th Century-Fox)

Shot in Greece's Aegean Sea and environs, with the interiors filmed in Rome's Cinecitta Studios, *Boy on a Dolphin* [from the novel by David Divine] develops into a 'chase' that is a pleasant blend of archaeological research, quasi-cloak & dagger stuff, and earthy, primitive acquisitiveness.

Alan Ladd is the archaeologist who has been engaged on several occasions in besting Clifton Webb's passion for antiquities. He has been invariably successful in restoring them to their rightful owners. The 'boy', in the same idiom, is historic Greek property. Sophia Loren's hunger for a home, the greed of an expatriate, alcohol-sotted British medico (Laurence Naismith) and the trickery of her Albanian lover (Jorge Mistral, a strong face in a chameleon role) conspire to thwart the American archaeologist and collaborate with the aesthetic, wealthy Webb in spiriting

73

the ancient treasure from Greek waters.

Director Jean Negulesco has not overextended any of the values, playing it in the right tempo for the locale and likewise playing down the neo-melodramatics. Ladd is the all-American boy archaeologist; Webb the suave dastard (because of his dollars); Loren a lustily appealing native Greek girl whose endowments fall automatically into character.

••••••••••••••••••••••••••••••

■ BOYS FROM BRAZIL, THE

1978, 123 MINS, US ◇ Ⓥ

Dir Franklin J. Schaffner   *Prod* Martin Richards, Stanley O'Toole   *Scr* Heywood Gould   *Ph* Henri Decae   *Ed* Robert E. Swink   *Mus* Jerry Goldsmith   *Art Dir* Gil Parrondo

● Gregory Peck, Laurence Olivier, James Mason, Lilli Palmer, Uta Hagen, Steven Guttenberg (Producer Circle/20th Century-Fox)

With two excellent antagonists in Gregory Peck and Laurence Olivier, *The Boys from Brazil* presents a gripping, suspenseful drama for nearly all of its two hours – then lets go at the end and falls into a heap.

In a fine shift from his usual roles, Peck plays the evil Josef Mengele, a real-life character who murdered thousands of Jews, including many children, carrying out bizarre genetic experiments at Auschwitz in Poland. Olivier, slipping completely into the role of an elderly Jewish gentleman, is the Nazi hunter who brings him to bay.

With the aid of James Mason, Peck is out to assassinate 94 fathers around the world. In a brief but lively part, Steven Guttenberg discovers the plot and tips Olivier, who sets out to find how the killings fit together. His search turns up three identical lads, all played menacingly by Jeremy Black, who are more than triplets.

What they are and whence they came are plausibly developed in Heywood Gould's script [from Iva Levin's novel] and director Franklin J. Schaffner builds the threatening menace well.

••••••••••••••••••••••••••••••

■ BOYS FROM SYRACUSE, THE

1940, 73 MINS, US

Dir A. Edward Sutherland   *Prod* Jules Levey   *Scr* Leonard Spigelgass, Charles Grayson   *Ph* Joseph Valentine   *Ed* Milton Carruth

● Allan Jones, Joe Penner, Martha Raye, Rosemary Lane, Charles Butterworth, Irene Hervey (Mayfair/Universal)

Writers Leonard Spigelgass and Charles Grayson have transformed the legiter – which George Abbott authored in collaboration with Richard Rodgers and Lorenz Hart (with a plot copped from Bill Shakespeare's *Comedy of Errors*) – from a satire to plain burlesque.

Martha Raye and Joe Penner are particularly outstanding in the comedy leads. Penner, away from the stereotyped 'wanna buy a duck?' characterization, makes a droll slave. Raye, provided with the swell Rodgers and Hart tunes, gets good opportunity to use her pipes as well as exhibit her broad comedy style. Charles Butterworth and Eric Blore, in lesser roles, turn in plenty of additional laughs, while Allan Jones capably acts and warbles his way through the top characterization.

Four of the tunes have been retained and two new ones have been provided by R&H to sub for three that were dropped. 'Who Are You?', romantic ballad sung by Jones, is one of the new ones, and 'The Greeks Had No Word for It', a specialty for Martha Raye, is the other. Both are equal to the originals.

Writers have done everything possible to further the basically ludicrous idea of the stage show, in which all sorts of modernisms surround the toga-clad populace of ancient Greece. It gives plenty of opportunity for gags, and none is missed, even to the checkered chariot, with a meter. Stone 'newspapers' announce that 'Ephesus Blitzkriegs Syracuse,' while the gladiators' union pickets and a voice strangely like that of Winchell's gives gossip on station EBC.

Tale concerns twin brothers and their twin slaves. One brother and one slave are parted from the other brother and his slave as babies. One brother becomes ruler of Ephesus and conqueror of Syracuse, town in which he doesn't know he was born. The other son comes to Ephesus, also, in search of his father. Neither twin knows the other exists and the resultant mixup of identity makes plenty of base for laughs.

••••••••••••••••••••••••••••••

■ BOYS IN COMPANY C, THE

1978, 125 MINS, US ◇ Ⓥ

Dir Sidney J. Furie   *Prod* Andre Morgan   *Scr* Rick Natkin, Sidney J. Furie   *Ph* Godfrey A. Godar   *Ed* Michael Berman, Frank J. Urioste, Alan Pattillo, James Benson   *Mus* Jaime Mendoza-Nava   *Art Dir* Robert Lang

● Stan Shaw, Andrew Stevens, James Canning, Michael Lembeck, Craig Wasson, Scott Hylands (Golden Harvest)

The Boys in Company C is a spotty but okay popcorn trade drama about five young Marines and how their lives were changed by duty in the Vietnam war. Laden with barracks dialog and played at the enlisted man's level, the Raymond Chow production, directed well by Sidney J. Furie, features strong performances by some very fine actors.

Not that *The Boys in Company C* is anywhere near a definitive film about the Vietnam debacle. No geopolitics or other cosmic matters intrude; instead, it's a deliberate action programmer (shot in the Philippines).

Stan Shaw heads the cast as a dope pusher who sees Vietnam as a major new connection, until he matures into a natural leader. Andrew Stevens, son of Stella Stevens, is a Southern athlete who turns junkie in action. James Canning is an aspiring writer who records the bewildering and unnatural warfare.

••••••••••••••••••••••••••••••

■ BOYS IN THE BAND, THE

1970, 117 MINS, US ◇ Ⓥ

Dir William Friedkin   *Prod* Mart Crowley   *Scr* Mart Crowley   *Ph* Arthur J. Ornitz   *Ed* Jerry Greenburg   *Art Dir* John Robert Lloyd

● Kenneth Nelson, Frederick Combs, Leonard Frey, Cliff Gorman, Reuben Greene, Robert La Tourneaux (Leo/Cinema Center)

Boys in the Band drags. But despite its often tedious postulations of homosexual case histories instead of realistic dialog, and the stagey posturing of the actors, the too literally faithful adaptation of Mart Crowley's off-Broadway swish-set piece has bitchy, back-biting humor, fascinating character studies, melodrama and, most of all, perverse interest.

As queen and host of the gay birthday party that is the film's only setting, Kenneth Nelson tells straight Peter White, it's like watching an accident, one is horrified and repulsed, but can't take his eyes away.

Crowley takes the fault for the self-indulgent dialog with prolonged speeches.

••••••••••••••••••••••••••••••

■ BOYS NEXT DOOR, THE

1985, 88 MINS, US ◇ Ⓥ

Dir Penelope Spheeris   *Prod* Keith Rubinstein, Sandy Howard   *Scr* Glen Morgan, James Wong   *Ph* Arthur Albert   *Ed* Andy Horvitch   *Mus* George S. Clinton   *Art Dir* John Tarnoff

● Maxwell Caulfield, Charlie Sheen, Christopher McDonald, Hank Garrett, Patti D'Arbanville, Paul C. Dancer (New World/Republic Entertainment)

A before-credits sequence of *The Boys Next Door* helps explain the motives for making the film. Stills are shown of notorious figures in the US who, for no apparent reason, have gone on killing sprees. One commentator suggests young criminals are so brutalized by their own upbringing that they can't see other people as human beings.

Unfortunately the film itself doesn't live up to the expectations. Even if intentions are worthy, it emerges glib and uninvolving.

Two alienated and disturbed 18-year-olds, Roy Alston (Maxwell Caulfield) and Bo Richards (Charlie Sheen), graduate from a small high school in California. Before taking up factory jobs, they decide to have a weekend in LA in which 'anything goes'.

An eruption of violence begins with the brutal beating of a gas station attendant. It ends with one boy shooting the other as the police close in on the pair in a shopping mall. In between there are beatings and killings of a homosexual, a young couple and a woman.

With conventional clean-cut good looks, Caulfield and Sheen clearly resemble the title, but they fail to adequately project the 'angry stuff' within.

••••••••••••••••••••••••••••••

■ BOYS TOWN

1938, 96 MINS, US Ⓥ

Dir Norman Taurog   *Prod* John W. Considine Jr   *Scr* John Meehan, Dore Schary   *Ph* Sidney Wagner   *Ed* Elmo Veron   *Mus* Edward Ward

● Spencer Tracy, Mickey Rooney, Henry Hull, Leslie Fenton, Gene Reynolds, Bobs Watson (M-G-M)

The story of Father Flanagan's struggle to make a successful boy's home and then an entire community near Omaha, Neb, is the motivating theme throughout. Producers shrewdly have not made it entirely a paean of praise for Boys Town, but rather a realistic portrayal of Father Flanagan's untiring efforts to make something of wayward youngsters who otherwise might wind up in the electric chair.

With Spencer Tracy and Mickey Rooney as the priest and the incorrigible lad, in tailor-made roles, *Boys Town* is a tear-jerker of the first water. Yet it has equal distribution of humorous and bitter moments. Rooney virtually takes the production away from the capable and veteran Tracy, though not appearing until feature is half-finished.

Rooney is the toughie whose repartee is as laughable as his cocky walk and mannerisms. Slow curbing of his desires as he bucks Boys Town customs and rules is a transition of character that is logically worked out. Tracy, showing necessary restraint, makes his portrayal of Flanagan sincere and human. It is not the first time he has played the role of a priest on the screen.

Henry Hull, the money-supplying pawnbroker who makes possible the boys home, builds this comparatively minor role into an impressive assignment.

☐ 1938: Best Picture (Nomination)

••••••••••••••••••••••••••••••

■ BOY WHO STOLE A MILLION, THE

1961, 81 MINS, UK

Dir Charles Crichton   *Prod* George H. Brown   *Scr* John Eldridge, Charles Crichton   *Ph* Douglas Slocombe   *Ed* Peter Bezencenet   *Mus* Tristram Cary   *Art Dir* Maurice Carter

● Virgilio Texera, Maurice Reyna, Marianne Benet, Harold Kasket, Curt Christian, Bill Nagy (British Lion-Bryanston)

It's difficult to go wrong with the combo of an appealing kid, the inevitable pooch and a chase in which the youngster's up against the world. This one is marred by some slightly uneasy dubbing and an occasional lapse into

B

slapstick when only light comedy was needed, but overall it's a warm little piece.

Though a British film, it was mainly shot in locations in Valencia, Spain. The yarn concerns a likeable youngster who lives with his widowed father and works as a bank messenger. He finds that his taxi-driver father needs money to get his cab out of hock and decides to borrow some from the bank. His haul, however, turns out to be a million pesetas (roughly $28,000) and that sets the city on its ears. At the drop of a peseta he is being chased by half the thugs in Valencia, the police and his father.

Young Maurice Reyna, making his screen debut, goes through the motions of thesping admirably. Harold Kasket is breezily effective as the friend of the kid's father, who is rather glumly played by Virgilio Texera.

. . . .

■ BOY WITH GREEN HAIR, THE

1948, 82 MINS, US ◇ ⓥ

Dir Joseph Losey   *Prod* Stephen Ames   *Scr* Ben Barzman, Alfred Lewis Levitt   *Ph* George Barnes   *Ed* Frank Doyle   *Mus* Leigh Harline   *Art Dir* Albert S. D'Agostino, Ralph Berger

● Pat O'Brien, Robert Ryan, Barbara Hale, Dean Stockwell (RKO)

RKO has turned out an absorbing, sensitive story of tolerance and child understanding in *The Boy with Green Hair*.

Story is that of a war orphan, shifted around from one relative to another, who finally finds haven and security with a waiter in a small town. Then, one morning, he wakes to find his hair has turned green – and the world turns topsy-turvey about him. Other kids jeer at him; adults are perturbed; even the kindly milkman turns against him when accused of bringing it about through his product.

Film was made by Dore Schary for RKO before Howard Hughes gained control of the studio, and in its small way was one of the things that caused Schary to step out of the RKO setup. Pic had been completed, but Hughes ordered it re-edited and the tolerance theme taken out, on Hughes' general theory that films should entertain only and eschew social significance. Studio found that pic couldn't be re-edited, although it's reported to be toned down somewhat.

Through this parable about the unconscious cruelty of people to what is different, and the need of tolerance, runs another theme, that of anti-war preachment. When the boy meets children from war-orphan posters in a dream scene in the woods, and returns to annoy the townsfolk with the message that war is very bad – his green hair has thus acquired a meaning, to preach pacifism – the film hits a well-intentioned but false note.

. . . .

■ BRAINSTORM

1983, 106 MINS, US ◇ ⓥ

Dir Douglas Trumbull   *Prod* Douglas Trumbull   *Scr* Robert Stitzell, Philip Frank Messina   *Ph* Richard Yuricich   *Ed* Edward Warschilka, Freeman Davies   *Mus* James Horner   *Art Dir* John Vallone

● Christopher Walken, Natalie Wood, Louise Fletcher, Cliff Robertson, Jordan Christopher, Joe Dorsey (M-G-M/JF Prod.)

Shaken and embattled during its completion phase, and carrying the memory of Natalie Wood's death *Brainstorm* is a high-tech $18 million movie dependent on the visualization of a fascinating idea.

Producer-director Douglas Trumbull's effects wizardry – and the concept behind it – is the movie. The fetching idea is a brain-wave device that gives characters the power to record and experience the physical, emotional and intellectual sensations of another human being.

On the downside, majority of players, including stars Christopher Walken and Wood as a married couple in a research environment, seem merely along for the ride. The film's acting surprise is Louise Fletcher, whose flinty, career scientist is a strong flavorful, workaholic portrait.

The film offers irrefutable evidence that Natalie Wood's drowning (in November 1981) did not cause the filmmakers to drastically re-write or re-shoot scenes. Her work appears intact and, reportedly, only one scene had to be changed (with actor Joe Dorsey replacing Wood in a scene with Walken).

Cliff Robertson earnestly plays the compromising head of a vast research complex that employs colleagues Walken and Fletcher. Predictably, a government bogeyman is trying to gum up pure science for the sake of national security.

. . . .

■ BRAINWAVES

1983, 81 MINS, US ◇ ⓥ

Dir Ulli Lommel   *Prod* Ulli Lommel   *Scr* Ulli Lommel, Buz Alexander, Suzanna Love   *Ph* Jon Kranhouse, Ulli Lommel   *Ed* Richard Brummer   *Mus* Robert O. Ragland   *Art Dir* Stephen E. Graff

● Keir Dullea, Suzanna Love, Vera Miles, Percy Rodrigues, Tony Curtis, Paul Willson (CinAmerica)

Brainwaves is a briskly-told, engaging psychological thriller dealing with the sci-fi concept of transferring thought processes and memories electronically between different people.

Suzanna Love toplines as Kaylie Bedford, a young San Francisco housewife who suffers a severe brain trauma (leaving her in a coma-like trance) in an auto accident. Her husband, Julian (Keir Dullea), and mother (Vera Miles) agree to an experimental medical procedure, unaware that it has not yet been tested on humans.

Designed to transfer corrective patterns by computer from a donor brain to the victim's damaged brain areas, process goes awry when the donor turns out to be a murdered girl (Corinne Alphen). Kaylie is physically and mentally rehabilitated, but plagued with traumatic first-person memories of the murder. Worse yet, the murderer is now after her.

Well-edited by Richard Brummer, picture zips along with admirable verisimilitude.

. . . .

■ BRANDED

1950, 50 MINS, US ◇

Dir Rudolph Mate   *Prod* Mel Epstein   *Scr* Sydney Boehm, Cyril Hume   *Ph* Charles B. Lang Jr   *Ed* Alma Macrorie   *Mus* Roy Webb

● Alan Ladd, Mona Freeman, Charles Bickford, Robert Keith, Joseph Calleia, Peter Hanson (Paramount)

Branded is a pleasing western that has a bit more plot and appeal than the average.

Rudolph Mate, photographer-turned-director, demonstrates he has not lost his hand at his former art. He and cameraman Charles B. Lang Jr must be given a score for at least part of *Branded's* appeal on basis of the Technicolor scenic work along the Rio Grande.

Yarn [from a novel by Evan Evans] finds Alan Ladd a no-good who figures on stealing the fortune of a cattle family by making like he's the long-lost son who was kidnapped at five. He doesn't figure, however, on falling for his 'sister' and getting right fond of mom and pop. Ladd's inability to indicate successfully a transition from scoundrel to a kid with a 24-karat heart makes the story at times harder to digest than it should be.

. . . .

■ BRANNIGAN

1975, 111 MINS, UK ◇

Dir Douglas Hickox   *Prod* Jules Levy, Arthur Gardner   *Scr* Christopher Trumbo, Michael Butler, William P. McGivern, Michael Butler   *Ph* Gerry Fisher

Ed Malcolm Cooke   *Mus* Dominic Frontiere   *Art Dir* Ted Marshall

● John Wayne, Richard Attenborough, Judy Geeson, Mel Ferrer, John Vernon, Daniel Pilon (United Artists)

Okay John Wayne actioner, as a contemporary cop in London tracking down Chicago fugitive John Vernon, whose lawyer Mel Ferrer has concocted a bewildering escape cover. Richard Attenborough plays well against Wayne as an urbane Scotland Yard detective.

Judy Geeson, as Wayne's policewoman escort, and Daniel Pilon, as a hired gun carrying Vernon's contract on Wayne's life, round out the principal players. Car chases, booby traps, etc round out the formula plot turns.

. . . .

■ BRASS TARGET

1978, 111 MINS, US ◇ ⓥ

Dir John Hough   *Prod* Arthur Lewis   *Scr* Alvin Boretz   *Ph* Tony Imi   *Ed* David Lane   *Mus* Laurence Rosenthal   *Art Dir* Rolf Zehetbauer

● Sophia Loren, John Cassavetes, George Kennedy, Robert Vaughn, Patrick McGoohan, Max Von Sydow (M-G-M)

Brass Target, like *The Eagle has Landed*, speculates on what might have happened to an historical figure in World War II had a given set of circumstances taken place.

This time, instead of Winston Churchill getting bumped off, it's General George Patton's turn. Writer Alvin Boretz has turned Frederick Nolan's speculative novel, *The Algonquin Project*, into a seemingly true-to-life revelation of how Patton actually died, not in a car accident, but at the hands of a clever paid assassin.

Robert Vaughn, Edward Herrman and Ed Bishop play three officers in occupied Germany who concoct a plan to steal the Third Reich's gold stores with the help of OSS head Patrick McGoohan.

Patton, as played by George Kennedy, gets into a snit when the Russian Allies taunt him about the theft, and personally supervises the investigation, joined by OSS vet John Cassavetes. Gradually, just about every cast member is eliminated by one side or the other, until only Cassavetes, assassin Max Von Sydow, and mutual lover Sophia Loren remain for the predictable finale.

Hough manages to interject some excitement into the action scenes, but these come few and far between. A generally competent cast is hamstrung by the material at hand.

. . . .

■ BRAZIL

1985, 142 MINS, UK ◇ ⓥ

Dir Terry Gilliam   *Prod* Arnon Milchan, Patrick Cassavetti   *Scr* Terry Gilliam, Tom Stoppard, Charles McKeown   *Ph* Roger Pratt   *Ed* Julian Doyle   *Mus* Michael Kamen   *Art Dir* Norman Garwood

● Jonathan Pryce, Robert De Niro, Michael Palin, Kim Greist, Katherine Helmond, Ian Holm (Embassy)

Brazil offers a chillingly hilarious vision of the near-future, set 'somewhere in the 20th Century.'

Director Terry Gilliam reportedly wanted to call the film *1984¹/₂*. As in Orwell's classic, society is monitored by an insidious, tentacular ministry, and the film's protagonist, a diligent but unambitious civil servant, Sam Lowry – played with vibrant comic imagination by Jonathan Pryce – becomes a victim of his own romantic delusions, and is crushed by a system he had never before thought of questioning.

He sees himself as a winged super-hero, part-Icarus, part-Siegfried, soaring lyrically through the clouds to the tune of 'Brazil', the old Xavier Cugat favorite, which as the film's ironic musical leitmotif, recurs in numerous mock variations.

Robert De Niro shows delightful comic flair in a small, but succulent characterization of a proletariat superhero, who disposes of some obnoxious rival repairmen in a disgustingly original manner, but meets a most bizarre end in the film's nightmare climax.

Gilliam has assembled a brilliant supporting cast of character actors, notably Ian Holm, as the edgy, paranoid ministry department chief hopelessly dependent on Pryce to untie bureaucratic knots.

••••••••••••••••••••••••••••••••••

■ BREAKER MORANT

1980, 106 MINS, AUSTRALIA ◇ ⓥ

Dir Bruce Beresford   *Prod* Matt Carroll   *Scr* Bruce Beresford, Jonathon Hardy, David Stevens   *Ph* Don McAlpine   *Ed* William Anderson   *Mus* Phil Cunneen   *Art Dir* David Copping

● Edward Woodward, Jack Thompson, John Waters, Bryan Brown, Charles Tingwell, Lewis Fitz-Gerald (South Australian Film)

Harry 'The Breaker' Morant (Edward Woodward) was an Englishman who went to Australia in the last century. When Britain and the Boers squared off against each other in South Africa, he and a number of other Australians volunteered and were absorbed into the non-regular army contingent.

The nature of the war made prisoner-taking a difficult business logistically, and while the film [from a play by Kenneth Ross] in no way tries to justify the killing of them, it does make clear that the Establishment's blind-eye can become very quickly healed.

As an example to others, Morant and two other Australians, Handcock (Bryan Brown) and Witton (Lewis Fitz-Gerald) were tried by court martial. Morant and Handcock were convicted and sentenced to death by firing-squad.

The execution sequence as handled by Bruce Beresford and the two actors is profoundly affecting. Beresford then turns his audience into an unwitting jury; as a sheer exercise in manipulation, it approaches the masterful and is extremely effective.

••••••••••••••••••••••••••••••••••

■ BREAKFAST AT TIFFANY'S

1961, 115 MINS, US ◇ ⓥ

Dir Blake Edwards   *Prod* Martin Jurow, Richard Shepherd   *Scr* George Axelrod   *Ph* Franz F. Planer   *Ed* Howard Smith   *Mus* Henry Mancini   *Art Dir* Hal Pereira, Roland Anderson

● Audrey Hepburn, George Peppard, Patricia Neal, Buddy Ebsen, Martin Balsam, Mickey Rooney (Paramount)

Out of the elusive, but curiously intoxicating Truman Capote fiction, scenarist George Axelrod has developed a surprisingly moving film, touched up into a stunningly visual motion picture. Capote buffs may find some of Axelrod's fanciful alterations a bit too precocious, pat and glossy for comfort, but enough of the original's charm and vigor has been retained.

What makes *Tiffany's* an appealing tale is its heroine, Holly Golightly, a charming, wild and amoral 'free spirit' with a latent romantic streak. Axelrod's once-over-go-lightly erases the amorality and bloats the romanticism, but retains the essential spirit ('a phony, but a real phony') of the character, and, in the exciting person of Audrey Hepburn, she comes vividly to life on the screen.

Hepburn's expressive, 'top banana in the shock department' portrayal is complemented by the reserved, capable work of George Peppard as the young writer whose love ultimately (in the film, not the book) enables the heroine to come to realistic terms with herself.

Excellent featured characterizations are contributed by Martin Balsam as a Hollywood agent, Buddy Ebsen as Hepburn's deserted husband, and Patricia Neal as Peppard's wealthy 'sponsor'. Mickey Rooney as a much-harassed upstairs Japanese photographer adds an unnecessarily incongruous note to the proceedings.

The film is a sleek, artistic piece of craftsmanship, particularly notable for Franz F. Planer's haunting photography and Henry Mancini's memorably moody score. The latter's 'Moon River', with lyrics by Johnny Mercer, is an enchanting tune.

••••••••••••••••••••••••••••••••••

■ BREAKFAST CLUB, THE

1985, 97 MINS, US ◇ ⓥ

Dir John Hughes   *Prod* Ned Tanen, John Hughes   *Scr* John Hughes   *Ph* Thomas Del Ruth   *Ed* Dede Allen   *Mus* Keith Forsey   *Art Dir* John W. Corso

● Emilio Estevez, Judd Nelson, Molly Ringwald, Anthony Michael Hall, Ally Sheedy, Paul Gleason (A&M/Universal)

In typical Shermer High in Chicago, a cross-section of five students – the jock, Miss Popularity, the ruffian, the nerd and Miss Weirdo – are thrown together under adverse circumstances and cast aside all discord and unite under the sudden insight that none would be such a despicable little twit if mom or dad or both weren't so rotten. The querulous quintet are actually being forced to *spend the entire day at school on Saturday* for some previous infraction of the rules.

Coming together as strangers, none of the group initially likes thuggish loudmouth Judd Nelson, who taunts pretty Molly Ringwald, torments dorkish Anthony Michael Hall and challenges champ athlete Emilio Estevez while the odd lady, Ally Sheedy, looks on from a different space.

When the causes of the Decline of Western Civilization are finally writ, Hollywood will surely have to answer why it turned one of man's most significant art forms over to the self-gratification of high-schoolers. Or does director John Hughes really believe, as he writes here, that 'when you grow up, your heart dies.' It may. But not unless the brain has already started to rot with films like this.

••••••••••••••••••••••••••••••••••

■ BREAKHEART PASS

1976, 95 MINS, US ◇ ⓥ

Dir Tom Gries   *Prod* Jerry Gershwin   *Scr* Alistair MacLean   *Ph* Lucien Ballard   *Ed* Buzz Brandt   *Mus* Jerry Goldsmith

● Charles Bronson, Ben Johnson, Jill Ireland, Richard Crenna, Charles Durning, Roy Jenson (United Artists)

Production has Charles Bronson as a government undercover agent who trips up a gang of gun runners, and a marvellous old steam train as setting for most of the plot.

Working from a lean Alistair MacLean script (based on his own novel), director Tom Gries forges a brisk and polished cinematic tale in which the mysteries pile up as old No. 9 steams with troops and medical supplies to an army post gripped by a killer epidemic.

Even before embarkation, a couple of officers go missing. Then, along the journey, telegraphic contact is lost, bodies hurtle out of the train into gorges, and the train's rear section containing the relief troops becomes detached.

Seasoned support in stock turns is furnished by Ben Johnson as a crooked marshal, and Ed Lauter as an honest army colonel.

••••••••••••••••••••••••••••••••••

■ BREAKIN'

1984, 87 MINS, US ◇ ⓥ

Dir Joel Silberg   *Prod* Allen DeBevoise, David Zito   *Scr* Charles Parker, Allen DeBevoise, Gerald Scaife   *Ph* Hannania Baer   *Ed* Mark Helfrich   *Mus* Gary Remal, Michael Boyd   *Art Dir* Ivo G. Crisante

● Lucinda Dickey, Adolfo 'Shabba-Doo' Quinones, Michael 'Boogaloo Shrimp' Chambers, Ben Lokey, Christopher McDonald, Phineas Newborn III (Golan-Globus)

Breakin' is the first feature film entirely devoted to the breakdancing craze.

On a plot level, concoction is too derivative of *Flashdance* for its own good, as the premise once again is untrained, but highly skilled and imaginative, street dancers versus the stuffy, inflexible dance establishment.

Filmmakers have also played it safe in focusing the action on a nice, middle-class white girl, whereas breakdancing is almost exclusively the domain of blacks and Latinos.

Aside from these fainthearted choices, however, film is quite satisfactory and breezily entertaining on its own terms.

••••••••••••••••••••••••••••••••••

■ BREAKIN' 2 ELECTRIC BOOGALOO

1984, 94 MINS, US ◇ ⓥ

Dir Sam Firstenberg   *Prod* Menahem Golan, Yoram Globus   *Scr* Jan Ventura, Julie Reichert   *Ph* Hanania Baer   *Ed* Marcus Manton   *Mus* Mike Linn   *Art Dir* Joseph T. Garrity

● Lucinda Dickey, Adolfo Quinones, Michael Chambers, Susie Bono, Harry Caesar, Jo de Winter (Cannon)

Breakin' 2 is a comic book of a film, and, as in a cartoon, kids can get away with anything to have a good time.

As a phenomenon, the hip-hop, break-dancing, sidewalk graffiti and rap music culture lends itself well to a comic book approach and to his credit director Sam Firstenberg doesn't try to interject too much reality into the picture.

This time around Ozone (Adolfo 'Shabba-Doo' Quinones) and Turbo (Michael 'Boogaloo Shrimp' Chambers) have turned their street dancing talents to teaching other disadvantaged youths at a rundown community club they've dubbed Miracles.

When a developer (Peter MacLean) and a corrupt politician (Ken Olfson) try to put up a shopping center where the community center stands, the kids decide to put on a show to raise the necessary $200,000.

••••••••••••••••••••••••••••••••••

■ BREAKING AWAY

1979, 100 MINS, US ◇ ⓥ

Dir Peter Yates   *Prod* Peter Yates   *Scr* Steve Tesich   *Ph* Matthew F. Leonetti   *Ed* Cynthia Scheider   *Mus* Patrick Williams   *Art Dir* Patrizia Von Brandenstein

● Dennis Christopher, Dennis Quaid, Daniel Stern, Jackie Earle Haley, Barbara Barrie, Robyn Douglass (20th Century-Fox)

Though its plot wins no points for originality, *Breaking Away* is a thoroughly delightful light comedy, lifted by fine performances from Dennis Christopher and Paul Dooley. The story is nothing more than a triumph for the underdog through sports, this time cycle racing.

Christopher, Dennis Quaid, Daniel Stern and Jackie Earle Haley are four recent high-school graduates with no particular educational ambitions, yet stuck in a small college town – and a fairly snooty college at that. But Christopher is a heck of a bike rider and such an adulator of Italian champions that he pretends to be Italian himself, even at home.

Pretending to be an Italian exchange student, Christopher meets pretty coed Robyn Douglass (an able film debut for her) and this ultimately brings the boys into conflict with the big men on campus that must finally be resolved in a big bike race.

The relationship among the four youths is warm and funny, yet full of different kinds of conflicts. Quaid is very good as the ex-quarterback facing a life with no more cheers; Haley is good as a sawed-off romantic; and

Stern is superb as a gangly, wise-cracking mediator.

Though pic sometimes seems padded with too much cycle footage, the climax is exciting, even though predictable.

□ 1979: Best Picture (Nomination)

....

■ BREAKING GLASS

1980, 104 MINS, UK ◇ Ⓥ

Dir Brian Gibson *Prod* Davina Belling, Clive Parsons *Scr* Brian Gibson *Ph* Stephen Goldblatt *Ed* Michael Bradsell *Mus* Tony Visconti (dir.) *Art Dir* Evan Hercules

● Phil Daniels, Hazel O'Connor, Jon Finch, Jonathan Pryce (Allied Stars/Film & General)

Breaking Glass presents a cynical, off-the-peg, view of the post-punk record business.

Cast opposite Hazel O'Connor, who's seen initially as a two-bit teenage performer playing a handful of her own numbers around lousy London gigs, is Phil Daniels, a hustling would-be manager who teams with O'Connor.

Ensuing success undermines the pair's tentative romantic partnership and, with the arrival on the scene of Jon Finch as an overly smooth-mannered producer, their professional interdependence as well.

Relentlessly fast-paced, the yarn relates to reality in much the same way as a fashion photo – that is, it works as an image-conscious reflection of a time and milieu, but does not purport to portray life as it really is.

....

■ BREAKING IN

1989, 91 MINS, US ◇ Ⓥ

Dir Bill Forsyth *Prod* Harry Gittes *Scr* John Sayles *Ph* Michael Coulter *Ed* Michael Ellis *Mus* Michael Gibbs *Art Dir* Adrienne Atkinson

● Burt Reynolds, Casey Siemaszlo, Sheila Kelley, Lorraine Toussant, Albert Salmi, Harry Carey (Act III/Goldwyn)

Burt Reynolds plays Ernie Mullins, a 61-year-old, graying, professional burglar with a gammy leg and the beginning of a pot belly, in this charming buddy-caper movie.

He teams up with young Mike Lefebb (Casey Siemaszko), a garage hand who likes to break into houses to raid the fridge and read the mail, when they both hit the same place one night. They become partners, with the oldtimer teaching the youngster the tricks of the trade.

What follows is a gentle comedy, filled with incisive observation, which builds to a wry conclusion which won't set well with action fans.

Reynolds plays the old-timer with a relaxed charm that's wholly delightful. Siemaszko is fine, too, as the initially nervous and ultimately relaxed and confident young criminal. Sheila Kelley is fun as a prostie who favors colored condoms and likes to be known as an actress.

....

■ BREAKOUT

1975, 96 MINS, US ◇

Dir Tom Gries *Prod* Robert Chartoff, Irwin Winkler *Scr* Howard B. Kreitsek, Marc Norman, Elliott Baker *Ph* Lucien Ballard *Ed* Bud Isaacs *Mus* Jerry Goldsmith *Art Dir* Alfred Sweeney Jr

● Charles Bronson, Robert Duvall, Jill Ireland, John Huston, Randy Quaid, Sheree North (Columbia)

Breakout is a cheap exploitation pic with Charles Bronson as a carefree aviator who rescues Robert Duvall from the Mexican prison frameup engineered by his father-in-law, John Huston. Jill Ireland, Duvall's wife, wants him back badly.

The spitball plot [from the novel by Warren Hinckle, William Turner and Eliot Asinof] is the sort of thing Columbia made

before Frank Capra. Director Tom Gries and the entire cast perform as though they all had better things to do.

....

■ BREATHLESS

1983, 100 MINS, US ◇ Ⓥ

Dir Jim McBride *Prod* Martin Erlichman *Scr* L.M. Kit Carson, Jim McBride *Ph* Richard H. Kline *Ed* Robert Estrin *Mus* Jack Nitzsche *Art Dir* Richard Sylbert

● Richard Gere, Valerie Kaprisky, Art Metrano, John P. Ryan, William Tepper, Robert Dunn (Orion/Miko)

More than a little guts was required to remake such a certified film classic as Jean-Luc Godard's *Breathless*, and the generation of film critics that had their lives changed by the 1959 film will easily be able to argue on behalf of the artistic superiority of the original. But the comparison remains virtually irrelevant to youthful audiences, who should find this update a suitably jazzy, sexy, entertainment.

On his way back from Las Vegas in a stolen car, Richard Gere accidentally mortally wounds a cop, then heads for the LA apartment of French UCLA student Valerie Kaprisky, with whom he's had just a brief fling but whom he is also convinced he loves.

A real romantic who dreams of escaping down to Mexico with his inamorata, Gere behaves as if he's oblivious to the heat closing in on him after the cop dies.

Gere's status as a sex star is certainly reaffirmed here, and not only does he appear with his shirt off through much of the pic, but he does some full-frontal scenes. Fresh and attractive, Kaprisky also does numerous scenes semi-clad or less.

....

■ BREED APART, A

1984, 101 MINS, US ◇ Ⓥ

Dir Philippe Mora *Prod* John Daly, Derek Gibson *Scr* Paul Wheeler *Ph* Geoffrey Stephenson *Ed* Chris Lebenzon *Mus* Maurice Gibb *Art Dir* Bill Barclay

● Rutger Hauer, Powers Boothe, Kathleen Turner, Donald Pleasence, John Dennis Johnston, Brion James (Hemdale/Sagittarius)

The visual splendors of North Carolina deserve top billing in *A Breed Apart*. The tale of romance and chicanery in the backwoods simply lacks reason, dramatic tension or emotional involvement.

The core of the story centers on an obsessive bird egg collector's passion to secure specimens of a newly discovered breed of bald eagle. As the bird is protected by law, he has to hire a noted climber (Powers Boothe) to illegally pilfer the shells. However, apart from the physical danger of reaching their lofty peak, he must contend with their protector, a reclusive mystery man (Rutger Hauer) who inhabits a secluded island.

Also figuring into the story is the unstated emotional bond between Hauer and the storekeeper, played by Kathleen Turner, and her son who worships his independent ways.

....

■ BREEZY

1973, 106 MINS, US ◇

Dir Clint Eastwood *Prod* Robert Daley *Scr* Jo Heims *Ph* Frank Stanley *Ed* Ferris Webster *Mus* Michel Legrand *Art Dir* Alexander Golitzen

● William Holden, Kay Lenz, Roger C. Carmel, Mari Dusay, Joan Hotchkis, Jamie Smith Jackson (Malpaso/Universal)

Clint Eastwood's third directorial effort is an okay contemporary drama about middle-aged William Holden falling for teenage Kay Lenz. Associate producer Jo Heims' script works the problem over with perhaps too much ironic, wry or broad humor for solid impact.

Story has divorced Holden, embittered at

women (sequence with Joan Hotchkis is a dramatic highlight), falling for Lenz, a persistent overly precocious teenage drifter in the Hollywood Hills. Roger C. Carmel and wife Shelley Morrison provide sounding boards for Holden's misgivings, before and after Holden begins having sex with Lenz.

The script doesn't help Eastwood out: too much laugh/smile/chuckle sitcom patter and situation make the film more like a TV feature than a gripping and certainly relevant sudser.

....

■ BREWSTER MCCLOUD

1970, 104 MINS, US ◇ Ⓥ

Dir Robert Altman *Prod* Lou Alder *Scr* Doran William Cannon *Ph* Lamar Boren, Jordan Cronenweth *Ed* Louis Lombardo *Mus* Gene Page *Art Dir* George W. Davis, Preston Ames

● Bud Cort, Sally Kellerman, Michael Murphy, William Windom, Shelley Duvall, Rene Auberjonois (M-G-M/Lion's Gate)

Brewster McCloud spares practically nothing in contemporary society. Literate original screenplay is a sardonic fairy tale for the times, extremely well cast and directed.

Bud Cort heads the cast as a young boy, hiding in the depths of Houston's mammoth Astrodome where he is building wings. He is, or is not, in reality a bird in human form.

His guardian angel is Sally Kellerman, always in the right spot to foil some nefarious person about to take advantage of Cort. Trouble is, her protection involves a series of unexplained murders.

Michael Murphy is the sleuth brought in from Frisco to help oldfashioned gumshoe G. Wood.

Kellerman, gets sensational results from her part. She can project more ladylike sensuality and emotion in a look than most actresses can in an hour.

....

■ BREWSTER'S MILLIONS

1945, 79 MINS, US Ⓥ

Dir Allan Dwan *Prod* Edward Small *Scr* Siegfried Herzig, Charles Rogers, Wilkie Mahoney *Ph* Charles Lawton *Ed* Richard Heermance *Mus* Hugo Friedhofer *Art Dir* Joseph Sternad

● Dennis O'Keefe, Helen Walker, Eddie 'Rochester' Anderson, June Havoc, Mischa Auer (United Artists)

Play [by Winchell Smith and Byron Ongley based on the novel by George Barr McCutcheon], first produced in 1907, remains somewhat dated despite efforts to refurbish background through introduction of wartime atmosphere.

The young, handsome soldier returns home to a swell girl waiting to marry him. He finds he's inherited $8 million bucks. Now here's the problem – he's got to spend $1 million in two months, or lose the entire estate. Even with the help of a flop musical, a bankrupt banker, the stock market, the racetrack and a spending society gal he has trouble. *Millions* is a broad farce, of course, and gets over as such.

....

■ BREWSTER'S MILLIONS

1985, 97 MINS, US ◇ Ⓥ

Dir Walter Hill *Prod* Lawrence Gordon, Joel Silver *Scr* Herschel Weingrod, Timothy Harris *Ph* Ric Waite *Ed* Freeman Davies, Michel Ripps *Mus* Ry Cooder *Art Dir* John Vallone

● Richard Pryor, John Candy, Lonette McKee, Stephen Collins, Jerry Orbach, Pat Hingle (Universal)

It's hard to believe a comedy starring Richard Pryor and John Candy is no funnier than this one is, but director Walter Hill has overwhelmed the intricate genius of each with constant background action, crowd confusions and other endless distractions.

All the frenetic motion, unfortunately, never disguises the fact that the writers haven't done much of distinction with the familiar story [a 1902 novel by George Barr McCutcheon] that has been produced in many forms, dating back to a 1906 stage version. [Previous film versions were in 1914, 1921, 1935, 1945 and 1961.]

In one incarnation or another, the yarn always involves somebody who stands to inherit a huge fortune, but first must squander a small one over a short time. In order to enjoy the fantasy, the audience must be given good reason to root for the hero.

Though Pryor plays it likeably enough, he never seems particularly deserving of the fun, excitement and brief luxury he falls into in having to spend $30 million in 30 days, much less the $300 million inheritance he stands to receive if he succeeds.

■ BRIDE, THE

1985, 118 MINS, US ◇ ⓥ

Dir Franc Roddam   *Prod* Victor Drai, Christ Kenny   *Scr* Lloyd Fonvielle   *Ph* Stephen H. Burum   *Ed* Michael Ellis   *Mus* Maurice Jarre   *Art Dir* Michael Seymour
● Sting, Jennifer Beals, Clancy Brown, David Rappaport, Geraldine Page, Alexei Sayle (Columbia-Delphi III)

Production departs from the host of other *Frankensteins* in its bright visual look, its lush Maurice Jarre score, its view of women, its younger characters, and its romantic scope.

Pic opens with a jolting laboratory sequence, when Sting as Baron Frankenstein brings to life the gauze-wrapped Jennifer Beals as the doctor's original monster creation looks on with frothing agitation.

In opting to tone down the horror aspect of the genre, producer Victor Drai and his team have created another kind of monster: a *Frankenstein* movie that's not scary.

While there is deliberate humor at times, most of it successfully produced by a lilting dwarf character who steals the movie (David Rappaport), the intention of the filmmakers is not camp. That's both the pic's virtue and, at the conclusion, its downfall.

■ BRIDE FOR SALE

1949, 87 MINS, US

Dir William D. Russell   *Prod* Jack H. Skirball   *Scr* Bruce Manning, Islin Auster   *Ph* Joseph Valentine   *Ed* Frederic Knudtson   *Mus* Frederick Hollander
● Claudette Colbert, Robert Young, George Brent, Max Baer, Gus Schilling (RKO/Crest)

Bride for Sale is a lot of escapist nonsense that manages to be generally amusing, and sometimes hilariously so. Screwball angles are played up for laughs, the pacing is good and the playing enjoyable, making it entirely acceptable for light entertainment.

Kingpinning the slapstick are Claudette Colbert, Robert Young and George Brent. Colbert does glib work as a tax expert for the accounting firm conducted by Brent. She figures to find the perfect husband, with suitable bankroll, by casing the returns the firm makes out. Brent wants to keep her on the job so enlists aid of Young to make like an eligible male, and woo the maiden.

On that basis of fun, William D. Russell's direction marches the plot and the players along a broad path of antics.

■ BRIDE OF FRANKENSTEIN, THE

1935, 73 MINS, US ⓥ

Dir James Whale   *Prod* Carl Laemmle Jr   *Scr* William Hurlbut, John L. Balderston   *Ph* John Mescall   *Ed* Ted Kent   *Mus* Franz Waxman   *Art Dir* Charles D. Hall
● Boris Karloff, Colin Clive, Elsa Lanchester, Valerie Hobson, Ernest Thesiger, O.P. Heggie (Universal)

In the previous Frankenstein film's finale the monster was burned in a huge fire. Here it's started off with the same fire scene, except that in a few moments he is revealed to have bored through the earth to a subterranean stream, which saved him from death. From there on, of course, it's a romp.

Perhaps a bit too much time is taken up by the monster and too little by the woman created to be his bride. Frankenstein, the monster's creator, is this time sorry and tries to crawl out but Dr Pretorious forces him to go into more life manufacturing, having conceived the idea of a woman to act as the monster's playmate. The woman is finally evolved, but she's just as horrified at him as everyone else.

Karloff manages to invest the character with some subtleties of emotion that are surprisingly real and touching. Especially is this true in the scene where he meets a blind man who, not knowing that he's talking to a monster, makes a friend of him.

Runner-up position from an acting standpoint goes to Ernest Thesiger as Dr Pretorious, a diabolic characterization if ever there was one. Elsa Lanchester handles two assignments, being first in a preamble as author Mary Shelley and then the created woman. In latter assignment she impresses quite highly, although in both spots she has very little to do.

■ BRIDE WORE BOOTS, THE

1946, 85 MINS, US

Dir Irving Pichel   *Prod* Seton I. Miller   *Scr* Dwight Mitchell Wiley   *Ph* Stuart Thompson   *Ed* Ellsworth Hoagland   *Mus* Frederick Hollander   *Art Dir* Hans Dreier, John Meehan
● Barbara Stanwyck, Robert Cummings, Diana Lynn, Patric Knowles, Robert Benchley, Natalie Wood (Paramount)

The Bride Wore Boots is never as funny as its makers intended. It is only in the final 10 minutes or so when the story casts off all restraint and goes slapstick with a vengeance that comedy rates a genuinely hearty response.

Barbara Stanwyck and Robert Cummings are seen as married couple with divided interests. Stanwyck loves horses, in fact operates a breeding farm. Cummings is an author and hates horses. The wife hates the stuffy Civil War relics wished off on her husband by adoring Confederate Dames societies.

Star trio, which has Diana Lynn as a young southern vamp, make frantic efforts to put the material over, but often fail. Patric Knowles has a thankless spot as near-rival for Stanwyck's attention. Peggy Wood and Robert Benchley team for more adult chuckles and Willie Best is good as Cummings' handyman. Natalie Wood and Gregory Muradian are seen as the obnoxious offspring of the married couple.

■ BRIDGE AT REMAGEN, THE

1969, 116 MINS, US ◇ ⓥ

Dir John Guillermin   *Prod* David L. Wolper   *Scr* Richard Yates, William Roberts   *Ph* Stanley Cortez   *Ed* William Cartwright   *Mus* Elmer Bernstein   *Art Dir* Alfred Sweeney
● George Segal, Robert Vaughn, Ben Gazzara, Bradford Dillman, E.G. Marshall, Peter Van Eyck (United Artists)

The taking of a bridge provides the basis for an actionful World War II melodrama. This time out it's the Ludendorff Bridge over the Rhine in the Remagen area, scene of desperate fighting for its control by both American and German forces.

Certain confusion in plot content exists, as it never appears overly clear the exact purpose of American and Nazi military thinking.

Against this background chief interest rests in the performance of George Segal, a hard-boiled American platoon leader, as he and his men attempt to accomplish the orders of their high command.

Director John Guillermin succeeds in realistic movement as he attempts to overcome deficiencies of script and generally manages strong characterizations from his cast.

■ BRIDGE ON THE RIVER KWAI, THE

1957, 161 MINS, UK/US ◇ ⓥ

Dir David Lean   *Prod* Sam Spiegel   *Scr* Pierre Boulle   *Ph* Jack Hildyard   *Ed* Peter Taylor   *Mus* Malcolm Arnold   *Art Dir* Donald M. Ashton
● William Holden, Alec Guinness, Jack Hawkins, Sessue Hayakawa, Geoffrey Horne, James Donald (Columbia/Horizon)

The Bridge on the River Kwai is a gripping drama, expertly put together and handled with skill in all departments. From a technical standpoint, it reflects the care and competence that went into the $3 million-plus venture, filmed against the exotic background of the steaming jungles and mountains of Ceylon [repping Burma]. A story of the futility of war in general [adapted, uncredited, by Carl Foreman, Michael Wilson and Calder Willingham from the novel by Pierre Boulle], the underlying message is never permitted to impede.

Story is 'masculine'. It's about three men, William Holden, Alec Guinness and Sessue Hayakawa. Latter is the commandant of a Japanese prison camp in which Holden, a Yank sailor posing as a commander, is a prisoner. Guinness is a British colonel who commands a new group of prisoners. He's a strict rules-of-war man who clashes immediately with Hayakawa over the latter's insistence that officers as well as men must work on the railroad bridge being built over the River Kwai.

Guinness wins and then proceeds to guide his men in building a superb bridge to prove the mettle of British soldiers under any conditions. Holden, meanwhile, escapes to safety but is talked into leading Jack Hawkins and British commandos back to the bridge to blow it up.

There are notable performances from the key characters, but the film is unquestionably Guinness'. He etches an unforgettable portrait of the typical British army officer, strict, didactic and serene in his adherence to the book. It's a performance of tremendous power and dignity. Hayakawa, once a star in American silents and long absent from the screen, also is solidly impressive as the Japanese officer, limning him as an admixture of cruelty and correctness.

□ 1957: Best Picture

■ BRIDGES AT TOKO-RI, THE

1954, 102 MINS, US ◇ ⓥ

Dir Mark Robson   *Prod* William Perlberg, George Seaton   *Scr* Valentine Davies   *Ph* Loyal Griggs   *Ed* Alma Macrorie   *Mus* Lyn Murray   *Art Dir* Hal Pereira, Henry Bumstead
● William Holden, Grace Kelly, Fredric March, Mickey Rooney, Robert Strauss, Charles McGraw (Paramount)

James A. Michener's hard-hitting novel of the Korean conflict finds slick translation in this topflight war spectacle.

In taking advantage of the navy's resources, aboard an aircraft carrier off the coast of Korea and through the use of planes and equipment, Mark Robson in his taut direction catches the spirit of the navy and what it stood for in the Korean War, never losing sight, however, of the personalized story of a Navy combat flier.

Narrative drives toward the climactic bombing by US fliers of the five bridges at

B

Toko-Ri, which span a strategic pass in Korea's interior. Here the story of William Holden, a reserve officer recalled to service, unfolds. A fine flier, he is taken under the wing of the admiral, played by Frederic March, who understands his gripe of having been forced to leave his wife and children to return to the Navy.

Practically every principal performance is a standout. Holden lends conviction to his character, and March delivers a sock portrayal of the admiral, who is drawn to Holden beause he reminds him of his two sons lost in war. As Holden's wife who brings their two daughters to Tokyo so they may be near the flier, Grace Kelly is warmly sympathetic.

• •

■ BRIDGE TOO FAR, A

1977, 175 MINS, UK ◇ ⓥ
Dir Richard Attenborough   *Prod* Joseph E. Levine, Richard P. Levine   *Scr* William Goldman   *Ph* Geoffrey Unsworth   *Ed* Anthony Gibbs   *Mus* John Addison   *Art Dir* Terry Marsh
● Dirk Bogarde, James Caan, Michael Caine, Sean Connery, Edward Fox, Elliott Gould (United Artists)

Futility and frustration are the overriding emotional elements in *A Bridge Too Far*, Joseph E. Levine's sprawling Second World War production [from the novel by Cornelius Ryan] about a 1944 military operation botched by both Allied and German troops.

Film opens with some vintage black and white newsreel footage in original frame ratio, setting up the falls. 1944, attempt to expedite the end of the Second World War by an enormous paratroop operation involving a series of bridges leading to Germany.

As operations begin, periodic appearances are made by cocky Robert Redford, wise-cracking Elliott Gould, stolid Ryan O'Neal and James Caan.

• •

■ BRIEF ENCOUNTER

1945, 83 MINS, UK ⓥ
Dir David Lean   *Prod* Noel Coward   *Scr* Noel Coward, David Lean, Ronald Neane   *Ph* Robert Krasker   *Ed* Jack Harris   *Mus* Rachmaninov   *Art Dir* L.P. Williams
● Celia Johnson, Trevor Howard, Stanley Holloway, Joyce Carey, Cyril Raymond Valentine Dyall (Cineguild)

Based on his playlet, *Still Life* from *Tonight at 8.30*, *Brief Encounter* does more for Noel Coward's reputation as a skilled film producer than *In Which We Serve*. His use of express trains thundering through a village station coupled with frantic, last-minute dashes for local trains is only one of the clever touches masking the inherent static quality of the drama.

Celia Johnson as the small-town mother whose brief encounter with a doctor, encumbered with a wife and kids, plunges her into a love affair from which she struggles vainly to escape, is terrific. Co-starred with her, Trevor Howard, as the doctor, gives a performance calculated to win the sympathy of femmes of all ages. As for the dumb husband whose idea of marital happiness is summed up in his parrot-like iteration, 'Have it your own way, my dear', Cyril Raymond manages to invest the stodgy character with a lovable quality.

• •

■ BRIGADOON

1954, 108 MINS, US ◇ ⓥ
Dir Vincente Minnelli   *Prod* Arthur Freed   *Scr* Alan Jay Lerner   *Ph* Joseph Ruttenberg   *Ed* Albert Akst   *Mus* Johnny Green (dir.)   *Art Dir* Cedric Gibbons, Preston Ames
● Gene Kelly, Van Johnson, Cyd Charisse, Elaine Stewart, Barry Jones, Hugh Laing (M-G-M)

In transferring *Brigadoon*, a click as a [1947] Broadway musical play, to the screen, Metro

has medium success. It's a fairly entertaining tunefilm of mixed appeal.

Among the more noteworthy points are the score, as directed by Johnny Green, and the stage-type settings that represent the plot's Highland locale. The latter are striking, even though they are the major contribution to the feeling that this is a filmed stage show, rather than a motion picture musical.

Less noteworthy is the choreography by Gene Kelly, who also plays the lead male role, and his singing of the Alan Jay Lerner-Frederick Loewe songs.

The Lerner musical play tells of two New Yorkers who become lost while hunting in Scotland and happen on Brigadoon on the one day that it is visible every 100 years. Besides, a wedding is to take place and Kelly and Van Johnson, the modern-day males, join in the fun. Particularly Kelly, who falls for Cyd Charisse hard enough to be willing to join his sweetheart in the long ago.

• •

■ BRIGHAM YOUNG

1940, 112 MINS, US
Dir Henry Hathaway   *Prod* Kenneth Macgowan   *Scr* Lamar Trotti   *Ph* Arthur Miller   *Ed* Robert Bischoff   *Mus* Alfred Newman   *Art Dir* William Darling, Maurice Ransford
● Tyrone Power, Linda Darnell, Dean Jagger, Brian Donlevy, Jane Darwell, John Carradine (20th Century-Fox)

Taking the favorable factual aspects of the trek of Mormons to the west, and combining them with well-concocted fictional ingredients, picture emerges as an epic filmization of early American history.

There's dramatic power in the persecution of the Mormons in their settlement at Nauvoo, Illinois; the conviction and murder of Joseph Smith; and the resultant decision of Brigham Young to lead his flock across the plains to their eventual home on the shores of Salt Lake. Adversity hits the entourage at every turn, but, despite recalcitrants in the ranks, Young commands attention with a most dominating personality which is most vividly depicted.

Through it all runs a minor romance between Tyrone Power and Linda Darnell; and a more important impress of man and wife on the parts of Young (Dean Jagger) and his first and favorite spouse, Mary Ann (Mary Astor). Latter is decidedly sympathetic and carries prominent appeal as standing solidly behind the leader through adversity.

Jagger brings to the character of the Mormon leader a personable humaness and sympathy. Astor turns in one of the finest performances of her career. Power and Darnell are overshadowed by the above twain.

• •

■ BRIGHT ANGEL

1990, 94 MINS, US ◇ ⓥ
Dir Michael Fields   *Prod* Paige Simpson, Robert MacLean   *Scr* Richard Ford   *Ph* Elliott Davis   *Ed* Melody London, Clement Barclay   *Mus* Christopher Young   *Art Dir* Marcia Hinds Johnson
● Dermot Mulroney, Lili Taylor, Sam Shepard, Valerie Perrine, Sheila McCarthy, Burt Young (Hemdale-Northwood/Bright Angel)

Bright Angel is one of those films that breathe freshness and life into familiar genres. Basically a road movie about a pair of young lovers who become involved in crime, Michael Fields' first feature as a director boasts a full cast-list of near-perfect performances. The intelligent and spare screenplay is by Richard Ford, who based it on two of his short stories [*Children* and *Great Falls*].

The setting is Montana, 'where the Great Plains begin'. George Russell (Dermot Mulroney), 18, lives with his parents (Sam Shepard and Valerie Perrine) who separate violently when his father finds his mother

with another man. George is attracted to Lucy (Lili Taylor), who has spent an afternoon in a motel with the father of his best friend, an Indian. She needs to get to the Wyoming town where her brother's in prison, and George offers to drive her.

Much of the film is taken up with the relationship between the naive and good-hearted George and the old-beyond-her-years Lucy as they journey to their destination, and with the characters they become involved with.

Fields and Ford deal with a familiar genre here, but they avoid cliches: no sex scenes (but a great deal of sexual tension); no shoot-outs (but an agonizing sequence of suspense); no neat ending.

• •

■ BRIGHT LIGHTS, BIG CITY

1988, 110 MINS, US ◇ ⓥ
Dir James Bridges   *Prod* Mark Rosenberg, Sydney Pollack   *Scr* Jay McInerney   *Ph* Gordon Willis   *Ed* John Bloom   *Mus* Donald Fagen   *Art Dir* Santo Loquasto
● Michael J. Fox, Kiefer Sutherland, Phoebe Cates, Swoosie Kurtz, Frances Sternhagen, Tracy Pollan (United Artists)

This novel-cum-feature film (from Jay McInerney's book) is a distinctly morose and maudlin journey through one man's destructive period of personal loss.

Opening scene establishes Michael J. Fox as a lonesome barfly with a cocaine habit in the Big Apple. First reason given is that his wife (Phoebe Cates) has dumped him to pursue modeling in Paris. It's later learned that he's also grieving over the death of his mother (Dianne Wiest) a year earlier.

Fox is cast here as Jamie, a would-be writer marking time as a fact checker for literary giant *Gotham* magazine. Jamie quickly slides so badly that he's fired during a scene with editorial chief, Frances Sternhagen – an exchange that points up the benefit of placing the youthful Fox in situations with seasoned veterans.

Jason Robards' appearance as a drunken fiction writer is all too familiar and a brief encounter with the fascinating William Hickey and a pittance of time with Wiest round out these cameos.

• •

■ BRIGHTON BEACH MEMOIRS

1986, 108 MINS, US ◇ ⓥ
Dir Gene Saks   *Prod* Ray Stark   *Scr* Neil Simon   *Ph* John Bailey   *Ed* Carol Littleton   *Mus* Michael Small   *Art Dir* Stuart Wurtzel
● Blythe Danner, Bob Dishy, Brian Dillinger, Stacey Glick, Judith Ivey, Lisa Waltz (Rastar)

The first of Neil Simon's semi-autobiographical trilogy, *Brighton Beach* bowed in Los Angeles in late 1982 and opened in New York in March, 1983.

Set in 1937 in a lower-middle class section of Brooklyn, story details assorted life crises of members of the Jerome family, hard-working moral Jews whose problems are all taken to heart by Mama Kate, played by Blythe Danner.

Despite the assurance of verbal reprisals, all family members are expected to speak their minds and share their difficulties (there can be no secrets anyway, since nothing can escape Mama's notice). Emotions are fully felt, responsibilities accepted and decisions taken, not avoided.

Performances are skilled all the way through.

• •

■ BRIGHTON ROCK

1948, 92 MINS, UK ⓥ
Dir John Boulting   *Prod* Roy Boulting   *Scr* Graham Greene, Terence Rattigan   *Ph* Harry Waxman   *Ed* Peter Graham Scott   *Mus* Hans May   *Art Dir* John Howell

● Richard Attenborough, Hermione Baddeley, William Hartnell, Carol Marsh (Boulting Brothers)

British producers are competing with each other in rushing mobster yarns to the screen. This tends to prove that Britain can turn out a gangster picture as brutal as any Hollywood had devised.

With Graham Greene and Terence Rattigan responsible for the screenplay [based on Greene's own novel], something more exciting might reasonably have been expected. Some of blame goes to director John Boulting whose tempo is much too leisurely for this type of picture.

Story is laid in pre-war seaside resort Brighton, where two razor-slashing race gangs are feuding.

It is difficult to believe that any gang which included William Hartnell could be led by Richard Attenborough. Hartnell is so much more the gangster type than Attenborough that it is obvious that an exchange of parts would have made the film more credible.

Acting honors are collared by that seasoned actress, Hermione Baddeley. She steals every scene in which she appears, making Ida, the concert artist, a sympathetic character. Carol Marsh (formerly Norma Simpson) plays the waitress and gangster's wife with modesty.

■ BRINGING UP BABY

1938, 102 MINS, US Ⓥ

Dir Howard Hawks   *Prod* Howard Hawks   *Scr* Dudley Nichols, Hagar Wilde   *Ph* Russell Metty   *Ed* George Hively   *Mus* Roy Webb (dir.)
● Katharine Hepburn, Cary Grant, Charlie Ruggles, Barry Fitzgerald, May Robson, Walter Catlett (RKO)

This harum-scarum farce comedy, Katharine Hepburn's first of the type, is constructed for maximum of laughs. Opposite her is Cary Grant, who is perfectly at home as a farceur after his work in *The Awful Truth* (1937).

Wacky developments [story by Hagar Wilde] include pursuit of an heiress after a zoology professor who expects to wed his femme assistant in the museum on the same day he plans to complete a giant brontosaurus; a pet leopard, 'Nissa', who makes a playmate of 'Asta', a redoubtable Scots terrier; a wealthy woman who may endow the prof's museum with $1 million; an escaped wild leopard from the circus; a stupid town constable; a forgetful ex-big game hunter; a scientifically-minded brain specialist; and a tippling gardener.

Hepburn is invigorating as the madcap deb. Grant, who thinks more of recovering the priceless missing bone for his uncompleted brontosaurus than his impending wedding and the companionship of the playful heiress, performs his role to the hilt. Charlie Ruggles, as the former African game hunter, does wonders with a minor characterization brought in late in the picture.

Chief shortcoming is that too much time is consumed with the jail sequence. Prime reason for it, of course, is that it gives Hepburn a chance to imitate a gunmoll.

■ BRING ME THE HEAD OF ALFREDO GARCIA

1974, 112 MINS, US ◇ Ⓥ

Dir Sam Peckinpah   *Prod* Martin Baum   *Scr* Gordon Dawson, Sam Peckinpah   *Ph* Alex Phillips   *Ed* Garth Craven, Robbe Roberts, Sergio Ortega, Dennis E. Dolan   *Art Dir* Enrique Estevez
● Warren Oates, Isela Vega, Gig Young, Robert Webber, Helmut Dantine, Kris Kristofferson (United Artists)

Bring Me the Head of Alfredo Garcia is turgid melodrama [from a story by Frank Kowalski and Sam Peckinpah] at its worst. Warren Oates stars as an expatriate American piano bar musician making a stab for riches in Mexico by finding the never-seen title character sought by an outraged Mexican father. Naturally the search brings unhappiness, and, being a Peckinpah film, naturally lots and lots of people get killed along the way, as well as audience interest.

The title derives from the command of wealthy Emilio Fernandez to find the father of his unwed daughter's child. Gig Young, Helmut Dantine and Robert Webber are the private detectives engaged. They meet Oates whose girl (Isela Vega) had been intimate with the stud. He is dead, so Oates and Vega head off to steal the guy's head from a grave.

■ BRITANNIA HOSPITAL

1982, 115 MINS, UK ◇ Ⓥ

Dir Lindsay Anderson   *Prod* Davina Belling, Clive Parsons   *Scr* David Sherwin   *Ph* Mike Fash   *Ed* Michael Ellis   *Mus* Alan Price   *Art Dir* Norris Spencer
● Leonard Rossiter, Graham Crowden, Malcolm McDowell, Joan Plowright, Jill Bennett, Marsha Hunt (EMI/General)

Britannia Hospital is a witty, unsparing expose of British manners and mores.

The film revolves around a strike at a hospital where a royal personage is expected. This gives rise to union complaints about privileges showered on monied notables when the National Health system was supposed to make medicine equally available for all.

Medics' own misuse of National Health funds is pilloried in no uncertain style. A mad doctor experiments, from funds meant for socialized medicine, to create Frankenstein-type creatures.

A zealous reporter with a small video camera sneaks in to tape the mad doctor's creature-building only to end up as the head of the Frankenstein figure.

Through it all, the hospital director tries to cope with typical British phlegm, assured by a Scotland Yard top cop that crowds and unions will be kept in check.

Malcolm McDowell is rightly overacting as the reporter who loses his head. Leonard Rossiter copes staunchly as the beset hospital director. Marsha Hunt, Jill Bennett and Joan Plowright do fine cameo work as nurse, doctor and the union head.

■ BROADCAST NEWS

1987, 131 MINS, US ◇ Ⓥ

Dir James L. Brooks   *Prod* James L. Brooks, Penney Finkelman Cox   *Scr* James L. Brooks   *Ph* Michael Ballhaus   *Ed* Richard Marks   *Mus* Bill Conti   *Art Dir* Charles Rosen
● William Hurt, Albert Brooks, Holly Hunter, Robert Prosky, Lois Chiles, Joan Cusack (20th Century-Fox)

Enormously entertaining *Broadcast News* is an inside look at the personal and professional lives of three TV journlists.

Brooks gently punctures the self-importance of his characters with a sly satirical edge. When veteran reporter Aaron Altman (Albert Brooks) and hard-nosed producer Jane Craig (Holly Hunter) go to the jungles of Central America to report on the revolution, the results are too humorous and self-serving to take seriously.

Where Craig and Altman are seasoned professionals with great talent, Tom Grunick (William Hurt) is a slick ex-sportscaster who knows how to turn on the charm and seduce an audience. But is it news, his colleagues wonder.

Grunick forms the third corner of a latent love traingle. Jane loves Tom but hates his work. Aaron loves his work and loves Jane and hates Tom. Tom loves himself and loves Jane. In short it's a case of scrambled emotions among people who heretofore have substituted work for pleasure.

Hunter is simply superb barking out orders from a mouth contorted with who-knows-what emotions. As the neurotic but brilliant reporter, Brooks gives an insightful performance while communicating his character's guardedness and anguish. As the hardest of the characters to read, Hurt does a good job keeping up the mystery so one never knows when he's sincere or faking, and maybe he doesn't either.

☐ 1987: Best Picture (Nomination)

■ BROADWAY

1942, 89 MINS, US

Dir William A. Seiter   *Prod* Bruce Manning   *Scr* Felix Jackson, John Bright   *Ph* George Barnes   *Ed* Ted Kent   *Mus* Charles Previn
● George Raft, Pat O'Brien, Broderick Crawford, Janet Blair, Anne Gwynne, Marjorie Rambeau (Universal)

Universal's modernized presentation of *Broadway* retains the thrilling tenseness and dramatic suspense of both the original Philip Dunning-George Abbott play and the first film version turned out by Universal in 1929.

As modernized, *Broadway* could easily be the autobiography of George Raft – and this impression is carried through the unreeling via the medium of a prolog deftly contrived. Picture opens with Raft airlining to New York with companion-bodyguard-shadow, Mack Gray, for a short visit between pictures. Wandering onto Broadway, alone, he stops at a cellar being remodelled into a bowling alley. Looking around, he starts reminiscing to the old night-watchman about the heyday of the spot as a cabaret during the lush prohibition era – when Raft got his start as a hoofer in the place.

In addition to swift dramatic pace, provided both in script and direction, picture is studded with a group of excellent performances. Raft justifies his casting for the lead, and clicks solidly. Sharing honors with him is Pat O'Brien.

■ BROADWAY DANNY ROSE

1984, 86 MINS, US Ⓥ

Dir Woody Allen   *Prod* Robert Greenhut   *Scr* Woody Allen   *Ph* Gordon Willis   *Ed* Susan E. Morse   *Mus* Dick Hyman   *Art Dir* Mel Bourne
● Woody Allen, Mia Farrow, Nick Apollo Forte, Milton Berle, Sandy Baron, Corbett Monica (Orion)

Broadway Danny Rose is a delectable diversion which allows Woody Allen to present a reasonably humane, and amusing gentle character study without sacrificing himself to overly commercial concerns.

Allen's perfect as a small-time, good-hearted Broadway talent agent, giving his all for a roster of hopeless clients.

Agent's career is fondly recalled here by a group of Catskill comics (all played by themselves) sitting around over coffee, focusing mainly on Allen's attempt to revive the career of an aging, overweight, boozing lounge singer, beautifully played by Nick Apollo Forte.

One of Forte's many problems that Allen must deal with is a floozy of a girlfriend. And it's truly one of the picture's early delights that this sunglassed bimbo is actually on screen for several minutes before most of the audience catches on that she's Mia Farrow.

Through Forte and Farrow, Allen becomes the target of a couple of hit men.

■ BROADWAY MELODY

1929, 104 MINS, US ◇ Ⓥ

Dir Harry Beaumont   *Scr* Edmund Goulding, James Gleason, Norman Houston   *Ph* John Arnold   *Mus* Herb Nacio Brown, Arthur Freed   *Art Dir* Cedric Gibbons

B

● Anita Page, Bessie Love, Charles King, Jed Prouty, Kenneth Thomson, Edward Dillon (M-G-M)

Broadway Melody, the first screen musical, tells of a vaudeville sister team coming in from the middle west, with the older girl engaged to a song-and-dance boy in a Broadway revue. Latter goes for the kid sister, now grown up, who starts playing with one of the show's backers to stand off the boy and spare the blow to her sister, despite that she, too, is in love with her prospective brother-in-law.

In between are the troubles of the femme team making the revue grade.

Both girls, Bessie Love as the elder sister and Anita Page as the youngster, are great in their respective climaxes, especially Love. Charlie King looks as good as he plays and plants comedy lines as they should be delivered. Other cast support is up to the mark with the exception of Kenneth Thomson, as the chaser, who plays too slow and doesn't convince.

Excellent bits of sound workmanship are that of camera and mike following Page and the heavy along the dance floor to pick up their conversation as they glide.

☐ 1928/29: Best Picture

· ·

■ **BROADWAY MELODY OF 1936**

1935, 102 MINS, US
Dir Roy Del Ruth *Prod* John W. Considine Jr *Scr* Jack McGowan, Sid Silvers *Ph* Charles Rosher *Ed* Blanche Sewell *Mus* Alfred Newman (dir.)
● Jack Benny, Eleanor Powell, Robert Taylor, Una Merkel, Sid Silvers, Buddy Ebsen (M-G-M)

Everything revolves about Eleanor Powell, Robert Taylor and June Knight, the menace. She's the Park Avenue bankroll ($60,000) for the forthcoming musical comedy. Columnist Jack Benny had been building up a phoney French comedienne, and so when Taylor fails to recognize his adolescent sweetheart from Albany she (Powell) essays an accent, bizarre make-up and goals everybody with her personality and her stepping as the pseudo-French star.

Story is a curious hodge-podge of fantasy, realism and just hokum musical comedy. When the Ebsens (Vilma and Buddy) are doing their 'Sing Before Breakfast', it's quite Rene Clair-ish in the whimsical mating of the tempo with the attic time-stepping. In other spots it goes Busby Berkeley with overhead ballet shots, or the sequence in what looks like the Rainbow Room at Radio City.

Songs are all good. 'Broadway Rhythm', sung by Frances Langford and with dance specialties by Powell, Nick Long Jr, Knight and the Ebsens, is a corking creation.

☐ 1935: Best Picture (Nomination)

· ·

■ **BROADWAY MELODY OF 1938**

1937, 115 MINS, US
Dir Roy Del Ruth *Prod* Jack Cummings *Scr* Jack McGowan *Ph* William Daniels *Ed* Blanche Sewell *Mus* George Stoll (dir.)
● Robert Taylor, Eleanor Powell, George Murphy, Binnie Barnes, Judy Garland, Sophie Tucker (M-G-M)

Much better than its predecessor of 1936, and not far behind the original 1929 *Broadway Melody*.

No use getting into the details until Sophie Tucker and Judy Garland are disposed of. Former is somewhere past 40, but when she walks on the screen something happens. Then she steps back and pushes Garland, still in her teens, into the camera foreground. Young Garland gives them 'Everybody sing', with a letter to the homefolks.

Each does numbers solo later on. Judy sings a plaint to Clark Gable's photograph which is close to great screen acting. Then, to top it off, Soph does 'Your Broadway and My

Broadway', with lyrics which bring in the great names of the past generation.

Most of the rest is just filler-in between the Tucker and the Garland numbers. There is a lot of plot [by Jack McGowan and Sid Silvers] about a racehorse which is owned by Eleanor Powell, and a Broadway musical show which Robert Taylor is trying to produce on a short bankroll.

Buddy Ebsen handles some first-class comedy bits on his own in addition to his eccentric dancing.

Music and lyrics by Nacio Herb Brown and Arthur Freed are first rate.

· ·

■ **BROADWAY MELODY OF 1940**

1940, 102 MINS, US
Dir Norman Taurog *Prod* Jack Cummings *Scr* Leon Gordon, George Oppenheimer *Ph* Oliver T. Marsh, Joseph Ruttenberg *Ed* Blanche Sewell *Mus* Alfred Newman (dir.)
● Fred Astaire, Eleanor Powell, George Murphy, Frank Morgan, Ian Hunter, Florence Rice (M-G-M)

Long on its display of corking dance routines and numbers by Fred Astaire, Eleanor Powell and George Murphy, mounted against elaborate production backgrounds, *Broadway Melody of 1940* slides through as moderately satisfying entertainment.

The story is a typical backstage yarn. Astaire and Murphy are an ambitious team of hoofers working in a dance hall for coffee and cakes. Mistake in names shoots Murphy instead of Astaire into the lead of a Broadway musical opposite the star (Eleanor Powell). Murphy hits the bottle for the opening night, Astaire taking his place to protect his former partner.

This is the first teaming of Astaire and Powell in a filmusical. The result is as to be expected, both presenting several new and applause-generating numbers. But the numbers are too many and too extended for general purposes. This is particularly true of the finale, a super-lavish production background in which Astaire and Powell dance tap and whirl for six minutes. It's not sufficient to maintain interest for that length of time.

Murphy gains attention with a top performance as the hoofer-partner of Astaire. Latter is adequate in the role of the dance expert who goes to town when he starts stepping out with his new routines. Powell is an eyeful in her dances, and okay for the story sequences. Frank Morgan provides plenty of laughs in characterization of the musical show producer, while Ian Hunter is his partner who really stages the shows.

· ·

■ **BROADWAY RHYTHM**

1944, 115 MINS, US ◇
Dir Roy Del Ruth *Prod* Jack Cummings *Scr* Dorothy Kingsley, Harry Clork *Ph* Leonard Smith *Ed* Albert Akst *Mus* Johnny Green (dir) *Art Dir* Cedric Gibbons, Jack Martin Smith
● George Murphy, Ginny Simms, Charles Winninger, Gloria DeHaven, Lena Horne (M-G-M)

Broadway Rhythm is a typical backstage filmusical wheeled out in the usual Metro elaborate and colorful style. Displaying group of toprank specialties and names among the entertainers, the fragile and hodge-podge yarn [based on the 1939 Kern-Hammerstein musical *Very Warm for May*] stops periodically while the guest stars appear.

Story follows run-of-mill formula for a backstager. George Murphy is a top musical comedy producer readying his next show for Broadway. Ginny Simms, Hollywood film star, hits town for a whirl at the stage after being stymied on new contract in films. Charles Winninger, veteran song-and-dance man, is Murphy's dad, while Gloria

DeHaven is the young sister with stage ambitions.

Tommy Dorsey and his orchestra provide the musical backgrounds, and are spotlighted for opening number to get picture away to a good start and one other number later. Lena Horne socks over two songs – the Gershwins' 'Somebody Loves Me', and 'Brazilian Boogie', by Hugh Martin and Ralph Blane – and both are smartly presented for maximum effect.

· ·

■ **BROADWAY TO HOLLYWOOD**

1933, 88 MINS, US
Dir Willard Mack *Prod* Harry Rapf *Scr* Willard Mack, Edgar Allan Woolf *Ph* William Daniels, Norbert Brodine *Mus* William Axt (arr.) *Art Dir* Stanford Rogers
● Alice Brady, Frank Morgan, Madge Evans, Russell Hardie, Jackie Cooper, Mickey Rooney (M-G-M)

Little from Metro's costly *March of Time* Technicolor musical has actually been resuscitated, although Metro's now historic and costly floppo venture inspired this combined effort by Harry Rapf, Willard Mack and Edgar Allan Woolf to retrieve something from the celluloid wreckage.

Patently it was primed to trace the hoofing variety Hacketts from their Tony Pastor's days until the third-generation success of grandson Ted Hackett III as a film juvenile star. Dovetailed in is all the array of venerable variety talent which Metro assembled for its *March of Time* production four years earlier.

It's all Alice Brady and Frank Morgan's picture in sterling characterizations as the original hoofing Hacketts of Tony Pastor's time and down through the years into the third generation. Madge Evans and Russell Hardie (Ted Hackett Jr) sustain the sub-romance interest.

The third generation has Jackie Cooper as Ted III as a child, and Eddie Quillan playing the matured Ted III when he becomes an overnight Hollywood click.

Cast names which are also included are dragged in by the heels, strictly for ballyhoo value. Among 'em are Jimmy Durante, whose brief appearance in a studio ante-room, as a would-be film aspirant, is strictly a one-to-fill; Fay Templeton and May Robson in the resurrected Technicolor stuff; Una Merkel in an anonymous bit merely shown flirting with the stage actor.

· ·

■ **BROKEN ARROW**

1950, 92 MINS, US ◇ ◇ ▼
Dir Delmer Daves *Prod* Julian Blaustein *Scr* Michael Blankfort *Ph* Ernest Palmer *Ed* J. Watson Webb Jr *Mus* Hugo Friedhofer
● James Stewart, Jeff Chandler, Debra Paget, Basil Ruysdael, Will Geer, Joyce MacKenzie (20th Century-Fox)

Broken Arrow is a western with a little different twist – the story of the attempt of whites and Apaches to learn to live together in the Arizona of 1870. Essentially it's an appealing, sentimental Indian romance, with plenty of action.

Pic has a quality of naive charm that peculiarly fits. There are colorful Indian tribal ceremonies that ring true.

Story [from a novel by Elliott Arnold] concerns a far-sighted young frontiersman (James Stewart) who, tired of the mutual killings of whites and redskins, boldly plans a visit to the feared Apache leader Cochise (Jeff Chandler) to propose a truce. Meeting not only succeeds, but Stewart falls in love with an Indian maiden (Debra Paget). Both truce and troth are impeded by treachery on the part of whites and Indians.

· ·

BROKEN BLOSSOMS OR THE YELLOW MAN AND THE GIRL

1919, 107 MINS, US ◇ ⊗ ⊛

Dir D.W. Griffith *Prod* D.W. Griffith *Scr* D.W. Griffith *Ph* Billy Bitzer, Herdrik Sartor, Karl Brown *Ed* James E. Smith, Rose Smith *Mus* Louis Gottschalk, D.W. Griffith *Art Dir* Charles E. Baker
● Lillian Gish, Donald Crisp, Richard Barthelmess, Edward Peil, Arthur Howard, George Beranger (Artcraft)

Although the picture consumes only 90 minutes, it somehow seems draggy, for the reason that everything other than the scenes with the three principals seems extraneous and tends to clog the progression of the tale.

Broken Blossoms is adapted from a story by Thomas Burke entitled *The Chink and the Child*. The footage allotted the titles is a point to be commended, ample time being allowed to read them slowly and digest their meaning.

The story is a drama of pathos, culminating in tragedy. A pure-minded young Chinaman, reared in the beautiful teachings of Buddha, journeys to London with the altruistic idea of civilizing the white race.

In London there resides in his vicinity a brutish prize-fighter who beats his child into helplessness and she crawls away, half dead, falling insensible into the shop of the Mongolian. With perhaps a whiff of the lilied pipe still in his brain, he finds her on the floor, carries her to his living room above and watches over her with a love so pure as to be wholly unnatural and inconsistent.

Lillian Gish as the girl, shrinking, self-effacing, timid, fearful and wistful, has never before done anything so fine. Donald Crisp is the brutal father, as great a triumph of histrionic artistry as that registered by Gish.

Yet not one whit behind these two masterful portrayals is that of Richard Barthelmess as the young Chinaman, idealized, necessarily, in the matter of facial attractiveness, yet visualizing to the full the gentle delicacy of the idyllic Oriental youth.

BROKEN LANCE

1954, 96 MINS, US ◇ ⊛

Dir Edward Dmytryk *Prod* Sol C. Siegel *Scr* Richard Murphy *Ph* Joe MacDonald *Ed* Dorothy Spencer *Mus* Leigh Harline
● Spencer Tracy, Robert Wagner, Jean Peters, Richard Widmark, Katy Jurado, Hugh O'Brian (20th Century-Fox)

Broken Lance is topnotch western drama. Seems too bad so much of the story is told via an unnecessary flashback. However, there is enough force in the trouping and direction to sustain mood and interest. This is particularly true of Spencer Tracy's performance, since he has the difficult task of making alive a character already dead when the picture opens.

Film starts with Robert Wagner's release from an Arizona prison after serving a three-year sentence. The enmity that lies between him and his three half-brothers (Richard Widmark, Hugh O'Brian and Earl Holliman) is quickly established.

The scene shifts from this strong early sequence, taking place in the office of the governor (E.G. Marshall), where they all try to get him to leave the state, to the once proud family ranch, now decayed from neglect. There Wagner recalls the events that led to his imprisonment.

Within the flashback Tracy is shown as a domineering cattle baron, who rules his four sons and vast empire ruthlessly by his own laws. However, time is running out for him as civilization advances, and he takes the law into his own hands once too often in destroying mining property and injuring miners.

BRONCO BILLY

1980, 119 MINS, US ◇ ⊛

Dir Clint Eastwood *Prod* Dennis Hackin, Neal Dobrofsky *Scr* Dennis Hackin *Ph* David Worth *Ed* Ferris Webster, Joel Cox *Mus* Snuff Garrett *Art Dir* Gene Lourie
● Clint Eastwood, Sondra Locke, Scatman Crothers, Bill McKinney, Sam Bottoms, Geoffrey Lewis (Warner)

In the title role, Clint Eastwood plays an ex-NJ shoe salesman who has trained himself to live out a fantasy as a sharpshooting, knife-throwing, stunt-riding cowboy. There's no place to practice it except as the leader of a run-down Wild West show touring tank towns and county fairs. The others in the troupe are also definitive losers of varying talents.

Along the same highways, however, comes Sondra Locke, an arrogant spoiled heiress, and Geoffrey Lewis, delightful as the idiotic husband she has just married. Fed up with Locke's mistreatment, Lewis abandons her without a dime and she winds up – quite reluctantly – as Eastwood's helper.

Bronco Billy is a caricature of many of the strong heroes whom Eastwood has played in other pix and he's obviously having a wonderful time with the satire.

BRONCO BULLFROG

1970, 86 MINS, UK ◇

Dir Barney Platts-Mills *Prod* Andrew St John *Scr* Barney Platts-Mills *Ph* Adam Barker-Mill *Ed* Jonathan Gili *Mus* Howard Werth, Tony Connor, Keith Gemmell, Trevor Williams
● Del Walker, Anne Gooding, Sam Shepherd, Roy Haywood, Freda Shepherd, Dick Philpott (British Lion)

Producer Andrew St John and director-writer Barney Platts-Mills assembled a bunch of East End amateurs and, with a thin storyline and dialog that seems mainly improvised, let them loose in 'their own scene'. Made for only $48,000, film is a praiseworthy attempt to show the drab environment of an area and to indicate how boredom in that environment can drive youngsters into being layabouts, petty thieves, etc and how such trapped youngsters can develop into more hardened criminals.

Through the film is woven an inarticulate, but frequently touching Romeo and Juliet theme, about two minors who run away from home because there is nowhere to go and nothing to do.

It would be pointless to comment on the non-existent acting. There is behavior, instead.

BROOD, THE

1979, 91 MINS, CANADA ◇ ⊛

Dir David Cronenberg *Prod* Claude Heroux *Scr* David Cronenberg *Ph* Mark Irwin *Ed* Alan Collins *Mus* Howard Shore *Art Dir* Carol Spier
● Oliver Reed, Samantha Eggar, Art Hindle, Cindy Hinds (New World)

A horror entry which casts children in the role of malevolent little monsters, *The Brood* is an extremely well made, if essentially unpleasant, shocker.

Cronenberg's helming is skillful enough to command attention even through his script's needlessly long stretches of dialog.

Action is relatively plodding stuff, with young parent Art Hindle trying to keep his daughter away from mother Samantha Eggar, who's supposedly in psychotherapy at the posh forested retreat of analyst Oliver Reed. Action is spiked with the mysterious murders of Eggar's parents.

Reed registers forcefully as the egotistical doctor and Eggar is appropriately flipped out but, unfortunately, most of the running time is spent with Hindle center stage and the

actor is just too morose to enlist much sympathy, despite his plight.

BROTHER FROM ANOTHER PLANET, THE

1984, 104 MINS, US ◇ ⊛

Dir John Sayles *Prod* Peggy Rajski, Maggie Renzi *Scr* John Sayles *Ph* Ernest R. Dickerson *Ed* John Sayles *Mus* Mason Daring *Art Dir* Steve Lineweaver
● Joe Morton, Darryl Edwards, Steve James, Leonard Jackson, Bill Cobbs, Maggie Renzi (A-Train)

John Sayles takes a turn toward offbeat fantasy in *The Brother from Another Planet*, a vastly amusing but progressively erratic look at the Harlem adventures of an alien, a black E.T.

Brother begins with a tall, mute, young black fellow seeming to be dumped unceremoniously in New York harbor. Within minutes, he makes his way to Harlem, where his unusual, but not truly bizarre, behavior raises some cackles but in most respects blends into the neighborhood.

Pic is essentially a series of behavioral vignettes, and many of them are genuinely delightful and inventive. Once the Brother discovers the Harlem drug scene, however, tale takes a rather unpleasant and, ultimately, confusing turn.

BROTHER SUN SISTER MOON

1973, 121 MINS, ITALY/UK ◇ ⊛

Dir Franco Zeffirelli *Prod* Luciano Perugia *Scr* Suso Cecchi D'Amico, Kenneth Ross, Lina Wertmuller, Franco Zeffirelli *Ph* Ennio Guarnieri *Ed* Reginald Hills, John Rushton *Mus* Donovan *Art Dir* Lorenzo Mongiardino
● Graham Faulkner, Judi Bowker, Alec Guinness, Leigh Lawson, Kenneth Cranham, Michael Feast (Euro International/Vic)

Brother Sun, Sister Moon is a delicate, handsome quasi-fictional biography of one of the great saints of the Catholic Church, Francis of Assisi. Franco Zeffirelli has utilized a style of simple elegance, befitting both the period and the subject.

Graham Faulkner makes an important film debut as Francis of Assisi. Judi Bowker, cast as a young girl who eventually sheds her materialistic existence for religious poverty, is stunningly beautiful, projecting the very essence of innocence.

Evidently edited from original form, the film utilizes flashback to establish briefly Faulkner's early life as a spoiled wastrel, indulged by parents Valentina Cortese and Lee Montague until a rude spiritual awakening in the fevers of wartime pestilence.

Faulkner's character evolution slowly recruits to the humble life of his friends. The illwill of older characters against the growsing band of mystics is portrayed with strength.

BROTHERHOOD, THE

1968, 96 MINS, US ◇ ⊛

Dir Martin Ritt *Prod* Kirk Douglas *Scr* Lewis John Carlino *Ph* Boris Kaufman *Ed* Frank Bracht *Mus* Lalo Schifrin *Art Dir* Tambi Larsen
● Kirk Douglas, Alex Cord, Irene Papas, Luther Adler, Susan Strasberg, Murray Hamilton (Paramount/Bryna)

Mafia-themed story pits Kirk Douglas, as a middle-aged New Jersey syndicate chief, against Alex Cord, his ambitious younger brother not as attuned to the curious, but rigidly-structured old underworld code.

Martin Ritt's topnotch direction of an excellent cast maximizes the tragedy inherent in original screenplay.

Goading Douglas to progress are syndicate partners Luther Adler, Murray Hamilton, Val Avery and Alan Hewitt, repping in dialog and acting the commingling of Irish gangsters and Jewish gangsters with Sicilian-Italian gangsters.

Cord is excellent as the product of an environment which has smoothed out not only the rough edges of immigrant assimilation into the US, but also the surface emotions, noble and ignoble, which marked earlier generations. Urbane, cold, ambitious, unfeeling – Cord's character is chilling.

Since a prolog telegraphs some tragic climax, there is not much suspense in the usual sense of the word.

....

■ BROTHERS

1977, 105 MINS, US ◇

Dir Arthur Barron *Prod* Edward Lewis, Mildred Lewis
Scr Edward Lewis, Mildred Lewis *Ph* John Morrill
Ed William Dornisch *Mus* Taj Mahal *Art Dir* Vince
Cresciman
● Bernie Casey, Vonetta McGee, Ron O'Neal, Renny
Roker, Stu Gilliam, John Lehne (Soho)

Most favorably judged, *Brothers* is an excellent dramatization of a contemporary dispute from one angry viewpoint. It's also a cheapshot, racist picture.

Though labeled 'fiction', pic only makes barest effort to differ from the true story of San Quentin inmate George Jackson, whose younger brother Jonathan and a judge were killed during a wild shoot out at the Marin County Courthouse.

Jackson himself was later killed in prison and black activist Angela Davis was arrested – and acquitted – of charges of helping to plan the break out.

As seen by scripters Edward and Mildred Lewis, American prisons are torture chambers for blacks forced into them by white society. Once behind bars, blacks are dehumanized by guards (all white) and other white prisoners.

....

■ BROTHERS IN LAW

1957, 94 MINS, UK

Dir Roy Boulting *Prod* John Boulting *Scr* Frank
Harvey, Jeffrey Dell, Roy Boulting *Ph* Max Greene
Ed Anthony Harvey *Mus* Benjamin Frankel *Art
Dir* Albert Witherick
● Richard Attenborough, Ian Carmichael,
Terry-Thomas, Jill Adams, Miles Malleson, Eric Barker
(Tudor/British Lion)

The three stars in *Private's Progress* are reunited in this Roy Boulting comedy. This time it's making fun of the law, doing full justice to a laugh-loaded script.

The witty and lighthearted yarn [from the novel by Henry Cecil] traces the experiences of a young lawyer from the day of his graduation until he achieves his first legal victory.

The raw legal recruit is Ian Carmichael, who through the good offices of his roommate and fellow attorney, is accepted as a pupil barrister by Miles Malleson, a distinguished but absent-minded Queen's Counsel. Within a few minutes of his appointment he accompanies his senior to the High Court, and is left to plead the case without even knowing which side he's on. This unhappy start to his career affects Carmichael's confidence. He gets his chance from Terry-Thomas, a seasoned swindler with 17 appearances at the Criminal Court to his credit – and gets his first practical lesson in how to beat the law.

....

■ BROTHERS KARAMAZOV, THE

1958, 149 MINS, US ◇ ▼

Dir Richard Brooks *Prod* Pandro S. Berman
Scr Richard Brooks *Ph* John Alton *Ed* John
Dunning *Mus* Bronislau Kaper *Art Dir* William A.
Horning, Paul Groesse
● Yul Brynner, Maria Schell, Claire Bloom, Lee J. Cobb,
Richard Basehart, William Shatner (M-G-M/Avon)

Bold handling of crude unbridled passion, of violently conflicting ideas, and of earthy

humor makes up *The Brothers Karamazov*. Sex and Salvation are the twin obsessions of the brothers and father, and they are the two themes that are hammered relentlessly home by Richard Brooks, who directs his own screenplay.

Brooks wrote his screenplay from an adaptation by Julius J. and Philip G. Epstein of the Dostoievsky novel. Lee J. Cobb is the father of the Karamazov brothers, a lecherous old buffoon who taunts, tantalizes and frustrates his sons into violence, despair and apathy. Yul Brynner is the handsome, cruel, profligate army officer, a combination of adult power and childish pleasure. He is in conflict with his father partly because they both lust after the same woman, Maria Schell as Grushenka.

Richard Basehart is in revolt because of his intellectual coldness, a rigidity brought on by revulsion at the open and untrammeled sexuality of the old rogue. The third son, William Shatner, has chosen his way of survival in contest with his father; he has retreated into the church as a monk. The explosion that these figures ignite comes when Brynner imagines Schell has gone to his father in preference to him.

Brynner succeeds in making his Dmitri a hero despite the fact that every facet of his character is against it. Schell, in her American motion picture debut, illumines her role, seemingly able to suggest innocence and depravity with the same sweet face. Claire Bloom, as the alabaster beauty who saves Brynner from debtors' prison, is very moving particularly in the court scene as her facade cracks from within, rent by bitterness and despair. It is Lee J. Cobb, however, who walks – or rather gallops – away with the picture. The part is gargantuan and it is not a bit too big for the actor.

The Metrocolor used by Brooks and cameraman John Alton is rich in purples, reds and blues.

....

■ BROWNING VERSION, THE

1951, 90 MINS, UK ▼

Dir Anthony Asquith *Prod* Teddy Baird *Scr* Terence
Rattigan *Ph* Desmond Dickinson *Ed* John D.
Guthridge *Art Dir* Carmen Dillon
● Michael Redgrave, Jean Kent, Nigel Patrick, Wilfrid
Hyde-White, Brian Smith, Bill Travers (Javelin)

Terence Rattigan's play, which had a big success in the West End in 1948, has been faithfully translated to the screen. The celluloid version is crammed with emotional incidents and has two noteworthy tear-jerker scenes.

The background of the story is an English public school with the action spanning barely 48 hours. It is the last day of term, and Andrew Crocker-Harris, an austere disciplinarian, is retiring because of ill health without a pension. The events leading up to the final, powerful valedictory address make up a plot which is rich in incident and human understanding.

The role of the retiring master is not an easy one, but a prize in the right hands. Michael Redgrave fills it with distinction. Almost matching this performance is the role of his wife, played with a mixture of callousness and coyness by Jean Kent.

Nigel Patrick, in a less bombastic part than usual, chalks up another personal success as the science master who becomes ashamed of the intrigue he has had with Kent. Wilfrid Hyde-White is as smooth as ever as the headmaster.

....

■ BRUBAKER

1980, 130 MINS, US ◇ ▼

Dir Stuart Rosenberg *Prod* Ron Silverman *Scr* W.D.
Richter *Ph* Bruno Nuytten *Ed* Robert Brown
Mus Lalo Schifrin *Art Dir* J. Michael Riva

● Robert Redford, Yaphet Kotto, Jane Alexander,
Murray Hamilton, David Keith, Morgan Freeman
(20th Century-Fox)

Even with a sharp cast topped by the star power of Robert Redford, it's hard to imagine a broad audience wanting to share the two hours of agony in this one.

For the squeamish, the first half hour is rough going, indeed, as Redford is inducted into a small state prison, isolated in the farmlands near a hamlet.

Joining the ranks, Redford discovers one horror after another. The prison administration is in corrupt cahoots with townspeople, leasing prisoners as slave labor; brutal trustees administer the discipline to fellow convicts, gaining good time for killing some off; minimally decent food and privileges must be bought for cash, with wormy gruel going to those who can't afford it.

....

■ BRUTE FORCE

1947, 94 MINS, US

Dir Jules Dassin *Prod* Mark Hellinger *Scr* Richard
Brookes *Ph* William Daniels *Ed* Edward Curtiss
Mus Miklos Rozsa *Art Dir* Bernard Herzbrun, John F.
De Cuir
● Burt Lancaster, Hume Cronyn, Charles Bickford,
Yvonne De Carlo, Ann Blyth, Howard Duff (Universal)

A closeup on prison life and prison methods, *Brute Force* is a showmany mixture of gangster melodramatics, sociological exposition, and sex. The s.a. elements are plausible and realistic, well within the bounds, but always pointing up the femme fatale. Thus Yvonne DeCarlo, Ann Blyth, Ella Raines and Anita Colby are the women on the 'outside' whose machinations, wiles or charms accounted for their men being on the 'inside'.

Burt Lancaster, Charles Bickford, Sam Levene, Howard Duff, Art Smith and Jeff Corey, along with Hume Cronyn as the machinating prison captain (later warden), are the 'inside' cast.

Each of the more prominent criminals has a saga. The flashback technique shows how bookkeeper Whit Bissell embezzled $3,000 to give his ambitious wife (Raines) that mink coat; how soldier Duff got jammed with the Military Police because of his love for his Italian bride (DeCarlo) and through the snivelling skullduggery of her fascistic father; how the sympathetic Lancaster is in love with the invalided Blyth.

Bristling, biting dialog by Richard Brooks paints broad cameos as each character takes shape under existing prison life. Bickford is the wise and patient prison paper editor whose trusty (Levene), has greater freedom in getting 'stories' for the sheet. Cronyn is diligently hateful as the arrogant, brutal captain, with his system of stoolpigeons and bludgeoning methods.

The aspect of an audience rooting for the prisoners plotting a jailbreak is given a sharp turnabout, at the proper time, to point up that brute force by prisoners is as wrong as the brute force exercised by their keepers.

....

■ BUCCANEER, THE

1958, 121 MINS, US ◇ ▼

Dir Anthony Quinn *Prod* Henry Wilcoxon *Scr* Jesse
L. Lasky Jr, Bernice Mosk *Ph* Loyal Griggs *Ed* Archie
Marshek *Mus* Elmer Bernstein *Art Dir* Hal Pereira,
Walter H. Tyler, Albert Nozako
● Yul Brynner, Charlton Heston, Claire Bloom, Charles
Boyer, Inger Stevens, E.G. Marshall (Paramount)

Romance is effectively brought in the Cecil B. DeMille-supervised production that focuses on the colorful historical character of Jean Lafitte. On the deficit side is a wordy script that lacks any large degree of excitement.

It's a first-time-out for Henry Wilcoxon as producer, after several credits as associate to

DeMille, with the latter in the role of 'supervisor'. It marks the debut for Anthony Quinn as director.

DeMille appears in a prologue to cite chapter and verse about the role Lafitte played in American history.

Continuity-wise, *Buccaneer* is a scrambled affair in the early reels. Open to question, also, are the story angles in the screenplay which derives from a previous *Buccaneer* scenario put out by DeMille in 1938 and, in turn, from an adaptation of the original book, *Lafitte the Pirate*, by Lyle Saxon.

It's the War of 1812 against Britain and the battle area in New Orleans. The action takes place on land except for the sinking of one ship, which is curiously underplayed, by a renegade buccaneer. Highpoint is the land battle between Andrew Jackson's forces and the British, with Jackson aided by Lafitte's personnel and ammunition. The British, like so many toy soldiers, go down in defeat as Lafitte rules the mast.

Yul Brynner is masterly as the pirate. Charlton Heston is a hard, firm Andrew Jackson, who, while mounted on horse, sees the wisdom of making a deal with the pirate Lafitte. Claire Bloom is a fiery creation who alternately hates and loves Lafitte; Charles Boyer is light as Lafitte's aide (a role basically inconsequential), and Inger Stevens is properly attractive as Lafitte's true love and daughter of the governor.

....

■ BUCHANAN RIDES ALONE

1958, 89 MINS, US ◇

Dir Budd Boetticher   *Prod* Harry Joe Brown
Scr Charles Lang   *Ph* Lucien Ballard   *Ed* Al Clark
● Randolph Scott, Craig Stevens, Barry Kelley, Peter Whitney, Manuel Rojas, L.Q. Jones (Columbia)

Buchanan Rides Alone is one of those workhorses of saddle opera. Turned out on a relatively modest budget, still it is an honest picture, made with skill and craftsmanship.

Well-paced screenplay, based on a novel [*The Name's Buchanan*] by Jonas Ward, has Randolph Scott as a man more or less innocently involved in the problems of a frontier western border town, as he is passing through to his home in Texas from making his stake in Mexico. He befriends a young Mexican (Manuel Rojas), who kills the town bully. Scott is thrown in jail with Rojas and both are threatened with lynching.

The plotting is tricky, with the local First Family divided among itself by greed and lust for power. Scott plays one member off against another, until the final blow-off.

Scott gives an understated performance, taciturnity relieved by humour and warmth. Craig Stevens is intriguing as a man of mystery; L.Q. Jones is picturesque as an offbeat gunman, and Rojas handles his role with finesse.

....

■ BUDDY HOLLY STORY, THE

1978, 113 MINS, US ◇ ▼

Dir Steve Rash   *Prod* Fred Bauer   *Scr* Robert Gittler
Ph Stevan Larner   *Ed* David Blewitt   *Mus* Joe Renzetti   *Art Dir* Joel Schiller
● Gary Busey, Don Stroud, Charles Martin Smith, Bill Jordan, Maria Richwine, Conrad Janis (Innovisions/ECA)

The Buddy Holly Story smacks of realism in almost every respect, from the dramaturgy involving Holly and his back-up band, The Crickets, to the verisimilitude of the musical numbers. Latter were recorded live, using 24 tracks, and there was no studio rerecording. It was a gamble that pays off in full, and the Holly repertoire (an extensive one) gives the pic its underlying structure.

Gary Busey not only imparts the driven, perfectionist side of Holly's character, but his vocal work is excellent, as is his instrumentation.

Robert Gittler's screenplay [from a story by Alan Swyer] takes Holly from his early days in Lubbock, Texas, where he churns out be-bop for the roller rink crowd, through his disastrous recording career (he punches out a Nashville producer), and up through national recognition on the heels of his big hit, 'That'll Be the Day'.

Along the way, director Steve Rash zeroes in on the growing conflict between Busey, drummer Don Stroud and bassist Charles Martin Smith, and the love relationship of Busey and Maria Richwine as his Puerto Rican bride. All principals register strongly.

....

■ BUFFALO BILL AND THE INDIANS OR SITTING BULL'S HISTORY LESSON

1976, 123 MINS, US ◇ ▼

Dir Robert Altman   *Prod* Robert Altman   *Scr* Alan Rudolph, Robert Altman   *Ph* Paul Lohmann   *Ed* Peter Appleton, Dennis Hill   *Mus* Richard Baskin
Art Dir Tony Masters
● Paul Newman, Joel Grey, Kevin McCarthy, Harvey Keitel, Allan Nicholls, Geraldine Chaplin (De Laurentiis/Lion's Gate/Talent)

It appears that the idea here is to expose and debunk the Buffalo Bill legend, revealing it for the promotional distortion which, in some ways, it most certainly has to have been. Project was shot completely in Alberta.

Film [based on the play *Indians* by Arthur Kopit] shows Paul Newman bumbling through the challenge of living up to a legend created by Burt Lancaster, regularly popping up with bartender Bert Remsen in scenes of verbal recall. Joel Grey is Newman's current showman partner, while Kevin McCarthy grinds out the press agent claptrap.

The serious plot note is the determination of Sitting Bull (played very well in total silence by Frank Kaquitts) and interpreter Will Sampson not to debase history through cheap carny melodrama.

....

■ BUG

1975, 99 MINS, US ◇

Dir Jeannot Szwarc   *Prod* William Castle   *Scr* William Castle, Thomas Page   *Ph* Michael Hugo   *Ed* Allan Jacobs   *Mus* Charles Fox   *Art Dir* Jack Martin Smith
● Bradford Dillman, Joanna Miles, Richard Gilliland, Jamie Smith Jackson, Alan Fudge, Jesse Vint (Paramount)

Bug concerns some mutated cockroaches liberated by an earthquake from the earth's core. Adapted from Thomas Page's book, *The Hephaestus Plague*, it starts off well with an earthquake in a farmland town, after which mysterious fires begin breaking out. The bugs, being from underground areas, are hot and eat carbon.

Bradford Dillman, an animal scientist, gets intrigued with them, so much so that, after wife Miles is incinerated in a bug attack, he becomes a recluse with the creatures and communicates with them. At the same time Dillman goes into seclusion, so does the film; its last half is largely static, and the film never revives much interest.

....

■ BUGSY MALONE

1976, 93 MINS, UK ◇ ▼

Dir Alan Parker   *Prod* Alan Marshall   *Scr* Alan Parker   *Ph* Michael Seresin, Peter Biziou   *Ed* Gerry Hambling   *Mus* Paul Williams   *Art Dir* Geoffrey Kirkland
● Scott Baio, Jodie Foster, Florrie Dugger, John Cassisi, Martin Lev, Paul Murphy (Rank/Bugsy Malone/NFFC)

Set in 1929 Gotham, pic is a compendium of gangster/Prohibition pic situations and cliches, played tongue-in-cheek by a splendid cast of juves, a veritable casting treasure trove.

Jodie Foster is outstanding as a moll, but so are Scott Baio as Bugsy, John Cassisi as Fat Sam, Florrie Dugger as Blousey, Martin Lev as Dandy Dan, Paul Murphy and Albin Jenkins as, respectively, Leroy and Fizzy. Plus many others.

Writer-director Alan Parker deserves much of the credit for concept and execution, with Paul Williams sharing the spotlight on the strength of his songs (music and lyrics), all pleasantly reminiscent and tinkly.

In short, it's a brave, funny and winning pic which is nearly – but regrettably not quite – a triumph.

....

■ BULL DURHAM

1988, 108 MINS, US ◇ ▼

Dir Ron Shelton   *Prod* Thom Mount, Mark Burg
Scr Ron Shelton   *Ph* Bobby Byrne   *Ed* Robert Leighton   *Mus* Michael Convertino   *Art Dir* Armin Ganz
● Kevin Costner, Susan Sarandon, Tim Robbins, Trey Wilson, Robert Wuhl (Mount/Orion)

Bull Durham is a fanciful and funny bush league sports story where the only foul ball is its overuse of locker-room dialog. Kevin Costner is the quintessential American male who loves romance, but loves baseball even more.

The Durham Bulls of North Carolina dream of getting called up to be 'in the show' as they endure another season of riding town to town on the team bus and suffering the dubious distinction of being one of the losingest clubs in Carolina league history.

Sent over from another 'A' farm team to instruct, insult and inspire the Bulls' bulletfast pitcher Ebby Calvin 'Nuke' Laloosh (Tim Robbins) is embittered veteran catcher Crash David (Kevin Costner). His job is to get the cocky kid's arm on target by game time.

Costner is a natural as the dyed-in-the-wool ballplayer. His best lines are when he's philosophizing, like on being an All-American male who hates anything by Susan Sontag.

Susan Sarandon is never believable as a community college English lit teacher who, at the start of every season, latches on to the most promising rookie – in this case Robbins.

....

■ BULLITT

1968, 113 MINS, US ◇ ▼

Dir Peter Yates   *Prod* Philip D'Antoni   *Scr* Alan R. Trustman, Harry Kleiner   *Ph* William A. Fraker
Ed Frank P. Keller   *Mus* Lalo Schifrin   *Art Dir* Albert Brenner
● Steve McQueen, Robert Vaughn, Jacqueline Bisset, Don Gordon, Robert Duvall, Simon Oakland (Warner/Seven Arts/Solar)

Conflict between police sleuthing and political expediency is the essence of *Bullitt*, an extremely well-made crime melodrama filmed in Frisco. Steve McQueen delivers a very strong performance as a detective seeking a man whom Robert Vaughn, ambitious politico, would exploit for selfish motives. Good scripting and excellent direction by Peter Yates maintain deliberately low-key but mounting suspense.

Arrival in Frisco of a Chi hood cues assignment of McQueen, plus assistants Don Gordon and Carol Reindel, to protect his life until headline-hunting Vaughn produces him dramatically before a senate crime committee. Hood's death, at the hands of Paul Genge, provokes the primary dramatic conflict: Vaughn wants a live witness, while McQueen is interested in apprehending the killer.

Simon Oakland, McQueen's superior, lets him pursue the case independently, while

B

Vaughn, with aid from another senior detective, Norman Fell, is after independent sleuth's scalp.

. . . .

■ BUNNY LAKE IS MISSING

1965, 107 MINS, UK ⓥ
Dir Otto Preminger *Prod* Otto Preminger *Scr* John Mortimer, Penelope Mortimer *Ph* Denys Coop *Ed* Peter Thornton *Mus* Paul Glass
● Carol Lynley, Keir Dullea, Laurence Olivier, Noel Coward, Martita Hunt, Anna Massey (Columbia)

Bunny Lake is about the only thing missing from Otto Preminger's exercise in suspense and the viewer is kept in uncertainty about her for most of the film. What Preminger has achieved is an entertaining, fast-paced exercise in the exploration of a sick mind. Evelyn Piper's 1957 novel dealt entirely with the unpredictable actions of a mother searching for her child (real or imaginary) who had disappeared. To this plot skeleton Preminger has added an equally important character whose predictable actions provide the search's principal obstacles.

Carrying much of the film on her shoulders, Carol Lynley, as the mother shoved into a state of near hysteria almost from the beginning, is outstanding.

Keir Dullea, as her brother, most effective in earlier scenes where he conveys the natural, if easily-aroused, anger of a devoted brother.

Laurence Olivier's police inspector, is played in the manner of a psychiatrist. While nothing more than a routine role, Olivier does give it dignity and purpose and makes it a calm and restful contrast to the highly-strung emoting of Dullea and Lynley.

. . . .

■ BUONA SERA, MRS. CAMPBELL

1968, 111 MINS, ITALY ◇
Dir Melvin Frank *Prod* Melvin Frank *Scr* Melvin Frank, Shelden Keller, Dennis Norden *Ph* Gabor Pogany *Ed* William Butler *Mus* Riz Ortolani *Art Dir* Arrigo Equini
● Gina Lollobrigida, Shelley Winters, Phil Silvers, Peter Lawford, Telly Savalas, Janet Margolin (United Artists/Connaught)

Buona Sera, Mrs. Campbell is a very entertaining comedy with solid, personal, human values. Story is about an Italian woman who has conned three American bed partners from World War II into support of her and an illegitimate daughter for more than 20 years.

Gina Lollobrigida, Shelley Winters, Phil Silvers, Peter Lawford, Telly Savalas and Lee Grant head an excellent cast.

Story is economically laid forth: Lollobrigida has fooled her neighbors into believing daughter Janet Margolin was by a deceased US Air Force pilot. However, a reunion of the airmen, in the town where they were based, precipitates a potential crisis, since, in truth, the real father could have been Silvers, Lawford or Savalas.

Performances are strong: Lollobrigida, no comedy actress, is one here. Winters and Grant are great; Silvers and all the others are just right.

. . . .

■ 'BURBS, THE

1989, 103 MINS, US ⓥ
Dir Joe Dante *Prod* Larry Brezner, Michael Finnell *Scr* Dana Olsen *Ph* Robert Stevens *Ed* Marshall Harvey *Mus* Jerry Goldsmith *Art Dir* James Spencer
● Tom Hanks, Bruce Dern, Carrie Fisher, Rick Ducommun, Corey Feldman (Imagine/Universal)

Director Joe Dante funnels his decidedly cracked view of suburban life through dark humour in *The 'Burbs*. The action never strays beyond the cozy confines of the nightmarish

block everyman Ray (Tom Hanks) inhabits along with an uproarious assemblage of wacky neighbors.

Poor Ray has a week off and just wants to spend it quietly at home with his wife Carol (Carrie Fisher). Instead, he's drawn into an increasingly elaborate sleuthing game involving the mysterious Klopeks, who reside in a 'Munsters'-esque house rife with indications of foul play.

Ray's more familiar neighbors are equally bizarre: the corpulent Art (Rick Ducommun), convinced the Klopeks are performing satanic sacrifices; Rumsfield (Bruce Dern), a shell-shocked ex-GI; Walter (Gale Gordon), who delights in letting his dog relieve himself on Rumsfield's lawn; and Ricky (Corey Feldman) a teenager who sees all the strange goings-on as viewing fodder for parties with his friends.

Hanks does a fine impersonation of a regular guy on the verge of a nervous breakdown, while Dern adds another memorable psychotic to his resume. The big breakthroughs, however, are Ducommun, superb in a role that would have well-suited John Candy; and Wendy Schaal as Dern's airhead wife.

. . . .

■ BURKE AND WILLS

1985, 140 MINS, AUSTRALIA ◇ ⓥ
Dir Graeme Clifford *Prod* Graeme Clifford *Scr* Michael Thomas *Ph* Russell Boyd *Ed* Tim Wellburn *Mus* Peter Sculthorpe *Art Dir* Ross Major
● Jack Thompson, Nigel Havers, Greta Scacchi, Matthew Fargher, Ralph Cotterill, Drew Forsythe (Hoyts Edgley)

Big in scope, and emotionally stimulating, this Australian pic about the doomed 1860 expedition of explorers Burke and Wills to cross the continent and back, is satisfying entertainment despite its length and seemingly downbeat subject.

That the story emerges quite differently on film is very much to the credit of director Graeme Clifford and screenwriter Michael Thomas, two expatriate Australians.

Russell Boyd's superior cinematography, on the locations originally traversed by the explorers, is quite ravishing. Clifford shrewdly inserts flashbacks into the desert material evoking scenes of Wills at home in England and Burke's dalliance with a comely opera singer.

Jack Thompson, with full beard, is an imposing Burke, a fiery-tempered Irishman whose determination to succeed clouds his judgment. This is one of Thompson's best performances. British actor Nigel Havers is excellent as the scientist, Wills, stubbornly following his friend into the unknown while barely concealing his fears for the outcome.

. . . .

■ BUS RILEY'S BACK IN TOWN

1965, 93 MINS, US ◇
Dir Harvey Hart *Prod* Elliott Kastner *Scr* Walter Gage *Ph* Russell Metty *Ed* Folmar Blangsted *Mus* Richard Markowitz *Art Dir* Alexander Golitzen, Frank Arrigo
● Ann-Margret, Michael Parks, Janet Margolin, Brad Dexter, Jocelyn Brando, Larry Storch (Universal)

Where to pinpoint the blame for this well-intended major feature's failure is difficult. Certainly some of it must be allotted to former TV-director Harvey Hart's inexperience with the bigger-screen medium, and his lack of control over several of the thespians involved, but the erratic, chopped-up screenplay is also a major fault. Originally announced as the work of William Inge, screen credit is now given to Walter Gage, evidently a pseudonym for the several studio writers who had a go at it. Bits of Inge remain.

The story centers on the title character, played by newcomer Michael Parks. He tends to rely overmuch on 'method' methods – the tightly-constricted gesture, the stammer, the withdrawn, hunched-shoulder, hooded-eye type of acting that is rarely effective on the wide screen. Fortunately, Parks responds to the interplay provided by a bona fide talent. His scenes with Janet Margolin are his best, those with Ann-Margret, his poorest.

A simple plot – young ex-serviceman seeking an identity and faced with the problem of succumbing to the wiles of bad girl (Ann-Margret) or meeting responsibility head on (with implied support of good girl).

. . . .

■ BUS STOP

1956, 96 MINS, US ◇ ⓥ
Dir Joshua Logan *Prod* Buddy Adler *Scr* George Axelrod *Ph* Milton Krasner *Ed* William Reynolds *Mus* Alfred Newman, Cyril Mockridge, Ken Darby
● Marilyn Monroe, Don Murray, Arthur O'Connell, Betty Field, Eileen Heckart, Hope Lange (20th Century-Fox)

William Inge's rowdy play about a cowboy and a lady (sic) gets a raucous screen treatment. Both the scripter and director, George Axelrod and Joshua Logan respectively, were brought from the legit field to get the Inge comedy on film and, with a few minor exceptions, bring the chore off resoundingly.

New face Don Murray is the exuberant young cowhand who comes to the city to win some rodeo money and learn about women.

Marilyn Monroe fans will find her s.a. not so positive, but still potent, in her *Bus Stop* character, but this goes with the type of well-used saloon singer and would-be actress she portrays. Monroe comes off acceptably, even though failing to maintain any kind of consistency in the Southern accent.

Murray is a 21-year-old Montana rancher who comes to Phoenix for the rodeo, meets and kisses his first girl and literally kidnaps her. The girl, a 'chantoosie' in a cheap restaurant patronized by rodeo performers, is reluctant about marriage, but by the time Murray ropes her, shouts at her, and gets beat up for her, she gives in, both because love has set in, as well as physical exhaustion.

Arthur O'Connell milks everything from his spot as Murray's friend and watchdog and Betty Field clicks big as the amorous operator of the roadside bus stop.

. . . .

■ BUSTER AND BILLIE

1974, 98 MINS, US ◇ ⓥ
Dir Daniel Petrie *Prod* Ron Silverman *Scr* Ron Turbeville *Ph* Mario Tosi *Ed* Michael Kahn *Mus* Al De Lory
● Jan-Michael Vincent, Joan Goodfellow, Pamela Sue Martin, Clifton James, Robert Englund, Jessie Lee Fulton (Columbia)

Nostalgia gets another workout in *Buster and Billie*. Screenplay, conventionally directed by Daniel Petrie, has a good deal of charm and veristic detail until its romantic tale crashes in a last-reel melee of unmotivated violence.

On the surface pic is just 1948 Georgia graffiti. Jan-Michael Vincent and Pamela Sue Martin are the town sweethearts, petting heavily in his truck but delaying further action until their imminent wedding day. Meanwhile, the stags all get theirs from Joan Goodfellow, a rather dumpy blonde from the other side of the tracks.

Feeling more frustrated than usual, Vincent also pays the glumly obliging Goodfellow a visit one night, then finds himself falling in love with her.

The slim plot raises psychological questions that could have been profitably explored.

. . . .

■ BUSTIN' LOOSE

1981, 94 MINS, US ◇
Dir Oz Scott *Prod* Richard Pryor, Michael S. Glick
Scr Roger L. Simon *Ph* Dennis Dalzell *Ed* David
Holden *Mus* Mark Davis *Art Dir* Charles R. Davis,
John Corso
● Richard Pryor, Cicely Tyson, Robert Christian
(Universal)

Bustin' Loose is obviously a personal project
for Pryor, who produced and wrote the story,
which has admirable ambitions but is also
the film's greatest weakness.

Still, Pryor is an infectious comedian and a
master of body language, keeping the picture
on the move with sheer energy. He's a bungling burglar but good mechanic whose
parole officer (Robert Christian) forces him
to go to the aid of Cicely Tyson, the director
of a school for emotionally disturbed children
about to close for lack of money.

She wants to flee Philly with eight of the
kids and get to her family farm near Seattle.
There's a bit of the *African Queen* to this journey as the prissy, prim and dominant Tyson
and vulgar, unkempt Pryor find their initial
hostility turning to romance.

On the way, it's the constant breakdowns of
the bus, the impatience with the kids and
other obstacles – including a hilarious
encounter with the Ku Klux Klan – that feed
Pryor his material and he makes the most of
it.

This is a feature debut for Broadway director Oz Scott and he handles the chore
comfortably.

■ BUSTING

1974, 91 MINS, US ◇
Dir Peter Hyams *Prod* Irwin Winkler, Robert Chartoff
Scr Peter Hyams *Ph* Earl Rath *Ed* James Mitchell
Mus Billy Goldenberg *Art Dir* Ray Molyneaux
● Elliott Gould, Robert Blake, Allen Garfield, John
Lawrence, Cornelia Sharpe, Erin O'Reilly (United
Artists)

Elliott Gould and Robert Blake star as
vagrant vice squad detectives, the kind who
in real life set law and order back decades.
Production is confused, compromised and
clumsy.

The plot eventually gets around to blaming
nearly every criminal activity in town on
Allen Garfield, cast as a local crime lord.
Garfield, as ever an outstanding performer,
brings dignity and a sense of being totally
together to the part.

Atop the script problems is overlaid some
embarrassingly forced direction by debuting
Peter Hyams, a former TV newsman. In
particular the crutch of an incessant slowly
tracking camera, as though a pile of debris
looks any different (or better) from assorted
angles. There are a couple of well-staged
vehicle chases which for a few minutes divert
attention from the story.

■ BUTCH AND SUNDANCE
THE EARLY DAYS

1979, 110 MINS, US ◇ ⓥ
Dir Richard Lester *Prod* Gabriel Katzka, Steven Bach
Scr Allan Burns *Ph* Laszlo Kovacs *Ed* Antony Gibbs,
George Trirogoff *Mus* Patrick Williams *Art Dir* Brian
Eatwell
● William Katt, Tom Berenger, Brian Dennehy, Peter
Weller, Jeff Corey, Jill Eikenberry
(20th Century-Fox/Pantheon)

This prequel doesn't match its progenitor in
either casting or style. Without Paul Newman or Robert Redford in the title roles, it
doesn't matter whether *Butch* dwells on the
pair's infancy or senility – there's no star
chemistry. Tom Berenger and William Katt
acquit themselves admirably, but they simply
can't compete with the ghosts of two
superstars.

Butch is standard sagebrush material, with
few of the comic misadventures that characterized the original. There are some patented
Richard Lester hijinks in the first half-hour of
the prequel, but these peter out surprisingly
soon.

■ BUTCH CASSIDY AND THE SUNDANCE
KID

1969, 112 MINS, US ◇ ⓥ
Dir George Roy Hill *Prod* John Foreman *Scr* William
Goldman *Ph* Conrad Hall *Ed* John C. Howard,
Richard C. Meyer *Mus* Burt Bacharach *Art Dir* Jack
Martin Smith, Philip Jefferies
● Paul Newman, Robert Redford, Katharine Ross,
Strother Martin, Jeff Corey, Cloris Leachman (20th
Century-Fox/Campanile)

Lighthearted treatment of a purportedly-true
story of the two badmen who made Wyoming
outlaw history, film emerges a near-comedy
of errors.

Newman plays Butch, one of the most
deadly outlaws of the West whose gang variously was known as The Wild Bunch and
Hole-in-the-Wall Gang. Robert Redford,
portrays the Kid, wizard with a gun.

Butch is an affable, almost gay, individual
who can turn on the power when he wishes
but usually is a sociable, talkative sort of
cuss; Redford, silent, menacing in the power
of his fabled guns, displays no evidence of the
evil temper which gained him his reputation.
Together, they make a fine team, accompanied by frequent banter.

Narrative starts in Wyoming where Butch
and his gang are involved in various train
holdups and pursuits by posses after bank
robberies.

This leads to Butch and the Kid trying
their luck in Bolivia.
□ 1969: Best Picture (Nomination)

■ BUTLEY

1974, 129 MINS, UK/US/CANADA ◇
Dir Harold Pinter *Prod* Ely Landau *Scr* Simon Gray
Ph Gerry Fisher *Ed* Malcolm Cooke *Art Dir* Carmen
Dillon
● Alan Bates, Jessica Tandy, Richard O'Callaghan,
Susan Engel, Michael Byrne, Georgina Hale
(American Express/Landau/Cinevision)

Alan Bates' stage triumph in Simon Gray's
Butley has been superbly recreated on the
screen, with the added excellence of Harold
Pinter's topnotch film directorial debut. It
reunites both Richard O'Callaghan and
Michael Byrne from the original London
production.

The plot basically is one horrendous day in
the life of an embittered teacher, who loses
his estranged wife to a lesser professional
colleague, his lover to another man, and his
sense of superiority over a female associate
whose lifelong book project has been
accepted for publication while his lies
unfinished.

Jessica Tandy, a middle-aged teacher who
doesn't seem to understand her modern
students, is excellent in projection of both a
dedicated instructor and a skilled academic
politician.

■ BUTTERCUP CHAIN, THE

1970, 95 MINS, UK ◇
Dir Robert Ellis Miller *Prod* John Whitney, Philip
Waddilove *Scr* Peter Draper *Ph* Douglas
Slocombe *Ed* Thelma Conneli *Mus* Richard Rodney
Bennett *Art Dir* Wilfrid Shingleton
● Hywel Bennett, Leigh Taylor-Young, Jane Asher,
Sven-Bertil Taube, Clive Revill, Roy Dotrice (Columbia)

The story's somewhat contrived and over
glib. Even superficial. But it is directed and

written with sympathy and tact and acted by
a small cast that could hardly be bettered.

Film, based on Janice Elliott's graceful
novel, concerns four individualistic young
people who develop as intense friendship
among themselves which, during one frenzied
summer, strays into dangerous ground
obviously aimed for tragedy.

Hywel Bennett is the catalyst, a brooding,
withdrawn young man who inevitably sets
things in motion. His cousin, a disturbed
wary young woman, from whom he's
inseparable is Jane Asher.

Leigh Taylor-Young has a radiant personality which gives life to all her scenes.
Asher is a shade less effective in a more complicated role.

■ BUTTERFIELD 8

1960, 109 MINS, US ◇ ⓥ
Dir Daniel Mann *Prod* Pandro S. Berman
Scr Charles Schnee, John Michael Hayes *Ph* Joseph
Ruttenberg, Charles Harten *Ed* Ralph E. Winters
Mus Bronislau Kaper *Art Dir* George W. Davis, Urie
McCleary
● Elizabeth Taylor, Laurence Harvey, Eddie Fisher,
Dina Merrill, Mildred Dunnock, Betty Field (M-G-M)

Alterations made on John O'Hara's 1935
novel by the scenarists (among other things,
they have updated it from the Prohibition
era, spectacularized the ending and refined
some of the dialog) have given *Butterfield 8*
the form and pace it needs, but the story itself
remains a weak one, the behavior and motivations of its characters no more tangible than
in the original work.

Under director Daniel Mann's guidance it
is an extremely sexy and intimate film, but
the intimacy is only skin deep, the sex only a
dominating behavior pattern.

It is the tragic tale of a young woman
(Elizabeth Taylor) tormented by the contradictory impulses of flesh and conscience.

Victim of traumatic childhood experiences,
a fatherless youth, a mother's refusal to face
facts and, most of all, her own moral irresponsibility, she drifts from one illicit affair to
another until passion suddenly blossoms into
love on a six-day sex spree with Laurence
Harvey, who's got the sort of 'problems' (loving, devoted wife, oodles of money via marriage, soft, respectable job) non-neurotic men
might envy.

The picture's major asset is Taylor. It is a
torrid, stinging portrayal with one or two
brilliantly executed passages within. Harvey
seems ill-at-ease and has a tendency to exaggerate facial reactions. Eddie Fisher, as Taylor's long-time friend and father image,
cannot unbend and get any warmth into the
role. Dina Merrill's portrayal of the society
wife is without animation or depth. But there
is better work from Mildred Dunnock as Taylor's mother and Susan Oliver as Fisher's impatient girl friend.

■ BUTTERFLIES ARE FREE

1972, 109 MINS, US ◇ ⓥ
Dir Milton Katselas *Prod* Mike Frankovich
Scr Leonard Gershe *Ph* Charles B. Lang *Ed* David
Blewitt *Mus* Bob Alcivar *Art Dir* Robert Clatworthy
● Goldie Hawn, Edward Albert, Eileen Heckart,
Michael Glasser, Mike Warren (Columbia)

Although the setting has been changed from
New York to San Francisco for no apparent
reason, Leonard Gershe's screen adaptation
of his successful Broadway play, is an excellent example of how to switch from one
medium to another.

Several other carryovers – Eileen Heckart
and director Milton Katselas – from the stage
production were also brilliant moves. In the
move a slight change of emphasis has
resulted, moving the center of attention from
the blind boy, handsomely played by Edward

Albert to the girl (Goldie Hawn). What comes over with great strength is Gershe's intimate tale of the interrelationships of three individuals, all of whom gain from their contacts with each other.

Hawn, funny and touching, is a delight throughout and Heckart gets a film role that enables her to display versatility.

. . . .

■ **BUTTERFLY**

1981, 107 MINS, US ◇

Dir Matt Cimber *Prod* Matt Cimber *Scr* John Goff, Matt Cimber *Ph* Eddy Van Der Enden *Mus* Ennio Morricone *Art Dir* Dave De Carlo

● Stacy Keach, Pia Zadora, Orson Welles, Lois Nettleton, James Franciscus, Stuart Whitman (Riklis/Par-Par)

Pia Zadora plays Kady, a nymphet who's been searching for her father in the Nevada silver mines. She tracks him down at an abandoned mine where he (Stacy Keach) is serving as a guard.

The headstrong young woman brings out incestuous desires in her God-fearing father. Eventually, his inner passions overcome his honest instincts. In an effort to keep Kady close to him, he agrees to work the almost depleted mine and cash in the remaining ore.

For Kady, the act is motivated by revenge. The mineowner's son got her pregnant and refused to marry her. However, the son reconsiders his cowardice and agrees to marry.

Keach plays his role without shadings and this self-righteousness is difficult to swallow even with the picture's old-fashioned underpinnings. Zadora, in her screen debut, has most of the picture's best moments and registers well with her little girl looks and Lolita sensuality.

Orson Welles as a corrupt judge provides the film with a few comic but misplaced moments. The final courtroom session sinks into a farce better suited to a comedy of manners on stage. Transferring novelist James M. Cain's narrative and eroticism proves too great a task for the filmmakers and the picture remains a series of partially realized sketches.

The film, however, does not betray its modest budget. Made for $2 million, *Butterfly* has the look of a studio production of three to four times its cost.

. . . .

■ **BWANA DEVIL**

1952, 79 MINS, US ◇

Dir Arch Oboler *Prod* Arch Oboler *Scr* Arch Oboler *Ph* Joseph F. Biroc *Ed* John Hoffman *Mus* Gordon Jenkins

● Robert Stack, Barbara Britton, Nigel Bruce, Ramsay Hill, Paul McVey (Oboler/United Artists)

This novelty feature boasts of being the first full-length film in Natural Vision 3-D. Although adding backsides to usually flat actors and depth to landscapes, the 3-D technique still needs further technical advances.

Without the paper-framed, polaroid glasses Natural Vision looks like a ghosty television picture. While watching 3-D, viewers are constantly forced to refocus their vision as the focus of the film changes, resulting in a tiring eye workout.

The Oboler production is full of tricks devised to show off the process, rather than to tell the screen story effectively. The much-ballyhooed point of a lion seemingly leaping out of the screen into the auditorium comes off very mildly. The single gasper is the throwing of a spear by a native, which has the illusion of coming right into the audience.

With banal dialog, stilted sequences and impossibly-directed players, Oboler tells a story, based on fact, of how two lions halt the building of a railroad in British East Africa.

. . . .

■ **BYE BYE BIRDIE**

1963, 120 MINS, US ◇ ▼

Dir George Sidney *Prod* Fred Kohlmar *Scr* Irving Brecher *Ph* Joseph Biroc *Mus* Johnny Green (sup.)

● Janet Leigh, Dick Van Dyke, Ann-Margret, Maureen Stapleton, Bobby Rydell, Jesse Pearson (Columbia)

Credit George Sidney with directing one of the better fun and frolic tune packages. The adaptation of the successful legit musical comedy clearly called for lots of visuals, rather than just dialog and straight storytelling. Additionally, there's apparently more emphasis on the dance (interesting choreography by Onna White) – more so perhaps than in the original.

Strikingly important in *Bye Bye Birdie* is Ann-Margret. Singer, hoofer and cutie-pie, all wrapped up into one, she has the magnetism of early-vintage Judy Garland.

Story is the wacky thing about an Elvis Presley type (Jesse Pearson) who's subject to immediate army call. Goes by the name of Conrad Birdie and he swoons the girls no end, what with all that guitar and hipnotism. Songwriter Dick Van Dyke, trying to make time with Janet Leigh, while his mother, Maureen Stapleton, interferes, also is engaged in having Presley-type appear on the Ed Sullivan TV show while doing his farewell song in Sweet Apple, Iowa. Sullivan is on view, playing the part of Ed Sullivan with remarkable authenticity.

There's lots of talent involved. The songs as penned by Charles Strouse and Lee Adams, fit in nicely. Van Dyke displays a showbiz knowhow far more extensive than his television outings communicate. Leigh is called upon to play it straight, and does so attractively. Stapleton is a comedienne of the first order. Young songster Rydell gets the right kind of chance to warble. Ann-Margret, to repeat, is a wow.

. . . .

■ **BYE BYE BRAVERMAN**

1968, 94 MINS, US ◇

Dir Sidney Lumet *Prod* Sidney Lumet *Scr* Herbert Sargent *Ph* Boris Kaufman *Ed* Gerald Greenberg *Mus* Peter Matz *Art Dir* Ben Kasazkow

● George Segal, Jack Warden, Joseph Wiseman, Sorrell Booke, Phyllis Newman, Jessica Walter (Warner/Seven Arts)

Bye Bye Braverman is a curious mixture of tasty and tasteless jokes, all at the expense of Jewish people. Pic describes, in padded vignette and travelog transition, the hypocritical mourning of a deceased man by four alleged friends.

Herbert Sargent has taken the 'dark comedy' approach; were it black comedy, or straight comedy, it might have worked better. As it is, the curious and erratic use of Jewish ruggedness of spirit and the native non-sequitur humor makes for a plot stew which will offend the sensibilities of many, and titillate the prejudices of others.

George Segal, Jack Warden, Joseph Wiseman and Sorrell Booke are the mourners of never-seen Braverman. Jessica Walter, the less-than-bereaved widow, has the yen for Segal (married to Zohra Lampert).

If the film meant to portray the four principals as basically clod characters, with some good points, it missed. If the idea was to portray them as basically good, with human frailties, insufficient depth was given along these lines, too.

. . . .

■ **CABARET**

1972, 124 MINS, US ◇ ▼

Dir Bob Fosse *Prod* Cy Feuer *Scr* Jay Presson Allen, Hugh Wheeler *Ph* Geoffrey Unsworth *Ed* David Bretherton *Mus* Ralph Burns (dir.) *Art Dir* Rolf Zehetbauer, Jurgen Kiebach

● Liza Minnelli, Michael York, Helmut Griem, Marisa Berenson, Fritz Wepper, Joel Grey (AA-ABC)

The film version of [the 1966 John Kander-Fred Ebb Broadway musical] *Cabaret* is most unusual: it is literate, bawdy, sophisticated, sensual, cynical, heart-warming, and disturbingly thought-provoking. Liza Minnelli heads a strong cast. Bob Fosse's generally excellent direction recreates the milieu of Germany some 40 years ago.

The adaptation of the stage book is expertly accomplished. The basic material derives from Christopher Isherwood's Berlin stories, and a 1951 dramatic play by John Van Druten, filmed in 1955, *I Am a Camera*.

The screenplay, which never seems to talk down to an audience while at the same time making its candid points with tasteful emphasis, returns the story to a variety of settings. The sleazy cabaret remains a major recurring set.

The choice of Minnelli for the part of Sally Bowles was indeed daring. Good-hearted, quasi-sophisticated amorality and hedonism are not precisely Minnelli's professional bag, and within many scenes she seems to carom from golly-gee-whiz-down-home rusticity to something closer to the mark.

□ 1972: Best Picture (Nomination)

. . . .

■ **CABIN IN THE COTTON**

1932, 76 MINS, US

Dir Michael Curtiz *Prod* Jack L. Warner *Scr* Paul Green *Ph* Barney McGill *Ed* George Amy

● Richard Barthelmess, Dorothy Jordan, Bette Davis, Henry B. Walthall, Berton Churchill (First National)

Picture proves that a book that attracts a good deal of attention isn't necessarily screen material. Conflict is the feud between a southern cotton planter (landowner) and tenant farmer (here described as 'peckerwoods'). It's the industrial capital vs labor wrangle in another setting, and not a particularly fascinating one at that.

Picture is not well done and it presents Richard Barthelmess in another lukewarm role, a role which he plays without vigor. Nub of the drama is that Marvin Blake (Barthelmess) belongs to the underdog tenant farmer class, but is befriended by the planter and finds himself between two fires – torn by loyalty to his class and an obligation to their enemy who also is his benefactor. Also Marvin falls in love with the planter's daughter.

Bette Davis is the naughty-naughty planter's daughter. Dorothy Jordan, as a humble farm girl, is just a shadow. Indeed, most of the people are puppet-like, including the Barthelmess character.

. . . .

■ **CABIN IN THE SKY**

1943, 98 MINS, US ▼

Dir Vincente Minnelli *Prod* Arthur Freed *Scr* Joseph Schrank *Ph* Sidney Wagner *Ed* Harold F. Cress *Mus* Vernon Duke, Harold Arlen

● Ethel Waters, Eddie 'Rochester' Anderson, Lena Horne, Louis Armstrong, Rex Ingram (M-G-M)

The picture version of *Cabin in the Sky* is little

87

changed from the original stage show. It still tells of Little Joe Jackson's weakness for dice, likker and the seductive Georgia Brown, of his mortal wound in a barroom brawl, and of his six-month period of grace obtained by his eternally-devoted wife, Petunia. It still shows the contest between Lucifer Jr and the General for Little Joe's soul.

In the legit version *Cabin* seemed constantly to be constricted by the limitations of the stage. But difficulty has not been solved in the present film adaptation. The yarn still appears weighed down by unimaginative conception, the few changes in the screen medium merely filling out the story, without expanding or developing its fantasy. In only one of two moments, such as the stairway to heaven finale, is there any apparent effort to utilize the facilities of the camera. There are far too many closeups, particularly in the vocal numbers.

Ethel Waters remains the one transcendant asset of the film *Cabin*, just as she was in the original. Her sincerity, compassion, personal warmth and dramatic skill, plus her unique talent as a singer make her performance as Petunia an overpowering accomplishment.

● ●

■ **CACTUS FLOWER**

1969, 103 MINS, US ◇ ⓥ

Dir Gene Saks   *Prod* Mike Frankovich   *Scr* I.A.L. Diamond   *Ph* Charles E. Lang   *Ed* Maury Winetrobe   *Mus* Quincy Jones   *Art Dir* Robert Clatworthy

● Walter Matthau, Ingrid Bergman, Goldie Hawn, Jack Weston, Rick Lenz, Vito Scotti (Columbia)

Cactus Flower drags, which is probably the worst thing that can be said of a light comedy. It's due to sloppy direction by Gene Saks and the miscasting of Walter Matthau opposite Ingrid Bergman.

The plot [from the play by Abe Burrows, based on a French play by Barillet & Gredy] is minimal and the lines are somewhat stilted and hollow, but if the direction was tighter and the mood kept light and airy it might have worked.

Matthau is cast as a dentist ready to marry his young mistress who enlists the aid of his stuffy but organized secretary. This too, might have worked had they found a suitable foil for him. Bergman, more believable in her role as the nurse, is too reserved and sophisticated opposite Matthau.

There are some laughs and Goldie Hawn, as the Greenwich Village kook with whom Matthau contemplates marriage, makes a credible screen debut.

● ●

■ **CADDIE**

1976, 107 MINS, AUSTRALIA ◇ ⓥ

Dir Donald Crombie   *Prod* Tony Buckley   *Scr* Joan Long   *Ph* Peter James   *Ed* Tim Wellburn   *Mus* Patrick Flynn   *Art Dir* Owen Williams

● Helen Morse, Takis Emmanuel, Jack Thompson, Jacki Weaver, Melissa Jaffer, Ron Blanchard (Buckley)

Caddie is based on the autobiography of a Sydney barmaid who, adandoned by her husband, struggled through the Depression to bring up two children. It is a sensitively-told story of one woman's fight – not a militant, but rather one of the masses; an unsung heroine.

Helen Morse, in the title role, maintains a wonderful dignity that is typical of the character's social class and aspirations. She never slips, and her scenes with the children are natural, especially at the fade out when despite a crushing personal disappointment, she rallies as soon as they appear.

But it is in her scenes with Takis Emmanuel that Caddie's story takes on fire. Emmanuel, a Greek actor imported for the production, registers power immediately his face hits the screen.

● ●

■ **CADDYSHACK**

1980, 90 MINS, US ◇ ⓥ

Dir Harold Ramis   *Prod* Douglas Kenney   *Scr* Brian Doyle-Murray, Harold Ramis, Douglas Kenney   *Ph* Steven Larner   *Ed* William Carruth   *Mus* Johnny Mandel   *Art Dir* Stan Jolley

● Chevy Chase, Rodney Dangerfield, Bill Murray, Michael O'Keefe, Ted Knight (Orion/Peters)

In its unabashed bid for the mammoth audience which responded to the anti-establishment outrageousness of *National Lampoon's Animal House*, this vaguely likable, too-tame comedy falls short of the mark.

This time, the thinly plotted shenanigans unfold against the manicured lawns and posh backdrop of a restricted country club, generally pitting the free-living youthful caddies against the uptight gentry who employ them.

Stock characters include Chevy Chase as resident golf-pro; club prexy and jurist Ted Knight; and Rodney Dangerfield as the perfectly cast and very funny personification of anti-social, nouveau riche grossness.

Beyond Chase, prime lure is Bill Murray as a foul-habited, semi-moronic groundskeeper, constantly aroused by the older femme golfers.

● ●

■ **CADILLAC MAN**

1990, 97 MINS, US ◇ ⓥ

Dir Roger Donaldson   *Prod* Charles Roven, Roger Donaldson   *Scr* Ken Friedman   *Ph* David Gribble   *Ed* Richard Francis-Bruce   *Mus* J. Peter Robinson   *Art Dir* Gene Rudolf

● Robin Williams, Tim Robbins, Pamela Reed, Annabella Sciorra, Zack Norman (Donaldson-Roven/Cavallo)

Denied an opportunity to showcase his deft rapid-fire comic skills, Robin Williams produces few laughs amid wreckage of the screenplay and poorly paced direction. Only Tim Robbins gets out alive as a crazed, simple-minded, cuckolded husband who ultimately makes hostages of the womanizing Joey (Williams) and everyone else in the car dealership where he works, suspecting correctly that his wife (Annabella Sciorra) is having an affair.

Williams lapses in and out of a what seems to be a New York-Italian street accent. Aside from being a smart aleck, however, he's rarely funny and shows little depth until the predictable ending. Some minor pleasures can be found in smaller roles drawn from the N.Y. street scene, especially Lauren Tom as a pushy and abusive waitress in a neighbourhood dim sum restaurant.

● ●

■ **CAESAR AND CLEOPATRA**

1946, 135 MINS, UK ◇ ⓥ

Dir Gabriel Pascal   *Prod* Gabriel Pascal   *Scr* George Bernard Shaw   *Ph* Freddie Young, Robert Krasker, Jack Hildyard, Jack Cardiff   *Mus* Georges Auric   *Art Dir* Oliver Messel, John Bryan

● Vivien Leigh, Claude Rains, Stewart Granger, Flora Robson, Francis L. Sullivan, Cecil Parker (Eagle Lion)

Caesar and Cleopatra is a disappointment. In spite of its prodigal magnificence, indeed because of its production values, such vague story interest as it has is hopelessly swamped.

Claude Rains' Caesar – thanks to Shaw and Gabriel Pascal, director – is accurately and succinctly pinpointed by Vivien Leigh as Cleopatra when she calls him 'a nice old gentleman'. As for her portrayal of the Queen of Queens – again the responsibility of author and director – Rains calls the turn when he tells her with justifiable incredulity she is not Queen of Egypt, but a queen of the gypsies.

Sketchy references to an earlier visit of a young Roman 'with strong, round, gleaming arms' elicit his identification by Caesar as being Marc Antony. Apart from this vague,

soft-pedal reference to the possibility of her knowing what passion means, Leigh's Cleopatra is as lacking in sex consciousness as the boy actor (Anthony Harvey) who plays the part of her brother, Ptolemy, whose throne she seizes.

Seemingly just to make things more irritating there appears halfway through the pic Stewart Granger as Apollodorus, a Sicilian with flashing eyes, dazzling white teeth and a torso of burnished bronze. But nix on anything like that, says Shaw. So Cleopatra passes Granger up as if he were a dirty deuce – instead of being what he so obviously, so vibrantly is, a grand chunk of three-quarters nude male s.a.

In a cast of more than 100 of Britain's finest stage actors individual performances of bits are all flawless. And make no mistake about it, the prodigality of this $6 million spectacle makes Griffith and DeMille and Von Stroheim look like niggards.

● ●

■ **CAHILL, UNITED STATES MARSHAL**

1973, 103 MINS, US ◇ ⓥ

Dir Andrew V. McLaglen   *Prod* Michael Wayne   *Scr* Harry Julian Fink, Rita M. Fink   *Ph* Joseph Biroc   *Ed* Robert L. Simpson   *Mus* Elmer Bernstein   *Art Dir* Walter Simonds

● John Wayne, Gary Grimes, George Kennedy, Neville Brand, Clay O'Brien, Marie Windsor (Batjac/Warner)

John Wayne combines the problems of fatherhood with his activities as a lawman in *Cahill, United States Marshal* to give different motivation from the usual western theme.

Crux of the strained relationship between Wayne and his two young sons is his continued absence tracking down criminals, which leads to the boys, 17 and 12, becoming involved in a bank robbery and murder.

Script, based on a story by Barney Slater, opens strongly with Wayne catching up to a band of outlaws and shooting it out with them. When he returns to town he finds the bank has been robbed, sheriff and deputy murdered and four new prisoners in jail, including his elder son. Boys have been lured into crime by smooth-talking outlaw George Kennedy.

Wayne carries out characterization realistically and gets firm support right down the line. Kennedy is menacing.

● ●

■ **CAINE MUTINY, THE**

1954, 123 MINS, US ◇ ⓥ

Dir Edward Dmytryk   *Prod* Stanley Kramer   *Scr* Stanley Roberts   *Ph* Franz Planer   *Ed* William A. Lyon, Henry Batista   *Mus* Max Steiner   *Art Dir* Rudolph Sternad

● Humphrey Bogart, Jose Ferrer, Van Johnson, Fred MacMurray, Robert Francis, May Wynn (Columbia)

The Caine Mutiny is highly recommendable motion picture drama, told on the screen as forcefully as it was in the Herman Wouk bestselling novel. The intelligently adapted screenplay retains all the essence of the novel.

The Caine Mutiny is the story of a war-weary destroyer-minesweeper and its personnel, over which presides – by the book – Captain Queeg, a man beginning to crack from the strain of playing hero over the years while he hides deep his inferiority complex. Lt Tom Keefer is the first to spot the crack in Queeg's armor and he needles Maryk and the other officers into seeing it, too.

Little incidents of faulty command build until, during a raging typhoon when the tired ship is in extreme danger of foundering Maryk relieves the captain, using Navy Article 184, which permits the executive officer taking over under certain emergency conditions, to do so.

Scene after scene in the picture during the

hour and one-half buildup to the court martial stand out, either for high action, drama or the beauty and grace of ships making their way proudly through the seas.
□ 1954: Best Picture (Nomination)

....

■ **CALAMITY JANE**

1953, 100 MINS, US ◇ ▼
Dir David Butler *Prod* William Jacobs *Scr* James O'Hanlon *Ph* Wilfrid M. Cline *Ed* Irene Morra *Mus* Ray Heindorf (dir.) *Art Dir* John Beckman
● Doris Day, Howard Keel, Allyn McLerie, Philip Carey, Dick Wesson (Warner)

Giving such Wild West characters as Calamity Jane and Wild Bill Hickok a workout in a tuned-in western doubtless had strong possibilities but Warners comes close to missing the stagecoach. Colorful settings and costumes add the entry some sparkle but the 'book' is lacking in originality and the players simply are uneasy.

Compensating factor is the total of 11 songs (music by Sammy Fain, lyrics by Paul Francis Webster) which gives the production some entertainment wallop.

Doris Day works very, very hard at being Calamity and is hardly realistic at all. She'd register fine as a country girl in calico or a cutie from the chorus line but strain shows through in her essaying the hard and dynamic Calamity character. Howard Keel handles the Bill Hickok assignment with listless amiability.

While flavorful, a number of the *Calamity* songs suggest other scores of other years. As a matter of fact, the entire film seems a little familiar, having some ingredients in common with *Annie Get Your Gun* and *Oklahoma!*. The dialog throughout is commonplace.

....

■ **CALIFORNIA SPLIT**

1974, 108 MINS, US ◇ ▼
Dir Robert Altman *Prod* Robert Altman, Joseph Walsh *Scr* Joseph Walsh *Ph* Paul Lohmann *Ed* Lou Lombardo *Mus* Phyllis Shotwell *Art Dir* Leon Ericksen
● George Segal, Elliott Gould, Ann Prentiss, Gwen Welles, Edward Walsh, Joseph Walsh (Columbia)

California Split is an aimless, strung-out series of vignettes starring George Segal and Elliott Gould as compulsive gamblers. The film is technically and physically handsome, all the more so for being mostly location work, but lacks a cohesive and reinforced sense of story direction.

The pic is well cast – Segal and Gould contrast well, while Ann Prentiss and Gwen Welles play happy hookers to good effect. Bert Remsen, an Altman stock player, herein does a drag number. Edward Walsh (the writer's father) is very good as a mean poker adversary, and the writer himself has a good scene as Segal's loan shark.

....

■ **CALIFORNIA SUITE**

1978, 103 MINS, US ◇ ▼
Dir Herbert Ross *Prod* Ray Stark *Scr* Neil Simon *Ph* David M. Walsh *Ed* Michael A. Stevenson, Margaret Booth *Mus* Claude Bolling *Art Dir* Albert Brenner
● Alan Alda, Michael Caine, Bill Cosby, Jane Fonda, Walter Matthau, Elaine May (Columbia)

Neil Simon and Herbert Ross have gambled in radically altering the successful format of *California Suite* as it appeared on stage. Instead of four separate playlets, there is now one semi-cohesive narrative revolving around visitors to the Beverly Hills Hotel.

Alan Alda and Jane Fonda portray a divorced couple wrangling over possession of their child, while Michael Caine and Maggie Smith play a showbiz couple with varying

sexual tastes holed up at the Bev-Hills prior to the Academy Awards. Walter Matthau has to explain his unwitting infidelity to spouse Elaine May in a third segment, and Richard Pryor and Bill Cosby, accompanied by their wives (Gloria Gifford and Sheila Frazier), manage to turn a vacation into a series of disastrous mishaps.

Ross and Simon have set up as counterpoint to the more tragicomic episodes (those involved Alda and Fonda, and Caine and Smith) some farcical moments around Matthau and blitzed floozy Denise Galik, along with the Pryor-Cosby shenanigans. The technique is less than successful, veering from poignant emotionalism to broad slapstick in sudden shifts.

Fonda demonstrates yet another aspect of her amazing range, although her brittle quips with Alda seem very stage-bound. Smith and Caine interplay wonderfully, as do Pryor and Cosby. The latter duo get the worst break, however, as their seg is chopped up, spread around and generally given short shrift.

....

■ **CALIGULA**

1979, 150 MINS, ITALY/US ◇ ▼
Dir Tinto Brass *Prod* Bob Guccione, Franco Rossellini *Scr* [uncredited] *Ph* Silvano Ippoliti *Ed* Nino Baragli *Mus* Paul Clemente *Art Dir* Danilo Donati
● Malcolm McDowell, Teresa Ann Savoy, Helen Mirren, Peter O'Toole, John Gielgud (Penthouse/Felix)

With the biggest investment ever in porn to play with, Tinto Brass in a creative fit of paranoic obsession, sifts through the pages of first century Rome under syphilitic Tiberius and epileptic Caligula to demonstrate the unlimited baseness of the human condition [from a story by Gore Vidal].

Such established names as John Gielgud and Peter O'Toole will have to be seen to be believed. Malcolm McDowell as the sick and/or insane emperor runs the gamut of cardboard emotions from grand guignol to hapless pathos.

Paid off to yield final cut and end two years of film freeze litigation, Brass gets a kind of ambiguous director credit ('scenes directed by'). He filmed everything on screen; though some reports mention added porno inserts during the post-Brass completion period. (A 210-minute version was clandestinely screened at Cannes earlier in the year.)

....

■ **CALL ME BWANA**

1963, 93 MINS, UK ◇
Dir Gordon Douglas *Prod* Harry Saltzman, Albert R. Broccoli *Scr* Nate Monaster, Johanna Harwood *Ph* Ted Moore *Ed* Peter Hunt *Mus* Monty Norman
● Bob Hope, Anita Ekberg, Edie Adams, Lionel Jeffries, Percy Herbert (Eon)

Bob Hope's gags are tossed off in his usual slick fashion. And a great number of them are slyly but pointedly directed at Anita Ekberg's stimulating sculpture. The visual situations and incidents need spacing out a little more but they invariably crop up just in time to disguise the occasional repetition of plot.

Hope has built up a phoney reputation as an intrepid explorer of the jungles of Darkest Africa, by writing successful books based on old, secret diaries of his uncle. Actually, the nearest the timid character has ever been to Africa is to visit his aunt in Cape Cod. When an American moon-probe capsule is lost in the jungle and it's necessary to locate it before foreign powers get their thieving mitts on it, Hope is detailed for the task because of his supposed expert knowledge of the locale.

Overall, there's enough fun to keep this bubbling along merrily. There is Hope going through bravery tests to escape the native tribe, getting mixed up with a rogue ele-

phant, a lion in his tub, having his pants repaired by Ekberg while he's wearing 'em (and with the poisoned needle from his suicide kit), and eventually becoming airborne in the moon-capsule.

Though most of the responsibility falls on Hope and his personality, Edie Adams gives a pleasantly unobtrusive performance and La Ekberg, though an unlikely Mata Hari, is a sound and decorative foil for Hope. Only the most fastidious carper will protest that the jungle often reeks of Pinewood Studio.

....

■ **CALL ME MADAM**

1953, 114 MINS, US ◇
Dir Walter Lang *Prod* Sol C. Siegel *Scr* Arthur Sheekman *Ph* Leon Shamroy *Ed* Robert Simpson *Mus* Irving Berlin *Art Dir* Lyle R. Wheeler, John De Cuir
● Ethel Merman, Donald O'Connor, Vera-Ellen, George Sanders, Billy De Wolfe, Helmut Dantine (20th Century-Fox)

A [1950] hit musical on Broadway, *Call Me Madam* scored a run of close to two years in Gotham with Ethel Merman, as Ambassador Sally Adams, the fabulous femme diplomat, representing the US in the mythical Grand Duchy of Lichtenburg. Merman still reigns in the cinematic version.

In key spots, George Sanders is the tiny country's foreign department chief, and Donald O'Connor is the US press attache, Billy De Wolfe is the American charge d'affaires, Vera-Ellen plays the princess and Helmut Dantine is on hand as the prince who's spurned by the princess in favor of the American press rep.

Madam offers an ingratiating book loosely fashioned after the career of Perle Mesta, former US Minister to Luxembourg. Added plusses are via the widened scope and richness of the production, lush mountains and extra trimmings for the delightful Irving Berlin score. Also, there's the fresh, inventive choreography staged by Robert Alton, with O'Connor and Vera-Ellen as a terping combo of top calibre.

The screenplay, from the Howard Lindsay-Russel Crouse book, is imaginative and whimsical. Merman is at her robust best with a tune. At the opening, she gives 'Hostess with the Mostest on the Ball' a powerhouse delivery and it's a cinch to provoke heavy mitting. Her 'You're Just in Love' duet with O'Connor also is standout.

....

■ **CALL NORTHSIDE 777**

1948, 111 MINS, US
Dir Henry Hathaway *Prod* Otto Lang *Scr* Jerome Cady, Jay Dratler *Ph* Joe MacDonald *Ed* J. Watson Webb Jr, Lyle R. Wheeler, Mark-Lee Kirk
● James Stewart, Richard Conte, Lee J. Cobb, Helen Walker (20th Century-Fox)

Call Northside 777 has all the separate ingredients for a sock film but registers only with a mild impact due to a lack of integration. Although following the surface pattern of such clicks as *The House on 92nd Street* and *Boomerang!*, this pic has a faltering pace, an uneven realistic focus and only a thin dramatic point.

Among the film's principal drawbacks is James Stewart's jarring and unpersuasive performance in the key role. As a Chicago reporter who's assigned to dig up a human-interest angle out of an 11-year-old murder case, Stewart shuttles between a phoney cynicism and a sob-sister sentimentalism into a recognizable newspaperman.

Henry Hathaway's direction marks a retreat from the documentary form. Instead of consistent realism, he lapses into a hybrid technique with plenty of hokey melodramatic tones.

Based on a celebrated miscarriage of justice

in 1932, when two innocent men were sentenced to 99 years apiece for killing a cop, the screenplay constructs a serviceable plot on the factual groundwork. Film, however, tends to wander aimlessly in an over-sized running time. Hathaway is forced to pad the pic with some highly interesting visual gimmicks, such as the operation of a lie detector machine, a photo facsimile unit, a photo-developing tank, etc.

Title is derived from a personal ad placed in the *Chicago Times-Herald* by the mother of one of the prisoners offering a $5,000 reward for information leading to the release of her son. Answering the ad, Stewart uses it as a peg for a series of human interest stories about the case. Initially skeptical, he's progressively drawn to a belief in the man's innocence and finally commits himself to plead the convict's case in his paper.

Richard Conte gives an intensely sincere performance as the young Polish-American who is railroaded to jail.

● ●

■ **CALL OF THE WILD**

1935, 89 MINS, US

Dir William Wellman *Prod* William Goetz, Raymond Griffith *Scr* Gene Fowler, Leonard Praskins *Ph* Charles Rosher *Ed* Hanoon Fritch *Mus* Alfred Newman *Art Dir* Richard Day, Alexander Golitzen
● Clark Gable, Loretta Young, Jack Oakie, Frank Conroy, Reginald Owen, Sidney Toler (20th Century/United Artists)

The lion-hearted dog that was Jack London's creation as the leading character of *Call of the Wild* emerges now as a stooge for a rather conventional pair of human love birds. Changes have made the canine classic hardly recognizable, but they have not done any damage.

The big and exceptionally wild St Bernard, known as Buck, is not entirely submerged, since such of his feats as the haul of a 1,000-pound load over the snow and his mating with a femme wolf are included, but he has been decidedly picture-house broken.

Clark Gable strong-and-silents himself expertly and Loretta Young, in the opposite corner of the revised love affair, is lovely and competent. But Jack Oakie has the laughs, and they land him on top.

It's a story of treachery, hardship, violence and unrequited love in Alaska, so anything that does away with sadness for a momentary giggle is highly welcome. Gable and Oakie's rescue of Young, whose husband has apparently lost his way and perished; their finding of the gold mine; their encounter with the villainous Reginald Owen; the return of Young's husband, lending a bitter-sweet finish to the romance, are the highlights of the story's human element.

This is the second trip for the London novel to the screen. Pathe made it silent in 1923.

● ●

■ **CALL OF THE WILD**

1973, 100 MINS, W. GERMANY/SPAIN/ITALY/FRANCE ◇ ⑱

Dir Ken Annakin *Prod* Arthur Brauner *Scr* Hubert Frank, Tibor Reves *Ph* John Cabrera *Mus* Carlo Rustincelli
● Charlton Heston, Raimund Harmsdorf, Michele Mercier, George Eastman, Sancho Garcia, Rik Battaglia (CCC-Berlin)

Jack London's thrilling, often-filmed tale trails a couple of roughnecks, John and Pete, on their gold-digging, mail-hopping, and booze-deal fortune hunts in Alaska's snow-bound wilderness. Time and again, they are outsmarted and outroughed by an assorted pack of rivals.

Director Ken Annakin picked a few good actors (Charlton Heston and Italo-western hero George Eastman) and some others capable of no more than looking their parts (Raimund Harmsdorf, Michele Mercier). But everybody appears to play merely along action line on his own and create a vacuum around him.

Thus lacking the density of London's original, the picture falls to pieces with all that frozen gore, dog fights, sled chases, saloon brawls and other knock-down melodramatics.

● ●

■ **CAMELOT**

1967, 179 MINS, US ◇ ⑱

Dir Joshua Logan *Prod* Jack L. Warner *Scr* Alan Jay Lerner *Ph* Richard H. Kline *Ed* Folmar Blangsted *Mus* Alfred Newman (dir.) *Art Dir* John Truscott
● Richard Harris, Vanessa Redgrave, Franco Nero, David Hemmings, Lionel Jeffries, Estelle Winwood (Warner/Seven Arts)

On the sumptuous face of it, *Camelot* qualifies as one of Hollywood's alltime great screen musicals. While most big musicals have fine production, dazzling costumes and all that, what gives *Camelot* special value is a central dramatic conflict that throbs with human anguish and compassion.

Camelot never need resort to the more obvious kind of added action. The focus is kept on the three mentally-tortured people, the cuckolded king, the cheating queen, the confused knight.

All of this is against the often exquisite sets and costumes of John Truscott, the creative use of research that is constantly visible. The fine camera work of Richard H. Kline, the clever screenplay by Alan Jay Lerner, the singular appropriateness to time and place of the Frederick Loewe score as lovingly managed by Alfred Newman are all major contributions.

Joshua Logan rates extraordinary tribute for the performances he elicits from Richard Harris as King Arthur, Vanessa Redgrave as Guinevere, and Franco Nero as the knight whose idealism succumbs to passion.

● ●

■ **CAMILLE**

1921, 90 MINS, US ⊗

Dir Ray C. Smallwood *Prod* Nazimova *Scr* June Mathis *Ph* Rudolph Bergquist *Art Dir* Natacha Rambova
● Nazimova, Rudolph Valentino, Arthur Hoyt, Zeffie Tilbury, Edward Connelly, Patsy Ruth Miller (Nazimova/Metro)

This production of Nazimova in *Camille* proves to be a modernized version of the story of *The Lady with the Camellias*, which fact is welcome for the major part, but not so felicitous as the concluding parts are reached. For, wonder of wonders, the director has entirely omitted the scene of Armand at the bedside of his beloved as she breathes her last. Perhaps this big moment was eliminated in the thought the picture fans, if unable to witness a happy ending, wanted one as happy as possible under the circumstances. Nothing could be further from the fact.

Nazimova totally immerses her own distinct personality into that of the famed heroine. Instead of the sinuous, clinging Nazimova, she appears an actress almost new-born for the part.

The surrounding company is excellent. Second to the star is the Armand of Rudolph Valentino. There are many opportunities for obtrusiveness in the role, but he keeps it correct to the minutest detail.

● ●

■ **CAMILLE**

1927, 96 MINS, US ⊗

Dir Fred Niblo *Scr* Fred De Gresac, Olga Printzlau, Chandler Sprague, George Marion Jr. *Ph* Oliver T. Marsh
● Norma Talmadge, Gilbert Roland, Lilyan Tashman, Maurice Costello, Harvey Clark, Alec B. Francis (Talmadge/First National)

Fred Niblo and Norma Talmadge have dedicated a pretty love story [from the novel by the younger Alexandre Dumas] to the screen that lacks the punch to make it a standout. Dramatic intensity only twice arises to make an audience forget it is watching a picture. This is when Armand returns to his suburban cottage to find Camille has left him, and when he next meets her in a gambling parlor escorted by her first financial amour, the Baron.

For some reason Niblo omitted the traditional sympathy that goes with Camille's death or a pull on the heart strings where she gives up Armand at the instigation of his father. For a demi-mondaine supposedly in the throes of the first and only real love of her life. Talmadge gives in much too easily as Niblo has screened it.

And through it all Talmadge looks beautiful. Never better, besides giving a sterling performance. Opposite Talmadge is Gilbert Roland. Other than Talmadge and Roland, no one shines except Harvey Clark.

● ●

■ **CAMILLE**

1937, 108 MINS, US ⑱

Dir George Cukor *Prod* David Lewis *Scr* Zoe Akins, Francis Marion, James Hilton *Ph* William Daniels, Karl Freund *Ed* Margaret Booth *Mus* Herbert Stothart *Art Dir* Cedric Gibbons, Fredric Hope
● Greta Garbo, Robert Taylor, Lionel Barrymore, Elizabeth Allan, Jessie Ralph, Henry Daniell (M-G-M)

George Cukor directs this famous play [by Alexandre Dumas] with rare skill. Interior settings, costumes and exteriors are lavish and beautiful. The film shows the great care which went into its preparation and making.

Robert Taylor plays with surprising assurance and ease. He never seems to be striving for a point. He speaks with a moderately modulated voice, never hurriedly, and in all the familiar Armand scenes, such as the first meeting, the parting from his mistress, the accusation in the gambling hall and, finally, the death chamber sequence, Taylor holds up his end of the story with distinction.

Garbo's impersonation of Marguerite Gautier is one of her best portraits. She wears striking clothes, white usually, and while she looks older than the ardent young Armand, the disparity does not mitigate against the illusion.

The two principals play the love scenes for full worth. There is much talk of their affection for each other, but Cukor, with wisdom, shows a minimum of embrace footage.

Of the support players, Henry Daniell, as Baron de Varville, turns in a performance of unusual interest. He is the menace in the background, the lover whom Camille deserts for Armand and the one to whom she returns. Daniell is suave and properly elegant without being too obvious.

● ●

■ **CAN-CAN**

1960, 134 MINS, US ◇ ⑱

Dir Walter Lang *Prod* Jack Cummings *Scr* Dorothy Kingsley, Charles Lederer *Ph* William H. Daniels *Ed* Robert Simpson *Mus* Nelson Riddle (arr.) *Art Dir* Lyle Wheeler, Jack Martin Smith
● Frank Sinatra, Shirley MacLaine, Maurice Chevalier, Louis Jourdan, Juliet Prowse, Marcel Dalio (20th Century-Fox)

Can-Can [based on the musical by Abe Burrows] is a serviceable musical. The more discriminating will find it wanting. It's Las Vegas, 1960; not Montmartre, 1896. The production somehow conveys the feeling that Clan members Frank Sinatra and Shirley MacLaine will soon be joined by other members of the group for another 'summit' meeting.

MacLaine is bouncy, outgoing, scintillating, vivacious and appealing – but French she ain't. Sinatra is, well, Sinatra, complete with the ring-a-ding-ding vocabulary of the insiders. The juxtaposition of Sinatra and MacLaine on the one hand, and authentic Parisians Maurice Chevalier and Louis Jourdan on the other is jarring.

As the proprietor of a cafe that pays off the gendarmes so that the imbibers can witness the illegal dance, MacLaine has the opportunity to indulge in uninhibited and brash clowning and frenzied dancing. Sinatra is her wisecracking playboy-lawyer who aptly handles her legal and private affairs. Both Chevalier and Jourdan, who clicked so strongly in *Gigi*, are wasted in thankless roles as corruptible and incorruptible judges, respectively.

The musical score has been enhanced with three Cole Porter songs that were not in the original Broadway musical – 'Let's Do It', 'Just One of Those Things' and 'You Do Something to Me.' The best tune from the original, as sung by Sinatra, is still 'C'est Magnifique.'

The dance numbers, for the most part, are the highlights of the film, particularly MacLaine's Apache dance. The famous 'Adam and Eve' ballet falls somewhat flat, although it does show off to good advantage Marc Wilder and Juliet Prowse. The can-can is fun, but about as lewd and lascivious as a Maypole dance.

● ●

■ **CANDIDATE, THE**

1972, 109 MINS, US ◇ Ⓥ
Dir Michael Ritchie   *Prod* Walter Coblenz   *Scr* Jeremy Larner   *Ph* Victor J. Kemper   *Ed* Richard A. Harris, Robert Estrin   *Mus* John Rubinstein   *Art Dir* Gene Callahan
● Robert Redford, Peter Boyle, Don Porter, Allen Garfield, Karen Carlson, Melvyn Douglas (Warner)

The Candidate is an excellent drama starring Robert Redford as a naive liberal political novice who wises up fast. Walter Coblenz produced the zesty, gritty film, directed and paced superbly by Michael Ritchie. Peter Boyle and Allen Garfield are tops as campaign supervisors.

The well-structured and developed screenplay takes Redford from a rural legal assistance vocation through the temptations and tortures of mass-merchandising politics, to an upset victory over longtime California Senator Don Porter. Redford's superior acting talents, which not-often-enough are tapped by the scripts he decides to do, are nearly all on display herein in a virtuoso peformance.

Intercutting of some actual political banquet footage is excellent, and the entire film often seems like a documentary special in the best sense of the word.

● ●

■ **CANDY**

1968, 123 MINS, US/ITALY/FRANCE ◇
Dir Christian Marquand   *Prod* Robert Haggiog   *Scr* Buck Henry   *Ph* Giuseppe Rotunno   *Ed* Frank Santillo, Giancarlo Cappelli   *Mus* Dave Grusin   *Art Dir* Dean Tavoularis
● Charles Aznavour, Marlon Brando, Richard Burton, James Burton, John Huston, Ewa Aulin (Selmur/Dear/ Corona)

Candy is a mixed bag of goodies. Based on a novel [by Terry Southern and Mason Hoffenberg] which was a successful satire on pornographic stories, film is at times hilarious, delightfully outrageous, silly, flat, and routine. Director Christian Marquand utilizes a Buck Henry adaptation, a very fine comedy sexpot newcomer (Ewa Aulin) and a strong cast of cameo stars and character thesps.

Candy tells of the unbelievably naive and innocent sexpot heroine, whose adventures were setups for the de rigeur sexual incidents found in most pornography.

The continuing characters are excellent. Aulin's performance in the title role is a delight. John Astin plays both her square father and lecherous uncle, and he is terrific. Elsa Martinelli also is excellent as Aunt Livia.

In retrospect, a prime flaw in *Candy* is the over-exposition of the vignettes. Nearly every episode suffers from the temptation to get one or two more gags out of the material before cutting.

Richard Burton, first cameo star, comes across as the most effective. Ringo Starr, as the Mexican gardener, is very good.

● ●

■ **CAN HEIRONYMUS MERKIN EVER FORGET MERCY HUMPPE AND FIND TRUE HAPPINESS?**

1969, 117 MINS, UK ◇
Dir Anthony Newley   *Prod* Anthony Newley   *Scr* Herman Raucher, Anthony Newley   *Ph* Otto Heller   *Ed* Bernard Gribble   *Mus* Anthony Newley   *Art Dir* William Constable
● Anthony Newley, Joan Collins, Milton Berle, George Jessel, Connie Kreski, Bruce Forsyth (Universal/Taralex)

This film is the work of Anthony Newley, who not only produced and directed from the script on which he collabed with Herman Raucher, and wrote the music, but stars as well in the title role.

Newley plays an introspective film singing idol who re-lives his part-real, part-illusionary past in a movie within a movie, drawing on strange characters to people this past as well as lovelies who line up in wild expectancy as Heironymus plucks them one by one.

Milton Berle in the fetching character-name of Good Time Eddie Filth is his agent who lures him into his career of concupiscence, and George Jessel as The Presence, perhaps an advance angel of death, occasionally emerges out of the blue before disappearing again to spout shaggy jokes as pointless parables.

Married to Polyester Poontang (Joan Collins), Heironymus cannot forget Mercy Humppe, the beautiful innocent so deliciously cavorted by Connie Kreski, onetime Playboy bunny.

● ●

■ **CANNERY ROW**

1982, 120 MINS, US ◇ Ⓥ
Dir David S. Ward   *Prod* Michael Phillips   *Scr* David S. Ward   *Ph* Sven Nykvist   *Ed* David Bretherton   *Mus* Jack Nitzsche   *Art Dir* Richard MacDonald
● Nick Nolte, Debra Winger, Audra Lindley, Frank McRae, M. Emmet Walsh, Tom Mahoney (M-G-M/United Artists)

Maybe Raquel Welch will have the last laugh after all. *Cannery Row*, pic from which she was ignominiously dismissed, gets somewhat better as it lurches along from vignette to vignette, but this long-in-the-works adaptation of John Steinbeck's waterfront tomes [*Cannery Row* and *Sweet Thursday*] displays more appreciation for the values inherent in the material than it does ability to breathe life into it.

Highly anecdotal in nature and tied together by some personable, literary narration by John Huston, 1940s tale centers mostly upon the sketchy activities of a self-employed marine biologist named Doc (Nick Nolte), who lives at ocean's edge, consorts with floozies, counts local bums as his best friends and conceals a troubled past behind his handsome physique.

Across the way stands the neighborhood bordello, into which comes mixed-up drifter

girl Suzy (Debra Winger), who has eyes for Doc but little knowledge of how to pursue him or improve her lot in life. The two sort of get together and break up numerous times.

Nolte seems ideally cast as Doc and has no trouble carrying the film, but is nevertheless hampered by incomplete nature of the part as written. Winger's winning personality and great cracking voice carry her through here, but she relies unduly on a few pat mannerisms.

● ●

■ **CANNONBALL**

1976, 93 MINS, US/HONG KONG ◇ Ⓥ
Dir Paul Bartel   *Prod* Samuel W. Gelfman   *Scr* Paul Bartel, Donald C. Simpson   *Ph* Tak Fujimoto   *Ed* Morton Tubor   *Mus* David A. Axelrod   *Art Dir* Michel Levesque
● David Carradine, Bill McKinney, Veronica Hamel, Gerrit Graham, Robert Carradine, Martin Scorsese (New World/Shaws)

Cannonball will please those who won't rest until they see every car in creation destroyed and aflame.

The sophisticated story line puts David Carradine, Bill McKinney and various other drivers and characters in autos in Los Angeles and promises $100,000 to the first to arrive in New York. Surely, goodness, mercy and high octane will triumph over villainy with lead in their guns, if not in their gas.

That's not to say *Cannonball* has no appeal beyond the crash crowd. It's full of handy highway hints, like what to do when someone steals your jack and then blasts your back tire apart with a pistol.

Best of all, though, is Carradine's inspirational automotive fortitude. When frustrated, he spins in circles, kicks his wheels, mutters oaths – just like the average weekend driver.

● ●

■ **CANNONBALL RUN, THE**

1981, 93 MINS, US ◇
Dir Hal Needham   *Prod* Albert S. Ruddy   *Scr* Brock Yates   *Ph* Michael Butler   *Ed* Donna Cambern, William D. Gordean   *Mus* Snuff Garrett (sup.)   *Art Dir* Carol Wenger
● Burt Reynolds, Roger Moore, Farrah Fawcett, Dom DeLuise, Dean Martin, Sammy Davis Jr (20th Century-Fox)

Full of terribly inside showbiz jokes and populated by what could be called Burt and Hal's Rat Pack, film takes place in that redneck never-never land where most of the guys are beer-guzzling good ole boys and all the gals are fabulously built tootsies.

Cross-country race of the title comes off as almost entirely incidental to the star turns. Overall effect is akin to watching the troupe take a vacation.

Reynolds doesn't even lay a finger on Farrah Fawcett, settling instead for a nice chat in the back of his speedy ambulance. Tuxedoed Roger Moore drives around in his Aston-Martin and tries to convince everyone he's really Roger Moore and not one Seymour Goldfarb. Oriental driver Jackie Chan distracts (and almost kills) himself by putting on a videotape of *Behind the Green Door*, one way to stay awake on a coast-to-coast trip. Partner Michael Hui plays it straight

● ●

■ **CAN SHE BAKE A CHERRY PIE?**

1983, 90 MINS, US ◇ Ⓥ
Dir Henry Jaglom   *Prod* M.H. Simonson   *Scr* Henry Jaglom   *Ph* Bob Fiore   *Mus* Karen Black
● Karen Black, Michael Emil, Michael Margotta, Frances Fisher, Martin Frydberg (Jaglfilm)

Henry Jaglom follows his *Sitting Ducks* [1981] with a similar opus. This is once again a talky comedy, in which the scripter-director puts his characters in a number of sitcom situations, feeds them the opening lines of their scenes and lets them embroider the rest on their own.

Starting from the basic premise that human beings suffer from their inability to communicate with their fellow men, Jaglom builds up a romance of sorts between a fresh divorcee who is still not emotionally rid of her husband, and a man who has been living on his own for some years.

Characters are built very much around the personality of the two main actors, Karen Black giving a beautiful performance, humorous, edgy, nervous and implying deep fears and pains hidden barely under the surface, and Michael Emil brings back many of the peculiarities of his part in *Sitting Ducks*.

■ CANTERBURY TALE, A

1944, 124 MINS, UK

Dir Michael Powell, Emeric Pressburger *Prod* Michael Powell, Emeric Pressburger *Scr* Michael Powell, Emeric Pressburger *Ph* Erwin Hillier *Ed* John Seabourne *Mus* Allan Gray *Art Dir* Alfred Junge
● Eric Portman, Sheila Sim, Dennis Price, John Sweet, Charles Hawtrey, Freda Jackson (Archers)

Sincerity and simplicity shine through every foot of this oversized modern version of the Chaucer epic tale. Here is rare beauty.

Without belittling the highly imaginative genius inspiring the two directors, Michael Powell and Emeric Pressburger, first honors go to Erwin Hillier, whose camerawork is superb. Nothing more effective by way of a time transition shot has been conceived than the way he carries his audience through nine centuries in a few seconds. Beginning with a close-up of a hooded falcon on the wrist of an ancient Canterbury pilgrim (400 years before Columbus discovered America), he follows the graceful bird as it soars aloft on speedy wings. When it becomes a mere speck, it turns and comes gliding back. On coming nearer, it is seen to be a Spitfire.

Sheila Sim is the sole femme in the story. As a London shop girl, turned farmeret for the duration, she turns in a polished performance. Although giving the American GI all the best of it, there is an equally well-drawn characterization, the British tank sergeant, done so well by Dennis Price. For him the cathedral works a miracle.

Star of the film, Eric Portman, gives a splendid, restrained performance as a small-town justice of the peace. Four miracles occur in this story, one to each of the four principal characters.

■ CANTERVILLE GHOST, THE

1944, 95 MINS, US

Dir Jules Dassin *Prod* Arthur L. Field *Scr* Edwin Harvey Blum *Ph* Robert Planck *Ed* Chester W. Schaeffer *Mus* George Bassman *Art Dir* Cedric Gibbons, Edward Carfagno
● Charles Laughton, Robert Young, Margaret O'Brien, Peter Lawford (M-G-M)

The Canterville Ghost is entertaining comedy-drama, with the accent on comedy despite the mystery-chiller emphasis in the title. Tight scripting, nimble direction and excellent casting are about equally responsible for the satisfactory results.

Margaret O'Brien and Charles Laughton come through with topnotch performances, with the clever moppet a solid smash and topping everything. One of her outstanding bits is in a jitterbug terping number with an American soldier and her sedately demure dancing with Robert Young. Her solemn, dignified interpretation as the youthful Lady Jessica de Canterville, head of one of the great English landowning families, is terrific.

Yarn [from the Oscar Wilde short story] is about a 300-year-old ghost (Laughton), once

walled up alive in the castle by his father because he proved a coward on the field of battle, who is looking for a kinsman to perform an act of bravery in his name so that he can be freed from his miserable existence.

■ CAN'T STOP THE MUSIC

1980, 118 MINS, US ◇ ⓥ

Dir Nancy Walker *Prod* Allan Carr, Jacques Morali, Henri Belolo *Scr* Bronte Woodard, Allan Carr *Ph* Bill Butler *Ed* John F. Burnett *Mus* Jacques Morali *Art Dir* Harold Michelson
● Valerie Perrine, Steve Guttenberg, June Havoc, Barbara Rush, Leigh Taylor-Young, The Village People (AFD/Allan Carr)

Writers have recreated the old 'I know, we'll put on a show' gimmick to hinge their story on. Valerie Perrine plays the ex-model with a heart of gold. Her room-mate is an aspiring pop composer (Steve Guttenberg) whom she helps.

She recruits various friends (The Village People) to sing on a demo tape she's going to present to ex-lover and president of Marrakesh Records.

Among the standout sequences is the 'Y.M.C.A.' number, replete with a chorus line of young males side-diving just like in an Esther Williams aquastravaganza in the 1950s.

Director Nancy Walker clearly had trouble with the non-actors in the cast. The Village People, along with ex-Olympic decathlon champion Bruce Jenner, have a long way to go in the acting stakes.

■ CAPE FEAR

1962, 105 MINS, US ⓥ

Dir J. Lee Thompson *Prod* Sy Bartlett *Scr* James R. Webb *Ph* Samuel Leavitt *Ed* George Tomasini *Mus* Bernard Herrmann *Art Dir* Alexander Golitzen, Robert Boyle
● Gregory Peck, Robert Mitchum, Polly Bergen, Lori Martin, Martin Balsam, Telly Savalas (Universal)

As a forthright exercise in cumulative terror *Cape Fear* is a competent and visually polished entry.

Taken from John D. MacDonald's magazine-serialized novel, *The Executioners* the screenplay deals with the scheme of a sadistic ex-convict (Robert Mitchum) to gain revenge against a smalltown Georgia lawyer (Gregory Peck), his wife and daughter. Peck, it seems, had testified against him eight years earlier for the savage assault on a woman in a parking lot.

Mitchum's menacing omnipresence causes the family much mental anguish. Their pet dog is poisoned, the daughter has a harrowing encounter with the degenerate, and there is the culminating terror in Georgia swampland.

What ails Mitchum obviously requires violent sexual expression – the woman he takes have to be clobbered as well as violated. But in the undiluted flow of evil, there is nothing in the script or J. Lee Thompson's direction which might provide audiences with some insight into Mitchum's behavior.

Peck, displaying his typical guarded self, is effective, if perhaps less distraught over the prospect of personal disaster than his character might warrant. Granting the shallowness of his motivation, Mitchum has no trouble being utterly hateful. Wearing a Panama fedora and chomping a cocky cigar, the menace of his visage has the hiss of a poised snake. Polly Bergen, breaking an eight-year screen absence, turns in a sympathetic job as Peck's wife.

■ CAPONE

1975, 101 MINS, US ◇

Dir Steve Carver *Prod* Roger Corman *Scr* Howard Browne *Ph* Vilis Lapenieks *Ed* Richard Meyer *Mus* David Grisman *Art Dir* Ward Preston
● Ben Gazzara, Susan Blakely, Harry Guardino, John Cassavetes, Sylvester Stallone, Peter Maloney (20th-Century Fox)

Capone, a somewhat crude, violent and deja vu actioner, focusses on Ben Gazzara as Capone, showing his brutish, casual arrogance in a climb from neighborhood punk to a Chi rackets kingpin, then his decline via an income tax rap (arranged, it is claimed by his own aide, Frank Nitti, very well played by Sylvester Stallone).

Susan Blakely again shows her sensual sparkle as a slumming rich chick taken to Capone; while John Cassavetes has a good cameo as the NY hood who discovers Capone's potential.

Gazzara has evidently gone to great lengths to attempt a full characterization of Capone, but it's hard to shoehorn developed drama between machine gun bullets.

■ CAPRICE

1967, 97 MINS, US ◇

Dir Frank Tashlin *Prod* Aaron Rosenberg, Martin Melcher *Scr* Jay Jayson, Frank Tashlin *Ph* Leon Shamroy *Ed* Robert Simpson *Mus* Frank DeVol *Art Dir* Jack Martin Smith, William Creber
● Doris Day, Richard Harris, Ray Walston, Jack Kruschen, Edward Mulhare (20th Century-Fox)

Caprice is one of those occasional pictures about which it can be said fairly that it could have been better than it is. A timely and inventive plot – industrial espionage – is never fully developed in either writing, acting or direction.

Doris Day and Richard Harris are double-crossing double agents working, variously, for US cosmetics king Jack Kruschen, British counterpart Edward Mulhare, or Interpol.

Ray Walston plays Kruschen's inventive genius, although it turns out that Lilia Skala, Walston's mother-in-law in Switzerland, is the creative brain.

Elements of comedy, murder, satire and psychology are blended uncertainly in the never-boiling pot.

■ CAPRICORN ONE

1978, 127 MINS, US ◇ ⓥ

Dir Peter Hyams *Prod* Paul N. Lazarus III *Scr* Peter Hyams *Ph* Bill Butler *Ed* James Mitchell *Mus* Jerry Goldsmith *Art Dir* Albert Brenner
● Elliott Gould, James Brolin, Brenda Vaccaro, Sam Waterston, O.J. Simpson, Hal Holbrook (Associated General)

Capricorn One begins with a workable, if cynical cinematic premise: the first manned space flight to Mars was a hoax and the American public was fooled through Hollywood gimmickry into believing that the phony landing happened. But after establishing the concept, Peter Hyams' script asks another audience – the one in the theatre – to accept something far more illogical, the uncovering of the hoax by reporter Elliott Gould.

The astronaut trio of James Brolin, Sam Waterston and O.J. Simpson together add up to nothing; there's no group chemistry. Still, scattershot casting means once in a while you hit and in the final scene Gould and Telly Savalas are teamed. The duo is a bullseye. Savalas, in a delightful cameo as a crop duster hired to help rescue Brolin in the desert and uncover the plot, is a marvelous complement to Gould.

Hal Holbrook plays the mission commander who calls off the Mars shot and engineers the dupe. His character must change from sincere – he believes he's doing the right thing by fooling the public – to menacing. In general, it is a script of conveniences.

．．．．．．．．．．．．．．．．．．．．．．．

■ CAPTAIN BLOOD

1935, 119 MINS, US ⓥ

Dir Michael Curtiz   *Scr* Casey Robinson   *Ph* Hal Mohr   *Ed* George Amy   *Mus* Erich Wolfgang Korngold   *Art Dir* Anton Grot

● Errol Flynn, Olivia de Havilland, Basil Rathbone, Lionel Atwill, Ross Alexander, Guy Kibbee (Cosmopolitan/Warner)

Captain Blood, from the Rafael Sabatini novel, is a big picture. It's a spectacle which will establish both Errol Flynn and Olivia de Havilland. Director Michael Curtiz hasn't spared the horses. It's a lavish, swashbuckling saga of the Spanish main.

The engaging Flynn is the titular Peter Blood, erstwhile physician, later sold into West Indian slavery, to emerge thereafter as a peer among Caribbean pirates, Capt Blood, only later to be pardoned, his crew of runaway slaves likewise granted their freedom, and sworn into the King's navy.

Flynn impresses favorably from the start. One lives with him in the unfairness of a tyrant King Charles which causes him and his fellow Englishmen to be sold into slavery. One suffers with their travail; the audience roots with them in their ultimately fruitless plot for escape from the island. And then he is catapulted into leadership of a pirate ship.

De Havilland, who came to attention in Warner's *A Midsummer Night's Dream*, is romantically beauteous as the unsympathetic plantation owner's (later governor's) niece. This supplies a modicum of romantic interest, although it all too paltry. It's one of the prime shortcomings of the production. Lionel Atwill is sufficiently hateful as the uncle. Basil Rathbone is an effective co-pirate captain (French brigands, this time), he and Flynn engaging in an arresting duel in the course of events.

□ 1935: Best Picture (Nomination)

．．．．．．．．．．．．．．．．．．．．．．．

■ CAPTAIN FROM CASTILE

1947, 140 MINS, US ◇

Dir Henry King   *Prod* Lamar Trotti   *Scr* Lamar Trotti   *Ph* Charles Clarke, Arthur E. Arling   *Ed* Barbara McLean   *Mus* Alfred Newman   *Art Dir* Richard Day, James Basen

● Tyrone Power, Jean Peters, Cesar Romero, Lee J. Cobb, Antonio Moreno (20th Century-Fox)

Based on Samuel Shellaberger's 1945 best-selling historical novel, the cinema adaptation hews closely to the structure of the book, capturing the vast sweep of its story and adding to it an eye-stunning Technicolor dimension. The coin poured into this production, reported to be around $4.5 million, is visible in every inch of the footage.

For this plume-and-sabre epic of 16th-century Spanish imperial conquerors, producer and production chief have assembled a group of thespers who are cleanly tailored for the various parts. Led by Tyrone Power, who's rarely been shown to better advantage, the roster is buttressed by Cesar Romero, in a stirringly virile protrait of Cortez; Lee J Cobb, as a fortune hunter; John Sutton, as a velvety villain, and newcomer Jean Peters, a buxom, appealing wench for the romantic byplay.

From one viewpoint, this picture is constructed like a self-contained double feature. In the first half, the locale is Spain during the Inquisition, with Power and his family unjustly persecuted for heresy. Escaping from Spain, Power finds himself during the second half in Mexico as a recruit in Cortez's expedition of plunder against the Aztec empire ruled by Montezuma.

There are, however several soft spots in the story that interfere with credibility. There is, for instance, the fact that Power narrowly escapes death no less than three times under the most extreme circumstances. Sutton, likewise, cheats death two times despite his being stabbed through the heart with a foot of steel one time and near-strangled the next.

．．．．．．．．．．．．．．．．．．．．．．．

■ CAPTAIN HORATIO HORNBLOWER, R.N.

1951, 116 MINS, UK ◇

Dir Raoul Walsh   *Prod* Raoul Walsh   *Scr* C.S. Forester, Ivan Goff, Ben Roberts   *Ph* Guy Green   *Ed* Jack Harris   *Mus* Robert Farnon   *Art Dir* Tom Morahan

● Gregory Peck, Virginia Mayo, Robert Beatty, James Kenney, James Robertson Justice, Stanley Baker (Warner)

The exploits of one of Britain's greatest fictional naval adventurers have been filmed by Warner with spectacular success. *Captain Horatio Hornblower* has been brought to the screen as effervescent entertainment with action all the way.

Three C.S. Forester stories provide the basis for the pic, and the author, in preparing his own adaptation, has selected the best material from these. It is an incisive study of a man who is dispassionate, aloof and remote, yet often capable of finer feelings.

In his interpretation of the title role, Gregory Peck stands out as a skilled artist, capturing the spirit of the character and atmosphere of the period. Whether as the ruthless captain ordering a flogging as a face-saving act for a junior officer or tenderly nursing Virginia Mayo through yellow fever, he never fails to reflect the Forester character.

The film is divided into two halves. In the opening, Hornblower (Peck) is commanding the frigate Lydia through Pacific waters to fulfill a British mission to provide arms to enemies of Spain. On his return to England, he participates in an exciting adventure against Napoleon's fleet, eventually becoming a national hero. The major action sequences have been lensed with great skill.

．．．．．．．．．．．．．．．．．．．．．．．

■ CAPTAIN KRONOS – VAMPIRE HUNTER

1974, 91 MINS, UK ◇ ⓥ

Dir Brian Clemens   *Prod* Albert Fennell, Brian Clemens   *Scr* Brian Clemens   *Ph* Ian Wilson   *Ed* James Needs   *Mus* Laurie Johnson   *Art Dir* Robert Jones

● Horst Janson, John Carson, Shane Briant, Caroline Munro, John Cater, Ian Hendry (Hammer)

Captain Kronos – Vampire Hunter, as played by Horst Janson, is a prototype blond Germanic, superstud caped like an operetta leading man. Accompanied by faithful friend John Cater, playing a hunchback professor, Kronos solves a vampire mystery with a lot of swash and buckle.

Story is unusual in that the vampire, who turns out to be an elderly woman (her ladyship in the castle, halfway up the next hill), sucks blood to get a youthful appearance. Being a new horror character, Kronos naturally has a groupie in tow (Caroline Munro) who caters to his earthier needs between random jousts with bad guys and bad vampires.

Ian Hendry has one scene as a heavy, got up like an aging leather gang leader solely for the purpose of Kronos showing off his swordsmanship.

．．．．．．．．．．．．．．．．．．．．．．．

■ CAPTAIN NEWMAN, M.D.

1963, 126 MINS, US ◇ ⓥ

Dir David Miller   *Prod* Robert Arthur   *Scr* Richard L. Breen, Henry Ephron   *Ph* Russell Metty   *Ed* Alma Macrorie   *Mus* Frank Skinner   *Art Dir* Alexander Golitzen, Alfred Sweeney

● Gregory Peck, Tony Curtis, Angie Dickinson, Eddie Albert, Bobby Darin, Robert Duvall (Universal)

Captain Newman, M.D. oscillates between scenes of great dramatic impact and somewhat strained and contrived comedy of the heartwarming variety. Thus, what might have been a provocatively realistic dramatization of a dedicated psychiatric doctor's attempts to heal the emotional injuries of servicemen scarred by war is reduced to the common denominator of lukewarm popular entertainment.

Leo Rosten's novel is the source of the hot-and-cold scenario. Hero of the story is Capt. Newman (Gregory Peck), chief of the neuro-psychiatric ward of a wartime (1944) army hospital who places his medical obligations above military duty. Newman's treatment of three cases is illustrated. One involves a decorated corporal (Bobby Darin) who believes himself a coward for having deserted a buddy in a burning aircraft. Another concerns a colonel (Eddie Albert) who has gone berserk with a sense of guilt at having sent so many men to their deaths in aerial combat. The third (Robert Duvall) feels shame over having hidden alone in a cellar for over a year in Nazi-occupied territory.

In between all of this, Newman gets his kicks in a romance with his nurse (Angie Dickinson) and by observing the antics of his number one orderly (Tony Curtis), a glib, resourceful operator from Jersey City with a streak of Bergen County larceny.

Peck's portrayal of the title figure is characteristically restrained and intelligent. Perhaps his best scene, oddly enough, is the one in which he is quietly but expressively reacting to Darin's high-powered histrionics. It is also the film's most deeply moving passage.

Curtis has some good moments, but essentially he is the pivotal figure in the film's secondary comic shenanigans. Dickinson is sweet, sometimes too darned sweet, as the nurse.

．．．．．．．．．．．．．．．．．．．．．．．

■ CAPTAINS COURAGEOUS

1937, 115 MINS, US ⓥ

Dir Victor Fleming   *Prod* Louis D. Lighton   *Scr* John Lee Mahin, Marc Connelly, Dale Van Every   *Ph* Harold Rosson   *Ed* Elmo Vernon   *Mus* Franz Waxman

● Spencer Tracy, Freddie Bartholomew, Lionel Barrymore, Melvyn Douglas, Charley Grapewin, Mickey Rooney (M-G-M)

Taking this Rudyard Kipling story, written when he visited America some years earlier, the producers have made the central character of the spoiled child younger than he was in the book, and for the purposes of the screen have indulged in other slight, unimportant alterations. Spencer Tracy is a Portuguese fisherman with an accent and a flair for singing songs of the briny. Lionel Barrymore is the happy-go-lucky but stern captain of a fishing schooner while Bartholomew, of course, is the boy.

The Kipling yarn, built around a wealthy, motherless brat who accidentaly lands with a cod-fishing fleet, and undergoes regeneration during an enforced three months' piscatorial quest, has been given splendid production, performance, photography and dramatic composition.

Young Bartholomew plays the spoiled kid, only son of wealthy father, who falls off a liner bound for Europe and is picked up by Tracy, the fisherman to whom the recalcitrant boy finally becomes deeply attached. Bartholomew's transition from a brat to a lovable child is done with convincing strokes.

His performance is matched by Tracy, who also doesn't seem right doing an accent and singing songs, but he, too, later gets under the skin of the character. Barrymore is himself, as usual. As the father of the boy, Mel-

vyn Douglas gives a smooth, unctuous performance. One of the fishermen is deftly portrayed by John Carradine.
□ 1937: Best Picture (Nomination)

••••••••••••••••••••••••••••••••••

■ **CAPTIVE**

1986, 95 MINS, UK/FRANCE ◇ ⓥ
Dir Paul Mayersberg   *Prod* Don Boyd   *Scr* Paul Mayersberg   *Ph* Mike Southon   *Ed* Marie-Therese Boiche   *Mus* The Edge, Michael Berkeley   *Art Dir* George Djurkovic
● Irina Brook, Oliver Reed, Xavier Deluc, Corinne Decla, Hiro Arai, Nic Reding (Virgin/World Audio)

The kidnapping of a beautiful rich young girl, not for money, nor for sex, but just for the joy of doing it is the theme intricately developed by Paul Mayersberg in *Captive*.

A trio of kidnapers – a French boy, a Japanese boy and an English girl – imprison a rich girl. She's drugged, handcuffed, blindfolded and gagged before being locked up in a chest for the night. As the action proceeds it becomes evident the object of the mission is a brainwashing exercise, to mold the girl to their mode of life. Gradually, they succeed.

Irina Brook (daughter of Peter Brook) is a handsome girl with a firm young body, and willing to show it off. Fortunately, she's also a competent actress in the difficult role of the captive. Oliver Reed gives a commanding performance as the girl's father.

••••••••••••••••••••••••••••••••••

■ **CAPTIVE CITY, THE**

1952, 91 MINS, US
Dir Robert Wise   *Prod* Theron Warth   *Scr* Karl Kamb, Alvin Josephy Jr   *Ph* Lee Garmes   *Ed* Ralph Swink   *Mus* Jerome Moross
● John Forsythe, Joan Camden, Harold J. Kennedy, Marjorie Crossland, Victor Sutherland, Ray Teal (Aspen/United Artists)

The Captive City is a tense, absorbing drama of a small town editor's fight against corruption. It has a documentary quality that rings with authenticity. Based on facts uncovered by probes of the Senate Crime Investigation Committee, it contains a cleverly interwoven epilog by Sen Estes Kefauver, who headed the latter group.

John Forsythe and Harold J. Kennedy, as former GI buddies, are co-owners of a newspaper in a city called Kennington. Then a local private detective, working on an apparently harmless divorce case, discovers the existence of a big-time gambling syndicate operating with the knowledge of the city fathers, the local police and the respectable elements of the community.

Forsythe succeeds in uncovering the whole mess. However, he is powerless to do anything.

••••••••••••••••••••••••••••••••••

■ **CAPTIVE HEART, THE**

1946, 108 MINS, UK
Dir Basil Dearden   *Prod* Michael Balcon   *Scr* Angus MacPhail, Guy Morgan   *Ph* Douglas Slocombe   *Ed* Charles Hasse   *Mus* Alan Rawsthorne   *Art Dir* Michael Relph
● Michael Redgrave, Rachel Kempson, Mervyn Johns, Jack Warner, Basil Radford (Ealing)

Second only to the unrelieved grim reality of life as it was lived in Stalags, the outstanding merit of *The Captive Heart* is the number of superlatively good performances turned in. To Michael Balcon as producer must go chief credit for the newsreel fidelity of the prison camp sequences.

Michael Redgrave, as a Czech, educated in England and fleeing from the Gestapo, takes on the identity of a dead English army officer and is jailed in a Stalag with British soldiers. He escapes lynching only to find himself marked down for a visit to a Nazi gas chamber.

Even when he convinces the British of the truth of his story, and after he has won freedom through repatriation, he's up against the task of squaring himself with the wife of the dead man whose identity he has assumed. The fact that this final sequence holds one's attention says something for the writing, acting, and directing.

••••••••••••••••••••••••••••••••••

■ **CARAVANS**

1978, 127 MINS, US/IRAN ◇ ⓥ
Dir James Fargo   *Prod* Elmo Williams   *Scr* Nancy Voyles Crawford, Thomas A. McMahon, Lorraine Williams   *Ph* Douglas Slocombe   *Ed* Richard Marden   *Mus* Mike Batt   *Art Dir* Ted Tester, Peter Williams, Peter James
● Anthony Quinn, Michael Sarrazin, Jennifer O'Neill, Christopher Lee, Joseph Cotten, Behrooz Vosoughi (Ibex/FIDCI)

The main trouble with this tale of 1948 Persia isn't the Iranians, it's Hollywood. Almost every fake moment in the film, and there are lots of them, has the touch of Hollywood laid on with a heavy coating. Fortunately for the average viewer, the scenic scope of the film, based on James Michener's epic story, and shot entirely on locations in Iran, is so sweeping that the tale that is told is almost palatable. But barely.

Briefly, the film deals with the search of a minor American consular employee (Michael Sarrazin) for an American woman (Jennifer O'Neill) who has married an Iranian colonel (Behrooz Vosoughi) but deserted him for a Kochi chieftain (Anthony Quinn) and has disappeared. Sarrazin finds her in short order. That's when the real trouble begins. She won't go back and he won't go back without her and off everyone goes into the desert.

Sarrazin, Quinn and O'Neill carry most of the story. The other non-Persians – Christopher Lee, Barry Sullivan, Jeremy Kemp and Joseph Cotten – are seen so briefly they may have done their roles over a long weekend. Histrionically, only Quinn is believable, followed closely by Vosoughi.

••••••••••••••••••••••••••••••••••

■ **CARAVAN TO VACCARES**

1974, 98 MINS, UK/FRANCE ◇ ⓥ
Dir Geoffrey Reeve   *Prod* Geoffrey Reeve, Richard Morris-Adams   *Scr* Paul Wheeler   *Ph* John Cabrera, David Bevan, Ted Deason   *Mus* Stanley Myers   *Art Dir* Frank White
● Charlotte Rampling, David Birney, Michel Lonsdale, Marcel Bozuffi, Michael Bryant, Manitas de Plata (Reeve/Prodis)

There's good, reliable stuff in this Alistair MacLean action-adventure item, colorfully location-set in Southern France's Camargue area and well acted by a carefully chosen Franco-British cast.

Plot basics involve the attempt to smuggle an East European scientist out of France and into the US, attempt which is hampered by repeated harassment and kidnappings by a scruple-less rival gang bent on gleaning the fugitive's secrets for resale to the highest bidder.

Principally involved are a footloose young American (David Birney), hired by a French Duke (Michel Lonsdale) to whisk the scientist onto a US-bound plane, and a pretty young British photographer (Charlotte Rampling) who gets involved when she hitches a ride with Birney.

••••••••••••••••••••••••••••••••••

■ **CARBON COPY**

1981, 92 MINS, US ◇
Dir Michael Schultz   *Prod* Carter De Haven, Stanley Shapiro   *Scr* Stanley Shapiro   *Ph* Fred Koenekamp   *Ed* Marion Segal   *Mus* Bill Conti   *Art Dir* Ted Howorth

● George Segal, Susan Saint James, Denzel Washington, Jack Warden, Paul Winfield, Dick Martin (Hemdale/RKO)

Carbon Copy is a comedy which attempts to deal with racial issues much in the way that *Watermelon Man* did. This time the story is rooted in reality. *Carbon Copy* has business executive George Segal faced with the arrival of a long-lost and heretofore unknown son whom he describes as 'Hickory Bronze.'

Segal attempts to pass off son Denzel Washington as a social experiment in his all-white suburb, but paternal instincts force him to reveal the truth to his straight-laced wife Susan Saint James. Abruptly, he loses his job, credit cards and Saint James throws him out of the house.

Suddenly, without allies, Segal is forced to accept the lot of the racial minorities. Cut off from his money and powerful contacts, he accepts manual labor jobs and begins to experiment and appreciate the lot of his son. The Segal character, a Jew, could hide behind a name, but his son can't adopt a new color.

Segal is particularly effective as he begins to realize just how complacent he is under his liberal values.

Carbon Copy is admittedly a fairy tale, just as the Capra films of the 1930s were. However, director Michael Schultz maintains a convincing balance between the film's broad humor and its genuinely poignant moments.

••••••••••••••••••••••••••••••••••

■ **CARD, THE**

1952, 91 MINS, UK ⓥ
Dir Ronald Neame   *Prod* John Bryan   *Scr* Eric Ambler   *Ph* Oswald Morris   *Ed* Clive Donner   *Mus* William Alwyn   *Art Dir* T. Hopwell Ash
● Alec Guinness, Petula Clark, Glynis Johns, Valerie Hobson, Edward Chapman, Gibb McLaughlin (British Film Makers/Rank)

The principal character in Arnold Bennett's novel *The Card*, depicting the progression of a washer-woman's son from poverty to wealth, from humble beginnings to the top of the civic tree, provides a made-to-measure part for Alec Guinness in a capital performance.

Set in the Potteries, without any attempt to glamorize the grimy, smoky, slum-ridden district, Eric Ambler's script keeps the focus entirely on Guinness.

The rise of the young lad is depicted in all its stages, from his dishonest beginning, when he alters examination results to ensure a place in high school. And from there he gradually makes his name in the world, advancing from a humble lawyer's clerk to rent collector and to big business as head and founder of a loan club.

••••••••••••••••••••••••••••••••••

■ **CARDINAL, THE**

1963, 175 MINS, US ◇ ⓥ
Dir Otto Preminger   *Prod* Otto Preminger   *Scr* Robert Dozier   *Ph* Leon Shamroy   *Ed* Louis R. Loeffler   *Mus* Jerome Moross   *Art Dir* Lyle Wheeler
● Tom Tryon, Carol Lynley, Romy Schneider, John Huston, Raf Vallone (Columbia)

Otto Preminger's *The Cardinal* is a long motion picture but for most of the way it is superlative drama, emotionally stirring, intellectually stimulating and scenically magnificent.

Like the Henry Morton Robinson novel that it lives up to more in spirit than plot-wise, it is a skillful, fascinating blend of fact and fiction. The story concerns the development of a Rome-educated American priest who has aspirations of clerical high office. However, he experiences shattering doubt of his ability to be a good priest and, indeed, if he ever had a true 'call', having from his ear-

C

liest memory been destined, according to his parents, for the priesthood.

Without faulting scenarist Robert Dozier, *The Cardinal* is Preminger's picture for it moves on such a vast canvas – Rome, Boston and environs, New York (dockside scene only), Georgia, Vienna and back to Rome – with all the richly pictorial ritual of the ordination of a priest, the consecration of a Bishop, later a Cardinal, and the vast public excitement in St Peter's Square for the election of a Pope.

Preminger also selected his cast wisely. Tom Tryon, who has the title role, plays it very well indeed, although there are shadings to the character which do not surface as might be desired. Romy Schneider is captivating as the Viennese girl who cannot disguise her feelings toward Tryon. Carol Lynley is effective as his troubled sister and also in a subsequent role as the latter's illegitimate daughter.

There are, however, two who steal the picture as far as acting goes. They are John Huston and Raf Vallone. Both play the roles of cardinals on distinctive, captivating levels.

. . . .

■ CAREER

1959, 105 MINS, US

Dir Joseph Anthony *Prod* Hal Wallis *Scr* James Lee *Ph* Joseph LaShelle *Ed* Warren Low
● Dean Martin, Anthony Franciosa, Shirley MacLaine, Carolyn Jones, Joan Blackman, Donna Douglas (Paramount)

This feature is so limited in production scope as to suggest the possibility that the producer was out to save money the hard way – that is, stinting on the pictorial values. But a closer look is reassuring, for it genuinely appears that Hal Wallis, in placing on the screen James Lee's off-Broadway play of the same name, and director Joseph Anthony were bent on preserving the intimacy of the original.

It's a show business story done in honest-to-goodness fashion. It centers on the ambition-driven but nonetheless agreeable aspiring actor. Whether he's maladjusted husband or insignificant waiter he's where he is because, in his free time, he's out to become a star and his other roles in life are unimportant.

It's a serious theme, to be sure, but somewhere there must have been opportunity to get a little lighthearted. A couple of Lee's story angles hardly seem to fit in, and this is no help in the secondary last-half that follows the attention-getting earlier episodes. Anthony Franciosa's call to the Korean war, with a brief glimpse of same, is not correctly integrated. Neither is the exposure of Dean Martin, as a smalltime director on the way up, as a onetime Communist because, as he puts it, '*I was ambitious.*'

Otherwise, Franciosa and Martin, however sombre their parts, perform convincingly. Shirley MacLaine as a producer's free-wheeling daughter has some misfitting dialog and story situations to cope with but gets across all right, and Carolyn Jones plays it straight as an agent.

. . . .

■ CAREER OPPORTUNITIES

1991, 85 MINS, US ◇ ▼

Dir Bryan Gordon *Prod* John Hughes *Scr* John Hughes *Ph* Don McAlpine *Ed* Glenn Farr, Peck Prior *Mus* Thomas Newman *Art Dir* Paul Sylbert
● Frank Whaley, Jennifer Connelly, Dermot Mulroney, Kieran Mulroney, Barry Corbin, John Candy (Universal/ Hughes)

Writer-producer John Hughes' followup to *Home Alone* lacks the spit-polish and magic of the blockbuster but still has plenty of absorbing characters, smart, snappy dialog and delightful stretches of comic foolery.

Like *Home Alone*, story has a young man on his own to defend a fortress against bungling burglars, but in this case he's a 21-year-old trapped in a job he hates (night janitor at a discount store) and pitted against gun-toting hoods out to clean out, not clean up, the store.

Jim (Frank Whaley) is a ne'er-do-well fast talker and nonstop liar bounced from as many deadend jobs as his humble hometown of Munroe, Ill, has to offer. He's been given his last chance to succeed by his blue-collar father – or get kicked out of the house.

That's when he discovers he's not alone. Darkly voluptuous Josie (Jennifer Connelly), princess daughter of the town land baron, is locked in after falling asleep during a shoplifting spree.

Trapped together, the misfits discover each other, and, in the type of scenes Hughes writes best, sort out their differences and common ground from their horrifying high school years. But the guntoting hoods (Dermot and Kieran Mulroney) show up and they must turn their specialties to more immediate escape.

. . . .

■ CAREFUL HE MIGHT HEAR YOU

1983, 116 MINS, AUSTRALIA ◇ ▼

Dir Carl Schultz *Prod* Jill Robb *Scr* Michael Jenkins *Ph* John Seale *Ed* Richard Francis Bruce *Mus* Ray Cook *Art Dir* John Stoddart
● Wendy Hughes, Robyn Nevin, Nicholas Gledhill, John Hargreaves, Geraldine Turner, Isabelle Anderson (Syme)

A top quality production about the struggle between two sisters for custody of an eight-year-old boy, their nephew, *Careful He Might Hear You* is a completely involving emotional experience.

The Summer Locke Elliott novel on which Michael Jenkins' excellent screenplay is based was, for many years, a project for Joshua Logan with, at one point, Elizabeth Taylor announced for the role of Vanessa Scott, the lonely frigid spinster whose causes all the trouble, and who is played, commandingly, here by Wendy Hughes.

Story is set in the Depression in Sydney. The boy, nicknamed 'PS' by everyone, is homeless after the death of his mother and the departure of his feckless father, Logan, for the goldfields. He's taken in by a loving but impoverished aunt and uncle (Robyn Nevin and Peter Whitford).

Their lives are disrupted, however, by the arrival of Vanessa, another sister, but from the moneyed side of the family. She wants custody of the child.

. . . .

■ CARETAKER, THE

1964, 105 MINS, UK

Dir Clive Donner *Prod* Michael Birkett *Scr* Harold Pinter *Ph* Nicolas Roeg *Ed* Fergus McDonnell *Mus* Ron Grainer *Art Dir* Reece Pemberton
● Alan Bates, Donald Pleasence, Robert Shaw (Caretaker)

Harold Pinter adapted his own three-character play for the screen, but made little attempt to broaden the canvas and its stage origins are barely disguised.

This production of *The Caretaker*, was financed by 10 prominent showbiz personalities, each of whom has a $14,000 stake in it, while the author, producer, director and three stars are all on deferment. Among its backers were stars, film producers and legit impresarios, including Elizabeth Taylor, Richard Burton, Peter Sellers, Noel Coward, Harry Saltzman and Peter Bridge.

Instead of using a conventional studio, the unit took over a house in a northeast London suburb, and that provides an ideal, shabby setting for Pinter's offbeat theme. Basically,

it's a one-set play, and that made it a tough assignment for director Clive Donner. His fluent treatment, however, makes the most of the macabre verbal exchanges, and overcomes many of the static handicaps of the subject.

The three characters are two brothers and a tramp. One of the brothers, a building worker, owns a house, but it is his brother who lives in it, though just in one room, cluttered with furniture from the remainder of the house. The tramp, homeless and unemployed, is invited to stay the night, and finds himself being tossed around like a shuttlecock, in favor with one brother, and out of favor with the other.

Donald Pleasence's standout performance as the tramp is the acting highlight, but he easily has the choicest role. Robert Shaw gives an intelligent study as the brother who offers the tramp shelter, while Alan Bates completes the stellar trio with another forceful portrayal.

. . . .

■ CARMEN JONES

1954, 105 MINS, US ◇ ▼

Dir Otto Preminger *Prod* Otto Preminger *Scr* Harry Kleiner *Ph* Sam Leavitt *Ed* Louis R. Loeffler *Mus* Georges Bizet *Art Dir* Edward L. Ilou
● Dorothy Dandridge, Harry Belafonte, Olga James, Pearl Bailey, Diahann Carroll, Roy Glenn (20th Century-Fox)

As a wartime [1943] legit offering *Carmen Jones* – the modernized, all-Negro version of [Georges Bizet's] opera *Carmen* – was a long-run hit both on Broadway and on the road. Otto Preminger has transferred it to the screen with taste and imagination in an opulent production.

The screenplay closely follows the lines of the stage libretto by Oscar Hammerstein II in which Carmen is a pleasure-loving southern gal who works in a Dixie parachute factory, where Joe (Jose) is a member of the army regiment on guard duty. She lures him away from Cindy Lou (Micaela) and he deserts with her. Eventually Carmen tires of him and takes up with Husky Miller (Escamillo) the fighter and Joe kills her when she refuses to return to him.

Preminger directs with a deft touch, blending the comedy and tragedy easily and building his scenes to some suspenseful heights. He gets fine performances from the cast toppers, notably Dorothy Dandridge, a sultry Carmen whose performance maintains the right hedonistic note throughout.

. . . .

■ CARNAL KNOWLEDGE

1971, 97 MINS, US ◇ ▼

Dir Mike Nichols *Prod* Mike Nichols *Scr* Jules Feiffer *Ph* Giuseppe Rotunno *Ed* Sam O'Steen *Art Dir* Richard Sylbert
● Jack Nicholson, Art Garfunkel, Candice Bergen, Ann-Margret, Cynthia O'Neal, Rita Moreno (Avco Embassy)

Mike Nichols' *Carnal Knowledge* is a rather superficial and limited probe of American male sexual hypocrisies. Jules Feiffer's episodic story follows for over 20 years the diverse paths of Jack Nicholson and Art Garfunkel as each tries to match their sexual fantasies with an uncooperative reality.

First, Nicholson and Garfunkel are college roommates in the 1940s, where Candice Bergen is the object of attention. Garfunkel, the more sensitive, wins her heart over Nicholson, whose ability to betray close friends is neatly established.

Time jumps ahead about a decade to the late 1950s. Nicholson falls in his own way for Ann-Margret, a sexpot who really would like to get married and have kids. Nicholson still can't cope, and at the same time introduces

Garfunkel – now a slightly bored suburban husband – to Cynthia O'Neal.

The final 13 minutes are set in the late 1960s. Garfunkel has gone mod, latching onto Carol Kane, a hippie nymphet, while Nicholson has been reduced to periodic visits to Rita Moreno, a for-hire playmate who helps him play out his fantasies.

The story pussyfoots round some underlying psychological and psychiatric hangups. Nicholson's compulsive stud character is the type that hates women. The film fails by avoiding confrontation with his character.

· ·

■ CARNY

1980, 105 MINS, US ◇ ⓥ

Dir Robert Kaylor *Prod* Robbie Robertson *Scr* Thomas Baum *Ph* Harry Stradling Jr *Ed* Stuart Pappe *Mus* Alex North *Art Dir* William J. Cassidy
● Gary Busey, Jodie Foster, Robbie Robertson, Elisha Cook, Meg Foster, Kenneth McMillan (United Artists)

Edgy tale [from a story by Phoebe and Robert Kaylor and Robbie Robertson] of three born outsiders living on a tightrope vividly recalls, both in style and content, the doom-laden films noir of the late 1940s.

Gary Busey plays a slightly demented bozo in a cage who mercilessly taunts spectators trying to dump him into water by throwing baseballs. Busey hooks up with runaway Jodie Foster.

As the carny makes its way through the South, Foster is gradually assimilated into the band of outcasts and a three-way relationship develops.

Busey is tremendous. Foster, ostensibly playing her first 'adult' role, works wonders with a somewhat underwritten part.

Director Kaylor displays an unerring eye for atmosphere and detail.

· ·

■ CAROUSEL

1956, 128 MINS, US ◇

Dir Henry King *Prod* Henry Ephron *Scr* Phoebe Ephron, Henry Ephron *Ph* Charles G. Clarke *Ed* William Reynolds *Mus* Alfred Newman (sup.) *Art Dir* Lyle Wheeler, Jack Martin Smith
● Gordon MacRae, Shirley Jones, Cameron Mitchell, Barbara Ruick, Gene Lockhart, Susan Luckey (20th Century-Fox)

Carousel, presented by the Theatre Guild in April 1945, ran 890 performances at the Majestic Theatre. It here gets the supertreatment in 55mm CinemaScope. There are two production numbers in the picture that are close to classic. Add the staging of the famed 'Soliloquy', as sung by Gordon MacRae for strong impact. Musical numbers are all in extremely good taste. Reservations as to some scenes and a certain slowness in pace are minor.

The stars of *Carousel* remain Rodgers & Hammerstein. The cast is uniformly attractive, from MacRae as the shiftless ne'er-do-well Billy Bigelow, to pretty Shirley Jones as Julie.

Production number that precedes the gay clambake is a tribute to the ingenuity of choreographer Rod Alexander.

If this scene is great, the finale, when Julie's daughter, Louise (danced by Susan Luckey), does a number with handsome Jacques D'Amboise, is even more of a rocking production success.

Carousel keeps elements of drama, humor and sentiment but starts out with MacRae already dead and in heaven, his courtship and marriage are then told in flashback.

· ·

■ CARPETBAGGERS, THE

1964, 150 MINS, US ◇ ⓥ

Dir Edward Dmytryk *Prod* Joseph E. Levine *Scr* John Michael Hayes *Ph* Joseph MacDonald *Ed* Frank Bracht *Mus* Elmer Bernstein *Art Dir* Hal Pereira, Walter Tyler
● George Peppard, Alan Ladd, Bob Cummings, Martha Hyer, Elizabeth Ashley, Carroll Baker (Paramount)

Joseph E. Levine's screen version of *The Carpetbaggers* is lusty, vulgar and gusty and, on one notable occasion, painfully brutal.

The story of a ruthless, emotionally unstable chemical-aircraft-film tycoon is told in vague, often lurching manner in the scenario out of Harold Robbins' tome. The career of the 'hero' – a heel in fact – is traced sketchily from the point at which he succeeds his just-deceased father (whom he detests) in business to the phase in which he manages to pull himself together emotionally after an unbroken string of brutally cold-blooded dealings, business and personal.

George Peppard growls and glowers his way through the pivotal role, wearing one basic expression – a surly, like-it-or-lump-it look – but there is an underlying animal magnetism to this performance. The late Alan Ladd limns with conviction one of the few appealing characters – the cowboy star who ultimately restores Peppard to his senses. Carroll Baker has the flashy role of a Harlowesque sexpot, and makes the most of it.

· ·

■ CARRIE

1952, 118 MINS, US ⓥ

Dir William Wyler *Prod* William Wyler *Scr* Ruth Goetz, Augustus Goetz *Ph* Victor Milner *Ed* Robert Swink *Mus* David Raksin *Art Dir* Hal Pereira, Roland Anderson
● Laurence Olivier, Jennifer Jones, Eddie Albert, Miriam Hopkins, Basil Ruysdael, Ray Teal (Paramount)

Theodore Dreiser's novel of another era, *Sister Carrie*, has been given a literal adaptation for films and the result is a sometimes mawkish, frequently dated drama. As just plain *Carrie*, with such stars as Jennifer Jones and Laurence Olivier, it is a somber, low-key entertainment.

Carrie is the turn-of-the-century story of the small-town girl who goes to Chicago to make good. It is the story of her meeting a traveling salesman and of how he becomes her 'benefactor'. The big love of her life, however, is the manager of a swank restaurant whom she meets while living with the salesman.

Jones gives one of the bright performances of her career. For Olivier, it is a role that gives him little opportunity for shading or dramatic intensity. Eddie Albert is excellent as the traveling salesman.

· ·

■ CARRIE

1976, 97 MINS, US ◇ ⓥ

Dir Brian De Palma *Prod* Paul Monash *Scr* Lawrence D. Cohen *Ph* Mario Tosi *Ed* Paul Hirsch *Mus* Pino Donaggio *Art Dir* William Kenny, Jack Fisk
● Sissy Spacek, Piper Laurie, Amy Irving, William Katt, John Travolta, Nancy Allen (United Artists)

Carrie is a modest but effective shock-suspense drama about a pubescent girl, her evangelical mother and cruel schoolmates.

Stephen King's novel, adapted by Lawrence D. Cohen, combines in unusual fashion a lot of offbeat story angles. Sissy Spacek heads cast in title role of an ugly duckling type schoolgirl.

Nancy Allen and other classmates, who normally berate her anyway, really go to town on the girl, until gym teacher Betty Buckley comes to her rescue.

At home, Carrie's mother is a dried-up, abandoned wife-turned-religious freak, played superbly by Piper Laurie, which explains in part the girl's ignorance. At the same time, Carrie discovers that, with intense concentration, she can make physical objects move.

· ·

■ CARRINGTON V.C.

1954, 105 MINS, UK ⓥ

Dir Anthony Asquith *Prod* Teddy Baird *Scr* John Hunter *Ph* Desmond Dickinson *Ed* Ralph Kemplen *Art Dir* Wilfrid Shingleton
● David Niven, Margaret Leighton, Noelle Middleton, Laurence Naismith, Clive Morton, Mark Dignam (British Lion/Remus)

Carrington V.C. by Dorothy and Campbell Christie, made a definite impact on the West End scene as a subject of dramatic intensity. In its translation to the screen, the drama loses none of the basic qualities.

The plot focusses on the title character, a wartime hero who has the routine job of commanding an artillery battery in peacetime. It's so secret that he is constantly feuding with his regimental commander, is in serious financial difficulties and is harassed by a wife who is desperately clamoring for money.

The army authorities owe him a substantial sum on his expense account, but this cash is not forthcoming. And in a moment of crisis, he helps himself to army funds 'to advertise a grievance'. His commander orders a court-martial and the main incident of the pic is concerned with this trial.

David Niven gives one of his best performances in recent times as the accused V.C. Some of his courtroom exchanges are dramatic high-spots of the plot.

· ·

■ CARRY ON CLEO

1964, 92 MINS, US ◇ ⓥ

Dir Gerald Thomas *Prod* Peter Rogers *Scr* Talbot Rothwell *Ph* Alan Hume *Ed* Archie Ludski *Mus* Eric Rogers *Art Dir* Bert Davey
● Sidney James, Kenneth Williams, Kenneth Connor, Charles Hawtrey, Joan Sims, Amanda Barrie (Anglo Amalgamated)

Intended as a parody of the expensive *Cleopatra*, this entry from the *Carry On* stables relies on the bludgeon rather than the rapier, so isn't entirely successful in its purpose.

Accent in this frolic is less on situation than on dialog and so there is less action to hold the audience. Talbot Rothwell's dialog is unabashedly corny but this doesn't much matter. But it is also unusually bristling with plodding double entendres. Gags, both verbal and visual, suffer from repetition and few are as neat as Julius Caesar's woeful complaint, 'Infamy! Infamy! Everybody's got it in for me!'

The practised cast of Old Regulars are also, mainly, up to form, with Sidney James as Mark Anthony and Kenneth Connor as Hengist the Wheelmaker particularly prominent as they disport among the vestal virgins. Kenneth Williams has a few twittering moments as Caesar but again irritatingly overplays. Charles Hawtrey's main function is to look incongruous and carry the weight of some of the least subtle sex patter.

On the femme side, Joan Sims is a hearty gal as Caesar's wife, Sheila Hancock is a shrill one as Hengist's spouse. Best discovery is Amanda Barrie as the poor man's Cleopatra. Her takeoff of the Queen of the Nile gets nearer to the tongue-in-cheek sense of what filmmakers were aiming at than any of her more experienced colleagues.

· ·

■ CARRY ON DOCTOR

1968, 95 MINS, UK ◇ ⓥ

Dir Gerald Thomas *Prod* Peter Rogers *Scr* Talbot Rothwell *Ph* Alan Hume *Ed* Alfred Roome *Mus* Eric Rogers
● Frankie Howerd, Sidney James, Kenneth Williams, Charles Hawtrey, Jim Dale, Barbara Windsor (Rank)

Usual unabashed mixture of double meanings, down-to-earth vulgarity, blue jokes about hypodermic syringes, etc., and slapstick situations. This time the Carry On team returns to hospital life for its farcical goings-on.

Inevitably, the gags and situations waver in comic impact but the general effect is artless yocks in which audience participation is carried to fullest extent, in that part of the fun is anticipating the verbal and physical jokes.

Added zest is given by the inclusion of Frankie Howerd as a quack 'mind-over-matter' doctor who becomes a reluctant patient. Howerd's brilliantly droll sense of comedy is given plenty of scope.

Among the grotesque patients are Sidney James, very funny as a cheerful malingerer; Bernard Bresslaw, Charles Hawtrey (more subdued than usual) and Peter Butterworth. The hospital staff is equally energetic and resourceful in providing simple-minded yocks, with Kenneth Williams as a supercilious chief physician.

■ CARRY ON SPYING

1964, 87 MINS, UK

Dir Gerald Thomas *Prod* Peter Rogers *Scr* Talbot Rothwell, Sid Colin *Ph* Alan Hume *Ed* Archie Ludski *Mus* Eric Rogers *Art Dir* Alex Vetchinsky
● Kenneth Williams, Bernard Cribbins, Charles Hawtrey, Barbara Windsor, Eric Pohlmann, Eric Barker (Anglo Amalgamated)

The Society for Total Extinction of Non-Conforming Humans (STENCH for short) has grabbed a secret formula and the British Operational Security Headquarters (BOSH in brief) tackles the job of getting back Formula X and outwitting its arch enemy, Doctor Crow. Through shortage of personnel, the assignment is handed to Simkins (Kenneth Williams), an agent in charge of training new spies, and three of his pupils.

Best knockabout sequences take place on the Orient Express, in a Viennese restaurant, a murky quarter of the Casbah and in the Automatum Plant where the inept foursome nearly come to a sticky end, but are rescued by good luck and the intervention of a beautiful spy.

Kenneth Williams' brand of camp comedy, while very funny in smallish doses, can pall when he has a lengthy chore as here. But Bernard Cribbins brings some useful virility to his fatuous role, Charles Hawtrey contributes his now familiar performance as the guileless one and Barbara Windsor proves a well-upholstered and perky heroine as the girl spy with a photogenic memory.

■ CARRY ON, SERGEANT

1958, 85 MINS, UK

Dir Gerald Thomas *Prod* Peter Rogers *Scr* Norman Hudis *Ph* Peter Hennessy *Ed* Peter Boita *Mus* Bruce Montgomery *Art Dir* Alex Vetchinsky
● William Hartnell, Bob Monkhouse, Shirley Eaton, Eric Barker, Dora Bryan, Kenneth Connor (Anglo Amalgamated)

Carry On Sergeant is an army farce [from a story by R.F. Delderfield, *The Bull Boys*] exploiting practically every army gag, but while some of the writing is careless and there is no attempt to develop a reasonable story, it is by no means sloppily produced.

William Hartnell is a training sergeant who is about to retire from the service and has one more chance to fulfill his life ambition, which is to train the champion troop of the intake. Moreover, he has a $140 bet on the outcome. He is handed a bunch of rookies which is believable only in farce. The barrack-room attorney, the young man in love, the hypochondriac malingerer, the man always out of step . . . in fact, the repertory company of

trainees. There's the sergeant with the bark, the fussy officer.

Kenneth Connor steals most of the honors as the hypochondriac being chased by a love-starved army waitress, played characteristically by Dora Bryan. He has a shade too much to do, but never misses a trick. Bob Monkhouse, called up on his wedding day, Shirley Eaton as his frustrated wife who crops up in camp, Eric Barker as a fussy officer, William Hartnell as the gravelly-voiced sergeant and Bill Owen as his faithful corporal add their quota.

■ CARS THAT ATE PARIS, THE

1974, 91 MINS, AUSTRALIA ◇ ▽

Dir Peter Weir *Prod* Jim McElroy, Howard McElroy *Scr* Peter Weir, Keith Gow, Piers Daries *Ph* John McLean *Ed* Wayne LeClos *Mus* Bruce Smeaton
● Terry Camilleri, John Meillon, Melissa Jaffa, Kevin Miles, Max Gillies, Peter Armstrong
(Australian Film Development/Royce Smeal)

Paris is a tiny Australian township with a surprising number of car accidents on its outskirts. Involved in one is Arthur, whose brother, driving a caravan-towing car, is killed.

Gradually it becomes evident that the car accidents are planned affairs. As each one occurs the townspeople swoop like vultures on the cars and retrieve any personal effects for themselves, whilst the doctor carries out strange experiments of his own upon the victims.

Attempting to preserve an air of normality, the mayor orders a scheduled dance to take place, which becomes macabre when the doctor brings his patients along.

Much of the pic is brilliant, although it does not always seem certain of the direction it is taking. At first it seems satirical, then black comedy, degenerating into a thriller.

■ CARVE HER NAME WITH PRIDE

1958, 119 MINS, UK ▽

Dir Lewis Gilbert *Prod* Daniel M. Angel *Scr* Vernon Harris, Lewis Gilbert *Ph* John Wilcox *Ed* John Shirley *Mus* William Alwyn *Art Dir* Bernard Robinson
● Virginia McKenna, Paul Scofield, Jack Warner, Denise Grey, Alain Saury, Maurice Ronet (Rank)

The film pays tribute to the real life exploits of Violette Szabo, a beautiful young woman who became a British cloak-and-dagger agent in France and won a posthumous George Cross after being tortured and executed in Ravensbruck Camp. Part of the pic's attraction is its lack of hysteria. It keeps resolutely to the facts [from a book by R.J. Minney] and refuses to allow the espionage and torture sequences to go past the bounds of credulity.

Virginia McKenna is topnotch. She runs the gamut of humor, charm and toughness. By skillful playing and equally skillful makeup, McKenna's ordeal is expertly revealed. Paul Schofield, as the officer colleague who falls in love with his gallant young comrade, and Alain Saury, as her young husband; Jack Warner and Denise Grey, as her stolid middle-aged parents; Bill Owen, a standout as McKenna's sergeant instructor, all contribute admirably to the thesping.

■ CAR WASH

1976, 97 MINS, US ◇ ▽

Dir Michael Schultz *Prod* Art Linson, Gary Stromberg *Scr* Joe Schumacher *Ph* Frank Stanley *Ed* Christopher Holmes *Mus* Norman Whitfield *Art Dir* Robert Clatworthy
● Franklyn Ajaye, Sully Boyar, Richard Brestoff, George Carlin, Irwin Corey, Ivan Dixon (Universal

Car Wash uses gritty humor to polish clean the souls of a lot of likeable street people.

The setting is Sully Boyar's downtown car wash, where the colorful ethnic crew contends as much with oddball customers as with themselves.

Perhaps the best known of the players is Richard Pryor, shining it on as a fancy-dressed preacher, complete with flashy car and retinue that includes The Pointer Sisters. Pryor's license plate spells out 'tithe', a sure evocation of the real-life character he suggests.

Woven into the main proceedings is the lonely sidewalk vigil of a streetwalker, Lauren Jones, which, combined with Bill Duke's equally sensitive portrayal of a frightened black militant, keeps the film in fine balance of humanism.

■ CASABLANCA

1942, 99 MINS, US

Dir Michael Curtiz *Prod* Hal B. Wallis *Scr* Julius J. Epstein, Philip G. Epstein, Howard Koch *Ph* Arthur Edeson *Ed* Owen Marks *Mus* Max Steiner *Art Dir* Carl Jules Weyl
● Humphrey Bogart, Ingrid Bergman, Paul Henreid, Claude Rains, Conrad Veidt, Sydney Greenstreet (Warner)

Although the title and Humphrey Bogart's name convey the impression of high adventure rather than romance, there's plenty of the latter. Adventure is there, too, but it's more as exciting background to the Bogart-Ingrid Bergman heart department. Bogart, incidentally, as a tender lover (in addition to being a cold-as-ice nitery operator) is a novel characterization.

Casablanca is pictured as a superficially gay town to which flee the monied refugees from Axis terror. There they await visas to Lisbon and then transportation to the United States. The waits are frequently interminable while arrangements for papers are being made with corrupt Vichy officials and the wealthy help to allay their impatience with chemin-de-fer and other games at Rick's. Rick is Bogart, who has opened his fancy joint after being 'jilted' by Bergman in Paris.

Bergman turns up one evening with her husband (Paul Henreid) whom she thought was dead during the period of her romance with Bogart. Henreid is leader of the underground in Europe and it is vital that he get to America. Bogart has two visas that will do the trick and the choice is between going off himself with Bergman – their torch still aflame – or sending her off with Henreid, who can do so much for the United Nations cause.

Bogart, as might be expected, is more at ease as the bitter and cynical operator of a joint than as a lover, but handles both assignments with superb finesse. Bergman, in a torn-between-love-and-duty role, lives up to her reputation as a fine actress. Henreid is well cast and does an excellent job too.

Superb is the lineup of lesser players. Some of the characterizations are a bit on the overdone side, but each is a memorable addition to the whole [adapted from the play *Everybody Comes to Rick's* by Murray Burnett and Joan Alison].
☐ 1943: Best Picture

■ CASINO ROYALE

1967, 131 MINS, UK ◇ ▽

Dir John Huston, Ken Hughes, Val Guest, Robert Parrish, Joe McGrath *Prod* Charles K. Feldman, Jerry Bresler *Scr* Wolf Mankowitz, John Law, Michael Sayers *Ph* Jack Hildyard *Ed* Bill Lenny *Mus* Burt Bacharach *Art Dir* Michael Stringer
● Peter Sellers, Ursula Andress, David Niven, Orson Welles, Woody Allen, William Holden (Columbia/Famous Artists)

Wacky comedy extravaganza, *Casino Royale* is an attempt to spoof the pants off James Bond. The $12 million film is a conglomeration of frenzied situations, gags and special effects, lacking discipline and cohesion. Some of the situations are very funny, but many are too strained.

Based freely on Ian Fleming's novel, the story line defies sane description. Sufficient to say that the original James Bond (David Niven), now knighted and living in eccentric retirement, is persuaded back into the Secret Service to help cope with a disastrous situation.

Niven seems justifiably bewildered by the proceedings, but he has a neat delivery of throwaway lines and enters into the exuberant physical action with pleasant blandness. Peter Sellers has some amusing gags as the gambler, the chance of dressing up in various guises and a neat near-seduction scene with Ursula Andress.

....

■ **CASS TIMBERLANE**

1947, 119 MINS, US

Dir George Sidney   *Prod* Arthur Hornblow Jr
Scr Donald Ogden Stewart   *Ph* Robert Planck
Ed John Dunning   *Mus* Roy Webb   *Art Dir* Cedric Gibbons, Daniel B. Cathcart
● Spencer Tracy, Lana Turner, Zachary Scott, Tom Drake, Mary Astor (M-G-M)

Metro has accomplished a highly successful translation to the screen of Sinclair Lewis' bookstore boff. Lana Turner is the surprise of the picture via her top performance thespically. In a role that allows her the gamut from tomboy to the pangs of childbirth and from being another man's woman to remorseful wife, she seldom fails to acquit herself creditably. Spencer Tracy, as a matter of fact, is made to look wooden by comparison.

What fault the picture has is its overlong running time. Director George Sidney is unable to hold the pace for two hours and the film lags in the midsection.

This is a love story all the way. Essentially, it's the tenderness of an older man – 41, not too old, of course – for a young girl. Tracy, respected small-town judge, pays tender court to Turner, who's strictly out of his class socially as well as chronologically, until he wins her. She adapts herself to local society and the new life until she thinks she can stand it no more and then is off with the husband's best-friend, Zachary Scott. Scott, of course, doesn't want her when he can have her.

Tracy's meeting and early courting of the gal is difficult to accept, but once that's passed, the only misgiving is that the yarn telegraphs its punches so far ahead.

....

■ **CASSANDRA CROSSING, THE**

1977, 126 MINS, US ◇ ⓥ

Dir George P. Cosmatos   *Prod* Carlo Ponti   *Scr* Tom Mankiewicz, Robert Katz   *Ph* Ennio Guarnieri
Ed Francois Bonnot, Roberto Silvi   *Mus* Jerry Goldsmith   *Art Dir* Aurelio Crugnola
● Sophia Loren, Richard Harris, Ava Gardner, Burt Lancaster, Martin Sheen, Ingrid Thulin (Associated General)

The Cassandra Crossing is a tired, hokey and sometimes unintentionally funny disaster film in which a trainload of disease-exposed passengers lurch to their fate.

One is asked to accept the premise that a terrorist bomber, accidentally exposed to some awesome plague, spreads the disease aboard a European express train. Mismatched leading players, all play directly to the camera, for themselves only, without betraying a hint of belief in their script.

While Richard Harris, cast as a brilliant doctor, is active among those posturing leads

on the train, Burt Lancaster and Ingrid Thulin hold down a command post where desperate efforts are made to isolate the train from the rest of civilization.

....

■ **CAST A GIANT SHADOW**

1966, 144 MINS, US ◇

Dir Melville Shavelson   *Prod* Melville Shavelson, Michael Wayne   *Scr* Melville Shavelson   *Ph* Aldo Tonti   *Ed* Bert Bates, Gene Ruggiero   *Mus* Elmer Bernstein   *Art Dir* Michael Stringer
● Kirk Douglas, Senta Berger, Angie Dickinson, Frank Sinatra, Yul Brynner, John Wayne (Mirisch/Llenroc/Batjac)

Cast a Giant Shadow exemplifies the problems in contemporary film biography, particularly when the subject is less well known than the events which brought him honor. Some complete fiction and fuzzy composites melodramatize the career of an American Jew who assisted in the fight for the creation of the State of Israel.

Story concerns Col David ('Mickey') Marcus, West Point grad, NY lawyer and cop, and participant in many facets of World War II, who, in the late 1940s, is recruited to volunteer military help in the establishment of Israel, at that time still a dream subject to United Nations equivocation, militant Arab threats and uncertain world support.

Kirk Douglas stars as Marcus in a very good portrayal of a likeable, adventurous soldier-of-fortune who cannot get used to domestic inactivity even when wife Angie Dickinson is sitting by the hearth.

Unfortunately for the overall impact of the film, it is found necessary to go into World War II flashbacks to establish the Marcus character. John Wayne, in one of three featured special appearances, is a composite of every superior officer under whom Marcus served in those days.

....

■ **CASTAWAY**

1987, 118 MINS, UK ◇ ⓥ

Dir Nicolas Roeg   *Prod* Rick McCallum   *Scr* Allan Scott   *Ph* Harvey Harrison   *Ed* Tony Lawson
Mus Stanley Myers   *Art Dir* Andrew Sanders
● Oliver Reed, Amanda Donohoe, Georgina Hale, Frances Barber (Cannon/United British Artists)

Picture this: London is cold, wet and miserable. What else does a girl do but answer an ad from a man looking for a 'wife' to take to a tropical island for a year?

Newcomer Amanda Donohoe spends most of the pic displaying the absence of bikini marks on her body (palm trees always seem to obscure the vital parts of Oliver Reed as Gerald Kingsland), and she copes well with a character whose motives and methods for going to the tiny desert island remain dubious.

Castaway is based on two nonfiction books – Lucy Irvine's version, also called *Castaway*, and Gerald Kingsland's *The Islander* – and tries to tread a path between the two conflicting versions of their sojourn.

Reed gives the performance of his career as a sexually frustrated middle-aged man in search of sun and sex, and is admirably complemented by Amanda Donohoe as the determined but fickle object of his lust.

Photography is excellent (especially underwater scenes) but though *Castaway* is a great ad for the tropical Seychelles, it won't be remembered as a Nicolas Roeg classic.

....

■ **CASTLE KEEP**

1969, 106 MINS, US ◇ ⓥ

Dir Sydney Pollack   *Prod* Martin Ransohoff
Scr Daniel Taradash, David Rayfiel   *Ph* Henri Decae
Ed Malcolm Cooke   *Mus* Michael Legrand
Art Dir Rino Mondellini

● Burt Lancaster, Patrick O'Neal, Jean-Pierre Aumont, Peter Falk, Scott Wilson (Columbia)

Film carries fast and savage action once the actual battle sequences are reached, but it's strictly a conversational war in footage leading up to these moments. Apparent efforts to insert a fresh side of war by concentrating on some of its grim humor act more as a deterrent than a booster to interest. Screenplay is based on William Eastlake's novel *Castle Keep*.

Burt Lancaster is a realistic, one-eyed major who leads a group of eight war-weary infantrymen come to occupy a Belgian castle in 1944 in the Ardennes Forest, which becomes a haven away from war for the men, who get up to all manner of frolics.

Lancaster enacts one of his fast-talking roles with a glib, almost tongue-in-cheek approach, and gets good mileage out of it. Patrick O'Neal as an art-loving captain out to save the treasures of the castle does a good job, as do Jean-Pierre Aumont and Peter Falk.

....

■ **CASUALTIES OF WAR**

1989, 113 MINS, US ◇ ⓥ

Dir Brian De Palma   *Prod* Art Linson, Fred Caruso
Scr David Rabe   *Ph* Stephen H. Burum   *Ed* Bill Pankow   *Mus* Ennio Morricone   *Art Dir* Wolf Kroeger
● Michael J. Fox, Sean Penn, Don Harvey, John C. Reilly, John Leguizamo, Thuy Thu Le (Columbia)

A powerful metaphor of the national shame that was America's orgy of destruction in Vietnam, Brian De Palma's film deals directly with the harrowing rape and murder of a Vietnamese woman by four GIs.

Journalist Daniel Lang's account of the actual 1966 atrocity first appeared in 1969 as a *New Yorker* article and was later reprinted in book form.

Screen newcomer Thuy Thu Le is the Vietnamese woman kidnapped by a reconnaissance patrol as what the deranged sergeant (Sean Penn) calls 'a little portable R&R to break up the boredom, keep up morale.' When the men are through using her sexually, they stab and shoot her to death, over the futile objections of the lone holdout, a 'cherry' private played by Michael J. Fox.

Casting Fox was a brilliant coup on De Palma's part, since he brings with him an image of all-American boyishness and eager-beaver conservatism. Fox's beautifully acted cowardly passivity in the face of the unthinkable challenges and implicates the viewer to examine his own conscience on the subject of Vietnam.

Wolf Kroeger's production design turns the Thailand locations into a convincing evocation of Vietnam's Central Highlands in 1966.

....

■ **CAT AND THE CANARY, THE**

1939, 72 MINS, US

Dir Elliott Nugent   *Prod* Arthur Hornblow Jr
Scr Walter De Leon, Lynn Starling   *Ph* Charles Lang
Ed Archie Marshek   *Mus* Ernst Toch   *Art Dir* Hans Dreier, Robert Usher
● Bob Hope, Paulette Goddard, John Beal, Douglass Montgomery, Gale Sondergaard (Paramount)

In *Canary* Bob Hope carries a straight dramatic characterization, with comedy quips and situations dropping into the plot naturally to accentuate the laughs.

Paulette Goddard gets her first co-star billing, displaying confidence and assurance in her role as the heir to the eccentric millionaire's fortune.

To provide chills and thrills, prospective heirs to the fortune assemble at the bayou home of the deceased 10 years after his death. Will is read, leaving estate to Goddard, when spooky manipulations start from strange

C

sources. There's the low key lighting, eerie music, and secret passages – all utilized to fullest extent to accentuate the chiller aspect of the piece. After three murders during the night, Hope solves the mystery – but only after Goddard has been placed in constant jeopardy.

Script [from the play by John Willard] is a well-knit and workmanlike job of writing.

....

■ CAT BALLOU

1965, 97 MINS, US ◇ ⓥ

Dir Elliot Silverstein *Prod* Harold Hecht *Scr* Walter Newman, Frank R. Pierson *Ph* Jack Marta *Ed* Charles Nelson *Mus* Frank DeVol
● Jane Fonda, Lee Marvin, Michael Callan, Dwayne Hickman, Nat 'King' Cole, Stubby Kaye (Columbia)

Cat Ballou spoofs the Old West, whose adherents take their likker neat, and emerges middlingly successful, sparked by an amusing way-out approach and some sparkling performances.

Cat is a girl – Jane Fonda – and she's a young lady (educated to be a schoolteacher) vendetta-minded in Wyoming of 1894 when town baddies murder her father for his ranch. She turns into a rootin', tootin', lovin' gun-lady, rounds up a gang of devoted followers and stages a train holdup, getting away with a payroll fortune, and holes up in the old Hole in the Wall outlaw lair.

Script juggles the elements of the Roy Chanslor novel producing a set of characters who fit the mood patly. A novel device has Stubby Kaye and Nat 'King' Cole as wandering minstrels of the early west, telling the story of the goings-on via a flock of spirited and tuneful songs composed by Mack David and Jerry Livingston.

Fonda delivers a lively interpretation as Cat. Lee Marvin doubles in brass, playing the gunman who shoots down her father and the legendary Kid Shelleen, a terror with the gun, whom she earlier called in to protect her father. In latter character, Marvin is the standout of the picture.

....

■ CAT CHASER

1989, 90 MINS, US ◇ ⓥ

Dir Abel Ferrara *Prod* Peter Davis, William Panzer *Scr* Elmore Leonard, Jim Borrelli, Alan Sharp *Ph* Anthony Richmond *Ed* Anthony Redman *Mus* Chick Corea *Art Dir* Dan Leigh
● Peter Weller, Kelly McGillis, Charles Durning, Frederic Forrest, Tomas Milian (Vestron/Whiskers)

Cat Chaser is another example of how difficult it is to transform a sharp and racy novel into a classy movie. Despite a fine cast and atmospheric direction by Abel Ferrara, the pic [from the novel by Elmore Leonard] doesn't quite make the grade, though it certainly is worth a look.

Peter Weller plays Miami hotel owner George Moran who fought during the American intervention of Santo Domingo. Years later he is drawn back to try and find the woman who taunted him with the name *Cat Chaser*.

He instead is joined by Mary (Kelly McGillis). Ensuing affair convinces Mary that she must end her marriage. Unfortunately she is married to Tomas Milian, former head of the Santo Domingo secret police, who has other thoughts on the matter.

Weller is fine as the intelligent, self-contained hero, but best of all is McGillis, seemingly relishing the part of a sexually charged femme fatale. Charles Durning, as always, gives the pic a dose of class, and manages to make his manipulative killer vaguely charming. Frederic Forrest, however, blusters badly and thankfully comes to a sticky end halfway through.

....

■ CATCH ME A SPY

1971, 94 MINS, UK/FRANCE ◇ ⓥ

Dir Dick Clement *Prod* Steven Pallos, Pierre Braunberger *Scr* Dick Clement, Ian Le Frenais *Ph* Christopher Challis *Ed* John Bloom *Mus* Claude Bolling
● Kirk Douglas, Marlene Jobert, Trevor Howard, Tom Courtenay, Patrick Mower, Bernadette Lafont (Ludgate/Pleiade/Capitole)

Catch Me a Spy is a straight-forward spy thriller. Gimmicks are out but the whole has been put over with tongue nicely in cheek and an impish sense of humor. The cast play their parts for all they are worth.

Kirk Douglas, a smuggler of literary works from Iron Curtain countries, is mistaken for a spy and gets involved in devious situations. Most are provided by Marlene Jobert who resides with a rakish British cabinet minister (Trevor Howard) and is games mistress at a boys' school. Tom Courtenay is the counter-espionage officer who is helplessly inept.

It is all highly improbable and involved but thanks to lively performances and Dick Clement's sharp direction, interest is continually held. The whole is climaxed with an exciting speedboat chase.

....

■ CATCHFIRE

1991, 98 MINS, US ◇ ⓥ

Dir Alan Smithee [=Dennis Hopper] *Prod* Dick Clark, Dan Paulson *Scr* Rachel Kronstadt Mann, Ann Louise Bardach *Ph* Ed Lachman *Ed* David Rawlins *Mus* Curt Sobel *Art Dir* Ron Foreman
● Dennis Hopper, Jodie Foster, Dean Stockwell, Vincent Price, Fred Ward, Joe Pesci (Vestron/Precision/Mack-Taylor/Clark)

A quirky comedy-thriller about a hitman who falls for his femme target, scrambled pic [story by Rachel Kronstadt Mann] has an LA artiste (Jodie Foster) accidentally witnessing a mob killing when her car breaks down one night. The cops (Fred Ward, Sy Richardson) want her to talk, and the hoods (Joe Pesci, Dean Stockwell, Vincent Price) want her dead. So she dons a blond wig and an alias and goes AWOL.

Meanwhile, Pesci hires a top-league hitman (Dennis Hopper) to do the job his own goons can't, and after months of tracking her around the States finally runs her aground in an ad agency.

Hopper 'kidnaps' his quarry, possesses her for himself, and the dynamic duo set of on a weird road-movie-to-nowhere, with the mob and the law in hot pursuit.

Somewhere in here is a dark, sassy picture, but final product is more like a jigsaw with half the pieces. Pic was lensed in LA, Seattle and Taos, NM, in summer 1988 under Hopper's direction and the title *Backtrack*. After postproduction squabbles (reportedly over Hopper's three-hour cut), he opted for the Director's Guild of America moniker 'Alan Smithee'.

Apart from Foster, who's strong, shrewd and sexy, thesping is vaudeville all the way. Pesci rants and raves, Stockwell shows a nice line in low-key comedy, Ward looks like he hasn't been shown the whole script, and Hopper has a go at Humphrey Bogart in shades.

....

■ CATCH-22

1970, 121 MINS, US ◇ ⓥ

Dir Mike Nichols *Prod* John Calley *Scr* Buck Henry *Ph* David Watkin *Ed* Sam O'Steen *Art Dir* Richard Sylbert
● Alan Arkin, Martin Balsam, Richard Benjamin, Arthur Garfunkel, Jack Gilford, Buck Henry (Paramount/Filmways)

Catch 22 stumbles its way through distended burlesque, and contrived stylism to its

ultimate root theme: antisocial nihilism.

Alan Arkin heads a large cast of familiar names, playing characters scooped from Joseph Heller's famed novel by adapter Buck Henry. Low, cheap comedy mingles nervously with slick, high-fashion technical polish in a slow-boiling stew of specious philosophy and superficial characterization.

A technical filmmaking brilliance plus a few effective low-comedy gags constitute the pic's assets. Its major liabilities are the script and the directorial concept.

Arkin is Capt Yossarian, the generally reactive character who perceives all the sham and hypocrisy around him; befuddled laundry officer Bob Newhart, elevated to bewildering status as a squadron leader; urbane operations officer Richard Benjamin; simpering medic Jack Gilford; hard-boiled, sex-teasing nurse Paula Prentiss; and Norman Fell, as the good-ole-sarge type.

....

■ CAT FROM OUTER SPACE, THE

1978, 103 MINS, US ◇ ⓥ

Dir Norman Tokar *Prod* Ron Miller, Norman Tokar *Scr* Ted Key *Ph* Charles F. Wheeler *Ed* Cotton Warburton *Mus* Lalo Schifrin *Art Dir* John B. Mansridge
● Ken Berry, Sandy Duncan, Harry Morgan, Roddy McDowall, McLean Stevenson, Jesse White (Walt Disney)

Cartoonist Ted Key turns to noodling over a spaceship commanded by a cat, forced to land on earth for emergency repairs. For help, the cat turns to a likeable physicist, Ken Berry, to help him get $120,000 in gold needed to repair his saucer in time to rendezvous with the space fleet.

Before long, Berry's girlfriend Sandy Duncan and buddy McLean Stevenson are in on the problem and planning to parlay the cat's extra-terrestrial powers into a series of winning bets with bookie Jesse White. But veterinarian Alan Young mistakenly puts pussy to sleep in the middle of the wagering.

The fun, as usual with Disney pix, comes in the believable sight gags provided along the way. Also as usual, it's a good cast of veterans and nothing to tax them beyond their abilities, all ably kept in pace by director Norman Tokar.

....

■ CATHERINE THE GREAT

1934, 95 MINS, UK

Dir Paul Czinner *Prod* Alexander Korda *Scr* Marjorie Deans, Arthur Wimperis, Lajos Biro, Melchior Lengyel *Ph* Georges Perinal *Ed* Stephen Harrison *Mus* Muir Mathieson (dir.) *Art Dir* Vincent Korda
● Douglas Fairbanks Jr, Elisabeth Bergner, Flora Robson, Gerald du Maurier, Irene Vanbrugh, Joan Gardner (London/United Artists)

A nice rather than a good-looking girl, with beautiful eyes, Elisabeth Bergner charms as she progresses and is altogether believable as the minor German princess of moderate circumstances summoned to Russia by the Empress Elizabeth to wed her erratic nephew, the Grand Duke Peter, sometimes called Peter the Impossible. The throne needs an heir.

Theatrical license has been liberally taken. This story makes the marriage the culmination of the blue-blooded Cinderella's childhood dream and almost places her upon the throne despite herself, except that she rises to meet the obligation upon realizing how unequipped her dissolute husband is to meet the responsibility.

Bergner's scene with the dying empress (Flora Robson) is a gem of expert playing by both women and there are other highlight sequences, particularly a banquet, which stand out for direction, portrayal and dialog. The story is principally in the hands of Bergner, Robson and Douglas Fairbanks. Robson gives a fine performance, while Fairbanks' definition of the fuming Peter is one of the best he has ever done.

Catherine is reported to have cost close to $400,000 which, for England, is the theoretical equivalent of a $1 million Hollywood effort. It is certainly one of the most expensive pictures ever made there.

■ CATHY'S CHILD

1979, 89 MINS, AUSTRALIA ◇

Dir Donald Crombie   *Prod* Pom Oliver, Errol Sullivan   *Scr* Ken Quinnell   *Ph* Gary Hansen   *Ed* Tim Wellburn   *Art Dir* Ross Major

● Michelle Fawdon, Alan Cassell, Bryan Brown, Harry Michael, Anna Hruby, Bob Hughes (CB Films)

Cathy's Child is based on a true story [and the book by Dick Wordley] in which a young Greek mother living in Sydney had her three-year-old daughter abducted by the child's father who returned to Greece with it. The incident was made into a cause celebre by one of the local afternoon newspapers whose reporters turned the spotlight on bureaucracy's mishandling of the situation.

Michelle Fawdon turns in a super performance as the young migrant mother. To her aid comes battered old pro journalist Wordley (Alan Cassell) who with the help of his tough young city editor forces the story onto the front page. Bryan Brown is standout as the embittered editor who some years before had been through a similar experience.

Production values are excellent for the budget of less than $800,000, with shooting on location in Greece and in the Sydney area. Pic has an undeniable aura of soap opera; but that is no put down in this case since director Donald Crombie and the players keep interest up even though it's clear there'll be a happy ending come fadeout.

■ CAT ON A HOT TIN ROOF

1958, 108 MINS, US ◇ Ⓥ

Dir Richard Brooks   *Prod* Lawrence Weingarten   *Scr* Richard Brooks, James Poe   *Ph* William Daniels   *Ed* Ferris Webster   *Art Dir* William A. Horning, Urie McCleary

● Elizabeth Taylor, Paul Newman, Burl Ives, Jack Carson, Judith Anderson, Madeleine Sherwood (M-G-M/Avon)

Cat on a Hot Tin Roof is an intense, important motion picture. By no means is this a watered-down version, though 'immature dependence' has replaced any hint of homosexuality. Motivations remain psychologically sound.

Cat, per Tennessee Williams, is set in the South, but the land is not as decadent as he has so often pictured it. The earth is fertile, the plantation is large and Big Daddy's wealth now amounts to $10 million. Burl Ives, playing Big Daddy, unknowingly is dying of cancer, and his first son (Jack Carson) is out for more than his share of the estate. He and his obnoxious wife (Madeleine Sherwood) make capital of the problems besetting Big Daddy's favorite son (Paul Newman) and his wife (Elizabeth Taylor), he being a drunk and she being childless. It's an often gruesome, often amusing battle.

Taylor has a major credit with her portrayal of Maggie. The frustrations and desires, both as a person and a woman, the warmth and understanding she molds, the loveliness that is more than a well-turned nose – all these are part of a well-accented, perceptive interpretation.

Newman plays cynical underacting against highly developed action. His command of the articulate, sensitive sequences is unmistakable, and the way he mirrors his feelings is

basic to every scene. Ives, repeating his legit role, is a vibrant and convincing plantation king.

□ 1958: Best Picture (Nomination)

■ CAT PEOPLE

1942, 73 MINS, US Ⓥ

Dir Jacques Tourneur   *Prod* Val Lewton   *Scr* DeWitt Bodeen   *Ph* Nicholas Musuraca   *Ed* Mark Robson   *Mus* Roy Webb

● Simone Simon, Kent Smith, Tom Conway, Jane Randolph, Jack Holt, Alan Napier (RKO)

This is a weird drama of thrill-chill caliber, with developments of surprises confined to psychology and mental reactions, rather than transformation to grotesque and marauding characters for visual impact on the audiences. Picture is well-made on moderate budget outlay.

Story is one of those it-might-happen dramas, if an old Serbian legend be true. Fable has it that women descendants of a certain tribe, when projected into a jealous rage, change into panthers or other members of the cat family for attack, later reverting to human form.

Script, although hazy for the average audience in several instances, carries sufficient punch in the melodramatic sequences to hold it together in good style. Picture is first feature directed by Jacques Tourneur. He does a fine job with a most difficult assignment.

■ CAT PEOPLE

1982, 118 MINS, US ◇ Ⓥ

Dir Paul Schrader   *Prod* Charles Fries   *Scr* Alan Ormsby   *Ph* John Bailey   *Ed* Bud Smith   *Mus* Giorgio Moroder, David Bowie   *Art Dir* Edward Richardson

● Nastassja Kinski, Malcolm McDowell, John Heard, Annette O'Toole, Ruby Dee, Ed Begley Jr (RKO-Universal)

Paul Schrader's reworking of the 1942 Val Lewton-Jacques Tourneur *Cat People* is a super-chic erotic horror story of mixed impact.

DeWitt Bodeen's original story held that there is a breed of people descended from ancient coupling of women with big cats, and that when one of their number engages in sex, he or she physically reverts to the animalistic state and must kill before becoming human again. It is therefore 'safe' to mate only with relatives.

Reunited in New Orleans with her long-lost brother Malcolm McDowell, Nastassja Kinski meets zoo curator John Heard, takes a job there and soon moves into his home.

At the same time, the Louisiana community is being terrorized by a big black panther. Having repressed her sexuality for a long time, Kinski finally gives in to the genuine love of Heard and condemns herself to repeat the pattern of her brother and ancestors.

Kinski was essential to the film as conceived, and she's endlessly watchable.

■ CAT'S EYE

1985, 93 MINS, US ◇ Ⓥ

Dir Lewis Teague   *Prod* Martha J. Schumacher   *Scr* Stephen King   *Ph* Jack Cardiff   *Ed* Scott Conrad   *Mus* Alan Silvestri   *Art Dir* Giorgio Postiglione

● Drew Barrymore, James Woods, Alan King, Kenneth McMillan, Robert Hays, Candy Clark (De Laurentiis)

The idea for this three-parter was hatched during Dino De Laurentiis' production of King's *Firestarter*, which also starred little Drew Barrymore. Asked to do another script for Barrymore, King sketched out an idea about a cat who protects a young girl from a threatening troll in her bedroom wall.

Unfortunately, that idea got tacked onto

two other King short stories that De Laurentiis had film rights to, *Quitters, Inc.* and *The Ledge*, lighting the fuse for the ultimate bomb.

The three stories just don't connect and efforts to join them never work. However, an excellent roster of talent does try its best.

■ CATTLE ANNIE AND LITTLE BRITCHES

1981, 79 MINS, US ◇

Dir Lamont Johnson   *Prod* Rupert Mitzig, Alan King   *Scr* David Eyre, Robert Ward   *Ph* Larry Pizer   *Ed* William Haugse   *Mus* Sanh Berti   *Art Dir* Stan Jolley

● Burt Lancaster, John Savage, Rod Steiger, Scott Glenn, Amanda Plummer, Diane Lane (Universal)

'*Cattle Annie and Little Britches*' is as cutesy and unmemorable as its title. Primary focus falls upon two teenaged girls, the gutsy and rather reckless Amanda Plummer and the more demure Diane Lane, who aspire to become what might be called outlaw groupies.

They get their chance when the Doolin-Dalton gang, headed up by an aging but still vigorous Burt Lancaster, rides into town, Plummer taking up with dashing John Savage and Lane coming under the fatherly wing of Lancaster himself.

The girls more or less get lost in the shuffle, however, during the central stretch of the film, which has Lancaster and his roaming bank robbers pursued by determined lawman Rod Steiger. Story's only potential resonance rests in the mutual respect-hate relationship between these two veterans of the range.

In fact, whole film [from the novel by Robert Ward] washes over the viewer, with no images or moments sticking in the mind. Effect is partially due to director Lamont Johnson's exceedingly distanced visual style.

■ CAUGHT

1949, 88 MINS, US Ⓥ

Dir Max Ophuls   *Prod* Wolfgang Reinhardt   *Scr* Arthur Laurents   *Ph* Lee Garmes   *Ed* Robert Parrish   *Mus* Frederick Hollander

● James Mason, Barbara Bel Geddes, Robert Ryan, Ruth Brady, Curt Bois, Art Smith (Enterprise/M-G-M)

Caught is an out-and-out soap opera on film. The performances are topnotch and consistent. So is the direction and physical production dressing. Where film falls down is in the rather ordinary story [from the novel *Wild Calendar* by Libbie Block] that doesn't take to the twists introduced in an effort to lift it above romantic pulp fiction.

It's the saga of the carhop who aspires to marry a millionaire. She goes to a charm school, becomes a model, and meets and marries her man. A life of riches isn't everything, so she gives it up, goes to work in the office of an East Side medico. They fall in love.

The millionaire is better developed than usual in this type story. He's a tall, dark man of many business interests, odd hours, playboy tendencies and a reluctance to wedlock. Robert Ryan plays him to the hilt.

The shopgirl as played by Barbara Bel Geddes is more rounded and without the empty-headedness such characters usually display. James Mason gives an impressive, underplayed characterization to a not too impressive role.

■ CAVALCADE

1933, 110 MINS, US

Dir Frank Lloyd   *Prod* Winfield Sheehan   *Scr* Reginald Berkeley, Sonya Levien   *Ph* Ernest Palmer   *Ed* Margaret Clancy   *Mus* Louis de Francesco (dir.)

● Clive Brook, Diana Wynyard, Herbert Mundin, Una O'Connor, Ursula Jeans, Beryl Mercer (Fox)

Noel Coward concocted the original stage

C

pageant the film was made from. In that London production it was all Coward. In the filmization Coward steps somewhat into the background.

Very good performances by almost the entire cast, especially the acting job by Diana Wynyard. But above everything recurs the unison and tenseness created by W.R. Sheehan as producer, and Frank Lloyd as director.

Coward's pageant begins at the birth of the 20th century and the beginning of the Boer War. From that it swells along on through three decades, up and through the World War, and to today. Nothing of world importance is lost sight of, including the sinking of the *Titanic*. And through it all is a strong, wistful story of the growth of a family, and the clinging through years of a loving couple.

The first couple of reels, from an American standpoint, at least, seem slow. The establishment of Jane and Robert Marryot (Wynyard and Clive Brook) as the family who are to be watched through 30 years, is a bit slow of development. The first thrill comes at the sailing of the troop ship for Africa.

Then, a half reel or so later, an interior of a London music hall, another big scene as the antiquated show is reproduced and then broken up by the audience and actors going wild with enthusiasm at the announcement the war is over. It's the second big scene in the picture, the biggest scene in the original London play, and so well done in the film that from that point on the audience is completely won.

□ 1932/33: Best Picture

C.C. AND COMPANY

1970, 94 MINS, US ◇ ▼
Dir Seymour Robbie *Prod* Allan Carr, Roger Smith
Scr Roger Smith *Ph* Charles Wheeler *Ed* Fred Chulack *Mus* Lenny Stack
● Joe Namath, Ann-Margret, William Smith, Jennifer Billingsley, Don Chastain, Teda Bracci
(Avco Embassy/Rogallan)

Joe Namath frolics with Ann-Margret against a sordid milieu of motorbikes and an uneasy riders' commune in *C.C. and Company*.

Namath and Ann-Margret encounter by chance on the road and he rescues her from a rape attempt by a few of his hippie gang. This leads to sex in the raw between him and her as consenting partners, and then, for Namath, some violent clashes with cult leader William Smith.

It's all put together ineffectually with one exception: Smith is impressive as the motorcyclists' guru; he's a big and handsome young guy who knows how to project. Ann-Margret is cute and Namath is clumsy.

CELIA

1989, 102 MINS, AUSTRALIA ◇ ▼
Dir Ann Turner *Prod* Timothy White, Gordon Glenn
Scr Ann Turner *Ph* Geoffrey Simpson *Ed* Ken Sallows *Mus* Chris Neal *Art Dir* Peta Lawson
● Rebecca Smart, Nicholas Eadie, Maryanne Fahey, Victoria Longley, William Zappa (Seon)

Celia starts out a a likeable family pic about the traumas of a sensitive 9-year-old girl growing up in a Melbourne suburb in the conservative late 1950s. It winds up as something quite different.

Celia, 9, played by Rebecca Smart is an only child; when she discovers her grandmother's body, it's the first of several traumas. Troubled by nightmares featuring monsters from a book read to her at school, Celia is delighted when newcomers, with three children, come to live next door; and finds Alice (Victoria Longley) far more sympathetic than her own mother.

Trouble is, Alice and her husband are active members of the Communist Party, and before long Celia is forbidden to see her new friends.

The child's other obsession is her pet rabbit. When a national plague of rabbits results in the Victoria state government calling for the handing over of all domestic bunnies, she blames her uncle, the local policeman, for enforcing the law, and when her beloved rabbit dies in Melbourne Zoo, she takes a surprisingly violent revenge.

Rebecca Smart, on-screen throughout, is effective as the ultimately scary Celia, but the film's best performance comes from Victoria Longley as the warm-hearted neighbor.

CEREMONY, THE

1963, 106 MINS, US
Dir Laurence Harvey *Prod* Laurence Harvey *Scr* Ben Barzman, Laurence Harvey *Ph* Brian West *Ed* Ralph Kemplen *Mus* Gerard Schurmann
● Laurence Harvey, Sarah Miles, Robert Walker, John Ireland (United Artists)

Ben Barzman's screenplay relates the dreary tale of a man (Laurence Harvey) about to be executed in a Tangier prison for a crime he did not commit, a murder that actually he'd tried to prevent but for which he is paying the supreme penalty as a kind of scapegoat. An elaborate escape scheme cooked up by his brother (Robert Walker) succeeds, but Harvey then discovers that little brother has been making time with his girl (Sarah Miles).

Concern is never aroused for any of the characters. The audience is thrust into the heart of the situation and never really allowed to get its bearings. The players are all snowed under by ill-defined, unappealing roles and lack of proper direction. *The Ceremony* is a depressingly dark film.

CERTAIN SMILE, A

1958, 105 MINS, US ◇
Dir Jean Negulesco *Prod* Henry Ephron *Scr* Frances Goodrich, Albert Hackett *Ph* Milton Krasner *Ed* Louis Loeffler *Mus* Alfred Newman *Art Dir* Lyle R. Wheeler, John F. DeCuir
● Rossano Brazzi, Joan Fontaine, Bradford Dillman, Christine Carere, Eduard Franz, Kathryn Givney (20th Century-Fox)

In the second of Francoise Sagan's novels to be filmed, once again the principal character is a young and attractive girl, only this time the 'shocker' involves her week-long affair with an older man.

Only the very basic elements in the slim Sagan book have been retained in this glossy, emotional yarn. None of the moody disenchantment of the girl in the book comes through and of course the ending has been totally changed. In Sagan's original the heroine blithely continued her affairs both with regular boyfriend and older lover.

As a film *A Certain Smile* is well made, reasonably well acted and quite magnificently photographed. Having so strenuously toned down the amoral aspects of their story, producer and director apparently decided to go whole hog for the visual aspects. As a result, the film abounds with mouth-watering vistas of the French Riviera, which is photographed from every possible vantage point, providing an idyllic setting for the romantic goings-on between Rossano Brazzi and Christine Carere. Scenes in the Paris streets also come alive temptingly.

Carere is charming and petite, turning in a capable performance that's just a shade too much on the wholesome side. Boyfriend Bradford Dillman, also a newcomer, is good-looking in an unconventional way. He does well in a frustrating role. Brazzi is suavely Continental as the middle-aged Don Juan,

and wife Joan Fontaine suffers as required by script.

CHAINED HEAT

1983, 95 MINS, US/W. GERMANY ◇ ▼
Dir Paul Nicolas *Prod* Billy Fine *Scr* Vincent Mongol, Paul Nicolas *Ph* Mac Ahlberg *Ed* Nino di Marco *Mus* Joseph Conlon *Art Dir* Bob Ziembicki
● Linda Blair, John Vernon, Sybil Danning, Tamara Dobson, Stella Stevens, Henry Silva
(Heat/TAT/Intercontinental)

Chained Heat is a silly, almost campy follow-up to producer Billy Fine's women's prison hit, *The Concrete Jungle*, that manages to pack in enough sex tease and violent action to satisfy undiscriminating action fans.

Linda Blair toplines as Carol, an innocent young girl serving an 18-month stretch in a California prison run by Warden Backman (John Vernon) and Captain Taylor (Stella Stevens), as corrupt a pair as the scripters can imagine. Real power in stir is shared by statuesque Ericka (Sybil Danning) and Duchess (Tamara Dobson), lording it over the white and black prison populations, respectively.

German director Paul Nicolas displays little feel for the prison genre, emphasizing archaic sex-for-voyeurs scenes.

CHAIRMAN, THE

1969, 104 MINS, US ◇ ▼
Dir J. Lee Thompson *Prod* Mort Abrahams *Scr* Ben Maddow *Ph* John Wilcox *Ed* Richard Best *Mus* Jerry Goldsmith *Art Dir* Peter Mullins
● Gregory Peck, Anne Heywood, Arthur Hill, Alan Dobie, Conrad Yama, Zienia Merton (20th Century-Fox)

A quality film, made at Pinewood Studios and on location in the Far East, introducing improbable mission wrapped up in such style it becomes engrossing.

Nobel Prize winning American scientist Gregory Peck, teaching at the University of London, receives a letter from his former instructor, Professor Soong Li (Keye Luke), telling him it would be impossible for Peck to visit Red China.

Since Peck has no intentions of visiting China, he is further mystified when the President, urges him to slip out of London and into the Chinese mainland.

Peck is finally convinced when shown food growing in formerly arid or snowcovered areas inside China.

Task of presenting the film [from a novel by Jay Richard Kennedy] on screen was stupendous, and it has been accomplished with imagination and taste. Peck performs well in a part far more demanding than appears on the surface, while Heywood is totally wasted in what is hardly more than a bit part.

CHALK GARDEN, THE

1964, 106 MINS, UK ◇ ▼
Dir Ronald Neame *Prod* Ross Hunter *Scr* John Michael Hayes *Ph* Arthur Ibbetson *Ed* Jack Harris *Mus* Malcolm Arnold *Art Dir* Carmen Dillon
● Deborah Kerr, Hayley Mills, John Mills, Edith Evans, Elizabeth Sellars, Felix Aylmer (Rank/Quota Rentals)

The Chalk Garden makes no bones about its legit background. Enid Bagnold's drama had a healthy 17 months' run at the Haymarket in 1956 and producer and director have not done much to disguise the original.

Hayley Mills vigorously plays a 16-year-old girl, in some ways perceptive beyond her years. But audiences will feel that a well-applied hairbrush on her derriere could have swiftly ironed out some of the problems that beset her and the surrounding adults.

The child suffers from the feeling that she is

not loved. Her mother has remarried and her grandmother is more obsessed with her arid garden. So the confused, unhappy girl grows up in a world of fantasy and lying. On to the scene comes a mystery woman as governess. Deborah Kerr's background turns out to be that of a woman straight from prison after a suspended sentence for bumping off her stepsister.

On paper, this sounds like a ripe old piece of Victoriana, but curiously it works, largely because of confident, smooth performances by all concerned.

● ●

■ CHAMP, THE

1931, 85 MINS, US
Dir King Vidor   *Scr* Frances Marion, Leonard Praskins, Wanda Tuchock   *Ph* Gordon Avil   *Ed* Hugh Wynn
Art Dir Cedric Gibbons
● Wallace Beery, Jackie Cooper, Irene Rich, Roscoe Ates, Edward Brophy, Hale Hamilton (M-G-M)

A good picture, almost entirely by virtue of an inspired performance by a boy, Jackie Cooper. There is none of the usual hammy quality of the average child actor in this kid.

What also makes *The Champ* a good talker is a studied, understanding adult piece of work by the costar, Wallace Beery, who had to step to keep up with Jackie, and a Frances Marion original story that isn't bad for a boxing story.

Beery plays a broken down ex-heavyweight champ. He's anchored in Tiajuana with his kid and a couple of training camp leeches, and training for a comeback between stews. When not stewing he's gambling and the comeback always seems more distant. He wins enough to buy the kid a race horse. Then he loses the horse in a crap game.

In the attempts of the Champ's former wife and the boy's mother to regain her son there is some menace, though Irene Rich as the mother and Hale Hamilton as her second husband are painted lily white by the script.
□ 1931/32: Best Picture (nomination)

● ●

■ CHAMP, THE

1979, 121 MINS, US ◇ ▽
Dir Franco Zeffirelli   *Prod* Dyson Lovell   *Scr* Walter Newman   *Ph* Fred J. Koenekamp   *Ed* Michael J. Sheridan   *Mus* Dave Grusin   *Art Dir* Theoni V. Aldredge
● Jon Voight, Faye Dunaway, Ricky Schroder, Jack Warden, Strother Martin, Joan Blondell
(United Artists/M-G-M)

Walter Newman's script adroitly updates Frances Marion's original scenario, placing down-and-out boxer Jon Voight as a horse handler in Florida, accompanied by sprig Ricky Schroder. An inveterate gambler and drinker, Voight doesn't hit the comeback trail until ex-wife Faye Dunaway, now a society matron, reappears to threaten his and Schroder's buddy-buddy relationship.

Even those unfamiliar with the 1931 pic will feel resonances in the current *Champ* and in this edition Schroder projects a comparable emotional range and depth.

Most debatable, and in some respects unsettling, aspects of the update concern the Voight-Dunaway characters and relationships.

But Voight, under Italian director Franco Zeffirelli, has adopted an accent and outlook that seems at odds with the setting, and seriously weakens the credibility of a relationship between him and the elegant Dunaway.

● ●

■ CHAMPION

1949, 90 MINS, US ▽
Dir Mark Robson   *Prod* Stanley Kramer   *Scr* Carl Foreman   *Ph* Franz Planer   *Ed* Harry Gerstad
Mus Dimitri Tiomkin

● Kirk Douglas, Marilyn Maxwell, Arthur Kennedy, Paul Stewart, Ruth Roman (Screen Plays)

Adapted from a Ring Lardner short story of the same title, *Champion* is a stark, realistic study of the boxing rackets and the degeneracy of a prizefighter.

Fight scenes, under Franz Planer's camera, have realism and impact. Unrelenting pace is set by the opening sequence.

Cast, under Mark Robson's tight direction, is fine. Kirk Douglas is the boxer and he makes the character live. Second honors go jointly to Arthur Kennedy, the fighter's crippled brother, and Paul Stewart as the knowing manager.

Where the Lardner story made the boxer a no-good from the start, Foreman's screenplay casts him as an appealing Joe in the earlier reels. Already stuck with a persecution complex because of his boyhood poverty, it doesn't take long for him to become a real heel.

● ●

■ CHANGELING, THE

1980, 107 MINS, CANADA ◇ ▽
Dir Peter Medak   *Prod* Joel B. Michaels, Garth H. Drabinsky   *Scr* William Gray, Diana Maddox
Ph John Coquillon   *Ed* Lilla Ledersen   *Mus* Rick Wilkins   *Art Dir* Trevor Williams
● George C. Scott, Trish Van Devere, Melvyn Douglas, John Colicos, Jean Marsh, Barry Morse
(Michaels-Drabinsky)

The Changeling is a superior haunted house thriller. The story [by Russell Hunter] centers on George C. Scott, a recently widowed music professor, who has moved to Seattle to forget his personal tragedy. His new residence is an old home owned by the local historic society. After moving in, the house begins to do strange things.

It turns out that the noisy spirit is a young sickly boy who was murdered at the turn of the century. The child's father could not collect an inheritance unless the boy reached the age of 21. After the murder a changeling was put in the boy's place. The changeling is still alive and the dead child wants to wreak his vengeance on him.

Scott and Melvyn Douglas (as a powerful industrialist) register the strongest performances with Trish Van Devere as coming off rather wooden.

● ●

■ CHANGE OF SEASONS, A

1980, 102 MINS, US ◇ ▽
Dir Richard Lang, [Noel Black]   *Prod* Martin Ransohoff   *Scr* Erich Segal, Ronni Kern, Fred Segal   *Ph* Philip Lathrop   *Ed* Don Zimmerman   *Mus* Henry Mancini   *Art Dir* Bill Kenney
● Shirley MacLaine, Anthony Hopkins, Bo Derek, Mary Beth Hurt, Michael Brandon, Ed Winter
(Film Finance/Ransohoff)

It would take the genius of an Ernst Lubitsch to do justice to the incredibly tangled relationships in *A Change of Seasons*, and director Richard Lang is no Lubitsch. The switching of couples seems arbitrary and mechanical, and more sour than amusing.

Shirley MacLaine emerges as the most sympathetic person in the film, the wife of college professor Anthony Hopkins, whose philandering with coed Bo Derek shatters the complacency of their marriage. MacLaine retaliates by taking a young lover (Michael Brandon) and they all head off on a Vermont skiing vacation together in a dubious demonstration of open-mindedness.

Derek and Hopkins romp in slow-motion in a hot tub but that's about all the sexual charge the film carries.

Hopkins comes off as a totally self-centered boor who never engages audience sympathy.

● ●

■ CHAN IS MISSING

1982, 80 MINS, US
Dir Wayne Wang   *Prod* Wayne Wang   *Scr* Wayne Wang   *Ph* Michael Chin   *Ed* Wayne Wang
Mus Robert Kikuchi-Yngojo
● Marc Hayashi, Wood May, Laureen Chew, Judy Mihei, Peter Wang (Wang)

Rather roughly lensed in b&w and 16mm tale traces the odyssey of two San Francisco Chinese taxi drivers as they search for an older partner who's vanished with their funds. As in Antonioni's *L'Avventura*, the object of their quest is never found, but suspense in this regard couldn't be further from the point.

Instead, Chan's relatives, local businessmen, politicos and citizens-at-large who are interviewed by the pair constitute a fascinating and often amusing gallery of portraits of contempo Chinese Americans.

Joe, the elder cabbie who serves as narrator, is like a solid working stiff of any race. His youthful cohort, Steve, seems to have fashioned his looks after Burt Reynolds, hiply speaks in a sort of black jive lingo and has little patience for the caution, moderation and discretion widely found in the older generations of Chinese immigrants.

Any filmmaker who can so thoroughly force the viewer to look at the world through his eyes possesses a talent to reckon with.

● ●

■ CHANT OF JIMMIE BLACKSMITH, THE

1978, 122 MINS, AUSTRALIA ◇
Dir Fred Schepisi   *Prod* Fred Schepisi   *Scr* Fred Schepisi   *Ph* Ian Baker   *Ed* Brian Kavanaugh
● Tommy Lewis, Freddy Reynolds, Ray Barrett, Jack Thompson, Peter Carroll, Elizabeth Alexander
(Filmhouse/Australia Party)

Fred Schepisi, for his second film, reveals a sure hand, a dynamic thrust in using a true turn-of-the-century happening [from a book by Thomas Keneally] to delve into the racism of the times against aborigines and the beginnings of governmental federation of its many regions.

The tale of a mulatto aborigine, raised by a Methodist minister, and torn between his people and his Christian teachings, has sweep and interesting insights into the loss of the aborigine culture and the life of a man who does not belong to either culture anymore.

Tommy Lewis, a non-actor, is well utilized as Jimmie Blacksmith. He works for a white family who allow him to build a hut for his family. When there is no food and no pay, he and his uncle go to the house, where the men are absent. The refusal of food leads to a sudden explosion of all the smoldering resentments and they slaughter the wife, two teenage daughters, a school teacher living with them and a young boy.

The violence is instinctive, harrowing but not exploited. It is masterfully handled by Schepisi. Jimmie and his brother leave the old uncle and the wife and child and go on the lam as a great manhunt begins.

● ●

■ CHAPMAN REPORT, THE

1962, 125 MINS, US ◇
Dir George Cukor   *Prod* Richard D. Zanuck
Scr Wyatt Cooper, Don M. Mankiewicz   *Ph* Harold Lipstein   *Ed* Robert Simpson   *Mus* Leonard Rosenman   *Art Dir* Gene Allen
● Efrem Zimbalist Jr, Shelley Winters, Jane Fonda, Claire Bloom, Glynis Johns, Ray Danton (Warner)

The Chapman Report is a talky melodramatization of several abnormal patterns in the sexual behaviour of the upper middleclass American female. The scenario, from an adaptation by Grant Stuart and Gene Allen of Irving Wallace's novel, attempts the feat of dramatically threading together the stories of four sexually unstable women who become voluntary subjects for a scientific sex survey conducted by a noted psychologist and his staff.

One (Claire Bloom) is a hopeless nympho and alcoholic. Another (Jane Fonda) suffers from fears of frigidity. The third (Glynis Johns), a kind of comedy relief figure, is an intellectual who feels there may be more to sex than she has realized in her smugly satisfied marital relationship. The last (Shelley Winters) enters into a clandestine extramarital affair with an irresponsible little theatre director.

Johns does the best acting in the film, rising above the flimsiest of the four episodes with a spirited and infectious performance. Fonda seems miscast and is affected and unappealing in her role. Bloom suffers up a storm. Winters plays with conviction. The men are all two-dimensional pawns.

· ·

■ CHAPTER TWO

1979, 124 MINS, US ◇

Dir Robert Moore *Prod* Ray Stark *Scr* Neil Simon *Ph* David M. Walsh *Ed* Michael A. Stevenson *Mus* Marvin Hamlisch *Art Dir* Gene Callahan
● James Caan, Marsha Mason, Joseph Bologna, Valerie Harper, Judy Farrell, Debra Mooney (Columbia)

Chapter Two represents Neil Simon at his bigscreen best. Film version of his successful and loosely autobiographical play is tender, compassionate and gently humorous all at once. Marsha Mason's tremendous performance under Robert Moore's sensitive direction gives the pic another boost.

Simon, producer Ray Stark and Moore, in their third film collaboration, have dared to alter the entire focus of the legit version of *Chapter Two*, by subtly but inalterably concentrating on Jennie MacLaine, the actress being wooed by author Schneider, rather than Schneider himself.

Result is to downplay the unusual casting of James Caan as Schneider (the choice still pays off richly), and affords Mason the opportunity for her best-realized film work to date.

· ·

■ CHARADE

1963, 113 MINS, US ◇ ▼

Dir Stanley Donen *Prod* Stanley Donen *Scr* Peter Stone *Ph* Charles Lang Jr *Ed* James Clark *Mus* Henry Mancini
● Cary Grant, Audrey Hepburn, Walter Matthau, James Coburn, Ned Glass, George Kennedy (Universal)

Basically a suspenser or chase film, *Charade* has several moments of violence but they are leavened with a generous helping of spoofery. Director Stanley Donen plays the taut tale against a colorful background of witty dialogue, humorous situations and scenic beauty.

While vacationing at a French Alps ski resort, Audrey Hepburn meets Cary Grant casually. Returning to Paris, she finds herself a widow, her husband having been murdered. Aware that her own life may be in danger, she appeals for help to the US Embassy. There she learns that former World War II associates of her husband, his accomplices in the theft of $250,000 in gold, believe that she knows the money's whereabouts. Walter Matthau, her informant, advises her, for her own safety, to find the money (property of the US government) and turn it over to him.

The two stars carry the film effortlessly, with the only acting competition coming from the versatile Matthau. James Coburn, Ned Glass and George Kennedy make an effective trio of villainous cutthroats. Kennedy's fight

with Grant on a slippery rooftop is a real gasper.

Fast-paced, from the pre-title shot of a body tossed from a train to the finale under a theatre stage, *Charade* seldom falters (amazing, considering its almost two-hour running time). Repartee between the two stars is sometimes subtle, sometimes suggestive, sometimes satirical but always witty.

· ·

■ CHARGE OF THE LIGHT BRIGADE, THE

1936, MINS, US ▼

Dir Michael Curtiz *Prod* Sam Bischoff *Scr* Michel Jacoby, Rowland Leigh *Ph* Sol Polito *Ed* George Amy *Mus* Max Steiner *Art Dir* John Hughes
● Errol Flynn, Oliva de Havilland, Patric Knowles, Henry Stephenson, Donald Crisp, David Niven (Warner)

Warner has turned out a magnificent production in this story based on Tennyson's immortal poem and historical facts. Foreword explains that history was consulted for background, but characters and development are fictionized.

Before the climactic sweeping drive of the cavalry there is the dramatic defense of the Chukoti garrison and the ruthless massacre of soldiers, wives and children after they have surrendered. The major who witnessed the slaughter is depicted as switching an order of the British high command. This results in the 600 cavalrymen riding into 'the valley of death' in the face of cannon fire and a force four or five times their number.

The tremendous sweep of this surging charge constitutes the feature's highlight. It has been skillfully done by means of closeups, a traveling camera shot depicting the changing pace of the horses as column after column races towards the enemy, and via some truly extraordinary process shots.

The dual love affair, two brothers seeking the hand of the colonel's daughter, is nicely intertwined with the more adventurous moments of the story.

Errol Flynn lives up to the promise of previous film efforts as the youthful major who sacrifices all to avenge the slaughter of his comrades. Donald Crisp is strong in the character portrayal of the colonel.

· ·

■ CHARGE OF THE LIGHT BRIGADE, THE

1968, 145 MINS, UK ◇

Dir Tony Richardson *Prod* Neil Hartley *Scr* Charles Wood *Ph* David Watkin *Ed* Kevin Brownlow, Hugh Raggett *Mus* John Addison *Art Dir* Edward Marshall
● Trevor Howard, Vanessa Redgrave, John Gielgud, Harry Andrews, Jill Bennett, David Hemmings (United Artists)

Thanks mainly to Lord Tennyson's piece of durable doggerel millions of people have at least a sketchy idea of the historical incident, though director Tony Richardson's treatment is almost disdainfully indifferent to the actual physical charge.

He is more concerned with analysing the reasons behind one of the most notorious blunders in military history. He's also intent on attacking by ridicule the class war and bigotry of the British mid-19th-century regime, and the futility of the Crimean War as a whole.

Those fascinated by the class distinction, crass stupidity, muddled thinking and old school tie snobbishness then prevailing will find richness in the earthy screenplay.

Film starts leisurely, carefully building up to the atmosphere of the times. In fact, despite Richardson's frequently lively direction and the brisk, electric editing, the pace of the film is remarkably easygoing, building up in a vague story line to the crass Charge as a finale which comes almost as an anti-climax.

Apart from some masterly directorial touches Richardson has made clever use of

animated sequences wittily drawn by Richard Williams, living caricatures based on broadsides and cartoons of the mid-Victorian period.

They are not only consistently amusing but also deftly link the action, explain the historical background and compress what would be unwieldy scenes into quick, understandable comment.

· ·

■ CHARIOTS OF FIRE

1981, 123 MINS, UK ◇

Dir Hugh Hudson *Prod* David Puttnam *Scr* Colin Welland *Ph* David Watkin *Ed* Terry Rawlings *Mus* Vangelis *Art Dir* Roger Hall
● Ben Cross, Ian Charleson, Nigel Havers, Alice Krige, John Gielgud, Lindsay Anderson (Allied Stars/Enigma)

Chariots of Fire, which weaves the stories of two former British track aces who both won major events at the 1924 Paris Olympics, is about the will to win and why. It's also a winner for director Hugh Hudson in his theatrical bow after an apprenticeship in commercials.

The Colin Welland script has a lot to admire in the engrossing way it counterpoints the progress of its two sporting heroes, each driven by impulse that has little to do with mere fame per se and even less with national honor.

Ian Charleson and Ben Cross are both exemplary as the respective super-runners, Eric Liddell and Harold Abrahams, the first a Christian Scot who believes that by winning can he best honor the Lord; the latter an English Jew with a chip on the shoulder for whom over-achieving is his ticket to acceptance in a prejudiced society.

What with two social outsiders hogging the glory for dear old Albion, the snobby establishment doesn't come off to raves.

Hudson's direction gets it all together with admirable assurance and narrative style. No arty tricks, no self-conscious posturing. His use of slow motion and freeze frames for the various racing sequences turns out to be a valid device for sharpening emotional intensity.

· ·

■ CHARLEY VARRICK

1973, 111 MINS, US ◇ ▼

Dir Don Siegel *Prod* Don Siegel *Scr* Howard Rodman, Dean Riesner *Ph* Michael Butler *Ed* Frank Morriss *Mus* Lalo Schifrin *Art Dir* Fernando Carrere
● Walter Matthau, Joe Don Baker, Felicia Farr, Andy Robinson, John Vernon, Sheree North (Universal)

Charley Varrick is a sometimes-fuzzy melodrama but so well put together that it emerges a hardhitting actioner with a sock finale.

Based on the John Reese novel, *The Looters*, narrative carries the unusual twist of Walter Matthau, a small-time bank robber, trying to return his heist of a smalltown New Mexico bank after later discovering his $750,000 take belongs to the Mafia and he wants none of it. He is opposed by a young companion who doesn't see eye-to-eye, and menaced by a Mafia hit-man who arrives on the scene.

Director Don Siegel overcomes deficiencies in part by his rugged handling of action and making handsome use of the Nevada landscape where pic was filmed and which provided stuntmen with a field day.

Matthau delivers strongly as a man who wants to limit his heisting to small banks because legal heat isn't so hot. Joe Don Baker scores solidly as Mafia man.

· ·

■ CHARLIE BUBBLES

1968, 89 MINS, UK ◇

Dir Albert Finney *Prod* Michael Medwin *Scr* Shelagh Delaney *Ph* Peter Suschitsky *Ed* Fergus McDonnell *Mus* Misha Donat *Art Dir* Edward Marshall

● Albert Finney, Colin Blakely, Billie Whitelaw, Liza Minnelli, Timothy Garland, Richard Pearson (Memorial)

Albert Finney stars as, and makes his directorial debut in, *Charlie Bubbles*. Comedy-drama concerns a materially successful man, fighting vainly the old ennui. Unfortunately, audiences also are bound to experience the same tedium, via underplaying and limp direction.

Finney's boredom is shown in biz relations, brief encounter with secretary Liza Minnelli, and disintegrating ties to his estranged wife (Billie Whitelaw) and alienated child (Timothy Garland).

This type screenplay which, essentially, is little more than exposition of a point made obvious in the first 10 minutes, requires direction which is dynamic both physically and artistically. Finney provides little of the required animation, thereby setting a plodding pace.

Among the cast, Whitelaw scores best. Minelli gets a trifle cloying, but is okay. Colin Blakely, Finney's booze companion, has some bright moments, and Alan Lake as a pushy hitchhiker, scores neatly.

■ **CHARLY**

1968, 103 MINS, US ◇ ▼
Dir Ralph Nelson *Prod* Ralph Nelson *Scr* Stirling Silliphant *Ph* Arthur Ornitz *Ed* Fredric Steinkamp *Mus* Ravi Shankar *Art Dir* Chas Rosen
● Cliff Robertson, Claire Bloom, Leon Janney, Lilia Skala, Dick Van Patton, Ed McNally (Selmur)

Charly boasts a most intriguing premise – a variation on the Pygmalion theme in which a mentally retarded adult 'grows up' as the result of a brain operation.

Recognizing that this idea [from the short story and novel *Flowers for Algernon* by Daniel Keyes] could be developed along several different lines, producer-director Ralph Nelson and screenwriter Stirling Silliphant try them all, with the result that *Charly* merges a peculiar combination of sentimentalized documentary, romance, science fiction and social drama.

Instead of frittering away time on an unmotivated romance, it would have been interesting if the reasons for this psychologically complicated affair were explored.

Considering the innumerable stumbling blocks, cast does well. Cliff Robertson seems to overdo the external manifestations of retardation, but he is excellent in the post-operative scenes. With more help from the script he could have been a movingly tragic figure.

■ **CHASE, THE**

1946, 86 MINS, US ▼
Dir Arthur Ripley *Prod* Seymour Nebenzal *Scr* Philip Yordan *Ph* Franz Planer *Ed* Ed Mann *Mus* Michel Michelet *Art Dir* Robert Usher
● Robert Cummings, Michele Morgan, Peter Lorre, Steve Cochran (United Artists)

The Chase is a meller that's taut as sprung steel for 75 minutes of its running time then slackens limply into the commonplace. Yarn [from a story by Cornell Woolrich] concerns the attempt of a killer's wife and his chauffeur to make their getaway from his household and henchman.

Through a series of adroit directorial strokes, in the Hitchcock tradition, the pic's momentum is made to mount in a steady, ascending line. Terror stalks the pair in their flight to Havana then explodes with the shocking stillness of a gun with a silencer on it.

Robert Cummings handles himself nicely but, though he tops the cast, is over-shadowed by the dominating personality and looks of a newcomer, Steve Cochran, who plays the killer. Cochran is handsome, suave, confident, and menacing in the manner of a Humphrey Bogart. Peter Lorre, in one of his best roles, comes through with a solid assist as the killer's aide-de-camp. Michele Morgan registers nicely, although she isn't given much to do besides modelling a few flashy gowns.

■ **CHASE, THE**

1966, 138 MINS, US ◇ ▼
Dir Arthur Penn *Prod* Sam Spiegel *Scr* Lillian Hellman *Ph* Joseph LaShelle *Ed* Gene Milford *Mus* John Barry *Art Dir* Richard Day
● Marlon Brando, Jane Fonda, Robert Redford, James Fox, E.G. Marshall, Angie Dickinson (Horizon/Columbia)

Only the framework of Horton Foote's novel (but little of his play, which preceded it), has been utilized by Lillian Hellman in her screenplay. The original plot centered on an escaped convict seeking revenge on the sheriff who had sent him up but Hellman makes them only two of the many characters with which she has populated her sociologically sick Texas town.

Through introduction of various other types she manages to provide most of the social grievances which trouble the world today.

Robert Redford, as the escaped convict whose impending return to his hometown gives many of its citizens the jitters, gives the film's best performance. Marlon Brando, in the comparatively small but important role of the sheriff, has obviously given much time and study to the part, but such detailed preparation as a carefully-delivered Texas accent means little when other cast members read their lines with a mixture of regional accents.

Jane Fonda, as Redford's wife and the mistress of wealthy oilman James Fox, makes the most of the biggest female role.

■ **CHATO'S LAND**

1972, 100 MINS, US ◇ ▼
Dir Michael Winner *Prod* Michael Winner *Scr* Gerald Wilson *Ph* Robert Paynter *Ed* Freddie Wilson *Mus* Jerry Fielding *Art Dir* Manolo Manpaso
● Charles Bronson, Jack Palance, Richard Basehart, James Whitmore, Simon Oakland, Ralph Waite (United Artists/Scimitar)

British producer-director Michael Winner in his second western takes a hard look at the early American West and comes up with a violence-drenched meller.

Writer Gerald Wilson, adopting and-then-there-were-none theme, plots an Apache half-breed relentlessly pursued by a ragtag white posse headed by an ex-Confederate officer after the Indian has killed a white sheriff. Charles Bronson portrays the Apache – Chato – and Jack Palance the posse leader.

Action too often slows during an overage of dialog between posse members and an apparent attempt to build characterization defeats its purpose as bickering among posse detracts from the real objective of story. Narrative is fleshed out when the Indian reverts to a savage vengeful warrior after a few members of posse rape his squaw and the roles of hunter and hunted are reversed.

■ **CHE**

1969, 96 MINS, US ◇ ▼
Dir Richard Fleischer *Prod* Sy Bartlett *Scr* Michael Wilson, Sy Bartlett *Ph* Charles Wheeler *Ed* Marion Rothman *Mus* Lalo Schifrin *Art Dir* Jack Martin Smith, Arthur Lonergan
● Omar Sharif, Jack Palance, Cesare Danova, Robert Loggia, Woody Strode, Barbara Luna (20th Century-Fox)

Producer Sy Bartlett and director Richard Fleischer claimed to have made an 'impartial, objective' film about Fidel Castro's Cuban Revolution and of subsequent events in that country. But it's emphatically not true about their viewpoint of Ernesto Che Guevara himself: to them, he was an evil genius who tried to lead Castro down wrong paths, a man whose revolutionary zeal took violent turns which ignored social reality.

As presented, Castro, played smokehouse by Jack Palance, is innocent not only of winning the initial revolution, but also of the deeds afterwards which condemn him in many American eyes. It was Guevara, adequately portrayed by Omar Sharif, who planned the military strategy which resulted in the fall of Havana, who maintained discipline within the rebel forces and who conducted executions after Castro took over.

Pic has been made in a mock-documentary style which comes out poorly. Supposedly, 'real' people are being interviewed who are telling Che's story in flashback.

■ **CHEAP DETECTIVE, THE**

1978, 92 MINS, US ◇ ▼
Dir Robert Moore *Prod* Ray Stark *Scr* Neil Simon *Ph* John A. Alonzo *Ed* Sidney Levin, Michael A. Stevenson *Mus* Patrick Williams *Art Dir* Robert Luthardt
● Peter Falk, Ann-Margret, Eileen Brennan, Sid Caesar, Stockard Channing, James Coco (Columbia)

The Cheap Detective, which might also be called *Son Of Casablanca*, is a hilarious and loving takeoff on all 1940s Warner Bros private eye and foreign intrigue mellers.

The time is 1940, San Francisco, where clumsy gumshoe Peter Falk is accused of murdering his partner, whose wife Marsha Mason (in early Janet Leigh curls) has been Falk's mistress. Detective Vic Tayback and assistants regularly blunder into matters.

Madeline Kahn, with as many smart clothes changes as aliases, appears in Falk's office. She's in league with John Houseman (Sydney Greenstreet to the core), Paul Williams (Elisha Cook Jr was never like this) and Dom DeLuise (a fat Peter Lorre) in search of ancient treasure – a dozen diamond eggs.

Amidst the confusing threads of mystery, Falk is regularly affronted by the overly explicit descriptions of sexual torture inflicted on all the dames. But at fadeout he's got a lot more going for him than Bogart did in the final dissolve.

■ **CHECKING OUT**

1989, 93 MINS, US ◇ ▼
Dir David Leland *Prod* Ben Myron *Scr* Joe Eszterhas *Ph* Ian Wilson *Ed* Lee Percy *Mus* Carter Burwell *Art Dir* Barbara Ling
● Jeff Daniels, Melanie Mayron, Michael Tucker, Kathleen York, Allan Havey (HandMade/Warner)

A dreadfully unfunny one-joke black comedy about hypochondria and mortality, *Checking Out* depends almost entirely for suspense of Jeff Daniels' 'Why don't Italians have barbecues?' Sadly, some 90 minutes elapse before he finds out.

In the interim Daniels, as budget airline executive Ray Macklin, witnesses the death by coronary of his irreverent best buddy Allan Havey. This trauma triggers the onset of a hysterical, fetishistic hypochondria that propels him through a series of discombobulating misadventures.

Daniels live in a tacky California suburb with wife Melanie Mayron and two kids. The blue-sky normalcy of his middle-class lifestyle is clearly intended to set up a big soft target for satirical demolition. Potshots also are misfired at American big business funeral homes, medicine and sexual hypocrisy.

Seeds of a more interesting film are scattered here and there, especially in a dazzlingly photographed dream sequence that imagines heaven as a cloyingly hellish redneck cabana club in a desert oasis.

• •

■ **CHELSEA GIRLS, THE**

1967, 210 MINS, US ◇
Dir Andy Warhol   *Prod* Andy Warhol
● Robert Olivio, Ondine, Mary Might, Nico, Ingrid Superstar, Mario Montez (Warhol)

The Chelsea Girls, perhaps the first Underground film to be accorded specifically non-Underground screenings, is a pointless, excruciatingly dull three-and-a-half hours spent in the company of Andy Warhol's friends. Warhol has attempted to counter all conventional methods of filmmaking, and the result is an anti-film or, more accurately, a non-film.

There is no plot-line. The single unifying device is that the film takes place in several rooms of a downtown hotel. Typical scenes include a blank-looking blonde trimming and combing her hair, a lesbian bullying her roommates, another lesbian talking endlessly on the phone, a homosexual eating an orange, a middle-aged homosexual and a girl competing for the attentions of a half-nude male, a girl on LSD confessing to a homosexual priest.

• •

■ **CHERRY, HARRY & RAQUEL!**

1969, 71 MINS, US ◇
Dir Russ Meyer   *Prod* Russ Meyer   *Scr* Tom Wolfe, Russ Meyer   *Ph* Russ Meyer   *Ed* Russ Meyer, Richard Serly Brummer   *Mus* William Loose
● Larissa Ely, Linda Ashton, Charles Napier, Bert Santos, Franklin H. Bolger, Astrid Lillimor (Eve/Panamint)

Film focuses on the narcotics traffic on the Mexican border, where Charles Napier is a sheriff in the pay of the drug operator.

Linda Ashton plays Cherry, his girlfriend, and Larissa Ely portrays Raquel, who takes on all comers. When the two ladies of the title get tired of it all with men, they try some Lesbian clinches. Flashes of nudes intersperse the unreeling every minute or so. Mebbe they're symbolic, they have no connection with the story.

Meyer inserts plenty of violence in Harry's search for a Yaqui Indian who is leaving the gang for private enterprise. The Yaqui shoots it out with the sheriff in a bloody sequence, and kills a Mexican member of the gang in another bloody encounter after an exciting and suspenseful auto chase. Dialog is on the stag side. Cost was $90,000, up from Meyer's previous $70,000 budgets.

• •

■ **CHERRY 2000**

1988, 93 MINS, US ◇ ▼
Dir Steve de Jarnatt   *Prod* Edward R. Pressman
Scr Michael Almereyda   *Ph* Jacques Haitkin
Ed Edward Abroms   *Mus* Basil Poledouris
Art Dir John J. Moore
● Melanie Griffith, David Andrews, Ben Johnson, Tim Thomerson, Harry Carey Jr, Pamela Gidley (ERP/Orion)

A tongue-in-cheek sci-fi action pic which owes a considerable debt to the *Mad Max* movies, *Cherry 2000*'s greatest asset is top-billed Melanie Griffith, who lifts the material whenever she's on screen.

Griffith plays E. Johnson, a tracker who lives at the edge of a desert known as The Zone. The year is 2017, and white-collar yuppie Sam Treatwell (David Andrews) seeks Johnson's help in replacing his beloved Cherry 2000 (Pamela Gidley), a robot sex-object who suffered internal meltdown when Treadwell unwisely tried to make love to her in soapsuds.

For obscure reasons, replacement Cherry clones are stored far out in the Zone, which is ruled over by the psychotic Lester (Tim

Thomerson) and his gang. Bulk of the film [story by Lloyd Fonvielle] consists of efforts of Johnson and Treadwell to avoid capture by Lester and reach the robot warehouse.

Along the way they meet Ben Johnson as a philosophical old-timer and Harry Carey Jr as a treacherous gas-station owner.

Technically, pic is quite lavish and the Nevada locations suitably rugged.

• •

■ **CHEYENNE AUTUMN**

1964, 161 MINS, US ◇ ▼
Dir John Ford   *Prod* Bernard Smith   *Scr* James R. Webb   *Ph* William Clothier   *Ed* Otho Lovering
Mus Alex North   *Art Dir* Richard Day
● Richard Widmark, Carroll Baker, James Stewart, Edward G. Robinson, Karl Malden, Sal Mineo (Warner)

Cheyenne Autumn is a rambling, episodic account of a reputedly little-known historic Cheyenne Indian migration 1,500 miles through almost unbelievable hardships and dangers to the tribe's home near the Yellowstone in Wyoming. Somewhere in the telling, the original premise of the Mari Sandoz novel is lost sight of in a wholesale insertion of extraneous incidents which bear little or no relation to the subject.

Action follows a small band of Cheyennes attempting to escape from their barren Oklahoma reservation to their own lush Wyoming lands, from which they were transported after having surrendered to the army in 1877. Originally more than 900, their number now has been decimated to 286 through starvation and lack of medical attention.

Richard Widmark in one of his hardboiled roles is persuasive as a cavalry captain sympathetic to the Indians, detailed to bring them back to the reservation and finally going to Washington to see the Secretary of the Interior in charge of Indian affairs. Gilbert Roland and Ricardo Montalban portray the historic Dull Knife and Little Wolf, leaders of the Cheyennes, and carry off their work with honors. Carroll Baker is somewhat lost as a Quaker schoolteacher who accompanied the Cheyennes because of her love for the children.

James Stewart as Wyatt Earp is in strictly for laughs, not for plot motivation, and Arthur Kennedy also is in briefly as Doc Holliday, neither having much to do. Karl Malden scores as a German captain of US cavalry; Dolores Del Rio plays an Indian woman with conviction; Edward G. Robinson does well by the Interior Secretary part and Patrick Wayne plays a brash young lieutenant with feeling.

• •

■ **CHEYENNE SOCIAL CLUB, THE**

1970, 103 MINS, US ◇ ▼
Dir Gene Kelly   *Prod* Gene Kelly   *Scr* James Lee Barrett   *Ph* William Clothier   *Ed* Adrienne Fazan
Mus Walter Scharf   *Art Dir* Gene Allan
● James Stewart, Henry Fonda, Shirley Jones, Sue Ane Langdon, Elaine Devry, Jackie Russell (National General)

James Stewart and Henry Fonda are long-time cowpoke buddies, and when the former finds he has inherited from his brother a business in Cheyenne, the latter follows. Turns out the business is the town's pleasure dome, inhabited by Sue Ane Langdon, Elaine Devry, Jackie Russell, Jackie Joseph and Sharon De Bord, under Shirley Jones' supervision. Each girl has her own doorbell signal, so Stewart never can talk to them for long without callers interrupting.

When Stewart learns the truth and plans to shutter the place, the whole male population turns against him, but Fonda works his way through the house, room by room.

The story is a flimsy, one-joke affair, and Gene Kelly's direction is too sluggish to make

it perk at the fast pace required to sustain momentum.

• •

■ **CHICAGO JOE AND THE SHOWGIRL**

1990, 103 MINS, UK ◇ ▼
Dir Bernard Rose   *Prod* Tim Bevan   *Scr* David Yallop   *Ph* Mike Southon   *Ed* Dan Rae   *Mus* Hans Zimmer, Shirley Walker   *Art Dir* Gemma Jackson
● Emily Lloyd, Keifer Sutherland, Patsy Kensit, Keith Allen, Liz Fraser, Alexandra Pigg (Polygram/Working Title)

Scripter David Yallop was inspired and intrigued by the sensational Hulten/Jones murder case of 1944, which became known as the 'Cleft Chin Murder Case' after the disappearance of a London taxi driver. It made household names of American serviceman Karl Hulten and British showgirl Elizabeth Maud Jones, beating war news to the headlines. Shame is Yallop was unable to ignite anything sensational in the finished product.

The trial, which resulted in the hanging of Hulten (the only execution of a Yank by the British) and the reprieve of Jones, is passed up. Yallop instead focuses on duo's six-day London crime spree, beginning with theft of an army truck and a fur, and finishing with murder of the cabbie.

Problem is that Emily Lloyd totally fails to deliver the necessary allurement, and Kiefer Sutherland is weak in playing a weak character. End result is a pair of languid leads fumbling their way through a passionless picture.

Whole pic was shot on sets rather than location, and despite Gemma Jackson's thoughtful designs, the overall look is cheap.

• •

■ **CHILD IS WAITING, A**

1963, 104 MINS, US
Dir John Cassavetes   *Prod* Stanley Kramer   *Scr* Abby Mann   *Ph* Joseph LaShelle   *Ed* Gene Fowler
Mus Ernest Gold
● Burt Lancaster, Judy Garland, Gena Rowlands, Steven Hill, Bruce Ritchey (United Artists)

As in *Judgment at Nuremberg*, producer Stanley Kramer dips into productive source of live television drama and comes up with a poignant, provocative, revealing dramatization. Again it is writer Abby Mann whose original work spawns the effort. This time it is the subject of mentally retarded children.

The film focuses on one profoundly touching case, around which are woven heartrending and often shocking illustrations of behavior and activity in institutions for the mentally retarded as well as academic discussions of the role in society to be played by the afflicted, and society's responsibility to them. There is no hokiness in the dramatization.

Burt Lancaster delivers a firm, sincere, persuasive and unaffected performance as the professionally objective but understanding psychologist who heads the institution. Judy Garland gives a sympathetic portrayal of an overly involved teacher who comes to see the error of her obsession with the plight of one child.

That child, a deeply touching 'borderline case', is played superbly by young Bruce Ritchey, a professional actor who manages to fit believably into a youthful cast that consists, for the most part, of actual retarded children who are patients of Pacific State Hospital in Pomona. As the lad's two troubled parents, Gena Rowlands (director John Cassavetes' wife) and Steven Hill pitch in with two exceptionally vivid and convincing performances.

• •

■ **CHILDREN, THE**

1990, 115 MINS, UK/W. GERMANY ◇
Dir Tony Palmer   *Prod* Andrew Montgomery, Harald Albrecht   *Scr* Timberlake Wertenbaker   *Ph* Nic Knowland   *Ed* Tony Palmer   *Art Dir* Chris Bradley

● Ben Kingsley, Kim Novak, Siri Neal, Geraldine Chaplin, Joe Don Baker, Karen Black (Isolde/Film Four/Arbo-Maram)

Previously filmed in 1929 by Paramount as *The Marriage Playground*, Edith Wharton's 1928 novel *The Children* comes to the screen as a somewhat dated enterprise. Story of a middle-aged man's infatuation for a teenage girl unfolds at a snail's pace.

Ben Kingsley is Martin Boyne, a middle-aged engineer returning to Europe after years in Brazil. He hopes to marry Rose Sellars (Kim Novak, looking ageless), his lifelong love recently widowed and living in an Alpine village. On the voyage home, he meets a group of seven children, the oldest of which is the budding Judith (Siri Neal).

Martin lingers on in Venice with the children, who seem to fascinate him, but eventually heads for the hills and Rose. The children soon follow. The rest of the film depicts Martin's indecision and his gradual emotional shift away from the demanding Rose to the guileless, appealing Judith, who appears to encourage him.

Kingsley gives one of his most affecting performances as the confused protagonist, and young Siri Neal is a find as the child-woman.

■ CHILDREN OF A LESSER GOD

1986, 110 MINS, US ◇ ⓥ
Dir Randa Haines   *Prod* Burt Sugarman, Patrick Palmer   *Scr* Hesper Anderson, Mark Medoff   *Ph* John Seale   *Ed* Lisa Fruchtman   *Mus* Michael Convertino   *Art Dir* Gene Callahan
● William Hurt, Marlee Matlin, Piper Laurie, Philip Bosco, Alison Gompf, John F. Cleary (Paramount)

Children of a Lesser God is the kind of good intentioned material that often gets weighed down with sentimentality on the screen. Fortunately, the translation of Mark Medoff's Tony Award-winning [1980] play avoids many of those traps by focusing on a touching and universal love story between a deaf woman and a hearing man.

At the heart of the picture is the attraction between William Hurt and Marlee Matlin. Their need and feeling for each other is so palpable that it is almost impossible not to share the experience and recognize it in one's own life.

It's another seamless performance for Hurt. Matlin, who makes her professional acting debut here and is in real life hearing impaired, is as much of the cast, is simply fresh and alive with fine shadings of expression.
□ 1986: Best Picture (Nomination)

■ CHILDREN OF THE CORN

1984, 93 MINS, US ◇ ⓥ
Dir Fritz Kiersch   *Prod* Donald P. Porchers, Terrence Kirby   *Scr* George Goldsmith   *Ph* Raoul Lomas   *Ed* Harry Keramidas   *Mus* Jonathan Elias   *Art Dir* Craig Stearns
● Peter Horton, Linda Hamilton, R.G. Armstrong, John Franklin, Courtney Gains, Robby Kiger (Gatlin/Angeles/Iverness)

Children of the Corn presents a normal couple, played by Peter Horton and Linda Hamilton, thrust into supernatural occurrences while on a cross-country trip. Horton is a newly graduated doctor on his way to start his internship in Seattle. Somewhere in Nebraska the couple happen on the children of the corn, a band of vicious youngsters who have murdered the adults and established a religious community worshipping a mysterious deity of the corn fields.

Led by Isaac (John Franklin), an adolescent with an old man's demeanor, the band of outsiders displays a sinister attraction. Shrouded in pseudo-Christian mythology, the children are more appealing than the mundane reality of the adults.

Director Fritz Kiersch and/or author Stephen King seem to play both ends against the middle, neither accepting nor denying the supernatural occurrences.
Children of the Corn does have a few good scare scenes but special effects are surprisingly disappointing.

■ CHILDREN OF THE DAMNED

1964, 90 MINS, UK
Dir Anton Leader   *Prod* Lawrence P. Bachmann   *Scr* Jack Briley   *Ph* Davis Boulton   *Ed* Ernie Walter   *Mus* Ron Goodwin   *Art Dir* Elliot Scott
● Ian Hendry, Alan Badel, Barbara Ferris, Alfred Burke, Sheila Allen, Clive Powell (M-G-M)

Like most sequels *Children Of The Damned* isn't nearly as good as its predecessor – Metro's 1960 *Village of the Damned*. What weakens this sequel is the fact that, unlike the original, it is burdened with a 'message'.

Jack Briley's screenplay broadens the scope to an international scale of what was originally a taut little sci-fi shocker. This time those strange, handsome parthenogenetic children the genius IQs, destructive dispositions and raygun eyes are not mere invaders from the outer limits bent on occupying earth, but are actually premature samplings of man as he will be in, say, a million years. And they have arrived for a curious purpose – to be destroyed, presumably to enable the silly, warlike contemporary man to learn some sort of lesson.

There are one or two genuinely funny lines in Briley's scenario and they are inherited by the character of a geneticist played engagingly by Alan Badel. A few of Badel's scenes with Ian Hendry, who plays an idealistic psychologist, are the best in the picture. Otherwise it's tedious going, and Anton Leader's lethargic direction doesn't help any.

■ CHILDREN'S HOUR, THE

1961, 109 MINS, US
Dir William Wyler   *Prod* William Wyler   *Scr* John Michael Hayes   *Ph* Franz F. Planer   *Ed* Robert Swink   *Mus* Alex North   *Art Dir* Fernando Carrere
● Audrey Hepburn, Shirley MacLaine, James Garner, Miriam Hopkins, Fay Bainter, Karen Balkin (United Artists)

Lillian Hellman's study of the devastating effect of malicious slander and implied guilt comes to the screen for the second time in this crackling production of *The Children's Hour*. William Wyler, who directed the 1936 production (*These Three*), which veered away from the touchier, more sensational aspects of Hellman's Broadway play, this time has chosen to remain faithful to the original source.

Story deals with an irresponsible, neurotic child who spreads a slanderous rumor of a lesbian relationship between the two head-mistresses of the private school for girls she attends.

Audrey Hepburn and Shirley MacLaine, in the leading roles, beautifully complement each other. Hepburn's soft sensitivity, marvelous projection and emotional understatement result in a memorable portrayal. MacLaine's enactment is almost equally rich in depth and substance. James Garner is effective as Hepburn's betrothed, and Fay Bainter comes through with an outstanding portrayal of the impressionable grandmother who falls under the evil influence of the wicked child.

■ CHILD'S PLAY

1972, 100 MINS, US ◇
Dir Sidney Lumet   *Prod* David Merrick   *Scr* Leon Prochnik   *Ph* Gerald Hirschfeld   *Ed* Edward Warschilka, Joanne Burke   *Mus* Michael Small   *Art Dir* Philip Rosenberg

● James Mason, Robert Preston, Beau Bridges, Ronald Weyand, Charles White, David Rounds (Paramount)

Child's Play, a taut and suspenseful drama of a Catholic boys' school, which won critical acclaim on Broadway, repeats in interest as a film production. Unfoldment often carries the aspects of a chiller as mysterious malevolent forces create a reign of terror and build to a powerful climax.

David Merrick gives the same meticulous care to script, written by Leon Prochnik in adapting the Robert Marasco original, and what emerges is compelling.

Situation revolves around deliberate violence as practised by some of the students on others, senseless incidents which cause fear and suspicion.

James Mason delivers a solid performance as a man whose hate of his fellow professor is exceeded, he says, only by Robert Preston's hate of him. Role is deeply dramatic, and Preston, in a different type of characterization, lends equal potency.

■ CHIMES AT MIDNIGHT

1966, 113 MINS, SPAIN/SWITZERLAND ◇
Dir Orson Welles   *Prod* Emiliano Piedra, Angel Escolano   *Scr* Orson Welles   *Ph* Edmond Richard   *Ed* Fritz Mueller   *Mus* Angelo Francesco Lavagnino   *Art Dir* Jose Antonio de la Guerra, Mariano Erdoza
● Orson Welles, John Gielgud, Jeanne Moreau, Norman Rodway, Keith Baxter, Margaret Rutherford (Internacional Films Espanola/Alpine)

This Swiss-Spanish pic chronicles the story of Shakespeare's Falstaff. Taken from several plays, it details the last days of Falstaff's relationship with the Prince of Wales, the future King Henry V of England. A personal viewpoint, it mixes the grotesque, bawdy, comic and heroic, and does have a melancholy under its carousing and battles.

Orson Welles has tried to humanize Falstaff in dwelling on his intimations of old age that make him accept a buffoonish part in the young prince's life. He contrasts this with the sombre reflections of the real father (Henry IV) on whose uneasy head lies the new crown of England. The prince finally has to choose between an indulgent father figure, Falstaff, and the real adult father who means responsibility, dedication and adulthood.

Welles himself is gigantically bloated and full of swagger that yet shows glints of lonely pride and fear of rejection under a pompous exterior. John Gielgud, on the other hand, is sombre, suffering and stately as the King Henry IV trying to sort out of the problems of the court and his vassals in order to unite his nobles.

■ CHINA

1943, 78 MINS, US
Dir John Farrow   *Prod* Richard Blumenthal   *Scr* Frank Butler   *Ph* Leo Tover   *Ed* Eda Warren   *Mus* Victor Young
● Loretta Young, Alan Ladd, William Bendix, Philip Ahn, Iris Wong, Sen Yung (Paramount)

Tale opens in an interior China town, with Jap planes attacking the spot and populace. Among quick evacuees is Alan Ladd, who's been trucking gasoline to the Jap armies out of Shanghai. William Bendix is his sidekick. Along the road, truck is stopped and Ladd is forced to take aboard group of Chinese femme university students in the charge of American instructress Loretta Young. Ladd is arrogant and unconcerned over the Jap atrocities against the Chinese, but wakes up when a Jap plane strafes his truck.

Frank Butler generates authenticity in the dramatic evolvement of his screenplay [from a play by Archibald Forbes], while director John Farrow neatly blends the human and melodramatic elements of the yarn. Interest is hyped in the early reels with pickup of a Chinese baby by Bendix at the bombed town, and gradual breakdown of Ladd's attitude towards the youngster until the point where the latter is murdered by the Jap soldiers and Ladd is transformed into a battler for the Chinese cause.

....

■ CHINA DOLL

1958, 99 MINS, US

Dir Frank Borzage   *Prod* Frank Borzage   *Scr* Kitty Buhler   *Ph* William Clothier   *Ed* Jack Murray   *Mus* Henry Vars   *Art Dir* Howard Richmond
● Victor Mature, Li Li-hua, Ward Bond, Bob Mathias, Johnny Desmond, Danny Chang (Romina/United Artists)

About average in its war story telling, *China Doll* has a field day with the warmth and humor of a romance between a burly air corps captain and a fragile oriental beauty.

The script, from a story by James Benson Nablo and Thomas F. Kelly, often is highly interesting, often humorous and sometimes corny. It's a tale of China in 1943, at a time when the Japanese had cut off all supply lines and American airmen took to flying the hump. Smack in the middle is Victor Mature, a lonely leader who has dropped good books and bad women and has taken to the bottle. In one of his most alcoholic states, he unknowingly purchases a young Chinese girl as a housekeeper, and she ends up carrying his child, drawing his love and marrying him, in that order.

Mature displays his share of love, emotion and humor. Highlight of the picture is sumptuous femme Li Li-hua in the title role. Ward Bond is excellent as an understanding man of the cloth, and Danny Chang is fine as the barracks' boy.

....

■ CHINA GATE

1957, 96 MINS, US

Dir Samuel Fuller   *Prod* Samuel Fuller   *Scr* Samuel Fuller   *Ph* Joseph Biroc   *Ed* Gene Fowler Jr   *Mus* Victor Young, Max Steiner   *Art Dir* John Mansbridge
● Gene Barry, Angie Dickinson, Nat 'King' Cole, Lee Van Cleef, Warren Hsieh, Paul Dubov (20th Century-Fox)

China Gate is an over-long but sometimes exciting story of the battle between Vietnamese and Red Chinese, told through the efforts of a small band of French Legionnaires to reach and destroy a hidden Communist munitions dump.

Samuel Fuller gives his indie good production values, early use of Oriental war footage clips establishing an interesting story setting. The dominating character is a beautiful Eurasian woman, who leads the Legion demolition patrol to its objective through enemy territory. An added exploitation turn is the casting of Nat 'King' Cole in dual assignment of a straight role and warbling title song.

Gene Barry and Angie Dickinson top the cast, former an American in the Legion, in charge of dynamiting operations of the Red ammunition cache; latter the Eurasian who is trusted by the Communists but on the side of the patriots. Romantic conflict is realized through their having once been married.

Dickinson does yeoman service with her colorful role. Barry also handles himself well but part sometimes is negative. Cole as the only other American in Legion patrol shows he can act as well as sing.

....

■ CHINA GIRL

1942, 98 MINS, US

Dir Henry Hathaway   *Prod* Ben Hecht   *Scr* Ben Hecht   *Ph* Lee Garmes   *Ed* James B. Clark   *Mus* Hugo Friedhofer

● Gene Tierney, George Montgomery, Lynn Bari, Victor McLaglen (20th Century-Fox)

Ben Hecht is listed as producer and scripter of this original by Melville Crossman, which is usually Darryl Zanuck's nom de plume when screen-scripting.

Plot has George Montgomery, as an American newsreel cameraman in Mandalay, falling in love with an American-educated Chinese girl (Gene Tierney). There are the usual Jap intrigue and paid spies in persons of Lynn Bari and Victor McLaglen, who try to get Montgomery into their clutches to turn over to the Japs.

Only angle for audience attention is the setting of China under Jap rule and bombing prior to Pearl Harbor, with romance of minor interest due to inadequacies of the script and original yarn. Otherwise, it's regulation stuff that has been re-told many times.

....

■ CHINA GIRL

1987, 88 MINS, US ◇ ⓥ

Dir Abel Ferrara   *Prod* Michael Nozik   *Scr* Nicholas St. John   *Ph* Bojan Bazelli   *Ed* Anthony Redman   *Mus* Joe Delia   *Art Dir* Dan Leigh
● James Russo, Sari Chang, Richard Panebianco, David Caruso, Russell Wong, Joey Chin (Great American/Street Life)

China Girl is a masterfully directed, uncompromising drama and romance centering on gang rumbles (imaginary) between the neighboring Chinatown and Little Italy communities in New York City.

Screenplay hypothesizes an outbreak of a gang war when a Chinese restaurant opens in Italian territory. In the midst of the battling, a beautiful Chinese teenager (Sari Chang) falls in love with a pizza parlor gofer (Richard Panebianco). A la *West Side Story*, the adults oppose the relationship and, more to the point, the Mafia dons and Chinese elder gansters are in cahoots to maintain peace in their bordered territory.

Russell Wong (as handsome as a shirt ad model) and sidekick Joey Chin dominate their scenes as the young Chinese gang leaders. Title roler Sari Chang is called upon merely to be an idealized porcelain beauty and she fills the bill.

....

■ CHINA 9 LIBERTY 37

1978, 94 MINS, ITALY ◇

Dir Monte Hellman   *Prod* Gianni Bozzacchi, Valerio De Paolis   *Scr* Ennio De Concini, Vicente Soriano   *Ph* Giovanni Fiore   *Ed* Cesare D'Amico   *Mus* Pino Donaggio
● Fabio Testi, Warren Oates, Jenny Agutter, Sam Peckinpah (CEA)

An oater made in Spain with Italo backing and American and English thesps in the main roles. Though the director, Monte Hellman, is American, this is a strange western that eschews Italo pasta violence and camp, Hispano romantics or more robust Yank counterparts.

Fabio Testi is a gunman who runs off after having raped the wife of a gunslinger he was sent by railroad reps to kill. But she follows him and there is love, until railroad men are sent after the gunslinger and the husband reappears with his brothers.

Warren Oates is gruff as the husband, Jenny Agutter pliant as the torn wife who finally ends up again with her husband when the gunman will not kill him.

The old west looks a bit flat. One cameo scene is done by Sam Peckinpah, a writer selling the legend rather than the reality of the west and who offers his services to the woman in the gunfighters' life but is refused.

....

■ CHINA SEAS

1935, 87 MINS, US ⓥ

Dir Tay Garnett   *Prod* Irving G. Thalberg, Albert Lewin   *Scr* Jules Furthman, James Kevin McGuinness   *Ph* Ray June   *Ed* William Levanway   *Mus* Herbert Stothart
● Clark Gable, Jean Harlow, Wallace Beery, Rosalind Russell, Lewis Stone, Dudley Digges (M-G-M)

This is a story of love – sordid and otherwise – of piracy and violence and heroism on a passenger boat run from Shanghai to Singapore [from a novel by Crosbie Garstin]. Clark Gable is a valiant sea captain, Wallace Beery a villainous pirate boss, and Jean Harlow a blond trollop who motivates the romance and most of the action. All do their jobs expertly.

Harlow is crossed in love when Gable, who has been her sweetheart in a sort of sparring partner but true-love affair, is tempted to return to English aristocracy. Temptation arrives in the form of the refined Rosalind Russell, a home town acquaintance. The social gap between Harlow and Rosalind touches off the fireworks.

Spurned by Gable, Harlow seeks to get hunk by slipping Beery the key to the ship's arsenal which makes it a cinch for the raiding pirates. But the raid fails, for Gable refuses to reveal the hiding place of a cargo of gold.

The pirate raid and its unsuccessful termination (for the pirates) is full of shooting, suspense and action. Add a running atmosphere of suspense through the picture, and there's plenty of excitement.

....

■ CHINA SKY

1945, 78 MINS, US

Dir Ray Enright   *Prod* Maurice Geraghty   *Scr* Brenda Weisberg, Joseph Hoffman   *Ph* Nicholas Musuraca   *Ed* Gene Milford   *Mus* Roy Webb   *Art Dir* Albert S. D'Agostino, Ralph Berges
● Randolph Scott, Ruth Warrick, Ellen Drew, Anthony Quinn, Carol Thurston, Philip Ahn (RKO)

Pearl Buck's novel of the tenacity of Chinese guerrillas who harass the Japanese advance, and the American medico who runs the hospital in the key Chinese village, turns out far from the spectacular production it might have been. The guerrilla and fighting angle is played down, while stress is laid on interior sets and romantic conflict. As often happens, this lack of action wears the interest thin.

Scripters and director are so concerned with the triangle between Randolph Scott, as the American doctor, his devoted hospital co-worker (Ruth Warrick), and his wife (Ellen Drew) that they neglect the story's movement. There finally is a bangup battle at the end between Jap paratroopers and the guerrillas as a wounded Jap officer wangles info out to his forces, but it's too late.

Scott is routine as the hospital head while Warrick is superb, but her role of the doctor's assistant is not sufficient to carry the whole load.

....

■ CHINA SYNDROME, THE

1979, 122 MINS, US ◇ ⓥ

Dir James Bridges   *Prod* Michael Douglas   *Scr* Mike Gray, T.S. Cook, James Bridges   *Ph* James Crabe   *Ed* David Rawlins   *Art Dir* George Jenkins
● Jane Fonda, Jack Lemmon, Michael Douglas, Scott Brady, James Hampton (Columbia)

The China Syndrome is a moderately compelling thriller about the potential perils of nuclear energy, whose major fault is an overweening sense of its own self-importance.

Jane Fonda limns a TV anchorwoman stuck in a 'happy news' rut, who hires freelance cameraman Michael Douglas for a series on energy that she hopes will break her into the world of hard news.

While filming at a nuclear energy plant, they witness a control room crisis involving supervisor Jack Lemmon, which is surreptitiously lensed by Douglas. The resulting footage becomes a political hot potato, as station manager Peter Donat buckles under pressure from power company exec Richard Herd.

It's not until the final half-hour of *China Syndrome* that its promise catches up to its punch, and the wind-up packs a solid wallop.

●●●●●●●●●●●●●●●●●●●●●●●●●●●●●●●

■ CHINATOWN

1974, 130 MINS, US ◇ ⓥ
Dir Roman Polanski *Prod* Robert Evans *Scr* Robert Towne *Ph* John A. Alonzo *Ed* Sam O'Steen *Mus* Jerry Goldsmith *Art Dir* Richard Sylbert
● Jack Nicholson, Faye Dunaway, John Huston, Perry Lopez, John Hillerman, Diane Ladd (Paramount)

Chinatown is an outstanding picture. Robert Towne's complex but literate and orderly screenplay takes gumshoe Jack Nicholson on a murder manhunt all over the Los Angeles of the late 1930s, where Faye Dunaway is the wife of a dead city official.

Towne, director Roman Polanski and Nicholson have fashioned a sort of low-key Raymond Chandler hero who, with assistants Joe Mantell and Bruce Glover, specializes in matrimonial infidelities. When Diane Ladd, posing as Dunaway, commissions a job on Darrell Zwerling, the city's water commissioner, Nicholson becomes involved in a series of interlocking schemes.

He is in disfavor with the local police, hounded by goons (Roy Jenson and Polanski, in a bit role) in the employ of John Huston, and partially conned by Dunaway despite a romantic vibration between the two.
☐ 1974: Best Picture (Nomination)

●●●●●●●●●●●●●●●●●●●●●●●●●●●●●●●

■ CHISUM

1970, 110 MINS, US ◇ ⓥ
Dir Andrew V. McLaglen *Prod* Andrew J. Fenady *Scr* Andrew J. Fenady *Ph* William H. Clothier *Ed* Robert Simpson *Mus* Dominic Frontiere *Art Dir* Carl Anderson
● John Wayne, Forrest Tucker, Christopher George, Ben Johnson, Glenn Corbett, Andrew Prine (Batjac)

John Wayne plays a rugged character set down in New Mexico Territory, circa 1878, as King of the Pecos, its greatest landholder and biggest cattle owner. Andrew J. Fenady, who scripted, has taken the events of the bloody Lincoln County cattle war which ended in 1878 to background his story.

Forrest Tucker plays Lawrence Murphy, the ambitious, land-grabbing and power-hungry newcomer who was one of the principals of the infamous cattle war.

Basis of picture is his move in on Chisum, who didn't create his empire through any lack of fighting, and the cattleman's powerful resistance.

Wayne clothes his interpretation of the early West figure with vigor and warmth.

●●●●●●●●●●●●●●●●●●●●●●●●●●●●●●●

■ CHITTY CHITTY BANG BANG

1968, 156 MINS, UK ◇ ⓥ
Dir Ken Hughes *Prod* Albert R. Broccoli *Scr* Roald Dahl, Ken Hughes *Ph* Christopher Challis *Ed* John Shirley *Mus* Richard M. Sherman, Robert B. Sherman *Art Dir* Harry Pottle
● Dick Van Dyke, Sally Ann Howes, Lionel Jeffries, Gert Frobe, Anna Quayle, Benny Hill (United/Warfield)

Dick Van Dyke is starred as the widowed, absent-minded, unsuccessful inventor whose children convince him to save the pioneer racing auto from destruction. Turned into a spanking and sleek vehicle by Van Dyke, car develops ability to float on water and fly.

Brought into the story by this point are Sally Ann Howes, daughter of a wealthy candy manufacturer (James Robertson Justice), and Lionel Jeffries, Van Dyke's father who likes to imagine that he's still in India fighting the natives.

Gert Frobe, the bullyish, temperamental, childlike prince of a middle European nation, proceeds to kidnap auto and its inventor. He gets wrong car and wrong man, Jeffries, with result that Van Dyke, Howes and the kids fly off to the principality on a rescue mission.

The $10 million film lacks warmth. No real feeling is generated between any two characters.

Howes goes through the romantic motions with Van Dyke and the maternal ones with the kids, but there is no real sentiment between players.

●●●●●●●●●●●●●●●●●●●●●●●●●●●●●●●

■ CHOICES

1981, 90 MINS, US ◇
Dir Silvio Narizzano *Prod* Alicia Rivera Alon, Rami Alon *Scr* Rami Alon *Ph* Hanania Baer *Mus* Sonny Gordon, Paul Carafotes *Art Dir* Nancy Auburn
● Paul Carafotes, Victor French, Lelia Goldoni, Val Avery, Demi Moore (Oaktree)

Director Silvio Narizzano's first US film in 13 years is an engaging feature that confronts its young hero with an unwanted tag of a physical handicap.

Paul Carafotes appears to be an average high schooler whose world consists of football and music. His family attempts to nurture the latter aspect. However, Carafotes is partially deaf and a school medical examiner rules this precludes him from the football team.

Carafotes resents his sudden freak status and his seeming lack of choices. His helplessness manifests itself in his behavior as he adopts an 'I don't care' attitude and falls in with a tough gang.

Choices has all its sympathies in the right place and one can't help but warm to its message even if its manipulation often lacks subtlety. At times its moralistic views and approach give the picture the feel of a propaganda piece commissioned by a handicapped rights organization.

Writer-co-producer Rami Alon provides a functional script in his maiden screen effort which has a dash too much preachiness.

●●●●●●●●●●●●●●●●●●●●●●●●●●●●●●●

■ CHOIRBOYS, THE

1977, 119 MINS, US ◇ ⓥ
Dir Robert Aldrich *Prod* Merv Adelson, Lee Rich *Scr* Christopher Knopf *Ph* Joseph Biroc *Ed* Maury Winetrobe, William Martin, Irving Rosenblum *Mus* Frank DeVol *Art Dir* Bill Kenney
● Charles Durning, Louis Gossett Jr, Perry King, Clyde Kusatsu, Stephen Macht, Randy Quaid (Lorimar/Airone)

When Robert Aldrich's filmmaking is good, it's very, very good; and when it's bad it's awful. This cheap-looking ultra-raunchy alleged comedy about policemen leaves no stone unturned in its exploitation of vulgarity.

The story peg apparently is that, underneath the public image of callousness, which many urban police departments today exude, lies the real callousness – bigoted, sexist, unfeeling, alienated, etc.

The leading characters represent a formula cross section of people – old-style cop Charles Durning all the way down through minorities, troubled Vietnam veterans (again!), naive twerps, sexually kinky All-American Boy type, and a special mention of Tim McIntyre who is terrific in portrayal of a person audiences will come to hate.

●●●●●●●●●●●●●●●●●●●●●●●●●●●●●●●

■ CHOPPER CHICKS IN ZOMBIETOWN

1990, 89 MINS, US ◇ ⓥ
Dir Dan Hoskins *Prod* Maria Snyder *Scr* Dan Hoskins *Ph* Tom Fraser *Ed* W.O. Garrett *Mus* Daniel May
● Jamie Rose, Catherine Carlen, Kristina Loggia, Martha Quinn, Don Calfa, Whitney Reis (Chelsea Partners)

Chopper Chicks in Zombietown is a surprisingly funny B-movie spoof with a feminist edge. Writer-director Dan Hoskins has a great deal of fun scrambling genres. It's a classic story of bikers invading a secluded town and rattling the suspicious populace.

At the same time, it's another classic story: the local mad scientist is killing off citizens, reviving them as zombie slaves, and generally making the town a miserable place to live. The bikers are leather-and-chain-wearing women.

Leader of the pack Rox (Catherine Carlen) is a hard-bitten (but not bad-looking) motorcycle mama who proudly proclaims herself 'a big, bad bulldyke'. Her gang, the Cycle Sluts, includes an ex-homecoming queen (Jamie Rose), an AWOL demolitions expert (Kristina Loggia) and a sex-crazed 'nymfomaniac' (Whitney Reis). The mad scientist is played by Don Calfa.

Hoskins isn't able to sustain the level of lunacy and several scenes suggest the Harley-riding actresses have been asked to vamp until a funny line comes along. Still, there is a lot to laugh about, and dialog that moviegoers will quote for days afterward.

●●●●●●●●●●●●●●●●●●●●●●●●●●●●●●●

■ CHORUS LINE, A

1985, 113 MINS, US ◇ ⓥ
Dir Richard Attenborough *Prod* Cy Feuer, Ernest Martin *Scr* Arnold Schulman *Ph* Ronnie Taylor *Ed* John Bloom *Mus* Marvin Hamlisch *Art Dir* Patrizia Von Brandenstein
● Michael Douglas, Terrence Mann, Alyson Reed, Cameron English, Vicki Frederick, Audrey Landers (Embassy/PolyGram)

Director Richard Attenborough has not solved the problem of bringing the 1975 musical *A Chorus Line* to the screen, but he at least got it there after nearly a decade of diddling around by others.

There's a common wisdom, of course, that a stage show must be 'opened up' for the camera, but *Chorus* often seems static and confined, rarely venturing beyond the immediate. Attenborough merely films the stage show as best he could.

Nonetheless, the director and lenser Ronnie Taylor have done an excellent job working within the limitations, using every trick they could think of to keep the picture moving. More importantly, they have a fine cast, good music and a great, popular show to work with. So if all they did was get it on film, that's not so bad.

Michael Douglas is solid as the tough choreographer and Terrence Mann is good as his assistant. Alyson Reed also is sympathetic as Douglas' dancing ex-girlfriend.

Worth special note, too, are Cameron English as the troubled young gay, Vicki Frederick as the older hoofer and Audrey Landers, who romps delightfully through the 'T&A' number.

●●●●●●●●●●●●●●●●●●●●●●●●●●●●●●●

■ CHORUS OF DISAPPROVAL, A

1989, 100 MINS, US ◇ ⓥ
Dir Michael Winner *Prod* Michael Winner *Scr* Michael Winner, Alan Ayckbourn *Ph* Alan Jones *Ed* Chris Barnes *Mus* John DuPrez *Art Dir* Peter Young
● Jeremy Irons, Anthony Hopkins, Prunella Scales, Jenny Seagrove, Sylvia Sims, Patsy Kensit (South Gate)

It's tricky trying to convert stage to screen,

and this is one play that suffers in translation. As a movie, *A Chorus of Disapproval*, chugs along when Alan Ayckbourn's play raced.

Jeremy Irons shines as Jones, a shy, rather nervous widower who comes to work in the small English seaside town of Scarborough. He is lonely and, to meet people, he joins the local amateur group, which is practicing *A Beggar's Opera*.

The production is directed by Dafydd Llewellyn (Anthony Hopkins), a scruffy solicitor whose only passion is the theatre and who only really comes alive when he is directing a new play.

Jones, without really trying, soon becomes a small Lothario, his actions having hilarious effects on the various members of the drama group. Jones becomes involved with Llewellyn's lonely wife, Hannah (Prunella Scales), but she finds she is not alone in his affections.

Pic is a fine, if uninspired, first screen adaptation of one of Great Britain's favorite playwrights.

• •

■ CHOSEN, THE

1981, 108 MINS, US ◇

Dir Jeremy Paul Kagan   *Prod* Edie Landau, Ely Landau   *Scr* Edwin Gordon   *Ph* Arthur Ornitz   *Ed* David Garfield   *Mus* Elmer Bernstein   *Art Dir* Stuart Wurtzel
● Maximilian Schell, Rod Steiger, Robby Benson, Barry Miller (Landau)

The Chosen is a first-rate adaptation of Chaim Potok's novel of friendship between two young Jewish men of widely different religio-cultural upbringings and their individual relationships with strong fathers.

Set in the latter years of World War II, the story has the principles, cultural Jew Barry Miller and orthodox Hassidic Jew Robby Benson, meeting as opponents in a baseball game. To Miller, a typical American kid, Benson's Hassidic upbringing complete with 19th-century attire and long side-curls makes him akin to a creature from outer space.

Yet the relationship grows and Miller is asked to meet with Benson's legendary father, an orthodox rabbi portrayed by Rod Steiger. In full-bearded Hassidic tradition, Steiger must approve of his son's non-sect friends.

Director Kagan and writer Gordon do wonders with the poignant material. Despite the obvious ethnic slant this is a picture which communicates universally.

Steiger gives an exceptional performance as the somewhat tyranical but loving patriarch whose primary concern is his son's welfare. Maximilian Schell provides an interesting contrast as a Jewish intellectual, reacting to the Holocaust and he instills his son with deep moral values.

• •

■ CHRISTMAS HOLIDAY

1944, 98 MINS, US

Dir Robert Siodmak   *Prod* Felix Jackson   *Scr* Herman J. Mankiewicz   *Ph* Woody Bredell   *Ed* Ted Kent   *Mus* Hans J. Salter   *Art Dir* John B. Goodman, Robert Clatworthy
● Deanna Durbin, Gene Kelly, Dean Harens, Gale Sondergaard, Richard Whorf (Universal)

The story is Somerset Maugham's tale of a boy who grew up emotionally during a holiday in France (with the locale changed to New Orleans) and the plot switched around. A young army lieutenant, disappointed in love, finds himself stranded in the southern city, and meets up with another heartsick kid in a sad-faced singer at a cheap nightclub. From then on the story is told in flashbacks, as the singer (Deanna Durbin) tells the lieutenant of her brief happy marriage to a young ne'er-do-well, her husband's arrest for murder, and his imprisonment for life.

As the nitery thrush, Durbin has two incidental songs. 'Spring Will Be a Little Late This Year' (Frank Loesser) and the Irving Berlin oldie, 'Always'. But otherwise the dramatic role is unrelieved except by a few glimpses of a happy, smiling past.

• •

■ CHRISTMAS IN JULY

1940, 67 MINS, US ▼

Dir Preston Sturges   *Prod* Paul Jones   *Scr* Preston Sturges   *Ph* Victor Milner   *Ed* Ellsworth Hoagland   *Mus* Sigmund Krumgold   *Art Dir* Hans Dreier, Earl Hedrick
● Dick Powell, Ellen Drew, Raymond Walburn, Alexander Carr, William Demarest, Ernest Truex (Paramount)

This is the second combined writer-producer effort of Preston Sturges following his initial dual chore on *Great McGinty*. A mildly diverting programmer, *Christmas in July* lacks both the overall spontaneity and entertainment impress of Sturges' first picture.

Sturges' original script details the adventures of a young romantic pair living on the East Side and hoping for the day when fortune will smile broadly enough for them to get hitched. Boy is victim of office joke that advises he won $25,000 in a slogan contest, even though the jury is still fighting over the winner. But he collects the check and proceeds to run up a heavy charge account before cashing the winnings, plays Santa Claus to everyone on the block, including his sweetheart, and then is presented with the payoff that it's a phoney.

Picture has its moments of comedy and interest, but these are interspersed too frequently by obvious and boresome episodes that swing too much to the talkie side. There are flashes of the by-play and incidental intimate touches displayed by Sturges in his first picture, but not enough to bridge over the tedious episodes.

Dick Powell progresses as a straight lead without benefit of vocalizing, providing a dominating performance as the slogan award victim.

• •

■ CHUCK BERRY: HAIL! HAIL! ROCK 'N' ROLL!

1987, 120 MINS, US ◇ ▼

Dir Taylor Hackford   *Prod* Stephan Bennett   *Ph* Oliver Stapleton   *Ed* Lisa Day   *Mus* Keith Richards (prod.)
● Chuck Berry, Eric Clapton, Robert Cray, Etta James, Julian Lennon, Keith Richards (Delila)

'If you had tried to give rock 'n' roll another name, you might call it Chuck Berry,' pronounces John Lennon in an old interview at the outset of Taylor Hackford's glowing two-hour love letter to the kingpin of rock 'n' roll.

Chuck Berry: Hail! Hail! Rock 'n' Roll! is a joyous docu that effortlessly weaves luminary rock interviews with performance footage mostly shot at Berry's 60th birthday bash concert at the Fox Theatre St Louis.

Talking heads interviews with such rockers at Phil and Don Everly, Jerry Lee Lewis, Bo Diddley, Little Richard, Keith Richards, Roy Orbison and Bruce Springsteen testify to the fact that Berry's influence is all-pervasive in rock. As a singer songwriter, guitarist, and bop-till-you-drop performer, Berry was real 'troubadour.'

Berry's ruminations cover everything from his love of cars, to breaking the color code, payola, his 40-year marriage, and how he chose to adapt his lyrics and subjects to cross over to white audiences.

• •

■ CHUMP AT OXFORD, A

1940, 63 MINS, US

Dir Alfred Goulding   *Prod* Hal Roach   *Scr* Charles Rogers, Felix Adler, Harry Langdon   *Ph* Art Lloyd   *Ed* Bert Jordan   *Mus* Marvin Hatley   *Art Dir* Charles D. Hall

● Stan Laurel, Oliver Hardy, James Finlayson, Forrester Harvey, Peter Cushing, Sam Lufkin (Roach/United Artists)

Stan Laurel and Oliver Hardy's farce is mildly comical without offending. Time-worn gags clutter up the earlier footage and only when Laurel and Hardy, as new initiates into Oxford, actually move into the dean's home does the action speed up.

Early episodes have Laurel as a maid and Oliver Hardy as butler in a rich man's home. It looks as though it had been tacked on in order to make up footage. James Finlayson is the wealthy host in this episode but not given any cast credit.

A dinner party brings in all the familiar dress-tearing, pastry-flinging, corkpopping and shot-gun gags. Even that venerable nifty where the cop says 'you are liable to blow my brains out' and then exhibits the bullet-marked seat of his trousers is left in.

But once the comedians land in England they fare better. Outside of the lost-in-the-woods stunt and ghost-at-midnight routine, the gagging and all-round material brightens up.

• •

■ CIAO, FEDERICO!

1970, 60 MINS, US/ITALY ◇

Dir Gideon Bachmann   *Prod* Victor Herbert   *Scr* Gideon Bachmann   *Ph* Gideon Bachmann, Harvey Felderbaum, Anton Haakma   *Ed* Regine Heuser
● (Herbert)

Yank critic-filmmaker Gideon Bachmann, a longtime Rome resident, made this 16mm docu on Italian director Federico Fellini making *Satyricon*.

Pic's glue-like coverage of the sly, wry Fellini, and the latter's charm and interest shows him as a chameleon-like figure. He rages, but with an underlying lack of true anger, and a seeming watching of his own actions. So he rarely reveals himself in words but may do so in actions, even if they appear often calculated.

Pic is as airy, unrevealing but picturesque as Fellini's symbolical, circusy pix and his tender choosing of grotesques and beauty to limn his own fantasy world on film.

• •

■ CIAO MANHATTAN

1973, 90 MINS, US ◇ ▼

Dir John Palmer, David Weisman   *Prod* Robert Margouleff   *Mus* John Phillips, Richie Havens, Kim Milford, Skip Batten, Kim Fowley
● Edie Sedgwick, Wesley Hayes, Isabel Jewell, Paul America, Viva, Roger Vadim (Maron/Margouleff)

Ciao Manhattan is Edie Sedgwick's filmed swansong – she died of acute barbiturate intoxication in 1971. Monotonous and nearly incomprehensible, *Ciao* consists chiefly of pieced-together short ends from two Sedgwick vehicles, one begun with great fanfare by undergrounder Chuck Wein in 1987 when the Andy Warhol 'superstar' was at the peak of her celebrity, and the second started three years later in California by John Palmer and David Weisman, who evidently believed they could reconstruct the ruin.

In the last years of her life, says this intendedly anti-dope film, Sedgwick took up residence at the bottom of a tented Santa Barbara pool, narcissistically surrounded by giant blowups of herself. It is here that the film dwells, cruelly exploiting her dope and booze bloated visage, her siliconed breasts (for at least half the pic she is topless, so proud is she of these new ornaments) and most of the non-plot consists of her drug-zonked recollections of her halcyon days.

• •

■ CIMARRON

1931, 124 MINS, US ▼

Dir Wesley Ruggles   *Prod* William Le Baron
Scr Howard Estabrook   *Ph* Edward Cronjager
Ed William Hamilton   *Mus* Max Steiner   *Art Dir* Max Ree

● Richard Dix, Irene Dunne, Estelle Taylor, Nance O'Neil, William Collier Jr, Roscoe Ates (Radio)

An elegant example of super film making, this spectacular western [from the book by Edna Ferber] holds action, sentiment, sympathy, thrills and comedy.

Two outstanders in the playing, Richard Dix and Edna May Oliver, each surprisingly excellent; Dix with his straight character playing of a westerner and an Oklahoma pioneer who dies before his statue is unveiled in that state, while Oliver is nothing less than exquisite in her eccentric comedy role of a Colonial dame in the wilds.

Perhaps nothing will draw more attention than the skillful aging of the main role players, from 1888 to 1929, a period they pass through of over 40 years on the screen.

Wesley Ruggles' direction misses nothing in the elaborate scenes, as well as in the usual film making procedure.

Big production bits start with the land rush into Oklahoma in 1888, then the gospel meeting in a frontier gambling hall where Dix makes his biggest mark, an attmepted bank robbery and the court room trial of Dixie Lee, the harlot.

The land rush starts the action, men on horses and in wagons racing to capture some part of the two million acres released by the government to the first comers after the boom of a cannon at noon.

Estelle Taylor as Dixie Lee somewhat fades Irene Dunne as Dix's young and old wife. Taylor's showings are few but she makes them impressive. Dunne does nicely enough in a role of a loving wife and mother, which does not permit her to be much else. What she later accomplishes in a political way is suggested rather than acted. Roscoe Ates as a stuttering printer lands several laughs.

☐ 1930/31: Best Picture

■ CIMARRON

1960, 140 MINS, US ◇

Dir Anthony Mann   *Prod* Edmund Grainger
Scr Arnold Schulman   *Ph* Robert L. Surtees   *Ed* John Dunning   *Mus* Franz Waxman   *Art Dir* George W. Davis, Addison Hehr

● Glenn Ford, Maria Schell, Anne Baxter, Arthur O'Connell, Russ Tamblyn, Mercedes McCambridge (M-G-M)

Edna Ferber's novel of the first Oklahoma land rush (1889) shapes up in its second film translation as a good balance between rousing action and the marriage of Glenn Ford and Maria Schell as Yancey and Sabra Cravet.

There are many subtle shadings in Schell's performance as she transforms over period of 25 years from adoring, lovable bride to embittered, abandoned wife, successful newspaper publisher and bigoted mother-in-law when son Cim marries a childhood friend Indian girl. Latter and her mother were taken into the Cravet family by Yancey during the homestead run when the father was lynched by an Indian-hating scoundrel, played in grand bullboy style by Charles McGraw.

Ford emerges a strong and thoroughly likeable adventurer-idealist as the restless rover, Yancey, who is loving and devoted after his own fashion and spurns opportunity to become governor by helping to defraud Indians of their oil rights. Pic pulls no punches in pointing up the greed that discovery of black gold brought out in the rags-to-riches Oklahoma pioneers.

Cimarron starts off with a bang. Spectacle of thousands of land seekers lined up in Conestoga wagons, buck-boards and even a surrey with the fringe on top, straining to dash into the new territory at high noon on 22 April 1889, is masterfully handled by director Anthony Mann. This is grand-scale action in spades. Fortunately Arnold Schulman's adaptation doesn't let the performers down after the whirlwind start.

As was the case with *Oklahoma!*, *Cimarron* was photographed on location in Arizona. Producer Edmund Grainger, apparently being more concerned about pictorial composition than actual topography, has permitted mountains to show in backgrounds alien to Oklahoma.

■ CINCINNATI KID, THE

1965, 102 MINS, US ◇ ▼

Dir Norman Jewison   *Prod* Martin Ransohoff
Scr Ring Lardner Jr, Terry Southern   *Ph* Philip H. Lathrop   *Ed* Hal Ashby   *Mus* Lalo Schifrin   *Art Dir* George W. Davis, Edward Carfagno

● Steve McQueen, Edward G. Robinson, Ann-Margret, Karl Malden, Tuesday Weld, Joan Blondell (M-G-M)

The Cincinnati Kid is the fastmoving story of a burningly-ambitious young rambling-gambling man who challenges the king of stud poker to a showdown for the champ title of The Man. Adapted from Richard Jessup's realistically-written novel, it emerges a tenseful examination of the gambling fraternity.

Martin Ransohoff has constructed a taut, well-turned-out production. In Steve McQueen he has the near-perfect delineator of the title role. Edward G. Robinson is at his best in some years as the aging, ruthless Lancey Howard, champ of the poker tables for more than 30 years and determined now to defend his title against a cocksure but dangerous opponent. The card duel between the pair is dramatically developed through gruelling action, building in intensity as the final and deciding hand is played.

Ring Lardner Jr and Terry Southern have translated the major elements of the book, changing, however, tome's St Louis locale to a more picturesque New Orleans background. They have added a key situation, too, to point up the game – Karl Malden, in part of Shooter, dealer for the game, is forced by another gambler holding his markers to slip cards to the Kid so he'll cinch his victory. The Kid senses what's going on and eases Malden from his post.

■ CINDERELLA LIBERTY

1973, 117 MINS, US ◇ ▼

Dir Mark Rydell   *Prod* Mark Rydell   *Scr* Darryl Ponicsan   *Ph* Vilmos Zsigmond   *Ed* Donn Cambera, Patrick Kennedy   *Mus* John Williams   *Art Dir* Leon Ericksen

● James Caan, Marsha Mason, Kirk Calloway, Eli Wallach, Allyn Ann McLerie, Burt Young (20th Century-Fox)

Cinderella Liberty is an earthy but very touching story of a sailor's love for a prostitute. James Caan stars in an outstanding performance, and Marsha Mason, in her second picture, is equally superb.

The title comes direct from navy slang, referring to enlisted men's ashore time cut off at midnight, the one here being Caan's temporary hospitalization and pending transfer to a new ship. In a most realistic bar setting, he meets Mason, who takes him home where the first of many surprises for Caan is the existence of a partially-black son (Kirk Calloway). The next surprise is Caan's infatuation, to the extent of busting in on her to eject another trick.

Eli Wallach's strong featured role is that of Caan's long-ago boot camp drill instructor, whose harsh methods provoke a fight years later.

■ CINERAMA HOLIDAY

1955, 119 MINS, US ◇

Dir Robert Bendick, Philippe de Lacey   *Prod* Louis de Rochemont   *Scr* Otis Carney, Louis de Rochemont   *Ph* Joseph Brun, Harry Squire   *Ed* Jack Murray, Leo Zochling, Frederick Y. Smith   *Mus* Morton Gould, Van Cleave

● (Stanley-Warner Cinerama)

The Fred Waller Cinerama process is seen in its second mounting. Much of the excitement [of the first, *This Is Cinerama*] remains, although there is some feeling of repeating tried-and-true pictorial effects.

Right off, one thing stands out. Here is the greatest trailer for travel ever produced. There is a wisp of continuity in *Holiday*, unlike the predecessor film. Betty and John Marsh of Kansas City and Beatrice and Fred Troller of Zurich do an exchange student type of act, each pair of newlyweds visiting the other's hemisphere.

Since the second part of the show, after a 15-minute intermission, is largely made up of an extended visit to Paris, the impression grows into a conviction that the American couple really went places, did things and met people far beyond the arrangements for the Swiss pair.

■ CIRCUS WORLD

1964, 135 MINS, US/SPAIN ◇ ▼

Dir Henry Hathaway   *Prod* Samuel Bronston   *Scr* Ben Hecht, Julian Halevy, James Edward Grant   *Ph* Jack Hildyard   *Ed* Dorothy Spencer   *Mus* Dimitri Tiomkin   *Art Dir* John F. DeCuir

● John Wayne, Claudia Cardinale, Rita Hayworth, Lloyd Nolan, Richard Conte, John Smith (Bronston-Roma)

Samuel Bronston's made-in-Spain *Circus World* is a bigscreen wedding of spectacle and romance. The pace, as directed by Henry Hathaway, is unslackening.

A major value throughout is the photography of Jack Hildyard, working harmoniously with Hathaway (after Frank Capra Sr. departed). A second unit directed by Richard Talmadge had Claude Renoir on camera.

Special effects are numerous, perhaps the most memorable being Alex Weldon's capsizing on cue of a 4,000-ton freighter, loaded with the American circus folk, gear and animals, at Barcelona dockside. Barcelona's opera house was planked over to simulate the Hansa Circus Theatre of Hamburg, circa 1910. The plaza at Chinchon, used for the bullfight scene in *Around the World in 80 Days*, may also be recognized. Negative cost was around $8.5 million.

The basic story, by Philip Yordan and Nicholas Ray, is about a runaway aerialist (Rita Hayworth) who returns to watch her daughter (Claudia Cardinale) rehearsing on the lot, like Madame X of long ago, but this time there is a happy reunion of all, the final scene being the performance given hours after a terrible fire in which mother and daughter costar in a two-act.

Hayworth looks very good and acts with warmth and authority. Cardinale, in her fifth English-language film, is ideal for the girl-bursting-into-womanhood. The relationship to foster father John Wayne is developed with a steady sense of the interplay of the stern heman and the passionate-natured ward.

Wayne is the center-pole, the muscle, the virility and the incarnate courage of this often down but never out circus. The role has been tailored to his talents and personality, a rooting-tooting-shooting figure.

C

CISCO PIKE

1971, 94 MINS, US ◇

Dir Bill L. Norton   *Prod* Gerald Ayres   *Scr* Bill L. Norton   *Ph* Vilis Lapenieks   *Ed* Robert C. Jones   *Mus* Bob Johnston (sup.)   *Art Dir* Alfred Sweeney
● Gene Hackman, Karen Black, Kris Kristofferson, Harry Dean Stanton, Viva, Joy Bang (Columbia)

Kris Kristofferson in title role makes an excellent formal acting debut as a faded and drug-busted rock star forced by corrupt cop Gene Hackman into selling marijuana. Well-written and directed by Bill L. Norton, the handsome Gerald Ayres production sustains a good plot while providing proper amounts of environmental color.

The weakest plot angle is Hackman's motivation: not until the surprise climax is it made clear that he wants some extra money since police are underpaid. There's a lot more breadth in that angle that writer Norton fails to make viable.

Principal supporting players include Karen Black in another Karen Black role as Pike's amiable but confused girl; the totally delightful Viva; Harry Dean Stanton, excellent as Pike's old partner, pitiably wasted on hard drugs; and Joy Bang, Viva's cruising partner.

Kristofferson's screen presence is very strong. There's a look in his eyes – a combination of resignation, optimism and torture – that sticks in the memory long after the film has ended.

CITADEL, THE

1938, 112 MINS, UK ▼

Dir King Vidor   *Prod* Victor Saville   *Scr* Ian Dalrymple, Frank Wead, Elizabeth Hill   *Ph* Harry Stradling   *Ed* Charles Frend   *Mus* Louis Levy   *Art Dir* Lazare Meerson, Alfred Junge
● Robert Donat, Rosalind Russell, Ralph Richardson, Rex Harrison, Emlyn Williams, Penelope Dudley Ward (M-G-M)

The Citadel is Metro's second British-made production. It's an effective drama based on A.J. Cronin's novel which generated quite a controversy in medical circles due to presentation of its subject matter. Major change for picture is a switch to a happy ending.

Story details the adventures of a young physician (Robert Donat) who starts out with high ideals and determination to help humanity. When Welsh miners object to his research to prevent tuberculosis in the community, he goes to London, gets in with a coterie of mulcting doctors who brush aside medical ethics in their chase for money. Snapped out of his new surroundings by a bungling operation on his best friend, the young physician discards the shams of money for his original ideals.

Donat gives a most seasoned performance. Rosalind Russell turns in a sympathetic portrayal of the young wife who struggles through at his side, and gets him back to his ideals after the London experiences.

Picture is studded with many brilliantly human and dramatic sequences. Success of Donat in reviving a stillborn baby in a worker's home is a real heart-puller; chiller is episode where entrapped miner's arm is amputated in cave-in; and vivid drama springs forth when Donat stands by while his best friend dies during bungled operation performed by the incompetent, social-climbing surgeon.
□ 1938: Best Picture (Nomination)

CITIZEN KANE

1941, 120 MINS, US ▼

Dir Orson Welles   *Prod* Orson Welles   *Scr* Herman J. Mankiewicz, Orson Welles, [Joseph Cotten, John Houseman]   *Ph* Gregg Toland   *Ed* Robert Wise, [Mark Robson]   *Mus* Bernard Herrmann   *Art Dir* Van Nest Polglase

● Orson Welles, Joseph Cotten, Ray Collins, Paul Stewart, Dorothy Comingore, Everett Sloane (RKO/Mercury)

Citizen Kane is a film which distinguishes every daring entertainment venture that is created by a workman who is master of the technique and mechanics of his medium. It is a two-hour show, filled to the last minute with brilliant incident, unreeled in method and effects that sparkle with originality and invention.

In the film's story of a multi-millionaire newspaper publisher, political aspirant and wielder of public opinion there are incidents that may be interpreted as uncomplimentary to William Randolph Hearst. Protests against the film release were made by executives and employees in his organization.

Story is credited jointly to Herman J. Mankiewicz and Welles. The early, rebellious, youthful years of the powerful Kane are described by the family attorney, who neither understood nor had any deep affection for the young man. The thread is picked up by Kane's faithful business manager, then by his second wife, by his only earnest friend and finally by his butler. Pieced together, like a jigsaw puzzle, the parts and incidents omitted by earlier narrators are supplied by others.

When completed the authors' conception of Kane is a man who had every material advantage in life, but who lacked a feeling of human sympathy and tolerance. It is a story of spiritual failure. So intent is the effort to prove Kane a frustrate that no allowance is made to picture him as a human being. On this account he is not wholly real. Neither he nor his associates is blessed with the slightest sense of humor.

Welles portrays the chief character with surprising success, considering that the picture marks his debut as a film actor. His associates are selected from his Mercury Theatre's actors, few of whom had previous screen experience. Whatever else *Citizen Kane* may be, it is a refreshing cinematic novelty, and the general excellence of its acting is not the least of its assets.
□ 1941: Best Picture (Nomination)

CITIZENS BAND

1977, 98 MINS, US ◇ ▼

Dir Jonathon Demme   *Prod* Shep Fields   *Scr* Paul Brickman   *Ph* Jordon Cronenweth   *Ed* John F. Link II   *Mus* Bill Conti   *Art Dir* Bill Malley
● Paul Le Mat, Candy Clark, Ann Wedgeworth, Bruce McGill, Marcia Rodd, Charles Napier (Fields)

Plot peg is the truck accident of philandering husband Charles Napier, who's got Ann Wedgeworth in Dallas and Marcia Rodd in Portland, both with homes and children.

While he is recovering at the hands of Alix Elias (whose charms are mobile), the two suspicious women arrive in a small town where Paul Le Mat and estranged brother Bruce McGill are both courting Candy Clark. Roberts Blossom is the boy's irascible widower-father. Linking all their lives is the CB radio, buzzing away like a verbal Muzak.

The CB dialog exemplifies the good-natured horsing around that marks those channels, at the same time the serious emergency traffic that often saves lives.

CITY BENEATH THE SEA

1953, 87 MINS, US ◇

Dir Budd Boetticher   *Prod* Albert J. Cohen   *Scr* Jack Harvey, Ramon Romero   *Ph* Charles P. Boyle   *Ed* Edward Curtiss   *Mus* Joseph Gershenson   *Art Dir* Alexander Golitzen, Emrich Nicholson
● Robert Ryan, Mala Powers, Anthony Quinn, Suzan Ball, George Mathews, Karel Stepanek (Universal)

High romance of the pulp-fiction variety is

niftily shaped in *City Beneath the Sea*. The film stages a thrilling underseas 'earthquake' as a capper to the derring-do yarn laid in the West Indies.

A couple of lusty, adventurous deep-sea divers, a sunken treasure, comely femmes and the earthquake are expertly mixed to provide chimerical film entertainment. The direction by Budd Boetticher is slanted to take the most advantage of the action, amatory and thrill situations in the story based on Harry E. Reiseberg's *Port Royal – Ghost City Beneath the Sea*. Picture is not necessarily logical, but it tells its tale with a robust sense of humor.

The earthquake sequence is a real thriller. Scene is the historic sunken city of Port Royal, Jamaica, which went to the bottom of the Caribbean during a 1692 earthquake. Robert Ryan and Anthony Quinn team excellently as the daring divers, ever ready for the adventures offered by sunken treasure or shapely femmes. They come to Kingston, Jamaica, to dive for $1 million in gold bullion that went down with a freighter, without knowing their employer (Karel Stepanek) doesn't want the treasure found just yet.

Plot tangents boil along while Ryan woos Mala Powers, owner of a small, coastwise ship, and Quinn makes time with Suzan Ball, singer in a waterfront nitery.

CITY GIRL, THE

1984, 85 MINS, US ◇

Dir Martha Coolidge   *Prod* Martha Coolidge   *Scr* Judith Tompson, Leonard-John Gates   *Ph* Daniel Hainey   *Ed* Linda Leeds, Eva Gardos   *Mus* Scott Wilk, Marc Levinthal   *Art Dir* Ninkey Dalton
● Laura Harrington, Joe Mastroianni, Carole McGill, Peter Riegert, Jim Carrington, Lawrence Phillips (Moon)

Martha Coolidge's *The City Girl* reps a hard-nosed, if frequently funny, look at a young woman's attempt to forge a career and self-esteem. It's a predecessor to same director's 1983 indie hit, *Valley Girl*.

Lead character of Anne is a young lady who, in an awfully serious way, is trying to get a foot up as a professional photographer. Joey, her sympathetic but very straight boyfriend, indulges her to a point but would rather have her fill the conventional woman's role, something it's obvious she won't do.

Most bracing aspect of Coolidge's treatment of the relatively plain material is her rigorously objective, unindulgent perspective.

In line with the director's approach, Laura Harrington, who plays Anne, does not sentimentalize her character.

CITY HEAT

1984, 97 MINS, US ◇ ▼

Dir Richard Benjamin   *Prod* Fritz Manes   *Scr* Sam O. Brown [= Blake Edwards], Joseph C. Stinson   *Ph* Nick McLean   *Ed* Jacqueline Cambas   *Mus* Lennie Niehaus   *Art Dir* Edward Carfagno
● Clint Eastwood, Burt Reynolds, Jane Alexander, Madeline Kahn, Rip Torn, Richard Roundtree (Malpaso/Deliverance/Warner)

City Heat is an amiable but decidedly lukewarm confection geared entirely around the two star turns.

Set in an unnamed city around the end of Prohibition, Clint Eastwood and Burt Reynolds were old pals in their early days as cops, but the former has taken a dim view of the latter's jump over to the private detective business, resulting in a certain tension between them.

Reynolds' partner, Richard Roundtree, gets bumped off in the early going, and Reynolds spends the remainder of the picture attempting to play two mobster kingpins off one another.

Some of the repartee is relatively amusing, and the two stars with tongues firmly in cheek, easily set the prevailing tone of low-keyed facetiousness.

••••••••••••••••••••••••••••

■ CITY LIGHTS

1931, 87 MINS, US Ⓥ
Dir Charles Chaplin   *Prod* Charles Chaplin
Scr Charles Chaplin   *Ph* Roland Totheroh   *Ed* Charles Chaplin   *Mus* Charles Chaplin   *Art Dir* Charles D. Hall
● Charles Chaplin, Virginia Cherrill, Harry Myers, Allan Garcia, Hank Mann, Florence Lee (United Artists)

It's not Chaplin's best picture, because the comedian has sacrificed speed to pathos, and plenty of it. This is principally the reason for the picture running some 1,500 or more feet beyond any previous film released by him. But the British comic is still the consummate pantomimist.

All through Chaplin schemes how to procure money for a blind flower girl (Virginia Cherrill).

Script is something of a fable in discovering the comic asleep in the lap of a statue when it is unveiled and then having him in and out of trouble through the means of a millionaire (Harry Myers), whom Chaplin prevents from a drunken suicide, and who thereafter only recognizes the comic when drunk.

It can be imagined how much stuff has been tossed away in getting this picture down to its present length, after spasmodically shooting on it over a period of 18 months or more. As previously, Chaplin mainly paints in broad strokes, with his most subtle maneuvering here being the sly turning of the sympathy away from the girl to himself as the picture draws to a close.

••••••••••••••••••••••••••••

■ CITY LIMITS

1985, 85 MINS, US ◇ Ⓥ
Dir Aaron Lipstadt   *Prod* Rupert Harvey, Barry Opper   *Scr* Don Opper   *Ph* Timothy Suhrstedt   *Ed* Robert Kizer   *Mus* John Lurie   *Art Dir* Cyd Smilie
● Darrell Larson, John Stockwell, Kim Cattrall, Rae Dawn Chong, Robby Benson, James Earl Jones (Sho/Videoform)

Elements of *City Limits* fit it into the category of the post-holocaust pic, but the historical disaster is a plague which has wiped out an older generation. The young survive in a condition of controlled anarchy and resist attempts to impose a centralized government.

Most successful aspect of the film [based on a story by James Reigle and Aaron Lipstadt] is its depiction of a tribal lifestyle regulated according to rules learned from comic strips. Two gangs of bikers, the Clippers and the DAs, have divided up the city and live under a truce. Infractions of their pact are regulated with competitive jousting or acts of reciprocal revenge. The dead are cremated with their vehicles like Vikings in their boats. The two groups may unite against outside threats.

Less convincing is the portrayal, with allusions to Fritz Lang's classic *Metropolis*, of the totalitarian-inclined Sunya Corp., which attempts to take over the city with the initial cooperation of the DAs.

Film features an ace ensemble cast. Action scenes are well-executed and there's a vibrant score.

••••••••••••••••••••••••••••

■ CITY SLICKERS

1991, 112 MINS, US ◇ Ⓥ
Dir Ron Underwood   *Prod* Irby Smith   *Scr* Lowell Ganz, Babaloo Mandel   *Ph* Dean Semler   *Ed* O. Nicholas Brown   *Mus* Marc Shaiman, Hummie Mann   *Art Dir* Lawrence G. Paull
● Billy Crystal, Daniel Stern, Bruno Kirby, Patricia Wettig, Helen Slater, Jack Palance (Columbia/Castle Rock/Nelson/Face)

The setup is sheer simplicity, as Billy Crystal, coming to grips with the doldrums of midlife thanks to his 39th birthday, is convinced by his wife (Patricia Wettig) and two best friends (Daniel Stern, Bruno Kirby) to take off for two weeks on a ranch driving cattle across the west.

The childhood fantasy comes to life in a number of ways, perhaps foremost in the presence of gnarled trail boss Curly (Jack Palance), a figure always seemingly backlit in larger-than-life silhouettes.

The other cowboy wannabes include a father-and-son dentist team (Bill Henderson, Phill Lewis), fraternal ice-cream tycoons (David Paymer, Josh Mostel) a beautiful woman (Bonnie Rayburn) who braved the trip on her own. A series of increasingly absurd events lead to central trio toward an ultimate challenge that turns the vacation into a journey of self-discovery.

Crystal gets plenty of chance to crack wise while he, Stern and Kirby engage in playful and not-so-playful banter – Stern coming off a recently (and publicly) failed marriage while the womanizing Kirby grapples with his own fear of fidelity. Director Ron Underwood (who made his feature debut on *Tremors*) generally keeps the herd moving at a fine pace.

••••••••••••••••••••••••••••

■ CITY STREETS

1931, 83 MINS, US
Dir Rouben Mamoulian   *Scr* Oliver H.P. Garrett, Max Marcin   *Ph* Lee Garmes
● Gary Cooper, Sylvia Sidney, Paul Lukas, William Boyd, Guy Kibbee, Stanley Fields (Paramount)

Probably the first sophisticated treatment of a gangster picture. Story is the usual love-redeeming tale of two kids caught in a gangster vortex.

Picture is lifted from mediocrity through the intelligent acting and appeal of Sylvia Sidney. This legit girl makes her first screen appearance here as co-star with Gary Cooper. From a histrionic standpoint she's the whole works, and that's not detracting from the others who perform ably.

Gang chieftain is shown controlling everything from his henchmen's women to his sidekicks' lives. He doesn't control his own life, though, and a jealous girl sends him low when he tries to shelve her for Babe (Sidney).

Final has Babe and her boy friend (Cooper) make the heights of dececency when they trick three badmen executioners, trailing them, into a long and speedy ride thru the great outdoors.

Camera angles are piled on thick. Most of the time these shots serve to slow up the film and confuse.

••••••••••••••••••••••••••••

■ CITY THAT NEVER SLEEPS

1953, 90 MINS, US Ⓥ
Dir John H. Auer   *Prod* John H. Auer   *Scr* Steve Fisher   *Ph* John L. Russell Jr   *Ed* Fred Allen   *Mus* R. Dale Butts   *Art Dir* James Sullivan
● Gig Young, Mala Powers, William Talman, Edward Arnold, Chill Wills, Marie Windsor (Republic)

Production and direction loses itself occasionally in stretching for mood and nuances, whereas a straightline cops-and-robbers action flavor would have been more appropriate. Same flaw is found in the Steve Fisher screen original.

Playing of the four cast toppers, Gig Young, a crazy, mixed-up cop; Mala Powers, a cheap saloon dancer; William Talman, a magician turned hood; and Edward Arnold, suave, crooked attorney, is adequate to script and directorial demands. Chill Wills, principal featured player, walks through the film without any definition, presumably being a cha-

racter that represents the city of Chicago itself.

One night in life on the Chicago police force finds Young ready to blow his job and wife (Paula Raymond) to run away with Powers. He accepts an assignment from Arnold to take Talman over the state line in order to get money for the flight from reality.

John L. Russell's photography makes okay use of Chicago streets and buildings for the low-key, night-life effect required to back the melodrama.

••••••••••••••••••••••••••••

■ CIVILIZATION

1916, 121 MINS, US ⊗ Ⓥ
Dir Raymond B. West   *Prod* Thomas H. Ince   *Scr* C. Gardner Sullivan   *Ph* Joseph August, Clyde de Vinna, Irvin Willat   *Ed* Thomas H. Ince   *Mus* Victor Schertzinger
● Howard Hickman, Enid Markey, Herschel Mayall, George Fisher, J. Frank Burke (Triangle/KayBee)

Master producer Thomas H. Ince was handicapped here by the limitations of C. Gardner Sulivan's scenario, designed as a strong protest against the horrors of war.

The entertainment opens showing a nation at peace, suddenly plunged headlong into war by its king (Herschel Mayall), due wholly to his selfish desire for conquest. He is dependent for success upon Count Ferdinand (Howard Hickman), who has invented a submarine calculated to destroy the enemy's fleet, thus insuring victory. The count is in love with Katheryn, 'a woman of the people'. Katheryn (Enid Mardey) belongs to a secret society, which is opposed to war. She takes him to one of the meetings and he becomes a convert.

When the count receives a wireless to blow up an enemy vessel carrying innocent passengers, he refuses to obey orders and, as his own crew attacks him, sinks his own vessel and deliberately drowns himself and crew. His body is picked up and the king sends for his scientists to restore life in order to secure the secrets of the death-dealing submarine. But it is only the count's body with the soul of Christ who resolves to return to earth to teach the message of Love not Hate.

There is very little opportunity to criticise Ince's magnificent effort, but Sullivan's captions are altogether too preachy. In his effort to project pathos he slops over to bathos.

••••••••••••••••••••••••••••

■ CLAN OF THE CAVE BEAR, THE

1986, 98 MINS, US ◇ Ⓥ
Dir Michael Chapman   *Prod* Gerald I. Isenberg   *Scr* John Sayles   *Ph* Jan De Bont   *Ed* Wendy Greene Bricmont   *Mus* Alan Silvestri   *Art Dir* Kelly Kimball
● Daryl Hannah, Pamela Reed, James Remar, Thomas G. Waites, John Doolittle (PSO/Guber-Peters/Jozak/Decade/Jonesfilm)

The Clan of the Cave Bear is a dull, overly genteel rendition of Jean M. Auel's novel. Handsomely produced on rugged Canadian exteriors, this is the story of pre-history's first feminist.

Although set 35,000 years ago, pic could more or less have been set in any time, as it displays little of the anthropological ambition of *Quest for Fire* and is pitched to appeal to the same sensibilities that responded to *The Blue Lagoon*.

Little imagination is in evidence here. A primitive language has been invented for these early humans to speak (subtitles run throughout), but nothing in their customs, habits or attitudes proves very interesting. Daryl Hannah, at least, is a fetching and sympathetic center of attention, but emoting of the entire cast is limited to expressive grunting.

••••••••••••••••••••••••••••

CLASH BY NIGHT

1952, 105 MINS, US Ⓥ

Dir Fritz Lang *Prod* Harriet Parsons *Scr* Alfred Hayes *Ph* Nicholas Musuraca *Ed* George J. Amy *Mus* Ray Webb *Art Dir* Albert S. D'Agostino, Carroll Clark

● Barbara Stanwyck, Paul Douglas, Robert Ryan, Marilyn Monroe, J. Carrol Naish, Keith Andes (Wald-Krasna/RKO)

Clifford Odets' *Clash by Night*, presented on Broadway over a decade earlier, reaches the screen in a rather aimless drama of lust and passion.

Clash captures much of the drabness of the seacoast fishing town, background of the pic, but only occasionally does the narrative's suggested intensity seep through. It is the story of a woman, buffeted by life's realities, who returns to her hometown after 10 years, only to find that the escapism she has sought is still beyond her reach. She marries a fisherman for security reasons, ultimately being forced to choose between two men.

Barbara Stanwyck plays the returning itinerant with her customary defiance and sullenness. It is one of her better performances. Robert Ryan plays the other man with grim brutality while Marilyn Monroe is reduced to what is tantamount to a bit role.

CLASH OF THE TITANS

1981, 118 MINS, UK ◇

Dir Desmond Davis *Prod* Charles H. Schneer, Ray Harryhausen *Scr* Beverly Cross *Ph* Ted Moore *Ed* Timothy Gee *Mus* Laurence Rosenthal *Art Dir* Frank White

● Laurence Olivier, Harry Hamlin, Claire Bloom, Maggie Smith, Burgess Meredith, Ursula Andress (United Artists/M-G-M)

Clash of the Titans is an unbearable bore that will probably put to sleep the few adults stuck taking the kids to it. This mythical tale of Perseus, son of Zeus, and his quest for the 'fair' Andromeda, is mired in a slew of corny dialog and an endless array of flat, outdated special effects.

Watching acclaimed actors like Laurence Olivier, Maggie Smith and Claire Bloom wandering through the clouds in long white gowns as Greek gods is funny enough. But when they start to utter the stylized dialog about what they're going to do to the mortals on the earth below, one wants to look to the Gods for help. But obviously, that's impossible here.

Unfortunately, none of the creatures of effects that famed expert Ray Harryhausen (who also co-produced) designed seem anything more than rehashes from B-pictures.

Desmond Davids directs with a tired hand, not helped much by the lackadaisical writing.

CLASS

1983, 98 MINS, US ◇ Ⓥ

Dir Lewis John Carlino *Prod* Martin Ransohoff *Scr* Jim Kouf, David Greenwalt *Ph* Ric Waite *Ed* Stuart Pappe, Dennis Dolan *Mus* Elmer Bernstein *Art Dir* Jack Poplin

● Rob Lowe, Jacqueline Bisset, Andrew McCarthy, Stuart Margolin, Cliff Robertson, John Cusack (Orion)

Class is anything but classy. About a brainy but virginal prep school student (Andrew McCarthy) who unwittingly begins an affair with his upper-class roommate's sexy mother (Jacqueline Bisset), film seems something like an unofficial remake of one of Bisset's first Hollywood efforts, the 1969 *The First Time*, in which she initiated the nerdy Wes Stern in the pleasures of the flesh. Throw in aspects of *The Graduate*, with the young fellow's best friend, instead of girlfriend, getting mad at the betrayal, and you get the idea.

McCarthy and Rob Lowe (as his roommate) carry most of the picture, and both acquit themselves reasonably well under the circumstances. Lewis John Carlino's direction is frequently awkward notably in the nudity-less sex scenes.

CLASS ACTION

1991, 109 MINS, US ◇ Ⓥ

Dir Michael Apted *Prod* Ted Field, Scott Kroopf, Robert W. Cort, Carolyn Shelby, Christopher Ames *Scr* Carolyn Shelby, Christopher Ames, Samantha Shad *Ph* Conrad Hall *Ed* Ian Crafford *Mus* James Horner *Art Dir* Todd Hallowell

● Gene Hackman, Mary Elizabeth Mastrantonio, Colin Friels, Joanna Merlin, Larry Fishburne, Donald Moffat (20th Century-Fox/Interscope)

Winning performances by Gene Hackman and Mary Elizabeth Mastrantonio and potent direction by Michael Apted pump life into the sturdy courtroom drama formula once again.

Hackman plays Jed Ward, a veteran civil rights lawyer still dedicated to defending the underdog, though his record, both professional and personal, is not without blotches.

Mastrantonio is his daughter Maggie, a ruthlessly effective corporate advocate and ladder-climber, whose disdain for her father has more to do with his amorous indiscretions than his politics.

They wind up on opposite sides of a class action suit filed against an auto company by the maimed survivors of crashes in which the cars exploded on impact.

For the first half, much of the script is by the numbers, as characters deliver plodding dialog to lay out the situation, but things pick up. Viewer sympathy accumulates quickly for Hackman, the charismatic, if flawed, man of the people, but Mastrantonio carves out her own turf and hangs on to it, truly taking on the senior actor.

CLASS OF '44

1973, 95 MINS, US ◇ Ⓥ

Dir Paul Bogart *Prod* Paul Bogart *Scr* Herman Raucher *Ph* Andrew Laszlo *Ed* Michael A. Hoey *Mus* David Shire *Art Dir* Ben Edwards

● Gary Grimes, Jerry Houser, Oliver Conant, William Atherton, Sam Bottoms, Deborah Winters (Warner)

Class of '44 is an okay follow-up to *Summer of '42* [1971], taking the three juveniles of the first film through their early college years at the end of World War II. Paul Bogart's production and direction are slightly better than Herman Raucher's script, in which nostalgia pellets fall like hailstones on an essentially programmer plot.

Encoring in the lead roles are Gary Grimes, Jerry Houser and Oliver Conant, all introduced graduating from high school. Conant joins the Marines and virtually disappears from the plot, leaving Houser and Grimes to head for college. Deborah Winters is Grimes' campus sweetheart, and William Atherton is very good as a fraternity president supervising the hazing of pledges.

CLASS OF MISS MACMICHAEL, THE

1978, 100 MINS, UK/US ◇ Ⓥ

Dir Silvio Narizzano *Prod* Judd Bernard *Scr* Judd Bernard *Ph* Alex Thomason *Ed* Max Benedict *Mus* Stanley Myers

● Glenda Jackson, Oliver Reed, Michael Murphy, Rosalind Cash, John Standing, Phil Daniels (Kettledrum/Brut)

This pic [from the book by Sandy Hutson] is about dippy doings at a special school for unruly teenagers whose next steps may be reformatories. Treading the usual character-izations and situations, film adds a more permissive tone in language and freewheeling sex of the students not to forget the harassed teachers and a scheming head master.

Though predictable, and the script serviceable for this of-treated theme, with direction average, it has Glenda Jackson adding her presence to the part of a dedicated teacher who eschews a second marriage to stay with her impossible charges.

Jackson's dedicated but world weary air gives an edge to her character as she is the rare teacher who gets through to her charges. Michael Murphy's nice guy playing, but with hints of stodginess, make his boyfriend of Jackson role acceptable.

Oliver Reed overcharges his role of the martinet, hypocritical, mean principal who uses a false front to visitors and a mailed fist at the school.

CLASS OF 1984

1982, 96 MINS, CANADA ◇ Ⓥ

Dir Mark L. Lester *Prod* Arthur Kent *Scr* Tom Holland, John Saxton, Mark L. Lester *Ph* Albert Dank *Ed* Howard Kunin *Mus* Lalo Schifrin

● Perry King, Timothy Van Patten, Merrie Lynn Ross, Roddy McDowall, Al Waxman, Michael J. Fox (Guerrilla High)

Class of 1984 is pure exploitation with plenty of action and a manipulative plot [from a story by Tom Holland] designed to have audiences cheering on the blood.

The Canadian production is set at Abraham Lincoln High School in a large American city. Newcomer music teacher Perry King finds his views on education rapidly altered at the school: students are frisked for weapons, teachers carry guns and the hallways are monitored by guards and cameras.

The chief purveyors of terror are a gang led by Timothy Van Patten. They run a drug and prostitution ring and wield a heavy blow to anyone obstructing their activities.

King refuses to buckle to their strongarm tactics and finds his car first vandalized and later fire-bombed. Walking into a cocaine deal in the school bathroom, King takes Van Patten to the principal, but lack of evidence places the teacher's actions in question.

Performances are generally good with King in fine form as the hard pressed hero while Van Patten is effectively chilling as Stegman.

CLASS OF 1999

1990, 98 MINS, US ◇ Ⓥ

Dir Mark L. Lester *Prod* Mark L. Lester *Scr* C. Courtney Joyner *Ph* Mark Irwin *Ed* Scott Conrad *Mus* Michael Hoenig

● Bradley Gregg, Traci Lind, Malcolm McDowell, Stacy Keach, Pam Grier, John P. Ryan (Original/Lightning/Vestron)

A followup to the 1981 pic *Class of 84* this violent exploitation film is too pretentious for its own good. Director Mark L. Lester takes a cynical, fake-hip view of young people's future.

The inconsistent screenplay posits high-schoolers out of control. So-called free-fire zones have been set up in urban areas around the schools as no man's land, and are literally under the control of youth gangs.

Hamming it up as an albino megalomaniac, Stacy Keach is carrying out an experiment sending three androids reconverted from army surplus to serve as teachers at Kennedy H.S. in Seattle and whip the students into shape. Simultaneously, hero Bradley Gregg has been let out of jail and returned to class at Kennedy in an experimental furlough program.

John P. Ryan and Pam Grier are loads of fun as the androids, latter mocking her image when not only her breasts but inner works are revealed for the final reel through hokey makeup effects.

....

■ **CLASS OF NUKE 'EM HIGH**

1986, 81 MINS, US ◇ ⓥ

Dir Richard W. Haines, Samuel Weil [=Lloyd Kaufman]   *Prod* Lloyd Kaufman, Michael Hertz   *Scr* Richard W. Haines, Mark Rudmitsky, Lloyd Kaufman, Stuart Strotin   *Ph* Michael Mayers   *Ed* Richard W. Haines   *Mus* Michael Lattanzi
● Janelle Brady, Gilbert Brenton, Robert Pritchard, R.L. Ryan (TNT/Troma)

Class of Nuke 'Em High is a misguided attempt to extract grossout humor from the very real concerns about nuclear power plants.

Students at Tromaville High School are exposed to nuclear waste from a nearby power plant. Attractive couple Chrissy (Janelle Brady) and Warren (Gilbert Brenton) are exposed to a mild dose of radiation in the form of tainted reefers.

First effect is to cause them to make love at a party. Next day, both go through temporary physical transformations (expanding stomachs and necks), with Chrissy emitting a small, lizardlike creature.

Level of violence is extreme with slapstick overtures that are intended to be funny.

....

■ **CLAUDINE**

1974, 92 MINS, US ◇ ⓥ

Dir John Berry   *Prod* Hannah Weinstein   *Scr* Tina Pine, Lester Pine   *Ph* Gayne Rescher   *Ed* Luis San Andres   *Mus* Curtis Mayfield   *Art Dir* Ted Haworth
● Diahann Carroll, James Earl Jones, Lawrence Hinton-Jacobs, Tamu, David Kruger, Yvette Curtis (Third World)

Claudine is an outstanding film. A gritty, hearty, heartful and ruggedly tender story of contemporary urban black family life avoiding blaxploitation genre.

Here we have some too-real problems – Diahann Carroll as a 36-year-old mother of six trying to keep a family together without a man around; James Earl Jones as her garbage collector-boyfriend trapped in the immorality of the welfare system which encourages impropriety and discourages decency.

The affair between Carroll and Jones is further complicated by various real problems with her kids. Eldest son Lawrence Hinton-Jacobs is tórn apart by maturing black pride; daughter Tamu is experiencing her first adult female impulses; son David Kruger is on the verge of teenage dropout status.

....

■ **CLEAN AND SOBER**

1988, 124 MINS, US ◇ ⓥ

Dir Glenn Gordon Caron   *Prod* Tony Ganz, Deborah Blum   *Scr* Tod Carroll   *Ph* Jan Kiesser   *Ed* Richard Chew   *Mus* Gabriel Yared   *Art Dir* Joel Schiller
● Michael Keaton, Kathy Baker, Morgan Freeman, M. Emmet Walsh, Brian Benben (Warner)

Covering the first 30 days of attempted recovery by middle-class cocaine addict Michael Keaton, *Sober* is sobering indeed, perhaps too grim.

Keaton carries his heavy load well enough, on screen a vast majority of time as a hotshot real estate executive whose cocaine use has gotten him $92,000 into hock on embezzled company money and into bed with a young girl dying of an overdose.

On the run, Keaton decides to hide out in a recovery hospital, attracted more by its policies of strict confidentiality than any desire for rehabilitation. There, he falls under the strict supervision of ex-junkie Morgan Freeman, which will do him good, but also develops a romantic interest in fellow recovering

addict Kathy Baker, which won't.

Sober chooses to focus on the couple's shared attraction for each other (and cocaine), and follows them to a predictable end.

....

■ **CLEOPATRA**

1934, 102 MINS, US

Dir Cecil B. DeMille   *Prod* Cecil B. DeMille   *Scr* Bartlett Cormack, Waldemar Young, Vincent Lawrence   *Ph* Victor Milner   *Ed* Anne Bauchens   *Mus* Rudolph Kopp
● Claudette Colbert, Warren William, Henry Wilcoxon, Gertrude Michael, Joseph Schildkraut, Ian Keith (Paramount)

Splendor and intimacy do not blend any more than the traditional oil and water. Each treads on the other's toes. Cecil B. DeMille adds nothing to his directorial rep in this one other than to again demonstrate his rare skill in the handling of mass action.

Another tribute ought to go to C. Aubrey Smith as a soldier in one of the few sincerely written bits. Claudette Colbert's best moment is the death of Cleo. The rest of the time she's a cross between a lady of the evening and a rough soubrette in a country melodrama. It is not so much her fault as the shortcoming of the scenarists.

In an effort to avoid the blank verse of Shakespeare, from which this story derives, the dialog is made to become colloquial with disastrous results. When Cleopatra stabs a man hiding behind the drapings she explains to Caesar that the eavesdropper was plotting against her life or his. The imperial Julius then strides to the door, throws it open and commands a couple of guards to 'take it away', referring to the body. The blankest of blank verse would have been better. The entire dialog, save for a few moments, is of like calibre.

Warren William, as Caesar, and Henry Wilcoxon, as Antony, play in the drawing room style, and a not too select drawing room at that. Joseph Schildkraut is a fair Herod.
□ 1934: Best Picture (Nomination)

....

■ **CLEOPATRA**

1963, 243 MINS, US ◇ ⓥ

Dir Joseph L. Mankiewicz   *Prod* Walter Wanger   *Scr* Joseph L. Mankiewicz, Ranald MacDougall, Sidney Buchman   *Ph* Leon Shamroy   *Ed* Dorothy Spencer   *Mus* Alex North   *Art Dir* John de Cuir
● Elizabeth Taylor, Richard Burton, Rex Harrison, Roddy McDowell, Martin Landau, Hume Cronyn (20th Century-Fox)

Cleopatra is not only a supercolossal eye-filler (the unprecedented budget shows in the physical opulence throughout), but it is also a remarkably literate cinematic recreation of an historic epoch.

Director and coauthor Mankiewicz and producer Walter Wanger's most stunning achievement is that they have managed to tell a story of such scope and complexity in such comparatively brief terms. The film covers the 18 turbulent years leading to the foundation of the Roman Empire, from Cleopatra's first meeting with Julius Caesar until her death in defeat with Mark Antony. The result is a giant panorama, unequalled in the splendor of its spectacle scenes and, at the same time, surprisingly acute in its more personal story.

This is due not only to the quality and focus of the screenplay, but to the talents of the three leading players. In the title role, one of the most difficult ever written, Elizabeth Taylor is a woman of continuous fascination. Though not fully at ease as the child-queen of the film's first part, she grows as the story progresses to become the mature queen who matches the star's own voluptuous assurance.

Rex Harrison is superb as Caesar, shrewd, vain and wise, formed somewhat in the image of the G.B. Shaw conception, but also unexpectedly ruthless and ambitious. His are the film's most brilliant lines, and something is lost with his assassination, which closes the film's first half.

Richard Burton then comes to the fore in the second half. Oddly he does not seem the romantic figure expected and plot-implied, partly perhaps because as a lover he is visibly overweight. The role is of a man of military competence consumed by envy of Caesar's genius and exposed in the end as self-pitying and drunken by the demands of Cleopatra's needs for a man in a larger sense than boudoir. Ironically some of the weakest moments in the film are the love scenes between Liz and Dickie.

Happily, however, the film sweeps along with a very real sense of time and place, building to a climax that is one of inevitable, tragic relief. Responsible to no little extent is the quality of the 'big' scenes – Cleopatra's triumphant entry into Rome, a dazzling display of color and sound and ancient pageantry; the grandeur of Cleopatra's barge, sailing into Tarsus; the crucial Battle of Actium, recreated on a scale perhaps unmatched in any spectacle.

The long windup of the story has Cleopatra taking longer to die than Camille. That Fox may still excise more footage is likely, and the second half is the place to do it. [The film was cut by 21 minutes very early in its New York run. No scenes were eliminated in their entirety, but cuts were made to shorten scenes and bridges.]

The real star of *Cleopatra*, however, is Mankiewicz, who brought order out of what had been production chaos. As Caesar observes to Cleopatra, early on: 'You have a way of mixing politics and passion'. So does Mankiewicz.
□ 1963: Best Picture (Nomination)

....

■ **CLEOPATRA JONES**

1973, 89 MINS, US ◇ ⓥ

Dir Jack Starrett   *Prod* William Tennant, Max Julien   *Scr* Max Julien, Sheldon Keller   *Ph* David Walsh   *Ed* Allan Jacobs   *Mus* J.J. Johnson, Carl Brandt, Brad Shapiro   *Art Dir* Peter Wooley
● Tamara Dobson, Bernie Casey, Brenda Sykes, Antonio Fargas, Bill McKinney, Shelley Winters (Warner)

Cleopatra Jones is a good programmer with the offbeat twist of having a sexy woman detective as the lead character. The script incorporates a slew of action set pieces, capably directed by Jack Starrett.

Tamara Dobson makes a smart starring debut, after fashion model and teleblurb work, as the title character, a sophisticated undercover agent working to stamp out the world drug trade. But a phony raid on lover Bernie Casey's ghetto halfway house, in which Dobson has a great interest, draws her home to unravel the plot.

Behind Casey's problems, and serving as Dobson's arch-enemy, is Shelley Winters in vulgar characterization as a lesbian-type gangleader. The line between offbeat cameo and repulsive casting is wider than a freeway, but Winters crosses it with felicity.

....

■ **CLIVE OF INDIA**

1935, 90 MINS, US

Dir Richard Boleslavski   *Scr* W.P. Lipscomb, R.J. Minney   *Ph* Peverell Marley   *Mus* Alfred Newman
● Ronald Colman, Loretta Young, Colin Clive, Francis Lister, C. Aubrey Smith, Cesar Romero (20th Century/ United Artists)

The Black Hole of Calcutta, the battle elephants (with their gargantuan and murderous barbed armor), the famous hindustani monsoons and, of course, the basically courageous warrior, Robert Clive, and his rise from an obscure clerkship with the East India Company – all these elements of fictionized fact and glorified history are recreated here vividly for the screen.

After the first three-quarters of an hour or so, the film plot veers to the personal romantic troubles besetting Clive and Margaret Maskelyne (later Lady Clive), whom he periodically deserts or ignores whenever trouble in the Far East summons him.

Ronald Colman is an excellent Clive sans his familiar mustache. The powdered wigs of the day do their bit in maintaining romantic illusion. Perhaps Loretta Young's spanning of the years is achieved somewhat too idealistically, but changing of the hairdressing with each period authentically gets across the idea of gracefully growing old.

Performances are consistently fine, notably Mischa Auer as the tyrannical native ruler, and Cesar Romero as the ambitious but friendly-to-Britain rival maharajah who double-crosses Auer.

■ CLOCK, THE

1945, 90 MINS, US

Dir Vincente Minnelli *Prod* Arthur Freed *Scr* Robert Nathan, Joseph Schrank *Ph* George Folsey *Ed* George White *Mus* George Bassman *Art Dir* Cedric Gibbons, William Ferrari
● Judy Garland, Robert Walker, James Gleason, Keenan Wynn (M-G-M)

Producer Arthur Freed and director Vincente Minnelli, the combination that scored so heavily with the Judy Garland musical, *Meet Me in St. Louis*, show their versatility in this picture which is straight drama sans any music. It's her first straight dramatic role. The entire story takes place in the 48 hours that Cpl Joe Allen (Walker) is on furlough in NY City.

Minnelli has the knack of getting deep meaning into little footage. For instance, the beanery scene where the jolly inebriate (Keenan Wynn) spouts about life and America. The entire sequence is probably four minutes long, but it is real meat.

Then there's a sequence after the boy and girl get hitched at City Hall. They're sitting in a self-service restaurant, and Garland is weeping because of the unattractiveness of the entire ceremony. The camera keeps concentrated on a lone diner, an unbilled character who just sits there and chews away, staring at the embarrassed couple, but not uttering a word. It is memorable humor.

■ CLOCKWISE

1986, 97 MINS, UK

Dir Christopher Morahan *Prod* Michael Codron *Scr* Michael Frayn *Ph* John Coquillon *Ed* Peter Boyle *Mus* George Fenton *Art Dir* Roger Murray-Leach
● John Cleese, Alison Steadman, Penelope Wilton, Stephen Moore, Joan Hickson, Sharon Maiden (Thorn EMI/Moment)

Clockwise is a somewhat uneven comic road film. John Cleese plays the headmaster of a secondary school whose main trait, obsessive timewatching, turns out to be a strategy to dam up the natural disarray of his personality.

Film's plot is triggered when Stimpson (Cleese) misses the train for a headmaster's conference over which he has been invited to preside. Immediately panic-struck, he seeks some other way to get to the meeting on time.

The best moments depict his gradually going to pieces as he struggles to complete his journey in the company of an abducted schoolgirl (Sharon Maiden) and former girlfriend (Penelope Wilton).

Clockwise would be a bore were it not for Cleese's comic ability, which derives from broad expressive gesticulations and expressions which mark the simple man still trying to control his world long after he has gone over the edge. Christopher Morahan's direction, in his first feature since the late 1960s, is adequate.

■ CLOCKWORK ORANGE, A

1971, 137 MINS, UK

Dir Stanley Kubrick *Prod* Stanley Kubrick *Scr* Stanley Kubrick *Ph* John Alcott *Ed* Bill Butler *Mus* Walter Carlos *Art Dir* John Barry
● Malcolm McDowell, Patrick Magee, Michael Bates, Miriam Carlin, Adrienne Corri, Aubrey Morris (Warner)

A Clockwork Orange is a brilliant nightmare. Stanley Kubrick's film takes the heavy realities of the 'do-your-thing' and 'law-and-order' syndromes, runs them through a cinematic centrifuge, and spews forth the commingled comic horrors of a regulated society. The film employs outrageous vulgarity, stark brutality and some sophisticated comedy to make an opaque argument for the preservation of respect for man's free will – even to do wrong.

Kubrick's screenplay, based on the 1962 Anthony Burgess novel, postulates a society composed of amoral young hedonists, an older generation in retreat behind locked doors, and a political-police government no longer accountable to anyone or to any principles except expediency and tenure.

In this world where youthful gangs control the street by night and disperse by dawn, lives anti-hero and narrator Malcolm McDowell and his sidekicks – Warren Clarke, James Marcus, and Michael Tarn. They have an Orwellian argot not difficult to grasp. Their escapades include beatings, rape and a bizarre murder.

The resolution is ambiguous to say the least. Is McDowell at last the subdued 'Orange' that runs like 'Clockwork' or has human nature begun to heal itself?
□ 1971: Best Picture (Nomination)

■ CLOSE ENCOUNTERS OF THE THIRD KIND

1977, 135 MINS, US

Dir Steven Spielberg *Prod* Julia Phillips, Michael Phillips *Scr* Steven Spielberg *Ph* Vilmos Zsigmond *Ed* Michael Kahn *Mus* John Williams *Art Dir* Joe Alves
● Richard Dreyfuss, Francois Truffaut, Teri Garr, Melinda Dillon, Cary Guffey, Bob Balaban (Columbia)

Close Encounters of the Third Kind is a daring film concept which in its special and technical effects has been superbly realized. Steven Spielberg's film climaxes with a confrontation with life forms from another world.

Story involves a series of UFO appearances witnessed by Richard Dreyfuss, Indiana power company technician, and Melinda Dillon and her son Cary Guffey. Concurrent with this plot line are the maneuverings of a seemingly international and secret team of military and scientific personnel.

But there's no denying that the climax is an absolute stunner, literate in plotting, dazzling in execution and almost reverent in tone.

[In 1980 film was replaced with a 132-minute version, re-edited and with extra material. On posters, but not on prints, this was subtitled *The Special Edition*].

■ CLOSET LAND

1991, 89 MINS, US

Dir Radha Bharadwaj *Prod* Janet Meyers *Scr* Radha Bharadwaj *Ph* Bill Pope *Ed* Lisa Churgin *Mus* Philip Glass (sup.), Richard Einhorn *Art Dir* Eiko Ishioka
● Madeleine Stowe, Alan Rickman (Imagine

The highly theatrical *Closet Land*, imaginatively produced on a modest $2.5 million, addresses the horror of political torture. It's a harrowing, focused two-character piece by first-time director Radha Bharadwaj.

Entire thing takes place in a gleaming, stylish, high-tech chamber, with a man (Alan Rickman) trying to break the will of a woman (Madeleine Stowe). Despite the claustrophobic setup, a great deal occurs to hold one's interest.

Rickman as interrogator is no ordinary brute but a complex, highly civilized man who displays a range of emotions and talents, including the ability to voice-act other people to confuse his blindfolded victim.

Stowe is a physically captivating victim with a fierce attachment to justice. Given a chance early on to escape, she stays and demands an apology. It's a costly error.

Story has Stowe, an author of children's books, dragged from her bed to face a servant of the government (Rickman) who accuses her of peddling subversive ideas to children in the guise of innocent stories. At issue is her work in progress, *Closet Land*, about a little girl whose mother leaves her locked in a closet.

Rickman deserves a great deal of notice for his powerfully controlled, multifaceted performance. Stowe displays some flash and backbone, but not enough to make this a truly engaging match.

■ CLOUDED YELLOW, THE

1950, 95 MINS, UK

Dir Ralph Thomas *Prod* Betty E. Box *Scr* Janet Green *Ph* Geoffrey Unsworth *Ed* Gordon Hales
● Jean Simmons, Trevor Howard, Sonia Dresdel, Kenneth More, Maxwell Reed (Carillon)

Although the plot breaks little new ground, the film grips consistently. Jean Simmons and Trevor Howard make a strong team.

Yarn describes the adventures of an ex-secret service agent who helps an innocent girl to escape from a murder charge. On the theory of setting a thief to catch a thief, Scotland Yard puts another secret agent on his tracks. There follows an exciting chase across England into the dockland area of Liverpool, where the hunted pair are hoping to board a ship for Mexico.

The build-up until the man-hunt begins is done with a nice mixture of humor, sentiment and drama. But once the chase is on, the suspense is sustained solidly.

■ CLUB, THE

1980, 99 MINS, AUSTRALIA

Dir Bruce Beresford *Prod* Matt Carroll *Scr* David Williamson *Ph* Don McAlpine *Ed* William Anderson *Mus* Mike Brady *Art Dir* David Copping
● Jack Thompson, Graham Kennedy, Frank Wilson, Harold Hopkins, John Howard, Alan Cassell (South Australia Film/New South Wales Film)

Based on his play of the same name, David Williamson's screen adaptation opens out the action, but in so doing somehow manages to close down the characters. The plot has to do with a football club and the behind-the-scenes machinations: ruthless powerplays that make what takes place on the field seem relatively tame.

The game in this case is a local aberration, confined to the State of Victoria mostly, called Australian Rules. Actually the game itself plays a background role and director Bruce Beresford has shrewdly kept the thrust of his film in the hands of his main characters.

Williamson's plays have been described as life at the top of your lungs, and *The Club* is no exception; there are few quiet passages.

■ CLUB PARADISE

1986, 104 MINS, US ◇ ⓥ
Dir Harold Ramis   *Prod* Michael Shamberg
Scr Harold Ramis, Brian Doyle-Murray   *Ph* Peter
Hannan   *Ed* Marion Rothman   *Mus* David
Mansfield   *Art Dir* John Graysmark
● Robin Williams, Peter O'Toole, Rick Moranis, Jimmy
Cliff, Twiggy, Adolph Caesar (Warner)

There are enough funny skits in *Club Paradise*
to make for a good hour of SCTV, where
most of the cast is from, but too few to keep
this Club Med satire afloat for 104 minutes.

Screenplay by Harold Ramis (*Ghost Busters*)
and Brian Doyle-Murray was originally written with Doyle-Murray's comedian brother,
Bill Murray, in mind as the lead.

Murray reportedly was unavailable and
Robin Williams was signed to head the cast
as a disabled Chicago fireman who uses his
insurance settlement to become partners with
a reggae musician (Jimmy Cliff) in a seedy
Caribbean club they hope to turn into a first-
class resort.

Williams can be a terrific actor/comedian,
but the spark isn't there.

Somehow, Murray might have come up
with cleverer ways of getting back at complaining guests (Andrea Martin, Steven
Kampmann), nerdy, sex-crazed weaklings
(Rick Moranis and Eugene Levy, respectively) and the other expected amalgam of
folks.

■ CLUE

1985, 87 MINS, US ◇ ⓥ
Dir Jonathan Lynn   *Prod* Debra Hill   *Scr* Jonathan
Lynn   *Ph* Victor J. Kemper   *Ed* David Bretherton,
Richard Haines   *Mus* John Morris   *Art Dir* John Lloyd
● Eileen Brennan, Tim Curry, Madeline Kahn,
Christopher Lloyd, Michael McKean, Martin Mull
(Paramount)

Clue is campy, high-styled escapism. In a
short 87 minutes that just zip by, the well-
known board game's one-dimensional card
figures like Professor Plum and others
become multi-dimensional personalities with
enough wit, neuroses and motives to intrigue
even the most adept whodunnit solver. Film
is released with three endings.

Tim Curry plays the loquacious organizer
of the evening's murder game, which takes
place in a Gothic hilltop mansion in New
England in 1954 during a storm (of course).

He sends six individuals a letter providing
the incentive to attend dinner at the mansion
and when each arrives, assigns them a
pseudonym – Professor Plum, Mr Green,
Mrs White and so on.

The unlikely assemblage of characters is
mostly portrayed by well-known actors and
comedians of which Lesley Ann Warren's
Miss Scarlet, Martin Mull's Colonel Mustard and Eileen Brennan's Mrs Peacock performances stand out.

Terrific performances also are given by
relative unknowns: Michael McKean as Mr
Green and Colleen Camp as the French
maid, Yvette.

■ COAL MINER'S DAUGHTER

1980, 125 MINS, US ◇ ⓥ
Dir Michael Apted   *Prod* Bernard Schwartz   *Scr* Tom
Rickman   *Ph* Ralf D. Bode   *Ed* Arthur Schmidt
Mus Owen Bradley   *Art Dir* John D. Bode
● Sissy Spacek, Tommy Lee Jones, Beverly D'Angelo,
Levon Helm, Phyllis Boyens (Universal)

Coal Miner's Daughter is a thoughtful, endearing film charting the life of singer Loretta
Lynn from the depths of poverty in rural
Kentucky to her eventual rise to the title of
'queen of country music'. Thanks in large

part to superb performances by Sissy Spacek
and Tommy Lee Jones, film [based on
Lynn's autobiography, with George Vescey]
mostly avoids the sudsy atmosphere common
to many showbiz tales.

There is seldom a slow moment in the picture, although towards the end short shrift is
given to Spacek's bout with drugs, nervous
breakdown, marriage troubles and death of
her best friend, Beverly D'Angelo, as country
singer Patsy Cline.

Both Spacek and D'Angelo deserve a
special nod for doing all of their own singing
with style and accuracy.
□ 1980: Best Picture (Nomination)

■ COBRA

1986, 87 MINS, US ◇ ⓥ
Dir George Pan Cosmatos   *Prod* Menahem Golan,
Yoram Globus   *Scr* Sylvester Stallone   *Ph* Ric Waite
Ed Don Zimmerman   *Mus* Sylvester Levay   *Art Dir* Bill
Kenney
● Sylvester Stallone, Brigitte Nielsen, Reni Santoni,
Andrew Robinson, Lee Garlington, John Herzfeld
(Cannon)

Cobra is a sleek, extremely violent and exciting police thriller.

Sylvester Stallone is cast as unconventional
cop Marion Cobretti, nickname Cobra, who
with partner Gonzales (Reni Santoni) works
the LA zombie squad, doing jobs no other
cops will do. They're called in to track down
a serial killer who's claimed 16 victims in a
month. They protect the one surviving witness, a beautiful model (Brigitte Nielsen) and
discover that the killer is actually a neo-fas-
cist army of killers.

Director George Pan Cosmatos tightens the
screws for a very fast ride. His low-key personality defined by his funny throwaway lines
of dialog, Stallone's Cobra is a far more
ingratiating character than his recent Rocky
and Rambo guises.

■ COBRA WOMAN

1944, 70 MINS, US ◇
Dir Robert Siodmak   *Prod* George Waggner
Scr Gene Lewis, Richard Brooks   *Ph* George Robinson,
W. Howard Greene   *Ed* Charles Maynard
Mus Edward Ward   *Art Dir* John B. Goodman,
Alexander Golitzen
● Maria Montez, Jon Hall, Sabu, Lon Chaney
(Universal)

Cobra Woman is a super-fantastic melodrama
backgrounded on a mythical island that
might exist somewhere in the Indian Ocean.
Elaborately and colorfully mounted for constant eye-appeal, and with the starring trio of
Maria Montez, Jon Hall and Sabu, picture
unfolds at fast pace to concentrate on action
features of the tale.

Plot combines jungle-island romance with
melodramatic complications, temple rituals,
chases and fights. Montez is kidnapped on
eve of wedding to Hall and carried back to an
island where her twin sister rules ruthlessly
as high priestess and preys on religious super-
stitions of the natives to keep latter under
control. Hall follows his betrothed to the forbidden island, accompanied by native boy
(Sabu) to rescue Montez.

Montez is decidedly shapely as sarong-
draped native girl and dazzlingly gowned as
the high priestess. She handles the dual
assignment very well. Hall and Sabu are
typed in regular characterizations.

■ COBWEB, THE

1955, 122 MINS, US ◇
Dir Vincente Minnelli   *Prod* John Houseman   *Scr* John
Paxton, William Gibson   *Ph* George Folsey
Ed Harold F. Kress   *Mus* Leonard Rosenman

● Richard Widmark, Lauren Bacall, Charles Boyer,
Gloria Grahame, Lillian Gish, John Kerr (M-G-M)

The neuroses of the staff and patients in a
psychiatric clinic serve for drama in this
filmization of William Gibson's novel,
The Cobweb.

The screenplay gives a wordy account of
the controversy developed around the hanging of a new set of drapes in the clinic's
library, and the reactions of staff and patients
sometime make wonder if identities should
not be reversed. Gloria Grahame, the
neglected wife of Richard Widmark, top doc
at the clinic, wants to select the drapes. Lillian Gish, waspish old maid who directs the
clinic's business affairs, wants to use cheap
muslin to save money. Widmark wants John
Kerr, young patient with a suicide complex,
to design the drapes.

Screen newcomers Kerr and Susan Strasberg, fellow patient, are responsible for one of
the few touching sequences in the film – the
simple act of his looking after her on a trip to
a film theater has a great deal of heart, an
ingredient generally lacking in the footage.

■ COCKTAIL

1988, 104 MINS, US ◇ ⓥ
Dir Roger Donaldson   *Prod* Ted Field, Robert W. Cort
Scr Heywood Gould   *Ph* Dean Semler   *Ed* Barbara
Dunning   *Mus* J. Peter Robinson   *Art Dir* Mel Bourne
● Tom Cruise, Bryan Brown, Elisabeth Shue, Lisa
Banes, Laurence Luckinbill, Kelly Lynch
(Touchstone/Silver Screen Partners III/Interscope)

Heywood Gould's script, based upon his
book inspired by some years as a New York
bartender, contains nary a surprise, as Tom
Cruise hits Manhattan after a hitch in the
army and immediately catches on as the hottest thing the uptown girls have seen in a
saloon in years.

Under the tutelage of old pro Bryan Brown,
Cruise learns every trick in the book, and the
pair soon move to the club scene downtown,
where Cruise becomes poetaster to the too-
hip crowd in addition to taking his pick of
trendy ladies.

In Jamaica, Brown goads his buddy into
setting his sights on one of the many women
with big bucks who patronize the resort,
which gets Cruise into trouble with the girl
he's becoming sweet on (Elisabeth Shue).

Under Roger Donaldson's impeccably slick
direction, film continually plays on Cruise's
attractiveness, as women make googoo eyes
at him throughout as he does his juggling act
with liquor bottles, serves up drinks like a
disco dancer and charms his way through
every situation.

■ COCOANUTS, THE

1929, 90 MINS, US ⓥ
Dir Robert Florey, Joseph Santley   *Prod* Walter
Wanger   *Scr* Morrie Ryskind   *Ph* George Folsey
Ed Barney Rogan   *Mus* Frank Tours (dir)
● Groucho Marx, Harpo Marx, Chico Marx, Zeppo
Marx, Mary Eaton, Oscar Shaw (Paramount)

Here is a musical talker, with the musical
background, music, songs and girls, taken
from the [1925] Broadway stage success [by
George S. Kaufman and Morrie Ryskind]
with the Marxes.

Cocoanuts is set in a Florida development
hotel barren of guests. Groucho is the fast-
thinking and talking boniface. A couple of
slickers, girls, bathing beach, etc, some
undressing but no s.a.

Groucho is always around and talking as he
did in the stage show. Harpo does his work
with craftsmanship. Chico has more of the
comedy end than usually falls to this foil.
Zeppo has to be straight here all of the while.

Only Irving Berlin song of merit is the

theme number, 'When Our Dreams Come True', good enough musically but as trite in idea as the title suggests.

■ COCOON

1985, 117 MINS, US ◇ ⓥ

Dir Ron Howard *Prod* Richard D. Zanuck, David Brown, Lili Fini Zanuck *Scr* Tom Benedek *Ph* Don Peterman *Ed* Daniel Hanley, Michael J. Hill *Mus* James Horner *Art Dir* Jack T. Collis

● Don Ameche, Wilford Brimley, Hume Cronyn, Brian Dennehy, Jack Gilford, Steve Guttenberg (20th Century-Fox/Zanuck-Brown)

A fountain of youth fable [from a novel by David Saperstein] which imaginatively melds galaxy fantasy with the lives of aging mortals in a Florida retirement home, *Cocoon* weaves a mesmerizing tale.

Film inventively taps a wellspring of universal desire: health and youth, a parable set, in this case, among a pallid group of denizens shuffleboarding their twilight days away until a mysterious quartet of normal-looking visitors shows up on their Floridian shores. They are arrivals from another galaxy, led by friendly Brian Dennehy and attractive Tahnee Welch (Raquel's daughter, in her first US film). Another nearly-silent member of the party is a debuting Tyrone Power Jr.

Dennehy hires a young, out-of-pocket charter boat skipper (engagingly played by Steve Guttenberg) for a plan to scuba dive for what appear to be weird, gigantic oyster shells. Dennehy rents an abandoned estate with a big indoor pool and rests the big pods in the pool's bottom.

Effectively intercut with these scenes is the life of the tight circle of nearby retirees, three of whom, played by Don Ameche, Wilford Brimley and Hume Cronyn, one day discover the cocoon-like shells and after a frolic in the water are soon diving in like 18-year-olds.

The effect of rejuvenation on the gray people, the inevitable mania when the whole retirement hospital wants in on the public bath, and the effect of this on the plans of the visitors from outer space propel the feature toward a suspenseful, ironic conclusion.

■ COCOON: THE RETURN

1988, 116 MINS, US ◇ ⓥ

Dir Daniel Petrie *Prod* Richard D. Zanuck, David Brown, Lili Fini Zanuck *Scr* Stephen McPherson *Ph* Tak Fujimoto *Ed* Mark Roy Warner *Mus* James Horner *Art Dir* Lawrence G. Paull

● Don Ameche, Wilford Brimley, Hume Cronyn, Steve Guttenberg, Maureen Stapleton, Jessica Tandy (Zanuck-Brown/20th Century-Fox)

Not altogether charmless, *Cocoon: The Return* still is far less enjoyable a senior folks' fantasy than *Cocoon*. An overdose of bathos weighs down the sprightliness of the characters, resulting in a more maudlin than magic effort.

Quandary begins with the return to St Petersburg, Fla, of the plucky group lead by the twinkle-eyed Don Ameche for a four-day visit from the utopian extra-terrestrial world of Antarea. Upon being reunited with family and friends, each questions his own choice for leaving in the first place and, at the end of the picture, the rationale for either returning to space or remaining on terra firma.

Jack Gilford as irascible widower Bernie Lefkowitz and Steve Guttenberg as Jack, the glass-bottom boat tour guide cum shlocky seashell merchandise salesman, keep this overly sappy production afloat.

Ameche, Gwen Verdon and occasionally Hume Cronyn want to play funny and loose but are restrained by Daniel Petrie's direction, which too often is unfocused.

■ CODE OF SILENCE

1985, 101 MINS, US ◇ ⓥ

Dir Andy Davis *Prod* Raymond Wagner *Scr* Michael Butler, Dennis Shryack, Mike Gray *Ph* Frank Tidy *Ed* Peter Parasheles, Christopher Holmes *Mus* David Frank *Art Dir* Maher Ahmed

● Chuck Norris, Henry Silva, Bert Remsen, Molly Hagan, Joseph Guzaldo, Mike Genovese (Orion)

With 27 stuntmen and Chuck Norris in the credits, *Code of Silence* is a predictability cacophonous cops-and-crooks yarn that is actually quite good for the type.

The best thing about Norris is he never gets involved in all that romance stuff. Granted, there's a pretty girl (Molly Hagan) whose life is at stake, but Norris never does more than hold her hand, lend his brawny chest for her to cry on, and – finally in a fit of passion – kiss her on the forehead.

Norris plays a police sergeant leading a raid on a drug den, who arrives a step behind another gang which gets away with all the dope and money, leaving a bloody mess behind. This sets off a gang war between forces led by properly menacing Henry Silva on one side and less prominent Mike Genovese on the other.

■ COFFY

1973, 91 MINS, US ◇ ⓥ

Dir Jack Hill *Prod* Robert A. Papazian *Scr* Jack Hill *Ph* Paul Lohmann *Ed* Charles McClelland *Mus* Roy Ayers *Art Dir* Perry Ferguson

● Pam Grier, Booker Bradshaw, Robert DoQui, William Elliott, Allan Arbus, Sid Haig (American International)

Coffy is the story of a black tart, vengeance-minded, who sets out to kill everyone she holds responsible for her 11-year-old sister losing her mind by the dope habit. She blasts her victims, most of them lured into sex, with a shotgun that never misses.

Jack Hill, who wrote and directs with an action-atuned hand, inserts plenty of realism in footage in which Pam Grier in title role ably acquits herself. She takes on her prey, including pushers, crooked cops and politicians, pimps, gangsters et al, with a ferocity which builds into often-suspenseful sequence.

Grier, a statuesque actress with a body she doesn't hesitate to show, is strongly cast. Booker Bradshaw as a city politician and William Elliott as an honest cop score well.

■ COLDITZ STORY, THE

1955, 97 MINS, UK ⓥ

Dir Guy Hamilton *Prod* Ivan Foxwell *Scr* Guy Hamilton, Ivan Foxwell, William Douglas Home *Ph* Gordon Dines *Ed* Peter Mayhew *Mus* Francis Chagrin *Art Dir* Alex Vetchinsky

● John Mills, Eric Portman, Christopher Rhodes, Lionel Jeffries, Bryan Forbes, Ian Carmichael (Foxwell/British Lion)

Easily one of the best prisoner-of-war yarns to come from any British studio, *The Colditz Story* is a taut real-life meller, based on the personal experiences of the author, Pat Reid.

Colditz Castle, in the heart of Saxony, was the fortress to which the German High Command sent officers who had attempted to escape from conventional prison camps. They regarded it as impregnable although they threatened the death penalty for anyone attempting to break out.

Film is loaded with meaty suspense situations and neatly leavened with good-natured humor to strike an excellent balance between the grim and the natural. The all-male cast keeps the yarn rolling at a lively pace.

Eric Portman turns in a distinguished performance as the British colonel.

■ COLD ROOM, THE

1984, 92 MINS, UK ⓥ

Dir James Dearden *Prod* Mark Forstater *Scr* James Dearden *Ph* Tony Pierce-Roberts *Ed* Mick Audley *Mus* Michael Nyman *Art Dir* Tim Hutchinson

● George Segal, Amanda Pays, Renee Soutendijk, Warren Clarke, Anthony Higgins, Ursula Howells (Jethro)

The Cold Room, a modestly intriguing psychological thriller, marks the feature debut (after a couple of interesting shorts) of director James Dearden. It's a very confident first feature, intelligently directed and always interesting to look at.

Story centers around an attractive if sulky British teenager (Amanda Pays), who joins her father (George Segal) for a vacation in (of all places) East Berlin.

Spending time in her tiny room in an old-fashioned hotel, she gradually comes under the spell of another girl who lived in the same house during the war.

Segal is relaxed as the baffled father who can't get through to his daughter and fears she may be going insane. Pays is a find as the possessed girl, but Dutch actress Renee Soutendijk has almost nothing to do as Segal's girlfriend.

■ COLD WIND IN AUGUST, A

1961, 79 MINS, US

Dir Alexander Singer *Prod* Phillip Hazelton *Scr* Burton Wohl *Ph* Floyd Crosby *Ed* Jerry Young *Mus* Gerald Fried

● Lola Albright, Scott Marlowe, Herschel Bernardi, Joe De Santis, Clark Gordon, Janet Brandt (United Artists/Troy)

No matter how well Vladimir Horowitz might play 'Chopsticks', it would still be 'Chopsticks'. By roughly the same token, all the exceptional ability that went into *A Cold Wind in August* is levelled to the common denominator of its subject – a short course in the seduction, care and feeding of a healthy 17-year-old boy by a nymphomaniacal 28-year-old stripper. This is a hormone opera of considerable quality.

Burton Wohl's screenplay, from his novel, plants the handsome super's son (Scott Marlowe) in the flashy upstairs apartment of a sultry body-goddess (Lola Albright) who is on a kind of annual three-month vacation in respectable anonymity from the questionable life she leads the other nine. Passion matures into love, but the romance goes ker-plop for the lad when he discovers she is not the madonna he naively believed her to be.

Director Alexander Singer has endowed his picture with a blunt and powerful realism. His actors seem perfectly at home in the NY environment. Their language (via Wohl) is the language of hip New Yorkers, their actions (via Singer) the natural actions of the Manhattan street scene and private realms a few stories above or one flight below street level.

Another factor in the film's visual impact is the extraordinarily active, inventive camerawork by Floyd Crosby. There is a strip scene (Albright as object) that rivals in sensuality any strip scene ever put on non-stag celluloid – darting images of undulating sections of Albright's partially exposed and admirable epidermis formation.

■ COLLECTOR, THE

1965, 117 MINS, US ◇ ⓥ

Dir William Wyler *Prod* William Wyler, Jud Kinberg, John Kohn *Scr* Stanley Mann, John Kohn *Ph* Robert L. Surtees, Robert Krasker *Ed* Robert Swink *Mus* Maurice Jarre *Art Dir* John Stoll

● Terence Stamp, Samantha Eggar, Maurice Dallimore, Mona Washbourne (Columbia)

William Wyler undertakes a vastly difficult

117

assignment, and carries it off with rare artistry, in bringing to the screen a solid, suspenseful enactment of John Fowles' bestselling novel.

As a character study of two persons – an inferiority-ridden young Englishman with an uncontrollable sex obsession and the young woman he abducts and holds prisoner in the cellar of his secluded farmhouse – the feature is adroitly developed and bears the stamp of class.

Color photography frequently is stunning, always of high quality, picture opening on a visually beautiful note as the leading male character (Terence Stamp) is introduced as a butterfly collector. The screenplay expands on this premise; he broadens his collecting to girls. He falls in love with a young art student, and has an uncontrollable desire to force her to reciprocate his feelings.

Both Stamp and Samantha Eggar turn in remarkably restrained performances under Wyler's guiding dramatic helmsmanship. Stamp makes his character of an insignificant London bank clerk entirely believable and carefully shades his characterization.

■ COLOR OF MONEY, THE

1986, 119 MINS, US ◇ ⓥ
Dir Martin Scorsese   *Prod* Irving Axelrad, Barbara De Fina   *Scr* Richard Price   *Ph* Michael Ballhaus   *Ed* Thelma Schoonmaker   *Mus* Robbie Robertson   *Art Dir* Boris Leven
● Paul Newman, Tom Cruise, Mary Elizabeth Mastrantonio, Helen Shaver, John Turturro, Bill Cobbs (Touchstone)

The Color of Money is another inside look at society's outsiders from director Martin Scorsese. This time out it's the subculture of professional pool hustlers that consumes the screen with a keenly observed and immaculately crafted vision of the raw side of life. Pic has a distinctive pulse of its own with exceptional performances by Paul Newman and Tom Cruise.

Based on a reworking of Walter Tevis' novel by scripter Richard Price, *The Color of Money* is a continuation of the 1961 film, *The Hustler*, 25 years later.

Back as Fast Eddie Felson, Paul Newman is a self-proclaimed 'student of human moves' – a hustler. When he happens on Vincent Lauria (Tom Cruise) in a nondescript midwest pool hall, Eddie's juices start flowing and the endless cycle starts again.

As Vincent's girlfriend Carmen, Mary Elizabeth Mastrantonio is working on her own short fuse and is learning how to use her main talent too – her sexuality. It's a hot and disturbing performance as her actions contradict her choirgirl good looks.

■ COLOR PURPLE, THE

1985, 152 MINS, US ◇ ⓥ
Dir Steven Spielberg   *Prod* Steven Spielberg, Kathleen Kennedy, Frank Marshall, Quincy Jones   *Scr* Menno Meyjes   *Ph* Allen Daviau   *Ed* Michael Kahn   *Mus* Quincy Jones   *Art Dir* J. Michael Riva
● Danny Glover, Whoopi Goldberg, Margaret Avery, Oprah Winfrey, Willard Pugh, Akosua Busia (Amblin/Warner)

There are some great scenes and great performances in *The Color Purple*, but it is not a great film. Steven Spielberg's turn at 'serious' filmmaking is marred in more than one place by overblown production that threatens to drown in its own emotions. But the characters created in Alice Walker's novel are so vivid that even this doesn't kill them off and there is still much to applaud (and cry about) here.

Walker's tale is the story of a black family's growth and flowering over a 40-year period in the south starting around 1909. At the center

of everything is Celie, who as a young girl gives birth to two children and is then married into a life of virtual servitude to a man she can refer to only as Mr (Danny Glover).

Above all *The Color Purple* is a love story between Celie and her sister, Nettie, from whom she is separated at childhood, and, later in life, the blues singer Shug Avery.

Saving grace of the film are the performances. As the adult Celie debuting Whoopi Goldberg uses her expressive face and joyous smile to register the character's growth. Equally good is Glover who is a powerful screen presence.
□ 1985: Best Picture (Nomination)

■ COLORS

1988, 120 MINS, US ◇ ⓥ
Dir Dennis Hopper   *Prod* Robert H. Solo   *Scr* Michael Schiffer   *Ph* Haskell Wexler   *Ed* Robert Estrin   *Mus* Herbie Hancock   *Art Dir* Ron Foreman
● Sean Penn, Robert Duvall, Maria Conchita Alonso, Randy Brooks, Grand Bush (Orion)

Colors is a solidly crafted depiction of some current big-city horrors and succeeds largely because of the Robert Duvall-Sean Penn teaming as frontline cops. They're terrific together as members of the gang crime division of the LAPD.

Filmmakers alert the uninitiated right off that theirs is a tale [story by Michael Schiffer and Michael DiLello] of unequal odds, pointing out that 600 street gangs roam America's second-largest city while local and county police directly assigned to the problem number only 250.

Drawn into this fracas is officer Bob Hodges (Duvall), married, the father of three, who's inexpicably been forced back into the action. He's savvy about his dealings with punks in 'bozoland', as Hodges calls the streets, and is unhappy about getting greenhorn Danny McGavin (Penn) as his sidekick.

Latter is a high strung and cocksure volunteer. He not only busts them with bravado but roughs 'em up out there.

Plot takes Duvall and Penn through investigation of the latest offing of a 'Blood' gang-member by the rival 'Crips' and shows the police frustrations in working the case against nearly insurmountable obstacles. While nicely avoiding the feel of a docu, film seems to effectively capture the gang 'culture'.

■ COMA

1978, 113 MINS, US ◇ .ⓥ
Dir Michael Crichton   *Prod* Martin Erlichman   *Scr* Michael Crichton   *Ph* Victor J. Kemper, Gerald Hirschfeld   *Ed* David Bretherton   *Mus* Jerry Goldsmith   *Art Dir* Albert Brenner
● Genevieve Bujold, Michael Douglas, Elizabeth Ashley, Rip Torn, Richard Widmark, Lois Chiles (M-G-M)

Coma is an extremely entertaining suspense drama in the Hitchcock tradition. Director-adapter Michael Crichton neatly builds mystery and empathy around star Genevieve Bujold, a doctor who grows to suspect her superiors of deliberate surgical error. Michael Douglas also stars as her disbelieving lover.

Robin Cook's novel is adapted by Crichton into a smartly-paced tale which combines traditional Hitchcock elements with contemporary personal relationships. Thus Bujold and Douglas wrestle in sub-plot with separate identity and mutual romantic problems while she becomes the innocent enmeshed in suspicious medical wrongdoing. When lifelong friend Lois Chiles goes into permanent coma during an otherwise routine operation, Bujold begins probing a series of similar incidents.

Arrayed against her are hospital superiors Richard Widmark and Rip Torn, and even

Douglas himself. Lance Le Gault is a hired killer whom Bujold outwits to the relief of the entire audience.

Elizabeth Ashley is notable as the head of a dubious medical experimental centre where the comatose victims vegetate pending ghoulish, but all-too-plausible disposition.

■ COMANCHEROS, THE

1961, 107 MINS, US ◇ ⓥ
Dir Michael Curtiz   *Prod* George Sherman   *Scr* James Edward Grant, Clair Huffaker   *Ph* William H. Clothier   *Ed* Louis Loeffler   *Mus* Elmer Bernstein   *Art Dir* Jack Martin Smith, Alfred Ybarra
● John Wayne, Stuart Whitman, Ina Balin, Nehemiah Persoff, Lee Marvin, Michael Ansara (20th Century-Fox)

The Comancheros is a big, brash, uninhibited action-western of the old school about as subtle as a right to the jaw.

The screenplay, based on the novel by Paul I. Wellman, is a kind of cloak-and-dagger yarn on horseback. It is set against the Texas of the mid-19th century, a troubled time prior to its statehood when the Comanches were on the warpath and renegade white men, or 'Comancheros', were aiding the Indian cause with fighting equipment. The film relates the story of a Texas Ranger (John Wayne) and an itinerant gambler (Stuart Whitman) who team up to detect and destroy the renegade, parasitic society.

Wayne is obviously comfortable in a role tailor-made to the specifications of his easy-going, square-shooting, tight-lipped but watch-out-when-I'm-mad screen personality. Whitman and Ina Balin (daughter of the Comanchero chieftain) both seem at home in the western idiom. Lee Marvin makes a vivid impression in a brief, but colorful, role as a half-scalped, vile-tempered Comanchero agent.

Director Michael Curtiz was fortunate in having aboard some excellent stuntmen whose hard falls, leaps and maneuvers during the raid and battle sequences (directed by Cliff Lyons) are something to see. Their tactics help in diverting attention from the annoying fact that neither Comancheros nor Comanches seem able to hit the side of a barn with their absurdly errant gunfire. Cameraman William H. Clothier's sweeping panoramic views of the Moab, Utah site are something to behold.

■ COME BACK CHARLESTON BLUE

1972, 100 MINS, US ◇ ⓥ
Dir Mark Warren   *Prod* Samuel Goldwyn Jr   *Scr* Bontche Schweig, Peggy Elliott   *Ph* Dick Kratina   *Ed* Gerald Greenberg, George Bowers   *Mus* Donny Hathaway   *Art Dir* Robert Gundlach
● Godfrey Cambridge, Raymond St Jacques, Peter De Anda, Percy Rodrigues, Jonelle Allen, Maxwell Glanville (Warner/Goldwyn)

Come Back Charleston Blue is an okay followup [from the novel *The Heat's On* by Chester Himes] by producer Samuel Goldwyn Jr to his successful 1970 *Cotton Comes to Harlem*, again featuring Godfrey Cambridge and Raymond St Jacques as offbeat, comedic Harlem gumshoes.

Cambridge and St Jacques find themselves caught between fading black drug king and mobster Maxwell Glanville, and Peter De Anda, ostensibly a successful photographer out to rid Harlem of drugs, but in reality eyeing the area for himself.

De Anda creates the impression that a series of gangland deaths has been caused by the ghost of Charleston Blue, a Depression-era hood, long dead.

The film lacks punch. The gags just don't quite add up to solid laughs or excitement.

COME BACK, LITTLE SHEBA

1952, 95 MINS, US
Dir Daniel Mann   *Prod* Hal B. Wallis   *Scr* Ketti Frings
Ph James Wong Howe   *Ed* Warren Low   *Mus* Franz
Waxman   *Art Dir* Hal Pereira, Henry Bumstead
● Burt Lancaster, Shirley Booth, Terry Moore, Richard
Jaeckel, Philip Ober (Paramount)

The Broadway legit success, *Come Back, Little Sheba*, has become a potent piece of screen entertainment. The production is faithful to the William Inge play.

Shirley Booth has the remarkable gift of never appearing to be acting. Opposite her is Burt Lancaster, bringing an unsuspected talent to his role of the middle-aged, alcoholic husband.

The story interest centers on the somewhat dull, middle-aged and middle-class husband and wife portrayed by Lancaster and Booth. She is a frowzy, talkative, earnestly pleasant woman continually living in the past, while he is a man almost beaten by life and a great thirst. Their stoogy, routine existence is brightened one day when a student boarder (Terry Moore) rents a room in their home.

Her cheery, comely presence gives the couple renewed interest, but also brings about the film's climactic punch when Lancaster's fondness for her is jolted by believing the girl is going too far in an affair with another student and amateur romeo (Richard Jaeckel).

COME BACK TO THE FIVE & DIME, JIMMY DEAN, JIMMY DEAN

1982, 109 MINS, US
Dir Robert Altman   *Prod* Scott Bushnell   *Scr* Ed
Graczyk   *Ph* Pierre Mignot   *Ed* Jason Rosenfield
Art Dir David Cropman
● Sandy Dennis, Cher, Karen Black, Sudie Bond, Marta
Heflin, Kathy Bates (Sandcastle 5)

Story is set in a small Texas town in 1975. Five women, who were part of a James Dean fan club, hold a 20th anniversary reunion, in the local Woolworth 5 and Dime. Sandy Dennis and Cher play characters who remained in the town and at the outset are anxious about which of the old crowd will appear.

Robert Altman had previously directed the story on Broadway with the same cast. However, while the location remains the area of the store, the action is far from claustrophobic.

The action occurs on two levels with incidents of the reunion run parallel to events of 20 years earlier. Altman uses a wall-length mirror to effect the time changes.

The women arrive and each offers her memories of the earlier time. The recollections are, at first, comical and innocent but eventually the characters reveal their most painful secrets. The material is told with great emotion and Altman gets wonderful performances from his female ensemble.

COME BLOW YOUR HORN

1963, 112 MINS, US
Dir Bud Yorkin   *Prod* Norman Lear, Bud Yorkin
Scr Norman Lear   *Ph* William H. Daniels   *Ed* Frank P.
Keller   *Mus* Nelson Riddle   *Art Dir* Hal Pereira,
Roland Anderson
● Frank Sinatra, Lee J. Cobb, Molly Picon, Barbara
Rush, Jill St John, Tony Bill (Paramount)

Art it ain't, fun it is. That about sums up *Come Blow Your Horn*. Like its legit parent, the screen version of Neil Simon's Jewish-oriented family comedy is a superficial but diverting romp.

The simple yarn is concerned with two brothers at opposite extremities of bachelorhood, the older one (Frank Sinatra) ultimately passing into a more mature, responsible phase of life when he sees in his younger brother's (Tony Bill) sensual excesses the reflection of a ferocious personality no longer especially becoming or appealing to him. This is mighty good news to his long-suffering father, a wax fruit manufacturer from Yonkers for whom any unmarried man over 30 is a bum.

Sinatra's role is perfectly suited to his rakish image. It also affords him an opportunity to manifest his most consummate talent – that of singer. He warbles the lilting title tune.

But it's Lee J. Cobb who steals the show (albeit in the juiciest part) with what might be described as a 'bum'-bastic portrayal of the explosively irascible old man who is forever appearing at the front door of his son's apartment when more glamorous company is expected.

Tony Bill makes a fairly auspicious screen bow as the younger brother. Barbara Rush is attractive as the girl who eventually gets Sinatra, and Jill St John is flashy as a guilelessly accommodating sexpot.

COMEDIANS, THE

1967, 156 MINS, US
Dir Peter Glenville   *Prod* Peter Glenville   *Scr* Graham
Greene   *Ph* Henri Decae   *Ed* Francoise Javet
Mus Laurence Rosenthal   *Art Dir* Francois De Lamothe
● Richard Burton, Elizabeth Taylor, Alec Guinness,
Peter Ustinov, Paul Ford, Lillian Gish (M-G-M)

The despair of people living under a despot may, indeed, be a sort of living death. Producer-director Peter Glenville's pic, scripted by Graham Greene [from his own novel], is a plodding, low-key, and eventually tedious melodrama.

Greene's screenplay rambles on through a seemingly interminable 156 minutes. Not the least of film's flaws is the role played by Elizabeth Taylor (wife of South American ambassador Peter Ustinov), who has a recurring, deteriorating affair with hotel-owner Richard Burton.

The very poorly-made story point is that Burton gradually, finds something to live for, in his eventual flight to join mountain rebels, pitiably equipped and pitilessly portrayed. Alec Guinness is a society-type arms promoter who fakes a military background. In a climactic scene where he confesses the fraud to Burton, Guinness excels.

COMEDY MAN, THE

1964, 92 MINS, UK
Dir Alvin Rakoff   *Prod* Jon Penington   *Scr* Peter
Yeldham   *Ph* Ken Hodges   *Mus* Bill McGuffie   *Art
Dir* John Blezard
● Kenneth More, Cecil Parker, Dennis Price, Billie
Whitelaw, Norman Rossington, Angela Douglas (British
Lion)

Douglas Hayes' lightweight novel about the struggle of a stock actor who has just passed the dangerous 40s, without making the grade, hardly scratches new ground. But the authenticity and atmosphere are complete and this well made little film recreates that atmosphere splendidly on the screen. A well drawn performance by Kenneth More adds greatly to the entertainment value of the film.

Fired from a stock company in the sticks for being found with the leading lady, who happens to be the producer's wife, More comes to London for one more crack at making good in the big time. In the seedy atmosphere of theatrical digs, promiscuous affairs, doing the agents' rounds he suffers all the humiliations and disappointments. Eventually pride breaks down, he takes a job doing TV commercials as 'Mr Honeybreath', which brings him dough and recognition.

COME FLY WITH ME

1963, 107 MINS, US
Dir Henry Levin   *Prod* Anatole de Grunwald
Scr William Roberts   *Ph* Oswald Morris   *Ed* Frank
Clarke   *Mus* Lyn Murray   *Art Dir* William Kellner
● Dolores Hart, Hugh O'Brian, Karl Boehm, Pamela
Tiffin, Karl Malden, Lois Nettleton (M-G-M)

Sometimes one performance can save a picture and in *Come Fly with Me* it's an engaging and infectious one by Pamela Tiffin. The production has other things going for it like an attractive cast, slick pictorial values and smart, stylish direction by Henry Levin, but at the base of all this sheer sheen lies a frail, frivolous and featherweight storyline that, in trying to take itself too seriously, flies into dramatic air pockets and crosscurrents that threaten to send the entire aircraft into a tailspin.

Fortunately Tiffin is around to bail it out almost every time the going gets too bumpy for passenger comfort.

Airline hostesses and their romantic pursuits provide the peg upon which William Roberts has constructed his erratic screenplay from a screen story he concocted out of Bernard Glemser's *Girl on a Wing*. The affairs of three hostesses are described.

One (Dolores Hart) is looking for a wealthy husband and thinks she's found the fellow in a young Continental baron (Karl Boehm). Another (Lois Nettleton) is a nice girl type who succeeds in winning the heart and hand of yon multi-millionaire Texas businessman (Karl Malden). The third (Tiffin), after a series of cockpitfalls and hotelroominations, decides that flying so high with some guy in the sky is her idea of something to do. The 'some guy' is first flight officer Hugh O'Brian.

Hart and Nettleton, Boehm and Malden have the misfortune to be implicated in affairs one and two, which are utterly absurd. The four characters are all stereotypes. O'Brian has the good fortune to be bouncing his characterization off Tiffin, and gets by. Much of the film was shot in Paris and Vienna.

COMES A HORSEMAN

1978, 118 MINS, US
Dir Alan J. Pakula   *Prod* Gene Kirkwood, Dan
Paulson   *Scr* Dennis Lynton Clark   *Ph* Gordon Willis
Ed Marion Rothman   *Mus* Michael Small
Art Dir George Jenkins
● James Caan, Jane Fonda, Jason Robards, George
Grizzard, Richard Farnsworth, Jim Davis
(United Artists/Chartoff-Winkler)

Alan Pakula's *Comes a Horseman* is so lethargic not even Jane Fonda, James Caan and Jason Robards can bring excitement to this artificially dramatic story of a stubborn rancher who won't surrender to the local land baron.

The real star of the film doesn't get billing. It's a stretch of verdant land in Colorado known as the Wet Mountain Valley. Gordon Willis photographs this location with so much love and awe that talk by oil explorers about ripping it up is both moving and repulsive.

Robards' part is the most troublesome. He's the land baron who wants both Fonda and Caan to sell their parcels to complete his empire. Every one of Robards' lines is shaded by a black hat. He is Evil in the most convenient way.

Caan, also an independent rancher who recently returned from serving in World War II, teams up with Fonda after his partner is killed (presumably on orders from Robards). When Fonda realizes what an accomplished cowboy Caan is and how much she needs him their relationship warms.

The only really good part in the film is Richard Farnsworth's Dodger, Fonda's aging hand. He's an altogether sympathetic character, close to the land and one of the few who really understands Fonda.

••••••••••••••••••••••••••••••••••

■ COME SEE THE PARADISE

1990, 138 MINS, US ◇ Ⓥ

Dir Alan Parker   *Prod* Robert F. Colesberry   *Scr* Alan Parker   *Ph* Michael Seresin   *Ed* Gerry Hambling   *Mus* Randy Edelman   *Art Dir* Geoffrey Kirkland
● Dennis Quaid, Tamlyn Tomita, Sab Shimono, Shizuko Hoshi, Stan Egi (20th Century-Fox)

In Alan Parker's richly mounted romantic saga of the Second World War relocation camps, the Asian-American cast is exemplary and Dennis Quaid has never been better. Noble if overlong effort depicts the love affair between the Irish-American labor activist and a woman from a well-established Japanese family ripped from its Los Angeles roots.

Quaid plays Jack McGurn, a newcomer to LA in 1936 who gets a job as a projectionist in a Little Tokyo theater and falls in love with the boss' daughter (Tamlyn Tomita). After he's fired and forbidden to see her again, they elope to Seattle, where, unlike in California, it was legal for a Japanese-American and a Caucasian to marry.

In general, Parker avoids most of the complexities behind the internment in favor of a broad, sentimental tale that emphasizes emotions.

Quaid gives a wonderfully open and unaffected performance, putting across romance, charm and integrity without resorting to any of the gimmicks he's used in earlier films. Tomita is a lovely, if under-nuanced, actress, and Egi as her brother is particularly interesting among the large supporting cast.

••••••••••••••••••••••••••••••••••

■ COME SEPTEMBER

1961, 112 MINS, US ◇

Dir Robert Mulligan   *Prod* Robert Arthur   *Scr* Stanley Shapiro, Maurice Richlin   *Ph* William Daniels   *Ed* Russell F. Schoengarth   *Mus* Hans J. Salter   *Art Dir* Henry Bumstead
● Rock Hudson, Gina Lollobrigida, Sandra Dee, Bobby Darin, Walter Slezak, Brenda De Banzie (Universal)

A rich US businessman (Rock Hudson), who ordinarily spends only one month (September) annually at his Italian villa, abruptly puts in a July appearance to the dismay of his enterprising major domo (Walter Slezak) who has been converting the private abode into a very public hotel for 11 months out of every year.

Even in the film's lesser spans there are occasional kicks and spurts of high good humor, but too often, in manipulating the plot for the purposes of introducing incongruous comedy spectacles (Hudson chasing after La Lollo at the wheel of a battered chicken truck, or the latter, garbed in full wedding gown regalia, chasing after the former in an old jeep), the writers seem inclined to telegraph, repeat and pile it on.

Under director Robert Mulligan's generally keen command, Hudson comes through with an especially jovial performance. Gina Lollobrigida need just stand there to generate sparks, but here she abets her eye-to-eye appeal with plenty of comedy savvy. Slezak is excellent. His scenes with Hudson are the best in the picture.

Sandra Dee has the misfortune to be overshadowed in the glamor department by La Lollo, but the young actress is plenty decorative and capable in her own right. In his first cinematic exposure, Bobby Darin does a workmanlike job.

••••••••••••••••••••••••••••••••••

■ COMFORT AND JOY

1984, 90 MINS, UK ◇ Ⓥ

Dir Bill Forsyth   *Prod* Davina Belling, Clive Parsons   *Scr* Bill Forsyth   *Ph* Chris Menges   *Ed* Michael Ellis   *Mus* Mark Knopfler   *Art Dir* Adrienne Atkinson
● Bill Paterson, Eleanor David, C.P. Grogan, Alex Norton, Patrick Malahide, Rikki Fulton (Kings Road)

In *Comfort and Joy* director-scripter Bill Forsyth again sets up a wacko scenario about zany, off-center characters.

But evincing much laughter over an unexpectedly funny couple living together, Forsyth abruptly switches into a more conventional plot.

Pic opens with a well-dressed kleptomaniac (Eleanor David) lifting goods at a department store, followed by a man (Bill Paterson). It turns out he's her lover and aware of her stealing. They return home, make love off camera and after a meal she announces she's leaving.

Depressed, he adopts a stiff upperlip attitude and goes to his job as an MOR radio station early morning deejay. He then becomes, innocently at first, a go-between as two warring Mafia families fight for territorial control of selling ice cream by van.

David and Paterson are terrific together and almost every line between them is a joy. From the point she departs with no explanation the pic flashes a sparky moment or two, but it doesn't reach the high spots again.

••••••••••••••••••••••••••••••••••

■ COMFORT OF STRANGERS, THE

1990, 107 MINS, ITALY/US ◇ Ⓥ

Dir Paul Schrader   *Prod* Angelo Rizzoli   *Scr* Harold Pinter   *Ph* Dante Spinotti   *Ed* Bill Pankow   *Mus* Angelo Badalamenti   *Art Dir* Gianni Quaranta
● Christopher Walken, Rupert Everett, Natasha Richardson, Helen Mirren (Erre/Sovereign/Reteitalia)

Neither the beguiling romance of Venice nor the undraped bodies of Natasha Richardson and Rupert Everett can disguise the hollowness of *The Comfort of Strangers*.

Mary (Richardson) and Colin (Everett) are an unmarried, liveapart couple who have returned to Venice in an attempt to rekindle their romance and assess their relationship. While both actors are paradigms of beauty, Harold Pinter's labored scenario [from the novel by Ian McEwan] would have us believe that all of Venice is transfixed by the heart-stopping magnificence of – Everett.

Among the many Venetian souls smitten by Everett's Apollonian magnetism is a man in an icecream suit, Robert (Christopher Walken), the grave, courtly son of an Italian diplomat. Unbeknownst to the English tourists, Walken has been photographing Everett obsessively since their arrival. The couple are easy prey for Walken's blandishments.

Undermined by the script, the actors are constantly upstaged by the timeless glories of Venice.

••••••••••••••••••••••••••••••••••

■ COMING HOME

1978, 126 MINS, US ◇ Ⓥ

Dir Hal Ashby   *Prod* Jerome Hellman   *Scr* Waldo Salt, Robert C. Jones   *Ph* Haskell Wexler   *Ed* Don Zimmerman   *Art Dir* Mike Haller
● Jane Fonda, Jon Voight, Bruce Dern, Robert Ginty, Penelope Milford, Robert Carradine (United Artists)

Coming Home is in general an excellent Hal Ashby film which illuminates the conflicting attitudes on the Vietnam debacle from the standpoint of three participants. Jerome Hellman's fine production has Jane Fonda in another memorable and moving performance; Jon Voight, back on the screen much more matured, assured and effective; Bruce Dern, continuing to forge new career dimension.

Nancy Dowd's story was adapted by Waldo

Salt and former film editor Robert C. Jones into a home-front drama. Gung-ho Marine officer Dern goes to Vietnam while loyal wife Fonda decides to work in a veterans' hospital where she meets high-school classmate Voight, now an embittered cripple from the war. Their lives become transformed completely.

Fonda and Ashby have reined in any tendencies to be smug or pedantic. Instead, she provides a superb characterization. Voight's character evolves as he and Fonda become lovers. A sex scene between the two is a masterpiece of discreet romantic eroticism.

Dern's character is the trigger for certain major events, but there remains enough exposure for him to be convincing as a career soldier disillusioned by Vietnam. Among the large supporting cast are Penelope Milford, excellent as another hospital worker keeping an eye on brother Robert Carradine, very effective as a pitiful, freaked-out and ultimately suicidal case.

□ 1978: Best Picture (Nomination)

••••••••••••••••••••••••••••••••••

■ COMING TO AMERICA

1988, 116 MINS, US ◇ Ⓥ

Dir John Landis   *Prod* George Folsey Jr., Robert D. Wachs   *Scr* David Sheffield, Barry W. Blaustein   *Ph* Woody Omens   *Ed* Malcolm Campbell, George Folsey Jr.   *Mus* Nile Rodgers   *Art Dir* Richard MacDonald
● Eddie Murphy, Arsenio Hall, John Amos, James Earl Jones, Shari Headley, Eriq LaSalle (Paramount)

Coming to America starts on a bathroom joke, quickly followed by a gag about private parts, then wanders in search of something equally original for Eddie Murphy to do for another couple of hours. It's a true test for loyal fans.

Murphy has no difficulty creating a pampered young prince of Zamunda who would like a chance to live a little real life and select his own bride instead of being forced into a royal marriage of convenience. Murphy even makes the prince sympathetic and genuine, complete to his stilted English. He and courtly sidekick Arsenio Hall venture to Queens to find a queen.

Longing for someone to love him for himself, Murphy discovers beautiful Shari Headley and goes to work mopping floors in father John Amos' hamburger emporium to be near her.

She, no surprise, already has a well-to-do, insufferable boyfriend (Eriq LaSalle) that dad is anxious for her to marry. How does a janitor capture the heart of such a maiden?

••••••••••••••••••••••••••••••••••

■ COMMANDO

1985, 88 MINS, US ◇ Ⓥ

Dir Mark L. Lester   *Prod* Joel Silver   *Scr* Steven de Souza   *Ph* Matthew F. Leonetti   *Ed* Mark Goldblatt, John F. Link, Glenn Farr   *Mus* James Horner   *Art Dir* John Vallone
● Arnold Schwarzenegger, Rae Dawn Chong, Dan Hedaya, Vernon Wells, David Patrick Kelly, Alyssa Milano (Silver/20th Century-Fox)

In *Commando*, the fetching surprise is the glancing humor between the quixotic and larky Rae Dawn Chong and the straight-faced killing machine of Arnold Schwarzenegger. Chong lights up the film like a firefly, Schwarzenegger delivers a certain light touch of his own, the result is palatable action comics.

Director Mark L. Lester, compelled to deal with an absurd plot [by Joseph Loeb III, Matthew Weisman and Steven de Souza], is blessed by the decision to cast Chong, who enjoys an offbeat sexuality and an insouciance that is irresistible.

Credit Lester with chiseling the quick, subtly romantic byplay between the two stars – unlikely mates thrown together in pursuit of

C

a deadly Latin neo-dictator – and pulling off a terrific series of tracking shots during a riotous chase in a crowded galleria complex.

Heavies are vividly drawn in the cases of the obsessed Vernon Wells, the punk David Patrick Kelly, and sullen, ice-cold Bill Duke.

■ COMPANY OF WOLVES, THE

1984, 95 MINS, UK ◇ ⓥ
Dir Neil Jordan *Prod* Chris Brown, Stephen Woolley
Scr Angela Carter, Neil Jordan *Ph* Bryan Loftus
Ed Rodney Holland *Mus* George Fenton
Art Dir Anton Furst
● Angela Lansbury, David Warner, Stephen Rea, Tusse Silberg, Sarah Patterson, Graham Crowden (Palace)

Admirably attempting an adult approach to traditional fairy tale material, *The Company of Wolves* nevertheless represents an uneasy marriage between old-fashioned storytelling and contemporary screen explicitness.

Virtually the entire film is the dream of the gravely beautiful adolescent Sarah Patterson. Within her dream are other dreams and stories told by others, all of which gives director Neil Jordan, who penned the screenplay with story originator Angela Carter, free imaginative rein, but which also gives the tale a less than propulsive narrative.

Anton Furst's elaborate forest settings, all created within studio-confines, are lovely. Jordan maneuvers well within them, even if Bryan Loftus' lush lensing is sometimes so dark that a claustrophobic feeling sets in.

■ COMPETITION, THE

1980, 129 MINS, US ◇ ⓥ
Dir Joel Oliansky *Prod* William Sackheim *Scr* Joel Oliansky *Ph* Richard H. Kline *Ed* David Blewitt
Mus Lalo Schifrin *Art Dir* Dale Hennesy
● Richard Dreyfuss, Amy Irving, Lee Remick, Sam Wanamaker (Columbia/Rastar)

The Competition is a disappointment. Writer-director Joel Oliansky's glibly cynical view of the performing world and his dreary character portraits are matched in clumsiness by his ugly visual style and lack of genuine feeling for music.

The film needed a conductor and composer of background music with a sensitivity to the classical field, but instead it has Lalo Schifrin.

Richard Dreyfuss, an aging piano wunderkind, is reunited at a San Francisco music competition with Amy Irving, a less driven but more gifted young woman he had impressed briefly at an earlier festival. She tries to rekindle their attraction, but Dreyfuss is too absorbed in his music at first to respond.

The film is tedious and predictable, curiously portraying music as a grim and joyless profession for these youngsters.

■ COMPROMISING POSITIONS

1985, 98 MINS, US ◇ ⓥ
Dir Frank Perry *Prod* Frank Perry *Scr* Susan Issacs
Ph Barry Sonnenfeld *Ed* Peter Frank *Mus* Brad Fiedel *Art Dir* Peter Larkin
● Susan Sarandon, Raul Julia, Edward Herrmann, Judith Ivey, Mary Beth Hurt, Joe Mantegna (Paramount)

Falling midway between a campy send-up of suburban wives soap operas and a legitimate thriller, *Compromising Positions*, from the 1978 novel by Susan Isaacs, emerges as a silly little whodunnit that's a mild embarrassment to all involved.

Unlikely material, about the murder of a philandering Long Island dentist, the reactions of his many mistresses, and the official and unofficial investigations into it, has hardly been approached with a straight face. The victim is a loathesome gold chain type, and most of his conquests are ladies who

lunch with little redeeming social or intellectual value.

Intrigued and naively amazed that nearly everyone she knows has been involved with the late Dr Fleckstein, upper-middle-class housewife Susan Sarandon undertakes some amateur sleuthing with an eye toward reviving her old profession of newspaper reporter.

Action moves along snappily enough. Supporting players such as Judith Ivey and Josh Mostel contribute some tolerably amusing comedy turns, and Sarandon is, as always, highly watchable.

■ COMPULSION

1959, 103 MINS, US
Dir Richard Fleischer *Prod* Richard D. Zanuck
Scr Richard Murphy *Ph* William C. Mellor *Ed* William Reynolds *Mus* Lionel Newman
● Orson Welles, Dean Stockwell, Bradford Dillman, Diane Varsi, E.G. Marshall, Martin Milner (20th Century-Fox)

Compulsion, from Meyer Levin's novel, is almost a literal case study of the notorious Leopold-Loeb murder of Bobby Franks.

The two protagonists, here called Artie and Judd, both have highly neurotic, seething minds bent on destruction as twisted proof of their superiority. That the boys have a homosexual relationship is quite clear, though the subject is not overstressed. Both come from wealthy families that spoiled them.

As Artie Straus, the sneering, arrogant youth who can no longer distinguish between reality and his dreams, but who knows how to hide under the veneer of smooth politeness, Bradford Dillman turns in a superb performance. Opposite him, as Judd Steiner, Dean Stockwell plays an impressionable, sensitive youth, caught up in the spell of his strong-willed companion.

Director Richard Fleischer establishes the characters' from the terrifying opening shot when the two try to run down a drunk on the road to their appearance in court, where lawyer Orson Welles pleads for their life in the same idiom that Clarence Darrow used to save Nathan Leopold Jr and Richard Loeb from the Illinois gallows. The lines he speaks become part of the man himself, an almost classic oration against capital punishment.

As the girl who understands more than she knows, and who reaches out for Stockwell, Diane Varsi seems at times awkward. It's not an easy part, and she brings to it a tenseness that doesn't always register.

■ COMRADES

1987, 160 MINS, UK ◇ ⓥ
Dir Bill Douglas *Prod* Simon Relph *Scr* Bill Douglas *Ph* Gale Tattersall *Ed* Mick Audsley *Mus* Hans Werner Henze, David Graham *Art Dir* Michael Pickwood
● Robin Soans, William Gaminara, Stephen Bateman, Philip Davis, Jeremy Flynn, Keith Allen (Skreba/NFFC/Curzon/Film Four)

Bill Douglas has an eye for fresh detail, the rituals of rural life, and the dignity of countryfolk. Rarely before have the poverty, the pains and the pleasures, the oppressiveness of the work routine, even of the weather, been so well conveyed on film.

However, because so much time is spent on building up this rich tapestry of rural England in the 1830s, the focus is lost.

Eventually one pieces together that the Tolpuddle Martyrs, film's subject, were a small group of peasant craftsmen who dared to form a union and ask for higher wages. They were singled out for their subversion by the British authorities and transported to Australia. After a public outcry they were subsequently recalled to England.

Although there is a unique vision at work in

Comrades it's a pity that more ruthlessness in scripting and editing was not exercised.

■ COMRADE X

1940, 87 MINS, US
Dir King Vidor *Prod* Gottfried Reinhardt *Scr* Ben Hecht, Charles Lederer, Walter Reisch *Ph* Joseph Ruttenberg *Ed* Harold F. Kress *Mus* Bronislau Kaper
● Clark Gable, Hedy Lamarr, Oscar Homolka, Felix Bressart, Eve Arden, Natasha Lytess (M-G-M)

As title implies, action is laid in Russia, with Clark Gable, a love-'em-and-leave-'em, elbow-bending American reporter cutting a wide swath as a carefree Lothario and out-witter of the censors in coding stories through to the outside. Gable hits a hurdle in maintaining his secret when simple-minded Felix Bressart, hotel porter, threatens exposure of the reporter's true identity unless Gable gets Bressart's daughter out of the country immediately.

Seems the girl, although a rabid Communist, is slated to be liquidated by the Kremlin. Matter-of-fact agreement of the girl to the plan, with ritual of typical Russian marriage ceremony and her quick breakdown under Gable's embraces, sets the stage for a continual series of laugh situations before the pair finally get out of the country.

Picture resembles Garbo's *Ninotchka* only in that it again directs well-aimed shafts of humor at Communist actions and preachments, for plenty of rousing humor.

Gable provides a strong characterization of the ever-resourceful American newspaperman. Hedy Lamarr is handed her strongest role and demonstrates she can be more than decorative by a good display of both deadpan comedy and romantic antics. Natasha Lytess shines as a Russian secretary. Hair-pulling battle between latter and Lamarr over Gable's affections is a honey.

■ CONAN THE BARBARIAN

1982, 129 MINS, US ◇ ⓥ
Dir John Milius *Prod* Buzz Feitshans, Raffaella De Laurentiis *Scr* John Milius, Oliver Stone *Ph* Duke Callaghan *Ed* C. Timothy O'Meara *Mus* Basil Poledouris *Art Dir* Ron Cobb
● Arnold Schwarzenegger, James Earl Jones, Max Von Sydow, Sandahl Bergman, Mako, Gerry Lopez (De Laurentiis)

The opening is promising enough as child Conan witnesses the brutal deaths of his father and mother at the whim of the evil Thulsa Doom (James Earl Jones). Conan Jr grows up as a slave who eventually has the good fortune of turning into Arnold Schwarzenegger.

It's the baddies' fatal flaw that they shove Conan into an arena to fight chosen competitors to the death. The guy naturally realizes he's pretty strong and decides to strike out on his own to see how far his muscles can take him.

In those days it was pretty far. On the road he meets up with a fellow drifter (Gerry Lopez), beautiful cohort and eventual lover Sandahl Bergman, needy king Max Von Sydow and goofy wizard Mako.

Director John Milius does a nice job of setting up the initial story. There is a real anticipation as Schwarzenegger is unveiled as the barbarian and sets off on the road to independence. But for whatever reasons, the actor has a minimum of dialog and fails to convey much about the character through his actions.

This is compounded by the script by Milius and Oliver Stone, which is nothing more than a series of meaningless adventures and ambiguous references until the final expected confrontation with Jones.

■ CONAN THE DESTROYER

1984, 103 MINS, US ◇ Ⓥ

Dir Richard Fleischer *Prod* Raffaella De Laurentiis
Scr Stanley Mann *Ph* Jack Cardiff *Ed* Frank J.
Urioste *Mus* Basil Poledouris *Art Dir* Pier Luigi Basile
● Arnold Schwarzenegger, Grace Jones, Wilt
Chamberlain, Mako, Tracey Walter, Sarah Douglas
(De Laurentiis)

Conan the Destroyer is the ideal sword and
sorcery picture. Plot is appropriately
elemental. Conan is recruited by sexy queen
Sarah Douglas to accompany teenage
princess Olivia D'Abo to a distant castle,
wherein lies a gem that will supposedly
unleash many secret powers.

Unbeknownst to Conan, Douglas has
instructed her henchman Wilt Chamberlain
to kill the muscleman once the mission is
accomplished, and to deliver D'Abo back
home with her virginity intact so that she can
be properly sacrificed.

Along the way, group also picks up fiery
warrioress Grace Jones.

As Conan, Arnold Schwarzenegger seems
more animated and much funnier under
Fleischer's direction than he did under John
Milius' in the original – he even has an
amusing drunk scene. Jones just about runs
off with the picture. Coming on like a full-
fledged star from her very first scene, singer
throws herself into her wild woman role with
complete abandon.

■ CONCORDE – AIRPORT '79, THE

1979, 123 MINS, US ◇ Ⓥ

Dir David Lowell Rich *Prod* Jennings Lang *Scr* Eric
Roth *Ph* Philip Lathrop *Ed* Dorothy Spencer
Mus Lalo Schifrin *Art Dir* Henry Bumstead
● Alain Delon, Susan Blakely, Robert Wagner, Sylvia
Kristel, George Kennedy, Eddie Albert (Paramount)

Unintentional comedy still seems the *Airport*
series' forte, although excellent special effects
work, and some decent dramatics help
Concorde take off.

This time out, the title entity is pursued by
a dogged electronic missile, avoids an attack
by a French fighter jet, barely makes a
runway landing with no brakes, suffers a lost
cargo door that rips open the bottom of the
plane, manages a crash landing in an Alpine
snow bank, and explodes just as its chic
passengers disembark. That's all just
part of a couple of days' work for pilots
George Kennedy, Alain Delon and flight
engineer David Warner.

Concorde does feature some better-than-
average thesping from Delon, who survives
the transition to American pix surprisingly
well.

■ CONDEMNED OF ALTONA, THE

1963, 112 MINS, ITALY

Dir Vittorio De Sica *Prod* Carlo Ponti *Scr* Abby
Mann, Cesare Zavattini *Ph* Roberto Gerardi
Ed Adriana Novelli *Mus* Nino Rota *Art Dir* Elvezio
Frigerio
● Sophia Loren, Maximilian Schell, Fredric March,
Robert Wagner, Francoise Prevost (Titanus)

Filmed on location in Hamburg, with interiors in Italy, this tale of post-war Germany, as symbolized by the members of one
family, is undoubtedly anti-German. Where
Jean-Paul Sartre's play was written from the
point of view of a French writer, scripters
Abby Mann and Cesare Zavattini have
changed these observations to Italian orientation. Here lies the film's chief controversy;
that Germany is painted black, while her collaborators (which did include Italy) are not
painted, period.

The title refers to the Gerlachs, a wealthy
Hamburg shipbuilding family, or what is left
of it, and Altona, the Hamburg suburb in

which they live. Director Vittorio De Sica
spins the tale as a series of disclosures about
the family and the resultant emotional effect
on Johanna (Sophia Loren), the actress-wife
of the younger son (Robert Wagner).

This throws the major dramatic responsibility on Loren, who creates a shudderingly
magnificent portrait of a beautiful, intelligent
woman just beginning to recover her dignity
and self-respect from the shambles of her
country's militaristic past, only to have them
threatened by 'secrets' of her husband's
family.

Striking flames is Maximilian Schell as
Franz, the eldest son whose personal war
guilt has kept him a self-imposed prisoner in
the attic of the Gerlach manor for 15 years
until, bordering on insanity, he is roused
from his self-delusion by Johanna, at first
sympathetic. Reported as dead by his family,
even to Johanna, Franz' self-delusion has
been supported by his family, particularly his
tycoon father (Fredric March), whose own
war guilt has been kept subservient to his
indomitable will and industrial genius.

March, whose impending death from cancer, brings the family together, creates Gerlach as much through visualization as
through dialog. Wagner, on the screen a comparatively short time and dropped entirely
after an important self-revealing speech,
makes one weak member of a strong family a
memorable character.

■ CONDUCT UNBECOMING

1976, 107 MINS, UK ◇

Dir Michael Anderson *Prod* Michael Deeley, Barry
Spikings *Scr* Robert Enders *Ph* Bob Huke *Ed* John
Glen *Mus* Stanley Myers *Art Dir* Ted Tester
● Michael York, Richard Attenborough, Trevor
Howard, Stacy Keach, Christopher Plummer, Susannah
York (Lion/Crown)

Based on a play by Barry England, this has
all the ingredients of good, sllightly old-fashioned courtroom drama transposed to 19th-
century, British-dominated India to give it an
added dimension.

Basically, action centers around a secret
trial by his fellow officers of a young lieutenant accused of assaulting an officer's widow
in a colonial outpost. In defending the
accused, a new arrival slowly uncovers not
only the real assaulter, but more especially
the hypocrisy which rules and motivates the
garrison officers' lives.

Acting is uniformly excellent. Michael York
as the defender and James Faulkner as the
defendant get top-notch backing. But, perhaps because of his seemingly offbeat casting
as a British officer, it's Stacy Keach who surprises and steals acting honors.

■ CONFESSIONS OF A NAZI SPY

1939, 110 MINS, US

Dir Anatole Litvak *Prod* Robert Lord *Scr* Milton
Krims, John Wexley *Ph* Sol Polito *Ed* Owen Marks
Mus Max Steiner *Art Dir* Carl Jules Weyl
● Edward G. Robinson, Francis Lederer, George
Sanders, Paul Lukas, Lya Lys (Warner)

The story itself is told for maximum mass
comprehension. Based on articles by Leon G.
Turrou, former G-man, it is an adaptation of
the spy trials of 1937 which resulted in the
conviction of four persons.

Its thesis is that espionage directed from
Berlin is tied up with the German-American
Bunds, their rallies and summer camps and
general parading around in uniforms. The
German goal is destruction of democracy.

The cast numbers a fine collection of scarfaced Gestapo agents, guys with crew hair-
cuts and assorted livid sneerers.

Edward G. Robinson comes in very late in
the film. Paul Lukas carries through as the

Bund leader who finally falls out with the
Gestapo. The missing motivation, anti-Semitism, is the one thing not named and
ticketed.

■ CONFIDENTIAL AGENT

1945, 113 MINS, US

Dir Herman Shumlin *Prod* Robert Buckner
Scr Robert Buckner *Ph* James Wong Howe
Ed George Amy *Mus* Franz Waxman *Art Dir* Leo
Kuter
● Charles Boyer, Lauren Bacall, Wanda Hendrix, Peter
Lorre, Katina Paxinou, George Coulouris (Warner)

The story attempts to show how in 1937 the
success of Franco adherents was to become
the prelude to an even greater conflict. The
yarn's development is inept, and the link of
the romance with the basic story [from a
novel by Graham Greene] is too pat, at the
expense of the major story line.

Charles Boyer plays a Spanish concert
musician who has given up his career to fight
the fascists. He's detailed to go to England
and outbid the Francoites for British coal.
The coal can be the difference between victory and defeat. The plot specifically deals
with the obstacles that confront him, including the British fascists, and secondary to this
is the romance that evolves between a British
coal tycoon's daughter and Boyer.

Boyer, as usual, underplays to gain an
effect as adequate as possible under the
circumstances. Lauren Bacall suffers from a
monotony of voice and an uncertainty of performance. Her s.a., however, is still plenty
evident.

■ CONNECTICUT YANKEE, A

1931, 93 MINS, US

Dir David Butler *Scr* William Conselman *Ph* Ernest
Palmer *Mus* Erno Rapee
● Will Rogers, William Farnum, Myrna Loy, Maureen
O'Sullivan, Frank Albertson, Mitchell Harris (Fox)

The [Mark Twain] story was originally
turned down by Doug Fairbanks, after which
Fox made it with Harry Myers. It was released late in 1920. The staff working on this
sound version must have run off the silent
print plenty. William Conselman gets the
credit for the modern adaptation, but there's
no telling how many writers worked on the
script. Neither the beginning nor the end is
entirely satisfactory, especially the finish. But
the main section is a dream, and there are
more than sufficient laughs to compensate.

Opening has Will Rogers as a smalltown
radio store proprietor, called to a mysterious
house to install a battery. An armored figure
falls over, knocks Rogers out and thence into
the dream. The change back to the modern
story and finish is decidedly weak.

Rogers' main cast support comes from William Farnum as King Arthur. Mitchell Harris as Merlin, the magician, and Brandon
Hurst playing the menace. Myrna Loy does
not do much with her femme heavy, while
Maureen O'Sullivan has nothing much more
than a bit. Frank Albertson, supplying the
other half of the love interest, appears to be at
a loss in not being able to chatter at his generally furious rate.

■ CONNECTICUT YANKEE IN KING ARTHUR'S COURT, A

1949, 106 MINS, US ◇ Ⓥ

Dir Tay Garnett *Prod* Robert Fellows *Scr* Edmund
Beloin *Ph* Ray Rennahan *Ed* Archie Marshek
Mus Victor Young
● Bing Crosby, Rhonda Fleming, Cedric Hardwicke,
William Bendix, Henry Wilcoxon (Paramount)

Bing Crosby, songs and color make pleasant
entertainment out of *A Connecticut Yankee in*

C

King Arthur's Court. It's not high comedy and there's little swashbuckling but it is pleasant.

A footnote emphasizes that this latest version of Mark Twain's gentle tale of a Yankee blacksmith who's knocked on the head and awakes in King Arthur's court is adapted strictly from the book as written by the author.

A bit more vigor in the handling would have sharpened the pace. Film also falls down in some of the technical work, which doesn't help to carry out the illusion of the romantic days of 528.

Rhonda Fleming's vocals please and her physical charms as Alisande, King Arthur's niece, are expressive enough to illustrate why the Yankee would develop a yen for her.

....

■ **CONQUEROR, THE**

1956, 111 MINS, US ◇ ⊛

Dir Dick Powell   *Prod* Dick Powell   *Scr* Oscar Millard   *Ph* Joseph LaShelle, Leo Tover, Harry J. Wild, William Snyder   *Ed* Robert Ford, Kennie Marstella   *Mus* Victor Young   *Art Dir* Albert S. D'Agostino, Carroll Clark

● John Wayne, Susan Hayward, Pedro Armendariz, Agnes Moorehead, Thomas Gomez, William Conrad (RKO)

Just so there will be no misunderstanding about *The Conqueror*, a foreword baldly states that it is fiction, although with some basis in fact. With that warning out of the way, the viewer can sit back and thoroughly enjoy a huge, brawling, sex-and-sand actioner purporting to show how a 12th Century Mongol leader became known as Genghis Khan.

The marquee value of the John Wayne-Susan Hayward teaming more than offsets any incongruity of the casting, which has him as the Mongol leader and she as the Tartar princess he captures and forcibly takes as mate.

Costarring with Wayne and Hayward is excellent Mexican actor, Pedro Armendariz, who makes believable his role of Wayne's blood-brother and is an important essential in the entertainment.

The s.a. pitch is in a harem dance choreographed by Robert Sidney, in which a covey of lookers give the appearance of being almost completely bare while gyrating to the Oriental strains of Victor Young's firstrate music.

....

■ **CONQUEST OF THE PLANET OF THE APES**

1972, 87 MINS, US ◇ ⊛

Dir J. Lee Thompson   *Prod* Arthur P. Jacobs   *Scr* Paul Dehn   *Ph* Bruce Surtees   *Ed* Marjorie Fowler, Allan Jaggs   *Mus* Tom Scott   *Art Dir* Philip Jefferies

● Roddy McDowall, Don Murray, Ricardo Montalban, Natalie Trundy, Hari Rhodes, Severn Darden (20th Century-Fox)

The *Planet of the Apes* series takes an angry turn in the fourth entry, *Conquest of the Planet of the Apes.*

The story begins about 20 years in the future, after a world epidemic has destroyed all dogs. People first had turned to apes as pets, but because of their intelligence the apes have become servants under civil regulation of computer-age overseer Don Murray. Into this milieu comes traveling circus operator Ricardo Montalban who, at the end of the prior film, had concealed the nearly-human offspring of the murdered Roddy McDowall and Kim Hunter. McDowall now has shifted to the role of his son.

In the new world, McDowall has to Uncle-Tom his way through the prevailing slave environment, until Murray's inexorable search for the long-missing ape-human child leads to Montalban's death under torture-grilling by Severn Darden. McDowall then

organizes a bloody revolt which occupies the last third of the film.

....

■ **CONRACK**

1974, 107 MINS, US ◇ ⊛

Dir Martin Ritt   *Prod* Martin Ritt, Harriet Frank Jr   *Scr* Irving Ravetch, Harriet Frank Jr   *Ph* John Alonzo   *Ed* Frank Bracht   *Mus* John Williams   *Art Dir* Walter Scott Herndon

● Jon Voight, Paul Winfield, Madge Sinclair, Tina Andrews, Antonio Fargas, Hume Cronyn (20th Century-Fox)

Jon Voight stars as a young Southerner who treks off to an isolated South Carolina island in 1969 for a teaching post, only to find the black children there uniformly illiterate and/or retarded. Through a combination of love and pedagogical razzmatazz, he opens their eyes to the wonders of yoga, Beethoven, Babe Ruth, Ho Chi Minh, and Halloween.

Some may resent the inadvertent white-liberal condescension evident in the initially one-dimensional portrait of the deprived youngsters. Others may be momentarily confused by the lack of explicit data – time, place, personal factors behind the teacher's willingness to submerge obvious intellectual gifts in a backwoods community.

But few will totally resist the surefire appeal of this latest variation on Pygmalion mythology.

....

■ **CONSTANCE**

1984, 103 MINS, NEW ZEALAND ◇ ⊛

Dir Bruce Morrison   *Prod* Larry Parr   *Scr* Jonathan Hardy   *Ph* Kevin Hayward   *Ed* Philip Howe   *Mus* John Charles   *Art Dir* Ric Kifoed

● Donogh Rees, Shane Briant, Judie Douglass, Martin Vaughan, Donald MacDonald, Marc Wignall (Mirage)

Constance is a highly stylized film about a beautiful young woman living in Auckland in 1946 who dreams she is a Hollywood superstar.

Constance (Donogh Rees) is given to such contrived charades as dressing as Marlene Dietrich at parties and singing along to a recording of Dietrich's hit, 'Falling in Love Again.'

Rees' stiffness of manner may be director Bruce Morrison's idea of the artificiality of the concept as a whole.

Imported actor Shane Briant has the right air of handsome, predatory decadence as a visiting Hollywood still-photographer. There is an outburst of sexual violence during a photo session which is given the blurred-lens, freeze-frame, jump-cut treatment, and it makes an effective contrast to the film's otherwise sharply focused sedate pace.

....

■ **CONSTANT HUSBAND, THE**

1955, 88 MINS, UK ◇

Dir Sidney Gilliat   *Prod* Frank Launder, Sidney Gilliat   *Scr* Sidney Gilliat, Val Valentine   *Ph* Ted Scaife   *Ed* G. Turney-Smith   *Mus* Malcolm Arnold   *Art Dir* Wilfrid Shingleton

● Rex Harrison, Margaret Leighton, Kay Kendall, Cecil Parker, Nicole Maurey, George Cole (London)

A frothy comedy, *The Constant Husband* is one of the brightest efforts from the Frank Launder and Sidney Gilliat partnership. The screenplay is light and amusing, and none of the sparkle has been lost in the translation to the screen.

The story could not be more slender. Rex Harrison, an amnesia victim, learns, to his horror, that he has seven wives to his credit. A bigamy charge follows, but rather than face seven eager ex-spouses, he pleas in favor of jail.

Harrison is thoroughly diverting as the amnesia victim. Margaret Leighton makes a

belated appearance on the screen, but her impact as the last of the seven wives, gives a sparkling portrayal. Cecil Parker is typically buoyant and Nicole Maurey is sufficiently alluring as another of the ex-wives.

....

■ **CONSTANT NYMPH, THE**

1934, 85 MINS, UK

Dir Basil Dean   *Scr* Dorothy Farnum, Basil Dean, Margaret Kennedy   *Ph* Mutz Greenbaum   *Mus* Eugene Goosens, John Greenwood   *Art Dir* Alfred Junge

● Brian Aherne, Victoria Hopper, Peggy Blythe, Jane Baxter, Lyn Harding, Mary Clare (Gaumont-British)

Story [by Margaret Kennedy] opens in the Austrian mountains where a slightly mad composer and his daughters, all half-sisters and all hoydens, live a carefree life of idyllic sweetness. There is a younger composer (Brian Aherne) and for him one of the girls (Victoria Hopper) conceives an undying passion.

He marries a respectability-minded English cousin (Leonora Corbett) and moves to London. Ultimately he realizes he should have waited for the girl to add a year or two to her age and married her instead of the older woman.

It is a soft, delicate, fragile, meandering yarn, beautifully directed by Basil Dean.

....

■ **CONSTANT NYMPH, THE**

1943, 106 MINS, US

Dir Edmund Goulding   *Prod* Henry Blanke   *Scr* Kathryn Scola   *Ph* Tony Gaudio   *Ed* David Weisbert   *Mus* Erich Wolfgang Korngold

● Charles Boyer, Joan Fontaine, Alexis Smith, Charles Coburn, Peter Lorre, Joyce Reynolds (Warner)

This is the film version of the novel and play of same title [by Margaret Kennedy and Basil Dean]. Devoting plenty of footage to character delineations and incidental episodes, it results in a bumpy screen tale with interlay of both draggy and interesting sequences. Major portion of excess footage is on the front end, where 40 minutes is consumed in setting up detailed background for the final event, which is a love triangle, with Charles Boyer the focal point for conflict between teenager played by Joan Fontaine and the older Alexis Smith. The stretch hits yawning periods.

This early portion serves to detail movement of Boyer, composer of promise but lacking the necessary fire to write his outstanding composition, from Brussels to home of his friend and mentor (Montagu Love) in Switzerland. Of the four daughters in the house, Fontaine is next to the youngest, with adolescent adoration for Boyer. When Love dies and girls' uncle (Charles Coburn) arrives from England with his own daughter (Smith), Boyer and latter embark on romance culminating in marriage.

Script covers plenty of ground and detail, but general tightening would have helped materially. There's a tang of the stage in the unfolding, which director Edmund Goulding found impossible to overcome with his careful and even-tempoed direction.

....

■ **CONTINENTAL DIVIDE**

1981, 103 MINS, US ◇

Dir Michael Apted   *Prod* Bob Larson   *Scr* Lawrence Kasdan   *Ph* John Bailey   *Ed* Dennis Virkler   *Mus* Michael Small   *Art Dir* Peter Jamison

● John Belushi, Blair Brown, Allen Garfield, Carlin Glynn (Universal/Amblin)

For a picture that you can't really believe for a second, *Continental Divide* still comes off as a reasonably engaging entertainment thanks to some lively performances and a liberal dose of laughs throughout the script.

John Belushi plays a star columnist for the *Chicago Sun Times* who loves dishing the dirt about the latest doings down at city hall. When his stories on a certain corrupt alderman get too hot, Belushi is sent to the Rocky Mountains to track down a crazy bird lady known for her reclusiveness and particular hatred of nosey reporters.

At first, beauteous Blair Brown orders the interloper from her mountaintop retreat but, as his guide won't be back to fetch him for two weeks, they gradually learn to cope and, finally, love together.

The problem is that these two just don't seem made for each other. When Tracy and Hepburn sparred for two hours in films like *Adam's Rib* and *Pat and Mike*, airing every possible reason they shouldn't get, or remain, together, the inevitability of their ultimate match-up was crystal clear.

Lawrence Kasdan displays a keen ability to write sparkling male-female repartee and also creates a believable context for Belushi's beat on the Windy City streets. Michael Apted's direction is solid.

■ CONVERSATION, THE

1974, 113 MINS, US ◇ Ⓥ
Dir Francis Coppola *Prod* Francis Coppola, Fred Roos *Scr* Francis Coppola *Ph* Bill Butler *Ed* Walter Murch, Richard Chew *Mus* David Shire *Art Dir* Dean Tavoularis
● Gene Hackman, John Cazale, Allen Garfield, Frederic Forrest, Cindy Williams, Harrison Ford (Paramount)

Francis Coppola's *The Conversation* stars Gene Hackman as a professional surveillance expert whose resurgent conscience involves him in murder and leads to self-destruction.

He is introduced in SF's Union Square at midday, teamed with John Cazale and Michael Higgins in tracking the movements and voices of Frederic Forrest and Cindy Williams. The cleaned-up sound tapes, along with photographs, are to be delivered to a mysterious businessman, played in an unbilled part by Robert Duvall. What appears to be a simple case of marital infidelity suddenly shifts to a possible murder plot.

A major artistic asset to the film – besides script, direction and the top performances – is supervising editor Walter Murch's sound collage and re-recording. Voices come in and out of aural focus in a superb tease.
□ 1974: Best Picture (Nomination)

■ CONVERSATION PIECE

1975, 120 MINS, ITALY/FRANCE ◇
Dir Luchino Visconti *Scr* Luchino Visconti, Suso Cecchi D'Amico *Ph* Pasqualino De Santis *Ed* Ruggero Mastroianni *Art Dir* Mario Garbuglia
● Burt Lancaster, Silvana Mangano, Helmut Berger, Claudia Marsani, Dominique Sanda, Claudia Cardinale (Rusconi/Gaumont)

Conversation Piece eschews the usually operatic, museum-like pix of Luchino Visconti for a touching tale of the generation gap and the loss of life-contact of an intellectual.

A prof (Burt Lancaster) is addicted to collecting 18th-century British paintings of families called Conversation Pieces. Into this comes a haughty, middleaged, but still beautiful Italian woman who wants to rent his upstairs apartment.

Lancaster is finally persuaded by her, her cute teenage daughter and her rich fiance. There is also the mother's lover, a young German (Helmut Berger). The professor gets tangled up with the young people despite himself.

Visconti has kept this talky but rarely ver-

bose pic in the two apartments with only an outside studio view of Rome. The assorted accents are justified andeven the peppering of blue lingo Americanisms fit these jet setters Lancaster is highly effective as the professor.

■ CONVOY

1978, 110 MINS, US ◇ Ⓥ
Dir Sam Peckinpah *Prod* Robert M. Sherman *Scr* B.W.L. Norton *Ph* Harry Stradling Jr *Ed* Graeme Clifford, John Wright, Garth Craven *Mus* Chip Davis *Art Dir* Fernando Carrere
● Kris Kristofferson, Ali MacGraw, Ernest Borgnine, Burt Young, Madge Sinclair, Franklyn Ajaye (United Artists)

Sam Peckinpah's *Convoy* starts out as *Smokey and the Bandit*, segues into either *Moby Dick* or *Les Miserables*, and ends in the usual script confusion and disarray, the whole stew peppered with the vulgar excess of random truck crashes and miscellaneous destruction. Kris Kristofferson stars as a likeable roustabout who accidentally becomes a folk hero, while Ali MacGraw recycles about three formula reactions throughout her nothing part.

B.W.L. Norton gets writing credit using C.W. McCall's c&w poptune lyric as a basis. No matter. Peckinpah's films display common elements and clumsy analogies, overwhelmed with logistical fireworks and drunken changes of dramatic emphasis.

This time around, Kristofferson (who, miraculously, seems to survive these banalities) is a trucker whose longtime nemesis, speed-trap-blackmailer cop Ernest Borgnine, pursues him with a vengeance through what appears to be three states. Every few minutes there's some new roadblock to run, alternating with pithy comments on The Meaning Of It All. There's a whole lot of nothing going on here.

■ COOGAN'S BLUFF

1968, 93 MINS, US ◇ Ⓥ
Dir Don Siegel *Prod* Don Siegel *Scr* Herman Miller, Dean Reisner, Howard Rodman *Ph* Bud Thackery *Ed* Sam E. Waxman *Mus* Lalo Schifrin *Art Dir* Alexander Golitzen, Robert C.MacKichan
● Clint Eastwood, Lee J. Cobb, Susan Clark, Tisha Sterling, Don Stroud, Betty Field (Universal)

Story of the clash between sophisticated law enforcement and frontier-style simplistics, which is perhaps one of the major internal American problems. Clint Eastwood stars as a laconic, taciturn stranger, this time a deputy sheriff from Arizona in NY City.

Herman Miller's story establishes Eastwood as a cold, selfish desert lawman sent to NY to extradite hippie Don Stroud, whose Arizona offense is never mentioned. Lee J. Cobb, a city detective, tries to explain to Eastwood that things are done differently.

Susan Clark is very good as a probation officer who falls for Eastwood. Tisha Sterling does well as Stroud's hippie girl friend. Betty Field has an excellent scene as Stroud's mother, impact being second only to Cobb's terrific work.

■ COOK, THE THIEF, HIS WIFE AND HER LOVER, THE

1989, 126 MINS, NETHERLANDS/FRANCE ◇ Ⓥ
Dir Peter Greenaway *Prod* Kees Kasander *Scr* Peter Greenaway *Ph* Sacha Vierny *Ed* John Wilson *Mus* Michael Nyman *Art Dir* Ben Van Os, Jan Roelfs
● Richard Bohringer, Michael Gambon, Helen Mirren, Alan Howard, Tim Roth, Gary Olsen (Allarts Cook/ Erato/Films Inc)

Peter Greenaway's grim sense of humor and cheerful assault on all our sacred cows is evident in this new outing from the iconoclastic filmmaker.

Setting is a smart restaurant, La Hollandaise, where Richard, the chef (Richard Bohringer) prepares a lavish menu every night. Among his regular customers are Albert Spica (Michael Gambon), a loud-mouthed, vulgar, violent gangster, who dines with his entourage of seedy yes-men, and his bored, beautiful wife, Georgina (Helen Mirren).

At another table each night sits Michael, a quiet, diffident man who's always reading books. He and Georgina make eye contact, and soon they're having a series of secret rendezvous. Eventually Albert discovers his wife's infidelity, and takes a typically violent revenge, triggering a more unusual retaliation from her.

Albert is one of the ugliest characters ever brought to the screen. Ignorant, over-bearing and violent, it's a gloriously rich performance by Gambon.

In contrast, Helen Mirren (in a role which was originally to have been played by Vanessa Redgrave) is all calm politeness and mute acceptance until her passion is aroused by the (far from handsome) Michael.

■ COOKIE

1989, 93 MINS, US ◇ Ⓥ
Dir Susan Seidelman *Prod* Laurence Mark *Scr* Nora Ephron, Alice Arlen *Ph* Oliver Stapleton *Ed* Andrew Mondshein *Mus* Thomas Newman *Art Dir* Michael Haller
● Peter Falk, Dianne Wiest, Emily Lloyd, Michael V. Gazzo, Brenda Vaccaro (Lorimar/Warner)

Half-baked, bland and flat as a vanilla wafer, *Cookie* rolls out the tired marriage of comedy and organized crime to produce a disorganized mess with little nutritional or comedic value.

The story gets set in motion, such as it is, when mobster Dino Capisco (Peter Falk) is released from prison after 13 years, rejoining his wife (Brenda Vaccaro), mistress (Dianne Wiest) and the headstrong daughter he had with the latter, played by Emily Lloyd.

Sadly, about the only thing Lloyd gets to do here is prove she can affect a New York accent and chew gum at the same time. Thrown together with Falk as his driver, the two fail to build any of the warmth or even grudging admiration they display in the final reel.

The film ultimately turns into an elaborate scheme by which Falk can get even with his treacherous former partner (played by Michael V. Gazzo), and the payoff is hardly worth the protracted build-up.

Only Wiest emerges in top form with her brassy portrayal of a weepy red-haired gun moll in the Lucille Ball mode.

■ COOLEY HIGH

1975, 107 MINS, US ◇
Dir Michael Schultz *Prod* Steve Krantz *Scr* Eric Monte *Ph* Paul vom Brack *Ed* Christopher Holmes *Mus* Freddie Perren *Art Dir* William B. Fosser
● Glynn Turman, Lawrence-Hilton Jacobs, Garrett Morris, Cynthia Davies (American International)

Cooley High is pitched as a black *American Graffiti*, and the description is apt. Furthermore, you don't have to be black to enjoy it immensely. The Steve Krantz production is a heartening comedy-drama about urban Chicago high school youths, written by Eric Monte.

The story focusses mainly on two frisky students, Glynn Turman and Lawrence-Hilton Jacobs. Girl trouble (principally charming Cynthia Davis), school trouble (with empathetic teacher Garrett Morris), and law trouble (via involvement with toughs Sherman Smith and Norman Gibson) lead the pair through experiences which range from broadly comic to deathly serious. The plot is simply about a lot of believable people and of course that's the way it should be.

. . . .

■ COOL HAND LUKE

1967, 126 MINS, US ◇ ▼

Dir Stuart Rosenberg *Prod* Gordon Carroll *Scr* Donn Pearce, Frank R. Pierson *Ph* Conrad Hall *Ed* Sam O'Steen *Mus* Lalo Schifrin *Art Dir* Cary Odell
● Paul Newman, George Kennedy, J.D. Cannon, Lou Antonio, Robert Drivas, Jo Van Fleet (Warner)

Paul Newman is *Cool Hand Luke*, a loner role in a film that depicts the social structure of a Dixie chain gang. Versatile and competent cast maintains interest throughout rambling exposition to a downbeat climax.

Luke, obviously supposed to be set in the South, was shot near Stockton, California, where the desired flat land, occasionally broken by gentle rolls, makes for an effective physical backdrop. In this case, it is a chain-gang compound, ruled by some patronizing, sadistic guards, to which Newman will not conform.

Newman gives an excellent performance, assisted by a terrif supporting cast, including George Kennedy, outstanding as the unofficial leader of the cons who yields first place to Newman.

Strother Martin's camp chief is chilling, a firstrate characterization. His goon squad likewise delivers strong performances: Morgan Woodward, Luke Askew, Robert Donner, John McLiam, Charles Tyner. Clifton James, the burly building overseer, is appropriately warmer.

. . . .

■ COOL WORLD, THE

1963, 125 MINS, US

Dir Shirley Clarke *Scr* Shirley Clarke, Carl Lee *Ph* Baird Bryant *Ed* Shirley Clarke *Mus* Mal Waldron
● Hampton Clayton, Yolanda Rodriguez, Carl Lee (Wiseman)

The Cool World is the world of Harlem. Film deals generally with its physical and human aspects and also comment on the personal feel and outlook of its characters. Both elements are well blended to make this a telling look at Harlem and probably one of the least patronizing films ever made on Negro life in New York.

A sharp, restless, whiplike camera picks up a Black Muslim spouting hate against the white man and claiming supremacy. Then the Harlem streets and the people listening, or letting the fanatic words float by, come to life and out of the crowd is picked a young teenager, Duke, whose one desire seems to be to own a gun that would give him standing in his own gang. Film [from the novel by Warren Miller] alternates Duke's story with general scenes of Harlem life.

The natural thesping is by a mainly non-pro cast. But it is chiefly the virile, well observed direction of Shirley Clarke that keeps this long film engrossing and revealing most of the way. She creates a tenseness around the familiar characters by a knowing look at Harlem rhythms, gaiety, lurking desperation, boredom tempered with joviality, and the general oppressiveness of bad housing and employment conditions.

Sometimes the characters get a bit lost in the general schematics of the pic, which at times waters down its underlying irony. But, overall, Clarke has a firm hold on her characters and story.

. . . .

■ CORN IS GREEN, THE

1945, 114 MINS, US ▼

Dir Irving Rapper *Prod* Jack Chertok *Scr* Casey Robinson, Frank Cavett *Ph* Sol Polito *Ed* Frederick Richards *Mus* Max Steiner *Art Dir* Carl Jules Weyl

● Bette Davis, Nigel Bruce, John Dall, Joan Lorring, Mildred Dunnock (Warner)

The performances, not only of Bette Davis but of newcomers John Dall and Joan Lorring, together with those of Nigel Bruce and others, capture attention and admiration far and above that of the story itself, which is somewhat slow in the first half. Several sequences could have been edited more sharply. While the exteriors of the Welsh countryside are almost entirely dreary and depressing, they reflect the mood of the Emlyn Williams play and its locale.

Davis, doing the emotional and serious-minded school mistress of the story, whose sociological ideals spur her to untiring efforts in raising the IQ of lowly Welsh mining folk, is cast in the kind of role she does well. Dall, her protege, is much less an admirable character, though interest stays with him all the way.

The youthful Lorring is also a very intriguing type. As the trollop Bessie Watty, she is particularly socko in the final reel, when returning to the village with the news that she has borne Dall's illegitimate child.

. . . .

■ CORPSE GRINDERS, THE

1971, 72 MINS, US ◇ ▼

Dir Ted V. Mikels *Prod* Ted V. Mikels *Scr* Arch Hall, Joseph L. Cranston *Ph* Bill Anneman *Ed* Ted V. Mikels *Art Dir* John Robinson, Laura Young
● Sean Kenney, Monika Kelly, Sanford Mitchell, J. Byron Foster, Warren Ball, Ann Noble (Mikels)

The Corpse Grinders revolves around the grinding of stolen cadavers into canned cat food which turns a gentle pussy into a raging man-eater. Film carries enough blood to satisfy any cravings for this type of divertissement but it's a cheapie in every respect.

Most of the chills are in the factory where bodies, supplied by a cemetery caretaker, are fed into a machine and the product comes out feline puree. Ted V. Mikels, who produced and directed, manages a few horror shots. Script builds as a young doctor and his nurse suspect that cat attacks are tied in with food which tests indicate might be human flesh.

Sean Kenney and Monika Kelly portray these two, and Sanford Mitchell and J. Byron Foster the diabolical food operators, all delivering pedestrian performances.

. . . .

■ COTTON CLUB, THE

1984, 127 MINS, US ◇ ▼

Dir Francis Coppola *Prod* Robert Evans *Scr* William Kennedy, Francis Coppola *Ph* Stephen Goldblatt *Ed* Barry Malkin, Robert Lovett *Mus* John Barry, Bob Wilbur *Art Dir* Richard Sylbert
● Richard Gere, Gregory Hines, Diane Lane, Lonette McKee, Bob Hoskins, Nicolas Cage (Zoetrope)

The Cotton Club certainly doesn't stint on ambition. Four stories threat through and intertwine in the $47 million picture. While the earlier Francis Coppola gangster efforts had a firm hand on the balance between plot elements and characters, *The Cotton Club* emerges as uneven and sometimes unfocused.

Focus is on Dixie Dwyer (Richard Gere), a cornet player in a small Gotham club. As the film opens in 1928, Dixie interrupts a solo to push a patron out of the way of a gunman's bullet. The thankful target turns out to be nightclub owner Dutch Schultz (James Remar).

Schultz is soon throwing work Dixie's way and hires his brother, Vincent (Nicolas Cage), as a bodyguard.

Another thread involves club tap star Sandman Williams (Gregory Hines) who partners with his brother Clay (Maurice Hines) and has his eyes and heart set on chorus girl Lila Rose Oliver (Lonette McKee).

Dramatically, Coppola and coscreenwriter

William Kennedy, juggle a lot of balls in the air. The parallel stories of Gere and Hines' professional rise prove more potent, thanks largely to a mixture of romance, music and gangland involvement. Hines and McKee generate real sparks in their relationship and latter adds an interesting dimension as a light-skinned singer trying to hide her racial origins.

. . . .

■ COUCH TRIP, THE

1988, 98 MINS, US ◇ ▼

Dir Michael Ritchie *Prod* Lawrence Gordon, Gordon A. Webb *Scr* Steven Kampmann, Will Porter, Sean Stein *Ph* Donald E. Thorin *Ed* Richard A. Harris *Mus* Michel Colombier *Art Dir* Jimmie Bly
● Dan Aykroyd, Walter Matthau, Charles Grodin, Donna Dixon, Richard Romanus (Orion)

The Couch Trip is a relatively low-key Dan Aykroyd vehicle that restores some of the comic actor's earlier charm simply by not trying too hard. Relying as much on character as shtick, Aykroyd is a likable everyman here out to right the minor indignities and injustices in the world.

As an obstreperous prisoner biding his time in a Cicero, Ill, loony bin, Aykroyd trades places with his attending shrink, Dr Baird (David Clennon), and moves to LA to fill in for radio therapist Dr Maitlin (Charles Grodin) who is having a mental breakdown of his own.

Screenplay [from the novel by Ken Kolb] doesn't break any new ground in suggesting there is a thin line between the certifiably crazy and certifiably sane, but it still manages some gentle jabs at the pretensions of the psychiatric profession.

As a mock priest and another fringe member of society, Walter Matthau is Aykroyd's soulmate, but the connection between the men is too thinly drawn to have much meaning. Donna Dixon, stunningly beautiful though she is, is impossible to swallow as a brilliant psychiatrist, particularly since her duties include signaling commercial breaks on radio and standing around posing.

. . . .

■ COUNTDOWN

1968, 101 MINS, US ◇ ▼

Dir Robert Altman *Prod* William Conrad *Scr* Loring Mandel *Ph* William W. Spencer *Ed* Gene Milford *Mus* Leonard Rosenman *Art Dir* Jack Poplin
● James Caan, Joanna Moore, Robert Duvall, Barbara Baxley, Charles Aidman, Steve Ihnat (Warner/Seven Arts)

Countdown, a story about a US space shot to the moon, is a literate and generally excellent programmer. Strong script [based on a novel by Hank Searls], emphasizing human conflict, is well developed and neatly resolved on a note of suspense.

James Caan is a civilian scientist, chosen because of political implications, to replace military officer Robert Duvall as the moonshot man. Added to this conflict is that between Steve Ihnat, project boss, and Charles Aidman, flight surgeon, who carry on the struggle between safety of life considerations and those of beating the Russians.

Although the emphasis is on personal interactions, pic interpolates some stock footage plus specially-shot technical mock-up scenes.

. . . .

■ COUNTERPOINT

1967, 105 MINS, US ◇

Dir Ralph Nelson *Prod* Dick Berg *Scr* James Lee, Joel Oliansky *Ph* Russel Metty *Ed* Howard G. Epstein *Mus* Bronislau Kaper *Art Dir* Alexander Golitzen, Carl Anderson
● Charlton Heston, Maximilian Schell, Kathryn Hays, Leslie Nielsen, Anton Diffring, Linden Chiles (Universal)

Counterpoint is the story of an American symphony orchestra – on a USO tour in Belgium – taken prisoner by the Germans during the Battle of the Bulge. Some of the incidents are contrived and characterizations of its two leads, as developed in trying to make them strong, are sometimes confusing. But in the main subject has been well handled.

Script, based upon Alan Sillitoe's novel, *The General*, packs suspense as fate of the martinet symph conductor and his 70 musicians at hands of the Germans, under order to execute every prisoner, remains uncertain.

Something new has been added here for a war film; parts of five major music works, recorded by Los Angeles Philharmonic Orchestra for the action, which should have particular appeal for music lovers.

COUNTESS FROM HONG KONG, A

1967, 120 MINS, UK ◇

Dir Charles Chaplin *Prod* Jerome Epstein
Scr Charles Chaplin *Ph* Arthur Ibbetson *Ed* Gordon Hales *Mus* Charles Chaplin *Art Dir* Bob Cartwright
● Marlon Brando, Sophia Loren, Sydney Chaplin, Tippi Hedren, Patrick Cargill, Michael Medwin
(Universal)

Charles Chaplin says the story was inspired by a trip he made to Shanghai in 1931 but, though the period has been updated, the style of his screenplay and direction are obstinately reminiscent of the 1930s.

Countess is what may be described as a romantic comedy. It has a nebulous plot, slim characterizations and all the trappings of an old-fashioned bedroom farce.

Sophia Loren, who radiates an abundance of charm, plays a Russian emigree countess who, after a night out on the town in Hong Kong with Marlon Brando, stows away in his cabin with the intention of getting to New York. Although the story barely taxes her acting resources, Loren adds a quality to every scene in which she appears. She is stylish, classy and striking. Brando, on the other hand, appears ill at ease in what should have been a light comedy role.

Sydney Chaplin as Brando's cruising companion gives a thoroughly reliable performance, while Tippi Hedren, as Brando's wife, is superb in her few scenes at the tail-end of the picture.

COUNT OF MONTE CRISTO, THE

1976, 103 MINS, UK ◇ ▼

Dir David Greene *Prod* Norman Rosemart
Scr Sidney Carroll *Ph* Aldo Tonti *Ed* Gene Milford
Mus Allyn Ferguson *Art Dir* Walter Patriarca
● Richard Chamberlain, Tony Curtis, Trevor Howard, Louis Jourdan, Donald Pleasence, Kate Nelligan (ITC)

Richard Chamberlain is Edmond Dantes, the romantic young sailor railroaded to prison for 15 years. After his escape, aided by an old fellow prisoner, the story gets down to his obsessive revenge against the four money and/or power-hungry men who conspired against him.

All this is retailed in a most workmanlike fashion. Script and moral values appear respectful of the original text, and the Alexandre Dumas saga is performed with ample conviction and polish. But it's developed with more sincerity than interest or dramatic originality, and with no style of its own.

Chamberlain is appealing and reasonably persuasive as the hero robbed of both his best years and his betrothed, the latter played touchingly in a promising feature bow by British-based Canadian Kate Nelligan.

COUNTRY

1984, 109 MINS, US ◇ ▼

Dir Richard Pearce *Prod* William D. Wittliff, Jessica Lange *Scr* William D. Wittliff *Ph* David M. Walsh *Ed* Bill Yahraus *Mus* Charles Gross *Art Dir* Ron Hobbs

● Jessica Lange, Sam Shepard, Wilford Brimley, Matt Clark, Therese Graham, Levi L. Knebel (Touchstone)

Jessica Lange's pet project took a while to get produced, but it winds up firmly on the right track, with its basic theme of the classic struggle of the working man against the forces of government.

Screenplay recalls recent real-life events of how farmers have taken on loans with the government's blessing in order to expand and wind up faced with foreclosure when unable to keep up with the payments.

Lange is the focal point, essaying the mother of the family faced with losing the farm which had been in her lineage for some 100 years.

The family, like 40% of the farmers in the area, is about to be victimized by get-tough government policies.

Almost overshadowed by Lange, is Sam Shepard the husband, though he gives a quietly effective portrayal of the husband dealt a humiliating blow to his pride when the farm is fingered for liquidation.

COUNTRY DANCE

1970, 112 MINS, UK ◇ ▼

Dir J. Lee Thompson *Prod* Robert Emmett Gianna
Scr James Kennaway *Ph* Ted Moore *Ed* Willy Kemplen *Mus* John Addison *Art Dir* Maurice Fowler
● Peter O'Toole, Susannah York, Michael Craig, Harry Andrews, Cyril Cusack, Judy Cornwell
(Windward/Keep/M-G-M)

Country Dance is a confusing love triangle film, focusing on a woman and the two men in her life, one her husband and the other her brother.

Interiors were lensed at Ardmore Studios, Ireland, and exteriors in Ireland's Wicklow County and in Perthshire, Scotland. The James Kennaway screenplay is based upon both his play, *Country Dance*, and his novel *Household Ghosts*.

Limning the decline and fall of Sir Charles Ferguson (Peter O'Toole), last scion of a noble Scottish family, there is in this descent the distasteful subject of the brother's unhealthy love for his sister (Susannah York), who has left her husband (Michael Craig) to make her home with her brother on their family estate.

O'Toole's enactment of the character who cannot face the reality of either losing his sister or the destruction of his traditional way of life on his dwindling estate is whimsically constructed.

COUNTRY GIRL, THE

1954, 104 MINS, US ▼

Dir George Seaton *Prod* William Perlberg
Scr George Seaton *Ph* John F. Warren *Ed* Ellsworth Hoagland *Mus* Victor Young
● Bing Crosby, Grace Kelly, William Holden, Anthony Ross, Gene Reynolds, Jacqueline Fontaine (Paramount)

An exceptionally well-performed essay on an alcoholic song man, with Bing Crosby carrying on a bottle romance, *Country Girl* is a show business story that has depth and movement.

Adapted from the 1950 Clifford Odets play of the same title, its key player, a quondam star induced into trying a painful comeback, is a weak, lying, excessive drinker. Grace Kelly is resolute to the hilt, conveying a certain feminine strength and courage that enable her to endure the hardships of being the boozer's wife. William Holden registers in sock style as the legit director determined that Crosby can stand up to the demands of the starring role in a new play.

Crosby pulls a masterly switch, immersing himself into the part with full effect. The film has four songs by Ira Gershwin and Harold Arlen. The bare NY theatre where the show

within the show is rehearsed, the Boston house which is the scene of the play's break-in, the squalid tenement apartment where Kelly and Crosby are first found – these are realistically staged. Robert Alton's staging of the musical numbers is adequate.
☐ 1954: Best Picture (Nomination)

COURT JESTER, THE

1956, 101 MINS, US ◇ ▼

Dir Norman Panama, Melvin Frank *Prod* Norman Panama, Melvin Frank *Scr* Norman Panama, Melvin Frank *Ph* Ray June *Ed* Tom McAdoo *Mus* Victor Shoen *Art Dir* Hal Pereira, Roland Anderson
● Danny Kaye, Glynis Johns, Basil Rathbone, Angela Lansbury, Cecil Parker, Mildred Natwick (Paramount/Dena)

Costumed swashbucklers undergo a happy spoofing in *The Court Jester* with Danny Kaye heading the fun-poking. Norman Panama and Melvin Frank drag in virtually every time-honored, and timeworn, medieval drama cliche for Kaye and cast to re-play for laughs via not-so-subtle treatment.

A major assist comes from the Sylvia Fine-Sammy Cahn songs, of which there are five all tuned to the Kaye talent. There's the quite mad 'Maladjusted Jester'; a lullaby, 'Loo-Loo-Loo I'll Take You Dreaming'; a ballad, 'My Heart Knows a Lovely Song'; the comedic 'They'll Never Outfox the Fox', and 'Life Could Not Better Be.'

Glynis Johns, fetched from England for the hoydenish Maid Jean role opposite Kaye, does exceedingly well. The same is true of Basil Rathbone, a many-seasoned chief heavy; Angela Lansbury, cutting a pretty picture as the Princess Gwendolyn; Cecil Parker, the not-so-bright King Roderick who has ousted the real royal family; and Mildred Natwick, the princess's evil-eyed maid.

COURT-MARTIAL OF BILLY MITCHELL, THE

1955, 100 MINS, US ◇ ▼

Dir Otto Preminger *Prod* Milton Sperling *Scr* Milton Sperling, Emmett Lavery *Ph* Sam Leavitt *Ed* Folmar Blangsted *Mus* Dimitri Tiomkin *Art Dir* Malcolm Bert
● Gary Cooper, Charles Bickford, Ralph Bellamy, Rod Steiger, Elizabeth Montgomery, Fred Clark
(United States/Warner)

Dealing with real-life events of 1925, the subject-matter spotlights something which is always present tense, namely, official rigidity, redtape and intellectual hardening of the arteries in the brains of aging bureaucrats.

The picture is a real kick in the shins for the cult of blind military obedience and the lesson which is laid on the line relates to Pearl Harbor. The picture shows Mitchell predicting the Japanese sneak attack on Pearl Harbor, and describing American vulnerability, all this 16 years before that catastrophic Sunday and in the presence of Douglas MacArthur.

The main trouping is by Gary Cooper, Ralph Bellamy as a congressman counsel with yellow journalistic instincts, Charles Bickford, Fred Clark and Rod Steiger. All are standout in professionalism though this is a writer's, not an actor's, picture.

COURTNEYS OF CURZON STREET, THE

1947, 120 MINS, UK ▼

Dir Herbert Wilcox *Prod* Herbert Wilcox
Scr Nicholas Phipps *Ph* Max Greene *Ed* Flora Newton, Vera Campbell *Mus* Tony Collins *Art Dir* William C. Andrews
● Anna Neagle, Michael Wilding, Gladys Young, Coral Browne, Michael Medwin, Bernard Lee
(British Lion)

Wilcox hasn't worried about any significant

theme in this. He tells his four-generation story with smiles and tears, and obviously enjoys seeing two people in love.

Story runs from 1900 to 1945, Michael Wilding plays the soldier son and heir of a baronet. He is in love with his mother's maid (Anna Neagle). Ignoring his mother's warning that he is risking social ostracism, he flouts tradition and marries the girl. Climax to society's persecution comes at a snobbish function with Queen Victoria present to hear first performance of Tchaikovsky's *Symphonie Pathetique*. His wife, nervous, does not behave with conventional stoicism and has to listen to catty remarks about her lowly beginning.

From then on the story tells of the joys and sorrows of the Courtneys, ending in 1945 when their grandson brings home his girl who hopes her humble family won't object to her marrying into the aristocracy.

••••••••••••••••••••••••••••

■ COURTSHIP OF ANDY HARDY, THE

1942, 94 MINS, US

Dir George B. Seitz   *Scr* Agnes Christine Johnston
Ph Lester White   *Ed* Elmo Veron
● Lewis Stone, Mickey Rooney, Donna Reed, William Lundigan (M-G-M)

Picture is studded with laugh lines throughout, and displays general effervescing tempo for maximum reaction. Mickey Rooney – between adolescence and manhood – successfully balances the assignment in excellent style. His is a strong performance with accent on straight acting ability and without recourse to the mugging antics that he called on previously.

Story [from characters created by Aurania Rouverol] opens with Judge Hardy endeavoring to reconcile a couple with an adolescent daughter. He invokes the aid of Andy to date the girl and break her of a haughty complex and Andy's campaign is successful in this respect.

Donna Reed is the girl who is turned over to Andy for regeneration, and how he finally succeeds is neatly contrived in the screenplay, with substance in both lines and situations provided by the script.

••••••••••••••••••••••••••••

■ COURTSHIP OF EDDIE'S FATHER, THE

1963, 118 MINS, US ◇

Dir Vincente Minnelli   *Prod* Joe Pasternak   *Scr* John Gay   *Ph* Milton Krasner   *Ed* Adrienne Fazan
Mus George Stoll   *Art Dir* George W. Davis, Urie McCleary
● Glenn Ford, Shirley Jones, Stella Stevens, Dina Merrill, Roberta Sherwood, Jerry Van Dyke (M-G-M)

The story of a dad and a lad and their divergent views on what constitutes desirable stepmotherhood, the production is richly mounted, wittily written and engagingly played by an expert, spirited and attractive cast.

In adapting the novel by Mark Toby, John Gay has penned an aware, clever and generally well-constructed scenario. Glenn Ford portrays a widower who, in rearing his precocious six-and-a-half-year-old son (Ronny Howard) must, in the course of his romantic pursuits, take into account the future maternal preferences of the boy, whose comic-book-eye-view of candidate wives is inclined to judge statistically on the basis of bustlines and eyesockets.

Ford creates a warm, likeable personality and is especially smooth in his reaction takes in scenes with his charge.

Never any question about Shirley Jones' credentials as the kind of woman any red-blooded American type would love to call mommy, bustline notwithstanding. Dina Merrill is an attractive loser. Stella Stevens comes on like gangbusters in her enactment of a brainy but inhibited doll from Montana.

It's a sizzling comedy performance of a kook.

Vincente Minnelli's direction tends toward melodramatic heaviness in some of the early 'serious' going and some exaggeration in several comic passages, but overall he has managed well enough, coaxing some bright performances from his cast.

••••••••••••••••••••••••••••

■ COUSINS

1989, 110 MINS, US ◇ Ⓥ

Dir Joel Schumacher   *Prod* William Allyn   *Scr* Stephen Metcalfe   *Ph* Ralf D. Bode   *Ed* Robert Brown
Mus Angelo Badalamenti   *Art Dir* Mark S. Freeborn
● Ted Danson, Isabella Rossellini, Sean Young, William Petersen, Lloyd Bridges, Norma Aleandro (Paramount)

As derivative as it is, *Cousins* still is a hugely entertaining Americanized version of the French film *Cousin, cousine*, with nearly the same insouciant tone as the Jean-Charles Tacchella comedy of 1975. It's been spiced with a dash of 1980s social commentary and a dollop of Italian ethnic flavoring.

Isabella Rossellini and Ted Danson's sappy, overly sentimental series of rendezvous are well compensated by their relatives' caustic comments, irreverent asides and other antics at the three weddings, one funeral and other functions all attend during the course of the picture.

Object of most of the ridicule is William Petersen, the unctuous BMW car salesman and Don Juan pretender who starts everything off in the opening wedding scene drooling at Danson's flamboyantly dressed wife (Sean Young).

It's obvious enough that Rossellini, the martyred Madonna type who knows of her husband's philandering, represents prudishness and purity as much as Young, dressed in outlandish high-fashion ruffles of red and black, represents the opposite.

What's most fun is to get everyone else's thoughts on the matter. There's Rossellini's wealthy mother Edie (Norma Aleandro), cranky old Aunt Sofia (Gina De Angelis) and Danson's son Mitchell (Keith Coogan), who has a penchant for videotaping family gatherings.

Best of all is Lloyd Bridges, Danson's irascible, sporting uncle, who has as much pep in his step and gleam in his eye for Aleandro as the two main couples have combined.

••••••••••••••••••••••••••••

■ COVER GIRL

1944, 105 MINS, US ◇

Dir Charles Vidor   *Prod* Arthur Schwartz   *Scr* Virginia Van Upp   *Ph* Rudolph Mate, Allen M. Davey   *Ed* Viola Lawrence   *Mus* Morris W. Stoloff (dir.)   *Art Dir* Lionel Banks, Cary Odell
● Rita Hayworth, Gene Kelly, Lee Bowman, Phil Silvers (Columbia)

Arthur Schwartz, in his initial film producer spot after years of experience with stage musicals, deftly injects surefire showmanship into the picture, neatly blending the talents of the players with an inspired script by Virginia Van Upp, fine and consistently-paced direction by Charles Vidor, and taking full advantage of the technical contributions.

Plot is neatly concocted to get over idea of sudden rise to theatrical fame of Rita Hayworth as result of winning a Cover Girl contest. Gene Kelly, operating the modest Brooklyn nightspot where he stages the floorshows, is in love with Hayworth, a dancer. Latter wins the contest to give the room immediate fame with the upper-crust customers from Manhattan.

Otto Kruger, responsible for her prominence, figures she should be lifted out of the lowly nightspot to a Broadway show. Result is break between the girl and Kelly when latter stubbornly blows off steam.

Dance sequences spotlighting the terping

abilities of Hayworth and Kelly are expertly staged. Kelly devised his own routines for the picture. Score by Jerome Kern and Ira Gershwin, comprising seven tunes, is of high caliber.

••••••••••••••••••••••••••••

■ COWBOYS, THE

1972, 128 MINS, US ◇ Ⓥ

Dir Mark Rydell   *Prod* Mark Rydell   *Scr* Irving Ravetch, Harriet Frank Jr, William Dale Jennings   *Ph* Robert Surtees   *Ed* Robert Swink, Neil Travis   *Mus* John Williams   *Art Dir* Philip Jefferies
● John Wayne, Roscoe Lee Browne, Bruce Dern, Colleen Dewhurst, Sarah Cunningham, Allyn Ann McLerie (Warner)

The Cowboys stars John Wayne as a tough cattleman forced to use some green teenagers to get the beef to market. Handsome, placid and pastoral, the film is a family-type entry, produced and directed by Mark Rydell.

Rustler Bruce Dern fights with Wayne and eventually shoots him dead. This foul deed gives the boys enough courage to plot vengeance under the leadership of Roscoe Lee Browne, an urbane black wagon-train cook who previously had exchanged some pithy comments with Wayne and the kids.

The story [from a novel by William Dale Jennings] is long and episodic, and its gentle treatment makes the length something of a hindrance to maximum enjoyment. Cast includes Colleen Dewhurst in an effective cameo as a travelling bordello madam.

••••••••••••••••••••••••••••

■ CRACKERS

1984, 92 MINS, US ◇ Ⓥ

Dir Louis Malle   *Prod* Edward Lewis, Robert Cortes
Scr Jeffrey Fiskin   *Ph* Laszlo Kovacs   *Ed* Susanne Baron   *Mus* Paul Chihara   *Art Dir* John J. Lloyd
● Donald Sutherland, Jack Warden, Sean Penn, Wallace Shawn, Larry Riley, Trinidad Silva (Universal)

A mild little caper comedy with plenty of sociological overtones, *Crackers* comes as a letdown from director Louis Malle. With a flimsy plot that is perhaps rightly treated in a throwaway manner, film basically consists of a wide assortment of character riffs which are offbeat enough to provide moment-to-moment amusement but don't create a great deal of comic impact.

As in dozens of tenement-set plays from *Street Scene* on, virtually all the action takes place within or very near the central setting, in this case a pawnshop owned by shameless profiteer Jack Warden. His buddy, Donald Sutherland, is out of work, and all but a few of the other characters make up a rainbow microcosm of today's unemployed.

••••••••••••••••••••••••••••

■ CRACK IN THE MIRROR

1960, 97 MINS, US

Dir Richard Fleischer   *Prod* Darryl F. Zanuck
Scr Mark Canfield   *Ph* William C. Mellor   *Ed* Roger Dwyre   *Mus* Maurice Jarre   *Art Dir* Jean d'Eaubonne
● Orson Welles, Juliette Greco, Bradford Dillman, Alexander Knox, Catherine Lacy, William Lucas (DFZ/20th Century-Fox)

The screenplay, based on a novel by Marcel Haedrich, tells two parallel stories, both age-old triangle situations in which a not-so-young woman throws over her elderly lover for a much younger man. The first situation involves three working class people and the second, three members of the Paris haute monde. The stories come together when the working class dame and her young paramour are brought to trial for the murder of the older man.

By casting Orson Welles as both the tyrannical old construction worker who is murdered and as the cuckolded lawyer, Juliette Greco as the mistress in both situations and

Bradford Dillman as the young laborer and the young lawyer in-a-hurry, producer and director have obviously intended to make some pertinent statements about guilt and the ironies of justice.

This irony, however, is telegraphed early in the film when the audience first is let in on the fact that the two stories are essentially the same. Another problem is that about halfway through, film's focal point switches from the working class triangle to the problems of the upperclass trio, with the result that audience interest and emotional involvement are put to a severe test.

Welles is fine as the drunken old slob and close to superb as the elderly lawyer. Dillman is also good as the two young men, both equally opportunistic. However, it's Greco who comes off best – whether it's because of performance or the projection of a unique cinema personality, is hard to say. She's all-girl.

Produced entirely in Paris, picture has a thoroughly French look and sound.

● ●

■ CRAZY MAMA

1975, 82 MINS, US ◇

Dir Jonathan Demme   *Prod* Julie Corman   *Scr* Robert Thom   *Ph* Bruce Logan   *Ed* Allan Holzman, Lewis Teague   *Mus* Marshall Lieb (co-ord.)   *Art Dir* Peter Jamison

● Cloris Leachman, Stuart Whitman, Ann Sothern, Tisha Sterling, Jim Backus, Donn Most (New World)

Spanning nearly three decades, Cloris Leachman stars as she starts in Jerusalem, Ark, 1932, when lawmen kill papa (Clint Kimbrough), making mother Ann Sothern a widow. They jump the 60-acres farm, next are in Long Beach, Calif, circa 1958, where the pair are evicted from their beauty salon for back rent, and Leachman has a pretty, pregnant teenage daughter (Linda Pure) with a boy friend (Donn Most). The three femmes, upset, steal cars and shoot their way across the US.

Next the sextet robs a motorcycle race box-office, then a bank heist, shooting all the way.

This *Bonnie and Clyde*-style, sadistic, sordid unveiling of wasted lives ends in 1959, with Leachman, her daughter and their studs running a Miami Beach snack bar. With good performances from familiar players, *Crazy Mama* appears a waste of top talent in a mindless life of crime.

● ●

■ CRAZY PEOPLE

1990, 90 MINS, US ◇ ⓥ

Dir Tony Bill   *Prod* Tom Barad   *Scr* Mitch Markowitz   *Ph* Victor J. Kemper   *Ed* Mia Goldman   *Mus* Cliff Eidelman   *Art Dir* John J. Lloyd

● Dudley Moore, Daryl Hannah, Paul Reiser, Mercedes Ruehl, J.T. Walsh, David Paymer (Paramount)

Crazy People combines a hilarious dissection of advertising with a warm view of so-called insanity. Pic had a rocky production history as two weeks into lensing John Malkovich was replaced by Dudley Moore, and screenwriter Mitch Markowitz ceded his directing chair to Tony Bill. Finished film is a credit to all hands.

Moore toplines as a burnt-out ad man working with fast-talking Paul Reiser (perfect as a type commonplace in business) for a tyranical boss, J.T. Walsh. Under deadline pressure, he turns in campaigns that attempt an honest approach.

This raises more than eyebrows, but when Moore hands in 'Most of our passengers get there alive' to promote United Air Lines, the film jumpcuts emphatically to Bennington Sanitarium, his new home.

Director Bill envisions this looney bin as an idyllic retreat, with a natural, warm and beautiful Daryl Hannah as Moore's nutty

playmate there. The visual mismatch (she towers over the diminutive star) pays off.

Markowitz's ingenious twists overcome the gag-driven nature of the film. Moore's oddball ads accidentally get printed and create a consumer rush. Walsh hires Moore back and soon the inmates are virtually running the asylum.

● ●

■ CREATURE FROM THE BLACK LAGOON

1954, 79 MINS, US ⓥ

Dir Jack Arnold   *Prod* William Alland   *Scr* Harry Essex, Arthur Ross   *Ph* William E. Snyder   *Ed* Ted J. Kent   *Mus* Joseph Gershenson

● Richard Carlson, Julie Adams, Richard Denning, Antonio Moreno, Nestor Paiva, Whit Bissell (Universal)

This 3-D hackle-raiser reverts to the prehistoric. After the discovery of a web-fingered skeleton hand in the Amazon region, a scientific expedition heads into the steaming tropics to hunt more fossils. In the back-washes of the Amazon they come across a still living Gill Man, half-fish, half-human.

The 3-D lensing adds to the eerie effects of the underwater footage, as well as to the monster's several appearances on land. The below-water scraps between skin divers and the pre-historic thing are thrilling and will pop goose pimples on the susceptible fan, as will the closeup scenes of the scaly, gilled creature. Jack Arnold's direction does a first-rate job of developing chills and suspense, and James C. Havens rates a good credit for his direction of the underwater sequences.

Richard Carlson and Julie Adams co-star in the William Alland production and carry off the thriller very well. As befitting the Amazonian setting, Adams appears mostly in brief shorts or swim suits.

● ●

■ CREEPSHOW

1982, 129 MINS, US ◇ ⓥ

Dir George Romero   *Prod* Richard Rubinstein   *Scr* Stephen King   *Ph* Michael Gornick   *Ed* Pat Buba, Paul Hirsch, Michael Spolan, George Romero   *Mus* John Harrison   *Art Dir* Cletus Anderson

● Hal Holbrook, Adrienne Barbeau, Fritz Weaver, Leslie Nielsen, Carrie Nye, E.G. Marshall (Laurel)

George Romero, collaborating with writer Stephen King, again proves his adeptness at combining thrills with tongue-in-cheek humor. He links five tales with animated bridges in the style of the comics.

The gimmick is used with reserve and the segments work fine on their own merits. The first *Father's Day*, is a shaggy dog tale of a despised patriarch who returns from the grave to collect his holiday cake.

In *The Lonesome Death of Jordy Verrill*, author King takes on the title role. He's a dull hillbilly who sees dollar signs when a meteor falls on his property. However, his fate is to turn into a plant.

In *Something to Tide You Over*, Leslie Nielsen plans a slow watery death for his wife and her lover. This is followed by *The Crate*, about a malevolent creature in a box from an Arctic expedition and the program finishes off with *They're Creeping Up on You*, in which millionaire E.G. Marshall is literally bugged to death by his phobia of insects.

● ●

■ CREEPSHOW 2

1987, 89 MINS, US ◇ ⓥ

Dir Michael Gornick   *Prod* David Ball   *Scr* George A. Romero   *Ph* Dick Hart, Tom Hurwitz   *Ed* Peter Weatherly   *Mus* Les Reed, Rick Wakemen   *Art Dir* Bruce Miller

● Lois Chiles, George Kennedy, Dorothy Lamour, Tom Savini, Domenick John (Laurel)

Tied together with some humdrum animated sequences, three vignettes on offer obviously

were produced on the absolute cheap, and are deficient in imagination and scare quotient.

Whatever interest some might have in seeing George Kennedy and Dorothy Lamour is undercut by their roles as helpless vicims of a smalltown robbery and double murder in the first tale, *Old Chief Wood'nhead*, a lifeless and listless yarn about a storefront Indian who comes to life to avenge the crimes.

The Raft concerns four goodtime teens trapped on a platform in the middle of a small lake, then eaten alive by what looks like tarpaulin covered with black goo.

The Hitchhiker is a painfully protracted telling of how rich gal Lois Chiles hits and runs from a hitchhiker on the highway at night and is then haunted by the bloodied but far-from-dead fellow.

● ●

■ CRIME AND PUNISHMENT

1935, 85 MINS, US

Dir Josef von Sternberg   *Prod* B.P. Schulberg   *Scr* S.K. Lauren, Joseph Anthony   *Ph* Lucien Ballard   *Mus* Arthur Honegger   *Art Dir* Stephen Goosson

● Edward Arnold, Peter Lorre, Marian Marsh, Tala Birell, Elisabeth Risdon, Douglass Dumbrille (Columbia)

The murder of the miserly pawnbroker (Mrs Patrick Campbell in a ruthless, unsympathetic characterization) is the premeditated crime by Peter Lorre. Edward Arnold's old-fashioned police methods, combined with psychological auto-suggestion and ultimate self-destruction, is the reincarnation of the punishment. Both contribute capital performances.

Sometimes the situations get out of hand and even Sternberg's directorial and camera genius can't cope with them. Usually it's a script deficiency [from the novel by Dostoievsky] when that occurs.

One is permitted to become a bit too conscious of the incongruity of a Bible-totin' harlot, an ingenue of a prostie with a Dietrichesque physiognomy and hair-dress. When that realization comes, the audience starts thinking of the past Sternberg and Dietrich pictures. That's when the too pretty Marian Marsh, as the St Petersburg street-walker, doesn't assist in the romance chores she's been endowed to sustain.

● ●

■ CRIME IN THE STREETS

1956, 91 MINS, US

Dir Don Siegel   *Prod* Vincent M. Fennelly   *Scr* Reginald Rose   *Ph* Sam Leavitt   *Ed* Richard C. Meyer   *Mus* Franz Waxman

● James Whitmore, John Cassavetes, Sal Mineo, Mark Rydell, Denise Alexander, Virginia Gregg (Lindbrook/Allied Artists)

Crime in the Streets, in its jump from a TV origin, sets out to be a gutsy melodrama about slum area delinquents and, within the framework of Reginald Rose's highly contrived story, succeeds in making its shock points under Don Siegel's pat directorial handling.

Plot poses the pitch that the young bums shown here need love and understanding to offset their squalid surroundings. However, as characterized by story and acting, it's likely they would be just as unpleasant and unwholesome in any setting.

John Cassavetes is the bitter, unlovable young tough who leads the street rat pack. When an adult (Malcolm Atterbury) slaps the young bum across the mouth for getting too uppity, the juve hood plots murder. Only two of the gang (Sal Mineo and Mark Rydell latter repeating from TV) go along with the scheme to kill Atterbury.

James Whitmore heads the cast as a settlement worker who does little more than observe and offer unheeded counsel.

● ●

■ CRIMES AND MISDEMEANORS

1989, 104 MINS, US ◇ Ⓥ
Dir Woody Allen   *Prod* Robert Greenhut   *Scr* Woody
Allen   *Ph* Sven Nykvist   *Ed* Susan E. Morse
Art Dir Santo Loquasto
● Martin Landau, Woody Allen, Mia Farrow, Alan
Alda, Anjelica Huston, Sam Waterston (Rollins/Joffe)

Woody Allen ambitiously mixes his two
favoured strains of cinema, melodrama and
comedy, with mixed results in *Crimes and
Misdemeanors.*

Two loosely linked stories here concern eye
doctor Martin Landau and documentary
director Allen, each facing moral dilemmas.
The structural and stylistic conceit is that
when Landau is onscreen, the film is dead
serious, even solemn, while Allen's own
appearance onscreen signals hilarious satire
and priceless one-liners.

Landau's problem is simple: his mistress
(Anjelica Huston, shrill in an underwritten
role) threatens to go to his wife (Claire
Bloom) and reveal all, including Landau's
previous embezzlement activities. At wit's
end, he seeks the assistance of his ne'er-do-
well brother (Jerry Orbach), who orders up a
hitman from out of town to waste Huston.

Meanwhile, Allen, unhappily married to
Joanna Gleason, has fallen in love with TV
documentary producer Mia Farrow, whom
he meets while directing a TV docu profiling
his enemy and brother-in-law, (Alan Alda).
Alda is perfect casting as a successful TV
comedy producer, whose pompous attitude
and easy romantic victories with women
(including Farrow) exasperate Allen.
Though portrayed as filled with sour grapes
and envy, Allen's plight is basically sympathetic.

■ CRIMES OF PASSION

1984, 101 MINS, US ◇ Ⓥ
Dir Ken Russell   *Prod* Barry Sandler, Donald P.
Borchers   *Scr* Barry Sandler   *Ph* Dick Bush   *Ed* Brian
Tagg   *Mus* Rick Wakeman   *Art Dir* Richard
Macdonald
● Kathleen Turner, Anthony Perkins, John Laughlin,
Annie Potts (New World)

The evocative Kathleen Turner thuds into a
wall of inanity in this dismally written, Ken
Russell-directed serio-comic examination of
sexual morality among American savages.

Painfully pretentious screenplay deflects
the usual Russell outrageousness and traps
the four principals (all other roles are
momentary) into the most superficial of
characterizations.

Turner leads two lives. By day she is
Joanna, a compulsively laboring sportswear
designer. She is divorced and, according to
her employer, frigid. But by night she is,
under a blond-banged wig, China Blue, the
hottest $50 a trick hooker in the local combat
zone.

Anthony Perkins' past also goes undetailed.
So he has to lean on 'psycho'-somatic
credentials to portray a glib, sweaty,
presumably ministerial, homicidal wacko
who would like to be China Blue if only he
had the right hormones.

Whatever the intention, and despite the
technical efficiency, *Crimes of Passion* falls
between the cracks. The fault line here is
quite identifiable – it's in the screenplay.

■ CRIMES OF THE FUTURE

1970, 63 MINS, CANADA ◇
Dir David Cronenberg   *Prod* David Cronenberg
Scr David Cronenberg   *Ph* David Cronenberg
Ed David Cronenberg
● Ronald Mlodzik, Jon Lidolt, Tania Zolty, Paul
Mulholland, Jack Messinger, Iain Ewing (Emergent)

Made on a $20,000 budget, David Cronen-

berg's second feature film, *Crimes of the Future,*
bears a strong similarity to his first outing,
Stereo, produced the year before.

Cronenberg's obsession for such matters as
bodily mutation and grotesque growths, aberrant medical experiments, massive plagues
and futuristic architecture are all here in a
convoluted look at a future gone perverse.

The world's entire female population has
evidently been wiped out, and the male population has turned to various, and disappointingly tame, alternative sexual fixations.
Prime symptom of the illness is Rouge's
Foam, a substance which leaks from bodily
orifices and is sexually exciting in its initial
stage, but deadly later on.

As he moves through the bleak but archi-
tecturally striking settings, the main character Tripod begins to take on the dimensions
of an Edgar Allan Poe hero, a doomed figure
traversing a devastated landscape.

■ CRIMES OF THE HEART

1986, 105 MINS, US ◇ Ⓥ
Dir Bruce Beresford   *Prod* Freddie Fields   *Scr* Beth
Henley   *Ph* Dante Spinotti   *Ed* Anne Goursand
Mus Georges Delerue   *Art Dir* Ken Adam
● Diane Keaton, Jessica Lange, Sissy Spacek, Sam
Shepard, Tess Harper (Fields/Sugarman/De Laurentiis)

Thoughtfully cast, superbly acted and masterfully written and directed, *Crimes of the
Heart* is a winner. Diane Keaton, Jessica
Lange and Sissy Spacek are a delight in their
roles as southern sisters attempting to come
to grips with the world, themselves and the
past.

Based on Beth Henley's 1980 play, Lenny
(Keaton) is the eldest of three sisters and the
only one still living in the large North
Carolina home of their youth. It is Lenny's
birthday, a day marked by youngest sister
Babe's (Spacek) jailing for shooting her husband and the arrival of middle sister Meg
(Lange), visiting from LA where she pursues
a singing career.

Far from being downbeat, the interplay
between Keaton's nervously frantic Lenny,
Spacek's unpredictable Babe and Lange as
the hard-living Meg is as funny as it is
riveting.

Bruce Beresford's direction within the
house is graceful, effortlessly following the action from room to room. Sam Shepard
notches a strong performance in the relatively
small part of Doc, and Tess Harper shows
her ability as a comic actress in the role of
neighbor/relative Chick.

■ CRIMINAL CODE, THE

1931, 97 MINS, US Ⓥ
Dir Howard Hawks   *Scr* Seton I. Miller, Fred Niblo Jr.
Ph James Wong Howe, L. William O'Connell
Ed Edward Curtiss   *Art Dir* Edward Jewell
● Walter Huston, Phillips Holmes, Constance
Cummings, Mary Doran, DeWitt Jennings, Boris Karloff
(Columbia)

A prison picture but an excellent interpretation of the play of the same name [by Martin
Flavin]. Howard Hawks' direction makes
everything count, while Walter Huston here
probably turns in his most modern characterization to date as a district attorney with a
daughter who becomes warden of a prison.
The love theme is taken care of by the girl
and a young prisoner whom Huston has previously sent away for manslaughter while
knowing a smart defense could have saved
him.

The transposition from stage to screen has
taken the proverbial liberties in dissolving the
tragedy of the play into a happy ending.

Plenty of action all the way, in and out of
the prison yard, with the performances of
Huston, Phillips Holmes, and Boris Karloff

always holding it together. Karloff is from the
stage cast.

■ CRIMSON PIRATE, THE

1952, 104 MINS, UK/US ◇ Ⓥ
Dir Robert Siodmak   *Prod* Harold Hecht   *Scr* Roland
Kibbee   *Ph* Otto Heller   *Ed* Jack Harris   *Mus* William
Alwyn
● Burt Lancaster, Eva Bartok, Nick Cravat, Torin
Thatcher, James Hayter, Margot Grahame
(Norma/Warner)

Swashbucking sea fables get a good-natured
spoofing in *The Crimson Pirate,* with Burt Lancaster providing the muscles and dash for the
takeoff.

The screen story is cloaked with a sense of
humor as it pictures Lancaster, the famed
Crimson Pirate, plying his trade on the high
seas. Opening finds the pirates capturing a
30-gun galleon by trickery and then scheming
to sell its cargo of cannon to rebels trying to
shake off the shackles of the King of Spain.
The buccaneers also plan to then reveal the
rebel group's whereabouts to the crown for
more gold, but there are a girl and such complications as an awakening to right and
wrong.

Lancaster and his deaf-mute pal (Nick Cravat) sock the acrobatics required of hero and
partner to a fare-thee-well under Robert
Siodmak's direction.

■ CRISS CROSS

1949, 87 MINS, US Ⓥ
Dir Robert Siodmak   *Prod* Michael Kraike   *Scr* Daniel
Fuchs   *Ph* Franz Planer   *Ed* Ted J. Kent   *Mus* Miklos
Rozsa
● Burt Lancaster, Yvonne De Carlo, Dan Duryea,
Stephen McNally, Richard Long (Universal)

Utilizing liberal flashbacks, the film [from a
novel by Don Tracy] unreels the relentless,
unswerving devotion of Burt Lancaster for
his divorced wife (Yvonne De Carlo). Basically he's an honest guy in contrast to the
shaky character of his ex-spouse, who has
become the moll of bigtime crook Dan
Duryea.

Caught in a rendezvous with his old flame
by Duryea, Lancaster fends off the jealousy of
his rival by suggesting the group pull off an
armored car holdup. As the driver of the payroll truck, he'll secretly work with the crooks.

Under Robert Siodmak's knowing direction, the flashbacks blend into a cohesive unit
and are never confusing or draggy. His staging of the holdup scene is a masterful job.

Lancaster's role is a made-to-order part of a
two-fisted square-shooter who gets fouled up
in a jam through no fault of his own.

■ CRITTERS

1986, 86 MINS, US ◇ Ⓥ
Dir Stephen Herek   *Prod* Rupert Harvey   *Scr* Stephen
Herek, Domonic Muir   *Ph* Tom Suhrstedt   *Ed* Larry
Bock   *Mus* David Newman   *Art Dir* Gregg Fonseca
● Dee Wallace, M. Emmet Walsh, Billy Green Bush,
Scott Grimes (Sho/Smart Egg)

Critters resemble oversize hairballs and roll
like tumbleweeds when prodded into action,
the perfect menace for this irritatingly insipid
and lightweight film which unfolds with plodding predictability and leaves few cliches
unturned.

Within minutes of film's start, a small band
of voracious Krites (a.k.a. Critters) easily
escape from a 'maximum security asteroid'
and are whizzing toward Kansas with two
crack bounty hunters in pursuit.

Establish the sleepy life of farmer (yes)
Brown and his wife Helen, as credibly performed by Billy Green Bush and Dee Wallace
as can be expected with such material, ram-

bunctious son Brad and sexually budding daughter April. There's also M. Emmet Walsh as the familiar smalltown sheriff.

Co-writers Domonic Muir and Stephen Herek, latter doubling as film's director, manage to deflate what little suspense is created by subtitling the Critters' chatter. The final result is neither scary nor humorous.

....

■ CRITTERS 2
THE MAIN COURSE

1988, 87 MINS, US ◇ ▽
Dir Mick Garris *Prod* Barry Opper *Scr* D.T. Twohy, Mick Garris *Ph* Russell Carpenter *Ed* Charles Bornstein *Mus* Nicholas Pike *Art Dir* Philip Dean Foreman
● Scott Grimes, Liane Curtis, Don Opper, Barry Corbin, Tom Hodges (New Line/Sho)

All concerned are back in small Grovers Bend, where Krites terrorized residents just two years earlier. Tipoff that they've returned is appearance of dozens and dozens of large eggs with colorful patterns on them.

Outer space bounty hunters Ug and Lee (Terrence Mann and Roxanne Kernohan), as well as Charlie (Don Opper), are dispatched to planet Earth to complete their earlier attempt to obliterate the nasty little killers.

Coincidentally, young Brad Brown (Scott Grimes) comes to visit his Nana (Herta Ware) and gets blamed again by some townfolk for arrival of the criters, which are now hatching and eating at a furious pace.

Film perfectly weaves together the gruesome behaviour of these bloodthirsty creatures and the comic asides that keep things gliding along.

....

■ 'CROCODILE' DUNDEE

1986, 102 MINS, AUSTRALIA ◇ ▽
Dir Peter Faiman *Prod* John Cornell *Scr* Paul Hogan, Ken Shadie *Ph* Russell Boyd *Ed* David Stiven *Mus* Peter Best *Art Dir* Graham Walker
● Paul Hogan, Linda Kozlowski, John Meillon, Mark Blom, Michael Lombard, David Gulpilil (Rimfire)

As the title character, Paul Hogan limns a laconic if rather dim crocodile hunter who achieves some notoriety after surviving an attack by a giant croc. New York reporter Linda Kozlowski journeys to the Northern Territory to cover the story.

Plot bogs down somewhat as Hogan and Kozlowski trudge through the outback. However, proceedings are intermittently enlivened by John Meillon who is slyly humorous as Dundee's manager and partner in a safari tour business.

Rather implausibly, Kozlowski persuades Hogan to return to Gotham with her. Here he is initiated into the delights of the Big Apple.

Director Peter Faiman, essaying his first theatrical venture after an impressive career in Australian TV, directing Hogan's shows among others, has problems with the pacing and a script that has its flat, dull spots.

Hogan is comfortable enough playing the wry, irreverent, amiable Aussie that seems close to his own persona, and teams well with Kozlowski, who radiates lots of charm, style and spunk.

....

■ 'CROCODILE' DUNDEE II

1988, 111 MINS, US ◇ ▽
Dir John Cornell *Prod* John Cornell, Jane Scott *Scr* Paul Hogan, Brett Hogan *Ph* Russell Boyd *Ed* David Stiven *Mus* Peter Best *Art Dir* Lawrence Eastwood
● Paul Hogan, Linda Kozlowski, Charles Dutton, Hechter Ubarry (Paramount)

'Crocodile' Dundee II is a disappointing fol-

lowup to the disarmingly charming first feature with Aussie star Paul Hogan. Sequel is too slow to constitute an adventure and has too few laughs to be a comedy.

Story unfolds with Hogan making a passable attempt to find gainful employment at just about the time Linda Kozlowski's ex-lover is killed in Colombia for taking photos of a cocaine king as he shoots one of his runners. The nefarious Rico (Hechter Ubarry is much too cute for this role) learns the photos were sent to Kozlowski and in a flash he sets up an operation in a Long Island fortress with a handful of stereotypical Latino henchmen to get the incriminating evidence back. Hogan has the photos, which means Rico has Kozlowski kidnaped.

Using outback strategy, that is, getting the punks to yelp like a pack of wild dogs, Hogan gains entrance and frees his woman. Kozlowski basically does little but wait at the sidelines as Hogan flies into action.

....

■ CROMWELL

1970, 139 MINS, UK ◇ ▽
Dir Ken Hughes *Prod* Irving Allen *Scr* Ken Hughes *Ph* Geoffrey Unsworth *Ed* Bill Lenny *Mus* Frank Cordell *Art Dir* John Stoll
● Richard Harris, Alec Guinness, Robert Morley, Dorothy Tutin, Frank Finlay, Timothy Dalton (Columbia)

The nub of director Ken Hughes' $9 million film (from his own screenplay, with Ronald Harwood as 'script consultant') is the confrontation of the two complex leading characters, Oliver Cromwell and King Charles I. Richard Harris and Alec Guinness, respectively, give powerhouse performances.

Harris plays the idealistic, dedicated Cromwell with cold eyes, tortured, rasping voice and an inflexible spirit. He is the man who regarded Jehovah as his main ally and was determined at all costs to rescue the England he loved from the corruption of a weak, greedy court and to set up a Parliament that would be truly democratic, speaking for the people and not be the puppets of the King.

The battle scenes (shot in Spain and using the Spanish Army) at Nazeby and Edgehill are excitingly drawn.

....

■ CROSS CREEK

1983, 122 MINS, US ◇ ▽
Dir Martin Ritt *Prod* Robert B. Radnitz *Scr* Dalene Young *Ph* John Alonzo *Ed* Sidney Levin *Mus* Leonard Rosenman *Art Dir* Walter Scott Herndon
● Mary Steenburgen, Rip Torn, Peter Coyote, Dana Hill, Alfre Woodard, Joanna Miles (Thorn-EMI)

Cross Creek, based on the memoirs of *The Yearling* author Marjorie Kinnan Rawlings, offers a sanitized vision of her early struggle to publish a novel and the Florida backwoods which inspired her prose.

It's an uncompelling, yet warm, tale which lightly skips over the woman's travails by illustrating a series of vignettes of rural humanity. The overall effect trivializes a life and provides little insight into the artistic process.

Story opens in 1928 with Rawlings (Mary Steenburgen) deciding to leave the security of a marriage to a wealthy New Yorker for the uncertainty of life in a remote region of Florida.

The drama, what little exists in the film, centers on Rawlings' inability to sell her work until she begins writing about the events of the Florida swamp folk.

Remainder of the film focuses on Rawlings' relationship with local hotelier Norton Baskin (Peter Coyote), the recovery of her land and the warm relationship between the author and her young black housekeeper.

....

■ CROSSFIRE

1947, 84 MINS, US ▽
Dir Edward Dmytryk *Prod* Dore Schary *Scr* John Paxton *Ph* J. Roy Hunt *Ed* Harry Gerstad *Mus* Roy Webb *Art Dir* Albert S. D'Agostino, Alfred Herman
● Robert Young, Robert Mitchum, Robert Ryan, Gloria Grahame, Paul Kelly, Sam Levene (RKO)

Crossfire is a frank spotlight on anti-Semitism. Producer Dore Schary, in association with Adrian Scott, has pulled no punches. There is no skirting such relative fol-de-rol as inter-marriage or clubs that exclude Jews. Here is a hard-hitting film [based on Richard Brooks' novel, 'The Brick Foxhole'] whose whodunit aspects are fundamentally incidental to the overall thesis of bigotry and race prejudice.

There are three Roberts (Young, Mitchum and Ryan) all giving capital performances. Young is unusual as the detective captain; Mitchum is the 'right' sort of cynical GI; and Ryan a commanding personality, in this instance the bigoted soldier-killer, whose sneers and leers about Sam Levene and his tribe are all too obvious.

The pic opens with the fatal slugfest in Levene's apartment, when his hospitality is abused and Ryan kills him. Director Edward Dmytryk has drawn gripping portraitures. The flashback technique is effective as it shades and colors the sundry attitudes of the heavy, as seen or recalled by the rest of the cast.

☐ 1947: Best Picture (Nomination)

....

■ CROSSING DELANCEY

1988, 97 MINS, US ◇ ▽
Dir Joan Micklin Silver *Prod* Michael Nozik *Scr* Susan Sandler *Ph* Theo Van de Sande *Ed* Rick Shaine *Mus* Paul Chihara *Art Dir* Dan Leigh
● Amy Irving, Reizl Bozyk, Peter Riegert, Jeroen Krabbe, Sylvia Miles (Warner)

In an unexpectedly enjoyable way, *Crossing Delancey* addresses one of the great societal issues of our day – the dilemma of how the 30-ish, attractive, successful, intelligent and unmarried female finds a mate she can be happy with.

Off-off-Broadway fans may remember the title from playwright Susan Sandler's semi-autobiographical 1985 comedy about how her loving, old-worldly and slightly over-bearing Lower East Side NY Jewish grandmother engages the services of a matchmaker to find her a suitable marriage partner.

Amy Irving is the dutiful granddaughter who works in a pretentious Manhattan bookstore by day, keeps her own apartment and always finds time to make frequent visits to her precious Bubbie (Yiddish actress Reizl Bozyk).

Matchmaker (Sylvia Miles) brings Irving together with an unlikely candidate, pickle maker Sam Posner (Peter Riegert). The major set-ups focus on Irving's torn affections between the rakish, smooth-talking charm of pulp novelist Anton Maes (Jeroen Krabbe), who gives good readings on rainy days at the bookstore, and earnest, straight-forward, vulnerable Riegert, who unabashedly holds his heart in his hand for her. To the credit of most of the actors, the sentimentality doesn't sink the story.

....

■ CROSS OF IRON

1977, 130 MINS, UK/W. GERMANY ◇ ▽
Dir Sam Peckinpah *Prod* Wolf C. Hartwig *Scr* Julius J. Epstein, Herbert Asmodi *Ph* Ted Haworth, Brian Ackland Snow *Ed* Tony Lawson, Mike Ellis, Herbert Taschner *Mus* Ernest Gold
● James Coburn, Maximilian Schell, James Mason, David Warner, Klaus Lowitsch, Roger Fritz (EMI/Rapid/Terra)

Cross of Iron more than anything else affirms

director Sam Peckinpah's prowess as an action filmmaker of graphic mayhem.

Told from the German viewpoint as the Wehrmacht's cream were being clobbered on the Russian front circa 1943, the production [from the book by Willi Heinrich] is well but conventionally cast, technically impressive, but ultimately violence-fixated.

The film efficiently employs James Coburn, Maximilian Schell, James Mason and David Warner as frontline Germans. Coburn plays a platoon sergeant of style, ability and soul, contemptuous of the military and sick of the war.

Cross of Iron's overwhelming image is not disillusion, even less war's absurdity, but the war itself.

....

■ CROSSPLOT

1969, 97 MINS, UK ◇

Dir Alvin Rakoff   *Prod* Robert S. Blake   *Scr* Leigh Vance, John Kruse   *Ph* Brendan J. Stafford   *Ed* Bert Rule   *Mus* Stanley Black   *Art Dir* Ivan King
● Roger Moore, Martha Hyer, Claudie Lange, Alexis Kanner, Francis Matthews, Bernard Lee (United Artists/Tribune)

A thriller with a few good jokes, red herrings, a few quick genuine thrills, chases, and some mystery. It doesn't jell because the mystery is too cloudy. Motivation of most characters is indecisive and some are badly undeveloped.

Roger Moore plays a debonair ad exec with a flair for his job and a roving eye for the chicks. When a flash, swinging campaign is okayed by a client, he has little time to find the girl around whom it will centre. His only clue is a portrait with her name on it.

His problem sparks off a search for the girl, a mysterious Hungarian, which lands him up to his neck in a bewildering political ploy involving Marchers of Peace members and some anarchists.

Some bright thesps keep the often puzzling events moving deftly and breezily. Moore is not wholly convincing as a man of action.

....

■ CROSSROADS

1986, 96 MINS, US ◇ Ⓥ

Dir Walter Hill   *Prod* Mark Carliner   *Scr* John Fusco   *Ph* John Bailey   *Ed* Freeman Davies   *Mus* Ry Cooder   *Art Dir* Jack T. Collis
● Ralph Macchio, Joe Seneca, Jami Gertz, Joe Morton, Robert Judd, Steve Vai (Carliner/Columbia-Delphi IV)

Penned partly on the basis of actual experiences he had as a teenager touring the South as a musician, John Fusco's screenplay makes ample use of the legend of the late bluesman Robert Johnson, who left behind a tiny but potent legacy.

Ralph Macchio, a classical guitar student at Juilliard, discovers an old travelling and playing companion of Johnson's in a New York hospital. Hoping to make his reputation by finding and recording Johnson's alleged 'unknown 30th song', Macchio springs old Joe Seneca from the facility, and the unlikely pair hit the road for Mississippi Delta country.

Seneca acquits himself very nicely, while director Walter Hill pulls of the expected professional mob, but he pushes so hard for pace that he skates right over the opportunities for thought that the subject calls for.

....

■ CROWD, THE

1928, 98 MINS, US Ⓥ

Dir King Vidor   *Scr* John V.A. Weaver, King Vidor, Harry Behn, Joe Farnham   *Ph* Henry Sharp   *Ed* Hugh Wynn   *Art Dir* Cedric Gibbons, A. Arnold Gillespie
● Eleanor Boardman, James Murray, Bert Roach, Daniel G. Tomlinson, Dell Henderson, Lucy Beaumont (M-G-M

A drab actionless story of ungodly length and apparently telling nothing. The longness of the picture suggests it was designed for a Metro special, but on what, only its authors, John V.A. Weaver and King Vidor, must know. Superficially it reels off as an analytical insight into the life, worries and struggles of two young, ordinary people, who marry and become parents.

The husband is a plodder and dreamer, achieving nothing but two children and an $8 raise of salary in five years. For this he seems in constant reprimand from his wife and her family. Casting aside his permanent desk job through mental strain over the death by a truck of his little daughter, the young husband tries other jobs in vain, until his wife, disgusted, finally slaps him in the face and walks out.

James Murray is the young husband and catches the spirit at times, more in looks than anything else. Both he and Eleanor Boardman have the opportunity for a big scene when seeing their child trampled by a moving truck while walking toward their home. Both parents muff the chance by a mile.

....

■ CROWD ROARS, THE

1932, 84 MINS, US

Dir Howard Hawks   *Scr* Howard Hawks, Seton I. Miller, Kubec Glasmon, John Bright   *Ph* Sid Hickox   *Ed* John Stumar, Thomas Pratt   *Mus* Leo Forbstein (dir.)   *Art Dir* Jack Okey
● James Cagney, Joan Blondell, Ann Dvorak, Eric Linden, Guy Kibbee, Frank McHugh (Warner)

All auto-race pictures lead to Indianapolis, and there is no deviation from that schedule here.

Script doesn't unfold unusual acting opportunities for any of the principals. In this instance James Cagney's a front rank pilot who likes his grog and is mixed up with a girl by the time he revisits the old home town after achieving sport-page fame. The kid brother (Eric Linden) has caught the racing bug, too, and this provides the complication which has its source in the feminine angle.

Cagney, having added the brother to his crew, can't reconcile himself to having the kid on too friendly terms with the girl with whom he's been living (Ann Dvorak). To retaliate she sics his girlfriend (Joan Blondell), also of the same stripe, onto the brother, with this latter situation developing into a romance which splits the brothers.

Howard Hawks has received valiant service from his cameramen. The director doesn't seem to have taken his own story too seriously, and the picture is cut so that it just about holds the continuity together, always with the hint that it's anxious to get back to the track.

....

■ CROWD ROARS, THE

1938, 87 MINS, US

Dir Richard Thorpe   *Prod* Sam Zimbalist   *Scr* Thomas Lennon, George Bruce, George Oppenheimer   *Ph* John Seitz   *Mus* Edward Ward
● Robert Taylor, Edward Arnold, Frank Morgan, Maureen O'Sullivan, William Gargan, Lionel Stander (M-G-M)

The manly art of self-defense, otherwise known as the cauliflower industry, alias prize-fighting, is a rough-and-tumble racket operated by big time gamblers with small time ethics, according to the film, *The Crowd Roars* in which Robert Taylor leads with his left hand. It's exciting melodrama with plenty of ring action, some plausible romance and several corking good characterizations.

There are moments early in the film when it appears that George Bruce, the author, intends to dwell on the angle of mob psychol-

ogy. He steers away from any depth in the treatment of his theme, however, and holds to a plot about a choir boy who becomes a contender for the light heavyweight championship.

Frank Morgan creates something interesting out of the role of the pug's father, a drunkard and braggart. Edward Arnold is the conventional bookmaker and fight manager, who works successfully on the theory that the smartest gamblers are the biggest suckers. Heart interest is centred in a love affair between Taylor and Maureen O'Sullivan.

....

■ CRUEL SEA, THE

1953, 120 MINS, UK Ⓥ

Dir Charles Frend   *Prod* Leslie Norman   *Scr* Eric Ambler   *Ph* Gordon Dines   *Ed* Peter Tanner   *Mus* Alan Rawsthorne   *Art Dir* Jim Morahan
● Jack Hawkins, Donald Sinden, John Stratton, Denholm Elliott, Stanley Baker, Virginia McKenna (Ealing)

Ealing breaks from its traditional light comedies to offer a serious, authentic reconstruction of the battle of the Atlantic, based on Nicholas Monsarrat's bestseller. Production, despite its overlong running time, emerges as a picture of dramatic intensity.

Much of the original novel's action has been telescoped and quite a few major incidents have been omitted. As the commentator explains, the heroes are the men, the heroines are the ships, and the villain is the cruel sea.

These three elements are put into focus via the activities of a corvette which puts to sea with only one experienced officer – the captain – aboard. The others are the normal wartime recruits from civilian life, including a freelance journalist, lawyer, bank clerk and second-hand car salesman. Their first operational duties land them into a storm, but subsequently they encounter enemy activity and are harassed by U-boats.

Notable thesping comes from Jack Hawkins, who plays the captain with requisite authority. Surrounding cast is well matched, with sterling work contributed by Donald Sinden, John Stratton, Denholm Elliot and Stanley Baker at the head of a handpicked cast. Charles Frend directs with a sure touch.

....

■ CRUISING

1980, 106 MINS, US ◇ Ⓥ

Dir William Friedkin   *Prod* Jerry Weintraub   *Scr* William Friedkin   *Ph* James Contner   *Ed* Bud Smith   *Mus* Jack Nitzsche   *Art Dir* Bruce Weintraub
● Al Pacino, Paul Sorvino, Karen Allen (Lorimar)

In *Cruising* writer-director William Friedkin explores the S & M life of New York City. Like any approach to the bizarre, it is fascinating for about 15 minutes.

In many respects, *Cruising* [from the novel by Gerald Walker] resembles the worst of the 'hippie' films of the 1960s.

Taking away the kissing, caressing and a few bloody killings, Friedkin has no story, though picture pretends to be a murder mystery combined with a study of Al Pacino's psychological degradation.

Pacino is an innocent young cop chosen to go underground in search of a killer. He ultimately zeroes in on the culprit but by now is almost as far around the bend as his prey. But that's not saying much more than the old maxim: 'he who lies down with dogs gets up with fleas.'

....

■ CRUSADES, THE

1935, 124 MINS, US

Dir Cecil B. DeMille   *Prod* Cecil B. DeMille   *Scr* Harold Lamb, Dudley Nichols, Waldemar Young   *Ph* Victor Milner   *Ed* Anne Bauchens   *Mus* Rudolph Kopp

● Loretta Young, Henry Wilcoxon, Ian Keith, C. Aubrey Smith, Katherine DeMille, Joseph Schildkraut (Paramount)

Probably only Cecil B. DeMille could make a picture like *The Crusades* – and get away with it. It's long, and the story is not up to some of his previous films, but the production has sweep and spectacle.

DeMille patently intended his puppets to be subjugated by the generally transcendental theme of this holy war on the infidels. The loose footage at times defeats that. There is no great surge of human sympathy for the ecclesiastic offensive. Only the pious wandering hermit (capably done by C. Aubrey Smith) stands out as the sole symbol of the faith in the invasion of Acre and Jerusalem. Richard-the-Lion-Hearted frankly accepts the call to arms for selfish reasons – the only out he has to sidestep the state marriage to the French king's sister (Loretta Young).

Henry Wilcoxon plays Richard. Full weight of *The Crusades* falls on his performance. For sheer versatility, ranging from horsemanship to boudoir, there are few players who could have done as well.

■ **CRY-BABY**

1990, 85 MINS, US ◇ ⓥ

Dir John Waters   *Prod* Rachel Talalay   *Scr* John Waters   *Ph* David Insley   *Ed* Janice Hampton   *Mus* Patrick Williams   *Art Dir* Vincent Peranio
● Johnny Depp, Amy Locane, Susan Tyrrell, Polly Bergen, Iggy Pop, Ricki Lake (Imagine)

John Waters' mischievous satire of the teen exploitation genre is entertaining as a rude joyride through another era, full of great clothes and hairdos.

Set on Waters' Baltimore turf, *Cry-Baby* returns to the nascent days of rock 'n' roll when teens were king, where the cleancut 'squares' are pitted against the hoodlum 'drapes'. Cry-Baby (Johnny Depp), a handsome delinquent with a perpetual tear in his eye (in memory of his criminal parents who died in the electric chair), takes the bait from a pony-tailed blonde from the well-bred set (Amy Locane).

Once it's clear the plot is just a raucous rebel without a cause with a handful of inspired elements clipped to a wornout *Romeo and Juliet* storyline, a lot of the foolery begins to wear thin. There's so much commotion in the pic, with its 11 full-fledged dance numbers and elaborate production values, that one can't help but catch on that a story's missing.

Depp is great as the delinquent juve, delivering the melodramatic lines with straight-faced conviction and putting some Elvis-like snap and wiggle into his moves.

■ **CRY DANGER**

1951, 79 MINS, US ⓥ

Dir Robert Parrish   *Prod* Sam Wiesenthal, W.R. Frank   *Scr* William Bowers   *Ph* Joseph F. Biroc   *Ed* Bernard W. Burton   *Mus* Emil Newman, Paul Dunlap   *Art Dir* Richard Day
● Dick Powell, Rhonda Fleming, Richard Erdman, William Conrad, Regis Toomey, Jean Porter (Olympic)

All the ingredients for a suspenseful melodrama are contained in *Cry Danger*. Plot [from a story by Jerome Cady] opens with Dick Powell returning after five years in prison, having been pardoned from a life sentence when new evidence turns up that clears him of a robbery rap. Evidence was manufactured by a crippled Marine vet (Richard Erdman) who figures Powell will be grateful enough to cut up some of the $100,000 loot he is supposed to have hidden.

Powell sees the pardon as an opportunity to bring the guilty parties to justice and free a friend still in prison. Scene of all the plot

movement is the poorer section of Los Angeles, where Powell and Erdman have holed up in a crummy trailer camp to be near Rhonda Fleming, wife of the friend still in prison.

Robert Parrish, erstwhile film editor, makes a strong directorial bow.

■ **CRY FREEDOM**

1987, 157 MINS, US ◇ ⓥ

Dir Richard Attenborough   *Prod* Richard Attenborough   *Scr* John Briley   *Ph* Ronnie Taylor   *Ed* Lesley Walker   *Mus* George Fenton, Jonas Gwangwa   *Art Dir* Stuart Craig
● Kevin Kline, Penelope Wilton, Denzel Washington, Kevin McNally, John Thaw, Timothy West (Marble Arch/Universal)

Cry Freedom personifies the struggle of South Africa's black population against apartheid in the evolving friendship of martyred black activist Stephen Biko and liberal white newspaper editor Donald Woods. It derives its impact less from epic scope than from the wrenching immediacy of its subject matter and the moral heroism of its appealingly played, idealistic protagonists.

John Briley's screenplay is based on two books by Woods, who could publish them only by escaping South Africa (where he was under virtual house arrest as a 'banned' person) with his family in harrowing fashion. This produces the singular flaw of *Cry Freedom* – an overemphasis in the film's final hour on the Woods family's escape to exile in England.

Film opens in 1975 with a pitiless dawn raid by bulldozers and armed police on an illegal shantytown of black squatters. Stephen Biko is at first an offscreen presence, revered by blacks as a charismatic advocate of racial self-worth and self-determination, but distrusted by whites – including liberals like Woods – as a dangerous reverse racist whose condemnation of white society carries an implicit threat of violence.

Realizing he needs to form an alliance with the liberals he so dislikes, Biko (Denzel Washington) arranges to meet Woods (Kevin Kline), an invitation that dedicated newshound cannot afford to turn down.

Kline's familiar low-key screen presence serves him well in his portrayal of the strong-willed but even-tempered journalist. Washington does a remarkable job of transforming himself into the articulte and mesmerizing black nationalist leader, whose refusal to keep silent led to his death in police custody and a subsequent coverup.

■ **CRY IN THE DARK, A**

1988, 121 MINS, US ◇ ⓥ

Dir Fred Schepisi   *Prod* Verity Lambert   *Scr* Robert Caswell, Fred Schepisi   *Ph* Ian Baker   *Ed* Jill Bilcock   *Mus* Bruce Smeaton   *Art Dir* Wendy Dickson
● Meryl Streep, Sam Neill, Bruce Myles, Charles Tingwell, Nick Tate (Cannon/Cinema Verity)

One of the oddest and most illogical murder cases of modern times is recounted in intimate, incredible detail in the classy, disturbing drama *A Cry in the Dark*.

The saga of Lindy Chamberlain's harassment, trial and imprisonment for having allegedly murdered her baby daughter, when there was literally no evidence against her, was the biggest news story in Australia of the 1980s.

In 1980, the Chamberlains visit the monumental Ayers Rock in the outback. With the baby put to sleep in a tent, the family begins enjoying a nighttime barbeque when a cry is heard. Checking the tent, Lindy briefly glimpses a dingo slipping out of it and then, to her horror, finds Azaria missing from her bed.

No trace of the infant is found, and the conclusion appears to be that the dingo made off with her. Astonishingly, however, sentiment begins to grow throughout the country to the effect that Lindy killed her daughter. From there, the press can't let the story die. Lindy is charged with murder and Michael named as accessory after the fact.

If one didn't know who Meryl Streep is, one could easily guess Lindy was played by a fine, unknown Australian actress. Sam Neill, who here looks remarkably like the real Michael Chamberlain, well conveys the tentative strengths and very real weaknesses of a man thrust into an unimaginable situation.

■ **CRY OF THE CITY**

1948, 96 MINS, US

Dir Robert Siodmak   *Prod* Sol C. Siegel   *Scr* Richard Murphy   *Ph* Lloyd Ahern   *Ed* Harmon Jones   *Mus* Alfred Newman   *Art Dir* Lyle R. Wheeler, Albert Hogsett
● Victor Mature, Richard Conte, Fred Clark, Shelley Winters, Debra Paget, Hope Emerson (20th Century-Fox)

The hard-hitting suspense of the chase formula is given topnotch presentation in *Cry of the City*. It's an exciting motion picture, credibly put together to wring out every bit of strong action and tension inherent in such a plot. Robert Siodmak's penchant for shaping melodramatic excitement that gets through to an audience is realistically carried out in this one.

The telling screenplay by Richard Murphy, based on a novel, *The Chair for Martin Rome* by Henry Edward Helseth, presents Victor Mature as a police lieutenant in homicide and Richard Conte as a cop-killer – antagonists, although both sprung from New York's Italian sector.

Shelley Winters sparks small assignment of a girl who drives the killer through the New York streets while an unlicensed doctor works desperately to patch up his wounds.

■ **CRY, THE BELOVED COUNTRY**

1952, 103 MINS, UK

Dir Zoltan Korda   *Prod* Zoltan Korda   *Scr* Alan Paton   *Ph* Robert Krasker   *Ed* David Eady   *Mus* R. Gallois-Montbrun   *Art Dir* Wilfrid Shingleton
● Canada Lee, Charles Carson, Sidney Poitier, Joyce Carey, Geoffrey Keen, Michael Goodliffe (London/British Lion)

Alan Paton's best-selling novel which was made into a Broadway musical *Lost in the Stars* [1949], has been turned into an absorbing pic. Filmed in its native South African locale, and in London, the pic emerges as a very moving film, full of simplicity and charm.

The picture is a strong social document in its study of the perplexed conditions of a submerged native population ruled by the whites in South Africa.

More particularly, *Cry* is the story of a simple, native Negro country preacher (Canada Lee), who goes to the big city of Johannesburg to seek a missing sister and wayward son, and who finds both in the crime-ridden, slum elements of the city.

Lee's performance, restrained and underplayed, is a rich, heartwarming portrayal, dominating the film. Sidney Poitier is manly and striking as a young Negro preacher.

■ **CUBA**

1979, 122 MINS, US ◇

Dir Richard Lester   *Prod* Arlene Sellers   *Scr* Charles Wood   *Ph* David Watkin   *Ed* John Victor Smith   *Mus* Patrick Williams   *Art Dir* Gil Parrondo
● Sean Connery, Brooke Adams, Jack Weston, Hector Elizondo, Denholm Elliott, Martin Balsam (United Artists)

Cuba is a hollow, pointless non-drama. Cynical and evasive about politics, pic displays uniformly unsympathetic characters enacting a vague plot amidst a splendid re-creation of Havana at the very end of the Batista regime.

Basic *Two Weeks in Another Town* situation has had all conventional melodrama calculatedly drained from it. Revolution is closing in on the upper-crust-types who serve as story focus, and Brooke Adams is torn between two men, but treatment deliberately goes against the grain of sentiments normally encountered in such potent dramatic set-ups.

Given the worthless, motley crew seen to populate Havana – including gross American profiteer Jack Weston and cynical gentleman Denholm Elliott – political outlook would seem to be that things couldn't get much worse, and maybe Castro will be a little bit better.

■ **CUJO**

1983, 91 MINS, US ◇ ⓥ

Dir Lewis Teague *Prod* Daniel H. Blatt, Robert Singer *Scr* Don Carlos Dunaway, Lauren Currier *Ph* Jan De Bont *Ed* Neil Travis *Mus* Charles Bernstein *Art Dir* Guy Comtois

● Dee Wallace, Danny Pintauro, Daniel Hugh-Kelly, Christopher Stone, Ed Lauter, Kaiulani Lee (Taft/Warner)

Although well-made, this screen adaptation of Stephen King's *Cujo* emerges as a dull, uneventful entry in the horror genre. Novel about a mad dog on the rampage occupies a low place in the King canon, which is understandable if the film's stupefying predictability is an accurate reflection of the book.

Opening sequence has a lovable looking St. Bernard bitten on the nose by a bat, whereupon audience is introduced to the Trentons, a family of young parents and a son which is disintegrating, mostly thanks to Dee Wallace's sideline affair with a local worker. Story basically marks time until, at least halfway through, the dog begins attacking Maine seacoast locals (pic was shot in Northern California).

Except for the appealing kid played by Danny Pintauro, the characters are of little interest.

■ **CUL-DE-SAC**

1966, 111 MINS, UK

Dir Roman Polanski *Prod* Gene Gutowski *Scr* Roman Polanski, Gerard Brach *Ph* Gilbert Taylor *Ed* Alastair McIntyre *Mus* Krzysztof Komeda *Art Dir* Voytek Roman

● Donald Pleasence, Francoise Dorleac, Lionel Stander, Jack McGowran, William Franklyn, Jacqueline Bisset (Compton)

As a study in kinky insanity, *Cul-de-Sac* creates a tingling atmosphere. This sags riskily at times when the director unturns the screws and does not keep control of his frequently introduced comedy.

Film was shot on location in and around a lonely castle on remote Holy Island off the northeast coast of Britain. Gill Taylor's camera bleakly catches the loneliness and sinister background that sparks the happenings.

Donald Pleasence, with steel-rimmed glasses and head completely shaven, is an obvious neurotic. A retired businessman, he is living like a hermit with his young, bored and flirtatious French wife (Francoise Dorleac), who is blatantly contemptuous of him. Suddenly, two wounded gangsters on the run descend upon them. From then on it's a battle of nerves, a cat-and-mouse psychological tightrope walk, as an uneasy truce develops between Pleasence and Stander, while the latter waits to be rescued by the boss of his gang, who never shows.

Pleasence pours some exaggerated but dis-

tinctive thesping into his pathetic role while Lionel Stander, obviously more flamboyant, blends nicely with him, turning in a far more subtle performance of latent brutality, mixed with surface geniality, than the screenplay may have promised.

■ **CULPEPPER CATTLE CO., THE**

1972, 92 MINS, US ◇ ⓥ

Dir Dick Richards *Prod* Paul A. Helmick *Scr* Eric Bercovici, Gregory Prentiss *Ph* Lawrence Edward Williams, Ralph Woolsey *Ed* John F. Burnett *Mus* Tom Scott, Jerry Goldsmith *Art Dir* Jack Martin Smith, Carl Anderson

● Gary Grimes, Billy 'Green' Bush, Luke Askew, Bo Hopkins, Geoffrey Lewis, Wayne Sutherlin (20th Century-Fox)

The Culpepper Cattle Co. is an unsuccessful attempt to mount a poetic and stylistic ballet of death in the environment of a period western. Gary Grimes is featured as a teenager who matures in the course of a hard, violent and bloody cattle drive.

Director Dick Richards' story has been scripted into a pallid, stilted plot, where the characters mutter and grunt empty aphorisms. Clearly, we have here one of those 'important-statement-on-the-human-condition' rationalizations for a gruesome series of blood-lettings.

Billy 'Green' Bush plays Culpepper, hard-bitten range boss who takes on Grimes, whose likeable, easy-going and natural manner come across as the only effective performance. Everyone else is saddled with limp dialog and unrestrained posturing. Lots of people are killed.

■ **CURSE OF THE CAT PEOPLE, THE**

1944, 70 MINS, US ⓥ

Dir Gunther von Fritsch, Robert Wise *Prod* Val Lewton *Scr* DeWitt Bodeen *Ph* Nicholas Musaraca *Ed* J.R. Whittredge *Mus* Roy Webb *Art Dir* Albert S. D'Agostino, Walter E. Keller

● Simone Simon, Kent Smith, Jane Randolph, Ann Carter, Elizabeth Russell (RKO)

Made as sequel to the profitable *Cat People*, this is highly disappointing because it fails to measure up as a horrific opus. Even though having the same principals as in the original chiller, this is an impossible lightweight. Chief trouble seems to be the over-supply of palaver and concern about a cute, but annoying child.

Two directors worked on *Curse of The Cat People*, suggesting production headaches. Pair has turned out a strange cinema stew that is apt to make audiences laugh at the wrong scenes. Many episodes are unbelievably bad, with hardly anything happening in the first three reels.

Plot has the offspring of the first wife of a naval architect (Kent Smith) apparently suffering from the same supernatural beliefs that brought the death of the child's mother. Yarn tries to show the child living in a dream world and imagining she is playing with her mother (Simone Simon). Youngster's visit to a supposedly haunted house where a half-crazed character actress (Julia Dean) lives with her daughter (Elizabeth Russell) builds into the slight horrific angle of film, resulting in the best episodes in the production.

■ **CURSE OF THE MUMMY'S TOMB, THE**

1964, 80 MINS, UK ◇

Dir Michael Carreras *Prod* Michael Carreras *Scr* Henry Younger *Ph* Otto Heller *Ed* Eric Boyd Perkins *Mus* Carlo Martelli *Art Dir* Bernard Robinson

● Terence Morgan, Fred Clark, Ronald Howard, Jeanne Roland, George Pastell, John Paul (Hammer)

It needs a crystal ball to sort out the reasons

for some of the contrived goings on in this modest and rather slapdash horror pic. But it doesn't need a soothsayer to guess, early, the identity of the heavy.

Plot hinges around the discovery of an ancient tomb in the Egyptian desert, with a curse on anybody who opens it. Leader of the expedition intends giving the archaeological discoveries to the Egyptian government for its National Museum. But the expedition's smooth backer, a slick talking American showman, sees it as a coast-to-coast peepshow.

Murder and mayhem begins its gory trail and the motivation comes from a plausible stranger (Terence Morgan) who turns out to be a murderous descendant of the ancient Egyptian dynasty.

Morgan performs smoothly enough as the villain but is too patently up to no good from the start. Ronald Howard, Jack Gwillim and George Pastell are among those who provide sound support but the liveliest performance comes from Fred Clark.

■ **CURSE OF THE PINK PANTHER**

1983, 109 MINS, UK ◇ ⓥ

Dir Blake Edwards *Prod* Blake Edwards, Tony Adams *Scr* Blake Edwards, Geoffrey Edwards *Ph* Dick Bush *Ed* Ralph E. Winters, Bob Hathaway, Alan Jones *Mus* Henry Mancini *Art Dir* Peter Mullins

● Ted Wass, David Niven, Robert Wagner, Herbert Lom, Capucine, Roger Moore (Titan/Edwards/United Artists)

The eighth in the hit comedy series, *Curse of the Pink Panther* resembles a set of gems mounted in a tarnished setting. Abetted by screen newcomer Ted Wass' flair for physical comedy, filmmaker Blake Edwards has created genuinely funny sight gags but the film's rickety, old-hat story values waste them.

Lensed simultaneously with *Trail of the Pink Panther*, *Curse* boasts all-new footage but virtually repeats the prior release's storyline. Instead of a newshen tracking down the missing Inspector Clouseau, this time Interpol's Huxley 600 computer (an uppity machine named Aldous) is secretly programmed by Clouseau's boss (Herbert Lom) to select the world's worst detective to search for his unwanted employee.

NY cop Clifton Sleigh (Ted Wass) is the bumbling man for the job, simultaneously trying to discover who has stolen (again) the Pink Panther diamond. As with *Trail*, format has him encountering and interviewing characters from earlier films in the series.

Guest stars David Niven (in his final film appearance), Robert Wagner and Capucine have little to do, while pert British blonde Leslie Ash is briefly impressive as a lethally-kicking martial arts partner for Wass.

■ **CUSTER OF THE WEST**

1968, 143 MINS, US/SPAIN ◇

Dir Robert Siodmak *Prod* Louis Dolivet, Philip Yordan *Scr* Bernard Gordon, Julian Halevy *Ph* Cecilio Paniagua *Ed* Maurice Rootes *Mus* Bernardo Segall *Art Dir* Jean-Pierre D'Eaubonne, Eugene Lourie, Julio Molina

● Robert Shaw, Mary Ure, Jeffrey Hunter, Ty Hardin, Charles Stanlaker, Robert Hall (Cinerama/Security)

Capable, audience-involving adventure on the visual level which doesn't rise to the epic stature but is content to resume the 'facts' about the Seventh Cavalry without taking a coherent attitude to them.

The arid, rock Spanish vistas stand in okay for old Indian territory – especially for those not overly familiar with them.

At the end of the Civil War, Custer is assigned to tame the Cheyenne, whose rights under government treaty are being whittled away by white depredations. He is at first content with his commission, and carries out his orders with zest and zeal. Conscience is represented by one of his junior officers, who looks mighty anxious about the moral probity of this constant onslaught on the Indians.

Robert Shaw gives Custer a simple forthrightness and dash that is effective, despite its naive context. Other thesp support is adequate within its straightforward idiom, with Jeffrey Hunter and Ty Hardin contrasting neatly as the troubled and dedicated junior officers respectively, Mary Ure as Custer's nebulous wife, and Robert Ryan guesting as the deserting gold-hungry soldier with a forceful cameo.

■ CYRANO DE BERGERAC

1950, 112 MINS, US ⓥ
Dir Michael Gordon   *Prod* Stanley Kramer   *Scr* Carl Foreman   *Ph* Franz Planer   *Ed* Harry Gerstad   *Mus* Dimitri Tiomkin
● Jose Ferrer, Mala Powers, William Prince, Morris Carnovsky, Lloyd Corrigan (United Artists)

More stage play than motion picture, Carl Foreman's screenplay is wisely concerned with letting the Brian Hooker words speak for themselves.

Interpreting the rhyme and prose of the play is Jose Ferrer. It comes to the screen as an outstanding achievement in histrionics, quick with humor and sadness.

The *Cyrano* plot needs little reprising. A man, made a clown by a great peninsular of a nose, supplies the love words so that another, more handsome of profile, may woo the girl to whom he has lost his heart.

Michael Gordon's direction doesn't always fulfill the romantic, tragic, comedic and action possibilities, but permits a number of players to account for solid moments in a story that, essentially, belongs to one performer, Ferrer.

■ DA

1988, 102 MINS, US ◇ ⓥ
Dir Matt Clark   *Prod* Julie Corman   *Scr* Hugh Leonard   *Ph* Alar Kivilo   *Ed* Nancy Nuttal Beyda   *Mus* Elmer Bernstein   *Art Dir* Frank Hallinan-Flood
● Barnard Hughes, Martin Sheen, William Hickey, Karl Hayden, Doreen Hepburn (Dallas)

This adaptation of Hugh Leonard's autobiographical play and book, *Home before Night* about an Irish-American playwright's journey of self-discovery from New York to his father's funeral in the Old Sod casts a beguiling spell, thanks to the playful richness of its language and the finely knit acting of Martin Sheen, Barnard Hughes and their supporting cast.

The linchpin of the affecting story is providing by Leonard's dramaturgic sleight of hand in presenting Charlie's (Sheen) dead father, Da (Hughes), and mother (Doreen Hepburn) as living, breathing temporal characters animated by the successful playwright's grief-catalyzed imagination.

Sheen's performance is distinguished by its subtlety, as he's swept up in the conflicting emotions that attend his wry encounters with his stubborn adolescent self (very capably rendered by Karl Hayden), his domineering mother and, most indelibly, the hard-headed, lyrically aphoristic gardener whose failings as an adoptive father the mature playwright

must reconcile with his own hard-earned knowledge of human fallibility.

■ DAD

1989, 117 MINS, US ⓥ
Dir Gary David Goldberg   *Prod* Joseph Stern, Gary David Goldberg   *Scr* Gary David Goldberg   *Ph* Jan Kiesser   *Ed* Eric Sears   *Mus* James Horner   *Art Dir* Jack DeGovia
● Jack Lemmon, Ted Danson, Olympia Dukakis, Kathy Baker, Kevin Spacey (Amblin/Universal)

Pic represents a promising feature directorial debut for TV producer Gary David Goldberg. There's certainly much that's funny, warm and endearing about *Dad*, which, based on William Wharton's novel, deals with the familiar theme of a grown child resolving his sense of duty toward an ageing parent.

Unfortunately, prolonged tilling of that emotional terrain and seemingly endless verbalization of feelings diminish most of what's good about the film.

Ted Danson has the pivotal role of Jack Lemmon's somewhat estranged son, who returns from his sheltered world of Wall Street opulence to find his parents failing and infirm. Danson moves in with his parents to ease their final days, in the process finding new meaning in his relationship with his own college-age son (Ethan Hawke).

There's some repartee nicely delivered by the principals, including Kathy Baker and Kevin Spacey as Danson's sister and brother-in-law.

■ DADDY LONG LEGS

1955, 126 MINS, US ◇
Dir Jean Negulesco   *Prod* Samuel G. Engel   *Scr* Phoebe Ephron, Henry Ephron   *Ph* Leon Shamroy   *Ed* William Reynolds   *Mus* Alfred Newman, Johnny Mercer
● Fred Astaire, Leslie Caron, Terry Moore, Thelma Ritter, Fred Clark, Charlotte Austin (20th Century-Fox)

Mary Pickford was the American sweetheart of an actress who suffered the orphanage hardships when First National made *Daddy Long Legs* in 1919. With Leslie Caron and Fred Astaire in the leads, the property was completely rewritten and fashioned into an appealing musical.

Astaire was a good choice and works well as the undisciplined and friendly moneybags who develops a wanna-get-married crush on the girl he sends through college, this despite the acknowledged difference in age. And he's still the agile hoofer, although the choreography he and David Robel blue-printed doesn't require too robust a workout. Caron is beguiling all the way.

Thelma Ritter and Fred Clark, as social and business aides to Astaire, team up for laughs – the Phoebe and Harry Ephron screenplay has some crackling dialog.

■ DADDY'S DYIN' ... WHO'S GOT THE WILL?

1990, 95 MINS, US ◇ ⓥ
Dir Jack Fisk   *Prod* Sigurjon Sighvatsson, Steve Golin, Monty Montgomery   *Scr* Del Shores   *Ph* Paul Elliott   *Ed* Edward Warschilka Jr   *Mus* David McHugh   *Art Dir* Michelle Minch
● Beau Bridges, Beverly D'Angelo, Tess Harper, Judge Reinhold, Amy Wright, Keith Carradine (Propaganda)

Del Shores' hit play about squabbling Texas siblings is brought to the screen with panache. Shores' script presents a bittersweet family reunion, as three sisters and a brother who don't like each other convene in tiny Loakie, Texas, to find out who got what in the will.

Since dotty dad, who hasn't quite slipped away yet, can't remember where he put it, they're stuck together while they ransack the rambling old farmhouse looking for it.

Amy Wright as the pious, mothering sister who became a preacher's wife, Tess Harper as the salty-tongued single gal who wound up taking care of dad, and Molly McClure as righteous Mama Wheelis are all excellent.

Beau Bridges has an uncanny bead on blind, dumb cruelty as Orville, the boorish younger brother, an obstinate redneck garbage collector who keeps his hefty wife Marlene (Patrika Darbo) pinned under his meaty thumb with constant put-downs. Beverly D'Angelo steals scenes as the spoiled, scattered little runaround sister who's brought home a beatific California hippie-musician (Judge Reinhold) as the latest in a long line of consorts.

■ DAISY KENYON

1947, 100 MINS, US
Dir Otto Preminger   *Prod* Otto Preminger   *Scr* David Hertz   *Ph* Leon Shamroy   *Ed* Louis Loeffler   *Mus* David Raksin   *Art Dir* Lyle R. Wheeler, George Davis
● Joan Crawford, Dana Andrews, Henry Fonda, Ruth Warrick, Peggy Ann Garner (20th Century-Fox)

Triangle, in which Dana Andrews and Henry Fonda fight it out for the love of Joan Crawford, is basically a shallow lending-library affair [based on the novel by Elizabeth Janeway], but it's made to seem important by the magnetic trio's slick-smart backgrounds – plus, of course, excellent direction, sophisticated dialog, solid supporting cast and other flashy production values.

Crawford, a fashion illustrator living in a glamorized Greenwich Village walkup, plays Andrews' reluctant mistress. He's a wealthy, ruthless attorney who refuses to give up his wife (Ruth Warrick) and two kids (Peggy Ann Garner and Connie Marshall) to make an honest woman of Crawford (in the title role). Fonda, an ex-soldier but somewhat less of a he-man than Andrews, comes along and talks her into marrying him and going to live in a Cape Cod hideaway. But Andrews doesn't give up that easily.

There are some torrid love scenes, a violent sequence in which Crawford musses up Andrews when he tries to break up her marriage, and the several scenes in which the three get together for 'civilized discussions' of their affairs. Charles LeMaire's wardrobe for Crawford, Warrick and Martha Stewart, playing Crawford's girl friend, are knockouts.

Title role is a thesping plum, with the audience never knowing which guy Daisy is going to wind up with, and Crawford really makes the most of it.

■ DAISY MILLER

1974, 90 MINS, US ◇ ⓥ
Dir Peter Bogdanovich   *Prod* Peter Bogdanovich   *Scr* Frederic Raphael   *Ph* Alberto Spagnoli   *Ed* Verna Fields   *Art Dir* Ferdinando Scarfiotti
● Cybill Shepherd, Barry Brown, Cloris Leachman, Mildred Natwick, Eileen Brennan, Duilio Del Prete (Paramount)

Daisy Miller is a dud. Cybill Shepherd is miscast in the title role. Frederic Raphael's adaptation of the Henry James story doesn't play. The period production by Peter Bogdanovich is handsome. But his direction and concept seem uncertain and fumbled. Supporting performances by Mildred Natwick, Eileen Brennan and Cloris Leachman are, respectively, excellent, outstanding, and good.

The story has Shepherd flirting all over Europe, shocking the mannered society there as well as Barry Brown, very good as a captivated young man with a fondness for her. But his aunt (Natwick) quietly disapproves, her mother (Leachman) nervously tolerates it, while a Rome socialite (Brennan) is vocally offended. All form (much of it bad), no substance.

• •

■ DAM BUSTERS, THE

1955, 125 MINS, UK Ⓥ

Dir Michael Anderson *Prod* Robert Clark, W.A. Whitaker *Scr* R.C. Sherriff *Ph* Erwin Hillier *Ed* Richard Best *Mus* Eric Coates, Leighton Lucas *Art Dir* Robert Jones
● Richard Todd, Michael Redgrave, Ursula Jeans, Derek Farr, Patrick Barr, John Fraser (Associated British)

As a record of a British operational triumph during the last war, *The Dam Busters* [adapted from Paul Brickhill's *Enemy Coast Ahead*] is a small slice of history, told with painstaking attention to detail and overflowing with the British quality of understatement.

This is the story of the successful raid on the Ruhr dams, when a small fleet of British bombers, using a new type of explosive, successfully breached the water supplies, which fed the Ruhr factories and caused desolation and havoc to the German war machine.

For more than 90 minutes, the film is devoted to the planning and preparation, and very absorbing material this proves to be. The reconstruction of the raid and the pounding of the dams is done with graphic realism. The aerial photography is one of the major technical credits.

The production is a personal triumph for Michael Anderson. Michael Redgrave, particularly, gives a vividly human portrayal of Dr Barnes Wallis the scientist while Richard Todd makes a distinguished showing as Guy Gibson the RAF commander.

• •

■ DAMES

1934, 90 MINS, US

Dir Ray Enright, Busby Berkeley *Scr* Delmer Daves *Ph* Sid Hickox, George Barnes *Ed* Harold McLernon *Art Dir* Robert Haas, Willy Pogany
● Joan Blondell, Dick Powell, Ruby Keeler, ZaSu Pitts, Guy Kibbee, Hugh Herbert (Warner)

Heavier on the comedy but lighter on the story than WB's predecessors. There are five song numbers and all amazingly well done. Busby Berkeley pyramids attention in spectacular manner, at times making 'em wide-eyed with his choreographic mating of rhythmic formations with the camera.

Three sets of songwriters fashioned a corking score. Al Dubin and Harry Warren have the cream of the crop with the title song, 'I Only Have Eyes for You', and 'The Girl at the Ironing Board'. Mort Dixon and Allie Wrubel are responsible for 'Try and See It My Way', and Irving Kahal and Sammy Fain (latter a personable youth who plays himself in a songwriter's bit) contributed 'When You Were a Smile on Your Mother's Lips'.

'I Only Have Eyes for You' is one of the two most spectacular numbers with the entire chorus in Benda masks of Ruby Keeler. 'Dames' is the spectacular topper-offer with the girls in opera length black tights and white blouses.

Ruby Keeler and Dick Powell again are the romantic interest, and again he is the ambitious songwriter who has just written a surefire musical comedy hit that's only begging for a backer, and again Keeler is the sympathetic and romantic inspiration. Joan Blondell is prominent in a decorously subdued but otherwise flip chorine who perpetrates a mild 'shake' on Guy Kibbee.

• •

■ DAMNATION ALLEY

1977, 95 MINS, US ◇ Ⓥ

Dir Jack Smight *Prod* Jerome M. Zeitman, Paul Maslansky *Scr* Alan Sharp, Lukas Heller *Ph* Harry Stradling Jr *Ed* Frank J. Urioste *Mus* Jerry Goldsmith *Art Dir* Preston Ames
● Jan-Michael Vincent, George Peppard, Dominique Sanda, Paul Winfield, Jackie Earle Haley, Kip Niven (20th Century-Fox)

Damnation Alley is dull, stirred only occasionally by prods of special effects that only seem exciting compared to the dreariness that proceeded it. What's worse, it's dumb, depending on its stereotyped characters to do the most stupid things under the circumstances in order to keep the story moving.

Jan-Michael Vincent and George Peppard are air force officers on duty in a desert missile bunker when World War III comes with a lot of stock shots of mushroom explosions.

Skip forward a couple of years through titled explanations that most of the country was destroyed and Earth tilted on its axis. But Vincent and Peppard are still in the desert with the other troops.

• •

■ DAMNED, THE

1963, 87 MINS, UK

Dir Joseph Losey *Prod* Anthony Hinds *Scr* Evan Jones *Ph* Arthur Grant *Ed* Reginald Mills, James Needs *Mus* James Bernard *Art Dir* Bernard Robinson
● Macdonald Carey, Shirley Anne Field, Viveca Lindfors, Alexander Knox, Oliver Reed, Walter Gotell (Hammer/Swallow)

'What is a director's picture?' This one is. Although the cast is excellent, no one character dominates the action or overshadows the others. Joseph Losey's hand is so apparent that the film's considerable effectiveness must be accredited to him as must its few faults and the fearsome message it conveys.

Much of the film's appeal is visual, although the dialog is a credit to the scripter Evan Jones, [from H.L. Lawrence's novel *The Children of Light*]. The only objection is in its failure to take a stand.

Macdonald Carey, Shirley Anne Field, Alexander Knox (particularly good), Viveca Lindfors and Oliver Reed have principal roles in the quasi-sci-fi story which centers on a group of children being exposed to radiation in preparation for the day predicted by Knox when global nuclear warfare will destroy all living things – except these few.

All the principals are excellent, with Reed playing a Teddy boy and brother of Field although his interest in her is strongly incestuous.

• •

■ DAMNED, THE

1969, 163 MINS, ITALY/W. GER ◇ Ⓥ

Dir Luchino Visconti *Prod* Alfred Levy, Ever Haggiag *Scr* Nicola Badalucco, Enrico Medioli, Luchino Visconti *Ph* Armando Nannuzzi, Pasquale De Santis *Mus* Maurice Jarre *Art Dir* Pasquale Romano
● Dirk Bogarde, Ingrid Thulin, Helmut Berger, Charlotte Rampling, Florinda Bolkan, Rene Kolldehoff (Pegaso/Praesidens)

Luchino Visconti pulls out all stops to detail the progress of Nazism in the 1930s as seen via one upperclass family. This has got to be the most violent family since the Borgias. Screaming, yelling, scheming, and conniving over factory ownership is but part of it: they murder each other with no hesitation to achieve their ends, they have perverse sexual hang-ups, they are dope-fiends, and, in film's most spectacular sequence, a mother amongst them sleeps with her son.

Although obviously based on the Krupp family of steel magnates, the family in *The Damned* could never really exist in quite this

way, and it seems clear that Visconti knows that it serves as a microcosm of Germany in the 1930s, a symbol of a country that began a world war.

The acting is so much in an older tradition that it becomes very hard to judge, but Helmut Berger's progress from meek son to matricidal Nazi is clearly a superior job. Ingrid Thulin is able to handle the violent emotions required for her role as Berger's mother, although Dirk Bogarde is sometimes uncomfortable as her lover.

• •

■ DAMN YANKEES

1958, 110 MINS, US ◇ Ⓥ

Dir George Abbott, Stanley Donen *Prod* George Abbott, Stanley Donen *Scr* George Abbott *Ph* Harold Lipstein *Ed* Frank Bracht *Mus* Richard Adler, Jerry Ross *Art Dir* William Eckart, Jean Eckart, Stanley Fleischer
● Tab Hunter, Gwen Verdon, Ray Walston, Russ Brown, Shannon Bolin, Nathaniel Frey (Warner)

The *Damn Yankees* team, which ran the score high for three seasons in Broadway's legit ballpark, was reassembled to go to bat in this sparkling film version. Sole 'newcomers' in the trek from Broadway to Burbank are Stanley Donen, who co-produced and co-directed, and Tab Hunter, who stars. Ten of the top 11 players, plus creators from writer to costume designer, were transferred en masse from Broadway.

Story, based on the Faust legend and Douglass Wallop's novel, *The Year the Yankees Lost the Pennant*, revolves around a Washington Senator fan who would give his soul for a long-ball hitter and a chance to beat the New York Yankees. Given his chance by the devil himself, the fan is wooshed into a 22-year-old who proceeds to become the national hero of the national pastime in the national capital, thus giving the Senators a pennant and the Yankees a bad name.

Gwen Verdon makes a sprightly 172-year-old witch who has been sumptuously embodied to stalk Tab Hunter. Her eccentric dancing and singing are stylishly engrossing. Ray Walston, with exaggerated widow's peak and devilish red accessories, makes a perfect comedy Satan. Whereas much of the action is superficial, Walston does a great job of tying up loose ends and moving the satire to its logical conclusion. Hunter [substituting for Broadway's Stephen Douglass] is sympathetic as the young baseball great, confused by all that's happening to him.

Still held in prominence is the Richard Adler-Jerry Ross musical score – a tuneful, storytelling assortment of gag songs and ballads. Top production goes to 'Two Lost Souls' (a la 'Hernando's Hideaway' from same pair's *Pajama Game*) and 'Shoeless Joe from Hannibal, Mo.' 'You've Gotta Have Heart' remains a standout, with a seductive 'Whatever Lola Wants' and a fast-moving 'Who's Got the Pain', danced with choreographer Bob Fosse, himself a fine hoofer. To add to the original score is one new tune, 'The Empty Chair', a sorrowful creation that makes little impression.

• •

■ DANCE OF THE VAMPIRES
PARDON ME, BUT YOUR TEETH ARE IN MY NECK

1967, 107 MINS, UK ◇ Ⓥ

Dir Roman Polanski *Prod* Gene Gutowski *Scr* Gerard Brach, Roman Polanski *Ph* Douglas Slocombe *Ed* Alastair McIntyre *Mus* Christopher Komeda *Art Dir* Wilfrid Shingleton
● Roman Polanski, Jack MacGowran, Alfie Bass, Jessie Robins, Sharon Tate, Ferdy Mayne (M-G-M/Cadre/Filmways)

Dance of the Vampires is a spoof on the Dracula theme. Roman Polanski is on a quadruple assignment. He produced, directed and collabed on story and screenplay with Gerard Brach and costars. Brach and Polanski wrote script in French and piece then was translated into English by Gillian and John Sutton [version reviewed is 91-minute US one, cut by Martin Ransohoff and disowned by Polanski.]

Plotline (?) deals with an old professor and his assistant who arrive at a Central Europe inn in dead of winter on a crusade to hunt down and destroy the chilling mystery figures of generations of legends, the dreaded vampires who stalk Slovania.

Jack MacGowran cavorts as the nimble oldster and Polanski plays his somewhat-dimwitted assistant, both up to the demands (?) of their roles. Ferdy Mayne is the menacing Dracula, and Sharon Tate, lady in question, looks particularly nice in her bath. Alfie Bass, the innkeeper; Iain Quarrier as the count's effeminate son, who has some fangs all his own; Terry Downes, the toothy hunchback castle handyman (who might be Quasimodo returned), and Jessie Robbins, innkeeper's spouse, lend proper support.

. . . .

■ DANCE WITH A STRANGER

1985, 101 MINS, UK ◇ Ⓥ

Dir Mike Newell *Prod* Roger Randall-Cutler
Scr Shelagh Delaney *Ph* Peter Hannan *Ed* Mick Audsley *Mus* Richard Hartley *Art Dir* Andrew Mollo
● Miranda Richardson, Rupert Everett, Ian Holm, Matthew Carroll, Tom Chadbon, Jane Bertish (First Picture/Goldcrest/NFFC)

Dance with a Stranger is a tale of dark passions based on a true story of the London underworld during the 1950s.

Film charts the rocky course of the relationship between Ruth Ellis, a divorcee and prostitute-turned-nightclub manageress, and the upper-class dropout David Blakeley. He's too emotionally immature to care while she's too infatuated to take the commonsense course of ending the affair. Film ends with Ellis entering mythology as the last woman to be hanged under British law, for her shooting of Blakeley.

The script is densely packed with social and psychological nuances. Audiences are left largely to draw their own conclusions as to what drew the seemingly ill-matched couple together.

Miranda Richardson's performance as Ruth Ellis is firstrate. With her rolling eyes and impulsive gestures, she captures the delicate nuances of an attractive girl who's both cool and coquettish. Major flaw is Rupert Everett's inability to convey more about David Blakeley than that he's set to fail consistently in work and life.

. . . .

■ DANCES WITH WOLVES

1990, 183 MINS, US ◇ Ⓥ

Dir Kevin Costner *Prod* Jim Wilson, Kevin Costner
Scr Michael Blake *Ph* Dean Semler *Ed* Neil Travis
Mus John Barry *Art Dir* Jeffrey Beecroft
● Kevin Costner, Mary McDonnell, Graham Greene, Rodney A. Grant (Tig/Orion)

In his directorial debut, Kevin Costner brings a rare degree of grace and feeling to this elegiac tale of a hero's adventure of discovery among the Sioux Indians on the pristine Dakota plains of the 1860s.

Costner stars as Lt John Dunbar, a Union officer in the Civil War invited to choose his own post after an act of heroism. Opting for the farthest reaches of the frontier because he 'wants to see it before it disappears', he transplants himself from a weary and cynical war culture to the windswept clarity of the Dakota plains.

His only company as he passes the days are his horse, a gangling wolf who keeps a ner-

vous distance, and finally, a Sioux Indian who tries to steal the horse and is frightened off by Dunbar.

He discovers a culture so deeply refreshing to his spirit, compared with the detritus he's left behind, that, by the time the US Army bothers to look for him, he has become a Sioux and his name is Dances With Wolves.

Lensed on location in South Dakota over 17 weeks, pic is infused with the natural grandeur of the plains and sky. Score by John Barry makes a major contribution, varying from the elegiac tone of the main theme to the heart-racing primal rhythms of the buffalo and scalp dances.

From its three-hour length, which amazingly does not become tiresome, to its bold use of subtitled Lakota language (the Sioux tongue) for at least a third of the dialog, it's clear the filmmakers were proceeding without regard for the rules.

Mary McDonnell is impressive as Stands With A Fist, an emotionally traumatized white woman adopted by the Sioux who helps Dunbar communicate with them.
☐ 1990: Best Picture

. . . .

■ DANCIN' THRU THE DARK

1990, 95 MINS, UK ◇

Dir Mike Ockrent *Prod* Andree Molyneux, Annie Russell *Scr* Willy Russell *Ph* Philip Bonham-Carter *Ed* John Stothart *Mus* Willy Russell *Art Dir* Paul Joel
● Claire Hackett, Con O'Neill, Angela Clarke, Mark Womack, Julia Deakin, Simon O'Brien (Palace/British Screen/BBC/Formost)

Shirley Valentine writer Willy Russell returns to his native Liverpool with a gritty low-budget comedy.

Pic started life as the play *Stags and Hens* in 1978 and retains many stagebound aspects, especially the male and female toilets where much of the action takes place. Most of the Liverpudlian cast have been in Russell plays before, while tyro helmer Ockrent directed the original West End and US stage versions of Russell's *Educating Rita*.

The strong femme role is Linda (Claire Hackett), who is out on the town with friends on the night before her wedding. Unfortunately her hubbie-to-be and his friends also end up at the same nightspot. Arriving back in Liverpool for a gig is now successful popster Peter (Con O'Neill), Linda's ex-boyfriend. His friends in the band can't believe the seedy side of Liverpool ('Like Beirut without the sun') and the bad news is they're signed to perform at that same nightspot.

Pic is an amusingly accurate look at Liverpool lifestyles amongst the young and aimless, and while the transition from humor to drama is a bit uncomfortable *Dancin' thru the Dark* is ultimately satisfying and enjoyable.

. . . .

■ DANDY IN ASPIC, A

1968, 107 MINS, UK ◇ Ⓥ

Dir Anthony Mann, [Laurence Harvey] *Prod* Anthony Mann *Scr* Derek Marlowe *Ph* Christopher Challis *Ed* Thelma Connell *Mus* Quincy Jones, Ernie Sheldon *Art Dir* Carmen Dillon, Patrick McLoughlin
● Laurence Harvey, Tom Courtenay, Mia Farrow, Harry Andrews, Peter Cook, Lionel Stander (Columbia)

A routine, poorly-titled espionage meller loaded with uninteresting, cardboard characters. Laurence Harvey, who finished pic after sudden death in Europe of producer-director Anthony Mann, and Tom Courtenay, both evidently working off pix commitments, are stiff and dull.

All-location lensing, in London and West Berlin, provides some documentary flavor as well as excuse for irrelevant plot setups, interestingly photographed.

Dandy was adapted by Derek Marlowe from his book. Harvey, it seems, is a double agent

and everyone in British Intelligence, except Courtenay, knows about it.

All of which leaves an audience wondering what Mia Farrow had to do with the film. Good question. She looks like a combination of Twiggy and the archetypical Hollywood girl-next-door. Farrow's footage is limited and so, unfortunately, is her apparent acting range.

. . . .

■ DANGEROUS LIAISONS

1988, 120 MINS, US ◇ Ⓥ

Dir Stephen Frears *Prod* Norma Heyman, Hank Moonjean *Scr* Christopher Hampton *Ph* Philippe Rousselot *Ed* Mick Audsley *Mus* George Fenton *Art Dir* Stuart Craig
● Glenn Close, John Malkovich, Michelle Pfeiffer, Swoosie Kurtz, Mildred Natwick, Uma Thurman (NFH/Lorimar)

A scandalous, often-censored literary sensation for two centuries and a highbrow international theatrical hit, *Les Liaisons Dangereuses* has been turned into a good but incompletely realized film.

This incisive study of sex as an arena for manipulative power games takes too long to catch fire and suffers from a deficient central performance.

Choderlos de Laclos' 1782 epistolary novel expertly chronicled the cunning, cold-blooded sexual calculations of the French pre-revolutionary upper class as represented by two of its idle, brilliant members, the Marquise de Merteuil and the Vicomte de Valmont. Former lovers, these two ideally matched players hatch schemes of deceit, revenge and debauchery.

The classic rake, Valmont (John Malkovich) at the outset is challenged by Merteuil (Glenn Close) to deflower a 16-year-old virgin, Cecile de Volanges (Uma Thurman), before Merteuil's former lover can go through with his marriage to the exquisite adolescent.

Valmont considers this too easy, however, and instead proposes to seduce Madame de Tourvel (Michelle Pfeiffer), a virtuous, highly moral married woman.

Glenn Close is admirably cast as the proud, malevolent Merteuil while the real problem is Malkovich's Valmont. This sly actor conveys the character's snaky, premeditated Don Juanism. But he lacks the devilish charm and seductiveness one senses Valmont would need to carry off all his conquests.
☐ 1988: Best Picture (Nomination)

. . . .

■ DANGEROUS MOONLIGHT

1941, 90 MINS, UK

Dir Brian Desmond Hurst *Prod* William Sistrom
Scr Terence Young *Ph* George Perinal *Mus* Richard Addinsell
● Anton Walbrook, Sally Gray, Derrick de Marney, Cecil Parker (RKO)

Terence Young's screenplay glosses a lot, dialog is okay, but plot is short on action apart from a zingy air battle in last few hundred feet. The same prosaic line is taken by Brian Desmond-Hurst in directing tale of a young Polish composer with the hands of a musician and the heart of a flyer. Piloting is slow and methodical, sans highlights.

Fighting a losing air battle when Nazis invade Poland, Stefan Radetzky (Anton Walbrook) is fixed for an escape to Roumania since fellow pilots deem his music-making of more use to their country. Prior to winging he meets Carole Peters (Sally Gray), a newsgirl from the US. When booked later for a fund-raising concert tour of America, the pair's paths cross again. This time they marry, but Walbrook is unable to repress the pilot urge.

Walbrook enacts with his customary underplaying, this time almost to a point of self-suffocation. Similarly, Gray is screened for

D

glamor that palls after too much of such footage. She's a nifty looker, but over-poses. Effect is something like a series of screentests.

DANGEROUS WHEN WET

1953, 95 MINS, US ◇ ▽
Dir Charles Walters   *Prod* George Wells   *Scr* Dorothy Kingsley   *Ph* Harold Rosson   *Ed* John McSweeney Jr   *Mus* George Stoll (dir.)   *Art Dir* Cedric Gibbons, Jack Martin Smith
● Esther Williams, Fernando Lamas, Jack Carson, Charlotte Greenwood, Denise Darcel, Donna Corcoran (M-G-M)

A light mixture of tunes, comedy, water ballet and Esther Williams in a bathing suit are offered in *Dangerous When Wet*. Best of the musical stints is an underwater cartoon sequence involving Williams and Tom and Jerry to a reprise of 'In My Wildest Dreams'.

Plot deals with a swimming family that falls in with Jack Carson, a salesman of a liquid vitamin, and decides to swim the English Channel en masse, so they can get enough money to buy a prize bull for their Arkansas farm. Romance comes Williams' way in the person of Fernando Lamas, wealthy peddler of French champagne, when he rescues her after she has lost her bearings in a heavy Channel fog while practicing.

Williams becomes the costumes designed by Helen Rose and looks good in her water work. Also, she handles dialog easily in scenes with Lamas and Carson. Lamas charms his way through a role that, essentially, requires that type of emphasis. Carson is topnotch as the producer, a sort of travelling salesman with an interest in the farmer's daughter that gets nowhere. Instead, he gets Denise Darcel, a French entry in the Channel swim, and she's worth getting.

DANGER ROUTE

1968, 92 MINS, UK ◇
Dir Seth Holt   *Prod* Max J. Rosenberg, Milton Subotsky   *Scr* Meade Roberts   *Ph* Harry Waxman   *Ed* Oswald Hafenrichter   *Mus* John Mayer   *Art Dir* Bill Constable
● Richard Johnson, Carol Lynley, Barbara Bouchet, Sylvia Syms, Diana Dors, Harry Andrews (United Artists)

Another Secret Agent a la 007 – British operative authorized to kill. The agent here, however, is sent on missions where his assignment is to dispose of his victims, usually by breaking their necks.

Overly confused in unfoldment, production winds on a rather indefinite note, as though the character of Jonas Wilde, portrayed by Richard Johnson, is to be called in again by the British government to pull chestnuts out of the fire.

Script is too vague to be conclusive and footage abounds in such plot and counterplot that audience is uncertain as to actual happenings.

Story thread focuses on Johnson, assigned to kill a Soviet scientist who has defected to the West. He is to do away with him before the Americans, who have him in custody, can question him.

Johnson makes a good impression with his role of an ex-Marine Commando and a karate expert, and lends conviction to his hard-hitting character. Carol Lynley as his girlfriend is pretty, but distaff interest rests primarily on Barbara Bouchet, as another secret agent.

DANIEL

1983, 129 MINS, US ◇ ▽
Dir Sidney Lumet   *Prod* Burtt Harris   *Scr* E.L. Doctorow   *Ph* Andrzej Bartkowiak   *Ed* Peter C. Frank   *Art Dir* Philip Rosenberg
● Timothy Hutton, Mandy Patinkin, Lindsay Crouse, Edward Asner, Ellen Barkin, Julie Bovasso (World Film Services)

Faithfully adapted by E.L. Doctorow from his own acclaimed novel, *The Book of Daniel* and directed by Sidney Lumet with his customary intensity, *Daniel* is nonetheless a curiously detached filmization of the highly charged book.

It's generally well acted and occasionally evokes the sense of tragedy surrounding the effect of Julius and Ethel Rosenberg's trial and eventual execution as Russian atom spies.

Taking its form from the novel, the film flashes back and forth in time between 1967 – as Daniel Isaacson (Timothy Hutton) an aloof, uncommitted grad student is prodded by the near-suicide of his activist sister (Amanda Plummer) into probing the events behind his parents' execution – and the period of his parents' last years from the 1930s to 1953.

Most effective portions of the film are those chronicling the parents (Lindsay Crouse in a staggeringly subtle performance as Daniel's mother, Mandy Patinkin superb as his father).

DARK ANGEL, THE

1935, 105 MINS, US
Dir Sidney Franklin   *Prod* Samuel Goldwyn   *Scr* Lillian Hellman, Mordaunt Shairp   *Ph* Gregg Toland   *Ed* Sherman Todd   *Mus* Alfred Newman   *Art Dir* Richard Day
● Fredric March, Merle Oberon, Herbert Marshall, Janet Beecher, John Halliday, Henrietta Crosman (Goldwyn/United Artists)

A sockeroo woman's picture. Has Fredric March, Merle Oberon and Herbert Marshall and a forthright sentimental romance, well directed by Sidney Franklin to sustain almost every element [from the play by Guy Bolton, a.k.a. R.B. Trevelyan].

Grown up together from childhood, the war throws Kitty Vane (Oberon) to March as her natural romantic choice. Marshall and Oberon later berate themselves in mistaken belief they have sent March to his doom. Instead, after nursing in a German prison camp and later back in his native England, March turns up under a nom-de-plume, an author of best sellers for juveniles, but permanently blind and in constant mental dread of becoming a burden to his bride without benefit of clergy.

Oberon is a revelation as a reformed vamp. In simple hairdo and sans any great sartorial display, her emotional opportunities are fully met upon every occasion. Marshall and March are superb as the war-torn, love-torn boyhood chums, mutually in love with Oberon. Both refuse to avail themselves of any opportunities to stretch the emotional tension.

DARK AT THE TOP OF THE STAIRS, THE

1960, 123 MINS, US ◇
Dir Delbert Mann   *Prod* Michael Garrison   *Scr* Harriet Frank Jr, Irving Ravetch   *Ph* Harry Stradling Sr   *Ed* Folmar Blangsted   *Mus* Max Steiner   *Art Dir* Leo K. Kuter
● Robert Preston, Dorothy McGuire, Eve Arden, Angela Lansbury, Shirley Knight, Lee Kinsolving (Warner)

The William Inge play on which the picture is based is a poignant study of an Oklahoma family torn by internal conflicts. Its relationships are barred with perception and penetration, and the problems of the parents, described in frank terms but handled in good taste, center on the bed and the activities which do, or more accurately, do not, take place in it.

The film is well cast and persuasively acted. Its chief cast value lies in Robert Preston, whose newly-won fame via *The Music Man* can be used to spur boxoffice for the WB picture. Easily detectable is the similarity in manner and speech between his Harold Hill of *The Music Man* and Robin Flood of *Dark*. Each is a high-powered salesman – one flamboyant, the other serious. But there's a strength and an independence that's the same.

Dorothy McGuire is tops as the mother caught between devotion to her children and the knowledge she must sever the cord. Eve Arden is convincing and highly effective as the sister, performing with spirit and proving she could have done even more with her big scene if given the chance. Angela Lansbury plays one of her better and more sympathetic roles as the woman who wants Robin, and she fills it well. Shirley Knight is fine as the daughter.

DARK CITY

1950, 97 MINS, US
Dir William Dieterle   *Prod* Hal B. Wallis   *Scr* John Meredyth Lucas, Larry Marcus   *Ph* Victor Milner   *Ed* Warren Low   *Mus* Franz Waxman
● Charlton Heston, Lizabeth Scott, Viveca Lindfors, Dean Jagger, Jack Webb, Ed Begley (Paramount)

Picture serves to introduce Charlton Heston, from legit, and his film debut is impressive. The script leans towards psychosis to make its character tick.

Heston has turned to gambling. He and two associates trim Don DeFore in a fixed card game. DeFore hangs himself. A crazy older brother starts stalking the gamblers, intent on giving them the same kind of death suffered by DeFore.

Heston takes off to Los Angeles to see DeFore's widow so that he may get a clue to the killer's appearance.

Lizabeth Scott, nitery chirp and in love with Heston, gives a fine portrayal of the character.

Viveca Lindfors as the widow has decided worth. Dean Jagger registers strongly as a police captain.

DARK CRYSTAL, THE

1983, 94 MINS, UK ◇ ▽
Dir Jim Henson, Frank Oz   *Scr* David Odell   *Ph* Oswald Morris   *Ed* Ralph Kemplen   *Mus* Trevor Jones   *Art Dir* Brian Froud, Harry Lange
● (ITC)

The Dark Crystal, besides being a dazzling technological and artistic achievement by a band of talented artists and performers, presents a dark side of *Muppet* creators Jim Henson and Frank Oz that could teach a lesson in morality to youngsters at the same time it is entertaining their parents.

While there is plenty of humor in the film, it is actually an allegory of the triumph of good over evil, of innocence over the wicked. This world is inhabited with monstrously evil Skeksis, who are temporarily in command of the world wherein only a handful of wise and virtuous creatures manage to stay alive.

Until, of course, Jen and Kira, a boy and girl gelfling, set out to defeat the Skeksis by replacing a shard that has been taken from the Dark Crystal, which awaits its return before Doomsday is due.

The creation of a small world of memorable characters is the main contribution of Henson and Oz. The outstanding character is the Aughra, an ancient one-eyed harridan of an oracle who somehow reminds one of a truly blowsy Shelley Winters.

■ DARKMAN

1990, 95 MINS, US ◇ Ⓥ

Dir Sam Raimi *Prod* Robert Tapert *Scr* Chuck Pfarrer,
Sam Raimi, Ivan Raimi, Daniel Goldline, Joshua
Goldin *Ph* Bill Pope *Ed* Bud Smith, Scott Smith, David
Stiven *Mus* Danny Elfman *Art Dir* Randy Ser
● Liam Neeson, Frances McDormand, Colin Friels,
Larry Drake, Nelson Mashita, Jenny Agutter
(Universal/Darkman)

Despite occasional silliness, Sam Raimi's
Darkman has more wit, pathos and visual
flamboyance than is usual in contemporary
shockers. Universal, studio that first brought
the Phantom of the Opera to the screen,
returns to its hallowed horror-film traditions
with this tale of a hideously disfigured scientist (Liam Neeson) seeking revenge on LA
mobsters.

Raimi's gripping story (unevenly scripted
by the director and others) more closely
echoes the 1941 Peter Lorre chiller *The Face
behind the Mask* in its nightmarish tale of a
man whose burned face makes him a social
pariah and brutal criminal.

Neeson, working on a holographic technique to synthetically re-create damaged skin
and body parts, is the innocent victim of
sadistic thug Larry Drake, who likes to snip
people's fingers off with his cigar cutter. He
orders his minions to dip Neeson's head into
an acid vat before blowing up his lab.

Drake's expertly vicious and campy villain
is after an incriminating document left in
Neeson's lab by the scientist's lawyer/g.f.
(Frances McDormand) who has caught a
client, real estate developer Colin Friels, in
corrupt practices.

Director Raimi, lenser Bill Pope and production designer Randy Ser conjure up a
flamboyantly expressionistic world out of
downtown LA's bizarre architectural mix of
gleaming skyscrapers and decaying
warehouses.

■ DARK MIRROR, THE

1946, 85 MINS, US Ⓥ

Dir Robert Siodmak *Prod* Nunnally Johnson
Scr Nunnally Johnson *Ph* Milton Krasner *Ed* Ernest
Nims *Mus* Dimitri Tiomkin *Prod Des* Duncan Cramer
● Olivia de Havilland, Lew Ayres, Thomas Mitchell
(Universal)

The Dark Mirror runs the full gamut of themes
currently in vogue at the box office – from
psychiatry to romance back again to the
double identity gimmick and murder mystery. But, despite the individually potent ingredients, somehow the composite doesn't
quite come off.

Opening with a promising gait, the pic gets
lost in a maze of psychological gadgets and
speculation that slow it down. Olivia de
Havilland, playing a twin role, carries the
central load of the picture. She's cast simultaneously as a sweet, sympathetic girl and
her vixenish, latently insane twin sister. A
murder is committed and while one girl has
been positively identified as coming out of the
man's apartment on the night of the murder,
the other establishes a fool-proof alibi.

Lew Ayres is cast in his familiar role as a
medico – a specialist on identical twins.
Slightly older looking and sporting a mustache, Ayres still retains much of his appealing boyish sincerity. But in the romantic
clinches, Ayres is stiff and slightly embarrassed looking. Copping thespic honors, despite a relatively light part, Thomas Mitchell
plays the baffled dick with a wry wit and
assured bearing that carries belief.

■ DARK PASSAGE

1947, 106 MINS, US Ⓥ

Dir Delmer Daves *Prod* Jerry Wald *Scr* Delmer
Daves *Ph* Sid Hickox *Ed* David Weisbart
Mus Franz Waxman *Art Dir* Charles Clarke
● Humphrey Bogart, Lauren Bacall, Bruce Bennett,
Agnes Moorehead (Warner)

The film [from the novel by David Goodis]
has a sharp, brutal opening, macabre touches
throughout, and a thick, gruesome quality.
What starts out as a thriller switches en route
into a sagging, psychological drama, but
recovers in time to give out with the satisfying
gory stuff. Lauren Bacall's charm and Humphrey Bogart's ruggedness count heavily in a
strange treatment of a murder story, which if
it doesn't withstand scrutiny, does sustain
mood and interest.

Scripting is superior and dialog frequently
crackles. Direction is smart, with suggestion
of the impressionistic approach. What begins
as an apparent imitation of the *Lady in the
Lake* technique with the central figure speaking but not being visible to the audience,
explains itself part way into the film in a
clever fashion. Bogart isn't shown at the start
because he's supposed to look like someone
else. When a doctor has done a plastic surgery job on him to hide him from the police,
and he looks the familiar Bogart, the point of
his late appearance in the film is evident.

Pic is a story of a man imprisoned on circumstantial evidence for the murder of his
wife, his escape from jail, and the efforts of a
girl to help him, because her father similarly
had suffered unjust imprisonment.

Bacall, in a simple, unglamorous pose at
the start, even then has a pleasant appeal,
that hypoes intensely as soon as the old, sultry makeup and sexy charm are turned on.
Bogart is impressive in something of a lacklustre character for him. Agnes Moorehead is
sufficiently vicious as the discarded femme
who turns killer, giving the film some of its
most vivid moments.

■ DARK STAR

1974, 83 MINS, US ◇ Ⓥ

Dir John Carpenter *Prod* John Carpenter *Scr* John
Carpenter, Dan O'Bannon *Ph* Douglas Knapp
Ed Dan O'Bannon *Mus* John Carpenter *Art Dir* Dan
O'Bannon
● Brian Narelle, Andreijah Pahich, Carl Duniholm, Dan
O'Bannon (Carpenter/Harris)

Dark Star is a limp parody of Stanley
Kubrick's *2001: A Space Odyssey* that
warrants attention only for some remarkably
believable special effects achieved with
very little money. [Pic began in 1970
as 45-minute USC Film School short.
Final budget was $60,000.]

The screenplay cloisters four astronauts
together on a lengthy extraterrestrial jaunt.
To pass the time, the men joke, record their
diaries on videotape, take sunlamp treatments, reminisce about their past earth
lives and play with their alien mascot
(an inflated beach ball with claws).
Eventually their talking female computer
misfires, the spaceship conks out and
only one, an ex-surfer, manages to careen
back to earth on an improvised board.

The dim comedy consists of sophomoric
notations and mistimed one-liners.

■ DARK VICTORY

1939, 105 MINS, US Ⓥ

Dir Edmund Goulding *Prod* David Lewis *Scr* Casey
Robinson *Ph* Ernest Haller *Ed* William Holmes
Mus Max Steiner *Art Dir* Robert M. Haas
● Bette Davis, George Brent, Humphrey Bogart,
Geraldine Fitzgerald, Ronald Reagan, Henry Travers
(Warner)

Intense drama, with undercurrent of tragedy

ever present, *Dark Victory* is a nicely produced
offering. It presents Bette Davis in a powerful
and impressive role.

In play form [by George Emerson Brewer
Jr and Bertram Bloch] Tallulah Bankhead
was not able to overcome the morbid dramatics of the piece and *Dark Victory* had a brief
Broadway run. Film rights were originally
purchased by David Selznick, but he shelved
production plans some weeks before picture
was due to hit the production stages.

Story unfolds the tragic circumstances of
Davis, gay heiress, afflicted with a malignant
brain tumor. A delicate operation by specialist George Brent is temporarily successful,
but when the girl finally accidentally discovers her true condition, she embarks on a
wild whirl of parties. In love with Brent,
Davis quickly marries the medic for a brief
happiness on his Vermont farm.

Important is the uncovering of Geraldine
Fitzgerald in her first effort, as Davis' confidential secretary. Seems rather unnecessary
to toss away the ability of Humphrey Bogart,
himself satisfactory, but role is extraneous.
□ 1939: Best Picture (Nomination)

■ DARLING ...

1965, 128 MINS, UK Ⓥ

Dir John Schlesinger *Prod* Joseph Janni *Scr* Frederic
Raphael *Ph* Ken Higgins *Ed* James Clarke
Mus John Dankworth *Art Dir* Pay Sim
● Julie Christie, Dirk Bogarde, Laurence Harvey,
Roland Curran, Jose Villalonga, Basil Henson (Vic/
Anglo-Amalgamated)

In many ways, this Joseph Janni production
can be described as a British *Dolce Vita*. Its
central character is a lovely, young, irresponsible and completely immoral girl, who can
see little wrong in jumping in and out of bed
with a complete lack of discrimination, and
who goes on a shop-lifting expedition in one
of London's more famous stores just for kicks.

While a fair slice of the credit must go to the
three stars and scripter Frederic Raphael,
the lion's share is due to John Schlesinger, a
documentary-trained director who skillfully
uses that technique to give in-depth portraits
to three principals.

Everyone calls Diana Scott (Julie Christie)
'darling'. She's that kind of girl – gay, good-
looking, amusing company. She is married to
a young, immature man, and once she has
met the more sophisticated Robert (Dirk
Bogarde) there is little doubt that the marriage will go on the rocks. He, too, is married,
but leaves his family to set up house with her.
But no sooner has she met Miles (Laurence
Harvey) than she hops into bed with him.

Christie almost perfectly captures the character of the immoral Diana, and very rarely
misses her target.
□ 1965: Best Picture (Nomination)

■ DARLING LILI

1970, 139 MINS, US ◇

Dir Blake Edwards *Prod* Blake Edwards *Scr* Blake
Edwards, William Peter Blatty *Ph* Russell Harlan
Ed Peter Zinner *Mus* Henry Mancini
Art Dir Fernando Carrere
● Julie Andrews, Rock Hudson, Jeremy Kemp, Lance
Percival, Michael Witney, Jacques Marin
(Paramount/Geoffrey)

Darling Lili is a conglomerate. In its World
War I expanse, the Blake Edwards presentation has comedy, adventure melodrama,
aerial dogfights, spectacular production
numbers, nostalgia, Julie Andrews and Rock
Hudson, lush trappings, lack of a decisive
hand, and smash moments. These elements
are juggled sometimes with eclat and a flair,
on other occasions abruptly and none too
successfully.

Andrews is a German spy whose mission is
to ferret out war secrets. She latches onto a

D

relationship with Hudson, in role of a dashing American air squadron commander, who knows all.

Andrews' best moments are her singing sequences, in which she does full justice to five numbers cleffed by Johnny Mercer and Henry Mancini.

••••••••••••••••••••••••••••••••

■ **D.A.R.Y.L.**

1985, 99 MINS, US ◇ ⓥ

Dir Simon Wincer   *Prod* John Heyman   *Scr* David Ambrose, Allan Scott, Jeffrey Ellis   *Ph* Frank Watts   *Ed* Adrian Carr   *Mus* Marvin Hamlisch   *Art Dir* Alan Cassie

● Mary Beth Hurt, Michael McKean, Kathryn Walker, Colleen Camp, Josef Sommer, Ron Frazier (Paramount)

Pic manages to get off to a strong start with a scenic chase through a curving mountain road as a chopper bears down on a racing car. Just before crashing, the driver pushes out a young boy who is rescued and taken into a foster home by the Richardsons (Mary Beth Hurt and Michael McKean). The Richardsons later find that this strange young man is a robot.

After establishing a cozy domestic situation the film takes off in a different direction when his 'parents' come to take Daryl home. Home is a top security research facility where scientists Josef Sommer and Kathryn Walker have given birth to D.A.R.Y.L. Acronym stands for Data Analyzing Robot Youth Lifeform and Daryl is described as 'an experiment in artificial intelligence.'

Second half of the picture is the most farfetched and also the most fun as the young robot gets to show off some of his powers.

••••••••••••••••••••••••••••••••

■ **DAUGHTERS OF DARKNESS**

1971, 87 MINS, US/FRANCE ◇

Dir Harry Kumel   *Prod* Paul Collet, Alain C. Guilleaume   *Scr* Pierre Drouot, Harry Kumel   *Ph* Edward Van Der Enden   *Ed* Gust Verschueren, Denis Bonan   *Mus* Francois de Roubiax

● Delphine Seyrig, Daniele Ouimet, John Karlen, Andrea Rau, Paul Esser, Fons Rademakers (Gemini/Maya)

Delphine Seyrig's silver lame presence and Harry Kumel's evocative direction make this an above-par vampire tale. Updating the old chestnut about the butch countess who remains forever young by drinking and bathing in the blood of maidens, *Daughters of Darkness* is so intentionally perverse that it often slips into impure camp, but Kumel and Seyrig hold interest by piling twists on every convention of the vampire genre.

Spending their honeymoon at a mammoth but deserted seaside resort hotel in Belgium, newlyweds John Karlen and Daniele Ouimet are marked by the countess (Seyrig) and her lesbian 'secretary' (Andrea Rau). Karlen is actually a sadistic mama's boy, but 'Mother' (played by Dutch film director Fons Rademakers) is an aging homosexual who's been keeping him in London. When Karlen vents his belt-wielding sexuality on his bride, she seeks refuge with the countess.

Avoiding standard fang-in-the-neck fright, Kumel keeps the gore limited to the two death sequences, but there he goes all out. Both are stunningly directed and edited.

••••••••••••••••••••••••••••••••

■ **DAVID AND BATHSHEBA**

1951, 153 MINS, US ◇ ⓥ

Dir Henry King   *Prod* Darryl F. Zanuck   *Scr* Philip Dunne   *Ph* Leon Shamroy   *Ed* Barbara McLean   *Mus* Alfred Newman   *Art Dir* Lyle Wheeler, George Davis

● Gregory Peck, Susan Hayward, Raymond Massey, Kieron Moore, James Robertson Justice, Jayne Meadows (20th Century-Fox)

This is a big picture in every respect. The reign of King David projects the Old Testament in broad sweeps, depicting the obligation of David (Gregory Peck) to his subjects while at the same time spotlighting his frailties, namely his relationship with the beauteous Bathsheba (Susan Hayward). He is shown forsaking his first wife (of his harem) for Bathsheba, and pinpointed is the stoning of an adultress for the same crime – her faithlessness while her husband was off to the wars with the Ammonites.

Expert casting throughout focuses on each characterization. Raymond Massey plays the prophet Nathan, whom Jehovah sends to King David to hold him up to judgment. The parable of David's atonement for his lechery and treachery is capped by the 23rd Psalm which he, in his poetic youth, had conjured along with his other psalms.

Peck is a commanding personality as the youth destined to rule Israel. He shades his character expertly. His emotional reflexes are not as static as the sultry Hayward in the femme lead. Kieron Moore is earnest as the Hittite whom David betrays because he covets his wife, Bathsheba. Massey, as the prophet, is a dominant personality throughout.

••••••••••••••••••••••••••••••••

■ **DAVID AND LISA**

1963, 85 MINS, US ⓥ

Dir Frank Perry   *Prod* Paul M. Heller   *Scr* Eleanor Perry   *Ph* Leonard Hirschfield   *Ed* Irving Oshman   *Mus* Mark Lawrence   *Art Dir* Paul M. Heller

● Keir Dullea, Janet Margolin, Howard Da Silva, Neva Patterson (Continental)

Tact, taste, insight and forthrightness make this one of the most incisive and original films treating mental problems.

A young man is brought to a mental home by his doting mother. He seems intelligent, haughty and sensitive. But he cannot bear to be touched by anybody.

He is worshipped by a younger boy and becomes interested in the case of a schizophrenic girl called Lisa who talks backwards in rhyme and takes herself for two girls. He manages to get to her and both are aware of each other's weak spots.

Film appears clinically observant and authentic and is refreshingly free of jargon and pseudo-psycho dramatics. It does have a tendency to be too spare and make each scene a point about psychotic behaviour or reactions to it by outsiders.

But there is no forced love affair or cliche suspense aspects. Keir Dullea has the knifelike, frigid presence that is right in his case of bottled up feelings that have made him fear death and any human emotion. And Janet Margolin has the touching disorder and mute need for help required for the part of the girl.

For a first film Frank Perry shows a concise feel for making the telling points in each scene. A tight ordered script by Eleanor Perry also helps. It was taken from a book by a practicing psychiatrist [Theodore Isaac Rubin].

••••••••••••••••••••••••••••••••

■ **DAVID COPPERFIELD**

1935, 129 MINS, US ⓥ

Dir George Cukor   *Prod* David O. Selznick   *Scr* Howard Estabrook, Hugh Walpole   *Ph* Oliver T. Marsh   *Ed* Robert J. Kern   *Mus* Herbert Stothart

● W.C. Fields, Lionel Barrymore, Freddie Bartholomew, Frank Lawton, Edna May Oliver, Roland Young (M-G-M)

Charles Dickens did not write with the idea of being dramatized. The strange charm of his characters is more important than the fidelity of his characterizations. It was almost an adventure to try to bring to the screen the expansively optimistic Micawber, but he

lives again in W.C. Fields, who only once yields to his penchant for horseplay. In the main he makes Micawber as real as David. The same may be said for Edna May Oliver, who does low comedy in the high comedy manner and shows flashes of the underlying tenderness of Aunt Betsey.

The adapters have not always been as successful. Now and then they linger too elaborately in a scene and they put the play completely off the track in introducing the mechanically melodramatic shipwreck scene, which might easily have been left undone.

Lionel Barrymore, as Dan Peggotty, proves again that it is possible to wear chin whiskers and still not be a comic, and Herbert Mundin does well by the willing Barkis.

A fine performance is that of Freddie Bartholomew as the child David. He is acceptable in his more quiet moments, but in times of stress he seems to be spurred up to the situation, and with Basil Rathbone, the Murdstone, he raises the whipping scene to a high point. Rathbone is not as happily cast as the others. Frank Lawton is a believable grown David and Maureen O'Sullivan, Madge Evans and Elizabeth Allan, as the three chief women, all rate bows.

☐ 1935: Best Picture (Nomination)

••••••••••••••••••••••••••••••••

■ **DAVID COPPERFIELD**

1970, 118 MINS, UK ◇

Dir Delbert Mann   *Prod* Frederick Brugger   *Scr* Jack Pulman   *Ph* Ken Hodges   *Ed* Peter Boita   *Mus* Malcolm Arnold   *Art Dir* Alex Vetchinsky

● Robin Phillips, Susan Hampshire, Edith Evans, Michael Redgrave, Ralph Richardson, Laurence Olivier (Omnibus)

Director Delbert Mann and his scriptwriter, Jack Pulman, elected to tell this version of *David Copperfield* through the eyes of David as a young man. A very woebegone chap he is. Just returned from a self-imposed exile abroad he wanders up and down a deserted beach, pondering over the last few years of his life and what went so despairingly wrong with them.

The story is jerkily and bitterly related, mainly in flashbacks, but the constant return to the brooding, self-pitying Copperfield makes for a melancholy drag.

It also means that through constant flashbacks few of Dickens' wonderful array of characters get much opportunity to develop their roles.

Notably, Laurence Olivier, as the schoolmaster Creakle, and Richard Attenborough, as his cringing, one-legged assistant, Tungay. Their brilliant brief appearances light up the screen in about 60 seconds flat. Then they disappear.

••••••••••••••••••••••••••••••••

■ **DAWN OF THE DEAD**

1979, 125 MINS, US ◇ ⓥ

Dir George Romero   *Prod* Richard Rubinstein   *Scr* George Romero   *Ph* Michael Gornick   *Ed* George Romero, Kenneth Davidow

● Scott Reiniger, Ken Foree, David Emge, Gaylen Ross (Laurel/Cuomo-Argento)

Dawn pummels the viewer with a series of ever-more-grisly events – decapitations, shootings, knifings, flesh tearings – that make Romero's special effects man, Tom Savini, the real 'star' of the film – the actors are as woodenly uninteresting as the characters they play. Romero's script is banal when not incoherent – those who haven't seen *Night of the Living Dead* may have some difficulty deciphering exactly what's going on at the outset of *Dawn*.

The plot isn't worth detailed description. Enough said those carnivorous corpses that stalked through *Night* return in sufficient numbers to threaten extinction of the entire US population.

Pic was shot for under $1.5 million in the Pittsburgh area, Romero's professional base. Michael Gornick's photography warrants a special nod.

■ **DAWN PATROL, THE**

1930, 90 MINS, US

Dir Howard Hawks   *Prod* Robert North   *Scr* Dan Totheroh, Seton I. Miller   *Ph* Ernest Haller   *Ed* Ray Curtiss   *Mus* Leo F. Forbstein   *Art Dir* Jack Okey

● Richard Barthelmess, Douglas Fairbanks Jr, Neil Hamilton, Gardner James, Clyde Cook (First National)

Dawn Patrol finds well-bred English gentlemen running up against the grim realities of war and always remaining true to the best Oxford traditions.

At the start, the air exploits are more talked about than revealed, but as the woman-less chronicle unfolds the fighting becomes more visual and less commented upon. Richard Barthelmess and Douglas Fairbanks Jr in one sequence raid the home ground of the Germans and spend 10 minutes dropping bombs and ploughing the helpless German air squadron with machine-gun fire.

This little mission of death and destruction is in the nature of a boyish lark because the Germans had taunted them on the quality of their aviatory. Neil Hamilton, the commanding officer, awaits their return in fury.

Howard Hawks has handled his material intelligently. Camerawork is excellent throughout and the effects are vivid.

■ **DAWN PATROL, THE**

1938, 103MINS, US

Dir Edmund Goulding   *Prod* Hal B. Wallis, Robert Lord   *Scr* Seton I. Miller, Dan Totheroh   *Ph* Tony Gaudio   *Ed* Ralph Dawson   *Mus* Max Steiner   *Art Dir* John Hughes

● Errol Flynn, David Niven, Basil Rathbone, Donald Crisp, Melville Cooper (Warner)

Dawn Patrol sparkles because of vigorous performances of the entire cast and Edmund Goulding's sharp direction. Story [by John Monk Saunders] is reminiscent of previous yarns about the flying service at the front during the World War. Yet it is different in that it stresses the unreasonableness of the 'brass hats' – the commanders seated miles from the front who dispatched the 59th Squadron to certain death in carrying out combat assignments.

Picture emphasizes the routine of the 'dawn patrol', as day after day new replacements, each time consisting of younger men, come up to take the place of those killed in action.

Director Goulding maintains an even pace, alternating the happier, drinking scenes in barracks with the ill-fated takeoffs at dawn and battle gyrations in the sky.

Errol Flynn is Courtney, squadron flight commander. It is a character made to order for him. Even where he deliberately gets his junior officer intoxicated to take his place on a daring single-handed exploit, he makes the action appear life-like.

David Niven makes the character of Flynn's great friend stand out. Basil Rathbone is superb as the aviator who suffers inwardly the loss of every man while he is forced to remain in command on the ground.

■ **DAY AT THE RACES, A**

1937, 100 MINS, US

Dir Sam Wood   *Prod* Max Siegel   *Scr* Robert Pirosh, George Seaton, George Oppenheimer   *Ph* Joseph Ruttenberg   *Ed* Frank Hull   *Mus* Bronislau Kaper, Walter Jurmann   *Art Dir* Cedric Gibbons, Stan Rogers

● Groucho Marx, Chico Marx, Harpo Marx, Allan Jones, Maureen O'Sullivan, Margaret Dumont (M-G-M)

Surefire film fun and up to the usual parity of the madcap Marxes, even though a bit hectic in striving for jolly moments and bright quips.

This is the picture which the late Irving Thalberg started and Max Siegel, Sam Harris' former legit production associate, completed as his initial Hollywood chore at Metro.

Obviously painstaking is the racehorse code-book sequence, a deft switch on the money-changing bit; the long-distance telephoning between the horse doctor (Groucho) and the light-heavy; the midnight rendezvous business between Groucho and Esther Muir, including the paper-handing slapstickery; the orchestra pit hokum, which permits the standard virtuosity by Chico at the Steinway and Harpo at the harp, including a very funny breakaway piano.

Allan Jones and Maureen O'Sullivan sustain the romance and Jones gets his baritone opportunities during a water carnival which is cameraed in light brown sepia.

Esther Muir is a good foil, topped only by Margaret Dumont as the moneyed Mrs Upjohn, who is stuck on Groucho and stands for much of his romantic duplicity, even unto paying off the mortgage on the sanatorium owned by O'Sullivan.

■ **DAYBREAK**

1931, 73 MINS, US

Dir Jacques Feyder   *Scr* Ruth Cumming, Zelda Sears, Cyril Hume   *Ph* Merritt B. Gerstad

● Ramon Novarro, Helen Chandler, Jean Hersholt, C. Aubrey Smith, William Bakewell, Karen Morley (M-G-M)

Lack of action stands against *Daybreak*, that gets its title because the two principals stay out all night the first time they met. Both of them, Ramon Novarro and Helen Chandler, give a perfectly blah performance.

With the locale apparently in Vienna and its Imperial Guard, Novarro speaks with his Latin accent.

In the Imperial Guards you pay your honor debts like an officer and a gentleman, which is in cash or suicide. And when Novarro goes in hock to Jean Hersholt for 14,000 guilders, Navarro has to either pay off or bump off. He is about ready to bump when his uncle comes across with his last 14,000 to save the lad, who thereupon resigns his lieutenant in the Guards and doubles up with the dame who has become Hersholt's mistress.

The picture dies all the way through the playing. Chandler starts wrong and never rights herself. Novarro tries the light juvenile style as the lieutenant but it flattens at every try.

■ **DAY IN THE DEATH OF JOE EGG, A**

1972, 108 MINS, UK

Dir Peter Medak   *Prod* David Deutsch   *Scr* Peter Nichols   *Ph* Ken Hodges   *Ed* Ray Lovejoy   *Mus* Marcus Dods   *Art Dir* Ted Tester

● Alan Bates, Janet Suzman, Peter Bowles, Sheila Gish, Joan Hickson, Murray Melvin (Domino/Columbia)

A splendid adaptation by Peter Nichols from his play, simpatico direction by Peter Medak and stellar playing combine to make *A Day in the Death of Joe Egg* a superior black comedy-drama about a young couple trying to cope with a spastic child.

Lachrymal but unsentimentalized, the gut moral issue is euthanasia. The almost surreal narrative unfolds yo-yo style – from bitter or hilarious (or both) humor to emotional wrench and back again, repeatedly. Medak achieves this with seemingly unerring timing and balance.

Alan Bates and Janet Suzman as the couple who play games to survive their nightmare are firstrate in their sardonic despair. *Joe Egg*

is less about their defective moppet than the struggle of their own connubial existence, the often foiled appetite for carnal contact, and their very sanity.

■ **DAY OF THE DEAD**

1985, 102 MINS, US ◇ ▼

Dir George A. Romero   *Prod* Richard P. Rubinstein   *Scr* George A. Romero   *Ph* Michael Gornick   *Ed* Pasquale Buba   *Mus* John Harrison   *Art Dir* Cletus Anderson

● Lori Cardille, Terry Alexander, Joseph Pilato, Jarlath Conroy, Antone DiLeo Jr, Richard Liberty (Laurel)

Day of the Dead is an unsatisfying part three in George A. Romero's zombie saga.

Set in Florida (but filmed mainly in Pennsylvania plus Fort Myers, Fla.), *Day* postulates that the living dead have now taken over the world with only a handful of normal humans still alive, outnumbered by about 400,000 to one. In a claustrophobic format reminiscent of early 1950s science fiction films, the human protagonists debate and fight among themselves in an underground missile silo while the common enemy masses topside.

Representing the scientific community are stalwart heroine Sarah (Lori Cardille), who is working on long-range research to find a way to reverse the process whereby dead humans become unreasoning, cannibalistic zombies, and loony Dr Logan (Richard Liberty), engaged in conditioning experiments on captured zombies to domesticate them.

The acting here is generally unimpressive and in the case of Sarah's romantic partner, Miguel (Antone DiLeo Jr), unintentionally risible.

■ **DAY OF THE DOLPHIN, THE**

1973, 104 MINS, US ◇ ▼

Dir Mike Nichols   *Prod* Robert E. Relyea   *Scr* Buck Henry   *Ph* William A. Fraker   *Ed* Sam O'Steen   *Mus* Georges Delerue   *Art Dir* Richard Sylbert

● George C. Scott, Trish Van Devere, Paul Sorvino, Fritz Wearer, Jon Korkes, Edward Herrmann (Avco Embassy)

Mike Nichols' film of *The Day of the Dolphin* is a rare and regrettably uneven combination of ideas and action. George C. Scott stars as a marine scientist whose work with dolphins faces corruption by his own sponsors. The story climax strains belief, but Nichols is one of a handful of directors who can get away with occasional improbability.

Robert Merle's novel has been adapted into a screenplay which commingles creative obsession, materialism, covert espionage and overt skulduggery. This rich mixture eventually turns to lead, but while it works it is very mind boggling.

Scott and wife Trish Van Devere are conducting advanced research into dolphins, under the sponsorship of a foundation where Fritz Weaver is a senior executive. Paul Sorvino, at first an apparent blackmailing writer, emerges in time as a government agent investigating Weaver's outfit. Scott's scientific breakthrough – communicating verbally with the mammals – becomes the means by which Weaver and associates would blow up the yacht of the US President.

A major asset of the film is the magnificent score by Georges Delerue.

■ **DAY OF THE JACKAL, THE**

1973, 141 MINS, UK/FRANCE ◇ ▼

Dir Fred Zinnemann   *Prod* John Woolf   *Scr* Kenneth Ross   *Ph* Jean Tournier   *Ed* Ralph Kemplen   *Mus* Georges Delerue   *Art Dir* Willy Holt, Ernest Archer

● Edward Fox, Alan Badel, Tony Britton, Cyril Cusack, Michel Lonsdale, Delphine Seyrig (Universal)

Fred Zinnemann's film of *The Day of the Jackal* is a patient, studied and quasi-documentary translation of Frederick Forsyth's big-selling political suspense novel. Film appeals more to the intellect than the brute senses as it traces the detection of an assassin hired to kill French President Charles de Gaulle.

The recruitment of Edward Fox as the assassin and his planning of the murder is a sort of carrier frequency for the story. Around this is the mobilization of French and other national law enforcement agencies to discover and foil the plot. The final confluence of the plot lines is somewhat brief and anti-climactic.

The major asset of the film is that it succeeds in maintaining interest and suspense despite obvious viewer foreknowledge of the outcome.

Fox does very well as the innocent-looking youth who plans his stalk with meticulous care.

．．．．．．．．．．．．．．．．．．．．．．．．．．．．

■ **DAY OF THE LOCUST, THE**

1975, 144 MINS, US ◇

Dir John Schlesinger   *Prod* Jerome Hellman
Scr Waldo Salt   *Ph* Conrad Hall   *Ed* Jim Clark
Mus John Barry   *Art Dir* Richard MacDonald
● Donald Sutherland, Karen Black, Burgess Meredith, William Atherton, Geraldine Page, Richard A. Dysart (Paramount)

Magnificent production, combined with excellent casting and direction, make *The Day of the Locust* as fine a film (in a professional sense) as the basic material lets it be. Nathanael West's novel about losers on the Hollywood fringe has lost little of its verisimilitude in adaptation.

The Day of the Locust puts its focus on the loser, the never-was and the never-will-be. The story of destined failure features Karen Black in a fine performance as an aspiring, selfish would-be starlet, the daughter of broken down vaudevillian Burgess Meredith (a brilliant characterization). Donald Sutherland, laboring under the most striking burden of fuzzy writing, still evokes a good measure of pity as the hick whose immature love for Black is abused by her.

The principals are surrounded by a truly superb supporting cast: and the physical and technical support is beyond belief.

．．．．．．．．．．．．．．．．．．．．．．．．．．．．

■ **DAY OF THE TRIFFIDS, THE**

1963, 93 MINS, UK ⓥ

Dir Steve Sekely   *Prod* George Pitcher   *Scr* Philip Yordan   *Ph* Ted Moore   *Ed* Spencer Reeve   *Mus* Ron Goodwin
● Howard Keel, Kieron Moore, Janette Scott, Nicole Maurey, Mervyn Johns (Allied Artists)

Basically, this is a vegetarian's version of *The Birds*, a science-fiction-horror melodrama about a vile people-eater of the plant kingdom with a voracious appetite. Although riddled with script inconsistencies and irregularities, it is a more-than-adequate film of its genre.

John Wyndham's novel served as the source for exec producer Philip Yordan's screenplay. The proceedings begin with a spectacular display of celestial fireworks, a meteorite shower that leaves the earth's population heir to two maladies: blindness and the sinister company of a fast-multiplying plant aptly called Triffidus Celestus that looks like a Walt Disney nightmare and sounds like a cauldron of broccoli cooking in Margaret Hamilton's witchin' kitchen.

Hero of the piece is Howard Keel as a Yank seaman who, ironically spared the ordeal of blindness by having had his ill optics bandaged during the meteorite invasion, makes his way through a world haplessly engaged in a universal game of blind man's buff while under mortal threat of the carnivorous chlorophyll. Ultimately a marine biologist (Kieron Moore) stranded in a lighthouse with his wife (Janette Scott) discovers the means to dissolve and destroy the triffid.

The acting is generally capable. Steve Sekely's otherwise able direction has a bothersome flaw in the contradictory manner in which the triffids seem to approach and assault their victims.

．．．．．．．．．．．．．．．．．．．．．．．．．．．．

■ **DAYS OF HEAVEN**

1978, 95 MINS, US ◇

Dir Terrence Malick   *Prod* Bert Schneider, Harold Schneider   *Scr* Terrence Malick   *Ph* Nestor Almendros, Haskell Wexler   *Ed* Billy Weber
Mus Ennio Morricone, Leo Kottke   *Art Dir* Jack Fisk
● Richard Gere, Brooke Adams, Sam Shepard, Linda Manz, Robert Wilke, Stuart Margolin (OP/Paramount)

Days of Heaven is a dramatically moving and technically breathtaking American art film, one of the great cinematic achievements of the 1970s. Told through the eyes and words of an innocent but wise teenage migrant worker (Linda Manz), it traces a trio of nomads as their lives intersect with a wealthy wheat farmer.

The story opens in Chicago with Richard Gere shoveling coal in a steel mill. After an altercation with a foreman he's fired. He, his sister (Manz) and girlfriend (Brooke Adams), hit the road to find work in the fields, traveling as brother and sisters.

They find employment on a farm owned by a young, wealthy Sam Shepard. Like the other performances Shepard's is quiet – this isn't from the tour de force school – but it is a marvel nonetheless.

The trio become entangled with Shepard when he falls in love with Adams and marries her. Suddenly the threesome – once so poor they travelled in freight cars like cattle – are rich. And it seems that the days of heaven have arrived. But with wealth, they learn, also comes idleness. And with idleness boredom.

Told in 95 minutes, it is an efficient, meaningful story filled with some offbeat touches, literary references and beautifully developed characters.

．．．．．．．．．．．．．．．．．．．．．．．．．．．．

■ **DAYS OF THUNDER**

1990, 107 MINS, US ◇ ⓥ

Dir Tony Scott   *Prod* Don Simpson, Jerry Bruckheimer
Scr Robert Towne   *Ph* Ward Russell   *Ed* Billy Weber, Chris Lebenzon   *Mus* Hans Zimmer   *Art Dir* Benjamin Fernandez
● Tom Cruise, Robert Duvall, Nicole Kidman, Randy Quaid, Michael Rooker, Cary Elwes (Paramount)

This expensive genre film about stock car racing has many of the elements that made the same team's *Top Gun* a blockbuster, but the producers recruited scripter Robert Towne to make more out of the story than junk food.

There's the cocky but insecure young challenger (Tom Cruise) breaking into the big time, the hardened champion he's trying to unseat (Michael Rooker), the grizzled manager who dispenses fatherly wisdom (Robert Duvall), the crass promoter (Randy Quaid), and the sexy lady from outside (Nicole Kidman) who questions the point of it all.

Director Tony Scott plunges the viewer into the maelstrom of stock car racing. A highly effective blending of car-mounted camerawork and long lenses imparts documentary credibility and impact.

Days of Thunder zigzags between exploiting Cruise's likable grin and charming vulnerability and portraying him as an emotional loser. It's an uncertain and unsatisfying mix.

The film's real glory is Duvall. His duplicitous, ruthless streak hovers just below the surface, giving a sense of inner danger to the racing scenes in which he coaches the untrusting Cruise by radio from trackside.

．．．．．．．．．．．．．．．．．．．．．．．．．．．．

■ **DAYS OF WINE AND ROSES**

1962, 116 MINS, US ⓥ

Dir Blake Edwards   *Prod* Martin Manulis   *Scr* J.P. Miller   *Ph* Philip Lathrop   *Ed* Patrick McCormack
Mus Henry Mancini   *Art Dir* Joseph Wright
● Jack Lemmon, Lee Remick, Charles Bickford, Jack Klugman (Warner)

Days of Wine and Roses hails from television's *Playhouse 90* series, and has been faithfully and painstakingly translated to the screen by two of the men responsible for the praised TV version – producer Martin Manulis and writer J. P. Miller.

Miller's gruelling drama illustrates how the unquenchable lure of alcohol can supersede even love, and how marital communication cannot exist in a house divided by one-sided boozing. The wife (Lee Remick), originally a non-drinker with a yen for chocolates that is a tip-off of her vulnerability to the habit pattern, begins to drink when her husband (Jack Lemmon), a p.r. man and two-fisted belter whose career is floundering, is dismayed by a gap in their togetherness. Upshot is the disastrous compatibility of mutual alcoholism.

Lemmon gives a dynamic and chilling performance. Scenes of his collapse, particularly in the violent ward, are brutally realistic and terrifying. Remick, too, is effective, and there is solid featured work from Charles Bickford and Jack Klugman and a number of fine supporting performances.

．．．．．．．．．．．．．．．．．．．．．．．．．．．．

■ **DAY THE EARTH CAUGHT FIRE, THE**

1961, 99 MINS, UK ⓥ

Dir Val Guest   *Prod* Val Guest   *Scr* Wolf Mankowitz, Val Guest   *Ph* Harry Waxman   *Ed* Bill Lenny
Mus Stanley Black   *Art Dir* Tony Masters
● Janet Munro, Leo McKern, Edward Judd, Bernard Braden, Michael Goodliffe, Peter Butterworth (British Lion/Pax)

Val Guest's production has a fascinating yarn, some very sound thesping and an authentic Fleet Street (newspaper) background.

By mischance, an American nuclear test at the South Pole is conducted on the same day as a Russian one at the North Pole. It first causes a sinister upheaval in the world's weather and then it is discovered that the globe has been jolted out of orbit and is racing towards the sun and annihilation. It's figured that four giant bombs exploded simultaneously might save the grave situation and the world's powers unite, for once, to help a possibly doomed civilization.

Drama of this situation is played out as a newspaper scoop. Picture was shot largely in the building of the *Daily Express*. Arthur Christiansen, ex-editor of the *Express*, acted as technical advisor as well as playing the editor.

Guest's direction is brisk and makes good use of newsreel sequences and special effects, designed by Les Bowie. Dialog is racy and slick without being too parochial for the layman.

The acting all round is effective. Edward Judd, making his first star appearance, clicks as the hero, the reporter who brings in the vital facts that make the story take shape. He shows rugged charm in his lightly romantic scenes with Janet Munro, who is pert and pleasant in the only considerable distaff role. Outstanding performance comes from Leo McKern, who is tops as a dependable gruff and understanding science reporter.

．．．．．．．．．．．．．．．．．．．．．．．．．．．．

■ DAY THE EARTH STOOD STILL, THE

1951, 92 MINS, US ⓥ

Dir Robert Wise   *Prod* Julian Blaustein   *Scr* Edmund H.
North   *Ph* Leo Tover   *Ed* William Reynolds
Mus Bernard Herrmann   *Art Dir* Lyle Wheeler, Addison
Hehr
● Michael Rennie, Patricia Neal, Hugh Marlowe, Sam
Jaffe, Billy Gray (20th Century-Fox)

Screenplay, based on a story by Harry Bates,
tells of an invasion of the earth by a single
spaceship from an unidentified planet in
outer space. Ship has two occupants, an
eight-foot robot, and an earth-like human.
They have come to warn the earth's people
that all other inhabited planets have banded
together into a peaceful organization and that
peace is being threatened by the wars of the
earth-people. If that happens, the inter-
planetary UN is prepared to blast the earth
out of the universe.

Spaceship lands in Washington and the
man, leaving the robot on guard, leaves to
hide among the people, to discover for
himself what they are like. His findings of
constant bickerings and mistrust aren't too
favorable for the earth's humans. Situation
naturally creates fear throughout the world
and the US brings out army tanks, howitzers,
etc, to guard the ship and the robot, while a
frantic search goes on for the man.

Cast, although secondary to the story,
works well. Michael Rennie is fine as the man
from space. Patricia Neal is attractive and
competent as the widowed mother of the
young boy whom he befriends and who is the
first to know his secret.

■ DEAD, THE

1987, 83 MINS, US ◇ ⓥ

Dir John Huston   *Prod* Wieland Schulz-Keil   *Scr* Tony
Huston   *Ph* Fred Murphy   *Ed* Roberto Silvi   *Mus* Alex
North   *Art Dir* Stephen Grimes
● Anjelica Huston, Donal McCann, Rachael Dowling,
Cathleen Delany, Helena Carroll (Vestron Zenith/Liffey)

A well-crafted miniature, this dramatization
of the Joyce story directly addresses the
theme of how the 'shades' from 'that other
world' can still live in those who still walk the
earth.

Opening hour is set exclusively in the warm
Dublin town house of two spinster sisters,
who every winter holiday season throw a festive party and dinner for their relatives and
friends. Time is 1904.

By evening's end, the focus clearly has been
placed upon the handsome couple of Gretta
and Gabriel (Anjelica Huston and Donal
McCann). Back at their hotel, Gabriel
attempts some rare intimacy with his
distracted wife, who throws him into deep
melancholy by telling him a secret of a youthful love. Gabriel sets upon a profound dis-
course about the living and the dead to the
visual accompaniment of snow falling on
bleak Irish landscapes.

Brought in for the California shoot, the virtually all-Irish cast brings the story to life
completely and believably, with Helena
Carroll's big-hearted Aunt Kate and Donal
Donnelly's drunken Freddy Malins being
special delights. Huston proves fully up to the
demands of her emotionally draining monolog, and McCann simply is ideal as the
thoughtful husband.

■ DEAD CALM

1989, 96 MINS, AUSTRALIA ◇ ⓥ

Dir Phillip Noyce   *Prod* Terry Hayes, Doug Mitchell,
George Miller   *Scr* Terry Hayes   *Ph* Dean Semler
Ed Richard Francis-Bruce   *Mus* Graeme Revill
Art Dir Graham (Grace) Walker
● Sam Neill, Nicole Kidman, Billy Zane (Kennedy
Miller)

Though not always entirely credible, *Dead*

Calm is a nail-biting suspense pic [from the
novel by Charles Williams] handsomely produced and inventively directed.

It's basically a three-hander: a happily
married couple John and Rae Ingram (Sam
Neill and Nichole Kidman), have found
peace alone on the Pacific on their well-
equipped yacht after the trauma of the death
of their baby son in a car accident when
they're threatened by a vicious, unstable
young killer, Hughie (Billy Zane).

They come to Hughie's aid initially, when
he seeks help, but Ingram doesn't believe his
story that the passengers and crew on the
decrepit yacht he's abandoned all died from
food poisoning. Leaving Hughie asleep,
Ingram goes across to the delapidated vessel
to discover dead bodies in the bilges and a
video tape indicating that a deranged Hughie
killed them.

While he's away, Hughie awakens, overpowers Rae, and sets sail in the opposite
direction, abandoning Ingram.

Throughout the film, Kidman is excellent.
She gives the character of Rae real tenacity
and energy. Neill is good, too, as a husband
who spends most of the film unable to contact
his wife, and Yank newcomer Zane is suitably manic and evil as the deranged Hughie.

■ DEAD END

1937, 90 MINS, US ⓥ

Dir William Wyler   *Prod* Samuel Goldwyn   *Scr* Lillian
Hellman   *Ph* Greg Toland   *Ed* Daniel Mandell
Mus Alfred Newman (dir.)   *Art Dir* Richard Day
● Sylvia Sidney, Joel McCrea, Humphrey Bogart,
Wendy Barrie, Claire Trevor, Allen Jenkins
(Goldwyn/United Artists)

Producer Samuel Goldwyn has made a near-
literal film translation of Sidney Kingsley's
play *Dead End*, the New York stage success.
The Kingsley theme is that tenements breed
gangsters, and no one does anything about it.
The play whammed the idea across the footlights; the picture says and does everything
the play said and did, and stops right there.

All the action is limited merely to a larger
background setting of the river front in the
East 50s (NY) than the Belasco theatre stage
could contain. Only material plot change is
to heroize the character of Dave, the student
architect (Joel McCrea).

Performances are uniformly fine, topped by
the acting of the boy players from the New
York production who seem better in the film
because they do not crowd their lines so fast.
Sylvia Sidney is excellent. Her sister-and-
brother scenes with the wild Tommy (Billy
Halop) are tender, moving and tragic.
McCrea does a fine bit in a scene with Wendy
Barrie, the keptive in the fashionable apart-
ment, when he turns down her proposition.
The Barrie role is indefinite in outline, due to
censoring.

Humphrey Bogart looks the part of Baby
Face Martin and plays with complete understanding of the character. Claire Trevor is
Francey, the street walker. In this instance
also censorship has stripped the role of the
shocking features which made it stand out in
the play.

□ 1937: Best Picture (Nomination)

■ DEADFALL

1968, 120 MINS, UK ◇

Dir Bryan Forbes   *Prod* Paul Monash   *Scr* Bryan
Forbes   *Ph* Gerry Turpin   *Ed* John Jympson
Mus John Barry   *Art Dir* Ray Simm
● Michael Caine, Giovanna Ralli, Eric Portman,
Nanette Newman, David Buck, Carlos Pierre
(Salamander)

An apparent attempt to pull off an Alfred
Hitchcock suspenser, with added Freudian
schleps, *Deadfall* falls dead as little more than

ponderous, tedious trivia. Adapted from Desmond Cory's novel, the talky, convoluted
writing is hurt by hyped-up cinematics.

Michael Caine is introduced in a sanito-
rium as a cured alcoholic; Giovanna Ralli
lures him to the home she shares with husband Eric Portman, who plays a homosexual,
a point hammered home incessantly by dialog, plus the presence of Carlos Pierre, a
pretty-boy-for-hire. The three principals join
in a jewel heist, a 23-minute sequence which
brings a halting pace to a complete stop. The
'real' story is Caine's love for Ralli, complicated by the presence of Portman.

Composer John Barry appears as a symphony conductor in that 23-minute sequence
of cross-cuts between guitarist Renata Tar-
rago, and Caine-Portman at work stealing
somebody's loot.

■ DEAD HEAT ON A MERRY-GO-ROUND

1966, 107 MINS, US ◇ ⓥ

Dir Bernard Girard   *Prod* Carter DeHaven
Scr Bernard Girard   *Ph* Lionel Lindon   *Ed* William
Lyon   *Mus* Stu Phillips   *Art Dir* Walter M. Simonds
● James Coburn, Camilla Sparv, Aldo Ray, Nina
Wayne, Robert Webber, Rose Marie (Columbia)

The idea and the premise of *Dead Heat on a
Merry-Go-Round* is okay but it doesn't jell, and
the title, a deliberate attempt to be cute, is
meaningless. What leads up to the comedy-
melodrama O. Henry finale most likely was
very funny in the producers' minds, but
much of the action is so fragmentary and episodic that there is not sufficient exposition
and the treatment goes overboard in striving
for effect.

James Coburn, who charms his way out of
a prison into a parole via an affair with a
femme psychologist (a nice trick if you know
how to do it), has in mind the burglary of a
bank at LA International Airport. Date set
for the heist coincides with arrival of the Russian premier, when security will engage full
attention of all arms of the law.

Coburn plays a rather sardonic character
who is capable of meeting every situation
successfully and with what is given him
comes through with a deft performance.
Camilla Sparv, whom he weds and is an
innocent accomplice, rivals him in interest,
displaying a fresh note which communicates
engagingly.

■ DEADLIER THAN THE MALE

1967, 98 MINS, UK ◇

Dir Ralph Thomas   *Prod* Betty E. Box   *Scr* Jimmy
Sangster, David Osborn, Liz Charles-Williams
Ph Ernest Steward   *Ed* Alfred Roome   *Mus* Malcolm
Lockyer   *Art Dir* Alex Vetchinsky
● Richard Johnson, Elke Sommer, Sylva Koscina, Nigel
Green, Suzanna Leigh, Steve Carlson (Universal/Rank/
Inflight)

There is no doubt that *Deadlier than the Male* is
loaded with colorful and exciting production
values. Opinion thereafter is likely to divide,
however, for the film will strike some as okay
dual-bill escapism, and others as overly raw
and single entendre. Sadism, sex and
attempted sophistication mark this Bulldog
Drummond pic.

David Osborn, Liz Charles-Williams and
Jimmy Sangster scripted the latter's original
story, in which Elke Sommer and Sylva Koscina are two cohorts of Nigel Green in his industrial deal-making.

Green's modus operandi is simple: intervene in major deals and promise consumma-
tion, then kill off all opposition and collect the
promised fee. Scripters had a major task in
making explicit murder appear as nonchalant
as taking tea, and they rarely achieve the
goal.

D

DEADLINE U.S.A.

1952, 87 MINS, US

Dir Richard Brooks   *Prod* Sol C. Siegel   *Scr* Richard
Brooks   *Ph* Milton Krasner   *Ed* William B. Murphy
Mus Cyril J. Mockridge   *Art Dir* Lyle Wheeler, George
Patrick
● Humphrey Bogart, Ethel Barrymore, Kim Hunter, Ed
Begley, Warren Stevens, Paul Stewart (20th Century-
Fox)

Humphrey Bogart is the traditionally intrepid big-city, big-sheet editor whose responsibility to his job, his corps of 1,500
fellow-workers on *The Day* (as this composite
but mythical rag is called), and his moxie in
locking horns with the No. 1 mobster, is
chiefly sparked when one of his news staff
gets beaten up by Martin Gabel's gang.

Complicating this is the projected sale of
the paper by the founder-publisher's heirs. In
midst of the imminence of job layoffs, Bogart
proceeds to break the mob, stall the courts'
approval of the sale, on his impassioned,
informal plea in the surrogate's court that a
newspaper, its functions, and its relation to
its 300,000 faithful daily readers, is more than
that of just another chattel. Much of the footage was shot in the NY *Daily News*
press-rooms.

Bogart gives a convincing performance all
the way, from his constantly harassed deadline existence, his personal romantic stalemate, and his guts in avenging the beating
given his crime reporter.

DEADLY AFFAIR, THE

1967, 107 MINS, UK ◇ Ⓥ

Dir Sidney Lumet   *Prod* Sidney Lumet   *Scr* Paul
Dehn   *Ph* Freddie Young   *Ed* Thelma Connell
Mus Quincy Jones   *Art Dir* John Howell
● James Mason, Simone Signoret, Maximilian Schell,
Harriet Andersson, Lynn Redgrave, Harry Andrews
(Columbia)

The Deadly Affair is based on *Call for the Dead*
by John le Carre. Shrewd and powerful development is given this tale of a British Home
Office intelligence officer seeking to unravel
the supposed suicide of a high Foreign Office
diplomat.

Mason is cast as an unromantic civil servant whose official problems are further complicated by his being wed to a compulsively
sexual young woman who has many affairs.
His is a thorough acting job as he conducts
his investigation in which he delivers one of
his best performances.

Harry Andrews, as a retired CIP inspector
called in to assist the intelligence officer, gives
a rugged portrayal of police methods in dealing with criminals, which in this instance is a
buildup to learning the identity of a foreign
spy responsible for the death of the diplomat.

DEADLY COMPANIONS, THE

1961, 90 MINS, US ◇ Ⓥ

Dir Sam Peckinpah   *Prod* Charles B. FitzSimons
Scr A.S. Fleischman   *Ph* William B. Clothier
Ed Stanley E. Rabjon   *Mus* Marlin Skiles
● Maureen O'Hara, Brian Keith, Steve Cochran, Chill
Wills, Strother Martin (Pathe-America)

A.S. Fleischman's adaptation of his own
novel is the dramatic tale of four characters
who encounter their respective moments of
truth in a ghost town smack dab in the heart
of Apache country. One (Maureen O'Hara)
is a dancehall woman heading for the ghost
town to bury her son next to her late husband, thus erasing the stigma of her shady
reputation. Another is Brian Keith, whose
motivation is revenge against Chill Wills, an
unstable galoot with whom he has an old
score to settle. Fourth member of the odd
party is Steve Cochran, a gunslinger with
eyes for O'Hara.

Fleischman's screenplay is pretty far-
fetched and relies heavily on coincidence but,
for the most part, it plays. This thanks to
superior emoting by the four principals and
an auspicious debut as director by Sam
Peckinpah, a fine TV helmsman.

Keith plays with customary reserve and
masculine authority a character refreshingly
different from the usual impregnable western
'tall man'.

DEADLY FRIEND

1986, 99 MINS, US ◇ Ⓥ

Dir Wes Craven   *Prod* Robert M. Sherwood
Scr Bruce Joel Rubin   *Ph* Philip Lathrop   *Ed* Michael
Eliot   *Mus* Charles Bernstein   *Art Dir* Daniel Lomino
● Matthew Laborteaux, Kristy Swanson, Michael
Sharrett, Anne Twomey, Anne Ramsey, Richard Marcus
(Pan Arts/Layton)

Pic has enough gore, suspense and requisite
number of shocks to keep most hearts pounding through to the closing credits.

Paul (Matthew Laborteaux) is a bit accelerated for his age, having built a semi-intelli-
gent robot named BB.

One night, neighbour Richard Marcus goes
a bit too far slapping his daughter (Kristy
Swanson) around and she ends up having to
be hospitalized. Just when the doctors determine she's brain-dead, Laborteaux steals her
body and transplants BB's 'brain' into her
gray matter.

That's when the fun begins.

Viewers can just as easily scream as laugh
through *Deadly Friend* watching the obviously
made-up Swanson come back to life and walk
around like a robot, crushing her enemies one
by one.

DEAD MEN DON'T WEAR PLAID

1982, 89 MINS, US Ⓥ

Dir Carl Reiner   *Prod* David V. Picker, William E.
McEuen   *Scr* Carl Reiner, George Gipe, Steve Martin
Ph Michael Chapman   *Ed* Bud Molin   *Mus* Miklos
Rozsa   *Art Dir* John DeCuir
● Steve Martin, Rachel Ward, Reni Santoni, Carl
Reiner, George Gaynes, Frank McCarthy
(Universal/Aspen)

Lensed in black-and-white and outfitted with
a 'straight' mystery score by Miklos Rozsa
and authentic 1940s costumes by Edith
Head, this spoof of film noir detective yarns
sees Steve Martin interacting with
18 Hollywood greats by way of intercutting
of clips from some 17 old pictures.

Thus, when sultry, Rachel Ward enters his
seedy LA office to discuss her father's murder,
$10-per-day sleuth Martin is able to call
Bogart's Philip Marlowe for assistance on the
case. And so it goes with such additional
tough guys as Burt Lancaster, Kirk Douglas
and Edward Arnold and such dames as
Barbara Stanwyck, Ingrid Bergman, Veronica Lake, Bette Davis, Lana Turner and Joan
Crawford.

Film is most engaging in its romantic sparring between Martin and his gorgeous client,
Ward. Latter looks sensational in period garb
and is not above such Martinesque gags as
removing bullets from his wounds with her
teeth or having her breasts 'rearranged' by
the hardboiled detective.

Sporting dark hair and facetious
confidence, Martin also looks spiffy in
trenchcoat and hat. Only other roles off note
see Carl Reiner essentially essaying Otto
Preminger as a Nazi, and Reni Santoni
as a zealous Peruvian officer.

DEAD OF NIGHT

1945, 103 MINS, UK Ⓥ

Dir Alberto Cavalcanti, Basil Dearden, Robert Hamer,
Charles Crichton   *Prod* Michael Balcon   *Scr* John V.
Baines, Angus MacPhail, T.E.B. Clarke   *Ph* Jack Parker,

H. Julius   *Ed* Charles Hasse   *Mus* Georges Auric
Art Dir Michael Relph
● Googie Withers, Michael Redgrave, Sally Ann
Howes, Mervyn Johns, Roland Culver, Frederick Valk
(Ealing)

Tightly-woven script [from stories by John
V. Baines, Angus MacPhail, E.F. Benson
and H.G. Wells] tells the story of a man who
has foreknowledge of the future through his
dreams. Summoned on business to a British
estate, he's shocked to find that the place and
people have all been in his dreams. When he
tells his dream, one of the house-guests, a
psychiatrist, scoffs at the story and attempts
to find a scientific explanation for it all. Other
guests, however, are more sympathetic and
each then tells of a strange, similarly psychic
situation in which he's been involved.

Producer Michael Balcon turned each individual episode over to a different director
and, told via flashback, they're equally good.
Best is the one featuring Redgrave as a ventriloquist whose dummy seemed imbued with
a human brain and soul. Redgrave turns in a
masterful piece of acting as he's driven to
'kill' the dummy.

DEAD OF WINTER

1987, 100 MINS, US ◇ Ⓥ

Dir Arthur Penn   *Prod* John Bloomgarden, Marc
Shmuger   *Scr* Marc Shmuger   *Ph* Jan Weincke
Ed Rich Shaine   *Mus* Richard Einhorn   *Art Dir* Bill
Brodie
● Mary Steenburgen, Roddy McDowall, Jan Rubes,
William Russ, Mark Malone (M-G-M)

Mary Steenburgen is first-rate as the struggling actress hired by an unusually accommodating casting director (Roddy
McDowall) to audition as a double for an
actress removed from a film-in-progress
because of an alleged nervous breakdown.

She's taken to the isolated country estate of
a psychiatrist-turned-producer during a violent snowstorm (hence the title *Dead of Winter*)
where she undergoes a complete makeover
until she – quite uncannily – resembles the
stricken actress.

Little does she know she's become the patsy
for a couple of blackmailers who have
bumped off the other actress, as revealed in
the very first scene of the film.

Suspense is built artfully around her gradual realization that she's trapped with a sly
shrink and his obsequious factotum,
McDowall, considerably more malevolent
than he first appeared.

Steenburgen and McDowall are the adversaries to follow, even though it would seem
more likely that the wheel-chair bound doctor (Jan Rubes) should be the one to watch.
Rubes is simply not sinister enough to be the
mastermind behind this scheme.

DEAD POETS SOCIETY

1989, 128 MINS, US ◇ Ⓥ

Dir Peter Weir   *Prod* Steven Haft, Paul Junger Witt,
Tony Thomas   *Scr* Tom Schulman   *Ph* John Seale
Ed William Anderson   *Mus* Maurice Jarre
Art Dir Wendy Stites
● Robin Williams, Robert Sean Leonard, Ethan Hawke,
Josh Charles, Gale Hansen (Touchstone/Silver Screen
Partners IV)

Pic is not so much about Robin Williams, as
unconventional English teacher John Keating at a hardline New England prep school,
as it is about the youths he teaches and how
the creative flames within them are kindled
and then stamped out.

Director Peter Weir fills the screen with a
fresh gang of compelling teenagers, led by
Robert Sean Leonard as outgoing Neil Perry
and balanced by Ethan Hawke as deeply
withdrawn Todd Anderson.

Keating enters their rigidly traditional world and has them literally rip out the pages of their hidebound textbooks in favor of his inventive didactics on the spirit of poetry.

Captivated by Keating's spirit, the influential Neil provokes his mates into reviving a secret club, the Dead Poets Society, that Keating led in his prep school days.

Meanwhile the gifted, medical-school-bound Neil begins to pursue acting, his true aspiration, against the strenuous objections of his domineering father (Kurtwood Smith).

Story sings whenever Williams is onscreen. Screen belongs just as often to Leonard, who as Neil has a quality of darting confidence mixed with hesitancy. Hawke, as the painfully shy Todd, gives a haunting performance.

□ 1989: Best Picture (Nomination)

．．．．．．．．．．．．．．．．．．．．．．．．．．．

■ **DEAD RECKONING**

1947, 100 MINS, US ⓥ

Dir John Cromwell *Prod* Sidney Biddell *Scr* Oliver H.P. Garrett, Steve Fisher *Ph* Leo Tover *Ed* Gene Havlick *Mus* Marlin Skiles *Art Dir* Stephen Goosson, Rudolph Sternad

● Humphrey Bogart, Lizabeth Scott, Morris Carnovsky (Columbia)

Humphrey Bogart's typically tense performance raises this average whodunit quite a few notches. Film has good suspense and action, and some smart direction and photography.

Columbia borrowed Bogart from Warners to play the role of a tough ex-paratrooper captain returning home with a pal to be honored by the War Dept for their achievements. When the pal jumps the DC train, to go home instead, the perplexed captain follows to find himself enmeshed in gangland, murders and romance. His pal, he learns, had enlisted under an alias because he was convicted of a killing. Two days after said pal arrives home, he gets bumped off.

Determined to solve the mystery and avenge his friend, the captain digs into his pal's haunts. Script uses a flashback method for part of the telling, to add variety.

Bogart absorbs one's interest from the start as a tough, quick-thinking ex-skyjumper. Lizabeth Scott stumbles occasionally as a nitery singer, but on the whole gives a persuasive sirenish performance.

．．．．．．．．．．．．．．．．．．．．．．．．．．．

■ **DEAD RINGERS**

1988, 115 MINS, CANADA ◇ ⓥ

Dir David Cronenberg *Prod* David Cronenberg, Marc Boyman *Scr* David Cronenberg, Norman Snider *Ph* Peter Suschitzky *Ed* Ronald Sanders *Mus* Howard Shore *Art Dir* Carol Spier

● Jeremy Irons, Genevieve Bujold, Heidi Von Palleske, Barbara Gordon, Shirley Douglas (Mantle Clinic II)

Dead Ringers is about identical twin gynecologists, both expertly played by Jeremy Irons, whose intense bond is fatally sliced when they both fall in love with the same internationally known actress (Genevieve Bujold).

The doctors are renowned, interchangeably taking on the same patients and making public appearances, with no one guessing who's who.

Yet one is outgoing, a smooth talker and a ladies man, and the other, more dependent and less sociable.

Bujold chooses the shy twin, and from that point, disintegration of the twins bond and their careers sets in.

Director David Cronenberg handles his usual fondness for gore in muted style; a brief scene has the shy twin dreaming of biting apart the skin joining Siamese twins; and the final operation, though bloody, is not lingered over.

．．．．．．．．．．．．．．．．．．．．．．．．．．．

■ **DEAD ZONE, THE**

1983, 102 MINS, US ◇ ⓥ

Dir David Cronenberg *Prod* Debra Hill *Scr* Jeffrey Boam *Ph* Mark Irwin *Ed* Ronald Sanders *Mus* Michael Kamen *Art Dir* Carol Spier

● Christopher Walken, Brooke Adams, Tom Skerritt, Herbert Lom, Anthony Zerbe, Martin Sheen (Dino De Laurentiis)

Joining the half-dozen shock-oriented directors who have filmed novelist Stephen King's horror and suspense yarns, David Cronenberg turns *The Dead Zone* into an accomplished psychological thriller.

Focus is Johnny Smith, a shy schoolteacher who snaps out of a long coma with the questionable gift of second sight. Convincingly played by Christopher Walken, Johnny can see into anybody's past or future merely by grasping the person's hand. The 'dead zone' seems to refer to the brain damage that enables him to change the outcome of events he 'sees'.

His first premonition enables a nurse to save her daughter from a domestic conflagration. The news of the patient's ESP spreads quickly and he experiences some pretty horrible incidents, inside and outside his head.

A lot happens in the 102-minute suspenser. There's the girlfriend (Brooke Adams) Johnny loses to his near-fatal accident and regains for awhile. There's also a sheriff (Tom Skerritt) who desperately needs a psychic solution to crack a murder case, and the wealthy businessman (Anthony Zerbe) who hires Johnny to tutor his problem son (Simon Craig).

．．．．．．．．．．．．．．．．．．．．．．．．．．．

■ **DEALERS**

1989, 89 MINS, UK ◇ ⓥ

Dir Colin Bucksey *Prod* William P. Cartlidge *Scr* Andrew MacLear *Ph* Peter Sinclair *Ed* Jon Costelloe *Mus* Richard Hartley *Art Dir* Peter J. Hampton

● Paul McGann, Rebecca DeMornay, Derrick O'Connor, John Castle (Euston)

Dealers though well produced, is a less than enthralling pic about a yuppie high-flyer and his glamorous mistress.

Paul McGann is a dollar dealer in a London bank, set for promotion when his superior suicides after a botched deal. To his chagrin, McGann's boss brings in an outsider over his head, beautiful Rebecca DeMornay, the latest whizkid in the banking business (and the boss' mistress to boot). Before long, though, McGann is romancing his rival and taking her home for a nightcap in his seaplane, which he parks near Tower Bridge.

Pic's most interesting character is Derrick O'Connor as a cockney dealer who's pink-slipped from the bank and sinks into a coke-snorting decline.

．．．．．．．．．．．．．．．．．．．．．．．．．．．

■ **DEAR BRIGITTE**

1965, 100 MINS, US ◇ ⓥ

Dir Henry Koster *Prod* Henry Koster *Scr* Hal Kanter *Ph* Lucien Ballard *Ed* Marjorie Fowler *Mus* George Duning *Art Dir* Jack Martin Smith, Malcolm Brown

● James Stewart, Fabian, Glynis Johns, Cindy Carol, Billy Mumy, Brigitte Bardot (20th Century-Fox)

An entertaining comedy with something for everyone, *Dear Brigitte* shapes up as an excellent family pic.

Hal Kanter's screenplay, based on John Haase's novel *Erasmus with Freckles*, focuses on poet-professor Robert Leaf who's not only pro-humanities but very much anti-science. James Stewart is perfect in characterization of the idealistic voice in academic wilderness, as nuclear labs and computer setups encroach upon his domain of arts and letters at mythical modern university.

Complications arise when eight-year-old son Erasmus turns tone-deaf, then color-blind (hence unsuited for artistic career) but displays mathematical genius which indicates great scientific future. Kanter's yarn is lightweight, but a sufficiently strong fiber to support a string of varied and effective comedy situations, including Erasmus' puppy love for Brigitte Bardot to whom he secretly writes letters from Sausalito riverboat home.

In role of Stewart's wife, Glynis Johns is standout as steadying influence on hubby, son Billy Mumy, teenage daughter Cindy Carol and latter's boyfriend Fabian.

．．．．．．．．．．．．．．．．．．．．．．．．．．．

■ **DEATH GAME**

1977, 89 MINS, US ◇ ⓥ

Dir Peter Traynor *Prod* Larry Spiegel, Peter Traynor *Scr* Anthony Overman *Ph* David Worth *Mus* Jimmie Haskell

● Sondra Locke, Colleen Camp, Seymour Cassel, Beth Brickell, Michael Kalmansohn, Ruth Warshawsky (Levitt-Pickman)

Plot places the utmost strain on credibility. Two young lesbians (Sondra Locke and Colleen Camp) show up one thunderously rainy night at the plush, suburban home of a San Francisco business exec (Seymour Cassel), just turned 40.

After being allowed to use the telephone (they claim they're lost), pair admire the house appointments, seduce the man into a sexual threesome, and proceed to move in (the man's wife is away with the two children for the weekend).

All this, given some restraint, might have been packed into a passable feature. But director Peter Traynor opts for the obvious both in the acting and special effects. Cassel appears as hysterical as a middle-manager whose luncheon plans have gone askew. Locke and Camp scream and lick their lips a lot.

．．．．．．．．．．．．．．．．．．．．．．．．．．．

■ **DEATH IN VENICE**

1971, 130 MINS, ITALY ◇ ⓥ

Dir Luchino Visconti *Prod* Luchino Visconti *Scr* Luchino Visconti, Nicola Badalucco *Ph* Pasquale de Santis *Mus* Gustav Mahler *Art Dir* Ferdinand Scarfiotti, Piero Tosi

● Dirk Bogarde, Bjorn Andresen, Silvana Mangano, Marisa Berenson, Mark Burns (Warner)

Based on Thomas Mann's novella, *Death in Venice* could have been no easy task to translate to the screen. But Visconti and Dirk Bogarde clearly have a rapport and Bogarde gives a subtle and moving performance which fits beautifully into the atmospheric realism of [pre-World War I] Venice.

Bogarde plays a German composer and conductor (made up to look very like Gustav Mahler, whose music is used for the score) who visits Venice on vacation when on the verge of a mental and physical collapse. He is concerned with the violent accusations of his friend (Mark Burns) that he has dodged the issue of emotion until he is now no longer capable of feeling it.

He is fastidious and will not react to the uncouth behavior of the people he meets until, at his hotel, he sees a young boy with his family. The lad looks to Bogarde to be the most beautiful thing he has ever seen. He never seeks to contact the lad but follows him and watches him with a hunger which, thanks to Bogarde's performance, is clearly more intellectual and emotional than homosexual.

The story has its troubles. It attempts to show how innocence can cause problems of corruption and yet there is a pervading air over the film that is far from innocent.

Bogarde is both pathetic and compelling. Bjorn Andresen undoubtedly is a remarkably attractively-featured lad and gives a memor-

D

able performance. Silvana Mangano plays his mother with a haughty charm.

DEATH OF A SALESMAN

1951, 115 MINS, US

Dir Laslo Benedek *Prod* Stanley Kramer *Scr* Stanley Roberts *Ph* Franz P. Planer *Ed* William Lyon *Mus* Alex North *Art Dir* Rudolph Sternad, Cary Odell
● Fredric March, Mildred Dunnock, Kevin McCarthy, Cameron Mitchell, Howard Smith, Royal Beal
(Kramer/Columbia)

The vise-like grip with which *Death of a Salesman* held Broadway theatregoers for almost two years continues undiminished in Stanley Kramer's production of the film version. Arthur Miller's Pulitzer Prize-winner has been closely followed in the screen adaptation.

Salesman starkly reveals how Willy Loman's disillusionments catch up with him, his sons, his wife Linda; of how, after 34 years selling for the same house, he is finally fired, thus bringing about his complete mental collapse. During the period when his mental processes are breaking down, the film images Willy's memories of the past 20 years in illustrating how his desire for importance somehow became enmeshed in his confused dreams.

Fredric March, in the part created on the New York stage by Lee Cobb, gives perhaps the greatest performance of his career. Mildred Dunnock, in her original Broadway part, is superb as Willy's wife Linda. Kevin McCarthy, as Biff, is a film newcomer who entrenches himself strongly in the role performed on Broadway by Arthur Kennedy, Cameron Mitchell is an engaging 'Happy' Loman, the other brother, which he played on Broadway.

DEATH ON THE NILE

1978, 140 MINS, UK

Dir John Guillermin *Prod* John Brabourne, Richard Goodwin *Scr* Anthony Shaffer *Ph* Jack Cardiff *Ed* Malcolm Cooke *Mus* Nino Rota *Art Dir* Peter Murton
● Peter Ustinov, Jane Birkin, Lois Chiles, Bette Davis, Mia Farrow, Jon Finch (EMI)

Death on the Nile is a clever, witty, well-plotted, beautifully-produced and splendidly acted screen version of Agatha Christie's mystery. It's old-fashioned stylized entertainment with a big cast and lush locations. Peter Ustinov is the fourth actor to play Belgian sleuth Hercule Poirot.

Anthony Shaffer's adaptation doesn't have a hole. When Ustinov reveals the killer in the final drawing room scene it comes as a complete surprise. Every one of the dozen characters floating down the Nile is a suspect. Every one on board could have and might have murdered Lois Chiles, the arrogant million-airess who has stolen her best friend's fiance.

Shaffer has also created a number of purposely exaggerated characters to complement Ustinov. There's Angela Lansbury's tipsy portrayal of a romantic novelist; Bette Davis as a stuffy and overbearing Washington socialite and Maggie Smith as her bitter companion; Jack Warden as an hysterical Swiss physician; I.S. Johar in a marvelously offbeat performance as the manager of the ship on which the murders take place; David Niven as Poirot's sidekick Colonel Race; and Jon Finch as a Marxist spouting rebel.

But the star is Ustinov and the penetrating mind of his character, Hercule Poirot.

DEATH RACE 2000

1975, 78 MINS, US

Dir Paul Bartel *Prod* Roger Corman *Scr* Robert Thom, Charles Griffith *Ph* Tak Fujimoto *Ed* Tina Hersch *Mus* Paul Chihara *Art Dir* Robinson Royce, B.B. Neel

● David Carradine, Simone Griffeth, Sylvester Stallone, Mary Woronov, Roberta Collins, Martin Kove (New World)

Roger Corman's quickie production deals with ultra-violent sport in a futuristic society, in this case an annual cross-country road race with drivers scoring points by running down pedestrians.

Script, from an Ib Melchior story, makes its satirical points economically, and director Paul Bartel keeps the film moving quickly. Almost all of the film takes place on the road, with carnage and crashes occurring like clockwork.

David Carradine, clad in a spooky black leather outfit, is the national champion driver, challenged by thug-like Sylvester Stallone and four other drivers, including Amazon-like Mary Woronov. While fending off Stallone's attacks, Carradine also has to deal with radicals trying to sabotage the race.

DEATHSPORT

1978, 83 MINS, US

Dir Henry Suso, Allen Arkush *Prod* Roger Corman *Scr* Henry Suso, Donald Stewart *Ph* Gary Graver *Ed* Larry Bock *Mus* Andrew Stein *Art Dir* Sharon Compton
● David Carradine, Claudia Jennings, Richard Lynch, William Smithers, Will Walker, David McLean (New World)

Deathsport is Roger Corman's futuristic science fiction gladiator picture. And what is a futuristic science fiction gladiator picture? It's a film set 1,000 years into the future, post neutron wars, where the good warriors ride horses and wield see-through sabres fighting bad guys known as Statesmen who drive lethal motorcycles known as 'Death Machines'.

The good guys, Ranger Guides, are quiet, live by a code, make temporary unions and roam desert wastelands trying to avoid the cannibal mutants and those motorcycles, which are very noisy.

Statesmen have other plans. They have two ways of amusing themselves: beating up Ranger Guides – no easy task since Ranger Guides are superior warriors – and capturing female rangers, who they strip, lock up in dark room with metal chandeliers and then apply electricity and special effects. Nice guys.

David Carradine is the quiet good guy and the best thing that can be said about his acting and his part is that he doesn't say much. Claudia Jennings is his partner good guy, the one who gets to amuse the bad guy in the dark room. The best thing that can be said about her performance is that she gets to take off her clothes, twice.

DEATHTRAP

1982, 115 MINS, US

Dir Sidney Lumet *Prod* Burtt Harris *Scr* Jay Presson Allen *Ph* Andrzej Bartkowiak *Ed* John J. Fitzstephens *Mus* Johnny Mandel *Art Dir* Tony Walton
● Michael Caine, Christopher Reeve, Dyan Cannon, Irene Worth, Henry Jones, Joe Silver (Warner)

Sidney Lumet is no stranger to stage adaptations. Despite its intermittently amusing dialog, however, *Deathtrap* comes across as a minor entertainment, cleverness of which cannot conceal its essential artificiality when blown up on the big screen.

There are countless twists and turns in the plot of Ira Levin's 1978 play and the dramatic surprises are not necessarily easy to predict.

Michael Caine essays a writer who was once the Neil Simon of Broadway mystery writers but has now cranked out a quartet of

clinkers. Into his lap falls the manuscript of a perfect suspenser penned by unknown Christopher Reeve. Desperate for a hit, Caine invites Reeve over one evening in the guise of potential collaborator, while in fact he intends to kill him and then present the work as a new effort of his own.

Actors turn in pro jobs in a technical sense, with Reeve skillfully walking the fine line of his pretty boy part. But actors' charm just doesn't balance out the distastefulness of their characters.

DEATHWATCH

1980, 128 MINS, FRANCE/W. GERMANY

Dir Bertrand Tavernier *Prod* Gabriel Boustani, Janine Rubeiz *Scr* Bertrand Tavernier, David Rayfiel *Ph* Pierre-William Glenn *Ed* Armand Psenny, Michael Ellis *Mus* Antoine Duhamel *Art Dir* Tony Pratt
● Romy Schneider, Harvey Keitel, Harry Dean Stanton, Therese Liotard, Max Von Sydow (Selta/Little Bear/Antenne 2/Sara)

The story, shrewdly crafted by Bertrand Tavernier and American screenwriter David Rayfiel from a novel by David Compton [*The Unsleeping Eye*], is a throat-catcher. In a future society people die of old-age, science having almost completely banished disease.

A cunning TV producer, Vincent Ferriman, played with chillingly unctuous serenity by Harry Dean Stanton, hits on the idea of a program that would cover live the last days of an individual who has managed to contract a terminal illness.

Ferriman's proposed subject is Katherine Mortenhoe (finely played by Romy Schneider), whose fierce independence and sensitivity would seem to provide poignant fodder for the camera eye. But Katherine, after signing a contract, flees the city.

Deathwatch is a compelling drama centered on the human implications of its fanciful premise, as well as a harsh indictment of the media's role in society.

DEATH WISH

1974, 92 MINS, US

Dir Michael Winner *Prod* Hal Landers, Bobby Roberts, Michael Winner *Scr* Wendell Mayes *Ph* Arthur J. Ornitz *Ed* Bernard Gribble *Mus* Herbie Hancock *Art Dir* Robert Gundlach
● Charles Bronson, Hope Lange, Vincent Gardenia, Steven Keats, William Redfield, Stuart Margolin (Paramount/De Laurentiis)

Poisonous incitement to do-it-yourself law enforcement is the vulgar exploitation hook on which *Death Wish* is awkwardly hung. Charles Bronson stars as a husband-turned-assassin after his wife is killed and daughter raped by muggers.

Adaptation of Brian Garfield's novel is functionally simplistic, which is precisely the intellectual level desired for straightout exploitation treatment. Hope Lange and daughter Kathleen Tolan are victims of assault, after which husband Bronson freaks out in vengeance.

Plot angles are mostly overwhelmed by the easier, conventional cutting to the action, in this case one killing about every 10 minutes.

DEATH WISH II

1982, 93 MINS, US

Dir Michael Winner *Prod* Menahem Golan, Yoram Globus *Scr* David Engelbach *Ph* Richard H. Kline, Tom Del Ruth *Ed* Arnold Crust [=Michael Winner], Julian Semilian *Mus* Jimmy Page *Art Dir* William Hiney
● Charles Bronson, Jill Ireland, Vincent Gardenia, J.D. Cannon, Anthony Franciosa, Ben Frank (Columbia/Cannon)

Director Michael Winner, who usually leaves

nothing to the imagination (censors permitting), does it again with *Death Wish* revisited. Charles Bronson, as the avenging vigilante Paul Kersey, is turned loose this time on the creeps of Los Angeles and the results are every bit as revolting as in the original 1974 jackpot fantasy.

For openers, Bronson's Spanish cook is gangbanged and killed, and his catatonic daughter (still unrecovered from the first assault in Gotham) is raped yet again before winding up impaled on an iron railing pike as she tries to elude her savage captors.

What little performing style pic offers comes from Vincent Gardenia encoring from the original edition as a NY gumshoe who finally gets knocked off for his trouble coming to the aid of Bronson in an LA ravine.

■ DEATH WISH 3

1985, 90 MINS, US ◇ Ⓥ

Dir Michael Winner *Prod* Menahem Golan, Yoram Globus *Scr* Michael Edmonds *Ph* John Stanier *Ed* Arnold Crust [= Michael Winner] *Mus* Jimmy Page *Art Dir* Peter Mullins
● Charles Bronson, Deborah Raffin, Ed Lauter, Martin Balsam, Gavan O'Herlihy, Kirk Taylor (Cannon)

Death Wish 3 adds significantly to the body count scored to date in this street-rampant series. Thrills, however, are way down due to script's failure to build motivation for Paul Kersey's latest killing spree.

Set in NY, but lensed mostly in London, pic's release was timed to capitalize on the controversy around subway vigilante Bernhard Goetz.

Attempts to justify the ensuing mass-murder are perfunctory. Film opens with the butchering of an old man who turns out to be an old mate of Kersey, but there's no suggestion that the relationship was intimate. Kersey's response, like Bronson's acting, is automaton-like. Mystery is why he came to New York in the first place without the tools of his brutal trade and has to make regular visits to the post office to accumulate firepower.

Michael Winner directs with customary tongue-in-cheek panache. There are occasional moments of wit as when apartment resident Bennett (Martin Balsam) wields his rusty machine gun.

■ DEATH WISH 4
THE CRACKDOWN

1987, 99 MINS, US ◇ Ⓥ

Dir J. Lee Thompson *Prod* Menahem Golan, Yoram Globus *Scr* Gail Morgan Hickman *Ph* Gideon Porath *Ed* Peter Lee Thompson *Mus* Paul McCallum, Valentine McCallum, John Bisharat *Art Dir* Whitney Brooke Wheeler
● Charles Bronson, Kay Lenz, John P. Ryan, Perry Lopez (Cannon)

It's a risky business getting close to Charles Bronson. His wife, daughter and friends have been blown away in the first three installments of *Death Wish*. Now the vigilante is back to revenge the death of his girlfriend's daughter.

What raises *Death Wish 4* above the usual blowout is a semi-engaging script and sure pacing by veteran action director J. Lee Thompson.

As architect turned crusader, Paul Kersey (Bronson) is a curious blend of soft-spoken family man and detached seeker of justice. When he turns up the heat he does so with a measured, methodical passion as if it were his true calling in life to measure out justice in his corner of the world.

Bronson's treatment of drug trafficking is akin to chopping off the weeds and thinking that they won't grow back. It's a good excuse for him to break out some heavy ammunition

in pursuit of the two rival gangs who supposedly supply 90% of the cocaine in Los Angeles.

■ DECEPTION

1946, 111 MINS, US Ⓦ

Dir Irving Rapper *Prod* Henry Blanke *Scr* John Collier, Joseph Than *Ph* Ernest Haller *Ed* Alan Crosland Jr *Mus* Erich Wolfgang Korngold *Art Dir* Anton Grot
● Bette Davis, Paul Henreid, Claude Rains (Warner)

Deception, a story of matrimonial lies that builds to a murder climax, gives Bette Davis a potent vehicle. Plot is backed with lavish production, strong playing of a story loaded with femme interest, and bright direction.

Davis plays to the hilt, using full dramatic talent. It's not all her show, though. Claude Rains as her elderly teacher and sponsor walks off with considerable portion of the picture in a fine display of acting ability. By contrast, Paul Henreid suffers although turning in a smooth performance in a role with not too much color.

Plot [from the play by Louis Verneuil] concerns deception practiced by Davis to prevent husband Henreid from discovering that she had been the mistress of Rains before her marriage. Henreid, refugee cellist, is a jealous man whose temperamental instability is reason for the wife's deception. Pickup to story comes with Rains' entrance and his mad jealousy over his desertion by his mistress. To him falls juicy plums in the form of dialog and situations that carry the story along.

Music importance is emphasized by Erich Wolfgang Korngold's score and staging of orchestral numbers by LeRoy Prinz. Korngold's original music and the Cello Concerto are outstanding highlights.

■ DECISION AT SUNDOWN

1957, 77 MINS, US ◇

Dir Budd Boetticher *Prod* Harry Joe Brown *Scr* Charles Lang Jr *Ph* Burnett Guffey *Ed* Al Clark *Mus* Heinz Roemheld *Art Dir* Robert Peterson
● Randolph Scott, John Carroll, Karen Steele, Valerie French, Noah Beery, Andrew Duggan (Columbia/Ranown)

Complex screenplay from Vernon L. Fluherty tale spans a single day in cow town of Sundown. Randolph Scott, a mysterious, revengeful gunman, rides into town. He's after unsavory local wheel John Carroll, who's slated to marry local belle Karen Steele on that day. Scott breaks up the wedding and is besieged with sidekick Noah Beery by Carroll's henchmen. Step by step, it develops that Carroll, in his none-too-scrupulous past, had stolen and later discarded Scott's wife (since dead); and that she hadn't been unwilling, a fact Scott cannot face.

Role is an offbeat one for Scott, but he carries off the gunman's frustrated rage very well. Carroll makes convincingly menacing heavy in the suave tradition. Steele, as his understandably confused fiancee, shows much promise of things to come.

■ DECISION BEFORE DAWN

1951, 119 MINS, US

Dir Anatole Litvak *Prod* Anatole Litvak, Frank McCarthy *Scr* Peter Viertel *Ph* Franz Planer *Ed* Dorothy Spencer *Mus* Franz Waxman
● Richard Basehart, Gary Merrill, Oskar Werner, Hildegarde Neff, O.E. Hasse, Hans Christian Blech (20th Century-Fox)

Anatole Litvak gives this Second World War spy thriller a strong feeling of reality through a semi-documentary treatment, the use of mostly unknown faces, and by location lensing entirely in Germany, where the scars

of the War still fit graphically into the story's 1945 period.

Story [from the novel *Call It Treason* by George Howe] really gets going when Oskar Werner, a sensitive Allied prisoner, volunteers to aid his captors by obtaining information behind the lines in his own country. He believes his actions will help, rather than betray, Germany. Werner's excursion is fraught with danger, and his playing and Litvak direction milk the situation of drama while drawing a rather clear picture of events within Germany at that stage of the war and of how the people were taking it.

Richard Basehart and Gary Merrill, latter the commander of the intelligence unit using prisoners of war, are excellent. Hildegarde Neff creates a fine portrait of a German woman made a victim of war, and Dominique Blanchar is equally good as a French girl aiding the Allies.
☐ 1951: Best Picture (Nomination)

■ DECKS RAN RED, THE

1958, 97 MINS, US

Dir Andrew Stone *Prod* Andrew Stone, Virginia Stone *Scr* Andrew Stone *Ph* Meredith M. Nicholson *Ed* Virginia Stone
● James Mason, Dorothy Dandridge, Broderick Crawford, Stuart Whitman, Katharine Bard (M-G-M)

The Decks Ran Red is a descriptive title for this story, presented as fact, of an attempted mutiny at sea. Before the mutineers have been beaten down, they have spilled enough blood to make the decks sticky, if not running, with gore.

The plot is a plan by Broderick Crawford and Stuart Whitman, crew members of a chartered freighter, to kill off other members of the crew, rig the ship to make it look like an abandoned derelict, and then bring it in as salvage. According to maritime law, it's said, they will get half the ship's value – $1 million – as prize money.

James Mason, who has been first officer on a trim Matson liner, is flown to Australia to take charge of this dingy vessel when its captain mysteriously dies. He quickly discovers he is in for trouble from a lacklustre and sullen crew, trouble that is compounded by taking aboard a native Maori cook and his wife, latter being Dorothy Dandridge.

The story is faintly incredible at times and there is a tendency to impose dialog on a scene when the action has already spoken for itself. But the picture moves swiftly and absorbingly.

■ DECLINE AND FALL

1968, 90 MINS, US ◇

Dir John Krish *Prod* Ivan Foxwell *Scr* Ivan Foxwell, Alan Hackney, Hugh Whitemore *Ph* Desmond Dickinson *Ed* Archie Ludski *Mus* Ron Goodwin *Art Dir* John Barry
● Robin Phillips, Genevieve Page, Donald Wolfit, Colin Blakely, Patience Collier, Leo McKern (20th Century-Fox)

This humorous and elegantly-confectioned adaptation of Evelyn Waugh's first (1928) literary success makes for a witty bundle of entertainment for discriminating audiences in search of tongue-in-cheek entertainment.

Writer-producer Ivan Foxwell has opted for a lightweight, spoofy approach to the Waugh story, with the result that everything is played one stop further out than normal. Consequently, some of the story's absurdities become almost acceptable in the context.

Pace is sprightly as we follow Paul Pennyfeather, the schoolboy who becomes teacher, then foil for a dazzling white slaver, then jailbird until his final rebirth as, literally, a different man.

Robin Phillips, in his first pic role, is excellent as the scapegoat predestined to a bitter-

D

sweet fate. Genevieve Page is as elegant and alluring as ever in another tailor-cast role as the source of most of Paul's troubles.

John Krish's direction helps underline the spoofish plot elements.

．．．．．．．．．．．．．．．．．．．．．．．．．．．．．

■ **DECLINE OF WESTERN CIVILIZATION, THE**

1981, 100 MINS, US ◇

Dir Penelope Spheeris   *Prod* Penelope Spheeris   *Ph* Steve Conant   *Ed* Charles Mullin, Peter Wiehl
(Spheeris)

A bracing, stimulating and technically superb close-up look at the LA punk scene, pic is pitched at a perfect distance to allow for simultaneous engagement in the music and spectacle, and for rueful contemplation of what it all might mean.

Artistic strategy here is to combine provocative performance footage with 'at home' interviews with punk group members and talks with club owners, managers, critics and hardcore fans.

Film constitutes a 100-minute total immersion in the indigenous California punk world.

While a few of the rockers come off as artificial poseurs, many more surprise through revealing articulation of whys and wherefores of their lifestyle, and what comes through most strongly is purity of their dedication to their music.

Given top-notch craftsmanship, it's hard to believe effort was made independently for $100,000, and well-nigh impossible to detect that 35mm print is a 16mm blowup.

．．．．．．．．．．．．．．．．．．．．．．．．．．．．．

■ **DEEP, THE**

1977, 124 MINS, US ◇ Ⓥ

Dir Peter Yates   *Prod* Peter Guber   *Scr* Peter Benchley, Tracy Keenan Wynn   *Ph* Christopher Challis   *Ed* David Berlatsky   *Mus* John Barry   *Art Dir* Tony Masters
● Robert Shaw, Jacqueline Bisset, Nick Nolte, Louis Gossett, Eli Wallach, Robert Tessier (Columbia-EMI)

The Deep is an efficient but rather colorless film based on the Peter Benchley novel about a perilous search for treasure in the waters off Bermuda.

Fully 40% of the film takes place underwater, and the actors and crew learned how to dive, playing long scenes without dialog on the ocean floor. Director Peter Yates keeps up the tension in a low-key way – with a few shocker moments thrown in from time to time – and these scenes are more involving than the ones above the surface.

It's possible that inside this slick piece of engineering there is a genuinely mordant satire of human greed struggling to get out, but it never quite gets to the surface.

．．．．．．．．．．．．．．．．．．．．．．．．．．．．．

■ **DEEP END**

1970, 90 MINS, W. GERMANY/US ◇ Ⓥ

Dir Jerzy Skolimowski   *Prod* Maran Film-COKG-Kettledrum   *Scr* Jerzy Skolimowski, Jerzy Gruza, B. Sulik   *Ph* Charly Steinberger   *Mus* Cat Ten
● Jane Asher, John Moulder-Brown, Karl Michael Vogler, Christopher Sandford (Maran/COKG/Kettledrum)

Though its main locale is a rather seamy London public bath, director Jerzy Skolimowski has avoided tawdriness by a sympathy in, and awareness of, the excessive but essentially pure actions of his love-smitten boy whose good looks make him prey for all types of women who come for their public ablutions.

Film gives the British scene a twist due to Skolimowski's treatment of the tangled desires of a young boy whose need for love goes to a rather vulgar, but enticing fellow worker at the baths.

John Moulder-Brown has the deep voice of the time between puberty and manhood and the childish yet dedicated pursuit of his first deeply troubled reaction to a woman.

Skolimowski keeps the film alive with quirky incidents.

．．．．．．．．．．．．．．．．．．．．．．．．．．．．．

■ **DEEP THROAT**

1972, 73 MINS, US ◇

Dir Jerry Gerard [=Gerard Damiano]   *Prod* Lou Perry   *Scr* Jerry Gerard   *Ph* Harry Flecks   *Ed* Jerry Gerard   *Art Dir* Len Camp
● Linda Lovelace (Vanguard)

While *Deep Throat* doesn't quite live up to its reputation as the *Ben-Hur* of porno pix, it is a superior piece which stands a head above the competition.

Pic takes a tongue-in-cheek approach to conventional hetero hardcore, dishing out enough laughs with the main course to prove sexpo features need as much comic relief as suspenders.

Plot centers on a young lady disappointed because she fails to 'hear bells' during her repeated sex bouts with as many as 14 men at a time.

Pic's technical quality is above par, including sharp color photography and a satirical musical score which spoofs, among other things, Coca-Cola's 'It's the Real Thing' television commercial.

Performances are spirited, especially that of the femme lead, and writer-director-editor Jerry Gerard puts it all together with some style.

．．．．．．．．．．．．．．．．．．．．．．．．．．．．．

■ **DEEPSTAR SIX**

1989, 100 MINS, US ◇ Ⓥ

Dir Sean S. Cunningham   *Prod* Sean S. Cunningham, Patrick Markey   *Scr* Lewis Abernathy, Geof Miller   *Ph* Mac Ahlberg   *Ed* David Handman   *Mus* Harry Manfredini   *Art Dir* John Reinhart
● Taurean Blacque, Nancy Everhard, Greg Evigan, Miguel Ferrer, Nia Peeples, Cindy Pickett (Carolco)

Director-producer Sean Cunningham molds this tale of a sea monster attacking an ocean-bottom research team [story by Lewis Abernathy].

Crew, while trying to create a level launch site for some ocean-floor navy missiles, blows up a cavern in which the creature has been dwelling for eons. Enraged, it attacks their craft, manages to get inside, and more or less picks them off one by one.

But effect is diluted by implausibility, as creature never seems real – more like a goof on a 1950s horror movie monster than a true threat.

Pic's cast is a grab-bag ensemble with no real center (topliers Taurean Blacque is killed early on). It eventually finds its emotional core in an affair between crewmen Greg Evigan and Nancy Everhard. A sharp performance by Miguel Ferrer as a punchy, smartmouthed crewmen is diluted when character goes campily berserk.

．．．．．．．．．．．．．．．．．．．．．．．．．．．．．

■ **DEER HUNTER, THE**

1978, 183 MINS, US ◇ Ⓥ

Dir Michael Cimino   *Prod* Barry Spikings, Michael Deeley, Michael Cimino, John Peverall   *Scr* Deric Washburn   *Ph* Vilmos Zsigmond   *Ed* Peter Zinner   *Mus* Stanley Myers   *Art Dir* Ron Hobbs, Kim Swados
● Robert De Niro, John Cazale, John Savage, Christopher Walken, Meryl Streep, George Dzundza (Universal/EMI)

Among the considerable achievements of Michael Cimino's *The Deer Hunter* is the fact that the film remains intense, powerful and fascinating for more than three hours.

The picture is a long, sprawling epic-type in many ways more novel than motion picture. It employs literary references stylistically, forecasting events which will happen in the film.

It is a brutal work. Robert De Niro, John Cazale, John Savage and Christopher Walken head cast as friends living in a small Pennsylvania town. They attend a Russian Orthodox wedding at the beginning of the film. Directly afterwards three of them go deer hunting and soon afterwards they are to serve in Vietnam.

While in Southeast Asia, the trio is reunited during a battle scene and later captured by the Vietcong. As POWs they are forced to play a form of Russian roulette.

Throughout the film various ceremonies and cultural rituals are explored, compared and juxtaposed – the wedding, the game and the deer hunt. It is up to the viewer to decide how these rituals fit together and it is a big comprehension demand.

Many will wish that the screenplay by Deric Washburn were a bit more straightforward. Still, the film is ambitious and it succeeds on a number of levels and it proves that Cimino is an important director.
□ 1978: Best Picture

．．．．．．．．．．．．．．．．．．．．．．．．．．．．．

■ **DEFECTOR, THE**

1966, 108 MINS, W. GERMANY/FRANCE ◇

Dir Raoul Levy   *Prod* Raoul Levy   *Scr* Robert Guenette, Raoul Levy   *Ph* Raoul Coutard   *Ed* Albert Jurgenson, Roger Dwyre   *Mus* Serge Gainsbourg   *Art Dir* Pierre Guffroy
● Montgomery Clift, Hardy Kruger, Macha Meril, Roddy McDowall, David Opatoshu, Christine Delaroche (PECF/Rhein-Main)

The last motion picture made by Montgomery Clift prior to his death, *Defector* provides a part that allows him to substitute action of body and mind for the immobility of facial expression that clouded this fine actor's performances during his last years. His taut, troubled face is perfect for the role of a scientist pushed into espionage by his own country and almost erased from it by enemy agents.

Levy and Robert Guenette's collaboration on an adaptation of Paul Thomas's *The Spy* has gone for 'suspense' at the sacrifice of logic. Just plain logical loopholes appear that may escape most viewers but will disturb some.

Most of the intellectual byplay is between Clift, as an American scientist, and Hardy Kruger, as the German-born Russian agent given the assignment of getting Clift to defect. The physical action comes from Clift's evasion of the security police and his attempt to escape from East Germany. Kruger makes an excellent contrast, in his cool behavior, to Clift's nervousness.

．．．．．．．．．．．．．．．．．．．．．．．．．．．．．

■ **DEFENCE OF THE REALM**

1985, 96 MINS, UK ◇ Ⓥ

Dir David Drury   *Prod* Robin Douet, Lynda Myles   *Scr* Martin Stellman   *Ph* Roger Deakins   *Ed* Michael Bradsell   *Mus* Richard Hartley   *Art Dir* Roger Murray-Leach
● Gabriel Byrne, Greta Scacchi, Denholm Elliott, Ian Bannen, Fulton MacKay, Bill Paterson (Enigma/NFFC)

The state of the nation's press and the evil antics of its secret services in the nuclear age are combined in this fast-paced thriller.

Script unravels a relatively uncomplicated story of events following the near crash of a nuclear bomber on an American airforce base in the English countryside. A left-wing MP who gets wind of the event is framed as a Russian spy and forced to resign. His journalist friend is bumped off secretly shortly before publishing details of the incident.

The story centers on a younger hack who enjoys the triumph of cracking the link between parliamentarian Markham and a Russian agent, only to discover after the death of his friend that he has been set up by the secret services.

A female character, Nina Beckman (Greta Scacchi), is strangely marginal. By the time she enters center stage as Mullen's journalistic accomplice, her only function is to tie up a few loose ends.

Gabriel Byrne is somewhat one-dimensional as Mullen. He's a perfect foil, however, to the older journalist caught between friendship, the truth and his career. Denholm Elliott gives an extraordinary performance in that role.

■ **DEFIANT ONES, THE**

1958, 97 MINS, US Ⓥ

Dir Stanley Kramer   *Prod* Stanley Kramer
Scr Nathan E. Douglas, Harold Jacob Smith   *Ph* Sam
Leavitt   *Ed* Frederic Knudtson   *Mus* Ernest Gold
Prod Des Rudolph Sternad
● Tony Curtis, Sidney Poitier, Theodore Bikel, Charles
McGraw, Cara Williams, Claude Akins (United Artists)

The theme of *The Defiant Ones* is that what keeps men apart is their lack of knowledge of one another. With that knowledge comes respect, and with respect comradeship and even love. This thesis is exercised in terms of a colored and a white man, both convicts chained together as they make their break for freedom from a Southern prison gang.

The performances by Tony Curtis and Sidney Poitier are virtually flawless. Poitier captures all of the moody violence of the convict, serving time because he assaulted a white man who had insulted him. It is a cunning, totally intelligent portrayal that rings powerfully true.

As 'Jocker' Jackson, the arrogant white man chained to a fellow convict whom he hates, Curtis delivers a true surprise performance. He starts off as a sneering, brutal character, willing to fight it out to-the-death with his equally stubborn companion. When, in the end, he sacrifices a dash for freedom to save Poitier, he has managed the transition with such skill that sympathy is completely with him.

Picture has other surprises, not the least of which is Kramer's sensitive and skilled direction, this being only his third try at calling the scenes. The scenes of Poitier and Curtis groping their way painfully out of a deep clay pit, their perilous journey down the river, as well as their clumsy attempt to break into a store and the subsequent near-lynch scene, become integral parts of the larger chase, for the posse is never far behind.

☐ 1958: Best Picture (Nomination)

■ **DELINQUENTS, THE**

1989, 101 MINS, AUSTRALIA ◇ Ⓥ

Dir Chris Thomson   *Prod* Alex Cutler, Michael Wilcox
Scr Clayton Frohman, Mac Gudgeon   *Ph* Andrew
Lesnie   *Ed* John Scott   *Mus* Miles Goodman
Art Dir Laurence Eastwood
● Kylie Minogue, Charlie Schlatter, Angela Punch-
McGregor, Bruno Lawrence, Desiree Smith, Todd Boyce
(Village-Roadster/Silver Lining)

The story, set in the late 1950s, about the passionate love affair of a couple of teens, is trite stuff. Lola (Kylie Minogue) and Brownie (Charlie Schlatter) live in the small town of Bundaberg in Queensland. She's still at school when they become lovers and she gets pregnant. The youngsters plan to elope, but are parted by Lola's alcoholic mother (Angela Punch-McGregor), who forces her daughter to have a backstreet abortion (offscreen).

Brownie goes to sea in despair. However, he happens to walk into a Melbourne bar one night and sees Lola, her hair bleached, sadder but wiser. Love blossoms again but, once more, the lovers are parted by the authorities.

The screenplay [from a novel by Criena Rohan] is repetitive and tame. There's no hint of genuine passion between the young lovers. Far more interesting characters are Mavis (Desiree Smith) and Lyle (Todd Boyce), who befriend Lola and Brownie. Their scenes have a warmth that's lacking in the central relationship.

Technically, pic is good, with great care taken to make the late 1950s setting as authentic as possible.

■ **DELIVERANCE**

1972, 109 MINS, US ◇

Dir John Boorman   *Prod* John Boorman   *Scr* James
Dickey   *Ph* Vilmos Zsigmond   *Ed* Tom Priestley   *Art
Dir* Fred Harpman
● Jon Voight, Burt Reynolds, Ned Beatty, Ronny Cox,
Billy McKinney, James Dickey (Warner)

Deliverance can be considered a stark, uncompromising showdown between basic survival instincts against the character pretensions of a mannered and material society. Unfortunately for John Boorman's heavy film of James Dickey's first novel, it can just as easily be argued as a virile, mountain country transposition of nihilistic, specious philosophising which exploits rather than explores its moments of violent drama.

Against the majestic setting of a river being dammed, Dickey's story takes four city men out for a last weekend trip down the river. Unexpected malevolence forces each to test his personal values in order to survive.

It is, however, in the fleshing out that the script fumbles, and with it the direction and acting. The unofficial group leader of the sailing trip is Burt Reynolds, a volatile, calculating, aggressive and offensive tempter of fate.

Why the best friend Jon Voight would maintain an apparent longstanding relationship with Reynolds' character is an early plot chuck-hole.

What makes for a pervading uneasiness is the implication of the story: the strongest shall survive. The values of Reynolds' character are repulsive; Ronny Cox is a cardboard-cutout as an intellectual type; Ned Beatty is the easy-going, middle-class figurehead patronized by both the 'doers' and the 'thinkers' of the world; leaving Voight apparently as the one to lead them out of travail.

In the depiction of sudden, violent death, there is the rhapsodic wallowing in the deadly beauty of it all: protruding arrows, agonizing expiration, etc. It's the stuff of which slapdash oaters and crime programmers are made but the obvious ambitions of *Deliverance* are supposed to be on a higher plane.

☐ 1972: Best Picture (Nomination)

■ **DELTA FORCE, THE**

1986, 129 MINS, US ◇ Ⓥ

Dir Menahem Golan   *Prod* Menahem Golan, Yoram
Globus   *Scr* James Bruner, Menahem Golan
Ph David Gurfinkel   *Ed* Alain Jakubowicz   *Mus* Alan
Silvestri   *Art Dir* Luciano Spadoni
● Chuck Norris, Lee Marvin, Martin Balsam, Joey
Bishop, Robert Forster, Lainie Kazan (Cannon)

Directed with the throttle wide open, pic roots itself firmly in very fresh history, then proceeds to brashly rewrite it, thereby turning itself into an exercise in wish fulfilment for those who favor using force instead of diplomacy.

First hour is mostly devoted to what seems to be a quite accurate rendition of the 1985 TWA Athens hijacking.

From here, film is purest fantasy pitting the noble Yankees against the dirty, low-down Palestinians. In an attempt at 'make my day' immortality, Chuck Norris growls at one of them, 'Sleep tight, sucker,' before blowing

him away, and gets a chance to make ample use of his martial arts skills.

■ **DELTA FORCE 2**
THE COLOMBIAN CONNECTION

1990, 105 MINS, US ◇ Ⓥ

Dir Aaron Norris   *Prod* Yoram Globus, Christopher
Pearce   *Scr* Lee Reynolds   *Ph* Joao Fernandes
Ed Michael J. Duthie   *Mus* Frederic Talgorn
● Chuck Norris, Billy Drago, Bobby Chavez, John R.
Ryan, Richard Jaeckel (Cannon)

Chuck Norris fans have all they could ask for with *Delta Force 2*. Norris and a dozen US marines fly into the South American drug capital San Carlos, destroy half the country's cocaine production, and rub out the land's untouchable drug czar, in a carthartic blaze of exploding missiles and flying fists.

(During the filming, five people were killed in a 15 May 1989, helicopter crash in the Philippines: pilot Jo Jo Imperial, stuntmen Geoffrey Brewer, Mike Graham and Gadi Danzig, and gaffer Don Marshall. Three others were injured.)

Production values are high with an endless stream of ammunition and extras. Lensing is pro, and score has a tropical flavor that stays pleasantly in the background.

Norris is a minimalist actor, rightly concentrating on the action. As the sadistic Coda, Billy Drago has a Medusa-like presence that produces shivers just from looking at him.

■ **DEMETRIUS AND THE GLADIATORS**

1954, 101 MINS, US ◇ Ⓥ

Dir Delmer Daves   *Prod* Frank Ross   *Scr* Philip
Dunne   *Ph* Milton Krasner   *Ed* Dorothy Spencer,
Robert Fritch   *Mus* Franz Waxman
● Victor Mature, Susan Hayward, Michael Rennie,
Debra Paget, Anne Bancroft, Jay Robinson (20th
Century-Fox)

Demetrius and the Gladiators is 20th-Fox's answer and followup to its tremendously successful *The Robe*. While Lloyd C. Douglas's fine novel from which 20th-Fox and Frank Ross filmed *The Robe* springboards this followup, it is a completely new story.

In the compelling screen story, and under the equally compelling direction by Delmer Daves, *Demetrius* swings from *The Robe*'s mysterious, religious miracle theme of the crucifixion, to a story of the trial of a man's faith by the temptations of an attractive, amoral woman and a pagan Rome.

Victor Mature again scores with the character of the slave. A mighty man is he battling three huge tigers in the Roman arena to satisfy the mad urges of the crazy Emperor Caligula and the wicked Messalina, dueling to the death with five of Rome's best gladiators, or making love to the same wicked temptress who has temporarily caused him to forget his God.

With Mature easily winning top acting honors for his splendidly projected Demetrius, he is pressed by Susan Hayward as the evil Messalina, and Jay Robinson, repeating his mad, effeminate Caligula.

■ **DEMON SEED**

1977, 94 MINS, US ◇ Ⓥ

Dir Donald Cammell   *Prod* Herb Jaffe   *Scr* Ronald
Jaffe, Roger O. Hirson   *Ph* Bill Butler   *Ed* Francisco
Mazzola   *Mus* Jerry Fielding   *Art Dir* Edward C.
Carfagno
● Julie Christie, Fritz Weaver, Gerrit Graham, Berry
Kroeger, Lisa Lu, Larry J. Blake (M-G-M)

Demon Seed tells of the impregnation of a female by a master computer system which seeks to perpetuate itself in human form.

D

Julie Christie stars as the electronic Eve, along with Fritz Weaver as her scientist husband.

Excellent performances and direction (Donald Cammell), from a most credible and literate screenplay [from a novel by Dean R. Koontz], make production an intriguing achievement in story-telling.

Christie and Weaver live adjacent to an advanced computer center. Their marriage is crumbling because of his commitment to a new machine, Proteus IV, designed to do almost everything but think.

The burden of the story falls on Christie and she does indeed make the film come off.

....

■ **DE SADE**

1969, 113 MINS, US/W. GERMANY ◇

Dir Cy Endfield   *Prod* Samuel Z. Arkoff   *Scr* Richard Matheson   *Ph* Richard Angst   *Ed* Max Benedict, Hermann Haller   *Mus* Billy Strange   *Art Dir* Juergen Kiebach

● Keir Dullea, Senta Berger, Lilli Palmer, Anna Massey, Sonja Ziemann, Uta Levka (American International/ CCC/TransContinental)

Pseudo-biography of the young French whippersnapper whose name became a household word. The film transcends reality. Chronology is warped in a continuum of time, fantasy, madness, staged drama and historical incidents.

Dullea's idea of a good time is to dive into a pile of nude women with his pants on, spank a few bottoms, pour wine over everybody, and howl his head off.

De Sade's rather exotic tastes were aggravated by a family-arranged marriage to a very rich girl (Anna Massey) with whose sister (Senta Berger) Dullea is in love.

Lilli Palmer is the mother of both girls, struggling to uphold the family respectability in the midst of her son-in-law's now publicly known debauches. She imparts dignity, strength and, in the end, sympathy to what is written as an unsympathetic role.

....

■ **DESERT BLOOM**

1986, 104 MINS, US ◇ Ⓥ

Dir Eugene Corr   *Prod* Michael Hausman   *Scr* Eugene Corr   *Ph* Reynaldo Villalobos   *Ed* David Garfield, John Currin, Cari Coughlin   *Mus* Brad Fiedel   *Art Dir* Lawrence Miller

● Jon Voight, JoBeth Williams, Ellen Barkin, Allen Garfield, Annabeth Gish (Carson/Columbia Delphi IV)

Desert Bloom emerges a muted, intelligently observed story of a girl's growing pains in an emotionally deprived and politically warped environment.

Arid setting in question is Las Vegas, 1950, where Second World War vet Jon Voight runs a gas station and is stepfather to JoBeth Williams' three daughters, the oldest of whom is the 13-year-old Rose, played by Annabeth Gish.

Big events in the household are the arrival of the girls' Aunt Starr (Ellen Barkin), a glamorous showgirl type who will live with the family for the 42 days necessary to obtain a quickie divorce, and the impending atmospheric A-bomb test, for which the entire community is preparing as if it were the second coming.

Due to her good housewife role, Williams can do little but be overshadowed by Barkin, who delivers a wonderfully splashy turn as the unlucky but resilient sexpot. Gish is a find as Rose. Obviously bright and physically reminiscent of another actress of about the same age, Jennifer Connelly, she almost singlehandedly lends the film its intelligent air and makes one root for Rose to survive her squalid upbringing.

....

■ **DESERT FOX, THE**

1951, 88 MINS, US Ⓥ

Dir Henry Hathaway   *Prod* Nunnally Johnson   *Scr* Nunnally Johnson   *Ph* Norbert Brodine   *Ed* James B. Clark   *Mus* Daniele Amfitheatrof   *Art Dir* Lyle Wheeler, Maurice Ransford

● James Mason, Cedric Hardwicke, Jessica Tandy, Luther Adler, Everett Sloane, Leo G. Carroll (20th Century-Fox)

The story of Field Marshal Erwin Rommel, as biographed by Brigadier Desmond Young, comes to the screen as an episodic documentary difficult to follow or understand. A controversial angle is posed by the sympathetic pitch made for Rommel by Young, and the whitewashing given a number of Nazi military leaders previously charged with being war criminals by the British.

Battle action in the film is very good, both that concocted in the studio and that snatched from actual war footage. Picture gets off to an unusually sock opening, depicting the November 1941 raid on Rommel's North African headquarters by British Commandos. This all takes place before the title and credits are flashed but the promise is not borne out for a solid war film after narration and episodic character study take over.

Performances are good, with James Mason's portrait of the Desert Fox extremely able within the shadowy confines of the script. His scenes with Jessica Tandy, playing Frau Rommel, have sound emotional value through the underplaying of both performers. Luther Adler's screaming, hysterical Hitler also is good, although confined to brief footage.

....

■ **DESERT HEARTS**

1985, 93 MINS, US ◇ Ⓥ

Dir Donna Deitch   *Prod* Donna Deitch   *Scr* Natalie Cooper   *Ph* Robert Elswit   *Ed* Robert Estrin   *Mus* Robert Estrin (sup.)   *Art Dir* Jeannine Oppewall

● Helen Shaver, Patricia Charbonneau, Audra Lindley, Andra Akers, Dean Butler, Katie La Bourdette (Goldwyn/Desert Hearts)

The plot focuses on a guest at a Nevada ranch, Vivian Bell, an English Literature lecturer from New York, frozen stiff by middle class morality and inbred prejudices, and totally confused by the drastic step she is about to take at the age of 35. She is about to get divorced.

To make matters much worse for her, once on the ranch she catches the fancy of the owner's adoptive daughter, who starts making advances, first timidly and then in a pressing fashion, until the prim, respectable East Coast intellectual has to drop her armour and face her own latent homosexuality.

Since the story [from the novel *Desert of the Heart* by Jane Rule] is placed in the 1950s, it is clear that what, by today's standards, would have been an unconventional but by no means an exceptional case, becomes an act of defiance against the accepted rules of society.

Helen Shaver, playing the lead, does a most commendable job as a character who starts by being all tied up inside, and ends up by melting and opening up to emotions she couldn't even conceive before.

Patricia Charbonneau, as the avowed lesbian desperate for true affection in female companionship, tends to look too much like the spoiled brat who will have her own way.

....

■ **DESERT RATS, THE**

1953, 88 MINS, US Ⓥ

Dir Robert Wise   *Prod* Robert L. Jacks   *Scr* Richard Murphy   *Ph* Lucien Ballard   *Ed* Barbara McLean   *Mus* Leigh Harline   *Art Dir* Lyle R. Wheeler, Addison Hehr

● Richard Burton, Robert Newton, Robert Douglas,

James Mason, Torin Thatcher, Chips Rafferty (20th Century-Fox)

Battle of Tobruk is fought in *The Desert Rats* as a followup, but not a sequel, to *The Desert Fox*, the 1951 Field Marshal Rommel feature. Picture is a rather impersonal account of warfare that lacks the controversial flavor of the Rommel treatment. War scenes are realistically staged under Robert Wise's direction, and a high spot in this action is a commando raid on a Nazi ammunition dump.

James Mason is back to repeat his Rommel characterization, but appears only in a few scenes to tie the Tobruk battle in with the Nazi plan of conquest that fell in the desert because of the stubbornness of men on the other side who fought back against terrific odds. Mason's work is good, and Richard Burton is excellent as the British captain in charge of the Australian troops that resist attacks on Tobruk. Robert Newton figures as the third star, playing a drunken old schoolteacher of Burton's, whose cowardice poses a problem for the young officer.

....

■ **DESERT SONG, THE**

1943, 90 MINS, US ◇

Dir Robert Florey   *Prod* Robert Florey   *Scr* Robert Buckner   *Ph* Bert Glennon   *Ed* Frank Magee   *Mus* Sigmund Romberg   *Art Dir* Charles Novi

● Dennis Morgan, Irene Manning, Bruce Cabot, Victor Francen, Lynn Overman (Warner)

In modernizing story, German agents and plans to construct new railroad in North Africa for terminus at Dakar provide motivation for Riff uprising and leadership by Dennis Morgan, an American piano player in Morocco nightspot, who's been fighting Franco in Spain prior to moving across the Mediterranean to Africa. Irene Manning is the new singer at the cafe, with mutual romance developing.

Riffs are rounded up by French officers to work on the railroad, with native Victor Francen, a tool of the Nazis, impressing the natives to work. But Morgan, as El Khobar, leader of the Riffs, circumvents the plans by periodic appearances on the desert and in Morocco to lead the natives in revolt against the forced labor regulations. From there on it's series of chases across the desert sands, pitched battles, and wild adventure.

Despite modernization to provide film technique and movement to the operetta, basic entertainment qualities of *Desert Song* are retained to provide most diverting audience reaction at this time.

Morgan is neatly cast as the Red Rider, delivering both dramatic and vocal assignments in top style. Manning capably handles the girl spot as singer and actress.

....

■ **DESERT SONG, THE**

1953, 110 MINS, US ◇

Dir Bruce Humberstone   *Prod* Rudi Fehr   *Scr* Roland Kibbee   *Ph* Robert Burks   *Ed* William Ziegler   *Mus* Max Steiner (adapt.)   *Art Dir* Stanley Fleischer

● Kathryn Grayson, Gordon MacRae, Steve Cochran, Raymond Massey (Warner)

After two times around as a film vehicle, once in 1929 and again in 1943, this venerable romantic musical has just about run out of entertainment vitamins. Both story and the songs are well-worn. Latter wear their age with charm and are nicely delivered by Kathryn Grayson and Gordon MacRae, but aren't of sufficient impact to create much of a stir in this era. Listening best are the title number, 'The Riff Song' and 'One Alone', as well as added Jack Scholl-Serge Walter cleffing, 'Gay Parisienne', which Grayson uses as a special piece.

Making a pretty picture is Grayson, and she serves up her tunes well. MacRae is unbelievable as the mysterious Riff leader, but fares better on the songs. Steve Cochran also has a hard time making anything out of his French legionnaire role, a character who is bothered by Grayson, the general's flighty daughter, and by the fact he can't capture the Riff hero who plays Robin Hood to the natives oppressed by Raymond Massey, a cruel sheik who is plotting to overthrow the French.

....

■ DESIGN FOR LIVING

1933, 90 MINS, US

Dir Ernst Lubitsch   *Prod* Ernst Lubitsch   *Scr* Ben Hecht   *Ph* Victor Milner   *Ed* Francis Marsh
● Fredric March, Gary Cooper, Miriam Hopkins, Edward Everett Horton, Franklin Pangborn, Isabel Jewell (Paramount)

Ben Hecht's screen treatment has transmuted Noel Coward's idea better than Coward's original play. It's a competent job in every respect. What matter it – or perhaps it does – if Hecht threw Coward's manuscript out the window and set about writing a brand new play? The dialog is less lofty, less epigramatic, less artificial. There's more reality.

Coward, of course, has contributed a basic premise that's arresting – a girl and two men all of whom are very fond of each other. Edward Everett Horton, as the patient mentor of the girl (or, as the dialog puts it, 'in other words, you never got to first base'), is built up here, as much by the script as his own personal histrionic dominance.

Miriam Hopkins' expert handling of the delicate premise which motivates the other three men is a consummate performance in every respect. She glosses over the dirt, but gets the punch over none the less. She confesses quite naively she is stumped – she likes both Tom and George (Fredric March and Gary Cooper).

Hecht patterns Cooper to a rugged chapeau and March to a more formal top-piece, and Hopkins interprets her reactions in relation to wearing one type of hat or another with the shifting moods.

....

■ DESIRE

1936, 95 MINS, US

Dir Frank Borzage   *Prod* Ernst Lubitsch   *Scr* Edwin Justus Mayer, Waldemar Young, Samuel Hoffenstein   *Ph* Charles Lang   *Ed* William Shea   *Mus* Frederick Hollander   *Art Dir* Hans Dreier, Robert Usher
● Marlene Dietrich, Gary Cooper, John Halliday, William Frawley, Ernest Cossart (Paramount)

Desire is the first Marlene Dietrich and Gary Cooper picture since *Morocco* (1930). The two stars work unusually well as a pair.

The direction is subtle and inspired, with many smart little Lubitschian touches adding to the general appeal of the yarn [by Hans Szekely and R.A. Stemmle] and its plot. Dietrich plays a jewel thief who gains possession of a valuable string of pearls. About half the footage is concerned with the efforts of Dietrich and a confederate to retrieve the pearls from Cooper who unknowingly has become their custodian.

The love scenes are excellently handled and written. A very good sequence is framed for the meeting between Cooper and the bogus nobleman, her accomplice, while another occurs later when efforts are made to get the two stars out of their beds one morning. The hand of producer Ernst Lubitsch is apparent here and in many other portions of the smartly-piloted romantic comedy.

....

■ DESIRE ME

1947, 90 MINS, US

Dir [George Cukor, Mervyn LeRoy, Jack Conway]   *Prod* Arthur Hornblow Jr   *Scr* Marguerite Roberts, Zoe Akins   *Ph* Joseph Ruttenberg   *Ed* Joseph Dervin

Mus Herbert Stothart   *Art Dir* Cedric Gibbons, Urie McCleary
● Greer Garson, Robert Mitchum, Richard Hart (M-G-M)

Against the technical excellence of mounting, a confused flashback plot [based on the novel, '*Karl und Anna*', by Leonhard Frank] is unfolded. Offered is a story of a wife who, after long years of faithful waiting, succumbs to lonesomeness on the eve of her supposedly dead husband's return from war. The husband kills his rival in a struggle. Locale is a small fishing village on the coast of Normandy and catches interest with colorful settings and seascapes.

Flashbacks within flashbacks make plot hard to follow as the wife talks over her story – and what caused it – with a doctor. There is no director credit, picture having had several during its long camera career, so kudos for some topnotch atmospheric effects, a number of strong, emotional scenes and occasional suspense go uncredited. George Cukor started it and Mervyn LeRoy finished it, but neither wants the credit apparently. Otherwise pace is slow and interest slack.

Greer Garson's role requires continual emotional stress that makes for a heavy job but she is capable. Robert Mitchum has too little footage as the husband but he makes every scene count. Richard Hart, the betrayer of the faithful wife, is permitted to overstress his designs where underplaying would have aided.

....

■ DESIRE UNDER THE ELMS

1958, 111 MINS, US

Dir Delbert Mann   *Prod* Don Hartman   *Scr* Irwin Shaw   *Ph* Daniel L. Fapp   *Ed* George Boemler   *Mus* Elmer Bernstein   *Art Dir* Hal Pereira, J. McMillan Johnson
● Sophia Loren, Anthony Perkins, Burl Ives, Frank Overton, Pernell Roberts, Rebecca Welles (Paramount)

Despite all the plus factors, *Desire under the Elms* is not satisfactory entertainment. It is painfully slow in getting underway, the characters are never completely understandable or believable, and the ghastly plot climax (of infanticide) plays with disappointingly little force.

Eugene O'Neill's play has been given a reverent translation. But Irwin Shaw, who did the screenplay, has not improved the story. O'Neill wrote a modern version of a Greek tragedy, as raw and chilling as anything in *Oedipus* or *Medea*. He chose the craggy New England of 1840 and its flinty characters with care. The casting of Sophia Loren in the role of the young (third) wife of farmer Burl Ives is a key error because it injects an alien-to-the-scene element that dislocates the drama permanently.

The passion of greed and lust that takes place, in which Anthony Perkins and Loren embark on a semi-incestuous love affair that ends with Loren's having a child that Ives thinks is his, has been handled with discretion. Too much, perhaps.

O'Neill saw it as men fighting the gods and losing. Shaw apparently sees it as men understood through modern psychology, still doomed and damned, but for different reasons.

Despite Loren's unsuitability for the play, she exposes a great variety of emotion and manages the scenes of tenderness with special value. Perkins' character is not as exciting or vivid as it should be. Ives is the best, a bull of a man, cold in emotion and hot in passion.

....

■ DESPAIR

1978, 119 MINS, W. GERMANY ◇ ⓥ

Dir Rainer Werner Fassbinder   *Scr* Tom Stoppard   *Ph* Michael Ballhaus   *Ed* Juliane Lorrenz, Franz Walsch   *Mus* Peer Raben   *Art Dir* Rolf Zehetbauer

● Dirk Bogarde, Andrea Ferreol, Volker Spengler, Klaus Lowitsch (Bavaria Atelier/SFP/Geria)

Despite a witty, albeit theatrical, script by Tom Stoppard, prolific German director Rainer Werner Fassbinder does not quite bring off the spirited linguistic innovations, wit and penetrating insights of Vladimir Nabokov's novel; but it is a good try. This tale of an exiled Russian in Germany in the late 1920s, who is driven to a weird murder, emerges over-long.

Dirk Bogarde, using a generally satisfactory Russo accent, has a pulpy, dim-witted, sensual wife, played in campy period style by Andrea Ferreol. He runs a chocolate factory that is going on the rocks as the Depression hits the world.

He has strange delusions of seeing another replica of himself watching his carryings-on with his wife or even imagining himself dressed as a budding Nazi going in for macho sadistic sexual actions.

He insures himself and then, on a business trip, meets a down-and-out whom, he thinks, looks just like him. He decides to use this man in a trumped-up action that may be a holdup but is aimed at killing the man, passing him off as himself and collecting his insurance.

....

■ DESPERATE HOURS, THE

1955, 112 MINS, US ⓥ

Dir William Wyler   *Prod* William Wyler   *Scr* Joseph Hayes   *Ph* Lee Garmes   *Ed* Robert Swink   *Mus* Gail Kubik   *Art Dir* Hal Pereira, Joseph MacMillan Johnson
● Humphrey Bogart, Fredric March, Arthur Kennedy, Martha Scott, Dewey Martin, Gig Young (Paramount)

Desperate Hours is an expert adaptation by Joseph Hayes of his own novel about three escaped desperadoes who gunpoint their way to temporary refuge in the suburban Indianapolis home of a respectable middleclass family.

This is a first for VistaVision in black and white. Wise, too, for color might have rendered less effective the strong fact-like appearance of *Hours*.

Wyler worked with major-league performers. This is Humphrey Bogart in the type of role that cues comics to caricature takeoffs. Here he's at his best, a tough gunman capable of murder, snarling delight with the way his captives must abide by his orders, and wise in the ways of self-preservation strategy.

Fredric March is powerful as head of the family, never before cited for bravery but now bent on protecting his family from the three intruders.

....

■ DESPERATE HOURS

1990, 105 MINS, US ◇ ⓥ

Dir Michael Cimino   *Prod* Dino De Laurentiis, Michael Cimino   *Scr* Laurence Konner, Mark Rosenthal, Joseph Hayes   *Ph* Doug Milsome   *Ed* Peter Hunt   *Mus* David Mansfield   *Art Dir* Victoria Paul
● Mickey Rourke, Anthony Hopkins, Mimi Rogers, Lindsay Crouse, Kelly Lynch, David Morse (De Laurentiis)

Desperate Hours is a coldly mechanical and uninvolving remake of the 1955 Bogart pic *The Desperate Hours*, with Mickey Rourke as the hood terrorizing a suburban family.

Joseph Hayes' plot (first written as a novel, then as a [1955] play) is pure 1950s paranoia about three scruffy guys who invade the sanctity of the home, mocking a family's helplessness until Dad reasserts his control. Despite being minimally updated with intensified blood and brutality on the part of the hoods and the authorities, *Desperate Hours* has no new insights to offer.

The clunky script doesn't permit any vestige of humanity to Rourke, who's portrayed as a simple psycho with a low flashpoint, viciously brutalizing his improbably gorgeous pro-bono lawyer (Kelly Lynch) even as she helps him escape from prison.

Anthony Hopkins, in the Fredric March role of the initially weak-seeming father, brings his formidable skills to the task of involving the audience in the family's terror, but he seems mismatched with his estranged wife Mimi Rogers and implausibly reckless in his defiance of Rourke.

In place of the original film's sheriff (Arthur Kennedy), who made it a priority to avoid endangering the lives of the hostages, the Cimino version has a demented FBI agent (Lindsay Crouse).

Doug Milsome contributes handsome lensing of the autumnal locations of the Colorado wilderness and suburban Salt Lake City (substituting for the Indianapolis setting of the original).

....

■ DESPERATELY SEEKING SUSAN

1985, 104 MINS, US ◇ ⓥ

Dir Susan Seidelman *Prod* Sarah Pillsbury, Midge Sanford *Scr* Leora Barish *Ph* Edward Lachman *Ed* Andrew Mondshein *Mus* Thomas Newman *Art Dir* Santo Loquasto
● Rosanna Arquette, Madonna, Aidan Quinn, Mark Blum, Robert Joy, Laurie Metcalf (Orion)

Rosanna Arquette does more than her share in the pivotal part of a bored Yuppie housewife who follows the personal ads, wondering about the identities behind a 'desperately seeking Susan' item that runs from time to time.

The ads are the way one boyfriend (Robert Joy) communicates with free-spirited Madonna between her street-life liaisons with other men, one of whom has been bumped off after stealing a pair of rare Egyptian earrings. Before his demise, Madonna has lifted the jewelry, thinking they are trinkets.

Drawn by curiosity to spy on Madonna, Arquette winds up with a bump on the head and a case of amnesia, complicated by the fact that Joy's pal Aidan Quinn thinks Arquette is Madonna and Arquette doesn't know she isn't.

All of this is cause for consistent smiling and a few outright laughs, without ever building to complete comedy. It's not clear either that director Susan Seidelman and writer Leora Barish ever intend for it to be funnier, so that can't be faulted.

....

■ DESTRY RIDES AGAIN

1939, 90MINS, US ⓥ

Dir George Marshall *Prod* Joseph Pasternak *Scr* Felix Jackson, Henry Meyers, Gertrude Purcell *Ph* Hal Mohr *Ed* Milton Carruth *Mus* Frank Skinner *Art Dir* Jack Otterson
● Marlene Dietrich, James Stewart, Charles Winninger, Mischa Auer, Brian Donlevy (Universal)

Destry Rides Again is anything but a super-western. It's just plain, good entertainment [from a novel by Max Brand], primed with action and laughs and human sentiment.

Marlene Dietrich's work as the hardened, ever-scrapping ginmill entertainer serves pretty much as the teeterboard from which this picture flips itself from the level of the ordinary western into a class item.

This gangster fable with an early West background revolves for the most part around the rowdy, gaudy ginmill and dance-hall which Brian Donlevy operates in the frontier town of Bottle Neck. With the aid of his No. 1 entertainer (Dietrich), Donlevy cuts a wide swath cheating the townsmen at cards and working a waterhole racket until he makes the mistake of appointing the town rumpot (Charles Winninger) the local sheriff.

....

■ DETECTIVE, THE

1968, 114 MINS, US ◇

Dir Gordon Douglas *Prod* Aaron Rosenberg *Scr* Abby Mann *Ph* Joseph Biroc *Ed* Robert Simpson *Mus* Jerry Goldsmith *Art Dir* Jack Martin Smith, William Creber
● Frank Sinatra, Lee Remick, Ralph Meeker, Jaqueline Bisset, Jack Klugman, Horace McMahon (20th Century-Fox)

Although extremely well cast, and fleshed out with some on-target dialog, Abby Mann's script is strictly potboiler material.

Homosexuality, police brutality, corruption in high places, and nymphomania are the peas in this literary shell game, which the admirable professional razzle-dazzle of direction, acting and, to an extent, editing, cannot sufficiently legitimize.

Jack Klugman and Frank Sinatra are the only honest cops portrayed. Ralph Meeker is on the take, Robert Duvall likes to bust 'queers,' and Al Freeman Jr decides in time that Nazi-style interrogation produces desired results.

Repeated plot digression – made bearable by the fact that it involves Lee Remick – explores Sinatra's unstable married life.

The promise of erudition in the first reel gives way to programmer superficiality about the two main themes. For one thing, homosexuality is depicted as rampant in either truck stops, or else cheaply elegant salons. Also, the plot is heavily weighted against the police.

....

■ DETECTIVE STORY

1951, 105 MINS, US ⓥ

Dir William Wyler *Prod* William Wyler *Scr* Philip Yordan, Robert Wyler *Ph* Lee Garmes *Ed* Robert Swink *Art Dir* Hal Pereira, Earl Hedrick
● Kirk Douglas, Eleanor Parker, William Bendix, Lee Grant, Cathy O'Donnell, Joseph Wiseman (Paramount)

William Wyler has polished the legit hit by Pulitzer-prizewinner Sidney Kingsley into a cinematic gem. Scripters have stuck almost to the letter of the original play. Even the location seldom changes from Kingsley's single set, the realistic headquarters room of the detective squad.

Kirk Douglas is the tortured detective determined unswervingly to do his duty as he sees it. Hunting an illicit doctor who has been delivering illegitimate children, Douglas suddenly finds himself being virtually blackmailed by the medico. Douglas' wife, long before she married him, had occasion to use the charlatan's services – and the doctor hadn't forgotten.

Eleanor Parker plays the wife with a dignity and emotional depth that makes a dramatic highlight of the scene in which she is forced to reveal her past. The personal drama is played against a broad and entertaining mosaic of other drama, humor and young love in the busy squad room. Lee Grant repeats one of the memorable stage roles of recent years as a pathetic albeit amusing little Brooklynesque femme shoplifter. Another holdover from the legiter, Joseph Wiseman, is tops as a sneering, dope-filled larcenist.

The unfrocked physician was an abortionist in the original. Screen version has him actually delivering the illicit children.

....

■ DEVIL AND DANIEL WEBSTER, THE

1941, 100 MINS, US

Dir William Dieterle *Prod* William Dieterle *Scr* Dan Totheroh, Stephen Vincent Benet *Ph* Joseph August *Ed* Robert Wise *Mus* Bernard Herrmann
● Edward Arnold, Walter Huston, Jane Darwell, Simone Simon, Anne Shirley (RKO)

Material for the screenplay is taken from Stephen Vincent Benet's short story, an O.

Henry prize-winner, and the author had a hand in the film version with Dan Totheroh.

The locale is New Hampshire, in 1840, a background of muddy roads, Currier & Ives farm settings, and peopled with struggling American peasantry. The legend is about the rise, fall and regeneration of a young farmer, Jabez Stone, who is alleged to have sold his soul to the devil for a pittance of gold and seven years of good luck. It's a twist on the Faust theme, but Benet isn't Goethe.

James Craig plays the youth who discovers that crime doesn't pay. He is a quite capable young actor, of pleasing appearance. Anne Shirley is the wife, who gets all the worst of it, and Jane Darwell is the rock-bound New England mother.

Trouble for Dieterle (and the audience) starts when Walter Huston appears on the scene via double-exposure and whispers beguiling temptations into the ear of the young husband-farmer. That's when gold coins appear from strange places and the boy pays off the mortgage. From there to the finish it's mostly symbols and morality play.

....

■ DEVIL AND MISS JONES, THE

1941, 92 MINS, US ⓥ

Dir Sam Wood *Prod* Frank Ross *Scr* Norman Krasna *Ph* Harry Stradling *Ed* Sherman Todd
● Jean Arthur, Charles Coburn, Robert Cummings, Edmund Gwenn, S.Z. Sakall, Spring Byington (RKO)

In a foreword, audiences are informed that this is a fanciful and imaginative story, put on the record mainly for amusement purposes. *The Devil and Miss Jones* then unwinds a light and fluffy tale of the richest man in the world who loses his stern front through association with the employees of one of his enterprises – a department store.

Jean Arthur is the Miss Jones, a decidedly personable salesgirl who takes the elderly shoe clerk under her wing to guide him through the intricacies of store routine. Charles Coburn is the richest man who steps into the store job incognito to ferret out the leaders of a union organization.

Coburn's performance as the millionaire who gradually unbends stands out as a fine characterization. Arthur excellently grooves as the salesgirl, but Robert Cummings' characterization is over-sketched in the main as a union organiser. Sam Wood injects deft direction with human byplay to lift the script considerably.

....

■ DEVIL AT 4 O'CLOCK, THE

1961, 125 MINS, US ◇ ⓥ

Dir Mervyn LeRoy *Prod* Fred Kohlmar *Scr* Liam O'Brien *Ph* Joseph Biroc *Ed* Charles Nelson *Mus* George Duning *Art Dir* John Beckman
● Spencer Tracy, Frank Sinatra, Kerwin Mathews, Jean-Pierre Aumont, Gregoire Aslan, Barbara Luna (Columbia)

A small volcanic South Seas isle makes a colorful setting for this tale of heroism and sacrifice, but vying with interest in characterizations are the exceptional special effects of an island being blown to pieces.

Based on a novel by Max Catto, plot is off the beaten path for an adventure yarn. Story is of a priest (Spencer Tracy) who with three convicts (Frank Sinatra, Gregoire Aslan, Bernie Hamilton) saves the lives of the children in a mountain-top leper hospital by leading them through fire and lava flow to the coast and a waiting schooner after the volcano erupts and island is doomed to certain destruction.

Tracy delivers one of his more colorful portrayals in his hard-drinking cleric who has lost faith in his God, walloping over a character which sparks entire action of film. Sinatra's role, first-class but minor in comparison, is overshadowed in interest by Aslan, one of the convicts in a stealing part who lightens some of the more dramatic action. Third con, Hamilton, also delivers solidly as the strong man who holds up a tottering wooden bridge over a deep gorge while the children and others from hospital cross to safety.

Special effects of Larry Butler and Willis Cook highlight the picture, filmed impressively by Joseph Biroc on the vivid island of Maui in the Hawaiian group.

．．．．．．．．．．．．．．．．．．．．．．．．．．．．．．

■ **DEVIL DOLL**

1964, 80 MINS, UK ▽
Dir Lindsay Shonteff   *Prod* Kenneth Rive, Richard Gordon, Lindsay Shonteff   *Scr* George Barclay, Lance Z. Hargreaves   *Ph* Gerald Gibbs   *Ed* Ernest Bullingham   *Art Dir* Stan Shields
● Bryant Halliday, William Sylvester, Yvonne Romain, Karel Stepanek (Gala/Galaworld/Gordon)

This slow-paced pic never comes up to its title in the way of shocks, thrills, scares, sex or other dividends for meller regulars. Filmed in England, its gimmick – a ventriloquial dummy's revenge on his manipulator – has been done before and better by Cavalcanti and Michael Redgrave in a real horror classic – *Dead of Night* – and *The Great Gabbo* of 1929.

American newspaperman William Sylvester, assigned to do a story of a hypnotist-ventriloquist suspected of being a fake, takes his girlfriend (Yvonne Romain), along but both are impressed by the act. The hypnotist (Bryant Halliday), invited to perform at a charity affair at the home of Romain's aunt, hypnotizes the girl and, without the others knowing it, leaves her in a trance.

Haliday plans to repeat, with the girl, an experiment he had done years previously in Berlin, transferring a human soul to the body of a dummy, which he will keep subservient and force it to carry out his demands. While Sylvester is tracking down the truth, Halliday's dummy, Hugo, takes matters into his own hands.

Sylvester gives an honest, realistic touch to the role of the newspaperman. Halliday, however, burdened with a messy beard and one expression, the hypnotic stare, depends on his resonant voice to make the role credible.

．．．．．．．．．．．．．．．．．．．．．．．．．．．．．．

■ **DEVIL-DOLL, THE**

1936, 70 MINS, US ▽
Dir Tod Browning   *Prod* Edward J. Mannix
Scr Garrett Fort, Guy Endore, Erich von Stroheim
Ph Leonard Smith   *Ed* Frederick Y. Smith   *Mus* Franz Waxman
● Lionel Barrmore, Maureen O'Sullivan, Frank Lawton, Robert Greig, Lucy Beaumont, Henry B. Walthall (M-G-M)

The premise [from the novel *Burn, Witch, Burn* by Abraham Merritt] is a scientist's discovery of a process by which all living things, including humans, can be reduced to one-sixth their normal size. The director, cameraman and art department make the most of it, but the writers' contribution is lacking in originality and seldom is equal to the idea in back of it.

Lionel Barrymore, as a framed convict named Lavond and later in the disguise of old Madam Mandelip, is a scientific Count of Monte Cristo who avenges his false imprisonment. His companion in a prison escape is the inventor of the atom-shrinking process. The inventor dies on the first night of freedom and Barrymore carries on the 'great work' with the man's crazy widow.

Two of the big moments derive their power from camerawork, while the third is a remake by Tod Browning of the scene which highlighted his *Unholy Three* (1925). Once again

the stolen jewels are concealed in a toy doll and the police inspector has them in his grasp without knowing it.

For Barrymore the leading part is a field day. Rafaela Ottiano, with a white streak in her hair and hobbling on a crutch, is convincing as the scientist's wacky widow. Capable ingenue that she is, Maureen O'Sullivan had no trouble as Barrymore's daughter, but Frank Lawton, her opposite in the romantic secondary theme, is much too British and refined for a cab driver assignment.

．．．．．．．．．．．．．．．．．．．．．．．．．．．．．．

■ **DEVIL IN MISS JONES, THE**

1973, 74 MINS, US ◇
Dir Gerard Damiano   *Prod* Gerard Damiano
Scr Gerard Damiano   *Ph* Harry Flecks   *Ed* Gerard Damiano   *Mus* Alden Shuman
● Georgina Spevlin, John Clemens, Harry Reams, Albert Gork [=Gerard Damiano], Rick Livermore, Sue Flaken (Marvin/Damiano)

With *The Devil in Miss Jones*, the hardcore porno feature approaches an 'art form'. For its genre, the pic is a sensation, marked by a technical polish that pales some Hollywood product and containing some of the most frenzied and erotic sex sequences in porno memory.

Written, directed and edited by Gerard Damiano, the man who dittoed on *Deep Throat* (under his Jerry Gerard pseudonym), this ambitious meller delivers in spades.

A thirtyish virgin, Justine Jones (Georgina Spevlin), commits suicide and is condemned to eternal damnation. Her suicide has been the only damnable act in a lonely, despairing life, and to make herself 'worthy' of the punishment meted out to her, Jones requests a little more time in which to experiment with and to be consumed by lust.

Georgina Spevlin lacks the specific sexpertise of Linda Lovelace and she's no conventional beauty. Male performers are familiar porno vets, with the exception of Damiano himself who appears, under the name of Albert Gork, in pic's hellish finale.

．．．．．．．．．．．．．．．．．．．．．．．．．．．．．．

■ **DEVIL IS A WOMAN, THE**

1935, 76 MINS, US
Dir Josef von Sternberg   *Scr* John Dos Passon, Sam Winston   *Ph* Josef von Sternberg, Lucien Ballard   *Ed* Sam Winston   *Mus* Ralph Rainger, Andrea Setaro (arr.)   *Art Dir* Hans Dreier
● Marlene Dietrich, Cesar Romero, Lionel Atwill, Edward Everett Horton, Alison Skipworth, Don Alvarado (Paramount)

Josef von Sternberg both directed and photographed *The Devil Is a Woman*, working with a Pierre Louys classic *The Woman and the Puppet* which gives the reader a cross-section of a ruthless courtesan and not much else. While *Devil* is a somewhat monotonous picture, Sternberg has given it clever photography and background. Marlene Dietrich has done the rest in playing the Louys trollop, turning in a fine performance.

Story is told in a background of southern Spain during a fiesta, this permitting Sternberg some big mob scenes and color, plus music. It opens on la Dietrich of today as a gorgeously desirable woman who has caught the eye of a young visitor. He is about to stage a rendezvous with her when he meets an old friend (Atwill), who tells him of his sad experience with the same woman, most of the story then being told by flashback.

Edward Everett Horton is in on a couple of sequences at opening and near close, and his political associates raising the only laughs that occur. *Caprice Espagnol*, vet classic, and other Spanish music is employed for melodic background in an effective manner.

．．．．．．．．．．．．．．．．．．．．．．．．．．．．．．

■ **DEVIL MAKES THREE, THE**

1952, 89 MINS, US
Dir Andrew Marton   *Prod* Richard Goldstone
Scr Jerry Davis   *Ph* Vaclav Vich   *Ed* Ben Lewis
Mus Rudolph G. Kopp (dir.)
● Gene Kelly, Pier Angeli, Richard Rober, Richard Egan, Claus Clausen, Wilfried Seyferth (M-G-M)

Postwar Germany provides the background for an interesting chase thriller. Snow-covered Munich, Salzburg, Berchtesgaden and Hitler's bombed-out Adlerhorst are the plot settings.

Lawrence Bachmann's story, *Autobahn*, supplies the basis for the script. Story deals with an underground movement to revive the Nazi Party and how Counter-Intelligence, with the aid of Gene Kelly's Air Force captain, and Pier Angeli's German B-girl, put down the aspirations of one would-be fuehrer.

The chase thrills and suspense moments come across expertly under Andrew Marton's direction, but he is inclined to pace the film a bit too slowly in other spots. One of the top thriller sequences is the motorcycle race on a frozen lake, during which the villain is revealed.

．．．．．．．．．．．．．．．．．．．．．．．．．．．．．．

■ **DEVIL RIDES OUT, THE**

1968, 95 MINS, UK ◇
Dir Terence Fisher   *Prod* Anthony Nelson-Keys
Scr Richard Matheson   *Ph* Arthur Grant   *Ed* James Needs   *Mus* James Bernard   *Art Dir* Bernard Robinson
● Christopher Lee, Charles Gray, Nike Arrighi, Leon Greene, Patrick Mower, Sarah Lawson (Hammer)

Director Terence Fisher has a ball with this slice of black magic, based on the Dennis Wheatley novel. He has built up a suspenseful pic, with several tough highlights, and gets major effect by playing the subject dead straight and getting similar serious performances from his capable cast.

Christopher Lee is for once on the side of the goodies. As the Duc de Richleau, he and his buddy (Leon Greene) are intent on saving the soul of a young man (Patrick Mower) caught up in black magic and at the mercy of Charles Gray, chief apostle of the evil. Also involved is a mysterious young girl (Nike Arrighi), in the thrall of the black sin.

Lee plays the Duc with his usual authority and Gray turns out another of his bland, cold essays in villainy. The weakness lies in the fact that these two rarely confront each other.

Arrighi as a slightly hysterical lass, Mower and Greene are all adequate.

Fisher's direction makes one of the Satanic orgies a production highspot, aided by some frenzied choreography by David Toguri and apt mood music.

．．．．．．．．．．．．．．．．．．．．．．．．．．．．．．

■ **DEVILS, THE**

1971, 109 MINS, UK ◇ ▽
Dir Ken Russell   *Prod* Robert H. Solo, Ken Russell
Scr Ken Russell   *Ph* David Watkin   *Ed* Michael Bradsell   *Mus* Peter Maxwell Davies   *Art Dir* Robert Cartwright
● Vanessa Redgrave, Oliver Reed, Dudley Sutton, Max Adrian, Gemma Jones, Murray Melvin (Warner)

Working from John Whiting's play of the same title, and Aldous Huxley's book, *The Devils of Loudun*, Ken Russell has taken some historical liberties in fashioning the story of Father Grandier (Oliver Reed), sensually liberated priest in 17th-century France whose ethics brought him into conflict with the political ambitions of Cardinal Richelieu and the Catholic Church, and whose virile presence and backstairs reputation cued the erotic fantasies of a humpbacked nun, Sister Jeanne (Vanessa Redgrave).

When this sister's lustful ravings begin to infect other nuns in her convent, the Church, through its military agent (Dudley Sutton), brings in an exorcist (Michael Gothard) to stage circus-like public purges of the naked, foulmouthed nuns which result in Grandier's conviction on heresy charges, his torture and burning at the stake.

As if the story alone weren't bizarre enough, Russell has spared nothing in hyping the historic events by stressing the grisly at the expense of dramatic unity.

Given Russell's frantic pacing, performances tend to get lost amid the savagery. Reed carries the film with an admirably restrained portrayal of the doomed priest. Redgrave, on screen only sporadically, is stunning as the salacious sister.

■ DEVIL'S DISCIPLE, THE

1959, 82 MINS, US/UK ◇
Dir Guy Hamilton   *Prod* Harold Hecht   *Scr* John Dighton, Roland Kibbee   *Ph* Jack Hildyard   *Ed* Alan Osbiston   *Mus* Richard Rodney Bennett
● Burt Lancaster, Kirk Douglas, Laurence Olivier, Jeanette Scott, Eva LeGallienne, Harry Andrews (Bryna/ United Artists)

The Devil's Disciple by George Bernard Shaw is better than this film version would indicate to those unfamiliar with the stage original. The final third of the picture is superb Shaw-manship, but the major portion preceding it is fumbling and unsatisfactory.

That all is not lost may be credited almost entirely to Laurence Olivier. His character, that of General 'Gentleman Johnny' Burgoyne, is a witty, mocking figure and mouthpiece for Shaw's wicked shafts into convention and history, in this case the American Revolution.

The other two stars, Burt Lancaster and Kirk Douglas, fare less well. Lancaster is Anthony Anderson, the peace-spouting person who eventually becomes a fiery rebel. Douglas is Dick Dudgeon, self-proclaimed, a shameless, cowardly scoundrel, who in turn displays the truest Christian attitudes.

Shaw's play is the ironic Irishman's version of how the British, bumbling and fumbling, lost the American colonies. The reason, says Shaw, is that due to the long British weekend someone at the War Office forgot to notify Lord North to join forces with General Burgoyne and pinch off the Colonials.

Directors were changed in mid-filming and there seems in the finished product to be a division of style. Guy Hamilton must bear the blame for the uncertain mood and pace.

■ DEVIL'S PLAYGROUND, THE

1976, 107 MINS, AUSTRALIA ◇ Ⓥ
Dir Fred Schepisi   *Prod* Fred Schepisi   *Scr* Fred Schepisi   *Ph* Ian Baker   *Ed* Brian Kavanagh   *Mus* Bruce Smeaton
● Arthur Dignam, Nick Tate, Simon Burke, Charles McCallum, John Frawley, Jonathon Hardy (Film House)

The Devil's Playground is a Roman Catholic boys' boarding school were the pupils are seen at their everyday work, play and worship. Stressed are the problems of puberty in such a community, and the evils of succumbing to self-abuse; one boy for instance is chastised for taking off his bathers whilst under a shower.

The more sensitive boys take such things to heart, others merely shrug it off and go their own way. In one quarter it breeds a cell where boys indulge in homosexual, masochistic and sadistic practices while the teachers react in different ways.

Film, almost like a factual documentary at times, has obviously been made with great sincerity. Lensing is fine, with some superb outdoor photography. The direction is always competent and most of the scenes involving the boys, organized and natural.

■ DIAL M FOR MURDER

1954, 105 MINS, US ◇ Ⓥ
Dir Alfred Hitchcock   *Prod* Alfred Hitchcock   *Scr* Frederick Knott   *Ph* Robert Burks   *Ed* Rudi Fehr   *Mus* Dimitri Tiomkin   *Art Dir* Edward Carrere, George James Hopkins
● Ray Milland, Grace Kelly, Robert Cummings, John Williams, Anthony Dawson, Patrick Allen (Warner)

The melodramatics in Frederick Knott's legit hit, *Dial M for Murder*, have been transferred to the screen virtually intact, but they are not as impressive on film. *Dial M* remains more of a filmed play than a motion picture, unfortunately revealed as a conversation piece about murder which talks up much more suspense than it actually delivers. The 3-D camera's probing eye also discloses that there's very little that's new in the Knott plotting.

Co-starring with Ray Milland are Grace Kelly, his wife and the intended murder victim, and Robert Cummings, her lover, who has a rather fruitless part in the resolution of the melodramatics.

Milland plots his wife's death, figuring on using Anthony Dawson for the actual killing while he has an alibi established elsewhere. The scheme goes awry.

There are a number of basic weaknesses in the setup that keep the picture from being a good suspense show for any but the most gullible. Via the performances and several suspense tricks expected of Hitchcock, the weaknesses are glossed over but not enough to rate the film a cinch winner.

■ DIAMOND HEAD

1962, 107 MINS, US ◇ Ⓥ
Dir Guy Green   *Prod* Jerry Bresler   *Scr* Marguerite Roberts   *Ph* Sam Leavitt   *Ed* William A. Lyon   *Mus* John Williams   *Art Dir* Malcolm Brown
● Charlton Heston, Yvette Mimieux, George Chakiris, France Nuyen, James Darren (Columbia)

Improbabilities and inconsistencies galore reside in Marguerite Roberts heavyhanded screenplay, from Peter Gilman's novel, about a Hawaiian agricultural tycoon, or King Bwana of Pineappleville, hellbent on holding-that-bloodline. When the baron's (Charlton Heston) baby sister (Yvette Mimieux) defiantly announces her engagement to a full-blooded Hawaiian lad (James Darren), the battle lines are drawn.

Heston etches a swaggering portrait of the bullying bigot. Mimieux is spirited as the liberal-minded sister, Chakiris is glum and inexpressive as the half-breed medic who captures the fair sister's heart. He also seems to be the only doctor on the Islands. Nuyen is sweet as Heston's unlikely heartthrob. Darren, despite a rich tan, seems about as 100% Hawaiian as Paul Revere.

Guy Green's direction, at any rate, is high-spirited, and production ingredients are slickly eye-appealing. Sam Leavitt's photography is Eastman colorful and dramatically calculating and alert.

■ DIAMONDS

1975, 106 MINS, US/ISRAEL ◇
Dir Menahem Golan   *Prod* Menahem Golan, Yoram Globus   *Scr* David Paulsen, Menahem Golan   *Ph* Adam Greenberg   *Ed* Dov Hoenig   *Mus* Roy Budd   *Art Dir* Kuli Sander
● Robert Shaw, Richard Roundtree, Barbara Hershey, Shelley Winters, Shai K. Ophir, Gadi Yageel (Avco Embassy/Golan-Globus)

The thin screenplay has Robert Shaw playing a jaded London aristocrat who turns diamond thief because of rivalry with his brother (also Shaw), a security expert who constructed the intricate vault in Israel where the rocks are stashed.

Along on the heist are Richard Roundtree and Barbara Hershey, but no one in the cast

gets much chance to develop a characterization. Shelley Winters has an estraneous role of an American widow putting the make on Shaw.

Diamonds is almost exclusively concerned with the technique of thievery, and there are some enjoyable scenes showing how the vault is cracked, but audiences surely demand more from a heist pic these days.

■ DIAMONDS ARE FOREVER

1971, 119 MINS, UK ◇ Ⓥ
Dir Guy Hamilton   *Prod* Albert R. Broccoli, Harry Saltzman   *Scr* Richard Maibaum, Tom Mankiewicz   *Ph* Ted Moore   *Ed* Bert Bates, John W. Holmes   *Mus* John Barry   *Art Dir* Ken Adam
● Sean Connery, Jill St John, Charles Gray, Lana Wood, Jimmy Dean, Bruce Cabot (United Artists)

James Bond still packs a lethal wallop in all his cavortings, still manages to surround himself with scantily-clad sexpots. Yet *Diamonds Are Forever* doesn't carry the same quality or flair as its many predecessors.

Sean Connery is back in the role as in five previous Bond entries, and he still has his own way both with broads and deeds. Jill St John is an agent for the smuggling ring in an attempt to smuggle a fortune in diamonds into the US, and Charles Gray the head of the organization with all the most advanced stages of nuclear energy at its disposal. Somewhere in the telling, diamonds are forgotten, never to be recalled, while Bond valiantly tries to save the world – one guesses.

The diamond caper takes Bond and his lovely companion to Las Vegas, where one of the funniest sequences in memory focuses on Bond trying to elude the police in downtown Vegas. Up-to-the-minute scientific gadget use is made again when Bond steals a moon machine at a simulated lunar testing-ground in a wild drive across the Nevada desert dunes.

■ DIAMONDS FOR BREAKFAST

1968, 102 MINS, UK ◇
Dir Christopher Morahan   *Prod* Carlo Ponti, Pierre Rouve   *Scr* N.F. Simpson, Pierre Rouve, Ronald Harwood   *Ph* Gerry Turpin   *Ed* Peter Tanner   *Mus* Norman Kaye   *Art Dir* Reece Pemberton
● Marcello Mastroianni, Rita Tushingham, Elaine Taylor, Maggie Blye, Francesca Tu, Warren Mitchell (Paramount)

Potentially amusing, light-comedy, crime idea is marred by uncertain steering by director Christopher Morahan, making his feature debut, and clashing styles of the three scripters. Comedy is never fully developed and Marcello Mastroianni, debuting in British pix, lacks his usual elegant confidence.

Mastroianni is a London boutique owner who, happening to be fourth in succession to the Throne of All the Russians, hits on the idea of lifting the Imperial Jewels which he figures belong to him, anyway.

He rustles up a gang of eyeworthy and skilful young femme crooks, cons the authorities into letting his girls wear the rocks at a charity fashion show but then runs into trouble as things go wrong.

Mastroianni is clearly not happy with his role in which he's too often the stooge, but the gals around him are good fun.

Femme star Rita Tushingham plays a nutty, Liverpool-Irish safecracker, who eventually gets the hero, but the part's skimpily developed and it's hardly Tushingham's league.

■ DIAMOND SKULLS

1990, 87 MINS, UK ◇ Ⓥ
Dir Nick Broomfield   *Prod* Tim Bevan   *Scr* Tim Rose Price   *Ph* Michael Coulter   *Ed* Rodney Holland   *Mus* Hans Zimmer   *Art Dir* Jocelyn James

● Gabriel Byrne, Amanda Donohoe, Michael Hordern, Judy Parfitt, Douglas Hodge (Film Four/British Screen/Working Title)

A stylish melodrama about sex and violence among the British aristocracy, *Diamond Skulls* never quite delivers the punches it promises.

Gabriel Byrne is Sir Hugo, an ex-guards officer, now in business. He has a lovely wife (the delectable Amanda Donohoe) of whom he's extremely jealous, suspecting her of having an affair with an Argentine business colleague.

One night, after a drunken dinner with his friends, Hugo is driving someone else's car when he hits a young woman, fatally injuring her. He and his friends leave her to die, though one of them, Jamie (Douglas Hodge), the car owner, wants to report the accident.

Jamie, who's having an affair with Hugo's sister Rebecca (Sadie Frost), threatens to spill the beans, and the friends are forced to silence him.

Donohoe gives another hot performance as the elegant Virginia whose name belies her actions. Veteran Michael Hordern is amusing as Hugo's titled father, though comedy actor Ian Carmichael is totally wasted as the family butler.

• •

■ DIARY OF A CHAMBERMAID

1946, 86 MINS, US ⊛

Dir Jean Renoir *Prod* Benedict Bogeaus, Burgess Meredith *Scr* Burgess Meredith *Ph* Lucien Andriot *Ed* James Smith *Art Dir* Eugene Lourie

● Paulette Goddard, Burgess Meredith, Hurd Hatfield, Francis Lederer, Judith Anderson (United Artists)

Diary is interesting from several angles, no less of which is its adaptation from the original French. The transition is certainly the most important factor in drawing a line on its entertainment values. This is an odd yarn, the type done so well by the French – and so falteringly by almost anyone else. *Diary* in its American form has not nearly the intrigue, nor the color, suggested by the original French version, but it has names and an interest all its own.

It is the yarn of a chambermaid who, tiring of her station in life, vows to achieve wealth whoever the man. The men in her life aren't too sharply defined, nor especially interesting. Nor is the murder of the aging captain by the valet, so he can get money to marry the chambermaid, committed with any degree of climactic excitement.

There is Paulette Goddard, as the chambermaid with a gold glint to her orbs; Burgess Meredith, a psychopathic, aging army captain; Hurd Hatfield, the sensitive consumptive whom the girl loves, and Francis Lederer, the glowering valet-murderer.

• •

■ DIARY OF A MAD HOUSEWIFE

1970, 85 MINS, US ◇ ⊛

Dir Frank Perry *Prod* Frank Perry *Scr* Eleanor Perry *Ph* Gerald Hirschfeld *Ed* Sidney Katz *Art Dir* Peter Dohanos

● Richard Benjamin, Frank Langella, Carrie Snodgress, Lorraine Cullen, Frannie Michel, Lee Addoms (Universal)

An engrossing story of the disintegration of a modern loveless marriage, with Richard Benjamin and Frank Langella effectively portraying the inadequacies of husband and lover, respectively, and Carrie Snodgress, as a frustrated, sensitive wife.

Story line [from a novel by Sue Kaufman] has Snodgress reach the breaking point under a marriage to Benjamin that has become sated with his selfish material values. She turns to Langella as an afternoon lover, only to find him just as bad.

Benjamin, who is top-billed, is saddled with the most unsympathetic role as a

disenchanted, post-JFK idealist now determined to rise in the middle-class flotsam, he is excellent in maintaining a character so delineated that one wants to throw something at the screen.

• •

■ DIARY OF ANNE FRANK, THE

1959, 170 MINS, US

Dir George Stevens *Prod* George Stevens *Scr* Frances Goodrich, Albert Hackett *Ph* William C. Mellor, Jack Cardiff *Ed* David Bretherton, Robert Swink, William Mace *Mus* Alfred Newman

● Millie Perkins, Joseph Schildkraut, Shelley Winters, Richard Beymer, Lou Jacobi, Diane Baker (20th Century-Fox)

The Diary of Anne Frank, first published in its original form, then made into a play by Frances Goodrich and Albert Hackett, is a film of often extraordinary quality. It manages, within the framework of a tense and tragic situation, to convey the beauty of a young and inquiring spirit that soars beyond the cramped confinement of the Frank family's hideout in Nazi-occupied Amsterdam.

And yet, with all its technical perfection, the inspired direction and the sensitivity with which many of the scenes are handled, *Diary* is simply too long. Everything possible is done to keep the action moving within its narrow, cluttered space, and a remarkable balance is achieved between stark terror and comedy relief, yet there are moments when the film lags and the dialog becomes forced. Unlike the play, the picture leaves too little to the imagination.

Millie Perkins plays Anne. It is her first film role and she turns in a charming and captivating performance. Whether Perkins, a model, is absolutely right for the part is open to question. It's certainly difficult to accept her as a 13-year-old, which was Anne's age at the time the Franks went into hiding.

As father Otto Frank, Joseph Schildkraut repeats his marvellous performance on the stage. There is dignity and wisdom in this man, a deep sadness too, and a love for Anne that makes the scene of his return to the hideout after the war a moment full of pain and compassion.

As the Van Daan couple, Shelley Winters and Lou Jacobi come up with vivid characterizations that score on all levels. As young Peter Van Daan, Richard Beymer is touchingly sincere and perfectly matched with Perkins, a boy who discovers in the girl the depth he has been seeking in himself. Diane Baker's sensitive face is pleasing in the comparatively small role of Margot Frank.

□ 1959: Best Picture (Nomination)

• •

■ DICK TRACY

1990, 103 MINS, US ◇ ⊛

Dir Warren Beatty *Prod* Warren Beatty *Scr* Jim Cash, Jack Epps Jr *Ph* Vittorio Storaro *Ed* Richard Marks *Mus* Danny Elfman *Art Dir* Richard Sylbert

● Warren Beatty, Charlie Korsmo, Glenne Headly, Madonna, Al Pacino, Dustin Hoffman (Touchstone/Silver Screen Partners IV)

Though it looks ravishing, Warren Beatty's longtime pet project is a curiously remote, uninvolving film. Beatty and his collaborators have created a boldly stylized 1930s urban milieu that captures the comic strip's quirky, angled mood, while dazzling the eye with deep primary colors.

Beatty – ultrastylish in yellow raincoat and snap-brim hat, black suit, red tie and crisp white shirts – is so cool he appears frozen. Torn between Madonna's allure – she's customed in black & white to look like a steamy low-rent version of Josef von Sternberg's Marlene Dietrich – and the more low-key beauty and sweetness of Glenne Headly's redhead Tess Trueheart, Beatty simply sits

there and mopes, occasionally rousing himself into bursts of action.

A large part of what fun there is in the pic comes from the inventive character makeup by John Caglione Jr and Doug Drexler, who mostly succeed in the difficult task of creating live-action cartoon figures. Dustin Hoffman takes an eerie turn as Mumbles, R.G. Armstrong is chilling as Pruneface, Paul Sorvino hilariously disgusting as Lips, William Forsythe spooky as Flattop.

Al Pacino, virtually runs away with the show in a sizable role as Tracy's nemesis, the Richard III-like hunchbacked villain Big Boy Caprice. His manic energy lifts the overall torpor.

Equally fine is young street urchin Charlie Korsmo who, together with the lovely Headly, gives the film a necessary counterbalance of normality.

• •

■ DICTATOR, THE

1935, 86 MINS, UK

Dir Victor Saville, Alfred Santell *Prod* Ludovico Toeplitz *Scr* Benn W. Levy *Ph* Franz Planer *Ed* Paul Weatherwax *Mus* Karol Rathaus *Art Dir* Andre Andrejev

● Clive Brook, Madeleine Carroll, Emlyn Williams, Alfred Drayton, Nicholas Hannen, Helen Hays (Toeplitz)

This is one of the most lavish costume pictures that has come out of England. Supposed to have cost $500,000. Sets and costumes give the impression of tremendous royal wealth; entire action takes place in gorgeous palaces; one banquet scene, with ballet music, is as good as anything ever seen on the screen.

Picture has other fine qualities, too. Clive Brook does an authoritative bit of acting, and imposes lots of femme appeal; Madeleine Carroll is attractive; Emlyn Williams is a splendid young debauchee and Helen Hays (not the American actress) a tough old queen mother. There is humor, particularly in the earlier scenes.

Trouble is with the story [by Ludovico Toeplitz]. It's a love tale of a beautiful queen and an ambitious young man – not developed in such a way as to be really dramatic.

Setting is 18th-century Danish royalty. Opens after the royal wedding, and shows the king (Williams) trying in vain to get into the bedroom of the queen (Carroll), whom he only met the day before. This, like the rest of the first dozen or so sequences, is effective. Then the king beats it to Hamburg to have a good time. Struensee, a Hamburg doctor (Brook), makes an impressive entry. He's called to attend the king, incognito, who has passed out after too much wine and women, and he wins the young man's favor by bringing him back to life unceremoniously.

Struensee, taken to Denmark, becomes the power behind the throne. In this he replaces the Queen mother, who, with her courtiers, sets out to get him.

• •

■ DIE HARD

1988, 131 MINS, US ◇ ⊛

Dir John McTiernan *Prod* Lawrence Gordon, Joel Silver *Scr* Jeb Stuart, Steven E. de Souza *Ph* Jan De Bont *Ed* Frank J. Urioste, John F. Link *Mus* Michael Kamen *Art Dir* Jackson De Govia

● Bruce Willis, Alan Rickman, Bonnie Bedelia, Alexander Godunov, Reginald Veljohnson (Gordon-Silver/20th Century-Fox)

Die Hard is as high tech, rock hard and souped up as an action film can be, a suspenser [based on the novel *Nothing Lasts Forever* by Roderick Thorpe] pitting a lone wolf cop against a group of terrorists that has taken over a highrise office tower.

Bruce Willis plays John McClane, an overworked New York policeman who flies into

D

Los Angeles at Christmas to visit his two daughters and estranged wife Holly (Bonnie Bedelia).

Planning a rather different holiday agenda are the terrorists led by Hans Gruber (Alan Rickman). The dastardly dozen invade the plush 30th floor offices of Nakatomi Corp during its Christmas party, and hold the employees hostage as a computer whiz cracks a code that will put the mainly German bad boys in possession of $600 million in negotiable bonds.

Slipping out of the party in the nick of time with nothing but his handgun, Willis is the fly in the ointment of the criminals' plans, picking off one, then two more of the scouts sent on pest control missions.

Beefed up considerably for his role, Willis is amiable enough in the opening stretch, but overdoes the grimacing and heavy emoting later on. The cooler and more humorous he is the better. Rickman has a giddy good time but sometimes goes over the top as the henchman.

. . . .

■ DIE HARD 2

1990, 124 MINS, US ◇ ⓥ
Dir Renny Harlin   *Prod* Laurence Gordon, Joel Silver, Charles Gordon   *Scr* Steven E. de Souza, Doug Richardson   *Ph* Oliver Wood   *Ed* Stuart Baird
Mus Michael Kamen   *Art Dir* John Vallone
● Bruce Willis, Bonnie Bedelia, William Atherton, Franco Nero, William Sadler (Gordon/Silver/20th Century-Fox)

Die Hard 2 lacks the inventiveness of the original but compensates with relentless action. The film [based on the novel *58 Minutes* by Walter Wager] works for the most part as sheer entertainment, a full-color comic book with shootouts, brutal fistfights and bloodletting aplenty.

Minding his own business, John McClane (Bruce Willis) is in DCs Dulles Airport to pick up wife Holly (Bonnie Bedelia) to spend Christmas with her folks. They've reconciled since the events in *Die Hard* and the Gotham cop has joined the LAPD. Unlike most domestic flights, the story takes off immediately, as terrorists seize control of the airport to free a Manuel Noriegaesque foreign dictator (Franco Nero) being transported to the US.

Director Renny Harlin does a creditable job with such a daunting large-scale assignment. But Harlin lacks *Die Hard* director John McTiernan's vicelike grip on action and strays into areas that derail certain scenes, using slow-motion in early sequences and sapping their energy.

. . . .

■ DILLINGER

1973, 107 MINS, US ◇ ⓥ
Dir John Milius   *Prod* Buzz Feitshans   *Scr* John Milius
Ph Jules Brenner   *Ed* Fred R. Feitshans   *Mus* Barry DeVorzon
● Warren Oates, Ben Johnson, Michelle Phillips, Cloris Leachman, Harry Dean Stanton, Richard Dreyfuss (American International)

The violent life and death of John Dillinger is graphically portrayed. With Warren Oates in title role, screenplay captures the various highlights of the killer's short-lived career as Public Enemy No. 1.

Oates is a good physical choice for role of the bank robber and killer who blazed his way to notoriety during 13 months of 1933 and 1934. Less known to the public was Melvin Purvis, the FBI man responsible for Dillinger's death in a Chicago alley, but as delineated by Ben Johnson he is as forceful a figure.

Actually, the tenor of the film is the FBI huntdown of Dillinger; Johnson acts as off-screen commentator as well as enacting him on screen. Pace is sometimes reduced during

events sandwiched in between actual gunfire sequences of Dillinger's career, but there can be no criticism of Milius' ability to keep such action sequences at top-heat.

Michelle Phillips, making her film bow after having been a member of The Mamas & The Papas singing group, scores heavily as Dillinger's girl friend.

. . . .

■ DIM SUM
A LITTLE BIT OF HEART

1985, 85 MINS, US ◇ ⓥ
Dir Wayne Wang   *Prod* Tom Sternberg, Wayne Wang, Danny Yung   *Scr* Terrel Seltzer   *Ph* Michael Chin
Ed Ralph Wikke   *Mus* Todd Boekelheide
Art Dir Danny Yung
● Laureen Chew, Kim Chew, Victor Wong, Ida F.O. Chung, Cora Miao, John Nishio (CIM)

Dim Sum offers up a few charming observations about cultural differences among assorted generations of Chinese Americans, but the dramatic situations are so underplayed as to be mostly ineffectual.

Taking a cue from countless earlier Asian family pictures that have dwelt upon the subject of family traditions and the responsibilities of children for their aging parents, director Wayne Wang and scripter Terrel Seltzer [working from a story by them and Laureen Chew] have focused upon the relationship between a traditional Chinese woman in her 60s and her 30-ish daughter, who unlike her brother and sister, is not yet hitched.

A great deal of the sought-after humor stems from the 'So when are you gonna get married?' attitudes of family friends.

The authenticity of Wang's depiction of San Francisco's Chinese need not be questioned, but the attitudes expressed are predictable in the extreme and are invested with little sense of dramatic urgency.

. . . .

■ DINER

1982, 110 MINS, US ◇ ⓥ
Dir Barry Levinson   *Prod* Jerry Weintraub   *Scr* Barry Levinson   *Ph* Peter Sova   *Ed* Stu Linder   *Art Dir* Leon Harris
● Steve Guttenberg, Daniel Stern, Mickey Rourke, Kevin Bacon, Timothy Daly, Ellen Barkin (M-G-M/United Artists)

It's easy to tell that *Diner* was chiefly conceived and executed by a writer. In his directorial debut, Barry Levinson takes great pains to establish characters.

The year is 1959 and the diner is in Baltimore, although the action could take place in any American city. Using the diner as the proverbial street corner hangout, Levinson centers on a close-knit group of guys in their early 20s and how their early adult lives are taking shape.

In this case there's lots to worry about. Among the characters is a young gambler just footsteps ahead of his loanshark; a thinking grad student whose pregnant career-wise girlfriend won't get married; a compulsive husband unhappy with his new wife; a handsome rich kid who gets drunk to escape his cold family; and a closet 'virgin' who won't marry his girlfriend until she can pass a football quiz.

Steve Guttenberg, Daniel Stern, Mickey Rourke, Kevin Bacon, Paul Reiser and Timothy Daly are terrific as the friends as are Ellen Barkin and Kathryn Dowling as the two females involved with different group members.

. . . .

■ DINNER AT EIGHT

1933, 110 MINS, US
Dir George Cukor   *Prod* David O. Selznick
Scr Frances Marion, Herman J. Mankiewicz, Donald Ogden Stewart   *Ph* William Daniels   *Ed* Ben Lewis

Mus William Axt   *Art Dir* Hobe Erwin, Fred Hope
● Marie Dressler, John Barrymore, Wallace Beery, Jean Harlow, Lionel Barrymore, Lee Tracy (M-G-M)

Play [by George S. Kaufman and Edna Ferber] was fine drama on the stage and has been translated to the screen in workmanlike manner, changes mostly being in the interest of condensation. For this reason the below stairs action among the servants has been deleted and the finish has been slightly changed to give a gag line to Marie Dressler, the latter being a first-rate device, handing the curtain to the principal two comedy characters – the ancient stage belle and the Jean Harlow role, who have been shrewdly emphasized in the film version.

The story grips from beginning to end with never-relaxing tension, its sombre moments relieved by lighter touches into a fascinating mosaic for nearly two hours. Play is a more searching document than *Grand Hotel* but not quite its equal in dramatic vividness.

Acting honors probably will go to Dressler and Harlow, the latter giving an astonishingly well-balanced treatment of Kitty, the canny little hussy who hooks a hard-bitten and unscrupulous millionaire and then makes him lay down and roll over.

Role of Carlotta doesn't find Dressler in her popular vein. It's a dressed-up part for one thing. But she handles this politer assignment with poise and aplomb.

John Barrymore's playing of the has-been picture star is a stark, uncompromising treatment of a pretty thorough-going blackguard and ingrate. Billie Burke is eminently suited for the role of a fluttering society matron immersed in social trivialities while tragedy stalks unknowing through her home. Wallace Beery is again at home as the millionaire vulgarian, made to order for his type.

. . . .

■ DIPLOMATIC COURIER

1952, 98 MINS, US ⓥ
Dir Henry Hathaway   *Prod* Casey Robinson
Scr Casey Robinson, Liam O'Brien   *Ph* Lucien Ballard
Ed James B. Clark   *Mus* Sol Kaplan   *Art Dir* Lyle Wheeler, John DeCuir
● Tyrone Power, Patricia Neal, Hildegarde Neff, Stephen McNally, Karl Malden, James Millican (20th Century-Fox)

A topnotch espionage yarn based on Peter Cheyney's novel, *Sinister Errand*, the script has Tyrone Power playing a diplomatic courier who is used by the Counter Intelligence Division to uncover the whereabouts of a missing Soviet timetable for invasion of Yugoslavia.

Power, the State Department's top postman, is sent to Salzburg to pick up vital secret papers from James Millican. At the arranged meeting place in a railway station, Millican refuses contact and is later killed. Aware the Soviets did not get the papers, Power is assigned to trace Hildegarde Neff, a Soviet agent in belief she will have some clue to the mystery. Power is hampered in his work by Patricia Neal, seemingly a slightly nutty American tourist.

. . . .

■ DIRIGIBLE

1931, 100 MINS, US
Dir Frank Capra   *Scr* Frank B. Wead, Jo Swerling
Ph Joseph Walker   *Ed* Maurice Wright
● Jack Holt, Ralph Graves, Fay Wray, Hobart Bosworth, Roscoe Karns, Clarence Muse (Columbia)

The big scene is a crack-up of the dirigible in the air; more interesting even than the explosion of the dirigible in *Hell's Angels*. The remainder of *Dirigible* is unconvincing, before or after the crack-up, the latter occurring about midway.

After the crack-up comes the South Pole expedition by plane and dirigible, the latter to rescue the survivors. As Ralph Graves

155

piloting the airplane to the pole is ready to return, the explorer aboard wants to drop an American flag to mark the spot. Graves says no, he will land and let the explorer do it in person. 'See that snow', says Graves, 'it's perfect for landing', and he lands, right on his neck with the others, while the plane burns. After that it's homeward bound, 6,000 miles away and getting there at the rate of seven miles daily. Trudging, starving, dying.

Of the actors Fay Wray looks the best, earnestly sincere as the wife of Graves' glory-seeking aviator. Graves early in the film is light enough to give the zest the story needs. Jack Holt is the dirigible's commander and pal of Graves.

● ●

■ DIRTY DANCING

1987, 97 MINS, US ◇ Ⓥ

Dir Emile Ardolino   *Prod* Linda Gottlieb   *Scr* Eleanor Bergstein   *Ph* Jeff Jur   *Ed* Peter C. Frank   *Mus* John Morris   *Art Dir* Mark Haack
● Jennifer Grey, Patrick Swayze, Jerry Orbach, Cynthia Rhodes, Jack Weston, Jane Brucker (Vestron)

It's summer 1963 and college kids carry copies of *The Fountainhead* in their back pocket and condoms in their wallet. It's also a time for *Dirty Dancing* and in her 17th summer, at a Borscht Belt resort, Baby Houseman (Jennifer Grey) learns how to do it in this skin-deep but inoffensive teen-throb pic designed to titillate teenage girls.

A headstrong girl bucking for a career in Peace Corps, Baby gets an education in life and loses her innocence when she befriends a young dancer (Cynthia Rhodes) in need of an abortion. She also gets involved with the hotel's maverick dance instructor Johnny Castle (Patrick Swayze).

Good production values, some nice dance sequences and a likable performance by Grey make the film more than watchable, especially for those acquainted with the Jewish tribal mating rituals that go on in the Catskill Mountain resorts. Swayze's character is played too soft to be convincing.

● ●

■ DIRTY DINGUS MAGEE

1970, 90 MINS, US ◇ Ⓥ

Dir Burt Kennedy   *Prod* Burt Kennedy   *Scr* Tom and Frank Waldman   *Ph* Harry Stradling Jr   *Ed* William B. Gulick   *Mus* Jeff Alexander   *Art Dir* George W. Davis
● Frank Sinatra, George Kennedy, Anne Jackson, Lois Nettleton, Jack Elam, Michele Carey (M-G-M)

Dirty Dingus Magee emerges as a good period western comedy, covering the spectrum from satire through double entendre to low slapstick, starring Frank Sinatra and George Kennedy as double-crossing buddies.

Burt Kennedy produced and directed a script [from the novel *The Ballad of Dingus Magee* by David Markson] which is loaded with effective vignette, and a strong supporting cast.

Sinatra plays an amiable roustabout, always eager but never quite able to satisfy the unending passions of Indian maiden Michele Carey. When old pal Kennedy shows up en route to California, Sinatra robs him, thus setting up the basic running, plot line of multiple compound double cross. The gag sub-plots move along at a good pace.

● ●

■ DIRTY DOZEN, THE

1967, 149 MINS, UK ◇ Ⓥ

Dir Robert Aldrich   *Prod* Kenneth Hyman   *Scr* Nunnally Johnson, Lukas Heller   *Ph* Edward Scaife   *Ed* Michael Luciano   *Mus* Frank DeVol   *Art Dir* W.E. Hutchinson
● Lee Marvin, Ernest Borgnine, Charles Bronson, Jim Brown, John Cassavetes, George Kennedy (M-G-M)

The Dirty Dozen is an exciting Second World War pre-D-Day drama about 12 condemned soldier-prisoners who are rehabilitated to serve with distinction. Lee Marvin heads a very strong, nearly all-male cast in an excellent performance.

E.M. Nathanson's novel was careful to disclaim any truth to the basic plot, for, if ever pressed, the US Army apparently can claim that no records exist on the subject. Still, Nathanson's book, as well as the very good screenplay, has a ring of authenticity to it.

Marvin delivers a top performance probably because he seems at his best in a role as a sardonic authoritarian. Herein, he is a major, handed the task of selecting 12 hardened, stockaded punks, training them for a guerrilla mission with just faintest hope of amnesty. Seeds of official conflict are sewn into plot: Marvin and Robert Ryan do not get along – but later they must.

John Cassavetes is firstrate as the tough Chicago hood who meets his match in Marvin. Charles Bronson stands out as a Polish-American who, once affixing his loyalty, does not shift under even physical brutality.

● ●

■ DIRTY HARRY

1971, 102 MINS, US ◇ Ⓥ

Dir Don Siegel   *Prod* Don Siegel   *Scr* Harry Julian Fink, R.M. Fink, Dean Riesner   *Ph* Bruce Surtees   *Ed* Carl Pingitore   *Mus* Lalo Schifrin   *Art Dir* Dale Hennesy
● Clint Eastwood, Harry Guardino, Reni Santoni, John Vernon, John Larch, Andy Robinson (Warner)

You could drive a truck through the plotholes in *Dirty Harry*, which wouldn't be so serious were the film not a specious, phony glorification of police and criminal brutality. Clint Eastwood, in the title role, is a super-hero whose antics become almost satire. Strip away the philosophical garbage and all that's left is a well-made but shallow running-and-jumping meller. Don Siegel produces handsomely and directs routinely.

Andy Robinson plays a mad sniper who attempts to hold up San Francisco for money to stop his random carnage. Mayor John Vernon is willing, police chief John Larch goes along, police lieutenant Harry Guardino unctuously follows the prevailing wind, and the work falls to supercop Eastwood.

Eastwood is dedicated – to his own violence. Perhaps his anger at Robinson is more at the delay in capturing him; after all, between bites on a hot dog, Eastwood foils a bank heist at midday, talks down a suicide jumper, and otherwise expedites assorted 'dirty work'. The character nearly drools, but Eastwood is far too inert for this bit of business.

There are several chase sequences – before the sadist-with-badge dispatches the sadist-without-badge. Thereupon, Eastwood flings his badge to the wind and walks away. At least Frisco is safe from his protection (but think of the rest of us).

● ●

■ DIRTY MARY CRAZY LARRY

1974, 93 MINS, US ◇ Ⓥ

Dir John Hough   *Prod* Norman T. Herman   *Scr* Leigh Chapman, Antonio Santean   *Ph* Mike Margulies   *Ed* Chris Holmes   *Mus* Jimmy Haskell
● Peter Fonda, Susan George, Adam Roarke, Vic Morrow, Ken Tobey, Roddy McDowall (Academy/20th Century-Fox)

Screenplay is from Richard Unekis novel *The Chase*, but what little narrative or characterization shows up on screen could barely fill an abridged short story. Racing enthusiasts Peter Fonda and Adam Roarke steal $150,000 from a supermarket manager (Roddy McDowall, strangely unbilled) in order to purchase a competition sports car. Joined by sluttish Susan George, they career around rural California with the law (demonic Vic Morrow) in pursuit.

With more than a third of the footage devoted to spectacular chases and collisions deftly staged by stunt coordinator Al Wyatt, there's little time left to hint at the reasons for Fonda's increasingly unappetizing monomania.

Cast performs ably. Fonda is less wooden than usual.

● ●

■ DISHONORED

1931, 91 MINS, US Ⓥ

Dir Josef von Sternberg   *Scr* Josef von Sternberg, Daniel N. Rubin   *Ph* Lee Garmes   *Art Dir* Hans Dreier
● Marlene Dietrich, Victor McLaglen, Lew Cody, Gustav von Seyffertitz, Warner Oland, Barry Norton (Paramount)

A secret service story [from *X-27* by Josef von Sternberg]. The start of the film, when Gustav von Seyffertitz as the Austrian intelligence chief picks up Dietrich on the street to make her a prize spy. But Dietrich rises above her director in this picture, as much as Sternberg smothered her while making *Morocco*. Dietrich is dominant in *Dishonored*. It is she who forces interest.

Her love for the Russian rival spy (Victor McLaglen) is made quite evident at the finish. Barring some silly dialog saddled upon him a couple of times, McLaglen gets through okay. Seyffertitz, always dependable, is more so than usual.

● ●

■ DISHONORED LADY

1947, 86 MINS, US Ⓥ

Dir Robert Stevenson   *Prod* Hunt Stromberg   *Scr* Edmund H. North   *Ph* Lucien Andriot   *Ed* John Foley   *Mus* Carmen Dragon   *Art Dir* Nicolai Remisoff
● Hedy Lamarr, Dennis O'Keefe, John Loder, William Lundigan, Margaret Hamilton (United Artists)

In this remake of the stage play [by Edward Sheldon and Margaret Ayer Barnes] Hedy Lamarr character is more psychological than immoral and the film approach lessens interest and clarity. Plot still gets in shadowy implications of character's promiscuous love life, mostly through dialog.

It tells of editor of fashionable femme mag who's not getting the best out of life although apparently enjoying it. Mental desperation drives her to attempted suicide, a visit with a psychiatrist, and renunciation of old way of living. She meets a young doctor, falls in love and becomes involved in a murder.

Male co-stars are Dennis O'Keefe and John Loder as the young doctor and an old love, respectively. O'Keefe character isn't always even and Loder's role is a bit too smooth. William Lundigan, Morris Carnovsky (psychiatrist), Paul Cavanagh (publisher) and Natalie Schafer are okay among other principals. Margaret Hamilton rates some chuckles in typical rooming housekeeper role.

● ●

■ DISORDERLY ORDERLY, THE

1964, 89 MINS, US ◇ Ⓥ

Dir Frank Tashlin   *Prod* Paul Jones   *Scr* Frank Tashlin   *Ph* W. Wallace Kelley   *Ed* John Woodcock   *Mus* Joseph J. Lilley   *Art Dir* Hal Pereira, Tambi Larsen
● Jerry Lewis, Glenda Farrell, Everett Sloane, Karen Sharpe, Kathleen Freeman, Susan Oliver (Paramount)

The Disorderly Orderly is fast and madcappish, with Lewis again playing one of his malaprop characters that seem to suit his particular talents.

As the orderly, Lewis is himself almost a mental patient as he takes on all the symptoms of the individual patients in the plush sanitarium where he's employed. Ambitious to be a doctor, he flunked out in medical school because of this particular attribute.

D

He's cured through some fancy script-figuring when Susan Oliver, one of the patients, offers him love and he discovers that he's really in love with Karen Sharpe, a nurse. Sandwiched within this premise is Lewis at work, at play, always in trouble.

Star is up to his usual comicking and Frank Tashlin's direction of his own screenplay is fast and vigorous in maintaining a nutty mood. Sharpe is pert and cute, Oliver ably transforms from a would-be suicide to a sex-pot, and Glenda Farrell, cast as head of the sanitarium, displays the talent which once made her a star.

. . . .

■ DISRAELI

1929, 90 MINS, US
Dir Alfred E. Green *Scr* Julian Josephson *Ph* Lee Garmes
● George Arliss, Joan Bennett, Florence Arliss, Anthony Bushell, David Torrence, Doris Lloyd (Warner)

Acting and characterization are a continuous delight, not to mention a plot that concerns the diplomatic imperativeness of possessing the Suez Canal.

To think of *Disraeli* without George Arliss is to shudder. The professional equipment of the central figure carries and dominates both plot and conversation [from the play by Louis N. Parker].

Warners have done it right. Production is unstinted, sedate, and colorful, in the style of 1874. Small bits as well as principal roles are equally meritorious. Florence Arliss, wife of the star, plays his wife in the picture and makes the family circle complete by attaching runner-up honors.

Doris Lloyd as a woman spy is interesting and plausible as she weaves her little net of intrigue. She proves the 'menace' to the plan to purchase the big ditch through Egypt.
□ 1929/30: Best Picture (Nomination)

. . . .

■ DISTANT VOICES, STILL LIVES

1988, 84 MINS, UK ◇
Dir Terence Davies *Prod* Jennifer Howarth
Scr Terence Davies *Ph* William Diver, Patrick Duval
Ed William Diver *Art Dir* Miki van Zwanenberg
● Freda Dowie, Pete Postlethwaite, Angela Walsh, Dean Williams, Lorraine Ashbourne (BFI/Film Four)

This is the first feature film of Liverpudlian Terence Davies, obviously autobiographical, dealing with a family called Davies and their lives during the 1940s and 1950s.

The film is divided into two parts: *Distant Voices* (45 mins) centers on the wedding of Eileen, eldest of the three Davies children, and the funeral of her father, events which spark memories of the past, including the frightening war years when the city was bombed frequently; *Still Lives* (39 mins) actually was filmed two years after the first part, with the same actors but with a substantially different crew. It's a seamless continuation which climaxes with the wedding of another of the clan, son Tony.

The film is full of singing, as the characters break into familiar songs at family gatherings or in the local pub. This isn't a film based on nostalgia, though; its very special qualities stem from the beautiful simplicity of direction, writing and playing, and the accuracy of the incidents depicted.

. . . .

■ DIVIDED HEART, THE

1954, 89 MINS, UK
Dir Charles Crichton *Prod* Michael Balcon *Scr* Jack Whittingham, Richard Hughes *Ph* Otto Heller
Ed Peter Bezencenet *Mus* Georges Auric
● Cornell Borchers, Yvonne Mitchell, Armin Dahlen, Alexander Knox, Geoffrey Keen, Liam Redmond (Ealing)

A human story taken from real life, *The Divided Heart* fails to tug the emotional heartstrings and ends up as little more than a conventional if convincing meller. Film is based on an actual story featured in '*Life*' in which a blood mother claims her son, who had legally been adopted during the war by German parents.

The narrative is sincerely developed from the actual documentation of the case. It spotlights the dilemma of the American tribunal which has to decide whether the boy should remain with his foster parents or be sent to his real mother. The circumstances are mainly depicted in flashback during the hearing by the American judges.

At no time does the script measure up to the real heartache of the actual incident and there is rarely more than a superficial approach to this postwar problem. The cast is more than adequate, however, and Cornell Borchers and Yvonne Mitchell give stirring performances as the two mothers involved in the dilemma.

. . . .

■ DIVINE MADNESS

1980, 94 MINS, US ◇ ▼
Dir Michael Ritchie *Prod* Michael Ritchie *Scr* Jerry Blatt, Bette Midler, Bruce Vilanch *Ph* William A. Fraker, Bobby Byrne *Ed* Glenn Farr *Mus* Tony Berg, Randy Kerber (arr.) *Art Dir* Albert Brenner
● Bette Midler, The Harlettes, Irving Sudrow (Ladd)

After years of honing her act in gay baths and on concert stages, Bette Midler in 1980 committed it to film in four days at the Pasadena, Calif, Civic Auditorium. 'Because this is the time capsule version of my show,' she tells the aud, 'I might as well do everything I know.' Well, she doesn't quite do everything but she does not stint on energy and showmanship.

The film has a more carefully designed and visually opulent look than most concert pix. Director Michael Ritchie and his supervising cameraman, William A. Fraker, employed a 30-man camera team to shoot more than one million feet of film.

Midler's monologs between songs, largely blue material familiar to devotees of her show, are uproariously funny and she delivers them with infectious physical panache.

As for her voice, Midler is no Streisand, but she has a solid personality to back up her songs, and her versatility is one of her strongest assets.

. . . .

■ DIVORCE AMERICAN STYLE

1967, 109 MINS, US ◇ ▼
Dir Bud Yorkin *Prod* Norman Lear *Scr* Norman Lear *Ph* Conrad Hall *Ed* Ferris Webster *Mus* Dave Grusin *Art Dir* Edward Stephenson
● Dick Van Dyke, Debbie Reynolds, Jason Robards, Jean Simmons, Van Johnson, Joe Flynn (Columbia)

Comedy and satire, not feverish melodrama, are the best weapons with which to harpoon social mores. An outstanding example is *Divorce American Style* [from a story by Robert Kaufman], which pokes incisive, sometimes chilling, fun at US marriage-divorce problems.

Amidst wow comedy situations, story depicts the break-up after 15 years of the Van Dyke-Debbie Reynolds marriage, followed by the economic tragedies exemplified by Jason Robards and Jean Simmons, caught in a vicious circle of alimony and remarriage problems.

Shelley Berman and Dick Gautier, two chummy lawyers, spotlight the occasional feeling by litigants that their personal problems are secondary to the games attorneys play.

. . . .

■ DIVORCEE, THE

1930, 80 MINS, US
Dir Robert Z. Leonard *Scr* Nick Grinde, Zelda Sears, John Meehan *Ph* Norbert Brodine *Ed* Hugh Wynn
● Norma Shearer, Chester Morris, Conrad Nagel, Robert Montgomery, Florence Eldridge, Helene Millard (M-G-M)

In its adaptation of *Ex-Wife*, the spicy 1929 novel by Ursula Parrott, Metro has taken liberties. Refinement has taken the upper hand here, with only the necessary touch of sauciness to satisfy readers of the novel, which was first published anonymously and later, after thousands of copies were sold, under the author's name.

Metro has even changed the names of the characters as they were in the Parrott story, given it a totally foreign opening, skipped much of the material that made *Ex-Wife* an interesting yarn, missed entirely the spirit with which the heroine accepts the futility of her marriage, suddenly broken off, and for a surprise ending takes the action to Paris and patches everything up.

Norma Shearer is excellent as the ad writer who in the novel finally despairs of ever getting her husband back, but in the picture does and with a very effective, formula-like clinch for the close. Opposite Shearer is Chester Morris, who is actually cast as a newspaper man. You only know that because he says so once. Audience figuring out things for the finish will probably be fooled to find that Conrad Nagel, the other man, doesn't successfully step in for the final fade, but that's the way it's been done here, the novel notwithstanding.

Besides good performances by Shearer, Morris and Nagel, unusually fine work is contributed by Robert Montgomery, the husband's friend, who helps himself to the wife as he would to an extended cocktail.
□ 1929/30: Best Picture (Nomination)

. . . .

■ DIVORCE OF LADY X, THE

1938, 92 MINS, UK ◇ ▼
Dir Tim Whelan *Prod* Alexander Korda *Scr* Ian Dalrymple, Arthur Wimperis, Lajos Biro *Ph* Harry Stradling *Ed* L.J.W. Stockviss, William Hornbeck *Mus* Miklos Rozsa *Art Dir* Lazare Meerson
● Merle Oberon, Laurence Olivier, Binnie Barnes, Ralph Richardson, Morton Selten, Gus McNaughton (London Films)

Alexander Korda's Technicolored comedy is rich, smart entertainment, a comedy built around several situations and a wrong-identity hoax. Picture takes unusually long in getting going into brisk action and the repetitions during the first half hour are many.

Robert E. Sherwood's deft writing is apparent in the screenplay job he did along with Lajos Biro, author of the play [*Counsel's Opinion*] from which the pic was evolved. Comedy lines have that Sherwood sting.

Merle Oberon attends a costume ball in a London hotel and after the manager can't persuade an annoyed young lawyer (Laurence Olivier) to part with some space in his suite, Oberon maneuvers in and wheedles him out of his bed.

Next day girl vamooses before chap can find out much about her; he's convinced she's married. On arrival at his office, he is plagued by a college classmate to get the latter a divorce. He claims his wife spent the night with an unknown man in the same hotel, after attending the same dance. Girl continues to interest the chap and when she knows the sort he believes her to be maintains the ruse.

Oberon impresses. Olivier does his role pretty well, retarded somewhat by an annoying bit of pouting business. Two key performances which sparkle are those of Ralph Richardson and Morton Selten. Former plays the man who wants the divorce; latter Oberon's grandfather, who is the judge sitting on most of the cases the young lawyer pleads.

■ **D.O.A.**

1950, 83 MINS, US ⓥ

Dir Rudolph Mate   *Prod* Harry M. Popkin   *Scr* Russell Rouse, Clarence Green   *Ph* Ernest Laszlo   *Ed* Arthur H. Nadel   *Mus* Dimitri Tiomkin   *Art Dir* Duncan Cramer

● Edmond O'Brien, Pamela Britton, Luther Adler, Beverly Campbell (United Artists)

D.O.A. poses the novel twist of having a man looking for his own murderer. That off-beat idea and a strong performance by Edmond O'Brien do a lot to hold it together. But script is difficult to follow and doesn't get into its real meat until about 35 minutes of footage have passed.

O'Brien is seen as a tax counselor who trips to San Francisco for a round of the fleshpots. During a visit of hot spots he is slipped deadly luminous poison in a drink, and he is told he only has a few days to live. He spends the next few days trying to find his murderer and why he had been made a victim.

Rudolph Mate's direction of the first portion of the story lingers too long over it, spreading the expectancy very thin, but when he does launch his suspense-building it comes over with a solid wallop.

■ **D.O.A.**

1988, 96 MINS, US ◇ ⓥ

Dir Rocky Morton, Annabel Jankel   *Prod* Ian Sander, Laura Ziskin, Cathleen Summers, Andrew J. Kuehn   *Scr* Charles Edward Pogue   *Ph* Yuri Neyman   *Ed* Michael R. Miller   *Mus* Chaz Jankel   *Art Dir* Richard Amend

● Dennis Quaid, Meg Ryan, Charlotte Rampling, Daniel Stern, Christopher Neame (Touchstone/Silver Screen Partners III)

An excessively morbid and unsubtle second remake of the 1949 film noir classic, *D.O.A.* remains unbelievable and unappealing despite a barnstorming central performance by Dennis Quaid.

Scripter uses two central MacGuffins to get the pot boiling. First Quaid is an English prof who's unwilling to read his precocious student Nick Lang's (played by Rob Knepper) novel. Just as hard-drinking Quaid marks an A on the still unread manuscript, Nick falls to his death past Quaid's window, an apparent suicide.

Second, pic's structure (bookended with black-&-white sequences at the police station) and catalyst are from Russell Rouse and Clarence Green's 1949 screenplay for *D.O.A.* In the third reel Quaid is diagnosed as having ingested a luminous poison, with only one to two days left to live. The protagonist who has given up on life since publishing his last novel four years back now has an obsession to live for: find his own killer.

Convoluted trail of murder and suicide teams Quaid with Meg Ryan, as a pretty coed with a crush on him.

Hailing from music videos and TV's *Max Headroom*, married helmers Rocky Morton and Annabel Jankel overload their maiden feature with visual gimmickry: lots of tilted, or swivelling first-person camerawork plus moire-patterned lighting to create distortion. Acting, particularly by Quaid, Ryan and Knepper, is fine, but Charlotte Rampling is very unflatteringly styled and photographed.

■ **DOC**

1971, 95 MINS, US ◇

Dir Frank Perry   *Prod* Frank Perry   *Scr* Pete Hamill   *Ph* Gerald Hirschfield   *Ed* Alan Helm   *Mus* Jimmy Webb   *Art Dir* Gene Callahan

● Stacy Keach, Faye Dunaway, Harris Yulin, Mike Witney, Denver John Collins, Dan Greenburg (United Artists)

Frank Perry in *Doc* attempts to remove the encrustations of myth and fantasy over the rough-hewn facts and persons of Wyatt Earp, Doc Holliday, Kate Elder and Tombstone.

Stacy Keach, Faye Dunaway and Harris Yulin star in good performances which may shock the naive, outrage the super-patriotic, offend those who prefer the cliches of the American West, but satisfy the well-adjusted.

Perry takes care to explore the reality of the situations, to recreate an earthy environment, and then to depict acts and events which, in their own time and morality, made sense. In order to achieve this, the first reel is as delicate as a kick in the groin; once over that pain the rest of the story evolves smoothly.

Earp (Yulin) emerges as a shifty politician of flexible motivation, by today's cynical standards a model pragmatic man of public life. His relationship with Holliday (Keach) has undertones left to the imagination (when little else is). Dunaway shakes her fashion-model fragility to become a believable frontier woman.

■ **DOCK BRIEF, THE**

1962, 88 MINS, UK

Dir James Hill   *Prod* Dimitri De Grunwald   *Scr* Pierre Rouve   *Ph* Edward Scaife   *Ed* Ann Chegwidden   *Mus* Ron Grainer   *Art Dir* Ray Simm

● Peter Sellers, Richard Attenborough, Beryl Reid, David Lodge, Tristram Jellinek (M-G-M)

This offbeat, arty film gets away to a good start with the stellar pull of Peter Sellers and Richard Attenborough. Originally a radio play by John Mortimer, it is a bold attempt to present something different and, on the whole, it's a fair try.

Sellers plays an aging, unsuccessful barrister who gets the chance of a lifetime when briefed to defend Attenborough, a mild bird-seed merchant who has murdered his wife because he wanted peace. He is bored with her because of her raucous sense of humour. It is the last straw when she doesn't elope with their equally raucous and boisterous lodger. Sellers plans his campaign optimistically and is quite undaunted when Attenborough admits the crime and shows the flaws in all Sellers' defense arguments.

The screenplay is a literate job, with a deft mixture of comedy and pathos. Sellers has the opportunity of showing many moods and much of his work is good. Attenborough comes out of the acting duel rather better.

■ **DOCKS OF NEW YORK, THE**

1928, 80 MINS, US ⊗ ⓥ

Dir Josef von Sternberg   *Scr* Jules Furthman, Julian Johnson   *Ph* Harold Rosson   *Art Dir* Hans Dreier

● George Bancroft, Betty Compson, Baclanova, Clyde Cook, Mitchell Lewis, Gustav von Seyffertitz (Paramount)

The Docks of New York is not Josef von Sternberg's greatest. But it's a corking program picture, thanks to George Bancroft, a good story and Julian Johnson's titles.

Sternberg's direction is excellent, but it is in the casting that the picture falls short of special classification. Betty Compson as an elliptical-heeled frail, who is punch drunk from life and attempts suicide, only to be rescued by Bancroft, a roughneck stoker, fails to get underneath the characterization. In real life she would probably have four husbands in the rack and be chalking up for the fifth.

Bancroft as Bill Roberts, the husky, hard-drinking, two-fisted stoker, has a role that he can make roll over. Roberts, on his one night ashore, saves the girl, and in a spirit of bra-

vado marries her in a waterfront dive operated by a crimp (Guy Oliver).

Next morning Roberts again is ready for sea. He is on his way to a ship when a crowd and the arrival of the police arouses his curiosity. He returns to find the girl about to be arrested for shooting the third engineer of the crew (Mitchell Lewis), who had entered her room and tried to force his attentions on her.

The scenario is adapted from the John Monk Saunders original, *The Dock Walloper*. Exquisite photography helps a lot. Foggy mystic water shots give the waterfront the same quality of *Street Angel*.

■ **DOC SAVAGE**
THE MAN OF BRONZE

1975, 100 MINS, US ◇

Dir Michael Anderson   *Prod* George Pal   *Scr* George Pal, Joe Morhaim   *Ph* Fred Koenekamp   *Ed* Thomas McCarthy   *Mus* Frank DeVol (adapt.)   *Art Dir* Fred Harpman

● Ron Ely, Paul Gleason, Bill Lucking, Michael Miller, Eldon Quick, Darrell Zwerling (Warner)

Execrable acting, dopey action sequences, and clumsy attempts at camp humor mark George Pal's *Doc Savage* as the kind of kiddie film that gives the G rating a bad name. Set in the 1930s and based on the Kenneth Robeson comic strip character, it is below the level of the *Batman* 1960s TV series, which it seems to be emulating.

Ron Ely looks impressive as the blond muscleman superhero, but doesn't do much beyond flexing his muscles and flashing smiles at the group of cronies who join him on an expedition into the South American jungles to avenge his father's murder.

Only thesp who survives the script with any dignity is Pamela Hensley, playing a native girl in love with the stolid hero.

■ **DOCTOR AT LARGE**

1957, 104 MINS, UK ◇ ⓥ

Dir Ralph Thomas   *Prod* Betty E. Box   *Scr* Nicholas Phipps   *Ph* Ernest Steward   *Ed* Frederick Wilson   *Mus* Bruce Montgomery   *Art Dir* Maurice Carter

● Dirk Bogarde, Muriel Pavlow, Donald Sinden, James Robertson Justice, Shirley Eaton, Michael Medwin (Rank)

This continues the adventures of the young medico who qualified in *Doctor in the House* and got his first appointment in *Doctor at Sea*. This time round he's on a job hunting spree and the film depicts his experiences and adventures while working for a mean provincial doctor and in a fashionable Park Lane practice.

The yarn develops with a blending of light comedy and a dash of sentiment, with punch comedy lines providing timely shots in the arm. They're welcome when they come, but they're too irregular.

Role of the young doctor again is played by Dirk Bogarde. The story opens at St Swithin's hospital where Bogarde hopes to achieve his vocational ambitions to practice surgery. But he falls foul of James Robertson Justice, who is the hospital's chief consultant. To gain experience (and pay the rent), he begins his job hunting trail.

Bogarde, of course, is the mainstay of the story, but Justice again emerges as the standout character, even though his role is reduced to more modest proportions.

■ **DOCTOR AT SEA**

1955, 93 MINS, UK ◇ ⓥ

Dir Ralph Thomas   *Prod* Betty E. Box   *Scr* Nicholas Phipps, Jack Davies   *Ph* Ernest Steward   *Ed* Frederick Wilson   *Mus* Bruce Montgomery

● Dirk Bogarde, Brigitte Bardot, Brenda De Banzie,

D

James Robertson Justice, Maurice Denham, Michael Medwin (Rank)

As their first British venture in VistaVision, the Rank studios play safe with a sequel to *Doctor in the House*, but *Doctor at Sea* does not rise to the same laugh-provoking heights as its predecessor.

James Robertson Justice is a gruff ship's captain on whose freighter the young medico has his first appointment at sea. The ship is obliged to take on board the daughter of the chairman of the line and her friend, a pert and attractive cabaret chanteuse.

By far the most dominating performance of the cast is given by Justice. He towers above the others and is the focal point of every scene in which he appears. Dirk Bogarde plays the medico with a pleasing quiet restraint and Brigitte Bardot has an acting talent to match her charm.

■ DOCTOR DOLITTLE

1967, 152 MINS, US ◇ Ⓥ

Dir Richard Fleischer *Prod* Arthur P. Jacobs *Scr* Leslie Bricusse *Ph* Robert Surtees *Ed* Samuel E. Beetley, Marjorie Fowler *Mus* Leslie Bricusse *Art Dir* Mario Chiari

● Rex Harrison, Samantha Eggar, Anthony Newley, Richard Attenborough, Peter Bull, Muriel Landers (20th Century-Fox/Apjac)

Rex Harrison, physically, is not at all the rotund original from Hugh Lofting's stories; but histrionically, he's perfect. Gentle and loving with animals, patient and kind with obtuse and very young friends, he can become a veritable holocaust when confronted with cruel and uncomprehending adults who threaten his animal world.

Leslie Bricusse's adaptation retains the delightful aspects while taking considerable liberty with the plot. His music and lyrics, while containing no smash hits, are admirably suited to the scenario.

Outstanding, considering his brief appearance, is Richard Attenborough as Albert Blossom, the circus owner. He comes on so strong in his one song-and-dance bit that it's nearly a perfect example of why important cameo roles should be turned over to important talents.

Most of the $16 million budget evidently went into the production and it shows.
□ 1967: Best Picture (Nomination)

■ DOCTOR EHRLICH'S MAGIC BULLET

1940, 103 MINS, US

Dir William Dieterle *Prod* Hal B. Wallis, Wolfgang Reinhardt *Scr* John Huston, Heinz Herald, Norman Burnside *Ph* James Wong Howe *Ed* Warren Low *Mus* Max Steiner *Art Dir* Carl Jules Weyl

● Edward G. Robinson, Ruth Gordon, Otto Kruger, Donald Crisp, Maria Ouspenskaya, Albert Basserman (Warner)

Here is a splendid production, with much care and attention to detail. Historical biography is based on the life of Paul Ehrlich, famed bacteriologist, whose most noteworthy contribution to medical science was the search for, and eventual discovery of, 606, which proved to be a positive cure for syphilis.

The social disease is intelligently handled for effective presentation of its disastrous effects on humans prior to Ehrlich's discovery. Despite its straightforward presentation of the scourge of syphilis during Ehrlich's research for a cure, there is nothing offensive in either action or dialog. Script, which necessitates care in combining the events of Ehrlich's career with scientific fact, is an excellently moulded screen biography.

Edward G. Robinson's portrayal of the famed Ehrlich is a distinguished performance. In tracing the scientist's accomplish-

ments, story traces through a span of about 35 years. Robinson makes the gradual transition down the years in great style.

Ruth Gordon is a most sympathetic and understanding wife of a scientist absorbed in his work; Otto Kruger is excellent as Ehrlich's close friend and colleague; Donald Crisp is the health minister, and Albert Basserman is the noted scientist, Koch, who takes Ehrlich on his staff in the early part. Albert Basserman, well-known German actor, gets his first American role here.

■ DOCTOR FAUSTUS

1967, 92 MINS, UK ◇ Ⓥ

Dir Richard Burton, Nevill Coghill *Prod* Richard Burton, Richard McWhorter *Scr* Nevill Coghill *Ph* Gabor Pogany *Ed* John Shirley *Mus* Mario Nascimbene *Art Dir* John F. DeCuir

● Richard Burton, Elizabeth Taylor, Andreas Teuber, Ian Marter, Elizabeth O'Donovan, David McIntosh (Columbia)

An oddity that may have some archive appeal, for at least it records a performance by Burton [at Oxford University in 1966] that gives an insight into his prowess in classical roles. He is obviously captivated by Christopher Marlowe's 400-year-old verse, and speaks it with sonorous dignity and sense.

The story concerns the medieval doctor's attempt to master all human knowledge by selling his soul to the devil, who dangles before him such delights as nights with Elizabeth Taylor, who flits through the film in various undraped poses as the Helen of Troy siren promising a fate worse than death.

One surprise is the general adequacy of the Oxford amateurs, with a good performance in any terms from Andreas Teuber as Mephistopheles. But the impersonation of the seven deadly sins is hardly likely to send good men off the rail. Production was filmed in Rome.

■ DOCTOR IN THE HOUSE

1954, 92 MINS, UK ◇ Ⓥ

Dir Ralph Thomas *Prod* Betty E. Box *Scr* Nicholas Phipps *Ph* Ernest Steward *Ed* Gerald Thomas *Mus* Bruce Montgomery

● Dirk Bogarde, Muriel Pavlow, Kenneth More, Donald Sinden, Kay Kendall, James Robertson Justice (Rank)

A topdraw British comedy, *Doctor in the House* is bright, diverting entertainment, intelligently scripted, and warmly played.

Background to the story is the medical school of a London hospital. Within 92 minutes, the film spans the five years in the life of a student group.

The new recruit to the school is Dirk Bogarde, who is taken under the protective wing of three old-timers who had all failed their preliminary exams. Kenneth More, Donald Sinden and Donald Houston make up a contrasted quartet who seem to have ideas on most subjects but not how to qualify as a medico.

Much of the comedy incident has been clearly contrived but it is nonetheless effective, particularly in the scenes featuring James Robertson Justice as a distinguished surgeon and More.

■ DOCTOR'S DILEMMA, THE

1959, 98 MINS, UK ◇

Dir Anthony Asquith *Prod* Anatole de Grunwald *Scr* Anatole de Grunwald *Ph* Robert Krasker *Ed* Gordon Hales *Mus* Joseph Kosma *Art Dir* Paul Sheriff

● Leslie Caron, Dirk Bogarde, Alastair Sim, Robert Morley, Felix Aylmer, Michael Gwynn (M-G-M/Comet)

George Bernard Shaw's stringent wit still shines in this film but, staged in 1903, his comments on Harley Street (London's medical row) and the doctoring profession have lost much of their impact. *Dilemma* remains, relentlessly, an easy-on-the-eye filmed version of an out-of-date play.

It concerns a young woman married to an artist who is a complete bounder – a sponger, a potential blackmailer and a man who can't resist other women. But she is blinded by hero-worship. He suffers from consumption, she pleads with a doctor to save his life. He thinks that he would do better to use his limited serum on a more worthwhile case.

Dirk Bogarde gives a stimulating performance as the selfish young artist and is particularly convincing in his final, highly theatrical death sequence. Leslie Caron is often moving in her blind belief in her man, but never suggests the strength necessary to fight the cynical doctors. These are played as caricatures.

■ DOCTOR ZHIVAGO

1965, 197 MINS, US ◇ Ⓥ

Dir David Lean *Prod* Carlo Ponti *Scr* Robert Bolt *Ph* Freddie Young *Ed* Norman Savage *Mus* Maurice Jarre *Art Dir* John Box

● Omar Sharif, Julie Christie, Tom Courtenay, Geraldine Chaplin, Rod Steiger, Alec Guinness (M-G-M)

The sweep and scope of the Russian revolution, as reflected in the personalities of those who either adapted or were crushed, has been captured by David Lean in *Doctor Zhivago*, frequently with soaring dramatic intensity.

Some finely etched performances by an international cast illuminate the diverse characters from the novel for which Boris Pasternak won but did not accept the Nobel Prize. The Pasternak novel turns on an introspective medic-poet who essentially reacts to the people and events before, during and after the Bolshevik takeover.

At the center of a universe of nine basic characters is Omar Sharif as Zhivago, the sensitive man who strikes different people in different ways. To childhood sweetheart Geraldine Chaplin he is a devoted (if cheating) husband; to Julie Christie, with whom he is thrown together by war, he is a passionate lover; to Tom Courtenay, once an intellectual but later a heartless Red general, he's a symbol of the personal life which revolution has supposedly killed; to lecherous, political logroller Rod Steiger he's the epitome of 'rarefied selfishness'; and to halfbrother Alec Guinness, the cold secret police official, he's a man who must be saved from himself.

Sharif, largely through expressions of indignation, compassion and tenderness, makes the character very believable. Christie is outstanding in a sensitive, yet earthy and full-blooded portrayal of a girl who is used and discarded by Steiger, then marries Courtenay only to lose him to his cause.

Lean has devoted as much care to physical values as he has to his players. The bitter cold of winter, the grime of Moscow, the lush countryside, the brutality of war, and the fool's paradise of the declining Czarist era are forcefully conveyed.
□ 1965: Best Picture (Nomination)

■ DODGE CITY

1939, 100 MINS, US ◇ Ⓥ

Dir Michael Curtiz *Prod* Robert Lord *Scr* Robert Buckner *Ph* Sol Polito, Ray Rennahan *Ed* George Amy *Mus* Max Steiner *Art Dir* Ted Smith

● Errol Flynn, Olivia de Havilland, Ann Sheridan, Bruce Cabot, William Lundigan (Warner)

Dodge City is a lusty western, packed with action, including some of the dandiest melee stuff screened.

Falling in the cycle of pioneering and American frontier days, *Dodge City* (Kansas) is essentially a bad man-and-honest-sheriff saga. However Michael Curtiz's forceful direction lifts this into the big league division.

Errol Flynn is a soldier of fortune, which explains his clipped English-Irish brogue as a Texas cattleman, transplanted to this Kansas frontier. Olivia de Havilland is the romance interest, and Ann Sheridan the dancehall girl.

Cabot's gambling saloon effectively typifies all the wickedness of the lawlessness that was Dodge City, as the basic excuse for Flynn's ultimate taking over of the sheriff's post. The street fighting, licentiousness and the skullduggery having to do with cattle trading typify the lusty atmosphere that backgrounds this actioner.

● ●

■ DODSWORTH

1936, 90 MINS, US ⊙

Dir William Wyler *Prod* Samuel Goldwyn *Scr* Sidney Howard *Ph* Ruldoph Mate *Ed* Danny Mandell *Mus* Alfred Newman *Art Dir* Richard Day
● Walter Huston, Ruth Chatterton, Paul Lukas, Mary Astor, David Niven, Gregory Gaye
(Goldwyn/United Artists)

Dodsworth is a superb motion picture and a golden borealis over the producer's name.

Sidney Howard transposes his own stage play version of Sinclair Lewis' novel into a picture that uses the camera to open up the vista a little and enrich a basically fertile theme. Picture has a steady flow and an even dramatic wallop from zippy start to satisfying finish.

Dodsworth was Walter Huston on the stage and is logically and perfectly the same actor on the screen. This is the kind of a role stars dream about.

It is also obvious that this is Ruth Chatterton's fanciest opportunity on the screen in a long while. Fran Dodsworth is a silly, vain, selfish, shallow kitten and in the playing of Chatterton comes to life with vividness and humanity.

Mary Astor is the sympathetic other woman to whom Dodsworth ultimately turns. Her footage is limited. Her performance is varied and mature.

Three men cross the path of the age-fearing wife on her grand fling. First an Englishman played by David Niven. Then a suave continental played by Paul Lukas. Last a sincere and youthful Austrian played by George Gaye. Each of the lovers is a case of slick casting. Mother of the Austrian who finally strikes home with the pampered American woman is beautifully performed by Maria Ouspenskaya.
□ 1936: Best Picture (Nomination)

● ●

■ DOG DAY AFTERNOON

1975, 130 MINS, US ◇

Dir Sidney Lumet *Prod* Martin Bregman, Martin Elfand *Scr* Frank Pierson *Ph* Victor J. Kemper *Ed* Dede Allen *Art Dir* Charles Bailey
● Al Pacino, John Cazale, Sully Boyar, Penny Allen, Charles Durning, James Broderick (Warner)

Dog Day Afternoon is an outstanding film. Based on a real life incident in NY it stars Al Pacino as the most unlikely bank robber ever to hit the screen.

The holdup was allegedly done for the purpose of financing a sex change operation for the male lover of one of the robbers. That incident is retained in the script, but it is just one of many key elements in a hilarious and moving story.

Pacino and laconic sidekick John Cazale take over the neighborhood bank branch managed by Sully Boyar. The malaprop heist gets the early laughs going, and then the film broadens and deepens as if re-enacting the Battle Of The Bulge.

The introduction of Pacino's lover (Chris Sarandon) is cleverly plotted, and comes as a surprise since Pacino's straight wife (Susan Peretz) has already appeared. The interactions between Pacino and other key characters are magnificently written, acted and directed.

The entire cast is excellent, top to bottom. *Dog Day Afternoon* is, in the whole as well as the parts, film-making at its best.

● ●

■ DOGS OF WAR, THE

1980, 122 MINS, UK ◇ ⊙

Dir John Irvin *Prod* Norman Jewison, Patrick Palmer *Scr* Gary DeVore, George Malko *Ph* Jack Cardiff *Ed* Antony Gibbs *Mus* Geoffrey Burgon *Art Dir* Peter Mullins
● Christopher Walken, Tom Berenger, Colin Blakely, Hugh Millais, Paul Freeman, JoBeth Williams
(United Artists)

The Dogs of War [from Frederick Forsyth's novel] is an intelligent and occasionally forceful treatment of a provocative but little-examined theme, that of mercenary warrior involvement in the overthrow of a corrupt black African dictatorship.

Script focuses almost exclusively on Christopher Walken, an 'irresponsible' American who is drawn to the mercenary's loner, adventurous life.

Film fails to really get at the heart of the whys and hows of mercenary life, and also rejects the idea of generating any sense of camaraderie among the men.

Details of life in a contempo African dictatorship country, from the bribery and censorship to the military strongarming and oppressive economic conditions, are effectively sketched. Pic displays the political realities without editorializing.

● ●

■ $

1971, 120 MINS, US ◇ ⊙

Dir Richard Brooks *Prod* M.J. Francovich *Scr* Richard Brooks *Ph* Petrus Schloemp *Ed* George Grenville *Mus* Quincy Jones *Art Dir* Guy Sheppard
● Warren Beatty, Goldie Hawn, Gert Frobe, Robert Webber, Scott Brady, Arthur Brauss (Columbia)

Richard Brooks wrote and directed $ with a sardonic twist to a caper plot. Bank security expert Warren Beatty, aided by friendly hooker Goldie Hawn, steal $1.5 million from three Hamburg safety-deposit boxes used by assorted criminals. An exhausting chase sequence is the ultimate destination of the production which features some good authentic locales.

The key subordinate characters, Las Vegas skimming courier Robert Webber, corrupt US Army black marketeer Scott Brady, and European narcotics dealer Arthur Brauss, are on a dramatic parity with the principals and often overpower them. Hawn's trademark kookiness keeps getting in the way, and Beatty's low-key sensitivity can hardly survive.

This film is obviously what is sometimes called 'an entertainment'. Paradoxically, Brooks maybe is too serious a filmmaker for this sort of thing. He wants his characters to have depth and motivation, but the principle does not work well herein.

● ●

■ DOLL'S HOUSE, A

1973, 95 MINS, UK ◇ ⊙

Dir Patrick Garland *Prod* Hillard Elkins *Scr* Christopher Hampton *Ph* Arthur Ibbetson *Ed* John Glen *Mus* John Barry *Art Dir* Elliott Scott
● Claire Bloom, Anthony Hopkins, Ralph Richardson, Denholm Elliott, Anna Massey, Edith Evans
(Elkins/Freeward)

What is good here is largely what was good in the 1971 Broadway production from which pic directly derives. The latter was produced by Hillard Elkins, topline his wife Claire Bloom, and was helmed and scripted by Patrick Garland and Christopher Hampton, respectively. All ditto for this film.

Package was assembled as though it were a legit production – two weeks of rehearsals preceded lensing, and scenes were shot in order.

Christopher Hampton's interpretation of Henrick Ibsen's text successfully plays down the original's creakier verbal anachronisms but leaves its excellent construction intact. Film, as does play, unfolds grippingly, like a first-rate murder mystery with a cosmic consciousness.

Bloom is topnotch as the childlike and pampered wife of a stuffy bank manager. Bloom's portrayal beautifully captures Nora's initial coquettishness and her emergence as an independent woman of strength and character.

● ●

■ DOLL'S HOUSE, A

1973, 108 MINS, UK ◇ ⊙

Dir Joseph Losey *Prod* Joseph Losey *Scr* David Mercer *Ph* Gerry Fisher *Ed* Reginald Beck *Mus* Michel Legrand *Art Dir* Eileen Diss
● Jane Fonda, David Warner, Trevor Howard, Delphine Seyrig, Edward Fox, Anna Wing (World)

The second version of the Henrik Ibsen classic to hit the screens in 1973, Joseph Losey's location-filmed (Norway) effort has the director's name plus that of Jane Fonda (playing the woman's lib pre-dating heroine, Nora) and a certain formal elegance to carry it.

Ironically, it is Fonda who appears miscast as the Ibsen heroine who dominates this Nordic drama, lacking as she does the vibrancy, depth and soul required to convey the transition of a fascinating character. The result, to all but Fonda die-hards, blurs the values of the film as a whole.

This is otherwise a rather striking if academic achievement: physically stunning, diligently acted, told in a linear style by a man who knows his cinema, unexcitingly effective here and there.

● ●

■ DOMINO PRINCIPLE, THE

1977, 97 MINS, US ◇ ⊙

Dir Stanley Kramer *Prod* Stanley Kramer *Scr* Adam Kennedy *Ph* Fred Koenekamp *Ed* John Burnett *Mus* Billy Goldenberg *Art Dir* William Greber
● Gene Hackman, Candice Bergen, Richard Widmark, Mickey Rooney, Edward Albert, Eli Wallach
(ITC/Associated General)

The Domino Principle is a weak and tedious potboiler starring Gene Hackman as a tool of mysterious international intrigue, and a barely recognizable Candice Bergen in a brief role as his perplexed wife. Stanley Kramer's film contains a lot of physical and logistical nonsense.

Adam Kennedy gets adaptation credit from his own novel. Hackman has been carefully spotted years earlier as an amoral and violent type, just the kind of guy that 'they' can use to assassinate selected public figures. We never know who 'they' are, but 'their' lower-level stooges include Richard Widmark, Eli Wallach and Edward Albert, each more or less archetypic organizational characters.

● ●

■ DON JUAN

1926, 100 MINS, US

Dir Alan Crosland *Scr* Bess Meredyth, Walter Anthony, Maude Fulton *Ph* Byron Haskin *Ed* Harold McCord *Mus* William Axt *Art Dir* Ben Carre
● John Barrymore, Mary Astor, Estelle Taylor, Warner Oland, Montagu Love, Myrna Loy (Warner

D

Several outstanders in this splendidly written, directed and produced feature. Not alone does John Barrymore's superb playing become one of them, but his athletics, as well. A chase scene is a bear. It's of Don Juan carrying his Adriana away, followed by about a dozen swordsmen on horses, with Barrymore placing his charge in a tree, to return and knock off all of the riders, one by one or in twos.

The complete surprise is the performance of Estelle Taylor as Lucretia Borgia. Her Lucretia is a fine piece of work. She makes it sardonic in treatment, conveying precisely the woman Lucretia is presumed to have been. The other outstanding performance is that of Mary Astor's Adriana. Astor has but comparatively little action, but fills the part so thoroughly that she is a dominating figure. Warner Oland is Cesare, the savage brother, and he looks the role.

■ **DO NOT DISTURB**

1965, 102 MINS, US ◇

Dir Ralph Levy *Prod* Aaron Rosenberg, Martin Melcher *Scr* Milt Rosen, Richard Breen *Ph* Leon Shamroy *Ed* Robert Simpson *Mus* Lionel Newman
● Doris Day, Rod Taylor, Hermione Baddeley, Sergio Fantoni, Reginald Gardiner, Maura McGiveney (20th Century-Fox)

Do Not Disturb is a light, entertaining comedy, set in England but filmed in Hollywood, with Doris Day teamed with a new screen hubby, Rod Taylor.

Milt Rosen and Richard Breen adapted a William Fairchild play, and Day and Taylor star as a Yank couple localed in London, where hubby runs a woolen mill.

Stars play extremely well together, Day as the loving, but slightly wacky wife who grapples with English currency problems, rescues a pursued fox, and never quite gets the home in order, while Taylor is busy getting his factory into the black.

Their lives diverge when Maura McGiveney becomes too much of an assistant to Taylor, and sales chief Reginald Gardiner spells out the key for biz success: getting on the good side of Leon Askin, big wool buyer who throws swinging parties, meaning no wives.

Action cross cuts from Taylor's problem to Day, who becomes innocently entangled with Sergio Fantoni, antique dealer and a prototype Continental charmer.

■ **DONOVAN'S REEF**

1963, 104 MINS, US ◇ Ⓥ

Dir John Ford *Prod* John Ford *Scr* Frank Nugent, James Edward Grant *Ph* William Clothier *Ed* Otho Lovering *Mus* Cyril Mockridge
● John Wayne, Lee Marvin, Jack Warden, Elizabeth Allen, Cesar Romero, Dorothy Lamour (Paramount)

Donovan's Reef for a director of John Ford's stature, is a potboiler. Where Ford aficianados will squirm is during that occasional scene that reminds them this effort-less effort is the handiwork of the men who made *Stagecoach* and *The Informer*.

John Wayne sailing along like a dreadnaught mothering a convoy of rowboats, conveys an exuberance to match the mayhem, moving from fracas to fracas, facing up to a gang of toughs or a belligerent Boston beauty with equal courage. The only demand made is on his muscles.

Lee Marvin, since their last excursion, has had his reins tightened by Ford. This is only a comic menace where once a malevolent terror smouldered. Jack Warden's role hints at earlier greater prominence, edited down to harmless support and irritating in its omissions.

Ford, best when he's faced with an unknown talent, brings out the ability of Elizabeth Allen, a darkling beauty. She's delightful as a Boston ice cube whose melting point is Wayne. Cesar Romero and Dorothy Lamour are the victims of acute scriptitis although Dick Foran is briefly impressive as an Australian naval officer.

The visual beauty of Kauai, in northern Hawaii, is captured by William Clothier's photography. Frank Nugent (an old Ford hand) and James Edward Grant's script has more holes in it than Liberty Valance. They've created a paradisical setting, 'somewhere in the South Pacific', ruled by a native princess; governed by the French; protected by the Australian navy; 'run' by expatriate Americans; and peopled by a league of national types.

■ **DON'S PARTY**

1976, 90 MINS, AUSTRALIA ◇ Ⓥ

Dir Bruce Beresford *Prod* Philip Adams *Scr* David Williamson *Ph* Don McAlpine *Ed* Bill Anderson *Art Dir* Rhoisin Harrison
● Ray Barrett, Claire Binney, Pat Bishop, Graeme Blundell, Jeannie Drynan, John Gorton (Double Head)

The eponymous get-together takes place in Australia on Election Night, 1969. The 11 characters are all friends who, save two, have assembled to cheer in a Labor Party victory. The election day atmosphere is added to by a walk-on appearance by John Gorton as the prime minister of the day – which, indeed, he was.

The central characters in David Williamson's play may be grotesque, uncouth, drunken louts, but they do represent a streak in the Australian character that exists. Bringing them together at that particular time and place increases the claustrophobic effect they have on the others.

Don's Party is a vicious and unrelenting attack on suburbia and a harsh look at these who help populate it. The entire cast turn in superlative performances.

■ **DON'T BOTHER TO KNOCK**

1952, 76 MINS, US

Dir Roy Ward Baker *Prod* Julian Blaustein *Scr* Daniel Taradash *Ph* Lucien Ballard *Ed* George A. Gittens *Mus* Lionel Newman
● Richard Widmark, Marilyn Monroe, Anne Bancroft, Donna Corcoran, Jeanne Cagney, Elisha Cook Jr (20th Century-Fox)

Marilyn Monroe, co-starred with Richard Widmark, gives an excellent account of herself in a strictly dramatic role which commands certain attention, but the story of a psycho baby-sitter lacks interest.

Femme star enters a NY hotel to take on a baby-sitting stint. Actually, she's newly released from a mental institution, sent there when her mind cracked after her fiance crashed in the Pacific and drowned. In Widmark, who glimpses her from his room across the court and comes calling with a bottle, she sees, in her dementia, the man she once loved.

Action progresses at a dull pace, and script by Daniel Taradash tries to juggle too many elements.

Monroe's role seems an odd choice, and in this she's anything but glamorous, despite her donning a negligee. Widmark doesn't appear too happy with his role. Anne Bancroft, making her screen bow, scores brightly as a torch singer.

■ **DON'T BOTHER TO KNOCK**

1961, 88 MINS, UK ◇

Dir Cyril Frankel *Prod* Richard Todd *Scr* Denis Cannan, Frederick Gotfurt, Frederic Raphael *Ph* Geoffrey Unsworth *Ed* Anne V. Coates

Mus Elisabeth Lutyens *Art Dir* Tony Masters
● Richard Todd, Nicole Maurey, Elke Sommer, June Thorburn, Judith Anderson, Eleanor Summerfield (Associated British/Haileywood)

Storyline has Richard Todd as an Edinburgh travel agent who goes off on a Continental business trip spree after quarreling with his fiancee (June Thorburn). He falls for a variety of charmers and hands out the key of his apartment to them with abandon. Having patched up his differences with his girl friend over the phone, he returns to Edinburgh and, of course, all the other feminine complications then arrive and take up residence.

Here is the basis of a spry bedroom farce, but the dialog [from a novel by Clifford Hanley] is heavy handed. And director Cyril Frankel has not been able to induce performances that disguise this sorry fact. Todd spends most of his time looking understandingly bewildered over the naive behavior of the character he is playing. Of the girls, Nicole Maurey is certainly the most attractive, June Thorburn the one who has to work hardest to make any effect and Elke Sommer the one who proves the biggest disappointment.

■ **DON'T LOOK BACK**

1967, 96 MINS, US ◇ Ⓥ

Dir D.A. Pennebaker *Prod* Albert Grossman, John Court *Ph* D.A. Pennebaker *Ed* D.A. Pennebaker
● (Leacock Pennebaker)

Don't Look Back is a cinema verite documentary by D. A. Pennebaker of Bob Dylan's spring 1965 concert tour of Britain. Pennebaker has fashioned a relentlessly honest, brilliantly edited documentary permeated with the troubador-poet's music.

During the month-long tour, Dylan was accompanied by Joan Baez, haunted by the rival reputation of Donovan, and badgered day and night by the press, teenie-boppers and hangers on. Pennebaker shot some 20 hours of film, and edited it chronologically to reveal a portrait that is not always flattering.

There is Dylan, faintly hostile, 'putting on' the press. In one classic scene he tells a *Time* magazine reporter exactly where *Time* and its readership are at, and if his outburst lacks tact, it seems to the point.

In one unique sequence Dylan's manager Albert Grossman and agent Tito Burns wheel, deal and bluff the BBC, playing them against Granada-TV to double the price for a Dylan appearance.

■ **DON'T LOOK NOW**

1973, 110 MINS, UK/ITALY ◇ Ⓥ

Dir Nicolas Roeg *Prod* Peter Katz *Scr* Allan Scott, Chris Bryant *Ph* Anthony Richmond *Ed* Graeme Clifford *Mus* Pino Donaggio *Art Dir* Giovanni Socol
● Julie Christie, Donald Sutherland, Hilary Mason, Clelia Matania, Massimo Serato, Renato Scarpa (Casey/Eldorado)

This British-Italian suspenser, in which the horror gets to one almost subliminally, as in *Rosemary's Baby*, is superior stuff. It can be 'read' on two levels: as simply a gripping tale of mysterious goings-on in a wintertime Venice or dealing with the supernatural and the occult as related to the established patterns of life and society.

Story itself is concocted from a Daphne du Maurier short story about a young British married couple who shortly after the accidental death – or was it? – of their daughter get involved in some strange happenings in a wintry Venice where the man is restoring a church.

A chance meeting in a restaurant with two sisters, one of them blind and suggesting she's 'seen' and spoken to the dead child, sets things moving, with puzzling detail following puzzling detail in a mosaic of mystery which crescendos right up to a twist finale.

It's the fillips, visually introduced by director Nicolas Roeg in glimpses and flashes, that make this much more than merely a well-made psycho-horror thriller.

The performances are right on the button; Donald Sutherland is (unusually) at his most subdued, top effectiveness as the materialist who ironically becomes the victim of his refusal to believe in the intangible; Julie Christie does her best work in ages as his wife; while a superbly-chosen cast of British and Italian supporting players etch a number of indelibly vivid portraits.

Editing too, is careful and painstaking (the classically brilliant and erotic love-making scene is merely one of several examples) and plays a vital role in setting the film's mood.

••••••••••••••••••••••••••••

■ DON'T MAKE WAVES

1967, 100 MINS, US ◇

Dir Alexander Mackendrick   *Prod* John Calley, Martin Ransohoff   *Scr* Ira Wallach, George Kirgo   *Ph* Philip H. Lathrop   *Ed* Rita Roland, Thomas Stanford   *Mus* Vic Mizzy   *Art Dir* George W. Davis, Edward Carfagno
● Tony Curtis, Claudia Cardinale, Robert Webber, Joanna Barnes, Sharon Tate, Mort Sahl (M-G-M/ Filmways-Reynard)

Don't Make Waves is a mildly amusing film which never gets off the ground in its intended purpose of wacky comedy. Based on Ira Wallach's novel, *Muscle Beach*, film stars Tony Curtis and Claudia Cardinale.

Script has a Southern California setting, mixing romance, infidelity, beach antics and sky diving with utter confusion as Curtis plays a frantic young man and Cardinale a peppery import with an accent.

Plot(?) gets underway as femme's car causes Curtis' Volkswagen to plunge down a hillside and burn, during which Curtis' pants and all his worldly possessions also go up in flames. Driving home with femme to look at her insurance policy, Curtis finds himself involved in her romance with a swimming pool operator, cheating on his wife.

••••••••••••••••••••••••••••

■ DON'T PLAY US CHEAP

1973, 104 MINS, US ◇

Dir Melvin Van Peebles   *Prod* Melvin Van Peebles   *Scr* Melvin Van Peebles   *Ph* Bob Maxwell   *Ed* Melvin Van Peebles   *Mus* Melvin Van Peebles
● Esther Rolle, Avon Long, Rhetta Hughes, George 'Ooppee' McCurn (Yeah)

Melvin Van Peebles' film of his play *Don't Play Us Cheap* offers some terrific musical numbers and an ebullient look at black culture.

Utilizing the same cast that he directed on Broadway [in 1972], Van Peebles creates the atmosphere of a house party in Harlem. His fantasy premise of an imp and little devil crashing the party to spoil it out of pure meanness allows the filmmaker's militant themes to be expressed in humor and whimsy.

Fantasy elements climax with black comedy of topliner Esther Rolle smashing the little devil in the form of a cockroach with a rolled up newspaper. Rolle is in great form as the party hostess, ably supported by an ensemble cast.

••••••••••••••••••••••••••••

■ DON'T RAISE THE BRIDGE, LOWER THE RIVER

1968, 99 MINS, UK ◇ ⓥ

Dir Jerry Paris   *Prod* Walter Shenson   *Scr* Max Wilk   *Ph* Otto Heller   *Ed* Bill Lenny   *Mus* David Whitaker   *Art Dir* John Howell
● Jerry Lewis, Terry-Thomas, Jacqueline Pearce, Bernard Cribbins, Patricia Routledge, Nicholas Parsons (Columbia)

Adapted by Max Wilk from his own novel, *Don't Raise the Bridge, Lower the River*, is a mildly diverting production, filmed at Britain's Shepperton Studios, and starring Jerry Lewis as a perennial dreamer. An initial lack of clarity in plot premise, followed by routine and not very exciting episodic treatment add up to a generally flat result.

Weaknesses are apparent at the very beginning: a series of disparate locations, after which it finally is established that Lewis is an eternal dreamer.

Subsequent to this revelation, story plods along in a dramatic monotone, progressing, but never building, towards an inevitable happy ending, after 99 slow minutes.

Featured players Terry-Thomas as the typical promoter; Bernard Cribbins as a garage mechanic who doubles as a steward on unscheduled airlines; and Patricia Routledge, a man-hungry Girl Scout leader, are quite excellent in their appearances.

Lewis comes across as uncertain of whether he is supposed to ham it up at times, play it down at others.

••••••••••••••••••••••••••••

■ DOORS, THE

1991, 141 MINS, US ◇ ⓥ

Dir Oliver Stone   *Prod* Bill Graham, Sasha Harari, A. Kitman Ho   *Scr* J. Randal Johnson, Oliver Stone   *Ph* Robert Richardson   *Ed* David Brenner, Joe Hutshing   *Art Dir* Barbara Ling
● Val Kilmer, Meg Ryan, Kevin Dillon, Kyle MacLachlan, Frank Whaley, Kathleen Quinlan (Carolco/Imagine)

The Doors is another trip into 1960s hell from Oliver Stone. This $40 million look at Jim Morrison's short, wild ride through a rock idol life is everything one expects from the filmmaker – intense, overblown, riveting, humorless, evocative, self-important and impossible to ignore.

As rendered with considerable physical accuracy by Val Kilmer, Morrison is drunk and/or stoned practically from beginning to end, providing an acute case study of ruinous excess. The singer's obsession with death and mysticism is rooted, via a sepia-tinged prolog, in a childhood experience in which he views the aftermath of a traffic accident involving some Indians.

Action proper begins in 1965, as Morrison the would-be poet and pretentious UCLA student filmmaker hooks up with flower child Pamela Courson (Meg Ryan) and launches a band in Venice Cal, with John Densmore, Ray Manzarek and Robby Krieger.

Outside of Morrison's abusive, drug-drenched relationship with Courson, only two of his innumerable sexual trysts are detailed – one with the exotic Velvet Underground star Nico, the other with the demonic Patricia Kennealy (Kathleen Quinlan).

Kilmer is convincing in the lead role, although he never allows the viewer to share any emotions. Morrison's own vocals have been skillfully augmented by Kilmer in some sequences.

The usually engaging Ryan brings little to a vaguely conceived part, whereas Quinlan commands the screen.

••••••••••••••••••••••••••••

■ DO THE RIGHT THING

1989, 120 MINS, US ◇ ⓥ

Dir Spike Lee   *Prod* Spike Lee   *Scr* Spike Lee   *Ph* Ernest Dickerson   *Ed* Barry Alexander Brown   *Mus* Bill Lee   *Art Dir* Wynn Thomas
● Danny Aiello, Ossie Davis, Ruby Dee, Richard Edson, Giancarlo Esposito, Spike Lee (40 Acres & a Mule)

Spike Lee combines a forceful statement on race relations with solid entertainment values in *Do the Right Thing*.

Lee adopts the durable theatrical format of *Street Scene* as his launching point, painstakingly etching an ensemble of neighborhood characters on a Bedford Stuyvesant block in Brooklyn. Centrepiece is Danny Aiello's pizza parlor, which he runs with his sons John Turturro and Richard Edson, with Lee delivering takeout orders.

On the hottest day of the summer, a myriad of contemporary issues covering personal, social and economic matters are laid on the table in often shrill but sometimes funny confrontations. Ossie Davis is perfect casting as a sort of conciliator, a hobo nicknamed the Mayor who injects folk wisdom into the discussion.

Standing out in a uniformly solid cast are Ruby Dee, the Earth Mother of the microcosmic community; Aiello, Turturro and Edson as three quite different variations on an ethnic theme; Paul Benjamin, Frankie Faison and Robin Harris as the funny trio of kibitzers on the block, and Roger Guenveur Smith as he creates an unusual, poetic figure of a stammering simpleton (who sells photos of black leaders) in the midst of such confident figures.

••••••••••••••••••••••••••••

■ DOUBLE INDEMNITY

1944, 103 MINS, US ⓥ

Dir Billy Wilder   *Prod* Joseph Sistrom   *Scr* Billy Wilder, Raymond Chandler   *Ph* John F. Seitz   *Ed* Doane Harrison   *Mus* Miklos Rozsa   *Art Dir* Hal Pereira, Hans Dreier
● Fred MacMurray, Barbara Stanwyck, Edward G. Robinson, Porter Hall, Jean Heather, Tom Powers (Paramount)

James M. Cain's movie *Double Indemnity*, apparently based on a sensational murder of the 1920s, is an absorbing melodrama in its Paramount adaptation. There are unmistakeable similarities between the pic and the famous Snyder-Gray murder wherein Albert Snyder was sash-weighted to death in 1927 in his Queens Village, NY, home by his wife, Ruth, and her lover, Judd Gray. Both the fictional and the real murders were for the slain men's insurance. Both were committed by the murdered men's wives and their amours.

The story's development revolves mainly around the characterizations of Fred MacMurray, Barbara Stanwyck and Edward G. Robinson, the first two as the lovers and Robinson as an insurance claims agent who balks the pair's 'perfect crime' from becoming just what they had intended it to appear – an accidental death from a moving train, for which there would have been a double indemnity.

Stanwyck plays the wife of an oilman, and when MacMurray, an insurance salesman, becomes her paramour, they sell to the husband, fraudulently, an accidental-death policy. They then kill him and place his body on the railway tracks.

It is a story told in flashback, film opening with MacMurray confessing voluntarily the entire setup into a dictaphone for use by the claims agent, from which the narrative then unfolds.

MacMurray has seldom given a better performance. It is somewhat different from his usually light roles, but is always plausible and played with considerable restraint. Stanwyck is not as attractive as normally with what is seemingly a blonde wig, but it's probably part of a makeup to emphasize the brassiness of the character. Robinson, as the infallible insurance executive quick to determine phoney claims, gives a strong performance, too.
☐ 1944: Best Picture (Nomination)

••••••••••••••••••••••••••••

■ DOUBLE LIFE, A

1947, 103 MINS, US ⓥ

Dir George Cukor   *Prod* Michael Kanin   *Scr* Ruth Gordon, Garson Kanin   *Ph* Milton Krasner   *Ed* Robert Parrish   *Mus* Miklos Rozsa   *Art Dir* Bernard Herzbrun, Harvey Gillett

● Ronald Colman, Signe Hasso, Edmond O'Brien, Shelley Winters (Universal)

Life is particularly distinguished for the manner in which the characters have been conceived and played. Each character rings true as the story goes into its play-within-a-play about actors and the theatre. There's murder, suspense, psychology, Shakespeare and romance all wrapped up into one polished package of class screen entertainment.

Plot poses an interesting premise – that an actor takes on some of the characteristics of the role he is playing if the run is long. In this instance Ronald Colman lives his roles without danger until he tackles *Othello*. Gradually, as the play goes into a second year, he is dominated more and more by the character he creates on the stage. It finally leads him to murder a chance acquaintance in the same manner in which Othello snuffs out the life of Desdemona each night on the stage.

Colman realizes on every facet of the demanding part in a performance that is flawless. It's a histrionic gem of unusual versatility. Signe Hasso, his stage co-star and former wife, is a solid click, revealing a talent that has rarely been called upon in her other film roles. Her Desdemona is brilliant and her interpretation of the understanding ex-wife perfect.

■ DOUBLE MAN, THE

1967, 105 MINS, UK ◇ ⑫

Dir Franklin J. Schaffner   *Prod* Hal. E. Chester
Scr Frank Tarloff, Alfred Hayes   *Ph* Denys Coop
Ed Richard Best   *Mus* Ernie Freeman   *Art Dir* Arthur Lawson
● Yul Brynner, Britt Ekland, Clive Revill, Anton Diffring, David Bauer, Lloyd Nolan (Warner-Pathe/Albion)

Frank Tarloff and Alfred Hayes have tailored a solid screenplay from Henry Maxfield's novel, *Legacy of a Spy*, in which intelligence agent Dan Slater (Yul Brynner) is plunged into strange problems when he goes to the Austrian Alps to investigate the death of his son on a ski-slope. The police write it off as an accident. Brynner suspects murder.

The film builds up an intriguing sense of tension with the motives of various people rating suspicion, Brynner being tailed by obvious enemy agents and a big payoff when he is confronted with his double.

Clive Revill, an ex-agent pal of Brynner's, though not fully trusted by him, also turns in an interesting show as an honest but weak, indecisive character who rallies at the critical moment. Anton Diffring is a suave enemy scientist and David Bauer does excellent work as an agent detailed to bring Brynner back to Washington.

■ DOVE, THE

1974, 105 MINS, UK ◇

Dir Charles Jarrott   *Prod* Gregory Peck   *Scr* Peter Beagle, Adam Kennedy   *Ph* Sven Nykvist   *Ed* John Jympson   *Mus* John Barry   *Art Dir* Peter Lamont
● Joseph Bottoms, Deborah Raffin, John McLiam, Dabney Coleman, John Anderson, Colby Chester (EMI/Peck)

The Dove is based on the book by round-the-world solo sailor Robin Lee Graham [with Derek Gill]. Though basically a yarn about Graham's five-year solo trip around the world in a small sailboat, an odyssey which provides nautical chills and thrills (as well as breathtaking scenics) aplenty, pic is also a tale of character development as the hero finds himself (and manhood) enroute, plus an unpreachy thesis on ecology.

Pic really takes off when he meets the girl (played with gauche hesitation at first, but then with beauty and considerable charm by Deborah Raffin) who is to provide the driving force behind his trek and on into manhood and maturity. Their yes-no yes-no-yes affair is nicely handled.

Fiji to Australia, South Africa and Madagascar to Panama and the Galapagos Isles, are simply breathtaking.

■ DOWN AND OUT IN BEVERLY HILLS

1986, 97 MINS, US ◇ ⑰

Dir Paul Mazursky   *Prod* Paul Mazursky   *Scr* Paul Mazursky, Leon Capetanos   *Ph* Donald McAlpine
Ed Richard Halsey   *Mus* Andy Summers   *Art Dir* Pato Guzman
● Nick Nolte, Richard Dreyfuss, Bette Midler, Little Richard, Tracy Nelson (Touchstone)

Down and Out in Beverly Hills continues Paul Mazursky's love-hate relationship with the bourgeoisie and its institutions, especially marriage. It's a loving caricature of the nouveau riche (Beverly Hills variety) and although it is more of a comedy of manners than a well-developed story, there are enough yocks and bright moments to make it a thoroughly enjoyable outing.

Mazursky and co-writer Leon Capetanos have cleverly taken the basic premise of Jean Renoir's 1932 classic *Boudu Saved from Drowning* and used it as a looking glass for the foibles of the rich and bored.

Head of the household is the aptly named David Whiteman (Richard Dreyfuss). Bette Midler is the lady of the house with their near anorexic daughter Tracy Nelson and son Evan Richards.

In short it's a household of unhappy people and the fly (perhaps flea is more accurate) in the ointment is Nick Nolte as the bum Jerry Baskin. A disheveled and dirty street person, Jerry is an artist of sorts, a con artist. For the Whitemans he becomes their idealized bum, the family pet.

■ DOWN BY LAW

1986, 106 MINS, US ⑰

Dir Jim Jarmusch   *Prod* Jim Jarmusch   *Scr* Jim Jarmusch   *Ph* Robby Muller   *Ed* Franck Kern
Mus John Lurie   *Art Dir* Roger Knight
● Tom Waits, John Lurie, Roberto Benigni, Nicoletta Braschi, Ellen Barkin (Black Snake/Grohenberger)

Zack (Tom Waits) is caught driving a car with a body in the trunk and Jack (John Lurie) is found by the cops in a hotel room with an unquestionably underage girl. Both men are framed. They wind up in the slammer, in the same cell. Third cell mate is Roberto (Roberto Benigni), who speaks fractured English but whose naive friendliness proves contagious.

After several funny scenes, the Italian proposes they escape, 'just like they do in American movies'. And so they do, out into the Louisiana swamps and eventually stumble on an isolated, unlikely diner where, surprise, surprise, the owner chef is a lonely Italian woman (Nicoletta Braschi) who immediately falls for Benigni.

The Jim Jarmusch penchant for off-the-wall characters and odd situations is very much in evidence. The black-and-white photography is a major plus, and so is John Lurie's score, with songs by Tom Waits. Both men are fine in their respective roles, but Benigni steals the film.

■ DOWNHILL RACER

1969, 101 MINS, US ⑰

Dir Michael Ritchie   *Prod* Richard Gregson   *Scr* James Salter   *Ph* Brian Probyn   *Ed* Nick Archer
Mus Kenyon Hopkins   *Art Dir* Ian Whittaker
● Robert Redford, Gene Hackman, Camilla Sparv, Kathleen Crowley, Jim McMullan (Paramount)

Downhill Racer is an intriguing film that balances skiing and the majesty of Alpine scenery with an absorbing story of hero Robert Redford, young American innocent abroad.

The picture was filmed in the Swiss, Austrian and French Alps. Screenplay [based on the novel *The Downhill Racers* by Oakley Hall] plunges into action when Colorado-born Redford, part of an American skiing team coached by tough Gene Hackman, asserts himself both with the personalities surrounding him and on the European slopes.

Redford contributes a sensitive, interesting portrayal. His interpretation is many-faceted and probing.

Hackman's characterization is virile and thoroughly human.

Filming of the downhill course, made with camera attached to the skier's helmet, was properly nervewracking. And a heart-in-the-throat Olympic downhill race as a finale tops everything that has gone before.

■ DOWN MEXICO WAY

1941, 72 MINS, US ⑰

Dir Joseph Santley   *Prod* Harry Grey   *Scr* Olive Cooper, Albert Duffy   *Ph* Jack Marta   *Ed* Howard O'Neill
● Gene Autry, Smiley Burnette, Fay McKenzie, Harold Huber (Republic)

After a pair of swindlers work over the small town of Sage City, Gene Autry discovers his townfolk have been bilked out of coin supposedly aimed for picture production. Accompanied by Smiley Burnette and reformed Mexican bad man (Harold Huber), Autry trails the crooks into Mexico, where the swindlers' confederates are repeating activities with a rich Mexican rancher as victim. From there on, it's up to Autry to uncover the machinations of the crooks, which he does with a rousing chase and gunfight for a finale.

Story carries along at a good pace, neatly intermingling action, romance and comedy. Autry carries his assignment as the hero in good style, singing several songs – including a couple of familiar pops – in usual fashion.

Picture carries ambitious production mounting in comparison to previous Autrys in the series; with climactic chase using an auto, horses and wildly careening motorcycles for variation.

■ DOWN TO EARTH

1947, 100 MINS, US ◇

Dir Alexander Hall   *Prod* Don Hartman   *Scr* Don Hartman, Edwin Blum   *Ph* Rudolph Mate   *Ed* Viola Lawrence   *Mus* George Duning, Heinz Roemheld
Art Dir Stephen Goosson, Rudolph Sternad
● Rita Hayworth, Larry Parks, Roland Culver, James Gleason, Edward Everett Horton (Columbia)

Yarn is one of those tricky ideas that look so much better on paper than celluloid. It picks up the characters from Harry Segall's play, *Heaven Can Wait*, filmed by Columbia in 1941 as the tremendously successful *Here Comes Mr Jordan*, and puts them down in a new setting. *Jordan* was about an angelized prizefighter who comes back to earth in someone else's body. *Down to Earth* is a typical backstage story – and putting it in the *Jordan* setting is certainly the hard way of getting a twist on the old, standard musical.

Producer Don Hartman has carried out his cute idea to the extent of using some of the same cast as *Jordan*. James Gleason is back as an agent and Edward Everett Horton is seen once again as the messenger who accompanies the spirit down to earth. Roland Culver subs for Claude Rains in the Jordan role, the guy who runs Heaven.

Rita Hayworth is pictured as Terpsichore, the Greek muse of the theatre. Looking down from Heaven she's unhappy over a Broadway musical about the nine muses, being done in jazz by producer Larry Parks. She makes a request to go down and help him so she can clean the show up. She lands in the star role and there's the usual falling-in-love with the vis-a-vis – in this case Parks.

Explanation necessary to get all this across takes interminable time and constantly slows even the angels to a lazy walk. Making things worse is the fact that all the gags which should give the yarn a bit of pepper fall flat.

Definitely on the credit side are the five tunes provided by Allan Roberts and Doris Fisher. Parks sings one tune. It's definitely a letdown. Hayworth does better in the vocal department and, of course is fine in the terp routines.

● ●

■ DRACULA

1931, 64 MINS, US Ⓥ

Dir Tod Browning   *Prod* Carl Laemmle Jr.   *Scr* Garrett Fort, Dudley Murphy   *Ph* Karl Freund   *Ed* Milton Carruth   *Art Dir* Charles D. Hall
● Bela Lugosi, Helen Chandler, Davis Manners, Dwight Frye, Edward Van Sloan, Herbert Bunston (Universal)

Treatment differs from both the stage version [by Deane and John Balderston] and the original novel [by Bram Stoker]. On the stage it was a thriller carried to such an extreme that it had a comedy punch by its very outre aspect. On the screen it comes out as a sublimated ghost story related with all surface seriousness and above all with a remarkably effective background of creepy atmosphere.

Early in the action is a barren rocky mountain pass, peopled only by a spectral coach driver and shrouded in a miasmic mist. Story proceeds thence into a tomb-like castle. In such surroundings the sinister figure of the human vampire, the living-dead Count Dracula who sustains life by drinking the blood of his victims, seems almost plausible.

It is difficult to think of anybody who could quite match the performance in the vampire part of Bela Lugosi, even to the faint flavor of foreign speech that fits so neatly. Helen Chandler is the blonde type for the clinging-vine heroine, and Herbert Bunston plays the scientist deadly straight, but with a faint suggestion of comedy that dovetails into the whole pattern.

● ●

■ DRACULA

1958, 82 MINS, UK ◇ Ⓥ

Dir Terence Fisher   *Prod* Anthony Hinds   *Scr* Jimmy Sangster   *Ph* Jack Asher   *Ed* Bill Lenny, James Needs   *Mus* James Bernard   *Art Dir* Bernard Robinson
● Peter Cushing, Christopher Lee, Melissa Stribling, Michael Gough, Carol Marsh, Valerie Gaunt (Hammer)

For those familiar with the original *Dracula* thriller, the screenplay has ably preserved the sanguinary aspects of the Bram Stoker novel. Here again we have Count Dracula sleeping in a coffin by day and plying his nefarious role of a blood-sucking vampire at night. Version has its usual quota of victims before his reign of terror is ended by a fearless doctor.

Both director Terence Fisher as well as the cast have taken a serious approach to the macabre theme that adds up to lotsa tension and suspense. Peter Cushing is impressive as the painstaking scientist-doctor who solves the mystery. Christopher Lee is thoroughly gruesome as Dracula, and Michael Gough is suitably skeptical as a bereaved relative who ultimately is persuaded to assist Cushing.

● ●

■ DRACULA

1979, 109 MINS, US ◇ Ⓥ

Dir John Badham   *Prod* Walter Mirisch   *Scr* W.D. Richter   *Ph* Gilbert Taylor   *Ed* John Bloom   *Mus* John Williams   *Art Dir* Peter Murton

● Frank Langella, Laurence Olivier, Donald Pleasence, Kate Nelligan, Trevor Eve, Jan Francis (Universal)

With this lavish retelling of an oft-told tale, *Dracula* puts the male vamp back in vampire. Director John Badham and Frank Langella pull off a handsome, moody rendition, more romantic than menacing [based on a stage play by Hamilton Deane and John L. Balderston, from Bram Stoker's novel].

Langella is the key in coming up with one more interpretation of the vampire out of hundreds previously presented. More humanly seductive, he's terrific with the ladies and the men would like him well-enough if he weren't so good-looking and arrogant.

Film gets under way slowly, bringing the count to England where he's introduced to Donald Pleasence, his daughter Kate Nelligan, her fiance Trevor Eve and visiting friend Jan Francis.

Finally, Francis is drained dry and the action starts to pick up.

● ●

■ DRACULA – PRINCE OF DARKNESS

1966, 90 MINS, UK ◇

Dir Terence Fisher   *Prod* Anthony Nelson-Keys   *Scr* John Sansom, Anthony Hinds   *Ph* Michael Reed   *Ed* Chris Barnes, James Needs   *Mus* James Bernard   *Art Dir* Bernard Robinson
● Christopher Lee, Barbara Shelley, Andrew Keir, Francis Matthews, Suzan Farmer, Charles Tingwell (Hammer/Seven Arts)

Four inquistive tourists are lured to Castle Dracula, met by a sinister butler and invited to dinner and to stay the night. The four treat this strange hospitality with incredibly bland acceptance. One of them (Charles Tingwell), wandering the castle at night, is killed and his blood used to reinfuse life into the Dracula ashes. Dracula then plunges his fangs into the neck of the corpse's wife, turning her into a vampire and the two are then arrayed against the other pair in the party.

This simple yarn [from an idea by John Elder (= Anthony Hinds)] is played reasonably straight and the main snag is that the thrills do not arise sufficiently smooth out of atmosphere. After a slowish start some climate of eeriness is evoked but more shadows, suspense and suggestion would have helped. Christopher Lee, an old hand at the horror business, makes a latish appearance but dominates the film enough without dialog.

● ●

■ DRAGNET

1954, 89 MINS, US ◇ Ⓥ

Dir Jack Webb   *Prod* Stanley Meyer   *Scr* Richard L. Breen   *Ph* Edward Colman   *Ed* Robert M. Leeds   *Mus* Walter Schumann
● Jack Webb, Ben Alexander, Richard Boone, Ann Robinson, Stacy Harris, Virginia Gregg (Warner/Mark VII)

In making the transition from radio-TV to the big screen and color, this is spotty in entertainment results. As on TV quite a bit is made of the long, tedious toil of thorough police methods. This can be kept in hand in a 30-minute period, but when that time is tripled the pace is bound to slow to a walk often.

Under Jack Webb's direction the film gets off on its melodramatic path with a brutal murder. Thereafter, the homicide and intelligence divisions of the LA Police Dept start a widespread hunt for evidence that will pin the killing on some redhot suspects.

Webb's direction of the screenplay is mostly a good job. He stages a four-man fight in which he and his police sidekick (Ben Alexander) are involved, rather poorly and it may invoke unwelcome laughs. Otherwise, when sticking to terse handling of facts, or in building honest emotion, such as in the splendidly-done drunk scene by Virginia Gregg,

grieving widow of the murdered hood, he brings his show off satisfactorily.

● ●

■ DRAGONSLAYER

1981, 108 MINS, UK ◇

Dir Matthew Robbins   *Prod* Hal Barwood   *Scr* Hal Barwood, Matthew Robbins   *Ph* Derek Vanlint   *Ed* Tony Lawson   *Mus* Alex North   *Art Dir* Elliot Scott
● Peter MacNicol, Caitlin Clarke, Ralph Richardson, John Hallam, Peter Eyre, Chloe Salaman (Paramount/Walt Disney)

A well intentioned fantasy with some wonderful special effects, *Dragonslayer* falls somewhat short on continuously intriguing adventure. Technically speaking, it is an expertly mounted period piece concerning a boy's attempt to slay a fire-breathing dragon in order to save an entire kingdom. However, the story line is often tedious and the major action sequences appear much too late in the picture.

Ralph Richardson limns the properly mysterious (and too seldom seen) sorcerer that members of a neighbouring kingdom seek as the only person who can slay the terrorizing dragon.

Early on Richardson's powers are put to the test by a representative of the king, who seems to kill the sorcerer. It is then up to his apprentice, newcomer Peter MacNicol, to fight the dragon with the magic at his disposal.

MacNicol has the proper look of innocence to be a little unnatural in his performance. Along the way he is given nice support by Caitlin Clarke as a spunky love interest.

The real stars (as expected) of this film are the fabulous special effects. Given the high failure rate, it's especially refreshing to see experts come up with the imaginative and effective devices.

● ●

■ DRAUGHTSMAN'S CONTRACT, THE

1982, 108 MINS, UK ◇ Ⓥ

Dir Peter Greenaway   *Scr* Peter Greenaway   *Ph* Curtis Clark   *Ed* John Wilson   *Mus* Michael Nyman   *Art Dir* Bob Ringwood
● Anthony Higgins, Janet Suzman, Anne Louise Lambert, Hugh Fraser (BFI/Channel 4)

Though seemingly a comedy of manners taking place in the country home of a rich man, Herbert, there is an underlying viciousness of these rich denizens that foreshadows coming upheavals. It is the end of the 17th century.

Film has fine costumes, florid headpieces for men and lovely surroundings on the big estate. Well-lensed, with a fine limpid narration that switches from observation of this landed class to a sort of foreboding tale of murder.

Herbert is almost estranged from his wife and goes off for two weeks of carousing. His wife beseeches a known draughtsman and landscape painter, a guest, Neville, to stay and make 12 drawings of the estate to surprise her husband. He refuses but finally says yes if the contract includes daily sexual dalliance with Mrs Herbert. It is accepted.

The daughter, still without a child and oblivious to her husband and his effete ways, also begins to dally with the shrewd, talented Neville.

On the day Neville is to leave, Herbert is found dead in the moat. Suspicions are aimed at Neville for it is felt he may have somehow given clues to the murder in his drawings.

● ●

■ DR. CYCLOPS

1940, 75 MINS, US ◇ Ⓥ

Dir Ernest Schoedsack   *Prod* Dale Van Every   *Scr* Tom Kilpatrick   *Ph* Henry Sharp, Winton C. Hoch   *Ed* Ellsworth Hoagland   *Mus* Ernest Toch, Gerard

D

Carbonara, Albert Hay Malotte   *Art Dir* Hans Dreier, Earl Hedrick
● Albert Dekker, Janice Logan, Thomas Coley, Charles Halton, Victor Kilian, Frank Yaconelli (Paramount)

In detailing the discoveries of a madman scientist wherein he is able to reduce the size of men and animals to miniature pygmies, story and direction both fail to catch and hold interest. Achieved through continual use of process and trick photography, idea gets lost in a jumble and pancakes off for a dull effort.

Albert Dekker, researching in the jungles of South America, finds a rich radium deposit from which he can draw concentrated energy for experimental use. He has already used the power to reduce animals to minute size, when a pair of mining engineers (Thomas Coley and Victor Kilian) and two biologists (Janice Logan and Charles Halton) arrive and soon discover his secret. Dekker gets the quartet, together with native Frank Yaconelli, into the radium machine room and reduces the group down to beings of a foot tall. From there on, it's an unexciting adventure to escape the madman.

- -

■ DREAM LOVER

1986, 104 MINS, US ◇ ⓥ
Dir Alan J. Pakula   *Prod* Alan J. Pakula, Jon Boorstin   *Scr* Jon Boorstin   *Ph* Sven Nykvist   *Ed* Trudy Ship   *Mus* Michael Small   *Art Dir* George Jenkins
● Kristy McNichol, Ben Masters, Paul Shenar, Justin Deas, John McMartin, Gayle Hunnicutt (M-G-M)

With the advice of a Yale University Sleep Laboratory consultant, *Dream Lover* firmly sets itself among some rather fascinating scientific notions. Specifically, some dream doctors believe that, while 'asleep', part of the brain reacts to dreams as if they were really happening and sends signals to the muscles to take appropriate action.

Kristy McNichol is an average young lady living alone in a NY apartment. She becomes victim to an intruder (Joseph Culp) whom she stabs in the back.

Was the stabbing really necessary for self-defense or did it leap out of some sub-conscious fury connected to her domineering father (Paul Shenar) or unfaithful lover (Justin Deas)? Only her brain knows for sure. Limps to a conclusion with no real excitement.

- -

■ DREAM OF KINGS, A

1969, 109 MINS, US ◇ ⓥ
Dir Daniel Mann   *Prod* Jules Schermer   *Scr* Harry Mark Petrakis, Ian Hunter   *Ph* Richard H. Kline   *Ed* Walter Hannemann, Ray Daniels   *Mus* Alex North
● Anthony Quinn, Irene Papas, Inger Stevens, Sam Levene, Val Avery (Schermer)

The adaptation of Harry Mark Petrakis' book about an epic Greek-American father, philanderer, and gambler whose dubious means of support is dispensing wisdom and wrestling instruction emerges as a warm, upbeat, artistically realized drama. It stars Anthony Quinn portraying super-mensch, the noble ethnic, and it is one of his most powerful and convincing performances.

In the Greek sector of Chicago, Quinn makes his hand-to-mouth living as a small time but honest gambler, since his counseling business is considerably less than a living. His wife (Irene Papas), two girls and his fatally ill son (Radames Pera) exist on the widowed mother-in-law's life insurance.

The film captures the gritty visual feel of the Hellenic quarter of a large American city with the winter air redolent with feta and baking Greek bread.

- -

■ DREAM OF PASSION, A

1978, 110 MINS, GREECE ◇ ⓥ
Dir Jules Dassin   *Prod* Jules Dassin   *Scr* Jules Dassin   *Ph* George Arvanitis   *Ed* George Klotz   *Mus* Iannis Markopoulos   *Art Dir* Dionysis Fotopoulos
● Melina Mercouri, Ellen Burstyn, Andreas Voutsinas, Despo Diamantidou, Dimitris Papamichael, Yannis Voglis (Brenfilm/Melina)

Two older women are caught up in a strange parallel. One, Melina Mercouri, is a film star who returns to her native Greece to do *Medea* on stage. The other, Ellen Burstyn, is an American living in Greece who has killed her three children 'just as Medea did' due to her husband's flaunting of her love and needs.

A misguided public relations idea, having Burstyn talk to Mercouri after seeing no one for a long time, backfires when photogs and press burst in. While Burstyn screams invectives, Mercouri feels cheapened, guilty and decides to take an interest in the case. She sees Burstyn again and gets her story.

Pic alternates two stories, as Mercouri's life and work are intertwined with her growing interest in Burstyn.

Burstyn is shattering as a religious, partially-educated woman caught up in a foreign land. At the end, Burstyn bursts into hysterical tears, which are intercut with Mercouri's dramatic finale in which she kills Medea's children in the play.

- -

■ DREAM TEAM, THE

1989, 113 MINS, US ◇ ⓥ
Dir Howard Zieff   *Prod* Christopher W. Knight   *Scr* Jon Connolly, David Loucka   *Ph* Adam Holender   *Ed* C. Timothy O'Meara   *Mus* David McHugh   *Art Dir* Todd Hallowell
● Michael Keaton, Christopher Lloyd, Peter Boyle, Stephen Frust, Dennis Boutsikaris (Imagine/Universal)

The Dream Team is a hokey comedy that basically reduces mental illness to a grab bag of quirky schtick. Yet with a quartet of gifted comic actors having a field day playing loonies on the loose in Manhattan, much of that schtick is awfully funny.

In an attempt to give his patients a taste of the real world, New Jersey hospital doctor Dennis Boutsikaris decides to treat four of his charges to a day game at Yankee Statium.

Going along for the ride are the certified oddballs: Keaton, who seems to have his wits about him but periodically displays extreme delusions of grandeur, as well as a mean violent streak; Christopher Lloyd, a prissy fuss-budget who enjoys posing as a member of the hospital staff; Peter Boyle, a man with a heavy Jesus complex given to undressing at moments of intense spirituality; and Stephen Furst, an uncommunicative simpleton who speaks mainly in baseball jargon.

As soon as they hit the Big Apple, however, the good doctor is seriously injured after witnessing a killing, and the boys are left to their own devices.

Keaton is at his manic best, Lloyd prompts numerous guffaws with his impersonation of a self-serious tidiness freak, and Furst quietly impresses as the sickest and most helpless of the lot.

- -

■ DREAMSCAPE

1984, 95 MINS, US ◇ ⓥ
Dir Joe Ruben   *Prod* Bruce Cohn Curtis, Jerry Tokofsky   *Scr* David Loughery, Chuck Russell, Joe Ruben   *Ph* Brian Tufano   *Ed* Richard Halsey   *Mus* Maurice Jarre
● Dennis Quaid, Max Von Sydow, Christopher Plummer, Eddie Albert, Kate Capshaw, David Patrick Kelly (Zupnick-Curtis)

Film centers on 'dreamlinking', the psychic projection of one person's consciousness into a sleeping person's subconscious, or his dreams. If that sounds far-fetched, it is.

Central character is played with gusto by Dennis Quaid as Alex Garland, a reluctant ex-psychic who hooks up with Dr Paul Novotny (Max Von Sydow), who runs a dream research project at the local college that has an elaborate laboratory setup to study the phenomena.

There he meets Dr Jane de Vries (Kate Capshaw), Von Sydow's chief assistant who secretly lusts after Quaid, but only until he 'eavesdrops' on her erotic dream that involves Quaid. Enter Christopher Plummer as Bob Blair, a secretive and despicable government type who finances and oversees Von Sydow's research, but covertly plans to use its results for sinister ends.

- -

■ DRESSED TO KILL

1980, 105 MINS, US ◇ ⓥ
Dir Brian De Palma   *Prod* George Litto   *Scr* Brian De Palma   *Ph* Ralf Bode   *Ed* Jerry Greenberg   *Mus* Pino Donaggio   *Art Dir* Gary Weist
● Michael Caine, Angie Dickinson, Nancy Allen, Keith Gordon (Arkoff/Cinema 77)

Brian De Palma goes right for the audience jugular in *Dressed to Kill*, a stylish exercise in ersatz-Hitchcock suspense-terror. Despite some major structural weaknesses, the cannily manipulated combination of mystery, gore and kinky sex adds up to a slick commercial package.

The film begins with a steamy auto-erotic shower scene and segues to a session between Angie Dickinson and psychiatrist Michael Caine.

Matters begin in earnest when Dickinson enters an elevator and is razor-sliced to death. Enter high-priced hooker Nancy Allen who finds the body and is caught razor-in-hand with no alibi, smack into the arch Hitchcockian position of a circumstantially involved 'innocent' forced to clear herself by discovering the real murderer.

Instances of patent manipulation or cheating (and the film's stolen ending from *Carrie*) are generally more annoying in retrospect than while they're happening.

Dickinson, who has an abdominal stand-in for the steamier segments, is used exceptionally well as the sexually torn, quickly disposed-of heroine. Caine, until the film's internal logic breaks down, is excellent as the suave shrink.

- -

■ DRESSER, THE

1983, 118 MINS, UK ◇ ⓥ
Dir Peter Yates   *Prod* Peter Yates   *Scr* Ronald Harwood   *Ph* Kevin Pike   *Ed* Ray Lovejoy   *Mus* James Horner   *Art Dir* Stephen Grimes
● Albert Finney, Tom Courtenay, Edward Fox, Zena Walker, Eileen Atkins, Michael Gough (Goldcrest/World Film Services)

Adapted by Ronald Harwood from his 1980 London comedy-drama, this is indisputably one of the best films every made about theatre. It's funny, compassionate, compelling, and in its final moments pulls off an uncanny juxtaposition between the emotionally and physically crumbling Albert Finney and the character he's playing on stage for the 227th time, King Lear.

Finney portrays an aging, spoiled, grandiloquent actor-manager of a traditional English touring company whose dedication to his art creates chaos for those around him. The only character who can handle the old actor is his gofer-valet Norman, played with an amazing dexterity and energy by Tom Courtenay.

Director Peter Yates brings to the film, much of it shot at Pinewood, a strong visual sense of the British experience in wartime. And the whiff of greasepaint, particularly notable when aide Courtenay goads Finney into his makeup for Lear, lends the tawdry dressing room world of touring theatre its most physically felt detail.

Harwood is said to have based much of his story on his experiences with flamboyant actor-manager Donald Wolfit (1902–68) and his troupe.

□ 1983: Best Picture (Nomination)

....

■ **DREYFUS**

1931, 80 MINS, UK

Dir F.W. Kraemer, Milton Rosmer *Scr* Reginald Berkeley, Walter Mycroft *Ph* W. Winterstein, J. Harvey Wheedon *Ed* John Harlow
● Cedric Hardwicke, Beatrix Thomson, Charles Carson, George Merritt, Sam Livesey, Garry Marsh (British International/Sudfilm)

British International, in making the picture, is understood to have followed closely along the lines of the original film as made by Sudfilm for German consumption. The film has more movement than the average British film.

The Dreyfus case revolved around a framed-up charge against Captain Alfred Dreyfus of the French Army of treason. Treason had been committed and Dreyfus was charged, largely because he was the only Jew on the staff. After making the charge, the army had to hold up its case or lose face, so they trumped up the evidence against him.

What made it a world-famous matter, rather than a forgotten incident in French army life, was that Emile Zola, one of the greatest of French writers, took to the Dreyfus case and fought it in the courts. Despite having as counsel Georges Clemenceau, Zola lost, but the story had gotten worldwide attention. After about 15 years Dreyfus was fully vindicated.

The film is not over-acted. If anything it's a little under-acted in parts. Cecil Hardwicke as Dreyfus gives a fine performance; George Merritt as Zola is exceptional. Another striking performance is that of Charles Carson as Col. Picquart, who was also degraded because he found proof, after Dreyfus was sent to Devil's Island, pointing to the fact that Major Esterhazy was the criminal and not Dreyfus. Beatrix Thomson as the wife is only so-so, largely because she's not given much to do.

....

■ **DRILLER KILLER**

1979, 90 MINS, US ◇ ⓥ

Dir Abel Ferrara *Prod* Rochelle Weisberg
Scr Nicholas St John *Ph* Ken Kelsch *Mus* Joseph Delia
● Carolyn Marz, Jimmy Laine, Bob De Frank, Baybi Day, Peter Yellen (Rochelle/Navaron)

This bit of gore was undoubtedly inspired by *The Texas Chain Saw Massacre*. It's hastily-shot and technically inept in every department operation.

An artist, living in a tenement near Union Square with two girlfriends who're not reluctant to turn to each other when his attentions are elsewhere, find it increasingly difficult to keep the wolf from the door. Things get worse. A punk rock band moves into the floor below him and the noise pushes him over the edge.

The most stupid thing about the film is why, when he turns into a murderer with an electric drill, he doesn't go downstairs and eliminate the band. No, he picks winos in doorways as his victims before turning to other targets – his girlfriends.

....

■ **DRIVE, HE SAID**

1971, 95 MINS, US ◇

Dir Jack Nicholson *Prod* Jack Nicholson, Steve Blauner, Bert Schneider *Scr* Jack Nicholson, Jeremy Larner *Ph* Bill Butler *Ed* Pat Somerset, Donn

Cambern, Christopher Holmes, Robert L. Wolfe
Mus David Shire *Art Dir* Harry Gittes
● William Tepper, Karen Black, Michael Margotta, Bruce Dern, Robert Towne, Henry Jaglom (BBS)

Director Jack Nicholson seems here to be making a sort of games-people-play charade which takes off on many of the would-be commitments of his characters.

William Tepper, as the central sports star character of the campus convolutions, reflects the changes and protest surrounding his simplistic existence.

His roommate (Michael Margotta) a Che-like student revolutionary wants to destroy all for he feels the draft, life around him, the war, will destroy him. Margotta leads a gag raid on a basketball game with guerrilla-clad friends that puts them all in custody, but later they are freed. He beats the draft by playing mad in a raucous induction physical scene, but winds up going mad for real, trying to kill his roommate's woman, who he feels is simply a lech.

Karen Black is the sensual older woman, who sexually grapples with the basketball hero but finally resents being used and tries to claim a personality of her own.

Nicholson deftly illustrates the background cynicism of big time sports against the more obvious cynicism of college life.

....

■ **DRIVER, THE**

1978, 91 MINS, US ◇ ⓥ

Dir Walter Hill *Prod* Lawrence Gordon *Scr* Walter Hill *Ph* Philip Lathrop *Ed* Tina Hirsch, Robert K. Lambert *Mus* Michael Small *Art Dir* Harry Horner
● Ryan O'Neal, Bruce Dern, Isabelle Adjani, Ronee Blakely, Matt Clark, Felice Orlandi (20th Century-Fox)

By the end of *The Driver* you can almost smell rubber burning, there are so many screeching tires. This may be the first film where the star of the show isn't an actor or even a machine but a sound effect.

Ryan O'Neal plays a master getaway driver who does most of his talking with his accelerator toe. Bruce Dern, departing only slightly from his maniac roles, plays an obsessed detective out to nab O'Neal. Isabelle Adjani is another reticent character, a gambler hired as an alibi for O'Neal. Ronee Blakely, in a supporting role, portrays O'Neal's connection; she sets up the jobs.

There's not much more to the plot than that. O'Neal is a great driver and Dern is a detective. They're enemies and one of them is going to win the game.

Director Walter Hill and stunt coordinator Everett Creach have engineered a number of car chases and they are fabulous, if you like car chases.

Because of the quiet and mysterious mood of this picture, it has a pretentious quality to it. Whenever someone does speak, the dialog seems precious, as if the last sentence of each speech were edited out.

....

■ **DRIVING MISS DAISY**

1989, 99 MINS, US ◇ ⓥ

Dir Bruce Beresford *Prod* Richard D. Zanuck
Scr Alfred Uhry *Ph* Peter James *Ed* Mark Warner *Mus* Hans Zimmer *Art Dir* Bruno Rubeo
● Morgan Freeman, Jessica Tandy, Dan Aykroyd, Patti LuPone, Esther Rolle (Zanuck/Warner)

Driving Miss Daisy is a touching exploration of 25 years of change in Southern race relations (1948-73) as seen through the relationship of an elderly Jewish widow and her stalwart black chauffeur.

Bruce Beresford's sensitive direction complements Alfred Uhry's skillful adapation of his Pulitzer Prize-winning play.

Set in the relatively tolerant city of Atlanta, Daisy effortlessly evokes the changing periods on a limited budget.

Jessica Tandy's Daisy is a captious and lonely old stick, living a bleakly isolated widow's life in her empty old house, and her inability to keep from tyrannizing Morgan Freeman, housekeeper Esther Rolle, and other black helpers gives the film a current of bitter truth, making her gradual friendship with Freeman a hard-won achievement.

Freeman's Hoke is the essence of tact, with a quiet, philosophical acceptance of his role in life and a secret sense of amusement toward whites' behavior.

□ 1989: Best Picture

....

■ **DR. JEKYLL AND MR. HYDE**

1932, 90 MINS, US ⓥ

Dir Rouben Mamoulian *Prod* Rouben Mamoulian *Scr* Samuel Hoffenstein, Percy Heath *Ph* Karl Struss
● Fredric March, Miriam Hopkins, Rose Hobart, Holmes Herbert, Edgar Norton, Halliwell Hobbes (Paramount)

The fundamental story is that a brilliant scientist turns himself into an ogre who goes upon orgies of lust and murder in peaceful London, all in a misguided frenzy of scientific research, and after murdering a number of other people by extremely horrifying means, destroys himself. That was the length and breadth of the stage play [from the novel by Robert Louis Stevenson], and it served in that form for years.

The picture is infinitely better art – indeed, in many passages it is an astonishing fine bit of interpreting a classic, but as popular fare it loses in vital reaction.

Camera trick of changing a central figure from the handsome Fredric March into the bestial, ape-like monster Hyde, carries a terrific punch, but in each successive use of the device – and it is repeated four times – it weakens in hair-raising effort.

March does an outstanding bit of theatrical acting. His Hyde make-up is a triumph of realized nightmare. Other people in the cast matter little, except that Miriam Hopkins plays Ivy, the London soiled dove, with a capital sense of comedy and coquetry that contributes to the subsequent horror build-up.

Settings and lighting alone are worth seeing as models of atmospheric surroundings.

....

■ **DR. JEKYLL AND MR. HYDE**

1941, 127 MINS, US ⓥ

Dir Victor Fleming *Prod* Victor Saville *Scr* John Lee Mahin *Ph* Joseph Ruttenberg *Ed* Harold F. Kress *Mus* Franz Waxman
● Spencer Tracy, Ingrid Bergman, Lana Turner, Ian Hunter (M-G-M)

In the evident striving to make *Jekyll* a 'big' film, by elaborating the theme and introducing new characters and situations, some of the finer psychological points are dulled. John Lee Mahin's screenscript is over-length.

Nevertheless, it has its highly effective moments, and Spencer Tracy plays the dual roles with conviction. His transformations from the young physician, bent on biological and mental research as an escape from his own moral weaknesses, to the demoniac Mr Hyde are brought about with considerably less alterations in face and stature than audiences might expect.

Ingrid Bergman plays the enslaved victim of Hyde's debauches. In every scene in which the two appear, she is Tracy's equal as a strong screen personality.

The script is meagre on the very important phase of Jekyll's inner struggle to free himself from his deadly alter ego. Millions of Stevenson readers have long found excitement and thrill in the angle that Jekyll's predicament was self-conceived to hide criminal and vicious desires. Mahin emphasizes that misdirected scientific research was the cause of the good doctor's downfall.

••••••••••••••••••••••••••••••

■ DR. JEKYLL AND SISTER HYDE

1971, 87 MINS, UK ◇ Ⓥ
Dir Roy Ward Baker *Prod* Albert Fennell, Brian Clemens *Scr* Brian Clemens *Ph* Norman Warwick *Ed* James Needs *Mus* David Whitaker *Art Dir* Robert Jones
● Ralph Bates, Martine Beswick, Gerald Sim, Lewis Fiander, Dorothy Alison, Neil Wilson (Hammer)

Scripter Brian Clemens had the highly imaginative idea of letting Robert Louis Stevenson's 19th-century Dr Jekyll turn into a homicidal, glamorous Sister Hyde instead of the original hairy monster. He then pinned on him/her the responsibility for the Jack the Ripper murders.

Here, Jekyll, played by Ralph Bates, murders to remove organs needed for his experiments to prolong life and then gets his hormones wrong. Testing the drug he knocks himself out. Coming round he finds he likes himself as a glamor girl in the person of Martine Beswick and starts to get the best of both sexes when not killing. As male, he attracts the pure young miss living next door and as female fascinates her brother.

Director Roy Ward Baker has set a good pace, built tension nicely and played it straight so that all seems credible. He tops chills and gruesome murders with quite a lot of subtle fun. Bates and Beswick, strong, attractive personalities, bear a strange resemblance to each other making the transitions entirely believable.

••••••••••••••••••••••••••••••

■ DR. NO

1962, 110 MINS, UK ◇ Ⓥ
Dir Terence Young *Prod* Harry Saltzman, Albert R. Broccoli *Scr* Richard Maibaum, Johanna Harwood, Berkeley Mather *Ph* Ted Moore *Ed* Peter Hunt *Mus* Monty Norman *Art Dir* Ken Adam
● Sean Connery, Ursula Andress, Joseph Wiseman, Jack Lord, Bernard Lee, Zena Marshall (United Artists/ Eon)

First screen adventure of Ian Fleming's hard-hitting, fearless, imperturbable, girl-loving Secret Service Agent 007, James Bond, is an entertaining piece of tongue-in-cheek action hokum. Sean Connery excellently puts over a cool, fearless, on-the-ball, fictional Secret Service guy. Terence Young directs with a pace which only occasionally lags.

The hero is exposed to pretty (and sometimes treacherous) gals, a poison tarantula spider, a sinister crook, flame throwers, gunshot, bloodhounds, beating up, near drowning and plenty of other mayhem and malarkey, and comes through it all with good humour, resourcefulness and what have you.

Connery is sent to Jamaica to investigate the murder of a British confidential agent and his secretary. Since both murders happen within three or four minutes of the credit titles the pic gets away to an exhilarating start. He becomes involved with the activities of Dr. No, a sinister Chinese scientist (Joseph Wiseman) who from an island called Crab Key is using a nuclear laboratory to divert off course the rockets being propelled from Cape Canaveral.

Among the dames with whom Connery becomes involved is easy-on-the-eye Ursula Andress, who shares his perilous adventures on Crab Key, and spends most of her time in a bikini, Zena Marshall as an Oriental charmer who nearly decoys him to doom via her boudoir and Eunice Gayson, whom he picks up in a gambling club in London and who promises to be the biggest menace of the lot.

••••••••••••••••••••••••••••••

■ DROP DEAD, DARLING

1966, 100 MINS, UK ◇
Dir Ken Hughes *Prod* Ken Hughes *Scr* Ken Hughes *Ph* Denys Coop *Ed* John Shirley *Mus* Dennis Farnon *Art Dir* Seamus Flannery
● Tony Curtis, Rosanna Schiaffino, Lionel Jeffries, Zsa Zsa Gabor, Nancy Kwan, Fenella Fielding (Paramount/ Seven Arts)

Pic is a silly sex comedy, as amusing at times as it is tasteless, in which Tony Curtis plays a contemporary Bluebeard.

Producer-director Ken Hughes scripted, from a Hughes-Ronald Harwood story, in turn suggested by Richard Deming's *The Careful Man*. Curtis stars as a gold-digging spouse-killer, who meets his match in Rosanna Schiaffino, a femme counterpart.

Story attempts to make likeable a character who arranges the death of his femme guardian, her sailor suitor, later his first two wives and, unsuccessfully, Schiaffino, bride-widow of an a.k. who expires in honeymoon excitement.

Withal, Curtis does a very good job, plotting with Lionel Jeffries to do in Schiaffino. Latter is by no means without acting ability, either.

Script abounds in lecherous one-liners, ably put over by Anna Quayle, palpitating in the Marilyn Monroe manner as Curtis' guardian; Zsa Zsa Gabor, the non-stop gabber whom Curtis locks in a space vehicle at blast-off, and Fenella Fielding, the English heiress of robust appetites and bank accounts.

••••••••••••••••••••••••••••••

■ DROWNING BY NUMBERS

1988, 118 MINS, UK/NETHERLANDS ◇ Ⓥ
Dir Peter Greenaway *Prod* Kees Kasander, Denis Wigman *Scr* Peter Greenaway *Ph* Sacha Vierny *Ed* John Wilson *Mus* Michael Nyman *Art Dir* Ben Van Os, Jan Roelfs
● Bernard Hill, Joan Plowright, Juliet Stevenson, Joely Richardson, Jason Edwards, Bryan Pringle (Film Four/Elsevier Vendex/Allarts/VPRO TV.Holland)

Drowning by Numbers deals with metaphorical game-playing of sex and death in the best traditions of black humor, all set in an idyllic English summer, and pays tribute to the games, landscape and especially a conspiracy of women.

Pic follows the darkly murderous acts of three women all named Cissie Colpitts (Joan Plowright, Juliet Stevenson and Joely Richardson) and their friend the local coroner Madgett (Bernard Hill) and his son Smut (Jason Edwards).

Pic opens with Plowright drowning her husband in a tin bath. The families and friends of the three murdered men suspect the three women of the killings and meet under a water tower.

When none of the three Colpitts women submit to Madgett's sexual advances he decides to admit his part in the murders. But his gameplaying instincts take the better of him, and he organizes a game of tug-of-war between the conspirators and the women.

As an aside Greenaway has placed the numbers 1–100 throughout the film (for example, 1 appears on a tree, 36 is on Joely Richardson's swimsuit) — yet another exercise in game-playing and a challenge for the viewer to spot all the numbers. The acting is uniformly excellent.

••••••••••••••••••••••••••••••

■ DROWNING POOL, THE

1975, 108 MINS, US ◇
Dir Stuart Rosenberg *Prod* Lawrence Torman, David Foster *Scr* Tracey Keenan Wynn, Lorenzo Semple Jr, Walter Hill *Ph* Gordon Willis *Ed* John Howard *Mus* Michael Small, Charles Fox *Art Dir* Paul Sylbert
● Paul Newman, Joanne Woodword, Anthony Franciosa, Murray Hamilton, Gail Strickland, Melanie Griffith (Warner)

Paul Newman again assumes the Lew Harper private eye role he first essayed in *Harper* (1966). *The Drowning Pool* [from Ross Mac-Donald's novel] is stylish, improbable, entertaining, superficial, well cast, and totally synthetic. Stuart Rosenberg's direction is functional and unexciting.

Newman is summoned by Joanne Woodward to her bayou home because of a blackmail letter to her husband Richard Derr alleging infidelity on her part; she's been unfaithful but the current rap is a bummer. Lots of interesting characters begin appearing. Melanie Griffith, Woodward's sexpot jailbait daughter; Murray-Hamilton, very good as an unscrupulous oil baron and Tony Franciosa, an old Woodward flame, now a police chief.

Title derives from an offbeat and exciting climactic sequence in an abandoned mental asylum hydro-therapy room where Hamilton has imprisoned his wife Gail Strickland and Newman to force disclosure of a black book which will explode lots of swampy intrigue.

••••••••••••••••••••••••••••••

■ DR. TERROR'S HOUSE OF HORRORS

1965, 98 MINS, UK ◇ Ⓥ
Dir Freddie Francis *Prod* Milton Subotsky, Max J. Rosenberg *Scr* Milton Subotsky *Ph* Alan Hume *Ed* Thelma Connell *Mus* Tubby Hayes
● Peter Cushing, Christopher Lee, Roy Castle, Donald Sutherland, Neil McCallum, Alan Freeman (Amicus)

Five short horror episodes, thinly linked, provide a usefully chilly package deal which will offer audiences several mild shudders and quite a lot of amusement. Even though occasional giggles set in, the cast, headed by experienced horror practitioners such as Peter Cushing, Michael Gough, Christopher Lee and Max Adrian, sensibly play it straight.

Five young men traveling on a routine train journey, meet up with the sixth passenger. He's a mysterious, bearded stranger (Cushing) who reveals himself as Dr Schreck. With the aid of a pack of Tarot cards, he foretells the grisly deaths in store for the quintet. The film emerges as a kind of Cinemagoers' Digest of how to come to a sticky end.

••••••••••••••••••••••••••••••

■ DR. PHIBES RISES AGAIN

1972, 88 MINS, UK ◇ Ⓥ
Dir Robert Fuest *Prod* Louis M. Heyward *Scr* Robert Fuest, Robert Blees *Ph* Alex Thomson *Ed* Tristan Cones *Mus* John Gale *Art Dir* Brian Eatwell
● Vincent Price, Robert Quarry, Valli Kemp, Hugh Griffith, John Thaw, Keith Buckley (American International)

Dr Phibes, that bizarre evil genius of *The Abominable Dr. Phibes*, is back with all his old diabolic devilry for another excusion into musical camp fantasy.

Dr Phibes, who went into a state of suspended animation at close of *Abominable*, rises three years later to restore life to his wife who died many years before.

Quest for the necessary elixir hidden in an ancient chamber below a mountain once used by the pharaohs takes him to Egypt, where Robert Quarry is his rival in race for the reincarnating drug. Phibes starts decimating Quarry's men who would prevent him from bringing his loved one back to life.

Vincent Price, as Phibes, delivers one of his priceless theatric performances, and Quarry is a properly ruthless rival who nearly matches Phibes in knowledge and cunning.

••••••••••••••••••••••••••••••

■ DR. SOCRATES

1935, 74 MINS, US
Dir William Dieterle *Scr* Robert Lord *Ph* Tony Gaudio *Ed* Ralph Dawson
● Paul Muni, Ann Dvorak, Barton MacLane, Raymond Brown, Ralph Remley, Robert Barrat (Warner

Arriving at the tail end of the G-man and gangster cycle, *Dr Socrates* hasn't the vigor of some of its predecessors, but the constant and basic threat of violence is always present.

Plot [from a story by W.R. Burnett, adapted by Mary C. McCall Jr] departs from what is customary in the gangster school, in that it stars neither the gunman nor the officer of the law, but makes both subservient to a country doctor.

The chief gangster in this case is a Dillinger type of gent who terrorizes a section of the middle west. The young physician is adopted as the gang's medical man, and he takes a chance because he needs the money. But when the gang grabs his girl he goes on the offensive.

For Muni, *Socrates* is an easy role, calling for little or no emotional work. For an actor of his calibre the soft-spoken doc seems a minor effort. Ann Dvorak plays a hitchhiking girl who gets innocently tangled with the mobsters and brings romance to the small town sawbones.

■ DR. STRANGELOVE
OR: HOW I LEARNED TO STOP WORRYING
AND LOVE THE BOMB

1964, 102 MINS, UK ⓥ

Dir Stanley Kubrick   *Prod* Stanley Kubrick   *Scr* Stanley Kubrick, Terry Southern, Peter George   *Ph* Gilbert Taylor   *Ed* Anthony Harvey   *Mus* Laurie Johnson   *Art Dir* Peter Murton
● Peter Sellers, George C. Scott, Sterling Hayden, Keenan Wynn, Slim Pickens, James Earl Jones (Columbia)

Nothing would seen to be farther apart than nuclear war and comedy, yet Kubrick's caper eloquently tackles a *Fail Safe* subject with a light touch.

Screenplay based on the book *Red Alert* by Peter George is imaginative and contains many an offbeat touch. Some of the characters have a broad brush in their depiction, but this is the very nature of satire.

It all begins when a Strategic Air Command general on his own initiative orders bomb-carrying planes under his command to attack Russia. From here on it's a hectic, exciting series of events, alternating between the General who has started it all, the planes en route to the USSR, and the Pentagon's war room, where the Chief Executive is trying his best to head off the nuclear war.

It would seem no setting for comedy or satire, but the writers have accomplished this with biting, piercing dialogue and thorough characterizations. Peter Sellers is excellent, essaying a trio of roles – a British RAF captain assigned to the US base where it all begins, the President and the title character, Dr Strangelove, a German scientist aiding the US whose Nazi mannerisms overcome him.

George C. Scott as the fiery Pentagon general who seizes on the crisis as a means to argue for total annihilation of Russia offers a top performance, one of the best in the film. Odd as it may seem in this backdrop, he displays a fine comedy touch. Sterling Hayden is grimly realistic as the General who takes it on his own to send our nuclear bomb-carrying planes to attack Russia. He is a man who blames the Communists for fluoridation of water, and just about everything else.

□ 1964: Best Picture (Nomination)

■ DRUGSTORE COWBOY

1989, 100 MINS, US ◇ ⓥ

Dir Gus Van Sant Jr   *Prod* Nick Wechsler, Karen Murphy   *Scr* Gus Van Sant Jr, Daniel Yost   *Ph* Robert Yeoman   *Ed* Curtiss Clayton   *Mus* Elliot Goldenthal   *Art Dir* David Brisbin

● Matt Dillon, Kelly Lynch, James Le Gros, Heather Graham, James Remar (Avenue)

No previous drug-themed film has the honesty or originality of Gus Van Sant's drama *Drugstore Cowboy*. Pic addresses the fact that people take drugs because they *enjoy* them.

Set in Portland, Ore. in the early 1970s, *Drugstore Cowboy* tells of one self-confessed and completely unrepentant 'drug fiend' (his own description), Bob Hughes (Matt Dillon). He robs drugstores, not for money – for drugs.

Backed up by a 'crew' consisting of his willowy but tough wife Dianne (Kelly Lynch), his dimwitted but true-blue pal Rick (James Le Gros) and Le Gros' weepy, bumbling girlfriend, Nadine (Heather Graham), Dillon revels in his self-described life of crime.

Dillon's world begins to sour when Graham dies of an overdose. The incident so frightens him he vows to give up drugs entirely. Unfortunately, Lynch refuses to go along with him.

It's a novel conflict. Dillon is kicking the habit for personal reasons – he still likes drugs. He and Lynch still love each other, but for junkies, drugs make every romance a triangle.

Van Sant draws fine performances from his cast, particularly Lynch, who up to now has appeared as the obligatory Sexy Girl. This is her *acting* debut. He also gets one truly great performance from Dillon.

■ DRUM, THE

1938, 101 MINS, US ◇ ⓥ

Dir Zoltan Korda   *Prod* Alexander Korda   *Scr* Lajos Biro, Arthur Wimperis, Patrick Kirwan, Hugh Gray   *Ph* Georges Perinal, Osmond Borradaile   *Ed* Henry Cornelius, William Hornbeck   *Mus* John Greenwood, Miklos Rozsa   *Art Dir* Vincent Korda, Ferdinand Bellan
● Sabu, Raymond Massey, Roger Livesey, Valerie Hobson, David Tree, Francis L. Sullivan (London)

Film is based on a story written specially for the screen by A.E.W. Mason. He supplies an excellent machine-made suspensive tale laid in India, with fine dialog.

Entire action is laid in the tribal territory of the northwest frontier of India. An elderly khan is anxious for British protection to ensure his throne for his son, Prince Axim (Sabu). Ruler's brother, Prince Ghul, is fanatically anti-British, kills the old man, and the plot involves the attempt to do away with the young prince.

Sabu, the 14-year-old Indian youth who came to attention in *Elephant Boy* (1937), lives up to the promise given in that film and conducts himself with requisite dignity. He now speaks very good English. Raymond Massey is sufficiently sinister as the throne usurper; Roger Livesey is excellent as the military commander.

■ DRUM

1976, 100 MINS, US ◇ ⓥ

Dir Steve Carver   *Prod* Ralph Serpe   *Scr* Norman Wexler   *Ph* Lucien Ballard   *Ed* Carl Kress   *Mus* Charlie Smalls   *Art Dir* Stan Jolley
● Warren Oates, Isela Vega, Ken Norton, Pam Grier, Yaphet Kotto, John Colicos (De Laurentiis)

Drum is a grubby followup to *Mandingo* [1975] which invites its own derisive audience laughter. Ham acting like you wouldn't believe, coupled with non-direction by Steve Carver and a correspondence-school script by Norman Wexler, add up to cinematic trash.

There's slave-breeder Warren Oates who buys Ken Norton and Yaphet Kotto from bordello queen Isela Vega, who in reality is Norton's real mother though her lesbian lover-maid Paula Kelly raised the boy; Pam Grier goes along with the deal as Norton's girl and occasional wench to Oates, though

Fiona Lewis, her eyes on Oates, has other plans.

Climax of the film is a slave revolt where lots of people get killed, including Royal Dano who manages to keep a straight face as a mean slaver.

■ DRUMS ACROSS THE RIVER

1954, 77 MINS, US ◇

Dir Nathan Juran   *Prod* Melville Tucker   *Scr* John K. Butler, Lawrence Roman   *Ph* Harold Lipstein   *Ed* Virgil Vogel   *Mus* Joseph Gershenson
● Audie Murphy, Walter Brennan, Lyle Bettger, Lisa Gaye, Hugh O'Brian, Mara Corday (Universal)

Plenty of rough and ready action keeps this regulation western rolling over its course.

The script has Lyle Bettger trying to stir up trouble between the Utes and the whites for personal profit. He'd like to open up the Ute territory and its gold deposits, closed to the whites by treaty, on one hand and, on the other, he's scheming to rob the stage of a gold shipment and lay the blame at the doorstep of Audie Murphy and his dad (Walter Brennan).

■ DRUMS ALONG THE MOHAWK

1939, 100 MINS, US ◇ ⓥ

Dir John Ford   *Prod* Darryl Zanuck   *Scr* Lamar Trotti, Sonya Levien   *Ph* Bert Glennon   *Ed* Robert Simpson   *Mus* Alfred Newman   *Art Dir* Richard Day, Mark-Lee Kirk
● Claudette Colbert, Henry Fonda, Edna May Oliver, Arthur Shields, Ward Bond (20th Century-Fox)

Having great sweep and colorful backgrounding, with the photography unusually good, the picture is an outdoor spectacle which highly pleases the eye even if the story [from the novel by Walter D. Edmonds], on occasion, gets a bit slow and some incidents fail to excite.

While the backgrounding is beautiful, as photoged by Bert Glennon, it doesn't always look like the Mohawk Valley (upstate New York) region with wheat fields, evergreens, big birches, etc. as atmosphere.

The story deals with farming pioneers of the Mohawk Valley sector at the time of the Revolutionary war, with Indian terror and English intrigue, plus hardship, testing the stamina of the colonists. Romance of Henry Fonda and Claudette Colbert, who have married and are forging ahead to new frontiers, has pull.

■ DRY WHITE SEASON, A

1989, 97 MINS, US ◇ ⓥ

Dir Euzhan Palcy   *Prod* Paula Weinstein   *Scr* Colin Welland, Euzhan Palcy   *Ph* Kelvin Pike, Pierre-William Glenn   *Ed* Sam O'Steen, Glenn Cunningham   *Mus* Dave Grusin   *Art Dir* John Fenner
● Donald Sutherland, Winston Ntshona, Zakes Mokae, Jurgen Prochnow, Susan Sarandon, Marlon Brando (M-G-M)

A wrenching picture about South Africa that makes no expedient compromises with feel-good entertainment values, *A Dry White Season* displays riveting performances and visceral style.

Filmmaker Euzhan Palcy – who is black – never tempers her outrage, but the film [from the novel by Andre Brink] drives home the point that the story of South Africa is a story of two races that's unlikely to be resolved by either one alone.

Set in 1976, the film moves quickly to a searing sequence in which a demonstration by black schoolchildren of Soweto is broken up with gratuitous lethal force. Many are brutally beaten and arrested, including the son of Gordon Ngubene (Winston Ntshona),

D

a gardener who works at the comfortable home of naive prep school teacher Ben du Toit (Donald Sutherland).

Du Toit is a basically decent man who cares enough to pay for the missing boy's schooling but not enough to question society's blatantly unjust status quo.

With mounting astonishment this community pillar comes to discover what he's always closed his eyes to: South African 'justice and law could be described as distant cousins – not on speaking terms.'

Those words are spoken by Ian McKenzie (Marlon Brando), rising with a world-weary magnificence to the role of a prominent human rights attorney whose idealism has been battered into resignation. Sarcasm is his only tactic, the moral high ground his only refuge as McKenzie proves Cpt Stolz (Jurgen Prochnow) a murderer, but loses his case before a judge who makes no effort to hide his disgraceful bias.

· ·

■ **DU BARRY WAS A LADY**

1943, 96 MINS, US ◇ ⒱
Dir Roy Del Ruth   *Prod* Arthur Freed   *Scr* Irving Brecher   *Ph* Karl Freund   *Ed* Blanche Sewell
● Red Skelton, Lucille Ball, Gene Kelly, Virginia O'Brien, Zero Mostel (M-G-M)

In sapolioing the script for celluloid, the studio has taken Red Skelton out of the men's room and put him in the coat room. Otherwise it follows the general outlines of the original 1939 Broadway show by Herbert Fields and B.G. DeSylva: the club caddy falls for the top warbler at the spot (Lucille Ball).

She pays no attention to him, being enamored of a broke songsmith (Gene Kelly), while she plays Douglas Dumbrille for his chips. Then Skelton wins a Derby pot and some attention from Ball, only to get a Mickey intended for Kelly mixed up with his own drink, which sends him into a dream sequence. He finds himself Louis XV and Ball his Du Barry.

With the weak plot and weaker dialog, Skelton has a tough time living up to his rep as a funnyman. Ball does a bit better, while Gene Kelly, whose forte is terping, suffers from the histrionic and singing demands of his role and lack of opportunity to make with the feet. O'Brien is disappointing, too, except for the one tune she's given, 'Salome Was the Grandma of Them All,' in which she literally sparkles.

· ·

■ **DUCHESS AND THE DIRTWATER FOX, THE**

1976, 104 MINS, US ◇ ⒱
Dir Melvin Frank   *Prod* Melvin Frank   *Scr* Melvin Frank, Barry Sandler, Jack Rose   *Ph* Joseph Biroc   *Ed* Frank Bracht, William Butler   *Mus* Charles Fox   *Art Dir* Trevor Williams, Robert Emmet Smith
● George Segal, Goldie Hawn, Roy Jenson, Thayer David, Pat Ast, Sid Gould (20th Century-Fox)

The Duchess and the Dirtwater Fox is a generally pleasant and amiable period western comedy starring George Segal as a fumbling gambler and Goldie Hawn as a singing-dancing frontier chick.

Pair get involved with Roy Jenson's robber gang, Thayer David's group of Mormons, a Jewish wedding, some good gags here, some forced humor there.

Barry Sandler's story has been scripted into sketches which tend to a predictably upbeat curtain. The Colorado scenery vies with the interactions of Hawn and Segal; the other players are more or less backdrop.

The stars work well together; Segal's comedy abilities seem in fullest flower when Mel Frank is directing, while Hawn's talents are showcased quite nicely.

· ·

■ **DUCK SOUP**

1933, 70 MINS, US
Dir Leo McCarey   *Scr* Bert Kalmar, Harry Ruby, Arthur Skeekman, Nat Perrin   *Ph* Henry Sharp   *Ed* LeRoy Stone   *Mus* Arthur Johnston (advisor)   *Art Dir* Hans Dreier, Wiard B. Ihnen
● Groucho Marx, Chico Marx, Harpo Marx, Zeppo Marx, Margaret Dumont, Louis Calhern (Paramount)

The laughs come often, too often sometimes, which has always been the case with Marx talkers, although in this instance more care appears to have been taken with the timing, since the step-on gags don't occur as frequently as in the past.

In place of the constant punning and dame chasing, *Duck Soup* has the Marxes madcapping through such bits as the old Schwartz Bros mirror routine, so well done in the hands of Groucho, Harpo and Chico that it gathers a new and hilarious comedy momentum all over again.

Story is a mythical kingdom burlesque that could easily have been written by a six-year-old with dust in his eyes, but it isn't so much the story as what goes with and on within it. Groucho is the prime minister. For his customary dowager-foil he has the high, wide and handsome Margaret Dumont, making it perfect for Groucho.

While Groucho soft pedals the verbal clowning for more physical effort this time the other boys also make a quick change. Chico and Harpo omit their musical specialties, which should make it much easier for the piano and harp numbers the next time, if needed. Zeppo is simply Zeppo.

Music and lyrics [by Bert Kalmar and Harry Ruby] through which much of the action is in rhyme and song, serve to carry the story along rather than to stand out on pop song merit on their own. Everything's in keeping with the tempo of the production.

· ·

■ **DUDES**

1987, 90 MINS, US ◇ ⒱
Dir Penelope Spheeris   *Prod* Herb Jaffe   *Scr* J. Randal Johnson   *Ph* Robert Richardson   *Ed* Andy Horvitch   *Art Dir* Robert Ziembicki
● Jon Cryer, Daniel Roebuck, Flea, Lee Ving, Catherine Mary Stewart (Vista)

How can a film that brings punk rockers from Queens, cowboys, Indians and crazed homicidal villains together in Utah be taken seriously? The answer, of course, is that it can't.

Dudes tells the story of three punked-out New Yorkers – Milo, Grant and Biscuit – who set out for Hollywood in a Volkswagen and get attacked while camping out in Big Sky country. Milo is murdered by Missoula, leader of a wild-eyed gang that roams the west killing Mexicans. Grant and Biscuit vow to avenge Milo's death.

Even if one were inclined to overlook the derivative story line, *Dudes* still manages to throw itself from the saddle so many times it bruises the sensibilities. The humor, when intentional, is slapstick. The dialog is hopelessly adolescent, the music incredibly loud and the plot is dependent on a bizarre sequence of coincidences.

· ·

■ **DUEL AT DIABLO**

1966, 105 MINS, US ◇ ⒱
Dir Ralph Nelson   *Prod* Fred Engel, Ralph Nelson   *Scr* Marvin Alpert, Michel Grilikhes   *Ph* Charles F. Wheeler   *Ed* Fredric Steinkamp   *Mus* Neal Hefti   *Art Dir* Alfred Ybarra
● James Garner, Sidney Poitier, Bibi Andersson, Dennis Weaver, Bill Travers, William Redfield (United Artists)

Duel at Diablo packs enough fast action in its cavalry-Indians narrative to satisfy the most

avid follower of this type of entertainment. Produced with knowhow, and directed with a flourish by Ralph Nelson, the feature is long on exciting and well-staged battle movement and carries a story that while having little novelty still stands to good effect.

Based on the Marvin Albert novel, *Apache Rising*, screenplay stars James Garner as a scout and Sidney Poitier as a former trooper who now makes his living breaking in horses for the service. Rivalling them in interest and importance, however, is Bill Travers, a cavalry lieutenant who heads the column of raw recruits to a distant fort and is attacked en route by the Apaches.

Garner is properly rugged and acquits himself handsomely, convincing as a plainsman who knows his Indians. Poitier tackles a new type of characterization here, far afield from anything he has essayed in the past. Travers in a strong character part is vigorous and appealing and endears himself with his light and human touch.

· ·

■ **DUEL IN THE SUN**

1946, 134 MINS, US ◇ ⒱
Dir King Vidor   *Prod* David O. Selznick   *Scr* David O. Selznick   *Ph* Lee Garmes, Hal Rosson, Ray Rennahan   *Ed* Hal C. Kern   *Mus* Dimitri Tiomkin   *Art Dir* J. McMillan Johnson
● Jennifer Jones, Gregory Peck, Joseph Cotten, Lionel Barrymore, Lillian Gish, Walter Huston (Selznick)

The familiar western formula reaches its highest commercialization in *Duel in Sun*. It is raw, sex-laden, western pulp fiction, told in 10-20-30 style. The star lineup is impressive. Vastness of the western locale is splendidly displayed in color by mobile cameras. Footage is overwhelmingly expansive, too much so at times considering its length.

Single scenes that stand out include Jennifer Jones' peril in riding bareback on a runaway horse, filmed against the vast scope of the western scene; Gregory Peck's taming of a sex-maddened stallion; the tremendous sweep of hundreds of mounted horsemen riding to do battle with the invading railroad.

King Vidor's direction keeps the playing in step with production aims. He pitches the action to heights in the top moments and generally holds the overall mood desired. Sharing director credit on the mass sequences are Otto Brower and Reaves Eason.

Plot, suggested by a novel by Niven Busch, adapted by Oliver H. P. Garrett, concerns a half-breed girl who goes to the ranch of a Texas cattle baron to live after her father has killed her adulterous mother and lover. The baron's two sons fall for her but the unrestrained younger one captures her emotions. So strong is physical desire that he murders one man who wants to marry her and tries to kill the brother, shown in latter attempts to make the girl a lady.

Jones as the half-breed proves herself extremely capable in quieter sequences but is overly meller in others. Same is true of Peck as the virile younger Texan raised to love 'em and leave 'em. Contrasting is Joseph Cotten as the older son. Role in his hands is believable and never overdrawn.

· ·

■ **DUELLISTS, THE**

1977, 95 MINS, UK ◇ ⒱
Dir Ridley Scott   *Prod* David Puttnam   *Scr* Gerald Vaughan-Hughes   *Ph* Frank Tidy   *Ed* Pamela Power   *Art Dir* Bryan Graves
● Keith Carradine, Harvey Keitel, Cristina Raines, Edward Fox, Robert Stephens, Albert Finney (Enigma)

The Napoleonic Wars are behind this stubborn sword slashing and then pistols of two men whose personalities are caught up in their own personal vendetta within the epic European battles of the times.

Harvey Keitel is an almost obsessed dueller who is asked to appear before the general due to his duels, by Keith Carradine who practically volunteers for the job.

Keitel is jaunty and menancing and Carradine more determined and a bit troubled but also caught up in this strange need of one to prove honor and the other slaking a twisted nature.

It does not quite achieve a more lusty visual feel for the times and the strange relations of these two men to themselves and to the women in and out of their lives.

Fine thesps in smaller roles help with even Albert Finney in as the Napoleonic head of the Paris police.

....

■ **DUET FOR ONE**

1986, 107 MINS, US ◇ Ⓥ

Dir Andrei Konchalovsky *Prod* Menahem Golan, Yoram Globus *Scr* Tom Kempinski, Jeremy Lipp, Andrei Konchalovsky *Ph* Alex Thomson *Ed* Henry Richardson *Mus* Michael Linn *Art Dir* John Graysmark

● Julie Andrews, Alan Bates, Max Von Sydow, Rupert Everett, Margaret Courtenay, Cathryn Harrison (Cannon)

The story of a world-class violinist who contracts multiple sclerosis and is forced to abandon her career, as long as *Duet for One* [from the 1980 stage play by Tom Kempinski] stays personal and specific it is a moving portrait of a life in turmoil.

Initially the film is not really about illness but the relationship of an artist to her art. Film is full of lovely musical interludes, both in concert and practice, and Julie Andrews actually looks credible stroking her violin. At the same time Andrews approaches her predicament in a pragmatic, overly rational manner as she plans out her recording schedule and the remaining days of her career.

In addition to the suggestion of a story, first half of the film offers an array of eccentric characters swirling around Andrews' life. As the philandering husband, Bates is a complex and restless soul afraid to face his own failings, whose vulnerability and physical deterioration bring an added and welcome dimension to the film.

....

■ **DUFFY**

1968, 101 MINS, UK ◇

Dir Robert Parrish *Prod* Martin Manulis *Scr* Donald Cammell, Harry Joe Brown Jr *Ph* Otto Heller *Ed* Willie Kemplen *Mus* Ernie Freeman *Art Dir* Phillip Harrison

● James Coburn, James Mason, James Fox, Susannah York, John Alderton (Columbia)

Duffy is the story of two alienated sons stealing from their wealthy father. Weak writing and heavy-handed direction by Robert Parrish, eliciting only tepid performances, combine to snuff out much interest before the genuinely perky climax.

James Mason is a cold, calculating industrialist, loathed heartily by his sons, James Fox (who feeds dad's money to pay for his hedonistic excesses) and John Alderton (who simply needs someone to rescue him from stupid blunders). Susannah York has some sort of affair going with Fox. Trio recruits drifter James Coburn to help with a money heist, designed to make them independently wealthy and also to embarrass Mason.

Fox's interpretation of his role is so swish (with costumes to match) that one wonders what attractions he holds for York. York in addition looks different in practically every setup. Only Alderton, who plays broadly to the pit, has what seems a definite concept of his part. Coburn tries awfully hard to be a hippie.

....

■ **DUMBO**

1941, 64 MINS, US ◇ Ⓥ

Dir Ben Sharpsteen *Prod* Walt Disney *Scr* Joe Grant, Dick Huemer *Mus* Oliver Wallace, Frank Churchill
● (Walt Disney)

Walt Disney returns in *Dumbo* to the formula that accounted for his original success – simple animal characterization.

There's a pleasant little story, plenty of pathos mixed with the large doses of humor, a number of appealing new animal characters, lots of good music, and the usual Disney skillfulness in technique.

Defects are some decidedly slow spots and that the film is somewhat episodic in nature.

Story [from a book by Helen Aberson and Harold Pearl] points a nice moral, although not one that gets in the way. Dumbo is a little elephant who is jeered at because of his big ears. But he is shown how to make use of his ears, they enable him to fly, and his handicap thereby becomes his greatest asset.

Yarn is set to a circus background, complete with clowns, the big top and all the rest. There is also a neatly contrived comedy characterization of gossipy lady elephants, and the even more earthy humor of a typical Disney locomotive being spurred to speed by a goose from the car behind it.

....

■ **DUNE**

1984, 140 MINS, US ◇ Ⓥ

Dir David Lynch *Prod* Raffaella De Laurentiis *Scr* David Lynch *Ph* Freddie Francis *Ed* Antony Gibbs *Mus* Toto, Marty Paich, Brian Eno *Art Dir* Anthony Masters
● Francesca Annis, Brad Dourif, Kyle MacLachlan, Sian Phillips, Sting, Max Von Sydow (De Laurentiis)

Dune is a huge, hollow, imaginative and cold sci-fi epic. Visually unique and teeming with incident, David Lynch's film holds the interest due to its abundant surface attractions but won't, of its own accord, create the sort of fanaticism which has made Frank Herbert's 1965 novel one of the all-time favorites in its genre.

Set in the year 10,991, *Dune* is the story of the coming to power of a warrior savior and how he leads the lowly inhabitants of the Dune planet to victory over an evil emperor and his minions.

Lynch's adaptation covers the entire span of the novel, but simply setting up the various worlds, characters, intrigues and forces at work requires more than a half-hour of expository screen time.

The anointed one, Paul Atreides, travels with his regal mother and father to the desert planet, where an all-powerful 'spice' is mined from beneath the sands despite the menace provided by enormous worms which gobble up harvesters in a single gulp.

The horrid Harkonnens conquer the city on Dune, but Paul and his mother escape to the desert. There Paul trains native warriors and achieves his full mystic powers.

Francesca Annis and Jurgen Prochnow make an outstandingly attractive royal couple, Sian Phillips has some mesmerizing moments as a powerful witch, Brad Dourif is effectively loony, and best of all is Kenneth McMillan, whose face is covered with grotesque growths and who floats around like the Blue Meanie come to life.

....

■ **DUNKIRK**

1958, 135 MINS, UK

Dir Leslie Norman *Prod* Michael Balcon *Scr* David Divine, W.P. Lipscomb *Ph* Paul Beeson *Ed* Gordon Stone *Mus* Malcolm Arnold *Art Dir* Jim Morahan
● John Mills, Bernard Lee, Richard Attenborough, Robert Urquhart, Ray Jackson, Maxine Audley (Ealing)

Eighteen years after the event, Ealing Films

tackled the mammoth task of committing Dunkirk to the screen. The story of a defeat which, miraculously, blossomed into ultimate victory because it stiffened Britain's resolve and solidarity, offered Michael Balcon and his team many challenging problems. *Dunkirk* is a splendid near-documentary which just fails to reach magnificence.

Director Leslie Norman planned his film [based on a novel by Elleston Trevor and also on a factual account] through the eyes of three men. John Mills, a spry Cockney corporal who with a few men becomes detached from his unit and leads them to the beaches without quite knowing what is happening. Bernard Lee, a newspaper correspondent who is suspicious of the red tape of the higher-ups. Richard Attenborough as a civilian having an easy time in a reserved occupation.

The film throughout is deliberately underplayed, with no false heroics and with dialog which has an almost clinical authenticity. On the whole, it is an absorbing rather than an emotion-stirring film.

....

■ **DUTCHMAN**

1967, 55 MINS, UK

Dir Anthony Harvey *Prod* Gene Persson *Scr* Le Roi Jones *Ph* Gerry Turpin *Ed* Anthony Harvey *Mus* John Barry *Art Dir* Herbert Smith
● Shirley Knight, Al Freeman Jr (Persson)

Dutchman is a literal filming of Le Roi Jones' 1964 off-Broadway play, pitting a white slut against a middle-class Negro youth who is, in turn, seduced, disgraced and killed. Excellent direction and performances are enhanced by realistically grim production values.

Producer Gene Persson casts wife Shirley Knight and Al Freeman Jr as the leads, actually a re-teaming since both starred in his 1965 LA and Frisco legit mountings of the property.

Anthony Harvey makes his directorial debut after a long career as a film editor. It is a challenging debut, since there is no screenplay, only Jones' legit dialog, and the action is confined to a NY subway car, except for some second-unit lensing by Edward R. Brown. Withal, Harvey's work is impressive, in eliciting adroit performances, in camera setups, and in overall editing pace.

Knight, a red-neck Jezebel if there ever was one, is outstanding as she deliberately debases Freeman, dragging him down from insecure middle class status to that of an embittered, violent youth.

....

■ **EAGLE, THE**

1925, 72 MINS, US ⊗ Ⓥ

Dir Clarence Brown *Scr* Hans Kraly, George Marion Jr. *Ph* George Barnes, Dev Jennings *Ed* Hal C. Kern *Art Dir* William Cameron Menzies
● Rudolph Valentino, Vilma Banky, Louise Dresser, Albert Conti, James Marcus (Art Finance/United Artists)

Rudolph Valentino as a Russian Robin Hood of more modern times. In *The Eagle*, he really goes out and does some 'he-man' stuff.

Louise Dresser as the Czarina handles herself superbly. She is the old girl of the Russians who liked the boys. Vilma Banky makes a most charming heroine opposite the star, but Louise Dresser is about as much the picture as the star himself.

....

E

EAGLE HAS LANDED, THE

1977, 134 MINS, UK ◇ Ⓥ

Dir John Sturges   *Prod* Jack Winer, David Niven Jr
Scr Tom Mankiewicz   *Ph* Tony Richmond   *Ed* Irene
Lamb   *Mus* Lalo Schifrin   *Art Dir* Peter Murton
● Michael Caine, Donald Sutherland, Robert Duvall,
Jenny Agutter, Donald Pleasence, Anthony Quayle
(ITC/Assoc. General)

In November 1943 Winston Churchill is due
to spend a weekend at a country house in
Norfolk – and the Germans propose to kid-
nap him there. Under orders from Heinrich
Himmler (Donald Pleasence), purportedly
coming from Hitler himself, a Nazi colonel,
Robert Duvall, organizes the smuggling into
Britain of the English-hating Irishman
Donald Sutherland and the parachuting of a
16-man task force of Germans under the
command of another colonel (Michael
Caine).

The events take place in the small village of
Studley Constable.

Most performances [in this adaptation of
Jack Higgins' novel] are first rate with
Sutherland exuding great credibility as the
Irishman, and Caine thoroughly convincing
as the Nazi commander. Pleasence gives a
stand-out lifelike interpretation of Himmler.

EAGLE'S WING

1979, 104 MINS, UK ◇ Ⓥ

Dir Anthony Harvey   *Prod* Peter Shaw   *Scr* John
Briley   *Ph* Billy Williams   *Ed* Lesley Walker
Mus Marc Wilkinson   *Art Dir* Herbert Westbrook
● Martin Sheen, Sam Waterston, Harvey Keitel,
Stephane Audran, Caroline Langrishe, John Castle
(Rank)

Claiming to evoke 'the West, the way it really
was, before the myths were born', British
director Anthony Harvey's poised, loving linger in the 1830s badlands of New Mexico is
primarily an art film – resolutely romantic,
high on production values, low on grit.

Ostensibly a tussle for possession of a
uniquely fleet white horse (poetically described by the title), the distinctly allegorical
plot [from an original story by Michael
Syson] pits Martin Sheen as a city-bred,
novice trapper against a no-longer-so-young
Indian brave, played with remarkable
success by Sam Waterston.

Sheen, wild-eyed and vulnerable, is good
casting and copes well with the central
character's awkward soliloquizing. Harvey
Keitel is lowkey but impressive as Sheen's
companion and mentor.

EARTH GIRLS ARE EASY

1988, 100 MINS, US ◇ Ⓥ

Dir Julien Temple   *Prod* Tony Garnett   *Scr* Julie
Brown, Charlie Coffey, Terence E. McNally   *Ph* Oliver
Stapleton   *Ed* Richard Halsey   *Mus* Nile Rodgers
Art Dir Dennis Gasner
● Geena Davis, Jeff Goldblum, Julie Brown, Jim
Carrey, Damon Wayans (Earth Girls Are Easy/Vestron)

Earth Girls Are Easy is a dizzy, glitzy fish-out-
of-water farce about three horny aliens on the
make in LA.

Julie (Geena Davis), a gorgeous Valley
Girl, works as a manicurist in high-tech
beauty salon operated by Candy (Julie
Brown) a Val-Queen supreme who likes good
times and good sex.

Meanwhile in outer space, three aliens who
look like tie-dyed werewolves are wandering
around our solar system going bonkers with
randiness. In keeping with the film's hot-
pastel, contempo-trash design motif, their
spacecraft looks like the inside of a pinball
machine. When it lands in Julie's swimming
pool, the broken-hearted girl who's just broken off with her nogoodnik lover takes it for
an oversized hair dryer.

Julie brings this gruesome threesome to
Candy's beauty parlor for a complete 'makeover.' They emerge as three hairless hunky
dudes: the captain, Jeff Goldblum and two
flaked-out crewman, Jim Carrey and Damon
Wayans. The two val-gals and their alien
'dates' take off for a weekend of LA nightlife,
where the visitors' smooth adaptation to
Coast culture is intended by director Julian
Temple and his screenwriters to affectionately skewer Tinseltown lifestyles.

EARTHQUAKE

1974, 122 MINS, US ◇ Ⓥ

Dir Mark Robson   *Prod* Mark Robson   *Scr* George
Fox, Mario Puzo   *Ph* Philip Lathrop   *Ed* Dorothy
Spencer   *Mus* John Williams   *Art Dir* Alexander
Golitzen
● Charlton Heston, Ava Gardner, George Kennedy,
Lorne Greene, Genevieve Bujold, Richard Roundtree
(Universal)

Mark Robson's *Earthquake* is an excellent dramatic exploitation extravaganza, combining
brilliant special effects with a multi-character
plot line which is surprisingly above average
for this type film. Large cast is headed by
Charlton Heston, who comes off better than
usual because he is not Superman, instead
just one of the gang.

Ava Gardner, ravishingly beautiful, plays
Heston's jealous wife, who also is the
daughter of Lorne Greene, Heston's architect
boss. Gardner's fits of pique concern
Genevieve Bujold.

The film spends its first 53 minutes establishing most of the key plot situations, but
regularly teases with some foreshocks the big
quake. When that occurs, the first big special
effects sequence provides an excellent,
unstinting panorama of destruction.

EASTER PARADE

1948, 102 MINS, US ◇ Ⓥ

Dir Charles Walters   *Prod* Arthur Freed   *Scr* Frances
Goodrich, Albert Hackett, Sidney Sheldon   *Ph* Harry
Stradling   *Ed* Albert Akst   *Mus* Irving Berlin   *Art
Dir* Cedric Gibbons, Jack Martin Smith
● July Garland, Fred Astaire, Peter Lawford, Ann
Miller, Jules Munshin (M-G-M)

Easter Parade is a musical with old and new
Irving Berlin tunes and standout dance numbers. The Berlin score includes 17 songs,
seven new and 10 from his extensive catalog.

The light story by Frances Goodrich and
Albert Hackett, scripted in conjunction with
Sidney Sheldon, makes a perfect backing for
the Berlin score and playing. Plot opens on
Easter 1911 and carries through to Easter
1912. It deals with splitup of Astaire and
Miller as partners and recruiting of Garland
by the dancer, who is determined to make her
outdraw his former hoofer.

Astaire's standout solo is the elaborate production piece 'Stepping Out with My Baby',
during which he does a slow-motion dance in
front of a large chorus terping in regular time.

·Highpoint of comedy is reached when
Astaire and Garland team for vocals and foot
work on 'A Couple of Swells'.

EAST OF EDEN

1955, 114 MINS, US ◇ Ⓥ

Dir Elia Kazan   *Prod* Elia Kazan   *Scr* Paul Osborn
Ph Ted McCord   *Ed* Owen Marks   *Mus* Leonard
Rosenman   *Art Dir* James Basevi, Malcolm Bert
● Julie Harris, James Dean, Raymond Massey, Burl
Ives, Jo Van Fleet, Albert Dekker (Warner)

Powerfully somber dramatics have been
captured from the pages of John Steinbeck's
East of Eden and put on film by Elia Kazan. It
is a tour de force for the director's penchant
for hard-hitting forays with life.

It is no credit to Kazan that James Dean
seems required to play his lead character as
though he were straight out of a Marlon
Brando mold, although he has a basic appeal
that manages to get through to the viewer
despite the heavy burden of carboning another's acting style in voice and mannerisms.

Only the latter part of the Steinbeck novel
is used in the screenplay, which picks up the
principals in this Salinas Valley melodrama
at the time the twin sons of a lettuce farmer
are graduating in the 1917 class at high
school.

Julie Harris gives her particular style to an
effective portrayal of the girl.

EASY LIVING

1937, 88 MINS, US

Dir Mitchell Leisen   *Prod* Arthur Hornblow Jr
Scr Preston Sturges   *Ph* Ted Tetzlaff   *Ed* Doane
Harrison   *Mus* Boris Morros (dir.)   *Art Dir* Hans Dreier,
Ernst Fegte
● Jean Arthur, Edward Arnold, Ray Milland, Luis
Alberni, Mary Nash, Franklin Pangborn (Paramount)

Slapstick farce, incredible and without rhyme
or reason, is Paramount's contribution to the
cycle of goofy pictures which started with *My
Man Godfrey* (1936). This one is a poor imitation, lacking spontaneity and cleverness.

Screenplay by Preston Sturges [from a
story by Vera Caspary] is a trivia of nonsense. Mitchell Leisen, who directs, tries to
overcome the story faults with elaborate settings and Keystone gags.

Opening portrays Edward Arnold as a
Wall Street speculative genius whose mad
selling and buying has the street agog with
his financial didoes. Conflict starts with an
altercation between him and his wife over the
purchase of a fur coat. Garment is tossed out
of the window and strikes a young stenographer (Jean Arthur) on her way to work. In
a jealous fit, Arnold insists the young woman
retain the coat and whisks her to the milliner
to buy a hat to match.

Meanwhile, the news spreads quickly that
the big Wall Street man has a mistress, and
Arthur, whose resources are measured in
nickels, accepts an elaborate suite in the leading hotel. What she wants most is a cup of
coffee, and she goes to the automat to get it.
There she meets Ray Milland, son of the
Wall Street wizard. He is a waiter in the
joint.

Yarns of this sort are likely to get out of
hand by introducing low slapstick comedy.
When the food throwing ends there is nothing
left for the players to do. All semblance of
probability has vanished.

EASY RIDER

1969, 94 MINS, US ◇ Ⓥ

Dir Dennis Hopper   *Prod* Peter Fonda   *Scr* Peter
Fonda, Dennis Hopper, Terry Southern   *Ph* Laszlo
Kovacs   *Ed* Donn Cambren   *Mus* The Byrds, The
Band, Jimi Hendrix, Steppenwolf   *Art Dir* Jerry Kay
● Peter Fonda, Dennis Hopper, Jack Nicholson, Robert
Walker Jr, Luana Anders, Phil Spector (Pando/Raybert)

Film deals with two dropouts on a long trip
from Los Angeles to New Orleans' Mardi
Gras, a search for freedom thwarted by that
streak of ingrained, bigoted violence in the
US and their own hangups.

Pic chronicles their trip that ends in tragedy. Their bikes whisk them through the
good roads surrounded by all the stretches of
land that have housed that mythic American
creation of the western.

Script is literate and incisive and Hopper's
direction is fluid, observant and catches the
pictorial poetics with feeling.

Fonda exudes a groping moral force and
Hopper is agitated, touching and responsive
as the sidekick, hoping for that so-called freedom their stake should give them.

Jack Nicholson is excellent as an articulate alcoholic who fills in the smothered needs in a verbal way that the others feel but cannot express.

. . . .

■ EAT A BOWL OF TEA

1989, 102 MINS, US ◇ ⓥ

Dir Wayne Wang *Prod* Tom Sternberg *Scr* Judith Rascoe *Ph* Amir Mokri *Ed* Richard Candib *Mus* Mark Adler *Art Dir* Bob Ziembicki
● Cora Miao, Russell Wong, Victor Wong, Lee Sau-kee, Eric Tsang (American Playhouse)

Wayne Wang returns to Chinatown with *Eat a Bowl of Tea*, and recaptures the relaxed humor and deep emotions of his earlier *Dim Sum* in the process.

Pic starts off with Wah Gay (Victor Wong), who runs a New York gambling club, deciding to send his soldier son Ben Loy (Russel Wong) to China to marry the daughter of his best friend. Fortunately, it's love at first sight between Ben and Mei Oi (Cora Miao), and they marry and return to the States.

Unfortunately, Ben finds the pressures of running a business so severe that his lovelife suffers. Basically, poor Ben is impotent, causing grief to his wife as well as to the couple's fathers, who eagerly want to become grandfathers.

Enter Ah Song (Eric Tsang), a cheerful, rascally gambler who becomes Mei's secret lover, and who succeeds in getting her pregnant. But when words gets out that Ben isn't the father, it's Wah Gay who tries to restore family honor by attacking Ah Song with a meat ax.

Typically, the aforementioned scene is played for laughs, and indeed is the comic high point of a generally charming and amusing film [from a novel by Louis Chu].

. . . .

■ EATING RAOUL

1982, 83 MINS, US ◇ ⓥ

Dir Paul Bartel *Prod* Anne Kimmel *Scr* Richard Blackburn, Paul Bartel *Ph* Gary Thieltges *Ed* Alan Toomayan *Mus* Arlon Ober *Art Dir* Robert Schulenberg
● Paul Bartel, Mary Woronov, Robert Beltram, Susan Salger, Ed Begley Jr, Buck Henry (Bartel)

All poor Paul and Mary Bland want in life is enough money to buy their own restaurant in Valencia, California and call it Paul and Mary's Country Kitchen. But they have little hope of raising the $20,000 they need to make their dreams come true.

To compound matters, the proper couple, who sleep in separate beds and find sex particularly dirty, live in a tacky Hollywood apartment building chock full of all kinds of crazies. When one of the 'low lifes' tries to rape Mary, Paul kills him by a blow to the head with a frying pan.

Alas, the victim had all kinds of money and both Paul and Mary soon realize they have a potential answer to their financial worries. They put an ad in a local sex publication and decide to lure new 'perverts' to their home. That way they can get the money for their restaurant and help clean up society in one sweeping stroke.

The appeal of Paul Bartel's tongue-in-cheek approach is that he manages to take his story to such a ridiculous extreme, remain genuinely funny and successfully tell his perverse story.

. . . .

■ EDDIE AND THE CRUISERS

1983, 92 MINS, US ◇ ⓥ

Dir Martin Davidson *Prod* Joseph Brooks, Robert K. Lifton *Scr* Martin Davidson, Arlene Davidson *Ph* Fred Murphy *Ed* Priscilla Nedd *Mus* John Cafferty *Art Dir* Gary Weist

● Tom Berenger, Michael Pare, Joe Pantoliano, Matthew Laurance, Helen Schneider, Ellen Barkin (Aurora)

Eddie and the Cruisers is a mish-mash of a film, combining elements of the ongoing nostalgia for rock music of previous decades with an unworkable and laughable mystery plotline.

Eddie opens in strict *Citizen Kane* fashion as TV news mag reporter Maggie Foley (Ellen Barkin) is using old clips to pitch her investigative story on the early 1960s rock group Eddie and The Cruisers. Unit disbanded in 1964 with the suicide of its leader Eddie Wilson (Michael Pare).

She needs a news hook, and settles on the unlikely gimmick that Eddie (whose body was never found) is still alive and that a search for the missing tapes of his final, unreleased recording session will solve the mystery of his disappearance.

Foley interviews other surviving group members, including the lyricist-keyboard man Frank Ridgeway (Tom Berenger), who is prompted to remember (in frequent flashbacks) those glory days of 1962-63.

Under Martin Davidson's tedious direction (he also coscripted with his sister Arlene), *Eddie* only comes alive during the flashbacks when John Cafferty's songs provide a showcase for the magnetic screen presences of Pare and Helen Schneider. Real life rock singer Schneider is very sexy on screen, but her contemporary scenes are ruined by unplayable dialog.

. . . .

■ EDDIE MACON'S RUN

1983, 95 MINS, US ◇ ⓥ

Dir Jeff Kanen *Prod* Louis A. Stroller *Scr* Jeff Kanen *Ph* James A. Contner *Ed* Jeff Kanen *Mus* Norton Buffalo *Art Dir* Bill Kenney
● Kirk Douglas, John Schneider, Lee Purcell, Leah Ayres, Lisa Dunsheath, Tom Noonan (Bregman)

Macon is an involving, enjoyable picture [based on a novel by James McLendon]. Most of the credit for that, however, goes to Kirk Douglas who brings interesting nuances to his part as the policeman in pursuit of John Schneider, and Lee Purcell as a bored but influential rich girl who gets more involved than she wants to in helping Schneider elude Douglas.

Schneider himself is okay and certainly brings more to his role than anything required of him on television. Without reaching towering dramatic heights, he nonetheless ably portrays the anguish of a young husband/father wrongly sent to prison and determined to escape to rejoin his family in Mexico.

With Schneider fleeing on foot for most of the picture, *Macon* has a tendency to drag in spots, especially in the beginning, but writer-director Jeff Kanen wisely keeps cutting back to Douglas in plotting his chase and figuring out the angles.

. . . .

■ EDGE OF DARKNESS

1943, 120 MINS, US

Dir Lewis Milestone *Prod* Henry Blanke *Scr* Robert Rossen *Ph* Sid Hickox *Ed* David Weisbart *Mus* Franz Waxman
● Errol Flynn, Ann Sheridan, Walter Huston, Judith Anderson, Helmut Dantine, Ruth Gordon (Warner)

In *Darkness*, as in *The Moon Is Down* the story treats with internal conditions and unrest, and, more important, the ruthlessness of the Nazis. The populace of Trollness in Norway seethes under the yoke of the Germans and finally erupts into a bloody revolt.

Best feature of this film is its cast. Errol Flynn and Ann Sheridan, as the stars, provide the proper romantic note, plus the necessary dash as the leaders of the Trollness underground. Both turn in some of their best

film acting, yet some of the cast's lesser-knowns eclipse them in dramatic power. Notable in this respect are Morris Carnovsky, Ruth Gordon, Judith Anderson, Charles Dingle and Nancy Coleman.

Carnovsky, as an aged schoolmaster, is outstanding in a throat-catching scene when he pits his culture and kindliness against the brutish thinking of the Nazi commander, played by Helmut Dantine, who is guilty of most of the film's over-acting.

There's one other particularly outstanding scene – the meeting of the underground in the church under the guise of a religious service. Original in concept, it's emotion-gripping in execution.

. . . .

■ EDGE OF THE CITY

1957, 85 MINS, US

Dir Martin Ritt *Prod* David Susskind *Scr* Robert Alan Aurthur *Ph* Joseph Brun *Ed* Sidney Meyers *Mus* Leonard Rosenman *Art Dir* Richard Sylbert
● John Cassavetes, Sidney Poitier, Jack Warden, Kathleen Maguire, Ruby Dee, Robert F. Simon (M-G-M)

The first film venture for producer David Susskind, writer Robert Alan Aurthur and director Martin Ritt is an auspicious bow. Trio, whose roots are in TV and legit, come up with a courageous, thought-provoking and exciting film.

Based on Aurthur's [1955] teleplay, *A Man Is Ten Feet Tall*, it marks a milestone in the screen presentation of an American Negro.

The peculiar aspect of *Edge* is that it is not a film dealing with the Negro problem. The protagonist is a guilt-ridden, psychologically mixed-up white youth, sensitively played by John Cassavetes. Plagued by the memory of his part in the accidental death of his brother and his inability to 'belong' either to his family or society, he AWOLs the army. He finds employment in a New York railroad yard where he immediately is befriended by a goodnatured, philosophical Negro lad (Sidney Poitier) and incurs the enmity of a vicious and tough hiring boss.

Filmed on location in New York, the film has a real-life flavor as it roams among New York's railroad yards and upper Manhattan's apartment house district.

. . . .

■ EDUCATING RITA

1983, 110 MINS, UK ◇ ⓥ

Dir Lewis Gilbert *Prod* Lewis Gilbert *Scr* Willy Russell *Ph* Frank Watts *Ed* Garth Craven *Mus* David Hentschel *Art Dir* Maurice Fowler
● Michael Caine, Julie Walters, Maureen Lipman, Jeananne Crowley, Malcolm Douglas, Godfrey Quigley (Rank/Acorn)

Producer-director Lewis Gilbert has done a marvelous job of bringing the charming British play, *Educating Rita*, to the big screen. Aided by an expert film adaptation by its playwright, Willy Russell, Gilbert has come up with an irresistible story about a lively, lower-class British woman hungering for an education and the rather, staid, degenerating English professor who reluctantly provides her with one.

Witty, down-to-earth, kind and loaded with common sense, Rita is the antithesis of the humorless, stuffy and stagnated academic world she so longs to infiltrate. Julie Walters injects her with just the right mix of comedy and pathos. Michael Caine is the sadly smart, alcoholic teacher who knows the fundamentals of English literature, but long ago lost the ability to enjoy life the way his uneducated pupil does.

The contradictions of the two characters are at the core of the picture, as Walters goes from dependent housewife to intelligent student and Caine begins to learn what it's like to feel again.

. . . .

E

EDWARD SCISSORHANDS

1990, 98 MINS, US ◇ ⓥ
Dir Tim Burton   *Prod* Denise De Novi, Tim Burton
Scr Caroline Thompson   *Ph* Stefan Czapsky
Ed Richard Halsey   *Mus* Danny Elfman   *Art Dir* Bo
Welsh
● Johnny Depp, Winona Ryder, Dianne Wiest,
Anthony Michael Hall, Alan Arkin, Kathy Baker (20th
Century-Fox)

Director Tim Burton takes a character as
wildly unlikely as a boy whose arms end in
pruning shears, and makes him the center of
a delightful and delicate comic fable.

Johnny Depp plays Edward, who lives in
isolation in a gloomy mansion on the hill
until a sunny Avon lady (Dianne Wiest) discovers him and takes him into her suburbia
home and mothers him like a crippled bird.
The creation of an inventor (Vincent Price)
who died and left him unfinished, Edward
sports an astonishing pair of hands – five-
fingered, footlong blades that render him
either lethal or extraordinarily skillful.

For the bevy of bored housewives in the
pastel-colored nabe, gentle and exotic
Edward becomes an instant celeb who
amuses them by artistically pruning their
hedges, their dogs and their coiffures.

But when he's wrongly accused in a burglary, his star falls and they turn on him.
Meanwhile his wistful and impossible attraction to Kim (Winona Ryder), the Avon lady's
teenage daughter, adds another level of
tension.

Depp, former TV teen idol in his second
starring screen role, gives a sensitive reading
of Edward. With Ryder kept mostly in the
background, Wiest's mother figure shares the
screen with Depp, and she's a smash. Also a
hoot is Alan Arkin as her unexcitable husband, and Kathy Baker as a sex-starved
vixen.

EFFECT OF GAMMA RAYS ON MAN-IN-THE-MOON MARIGOLDS, THE

1972, 100 MINS, US ◇
Dir Paul Newman   *Prod* Paul Newman   *Scr* Alvin
Sargent   *Ph* Adam Holender   *Ed* Evan Lottman
Mus Maurice Jarre   *Art Dir* Gene Callahan
● Joanne Woodward, Nell Potts, Roberta Wallach,
Judith Lowry, Richard Venture, Estelle Omens (20th
Century Fox)

Producer-director Paul Newman has made
his finest behind-the-camera film to date in
the screen version of Paul Zindel's play. As
the slovenly, introverted mother of two young
girls, Joanne Woodward brilliantly projects
the pitiable character.

Alvin Sargent's adaptation provides Woodward with a full complement of the despicable dimensions which make the focal
character both a monster and an object of
genuine pity.

Roberta Wallach is excellent as the elder
daughter, Ruth, an epilepsy-prone, hardening creature almost destined to become her
mother. As the younger star, whose school experiments give the play its title, Nell Potts is
equally impressive, with a sensitive screen
presence most rare in young actresses.

Newman has gotten it all together as a
director, letting the story and the players
unfold with simplicity, restraint and
discernment.

EGG AND I, THE

1947, 108 MINS, US ⓥ
Dir Chester Erskine   *Prod* Chester Erskine, Fred F.
Finklehoffe   *Scr* Chester Erskine, Fred F. Finklehoffe
Ph Milton Krasner   *Ed* Russell Schoengarth
Mus Frank Skinner   *Art Dir* Bernard Herzbrun
● Claudette Colbert, Fred MacMurray, Marjorie Main,
Percy Kilbride, Louise Allbritton (Universal)

In this picturization of Betty MacDonald's

best-selling book Chester Erskine and Fred
Finklehoffe tamper very little with the load of
amusing situations MacDonald gets herself
into when her husband snaps her out of a
Boston finishing school and takes her off to
the modern-day frontier of the Pacific Northwest to embark on chicken farming.

Shortcoming is in an evenness of treatment
– partially in the writing but more importantly in Erskine's direction – that fails to suck
the drama out of the situations presented in
the book. Even the supposedly big scene
where a forest fire licks down at all that the
chicken-raising couple have in the world –
their home, barn and henhouses – fails to
achieve suspense or deep-seated emotional
drama.

Claudette Colbert is appealing but not
entirely believable as the city gal who accepts
so willingly out of wifely love the rugged life
husband Fred MacMurray lays out for her.
MacMurray runs through his role in his routine, superficial fashion – which is unfortunately accentuated by the impassive manner
of the telling of the story itself. Percy Kilbride
and Marjorie Main, as the Kettles, the
tobacco-road-like neighbors of Colbert and
MacMurray, are literally tops as character
players, accounting, by their feeling and
understanding of their roles, for high points
in the film every time they're on the screen.

EGYPTIAN, THE

1954, 140 MINS, US ◇ ⓥ
Dir Michael Curtiz   *Prod* Darryl F. Zanuck   *Scr* Casey
Robinson, Philip Dunne   *Ph* Leon Shamroy
Ed Barbara McLean   *Mus* Alfred Newman, Bernard
Herrmann
● Jean Simmons, Victor Mature, Gene Tierney,
Michael Wilding, Bella Darvi, Peter Ustinov (20th
Century-Fox)

The decision to bring Mika Waltari's masterly scholarly-detailed [novel] *The Egyptian*
to the screen must have taken a lot of courage, for this is a long way off the standard
spectacle beat. The book tells a strange and
unusual story laid against the exotic and yet
harshly realistic background of the Egypt of
33 centuries ago, when there was a Pharaoh
who believed in one god, and a physician who
glimpsed a great truth and tried to live it.

Big coin – around $4.2 million – was
splurged on bringing ancient Egypt to life
again and the results justify the expense.

A big cast with good marquee appeal goes
through its paces with obvious enjoyment. In
the title part, Edmund Purdom etches a
strong handsome profile. As the truth-seeking
doctor who grows from weakness to the maturity of a new conviction, Purdom brings *The
Egyptian* to life and makes him a man with
whom the audience can easily identify and
sympathize. Jean Simmons is lovely and
warm as the tavern maid. Victor Mature as
the robust Horemheb, the soldier who is to
become ruler, is a strong asset to the cast.

EIGER SANCTION, THE

1975, 125 MINS, US ◇
Dir Clint Eastwood   *Prod* Robert Daly   *Scr* Hal
Dresner, Warren B. Murphy, Rod Whitaker   *Ph* Frank
Stanley   *Ed* Ferris Webster   *Mus* John Williams   *Art
Dir* George Webb, Aurelio Cruguola
● Clint Eastwood, George Kennedy, Vonetta McGee,
Jack Cassidy, Herdi Bruhl, Thayer David
(Universal/Malpaso)

The Eiger Sanction, based on the novel by Tre-
vanian, focuses on Clint Eastwood, a retired
mountain climber and hired assassin, being
recalled from retirement by head of a secret
intelligence organization for another lethal
assignment.

Pic takes its title from the leader's euphe-
mism for assassination, to be carried out on

Switzerland's Eiger Mountain during an
international team's climb.

To condition himself for the ascent Eastwood flies to the Arizona ranch of George
Kennedy, an old climbing friend, who puts
him through his paces in the magnificent
reaches of Monument Valley.

Eastwood, who also directs and according
to studio did his own mountain climbing
without doubles, manages fine suspense. His
direction displays a knowledge that permits
rugged action.

EIGHT MEN OUT

1988, 119 MINS, US ◇ ⓥ
Dir John Sayles   *Prod* Sarah Pillsbury, Midge
Sanford   *Scr* John Sayles   *Ph* Robert Richardson
Ed John Tintori   *Mus* Mason Daring   *Art Dir* Nora
Chavooshian
● John Cusack, Clifton James, Michael Lerner,
Christopher Lloyd, Charlie Sheen (Orion)

Perhaps the saddest chapter in the annals of
professional American sports is recounted in
absorbing fashion in *Eight Men Out*.

Story tells of how the 1919 Chicago White
Sox threw the World Series in cahoots with
professional gamblers, in what became
known as the Black Sox Scandal.

Based on Eliot Asinof's 1963 bestseller,
John Sayles' densely packed screenplay lays
out how eight players for the White Sox, who
were considered shoo-ins to beat the Cincinnati Reds in the World Series, committed an
unthinkable betrayal of the national pastime
by conspiring to lose the Fall Classic.

The most compelling figures here are
pitcher Eddie Cicotte (David Strathairn), a
man nearing the end of his career who feels
the twin needs to insure a financial future for
his family and take revenge on his boss, and
Buck Weaver (John Cusack), an innocent
enthusiast who took no cash for the fix but,
like the others, was forever banned from
baseball.

8 MILLION WAYS TO DIE

1986, 115 MINS, US ◇ ⓥ
Dir Hal Ashby   *Prod* Steve Roth   *Scr* Oliver Stone,
David Lee Henry   *Ph* Stephen H. Burum   *Ed* Robert
Lawrence, Stuart Pappe   *Mus* James Newton
Howard   *Art Dir* Michael Haller
● Jeff Bridges, Rosanna Arquette, Alexandra Paul,
Randy Brooks, Andy Garcia (PSO)

What could have been a better film delving
into complexities of one tough-but-vulnerable
alcoholic sheriff out to bust a cocaine ring,
instead ends up an oddly-paced work that is
sometimes a thriller and sometimes a love
story, succeeding at neither.

A former LA Sheriff named Scudder (Jeff
Bridges) comes close to death less than a
handful of times while trying to dismantle a
scummy Latino drug smuggler's empire and
at the same time winning his girl (Rosanna
Arquette).

Respected director Hal Ashby was reportedly fired from this picture before it was finished, which could explain its unevenness as
he wasn't privy to what happened in the editing room.

In isolated scenes, the actors manage to rise
above it all to bring some nuances to their
fairly stereo-typical roles. Arquette is best as
the hooker with a heart, coyly playing off
main squeeze Angel (Andy Garcia), the ultra
chic cocaine dealer, until she goes over to
Scudder's side.

84 CHARING CROSS ROAD

1987, 97 MINS, US ◇ ⓥ
Dir David Jones   *Prod* Geoffrey Helman   *Scr* Hugh
Whitemore   *Ph* Brian West   *Ed* Chris Wimble
Mus George Fenton   *Art Dir* Eileen Diss, Edward Pisoni

● Anne Bancroft, Anthony Hopkins, Judi Dench, Jean De Baer, Maurice Denham (Brooksfilms)

An uncommonly and sweetly civilized adult romance between two transatlantic correspondents who never meet, *84 Charing Cross Road* is an appealing film on several counts, one of the most notable being Anne Bancroft's fantastic performance in the leading role.

Helene Hanff's slim volume of letters between herself and a dignified antiquarian bookseller in London [originally adapted for the stage by James Roose-Evans] is the basis of the film. They began in 1949 as formal requests by the New Yorker Hanff for old books over a 20-year period into a warm, loving exchange of missives and gifts between her and much of the staff of the bookshop of Marks & Co.

Built on a basis of mutually held taste, knowledge, interests and consideration, the bond between Hanff (Bancroft) and Frank Doel (Anthony Hopkins) becomes a form of pure love, which is why the film is so touching in spots.

Although well balanced between events on both sides of the pond, story suffers from an imbalance between the active, initiating Hanff, who occasionally addresses the camera directly, and the relatively passive, inexpressive Doel. At the end, the man's humor and high intelligence are described, but these traits are never revealed.

Anne Bancroft brings Helene Hanff alive in all her dimensions, in the process creating one of her most memorable characterizations.

. . . .

■ 80,000 SUSPECTS

1963, 113 MINS, UK

Dir Val Guest   *Prod* Val Guest   *Scr* Val Guest
Ph Arthur Grant   *Ed* Bill Lenny   *Mus* Stanley Black
Art Dir Geoffrey Tozer
● Claire Bloom, Richard Johnson, Yolande Donlan, Cyril Cusack, Michael Goodliffe (Rank)

Based on the novel by Elleston Trevor, the drama concerns a city supposedly gripped by an epidemic of smallpox. Director Val Guest chose the city of Bath and, with complete co-operation from local authorities, the film has a vital authenticity which gives a fine assist to the production.

The killer epidemic sparks intense activity by local health authorities as they try to trace potential smallpox carriers. It's a painstaking process, carefully reproduced by Guest.

Guest also plays up some human emotional angles. Dedicated doctor (Richard Johnson) is trying to keep together his marriage with an equally dedicated nurse (Claire Bloom). Another medico (Michael Goodliffe) despairs of saving his own marriage to a nymphodipso who has had an affair with Johnson, and eventually becomes a key figure in the search for the ultimate germ carrier.

The documentary and the fictional elements do not entirely jell. But Guest juggles adroitly enough with the problems to keep interest alert. The thesping is okay.

. . . .

■ EL CID

1961, 180 MINS, US/SPAIN/ITALY ◇ ⑫

Dir Anthony Mann   *Prod* Samuel Bronston
Scr Fredric M. Frank, Philip Yordan   *Ph* Robert Krasker   *Ed* Robert Lawrence   *Mus* Miklos Rozsa
Art Dir Veniero Colasanti, John Moore
● Charlton Heston, Sophia Loren, Raf Vallone, Gary Raymond, John Fraser, Genevieve Page (Bronston/Dear)

El Cid is a fast-action color-rich, corpse-strewn, battle picture. The Spanish scenery is magnificent with a kind of gaunt beauty. The costumes are vivid, the chain mail and Toledo steel gear impressive. Perhaps the 11th century of art directors Veniero Cola-

santi and John Moore exceeds reality, but only scholars will complain of that. Action rather than acting characterizes this film.

Yet the film creates respect for its sheer picturemaking skills. Director Anthony Mann, with assists from associate producer Michael Waszynski who worked closely with him, battle manager Yakima Canutt, and a vast number of technicians, have labored to create stunning panoramic images.

Of acting there is less to say after acknowledging that Charlton Heston's masculine personality ideally suits the title role. His powerful performance is the central arch of the narrative. Sophia Loren, as first his sweetheart and later his wife, has a relatively passive role, in the Spanish preference. While Heston is out doing the picture's business – fighting, fighting, fighting – the glamorous Italian has little to do in the last half but keep the lamp in the window.

Two actors in *King of Kings* who remained over in Spain to appear in *El Cid* ended up as bit actors. Hurd Hatfield is the court herald in a couple of scenes, Frank Thring is a most unconvincing Moorish emir with a shaved noggin who lolls about in a harem registering a kind of sulky impatience.

Italy's Raf Vallone is the other man who never has a chance with Chimene. After betraying El Cid he is spared and, at a later period, becomes a follower only to die, tortured, by the invading North African monster, Britain's Herbert Lom. Lom has the curious experience of doing almost all his acting with his face covered to the eyes by a black mask.

Most provocative performance among the supporting players is that of Genevieve Page, as the self-willed princess who protects the weakling brother who becomes king after she, sweet sibling, has the older brother slain. As the sniveling prince, John Fraser starts slowly but ends up creating some conviction.

. . . .

■ EL DORADO

1967, 126 MINS, US ◇ ⑫

Dir Howard Hawks   *Prod* Howard Hawks   *Scr* Leigh Brackett   *Ph* Harold Rosson   *Ed* John Woodcock
Mus Nelson Riddle   *Art Dir* Hal Pereira, Carl Anderson
● John Wayne, Robert Mitchum, James Caan, Charlene Holt, Michele Carey, Ed Asner (Paramount)

Technical and artistic screen fads come and go, but nothing replaces a good story, well told. And Howard Hawks knows how to tell a good story. *El Dorado* [from the novel *The Stars in Their Courses* by Harry Brown] stars John Wayne and Robert Mitchum in an excellent oater drama, laced with adroit comedy and action relief, and set off by strong casting, superior direction and solid production.

Wayne, a hired gun, is dissuaded from working for land-grabber Ed Asner by Mitchum, a reformed gunslinger now a sharp-looking, disciplined sheriff.

. . . .

■ ELECTRA GLIDE IN BLUE

1973, 106 MINS, US ◇ ⑫

Dir James William Guercio   *Prod* James William Guercio, Rupert Hitzig   *Scr* Robert Boris, Michael Butler   *Ph* Conrad Hall   *Ed* Jim Benson, John F. Link II, Jerry Greenberg   *Mus* James William Guercio
● Robert Blake, Billy 'Green' Bush, Mitchell Ryan, Jeannine Riley, Elisha Cook, Royal Dano (United Artists)

Director-producer James William Guercio comes on tall in a first pic about a motorcycle cop in the US west, who is done in by the corruption, change and violence about him.

Guercio at one time played with the rock group of Frank Zappa and brings that ballad-like, terse feel of rock to this extremely well-played and mounted pic.

Robert Blake is effective as a small motorcycle cop in Arizona who has a certain hard-headed dignity and feels he can help people and also wants to graduate to higher police echelons. He is a Viet vet without bitterness and expecting no condescension from anybody.

Billy 'Green' Bush as his slightly violent sidekick, Mitchell Ryan as a flamboyant, sadistic sheriff, Jeannine Riley as a disillusioned starlet all keep up with Blake's fine character composition.

Conrad Hall's extraordinary controlled hues are an asset to this look at the life of a motorized cop.

. . . .

■ ELECTRIC HORSEMAN, THE

1979, 120 MINS, US ◇ ⑫

Dir Sydney Pollack   *Prod* Ray Stark   *Scr* Robert Garland   *Ph* Owen Roizman   *Ed* Sheldon Kahn
Mus Dave Grusin   *Art Dir* Stephen Grimes
● Robert Redford, Jane Fonda, Valerie Perrine, John Saxon, Willie Nelson, Allan Arbus (Columbia)

The Electric Horseman is a moderately entertaining film, but no screen magic from Robert Redford and Jane Fonda.

The pic is overlong, talky and diffused.

Even though Redford, as an ex-rodeo champ, and Fonda don't create the romantic sparks that might be expected, it's their dramatic professionalism that salvages *Horseman* and makes it a moving and effective film by the time the final credits roll by.

What *Electric Horseman* is peddling is the virtue of 'freedom', morally, economically and socially. Redford's attempt to liberate the prize-winning horse of the AMPCO conglomerate from an overabundance of steroids and pain-killing is presumably intended as an analogy for the way the American public is force-fed consumerism from today's corporate giants.

. . . .

■ ELEPHANT BOY

1937, 81 MINS, UK ⑫

Dir Zoltan Korda, Robert Flaherty   *Prod* Alexander Korda   *Scr* John Collier, Akos Tolnay, Marcia De Silva   *Ph* Osmond Borradaile   *Ed* Charles Crichton
Mus John Greenwood   *Art Dir* Vincent Korda
● Sabu, Walter Hudd, Allan Jeayes, W.E. Holloway, Bruce Gordon, Wilfrid Hyde-White (London)

Elephant Boy is a legendary and rather fantastic tale built around the affection which grows up between a native Indian boy and his elephant, an animal which is tops as a hunter. It is a Rudyard Kipling story which reads better than it films, same as the Tarzan yarns, having nothing particularly exciting for the camera, nor any plot to speak of.

Kipling wrote the story under the title of *Toomai of the Elephants*. Toomai is the Indian lad whose great ambition is to be a hunter. Played by a native Indian boy named Sabu and he imparts to it as much charm and naivete as can be expected. Child has a pronounced native dialect which doesn't hurt, but many of the other characters are entirely too British to be convincing.

Walter Hudd, with the exception of a couple who appear only in brief scenes, is the only person cast as a white, he being the hunter commissioned by the government to round up much-needed pachyderms.

Aside from the footage used to emphasize the strong affection between the boy and his mammoth pal, the action concerns the routine job of rounding up men and animals for the big hunt, pitching of camp, killing by a tiger of one of the crew, and the rather accidental success of little Sabu in leading his trusty elephant to the big herd they're despairing of finding.

. . . .

E

ELEPHANT MAN, THE

1980, 125 MINS, US/UK Ⓥ

Dir David Lynch *Prod* Jonathan Sanger
Scr Christopher DeVore, Eric Bergren, David Lynch
Ph Freddie Francis *Ed* Anne V. Coates *Mus* John
Morris *Art Dir* Stuart Craig
● Anthony Hopkins, John Hurt, Anne Bancroft, John
Gielgud, Wendy Hiller, Freddie Jones
(Paramount/Brooksfilms)

Director David Lynch has created an eerily
compelling atmosphere in recounting a
hideously deformed man's perilous life in
Victorian England.

Screenplay was based on two books about
the real-life Elephant Man, one [*The Elephant
Man and Other Reminiscences*] written by his
protector, Sir Frederick Treves, played in the
film by Anthony Hopkins [and the other, *The
Elephant Man: A Study in Human Dignity* by
Ashley Montagu].

Hopkins is splendid in a subtly nuanced
portrayal of a man torn between humani-
tarianism and qualms that his motives in
introducing the Elephant Man to society are
no better than those of the brutish carny.
The center-piece of the film, however, is
the virtuoso performance by the almost
unrecognizable John Hurt.

Like Quasimodo in *The Hunchback of Notre
Dame*, the Elephant Man gradually reveals
suppressed depths of humanity.

Lynch commendably avoids summoning
up feelings of disgust.
□ 1980: Best Picture (Nomination)

ELEPHANT WALK

1954, 102 MINS, US ◇

Dir William Dieterle *Prod* Irving Asher *Scr* John Lee
Mahin *Ph* Loyal Griggs *Ed* George Tomasini
Mus Franz Waxman
● Elizabeth Taylor, Dana Andrews, Peter Finch,
Abraham Sofaer, Abner Biberman, Noel Drayton
(Paramount)

The novelty of the Ceylon backgrounds and
pictorial beauty are recommendable points in
Elephant Walk, an otherwise leisurely-paced
romantic drama.

Robert Standish's novel about life among
the pekoe-planters rates a sprawling script
and direction that lacks attention-holding
pace from William Dieterle. Of interest is the
fact that in some of the Ceylon-filmed long-
shots, Vivien Leigh is still seen, although not
noticeably so. Illness forced the English star
out of the picture after about a month of lensing, with Elizabeth Taylor replacing.

Elephants are the sympathetic heavies in
this story of a bride who comes to Ceylon
from England and finds her husband, the
natives and the tea plantation still under the
dominance of a dead man's memory. Added
to this tradition worship is the always present
threat that the pachyderms may eventually
succeed in wrestling back from the white
usurpers the trail they had used for centuries
in coming down from the wilds to water. The
plantation mansion had been built across the
trail by the bridegroom's strong-willed late
father, who had bowed to nothing, man or
beast.

11 HARROWHOUSE

1974, 95 MINS, UK ◇ Ⓥ

Dir Aram Avakian *Prod* Elliott Kastner *Scr* Jeffrey
Bloom, Charles Grodin *Ph* Arthur Ibbetson *Ed* Anne
V. Coates *Mus* Michael J. Lewis *Art Dir* Peter Mullins
● Charles Grodin, Candice Bergen, John Gielgud,
Trevor Howard, James Mason, Helen Cherry
(20th Century-Fox)

Charles Grodin stars in, adapted for the
screen, and just about ruins *11 Harrowhouse*, a
comedy-caper film about a theft of billions in
diamonds. Cast as a low-key diamond sales-

man who wreaks vengeance on the diamond
establishment, Grodin messes up the film
with ineffective shy-guy acting, and clobbers
it with catatonic voice-over that is supposed
to be funny.

Gerald A. Browne wrote the novel. The
main story, which takes a long time to get
going, involves eccentric billionaire Trevor
Howard commissioning Grodin and wealthy
girl friend Candice Bergen to rob the diamond vaults presided over by dissatisfied
James Mason, who is resentful of his pension
treatment at the hands of John Gielgud.

Howard and Mason appear close to
embarrassed in their roles.

ELMER GANTRY

1960, 146 MINS, US ◇ Ⓥ

Dir Richard Brooks *Prod* Bernard Smith *Scr* Richard
Brooks *Ph* John Alton *Ed* Marge Fowler
Mus Andre Previn *Art Dir* Edward Carrere
● Burt Lancaster, Jean Simmons, Dean Jagger, Arthur
Kennedy, Shirley Jones, Edward Andrews (United
Artists)

In filming Sinclair Lewis' contentious 1927
study of a scandalous evangelist, *Elmer Gantry*, Richard Brooks has framed a big story
and bold religioso subject for the old-fashioned rectangular screen (aspect ratio
1.33:1).

Brooks honors the spirit of Lewis' cynical
commentary on circus-type revivalist exhortation with pictorial imagery that is always
pungent. He also has written dialog that is
frank and biting.

From the standpoint of technique this production plays like a symphony, with expertly
ordered pianissimo and fortissimo story passages which build to a smashing crescendo in
the cremation of Sister Sharon Falconer, an
evangelist of questionable sincerity and propriety. The film ends roughly about the halfway mark in Gantry's life, whereas in the
book he went on to become an influential
Methodist minister, who married and raised
a family but continued to indulge in the carnal pleasures he denounced vehemently from
the pulpit.

Burt Lancaster pulls out virtually all the
stops as Gantry to create a memorable characterization. He acts with such broad and
eloquent flourish that a finely balanced, more
subdued performance by Jean Simmons as
Sister Sharon seems pale by comparison.
□ 1960: Best Picture (Nomination)

EMBRYO

1976, 108 MINS, US ◇ Ⓥ

Dir Ralph Nelson *Prod* Arnold H. Orgolini, Anita
Doohan *Scr* Anita Doohan, Jack W. Thomas *Ph* Fred
Koenekamp *Ed* John Martinelli *Mus* Gil Melle
Art Dir Joe Alves
● Rock Hudson, Diane Ladd, Barbara Carrera, Roddy
McDowall, Ann Schedeen, John Elerick (Cine Artists)

The story has doctor Rock Hudson grow a
beautiful young woman (Barbara Carrera) in
his laboratory from fetal beginnings. It's kind
of a *Bride of Frankenstein* tale, cast in terms of
scientific mumbo-jumbo, an effective blending of old and new plot elements.

Hudson plays with gentleness and restraint, and Carrera's pristine fashion-model
beauty is perfect for the role, but there's little
feeling of genuine passion or eroticism.

The script [from a story by Jack W.
Thomas] is much stronger on plot than it
is on character relationships. Suspense
built up before Carrera's birth is dissipated
in clumsy dramatic confrontations when she
and Hudson set out in society.

Diane Ladd is wasted as Hudson's jealous
housekeeper.

EMERALD FOREST, THE

1985, 113 MINS, US ◇ Ⓥ

Dir John Boorman *Prod* John Boorman *Scr* Rospo
Pallenberg *Ph* Philippe Rousselot *Ed* Ian Crafford
Mus Junior Homrich, Brian Gascoigne *Art Dir* Simon
Holland
● Powers Boothe, Meg Foster, Charley Boorman, Dira
Pass, Rui Polonah, Claudio Moreno (Embassy)

Based on an uncredited true story about a
Peruvian whose son disappeared in the
jungles of Brazil, screenplay trades on numerous enduring myths and legends about
the return to nature and growing up in the
wild.

Powers Boothe, an American engineer and
designer assigned to build an enormous dam
in Brazil, loses his young son in the wilderness and, against seemingly hopeless odds,
sets out to find him.

Ten years later, the two finally meet up
under perilous circumstances. By this time,
the son, played by the director's own sprog,
Charley Boorman, has become well integrated into the ways of a friendly Indian tribe
and has little desire to return to the outside
world.

Once he has been exposed to the simple
virtues of 'uncivilized' life, Boothe begins to
have serious doubts about the nature of his
work in the area.

Despite some lumps in the narrative and
characterization and some occasionally
awkward tension between the documentary
realism enforced by the subject and the heavy
stylization of the director's approach, film
proves engrossing and visually fascinating.

EMMA

1932, 70 MINS, US

Dir Clarence Brown *Scr* Leonard Praskins, Frances
Marion, Zelda Sears *Ph* Oliver Marsh *Ed* William
LeVanway
● Marie Dressler, Richard Cromwell, Jean Hersholt,
Myrna Loy, John Miljan, Barbara Kent (M-G-M)

There are probably 20 actresses who would
have fitted the role of the old servant who
spent a lifetime with the Smith family,
watching the children grow up and then turn
against her in her old age. But there is only
one Marie Dressler, a trouper with a genius
for characters of comic surface but profound
pathos.

The whole *Emma* affair is synthetic, in its
comedy as well as in its sentiment the purest
of hoke, sometimes skillfully wrought, but
often far from clever in its manipulation.
Dressler's acting alone gives it vitality. There
are bits that drag sadly. Such a sequence is
the old servant's departure for Niagara Falls
on a long deferred vacation.

There is a courtroom scene that is the
height of strong arm bathos and some of the
passages toward the end are absurd in their
determination to pull tears. Nothing but
Dressler's astonishing ability to command
conviction saves some of these sequences
from going flat.

Jean Hersholt delivers a well-paced and
nicely restrained performance as an absent
minded inventor; Myrna Loy and Barbara
Kent help to decorate the picture with grace;
and Richard Cromwell gives just the right
feeling of a loveable adolescent boy.

EMPEROR OF THE NORTH

1973, 118 MINS, US ◇ Ⓥ

Dir Robert Aldrich *Prod* Stan Hough *Scr* Christopher
Knopf *Ph* Joseph Biroc *Ed* Michael Luciano
Mus Frank DeVol *Art Dir* Jack Martin Smith
● Lee Marvin, Ernest Borgnine, Keith Carradine,
Charles Tyner, Malcolm Atterbury, Simon Oakland
(Inter-Hemisphere/20th Century-Fox)

Premise of a challenge by an easy going

175

tramp to ride the freight train of a sadistic conductor reputed to kill non-paying passengers (as his hobo associates and train men lay bets on the outcome) is limited in scope.

The production takes its title from hobos crowning Lee Marvin 'Emperor' for riding Ernest Borgnine's train even a mile, something no other hobo has ever accomplished. While there is a wealth of violence under Robert Aldrich's forceful direction , the motivating idea is bogged down frequently with time out while Marvin expounds the philosophy and finer points of hobodom to a brash young kid (Keith Carradine).

Marvin scores again in one of his uncolorful but commanding characterizations. Borgnine's interpretation borders on a caricature of the heavies of the past. [Film was initially released as *The Emperor of the North Pole*.]

....

■ EMPIRE OF THE ANTS

1977, 89 MINS, US ◇ ⓥ

Dir Bert I. Gordon   *Prod* Bert I. Gordon   *Scr* Jack Turley   *Ph* Reginald Morris   *Ed* Michael Luciano   *Mus* Dana Kaproff   *Art Dir* Charles Rosen
● Joan Collins, Robert Lansing, John David Carson, Albert Salmi, Jacqueline Scott, Pamela Shoop (American International)

The H.G. Wells-inspired exploitationer *Empire of the Ants*, is an above-average effort about ants that grow big after munching on radioactive waste, and terrorize a group headed by Joan Collins, Robert Lansing and John David Carson.

Periodic moments of good special effects are separated by reels of dramatic banality as players flounder in flimsy dialog and under sluggish direction.

Collins is a sharpie Florida real estate agent who takes a group of potential suckers on Lansing's boat to remote swampland. There the big ants attack.

....

■ EMPIRE OF THE SUN

1987, 152 MINS, US ◇ ⓥ

Dir Steven Spielberg   *Prod* Steven Spielberg, Kathleen Kennedy, Frank Marshall   *Scr* Tom Stoppard   *Ph* Allen Daviau   *Ed* Michael Kahn   *Mus* John Williams   *Art Dir* Norman Reynolds
● Christian Bale, John Malkovich, Miranda Richardson, Nigel Havers, Joe Pantoliano, Leslie Phillips (Amblin/Warner)

Story of an 11-year-old boy stranded in Japanese-occupied China during World War II is based on J.G. Ballard's autobiographical 1984 novel which marked the first non-science-fiction book by author. Both it and the film clearly are the work of sci-fi artists channelling their imaginations into a more traditional framework.

Leading the first troupe of Hollywood studio filmmakers ever into Shanghai, Steven Spielberg turns the grey metropolis into a sensational film set as he delineates the edginess and growing chaos leading up to Japan's entry into the city just after Pearl Harbor.

Jim (Christian Bale) is in every way a proper upper-class English lad but for the fact he has never seen England. Separated from his parents during the spectacularly staged evacuation of Shanghai, Jim hooks up with a pair of Amerian scavengers, with whom in due course he is rounded up and sent to a prison camp for the duration of the war.

It is there that Jim flourishes, expending his boundless energy on creative projects and pastimes that finally land him a privileged place among the entrepreneurially minded Americans.

John Malkovich's Basie, an opportunistic King Rat type, keeps threatening to become a fully developed character but never does. Other characters are complete blanks, which

severely limits the emotional reverberation of the piece. No special use is made of the talents of Miranda Richardson, Nigel Havers, Joe Pantoliano and the others, so it is up to young English thesp Bale to engage the viewer's interest, which he does superbly.

....

■ EMPIRE STRIKES BACK, THE

1980, 124 MINS, US ◇ ⓥ

Dir Irvin Kershner   *Prod* Gary Kurtz   *Scr* Leigh Brackett, Lawrence Kasdan   *Ph* Peter Suschitzy   *Ed* Paul Hirsch   *Mus* John Williams   *Art Dir* Leslie Dilley, Harry Lange, Alan Tomkins
● Mark Hamill, Harrison Ford, Carrie Fisher, Billy Dee Williams, Frank Oz, Alec Guinness (20th Century-Fox)

The Empire Strikes Back is a worthy sequel to *Star Wars*, equal in both technical mastery and characterization, suffering only from the familiarity with the effects generated in the original and imitated too much by others.

From the first burst of John Williams' powerful score and the receding opening title crawl, we are back in pleasant surroundings and anxious for a good time.

This is exec producer George Lucas' world. Though he has turned the director's chair and his typewriter, there are no recognizable deviations from the path marked by Lucas and producer Gary Kurtz.

They're assisted again by good performances from Mark Hamill, Harrison Ford and Carrie Fisher. And even the ominous Darth Vader (David Prowse [voiced by James Earl Jones]) is fleshed with new – and surprising – motivations.

Among the new characters, Billy Dee Williams gets a good turn as a duplicitous but likeable villain-ally and Frank Oz is fascinating as sort of a guru for the Force.

Vader's admirals now look even more dressed like Japanese admirals of the fleet intercut with Hamill's scrambling fighter pilots who wouldn't look too out of place on any Marine base today.

....

■ ENCHANTED COTTAGE, THE

1945, 91 MINS, US ⓥ

Dir John Cromwell   *Prod* Harriet Parsons   *Scr* DeWitt Bodeen, Herman J. Mankiewicz   *Ph* Ted Tetzlaff   *Ed* Joseph Noriega   *Mus* Roy Webb   *Art Dir* Albert S. D'Agostino, Carroll Clark
● Dorothy McGuire, Robert Young, Herbert Marshall, Mildred Natwick, Spring Byington (RKO)

Sensitive love story of a returned war veteran with ugly facial disfigurements, and the homely slavey – both self-conscious of their handicaps – is sincerely told both in the script [based on the play by Arthur Wing Pinero] and outstanding direction of John Cromwell.

Brief prolog establishes Robert Young as the flyer who leases a cottage for his honeymoon, but is called to service on eve of his wedding. Two years later he returns to hide his war disfigurements from his family at the cottage, where Dorothy McGuire is hiding from people because of her ugliness. But the girl's tender attention to the flyer results in idyllic love, with each appearing beautiful to the other and pair sincerely believing that the cottage is enchanted and responsible for the transformations.

McGuire turns in an outstanding performance, with Young also sharing the limelight. Herbert Marshall is excellent, while Mildred Natwick scores as the housekeeper.

....

■ ENCORE

1951, 89 MINS, UK ⓥ

Dir Pat Jackson, Anthony Pelissier, Harold French   *Prod* Anthony Darnborough   *Scr* T.E.B. Clarke, Arthur Macrae, Eric Ambler   *Ph* Desmond Dickinson   *Ed* Alfred Roome   *Mus* Richard Addinsell   *Art Dir* Maurice Carter

● Nigel Patrick, Roland Culver, Kay Walsh, Glynis Johns, Terence Morgan (Two Cities)

For the third time, a group of Somerset Maugham short stories have been collated to make a quality British film. *Quartet* (1948), was followed by *Trio* (1950). *Encore*, a co-production between Paramount and Rank, is also based on three of the writer's vignettes.

First of the stories is *The Ant & The Grasshopper*, in which Nigel Patrick is a ne'er-do-well who soaks his lawyer brother for cash until he lands a wealthy heiress. Acting of Patrick and Roland Culver, as his brother, sets a high standard.

Winter Cruise is another light piece, but of a contrasting type. Kay Walsh plays a middle-aged garrulous spinster who takes a trip by cargo boat to Jamaica, but whose non-stop chattering drives the captain and crew to distraction. Fine acting and a flawless script keeps the fun rolling in this.

The drama and tension of the series is provided by the third subject, *Gigolo & Gigolett*. This is a dramatic piece about a young vaudeville artist whose specialty is diving from an 80-foot platform into a five-foot lake of flames. When the girl begins to feel that her husband is persisting with the act because of the money that goes with it, she loses her nerve. Glynis Johns makes a deep impression as the girl, and Terence Morgan aptly suggests the weak, scheming husband.

....

■ END, THE

1978, 100 MINS, US ◇ ⓥ

Dir Burt Reynolds   *Prod* Lawrence Gordon   *Scr* Jerry Belson   *Ph* Bobby Byrne   *Ed* Donn Cambern   *Mus* Paul Williams   *Art Dir* Jan Scott
● Burt Reynolds, Dom DeLuise, Sally Field, Strother Martin, David Steinberg, Joanne Woodward (United Artists)

The rather complete failure of Jerry Belson's script makes 'The End' of *The End* come none too soon. Star-director Burt Reynolds, as a medically-doomed sharpie, exercises and exorcises his fears while milking sympathy from everyone available. Production is a tasteless and overripe comedy that disintegrates very early into hysterical, undisciplined hamming.

For a few frames of the film, Reynolds' bearded face suggests that there was some effort to project a different image; to transform his familiar and likable charisma into something different, befitting the last days of a carefree, selfish person who has been informed of fatal illness.

There's little more to do than list the featured players: Dom DeLuise, absolutely dreadful; Sally Field, phoning in a kooky-pretty role; David Steinberg, an outtake that crept back into the print; Joanne Woodward, poorly utilized though adroitly cast.

....

■ ENDLESS LOVE

1981, 115 MINS, US ◇

Dir Franco Zeffirelli   *Prod* Dyson Lovell   *Scr* Judith Rascoe   *Ph* David Watkin   *Ed* Michael J. Sheridan   *Mus* Jonathan Tunick   *Art Dir* Ed Witlstein
● Brooke Shields, Martin Hewitt, Shirley Knight, Don Murray, Beatrice Straight (Universal)

A Cotton-candy rendition of Scott Spencer's powerful novel, *Endless Love* is a manipulative tale of a doomed romance which careens repeatedly between the credible and the ridiculous.

With a nod to *Romeo and Juliet*, with which director Franco Zeffirelli enjoyed such success in 1968, plot concerns the scorching love affair between a 17-year-old boy, from a social-activist Chicago family, and a 15-year-old girl. Normally braod-minded, girl's father finally can't take it anymore when the boy

E

more or less moves into his daughter's bedroom, and banishes him from the household for a month.

Since he's center stage most of the time, it's fortunate that newcomer Martin Hewitt registers so strongly. Zeffirelli has dressed and photographed his find almost in the style of some of his mentor Luchino Visconti's neo-realist heroes, with two-day beard growths and anachronistic Clark Gable undershirts.

Despite top billing, Brooke Shields disappears during entire center section of the film, which reduces extent to which film stands or falls by her work. One can never really tell what her responses to sex are because she's smiling all the time.

• •

■ END OF INNOCENCE, THE

1990, 102 MINS, US ◇ ⓥ

Dir Dyan Cannon   *Prod* Thom Tyson, Vince Cannon
Scr Dyan Cannon   *Ph* Alex Nepomniaschy   *Ed* Bruce Cannon   *Mus* Michael Convertino   *Art Dir* Paul Eads
● Dyan Cannon, John Heard, George Coe, Lola Mason, Rebecca Schaeffer, Steve Meadows (Skouras)

A moralistic drama about a woman's struggle for self-determination, *The End of Innocence* is a well-intentioned vehicle for writer-director-star Dyan Cannon.

In its peppy opening, Cannon time-telescopes the childhood, adolescence (played by the late Rebecca Schaeffer) and young womanhood of Stephanie Lewis, a lovely if malleable only child of querulous middle-class Jewish parents.

Predictably enough, selfish struggling writer Michael (Steve Meadows), turns out to be not much different than the boorish cad who deflowered Stephanie on her prom night long ago.

A caring platonic male friend, lost in the narrative shuffle, tries to warn her off Michael to no avail. Drifting through life with no real career or focus, Stephanie (Cannon) deals with her deep unhappiness with junk food, mood pills and marijuana.

Cannon, looking remarkably good, has a field day dominating the film. But the auteur/star gets too carried away with a sense of mission here.

• •

■ ENEMIES, A LOVE STORY

1989, 119 MINS, US ◇ ⓥ

Dir Paul Mazursky   *Prod* Paul Mazursky   *Scr* Roger L. Simon   *Ph* Fred Murphy   *Ed* Stuart Pappe
Mus Maurice Jarre   *Art Dir* Guzman
● Ron Silver, Anjelica Huston, Lena Olin, Margaret Sophie Stein, Alan King, Paul Mazursky (Morgan Creek)

Haunting, mordantly amusing, deliciously sexy, *Enemies, a Love Story* is Paul Mazursky's triumphant adapation of the Isaac Bashevis Singer novel about a Holocaust survivor who finds himself married to three women in 1949 New York.

Ron Silver is fascinatingly enigmatic in the lead role of Herman Broder. He's a quietly charming, somewhat withdrawn man whose cushy job as a ghostwriter for a very reformed rabbi (Alan King) gives him plenty of time to attend to his deliriously complicated love life.

The character simultaneously is married to a devoted but cloddish woman (Margaret Sophie Stein), is carrying on a passionate affair with a sultry married woman (Lena Olin), and also finds himself back in the arms of his long-vanished wife (Anjelica Huston), who was thought to be lost in the war.

Like Silver, the audience will find it difficult to prefer one of his three women over the others, since Stein, Olin, and Huston are equally captivating. Olin is sensational here as the doomed Masha, for whom lovemaking is the best assertion of life over the inevitability of self-destruction.

• •

■ ENEMY MINE

1985, 108 MINS, US ◇ ⓥ

Dir Wolfgang Petersen   *Prod* Stephen Friedman
Scr Edward Khmara   *Ph* Tony Imi   *Ed* Hannes Nikel
Mus Maurice Jarre   *Art Dir* Rolf Zehetbauer
● Dennis Quaid, Louis Gossett Jr, Brion James, Richard Marcus, Carolyn McCormick, Bumper Robinson (Kings Road/20th Century-Fox)

Enemy Mine is a friendship story between two disparate personalities carried to extreme lengths. It may be a long way to go to a distant sun system to get to a familiar place, but the $33 million project is largely successful in establishing a satisfying bond.

Story is set up by a kind of videogame battle between the Earth forces and the warring Dracs from the distant planet of Dracon. Space pilot Willis Davidge (Dennis Quaid) goes down with a Drac ship and is the only survivor on a desolate planet. His initial response to the half-human, half-reptilian is inbred hatred, distrust and combativeness, all recognizable human triggers.

Hostility soon gives way to a common goal – survival. Davidge and the Drac (Louis Gossett Jr) peel away their outer layers and reveal two similar beings. It's an anthropomorphic view of life but touching nonetheless.

• •

■ ENEMY OF THE PEOPLE, AN

1978, 103 MINS, US ◇

Dir George Schaefer   *Prod* George Schaefer
Scr Alexander Jacobs   *Ph* Paul Lohman   *Ed* Sheldon Kahn   *Mus* Leonard Rosenman   *Art Dir* Eugene Lourie
● Steve McQueen, Charles Durning, Bibi Andersson, Eric Christmas, Michael Cristofer, Richard Dysart (First Artists/Solar)

Transferring stage works to the screen has always been a procedure fraught with peril, and *An Enemy of the People* fails to avoid the obvious pitfalls.

The Henrik Ibsen drama, which was first performed in 1883, concerns a smalltown doctor who discovers that his village's new hot springs spa is contaminated by tannery waste. Over the objections of the town leaders (particularly his brother, the mayor), he attempts to publicize the scandal, only to be declared a social outcast, his family and career ruined.

Steve McQueen wanted to do the Ibsen work itself, and that was his undoing. While *Enemy of the People* has much relevance to current ecological dilemmas, the script, based on an Arthur Miller adaptation, isn't content to simply raise the issues. They are proclaimed in ringing tones, intensifying the preachiness of a work that is already condescending to its audience.

The imbalance wouldn't be so pronounced were Charles Durning not so magnificent in the role of the harshly realistic brother. Without an adequate presence to balance Durning's domination of the proceedings, *Enemy* founders in a sea of verbiage.

• •

■ ENFORCER, THE

1951, 86 MINS, US ⓥ

Dir Bretaigne Windust   *Prod* Milton Sperling
Scr Martin Rackin   *Ph* Robert Burks   *Ed* Fred Allen
Mus David Buttolph   *Art Dir* Charles H. Clarke
● Humphrey Bogart, Zero Mostel, Ted De Corsia, Everett Sloane, Roy Roberts, King Donovan (United States/Warner)

The film plays fast and excitingly in dealing with Humphrey Bogart's efforts to bring the head of a gang of killers to justice. The script uses the flashback technique to get the story on film, but it is wisely used so as not to tip the ending and spoil suspense.

Footage kicks off with a brief prolog by Senator Estes Kefauver, crime investigation committee head, explaining necessity of bringing crooks to justice. Story starts with Bogart ready to crack a case on which he has worked four years; he has a witness who can pin a murder rap on the gang head. However, the witness, in fear, escapes and falls to his death. Seeking to find some other tiny clue in the bulk of evidence, Bogart reviews the material gathered over the long years, permitting flashbacks into the past, and finally picks a single twist that gives him his lead and sets up an exciting finale.

Bretaigne Windust's direction is thorough, never missing an opportunity to sharpen suspense values, and the tension builds constantly.

• •

■ ENFORCER, THE

1976, 96 MINS, US ◇ ⓥ

Dir James Fargo   *Prod* Robert Daley   *Scr* Stirling Silliphant, Dean Reisner   *Ph* Charles W. Short
Ed Ferris Webster, Joel Cox   *Mus* Jerry Fielding
Art Dir Allen E. Smith
● Clint Eastwood, Harry Guardino, Bradford Dillman, John Mitchum, DeVeren Bookwalter, Tyne Daly (Warner)

The bad guys in this third installment from Dirty Harry's life include not only the archly defined criminals (here, DeVeren Bookwalter and a group of post-Vietnam gun crazies), but also his police and political superiors – like Bradford Dillman, captain of detectives, and John Crawford, whose characterization of the mayor is one of the few highlights. Harry Guardino has the role of a weak-kneed detective.

Tyne Daly's casting as a femme cop injects some predictable, but enjoyable, male chauvinism sparks in dialog between her and Clint Eastwood.

The spitball script [from a story by Gail Morgan Hickman and S.W. Schurr] lurches along, stopping periodically for the bloodlettings and assorted running and jumping and chasing stuff.

• •

■ ENGLAND MADE ME

1973, 100 MINS, UK ◇

Dir Peter Duffell   *Prod* Jack Levin   *Scr* Peter Duffell, Desmond Cory   *Ph* Ray Parslow   *Ed* Malcolm Cooke   *Mus* John Scott   *Art Dir* Tony Woollard
● Peter Finch, Michael York, Hildegard Neil, Michael Hordern, Joss Ackland, Tessa Wyatt (Atlantic)

England Made Me is the symbolic title for a tale of moral conflict set in prewar Germany, circa 1935. Based on an early Graham Greene novel, the film is also a well-observed evocation of time, place and mood, directed and co-authored by Peter Duffell with evident intelligence and sensitivity, if not optimum success.

Michael York plays an innocent idealist ultimately snuffed out by the intrigues and ruthlessness that marked Nazi Germany. The title is a reference to his character, his fairness and morality as shaped by a society where they were and are esteemed. Superficially he runs afoul of rascally Peter Finch's great financial empire based in Germany, but his goodness is in wider conflict with the coarsened values of decadence and nihilism.

Finch plays the ruthless financier with competence and physical presence while Hildegard Neil scores well as York's dominating older sister and Finch's mistress.

• •

■ ENIGMA

1983, 101 MINS, UK/FRANCE ◇ ⓥ

Dir Jeannot Szwarc   *Prod* Peter Shaw, Ben Arbeid, Andre Pergament   *Scr* John Briley   *Ph* Jean-Louis Picavet   *Ed* Peter Weatherley   *Mus* Marc Wilkinson
Art Dir Francois Comtat

● Martin Sheen, Brigitte Fossey, Sam Neill, Derek Jacobi, Michael Lonsdale, Frank Finlay (Archerwest/SFPC)

Enigma is a well-made but insufficiently exciting spy thriller which rather pleasingly emphasizes the emotional vulnerabilities of the pawns caught up in East-West intrigue.

Martin Sheen ably portrays an East German refugee who, after working as a Radio Free Europe-type broadcaster out of Paris, is recruited by the CIA to return to East Berlin. Assignment: steal a coded microprocessor, or scrambler, from the Russians before the KGB proceeds with the assassination of five Soviet dissidents in the West.

After neatly making his way to his destination. Sheen locates old flame Brigitte Fossey who, while resisting the idea of resuming their romance, sympathizes with his unexplained cause.

John Briley's screenplay [from the novel by Michael Barak] keeps everything coherent, not always easy with this sort of fare, and Jeannot Szwarc's direction is very handsome indeed.

....

■ ENORMOUS CHANGES AT THE LAST MINUTE

1983, 110 MINS, US ◇ ⓥ

Dir Mirra Bank, Ellen Hovde, Muffie Meyer   *Prod* Mirra Bank   *Scr* John Sayles, Susan Rice   *Ph* Tom McDonough   *Ed* Mirra Bank, Ellen Hovde, Muffie Meyer   *Mus* Peter Link
● Ellen Barkin, Kevin Bacon, Maria Tucci, Lynn Milgrim, Sudie Bond (Ordinary Lives)

Enormous Changes at the Last Minute is an enormously uneven trilogy of modern urban woman's dilemma in the precarious area of relationships with men.

Pic is first fictional feature for the three producer/directors, Mirra Bank, Ellen Hovde, and Muffie Meyer, all film editors. First vignette pits Virginia (Ellen Barkin) as a housewife with three kids who is newly deserted by her husband. Barkin succumbs to the advances of a former boyfriend (now married with kids), who is also the landlord's son.

In second entry, Faith (Lynn Milgrim) makes a trek to visit her artsy, literary parents in an old-age Jewish residence, to tell her father that she's separated from her husband Ricardo. This is the weakest and least successful section, failing to capture the potential intimacy and poignancy of the encounter. [Seg was shot earliest, in 1978].

Alexandra (Maria Tucci) is a middle-aged, divorced, social worker who has a ludicrous affair with frenetic cab driver/punk rocker Dennis (Kevin Bacon). When Alexandra becomes pregnant by Dennis she vehemently decides to go it alone and raise it herself. Dennis is hurt and confused by his forced exclusion from the event.

....

■ ENTER ARSENE LUPIN

1944, 72 MINS, US

Dir Ford Beebe   *Prod* Ford Beebe   *Scr* Bertram Millhauser   *Ph* Hal Mohr   *Ed* Saul A. Goodkind   *Mus* Milton Rosen   *Art Dir* John B. Goodman, Abraham Grossman
● Charles Korvin, Ella Raines, J. Carrol Naish, George Dolenz, Gale Sondergaard (Universal)

Enter Arsene Lupin a Universal cops-and-robbers saga, French style, is a slick enough combination of romance, action and suspense and offset phony, far-fetched plot.

Part of appeal is romantic team of Charles Korvin and Ella Raines in some torrid moments. Korvin isn't much of an actor, but he has the Continental ease of manner and attractive face to catch the femme trade. Also a draw is the flavorsome caricature of a stupid French detective which J. Carrol Naish,

in a change of pace from gangster roles, plays very amusingly, even if he does milk role.

Yarn concerns [Maurice LeBlanc's character] Lupin, renowned suave French thief, who robs a lady of her fabulous emerald on the Paris-Constantinople express. Pic is produced on good scale, with some rich interiors, to help illusion. Raines adds glamor and beauty to role of heiress, and Gale Sondergaard is menacing enough as one of sleek, murderous cousins.

....

■ ENTER THE DRAGON

1973, 98 MINS, US/HONG KONG ◇ ⓥ

Dir Robert Clouse   *Prod* Fred Weintraub, Paul Heller, Raymond Chow   *Scr* Michael Allin   *Ph* Gilbert Hubbs   *Ed* Kurt Hirshler, George Watters   *Mus* Lalo Schifrin   *Art Dir* James Wong Sun
● Bruce Lee, John Saxon, Jim Kelly, Shih Kien, Bob Wall, Angela Mao (Warner/Concord)

Enter the Dragon marks the final appearance of Bruce Lee, who died suddenly in Hong Kong on 20 July 1973, only a few weeks after he completed the film.

Film is rich in the atmosphere of the Orient, where it was lensed in its entirety, and brims with frequent encounters in the violent arts. Lee plays a James Bond-type of super-secret agent, past-master in Oriental combat, who takes on the assignment of participating in brutal martial arts competition as a cover for investigating the suspected criminal activities of the man staging this annual tournament.

Lee socks over a performance seldom equalled in action. John Saxon, as an American expert drawn to the tournament, is surprisingly adept in his action scenes. Robert Clouse's realistic direction results in constant fast play by all the principals.

....

■ ENTER THE NINJA

1982, 99 MINS, US ◇ ⓥ

Dir Menahem Golan   *Prod* Judd Bernard, Yoram Globus   *Scr* Dick Desmond   *Ph* David Gurfinkel   *Ed* Mark Goldblatt, Michael Duthie   *Mus* W. Michael Lewis, Laurin Rinder
● Franco Nero, Susan George, Sho Kosugi, Alex Courtney, Will Hare, Christopher George (Cannon)

Enter the Ninja represents an unusual hybrid action film, an Italian Western-type story filmed as a contemporary Japanese martial arts action film in the Philippines. Results are pleasant though unspectacular.

After a misjudged opening consisting of a series of bloody one-on-one battles later revealed to be just a phony graduation exercise for American ninjitsu student Cole (Franco Nero), pic settles down to a simple landgrabbers story.

Cole arrives to help his old mercenary fighter buddy Landers (Alex Courtney) fight off various nasties out to steal away his plantation to exploit its oil rights. Landers's tough cookie wife (Susan George sporting a very sexy and giggly bra-less look) is on hand to help out.

Well-photographed pic is heavy on the chop-socky stuff, with baddie Venarius (Christopher George) hiring a real Japanese ninja (Sho Kosugi) to neutralize Cole.

....

■ ENTERTAINER, THE

1960, 96 MINS, UK ⓥ

Dir Tony Richardson   *Prod* Henry Saltzman   *Scr* John Osborne, Nigel Kneale   *Ph* Oswald Morris   *Ed* Alan Osbiston   *Mus* John Addison
● Laurence Olivier, Brenda De Banzie, Joan Plowright, Roger Livesey, Alan Bates, Albert Finney (Woodfall/Bryanston)

There was a bit of a hassle over [the release of] *The Entertainer* what with arguments with

the censor, the film having to be re-dubbed and cut from 104 to 96 minutes, and held over for three months before its West End showing. This version of John Osborne's play is raw, but vital stuff, which you'll either like or loathe.

The yarn is mainly a seedy character study of a broken-down, disillusioned vaude artiste with more optimism than talent, and of the various members of his family and their reactions to his problems. So it depends mainly on the thesping and the direction.

Tony Richardson, the director, makes several mistakes. But he has a sharp perception of camera angles, stimulates some good performances and, particularly, whips up an excellent atmosphere of a smallish British seaside resort.

Mainly, the interest is held by the acting and here there is a lot to praise, if some that may be condemned. The stage sequences in which the third-rate comedian, Archie Rice (Laurence Olivier), has to put over some tatty material in a broken down show, does not come over as effectively as it did on the stage. He is far happier in other sequences. The way he allows his sleazy facade to slip by a twist of the mouth, a throwaway line or a look in the eyes is quite brilliant.

Joan Plowright brings warmth and intelligence to the role of the loyal daughter while Roger Livesey, as Olivier's father, is sympathetic and completely believable. Brenda Da Banzie's role, as Olivier's wife, is at times irritating.

....

■ ENTERTAINER, THE

1975, 105 MINS, US/AUSTRALIA ◇

Dir Donald Wrye   *Prod* Beryl Vertue, Marvin Hamlisch   *Scr* Elliott Baker   *Ph* James Crabe   *Mus* Marvin Hamlish   *Art Dir* Bob Mackichan
● Jack Lemmon, Ray Bolger, Sada Thompson, Tyne Daly, Michael Cristofer, Annette O'Toole (Stigwood/Persky-Bright)

This basically is the John Osborne play in which Laurence Olivier made such an impact. Setting is now America instead of England and period switched from Suez crisis days to 1944.

This time around it's Jack Lemmon as secondrate vaudevillian Archie Rice, desperately trying for laughs from nearly empty houses.

With debt problems, Archie meets Bambi Pasko, a young beauty with little talent but a rich father and starstruck mother. Archie persuades them to back a new show which will feature Bambi, whom he seduces, promising to marry.

Archie's father, Billy hears of the plan and he informs the Paskos Archie is already married; they immediately pull out of the new show, and when Billy realizes Archie will face prison, he agrees to return to the stage and saves the day.

Lemmon gives a fine performance as Archie, though is not so awful as he should be on stage.

....

■ ENTERTAINING MR SLOANE

1970, 94 MINS, UK ◇ ⓥ

Dir Douglas Hickox   *Prod* Douglas Kentis   *Scr* Clive Exton   *Ph* Wolfgang Suschitzky   *Ed* John Trumper   *Mus* Georgie Fame   *Art Dir* Michael Seymour
● Beryl Reid, Peter McEnery, Harry Andrews, Alan Webb (Canterbury)

The sacred cow of 'good taste' is in for a battering with *Entertaining Mr Sloane*, based on Joe Orton's play. *Sloane* blends morbid humor, an obsession with sex, and an underlying pathos and result is interest that is always held.

It's no detraction from the rest of the cast to say that it is firmly Beryl Reid's picture. She gives a memorable study of a middle-aged, flabby, arch 'nymphette', hazily pining for a lost love.

Her brother (Harry Andrews) also falls for Sloane's superficial charm and makes him his chauffeur, clearly with more furtive and kinky motives.

Director Douglas Hickox, who does an astute job, though sometimes his direction meanders slightly, has opened up the play a little, though not at the expense of the claustrophobic atmosphere.

....

■ ENTITY, THE

1982, 125 MINS, US ◇ Ⓥ

Dir Sidney J. Furie *Prod* Harold Schneider *Scr* Frank DeFelitta *Ph* Stephen H. Burum *Ed* Frank J. Urioste *Mus* Charles Bernstein *Art Dir* Charles Rosen
● Barbara Hershey, Ron Silver, David Lablosa, George Coe, Margaret Blye, Jacqueline Brookes (Pelleport Investors/20th Century-Fox)

Theoretically, at least, *The Entity* would have made a fine drama-docu. As is, a fascinating fact-based tale of the supernatural is reduced by cliches of narrative and characterization to routine exploitation fare.

Pic's disappointment rests with Sidney J. Furie's insipid direction and Frank DeFelitta's trite screen treatment, based on his own novel of the actual paranormal case history of a California woman who was 'violated' and otherwise terrorized over an extended period by an invisible something.

Aside from creditable acting by Barbara Hershey as the female in question and Ron Silver as a psychiatrist who presumes she's a victim of her own childhood-rooted hysteria, film's most inspired elements are the visual effects. These range from standard poltergeist effects to a climactic eruption by the 'entity'.

....

■ EQUUS

1977, 137 MINS, US ◇ Ⓥ

Dir Sidney Lumet *Prod* Lester Persky *Scr* Peter Shaffer *Ph* Oswald Morris *Ed* John Victor-Smith *Mus* Richard Rodney Bennett *Art Dir* Tony Walton
● Richard Burton, Peter Firth, Colin Blakely, Joan Plowright, Harry Andrews, Eileen Atkins (United Artists)

Equus is an excellent example of film-as-theatre. Peter Shaffer's play, which he adapted for the screen, has become under Sidney Lumet's outstanding direction a moving confrontation between a crudely mystical Peter Firth and the psychiatrist (Richard Burton), who is trying to unravel the boy's mind.

The (screen) story is properly oriented to that of a suspense yarn: why did Firth blind Harry Andrews' horses? Judge Eileen Atkins wants Burton to find out. In the process, Burton discerns the boy's transference of extremely physical religious devotion to Jesus, to the spirit Equus as embodied in horses.

Jenny Agutter is excellent as the young girl whose plausible emotional attitudes trigger the boy's outrage at his personal deity.

....

■ ERASERHEAD

1977, 100 MINS, US Ⓥ

Dir David Lynch *Prod* David Lynch *Scr* David Lynch *Ph* Fred Elms *Ed* David Lynch *Mus* Fats Waller *Art Dir* David Lynch
● Jack Nance, Charlotte Stewart, Jeanne Bates, Allen Josephs, Judith Anna Roberts, Laurel Near (AFI/Lynch)

Eraserhead is a sickening bad-taste exercise made by David Lynch under the auspices of the American Film Institute.

Set, apparently, in some undefined apocalyptic future era, *Eraserhead* consists mostly of a man sitting in a room trying to figure out what to do with his horribly mutated child.

Lynch keeps throwing in graphic close-ups of the piteous creature, and pulls out all gory stops in the unwatchable climax.

Like a lot of AFI efforts, the pic has good tech values (particularly the inventive sound mixing), but little substance or subtlety. The mind boggles to learn that Lynch labored on this pic for five years.

....

■ ERIC THE VIKING

1989, 103 MINS, UK ◇ Ⓥ

Dir Terry Jones *Prod* John Goldstone *Scr* Terry Jones *Ph* Ian Wilson *Ed* George Akers *Mus* Neil Innes *Art Dir* John Beard
● Tim Robbins, Gary Cady, Mickey Rooney, Eartha Kitt, Terry Jones, John Cleese (Prominent)

The idea of telling the story of a Viking warrior who thought there must be more to life than rape and pillage is an amusing one, and for the most part *Erik the Viking* is an enjoyable film.

Pic opens with Erik (Tim Robbins) falling in love with a girl just as he kills her. Spurred by her death he decides to try and bring the Age of Ragnarok – where men fight and kill – to an end.

He sets off with an unruly band of followers – including the local blacksmith who wants Ragnarok to continue as it helps his sword-making business – and is pursued by Halfdan the Black (John Cleese), the local warlord who quite enjoys Ragnarok and wants it to continue.

American Tim Robbins is fine as the softly spoken and sensitive Erik, and especially seems to enjoy himself in the battle scenes. The film's great strength, though, is the Viking crew, which is full of wonderful characters, such as Tim McInnerny's manic Sven the Berserk, heavily disguised Antony Sher's scheming Loki and best of all Freddie Jones' put-upon missionary.

....

■ ESCAPE ARTIST, THE

1982, 93 MINS, US ◇ Ⓥ

Dir Caleb Deschanel *Prod* Doug Claybourne, Buck Houghton *Scr* Melissa Mathison, Stephen Zito *Ph* Stephen H. Burum *Ed* Arthur Schmidt *Mus* Georges Delerue *Art Dir* Dean Tavoularis
● Griffin O'Neal, Raul Julia, Teri Garr, Joan Hackett, Gabriel Dell, Jackie Coogan (Zoetrope)

The Escape Artist is a muted fable [from the novel by David Wagoner] about a gifted child in a never-never-land America. Treatment frequently pushes past the careful to the precious, and the quiet, odd tale never becomes more than mildly intriguing.

After brash but not arrogant youth Griffin O'Neal issues a challenge to the police department that he can break out of their jail in one hour, story flips into an hour-long flashback.

O'Neal imposes himself on his aunt and uncle, small-time vaudevillians, essayed by Joan Hackett and Gabriel Dell, and begins making trouble for himself and the entire Midwestern town by making off with the loot-filled wallet of the corrupt mayor's son, played as a real looney tune by Raul Julia.

It all ends with O'Neal royally turning the tables on Julia and mayor Desiderio (Desi) Arnaz.

In his film debut, O'Neal, who is Ryan's son and Tatum's brother, comes across as spry and able, but seems to come fully alive only in the confrontation scenes with Julia and in a nice flirtation with young waitress Elizabeth Daily.

....

■ ESCAPE FROM ALCATRAZ

1979, 112 MINS, US ◇ Ⓥ

Dir Don Siegel *Prod* Don Siegel *Scr* Richard Tuggle *Ph* Bruce Surtees *Ed* Ferris Webster *Mus* Jerry Fielding *Art Dir* Allen Smith

● Clint Eastwood, Patrick McGoohan, Fred Ward, Roberts Blossom, Bruce M. Fischer, Paul Benjamin (Paramount)

Considering that the escape itself from rock-bound Alcatraz prison consumes only the film's final half-hour, screenwriter Richard Tuggle [adapting the book by J. Campbell Bruce] and director Don Siegel provide a model of super-efficient filmmaking. From the moment Clint Eastwood walks onto The Rock, until the final title card explaining the three escapees were never heard from again, *Escape from Alcatraz* is relentless in establishing a mood and pace of unrelieved tension.

Pic's only fault may be an ambiguous ending, tied, of course, to the historical reality of the 1962 escape, only successful one in Alcatraz' 29-year history as America's most repressive penal institution.

Key counterpoint to Eastwood's character comes from Patrick McGoohan as the megalomaniacal warden.

....

■ ESCAPE FROM NEW YORK

1981, 99 MINS, US ◇

Dir John Carpenter *Prod* Larry France, Debra Hill *Scr* John Carpenter, Nick Castle *Ph* Dean Cundey *Ed* Todd Ramsay *Mus* John Carpenter, Alan Howarth *Art Dir* Joe Alves
● Kurt Russell, Lee Van Cleef, Ernest Borgnine, Donald Pleasence, Isaac Hayes, Harry Dean Stanton (Avco Embassy)

Although execution doesn't quite live up to the fabulous premise, *Escape from New York* is a solidly satisfying actioner. Impressively produced for $7 million, it reps director John Carpenter's biggest budget to date.

In the 1997 New York City neatly turned out (mostly in St Louis) by production designer Joe Alves, Manhattan is a walled, maximum security prison inhabited by millions of felons and loonies. The president of the US has the misfortune of crash landing on the island and being taken hostage by the crazies, who demand their release in exchange for the leader.

Into this cesspool is sent tough criminal Kurt Russell, who is charged with extricating the prexy within 24 hours.

Pic only falls a little short in not taking certain scenes to their dramatic limits. For instance, Russell is finally captured by Isaac Hayes and his cronies and thrown, like a doomed gladiator, into an arena with a hulking behemoth. Instead of milking the confrontation for all it's worth, Carpenter keeps cutting away to parallel events elsewhere.

Model and matte work, executed at New World's special effects studio in Venice, is obvious but imaginatively fun enough to get by.

....

■ ESCAPE FROM THE PLANET OF THE APES

1971, 97 MINS, US ◇ Ⓥ

Dir Don Taylor *Prod* Arthur P. Jacobs *Scr* Paul Dehn *Ph* Joseph Biroc *Ed* Marion Rothman *Mus* Jerry Goldsmith *Art Dir* Jack Martin Smith, William Creber
● Roddy McDowall, Kim Hunter, Bradford Dillman, Natalie Trundy, Eric Braeden, William Windom (20th Century-Fox)

Escape from the Planet of the Apes is an excellent film, almost as good as the original *Planet of the Apes*. Arthur Jacobs' production is marked by an outstanding script, using some of the original Pierre Boulle novel characters; excellent direction by Don Taylor; and superior performances from a cast headed by encoring Roddy McDowall and Kim Hunter.

In the previous film one will recall that the world seemed to be ending in nuclear holocaust. Something that trivial never stopped a good writer, so this film opens with Hunter,

179

McDowall and Sal Mineo arriving on earth in a space vehicle.

After about half of the film's literate, suspenseful, delightful and thought-provoking 97 minutes, the story emphasis segues from broad comedic antics to a rather horrifying dilemma. Eric Braeden, scientific advisor to US President William Windom, suggests that, if indeed in our future apes would subdue humans, why not remove that distant threat by aborting the life of the child of McDowall and Hunter?

• •

■ ESCAPE ME NEVER

1935, 93 MINS, UK

Dir Paul Czinner   *Prod* Herbert Wilcox, Dallas Bower   *Scr* Margaret Kennedy, R.J. Cullen   *Ph* Georges Perinal, Sepp Allgeier   *Ed* Merrill G. White, David Lean   *Mus* William Walton   *Art Dir* Andre Andrejev, Wilfred Arnold

● Elisabeth Bergner, Hugh Sinclair, Irene Vanbrugh, Griffith Jones, Penelope Dudley-Ward, Lyn Harding (British & Dominions/United Artists)

Escape Me Never, produced as a play [by Margaret Kennedy] in London and New York with the same star, is a well-produced film transcription of a story of moods and morbidity.

Locale includes Venice, where the picture opens, the mountains, and finally London. At the outset Elisabeth Bergner is fashioned as an impish waif of immoral caste, who instantly becomes likable in spite of her character background. Further on, by degrees, she loses a part of this charm and becomes a helpless mother and wife who is figuratively kicked around by her musician husband.

Two brothers figure in the supporting cast, played by Hugh Sinclair and Griffith Jones. Story makes the brothers unreal to some extent, at the same time also stretching logic of actions of Bergner and the other girl (Penelope Dudley-Ward). Latter is unbelievably smitten with one brother, then with the other, and, though appealed to by Bergner, as the latter's wife, stolidly refuses to believe her second choice is married.

Some of the interiors tend to drabness, possibly to lend that touch to a depressing story.

• •

■ ESCAPE ME NEVER

1947, 101 MINS, US

Dir Peter Godfrey   *Prod* Henry Blanke   *Scr* Thames Williamson, Lenore Coffee   *Ph* Sol Polito   *Ed* Clarence Kolster   *Mus* Erich Wolfgang Korngold   *Art Dir* Carl Jules Weyl

● Errol Flynn, Ida Lupino, Eleanor Parker, Gig Young (Warner)

Errol Flynn is given plenty of opportunity to flash the old charm but there's hardly a touch of the usual swashbuckling or boudoir romance activities in his role of a serious composer. Under the capable direction of Peter Godfrey, he turns in one of the best jobs of his career. Ida Lupino, although she's seldom been typed so much as Flynn, has a role here that she can really sink her teeth into and she demonstrates once more her versatility as a serious actress.

Story [from a novel and play by Margaret Kennedy] is cut sharply in half between light romance and heavy drama and therin lie its only fault of note.

Tale is imbued with much of the nostalgic flavor of pre-World War I Europe. It tees off in Venice where Gig Young, a struggling young composer, wants to marry the wealthy Eleanor Parker. Through a misunderstanding, however, her parents think Young is living with Lupino, a widowed waif with an infant son, and so rush Parker off to a resort in the Alps. Seems, though, that it's been Flynn, Young's happy-go-lucky brother, who

took Lupino and child in off the streets. To set things right again, the two brothers, Miss Lupino and the moppet start off on foot through the Alps to find Parker and explain the mistake to her.

Chief production assist is lent by Erich Wolfgang Korngold's score, with both the ballet and theme music standout. Ballet sequences are tastefully staged by LeRoy Prinz and Milada Mladova sparkles in both terping and thesping as the prima ballerina.

• •

■ ESCAPE TO ATHENA

1979, 125 MINS, UK ◇ ▼

Dir George P. Cosmatos   *Prod* Jack Wiener   *Scr* Richard S. Lochte, Edward Anhalt   *Ph* Gil Taylor   *Ed* Ralph Kemplen   *Mus* Lalo Schifrin   *Art Dir* John Graysmark

● Roger Moore, Telly Savalas, David Niven, Claudia Cardinale, Richard Roundtree, Stefanie Powers (ITC/Grade)

Escape to Athena not only has the unabashed look of a cynical 'package' but also plays like one as well. It's a joke-up wartime action retread, feeble as to both humor and suspense, in which a group of Anglo-American prisoners of the Germans scramble to liberate (a) themselves and (b) some Greek art treasures.

Of those billed above the title, Roger Moore as the Nazi camp commander, Elliott Gould, David Niven, Sonny Bono, Stefanie Powers and Richard Roundtree as POWs (how's that for a motley bunch?), Telly Savalas as a Greek resistance leader, and Claudia Cardinale as a brothel madam, none has much scope to register with any dimension and most are as implausible as the hammy action [based on a story by Richard S. Lochte and George P. Cosmatos].

• •

■ ESCAPE TO WITCH MOUNTAIN

1975, 97 MINS, US ◇

Dir John Hough   *Prod* Jerome Courtland   *Scr* Robert Malcolm Young   *Ph* Frank Phillips   *Ed* Robert Stafford   *Mus* Johnny Mandel   *Art Dir* John B. Mansbridge, Al Roelofs

● Eddie Albert, Ray Milland, Donald Pleasence, Kim Richards, Ike Eisenmann, Walter Barnes (Buena Vista)

The two leading protagonists are a young orphaned brother and sister who are psychic.

Based on a book by Alexander Key and directed with a light and sure hand by John Hough, picks up the youngsters as they arrive at a children's home after the loss of their foster parents.

Their unusual powers, displayed early when they warn a man not to enter a car moments before it is demolished by a runaway truck, leads to an eccentric tycoon who craves a gifted clairvoyant who can make him omnipotent, arranging for their transfer to his palatial home where they are held prisoner.

Using their magical talents for an escape, they take up with a cranky oldtimer travelling in a motor home. Much of the action focuses on their efforts to elude the millionaire and his men who want the children returned.

Eddie Albert inserts just the proper type of crankiness as the camper-owner who gets entangled with them, and Ray Milland properly hams the multimillionaire. Donald Pleasence scores, too, as Milland's aide.

• •

■ E.T.
THE EXTRA-TERRESTRIAL

1982, 115 MINS, US ◇ ▼

Dir Steven Spielberg   *Prod* Steven Spielberg   *Scr* Melissa Mathison   *Ph* Allen Daviau   *Ed* Carol Littleton   *Mus* John Williams   *Art Dir* James D. Bissell

● Dee Wallace, Henry Thomas, Peter Coyote, Robert

MacNaughton, Drew Barrymore, K.C. Martel (Universal)

E.T. may be the best Disney film Disney never made. Captivating, endearingly optimistic and magical at times, Steven Spielberg's fantasy is about a stranded alien from outer space protected by three kids until it can arrange for passage home.

E.T. is highly fortunate to be found by young Henry Thomas who, after some understandable initial fright, takes the 'goblin' in, first as a sort of pet and then as a friend he must guard against the more preying elements of human society. Over time, Thomas teaches E.T. how to talk and includes his older brother (Robert MacNaughton) and younger sister (Drew Barrymore) in on the secret.

Ultimately, of course, the official representatives of society locate E.T., which seems to occasion a rapid decline in its health until it appears to die.

As superlatively created by Carlo Rambaldi, the creature manages to project both a wondrous childlike quality and a sense of superior powers. It even gets to play a drunk scene, perhaps a first for screen aliens.

All performers fulfill the requirements, and Thomas is perfect in the lead, playing the childhood equivalent of Spielberg's everyman heroes of his previous pics.
☐ 1982: Best Picture (Nomination)

• •

■ ETERNITY

1990, 125 MINS, US ◇ ▼

Dir Steven Paul   *Scr* Jon Voight, Steven Paul, Dorothy Koster Paul   *Ph* John Lambert   *Ed* Christopher Greenbury, Peter Zinner, Michael Sheridan   *Mus* Michel Legrand   *Art Dir* Martin Zboril

● Jon Voight, Armand Assante, Eileen Davidson, Wilford Brimley, Kaye Ballard, Joey Villa (Paul)

Written in collaboration with director Steven Paul and his mother Dorothy Koster Paul, Jon Voight's vision of mankind's dilemma revolves around mystical notions of reincarnation. Opening reel is a medieval prolog in which Voight wars with his brother Armand Assante over a kingdom, resulting in the death of his beloved Eileen Davidson.

Voight wakes up and, in true *Wizard of Oz* style, recognizes all the people in his life as reincarnations of relatives and other folks from the dream. Assante is now a megalomaniacal, right-wing industrialist out to control the media, the US presidency, and to push a vast weapons project he believes will deter war.

Voight is a self-professed do-gooder, who opposes Assante's militaristic approach. Assante attempts to buy out Voight's show to silence him and then co-opts his girlfriend (Davidson again) by making her a TV star on his network.

Voight invests equal measures of naturalism and quirks in his messianic role which goes over the top occasionally. Davidson stands out in the supporting cast, possessing an unusual beauty reminiscent of Polish star Joanna Pacula.

• •

■ EUREKA

1983, 129 MINS, UK ◇ ▼

Dir Nicolas Roeg   *Prod* Jeremy Thomas   *Scr* Paul Mayersberg   *Ph* Alex Thomson   *Ed* Tony Lawson   *Mus* Stanley Myers   *Art Dir* Michael Seymour

● Gene Hackman, Theresa Russell, Rutger Hauer, Jane Lapotaire, Ed Lauter, Mickey Rourke (JF Prods/Recorded Picture)

Even by his own standards, Nicolas Roeg's *Eureka* is an indulgent melodrama about the anticlimactic life of a greedy gold prospector after he has struck it rich.

Gene Hackman performs with predictable credit as the man whose jackpot fortune only leaves him bored, surly and suspicious of being ripped off, by one and all, family included.

Theresa Russell is the girl-woman daughter who rebelliously marries a putative gigolo (Rutger Hauer) whom paranoid papa psychs as a fortune hunter. Mother Jane Lapotaire, meanwhile, driven to the sauce by an uncaring husband, drifts through life in the tropics with sulky sarcasm.

Violent menace permeates pic, radiated by Joe Pesci as a Yiddish-speaking 'entrepreneur' who, foiled in his bid to buy a piece of Hackman's island in order to establish a casino, finally sends the hoods after Hackman, leading up to a gruesome pre-finale.

● ●

■ EUROPEANS, THE

1979, 90 MINS, UK ◇ Ⓥ

Dir James Ivory   *Prod* Ismael Merchant   *Scr* Ruth Prawer Jhabvala   *Ph* Larry Pizer   *Ed* Jeremiah Rusconi   *Mus* Richard Robbins
● Lee Remick, Robin Ellis, Wesley Addy, Lisa Eichhorn (Merchant-Ivory)

'The Europeans' are Americans who grew up in Europe in the mid-19th century. They come back to the US to visit rich cousins. Perhaps a bit down on their luck, the arrival leads to a mingling and interaction of cultures, that ends up with the more innocent Yankee outlooks holding their own with the worldly wiles of the European ways.

The European cousins are Lee Remick as a mid-30s baroness now estranged from her Austrian nobleman husband and her younger brother, a free-living portrait painter with bohemian attitudes.

Shot in the US, New England is a lovely backdrop with its languid, genteel ways and extraordinary houses that are a mixture of European and local influences.

Director James Ivory handles this roundelay [from the Henry James novel] with subtlety, delivering an engaging drama.

● ●

■ EVE

1962, 100 MINS, FRANCE/ITALY

Dir Joseph Losey   *Prod* Robert Hakim, Raymond Hakim   *Scr* Hugo Butler, Evan Jones   *Ph* Gianni Di Venanzo   *Ed* Reginald Beck, Franca Silvi   *Mus* Michel Legrand   *Art Dir* Richard MacDonald, Luigi Scaccianoce
● Jeanne Moreau, Stanley Baker, Virna Lisi, Giorgio Albertazzi, James Villiers, Lisa Gastoni (Paris/Interopa)

Made [from the novel by James Hadley Chase] by an American director in Italy using English, with French producers and French, British and Italo actors, this is a sleek, mannered look at an affair between a cold, almost psychotic, call girl and a writer, who is a fraught with overtones of masochism.

A blustering, self satisfied British writer, who has a bestseller and smash pic under his belt, has also amassed an Italian fiancee and lives in Venice and Rome. His film producer suspects him and, being in love with his fiancee, is having him investigated.

He has to come up with another story, and goes off to a posh secluded house on an isle near Venice. A broken rudder had let a boat in with an enigmatic, hard-looking French girl and an older man. They had broken into the house and she was calmly in the bathtub when the writer comes in. He wants to throw them out until he ogles the femme.

He throws out the older man who had paid off the girl in paintings for a night of love. The writer tries to get next to her but she knocks him cold with an ashtray. Thus starts an obsession.

Picture is reminiscent of pre-war Yank femme fatale films. But there is not enough character to give acceptance to the over-

indulgence in Jeanne Moreau as the cold-hearted harlot. Moreau speaks good English but is hampered by the over-decorated, over-stylized vamp she is called on to play. Stanley Baker acquits himself acceptably as the climbing ex-coal miner, and others are adequate.

● ●

■ EVERGREEN

1934, 92 MINS, UK

Dir Victor Saville   *Prod* Michael Balcon   *Scr* Emlyn Williams, Marjorie Gaffney   *Ph* Glen MacWilliams   *Ed* Ian Dalrymple   *Mus* Harry Woods   *Art Dir* Alfred Junge, Peter Pride
● Jessie Matthews, Sonnie Hale, Betty Balfour, Barry Mackay, Ivor McLaren (Gaumont-British)

Jessie Matthews has the name part, which she created on the stage. The screen adaptation and dialog is, for picture purposes, a better story than the stage version. It is more definite and coherent. Benn Levy and Lorenz Hart wrote the original musical for C. B. Cochran.

In 1909 (this is the plot) Harriet Green is London's pet singing comedienne, making her farewell appearance at the old Tivoli prior to her marriage to a marquis. That night the father of her child, whom she believed to be dead, turns up and demands blackmail. She places the baby girl in the charge of a faithful maid and disappears.

Twenty-five years later the daughter seeks a job in the chorus and is recognized by the mother's old understudy, now the widow of an ancient lord. Daughter is foisted on the public as the original Harriet Green and starred in an elaborate musical. This gives scope for Edwardian and modern costuming and ample advantage is taken of the opportunities.

It is the astonishingly competent performances by the principals that is most impressive. They embrace, in addition to Matthews, Sonnie Hale and Ivor McLaren, Betty Balfour and Barry MacKay, all good.

● ●

■ EVERYBODY WINS

1990, 97 MINS, UK/US Ⓥ

Dir Karel Reisz   *Prod* Jeremy Thomas, Ezra Swerdlow   *Scr* Arthur Miller   *Ph* Ian Baker   *Ed* John Bloom   *Mus* Mark Isham, Leon Redbone   *Art Dir* Peter Larkin
● Debra Winger, Nick Nolte, Will Patton, Judith Ivey, Jack Warden (Recorded Picture)

Everybody Wins is a very disappointing picture. Repping Arthur Miller's first feature film screenplay since *The Misfits* in 1961, the Karel Reisz-helmed film noir is obscure and artificial.

Overladen with pompous and frequently dated dialog, Miller's script (developed from his 1982 pair of one-act plays, *Two-Way Mirror*) is essentially a routine whodunit. Nick Nolte plays an investigator called in by seeming good Samaritan Debra Winger to get young Frank Military out of jail for a murder she claims he did not commit. Nolte doggedly pursues various leads, interviews odd people and discovers a web of corruption engulfing a small Connecticut town.

Winger as a schizo femme fatale copes uneasily with Miller's overblown dialog, which has her alternatively putting on airs to a bewildered Nolte or handing him non sequiturs. Not helping matters is the lack of chemistry between Nolte and Winger in their sex scenes.

● ●

■ EVERYTHING I HAVE IS YOURS

1952, 91 MINS, US ◇

Dir Robert Z. Leonard   *Prod* George Wells   *Scr* George Wells, Ruth Brooks Flippen   *Ph* William V. Skall   *Ed* Adrienne Fazan   *Mus* David Rose (dir.)
● Marge Champion, Gower Champion, Dennis

O'Keefe, Monica Lewis, Dean Miller, Eduard Franz (M-G-M)

The talents of Marge and Gower Champion get a flashy showcasing. The star team is extremely likeable and almost generates enough verve and audience response to carry off even the sagging spots.

Marge Champion, particularly, continues to show promise as an ingenue who can get by even without a dance or song. Champion gives a very pleasing account of himself.

The plot finds the Champions opening to a smash hit on Broadway in an O'Keefe-produced show, only to discover that the gal's dizziness is caused by pregnancy. Forced to retire with only one night in the show, Marge Champion becomes a successful mother for the next few years while Champion continues in show business partnered with Monica Lewis.

● ●

■ EVERYTHING YOU ALWAYS WANTED TO KNOW ABOUT SEX** BUT WERE AFRAID TO ASK

1972, 87 MINS, US ◇ Ⓥ

Dir Woody Allen   *Prod* Charles H. Joffe   *Scr* Woody Allen   *Ph* David M. Walsh   *Ed* James T. Heckart, Eric Albertson   *Mus* Mundell Lowe   *Art Dir* Dale Hennesy
● Woody Allen, John Carradine, Anthony Quayle, Tony Randall, Burt Reynolds, Gene Wilder (United Artists)

Borrowing only the title and some typically inane questions from Dr David Reuben's oft-ingenuous but widely read overview of sexual matters, Woody Allen writes his sixth screenplay and serves for the third time as his own director.

Pic is divided into seven segments – blackout sketches, really – that presumably are Allen's surrealistic answer to selected questions from the Reuben tome.

One of the episodes is a prolonged piece of nonsense involving a *2001*-inspired mission control centre that is engineering a bout of intercourse in a parked car. Idea of Allen as a reluctant sperm may sound funny on paper, but it plays like an adolescent jape.

Allen's gift is in the depiction of a contemporary intellectual shlump who cannot seem to make it with the chicks always tantalizingly out of reach. That persona could well have served him once more as the focus for a good bit of caustic comedy on today's sexual mores.

● ●

■ EVERY TIME WE SAY GOODBYE

1986, 95 MINS, US ◇ Ⓥ

Dir Moshe Mizrahi   *Prod* Jacob Kotzky, Sharon Harel   *Scr* Moshe Mizrahi, Rachel Fabien, Leah Appet   *Ph* Giuseppe Lanci   *Ed* Mark Burns   *Mus* Philippe Sarde   *Art Dir* Micky Zahar
● Tom Hanks, Cristina Marsillach, Benedict Taylor, Anat Atzmen (Tri-Star)

Every Time We Say Goodbye is a tale of star-crossed lovers played out against a backdrop of Jerusalem in 1942. Tom Hanks is featured as an American pilot recovering from an injury who falls in love with a girl from a traditional Sephardic Jewish family (Cristina Marsillach).

The film is not devoid of humor. Early scenes when Hanks is accepted to dinner by the family as a friend and not yet a suitor are funny and believable. Culturally rich story is aided throughout by the pic's all-Israel shoot, nicely highlighting the different worlds these two lovers come from.

● ●

■ EVERY WHICH WAY BUT LOOSE

1978, 119 MINS, US ◇ Ⓥ

Dir James Fargo   *Prod* Robert Daley   *Scr* Jeremy Joe Kronsberg   *Ph* Rexford Metz   *Ed* Ferris Webster   *Art Dir* Elayne Ceder

● Clint Eastwood, Sondra Locke, Geoffrey Lewis, Beverly D'Angelo, Ruth Gordon (Malpaso/Warner)

Screenplay has Clint Eastwood as a beer-guzzling, country music-loving truck driver who picks up spare change as a barroom brawler. When Sondra Locke, an elusive singer Eastwood meets at The Palomino Club, takes off for Colorado, Eastwood packs his pickup truck in pursuit.

Behind him are a motorcycle gang and an LA cop. Both have been victims of Eastwood's fists. They want revenge. Traveling with Eastwood is Geoffrey Lewis and Beverly D'Angelo, whom the two meet on the road.

There's also an orangutan. His name is Clyde. Eastwood won him a few years back in a fight. He goes everywhere with Eastwood. He drinks beer, finds a one-night stand at a zoo in New Mexico and cheers on his friend.

For Eastwood fans, the essential elements are there. Lots of people get beat up, Eastwood walks tall and looks nasty, cars are crashed. James Fargo directs limply.

EVIL, THE

1978, 89 MINS, US ◇ ⓥ

Dir Gus Trikonis *Prod* Ed Carlin *Scr* Donald G. Thompson *Ph* Mario Di Leo *Ed* Jack Kirshner *Mus* Johnny Harris *Art Dir* Peter Jamison
● Richard Crenna, Joanna Pettet, Andrew Prine, Cassie Yates, Lynne Moddy, Victor Buono (Rangoon)

Any satanic-oriented film that actually has the nerve to display the Wicked One in the flesh can't be all bad, and in fact, *The Evil* is quite good.

Screenplay has psychologist Richard Crenna, accompanied by wife (also a medico) Joanna Pettet, picking up a lease on the proverbial haunted house, despite real estate agent Milton Selzer's recounting of the grisly horrors that took place there.

Crenna and Pettet are soon joined by college prof Andrew Prine with student companion Mary Louise Weller, and several of Crenna's patients. Just what they're all up to is never clearly delineated, but once the house (or something in it) begins to act up, it really doesn't matter.

Throughout, there is a spirit on the loose (resembling the White Tornado) in communication with Pettet, trying to warn her of the dangers ahead. But Crenna is a stubborn skeptic, only admitting his own helplessness in dealing with the situation when there is no other recourse.

This type of psychological insight is rare in suspensers, and is a credit to both Crenna, who delivers a strong performance, and director Gus Trikonis. Fulcrum of pic's success or failure comes in final scenes, when Crenna and Pettet confront the devil himself, played with sinister angelicism by Victor Buono.

EVIL DEAD, THE

1983, 85 MINS, US ◇ ⓥ

Dir Sam Raimi *Prod* Robert Tapert *Scr* Sam Raimi *Ph* Tim Philo *Ed* Edna Ruth Paul *Mus* Joseph Lo Duca
● Bruce Campbell, Ellen Sandweiss, Betsy Baker, Hal Delrich, Sarah York (Renaissance)

The Evil Dead emerges as the ne plus ultra of low-budget gore and shock effects.

Story premise has five youngsters (in their 20s) holed up in a remote cabin where they discover a Book of the Dead. Archaeologist's tape recording reveals it having been found among the Khandarian ruins of a Sumerian civilization. Playing the taped incantations unwittingly summons up dormant demons living in the nearby forest, which possess the youngsters in succession until only Ash (Bruce Campbell) is left intact to fight for survival.

While injecting considerable black humor, neophyte Detroit-based writer-director Sam Raimi maintains suspense and a nightmarish mood in between the showy outbursts of special effects gore and graphic violence which are staples of modern horror pictures. Powerful camerawork suggests the lurking presence of the huge-scale demons in the forest.

Filmed in 1980 on Tennessee and Michigan locations for under $400,000, pic is a grainy blowup from 16mm. Cast is functional.

EVIL DEAD II

1987, 85 MINS, US ◇ ⓥ

Dir Sam Raimi *Prod* Robert Tapert *Scr* Sam Raimi, Scott Spiegel *Ph* Peter Deming *Ed* Kaye Davis *Mus* Joseph Lo Duca *Art Dir* Philip Duffin, Randy Bennett
● Bruce Campbell, Sarah Berry, Dan Hicks, Kassie Wesley, Theodore Raimi, Denise Bixler (Renaissance/De Laurentiis)

More an absurdist comedy than a horror film, *Evil Dead II* is a flashy good-natured display of special effects and scare tactics so extreme they can only be taken for laughs.

Action, and there's plenty, is centered around a remote cabin where Ash (Bruce Campbell) and girlfriend Linda (Denise Bixler) run into some unexpected influences. It isn't long before the forces of the Evil Dead have got ahold of Linda and her head winds up in a vise.

It seems Prof Knowby (John Peaks) has unleashed the spirits of the dead and they want to escape limbo by claiming possession of the living. They're a remarkably protean lot and take on all sorts of imaginative and grotesque forms almost instantaneously.

Story here is merely an excuse for director Sam Raimi to explore new ways to shock an audience and usually he keeps his sense of humor about it.

EVIL UNDER THE SUN

1982, 102 MINS, UK ⓥ

Dir Guy Hamilton *Prod* John Brabourne, Richard Goodwin *Scr* Anthony Shaffer *Ph* Christopher Challis *Ed* Richard Marden *Mus* Jack Larchbury (arr.) *Art Dir* Elliot Scott
● Peter Ustinov, Jane Birkin, Colin Blakely, James Mason, Diana Rigg, Maggie Smith (EMI)

Director Guy Hamilton admits to hating Agatha Christie's writing style. He finds it overcrowded with characters and passe in general. Apart from cutting down the number of characters, Hamilton and scripter Anthony Shaffer have also had the audacity to switch things around in the inevitable denouement scene. Poirot points right away at the guilty party, while the true suspense is put into the how's and why's that follow.

But fun it is to follow this cast of English and US characters in their stay at the elegantly old-fashioned resort hotel on a remote Tyrrhenian island (shot in Mallorca, original novel took place in Cornwall), where a famous stage actress gives them all a good motive for doing her in.

Through it all, Peter Ustinov's Poirot paddles about, being demanding of staff (beeswax for his shoes) and cuisine and happy about himself.

Next to Ustinov, Maggie Smith shines as the hotel proprietress in love with the murdered woman's husband, played with quiet gusto by Denis Quilley. Diana Rigg as the stage star makes it believable in one short song-and-dance scene that she really is such a star.

EXCALIBUR

1981, 140 MINS, US ◇

Dir John Boorman *Prod* John Boorman *Scr* John Boorman, Rospo Pallenberg *Ph* Alex Thomson *Ed* John Merritt *Mus* Trevor Jones *Art Dir* Anthony Pratt
● Nigel Terry, Nicol Williamson, Nicholas Clay, Helen Mirren, Cheri Lunghi, Corin Redgrave (Orion)

Excalibur is exquisite, a near-perfect blend of action, romance, fantasy and philosophy, finely acted and beautifully filmed by director John Boorman and cinematographer Alex Thomson.

Not surprisingly, *Excalibur* is essentially the legend of King Arthur, embellished a bit by Boorman and coscripter Rospo Pallenberg, working from the Malory classic, *Morte d'Arthur*.

Filmed in timeless Irish locales, the film rests solidly on a feeling that this, indeed, must have been what life was like in the feudal ages, even as it resists bing pinned to any historical point and accepts magic and sorcery on faith.

Nicol Williamson stands out early as the wizard Merlin, at times a magician, flim-flam artist and philosopher, always interesting. The tangle of lust and betrayal that leads to Arthur's conception, the planting of Excalibur in the stone and Arthur's rise to Camelot after extracting it, is followed by restlessness and more dark deeds.

If *Excalibur* has a major fault, it's a somewhat extended sequence of the Knights of the Round Table in search of the Grail, seemingly ill-established and overdrawn.

EXECUTIONER, THE

1970, 111 MINS, UK ◇ ⓥ

Dir Sam Wanamaker *Prod* Charles H. Schneer *Scr* Jack Pulman *Ph* Denys Coop *Ed* R. Watts *Mus* Ron Goodwin *Art Dir* E. Marshall
● George Peppard, Joan Collins, Judy Geeson, Oscar Homolka, Charles Gray, Nigel Patrick (Schneer/Columbia)

George Peppard is a British undercover agent out to prove that a colleague is really a double agent.

Supposedly a triple-cross suspenser, film [from a story by Gordon McDonell] just lies there so that interest fades fast in the overexposition and redundancy. Peppard is cast as an American-raised Briton whose latest spy caper has been aborted. Nigel Patrick and Charles Gray, Peppard's superiors, don't believe his charges that Keith Michell is a double agent.

Joan Collins appears occasionally as Michell's wife, and sometimes playmate of Peppard and also of George Baker. Judy Geeson appears even less frequently as Peppard's girl friend who helps him obtain secret information.

EXECUTIVE ACTION

1973, 91 MINS, US ◇ ⓥ

Dir David Miller *Prod* Edward Lewis, Dan Bessie *Scr* Dalton Trumbo *Ph* Robert Steadman *Ed* George Grenville, Irving Lerner *Mus* Randy Edelman *Art Dir* Kirk Axtell
● Burt Lancaster, Robert Ryan, Will Geer, Gilbert Green, John Anderson, Paul Carr (Lewis/Wakeford-Orloff)

The open lesion known as Watergate revealed a form of governmental-industrial syphilis, which in turn has made more plausible to millions the theory of an assassination conspiracy in 1963 against President John F. Kennedy. *Executive Action*, a part-fiction and documentary style film [from a story by Donald Freed and Mark Lane], dramatized with low key terror, is an emotional aftershock to the event.

Burt Lancaster, Robert Ryan and Will Geer star as informed men of industry and government service who concluded that JFK must be eliminated. Lancaster is the overall project officer. James MacColl, a remarkable look alike to Lee Harvey Oswald, depicts the alleged Oswald frameup. Oscar Oncidi plays Jack Ruby, Oswald's own assassin who, per this story, is wired into the plot.

• •

■ EX-MRS. BRADFORD, THE

1936, 80 MINS, US

Dir Stephen Roberts   *Scr* Anthony Veiller   *Ph* J. Roy Hunt   *Ed* Arthur Roberts   *Mus* Roy Webb (dir.)
● William Powell, Jean Arthur, James Gleason, Eric Blore, Robert Armstrong (RKO)

Another sprightly entry for the school of smart comedy, detective mystery yarns, *The Ex-Mrs Bradford* has a neat combo of names – William Powell and Jean Arthur – backed up by excellent support.

Comparison with *The Thin Man* is natural. But the film is much better than a copy.

Teaming of Powell and Arthur, as doctor and divorced wife, is a happy one. Story [by James Edward Grant] brings the wife right back to the doorstep of the busy physician, where she 'moves in' and resumes where she left off annoying him with her interest in writing detective stories.

While the romance between the pair is slowly revived, the whole affair is treated with smart flippancy. Much the same attitude is taken towards the doctor's tumbling efforts to solve a series of killings that has the police baffled, until they attempt to pin them on him. Here, his wife's sharp wit and impertinence help.

• •

■ EXODUS

1960, 212 MINS, US ◇ Ⓥ

Dir Otto Preminger   *Prod* Otto Preminger   *Scr* Dalton Trumbo   *Ph* Sam Leavitt   *Ed* Louis R. Loeffler   *Mus* Ernest Gold   *Art Dir* Richard Day
● Paul Newman, Eva Maria Saint, Ralph Richardson, Peter Lawford, Lee J. Cobb, Sal Mineo (United Artists)

Transposing Leon Uris' hefty novel to the screen was not an easy task. It is to the credit of director Otto Preminger and scenarist Dalton Trumbo that they have done as well as they have. One can, however, wish that they had been blessed with more dramatic incisiveness. (Estimated cost of pic was $3.5–4 million.)

The picture wanders frequently in attempting to bring into focus various political and personal aspirations that existed within the Jewish nationalist movement itself as well as in regards to Arab opposition to the partitioning of Palestine and the unhappy role that Great Britain played as custodian of the status quo while a young United Nations pondered the fate of a new nation.

One of the overwhelming moments is played aboard a rusty old freighter in which 611 Jews of all ages, from all over the face of Europe and spirited out of an internment camp on Cyprus under the nose of the British, attempt to sail to Palestine. The whole spirit that brought Israel into being is reflected in this particular sequence toward the end of the first part of the film. It's a real dramatic gem.

The romance that develops slowly between young, dedicated Hagana leader Paul Newman and Eva Marie Saint, as a widowed American who contributes her nursing abilities to Jewish refugees on Cyprus and later in Palestine, as Arabs attack the new settlers, is conventional. Techincally Newman gives a sound performance, but he fails to give the role warmth. Saint has several good scenes and makes the most of them, as does Ralph Richardson, a sympathetic British general.

Lee J. Cobb gives his customary dependable, thoroughly professinol performance as a conservative elder Hagana community leader, father of Newman and brother of the fanatical violence advocate played by David Opatoshu. The brothers' silent meeting after years of separation through a barred slot in a prison door is great pictorial drama.

Sal Mineo as a loyal Irgun youngster, who has been brutalized by the Nazis, is excellent and John Derek stands out too as an Arab whose friendship for Newman and his family goes back to boyhood.

• •

■ EXORCIST, THE

1973, 121 MINS, US ◇ Ⓥ

Dir William Friedkin   *Prod* William Peter Blatty   *Scr* William Peter Blatty   *Ph* Owen Roizman, Billy Williams   *Ed* Jordan Leondopoulos, Evan Lottman, Norman Gay, Bud Smith   *Mus* Jack Nitzsche   *Art Dir* Bill Malley
● Ellen Burstyn, Max Von Sydow, Lee J. Cobb, Kitty Winn, Jack MacGowran, Linda Blair (Warner)

William Friedkin's film of William Peter Blatty's novel *The Exorcist* is an expert telling of a supernatural horror story. The well cast film makes credible in powerful laymen's terms the rare phenomenon of diabolic possession.

Blatty's story is based on a 1949 incident of documented possession, atop which came Friedkin's own investigations. The joint effort is cohesive and compelling, gripping both the senses and the intellect.

A compendium of production delays, some of puzzling origin (shooting alone occupied more than 10 months [of the 16-month period]), and rush to completion upped final costs to $8 million-$10 million.

Jesuit priest Max Von Sydow is the leader of an archeological expedition. After unearthing some pagan hex symbol, several near fatal
accidents occur. Thence to Georgetown, Maryland.

Ellen Burstyn, a divorced film actress, is on location with daughter Linda Blair, the latter becoming aware of some apparent inner spiritual friend whom she calls 'Captain Howdy', and their rented house now filled with strange sounds and movements. Finally, Jason Miller is a psychiatrist-Jesuit.

The lives of these three gradually converge as Blair's fits become genuinely vicious and destructive, provoking a shocking series of psychiatric tests. At length, Von Sydow, who has exorcised before, is sent to perform the rare rites. The climactic sequences assault the senses and the intellect with pure cinematic terror.

□ 1973: Best Picture (Nomination)

• •

■ EXORCIST II
THE HERETIC

1977, 117 MINS, US ◇ Ⓥ

Dir John Boorman   *Prod* John Boorman, Richard Lederer   *Scr* William Goodhart   *Ph* William A. Fraker   *Ed* Tom Priestley   *Mus* Ennio Morricone   *Art Dir* Richard Macdonald
● Linda Blair, Richard Burton, Louise Fletcher, Max Von Sydow, Kitty Winn, Paul Henreid (Warner)

Since any title containing Roman numerals invites comparison, the answer is:
No, *Exorcist II* is not as good as *The Exorcist*. It isn't even close.

Gone now is the simple clash between Good and Evil, replaced by some goofy transcendental spiritualism.

Linda Blair is back as Regan, four years older and still suffering the residual effects of her demonic possession. For the most part, however, she's cheerful and good, seemingly no more bothered by her lingering devil than a chronic zit that keeps popping out on prom night.

She is under the kindly care of psychiatrist Louise Fletcher and Kitty Winn, mom's secretary from the old days. Another self-doubting priest (Richard Burton) is assigned to investigate the death of the old exorcist (Max Von Sydow).

• •

■ EXORCIST III, THE

1990, 110 MINS, US ◇ Ⓥ

Dir William Peter Blatty   *Prod* Carter DeHaven   *Scr* William Peter Blatty   *Ph* Gerry Fisher   *Ed* Todd Ramsay   *Mus* Barry DeVorzon   *Art Dir* Leslie Dilley
● George C. Scott, Ed Flanders, Brad Dourif, Jason Miller, Nicol Williamson, Scott Wilson (Morgan Creek/20th Century-Fox)

Since *The Exorcist* was one of the most frightening films ever and *Exorcist II* one of the goofiest, chances favored *The Exorcist III* to fall somewhere in between, though not nearly far enough up the scale to rival the original.

The Devil and the Church have clashed in too many other pics since with increasingly ingenious ways to burst bodies, leaving director-writer William Peter Blatty [adapting his own novel, *Legion*] with all mood and no meat. Much too often, he lingers under flickering lights in dark corridors where nothing happens.

It's been 15 years since Father Karras battled the Devil for the little girl and ended up dead at the bottom of the stairway. Now his old policeman friend (George C. Scott) is confronted with a series of sacrilegious murders bearing the trademarks of a killer executed about the same time the priest died.

Anyway, there's a guy in chains over at the nuthouse who sometimes appears to Scott as Karras (Jason Miller) and sometimes as the executed killer (Brad Dourif), and it's all very confusing.

It would be downright incomprehensible, in fact, if Dourif didn't do such a dandy job in explaining things in a couple of long, madman monologs.

• •

■ EXPERIMENT IN TERROR

1962, 123 MINS, US Ⓥ

Dir Blake Edwards   *Prod* Blake Edwards   *Scr* Mildred Gordon, Gordon Gordon   *Ph* Philip Lathrop   *Ed* Patrick McCormack   *Mus* Henry Mancini   *Art Dir* Robert Peterson
● Glenn Ford, Lee Remick, Stefanie Powers, Roy Poole, Ned Glass, Anita Loo (Columbia)

Written by Mildred and Gordon Gordon from their book and *Ladies' Home Journal* serial *Operation Terror*. The film treatment embraces a number of unnecessary character bits that merely extend the plot and, despite their striking individual reaction, deter from the suspense buildup.

Edwards' particular interest seems to lie in the camera angles. He concentrates on overhead shots and unusual perspective merely for visual effect. Only in the climactic scenes, which take place in San Francisco's Candlestick Park during an actual baseball game of capacity attendance, does the overhead filming become fully valuable.

The 'experiment' is a terrifying episode in which a bank teller is forced by a psychopathic killer into embezzling $100,000 under threat of murder. She goes to the FBI.

Glenn Ford and Lee Remick play the FBI agent and bank teller, respectively. For Remick it is a handsome role played with nicely-modulated control and a natural feeling that is devoid of the extreme emotional tension often exposed in such characters. Ford has solidarity, but his role is merely that of a staunch agent doing his job well.

Picture was shot extensively in San Francisco, though story could be placed in any area. However, Philip Lathrop's camera took fine advantage of known Bay City landmarks, giving the film a nice visual style.

••••••••••••••••••••••••••••••••

■ EXPLORERS

1985, 109 MINS, US ◇ ⓥ

Dir Joe Dante *Prod* Edward S. Feldman *Scr* Eric Luke *Ph* John Hora *Ed* Tina Hirsch *Mus* Jerry Goldsmith *Art Dir* Robert F. Boyle
● Ethan Hawke, River Phoenix, Jason Presson, Amanda Peterson, Dick Miller, Robert Picardo (Paramount/Industrial Light & Magic)

Two young boys, a dreamer (Ethan Hawke) and a nerdy science genius type (River Phoenix), manage, through combining their talents and happening upon an unusual discovery, to fashion a homemade spacecraft.

In league with a lower-class misfit (Jason Presson) who falls in with them, the lads inventively use a leftover Tilt-A-Whirl as their basic chassis and elaborate upon their design with spare parts of all kinds.

Along with their extracurricular Advanced Shop work, opening hour is occupied with passable but far from original stuff devoted to bullies vs nerds, puppy love and schoolroom antics.

Throughout, director Joe Dante and writer Eric Luke load the proceedings with references to sci-fiers of an earlier day, such as *War of the Worlds*, *This Island Earth*, *Journey to the Center of the Earth* and many others, but this is nothing compared to what happens when the trio of youngsters finally take off into outer space and make contact with an alien race.

••••••••••••••••••••••••••••••••

■ EXPOSED

1983, 100 MINS, US ◇ ⓥ

Dir James Toback *Prod* James Toback *Scr* James Toback *Ph* Henri Decae *Ed* Robert Lawrence, Annie Charvein *Mus* Georges Delerue *Art Dir* Brian Eatwell
● Nastassja Kinski, Rudolf Nureyev, Harvey Keitel, Ian McShane, Bibi Andersson, Ron Randell (M-G-M/United Artists)

Intelligent and illogical, beautiful and erratic, *Exposed* is a provocative, jet-setter's visit to the worlds of high fashion and international terrorism.

After a prolog in which a foxy blonde is observed blowing up a Paris cafe, writer-director James Toback himself, as a college English teacher, breaks up romantically with one of his students (Nastassja Kinski).

Kinski returns to her home in Wisconsin and, in one of the film's most striking, and convincing, sequences, is attending an exhibition of photos featuring her when her eye is caught by Rudolf Nureyev.

After a bizarre, cat-and-mouse courtship, the inevitable big love scene arrives. As it happens, Nureyev is also a dedicated terrorist fighter with intensely personal motives, and when Kinski follows him to Paris, she naively becomes involved with the very forces Nureyev is intent upon wiping out. Kinski is delivered into the lair of Carlos-type terrorist Harvey Keitel, a provocateur dedicated to random violence.

Performers seem to have been chosen mostly for their physical attributes, and Kinski and Nureyev lead the way in ably fleshing out characters who are meant to remain mysterious.

••••••••••••••••••••••••••••••••

■ EXPRESSO BONGO

1959, 111 MINS, UK ⓥ

Dir Val Guest *Prod* Val Guest *Scr* Wolf Mankowitz *Ph* John Wilcox *Ed* Bill Lenny *Mus* Monty Norman, Robert Farnon, Norrie Paramor, Bunny Lewis
● Laurence Harvey, Sylvia Syms, Yolande Donlan, Cliff Richard, Meier Tzelniker, Ambrosine Philpotts (British Lion/Britannia)

Soho, with its atmosphere of sleazy stripperies, gaudy coffee bars and frenetic teenagers, is the setting for this amusing satire on how a little talent can be boosted overnight as the result of a successful disk and a click TV appearance. Wolf Mankowitz's story [from his own play] is slight and not particularly original, but it has pungency, wit and a sharp sense of observation.

Laurence Harvey is a cheap, opportunistic promoter, always on the lookout for an easy buck. In a Soho expresso bar, he picks up an amateur singer and bongo player, signs him up on a dubious contract and boosts him to what is now regarded as stardom.

Harvey gives a brashly amusing, offbeat performance as the smalltime operator while Sylvia Syms is cast as a stripper with aspirations towards stardom as a singer. Expresso Bongo is played by Cliff Richard, a wrong piece of casting. The songs are intended to spoof the whole business of pop crooning but they come over, in Richard's larynx, as completely feasible entries into the pop market. Meier Tzelniker plays the part which he did so well on the stage. He's boss of a disk company and here's an excellent characterization – flamboyant, garrulous and only slightly exaggerated.

••••••••••••••••••••••••••••••••

■ EXTERMINATOR, THE

1980, 101 MINS, US ◇ ⓥ

Dir James Glickenhaus *Prod* Mark Buntzman *Scr* James Glickenhaus *Ph* Bob Baldwin *Ed* Corky O'Hara *Mus* Joe Renzetti
● Christopher George, Samantha Eggar, Robert Ginty, Steve James (Interstar)

For his second pic, writer-director James Glickenhaus commits the major sin of shooting an action film with little action. Contrived script instead opts for grotesque violence in a series of glum, distasteful scenes.

The Exterminator returns to New York City for a listlessly paced tale of Robert Ginty suddenly deciding to avenge his war buddy, paralyzed from an encounter with a youth gang. Absence of proper transition scenes and script's frequent reliance upon coincidence loses credibility for Ginty's actions early on.

Christopher George's walkthrough as a policeman is regrettable, while Samantha Eggar as both the buddy's doctor and George's girlfriend must have calculated that this travesty would never be released.

••••••••••••••••••••••••••••••••

■ EXTRAORDINARY SEAMAN, THE

1969, 79 MINS, US ◇

Dir John Frankenheimer *Prod* Edward Lewis, John H. Cushingham *Scr* Phillip Rock, Hal Dresner *Ph* Lionel Linden *Ed* Fredric Steinkamp *Mus* Maurice Jarre *Art Dir* George W. Davis, Edward Carfagno
● David Niven, Faye Dunaway, Alan Alda, Mickey Rooney, Jack Carter (M-G-M)

The Extraordinary Seaman is strictly steerage cargo. A tepid story keel, not entirely – but almost – devoid of amusement strength, has been ballasted with padding newsreel footage and other effect to yield an unstable comedy vessel. David Niven, Faye Dunaway, Alan Alda, Mickey Rooney and Jack Carter end up awash in the artistic debris.

Set in the Philippines where three US Navy men, in flight from the Japanese, discover an urbane Niven, as a Royal Navy officer, living in uncanny nattiness aboard a beached ship. Dunaway joins the crew as Niven sets sail for Australia.

To simulate the original environment, pic was shot in Baja, California, but what shows in the final cut could have been shot off Santa Barbara.

••••••••••••••••••••••••••••••••

■ EXTREME PREJUDICE

1987, 104 MINS, US ◇ ⓥ

Dir Walter Hill *Prod* Buzz Feitshans *Scr* Deric Washburn, Harry Kleiner *Ph* Matthew F. Leonetti *Ed* Freeman Davis *Mus* Jerry Goldsmith *Art Dir* Albert Heschong
● Nick Nolte, Powers Boothe, Michael Ironside, Maria Conchita Alonso, Rip Torn, Clancy Brown (Carolco)

Extreme Prejudice is an amusing concoction that is frequently offbeat and at times compelling. Taut direction and editing prevail despite overstaged hyper-violence that is so gratuitous to be farcical.

Story pivots on the adversarial relationship between small town Texas Ranger Nick Nolte and drug kingpin Powers Boothe. Originally childhood friends, they are now on opposite sides of the law and the US-Mexican border.

Presented as a severe and humorless straight arrow, Nolte's character is not easy to like but his acting nonetheless intrigues. Freewheeling and provocative, Boothe is the film's wild card as director Walter Hill signals right off that he's going to have some fun here.

Story proceeds through some interesting twists on the commando front while Nolte and Boothe try to reconcile their friendship and separate paths.

••••••••••••••••••••••••••••••••

■ EXTREMITIES

1986, 90 MINS, US ◇ ⓥ

Dir Robert M. Young *Prod* Burt Sugarman *Scr* William Mastrosimone *Ph* Curtis Clark *Ed* Arthur Coburn *Mus* J.A.C. Redford *Art Dir* Chester Kaczenski
● Farrah Fawcett, James Russo, Diana Scarwid, Alfre Woodard (Atlantic)

Playwright William Mastrosimone adapted his 1982 off-Broadway work for the screen, but it seems to be director Robert M. Young who is responsible for virtually exploiting cinema's power to propel the viewer into the on-screen action.

Marjorie (Farrah Fawcett) is a museum employee on her way home from work and a workout. A ski-masked assailant imprisons and terrorizes her in her own car.

Marjorie manages to escape but the attacker knows her identity and address. Successive events document the trials of any woman in a similar predicament: essentially unsympathetic police and friends.

Finally, Marjorie's worst nightmare comes true. She is visited at her secluded home by the man who attacked her (James Russo).

Fawcett, who acquainted herself with the role of Marjorie on stage, following Susan Sarandon and Karen Allen, acts with a confidence and control not often seen in her screen work.

••••••••••••••••••••••••••••••••

■ EYE FOR AN EYE, AN

1981, 106 MINS, US ◇

Dir Steve Carver *Prod* Frank Capra Jr *Scr* William Gray, James Bruner *Ph* Roger Shearman *Ed* Anthony Redman *Mus* William Golstein *Art Dir* Vance Lorenzini
● Chuck Norris, Christopher Lee, Richard Roundtree, Mako, Rosalind Chao, Maggie Cooper (Avco Embassy/Wescom)

An Eye for an Eye is an effective martial arts actioner vehicle for Chuck Norris.

Norris toplines as a San Francisco cop who quits the force and goes after revenge when his partner and partner's girlfriend are killed by drug traffickers. Aided by his former police boss Capt Stevens (Richard Roundtree),

Norris evens the accounts and takes care of the drug ring.

Making solid atmospheric use of SF locations, helmer Steve Carver segues from realistic violence and tension to comic strip hokum in the form of a huge oriental villain (Toru Tanaka) whose menacing antics tip the audience that the film is all in fun.

Format has Norris, in traditional Western genre fashion, helped and jeckled by an old pro 'master' James Chan (Mako), whose wise-cracks provide comic relief.

....

■ **EYE OF THE CAT**

1969, 102 MINS, US ◇

Dir David Lowell Rich *Prod* Bernard Schwartz, Phillip Hazelton *Scr* Joseph Stefano *Ph* Russell Metty, Ellsworth Fredricks *Ed* J. Terry Williams *Mus* Lalo Schifrin *Art Dir* Alexander Golitzen, William D. DeCinces

● Michael Sarrazin, Gayle Hunnicutt, Eleanor Parker, Tim Henry, Laurence Naismith, Jennifer Leak (Universal)

Pic has a few good jolts, successful buildups, and good looking people, but stilted dialog and plot shot through with holes keep mystery at a minimum, suspense overdue. Despite San Francisco as backdrop, with North Beach and Sausalito tossed in for spice, film trips over its own cliches and errors.

Beautician Kassia (Gayle Hunnicutt), after witnessing emphysema attack of wealthy San Francisco matron Danny (Eleanor Parker), finds Danny's runaway favorite nephew Wylie (Michael Sarrazin).

Kassia plans to re-establish Wylie in the house and, after Aunt Danny changes her will in his favor, murder her and split the fortune.

David Lowell Rich's direction often misleads, but he does manage to get actors to speak bad lines with straight faces.

....

■ **EYE OF THE DEVIL**

1968, 89 MINS, UK

Dir J. Lee Thompson *Prod* Martin Ransohoff, John Colley *Scr* Robin Estridge, Dennis Murphy *Ph* Erwin Hillier *Ed* Ernest Walter *Mus* Gary McFarland *Art Dir* Elliot Scott

● Deborah Kerr, David Niven, Donald Pleasence, Edward Mulhare, Flora Robson, Sharon Tate (M-G-M/Filmways)

Originally titled *13*, film has a production history far more interesting than the final cut. From files, names of Julie Andrews and Kim Novak appear, latter forced out by an accident, after production started, and replaced by Deborah Kerr. Script-wise, *Day of the Arrow*, a Philip Loraine novel, went from Terry Southern (unbilled) to Robin Estridge, who shares screen credit with Dennis Murphy, engaged just before shooting.

The directorial montage includes Sidney J. Furie, Arthur Hiller and Michael Anderson, latter dropping out on medic's orders, with J. Lee Thompson taking over reins.

David Niven, a vineyard manor lord, is called back to his property because of another dry season. Kerr, against his wishes, follows with their children (Suky Appleby and Robert Duncan), latter acting mysteriously at start and finish. At the gloomy ancestral home, characters include Donald Pleasence, the local 'priest', butler Donald Bisset, Flora Robson, Niven's aunt who knows (and finally tells) what is going on, and Emlyn Williams, Niven's father.

Sharon Tate and David Hemmings loom as paper threats who speak deadpan dialog about the goings on. Kerr is our only touch with reality, and she tries to carry the pic, to little avail.

....

■ **EYE OF THE NEEDLE**

1981, 111 MINS, UK ◇

Dir Richard Marquand *Prod* Stephen Friedman *Scr* Stanley Mann *Ph* Alan Hume *Ed* Sean Barton *Mus* Miklos Rozsa *Art Dir* Wilfrid Shingleton

● Donald Sutherland, Kate Nelligan, Ian Bannen, Christopher Cazenove (United Artists/Kings Road)

As a study of a ruthless, essentially unsympathetic killer, working for the wrong side, *Eye of the Needle* [from the 1978 best seller by Ken Follett] perhaps resembles *The Day of the Jackal*. Similarly, this tale of subtle intrigue and skilled maneuvers works rather better in print than on film.

Steely blue-eyed Donald Sutherland is introduced as a low-level British railway functionary in 1940. In prolog, Sutherland is shown murdering his friendly landlady when she discovers him working with a short-wave radio, and newlyweds Kate Nelligan and Christopher Cazenove suffer a horrible auto accident as they speed off on their honeymoon.

Cut to four years later, and Sutherland is soon revealed as perhaps Berlin's most reliable spy still working undetected within Britain. Armed with photos of a phony airbase in Eastern England, Sutherland makes his way to the aptly named Storm Island to rendezvous with a U-boat, waiting there to take him to Germany.

In the meantime, Nelligan and Cazenove have resettled on the bleak outpost of civilization. Formerly a dashing pilot, the latter has become a bitter paraplegic as a result of the accident, so his beauteous wife readily responds to the mysterious stranger when he temporarily lands in their household.

It's a good yarn, remindful of some of Alfred Hitchcock and Fritz Lang's wartime mellers as well as Michael Powell's 1939 tale of a World War I German agent in Scotland, *The Spy in Black*.

....

■ **EYE OF THE TIGER**

1986, 90 MINS, US ◇ Ⓥ

Dir Richard Sarafian *Prod* Tony Scotti *Scr* Michael Montgomery *Ph* Peter Collister *Ed* Greg Prange *Art Dir* Wayne Springfield

● Gary Busey, Yaphet Kotto, Seymour Cassel, Bert Remsen, William Smith (Scotti Bros)

Gary Busey is yet another lone vigilante out to avenge his wife's brutal murder in *Eye of the Tiger*. The pic opens with Buck Matthews' (Busey) release from prison. Matthews' hometown is being terrorized by a gang of motorcycle-riding drug peddlers, all of whom wear black with black helmets and ride in packs.

The motorcycle gang makes a visit to Matthews' house, killing his wife, beating him up and sending their daughter into a catatonic state. The rest of the film is about Matthews' one-man quest for vengeance, most of which is set to the pounding beat of rock music. The best character in the film is J.B. Deveraux (Yaphet Kotto), one of the sheriff's lackeys.

....

■ **EYES OF LAURA MARS**

1978, 104 MINS, US ◇ Ⓥ

Dir Irvin Kershner *Prod* Jon Peters *Scr* John Carpenter, David Zelag Goodman *Ph* Victor J. Kemper *Ed* Michael Kahn *Mus* Artie Kane *Art Dir* Gene Callahan

● Faye Dunaway, Tommy Lee Jones, Brad Dourif, Rene Auberjonois, Raul Julia, Frank Adonis (Columbia)

Eyes of Laura Mars is a very stylish thriller in search of a better ending.

Faye Dunaway stars as a chic fashion photographer with mysterious and accurate premonitions about a series of murders. All of the victims are either friends or associates.

Tommy Lee Jones, in an inspired bit of casting, plays a police lieutenant assigned to the case and an integral element in the mystery. Brad Dourif as Dunaway's driver, Rene Auberjonois as her trendy and obnoxious manager and Raul Julia as her ex-husband, add marvelous supporting performances.

Especially well handled are the screen realizations of Dunaway's premonitions. They look like a blurred videotape, as she explains to Jones at one point, a conception which works well on screen.

The relationships among the characters, Dunaway's portrayal of a chic and haggard photographer-artist and even the choice of Helmut Newton and Rebecca Blake's violent and stark photos as the work of the fictional Dunaway character are satisfying and engaging.

....

■ **EYEWITNESS**

1981, 102 MINS, US ◇

Dir Peter Yates *Prod* Peter Yates *Scr* Steve Tesich *Ph* Mathew F. Leonetti *Ed* Cynthia Scheider *Mus* Stanley Silverman *Art Dir* Philip Rosenberg

● William Hurt, Sigourney Weaver, Christopher Plummer, James Woods, Irene Worth, Morgan Freeman (20th Century-Fox)

Once an office-building janitor himself, writer Steve Tesich often wondered in the quiet of the night what evil deeds might be going on behind closed doors. Enter William Hurt on the night-shift discovering the murdered body of a mysterious Chinese businessman.

Tesich's other fantasy concerned a real-life infatuation with a lady reporter on CBS, wondering what she would be like and how far he would go to meet her. Hurt, too, has an obsession for newswoman Sigourney Weaver, so consuming he videotapes her every show to linger over.

When Weaver comes to his building to report on the murder, Hurt pretends to know something secret to prolong this unexpected encounter with his distant sweetheart. That in turn leads him into danger with assorted characters – Christopher Plummer in particular – who really do know something about the murder.

Weaver plays her part very well, but simply can't justify the character's actions, which ripple through the murder plot in several directions. Consequently, the story gets more and more strained before it's resolved.

....

■ **FABULOUS BAKER BOYS, THE**

1989, 113 MINS, US ◇ Ⓥ

Dir Steve Kloves *Prod* Paula Weinstein, Mark Rosenberg *Scr* Steve Kloves *Ph* Michael Ballhaus *Ed* William Steinkamp *Mus* Dave Grusin *Art Dir* Jeffrey Townsend

● Jeff Bridges, Michelle Pfeiffer, Beau Bridges, Elie Raab, Jennifer Tilly (Gladden/Mirage)

There's nothing startlingly original about this smoothly made little romantic comedy of two piano-playing brothers who find an attractive young singer to give some much needed CPR to their dying lounge act.

The first look at cynical, seen-it-all Jack Baker (Jeff Bridges) and his bubbling, ever-optimistic brother Frank (Beau Bridges) tells us that's necessary to know about them.

When they're joined by sexy-surly singer Susie Diamond (Michelle Pfeiffer), it's obvious exactly where the film is headed. Jack and Susie are on a romantic collision course, with Frank bound to be hurt by the explosion.

The fun part is seeing it all play out, thanks to a standout cast and first-time director Steve Kloves' skill in handling them.

The focus of all eyes is on Pfeiffer. The actress, who does all her own singing, is required to play a character whose vocal abilities are good, but not so good as to make a viewer wonder why she hasn't been signed to a major label. Pfeiffer hits the nail right on the head.

She also hits the spot in the film's certain-to-be-remembered highlight – a version of 'Makin' Whoopee' that she sings while crawling all over a piano in a blazing red dress. She's dynamite.

....

■ **FACE IN THE CROWD, A**

1957, 125 MINS, US ⑲

Dir Elia Kazan *Prod* Elia Kazan *Scr* Budd Schulberg *Ph* Harry Stradling, Gayne Rescher *Ed* Gene Milford *Mus* Tom Glazer *Art Dir* Richard Sylbert, Paul Sylbert
● Andy Griffith, Patricia Neal, Anthony Franciosa, Walter Matthau, Lee Remick (Newtown/Warner)

Elia Kazan and Budd Schulberg, who teamed to bring forth *On the Waterfront*, have another provocative and hardhitting entry, based on Schulberg's short story *The Arkansas Traveler*. It's a devastating commentary on hero-worship and success cults in America.

Its basic story is somewhat similar to that of *The Great Man* in that it exposes a beloved television personality as an unmitigated heel.

Story plucks an ignorant guitar-playing hillbilly from an Arkansas jail and converts him in a short space of time to America's most popular and beloved television personality. He is in private life an unsavory character, a libertine and an opportunist with loyalty to no one but himself. He enters the political arena, becomes aligned with an 'isolationist' senator, and pitches an extreme reactionary philosophy.

Andy Griffith makes his film debut as Lonesome Rhodes, the power-mad hillbilly. As his vis-a-vis, Patricia Neal is the girl who guides Griffith to fame and fortune. Anthony Franciosa plays the unprincipled personal manager, Walter Matthau a cynical writer.

....

■ **FACES**

1968, 130 MINS, US

Dir John Cassavetes *Prod* Maurice McEndree *Scr* John Cassavetes *Ph* Al Ruban *Ed* Maurice McEndree *Mus* Jack Ackerman *Art Dir* Phedon Papamichael
● John Marley, Gena Rowlands, Lynn Carlin, Fred Draper, Seymour Cassel (Maurice McEndree)

Faces is a long, long (at least an hour too long) look at a 36-hour splitup in the 14-year marriage of a middle-class couple. At least John Cassavetes, who also wrote the screenplay, describes them as middle-class.

As the result of tensions, inhibitions created by years of trying to adjust, and temporary clashes of personality, John Marley and his wife, played frigidly by Lynn Carlin, clash and Marley leaves the house for the temporary emotional warmth of an attractive prostitute (Gena Rowlands).

Most of the running time of the film is devoted to a melange of observing the husband and wife seeking emotional outlets outside their home; the husband with the prostitute, the wife in a discotheque.

The film uses two homes – that of the couple and that of the prostitute – for most of the action. Rowlands and a few other members of the cast are superior to their material but they're unable to breathe life into an overblown opus.

....

■ **FAHRENHEIT 451**

1966, 113 MINS, UK ◇ ⑲

Dir Francois Truffaut *Prod* Lewis M. Allen
Scr Francois Truffaut, Jean-Louis Richard *Ph* Nicolas Roeg *Ed* Thom Nobie *Mus* Bernard Herrmann *Art Dir* Syd Cain
● Oskar Werner, Julie Christie, Cyril Cusack, Anton Diffring, Jeremy Spenser, Bee Duffell (Anglo-Enterprise Vineyard/Universal)

With a serious and even terrifying theme, this excursion into science fiction has been thoughtfully directed by Francois Truffaut and there is adequate evidence of light touches to bring welcome and needed relief to a sombre and scarifying subject.

In author Ray Bradbury's glimpse into the future, books are considered the opium of the people. Their possession is a crime and the state has a squad of firemen to destroy the illicit literature with flame throwers. Fahrenheit 451, it is explained, is the temperature at which books are reduced to ashes.

The yarn develops just a handful of characters, emphasising the inevitable conflict between state and literate-minded citizens. One of the principals is Montag (Oskar Werner) an obedient and lawful fireman, who does his book destroying job with efficiency and apparent enthusiasm, while his equally law-abiding wife (Julie Christie) spends her days glued to the mural TV screen.

A young probationary school teacher (also played by Christie) whom Montag meets on the monorail while on the way to the fire station, plants the first seeds of doubt in his mind, and from then on he regularly steals the odd book which he reads secretly.

Werner, in the difficult role of the once diffident and ambitious fireman who finally challenges authority, plays the part in low key style which adds to the integrity of the character, and Christie is standout in her dual roles.

Cyril Cusack plays the fire station captain with horrifying dedication, and Anton Diffring is effectively cast as a heavy who has caught Montag in the book stealing act.

....

■ **FAIL SAFE**

1964, 112 MINS, US ⑲

Dir Sidney Lumet *Prod* Max E. Youngstein
Scr Walter Bernstein *Ph* Gerald Hirschfeld *Ed* Ralph Rosenblum *Mus* [none] *Art Dir* Albert Brenner
● Henry Fonda, Walter Matthau, Frank Overton, Dan O'Herlihy, Fritz Weaver, Larry Hagman (Columbia)

Fail Safe is a tense and suspenseful piece of filmmaking dealing with the frightening implications of accidental nuclear warfare. It faithfully translates on the screen the power and seething drama of the Eugene Burdick-Harvey Wheeler book, capturing the full menace of the Strategic Air Command's fail-safe device in respect to its possible malfunction, and paints a vivid canvas of an imaginary situation which conceivably could arise.

An earlier Columbia release, *Dr Strangelove* dealt with precisely the same situation: a US plane loaded with hydrogen bombs is flying toward Moscow and because of technical difficulties barring any communication it is impossible to recall the bomber before it can drop its deadly cargo which unquestionably will launch a world holocaust.

Identical basic premise and attendant situations between the two story properties led to Columbia and others attached to the production of *Strangelove* to file a Federal Court suit against the authors of *Fail Safe*, the book's publishers and the production company – ECA – which had announced it would film the tome. Charge was made that *Safe* was plagiarized from book on which *Strangelove* was based. Controversy was finally resolved when Columbia took over the financing-distribution of *Safe* and Max E. Youngstein,

whose ECA unit had planned its indie production before dissolving, swung over as producer.

Fail Safe is a gripping narrative realistically and almost frighteningly told as the US goes all-out to halt the plane carrying the bombs, even to the extent of trying to shoot it down and advising the Russians of their peril and urging them to destroy the plane. Particularly dramatic are the sequences in which the president – tellingly portrayed by Henry Fonda – talks with the Russian premier over the 'hot wire'.

Fonda is the only big name in the cast, which uniformly is topflight and socks over respective roles. Frank Overton, as the general in charge of the SAC base in Omaha, home of the fail-safe mechanism which fails to act properly, is a particular standout; Dan O'Herlihy, Edward Binns and Fritz Weaver score as army officers; Walter Matthau as a professor who urges that the US attack the Soviets, and Larry Hagman as the president's interpreter.

....

■ **FALCON AND THE SNOWMAN, THE**

1985, 131 MINS, US ◇ ⑲

Dir John Schlesinger *Prod* Gabriel Katzka, John Schlesinger *Scr* Steven Zaillian *Ph* Allen Daviau *Ed* Richard Marden *Mus* Pat Metheny *Art Dir* James D. Bissell
● Timothy Hutton, Sean Penn, David Suchet, Lori Singer, Pat Hingle, Dorian Harewood (Hemdale)

All the way through *The Falcon and the Snowman* director John Schlesinger and an exemplary cast grapple with a true story so oddly motivated it would be easily dismissed if fictional.

Working backwards from a 1977 espionage trial, newspaperman Robert Lindsey wrote a book examining how an idealistic 22-year-old college dropout and a wacked-out drug pusher carried off a successful scheme to sell US secrets to the Soviets. With one working with a mind confused by addled loyalties and the other with a mind confused by chemicals, it remains hard to fathom exactly what they hoped to achieve or how they managed to progress so far toward achieving it.

As the two lads, however, Timothy Hutton and Sean Penn are superb. As the one who comes into unexpected access to state secrets, Hutton has the tougher job in making treason at all sympathetic while Penn is left with the shallower part of the deteriorating druggie, to which he nonetheless adds necessary dimensions.

....

■ **FALLEN ANGEL**

1945, 97 MINS, US

Dir Otto Preminger *Prod* Otto Preminger *Scr* Harry Kleiner *Ph* Joseph LaShelle *Ed* Harry Reynolds *Mus* David Raksin *Art Dir* Lyle R. Wheeler, Leland Fuller
● Alice Faye, Dana Andrews, Linda Darnell, Charles Bickford, Anne Revere (20th Century-Fox)

There are lapses in *Angel* from the story viewpoint and character development, but these are few and unlikely to militate against the film's over-all entertainment values. Pic deals with a trollop (Linda Darnell) who gets a flock of guys on the string, then gets bumped off. The yarn [from a novel by Marty Holland] revolves around which of her admirers committed the deed.

Linked to the plot is the story's basic romantic tie up between Alice Faye and Dana Andrews, the former as a respectable, wealthy small-town gal who is ripe for the takings, and Andrews is the guy who starts out to do the taking, even marrying her to do it, his idea being to get enough moola so he can cop the other gal.

F

This is Faye's first straight dramatic part and she handles herself well, generally, though her one dramatic scene could have gotten better direction. Andrews remains one of the better young dramatic actors in this film though his character is not always too clearly defined in the writing. Darnell looks the trollop part and plays it well.

••••••••••••••••••••••••••••••

■ **FALLEN IDOL, THE**

1948, 94 MINS, UK ⓥ

Dir Carol Reed   *Prod* Carol Reed   *Scr* Graham Greene   *Ph* Georges Perinal   *Ed* Oswald Hafenrichter   *Mus* William Alwyn   *Art Dir* Vincent Korda

● Ralph Richardson, Michele Morgan, Bobby Henrey, Sonia Dresdel, Jack Hawkins, Dora Bryan (London)

A fine sensitive story, a brilliant child star and a polished cast, headed by Ralph Richardson and Michele Morgan, combine to make *The Fallen Idol* a satisfying piece of intelligent entertainment.

Based on a short story by Graham Greene, the script develops the triangle drama with powerful dramatic force. Briefly, it's a story of the frustrated marriage of a butler, working at a foreign embassy in London, who's in love with an embassy typist. While the lovers are together, the wife, who has pretended to be in the country, comes in and after a hysterical row with her husband, accidentally falls and is killed.

Dominating the entire theme is young Felipe, son of the ambassador, who is left in the servants' care while the parents are away. The butler, Baines, and the boy are great friends, but Mrs Baines and Felipe are not. When a police investigation suggests that the wife might have been murdered, Felipe lies for all he is worth to defend the butler.

There's hardly a scene in the picture in which the kid, played by Bobby Henrey, doesn't appear and he comes through like a seasoned trouper. Setting the high standard for the acting is Ralph Richardson, whose masterly portrayal of the butler is a gratifying piece of work.

••••••••••••••••••••••••••••••

■ **FALLING IN LOVE**

1984, 107 MINS, US ◊ ⓥ

Dir Ulu Grosbard   *Prod* Marvin Worth   *Scr* Michael Cristofer   *Ph* Peter Suschitzky   *Ed* Michael Kahn   *Mus* Dave Grusin   *Art Dir* Santo Loquasto

● Robert De Niro, Meryl Streep, Harvey Keitel, Jane Kaczmarek, George Martin, Dianne Wiest (Paramount)

Falling in Love is a polite little romance, the ambition and appeal of which are modestly slight. Dynamic starring duo of Robert De Niro and Meryl Streep keeps the film afloat most of the time.

Both De Niro, a construction engineer, and Streep, a graphic-designer, have marriages which, while not unhappy, have settled into the routine. Meeting in Manhattan and on the commuter train to and from Westchester County, they are compelled to continue seeing one another, but are unsure where it's all headed. More quickly than Streep, De Niro decides he wants to have an affair, but she can't make up her mind.

De Niro is charming and, like Streep, plenty of fun to watch, but he is very contained here compared to his usual work.

••••••••••••••••••••••••••••••

■ **FALLING IN LOVE AGAIN**

1980, 103 MINS, US ◊ ⓥ

Dir Steven Paul   *Prod* Steven Paul   *Scr* Steven Paul, Ted Allan, Susannah York   *Ph* Michael Mileham, Dick Bush, Wolfgang Suschitzky   *Ed* Bud Smith, Doug Jackson, Jacqueline Cambas   *Mus* Michel Legrand

● Elliott Gould, Susannah York, Michelle Pfeiffer, Kay Ballard, Robert Hackman, Steven Paul (OTA)

Elliott Gould is perfectly cast as Harry Lewis, a New Yorker entering middle age, suffering the usual crisis and recalling the good old days of his youth. On a cross-country trip by car with his family, Gould narrates flashbacks of his romance with Susannah York in the 1940s.

Lewis went after and married the beautiful, 'unattainable' rich girl. His hopes of career success did not materialize, with duo currently owning a clothing business.

Young actor-turned director Steven Paul shot *Falling in Love Again* in 1979 at age 20, but his feel for a past era and emphasis upon old-fashioned (but still effective) picture values bely his youthful status. Pic artfully captures the 1940s look and feel.

Michelle Pfeiffer makes a strong impression as York's younger self.

••••••••••••••••••••••••••••••

■ **FALL OF THE ROMAN EMPIRE, THE**

1964, 185 MINS, US ◊ ⓥ

Dir Anthony Mann   *Prod* Samuel Bronston   *Scr* Ben Barzman, Basilio Franchina, Philip Yordan   *Ph* Robert Krasker   *Ed* Robert Lawrence   *Mus* Dimitri Tiomkin   *Art Dir* Veniero Colasanti, John Moore

● Alec Guinness, Sophia Loren, Stephen Boyd, James Mason, Christopher Plummer, Omar Sharif (Bronston)

This made-in-Spain production is a giant-size, three-hour, sweepingly pictorial entertainment. It probably tells all that most film fans will want to know about the glory, grandeur and greed of Rome.

The production reeks of expense – harness and hay for all those horses, arroz con pollo for all those Spanish extras, annuities for all those stars. Attention will focus upon the marblesque replica of downtown Rome in pagan days with temples, squares, forums, statuary, mosaic floors, columned chambers, luxury suites and a plunge for Caesar. If these sets cost a fortune they pay off in stunning camera angles.

The story gets under way speedily. Marcus Aurelius (Alec Guinness) has been campaigning for years in the bleak northern frontiers of Rome. He is dying and knows it, intends to disinherit his undependable son and neglects to do so. Stephen Boyd, a true-blue Tribune, will not claim the succession but instead supports the son, his old wrestling club chum Commodus. The entire subsequent plot swings on the failure of intention of the noble and just emperor to assure the continued peace and prosperity of Rome. In all of which the daughter, played attractively by Sophia Loren, is a desperately unhappy witness and victim.

There is much dialog about the factors which favor, and which oppose, good relations among peoples. The arrogance and cynicism in the Senate is part and parcel of the decline, as much as the vain and cruel Commodus, a man quick with the torch to homes, merciless in the ordering of wholesale crucifixions.

This anti-intellectual sadist is played with smiling malice by Christopher Plummer. He, Guinness and James Mason as a cultivated and honorable Roman minister to Marcus Aurelius pretty much wrap up the acting honors.

••••••••••••••••••••••••••••••

■ **FALSE IDENTITY**

1990, 92 MINS, US ◊

Dir James Keach   *Prod* James Shavick   *Scr* Sandra Bailey   *Ph* Bernard Aurox   *Art Dir* Kevin Ryan

● Genevieve Bujold, Stacy Keach, Tobin Bell, Mike Champion, Veronica Cartwright (RKO)

This low-energy murder mystery, slow-moving and seamily produced, casts Stacy Keach as a man presumed dead who returns to his hometown after 17 years in prison. He tries to piece together his identity, but he's hampered by the fact that his face was carved up in a murder attempt. He also has a steel plate in his head.

Genevieve Bujold reprises her *Choose Me* assignment as a radio personality, but this time she's a terrier-like reporter who's gotten hold of a dirty bone involving the murder, some 20 years ago, of a local Vietnam vet.

Keach's role requires him to lurch around with a numbed brain in a project that has no discernible aspirations beyond its dubious entertainment value. Bujold, too, suffers some diminishment in these dim surroundings, although her performance surpasses the requirements.

••••••••••••••••••••••••••••••

■ **FAME**

1980, 134 MINS, US ◊ ⓥ

Dir Alan Parker   *Prod* David De Silva, Alan Marshall   *Scr* Christopher Gore   *Ph* Michael Seresin   *Ed* Gerry Hambling   *Mus* Michael Gore   *Art Dir* Geoffrey Kirkland

● Eddie Barth, Irene Cara, Paul McCrane, Laura Dean, Gene Anthony Ray, Anne Meara (M-G-M)

The idea behind Metro's *Fame* is that it is supposed to tell the story, via its actors, of New York's venerable High School of Performing Arts. In truth, the educational institution would have none of the project, so producers had to do with second best – the street outside the school.

Alan Parker has come up with an exposure for some of the most talented youngsters seen on screen in years. There isn't a bad performance in the lot.

The great strength of the film is in the school scenes – when it wanders away from the scholastic side as it does with increasing frequency as the overlong feature moves along, it loses dramatic intensity and slows the pace.

With all this talent, there are two individuals who are so outstanding that they dominate every scene they're in. Gene Anthony Ray, plays Leroy – a superb natural dancer, but resentful of anyone trying to help, especially a white. His continuing fight with English teacher Mrs Sherwood (Anne Meara) is the most believable plotline in the entire film.

••••••••••••••••••••••••••••••

■ **FAME IS THE SPUR**

1947, 116 MINS, UK

Dir Roy Boulting   *Prod* John Boulting   *Scr* Nigel Balchin   *Ph* Gunther Krampf   *Ed* Richard Best   *Mus* John Woodridge   *Art Dir* John Howell

● Michael Redgrave, Rosamund John, Bernard Miles (Twin Cities/F. Del Giudice)

Few writers can give poverty such an air of adventure as Howard Spring, and in the Boulting Bros he found the right producer and director. It was not an easy matter to translate Spring's workmanlike novel of a self-made politician to the screen, but the Boultings have done this with praiseworthy conscientiousness.

Having wisely discarded the flashback, the Boultings begin in 1870 when Hamer Radshaw, a lad in a north country slum, dedicates his life to better the lot of his fellow workers. The sword his grandfather picked up at Peterloo (1819), when soldiers cut down workers crying for 'bread and liberty', becomes his talisman and symbol.

Attractive, he becomes a grand rabble-rouser. With his sword he can incite men to their own death, all for the 'cause', and as a Labour Member of Parliament he takes the line of least resistance, shedding old friends when necessary, making new ones if they can help, as long as it all leads to glory and power.

Michael Redgrave gives a grand performance as the earnest young idealist who becomes the vain selfish politician. It is a difficult part, but he makes it wholly credible.

● ●

■ FAMILY BUSINESS

1989, 115 MINS, US ◇ ⊙

Dir Sidney Lumet   *Prod* Lawrence Gordon
Scr Vincent Patrick   *Ph* Andrzei Bartkowiak
Ed Andrew Mondshein   *Mus* Cy Coleman
Art Dir Robert Guerra
● Sean Connery, Dustin Hoffman, Matthew Broderick, Rosana DeSoto, Janet Carroll, Victoria Jackson (Regency/Gordon)

Sean Connery steals scenes as well as merchandise in an immensely charismatic turn in *Family Business*, a darkly comic tale about three generations brought together and torn apart by their common attraction to thievery.

Director Sidney Lumet has crafted a film with real pathos while writer Vincent Patrick (adapting his own novel) injects enough bawdy humor to create a delightful mixed bag spiced with almost a European sensibility.

The key, however, is Connery, who dives head-first into his part as amoral family patriarch Jessie.

He's an unabashed rogue well into his 60s who, when we meet him, must be bailed out of jail after savaging an off-duty cop in a bar fight. Connery cuts an irresistible figure to his sheltered Ivy League grandson (Matthew Broderick), who enlists the old man's aid to carry out a high-tech robbery.

Caught in the middle, literally and figuratively, is the boy's father (Dustin Hoffman), who once had the same relationship with his father and ended up doing hard time for it.

● ●

■ FAMILY PLOT

1976, 120 MINS, US ◇ ⊙

Dir Alfred Hitchcock   *Prod* [uncredited]   *Scr* Ernest Lehman   *Ph* Leonard J. South   *Ed* J. Terry Williams   *Mus* John Williams   *Art Dir* Henry Bumstead
● Karen Black, Bruce Dern, Barbara Harris, William Devane, Ed Lauter, Cathleen Nesbitt (Universal)

Family Plot is a dazzling achievement for Alfred Hitchcock masterfully controlling shifts from comedy to drama thoughout a highly complex plot. Witty screenplay, transplanting Victor Canning's British novel, *The Rainbird Pattern*, to a California setting, is a model of construction, and the cast is uniformly superb.

Bruce Dern and Barbara Harris are the couple who receive primary attention, a cabbie and a phony psychic trying to find the long-lost heir to the Rainbird fortune.

Dern is a more than slightly absurd figure, oddly appealing; Harris is sensational.

William Devane takes a high place in the roster of Hitchcockian rogues, while Karen Black, gives a deep resonance to her relationship with the mercurial Devane.

● ●

■ FAMILY VIEWING

1987, 86 MINS, CANADA ◇

Dir Atom Egoyan   *Scr* Atom Egoyan   *Ph* Robert Macdonald, Peter Mettler   *Ed* Atom Egoyan, Bruce Macdonald   *Mus* Michael Danna   *Art Dir* Linda Del Rosario
● David Hemblen, Aidan Tierney, Gabrielle Rose, Arsinee Khanjian, Selma Keklikian (Ego/Ontario FDC/ Canada Council/Ontario Arts Council)

He's something of a darling to the Canadian new wave cinema, but Atom Egoyan's second feature is particularly exasperating precisely because there are streaks of filmmaking talent visible through the pretentious murk of this disjointed story about a single-minded young man and his emotionally pulverized family life.

Egoyan's film stands shakily upon a glib foundation of familiar themes. These include ruptured familial communication in an impersonal urban society, the displacement of human feelings in an age of instant sensual gratification and the subsuming of modern life to the omnipresent value systems of the video tube.

At the center of all this is college graduate Van (Aidan Tierney), who lives in a high-rise co-op with his slightly kinky father Stan (David Hemblen) and dad's provocatively flirtatious mistress Sandra (Gabrielle Rose).

The devices of home movies (in which the family lives on in its happier nuclear past) and the tiresome use of b&w TV static patterns between scenes are clever mostly in the sophomoric sense. By the time Egoyan moves to bring this affair to a hopeful resolution the actors don't seem to care very much and neither should the audience.

● ●

■ FAMILY WAY, THE

1967, 114 MINS, UK ◇

Dir Roy Boulting   *Prod* John Boulting   *Scr* Bill Naughton   *Ph* Harry Waxman   *Ed* Ernest Hosler   *Mus* Paul McCartney   *Art Dir* Alan Withy
● Hayley Mills, Avril Angers, John Comer, Hywel Bennett, John Mills, Wilfred Pickles (British Lion)

Based on Bill Naughton's warm-hearted play, *All in Good Time*, and adapted by Roy Boulting and Jeffrey Dell, film is the story of an innocent young couple who marry and are unable to consummate their marriage.

The youngsters (Hayley Mills and Hywel Bennett) marry and because of circumstances have to live with the lad's parents. Even the honeymoon is a disaster since a flyaway travel agent cheats them out of their package deal trip to the Continent.

Hayley Mills gets away from her Disney image as the young bride, even essaying an undressed scene. Bennett is excellent as the sensitive young bridegroom. But it is the older hands who keep the film floating on a wave of fun, sentiment and sympathy.

John Mills is firstclass in a character role as the bluff father who cannot understand his son and produces the lower working-class man's vulgarity without overdoing it. Avril Angers as the girl's acid mother and John Comer as her husband are equally effective, but the best performance comes from Marjorie Rhodes as John Mills' astute but understanding wife.

● ●

■ FAN, THE

1949, 79 MINS, US ◇

Dir Otto Preminger   *Prod* Otto Preminger   *Scr* Walter Reisch, Dorothy Parker, Ross Evans   *Ph* Joseph LaShelle   *Ed* Louis Loeffler   *Mus* Daniele Amfitheatrof
● Jeanne Crain, Madeleine Carroll, George Sanders, Richard Greene, Martita Hunt (20th Century-Fox)

Screen adaptation [from Oscar Wilde's *Lady Windermere's Fan*] is refreshing and neatly uses the flashback technique in telling the 19th-century narrative.

Yarn of the attractive mother who moves in English society so as to be near her married daughter is deftly told. It shows her trying to prevent the daughter from making the same elopement mistake that she herself made only to become one of the most notorious women in Europe.

Madeleine Carroll makes of the young, attractive mother a vivid personality, a woman sought by wealth and nobility in nearly every European capital. Only when pictured as an elderly woman (in postwar London) does she seem a bit unconvincing. George Sanders, as her ardent lover, contributes a believable characterization. Jeanne Crain, as Lady Windermere, achieves further acting laurels.

● ●

■ FAN, THE

1981, 95 MINS, US ◇

Dir Edward Bianchi   *Prod* Robert Stigwood
Scr Priscilla Chapman, John Hartwell   *Ph* Dick Bush
Ed Alan Helm   *Mus* Pino Donaggio   *Art Dir* Santo Loquasto
● Lauren Bacall, James Garner, Maureen Stapleton, Michael Biehn, Hector Elizondo (Paramount)

Lauren Bacall makes the film [from a novel by Bob Randall] work with a solid performance as a stage star pursued by a pyschotic fan whose adoration turns to hatred. To be sure, the part doesn't test the broadest range of Bacall's abilities, but she and director Edward Bianchi achieve the essential element: they make the audience care what happens to her.

In his first major feature, TV commercials veteran Michael Biehn contributes solidly toward the picture's believability, gradually transforming his character's fantasies into a deadly delusion. The more his performance is acceptable, the more perilous is Bacall's plight.

Maureen Stapleton is also necessarily sympathetic as Bacall's likable secretary who stands between Biehn and what he perceives as true romance, setting herself up as his first victim.

James Garner is given less to do as Bacall's ex-husband, whom she still loves. Mainly, he's limited to standing around for moral support.

● ●

■ FANATIC

1965, 97 MINS, UK ◇ ⊙

Dir Silvio Narizzano   *Scr* Richard Matheson
Ph Arthur Ibbetson   *Ed* James Needs   *Mus* Wilfred Josephs
● Tallulah Bankhead, Stefanie Powers, Peter Vaughan, Maurice Kaufmann, Yootha Joyce, Donald Sutherland (Hammer)

Melodramatic script by Richard Matheson echoes with cliches from other stories set in sinister mansions in English countryside. But it provides Tallulah Bankhead with numerous chances to display virtuosity, from sweet-tongued menace to maniacal blood-lust, as religious-fanatic mother of Stefanie Powers' dead fiance.

Another standout in small cast is Peter Vaughan, ne'er-do-well major domo of manse, who has roving eye for Powers' trim figure and shapely legs, which are in sharp contrast to drabness of his housekeeper-wife, well-played by Yootha Joyce.

Story line has Powers, modern miss, paying courtesy call to former fiance's mother, only to be held prisoner while the mother tries to cleanse her soul so she will be fit to meet the son in the hereafter. Escape attempts are violently thwarted by Vaughan, Joyce and Donald Sutherland, who gives vivid portrayal of giant halfwit.

● ●

■ FANNY

1961, 133 MINS, US ◇ ⊙

Dir Joshua Logan   *Prod* Joshua Logan   *Scr* Julius J. Epstein   *Ph* Jack Cardiff   *Ed* William H. Reynolds   *Mus* Harold Rome   *Art Dir* Rino Mondellini
● Leslie Caron, Maurice Chevalier, Charles Boyer, Horst Buchholz, Salvatore Baccaloni, Lionel Jeffries (Warner)

Marcel Pagnol's enduring creation has a peculiar history. Center of a trilogy (*Marius, Fanny* and *Cesar*) penned around the early 1930s, it graduated from stage to screen in 1933 French film versions that, sans English titles, died after a week's exhibition in a New York theatre. Refurbished with titles and an additional 25 minutes in 1948, it became an unforgettable motion picture and an art

F

house click. Earlier, in 1938, Metro produced a film (a Wallace Beery starrer titled *Port of the Seven Seas*) based on the Pagnol yarn. Then, of course, there was the Broadway musical version in 1956.

Although the deep sentiment in Pagnol's tale constantly threatens to lapse into maudlinity in this film, it never quite does. Pagnol's story, skillfully adapted out of the original Marseilles Trilogy and the legit book by S. N. Behrman and Joshua Logan, focuses upon four people: a thrifty waterfront bar operator (Charles Boyer); his son (Horst Buchholz), who has a yen to sail away to the 'isles beneath the wind'; a fishmonger's daughter (Leslie Caron) in love with the wanderlustful lad; and an aging, wealthy widower (Maurice Chevalier), whose great wish is to add '& Son' to the sign above his shop.

The contribution of cameraman Jack Cardiff is enormous, ranging from great, sweeping panoramic views of the port of Marseilles and the sea to tight, intimate shots of the faces of the principals. Caron employs that Gallic gamin quality to full advantage again, Buchholz does a nice job as Marius, but a couple of old pros named Boyer and Chevalier walk off with the picture.

□ 1961: Best Picture (Nomination)

....

■ **FANNY BY GASLIGHT**

1944, 108 MINS, UK

Dir Anthony Asquith   *Prod* Edward Black   *Scr* Doreen Montgomery   *Ph* Arthur Crabtree   *Ed* R.E. Dearing   *Mus* Cedric Mallabey   *Art Dir* John Bryan
● Phyllis Calvert, James Mason, Wilfrid Lawson, Stewart Granger, Jean Kent, Nora Swinburne (Gainsborough)

Unfortunately, Anthony Asquith's direction is hurt by faulty film editing and irritatingly slow tempo. Although the script distorts the original story almost beyond recognition, there is still retained a lot of plot development in the house of ill-fame, which in the book is the main background. For all its being toned down from Michael Sadleir's frank treatment in the novel, the way the curvaceous femmes do their stuff in the underground joint hardly makes for best family trade.

As a matter of fact, the film would suffer little if all the bawdy-house sequences were removed. The main theme – the thorny path traveled by the true lovers because the man is 'well born' while the girl is an illegitimate child, foster-fathered by the bawdy housekeeper – would be preserved by the mid-Victorian pillorying they both receive.

With so many good performances, it is significant that Phyllis Calvert in the lead more than holds her own. She succeeds in portraying Fanny with girlish wistfulness and appeal.

....

■ **FANTASIA**

1940, 120 MINS, US ◇

Dir Ben Sharpsteen, Joe Grant, Dick Heumer   *Prod* Walt Disney   *Ed* Stephen Csillag   *Mus* Leopold Stokowski (dir.)
● (Walt Disney)

In *Fantasia* Walt Disney enlists the assistance of Leopold Stokowski, the Philadelphia Symphony Orchestra, and Deems Taylor as screen commentator. The result of mixing all these ingredients, including his own unique approach to things theatrical, is a two-hour $2 million-plus variety show, which spans the formidable entertainment categories ranging from a Mickey Mouse escapade in the title role of Dukas' *The Sorcerer's Apprentice* to a very lovely musical and visual interpretation of Schubert's *Ave Maria*.

The first offering is a flight of sheer fancy on the part of the Disney illustrators. The Bach number, *Toccata and Fugue in D Minor*, is nine minutes of pictorial kaleidoscope, in the course of which various gay and bizarre representations of musical instruments are flashed in grotesque shapes across the screen.

The familiar Tchaikovsky *Nutcracker Suite* is the second offering, somewhat longer, as it runs 14 minutes. Pictorially, it is a series of charming ballets, the leading and supporting characters of which are flowers, fish and fairies that cavort in whimsical surroundings.

Comes Mickey next as the mischievous apprentice in the Dukas number, in the telling of which he becomes highly and humorously involved with a broomstick.

First part closes with Stravinsky's *Rite of Spring*, the most ambitious number on the program and a 20-minute gasp for breath. Here is visualized the birth of creation, the heavenly nebulae and the placement of the solar system in the universe.

Reserved for the second part are the Beethoven *Pastoral Symphony* and Ponchielli's *Dance of the Hours*. Former is a mythological allegory, employing Zeus and others on Mt Olympus. Hamilton Luske, Jim Handley and Ford Beebe supervised the execution which is one of the loveliest tales from the Disney plant. In contrast, the studio tackles the *Dance of the Hours* in a facetious mood, burlesquing and satirizing the ballet traditions. Among the dancers are elephants, rhinos and ostriches.

Concluding film is a combination of Moussorgsky's *Night on Bald Mountain*, a terrifying exposition on evil, and the compensating *Ave Maria*, charmingly sung by Juliette Novis with appropriate decor.

....

■ **FANTASTIC VOYAGE**

1966, 100 MINS, US ◇ ▽

Dir Richard Fleischer   *Prod* Saul David   *Scr* Harry Kleiner   *Ph* Ernest Laszlo   *Ed* William B. Murphy   *Mus* Leonard Rosenman   *Art Dir* Jack Martin Smith, Dale Hennesy
● Stephen Boyd, Raquel Welch, Edmond O'Brien, Donald Pleasence, Arthur O'Connell, Arthur Kennedy (20th Century-Fox)

Fantastic Voyage is just that. The lavish production, boasting some brilliant special effects and superior creative efforts, is an entertaining, enlightening excursion through inner space – the body of a man.

The original Otto Klement-Jay Lewis Bixby story, adapted by David Duncan, has been updated and fashioned into an intriguing yarn about five people who undergo miniaturization for injection into the bloodstream of a scientist.

Action cross cuts from lifesize medics to the shrunken quintet who encounter, and are endangered by, the miracles of life.

The competent cast is headed by Stephen Boyd, the US agent who has brought scientist Jean Del Val to America, only to have a last-ditch attempt on latter's life cause the blood clot which necessitates the weird journey to come. Boyd is assigned to join the expedition under the command of Donald Pleasence, a medical specialist in circulatory systems, thus qualifying him as navigator for William Redfield's sub.

Richard Fleischer's fine direction maintains a zesty pace. Ernest Laszlo's outstanding lensing brings out every lush facet in the superb production values. Over half of the $6.5 million cost went into the special values.

....

■ **FAREWELL TO ARMS, A**

1932, 90 MINS, US ▽

Dir Frank Borzage   *Prod* Frank Borzage   *Scr* Benjamin Glazer, Oliver H. P. Garrett   *Ph* Charles Lang   *Ed* Otho Lovering   *Art Dir* Hans Dreier, Roland Anderson
● Gary Cooper, Helen Hayes, Adolphe Menjou, Mary Phillips, Jack La Rue, Henry Armetta (Paramount)

A Farewell to Arms is a corking flicker [from the novel by Ernest Hemingway]. Director Frank Borzage skims over two hyper-delicate situations with deftness and ingenuity. He makes wholly palatable (and highly believable) the premise that a fleeting one hour's meeting behind the front and the resulting seduction (Gary Cooper and Helen Hayes) is the culmination of a love which, in another sphere, would have followed only a long span of courtship and flowers.

Equally acute is the hospital situation where she, as one of the nurses, violates every regulation and remains with the convalescent Cooper in his room.

All this builds up to the finale where Cooper deserts his regiment, to brave frontiers and sentinels to ultimately reach the woman.

Casting Hayes as Catherine Barkley was a natural. Cooper and Adolphe Menjou are aces in the two other major roles. Menjou's suave Italian Major Rinaldi becomes distinguished more through personal histrionics than the script's generosities. Cooper's sincerity as the enlisted American lieut attached to the Italian army, who abjures the dashing Rinaldi's penchant of patronizing joy palaces, once the romance sequences get under way, is consistently impressive in a none too easy assignment.

□ 1932/33: Best Picture (Nomination)

....

■ **FAREWELL TO ARMS, A**

1957, 159 MINS, US ◇ ▽

Dir Charles Vidor   *Prod* David O. Selznick   *Scr* Ben Hecht   *Ph* Piero Portalupi, Oswald Morris   *Ed* James E. Newcom, Gerard J. Wilson, John M. Foley   *Mus* Mario Nascimbene   *Prod Des* Alfred Junge
● Rock Hudson, Jennifer Jones, Vittorio De Sica, Alberto Sordi, Kurt Kasznar, Mercedes McCambridge (20th Century-Fox)

New version of the Ernest Hemingway World War I story conveys some of the Hemingway spirit that speaks of the futility of war and a desperate love that grips two strangers in its midst. But sweep and frankness alone don't make a great picture; and *Farewell* suffers from an overdose of both.

Producer David O. Selznick and director Charles Vidor, shooting all of the film in Italy and a good part of it on location in the Dolomites, have concentrated heavily on nature and war. It's the more unfortunate that Ben Hecht's often mature dialog is also riddled with cliches, and that the relationship between Rock Hudson and Jennifer Jones never takes on real dimensions.

Story, briefly, has American Red Cross ambulance driver Hudson meeting up with nurse Jones and falling violently in love with her. When he's wounded on the front, he's brought back to the hospital, where she joins him. Their protracted affair ends when he's sent back to the front where he's caught up in the disastrous retreat from Caporetto.

Such a tragic story requires great performances to put it across. It gets only a few of them in this picture.

In the supporting roles, Selznick has cast a group of very good actors. Vittorio De Sica plays the cynical Major Rinaldi with dash, and in him the Hemingway spirit comes alive with full force.

....

■ **FAREWELL, MY LOVELY**

1975, 97 MINS, US ◇

Dir Dick Richards   *Prod* George Pappas, Jerry Bruckheimer   *Scr* David Zelag Goodman   *Ph* John Alonzo   *Ed* Walter Thompson, Joel Cox   *Mus* David Shire   *Art Dir* Dean Tavoularis
● Robert Mitchum, Charlotte Rampling, John Ireland, Sylvia Miles, Jack O'Halloran, Anthony Zerbe (EK-ITC)

Farewell, My Lovely is a lethargic, vaguely

campy tribute to Hollywood's private eye mellers of the 1940s and to writer Raymond Chandler, whose Phillip Marlowe character has inspired a number of features.

Despite an impressive production and some first-rate performances, this third version fails to generate much suspense or excitement.

The plot has the cynical but humane Marlowe (Robert Mitchum) searching in seedy LA for the missing girl friend of an ex-con. After a number of false leads and predictable murders, Marlowe winds up on a gambling ship for the final confrontation, shoot-out and body count.

Mitchum, who might appear a natural for the Marlowe role, seems a bit adrift here, underplaying to the point of inertia. Remainder of cast makes effective use of smaller roles.

■ FAREWELL TO THE KING

1989, 117 MINS, US ◇ ⓥ

Dir John Milius *Prod* Albert S. Ruddy, Andre Morgan *Scr* John Milius *Ph* Dean Semler *Ed* C. Timothy O'Meara, Anne V. Coates *Mus* Basil Poledouris *Art Dir* Bernard Hides, Gil Parrondo
● Nick Nolte, Nigel Havers, James Fox, Marilyn Tokuda, Frank McRae, Gerry Lopez (Vestron)

The cliches are as thick as the foliage in *Farewell to the King*, John Milius' adaptation of a novel by French author-filmmaker Pierre Schoendoerffer. Pic recycles familiar situations and stock characters in an overlong actioner that never builds to a spiritual climax.

Two British army officers (Nigel Havers and Frank McRae) are parachuted into the Borneo jungle to rally the tribes against imminent Japanese invasion in the latter days of World War II. They come across a virile and fulfilled Nick Nolte, playing a freedom-loving white man who's anxious to protect his natives from the barbarities of civilization.

Nolte, however, needs no further prompting to fight when the Japanese slaughter his own family. Hitting the Rambo warpath, the ex-Yank sergeant (who deserted after General MacArthur's defeat at Corregidor) performs a ruthless clean-up operation.

Nolte, in a purely exterior performance, never rises to the nobility and tragic majesty the at-first skeptical British officers finally see in him. Havers is a sympathetic presence in an equally empty role. Other performers, including James Fox as Havers' commanding officer, are treated as trite thumbnail portraits.

■ FAR FROM THE MADDING CROWD

1967, 169 MINS, UK ◇ ⓥ

Dir John Schlesinger *Prod* Joseph Janni *Scr* Frederic Raphael *Ph* Nicolas Roeg *Ed* Malcolm Cooke *Mus* Richard Rodney Bennett *Art Dir* Richard MacDonald
● Julie Christie, Terence Stamp, Peter Finch, Alan Bates, Prunella Ransome, Fiona Walker (M-G-M)

Literary classics or semi-classics traditionally provide pitfalls in adaptation, and faithfulness can often prove a double-edged sword.

In this case, scripter Frederic Raphael has perhaps hewn too closely to Thomas Hardy's original. Thus he has allowed director John Schlesinger only occasional – and principally mechanical – chances to forge his own film.

It is the story of Bathsheba Everdene's multifaceted love for the three men in her life, Sergeant Troy, Gabriel Oak and Boldwood. Julie Christie, Peter Finch, Terence Stamp and Alan Bates are variedly handsome and have their many effective moments, but there is little they can ultimately and lastingly do to overcome the basic banality of their characters and, to a certain degree, their lines.

Christie has few real opportunities to branch out of her rather muted and pouty lead. Finch struggles manfully against his role as Boldwood, but never really defeats it by convincing one. Stamp is the cocky, sneering Sergeant to the part born, but there's nary a glint of anything more. Nor does Bates have more of a chance as the ever-reliable Oak.

■ FARMER TAKES A WIFE, THE

1935, 91 MINS, US

Dir Victor Fleming *Prod* Winfield R. Sheehan *Scr* Edwin Burke *Ed* Harold Schuster *Mus* Oscar Bradley (dir.)
● Janet Gaynor, Henry Fonda, Charles Bickford, Slim Summerville, Andy Devine, Margaret Hamilton (Fox)

Too thin a plot trying to cover entirely too much area is a handicap to this screen adaptation of Walter Edmonds' novel *Rome Haul* [and the play by Frank B. Elser and Marc Connelly], of the Erie canal.

The plot proper is very simple. Molly (Janet Gaynor), cook on a canal boat, and bred in the belief that physical prowess is the only thing that counts and that all farmers are cravens, falls in love with Dan Harrow (Henry Fonda), who is driving a canal team to earn the money for the purchase of a farm.

Gaynor is given a part which permits her to get away from her sometimes too sweet assignments. She's a forthright young woman in this, and she plays the part extremely well. Fonda, as the farmer, is youthfully manly and shows nice personality, but he is made to dress as no York state farmer or canaler ever did. Charles Bickford, on the other hand, looks like the men who used to string along the Erie and the Champlain canals. Slim Summerville, out of his usual type of part, plays smoothly and with effect as a driver.

■ FARMER TAKES A WIFE, THE

1953, 80 MINS, US ◇ ⓥ

Dir Henry Levin *Prod* Frank P. Rosenberg *Scr* Walter Bullock, Sally Benson, Joseph Fields *Ph* Arthur E. Arling *Ed* Louis Loeffler *Mus* Lionel Newman *Art Dir* Lyle R. Wheeler, Addison Hehr
● Betty Grable, Dale Robertson, Thelma Ritter, John Carroll, Eddie Foy Jr (20th Century-Fox)

The Farmer Takes a Wife was first screened in 1935 as a straight drama, the same as it was on the stage, and it doesn't take smoothly to the injection of songs (by Harold Arlen-Dorothy Fields) and dances, probably because the tuning is unimpressive and the terp numbers are lacking in bounce.

The production tells the story of a farm boy who takes a job on the Erie Canal to save money for a farm, meets a barge cook, falls in love, and returns with her to the soil when the railroad puts the canal out of business. Henry Levin's direction hasn't much to work with in the screenplay [from the play by Frank B. Elser and Marc Connelly, based on the novel *Rome Haul* by Walter D. Edmonds] and he fails to add any punch that would keep up interest in the unfoldment.

Grable takes prettily to the Technicolor hues and the period costuming, latter being rather fancy for a canal boat cook. As the farmer turned boatman, Robertson is okay, but is out of his element in picture's musical requirements, light as they are. Carroll is asked to do little but bluster through his role of a rival boatman.

■ FAR NORTH

1988, 90 MINS, US ◇ ⓥ

Dir Sam Shepard *Prod* Carolyn Pfeiffer, Malcolm Harding *Scr* Sam Shepard *Ph* Robbie Greenberg *Ed* Bill Yahraus *Mus* The Red Clay Ramblers *Art Dir* Peter Jamison
● Jessica Lange, Charles Durning, Tess Harper, Donald Moffat, Ann Wedgeworth, Patricia Arquette (Alive/Nelson/Circle JS)

In his film directing debut, Sam Shepard forsakes the fevered elliptical prose flights of his plays, for a straightforward approach of surprising flatness and sentimentality that never gets airborne in this conventional tale of a Minnesota farm family coming to terms with its past and present in a time of accelerating change.

Bertrum (Charles Durning), a veteran of two wars and the railroad, is thrown from a cart by his rebellious runaway horse, and lands in the hospital obsessed with exacting revenge from the nag. His citified, unmarried pregnant daughter Kate (Jessica Lange) flies out from New York to comfort the curmudgeon in his crisis.

In what's meant to be taken as a profound gesture of filial obeisance, Lange reluctantly agrees to assassinate the horse. This mystifies Lange's slightly dotty mom (Ann Wedgeworth) and outrages her fiery farm-bound sister Rita (Tess Harper).

Adding to the emotional fireworks in this world without men is the post-pubescent defiance of Harper's daughter Jilly (Patricia Arquette), who plays fast and loose with the local boys for amusement in this nowhere town.

This loving but fractious litle family is intended by Shepard to represent the dislocation of fundamental American values in the socially vertiginous 80s.

■ FAST AND LOOSE

1930, 70 MINS, US

Dir Fred Newmeyer *Scr* Doris Anderson, Jack Kirkland, Preston Sturges *Ph* William Steiner
● Miriam Hopkins, Carole Lombard, Frank Morgan, Charles Starrett, Henry Wadsworth, Winifred Harris (Paramount)

A frothy bit of celluloid [from the play *The Best People* by Avery Hopwood and David Gray]. It is Miriam Hopkins' first picture. The stage artiste plays tick-tack-toe with the camera, sometimes winning, sometimes losing.

Cast principals are almost entirely from the stage, with Charles Starrett opposite Hopkins and Frank Morgan playing the financier father. Carole Lombard is the name lady.

Hopkins is engaged to a theatric silly-ass and titled Englishman, while Henry Wadsworth is in love with an on-the-level chorus girl (Lombard). Hopkins seeks an out on her prospective marriage for a title and grasps her chance when accidentally meeting Charles Starrett. Later discovery that he's merely a garage mechanic enhances the romance for her, and it's a grand mixup when the entire family meets in a roadhouse raid.

The direction and the players hold the much-used script together.

■ FASTER, PUSSYCAT! KILL! KILL!

1966, 84 MINS, US

Dir Russ Meyer *Prod* Russ Meyer, Eve Meyer *Scr* Jack Moran *Ph* Walter Schenk *Ed* Russ Meyer *Mus* Paul Sawtell, Bert Shefter
● Tura Satana, Haji, Lori Williams, Susan Bernard, Stuart Lancaster, Paul Trinka (Eve)

Faster, Pussycat! Kill! Kill! is a somewhat sordid, quite sexy and very violent murder-kidnap-theft meller which includes elements of rape, lesbianism and sadism, clothed in faddish leather and boots and equipped with sports cars. Some good performances emerge from a one-note script via very good Russ Meyer direction and his outstanding editing. It was brought in at $44,000 and uses California desert exteriors throughout.

Jack Moran's story concerns a trio of bosomy swingers led by Tura Satana, her

F

female lover Haji, and his ambiSEXtrous Lori Williams. Out for kicks, Satana does in Ray Barlow via explicit karate, then kidnaps latter's chick, a petite Susan Bernard. Greed takes them to crippled widower Stuart Lancaster's desert diggings, where he dominates his retarded, but muscular son, Dennis Busch, also Paul Trinka, a more sensitive offspring.

It is obvious that Meyer has a directorial talent which belongs in bigger and stronger films. His visual sense is outstanding, also his setups (executed by Walter Schenk's crisp camera). Meyer's editing has a zest and polish which, without being obvious post-production gimmickry, lends proper pace and emphasis. All he needs is stronger scripting and more adept performers.

....

■ FAST-WALKING

1982, 115 MINS, US ◇ ▽
Dir James B. Harris   *Prod* James B. Harris   *Scr* James B. Harris   *Ph* King Baggot   *Ed* Douglas Stewart   *Mus* Lalo Schifrin   *Art Dir* Richard Haman
● James Woods, Tim McIntire, Kay Lenz, Robert Hooks, M. Emmet Walsh, Timothy Agoglia Carey (Pickman)

A prison drama which focuses on guards rather than prisoners and which reeks of a sort of late-1960s, counter-culture existentialism, pic seems oddly out of time and place. Producer-director-writer James B. Harris, hasn't really pulled it all together into a meaningful finished work.

James Woods plays 'Fast-Walking' Miniver, a self-described redneck with little on his mind, who smokes dope even on his job as a prison guard. On the side he drums up business for small-time madam Susan Tyrrell. In due course, Woods becomes involved in two interconnecting plots brewing within the penitentiary walls. First, being engineered by his weird cousin Tim McIntire, involves the assassination of a newly-arrived Black militant (Robert Hooks), while the other is a competing scheme to spring Hooks.

He becomes at the same time implicated in McIntire's affairs when he takes up with his g.f. Kay Lenz, and in the blacks' plot by the promise of $50,000 once Hooks escapes. It's a dirty, no-good world, to be sure.

Woods is always interesting to watch, even if his character suffers most from not growing in the course of the drama. In a very strange part, McIntire again proves he's a commanding, offbeat actor, too little seen.

....

■ FATAL ATTRACTION

1987, 119 MINS, US ◇ ▽
Dir Adrian Lyne   *Prod* Stanley R. Jaffe   *Scr* James Dearden   *Ph* Howard Atherton   *Ed* Michael Kahn, Peter E. Berger   *Mus* Maurice Jarre   *Art Dir* Mel Bourne
● Michael Douglas, Glenn Close, Anne Archer, Ellen Hamilton Latzen, Stuart Pankin (Paramount)

The screws are tightened expertly in this suspenseful meller about a flipped-out femme who makes life hell for the married man who scorns her.

New York attorney Michael Douglas is happily married to the gorgeous Anne Archer and has a lovely daughter, but succumbs to Glenn Close's provocative flirtations while his wife is out of town.

It appears that these two sophisticated adults are in it just for fun and sport, but when Close slits her wrists in despair over the end of the affair, Douglas knows he's taken on more of a burden than he bargained for.

Michael Douglas, in a family man role, seems warmer and more sympathetic than before, and well conveys the evasiveness and anguish of his cornered character. Glenn

Close throws herself into the physical abandon of the early reels with surprising relish, and become genuinely frightening when it comes clear she is capable of anything.

Unusual credit to James Dearden for his (very good) screenplay 'based on his original screenplay' stems from the fact that pic is based on Dearden's 45-minute film *Diversion*, which he wrote and directed in 1979.
□ 1987: Best Picture (Nomination)

....

■ FAT CITY

1972, 100 MINS, US ◇ ▽
Dir John Huston   *Prod* Ray Stark   *Scr* Leonard Gardner   *Ph* Conrad Hall   *Ed* Margaret Booth   *Mus* Marvin Hamlisch (sup.)   *Art Dir* Richard Sylbert
● Stacy Keach, Jeff Bridges, Susan Tyrrell, Candy Clark, Nicholas Colasanto, Art Aragon (Rastar/Columbia)

John Huston has a terse, sharp, downbeat but compassionate look at the underside of smalltown American life in the west, actually in central California in the town of Stockton.

It is about boxing, about failures, about part-time agricultural workers, but really about those who, in defeat, still have meaning. The allusion stems from the old American dream of another chance, a reward for trying and for triumph in competition. Huston has been blessed by a brilliantly dialogued script by Leonard Gardner from his own much-praised novel.

Huston catches the feel of the community with a lean, no-nonsense economy, a hard-boiled but humanly alert feeling which raises the tale from a purely naturalistic lowlife depiction of the characters to make a statement on the life style of the drifters and those who accept a moderate place in the smalltown hierarchy.

....

■ FATE IS THE HUNTER

1964, 106 MINS, US
Dir Ralph Nelson   *Prod* Aaron Rosenberg   *Scr* Harold Medford   *Ph* Milton Krasner   *Ed* Robert Simpson   *Mus* Jerry Goldsmith   *Art Dir* Jack Martin Smith, Hilyard Brown
● Glenn Ford, Nancy Kwan, Rod Taylor, Suzanne Pleshette, Jane Russell, Wally Cox (20th Century-Fox)

Fate Is the Hunter based upon the Ernest K. Gann book, is a realistically-produced picture, sparked by good acting right down the line. Its greatest asset is a stirring climax which brings the story line to a satisfactory conclusion, but the buildup, while meeting expository requirements, frequently plods due to lack of significant line and situations.

The production deals with the cause of a spectacular plane crash in which 53 people are killed. As the various elements are considered, then discarded, the investigation finally centers on the dead pilot, reported to have been drinking a few hours before the tragedy. With the Civil Aeronautics Board and the FBI already on the case, the airline's director of flight operations and old friend of the pilot pursues his own line of inquiry.

Glenn Ford as the operations director who was a war flyer with the dead pilot (Rod Taylor) underplays his character for good effect. Part isn't as outgoing as Ford generally undertakes, but is dramatically forceful. Taylor's role is more flamboyant and colorful, most of it in flashback sequences as the Harold Medford screenplay limns the character of the man and what made him tick.

Ralph Nelson's taut direction gets the most out of his script, the crash emerging as a thrilling experience and with suspense mounting in Ford's reenactment of the fatality. Under his helming, too, Nancy Kwan, as Taylor's fiancee, and Suzanne Pleshette, the stewardess, register nicely, and Jane Russell

makes an appearance as herself playing a World War II army camp.

....

■ FATHER

1990, 100 MINS, AUSTRALIA ◇
Dir John Power   *Prod* Damien Parer, Tony Cavanaugh, Graham Hartley   *Scr* Tony Cavanaugh, Graham Hartley   *Ph* Dan Burstall   *Ed* Kerry Regan   *Mus* Peter Best   *Art Dir* Phil Peters
● Max Von Sydow, Carol Drinkwater, Julie Blake, Steve Jacobs, Tim Robertson (Barron/Latin Quarter)

Father is strikingly similar to Costa-Gavras' *Music Box*. The story unfolds in Melbourne where German-born Joe Mueller (Max Von Sydow) has lived since the war. Since his wife's death, and his retirement, he's lived with his devoted daughter, Anne (Carol Drinkwater), son-in-law Bobby (Steve Jacobs) and two granddaughters.

Their peaceful lifestyle is disrupted by a television program in which an old woman, Iya Zetnick (Julia Blake) accuses Mueller of wartime atrocities. Mueller vigorously denies the charges, but winds up in an Australian court.

Writers introduced an extra element into the drama, however: a more general war guilt. Son-in-law is a Vietnam vet and admits that he knows all about making war against civilians. 'It's in all of us,' he says. Steve Jacobs gives an impressive performance.

Von Sydow is a tower of strength as the accused German who may, or may not, be guilty, while Blake is extremely touching as the accusing survivor of Nazi atrocities.

....

■ FATHER GOOSE

1964, 115 MINS, US ◇ ▽
Dir Ralph Nelson   *Prod* Robert Arthur   *Scr* Peter Stone, Frank Tarloff   *Ph* Charles Lang Jr   *Ed* Ted J. Kent   *Mus* Cy Coleman   *Art Dir* Alexander Golitzen, Henry Bumstead
● Cary Grant, Leslie Caron, Trevor Howard, Jack Good, Sheryl Locke, Pip Sparke (Universal)

Cary Grant comes up with an about-face change of character in this World War II comedy. As a Japanese plane watcher on a deserted South Sea isle Grant plays an unshaven bum addicted to tippling and tattered attire, a long way from the suave figure he usually projects but affording him opportunity for nutty characterization. Leslie Caron and Trevor Howard are valuable assists to plottage which brings in a flock of refugee kids.

Under Ralph Nelson's shrewd helming the screenplay takes amusing form as Grant, who plies the South Seas in his own cruiser at the begining of the war, is pressed into service by Australian Navy Commander Howard to man a strategic watching station.

Into this harrassed existence comes further harrassment when Grant crosses 40 miles of open sea in an eight-foot dinghy to rescue another watcher, but ends up with Caron and seven young girls, marooned there when a pilot who was transporting them to safety from New Guinea was ordered to pick up survivors of a crashed bomber.

....

■ FATHERLAND

1986, 110 MINS, UK/W. GERMANY ◇ ▽
Dir Ken Loach   *Prod* Raymond Day   *Scr* Trevor Griffiths   *Ph* Chris Menges   *Ed* Jonathan Morris   *Mus* Christian Kunert, Gerulf Pannach   *Art Dir* Martin Johnson
● Gerulf Pannach, Fabienne Babe, Sigfrit Steiner, Cristine Rose (Film Four/MK2/Clasart/Kestrel II)

Fatherland is a major film from Ken Loach. He has created an ambiguous yet penetrating work about two opposing cultures and the way they both manipulate and control artistic expression, and about the response of two generations to those cultures.

Focus of the drama is Klaus Dritteman, a dissident folk singer first silenced by the East Germans, then allowed to leave quietly. He is greeted in West Berlin with lavish treatment all round, but he is unhappy being treated as a commodity in the West and doesn't know if he can be creative in his new environment.

As usual with Loach, performers are not encouraged to 'act' in the expected emotive way, and everyone, notably singer Gerulf Pannach, who plays Klaus, is quietly thoughtful and low-key.

■ **FATHER OF THE BRIDE**

1950, 92 MINS, US ⓥ

Dir Vincente Minnelli   *Prod* Pandro S. Berman
Scr Frances Goodrich, Albert Hackett   *Ph* John Alton
Ed Ferris Webster   *Mus* Adolph Deutsch
● Spencer Tracy, Joan Bennett, Elizabeth Taylor, Don Taylor, Billie Burke, Russ Tamblyn (M-G-M)

Father of the Bride as a pic smites the risibilities just as hard as it did in book form [by Edward Streeter].

Screenplay provides director Vincente Minnelli with choice situations and dialog, sliced right from life and hoked just enough to bring out the comedy flavor. Opening shot is a daybreak scene among the debris created by a wedding reception. Weary, but relieved, Spencer Tracey recounts the sorry lot of a bride's father, emotionally and financially devastating, and gives a case history of the events leading up to his present state.

On the critical side: Minnelli could have timed many of the scenes so that laughs would not have stepped on dialog tag lines. Also he permits the wedding rehearsal sequence to play too long, lessening the comedic effect.

□ 1950: Best Picture (Nomination)

■ **FATHOM**

1967, 100 MINS, US ◇

Dir Leslie Martinson   *Prod* John Kohn   *Scr* Lorenzo Semple Jr   *Ph* Douglas Slocombe   *Ed* Max Benedict
Mus John Dankworth   *Art Dir* Maurice Carter
● Raquel Welch, Anthony Franciosa, Ronald Fraser, Greta Chi, Richard Briers, Tom Adams (20th Century-Fox)

Fathom, lensed on location in Spain to take full advantage of scenic backdrops, is a melange of melodramatic ingredients personalized by the lush presence of Raquel Welsh. Actress stars with Tony Franciosa in this production, highlighted by some exciting parachute scenes.

Script, based on the Larry Forrester novel, was obviously triggered by the real-life incident of an American H-bomb accidentally lost off the coast of Spain.

Welch's services, as a parachute jumper, are enlised to help recover what is described as an electronic device which will fire the bomb, now in the possession of certain evil forces, and which was not retrieved at the time the bomb itself was salvaged.

■ **FAT MAN AND LITTLE BOY**

1989, 126 MINS, US ◇ ⓥ

Dir Roland Joffe   *Prod* Tony Garnett   *Scr* Bruce Robinson, Roland Joffe   *Ph* Vilmos Zsigmond
Ed Francoise Bonnot   *Mus* Ennio Morricone
Art Dir Gregg Fonseca
● Paul Newman, Dwight Schultz, Bonnie Bedelia, John Cusack, Laura Dern, Natasha Richardson (Light motive/Paramount)

The problems of this historical drama about the creation of the atom bomb are crystalized in its title. 'Fat Man' and 'Little Boy' were the nicknames given to the bombs dropped over Hiroshima and Nagasaki. These names aren't mentioned by any of the characters in the film, nor do the bombings figure in the action.

Film concentrates instead on Gen. Groves (Paul Newman), the man assigned to oversee the project, and J. Robert Oppenheimer (Dwight Schultz), the brilliant scientist with far-left-to-all-out-communist connections picked to lead it. This is all well and good, except that few dramatic sparks fly.

Newman has no trouble bringing the tough-talking 'can do' general to life. The trouble is the scriptwriters have no interest in exploring the man behind the mission.

This tends to tilt the dramatic balance toward Oppenheimer. The film falls short here, too, partially because of Schultz' lack-luster performance, but primarily because the script fails to give a clue to what made this man tick.

■ **FBI STORY, THE**

1959, 149 MINS, US ◇ ⑰

Dir Mervyn LeRoy   *Prod* Mervyn LeRoy   *Scr* Richard L. Breen, John Twist   *Ph* Joseph Biroc   *Ed* Philip W. Anderson   *Mus* Max Steiner
● James Stewart, Vera Miles, Murray Hamilton, Larry Pennell, Nick Adams, Diane Jergens (Warner)

Mervyn LeRoy takes the factual material of Don Whitehead's best-selling *The FBI Story* and makes of it a tense, exciting film story told in human terms. The method used is to show the work of the FBI through the life of one of its agents (James Stewart), a familiar enough device, but correct and rewarding in this instance.

The fictional story used as a framework sounds conventional enough. Stewart and his wife (Vera Miles), are torn between his dedication to his job with the FBI and the fact that he could give his family a more rewarding life outside the bureau. But Stewart believes what J. Edgar Hoover tells his agents when he takes over the service, that its men must be imbued not only with the service of justice but the love of justice.

The dialog is exemplary, economical in words despite the film's length. Too, the story does not run out of plot. It plunges directly into a revelatory incident before the main titles, and one of the most suspenseful sequences, a fine chase through New York streets, is used for the final crisis.

Stewart gives a restrained performance, wry and intelligent, completely credible as the film covers a span of about 25 years to show both the fledgling agent and the older man. Miles, who plays particularly well with Stewart, synchronizes her more direct attack smoothly with his underplaying. Murray Hamilton is memorable as Stewart's fellow agent, felled by gangsters. Larry Pennell and Diane Jergens supply the young love interest believably.

■ **FEAR AND DESIRE**

1953, 68 MINS, US

Dir Stanley Kubrick   *Prod* Stanley Kubrick
Scr Howard O. Sackler   *Ph* Stanley Kubrick
Ed Stanley Kubrick   *Mus* Gerald Fried
● Frank Silvera, Kenneth Harp, Paul Mazursky, Steve Coit, Virginia Leith (Kubrick)

Fear and Desire is a literate, unhackneyed war drama, outstanding for its fresh camera treatment and poetic dialog.

Pic is work of Stanley Kubrick, who produced, directed, photographed and edited the film on a $100,000 shoestring budget. Film was written by 23-year-old poet Howard O. Sackler who has confected a blend of violence and philosophy, some of it half-baked, and some of it powerfully moving.

Story deals with four GIs stranded six miles behind enemy lines and what happens to their moral fibre as they try to escape. Kenneth Harp is a glib intellectual, grows weary with his own sophistication. Paul Mazursky, over-sensitive to violence, is a weakling who tries to befriend a captured enemy girl, Virginia Leith (a toothsome dish), shoots her, and then goes insane.

Steve Coit is a level-headed Southerner who also winds up confused about his values. Frank Silvera plays the one character who fulfills himself – a tough, brave primitive, who purposely draws the fire of the enemy on himself on a river raft, so that Harp and Coit can shoot an enemy general and escape in a captured plane.

Kubrick shot the entire film in the San Gabriel Mts and at a river at Bakersfield on the Coast, and he uses mists and tree leaves with telling effect.

Fear and Desire is definitely out of the pot-boiler class one would expect from a shoe-string budget.

■ **FEAR CITY**

1984, 96 MINS, US ◇ ⓥ

Dir Abel Ferrara   *Prod* Bruce Cohn Curtis, Jerry Tokofsky   *Scr* Nicholas St John   *Ph* James Lemmo
Ed Jack Holmes, Anthony Redman   *Mus* Dick Halligan
● Tom Berenger, Billy Dee Williams, Jack Scalia, Melanie Griffith, Rossano Brazzi, Rae Dawn Cheong (Zupnik/Curtis)

Fear City lives up to its title as a tough, nasty, big-league meller by throwing every element from the exploitation cookbook – gory violence, straight and gay sex, multiple murders, martial arts, raw-dialog, mobsters, drugs and gobs of female nudity – into the pot and letting them stew.

Pic is set in the fleshpot of mid-town Manhattan and is populated by strippers and the sleazy men who run their lives. Hovering above them are organized crime types on the one side and the cops on the other, and soon a third menace is introduced, that of a roving sicko who launches a systematic genocidal assault on the girls who work at the nude clubs.

Teeming plot has B-girl talent agent Tom Berenger trying to get things started again with old flame Melanie Griffith.

■ **FEAR IN THE NIGHT**

1947, 71 MINS, US

Dir Maxwell Shane   *Prod* William H. Pine, William C. Thomas   *Scr* Maxwell Shane   *Ph* Jack Greenhalgh
Ed Howard Smith   *Mus* Rudy Schrager   *Art Dir* F. Paul Sylos
● Paul Kelly, DeForest Kelley, Ann Doran, Kay Scott (Paramount)

Fear in the Night is a good psychological melo-drama, unfolded at fast clip and will please the whodunit-and-how fans.

Maxwell Shane, who scripted from a William Irish [= Cornell Woolrich] story, also directed. It's his first directorial chore. He realizes on meller elements for full worth. Plot concerns young man who awakens one morning after dream that he has killed a man. Reality of dream is strengthened when he finds strange button and key in his pocket. He seeks aid from his detective brother-in-law.

Paul Kelly is a believable cop who aids DeForest Kelley solve nightmare riddle.

■ **FEAR IS THE KEY**

1973, 105 MINS, UK ◇

Dir Michael Tuchner   *Prod* Alan Ladd Jr, Jay Kanter
Scr Robert Carrington   *Ph* Alex Thomson   *Ed* Ray Lovejoy   *Mus* Roy Budd   *Art Dir* Syd Cain, Maurice Carter
● Barry Newman, Suzy Kendall, John Vernon, Dolph Sweet, Ben Kingsley, Ray McAnally (KLK/Anglo-EMI

Sustained interest and suspense mark *Fear Is the Key*, well-made action stuff [from the novel by Alistair MacLean] including the obligatory auto chase routine around the highways and byways of Louisiana where pic was shot.

Barry Newman and Suzy Kendall are top-featured, he as a deepsea salvage expert, she as an oil heiress and kidnap victim. When Newman's wife, brother and child are shot out of the sky while fetching a salvage cargo of priceless gems, he goes undercover in cahoots with the law to avenge the killings. An elaborate charade ensues wherein he feigns the murder of a cop and kidnap of Kendall from a courtroom, all designed to land him in the lair of the villains who are contriving to retrieve the gems from the aircraft on the floor of the Gulf of Mexico.

Michael Tuchner's direction, abetted by tight editing, unravels the yarn at a crisp clip. The auto pursuit sequence is superbly staged by stunt coordinator Carey Loftin and crew.

••••••••••••••••••••••••••••••

■ **FEAR NO EVIL**

1981, 99 MINS, US ◇
Dir Frank LaLoggia   *Prod* Frank LaLoggia, Charles LaLoggia   *Scr* Frank LaLoggia   *Ph* Fred Goodich   *Ed* Edna Ruth Paul   *Mus* Frank LaLoggia, David Spear
● Elizabeth Hoffman, Kathleen Rowe McAllen, Frank Birney (LaLoggia Productions)

Though the horror genre is sated with maniacs on the menace, 'Fear No Evil' stands out. Spooky and surreal, the ultimately hopeful film has its basis in religious morality.

A rotten seed, born to horrified parents, grows into a menacing 17-year-old. He's a hopeless baddie consumed with the power to destroy. At Andrew/Lucifer's wicked island domain, he summons the undead and tangles with Margaret, an old woman with the power of God behind her.

Strong on atmospherics, thanks to slick lensing by Fred Goodich, *Fear No Evil* is a studious chiller that works best in scenes featuring Elizabeth Hoffman, who fairly glows with devotional fervour as Margaret.

At a cost of $1.5 million, *Fear No Evil* is an admirable first feature by writer-director Frank LaLoggia, 27, who also co-wrote the lush music. The former U of Miami drama student previously made three award-winning shorts and acted in three television pilots.

••••••••••••••••••••••••••••••

■ **FEAR STRIKES OUT**

1957, 100 MINS, US ⊤
Dir Robert Mulligan   *Prod* Alan J. Pakula   *Scr* Ted Berkman, Raphael Blau   *Ph* Haskell Boggs   *Ed* Aaron Stell   *Mus* Elmer Bernstein   *Art Dir* Hal Pereira, Hilyard Brown
● Anthony Perkins, Karl Malden, Norma Moore, Adam Williams, Perry Wilson, Peter J. Votrian (Paramount)

Baseball is only a means to an end in this highly effective dramatization of the tragic results that can come from a father pushing his son too hard towards a goal that he, himself, was not able to achieve.

In trying to be the major leaguer his father had wanted to be, Jim Piersall so filled his life with pressure and tension that he went into a complete mental breakdown right after smashing a homerun for the Boston Red Sox. Confined to the Westborough State Hospital under restraint, Piersall gradually started to respond to electro-shock treatments and was eventually restored. When the 1953 season opened for the Red Sox, Piersall was back in right field.

Anthony Perkins, in the young Piersall role, delivers a remarkably sustained performance

of a sensitive young man, pushed too fast to the limits of his ability to cope with life's pressures. Karl Malden is splendid as the father who gets his own ambitions mixed up with love for his son.

••••••••••••••••••••••••••••••

■ **FEDORA**

1978, 110 MINS, W. GERMANY/FRANCE ◇ ⊤
Dir Billy Wilder   *Prod* Billy Wilder   *Scr* I.A.L. Diamond, Billy Wilder   *Ph* Gerry Fisher   *Ed* Stefan Arsten   *Mus* Miklos Rozsa
● William Holden, Marthe Keller, Jose Ferrer, Hildegard Knef, Frances Sternhagen, Mario Adorf (Geria/Bavaria/SFP)

With *Fedora* based on a tale from Tom Tryon's bestseller, *Crowned Heads*, Billy Wilder goes serenely back to Hollywood treatment of itself as legend, illusion and dreams rather than reality.

In his more successful, acerbic look at an over-the-hill star, *Sunset Boulevard* [1950], the star was a real oldtimer, Gloria Swanson. Neither Marthe Keller, as the once great star Fedora, or Hildegard Knef as a crusty Polish countess and the star's keeper, have that allusive, self absorbed but camera-loving look that stars possessed, though they are good.

William Holden tells most of the tale, as he did in *Boulevard*. But here he is an indie producer down on his luck trying desperately to get a script to the amazingly still youthful star, at 67, Fedora, in a hideaway on a Greek island. It appears she is being held captive by a quack doctor, once famed for keeping personalities youthful, well mimed by Jose Ferrer.

Wilder's directorial flair, the fine production dress, Holden's solid presence and Michael York playing himself as a narcissistic actor and Henry Fonda, also as himself as head of the Academy who delivers a belated Oscar to Fedora, add some flavor to this bittersweet bow to the old star system.

••••••••••••••••••••••••••••••

■ **FELLOW TRAVELLER**

1990, 97 MINS, UK/US ◇ ⊤
Dir Philip Saville   *Prod* Michael Wearing   *Scr* Michael Wearing   *Ph* John Kenway   *Ed* Greg Miller   *Mus* Colin Towns   *Art Dir* Gavin Davies
● Ron Silver, Hart Bochner, Imogen Stubbs, Daniel J. Travanti, Katherine Borowitz (BFI/BBC/HBO)

Fellow Traveller has the rare distinction of being a British film that actually looks international. Helmer Philip Saville shows a big-screen feel with the story of a blacklisted Hollywood screen-writer during the McCarthy era who is forced to Britain to find work.

Pic goes some way in covering the commie-bashing McCarthy Era 1950s, but eventually becomes rather simplistic when trying to debate the actual politics of the time.

Glossy opening is set beside a luxury swimming pool in Hollywood where film star Clifford Byrne (Hart Bochner) shoots himself. At the same time in London, his friend Asa Kaufman (Ron Silver) is escaping the McCarthyist witch-hunt and – illegally – looking for work.

A series of flashbacks shows that Bochner and Silver were best friends. In England Silver takes a false name, starts writing a TV series, *The Adventures of Robin Hood*, and searches for Bochner's English girlfriend (Imogen Stubbs), whom he has a brief affair with; he also mulls over politics with her leftie friends.

Silver is convincing as the cynical writer thrown into a strange English environment, and Hart Bochner looks the handsome leading man, replete with Errol Flynn mustache. Pic is excellent at re-creating the early heady days of independent TV in the UK.

••••••••••••••••••••••••••••••

■ **FEMALE TROUBLE**

1975, 95 MINS, US ◇
Dir John Waters   *Prod* John Waters   *Scr* John Waters   *Ph* John Waters   *Ed* Charles Roggero
● Divine, David Lochary, Mary Vivien Pearce, Mink Stole, Edith Massey, Cookie Mueller (Dreamland/New Line)

Female Trouble is the sordid tale of Dawn Davenport, who rises from high school hoyden to mistress of crime before frying in the electric chair. As she climbs the ladder of success, she is raped by a stranger, gives birth to an obnoxious child who later murders the father, marries a beautician whose mother she imprisons in a bird cage before cutting off her hand and opens a niteclub act during which she guns down members of the audience. A true original.

Repeating from *Pink Flamingos* in the stellar role is Divine, a mammoth 300-pound transvestite with a tinsel soul. Though Divine doesn't stoop to devouring dog excrement as at the *Flamingos* fade-out, he does everything else, from cavorting on a trampoline, to playing a rape scene opposite himself, and 'giving birth' on camera. Camp is too elegant a word to describe it all.

Sets, lighting, camerawork, editing and sound are all superior to their *Flamingos* counterparts and Waters makes the most of a reported $25,000 budget.

••••••••••••••••••••••••••••••

■ **FERRIS BUELLER'S DAY OFF**

1986, 103 MINS, US ◇ ⊤
Dir John Hughes   *Prod* John Hughes, Tom Jacobson   *Scr* John Hughes   *Ph* Tak Fujimoto   *Ed* Paul Hirsch   *Mus* Ira Newborn   *Art Dir* John W. Corso
● Matthew Broderick, Alan Ruck, Mia Sara, Jeffrey Jones, Jennifer Grey, Cindy Pickett (Paramount)

Ferris Bueller exhibits John Hughes on an off day. Paucity of invention here lays bare the total absence of plot or involving situations.

In a nutshell, the thin premise demonstrates the great lengths to which the irrepressible Ferris Bueller (Matthew Broderick) goes in order to hoodwink his parents and high school principal into thinking he's really sick when, in fact, all he wants to do is play hooky for a day.

Oddly, for a rich kid, Ferris doesn't have his own car, so he shanghais his best friend for the day, appropriates the vintage Ferrari of the buddy's father, spirits his girlfriend out of school and speeds off for downtown Chicago.

Broderick's essential likeability can't replace the loony anarchy of Hughes' previous leading man, Anthony Michael Hall. Alan Ruck can't do much with his underwritten second-banana role, and Mia Sara is fetching as Ferris' g.f.

Picture's one saving grace is the absolutely delicious comic performance of Jeffrey Jones as the high school principal.

••••••••••••••••••••••••••••••

■ **FEVER PITCH**

1985, 96 MINS, US ⊤
Dir Richard Brooks   *Prod* Freddie Fields   *Scr* Richard Brooks   *Ph* William A. Fraker   *Ed* Jeff Jones   *Mus* Thomas Dolby   *Art Dir* Raymond G. Storey
● Ryan O'Neal, Catherine Hicks, Giancarlo Giannini, Bridgette Andersen, Chad Everett, John Saxon (M-G-M)

Weak script, poor acting and miscasting aside, it's the power of the subject that makes this an enjoyable ride. Writer/director Richard Brooks thoroughly researched the territory of the compulsive gambler and captures the obsession with almost a documentary eye.

Unfortunately, plot is a totally unconvincing jumble and Ryan O'Neal as a sports reporter hooked on the gambling game is wooden and unsympathetic. Up to his ears in gambling debts, O'Neal just gets in deeper with loansharks and operators. He's already lost his wife due to gambling.

Most of the action takes place in Las Vegas where O'Neal wins and loses huge sums and gets involved with big-timer Giancarlo Giannini.

Rest of the cast is as stiff as the script. Catherine Hicks as a Vegas cocktail waitress and sometime call-girl goes through a few turns that don't quite fit.

....

■ F FOR FAKE

1973, 85 MINS, FRANCE ◇
Dir Orson Welles, Francois Reichenbach *Scr* Orson Welles, Oja Palinkas *Ph* Christian Odasso, Gary Graver *Ed* Marie Sophie Dubus, Dominique Enegerer *Mus* Michel Legrand
● (Prisme)

Orson Welles has reworked the docu material of Francois Reichenbach on noted art forger Elmyr De Houry, made for TV about 1968, into an intriguing, enjoyable look at illusion in general and his own, Clifford Irving's and De Houry's dealing with it in particular.

He has deftly added himself to the affair as he is seen doing some magico stints and winkingly admitting he is a charlatan.

Welles also brings in his early fakery of becoming an actor in passing himself off as a New York thesp to the Abbey Theatre in Ireland at 16 and his Mars radio scare, also a fake, which, unlike Irving, did not lead him to prison but to Hollywood. There, according to Joseph Cotten, interviewed, he was thinking of making a fictional film on Howard Hughes which finally became *Citizen Kane*, loosely based on W.R. Hearst.

Welles shows his shrewd flair for visuals and montage even if he has shot only a part of the footage.

....

■ FIDDLER ON THE ROOF

1971, 180 MINS, US ◇ Ⓥ
Dir Norman Jewison *Prod* Norman Jewison *Scr* Joseph Stein *Ph* Oswald Morris *Ed* Anthony Gibbs, Robert Lawrence *Mus* John Williams (arr.) *Art Dir* Michael Stringer
● Chaim Topol, Norman Crane, Leonard Frey, Molly Picon, Paul Mann, Rosalind Harris (United Artists/Mirisch)

Sentimental in a theatrical way, romantic in the oldfashioned way, nostalgic of immigration days, affirmative of human decency, loyalty, bravery and folk humor, here is the screen version of the long-running Hal Prince-Jerome Robbins stage musical smash.

Pictured is the Ukrainian village of pious and tradition-ruled Jews at the point the corrupt Czaristic regime was goading them to move out. A tight-lipped bigot, Vernon Dobtcheff drives into the village in his carriage with an escort of military horsemen and lays down to the reluctant constable (Louis Zorich) the obligatory political line, namely there must be a 'distractive' demonstration of the local peasants against 'those Christ-killers'.

Attention naturally falls on the Tevye. Norman Jewison chose the Israeli actor, Chaim Topol, who played the role on the London stage. An enormous man with sparkling (not melting) brown eyes, Topol has the necessary combination of bombast and compassion, vitality and doubts. His dialogs with God (and/or the audience) are more cautious and less in the chutzpah style of, say, Zero Mostel. Topol sings passably, but 'If I Were a Rich Man' is too serious, losing the fun.
□ 1971: Best Picture (Nomination)

■ FIELD, THE

1991, 110 MINS, UK Ⓥ
Dir Jim Sheridan *Prod* Noel Pearson *Scr* Jim Sheridan *Ph* Jack Conroy *Ed* J. Patrick Duffner *Mus* Elmer Bernstein *Art Dir* Frank Conway
● Richard Harris, John Hurt, Tom Berenger, Sean Bean, Frances Tomelty, Brenda Fricker (Granada)

Superb acting and austere visual beauty are offset by a somewhat overheated screenplay in this tragic tale [from the play by John B. Keane] about an indomitable Irish peasant's blood ties to the land.

Richard Harris is in the larger-than-life role of a patriarchal Irish tenant farmer with a ferocious temperament and blazing charisma. The time is the 1930s, when the memory of the great famine was fresh and feudal ways held sway in the Irish countryside.

For most of his life, Bull McCabe has farmed a field belonging to a wealthy widow (Frances Tomelty), who one day decides to sell the plot. Bull is outraged.

He holds in thrall his slow-witted son Tadgh (Sean Bean) and even slower-witted crony Bird O'Donnell (John Hurt). The suicide of another son during the famine still haunts Bull, and his wife Maggie (Brenda Fricker) has not spoken to him in the 20 years since.

'Who would insult me by bidding for my field?' he demands at the local pub. No one but an Irish-American from Boston (Tom Berenger), who has returned to his ancestral village with a plan to pave Bull's field for an access road to lucrative limestone deposits.

Harris gives a resonant, domineering performance as the prideful peasant, casting him as a pagan throwback who views God and nature as one. Incredibly disguised, Hurt is remarkable as the pathetic village idiot who lives for the reflected glory of the most fearsome man in town.

....

■ FIELD OF DREAMS

1989, 106 MINS, US ◇
Dir Phil Alden Robinson *Prod* Lawrence Gordon, Charles Gordon *Scr* Phil Alden Robinson *Ph* John Lindley *Ed* Ian Crafford *Mus* James Horner *Art Dir* Dennis Gassner
● Kevin Costner, Amy Madigan, Gaby Hoffman, Ray Liotta, James Earl Jones, Burt Lancaster (Gordon/Universal)

Alternately affecting and affected, *Field of Dreams* is a fable about redemption and reconciliation that uses the mythos of baseball as an organizing metaphor.

Kevin Costner plays Ray Kinsella, a new-age farmer who has come to Iowa's cornfields with his college sweetheart (Amy Madigan).

In the fields one day Costner hears a celestial voice that cryptically advises: 'If you build it, he will come.' Once he convinces himself and his family that he's not going crazy, Costner sets out to sculpt a beautiful baseball diamond from his precious cornfield.

The whole town thinks the outsider has gone bonkers, but one night Costner's faith is rewarded: the spirit of Shoeless Joe Jackson, the most precipitously fallen of the disgraced World Series fixers, the 1919 Chicago White Sox, materializes on his ballfield.

Fully in the grip of supernatural forces, Costner leaves the farm on a cross-country pilgrimage to find the Boston home of America's best-known reclusive writer (James Earl Jones) -- a cultural demigod depicted as a cross between J.D. Salinger and Bob Dylan.

Costner, Shoeless Joe, Jones and Burt Lancaster (a failed dead baseballer) are all haunted by regrets over failed relatonships, life-shattering mistakes and missed opportunities. All yearn for a collective second chance at inner peace. In spite of a script hobbled with cloying aphorisms and shameless sentimentality, *Field of Dreams* sustains a dreamy mood in which the idea of baseball is

distilled to its purest essence: a game that stands for unsullied innocence in a cruel, imperfect world.
□ 1989: Best Picture (Nomination)

....

■ FIFTH AVENUE GIRL

1939, 82 MINS, US Ⓥ
Dir Gregory LaCava *Prod* Gregory LaCava *Scr* Allan Scott *Ph* Robert de Grasse *Ed* William Hamilton, Robert Wise *Mus* Robert Russell Bennett *Art Dir* Van Nest Polglase, Perry Ferguson
● Ginger Rogers, Walter Connolly, Verree Teasdale, James Ellison, Tim Holt (RKO)

Fifth Avenue Girl, is a cleverly devised comedy drama, expertly guided by Gregory LaCava. Story is basically of Cinderella pattern – always good. Millionaire Walter Connolly, shunned by his family on his birthday, meets Ginger Rogers in Central Park. After a night club celebration, he hires her to pose as a golddigger, and takes her to his Fifth Avenue mansion.

Sock laughs are supplied by situations and surprise dialog. Rogers, bewildered by her sudden catapult into a swank home, carries it all off with a blankness that accentuates her characterization. Connolly deftly handles the assignment of the prosperous manufacturer.

Production is distinctly a LaCava achievement. In motivation, its unfolding lies between the wacky *My Man Godfrey* and the more serious *Stage Door*.

....

■ 55 DAYS AT PEKING

1963, 150 MINS, US ◇ Ⓥ
Dir Nicholas Ray *Prod* Samuel Bronston *Scr* Philip Yordan, Bernard Gordon *Ph* Jack Hildyard *Ed* Robert Lawrence *Mus* Dimitri Tiomkin *Art Dir* Veniero Colasanti, John Moore
● Charlton Heston, Ava Gardner, David Niven, Flora Robson, John Ireland, Leo Genn (Bronston)

Producer Samuel Bronston shows characteristic lavishness in the pictorial scope, the vivid and realistic sets and extras by the thousands in his reproduction of the capital of Imperial China in 1900. The lensing was in Spain where the company built an entire city.

The screenplay presumably adheres to the historical basics in its description of the violent rebellion of the 'Boxers' against the major powers of the period – Great Britain, Russia, France, Germany, Italy, Japan, and the United States – because of their commercial exploitation of tradition-bound and unmodern (backward) China. These market-seeking nations have in their Peking outpost gallant fighting men who, although only a few hundred in number, withstand the merciless 55-day siege. *55 Days at Peking* takes sides with imperialism.

While Ray is identified as director, some of the battle scenes actually were directed by Andrew Marton. This came to be in a period when Ray was ill.

David Niven is the British embassy head who stubbornly refuses to surrender, risking the safety of all about him, including his wife and two children. Both he and Charlton Heston perform with conviction, Heston as the American Marine major who commands the defense. Ava Gardner's role is not too well conceived. Hers is the part of the widow of a Russian bigshot who killed himself upon learning of his wife's infidelity with a Chinese official.

Lynne Sue Moon gives a poignant performance as an Oriental 12-year-old whose American father, an army captain, is killed in battle. Flora Robson appears strikingly authentic as the Dowager Empress Tzu Hsi whose sympathies lie with the outlaws.

Jack Hildyard's photography is excellent, particularly in getting on the big screen the savage attack scenes which take up the major

F

part of the picture. Dimitri Tiomkin provides engaging music.

••

■ **52 PICK-UP**

1986, 114 MINS, US ◇ Ⓥ
Dir John Frankenheimer   *Prod* Menahem Golan, Yoram Globus   *Scr* Elmore Leonard, John Steppling   *Ph* Jost Vacano   *Ed* Robert F. Shugrue   *Mus* Gary Chang   *Art Dir* Philip Harrison
● Roy Scheider, Ann-Margret, Vanity, John Glover, Robert Trebor, Kelly Preston (Cannon)

52 Pick-Up is a thriller without any thrills. Although director John Frankenheimer stuffs as much action as he can into the screen adaptation of Elmore Leonard's novel (previously filmed by Cannon in Israel in 1984 as *The Ambassador*), he can't hide the ridiculous plot and lifeless characters.

Roy Scheider is an all-American hero, married for 23 years to the still attractive Ann-Margret, who has worked his way up by his bootstraps and after many lean years now owns a successful business and a luxurious home in the Hollywood hills.

Caught in a blackmail scheme by an unlikely trio of porno operators who film him in bed with cute young Kelly Preston, Scheider balks at giving up his hard-earned wealth, but even more at being told what to do.

Chemistry between Scheider and Ann-Margret is minimal and undermines the film's foundation. More lively are the three thugs who are fingering Scheider. Ring-leader John Glover gives the role such a decadently sinister turn that he's far more interesting and lively to watch than Scheider.

••

■ **FIGHTING KENTUCKIAN, THE**

1949, 109 MINS, US Ⓥ
Dir George Waggner   *Prod* John Wayne   *Scr* George Waggner   *Ph* Lee Garmes   *Ed* Richard L. Van Enger   *Mus* George Antheil
● John Wayne, Vera Ralston, Philip Dorn, Oliver Hardy, Marie Windsor, Hugo Haas (Republic)

Whether the story of two Kentucky riflemen coming to the aid of French refugees starts a bit incongruous, it all pans out as swift-moving melodrama. Pic also introduces Oliver Hardy, better known as the rotund half of the Laurel-Hardy slapstick team, as a tough albeit corpulent Kentucky backwoods fighter. That he registers speaks well for his natural thespian ability, mugging and all.

A little known bit of American history, that Congress granted four townships of land in Alabama to French officers of Napoleon's defeated armies and their families, forms the background for the story. That is until Wayne, one of the Kentucky troopers returning from final battle of the war of 1812, falls in love with Vera Ralston, daughter of French general Hugo Haas.

••

■ **FIGURES IN A LANDSCAPE**

1970, 95 MINS, UK ◇
Dir Joseph Losey   *Prod* John Kohn   *Scr* Robert Shaw   *Ph* Henri Alekan   *Ed* Reginald Beck   *Mus* Richard Rodney Bennett   *Art Dir* Ted Tester
● Robert Shaw, Malcolm McDowell, Pamela Brown (Cinema Center)

The plight of two prisoners escaping from a relentless helicopter over '400 miles of hostile terrain' is the armature around which this yarn, which purposely never defines who the prisoners or the forces chasing them are, is spun.

MacConnachie, a 40-year-old 'coarse man born to kill' and young Ansell, who supposedly is 'propelled by reason and perception' have somewhere joined forces, are scrambling over the wastelands, and are being pursued by an acrobatic helicopter whose job it

is to spot them, and whose faceless pilot seems to enjoy swooping down to give them a scare.

It is difficult to get into the characters, who always remain as elusive as the country they are traveling over is supposed to be.

••

■ **FILE ON THELMA JORDON, THE**

1950, 100 MINS, US
Dir Robert Siodmak   *Prod* Hal B. Wallis   *Scr* Ketti Frings   *Ph* George Barnes   *Ed* Warren Low   *Mus* Victor Young   *Art Dir* Hans Dreier, Earl Hedrick
● Barbara Stanwyck, Wendell Corey, Paul Kelly, Joan Tetzel, Stanley Ridges (Paramount)

Thelma Jordon unfolds as an interesting, femme-slanted melodrama, told with a lot of restrained excitement.

Scripting is very forthright, up to the contrived conclusion, and even that is carried off successfully because of the sympathy developed for the misguided and misused character played by Wendell Corey.

Corey is seen as an assistant d.a., a husband and father. One night, after a quarrel with his wife Joan Tetzel, he is intrigued by the Barbara Stanwyck character. It leads him to further pursuit and a hot amour.

Stanwyck is pretending to be a poor cousin to her rich aunt. When the latter is killed by a house-breaker, Corey attempts to remove evidence which would point towards Stanwyck. Despite this, she is charged with murder.

Robert Siodmak's direction pinpoints many scenes of extreme tension.

••

■ **FINAL CONFLICT, THE**

1981, 108 MINS, US ◇
Dir Graham Baker   *Prod* Harvey Bernhard   *Scr* Andrew Birkin   *Ph* Robert Paynter, Phil Meheux   *Ed* Alan Strachan   *Mus* Jerry Goldsmith   *Art Dir* Herbert Westbrook
● Sam Neill, Rossano Brazzi, Don Gordon, Lisa Harrow (20th Century-Fox)

The Final Conflict is the last chapter in the *Omen* trilogy, which is too bad because this is the funniest one yet.

This time Sam Neill plays Damien Thorn, all grown up now after killing off two nice families in the previous chapters. Fear of orphanage, of course, never worries Damien because his real father is the Devil, who only wanted him to go to the best schools, get a job and take over the world for evil.

And now he has, or almost. He's running Thorn Industries and will soon be US Ambassador to England when the fellow who has the job sees a bad dog and goes back to the office and blows his head off, the single startling episode in the whole film.

Having memorized the Book of Hebron from The Apocrypha, plus several dopy soliloquies in Andrew Birkin's script. Neill knows the only obstacle to his plan is the baby born when three stars conjoin overhead.

There's also the matter of the daggers. If you remember the first two episodes, somebody or other, sometimes mom, sometimes dad, sometimes a stranger, was always trying to stab little Damien to death with the daggers.

This is the first feature for director Graham Baker, a veteran of British TV commercials, and it seems like he doesn't quite know what to do when the daggers don't have a brand name to hold toward the camera or the dialog stretches beyond two sentences.

••

■ **FINAL COUNTDOWN, THE**

1980, 103 MINS, US ◇ Ⓥ
Dir Don Taylor   *Prod* Peter Vincent Douglas   *Scr* David Ambrose, Gerry Davis, Thomas Hunter, Peter Powell   *Ph* Victor J. Kemper   *Ed* Robert K. Lambert

Mus John Scott   *Art Dir* Fernando Carrere
● Kirk Douglas, Martin Sheen, Katharine Ross, James Farentino, Ron O'Neal, Charles Durning (Bryna/United Artists)

As a documentary on the USS *Nimitz*, *The Final Countdown* is wonderful. As entertainment, however, it has the feeling of a telepic that strayed onto the big screen. The magnificent production values provided by setting the film on the world's largest nuclear-powered aircraft carrier can't transcend the predictable cleverness of a plot that will seem overly familiar to viewers raised on *Twilight Zone* reruns.

The liberal sympathies typical of the work of Kirk Douglas are evident in his characterization of the ship's commander as a man whose sense of military honor will not allow him to take the opportunity provided him by a mysterious storm – his ship and crew find themselves transported back in time to 6 December 1941, between Pearl Harbor and the Japanese fleet heading to destroy the American naval base and send the US into World War II.

The philosophical issues raised by the film hardly bear much examination, because the patchwork screenplay by two pairs of writers paints each character in too schematic a fashion. Martin Sheen has much more to work with than Douglas, who seems uncharacteristically subdued.

••

■ **FINDERS KEEPERS**

1966, 94 MINS, UK ◇
Dir Sidney Hayers   *Prod* George H. Brown   *Scr* Michael Pertwee   *Ph* Alan Hume   *Ed* Tristam Cones   *Mus* The Shadows   *Art Dir* Jack Sheripan
● Cliff Richard, The Shadows, Robert Morley, Peggy Mount, Viviane Ventura, Graham Stark (Interstate/United Artists)

George H. Brown's storyline about a mini-bomb dropped by accident from an American plane over Spain and subsequent attempts by various foreign 'spies' to locate it could have had a good astringent and satirical tang. The theme is not only largely frittered away but is hardly suitable for a relaxed, easygoing musicomedy designed to showcase a pop group such as Cliff Richard and The Shadows. Wit gets lost, and incidents are held up, to make room for inevitable song, dance and fiesta.

Richard and The Shadows hitchhike to a hotel in Spain and find it deserted. The dropped bomb has sent everybody scurrying away. The lads, with the help of a local charmer (Viviane Ventura), decide that it's in their interests to find it and hand it over to the US troops who have moved in on a similar mission.

Michael Pertwee's screenplay does not build up much urgency or suspense but provides opportunity for colorful fiesta, a gentle romance between Richard and Ventura, some verbal dueling between Robert Morley and Graham Stark.

••

■ **FINDERS KEEPERS**

1984, 96 MINS, US ◇ Ⓥ
Dir Richard Lester   *Prod* Sandra Marsh, Terence Marsh   *Scr* Ronny Graham, Terence Marsh, Charles Dennis   *Ph* Brian West   *Ed* John Victor Smith   *Mus* Ken Thorne   *Art Dir* J. Dennis Washington
● Michael O'Keefe, Beverly D'Angelo, Louis Gossett Jr, Ed Lauter, David Wayne, Brian Dennehy (CBS)

Director Richard Lester returns to his pell-mell trademark and the result is maddening. Interesting cast is wasted, with bright exception of Beverly D'Angelo.

Producers Sandra and Terence Marsh hang their frenetic tale of stolen money, chases and deceptions on several characters racing up and down a train en-route from California to Nebraska.

There's $5 million in a coffin in the baggage car, there's a sexy neurotic (D'Angelo, who steals the movie), a bumbling con man (top-lined Michael O'Keefe), a razor sharp con man (Louis Gossett Jr, on screen only briefly), a sweaty heavy (Ed Lauter), and a gregarious old train conductor (David Wayne). Its parts add up to pieces that artlessly lurch and hurtle around.

· ·

■ **FINE MADNESS, A**

1966, 104 MINS, US ◇ ⓥ

Dir Irvin Kershner   *Prod* Jerome Hellman   *Scr* Elliott Baker   *Ph* Ted McCord   *Ed* William Ziegler   *Mus* John Addison   *Art Dir* Jack Poplin

● Sean Connery, Joanne Woodward, Jean Seberg, Patrick O'Neal, Colleen Dewhurst, Clive Revill (Pan Arts/Warner)

A Fine Madness is offbeat, and downbeat, in many ways. Too heavyhanded to be comedy, yet too light to be called drama, the well-mounted production depicts a non-conformist poet-stud in an environment of much sex, some violence and modern headshrinking. Fine direction and some good characterizations enhance negative script outlook.

Sean Connery is a virile, headstrong poet, hung up in a dry spell of inspiration. He despises women in general, and to hammer home this point, all femme characters, except second wife Joanne Woodward, are shrews, battle-axes, or shallow broads.

Overdue back alimony cues an outburst, eventually leading Connery to psychiatric care, alternating with a running chase from the fuzz, and climaxed by a curiously ineffective brain lobotomy. A lot of sophisticated throwaway dialog is dispensed along with sight gags and slapstick.

Director Irvin Kershner has drawn effective performances from Connery, who makes a good comic kook in a switch from the somnambulism of his James Bond roles, and Woodward, almost unrecognizable in face and voice via a good characterization of the loud-mouthed, but loving, wife, done in the Judy Holliday style. Jean Seberg, bored wife of headshrinker Patrick O'Neal, is okay.

· ·

■ **FINE MESS, A**

1986, 88 MINS, US ◇ ⓥ

Dir Blake Edwards   *Prod* Tony Adams   *Scr* Blake Edwards   *Ph* Harry Stradling   *Ed* John F. Burnett   *Mus* Henry Mancini   *Art Dir* Rodger Maus

● Ted Danson, Howie Mandel, Richard Mulligan, Stuart Margolin, Maria Conchita Alonso, Paul Sorvino (BEE/Columbia-Delphi V)

Blake Edward's obsession with the slapstick comedy genre has produced some all-time comedy classics and some best-forgotten clinkers. *A Fine Mess* belongs in the latter category.

Neither Ted Danson and Howie Mandel nor Richard Mulligan and Stuart Margolin offer audiences much affection, or are likely to receive much.

Danson plays a small-time actor who, during location filming at a racing stable, overhears two crooks (Mulligan and Margolin) as they dope a horse on the instructions of their boss (Paul Sorvino). Before long, Danson and his buddy Mandel are being chased all over LA by the incompetent villains, cueing in plenty of over-familiar car chases.

A Fine Mess is light on plot and instead concentrates on strenuous, familiar comedy routines. Trouble is, the principal players are all quite charmless.

· ·

■ **FINE PAIR, A**

1969, 88 MINS, ITALY/US ◇

Dir Francesco Maselli   *Prod* Leo L. Fuchs   *Scr* Francesco Maselli, Luisa Montagnana, Larry Gelbart, Virgil C. Leone   *Ph* Alfio Contini   *Ed* Nicoletta

Nardi   *Mus* Ennio Morricone   *Art Dir* Luciano Puccino

● Rock Hudson, Claudia Cardinale, Tomas Milian, Leon Askin, Ellen Corby (Cinema Center)

A Fine Pair carries a promising original premise but film is so bogged down in contrived and confusing action that its impact is reduced to a minimum. Pic was lensed mostly in Italy. Script never rings true and Rock Hudson is called upon to enact an unconvincing character.

Film opens in NY, where Claudia Cardinale, a sexy 24-year-old who once knew Hudson when he visited her policeman-father in Italy 10 years before, arrives from her native country to enlist his assistance. She claims she's been involved with an international jewel thief and she wants Hudson's help in returning a fortune in jewels stolen from the winter villa of a rich American family in Austria.

Hudson plays his role in a grim manner and Cardinale is nice to look at even though difficult to understand.

· ·

■ **FINIAN'S RAINBOW**

1968, 145 MINS, US ◇ ⓥ

Dir Francis Coppola   *Prod* Joseph Landon   *Scr* E. Y. Harburg, Fred Saidy   *Ph* Philip Lathrop   *Ed* Melvin Shapiro   *Mus* Burton Lane   *Art Dir* Hilyard M. Brown

● Fred Astaire, Petula Clark, Tommy Steele, Don Francks, Keenan Wynn, Barbara Hancock (Warner/Seven Arts)

This translation of the 1947 legituner is a light, pastoral fantasy with civil rights angles, underscored by comedy values.

Film opens leisurely with Fred Astaire and Petula Clark, his daughter, on a montage tour of the US. The stars come to rest in Rainbow Valley, just as the police henchmen of racist judge Keenan Wynn are about to foreclose on property owned by vagabond Don Francks.

Astaire bails out Francks, and latter's romance with Clark develops. Tommy Steele arrives as the leprechaun searching for gold which Astaire has stolen.

Overall, the $4 million film has an ethereal quality: it's a blend of real elements, such as love, greed, compassion, prejudice, and other aspects of human nature both noble and otherwise; yet it's also infused with mystical elements of magic, leprechauns, pixies and wishes that come true.

Clark, in her American film debut, has a winsome charm, which comes through despite a somewhat reactive role.

· ·

■ **FIRE AND ICE**

1983, 81 MINS, US ◇ ⓥ

Dir Ralph Bakshi   *Prod* Ralph Bakshi, Frank Frazetta   *Scr* Roy Thomas, Gerry Conway   *Ed* A. Davis Marshall   *Mus* William Kraft

● (PSO)

Ralph Bakshi's newest animation feature is interesting for two special reasons: (1) the production represents a clear design on Bakshi's part to capture a wider and younger audience and (2) the animation marks the film debut of America's leading exponent of heroic fantasy art, Frank Frazetta, who coproduced.

Known for his classic comic book and poster art, Frazetta works some of his famous illustrations into the film, such as his *Death Dealer* painting portraying an axe-wielding figure on horseback. Populating an Armageddon embellished with subhumans and flying dragonhawks are a blond hero, Larn; a sensuous-vulnerable dream girl in distress, Teegra; and an icy sorcerer and his willful mother, Lord Nekron and Juliana. Bakshi shot live actors first, to lay the foundation for the animation, in a process called Rotoscope.

· ·

■ **FIRE BIRDS**

1990, 85 MINS, US ◇ ⓥ

Dir David Green   *Prod* William Badalato   *Scr* Nick Thiel, Paul F. Edwards   *Ph* Tony Imi   *Ed* Jon Poll, Norman Buckley, Dennis O'Connor   *Mus* David Newman   *Art Dir* Joseph T. Garrity

● Nicolas Cage, Tommy Lee Jones, Sean Young, Bert Rhine (Touchstone/Nova/Barish-Kopelson)

Originally titled *Wings of the Apache* for the Apache assault helicopters prominently featured, *Fire Birds* resembles a morale booster project leftover from the Reagan era. A paean to Yankee air power, it shows the US Army as a take-charge outfit able to kick the butt of those South American drug cartel jerks.

Not surprisingly, given changing times and politics, *Fire Birds* has a tongue-in-cheek aspect. Camaraderie and rat-a-tat-tat dialog may have started out as fun a la Howard Hawks' classic *Only Angels Have Wings* but emerges at times as a satire of the genre.

Formula script, which inevitably recalls *Top Gun*, has Nicolas Cage training to use the army's Apache aircraft while vainly trying to rekindle a romance with old flame Sean Young. Tommy Lee Jones is dead-on as the taskmaster instructor who cornily singles out Cage for rough treatment. Film's main novelty is having Young also sent into combat instead of being the woman sitting on the sidelines.

· ·

■ **FIRE DOWN BELOW**

1957, 116 MINS, US ◇ ⓥ

Dir Robert Parrish   *Prod* Irving Allen, Albert R. Broccoli   *Scr* Irwin Shaw   *Ph* Desmond Dickinson, Cyril Knowles   *Ed* Jack Slade   *Mus* Arthur Benjamin   *Art Dir* John Box

● Rita Hayworth, Robert Mitchum, Jack Lemmon, Herbert Lom, Bernard Lee, Anthony Newley (Warwick/Columbia)

Story [from a novel by Max Catto]: bad, bad girl (Rita Hayworth) meets youthful American, and finally agrees to marry him though warning him of her past – that of sort of a Mata Hari in Europe. Robert Mitchum, as Jack Lemmon's pal in a small fishing and smuggling boat operation, is vastly displeased with this development and tips off the Coast Guard on a smuggling trip so that Lemmon abandons the boat rather than be captured as a smuggler.

This lands him on a Greek freighter which crashes into a heavier ship in the fog. Lemmon is pinned down in the hold by a steel girder. Nearly all the second half of the film is centered on efforts to rescue him.

Hayworth is excellent as the comely femme who is always just one step ahead of the law. Lemmon (who takes a bow for composing the harmonica theme) shows plainly that he can handle a dramatic type role while Mitchum, as the tough man of the world, contributes one of his better portrayals.

· ·

■ **FIREFOX**

1982, 137 MINS, US ◇ ⓥ

Dir Clint Eastwood   *Prod* Clint Eastwood   *Scr* Alex Lasker, Wendell Wellman   *Ph* Bruce Surtees   *Ed* Ferris Webster, Ron Spang   *Mus* Maurice Jarre   *Art Dir* John Graysmark, Elayne Ceder

● Clint Eastwood, Freddie Jones, David Huffman, Warren Clarke, Ronald Lacey, Kenneth Colley (Warner)

Firefox is a burn-out. Lethargic, characterless and at least a half-hour too long, Cold War espionage saga [from the novel by Craig Thomas] about an American pilot smuggled into the USSR to steal an advanced fighter jet is a disappointment since it possessed the basic elements of a topflight, us vs them actioner.

It all sounded good on paper – Clint Eastwood, as a retired ace flyer, infiltrating

F

the Russian Air Force to spirit away the supposedly top-secret Firefox, a plane capable of Mach 5 speed and equipped with a thought-controlled weapons system.

But Eastwood, who generally displays astuteness when controlling his own projects has inexplicably dropped the ball here. Despite the tense mission being depicted, there's no suspense, excitement or thrills to be had, and laxidaisical pacing gives viewer plenty of time to ponder the gaping implausibilities.

. . . .

■ FIRE OVER ENGLAND

1937, 88 MINS, UK Ⓥ
Dir William K. Howard *Prod* Erich Pommer
Scr Clemence Dane, Sergei Nolbandov *Ph* James Wong Howe *Ed* Jack Dennis *Mus* Richard Addinsell *Art Dir* Lazare Meerson
● Flora Robson, Raymond Massey, Leslie Banks, Laurence Olivier, Vivien Leigh, Lyn Harding
(Pendennis London)

This is a handsomely mounted and forcefully dramatic glorification of Queen Bess. It holds a succession of brilliantly played scenes, a wealth of choice diction, pointed excerpts from English history and a series of impressive tableaux.

It projects Flora Robson in a conception of the British regent which holds the imagination. Her keen aptitude in dovetailing the strong and frail sides of Elizabeth's nature makes a solid keystone for the production.

Action ranges from cumbersomely dull to sharp, hardhitting flashes of excitement. Where director William K. Howard seems to get in his most telling dramatic effects are the sequences which build up to Laurence Olivier's undoing as an English spy and his subsequent escape, the queen's confronting of her coterie of exposed betrayers, and the burning of the Spanish armada.

Sprightly plied are the romantic passages. It's a two-cornered play for Olivier. First object of his deportment is his childhood sweetheart and lady-in-waiting to the queen, persuasively treated by Vivian Leigh. His other idyllic moments bring him in contact with the daughter of a Spanish nobleman. As the Spanish beauty Tamara Desni blends a compound of charm and sympathy.

. . . .

■ FIREPOWER

1979, 104 MINS, UK ◇ Ⓥ
Dir Michael Winner *Prod* Michael Winner
Scr Gerald Wilson *Ph* Robert Paynter, Dick Kratina *Ed* Arnold Crust *Mus* Gato Barbieri *Art Dir* John Stoll, John Blezard, Robert Gundlach
● Sophia Loren, James Coburn, O.J. Simpson, Eli Wallach, Anthony Franciosa, Vincent Gardenia
(Scimitar)

Firepower is one of those international action thrillers designed to combine a top-name cast with lots of shooting and explosions so the story can be followed regardless of whether you understand the language.

Though competent with chases and gunfire, producer-director Michael Winner handles the dialog scenes as if the most significant thing in the world were sunglasses.

Beautiful Sophia Loren believes her chemist husband was murdered at the order of Stegner (George Touliatos), a wealthy, seclusive industrialist. She persuades the Justice Department, who also wants Stegner, to put the pressure on mobster Eli Wallach to entice retired hitman James Coburn to get Stegner.

. . . .

■ FIRE SALE

1977, 88 MINS, US ◇
Dir Alan Arkin *Prod* Marvin Worth *Scr* Robert Klane *Ph* Ralph Woolsey *Ed* Richard Halsey *Mus* Dave Grusin *Art Dir* James H. Spencer

● Alan Arkin, Rob Reiner, Vincent Gardenia, Anjanette Comer, Kay Medford, Barbara Dana
(20th Century-Fox)

Fire Sale, Alan Arkin's alleged comedy is a consummate sophomoric vulgarity. Marvin Worth's production matches in crippled creativity the physical infirmities on which most of the forced and strident humor is based. Arkin and Rob Reiner head the cast as two harried sons of Vincent Gardenia, himself the henpecked husband of Kay Medford.

Gardenia owns a dumpy department store, Reiner his cowed assistant after Arkin years earlier departed the family circle to become a failure as a basketball coach.

Sid Caesar is appropriately offensive as a Veterans' Hospital basket case coaxed by Gardenia into burning the store for insurance, thinking it's a World War II German installation.

. . . .

■ FIRESTARTER

1984, 115 MINS, US ◇ Ⓥ
Dir Mark L. Lester *Prod* Frank Capra Jr *Scr* Stanley Mann *Ph* Giuseppe Ruzzolini *Ed* David Rawlins *Mus* Tangerine Dream *Art Dir* Giorgio Postiglione
● David Keith, Drew Barrymore, George C. Scott, Martin Sheen, Heather Locklear, Art Carney
(De Laurentiis)

Story of a nine-year-old girl who can enflame objects and people by power of her will balances human concern of a pursued and loving father and daughter (David Keith and Drew Barrymore) against a clandestine government agency that wants to use the girl's power for nefarious ends. Agency is headed by Martin Sheen, with Moses Gunn and George C. Scott as chilly support group.

Film marks the first major picture for director Mark L. Lester. But pic's stars are special effects team Mike Wood and Jeff Jarvis, whose pyrotechnics – flying fireballs, fire trenches, human balls of fire – create the film's impact.

Script by Stanley Mann is quite faithful to the Stephen King novel, but cinematically that loyalty is damaging. Picture's length can't sustain the material.

. . . .

■ FIRST A GIRL

1935, 92 MINS, UK
Dir Victor Saville *Prod* Michael Balcon *Scr* Marjorie Gaffney *Ph* Glen MacWilliams *Ed* A. Barnes *Art Dir* Oscar Werndorff
● Jessie Matthews, Sonnie Hale, Anna Lee, Griffith Jones, Alfred Drayton, Eddie Gray (Gaumont-British)

Jessie Matthews' admirers will love to see her rise from her humdrum niche in a dressmaking establishment to the giddy heights of thespian glory.

Though always longing for a stage career, her precipitous plunge comes about accidentally. She pals up with an aspiring Shakespearean actor, in reality a female impersonator. While sheltering her, he gets a wire giving him an unexpected date, which sudden loss of voice makes it impossible for him to accept. He coaches the bewildered girl and insists she take his place.

The variety hall is an awful dump. Billed, and trading, on the doubt concerning her sex, and carefully managed by her new partner, the act is a hit and she quickly makes a name.

The former wealthy customer, a 'princess' and her boyfriend become friendly with the couple, but suspect she is really a girl and trick her by stalling on a motor trip to the Riviera, forcing her to share a room at a wayside inn with the two men.

Sonnie Hale plays the impersonator and gives an air of sincerity to a rather dubious situation. The boyfriend (Griffith Jones) has charm and a quiet dignity. The starring role

is a natural for Jessie Matthews, where her dancing is unobtrusively displayed.

. . . .

■ FIRST BLOOD

1982, 94 MINS, US ◇ Ⓥ
Dir Ted Kotcheff *Prod* Buzz Feitshans *Scr* Michael Kozoll, William Sackheim, Sylvester Stallone *Ph* Andrew Laszlo *Ed* Tom Noble *Mus* Jerry Goldsmith *Art Dir* Stephane Reichel
● Sylvester Stallone, Richard Crenna, Brian Dennehy, David Caruso, Jack Starrett, Michael Talbot (Orion)

Sylvester Stallone plays a former Green Beret, a 'killing machine' who's so tough if there had been one more of him, the Viet Cong wouldn't have had a chance.

Arriving unshaven at the quiet community of Hope, he's greeted by sheriff Brian Dennehy, who does not invite him to join the local Lion's club. In fact, Dennehy won't even let him linger for a sandwich. This upsets the taciturn Stallone and he winds up at the slammer. Beating up the whole station house, he escapes into the woods.

Richard Crenna shows up, a Green Beret colonel who trained Stallone. They trap Stallone in a mine and blast the dickens out of it with a rocket. But our boy commandeers an army truck and machine gun and goes back to level Dennehy's quiet little town.

Director Ted Kotcheff has all sorts of trouble with this mess, aside from credibility. Supposedly, the real villain here is society itself, which invented a debacle like Vietnam and must now deal with its lingering tragedies. But *First Blood* cops out completely on that one, not even trying to find a solution to Stallone's problems.

. . . .

■ FIRST DEADLY SIN, THE

1980, 112 MINS, US ◇ Ⓥ
Dir Brian Hutton *Prod* George Pappas, Mark Shanker *Scr* Mann Rubin *Ph* Jack Priestley *Ed* Eric Albertson *Mus* Gordon Jenkins *Art Dir* Woody Mackintosh
● Frank Sinatra, Faye Dunaway, Brenda Vaccaro, James Whitmore, David Dukes, Martin Gabel
(Kastner/Artanis/Cinema 7)

Otherwise a fairly routine and turgid crime meller, *The First Deadly Sin* commands some interest as Frank Sinatra's first film in 10 years.

Pic presents audience with considerable barriers to involvement from the outset, as first few reels consist predominantly of a bloody operation, a violent murder, dialog conducted over mutilated bodies in an autopsy room and unappetizing hospital scenes.

Plot has Sinatra latching onto an apparent series of arbitrary murders.

Paralleling the crime-and-detection yarn, and slowing down the entire proceedings, are Sinatra's visits to wife Faye Dunaway, who's not recovering well from a kidney operation.

As for Sinatra, direct and not at all the wise guy, this amounts to a decent performance, even if the role might have called for a more desperate attitude.

. . . .

■ FIRST GREAT TRAIN ROBBERY, THE

1979, 110 MINS, UK ◇ Ⓥ
Dir Michael Crichton *Prod* John Foreman
Scr Michael Crichton *Ph* Geoffrey Unsworth *Ed* David Bretherton *Mus* Jerry Goldsmith *Art Dir* Maurice Carter
● Sean Connery, Donald Sutherland, Lesley-Anne Down, Wayne Sleep, Michael Elphick
(United Artists/De Laurentiis)

Based on fact, the story [from the novel by Michael Crichton] concerns the first recorded heist from a moving train. Suave arch-criminal Sean Connery enlists Donald

197

Sutherland, Wayne Sleep, in a bid to lift a payroll of gold bars destined for the Crimea in 1855. A vital part, or rather series of parts, in the plan is played by Lesley-Anne Down as Connery's versatile yet reliable mistress.

The actual theft is ingenious. The film's highpoint comes when Connery clambers from car roof to car roof as the steam train speeds smokily under low bridges.

Crichton's films drag in dialog bouts, but triumph when action takes over.

Handling of the train sequences by cinematographer Geoffrey Unsworth is a lesson in the superior effectiveness of a well-placed camera over fancy tricks. A final caption dedicates the film to his memory, stating: 'His friends miss him.' So will his audiences.

● ●

■ FIRST LOVE

1977, 91 MINS, US ◇ ⓥ
Dir Joan Darling   *Prod* Lawrence Turman, David Foster   *Scr* Jane Stanton Hitchcock, David Freeman   *Ph* Bobby Byrne   *Ed* Frank Morriss   *Mus* Joel Sill   *Art Dir* Robert Luthardt
● William Katt, Susan Dey, John Heard, Beverly D'Angelo, Robert Loggia, Tom Lacy (Paramount)

First Love is a sensitive and melancholy film about the impact of romance on college student William Katt when he falls for coed Susan Dey.

Harold Brodkey's *New Yorker* story, *Sentimental Education*, has been adapted into a script which takes Katt through the highs and lows of commplicated young love.

But an unfortunate element in the story is the never-ending pall of doom that hangs over everything. From frame one the mood is a downer, which dampens the several nice bright moments of exuberance and telegraphs the coming climactic ambiguity.

Katt is excellent. So is Dey, who has an appealing charisma of vivacious sensuality.

● ●

■ FIRST MONDAY IN OCTOBER

1981, 96 MINS, US ◇
Dir Ronald Neame   *Prod* Paul Heller, Martha Scott   *Scr* Jerome Lawrence, Robert E. Lee   *Ph* Fred J. Koenekamp   *Ed* Peter E. Berger   *Mus* Ian Fraser   *Art Dir* Philip M. Jefferies
● Walter Matthau, Jill Clayburgh, Jan Sterling (Paramount)

Amiable talents of Walter Matthau and Jill Clayburgh make *First Monday in October* a mildly engaging lovefest in which all serious issues serve as window dressing for an almost-romantic comedy.

Rumpled and as likeable as ever, Matthau here portrays the court's 'great dissenter,' an individualistic civil libertarian a la the late William O. Douglas. In theory he greatly welcomes the appointment of a woman, but his hair stands on end when he learns that America's first female Supreme Court justice is the arch-conservative Clayburgh, 'the Mother Superior of Orange County.'

Decorum of the widow's installment into the men's club atmosphere of the court provokes smiles, if not big laughs, but it's all a prelude to the civilized sparks which fly when the two tangle over two major cases on the docket.

Scripters, working from their own popular play, have opted for the light treatment, with issues of the day merely providing a means for this odd couple to (sort of) get together.

● ●

■ FIRST OF THE FEW, THE

1942, 118 MINS, UK ⓥ
Dir Leslie Howard   *Prod* Leslie Howard   *Scr* Anatole de Grunwald, Miles Malleson   *Ph* Jack Hildyard   *Ed* Douglas Myers   *Mus* William Walton   *Art Dir* Paul Sheriff
● Leslie Howard, David Niven, Rosamund John, Roland Culver, Anne Firth (British Aviation)

In interpreting the life of R.J. Mitchell, who designed the Spitfire plane, Leslie Howard's work ranks among his finest performances. And it is an epic picture.

Film portrays Mitchell's heartbreaking efforts to get his series of aircraft models accepted. His work was looked upon as too revolutionary, and the reluctance of Whitehall to sponsor anything new was most discouraging.

For big scenes there is the reproduction of a race for the Schneider Cup. For sweet domestic felicity there's Rosamund John as the wife of Mitchell. For a magnificent patriotic gesture there is Toni Edgar Bruce as Lady Houston, who contributed generously to the financing of the inventor. Finally (or should it be firstly?) there's Howard's young airman friend in the person of David Niven, as a lovable philanderer who shares the other's vicissitudes and glories.

● ●

■ FIRST TIME, THE

1983, 95 MINS, US ◇ ⓥ
Dir Charlie Loventhal   *Prod* Sam Irvin   *Scr* Charlie Loventhal, Susan Weiser-Finley, William Franklin Finley   *Ph* Steve Fierberg   *Ed* Stanley Vogel   *Mus* Lanny Meyers   *Art Dir* Tom Surgal
● Tim Choate, Krista Errickson, Marshall Efron, Wendy Fulton, Raymond Patterson, Jane Badler (New Line/Goldmine)

The First Time is a mild but entertaining first feature by writer-director Charlie Loventhal and producer Sam Irvin, former assistants to Brian De Palma. Dealing fictionally with Loventhal's growing-up adventures while a student at formerly all-girls school Sarah Lawrence, the comedy owes much to De Palma's freewheeling satires made in the 1960s.

Charlie (Tim Choate) is an odd-man-out at college: unable to score with the pretty (but believably so) girls there while his black room-mate Ronald (Raymond Patterson) shows off and gives him tips.

While pursuing an unattainable dream girl Dana (Krista Errickson), Charlie links up with another lonely soul Wendy (Wendy Fulton), and ultimately loses his virginity with the inevitable older woman Karen (Jane Badler).

Choate is very sympathetic in the lead role, matched by the sex appeal of Errickson, naturalism of Fulton and comedy sex-bomb Wendie Jo Sperber.

● ●

■ FISH CALLED WANDA, A

1988, 108 MINS, US ◇ ⓥ
Dir Charles Crichton   *Prod* Michael Shamberg   *Scr* John Cleese   *Ph* Alan Hume   *Ed* John Jympson   *Mus* John Du Prez   *Art Dir* Roger Murray-Leach
● John Cleese, Jamie Lee Curtis, Kevin Kline, Michael Palin, Tom Georgeson, Maria Aitken (M-G-M)

In *A Fish Called Wanda*, Monty Pythoners John Cleese and Michael Palin get caught up in a double-crossing crime caper with a mismatched and hilarious pair of scheming Yanks, Jamie Lee Curtis and Kevin Kline.

Though it is less tasteless, irreverent and satirical than the Python pics, film still is wacky and occasionally outrageous in its own, distinctly British way.

John Cleese is Archie Leach (Cary Grant's real name) an uptight, respected barrister who becomes unglued when Wanda (Jamie Lee Curtis), the girlfriend of a crook he's defending, comes on to him for no apparent reason.

Curtis fakes it as an American law student looking to learn about English law when really she just wants to get information out of Cleese about some diamonds she's recently heisted with his client George (Tom Georgeson) and two others – her 'brother' Otto (Kevin Kline), who's really no relation and a stuttering animal rights freak Ken (Michael Palin), the proud owner of a fish tank and a fish named Wanda.

Cleese takes an opportunity to poke fun at something ripe for ridicule – this time, the love-hate rivalry between the Brits and the Yanks. It's funny without being mean, since both sides gets their due. Curtis steals the show with her keen sense of comic timing and sneaky little grins and asides. Palin has too limited a role.

● ●

■ F.I.S.T.

1978, 145 MINS, US ◇ ⓥ
Dir Norman Jewison   *Prod* Norman Jewison   *Scr* Joe Eszterhas, Sylvester Stallone   *Ph* Laszlo Kovacs   *Ed* Tony Gibbs, Graeme Clifford   *Mus* Bill Conti   *Art Dir* Richard MacDonald
● Sylvester Stallone, Rod Steiger, Peter Boyle, Melinda Dillon, David Huffman, Tony Lo Bianco (United Artists)

In its superb telling of how a humble but idealistic young man escalates to the corrupt heights of unbridled power, *F.I.S.T.* is to the labor movement in the United States what *All the King's Men* was to an era in American politics.

The first hour of the film presents the milieu of unorganized labor circa 1937, a time when the phrase 'property rights' was as persistent (and often as shrill) a harangue as 'human rights' later became. Sylvester Stallone and lifelong friend David Huffman are among the workers in Henry Wilcoxon's trucking company. They drift into organizing drivers for local union rep Richard Herd, whose assassination during a brawl triggered by management goons drives Stallone into league with Kevin Conway, a local hood.

The next act depicts the militant labor response of Stallone and Conway, highlighted by a well-staged riot, after which the tentacles of mobsterism – Tony Lo Bianco personifying them well – parallel the growth and power of the truckers' union.

Action then cuts to the late 1950s, when Stallone pushes international union leader Peter Boyle out of office by some private blackmail, only to run head-on into Rod Steiger, crusading US senator.

● ●

■ FISTFUL OF DYNAMITE, A

1972, 139 MINS, ITALY ◇ ⓥ
Dir Sergio Leone   *Prod* Fulvio Morselli   *Scr* Luciano Vincenzoni, Sergio Donati, Sergio Leone   *Ph* Giuseppe Ruzzolini   *Ed* Nino Baragli   *Mus* Ennio Morricone   *Art Dir* Andrea Crisanti
● Rod Steiger, James Coburn, Romolo Valli, Maria Monti, Rik Battaglia, Franco Graziosi (Rafram/United Artists)

Sergio Leone comes up with a tale of the Mexican revolution. Rod Steiger plays a simple bandit who wants to rob a bank in a Mexican town but instead gets mixed up in a revolution in which he has no interest. He meets Coburn, a veritable storehouse of explosives on his person, and together they become involved in the peasants' revolt.

Leone occasionally inserts a light touch but generally action which includes firing squads, much shooting, a bridge which troops are crossing blown up and a climaxing train collision are realistically portrayed. A paralleling note is offered via flashbacks through Coburn comparing some of his past experiences in the Irish Rebellion to events at hand, but procedure sometimes is clumsy.

[Reviewed above as *Duck, You Sucker*. Film's English-language title was changed soon after to *A Fistful of Dynamite*.]

● ●

F

■ FITZWILLY

1967, 102 MINS, US ◇

Dir Delbert Mann   *Prod* Walter Mirisch   *Scr* Isobel
Lennart   *Ph* Joseph Biroc   *Ed* Ralph Winters
Mus John Williams   *Art Dir* Robert F. Boyle
● Dick Van Dyke, Barbara Feldon, Edith Evans, John
McGiver, Harry Townes, John Fiedler (United Artists)

An okay, but sluggish, comedy about a butler
who masterminds robberies. Potential in the
screenplay, the very good cast, and the handsome production, is not realized due to generally tame direction by Delbert Mann.

Isobel Lennart adapted Poyntz Tyler's
novel *A Garden of Cucumbers*, in which Dick
Van Dyke is the devoted butler to Edith
Evans, one of those lovable biddies who, in
this case, is not at all as wealthy as she thinks.
Van Dyke and crew keep planning heists in
order to support her fantasies, and philan-
thropies. Arrival of new secretary Barbara
Feldon upsets the smooth-running
machinery.

Results of the flat direction is a pic that, in
the main, draws smiles, not outright laughs,
until the department store panic scene,
staged in top fashion.

■ FIVE

1951, 93 MINS, US

Dir Arch Oboler   *Prod* Arch Oboler   *Scr* Arch
Oboler   *Ph* Louis Clyde Stoumen   *Ed* John Hoffman
Mus Henry Russell   *Art Dir* Arch Oboler
● William Phipps, Susan Douglas, James Anderson,
Charles Lampkin, Earl Lee (Oboler/Columbia)

Intriguing in theme, but depressing in its
assumption. *Five* ranks high in the class of
out-of-the-ordinary pix. It is the story of the
last five persons on earth, survivors of an
atom blast which turns thriving cities into
ghost towns.

Writer-producer-director Arch Oboler
has injected vivid imagination into the
production, but draws a little too much
on his radio technique. Principal criticism
lies in its dearth of action. However, interest
is sustained in suspenseful situations
and convincing dialog.

Oboler has selected his characters with
care. William Phipps and Susan Douglas are
effective as the love interest, with James
Anderson doing a commendable job as the
heavy. Charles Lampkin is competent as the
sole Negro in a minute white world. and
Earl Lee makes the most of his role as a bank
teller who because of his horror-stricken
mind, believes he's on 'vacation' from his job.

■ 5 CARD STUD

1968, 101 MINS, US ◇

Dir Henry Hathaway   *Prod* Hal Wallis
Scr Marguerite Roberts   *Ph* Daniel L. Fapp
Ed Warren Low   *Mus* Maurice Jarre   *Art Dir* Walter
Tyler
● Dean Martin, Robert Mitchum, Inger Stevens, Roddy
McDowall, Katherine Justice, Yaphet Kotto (Paramount)

Dean Martin is cast as a frontier gambler and
Robert Mitchum plays a frontier parson who
woos his congregation with a fast six-shooter.
Script [from a novel by Ray Gaulden] pits
them against one another in the unraveling of
whodunit murders, but dramatic buildup
suffers thru a premature disclosure of killer's
identity and subsequent lessening of what
should have been more potent impact.

Action follows the aftermath of a late night
poker game when a stranger is caught cheating and is lynched by five angry players.

Martin injects certain amount of humor
into his role and generally acquits himself
strongly. Mitchum's character at times seems
contrived but he handles himself well nevertheless. Inger Stevens, playing a gold-rush
Delilah who mistresses a stable of lady 'bar-

bers,' lends distaff interest, and Katherine
Justice is a nice addition as a ranch girl in
love with Martin.

■ FIVE CORNERS

1987, 92 MINS, UK ◇ ▼

Dir Tony Bill   *Prod* Forrest Murray, Tony Bill   *Scr* John
Patrick Shanley   *Ph* Fred Murphy   *Ed* Andy
Blumenthal   *Mus* James Newton Howard
Art Dir Adrianne Lobel
● Jodie Foster, Tim Robbins, Todd Graff, John Turturro,
Elizabeth Berridge (HandMade)

Five Corners starts out as an affectionate look
back at a Bronx neighborhood circa 1964 and
then about halfway through takes a darker
turn into urban violence.

In his first produced script, Patrick Shanley
clearly has drawn from his experience to
create the variety of personalities and swirl of
influences that make life in the boroughs of
New York City so distinctive.

Before would-be freedom fighter in
Mississippi Harry (Tim Robins) goes off to
save the world, there is business for him to
take care of in the old neighborhood. Local
no-goodnik Heinz (John Turturro) is out of
jail and looking to renew his old battle with
Harry and his old longing for Linda (Jodie
Foster).

They are marvelously drawn parts and
Robbins as the Irish working-class kid with a
social conscience gets into the heart and soul
of the character. Turturro is downright scary
but also sympathetic as the schoolyard psychotic. Foster is serviceable, but a little out of
her element as a tough Catholic kid.

■ FIVE DAYS ONE SUMMER

1982, 108 MINS, US ◇ ▼

Dir Fred Zinnemann   *Prod* Fred Zinnemann
Scr Michael Austin   *Ph* Giuseppe Rotunno   *Ed* Stuart
Baird   *Mus* Elmer Bernstein   *Art Dir* Willy Holt
● Sean Connery, Betsy Brantley, Lambert Wilson,
Jennifer Hilary, Isabel Dean, Anna Massey
(Ladd/Warner)

An attempt at an intimate personal drama
that just doesn't come off, *Five Days One
Summer* is so slow that it seems more like
Five Summers One Day. A tale of adultery,
mountain climbing and death that is as dramatically placid as the Swiss landscape it
inhabits, the $15 million production is Fred
Zinnemann's first film since *Julia* [1977].

Seeming hale and hearty, Sean Connery
plays a Scottish doctor off on an Alpine
vacation in 1932 with a twentyish woman he
introduces as his wife. He aims to introduce
her to his great sport, mountain climbing.

Gradually, flashbacks reveal that the girl is
not his wife at all, but his niece, that Connery
has a wife back home and that young Kate
has been not so secretly in love with Connery
since she was a child.

Ultimately, it all comes down to whether or
not the girl will stay or leave, and if Connery
and/or the guide will survive their climb of
one of the most difficult mountains in the
vicinity.

■ FIVE EASY PIECES

1970, 96 MINS, US ◇ ▼

Dir Bob Rafelson   *Prod* Bob Rafelson, Richard
Wechsler   *Scr* Adrien Joyce [=Carolyn Eastman]
Ph Laszlo Kovacs   *Ed* Christopher Holmes, Gerald
Sheppard   *Art Dir* Toby Rafelson
● Jack Nicholson, Karen Black, Lois Smith, Susan
Anspach, Helena Kallianiotes, Sally Ann Struthers
(Columbia/BBS)

Director Bob Rafelson has put together an
absorbing, if nerve-wracking, film.

Despite its solid American roots, this pic is
reminiscent of nothing so much as the French
films of the 1940s and 1950s.

Jack Nicholson is first seen on the job as a
Southern California oilrigger sporting a
'cracker' accent and consorting with three
members of the same breed especially his
dumb, sexy girlfriend Rayette (Karen Black).

It's clear from the beginning that he doesn't
think he belongs in this environment. But
only later, when he quits his job and goes
back home to the State of Washington does it
become clear that his hard hat and his accent
were a masquerade.

The film's nervewracking quality is
consistent with its content. Nicholson's
performance is a remarkably varied and daring exploration of a complex character,
equally convincing in its manic and sober
aspects.
☐ 1970: Best Picture (Nomination)

■ FIVE FINGER EXERCISE

1962, 108 MINS, US

Dir Daniel Mann   *Prod* Frederick Brisson   *Scr* Frances
Goodrich, Albert Hackett   *Ph* Harry Stradling
Ed William A. Lyon   *Mus* Jerome Moross   *Art Dir* Ross
Bellah
● Rosalind Russell, Jack Hawkins, Maximilian Schell,
Richard Beymer, Annette Gorman, Lana Wood
(Columbia)

Frederick Brisson, who transplanted this
1958 London stage hit to Broadway in 1959,
where it met with further success, has transplanted it into the more taxing idiom of the
screen. It appears that something has been
misplaced in the translation, as adapted by
Frances Goodrich and Albert Hackett, and
directed by Daniel Mann.

For one thing, the trimming to 108 minutes
apparently has taken its toll of both characterization and plot. Furthermore, although
there are two solid performances by Russell
and Hawkins, there are three equally weak
ones by Schell, Beymer and Annette
Gorman,

The title refers to the significance of five fingers operating in coordination to create harmonious music, as in a piano study for
beginners. The thoroughly uncoordinated
'five fingers' in this family melodrama, reset
in California from the original England, are
an uncultured, intolerant, self-made busi-
nessman-father (Hawkins), a culture-
obsessed, pseudo-intellectual mother (Russell), a confused, educated, 'mama's boy' son
(Beymer), an animated, highspirited
daughter (Gorman), and a young German
refugee (Schell), who has been employed by
the family as tutor, and yearns to become a
permanent part of it.

■ 5 FINGERS

1952, 107 MINS, US ▼

Dir Joseph L. Mankiewicz   *Prod* Otto Lang
Scr Michael Wilson   *Ph* Norbert Brodine   *Ed* James B.
Clark   *Mus* Bernard Herrmann   *Art Dir* Lyle Wheeler,
George W. Davis
● James Mason, Danielle Darrieux, Michael Rennie,
Walter Hampden, John Wengraf, Michael Pate (20th
Century-Fox)

A good, if somewhat overlong, cloak-and-
dagger thriller has been concocted from an
actual World War II espionage case. Screenplay is based on the novel *Operation Cicero*,
written by L.C. Moyzisch, Nazi agent in the
espionage dealings with 'Cicero', the fabulous spy.

Mason portrays Ulysses Diello known to
the Nazis as Cicero, a valet to the British Ambassador in Turkey. A cold, assured character, he decides to make himself a fortune by
selling Allied war plans to the Germans.
Cicero's operations are moving forward without a hitch until the British begin to suspect
someone within the Embassy and turn
Michael Rennie loose on a counter-espionage
job.

The script runs to considerable dialog in the first portions. However, pace quickens and becomes sock suspense drama, tight and tingling, when the story gets down to cases. Actual locations in Berlin, Ankara, Turkey, London and Istanbul were used for a documentary background effect.

· ·

■ FIVE GRAVES TO CAIRO

1943, 96 MINS, US

Dir Billy Wilder   *Prod* Charles Brackett   *Scr* Charles Brackett, Billy Wilder   *Ph* John Seitz   *Ed* Doane Harrison   *Mus* Miklos Rozsa
● Franchot Tone, Anne Baxter, Erich von Stroheim, Peter van Eyck, Akim Tamiroff, Fortunio Bonanova (Paramount)

Idea of making Field Marshal Rommel's campaign into an exciting fable is by Lajos Biro, Hungarian writer, who did so many successful Ernst Lubitsch screen hits. It affords a vivid picture of Rommel, Erich von Stroheim doing a capital job. The characterization is tailor-made for him.

Surprisingly for such a dynamic, moving vehicle, there is a minimum of actual battle stuff. Director Billy Wilder handles the varied story elements, countless suspenseful moments and vivid portrayals in excellent fashion. In some instances the absence of spoken word or muffled sentences have been pointed up through skilful pantomime and action.

Basically *Five Graves* is the story of a British corporal (Franchot Tone) who impersonates a Nazi spy to gain military information from the Germans as they sweep towards Cairo.

Crackling dialog and fine scripting by director Wilder and Charles Brackett enhance the Biro original [play]. Camerawork of John Seitz is outstanding, as is the film editing by Doane Harrison. Use of sound effects, indicating superb recording, especially during the running gun fight, also is topflight.

· ·

■ FIVE STAR FINAL

1931, 85 MINS, US

Dir Mervyn LeRoy   *Scr* Byron Morgan, Robert Lord   *Ph* Sol Polito   *Ed* Frank Ware   *Mus* Leo Forbstein (dir.)   *Art Dir* Jack Okey
● Edward G. Robinson, Marian Marsh, H.B. Warner, Anthony Bushell, George E. Stone, Boris Karloff (First National)

Playwright Louis Weitzenkorn's strong argument against the scandal type of tabloid newspaper makes a strong talker.

Edward G. Robinson means a lot to this entertainment. He represents the margin between Weitzenkorn's story on the stage and on the screen. The picture version had a head start with its unrestricted area foundation, but it needed someone like Robinson as the managing editor.

H.B. Warner and Frances Starr have a suicide scene that could have been botched very easily. But they play it. The experience in back of both stands up and gives its right age in this picture.

A bit of symbolism inserted in the picture is, for once, a help. The editor is given the habit of washing his hands often at the basin in his office. His first washing occurs during his introduction in a speak. Thereafter, as the job gets dirtier, he repeats the soap stunt more often. When Robinson finally washes his hands of the job, he does it with soap and water.

After the yellow tab, for circulation purposes, has caused two suicides by reviving a 20-year-old murder case, the picture starts to move speedily. The daughter of the unfortunate parents goes to the newspaper with a gun in her bag to ask 'Why did you kill my mother?'

Marion Marsh is as strong as the rest in the payoff scene. She stands with Georgie Stone, Warner, Starr and Robinson as punch members of the cast.
□ 1931/32: Best Picture (Nomination)

· ·

■ 5,000 FINGERS OF DR. T., THE

1953, 89 MINS, US ◇

Dir Roy Rowland   *Prod* Stanley Kramer   *Scr* Dr Seuss [= Ted Geisel], Allan Scott   *Ph* Franz Planer   *Ed* Al Clark   *Mus* Frederick Hollander   *Art Dir* Rudolph Sternad
● Peter Lind Hayes, Mary Healy, Hans Conried, Tommy Rettig (Columbia)

The mad humor of Dr Seuss (Ted Geisel) has been captured on film in this odd flight into chimerical fiction. Story and conception were shaped by Dr Seuss for the Stanley Kramer unit at Columbia, and he also contributed to the screenplay and did lyrics for the songs composed by Frederick Hollander. Results are sometimes fascinating, more often fantastic.

Of all the wild, weird happenings, the film's standout is the fantastically imaginative dungeon ballet – a mad creation.

Tommy Rettig is the kid who would rather be out playing with his baseball and dog than learning the scales under the tutelage of Hans Conried, the Dr Terwilliker who becomes the villain of the plot. Opening finds the youngster dreaming he is being pursued by strange creatures with butterfly nets in a land full of odd cylinders and mounds, eerie hues and fog.

This new land is a terrifying one, filled with a strong castle in which Dr T conducts a school of piano for the 500 boys he holds prisoner. In the dungeon, deep below the fortress, is a group of miserable creatures, grown green and moldy with age, who were imprisoned because they dared play instruments other than the piano.

Roy Rowland, an expert in the direction of kids, shows his skill in handling Rettig and does fairly well by most of the fantasy, although the material is such that it's hard to keep the interest from lagging at times.

· ·

■ FIXED BAYONETS

1951, 92 MINS, US ▼

Dir Samuel Fuller   *Prod* Jules Buck   *Scr* Samuel Fuller   *Ph* Lucien Ballard   *Ed* Nick De Maggio   *Mus* Roy Webb   *Art Dir* Lyle Wheeler, George Patrick
● Richard Basehart, Gene Evans, Michael O'Shea, Richard Hylton, Craig Hill, Skip Homeier (20th Century-Fox)

Story [suggested by a novel by John Brophy] revolves around a platoon left behind temporarily to fight a rearguard action for a retreating regiment in Korea.

The detail is supposed to be a hand-picked group of veterans. Yet among them is a corporal (Richard Basehart) who cannot bring himself to shoot an enemy soldier. How he shakes off this fixation and ultimately assumes command of the decimated platoon is an underlying theme that pervades the whole yarn.

Writer-director Samuel Fuller's platoon is a typical band of GIs. There's the sergeant (Gene Evans), a bearded vet of the last war who takes to his chores with a skill born of long experience. Sergeant Michael O'Shea is another hard-bitten '20-year man'. Privates include men of Italian, Polish and American Indian extraction, among others.

There's a wealth of suspense in the screenplay, for until the closing minutes filmgoers are unaware whether the platoon will succeed in its mission and rejoin the regiment.

· ·

■ FIXER, THE

1968, 130 MINS, US ◇

Dir John Frankenheimer   *Prod* Edward Lewis   *Scr* Dalton Trumbo   *Ph* Marcel Grignon   *Ed* Henry Berman   *Mus* Maurice Jarre   *Art Dir* Bela Zeichan
● Alan Bates, Dirk Bogarde, Georgia Brown, Hugh Griffith, Elizabeth Hartman, Ian Holm (M-G-M)

Much of the unfoldment is in the filthy prison cell of its chief protagonist, a Jew accused of the murder of a young boy but never formally charged.

Czarist Russia at the turn of the century is the period and the locality is Kiev, where a handyman is caught up in the wave of anti-Semitism. In his long suffering that follows his refusal to confess to a crime he did not commit, his case becomes known to the world.

Basic character is enacted by Alan Bates in an indefinite delineation frequently baffling to the spectator. Victim of the Russian government's persecution of all Jews and its dedication to his conviction, he is subjected to every form of mental and physical punishment to make him confess.

But reaction to violence is not alone sufficient for a fine sustained performance and overall Bates suffers from the writing.

Dirk Bogarde is fairly persuasive as a government lawyer who tries to help Bates, but his character isn't well developed.

Scoring more satisfactorily, histrionically, is Elizabeth Hartman, as a young woman who tries to seduce Bates.

· ·

■ FLAME AND THE ARROW, THE

1950, 89 MINS, US ◇ ▼

Dir Jacques Tourneur   *Prod* Harold Hecht   *Scr* Waldo Salt   *Ph* Ernest Haller   *Ed* Alan Crosland Jr   *Mus* Max Steiner
● Burt Lancaster, Virginia Mayo, Robert Douglas, Nick Cravat, Aline MacMahon, Frank Allenby (Warner)

The Flame and the Arrow is a romantic costume drama geared to attract action audiences. Setting is medieval Italy with a Robin Hood plot of how injustice is put down under the daring leadership of a heroic mountaineer.

Burt Lancaster does the latter, portraying the Arrow of the title with just the right amount of dash.

Virginia Mayo is the niece of the hated ruler. She figures romantically with Lancaster in the byplay and also gives an assist to the rebellion of the mountain people against Hessian cruelty.

Jacques Tourneur does not overlook the development of any number of interesting characters. Best of these is Cravat, partner of Lancaster during latter's circus-vaude tumbling days before entering films.

· ·

■ FLAME IN THE STREETS

1961, 93 MINS, UK ◇

Dir Roy Baker   *Prod* Roy Baker   *Scr* Ted Willis   *Ph* Christopher Challis   *Ed* Roger Cherrill   *Mus* Philip Green   *Art Dir* Alex Vetchinsky
● John Mills, Sylvia Syms, Brenda De Banzie, Earl Cameron, Johnny Sekka, Ann Lynn (Rank)

Story, which hasn't much dramatic bounce, concerns the dilemma of a staunch trade unionist who averts a threatened factory strike over a Negro foreman, swaying the staff by urging that the color of a man's skin is unimportant, only to find that his daughter has fallen in love with another colored man. How to reconcile his very different feelings over the two incidents is his problem.

John Mills makes a convincing figure as the father who has neglected his family because of his dedication to union work.

Brenda De Banzie, his wife, bitter and intolerant about colored people, has two telling scenes, one with her husband and one with her daughter. Sylvia Syms, the school-mistress daughter who outrages her parents by her determination to marry a young Negro schoolteacher, contributes a neat perform-ance in a role which is not developed fully.

Ann Lynn has a couple of neat cameos as a white girl married to the colored foreman, played with dignity and assurance by Earl Cameron. The Negro hero is Johnny Sekka, and he, too, has enough charm, dignity and good breeding to make it appear quite logical that Syms should fall in love with him.

The fact that *Flame in the Streets* is derived from a play *Hot Summer Night* is always obvious. However, by staging the film on Guy Fawkes' Night, the director is able to get his cameras out into well-filled streets for atmosphere. The street riot between the two factions is curiously anticlimactic, mainly because the film's appeal is largely the quiet-ness of its direction and playing.

■ FLAME OF THE BARBARY COAST

1945, 91 MINS, US ⓥ

Dir Joseph Kane   *Prod* Joseph Kane   *Scr* Borden Chase   *Ph* Robert de Grasse   *Ed* Richard L. Van Enger   *Mus* Morton Scott   *Art Dir* Gano Chittenden
● John Wayne, Ann Dvorak, Joseph Schildkraut, William Frawley, Virginia Grey, Russell Hicks   (Republic)

A Montana cattleman comes to scoff at the pre-earthquake Barbary Coast of San Francisco and stays to like it; a 'gentleman' gambler runs the most successful joint in the district until the guy from the tall grass decides to take over; and the gambler's sin-ger-sweetheart is also the toast of the town's haut monde.

Through dialog, songs and music that's dis-tinguished chiefly for the fact that it sounds like 1945 instead of 1906, the story winds a tortuous path until the earthquake breaks things up. But there is never any suspense in the piece, there is no juxtaposition of charac-ters, no inner logic. One is conscious con-stantly of the dragging proceedings.

John Wayne handles himself very well in the role of the man from the plains. Ann Dvorak not only sings well but looks and acts the part of the nitery queen, Joseph Schild-kraut as the gambler is socko.

■ FLAMINGO KID, THE

1984, 100 MINS, US ◇ ⓥ

Dir Garry Marshall   *Prod* Michael Phillips   *Scr* Neal Marshall, Garry Marshall   *Ph* James A. Contner   *Ed* Priscilla Nedd   *Art Dir* Lawrence Miller
● Matt Dillon, Richard Crenna, Hector Elizondo, Jessica Walter, Molly McCarthy, Janet Jones   (ABC/Mercury)

The Flamingo Kid, set in 1963, sports the amusing trappings connected with 18-year-old Matt Dillon working for a summer at the El Flamingo Beach Club in Far Rockaway, NY. At its heart, though, story has to do with the critical choices facing a youth of that age and how they will help determine the rest of one's life.

Taken out of his rundown Brooklyn neigh-borhood one day to play cards with friends at the club, Dillon ends up getting a job there parking cars. He is soon promoted to cabana boy, and also attracts the attention of blonde UCLA student Janet Jones, with whom he has a skin-deep summer fling, and her uncle Richard Crenna, a sharp-talking sports car dealer.

Dillon does a good job in his fullest, least narcissistic characterization to date.

■ FLAMINGO ROAD

1949, 94 MINS, US

Dir Michael Curtiz   *Prod* Jerry Wald   *Scr* Robert Wilder, Edmund H. North   *Ph* Ted McCord   *Ed* Folmar Blangsted   *Mus* Max Steiner   *Art Dir* Les Kuter

● Joan Crawford, Zachary Scott, Sydney Greenstreet, David Brian (Warner)

Flamingo Road is a class vehicle for Joan Crawford, loaded with heartbreak, romance and stinging violence. Film is hooped together by a smart, well-meshed screenplay and reinforced by a strong cast and sound direction.

Yarn [from a play by Robert and Sally Wil-der] swivels around a deadly antagonism be-tween Crawford and Sydney Greenstreet, a sinister small-town sheriff with a ruthless appetite for power. Film rapidly gathers momentum after Crawford, stranded by a bankrupt sideshow company, falls in love with Zachary Scott, the sheriff's protege.

Crawford imparts convincing personality shadings ranging from strength to tenderness with a continuous and convincing style. As the heavy, Greenstreet delivers a suavely powerful performance that surmounts his overdrawn role.

■ FLAMING STAR

1960, 92 MINS, US ◇

Dir Don Siegel   *Prod* David Weisbart   *Scr* Clair Huffaker, Nunnally Johnson   *Ph* Charles G. Clarke   *Ed* Hugh S. Fowler   *Mus* Cyril J. Mockridge   *Art Dir* Duncan Craimer, Walter M. Simonds
● Elvis Presley, Steve Forrest, Barbara Eden, Dolores Del Rio, John McIntire (20th Century-Fox)

Flaming Star has Indians-on-the-warpath for the youngsters, Elvis Presley for the teenagers and socio-psychological ramifications for adults who prefer a mild dose of sage in their sagebrushers. The plot – half-breed hope-lessly involved in war between white man and Red man [from a novel by Clair Huf-faker] – is disturbingly familiar and not alto-gether convincing, but the film is attractively mounted and consistently diverting.

Presley plays the half-breed, pivotal cha-racter in the conflict between a group of Texas settlers and the angry Kiowa tribe. Part of a heterogeneous family (full-blooded Indian mother, white father, half brother) resented and tormented by whites, taunted and haunted by Indian ties, Presley is buf-feted to and fro between enemy camps by the prevailing winds of prejudice and pride.

The role is a demanding one for Presley. But he lacks the facial and thespic sensitivity and projection so desperately required here. The standouts are the veterans, Dolores Del Rio and John McIntire. Del Rio brings dig-nity and delicacy to the role of Presley's full-blooded Indian mother. McIntire adds no-bility and compassion as the father of the doomed household. Steve Forrest is compe-tent as the brother, Barbara Eden decorative as his girl.

Director Don Siegel has packed plenty of excitement into the picture, notably some re-alistically-staged fistfight, battle and chase passages. But there are a few equally unre-alistic-looking scenes.

■ FLASHBACK

1990, 108 MINS, US ◇ ⓥ

Dir Franco Amurri   *Prod* Marvin Worth   *Scr* David Loughery   *Ph* Stefan Czapsky   *Ed* C. Timothy O'Meara   *Mus* Barry Goldberg   *Art Dir* Vincent Cresciman
● Dennis Hopper, Kiefer Sutherland, Carol Kane, Paul Dooley, Cliff De Young (Paramount)

Dennis Hopper does a delightful self-parody in *Flashback* as an Abbie Hoffman-like fug-itive 'radical jester' brought to farcical justice in 1989 by uptight FBI agent Kiefer Suther-land. Unfortunately, the film's promising premise is dissipated by character cliches, mechanical plot twists and an uncertain grasp on political satire.

The fun part is the Rip Van Winkle story of the gray-bearded Hopper, looking like he's been sleeping off a 20-year o.d., expounding on the political and sexual mores of the 1960s to Sutherland while en route to jail between San Francisco and the Pacific Northwest.

Scripter and director seem to be suffering from a serious case of cultural amnesia when it comes to remembering what was going on in the late 1960s.

When the pair find themselves back on the rundown commune in Oregon where Suther-land lived as a child, encountering dilapi-dated hippie Carol Kane dwelling among the portraits of martyred 1960s figures, the film taps briefly into the sadness of the time.

■ FLASHDANCE

1983, 96 MINS, US ◇ ⓥ

Dir Adrian Lyne   *Prod* Don Simpson, Jerry Bruckheimer   *Scr* Tom Hedley, Joe Eszterhas   *Ph* Don Peterman   *Ed* Bud Smith, Walt Mulconery   *Mus* Giorgio Moroder   *Art Dir* Charles Rosen
● Jennifer Beals, Michael Nouri, Lilia Skala, Sunny Johnson, Kyle T. Heffner, Belinda Bauer (PolyGram/Paramount)

Watching *Flashdance* is pretty much like look-ing at MTV for 96 minutes. Virtually plot-less, exceedingly thin on characterization and sociologically laughable, pic at least lives up to its title by offering an anthology of extraordinarily flashy dance numbers.

Appealing newcomer Jennifer Beals plays an 18-year-old come to Pittsburgh to toil in a steel mill by day and work off steam at night by performing wild, improvised dances in a local bar (much of Beals's dancing was reportedly done by an uncredited double [Marine Jahan]).

What story there is sees Beals trying to get up the courage to audition for formal dance study and dealing with the advances of her daytime boss Michael Nouri who, to her fury, secretly intervenes to get her admitted to the school.

Female performances all come off as if the sole directorial command was, "All right, girls, let's get physical!' Pic features better bodies and more crotch shots than *Personal Best*, and every effect is of the most vulgar and obvious variety.

■ FLASH GORDON

1980, 110 MINS, UK ◇ ⓥ

Dir Mike Hodges   *Prod* Dino De Laurentiis   *Scr* Lorenzo Semple Jr   *Ph* Gil Taylor   *Ed* Malcolm Cooke   *Mus* Howard Blake, Queen   *Art Dir* Danilo Donati
● Sam J. Jones, Melody Anderson, Topol, Max Von Sydow, Ornella Muti, Brian Blessed (Universal/De Laurentiis)

The expensive new version of *Flash Gordon* is a lot more gaudy, and just as dumb, as the original series starring Buster Crabbe. Sam J. Jones in the title role has even less thespic range than Crabbe, but the badness of his performance is part of the fun of the film.

This film cost around $20 million, a hefty outlay of money for such frivolity.

The big differences between this film and the old serial are the lavish sets and costumes, and the colorful lensing by Gil Taylor, who also did *Star Wars*.

Jones, a former *Playgirl* nude centerfold whose only previous film role was the hus-band of Bo Derek in '*10*', lumbers vacantly through the part of Flash Gordon with the naivete, fearlessness, and dopey line readings familiar from the 1930s serials.

Film benefits greatly from the adroit performance of Max Von Sydow as Emperor Ming.

F

■ FLATLINERS

1990, 111 MINS, US ◇ ⑦

Dir Joel Schumacher   *Prod* Michael Douglas, Rick Bieber   *Scr* Peter Filardi   *Ph* Jan De Bont   *Ed* Robert Brown   *Mus* James Newton Howard   *Art Dir* Eugenio Zanetti
● Kiefer Sutherland, Julia Roberts, Kevin Bacon, William Baldwin, Oliver Platt, Kimberly Scott (Stonebridge/Columbia)

Death, the ultimate rush, is the target experience for a group of daring young medical students who break on through to the other side – and live to tell about it. A cautionary tale that ends along fairly traditional horror-sci-fi lines, *Flatliners* is a strikingly original, often brilliantly visualized film from director Joel Schumacher and writer Peter Filardi.

Premise is that daring doctor-in-training Nelson (Kiefer Sutherland) decides to make his mark on medicine by stopping his heart and brain ('flatlining', as the lack of vital signs produces a flat line on the EKG and EEG monitors) and then having himself brought back by the gifted medical students he recruits to help him. Initially angry and reluctant, the others end up totally seduced, vying with each other for the chance to go next by offering to flatline the longest.

Problem is, as Nelson discovers, that the curtain of death, once penetrated, doesn't close behind you, and Nelson finds himself haunted by an aggressive demon from another world. Before he can bring himself to admit that his idea wasn't such a good one, all the others but one have gone over.

Sutherland, as always, registers real presence and pulls off a wildly demanding role, but the remarkably gifted Julia Roberts is the film's true grace note as the low-key, private and intensely focused Rachel.

■ FLEET'S IN, THE

1942, 93 MINS, US

Dir Victor Schertzinger   *Prod* Paul Jones   *Scr* Walter DeLeon, Sid Silvers, Ralph Spence   *Ph* William Mellor   *Ed* Paul Weatherwax   *Mus* Victor Schertzinger
● Dorothy Lamour, William Holden, Eddie Bracken, Betty Hutton, Cass Daley (Paramount)

Paul Jones, the producer of this musical version of *Sailor Beware*, has surrounded Dorothy Lamour with a miscellaneous collection of talent, including two first-starters who click strongly; but while he has turned out something that generally pleases, it falls short of being a smash.

Holden handles himself well opposite Lamour as the sailor who falls for her while the battleship crew is on furlough in Frisco.

The quarrel is less with the story itself than the musical side. There are no production numbers but an overdose of vocalists, backed by the Dorsey band.

■ FLESH

1932, 95 MINS, US

Dir John Ford   *Scr* Leonard Praskins, Edgar Allan Woolf, Moss Hart   *Ph* Arthur Edeson   *Ed* William S. Gray
● Wallace Beery, Karen Morley, Ricardo Cortez, Jean Hersholt, John Miljan (M-G-M)

Wallace Beery plays a big-hearted, big-muscled, small-brained guy with lovable qualities, a sort of cross between Emil Jannings of *Variety* (1926) and the same Beery of *The Champ* (1931). Instead of being an acrobat or a punch drunk fighter, he's a wrestler. He goes chump for a faithless woman, according to pattern, and the finish is sad, only this time there's a suggestion of ultimate happiness to deaden the pain.

As an inside on the honorable profesh of grappling, the original yarn by Edmund Goulding takes huge Polikai (Beery) out of a waiter's suit in a German beer garden to the wrassling championship of that country, and then to America where he has to play ball with the gamblers. He wins the world's title when he's supposed to lose.

Karen Morley is with him all through the climb as the double-crossing lady who loves her man on the side. Latter, and doing a perfect job of an 100% unsympathetic character, is Ricardo Cortez.

■ FLESH

1968, 105 MINS, US ◇ ⑦

Dir Paul Morrissey   *Prod* Andy Warhol   *Scr* Paul Morrissey   *Ph* Paul Morrissey
● Joe Dallesandro, Geraldine Smith, John Christian, Maurice Bardell, Candy Darling, Patti D'Arbanville (Warhol)

Blithely, as if it were as natural a romantic yarn as would appear in a popular magazine, the synopsis of Andy Warhol's opus reads: 'The story of a young married couple and the efforts of the husband, Joe, to sell himself to earn money for his wife's girl friend's abortion.'

Paul Morrissey wrote, directed and lensed this hapless erotica freakout as Warhol was recuperating from gunshot wounds inflicted by Gloria Solanis. Morrisey's efforts, true to the master, are pedestrian in both form and content, but much worse is the technical amateurishness with camera and sound.

Half sentences are abundant. But it probably doesn't matter to any great extent since the wild sound recorded during the action bounces off the walls, rendering most interchanges between characters largely incoherent.

The principal character Joe concerns himself mainly with floating from one homosexual encounter to the next in order to make the required coin, sporting an abundance of frontal nudity. The anti-climax comes when Joe finds his wife in bed with her girlfriend.

■ FLESH AND FANTASY

1943, 92 MINS, US

Dir Julien Duvivier   *Prod* Charles Boyer, Julien Duvivier   *Scr* Ernest Pascal, Samuel Hoffenstein, Ellis St Joseph   *Ph* Paul Ivano, Stanley Cortez   *Ed* Arthur Hilton   *Mus* Alexandre Tansman
● Edward G. Robinson, Charles Boyer, Barbara Stanwyck, Betty Field, Robert Cummings, Thomas Mitchell (Universal)

This is a decidedly novel and unusual picture, displaying the impress on individuals of dreams, fortune-telling and other supernatural phenomena. Picture idea was contrived by Charles Boyer and Julien Duvivier and sold to Universal, with pair combining as producers, Duvivier also directing, and Boyer handling a major acting assignment.

Clubmen Robert Benchley and David Hoffman discuss dreams, predictions and the supernatural to provide necessary interweave of the three episodes on display.

First delves into romance of Betty Field, who's become calloused, bitter and defeated through ugly looks. But on Mardi Gras night she is handed a beautiful face mask and romances with Robert Cummings and finally discovers truth in the moral: faith in yourself is the main thing.

Second episode presents Thomas Mitchell as a palmist at a socialite group, and after attorney Edward G. Robinson scoffs at the predictions, latter nevertheless submits to a reading, and becomes intrigued when he's told he will commit murder.

Boyer shares starring honors with Barbara Stanwyck in the final episode, which has the former upset by dream which predicts disaster to himself while performing as a circus high-wire artist.

■ FLESH + BLOOD

1985, 126 MINS, US ◇ ⑦

Dir Paul Verhoeven   *Prod* Gys Versluys   *Scr* Gerard Soeteman, Paul Verhoeven   *Ph* Jan de Bont   *Ed* Ine Schenkkan   *Mus* Basil Poledouris   *Art Dir* Felix Murcia
● Rutger Hauer, Jennifer Jason Leigh, Tom Burlinson, Jack Thompson, Susan Tyrrell, Ron Lacey (Orion/Riverside)

Flesh + Blood is a vivid and muscular, if less than fully startling, account of lust, savagery, revenge, betrayal and assorted other dark doings in the Middle Ages.

Drama opens with a successful siege on a castle by Lord Arnolfini (Fernando Hillbeck), who has recently been ousted from the premises. After promising them loot, Hillbeck goes back on his word and banishes the mercenaries who have helped him in his conquest.

Before long, warrior leader Martin (Rutger Hauer) and his ragtag band gets theirs back by nearly killing Hillbeck in an ambush and capturing lovely young Agnes (Jennifer Jason Leigh), the intended bride of Hillbeck's studious son Steven (Tom Burlinson).

Director Paul Verhoeven has told his tale in visceral, involving fashion and, for the amount of carnage that piles up, explicit gore is kept to a minimum.

Fine use is made of Belmonte Castle (on view in *El Cid*) and other Spanish locales.

■ FLESH AND THE DEVIL

1926, 91 MINS, US ⊗ ⑦

Dir Clarence Brown   *Scr* Benjamin F. Glazer, Marian Ainslee   *Ph* William Daniels   *Ed* Lloyd Nosler   *Art Dir* Cedric Gibbons, Frederic Hope
● John Gilbert, Greta Garbo, Lars Hanson, Barbara Kent, William Orlamond (M-G-M)

This film [based on *The Undying Past* by Hermann Sudermann] is a battle between John Gilbert, starred, and Greta Garbo, featured, for honors. Gilbert has to keep moving to overshadow her, even though she has a most unsympathetic role.

The story is laid in a small German or Austrian town. Two boys have, as kids, sworn eternal friendship through a blood bond. They are both at military school when the picture opens. Back home there is a ball and Lee (Gilbert), the more sophisticated of the two, sees a girl that he admired at the station. He dances with her, but fails to learn her name. Her husband walks in on the picture and the youngster then knows for the first time that she is married. The husband strikes the boy, and it calls for a duel. The husband is killed. The military authorities 'advise' foreign service for five years for the youngster. Before going he asks his bloodbound friend to seek out the widow and console her.

After three years away, Leo discovers that she has wed the friend. Then a series of incidents occurs that almost brings on a duel between the friends.

A corking story, exceptionally acted and cleverly directed. A lot of glory to be distributed among all concerned.

■ FLESH FOR FRANKENSTEIN

1974, 95 MINS, FRANCE/ITALY ◇ ⑦

Dir Paul Morrissey   *Prod* Andrew Braunsberg   *Scr* Paul Morrissey   *Ph* Luigi Kueveillier   *Ed* Ted Johnson   *Mus* Carlo Gizzi
● Joe Dallesandro, Udo Kier, Monique Van Vooren, Arno Juerging, Srdjan Zelenovic, Dalila Di Lazzaro (CC-Champion & 1/Ponti/Yanne/Rassam)

Paul Morrissey of the Andy Warhol stable made this pic back to back with *Blood for Dracula*, with an added gimmick of 3-D and more skillfully directed. Morrissey plays some variations on the old Prometheus myth. He adds plenty of gore, with some dollops of sex.

Morrissey otherwise plays this for neat Gothic atmosphere in Frankenstein's castle where his nympho sister (Monique Van Vooren), also mother of his children, carries on with servants as the kids and Frankenstein (Udo Kier) look on.

Joe Dallesandro is a servant who suspects foul doings, especially when he sees the head of his friend on one of Frankenstein's monsters and breaks up things to find he may be a victim of the Baron's two children as he hangs helplessly by his hands.

. . . .

■ FLESH GORDON

1974, 78 MINS, US ◇ ⊙
Dir Howard Ziehm, Michael Benveniste *Prod* Howard Ziehm, Bill Osco *Scr* Michael Benveniste *Ph* Howard Ziehm *Mus* Ralph Ferraro *Art Dir* Donald Harris
● Jason Williams, Suzanne Fields, Joseph Hudgins, John Hoyt, William Hunt (Graffiti)

Puerile is the word for this softcore spoof of the sci-fi serials of the 1930s which, for their time, had genuine merit as audience hair-raisers. By attempting to combine sexplicity and low-level camp, pic emerges as an expensive-looking mish-mash of obvious double entendres, idiotic characterizations and dull situations. Only compensation is flash of bawdy humor.

Title character (Jason Williams) heads a group of earthlings out to defeat evil forces on the planet Porno, bent on flooding the universe with chaos-inducing sex rays. Porno is manned by sinister Emperor Wang (William Hunt). Flesh, his girl (Suzanne Fields) and sidekick (Joseph Hudgins) rocket to Porno and encounter various of the emperor's evil minions and a mildly entertaining series of monsters.

. . . .

■ FLETCH

1985, 96 MINS, US ◇ ⊙
Dir Michael Ritchie *Prod* Alan Greisman, Peter Douglas *Scr* Andrew Bergman *Ph* Fred Schuler *Ed* Richard A. Harris *Mus* Harold Faltermeyer *Art Dir* Boris Leven
● Chevy Chase, Dana Wheeler-Nicholson, Tim Matheson, Joe Don Baker, Richard Libertini, Geena Davis (Universal)

What propels this contempo LA yarn about a dissembling newspaper columnist on the trail of a nefarious con man (Tim Matheson) is the obvious and successful byplay between Chevy Chase's sly, glib persona and the satiric brushstrokes of director Michael Ritchie. Their teamwork turns an otherwise hair-pinned, anecdotal plot into a breezy, peppy frolic and a tour de force for Chase.

Most supporting players have little to do, such as M. Emmet Walsh as an inane MD. The film is sparked by some hilarious moments, among them Chase as an unwitting surgeon in attendance at an autopsy conducted by a cackling pathologist and, in the script's funniest scene, Chase donning the guise of a legionnaire in a hall full of VFW stalwarts.

. . . .

■ FLETCH LIVES

1989, 95 MINS, US ◇ ⊙
Dir Michael Ritchie *Prod* Alan Greisman, Peter Douglas *Scr* Leon Capetanos *Ph* John McPherson *Ed* Richard A. Harris *Mus* Harold Faltermeyer *Art Dir* Cameron Birnie, Jimmie Bly, W. Steven Graham, Donald B. Woodruff
● Chevy Chase, Hal Holbrook, Julianne Phillips, Cleavon Little, R. Lee Ermey, Patricia Kalember (Universal)

Chevy Chase is perfectly suited to playing a smirking, wisecracking, multiple-identitied reporter in *Fletch Lives*.

Ridiculous and anecdotal plot that transports Chase from his beloved LA base to Louisiana's bayou country to take over his dead aunt's crumbling plantation works for the simple reason that Chase's sly, glib persona is in sync with Michael Ritchie's equally breezy direction.

From Gregory McDonald's popular novel, script works out an excessive and cliche-ridden portrait of a Southern, insular town. Dimwits abound as if inbreeding has been going on since the days of slavery.

The night Chase arrives, he beds the sexy executor/lawyer of his aunt's estate (Patricia Kalember as a convincing belle), who is then murdered while they're slumbering.

Chase tracks the murderer through some inane sequences as only he could do. Film's saving grace is its scathing satirical sketches of fictional televangelist preacher Jimmy Lee Farnsworth.

. . . .

■ FLIGHT OF THE DOVES

1971, 101 MINS, US ◇
Dir Ralph Nelson *Prod* Ralph Nelson *Scr* Frank Gabrielson, Ralph Nelson *Ph* Harry Waxman *Ed* John Jympson *Mus* Roy Budd *Art Dir* Frank Arrigo
● Ron Moody, Jack Wild, Dorothy McGuire, Stanley Holloway, William Rushton, Dana (Columbia)

Ralph Nelson's film version of Walter Macken's story, *Flight of the Doves*, is a heartwarming, often funny, often suspenseful story of two runaway children, fleeing from a cruel stepfather (British) to their grandmother (Irish) who lives 'somewhere in Ireland'.

The screenplay, takes some liberties in casting. Dorothy McGuire is a delight as a bright-eyed, most articulate grandmother, standing up to authority, both Irish and British, on behalf of the young runaways, but is much too young looking to make anyone believe that she could have a grandson as large as Jack Wild.

It allows Ron Moody to dominate the film from his first appearance. With almost as many character changes as Alec Guinness had in *Kind Hearts and Coronets*, Moody is so good at his disguises that the audience starts imagining that each new character who appears might be the irresponsible Moody. Ostensibly the villain, he's so captivating that no one really believes that he won't survive (even after seeing him plunged into a wild Irish sea).

As the uncle of Wild and Helen Raye, he's described as the eventual heir to money left by the children's grandfather should they die before he does.

. . . .

■ FLIGHT OF THE INTRUDER

1991, 113 MINS, US ◇ ⊙
Dir John Milius *Prod* Mace Neufeld *Scr* Robert Dillon, David Shaber *Ph* Fred J. Koenekamp *Ed* C. Timothy O'Mears, Steve Mirkovich, Peck Prior *Mus* Basil Poledouris *Art Dir* Jack T. Collis
● Danny Glover, Willem Dafoe, Brad Johnson, Rosanna Arquette, Tom Sizemore, J. Kenneth Campbell (Paramount)

Flight of the Intruder is the most boring Vietnam War pic since *The Green Berets* (1968), but lacks the benefit of the latter's political outrageousness to spark a little interest and humor.

Set mostly aboard a giant aircraft carrier, yarn [from the novel by Stephen Coonts] unspools in 1972. Prevented from bombing Hanoi and other strategic spots while the Paris peace talks are in progress, fighter pilots are reduced to assaulting meaningless targets and facing the likelihood that the massive US war effort will have been in vain.

Nonetheless, officers have to keep discipline and morale up, a task that falls to Danny Glover, the tough-talking but humorous squadron leader.

Title refers to the A-6, a small, low-altitude bomber designed for quick in-and-out strikes. Ace of the outfit is Brad Johnson, who loses a bombardier in an elaborate credit sequence and is thereafter interested in 'payback'.

Opportunity presents itself with the arrival of a vet bombardier (Willem Dafoe) not averse to hijinks. Johnson and Dafoe cook up a scheme to devastate People's Resistance Park in downtown Hanoi, a.k.a. SAM City, where captured US artillery is on display.

Glover brings energy and glee to his reams of dialog. Dafoe puts a few cynical spins on his delivery, but his character pales next to his role in *Platoon*. Johnson, again playing a flier, is even more lackluster than in *Always*. Hawaiian locations, when viewed from the air, are too lushly recognizable to be an entirely credible Vietnam.

. . . .

■ FLIGHT OF THE PHOENIX, THE

1965, 149 MINS, US ◇ ⊙
Dir Robert Aldrich *Prod* Robert Aldrich *Scr* Lukas Heller *Ph* Joseph Biroc *Ed* Michael Luciano *Mus* Frank DeVol *Art Dir* William Glasgow
● James Stewart, Richard Attenborough, Peter Finch, Hardy Kruger, Ernest Borgnine, Ian Bannen (Associates & Aldrich/20th Century-Fox)

The Flight of the Phoenix is a grim, tenseful, realistic tale of a small group of men forced down on the North African desert and their desperate efforts to build a single-engine plane out of the wreckage of the twin job in which they crashed during a sandstorm. Robert Aldrich's filmic translation of the Elleston Trevor book is an often-fascinating and superlative piece of filmmaking highlighted by standout performances and touches that show producer-director at his best.

James Stewart, as the pilot of a desert oil company cargo-passenger plane who flies by the seat of his pants, is strongly cast in role and is strongly backed by entire cast. Each, seemingly hand-picked for the individual parts, are every-day persons who might either be employees of an oil company or business visitors.

A young aircraft designer, who had been visiting his brother at the oil camp, comes up with the extraordinary idea that a make-shift plane might be fashioned to fly the survivors to safety. So work starts, and it is this endeavor in its various phases that makes the story.

. . . .

■ FLIM-FLAM MAN, THE

1967, 104 MINS, US ◇ ⊙
Dir Irvin Kershner *Prod* Lawrence Turman *Scr* William Rose *Ph* Charles Lang *Ed* Robert Swink *Mus* Jerry Goldsmith *Art Dir* Jack Martin Smith
● George C. Scott, Sue Lyon, Michael Sarrazin, Harry Morgan, Jack Albertson, Alice Ghostley (20th Century-Fox)

An outstanding comedy starring George C. Scott as a Dixie drifter. Socko comedy-dramatic direction by Irvin Kershner makes the most of a very competent cast and a superior script. Michael Sarrazin, as Scott's fellow-traveler, makes an impressive feature film bow.

Guy Owen's novel, *The Ballad of the Flim-Flam Man*, has been adapted into a finely balanced screenplay which exploits inherent comedy situations while understating, appropriately, the loneliness of a rootless man. A series of flim-flams are pulled off only on people who seemingly deserve to be stiffed, thus minimizing any complaint that lawlessness is being made attractive.

. . . .

■ FLIPPER

1963, 87 MINS, US ◇ ⊙
Dir James B. Clark *Prod* Ivan Tors *Scr* Arthur Weiss *Ph* Lamar Bowen, Joseph Brun *Ed* Warren Adams *Mus* Henry Vars

● Chuck Connors, Luke Halpin, Connie Scott, Kathleen Maguire (M-G-M)

Boy meets dolphin, boy loses dolphin, boy wins dolphin. Thus substituting gill for gal, producer Ivan Tors has fashioned a serviceable little family picture that to all intents and porpoises, should satisfy aquabrats everywhere.

Actually this little fish story, or Tors opera, amounts to a kind of bubbly variation on *Androcles and the Lion*. Arthur Weiss' screenplay, from a story by Ricou Browning and Jack Cowden, has a boy (Luke Halpin) rescuing an eight-foot dolphin from permanent residence in that big fish tank in the sky by removing a skin diver's spear from its torso and nursing it back to health in his dad's Florida Keys fish pen.

Chuck Connors limns the father firmly but agreeably, and young Halpin, in his screen bow, demonstrates keen acting instincts as the boy on a dolphin.

• •

■ **FLIRTATION WALK**

1934, 95 MINS, US

Dir Frank Borzage   *Prod* Frank Borzage   *Scr* Delmer Daves, Lou Edelman   *Ph* Sol Polito, George Barnes   *Ed* William Holmes   *Art Dir* Jack Okey
● Dick Powell, Ruby Keeler, Pat O'Brien, Ross Alexander, John Eldredge (First National)

Flirtation Walk is bright and diverting entertainment in which the musical sequences [dance numbers directed by Bobby Connolly, music and lyrics by Allie Wrubel and Mort Dixon] are logically worked in , albeit with the usual Hollywood flair for exaggeration. Background of West Point allows the picture to possess some snappy drill and brass-button stuff. Deft direction of Frank Borzage gives the production the tempo and zing that stamps it swell amusement.

Dick Powell, in his plebe year at the Point, plays the situations for excellent natural comedy. Ruby Keeler does not dance. She has a lot to do and does it with considerable assurance. Ross Alexander as Powell's roommate will be liked, a personable young man with a knack for light comedy and horseplay.

Laughs and drama of the story are derived from the interplay of officer-private class distinctions and military discipline. The quiet competence of John Eldredge's performance as the disappointed suitor rates a few merit stripes.
□ 1934: Best Picture (Nomination)

• •

■ **FLOWER DRUM SONG**

1961, 133 MINS, US ◇ ⓥ

Dir Henry Koster   *Prod* Ross Hunter   *Scr* Joseph Fields   *Ph* Russell Metty   *Ed* Milton Carruth   *Mus* Alfred Newman (sup.)   *Art Dir* Alexander Golitzen, Joseph Wright
● .Nancy Kwan, James Shigeta, Juanita Hall, Jack Soo, Miyoshi Umeki, Benson Fong (Universal)

Much of the fundamental charm, grace and novelty of Rodgers & Hammerstein's *Flower Drum Song* has been overwhelmed by the sheer opulence and glamour with which Ross Hunter has translated it to the screen. As a film, it emerges a curiously unaffecting, unstable and rather undistinguished experience, lavishly produced but only sporadically rewarding.

The dominant issue in the screenplay, based on the novel by C. Y. Lee and adapted from the legit book by Joseph Fields and Oscar Hammerstein, is the clash of East-West romantic-marital customs as it affects the relationships of four young people of Chinese descent living in a state of social flux between two worlds in San Francisco's Chinatown.

The four are Nancy Kwan, a gold-digging, husband-hungry nightclub dancer; Jack Soo,

a kind of Chinese Nathan Detroit; James Shigeta, most eligible bachelor in Chinatown – the student prince of Grant Avenue; and Miyoshi Umeki, 'picture (or mail-order) bride' fresh (and illegally) off a slowboat from China and ticketed for nuptials with Soo.

As in most R&H enterprises, the meat is in the musical numbers. There are some bright spots in this area but even here the effect isn't overpowering.

Kwan demonstrates plenty of dance savvy, and gets by histrionically here. Shigeta handles his number one song role capably and exhibits vocal prowess. Umeki re-creates her Broadway role with the same winning China-doll-like quality. Music supervisor-conductor Alfred Newman has fashioned some rousing orchestrations, with the assistance of Ken Darby. Dong Kingman's watercolored title paintings are a delight.

• •

■ **FLY, THE**

1958, 94 MINS, US ◇ ⓥ

Dir Kurt Neumann   *Prod* Kurt Neumann   *Scr* James Clavell   *Ph* Karl Struss   *Ed* Merrill G. White   *Mus* Paul Sawtell   *Art Dir* Lyle R. Wheeler, Theobold Holsopple
● Al Hedison, Patricia Owens, Vincent Price, Herbert Marshall, Kathleen Freeman, Betty Lou Gerson (20th Century-Fox)

The Fly is a high-budget, beautifully and expensively mounted exploitation picture [derived from a story by George Langelaan. Al Hedison plays a scientist who has invented a machine that reduces matter to disintegrated atoms and another machine that reassembles the atoms. He explains to his wife (Patricia Owens) that this will enable humans to travel – disintegrated – anywhere in the world at the speed of light. In experimenting on himself, however, a fly gets into the disintegration chamber with him.

When Hedison arrives in the integration chamber, he discovers some of his atoms have been scrambled with the fly's. Hedison has the head and 'arm' of a fly; the fly has the head and arm of the man – each, of course, in his own scale of size. The problem is to catch the fly and rescramble. But before this can happen, Hedison finds the predatory instincts of the insect taking over.

One strong factor of the picture is its unusual believability. It is told as a mystery suspense story, so that it has a compelling interest aside from its macabre effects. There is an appealing and poignant romance between Owens and Hedison, which adds to the reality of the story, although the flashback technique purposely robs the picture of any doubt about the outcome.

• •

■ **FLY, THE**

1986, 100 MINS, US ◇ ⓥ

Dir David Cronenberg   *Prod* Stuart Cornfeld   *Scr* Charles Edward Pogue, David Cronenberg   *Ph* Mark Irwin   *Ed* Ronald Sanders   *Mus* Howard Shore   *Art Dir* Carol Spier
● Jeff Goldblum, Geena Davis, John Getz, Joy Booshel, Les Carlson (Brooksfilms)

David Cronenberg's remake of the 1958 horror classic *The Fly* is not for the squeamish. Casting Jeff Goldblum was a good choice as he brings a quirky, common touch to the spacey scientist role. Cronenberg gives him a nice girlfriend (Geena Davis), too.

But there's trouble in paradise. Goldblum's got a set of teleporters that he promises will 'change the world as we know it', and indeed, it changes his.

Even though the machinery is not yet perfected, Goldblum, in a moment of drunken jealousy, throws himself in the works. Unbeknownst to him a fly accompanies him on the journey and he starts to metamorphise.

Chris Walas' design for *The Fly* is never less than visually intriguing. Production design

by Carol Spier, particularly for Goldblum's warehouse lab, is original and appropriate to the hothouse drama. Cronenberg contains the action well in a limited space with a small cast.

• •

■ **FLY II, THE**

1989, 105 MINS, US ◇ ⓥ

Dir Chris Walas   *Prod* Steven-Charles Jaffe   *Scr* Mick Garris, Jim Wheat, Ken Wheat, Frank Darabont   *Ph* Robin Vidgeon   *Ed* Sean Barton   *Mus* Christopher Young   *Art Dir* Michael S. Bolton
● Eric Stoltz, Daphne Zuniga, Lee Richardson, John Getz, Frank Turner (Brooksfilm)

The Fly II is an expectedly gory and gooey but mostly plodding sequel to the 1986 hit that was a remake of the 1958 sci-fier that itself spawned two sequels.

After a shock opening in which the late man-fly's son is born within a horrible insect-like encasement, slickly produced pic [story by Mick Garris] generates some promise as little Martin Brundle is raised in laboratory conditions provided by scientific tycoon Anton Bartok (Lee Richardson).

Afflicted with a dramatically accelerated lifecycle, Martin quickly demonstrates genius, and by the age of five emerges fully grown in the person of Eric Stoltz. Martin becomes determined to perfect his father's teleportation machine, which Bartok controls, and also takes an interest in researcher Beth Logan (Daphne Zuniga).

Martin gradually becomes aware that Bartok's motives are far from benign, and simultaneously begins mutating into a hideous beast while retaining his human sensibility.

By the climax, the film more closely comes to resemble *Aliens* than the previous *Fly*, as the transformed Martin hides behind walls and in the ceiling before pouncing on Bartok's goons, spitting on them, chewing them up and spitting them out.

• •

■ **FLYING DOWN TO RIO**

1933, 88 MINS, US

Dir Thornton Freeland   *Prod* Merian C. Cooper, Louis Brock   *Scr* Cyril Hume, H. W. Hanemann, Erwin Gelsey   *Ph* J. Roy Hunt   *Ed* Jack Kitchin   *Mus* Max Steiner (dir.)   *Art Dir* Van Nest Polglase, Carroll Clark
● Dolores Del Rio, Gene Raymond, Raul Roulien, Ginger Rogers, Fred Astaire, Blanche Friderici (RKO)

The main point of *Flying down to Rio* is the screen promise of Fred Astaire. He's distinctly likeable on the screen, the mike is kind to his voice and as a dancer he remains in a class by himself.

This picture makes its bid via numbers staged by Dave Gould to Vincent Youman melodies. But *Rio*'s story [by Louis Brock] lets it down. It's slow and lacks laughs to the point where average business seems its groove. From the time of the opening melody ('Music Makes Me' – and hot) to the next number, 'Carioca', almost three reels elapse and anybody can take a walk, come back and be that much ahead.

It takes all that time for Gene Raymond, as a band leader, to be enticed by Dolores Del Rio, as a South American belle, and frame her into a plane ride to Rio de Janeiro. This hop includes a faked overnight forced landing on a beach, strictly in the platonic manner. When they finally get off the sand and to Rio, Raymond finds his Brazilian pal is engaged to the girl, but the Latin member gives the damsel to him and takes a novel way out via a parachute dive at the finish. Meanwhile, the opening of a new hotel by the girl's father, for which Raymond's band has been engaged, is the premise for continuing the musical portion below the Equator.

• •

F

FLYING LEATHERNECKS

1951, 103 MINS, US ◇ ⓥ

Dir Nicholas Ray *Prod* Edmund Grainger *Scr* James
Edward Grant *Ph* William E. Snyder *Ed* Sherman
Todd *Mus* Roy Webb *Art Dir* Albert S. D'Agostino,
James W. Sullivan
● John Wayne, Robert Ryan, Don Taylor, Janis Carter,
Jay C. Flippen, William Harrigan (RKO)

Marquee pull of John Wayne and Robert
Ryan in the action market has been teamed
with a story of Marine fighter pilots.

Actual color footage of battle action in the
Pacific has been smartly blended with studio
shots to strike a note of realism.

James Edward Grant scripted the Kenneth
Gamet story, which deals with a small
squadron of flying leathernecks stationed in
the Pacific and the frictions that develop between its commander (Wayne) and its executive officer (Ryan) when they are not busy
fighting the war. Ryan is disappointed
because he has not been recommended for
command of the squadron but works with
Wayne until latter's rigid discipline and im-
partiality build a bitter friction between
them.

This purely masculine yarn sidetracks
when Wayne goes on leave to the States for
time with his wife, (Janis Carter) and small
son. These scenes are excellently done, both
in playing, direction and writing, but do have
the effect of ending the action. This starts in
again, however, when Wayne is re-assigned
to the Pacific.

FLYING TIGERS

1942, 96 MINS, US ⓥ

Dir David Miller *Prod* Edmund Grainger
Scr Kenneth Gamet, Barry Trivers *Ph* Jack Marta
Ed Ernest Nims *Mus* Victor Young
● John Wayne, John Carroll, Anna Lee, Paul Kelly
(Republic)

Flying Tigers is based on exploits of American
flyers in China who took up the cudgels
against the Japs long before Pearl Harbor.

Aside from a foreword written by Gener-
alissimo Chiang Kai-shek, paying tribute to
the American Volunteer Group who 'have
become the symbol of the invincible strength
of the forces now upholding the cause of
humanity and justice', there is nothing to distinguish this film from other conventional
aviation yarns.

Handicapped primarily by a threadbare
script, production also suffers from slow pacing while John Wayne, John Carroll, Anna
Lee and Paul Kelly are barely adequate in
the major acting assignments. Some of the
scenes look repetitious, the same Jap flyers
apparently being shot down and killed three
or four times over.

FOG, THE

1980, 91 MINS, US ◇ ⓥ

Dir John Carpenter *Prod* Debra Hill *Scr* John
Carpenter, Debra Hill *Ph* Dean Cundey *Ed* Tommy
Wallace, Charles Bornstein *Mus* John Carpenter
Art Dir Tommy Wallace
● Adrienne Barbeau, Hal Holbrook, Janet Leigh, Jamie
Lee Curtis, John Houseman (Avco Embassy)

John Carpenter is anything but subtle in his
approach to shocker material. Premise is
obvious from almost the first frame, as a
grizzled John Houseman tells youngsters
grouped around a campfire about a foggy
curse that surrounds a coastal town where a
horrible shipwreck took place 100 years ago.

Story exposition and setting are well-
established before the opening titles are over,
and *The Fog* proceeds to layer one fright
atop another.

Adrienne Barbeau makes her film debut as
the husky-voiced deejay of the town's sole
radio station, perched atop a lighthouse from
which the title phenomenon becomes
increasingly apparent.

Thesping is okay in all departments
although Janet Leigh isn't given much to do,
nor is daughter Jamie Lee Curtis.

FOLIES BERGERE

1935, 83 MINS, US

Dir Roy Del Ruth *Prod* William Goetz, Raymond
Griffith *Scr* Bess Meredyth, Hal Long *Ph* Barney
McGill *Mus* Alfred Newman (dir.)
● Maurice Chevalier, Ann Sothern, Merle Oberon, Eric
Blore, Ferdinand Munier, Walter Byron (20th Century/
United Artists)

Picture has nothing whatever to do with the
Folies Bergere of Paris, except that one of the
characters is supposed to be the head comic
of the show at the Paris music hall, and that
allows for three musical numbers on the stage
thereof. For plot and continuity purposes studio has taken an old continental farce, *The
Red Cat* [by Rudolph Lothar and Hans Adler]
and switched it about a bit.

Maurice Chevalier does excellent work. He
handles the double assignment of Charlier,
the Folies comic, and the Baron Cassini.
Baron gets into a financial jam so Charlier is
hired to impersonate him while he's off to
London to dig up some coin. Baron has been
having marital difficulties with his wife, too,
and Charlier manages to fix up both the
home work and the office work for the baron
with happy fadeout all around.

Chevalier shows, perhaps for the first time
in films, that he has range as an actor. Ann
Sothern as Charlier's wife is pretty and effective. She sings and dances with Chevalier and
makes a definite sock impression. Merle
Oberon, as the baron's wife, on the other
hand, gets a tough break.

Dance routines by Dave Gould are nifty.

FOLLOW THAT DREAM

1962, 109 MINS, US ◇ ⓥ

Dir Gordon M. Douglas *Prod* David Weisbart
Scr Charles Lederer *Ph* Leo Tover *Ed* William B.
Murphy *Mus* Hans J. Salter *Art Dir* Mal Bert
● Elvis Presley, Arthur O'Connell, Anne Helm, Joanne
Moore (United Artists)

Follow That Dream is a kind of second cinematic cousin to *Tammy* with Elvis Presley as
the hinterland's answer to the supposed
advantages of formal booklarnin'. Scenarist
Charles Lederer has constructed several
highly amusing scenes in tailoring Richard
Powell's novel, *Pioneer, Go Home*, to fit the
specifications of the screen. There are lags
and lapses in the picture, to be sure, but, by
Presley pix standards, it's above average.

Presley portrays what amounts to a cross
between Li'l Abner and male counterpart of
Tammy, a sort of number one son in a
makeshift, itinerant brood of Real McCoy
types who plant themselves on a strip of
unclaimed Florida beach and proceed to play
homesteaders whilst befuddled officials of
city and state, welfare workers and thugs
haplessly attempt to unsquat them from their
profitable perch.

FOLLOW THE FLEET

1936, 110 MINS, US ⓥ

Dir Mark Sandrich *Prod* Pandro S. Berman
Scr Dwight Taylor, Allan Scott *Ph* David Abel
Ed Henry Berman *Mus* Max Steiner (dir.) *Art Dir* Van
Nest Polglase, Carroll Clark
● Fred Astaire, Ginger Rogers, Randolph Scott, Harriet
Hilliard, Astrid Allwyn, Betty Grable (RKO)

With Ginger Rogers again opposite, and the
Irving Berlin music to dance to and sing,
Astaire once more legs himself and his pic-
ture into the big-time entertainment class.

Imperfections in *Fleet* are confined to story.
That's usual with musicals, stage or screen.
This is a rather free adaptation of *Shore Leave*,
a David Belasco oldie. Yet the story never
detracts from the important element – the
Astaire-Rogers musical efforts.

There are seven songs which is a bit too
much – all by Irving Berlin, with 'Face the
Music', a cross between 'Piccolino' and
'Lovely Day', easily the leader. The score on
the whole is pleasant but save for 'Face the
Music', the last number, not particularly
distinguished.

Story is a double romance involving the
starred duo and Harriet Hilliard-Randolph
Scott. Yarn breaks them up and teams them
again for the finish.

This is Hilliard's first picture. She's from
radio, having sung mostly with the Ozzie
Nelson band and chiefly on the Joe Penner
programs. A blonde originally, she's in brunet wig in this film, presumably in deference
to Rogers.

FOOL, THE

1991, 135 MINS, UK ⓥ

Dir Christine Edzard *Prod* Richard Goodwin, Christine
Edzard *Scr* Christine Edzard, Olivier Stockman
Ph Robin Vidgeon *Ed* Olivier Stockman *Mus* Michel
Sanvoisin
● Derek Jacobi, Cyril Cusack, Ruth Mitchell, Paul
Brooke, Corin Redgrave, John McEnery (Sands/Film
Four/British Screen/Tyler)

Three years after their marathon, *Little
Dorrit*, husband-and-wife producers Richard
Goodwin and Christine Edzard tread the
same streets to lesser effect in *The Fool*.

In 1857, an obscure theater clerk (Derek
Jacobi) engineers a financial scam to show up
the monied classes. Problems start when,
posing as the carefree Sir John, he's recognized by some theater folk, and he starts taking his alter ego too seriously.

Later scenes, with their *Wall Street* lingo and
Jacobi's crisis of conscience, are an obvious
allegory of the me-too 1980s. But they're a
long time coming, and the thrill of the paper
chase is lacking. Without a strong central
yarn like Dickens' *Dorrit*, pic becomes a series
of one-off routines by w.k. Brit thesps.

Helmer and co-scripter Edzard shows off
her research and topnotch design with street
characters based on interviews by 19th-
century social journalist Henry Mayhew.
They're fine on their own terms, right down
to the dirt under their fingernails, but Edzard
needs to make up her mind whether she's
building a museum or making a movie.

FOOL FOR LOVE

1985, 106 MINS, US ◇ ⓥ

Dir Robert Altman *Prod* Menahem Golan, Yoram
Globus *Scr* Sam Shepard *Ph* Pierre Mignot
Ed Luce Grunenwaldt *Mus* George Burt
Art Dir Stephen Altman
● Sam Shepard, Kim Basinger, Harry Dean Stanton,
Randy Quaid, Martha Crawford, Louise Egolf (Cannon)

Robert Altman directs a fine cast with all the
authority and finesse a good play deserves, so
it's too bad the play fooled them all. Sam
Shepard's drama of intense, forbidden love in
the modern West is made to seem like specious stuff filled with dramatic ideas left over
from the 1950s.

Opening up the play, which was set entirely
in a dingy motel room, Shepard and Altman
have spread out the action all around a rundown motel complex on the edge of the
desert.

Eddie, a rangy, handsome cowboy, returns
after a long absence to try to get back with
the sexy May, with whom he has a can't-live-
with-or-without-her relationship. The two
shout, argue, make up, make out, split up,

205

pout, dance around each other and start up all over again, while an old drunk observer takes it all in. Finally, the arrival of another fellow to take May out prompts a nocturnal spilling of the beans about Eddie and May's taboo love affair.

Beginning with the impressive Shepard, cast is handpicked with care. As the saucy May, Kim Basinger alternately conjures up Marilyn Monroe in *The Misfits* and *Bus Stop* and Brigitte Bardot in *And God Created Woman*. Harry Dean Stanton is excellent as the washed-up cause of all the problems.

●●●●●●●●●●●●●●●●●●●●●●●●●●

■ FOOLISH WIVES

1922, 180 MINS, US ⊗ Ⓥ

Dir Erich von Stroheim *Scr* Erich von Stroheim
Ph Ben Reynolds, William Daniels *Mus* Sigmund Romberg *Art Dir* E.E. Sheeley, Richard Day
● Erich von Stroheim, Rudolph Christians, Miss Du Pont, Maude George, Mae Busch, Louis K. Webb (Universal)

According to the Universal's press department, the picture cost $1,103,736.38; was 11 months and six days in filming; six months in assembling and editing; consumed 320,000 feet of negative, and employed as many as 15,000 extras for atmosphere.

Foolish Wives shows the cost – in the sets, beautiful backgrounds and massive interiors that carry a complete suggestion of the atmosphere of Monte Carlo, the locale of the story. And the sets, together with a thoroughly capable cast, are about all the picture has for all the heavy dough expended.

Obviously intended to be a sensational sex melodrama, *Foolish Wives* is at the same time frankly salacious.

Erich von Stroheim wrote the script, directed, and is the featured player. He's all over the lot every minute. His character is a Russian Captain of Hussars. The uniform may be Russian, but von Stroheim's general facial and physical appearance clearly suggests the typical Prussian military officer.

The story starts with a flirtation between the Count (Von Stroheim) and the American diplomat's wife, continues along with his obvious attempts to possess her, right under her husband's nose, and with the woman's evident liking for the count's attentions.

●●●●●●●●●●●●●●●●●●●●●●●●●●

■ FOOLS OF FORTUNE

1990, 104 MINS, UK ◇ Ⓥ

Dir Pat O'Connor *Prod* Sarah Radclyffe *Scr* Michael Hirst *Ph* Jerzy Zielinski *Ed* Michael Bradsell
Mus Hans Zimmer *Art Dir* Jamie Leonard
● Mary Elizabeth Mastrantonio, Iain Glen, Julie Christie, Michael Kitchen, Sean T. McClory, Niamii Cusack (Polygram/Working Title/Film Four)

Fools of Fortune is an historical saga written with lucidity and performed with sensitivity, but tending to melodrama.

The Irish war of independence is the starting point for the story [from the novel by William Trevor] of a family's destruction and the survival of an unlikely love. The Quinton family seem sheltered in their grand rural home until the British-employed soldiers, the Black and Tans, burn down the house. The only survivors of the massacre are Quinton's wife (Julie Christie), her son Willie (first, Sean T. McClory, and then as an adult, Iain Glen), and their maid (Niamii Cusack).

Willie becomes an introspective and withdrawn young man, while his mother becomes a manic depressive and chronic alcoholic, a role which Christie relishes in.

When Christie finally commits suicide, Willie is comforted by childhood playmate Marianne, who's grown into an exquisitely beautiful woman (Mary Elizabeth Mastrantonio). Result of this comfort is a child.

●●●●●●●●●●●●●●●●●●●●●●●●●●

■ FOOTLIGHT PARADE

1933, 102 MINS, US

Dir Lloyd Bacon, Busby Berkeley *Scr* Manuel Seff, James Seymour *Ph* George Barnes *Ed* George Amy *Art Dir* Anton Grot, Jack Okey
● James Cagney, Joan Blondell, Ruby Keeler, Dick Powell, Guy Kibbee, Ruth Donnelly (Warner)

Footlight Parade is not as good as *42nd Street* and *Gold Diggers* but the three socko numbers here eclipse some of the preceding Busby Berkeley staging for spectacle.

The first hour is a loose, disjointed plot to plant the Fanchon & Marco presentation production stuff. F&M isn't mentioned but that's the setting, with James Cagney as the unit stager who's being rooked by his partners.

As in *Gold Diggers*, where Ned Sparks puts on a Ziegfeld production with a $15,000 budget, similarly no picture house ever saw such tabs as Cagney gives 'em here. But that's cinematic license.

That water ballet, the hokum 'Honeymoon Hotel' and 'Shanghai Lil' are punchy and undeniable. They more than offset the lethargy of what has preceded and sweeps the spectator away.

Characters are formula. Ruby Keeler is again the mousey type who becomes a swell number, and Dick Powell again is the juve lead. Cagney is the dynamic stager of units and Joan Blondell is his overly efficient secretary who contributes an element of unrequited love while Cagney gets rid of one wife and falls for another phoney dame.

●●●●●●●●●●●●●●●●●●●●●●●●●●

■ FOOTLIGHT SERENADE

1942, 81 MINS, US Ⓥ

Dir Gregory Ratoff *Prod* William Le Baron
Scr Richard Ellis, Helen Logan, Lynn Starling *Ph* Lee Garmes *Ed* Robert Simpson *Mus* Lee Robin, Ralph Rainger
● John Payne, Betty Grable, Victor Mature, Jane Wyman, Phil Silvers, James Gleason (20th Century-Fox)

Footlight Serenade is a typical backstage number. New twist of minor importance has been provided for the boy-meets-girl-and-both-get-into-Broadway-show formula. Victor Mature is the champ, with the show built around him by producer James Gleason. His characterization is decidedly reminiscent of a heavyweight champ of the 1930s. Betty Grable gets a chorine job, while her fiance John Payne is projected into a line of candidates for stumble-bum for the champ in the show.

Although Mature successfully pictures the egoistic and swaggering fight champ for reverse angles, he's painted with lily-white duco for the finish.

Gregory Ratoff carries the direction at a good pace. With the backstage filmusical angles well culled, there was nothing new for the scripters to devise on their own.

●●●●●●●●●●●●●●●●●●●●●●●●●●

■ FOOTLOOSE

1984, 107 MINS, US ◇ Ⓥ

Dir Herbert Ross *Prod* Lewis J. Rachmil, Craig Zadan
Scr Dean Pitchford *Ph* Ric Waite *Ed* Paul Hirsch
Mus Miles Goodman, Becky Shargo *Art Dir* Ron Hobbs
● Kevin Bacon, Lori Singer, John Lithgow, Dianne Wiest, Christopher Penn, Sarah Jessica Parker (Paramount)

In addition to his usual directorial skill and considerable choreographic experience, Herb Ross brings to *Footloose* an adult sensibility often lacking in troubled-teen pics.

To be sure, from its toe-tapping titles onward, *Footloose* is mainly a youth-oriented rock picture, complete with big-screen reminders of what's hot today in music video. And there's usually a stereo in sight to explain where the music's coming from, even on the

side of tractors. But by writing both the screenplay and contributing lyrics to nine of the film's songs, Dean Pitchford has come up with an integrated story line that works.

Essential to the result is young Kevin Bacon, superb in the lead part. Bacon really just wants to get along in the small town he's been forced to move to from Chicago. Sure to complicate his life, however, is pretty Lori Singer, a sexually and otherwise confused preacher's daughter.

●●●●●●●●●●●●●●●●●●●●●●●●●●

■ FOOTSTEPS IN THE DARK

1941, 96 MINS, US

Dir Lloyd Bacon *Scr* Lester Cole, John Wexley
Ph Ernie Haller *Ed* Owen Marks *Mus* Frederick Hollander
● Errol Flynn, Brenda Marshall, Ralph Bellamy, Alan Hale, Lee Patrick, Lucile Watson (Warner/First National)

Errol Flynn becomes a detective book author and amateur Sherlock in *Footsteps in the Dark*, his first comedy in years. Not his best picture, this modest budgeter gives the star a chance to appear in a role different from his usual costume or military films. Lloyd Bacon's direction furnishes the film with plenty of suspense and hokey but socko absurdities.

Flynn is depicted as an investment banker, leading a double life as a writer under the nom-de-plume of F.X. Pettijohn. His search for story material takes him on nightly prowls which get him into hot water in his own home.

Flynn does well enough as the amateur Sherlock. It's a role that calls for much action, with the plot [from a play by Laslo Fodor] centered about him in almost every scene. His portrayal indicates he could do better in future semi-comic roles, especially if given brighter material.

●●●●●●●●●●●●●●●●●●●●●●●●●●

■ FORBIDDEN PLANET

1956, 98 MINS, US ◇ Ⓥ

Dir Fred McLeod Wilcox *Prod* Nicholas Nayfack
Scr Cyril Hume *Ph* George J. Folsey *Ed* Ferris Webster *Mus* Louis Barron, Bebe Barron *Art Dir* Cedric Gibbons, Arthur Lonergan
● Walter Pidgeon, Anne Francis, Leslie Nielsen, Warren Stevens, Jack Kelly, Earl Holliman (M-G-M)

Imaginative gadgets galore, plus plenty of suspense and thrills, make the production a top offering in the space travel category. Best of all the gadgets is Robby, the Robot, and he's well-used for some comedy touches.

The conception of space cruisers, space planet terrain, the monstrous self-operating power plant, and of the terribly frightening spectre that threatens the human principals in the story are weird and wonderful.

With all the technical gadgetry on display and carrying the entertainment load, the players are more or less puppets with no great acting demands made. Leslie Nielsen, space cruiser commander, lands on Altair-4 to search for survivors from a previous flight. He finds Walter Pidgeon, super-scientist, and the latter's daughter (Anne Francis) who, with Robby, are the planet's only inhabitants.

Pidgeon, who has gained knowledge beyond usual human limits, wants the rescuers to be gone. Nielsen takes to Francis and she to him, so he determines to seek out the unseen menace.

Credited for the special effects that add the punch to the show are A. Arnold Gillespie, Warren Newcombe, Irving G. Ries and Joshua Meador.

●●●●●●●●●●●●●●●●●●●●●●●●●●

■ FORCE 10 FROM NAVARONE

1978, 118 MINS, UK ◇ Ⓥ

Dir Guy Hamilton *Prod* Oliver A. Unger *Scr* Robin Chapman *Ph* Christopher Challis *Ed* Ray Poulton
Mus Ron Goodwin *Art Dir* Geoffrey Drake

F

● Robert Shaw, Harrison Ford, Edward Fox, Barbara Bach, Franco Nero, Richard Kiel (American International)

This is not a sequel to the 1961 hit, *Guns of Navarone*, although *Force 10* opens with the bangup conclusion of the earlier exercise in World War II commando heroics.

Two survivors of the spiking of the guns, British Major Mallory (now played by Robert Shaw) and demolitions expert Miller (Edward Fox) provide the link that gives some purpose to the title.

Director Guy Hamilton manages over the course of almost two hours to keep his audience on edge. For a finale he has a double whammy destruction of a giant Yugoslav dam which sets loose forces of nature that crumble a seemingly indestructible bridge.

This next-to-last film appearance of Robert Shaw is not his glory farewell. He is very good in what he is called upon to do, but the role is not one that makes any particular demand upon an exceptionally talented person.

Harrison Ford does a creditable job as the American Colonel; Fox is excellent as the British demolitions expert; Carl Weathers gives a powerful performance as the unwanted black GI who proves himself in more ways than one. Barbara Bach, lone femme, does fine in a tragic, patriotic role as a Partisan. Franco Nero as a Nazi double agent who fools the Partisans is slickly nefarious.

■ FOREIGN AFFAIR, A

1948, 113 MINS, US

Dir Billy Wilder   *Prod* Charles Brackett   *Scr* Charles Brackett, Billy Wilder, Richard Breen, Robert Harari   *Ph* Charles B. Lang Jr   *Ed* Doane Harrison   *Mus* Frederick Hollander   *Art Dir* Hans Dreier, Walter Tyler
● Jean Arthur, Marlene Dietrich, John Lund, Millard Mitchell (Paramount)

A Foreign Affair is a witty satire developed around a Congressional investigation of GI morals in Germany. Much of the action is backgrounded against actual Berlin footage. The humor to which such a theme lends itself has been given a stinging bite, even though presented broadly to tickle the risibilities.

While subject is handled for comedy, Charles Brackett and Billy Wilder have managed to underlay the fun with an expose of human frailties and, to some extent, indicate a passive bitterness among the conquered in the occupied areas.

Jean Arthur is in a topflight characterization as a spinsterish congresswoman, who furnishes the distaff touch to an elemental girl-meets-boy angle in the story. The boy is John Lund, and Marlene Dietrich personifies the eternal siren as an opportunist German femme who furnishes Lund with off-duty diversion. Also, she gives the Dietrich s.a. treatment to three Frederick Hollander tunes, lyrics of which completely express the cynical undertones of the film.

■ FOREIGN BODY

1986, 108 MINS, US/UK ◇ ⓥ

Dir Ronald Neame   *Prod* Colin M. Brewer   *Scr* Celine La Freniere   *Ph* Ronnie Taylor   *Ed* Andrew Nelson   *Mus* Ken Howard   *Art Dir* Roy Stannard
● Victor Banerjee, Warren Mitchell, Geraldine McEwan, Denis Quilley, Amanda Donohoe, Anna Massey (Neame/Brewer)

If *Foreign Body* [based on the novel by Roderick Mann] doesn't have quite the comic and narrative richness of Ronald Neame's Ealing Studios classics, this variation on the 'great impostor' plot device is still an unalloyed pleasure to watch.

Built solidly upon a fluid, comic virtuoso performance by Victor Banerjee, the picaresque fable of an impoverished refugee from Calcutta faking it as a doctor to London's upper crust makes some jaunty points about racism, gullibility and pluck.

Even though he's a deceiver, sincerity is a bedrock trait of the *Foreign Body* hero, Ram Das, and Banerjee is free to romp with bug-eyed zaniness through the improbable adventures of this Asian naif abroad.

■ FOREIGN CORRESPONDENT

1940, 119 MINS, US ⓥ

Dir Alfred Hitchcock   *Prod* Walter Wanger   *Scr* Charles Bennett, Joan Harrison, James Hilton, Robert Benchley   *Ph* Rudolph Mate   *Ed* Dorothy Spencer, Otho Lovering   *Mus* Alfred Newman   *Art Dir* Alexander Golitzen
● Joel McCrea, Laraine Day, Herbert Marshall, George Sanders, Albert Basserman, Edmund Gwenn (Wanger/United Artists)

Story is essentially the old cops-and-robbers. But it has been set in a background of international political intrigue of the largest order. It has a war flavor, the events taking place immediately before and at the start of World War II; yet it can in no sense be called a war picture. Mystery and intrigue march in place.

Add to all this a cast carefully selected to the last, unimportant lackey. Joel McCrea neatly blends the self-confidence and naivete of the reporter-hero, while Laraine Day, virtually a fledgling in pictures, only in the most difficult sequences misses out as a top-grade dramatic player. Vet Herbert Marshall as the heavy, George Sanders as McCrea's fellow-reporter, 72-year-old refugee Albert Basserman as a Dutch diplomat, Edmund Gwenn as a not-to-be-trusted bodyguard, Eduardo Ciannelli as the usual hissable villain, are all tops. Comic touch is provided by Robert Benchley and Eddie Conrad.

Story uncorks with the editor of a New York paper going nuts because his foreign correspondents cable nothing but rumor and speculation. He hits on the idea of sending one of his police reporters to dig factual material out of the Europe of August 1939. McCrea, who knows nothing of foreign affairs, immediately runs into the tallest story a reporter can imagine – a big-league peace organization, headed by Marshall, which is operating as nothing but a spy ring.

McCrea runs into the double-cross organization when it kidnaps an honest Dutch diplomat (Basserman) and assassinates his imposter to give the impression that he is dead. Assassination sequence in the rain on the broad steps of an Amsterdam building (set is a tremendous and excellent re-creation of a whole block in Amsterdam) is virtually a newsreel in its starkness.
□ 1940: Best Picture (Nomination)

■ FOREVER AMBER

1947, 140 MINS, US ◇

Dir Otto Preminger   *Prod* William Perlberg   *Scr* Philip Dunne, Ring Lardner Jr   *Ph* Leon Shamroy   *Ed* Louis Loeffler   *Mus* David Raksin   *Art Dir* Lyle R. Wheeler
● Linda Darnell, Cornel Wilde, Richard Greene, George Sanders, Jessica Tandy, Anne Revere (20th Century-Fox)

Here is a $4 million (and claimed to be more) picture that looks its cost. That goes even for the lost footage through mishap with Peggy Cummins, the original candidate until Linda Darnell replaced. And she does quite well.

The lusty yarn [from the novel by Kathleen Winsor] is treated for what it is. Darnell runs the gamut from romantic opportunist to prison degradation and up again to being the king's favorite and finally a discarded mis-

tress, grateful that the royal equerry invites her to supper after Charles II gives her the brush-off.

In between there's a wealth of derring-do, 17th-century knavery and debauchery, the love of a good woman (Jane Ball), and the rest of a depraved court's atmosphere. It's solid escapology.

Darnell manages her chameleon Amber character very well. Her blonde beauty shows off well in Technicolor, and she is equally convincing when she is thrown in a pauper's gaol.

Cornel Wilde is the No. 1 juve, although Glenn Langan suggests he might have made an excellent choice for that role instead of a secondary swain. Richard Haydn plays his a.k. role well as the arrogant earl who Amber premeditatedly weds in order to gain a title. John Russell is convincing as the highwayman; Anne Revere is sufficiently despicable as a keeper of a thieves' den; Jessica Tandy does all right as Amber's maid; George Sanders turns a neat character when chiding Amber for thinking he could be played for a sucker in a supposedly compromising rendezvous.

■ FOREVER AND A DAY

1943, 104 MINS, US

Dir Rene Clair, Edmund Goulding, Cedric Hardwicke, Frank Lloyd, Victor Saville, Robert Stevenson, Herbert Wilcox   *Scr* Charles Bennett, C.S. Forrester, Lawrence Hazard, Michael Hogan, W.P. Lipscomb, Alice Duer Miller, John Van Druten, Alan Campbell, Peter Godfrey, S.M. Herzig, Christopher Isherwood, Gene Lockhart, R.C. Sherriff, Claudine West, Norman Corwin, Jack Hartfield, James Hilton, Emmet Lavery, Frederick Lonsdale, Donald Ogden Stewart, Keith Winter   *Ph* Robert de Grasse, Lee Garmes, Russell Metty, Nicholas Musuraca   *Ed* Elmo J. Williams, George Crone   *Mus* Anthony Collins
● Merle Oberon, Gladys Cooper, C. Aubrey Smith, Claude Rains, Anna Neagle, Ray Milland (RKO)

Forever and a Day is a sentimental romantic-adventure yarn, encompassing in cavalcade manner Britain's epochal struggles to retain the integrity of an empire and the freedom of its people in face of periodical threats of would-be world conquerors. Interwoven is the quaint history of a picturesque London mansion – its illustrious builder and his descendants – built during the Napoleonic period, that withstands the ravages of time and world-shattering conflict until the days of the Nazi blitz.

In a star-studded cast, including some 45 name players, a number of topnotchers are necessarily limited. However, a large proportion of the subordinate sequences have been handled with telling effect.

Picture, in the making for about a year, rolled up a negative cost of around $500,000 at RKO, which financed the production. This is exclusive of the players, who undertook the assignment on a gratis basis, some 21 writers and the seven accredited directors who also contributed their services.

Yarn revolves about the fusing of two families after a feud dating back to the early part of the 19th century when C. Aubrey Smith, as the robust, swashbuckling British admiral first built the house. Claude Rains, as the vindictive guardian of Anna Neagle, who runs away to marry one of the Smith tribe, does not impress as the menace.

■ FORMULA, THE

1980, 117 MINS, US ◇ ⓥ

Dir John G. Avildsen   *Prod* Steve Shagan   *Scr* Steve Shagan   *Ph* James Crabe   *Ed* David Bretherton, John G. Avildsen, John Carter   *Mus* Bill Conti   *Art Dir* Herman A. Blumenthal
● George C. Scott, Marthe Keller, Marlon Brando, John Gielgud, Beatrice Straight (M-G-M)

207

M-G-M refused to let director John Avildsen take his name off this picture. According to Avildsen, it was not his original cut, nor producer-writer Steve Shagan's cut, but sort of a combination of the two, plus a few snips and patches by M-G-M president David Begelman.

Given the combined efforts of 14 Oscar nominees and a solid bestseller [by Shagan] to start from, it's truly amazing that *The Formula* is such a clump of sludge, impossible to understand for at least an hour before it grinds to a halt.

Initial sequences solidly establish the closing hours of World War II when a German general (Richard Lynch) is entrusted with top secret documents to take to Switzerland in hopes the Nazis can use them to bargain for amnesty. But Lynch is captured by a US major (Robin Clarke) who recognizes what the secrets will be worth in the postwar world of commerce.

Cut forward 35 years and Clarke is a fresh corpse, murdered in his bed. George C. Scott is called in to investigate the murder of his old friend and before long establishes Clarke had some mysterious dealings with oil supertycoon Marlon Brando.

Appearing grotesquely fat and ridiculous, Brando apparently thinks he's making some visual comment on the nature of his character.

....

■ FOR PETE'S SAKE

1974, 90 MINS, US ◇ ⓥ

Dir Peter Yates   *Prod* Martin Erlichman, Stanley Shapiro   *Scr* Stanley Shapiro, Maurice Richlin   *Ph* Laszlo Kovacs   *Ed* Frank Keller   *Art Dir* Gene Callaghan
● Barbra Streisand, Michael Sarrazin, Estelle Parsons, William Redfield, Molly Picon, Louis Zorich (Rastar/Columbia)

For Pete's Sake is a flaccid, relentlessly 'zany' comedy that in the 1960s might have been offered Doris Day.

Co-scripter and co-producer Stanley Shapiro, who penned those Doris Day-Rock Hudson comedies of yore, has tailormade this tale of a brash Brooklyn housewife (Barbra Streisand) married to a poor taxi driver (Michael Sarrazin) who yearns to return to school. Sarrazin is given inside info about a pending meat deal between the US and the Soviet Union which promises to zoom the price of pork bellies. (Pic's original title was *July Pork Bellies*.)

To get the $3,000 necessary to invest in pork belly futures on the stock exchange, Streisand secretly goes to a loan shark. When the Soviet deal is delayed and she can't pay up, her 'contract' is sold. Each contract sale increases the debt while allowing maximum opportunity for broad comedy schtik.

....

■ FORT APACHE

1948, 127 MINS, US ⓥ

Dir John Ford   *Prod* Merian C. Cooper, John Ford   *Scr* Frank S. Nugent   *Ph* Archie J. Stout   *Ed* Jack Murray   *Mus* Richard Hageman   *Art Dir* James Basevi
● John Wayne, Henry Fonda, Shirley Temple, John Agar, Pedro Armendariz, Victor McLaglen (Argosy/RKO)

Mass action, humorous byplay in the western cavalry outpost, deadly suspense, and romance are masterfully combined in this production [based on a story by James Warner Bellah]. Integrated with the tremendous action is a superb musical score by Richard Hageman, Score uses sound effects as tellingly as the music notes to point up the thrills. In particular, the massacre scene where the deadly drumming of the Indian ponies makes more potent the action that transpires.

Cast is as tremendous as the scope achieved by Ford's direction and, as a consequence, some of the roles are very short but all effective. Henry Fonda is the colonel, embittered because he has been assigned to the remote fort after a brilliant war record.

John Wayne makes a virile cavalry captain, wise in the way of the Indian. Shirley Temple, the colonel's daughter, perks her sequences in romance with John Agar, West Point graduate. Latter impresses. Pedro Armendariz is excellent as a sergeant. Making up a group of tough topkicks that are responsible for the film's humor are Victor McLaglen, Dick Foran and Jack Pennick.

....

■ FORT APACHE, THE BRONX

1981, 123 MINS, US ◇

Dir Daniel Petrie   *Prod* Martin Richards, Tom Fiorella   *Scr* Heywood Gould   *Ph* John Alcott   *Ed* Rita Roland   *Mus* Jonathan Tunick   *Art Dir* Ben Edwards
● Paul Newman, Edward Asner, Danny Aiello, Rachel Ticotin, Pam Grier (20th Century-Fox)

Driving relentlessly to make points that are almost pointless. *Fort Apache, The Bronx* is a very patchy picture, strong on dialog and acting and exceedingly weak on story.

Even while shooting, *Apache* drew protests from neighborhood factions claiming it would show only the bad about the Bronx and ignore the good. Because of that, the pic starts with a tip-of-the-hat title card to the 'law abiding' citizens of the community. But that's the last to be seen of them.

Title is taken from the nickname for a real police station uptown, literally surrounded and often under siege from thieves, murderers, hookers, junkies, dealers.

One of the cops (Danny Aiello) is a murderer himself and even the heroes. (Paul Newman and Ken Wahl) aren't all that admirable in their feeble attempts to control crime in the streets, their abject cynicism about life in the station house and vacillation over whether to snitch on Aiello after they watch him kill a kid.

Typical of the problem director Daniel Petrie creates for himself, he introduces Pam Grier right away as a drug-crazed cop killer and brings her back a couple of more times for additional murders, effectively grizzly in detail. But she never says much and there's never an inkling of what motivates her, other than dope.

....

■ FORTUNE, THE

1975, 88 MINS, US ◇

Dir Mike Nichols   *Prod* Nichols, Don Devlin   *Scr* Adrien Joyce [= Carol Eastman]   *Ph* John A. Alonzo   *Ed* Stu Linder   *Mus* David Shire   *Art Dir* Richard Sylbert
● Jack Nicholson, Warren Beatty, Stockard Channing, Florence Stanley (Columbia)

The Fortune is an occasionally enjoyable comedy trifle, starring Jack Nicholson and Warren Beatty as bumbling kidnappers of heiress Stockard Channing, who is excellent in her first major screen role. Very classy 1920s production values often merit more attention than the plot.

Beatty elopes with Channing but, not yet free of a former wife, Nicholson actually marries her. Trio sets up housekeeping in Los Angeles, and after Channing is disinherited, the guys try to kill her. If lugging around a passed-out intoxicated girl in clumsy murder attempts does not offend sensibilities, then the alleged fun may be passable.

David Shire superbly recreates some old Joe Venuti-Eddi Lang jazz band arrangements.

....

■ FORTUNE COOKIE, THE

1966, 125 MINS, US ⓥ

Dir Billy Wilder   *Prod* Billy Wilder   *Scr* Billy Wilder, I.A.L. Diamond   *Ph* Joseph LaShelle   *Ed* Daniel Mandell   *Mus* Andre Previn   *Art Dir* Robert Luthardt
● Jack Lemmon, Walter Matthau, Ron Rich, Cliff Osmond, Judi West, Lurene Tuttle (United Artists/Mirisch)

Producer-director-writer Billy Wilder presents in *The Fortune Cookie* another bittersweet comedy commentary on contemporary US mores. Generally amusing (often wildly so) but overlong, the pic is pegged on an insurance fraud in which Jack Lemmon and Walter Matthau are the conspirators.

Original screenplay is by Wilder, paired for seventh time with I.A.L. Diamond. Plot turns on the complications following TV cameraman Lemmon's accidental injury at the hands of grid star Ron Rich. Matthau, shyster lawyer and Lemmon's brother-in-law, sees fancy damages in the injury, and exwife Judi West smells money in a fake reunion with Lemmon.

Lemmon, confined perforce to sickroom immobility (bandages, wheelchair, etc) is saddled most of the time with the colorless image of a man vacillating with his conscience over the fraud, and its effect on Rich, whose playing has deteriorated from remorse.

Title derives from a scene where Lemmon breaks a fortune cookie, only to find inside Abraham Lincoln's famous aphorism about fooling all/some people all/some of the time.

....

■ FORTY GUNS

1957, 76 MINS, US

Dir Samuel Fuller   *Prod* Samuel Fuller   *Scr* Samuel Fuller   *Ph* Joseph Biroc   *Ed* Gene Fowler Jr   *Mus* Harry Sukman   *Art Dir* John Mansbridge
● Barbara Stanwyck, Barry Sullivan, Dean Jagger, John Ericson, Gene Barry, Eve Brent (20th Century-Fox)

Samuel Fuller in triple capacity of producer-scripter-director has devised a solid piece of entertainment which has femme star Barbara Stanwyck playing a ruthless Arizona ranch owner, the boss of Cochise County. Into her realm rides Barry Sullivan and his two brothers, former an ex-gun slinger now working for the US Attorney General, his fame with a gun preceding him.

He's in Tombstone on official business, which means conflict with femme, who rules her domain, including the sheriff, with an iron hand. Further complications arise between the two, even as a romance develops, over Stanwyck's brother (John Ericson), a brawling, would-be killer.

Stanwyck socks over her role in experienced style and Sullivan is persuasive as the marshal who loses his 10-year record for non-killing by gunning down Ericson after latter has murdered his brother (Gene Barry).

....

■ 40 POUNDS OF TROUBLE

1962, 106 MINS, US ◇

Dir Norman Jewison   *Prod* Stan Margulies   *Scr* Marion Hargrove   *Ph* Joe MacDonald   *Ed* Marjorie Fowler   *Mus* Mort Lindsey   *Art Dir* Alexander Golitzen, Robert Clatworthy
● Tony Curtis, Phil Silvers, Suzanne Pleshette, Claire Wilcox, Stubby Kaye, Larry Storch (Universal)

Marion Hargrove's 'original' screenplay actually owes a little something to the Little Miss Marker-Sorrowful Jones school of screen comedy, but it's a precocious and likeable offspring. The troublesome 40-pounder of the title is moppet Claire Wilcox, who makes her screen debut as an orphaned youngster who gradually melts the heart of the businesslike, efficient manager of a Lake Tahoe, Nevada gambling resort (Tony Curtis).

F

In the course of her conquest, she also aids the cause of husband-hunting nitery canary Suzanne Pleshette, whose romance with Curtis is complicated by the latter's relationship with his ex-wife, to whom he refuses to pay alimony, a stubborn stance that places him in jeopardy every time he leaves his Nevada legal sanctuary and crosses the border to California.

Curtis dispatches his role with comic savvy. Pleshette, whose manner is reminiscent of Joan Bennett's, handles her romantic assignment with finesse. Little Miss Wilcox is an appealing youngster, although director Jewison (in his first screen assignment after TV credits) might have obtained even better results from her by striving for more spontaneous, less practiced, childish reactions.

Phil Silvers has some memorable moments as the owner of the gambling establishment, notably one sequence in which he grandly strides into his domain, gruffly urging his customers to 'play, play.'

■ **48HRS.**

1982, 96 MINS, US ◇ Ⓥ

Dir Walter Hill *Prod* Lawrence Gordon, Joel Silver *Scr* Roger Spottiswoode, Walter Hill, Larry Gross, Steven E. De Souza *Ph* Ric Waite *Ed* Freeman Davies, Mark Warner, Billy Weber *Mus* James Horner *Art Dir* John Vallone

● Nick Nolte, Eddie Murphy, Annette O'Toole, Frank McRae, James Remar, David Patrick Kelly (Paramount)

48HRS. is a very efficient action entertainment which serves as a showy motion picture debut for Eddie Murphy. Pairing of Nick Nolte as a rough-and-tumble San Francisco cop and Murphy as a small-time criminal sprung for two days to help track down former associates makes for a throwback to the buddy-buddy pics of the 1970s.

It's all pretty predictable stuff, but done with plenty of savvy and professionalism. Director Walter Hill has always worked within traditional action genres, but has generally applied an artier, more philosophical slant to them.

Speaking with a voice sanded by a constant supply of booze and cigarettes, Nolte lays on the gruff Wallace Beery stuff a little thick and is generally willing to play second fiddle to Murphy's more kinetic shtick, but registers strongly withal. For his part, Murphy has a lot to do and gets through it amusingly.

■ **42ND STREET**

1933, 89 MINS, US

Dir Lloyd Bacon, Busby Berkeley *Scr* James Seymour, Rian James *Ph* Sol Polito *Ed* Thomas Pratt, Frank Ware *Art Dir* Jack Okey

● Warner Baxter, Bebe Daniels, George Brent, Ruby Keeler, Guy Kibbee, Ginger Rogers (Warner)

Everything about the production rings true. It's as authentic to the initiate as the novitiate.

There are good performances by Warner Baxter, as the neurotic showman who whips *Pretty Lady* into a hit musical comedy, and Bebe Daniels in a not particularly sympathetic assignment as the outmoded musical comedy ingenue whose unrequited association with a sap kiddie car manufacturer angels the production.

Una Merkel and Ginger Rogers, as a pair of dumb and not-so chorines, are types. George E. Stone, as the dance stager, is likewise a believable reflection of the type. Harry Akst is the piano rehearser, and Al Dubin and Harry Warren, who fashioned the film's song ditties, play themselves.

Ruby Keeler, as the unknown who comes through and registers a hit, is utterly convincing.

Not the least of the total belongs to the direction by Lloyd Bacon, who fashioned

some novelties in presentation, with Busby Berkeley an excellent aide on the terp mountings. The same overhead style of camera angles, which Berkeley introduced in the Eddie Cantor pictures and elsewhere, are further advanced.

☐ 1932/33: Best Picture (Nomination)

■ **49TH PARALLEL**

1941, 123 MINS, UK Ⓥ

Dir Michael Powell *Prod* John Sutro, Michael Powell *Scr* Emeric Pressburger, Rodney Ackland *Ph* Frederick Young *Ed* David Lean *Mus* Ralph Vaughan Williams *Art Dir* David Rawnsley

● Leslie Howard, Raymond Massey, Laurence Olivier, Anton Walbrook, Glynis Johns, Eric Portman (Ortus/Min. of Information)

This is an important and effective propaganda film. Picture, started in April 1940 and took 18 months to complete. The British Government invested over $100,000 in the venture.

The locales depict Canadian life from an Eskimo village to a Hutterite settlement in the Canadian wheatfields. Story is the strongest possible indictment against Nazism. Plot concerns six Nazi U-boat men whose craft is blown up in the Hudson Bay Straits. They reach land and commit every sort of crime up to murder in their efforts to reach the neutral territory of the US. The script of Emeric Pressburger is direct and forceful.

The stars are Leslie Howard, with his comedy gifts at high tide; Laurence Olivier (a bit, but best thing he has ever done); Raymond Massey (also a bit, but outstanding) and Anton Walbrook, as a dignified Hitlerite leader. Despite the heartbreaking difficulties encountered, such as the defection of Elisabeth Bergner after the picture was well on its way, Michael Powell, the director, has managed to maintain his stature among the top directors.

■ **FOR WHOM THE BELL TOLLS**

1943, 166 MINS, US ◇

Dir Sam Wood *Prod* Sam Wood *Scr* Dudley Nichols *Ph* Ray Rennahan *Ed* Sherman Todd, John Link *Mus* Victor Young *Art Dir* William Cameron Menzies

● Gary Cooper, Ingrid Bergman, Akim Tamiroff, Katina Paxinou, Arturo de Cordova, Vladimir Sokoloff (Paramount)

For Whom the Bell Tolls is one of the important pictures of all time although almost three hours of running time can overdo a good thing. Running sans intermission, the saga of Roberto and Maria (Gary Cooper and Ingrid Bergman) asks for too much concentrated attention on what is basically one dramatic episode, that of blasting a crucial bridge, in order to foil the Nationalists.

On a beautiful Technicolor canvas is projected an equally beautiful romance which, perhaps, lays a little too much emphasis on the amorous phase. It's one thing to punch up boy-meets-girl sequencing, but the nature of Ernest Hemingway's bestseller, of course, was predicated on a political aura resulting in the Spanish civil war.

Histrionically, *Bell Tolls* is a triumph for the four sub-featured players. Katina Paxinou, onetime foremost in her native Greek theatre, dominates everything by a shade. A masculine woman who, however, has known of love and beauty, despite her realistic self-abnegation that she is ugly, is standout in everything she does.

For the record *Bell* cost around $150,000 for the screen rights (Hemingway's book sales determined the overage on top of the basic $100,000 price) and the production cost was officially a few thousands under $3 million.

☐ 1943: Best Picture (Nomination)

■ **FOR YOUR EYES ONLY**

1981, 127 MINS, UK ◇

Dir John Glen *Prod* Albert R. Broccoli *Scr* Richard Maibaum, Michael G. Wilson *Ph* Alan Hume *Ed* John Grover *Mus* Bill Conti *Art Dir* Peter Lamont

● Roger Moore, Carole Bouquet, Chaim Topol, Jill Bennett, Lois Maxwell, Lynn-Holly Johnson (United Artists/Eon)

For Your Eyes Only bears not the slightest resemblance to the Ian Fleming novel of the same title, but emerges as one of the most thoroughly enjoyable of the 12 Bond pix [to date] despite fact that many of the usual ingredients in the successful 007 formula are missing.

The film is probably the best-directed on all levels since *On Her Majesty's Secret Service*, as John Glen, moving into the director's chair after long service as second unit director and editor, displays a fine eye.

Story also benefits from presence of a truly sympathetic heroine, fetchingly portrayed by Carole Bouquet, who exhibits a humanity and emotionalism not frequently found in this sort of pop adventure and who takes a long time (the entire picture, in fact) to jump into the sack with him.

M is gone, due to Bernard Lee's death; Bond doesn't make his first feminine conquest until halfway through the picture; there's no technology introduced by Q which saves the hero in the end; no looming supervillain dominates the drama; Bond bon mots are surprisingly sparse, and the fate of the whole world isn't even hanging in the balance at the climax.

■ **FOUL PLAY**

1978, 116 MINS, US ◇ Ⓥ

Dir Colin Higgins *Prod* Thomas L. Miller, Edward K. Milkis *Scr* Colin Higgins *Ph* David M. Walsh *Ed* Pembroke J. Herring *Mus* Charles Fox *Art Dir* Alfred Sweeney

● Goldie Hawn, Chevy Chase, Burgess Meredith, Rachel Roberts, Eugene Roche, Dudley Moore (Paramount)

Foul Play revives a relatively dormant film genre – the crime-suspense-romantic comedy in which low-key leading players get involved with themselves while also caught up in monumental intrigue. The name missing from the credits is Alfred Hitchcock. Writer Colin Higgins makes a good directorial bow.

If you think you've been through the plot before, you have: Goldie Hawn, likable librarian, picks up undercover agent Bruce Solomon who passes her film evidence of how Rachel Roberts, Eugene Roche and other heavies are going to assassinate visiting Pope Pius XIII (played by SF socialite Cyril Magnin) at a performance of *The Mikado* in the Opera House. Chevy Chase, a detective, eventually believes Hawn's stories about attempts on her life. Car chases and theatre shootout climax the film's 116 minutes.

Entire cast comes off very well. In prominent support are Burgess Meredith as Hawn's landlord; Dudley Moore, a dedicated swinger who turns out to be the opera conductor; Marilyn Sokol, Hawn's girlfriend who carries anti-rapist tools in her handbag.

■ **FOUNTAINHEAD, THE**

1949, 112 MINS, US Ⓥ

Dir King Vidor *Prod* Henry Blanke *Scr* Ayn Rand *Ph* Robert Burks *Ed* David Weisbart *Mus* Max Steiner

● Gary Cooper, Patricia Neal, Raymond Massey, Kent Smith (Warner)

Because the plot is completely devoted to hammering home the theme that man's personal integrity stands above all law, the picture develops a controversial element.

The garrulous script which Ayn Rand did from her novel calls for a great deal of posturing by the cast and King Vidor's direction permits much over-acting where underplaying might have helped develop a better emotional feeling and a truer sense of reality. Gary Cooper has an uneasy time in the miscasting as the plot's hero, an architect who is such an individualist that he dynamites a charity project when the builders alter his plans.

As Cooper's co-star, Patricia Neal makes a moody heroine, afraid of love or any other honest feeling. Raymond Massey is allowed to be too flamboyant as the publisher.

....

■ **FOUR FEATHERS**

1929, 80 MINS, US ⊗
Dir Merian C. Cooper, Ernest B. Schoedsack
Prod Merian C. Cooper, Ernest B. Schoedsack
Scr Howard Estabrook, Hope Loring *Mus* William Frederick Peters
● Richard Arlen, Fay Wray, Clive Brook, William Powell, Theodore von Eltz, Noah Beery (Paramount)

Four Feathers is a good picture. Merian C. Cooper and Ernest B. Schoedsack were the producers. They made *Chang*. It is no secret that *Feathers'* treatment was primarily photographic. The dramatics followed. Cooper and Schoedsack must also have been the directors of the story part, for no one else is credited. Nor is a photographer named.

Ever see a herd of hippo slide down a steep bank of a jungle watering place? Ever see a large family of baboons hop from limb to limb to escape a forest fire? Or a huge army of black savages dashing to battle on white camels? These three items are *Four Feathers*.

The white feather is the symbol of cowardice in the British army. The principal character and subsequent hero of A.W. Mason's novel receives four white feathers.

Tale is set late in the last century. *Four Feathers* is highly reminiscent of *Beau Geste*. Pictorially they are much the same.

Richard Arlen's performance is good most of the while, excellent at times. William Powell is next with the most to do and does it like Powell. Clive Brook is not handed his usual weighty part and isn't impressive because of that, while Theodore von Eltz, as the lesser of the four chums, has no opportunity to be more than satisfactory. Fay Wray only has to look good.

....

■ **FOUR FEATHERS, THE**

1939, 130 MINS, UK ◇ ▼
Dir Zoltan Korda *Prod* Alexander Korda *Scr* R.C. Sherriff, Lajos Biro, Arthur Wimperis *Ph* Georges Perinal, Osmond Borrodaile *Ed* William Hornbeck, Henry Cornelius *Mus* Miklos Rozsa *Art Dir* Vincent Korda
● John Clements, Ralph Richardson, C. Aubrey Smith, June Duprez (London)

The Four Feathers has been filmed before, with the book [by A.E.W. Mason] from which it was adapted having enjoyed big world sale.

A young British officer resigns from his regiment the night before it embarks for an Egyptian campaign. Three of his pals and his fiancee hand him white feathers, indicative of cowardice. The next day he disappears. Alone and unaided in Egypt, he goes through harrowing ordeals to gain his reinstatement in their eyes.

June Duprez, the fiancee, is the only woman in the cast. She postulates prettily and attractively, with little else to do. Rest of the cast is excellent, with C. Aubrey Smith, enacting a lovable, elderly bore. John Clements, the hero, is excellent.

Photography is excellent along with the direction by Zoltan Korda.

....

■ **FOUR HORSEMEN OF THE APOCALYPSE, THE**

1921, 130 MINS, US ⊗
Dir Rex Ingram *Scr* June Mathis *Ph* John F. Seitz
Ed Grant Whytock *Mus* Louis F. Gottschalk *Art Dir* Joseph Calder, Amos Myers
● Rudolph Valentino, Alice Terry, Alan Hale, Nigel de Brulier, Jean Hersholt, Wallace Beery (Metro)

The magnitude of *The Four Horsemen* is staggering, and it is not hard to believe the statistics relative to the production. It is said to have cost approximately $800,000; director Rex Ingram had 14 assistants, each with a cameraman; more than 12,000 persons were used, and 125,000 tons of masonry and other material employed; $375,000 insurance was carried on the art works, furniture, etc, used in the picture, which was six months in the making.

Horror stalked grinningly bold through the book of Vicente Blasco Ibanez, the greatest of the World War I romances. Ingram has mercifully cloaked it with distance and delicacy of treatment. This is a characteristic of the director's handling of the entire subject. It is a production of many nuances, shadings so artistic and skillful as to intrigue the mind of the spectator.

....

■ **FOUR HORSEMEN OF THE APOCALYPSE, THE**

1962, 153 MINS, US ◇ ▼
Dir Vincente Minnelli *Prod* Julian Blaustein
Scr Robert Ardrey, John Gay *Ph* Milton Krasner
Ed Adrienne Fazan, Ben Lewis *Mus* Andre Previn
Art Dir George W. Davis, Urie McCleary, Elliot Scott
● Glenn Ford, Ingrid Thulin, Charles Boyer, Lee J. Cobb, Paul Henreid, Yvette Mimieux (M-G-M)

Although *The Four Horsemen of the Apocalypse* is a screen spectacle of dynamic artistic proportions, it gradually becomes a victim of dramatic anemia – a strapping hulk of cinematic muscle rendered invalid by a weak heart. Lamentably, the romantic nucleus of this tragic chronicle of a family divided and devoured by war fails in the adaptation to achieve a realistic and compassionate relationship between the lovers.

Director Minnelli and leads Glenn Ford and Ingrid Thulin must share responsibility with the writers for this fundamental weakness.

It is quite possible that Ford's characterization was plagued by the ghost of Valentino, whose enactment of the leading role in 1921 was his first screen triumph. There is, for instance, a tight eyeball shot of Ford's orbs reminiscent of Valentinography. At any rate, Ford's performance is without warmth, without passion, without magnetism. Warmth is also missing in the performance of Ingrid Thulin.

However, the film shines in other areas. Frank Santillo's montages contribute touches of art and explanation to a picture that is sometimes wobbly, choppy and incomplete in the area of exposition. The device of veiling black-and-white newsreel photography in a splash of hot, vivid color registers with great emotional effect, notably in passages utilizing the novel technique of quadruple image superimposition.

Another major assist is that of Andre Previn, who has composed a tearing, soaring, emotionally affecting score to take up some of the slack in the love story.

....

■ **FOUR IN THE MORNING**

1966, 94 MINS, UK
Dir Anthony Simmons *Prod* John Morris *Scr* Anthony Simmons *Ph* Larry Pizer *Ed* Fergus McDonnell
Mus John Barry
● Ann Lynn, Brian Phelan, Judi Dench, Norman Rodway, Joe Melia (West One)

Writer-director Anthony Simmons shows two couples in crisis, tying them in with a gimmick, which works. There's an unidentified girl found in a river. Simmons gives the scene of the discovery and study of the drowned girl a metallic, sombre documentary flavor.

A seemingly rootless young man picks up a singer he knows after her work. At four in the morning they romp around the Thames' shores, steal a boat, leave it, almost touch each other emotionally but part still uncommitted. Hints of the instability of both are carefully and intelligently suggested.

The other couple is shown as a woman waiting for her husband, out on the town with a bachelor crony. The baby cries and exasperates her. The growing incompatibility of the couple is deftly outlined in bold, dramatic strokes.

Judi Dench has the right checked hysteria for her role of the wife with a disposition towards love that makes her poignant. Ann Lynn and Brian Phelan are also effective as the other couple with Joe Melia a pointed counterpoint to the married couple with his personal problems.

....

■ **FOUR JUST MEN, THE**

1939, 85 MINS, UK
Dir Walter Forde *Prod* Michael Balcon *Scr* Angus MacPhail, Sergei Nolbandov, Roland Pertwee
Ph Ronald Neame *Mus* Ernest Irving (dir.) *Art Dir* Wilfrid Shingleton
● Hugh Sinclair, Griffith Jones, Francis L. Sullivan, Frank Lawton, Anna Lee, Alan Napier (Associated British)

A skilled and dramatic filmization of one of Edgar Wallace's best known novels. Murder, sabotage and international troublemaking form the basis of this exploit of the Four Just Men who, incognito, spend their lives breaking up dope rings and foiling plots of foreign agitators.

While incarcerated in a foreign prison, the youngest member of the quartet escapes execution by a few seconds, being rescued by two of the others disguised as higher officials. He has learned the name of an eastern conspirator; also that one of the members of parliament is responsible for a leakage of state secrets.

The casting is superb, Frank Lawton making a wistful and pathetic figure of the youngest patriot. Francis L. Sullivan as a French designer, playing one of his rare non-villainous roles, is his usual suave self as one of the four.

....

■ **FOUR MUSKETEERS, THE**

1975, 108 MINS, PANAMA ◇
Dir Richard Lester *Prod* Alexander Salkind
Scr George MacDonald Fraser *Ph* David Watkins
Ed John Victor Smith *Mus* Lalo Schifrin *Art Dir* Brian Eatwell
● Oliver Reed, Raquel Welch, Richard Chamberlain, Michael York, Frank Finlay, Christopher Lee (20th Century-Fox)

The Four Musketeers continues the story of Oliver Reed, Richard Chamberlain, Frank Finlay and Michael York as they joust with evil plotter Charlton Heston and evil seductress Faye Dunaway, defend fair lady queen Geraldine Chaplin, bypass imbecile King Jean Pierre Cassel, and eventually triumph over arch fiend Christopher Lee.

The same mixture of teenybopper naughtiness, acne spiciness, contrived tastelessness and derring don't as found in the earlier film (*The Three Musketeers*) are laid on with the same deft trowel herein. Perhaps the film is a triumph of controlled and deliberate mediocrity, but it still closer resembles a clumsy carbon of a bad satire on the original.

....

F

FOUR POSTER, THE

1952, 103 MINS, US

Dir Irving Reis   *Prod* Stanley Kramer   *Scr* Allan Scott
Ph Hal Mohr   *Ed* Henry Batista, Harry Gerstad
Mus Dimitri Tiomkin   *Art Dir* Rudolph Sternard, Carl
Peterson
● Rex Harrison, Lilli Palmer (Kramer/Columbia)

The Four Poster as a pic is still limited to the
same two characters of the play, with nary
the suggestion of an interloper. Though the
stars' performances are excellent, they are
unable to salvage audience interest during
the film's lesser moments. In fact, the major
fault is the inability of the two characters to
cope with the lack of incident.

With the four poster bed in the background
as the common denominator of their marital
relationship, pic traces the lives of a couple
from the day the groom carries his bride
across the threshold. From then on are
detailed his struggles as a writer, the bride's
faith in his ability, his success, their children,
the son's death in World War I, the romantic
escapades of the husband and wife, and
finally their deaths.

Lilli Palmer imparts s.a. and natural
beauty to the role of the wife.

FOUR SEASONS, THE

1981, 107 MINS, US ◇

Dir Alan Alda   *Prod* Martin Bregman   *Scr* Alan Alda
Ph Victor J. Kemper   *Ed* Michael Economou
Mus Antonio Vivaldi   *Art Dir* Jack Collis
● Alan Alda, Carol Burnett, Len Cariou, Sandy Dennis,
Rita Moreno, Jack Weston (Universal)

If *The Four Seasons* was never a play, it should
have been, since it's based on the most stagey, dialog-bound original screenplay in
memory. A lightweight, overly contrived
examination of the relationship among three
couples who vacation together four times
over course of story, Alan Alda's feature
directorial debut is middle-brow, middle-
aged material.

Pic's structure is too strikingly similar to
that of *Same Time Next Year* to ignore the fact
that Alda starred in screen adaptation of that
Broadway hit.

Tale is populated strictly with *Ordinary
People*, but Alda's script doesn't begin to
scratch the surface to discover what makes
them tick and is particularly stingy in giving
Carol Burnett and Rita Moreno anything to
work with.

New England and Virgin Islands locations
are fresh and well chosen, and Vivaldi background score helps lend a tony atmosphere to
the proceedings.

FOURTEEN HOURS

1951, 92 MINS, US

Dir Henry Hathaway   *Prod* Sol C. Siegel   *Scr* John
Paxton   *Ph* Joe MacDonald   *Ed* Dorothy Spencer
Mus Alfred Newman   *Art Dir* Lyle Wheeler, Leland
Fuller
● Richard Basehart, Paul Douglas, Barbara Bel
Geddes, Agnes Moorehead, Robert Keith, Grace Kelly
(20th Century-Fox)

Suspense elements in a situation that has a
would-be suicide swaying precariously on a
high window ledge are fully realized in
Fourteen Hours. Story [by Joel Sayre] is based
on an actual suicide case in New York.

Paul Douglas is the traffic policeman who
becomes a hero when his routine duties are
interrupted one morning by the sight of
Richard Basehart perched on a 14-storey
high window ledge.

Tension reaches the screaming point often
as Douglas and the others try to talk Basehart
back into the building, while the citizens of
New York make a Roman holiday of the
event.

Douglas wallops his policeman role by
sound underplaying. Basehart comes over
solidly. Barbara Bel Geddes is his girlfriend,
adding worth to the character. Agnes
Moorehead scores as the selfish mother, and
Robert Keith matches her excellence in his
playing of the father.

A romance with a nice fresh touch is born
in the chance meeting of Debra Paget and
Jeffrey Hunter in the crowd. Grace Kelly,
drawing a divorce property settlement in a
nearby building, decides to make another try
at marriage.

FOURTH PROTOCOL, THE

1987, 119 MINS, UK ◇ Ⅴ

Dir John Mackenzie   *Prod* Timothy Burrill
Scr Frederick Forsyth   *Ph* Phil Meheuy   *Ed* Graham
Walker   *Mus* Lalo Schifrin   *Art Dir* Alan Cameron
● Michael Caine, Pierce Brosnan, Joanna Cassidy,
Ned Beatty, Ray McAnally, Ian Richardson (Rank)

The Fourth Protocol is a decidedly contempo
thriller, a tale of vying masterspies and a
chase to head off a nuclear disaster. Its edge
is a fine aura of realism.

Novelist Frederick Forsyth, who also was
an executive producer, adapted the pic from
his book.

The story is pretty straightforward. A ruthless KGB head plans to detonate a nuclear
bomb close to a US airbase in England so the
Brits blame the Yanks and the NATO
alliance will collapse.

What follows is a good old-fashioned race
against time as Caine tracks down his Russian alter ego Major Petrofsky (Pierce
Brosnan) and after a hand-to-hand scuffle
manages to defuse the bomb.

Michael Caine as a maverick counter-
espionage expert gives a thorough performance in a part that doesn't really stretch his
abilities.

FOURTH WAR, THE

1990, 91 MINS, US ◇ Ⅴ

Dir John Frankenheimer   *Prod* Wolf Schmidt
Scr Stephen Peters, Kenneth Ross   *Ph* Gerry Fisher
Ed Robert F. Shugrue   *Mus* Bill Conti   *Art Dir* Alan
Manzer
● Roy Scheider, Jurgen Prochnow, Tim Reid, Lara
Harris, Harry Dean Stanton (Kodiak)

The Fourth War is a well-made Cold War
thriller about private battling that might
escalate out of control. Opening title sets the
tale in November 1988 on the border of
Czechoslovakia and East Germany.

Roy Scheider is well-cast as a hardline colonel who's caused nothing but trouble in his
career and is now stationed at a post near the
border by his general, Harry Dean Stanton.
Scheider witnesses the murder of a fleeing
defector through no man's land. He rightly
blames the Soviet colonel (Jurgen Prochnow)
for this dastardly deed and from this minor
act of outrage ensues a man-to-man feud of
Laurel & Hardy proportions.

Tightly directed by Frankenheimer with an
eye for comic relief as well as tension maintenance, *The Fourth War* holds the fascination
of eyeball-to-eyeball conflict.

Besides the two stars, Tim Reid is very
effective as the man on the spot (his commanding officer is out of control), and Lara
Harris is convincing as a duplicitous femme
fatale.

FOX, THE

1968, 110 MINS, US/CANADA ◇

Dir Mark Rydell   *Prod* Raymond Stross   *Scr* Lewis
John Carlino   *Ph* William Fraker   *Ed* Thomas
Stanford   *Mus* Lalo Schifrin   *Art Dir* Charles Bailey
● Sandy Dennis, Keir Dullea, Anne Heywood, Glyn
Morris (Warner/Seven Arts/Motion Pictures Intl

D.H. Lawrence's lesbian-themed novella
The Fox is turned into a beautifully photographed, dramatically uneven Canadian-
made film.

Sandy Dennis and Anne Heywood are cast
as lesbian lovers who have exiled themselves
to a lonely farm. Arrival of Keir Dullea cues a
disintegration of the femme relationship and
eventual tragedy.

In early reels, Anne Heywood seems the
dominant female. She is inwardly uneasy,
perhaps afraid of eventual old age.

Dennis has the greater acting burden, and
her performance is uneven. Her daffiness in
early reels seems overdone, result of which is
that her later remarks may draw unwanted
smiles, even chuckles, from audiences.

Dullea plays his part with quiet determination to snare Heywood. Whether or not he
suspects or comprehends the lesbian relationship is debatable, from script and actions.

First sexual encounter between him and
Heywood is awkward – the gaspings, the
clutching of turf, etc. A later romantic scene
between the two gals, by contrast, is
excellent.

FOXES

1980, 106 MINS, US ◇ Ⅴ

Dir Adrian Lyne   *Prod* David Puttnam, Gerald Ayres
Scr Gerald Ayres   *Ph* Leon Bijou   *Ed* Jim Coblentz
Mus Giorgio Moroder   *Art Dir* Michael Levesque
● Jodie Foster, Scott Baio, Sally Kellerman, Randy
Quaid (Filmworks/Casablanca)

Foxes is an ambitious attempt to do a film
relating to some of the not-so-acceptable
realities among teenagers that ends up
delivering far less than it is capable of.

Story of four teenage girls and their battles
often becomes a depressing, one-sided and
melodramatic treatise on American youth.

It soon becomes clear this is not the usual
gaggle of girls portrayed as typical American
teenagers. Cherie Currie is a stoned-out
former hooker, Marilyn Kagan is an unhappy, overweight fat girl longing to shed her
parents' protective shell, Kandice Stroh is a
lying, confused flirt and Jodie Foster is a
level-headed intellect.

Constant switching of action between the
girls causes Stroh's character to be lost midway and Foster's identity to never fully be
explored despite the fact she's the focal point.

FOXES OF HARROW, THE

1947, 115 MINS, US

Dir John M. Stahl   *Prod* William A. Bacher
Scr Wanda Tuchock   *Ph* Joseph La Shelle   *Ed* James
B. Clark   *Mus* Alfred Newman   *Art Dir* Lyle R.
Wheeler, Maurice Ransford
● Rex Harrison, Maureen O'Hara, Richard Haydn,
Victor McLaglen, Patricia Medina (20th Century-Fox)

The Foxes of Harrow is an elaborate filmization
of Frank Yerby's novel. Invested with the
polished direction of John M. Stahl, it builds
into a powerful drama of an adventurer's rise
to fame and fortune in New Orleans of the
19th century. Exciting story has strong production, vivid developments and helped
along with excellent pace most of the time.

Technically, *Foxes* runs too long. It contains
passages at the outset and near the end that
appear superfluous. But because there are so
many meaty scenes, even the more tedious
ones overflow with nice performances.

Rex Harrison, the child born out of
wedlock, rises to the heights in New Orleans
business even though his first money is won
gambling. Plot shows Harrison being put off
a Mississippi steamboat for cheating at cards
but being rescued from a sandbar by Victor
McLaglen, captain of a pigboat. Harrison's
audacity both at cards and with women cata-

pult him to riches. His main ambition is to build another Harrow estate like his mother had known in Ireland. He finally persuades Maureen O'Hara, daughter of one of New Orleans' aristocrats, to become his wife.

Harrison is perfect as the suave gambler and O'Hara carries the highly dramatic scenes with surprising skill, but it seems a pity that she is not permitted to smile more often.

■ FOXY BROWN

1974, 91 MINS, US ◇ Ⓥ

Dir Jack Hill   *Prod* Buzz Feitshans   *Scr* Jack Hill   *Ph* Brick Marquand   *Ed* Chuck McClelland   *Mus* Willie Hutch   *Art Dir* Kirk Axtel

● Pam Grier, Antonio Fargas, Peter Brown, Terry Carter, Kathryn Loder, Harry Holcombe (American International)

Bosomy black starlet Pam Grier plays a gal whose dope-dealing brother (Antonio Fargas) rats on her undercover-narc boyfriend (Terry Carter), cuing latter's gangland murder on her doorstep. Not one to take romantic disappointment lightly, she sets her vengeful eye on the leaders of the local vice ring (Kathryn Loder and Peter Brown).

Before femme might makes right, Grier and callgirl Juanita Brown have a brawl in a lesbian bar, Fargas writhes to his gunned-down death, doxy Sally Ann Stroud has her throat slashed, two degenerate thugs who've raped Grier are burned to death, and Brown is castrated.

Even by the gutter-high standards of the genre, *Foxy Brown* is something of a mess. Jack Hill's screenplay has peculiar narrative gaps.

■ FRANCES

1982, 140 MINS, US ◇ Ⓥ

Dir Graeme Clifford   *Prod* Jonathan Sanger   *Scr* Eric Bergren, Christopher DeVore, Nicholas Kazan   *Ph* Laszlo Kovacs   *Ed* John Wright   *Mus* John Barry   *Art Dir* Richard Sylbert

● Jessica Lange, Kim Stanley, Sam Shepard, Bart Burns, Jeffrey DeMunn, Jordan Charney (EMI/Brooksfilms)

Rare to the memory is a film like *Frances* which runs 140 minutes and its star is on the screen 85% of the time in one intense scene after another. It's quite an accomplishment for Jessica Lange and it's too bad a better film didn't come of it.

Though her troubled life made headlines around the world, Frances Farmer is still much a mystery. What is agreed is that Farmer was a rebellious young girl in Seattle who first shocked the 1930s with a high-school essay questioning God, then outraged conservatives again a few years later with a visit to Moscow. The publicity, plus her talent, led to a successful Broadway and Hollywood career, followed by some kind of a breakdown and many years in mental institutions.

Resolving the doubts that haunt Farmer's life, the film presents her basically as a woman to be admired for standing behind her convictions regardless of the consequences.

As a directorial debut by editor Graeme Clifford, however, *Frances* tends to trivialize. It's hard to shake the persistent feeling that she brought a lot of woe on herself.

■ FRANKENSTEIN

1931, 71 MINS, US Ⓥ

Dir James Whale   *Prod* Carl Laemmle Jr.   *Scr* John L. Balderston, Garrett Fort, Francis Edward Faragoh   *Ph* Arthur Edeson   *Ed* Clarence Kolster   *Mus* David Broekman   *Art Dir* Charles D. Hall

● Colin Clive, Mae Clarke, John Boles, Boris Karloff, Edward Van Sloan, Dwight Frye (Universal)

Frankenstein looks like a *Dracula* plus, touching a new peak in horror plays and handled in production with supreme craftsmanship.

Picture [from the play by Peggy Webling, based on the novel by Mary W. Shelley] starts with a wallop. Midnight funeral services are in progress on a blasted moor, with the figure of the scientist and his grotesque dwarf assistant hiding at the edge of the cemetery to steal the newly-buried body. Sequence climaxes with the gravedigger sending down the clumping earth upon newly-laid coffin. Shudder No. 1.

Shudder No. 2, hard on its heels is when Frankenstein cuts down his second dead subject from the gallows, presented with plenty of realism. The corpses are to be assembled into a semblance of a human body which Frankenstein seeks to galvanize into life, and to this end the story goes into his laboratory, extemporized in a gruesome mountain setting out of an abandoned mill.

Laboratory sequence detailing the creation of the monster patched up of human odds-and-ends is a smashing bit of theatrical effect, taking place during a violent mountain storm.

Playing is perfectly paced. Colin Clive, the cadaverous hero of *Journey's End* (1930), is a happy choice for the scientist driven by a frenzy for knowledge. He plays it with force, but innocent of ranting. Boris Karloff makes a memorable figure of the bizarre monster with its indescribably terrifying face of demoniacal calm.

■ FRANKENSTEIN CREATED WOMAN

1967, 92 MINS, UK ◇ Ⓥ

Dir Terence Fisher   *Prod* Anthony Nelson Keys   *Scr* John Elder [= Anthony Hinds]   *Ph* Arthur Grant   *Ed* James Needs   *Mus* James Bernard   *Art Dir* Don Mingaye

● Peter Cushing, Susan Denberg, Thorley Walters, Robert Morris, Peter Blythe, Barry Warren (Hammer/Seven Arts)

In *Frankenstein Created Woman* the good doctor, as usual, played by Peter Cushing, doesn't really create woman, he just makes a few important changes in the design. Considering the result is beautiful blonde Susan Denberg, most film fans would like to see the doctor get a grant from the Ford Foundation, or even the CIA.

In this version, Frankenstein dabbles as much in transmigration of souls as actual patchwork surgery, capturing the psyche of an executed young man and instilling it in the body of a drowned young woman (Denberg). The girl, originally a disfigured, shy maiden, is rejuvenated as a beautiful femme whose touch proves tres fatale when the male soul uses the female body to wreak vengeance on the trio of young wastrels responsible for his execution (Peter Blythe, Barry Warren, Derek Fowlds).

■ FRANKENSTEIN MEETS THE WOLF MAN

1943, 72 MINS, US Ⓥ

Dir Roy William Neill   *Prod* George Waggner   *Scr* Curt Siodmak   *Ph* George Robinson   *Ed* Edward Curtiss   *Mus* Hans J. Salter

● Lon Chaney, Ilona Massey, Patric Knowles, Lionel Atwill, Bela Lugosi, Maria Ouspenskaya (Universal)

In order to put the Wolf Man and the Monster through further film adventures, scripter Curt Siodmak has to resurrect the former from a tomb, and the Frankenstein creation from the ruins of the castle where he was purportedly killed. But he delivers a good job of fantastic writing to weave the necessary thriller ingredients into the piece, and finally

brings the two legendary characters together for a battle climax.

Eerie atmosphere generates right at the start, when Lon Chaney, previously killed off with the werewolf stain on him, is disinterred and returns to life. After one transformation, he winds up in a hospital to gain the sympathetic attention of medico Patric Knowles, then seeks out gypsy Maria Ouspenskaya for relief, and she takes him to the continent and the village where Frankenstein held forth. This allows Chaney to discover and revive the monster, role handled by Bela Lugosi, and from there on it's a creepy affair in grand style.

■ FRANKENSTEIN MUST BE DESTROYED

1969, 97 MINS, UK ◇

Dir Terence Fisher   *Prod* Anthony Nelson Keys   *Scr* Bert Batt   *Ph* Arthur Grant   *Ed* Gordon Hales   *Mus* James Bernard   *Art Dir* Bernard Robinson

● Peter Cushing, Veronica Carlson, Freddie Jones, Simon Ward, Thorley Walters, Maxine Audley (Hammer)

Frankenstein's (Peter Cushing) diabolical plan is, in the cause of science, to preserve the medical knowledge of a brilliant but insane surgeon. This he'll do by murdering the medico, removing his brain and inserting it in the body of a kidnapped man.

With the help of two young accomplices (a doctor, Simon Ward, and his girl friend, Veronica Carlson), drawn into the plot because Frankenstein is blackmailing them over a drug robbery offense, the mad scientist is hijacked from an asylum, operated on and the brains switched.

The film is a good-enough example of its low-key type, with artwork rather better than usual (less obvious backcloths, etc.), a minimum of artless dialog, good lensing by Arthur Grant and a solid all round cast.

■ FRANKENSTEIN UNBOUND

1990, 85 MINS, US ◇ Ⓥ

Dir Roger Corman   *Prod* Roger Corman, Thom Mount, Kabi Jaeger   *Scr* Roger Corman, F.X. Feeney, Ed Neumeir   *Ph* Armando Nannuzzi, Michael Scott   *Ed* Jay Cassidy   *Mus* Carl Davis   *Art Dir* Enrico Tovaglieri

● John Hurt, Raul Julia, Bridget Fonda, Nick Brimble, Catherine Rabett, Catherine Corman (Mount)

Roger Corman's *Frankenstein Unbound* is a competent but uninspired riff on the venerable legend. For Corman, it's also a return trip to modern British sci-fi, adapting a Brian W. Aldiss novel.

John Hurt toplines as a mad scientist in New Los Angeles of 2031, trying to develop a laser weapon that causes objects to implode. Unfortunately, his experiments are causing time slips, violent dislocations including one that suddenly transports Hurt to Switzerland in 1817.

Hurt chances upon Dr Frankenstein in a local pub and he's soon visiting gothic folk Mary Godwin (soon to be Shelley), Lord Byron and Percy Shelley. Out on the rampage is Frankenstein's monster, killing people until his creator fabricates a mate for him.

While warring with Frankenstein and his monster, Hurt ultimately identifies with them, leading to an interesting, somber climax set in icy wastes as in Shelley's original novel.

Though some of the dialog is clutzy, acting is generally good with top honors to Raul Julia as a thoughtful Frankenstein. More single-minded is Hurt's sketchy role.

Bridget Fonda is attractive in the Mary Godwin role, overshadowed by British actress Catherine Rabett, who brings panache to the role of Frankenstein's fiancee, later resurrected as bride for the monster.

F

FRANTIC

1988, 120 MINS, US ◇ ▽

Dir Roman Polanski   *Prod* Thom Mount, Tim
Hampton   *Scr* Roman Polanski, Gerard Brach
Ph Witold Sobocinski   *Ed* Sam O'Steen   *Mus* Ennio
Morricone   *Art Dir* Pierre Guffroy
● Harrison Ford, Emmanuelle Seigner, Betty Buckley,
John Mahoney, Jimmie Ray Weeks (Mount/Warner)

Frantic, is a thriller without much surprise,
suspense or excitement. Drama about an
American doctor's desperate search for his
kidnapped wife through the demi-monde of
Paris reveals director Roman Polanski's personality and enthusiasm only in brief humorous moments.

San Francisco medic Harrison Ford arrives
in Paris with wife Betty Buckley to deliver a
paper at a conference and, incidentally, to
revisit the scene of their honeymoon 20 years
before. While Ford is showering, Buckley disappears from the hotel room, thus setting off
an urgent woman-hunt that takes the distraught husband to young Emmanuelle
Seigner, a sleek, punky drugette and night-
clubber who appears to be the only lead to
the kidnappers.

The McGuffin, or object of everyone's pursuit, here is a miniature Statue of Liberty
which contains an object that, predictably,
could endanger the Free World. Action
climax takes place alongside the small-scale
replica of France's gift to New York Harbor.

Ford sweats a lot while conveying Polanski's view that anxiety is the natural state of
the human condition. His latest discovery,
Seigner, certainly is eye-catching and proves
servicable in her part.

FREAKS

1932, 61 MINS, US ▽

Dir Tod Browning   *Prod* Tod Browning   *Scr* Willis
Goldbeck, Leon Gordon, Edgar Allan Woolf, Al
Boasberg   *Ph* Merritt B. Gerstad   *Ed* Basil Wrangell
● Wallace Ford, Leila Hyams, Olga Baclanova, Rosco
Ates, Harry Earles, Daisy Earles (M-G-M)

Freaks is sumptuously produced, admirably
directed, and no cost was spared. But Metro
failed to realize that even with a different sort
of offering the story still is important. Here it
is not sufficiently strong to get and hold the
interest, partly because interest cannot easily
be gained for a too fantastic romance.

The plot outline is the love of a midget in a
circus for a robust gymnast, her marriage
with the idea of getting his fortune and
putting him out of the way through poisoning
and effecting a union with the strongman of
the show.

The story [from *Spurs* by Tod Robbins] is
laid in a European touring circus. It is only a
one-ring affair, but it carries three times as
many high-class freaks as the Ringling show
ever trouped in one season, and the dressing
tent is larger than the main top.

No effort is made to show the ring performance, most of the action occurring in the
dressing tent and much of it while the show is
closed. The midget leads are Harry and
Daisy Earles. Earles builds on his fine
performance in *The Unholy Three* (1930) but
he fails in the stronger scenes, when he seeks
to gain sympathy through his despair.

Daisy Earles is less successful as the midget
rival to Olga Baclanova. She is a doll-like
little woman who reads her lines with
extreme care, but seldom succeeds in acting.
Baclanova as the rather rowdy gymnast has
several fine opportunities but at other times is
handicapped by action too obvious and her
cheerful effort to poison her tiny spouse carries no suggestion of menace. Harry Victor,
as the strongman, is conventional and
Wallace Ford and Leila Hyams, heading
the cast, have little more than walk-through

parts. The one sincere human note is Rose
Dione in an unfortunately brief bit.

FREEBIE AND THE BEAN

1974, 112 MINS, US ◇ ▽

Dir Richard Rush   *Prod* Richard Rush   *Scr* Robert
Kaufman   *Ph* Laszlo Kovacs   *Ed* Fredric Steinkamp,
Michael McLean   *Mus* Dominic Frontiere
Art Dir Hilyard Brown
● Alan Arkin, James Caan, Loretta Swit, Jack Kruschen,
Mike Kellin, Valerie Harper (Warner)

Freebie and the Bean stars Alan Arkin and
James Caan as two allegedly 'funny' lawless
lawmen. Richard Rush's tasteless film, from
a spitball script by Robert Kaufman, utilized
lots of stunt and action crews disturbing the
peace all over San Francisco.

The purported 'humor' between the two
stars largely hinges on Caan's delivery of
what are nothing more than repeated racist
slurs on Arkin's character's Chicano ancestry. Arkin's performance adds even more
concrete nuances to this characterization.
What passes for a basic story line is
something about their nabbing bigtime
gangster Jack Kruschen, and between
car chases and mindless destruction of cars
and other things, the plot lurches forward.

FRENCH CONNECTION, THE

1971, 104 MINS, US ◇ ▽

Dir William Friedkin   *Prod* Philip D'Antoni   *Scr* Ernest
Tidyman   *Ph* Owen Roizman   *Ed* Jerry Greenberg
Mus Don Ellis   *Art Dir* Ben Kazaskow
● Gene Hackman, Fernando Rey, Roy Scheider, Tony
LoBianco, Marcel Bozzuffi, Frederic De Pasquale
(20th Century-Fox)

So many changes have been made in Robin
Moore's taut, factual reprise of one of the
biggest narcotics hauls in New York police
history that only the skeleton remains, but
producer and screenwriter have added
enough fictional flesh to provide director
William Friedkin and his overall topnotch
cast with plenty of material, and they make
the most of it.

Gene Hackman and Roy Scheider are very
believable as two hard-nosed narcotics
officers who stumble onto what turned out to
be the biggest narcotics haul to date. As
suave and cool as the two cops are overworked, tired and mean, Fernando Rey is the
French mastermind of the almost-perfect
plan.

Friedkin includes a great elevated train-
automobile chase sequence that becomes
almost too tense to be enjoyable, especially
for New Yorkers who are familiar with such
activities.

Shot almost entirely in and around New
York, Owen Roizman's fluid color camera
explores most of Manhattan and much of
Brooklyn without prettifying the
backgrounds.
☐ 1971: Best Picture

FRENCH CONNECTION II

1975, 119 MINS, US ◇

Dir John Frankenheimer   *Prod* Robert L. Rosen
Scr Robert Dillon, Laurie Dillon, Alexander Jacobs
Ph Claude Renoir   *Ed* Tom Rolf   *Mus* Don Ellis   *Art
Dir* Jacques Saulnier
● Gene Hackman, Fernando Rey, Bernard Fresson,
Jean-Pierre Castaldi, Charles Millot, Cathleen Nesbitt
(20th-Century Fox)

John Frankenheimer's *French Connection II* is
both complementary to, yet distinctly different from, William Friedkin's *The French
Connection*.

Gene Hackman as Popeye Doyle goes to
Marseilles in search of heroin czar Fernando
Rey (also encoring from the first pic). The
assignment in reality is a setup (thereby im-

plying that high-level law enforcement corruption still exists), and Hackman is duly
kidnapped, drugged and left for dead by Rey.

Hackman's addiction and withdrawal sequences are terrifyingly real and make
uncompromisingly clear the personal and
social horror of drug abuse.

This plot turn is both intelligent and clever.
Bernard Fresson is excellent as the French
narc who must cope not only with his country's dope problem, but also Hackman's
unruly presence.

Hackman's performance is another career
highlight, ranging from cocky narc, Ugly
American, helpless addict, humbled ego and
relentless avenger.

FRENCH DRESSING

1964, 86 MINS, UK

Dir Ken Russell   *Prod* Kenneth Harper   *Scr* Peter
Myers, Ronald Cass, Peter Brett   *Ph* Ken Higgins
Ed Jack Slade   *Mus* Georges Delerue   *Art Dir* Jack
Stephens
● James Booth, Roy Kinnear, Marisa Mell, Alita
Naughton, Bryan Pringle, Robert Robinson (Associated
British)

It's a pity to see a promising comedy idea go
busted through sheer lack of bright wit and
irony. *French Dressing* is a light comedy which
needed the satirical touch, but instead suffers
from a flat, heavy treatment. This squelches
many of the lighter, more promising
moments.

Gormleigh-on-Sea is one of those British
holiday resorts that suffer from acute dull-
itis. A bright young deckchair attendant
(James Booth) cons the local entertainments
manager and the mayor into running a film
festival. They persuade an ambitious young
French actress to be the star of the proceedings which lead to some inevitable disasters
and coy jokes such as a total washout at the
opening of a new Nudist Beach and a riot at a
premiere. Only quick thinking by the young
American journalist girl friend of James
Booth saves the situation.

Too much stodgy joking does not aid predictable slapstick situations. Quick cutting
and speeding up of camerawork are not
enough to disguise the fact that this is not a
souffle but mainly an indigestible pancake.

FRENCH LIEUTENANT'S WOMAN, THE

1981, 127 MINS, UK ◇

Dir Karel Reisz   *Prod* Leon Clore   *Scr* Harold Pinter
Ph Freddie Francis   *Ed* John Bloom   *Mus* Carl Davis
Art Dir Assheton Gorton
● Meryl Streep, Jeremy Irons, David Warner, Leo
McKern, Charlotte Mitchell (United Artists/Junipaer)

Diverse directing talents including Fred Zinnemann, Richard Lester and Mike Nichols
all tried and failed to conquer the complicated narrative of John Fowles' epic romantic
novel, *The French Lieutenant's Woman*.

Finally, it took director Karel Reisz and
playwright Harold Pinter to develop an ingenious method to convey the essence of Fowles' book. The film retells the novel's story,
set in 1867, of a strange young woman dishonored by her involvement with a French
soldier and the English gentleman who finds
her mystery and sadness irresistible. Simultaneously, a parallel story of the affair between the two actors portraying the central
roles in a film within-a-film unfolds on
screen.

The effect of the two interwoven stories is at
times irritating and confusing, but ultimately
most affecting. This is due in large part to the
strong performances of Meryl Streep as Sara
Woodruff/Anna and Jeremy Irons as Charles
Smithson/Mike.

The action flip-flops between the two tales,
but favors the historic story. Reisz employs

213

several lightning mixes to bridge the action, but more often abruptly moves from past to present.

The unconventional approach to Fowles' novel takes some getting used to but succeeds in conveying the complexity of the original in the final analysis.

Cameraman Freddie Francis deserves special mention for his painterly skill of recreating 19th-century Dorset and the contrasting sheen of the contemporary segments.

The casting of Meryl Streep as Sarah/Anna could not have been better. Sarah comes complete with unbridled passions and Anna is the cool, detached professional. There is never a false note in the sharply contrasting characters.

■ **FRENCH LINE, THE**

1954, 102 MINS, US ◇ Ⓥ

Dir Lloyd Bacon *Prod* Edmund Grainger *Scr* Mary Loos, Richard Sale *Ph* Harry J. Wild *Ed* Robert Ford *Mus* Constantin Bakaleinikoff
● Jane Russell, Gilbert Roland, Arthur Hunnicutt, Mary McCarty, Joyce Mackenzie, Paula Corday (RKO)

Except for a four-minute, censorably costumed dance by Jane Russell, this is a rather mild, gabby, fashion parade in 3-D.

The plot is the long-worked one about a rich girl who wants to be loved for herself and goes incognito as a working frail to find the right man. It's an okay basis for a musical if ingenuously handled, but there is little of the imaginative displayed in Lloyd Bacon's direction or in the screenplay by Mary Loos and Richard Sale [based on a story by Matty Kemp and Isabel Dawn]. Once in a while a snappy quip breaks through the long passages of verbiage that strain too hard to be smart talk. And in line with the film's principal concern, these snappy quips are bosom-conscious.

Russell is an eye-pleaser, and she can be a good musical comedy actress (*Gentlemen Prefer Blondes*) when given material and direction. Gilbert Roland's suave way with the ladies helps his character of the French lover who pursues oil-rich Russell for herself, not her millions.

■ **FRENCHMAN'S CREEK**

1944, 113 MINS, US ◇

Dir Mitchell Leisen *Prod* Mitchell Leisen *Scr* Talbot Jennings *Ph* George Barnes *Ed* Alma Macrorie *Mus* Victor Young *Art Dir* Hans Dreier, Ernst Fegte
● Joan Fontaine, Arturo de Cordova, Basil Rathbone, Nigel Bruce, Cecil Kellaway, Ralph Forbes (Paramount)

Frenchman's Creek is a 17th-century romance about the lady and the pirate, beautifully Technicolored and lavishly mounted. Film reputedly cost over $3 million to produce, Paramount's costliest investment [at the time].

The romantic pirate from France who invades the Cornish coast of England, hiding his frigate in what thus becomes known as Frenchman's Creek, plays his role with all the musical comedy bravado the part calls for.

The romance is supposedly forthright and played straight. Joan Fontaine seeks refuge in the Cornish castle to get away from a stupid husband (Ralph Forbes) and a ducal menace. The scoundrelly servant at the Cornish retreat is actually the pirate chief's hireling, and the romance between the two, is but one of a sequence of similar adventures.

The performances are sometimes unconsciously tongue-in-cheek, but withal come off well. Cecil Kellaway is particularly good as the servant.

The scripting [from the novel by Daphne du Maurier] at times borders on the ludicrous, especially when almost all the

sympathetic figures wax near hysteria in their scoffing at the dangers which may beset them. Productionally it is ultra. And no minor assist is an excellent Victor Young score.

■ **FRENZY**

1972, 116 MINS, UK ◇ Ⓥ

Dir Alfred Hitchcock *Prod* Alfred Hitchcock *Scr* Anthony Shaffer *Ph* Gil Taylor *Ed* John Jympson *Mus* Ron Goodwin *Art Dir* Syd Cain
● Jon Finch, Barry Foster, Barbara Leigh-Hunt, Anna Massey, Alec McCowen, Vivien Merchant (Universal)

Armed with a superior script by Anthony Shaffer, an excellent cast, and a top technical crew, Alfred Hitchcock fashions a firstrate melodrama about an innocent man hunted by Scotland Yard for a series of sex-strangulation murders.

Working from Arthur La Bern's novel, *Goodbye Piccadilly, Farewell Leicester Square*, Shaffer develops a finely-structured screenplay. Jon Finch heads the cast as something of a loser who becomes trapped by circumstantial evidence in the sordid murders of several women, including his former wife (Barbara Leigh-Hunt), and current girlfriend (Anna Massey). The audience knows early who the real culprit is – in this case, Finch's friend, Barry Foster – so the interest lies in hoping for the rescue of the hero. Hitchcock has used this basic dramatic situation before.

■ **FRESHMAN, THE**

1990, 102 MINS, US ◇ Ⓥ

Dir Andrew Bergman *Prod* Mike Lobell *Scr* Andrew Bergman *Ph* William A. Fraker *Ed* Barry Malkin *Mus* David Newman *Art Dir* Ken Adam
● Marlon Brando, Matthew Broderick, Bruno Kirby, Penelope Ann Miller, Paul Benedict, Maximilian Schell (Tri-Star)

Marlon Brando's sublime comedy performance elevates *The Freshman* from screwball comedy to a quirky niche in film history – among films that comment on cult movies.

Mario Puzo and Francis Coppola's *The Godfather* is director Andrew Bergman's starting point. Incoming NYU film student Matthew Broderick is exposed not only to that Paramount film (and its sequel) in pretentious prof Paul Benedict's classroom but meets up with a virtual doppelganger for Don Vito Corleone in the form of mobster Carmine Sabatini (Brando).

The ornate and intentionally screwy plotline has Brando making an irresistible offer to Broderick to work for him part-time as a delivery boy. Broderick's first assignment is transporting a huge (but real) lizard from the airport. Broderick quickly tumbles to the criminality of Brando and his nutty partner Maximilian Schell, but is unable to extricate himself.

Pic's weakest element is the recurring satire of film studies. Although Benedict is droll as an academic poseur, the mocking of film analysis is puerile and obvious. Broderick is ably abetted by two previous costars: Penelope Anne Miller (*Biloxi Blues*), winning as an offbeat form of mafia princess; and B.D. Wong (who popped up in *Family Business*) as Schell's goofy partner in culinary crime. Tech credits on the mixed New York and Toronto shoot are good, capturing the right amount of Greenwich Village ambience.

■ **FREUD**

1962, 140 MINS, US

Dir John Huston *Prod* Wolfgang Reinhardt *Scr* Charles Kaufman, Wolfgang Reinhardt *Ph* Douglas Slocombe *Ed* Ralph Kemplen *Mus* Jerry

Goldsmith *Art Dir* Stephen B. Grimes
● Montgomery Clift, Susannah York, Larry Parks, Susan Kohner, Eric Portman, David McCallum (Universal)

Intricate scenario by Charles Kaufman and producer Reinhardt, from the former's story, translates into dramatic, not biographical, terms the events of five key years (1885-90) in Freud's life, the years during which he formulated his principal theory – that sexual instinct is the basic one in the human personality – and led him to discover and describe the presence of sexual behavior even in infancy.

The drama revolves around Freud's (Montgomery Clift) treatment of a young patient (Susannah York) who has broken down mentally and physically upon the death of her father. In treating her, and relating her neuroses to his own, he is able not only to cure her, but to formulate the Oedipus Complex theory – the child's fixation on the parent of the opposite sex. This is the dramatic nucleus of the film.

The appropriately bewhiskered Clift delivers an intense, compassionate and convincing personification of Freud. York is vivid and true as his agitated patient, although the character is not always in sharp focus. Larry Parks etches a warm and appealing portrait of Freud's friend, colleague and associate. Susan Kohner is fine as Freud's understanding wife. Among the supporting players, Eric Portman stands out with a crisp, biting enactment of Freud's orthodox superior who reveals the contradictory nature of his inner personality only when he is dying.

■ **FRIDAY FOSTER**

1975, 89 MINS, US ◇

Dir Arthur Marks *Prod* Arthur Marks *Scr* Orville Hampton *Ph* Harry May *Ed* Stanley Fragen *Mus* Luchi De Jesus
● Pam Grier, Yaphet Kotto, Godfrey Cambridge, Thalmus Rosulala, Eartha Kitt, Jim Backus (American International)

Friday Foster, is based on a comic strip of the same name; Pam Grier is a fearless magazine fotog, sort of a female Clark Kent, who stumbles onto a St Valentine's Day-type massacre involving black millionaire Thalmus Rasulala and lots of political and underworld opponents mixed up on both sides.

There's a truly impressive credit sheet, including Yaphet Kotto as a cop, Godfrey Cambridge as a swishy criminal type, Eartha Kitt as an outrageously camp fashion designer, Seatman Crothers as a dirty-minded minister, Ted Lange as a sardonic pimp, and Jim Backus as the Mr Big who pulls the strings behind the action.

Grier has some steamy sex scenes and a lot of rugged action, though she isn't totally macho and radiates a lot of traditional feminine charm along the way.

■ **FRIDAY THE 13TH**

1980, 95 MINS, US ◇ Ⓥ

Dir Sean S. Cunningham *Prod* Sean S. Cunningham *Scr* Victor Miller *Ph* Barry Abrams *Ed* Bill Freda *Mus* Harry Manfredini *Art Dir* Virginia Field
● Betsy Palmer, Adrienne King, Harry Crosby, Laurie Bartram, Robbi Morgan (Paramount)

Lowbudget in the worst sense – with no apparent talent or intelligence to offset its technical inadequacies – *Friday the 13th* has nothing to exploit but its title.

Another teenager-in-jeopardy entry, contrived to lure the profitable *Halloween* audience, this one is set at a crumbling New Jersey summer camp, shuttered for 20 years after a history of 'accidental' deaths and other spooky stuff, and about to be reopened for the summer.

F

Six would-be counselors arrive to get the place ready, then are progressively dispatched by knife, hatchet, spear and arrow.

Producer-director Sean S. Cunningham telegraphs the six murders too far ahead to keep anyone in even vague suspense, and without building a modicum of tension in between.

● ●

■ **FRIDAY THE 13TH PART 2**

1981, 87 MINS, US ◇

Dir Steve Miner   *Prod* Steve Miner   *Scr* Ron Kurz   *Ph* Peter Stein   *Ed* Susan E. Cunningham   *Mus* Harry Manfredini   *Art Dir* Virginia Field

● Amy Steel, John Furey, Warrington Gillette, Adrienne King (Paramount)

Horror fans will probably delight in seeing yet another group of sexy, teen camp counselors gruesomely executed by yet another unknown(?) assailant, but the enthusiasm will dampen once they recognize too many of the same twists and turns used in the original.

When we last left Camp Crystal Lake one nubile counselor (Adrienne King) managed to survive the murderous spree of surprise villain Betsy Palmer who, it might be remembered, was killing all of the counselors as a symbolic revenge for her son drowning in camp years earlier.

Now five years have gone by and a new group of counselors (that seems to be the operating vocation here) have returned next door to the legendary camp. They know about the past violence and are even told of the legend of Palmer's son Jason, who supposedly lives on in the woods.

Producer-director Steve Miner doesn't move in and out of scenes with the flair of original producer-director Sean Cunningham nor is he able to create the same nauseatingly realistic murder situations (perhaps he's better off for the latter).

● ●

■ **FRIDAY THE 13TH PART 3**

1982, 95 MINS, US ◇

Dir Steve Miner   *Prod* Frank Mancuso Jr   *Scr* Martin Kitrosser, Carol Watson   *Ph* Gerald Feil   *Ed* George Hively   *Mus* Harry Manfredini   *Art Dir* Robb Wilson King

● Dana Kimmell, Richard Brooker, Catherine Parks, Paul Kratka, Jeff Rogers, Larry Zerner (Paramount)

Friday the 13th was dreadful and took in more than $17 million. *Friday the 13th Part 2* was just as bad and took in more than $10 million. *Friday the 13th Part 3* is terrible, too.

This time it's Dana Kimmell who leads the gang up to evil Lake Crystal for an outing. Crazy Jason is still there, though played this time by Richard Brooker instead of Warrington Gillette.

Kimmel has had some previous contact with Jason but doesn't quite remember it. All the kids are just about that bright, especially her boyfriend Paul Kratka. The most shocking scene in the film, in fact, is when Kratka gets his brains squeezed out; up until then, you would have sworn he didn't have any brains.

There are some dandy 3-D sequences, however, of a yo-yo going up and down and popcorn popping.

● ●

■ **FRIDAY THE 13TH PART VIII JASON TAKES MANHATTAN**

1989, 100 MINS, US ◇

Dir Rob Hedden   *Prod* Randolph Cheveldave   *Scr* Rob Hedden   *Ph* Bryan England   *Ed* Steve Mirkovich   *Mus* Fred Mollin   *Art Dir* David Fischer

● Jensen Daggett, Scott Reeves, Peter Mark Richman, Barbara Bingham, V. C. Dupree, Kane Hodder (Horror/Paramount)

Paramount's latest cynical excursion into sadistic violence is lifted slightly above its generic mire by the stylish efforts of debuting director Rob Hedden.

The minimal variation this time in Hedden's script is to have most of the action take place on a cruise ship taking the Crystal Lake high school grads to Manhattan, where some humor naturally arises from the locals' indifference to the madman in their midst.

The film devotes its energies to recycling all the tried-and-true methods of dispatching teens by stabbing, strangling, electrocuting, burning, head-smashing, slashing and spearing.

Jensen Daggett is a standout as the troubled young girl on whom Jason is fixated. V.C. Dupree has vibrant energy in his boxing scenes, Sharlene Martin has a fine time with the bitch role, and Martin Cummins is funny as a video freak who compulsively films the proceedings.

● ●

■ **FRIDAY THE 13TH THE FINAL CHAPTER**

1984, 91 MINS, US ◇

Dir Joseph Zito   *Prod* Frank Mancuso Jr   *Scr* Barney Cohen   *Ph* Joao Fernandes   *Ed* Joel Goodman   *Mus* Harry Manfredini   *Art Dir* Shelton H. Bishop III

● Crispin Glover, Kimberly Beck, Barbara Howard, E. Erich Anderson, Corey Feldman, Alan Hayes (Paramount)

Opening line of film – 'I don't want to scare anyone, but Jason is still out there' – is film's only laugh, aside from unintended chuckle in the credit roll for First Aid. Everyone in sight of the lake gets it this time, except for a little boy with a fetish for masks who slaughters the crazed Jason and the boy's older sister (Corey Feldman and Kimberly Beck).

That leaves a dozen others who don't make it. More accurately, most are butchered after making it.

Of course, nobody is expected to take this stuff seriously. Given, however, the consistent pro production value, the evisceration on parade is not campy. Implausibilities abound as ever, and several *Friday the 13th* veteran players make brief appearances in an opening flashback compilation of old footage.

● ●

■ **FRIENDLY PERSUASION**

1956, 137 MINS, US ◇

Dir William Wyler   *Prod* William Wyler   *Scr* [Michael Wilson]   *Ph* Ellsworth Fredricks   *Ed* Robert Swink, Edward Biery Jr   *Mus* Dimitri Tiomkin   *Art Dir* Edward S. Haworth

● Gary Cooper, Dorothy McGuire, Anthony Perkins, Marjorie Main, Robert Middleton, Richard Eyer (Allied Artists)

While it is the simple story [from a novel by Jessamyn West] of a Quaker family in Indiana back in the 1860s, the footage contains just about everything in the way of comedy and drama, suspense and action.

Producer-director William Wyler had the project in mind for eight years and brought the property to Allied Artists from Paramount. Production cost was reportedly over $3 million. Film is without a screenplay credit.

After many warm, beguiling vignettes of family life, story works into its key dramatic point tying onto the Quaker feeling against bearing arms against a fellow man.

Role of the Quaker father, a man touched with gentle humor and inward strength, is glove-fit for Gary Cooper and he carries it off to an immense success. So does Dorothy McGuire in playing the mother of the family. Marjorie Main tops an extremely broad comedy episode involving Cooper's yen for a faster horse so he can beat a friend to church each Sunday, and three out-sized daughters

who go on the make for Cooper's unworldly son (Anthony Perkins).

Figuring importantly in the way the picture plays is Dimitri Tiomkin's conducting of his own score.

□ 1956: Best Picture (Nomination)

● ●

■ **FRIENDS OF EDDIE COYLE, THE**

1973, 100 MINS, US ◇

Dir Peter Yates   *Prod* Paul Monash   *Scr* Paul Monash   *Ph* Victor J. Kemper   *Ed* Patricia Lewis Jaffe   *Mus* Dave Grusin   *Art Dir* Gene Callahan

● Robert Mitchum, Peter Boyle, Richard Jordan, Steven Keats, Alex Rocco, Joe Santos (Paramount)

The Friends of Eddie Coyle is a very fine film about real people on the fringes of both crime and law enforcement. Shot in Boston, Paul Monash's top adaptation of a first novel by Mass asst attorney general George V. Higgins, stars Robert Mitchum and Peter Boyle as middle-aged, smalltime hoods.

Mitchum is very effective as an aging smalltimer, complete with a most believable Boston-area accent (as are all the players), who retails in guns obtained from younger hotshot supplier Steven Keats. Boyle, ostensibly a bartender, is a conduit for murder contracts, criminal contacts, and, for weekly pay, tipoffs to Richard Jordan, terrific in a true 'Southie' evocation of a plainsclothes narc. Alex Rocco heads a bank heist gang which also includes Joe Santos.

The plot is electric with the endless, daily trading of favors and betrayals which are necessary for survival in this gray jungle.

● ●

■ **FRIGHTENED CITY, THE**

1961, 97 MINS, UK

Dir John Lemont   *Prod* John Lemont, Leigh Vance   *Scr* Leigh Vance   *Ph* Desmond Dickinson   *Ed* Bernard Gribble   *Mus* Norrie Paramor   *Art Dir* Maurice Carter

● Herbert Lom, John Gregson, Sean Connery, Alfred Marks, Yvonne Romain, Kenneth Griffiths (Anglo-Amalgamated/Zodiac)

The Frightened City is a conventional but brisk gangster yarn. Accent of the film is tough and hard-hitting and concerns intergang warfare plus the clash between the cops and the crooks, the cops, as a spokesman bitterly says, finding themselves hampered by outdated laws. 'We're trying to fight 20th-century crime with 19th-century legislation.'

Six main gangs are running the protection racket and a bent accountant hits on the idea of organizing the gangs into one all-powerful syndicate. All goes well for awhile but then the boss of the organization makes a successful play for a deal involving a $560,000 block of offices being built. One of the gangsters fights shy of this bigger game, backs out of the organization and re-forms his own gang. This sparks off gang warfare.

Herbert Lom plays the brains of the crooked organization with urbane villainy and equally reliable John Gregson makes a solid, confident job of the dedicated cop. Alfred Marks is cast offbeat as Lom's gangster lieutenant. Marks gives a rich, oily, sinister and yet often amusing portrayal of an ambitious thug who is prepared to turn killer to get his own way. Comparative newcomer, rugged Sean Connery makes a distinct impression as an Irish crook, with an eye for the ladies. Connery combines toughness, charm and Irish blarney.

● ●

■ **FRIGHT NIGHT**

1985, 105 MINS, US ◇

Dir Tom Holland   *Prod* Herb Jaffe   *Scr* Tom Holland   *Ph* Jan Kiesser   *Ed* Kent Beyda   *Mus* Brad Fiedel   *Art Dir* John DeCuir Jr

● Chris Sarandon, William Ragsdale, Amanda Bearse, Roddy McDowall, Stephen Geoffreys, Jonathan Stark (Columbia)

Director Tom Holland keeps the picture wonderfully simple and entirely believable (once the existence of vampires is accepted, of course). In a quick 105 minutes, the film simply answers the question of what would probably happen if a charming, but deadly sinister, vampire moved in next door to a likable teenager given to watching horror films on the late show – and the only one the kid can turn to for help is a washed-up actor who hosts the show.

Chris Sarandon is terrific as the vampire, quite affable and debonair until his fingernails start to grow and his eyes get that glow. William Ragsdale superbly maintains due sympathy as a fairly typical youngster who can't get anybody to believe him about the odd new neighbor next door.

Roddy McDowall hams it up on the telly as the 'fearless vampire killer.' Naturally, when Ragsdale comes looking for help, McDowall is more than aware of his humanly limitations, becoming a consistently amusing, unwilling ally in invading Sarandon's lair.

■ FRISCO KID, THE

1979, 122 MINS, US ◇ ⓥ
Dir Robert Aldrich *Prod* Mace Neufeld *Scr* Michael Elias, Frank Shaw *Ph* Robert B. Hauser *Ed* Maury Winetrobe, Irving Rosenblum, Jack Horger *Mus* Frank DeVol *Art Dir* Terence Marsh
● Gene Wilder, Harrison Ford, Ramon Bieri, William Smith (Warner)

Director Robert Aldrich has always adroitly mixed comedic and dramatic aspects in his films, and *Frisco Kid* is no exception. For audiences expecting Mel Brooks belly-laughs amidst the Yiddishisms, however, there's bound to be disappointment.

As Avram Belinsky, Yeshiva flunky packed off to an American rendezvous with a leaderless 1850s San Francisco congregation, Gene Wilder has his best role in years. The manic gleam featured in early Wilder pix has now turned into a mature twinkle.

Excellent counterpoint is provided by Harrison Ford, as the cowboy, who proves the perfect foil for Wilder's gaffes.

Frisco Kid remains a series of set pieces, however, and not a cohesive film. For all his skills, Wilder is given too many solo shots. As is his practice, Aldrich has also inserted some action sequences that are jarring in their sadistic intensity.

■ FRITZ THE CAT

1972, 77 MINS, US ◇ ⓥ
Dir Ralph Bakshi *Prod* Steve Krantz *Scr* Ralph Bakshi *Ed* Renn Reynolds *Mus* Ed Bogas, Ray Shanklin
● (Krantz/Cinemation)

Fritz the Cat, X-rated cartoon feature based on the characters created by Robert Crumb, is an amusing, diverting, handsomely executed poke at youthful attitudes. Production follows the title character through a series of bawdy and playpen-political encounters. Excellent animation and montage shore up a plot which has a few howls, several chuckles and many smiles.

With an excellent vocal characterization by Skip Hinnant, Fritz lurches his amiable way through group sex encounters, police chases, black ghettos, motorcycle revolutionaries and assorted devastation of property. Rosetta Le Noire, John McCurry and Judy Engles vocalize the other characters, with as much success as Hinnant.

■ FROGS

1972, 90 MINS, US ◇ ⓥ
Dir George McCowan *Prod* George Edwards, Peter Thomas *Scr* Robert Hutchison, Robert Blees *Ph* Mario Tosi *Ed* Fred R. Feitshans *Mus* Les Baxter
● Ray Milland, Sam Elliott, Joan Van Ark, Adam Roarke, Judy Pace, Lynn Borden (American International)

Frogs is a story [from an original by Robert Hutchison] of Nature striking back at man. Snakes, giant lizards, alligators, quicksand, frogs and toads, savage fish, granddad turtles.

Action takes place on a private island in the Deep South where great-grandfather Ray Milland has gathered his family at the ancestral mansion to celebrate his birthday and the Fourth of July. Instead of the usual joyousness a sense of strangeness pervades the air. Growing numbers of large frogs are beginning to appear, large lizards and strange crawling life are converging onto the estate, right up to the windows.

One by one different members of the family meet their tragic fate through violent attack. In each case it is a frightening finish.

Cast is generally firstclass and Milland's presence, though comparatively brief, is always commanding.

■ FROM HERE TO ETERNITY

1953, 118 MINS, US ⓥ
Dir Fred Zinnemann *Prod* Buddy Adler *Scr* Daniel Taradash *Ph* Burnett Guffey *Ed* William Lyon *Mus* George Duning *Art Dir* Cary Odell
● Burt Lancaster, Montgomery Clift, Deborah Kerr, Donna Reed, Frank Sinatra, Ernest Borgnine (Columbia)

The James Jones bestseller is an outstanding motion picture in this smash screen adaptation. The bawdy vulgarity and the outhouse vocabulary, the pros and non-pros among its easy ladies, and the slambang indictment of army brass have not been emasculated in the transfer to the screen.

Burt Lancaster wallops the character of Top Sergeant Milton Warden, the professional soldier who wetnurses a weak, pompous commanding officer and the GIs under him. Montgomery Clift, with a reputation for sensitive, three-dimensional performances, adds another to his growing list as the independent GI who refuses to join the company boxing team, taking instead the 'treatment' dished out at the c.o.'s instructions. Frank Sinatra scores a decided hit as Angelo Maggio, a violent, likeable Italo-American GI.

Additional performance surprises are in the work turned in by Deborah Kerr, the nymphomaniac wife of the faithless c.o., and Donna Reed as a hostess (sic) in the New Congress Club, which furnished femme and other entertainment for relaxing soldiers.

The story opens in the summer of 1941 before Pearl Harbor with the setting Schofield Barracks, Honolulu, where much of the footage was taken. It deals with the transfer of Clift to the company under Philip Ober, the pompous, unfaithful husband of Kerr, who is interested only in getting a promotion to major, in his boxing team and extra-curricular affairs. When Clift refuses to join the boxing team, he is subjected to all the unpleasantness the idle GI mind can think up.

Eyes will moisten and throats will choke when Clift plays taps on an army bugle for his friend Sinatra after the latter dies from the brutality administered by Ernest Borgnine, the sadist sergeant in charge of the prison stockade.

□ 1953: Best Picture

■ FROM NOON TILL THREE

1976, 98 MINS, US ◇ ⓥ
Dir Frank D. Gilroy *Prod* Mike Frankovich *Scr* Frank D. Gilroy *Ph* Lucien Ballard *Ed* Maury Winetrobe *Mus* Elmer Bernstein *Art Dir* Robert Clatworthy
● Charles Bronson, Jill Ireland, Douglas V. Fowley, Stan Haze, Damon Douglas, Hector Morales (United Artists)

From Noon till Three is an offbeat and amiable, if uneven and structurally awkward, western comedy. Frank D. Gilroy scripted his novel and directed the good-looking production.

Film stars Charles Bronson as an amateur bank robber whose mistaken death supports a worldwide romantic legend, and Jill Ireland, beneficiary of the fantasy.

Bronson is a frontier drifter recruited into the bank robber gang headed by Douglas V. Fowley. En route, Bronson has a dream of a heist, later spoiled by an aware townsfolk. That's enough for him to stay behind at widow Ireland's prairie home when his horse goes lame.

He and the widow evolve from antagonism to the beginning of love, when news arrives that the Fowley gang is caught.

■ FROM RUSSIA WITH LOVE

1963, 110 MINS, UK ◇ ⓥ
Dir Terence Young *Prod* Harry Saltzman, Albert R. Broccoli *Scr* Richard Maibaum *Ph* Ted Moore *Ed* Peter Hunt *Mus* John Barry *Art Dir* Ken Adam
● Sean Connery, Daniela Bianchi, Pedro Armendariz, Lotte Lenya, Robert Shaw, Bernard Lee (Eon)

From Russia with Love is a preposterous, skillful slab of hardhitting, sexy hokum. After a slowish start, it is directed by Terence Young at zingy pace.

This one has to do with Sean Connery being detailed to go to Istanbul and lift a top secret Russian decoding machine from the embassy. British Intelligence senses that this may be a trap, but getting the machine is important. Connery can pull it off if he will help a young Russian cipher clerk (Daniela Bianchi) to escape to the West. She thinks she is working for her Russian government, but actually she is a pawn of Spectre, an international crime syndicate.

Bond has a glorious slapup fight to the death with Robert Shaw, the killer detailed to bump him off. He is hounded by a helicopter as he runs across moorland clutching the decoding machine. He beats off his pursuers in a motor boat by setting fire to the sea. He referees a fight between two jealous gypsy girls just before the encampment is invaded by the crime gang.

Connery is well served by some crisp wisecracking dialog by Richard Maibaum. Robert Shaw is an impressive, icy, implacable killer and the late Pedro Armendariz weighs in with a formidable, yet lightly played, performance as the man who knows the sinister secrets of Istanbul.

The distaff side is less well served. Newcomer Daniela Bianchi is a good looking Italian girl with shapely legs and promising smile. But only in one bedroom sequence is she able to give evidence that she has some thespian talent. Lotte Lenya has been lumbered with a part that doesn't fully come off. Disguised with an Eaton Crop and heavy pebble spectacles, she stands out as somebody up to no good from the first glimpse.

■ FROM THE TERRACE

1960, 144 MINS, US ◇
Dir Mark Robson *Prod* Mark Robson *Scr* Ernest Lehman *Ph* Leo Tover *Ed* Dorothy Spencer *Mus* Elmer Bernstein *Art Dir* Lyle R. Wheeler, Maurice Ransford, Howard Richman
● Paul Newman, Joanne Woodward, Myrna Loy, Ina Balin, Leon Ames, Felix Aylmer (20th Century-Fox)

It's apparent that scripter Ernest Lehman faced a Herculean task in condensing John O'Hara's fat novel to the exigencies of the screen. On the assumption that Lehman followed the O'Hara story closely, the blame must be placed squarely on the novelist, for *From The Terrace* builds up to one big cliche.

The picture is the study of one man's pursuit of success and money. During his climb up the Wall Street ladder, he neglects his wife, sacrifices his integrity, and unrelentingly pursues his goal. But in keeping with American popular culture, he is overcome at end by the moment of truth.

Mark Robson's old-fashioned approach to the direction is no help. He has his characters speaking in sepulchral tones, particularly in the scenes between Paul Newman and Ina Balin, as if to give their conversations a world-shaking meaning. They seem to be reciting blank verse in a background of soft hearts-and-flowers music.

Why the picture tries to depict Joanne Woodward as some sort of villainess is unclear. She is wholly devoted to her husband until it becomes clear that he is uninterested in her. Yet Newman, playing the leading role in a weltschmertz manner, emerges as the hero. He seems more like a pawn being pushed than an individual who knows what he is doing.

Woodward is excellent as the wife who married Newman despite the objections of her socially-prominent family. There is a strong indication that the marriage is based more on sexual attraction than on deeper love. Balin, a dark-haired beauty, makes a nice contrast to blonde Woodward. However, she plays her role with such a dedicated seriousness that it is difficult to believe.

■ FROM THIS DAY FORWARD

1946, 96 MINS, US
Dir John Berry *Prod* William L. Pereira *Scr* Hugo Butler *Ph* George Barnes *Ed* Frank Doyle *Mus* Leigh Harline *Art Dir* Albert S. D'Agostino, Alfred H. Herman
● Joan Fontaine, Mark Stevens, Rosemary DeCamp, Bobby Driscoll (RKO)

Story unfolds in flashback. This makes it sometimes difficult to follow as a whole, but there can be no quarrel with the merit of presentation and acting of the individual sequences. Plot deals with marriage of a young couple, fear for their security, the draft and the husband's return to establish himself again. Scenes show a soldier's mind as he goes through the redtape of government employment centers for the veteran.

Joan Fontaine and Mark Stevens are the young couple. Under John Berry's direction they make real the courtship, marriage and marital existence of the two young people.

Hugo Butler rates smart credit for his scripting job, working from adaptation by Garson Kanin, based on Thomas Bell's novel, *All Brides Are Beautiful*.

■ FRONT, THE

1976, 94 MINS, US ◇ Ⓥ
Dir Martin Ritt *Prod* Martin Ritt *Scr* Walter Bernstein *Ph* Michael Chapman *Ed* Sidney Levin *Mus* Dave Grusin *Art Dir* Charles Bailey
● Woody Allen, Zero Mostel, Herschel Bernardi, Michael Murphy, Andrea Marcovicci, Remak Ramsay (Columbia)

The Front is a disappointing drama about showbiz blacklisting. The offbeat casting of Woody Allen, as a perennial loser who lends his name and person to blacklisted writers, is far more showmanlike than successful.

Michael Murphy, very good as an Allen chum from high-school days, gets Allen to put his name on scripts for live TV producer Herschel Bernardi and story editor Andrea Marcovicci, latter becoming the target of Allen's emotions. Lloyd Gough and David Margulies also feed their scripts through Allen. This attracts the attention of Remak Ramsay, professional 'clearance consultant' to the network where Scott McKay is the liaison exec.

The real-life story of the blacklist in NY-based broadcasting is certainly not unfamiliar to several of the filmmakers here.

■ FRONT PAGE, THE

1931, 100 MINS, US Ⓥ
Dir Lewis Milestone *Prod* Howard Hughes *Scr* Bartlett Cormack, Charles Lederer *Ph* Glen MacWilliams, Hal Mohr, Tony Gaudio *Ed* W. Duncan Mansfield *Art Dir* Richard Day
● Adolphe Menjou, Pat O'Brien, Mary Brian, Edward Everett Horton, Walter Catlett, George E. Stone (Caddo/United Artists)

A very entertaining picture. Action is here all of the time, even with and during the dialog. All of it is contained within a single setting, the press room at the court house. It's of newspaper men, waiting in the press room for a hanging the following morning at 7a.m. General tenor may be taken from one of the reporters asking the sheriff if he can't advance the hanging to 5a.m. so the story can make the first edition.

The star reporter for the *Post* is between love and a good story all the while. He has arranged for a wedding in New York, bought the tickets, but is obliged through the breaks and conniving of his managing editor to keep the girl and her mother waiting while he continues to be the reporter.

Lewis Milestone's big idea appears to have been to keep it moving, and he does. It's a panorama of blended action without fireworks.

A standout performance, one of three, is by Adolphe Menjou as the managing editor. He's the cold-blooded story man, knowing only news and believing nothing should ever get in its way. Next is Mae Clarke as Molly, a prostie who is the murderer's only sympathizer. The third is Pat O'Brien as the star reporter, who maintains the same even tempo of liveliness in his work and love making.

Ben Hecht and Chalres MacArthur turned out a stage wallop that lasted a long while through George Kaufman's stage direction, but Bartlett Cormack's adaptation for the screen, with Milestone, improves the original.

□ 1930/31: Best Picture (Nomination)

■ FRONT PAGE, THE

1974, 105 MINS, US ◇
Dir Billy Wilder *Prod* Paul Monash *Scr* Billy Wilder, I.A.L. Diamond *Ph* Jordan S. Cronenweth *Ed* Ralph E. Winters *Mus* Billy May *Art Dir* Henry Bumstead
● Jack Lemmon, Walter Matthau, Carol Burnett, Susan Sarandon, Vincent Gardenia, David Wayne (Universal)

The reteaming of Jack Lemmon and Walter Matthau, in a Billy Wilder remake of a famous 1920s period newspaper story, *The Front Page*, with a featured spot by Carol Burnett, sure looks good on paper. But that's about the only place it looks good. The production has the slick, machine-tooled look of certain assembly line automobiles that never quite seem to work smoothly.

The 1928 play by Ben Hecht and Charles MacArthur has, in this third screen version, been 'liberated' from old Production code restraints. The extent of the liberation appears to be in the tedious use of undeleted expletives.

The basic story takes place in a Chicago police press room on the eve of a politically-railroaded execution of a supposed radical who killed a cop in a scuffle.

Matthau and Lemmon again demonstrate their fine screen empathy.

■ FRONT PAGE WOMAN

1935, 80 MINS, US
Dir Michael Curtiz *Prod* Samuel Bischoff *Scr* Laird Doyle *Ph* Tony Gaudio *Ed* Terry Morse *Mus* Heinz Roemheld *Art Dir* John Hughes
● Bette Davis, George Brent, June Martel, Dorothy Dare, Joseph Crehan, Winifred Shaw (Warner)

As the title indicates, this is a newspaper yarn and a completely screwy one. Lacks authenticity and is so far fetched it'll hand newsscribes around the country a constant run of ripples. But it's light and has some funny lines and situations [from a story by Richard Macauley, adapted by Roy Chanslor and Lillie Hayward].

George Brent and Bette Davis are working for opposition papers. They're in love but always trying to outdo each other on stories. They keep topping each other on one story or another for the entire length of the film and then clinch in a truce.

But there are some laughs. And there are grand performances by Davis, Brent, Winifred Shaw and Joseph Crehan. And nice bit work by Roscoe Karns, J. Farrell MacDonald, Addison Richards, Walter Walker, Dorothy Dare, June Martel and Mike Morita.

■ FUGITIVE KIND, THE

1960, 119 MINS, US
Dir Sidney Lumet *Prod* Martin Jarow, Richard A. Shepherd *Scr* Tennessee Williams, Meade Roberts *Ph* Boris Kaufman *Ed* Carl Lerner *Mus* Kenyon Hopkins
● Marlon Brando, Anna Magnani, Joanne Woodward, Maureen Stapleton, Victor Jory (United Artists)

Another helping from Tennessee Williams' seemingly inexhaustible closet of mixed-up southern skeletons is exposed here with only occasional flashes of cinematic power. The adaptation of his theatre piece, *Orpheus Descending*, will stimulate the morbidly curious.

The Fugitive Kind is not basically one of Williams' better works and, as directed by Sidney Lumet, it sputters more often than it sizzles. Aside from the fact that the screenplay is overlength and untidy, the combination of Marlon Brando and Anna Magnani fails to generate the electricity hoped for. Joanne Woodward, looking like a battered fugitive from skid row, pops in and out of the story to provide a distasteful and often ludicrous extra dash of degeneracy.

The only fully motivated character is that of Lady Torrance portrayed by Magnani with a faded veneer of lustfulness. At least one can understand her frustration and loneliness, being married to a dying older man she doesn't love, and her bitterness toward fellow townsfolk, her father having died trying to save his wine garden set afire by vigilantes because he sold liquor to Negroes.

Brando's role as a disillusioned guitar-singer, who becomes involved, as hired hand and lover, with Lady in a small Mississippi town while trying to put aside the wild life he experienced in New Orleans hot spots, is less clearly defined.

Brando is back to mumbling with marbles in his mouth too often, and Magnani's English is not always as distinguishable as could be desired. Frequently it is a strain to catch dialog and that doesn't help.

Much of the picture was filmed on location in Milton, New York, and at the Gold Medal Studios in the Bronx. Boris Kaufman's photography is good.

FULL METAL JACKET

1987, 116 MINS, US ◇ ▣

Dir Stanley Kubrick *Prod* Stanley Kubrick *Scr* Stanley Kubrick, Michael Herr, Gustav Hasford *Ph* Douglas Milsome *Ed* Martin Hunter *Mus* Abigail Mead *Art Dir* Anton Furst
● Matthew Modine, Adam Baldwin, Vincent D'Onofrio, Lee Ermey, Dorian Harewood, Arliss Howard (Warner)

Stanley Kubrick's *Full Metal Jacket* is an intense, schematic, superbly made Vietnam War drama.

Like the source material, Gustav Hasford's ultra-violent novel *The Short-Timers*, Kubrick's picture is strikingly divided into two parts. First 44 minutes are set exclusively in a Marine Corps basic training camp, while remaining 72 minutes embrace events surrounding the 1968 Tet Offensive and skirmishing in the devastated city of Hue.

While it doesn't develop a particularly strong narrative line, script is loaded with vivid, outrageously vulgar military vernacular that contributes heavily to the film's power.

Performances by the all-male cast (save for a couple of Vietnamese hookers) are also exceptional. Surrounded on one side by humorously macho types such as Cowboy and Rafterman, Matthew Modine holds the center effectively by embodying both what it takes to survive in the war and a certain omniscience.

FUNERAL IN BERLIN

1966, 102 MINS, UK ◇ ▣

Dir Guy Hamilton *Prod* Charles Kasher *Scr* Evan Jones *Ph* Otto Heller *Ed* John Bloom *Mus* Conrad Ellfers *Art Dir* Ken Adam
● Michael Caine, Paul Hubschmid, Oscar Homolka, Eva Renzi, Guy Doleman, Rachel Gurney (Paramount/Saltzman)

Funeral in Berlin is the second presentation of the exploits of Harry Palmer, the soft-sell sleuth, this time enmeshed in Berlin counterespionage. Michael Caine encores in the role that made him a star. Excellent scripting, direction and performances, plus colorful and realistic production, add up to surprise-filled suspense, relieved adroitly by subtle irony. Len Deighton's novel has been adapted by Evan Jones to a taut, economical screenplay, just right for the semi-documentary feel.

Herein, amidst a clutch of running gags which never wear out their appeal, Caine is sent to East Berlin, where Communist spy chief Oscar Homolka is making the motions of trying to defect. Paul Hubschmid is the local British contact for Caine, and Eva Renzi pops up as an undercover agent for Israel, tracking down Nazis before statutes of limitation run out.

This being a well-developed suspenser, few people are as they seem, including prissy-pedantic Hugh Burden, a secret documents clerk in Doleman's British spy group.

FUNHOUSE, THE

1981, 96 MINS, US ◇

Dir Tobe Hooper *Prod* Derek Power, Steven Bernhardt *Scr* Larry Block *Ph* Andrew Laszlo *Ed* Jack Hofstra *Mus* John Beal *Art Dir* Morton Rabinowitz
● Elizabeth Berridge, Cooper Huckabee, Sylvia Miles (Universal)

The Funhouse is a spitty movie, full of great expectorations. That is, there's more drool on view than blood, which is a new twist for the horror genre.

Set-up is a variation on the old dark house premise, as four pot-smoking teens work up the nerve to spend the night in the spooky funhouse of a traveling carnival. After some

hanky panky in the midst of goblins and skeletons, kids witness a carny Frankenstein being serviced by, then strangling, fortune teller Sylvia Miles, upon which malevolent barker Kevin Conway locks them in for a night of unanticipated chills and thrills.

For all the elegance of photography, pic has nothing in particular up its sleeves, and devotees of director Tobe Hooper's '*The Texas Chain Saw Massacre*' will be particularly disappointed with the almost total lack of shocks and mayhem.

FUN IN ACAPULCO

1963, 100 MINS, US ◇ ▣

Dir Richard Thorpe *Prod* Hal Wallis *Scr* Allan Weiss *Ph* Daniel L. Fapp *Ed* Stanley E. Johnson *Mus* Joseph J. Lilley *Art Dir* Hal Pereira, Walter Tyler
● Elvis Presley, Ursula Andress, Elsa Cardenas, Paul Lukas, Alejandro Rey (Paramount)

Elvis Presley fans won't be disappointed – he sings serviceable songs and wiggles a bit to boot. However, Presley is deserving of better material than has been provided in this screenplay in which he portrays an ex-trapeze catcher who has lost his nerve after a fatal mishap.

Arriving in Acapulco, he hires on as an entertainer-life guard at a resort, in hopes the latter job may afford him the opportunity to dive off the high board and erase his fear of heights. A romantic entanglement leads to the moment of truth.

The other three-fourths of the central romantic quartet are Ursula Andress, Elsa Cardenas and Alejandro Rey, fine-looking specimens, all. Others of note in the cast are Paul Lukas as an ex-duke-turned-chef and young Larry Domasin as a business-minded urchin more or less adopted by Presley.

Richard Thorpe's direction keeps the routine story on the move, a strong asset since opportunity for developing characterization is virtually nil.

FUNNY ABOUT LOVE

1990, 101 MINS, US ◇ ▣

Dir Leonard Nimoy *Prod* Jon Avnet, Jordan Kerner *Scr* Norman Steinberg, David Frankel *Ph* Fred Murphy *Ed* Peter E. Berger *Mus* Miles Goodman *Art Dir* Stephen Storer
● Gene Wilder, Christine Lahti, Mary Stuart Masterson, Robert Prosky, Anne Jackson, Susan Ruttan (Paramount)

Funny about Love is a not-so-funny Gene Wilder vehicle. Tale of the biological clock regarding procreation is told from a male point of view here. However, Wilder's problems as a would-be-daddy aren't interesting or compelling.

Inability to conceive with wife Christine Lahti bogs the film down in almost clinical detail. Funniest bit has Wilder sticking ice cubes in his jockey shorts on doctor's advice to get his sperm temperature down.

Film takes an absurd turn in the third reel when Wilder's child bride of a mother (Anne Jackson) is killed by a falling stove (meant to be black humor). Pic hardly recovers from this failed bit of whimsy.

Co-star Mary Stuart Masterson doesn't enter the scene until a full hour has elapsed. Wilder meets her at a convention of beautiful sorority girls where he's guest speaker. Another whirlwind romance ensues, and Masterson is pregnant.

Wilder has his moments in a role that overdoes the crying jags and self-pity. Both Lahti and Masterson remain most appealing actresses in search of challenging roles, not provided here.

FUNNY FACE

1957, 103 MINS, US ◇ ▣

Dir Stanley Donen *Prod* Roger Edens *Scr* Leonard Gershe *Ph* Ray June *Ed* Frank Bracht *Mus* George Gershwin, Roger Edens *Art Dir* Hal Pereira, George W. Davie
● Audrey Hepburn, Fred Astaire, Kay Thompson, Michel Auclair, Robert Flemyng, Suzy Parker (Paramount)

While it wears the title and bears several of the songs, *Funny Face*'s relationship to the Broadway musical [of 1927] stops right there. With a different book and new, added tunes, this is a lightly diverting, modish, Parisian-localed tintuner.

Originally slated for production at Metro, film moved to Paramount as a package so Audrey Hepburn could have the femme lead opposite Fred Astaire. This May-November pairing gives the production the benefits of Astaire's debonair style and terp accomplishments, and the sensitive acting talents of Hepburn.

Hepburn's plays a bookish introvert who is suddenly swept from her literary existence in a Greenwich Village shop to a heady, high fashion round of Paris when she's discovered by glamor photog Astaire.

Style runs rampant, with Hubert de Givenchy creating the Paris wardrobe worn by Hepburn as a model, while Edith Head takes care of things elsewhere. Tune-wise, there are six George and Ira Gershwin numbers from the stage musical and five from producer Roger Edens and scripter Leonard Gershe. All are either sung or used as backing for dance numbers, with director Stanley Donen handling the song staging while Astaire and Eugene Loring take care of the choreography.

FUNNY GIRL

1968, 145 MINS, US ◇ ▣

Dir William Wyler *Prod* William Wyler, Ray Stark *Scr* Isobel Lennart *Ph* Harry Stradling *Ed* Robert Swink *Mus* Walter Scharf (sup.) *Art Dir* Gene Callahan
● Barbra Streisand, Omar Sharif, Kay Medford, Anne Francis, Walter Pidgeon, Lee Allen (Columbia/Rastar)

Barbra Streisand in her Hollywood debut makes a marked impact. The saga of the tragi-comedienne Fanny Brice of the ungainly mien and manner, charmed by the suave card-sharp Nick Arnstein, is perhaps of familiar pattern, but it is to the credit of all concerned that it plays so convincingly.

Streisand's basic Grecian-profiled personality has not been photographically camouflaged.

The projection of Fanny Brice's rise from the pushcart-laden lower East Side to Ziegfeld stardom and a baronial Long Island estate is achieved in convincing broad strokes.

The durable Jule Styne-Bob Merrill songs, from the [1964] stage score, are given fuller enhancement under the flexibility of the cinematic sweep.

'People,' 'You Are Woman, I Am Man,' 'Don't Rain on my Parade,' 'I'm the Greatest Star' have been enhanced by the original Broadway songsmiths with 'Roller Skate Rag' a parody on 'The Swan' ballet and a title song, not part of the original score.
☐ 1968: Best Picture (Nomination)

FUNNY LADY

1975, 136 MINS, US ◇

Dir Herbert Ross *Prod* Ray Stark *Scr* Jay Presson Allen *Ph* James Wong Howe *Ed* Marion Rothman *Mus* Peter Matz (arr.) *Art Dir* George Jenkins
● Barbra Streisand, James Caan, Omar Sharif, Roddy McDowall, Ben Vereen, Carole Wells (Rastar/Columbia)

Barbra Streisand was outstanding as the

F

younger Fanny Brice in *Funny Girl*, and in *Funny Lady* she's even better. Ray Stark's extremely handsome period production also stars James Caan in an excellent characterization of Billy Rose, the second major influence in Brice's personal life.

The story picks up Brice in 1930, an established Ziegfeld star in a career lull as her mentor has trouble finding depression-era backing. Enter Rose, the brash comer who learns some showmanship savvy from her and marries her, after which the two drift apart as public careers and personal attachments diverge.

The plot is partially fictionalized in its apparent main thrust of showing how Brice finally purged her first love, for gambler Nick Arnstein (Omar Sharif), but in the process lost Rose as well. Thereafter, she was prepared to go it alone, a perfect hook for firstrate dramatic climax.

More than half a dozen older songs, on which Billy Rose's name appears as one of the authors, are used to good advantage.

The film cost about $8.5 million to which Columbia contributed about $4.9 million and the rest from one of those tax shelter consortia.

■ FUNNY THING HAPPENED ON THE WAY TO THE FORUM, A

1966, 99 MINS, US ◇ Ⓥ

Dir Richard Lester   *Prod* Melvin Frank   *Scr* Melvin Frank, Michael Pertwee   *Ph* Nicolas Roeg   *Ed* John Victor Smith   *Mus* Ken Thorne (arr.)   *Art Dir* Tony Walton

● Zero Mostel, Phil Silvers, Buster Keaton, Jack Gilford, Michael Crawford, Annette Andre (Quadrangle/United Artists)

A Funny Thing Happened on the Way to the Forum – after the [1962 Stephen Sondheim] stage musicomedy of the same name – will probably stand out as one of the few originals of two repetition-weary genres, the film musical comedy and the toga-cum-sandal 'epic'. Flip, glib and sophisticated, yet rump-slappingly bawdy and fast-paced, *Forum* is a capricious look at the seamy underside of classical Rome through a 20th-century hipster's shades.

Plot follows the efforts of a glib, con-man slave, Pseudolus (Zero Mostel), to cheat, steal or connive his freedom from a domineering mistress, Domina (Patricia Jessel), and his equally victimized master, the henpecked Senex (Michael Hordern). Unwilling ally, through blackmail, is the timorous toady Hysterium (Jack Gilford), another household slave.

Early instrument of Pseudolus' plot is the callow Hero (Michael Crawford), who, smitten by one of the luscious courtesans peddled by Lycus (Phil Silvers), local flesh supplier, promises Mostel his freedom if he can finagle the 'virgin's' purchase. Plot complications multiply like the film's pratfalls, however, and the winsome object of Hero's passion has already been sold to the egomaniacal Miles (Leon Greene), a legion captain of legendary ferocity, who thunders onto the scene to claim the girl.

Interwoven through the plot is the presence of Erronius (Buster Keaton) who, searching for his lost children, unties the knotted situation.

■ FUN WITH DICK AND JANE

1977, 95 MINS, US ◇ Ⓥ

Dir Ted Kotcheff   *Prod* Peter Bart, Max Palevsky   *Scr* David Giler, Jerry Belson, Mordecai Richler   *Ph* Fred Koenekamp   *Ed* Danford B. Greene   *Mus* Ernest Gold   *Art Dir* James G. Hulsey

● George Segal, Jane Fonda, Ed McMahon, Dick Gautier, Allan Miller, Hank Garcia (Columbia)

Fun with Dick and Jane is a great comedy idea [from a story by Gerald Gaiser] largely shot down by various bits of tastelessness, crudity and nastiness. Stars George Segal and Jane Fonda are an upper middle-class family which turns to armed robbery when hubby loses his aerospace job.

Fonda and Segal have all the basic comedy essentials necessary to fulfill the minimum demands of the story, and that seems to be the problem: they seem to have gotten no help from direction and/or writing in getting off the ground.

Ed McMahon is terrific as Segal's employer whose boozy bonhomie conceals the heart of a true Watergater. Making this essentially shallow and hypocritical character into a fascinating figure of corporate logrolling was a major challenge.

■ FURY

1936, 90 MINS, US Ⓥ

Dir Fritz Lang   *Prod* Joseph L. Mankiewicz   *Scr* Bartlett Cormack, Fritz Lang   *Ph* Joseph Ruttenberg   *Ed* Frank Sullivan   *Mus* Franz Waxman   *Art Dir* Cedric Gibbons, William Horning

● Sylvia Sidney, Spencer Tracy, Walter Abel, Bruce Cabot, Edward Ellis, Walter Brennan (M-G-M)

Punchy story [by Norman Krasna] has been masterfully guided by the skillfull direction of the Viennese Fritz Lang. It's his first in America and represents the culmination of a year and a half of waiting, while being carried on the Metro payroll, until finally finding something to his liking. It coincides also with the debut efforts of Joseph L. Mankiewicz as a Metro associate producer.

Spencer Tracy gives his top performance as the upright young man until he's involved in a kidnapping mess through mistaken identity. Escaping a necktie lynching party, the jailhouse is burned down, despite the meagre protective efforts of the constabulary, and legally he is dead. But somehow he had managed to escape and he is intent on vengeance on the 22 (including one woman who had whirled the igniting torch into the kerosened pyre at the jailhouse door), who are ultimately brought to trial.

Walter Abel, as the state attorney, virtually walks away with the proceedings during the courtroom scene. Sylvia Sidney, whose tender love scenes in the early motivations are relatively passive, rises to the proper heights in the dramatic testimony. Tracy is capital during the somewhat slowly pacing scenes up until the pseudo-lynching; then he becomes the dominating character in the scenes where he hides out and permits the trial to proceed.

■ FURY, THE

1978, 117 MINS, US ◇ Ⓥ

Dir Brian De Palma   *Prod* Frank Yablans   *Scr* John Farris   *Ph* Richard H. Kline   *Ed* Paul Hirsch   *Mus* John Williams   *Art Dir* Bill Malley

● Kirk Douglas, John Cassavetes, Carrie Snodgress, Charles Durning, Amy Irving, Fiona Lewis (20th Century-Fox)

The Fury features Kirk Douglas and John Cassavetes as adversaries in an elaborate game of mind control. Director Brian De Palma is on home ground in moving the plot pieces around effectively.

John Farris adapted his novel for the screen. Most viewers will enjoy the razzle-dazzle of the lengthy pursuit by Douglas of son Andrew Stevens, kidnapped by Cassavetes because of his mystical powers. But apart from a few throwaway references to government agencies and psychic phenomena, there is never, anywhere, a coherent exposition of what all the running and jumping is about.

Strong cast also includes Carrie Snodgress as a staffer in Charles Durning's research institute where Amy Irving (also blessed/cursed with psychic powers) is being readied as a substitute for Stevens. Seems that Stevens is freaking out, despite the attentions and care of Fiona Lewis, and he is targeted for elimination.

■ FUTURE SCHLOCK

1984, 75 MINS, AUSTRALIA ◇

Dir Barry Peak, Chris Kiely   *Prod* Barry Peak, Chris Kiely   *Scr* Barry Peak, Chris Kiely   *Ph* Malcolm Richards   *Ed* Robert Martin, Ray Pond   *Mus* John McCuubery, Doug Sanders   *Art Dir* John McWha

● Maryanne Fahey, Michael Bishop, Tracey Callander, Tiriel Mora, Simon Thorpe, Peter Cox (Ultimate Show)

A chaotic, anarchic punk comedy, made on a micro-budget, but with enough going for it to reach its target audience, *Future Schlock* is a mess, but fun.

Set in Melbourne in the 21st century, the pic posits a post-civil war society in which the middleclass suburbanites defeated the non-conformists and then walled them up in a huge ghetto. Action centers around a ghetto watering hole, Alvin's, where the locals meet to do their own thing. Leading lights are Sarah (Maryanne Fahey) and Bear (Michael Bishop) who do a brezzy nightclub act, often directing hostility against suburbanites who drop by on a slumming trip.

Film is a haphazard affair, with variable performances, uneven writing, and rough sound.

■ FUTUREWORLD

1976, 107 MINS, US ◇ Ⓥ

Dir Richard T. Heffron   *Prod* Paul Lazarus III, James T. Aubrey Jr   *Scr* Mayo Simon, George Schenck   *Ph* Howard Schwartz, Gene Polito   *Ed* James Mitchell   *Mus* Fred Karlin   *Art Dir* Trevor Williams

● Peter Fonda, Blythe Danner, Arthur Hill, Yul Brynner, Jim Antonio, John Ryan (American International)

Futureworld is a strong sequel to *Westworld* in which the rebuilt pleasure dome aims at world conquest by extending the robot technology to duplicating business and political figures.

Peter Fonda and Blythe Danner come across very well in their starring roles as investigative reporters on a junket to help promote the rebuilt and enlarged theme park.

The reporters are hosted by Arthur Hill, repping the theme park owners, and John Ryan, the chief scientist. Fonda and Danner eventually discover the world domination plot with the help of Stuart Margolin, one of the few non-robot technicians still employed.

Yul Brynner makes a cameo reappearance as the robot gunslinger so prominent in *Westworld*, a good bridging element between the two pix.

■ FUZZ

1972, 92 MINS, US ◇ Ⓥ

Dir Richard A. Colla   *Prod* Jack Farren   *Scr* Evan Hunter   *Ph* Jacques Marquette   *Ed* Robert Kimble   *Mus* Dave Grusin   *Art Dir* Hilyard Brown

● Burt Reynolds, Jack Weston, Tom Skerritt, Yul Brynner, Raquel Welch, James McEachin (Filmways)

Fuzz has an excellent screenplay by Evan Hunter, from his 87th Precinct series written under the name Ed McBain. The basic plot line is a search for a mysterious meticulous bomber, played by Yul Brynner, who keeps killing local officials. The search is conducted against a back-drop of an urban neighborhood police station where the cops are as humanized as those under arrest or suspicion.

The assorted people involved innocently or criminally with the police are neither patronized middle-class nor anointed low-life.

There is compassion in the treatment of all characters while at the same time their foibles are milked for both laughs and occasionally chilling reality.

Burt Reynolds is very good, Jack Weston and James McEachin are excellent, and Tom Skerritt is outstanding as the principal quartet of detectives.

· ·

■ **FX2**
THE DEADLY ART OF ILLUSION

1991, 109 MINS, US ◇ ▽

Dir Richard Franklin *Prod* Jack Wiener, Dodi Fayed *Scr* Bill Condon *Ph* Victor J. Kemper *Ed* Andrew London *Mus* Lalo Schifrin *Art Dir* John Jay Moore
● Bryan Brown, Brian Dennehy, Rachel Ticotin, Joanna Gleason, Philip Bosco, Kevin J. O'Connor (Orion)

With all the ingenuity that went into toys and gadgetry in this five-years-removed sequel, it's a shame no one bothered to hook a brain up to the plot. Beyond the engaging leads, there's little here on the level that made 1986's *F/X* so entertaining, as the sequel throttles a stale police-corruption setup loaded with genre cliches.

Because the pic's basic conceit is so simple – a film effects man using his 'reel' skills to thwart dense public officials and criminals – the story actually gets off to a rather slow start, as the semiretired Rollie Tyler (Bryan Brown) is talked into participating in a police sting operation by his g.f.'s ex-husband (Tom Mason).

The operation goes haywire, the ex-husband is killed and Tyler starts looking into the intrigue behind it. In over his head, he recruits the help of Leo (Brian Dennehy), the cop he teamed with at the end of the first pic.

The lack of an interesting villain also hurts. Philip Bosco is more a comic foil than anything else, while other bad guys are merely shadowy mob types left on the film's fringe.

Dennehy remains one of the more effortlessly likable actors around, while Brown may be a little too self-assured this time in using his fantasy skills in life-or-death situations.

· ·

■ **GABLE AND LOMBARD**

1976, 131 MINS, US ◇ ▽

Dir Sidney J. Furie *Prod* Harry Korshak *Scr* Barry Sandler *Ph* Jordan S. Cronenweth *Ed* Argyle Nelson *Mus* Michel Legrand *Art Dir* Edward C. Carfagno
● James Brolin, Jill Clayburgh, Allen Garfield, Red Buttons, Melanie Mayron, Carol McGinnis (Universal)

Gable and Lombard is a film with many major assets, not the least of which is the stunning and smashing performance of Jill Clayburgh as Carole Lombard. James Brolin manages excellently to project the necessary Clark Gable attributes while adding his own individuality to the characterization.

Sidney J. Furie's direction of handsome period production supplies zest as well as romance to the tragi-comedy aspects of the two stars' offscreen life together.

Barry Sandler's original screenplay conveys the excitement and fun of an era when everyone seemed to enjoy themselves in the profession of making pictures.

Gable and Lombard is candid without being prurient; delightful without being superficially glossy; heart-warming without being corny.

· ·

■ **GAILY, GAILY**

1969, 100 MINS, US

Dir Norman Jewison *Prod* Norman Jewison *Scr* Abram S. Ginnes *Ph* Richard Kline *Ed* Ralph Winters *Mus* Henry Mancini *Art Dir* Robert Boyle
● Beau Bridges, Melina Mercouri, Brian Keith, George Kennedy, Hume Cronyn, Margot Kidder (Mirisch-Cartier)

Ben Hecht's pseudo-reminiscences of a cub reporter in 1910 Chicago emerges on the screen as a lushly staged, handsomely produced, largely unfunny comedy.

Director-producer Norman Jewison seemingly works on the comedic theory that nothing succeeds like excess. The very basic decision to play *Gaily, Gaily* broadly as possible, lay it on with a trowel, divorces the film from the realities of 1910 Chicago.

Based on Hecht's book *Gaily, Gaily* the situations and characters are unbelievable, and because they are, they are unfunny. The paradox is that Jewison sets the stage and Richard Kline photographs it with a lover's eye for the richness, earthiness, brawling vitality and raw meat of the era. The sets, costuming and resurrected locations in Chicago and Milwaukee are a glorious period pageant.

· ·

■ **GALLIPOLI**

1981, 110 MINS, AUSTRALIA ◇

Dir Peter Weir *Prod* Robert Stigwood *Scr* David Williamson *Ph* Russell Boyd *Ed* Bill Anderson *Mus* Brian May *Art Dir* Wendy Weir
● Mark Lee, Bill Kerr, Mel Gibson, Robert Grubb, David Argue (Associated R & R)

Against a backdrop broader than his previous outings, Weir has fashioned what is virtually an intimate epic. A very big picture by Aussie standards, the film is all the same a finely-considered story focussing closely on the relationship that builds between Frank (Mel Gibson) and Archy (Mark Lee), and how it is affected by events on the battlefield of Gallipoli.

Gallipoli is as much an essential part of the Australian ethos as, say The Alamo is to Texas: a military defeat that became rationalized over the years into a moral victory. In April 1915 a combined force of Australian and New Zealand troops numbering about 35,000 joined an Allied attempt to control the Dardanelles waterway by capturing Istanbul. Bungling by the generals allowed the Turks time to dig in and the landings devolved into stalemate, but not before much bitter fighting.

The Australian-New Zealand Army Corps in great part bore the brunt of the bitterest exchanges. Thus Peter Weir's *Gallipoli* tackles a legend in human terms and emerges as a highly entertaining drama on a number of levels, none of them inaccessible to anyone unfamiliar with the actual events.

· ·

■ **GAMBIT**

1966, 107 MINS, US ◇ ▽

Dir Ronald Neame *Prod* Leo L. Fuchs *Scr* Jack Davies, Alvin Sargent *Ph* Clifford Stine *Ed* Alma Macrorie *Mus* Maurice Jarre *Art Dir* Alexander Golitzen, George C. Webb
● Shirley MacLaine, Michael Caine, Herbert Lom, Roger C. Carmel, Arnold Moss, John Abbott (Universal)

Shirley MacLaine and Michael Caine star in a firstrate suspense comedy, cleverly scripted, expertly directed and handsomely mounted.

Sidney Carroll's original story has been adapted into a zesty laugh-getter as MacLaine becomes Miss Malaprop in Caine's scheme to loot the art treasures of mid-East potentate Herbert Lom. An idealized swindle sequence lasting 27 minutes opens pic, after which the execution of the

plan shifts all characterizations and sympathies.

Director Ronald Neame has obtained superior characterizations from all hands. MacLaine, playing a Eurasian gal, displays her deft comedy abilities after the opening segment, in which she is stone-faced and silent. Caine socks over a characterization which is at first tightlipped and cold, then turning warm with human and romantic frailty.

Lom is excellent as the potentate, so assured of his security devices that audience sympathy encourages the machinations of Caine and MacLaine.

· ·

■ **GAMBLER, THE**

1974, 109 MINS, US ◇ ▽

Dir Karel Reisz *Prod* Irwin Winkler, Robert Chartoff *Scr* James Toback *Ph* Victor J. Kemper *Ed* Roger Spottiswoode *Mus* Jerry Fielding *Art Dir* Philip Rosenberg
● James Caan, Paul Sorvino, Lauren Hutton, Morris Carnovsky, Jacqueline Brookes, Burt Young (Paramount)

The Gambler, is a compelling and effective film. James Caan is excellent and the featured players are superb. However, it is somewhat overlong in early exposition and has one climax too many.

James Toback's script commingles candor and compassion, without hostility or superficial sociology or patronizing.

After getting off to a good start, film slows down in some redundant and/or sluggishly paced exposition, at least understandable considering the calibre of players such as Paul Sorvino, Jacqueline Brookes, Morris Carnovsky (Caan's wealthy grandfather who declines to bail him out) and Burt Young (a very cordial yet simultaneously merciless and brutal loan shark collection agent), whose roles provide full dimension and bitter irony to the story. The pace quickens towards the end.

Jerry Fielding's score, based on Mahler's Symphony No 1, is excellent, making the point that a contemporary urban drama can be underscored to great effect without tinny transistor radio source excerpts or mickey-mouse rock riffs.

· ·

■ **GAME IS OVER, THE**

1966, 95 MINS, FRANCE/ITALY ◇ ▽

Dir Roger Vadim *Scr* Jean Cau, Roger Vadim, Bernard Frechtman *Ph* Claude Renoir *Ed* Victoria Mercanton *Mus* J.P. Bourtayre, Jean Bouchety *Art Dir* Jean Andre
● Jane Fonda, Peter McEnery, Michel Piccoli, Tina Marquand (Marceau/Cocinor/Mega)

This melodrama is sleek and elegant if sometimes short on motivation. Updated version of an Emile Zola 19th-century novel [*La curee*] deals with a rich financier married to a very young woman (Jane Fonda). He also has a 22-year-old son (Peter McEnery). Love blossoms between this son and the young wife.

Director Roger Vadim has a glossy style that shows the aimless life of the bored wife and the drifting son that finally results in love only to be throttled by his weakness which ends in the woman's breakdown.

McEnery is effective as the weak son while Michel Piccoli does not have the right sort of role to be able to limn a strong and overpowering father figure to overcome love and desired freedom.

· ·

■ **GAMES, THE**

1970, 97 MINS, UK ◇ ▽

Dir Michael Winner *Prod* Lester Linsk *Scr* Erich Segal *Ph* Robert Paynter *Ed* Bernard Gribble *Mus* Francis Lai *Art Dir* Albert Witherick, Fred Carter, Roy Stannard

● Michael Crawford, Ryan O'Neal, Charles Aznavour, Jeremy Kemp, Elaine Taylor, Stanley Baker (20th Century-Fox)

Story turns on four runners from different nations who eventually compete in a climactic 26-mile marathon in the Rome Olympic Games.

Michael Crawford is the ex-milkman driven to prowess by Stanley Baker; Ryan O'Neal is a fun-loving American college kid – as only Hollywood can define and perpetuate this stereotype; Charles Aznavour is a Czech soldier, forced to return to running as a political pawn; and Athol Compton is the down-under Aborigine exploited by Jeremy Kemp.

Filmed in England, Italy, Austria, Czechoslovakia, Australia and Japan, the pic [from a novel by Hugh Atkinson] is long on production values and nothing else.

Technical adviser Gordon Pirie, a retired British track star and Olympics participant, did a creditable job in the exteriors.

Aznavour, Crawford and Jeremy Kemp come off best.

■ GANDHI

1982, 188 MINS, UK/INDIA ◇ ▼
Dir Richard Attenborough *Prod* Richard Attenborough, Rani Dube *Scr* John Briley *Ph* Billy Williams, Ronnie Taylor *Ed* John Bloom *Mus* Ravi Shankar, George Fenton *Art Dir* Stuart Craig
● Ben Kingsley, Candice Bergen, Edward Fox, John Gielgud, Trevor Howard, John Mills (Columbia/IFI/Goldcrest/NFDC/Indo-British)

The canvas upon which the turmoil of India, through its harshly won independence in 1947 from British rule, is, as depicted by Richard Attenborough, bold, sweeping, brutal; tender, loving and inspiring. He has juggled the varied emotional thrusts with generally expert balance.

Attenborough and scenarist John Briley agreed to attempt to capture the 'spirit' of the man and his times, and in this they succeed admirably.

Ben Kingsley, the British (half-Indian) actor, who portrays the Mahatma from young manhood as a lawyer in South Africa, is a physically striking Gandhi and has captured nuances in speech and movement which make it seem as though he has stepped through black and white newsreels into the present Technicolor reincarnation.

From the time he first experiences apartheid in being unceremoniously booted off a train in South Africa after obtaining his law degree in London, Mohandas Karamchand Gandhi becomes a man with a mission – a peaceful mission to obtain dignity for every man, no matter his color, creed, nationality.

While the focus of the drama is naturally on the person of Kingsley who gives a masterfully balanced and magnetic portrayal of Gandhi, the unusually large cast, some with only walkthrough roles, responds nobly.

Calling for individual mention are Edward Fox as General Dyer; Candice Bergen as Margaret Bourke-White, Geraldine James as devoted disciple Mirabehn, John Gielgud as Lord Irwin; Trevor Howard as Judge Broomfield; John Mills as The Viceroy; Rohini Hattangady as Mrs Gandhi; Roshan Seth as Nehru, and Athol Fugard as General Smuts.
□ 1982: Best Picture

■ GANG'S ALL HERE, THE

1939, 75 MINS, UK
Dir Thornton Freeland *Prod* Walter C. Mycroft, Jack Buchanan *Scr* Ralph Spence *Ph* Claude Friese-Greene *Ed* E.B. Jarvis *Art Dir* John Mead, Cedric Dawe
● Jack Buchanan, Googie Withers, Edward Everett Horton, Otto Kruger (Associated British

Jack Buchanan plays a private detective for a large insurance company, and never takes anything seriously, even murder. He's ably partnered with Edward Everett Horton as his brother in the farcical by-play.

The story and its method of telling have in it innumerable surefire farcical ingredients, is played by a carefully selected cast and is competently produced.

Story opens with a banquet given in honor of John Forrest (Buchanan), who's retiring from his post as chief investigator for the Stamford Assurance Co. He intends to devote himself to the writing of detective novels. When he learns that his former firm's safe has been robbed of more than $1 million in jewels belonging to a foreign prince, he returns to the scent.

■ GANG'S ALL HERE, THE

1943, 102 MINS, US ◇
Dir Busby Berkeley *Prod* William LeBaron *Scr* Walter Bullock *Ph* Edward Cronjager *Ed* Roy Curtiss *Mus* Alfred Newman, Charles Henderson (dir.)
● Alice Faye, Carmen Miranda, Charlotte Greenwood, Eugene Pallette, Edward Everett Horton, Phil Baker (20th Century-Fox)

A weak script is somewhat relegated by the flock of tuneful musical numbers that frequently punctuate the picture. Alice Faye has never been screened more fetchingly, and she still lilts a ballad for sock results. Carmen Miranda is given her fattest screen part to date, and she's a comedienne who can handle lines as well as put over her South American rhythm tunes. Phil Baker makes the most of invariably drab comedy lines, while Benny Goodman's orch is always prominently focused.

There's a supporting cast, notably Eugene Pallette, Charlotte Greenwood and Edward Everett Horton, that generally backs up the principals niftily in this yarn of a romantic tangle involving Faye, Sheila Ryan and James Ellison. Latter plays a wealthy doughboy who makes a pitch for Faye, a nitery chorine, though engaged to wealthy Ryan.

The Leo Robin-Harry Warren tunes include several potentially exploitable ones, namely 'A Journey to a Star', which Miss Faye reprises a couple of times.

Of the cast, Miranda is outstanding, and the way she kicks around the English lingo affords much of the film's comedy. Faye underplays as usual, but always clicko.

■ GARBO TALKS

1984, 103 MINS, US ◇ ▼
Dir Sidney Lumet *Prod* Burtt Harris, Elliott Kastner *Scr* Larry Grusin *Ph* Andrzej Bartkowiak *Ed* Andrew Mondshein *Mus* Cy Coleman *Art Dir* Philip Rosenberg
● Anne Bancroft, Ron Silver, Carrie Fisher, Catherine Hicks, Steven Hill, Hermione Gingold (United Artists)

Garbo Talks is a sweet and sour film clearly not for all tastes. Packed with New York in-jokes, not everyone will appreciate its aggressive charm. But beneath its cocky exterior, picture has a beat on some very human and universal truths.

Estelle Rolfe (Anne Bancroft) is a certifiable eccentric who has worshipped Garbo from afar since childhood, until the star has become woven into the fabric of her imagination. Her identification with Garbo has become a way for her to glamorize her day-to-day life.

Estelle is no ordinary housewife. Divorced from her husband (Steven Hill), she is continually arrested for defending any and all causes and fighting the everyday

indignities of life in NY. If not for Bancroft's spirited performance, Estelle would deteriorate into a caricature.

■ GARDEN OF ALLAH

1936, 80 MINS, US ▼
Dir Richard Boleslawski *Prod* David O. Selznick *Scr* W.P. Lipscomb, Lynn Riggs *Ph* W. Howard Greene, Hal Rossen *Ed* Hal C. Kern, Anson Stevenson *Mus* Max Steiner
● Marlene Dietrich, Charles Boyer, Basil Rathbone, C. Aubrey Smith, Joseph Schildkraut, John Carradine (Selznick)

Garden of Allah, sumptuously and impressively mounted by David O. Selznick, impresses in color production but is a pretty dull affair. It is optically arresting and betimes emotionally gripping but, after a spell, the ecclesiastic significance of the Trappist monk whose earthly love cannot usurp his prior secular vows [from the book by Robert Hichens] peters out completely.

Marlene Dietrich and Charles Boyer are more than adequately competent in the leads, although sometimes slurring their lines. Basil Rathbone, C. Aubrey Smith, Tilly Losch (making her screen debut in a Bagdad cafe dancing sequence, and okay in what she does), Joseph Schildkraut (who almost steals the picture with his exaggerated oriental ingratiations) and John Carradine as the sandseer leave nothing wanting.

The color is particularly flattering to Dietrich, who has also taken off a little weight. In the flowing capes to which she is so partial, the color camera has caught her at her photographic best.

■ GARDENS OF STONE

1987, 111 MINS, US ◇ ▼
Dir Francis Coppola *Prod* Michael I. Levy, Francis Coppola *Scr* Ronald Bass *Ph* Jordan Cronenweth *Ed* Barry Malkin *Mus* Carmine Coppola *Art Dir* Dean Tavoularis
● James Caan, Anjelica Huston, James Earl Jones, D.B. Sweeney, Dean Stockwell, Mary Stuart Masterson (Tri-Star)

Gardens of Stone, Francis Coppola's muddled meditation on the Vietnam War, seems to take its name not so much from the Arlington Memorial Cemetery, where much of the action takes place, but from the stiffness of the characters it portrays.

Structured around the small details and formal rituals of military life, pic opens and closes with a funeral and in between is supposed to be the emotional stuff that makes an audience care about the death of a soldier. But there is a hollowness at the film's core.

As a two-time combat vet biding his time training young recruits for the Old Guard, the army's ceremonial unit at Fort Myer, Va, Clell Hazard (James Caan) knows the war is wrong but cannot oppose it. Rather than protest, he feels it is his responsibility to prepare the young soldiers as best he can, especially young Private Willow (D.B. Sweeney), the son of an old Korean war buddy.

Script, from Nicholas Proffitt's novel, attempts to create sympathetic soldiers whose first loyalty is to their brothers in arms. Indeed it is a world unto itself as Caan swaps tales of horrors and heroism with his buddy 'Goody' Nelson (James Earl Jones).

Most contrived of the relationships is Caan's affair with Anjelica Huston who plays a Washington Post reporter vehemently opposed to the war. Basically the supportive woman waiting in the wings, she also has enough stilted dialog to destroy her character.

■ GASLIGHT

1940, 80 MINS, UK

Dir Thorold Dickinson *Prod* John Corfield *Scr* A.R.
Rawlinson, Bridget Boland *Ph* Bernard Knowles, Cyril
Knowles
● Anton Walbrook, Diana Wynyard, Cathleen Cordell,
Robert Newton, Frank Pettingell, Jimmy Hanley (British
National)

Patrick Hamilton's stageplay *Gaslight* had
considerable London success as a legit vehicle. Excellent direction by Thorold Dickinson retains all the psychological drama of the
original in presenting the tale of a woman
being driven steadily mad.

In transferring story to the screen, scripters
have embellished the action with an explanatory opening for the motive behind the
events, and stretched it with one or two incidents which neither add nor detract.

Anton Walbrook's study of the half insane
Paul Mallen, driven to further crime in a
search of a handful of ruby stones, is an obnoxious type of characterization. He successfully avoids overplaying. Diana Wynyard
brings a sympathy and understanding to her
portrayal of the woman who, once married to
Mallen, unwittingly stumbles on the secret of
his early days, and is influenced by him that
she is developing insanity.

■ GASLIGHT

1944, 114 MINS, US

Dir George Cukor *Prod* Arthur Hornblow Jr
Scr John Van Druten, Walter Reisch, John L.
Balderston *Ph* Joseph Ruttenberg *Ed* Ralph E.
Winters *Mus* Bronislau Kaper *Art Dir* Cedric
Gibbons, William Ferrari
● Charles Boyer, Ingrid Bergman, Joseph Cotten, May
Whitty, Angela Lansbury (M-G-M)

Patrick Hamilton's London stage melodrama, is given an exciting screen treatment
by Arthur Hornblow Jr's excellent
production starring Charles Boyer,
Ingrid Bergman and Joseph Cotten.

It is a faithful adaptation, conspicuously
notable for fine performances of the stars and
the screenplay by John van Druten, Walter
Reisch and John L. Balderston. There are
times when the screen treatment verges on a
type of drama that must be linked to the
period upon which the title is based, but this
factor only serves to hypo the film's dramatic
suspense where normally it might be
construed as corny theatrics.

Gaslight is the story of a murderer who
escaped detection for many years. He kills a
famous opera singer for her jewels but is
never able to uncover the baubles. Years later
he marries the singer's niece so that he can
continue his search for the gems in the late
singer's home, which has been inherited by
her niece and in which the newlyweds make
their home.

Director George Cukor keeps the film at an
even pace and is responsible for the film lacking the ten-twent-thirt element that was a
factor in the stage play.
□ 1944: Best Picture (Nomination)

■ GAS-S-S-S
OR IT BECAME NECESSARY TO DESTROY THE WORLD IN ORDER TO SAVE IT

1970, 79 MINS, US ◇

Dir Roger Corman *Prod* Roger Corman *Scr* George
Armitage *Ph* Ron Dexter *Ed* George Van Noy
Mus Country Joe and the Fish
● Robert Corff, Elaine Giftos, Pat Patterson, George
Armitage, Alex Wilson, Alan Braunstein
(American International)

Ostensibly about the actions of the under-25s
of the world, as displayed by a sample group
in Texas, when an experimental gas kills off
all those over that age, most of the screenplay

is devoted to moving a group of six young
people along the highways to a New Mexican
commune where they've heard 'a brave new
world' awaits them.

Obstacles appear in the form of automobile
rustlers, headed by a character who calls
himself Billy the Kid. After a night of rest,
recuperation and rocking at a drive-in
theatre, they encounter a gang of football
players who try to force them to join the team
(whose motto is loot, burn and rape),
but they escape.

A brief idyll at the commune is threatened
when the fascistic footballers lay siege, but
they're converted just in time.

Robert Corff and Elaine Giftos, despite
their top billing, devote most of their screen
time smiling at and admiring each other's
hair, which is almost of equal length.

■ GATOR

1976, 115 MINS, US ◇ ▼

Dir Burt Reynolds *Prod* Jules Levy, Arthur Gardner
Scr William Norton *Ph* William A. Fraker *Ed* Harold
F. Kress *Mus* Charles Bernstein *Art Dir* Kirk Axtell
● Burt Reynolds, Jack Weston, Lauren Hutton, Jerry
Reed, Alice Ghostley, Dub Taylor (United Artists)

This follow-up to *White Lightning* never takes
itself seriously, veering as it does through
many incompatible dramatic and violent
moods for nearly two hours.

William Norton's coloring books script
picks up Burt Reynolds' Gator McKlusky
character, now on parole from moonshining
time. State governor Mike Douglas can't
realize political ambitions until a notorious
back-water county, run by crime czar Jerry
Reed, gets cleaned up.

Enter Jack Weston as Dept of Justice
undercover agent, who (somewhat unclearly)
blackmails Reynolds into working against old
pal Reed.

Reynolds clearly was shot down as a
director by the story structure which also
works to defeat much of the time even his
screen charisma and credibility.

■ GAUNTLET, THE

1977, 108 MINS, US ▼

Dir Clint Eastwood *Prod* Robert Daley *Scr* Michael
Butler, Dennis Shryack *Ph* Rexford Metz *Ed* Ferris
Webster, Joel Cox *Mus* Jerry Fielding *Art Dir* Allen E.
Smith
● Clint Eastwood, Sondra Locke, Pat Hingle, William
Prince, Bill McKinney, Michael Cavanaugh (Warner)

In a major role reversal, Clint Eastwood stars
in *The Gauntlet* as a person who might be on
the receiving end of the violence epitomized
in his famed Dirty Harry film series.

Eastwood, a flop cop sent to extradite
hooker Sondra Locke, finds they are the
targets of both the underworld and law
enforcement elements tied to the mob.

William Prince is very good as a police
commissioner with mob ties who selects
Eastwood to bring Locke from Las Vegas as
a key witness in a trial which could embarrass a lot of highly-placed people.

Plot provides a series of narrow escapes in
van rides, motorcycle rides, train rides, car
rides and climactic bus ride. Chuck Gaspar's
special effects crew destroys a house, a
helicopter and a cross-country bus as the
film unfolds.

■ GAY CABALLERO, THE

1940, 58 MINS, US

Dir Otto Brower *Prod* Walter Morosco, Ralph
Dietrich *Scr* Albert Duffy, John Larkin, Walter Bullock
Ph Edward Cronjager *Ed* Harry Reynolds *Mus* Emil
Newman *Art Dir* Richard Day, Chester Cord
● Cesar Romero, Sheila Ryan, Robert Sterling, Chris-
Pin Martin, Janet Beecher (20th Century-Fox

The Cisco Kid [created by William Sydney
Porter (O. Henry)] continues his Robin Hoo-
dian adventures along the south-west border
in a story which grooves along familiar lines
of the series.

As usual, Cisco rides into the district with
sidekick Chris-Pin Martin to find a grave
marked with his name. Deciding to stick
around and find out what's going on, he discovers enough plot to step in to protect a
pretty girl and her father from nefarious
deeds.

Cesar Romero is in the familiar role of
Cisco, never losing his composure in the darkest situations. Chris-Pin Martin continues
as his Mexican stooge, while Sheila Ryan is
the girl in this instance. Edmund MacDonald
is the familiar moustached villain, aided by
conniving skullduggery by Janet Beecher.

■ GAY DIVORCEE, THE

1934, 107 MINS, US

Dir Mark Sandrich *Prod* Pandro S. Berman
Scr George Marion Jr, Dorothy Yost, Edward
Kaufman *Ph* David Abel, Vernon Walker *Ed* William
Hamilton *Mus* Max Steiner (dir.) *Art Dir* Van Nest
Polglase, Carroll Clark
● Fred Astaire, Ginger Rogers, Alice Brady, Edward
Everett Horton, Erik Rhodes, Eric Blore (Radio)

All through the picture there's charm,
romance, gaiety and eclat. There's a dash of
Continental spice in the situation of the
professional male co-respondent who is to
expedite Ginger Rogers' divorce.

The manner in which Fred Astaire taps
himself into an individual click with 'Looking
for a Needle in Haystack', a hoofing soliloquy
in his London flat, while his man hands him
his cravat, boutonniere and walking stick, is
something which he alone elevates and socks
over on individual artistry.

'The Continental', is the smash song and
dance hit. Cole Porter's 'Night and Day',
from the original show [*The Gay Divorce*, book
by Dwight Taylor], is alone retained and
worthily so, especially as Astaire interprets it.
After having done it for months on New York
and London stages it's natural that his celluloid translation must be enhanced by much
personable business and lyric mannerisms.

Rogers is also excellent, but the performances don't end there. Alice Brady and
Edward Everett Horton, as the sub-team, are
more than just good foils. Erik Rhodes and
Eric Blore, both from legit, also impress in no
small manner.

Mark Sandrich rates all sorts of bends on
the direction. He's colored the story values
with a flock of nifty business. His terp stager,
Dave Gould, displays considerable
imagination with the dance staging.
□ 1934: Best Picture (Nomination)

■ GAZEBO, THE

1959, 102 MINS, US

Dir George Marshall *Prod* Lawrence Weingarten
Scr George Wells *Ph* Paul C. Vogel *Ed* Adrienne
Fazan *Mus* Jeff Alexander *Art Dir* George W. Davis,
Paul Groesse
● Glenn Ford, Debbie Reynolds, Carl Reiner, John
McGiver, Doro Merande (Avon/M-G-M)

Gazebo is based on the Alec Coppel play
which starred Walter Slezak and Jayne Meadows on Broadway and Tom Ewell and Jan
Sterling on the road. In its transfer to the
screen, scripter George Wells has spiced the
often far-fetched devices of the play with a
number of his own delicacies, including a
gregarious pigeon named Herman. Director
George Marshall, achieving a frisky blend of
suspense and tomfoolery, puts it all together
with a bright, well-timed hand.

Glenn Ford plays a television writer who is married to a Broadway star (Debbie Reynolds). Several years earlier, Reynolds posed without proper attire, and now the possessor of said photographs is blackmailing Ford. Murder is his only out, Ford reasons, and he invites the blackmailer to his home and shoots him. He hides the body on the spot where a gazebo (summer house) is about to be positioned the following day.

The film is nearly all Ford, and he's up to every scene, earning both sympathy and laughs as he muddles through his farcical 'crime'. Reynolds is excellent, but her talents are beyond what her limited role requires. The part on Broadway was very minor and has not changed much. Carl Reiner, as the couple's district attorney friend, is good but also beyond the part.

••••••••••••••••••••••••••••••••

■ **GEISHA BOY, THE**

1958, 95 MINS, US ◇

Dir Frank Tashlin   *Prod* Jerry Lewis   *Scr* Frank Tashlin   *Ph* Haskell Boggs   *Ed* Alma Macrorie   *Mus* Walter Scharf   *Art Dir* Hal Pereira, Tambi Larsen
● Jerry Lewis, Marie McDonald, Sessue Hayakawa, Barton MacLane, Suzanne Pleshette, Nobu McCarthy (Paramount)

The Geisha Boy is a good Jerry Lewis comedy, one that rips along with never a backward glance at shattered remnants of plot behind it. Frank Tashlin, who wrote and directed, loads in wild sight and sound gags, parodies and takeoffs that relieve Lewis of some comic burden and show him in his best light.

Tashlin's screenplay, from a story by Rudy Makoul, has Lewis as a very low man on the show business totem pole. He is a magician who 'can't even get a job on daytime television'. He and his rabbit, Harry, join a USO tour of the Orient, because they couldn't get a job anywhere else.

Lewis first tangles with the troupe's headliner (Marie McDonald) who serves the picture as a kind of young Margaret Dumont; then with the army brass, represented by Barton MacLane, and finally with the Japanese themselves. There is a romance between Lewis and a Japanese widow (Nobu McCarthy) whose young son (Robert Hirano) 'adopts' Lewis as his father.

Lewis is at his best when he eschews some of the stock physical mannerisms that were originally his trademarks. He is more appealing and much funnier when he is playing more or less straight, using his timing and more restrained reactions for fine comedy effect. He is also effective in the few serious moments.

••••••••••••••••••••••••••••••••

■ **GENERAL DIED AT DAWN, THE**

1936, 98 MINS, US ▽

Dir Lewis Milestone   *Prod* William LeBaron   *Scr* Clifford Odets   *Ph* Victor Milner   *Mus* Werner Janssen   *Art Dir* Hans Dreier, Ernest Fegte
● Gary Cooper, Madeleine Carroll, Akim Tamiroff, Dudley Digges, Porter Hall, William Frawley (Paramount)

In Clifford Odets' first film attempt his hand is distinctly visible throughout. But without Gary Cooper and Madeleine Carroll to top an A-1 cast, all the splendid trouping, all the splendid imagery of direction, photography, music and general production might well have jelled into an artistic flop.

Story supplied by Charles G. Booth's novel is an old-fashioned piece of claptrap. It has to do with intrigue in the Far East, gun-runners, smugglers, and spies. Odets has left all that alone but has underlined Gary Cooper as the agent for the ammunition runners by making him engaged in the dangerous work not because of the adventure or money, but

because he's trying to help the downtrodden Chinese rid themselves of a money-grubbing, rapacious Chinese war lord, General Yang (Akim Tamiroff).

Cooper, as the daredevil American, is at top form throughout; Madeleine Carroll as his vis-a-vis in a very difficult assignment, impresses. Two comparatively unknowns, Tamiroff and Porter Hall, turn in exceptionally strong performances. Hall, as a sniveling, broken-down villain, handles an unusual job beautifully; John O'Hara, the novelist, does a bit as a newspaperman, looking the part. Allegedly Odets, director Milestone and Sidney Skolsky, Hollywood columnist, are also in for a shot or two, but if so it's their secret which scene it is.

••••••••••••••••••••••••••••••••

■ **GENEVIEVE**

1953, 86 MINS, UK ◇ ▽

Dir Henry Cornelius   *Prod* Henry Cornelius   *Scr* William Rose   *Ph* Christopher Challis   *Ed* Clive Donner   *Mus* Larry Adler   *Art Dir* Michael Stringer
● John Gregson, Dinah Sheridan, Kenneth More, Kay Kendall, Geoffrey Keen, Joyce Grenfell (Sirius)

The 'Genevieve' of the title is a vintage 1904 car which has been entered for the annual London-to-Brighton rally by its enthusiastic owner (John Gregson). His wife (Dinah Sheridan) hardly shares his enthusiasm but joins him on the run and there is constant good-natured bickering between them and their friendly rivals (Kenneth More) and his girlfriend (Kay Kendall). But the rivalry becomes intense on the return journey, ending up with a wager as to which car will be the first over Westminster Bridge.

First-rate direction by Henry Cornelius keeps the camera focused almost entirely on the four principals, and rarely has a starring foursome been so consistently good. Dinah Sheridan's sophisticated performance is a good contrast to John Gregson's more sullen interpretation. Kenneth More's exuberance is well-matched by Kay Kendall's effervescent portrayal.

••••••••••••••••••••••••••••••••

■ **GENGHIS KHAN**

1965, 124 MINS, US ◇

Dir Henry Levin   *Prod* Irving Allen   *Scr* Clarke Reynolds, Beverley Cross   *Ph* Geoffrey Unsworth   *Ed* Geoffrey Foot   *Mus* Dusan Radic   *Art Dir* Maurice Carter
● Stephen Boyd, Omar Sharif, James Mason, Eli Wallach, Francoise Dorleac, Telly Savalas (Allen/CCC/Avala)

Genghis Khan is an introspective biopic about the Mongol chief Temujin who unified Asia's warring tribes in the Dark Ages. An international cast delivers okay performances in occasionally trite script which emphasizes personal motivation rather than sweeping pageantry.

The screenplay, from story by Berkely Mather, hinges on continuing vendetta between tribal chieftain Stephen Boyd and Omar Sharif, once enslaved by Boyd but escaping to forge an empire that threatened western and eastern civilization some eight centuries out.

Sharif does a near-excellent job in projecting with ease the zeal which propelled Temujin from bondage to a political education in China, and finally to realizing at death his dream of Mongol unity. Boyd is less successful as the brutish thorn in Sharif's side, being overall too restrained for sustained characterization despite flashes of earthiness.

Most unusual characterization is essayed by James Mason, playing the neatly-contrasting urbane imperial counsellor who mentors political savvy.

••••••••••••••••••••••••••••••••

■ **GENTLEMAN JIM**

1942, 104 MINS, US ▽

Dir Raoul Walsh   *Prod* Robert Buckner   *Scr* Vincent Lawrence, Horace McCoy   *Ph* Sid Hickox   *Ed* Jack Killifer   *Mus* Heinz Roemheld
● Errol Flynn, Alexis Smith, Jack Carson, Alan Hale, John Loder, Ward Bond (Warner)

Warner Bros has managed to turn out a good film based on the life of James J. Corbett. In doing so, however, the scenarists have sacrificed a good deal of one of the best reputations the boxing game has ever known.

On celluloid, Corbett is a 'wise-guy', brash character oozing with braggadocio. In real life the heavyweight champ was a self-effacing, quiet personality so distinctly apart from the general run of mugg fighters of that day that the 'gentleman' tag was a natural.

Errol Flynn is the screen Corbett and is a real-life prototype only in the fact that Corbett was a bank clerk in Frisco and that his father was a bluff Irishman who operated a livery stable.

From there on, with the exception of some of Corbett's fights, the film is pure fiction. Corbett is shown as a young bachelor, who, because he got a prominent judge out of an embarrassing jam at an illegal bareknuckle fight, gets favored treatment at the bank where he's employed; meets the beauteous daughter of a millionaire miner and thus gains entrance to Frisco's famed Olympic club. At a party, according to the film, Corbett and his friend, Jack Carson, are tossed out of the Olympic when liquor makes Carson's mouth and feet misbehave.

This is so far removed from fact that it's ludicrous. Corbett was a revered member of the Olympic club to the very end.

All this fiction, plus the scenarists' depiction of Sullivan, after being kayoed by Corbett, calling on the latter to wish him well and present him with his championship belt, take this picture out of the biographical class and into fantasy.

••••••••••••••••••••••••••••••••

■ **GENTLEMAN'S AGREEMENT**

1947, 118 MINS, US

Dir Elia Kazan   *Prod* Darryl F. Zanuck   *Scr* Moss Hart   *Ph* Arthur Miller   *Ed* Harmon Jones   *Mus* Alfred Newman   *Art Dir* Lyle R. Wheeler, Mark Lee Kirk
● Gregory Peck, Dorothy McGuire, John Garfield, Celeste Holm, Anne Revere, Dean Stockwell (20th Century-Fox)

Just as Laura Z. Hobson's original novel of the writer (character), who poses as a Jew to write a magazine series on anti-Semitism was a milestone in modern fiction, the picture is vital and stirring.

The basic elements of the Hobson work are not only retained, but in some cases given greater dimension and plausibility. The picture is memorable for numerous vivid, impelling passages. For instance the breakfast scene, when Green tries to explain anti-Semitism to his innocent little son, stamps the picture's urgent theme on the spectator's mind virtually at once.

There are also disappointing or confusing scenes. One is the party given by Kathy's sister which remains as unresolved on the screen as in the book and as lacking in realistic atmosphere. In the same scene, the stupid Connecticut dowagers seem exaggerated. Celeste Holm, with some of the film's most pungent lines, frequently reads them too fast for intelligibility.

As Phil Green, the magazine writer, Gregory Peck gives a fine performance. He is quiet, almost gentle, progressively intense and resolute, with just the right suggestion of inner vitality and turbulence. Dorothy McGuire too, is dramatically and emotionally compelling as Kathy. The range from her somewhat flippant opening scene to the searing final one with John Garfield is impressive. Garfield is a natural in the part of Dave, giving it admirable strength and understated eloquence.

☐ 1947: Best Picture

....

GENTLEMEN PREFER BLONDES

1953, 91 MINS, US ◇ Ⓥ

Dir Howard Hawks *Prod* Sol C. Siegel *Scr* Charles Lederer *Ph* Harry J. Wild *Ed* Hugh S. Fowler *Mus* Lionel Newman (dir.) *Art Dir* Lyle R. Wheeler, Joseph C. Wright

● Jane Russell, Marilyn Monroe, Charles Coburn, Elliott Reid, Tommy Noonan, George Winslow (20th Century Fox)

An attractive screen tintuner has been fashioned from the musical stage hit, *Gentlemen Prefer Blondes*. The Joseph Fields-Anita Loos [1949] stage original has been modernized but the general theme and principal characters are intact. Only three of the stage tunes by Jule Styne and Leo Robin are used, but two numbers were cleffed by Hoagy Carmichael and Harold Adamson.

Together, the two femmes are the picture's outstanding assets. Jane Russell is a standout and handles the lines and songs with a comedy flair she has previously demonstrated. Marilyn Monroe matches with a newly displayed ability to sex a song as well as point up the eye values of a scene by her presence.

The big production number in the presentation is 'Diamonds Are a Girl's Best Friend', flashily presented by Monroe and a male line against a vivid red backdrop.

Monroe, a blonde who likes diamonds, and Russell, a brunet who likes men, sail for Paris and fun when Tommy Noonan, the blonde's lovesick millionaire, is unable to make the trip. Noonan's pop (Taylor Holmes), who would like to bust up the son's attachment, sends Elliott Reid, a private eye, along to keep an eye on the girls.

Charles Coburn is in fine form as the diamond tycoon with an eye for dames. Reid and Noonan carry off the romantic male spots nicely. Little George Winslow's big voice in a little body provides a comedy contrast to Monroe's little girl voice in a big girl's body for his two scenes with her.

....

GEORGE WHITE'S 1935 SCANDALS

1935, 83 MINS, US

Dir George White *Prod* Winfield Sheehan *Scr* Jack Yellen, Patterson McNutt *Ph* George Schneiderman *Mus* Louis De Francesco (dir.)

● George White, Alice Faye, James Dunn, Ned Sparks, Lyda Roberti, Eleanor Powell (Fox)

Once more George White presents himself in his very own conception of a film *Scandals*, the second of the series. Once more it is dull entertainment. Trouble is largely traceable directly to White.

From only one standpoint is the film worthy top-screen entertainment and that is the songs. There are six, two of them real outstanders from a tune standpoint, but all tops on lyrics. Even these numbers, however, are wasted because of poor staging [by White].

Cast is big and studded with featured players, many of them wasted. Most of the work is left to James Dunn and Alice Faye as the boy and girl. They're in a small town show in Georgia when White catches them. He brings 'em to New York and stars 'em immediately. Then follows the usual back-stage filmusical story. Inflated egos, pouting, quarrels, the kids leave the show. Girl's aunt from down Georgia way comes to catch the show, White digs them up; they've learned their lesson; all is well.

....

GEORGE WHITE'S SCANDALS

1934, 79 MINS, US

Dir George White, Thornton Freeland, Harry Lachman *Prod* Robert Kane *Scr* Jack Yellen, George White *Ph* Lee Garmes, George Schneiderman *Ed* Paul Weatherwax *Mus* Louis De Francesco (dir.)

● George White, Rudy Vallee, Alice Faye, Jimmy Durante, Dixie Dunbar, Adrienne Ames (Fox)

As the first musical talker turned out by an important eastern legit revue producer, this is an unintentional but flattering compliment to Hollywood's own stagers of musicals. George White contributes surprisingly little in the way of technique or ideas. *Scandals* follows the regulation Hollywood pattern. He not only borrows the backstage device, but weighs his production down with a dressing-room yarn that almost nullifies the picture's few meritorious moments.

Alice Faye is pretty much on the spot, and in an important part in her first picture. In looks and performance she is a pleasant surprise. She sings adequately, for that's her business. Rudy Vallee, a decidedly more versatile performer than the Vallee of a couple of years earlier, also enjoys more complimentary photography. The two make a pleasant team of singing leads.

Jimmy Durante, carrying the secondary love match with Dixie Dunbar, suffers from bad material most of the time. When he has something to work with, such as in his black-face number, he shines.

....

GEORGE WHITE'S SCANDALS

1945, 95 MINS, US

Dir Felix E. Feist *Prod* George White *Scr* Hugh Wedlock, Howard Snyder, Parke Levy, Howard J. Green *Ph* Robert de Grasse *Ed* Joseph Noriega *Mus* Leigh Harline (ballet) *Art Dir* Albert S. D'Agostino, Ralph Berges

● Joan Davis, Jack Haley, Martha Holliday, Philip Terry (RKO)

The George White 'Scandals' legit musicals, Ziegfeld's 'Follies' and Earl Carroll's 'Vanities' date back to the Prohibition era and the current picture, produced by George White, also dates back in that it is reminiscent of the backstage musicals of the early talker days. Though there are a few moments that hit home, on the whole the picture is a drawn-out affair.

Joan Davis and Jack Haley, starred, yeomanly try to overcome the assignments handed them, as do others, but the net result is still very negative. One of the drawbacks is the padding to 95 minutes and the dreary routine concerned with planning a George White's 'Scandals' show, the auditioning, the picking of chorines, costuming, etc.

Story, a weak one, concerns two romances in connection with the staging of a 'Scandals', Davis and Haley being paired on the one side and specialty dancer Martha Holliday and Philip Terry on the other.

....

GEORGY GIRL

1966, 100 MINS, UK Ⓥ

Dir Silvio Narizzano *Prod* Robert A. Goldston, Otto Plaschkes *Scr* Margaret Forster, Peter Nichols *Ph* Ken Higgins *Ed* John Bloom *Mus* Alexander Faris *Art Dir* Tony Woollard

● James Mason, Alan Bates, Lynn Redgrave, Charlotte Rampling, Rachel Kempson, Bill Owen (Columbia)

The role of a gawky ungainly plain Jane [in this adaptation of the novel by Margaret Forster] is a natural for Lynn Redgrave's talents, and she frequently overwhelms her costars by sheer force of personality.

She's sharing a slovenly apartment with an attractive, brittle and promiscuous girl friend (Charlotte Rampling). And whenever a lover is being entertained in the communal

bedroom, Redgrave takes herself off to the home of her parents' wealthy employer. Girl friend becomes pregnant, opts for marriage instead of another abortion, but when mother-to-be is in hospital, husband (Alan Bates) realizes he chose the wrong girl.

James Mason, as the wealthy employer, attempts to adopt a father figure in relations to the girl, but is actually nothing more than a conventional old roue.

Redgrave has a pushover of a part, and never misses a trick to get that extra yock, whether it's her first passionate encounter with Alan Bates or her fielding of Mason's amorous overtures.

....

GERONIMO

1962, 101 MINS, US ◇

Dir Arnold Laven *Prod* Arnold Laven *Scr* Pat Fielder *Ph* Alex Phillips *Ed* Marsh Hendry *Mus* Hugo Friedhofer *Art Dir* Roberto Silva

● Chuck Connors, Kamala Devi, Ross Martin, Pat Conway, Adam West (United Artists)

Time was when Indians on the warpath were known to claim a few scalps in their pursuits. Although Geronimo's band of idealistic warriors are acknowledged to be scalpers in Pat Fielder's screenplay, from the story she penned with producer Laven, there is no evidence of such menacing behaviour in this film. In fact, the Indians of Fielder's scenario are unbelievably henpecked, domesticated and generally wishy-washy – proud and arrogant in their war-making but meek enough to be bossed about by a frail, lone white woman in more intimate business.

The story describes the latter, leaner days of Geronimo's career, during which, denied humanitarian treatment by white supervisors on the reservation, he escaped and fled with some 50 tribesmen to Mexico, where he waged a courageous 'war' against the US to focus attention on the principle of the issue – treatment of the Indian as a human being.

Chuck Connors gives the film a decided lift with an impressive portrayal in the title role.

The picture was filmed in Mexico, and is a fine physical production.

....

GETAWAY, THE

1972, 122 MINS, US ◇ Ⓥ

Dir Sam Peckinpah *Prod* David Foster, Mitchell Brower *Scr* Walter Hill *Ph* Lucien Ballard *Ed* Roger Spottiswoode, Robert Wolfe *Mus* Quincy Jones *Art Dir* Edward S. Haworth, Angelo Graham

● Steve McQueen, Ali MacGraw, Ben Johnson, Sally Struthers, Al Lettieri, Slim Pickens (First Artists)

The Getaway has several things going for it: Sam Peckinpah's hard-action direction, this time largely channeled into material destruction, although fast-cut human bloodlettings occur frequently enough, and Steve McQueen and Ali MacGraw as stars.

Peckinpah's particular brand of storytelling comes through in the adaptation of a Jim Thompson novel. McQueen, denied parole despite four years of good behavior, gives in to crooked politico Ben Johnson's bank caper scheme in return for release from prison. MacGraw arranges and participates in the robbery plus the rambling escape which follows.

There is an overwritten secondary plot line involving Al Lettieri, so effective in projecting the greasy sadism of one of the robbery gang that his portion of the film eventually becomes vulgar overexposure.

....

GET CARTER

1971, 111 MINS, UK ◇

Dir Mike Hodges *Prod* Michael Klinger *Scr* Mike Hodges *Ph* Wolfgang Suschitzky *Ed* John Trumper *Mus* Roy Budd *Art Dir* Assheton Gorton

G

● Michael Caine, Ian Hendry, Britt Ekland, John Osborne, Tony Beckley, George Sewell (M-G-M)

Get Carter is a superior crime action meller. Michael Caine stars as an English hood seeking vengeance for the murder of his brother. Mike Hodges' top-notch adaptation of a Ted Lewis novel not only maintains interest but conveys with rare artistry, restraint and clarity the many brutal, sordid and gamy plot turns.

Lewis' novel, *Jack's Return Home*, is adapted by Hodges into a fast-moving screenplay in which episodes of compounded criminal double-crossing build gradually but steadily to a logical if ironic climax.

The curious death of Caine's brother triggers his departure from London, where he is a key torpedo for gangsters Terence Rigby and John Bindon, to his Newcastle home, where John Osborne (the playwright) appears the area crime boss. In tracking down his brother's murderer, Caine encounters the full spectrum of contemporary crime, including pornographic pix (in which his niece Petra Markham has been innocently compromised), drugs, high-stakes gambling, and vicious give-and-take retribution.

■ GETTING IT ON

1983, 96 MINS, US ◇ ▼
Dir William Olsen   *Prod* Jan Thompson, William Olsen   *Scr* William Olsen   *Ph* Austin McKinney   *Ed* William Olsen   *Mus* Ricky Keller   *Art Dir* James Eric
● Martin Yost, Heather Kennedy, Jeff Edmond, Kathy Brickmeier, Mark Alan Ferri, Charles King Bibby (Comworld)

This North Carolina-lensed teenage comedy nimbly pumps new life into the overdone high school hijinks genre.

Filmmaker William Olsen targets our consumerist and video-obsessed culture for some ribbing in this story of high school freshman Alex Carson (Martin Yost), with a crush on the girl next door, Sally (Heather Kennedy). Devising a video software business to earn money, Alex borrows his startup capital from his very businesslike dad, and with the help of his cutup classmate Nicholas (Jeff Edmond) uses the video equipment to record hidden camera footage of Heather and other pretty girls.

When Nicholas is kicked out of school by mean principal White (Charles King Bibby), the heroes enlist the services of a friendly prostitute (Kim Saunders) to record footage of White in flagrante delicto.

What makes this material work is a fresh, enthusiastic cast, witty writing, and direction by Olsen that bears no hint of malice.

■ GETTING OF WISDOM, THE

1977, 100 MINS, AUSTRALIA ◇ ▼
Dir Bruce Beresford   *Prod* Phillip Adams   *Scr* Eleanor Witcombe   *Ph* Don McAlpine   *Ed* William Anderson   *Art Dir* John Stoddart
● Susannah Fowle, Barry Humphries, John Waters, Sheila Helpmann, Patricia Kennedy, Julia Blake (Southern Cross)

The Getting of Wisdom was a bold choice as the subject of a feature film. The novel by Henry Handel Richardson was published in 1910, 13 years after the action depicted and was so shocking at the time that the author's name was stricken from the records of the school in which she set the lightly-disguised autobiography.

It is the story of a young girl's trials and adjustment to life in a strict, Victorian boarding school. Laura (Susannah Fowle) is strong-willed and rebellious, which creates conflicts with her peers and her teachers. The only real soulmate she finds is a senior girl (Hilary Ryan), but her possessiveness drives a wedge in the relationship.

The plotline is episodic, charting the development of the lead character over the years between her arrival and her graduation.

■ GETTING STRAIGHT

1970, 126 MINS, US ◇ ▼
Dir Richard Rush   *Prod* Richard Rush   *Scr* Robert Kaufman   *Ph* Laszlo Kovacs   *Ed* Maury Winetrobe   *Mus* Ronald Stein   *Art Dir* Sydney Z. Witwack
● Elliott Gould, Candice Bergen, Robert F. Lyons, Jeff Corey, Max Julien, Cecil Kellaway (Columbia)

Getting Straight is an outstanding film. It is a comprehensive, cynical, sympathetic, flip, touching and hilarious story of the middle generation [of the late 1960s] – those millions a bit too old for protest, a bit too young for repression.

The setting is a college campus where Elliott Gould is nearly through with an education course. Bergen is his girl. Both represent the post-JFK/RFK generation, who perceive the tremendous flaws in organized civilization, but scorn the often-puerile methods used in protest.

The episodic story [updated from a novel by Ken Kolb] covers lots of ground as it permits the very large and extremely competent supporting cast to limn the attitudes of an entire population.

While the film is a parade of accurately-hewn postures, the root story never strays too far.

■ GHOST

1990, 127 MINS, US ◇ ▼
Dir Jerry Zucker   *Prod* Lisa Weinstein   *Scr* Bruce Joel Rubin   *Ph* Adam Greenberg   *Ed* Walter Murch   *Mus* Maurice Jarre   *Art Dir* Jane Musky
● Patrick Swayze, Demi Moore, Whoopi Goldberg, Tony Goldwyn, Rick Aviles (Paramount/Koch)

An unlikely grab bag of styles that teeters, spiritlike, between life and death, this lightweight romantic fantasy delivers the elements a *Dirty Dancing* audience presumably hungers for.

Patrick Swayze and Demi Moore play Sam and Molly, a have-it-all Manhattan couple (he's a banker, she's an artist) who have just happily renovated their new Tribeca loft when he's shot and killed by a street thug. Unknown to her, he's walking around as a ghost, desperate to communicate with her because she's still in danger. He stumbles upon a spirit-world medium (Whoopi Goldberg) and drags her in to help him as a money-laundering and murder plot unfolds around them.

As the first dramatic film directed by Jerry Zucker (who collaborated on *Airplane! Ruthless People* and *The Naked Gun* with David Zucker and Jim Abrahams), *Ghost* is an odd creation – at times nearly smothering in arty somberness, at others veering into good, wacky fun.

Two-hour-plus film really takes its time unfolding, and it's not until Goldberg is brought in that the first laughs occur, but things do get wilder as Swayze explores his ghostly powers. Sporting a boyish haircut and her usual husky voice, Moore mostly has to spout tears and look vulnerable as she mourns Swayze and tries to avoid Goldberg, who she's convinced is a con artist.
□ 1990: Best Film (Nomination)

■ GHOST AND MRS MUIR, THE

1947, 103 MINS, US
Dir Joseph L. Mankiewicz   *Prod* Fred Kohlmar   *Scr* Philip Dunne   *Ph* Charles Lang Jr   *Ed* Dorothy Spencer   *Mus* Bernard Herrmann   *Art Dir* Richard Day, George Davis

● Gene Tierney, Rex Harrison, George Sanders, Edna Best (20th Century-Fox)

This is the story of a girl who falls in love with a ghost – but not an ordinary spook. As that girl, Gene Tierney gives, what undoubtedly is her best performance to date. It's warmly human and the out-of-this-world romance pulls audience sympathy with an infectious tug that never slackens. In his role as the lusty, seafaring shade, Rex Harrison commands the strongest attention.

Philip Dunne's script lards the R. A. Dick novel with gusty humor and situations that belie the ghostly theme. Dialog makes full use of salty expressions to point up chuckles.

Plot, briefly, deals with young widow who leaves London at turn of century for a seaside cottage. The place is haunted by the ghost of its former owner, Capt Daniel Gregg. The salty shade seeks to frighten the widow away but she's stubborn and stays. When her income is wiped out, the shade dictates to her his life story; she sells it as successful novel.

George Sanders is in briefly, and effectively, as a married lothario who makes a play for the widow, much to Capt Gregg's discomfort. Edna Best shows brightly as the widow's maid-companion. Natalie Wood, as the young daughter, is good, as is Vanessa Brown who becomes the grownup Anna.

■ GHOST BUSTERS

1984, 107 MINS, US ◇ ▼
Dir Ivan Reitman   *Prod* Ivan Reitman   *Scr* Dan Aykroyd, Harold Ramis   *Ph* Laszlo Kovacs   *Ed* Sheldon Kahn, David Blewitt   *Mus* Elmer Bernstein   *Art Dir* John DeCuir
● Bill Murray, Dan Aykroyd, Sigourney Weaver, Harold Ramis, Rick Moranis, Annie Potts (Columbia/Delphi)

Ghost Busters is a lavishly produced ($32 million) but only intermittently impressive all-star comedy lampoon of supernatural horror films.

Originally conceived as a John Belushi–Dan Aykroyd vehicle called *Ghostsmashers* before Belushi's death in 1982, *Ghost Busters* under producer-director Ivan Reitman makes a fundamental error: featuring a set of top comics but having them often work alone.

A Manhattan apartment building inhabited by beautiful Dana Barrett (Sigourney Weaver) and her nerd neighbor Louis Tully (Rick Moranis) becomes the gateway for demons from another dimension to invade the Earth.

To battle them come the Ghostbusters, a trio of scientists who have been kicked off campus and are now freelance ghost catchers for hire. Aykroyd is the gung-ho scientific type, Bill Murray is faking competency (he's had no higher education in parapsychology) and using the job to meet women, while Harold Ramis is the trio's technical expert.

Within the top-heavy cast, it's Murray's picture, as the popular comedian deadpans, ad libs and does an endearing array of physical schtick.

■ GHOSTBUSTERS II

1989, 102 MINS, US ◇ ▼
Dir Ivan Reitman   *Prod* Ivan Reitman   *Scr* Harold Ramis, Dan Aykroyd   *Ph* Michael Chapman   *Ed* Sheldon Kahn, Donn Cambern   *Mus* Randy Edelman   *Art Dir* Bo Welch
● Bill Murray, Dan Aykroyd, Sigourney Weaver, Harold Ramis, Rick Moranis, Peter MacNicol (Columbia)

Ghostbusters II is babyboomer silliness. Kids will find the oozing slime and ghastly, ghostly apparitions to their liking and adults will enjoy the preposterously clever dialog.

In *II*, the foe is slime, a pinkish, oozing substance that has odd, selective powers – all of them (humorously) evil. Its origins have something to do with a bad imitation Rembrandt painting, the lecherous art historian with an indecipherable foreign accent who's restoring it (Peter MacNicol), and all the bad vibes generated by millions of cranky, stressed-out New Yorkers. The worse their attitude, the worse the slime problem, which is very bad indeed.

The Ghostbusters, naturally, are the only guys for the job.

Bill Murray gets the plum central role (or he forced it by seemingly adlibbing dozens of wisecracks) at the same time his character also manages to skip out on a lot of the dirty ghostbusting work, leaving it to his pals Dan Aykroyd, Harold Ramis and Ernie Hudson.

While they are zapping Slimer, the main nasty creature from the original film, Murray's time is spent wooing back Sigourney Weaver, now a single mother.

It may be a first time, but Weaver get to play a softie, a nice break for the actress and her admirers (even if shots with her cute imperiled baby are scene-stealers).

■ GHOST DAD

1990, 84 MINS, US ◇ ▽
Dir Sidney Poitier   *Prod* Terry Nelson   *Scr* Chris Reese, Brent Maddock, S.S. Wilson   *Ph* Andrew Laszlo   *Ed* Pembroke Herring   *Mus* Henry Mancini   *Art Dir* Henry Bumstead
● Bill Cosby, Kimberley Russell, Denise Nicholas, Ian Bannen (SAH/Universal)

Cartoonish antics and ghostly special effects will entertain the kiddies but, like Bill Cosby's ghostly incarnation, this pic disappears when the lights come on.

Cosby plays a growly, funny, animated and lovable dad with lots of opportunities for physical, facial and vocal comedy. He dies and turns into a ghost 10 minutes into the picture; the story outlives him, but not by much.

Premise offers plenty of opportunity for optical illusions and gags, and they're abundant, but once the novelty of Cosby's plight wears off, it's the script that does the disappearing act. Overall thrust is that dad will learn it's more important to spend time with the kids (he's got only three days left before he'll be whisked off earth forever).

Sidney Poitier directs with vitality and punch, but when the script deserts him, things grow tedious.

■ GHOST STORY

1981, 110 MINS, US ◇
Dir John Irvin   *Prod* Burt Weissbourd   *Scr* Lawrence D. Cohen   *Ph* Jack Cardiff   *Ed* Tom Rolf   *Mus* Philippe Sarde   *Art Dir* Norman Newberry
● Fred Astaire, Melvyn Douglas, Douglas Fairbanks Jr, John Houseman, Craig Wasson, Alice Krige (Universal)

Authors like Peter Straub can take an essentially familiar spook story and make it work as a novel because of the solitary hold on the reader and ample time to embroider the details. But it's a real challenge to put the novel on screen where hundreds can share the flaws.

Helped by solid casting, writer and director make a valiant effort but come up with isolated and excellent moments separated by artful but ordinary stretches.

Even without reading Straub's novel, it's easy to guess early on that Fred Astaire, Melvyn Douglas, Douglas Fairbanks Jr and John Houseman share a dark secret that has prompted the appearance of Alice Krige in both bodily (sometimes very bodily) and ethereal forms. And whatever that secret is, they're going to pay for it.

Unfortunately, it then spins backward to an extremely long re-enactment of the events of long ago. By the time it gets back to the present to deal with the haunting menace, the mood is all wrong and the story riddled with questions that aren't answered.

■ GIANT

1956, 198 MINS, US ◇ ▽
Dir George Stevens   *Prod* George Stevens   *Scr* Fred Guiol, Ivan Moffat   *Ph* William C. Mellor   *Ed* William Hornbeck   *Mus* Dimitri Tiomkin   *Art Dir* Boris Leven
● Elizabeth Taylor, Rock Hudson, James Dean, Carroll Baker, Mercedes McCambridge, Sal Mineo (Warner)

Producers George Stevens and Henry Ginsberg spent freely to capture the mood of the Edna Ferber novel and the picture is fairly saturated with the feeling of the vastness and the mental narrowness, the wealth and the poverty, the pride and the prejudice that make up Texas.

Trio of Elizabeth Taylor, Rock Hudson and James Dean turns in excellent portrayals, with each character moulded in a strongly individual vein. Carroll Baker, in her first important part, proves herself a most competent actress.

Story starts when Hudson, as Bick Benedict, comes to Maryland and marries Taylor, a beautiful and strongwilled girl, who is transplanted from the gentle green of her state to the dusty gray of Texas in the early twenties.

Jett, a ranchhand, played by James Dean, antagonistic to Hudson, finds oil on his little plot and realizes an ambition to become rich. At the start of World War II he convinces Hudson to allow oil drilling also on Hudson's ranch and the millions come flowing in. But money only intensifies Dean's bad characteristics.

Giant isn't preachy but it's a powerful indictment of the Texas superiority complex. In fact, the picture makes that point even stronger than it's in the book.

As the shiftless, envious, bitter ranchhand who hates society, Dean delivers an outstanding portrayal. It's a sock performance. Taylor turns in a surprisingly clever performance that registers up and down the line. Hudson achieves real stature.

□ 1956: Best Picture (Nomination)

■ G.I. BLUES

1960, 115 MINS, US ◇ ▽
Dir Norman Taurog   *Prod* Hal Wallis   *Scr* Edmund Beloin, Henry Garson   *Ph* Loyal Griggs   *Ed* Warren Low   *Mus* Joseph L. Lilley (arr.)   *Art Dir* Hal Pereira, Walter Tyler
● Elvis Presley, Juliet Prowse, Robert Ives, Leticia Roman, James Douglas, Sigrid Maier (Paramount)

About the creakiest 'book' in musicomedy annals has been revived by the scenarists as a framework within which Elvis Presley warbles 10 wobbly songs and co-star Juliet Prowse steps out in a pair of flashy dances.

Plot casts Presley as an all-American-boy tank-gunner stationed in Germany who woos supposedly icy-hearted Prowse for what starts out as strictly mercenary reasons (if he spends the night with her, he wins a hunk of cash to help set up a nitery in the States). Needless to say, the ice melts and amor develops, only to dissolve when Miss Prowse learns of the heely scheme.

Responsibility for penning the 10 tunes is given no one on Paramount's credit sheet. Considering the quality of these compositions, such anonymity is understandable. Joseph J. Lilley is credited with scoring and conducting music for the film. It is not absolutely clear whether he had a hand in composing the pop selections, but it is doubtful. Presley sings them all as a slightly subdued pelvis.

Prowse is a firstrate dancer and has a pixie charm reminiscent of Leslie Caron. She deserves better roles than this.

■ GIDGET

1959, 95 MINS, US ◇ ▽
Dir Paul Wendkos   *Prod* Lewis J. Rachmil   *Scr* Gabrielle Upton   *Ph* Burnett Guffey   *Ed* William A. Lyon   *Mus* Morris Stoloff (sup.)
● Sandra Dee, Cliff Roberston, James Darren, Arthur O'Connell, Mary La Roche, Jo Morrow (Columbia)

Sandra Dee is the 'gidget' of the title, being a young woman, so slight in stature she is tagged with a nickname which is a contraction of girl and midget. Dee is in that crucial period of growing up where she doesn't like boys very much but is beginning to realize they are going to play a big part in her life.

The screenplay, based on the novel by Frederick Kohner, is played mostly out-of-doors on the ocean front west of Los Angeles that constitutes the play grounds and mating grounds for the young of the area.

The simple plot is a contemporary restatement of the *Student Prince* theme. The surf bum who Dee falls in love with (James Darren), turns out to be the respectable son of a business acquaintance of her father.

Paul Wendkos' direction is ingenious in delineating the youthful characters, not so easy in presenting normal youngsters of no particular depth or variety. Direction could have been more fluid, however, particularly in the musical numbers.

Dee makes a pert and pretty heroine, and Cliff Robertson, as the only adult of the beach group, is acceptable. Darren is especially effective as the young man torn between the carefree life and the problems of growing up.

■ GIG, THE

1985, 92 MINS, US ◇ ▽
Dir Frank D. Gilroy   *Prod* Norman I. Cohen   *Scr* Frank D. Gilroy   *Ph* Jeri Sopanen   *Ed* Rick Shaine   *Mus* Warren Vache
● Wayne Rogers, Cleavon Little, Andrew Duncan, Jerry Matz, Daniel Nalbach, Warren Vache (The Gig)

The Gig is a winning little film about a group of guys who try to fulfill their dream of being jazz players.

Wayne Rogers toplines as a New York businessman who has played Dixieland Jazz with his five pals for their own amusement once a week since 1970. He arranges a two-week pro engagement and talks the group into taking the step, the convincing argument being when their bass player George (Stan Lachow) drops out, promoting solidarity among the other five.

The replacement bassist, veteran player Marshall Wilson (Cleavon Little), causes friction in the group, because of his unfriendly personality and condescending attitude towards the budding amateurs.

Filmmaker Gilroy gets maximum comic mileage out of this contrast, while making good points concerning the snobism and purist stance that pervades many jazz circles.

Aided by a very entertaining portrait of life at a Catskills resort, Rogers and Little make a solid team.

■ GIGI

1958, 116 MINS, US ◇ ▽
Dir Vincente Minnelli   *Prod* Arthur Freed   *Scr* Alan Jay Lerner   *Ph* Joseph Ruttenberg   *Ed* Adrienne Fazan   *Mus* Frederick Loewe   *Art Dir* Cecil Beaton, William A. Horning, Preston Ames
● Leslie Caron, Maurice Chevalier, Louis Jourdan, Hermione Gingold, Eva Gabor, Jacques Bergerac (M-G-M)

Gigi is a naughty but nice romp of the hyper-romantic naughty 90s of Paris-in-the-spring, in the Bois, in Maxim's and in the boudoir. Alan Jay Lerner's libretto is tailor-made for an inspired casting job for all principals, and Fritz Loewe's tunes (to Lerner's lyrics) vie with and suggest their memorable *My Fair Lady* score.

Gigi is a French variation, by novelist Colette, of the *Pygmalion* legend. As the character unfolds it is apparent that the hoydenish Gigi has a greater preoccupation with a wedding ring than casual, albeit supercharged romance.

The sophistication of Maurice Chevalier (who well nigh steals the picture), Isabel Jeans, Hermione Gingold and Eva Gabor are in contrast to the wholesomeness of the Leslie Caron-Louis Jourdan romance. Caron is completely captivating and convincing in the title role.

Produced in France, *Gigi* is steeped in authentic backgrounds from Maxim's to the Tuileries, from the Bois de Boulogne to the Palais de Glace which sets the scene for Gabor's philandering with Jacques Bergerac, her skating instructor, and establishes the pattern of playing musical boudoirs, which was par for the circa 1890s Paris course.

The performances are well nigh faultless. From Chevalier, as the sophisticated uncle, to John Abbott, his equally suave valet; from Gingold's understanding role as Gigi's grandma to Isabel Jeans, the worldly aunt who could tutor Gigi in the ways of demimondaine love; from Jourdan's eligibility as the swain to Bergerac's casual courting of light ladies' loves. Caron's London experience in the stage version of Colette's cocotte (Audrey Hepburn did it in the US) stands her in excellent stead.

□ 1958: Best Picture

■ GILDA

1946, 110 MINS, US

Dir Charles Vidor   *Prod* Virginia Van Upp   *Scr* Marion Parsonnet   *Ph* Rudolph Maté   *Ed* Charles Nelson   *Mus* Morris Stoloff, Marlin Skiles   *Art Dir* Stephen Goosson, Van Nest Polglase
● Rita Hayworth, Glenn Ford, George Macready (Columbia)

Practically all the s.a. habiliments of the femme fatale have been mustered for *Gilda*, and when things get trite and frequently farfetched, somehow, at the drop of a shoulder strap, there is always Rita Hayworth to excite the filmgoer.

The story is a confusion of gambling, international intrigue and a triangle that links two gamblers and the wife of one of them. The setting is Buenos Aires. Sneaking in somehow is the subplot of a tungsten cartel operated by the husband, who also runs a swank gambling casino. A couple of Nazis are thrown in also.

Hayworth is photographed most beguilingly. The producers have created nothing subtle in the projection of her s.a., and that's probably been wise. Glenn Ford is the vis-a-vis, in his first picture part in several years.

There are a couple of songs ostensibly sung by Hayworth, and one of them, 'Put the Blame on Mame', piques the interest because of its intriguing, low-down quality.

Gilda is obviously an expensive production – and shows it. The direction is static, but that's more the fault of the writers.

■ GIMME SHELTER

1970, 90 MINS, US

Dir David Maysles, Albert Maysles, Charlotte Zwerin   *Prod* Porter Bibb   *Ed* Ellen Gifford, Robert Farren, Joanne Burke, Kent McKinney, Mirra Bank, Susan Steinberg, Janet Laurentano
● (Maysles)

Maysles Brothers' 16mm documentary on

1969 Rolling Stones' US concert tour which culminated in violence and death at the Altamont Speedway in California.

What precedes the satanic finale is a riveting close-up look at the Stones in performance. Contrary to the popular image, lead singer Mick Jagger emerges in off-stage footage as a withdrawn, almost catatonic individual totally involved in his music and virtually immune to events occurring around him.

Onstage it's another matter, and *Gimme Shelter* captures that petulant omnisexuality that made many adults consider Jagger a threat to their daughters, sons and household pets alike. Pouting and bumping through such numbers as 'I Can't Get No Satisfaction,' he is seldom less than mesmerizing.

■ GIRL CAN'T HELP IT, THE

1956, 96 MINS, US ◇ ⊛

Dir Frank Tashlin   *Prod* Frank Tashlin   *Scr* Frank Tashlin, Herbert Baker   *Ph* Leon Shamroy   *Ed* James B. Clark   *Mus* Lionel Newman
● Tom Ewell, Jayne Mansfield, Edmond O'Brien, Henry Jones, John Emery, Juanita Moore (20th Century-Fox)

The Girl Can't Help It is an hilarious comedy with a beat. On the surface, it appears that producer-director-scripter Frank Tashlin concentrated on creating fun for the juniors – a chore that he completes to a tee. However, the suspicion lurks that he also poked some fun at the dance beat craze. There are so many sight gags and physical bits of business, including Jayne Mansfield and a couple of milk bottles, that males of any age will get the entertainment message.

Mansfield doesn't disappoint as the sexpot who just wants to be a successful wife and mother, not a glamor queen. She's physically equipped for the role, and also is competent in sparking considerable of the fun. Nature was so much more bountiful with her than with Marilyn Monroe that it seems Mansfield should have left MM with her voice. However, the vocal imitation could have been just another part of the fun-poking indulged in.

Edmond O'Brien, rarely seen in comedy, is completely delightful as the hammy ex-gangster who thinks his position demands that his girl be a star name. Tom Ewell scores mightily as the has-been agent who is haunted by the memory of Julie London, another girl he had pushed to reluctant stardom.

■ GIRLFRIENDS

1978, 86 MINS, US ◇ ⊛

Dir Claudia Weill   *Prod* Claudia Weill, Jan Sanders   *Scr* Vicki Polon   *Ph* Fred Murphy   *Ed* Suzanne Pettit   *Mus* Michael Small   *Art Dir* Patrizia von Brandenstein
● Melanie Mayron, Eli Wallach, Anita Skinner, Bob Balaban, Christopher Guest, Viveca Lindfors (Cyclops)

This is a warm, emotional and at times wise picture about friendship. It's documentary film-maker Claudia Weill's first feature, although there's no reason to apologetically pigeonhole this movie as a 'promising first feature'. It's the work of a technically skilled and assured director.

Melanie Mayron is outstanding as a photographer fresh out of college maturing under the strains of professional insecurity and loneliness.

Down the line Weill has extracted first-rate performances. Anita Skinner is Mayron's best friend and until she suddenly marries Christopher Guest, her room mate. Eli Wallach portrays a rabbi and almost paramor for whom Mayron sometimes photographs Bar Mitzvahs and weddings. Bob Balaban is Mayron's slightly off-center boy friend and Viveca Lindfors is Beatrice, owner of a

Greenwich Village gallery who believes in Mayron and gives her a big break.

Each performance is a little gem and so are the characters developed by Vicki Polon from a story by her and Weill. They look and act like people, which is a relief. There are no false touches of glamour.

■ GIRL HUNTERS, THE

1963, 103 MINS, UK

Dir Roy Rowland   *Prod* Robert Fellows   *Scr* Mickey Spillane, Roy Rowland, Robert Fellows   *Ph* Ken Talbot   *Ed* Sidney Stone   *Mus* Phil Green   *Art Dir* Tony Inglis
● Mickey Spillane, Shirley Eaton, Lloyd Nolan, Hy Gardner, Scott Peters (Fellane)

A slick and entertaining adventure meller, *The Girl Hunters* also debuts author Mickey Spillane portraying his rough 'n' tumble hero Mike Hammer for the first time on the screen. He turns in a credible job.

Plot finds the private eye in the gutter from seven years of boozing and fretting because he believes that he sent his secretary and best gal to her doom when he gave her an assignment to do. It develops, however, that she may still be alive and Hammer straightens out and goes in search of her 'just like the old days', as one of the characters comments.

Along the line he finds himself in a romantic entanglement with one of his prime info sources, played cooly and with seductive restraint by Shirley Eaton who spends much of her time in the film wearing just a bikini.

Scott Peters is police captain Pat Chambers. The actor puts plenty of bite into the role but sometimes tends to overplay his obvious distaste for his ex-chum.

As a federal agent who's also interested in the case which has the foreign intrigue element of the murder of a US Senator which is linked to an international Commie plot, Lloyd Nolan turns in a pro and reliable job.

Pic was lensed in London but considerable care is taken to preserve Gotham locales where the action takes place. Several fave watering spots around town like Al & Dicks and the Blue Ribbon have been faithfully reproduced by art director Tony Inglis.

■ GIRL IN A SWING, THE

1988, 117 MINS, US/UK ◇

Dir Gordon Hessler   *Prod* Just Betzer, Benni Korzen   *Scr* Gordon Hessler   *Ph* Claus Loof   *Ed* Robert Gordon   *Mus* Carl Davis   *Art Dir* Rob Schilling
● Meg Tilly, Rupert Frazer, Nicholas Le Prevost, Elspet Gray, Lorna Heilbron (Panorama)

British writer-director Gordon Hessler has turned Richard Adams' 1980 psycho-chiller novel *The Girl in a Swing* into a smooth, fine-looking piece of romantic-erotic entertainment with many a fine Hitchcockian touch and a rather special star turn by Meg Tilly.

During their brief Florida honeymoon Karin's feelings of guilt and Alan's premonitions of disaster mount. They seek solace in their joy of sex. Karin also joins Alan in his hunt for ceramic treasures.

When she succeeds in finding, and buying for next to nothing, a third example of the porcelain rarity 'The Girl in the Swing', they are assured of instant wealth, and Karin tries to take Holy Communion from a vicar friend to make a clean break with the past.

Instead of absolution, Karin finds fear and guilt taking full possession of her, while Alan indulges her. It becomes more and more obvious that Karin must have killed the baby that came before the one she is now pregnant with.

The recurring theme of guilt, atonement and punishment is gently explored during the development of suspense.

G

GIRL NAMED TAMIKO, A

1962, 110 MINS, US ◇

Dir John Sturges   *Prod* Hal Wallis   *Scr* Edward
Anhalt   *Ph* Charles Lang Jr   *Ed* Warren Low
Mus Elmer Bernstein   *Art Dir* Hal Pereira, Walter Tyler
● Laurence Harvey, France Nuyen, Martha Hyer,
Gary Merrill, Michael Wilding, Miyoshi Umeki
(Paramount)

This has its share of shortcomings; there's
now and again a bit of fuzziness in character
development and plot detail. But these may
well be overlooked, for the story of emotional
conflicts in modern-day Japan is a fairly
arresting work.

Laurence Harvey's character is not one immediately easy to accept and this is one of the
flaws. As Ivan Kalin, he's a Chinese-Russian
photographer and looks, speaks and
romances like a British matinee idol.

The girl of the title is France Nuyen, thoroughly enchanting as the librarian whose
family adheres to the Japanese traditions
while she breaks away to engage in the
romance with Harvey. Martha Hyer, as an
American girl, very much on the loose in flit-
ting from man to man, handles the part
fittingly.

Gary Merrill fits in as a brooding business
man who cares and yearns for Hyer only to
have her walk out on him. Michael Wilding is
a British art dealer with a distaste for the
devious measures taken by Harvey in order
to get his much-wanted visa to go to the
United States. Miyoshi Umeki is a cutie who
does the co-habitat bit with Wilding. These
two make for a colorful pair and their East-
West mating game is rendered plausibly.

GIRL ON A MOTORCYCLE

1968, 91 MINS, UK/FRANCE ◇ ⓥ

Dir Jack Cardiff   *Prod* William Sassoon   *Scr* Ronald
Duncan, Jack Cardiff, Gillian Freeman   *Ph* Jack Cardiff,
Rene Guissart   *Ed* Peter Musgrave   *Mus* Les Reed
Art Dir Russell Hagg, Charles d'Eaubonne
● Alain Delon, Marianne Faithfull, Roger Mutton,
Marius Goring, Catherine Jourdan, Jean Leduc (Mid-
Atlantic/Ares)

A pretty young girl in a leather form-fitting
getup covering her nudity rides a powerful
motorcycle towards her lover after creeping
out of her young husband's bed. Her ride is
studded with flashbacks and even flash forwards and psychedelic inserts of torrid lovemaking. The ride gets a bit long and the film
lacks a true erotic flair. But it is well lensed
and has a shattering finale.

The motorcycle is a present from her lover
and is supposed to be an erotic symbol. But
treatment can rarely give the fiery dash to
make this acceptable except in the girl's final
mixing of metaphors as she literally makes
love to the bike.

Marianne Faithfull appears a bit too showy
and on the surface as the girl and uses facile
facial expressions rather than being able to
project the girl's feelings. Alain Delon is a
sort of hedonistic young college don who does
not believe in love in a romantic sense and is
mad about motorcycles.

GIRLS ABOUT TOWN

1931, 80 MINS, US

Dir George Cukor   *Scr* Raymond Griffith, Brian
Marlow   *Ph* Ernest Haller
● Kay Francis, Joel McCrea, Lilyan Tashman, Eugene
Pallette, Alan Dinehart, Lucile Webster Gleason
(Paramount)

There's an unwitting punch scene in this picture to draw laughter. It's where Kay Francis
shows off her figure in undies while explaining she's through with the gold-digger racket
and intends going straight because she's
found love with a rich rube.

When Francis falls for a young-looking
sucker from a hick town the burn is on. She's
the dame with a twisted virtue. Only the boy
friend would rather marry her than take her
unawares even if she's willing.

There's some additional sentiment brought
in between the elder of the two chumps, as
played ingenuously by Eugene Pallette, and
his middle-aged wife, as done by Lucile Gleason. He's a tightwad and practical joker from
Lansing. With the help of Lilyan Tashman,
who does the gold-digger role as natural as it
can seem, the bird's wife works the old boy
into a mad spree of jewelry buying.

GIRLS! GIRLS! GIRLS!

1962, 101 MINS, US ◇ ⓥ

Dir Norman Taurog   *Prod* Hal Wallis   *Scr* Edward
Anhalt, Allan Weiss   *Ph* Loyal Griggs   *Ed* Warren
Low   *Mus* Joseph J. Lilley   *Art Dir* Hal Pereira, Walter
Tyler
● Elvis Presley, Stella Stevens, Jeremy Slate, Laurel
Goodwin, Benson Fong (Paramount)

Girls! Girls! Girls! is just that – with Elvis
Presley there as the main attraction. Hal
Wallis' production puts the entertainer back
into the non-dramatic, purely escapist light
musical vein. The thin plot, scripted by
Edward Anhalt and Allan Weiss from an original story by Weiss, has him the romantic
interest of two girls. Hackneyed tale is of poor
boy fisherman who meets rich girl who
doesn't tell him she is rich but who, naturally, falls in love with him.

Weiss also penned story for the earlier *Blue
Hawaii*, which Norman Taurog also directed
for Wallis.

Most striking thing about the picture is the
introduction of new Paramount pactee Laurel Goodwin, who makes an auspicious film
bow. Youngster has the cute, home spun
potential of a Doris Day.

Stella Stevens, however, is wasted in a standard role as a sultry torch singer who has
given up ever really nailing the guy. She does
her best but, aside from singing three songs
(her first singing in a film) in a style suitable
for the character, there just isn't enough for
her to do.

GIRL WITH GREEN EYES

1964, 91 MINS, UK ⓥ

Dir Desmond Davis   *Prod* Oscar Lewenstein
Scr Edna O'Brien   *Ph* Manny Wynn   *Ed* Brian
Smedley-Aston   *Mus* John Addison   *Art Dir* Edward
Mashall
● Peter Finch, Rita Tushingham, Lynn Redgrave, Marie
Kean, Julian Glover, T.P. McKenna (United Artists/
Woodfall)

This first film by Desmond Davis, who was a
cameraman with Tony Richardson on *Loneliness of the Long Distance Runner* and *Saturday
Night, Sunday Morning*, has the smell of success. Davis is imaginative, prepared to take
chances and has the sympathy to draw perceptive performances from his cast.

Story [from the novel, *The Lonely Girl*, by
Edna O'Brien] is set in Dublin where two
shopgirls share a room. One (Rita Tushingham) is a quiet, withdrawn girl in the painful
throes of awakening. The other (Lynn Redgrave) is a vivacious, gabby, good-natured
colleen with a roving eye for the boys. But
when the two girls casually meet a quiet,
middle-aged writer (Peter Finch), the friendship that starts up is, naturally, between
Tushingham and Finch.

Finch does a standout job as the tolerant
writer who, despite occasional lapses into impatience, develops a fine understanding of the
problems of the girl. Tushingham is often
moving, sometimes spritely and always interesting to watch in her puzzled shyness. Redgrave makes an ebullient wench.

GIRO CITY

1982, 102 MINS, UK ◇ ⓥ

Dir Karl Francis   *Prod* Sophie Balhetchet, David
Payne   *Scr* Karl Francis   *Ph* Curtis Clark   *Ed* Neil
Thomson   *Mus* Alun Francis   *Art Dir* Jamie Leonard
● Glenda Jackson, Jon Finch, Kenneth Colley, James
Donnelly, Emrys James, Karen Archer (Silvercalm)

Giro City is a British thriller which examines
political corruption and media attitudes to
the rot on its doorstep. Story involves a documentary filmmaker and a reporter who work
for a successful TV magazine programme,
and their attempts to cover two controversial
news stories.

In breaking new ground, the film (shot on
Super-16) has to make up in freshness and
conviction for the superficiality with which
some of the many issues raised are treated.
But a hard-hitting and emotional core is provided by the story of a family in South Wales
who, alone but for the TV crew, take on the
local council in their determination to stay on
their land.

Glenda Jackson and Jon Finch as filmmaker and journalist are depicted as people
for whom work covers up a hollow emotional
core. Their pursuit of the corrupt councillor
is determined and thrilling.

GIVE MY REGARDS TO BROADWAY

1948, 89 MINS, US ◇

Dir Lloyd Bacon   *Prod* Walter Morosco   *Scr* Samuel
Hoffenstein, Elizabeth Reinhardt   *Ph* Harry Jackson
Ed William Reynolds   *Art Dir* Lyle R. Wheeler, J. Russell
Spencer
● Dan Dailey, Charles Winninger, Fay Bainter, Charles
Ruggles (20th Century-Fox)

Despite the mental images of lush production
numbers that might be conjured up by the
title, *Broadway* has none of that. Instead, it's a
simple story about an old vaude family that
lives in the hope that the Palace two-a-day
will some time be revived. Film has plenty of
showbiz nostalgia. Title song, cleffed by
George M. Cohan, runs through the film as
its theme.

Although he's backed by a fine supporting
cast that might otherwise steal his thunder,
Dan Dailey has a personal field day. He gets
a full chance to demonstrate his amazing
versatility.

In addition to Dailey, who's standout as the
son, the cast is excellent under the leisurely
directorial touch of Lloyd Bacon. Winninger
does one of his neatest characterizations as
the oldtimer who refuses to toss in the
sponge, and Bainter is fine as his understanding spouse.

GIVE US THIS DAY

1949, 120 MINS, UK

Dir Edward Dmytryk   *Prod* Rod Geiger, Nat A.
Bronsten   *Scr* Ben Barzman   *Ph* C. Pennington
Richards   *Ed* John Guthridge   *Mus* Benjamin Frankel
● Sam Wanamaker, Lea Padovani, Kathleen Ryan,
Bonar Colleano (Plantagenet)

The moving simplicity of the Pietro Di
Donato novel, *Christ in Concrete*, has been
brought to the screen with rare sincerity. It is
two hours of genuine human drama, which
makes no concession to convention.

This is one of the few occasions in which
British studios have embarked on a production with a New York setting. The expert
hand of Edward Dmytryk's direction ensures
faithful atmosphere.

Dmytryk presents the story of Geremio, an
Italian bricklayer who works in Brooklyn. It
is his wife's ambition to have a home of their
own, and carefully they save for the down-
payment. But the Depression overtakes them.
Then comes Geremio's opportunity to work
as a foreman on a job which he knows to be
unsafe and which culminates in tragedy.

Sam Wanamaker has never been better, investing the part with warmth and emotion.
• •

■ **GLASS BOTTOM BOAT, THE**

1966, 110 MINS, US ◇

Dir Frank Tashlin   *Prod* Martin Melcher, Everett Freeman   *Scr* Everett Freeman   *Ph* Leon Shamroy   *Ed* John McSweeney   *Mus* Frank DeVol   *Art Dir* George W. Davis, Edward Carfagno

● Doris Day, Rod Taylor, Arthur Godfrey, John McGiver, Paul Lynde, Edward Andrews (M-G-M)

Doris Day enters the world of rocketry and espionage in *The Glass Bottom Boat*, an expensively-mounted production given frequently to sight gags and frenzied comedy performances.

Star plays a conscientious public relations staffer in a space laboratory where Rod Taylor, the engineering genius heading the facility, has invented a device both the US government and the Soviets want. He falls for her and to keep her always by his side invents the idea of having her write a very definitive biography of him. She becomes a spy suspect because she has a dog named Vladimir, which she's always calling on the telephone so its ringing will give her pet exercise when she isn't there, and because she follows a standing order that every bit of paper should be burned.

Arthur Godfrey scores strongly as her father, operator of a glass-bottom sightseeing boat at Catalina. Taylor lends his usual masculine presence effectively, both as the inventor and romantic vis-a-vis.
• •

■ **GLASS KEY, THE**

1935, 77 MINS, US

Dir Frank Tuttle   *Prod* E. Lloyd Sheldon   *Scr* Kathryn Scola, Kubec Glasmon, Harry Ruskin   *Ph* Henry Sharp   *Ed* Hugh Bennett

● George Raft, Edward Arnold, Claire Dodd, Ray Milland, Rosalind Keith, Guinn Williams (Paramount)

This is a tale [from the story by Dashiell Hammett] of politics which involves murder, gangsterism and rocky romances. As murder mystery material, the story provides interesting plot situations. Performances by Raft and others are excellent, the direction is skilled and the dialog job leaves little to be desired, but too much has gone into the narrative that is up the alley of inconsistency.

It is a little unreasonable to expect that a daughter would dangerously turn against her father because of accusations that he murdered the man she loved, the son of a senator from whom the father was expecting patronage. It is equally implausible to expect that the politician would dig his own grave by shielding the senator.

Three romances are knitted into the murder mystery, but, in the main, the romantic aspects of the picture don't impress.

Raft gives a fine performance, as does Edward Arnold, playing the aspiring politician. Senator isn't much in the hands of Charles Richman, nor do Claire Dodd, Rosalind Keith or Ray Milland register any too well.
• •

■ **GLASS KEY, THE**

1942, 85 MINS, US ▼

Dir Stuart Heisler   *Prod* Fred Kohlmar   *Scr* Jonathan Latimer   *Ph* Theodor Sparkuhl   *Ed* Archie Marshek   *Mus* Victor Young   *Art Dir* Hans Dreier, Haldane Douglas

● Brian Donlevy, Veronica Lake, Alan Ladd, Bonita Granville, William Bendix, Joseph Calleia (Paramount)

Parading a murder mystery amidst background of politics, gambling czars, romance and lusty action, this revised version of Dashiell Hammett's novel – originally made in 1935 – is a good picture of its type.

Brian Donlevy is the political boss, a role similar to that he handled in *Great McGinty*. Alan Ladd is his assistant and confidant. Veronica Lake is the vacillating daughter of the gubernatorial candidate who first makes a play for Donlevy but winds up in the arms of Ladd, while Joseph Calleia has the gambling house concessions around the city. Mixed well, the result is an entertaining whodunit with sufficient political and racketeer angles to make it good entertainment for general audiences.

Donlevy makes the most of his role of the political leader who fought his way up from the other side of the tracks.
• •

■ **GLASS MENAGERIE, THE**

1950, 106 MINS, US

Dir Irving Rapper   *Prod* Jerry Wald, Charles K. Feldman   *Scr* Tennessee Williams, Peter Berneis   *Ph* Robert Burks   *Ed* David Weisbart   *Mus* Max Steiner

● Jane Wyman, Kirk Douglas, Gertrude Lawrence, Arthur Kennedy (Warner)

Spotting Jane Wyman as crippled Laura, Arthur Kennedy as her compassionate brother, Gertrude Lawrence as their frowzy mother and Kirk Douglas as the Gentleman Caller who unwittingly changes their lives, for better or worse, is a casting scoop.

Familiar plot [from Tennessee Williams' play] about the aging southern belle who holds her brood together in a St Louis tenement, only to lose her son when he decides he can take her nagging no longer, unreels engrossingly. Most remarkable is the subtle restraint employed to register Laura's awakening to the fact that life isn't a bust just because you've got a bum gam.

Kennedy, Wyman and Lawrence fight it out for thesp honors, and it would appear to be a draw.
• •

■ **GLASS MENAGERIE, THE**

1987, 130 MINS, US ◇ Ⓥ

Dir Paul Newman   *Prod* Burtt Harris   *Scr* [uncredited]   *Ph* Michael Ballhaus   *Ed* David Ray   *Mus* Henry Mancini   *Art Dir* Tony Walton

● Joanne Woodward, John Malkovich, Karen Allen, James Naughton (Cineplex Odeon)

Paul Newman's adaptation of *The Glass Menagerie* is a reverent record of Tennessee Williams's 1954 dream play, and one watches with a kind of distant dreaminess rather than an intense emotional involvement. It's a play of stunning language and brilliant performances creating living nightmares well defined by Newman's direction.

In this dreamscape Amanda (Joanne Woodward) is the center of a universe of her own making and her children are satellites. But she is every overbearing mother more than a specific character, and she and her children are drawn in broad strokes and dark colors that keep them at a distance and contain their emotional impact.

Newman has heightened this impression by framing the action at the beginning and the end with Tom (John Malkovich) returning years later to look back at the wreck of his life. Smack in the middle of Depression America, he, too, is any man who longs to escape the banality of his life and demands of his mother.

But the greater victim in this world is his crippled sister Laura (Karen Allen) who is doomed to live in perpetual waiting for a gentleman caller who will never come, and whose life is worthless because of it.

Woodward is a constantly moving center of nervous neurotic energy with her active hands and darting eyes always seeming to be reaching out for something to grab on to.
• •

■ **GLASS MOUNTAIN, THE**

1949, 97 MINS, UK

Dir Henry Cass   *Prod* George Minter   *Scr* Joseph Janni, John Hunter, Henry Case   *Ph* William McLeod   *Ed* Lister Laurence   *Mus* Vivian Lambelet, Nino Rota, Elizabeth Anthony

● Dulcie Gray, Michael Denison, Valentina Cortese, Tito Gobbi, Sebastian Shaw (Victoria)

The Glass Mountain has a theme inspired by a legend of the mountains in the Dolomites.

The romantic legend of thwarted love captivates an airman who is rescued in the Italian mountain district during the war. But on his return home to his wife, obsessed with writing an operatic piece on the theme, he cannot forget the girl he left behind.

Throughout, the story emphasis is placed on the frankly sentimental, but when the plot breaks away from its narrow limitations and gets out among the snow and the mountains it becomes alive and moving.

Dulcie Gray and Michael Denison, husband and wife in real life, have little difficulty in interpreting that role convincingly on the screen, but the standout performance comes from Valentina Cortese, who possesses a refreshing charm, and an ability to act.
• •

■ **GLASS SLIPPER, THE**

1955, 93 MINS, US ◇

Dir Charles Walters   *Prod* Edwin H. Knopf   *Scr* Helen Deutsch   *Ph* Arthur E. Arling   *Ed* Ferris Webster   *Mus* Bronislau Kaper

● Leslie Caron, Michael Wilding, Keenan Wynn, Estelle Winwood, Elsa Lanchester, Barry Jones (M-G-M)

Without making too strong a comparison with *Lili*, a previous click turned out by the principals connected with this offering, it is probable the makers figured on approaching the previous film's success. While *Slipper* has charm and a somewhat similar ugly duckling-love triumphant plot, it has neither the tremendous heart impact of *Lili* nor sufficient freshness of theme.

Leslie Caron, as drab and dirty as any scullery maid could have ever been, is the Cinderella who rides to the castle on her dreams, magically whisked into an enchantingly gowned, diademed princess fit for the prince played by Michael Wilding. Wilding does not seem happily cast in his character, nor does it get over to the viewer.

Where *Slipper* makes its best points is in the Bronislau Kaper score and in the ballets.
• •

■ **GLASS WEB, THE**

1953, 81 MINS, US

Dir Jack Arnold   *Prod* Albert J. Cohen   *Scr* Robert Blees, Leonard Lee   *Ph* Maury Gertsman   *Ed* Ted J. Kent   *Mus* Joseph Gershenson   *Art Dir* Bernard Herzbrun, Eric Orbom

● Edward G. Robinson, John Forsythe, Kathleen Hughes, Marcia Henderson, Richard Denning (Universal)

Albert J. Cohen's production is concerned with a TV crime show. A good cast, headed by Edward G. Robinson, a satisfactory murder-mystery script [based on a novel by Max Simon Ehrlich] and nicely valued direction by Jack Arnold make for an okay unfoldment of the melodramatics.

Robinson, frustrated researcher, and John Forsythe, writer, are responsible for the *Crime of the Week* program being televised each week. Both are being taken for money by Kathleen Hughes, TV actress, who is blackmailing Forsythe because of his summer dalliance with her while his wife was away, and bleeding Robinson on the strength of his infatuation for her.

The blonde blackmailer is killed and her death becomes the subject of a show, with her estranged husband apparently the patsy.

Robinson gives an excellent account of the frustrated researcher who feels his true worth isn't appreciated, and Forsythe comes over well as the writer. Hughes turns on the obvious s.a. for her hard-boiled role and brings it off neatly.

....

■ GLEAMING THE CUBE

1988, 105 MINS, US ◇ Ⓥ

Dir Graeme Clifford   *Prod* Lawrence Turman
Scr Michael Tolkin   *Ph* Reed Smoot   *Ed* John Wright
Mus Jay Ferguson   *Art Dir* John Muto
● Christian Slater, Steven Bauer, Min Luong, Art Chudabala, Le Tuan (Gladden)

A skateboarding-obsessed suburban kid (Christian Slater) goes about solving – exploitation style – the death of his adopted Vietnamese brother (Art Chudabala), who Slater knows in his heart was too smart to commit suicide.

Slater skateboards all over Little Saigon, going in and out of minimalls skillfully enough to elude Vietnamese hoods on his trail while conducting some Chuck Norris-inspired sleuthing.

Slater, who sounds as if he is trying to imitate Jack Nicholson, is the only character who has a shading of personality. His skateboarding buddies are funny, considering one needs a glossary to translate their dialog, while the Vietnamese are mostly sleazy cardboard figures. The police are inept and the mastermind villain (Richard Herd) seems to be right out of the Method acting school.

....

■ GLENN MILLER STORY, THE

1954, 115 MINS, US ◇ Ⓥ

Dir Anthony Mann   *Prod* Aaron Rosenberg
Scr Valentine Davies, Oscar Brodney   *Ph* William Daniels   *Ed* Russell Schoengarth   *Mus* Joseph Gershenson, Henry Mancini
● James Stewart, June Allyson, Charles Drake, George Tobias, Henry Morgan, Frances Langford (Universal)

Sentiment and swing feature in this biopic treatment on the life of the late Glenn Miller. The Miller music, heard in some 20 tunes throughout the production, is still driving, rhythmic swing at its best.

The Aaron Rosenberg supervision makes excellent use of the music to counterpoint a tenderly projected love story, feelingly played by James Stewart and June Allyson. The two stars, who clicked previously as a man-wife team in *The Stratton Story*, have an affinity for this type of thing.

The first 70 minutes of the picture is given over to Miller's search for a sound in music arrangement that would be his trademark and live after him. Remaining 45 minutes covers the rocketing Miller fame, his enlistment when World War II starts and the service band's playing for overseas troops.

To match the topflight performances of Stewart and Allyson, the picture has some strong thesping by featured and supporting players, as well as guest star appearances. Henry Morgan stands out as Chummy MacGregor. Charles Drake is good as Don Haynes, the band's manager.

....

■ GLEN OR GLENDA

1953, 65 MINS, US

Dir Edward D. Wood Jr   *Prod* George G. Weiss
Scr Edward D. Wood Jr   *Ph* William C. Thompson
Ed Bud Schelling
● Bela Lugosi, Daniel Davis [= Edward D. Wood Jr], 'Tommy' Haynes, Lyle Talbot, Dolores Fuller, Timothy Farrell (Screen Classics)

Glen or Glenda is an exploitation film dealing with transvestism and sex-change.

Told mainly in semi-documentary fashion, story unfolds as two case histories related by a psychiatrist. main story concerns Glen (Daniel Davis), a man who secretly dresses in women's clothes, much to the dismay of his fiancee Barbara (Dolores Fuller). Other story briefly deals with Alan ('Tommy' Haynes), identified as a 'pseudohermaphrodite', who is changed into Ann by a sex-change operation (presented tastefully without the explicit shock visuals common to such case study pics).

Though opening credits warn of film's *stark realism*, director Edward Wood's use of stock footage, cheap sets, perfunctory visuals and recited-lecture dialog gives the picture a phony quality. What distinguishes it from other low-budget efforts are the occasional mad flights of fancy.

Most involve a weird scientist, delightfully played by Bela Lugosi in eye-popping fashion. Also out of the ordinary is a suggestive (but far from pornographic) sequence of women writhing in their sexy undies, laden with bondage overtones, as well as a surrealist nightmare scene.

....

■ GLORIA

1980, 123 MINS, US ◇ Ⓥ

Dir John Cassavetes   *Prod* Sam Shaw   *Scr* John Cassavetes   *Ph* Fred Schuler   *Ed* George C. Villasenor   *Mus* Bill Conti
● Gena Rowlands, John Adames, Buck Henry, Julie Carmen (Columbia)

Gloria is a glorious broad perhaps pushing 40. She has been in prison but now has her nestegg and just wants to be let alone with her cat, friends and a fairly economically carefree life. But the way things happen, she has to put her neck out again, and for a precocious kid, half Puerto Rican, whom she has inadvertently pledged to help.

Director-actor John Cassavetes eases up on his unusually probing, darting camera and closeups studying human problems and disarray. Here instead he stands back and churns out a chase film that pits Gloria and the kid against the powerful Mafia no less.

Gena Rowlands is excellent as the tired woman who decides to take her chances for the boy.

The kid is a right blend of understanding and childish tantrums.

....

■ GLORY

1989, 122 MINS, US ◇ Ⓥ

Dir Edward Zwick   *Prod* Freddie Fields   *Scr* Kevin Jarre   *Ph* Freddie Francis   *Ed* Steven Rosenblum   *Mus* James Horner   *Art Dir* Norman Garwood
● Matthew Broderick, Denzel Washington, Cary Elwes, Morgan Freeman, Cliff DeYoung, Jane Alexander (Tri-Star)

A stirring and long overdue tribute to the black soldiers who fought for the Union cause in the Civil War, *Glory* has the sweep and magnificence of a Tolstoy battle tale or a John Ford saga of American history.

Glory tells the story of the 54th Regiment of Massachusetts Volunteer Infantry, the first black fighting unit raised in the North during the Civil War. As the war went on, 186,107 blacks fought for the Union and 37,300 of them died.

Matthew Broderick's starring role as Col. Shaw, the callow youth from an abolitionist family who proved his mettle in training and leading his black soldiers, is perfectly judged.

Broderick's boyishness becomes a key element of the drama, as the film shows him confiding his inadequacies in letters home to his mother (the unbilled Jane Alexander) and struggling to assert leadership of his often recalcitrant men.

The rage caused by ill treatment is searingly incarnated in a great performance by Denzel Washington, as an unbroken runaway slave whose combative relationship with Broderick provides the dramatic heart of the film.

....

■ GLORY GUYS, THE

1965, 111 MINS, US ◇

Dir Arnold Laven   *Prod* Arnold Laven, Arthur Gardner, Jules Levy   *Scr* Sam Peckinpah   *Ph* James Wong Howe   *Ed* Melvin Shapiro, Ernst R. Rolf   *Mus* Riz Ortolani
● Tom Tryon, Harve Presnell, Senta Berger, James Caan, Andrew Duggan, Slim Pickens (United Artists)

The Glory Guys is an entertaining US Cavalry-Indian conflict, sparked by an opportunist army general who sacrifices dedicated soldiers to his ambition. Brawling fisticuffs, comedy and romantic triangle mark a slightly forced plot until an exciting climax.

Adaptation by Sam Peckinpah of Hoffman Birney's novel, *The Dice of God*, finds Andrew Duggan very effective as a general again in responsible command despite prior goofs.

Senta Berger is an adequate but voluptuous frontier woman with an unspecified past, who provides romantic interest as Tryon and Presnell vie for her favors. Jeanne Cooper is good as Duggan's vicious and perfectly-matched wife who never fails to insult Berger.

Although Tryon is somewhat wooden and Presnell too refined for a frontier scout, director Arnold Laven has drawn some fine performances from supporting names. Slim Pickens brings a new life to the gruff humor and paternalism of a cliche role as non-com. James Caan makes a sharp impression as the stubborn recruit in an amusing running battle with shavetail Peter Breck.

....

■ G-MEN

1935, 84 MINS, US ◇

Dir William Keighley   *Prod* Louis F. Edelman
Scr Seton I. Miller   *Ph* Sol Polito   *Ed* Jack Killifer
Art Dir John J. Hughes
● James Cagney, Margaret Lindsay, Ann Dvorak, Robert Armstrong, Barton MacLane, Lloyd Nolan (First National/Warner)

This is red hot off the front page. But beyond that it has nothing but a weak scenario [from a story by Gregory Rogers] along hackneyed lines.

Little Caesar, *Scarface* and *Public Enemy* were more than portrayals of gangster tactics: they were biographies of curious mentalities. In the new idea of glorifying the government gunners who wipe out the killers there is no chance for that kind of character development and build-up.

This time James Cagney is a government man, he's in love with his chief's sister and she's thumbs down on him until the final clinch. And his chief rides him constantly, only to give in at the end.

Sprinkled through and around that is just about every situation from the Dillinger-Baby Face Nelson etcetera saga. The Kansas City depot massacre is paralleled, the Dillinger escape from a Chicago apartment, the Wisconsin resort roundup, the bank holdups throughout Kansas-Missouri, et al.

The acting throughout is A-1, and that helps consistently. Beyond Cagney and Robert Armstrong, both at their best, there is Ann Dvorak, a moll who tips off the cops to the final capture. Margaret Lindsay is Armstrong's sister and Cagney's gal. An easy assignment, and she romps off with it.

....

■ GO-BETWEEN, THE

1971, 118 MINS, UK ◇

Dir Joseph Losey   *Prod* John Heyman, Norman Priggen   *Scr* Harold Pinter   *Ph* Gerry Fisher
Ed Reginald Beck   *Mus* Michel Legrand
Art Dir Carmen Dillon
● Julie Christie, Alan Bates, Margaret Leighton,

Michael Redgrave, Michael Gough, Edward Fox
(M-G-M/EMI)

In its glimpse of the manners and mores of
the British socialites at the beginning of the
century, *The Go-Between* is both fascinating
and charming. Joseph Losey's direction sets a
pace in which incident and characterization
take precedence over action.

The Harold Pinter screenplay, based on the
L.P. Hartley novel, is, as one would naturally
expect, literate and penetrating, yet there are
certain obscurities in the treatment.

It is Michael Redgrave looking back at a
definitive event of his boyhood, an experience
which undoubtedly was largely responsible
for his remaining unmarried. For it is during
the long hot summer in the lavish country
home that the youngster becomes emotionally involved by acting as the contact (or go-
between) between the daughter of the house –
with whom he believes himself to be in love –
and the tenant farmer, although the girl is
already betrothed to a member of the aristocracy. And it is in that period that the boy gets
his first inkling of what sex is all about.

Though Julie Christie and Alan Bates are
starred as the girl and the farmer, it is the boy
who has the pivotal role, and Dominic
Guard, a screen newcomer, appears to play
his part effortlessly, with an absence of
precociousness.

■ **GODFATHER, THE**

1972, 175 MINS, US ◇ Ⓥ

Dir Francis Coppola   *Prod* Albert S. Ruddy   *Scr* Mario
Puzo, Francis Coppola   *Ph* Gordon Williams
Ed William Reynolds, Peter Zinner   *Mus* Nino Rota
Art Dir Dean Tavoularis
● Marlon Brando, Al Pacino, James Caan, Richard
Conte, Robert Duvall, Sterling Hayden (Paramount)

Paramount's film version of Mario Puzo's
sprawling gang-land novel has an outstanding performance by Al Pacino and a strong
characterization by Marlon Brando in the
title role. It also has excellent production
values, flashes of excitement, and a well-
picked cast.

Puzo and director Francis Coppola are credited with the adaptation which best of all
gives some insight into the origins and heritage of that segment of the population known
off the screen (but not on it) as the Mafia or
Cosa Nostra.

In *The Godfather* we have the New York-
New Jersey world, ruled by five 'families',
one of them headed by Brando. This is a
world where emotional ties are strong, loyalties are somewhat more flexible at times, and
tempers are short. Brando does an admirable
job as the lord of his domain.

It is Pacino who makes the smash impression here. Initially seen as the son whom
Brando wanted to go more or less straight,
Pacino matures under trauma of an assassination attempt on Brando, his own double-
murder revenge for that on corrupt cop Sterling Hayden and rival gangster Al Lettieri,
the counter-vengeance murder of his Sicilian
bride, and a series of other personnel re-
adjustments which at fadeout find him king
of his own mob.

Among the notable performances are Robert Duvall as Hagen, the non-Italian number-
two man, Richard Conte as one of Brando's
malevolent rivals and Diane Keaton as Pacino's early sweetheart, later second wife.
□ 1972: Best Picture

■ **GODFATHER PART II, THE**

1974, 200 MINS, US ◇ Ⓥ

Dir Francis Coppola   *Prod* Francis Coppola
Scr Francis Coppola, Mario Puzo   *Ph* Gordon Willis
Ed Peter Zinner, Barry Malkin, Richard Marks
Mus Nino Rota, Carmine Coppola   *Art Dir* Dean
Tavoularis

● Al Pacino, Robert Duvall, Diane Keaton, Robert De
Niro, John Cazale, James Caan (Paramount)

The Godfather Part II, far from being a spinoff
followup to its 1972 progenitor, is an excellent epochal drama in its own right providing
bookends in time to the earlier story. Al
Pacino again is outstanding as Michael
Corleone, successor to crime family
leadership. The $15 million production cost
about two-and-a-half times the original.

The film's 200 minutes could be broken
down into two acts and 10 scenes. The scenes
alternate between Pacino's career in Nevada
gambling rackets from about 1958 on and
Robert De Niro's early life in Sicily and New
York City. A natural break comes after 126
minutes when De Niro, involved with low
level thievery, brutally assassinates Gaston
Moschin the neighborhood crime boss
without a shred of conscience. It's the only
shocking brutality in the film.
□ 1974: Best Picture

■ **GODFATHER PART III, THE**

1990, 161 MINS, US ◇ Ⓥ

Dir Francis Coppola   *Prod* Francis Coppola
Scr Mario Puzo, Francis Coppola   *Ph* Gordon Willis
Ed Barry Malkin, Lisa Fruchtman   *Mus* Carmine
Coppola, Nino Rota   *Art Dir* Dean Tavoularis
● Al Pacino, Diane Keaton, Talia Shire, Andy Garcia,
Eli Wallach, Joe Mantegna (Zoetrope/Paramount)

The Godfather Part III matches its predecessors
in narrative intensity, epic scope, socio-political analysis, physical beauty and deep feeling
for its characters and milieu. In addition, the
$55 million-plus production is the most per-
sonal of the three for the director.

Like the original, Part III opens with a lengthy festival celebration punctuated by backroom dealings. It is 1979, and Michael
Corleone, having divested himself of his illegal
operations, is being honored by the Catholic
Church for his abundant charitable activities.

Hopeful of bringing his family closer
together, Michael dotes on his daughter
Mary (Sofia Coppola) and understandably
becomes perturbed by her affair with cousin
Vincent (Andy Garcia), hot-headed, viol-
ence-prone illegitimate son of Michael's late
brother Sonny. Vincent has been unhappily
working for slumlord and old-style thug Joey
Zasa (Joe Mantegna), who has taken on
Michael's less savory holdings.

Bad blood between the ruthless Zasa and
the Corleone family mounts just as Michael
tries, with $600 million, to buy a controlling
interest in the European conglomerate Im-
mobiliare, a move that would cement his
business legitimacy and financial future.

After 80 minutes, the action switches to
Italy, where it remains for the duration.
Pacino and Eli Wallach's old dons can't help
begin scheming against one another. In one
of the most masterful examples of sustained
intercutting in cinema, the performance on
opening night of Pacino's son in *Cavalleria
Rusticana* serves as the backdrop for several
murderous missions.

For the third time out in his career role,
Pacino is magnificent. Garcia brings much-
needed youth and juice to the ballsy Vincent,
heir apparent to the Corleone tradition,
much as James Caan sparked the first film
and Robert De Niro invigorated the second.

Diane Keaton proves a welcome, if brief,
presence in warming the film, and Talia
Shire seems pleased with the opportunity to
do some dirty work at long last.

Film's main flaw, unavoidably, is Sofia
Coppola in the important, but not critical,
role of Michael's daughter. Unfortunate casting decision was made after original actress
Winona Ryder had to bow out at the start of
production.
□ 1990: Best Picture (Nomination)

■ **GOD IS MY CO-PILOT**

1945, 83 MINS, US

Dir Robert Florey   *Prod* Robert Buckner   *Scr* Peter
Milne, Abem Finkel   *Ph* Sid Hickox   *Ed* Folmer
Blangsted   *Mus* Franz Waxman   *Art Dir* John Hughes
● Dennis Morgan, Dane Clark, Raymond Massey,
Alan Hale, Andrea King (Warner)

Narrative uses flashback technique to condense life of Col Robert Lee Scott Jr, army
ace who gained fame with General Chen-
nault's Flying Tigers.

Air fight sequences bear an authentic
stamp, although studio-made and the thrills
are good drama. Title derives from Scott's
realization that a pilot doesn't face danger
alone, and several of his real-life brushes with
death sustain the belief.

There has been considerable condensation
of Scott's story, taken from his best-selling
book of same title, and undoubtedly commercial license has pointed up some incidents for
better dramatic flavor. It's the story of a boy
born to fly and spans his days from the time
he first jumped off the barn with an umbrella,
through model planes, West Point, flying the
mail, instructing and his takeoff on a secret
mission to China after Pearl Harbor.

Condensation was evidently more in the
hands of the film editor than in the script.
Finished picture indicates there was considerable scissoring to hold footage to
reasonable length. Robert Florey's direction
manages authenticity and obtains excellent
performances from the cast headed by Dennis
Morgan.

■ **GOD'S LITTLE ACRE**

1958, 112 MINS, US Ⓥ

Dir Anthony Mann   *Prod* Sidney Harmon   *Scr* Philip
Yordan   *Ph* Ernest Haller   *Ed* Richard C. Meyer
Mus Elmer Bernstein   *Art Dir* John S. Poplin Jr
● Robert Ryan, Aldo Ray, Tina Louise, Buddy Hackett,
Jack Lord, Fay Spain (United Artists)

Rousing, rollicking and ribald, *God's Little
Acre* is a rustic revel with the kick of a Georgia
mule. The production of Erskine Caldwell's
novel is adult, sensitive and intelligent.

The direct, bucolic humor is virtually
intact, and so is Caldwell's larger scheme, the
morality play he told through the artless,
sometimes disastrous behavior of his foolish
and lovable characters. A changed ending
gives a different meaning to the story, but the
ending is sound, aesthetically and popularly.

The story remains that of a Georgia farmer
(Robert Ryan) who believes he can find gold
on his farm. In the book it was a gold mine; in
the picture it is buried treasure. Ryan has
spent years of his life digging for it, all his
energies and those of his two sons (Jack Lord
and Vic Morrow) go into the search and the
dream it represents. The hunt leads everywhere on their farm except on the one acre
Ryan has set aside, in the olden way of tith-
ing, for God.

Ryan dominates the picture, as his character should. Aldo Ray, as his son-in-law,
creates a moving characterization as the husband torn between his wife, sensitively
played by Helen Westcott, and the voluptuous barnyard Susannah, strikingly projected
by newcomer from legit Tina Louise.

■ **GODS MUST BE CRAZY, THE**

1984, 108 MINS, BOTSWANA ◇ Ⓥ

Dir Jamie Uys   *Prod* Jamie Uys   *Scr* Jamie Uys
Ph Jamie Uys, Buster Reynolds, Robert Lewis   *Ed* Jamie
Uys   *Mus* John Boshoff
● Marius Weyers, Sandra Prinsloo, N!xau, Louw
Verwey, Michael Thys, Jamie Uys (CAT)

The Gods Must Be Crazy is a comic fable by one-man-band South African filmmaker Jamie Uys, who shot the picture in Botswana in 1979.

Uys' basic storyline has Xi (N!xua), a bushman who lives deep in the Kalahari desert, setting off on a trek to destroy a Coca Cola bottle which fell from a passing airplane and by virtue of its strange usefulness as a utensil (thought to be thrown by the gods from heaven) has caused great dissension within his tribe.

Xi plans to throw the unwanted artifact of modern civilization off the edge of the world and in his trek encounters modern people.

Film's main virtues are its striking, wide-screen visuals of unusual locations, and the sheer educational value of its narration.

■ GODS MUST BE CRAZY 2, THE

1989, 99 MINS, BOTSWANA/US ◇ Ⓥ
Dir Jamie Uys   *Scr* Jamie Uys   *Ph* Buster Reynolds
Ed Renee Engelbrecht, Ivan Hall   *Mus* Charles Fox
● N!xau, Lena Farugia, Hans Strydom, Eiros, Nadies, Erick Bowen (Boet Troskie/Weintraub)

Jamie Uys has concocted a genial sequel to his 1983 international sleeper hit *The Gods Must Be Crazy* that is better than its progenitor in most respects.

His tongue-clicking Kalahari Bushman hero, again played by a real McCoy named N!xau, is once more unwittingly embroiled in the lunacies of civilization.

First plotline has N!xau's two adorable offspring getting innocently borne away on the trailer truck of a pair of unsuspecting ivory poachers. N!xau follows the tracks and comes across two other odd couples from the nutty outside world.

There is a New York femme lawyer (Lena Faragia), who is stranded in the middle of the Kalahari with a handsome, phlegmatic game warden (Hans Strydom) when their ultra-light plane is downed in a sudden storm.

Then there are two hapless mercenaries, an African and a Cuban, who keep taking one another prisoner in a series of table-turning pursuits through the brush.

Uys orchestrates a desert farce of criss-crossing destinies with more assured skill and charming sight-gags, marred only by facile penchant for speeded-up slapstick motion.

■ GODSPELL

1973, 103 MINS, US ◇
Dir David Greene   *Prod* Edgar Lansbury   *Scr* David Greene, John-Michael Tebelak   *Ph* Richard G. Heimann   *Ed* Alan Heim   *Mus* Stephen Schwartz   *Art Dir* Brian Eatwell
● Victor Garber, David Haskell, Jerry Sroka, Lynne Thigpen, Katie Hanley, Rubin Lamont (Columbia)

Godspell originated as a workshop production at off-off-Broadway's La Mama for a group of actor-graduates of Carnegie-Mellon Univ. Overall concept – a youth-slanted reworking of the gospel according to St Matthew – was that of director John-Michael Tebelak as part of a master's thesis.

Film follows original 1971 off-Broadway legit production closely but 'opens up' setting to include footage of virtually every New York City tourist landmark, graffiti and all.

Result is that original production's appealing aspects have remained intact – a strong Stephen Schwartz score and an infectious joie de vivre conveyed by an energetic, no-name cast. So also, unfortunately, have its flaws – a relentlessly simplistic approach to the New Testament interpreted in overbearing children's theatre-style mugging.

Story line merely consists of a series of ensemble interpretations of gospel parables as enunciated by a Christ figure (Victor Garber)in a superman sweatshirt and workman's overalls.

■ GOD'S WILL

1989, 100 MINS, US Ⓥ
Dir Julia Cameron   *Prod* Julia Cameron, Pam Moore
Scr Julia Cameron   *Ph* William Nusbaum
Mus Christopher (Hambone) Cameron
● Marge Kotlisky, Daniel Region, Laura Margolis, Domenica Cameron-Scorsese, Linda Edmond (Power & Light)

Veteran Hollywood screen writer Julia Cameron moved home to Chicago to produce and direct her first feature, *God's Will*, and discovered first-hand one of a filmmaker's worst nightmares: the production soundtrack was stolen after shooting wrapped.

As a consequence, the scenes' delicate at best under normal low-budget conditions, simply don't play right.

A plus for the Cameron family is an outstanding debut by pre-teen daughter Domenica Cameron-Scorsese (whose father is director Martin Scorsese).

Cameron's intent, obviously, was to create a lighthearted effort at family fun in which a divorced, self-centred show-business couple (Daniel Region and Laura Margolis) meet an untimely demise and wind up in heaven squabbling over what will happen now to their daughter.

The little girl has fallen into the custody of the couple's new spouses (Linda Edmond and Mitchell Canoff). Some ghostly haunting is therefore required to free Domenica into the hands of another couple preferred by the parents and the result is a romp.

■ GOING HOME

1971, 97 MINS, US ◇
Dir Herbert B. Leonard   *Prod* Herbert B. Leonard
Scr Lawrence B. Marcus   *Ph* Fred Jackman
Ed Sigmund Neufeld Jr   *Mus* Bill Walker   *Art Dir* Peter Wooley
● Robert Mitchum, Brenda Vaccaro, Jan-Michael Vincent (M-G-M)

Going Home is a most unusual and intriguing melodrama about a teenage boy's vengeance against his father for the long-ago killing of his mother. Robert Mitchum in an offbeat role gives an excellent performance as the crude but sensitive father. Jan-Michael Vincent is very effective as his son. Brenda Vaccaro, as Mitchum's sweetheart, makes a catalytic role into a memorable experience.

The script takes Vincent on a search from prison, where Mitchum was incarcerated, to the sleazy seashore environment where the paroled father is eking out a living. The boy's love-hate relationship with his father is developed neatly and often to a terrifying degree. Vaccaro, in the literal sense an innocent bystander who gets hurt for her trouble, fills in with human emotions the two men cannot express to each other.

As the undaunted but well worn-down Korean War hero 20 years later, fresh out of stir with a son who hates his guts, with a beer belly and a black future, Mitchum presents a characterization that combines a wide range of acting talents.

■ GOING MY WAY

1944, 126 MINS, US Ⓥ
Dir Leo McCarey   *Prod* Leo McCarey   *Scr* Frank Butler, Frank Cavett   *Ph* Lionel Lindon   *Ed* Leroy Stone   *Mus* Robert Emmett Dolan (dir)   *Art Dir* Hans Dreier, William Flannery
● Bing Crosby, Rise Stevens, Barry Fitzgerald, Gene Lockhart (Paramount)

Bing Crosby gets a tailor-made role in *Going My Way*, and with major assistance from Barry Fitzgerald and Rise Stevens, clicks solidly to provide topnotch entertainment for wide audience appeal.

Picture is a warm, human drama studded liberally with bright episodes and excellent characterizations accentuated by fine direction of Leo McCarey. Intimate scenes between Crosby and Fitzgerald dominate throughout, with both providing slick characterizations.

Crosby plays a young priest interested in athletics and music who's assigned as assistant to crusty Fitzgerald in an eastside church saddled with burdensome mortgage that might be foreclosed by grasping Gene Lockhart. Progressive youth and staid oldster clash continually, but Crosby gradually bends Fitzgerald to his way.

Major thread of gaiety runs through the proceedings, and McCarey has liberally sprinkled sparkling individual episodes along the way for cinch audience reaction. Rise Stevens comes on for the second half, introduced as a Metropolitan Opera star and old friend of Crosby when both were interested in music.

Crosby's song numbers include three new tunes by Johnny Burke and James Van Heusen – 'Going My Way', 'Would You Like to Swing On a Star' and 'Day after Forever'.
□ 1944: Best Picture

■ GOIN' SOUTH

1978, 101 MINS, US ◇ Ⓥ
Dir Jack Nicholson   *Prod* Harry Gittes, Harold Schneider   *Scr* John Herman Shaner, Al Ramus, Charles Shyer, Alan Mandel   *Ph* Nestor Almendros
Ed Richard Chew, John Fitzgerald Beck   *Mus* Van Dyke Parks, Perry Botkin Jr   *Art Dir* Toby Carr Rafelson
● Jack Nicholson, Mary Steenburgen, Christopher Lloyd, John Belushi, Veronica Cartwright, Danny DeVito (Paramount)

Jack Nicholson playing Gabby Hayes is interesting, even amusing at times, but Hayes was never a leading man, which *Goin' South* desperately needs.

Picture starts off promisingly enough with Nicholson as a hapless outlaw who makes it across the border but the posse cheats and comes across after him causing his horse to faint.

On his way to the gallows, Nicholson discovers an unordinary county ordinance that would allow him to go free if picked for marriage by a maiden lady in town. Up to now, *Goin' South* is still going strong. But here it stops as lovely young Mary Steenburgen steps out of the crowd and agrees to marry the bearded, dirty horse-thief.

Why she should do this is never satisfactorily established in the script carrying the names of four writers. Ostensibly, it's to get the manpower to help her mine her property for gold before the railroad takes over. But it never jells, as Nicholson continues to sputter and chomp, acting more like her grandfather than a handsome roue out to overcome her virginity.

■ GO INTO YOUR DANCE

1935, 92 MINS, US
Dir Archie Mayo   *Scr* Earl Baldwin, Bradford Ropes
Ph Tony Gaudio, Sol Polito   *Ed* Harold McLernon
● Al Jolson, Ruby Keeler, Glenda Farrell, Helen Morgan, Barton MacLane, Sharon Lynne (First National/Warner)

Go into Your Dance has much to recommend it as a lavishly produced, vigorously directed and agreeably entertaining musical picture. Besides everything else it has Al Jolson in top form, plus a nifty set of songs [by Al Dubin and Harry Warren].

Along with Jolson and for the first time his screen partner is the missus, Ruby Keeler. A sensible story setting, in which each is per-

G

mitted to adhere to type, makes them a nice film couple.

Jolson plays the role of a talented star who has broken up many a hit show by going off on bats. The star is finally barred from the musical stage by the combined votes of Actors Equity and an association of producers.

With the help of his devoted sister and a dancing girl with whom he teams up, the banished star starts his comeback via the night club field. The comeback is nearly interrupted by gangster bullets, but they miss the star and hit his girl partner.

Keeler is given plenty of footage for her dancing; perhaps more than any dancer, including Astaire, has been accorded in any one picture thus far. On the hoof she's a girl who can take good care of herself, and in the histrionic moments she's carried along by Jolson's aggressive trouping.

....

■ **GOLD**

1974, 118 MINS, UK ◇ ⓥ

Dir Peter Hunt *Prod* Michael Klinger *Scr* Wilbur Smith, Stanley Price *Ph* Ousama Rawi *Ed* John Glen *Mus* Elmer Bernstein *Art Dir* Alex Vetchinsky, Syd Cain

● Roger Moore, Susannah York, Ray Milland, Bradford Dillman, John Gielgud, Simon Sabela (Hemdale/Avton)

Power of a major physical disaster as theme for an exciting motion picture [based on Wilbur Smith's novel *Goldmine*] is evidenced in this British item, lensed entirely in the South Africa locale of its well-developed narrative. Punishing action is tempered by a modern love story.

Roger Moore plays a tough mine foreman unwittingly manipulated by an unscrupulous gang of financiers who want to flood the mine to raise the price of gold on the world market.

Particular attention has been given to the terrifying underground sequences, and tremendous realism is accomplished in an opening tragedy of men caught in the grip of a sudden flood and later in the climactic flooding.

Moore delivers in pat fashion and Susannah York is a love as the wife of the mine operator who is used by her husband in the web of deceit woven by an international syndicate whom he represents.

....

■ **GOLD DIGGERS OF BROADWAY**

1929, 105 MINS, US ◇

Dir Roy del Ruth *Scr* Robert Lord *Mus* Al Dubin, Joe Burke

● Nancy Welford, Conway Tearle, Winnie Lightner, Ann Pennington, Lilyan Tashman, Nick Lucas (Warner)

Lots of color – Technicolor – lots of comedy, girls, songs, music, dancing, production in *Gold Diggers of Broadway*.

When they got through with [Avery Hopwood's play] *Gold Diggers*, Warners had only the title left. Around that they built another show, on and off stage.

Somebody tossed the picture into Winnie Lightner's lap. Mugging, talking, singing or slapsticking, she can do them all, and does in this picture. Nancy Welford does nicely enough what she has to do.

Next to Lightner in work is her comedy opposite, Albert Gran, as a grey-haired heavyweight lawyer, whom Winnie lands. Lilyan Tashman is an upstage show dame rather well. Helen Foster and William Bakewell are the kids in a very slim love thread.

In the rewritten *Gold Diggers* the love thing is only the alibi. The new story is hung onto it, with just enough of the digging to hold up the title. Well worked out, with plenty of speed all of the time, and color all of the while.

....

■ **GOLD DIGGERS OF 1933**

1933, 94 MINS, US

Dir Mervyn LeRoy, Busby Berkeley *Scr* Erwin Gelsey, James Seymour, David Boehm, Ben Markson *Ph* Sol Polito *Mus* Leo Forbstein (dir.)

● Warren William, Joan Blondell, Aline MacMahon, Ruby Keeler, Dick Powell, Guy Kibbee (Warner)

Gold Diggers makes some sort of screen history in that it's the first of the 'second editions' of film musicals. In 1929 WB made *Gold Diggers of Broadway*. But the real feature of *Gold Diggers of 1933* are the numbers staged by Busby Berkeley.

The film's superiority to *42nd Street* lies in the greater romance interest with a multiplicity of amorous complications wherein Warren William and Joan Blondell, and Guy Kibbee and Aline MacMahon, are paired off as sub-interest to the Ruby Keeler-Dick Powell coupling. The subromances become mild menaces, for William and Kibbee are the Back Bay bluebloods who seek to quell the kid brother's (Powell) stage romance. Kibbee is the family attorney and William the elder brother. They both fall for show girls as well.

Adaptation from the Avery Hopwood-David Belasco-Ina Claire original is as liberal as was the 1929 version. At least, in 1933, they don't have Nick Lucas and Winnie Lightner warble numbers every other minute.

Once the numbers get going, nothing else matters. There are five impressive songs by Al Dubin and Harry Warren.

Some good trouping, especially where expert playing is necessary, to bolster the loose assignments, such as the difficult roles given William and Kibbee. Powell also overcomes the trite situation of the society blueblood with stage ambitions. For the rest, however, Keeler, Blondell and MacMahon are more or less faithful to their characters. Ned Sparks and Ginger Rogers also score.

....

■ **GOLD DIGGERS OF 1935**

1935, 95 MINS, US ⓥ

Dir Busby Berkeley *Scr* Manuel Seff, Robert Lord, Peter Milne *Ph* George Barnes

● Dick Powell, Gloria Stuart, Adolphe Menjou, Glenda Farrell, Grant Mitchell, Alice Brady (First National/Warner)

As in the previous *Diggers*, it's the spec that counts, and the story deficiencies are a bit more acute. Basically, the story lags for an hour before the fashionable charity show, which is the excuse for the spec, commences.

Dick Powell is the affable hotel clerk (no longer a songwriter) who falls for the stingy millionairess' daughter (Gloria Stuart). Frank McHugh, the scapegrace son, who's checked off three chorus-girl wives at the rate of $100,000 settlement to each, is the vis-a-vis of Dorothy Dare.

Adolphe Menjou does the best job as the irascible, chiseling entrepreneur, with Joe Cawthorn as comedy foil. Alice Brady is equally legit and effective in her skinflint assignment. Hugh Herbert's role of an eccentric snuffbox addict is rather hazy.

The Al Dubin-Harry Warren songs this time miss a bit. 'The Words Are In My Heart' is the waltz theme, reprised for the choreography with the baby grands – a highly effective ballet of the Steinways. 'Lullaby of Broadway' is the final musical elaboration. Latter number, led by Winifred Shaw, runs overboard in footage.

....

■ **GOLD DIGGERS OF 1937**

1936, 101 MINS, US

Dir Lloyd Bacon, Busby Berkeley *Scr* Warren Duff *Ph* Arthur Edeson *Mus* Leo F. Forbstein (dir.)

● Dick Powell, Joan Blondell, Victor Moore, Glenda Farrell, Lee Dixon, Osgood Perkins (Warner/First National)

Where some of the *Gold Digger* annuals from Warner have not been overburdened with heavy story material, the current musical opus gets moving with the advantage of a trim backstage yarn taken from *Sweet Mystery of Life*, the Broadway play by Richard Maibaum, Michael Wallace and George Haight.

Cast as a cocksure insurance salesman, Dick Powell breezes through the picture like he had been selling policies all his life. He has four outstanding songs, never overdoes them and breaks through with his ballads at the most opportune times.

Victor Moore enters the picture scene again back at his old trick of show thefting. In the role of the hypochondriac theatrical producer, he is the trouper of old and easily the comedy life of the party. Glenda Farrell, a typical gold-digging chorine in the story, works smoothly and for laughable results opposite the pompous show czar.

Joan Blondell, while not given her customary rowdy role, is effective as the chorine turned stenog. This spots her opposite Dick Powell again, with a modern-day romance deftly introduced and never permitted to go overboard.

....

■ **GOLDEN BRAID**

1990, 91 MINS, AUSTRALIA ◇ ⓥ

Dir Paul Cox *Prod* Paul Cox, Paul Ammitzboll, Santhana K. Naidu *Scr* Paul Cox, Barry Dickins *Ph* Nino Martinetti *Ed* Russell Hurley *Art Dir* Neil Angwin

● Chris Haywood, Gosia Dobrowolska, Paul Chubb, Norman Kaye, Marion Heathfield, Monica Maughan (AFC/Film Victoria/Illumination)

Australia's most interesting auteur, Paul Cox, has often dealt with obsession in his work, and his protagonist here, Bernard (Chris Haywood) fits well and truly into this obsessive pattern. Of Central European extraction, Bernard lives alone among a world of clocks. For him, clocks represent in the passing of time, and he's also haunted by thoughts of aging and death.

Bernard is also, we discover, something of a womanizer, and at present is involved in an affair with Terese (Gosia Dobrowolska), wife of an unsuspecting Salvation Army major (Paul Chubb). The lovers enjoy a guilt-free relationship which cools only when Bernard is sidetracked by a new obsession: a braid of hair he discovers in a 100-year-old, supposedly Venetian, cabinet.

Though the mood of the film – loosely based on a Guy de Maupassant short story – is generally somber, it is leavened by the intensity of its love story. Dobrowolska, in a radiant performance, makes Terese a complex woman whose passion for the reclusive Bernard is seen in sharp contrast to her dying marriage.

....

■ **GOLDEN CHILD, THE**

1986, 93 MINS, US ◇ ⓥ

Dir Michael Ritchie *Prod* Edward S. Feldman, Robert D. Wachs *Scr* Dennis Feldman *Ph* Donald E. Thorin *Ed* Richard A. Harris *Mus* Michel Colombier *Art Dir* J. Michael Riva

● Eddie Murphy, Charles Dance, Charlotte Lewis, Victor Wong, J.L. Reate (Feldman/Meeker/Murphy)

A strange hybrid of Far Eastern mysticism, treacly sentimentality, diluted reworkings of Eddie Murphy's patented confrontation scenes across racial and cultural boundaries, and dragged-in ILM (Industrial Light & Magic) special effects monsters, film makes no sense on any level.

Concoction has Murphy as a social worker specializing in tracking down missing children who is recruited to rescue the virtually

233

divine Golden Child. Eponymous character, a so-called perfect child with magical powers of good, has been kidnapped in an overblown opening sequence by an unmitigated villain portrayed by a bearded Charles Dance, who wears a long leather coat like a Sergio Leone baddie.

Much nonsense ensues involving assorted bikers, chop-socky-happy Orientals and a serpentine sorceress.

. . . .

■ GOLDEN RENDEZVOUS

1977, 103 MINS, US ◇ ⓥ

Dir Ashley Lazarus *Prod* Andre Pieters *Scr* Stanley Price *Ph* Ken Higgins *Ed* Ralph Kemplen
● Richard Harris, Ann Turkel, David Janssen, Burgess Meredith, John Vernon, Gordon Jackson
(Film Trust/Okun/Golden Rendezvous)

Despite an overabundance of plot, deaths, and explosions, there's virtually nothing in this puddle of a mid-ocean thriller that wouldn't make a 12-year-old cringe in embarrassment.

Pic [adapted from an Alistair MacLean novel] tells the tale of the Caribbean Star, a combination cargo ship and floating casino, hijacked by mercenary John Vernon. Following the orders of an unknown mastermind, he and his men, with the aid of an atomic device, plan to exchange the captured passengers and bomb for the golden contents of a US Treasury ship.

And so it goes, albeit not as simply, until First Officer Richard Harris, accompanied by Ann Turkel and Gordon Jackson, step in to save the day.

. . . .

■ GOLDEN VOYAGE OF SINBAD, THE

1974, 105 MINS, UK ◇ ⓥ

Dir Gordon Hessler *Prod* Charles H. Schneer, Ray Harryhausen *Scr* Brian Clemens *Ph* Ted Moore *Ed* Roy Watts *Mus* Miklos Rozsa *Art Dir* John Stoll
● John Phillip Law, Caroline Munro, Tom Baker, Douglas Wilmer, Martin Shaw, Gregoire Aslan (Columbia)

An Arabian Nightish saga told with some briskness and opulence for the childish eye, yet ultimately falling short of implied promise as an adventure spree.

As with producer Charles H. Schneer's *Jason and the Argonauts*, Ray Harryhausen encores as coproducer and special effects collaborator. Among his creations: an animated ship's figurehead, a grotesque centaur, a many-armed religious idol and swordplay adversary, and a couple of small bat-like creatures performing intelligence duty for the black artsy heavy of the piece. Good enough conjuring tricks to impress the kids.

Neither story nor running time are belabored under Gordon Hessler's capable direction. And the play-acting is up to snuff for this kind of throwback, in which John Phillip Law impersonates Sinbad with appealing understatement.

. . . .

■ GOLDFINGER

1964, 112 MINS, UK ◇ ⓥ

Dir Guy Hamilton *Prod* Harry Saltzman, Albert R. Broccoli *Scr* Richard Maibaum, Paul Dehn *Ph* Ted Moore *Ed* Peter Hunt *Mus* John Barry *Art Dir* Ken Adam
● Sean Connery, Honor Blackman, Gert Frobe, Shirley Eaton, Tania Mallet, Harold Sakata (United/Artists/Eon)

There's not the least sign of staleness in this third sample of the Bond 007 formula. Some liberties have been taken with Ian Fleming's original novel but without diluting its flavor. The mood is set before the credits show up, with Sean Connery making an arrogant pass at a chick and spying a thug creeping up from behind; he's reflected in the femme's eyeballs.

So he heaves the heavy into bathful of water and connects it deftly to a handy supply of electricity.

Thereafter the plot gets its teeth into the real business, which is the duel between Bond and Goldfinger. The latter plans to plant an atomic bomb in Fort Knox and thus contaminate the US hoard of the yellow stuff so that it can't be touched, and thus increase tenfold the value of his own gold, earned by hard international smuggling.

Connery repeats his suave portrayal of the punch-packing Bond, who can find his way around the wine-list as easily as he can negotiate a dame. But, if backroom boys got star billing, it's deserved by Ken Adam, who has designed the production with a wealth of enticing invention. There's a ray-gun that cuts through any metal, and threatens to carve Bond down the middle. There's Goldfinger's automobile – cast in solid gold. And his farm is stocked with furniture that moves at the press of a button.

Honor Blackman makes a fine, sexy partner for Bond. As Pussy Galore, Goldfinger's pilot for his private plane, she does not take things lying down – she's a judo expert who throws Bond until the final k.o. when she's tumbled herself.

Gert Frobe, too, is near-perfect casting as the resourceful Goldfinger, an amoral tycoon who treats gold-cornering as a business like any other.

. . . .

■ GOLD OF THE SEVEN SAINTS

1961, 89 MINS, US

Dir Gordon M. Douglas *Prod* Leonard Freeman *Scr* Leigh Brackett, Leonard Freeman *Ph* Joseph Biroc *Ed* Folmar Blangsted *Mus* Howard Jackson *Art Dir* Stanley Fleischer
● Clint Walker, Roger Moore, Leticia Roman, Robert Middleton, Chill Wills, Gene Evans (Warner)

By gold-and-rod western standards this is no *Treasure of the Sierra Madre* by a long shot, but it's a darned good imitation-heir apparent, expertly written and colorfully enacted by a polished cast headed by Clint Walker and Roger Moore.

A strong screenplay is the firm foundation upon which the picture remains erect and engrossing until its disappointingly shaky conclusion. Working with a novel by Steve Frazee, the writers have penned some frisky dialog and constructed several gripping situations. Walker and Moore are cast as trapping partners who strike it rich and are chased persistently over the sprawling desert and through craggy hill country by several marauding parties who have one thing in common – total disdain for the golden rule.

Unlike *Treasure*, this film lays a golden egg through the unconvincing nature and transparent spirit of the climactic laughing jag, for the gold did not corrupt these heroes as it did the gentlemen of *Sierra Madre*.

Utilizing his customary heroically-reserved approach Walker does well by the role of anchor man. Moore, as his faithful but emotionally-unsettled Irish mate, gives a most colorfully compelling screen characterization.

. . . .

■ GOLD RUSH, THE

1925, 120 MINS, US ⊗ ⓥ

Dir Charles Chaplin *Prod* Charles Chaplin *Scr* Charles Chaplin *Ph* Rollie H. Totheroh *Art Dir* Charles D. Hall
● Charles Chaplin, Mack Swain, Tom Murray, Georgia Hale (Chaplin)

The Gold Rush is a distinct triumph for Charlie Chaplin from both the artistic and commercial standpoints. Billed as a dramatic comedy, the story carries more of a plot than the rule with the star's former offerings.

Charlie is presented as a tramp prospector in the wilds of Alaska, garbed in his old familiar derby, cane, baggy pants and shoes. He seeks refuge from a raging Arctic storm in the cabin of Black Larson (Tom Murray), hunted outlaw, and is allowed to stay by the latter.

Big Jim McKay (Mack Swain), a husky prospector, discovers a huge vein of gold on his claim, but the storm uproots his tent and blows him to the hut of Larson. The latter objects to McKay's intrusion, and a struggle ensues between the two for possession of a rifle. Chaplin scores here with business in trying to keep out of line with the barrel of the gun. McKay finally subdues Larson and elects to stay till the storm subsides. But the blizzard continues for many days, and provisions give out.

The final scenes of Charlie and McKay journeying back to the States as multi-millionaires are unusual in that they show Chaplin out of his familiar attire. He is dressed in the height of fashion with evening dress and all the adornments.

Humor is the dominating force, with Chaplin reaching new heights as a comedian. Chaplin naturally carries practically the entire 10 reels of action and performs this task without difficulty.

. . . .

■ GOLD RUSH, THE

1942, 71 MINS, US ⓥ

Dir Charles Chaplin *Prod* Charles Chaplin *Scr* Charles Chaplin *Ph* Rollie Totheroh *Ed* Reginald McGahann *Mus* Charles Chaplin, Max Terr
● Charles Chaplin, Mack Swain, Georgia Hale (United Artists)

With music and narrative dialog added, Charlie Chaplin's *The Gold Rush* [1925] stands the test of time. Chaplin's inimitable cane, derby, hobble and moustache of early days still retain solid comedy for both the younger generation and older folks.

Chaplin did a remarkable job in the editing, background, music and narrative for the new version of his greatest grosser. Original two hours of running time has been edited down to 71 minutes.

Result is a technical achievement in speeding up action of a silent picture to the requirements of sound, and still not making apparent the increased speed in projection.

All the episodes of *Gold Rush* are retained to provide strong comedy reaction of original, like the prospector's cabin marooned in the storm with Chaplin stewing the shoe when food runs out; Chaplin's own narrative is crisply delivered, and he refers to his screen character as 'The Little Fellow' throughout.

. . . .

■ GOLDWYN FOLLIES, THE

1938, 113 MINS, US ◇ ⓥ

Dir George Marshall *Prod* Samuel Goldwyn *Scr* Ben Hecht *Ph* Gregg Toland *Ed* Sherman Todd *Mus* Alfred Newman (dir.) *Art Dir* Richard Day
● Adolphe Menjou, Ritz Brothers, Zorina, Kenny Baker, Andrea Leeds, Ella Logan (Goldwyn/United Artists)

The astute Samuel Goldwyn has assembled top names from grand opera, class terpsichore, music, radio and films. The mixture, in the brilliant hues of Technicolor, turns out to be a lavish production in which certain individual performances and ensembles erase the memory of some dull moments. Four of the musical numbers were composed by the late George Gershwin, with lyrics by Ira Gershwin; Vernon Duke completed the score.

Filmusical is reported to have cost $2 million. It doesn't parade such extravagance on the screen, which probably is due to some heavy blue penciling en route. Not-withstanding, it is a hefty eyeful.

Start shows Adolphe Menjou much concerned that his productions have lost mass appeal – the common touch. Country girl (Andrea Leeds) tells him what's the matter, takes the job of studio censor and passes on the script and casting of the production in progress.

Meanwhile, Edgar Bergen and 'Charlie' wait in the outer office of the casting director and exchange quips on the world as they see it and some of the people in it. The Ritz Bros, owners of a traveling animal circus, drive in the studio gates intent on film careers. Phil Baker dashes from stage to wardrobe in an effort to keep pace with script changes of his part. Jerome Cowan directs the revised version, sequences of which introduce Helen Jepson in scenes from *La Traviata*, and Zorina dances with the American Ballet troupe. That's how all of them, except Kenny Baker, get in front of the camera.

••••••••••••••••••••••••••

■ GONE TO EARTH

1950, 110 MINS, UK ◇

Dir Michael Powell, Emeric Pressburger *Prod* David O. Selznick *Scr* Michael Powell, Emeric Pressburger *Ph* Christopher Challis *Ed* Reginald Mills *Mus* Brian Easdale *Art Dir* Hein Heckroth
● Jennifer Jones, David Farrar, Cyril Cusack, Sybil Thorndike, Edward Chapman, Hugh Griffith (London/ Vanguard)

Powell and Pressburger freely adapted the novel by Mary Webb which has English fox-hunting as its background.

Principal character, Jennifer Jones, lives with her father in the mountains. A simple girl, steeped in local mysticisms, when asked by her father if she will marry the first man to propose, she agrees. The first proposal is from the local parson, but after the wedding, she is induced to run away with the squire and is brought back home by her husband.

Primarily a simple yarn about simple people, it is without finesse, polish or sophistication. Dialog just about emerges from the monosyllabic state.

Jones makes the character of Hazel Woodus a pathetic, winsome creature. It is a genuine and at times glowing performance.

••••••••••••••••••••••••••

■ GONE WITH THE WIND

1939, 217 MINS, US ◇ Ⓥ

Dir Victor Fleming *Prod* David O. Selznick *Scr* Sidney Howard *Ph* Ernest Haller, Ray Rennahan, Wilfrid M. Cline *Ed* Hal. C. Kern, James E. Newcom *Mus* Max Steiner *Prod Des* William Cameron Menzies
● Vivien Leigh, Clark Gable, Olivia de Havilland, Leslie Howard, Hattie McDaniel, Thomas Mitchell (M-G-M/ Selznick)

After nearly a year of actual filming, editing and scoring, David O. Selznick's production of *Gone with the Wind*, from Margaret Mitchell's novel of the Civil War and reconstruction period, is one of the truly great films. The lavishness of its production, the consummate care and skill which went into its making, the assemblage of its fine cast and expert technical staff combine in a theatrical attraction completely justifying the princely investment of $3.9 million.

In the leading roles, the casting of which was the subject of national debate and conjecture for many months, are Clark Gable, as Rhett Butler; Vivien Leigh, who gives a brilliant performance as Scarlett O'Hara; Leslie Howard and Olivia de Havilland, as Ashley and Melanie.

In the desire apparently to leave nothing out, Selznick has left too much in.

As in the book, the most effective portions of the saga of the destroyed South deal with human incident against the background of the war between the states and the impact of honorable defeat to the Southern forces. Director Victor Fleming has caught a series of memorable views of plantation life and

scenes and builds a strong case for a civilization of chivalry.

Among the players, Leigh's Scarlett commands first commendation as a memorable performance, of wide versatility and effective earnestness. Gable's Rhett Butler is as close to Mitchell's conception as might be imagined. He gives a forceful impersonation.

On the heels of these two, Hattie McDaniel, as Mammy, comes closest with a bid for top position as a trouper. It is she who contributes the most moving scene in the film, her plea with Melanie that the latter should persuade Rhett to permit burial of his baby daughter.

Of the other principals, de Havilland does a standout as Melanie, and Howard is convincing as the weak-charactered Ashley.

☐ 1939: Best Picture (Nomination)

••••••••••••••••••••••••••

■ GOODBYE CHARLIE

1964, 117 MINS, US

Dir Vincente Minnelli *Prod* David Weisbart *Scr* Harry Kumitz *Ph* Milton Krasner *Ed* John W. Holmes *Mus* Andre Previn *Art Dir* Jack Martin Smith, Richard Day
● Tony Curtis, Debbie Reynolds, Pat Boone, Joanna Barnes, Ellen Burstyn, Walter Matthau (Venice/20th Century-Fox)

Even by delving into fantasy for its wildly implausible premise this picturization of George Axelrod's not-so-successful 1960 Broadway play doesn't come off as anything but the mildest type of entertainment.

A joint effort of Curtis' indie Venice banner and 20th-Fox, story framework of the David Weisbart production takes form when a hot-shot Hollywood-writer Lothario named Charlie is thoroughly punctured by a gun-wielding Hungarian producer after catching him vis-a-vis with his wife, and writer is reincarnated as a luscious babe.

Debbie Reynolds takes on the task of creating an offbeat character as the reincarnated late-departed who combines the lecherous mind and mores of her former male self with a sexy exterior and newfound femininity while announcing to the world she is the writer's widow.

Tony Curtis plays another writer, victim's best friend who arrives from his Paris home to deliver the eulogy and finds himself saddled not only with a debt-plagued estate, as executor, but this reborn pal as well, now a blonde who decides to cash in on former affairs with filmdom wives and plays cozy with the producer who shot Charlie.

Pat Boone is an over-rich boy with a mother complex who falls for Debbie and wants to marry her, while Walter Matthau puts goulash in the producer role.

••••••••••••••••••••••••••

■ GOODBYE, COLUMBUS

1969, 104 MINS, US ◇ Ⓥ

Dir Larry Peerce *Prod* Stanley R. Jaffe *Scr* Arnold Schulman *Ph* Gerald Hirschfeld *Ed* Ralph Rosenblum *Mus* Charles Fox *Art Dir* Manny Gerard
● Richard Benjamin, Ali MacGraw, Jack Klugman, Nan Martin, Michael Meyers (Paramount/Willow Tree)

This adaptation of Philip Roth's National Book Award-winning novella is sometimes a joy in striking a boisterous mood, and otherwise handling action.

Castwise the feature excels. Richard Benjamin as the boy, a librarian after serving in the army, and Ali MacGraw, making her screen bow as the daughter of wealthy and socially-conscious parents, offer fresh portrayals seasoned with rich humor. Their romance develops swiftly after their meeting at a country-club pool.

As girl's hard-working father, Jack Klugman rates a big hand and there is a dramatic sequence between father and daughter at

wedding of the son of the house which is both tender and memorable.

Several outstanding sequences, among them the gaiety of a Jewish wedding, and hilarious dinner-table action as Benjamin first meets the family.

••••••••••••••••••••••••••

■ GOODBYE GIRL, THE

1977, 110 MINS, US ◇ Ⓥ

Dir Herbert Ross *Prod* Ray Stark *Scr* Neil Simon *Ph* David M. Walsh *Ed* Margaret Booth *Mus* Dave Grusin *Art Dir* Albert Brenner
● Richard Dreyfuss, Marsha Mason, Quinn Cummings, Paul Benedict, Barbara Rhoades, Theresa Merritt (M-G-M/Warner)

Richard Dreyfuss in offbeat romantic lead casting, and vibrant Marsha Mason head the cast as two lovers in spite of themselves.

Story peg finds Mason, once-divorced and now jilted, finding out that her ex-lover has sublet their NY pad to aspiring thesp Dreyfuss. Mason has two other problems: a precocious daughter, Quinn Cummings, and her own thirtyish age which will prevent a successful resumption of a dancing career necessary to make ends meet.

The Neil Simon script evolves a series of increasingly intimate and sensitive character encounters as the adults progress from mutual hostility to an enduring love.

Performances by Dreyfuss, Mason and Cummings are all great, and the many supporting bits are filled admirably.

☐ 1977: Best Picture (Nomination)

••••••••••••••••••••••••••

■ GOODBYE, MR. CHIPS

1939, 110 MINS, UK Ⓥ

Dir Sam Wood *Prod* Victor Saville *Scr* R.C. Sherriff, Claudine West, Eric Maschwitz *Ph* Frederick A. Young *Ed* Charles Frend *Mus* Richard Addinsell *Art Dir* Alfred Junge
● Robert Donat, Greer Garson, John Mills, Lyn Harding, Terry Kilburn (M-G-M)

A charming, quaintly sophisticated account [from the novel *Goodbye, Mr. Chips!* by James Hilton] of the life of a schoolteacher, highlighted by a remarkably fine performance from Robert Donat.

Donat's range of character carries him from youth when he begins to teach at a boys school, through to his middle 30s, then to around the half-century mark, and finally into the slightly doddering age. The character he etches creates a bloodstream for the picture that keeps it intensely alive.

The romance of the schoolteacher and the girl he meets is adroitly and fascinatingly developed. Greer Garson is Katherine, who becomes Donat's wife, only to die all too soon, leaving the schoolmaster nothing but his desire to go forward, with his work and with the boys he tutors.

☐ 1939: Best Picture (Nomination)

••••••••••••••••••••••••••

■ GOODBYE, MR CHIPS

1969, 151 MINS, UK ◇

Dir Herbert Ross *Prod* Arthur P. Jacobs *Scr* Terrence Rattigan *Ph* Oswald Morris *Ed* Ralph Kemplen *Mus* Leslie Bricusse *Art Dir* Ken Adam
● Peter O'Toole, Petula Clark, Michael Redgrave, George Baker, Michael Bryant, Sian Phillips (M-G-M)

Lightning seldom strikes in the same place twice, and Hollywood's record for remaking its classics is only slightly better. M-G-M's reproduction of *Goodbye, Mr Chips* as a big-budget musical with Peter O'Toole and Petula Clark is a sumptuous near-miss that trips on its own overproduction.

The film tells the love story of an English public school master for his work and wife. The scholarly, somewhat prissy and martinetish teacher who frets that his students

235

don't like him is a total departure from O'Toole's previous roles. But there is a curious lack of warmth and humor, a middle-aged bachelor crotchefiness in the opening sequences.

But as he transitions through his troubled love affair and unspectacular career, O'Toole creates a man of strength and dignity, whose tendency to appear ridiculous at times is endearing.

....

■ **GOODBYE PEOPLE, THE**

1984, 104 MINS, US ◇ ⓥ

Dir Herb Gardner   *Prod* David V. Picker   *Scr* Herb Gardner   *Ph* John Lindley   *Ed* Rick Shaine   *Art Dir* Tony Walton

● Judd Hirsch, Martin Balsam, Pamela Reed, Ron Silver, Michael Tucker, Gene Saks (Coney Island)

The Goodbye People marks stage author and director Herb Gardner's first foray into film direction. Based on his late 1960s stage flop of the same name, neither time nor the trans-feral of media has improved the story of three eccentric losers who band together in hopes of changing their luck.

Basically a one-set human comedy, the film centers on Arthur Korman (Judd Hirsch), a man in his 40s trapped in a job he cannot stand. To relieve the tension stemming from his inability to chuck working at a toy firm, he makes a daily early morning excursion to Coney Island to watch the sunrise. It is there he meets Max Silverman (Martin Balsam), the former owner of a boardwalk hot dog stand.

The uneasy alliance between the characters is treated in a glib fashion by Gardner.

....

■ **GOODBYE PORK PIE**

1981, 100 MINS, NZ ◇

Dir Geoff Murphy   *Prod* Geoff Murphy, Nigel Hutchinson   *Scr* Geoff Murphy   *Ph* Alan Bollinger   *Ed* Michael Horton   *Mus* John Charles (dir.)   *Art Dir* Kai Hawkins

● Kelly Johnson, Tony Barry, Claire Oberman (Pork Pie)

In *Goodbye Pork Pie*, *Easy Rider* meets the Keystone Kops. Following the classic road formula a car chase covers the length of the country and it is a major plus that the pace, fun and general mayhem are such that the pic does not get upstaged by the spectacular scenery.

In the breathing spells between, characters that might have been ciphers – the young punk on the run, the girl hitch-hiker and others whose paths intersect the speeding car – are given human dimensions.

Near the top of New Zealand's North Island Kelly Johnson steals a rental car and heads south, picking up a couple of passengers before he has gone very far. One is pursuing the wife who has walked out on him, and he persuades Johnson to extend what was to have been a short dash into a 1,000-mile marathon, taking in a car ferry crossing on the way.

Claire Oberman is a liberated blond whose frank confession that she is a virgin, given in the same breath with which she introduces herself, leads to a private $2 bet between the two men that this will be changed.

....

■ **GOOD COMPANIONS, THE**

1933, 110 MINS, UK

Dir Victor Saville   *Prod* Michael Balcon   *Scr* W. P. Lipscomb   *Ph* Bernard Knowles

● Jessie Matthews, Edmund Gwenn, John Gielgud, Mary Glynne, Percy Parsons, A. W. Baskcomb (Gaumont-British)

Picturization of the J. B. Priestley bestseller was difficult, the story texture being complex.

Story [with songs by George Posford and Douglas Furber] deals with a concert party that goes from bankruptcy to fame and fortune, helped by the stray people who flit across the canvas, the schoolmaster who writes jazz, the fading damsel who finances the show from a thirst for adventure, the little chorus girl who rises to be a great star, and so on.

In comparison to the book, picture may seem sketchy, but the interest is held. Characterizations are outstanding. Edmund Gwenn, as the carpenter who is really the center of the story, does the best bit of work. Mary Glynne is very good as Miss Trant, suggesting the pathetic side of the character with real skill. Jessie Matthews is not as boisterous as usual as the chorus girl.

Max Miller, the music-hall man, contributes an outstanding sketch as a salesman. Victor Saville's direction is straight but sound.

....

■ **GOOD COMPANIONS, THE**

1957, 105 MINS, UK ◇

Dir J. Lee Thompson   *Prod* Hamilton G. Inglis, J. Lee Thompson   *Scr* T.J. Morrison   *Ph* Gilbert Taylor   *Ed* Gordon Pilkington   *Mus* Laurie Johnson   *Art Dir* Robert Jones

● Eric Portman, Celia Johnson, Hugh Griffith, Janette Scott, John Fraser, Rachel Roberts (Associated British)

J.B. Priestley's homely and colorful yarn of a thirdrate touring company makes a pedestrian musical. Much of the characterization and writing quality of the original is lost in the conventional screenplay. An old-fashioned story line, without surprise twists, is not aided by the moderate quality of the score.

Opening shows some promise. In three short cameos it depicts the way in which Eric Portman, Celia Johnson and John Fraser throw in their lot with the Dinky Doos concert party, who are out of funds and facing disbandment. Johnson provides the cash to keep them in business and the rest of the film describes their unhappy experiences playing No. 3 dates to empty houses, until Janette Scott, the youthful star of the company, and Fraser get their big West End chance.

Scott makes a refreshing and appealing showing as the concert party star with ambitions. Fraser also turns in a sincere performance as a composer-accompanist, but it's also hard to accept his music as so good the publishers would be competing for it. Joyce Grenfell makes a typical contribution as a wealthy admirer.

....

■ **GOOD EARTH, THE**

1937, 140 MINS, US ⓥ

Dir Sidney Franklin   *Prod* Albert Lewin   *Scr* Talbot Jennings, Tess Schlesinger, Claudine West   *Ph* Karl Freund   *Ed* Basil Wrangell   *Mus* Herbert Stothart

● Paul Muni, Luise Rainer, Walter Connolly, Tillie Losch, Charley Grapewin, Jessie Ralph (M-G-M)

Transfer of the [Pearl S.] Buck novel from page to celluloid, with a stop-off via the stage [play by Owen and Donald Davis], is a tough adaptation job. The characters are 100% Chinese. In many scenes such occidentals as Paul Muni and Walter Connolly are mixed with genuine Orientals for direct conversational contact, and no harmful false note is struck. Luise Rainer's Viennese amidst this mumble-jumble of dialects is but slightly noticeable, and then only at the beginning.

The marriage of Wang and O-Lan, their raising of the family and care of their land, the drought, Wang's rise to wealth, his desertion of the farm and his taking of a second wife, his return to the farm and the earth are faithfully transcribed. There are some departures for brevity's sake and some additions,

such as the locust plague, which is a helpful contribution rather than a distraction, but the members of the House of Wang are Pearl Buck's original creations without change in this reported $3 million production.

Muni as Wang, with a great makeup, is a splendid lead. Rainer has more difficulty, since her features are not so receptive to Oriental makeup. Yet a good actress overcomes these things, and Luise Rainer is an actress. Connolly as the semi-villainous and greedy uncle, takes the few laughs in a picture which is very sparing with its lightness. Tilly Losch, a dancer by profession, does little dancing, but plenty of good playing, as the second wife, and Charley Grapewin is splendid as the father of Wang.

The slightly tinted and brownish sepia hues, shading some of the farm sequences, give a magnificent effect.

□ 1937: Best Picture (Nomination)

....

■ **GOODFELLAS**

1990, 146 MINS, US ◇ ⓥ

Dir Martin Scorsese   *Prod* Irwin Winkler   *Scr* Nicholas Pileggi, Martin Scorsese   *Ph* Michael Ballhaus   *Ed* Thelma Schoonmaker   *Art Dir* Kristi Zea

● Robert De Niro, Ray Liotta, Joe Pesci, Lorraine Bracco, Paul Sorvino (Warner)

Simultaneously fascinating and repellent, *GoodFellas* is Martin Scorsese's colorful but dramatically unsatisfying inside look at Mafia life in 1955–80 New York City. Working from the non-fiction book *Wiseguy* by Nicholas Pileggi, Scorsese returns to the subject matter of his 1973 *Mean Streets* but from a more distanced, older, wiser and subtler perspective.

First half of the film, introing Ray Liotta, as an Irish-Italian kid, to the Mafia milieu, is wonderful. Scorsese's perfectly cast friezes of grotesque hoodlum types are caricatures in the best sense of the word. There's a giddy sense of exploring a forbidden world.

The second half, however, doesn't develop the dramatic conflicts between the character and the milieu that are hinted at earlier.

Liotta starts as a gofer for laconic neighborhood godfather Paul Sorvino, gradually coming under the tutelage of Robert De Niro, cast as a middle-aged Irish hood of considerable ruthlessness and repute. The skewed concept of loyalty involved is intertwined with an adolescent obsession with machismo, most memorably captured in Joe Pesci's short-statured, short-fused psycho.

One of the film's major flaws is that De Niro, with his menacing charm, always seems more interesting than Liotta, but he isn't given enough screen time to explore the relationship fully in his supporting role.

□ 1990: Best Film (Nomination)

....

■ **GOOD MORNING, VIETNAM**

1987, 120 MINS, US ◇ ⓥ

Dir Barry Levinson   *Prod* Mark Johnson, Larry Brezner   *Scr* Mitch Markowitz   *Ph* Peter Sova   *Ed* Stu Linder   *Mus* Alex North   *Art Dir* Roy Walker

● Robin Williams, Forest Whitaker, Tung Thanh Tran, Chintara Sukapatana, Bruno Kirby (Touchstone/Silver Screen Partners III)

After airman Adrian Cronauer (Robin Williams) blows into Saigon to be the morning man on armed forces radio, things are never the same. With a machine-gun delivery of irreverencies and a crazed gleam in his eye, Cronauer turns the staid military protocol on its ear.

On the air he's a rush of energy, perfectly mimicking everyone from Gomer Pyle to Richard Nixon as well as the working grunt in the battlefields, blasting verboten rock'n'roll over the airwaves while doing James Brown splits in the studio. From the start, the film bowls you over with excitement and for those who can latch on, it's a nonstop ride.

Although the film is set in Vietnam in 1965 the fighting seems to take a backseat to William's joking. Instead of the disk jockey being the eyes and ears of the events around him Williams is a totally self-contained character, and despite numerous topical references, his comedy turns in on itself rather than opening on the scene outside.

Bruno Kirby as Cronauer's uptight immediate superior has a few priceless comic moments of his own as he takes to the airwaves with an array of polka music.

．．．．．．．．．．．．．．．．．．．．．．．．．．．．

■ GOOD NEIGHBOR SAM

1964, 130 MINS, US ◇ Ⓥ

Dir David Swift   *Prod* David Swift   *Scr* James Fritzell, Everett Greenbaum, David Swift   *Ph* Burnett Guffey   *Ed* Charles Nelson   *Mus* Frank DeVol   *Art Dir* Dale Hennesy

● Jack Lemmon, Romy Schneider, Dorothy Provine, Michael Connors (Columbia)

Jack Lemmon's farcial flair finds amusing exposure in this situation comedy. Lemmon topbills star lineup in his usual competent and zany fashion but it is the Viennese Romy Schneider, making her first Hollywood-lensed feature, who shines the brightest.

Narrative [based on the novel by Jack Finney] jumps with crazy, mixed-up situations, Lemmon playing low man on the totem pole of a San Francisco advertising agency until he suggests a new approach built around the average man in a campaign for a dissatisfied client about to ankle agency. Suddenly, he is important business-wise. He also finds himself called upon to play the 'husband' to his nextdoor neighbour, who is divorced and must come up with a spouse if she is to meet the provisions of her grandfather's will in bequeathing her his $15 million estate.

Edward G. Robinson gets chuckles as the client, who demands a wholesome campaign and a wholesome man to conduct it.

．．．．．．．．．．．．．．．．．．．．．．．．．．．．

■ GOOD WIFE, THE

1986, 92 MINS, AUSTRALIA ◇ Ⓥ

Dir Ken Cameron   *Prod* Jan Sharp   *Scr* Peter Kenna   *Ph* James Bartle   *Ed* John Scott   *Mus* Cameron Allan   *Art Dir* Sally Campbell

● Rachel Ward, Bryan Brown, Sam Neill, Steven Vidler (Laughing Kookaburra)

Ken Cameron's third feature, *The Good Wife* is a classy romantic drama set in the small Australian country town of Corrimandel in 1939. Rachel Ward toplines as the eponymous wife who's bored with her unexciting life in this rural backwater. She's married to a burly, well-intentioned logger (real-life hubby Bryan Brown) and spends her time cooking, cleaning and helping other women in childbirth; part of her problem is that she's childless herself.

Neville Gifford (Sam Neill) arrives in town. Marge becomes more and more obsessed with the handsome stranger, eventually openly chasing after him, bringing scandal and shame on herself and her uncomprehending spouse. Fine performances from Ward, Brown and Neill.

．．．．．．．．．．．．．．．．．．．．．．．．．．．．

■ GOONIES, THE

1985, 111 MINS, US ◇ Ⓥ

Dir Richard Donner   *Prod* Richard Donner, Harvey Bernhard   *Scr* Chris Columbus   *Ph* Nick McLean   *Ed* Michael Kahn   *Mus* Dave Grusin   *Art Dir* J. Michael Riva

● Sean Astin, Josh Brolin, Jeff Cohen, Corey Feldman, Kerri Green, Martha Plimpton (Amblin)

Territory is typical small town Steven Spielberg; this time set in a coastal community in

Oregon. Story is told from the kids' point-of-view and takes a rather long time to be set in motion.

Brothers Mikey (Sean Astin) and Brand (Josh Brolin) are being forced to leave their home because land developers are foreclosing on their house to build a new country club. The boys are joined by compulsive eater Chuck (Jeff Cohen) and mumbling Mouth (Corey Feldman) for one final adventure together.

Searching through the attic holding museum pieces under the care of their curator father, the boys uncover a pirate treasure map. Sidetracked only temporarily by the nefarious Fratelli family (Robert Davi, Joe Pantoliano, Anne Ramsey), the boys begin their fairy tale treasure hunt.

The pirate One-Eyed Willie, it seems, was no one's fool; he left a deadly obstacle course to the treasure.

Linking the kids together is their identification as 'Goonies', residents of the boondocks. Handle apparently imbues them with a mystical bond and idealized state of grace.

．．．．．．．．．．．．．．．．．．．．．．．．．．．．

■ GORGEOUS HUSSY, THE

1936, 103 MINS, US

Dir Clarence Brown   *Prod* Joseph L. Mankiewicz   *Scr* Ainsworth Morgan, Stephen Morehouse Avery   *Ph* George Folsey   *Ed* Blanche Sewell   *Mus* Herbert Stothart   *Art Dir* Cedric Gibbons, William A. Horning

● Joan Crawford, Robert Taylor, Lionel Barrymore, Franchot Tone, Melvyn Douglas, James Stewart (M-G-M)

Picture is primarily Lionel Barrymore's, and not particularly because the character of Andrew Jackson he portrays calls for it. His tenderness towards his backwoods wife, his rough-and-ready fighting spirit in the campaign for presidency, his opening address to Congress, his sorrow over his wife's death and his bitter encounter with his cabinet – all are portrayed with acting acumen.

Joan Crawford figures in four love affairs, two of which are prominent in the picture and two of which result in marriage. Her first two sweethearts are Robert Taylor and Melvyn Douglas, and later James Stewart is spotted as a suitor. Last in the line is Franchot Tone, the cabinet member she is married to at the finish.

Title [from the novel by Samuel Hopkins] obtains from the fact that the daughter of a tavern keeper (sneeringly called the Gorgeous Hussy) is the childhood friend of Andrew Jackson and his wife. When the latter dies, she promises to remain by Andy's side while he is President.

Crawford makes her debut in a costumer. Role naturally is more subdued and confining than generally associated with her. But she fills the role and the billing.

Melvyn Douglas, as John Randolph, the state-righter Virginian senator, clicks strongly. Next to Barrymore's, his is the film's striking portrayal. Tone contributes a smooth job as the war secretary who wins Joan as his bride after her first husband is killed in action. Stewart isn't given many opportunities but makes something of them.

．．．．．．．．．．．．．．．．．．．．．．．．．．．．

■ GORILLAS IN THE MIST

1988, 129 MINS, US ◇ Ⓥ

Dir Michael Apted   *Prod* Arnold Glimcher, Terence Clegg   *Scr* Anna Hamilton Phelan   *Ph* John Seale   *Ed* Stuart Baird   *Mus* Maurice Jarre   *Art Dir* John Graysmark

● Sigourney Weaver, Bryan Brown, Julie Harris, John Omirah Miluwi, Iain Cuthbertson (Guber-Peters/Glimcher)

The life story of the late anthropologist Dian Fossey posed considerable challenges to the filmmakers tackling it, and they have been

met in admirable fashion in *Gorillas in the Mist* [based on Fossey's work and an article by Harold T.P. Hayes].

Fossey devoted nearly 20 years to observing, and trying to protect, the gorillas who live in a small area in the Virunga mountain range, which extends into Rwanda, where Fossey established her Karisoke Research Center. Thanks to National Geographic and films made by Bob Campbell, her work became internationally known, but she alienated a number of people, and was murdered in 1985. (Although her research assistant was convicted in absentia, many feel guilt lies elsewhere.)

After a while, just as Fossey began making unprecedented physical contact with these imposing animals, Sigourney Weaver seems to establish an exceptional familiarity and rapport with the jungle inhabitants. The intense bond makes the later scenes relating to the gorilla slaughter by poachers all the more powerful.

Campbell, played by Bryan Brown, turns up unannounced to photograph her activities and, after initial resistance, Fossey not only welcomes his presence but takes the married man as her lover.

Weaver is utterly believable and riveting in the role. Her scenes with the apes are captivating. Brown lends a nice lilt to his sympathetic interloper. Lensed high in the mountains of Rwanda, the production looks impressive.

．．．．．．．．．．．．．．．．．．．．．．．．．．．．

■ GORKY PARK

1983, 128 MINS, US ◇ Ⓥ

Dir Michael Apted   *Prod* Gene Kirkwood, Howard W. Koch Jr   *Scr* Dennis Potter   *Ph* Ralf D. Bode   *Ed* Dennis Virkler   *Mus* James Horner   *Art Dir* Paul Sylbert

● William Hurt, Lee Marvin, Brian Dennehy, Ian Bannen, Joanna Pacula, Michael Elphick (Orion)

There's enough menace and romance in *Gorky Park* to appeal to many, especially those helped by the memory of Martin Cruz Smith's successful novel.

At the center, however, William Hurt is superb as a Moscow militia detective caught between his desires to be simply a good cop and the unfathomable motives of the secret Soviet government, all complicated by an unexpected love for Joanna Pacula.

Director Michael Apted sets Hurt up well with the discovery of three mutilated, faceless bodies in the city's Gorky Park, leading Hurt to suspect this is all the affair of the dangerous KGB and much to be avoided by plodding policemen such as himself.

Very quickly, Hurt's investigation brings him into contact with Lee Marvin, a wealthy American who enjoys high privilege in important Soviet circles, obviously not simply because he's a successful trader in sables.

Apted, cinematographer Ralf D. Bode and production designer Paul Sylbert do an excellent job in making Helsinki stand in for Moscow, where they were denied access for filming.

．．．．．．．．．．．．．．．．．．．．．．．．．．．．

■ GO TELL THE SPARTANS

1978, 114 MINS, US ◇ Ⓥ

Dir Ted Post   *Prod* Allan F. Bodoh, Mitchell Cannold   *Scr* Wendell Mayes   *Ph* Harry Stradling Jr   *Ed* Millie Moore   *Mus* Dick Halligan   *Art Dir* Jack Senter

● Burt Lancaster, Craig Wasson, Jonathan Goldsmith, Marc Singer, Joe Unger, Dennis Howard (Spartan)

A good war film needs heroes. But Vietnam had no heroes in the eyes of most Americans. Even a reasonably well-made and well-acted earnest effort like *Go Tell The Spartans*, set in 1964 when the US involvement was limited to 'military advisors', can't overcome that disadvantage.

Based on Daniel Ford's novel, *Incident at Muc Wa*, Wendell Mayes' script follows a detachment of Americans and Vietnamese mercenaries as they occupy an outpost abandoned by the French a decade ago. Burt Lancaster is the commander of an advisory group at Penang who must order the raw detachment into the jungle. When the Vietcong move in on the soldiers, Lancaster arranges for their evacuation.

Lancaster leads a mostly untried cast, including Marc Singer as his assistant, Jonathan Goldsmith playing a burned-out veteran, Joe Unger as a naive over-zealous lieutenant on his first mission and Evan Kim as the tough leader of the Vietnam mercenaries. All turn in fine performances.

．．．．．．．．．．．．．．．．．．．．．．．．．．．．．．

■ **GOTHIC**

1986, 90 MINS, UK ◇ ⓥ

Dir Ken Russell   *Prod* Penny Corke   *Scr* Stephen Volk   *Ph* Mike Southon   *Ed* Michael Bradsell   *Mus* Thomas Dolby   *Art Dir* Christopher Hobbs

● Gabriel Byrne, Julian Sands, Natasha Richardson, Myriam Cyr, Timothy Spall, Andreas Wisniewski (Virgin)

Ken Russell's films always have been very much an acquired taste, but with *Gothic* he is back to his theatrically extravagant best.

Set on a stormy June night in 1816 at the Villa Diodati in Switzerland, the drug-induced excesses of the poet Byron (Gabriel Byrne) and his four guests inspire both Mary Shelley to write *Frankenstein* and Dr Polidori *The Vampyre*, two gothic horrror classics.

As the group becomes more drug-soaked and terrified, the villa with its darkened passages, spiral staircases, shuttered rooms, and menacing candlelight, becomes a labyrinth of horror.

Ken Russell has made an unrelenting nightmare that is both uncomfortable and compulsive to watch. Gabriel Byrne and Natasha Richardson, as Mary Shelley, are powerful and hold the film together.

．．．．．．．．．．．．．．．．．．．．．．．．．．．．．．

■ **GO WEST**

1940, 79 MINS, US ⓥ

Dir Edward Buzzell   *Prod* Jack Cummings   *Scr* Irving Brecher   *Ph* Leonard Smith   *Ed* Blanche Sewell   *Art Dir* Cedric Gibbons, Stan Rogers

● Groucho Marx, Harpo Marx, Chico Marx, John Carroll, Diana Lewis, Walter Woolf King (M-G-M)

The three Marx Bros ride a merry trail of laughs and broad burlesque in a speedy adventure through the sagebrush country. Story is only a slight framework on which to parade the generally nonsensical antics of the trio. Attracted to the wide open spaces by tales of gold lining the street, Chico, Harpo, and Groucho get involved in ownership of a deed to property wanted by the railroad for its western extension, and the action flashes through typical dance hall, rumbling stagecoach and desert waste episodes – with a wild train ride for a climax to outwit the villains.

Material provided by tightly knit script is topnotch while direction by Edward Buzzell smacks over the gags and comedy situations for maximum laughs. The Marxes secured pre-production audience reaction through tour of key picture houses trying out various sequences, which undoubtedly aided in tightening the action and dialog.

Groucho, Chico and Harpo handle their assignments with zestful enthusiasm. There's a bill-changing routine in Grand Central Station, wild melee and clowning in the rolling stagecoach, and the train chase for a finish that winds up with the upper car structures dismantled by the silent Harpo to provide fuel for the engine. It's all ridiculous, but tuned for fun.

．．．．．．．．．．．．．．．．．．．．．．．．．．．．．．

■ **GRADUATE, THE**

1967, 105 MINS, US ◇ ⓥ

Dir Mike Nichols   *Prod* Lawrence Turman   *Scr* Calder Willingham, Buck Henry   *Ph* Robert Surtees   *Ed* Sam O'Steen   *Mus* Dave Grusin   *Art Dir* Richard Sylbert

● Anne Bancroft, Dustin Hoffman, Katharine Ross, William Daniels, Murray Hamilton, Elizabeth Wilson (Embassy)

The Graduate is a delightful, satirical comedy-drama about a young man's seduction by an older woman, and the measure of maturity which he attains from the experience. Anne Bancroft, Katharine Ross and Dustin Hoffman head a very competent cast.

An excellent screenplay, based on the Charles Webb novel, focuses on Hoffman, just out of college and wondering what it's all about. Predatory Bancroft, wife of Murray Hamilton, introduces Hoffman to mechanical sex, reaction to which evolves into true love with Ross, Bancroft's daughter.

In the 70 minutes which elapse from Hoffman's arrival home from school to the realization by Ross that he has had an affair with her mother, pic is loaded with hilarious comedy and, because of this, the intended commentary on materialistic society is most effective.

Only in the final 35 minutes, as Hoffman drives up and down the LA-Frisco route in pursuit of Ross, does film falter in pacing, result of which the switched-on cinematics become obvious, and therefore tiring.

☐ 1967: Best Picture (Nomination)

．．．．．．．．．．．．．．．．．．．．．．．．．．．．．．

■ **GRAND HOTEL**

1932, 105 MINS, US ⓥ

Dir Edmund Goulding   *Scr* William A. Drake   *Ph* William Daniels   *Ed* Blanche Sewell

● Greta Garbo, John Barrymore, Joan Crawford, Wallace Beery, Lionel Barrymore, Jean Hersholt (M-G-M)

Better than just a good transcription of the Vicki Baum stage play. Story is many angled in characters and incidents. There is the romantic grip of the actress-nobleman lovers; there is the triumph of the underdog in the figure of Kringelein, the humble bookkeeper doomed to approaching death and determined to spend his remaining days in a splurge of luxury in the Grand Hotel; and there is the everlasting Cinderella element in the not-so-good stenographer who at last finds a friend and protector in the dying Kringelein.

First honors again go to Lionel Barrymore for an inspired performance as the soon-to-die bookkeeper. Greta Garbo gives the role of the dancer something of artificiality, risking a trace of acting swagger, sometimes stagey. Her clothes are ravishing in the well-known Garbo style.

John Barrymore is back where he belongs as the down-at-heel but glamorous baron, going about debonairly in a career of crime but with a heart of gold that will not stoop to small meanness.

There remains the stenographer Miss Flaemmchen, not the most fortunate casting for Joan Crawford, who is rather too capable a type to successfully play an unhappy plaything of fate.

Wallace Beery is at home in the part of the German industrialist, a grandiose but pathetic figure in his struggles with business rivals.

☐ 1931/32: Best Picture

．．．．．．．．．．．．．．．．．．．．．．．．．．．．．．

■ **GRAND PRIX**

1966, 179 MINS, US ◇ ⓥ

Dir John Frankenheimer   *Prod* Edward Lewis   *Scr* Robert Alan Aurthur   *Ph* Lionel Lindon   *Ed* Fredric Steinkamp, Henry Berman, Stewart Linder, Frank Santillo   *Mus* Maurice Jarre   *Art Dir* Richard Sylbert

● James Garner, Eva Marie Saint, Yves Montand, Toshiro Mifune, Brian Bedford, Jessica Walter (Douglas & Lewis/M-G-M)

The roar and whine of engines sending men and machines hurtling over the 10 top road and track courses of Europe, the US and Mexico – the Grand Prix circuits – are the prime motivating forces of this action-crammed adventure that director John Frankenheimer and producer Edward Lewis have interlarded with personal drama that is sometimes introspectively revealing, occasionally mundane, but generally a most serviceable framework.

Frankenheimer has shrewdly varied the length and the importance of the races that figure in the film and the overplay of running commentary on the various events, not always distinct above the roar of motors, imparts a documentary vitality. The director, moreover, frequently divides his outsized screen into sectional panels for a sort of montage interplay of reactions of the principals – a stream of consciousness commentary – that adroitly prevents the road running from overwhelming the personal drama.

There is a curious thing, however, about the exposition of the characters in this screenplay. Under cold examination they are stock characters. James Garner, American competitor in a field of Europeans, is somewhat taciturn, unencumbered by marital involvement. Yves Montand has a wife in name and forms a genuine attachment for American fashion writer Eva Marie Saint, a divorcee. Brian Bedford is the emotionally confused Britisher competing against the memory of his champion-driver brother and whose compulsion to be a champion almost wrecks his marriage to whilom American actress-model Jessica Walter.

．．．．．．．．．．．．．．．．．．．．．．．．．．．．．．

■ **GRAPES OF WRATH, THE**

1940, 129 MINS, US ⓥ

Dir John Ford   *Prod* Darryl F. Zanuck   *Scr* Nunnally Johnson   *Ph* Gregg Toland   *Ed* Robert Simpson   *Mus* Alfred Newman   *Art Dir* Richard Day, Mark-Lee Kirk

● Henry Fonda, Jane Darwell, John Carradine, Charlie Grapewin, Dorris Bowdon, John Qualen (20th Century-Fox)

It took courage, a pile of money and John Ford to film the story of the dust bowl and the tribulations of its unhappy survivors, who sought refuge in inhospitable California. *The Grapes of Wrath*, adapted by Nunnally Johnson from John Steinbeck's best-seller, is an absorbing, tense melodrama, starkly realistic, and loaded with social and political fireworks. The film interprets the consequences of national disaster in terms of a family group – the Joads – who left their quarter-section to the wind and dust and started cross-country in an over-laden jalopy to the land of plenty.

It is not a pleasant story, and the pictured plight of the Joads, and hundreds of other dust bowl refugee families, during their frantic search for work in California, is a shocking visualization of a state of affairs demanding generous humanitarian attention. Neither book nor film gives any edge to citizens of California who are working diligently to alleviate suffering and conditions not of their origination. Steinbeck offers no suggestion. In this respect the film ends on a more hopeful note. Someway, somehow, Ma Joad declares 'the people' will solve the unemployment riddle.

It is all on the screen – everything except the unpalatable Steinbeck dialog, and such other portions of the book which good taste exclude. The characters are there, and under Ford's direction a group of actors makes them into living people, whose frustration catches at the heart and throat. There is humor, too, but the film as a whole scores as a gripping experience.

Henry Fonda does a swell job as Tom and John Carradine is excellent as Casey, the reformed preacher. Jane Darwell gives the family strength and leadership in the mother part. Charley Grapewin's grandpa is rich in humor and tragedy.
□ 1940: Best Picture (Nomination)

GRASSHOPPER, THE

1970, 96 MINS, US ◇ ⓥ
Dir Jerry Paris *Prod* Jerry Belson, Garry Marshall *Scr* Jerry Belson, Garry Marshall *Ph* Sam Leavitt *Ed* Aaron Stell *Mus* Billy Goldenberg *Art Dir* Tambi Larsen
● Jacqueline Bisset, Jim Brown, Joseph Cotten, Corbett Monica, Ramon Bieri, Christopher Stone (National General)

The Grasshopper is the dark side of the Hollywood story, every schoolgirl's American Dream gone sour [from the novel *The Passing of Evil* by Mark McShane]. Jacqueline Bisset is the good-looking, well-built, lively chick, bored with a bankteller's job and the prospects of a middle-class husband, suburban home and kids, who is attracted by the tinsel of Las Vegas.

Attractive and busty enough to make the chorus, but neither talented nor ambitious enough to go beyond, she drifts into a bad marriage, being kept by a rich old man and then into outright hustling, having run the gamut by age 22.

Bisset is on camera for almost the entire film, kept carefully within her dramatic depth by Director Jerry Paris, with unexpected outbreaks of a kooky humor.

GRAY LADY DOWN

1978, 111 MINS, US ◇ ⓥ
David Greene *Prod* Walter Mirisch *Scr* James Whittaker, Howard Sackler *Ph* Steven Larner *Ed* Robert Swink *Mus* Jerry Fielding *Art Dir* William Tuntke
● Charlton Heston, David Carradine, Stacy Keach, Ned Beatty, Stephen McHattie, Ronny Cox (Mirisch/Universal)

Charlton Heston is back in jeopardy. He's 60 miles off the coast of Connecticut stuck with 41 other sailors on the edge of an ocean canyon in a nuclear submarine, waiting for Stacy Keach to organize a rescue mission. If Keach doesn't hurry one of three disasters will soon happen: water pressure will crush the sub's hull, oxygen will run out, or the boat will slip off the ledge.

David Carradine and Ned Beatty enter the scene after Heston and crew suffer a pair of double setbacks. First their surfacing vessel is rammed by a Norwegian freighter and plunges straight down. Then an earth tremor covers the sub's escape hatch.

Up to this point things are fairly routine [in a story based on the novel *Event 1000* by David Lavallee]. Heston looks courageous; Ronny Cox, the second in command, freaks out; some crew members get sick, and a handful die; Heston's on-shore wife is informed of her husband's condition and adopts a visage of sadness; Keach, a very formal officer, promises Heston and crew that everything will be all right.

But the second disaster – the escape hatch burial – calls for special action. Enter Carradine, a subdued Navy captain and inventor of an experimental diving vessel known as the Snark, and his assistant, Beatty. They resemble a disaster movie's Laurel and Hardy. They're a nice twist.

GREASE

1978, 110 MINS, US ◇ ⓥ
Dir Randal Kleiser *Prod* Robert Stigwood, Allan Carr *Scr* Bronte Woodard, Allan Carr *Ph* Bill Butler *Ed* John F. Burnett *Mus* Bill Oakes (sup.) *Art Dir* Phillip Jefferies
● John Travolta, Olivia Newton-John, Stockard Channing, Jeff Conaway, Didi Conn, Jamie Donnelly (Paramount)

Grease has got it, from the outstanding animated titles of John Wilson all the way through the rousing finale as John Travolta and Olivia Newton-John ride off into teenage happiness.

Allan Carr is credited with adapting the 1950s style legituner of Jim Jacobs and Warren Casey, which Bronte Woodward then fashioned into an excellent screenplay that moves smartly. Director Randal Kleiser and choreographer Patricia Birch stage the sequences with aplomb, providing as necessary the hoke, hand or heart appropriate to the specific moment.

Plot tracks the bumpy romantic road of Travolta and Newton-John, whose summer beach idyll sours when he feels he must revert to finger-snapping cool in the atmosphere of the high school they both wind up attending. Stockard Channing provides a nice contrast to Newton-John in a hard but really nice characterization. Jeff Conaway is very good as the type guy for whom Travolta is a natural leader.

GREASE 2

1982, 114 MINS, US ◇ ⓥ
Dir Patricia Birch *Prod* Robert Stigwood, Allan Carr *Scr* Ken Finkleman *Ph* Frank Stanley *Ed* John F. Burnett *Mus* Louis St Louis (arr.) *Art Dir* Gene Callahan
● Maxwell Caulfield, Michelle Pfeiffer, Adrian Zmed, Christopher McDonald, Peter Frechette, Leif Green (Paramount)

It's 1961 now at Rydell High, a becalmed, upbeat time when JFK's photo has replaced Ike's on the school wall. In fact, hardly anything is happening socially or musically.

It's not even a question of will boy get girl, but how. Gorgeous Michelle Pfeiffer plays the leader of the foxy Pink Ladies, whose members are only supposed to go out with greasers from the T-Birds gang. Maxwell Caulfield, fresh from England and complete with accent, is the new boy in school, and it's made clear to him that Michelle is off limits until he proves himself as a leather-clad biker.

Where this film has a decided edge on its predecessor is in the staging and cutting of the musical sequences. Choreographer and director Patricia Birch has come up with some unusual settings (a bowling alley, a bomb shelter) for some of the scenes, and employs some sharp montage to give most of the songs and dances a fair amount of punch.

Pfeiffer is all anyone could ask for in the looks department, and she fills Olivia Newton-John's shoes and tight pants very well, thank you. Caulfield is a less certain choice.

GREASED LIGHTNING

1977, 96 MINS, US ◇ ⓥ
Dir Michael Schultz *Prod* Hannah Weinstein *Scr* Kenneth Vose, Lawrence DuKore, Melvin Van Peebles, Leon Capetanos *Ph* George Bouillet *Ed* Bob Wyman, Christopher Holmes, Randy Roberts *Mus* Fred Karlin *Art Dir* Jack Senter
● Richard Pryor, Beau Bridges, Pam Grier, Cleavon Little, Vincent Gardenia, Richie Havens (Third World)

Greased Lightning is a pleasant, loose and relaxed comedy starring Richard Pryor in an excellent characterization based on real-life racing driver Wendell Scott.

Beau Bridges plays a redneck driver who befriends Pryor's stolid efforts to break the color barrier in car racing. Pam Grier is smashingly decorous but wasted in a supportive wife role, while Cleavon Little is cast as Pryor's close friend.

Story covers about 25 years, from Pryor's release from Second World War Army service to championship race in 1971.

Another virtue of the film is its discreet conveyance of an important theme: In any large society, progress by any minority group is accomplished through particular individuals doing notable things.

GREAT AMERICAN BROADCAST, THE

1941, 90 MINS, US ◇ ⓥ
Dir Archie Mayo *Prod* Kenneth Macgowan *Scr* Don Ettlinger, Edwin Blum, Robert Ellis, Helen Logan *Ph* Leon Shamroy *Ed* Robert Simpson *Mus* Alfred Newman (dir.)
● Alice Faye, Jack Oakie, John Payne, Cesar Romero (20th Century-Fox)

The Great American Broadcast is light and breezy, a showmanly admixture of comedy, romance, drama and music woven around the extraordinary progress of radio broadcasting during the 1920s. Scripters fudge a few years in setting the year of the Dempsey-Willard heavyweight battle in Toledo. Original shots of the fight are utilized to accompany the radio account.

Picture has many attributes on the entertainment side despite its thin and sketchy story. Most prominent is the breezy and zestful performance of Jack Oakie, who works energetically throughout and holds audience attention every minute he is on the screen.

Story details the adventures of Oakie, John Payne, Faye and Cesar Romero as early pioneers in radio broadcasting. Oakie tinkers with a crystal set in his room, idea-minded Payne gets enthusiastic over wireless entertainment possibilities, Faye is radio's first singing star, and Romero supplies the early coin.

Direction by Archie Mayo carries the pace at good speed, and injects many surefire touches for laugh attention.

GREAT BALLS OF FIRE!

1989, 108 MINS, US ◇ ⓥ
Dir Jim McBride *Prod* Adam Fields *Scr* Jack Baran, Jim McBride *Ph* Affonso Beato *Ed* Lisa Day, Pembroke Herring, Bert Lovitt *Mus* Jack Baran, Jim McBride *Art Dir* David Nichols
● Dennis Quaid, Winona Ryder, John Doe, Stephen Tobolowsky, Trey Wilson (Orion)

Rock 'n' roll and its legendary characters have always been a tempting subject for filmmakers, but rare is the non-documentary that adds anything to the music. *Great Balls of Fire!* is no exception. It's a thin, cartoonish treatment of the hellbent, musically energetic young Jerry Lee Lewis.

Full-bore performance by Dennis Quaid as the kinetic piano-pumper stops at surface level, and 108 minutes of his gum-cracking smirks and cock-a-doodle-doo dandyism are hard to take.

Pic focuses on the years 1956-59, when Lewis' career took off with the provocative hit 'Whole Lotta Shakin' Goin' On' and was nearly destroyed by his marriage to 13-year-old cousin, Myra Gayle Brown (Winona Ryder), which shocked British fans and cut short his first overseas tour.

Mixed up in the Memphis milieu are the presence of Elvis Presley, who preceded Lewis at Sun Studios; Jimmy Swaggart, Lewis' Bible-thumping cousin; and the heady, devilish allure of the jumpin' black juke joints from which Lewis lifts his best music.

Script is based on a book by Myra Lewis and is by-the-numbers, suffering from a lack of grace or metaphor and relying on cash and flash as character motivations.

. . . .

■ **GREAT CARUSO, THE**

1951, 109 MINS, US ◇ Ⓥ

Dir Richard Thorpe   *Prod* Joe Pasternak, Jesse L. Lasky   *Scr* Sonya Levien, William Ludwig   *Ph* Joseph Ruttenberg   *Ed* Gene Ruggiero   *Mus* Johnny Green (sup.)   *Art Dir* Cedric Gibbons, Gabriel Scognamillo

● Mario Lanza, Ann Blyth, Dorothy Kirsten, Jarmila Novotna, Richard Hageman, Carl Benton Reid (M-G-M)

This highly fictionalized, sentimental biog of the late, great Metropolitan Opera tenor, Enrico Caruso, handsomely mounted in Technicolor, has a lot of popular ingredients, including a boy-and-girl-vs-disapproving-parent romance, the draw of Caruso's rep, glamor of the Met, a host of surefire, familiar operatic arias, and the pull of Mario Lanza.

Otherwise, the film is a superficial pic, bearing little relationship to Caruso's actual story, which was a much more dramatic one than emerges here. There are strong omissions and some falsifications.

Story is a casual recital of part of Caruso's career, with a few, brief scenes of him as a young Neapolitan cafe singer, then his quick rise as tenor in Milan, London, and other European music capitals, and his triumphs at the NY Met. The film centers early on Caruso's romance with Dorothy Benjamin, his difficulty with her father and their happy marriage. It shows him in some of his Met successes and touches briefly on his breakdown and death.

Lanza is handsome, personable and has a brilliant voice. He's a lyric tenor, like Caruso; has his stocky build, his Italianate quality and some of his flair. Dorothy Kirsten, who plays a Met soprano befriending Caruso, is a good actress as well as a gifted singer.

. . . .

■ **GREAT CATHERINE**

1968, 98 MINS, UK ◇

Dir Gordon Flemyng   *Prod* Jules Buck, Peter O'Toole   *Scr* Hugh Leonard   *Ph* Oswald Morris   *Ed* Anne V. Coates   *Mus* Dimitri Tiomkin   *Art Dir* John Bryan

● Peter O'Toole, Zero Mostel, Jeanne Moreau, Jack Hawkins, Akim Tamiroff, Kenneth Griffith (Warner/Seven Arts)

A foreword to this film, based on a George Bernard Shaw play, reads: 'Mr. Shaw stated that historical portraiture was not the motive of this story and the producers would like to add that any similarity to any historical event will be nothing short of a miracle'.

Atmosphere it has, mammoth and impressive sets, Zero Mostel as a wildman like you've never seen, Peter O'Toole as a stuffy Englishman like you've never imagined, all wrapped around the amorous yearnings of Catherine of Russia.

This is a souped-up version of the Russian Empress' romantics, focused on her going on the make for a slightly-imbecilic English Light Dragoons captain. Jeanne Moreau essays Catherine with humor.

O'Toole, as the beaddled captain on his way to seek an audience with the Empress, and finding himself tossed on her bed by Mostel, in a mad-Russian character, lends credence through underplaying his role.

. . . .

■ **GREAT DICTATOR, THE**

1940, 127 MINS, US Ⓥ

Dir Charles Chaplin   *Prod* Charles Chaplin   *Scr* Charles Chaplin   *Ph* Karl Struss, Roland Totheroh   *Ed* Willard Nico   *Mus* Meredith Willson   *Art Dir* J. Russell Spencer

● Charles Chaplin, Paulette Goddard, Jack Oakie, Reginald Gardiner, Henry Daniell, Billy Gilbert (Chaplin/United Artists

Chaplin makes no bones about his utter contempt for dictators like Hitler and Mussolini in his production of *The Great Dictator*. He takes time out to make fun about it, but the preachment is strong, notably in the six-minute speech at the finish.

Chaplin speaks throughout the film, but wherever convenient depends as much as he can on pantomime. His panto has always talked plenty.

Chaplin plays a dual role, that of a meek little Jewish barber in Tomania and the great little dictator of that country, billed as Hynkel. It's when he is playing the dictator that the comedian's voice raises the value of the comedy content of the picture to great heights. He does various bits as a Hitler spouting at the mouth in which he engages in a lot of double talk in what amounts to a pig-Latin version of the German tongue, with grunts thrown in here and there, plus a classical 'Democracy shtoonk'. On various occasions as Hitler he also speaks English. In these instances he talks with force, as contrasted by the mousey, half-scared way he speaks as the poor barber.

Somewhat of a shock is the complete transformation of the barber when he delivers the speech at the finish, a fiery and impassioned plea for freedom and democracy. It is a peculiar and somewhat disappointing climax with the picture ending on a serious rather than a comical note.

The vast majority of the action is built around Hynkel and the Jewish barber. Not so much is devoted to the dictator who is Napaloni (Mussolini). Jack Oakie plays the satirized Duce to the hilt and every minute with him is socko.

In making up the billing, Chaplin has displayed an unusually keen sense of humor. While Hynkel is the dictator of Tomania, Napaloni is the ruler of Bacteria. Tomania higher-ups include Garbitsch (Goebels) and Herring (Goering). These are played effectively by Henry Daniell and Billy Gilbert.

□ 1940: Best Picture (Nomination)

. . . .

■ **GREAT ESCAPE, THE**

1963, 169 MINS, US ◇ Ⓥ

Dir John Sturges   *Prod* John Sturges   *Scr* James Clavell, W. R. Burnett   *Ph* Daniel Fapp   *Ed* Ferris Webster   *Mus* Elmer Bernstein   *Art Dir* Fernando Carrere

● Steve McQueen, James Garner, Richard Attenborough, Charles Bronson, Donald Pleasence, James Coburn (United Artists)

From Paul Brickhill's true story of a remarkable mass breakout by Allied POWs during World War II, producer-director John Sturges has fashioned a motion picture that entertains, captivates, thrills and stirs.

The film is an account of the bold, meticulous plotting that led to the escape of 76 prisoners from a Nazi detention camp, and subsequent developments that resulted in the demise of 50, recapture of a dozen.

Early scenes depict the formulation of the mass break design. These are played largely for laughs, at the occasional expense of reality, and there are times when authority seems so lenient that the inmates almost appear to be running the asylum.

There are some exceptional performances. The most provocative single impression is made by Steve McQueen as a dauntless Yank pilot whose 'pen'-manship record shows 18 blots, or escape attempts. James Garner is the compound's 'scrounger', a traditional type in the *Stalag 17* breed of war-prison film. Charles Bronson and James Coburn do solid work, although the latter's character is anything but clearly defined.

British thespians weigh in with some of the finest performances in the picture. Richard Attenborough is especially convincing in a

stellar role, that of the man who devises the break. A moving portrayal of a prisoner losing his eyesight is given by Donald Pleasence. It is the film's most touching character.

Elmer Bernstein's rich, expressive score is consistently helpful. His martial, Prussianistic theme is particularly stirring and memorable.

. . . .

■ **GREATEST, THE**

1977, 101 MINS, US ◇ Ⓥ

Dir Tom Gries   *Prod* John Marshall   *Scr* Ring Lardner, Jr   *Ph* Harry Stradling Jr   *Ed* Byron Brandt   *Mus* Michael Masser   *Art Dir* Bob Smith

● Muhammad Ali, Ernest Borgnine, John Marley, Lloyd Haynes, Robert Duvall, David Huddleston (Columbia)

Muhammad Ali is a natural performer. More to the point, starring in his own autobiopic, *The Greatest*, he brings to it an authority and a presence that lift John Marshall's production above some of the limitations inherent in any film bio.

The film gets off to a fine start with newcomer Phillip MacAllister playing the young Cassius Clay Jr displaying the engaging affrontery of a young talent so sure of himself that discretion in self-description knows no bounds.

Plot follows Ali from his early career through formal discipline, professional conflicts and the controversial refusal to be inducted in the US Army. En route is Ali's deliberate public baiting of Sonny Liston.

Intercut are actual sequences from Ali's major fights.

. . . .

■ **GREATEST SHOW ON EARTH, THE**

1952, 151 MINS, US ◇ Ⓥ

Dir Cecil B. DeMille   *Prod* Cecil B. DeMille   *Scr* Fredric M. Frank, Barre Lyndon, Theodore St John   *Ph* George Barnes, Peverell Marley, Wallace Kelley   *Ed* Anne Bauchens   *Mus* Victor Young   *Art Dir* Hal Pereira, Walter Tyler

● Betty Hutton, Cornel Wilde, Charlton Heston, Dorothy Lamour, Gloria Grahame, James Stewart (Paramount)

The Greatest Show on Earth is as apt a handle for Cecil B. DeMille's Technicolored version of the Ringling Bros.-Barnum & Bailey circus as it is for the sawdust extravaganza itself. This is the circus with more entertainment, more thrills, more spangles and as much Big Top atmosphere as RB-B&B itself can offer.

As has come to be expected from DeMille, the story line is not what could be termed subtle. Betty Hutton is pictured as the 'queen flyer' who has a yen for Charlton Heston, the circus manager. Lad has sawdust for blood, however. To strengthen the show and thus enable it to play out a full season, he imports another aerialist, the flamboyant and debonair Sebastian (Cornel Wilde). Latter promptly falls for her and she rifts with Heston. That's quickly exploited by elephant girl Gloria Grahame, who also finds Heston a pretty attractive guy.

James Stewart is woven into the pic as an extraneous but appealing plot element. He's pictured as a police-sought medico who never removes his clown makeup.

□ 1952: Best Picture

. . . .

■ **GREATEST STORY EVER TOLD, THE**

1965, 225 MINS, US ◇

Dir George Stevens   *Prod* George Stevens   *Scr* George Stevens, James Lee Barrett   *Ph* William C. Mellor, Loyal Griggs   *Ed* Harold F. Kress, Argyle Nelson Jr, Frank O'Neill   *Mus* Alfred Newman   *Art Dir* Richard Day, William Creber

● Max Von Sydow, Dorothy McGuire, Robert Loggia, Claude Rains, Jose Ferrer, Charlton Heston (United Artists

The prophets should speak with respect of this $20 million Biblical epic. *The Greatest Story Ever Told* is the word made manifest. Producer-director George Stevens has elected to stick to the straight, literal, orthodox, familiar facts of the four gospels. He has scorned plot gimmicks and scanted on characterization quirks. What Stevens puts on view, overall, is panoramic cinema, cannily created backgrounds, especially the stupendous buttes of Utah.

Stevens is not particularly original in his approach to the galaxy of talent, some 60 roles. Hollywood's fad for cameo bits by featured players may suffer some discredit in the light of the triviality of footage and impact by such players as Carroll Baker, Pat Boone, Richard Conte, Ina Balin, Frank De Kova, Victor Buono, Marian Seldes, Paul Stewart. John Wayne is ill-at-ease and a waste of name, many may feel, as the captain of the soldiers who escort the Redeemer to the cross. Claude Rains is standout in the opening sequence [directed by David Lean] as the dying ruler of Judea.

Quite properly Stevens has focused on the birth, ministry, execution and resurrection of the Son of God. In the casting of Jesus there is occasion for compliment. The performance of the Swedish actor, Max Von Sydow, and his English diction are ideal.

The Baptist (Charlton Heston) is the only out-and-out fanatic in the picture but this takes the form of roaring demands that Herod 'repent'. Herod, in the remarkably curbed performance of Jose Ferrer, is no worse than a cynical administrative stooge for the Romans.

. . . .

■ GREAT EXPECTATIONS

1946, 110 MINS, UK ⓥ

Dir David Lean *Prod* Ronald Neame *Scr* David Lean *Ph* Guy Green *Ed* Jack Harris *Mus* Walter Goehr, Ronald Neame, Anthony Havelock-Allan *Art Dir* Wilfred Shingleton
● John Mills, Valerie Hobson, Francis L. Sullivan, Alec Guinness, Jean Simmons, Martita Hunt (Cineguild)

Only rabid Dickensians will find fault with the present adaptation, and paradoxically only lovers of Dickens will derive maximum pleasure from the film.

This adaptation tells how young Pip befriends an escaped convict, who, recaptured and transported to Australia, leaves Pip a fortune so he may become a gentleman with great expectations. Pip believes the unexpected fortune originated with the eccentric Miss Havisham at whose house he has met Estella the girl he loves.

To condense the novel into a two-hour picture meant sacrificing many minor characters. The period and people are vividly brought to life. But so particular have the producers been to avoid offending any Dickensian and every character is drawn so precise that many of them are puppets.

That's the great fault of the film. It is beautiful but lacks heart. It evokes admiration but no feeling.

With the exception of John Mills and Alec Guinness, only the secondary characters are entirely credible. Valerie Hobson, whose beauty is not captured by the camera, fails to bring Estella to life, and young Jean Simmons, who plays the role as a girl, is adequately heartless.
☐ 1947: Best Picture (Nomination)

. . . .

■ GREAT GABBO, THE

1929, 91 MINS, US ◇ ⓥ

Dir James Cruze *Prod* Henry D. Meyer, Nat Cordish *Scr* Ben Hecht, Hugh Herbert
● Erich von Stroheim, Betty Compson, Don Douglas, Margie Kane (Meyer-Cordish

The story is simplicity itself. Just a pair of show people – one a lovely, considerate girl and the other a ventriloquist with a hyperegotist complex. The expected break, followed by a rise from the grinds to the individual success of both. Then the too late realization of love by the dummy manipulator.

Erich von Stroheim, as the eccentric and arrogant performer who reveals a Pagliacci heart through the medium of Otto, the dummy, doubles the enhancement of a dominant screen personality with his lines. It is the voice, frenzied and then modulated to a pianissimo, that is one of the strongest threads, carrying the interest over sequences devoted to color and stage show that would be irrelevant gaps in productions less skillfully directed and enacted.

In part of the colored sequence the print is grainy and the characters blurred. But both of these conditions are too brief to be considered drawbacks.

. . . .

■ GREAT GATSBY, THE

1949, 91 MINS, US ⓥ

Dir Elliott Nugent *Prod* Richard Maibaum *Scr* Cyril Hume, Richard Maibaum *Ph* John F. Seitz *Ed* Ellsworth Hoagland *Mus* Robert Emmett Dolan
● Alan Ladd, Betty Field, Macdonald Carey, Ruth Hussey, Barry Sullivan, Shelley Winters (Paramount)

F. Scott Fitzgerald's story of the roaring '20s is peopled with shallow characters and the script stresses the love story rather than the hi-jacking, bootlegging elements.

Gatsby is a fabulous bootlegger who has parlayed his relentless drive into fortune. When the stack of blue chips is large enough, he turns his attention to winning back a girl he lost years ago to a wealthy man.

Alan Ladd handles his characterization ably, making it as well-rounded as the yarn permits and fares better than any other cast members in trying to make the surface characters come to life.

Elliott Nugent's direction skips along the surface of the era depicted. The script doesn't give him much substance to work with.

. . . .

■ GREAT GATSBY, THE

1974, 144 MINS, US ◇ ⓥ

Dir Jack Clayton *Prod* David Merrick *Scr* Francis Coppola *Ph* Douglas Slocombe *Ed* Tom Priestley *Mus* Nelson Riddle *Art Dir* John Box
● Robert Redford, Mia Farrow, Bruce Dern, Karen Black, Scott Wilson, Sam Waterston (Paramount)

Paramount's third pass at *The Great Gatsby* is by far the most concerted attempt to probe the peculiar ethos of the Beautiful People of the 1920s. The fascinating physical beauty of the $6 million-plus film complements the utter shallowness of most principal characters from the F. Scott Fitzgerald novel.

Robert Redford is excellent in the title role, the mysterious gentleman of humble origins and bootlegging connections; Mia Farrow is his long-lost love, married unhappily but inextricably to brutish Bruce Dern, who has a side affair going with restive working class wife Karen Black.

The Francis Coppola script and Jack Clayton's direction paint a savagely genteel portrait of an upper class generation that deserved in spades what it got circa 1929 and after.

. . . .

■ GREAT MAN, THE

1956, 92 MINS, US

Dir Jose Ferrer *Prod* Aaron Rosenberg *Scr* Al Morgan, Jose Ferrer *Ph* Harold Lipstein *Ed* Sherman Todd, Al Joseph *Mus* Herman Stein

● Jose Ferrer, Dean Jagger, Keenan Wynn, Julie London, Joanne Gilbert, Ed Wynn (Universal)

Like the novel by Al (NBC) Morgan, the film is a series of flash episodes adding into a character study as a probing reporter researches the background of a nationally-known and presumably revered radio figure who has died in an auto accident. The research brings out that, away from the mike, the late lamented was a stinker with no scruples. The 'great man' is never seen in person.

Jose Ferrer, who stars as the reporter, collaborated with author Morgan on the screenplay and directed. In each function he is extremely able, with particular emphasis on his direction which brings out several surprise performances.

Ed Wynn is outstanding as the pious owner of a small New England radio station who gave the 'morning man' his start. Julie London socks across the dramatic role of the singer who also must hold herself available as a part-time mistress if the Studio King is minded that way. Dean Jagger is fine as the network head and son Keenan Wynn scores, too, as the executive always looking out for himself.

. . . .

■ GREAT MCGINTY, THE

1940, 81 MINS, US ⓥ

Dir Preston Sturges *Prod* Paul Jones *Scr* Preston Sturges *Ph* William Mellor *Ed* Hugh Bennett *Mus* Frederick Hollander *Art Dir* Hans Dreier, Earl Hedrick
● Brian Donlevy, Muriel Angelus, Akim Tamiroff, Allyn Joslyn, William Demarest, Louis Jean Heydt (Paramount)

The Great McGinty initiates Preston Sturges into the directing ranks, after a long stretch as a film scenarist. Piloting an original story and screenplay of his own concoction, Sturges displays plenty of ability in accentuating both the comedy and dramatic elements of his material, withal maintaining a consistent pace in the unreeling.

Sturges' story departs radically from accepted formula. His main character is a tough, rowdy and muscular individual who creates more interest than sympathy in his career as a prototype of many political rascals of the American scene.

Story is unfolded by flashback. Brian Donlevy is introduced as the toughened bartender of a dive in a Central American banana republic. He's a fugitive from justice, the same as the young bank clerk who absconded with funds in a weak moment. Across the bar Donlevy tells the latter his story – a life of crookedness where the first honest thing he attempted chased him from the country. When he first finds that illegal voting brings coin, he becomes a repeater, gets into favor of political boss (Akim Tamiroff) and gradually rises to positions of alderman, mayor and finally governor of the state.

Portrayal of Donlevy as the slightly-educated political apprentice who learns the ropes fast, and wields his fists at every opportunity, is excellent. Tamiroff clicks as the political boss, while Muriel Angelus provides a charming and warmful personality in the role of the politico's wife. Bill Demarest provides attention as a political stooge.

. . . .

■ GREAT MOMENT, THE

1944, 83 MINS, US

Dir Preston Sturges *Prod* Preston Sturges *Scr* Preston Sturges *Ph* Victor Milner *Ed* Stuart Gilmore *Mus* Victor Young *Art Dir* Hans Dreier, Ernst Fegte
● Joel McCrea, Betty Field, Harry Carey, William Demarest (Paramount)

Preston Sturges brings to the screen the compelling biography of Dr W.T.G. Morton, who in 1844 discovered anaesthesia. The film [from the book by Rene Fulop-Muller] is the story of the romance, the trials and the ultimate victory of a Boston dentist, who experimented until he finally hit upon a painless means of extracting teeth, then passed on his discovery to the world of medicine. Performances of Joel McCrea and Betty Field, as well as a solid supporting cast, are well in keeping with the dignity of the yarn.

McCrea gives an excellent portrayal in the role of the impoverished medical student, forced to forego the study of medicine in lieu of a dental career because of lack of funds. Field, as the wife who sometimes gets on his nerves because of her lack of understanding of what he is endeavoring to accomplish, proves again that she is an actress with loads of talent.

Supporting roles of Harry Carey, the doctor who gives McCrea a chance to prove that anaesthesia is suitable for surgical operations, and William Demarest, as the first patient of McCrea, are expertly handled by them.

························

■ GREAT MUPPET CAPER, THE

1981, 95 MINS, UK ◇

Dir Jim Henson *Prod* David Lazar *Scr* Tom Patchett, Jay Tarses, Jerry Juhl, Jack Rose *Ph* Oswald Morris *Ed* Ralph Kemplen *Mus* Joe Raposo *Art Dir* Harry Lange
● Charles Grodin, Diana Rigg, John Cleese, Robert Morley, Peter Ustinov, Jack Warden (Universal/AFD)

Muppet creator Jim Henson took over the directorial reins this second time out and, buttressed by a $14 million budget and top professionalism down the line in the production department, shows a sure hand in guiding his appealing stars through their paces.

Story hook has hapless reporters Kermit, Fozzie Bear and The Great Gonzo literally plunked down in London Town to follow up on a major jewel robbery involving fashion world magnate Diana Rigg. Once there, Kermit mistakenly takes Miss Piggy for beautiful Lady Holiday and instantly falls in love with the rotund aspiring model.

At the same time, Rigg's sly brother Charles Grodin puts the make on Miss Piggy himself while also setting her up for arrest in the jewel robbery case.

As before, much of the dialog neatly walks the line between true wit and silly (and sometimes inside) jokes.

Grodin and Rigg are both fine, and cameo appearances are limited to nice turns by John Cleese, Robert Morley, Peter Ustinov and Jack Warden.

························

■ GREAT NORTHFIELD, MINNESOTA RAID, THE

1972, UK ⓥ

Dir Philip Kaufman *Prod* Jennings Lang *Scr* Philip Kaufman *Ph* Bruce Surtees *Ed* Douglas Stewart *Mus* Dave Grusin *Art Dir* Alexander Golitzen, George Webb
● Cliff Robertson, Robert Duvall, Luke Askew, R.G. Armstrong, Dana Elcar, Donald Moffat (Universal/Robertson & Associates)

The Great Northfield, Minnesota Raid – described as shedding 'new light' on Cole Younger and Jesse James – may be a valiant attempt but fails to come off.

Primarily, this is due to utter lack of sustained narrative, confused and inept writing, over-abundance of characters difficult for ready identification, often apparent indecision whether to make this drama or comedy and a mish-mash of irrelevant sequences.

Plottage bases its premise on the outlaws' decision to go from their native Missouri to Minnesota to rob what a newspaper ad claims to be the biggest bank west of the

Mississippi. Cliff Robertson plays Cole and Robert Duvall is Jesse.

Perhaps Philip Kaufman, who directs and provides the screenplay, accurately attains historic accuracy in his recital of events leading up to the raid, and afterwards, but his treatment is such that characters throughout are dull fellows indeed, and picture itself is in kind.

························

■ GREAT RACE, THE

1965, 157 MINS, US ◇ ⓥ

Dir Blake Edwards *Prod* Martin Jurow *Scr* Arthur Ross *Ph* Russell Harlan *Ed* Ralph E. Winters *Mus* Henry Mancini *Art Dir* Fernando Carrere
● Jack Lemmon, Tony Curtis, Natalie Wood, Peter Falk, Keenan Wynn, Arthur O'Connell (Warner)

The Great Race is a big, expensive, whopping, comedy extravaganza, long on slapstick and near-inspired tomfoolery whose tongue-in-cheek treatment liberally sprinkled with corn frequently garners belly laughs.

A certain nostalgic flavor is achieved, both in the 1908 period of an automobile race from New York to Paris and Blake Edwards' broad borrowing from *The Prisoner of Zenda* tale and an earlier Laurel and Hardy comedy for some of his heartiest action.

Characters carry an old-fashioned zest when it was the fashion to hiss the villain and cheer the hero. Slotting into this category, never has there been a villain so dastardly as Jack Lemmon nor a hero so whitely pure as Tony Curtis, rivals in the great race staged by an auto manufacturer to prove his car's worth.

Strongly abetting the two male principals is Natalie Wood as a militant suffragette who wants to be a reporter and sells a NY newspaper publisher on allowing her to enter the race and covering it for his sheet.

To carry on the overall spirit, Curtis always is garbed in snowy white, Lemmon in black, a gent whose every tone is a snarl, and whose laugh would put Woody Woodpecker to shame.

Lemmon plays it dirty throughout and for huge effect. Curtis underplays for equally comic effect. Wood comes through on a par with the two male stars.

························

■ GREAT ROCK 'N' ROLL SWINDLE, THE

1980, 103 MINS, UK ◇ ⓦ

Dir Julian Temple *Prod* Jeremy Thomas, Don Boyd *Scr* Julian Temple *Ph* A. Barker-Mills *Ed* R. Bedford, M.D. Maslin, G. Swire *Mus* The Sex Pistols
● Malcolm McLaren, Johnny Rotten, Sid Vicious, Steve Jones, Paul Cook, Jess Conrad (Kendon/Matrix Best/Virgin)

The Great Rock 'n' Roll Swindle is the *Citizen Kane* of rock 'n' roll pictures. An incredibly sophisticated, stupefyingly multi-layered portrait of the 1970s phenomenon known as The Sex Pistols, unstintingly cynical pic casts a jaundiced eye at the entire pop culture scene and, if nothing else, represents the most imaginative use of a rock group in films since The Beatles debuted in *A Hard Day's Night*.

Pic, which stars and is narrated after a fashion by Pistols' manager Malcolm McLaren, begins with the basic premise that the campaign of shock tactics was premeditated.

A bubbling brew of devices and styles somehow mesh under firsttime helmer Julian Temple's wizardly direction to amplify McLaren's thesis on how to create a rock sensation in 10 easy lessons. Among his dicta are: Demonstrate To Record Companies The Enormous Potential Of A Band That Can't Play; Make It As Hard As Possible For The Press To See It; Insult Your Audiences As Much As Possible, and Cultivate Hatred.

························

■ GREAT SANTINI, THE

1979, 115 MINS, US ◇ ⓥ

Dir Lewis John Carlino *Prod* Charles A. Pratt *Scr* Lewis John Carlino *Ph* Ralph Woolsey *Ed* Houseley Stevenson *Mus* Elmer Bernstein *Art Dir* Jack Poplin
● Robert Duvall, Blythe Danner, Michael O'Keefe, Lisa Jane Persky, Julie Anne Haddock (Orion)

Robert Duvall gives an excellent portrayal of a semi-psychotic, softened with a warmer side. But Duvall has to fight for every inch of footage against the overwhelming performances by several others in the cast – and that's the strength of *The Great Santini*.

Title is a nickname Duvall picks up as the finest fighter pilot in the US Marines. But this isn't a war picture. Quite the contrary, it's the compellingly relevant story of a super-macho peacetime warrior with nobody to fight except himself and those who love him.

As the sensitive son who strives to meet all of his father's supermasculine standards, Michael O'Keefe is terrific and emerges as the major star of the picture.

Blythe Danner is also strong as the wife who suffers Duvall's excesses.

························

■ GREAT SCOUT AND CATHOUSE THURSDAY, THE

1976, 102 MINS, US ◇ ⓥ

Dir Don Taylor *Prod* Jules Buck, David Korda *Scr* Richard Shapiro *Ph* Alex Phillips Jr *Ed* Sheldon Kahn *Mus* John Cameron *Art Dir* Jack Martin Smith
● Lee Marvin, Oliver Reed, Robert Culp, Elizabeth Ashley, Strother Martin, Sylvia Miles (American International)

Richard Shapiro's up-and-down screenplay uses the plot about former partners in crime (here Lee Marvin and Indian sidekick Oliver Reed) going back to get revenge on the partner who cheated them and went respectable with the loot (Robert Culp).

In the mid-section, the May-December romance between Marvin's aging cowpoke and Kay Lenz' young prostie rouses some dramatic interest, coming through the general hokiness like rays of sunshine on a smoggy day. Marvin, to his credit, resists the strong temptation to mug it up, playing with an amusing attempt at dignity, and Lenz is a very appealing and spunky actress.

Reed's role is a hammy embarrassment, Culp seems uncomfortable as a strident politico and Sylvia Miles is wasted as a madam.

························

■ GREAT ST. TRINIAN'S TRAIN ROBBERY, THE

1966, 94 MINS, UK ◇ ⓥ

Dir Frank Launder, Sidney Gilliat *Prod* Leslie Gilliat *Scr* Frank Launder, Ivor Herbert *Ph* Kenneth Hodges *Ed* Geoffrey Foot *Mus* Malcolm Arnold *Art Dir* Albert Witherick
● Frankie Howerd, Reg Varney, Stratford Johns, Eric Barker, Dora Bryan, George Cole (British Lion)

Ronald Searle's little schoolgirl demons from St. Trinian's are berserk again on the screen in a yarn with a topical twist, the [1963] Great Train Robbery.

Having pulled off a $7 million train robbery, a hapless gang of crooks stash the loot in a deserted country mansion. But when they go back to collect they find the St. Trinian's school has taken over, and they are completely routed by the hockey sticks and rough stuff handed out by the little she-monsters. When the gang returns on parents' day for a second attempt at picking up the loot they run into further trouble and complications and eventually get involved in a great train chase which is quite the funniest part of the film, having a great deal in common with the old silent slapstick technique.

Among the many performances which contribute to the gaiety are those of Frankie

Howerd as a crook posing as a French male hairdresser, Raymond Huntley as a Cabinet Minister with amorous eyes on the St. Trinian's headmistress (Dora Bryan), Richard Wattis in one of his typical harassed civil servant roles and Peter Gilmore as his confrere. George Cole crops up again as Flash Harry, the school bookie.

- -

■ **GREAT TEXAS DYNAMITE CHASE, THE**

1976, 90 MINS, US ◇ ▽
Dir Michael Pressman   *Prod* David Irving   *Scr* David Kirkpatrick   *Ph* Jamie Anderson   *Ed* Millie Moore   *Mus* Craig Safan   *Art Dir* Russel Smith
● Claudia Jennings, Jocelyn Jones, Johnny Crawford, Chris Pennock, Tara Strohmeier, Miles Watkins (Yasny Talking Pictures II)

The Great Texas Dynamite Chase is a well-made exploitation film which works on two levels, providing kicks for the ozoner crowd and tongue-in-cheek humor for the more sophisticated. The film had some initial playdates under the title *Dynamite Women*.

Claudia Jennings and Jocelyn Jones are stylish and attractive as a pair of brazen Texas bankrobbers. They stay firmly in character throughout as a loyal but very divergent criminal pair.

Jennings is a hardened prison escapee, while Jones goes on the road to avoid the boredom of being a smalltown bank teller. They use lots of dynamite along the way, but there's little bloodshed until the last part of the film, when the film's dominant spoof tone turns uncomfortably and unsuccessfully close to reality.

- -

■ **GREAT WALDO PEPPER, THE**

1975, 108 MINS, US ◇
Dir George Roy Hill   *Prod* George Roy Hill   *Scr* William Goldman   *Ph* Robert Surtees   *Ed* William Reynolds   *Mus* Henry Mancini   *Art Dir* Henry Bumstead
● Robert Redford, Bo Svenson, Bo Brundin, Susan Sarandon, Geoffrey Lewis, Edward Herrman (Universal)

The Great Waldo Pepper is an uneven and unsatisfying story of anachronistic, pitiable, but misplaced heroism. Robert Redford stars as an aerial ace, unable to cope with the segue from pioneer barnstorming to bigtime aviation.

George Roy Hill's original story was scripted by William Goldman into yet another stab at dramatizing the effect of inexorable social change on pioneers. In this case, Redford and Bo Svenson, two World War I airmen, scratch out a living, and feed their egos, via daring stunts in midwest fields. But Geoffrey Lewis has made the transition from cocky pilot to aviation official, and inventor Edward Herrmann unwittingly complements the shift through his technological advances.

The film stumbles towards its fuzzy climax.

- -

■ **GREAT WALL, A**

1986, 97 MINS, US ◇ ▽
Dir Peter Wang   *Prod* Shirley Sun   *Scr* Peter Wang, Shirley Sun   *Ph* Peter Stein   *Ed* Graham Weinbren   *Mus* David Liang
● Peter Wang, Sharon Iwai, Kelvin Han Yee, Li Qinqin (W&S)

A charming but unduly lightweight film, *A Great Wall* humorously accentuates the many cultural differences between the two giant nations of the US and China, but goes out of its way to avoid dealing with politics or any other issues of substance.

Peter Wang, who appeared in *Chan Is Missing*, himself portrays a San Francisco computer executive who takes advantage of the opening up of China to visit relatives there as well as to introduce his American-born wife and son to his native land.

Wang quickly sketches in his key players on both sides of the Pacific and deftly characterizes their differing lifestyles but he simply glosses over too many important issues for the film to be considered a true artistic success.

- -

■ **GREAT WALTZ, THE**

1938, 107 MINS, US
Dir Julien Duvivier   *Scr* Samuel Hoffenstein, Walter Reisch   *Ph* Joseph Ruttenberg   *Ed* Tom Held   *Mus* Dimitri Tiomkin (arr.)
● Luise Rainer, Fernand Gravet, Miliza Korjus, Hugh Herbert, Lionel Atwill, Curt Bois (M-G-M)

The Great Waltz is a field day for music lovers plus elegant entertainment. Producers were nearly two years on this film, but the extra effort shows in the nicety with which its many component parts fit together. It is Luise Rainer who makes the film.

While primarily a fanciful tale of Johann Strauss II's rise in the musical firmament [from an original story by Gottfried Reinhardt], entire plot has been constructed around his outstanding works.

The youthful Strauss (Fernand Gravet) is shown quitting his job in a Vienna banking house to carry on as a musician, first as a director of his own neighborhood orchestra playing his newest compositions, and then as a composer whose waltz tunes are recognized even in official court circles, something unheard of in those days.

Strauss marries the baker's daughter soon after he wins his first success. His part in the short-lived revolution serves to develop romance with the opera singer Carla Donner (Miliza Korjus). It is the sudden decision to fight for her mate, after months of self-sacrifice, that takes Mrs Strauss (Rainer) storming backstage after the successful premiere of his first opera.

Not cast in a thoroughly sympathetic role, operatic singer Korjus suffers at times from photographic angles and does not arouse as much excitement as obviously was intended [in her first American picture].

Besides Rainer's sterling portrayal of the adoring wife, Gravet does surprisingly well as the younger Strauss. Burden of romantic scenes rest on his shoulders and he comes through with elan. His singing measures up also.

- -

■ **GREAT WHITE HOPE, THE**

1970, 102 MINS, US ◇ ▽
Dir Martin Ritt   *Prod* Lawrence Turman   *Scr* Howard Sackler   *Ph* Burnett Guffey   *Ed* William Reynolds   *Mus* Lionel Newman   *Art Dir* John DeCuir
● James Earl Jones, Jane Alexander, Lou Gilbert, Joel Fluellen, Chester Morris, Robert Webber (20th Century-Fox)

In its telling of the quasi-fictionalized public life of famed black heavyweight champ, circa 1910, Jack Johnson, the film's pacing and gritty cynicism resembles the best of the old Warner Bros Depression dramas; but in the distended playout of the fighter's tragic private life via involvement with a white woman, the picture sags.

However, a superior cast, headed by James Earl Jones encoring in his stage role, a colorful and earthy script, plus outstanding production, render film quite palatable.

Jones' re-creation of his stage role is an eye-riveting experience. The towering rages and unrestrained joys of which his character was capable are portrayed larger than life.

- -

■ **GREAT ZIEGFELD, THE**

1936, 170 MINS, US ▽
Dir Robert Z. Leonard   *Prod* Hunt Stromberg   *Scr* William Anthony McGuire   *Ph* Oliver T. Marsh, George Folsey, Ray June, Merritt B. Gerstad, Karl Freund   *Ed* William S. Gray   *Mus* Arthur Lange (dir.), Frank Skinner (arr.)   *Art Dir* Cedric Gibbons, Merrill Pye
● William Powell, Myrna Loy, Luise Rainer, Frank Morgan, Fannie Brice, Virginia Bruce (M-G-M)

The Great Ziegfeld is the last gasp in filmusical entertainment. On its running time (10 minutes short of three hours), it is the record holder to date for length of a picture in the US. After two years, and a reported $1.5 million, Metro emerges with a picture whose sole shortcoming is its footage.

The production high mark of the numbers is 'Pretty Girl' as the first half finale. This nifty Irving Berlin tune becomes the fulcrum for one of Frank Skinner's best arrangements as Arthur Lange batons the crescendos into a mad, glittering pot-pourri of Saint-Saens and Gershwin, Strauss and Verdi, beautifully blended against the Berlinesque background.

Among riot of song and dance, Seymour Felix's dances and ensembles stand out for imagination and comprehensive execution.

William Powell's Zieggy is excellent. He endows the impersonation with all the qualities of a great entrepreneur and sentimentalist. Luise Rainer is tops of the femmes with her vivacious Anna Held. Myrna Loy's Billie Burke, perhaps with constant regard for a contemporaneous artiste, seems a bit under wraps. Frank Morgan almost pars Powell as the friendly enemy.

Fannie Brice is Fannie Brice; ditto Ray Bolger and Harriet Hoctor playing themselves. Character of Sampson is obviously the late Sam Kingston, long Zieggy's general manager who worried and fretted over the glorifyer's extravagances. Reginald Owen's personation here is capital.
□ 1936: Best Picture

- -

■ **GREED**

1924, 114 MINS, US ◇ ⊗ ▽
Dir Erich von Stroheim   *Prod* Erich von Stroheim   *Scr* June Mathis, Erich von Stroheim   *Ph* Ben F. Reynolds, William H. Daniels   *Ed* Frank Hull, Joseph W. Farnham   *Art Dir* Cedric Gibbons, Richard Day
● Gibson Gowland, ZaSu Pitts, Jean Hersholt, Chester Conklin, Sylvia Ashton, Austin Jewell (Metro-Goldwyn)

Greed, the screen adaptation of the Frank Norris story, *McTeague*, was directed by Erich von Stroheim. He utilized two years and over $700,000 of Goldwyn and possibly some Metro money in its making.

Stroheim shot 130 reels in the two years. He finally cut it to 26 reels and told Metro-Goldwyn executives that was the best he could do. It was then taken into hand and cut to 10 reels.

McTeague, a worker in a gold mine, serves an apprenticeship with an itinerant dentist and in years after sets up an office in Market street, San Francisco. A chum brings in his cousin as a patient. McTeague falls in love with her, but, before Mac and she are married, the girl wins a $5,000 lottery prize.

Several years afterward, the chum, revengeful because of his failure to share in the spoils, tips off the Dentists' Society that Mac is practicing without a license. Mac then drifts from bad to worse. With a few drinks of whiskey under his belt he walks out on the money-grabbing wife. Months later he runs across her. She is working as a scrubwoman. He tries to compel her to give him money, later murdering her to secure it.

After the crime Mac makes his way to the desert, in the direction of Death Valley. A posse starts after him from a small New Mexico town. In it is the former chum, still actuated by his greed for the $5,000.

The picture brings to light three great character performances by Gibson Gowland as McTeague, Jean Hersholt as the chum, and ZaSu Pitts as the wife. Chester Conklin is another who registers with a performance that is marked, although it is noticeable the part that Stroheim's direction plays in it.

••••••••••••••••••••••••••••••••••

■ GREEK TYCOON, THE

1978, 106 MINS, US ◇ ⓥ

Dir J. Lee Thompson   *Prod* Allen Klein, Ely Landau   *Scr* Mort Fine   *Ph* Tony Richmond   *Ed* Alan Strachan   *Mus* Stanley Myers   *Art Dir* Michael Stringer

● Anthony Quinn, Jacqueline Bisset, Raf Vallone, Edward Albert, James Franciscus, Camilla Sparv (Abkco)

As a thinly disguised biopic of Aristotle Onassis and Jacqueline Kennedy Onassis – accent on thinly disguised – *The Greek Tycoon* has the conviction of its subject. It's a trashy, opulent, vulgar, racy $6.5 million picture. You've watched the headlines, now you can read the movie.

Mort Fine's script begins with Anthony Quinn as Theo Tomasis returning from a business trip. He greets his wife, wades through the guests at his island manor searching for his son and quickly spots Jackie Bisset with her husband Senator James Cassidy.

The story moves quickly onto Quinn's yacht. The Cassidys are persuaded to join the affair and while the senator is immersed in conversation with a former British prime minister, Quinn lays the seeds for his own affair.

Quinn is fabulous as Tomasis, a charming, wealthy, conniving and influential tycoon. Raf Vallone as Quinn's brother, James Franciscus as President Cassidy, Edward Albert as Quinn's son and the always reliable Charles Durning as Quinn's lawyer and later attorney general, all turn in good performances. As Liz Cassidy, Bisset capitalizes on her looks, but her accent seems off for the part and much of the acting is just posing.

••••••••••••••••••••••••••••••••••

■ GREEN BERETS, THE

1968, 141 MINS, US ◇ ⓥ

Dir John Wayne, Ray Kellogg   *Prod* Michael Wayne   *Scr* James Lee Barrett   *Ph* Winston C. Hoch   *Ed* Otto Lovering   *Mus* Miklos Rozsa   *Art Dir* Walter M. Simonds

● John Wayne, David Janssen, Jim Hutton, Aldo Ray, Raymond St Jacques (Warner/Seven Arts/Batjac)

The Green Berets, based on Robin Moore's book about US Special Forces, sheds no light on the arguments pro and con US involvement in Vietnam. Cliche-cluttered plot structure and dialog, wooden performances by actors playing soldiers, pedestrian direction and lethargic editing dog this production. James Lee Barrett did the flat script, loaded with corn and cardboard.

John Wayne is a colonel sent to Vietnam, while David Janssen plays a hostile newspaper reporter who, from time-to-time, alters his thinking about the fighting.

Role is a shambles for Janssen, because it was a patent setup from the start, and nobody could buck the thankless, inarticulate development.

The interminable length permits about every hack character type to be introduced: Jim Hutton, the goofy kid who steals supplies; Aldo Ray, as 'good-old-Sarge' type; Raymond St. Jacques, the sensitive medic; Luke Askew, country-boy; Jason Evers, an all-American young officer type, and playing it like a toothpaste commercial; Mike Henry, beefy soldier who takes several enemy soldiers with him as he dies, and dies, and dies.

••••••••••••••••••••••••••••••••••

■ GREEN CARD

1991, 108 MINS, AUSTRALIA/FRANCE ◇ ⓥ

Dir Peter Weir   *Prod* Peter Weir   *Scr* Peter Weir   *Ph*

Geoffrey Simpson   *Ed* William Anderson   *Mus* Hans Zimmer   *Art Dir* Wendy Stites

● Gerard Depardieu, Andie MacDowell, Bebe Neuwirth, Gregg Edelman, Robert Prosky (Rio/UGC/DD/Sedif/Green Card)

Although a thin premise endangers its credibility at times, *Green Card* is a genial, nicely played romance. Gerard Depardieu is winning in the tailor-made role of a French alien who pairs up with New Yorker Andie MacDowell in a marriage of convenience in order to remain legally in the United States.

An Australian-French co-production shot in Gotham and completed Down Under, modest pic is essentially a two-character piece and looks to have been made on a very low budget. Plot is an inversion of the 1930s screwball comedies in which a divorcing couple spend the entire running time getting back together.

Green Card begins with Depardieu and MacDowell, who have scarcely been introduced, getting married, then charts the tricky weekend the two temperamental opposites spend getting to know each other in a hurry when faced with a government probe of their relationship.

Elements that might look hokey on paper – he's a freewheeling bohemian, she's an uptight prude; he's a smoker and enthusiastic carnivore, she practically faints upon exposure to a cigarette or a piece of meat – go down easily because the two leads incorporate these attitudes believably into generally well-rounded characters.

••••••••••••••••••••••••••••••••••

■ GREEN DOLPHIN STREET

1947, 140 MINS, US ⓥ

Dir Victor Saville   *Prod* Carey Wilson   *Scr* Samson Raphaelson   *Ph* George Folsey   *Ed* George White   *Mus* Bronislau Kaper   *Art Dir* Cedric Gibbons, Malcolm Brown

● Lana Turner, Van Heflin, Donna Reed, Richard Hart, Edmund Gwenn (M-G-M)

Metro throws the full weight of its moneybags into *Green Dolphin Street*. To salvage the $4 million or so that went into this epic [based on the novel by Elizabeth Goudge], it must primarily count on the eminent saleability of earthquakes, tidal waves and native uprisings. Its curiously unreal story offers no help.

Flaws in the novel, which verbiage may have made less perceptible, sore-thumb their way through the pic. There's the weak dramatic dodge, for one instance, of the wrong sister being married because she was mistakenly named by the suitor in a letter of proposal to her parents. And it's nothing but a hokey have-your-cake-and-eat-it device to confer happiness on the other by retiring her to a religious order.

Alternately localed in primitive New Zealand and one of the French channel isles (circa 1840), pic details how Lana Turner, mistaken for her sister Donna Reed, makes the perilous sea voyage to the Antipodes to marry a deserter from the British navy.

When Victor Saville's direction focuses on nature's vengeance on man's works, the handling is superb. The toppling of giant trees, the shuddering of splitting earth and, the sweep of a river rending everything in its path is simon-pure cinematology. Credit, too, the fetching grandeur of the New Zealand country.

Refusal by M-G's studio-ites to recognize the ravages of time and events on the human face hampers Turner in depicting her exacting and pivotal role. As the gentler of the sisters, Reed is bogged by the weight of the yarn. Patly performing in the early reels, she fails to turn the hazardous trick of making her later conversion credible.

••••••••••••••••••••••••••••••••••

■ GREEN FIRE

1954, 99 MINS, US ◇

Dir Andrew Marton   *Prod* Armand Deutsch   *Scr* Ivan Goff, Ben Roberts   *Ph* Paul Vogel   *Ed* Harold F. Kress   *Mus* Miklos Rozsa

● Stewart Granger, Grace Kelly, Paul Douglas, John Ericson, Murvyn Vye, Jose Torvay (M-G-M)

A good brand of action escapism is offered in *Green Fire*. Its story of emerald mining and romantic adventuring in South America is decorated with the names of Stewart Granger, Grace Kelly and Paul Douglas.

The location filming in Colombia ensured fresh scenic backgrounds against which to play the screen story. The script supplies believable dialog and reasonably credible situations, of which Andrew Marton's good direction, takes full advantage, and the picture spins off at a fast 99 minutes.

The adventure end of the plot is served by the efforts of Granger to find emeralds in an old mountain mine; in the face of halfhearted opposition from his partner, Douglas; the more active interference of Murvyn Vye, a bandit, and the danger of the mining trade itself. Romance is served through the presence of Kelly, whose coffee plantation lies at the foot of the mountain on which Granger is mining, and the attraction that springs up between these two.

••••••••••••••••••••••••••••••••••

■ GREENGAGE SUMMER, THE

1961, 100 MINS, UK ◇

Dir Lewis Gilbert   *Prod* Victor Saville   *Scr* Howard Koch   *Ph* Frederick A. Young   *Ed* Peter Hunt   *Mus* Richard Addinsell   *Art Dir* John Stoll

● Kenneth More, Danielle Darrieux, Susannah York, Jane Asher, Claude Nollier, Maurice Denham (Columbia/Saville-Small)

Here's a stylish, warm romantic drama which gets away to a flying start in that it's set in the leisurely champagne country of France. Pic is always a delight to the eye apart from its other qualities.

The screenplay, based on Rumer Godden's novel, works up to a holding emotional pitch. Story concerns four English schoolchildren, the oldest (Susannah York) being just over 16, who are enroute to a holiday in France's champagne-and-greengage country when their mother is taken ill and is whisked off to hospital.

Alone and dispirited they arrive at the hotel which is run by Danielle Darrieux and managed by Claude Nollier. The children get a frigid reception but Kenneth More, a debonair, charming, mysterious Englishman insists that they stay. He's having an affair with Miss Darrieux and she cannot resist her whims. During the long summer the atmosphere thickens.

The early part of the film, when the relationship between More and the children is developing, is particularly charming and pleasantly staged. York progresses delightfully from the resentful, gawky schoolgirl to the young woman eager to live. She handles some tricky scenes (as when she gets drunk with champagne and when she is assaulted by an amorous scullery boy) with assurance.

More's scenes with the moppets are great as are his rather more astringent skirmishes with Darrieux. She plays the jealous, fading mistress on rather too much of one note, but with keen insight. And there is a subtly drawn relationship of hinted lesbianism between her and Nollier.

••••••••••••••••••••••••••••••••••

■ GREEN MANSIONS

1959, 104 MINS, US ◇

Dir Mel Ferrer   *Prod* Edmund Grainger   *Scr* Dorothy Kingsley   *Ph* Joseph Ruttenberg   *Ed* Ferris Webster   *Mus* Bronislau Kaper, Heitor Villa-Lobos

● Audrey Hepburn, Anthony Perkins, Lee J. Cobb,

Sessue Hayakawa, Henry Silva, Nehemiah Persoff
(M-G-M)

Filmization of W.H. Hudson's novel has been approached with reverence and taste but fantastic elements puzzle and annoy. Hudson wrote an allegory of eternal love in his story of Rima, the bird-girl, who is discovered in the Venezuelan jungles by the political refugee, Abel. In the screenplay, Rima (Audrey Hepburn), is a real girl, but one with unusual communion with the forest and its wild life.

She is found by Abel (Anthony Perkins) when he hides out with an Indian tribe after fleeing a political uprising in which his father had been killed. Rumors of gold in the neighborhood stir Perkins' imagination because he needs money to avenge his father's assassination.

Director Mel Ferrer and his cameraman had done some good location work in South America. It is skillfully utilized, by process and editing, with backlot work. But Ferrer has been less successful in getting his characters to come alive, or in getting his audience to care about them.

Hepburn is pretty as the strange young woman, but with no particular depth. Perkins seems rather frail for his role, despite a trial by ordeal given him by Henry Silva's tribe. Silva, on the other hand, gives an exciting performance, fatally damaging to Perkins, the hero, overshadowing him in their dramatic conflict.

● ●

■ GREEN PASTURES

1936, 93 MINS, US Ⓥ

Dir Marc Connelly, William Keighley   *Prod* Henry Blanke   *Scr* Marc Connelly, Sheridan Gibney   *Ph* Hal Mohr   *Ed* George Amy   *Mus* Erich Wolfgang Korngold   *Art Dir* Allen Salburg, Stanley Fleischer
● Rex Ingram, Oscar Polk, Eddie Anderson, Frank Wilson, Abraham Gleaves (Warner Bros.)

Green Pastures is a simple, enchanting, audience-captivating all-Negro cinematic fable. The show [by Marc Connelly, suggested by Roark Bradford's novel *Ol' Man Adam an' His Chillun'*] made history by touring the hinterland for three years after two years on Broadway.

Rex Ingram's glowing personality is a thoroughly satisfying and convincing Lawd. Ingram's is a yeoman protean contribution, as he also personates Adam and Hezdrel, his images re-created on earth.

The very essence of *Green Pastures* is the Sabbath school. It's the Harlem version of the Old Testament, as the pastor word-paints the mood of De Lawd from Genesis to Exodus and beyond.

Oscar Polk as Gabriel – whom De Lawd colloquially addresses as Gabe – is a human and humorous archangel who efficiently and matter-of-factly sees that De Lawed's will be done, and without the slightest hitches.

Punctuating all the Biblical background are mundane references to gay fishfries, ten cent seegars, generous fishing and plenty of milk-and-honey for the good folks, yet it's all in fine taste and with due regard to proportions and standards of all races and creeds.

Marc Connelly and William Keighley – the latter the more remarkable in view of his previous specialization in gangster mellers – rate most of the bends for their distinguished transition of the play to the screen.

Frank Wilson's Moses; George Reed's Mr Deshee; Edna M. Harris and Al Stokes as Zeba and Cain, a couple of hot potatoes, she a uke-strumming slut and he a fancy man; Ernest Whitman, impressive as the regally arrogant Pharaoh; plus the Hall Johnson choir, are among other stand-outs.

● ●

■ GREEN YEARS, THE

1946, 127 MINS, US

Dir Victor Saville   *Prod* Leon Gordon   *Scr* Robert Ardrey, Sonya Levien   *Ph* George Folsey   *Ed* Robert J. Kern   *Mus* Herbert Stothart   *Art Dir* Cedric Gibbons, Hans Peters
● Charles Coburn, Tom Drake, Beverly Tyler, Hume Cronyn, Dean Stockwell, Jessica Tandy (M-G-M)

Metro, with the skill it has so often demonstrated in transforming a best-selling novel to a best-selling picture, turns the trick again with this filmization of A. J. Cronin's *The Green Years*.

Since this is essentially a yarn built on careful development of its various characters, a major contribution is in giving new stature and audience appeal to virtually every player in it. That's true all the way from vet Charles Coburn, who evidences his virtuosity in a new type role for him, to moppet Dean Stockwell and Beverly Tyler, both making their second screen appearances.

Ten-year-old Stockwell is the particularly bright spot in the well-turned cast. He gets real opportunity to demonstrate a sensitivity and true dramatic poignancy that definitely set him off from the usual studio moppets.

Young Stockwell plays an orphan boy in this Scottish-localed story of ambitious youth and amusing old age. The oldster, of course, is Coburn, as Dean's great-grandfather, a man of large heart and large desires for the native brew. While this not-so-venerable, but thoroughly enjoyable, citizen is getting himself into one minor scrape after another, the youth (later played by Tom Drake) goes through the process of growing up, going to school and falling in love.

The two principals are set against a household full of characters. Hume Cronyn wreaks every bit of tightfistedness and little man-meanness out of the role of head of the house that takes the small boy in. Tyler and Drake play the teenage romance.

● ●

■ GREGORY'S GIRL

1982, 91 MINS, UK ◇ Ⓥ

Dir Bill Forsyth   *Prod* Davina Belling, Clive Parsons   *Scr* Bill Forsyth   *Ph* Michael Coulter   *Ed* John Gow   *Mus* Colin Tully   *Art Dir* Adrienne Atkinson
● John Gordon Sinclair, Dee Hepburn, Jake D'Arcy, Clare Grogan, Robert Buchanan, William Greenlees (Lake/NFFC/Scottish TV)

Filmmaker Bill Forsyth, whose friendly, unmalicious approach recalls that of Rene Clair, is concerned with young students (in particular, a soccer team goalie, Gregory) seeking out the opposite sex. Much of the pic's peculiar fascination comes from tangential scenes, limning each character's odd obsession, be it food, girls, soccer, or just watching the traffic drive by.

Main narrative thread has Gregory becoming infatuated with the cute (and athletic) new girl on his soccer team, Dorothy (Dee Hepburn), while her schoolmates delightfully maneuver him into giving the out-going Susan (Clare Grogan) a tumble.

As Gregory, John Gordon Sinclair is adept at physical comedy. Hepburn is properly enigmatic as the object of his desire, with ensemble approach giving Greg's precocious 10-year-old sister played by Allison Forster a key femme role.

● ●

■ GREMLINS

1984, 111 MINS, US ◇ Ⓥ

Dir Joe Dante   *Prod* Michael Finnell   *Scr* Chris Columbus   *Ph* John Hora   *Ed* Tina Hirsch   *Mus* Jerry Goldsmith   *Art Dir* James H. Spencer
● Zach Galligan, Hoyt Axton, Frances Lee McCain, Phoebe Cates, Polly Holliday, Scott Brady (Amblin)

In what story there is, amiable Hoyt Axton comes across a mysterious creature in Chinatown and takes it home as a Christmas present for his likable teenage son, Zach Galligan. With the gift, he passes along a warning from the inscrutable Chinese that the creature must never get wet, be allowed into the sunshine or fed after midnight.

For a while, all is extremely precious as the little furry thing goes through an array of facial expressions and heart-warming attitudes.

Without giving away too much, suffice to say the creature spawns a townful of evil, snarling, drooling, maniacal killer-creatures who are bound to cause a lot of woe before their predictable downfall.

The humans are little more than dress-extras for the mechanics.

● ●

■ GREMLINS 2
THE NEW BATCH

1990, 105 MINS, US ◇ Ⓥ

Dir Joe Dante   *Prod* Michael Finnell   *Scr* Charlie Haas   *Ph* John Hora   *Ed* Kent Beyda   *Mus* Jerry Goldsmith, Alexander Courage, Fred Steiner   *Art Dir* James Spencer
● Zach Galligan, Phoebe Cates, John Glover, Robert Prosky, Robert Picardo, Christopher Lee (Amblin)

Joe Dante & Co. have concocted an hilarious sequel featuring equal parts creature slapstick for the small fry and satirical barbs for adults. Addition of Christopher Lee to the cast as a mad genetics engineering scientist is a perfect touch.

Film opens with a wrecking ball demolishing Keye Luke's old curiosity shop in downtown Manhattan to make way for another development project by megalomaniac Daniel Clamp, played with relish by John Glover.

The cuddly Mogwai creature Gizmo (wonderfully voiced by Howie Mandel) escapes but is immediately captured by twins Don & Dan Stanton as a research subject for Lee's science lab Splice of Life Inc. The lab is located in the new Clamp Center office building and, when Gizmo gets loose and exposed to water, the first of hundreds of horrific gremlins are unleashed to wreak mayhem.

Gremlins 2 is sans starpower, but its creatures more than make up for the lack of marquee lure. As realized by Rick Baker, the innumerable creations are quite an eyeful.

● ●

■ GREY FOX, THE

1982, 90 MINS, CANADA ◇ Ⓥ

Dir Phillip Borsos   *Prod* Peter O'Brian   *Scr* John Hunter   *Ph* Frank Tidy   *Ed* Ray Hall   *Mus* Michael Baker
● Richard Farnsworth, Jackie Burroughs, Wayne Robson, Ken Pogue, David Petersen (Mercury)

A graceful, stunningly-photographed bio of Bill Miner, a notorious train robber in Canada and the US at the turn of the century.

Director Phillip Borsos approaches his material – a stagecoach robber goes to jail for 30 years and is released into an unknown world where trains have started carrying the mail – as a kind of neo-western very much in sympathy with the bandit. Veteran Hollywood actor and western stunt man Richard Farnsworth was suggested for the role by Francis Coppola. His performance as the gentleman robber is one of the $3 million pic's strong points.

Until trapped by a Pinkerton detective, Miner lives a quiet life in a frontier town passing himself off as a gold-digger. Between train robberies, there is a delicately-handled love story with a cultured blue-stocking who makes a living as a photographer in the town.

● ●

■ GREYFRIARS BOBBY

1961, 91 MINS, US ◇ ⑦

Dir Don Chaffey   *Prod* Walt Disney   *Scr* Robert
Westerby   *Ph* Paul Beeson   *Ed* Peter Tanner
Mus Francis Chagrin   *Art Dir* Michael Stringer
● Donald Crisp, Laurence Naismith, Alexander
Mackenzie, Kay Walsh, Andrew Cruickshank, Gordon
Jackson (Walt Disney)

Greyfriars Bobby sets out to melt the heart and
does it skillfully. Central character is a little
Skye terrier, and this engaging little animal is
quite irresistible. He's a sort of Pollyanna
Pooch. Story is a true one, set in and around
Edinburgh some 100 years ago.

It tells of an old shepherd who died of old
age, exposure and starvation, and was buried
in the little Greyfriars Kirk in Edinburgh.
From the day of the funeral Bobby resolutely
refused to leave his beloved master. In the
end he won over all the local burghers and
was solemnly declared a Freeman of the City,
handed a collar by the Lord Provost and
adopted by the entire populace of Edinburgh.
Yes, a true, if odd story, and there's a statue
of Greyfriars Bobby in Edinburgh to prove it.

Patiently and brilliantly trained, Bobby
wraps up the stellar honors for himself and
the humans, knowing they don't stand a
chance, wisely are content to play chorus.
Nevertheless, there are some very effective
pieces of thesping, largely by Scottish actors.
Laurence Naismith gives a strong, likeable
performance as the kindly eating-house
owner who takes Bobby under his wing but,
by standing up for a principle, brings the
facts of the dog's case into court.

....

■ GREYSTOKE
THE LEGEND OF TARZAN LORD OF THE APES

1984, 129 MINS, US/UK ◇ ⑫

Dir Hugh Hudson   *Prod* Hugh Hudson, Stanley S.
Canter   *Scr* P.H. Vazak [= Robert Towne], Michael
Austin   *Ph* John Alcott   *Ed* Anne V. Coates   *Mus* John
Scott   *Art Dir* Stuart Craig
● Ralph Richardson, Ian Holm, James Fox, Christopher
Lambert, Andie MacDowell, Cheryl Campbell (Warner)

One of the main points of *Greystoke* is that the
$33 million pic adheres much more closely to
the original Edgar Rice Burroughs story than
have the countless previous screen tellings of
Tarzan stories.

While a little obligatory vine swinging is on
view, this is principally the tale of the education of the seventh Earl of Greystoke, first by
the family of apes which raises a stranded
white child and eventually accepts him as its
protector and leader, then by a Belgian
explorer who teaches him language, and
finally by the aristocracy of Britain, which
attempts to make him one of their own.

With the exception of the warm, slightly
batty Ralph Richardson, nearly all the
Englishmen on view are impossible, offensive
snobs.

Christopher Lambert is a different sort of
Tarzan. Tall, lean, firm but no muscleman,
he moves with great agility and mimics the
apes to fine effect.

Ian Holm is helpfully energetic as the
enterprising Belgian, James Fox is the
personification of stiff propriety, and Andie
MacDowell [voiced by actress Glenn Close]
smiles her way through as the eternally
sympathetic Jane.

On a production level, film is a marvel, as
fabulous Cameroon locations have been
seamlessly blended with studio recreations of
jungle settings.

....

■ GRIFTERS, THE

1990, 113 MINS, US ◇ ⑱

Dir Stephen Frears   *Prod* Martin Scorsese, Robert
Harris, James Painten, Peggy Rajski   *Scr* Donald
Westlake   *Ph* Oliver Stapleton   *Ed* Mick Audsley
Mus Elmer Bernstein   *Art Dir* Leslie McDonald
● John Cusack, Anjelica Huston, Annette Bening, Pat
Hingle, J.T. Walsh (Cineplex Odeon)

Jim Thompson's intriguing novel about the
subculture of smalltime hustlers is fashioned
into a curiously uneven movie in *The Grifters*.

John Cusack plays Roy Dillon, a Los
Angeles con man whose salesman's job is a
cover for his real vocation. Roy's mother,
Lilly (Anjelica Huston), gave birth at the tender age of 14, then fashioned a lucrative
career as a roving racetrack bag lady, putting
down bets for the Baltimore mob.

Roy is ministered to by his sexy girlfriend
Myra (Annette Bening), who lives by her
wits and her tightly wrapped body. Meanwhile, the mob boss travels west to teach
Lilly a painful lesson for skimming mob
money at the track.

When Roy and Myra take a holiday in La
Jolla, she reveals her true colors. Myra, is an
expert at the 'big con', elaborate swindles
geared to netting five- and six-figure scores.
Myra correctly suspects Roy's little secret: a
large horde of hidden cash accumulated from
years of grifting.

Cusack underplays Roy, making him an
unbelievable wiseguy, a colorless cipher too
akin to the saps he loves to fleece.

....

■ GRISSOM GANG, THE

1971, 127 MINS, US ◇ ⑱

Dir Robert Aldrich   *Prod* Robert Aldrich   *Scr* Leon
Griffiths   *Ph* Joseph Biroc   *Ed* Michael Luciano
Mus Gerald Fried   *Art Dir* James Vance
● Kim Darby, Scott Wilson, Tony Musante, Irene
Dailey, Robert Lansing, Connie Stevens
(ABC/Associates & Aldrich)

The Grissom Gang offers no sympathy at all for
the debased human beings it depicts. Rather,
it denies their existence as people, treating
them instead as the butts of a cruel joke.

The action takes place in Kansas City in
1931, and concerns the kidnapping of a
young heiress by an unbelievably depraved
gang presided over by venomous Ma Grissom (Irene Dailey) and her cretinous son
(Scott Wilson). It begins in a wash of blood,
opening the same vein throughout – and the
key to its debasing approach is the laughter
this mayhem often provokes.

Provided with a script [from a novel by
James Hadley Chase] that offers absolutely
no insight into the inner lives of its people,
director Robert Aldrich takes matters a step
further by directing his actors in performances that strain the bounds of credulity.
Wilson and Kim Darby, as the kidnapped
girl, make stabs at more than one dimension,
but when they indulge in caricatures of feeling, as they often do, they cancel out the rest
of their work. Dailey is the most persistent
mugger, while Robert Lansing, in one of the
few sympathetic roles, comes off best.

....

■ GROUNDSTAR CONSPIRACY, THE

1972, 95 MINS, CANADA ◇ ⑦

Dir Lamont Johnson   *Prod* Trevor Wallace
Scr Matthew Howard   *Ph* Michael Reed   *Ed* Edward
M. Abroms   *Mus* Paul Hoffert   *Art Dir* Cam Porteous
● George Peppard, Michael Sarrazin, Christine
Belford, Cliff Potts, James Olson, Tim O'Connor
(Universal/Roach)

George Peppard stars as a government agent
trying to break up a spy ring. Spectacular locations around Vancouver, plus some excellent and offbeat music by Paul Hoffert, only
partially compensate for a script that is as

often routine as it is bewildering. Lamont
Johnson's direction is one of his lesser efforts.

Matthew Howard adapted L. P. Davies'
[novel] *The Alien* into a diffused whodunit.
Michael Sarrazin is, or is not, a traitor who
worked in a super-secret lab trying to break a
computer code. The lab's destruction
launches the story.

Hard by the facility is the summer house
owned by Christine Belford who, before disappearing completely from the plot, plays an
important role in Peppard's trackdown of
Sarrazin. There is a lot of rough action and
violence, compounded intrigue, and confusing shifts of focus.

....

■ GROUP, THE

1966, 150 MINS, US ◇ ⑦

Dir Sidney Lumet   *Prod* Sidney Buchman   *Scr* Sidney
Buchman   *Ph* Boris Kaufman   *Ed* Ralph Rosenbloom
Mus Charles Gross   *Art Dir* Gene Callahan
● Candice Bergen, Joan Hackett, Elizabeth Hartman,
Shirley Knight, Joanna Pettet, Jessica Walter (Famous
Artists/United Artists)

The principal problem Sidney Buchman had
to face in adapting Mary McCarthy's very
successful college classmates novel was to
transfer its colorful characterizations and
story-telling without overloading his script
with the mass of novelistic detail. His script
does not completely solve this.

There's little tampering with the original
storyline but the filmscript concentrates on
the story of Kay (Joanna Pettet), the first girl
to be married and the one meeting the most
tragic end. Throughout, she and Larry Hagman, as her philandering playwright husband, have the longest roles. However, if less
important, the characters played by Joan
Hackett and Jessica Walter, thanks to their
performances, register as strongly as does
Pettet. Hackett, particularly, is provided with
a wide range of emotional changes.

Biggest letdown, and doubly so because her
few scenes are so effective and played so well,
is the part played by Candice Bergen. As
Lakey, the ambisextrous leader of the Group
(and the novel's most memorable character),
her treatment in Buchman's script will puzzle
the audience, as her few scenes at the beginning and at the end don't match with the billing she receives.

....

■ GUADALCANAL DIARY

1943, 90 MINS, US ⑦

Dir Lewis Seiler   *Prod* Bryan Foy   *Scr* Lamar Trotti
Ph Charles Clarke   *Ed* Fred Allen   *Mus* David Buttolph
● Preston Foster, Lloyd Nolan, William Bendix, Richard
Conte, Anthony Quinn (20th Century-Fox)

To anyone unfamiliar with the Richard Tra-
gaskis book, the picture version may or may
not be a faithful adaptation of the original.
But it is without question a painstaking, dignified and, in general, eloquent expression of
a heroic theme. It is at times a sobering film
and at other times an exalting one. It is also
an almost continuously entertaining one.

The diary form of the original book is utilized in the picture. Opening with a quiet
scene aboard a transport on a Sunday afternoon, as the Marine Corps task force steams
toward an as-yet undisclosed objective, the
story is narrated by an off-screen voice, fading in and out of the action sequences.

All this is admirably free from bombast and
chauvinistic boasting. Although the deeds of
the men are heroic, the men themselves
reveal no self-consciousness of heroism.

With minor exceptions, *Guadalcanal Diary*
is skillfully produced. A few of the incidents
seem synthetic and such scenes as the sinking
of the Jap submarine are rather obviously
faked, but in general both the action and the
manner of its presentation are genuinely
believable.

G

Of the cast, William Bendix stands out in a juicy comedy-straight part as a tough-soft taxi driver from Brooklyn, while Preston Foster and Lloyd Nolan give effective performances in the other principal leads.

● ●

■ **GUARDIAN, THE**

1990, 98 MINS, US

Dir William Friedkin   *Prod* Joe Wizan   *Scr* Steven Volk, Dan Greenburg, William Friedkin   *Ph* John A. Alonzo   *Ed* Seth Flaum   *Mus* Jack Hues   *Art Dir* Gregg Fonseca
● Jenny Seagrove, Dwier Brown, Carey Lowell, Brad Hall (Universal)

Who knows what possessed director William Friedkin to straight-facedly tell this absurd 'tree bites man' tale, but it's an impulse he should have exorcised.

The scant plot [from Dan Greenburg's story *The Nanny*] involves an attractive yuppie couple (Dwier Brown, Carey Lowell) who hire a live-in nanny to take care of their infant son. The nanny (Jenny Seagrove) turns out to be some sort of evil spirit that sacrifices newborns to this big, anthropomorphic tree, a species apparently indigenous to the canyon areas of metropolitan Los Angeles.

Friedkin's first horror film since *The Exorcist*, *The Guardian* is more likely to make viewers think at best of the wan film adaptation of *Pet Sematary*, at worst of the talking trees in *The Wizard of Oz*. The design is so shoddy one half expects it to start talking and pitching apples.

Seagrove looks properly bewitching but never brings much menace or mystery to her role. Lowell, a former Bond girl, has the least to do as the confused wife.

● ●

■ **GUESS WHO'S COMING TO DINNER**

1967, 108 MINS, US

Dir Stanley Kramer   *Prod* Stanley Kramer   *Scr* William Rose   *Ph* Sam Leavitt   *Ed* Robert C. Jones   *Mus* Frank DeVol   *Art Dir* Robert Clatworthy
● Spencer Tracy, Sidney Poitier, Katharine Hepburn, Katharine Houghton, Cecil Kellaway, Beah Richards (Columbia)

Problem: how to tell an interracial love story in a literate, nonsensational and balanced way. Solution: make it a drama with comedy. *Guess Who's Coming to Dinner* is an outstanding Stanley Kramer production, superior in almost every imaginable way, which examines its subject matter with perception, depth, insight, humor and feeling.

Spencer Tracy, Sidney Poitier and Katharine Hepburn head a perfect cast. Script is properly motivated at all times; dialog is punchy, adroit and free of preaching; dramatic rhythm is superb.

The story covers 12 hours, from arrival in, and departure from, Frisco of Poitier and Katharine Houghton (Hepburn's niece, in a whammo screen debut). Tracy and Hepburn are her parents, of longtime liberal persuasion, faced with a true test of their beliefs: do they approve of their daughter marrying a Negro.

Between the lovers and two sets of parents, every possible interaction is explored admidst comedy angles which range from drawingroom sophistication to sight gag, from bitter cynicism to telling irony. Film must be seen to be believed.

Apart from the pic itself, there are several plus angles. This is the ninth teaming of Tracy and Hepburn, and the last, unfortunately; Tracy died shortly after principal photography was complete. Also, for Poitier, film marked a major step forward, not just in his proven acting ability, but in the opening-up of his script character.

□ 1967: Best Picture (Nomination)

● ●

■ **GUIDE FOR THE MARRIED MAN, A**

1967, 89 MINS, US

Dir Gene Kelly   *Prod* Frank McCarthy   *Scr* Frank Tarloff   *Ph* Joe McDonald   *Ed* Dorothy Spencer   *Mus* John Williams   *Art Dir* Jack Martin Smith, William Glasgow
● Walter Matthau, Robert Morse, Inger Stevens, Sue Ane Langdon, Claire Kelly, Linda Harrison (20th Century-Fox)

Walter Matthau plays a married innocent, eager to stray under the tutelage of friend and neighbor Robert Morse. But this long-married hubby is so retarded in his immorality (it takes him 12 years to get the seven-year-itch) that, between his natural reluctance and mentor Morse's suggestions (interlarded with warnings against hastiness), he needs the entire film to have his mind made up.

Guide is packed with action, pulchritude, situations, and considerable (if not quite enough) laughs. Inger Stevens is beautiful as Matthau's wife, and so unbelievably perfect that it makes his reluctance most understandable.

Some of the guest talent have no more than one line (Jeffrey Hunter, Sam Jaffe), some are mimed (Wally Cox, Ben Blue) and others have several lines (Sid Caesar, Phil Silvers, Jack Benny, Hal March).

● ●

■ **GUILTY BY SUSPICION**

1991, 105 MINS, US

Dir Irwin Winkler   *Prod* Arnon Milchan, Alan C. Blomquist   *Scr* Irwin Winkler   *Ph* Michael Ballhaus   *Ed* Priscilla Nedd   *Mus* James Newton Howard   *Art Dir* Leslie Dilley
● Robert De Niro, Annette Bening, George Wendt, Patricia Wettig, Sam Wanamaker, Martin Scorsese (Warner)

First writing-directing effort by vet producer Irwin Winkler squarely lays out the professional, ethical and moral dilemmas engendered by the insidious political pressures brought to bear on filmmakers in the early 1950s. Robert De Niro is excellent as a top director brought down by reactionary paranoia. But the drama comes to life only fitfully.

De Niro portrays David Merrill, a director on a roll who lives only for his work. Arriving back in Hollywood in 1951 after a European sojourn, he soon finds the atmosphere changed. Charged by a colleague as having attended a couple of left-wing meetings years before, Merrill is asked by 20th Century-Fox boss Darryl F. Zanuck (Ben Piazza) to cooperate with the House Un-American Activities Committee before proceeding with his next big production.

After a disagreeable meeting with an attorney (Sam Wanamaker) and a HUAC rep, Merrill, refusing to cooperate, finds that the chill sets in almost immediately. He is yanked from the Fox film, listens to his agent demand back a $50,000 advance, looks to lose his house and hears his 10-year-old son doubting him. Worst of all, no one will return his calls.

Looking raffish and trim, De Niro perfectly conveys a charming, quiet confidence at the outset. During the extraordinary appearance before HUAC, he finally blossoms into a man of conviction and passion. The actor pulls off this last-minute transformation beautifully.

● ●

■ **GUMSHOE**

1971, 85 MINS, UK

Dir Stephen Frears   *Prod* Michael Medwin   *Scr* Neville Smith   *Ph* Christopher Menges   *Ed* Charles Rees   *Mus* Andrew Lloyd Webber
● Albert Finney, Billie Whitelaw, Frank Finlay, Janice Rule, Carolyn Seymour, Fulton Mackay (Memorial)

Gumshoe is an affectionately nostalgic and amusing tribute to the movie-fiction private-eye genre of yesteryear.

Story's about a smalltime Liverpool nitery emcee and would-be comedian with a buff's passion for Bogie and Dashiell Hammett who gets involved in a gun- and drug-running caper. Though often twistful, the tale's not the thing but its telling, and this, thanks to screenplay and direction, is an almost constantly chucklesome homage to the vintage sleuthing era – as the hero acts out his Mittyish adventure in Bogieland – with more reverence than outright spoof, for a curious and effective amalgam.

Albert Finney is brilliant as the key figure with just the right dose of tightlipped panache or – to bridge a plot gap – soliloquizing by quoting chapter and verse from his favorite authors or, again, tipping his hat to them with a look or a gesture. He's ably backed by Billie Whitelaw, Frank Finlay, Janice Rule and especially Fulton Mackay as Straker, another would-be eye.

● ●

■ **GUMSHOE KID, THE**

1990, 98 MINS, US

Dir Joseph Manduke   *Prod* Joseph Manduke   *Scr* Victor Bardack   *Ph* Harvey Genkins   *Ed* Richard G. Haines   *Mus* Peter Matz   *Art Dir* Batia Grafka
● Jay Underwood, Tracy Scoggins, Vince Edwards, Arlene Golonka, Pamela Springstein, Gino Conforti (Argus)

The Gumshoe Kid, alternately titled *The Detective Kid*, is a charming little comedy that pays homage to the private eye genre.

Jay Underwood, performing with the self-assurance of a younger Tom Hanks, carries the picture as a guy obsessed with Bogart who gets a job in Vince Edwards' agency through the efforts of his mom, Arlene Golonka. Finally assigned to a field case in surveillance, he's thrown together with femme fatale Tracy Scoggins. The two of them are on the lam for the rest of the film after Scoggins' boyfriend is nabbed by persons unknown.

This is breezy, light entertainment. Helmer Joe Manduke maintains a lighthearted mood, giving both principal players a chance to let their hair down engagingly.

● ●

■ **GUNFIGHT, A**

1971, 89 MINS, US

Dir Lamont Johnson   *Prod* A. Ronald Lubin, Harold Jack Bloom   *Scr* Harold Jack Bloom   *Ph* David M. Walsh   *Ed* Bill Mosher   *Mus* Laurence Rosenthal   *Art Dir* Tambi Larsen
● Kirk Douglas, Johnny Cash, Jane Alexander, Karen Black, Keith Carradine, Raf Vallone (Paramount)

A Gunfight is an offbeat western drama about two aging gunfighters who manipulate, and are manipulated by the blood lust of supposedly peaceful, average folks. Bankrolled by the Jicarilla Apache Tribe of American Indians, an investment-wealthy group making a first venture into pix, the handsome production stars Kirk Douglas and Johnny Cash. Lamont Johnson's very fine direction of the ruggedly sensitive script adds up to a fine depiction in discreet allegorical form of the darker sides of human nature.

Plot is essentially a three-acter. First the stars meet, fence nervously but with good humor, and at Douglas' suggestion, they decide to turn the town's unofficial speculation on the results of a shoot-out confrontation into personal profit for the survivor.

Next, intercut with the objections of Jane Alexander, excellent as Douglas' wife, and Karen Black, very good as a saloon dame who takes to Cash, the pair plan the carnival duel, aided by Raf Vallone, a shop-keeper whose eyes long have been on Alexander. Finally, the event itself, with the survivor really no better off than the deceased, a fact recognized by the friends of both men.

● ●

■ GUNFIGHT AT THE O.K. CORRAL

1957, 122 MINS, US ◇ ⓥ

Dir John Sturges   *Prod* Hal Wallis   *Scr* Leon Uris
Ph Charles Lang   *Ed* Warren Low   *Mus* Dimitri
Tiomkin   *Art Dir* Hal Pereira, Walter Tyler
● Burt Lancaster, Kirk Douglas, Rhonda Fleming, Jo
Van Fleet, John Ireland, Lyle Bettger (Paramount)

Producer Hal Wallis has taken the historic
meeting of Wyatt Earp, a celebrated lawman
of the West, his brothers and Doc Holliday,
with the Clanton gang in the O.K. Corral of
Tombstone, Arizona, and fashioned an absorbing yarn in action leading up to the gory
gunfight.

Burt Lancaster and Kirk Douglas enact the
respective roles of Earp and Holliday, story
opening in Fort Griffin, Texas, when the gun-
handy Dodge City marshal saves the other
from a lynch mob. Action moves then to the
Kansas town, where Holliday, at first
ordered to leave town but permitted to stay,
helps Earp in gunning three badmen. When
the marshal heeds the plea of one of his
brothers, marshal of Tombstone, for aid in
handling the dangerous Clanton gang,
Holliday accompanies him.

Both stars are excellently cast in their respective characters. Rhonda Fleming is in
briefly as a femme gambler whom Lancaster
romances, beautifully effective, and Jo Van
Fleet, as Holliday's constant travelling companion again demonstrates her ability in dramatic characterization.

■ GUNFIGHTER, THE

1950, 84 MINS, US ⓥ

Dir Henry King   *Prod* Nunnally Johnson   *Scr* William
Bowers, William Sellers   *Ph* Arthur Miller   *Ed* Barbara
McLean   *Mus* Alfred Newman
● Gregory Peck, Helen Westcott, Millard Mitchell, Karl
Malden, Skip Homeier, Jean Parker (20th Century-Fox)

The Gunfighter is a sock melodrama of the old
west. There's never a sag or off moment in
the footage as it goes about depicting a lightning draw artist, the fastest man with a gun
in the old west, and what his special ability
has done to his life.

Gregory Peck perfectly portrays the title
role, a man doomed to live out his span killing to keep from being killed. He gives it
great sympathy and a type of rugged individualism that makes it real. Peck is a man sad-
dened by his talent, forced to stay on the run
by all the young gunners seeking to make a
reputation by shooting down the great man.

Despite all the tight melodrama, the picture
[from a story by William Bowers and Andre
de Toth] finds time for some leavening
laughter.

■ GUNGA DIN

1939, 120 MINS, US ⓥ

Dir George Stevens   *Prod* Pandro S. Berman   *Scr* Joel
Sayre, Fred Guiol   *Ph* Joseph H. August   *Ed* Henry
Berman, John Lockert   *Mus* Alfred Newman   *Art
Dir* Van Nest Polglase, Perry Ferguson
● Cary Grant, Victor McLaglen, Douglas Fairbanks Jr,
Sam Jaffe, Joan Fontaine (RKO)

Aside from the feature's ability to tell a
swiftly-paced, exciting yarn about British
rule in India in the 1890s, it shows Cary
Grant, Victor McLaglen and Douglas Fairbanks Jr as a trio of happy-go-lucky British
army sergeants who typify the type of hard-
bitten non-coms described by Rudyard
Kipling in his famed poems *Barrack Room
Ballads*.

Basis of Ben Hecht and Charles MacArthur's original story, from the barrack ballad,
is the outbreak of the Thugs, cruel religious
marauders, who revolted against English
troops.

George Stevens employs superb change of
pace, going from action to character closeups
and then tossing in a romantic touch.

As Gunga Din, native water carrier, Sam
Jaffe contributes possibly his best screen portrayal since *Lost Horizon*. Eduardo Ciannelli
outdoes himself as ruthless native leader of
India's Thugs.

■ GUNG HO!

1943, 88 MINS, US ⓥ

Dir Ray Enright   *Prod* Walter Wanger   *Scr* Lucien
Hubbard, Joseph Hoffman   *Ph* Milton Krasner
Ed Milton Carruth   *Mus* Frank Skinner
● Randolph Scott, Grace McDonald, Noah Beery Jr, J.
Carrol Naish, Robert Mitchum, Rod Cameron
(Universal)

Randolph Scott has the lead in this story,
adapted from what is said to be a factual account written by Lieut W.S. Le Francois,
USMC.

Pertinently, it's the story of how, out of
thousands of trainees, a picked group of
Marines is slated for a special mission – the
first raid on [the tiny Pacific] Makin Island.
It's an at-times loosely written script. The
'boot training' preliminaries to the raid are
just so much of a wait, but the actual attack
has its compensating and exciting moments.

Scott gives one of his usually fine heroic
performances, while J. Carrol Naish is a
tough lieutenant who, somehow, doesn't look
the part. Noah Beery Jr and David Bruce
play half-brothers in a heat over the same
blonde (Grace McDonald). Sam Levene, in a
small role as a sergeant, is best of the support.

The direction has geared the pic for pace
but some of that dialog is strictly for the
younger element. The story has been needlessly glamorized, and it's here that it bogs
down. It has a love yarn where one need not
necessarily exist.

■ GUNG HO

1986, 111 MINS, US ◇ ⓥ

Dir Ron Howard   *Prod* Tony Ganz, Deborah Blum
Scr Lowell Ganz, Babaloo Mandel   *Ph* Don
Peterman   *Ed* Daniel Hanley, Michael Hill
Mus Thomas Newman   *Art Dir* James Schoppe
● Michael Keaton, Gedde Watanabe, George Wendt,
Mimi Rogers, John Turturro (Paramount)

Trying to save his town, auto worker Michael
Keaton journeys abroad to plead with Japanese industrialists to re-open the plant in
Hanleyville, Pa, that's been closed by foreign
competition. Soon after, the Japanese invasion begins. From the first morning of calisthenics, it's clear the American workers will
not adapt well to Japanese management.

Drawn from real life, the conflict between
cultures is good for both a laugh and a sober
thought along the way. Director Ron Howard
has problems straddling the two, sometimes
getting bogged down in the social significance.

Keaton can be funny as he puzzles the
Japanese. Gedde Watanabe is excellent as
the young Japanese exec whose career is
threatened by the lack of output by the
Americans.

■ GUNN

1967, 94 MINS, US ◇

Dir Blake Edwards   *Prod* Owen Crump   *Scr* Blake
Edwards, William Peter Blatty   *Ph* Philip Lathrop
Ed Peter Zinner   *Mus* Henry Mancini   *Art
Dir* Fernando Carrere
● Craig Stevens, Laura Devon, Ed Asner, Albert
Paulsen, Sherry Jackson, Helen Traubel (Paramount)

Blake Edwards has transplanted his three-
season *Peter Gunn* NBC-TV series (which
began in the 1959-60 season) to the screen in

Gunn, a well-made, but a trifle longish,
programmer.

Episodic scripting, as befits a murder suspense comedy, is combined with solid Owen
Crump production supervision, Henry Mancini music, and a surprise ending.

There's a prolog murder of a top-dog gangster. Albert Paulsen, successor to the gangland throne, is the natural suspect. M. T.
(Marion) Marshall, a seagoing madame,
hires Craig Stevens to prove Paulsen guilty.
Eventually, Paulsen forces Stevens to prove
him innocent.

Popping up at intervals are Laura Devon,
Gunn's occasional dame, Sherry Jackson, in
a standout sexpot part, J. Pat O'Malley,
excellent as a boozer informer who plays it
like Alfred Hitchcock's old TV show intros,
and skid-row topster Regis Toomey.

■ GUNS AT BATASI

1964, 102 MINS, UK

Dir John Guillermin   *Prod* George H. Brown
Scr Robert Holles   *Ph* Douglas Slocombe   *Ed* Max
Benedict   *Mus* John Addison   *Art Dir* Maurice Carter
● Richard Attenborough, Jack Hawkins, Flora Robson,
John Leyton, Mia Farrow, Cecil Parker (20th Century-
Fox)

Soldiering and politics don't mix, according
to this well developed screenplay and story
by Robert Holles [from his novel] which dis-
sects with a piercing personal touch the strict
disciplinary attitudes that govern a true British soldier and makes him retain his own individual pride in the face of political forces
unappreciative of his principles.

Producer and director come up with a
strong and frequently exciting piece of work,
the story of a British battalion caught in the
midst of the African struggle for
independence.

Performances throughout are excellent.
Richard Attenborough is tough, crisp and
staunch as the sergeant, playing with as
much starch as the character implies. Errol
John has intense qualities of fanaticism as the
lieutenant who seizes the government, and
Jack Hawkins, in essentially a cameo spot,
plays like the resigned warhorse he is meant
to be.

■ GUNS FOR SAN SEBASTIAN

1968, 100 MINS, FRANCE/MEXICO/ITALY ◇

Dir Henri Verneuil   *Prod* Jacques Bar   *Scr* James R.
Webb   *Ph* Armand Thirard   *Ed* Francoise Bonnot
Mus Ennio Morricone   *Art Dir* Robert Clavel
● Anthony Quinn, Anjanette Comer, Charles Bronson,
Sam Jaffe, Silvia Pinal, Jaime Fernandez (M-G-M)

Anthony Quinn stars as an outcast, assumed
to be a priest, in the Mexico of two centuries
ago. The production, a plodding mix of religious–themed action and comedy-romance,
has some good direction and battle scenes,
but the very poor dubbing (in dramatic
sense) is hard going.

Filmed entirely in Mexico, pic is a three-
way coproduction of Mexican, French and
Italian companies. Based on *A Wall for San
Sebastian*, by William Barby Faherty, story
concerns Quinn's influence on frightened
mountain peasants, by which they become a
cohesive town, instead of being terrorized by
Charles Bronson, in league with Indian chief
Jaime Fernandez.

Anjanette Comer plays a peasant gal, only
one in town with slit skirts, by the way.

Sam Jaffe, as a priest who dies early and
creates the situation whereby Quinn is
assumed to be a cleric, is saddled with
dubbed banalities. Of course, part of the fault
is in the writing, acting and directing of the
dubbing.

G

■ GUNS OF DARKNESS

1962, 102 MINS, UK
Dir Anthony Asquith   *Prod* Thomas Clyde   *Scr* John
Mortimer   *Ph* Robert Krasker   *Ed* Frederick Wilson
Mus Benjamin Frankel   *Art* John Howell
● Leslie Caron, David Niven, James Robertson Justice,
David Opatoshu (Cavalcade/Associated British)

Anthony Asquith is slightly off form with this
one. An advocate of anti-violence, he pursues
a theme that he has explored before, that violence is sometimes necessary to achieve
peace. But the film does not stand up satisfactorily as a psychological study. And as a
pure 'escape' yarn, its moments of tension are
only spasmodic.

John Mortimer's screenplay [from Francis
Clifford's novel *Act of Mercy*] is not positive
enough to enable Asquith to keep a firm grip
on the proceedings. There are times when the
film plods as laboriously as do the stars in
their escape to the frontier. It opens in Trib-
ulacion, capital of a South American republic, during a revolution. The president is
deposed in a swift coup and, wounded, has to
take off in a hurry.

Niven, a rather boorish PRO with a Brit-
ish-owned plantation, elects to smuggle him
across the border, for reasons which are not
even clear to Niven himself. Tagging along is
Niven's wife (Leslie Caron) with whom he is
having an emotional upheaval.

Niven's charm seeps through his mask of
boorishness but he manages skilfully to keep
up an illusion of high voltage danger. Opatoshu gives an excellent show as the disillusioned, yet philosophical president. Caron,
however, seems uncomfortable, with her role
coming over as curiously colorless.

■ GUNS OF NAVARONE, THE

1961, 157 MINS, UK ◇ ⓥ
Dir J. Lee Thompson   *Prod* Carl Foreman   *Scr* Carl
Foreman   *Ph* Oswald Morris   *Ed* Alan Osbiston,
Raymond Poulton, John Smith, Oswald Hafenrichter
Mus Dimitri Tiomkin   *Art Dir* Geoffrey Drake
● Gregory Peck, David Niven, Anthony Quinn, Stanley
Baker, Anthony Quayle, James Darren
(Columbia/Open Road)

A real heap of coin ($6 million), labor, sweat,
patience, tears, faith and enthusiasm went
into the making of *The Guns of Navarone*. It
faced the problem of a director-switch in mid-
stream. But with a bunch of weighty stars,
terrific special effects and several socko situations, producer Carl Foreman and director
J. Lee Thompson sired a winner.

Story, adapted by Foreman from Alistair
MacLean's novel, is set in 1943. The Axis has
virtually over-run Greece and its islands,
except for Crete and the tiny island of Kheros, both a few miles from Turkey. The only
chance for the worn-out garrison of 2,000
men is evacuation by sea, through a channel
between Kheros and another island. But this
channel is impregnably guarded by a couple
of huge, radar-controlled guns on Navarone.
A small bunch of saboteurs is detailed to
spike these guns.

The saboteur gang consists of Anthony
Quayle, Gregory Peck, David Niven, Stanley
Baker, Anthony Quinn and James Darren.
They all turn in worthwhile jobs. Of this sextet, Baker, playing a dour, war-sick expert
with a knife, and Darren, as a baby-faced
killer, get rather less opportunity for impact
than the others.

Quayle leads the expedition with conviction as the man who dreamed it up, a character who revels in war's danger kicks. Peck is
suitably laconic yet authoritative as the
officer who takes over when Quayle becomes
a casualty. Quinn is a dominating figure as a
Greek officer who is conducting all-out vendetta against the enemy and a half-hearted
personal one against Peck. And Niven, cast
as a satirical corporal with a genius for hand-

ling high explosives, scores with most of the
rare but wry humor in the film. Two women
have been written into the film who were not
in the novel, Greek partisans played very well
by Irene Papas and Gia Scala.

The cliff-scaling sequence, a scene when the
saboteurs are rounded up by the enemy, a
wonderfully directed and lensed storm
segment and the final boffo climax are just
a few of the nail-biting highlights.

□ 1961: Best Picture (Nomination)

■ GUNS OF THE MAGNIFICENT SEVEN

1969, 95 MINS, US ◇ ⓥ
Dir Paul Wendkos   *Prod* Vincent M. Fennelly
Scr Herman Hoffman   *Ph* Antonio Macasoli
Ed Walter Hannemann   *Mus* Elmer Bernstein   *Art
Dir* Jose Maria Tapiador
● George Kennedy, James Whitmore, Monte
Markham, Bernie Casey, Joe Don Baker (United/
Mirisch)

Guns of the Magnificent Seven is a handy follow-up to the 1960 original *Magnificent Seven*
and *Return of the Seven*. It rises above a routine
story line via rugged treatment and action
builds to a blazing gunplay climax.

George Kennedy takes on role played by
Yul Brynner in two previous films, the only
remaining character of the original seven.

Filmed entirely in Spain, as was *Return*,
director Paul Wendkos makes interesting use
of backgrounds.

Period is Mexico in the late 1890s, the narrative setting an attempt by Kennedy and his
men to rescue a patriot who is attempting to
assist helpless and downtrodden peasants.

Cast is well-chosen and Kennedy is a good
choice for the Brynner role.

■ GURU, THE

1969, 112 MINS, UK ◇
Dir James Ivory   *Prod* Ismail Merchant   *Scr* R. Prawer
Jhabvala, James Ivory   *Ph* Subrata Mitra
Ed Prabhakar Supare   *Mus* Ustad Vilaya Khan   *Art
Dir* Bansi Chandragupta
● Michael York, Utpal Dutt, Madhur Jaffrey, Rita
Tushingham, Aparna Sen (20th Century Fox/Arcadia/
Merchant-Ivory)

The Guru is a hazy study of how people can
transfer their own ideas about the value or
qualities of another person and in so doing
miss what the person is all about. Script is
never realized in concrete dramatic terms.

Michael York is cast as a young Englishman who comes to India to learn the secret of
playing the sitar at the house of a master
musician, Utpal Dutt. Dutt gives the film's
outstanding performance, with just the right
amount of annoying egotism and naive pomposity. He doesn't quite understand his guest
and tries, without success, to teach him the
'mystic' significance of the complicated
instrument and the Indian relationship between student and teacher or 'guru'.

At the same time that York comes into the
musical household a wandering 'hippie',
played by Rita Tushingham, talks her way
into staying and learning from the master.

■ GUY NAMED JOE, A

1943, 120 MINS, US ⓥ
Dir Victor Fleming   *Prod* Everett Riskin   *Scr* Dalton
Trumbo   *Ph* George Folsey, Karl Freund   *Ed* Frederick
Brennan   *Mus* Herbert Stothart
● Spencer Tracy, Irene Dunne, Van Johnson, Ward
Bond, Lionel Barrymore, Esther Williams (M-G-M)

In taking a fling at the spirit world, Metro
doesn't quite succeed in reaching the nebulous but manages to turn out an entertaining and excellently performed picture. Had
the fantasy been interpreted wholly in terms
of the sharp wit and dry humor which Spen-

cer Tracy, as a ghostly visitor, only occasionally injects, instead of investing it with
spiritual counselling, the film might have
attained smash proportions.

As it is, there hovers over too many scenes
in the cloudy strata a fogginess that isn't
made any more acceptable by the final solution. The latter only changes the mood of
the film from one of light cockiness to the
realm of metaphysics.

Tracy is cast as a squadron commander at
an English base who's in a constant jam
because of his foolhardy heroics.

Fulfilling a premonition felt by Dunne, he
crashes on his last heroic stunt, proceeding to
the land where all dead pilots go. There he
meets up with The Boss, and is assigned to
guide and instruct the new pilots in the
earthly world who are making a bid for their
wings. It's at this point that the serious overtones of the picture intrude themselves, with
the offering of the matter-of-fact solution that
'life must go on for the living' too abruptly
thrust into the story's continuity.

■ GUYS AND DOLLS

1955, 150 MINS, US ◇ ⓥ
Dir Joseph L. Mankiewicz   *Prod* Samuel Goldwyn
Scr Joseph L. Mankiewicz   *Ph* Harry Stradling
Ed Daniel Mandell   *Mus* Frank Loesser   *Art Dir* Oliver
Smith, Joseph Wright, Howard Bristol
● Marlon Brando, Jean Simmons, Frank Sinatra, Vivian
Blaine, Robert Keith, Stubby Kaye (M-G-M)

Guys and Dolls is a bangup filmusical in the
topdrawer Goldwyn manner, including a
resurrection of the Goldwyn Girls.

The casting is good all the way. Much
interest will focus, of course, around Marlon
Brando in the Robert Alda stage original and
Jean Simmons as the Salvation Army sergeant (created by Isabel Bigley), and they
deport themselves in inspired manner. They
make believable the offbeat romance between
the gambler and the spirited servant of the
gospel.

Vivian Blaine is capital in her original stage
role. Frank Sinatra is an effective vis-a-vis in
the Sam Levene original of Nathan Detroit
and among the four they handle the burden
of the score.

The action shifts from the Times Square
street scenes to the Havana idyll, where
Brando had taken the mission doll
('on a bet').

■ GYPSY

1962, 149 MINS, US ◇ ⓥ
Dir Mervyn LeRoy   *Prod* Mervyn LeRoy   *Scr* Leonard
Spigelgass   *Ph* Harry Stradling Jr   *Ed* Philip W.
Anderson   *Mus* Jule Styne   *Art Dir* John Beckman
● Rosalind Russell, Natalie Wood, Karl Malden, Paul
Wallace, Ann Jilliann (Warner)

There is a wonderfully funny sequence
involving three nails-hard strippers which
comes when *Gypsy* has been unreeling about
an hour. The sequence is thoroughly welcome and almost desperately needed to
counteract a certain Jane One-Note implicit
in the tale of a stage mother whose egotisms
become something of a bore despite the
canny skills of director-producer Mervyn
LeRoy to contrive it otherwise

Rosalind Russell's performance as the
smalltime brood-hen deserves commendation. It is cleverly managed all the way,
with much help from the camera angles of
Harry Stradling Sr.

Russell is less surprising than Karl Malden,
as the mother's incredibly loyal lover who
finally screams when he perceives that she
cares for nobody and nothing except her own
ego compulsions.

About Natalie Wood: it is not easy to credit
her as a stripper but it is interesting to watch

249

her, under LeRoy's guidance, go through the motions in a burlesque world that is prettied up in soft-focus and a kind of phony innocence. Any resemblance of the art of strip, and its setting, to reality is, in this film, purely fleeting.

There are some beguiling satirical touches in the re-creation of the hokey vaudeville routines starring 'Baby June' Havoc, well impersonated by Ann Jilliann, whose flight from the mother turns the latter's attention upon the previously neglected sister, Louise, the Gypsy Rose of later show biz. The film, of course, is based upon the autobiography of Gypsy Rose Lee and the musical comedy in which Ethel Merman starred.

More chronicle than musical, there are advantages still in some of the music (Jule Styne) and lyrics (Stephen Sondheim) and the choreography (Robert Tucker).

....

■ **GYPSY MOTHS, THE**

1969, 106 MINS, US ◇ ⑦
Dir John Frankenheimer *Prod* Hal Landers, Bobby Roberts *Scr* William Hanley *Ph* Philip Lathrop *Ed* Henry Berman *Mus* Elmer Bernstein *Art Dir* George W. Davis, Cary Odell
● Burt Lancaster, Deborah Kerr, Gene Hackman, Scott Wilson, Sheree North, Bonnie Bedelia (M-G-M)

The Gypsy Moths is the story of three barnstorming skydivers and subsequent events when they arrive in a small Kansas town to stage their exhibition. Pairing Burt Lancaster and Deborah Kerr, stars sometimes are lost in a narrative [from a novel] by James Drought] that strives to be a tale of smouldering inner conflicts and pent-up emotions.

At best, aside from exciting sky-diving episodes, picture is a lack-lustre affair insofar as the character relationships are concerned. The stars do not appear particularly happy with their roles. Lancaster seldom speaking, Kerr not particularly well cast.

Lancaster delivers well enough considering what the script requires of him, and Kerr is mostly grim. Hackman and Wilson are forceful, both giving excellent accounts of themselves.

....

■ **HAIL THE CONQUERING HERO**

1944, 101 MINS, US
Dir Preston Sturges *Prod* Preston Sturges *Scr* Preston Sturges *Ph* John F. Seitz *Ed* Stuart Gilmore *Mus* Werner Heymann *Art Dir* Hans Dreier, Haldane Douglas
● Eddie Bracken, Ella Raines, William Demarest, Bill Edwards, Raymond Walburn, Freddie Steele (Paramount)

The deft hand of Preston Sturges molded this film, further proof that he is one of the industry's best writer-directors. The numerous situations that lend themselves readily to comedy lines and business are taken advantage of by a cast that sparkles because of the swift pace they are put through.

Yarn finds Eddie Bracken, medically discharged from the Marines after only one month of service because of hay fever, befriended by six real Guadalcanal heroes. During the course of this friendship, Bracken is clothed in his old marine uniform, bodily taken back to his old home town, where he is welcomed as a hero.

Proof that a capable director can take an actor who is willing to listen and get a better-than-good performance out of him or her is amply displayed here. Sturges has a large cast of veterans supporting Bracken, and a former boxing champion, Freddie Steele, as Bugsy, one of the six marines. The vets all do a good job, but Steele's work is standout.

....

■ **HAIR**

1979, 118 MINS, US ◇ ⑦
Dir Milos Forman *Prod* Lester Persky, Michael Butler *Scr* Michael Weller *Ph* Miroslav Ondricek *Ed* Lynzee Klingman *Mus* Galt MacDermot *Art Dir* Stuart Wurtzel
● John Savage, Treat Wiliams, Beverly D'Angelo, Nicholas Ray, Annie Golden, Dorsey Wright (United Artists)

The storyline imposed on the original musical's book has large expository gaps. These are accentuated by director Milos Forman's determination to have free-form musical numbers evolve out of the tale of a draftee adopted by a bunch of New York hippies, who tune him into their uninhibited lifestyles.

John Savage plays the inductee, fascinated by the group he stumbles upon at a Central Park be-in, composed of Treat Williams, Annie Golden, Dorsey Wright and Don Dacus. They get him stoned, urge him on in his quest for debutante Beverly D'Angelo, and pursue him to his basic training camp in Nevada and a bittersweet finale.

The spirit and elan that captivated the Vietnam protest era are long gone, and what Forman tries to make up with splash and verve fails to evoke potent nostalgia.

....

■ **HAIRSPRAY**

1988, 90 MINS, US ◇ ⑦
Dir John Waters *Prod* Rachal Talalay, Stanley F. Buchthal, John Waters *Scr* John Waters *Ph* David Insley *Ed* Janice Hampton *Mus* Bonnie Greenberg *Art Dir* Vincent Peranio
● Sonny Bono, Ruth Brown, Divine, Colleen Fitzpatrick, Michael St Gerard, Debbie Harry (Buchthal/New Line Cinema)

John Waters' appreciation for the tacky side of life is in full flower in *Hairspray*, a slight but often highly amusing diversion about integration, big girls' fashions and music-mad teens in 1962 Baltimore.

Ricki Lake, chubette daughter of Divine and Jerry Stiller, overcomes all to become queen of an afternoon teenage dance show, much to the consternation of stuck-up blond Colleen Fitzpatrick, whose parents are Debbie Harry and Sonny Bono.

Divine spits out some choice bon mots while denigrating her daughter's pastime, but finally rejoicing in her success, takes Lake off for a pricelessly funny visit to Hefty Hideaway, where full-figure girls can shop to their hearts' content.

Divine, so big he wears a tent-like garment big enough for three ordinary mortals to sleep in, is in otherwise fine form in a dual role. Harry has little to do but act bitchy and sport increasingly towering wigs, while Pia Zadora is virtually unrecognizable as a beatnik chick. All the kids in the predominantly teenage cast are tirelessly enthusiastic.

....

■ **HALF A SIXPENCE**

1967, 148 MINS, UK ◇
Dir George Sidney *Prod* Charles H. Schneer, George Sidney *Scr* Beverley Cross *Ph* Geoffrey Unsworth *Ed* Bill Lewthwaite, Frank Santillo *Mus* David Heneker *Art Dir* Ted Haworth
● Tommy Steele, Julia Foster, Cyril Ritchard, Grover Dale, Elaine Taylor, Hilton Edwards (Paramount)

As with all good musicals, the story [from the stage musical adapted from H.G. Wells' novel *Kipps*] has a simple moral – that money can be a troublesome thing – and it is told in a straightforward narrative, without too much complication of character.

Thus Kipps is projected as a likable lad, temporarily aberrated by his coming into a fortune, and returning to the true common virtues when he loses it.

The cohesive force is certainly that of Tommy Steele, who takes hold of his part like a terrier and never lets go. His assurance is overwhelming, and he leads the terping with splendid vigor and elan.

Of course, the haunting title song and the ebullient 'Flash, Bang, Wallop!' remain the showstoppers, and David Heneker's score is a little short of socko tunes elsewhere.

....

■ **HALF MOON STREET**

1987, 90 MINS, UK/US ◇ ⑦
Dir Bob Swaim *Prod* Geoffrey Reeve *Scr* Bob Swaim, Edward Behr *Ph* Peter Hannan *Ed* Richard Marden *Mus* Richard Harvey *Art Dir* Anthony Curtis
● Sigourney Weaver, Michael Caine, Patrick Kavanagh, Keith Buckley, Nadim Sawalha, Angus MacInnes (RKO/Pressman/Showtime – Movie Channel)

Half Moon Street is a half-baked excuse for a film that is redeemed not a whit by having Sigourney Weaver and Michael Caine in the starring roles. Script, based on Paul Theroux' thriller *Dr Slaughter*, has been rendered nonsensical and incoherent by screenwriters.

Weaver plays Dr Slaughter, a scholar at the Middle East Institute in London who turns to working as an escort to supplement her paltry income. She manages to avoid any emotional attachments with her clients until she arrives one rainy night to be the paid guest of Lord Bulbeck, played competently if uninvolvingly by Caine.

Caine is somehow mixed up with Arabs in a convoluted scheme and somehow Weaver becomes inextricably and unwittingly wound up in his dealings.

....

■ **HALLELUJAH**

1929, 109 MINS, US
Dir King Vidor *Scr* Wanda Tuchock, Ransom Rideout *Ph* Gordon Avil *Ed* Hugh Wynn, Anson Stevenson *Art Dir* Cedric Gibbons
● Daniel L. Haynes, Nina Mae McKinney, William Fountaine, Harry Gray, Fannie Belle DeKnight, Victoria Spivey (M-G-M)

In his herculean attempt to take comedy, romance and tragedy and blend them into a big, gripping, Negro talker, King Vidor has turned out an unusual picture from a theme that is almost as ancient as the sun. Vidor's strict adherence to realism is so effective at times it is stark and uncanny.

The story is a plain one, the characters not too many and no fancy long-drawn-out monickers and thus the average screen fan can follow its theme without the slightest difficulty. This is all a big feather in Vidor's hat.

Nina Mae McKinney as the dynamic, vivacious girl of the colored underworld, who lives by her wits and enmeshes the males by her personality, sex appeal and dancing feet, never had a day's work before a camera.

Daniel L. Haynes as Zeke, the principal male, is the big, rough, lazylike colored boy, happiest when he sings and who loves his women.

Victoria Spivey is the blues singer who does a pretty naturalistic bit of acting as the girl who loves and waits. William Fountaine becomes a dominant figure as the heavy, and acquits himself creditably. Fannie Belle DeKnight is the mother of the film, and what a mammy!

A characteristic figure is Harry Gray as the white bewhiskered parson and daddy of the Johnson family.

. . . .

■ HALLELUJAH, I'M A BUM!

1933, 83 MINS, US

Dir Lewis Milestone   *Prod* Joseph M. Schenck
Scr S. N. Behrman, Ben Hecht   *Ph* Lucien Andriot
Mus Alfred Newman (dir.)   *Art Dir* Richard Day
● Al Jolson, Madge Evans, Frank Morgan, Harry Langdon, Chester Conklin   (United Artists)

Almost Barrie-ish in its whimsy, the ethereal quality of the Ben Hecht-S. N. Behrman script foundation is its primary deficiency. Lorenz Hart, while solely credited for the lyrics to Richard Rodgers' music, probably merits as much authorship credit because his lyrical dialog constitutes the main burden of the proceedings.

The whole thing is an unconvincing mixture of the fictional and factional. Ultra-modern realism with the playboy mayor of the city of New York and his weakness for the Central Park Casino and a pretty femme in particular (Madge Evans) is blended with such unconvincing detail as non-existing Central Park's hobos of which Al Jolson is the unofficial mayor.

The rollicking fun of an uncertain but not too unsteady story structure collapses utterly when Evans, a victim of aphasia or amnesia, later figures as the romance interest opposite Jolson, until recovering her senses for the finale with the mayor (Frank Morgan).

The 'rhythmic dialog' and the Lewis Milestonian method of wedding the tempo'd music to the action has its moments. The laity will doubtlessly compare this to the Ernst Lubitsch technique in *Trouble in Paradise*.

This must have been one of the toughest pictures to shoot and undoubtedly the most trying for the rest of the cast who had to talk in rhyme and rhythm rather than their accustomed dramatic prose.

Jolson's selling of the title song and 'You Are Too Beautiful', the former reprised more often, of course leaves little wanting. 'Bum' is a pip of a number with its odd-rhythmed style and tempo. 'I'll Do It Again' and 'What Do You Want with Money' are other songs.

. . . .

■ HALLELUJAH THE HILLS

1963, 88 MINS, US

Dir Adolfas Mekas   *Prod* David C. Stone   *Scr* Adolfas
Mekas   *Ph* Ed Emshwiller   *Ed* Adolfas Mekas
Mus Meyer Kupferman
● Peter H. Beard, Martin Greenbaum, Sheila Finn, Peggy Steffans   (Vermont)

Formerly this offbeat NY filmmaking group mainly made dramas. But this zesty unusual romp twits its subject with knowing insight and also packs in some inside film buff gags and allusions.

There is not much of a story. It is mainly a joyous rush of images by a new director who has assimilated his classics and regular run of films. Two clean-cut, adventurous young American stalwarts vie for the hand of a beauteous young girl only to have her snapped up by a bearded character. Small town life and the seasons pass in review as the two men camp out and take their turns at wooing the girl or trying to cope with outdoor life in the snow and sun.

Writer-director-editor Adolfas Mekas displays a flair for visual revelation, gags and shenanigans that manage to keep this stimulating throughout. The intimations of noted pix culminates with a bow to D. W. Griffith in showing the great ice flow rescue of Lillian Gish by Richard Barthlemess in *Way Down East*.

Mekas assimilates rather than imitates. The actors are all fresh, and cavort with grace and a lack of self-consciousness. Camerawork is clear with editing sharp and the music a counterpoint help. There are glimpses and incisive satiric shafts against war, courting habits, youthful shyness and self absorption in this madcap, bright pic.

. . . .

■ HALLELUJAH TRAIL, THE

1965, 152 MINS, US ◇ ⊽

Dir John Sturges   *Prod* John Sturges   *Scr* John Gay
Ph Robert Surtees   *Ed* Ferris Webster   *Mus* Elmer
Bernstein   *Art Dir* Cary Odell
● Burt Lancaster, Lee Remick, Jim Hutton, Pamela Tiffin, Donald Pleasance, Brian Keith   (United Artists)

It all begins with the burgeoning city of Denver facing the worst threat of its existence – becoming bone dry in 10 days in the approaching winter of 1867. This awesome situation paves the way for one of the nuttiest cinematic mishmashes you ever saw, in which thirsty miners, a worried US Cavalry, a band of whiskey-mad Sioux, a crusading temperance group and a train of 40 wagons carrying 600 barrels of hard likker become so thoroughly involved that even the off-screen narrator has a hard time trying to keep track of them and their proper logistics.

Producer-director John Sturges has pulled every plug in spoofing practically every western situation known to the scripter, and the whole is beautifully packaged. Screenplay, from Bill Gulick's novel, approaches the situations straight.

The cavalry, coloneled by Burt Lancaster, is constantly threatened with breaching the articles of war and the Constitution itself by the demands of temperance leader Lee Remick. Sioux, leaving their reservation when they get wind of the approaching whiskey, can't be attacked by the cavalry because they carry certain signed government papers.

Performances, like situations, are played straight, and therein lies their beauty. Lancaster does a bangup job as the harassed cavalry colonel plagued with having to offer safe conduct to the whiskey train and to the temperance ladies.

One of the standouts in pic is Martin Landau, as Chief Walks-Stooped-Over, as deadpan as any Injun ever lived but socking over his comedy scenes mostly with his eyes.

. . . .

■ HALLOWEEN

1978, 93 MINS, US ◇ ⊽

Dir John Carpenter   *Prod* Debra Hill   *Scr* John
Carpenter, Debra Hill   *Ph* Dean Cundey   *Ed* Tomy
Wallace, Charles Burnstein   *Mus* John Carpenter
Art Dir Tomy Wallace
● Donald Pleasance, Jamie Lee Curtis, Nancy Loomis, P.J. Soles, Charles Cyphers, Kyle Richards   (Falcon)

After a promising opening, *Halloween* becomes just another maniac-on-the-loose suspenser. However, despite the prosaic plot, director John Carpenter has timed the film's gore so that the 93-minute item is packed with enough thrills.

The picture opens 15 years earlier, on Halloween night in a small midwestern town. A young boy spies his sister necking with her boyfriend. As they mount the steps for her bedroom he slips on his Halloween mask, pulls out a butcher knife and does some cutting.

For the rest of the thriller the Hitchcockian influence remains, but the plot ambles along to a predictable conclusion. It is now the present, also Halloween. Donald Pleasance, a psychiatrist who has been caring for the killer during the years, is on his way to the state hospital to make sure that the maniac is never freed.

Of course, the maniac escapes, returns to the scene of the original crime and searches for suitable victims, in this case a trio of babysitting friends.

. . . .

■ HALLOWEEN II

1981, 92 MINS, US ◇

Dir Rick Rosenthal   *Prod* Debra Hill, John Carpenter
Scr John Carpenter, Debra Hill   *Ph* Dean Cundy
Ed Mark Goldblatt   *Mus* John Carpenter, Alan
Howarth   *Art Dir* Michael Riva
● Jamie Lee Curtis, Donald Pleasence, Charles Cyphers, Dick Warlock   (De Laurentiis)

This uninspired version amounts to luke-warm sloppy seconds in comparison to the original film that made director John Carpenter a hot property.

There are incredibly almost never any really terrific scares in 92 minutes – just multiple shots of violence and gore that are more gruesome than anything else.

Script commences with the finale from the original where concerned doctor Donald Pleasence shoots Jamie Lee Curtis' demented predator six times only to have him walk away and continue his killing spree. Young Curtis is rushed to the hospital for care where a whole set of young, nubile hospital staffers are primed as the next victims.

Meanwhile the zombie-like masked killer makes his way through the town, wandering in and out of houses slashing unsuspecting residents. So many people wander through the proceedings that it becomes difficult to care who is getting sliced or why.

. . . .

■ HALLOWEEN III
SEASON OF THE WITCH

1982, 96 MINS, US ◇ ⊽

Dir Tommy Lee Wallace   *Prod* John Carpenter, Debra
Hill   *Scr* Tommy Lee Wallace, [Nigel Kneale]
Ph Dean Cundey   *Ed* Millie Moore   *Mus* John
Carpenter, Alan Howarth   *Art Dir* Peter Jamison
● Tom Atkins, Stacey Nelkin, Dan O'Herlihy, Ralph Strait, Michael Currie, Jadeen Barbor   (De Laurentiis)

There's not much to say about *Halloween III* that hasn't already been said about either of the other two *Halloween* pics or a slew of imitators.

Interesting to note here is producer Debra Hill's earlier claim that this film would steer clear of gore and blood and instead go for the science fiction paranoia genre of *Invasion of the Body Snatchers*. Apparently, yanking someone's head off their shoulders, shoving fingers down a man's eyeballs or inserting a power drill in a woman's head don't qualify as particularly disgusting.

There is the tired old cliche of a crazed toy manufacturer (in this case he makes Halloween masks), the fearless couple out to figure what's 'really' going on, and plot holes big enough to shoot another film through. On the latter note, Nigel Kneale, credited screenwriter all through production, somehow managed to get his name removed from the credits.

. . . .

■ HALLOWEEN 4
THE RETURN OF MICHAEL MYERS

1988, 88 MINS, US ◇ ⊽

Dir Dwight H. Little   *Prod* Paul Freeman   *Scr* Alan B.
McElroy   *Ph* Peter Lyons Collister   *Ed* Curtiss
Clayton   *Mus* Alan Howarth   *Art Dir* Roger S.
Crandall
● Donald Pleasence, Ellie Cornell, Danielle Harris, George P. Wilbur, Michael Pataki   (Trancas)

Fourth entry in the *Halloween* horror series is a no-frills, workmanlike picture [story by Dhani Lipsius, Larry Rattner, Benjamin Ruffner and Alan B. McElroy].

Designed as a direct sequel to John Carpenter's 1978 hit, with no reference to the events chronicled in parts 2 and 3, pic resurrects monster Michael Myers (previously referred to mainly as The Shape), who escapes from a hospital to return home and wreak havoc, with the vague notion of getting to his niece Jamie (Danielle Harris).

His face scarred from an earlier altercation with the monster, Donald Pleasence reprises his role as Dr Loomis, now hell-bent on destroying the obviously unkillable Myers.

■ HALLS OF MONTEZUMA

1950, 113 MINS, US ◇

Dir Lewis Milestone *Prod* Robert Bassler *Scr* Michael Blankfort *Ph* Winton C. Hoch *Ed* William Reynolds *Mus* Sol Kaplan
● Richard Widmark, Jack Palance, Robert Wagner, Karl Malden, Richard Hylton, Richard Boone (20th Century-Fox)

Halls of Montezuma is an account of Marine heroism during the fierce South Pacific fighting of the Second World War.

Rather than a presentation of mass battle, film deals intimately with a small group of Marines under the command of Richard Widmark and how it fulfills a mission to take Jap prisoners for questioning. Footage is long but there is no feeling of great length.

Opening shots feature flashbacks to acquaint the audience with the Marines as civilians and show their strengths and weaknesses.

Widmark is exceptionally good as an officer who masks his fear and encourages his men. Reginald Gardiner adds lightness as a Marine sergeant who scoffs at regulations. Karl Malden stands out as the pharmacist's mate.

■ HAMBURGER HILL

1987, 110 MINS, US ◇ Ⓥ

Dir John Irvin *Scr* Jim Carabatsos *Ph* Peter MacDonald *Ed* Peter Tanner *Mus* Philip Glass *Art Dir* Austen Spriggs
● Anthony Barrile, Michael Patrick Boatman, Don Cheadle, Michael Dolan, Don James, Dylan McDermott (RKO/Nasatir-Carabatsos/Interaccess)

Well-produced and directd with an eye to documentary-like realism and authenticity, pic centers upon a military undertaking of familiar futility during the Vietnam War. It follows a squad of 14 recruits from initial R&R through 10 days' worth of hell, as the men make 11 agonizing assaults on a heavily fortified hill.

First 40 minutes attempt to show the developing relationships among the guys, and screenwriter-coproducer Jim Carabatsos has been particularly attentive to delineating the tensions between the blacks and whites in the group.

More than an hour is devoted to the protected effort to scale the indistinguished piece of Vietnamese real estate of the title. As physically impressive as some of it is, the action also proves dispiriting and depressing, as the soldiers slide helplessly down the muddy slopes in the rain and are inevitably picked off by enemy gunfire.

Director John Irvin, who shot a documentary in Vietnam in 1969, the year the action takes place, makes fine use of the Philippines locations and the verisimilitude supplied by the production team.

■ HAMLET

1948, 155 MINS, UK Ⓥ

Dir Laurence Olivier *Prod* Laurence Olivier *Scr* William Shakespeare *Ph* Desmond Dickinson *Ed* Helga Cranston *Mus* William Walton *Art Dir* Roger Furse, Carmen Dillon
● Laurence Olivier, Eileen Herlie, Basil Sydney, Jean Simmons, Norman Wooland, Felix Aylmer (Rank/Two Cities)

This is picture-making at its best. At a cost of $2 million it seems incredibly cheap compared with some of the ephemeral trash that is turned out.

Star-producer-director Laurence Olivier was the driving force behind the whole venture. Minor characters and a good deal of verse have been thrown overboard, and a four-and-a-quarter hour play becomes a two-and-a-half hour film.

Pundits may argue that Rosencrantz, Guildenstern and Fortinbras shouldn't have been sacrificed, and that many familiar gems are missing. They will argue about the bewildering crossing and intercrossing of motives. Scholars may complain that this isn't Hamlet as Shakespeare created him, but one that Olivier has made in his own image.

In his interpretation of Hamlet, Olivier thinks of him as nearly a great man, damned, as most people are, by lack of resolution. He announces it in a spoken foreword as 'the tragedy of a man who couldn't make up his mind'.

Special praise is due Eileen Herlie for her playing of the queen. She has made the character really live. Her love for her son, the consciousness of evil-doing, her grief and agony, her death – made by Olivier to appear as sacrificing herself for Hamlet – make her a very memorable, pitiful figure. Jean Simmons as Ophelia brings to the role a sensitive, impressionable innocence, perhaps too childlike.

Basil Sydney repeats his stage success as the king, of whom ambition and lust have taken possession, and rises to his greatest height in his soliloquy trying to pray and seeing himself accursed like Cain.

□ 1948: Best Picture (Nomination)

■ HAMLET

1990, 135 MINS, US ◇ Ⓥ

Dir Franco Zeffirelli *Prod* Dyson Lovell *Scr* Christopher De Vore, Franco Zeffirelli *Ph* David Watkin *Ed* Richard Marden *Mus* Ennio Morricone *Art Dir* Dante Ferretti
● Mel Gibson, Glenn Close, Alan Bates, Paul Scofield, Ian Holm, Helena Bonham-Carter (Warner/Nelson)

Mel Gibson's best moments come in the highly physical duelling scene that climaxes the Shakespeare play. Otherwise, Mel's Hamlet is blond and Franco Zeffirelli's *Hamlet* is bland.

By slicing the text virtually in half, and casting a matinee idol in the lead, the director clearly hoped to engage the masses. Unfortunately, this Hamlet seems no more modern or pertinent to contemporary concerns than any other on stage, screen or tube in recent decades. Nor does it possess the rugged freshness of Kenneth Branagh's *Henry V.*

Familiar story unfolds in and around a formidable fortress that is actually a combination of three ancient structures in the British Isles. Deeply aggrieved by the death of his father, Hamlet is commanded by his father to avenge his murder at the hands of his brother Claudius, who has since become king and married Hamlet's mother, Gertrude.

Performances all fall in a middle range between the competent and the lackluster. Gibson gets the dialog and soliloquies out decently, but rolls and bugs his eyes a lot. Best is probably Paul Scofield as the ghost, although Zeffirelli irritatingly cuts or pulls away from him midstream. Alan Bates is a solid Claudius. Glenn Close brings a juicy vigor to Gertrude.

■ HAMMERSMITH IS OUT

1972, 108 MINS, US ◇ Ⓥ

Dir Peter Ustinov *Prod* Alex Lucas *Scr* Stanford Whitmore *Ph* Richard H. Kline *Ed* David Blewitt *Mus* Dominic Frontiere *Art Dir* Robert Benton
● Elizabeth Taylor, Richard Burton, Peter Ustinov, Beau Bridges, Leon Ames, George Raft (Crean)

What is, apparently, an exercise in spoofery on the part of Elizabeth Taylor, Richard Burton and the even more energetic Peter Ustinov, starts as a variation on the Faust legend but almost immediately turns into a belabored antic.

The somewhat sketchy screenplay is no more than a line on which the three principals hang their rarely inspired improvisations.

Burton, as the lunatic Hammersmith who flees the asylum with the connivance of male nurse Beau Bridges by promising him unworldly riches, goes through the film with a single bored expression. Bridges is sleazy and repulsive and well deserving of his fate. Ustinov, as the asylum keeper, committed to recapturing Hammersmith, would be funnier if his lines, spoken with an unintelligible 'mad scientist' accent could be understood.

■ HAMMETT

1982, 94 MINS, US ◇ Ⓥ

Dir Wim Wenders *Prod* Fred Roos, Ronald Colby, Don Guest *Scr* Ross Thomas, Dennis O'Flaherty *Ph* Philip Lathrop, Joseph Biroc *Ed* Barry Malkin, Marc Lamb, Robert Q. Lovett, Randy Roberts *Mus* John Barry *Art Dir* Dean Tavoularis, Eugene Lee
● Frederic Forrest, Peter Boyle, Marilu Henner, Roy Kinnear, Elisha Cook, Lydia Lei (Zoetrope)

Wim Wenders' problems with this, his first Hollywood film, are many and well known. Reportedly hired by producer Francis Coppola on the strength of his complicated muder opus, *The American Friend* [1977], Wenders' *Hammett* was early on dubbed a rough diamond.

Now, overpolished by too many script rewrites, perhaps emasculated by massive footage scraps and belated re-shoots, project (all shot on interiors) emerges a rather suffocating film taking place in a rickety 'Chinatown'.

But *Chinatown* it is not. Film is a sort of homage to Dashiel Hammett. Based on a fiction by Joe Gores, it has Hammett far removed from his old private eye days and suffering from TB, eking out a precarious living with short stories penned for pulp detective magazines.

Frederic Forrest looks like Hammett, talks like Humphrey Bogart and is acceptable. His old boss from the Pinkerton Private Eye Co is played with force by Peter Boyle.

A Chinese prostitute has disappeared and must be found for she might be dangerous to top monied interests. After several chases, killings and muggings, it emerges that the Chinese girl has some incriminating porn pictures of all the men who really run the town.

■ HAND, THE

1981, 104 MINS, US ◇

Dir Oliver Stone *Prod* Edward R. Pressman *Scr* Oliver Stone *Ph* King Baggott *Ed* Richard Marks *Mus* James Horner *Art Dir* John Michael Riva
● Michael Caine, Andrea Marcovicci, Viveca Lindfors, Bruce McGill, Mara Hobel, Annie McEnroe (Orion)

Director-scripter Oliver Stone takes on a premise – that of an autonomous appendage wreaking havoc on anyone crossing the human it was previously attached to – that has in some form been effectively executed in many past pix.

Special visual effects consultant Carlo Rambaldi, who performed wonders on '*Alien,*' should probably share some of the blame for the ineffectiveness of the aforementioned villain.

There is little relief to be found from the relationships in the script [from the book *The Lizard's Tail*]. Cartoonist Michael Caine

H

evokes some sympathy after he loses his hand and particularly in scenes with daughter Mara Hobel, he spends most of his time sweating and grimacing into the camera lens. It's not a pretty sight.

James Horner has concocted an appropriately haunting score throughout.

. . . .

■ HANDFUL OF DUST, A

1988, 118 MINS, UK ◇ ▽

Dir Charles Sturridge *Prod* Derek Granger *Scr* Tim Sullivan, Derek Granger, Charles Sturridge *Ph* Peter Hannan *Ed* Peter Coulson *Mus* George Fenton *Art Dir* Eileen Diss
● James Wilby, Kristin Scott-Thomas, Rupert Graves, Anjelica Huston, Alec Guinness, Judi Dench (LWT/ Stagescreen)

A Handful of Dust is classy stuff based on an Evelyn Waugh novel, with a high production standard but an essentially empty story.

Kristin Scott-Thomas as a lovely but fickle aristocrat is excellent, with an appealing fey manner. The virtual cameo appearances of Alec Guinness, Anjelica Huston and Judi Dench go some way to giving *Dust* a pedigree it might otherwise not be able to claim.

Set in Britain of the 1930s, at the beautiful country house Hetton Abbey, James Wilby and Scott-Thomas and their young son seem content until the weekend visit of idle socialite Rupert Graves.

Scott-Thomas slips into an affair with the penniless Graves while Wilby happily wanders his estate unaware he is being cuckolded. When their son is killed in a freak riding accident, Scott-Thomas tells her husband she wants a divorce.

When Wilby finds the divorce settlement would mean selling Hetton he promptly sets sail for South America in search of a lost Amazonian city with an eccentric explorer.

Technically, *A Handful of Dust* cannot be faulted. Where the film disappoints is the story, which though it ably highlights the vacuous attitudes of the English upper classes, is essentially slight.

. . . .

■ HANDGUN

1983, 101 MINS, US ◇ ▽

Dir Tony Garnett *Prod* Tony Garnett *Scr* Tony Garnett *Ph* Charles Stewart *Ed* William Shapter *Mus* Mike Post *Art Dir* Lilly Kilvert
● Karen Young, Clayton Day, Suzie Humphreys, Helena Humann, Ben Jones (Kestrel)

Handgun takes a subject which is the stuff of exploitation and steers it towards social commentary. The result is an intelligent analysis of the political and sexual values of male society in Texas.

Pic is cast in three chapters that follow the maturing of a pretty young girl who goes to the midwest to teach history after a protected Catholic upbringing in Boston. She's just too soft to counter the approaches of a macho attorney who's obsessed with guns and hunting. It's only when he decides to have his own way with her that she realizes what she's up against.

Karen Young is sharp in her depiction of a nervy girl whose eyes are slowly opened. And Clayton Day plays all the subtleties of a decent chap who, nevertheless, has swallowed whole a value system that debases women and seeks to protect its integrity through violent confrontation.

. . . .

■ HANDMAID'S TALE, THE

1990, 109 MINS, US/W. GERMANY ◇ ▽

Dir Volker Schlondorff *Prod* Danny Wilson *Scr* Harold Pinter *Ph* Igor Luther *Ed* David Ray *Mus* Ryuichi Sakamoto *Art Dir* Tom Walsh
● Natasha Richardson, Robert Duvall, Faye Dunaway, Aidan Quinn, Elizabeth McGovern, Victoria Tennant (Cinecon/Bioskop)

The Handmaid's Tale is a provocative protrait of a future totalitarian theocracy where women have lost all human rights. The adaptation of Margaret Atwood's best seller belongs to that rare category of science fiction film dealing with dystopias.

Even rarer, *Handmaid's Tale* is sci-fi from a woman's point-of-view. Following a military coup, this future society called Gilead operates under martial law in a perpetual state of warfare (a la *1984*), with Old Testament religion the rule. The so-called sins of late 20th-century society, ranging from pollution to such activities as birth control and abortion are blamed by the authorities as causing God's plague of infertility, requiring drastic measures to preserve the race.

Natasha Richardson protrays a young mother who's rounded up by the authorities to serve as a breeder, or handmaid, assigned to the barren family of state security chief Robert Duvall and his wife Faye Dunaway. Her travails unfold in Harold Pinter's uncharacteristically staight-forward screenplay rather mechanically.

Though helmer Volker Schlöndorff succeeds in painting the bleakness of this extrapolated future, he fails to create a strong and persistent connection with the heroine's plight.

. . . .

■ HANG 'EM HIGH

1968, 114 MINS, US ◇ ▽

Dir Ted Post *Prod* Leonard Freeman *Scr* Leonard Freeman, Mel Goldberg *Ph* Leonard South, Richard Kines *Mus* Dominic Frontiere
● Clint Eastwood, Inger Stevens, Ed Begley, Pat Hingle, Arlene Golonka (United Artists/Malpaso)

Hang 'em High comes across as a poor-made imitation of a poor Italian-made imitation of an American western. It stars Clint Eastwood as a man bent on vengeance and is an episodic, rambling tale which glorifies personal justice, and mocks orderly justice.

Eastwood is hanged (but not killed) by do-it-yourself vigilantes, headed by Ed Begley; district judge Pat Hingle recruits Eastwood to be a deputy marshal, and part of the job is to round up those who wronged him. Inger Stevens drifts in and out as a forced romantic interest.

From then on, film drags along through at least a dozen killings and legal hangings, shown in meticulous, morbid detail. Plot makes Hingle practically psychotic in his pursuit of 'justice', and in the big hanging scene he fairly drools over the event.

Eastwood projects a likeable image, but the part is only a shade more developed over his Sergio Leone Italoaters. Begley goes way overboard in mugging the climactic shoot-out and hang-in.

. . . .

■ HANGING TREE, THE

1959, 106 MINS, US ◇

Dir Delmer Daves *Prod* Martin Jurow, Richard Shepherd *Scr* Wendell Mayes, Halstead Welles *Ph* Ted McCord *Ed* Owen Marks *Mus* Max Steiner
● Gary Cooper, Maria Schell, Karl Malden, Ben Piazza, George C. Scott (Warner)

Wendell Mayes and Halstead Welles did the screenplay from a long short story by Dorothy M. Johnson, who is a kind of western writers' western writer. Johnson's stories show the West as it was, not as it is often shown, with tinted romance or dubious Freudianism. Her west is a hard, cruel, lonely frontier, in which the humans were often stripped of the savagery of the country.

In essence, the story follows western classic form. Gary Cooper is the mysterious stranger, a taciturn and quixotic man who drifts into a Montana gold-mining town. He quickly establishes himself as a man equally handy with a scalpel, a Colt and an inside straight, tender in his professional role as MD, and a paradoxically tough man when dealing with gamblers and con men.

His first action is to rescue young Ben Piazza from a lynch-minded mob and make him his bond-servant under threat of exposure. His second is to take on the recovery of Maria Schell, a Swiss immigrant, who is ill and blinded from exposure. Stirring in these complicated relationships is the character of Karl Malden, an evil and lascivious gold prospector, who wants Piazza's life, Cooper's money and Schell's body, more or less in that order.

There are fine performances from a good cast, but the main contribution comes from the director. The natural splendor of the Washington location is thoroughly exploited in Technicolor, but Delmer Daves doesn't allow his characters to get lost in the forest or mountains. Daves uses one technique, of presenting his background scene and then letting his characters walk into it, that is intriguing.

Cooper has one of his best roles. His mystery and tight-lipped refusal to discuss it perfectly suit his laconic style. Schell is inspired casting, giving her role unusual sensitivity and strength. Malden, with an out-sized role of a leering and lewd sadist, gives it king-sized treatment.

. . . .

■ HANGMEN ALSO DIE

1943, 131 MINS, US

Dir Fritz Lang *Prod* Arnold Pressburger *Scr* John Wexley, Bert Brecht, Fritz Lang *Ph* James Wong Howe *Ed* Gene Fowley Jr *Mus* Hanns Eisler
● Brian Donlevy, Walter Brennan, Anna Lee, Gene Lockhart, Dennis O'Keefe (United Artists)

From a directorial standpoint this is a triumph for Fritz Lang, who succeeds with singular success in capturing the spirit of the Czech people in the face of the Nazi reign of terror.

UA sunk plenty of coin into the picture. Cameraman James Wong Howe, in particular, turns in a magnificent job.

The cast, topped by Brian Donlevy and Walter Brennan, is uniformly splendid, with the performances of Gene Lockhart, as a cowering Quisling Czech, and Alexander Granach, as a shrewd, calculating and ruthless inspector of the Gestapo, being particularly outstanding. Story continuity is fine and absorbing throughout, but essentially it's the incisive terms of the message propounded that sets *Hamgmen* apart and points up the fact that propaganda can be art.

Saga of the courageous spirit of the Czechs starts with the assassination of Heydrich, the hangman, by an appointed member of the underground (Donlevy), but the plans for his escape go awry and, due to the stringent curfew laws, he is forced to spend the night at the home of a professor and his daughter. In order to save her father, who is held as hostage along with several hundred others until the assassin will be given up, she goes to the Gestapo to reveal his identity, but realizes that the spirit of the Czech people has made of him a symbol of freedom and that the underground will protect him at all costs.

Both Donlevy and Brennan, as the professor, are excellent, the latter emerging in the film a figure of heroic proportions.

. . . .

■ HANGOVER SQUARE

1945, 77 MINS, US

Dir John Brahm *Prod* Robert Bassler *Scr* Barre Lyndon *Ph* Joseph La Salle *Ed* Harry Reynolds *Mus* Bernard Herrmann *Art Dir* Lyle R. Wheeler, Maurice Ransford
● Laird Cregar, Linda Darnell, George Sanders (20th Century-Fox)

Hangover Square is eerie murder melodrama of the London gaslight era – typical of Patrick Hamilton yarns, of which this is another. And it doesn't make any pretense at mystery. The madman-murderer is known from the first reel.

It is the story of a distinguished young composer-pianist with a Jekyll-Hyde personality. When he becomes over-wrought, he's a madman – and his lustful forages are always accompanied by a loss of memory for the periods during which he is murder-bent.

Laird Cregar as the madman-murderer shows markedly the physical decline, through dieting, said to have been a factor in [the actor's] death.

Linda Darnell and George Sanders are co-stars, the former as the two-timing girl and Sanders as a Scotland Yard psychiatrist who provides the tell-tale clues responsible for the denouement.

Production is grade A, and so is the direction by John Brahm, with particular bows to the music score by Bernard Herrmann.

■ **HANKY PANKY**

1982, 105 MINS, US ◇ ⓥ
Dir Sidney Poitier   *Prod* Martin Ransohoff   *Scr* Henry Rosenbaum, David Taylor   *Ph* Arthur Ornitz   *Ed* Harry Keller   *Mus* Tom Scott   *Art Dir* Ben Edwards
● Gene Wilder, Gilda Radner, Kathleen Quinlan, Richard Widmark, Robert Prosky, Josef Sommer (Columbia)

Hanky Panky is a limp romantic suspense comedy which manages to be neither romantic, suspenseful nor funny. What with Gene Wilder as a hapless Chicago architect caught up in a string of extraordinary coincidences involving government agents, a secret tape, and a big scene taking place at the Grand Canyon, pic appears to be an attempt to duplicate the classy thrills of *North by Northwest*.

Tale opens moodily with an unexplained suicide and then picks up Wilder, whose short cab ride with frantic Kathleen Quinlan plunges him into a web of intrigue obliging him to endure suspicion by the police for murder, beatings by agent Richard Widmark, and an attempt to kill him by a helicopter out in the desert.

He's an innocent, of course, but once he latches onto Gilda Radner, sister of the guy who hanged himself in the opening scene, he's committed to seeing the escapade through.

Casting of Wilder and Radner strikes no sparks. Quinlan, a serious actress who deserves greater challenges than this, disappears in the early going.

■ **HANNAH AND HER SISTERS**

1986, 106 MINS, US ◇ ⓥ
Dir Woody Allen   *Prod* Robert Greenhut   *Scr* Woody Allen   *Ph* Carlo Di Palma   *Ed* Susan E. Morse   *Art Dir* Stuart Wurtzel
● Woody Allen, Michael Caine, Mia Farrow, Carrie Fisher, Barbara Hershey, Dianne Wiest (Rollins/Joffe)

Hannah and Her Sisters is one of Woody Allen's great films. Indeed, he makes nary a misstep from beginning to end in charting the amorous affiliations of three sisters and their men over a two-year period.

Its structure is a successful mixture of outright comedy, rueful meditation and sexual complications.

Pic begins at a Thanksgiving dinner, and ends at one two years later, with most of the characters going through mate changes in the interim.

Hannah, played by Mia Farrow, was formerly married to TV producer Woody Allen but is now happily wed to agent Michael Caine, who, in turn, secretly lusts for his wife's sexy sister, Barbara Hershey, the live-in mate of tormented painter Max Von Sydow.

The third sister (Dianne Wiest) is by far the most neurotic of the bunch and, while waiting for her acting, singing or writing career to take off, runs a catering business with Carrie Fisher.
□ 1986: Best Picture (Nomination)

■ **HANNIBAL BROOKS**

1969, 101 MINS, UK ◇
Dir Michael Winner   *Prod* Michael Winner   *Scr* Dick Clement, Ian La Frenais   *Ph* Robert Paynter   *Ed* [uncredited]   *Mus* Francis Lai   *Art Dir* Jurgen Kiebach
● Oliver Reed, Michael J. Pollard, Karin Baal, Wolfgang Preiss, Helmut Lohner (United Artists/Scimitar)

A pleasant, tame tale about a British prisoner (Oliver Reed), assigned to nursemaid an elephant in a Munich Zoo. From here, it is a short jump into attempted escapes, with the elephant in tow, across some mountain passes (a la Hannibal, hence the title) into Switzerland.

The humorous vein which was evidently intended to be topmost throughout the film gets sidetracked by the excursion into action and there isn't a laugh in the second half of the film.

The British actor, playing a kindly, animal-loving and, for most of the film, pacifistic soldier carries the entire film on his admittedly broad shoulders but can't overcome the confused writing, or the even greater burden of a poor performance by costar Michael J. Pollard. The latter is simply dreadful as a cocky Yank prisoner.

Filmed almost entirely on location in Bavaria, the beautiful countryside is caught perfectly by Robert Paynter's color camera.

■ **HANNIE CAULDER**

1971, 85 MINS, UK ◇
Dir Burt Kennedy   *Prod* Patrick Curtis, Raquel Welch   *Scr* Z.X. Jones   *Ph* Edward Scaife   *Ed* Jim Connock   *Mus* Ken Thorpe
● Raquel Welch, Robert Culp, Ernest Borgnine, Strother Martin, Jack Elam, Diana Dors (Tigon British/Curtwel)

Raquel Welch plays Hannie Caulder who, having been widowed and raped by the Clemens brothers, determines to avenge these wrongs. With the aid of a bounty hunter she is soon showing that ladies shoot first and can be more deadly than the male.

The west may never have boasted so immaculate a markswoman but it seems highly unlikely that anyone is expected to take the film too seriously. Welch, with genteel modesty, makes the character for many rather ingratiating though others undoubtedly will find her plain ludicrous. All she has to wear after her farm has been set ablaze, while being raped by the drunken brothers, is a hastily-grabbed poncho. The avoidance of more than quick glimpses of a shapely thigh seems her main concern.

She is admirably supported by Ernest Borgnine as the meanest of the brothers and Robert Culp as the bounty hunter who befriends her. Christopher Lee, after his usual horror roles makes an unusual appearance as a sympathetic gunsmith.

■ **HANOI HILTON**

1987, 123 MINS, US ◇ ⓥ
Dir Lionel Chetwynd   *Prod* Menahem Golan, Yoram Globus   *Scr* Lionel Chetwynd   *Ph* Mark Irwin   *Ed* Penelope Shaw   *Mus* Jimmy Webb   *Art Dir* R. Clifford Searcy
● Michael Moriarty, Jeffrey Jones, Paul Le Mat, Stephen Davies, Lawrence Pressman, Aki Aleong (Cannon)

The Hanoi Hilton is a lame attempt by writer-director Lionel Chetwynd to tell the story of US prisoners in Hoa Lo Prison, in Hanoi during the Vietnam War. Pic is a slanted view of traditional prison camp sagas, injecting lots of hindsight and taking right-wing potshots that do a disservice to the very human drama of the subject.

Michael Moriarty heads a curiously bland cast. He's thrust into a position of authority when the ranking officer played by Lawrence Pressman is taken off to be tortured. Episodic structure introduces new prisoners as more pilots are shot down over a roughly 10-year span (including some comic relief such as one prisoner who says he fell off his ship accidentally and was captured).

Pic is desperately lacking side issues or subplots of interest with Chetwynd monotonously hammering away at the main issue of survival in the face of inhuman treatment.

■ **HANOVER STREET**

1979, 109 MINS, UK ◇ ⓥ
Dir Peter Hyams   *Prod* Paul N. Lazarus III   *Scr* Peter Hyams   *Ph* David Watkin   *Ed* James Mitchell   *Mus* John Barry   *Art Dir* Philip Harrison
● Harrison Ford, Lesley-Anne Down, Christopher Plummer, Alec McCowen, Max Wall, Patsy Kensit (Columbia)

Writer-director Peter Hyams has moved this tale of star-crossed lovers from 1940s MGM to World War II England, where American flying ace Harrison Ford and British hospital nurse Lesley Anne-Down meet during an air raid, and fall hopelessly in love.

But *Hanover Street* demonstrates that sugary dialog doesn't work any better than in the 1940s. Hyams has proven himself an adroit action-adventure director with *Capricorn One*, but his writing lags behind his other skills.

Only when Down takes a back seat, and Ford is thrown together with her cuckolded husband, British secret service topper Christopher Plummer, does *Hanover Street* manifest any vital life signs. The last third of the picture becomes a model of efficient war filmmaking, but then it's back to tears and stiff upper lips.

■ **HAPPENING, THE**

1967, 101 MINS, US ◇
Dir Elliot Silverstein   *Prod* Jud Kinberg   *Scr* Frank R. Pierson, James Buchanan, Ronald Austin   *Ph* Philip Lathrop   *Ed* Philip Anderson   *Mus* Frank DeVol   *Art Dir* Richard Day, Al Brenner
● Anthony Quinn, George Maharis, Michael Parks, Robert Walker, Martha Hyer, Faye Dunaway (Columbia/Horizon)

Intriguing offbeat item, *The Happening* attempts to blend various elements of kickhappy teeny-boppers, melodrama, pop culture, suburban tragedy, suspense, 'in' gags, 'black humor', Keystone Kops, 'beach party' pix, and alienation in the affluent society in a comedic potpourri, which, between expected laughs, seeks to offer satiric peeks at US life and values.

Well-tempered plotline, with several corkscrew twists, follows the weekend hegira of four ennui-laden but debauched Miami beachbums in search of some potent stimuli. They find it, albeit accidentally, by stumbling into an unlikely kidnapping.

What is bothersome about this tragi-farce is why it doesn't succeed, with all of the above and generally capable performers, going for it. George Maharis, playing a bull without horns, is spotty but fine, alternating swagger with weakness in his impersonation of a gigolo, while Michael Parks is less convincing but appropriately faceless as a blank-faced rich kid. Newcomer Faye Dunaway, though stunning to view and essaying her role with elan, is too womanly seductive for a teeny-bopper role.

• •

■ HAPPIEST DAYS OF YOUR LIFE, THE

1950, 81 MINS, UK

Dir Frank Launder   *Prod* Frank Launder, Sidney Gilliat   *Scr* Frank Launder, John Dighton   *Ph* Stan Pavey   *Ed* Oswald Hafenrichter   *Mus* Mischa Spoliansky

● Alastair Sim, Margaret Rutherford, Joyce Grenfell, Richard Wattis (London)

Bright script and brisk direction conceal the stage origin. The story is given a wider canvas and isn't wanting in action. In fact, the pace never lets up and one hilarious farcical incident only ends to give place to another.

Setting of the film is a college for boys, to which, as a result of a slip at the Ministry of Education, a girl's school is evacuated. The story builds up to a boisterous climax in which the principals are trying to conceal the real situation from visitors to the college.

There is no shortage of laughs, but the joke is a little too protracted and wears thin before the end. It's an ideal vehicle for Alastair Sim as the harassed headmaster, while Margaret Rutherford admirably suggests the overpowering headmistress.

• •

■ HAPPILY EVER AFTER

1990, 74 MINS, US ◇

Dir John Howley   *Prod* Lou Scheimer   *Scr* Robby London, Martha Moran   *Ph* Fred Ziegler   *Ed* Jeffrey C. Patch, Joe Gall   *Mus* Frank W. Becker   *Art Dir* John Grusd

● (Filmation)

An unauthorized sequel to the Walt Disney classic *Snow White*, *Happily Ever After* is a well-crafted but uninspired animated fantasy. Lou Scheimer's Filmation banner began work on the pic in 1986 simultaneously with another unauthorized sequel to a Disney masterpiece, *Pinocchio and the Emperor of the Night* (1987).

Action picks up here with the evil queen's brother Lord Maliss (drawn to resemble Basil Rathbone and voiced with gusto by Malcolm McDowell) in a vendetta to avenge sis' death by zonking Snow White and her handsome Prince. Snowy takes refuge in the seven dwarfs' cottage when the Prince is captured. The little fellows are away slaving in the mines, but their femme cousins, the seven dwarfelles, entertain Snowy with their fantastic control of natural phenomena.

Voice casting is pic's big plus. Irene Cara warbles a catchy, uptempo song 'Love Is the Reason' to bookend the film. Three other songs spotlight Ed Asner, Phyllis Diller and a very effective vocal from Tracey Ullman simulating a little girl's voice.

• •

■ HAPPY BIRTHDAY, WANDA JUNE

1971, 105 MINS, US ◇

Dir Mark Robson   *Prod* Lester Goldsmith   *Scr* Kurt Vonnegut Jr.   *Ph* Fred Koenekamp   *Ed* Dorothy Spencer   *Art Dir* Boris Leven

● Rod Steiger, Susannah York, George Grizzard, Don Murray, William Hickey, Steven Paul (Filmakers/Sourdough/Red Lions)

Imagine Ulysses' long voyage home with nothing on board to read but the collected writings of Ernest Hemingway. That must have been in the mind of novelist-turned playwright-turned screenwriter Kurt Vonnegut Jr when he dreamed up the hero for *Happy Birthday, Wanda June*.

Rod Steiger shines as the self-deceiving ultra-masculine hero, returned from eight years in the Amazon jungle, to find that not only has his loving wife, a former pinheaded

carhop (played brilliantly by Susannah York), become a levelheaded intellectual equal but has gone to his extreme opposite in seeking another soul mate.

She's trying to decide between a violin-playing doctor and practicing pacifist (George Grizzard) and a clumsy, eager vacuum-cleaner salesman (Don Murray). Only his son remembers him (resenting the non-observance of his supposedly dead father's birthday as a major catastrophe).

The treatment is too irreverent to be taken seriously for a moment, including Vonnegut's preachments.

• •

■ HAPPY ENDING, THE

1969, 117 MINS, US ◇ Ⓥ

Dir Richard Brooks   *Prod* Richard Brooks   *Scr* Richard Brooks   *Ph* Conrad Hall   *Ed* George Grenville   *Mus* Michel Legrand

● Jean Simmons, John Forsythe, Lloyd Bridges, Teresa Wright, Dick Shawn, Nanette Fabray (United Artists/PaxFilms)

The American Dream, the affluent upper middleclass marriage, is a conjugal bed of nails peopled by bored-to-tears alcoholic wives and hard working, but less than faithful hubbies, according to producer-director-writer Richard Brooks. A well-developed and acted and potentially significant 'woman's movie' unfortunately drowns in Brooks' over indulgences and over-writing.

As Mrs America, class of '53, Jean Simmons fortifies herself with vodka and tranquilizers for her 16th wedding anniversary with tax lawyer John Forsythe.

As the still attractive but anxiously middle-aged and self-pitying matron who is financially secure but personally bankrupted, Simmons gives a moving, emotionally wringing performance. Forsythe has the patience of Job with his spoiled, high-strung wife. His is a basically dull, one-dimensional role.

• •

■ HARD CONTRACT

1969, 106 MINS, US ◇

Dir S. Lee Pogostin   *Prod* Marvin Schwartz   *Scr* S. Lee Pogostin   *Ph* Jack Hildyard   *Ed* Harry Gerstad   *Mus* Alex North   *Art Dir* Ed Graves

● James Coburn, Lee Remick, Lilli Palmer, Burgess Meredith, Patrick Magee, Sterling Hayden (20th Century-Fox)

The principle of the loner, the individual in the jungle of society, the solitary predator, is emphatically portrayed in this skillfully-mounted film about the killer-for-hire who agrees to a hard contract to eliminate three men in Europe.

James Coburn, as Cunningham, accepts the deal dished out by Burgess Meredith. Leaving the US for Torremelinos, he meets the self-indulgent jet-set quartet who bloom in the Spanish sun.

Leader of the group is Lee Remick, who finds herself in love with Coburn but not his profession.

Scenery of Spain and Belgium is in sharp focus, which isn't always true of story. A shift of values has been initiated, but no one has raised a signpost to tell where we're going.

Coburn and Remick, effective in their roles, allow characters to develop naturally.

• •

■ HARDCORE

1979, 105 MINS, US ◇ Ⓥ

Dir Paul Schrader   *Prod* Buzz Feitshans   *Scr* Paul Schrader   *Ph* Michael Chapman   *Ed* Tom Rolf   *Mus* Jack Nitzsche   *Art Dir* Paul Sylbert

● George C. Scott, Peter Boyle, Season Hubley, Dick Sargent, Leonard Gaines (Columbia/A-Team)

George C. Scott, gives as fine a performance as he's ever done.

An unventuring Calvinist, Scott lives a contented small-town Michigan life until his daughter, Ilah Davis, disappears on a trip to LA. He hires seedy private-eye Peter Boyle who eventually finds her on film in a porno movie. Forced to watch, Scott's anguish at the sight bespeaks a clash of values still haunting the country.

For many, this will be the first up-close look at the world including nude-conversation encounters, massage parlors, bondage joints and the lowest degradation – 'snuff' films.

The easily shocked may want an exposé, or more a condemnation. The more sophisticated may grow tired of Scott's morality. But shocked, cynical or dissatisfied, nobody's going to be bored.

• •

■ HARD DAY'S NIGHT, A

1964, 83 MINS, UK Ⓥ

Dir Richard Lester   *Prod* Walter Shenson   *Scr* Alun Owen   *Ph* Gilbert Taylor   *Ed* John Jympson   *Mus* John Lennon, Paul McCartney   *Art Dir* Ray Simm

● John Lennon, Paul McCartney, George Harrison, Ringo Starr, Wilfrid Brambell, Norman Rossington (United Artists)

A Hard Day's Night is a wacky, offbeat piece of filming, charged with vitality, and inventiveness by director Dick Lester, slickly lensed and put over at a fair lick. No attempt has been paid to build the Beatles up as Oliviers; they are at their best when the pic has a misleading air of off-the-cuff spontaneity.

Running at 83 minutes, in black and white, it keeps Beatles within their ability. Alun Owen's screenplay merely attempts to portray an exaggerated 36 hours in the lives of the Beatles. But, though exaggerated, the thin story lines gives a shrewd idea of the pressure and difficulties under which they work and live.

Four set off by train to keep a live television date and, before taking off by helicopter for their next stint, they have some rum adventures. A skirmish with the police, mobbing by hysterical fans, then a press conference, riotous moments in a tavern, a jazz cellar, a gambling club and at TV rehearsals all work into the crazy tapestry and offer the Beatles a chance to display their sense of humor and approach to life.

To give the almost documentary storyline a boost scriptwriter Owen has introduced Paul's grandfather, a mischief making mixer with an eye on the main chance. Played by Wilfrid Brambell with sharp perception his presence is a great buffer for the boys' throwaway sense of comedy.

• •

■ HARD FEELINGS

1982, 104 MINS, CANADA ◇

Dir Daryl Duke   *Prod* Harold Greenberg   *Scr* W.D. Richter, John Herzfeld   *Ph* Harry Makin   *Ed* Tony Lower   *Mus* Mickey Erbe, Maribeth Solomon   *Art Dir* Douglas Higgins

● Carl Marotte, Charlaine Woodward, Vincent Bufano, Grand Bush, Lisa Langlois, Michael Donaghue (Astral)

Hard Feelings is an admirable, if flawed, look at the perils of growing up. Directed by Daryl Duke, the script, based on a novel by Don Bredes, is certainly not lacking ambition. Set on Long Island in 1963, it concerns an aimless high school senior played by Carl Marotte.

Superficially, he's much like his classmates with scholastic, athletic (tennis) and social interests. The major difference in Marotte's life is he's been singled out by school bully Vincent Bufano as an object of persecution.

He's also confused about sex and in this area the intensity of his family situation reflects poorly on his attitude toward his girlfriend (Lisa Langlois). The story takes an abrupt turn when the combination of anxieties lead Marotte to run away.

Duke's film is a highly perplexing tale which is really more concerned with questions than in providing neat answers.

● ●

■ HARD TO KILL

1990, 95 MINS, US ◇ ⓥ

Dir Bruce Malmuth   *Prod* Gary Adelson, Joel Simon, Bill Todmore Jr   *Scr* Steven McKay   *Ph* Matthew F. Leonetti   *Ed* John F. Link   *Mus* David Michael Frank *Art Dir* Robb Wilson King

● Steven Seagal, Kelly Le Brock, Bill Sadler, Frederick Coffin, Bonnie Burroughs, Branscombe Richmond (Warner)

The threadbare screenplay, which went into production as *Seven Year Storm*, uses a Rip van Winkle gimmick. As Mason Storm, cop Steven Seagal is nearly killed in the first reel after shooting surveillance film of corrupt politico Bill Sadler. His wife (Bonnie Burroughs) is murdered by Sadler's minions.

Cop buddy Frederick Coffin recognizes the danger and hides evidence of Seagal's last-minute recovery. Seven years later, under the tutelage of impossibly beautiful nurse (and real-life wife) Kelly Le Brock, Seagal comes out of his coma (sporting a laughable phony beard), uses Oriental methods of recovery and plots his revenge.

Sluggish direction by Bruce Mallmuth doesn't help, but whenever Seagal is allowed to whip into action the film is a crowdpleaser. Unlike other loner prototypes, he goes beyond merely ruthless into the realm of sadistic, breaking opponents' limbs just for starters (as in a memorable fight here with latino heavy Branscombe Richmond). It ain't pretty, but it gets the action fans off.

● ●

■ HARDWARE

1990, 92 MINS, UK/US ◇ ⓥ

Dir Richard Stanley   *Prod* Joanne Sellar, Paul Trybits *Scr* Richard Stanley   *Ph* Steven Chivers   *Ed* Derek Trigg   *Mus* Simon Boswell   *Art Dir* Joseph Bennett

● Dylan McDermott, Stacey Travis, John Lynch, William Hootkins, Iggy Pop (Palace/Miramax/British Screen/BSB)

A cacophonic, nightmarish variation on the postapocalyptic cautionary genre, *Hardware* has the makings of a punk cult film.

After the nuclear holocaust, vast reaches of incinerated North America have been reduced to an infrared desert ravaged by guerrilla warfare and littered with cybernetic scrapheaps. Moses (Dylan McDermott) and Shades (John Lynch) are 'zone tripper' soldiers of fortune who scavenge the corpse-strewn, irradiated wasteland for techno-detritus to black market in the big city.

Moses, wasting away from radiation cancer, wants to return to his woman, Julie (Stacey Travis). She's a fiercely cynical techno-alchemist, fond of smoking packaged dope, who keeps a fortress workshop in a blasted downtown apartment block. Reunited in a frenzied sexual collision of pulse-pounding eroticism, the couple ponder their outer-limits relationship of love in the ruins.

Hardware veers loonily out of control and becomes a black comic exercise in F/X tour-deforce that's ceaselessly pushing itself over the top.

● ●

■ HARD WAY, THE

1991, 111 MINS, US ◇ ⓥ

Dir John Badham   *Prod* William Sackheim, Rob Cohen, Peter R. McIntosh   *Scr* Daniel Pyne, Lem Dobbs *Ph* Don McAlpine, Robert Primes   *Ed* Frank Morriss, Tony Lombardo   *Mus* Arthur B. Rubinstein *Art Dir* Philip Harrison

● Michael J. Fox, James Woods, Stephen Lang,

Annabella Sciorra, LL Cool J, Penny Marshall (Universal/Badham-Cohen)

Too bad there's more method in the acting than the script, as John Badham's tired action-comedy formula squanders its best moments during the film's first act and wastes the nifty pairing of James Woods and Michael J. Fox.

Fox is a popular star of action fluff, like *Smoking Gunn II*, who yearns for a leading role in a film 'without a Roman numeral in it'. Determined to play a tough street cop, he decides to research the role by partnering New York cop John Moss (Woods), who's involved in hunting a lunatic serial killer (Stephen Lang).

The film exhausts its best Hollywood in-jokes during the first 20 minutes, with a Penny Marshall cameo as Fox's agent and lots of lines about cappuccino, personal trainers and Mel Gibson.

After the initial meeting of Fox and Woods, however, the pic degenerates into a series of random melees that will bring the buddies together – and introduce a stale subplot that has the actor helping Moss woo his sort-of girlfriend (Annabella Sciorra) as an added bonus.

Woods is appropriately gruff and nasty as the cop, and his trademark intensity makes a broad target for Fox to play off.

● ●

■ HAREM

1985, 113 MINS, FRANCE ◇ ⓥ

Dir Arthur Joffe   *Prod* Alain Sarde   *Scr* Arthur Joffe, Tom Rayfiel, Richard Prieur   *Ph* Pasqualino De Santis *Ed* Dominique Martin   *Mus* Philippe Sarde *Art Dir* Alexandre Trauner

● Nastassja Kinski, Ben Kingsley, Dennis Goldson, Zohra Segal, Michel Robin, Julette Simpson (Sara)

Harem is an album of gorgeous images, aligned to tell a story, but it's a poor excuse for a dramatic motion picture packaged for the international marketplace.

Despite an investment of $10 million, which afforded stars Ben Kingsley and Nastassja Kinski, producer has skimped on the essential – screenwriter. Instead he has disastrously allowed director Arthur Joffe, obviously not yet at ease with an elaborate full-length narrative, to develop his own original story idea.

Tale concerns a fabulously wealthy Arab prince who kidnaps a beautiful young New York girl and has her brought to his desert palace, where she joins his harem.

As played by Kingsley, the unscrupulous potentate turns out to be a hypersentive aesthete, trapped by tradition to maintain, for appearances' sake at least, a way of life he doesn't believe in.

The film is visually ravishing, often happily distracting the viewer from the emptiness of the script and the exasperating indigence of the main characters.

● ●

■ HARLAN COUNTY, U.S.A.

1976, 103 MINS, US ◇ ⓥ

Dir Barbara Kopple   *Prod* Barbara Kopple *Scr* Barbara Kopple   *Ph* Hart Perry, Kevin Keating, Phil Parmet, Flip McCarthy, Tom Hurwitz   *Ed* Nancy Baker, Mary Lampson, Lora Hays, Mirra Bank   *Mus* Merle Travis, David Morris, Nimrod Workman, Sarah Gunning, Hazel Dickens, Phyllis Boyens

● (Cabin Creek)

Harlan County, U.S.A. is in essence a straightforward cinema verite documentary about a coal miners' strike in Kentucky. Director Barbara Kopple began the project in 1972 in Kentucky and was on hand to record the year-plus battle of coal miners at the Brookside Mine in Harlan to join the United Mine Workers.

There is much emphasis on the predictable elements which give the pic the impact of a carefully-plotted fiction feature.

Actual strike events are fleshed out with vintage film and stills of mining conditions over the years, of previous labor battles and of current living (and dying) conditions in the industry.

The stars of the film are the men and women of Harlan County, portrayed here not as patronized mountain folks but as human beings.

● ●

■ HARLEM NIGHTS

1989, 118 MINS, US ◇ ⓥ

Dir Eddie Murphy   *Prod* Robert D. Wachs, Mark Lipsky   *Scr* Eddie Murphy   *Ph* Woody Omens *Ed* George Bowers   *Mus* Herbie Hancock *Art Dir* Lawrence G. Paull

● Eddie Murphy, Richard Pryor, Redd Foxx, Danny Aiello, Michael Lerner, Della Reese (Murphy)

This blatantly excessive directorial debut for Eddie Murphy is overdone, too rarely funny and, worst of all, boring.

The film features Richard Pryor as the sage Sugar Ray to Murphy's hot-tempered Quick, who risk losing their 1930s Harlem nightclub when a corpulent crime boss (Michael Lerner) sets his sights on it.

The pair hatches up a predictable scheme to turn the tables on the mobster, whose henchmen include a cold-hearted mistress (Jasmine Guy) and a crooked cop (Danny Aiello).

There's an obnoxious cameo by Murphy's chum Arsenio Hall that proves pointless and unnecessary, as well as a mean-spirited recurring gag involving the stuttering heavyweight champ (Stan Shaw).

But the film does have its moments, such as when Murphy dukes it out with Reese's growling club madam or beds the carnivorous Dominque (Guy).

● ●

■ HARLOW

1965, 107 MINS, US

Dir Alex Segal   *Prod* Lee Savin   *Scr* Karl Tunberg *Ph* Jim Kilgore   *Mus* Al Ham, Nelson Riddle   *Art Dir* Duncan Cramer

● Carol Lynley, Efrem Zimbalist Jr, Ginger Rogers, Barry Sullivan, Hurd Hatfield, Celia Lovsky (Sargent)

This first-to-market biopic lensed in the quick-filming Electronovision process is peopled with a set of characters not altogether convincing and even the star part making small impression. Carol Lynley, as the tragic, platinum-tressed queen of the 1930s, who was a sex symbol of her time, tries valiantly but the outcome is not altogether a triumph.

The script follows the major points of the Harlow tradition although dramatic licenses are taken. The Paul Bern incident figures prominently, a dramatic hook utilized to mold the entire later character of the star. Hurd Hatfield in the role of the producer-writer who weds the sexy blonde and then commits suicide when he discovers he's impotent, delivers a sincere performance. Celia Lovsky's is another honestly-offered delineation, as Maria Ouspenskaya, the veteran actress to whom Jean goes for dramatic instruction after she temporarily deserts her film career.

Technically, this third Electronovision production – preceded by *Hamlet* and *The TAMI Story* – and first to be shot under controlled conditions on a soundstage, still presents many problems. Photography continues to be a major difficulty, grainy and of general poor quality, and bad lighting heightens the effect of oldfashioned production. Filmed in eight days in the TV-type lensing process, picture very often looks it as action sketches the rise

H

of the star until her untimely death while still a young woman. Alex Segal's direction is as good as the script and fast-filming process will permit.

● ●

■ HARLOW

1965, 125 MINS, US ◇ Ⓥ

Dir Gordon Douglas *Prod* Joseph E. Levine *Scr* John Michael Hayes *Ph* Joseph Ruttenberg *Ed* Frank Bracht, Archie Marshek *Mus* Neal Hefti *Art Dir* Hal Pereira, Roland Anderson

● Carroll Baker, Martin Balsam, Red Buttons, Michael Connors, Angela Lansbury, Peter Lawford (Paramount/ Levine)

Second biopic of Jean Harlow is handsomely mounted. As the ill-fated Jean Harlow, Carroll Baker is a fairly reasonable facsimile although she lacks the electric fire of the original.

Script by John Michael Hayes is based on the questionable (at least in Hollywood) biog by Irving Shulman, who wrote tome in collaboration with Arthur Landau, the star's first agent. The part of Landau is fashioned almost on a par with the star character herself in the opening reels, past the needs of the story which essentially focuses on girl's rise to become one of the hottest properties in films of that era.

Several real-life characters are thinly veiled while parts of star's mother and stepfather are importantly projected. Angela Lansbury undertakes role of Mama Jean with quiet conviction, and Raf Vallone in the Marino Bello-stepfather role, also lends a persuasive presence.

Martin Balsam, head of Harlow's studio (here called Majestic Pictures) who gives her her chance at stardom, is the thinly-veiled Louis B. Mayer.

● ●

■ HAROLD AND MAUDE

1971, 90 MINS, US ◇ Ⓥ

Dir Hal Ashby *Prod* Colin Higgins, Charles B. Mulvehill *Scr* Colin Higgins *Ph* John Alonzo *Ed* William A. Sawyer, Edward Warschilka *Mus* Cat Stevens *Art Dir* Michael Haller

● Ruth Gordon, Bud Cort, Vivian Pickles, Cyril Cusack, Charles Tyner, Ellen Geer (Paramount)

Harold and Maude has all the fun and gaiety of a burning orphanage. Ruth Gordon heads the cast as an offensive eccentric who becomes a beacon in the life of a self-destructive rich boy, played by Bud Cort. Together they attend funerals and indulge in specious philosophizing.

Director Hal Ashby's second feature is marked by a few good gags, but marred by a greater preponderance of sophomoric, overdone and mocking humor.

Cort does well as the spoiled neurotic whose repeated suicide attempts barely ruffle the feathers of mother Vivian Pickles, whose urbane performance is outstanding. She solicits a computer dating service to provide three potential brides: Shari Summers and Judy Engles are frightened off by Cort's bizarre doings, but Ellen Geer is delightful as one who goes him one better.

One thing that can be said about Ashby – he begins the film in a gross and macabre manner, and never once deviates from the concept. That's style for you.

● ●

■ HARPER

1966, 121 MINS, US ◇ Ⓥ

Dir Jack Smight *Prod* Jerry Gershwin, Elliott Kastner *Scr* William Goldman *Ph* Conrad Hall *Ed* Stefan Arnsten *Mus* Johnny Mandel

● Paul Newman, Lauren Bacall, Julie Harris, Arthur Hill, Janet Leigh, Pamela Tiffin (Warner)

Harper is a contemporary mystery-comedy with Paul Newman as a sardonic private eye

involved in a missing person trackdown. Some excellent directorial touches and solid thesping are evident in the colorful and plush production. Abundance of comedy and sometimes extraneous emphasis on cameo characters make for a relaxed pace and imbalanced concept, resulting in overlength and telegraphing of climax.

Ross MacDonald's novel, *The Moving Target*, has Newman commissioned by Lauren Bacall to find her hubby (never seen until climax), although she has no love for either him or step-daughter Pamela Tiffin.

Complications include the spoiled Tiffin, casual companion of family pilot Robert Wagner, himself hung up on Julie Harris, a piano bar entertainer also a junkie. Shelley Winters is the aging actress failure who has known the missing man, and is married to Robert Webber, brains behind a wetback smuggling ring run by religious nut Strother Martin.

Director Jack Smight has inserted countless touches which illuminate each character to the highest degree. In this he complements William Goldman's sharp and often salty lingo. All principals acquit themselves admirably, including Newman, Bacall, Webber, and particularly Winters, who makes every second count as the once-aspiring film star now on the high-calorie sauce.

● ●

■ HARRY & SON

1984, 117 MINS, US ◇ Ⓥ

Dir Paul Newman *Prod* Paul Newman, Ronald L. Buck *Scr* Paul Newman, Ronald L. Buck *Ph* Donald McAlpine *Ed* Dede Allen *Mus* Henry Mancini *Art Dir* Henry Bumstead

● Paul Newman, Robby Benson, Ellen Barkin, Wilford Brimley, Judith Ivey, Joanne Woodward (Orion)

Fuzzily conceived and indecisively executed, *Harry & Son* represents a deeply disappointing return to the director's chair for Paul Newman. Cowritten and coproduced by the star as well, pic [suggested by the novel *A Lost King* by Raymond DeCapite] never makes up its mind who or what it wants to be about and, to compound the problem, never finds a proper style in which to convey the tragicomic events that transpire.

Opening scenes are perhaps the strongest, as Newman gets fired from his job as a Florida construction worker due to an ailment which momentarily blinds him. He goads his son into expanding his horizons beyond polishing cars and pretending to be a young Hemingway.

As presented, Newman's character is in a position either to give up on life or make a fresh start, and perhaps film's overriding frustration is that he goes nowhere. Structurally, it's a mess.

● ●

■ HARRY AND TONTO

1974, 115 MINS, US ◇ Ⓥ

Dir Paul Mazursky *Prod* Paul Mazursky *Scr* Paul Mazursky, Josh Greenfeld *Ph* Michael Butler *Ed* Richard Halsey *Mus* Bill Conti *Art Dir* Ted Haworth

● Art Carney, Ellen Burstyn, Chief Dan George, Geraldine Fitzgerald, Larry Hagman, Arthur Hunnicutt (20th Century-Fox)

Harry and Tonto stars Art Carney and a trained cat, respectively, in a pleasant film about an old man who rejuvenates himself on a cross-country trek. Script is a series of good human comedy vignettes, with the large supporting cast of many familiar names in virtual cameo roles.

Carney is excellent as an old NY widower, evicted by force from a building being torn down. The rupture in his life triggers an odyssey, with pet cat named Tonto, to LA, with family stopovers at the Jersey home of

son Phil Bruns, then to Chicago where Ellen Burstyn remains a warm antagonist, finally to LA where Larry Hagman emerges as a failure in life. En route, Carney picks up young hitchhiker Melanie Mayron, eventually paired off with grandson Joshua Mostel.

● ●

■ HARRY AND WALTER GO TO NEW YORK

1976, 120 MINS, US Ⓥ

Dir Mark Rydell *Prod* Don Devlin, Harry Gittes *Scr* John Byrum, Robert Kaufman *Ph* Laszlo Kovacs *Ed* Fredric Steinkamp, David Bretherton, Don Guidice *Mus* David Shire *Art Dir* Harry Horner

● James Caan, Elliott Gould, Michael Caine, Diane Keaton, Charles Durning, Lesley Ann Warren (Columbia)

Harry and Walter Go to New York is an alleged period comedy [from a story by Don Devlin and John Byrum] about two carnival types who get involved with a bigtime safecracker plus the femme leader of a radical movement. James Caan, Elliott Gould, Michael Caine and Diane Keaton are the respective stars in this two-hour embarrassment.

Busted for a carny ripoff, Caan and Gould are sent to prison where high-class, urbane Caine is doing time for bank robbery, but living so well that Keaton, repping an underground paper, interviews Caine for a big expose.

The principals' paths intertwine through miles and miles of forced comedic footage, a climactic bank heist, plus all manner of running and jumping and screaming and hollering.

● ●

■ HARRY IN YOUR POCKET

1973, 102 MINS, US ◇

Dir Bruce Geller *Prod* Bruce Geller *Scr* James David Buchanan, Ron Austin *Ph* Fred Koenekamp *Ed* Arthur L. Hilton *Mus* Lalo Schifrin *Art Dir* William Bates

● James Coburn, Michael Sarrazin, Trish Van Devere, Walter Pidgeon, Michael C. Gwynne, Tony Giorgio (United Artists)

Any earnest young man mulling a pickpocket career might pick up some valuable pointers in *Harry in Your Pocket*, story of a gang of slick dips. Producer-director Bruce Geller invades the underworld of cannons (master pickpockets) with a fast expose of how they operate.

Well-paced and credible script poses the situation of a novice with his girlfriend joining a couple of smooth pros to learn the biz. James Coburn and Walter Pidgeon are the experts – Coburn the cannon and Pidgeon his cocaine-sniffing associate – and Michael Sarrazin and Trish Van Devere the apprentices. Presence of Van Devere leads to romantic complications and an underlying feud between Coburn and Sarrazin.

To assure authenticity, Geller hired Tony Giorgio, sleight-of-hand artist well versed in all the dip tricks, who worked both as technical advisor and appears as a detective.

Coburn delivers convincingly as he instructs his amateurs in the art of lifting wallets.

● ●

■ HARVEY

1950, 103 MINS, US

Dir Henry Koster *Prod* John Beck *Scr* Mary Chase, Oscar Brodney *Ph* William Daniels *Ed* Ralph Dawson *Mus* Frank Skinner

● James Stewart, Josephine Hull, Peggy Dow, Charles Drake, Cecil Kellaway, Wallace Ford (Universal)

Harvey, Mary Chase's Pulitzer Prize play, loses little of its whimsical comedy charm in the screen translation.

Three of the principals, James Stewart, Josephine Hull and Jesse White, were seasoned in the wacky characters by playing them on stage.

The exploits of Elwood P. Dowd, a man who successfully escaped from trying reality when his invisible six-foot rabbit pal Harvey came into his life, continually spring chuckles, often hilarity, as the footage unfolds. Stewart would seem the perfect casting for the character so well does he convey the idea that escape from life into a pleasant half-world existence has many points in its favor. Josephine Hull, the slightly balmy aunt who wants to have Elwood committed, is immense, socking the comedy for every bit of its worth.

••••••••••••••••••••••••••••••••••

■ **HARVEY GIRLS, THE**

1946, 101 MINS, US ◇ ⊛

Dir George Sidney *Prod* Arthur Freed *Scr* Edmund Beloin, Nathaniel Curtis, Harry Crane, James O'Hanlon, Samson Raphaelson *Ph* George Folsey *Ed* Albert Akst *Mus* Lennie Hayton (dir.) *Art Dir* Cedric Gibbons, William Ferrari
● Judy Garland, John Hodiak, Ray Bolger, Angela Lansbury, Marjorie Main, Cyd Charisse (M-G-M)

The Harvey Girls [based on the novel by Samuel Hopkins Adams] is a curious blend of Technicolor wild-westernism, frontier town skullduggery and a troupe of Harvey restaurant waitresses who deport themselves in a manner that's a cross between a sorority and a Follies troupe.

John Hodiak is a curious casting in a musical of this nature. Judy Garland, however, makes much of it believable and most of it acceptable.

Angela Lansbury is prominent as the Mae West of the casino, Hodiak's No. 1 flame until Garland, Virginia O'Brien and Cyd Charisse, appear on the scene.

There's the usual fol-de-rol such as hijacking all the good steaks; snakes in the Harvey gals' closets; incendiary tactics and the like.

••••••••••••••••••••••••••••••••••

■ **HAS ANYBODY SEEN MY GAL?**

1952, 88 MINS, US ◇

Dir Douglas Sirk *Prod* Ted Richmond *Scr* Joseph Hoffman *Ph* Clifford Stine *Ed* Russell Schoengarth *Art Dir* Bernard Herzbrun, Hilyard Brown
● Piper Laurie, Rock Hudson, Charles Coburn, Gigi Perreau, Lynn Bari, William Reynolds (Universal)

A rather solid piece of nostalgic entertainment is offered in this comedy-drama of the 1920s 'flapper' era. While the younger Piper Laurie and Rock Hudson are starred over him, it is really Charles Coburn's vehicle.

He wallops the part of a rich old duffer who plans to leave his fortune to the family of a girl who had spurned his proposal of marriage years before.

Incognito, he travels to the small Vermont town where the family lives to find out what kind of people they are. Coburn arranges for the family to receive $100,000 from an 'unnamed' benefactor and sits back to observe the results.

Laurie and Hudson team well as the young lovers. She does things to a sweater that were not done during the time of the story, but otherwise the era is recreated rather faithfully.

••••••••••••••••••••••••••••••••••

■ **HASTY HEART, THE**

1949, 102 MINS, US/UK

Dir Vincent Sherman *Prod* Vincent Sherman *Scr* Ranald MacDougall *Ph* Wilkie Cooper *Ed* E.B. Jarvis *Mus* Jack Beaver
● Ronald Reagan, Patricia Neal, Richard Todd, Anthony Nicholls (Warner)

The John Patrick play has grown in range of feeling on the screen, although the essentials of the legit staging have not been changed. Its background is the Second World War and

the setting is an army hospital in Burma, in a ward where six assorted soldiers sweat out their injuries while awaiting shipment home.

Notable is the performance of Richard Todd in the role of the Scot who must die. Todd comes over with a performance that is star calibre in every facet.

Ronald Reagan plays the Yank with the exact amount of gusto such a character should have in a British outpost hospital. Patricia Neal gives feeling to her role as the nurse.

Vincent Sherman directed the production in England. Ranald MacDougall's scripting is wise to the humaness that marked the play and the tremendous heart that backgrounds the telling.

••••••••••••••••••••••••••••••••••

■ **HATARI!**

1962, 159 MINS, US ◇ ⊛

Dir Howard Hawks *Prod* Howard Hawks *Scr* Leigh Brackett *Ph* Russell Harlan *Ed* Stuart Gilmore *Mus* Henry Mancini *Art Dir* Hal Pereira, Carl Anderson
● John Wayne, Hardy Kruger, Elsa Martinelli, Gerard Blain, Red Buttons, Michele Girardon (Paramount)

Hatari! is an ambitious undertaking. Its cast is an international one, populated by players of many countries. Its wild animals do not come charging out of dusty stock footage studio libraries but have been photographed while beating around the bush of Tanganyika, East Africa. However, in this instance, the strapping physique of the film unhappily emphasizes the anemic condition of the story streaming within.

Leigh Brackett's screenplay, from an original story by Harry Kurnitz, describes at exhaustive length the methods by which a group of game catchers in Tanganyika go about catching wild animals for the zoo when not occupied at catching each other for the woo. Script lacks momentum. It never really advances toward a story goal.

John Wayne heads the colorful cast assembled for this zoological field trip. The vet star plays with his customary effortless (or so it seems) authority a role with which he is identified; the good-natured, but hard-drinking, hot-tempered, big Irishman who 'thinks women are trouble' in a man's world.

Germany's Hardy Kruger and French actor Gerard Blain manage, resourcefully, to pump what vigor they can muster into a pair of undernourished roles. Red Buttons and Elsa Martinelli emerge the histrionic stickouts, Buttons with a jovial portrayal of an excabbie who 'just pretends it's rush hour in Brooklyn' as he jockeys his vehicle through a pack of frightened giraffe, Martinelli as a sweet but spirited shutterbug and part time pachydermatologist.

••••••••••••••••••••••••••••••••••

■ **HATFUL OF RAIN, A**

1957, 109 MINS, US

Dir Fred Zinnemann *Prod* Buddy Adler *Scr* Michael V. Gazzo, Alfred Hayes *Ph* Joe MacDonald *Ed* Dorothy Spencer *Mus* Bernard Herrmann *Art Dir* Lyle R. Wheeler, Leland Fuller
● Eva Marie Saint, Don Murray, Anthony Franciosa, Lloyd Nolan, Henry Silva, William Hickey (20th Century-Fox)

The first film dealing with dope addiction made with the prior approval of the industry's self-governing Production Code, *A Hatful of Rain* is more than a story of a junkie. It touches knowingly and sensitively on a family relationship. Michael V. Gazzo has converted his Broadway play into a provocative and engrossing film drama.

The people involved in this web of narcotics are basically decent human beings. The story revolves about their reactions when one of them turns out to be a junkie. As the pregnant wife of a narcotics addict, Eva Marie

Saint handles the emotional peaks and tender moments with sensitive understanding. Don Murray scores, too, as the likeable junkie who desperately attempts to hide his secret from his wife and his obtusely devoted father.

The role of the brother who shares an apartment in a lower east side NY housing project with his dope-addicted relative and his wife is compellingly played by Anthony Franciosa, repeating his original stage assignment. Misunderstood and rejected by his father, Franciosa is moving as 'his brother's keeper' and sister-in-law's confidante. As the widowed father who left his sons in an orphanage at an early age, Lloyd Nolan turns in a topnotch portrayal. Henry Silva, also repeating his stage role, is convincingly unctuous and contemptible as the dope peddler.

••••••••••••••••••••••••••••••••••

■ **HAUNTED HONEYMOON**

1986, 82 MINS, US ◇ ⊛

Dir Gene Wilder *Prod* Susan Ruskin *Scr* Gene Wilder, Terence Marsh *Ph* Fred Schuler *Ed* Christopher Greenbury *Mus* John Morris *Art Dir* Terence Marsh
● Gene Wilder, Gilda Radner, Dom DeLuise, Jonathan Pryce, Paul L. Smith, Peter Vaughan (Orion)

Gene Wilder is back in the rut of sending up old film conventions in *Haunted Honeymoon*, a mild farce. Title is a misnomer, since set-up has radio actor Wilder taking his fiancee Gilda Radner out to his family's gloomy country estate to meet the kinfolk just before tying the knot. Clan is presided over by the tubby, genial Aunt Kate, played by Dom DeLuise, who maintains that a werewolf is on the loose in the vicinity.

In any event, Wilder is obliged to contend with numerous assaults on his health, and much of the blessedly brief running time is devoted to frantic running among different rooms in the mansion for reasons that occasionally prove faintly amusing but are singularly uncompelling. Pic provokes a few chuckles along the way, but no guffaws.

••••••••••••••••••••••••••••••••••

■ **HAUNTING, THE**

1963, 112 MINS, US ⊛

Dir Robert Wise *Prod* Robert Wise *Scr* Nelson Gidding *Ph* Davis Boulton *Ed* Ernest Walter *Mus* Humphrey Searle *Art Dir* Elliot Scott
● Julie Harris, Claire Bloom, Richard Johnson, Russ Tamblyn, Lois Maxwell (M-G-M)

The artful cinematic strokes of director Robert Wise and staff are not quite enough to override the major shortcomings of Nelson Gidding's screenplay from the Shirley Jackson novel.

Gidding's scenario is opaque in spots, but its cardinal flaw is one of failure to follow through on its thematic motivation. After elaborately setting the audience up in anticipation of drawing some scientific conclusions about the psychic phenomena field, the film completely dodges the issue in settling for a half-hearted melodramatic climax.

The story has to do with the efforts of a small psychic research team led by an anthropology professor (Richard Johnson) to study the supernatural powers that seem to inhabit a 90-year-old New England house with a reputation for evil. The group includes an unhappy spinster (Julie Harris) obsessed with guilt feelings over the recent death of her mother; a young woman (Claire Bloom) of unnatural instincts (she has lesbian tendencies coupled with an extraordinary sense of ESP); and a young man (Russ Tamblyn) who is to inherit the house.

The acting is effective all around. The picture excels in the purely cinematic departments. Davis Boulton has employed his camera with extraordinary dexterity in fashioning a visual excitement that keeps the pic-

H

ture alive with images of impending shock. As photographed by Boulton, the house itself is a monstrous personality, most decidedly the star of the film. The pity is that all this production savvy has been squandered on a screen yarn that cannot support such artistic bulk.

HAVANA

1990, 145 MINS, US ◇ ⓥ

Dir Sydney Pollack   *Prod* Sydney Pollack   *Scr* Judith Rascoe, David Rayfiel   *Ph* Owen Roizman   *Ed* Fredric Steinkamp, William Steinkamp   *Mus* Dave Grusin   *Art Dir* Terence Marsh
● Robert Redford, Lena Olin, Alan Arkin, Tomas Milian, Raul Julia, Mark Rydell (Mirage/Universal)

Much as the filmmakers would like to get there, *Havana* remains a long way from *Casablanca*. In their seventh outing over a 25-year period, director Sydney Pollack and star Robert Redford have lost their normally dependable quality touch as they slog through a notably uncompelling $45 million-plus tale of a gringo caught up in the Cuban revolution.

In a shipboard prolog, Redford's rogue gambler character, Jack Weil, strikes a few sparks with Lena Olin's mysterious Bobby Duran and agrees to smuggle into Havana a radio that will help Castro spread his word in the capital in the waning days of 1958.

Although the city is astir with rumors concerning the rebel leader's activities in the mountains, it's still business as usual under the Batista dictatorship.

Redford's eye for Olin leads him into dangerous political territory involving her wealthy left-wing husband Arturo (played suavely by an uncredited Raul Julia), a CIA spook posing as a food critic, and various military toughs.

Unfortunately, the tentative romance between the two is never really credible. As usual, Redford is cool, reserved and a bit bemused, while the striking Olin is mercurial and intense. The combination doesn't take.

Judith Rascoe's original script was written in the mid-1970s. As rewritten by David Rayfiel, yarn is a mishmash of old-hat Hollywood conventions, political pussyfooting and loads of bad dialog.

HAWAII

1966, 186 MINS, US ◇ ⓥ

Dir George Roy Hill   *Prod* Walter Mirisch   *Scr* Dalton Trimbo, Daniel Taradash   *Ph* Russell Harlan   *Ed* Stuart Gilmore   *Mus* Elmer Bernstein   *Art Dir* Cary Odell
● Julie Andrews, Max Von Sydow, Richard Harris, Carroll O'Connor, Elizabeth Cole, Gene Hackman (Mirisch)

Based on James A. Michener's novel, which embraced centuries of history, *Hawaii* focuses on a critical period – 1820-41 – when the islands began to be commercialized, corrupted and converted to Western ways. Superior production, acting and direction give depth and credibility to a personal tragedy, set against the clash of two civilizations.

Filmed at sea off Norway, also in New England, Hollywood, Hawaii and Tahiti, this vast production reps an outlay of about $15 million, including $600,000 for film rights, and seven years of work. Fred Zinnemann, originally set to produce-direct, worked four and a half years on it, after which Hill took over.

Dalton Trumbo and original adapter Daniel Taradash are both credited with the screenplay, which develops Max Von Sydow's character from a young and over-zealous Protestant missionary, through courtship of Julie Andrews, to their religious work in Hawaii. Richard Harris, an old beau, turns up occasionally at major plot turns.

Von Sydow's outstanding performance makes his character comprehensible, if never totally sympathetic. A less competent actor, with less competent direction and scripting, would have blown the part, and with that, the film. Andrews is excellent in a demanding dramatic role.

Hill's direction, solid in the intimate dramatic scenes, is as good in crowd shots which rep the major external events.

HAWAIIANS, THE

1970, 134 MINS, US ◇

Dir Tom Gries   *Prod* Walter Mirisch   *Scr* James R. Webb   *Ph* Phil Lathrop, Lucien Ballard   *Ed* Ralph Winters, Byron Brandt   *Mus* Henry Mancini   *Art Dir* Cary O'Dell
● Charlton Heston, Geraldine Chaplin, John Phillip Law, Tina Chen, Alec McCowen, Mako (United Artists/Mirisch)

While James A. Michener's monumental novel, *Hawaii*, contained enough material for half a dozen films, the earlier version in 1966 used up most of the first half. This followup film, devotes most of its time to the growth of Hawaii in the present century and the huge influx of other Orientals, particularly the Chinese and Japanese, into the islands as cheap labor.

Charlton Heston, as the American descendant of early settlers and the only man with the vision and steadfastness to make the Hawaiian Islands one of the garden spots of the world (he's credited with introducing the pineapple as a commercial crop), is less the larger-than-life hero and more a stereotyped islander.

HAWKS

1988, 107 MINS, UK ◇

Dir Robert Ellis Miller   *Prod* Steve Lanning, Keith Cavele   *Scr* Roy Clarke   *Ph* Doug Milsome   *Ed* Malcolm Cook   *Mus* Barry Gibb   *Art Dir* Peter Howitt
● Timothy Dalton, Anthony Edwards, Janet McTeer, Camille Coduri, Connie Booth (Gibb/English/PRO)

This black comedy about terminal cancer patients escaping for one last fling stares death in the face and laughs, but takes too long to get to the punch line.

From the start, it's clear that director Robert Ellis Miller is using the script about men facing an early death to examine how people deal with their fears and how they try or fail to disguise it from others.

In this instance, terminal bone cancer pits lawyer Bancroft (Timothy Dalton) and ex-football pro Decker (Anthony Edwards) together in a team effort to thwart their disease (and the ward nurses) with laughs, grit and a last pilgrimage to a Dutch bordello.

Dalton goes a bit overboard as Bancroft, occasionally stretching believability. Edwards plays it straight as the Yank jock, but brings out the laconic ladies' man in his character despite being nonambulatory much of the time.

HE WAS HER MAN

1934, 70 MINS, US

Dir Lloyd Bacon   *Scr* Robert Lord, Tom Buckingham, Niven Busch   *Ph* George Barnes   *Ed* George Amy   *Mus* Leo F. Forbstein (dir.)   *Art Dir* Anton Grot
● James Cagney, Joan Blondell, Victor Jory, Frank Craven, Harold Huber, Russell Hopton (Warner)

With Joan Blondell and James Cagney lending apt cast personalities, director Lloyd Bacon has woven from an original story by Robert Lord a forthright narrative about two pieces of human flotsam.

Most of the action is set against the background of a Portuguese fishing village on the Pacific coast. Both Blondell and Cagney turn in deftly confected performances.

Plot gets its motivation from the efforts of a double-crossing cracksman (Cagney) to escape the penalty of gang law. In his flight from the torpedoes Cagney winds up in San Francisco. There he is spotted by an underworld tipoff (Frank Craven) and the word is passed on to the mob back east. Meanwhile he meets the girl (Blondell), who has just decided to call it quits with the wayfaring life she's been leading and accept a proposal of marriage from a Portuguese fisherman located 100 miles south of Frisco. Cagney elects to join the girl on her trip to the groom.

Cagney settles down in the village and the fisherman, capably played by Victor Jory, goes about making the marriage arrangements. In the interim the girl falls for Cagney and there's talk between them of going away together. Overnight Cagney becomes leery of getting himself entangled and unbeknown to her prepares to scram. From here the action starts building to a tense climax.

HE WHO RIDES A TIGER

1966, 103 MINS, UK

Dir Charles Crichton   *Prod* David Newman   *Scr* Trevor Peacock   *Ph* John Von Kotze   *Ed* Jack Harris, John Smith   *Mus* Alexander Faris   *Art Dir* Richard Harrison, Seamus Flannery
● Tom Bell, Judi Dench, Paul Rogers, Kay Walsh, Ray McAnally, Jeremy Spenser (British Lion)

Legal and financial hassles upset the smooth production of this crime meller, but it does not show on the screen. Story concerns a young, nerveless cat burglar (specialty: rocks from stately homes) with a split personality. Kind to children and animals, suave, good-mannered on the one hand. But this personable young guy is equally prone to violent outbursts of impatience and hot temper. Released from the cooler, he sets out on a string of profitable crimes, with Superintendent Taylor (Paul Rogers) breathing down his neck.

Trevor Peacock's screenplay is crisp, and even in the love scenes and with the kids does not teeter overmuch towards the sentimental. Tom Bell as the anti-hero is one of the crop of young actors who emerged around the Finney, Courtenay, Lynch, O'Toole era. He has an easy style and diamond-hard personality which put him among the leading runners in this field.

Judi Dench, in a somewhat indecisive part, again shows her very bright talent and Rogers is fine as the determined, disgruntled cop.

HEAD OVER HEELS

1979, 97 MINS, US ◇ ⓥ

Dir Joan Micklin Silver   *Prod* Mark Metcalf   *Scr* Joan Micklin Silver   *Ph* Bobby Byrne   *Ed* Cynthia Schneider   *Mus* Ken Lauber   *Art Dir* Peter Jamison
● John Heard, Mary Beth Hurt, Peter Riegert, Kenneth McMillan, Gloria Grahame (United Artists/Triple Play)

Joan Micklin Silver's third directorial effort possesses moderate charm and shows some of the talent she's exhibited before, but ultimately emerges as somewhat thin and one-dimensional.

Based on Ann Beattie's novel *Chilly Scenes of Winter*, Silver's screenplay has affable John Heard reflecting back on his happy past with Mary Beth Hurt from the wistful present. Thrust of pic has him trying to win her back from the clutches of king-sized jock Mark Metcalf.

Ultimately, however, both characters rather wear out their welcome, Heard becoming almost oppressively absolutist in his feelings and Hurt seeming too confused and selfish to be worth all the trouble. After all the difficulties and anxieties that have preceded it, resolution comes off as a bit pat and conventional.

● ●

■ HEARTACHES

1981, 83 MINS, CANADA ◇

Dir Donald Shebib   *Prod* Pieter Kroonenburg, David J. Patterson, Jerry Ralbourn   *Scr* Terence Heffernan   *Ph* Vic Sarin   *Ed* Gerry Hambling, Peter Bolta   *Mus* Simon Michael Mastin
● Margot Kidder, Annie Potts, Robert Carradine (Rising Star)

Heartaches is a female buddy picture with actresses Margot Kidder and Annie Potts involved in a series of delightful misadventures in love. Film, plagued by its own financial heartaches, emerges unscathed from production delays and shut downs.

Potts is the wife of perennial juvenile Robert Carradine who spends most of his time racing cars and getting drunk. She splits rather than face him with the hard fact that he's not the father of the child she's carrying.

On her way to the big city for an abortion Potts reluctantly teams up with Kidder. Kidder in blond wig, tight pants, and outrageous jewelry looks the part of a kook. Her foulmouthed, man-hungry character is in sharp contrast to Potts' relative innocence.

Cast is outstanding with Kidder giving full performance. However, it is basically Potts' film as the runaway wife who's tired of her husband's immature attitude.

● ●

■ HEART BEAT

1979, 109 MINS, US ◇ ▼

Dir John Byrum   *Prod* Alan Greisman, Michael Shamberg   *Scr* John Byrum   *Ph* Laszlo Kovacs   *Ed* Eric Jenkins   *Mus* Jack Nitzsche   *Art Dir* Jack Fisk
● Nick Nolte, Sissy Spacek, John Heard, Ray Sharkey, Anne Dusenberry, Tony Bill (Orion)

Heart Beat never manages to expand its loosely biographical tale of Jack Kerouac, Neal and Carolyn Cassady beyond a very narrow scope.

Nick Nolte and Sissy Spacek, as the Cassadys enmeshed in a love-hate relationship, are standout in a film where performances dominate. Ditto Ray Sharkey, in a manic performance as a disguised Allen Ginsberg character. John Heard struggles manfully with the Kerouac character, but writer-director John Byrum has given him few compass points on which to base a reading.

Heat Beat fails to establish either a coherent story line, or a definitive treatment of the forces that shaped the literary and social explosion following publication of Kerouac's *On the Road* in 1957.

● ●

■ HEARTBREAK KID, THE

1972, 104 MINS, US ◇ ▼

Dir Elaine May   *Prod* Edgar J. Scherick   *Scr* Neil Simon   *Ph* Owen Roizman   *Ed* John Carter   *Mus* Garry Sherman   *Art Dir* Richard Sylbert
● Charles Grodin, Cybill Shepherd, Jeannie Berlin, Eddie Albert, Audra Lindley, William Prince (Palomar/20th Century Fox)

The Heartbreak Kid is the bright, amusing saga of a young NY bridegroom whose bride's maddening idiosyncrasies freak him and he leaves her at the end of a three-day Miami honeymoon to pursue and wed another doll. Scripted by Neil Simon from Bruce Jay Friedman's *Esquire* mag story [*A Change of Plan*], film has a sudden shut-off ending with no climax whatever.

Elaine May's deft direction catches all the possibilities of young romance and its tribulations in light strokes and cleverly accents characterization of the various principals. Most of the pace is as fast as Charles Grodin's speeding to his Florida honeymoon, and

falling for a gorgeous blonde on the beach the first day there.

Grodin is slick and able as the fast-talking bridegroom whose patience is worn thin and he's a natural for the charms of another.

● ●

■ HEARTBREAK RIDGE

1986, 130 MINS, US ◇ ▼

Dir Clint Eastwood   *Prod* Clint Eastwood   *Scr* James Carabatsos   *Ph* Jack N. Green   *Ed* Joel Cox   *Mus* Lennie Niehaus   *Art Dir* Edward Carfagno
● Clint Eastwood, Marsha Mason, Everett McGill, Moses Gunn, Eileen Heckart, Bo Svenson (Malpaso/Weston)

Heartbreak Ridge offers another vintage Clint Eastwood performance. There are enough mumbled half-liners in this contemporary war pic to satisfy those die-hards eager to see just how he portrays the consummate marine veteran.

Eastwood is Gunnery Sergeant Tom Highway – a man determined to teach some of today's young leathernecks how to behave like a few good men.

Eastwood's stern ways inevitably prevail as his platoon is called up for emergency overseas combat. Guns are blazing as Clint's cadre faces its first real action after hitting the beaches. As film moves towards its jingoistic peak in these sequences, Eastwood's insubordinate bent culminates in a final conflict with a modern major (Everett McGill).

● ●

■ HEARTBREAKERS

1984, 98 MINS, US ▼

Dir Bobby Roth   *Prod* Bob Weis, Bobby Roth   *Scr* Bobby Roth   *Ph* Michael Ballhaus   *Ed* John Carnochan   *Mus* Tangerine Dream
● Peter Coyote, Nick Mancuso, Carole Laure, Max Gail, James Laurenson, Carol Wayne (Jethro)

Amusing and dramatic, sexy and insightful, *Heartbreakers* is about contemporary relations between the sexes and men's emotional lives. Study of two male best friends in their mid-30s who experience convulsions in their careers, romances and their own relationship emerges as a potent portrait of modern mores and neuroses.

Peter Coyote is superb, managing to maintain viewer sympathy even when his character is unreasonable and wrong, and producing genuine joy for him when his long artistic struggle finally pays off.

Despite built-in limitations, Nick Mancuso is appealing and holds his own, and admirably registers his confusion and desperation in his scenes with Carole Laure, fine as the insecure but strong-minded art gallery assistant.

● ●

■ HEARTBURN

1986, 108 MINS, US ◇ ▼

Dir Mike Nichols   *Prod* Mike Nichols, Robert Greenhut   *Scr* Nora Ephron   *Ph* Nestor Almendros   *Ed* Sam O'Steen   *Mus* Carly Simon   *Art Dir* Tony Walton
● Meryl Streep, Jack Nicholson, Jeff Daniels, Maureen Stapleton, Stockard Channing, Richard Masur (Paramount)

Heartburn is a beautifully crafted film with flawless performances and many splendid moments, yet the overall effect is a bit disappointing.

From the start Meryl Streep and Jack Nicholson are never quite a couple. He's a Washington political columnist and she's a New York food writer. They meet at a wedding and he overpowers her. Soon they're having their own wedding.

Nora Ephron adapted her own novel for the screen which in turn borrowed heavily from her marriage with Watergate reporter Carl Bernstein.

While the day-to-day details are drawn with a striking clarity, Ephron's script never goes much beyond the mannerisms of middle-class life. Even with the sketchy background information, it's hard to tell what these people are feeling or what they want.

Where the film does excel is in creating the surface and texture of their life. Director Mike Nichols knows the territory well enough to throw in some subtle but biting satire and Nicholson (who replaced Mandy Patinkin during production) and Streep fill in the canvas.

● ●

■ HEART CONDITION

1990, 95 MINS, US ◇ ▼

Dir James D. Parriott   *Prod* Steve Tisch   *Scr* James D. Parriott   *Ph* Arthur Albert   *Ed* David Finter   *Mus* Patrick Leonard   *Art Dir* John Muto
● Bob Hoskins, Denzel Washington, Chloe Webb, Roger E. Mosley (New Line)

From what seems like a far-fetched premise – a cop who gets a heart transplant ends up depending on his worst enemy's ticker – writer-director James D. Parriott spins a most engrossing and rewarding tale in an auspicious feature debut.

Bob Hoskins plays vice detective Moony, an intense, crazy, racist slob who briefly has a girl in his life – a hooker, Crystal (Chloe Webb). She disappears and gets involved with her black lawyer, Stone (Denzel Washington), a handsome self-possessed smooth operator who becomes the object of Moony's obsessive rage.

Moony, who lives on greaseburgers and booze, has a heart attack the same night Stone is killed in a car crash. Thanks to expedient transplant surgery he ends up a 'blood brother' to his enemy. To Mooney's horror, the sarcastic, clever Stone appears in ghost-like form visible only to him, and becomes his constant, unwanted companion.

Washington creates a most compelling character in Stone, finding the rhythm of the role with an assurance that never flags; Hoskins is gutsy and amusing, exhibiting bug-eyed discomfort when he's manicured and barbered in a Stone-style transformation.

● ●

■ HEART IS A LONELY HUNTER, THE

1968, 122 MINS, US ◇ ▼

Dir Robert Ellis Miller   *Prod* Thomas C. Ryan, Marc Merson   *Scr* Thomas C. Ryan   *Ph* James Wong Howe   *Ed* John F. Burnett   *Mus* David Grusin   *Art Dir* LeRoy Deane
● Alan Arkin, Sondra Locke, Laurinda Barrett, Stacy Keach, Chuck McCann, Biff McGuire (Warner/Seven Arts)

Translating to the screen the delicate if specious tragedy of Carson McCuller's first novel was clearly not an easy matter. Nor an entirely successful one, either. *The Heart is a Lonely Hunter* emerges as a fragmented episodic melodrama, with uneven dramatic impact and formula pacing.

Alan Arkin's starring performance as a deaf-and-mute loner is erratic and mannered, but supporting cast generally is on target.

Story turns on Arkin and his influence on the lives of others. Pivotal character is little more than a prop, but, as rendered by Arkin, a destructive one.

Arkin's performance is marred by twitching mannerism. Result is slapstick at times, bathos at others. Suffice it to say that when the focus of attention returns to the main character, the pic has a tendency to fall apart.

The motivations of other characters are defined in better fashion, although the credibility of most is doubtful. Actors have an uphill fight, and to their personal credit they rise above the material.

● ●

■ HEARTLAND

1980, 98 MINS, US ◇ ⓥ
Dir Richard Pearce   *Prod* Annick Smith   *Scr* Beth
Ferris   *Ph* Fred Murphy   *Ed* Bill Yahrus   *Mus* Charles
Gross
● Conchata Ferrell, Rip Torn, Lilia Skala, Barry Primus
(Wilderness Women's Productions/Filmhaus)

Heartland is a film with heart about the
tribulations of homesteading life in Wyoming
circa 1910. The entire budget of $600,000 was
backed by the National Endowment for the
Humanities.

The ruggedness of ranch life is mainly
shown from the viewpoint of a hearty, strong
but never overbearing widow with a 10-year-
old child who goes to a ranch in an isolated
part of Wyoming to be the housekeeper for a
taciturn Scottish rancher.

The seasons are neatly etched by lenser
Fred Murphy and perceptive script, based on
the books of the real widow Elinore Randall
Stewart, is also an asset.

Richard Pearce, who made many docus
and some TV films, handles this simple tale
with a nice balance of regional feel and
elemental drama.

■ HEART LIKE A WHEEL

1983, 113 MINS, US ◇ ⓥ
Dir Jonathan Kaplan   *Prod* Charles Roven   *Scr* Ken
Friedman   *Ph* Tak Fujimoto   *Ed* O. Nicholas Brown
Mus Laurence Rosenthal   *Art Dir* James William
Newport
● Bonnie Bedelia, Beau Bridges, Leo Rossi, Hoyt Axton,
Bill McKinney, Anthony Edwards (Aurora/20th Century-
Fox)

Heart Like A Wheel is a surprisingly fine biopic
of Shirley Muldowney, the first professional
female race car driver. What could have been
a routine good ol' gal success story has been
heightened into an emotionally involving,
superbly made drama.

Winning prolog has pa Hoyt Axton letting
his little daughter take the wheel of his speeding sedan, an indelible experience which
prefigures Shirley, by the mid-1950s, winning
drag races against the hottest rods in town.

Happily married to her mechanic husband
Jack and with a young son, Shirley finds her
innate ability compelling her, by 1966, to
enter her first pro race. Roadblocked at first
by astonished, and predictably sexist, officials, Shirley proceeds to set the track
record in her qualifying run, and her career is
underway.

But her husband ultimately can't take her
career-mindedness, and she's forced to set
out on her own.

Director Jonathan Kaplan has served a
long apprenticeship but nothing he has
done before prepares one for his mature,
accomplished work here.

■ HEART OF MIDNIGHT

1988, 101 MINS, US ◇ ⓥ
Dir Matthew Chapman   *Prod* Andrew Gaty
Scr Matthew Chapman   *Ph* Ray Rivas   *Ed* Penelope
Shaw   *Mus* Yanni   *Art Dir* Gene Rudolf
● Jennifer Jason Leigh, Peter Coyote, Gale Mayron,
Sam Schact, Denise Dommont (Goldwyn)

Heart of Midnight is a twisted little sadoma-
sochistic outing whose plot centers on Carol
Rivers (Jennifer Jason Leigh), a young
woman with psychological problems. When
her uncle Fletcher (Sam Schact) dies of
AIDS, she inherits property being transformed into the 'Midnight' club.

Against the wishes of her mother Betty
(Brenda Vaccaro), Carol moves to the building, only to find a bizarre series of rooms
upstairs. They suggest Fletcher was hosting
sex parties for people of various persuasions.

Carol is plunged into her own hell as a
couple of workmen try to rape her. If the

assault wasn't problem enough, signs appear
that someone else is on the premises.

Events proceed to particularly sadistic
circumstances, in which the reason for
Carol's years of torment and her relationship
to her late uncle also come to light.

Performances are strong all around,
particularly by Leigh and Vaccaro.

■ HEARTS OF FIRE

1987, 95 MINS, US ◇ ⓥ
Dir Richard Marquand   *Prod* Richard Marquand,
Jennifer Miller, Jennifer Alward   *Scr* Scott Richardson,
Joe Eszterhas   *Ph* Alan Hume   *Ed* Sean Barton
Mus John Barry   *Art Dir* Kit Surrey, Barbara Dunphy
● Bob Dylan, Rupert Everett, Fiona, Julian Glover, Ian
Drury, Richie Havens (Phoenix/Lorimar)

It is unfortunate that the last film of helmer
Richard Marquand, who died shortly after
completing it, should be *Hearts of Fire*. As an
epitaph it leaves something to be desired, failing to fire on all cylinders despite a nimble
performance by the enigmatic Bob Dylan
typecast as a reclusive rock star.

Pic opens with would-be rock singer Molly
McGuire (exuberantly played by Yank singer
Fiona) meeting rock star Billy Parker
(Dylan) and agreeing to hop over to England
with him.

In Blighty she is spotted by British popster
James Colt (Rupert Everett), who takes her
under his wing – and into his bed – while a
drunken Dylan flies home to the security of
his chicken farm.

Fiona and Everett head off on tour together
and, while Fiona agonizes about the real
price of success and worries about which man
she prefers, the inevitable climax of the gig in
her hometown fast approaches.

Dylan performs well, though he looks a
mite uncomfortable during the musical numbers. He certainly appears fitter than Everett
whose voice is as wet and stilted as his
performance.

■ HEARTS OF THE WEST

1975, 102 MINS, US ◇
Dir Howard Zieff   *Prod* Tony Bill   *Scr* Rob
Thompson   *Ph* Mario Tosi   *Ed* Edward Wearschilka
Mus Ken Lauber   *Art Dir* Robert Luthardt
● Jeff Bridges, Andy Griffith, Donald Pleasance, Blythe
Danner, Alan Arkin, Richard B. Schull (M-G-M)

Hearts of the West is a pleasant, amusing
period comedy featuring Jeff Bridges in an
excellent characterization as a cliche-quoting
novice western pulp writer who discovers
that his correspondence school is no more
than a remote Nevada mailbox pickup operation, the swindle of Richard B. Shull and
Anthony James. Escaping their robbery
attempt, Bridges accidentally takes their cash
stash into the desert wastes where he is rescued by an oater quickie film location unit.

The casting is very adroit, with all principals complementing in style and charisma.
The structure of the film is notable in that it
tells its story in the manner of films of the
1930s, while in turn keeping separate the
ways in which they were then artistically conceived and executed.

■ HEAT

1972, 100 MINS, US ◇ ⓥ
Dir Paul Morrissey   *Prod* Andy Warhol   *Scr* Paul
Morrissey, John Hollowell   *Ph* Paul Morrissey   *Ed* Lara
Idel, Jed Johnson   *Mus* John Cale
● Sylvia Miles, Joe Dallesandro (Warhol)

Paul Morrissey, who made *Flesh* and *Trash* for
the Andy Warhol Factory Group, always had
a soft spot for the so-called Hollywood film.
In fact, he often claimed he was making Hollywood films, albeit impregnated by new per-

missiveness, plus scenes of drugs, sexual
freedom and his own kind of social
observation.

This one, main centered in Hollywood,
might be a sort of homage to Billy Wilder's
Sunset Blvd. Sex is more implicit here, if tactful, and it is about an out-of-work young actor and an ex-star with daughter troubles and
a turning point in her career.

Morrissey has given more fluidity than his
other pix but relies mainly on actors in a
series of well-meshed scenes as they play out
the drama and comedy of a Hollywood that is
sliding away.

■ HEAT AND DUST

1983, 133 MINS, UK ◇ ⓥ
Dir James Ivory   *Prod* Ismail Merchant   *Scr* Ruth
Prawer Jhabvala   *Ph* Walter Lassally   *Ed* Humphrey
Dixon   *Mus* Richard Robbins   *Art Dir* Wilfrid
Shingleton
● Julie Christie, Christopher Cazenove, Greta Scacchi,
Julian Glover, Susan Fleetwood, Shashi Kapoor
(Merchant-Ivory)

Scripted from her own novel by Ruth Prawer
Jhabvala, *Heat and Dust* intercuts the stories
of two women and of India past and present.
The device is sometimes irritating in its
jumps but ultimately successful in conveying
the essential immutability of India's mystic
character and ambivalent appeal.

Julie Christie, as a distinctly modern
Englishwoman researching and to some
extent reliving the Indian past of a late great
aunt, is the top name in a fine and well-
matched Anglo-Indian cast. But the
principal impact, partly by virtue of role,
is supplied by British newcomer
Greta Scacchi. Portraying the great aunt
as a young bride of scandalous behavior in
colonial India, she creates an impressive
study of classic underplayed well-bred
English turmoil as her affections oscillate between loyal husband and an Indian
potentate.

■ HEATHERS

1989, 102 MINS, US ◇ ⓥ
Dir Michael Lehmann   *Prod* Denise Di Novi
Scr Daniel Waters   *Ph* Francis Kenney   *Ed* Norman
Hollyn   *Mus* David Newman   *Art Dir* Jon Hutman
● Winona Ryder, Christian Slater, Shannen Doherty,
Lisanne Falk, Kim Walker (Cinemarque/New World)

Heathers is a super-smart black comedy about
high school politics and teenage suicide that
showcases a host of promising young talents.

Daniel Waters' enormously clever screenplay blazes a trail of originality through the
dead wood of the teen-comedy genre by
focusing on the *Heathers*, the four prettiest and
most popular girls at Westerburg High, three
of whom are named Heather.

Setting the tone for the group is founder
and queen bitch Heather No. 1, who has a
devastating put-down or comeback for every
occasion and could freeze even a heat-seeking
missile in its tracks with her icy stare.

Heathers No. 2 and 3 get off their own zingers once in a while, while the fourth nubile
beauty, Veronica (Winona Ryder), goes
along for the ride but seems to have a mind of
her own. She also has eyes for a rebellious-
looking school newcomer named J.D. (Christian Slater).

Goaded by the seductive J.D., Veronica
half-heartedly goes along with an attempt to
murder Heather No. 1, who has become irritating beyond endurance.

Winona Ryder is utterly fetching and winning as an intelligent but seriously divided
young lady. Oozing an insinuating sarcasm
reminiscent of Jack Nicholson, Christian
Slater has what it takes to make J.D. both
alluring and dangerous. The three Heathers

(Shannen Doherty, Lisanne Falk and Kim Walker) look like they've spent their lives practicing putdowns.

■ **HEAT'S ON, THE**

1943, 79 MINS, US

Dir Gregory Ratoff   *Prod* Milton Carter   *Scr* Fitzroy Davis, George S. George, Fred Schiller   *Ph* Franz E. Planer   *Ed* Otto Meyer

● Mae West, Victor Moore, Lloyd Bridges, Mary Roche (Columbia)

Picture opens on *Indiscretions*, a Broadway musical that's having trouble getting along, with Mae West singing 'I'm Just a Stranger in Town', done in the typical Westian manner, while for the close she is surrounded by a male chorus in 'Hello, Mi Amigo', which rates okay. 'There Goes That Guitar', used by the Xavier Cugat band as background for a Latinesque dance double, is also a part of the structure of this musical.

Story of *Heat's On*, with West as the actress-siren, her hips a-swinging in a familiar manner and arms akimbo for added familiar effect, plus the affected hard-boiled Westian diction, concerns the efforts of a legit producer, in love with his star, to wrest her from a rival producer after latter has been hoodwinked into believing she's been blacklisted by a reform society.

West looks well but her technique somehow seems dated. William Gaxton does well as the legit producer who's soft for his glamorous star, while Alan Dinehart does okay as a rival prod.

■ **HEATWAVE**

1981, 93 MINS, AUSTRALIA ◇ ▽

Dir Philip Noyce   *Prod* Hillary Linstead, Ross Matthews   *Scr* Marc Rosenberg, Phillip Noyce   *Ph* Vincent Monton   *Ed* John Scott   *Mus* Cameron Allan   *Art Dir* Ross Major

● Judy Davis, Richard Moir, Chris Haywood, Bill Hunter, John Gregg, Anna Jemison (Preston Crothers/M & L)

In his first feature film since the widely acclaimed *Newsfront* [1978] director Phillip Noyce projects Sydney as a cauldron in which hapless individuals are scalded by big business, organized crime, lawyers, police and journalists, working in an unholy alliance.

Noyce's chief protagonists are Richard Moir as a visionary young architect who has designed a $100 million residential complex, and Judy Davis as a radical activist in the forefront of the residents' resistance to its construction.

In part, pic takes on the trappings of the conventional mystery-thriller, pointing to a conspiracy involving the project's financial backer (Chris Haywood), his oily lawyer (John Gregg), Moir's boss (Bill Hunter), a journalist (John Meillon), and union official (Dennis Miller).

Davis, a formidable actress, wrestles with her ambiguous and enigmatic character, and does not quite jell. Moir, however, is a strong, sustaining force as the arrogant, moody, idealistic architect.

■ **HEAVEN**

1987, 80 MINS, US ◇ ▽

Dir Diane Keaton   *Prod* Joe Kelly   *Ph* Frederick Elmes, Joe Kelly   *Ed* Paul Barnes   *Mus* Howard Shore   *Art Dir* Barbara Ling

● (Perpetual/RVF)

Heaven represents an exercise in frivolous metaphysics, an engagingly light-hearted but ultimately light-headed inquiry into the nature of paradise. Diane Keaton's feature directorial debut is a small-scale, non-narra-

tive work using trendily shot interviews, snazzy optical effects and loads of film clips and songs to illustrate fanciful notions of the hereafter.

Close to 100 individuals, all unknown except for boxing promoter Don King, are quizzed on such matters as, 'What is Heaven?' and 'How do you get to Heaven?'

Peppering all these speculations are often goofy clips from old films and TV shows. Excerpts, none of which is identified, range from extravagant depictions of the afterlife, Hollywood-style, to the hilarious expostulations of early broadcast ministers and evangelists.

■ **HEAVEN CAN WAIT**

1943, 112 MINS, US ◇

Dir Ernst Lubitsch   *Prod* Ernst Lubitsch   *Scr* Samson Raphaelson   *Ph* Edward Cronjager   *Ed* Dorothy Spencer   *Mus* Alfred Newman

● Gene Tierney, Don Ameche, Charles Coburn, Marjorie Main, Laird Cregar, Louis Calhern (20th Century-Fox)

Provided with generous slices of comedy, skillfully handled by producer-director Ernst Lubitsch, this is for most of the 112 minutes a smooth, appealing and highly commercial production. Lubitsch has endowed it with light, amusing sophistication and heart-warming nostalgia. He has handled Don Ameche and Gene Tierney, in (for them) difficult characterizations, dexterously.

The Laszlo Bus-Fekete play covers the complete span of a man's life, from precocious infancy to in this case, the sprightly senility of a 70-year-old playboy. It opens with the deceased (Ameche) asking Satan for a passport to hell, which is not being issued unless the applicant can justify his right to it.

This is followed by a recital of real and fancied misdeeds from the time the sinner discovers that, in order to get girls, a boy must have plenty of beetles, through the smartly fashioned hilarious drunk scene with a French maid at the age of 15, to the thefting of his cousin's fiancee, whom he marries.

Charles Coburn as the fond grandfather who takes a hand in his favorite grandson's romantic and domestic problems, walks away with the early sequences in a terrific comedy performance.

☐ 1943: Best Picture (Nomination)

■ **HEAVEN CAN WAIT**

1978, 100 MINS, US ◇ ▽

Dir Warren Beatty, Buck Henry   *Prod* Warren Beatty   *Scr* Warren Beatty, Elaine May   *Ph* William A. Fraker   *Ed* Robert C. Jones, Don Zimmerman   *Mus* Dave Grusin   *Art Dir* Paul Sylbert

● Warren Beatty, Julie Christie, James Mason, Jack Warden, Charles Grodin, Dyan Cannon (Paramount)

Heaven Can Wait is an outstanding film. Harry Segall's fantasy comedy-drama play, made in 1941 by Columbia as *Here Comes Mr Jordan*, returns in an updated, slightly more macabre treatment.

Warren Beatty plays an aging football star, prematurely summoned to judgment after a traffic accident because celestial messenger (played by co-director Buck Henry) jumped the gun. This embarrasses James Mason into permitting Beatty to inhabit temporarily another body. The only available one is that of a wealthy industrialist whose death is plotted by floozy wife Dyan Cannon and Charles Grodin, the tycoon's nerd secretary.

Julie Christie falls for the rich guy, whose main ambition is to resume his football career in which coach Jack Warden plays an important part.

Script and direction are very strong, providing a rich mix of visual and verbal humor that is controlled and avoids the extremes of cheap vulgarity and overly esoteric whimsy.

☐ 1978: Best Picture (Nomination)

■ **HEAVEN HELP US**

1985, 104 MINS, US ◇ ▽

Dir Michael Dinner   *Prod* Dan Wigutow, Mark Carliner   *Scr* Charles Purpura   *Ph* Miroslav Ondricek   *Ed* Stephen A. Rotter   *Mus* James Horner   *Art Dir* Michael Molly

● Donald Sutherland, John Heard, Andrew McCarthy, Mary Stuart Masterson, Kevin Dillon, Malcolm Danare (HBO/Silver Screen Partners)

Heaven Help Us focuses upon several Catholic school boys, three in particular, who get into an increasing amount of trouble with the presiding priests. Andrew McCarthy, a new arrival at St Basil's, instantly latches onto reigning outsider in his class, Malcolm Danare, a chubby egghead who is constantly picked on by school bully Kevin Dillon.

It's virtually inconceivable that the intelligent, sensible McCarthy or Danare would have anything to do with the likes of ne'er-do-well Dillon in real life, but Dillon intimidates them into something resembling friendship. Along with a couple of other large, silent boys, they receive their share of corporal punishment for relatively harmless offenses, wreak havoc during confession and communion and ultimately inspire some helpful changes to be made in the school heirarchy.

Very funny in spots and wonderfully evocative of Brooklyn, circa 1965, pic suffers somewhat by dividing its attention between outrageous pranks and realistic sketches of the Catholic school experience.

■ **HEAVEN KNOWS, MR. ALLISON**

1957, 107 MINS, US ◇ ▽

Dir John Huston   *Prod* Buddy Adler, Eugene Frenke   *Scr* John Lee Mahin, John Huston   *Ph* Oswald Morris   *Ed* Russell Lloyd   *Mus* Georges Auric   *Art Dir* Stephen Grimes

● Deborah Kerr, Robert Mitchum (20th Century-Fox)

Behind the misleading title is an intriguing yarn [from a novel by Charles Shaw] about two people on opposite ends of the social ladder, thrown together in a highly unusual situation. It's about a marine, marooned on a small Pacific atoll [Tobago] with a nun. They divide their time dodging Japs and trying to steer clear of their emotions.

The film, directed by John Huston with something less than outstanding imagination, but with a good measure of humor and bravado, holds out an early promise which it doesn't keep. The parallel is drawn between the nun and her vocation and the marine with his, both subject to strong discipline. But – apart from a few remarks – the character and motivations of Deborah Kerr remain shrouded in mystery and she reveals very little of herself.

The high spots of the film involve Robert Mitchum's exploits – and fantastic ones they are – in the midst of the occupying Japanese force when he raids its supply depot for food. These scenes are staged with noise, gusto and a good deal of suspense.

■ **HEAVENS ABOVE!**

1963, 118 MINS, UK ▽

Dir John Boulting   *Prod* John Boulting, Roy Boulting   *Scr* Frank Harvey, John Boulting   *Ph* Max Greene   *Ed* Teddy Farvas   *Mus* Richard Rodney Bennett

● Peter Sellers, Bernard Miles, Eric Sykes, Irene Handl, Miriam Karlin, Isabel Jeans (British Lion/Romulus)

A measure of the merit of *Heavens Above!* is that its theme could have been just as acceptably used as a straight drama. But the Boulting Brothers effectively employ their favorite weapon, the rapier of ridicule. The screenplay is full of choice jokes, but the humor is often uneven.

H

Story concerns the appointment, by a clerical error, of the Reverend John Smallwood (Peter Sellers) to the parish of Orbiston Parva, a prosperous neighborhood ruled by the Despard family, makers of Tranquilax, the three-in-one restorative (Sedative! Stimulant! Laxative!). He's a quiet, down-to-earth chap who happens to believe in the scriptures and lives by them.

From the moment he gives his first sermon all hell breaks out, so to speak. He shocks the district by making a Negro trashman his warden and takes a bunch of disreputable evicted gypsies into the vicarage. Soon he makes his first convert, Lady Despard.

Within this framework there are some very amusing verbal and visual jokes, and both are largely aided by some deft acting. Sellers gives a guileful portrayal of genuine simplicity. Bernard Miles, as an acquisitive butler; Eric Sykes, Irene Handl, Miriam Karlin and Roy Kinnear (leader of the gypsies); and Isabel Jeans, a regal Lady Despard, all contribute heftily.

Those who expect to see church steeples crumble under a blistering attack will be unlucky. But there is enough amusement to satisfy even those who want to duck the film's unmistakable and uncomfortable conclusion: 'That in this material world anyone who tries to lead a truly Christian life is weighing himself down with socko odds.'

●●●●●●●●●●●●●●●●●●●●●●●●●●●●

■ **HEAVEN'S GATE**

1980, 219 MINS, US ◇ ▼

Dir Michael Cimino   *Prod* Joann Carelli   *Scr* Michael Cimino   *Ph* Vilmos Zsigmond   *Ed* Tom Rolf, William Reynolds, Lisa Fruchtman, Gerald Greenberg   *Mus* David Mansfield   *Art Dir* Tambi Larsen
● Kris Kristofferson, Christopher Walken, Isabelle Huppert, Sam Waterston, John Hurt, Jeff Bridges (United Artists)

The first scenes of *Heaven's Gate* are so energetic and beautiful that anyone who knows the saga of the $35 million epic might begin to think it was going to be worth every penny. Unfortunately the balance of director Michael Cimino's film is so confusing, so overlong at three-and-a-half hours and so ponderous at almost every level that it fails to work at almost every level.

What structure the film does have is based on the Johnson County wars which took place in the 1890s in Wyoming.

The story deals with a group of established cattlemen headed by Canton (Sam Waterston) who are convinced their herds are being looted by immigrant settlers. With the approval of the state, the operators of the large cattle ranches draw up a death list of 125 poor immigrants in Johnson County who are supposedly doing the 'rustling'. Kris Kristopherson plays the Federal marshall who turned against his class.

Cimino's attempts to draw a portrait of the plight of the immigrants in the west in that period are so impersonal that none of the victims ever get beyond pat stereotypes.

Cimino, who wrote the script himself, has simply not provided enough details for his story, leaving his audience guessing.

●●●●●●●●●●●●●●●●●●●●●●●●●●●●

■ **HEAVY METAL**

1981, 90 MINS, US ◇

Dir Gerald Potterton   *Prod* Ivan Reitman   *Scr* Dan Goldberg, Len Blum   *Ed* Janice Brown   *Mus* Elmer Bernstein   *Art Dir* Michael Gross

This technically firstrate six-segment animated anthology is an amalgam of science fiction, sword and sorcery, hip humor, violence, sex and a smidgen of drugs.

The film, which draws its title and sensibility from the adult fantasy magazine of the same name, tends to frontload its virtues. Initial segments have a boisterous blend of dynamic graphics, intriguing plot premises and sly wit that unfortunately slide gradually downhill.

Courtesy of a vastly overlong, relatively unrousing 27-minute end-piece that may be the technical highpoint of the film, but lacks the punch and tightness of the earlier segments, the venture tends to run out of steam. Still, the net effect is an overridingly positive one.

●●●●●●●●●●●●●●●●●●●●●●●●●●●●

■ **HEDDA**

1975, 104 MINS, UK ◇

Dir Trevor Nunn   *Prod* Robert Enders   *Scr* Trevor Nunn   *Ph* Douglas Slocombe   *Ed* Peter Tanner   *Mus* Laurie Johnson   *Art Dir* Ted Tester
● Glenda Jackson, Timothy West, Peter Eyre, Jennie Linden, Patrick Stewart, Constance Chapman (Brut)

Hedda is a gem, taking the Royal Shakespeare production of the Henrik Ibsen classic, complete with a fine cast headed by Glenda Jackson.

It's heady stuff, nearly every line to be relished, as one watches the destructively dominant Hedda torturing her friends and relations with rapier-sharp lines and stiletto-like glances.

So persuasively talented and self-assured a performer as Jackson is not everyone's cup of tea, but few should quibble with one of her best parts.

●●●●●●●●●●●●●●●●●●●●●●●●●●●●

■ **HEIRESS, THE**

1949, 115 MINS, US ◇

Dir William Wyler   *Prod* William Wyler   *Scr* Ruth Goetz, Augustus Goetz   *Ph* Leo Tover   *Ed* William Hornbeck   *Mus* Aaron Copland
● Olivia de Havilland, Montgomery Clift, Ralph Richardson, Miriam Hopkins (Paramount)

The Heiress is a meticulous reproduction of the Victorian scene, so faithful to its mores that it is a museum piece.

William Wyler, in his producer-director role, has seen fit to cling exactly to the period portrayed in the Ruth and Augustus Goetz script, based on their stage play suggested by Henry James' novel *Washington Square*.

Olivia de Havilland, in the title role, is the homely daughter of a wealthy physician. A social shyness that cloaks the quick wit and puckishness has kept her suitorless despite a sizeable wealth that will be augmented when her father passes. Montgomery Clift is the first male to show her attention. The father sees through his courting, tries to break up a quick engagement.

Clift plays the difficult part of an ambiguous character who is more opportunist than crook in his fortune-hunting. Ralph Richardson is grand as the stern, strait-laced father.
□ 1949: Best Picture (Nomination)

●●●●●●●●●●●●●●●●●●●●●●●●●●●●

■ **HELEN OF TROY**

1955, 118 MINS, US ◇

Dir Robert Wise   *Scr* John Twist, Hugh Gray   *Ph* Harry Stradling   *Ed* Thomas Reilly   *Mus* Max Steiner   *Art Dir* Edward Carrere
● Rossana Podesta, Jacques Sernas, Cedric Hardwicke, Stanley Baker, Niall MacGinnis, Robert Douglas (Warner)

The retelling of the Homeric legend, filmed in its entirety in Italy, makes lavish use of the CinemaScope screen.

WB and director Robert Wise piled on the extras in Greek and Trojan armies. Production values ride over shortcomings in John Twist and Hugh Gray's script and dialog. Like many tales of antiquity, the story is occasionally stilted.

As Helen and Paris, the love-smitten Trojan prince, Warners cast two unknowns – Rossana Podesta, an exquisite Italian beauty, and Jacques Sernas, a brawny and handsome Frenchman. Visually both meet the demands of the roles. Their voices have been dubbed.

The story opens with Paris' journey to Sparta to effect a peace treaty between the Greeks and Troy. He falls in love with Helen not knowing she is the queen of Sparta. His peace mission fails, and in making his escape from Sparta, takes Helen with him. The 'abduction' unites the Greeks and sends them off on a war against Troy.

●●●●●●●●●●●●●●●●●●●●●●●●●●●●

■ **HELL AND HIGH WATER**

1954, 103 MINS, US ◇

Dir Samuel Fuller   *Prod* Raymond A. Klune   *Scr* Jesse L. Lasky Jr, Samuel Fuller   *Ph* Joe MacDonald   *Ed* James B. Clark   *Mus* Alfred Newman
● Richard Widmark, Bella Darvi, Victor Francen, Cameron Mitchell, Gene Evans, David Wayne (20th Century-Fox)

CinemaScope and rip-roaring adventure mate perfectly in *Hell and High Water*, a highly fanciful, but mighty entertaining action feature.

As the male star, Richard Widmark takes easily to the rugged assignment, giving it the wallop needed. It is a further projection of the action-adventure type of hero he does quite often, and good. The picture introduces a new star Polish-born, French-raised Bella Darvi and she creates an interesting impression in her debut.

Plot has to do with a group of individuals of many nationalities who band together to thwart a scheme to start a new world war with an atomic incident that will be blamed on the United States. These private heroes hire Widmark, a former naval submarine officer, to command an underwater trip to the Arctic, where scientists on the voyage will check reports that a Communist atomic arsenal is being built on an isolated island.

●●●●●●●●●●●●●●●●●●●●●●●●●●●●

■ **HELL BENT**

1918, 77 MINS, US

Dir John Ford   *Scr* John Ford, Harry Carey   *Ph* Ben Reynolds
● Harry Carey, Neva Gerber, Duke Lee, Joseph Harris (Universal)

Hell Bent was rediscovered at the Czech Film Archives. Current print is presently the only one of two complete films surviving from the director's 1917-19 beginning years at Universal Studios.

Hell Bent was Ford's 14th film and his ninth feature. Its leading player, Harry Carey was Ford's most frequent early star and collaborator. Here, Carey again plays his laconic Cheyenne Harry protagonist.

Harry rides into the town of Rawhide where in a long winded comic turn he strikes up a friendship with Cimmaron Bill (Duke Lee) and is then smitten by love for Bess (Neva Gerber), a 'good girl' forced by circumstances to work in a dance hall. B-plot mechanics take over as Harry tries to rid town of outlaws but is stymied when he learns Bess' weak-willed brother is member of gang led by Bean Ross (Joseph Harris).

Film is enlivened by some of Ford's special moments. As his relationship with Bess develops Harry awkwardly carries her home in the rain while in the next shot his abandoned pal wanders through the darkened saloon.

●●●●●●●●●●●●●●●●●●●●●●●●●●●●

■ **HELLBOUND HELLRAISER II**

1988, 96 MINS, UK/US ◇ ▼

Dir Tony Randel   *Prod* Christopher Figg   *Scr* Peter Atkins   *Ph* Robin Vidgeon   *Mus* Christopher Young   *Art Dir* Mike Buchanan

● Clare Higgins, Ashley Laurence, Ken Cranham, Imogen Boorman (Film Futures)

Hellraiser II is a maggotty carnival of mayhem, mutation and dismemberment, awash in blood and recommended only for those who thrive on such junk.

Helmer Tony Randel returns to the off-the-wall tale of a psychotic psychiatrist's long struggle to get the better of something called the Lament Configuration, a kind of demonic, silver-filigreed Rubik's Cube whose solution opens the transdimensional doors into a parallel world of sinful pleasure and unspeakably hellish pain.

This fiendish shrink takes a special interest in a new patient, Kristy, whose family was massacred in appropriately gruesome fashion by box-sprung flesh-eating ghouls called Cenobites.

As Kristy and the shrink head toward the big showdown in Hades, the movie unfolds with a tableau of can-you-top-this gross-outs.

●●●●●●●●●●●●●●●●●●●●●●●●●●●●

■ **HELLER IN PINK TIGHTS**

1960, 100 MINS, US ◇ Ⓥ
Dir George Cukor *Prod* Carlo Ponti, Marcello Girosi *Scr* Dudley Nichols, Walter Bernstein *Ph* Harold Lipstein *Ed* Howard Smith *Mus* Daniele Amfitheatrof *Art Dir* Hal Pereira, Eugene Allen
● Sophia Loren, Anthony Quinn, Eileen Heckart, Ramon Novarro, Margaret O'Brien, Steve Forrest (Paramount)

With *Heller In Pink Tights* director George Cukor puts tongue in cheek to turn an ordinary story into a gaudy, old-fashioned western satire with gleeful touches of melodrama.

Taken from a novel by Louis L'Amour, *Heller* follows The Great Healy Dramatic and Concert Co in two red wagons through the wilds of Wyoming. The traveling theatre is fighting for its survival, and Sophia Loren and Anthony Quinn put up a strong enough battle to make things interesting and amusing. It's when the film's plottage dissolves into pure western that it becomes somewhat commonplace.

Loren dons blonde tresses for the role of an actress who has a knack for getting into situations. She looks fine with golden head and turns in a respectable, most believable performance. Quinn, as head of the Healy company, adeptly projects as the he-man, yet properly building a tender, calm characterization.

Eileen Heckart just about steals the whole shootin' match as an actress who has given up a 'promising' career for her daughter's chances on stage. It's real comedy, and Heckart carries it off with polish. Steve Forrest makes a lovable villain, evil but never evil enough to lose his attraction. Margaret O'Brien is fine in a role that offers her more chances to be seen than heard; Edmund Love is very good as a 'Shakespearean' actor; and Ramon Novarro is aptly sinister as a well-heeled banker.

●●●●●●●●●●●●●●●●●●●●●●●●●●●●

■ **HELL IN THE PACIFIC**

1968, 103 MINS, US ◇ Ⓦ
Dir John Boorman *Prod* Reuben Bercovitch *Scr* Alexander Jacobs, Eric Bercovici *Ph* Conrad Hall *Ed* Thomas Stanford *Mus* Lalo Schifrin *Art Dir* Anthony Pratt, Masao Yamazaki
● Lee Marvin, Toshiro Mifune (Selmur)

Tale of two warriors forced to co-exist. Lee Marvin and Toshiro Mifune comprise the entire cast of this World War II drama, directed with an uncertain hand by John Boorman.

Story takes off with the discovery by Mifune that he no longer is alone on a desolate Pacific island. Pair stalk each other, then attempt to outwit each other, finally collaborate on survival in the form of a raft.

Mifune's unrestrained grunting and running about create an outdated caricature of an Oriental. Marvin has sardonic lines which resemble wisecracks, intended for on-lookers. The subtle humor which was meant to exist becomes overpowering.

Lalo Schifrin could not have served worse the purposes of the film. Phony suspense bits – snapping twigs, etc. – are punched to death through maladroit composing. Net effect of this is the impression that there have got to be 50 musicians lurking just off-camera.

Marvin's arresting screen presence requires appreciative surrounding characters, none of which are present, or meant to be.

Mifune gets few chances to project three-dimensional characterization.

●●●●●●●●●●●●●●●●●●●●●●●●●●●●

■ **HELL IS A CITY**

1960, 98 MINS, UK
Dir Val Guest *Prod* Michael Carreras *Scr* Val Guest *Ph* Arthur Grant *Ed* John Dunsford *Mus* Stanley Black *Art Dir* Robert Jones
● Stanley Baker, John Crawford, Donald Pleasence, Maxine Audley, Billie Whitelaw, Joseph Tomelty (Hammer)

Hell Is a City is an absorbing film of a conventional cops and robbers yarn. Val Guest's taut screenplay [from a novel by Maurice Proctor], allied to his own deft direction, has resulted in a notable film in which the characters are all vividly alive, the action constantly gripping and the background of a provincial city put over with authenticity.

The film was shot largely in Manchester. Arthur Grant's camerawork has arrestingly caught the feel of the big city with its grey, sleazy backstreets, its saloons, the surrounding factory chimneys, the bleakness of the moors and the bustle of the city.

The yarn has Stanley Baker as a detective inspector who, married to a bored, unsympathetic wife (Maxine Audley) spends most of his time on his job. In this instance he is concerned with a dangerous escaped convict who, he suspects, will be returning to Manchester to pick up the stolen jewels that sent him to the cooler. When the girl clerk of the local bookie is attacked while on her way to the bank and then found murdered on the nearby moors, Baker suspects that the crook and a small gang are the criminals. Doggedly he starts to track them down.

From the moment when the killer (John Crawford) makes his sudden surprise entrance and sets the wheels of the robbery in motion, suspense rarely lets up. The robbery itself is briskly pulled off, there is a firstrate scene on the moors when the police raid an illegal gathering of gamblers and some down-to-earth police station sequences, with Baker pulling no punches in his determination to get at the truth. Acting all round is admirable.

●●●●●●●●●●●●●●●●●●●●●●●●●●●●

■ **HELLO, DOLLY!**

1969, 129 MINS, US ◇ Ⓥ
Dir Gene Kelly *Prod* Ernest Lehman *Scr* Ernest Lehman *Ph* Harry Stradling *Ed* William Reynolds *Mus* Jerry Herman *Art Dir* John De Cuir
● Barbra Streisand, Walter Matthau, Michael Crawford, Louis Armstrong, Marianne McAndrew, Tommy Tune (20th Century-Fox/Chenault)

Hello, Dolly! is an expensive, expansive, sometimes exaggerated, sentimental, nostalgic, wholesome, pictorially opulent $20 million filmusical [from the 1964 Broadway production] with the charisma of Barbra Streisand in the title role.

Streisand is a unique performer, with that inborn vitality which marks great personalities. She brings her own special kind of authority. There is a certain inconsistency, or even confusion, in the speech pattern.

Walter Matthau is hard to accept at first, his dancing being the step-counting sort and his singing somewhat awkward. Nonetheless his experience cannot be discounted.

The film 'opens cute' with a long-held still of the 14th St replica. Immensely and imaginatively detailed it intrigues the eye and mind directly. When the still 'wipes' into live action, the film is off in a flurry of promise and introducing the times (1890) and the heroine (Dolly) en route to Yonkers.
□ 1969: Best Picture (Nomination)

●●●●●●●●●●●●●●●●●●●●●●●●●●●●

■ **HELLRAISER**

1987, 90 MINS, UK ◇ Ⓥ
Dir Clive Barker *Prod* Christopher Figg *Scr* Clive Barker *Ph* David Worley *Mus* Christopher Young *Art Dir* Jocelyn James
● Andrew Robinson, Clare Higgins, Ashley Laurence, Sean Chapman, Oliver Smith (Film Futures)

Hellraiser is a well-paced sci-fi cum horror fantasy [from Clive Barker's own novel *The Hellbound Heart*].

Film concerns a dissipated adventurer who somewhere in the Orient buys a sort of magic music box which is capable of providing its owner hitherto undreamt of pains and pleasures, and which ultimately causes him to be torn to shreds in a temple which transforms itself into a torture chamber.

Back home, his brother has just moved into a rickety old house with his new wife or girlfriend; digs had formerly been the dwelling of the ill-fated adventurer. Latter returns, by rising through the floorboards, partly decomposed, seeking human flesh and blood which, when devoured, will enable him to regain his human form. Pic is well made, well acted, and the visual effects are generally handled with skill.

●●●●●●●●●●●●●●●●●●●●●●●●●●●●

■ **HELL'S ANGELS**

1930, 119 MINS, US ◇
Dir Howard Hughes *Scr* Joseph Moncure March, Howard Estabrook, Harry Behn *Ph* Tony Gaudio, Harry Perry, E.B. Steene, Harry Zach, Dewey Wrigley, Elmer Dyer, Pliny Goodfriend, Alvin Wyckoff, Sam Landers, William Tuers, Glenn Kershner, Donald Keyes, Roy Klaffki, Paul Ivano, Charles Boyle, Herman Schopp, L. Guy Wilky, John Silver, Edward Snyder, Ed Krull, Jack Greenhalgh, Henry Cronjager, Edward Cohen, Frank Breamer, Ernest Laszlo *Ed* Frank Lawrence, Douglas Biggs, Perry Hollingsworth *Mus* Hugo Riesenfeld *Art Dir* J. Boone Fleming, Carroll Clark
● Ben Lyon, James Hall, Jean Harlow, John Darrow, Lucien Prival, Frank Clarke (Caddo)

Howard Hughes' air film was advertised as costing $4 million, which likely means $3 million – plenty.

It's no sappy, imbecilic tale. One of the brothers (Ben Lyon) is strictly a 'good-time Charlie' continuously on the make and humanly afraid to die; the girl (Jean Harlow) is no good in the sense that she has and will try anything with either brother, but only does so with Lyon. This is because Jimmy Hall has ideals, idolizes her and wants to make everything official.

The first half of the film builds up to a Zeppelin raid on London which runs two reels and is given a big screen. Second half's main display is an aerial dog fight in which at least 30, maybe 40, planes simultaneously start diving and zooming at each other.

Story actually opens in Munich with Lyon trying to date every femme in town. Highly seasoned portion of the second half comes with Lyon and Hall on a spree. Hall finds Harlow half soused and entwined with another officer in a barroom booth.

Hughes spent three years working on his pet. The story was remade three times. Orig-

H

inally it was silent, with Greta Nissen as the girl; then it was made once in sound and remade again after that. Air shots were taken silent with the sound dubbed in afterward.

James Whale is programmed as having staged the dialog and does that smartly. The one color sequence [a London ball] runs just about a reel and is not important.

. . . .

■ **HELL'S HIGHWAY**

1932, 62 MINS, US

Dir Rowland Brown   *Prod* David O. Selznick
Scr Samuel Ornitz, Robert Tasker, Rowland Brown
Ph Edward Cronjager   *Art Dir* Carroll Clark
● Richard Dix, Tom Brown, Louise Carter, Rochelle Hudson, C. Henry Gordon, Warner Richmond (Radio)

In *Hell's Highway* the entire action, with the exception of one scene, occurs in and around a prison camp in some southern state; the preponderance of the convict labor is negro. The convicts have been hired to work on a new road. The contractor tells his foreman that he bid 50% under his nearest competitor and to win a profit he must get twice as much work out of the convicts.

To force their efforts recourse is had to the lash and the sweatbox, the latter a structure of corrugated iron barely large enough to contain a man, and placed so that the metal absorbs the full force of the burning sun. In this men are placed with a heavy leather collar about the neck and with feet strapped to the floor.

Richard Dix is one of the convicts. His brother (Tom Brown) is sent to the gang for having shot and wounded Dix's betrayer. Dix, who is planning an escape, has to prevent the kid from coming along.

The direction is remarkably good at most points. Some handsome scenic backgrounds are created during the hunt for the convicts.

The director is rather less successful in his effort to inject comedy. Once or twice a nance camp laborer is employed, once for a genuine if smutty laugh. Other humor is supposed to arise from the smug mouthings of the Hermit (Charles Middleton), a crazed religionist type.

Dix is wasted as the young convict, with Brown much more effective as the kid. Louise Carter is an almost total loss in her single scene, as is Rochelle Hudson. Clarence Muse, in a very small bit, strikes one of the few really human notes.

. . . .

■ **HELLZAPOPPIN**

1941, 92 MINS, US

Dir H.C. Potter   *Prod* Jules Levey   *Scr* Nat Perrin, Warren Wilson   *Ph* Woody Bredell   *Ed* Milton Carruth
● Ole Olsen, Chic Johnson, Martha Raye, Hugh Herbert, Mischa Auer (Universal/Mayfair)

There's the thinnest thread of a romantic story, but it's incidental to Olsen and Johnson's [1938] stage formula for *Hellzapoppin*.

The yarn itself can be summed up in a few words: the rich girl in love with the poor boy, who in turn doesn't want to cross his rich pal, favored by the girl's socially conscious parents. The poor boy stages a charity show for the girl, and his stagehand pals (O&J) think they can save him from the girl, by lousing it up.

One of the picture's saving graces is the originality of presentation of screwball comedy. The business of O&J talking from the screen to the comic projectionist (Shemp Howard) is one such detail; ditto the slide bit telling a kid in the audience, 'Stinky go home', with Jane Frazee and Robert Paige interrupting a duet until Stinky finally leaves.

Don Raye and Gene DePauf have contributed several nice songs for this film. There are some lavish production numbers. Jules Levey (Mayfair), producer, was obviously unstinting.

. . . .

■ **HELP!**

1965, 92 MINS, UK ◇ ⓥ

Dir Richard Lester   *Prod* Walter Shenson   *Scr* Marc Behm, Charles Wood   *Ph* David Watkin   *Ed* John Victor Smith   *Mus* Ken Thorne, John Lennon, Paul McCartney   *Art Dir* Ray Simm
● John Lennon, Paul McCartney, Ringo Starr, George Harrison, Leo McKern, Eleanor Bron (Subafilms)

The Beatles' second effort is peppered with bright gags and situations and throwaway nonsense. Richard Lester's direction is expectedly alert and the color lensing is a delight. But there are also some frantically contrived spots and sequences that flag badly. The simple good spirits that pervaded *A Hard Day's Night* are now often smothered as if everybody is desperately trying to outsmart themselves and be ultra-clever-clever. Nevertheless, *Help!* is a good, nimble romp with both giggles and belly-laughs.

Story concerns the efforts of a gang of Eastern thugs, led by Leo McKern, to get hold of a sacrificial ring which has been sent to Ringo by a fan and which he is innocently wearing. Also after the ring is a nutty, powerdrunk scientist who sees the ring as a key to world domination. The Beatles are given a heck of a runaround which takes them from London to Stonehenge, the Alps and the Bahamas.

The Beatles prove more relaxed in front of the camera but they have still to prove themselves to be actors; as screen personalities they are good material and have a touch of the Marx Bros in their similarly irreverent flights of fantasy.

. . . .

■ **HEMINGWAY'S ADVENTURES OF A YOUNG MAN**

1962, 145 MINS, US ◇

Dir Martin Ritt   *Prod* Jerry Wald   *Scr* A.E. Hotchner
Ph Lee Garmes   *Ed* Hugh S. Fowler   *Mus* Franz Waxman   *Art Dir* Jack Martin Smith, Paul Groesse
● Richard Beymer, Diane Baker, Paul Newman, Ricado Montalban, Dan Dailey, Arthur Kennedy (20th Century-Fox)

The formidable task of assembling the bits and pieces of Ernest Hemingway's autobiographical young hero, Nick Adams, and welding them into a single, substantial flesh-and-blood screen personality has nearly been accomplished in *Adventures of a Young Man*. But, while the film has been executed with concern, integrity and respect for the pen from which it flows, it has a disquieting tendency to oscillate between flashes of artistry and truth and interludes of mechanics and melodramatics.

Hotchner's scenario, gleaned from the prose of 10 of Hemingway's short stories, traced the path to maturity of Nick Adams. It follows him in his restless, searching pursuit of knowledge and worldly experience with which to build his character, advance his potential, shape his identity and prepare him for his destiny in the higher sphere to which he aspires.

There are a host of fine performances, and a few weak ones. Paul Newman, almost unrecognizable behind a masterfully grotesque yet realistic makeup mask by Ben Nye, re-creates the punchdrunk Battler character. It's a colorful and compassionate acting cameo.

Other important standouts are Ricardo Montalban as a perceptive Italian officer, Fred Clark as a slick but sympathetic burlesque promoter, Dan Dailey as a down-and-out advance man, Juano Hernandez as the Battler's devoted watchdog 'trainer', and Eli Wallach as a practical but kind Italian Army orderly. Probably the finest performance in the film is Arthur Kennedy's as Nick's peace-loving, recessive father. And Jessica Tandy is excellent as the fanatical, domineering mother who leads Kennedy to his self-destruction.

. . . .

■ **HENNESSY**

1975, 104 MINS, UK ◇

Dir Don Sharp   *Prod* Peter Snell   *Scr* John Gay
Ph Ernest Steward   *Ed* Eric Boyd-Perkins   *Mus* John Scott   *Art Dir* Ray Simm
● Rod Steiger, Lee Remick, Richard Johnson, Trevor Howard, Eric Porter, Peter Egan (American International)

Good suspense drama starring Rod Steiger as a man planning to blow up the British Parliament in revenge for his family's accidental death in Belfast.

Richard Johnson, who wrote the intriguing original story, plays a Scotland Yard inspector, well-versed (and earlier wounded) in Irish tumult, working under Trevor Howard in the attempt to find Steiger, who has come to London with a plan to substitute himself for MP Hugh Moxey on 5 November and, triggering himself as a human bomb, destroy the British power structure.

Ironically, IRA leader Eric Porter, knowing that event would lead to more British, rather than less, in Northern Ireland, sets out to kill Steiger. Steiger does very well in the title role.

. . . .

■ **HENRY & JUNE**

1990, 136 MINS, US ◇ ⓥ

Dir Philip Kaufman   *Prod* Peter Kaufman   *Scr* Rose Kaufman, Philip Kaufman   *Ph* Philippe Rousselot
Ed Vivien Hillgrove, William S. Scharf, Dede Allen
Art Dir Guy-Claude Francois
● Fred Ward, Uma Thurman, Maria de Medeiros, Richard E. Grant, Kevin Spacey, Jean-Philippe Ecoffey (Universal/Walrus)

Henry & June, will be considered liberating by some and obscene by others. The lovemaking scenes in his previous film, *The Unbearable Lightness of Being* (1988), proved that director Philip Kaufman was perhaps the best director to handle the story of the long-secret, passionate affair between writers Henry Miller and Anais Nin in Paris in 1931–32.

Pic's title, also the title of the Nin book, is actually a misnomer. This is the story of Henry and Anais; June, playing a marginal role, is offscreen much of the time.

The film opens with Anais and her banker husband, Hugo, establishing themselves in Paris. It quickly becomes clear that, although fond of the rather stuffy Hugo, Anais, who keeps a secret diary, isn't telling him everything, and is eager to experience the kind of things she imagines in her erotic dreams. Miller's arrival is the catalyst.

Anais is also attracted to Miller's wife, June, who visits occasionally from America, and dreams of erotic experiences in which June assumes the male role.

In its depiction of Depression Paris and sexual candor, *Henry & June* succeeds. The central performances of Fred Ward, as the cynical, life-loving Miller, and Maria de Medeiros, as the beautiful, insatiable Anais, splendidly fulfill the director's vision.

Pic is less successful in gaining audience sympathy for these hedonists. Also, the character of June (Uma Thurman) is ill-defined.

. . . .

■ **HENRY V**

1946, 127 MINS, UK ◇ ⓥ

Dir Laurence Olivier   *Prod* Laurence Olivier
Scr William Shakespeare   *Ph* Robert Krasker, Jack Hildyard   *Ed* Reginald Beck   *Mus* William Walton
Art Dir Paul Sheriff

● Laurence Olivier, Robert Newton, Renee Asherson, Esmond Knight, Leo Genn, Felix Aylmer (Two Cities)

Production cost ran to about $2 million and every cent of it is evident on the screen. The color, the sets, the expanse and the imaginative quality of the filming are unexcelled. *Henry V* as a picture, however, requires that the spectator takes more with him into the theatre in the way of mental preparedness than mere curiosity.

Story is considerably simpler than the boys from Hollywood turn out. Henry's a British king, hardly more than a moppet, when, with the aid of a couple of clergymen, he cons himself into believing that he ought to muscle his way into France and stake his royal claim there on the basis of ancestry. So he loads some 30,000 men and their horses on the 15th-century version of LSTs and hies across the channel.

There are many interesting scenes and one really exciting one – the battle. With thousands of horses, knights in armor and longbowmen in colorful costumes, it's a Technicolor setup. Strong contrast is made between the overstuffed French warriors in armor so heavy they have to be lowered onto their horses with block and tackle, and the British, who won the battle with the longbow, used by men afoot and unhindered by iron pants.

Memorable for their deft humor and poignancy are both scenes in which Renee Asherson, as Princess Katharine, appears. Even Olivier is put well back into the No. 2 spot in the scene in which he woos her.

Treatment is interesting and adds much to the general effect. Picture opens with the camera panning over London and coming into the Old Globe theatre. Heralds' horns announce the opening of the play as the camera gets to the stage – and the show is on.

Acting, at the beginning, is in the stylized pattern of the 16th century and it doesn't get far away from that even when the camera is given full sweep after the Old Globe has been left behind. Sets throughout also give a feeling that you haven't left the theatre for while tri-dimensional close to the camera, they fade into purposely obvious painted scenics in the background.

□ 1946: Best Picture (Nomination)

■ **HENRY V**

1989, 137 MINS, UK ◇ ⓥ
Dir Kenneth Branagh   *Prod* Bruce Sharman
Scr Kenneth Branagh   *Ph* Kenneth MacMillan
Ed Michael Bradsell   *Mus* Patrick Boyle   *Art Dir* Tim Harvey
● Kenneth Branagh, Derek Jacobi, Brian Blessed, Ian Holm, Paul Scofield, Emma Thompson (Renaissance/BBC/Curzon)

Henry V is a stirring, gritty and enjoyable pic which offers a plethora of fine performances from some of the U.K.'s brightest talents.

Laurence Olivier's *Henry V* (1944) was designed to rally the English with its glorious battle scenes and patriotic verse. Branagh's version is more realistic and tighter in scale, and is a contempo version of Shakespeare.

Pic opens with Derek Jacobi as the chorus wandering around a film studio setting the scene. Branagh (Henry V, King of England) prepares for an invasion of France to secure his legal claim to the French throne. Paul Scofield (the French king) sadly ponders his country's situation and is urged to enter in bloody battle by Michael Maloney (the Dauphin).

After many battles, Branagh's tired and bedraggled army prepares for the final conflict with the massive French forces. After wandering among his troops in disguise, Branagh makes an impassioned speech and his forces win.

One subplot has Emma Thompson (the French king's daughter Katherine) and her maid (Geraldine McEwan) playing at learning English. Branagh declares his love for Thompson after he has won the French throne.

■ **HENRY VIII AND HIS SIX WIVES**

1972, 125 MINS, UK ◇ ⓥ
Dir Waris Hussein   *Prod* Roy Baird   *Scr* Ian Thorne
Ph Peter Suschitzky   *Ed* John Bloom   *Mus* David Munro   *Art Dir* Roy Stannard
● Keith Michell, Frances Cuka, Charlotte Rampling, Jane Asher, Jenny Bos, Lynne Frederick (Anglo-EMI)

A beautifully crafted epic, *Henry VIII* is told in flashback form from the king's deathbed. Pic deals almost exclusively with Henry and his succession of wives, deliberately relegating historic events to backdrops, even though audiences are kept in touch at all times with what else was going on in the realm.

Thanks also to a fine, tight script and sensitive but firm direction, the king acquires many more dimensions than those usually credited him. Keith Michell gives an uppercase performance all the way, through a succession of equally very believable makeup transformations.

Somewhat over-stolid at times, and taking itself too seriously, it perhaps needs more amusing change-of-pace sequences such as the one which finds the king saddled, sightunseen, with the ugly Anne of Cleves.

■ **HER ALIBI**

1989, 94 MINS, US ◇ ⓥ
Dir Bruce Beresford   *Prod* Keith Barish   *Scr* Charlie Peters   *Ph* Freddie Francis   *Ed* Anne Goursaud
Mus Georges Delerue   *Art Dir* Henry Bumstead
● Tom Selleck, Paulina Porizkova, William Daniels, James Farentino, Hurd Hatfield, Patrick Wayne (Warner)

He's a mystery writer; she's a mystery; and it's also a mystery how TV fodder like this manages to get the high-gloss, top-talent treatment at studios.

Bestselling writer Phil Blackwood (Tom Selleck), out of stories and under pressure for his next book, decides to rescue drop-dead beautiful Nina (Czech-born model Pauline Porizkova) from court custody as a murder suspect.

He gives her an alibi by telling the canny d.a. (rigorously played by James Farentino) that they're having an affair and were together during the time of the alleged murder.

To maintain the facade, Selleck has to take the aloof Rumanian beauty out to his lush country estate to live while he pecks away at his new novel – about her, naturally, and his feverishly imagined version of their relationship.

Porizkova has the disconcerting habit of hurling kitchen knives at the wall and otherwise inviting Selleck's demise. He soon begins to suspect she is a murderer.

Mix of sexual tension, physical danger and quirky black humour has a certain appealing bouyancy, but ultimately it's deflated by general lack of credibility.

■ **HERBIE GOES TO MONTE CARLO**

1977, 105 MINS, US ◇ ⓥ
Dir Vincent McEveety   *Prod* Ron Miller   *Scr* Arthur Alsberg, Don Nelson   *Ph* Leonard J. South   *Ed* Cotton Warburton   *Mus* Frank DeVol   *Art Dir* John B. Mansbridge
● Dean Jones, Don Knotts, Julie Sommars, Jacques Marin, Roy Kinnear, Bernard Fox (Walt Disney)

Herbie, the spunky little Volks beetle with a mind of his own, gets romantic buildup when he becomes a Romeo on wheels infatuated with a flirty powder-blue Lancia named Giselle, as both participate in the annual Paris to Monte Carlo road rally. Herbie is reunited with his original owner and driver, Dean Jones, a former second-rate racer whom he once adopted and won a flock of races for in the US.

Together again, Jones finds once more he is at the mercy of Herbie, who time and again takes matters into his own hands for often slapstick and mirthful effect as they roar toward their destination.

Herbie performs in the qualifying races outside Paris where he falls hood over wheels in love with the smart Lancia, driven by Julie Sommars who takes Jones' eye as well.

■ **HERBIE RIDES AGAIN**

1974, 88 MINS, US ◇ ⓥ
Dir Robert Stevenson   *Prod* Bill Walsh   *Scr* Bill Walsh   *Ph* Frank Phillips   *Ed* Cotton Warburton
Mus George Bruns   *Art Dir* John B. Mansbridge, Walter Tyler
● Helen Hayes, Ken Berry, Stefanie Powers, John McIntire, Keenan Wynn (Walt Disney)

Herbie Rides Again is Disney's sequel to *The Love Bug*, and a team encore for producer Bill Walsh and director Robert Stevenson. Walsh also scripted from a Gordon Buford story. It adds up, natch, to another fat plug for the Volkswagen 'bug' as the runaway (literally) titular star.

Keenan Wynn is a San Francisco construction tycoon hellbent on putting up the tallest skyscraper yet, but the plan is frustrated and ultimately foiled by sweet little old widow lady Helen Hayes. She owns the ramshackle Victorian firehouse that stands in Wynn's greedy way, and she won't budge.

Ken Berry, as Wynn's hayseed nephew lawyer from the midwest, is enlisted to pull off the trick, but instead succumbs to the charms of widow and miniskirted friend, Stefanie Powers.

■ **HERCULES**

1983, 98 MINS, ITALY ◇ ⓥ
Dir Lewis Coates [=Luigi Cozzi]   *Prod* Menahem Golan, Yoram Globus   *Scr* Lewis Coates   *Ph* Alberto Spagnoli   *Ed* Sergio Montanari   *Mus* Pino Donaggio
● Lou Ferrigno, Mirella D'Angelo, Sybil Danning, Ingrid Anderson, William Berger, Rossana Podesta (Golan-Globus)

Golan and Globus have corralled 'The Incredible Lou Ferrigno' to topline in a cheesy epic that could just about be titled *Hercules in Outer Space*. Since a lumpy space suit would cover Ferrigno's mighty physique from view, the all-powerful one travels through the universe wearing nothing but his gladiatorial briefs.

A lot of it takes place on the moon, as Zeus and wife and daughter Hera and Athena toy from above with the fate of mortals. It is Hercules' tasks to try to rescue the Princess Cassiopea from the clutches of her evil kidnappers, and given the changing times, the muscleman doesn't have to battle cardboard monsters, but hi-tech mechanical beasts made of metal and which emit deadly laser blasts from their jaws.

Ferrigno is perfectly affable, and physically (if not physiognomally) he more than lives up to his billing. Sybil Danning, Mirella D'Angelo and Ingrid Anderson comprise a fetching trio of femmes.

■ **HERE COMES MR. JORDAN**

1941, 93 MINS, US ⓥ
Dir Alexander Hall   *Prod* Everett Riskin   *Scr* Sidney Buchman, Seton I. Miller   *Ph* Joseph Walker   *Ed* Viola Lawrence   *Mus* Frederick Hollander
● Robert Montgomery, Evelyn Keyes, Claude Rains,

Rita Johnson, Edward Everett Horton, James Gleason (Columbia)

Story [from Harry Segall's play *Heaven Can Wait*] humorously poses the theory of reincarnation of a personality and soul that has been snatched from its earthly body 50 years before the cosmic schedule. Robert Montgomery is an aggressive prizefighter, determined to be champ, with an airplane and saxophone as hobbies. Flying from training camp to New York, the plane crashes, and Montgomery is snatched by Heavenly messenger Edward Everett Horton from his earthly body, and taken to Heaven for celestial registration.

When it is found Montgomery's arrival is premature, and his earthly body has already been cremated to prevent replacement, it's up to registrar Claude Rains (Mr Jordan) to secure another body suitable to Montgomery. In this body, retaining his own soul, Montgomery falls in love with Evelyn Keyes, daughter of a duped financial agent. After wandering for weeks in search of another landing, under guidance of Rains, Montgomery lands permanently in the body of a contender for the boxing championship.

Montgomery's portrayal is a highlight in a group of excellent performances. Keyes displays plenty of charm. James Gleason scores as the fast-gabbing fight manager, who is bewildered by the proceedings. Direction by Alexander Hall sustains a fast pace throughout.

☐ 1941: Best Picture (Nomination)

● ●

■ HERE WE GO ROUND THE MULBERRY BUSH

1968, 94 MINS, UK ◇

Dir Clive Donner   *Prod* Clive Donner   *Scr* Hunter Davies   *Ph* Denis Lewiston   *Ed* Fergus McDonnell   *Mus* Spencer Davis Group, Stevie Winwood, The Traffic
● Barry Evans, Judy Geeson, Angela Scoular, Sheila White, Adrienne Posta (United Artists)

A lightfooted look at the teenagers with engaging performances from hitherto largely unknown youngsters, the film was made entirely on location in a new town near London. It has a nimble alertness to juve characteristics and a nice flair for comedy.

Story is based on a successful novel by journalist Hunter Davies. Its strength is the wit of characterization and it's pleasantly salted with lines about young sexual ambitions.

The hero is a final-year student at high school, absorbed with stalking gals but finding the hunt leaves him too often up a cul-de-sac.

Barry Evans wins both sympathy and laughs as the boy. Story is spliced with Mitty-type dream bits, which give additional bite to the gap between ideal and reality.

The girls are well chosen, with Angela Scoular scoring with fine comic precision as the uppercrust girl, Judy Geeson purveying easy charm as the final near-conquest, and Adrienne Posta and Sheila White making the most of their chances.

● ●

■ HER HUSBAND'S AFFAIRS

1947, 84 MINS, US

Dir S. Sylvan Simon   *Scr* Ben Hecht, Charles Lederer   *Ph* Charles Lawton Jr   *Ed* Al Clark   *Mus* George Dunning   *Art Dir* Stephen Goossen, Carl Anderson
● Lucille Ball, Franchot Tone, Edward Everett Horton, Mikhail Rasumny, Gene Lockhart, Jonathan Hale (Columbia)

Her Husband's Affairs is well-premised fun that has a laugh a minute. As a comedy team, Lucille Ball and Franchot Tone excel. Tone is a slightly screwball advertising-slogan genius while Ball is his ever-loving wife who somehow always winds up with the credit for his spectacular stunts.

Director S. Sylvan Simon's pace is perfect and he welds zany situations into socko laughs. Motivation for much of the comedy comes from Tone's sponsorship of a screwball inventor and the products that he develops while searching for the perfect embalming fluid. Gentle fun is poked at advertising agencies and bigshot sponsors and public figures.

Mikhail Rasumny is the crazy inventor and wraps up the role for honors, Edward Everett Horton, Gene Lockhart, a business tycoon, Nana Bryant, his wife, and Jonathan Hale are among others who keep the laughs busy.

● ●

■ HEROES

1977, 113 MINS, US ◇ Ⓥ

Dir Jeremy Paul Kagan   *Prod* David Foster, Lawrence Turman   *Scr* James Carabatsos   *Ph* Frank Stanley   *Ed* Patrick Kennedy   *Mus* Jack Nitzsche, Richard Hazard   *Art Dir* Charles Rosen
● Henry Winkler, Sally Field, Harrison Ford, Val Avery, Olivia Cole, Hector Elias (Universal)

Heroes is a poorly-written melodrama about a troubled Vietnam veteran and a girl who helps him work out his problems. The multi-location production stars Henry Winkler, in a good though flawed performance, and Sally Field.

Plot peg is standard – boy and girl, running from separate problems, meet 'cute' and fall in love with some ups and downs enroute.

Speaking of the writing 'cutes', there's a plague in this screenplay, mainly in the Winkler character and the actor's performance. Since the character has a history of mental malaise, the kooky bits are many and just awful. See Winkler confound his doctor, Hector Elias. See him escape from the hospital. See him run and jump and streak and shout.

● ●

■ HEROES OF TELEMARK, THE

1965, 131 MINS, UK ◇ Ⓢ

Dir Anthony Mann   *Prod* S. Benjamin Fisz   *Scr* Ivan Moffat, Ben Barzman   *Ph* Robert Krasker   *Ed* Bert Bates   *Mus* Malcolm Arnold   *Art Dir* Tony Masters
● Kirk Douglas, Richard Harris, Ulla Jacobsson, Michael Redgrave, Anton Diffring, Eric Porter (Benton/Rank)

Producer Benjamin Fisz and director Anthony Mann have made a $5.6 million motion picture that emerges as hefty, gripping and carefully made entertainment.

It's 1942 in Nazi-occupied Norway. The Germans are ahead of the Allies on atomic fission, as reports from the Norsk Hydro heavy water factory near Telemark reveal. It's the job of a tiny band of nine resistance workers to scotch the Nazi plans.

Kirk Douglas, as the scientist drawn unwillingly into the exploit, and Richard Harris, as the resistance leader, turn in powerhouse performances. They detest each other on sight (never satisfactorily explained) but learn to respect and grudgingly like each other during mutual danger. Ulla Jacobsson, as Douglas' ex-wife, also fighting for the resistance, has a sketchy role but plays it with charm and conviction.

Krasker's work over ice and snow-girt Norway is a joy. Craftily he used Helge Stoylen, a Norwegian ski coach, to help out on some lensing. Stoylen held a Panavision camera between his legs for some of the graceful and gripping ski shots.

● ●

■ HER WEDDING NIGHT

1930, 78 MINS, US

Dir Frank Tuttle   *Scr* Henry Myers   *Ph* Harry Fischbeck   *Ed* Denis Drought
● Clara Bow, Ralph Forbes, Charles Ruggles, Skeets Gallagher (Paramount)

Smart showmanship. Combination of jaunty comedy of the spicy Avery Hopwood type, [based on his play, *Little Miss Bluebeard*] generous flavoring of spice in title and action, and a wealth of gay romance in hoke farcical setting.

Whole production is deftly handled. Settings and atmosphere beautifully manage to set off the gay tone of the whole affair. And the cast surrounding the Paramount redhead has been fitted to tailor-made roles with nicety. Clara Bow plays the racy heroine with a vigor that compensates for some of her shortcomings of voice and diction.

Plot doesn't matter except that Larry (Ralph Forbes), composer of sentimental songs, persuades his friend, Bob (Skeets Gallagher), to impersonate him to escape hero-worshipping flappers. Bob goes off on a romantic spree under his pal's name, inadvertently marrying Norma (Bow) before a rural Italian magistrate.

● ●

■ HESTER STREET

1975, 90 MINS, US

Dir Joan Micklin Silver   *Prod* Raphael D. Silver   *Scr* Joan Micklin Silver   *Ph* Kenneth Van Sickle   *Ed* Katerine Wenning   *Mus* William Bolcon
● Steven Keats, Carol Kane, Mel Howard, Dorrie Kavanaugh (Midwest)

Hester Street deftly delves into Jewish emigration to the US just before the turn-of-the-century. Hester Street is a sort of mobile ghetto as Eastern European Jews pour in and go in for their Americanization before moving on to other NY boroughs or to further west US climes.

Adapted from Abraham Cahan's story *Yekl*, it concerns Jake who has gone in for Americanization.

He sends for his wife and son but their arrival first fills him with shame at their old world clodishness. However, the wife cannot keep up with her husband's ways as she goes another way towards becoming an American.

Joan Micklin Silver displays a sure hand for her first pic.

● ●

■ HICKEY AND BOGGS

1972, 111 MINS, US ◇ Ⓥ

Dir Robert Culp   *Prod* Fouad Said   *Scr* Walter Hill   *Ph* Wilmer Butler   *Ed* David Berlatsky   *Mus* Ted Ashford
● Bill Cosby, Robert Culp, Rosalind Cash, Carmen, Louis Moreno, Michael Moriarty (Film Guarantors/United Artists)

Title of this Bill Cosby-Robert Culp starrer might indicate comedy, but action pairs former stars of pop *I Spy* teleseries, making their first appearance together since they were down-at-the-heel private eyes operating just outside the law.

Culp makes his directorial bow and Fouad Said, who started in the industry as cameraman on *I Spy* series, debuts as a producer. Latter should have paid more attention to story line of the Walter Hill screenplay, which suffers through audience never being entirely certain as to the identity of some of the characters.

Dicks are employed to find a missing femme and become innocently involved in search for a $400,000 haul stolen from a Pittsburgh bank. Somehow, the femme is connected with missing loot but audience is never let in on secret.

● ●

■ HIDDEN AGENDA

1990, 108 MINS, UK ◇ Ⓥ

Dir Ken Loach   *Prod* Eric Fellner   *Scr* Jim Allen   *Ph* Clive Tickner   *Ed* Jonathan Morris   *Mus* Stewart Copeland   *Art Dir* Martin Johnson

● Brian Cox, Frances McDormand, Brad Dourif, Mai Zetterling (Hemdale)

Hidden Agenda is a hard-hitting attack on allegedly ruthless methods of the British police in Northern Ireland. Pic is set in 1982, and seems inspired by the notorious Stalker case. Stalker was a top-level British police officer sent to Northern Ireland to investigate the Royal Ulster Constabulary. His eventual highly critical report was hushed up, and he resigned and went public.

Brian Cox plays the Stalker-like Kerrigan, brought to Belfast to investigate the killings of an IRA sympathizer and an American lawyer (Brad Dourif in a tiny role). Kerrigan befriends Dourif's bereaved girlfriend (Frances McDormand, good in a Jane Fonda-type role). He quickly discovers the men were killed by members of the Royal Ulster Constabulary, and exposes a high-level coverup.

Jim Allen's provocative screenplay includes references to British secret service and their dirty tricks against the Heath and Wilson governments of the 1970s.

But though it attempts to make an acceptable theatrical entertainment out of a complex political saga, *Hidden Agenda* lacks bigscreen impact.

....

■ HIDE IN PLAIN SIGHT

1980, 92 MINS, US ◇ ⓥ
Dir James Caan   *Prod* Robert Christiansen, Rick Rosenberg   *Scr* Spencer Eastman   *Ph* Paul Lohmann   *Ed* Fredric Steinkamp, William Steinkamp   *Mus* Leonard Rosenman   *Art Dir* Pato Guzman
● James Caan, Jill Eikenberry, Danny Aiello, Robert Viharo (M-G-M)

Hide in Plain Sight has some of the makings of a good, honest film. It tells the true story of a working man's fight against the system, features several poignant moments, and makes a number of political messages in an effective yet unobtrusive manner. But in his directorial debut, James Caan never musters the energy or emotion needed to break the unbearably slow, dismal tone.

Caan is wonderfully accurate as the factory worker who becomes an innocent victim of a new witness relocation program that gives a new identity to any person (and his family) who informs on organized crime. In this case, two-bit mobster Robert Viharo testifies against his cronies and the authorities relocate him, his wife (who happens to be Caan's former spouse), and her two children by Caan to another state.

The frustration of the almost hopeless search Caan attempts could have been excellent fodder for a gripping, human drama. Screenplay, based on a book by Leslie Waller, seems true to its subject but somehow fails to create enough dramatic sparks.

....

■ HIGH AND THE MIGHTY, THE

1954, 147 MINS, US ◇
Dir William A. Wellman   *Scr* Ernest K. Gann   *Ph* Archie Stout, William Clothier   *Ed* Ralph Dawson   *Mus* Dimitri Tiomkin
● John Wayne, Claire Trevor, Laraine Day, Robert Stack, Jan Sterling, Phil Harris (Warner/Wayne-Fellows)

Ernest K. Gann's gripping bestseller *The High and the Mighty* has been turned into an equally socko piece of screen entertainment. It is a class drama, blended with mass appeal into a well-rounded show.

The plot has to do with human reactions to danger as a troubled plane, carrying 22 persons, limps through stormy skies en route from Honolulu to San Francisco. Shortly after the takeoff, suspense sets in when the audience is tipped there's trouble, maybe death, aboard. Gradually the crew and then the passengers become aware of danger.

Virtually every member of the large cast delivers a discerning performance but the lineup is too long to give each the individual credit rated. Especially good are John Wayne, the older co-pilot under the younger pilot captain, Robert Stack, Wally Brown and William Campbell, crew members, and Doe Avedon, very fine as the stewardess.

The technical departments deliver outstandingly. The same can't be said for the score composed and conducted by Dimitri Tiomkin.

....

■ HIGH ANXIETY

1977, 94 MINS, US ◇ ⓥ
Dir Mel Brooks   *Prod* Mel Brooks   *Scr* Mel Brooks, Ron Clark, Rudy DeLuca, Barry Levinson   *Ph* Paul Lohmann   *Ed* John C. Howard   *Mus* John Morris   *Art Dir* Peter Wooley
● Mel Brooks, Madeline Kahn, Cloris Leachman, Harvey Korman, Ron Carey, Howard Morris (Crossbow/20th Century-Fox)

High Anxiety is a straight Hitchcockian sendup – homage applies as well – with highs and lows ranging from a brilliant restaging of the shower scene in *Psycho* to childish bathroom humor.

Besides playing the role of a Harvard professor and psychiatrist with a fear of heights who takes over the Psycho-Neurotic Institute for the Very, Very Nervous, Mel Brooks dons the producer, director and cowriter caps.

Even more than the games he can play with the Hitchcock story, Brooks seems to enjoy toying with the technical references – the tight closeups, shots of hands and feet, stairway sequences and manipulation of the interaction between music and visuals. Nearly all of these gags, and none of them require the background of a buff, score.

....

■ HIGH BRIGHT SUN, THE

1965, 114 MINS, UK ◇
Dir Ralph Thomas   *Prod* Betty E. Box, Ralph Thomas   *Scr* Ian Stuart Black   *Ph* Ernest Steward   *Ed* Alfred Roome   *Mus* Angelo Lavagnino
● Dirk Bogarde, George Chakiris, Susan Strasberg, Denholm Elliott, Gregoire Aslan, Colin Campbell (Rank)

Betty E. Box and Ralph Thomas elected to make this film because they regarded it 'as a suspenseful drama which could be played against any background'. They certainly played safe. Though set in Cyprus during the 1957 troubles, this sits firmly on a fence and makes virtually no attempt to analyze the troubles, the causes or the attitudes of the cardboard characters.

Film comes out with the British looking at times rather silly and at others very dogged, the Cypriots clearly detesting the British occupation, the Turks shadowy almost to a point of non-existence and America, represented by Susan Strasberg, merely a bewildered intruder.

Strasberg, a dewy-eyed young American archeology student of Cypriot parentage, is visiting Cypriot friends who, unbeknown to her, are mixed up in the local terrorist racket. She gets to know more than is good for her and is torn between loyalty to the Cypriots and to the British, as represented by an intelligence major (Dirk Bogarde) whose job it is to keep alive the unhelpful young dame for whom he has fallen.

Strasberg brings intelligence and charm to a sketchy role while Bogarde has no trouble with a part as the major which scarcely strains his thesping ability.

....

■ HIGH HOPES

1988, 112 MINS, UK ◇
Dir Mike Leigh   *Prod* Victor Glynn, Simon Channing-Williams   *Scr* Mike Leigh   *Ph* Roger Pratt   *Ed* John Gregory   *Mus* Andrew Dixon   *Art Dir* Diana Charnley
● Philip Davis, Ruth Sheen, Edna Dore, Philip Jackson, Heather Tobias (Portman/Film Four/British Screen)

In the working-class London district of King's Cross, yuppies are moving into old houses, restoring them, and driving out the locals who've lived there for ages. Old Mrs Bender, a widow, lives in one house; her neighbors are the fearfully uppercrust Booth-Braines and they treat the old lady with ill-disguised contempt.

Mrs Bender's two children are an ill-assorted pair. Cyril, with long hair and beard, works as a courier, lives with his down-to-earth girlfriend Shirley, and despises the British establishment.

Daughter Valerie, on the other hand, is a would-be yuppie, married to a crass used-car dealer, and living in a garishly over-decorated home. She's completely self-centered and insensitive to her elderly mother's needs.

Around these characters, Leigh builds a slight story intended to be a microcosm of today's London.

....

■ HIGHLANDER

1986, 111 MINS, US ◇ ⓥ
Dir Russell Mulcahy   *Prod* Peter S. Davis, William N. Panzer   *Scr* Gregory Widen, Peter Bellwood, Larry Ferguson   *Ph* Gerry Fisher   *Ed* Peter Honess   *Mus* Michael Kamen   *Art Dir* Allan Cameron
● Christophe Lambert, Roxanne Hart, Clancy Brown, Sean Connery, Beatie Edney (20th Century-Fox)

Film starts out with a fantastic sword-fighting scene in the garage of Madison Square Garden and then jumps to a medieval battle between the clans set in 16th-century Scotland.

Adding to the confusion in time, director Russell Mulcahy can't seem to decide from one scene to the next whether he's making a sci-fi, thriller, horror, music video or romance – end result is a mishmash.

A visit by Sean Connery, playing a campy Obe Wan Kenobi-type character named Ramirez, teaches Connor MacLeod (Christophe Lambert) how to wield a sword like a warrior and understand his fate is to be immortal man who cannot have children, facing instead a life fending off other immortals like the evil Kurgan.

Lambert looks and acts a lot better in a tartan than as a nearly non-verbal antiques dealer. Clancy Brown never seems to frighten whether as the supposedly-terrifying Kurgan or as the shaven-headed punker.

....

■ HIGHLANDER II
THE QUICKENING

1991, 96 MINS, US ◇ ⓥ
Dir Russell Mulcahy   *Prod* Peter S. Davis, William Panzer   *Scr* Peter Bellwood   *Ph* Phil Meheux   *Ed* Herbert C. de la Boullerie   *Mus* Stewart Copeland   *Art Dir* Roger Hall
● Christopher Lambert, Sean Connery, Virginia Madsen, Michael Ironside, John C. McGinley, Allan Rich (Davis-Panzer/El Khoury-Defait/Lam Bear)

Audiences unfamiliar with the first film will be hard put to follow the action [from a story by Brian Clemens] as it incoherently hops about in time and space.

Original topliners Christopher Lambert and Sean Connery are back (as is Aussie director Russell Mulcahy). Lambert plays immortal Connor MacLeod, who, despite his Scottish ancestry, hails from the planet Zeist. He and partner Ramirez (Connery) were banished to Earth for participating in a failed rebellion.

H

One storyline involves assassins led by Michael Ironside, and the other concentrates on the disappearing ozone layer. Connor joins with scientists to devise a sun shield projected into space. The shield is controlled by a large, untrustworthy (natch) corporation, which keeps the later renewal of the ozone layer a secret.

Lambert manages to decapitate the villains arrayed against him while teaming up with attractive environmental terrorist Virginia Madsen. Connery, sporting long white hair in a ponytail, occasionally appears wielding a broadsword.

Highlander II comes alive during the action scenes, including an unexplained but nail-biting segment in which deranged Ironside takes over a subway train and drives it at 400 mph, sending its terrified passengers crashing through windows.

Pic was lensed in Argentina on an apparently generous budget.

■ **HIGH NOON**

1952, 84 MINS, US ⓥ

Dir Fred Zinnemann *Prod* Stanley Kramer *Scr* Carl Foreman *Ph* Floyd Crosby *Ed* Elmo Williams *Mus* Dimitri Tiomkin *Art Dir* Rudolph Sternad
● Gary Cooper, Grace Kelly, Thomas Mitchell, Lloyd Bridges, Katy Jurado, Ian MacDonald (Kramer/United Artists)

A basic western formula has been combined with good characterization in *High Noon*, making it more of a western drama than the usual outdoor action feature.

The production does an excellent job of presenting a picture of a small western town and its people as they wait for a gun duel between the marshal and revenge-seeking killer, an event scheduled for high noon. The mood of the citizens, of Gary Cooper the marshal, and his bride (Grace Kelly), a Quaker who is against all violence, is aptly captured by Fred Zinnemann's direction and the graphic lensing of Floyd Crosby, which perfectly pictures the heat and dust of the sun-baked locale.

Script is based on John W. Cunningham's mag story, *The Tin Star*, and is rather derisive in what it has to say about citizens who are willing to accept law and order if they do not have to put personal effort into obtaining it.

Cooper does an unusually able job of portraying the marshal, ready to retire with his bride and then, for his own self-respect, called upon to perform one last chore as a lawman even though it is the duty of the town's citizens. Kelly fits the mental picture of a Quaker girl nicely, but the femme assignment that has color and s.a. is carried by Katy Jurado, as an ex-girl friend of the marshal.

Throughout the film is a hauntingly-presented ballad that tells the story of the coming gun duel, and is tellingly sung by Tex Ritter.
☐ 1952: Best Picture (Nomination)

■ **HIGH PLAINS DRIFTER**

1973, 105 MINS, US ◇ ⓥ

Dir Clint Eastwood *Prod* Robert Daley *Scr* Ernest Tidyman *Ph* Bruce Surtees *Ed* Ferris Webster *Mus* Dee Barton *Art Dir* Henry Bumstead
● Clint Eastwood, Verna Bloom, Mariana Hill, Mitchell Ryan, Jack Ging, Stefan Gierasch (Malpaso/Universal)

High Plains Drifter is a nervously-humorous, self-conscious near satire on the prototype Clint Eastwood formula of the avenging mysterious stranger. Script has some raw violence for the kinks and some dumb humor for audience relief. Eastwood's second directorial effort is mechanically stylish.

Untidy patchwork script involves one of those towns with a collective guilt streak, having engineered the death-by-whipping of its honest marshal by some hoods who themselves were framed after getting out of hand. Into this setting rides Eastwood, emerging from heat waves (among other obvious evocations of films past) as a sort of archangel of retribution.

After establishing himself as a force to be reckoned with Eastwood is engaged by the town fathers to help defend them against the former local police who are being released from jail after their frame-up.

■ **HIGH PRESSURE**

1932, 72 MINS, US

Dir Mervyn LeRoy *Scr* Joseph Jackson *Ph* Robert Kurrle *Ed* Ralph Dawson *Mus* Leo Forbstein (dir.)
● William Powell, Evelyn Brent, George Sidney, Guy Kibbee, Evalyn Knapp, John Wray (Warner)

The phoney stock or 'wall paper' grift gets a pretty expert expose in this yarn [by S. J. Peters]. William Powell does a swell job as Gar Evans, a fast-talking and thinking promoter. He keeps his larceny just within the law, but it's when the racket is nearest the edge that the story becomes most interesting.

Powell is first found in a speak's backroom on the tail end of a five-day bender. He told his girl friend he was going out to the drug store for a dose of bicarbonate. The girl friend is interpreted by Evelyn Brent, who is called on to do little else than get mad at and make up with her racketeer sweetheart.

George Sidney teams with Powell in grabbing the picture most of the way, Sidney for laughs and Powell for the action. Rest of the cast very good, with still more excellent casting of salesmen types in the 'boiler-room' sequence. Whoever framed this scene must have had experience, for it's perfect.

■ **HIGH ROAD TO CHINA**

1983, 120 MINS, US ◇ ⓥ

Dir Brian G. Hutton *Prod* Fred Weintraub *Scr* Sandra Weintraub Roland, S. Lee Pogostin *Ph* Ronnie Taylor *Ed* John Jympson *Mus* John Barry *Art Dir* Robert Laing
● Tom Selleck, Bess Armstrong, Jack Weston, Wilford Brimley, Robert Morley, Brian Blessed (Golden Harvest/Warner)

High Road to China is a lot of old-fashioned fun, revived for Tom Selleck after his TV schedule kept him from taking the Harrison Ford role in *Raiders Of The Lost Ark*. Ford clearly got the better deal because *China* just isn't as tense and exciting.

But it has the same Saturday-matinee spirit, with director Brian G. Hutton nicely mixing a lot of action with a storyline [from a book by Jon Cleary] that never seems as absurd as it is, allowing the two hours to move by very quickly.

Selleck is perfect as a grizzled, boozing biplane pilot whom 1920s flapper Bess Armstrong is forced to hire to help her find her father before he's declared dead and her inheritance is stolen. Selleck and Armstrong make a cute couple, even though their bantering, slowly developing romance is deliberately predictable throughout.

■ **HIGH SIERRA**

1941, 100 MINS, US ⓥ

Dir Raoul Walsh *Prod* Hal B. Wallis *Scr* John Huston, W.R. Burnett *Ph* Tony Gaudio *Ed* Jack Killifer *Mus* Adolph Deutsch *Art Dir* Ted Smith
● Humphrey Bogart, Ida Lupino, Arthur Kennedy, Joan Leslie, Cornel Wilde (Warner)

High Sierra is something of a throwback to the gangster pictures of the prohibition era; purely and simply an action story that's partially salvaged by the fine performances of Humphrey Bogart and Ida Lupino. They ac-

tually carry a film that is weighted down by too much extraneous story and production matter.

Throwback nature of the yarn is evident in the semi-glorification of Bogart's gangster character. Story depicts him as a country boy who went wrong with John Dillinger's mob, but still retaining a soft spot for green fields and trees, a crippled girl and a stray dog.

The screenplay [from a novel by W.R. Burnett] brings in too many side issues that clutter up the picture. There's no logical reason why the migrant family of Henry Travers and Elizabeth Risdon, with granddaughter Joan Leslie, was included, except as an effort to pad out the yarn in showing Bogart to be a nice guy at heart.

If anything, the film now suffers from slowness, Raoul Walsh's direction evidently being unable to overcome the screenplay plotting.

■ **HIGH SOCIETY**

1956, 107 MINS, US ◇ ⓥ

Dir Charles Walters *Prod* Sol C. Siegel *Scr* John Patrick *Ph* Paul C. Vogel *Ed* Ralph E. Winters *Mus* Cole Porter *Art Dir* Cedric Gibbons, Hans Peters
● Bing Crosby, Grace Kelly, Frank Sinatra, Celeste Holm, John Lund, Louis Armstrong (M-G-M)

Fortified with a strong Cole Porter score, film is a pleasant romp for cast toppers Bing Crosby, Grace Kelly and Frank Sinatra. Their impact is almost equally consistent. Although Sinatra has the top pop tune opportunities, the Groaner makes his specialties stand up and out on showmanship and delivery, and Kelly impresses as a femme lead.

The original Philip Barry play, *The Philadelphia Story*, holds up in its transmutation from the Main Line to a Newport jazz bash. Casting of Louis Armstrong for the jazz festivities was an inspired booking also.

The unfolding of the triangle almost assumes quadrangle proportions, when Sinatra (as the *Life*-mag-type feature writer), sent with Celeste Holm, almost moves in as a romantic vis-a-vis to the slightly spoiled and madcap Tracy Lord (Kelly).

Crosby is her first, now ex-husband, a hip character with song-smithing predilections, hence the Armstrong band booking on the local scene. Satchmo is utilized as a sort of pleasant play moderator, opening with 'High Society Calypso', which sets the al fresco mood of the picture.

Porter has whipped up a solid set of songs with which vocal pros like the male stars and Holm do plenty. Latter and Sinatra have a neat offbeat number with 'Who Wants to Be a Millionaire?' Crosby makes 'Now You Has Jazz' (aided by Armstrong) as his standout solo, although he is also effective with Kelly on 'True Love'. Crosby and Sinatra milk 'Well, Did You Evah?' in a sophisticated smoking room sequence.

■ **HIGH SPIRITS**

1988, 97 MINS, UK/US ◇ ⓥ

Dir Neil Jordan *Prod* Stephen Woolley, David Saunders *Scr* Neil Jordan *Ph* Alex Thomson *Ed* Michael Bradsell *Mus* George Fenton *Art Dir* Anton Forst
● Daryl Hannah, Peter O'Toole, Steve Guttenberg, Beverly D'Angelo, Liam Neeson, Ray McAnally (Vision/Palace)

High Spirits is a piece of supernatural Irish whimsy with a few appealing dark underpinnings, but it still rises and falls constantly on the basis of its moment-to-moment inspirations.

Elaborate physical production is set almost entirely at Castle Plunkett, a rundown Irish edifice that proprietor Peter O'Toole opens as a tourist hotel in order to meet the mortgage payments. With the American market in mind, O'Toole bills the place as a haunted castle, to this end having his staff dress up like ghouls of various persuasions.

It comes as little surprise that the castle turns out to be actually haunted. Steve Guttenberg, who is not getting along with wife Beverly D'Angelo, comes to meet ghost Daryl Hannah, who was killed on the premises years ago on her wedding night by Liam Neeson, who takes a fancy to D'Angelo.

....

■ HIGH TIDE

1987, 104 MINS, AUSTRALIA ◇ ⓥ
Dir Gillian Armstrong *Prod* Sandra Levy *Scr* Laura Jones *Ph* Russell Boyd *Ed* Nicholas Beauman *Mus* Mark Moffiatt, Ricky Fataar *Art Dir* Sally Campbell
● Judy Davis, Jan Adele, Claudia Karvan, Colin Friels, Frankie J. Holden (FGH/SJL)

A powerful emotional, beautifully made film which will touch the hearts of all but the very cynical.

Setting is the small New South Wales coastal town of Eden where Judy Davis rents a cheap trailer by the sea while she awaits completion of the auto repairs. One night, when hopelessly drunk in the toilet block, she's helped by an adolescent girl (Claudia Karvan) who lives with her grandmother (Jan Adele) in another trailer.

Davis befriends the child; only when she meets the grandmother does she realize Karvan is her own daughter who she'd left years before in the aftermath of her husband's death.

Adele makes the grandmother, who still enjoys a sexual fling even though she has a regular lover, a wonderfully warm character. Karvan sharply etches the pain and insecurity hiding beneath the tough, tomboyish exterior of the child; and Judy Davis, always a consummate actress, provides great depth and subtlety, making her character come vividly alive.

....

■ HIGH WALL

1947, 98 MINS, US
Dir Curtis Bernhardt *Prod* Robert Lord *Scr* Sydney Boehm, Lester Cole *Ph* Paul Vogel *Ed* Conrad A. Nervig *Mus* Bronislau Kaper *Art Dir* Cedric Gibbons, Leonid Vasian
● Robert Taylor, Audrey Totter, Herbert Marshall, H.B. Warner (M-G-M)

High Wall [based on a play by Alan R. Clark and Bradbury Foote] garners a high score as a strong entry in the psycho-melodrama cycle. Unfolded credibly and with almost clinical attention to detail, film holds the interest and punches all the way.

Robert Lord has given the melodramatics fine production polish and able handling to spotlight best features in story of a man who believes he has murdered his wife during a mental blackout.

Robert Taylor is seen as a man believed homicidally insane, being treated at mental hospital pending trial for murder of his wife. His case seems hopeless until a femme doctor breaks down his reluctance to try treatment to penetrate details that occurred during the lapse of memory.

Taylor scores in his role, making it believable. Audrey Totter registers strongly as the doctor, displaying a marked degree of talent able to handle most any character. Herbert Marshall is another who clicks as the murderer who cloaks his sin behind the garb of a pious publisher of biblical tracts. H. B. Warner movingly creates a pathetic mental case.

....

■ HIGH, WIDE AND HANDSOME

1937, 110 MINS, US
Dir Rouben Mamoulian *Prod* Arthur Hornblow Jr *Scr* Oscar Hammerstein II *Ph* Victor Milner, Theodore Sparkuhl *Ed* Archie Marshek *Mus* Boris Morros (dir.) *Art Dir* Hans Dreier, John Goodman
● Irene Dunne, Randolph Scott, Dorothy Lamour, Elizabeth Patterson, Raymond Walburn, Charles Bickford (Paramount)

Film shapes up as a $1.9 million western, although possessed of all the elements to have made it a saga of Pennsylvania oilwell pioneering. Something went wrong on scripting and production from what was, undoubtedly, an intriguing script on paper.

Film's title sounds like a musical or operetta, but it's more of a melodramatic romance, with six songs by Jerome Kern and Oscar Hammerstein II, latter also credited for the original story and the screenplay. Wherein lies the film's principal deficiency. It's a cross-section of Americana tinged with too much Hollywood hokum.

As a result, *High, Wide*, after teeing off vigorously, flounders as it progresses, and winds up in a melodramatic shambles of fisticuffs, villainy and skullduggery which smacks of the serial film school.

Irene Dunne is too coy as the daughter of a medicine-show owner and Randolph Scott too forthright as her romantic vis-a-vis. And the menacing by Charles Bickford, at the helm of his hired plug-uglies, with Alan Hale as the villainous banker, is very tent-twent-thirt.

Dorothy Lamour is rather heavy eye-laden for the nitery gal who ultimately repays the Scott-Dunne combo for previous kindnesses.

Rouben Mamoulian's production is heavy-handed. While endowed with an elastic budget, save for the fighting scenes there's little that's spectacular or impressive about the result. The mob scenes are as much to the credit of the camera as to the direction.

....

■ HIGH WIND IN JAMAICA, A

1965, 104 MINS, UK ⓥ
Dir Alexander Mackendrick *Prod* John Croydon *Scr* Ronald Harwood, Denis Cannan, Stanley Mann *Ph* Douglas Slocombe *Ed* Derek Yorke *Mus* Larry Adler *Art Dir* John Howell, John Hoesli
● Anthony Quinn, James Coburn, Dennis Price, Gert Frobe, Lila Kedrova, Kenneth J. Warren (20th Century-Fox)

Anthony Quinn's penchant for grizzled characterization gets a colorful boost in this picturization of Richard Hughes' 1929 best-seller, which projects him as a Caribbean pirate. British production is a curious mixture of high melodrama and light overtones, the latter occasioned by presence of a flock of youngsters aboard a pirate ship.

Most of the action takes place at sea. Filmed on location around Jamaica, Alexander Mackendrick's direction keeps his movement alive within the somewhat limited confines of a schooner where Quinn, the Spanish pirate captain, is confronted with the disturbing question of what to do with seven children who unbeknownst to him have slipped from another ship he attacked and now are found in the hold of his own craft.

Quinn endows his role with a subdued humanness in which there is occasional humor.

James Coburn, costarred with Quinn as his English mate, socks over character in which he combines humor with dramatic strength.

....

■ HILL, THE

1965, 125 MINS, UK
Dir Sidney Lumet *Prod* Kenneth Hyman *Scr* Ray Rigby *Ph* Oswald Morris *Ed* Thelma Connell *Mus* Art Noel, Don Pelosi *Art Dir* Herbert Smith

● Sean Connery, Harry Andrews, Ian Bannen, Alfred Lynch, Ossie Davis, Michael Redgrave (Seven Arts)

Kenneth Hyman's production of *The Hill* is a tough, uncompromising look at the inside of a British military prison in the Middle East during the last war. It is a harsh, sadistic and brutal entertainment, superbly acted and made without any concessions to officialdom.

The 'hill' of the title is a man-made pile of sand up and down which the soldier-prisoners have to run with full kit, often until they are physically exhausted, as part of a punishment designed more to break a man's spirit rather than provide corrective treatment.

The screenplay [from a play by Ray Rigby and R.S. Allen] puts the spotlight on a new bunch of prisoners, one of whom (Sean Connery) is a 'busted' sergeant-major, and a natural target for the vindictive and sadistic treatment. Another is a Negro sent down for drinking three bottles of Scotch from the officers' mess.

One of the new intake collapses and dies, and that sparks off a mutiny, which is one of the most powerful and dramatic sequences of the pic.

Connery gives an intelligently restrained study, carefully avoiding forced histrionics. The juiciest role, however, is that of the prison regimental sergeant major, and Harry Andrews does a standout job.

....

■ HILLS HAVE EYES, THE

1978, 89 MINS, US ◇ ⓥ
Dir Wes Craven *Prod* Peter Locke *Scr* Wes Craven *Ph* Eric Sadrinen *Ed* Wes Craven *Mus* Don Peake *Art Dir* Robert Burns
● Susan Lanier, Robert Houston, Virginia Vincent, Russ Grieve, Dee Wallace, Martin Speer (Blood Relations)

Wes Craven's blood-and-bone frightener about an all-American family at the mercy of cannibal mutants is a satisfying piece of pulp.

Reputedly based on genuine 17th-century Scottish cave-dwellers, these savages terrorize a strip of Californian desert in which the Carters are stranded by a snapped axle. Hollywood movie-dog tradition is put to use in the forms of Beauty and the Beast, Carters' protective pets, which play their part in final outwitting of the marauders.

But there's plenty of death before then, survivors of the symbolic struggle being the teenagers on both sides, one dog and a baby, on whose future (in the world or in the pot) much of the rival hysterias have centered.

Gratifying aspects are Craven's businesslike plotting and pacy cutting, and a script which takes more trouble over the stock characters than it needs. There are plenty of laughs, in the dialog and in the story's disarming twists.

....

■ HILLS HAVE EYES PART II, THE

1985, 88 MINS, US/UK ◇ ⓥ
Dir Wes Craven *Prod* Barry Cahn, Peter Locke *Scr* Wes Craven *Ph* David Lewis *Ed* Richard Bracken *Mus* Harry Manfredini
● Michael Berryman, Tamara Stafford, Kevin Blair, John Bloom, Janus Blythe (Castle Hill/Fancey/New Realm/VTC)

The Hills Have Eyes Part II is a lower case followup by Wes Craven to his 1977 cult horror pic.

Film concerns two grownup survivors of the earlier pic. Young Bobby Carter (Robert Houston) is plagued by nightmares of the desert massacre that he survived. He has invented a super formula of gasoline which his local motor-cross club is testing in an upcoming race. Ruby (Janus Blythe), a nice-gal survivor, is taking the bikers to the race, when they foolishly try a shortcut across the desert.

From then on, it's dull, formula terror pic clichés, with one attractive teenager after another picked off by the surviving cannibals.

Acting is on the level of a formula shocker, featuring a winsome Candice Bergen-look-alike, Tamara Stafford, as a blind girl.

....

■ **HINDENBURG, THE**

1975, 125 MINS, US ◇

Dir Robert Wise   *Prod* [uncredited]   *Scr* Nelson Gidding   *Ph* Robert Surtees   *Ed* Donn Cambern   *Mus* David Shire   *Art Dir* Edward Carfagno
● George C. Scott, Anne Bancroft, William Atherton, Roy Thinnes, Gig Young, Burgess Meredith (Universal)

Michael Mooney's non-fiction compendium of the facts and theories behind the German zeppelin's 1937 air disaster at NAS, Lakehurst, new Jersey, was earlier dramatized for the screen by Richard A. Levinson and William Link, and both receive a screen story credit.

George C. Scott stars as an air ace assigned as special security officer on the fatal Atlantic crossing.

The array of characters is dealt boringly from a well-thumbed deck: Anne Bancroft, eccentric German countess; Roy Thinnes, Scott's nasty partner; Gig Young, mysterious and nervous ad agency exec; Burgess Meredith and Rene Auberjonois, an improbable and dull effort at comedy relief as tourist-trapping card cheats; Robert Clary, also bombing in cardboard comedy relief, the list goes on. William Atherton emerges as the good-guy crewman saboteur who plans to blow up the ship. A battle of mental wits ensues between Scott, Thinnes and Atherton; it's as exciting as watching butter melt.

....

■ **HIRED HAND, THE**

1971, 90 MINS, US ◇ Ⓥ

Dir Peter Fonda   *Prod* William Hayward   *Scr* Alan Sharp   *Ph* Vilmos Zsigmond   *Ed* Frank Mazzola   *Mus* Bruce Langhorne   *Art Dir* Lawrence G. Paull
● Peter Fonda, Warren Oates, Verna Bloom, Robert Pratt, Severn Darden, Ann Doran (Pando)

The Hired Hand doesn't work very well. An off-beat western, starring and directed by Peter Fonda, the film has a disjointed story, a largely unsympathetic hero, and an obtrusive amount of cinematic gimmickry which renders inarticulate the confused story subtleties. Warren Oates appears as Fonda's loyal and more mature friend, while Verna Bloom is Fonda's abandoned wife.

The script discovers Fonda en route to California with Oates, a fellow-wanderer in the seven years since Fonda abandoned his wife. Robert Pratt, pair's younger companion, is brutally murdered by Severn Darden's henchmen in a frame-up; Fonda and Oates exact an appropriate revenge, then Fonda returns home with Oates.

Film evidently is trying to show a truer picture of early western life, as opposed to formula plotting; but when one is trying to buck an entrenched cliche, extreme care and artfulness are required to persuade those few not already convinced.

....

■ **HIRELING, THE**

1973, 95 MINS, UK ◇ Ⓥ

Dir Alan Bridges   *Prod* Ben Arbeid   *Scr* Wolf Mankowitz   *Ph* Michael Reed   *Ed* Peter Weatherley   *Mus* Marc Wilkinson   *Art Dir* Natasha Kroll
● Robert Shaw, Sarah Miles, Peter Egan, Elizabeth Sellars, Caroline Mortimer, Patricia Lawrence (World)

Based on a novel by L.P. Hartley set in 1923, this heavily atmospheric, painstakingly accoutred and splendidly acted pic deals with the increasingly close relationship, on a conversational-companionship level at first, of a young widow (Sarah Miles) and the hired chauffeur (Robert Shaw) who drives her home after a spell in a clinic recovering from a nervous depression.

Temporarily, class barriers are down – or so he begins to believe. Shortly, however, as she recovers her equilibrium and social contacts, the barriers and demarcations return.

Item has quality written all over it, and patient viewers will savor its many plusses. Miles is splendid as the confused lady, Shaw fine as her momentarily blinded opposite.

....

■ **HIS GIRL FRIDAY**

1940, 92 MINS, US Ⓥ

Dir Howard Hawks   *Prod* Howard Hawks   *Scr* Charles Lederer   *Ph* Joseph Walker   *Ed* Gene Havlick   *Art Dir* Lionel Banks
● Cary Grant, Rosalind Russell, Ralph Bellamy, Gene Lockhart, Helen Mack, John Qualen (Columbia)

No doubt aiming to dodge the stigma of having *His Girl Friday* termed a remake, Columbia blithely skips a pertinent point in the credits by merely stating 'From a play by Ben Hecht and Charles MacArthur.' It's inescapable, however, that this is the former legit and pic smash *The Front Page*. The trappings are different – even to the extent of making reporter Hildy Johnson a femme – but it is still *Front Page*.

With more of the feminine-romance angle injected than was in the original, this new edition becomes more the modern-style sophisticated comedy than the hard, biting picture of newspapermen that Hecht and MacArthur painted in their stage play. Its remake in this revised form was a happy idea, especially since it still moves punchily, retains plenty of its laughs and almost all of its drama.

Casting is excellent, with Cary Grant and Rosalind Russell in the top roles. Grant is the sophisticated, hard-boiled, smart-alec managing editor who was portrayed by Adolphe Menjou in the earlier version. A newly-injected part, required by the switch in sex of Hildy, is taken by Ralph Bellamy.

Principal action of the story still takes place in a courthouse pressroom. All of the trappings are there, including the crew of newshawks who continue their penny-ante poker through everything and the practice of the sheriff's crew on the gallows for an execution in the morning. With the wider vista given the story, there is, in addition, the newspaper office.

Star-reporter Russell tells managing editor Grant, from whom she has just been divorced, that she is quitting his employ to marry another man. Grant neither wants to see her resign nor marry again, retaining hope of a rehitching. To prevent her escaping, he prevails upon her to cover one more story, that of a deluded radical charged with murder and whom the paper thinks is innocent. Escape of the convicted man, his virtual falling into Russell's lap as she sits alone in the pressroom, and attempts by Grant and Russell to bottle up the story, are w.k., but still exciting.

....

■ **HIS MAJESTY O'KEEFE**

1953, 89 MINS, US ◇

Dir Byron Haskin   *Prod* Harold Hecht   *Scr* Borden Chase, James Hill   *Ph* Otto Heller   *Ed* Manuel Del Campo   *Mus* Robert Farnon   *Art Dir* Edward S. Haworth, W. Simpson Robinson
● Burt Lancaster, Joan Rice, Andre Morell, Archie Savage, Benson Fong, Tessa Prendergast (Warner)

This swashbuckling South Seas adventure feature is ideally suited to Burt Lancaster's muscular heroics. The Fiji Islands location lensing is a plus factor for interest.

The island of Viti Levu in the South Pacific is the locale used. Lancaster is seen as a dare-devil Yankee sea captain, cast overboard off the island by a mutinous crew. Intrigued by the possibilities of making a fortune off the island's copra, he stays on to battle other traders, native idleness and superstition, becoming His Majesty O'Keefe with a beautiful Polynesian (Joan Rice) as queen.

The action emphasis of the screenplay, suggested by a novel by Lawrence Kingman and Gerald Green, provides Byron Haskin's direction innumerable opportunities for movement, so the film's pace is quick-tempoed. Rice is a sweet romantic foil for Lancaster's swashbuckling. Tessa Prendergast, as another island beauty, teases the eyes.

....

■ **HISTORY OF MR POLLY, THE**

1949, 94 MINS, UK

Dir Anthony Pelissier   *Prod* John Mills   *Scr* Anthony Pelissier   *Ph* Desmond Dickinson   *Ed* John Seabourne   *Mus* William Alwyn
● John Mills, Sally Ann Howes, Finlay Currie, Juliet Mills, Betty Ann Davies, Gladys Henson (Two Cities)

Faithful adherence to the original H. G. Wells story is one of the main virtues of *The History of Mr Polly* which is noted for its fine characterizations.

The story of Mr Polly is retold simply from the time of his father's death, his inheritance and marriage, subsequent failure as a shopkeeper and final happiness and freedom as a general handyman in a small country inn. Its success is a personal tribute to the sterling acting of John Mills.

Director Anthony Pelissier has put all the emphasis on the principal characters, and has extracted every ounce of human interest from the classic. Every part, right down to the smallest bit, has been selected with care and there is some notable work from an experienced cast.

....

■ **HISTORY OF THE WORLD – PART I**

1981, 92 MINS, US ◇

Dir Mel Brooks   *Prod* Mel Brooks   *Scr* Mel Brooks   *Ph* Woody Omens, Paul Wilson   *Ed* John Howard   *Mus* John Morris   *Art Dir* Harold Michelson, Stuart Craig
● Mel Brooks, Dom DeLuise, Madeline Kahn, Cloris Leachman, Gregory Hines, Sid Caesar (20th Century-Fox)

Boisterous cinematic vaudeville show is comprised of five distinct sections: the *2001* parody *Dawn of Man*, *The Stone Age*, featuring Brooks' acid comment on the role of the art critic, and a brief 'Old Testament' bit, which together run 10 minutes; *The Roman Empire*, the best-sustained and, at 43 minutes, longest episode; *The Spanish Inquisition*, a splashy nine-minute production number; *The French Revolution*, a rather feeble 24-minute sketch; and *Coming Attractions* which, with end credits, runs six minutes and at least punches up the finale with the hilarious *Jews in Space* inter-galactic musical action number.

Although Monty Python's *Life of Brian* went well beyond Brooks in the blasphemy department, many of the pic's most successful gags poke holes in religious pieties. When Brooks as Moses comes down from the mountain, he's carrying three tablets. Frightened by a lightning blast, he drops one of them and quickly switches to 10 commandments instead of 15.

The one interlude which really brings down the house has Brooks working as a waiter at the Last Supper and asking the assembled group. 'Are you all together or is it separate checks?'

As the old ad line said, there's something here to offend everybody, particularly the devout of all persuasions and homosexuals.

....

HITCHER, THE

1986, 97 MINS, US ◇ ⑦
Dir Robert Harmon   *Prod* David Bombyk, Kip
Ohman   *Scr* Eric Red   *Ph* John Seale   *Ed* Frank J.
Urioste   *Mus* Mark Isham   *Art Dir* Dennis Gassner
● Rutger Hauer, C. Thomas Howell, Jennifer Jason
Leigh, Jeffrey DeMunn (HBO/Silver Screen)

The Hitcher is a highly unimaginative slasher
that keeps the tension going with a massacre
about every 15 minutes.

Film proves mom's admonition not to pick
up hitchhikers, especially if they're anything
like John Ryder, a psychotic and diabolical
killer played with a serene coldness by Rutger
Hauer.

Along comes an innocent young man (C.
Thomas Howell), who is falling asleep at the
wheel and stops to pick Hauer up in the
hopes that having a companion will keep him
awake. What ensues for the rest of the film is
a cat and mouse game where Hauer eliminates just about everyone Howell comes in
contact with.

In addition to working with a script that
has many holes, filmmakers didn't allow for
one laugh in the entire 97 minutes.

HITLER
THE LAST TEN DAYS

1973, 108 MINS, UK/ITALY ◇ ⑦
Dir Ennio De Concini   *Prod* Wolfgang Reinhardt
Scr Ennio De Concini, Maria Pia Fusco, Wolfgang
Reinhardt, Ivan Moffat   *Ph* Ennio Guarnieri   *Ed* Kevin
Connor   *Mus* Mischa Spoliansky   *Art Dir* Roy Walker
● Alec Guinness, Simon Ward, Adolfo Celi, Diane
Cilento, Gabriele Ferzetti, Eric Porter (Reinhardt/West)

A major fault of the film is that there's no
German feeling to it. The cast, with the
exception of German actress Doris Kunst-
mann as Eva Braun, is made up of British
and Italian actors. The film's interiors (and a
few exteriors) were shot at Shepperton
Studios, England.

What is good about the film is the treatment of Hitler by Alec Guinness, who gives
perhaps the best portrayal yet of that bizarre
figure. Even he, however, never conveys the
fanaticism which Hitler certainly had and
which he so powerfully conveyed to millions
of susceptible German minds.

As the film [from Gerhard Boldt's *The Last
Days of the Chancellery*] revolves almost
entirely around him, other cast members
have to work hard to make even a momentary
impression. The talent most lost in the shuffle
is Simon Ward.

Most outstanding, considering her brief
appearance, is Diane Cilento as a test pilot
who gets across the authentic if misguided
obsessive devotion to Der Fuehrer of some
Germans.

HITLER'S CHILDREN

1943, 80 MINS, US ⑦
Dir Edward Dmytryk   *Prod* Edward A. Golden
Scr Emmett Lavey   *Ph* Russell Metty   *Ed* Joseph
Noriega   *Mus* Roy Webb
● Tim Holt, Bonita Granville, Kent Smith, Otto Kruger,
H.B. Warner, Lloyd Corrigan (RKO)

The philosophies of Nazism and the manner
in which the youth of Germany was moulded
to a militaristic order are forcefully brought
to the screen in *Hitler's Children* [from the
novel *Education for Death* by Gregor Zeimer].

Tim Holt essays the leading role of the German boy who grows up to become a Gestapo
officer, but cannot grow away from the childhood love he had for a girl who suffers the tortures of the Nazis.

Holt gives an excellent performance and
looks the part he plays. Opposite him, Bonita
Granville likewise acquits herself very creditably. An outstanding job is done by H.B.

Warner as a bishop, whose church service is
broken up by Gestapo agents on the hunt for
Granville, who has taken shelter there. The
dialog given Warner proves very trenchant.

HIT PARADE OF 1943

1943, 90 MINS, US
Dir Albert S. Rogell   *Prod* Albert J. Cohen   *Scr* Frank
Gill Jr, Frances Hyland   *Ph* Jack Marta   *Ed* Thomas
Richards   *Mus* Jule Styne, Harold Adamson
● John Carroll, Susan Hayward, Gail Patrick, Eve
Arden, Dorothy Dandridge (Republic)

Here's a little musical which is 'little' only
compared to some of the majors' past gargantuan efforts, but which actually blends a
fetching set of songs, a wealth of variety
talent, mostly colored, to a fair story.

The cast names aren't breath-taking as
some of the others stabled in the major league
studios, but from Al Cohen's production and
Al Rogell's direction to the dance-staging and
songsmithing it's a very satisfying confection
indeed.

You may get captious with the idea of making a thieving songwriter your hero, which is
what John Carroll personates, but thus is
Susan Hayward, talented young tunesmith,
thrown together with him. In fact, the characterization of Rick Farrell, who even continues to let Hayward ghost his songs, is never
wholly palatable, but Carroll's personal
charm glorifies the double-crossing, two-
timing lothario of Lindy's into a model swain
in time for the fadeout.

HIT THE DECK

1955, 112 MINS, US ◇ ⑦
Dir Roy Rowland   *Prod* Joe Pasternak   *Scr* Sonya
Levien, William Ludwig   *Ph* George Folsey   *Ed* John
McSweeney Jr   *Mus* Vincent Youmans
● Jane Powell, Tony Martin, Debbie Reynolds, Walter
Pidgeon, Vic Damone, Ann Miller (M-G-M)

The emphasis of youth, in the person of a
number of personable young players on the
Metro contract list, has been put on this
remake of the [1927] legit musical, *Hit the
Deck*.

There's not much producer Joe Pasternak
could do to refurbish the shopworn plot
about three sailors on the loose, with three
femmes on their mind, and the sundry complications that batter at the steadfast portals
of Navy redtape and credibility. With the
limitations, he has made it a pretty picture,
replete with songs from the old footlight
piece, complete with new lyrics and flashy
production numbers.

The vintage musical takes on its best semblance to life when Debbie Reynolds and
Russ Tamblyn are lending their enthusiasm,
either alone or together, to the action.

H.M.S. DEFIANT

1962, 101 MINS, UK ◇
Dir Lewis Gilbert   *Prod* John Brabourne   *Scr* Nigel
Kneale, Edmund H. North   *Ph* Christopher Challis
Ed Peter Hunt   *Mus* Clifton Parker   *Art Dir* Arthur
Lawson
● Alec Guinness, Dirk Bogarde, Anthony Quayle, Tom
Bell, Maurice Denham, Victor Maddern (Columbia)

H.M.S. Defiant is a strong naval drama about
the days of the Napoleonic wars, enhanced by
the strong appeal of Alec Guinness, Dirk
Bogarde and Anthony Quayle.

Based on Frank Tilsley's novel, *Mutiny*,
story is of the time of old press gangs. British
navy conditions were appalling and it was the
mutiny depicted in this pic which did much
to give the British naval men a new deal.
Guinness plays the skipper of the *Defiant*
which, when it sets out to help tackle the
Napoleonic fleet, is ruptured by a tussle for

power between Guinness and his first lieutenant (Bogarde).

Guinness is a humane man, though a stern
disciplinarian. Bogarde is a sadist, anxious to
jockey Guinness out of position.

Below deck the crew, led by Quayle and
Tom Bell, is plotting mutiny against the bad
food, stinking living conditions and constant
floggings ordered by Bogarde.

Guinness' role does not give this actor
scope for his fullest ability. Bogarde's is the
more showy portrayal. Quayle makes an impressive appearance as the leader of the
rebels, determined and tough, but realizing
that there is a right and a wrong way to stage
a mutiny, like anything else.

HOBSON'S CHOICE

1954, 107 MINS, UK ⑦
Dir David Lean   *Prod* David Lean   *Scr* David Lean,
Norman Spencer, Harold Brighouse, Wynyard
Browne   *Ph* Jack Hildyard   *Ed* Peter Taylor
Mus Malcolm Arnold
● Charles Laughton, John Mills, Brenda de Banzie,
Daphne Anderson, Prunella Scales, Richard Wattis
(British Lion/London)

There is a wealth of charm, humor and fine
characterization in David Lean's picture
made under the Korda banner. The period
comedy, with a Lancashire setting, is essentially British in its makeup. Charles
Laughton returned to his native country to
star.

Laughton plays the widower Hobson, a
shoemaker with three unmarried daughters,
one of whom is regarded as being permanently on the shelf. After all, as he is always
explaining to his cronies in the saloon, she is
past it at 30. But the daughter will have none
of it; she railroads one of her father's assistants into marriage.

Although Laughton richly overplays every
major scene, his performance remains one of
the film's highlights. Mills also makes a
major contribution in his interpretation of the
illiterate shoemaker's assistant who learns to
assert himself. Brenda de Banzie captures top
femme honors for her playing of the spirited
daughter who triumphs over the ridicule of
her father and sisters.

HOLD BACK THE DAWN

1941, 114 MINS, US
Dir Mitchell Leisen   *Prod* Arthur Hornblow
Scr Charles Brackett, Billy Wilder   *Ph* Leo Tover
Ed Doane Harrison   *Mus* Victor Young
● Charles Boyer, Olivia de Havilland, Paulette
Goddard, Victor Francen, Walter Abel (Paramount)

While *Hold Back the Dawn* is basically another
European refugee yarn, scenarists Charles
Brackett and Billy Wilder exercised some
ingenuity and imagination and Ketty Frings'
original emerges as fine celluloidia.

Charles Boyer is cast similarly to his role in
Algiers – a rogue of hypnotic charm over
women. A gigolo in Europe, he's washed up
in Mexico by the war and the quota laws
make his entry into the United States a
dream at least eight years distant. Caught
among numerous other Europeans likewise
waiting for the bars to be let down, Boyer is
rapidly going to seed in the Mexican town
when he meets up with Paulette
Goddard, his former partner in crime in
Paris, Vienna, etc.

She crashed the US by marrying an American jockey, ditching him later, and, still in
love with Boyer, she puts him wise to the simple gimmick for making the immigration
authorities relax. This sets the trap for Olivia
de Havilland, a romance-hungry school
teacher escorting a flock of young boys on an
excursion in Mexico over the 4 July holiday.

Mitchell Leisen's only visible mistake is a
tendency of the film to drag in spots, but this

H

might be unavoidable due to Boyer's slow delivery.
□ 1942: Best Picture (Nomination)

HOLIDAY

1938, 93 MINS, US ⓥ

Dir George Cukor *Prod* Everett Riskin *Scr* Donald Ogden Stewart, Sidney Buchman *Ph* Franz Planer *Ed* Otto Meyer, Al Clark *Mus* Morris Stoloff (dir.) *Art Dir* Stephen Goosson, Lionel Banks
● Katharine Hepburn, Cary Grant, Doris Nolan, Lew Ayres, Edward Everett Horton, Henry Kolker (Columbia)

Philip Barry's play, *Holiday*, in film form was a smash hit in the Depression's depth in 1930. Futility of riches is the topic and Donald Ogden Stewart and Sidney Buchman, who wrote this version, have tossed in a few timely shots which bolster the Barry original. Changes and interpolations are few, however.

Katharine Hepburn is in her best form and type of role in *Holiday*. Her acting is delightful and shaded with fine feeling and understanding throughout. Cary Grant plays this one straight.

George Cukor brings out the best from all the players. Lew Ayres is the despondent younger brother in the wealthy family who seeks some relief from the monotony of riches by resorting to strong liquor. Comedy by Edward Everett Horton and Jean Dixon is good, and Henry Kolker's portrait of the father is splendid.

HOLIDAY INN

1942, 100 MINS, US ⓥ

Dir Mark Sandrich *Prod* Mark Sandrich *Scr* Claude Binyon *Ph* David Abel *Ed* Ellsworth Hoagland *Mus* Irving Berlin, Robert Emmett Dolan (arr)
● Bing Crosby, Fred Astaire, Virginia Dale, Marjorie Reynolds, Walter Abel, Louise Beavers (Paramount)

Loaded with a wealth of songs, it's meaty, not too kaleidoscopic and yet closely knit for a compact 100 minutes of tiptop filmusical entertainment. The idea is a natural, and Irving Berlin has fashioned some peach songs to fit the highlight holidays.

Plot is a new slant on a backstage story. Bing Crosby is the crooner, Fred Astaire the hoofer, partnered with brunet and fickle Virginia Dale. Latter jilts Crosby for Astaire (who subsequently becomes No. 2 to a Texan millionaire) which thus leaves the frankly lazy Crosby to carry out his Holiday Inn idea on his own. The crooner has figured out there are some 15 holidays in the year and by operating a Connecticut roadhouse on those festive occasions only he can loaf the rest of the 340 days.

Thus are strung together these songs and ideas: 'White Christmas'; 'Let's Start the New Year Right'; 'Abraham', a modern spiritual for Lincoln's Birthday holiday; 'Be Careful, It's My Heart' (St Valentine's Day); 'I Gotta Say I Love You, 'Cause I Can't Tell a Lie' (Washington's birthday); 'Easter Parade', of course; 'I'm Singing a Song of Freedom', wherein Crosby, attired as the Freedom Man (with a snatch of 'Any Bonds Today?') introduces himself as an American Troubadour.

Mark Sandrich's production and direction are more than half the success of the picture.

HOLLYWOOD CANTEEN

1944, 124 MINS, US

Dir Delmer Daves *Prod* Alex Gottlieb *Scr* Delmer Daves *Ph* Bert Glennon *Mus* Ray Heindorf (adapt.) *Art Dir* Leo Kuter
● Robert Hutton, Joan Leslie, Bette Davis, John Garfield, Sydney Greenstreet, Joan Crawford (Warner)

Author-director Delmer Daves scripted *Stage*

Door Canteen for Sol Lesser in early 1943 and he parlayed himself into another smasheroo for Warners with *Hollywood Canteen*.

Robert Hutton and Joan Leslie emerge as the real stars of the filmusical. They carry the story and a human one it is, too. Hutton looks like the ideal GI Joe, back with a Purple Heart from the South Pacific, and his buddy (Dane Clark) looks the perfect Brooklynite.

Story has Hutton winding up not only meeting his dream-girl (Leslie) but is also the lucky winner as the millionth guest of the Hollywood Canteen. That entitles him to an Arabian Nights suite, car, gifts and his choice of actresses for his weekend date, Natch, it's Leslie. What's nice is that real-life Leslie plays herself with charm, poise and ease, and the plot is so glib one accepts the romance wholeheartedly.

HOLLYWOOD CAVALCADE

1939, 100 MINS, US ◇

Dir Irving Cummings *Prod* Darryl F. Zanuck *Scr* Ernest Pascal *Ph* Allen M. Davey *Ed* Walter Thompson *Mus* Louis Silvers (dir) *Art Dir* Richard Day, Wiard B. Ihnen
● Alice Faye, Don Ameche, Buster Keaton, Ben Turpin, Chester Conklin (20th Century-Fox)

Hollywood Cavalcade relates an interesting and sentimental story of film producing in California, beginning in the pie-throwing, Keystone era of 1913, and winding up when Al Jolson sang from the screen in *The Jazz Singer*, and the silent picture days were ended.

Mack Sennett plays an important off-screen role in the film, principal novelty of which is the successful and amusing introduction of oldtime Sennett comedy routines and formula.

Scenes from the older films are projected in black and white, sometimes framed in colored borders.

As for the yarn itself, it relates the rise, fall and rise again of an enthusiastic young director, played by Don Ameche. He sees a promising understudy (Alice Faye) who is substituting for the leading woman. He persuades her to make the jump to Hollywood and the films.

HOLLYWOOD HOT TUBS 2 EDUCATING CRYSTAL

1990, 100 MINS, US ◇

Dir Ken Raich *Prod* Mark Borde, Ken Raich *Scr* Brent V. Friedman *Ph* Areni Milo *Ed* Michael Hoggan *Mus* John Lombardo, Bill Bodine *Art Dir* Thomas Cost
● Jewel Shepard, Patrick Day, David Tiefen, Remy O'Neil, Bart Braverman, J.P. Bumstead (Alimar)

Beneath its come-on title, this sequel to Chuck Vincent's 1984 feature moves out of the exploitation film arena to a well-scripted comic look at west coast life styles.

The Crystal of the title, Jewel Shepard, encores as the bubbly, jiggly valley girl who heads for business school to learn how to run her mom Remy O'Neill's hot tubs/health spa establishment. Evil Bart Braverman (convincing with beard as a prince) is conspiring to take over the business, even planning to marry O'Neill to achieve his ends. Film is told from the point of view of handsome hero David Tiefen, who's working as a chauffeur to Braverman while writing a book about Shepard.

Under newcomer Ken Raich's direction, film works due to the quirky touches of Brent Frieman's screenplay. Previously wasted in purely decorative assignments, Shepard comes into her own here in a funny and sympathetic role. It's not quite *Educating Rita*, but the formula of gawky ingenue blossoming is a sure-fire one.

HOLLYWOOD OR BUST

1956, 94 MINS, US ◇ ⓥ

Dir Frank Tashlin *Prod* Hal Wallis *Scr* Erna Lazarus *Ph* Daniel Fapp *Ed* Howard Smith *Mus* Walter Scharf
● Dean Martin, Jerry Lewis, Anita Ekberg, Pat Crowley, Maxie Rosenbloom (Paramount)

Hollywood's in the label and does make a finale appearance, but most of this comedy caper takes place on a cross-country junket from New York, with way stops enroute, including Las Vegas.

Direction by Frank Tashlin scores enough comedy highspots to keep the pace fairly fast, even with the slow spots that his handling and the team's talent cannot overcome. One of the film's funniest bits comes before the title with Dean Martin introducing Jerry Lewis as different types of movie-watchers. Lewis' encounter with a bull and making like a matador is another fun-filled sequence, as is his champagne binge in Vegas after hexing the gambling devices into a big payoff.

By way of making the latter part of the title legit, Anita Ekberg appears as guest star on whom Lewis has a crush. She doesn't have much more to do than to display what nature has wrought in the fjords of Sweden, so it's still a big part. Enroute west Martin and Lewis will pick up Pat Crowley so that Martin will have someone to sing romantic songs to.

HOLOCAUST 2000

1977, 102 MINS, ITALY/UK ◇ ⓥ

Dir Alberto De Martino *Prod* Edmondo Amati *Scr* Sergio Donati, Aldo De Martino, Michael Robson *Ph* Enrico Menczer *Ed* Vincenzo Tomassi *Mus* Ennio Morricone *Art Dir* Umberto Betacca
● Kirk Douglas, Agostina Belli, Simon Ward, Anthony Quayle, Virginia McKenna, Alexander Knox (Embassy/Aston)

Take the threat of nuclear disaster, the ecological deterioration of the earth, the terror of an all-powerful Antichrist; mix it with an international cast topped by Kirk Douglas, Agostina Belli and a number of convincing British actors like Simon Ward, Anthony Quayle, Alexander Knox and Virginia McKenna and shake well.

The conflict is between Robert Caine (Douglas), an idealist in the realm of nuclear power plants and his demon son Angelo (Ward) with tenebrous plans to push dad's project for fission power to wipe out human life. The supernatural pushes superficial arguments about nuclear power to the side and gives the spectator a sense of human helplessness to contend with such an evil and destructive force as the Antichrist.

As striking a beauty as Belli is catapulted into the conflict with only symbolic story roots in a Biblical-like finale and with a slow, pronounced accent for her lines. The dramatic picture-long father-son duel between Douglas with a mid-American accent and Ward with a British lilt keeps the plot in place right up to the inconclusive finale.

HOMBRE

1967, 119 MINS, US ◇ ⓥ

Dir Martin Ritt *Prod* Martin Ritt, Irving Ravetch *Scr* Irving Ravetch, Harriet Frank Jr *Ph* James Wong Howe *Ed* Frank Bracht *Mus* David Rose *Art Dir* Jack Martin Smith, Robert E. Smith
● Paul Newman, Fredric March, Richard Boone, Diane Cilento, Cameron Mitchell, Barbara Rush (20th Century-Fox)

Hombre develops the theme that socially and morally disparate types are often thrown into uneasy, explosive alliance due to emergencies.

An unhurried, measured look at interacting human natures, caught up only for story purposes in a given situation, the characters speak truisms which, sometimes, are overdone platitudes.

Adapted from Elmore Leonard's novel, it tells the story of an Apache-raised white boy who becomes the natural leader of a group in its survival against a robber band headed by Richard Boone.

Paul Newman is excellent as the scorned (but only supposed) Apache. Fredric March, essaying an Indian agent who has embezzled food appropriations for his charges, also scores in a strong, unsympathetic – but eventually pathetic – role. Richard Boone is very powerful, yet admirably restrained as the heavy.

■ HOME ALONE

1990, 102 MINS, US ◇ ⓥ
Dir Chris Columbus *Prod* John Hughes *Scr* John Hughes *Ph* Julio Macat *Ed* Raja Gosnell *Mus* John Williams *Art Dir* John Muto
● Macauley Culkin, Joe Pesci, Daniel Stern, Catherine O'Hara, John Heard, John Candy (20th Century-Fox)

The family of poor little dumped-upon Kevin (Macauley Culkin) has rushed off to catch their holiday plane and accidentally left him behind. Now they're in Paris, frantically trying to reach him, and he's home alone, where a storm has knocked out the telephones, the neighbors are away for the holiday and the houses on the street are being systematically cleaned out by a team of burglars.

Generally perceived by his family as a helpless, hopeless little geek, Kevin is at first delighted to be rid of them, gorging on forbidden pleasures like junk food and violent videos, but when the bandits (Joe Pesci, Daniel Stern) begin circling his house, he realizes he's on his own to defend the place.

Kevin proves he's not such a loser by defending the fort with wits and daring and by the time Mom (Catherine O'Hara) comes rushing back from Europe, everything's in order.

A firstrate production in which every element contributes to the overall smartly realized tone, pic boasts wonderful casting, with Culkin a delight as funny, resilient Kevin, and O'Hara bringing a snappy, zesty energy to the role of mom. Pesci is aces in the role of slippery housebreaker Harry, who does a Two Stooges routine with lanky sidekick Stern.

■ HOME AT SEVEN

1952, 85 MINS, UK
Dir Ralph Richardson *Prod* Maurice Cowan *Scr* Anatole De Grunwald *Ph* Jack Hildyard, Edward Scaife *Ed* Bert Bates *Mus* Malcolm Arnold *Art Dir* Vincent Korda, Frederick Pusey
● Ralph Richardson, Margaret Leighton, Jack Hawkins, Campbell Singer, Michael Shepley, Margaret Withers (London/British Lion)

When *Home at Seven* was produced on the London stage in 1950, it proved to be one of the major successes of the legit season. Ralph Richardson repeats his starring role.

The production is notable for three 'firsts'. It was the first independent venture of Maurice Cowan; Richardson's first attempt at direction; and the first picture under the Alexander Korda banner to be produced under the speed-up technique of three weeks shooting schedule after extensive rehearsals.

The principal character, a bank clerk, loses a day in his life, and during the time he was an amnesia victim, the funds of his sports club are stolen and the steward is murdered. When the police starts its inquiries, he gives a false alibi, but that is soon exploded and he is convinced of his own guilt.

Richardson directs the piece with a straightforward competence.

■ HOME BEFORE DARK

1958, 137 MINS, US
Dir Mervyn LeRoy *Prod* Mervyn LeRoy *Scr* Eileen Bassing, Robert Bassing *Ph* Joseph F. Biroc *Ed* Philip W. Anderson *Mus* Franz Waxman *Art Dir* John Beckman
● Jean Simmons, Dan O'Herlihy, Rhonda Fleming, Efrem Zimbalist Jr, Mabel Albertson, Steve Dunne (Warner)

Home before Dark should give the Kleenex a vigorous workout. Based on one woman's battle to regain her slipping sanity, it is a romantic melodrama of considerable power and imprint.

The screenplay, based on Eileen Bassing's novel of the same name, sometimes seems rather skimpy in its character motivation. It is also difficult at times to understand the mental tone of the mentally ill heroine (Jean Simmons). But while the tale is unfolding it is made so gripping that factual discrepancies are relatively unimportant.

Simmons is the wife of Dan O'Herlihy, who has ceased to love her before mental breakdown and has not changed his attitude on her recovery. Living in their home, to which she returns on her release from hospitalization, are her stepmother (Mabel Albertson) and her stepsister (Rhonda Fleming). They are masterful females who could drive anyone to the edge of madness.

Her only real ally in the house is a stranger (Efrem Zimbalist Jr), who is also an alien in the setting of the inbred New England college community. Zimbalist is the only Jewish member of the faculty, and ostensibly a protege of O'Herlihy's.

The whole picture is seen from Simmons' viewpoint, which means she is 'on' virtually the whole time. Her voice is a vibrant instrument, used with thoughtful articulation and placement, the only vital part of her at times.

Joseph Biroc's photography is suited to the grim New England atmosphere. It is winter, a depressingly gray winter, and the locations in Massachusetts give the picture the authentic feel.

■ HOMECOMING

1948, 113 MINS, US
Dir Mervyn LeRoy *Prod* Sidney Franklin *Scr* Paul Osborn *Ph* Harold Rosson *Ed* John Dunning *Mus* Bronislau Kaper *Art Dir* Cedric Gibbons, Randall Duell
● Clark Gable, Lana Turner, Anne Baxter, John Hodiak, Ray Collins, Gladys Cooper (M-G-M)

Performances are of top quality all down the line, with Gable and Turner pacing the playing. Story line makes a direct play for the tear ducts and has heart. These two factors overcome some patness in resolving plot's problems.

Gable portrays a successful surgeon, happily married, who joins the Army. Three years of patching up the wounded in close association with his nurse, Turner, gradually changes the man's character from smug successfulness to an awareness of his obligations to others.

Story, scripted by Paul Osborn from an original by Sidney Kingsley, is told in flashback and draws its title from the surgeon's return home after his great war love. The dialog and the characters are made real by the forceful playing. There is strong sympathy for the love between Gable and Turner, even though the doctor's wife, Anne Baxter, waits at home.

A considerable portion of the footage is devoted to detailing heroic work done by doctors and nurses under fire at the front, but film does not class as a war picture. Combat medical scenes add punch.

■ HOME FROM THE HILL

1960, 150 MINS, US ◇ ⓥ
Dir Vincente Minnelli *Prod* Sol C. Siegel *Scr* Harriet Frank Jr, Irving Ravetch *Ph* Milton Krasner *Ed* Harold F. Kress *Mus* Bronislau Kaper
● Robert Mitchum, Eleanor Parker, George Peppard, George Hamilton, Everett Sloane, Luana Patten (M-G-M)

A full-blown melodrama, high-octane in situation and characters, *Home from the Hill* is like an over-taxed engine. The production throws a plot rod or two in its final moments, but when it is concluded the spectator is at least aware he has seen something.

Even though the screenplay, from William Humphrey's novel, is florid and complicated, in the customary Deep South literary manner, it does not neglect humor and the lighter touches. Vincente Minnelli's direction is rich and satisfying, especially adroit in the creation and direction of a fistful of important characters.

Illicit and illegitimate romance in two generations occupy the principals. Setting is Texas, a town of which Robert Mitchum is not only the richest citizen but the busiest stud. The latter characteristic has iced his marriage to Eleanor Parker since the birth of their now-grown son (George Hamilton). Mitchum has another son (George Peppard), born out of wedlock at about the same time as Hamilton. Hamilton has been so marked by his parents' relationship that when he falls in love with Luana Patten he lacks the courage to marry her.

Despite the intricacies, the story plays well, due to a fine cast and Minnelli's sure-handed direction. Minnelli uses a technique he tried in *Some Came Running*, of pacing his film like an orchestral composition, with a thunderous and complex climax. It does not altogether come off.

Among the things that do come off are some stunning travelling shots by Minnelli and his cameraman, Milton Krasner, of Hamilton on a boar hunt; the race through the vine-clotted forest is superb.

Mitchum delivers his strongest performance in years, and Parker handles her end of the conflict well, too, although her role is less interesting. But it is Peppard, from the NY stage, who shines through.

■ HOME MOVIES

1979, 90 MINS, US ◇ ⓥ
Dir Brian De Palma *Prod* Brian De Palma, Jack Temchin, Gil Adler *Scr* Robert Harders, Gloria Norris, Kim Ambler, Dana Edelman, Stephen Le May, Charles Loventhal *Ph* James L. Carter *Ed* Corky Ohara *Mus* Pino Donaggio *Art Dir* Tom Surgal
● Kirk Douglas, Nancy Allen, Keith Gordon, Gerrit Graham, Vincent Gardenia (SLC)

Home Movies, resulted from Brian De Palma teaching students at Sarah Lawrence College, New York, how to make films by making one with them.

The story has Kirk Douglas running a cult called Star Therapy. He exhorts each pupil to 'put you name above the title' in life. Practicing what he preaches, he has his own life continuously filmed, with himself as director and star. The sessions, filmed with a mask reducing the frame, as if by Douglas' own 16mm camera crew, are recurrently hilarious.

Singling out one pupil as an example of 'an extra in his own life', Douglas spurs the boy – engagingly played by Keith Gordon – into an ego-quest which involves a successful pursuit of his elder brother's fiancee and some laughably inept attempts to film himself doing not-so-dramatic things like falling asleep.

■ HOMER AND EDDIE

1989, 99 MINS, US ◇ ⑦

Dir Andrei Konchalovsky   *Prod* Moritz Borman, James Cady   *Scr* Patrick Cirillo   *Ph* Lajos Koltai   *Ed* Henry Richardson   *Mus* Edvard Artemyev   *Art Dir* Michel Levesque

● James Belushi, Whoopi Goldberg, Karen Black, John Waters (Kings Road/Borman/Cady)

This road film about a mentally deficient dishwasher and a homicidal escaped cancer patient is a downer from beginning to end.

Homer, a mentally retarded dishwasher in Arizona, decides to hitchhike up to Oregon to see his father, who is dying of cancer. He meets up with wacky vagabond Eddie in an old jalopy, and soon they become pals.

On the road Eddie tries to enlighten Homer to the ways of the world. She takes him to a brothel and gets the money to pay for it by holding up a store. Her criminal activities increase, and she winds up shooting people while robbing their stores. The twosome argue about the existence of God. Meanwhile, Eddie tells Homer that the doctors have only given her a month to live.

It is hard to feel much sympathy for these two mental patients. The image of two under-privileged people in a cruel world is rather too pat to be convincing.

■ HOMETOWN USA

1979, 93 MINS, US ◇ ⑦

Dir Max Baer   *Prod* Roger Comrass, Jesse Vint   *Scr* Jesse Vint   *Ph* [uncredited]   *Ed* Frank Morriss   *Mus* Marshall Leib

● Gary Springer, David Wilson, Brian Kerwin, Pat Delaney, Julie Parsons (Film Ventures)

In *Hometown USA* director Max Baer has drawn liberally from *American Graffiti*, but pic still contains generous amount of earthy wit that flows naturally from pic's characters and action.

Baer has obviously put some effort into establishing proper, circa 1957, atmosphere for story of adolescents fixated on hot rods, necking and cruising hometown boulevards all night.

Screenplay set pieces mostly deals with a meek, sexually naive teenager, Gary Springer, and his cronies, David Wilson and Brian Kerwin, who supposedly want to fix him up with a date, but who always seem to end up with the girls themselves.

Baer doesn't hesitate to satirise at kids whose story he's telling, adding an unexpected bit of depth to what is basically a piece of entertainment.

■ HOMICIDE

1991, 100 MINS, US ◇ ⑦

Dir David Mamet   *Prod* Michael Hausman, Edward R. Pressman   *Scr* David Mamet   *Ph* Roger Deakins   *Ed* Barbara Tulliver   *Mus* Aeric Jans   *Art Dir* Michael Merritt

● Joe Mantegna, William H. Macy, Natalija Nogulich, Ving Rhames, Rebecca Pidgeon (Pressman/Cinehaus)

David Mamet's first-rate writing and boldly idiosyncratic directing redeem this story of a toughened Jewish cop torn between two worlds. *Homicide* presents an urban hell in which stoic survivor Bobby Gold (Joe Mantegna) must negotiate through rotten politics, unpredictable violence and virulent racial tension just to get through a day of police work.

Gold sees a chance to regain his enthusiasm when he becomes a key player in a team effort to bring in a cop killer who's eluded the FBI. But he's callously reassigned to a routine investigation of an elderly Jewish woman shot down in her candy store in a black ghetto.

To the disgust of his cynical Irish partner (William H. Macy), Gold gets caught up in the family's claims that they are targets of a deep-rooted and violent anti-Semitic conspiracy. When his fellow cops need him to help bring down the killer, he's busy with initiation rites into his new sect.

Mamet's direction gives much of the film a bracing, refreshing tone as he works to express the shattering tensions of Gold's work.

Excellent work by Mantegna does much to enlist sympathies and interest. Macy is also strong as the flinty partner.

■ HONEY, I SHRUNK THE KIDS

1989, 86 MINS, US ◇ ⑦

Dir Joe Johnston   *Prod* Penney Finkelman Cox   *Scr* Ed Naha, Tom Schalman   *Ph* Hiro Narita   *Ed* Michael A. Stevenson   *Mus* James Horner   *Art Dir* Gregg Fonseca

● Rick Moranis, Matt Frewer, Marcia Strassman, Kristine Sutherland, Thomas Brown (Walt Disney)

Borrowing two good end elements from two 1950s sci-fi pics, *The Incredible Shrinking Man* and *Them*, scripters pit two sets of unfriendly neighbor kids, mistakenly shrunk to only ¼-inch high, against what ordinarily would be benign backyard fixtures, both alive and inanimate.

Their misfortune was to get caught in the beam of ne'er-do-well inventor Wayne Szalinski's (Rick Moranis) molecule-reducing contraption while he's out giving a lecture to a group of skeptical scientists.

He sweeps them into the dustplan along with the other flotsam that goes out with the trash.

Now, they must make it back to the house among towering vegetation, homungous bugs and fierce water showers on a quest that would be nightmarish except that it seems mostly like a lot of fun.

Pic [story by Stuart Gordon, Brian Yuzna and Ed Naha] is in the best tradition of Disney and even better than that because it is not so juvenile that adults won't be thoroughly entertained.

■ HONEYMOON KILLERS, THE

1969, 115 MINS, US ⑦

Dir Leonard Kastle   *Prod* Warren Steibel   *Scr* Leonard Kastle   *Ph* Oliver Wood   *Ed* Stan Warnow

● Shirley Stoler, Tony LoBianco, Mary Higbee, Kip McArdle, Barbara Cason (A.I.P./Roxanne)

Made on a very low budget by a writer-director Leonard Kastle, *The Honeymoon Killers*, based on the Lonely Hearts murder case of the late 1940s, is made with care, authenticity and attention to detail.

The acting throughout the film never falters, each of the lonely heart victims presented as a fully rounded character.

Theme, presented with perhaps a shade too heavy an underlining is the desperate search for love in the US, the idea that no woman is complete without a man beside her.

Fernandez has disappeared from the lives of a score of women, after receiving their 'dowries', when he meets Martha, but it is only when she becomes intimately involved in his life, bringing her fantastic jealousy to bear on his new targets, that murder enters the picture.

There are a few lapses, but the pic goes towards its harrowing climax without losing step.

■ HONEY POT, THE

1967, 150 MINS, UK ◇ ⑦

Dir Joseph L. Mankiewicz   *Prod* Joseph L. Mankiewicz, Charles K. Feldman   *Scr* Joseph L. Mankiewicz   *Ph* Gianni Di Venanzo   *Ed* David Bretherton

Mus John Addison   *Art Dir* John F. DeCuir

● Rex Harrison, Susan Hayward, Cliff Robertson, Capucine, Edie Adams, Maggie Smith (United Artists)

An elegant, sophisticated screen vehicle for more demanding tastes, previously billed as *Mr Fox of Venice* and *Anyone for Venice?* Vaguely drawing its inspiration from Ben Jonson's *Volpone*, film's updated plot centers around the fabulously rich Cecil Fox (Rex Harrison) who with the aid of a sometimes gigolo and secretary, William McFly (Cliff Robertson), plays a joke of sorts on three one-time mistresses by feigning grave illness and gauging their reactions as they come flocking to his bedside.

There is the wisecracking hypochondriac, Mrs Sheridan (Susan Hayward), who was Fox's first love, accompanied by the attractive nurse, Sarah Watkins (Maggie Smith). There's Princess Dominique, a glacially beautiful jetsetter played by Capucine. And there's the ebullient Merle McGill (Edie Adams), a Hollywood star without a care in the world – except for a massive debt to Uncle Sam.

The dialog is often a delight in its harkback to the days when the turn of a phrase and the tongue-in-cheek were a staple of better Hollywood product. The playing is all of a superior character.

■ HONEYSUCKLE ROSE

1980, 119 MINS, US ◇ ⑦

Dir Jerry Schatzberg   *Prod* Gene Taft   *Scr* Carol Sobieski, William D. Whitliff, John Binder   *Ph* Robby Muller   *Ed* Aram Avakian, Norman Gay, Mark Laub, Evan Lottman   *Mus* Willie Nelson, Richard Baskin   *Art Dir* Joel Schiller

● Willie Nelson, Dyan Cannon, Amy Irving, Slim Pickens (Warner)

This is not a picture for anybody who doesn't like Willie Nelson. But the picture adroitly blends his musical performances with a gently dramatic acting job in an old-fashioned love story.

Picture catches Nelson at that point in his career around 1970 when his touring band was wildly popular in Texas and nearby regions, but he had yet to break out with the big hit that would make him nationally famous.

Dyan Cannon and Joey Floyd nicely set up Nelson's approaching conflict as the wife and son who wait affectionately at home for him to finish his periodic tours.

Slim Pickens is right on target as the guitar-picking sidekick. Amy Irving is near perfect as the woman who has adored Nelson since girlhood.

■ HONKY TONK FREEWAY

1981, 107 MINS, US ◇

Dir John Schlesinger   *Prod* Don Boyd, Howard W. Koch Jr   *Scr* Edward Clinton   *Ph* John Bailey   *Ed* Jim Clark   *Mus* George Martin   *Art Dir* Edwin O'Donovan

● Beau Bridges, Hume Cronyn, Beverly D'Angelo, William Devane, Teri Garr, Geraldine Page (Universal/ AFD/EMI)

Veteran director John Schlesinger, who was responsible for such screen classics as *Midnight Cowboy* and *Sunday Bloody Sunday* has concocted a kind of *Nashville on Wheels* here.

The thin story line of this $26 million film revolves around the residents of a small Florida town. Ticlaw, who are miffed that the new super duper freeway won't have an exit for tourists to stop off and spend their money in the area.

Ticlaw's Mayor William Devane tries to bribe some officials for the exit but is double-crossed early on. Major portion of the picture then switches to the collection of people who travel the freeway and eventually (through no fault of their own) wind up in Ticlaw.

Only Hume Cronyn and Jessica Tandy as an offbeat elderly couple, and Deborah Rush as a discontented nun, brighten up the trip along the road. Rest of the cast falls victim to Edward Clinton's meandering script and dismal sense of humor.

. . . .

■ HONKYTONK MAN

1982, 122 MINS, US ◇ ⓥ

Dir Clint Eastwood *Prod* Clint Eastwood *Scr* Clancy Carlile *Ph* Bruce Surtees *Ed* Ferris Webster, Michael Kelly, Joel Cox *Mus* Steve Dorff *Art Dir* Edward Carfagno

● Clint Eastwood, Kyle Eastwood, John McIntire, Alexa Kenin, Verna Bloom, Matt Clark (Warner)

Honkytonk Man is one of those well-intentioned efforts that doesn't quite work. It seems that Clint Eastwood took great pains in telling this story of an aging, struggling country singer but he is done in by the predictability of the script [from Clancy Carlile's own novel] and his own limitations as a warbler.

It is initially funny to see a drunk Eastwood drive his spiffy car into the rural, Depression-era farm his sister and her burdened family live in. Though he is a breath of fresh air for them, especially his 14-year-old nephew, it soon becomes clear that he is more accurately an alcoholic on his last legs.

Eastwood does his best, though he never really manages to be fully convincing because of his own vocal limitations. His son, Kyle, who has limited acting experience, doesn't seem to know what to do with his key role of the emerging teenager.

. . . .

■ HOODLUM PRIEST, THE

1961, 100 MINS, US

Dir Irvin Kershner *Prod* Don Murray, Walter Wood *Scr* Don Deer [= Don Murray], Joseph Landon *Ph* Haskell Wexler *Ed* Maurice Wright *Mus* Richard Markowitz *Art Dir* Jack Poplin

● Don Murray, Larry Gates, Cindi Wood, Keir Dullea, Logan Ramsey (United Artists)

Biographically based on the offbeat activities of the Rev Charles Dismas Clark, a Jesuit priest in St Louis noted for his rehabilitation work with ex-cons, the screenplay pinpoints Clark's problems against the tragedy of a confused, but far from hopeless, youth who pays with his life for crimes of which he is not solely responsible. Along the way, the writers illustrate the necessity of meeting ex-cons on their own terms to urge them away from a life of crime, and even take a swipe at capital punishment, going right into the gas chamber to do so in the film's most powerful scene.

The picture, largely photographed in St Louis, is burdened with loose motivational ends and has a tendency to skip over key expository details. But it is a case of the whole justifying its parts. The moving parts are erratic, but the machine does its job.

Don Murray gives a vigorous, sincere performance in the title role. But the film's most moving portrayal is delivered by Keir Dullea as the doomed lad. Larry Gates manages to be effective as an attorney whose motivations aren't quite clear.

. . . .

■ HOOPER

1978, 99 MINS, US ◇ ⓥ

Dir Hal Needham *Prod* Hank Moonjean *Scr* Thomas Rickman, Bill Kerby *Ph* Bobby Byrne *Ed* Donn Cambern *Mus* Bill Justis *Art Dir* Hilyard Brown

● Burt Reynolds, Jan-Michael Vincent, Sally Field, Brian Keith, John Marley, James Best (Warner/Reynolds-Gordon)

Individually, the performances in this story of three generations of Hollywood stuntmen are a delight. And Hal Needham's direction and stunt staging are wonderfully crafted.

But it's the ensemble work of Burt Reynolds, Jan-Michael Vincent, Sally Field and Brian Keith, with an able assist from Robert Klein, which boosts an otherwise pedestrian story with lots of crashes and daredevil antics into a touching and likable piece.

Reynolds, in a further extension of his brash, off-handed wise guy screen persona, plays the world's greatest stuntman. He took over that position 20 years back from Brian Keith. His status is being challenged by newcomer Jan-Michael Vincent.

To cement a place in the stuntman's record books, Reynolds must perform one last stunt, in this case a 325-foot jump in a jet-powered car over a collapsed bridge. All this is to take place in a film, *The Spy Who Laughed At Danger*, some sort of a disaster James Bond type picture being directed by the deliciously obnoxious Klein.

Besides the final jump over the bridge, Needham and stunt coordinator Bobby Bass have arranged a smorgasbord of stunts – car crashes, barroom brawls, chariot races, helicopter jumps and motorcycle slides.

. . . .

■ HOOSIERS

1986, 114 MINS, US ◇ ⓥ

Dir David Anspaugh *Prod* Carter De Haven, Angelo Pizzo *Scr* Angelo Pizzo *Ph* Fred Murphy *Ed* C. Timothy O'Meara *Mus* Jerry Goldsmith *Art Dir* David Nichols

● Gene Hackman, Barbara Hershey, Dennis Hopper, Sheb Wooley, Fern Persons, Brad Boyle (Hemdale)

Hoosiers is an involving tale about the unlikely success of a smalltown Indiana high school basketball team that paradoxically proves both rousing and too conventional, centered around a fine performance by Gene Hackman as the coach.

During the opening reels, first-time feature director David Anspaugh paints a richly textured portrait of 1951 rural American life, both visually and through glimpses of the guarded reticence of the people. Dialog rings true, and the characters are neither sentimentalized nor caricatured. Tension is built nicely as the farmboys advance through the playoffs.

Pic belongs to Hackman, but Dennis Hopper gets another opportunity to put in a showy turn as a local misfit.

. . . .

■ HOPE AND GLORY

1987, 113 MINS, UK ◇ ⓥ

Dir John Boorman *Prod* John Boorman *Scr* John Boorman *Ph* Philippe Rousselot *Ed* Ian Crafford *Mus* Peter Martin *Art Dir* Anthony Pratt

● Sarah Miles, David Hayman, Derrick O'Connor, Susan Woolridge, Sammi Davis, Ian Bannen (Nelson/Goldcrest)

Essentially a collection of sweetly autobiographical anecdotes of English family life during World War II.

Tale is narrated from an adult perspective by Billy, an exquisite-looking nine-year-old who finds great excitement in the details of warfare but also has the air of a detached observer and, therefore, possible future writer.

Best scenes are those with Billy centerstage, and particularly those showing the unthinking callousness kids can display in the face of others' misfortune and tragedy.

Then the Rohan family's home is destroyed, and mom Sarah Miles takes the kids out to grandpa's idyllic home by a river in the country, where the raging conflict becomes an afterthought.

Happily, young Sebastian Rice-Edwards is a marvelous camera subject and holds the center well as Bill. His younger sister, played by Geraldine Muir, is even cuter, as is Sara Langton as the girl whose mother is killed.

The adults, however, come off rather less well, with Sarah Miles overdoing things and projecting little inner feeling and no one else making much of an impression.

☐ 1987: Best Picture (Nomination)

. . . .

■ HOPSCOTCH

1980, 104 MINS, US ◇ ⓥ

Dir Ronald Neame *Prod* Edie Landau, Ely Landau *Scr* Brian Garfield, Bryan Forbes *Ph* Arthur Ibbetson *Ed* Carl Kress *Mus* Ian Fraser *Art Dir* William Creber

● Walter Matthau, Glenda Jackson, Ned Beatty, Sam Waterston, Herbert Lom (Avco Embassy)

Hopscotch is a high-spirited caper comedy which, unfortunately, reaches its peak too soon.

Grizzled as usual, Walter Matthau plays CIA agent whose independent ways are too much for his finicky, double-dealing boss (Ned Beatty). So Matthau is put in charge of the files.

But he never shows up for the new assignment, deciding instead to hide out and write a book that will embarrass not only the CIA but spies in every country, making himself a target for extinction from several directions.

Hiding out, Matthau takes up with Glenda Jackson. They are old flames and their initial moments together serve up the same good bantering chemistry of *House Calls*.

It's all for laughs as Matthau evades the hunters while dreaming up additional ways to make fools of them.

. . . .

■ HORIZONS WEST

1952, 80 MINS, US ◇ ⓥ

Dir Budd Boetticher *Prod* Albert J. Cohen *Scr* Louis Stevens *Ph* Charles P. Boyle *Ed* Ted J. Kent *Mus* Joseph Gershenson *Art Dir* Bernard Herzbrun, Robert Clatworthy

● Robert Ryan, Julie Adams, Rock Hudson, John McIntire, Raymond Burr, James Arness (Universal)

Plot is laid in the post-War Between States period, opening with three Texans returning to their home state. Rock Hudson and James Arness welcome a resumption of ranching, but Robert Ryan's ambition is for a quick dollar. He turns his attention towards easy money and a desire to build a western empire.

From a rather slow start, it then becomes a session of pretentious, cliche-laden talk that even spurts of hardy action fail to enliven. Ryan does what he can with his character but beyond endowing it with a certain ruthless ruggedness can't make it believable enough to carry the tale.

Hudson turns in a sympathetic performance, and Arness is good as the brothers' soldiering buddy. Julie Adams makes a pretty picture as the widow with an eye for Ryan.

. . . .

■ HORN BLOWS AT MIDNIGHT, THE

1945, 80 MINS, US

Dir Raoul Walsh *Prod* Mark Hellinger *Scr* Sam Hellman, James V, Kern *Ph* Sid Hickox *Ed* Irene Morra *Mus* Franz Waxman *Art Dir* Hugh Reticker, Clarence Steensen

● Jack Benny, Alexis Smith, Guy Kibbee, Margaret Dumont, Dolores Moran, Reginald Gardiner (Warner)

This one is a lightweight comedy that never seems able to make up its mind whether to be fantasy or broad slapstick. There are some good laughs but generally *The Horn Blows at Midnight* is not solid.

Jack Benny works hard for his laughs and some come through with a sock, but generally the chuckles are dragged in and overworked. Biggest howls are the scenes depicting Benny and others dangling from atop a 40-story building.

Benny plays third trumpet in a radio station orch. Falling asleep during reading of

H

commercials, Benny dreams he's an angel in Heaven – and still playing third trumpet. The Big Chief, disgusted with conditions on the planet earth, dispatches Benny to earth to destroy it. The angel is to blow his special horn promptly at midnight, the blast to do away with the earth.

Heaven, as depicted, is certainly not a very soul-satisfying spot. It's portrayed as a satire on government and the many bureaus and sub-bureaus, etc.

■ **HORSE FEATHERS**

1932, 70 MINS, US Ⓥ
Dir Norman Z. McLeod *Scr* Bert Kalmar, Harry Ruby, S. J. Perelman, Will B. Johnstone *Ph* Ray June
● Groucho Marx, Chico Marx, Harpo Marx, Zeppo Marx, Thelma Todd, David Landau (Paramount)

The madcap Marxes, in one of their maddest screen frolics. The premise of Groucho Marx as the college prexy and his three aides and abettors putting Huxley College on the grid-iron map promises much and delivers more.

Zeppo is his usual straight opposite Thelma Todd as the college widow. She's a luscious eyeful and swell foil for the Marxian boudoir manhandling, which is getting to be a trade-marked comedy routine.

On the matter of formula, the harp and piano numbers were repeated against the Marxes' personal wishes but by exhibitor demands to the studio. The piano is oke, but the harp reprise of 'Everyone Says I Love You' (by Bert Kalmar and Harry Ruby) sub-stantiates the boys' opinion that it tends to slow up the comedy.

The plot, such as it is, is motivated around gambler David Landau's planting of two pros on the Darwin team which meets Huxley. Groucho visits the speak where the Darwin ringers have been engaged and mistakes dog-catcher Harpo and bootlegging iceman Chico as gridiron material.

■ **HORSEMEN, THE**

1971, 108 MINS, US ◇ Ⓥ
Dir John Frankenheimer *Prod* Edward Lewis
Scr Dalton Trumbo *Ph* Claude Renoir *Ed* Harold Kress *Mus* Georges Delerue *Art Dir* Pierre Thevenet
● Omar Sharif, Leigh Taylor-Young, Jack Palance, David De, Peter Jeffrey, Mohammed Shamsi (Columbia)

The Horsemen is a would-be epic stretched thin across Hollywood's 'profound peasant' tradition. It's a misfire, despite offbeat Afghanistan locations and some bizarre action sequences.

Omar Sharif, son of rural Afghanistan clan leader Jack Palance, is injured and humi-liated (he thinks) in a brutal ritual soccer-type game played with the headless carcass of a calf. Returning home in company of his now treacherous servant (David De) and a wandering 'untouchable' out for his money (Leigh Taylor-Young), Sharif's leg is ampu-tated below the knee in a remote mountain village. Back with his clan, Sharif forgives De and Taylor-Young for two attempts they made on his life and then trains hard to reestablish his honor and reputation as the greatest horseman in the area.

Dalton Trumbo's cliche script, based on the novel by Joseph Kessel, opts for the kind of mock-poetic dialog even Hugh Griffith might have trouble mouthing. Sharif, however, maintains his composure.

■ **HOSPITAL, THE**

1971, 103 MINS, US ◇
Dir Arthur Hiller *Prod* Howard Gottfried *Scr* Paddy Chayefsky *Ph* Victor J. Kemper *Ed* Eric Albertson
Mus Morris Surdin *Art Dir* Gene Rudolf
● George C. Scott, Diana Rigg, Barnard Hughes, Nancy Marchand, Stephen Elliott, Donald Harron (United Artists)

The Hospital is a civilian mis-*M*A*S*H*. George C. Scott stars as a NY medical center chief surgeon whose ruined personal life alternates with a daily routine of apparently inept, callous, bored, overworked and murdered staff members. Diana Rigg is the daughter of a deranged doctor-patient whose unmasking destroys most of author Paddy Chayefsky's basic premise.

In the plot's medico environment stands Scott, at 53 a washout as husband and father and on the verge of suicide. The heavily sprayed-on sociological angle is that hospitals today treat patients like baggage.

Rigg turns Scott on to the promise of a peaceful life in the western mountains; she is in the hospital because father Barnard Hughes, a gone-berserk Boston doctor, has been treated in bungled fashion by Richard Dysart, a medic whose eye is on the stock market more than his avowed profession.

The film is larded with vignettes strung on a series of mysterious murders: girl-chasing doctor Lenny Baker, internist Robert Anthony and nurse Angie Ortega.

■ **HOTEL**

1967, 124 MINS, US ◇ Ⓥ
Dir Richard Quine *Prod* Wendell Mayes
Scr Wendell Mayes *Ph* Charles Lang *Ed* Sam O'Steen *Mus* Johnny Keating *Art Dir* Cary Odell
● Rod Taylor, Catherine Spaak, Karl Malden, Melvyn Douglas, Merle Oberon, Richard Conte (Warner)

Hotel is a very well made, handsomely pro-duced drama about the guests and manage-ment of an old hostelry which must modernize or shutter. Uniformly strong per-formances, scripting and direction make for good pacing.

In an impressive debut as a film producer, Wendell Mayes has dressed the pic with lush settings and wardrobe, while not neglecting scripting chores in adapting Arthur Hailey's novel.

Merle Oberon, dripping in gems, registers well as the wife of Michael Rennie, whose hit-and-run driving cues a blackmail attempt by house gumshoe Richard Conte. Catherine Spaak, in her US film debut, is charming and sexy as Kevin McCarthy's mistress who drifts to Rod Taylor. Karl Malden has a choice role of a key thief who is frustrated at many turns by double-crossing accomplices.

■ **HOTEL BERLIN**

1945, 98 MINS, US
Dir Peter Godfrey *Prod* Louis F. Edelman *Scr* Jo Pagano, Alvah Bessie *Ph* Carl Guthrie *Ed* Frank Magee *Mus* Franz Waxman *Art Dir* John Hughes
● Helmut Dantine, Andrea King, Raymond Massey, Faye Emerson, Peter Lorre (Warner)

Grand Hotel in a 1945 Nazi setting, now known as *Hotel Berlin*, [both of them based on novels by Vicki Baum] is socko. The war's already lost – or, at least, there's that defeat-ist aura about Hotel Berlin – and the Nazi higherups are packing their loot for a South American getaway.

Producer Lou Edelman has guided his charges well. Productionally the lavishness is by suggestion rather than in reality. There are the periodic Allied air blitzes which chase everybody into the shelters, but otherwise it's a Grand Hotel in the lobby or on the sundry floors, but particularly in the apartments of a general (Raymond Massey), an informer (Faye Emerson), or a theatre darling (Andrea King).

There are many suspenseful touches right along. The footage is replete with arresting meller. Whether it's Dickie Tyler as the resourceful little bellboy of the underground, or the femme star who apparently first falls for Helmut Dantine (the escaped anti-Nazi) and later would turn him in, the situations are constantly intriguing.

■ **HOTEL IMPERIAL**

1927, 67 MINS, US ⊗
Dir Mauritz Stiller *Prod* Erich Pommer *Scr* Jules Furthman *Ph* Bert Glennon
● Pola Negri, James Hall, George Siegmann (Paramount)

In direction and camerawork the picture [based on a play by Lajos Biro] stands out, but the story isn't one that is going to give anyone a great thrill. Mauritz Stiller and Erich Pommer have done their work well, and they have made Pola Negri look like a gorgeous beauty in some shots, and effec-tively handled her in others, such as her scenes with the Russian general, but to what avail are good direction and supervision, plus acting, when the story isn't there?

It has to do with the advance of Russian armies into Galicia after their defeat of the Austrians. The Hotel Imperial is located in one of the border towns of Austria-Hungary. Here a fleeing Austrian hussar seeks rest and is caught behind the lines of the enemy when they move into the town.

Negri, as the hotel slavey, shelters him and suggests that he act as the waiter to cover himself. The Russian general makes the hotel his headquarters and falls for the girl. The waiter, in turn, loves her also and she recipro-cates his feeling.

A corking leading man is James Hall. He has an air that denotes that he is capable of real things in picture work. George Sieg-mann, as the Russian general, puts all that there should be into the heavy.

■ **HOTEL NEW HAMPSHIRE, THE**

1984, 110 MINS, US ◇ Ⓥ
Dir Tony Richardson *Prod* Neil Hartley *Scr* Tony Richardson *Ph* David Watkin *Ed* Robert K. Lambert
Mus Jacques Offenbach, Raymond Leppard
Art Dir Jocelyn Herbert
● Jodie Foster, Beau Bridges, Rob Lowe, Nastassja Kinski, Wilford Brimley, Dorsey Wright (Woodfall)

While it is decidedly not to all tastes, *The Hotel New Hampshire* is a fascinating, largely successful adaptation of John Irving's 1981 novel. Writer-director Tony Richardson has pulled off a remarkable stylistic tight-rope act, establishing a bizarre tone of morbid whimsicality at the outset and sustaining it throughout.

Tale concerns an eccentric New England family that, spurred on by an ever-searching father, establishes a new hotel in locale after locale and mutates in the process.

Among the unusual family members is Jodie Foster, who must endure a punishing gang rape and a prolonged fascination with the young man who did it; her brother, Rob Lowe, an impossibly good-looking fellow who takes on most of the women in the cast; their 'queer' brother Paul McCrane; and their little sister Jennie Dundas.

Also virtually part of the family by association, if not by blood, are black jock Dorsey Wright; voluptuous hotel waitress Anita Morris; and Nastassja Kinski, a girl so insecure that she hides most of the time inside an enormous bear suit.

■ **HOTEL PARADISO**

1966, 100 MINS, UK ◇
Dir Peter Glenville *Prod* Peter Glenville *Scr* Peter Glenville, Jean-Claude Carriere *Ph* Henri Decae
Ed Anne V. Coates *Mus* Laurence Rosen
Art Dir Francois de Lamothe

277

● Alec Guinness, Gina Lollobrigida, Robert Morley, Peggy Mount, Akim Tamiroff, Marie Bell (M-G-M)

Film version of Georges Feydeau's turn-of-the-century *L'hotel du libre echange* is a second generation production of Peter Glenville's legit revival of the French farceur in London.

Plot involves a complicated series of mishaps triggered by the 40-year-old 'itch' of M. Boniface, played with wearily glossy perfection by Alec Guinness, for the wife of his next-door neighbor, Henri Cot, assayed with appropriate bluster by Robert Morley. Miffed by her neglectful husband, Mme Cot, adequately acted by Gina Lollobrigida, succumbs to Boniface's suggestion that they rendezvous at the seedy Parisian assignation locale, Hotel Paradiso.

A concatenation of endless coincidences, laboriously contrived for the better part of the film, conspire to relegate the rendezvous to farce.

Main problem with the film is a bloodless script. Glenville, in an attempt to infuse theatrical brio into the play, only succeeds in over-stylizing it.

■ HOT ENOUGH FOR JUNE

1964, 98 MINS, UK ◇

Dir Ralph Thomas   *Prod* Betty E. Box   *Scr* Lukas Heller   *Ph* Ernest Steward   *Ed* Alfred Roome   *Mus* Angelo Lavagnino   *Art Dir* Syd Cain
● Dirk Bogarde, Sylva Koscina, Robert Morley, Leo McKern, Roger Delgado, John Le Mesurier (Rank)

A faster pace from director Ralph Thomas and a few more red herrings and surprise situations could have worked wonders in lifting this amiable enough spoof of espionage into a top league comedy-thriller.

June is by no means a skit on the Bond adventures. It is simply a genial leg-pull of some of the situations which, in tougher circumstances, Bond might easily be facing. Dirk Bogarde, who plays the hero with ingratiating efficiency, is an unsuccessful writer, content to live on national assistance. When the Labour Exchange unexpectedly sends him to take up a post as a trainee junior-executive in a glassworks, Bogarde finds the combination of a good salary and useful expenses irresistible. He is assigned to visit a Czech factory and bring back a written message which he guilelessly believes to be a simple commercial job. He does not know that he is now attached to the Espionage Department of the Foreign Office.

Most of the humor comes from witty prods at the expense of the Foreign Office and the Iron Curtain Party system. Robert Morley is superb as the boss of the department, with his old Etonian tie, benign plottings and general appearance of a well-poised walrus.

■ HOT ROCK, THE

1972, 105 MINS, US ◇ ⊽

Dir Peter Yates   *Prod* Hal Landers, Bobby Roberts   *Scr* William Goldman   *Ph* Ed Brown   *Ed* Frank P. Keller, Fred W. Berger   *Mus* Quincy Jones   *Art Dir* John Robert Lloyd
● Robert Redford, George Segal, Ron Leibman, Paul Sand, Zero Mostel, Moses Gunn (20th Century Fox)

With its mixture of courtship, satire and broad comedy, *The Hot Rock* emerges as an offbeat crime feature. Stars Robert Redford and George Segal head a quartet of thieves who usually miss the objective, here a famous diamond which inspired the title of the piece.

Peter Yates' direction and uniformly good cast partly overcome a William Goldman script [from Donald E. Westlake's novel] that has many exciting and funny bits, but lacks a clear, unifying thrust.

However, the plot involves four separate heists, and, given the deliberate exposition of the human frailty of the hoods, the sequential

capers lose a lot of momentum, giving the film as a whole the look of a spliced-together multi-episode TV show.

■ HOT SPOT, THE

1990, 120 MINS, US ◇ ⊽

Dir Dennis Hopper   *Prod* Paul Lewis   *Scr* Nona Tyson, Charles Williams   *Ph* Ueli Steiger   *Ed* Wende Pheiffer Mate   *Mus* Jack Nitzsche   *Art Dir* Cary White
● Don Johnson, Virginia Madsen, Jennifer Connelly, Charles Martin Smith, William Sadler, Barry Corbin (Orion)

Director Dennis Hopper just won't say no to kinky amorality, and that's all to the good in this twisting, languorous and very sexy thriller [based on Charles Williams' novel *Hell Hath No Fury*].

Hopper elicits a sharp, understated performance from *Miami Vice* star Don Johnson, who's neither a cop nor a good guy here. As the low-key, manipulative drifter Harry Madox, Johnson shakes things up in a godforsaken Texas town, where his job at a used car lot involves him with two restless women yearning to beat the heat.

Gloria Harper (Jennifer Connelly) is the sweetly stunning office girl; Dolly Harshaw (Virginia Madsen) is the irresistibly tempting boss' wife. This is the type of town, says Madsen, where there are 'only two things to do', and one of them is watching TV. Johnson charts a sexual collision course with both women. But he has another agenda. Once he's insinuated himself into the town, Johnson aims to con the yokels.

Hopper clearly was impressed by what he learned from working with David Lynch on *Blue Velvet*. *The Hot Spot* seeps with atmosphere, unfolds at a deceptively relaxed pace, steadily accumulates noirish grit, then dizzily plunges into a Lynch-like plumbing of the dark passions and nasty secrets at the heart of Main Street, USA.

■ HOUDINI

1953, 105 MINS, US ◇

Dir George Marshall   *Prod* George Pal   *Scr* Philip Yordan   *Ph* Ernest Laszlo   *Ed* George Tomasini   *Mus* Roy Webb   *Art Dir* Hal Pereira, Al Nozaki
● Tony Curtis, Janet Leigh, Torin Thatcher, Angela Clarke, Douglas Spencer (Paramount)

A typical screen biography, presenting a rather fanciful version of Houdini's life. Production does well by illusions and escapes on which Houdini won his fame, using these tricks to give substance to a plot that uses a backstage formula that follows pat lines. Under George Marshall's direction, story spins along nicely, with occasional emphasis on drama in several of escape sequences to keep interest up. Performances of two stars are likeable, although neither shows any aging in the time span that covers Houdini from 21 to death.

Screenplay, based on book by Harold Kellock, opens at the turn of the century to find Houdini performing as a 'wild man' and magician in Schultz' Dime Museum in New York. To this amusement spot comes a group of school girls, including Janet Leigh, and Houdini (Tony Curtis) is attracted to her. After an extremely brief courtship, they marry, try an act together, before she persuades him to take a job in a lock factory. Later, after winning a prize at a magicians' convention, Houdini and his bride go to Europe and he becomes a success with miracle escapes.

■ HOUND OF THE BASKERVILLES, THE

1939, 78 MINS, US ⊽

Dir Sidney Lanfield   *Prod* Gene Markey   *Scr* Ernest Pascal   *Ph* Peverell Marley   *Ed* Robert Simpson   *Mus* Cyril J. Mockridge   *Art Dir* Richard Day, Hans Peters

● Richard Greene, Basil Rathbone, Nigel Bruce, Lionel Atwill, John Carradine, Wendy Barrie (20th Century-Fox)

The Hound of the Baskervilles retains all of the suspensefully dramatic ingredients of Conan Doyle's popular adventure of Sherlock Holmes. It's a startling mystery-chiller developed along logical lines without resorting to implausible situations and over-theatrics.

Doyle's tale of mystery surrounding the Baskerville castle is a familiar one. When Lionel Atwill learns that Richard Greene, heir to the estate, is marked for death, he calls in Basil Rathbone.

Rathbone gives a most effective characterization of Sherlock Holmes. Greene, in addition to playing the intended victim of the murderer, is the romantic interest opposite Wendy Barrie.

Chiller mood generated by the characters and story is heightened by effects secured from sequences in the medieval castle and the dreaded fogbound moors. Low key photography by Peverell Marley adds to suspense.

■ HOUND OF THE BASKERVILLES, THE

1959, 88 MINS, UK ◇ ⊽

Dir Terence Fisher   *Prod* Anthony Hinds   *Scr* Peter Bryan   *Ph* Jack Asher   *Ed* James Needs   *Mus* James Bernard   *Art Dir* Bernard Robinson
● Peter Cushing, Andre Morell, Christopher Lee, Marla Landi, Miles Malleson, David Oxley (Hammer)

This first Sherlock Holmes pic in color takes place in the desolate setting of Dartmoor. The private eye and his faithful stooge, Doctor Watson, are called in following the mysterious slaying of Sir Charles Baskerville. It's thought that his successor, Sir Henry, may meet the same fate.

It is difficult to fault the performance of Peter Cushing, who looks, talks and behaves in precisely the way approved by the Sherlock Holmes Society. Andre Morell is also a very good Watson – stolid, reliable and not as stupidly bovine as he is sometimes depicted. Christopher Lee has a fairly colorless role as the potential victim of the legendary hound, but he plays it competently. Miles Malleson contributes most of the rare humor with one of his first class studies, as a bumbling bishop.

Terence Fisher's direction captures the eeriness of the atmosphere. Some of the settings are a shade stagey but Jack Asher's lensing also helps to build up the dank gloom of the Dartmoor area.

■ HOUR OF THE GUN

1967, 101 MINS, US ◇ ⊽

Dir John Sturges   *Prod* John Sturges   *Scr* Edward Anhalt   *Ph* Lucien Ballard   *Ed* Ferris Webster   *Mus* Jerry Goldsmith   *Art Dir* Alfred Ybarra
● James Garner, Jason Robards, Robert Ryan, Albert Salmi, Charles Aidman, Steve Ihnat (United Artists/Mirisch)

Edward Anhalt, using Douglas D. Martin's *Tombstone's Epitaph*, has fashioned a heavily-populated script which traces Wyatt Earp's moral decline from a lawman to one bent on personal revenge. Produced under earlier title of *The Law and Tombstone*, it continues the story of Earp after *Gunfight at the O.K. Corral*.

Unfortunately, for any filmmaker, probing too deeply into the character of folk heroes reveals them to be fallible human beings – which they are, of course – but to mass audiences, who create fantasies, such exposition is unsettling. Reality often makes for poor drama.

Jason Robards and James Garner play well together, the former supplying an adroit irony in that he, an admitted gambler as much outside the law as in, becomes more

H

moral as Garner lapses into personal vendetta. Robert Ryan is a perfect heavy.

....

■ HOUSEBOAT

1958, 112 MINS, US ◇ Ⓥ

Dir Melville Shavelson   *Prod* Jack Rose   *Scr* Melville Shavelson, Jack Rose   *Ph* Ray June   *Ed* Frank Bracht   *Mus* George Duning   *Art Dir* Hal Pereira, John Goodman

● Cary Grant, Sophia Loren, Martha Hyer, Harry Guardino, Eduardo Ciannelli, Murray Hamilton (Paramount/Scribe)

The voyage of *Houseboat* is to a nearly extinct era in motion pictures when screens and hearts bubbled over with the warmth of original family humor.

It's a perfect role for Cary Grant, who plays a government lawyer separated from his wife and who, upon her accidental death, is brought into contact with his three children, none of whom are very friendly toward him.

Enter Sophia Loren, a full-blown lass with lovely knees who's been kept in tow by her father, a noted Italian symphony conductor and who takes the first chance to get away from it all. Grant, though he takes her for a tramp, hires her as a maid at seeing her ability to handle his children upon first meeting. Off goes everyone to the country, and through living together begin to understand and love each other. This, of course, also goes for the two adults (by now, he's noticed her knees).

Grant mixes concern with disconcern and says more with a head tilt than most residents of situation comedy are able to say with an entire script. Loren acts better in irate Italian than in emotional English, but she is believable and sometimes downright warm as the lover of Grant and his children.

Harry Guardino is outstanding as a fiery wolf who will take anything but a wife, and Martha Hyer, as the rich 'other' woman, is beautiful and skillfully competent. As one might expect, the moppets steal the show.

....

■ HOUSE BY THE RIVER

1950, 88 MINS, US

Dir Fritz Lang   *Prod* Howard Welsch   *Scr* Mel Dinelli   *Ph* Edward Cronjager   *Ed* Arthur D. Hilton   *Mus* George Antheil   *Art Dir* Boris Leven

● Louis Hayward, Lee Bowman, Jane Wyatt, Dorothy Patrick (Republic/Fidelity)

House by the River is a fair mystery which lacks sufficient plot twists and suspense.

As screenplayed from an A.P. Herbert novel, the film departs from the conventional whodunit in that the audience knows the identity of the murderer from the opening reel. Subsequent footage is chiefly a character study of the three principals.

Bulk of the action takes place in a gloomy mansion and a courtroom.

Yarn revolves around a hack writer who strangles the maid when she rebuffs his advances. His brother, an accountant, realizes murder has been committed, but somehow lets his kin persuade him to assist in disposing of the body.

Role of the writer represents a meaty part for Louis Hayward who essays it with such gusto that he frequently overplays.

....

■ HOUSE CALLS

1978, 98 MINS, US ◇ Ⓥ

Dir Howard Zieff   *Prod* Alex Winitsky, Arlene Sellers   *Scr* Max Shulman, Julius J. Epstein   *Ph* David M. Walsh   *Ed* Edward Warschilka   *Mus* Henry Mancini   *Art Dir* Henry Bumstead

● Walter Matthau, Glenda Jackson, Art Carney, Richard Benjamin, Candice Azzara, Dick O'Neill (Universal)

Despite some horsepower casting, *House Calls* is overall a silly and uneven comedy about doctors which wants to be as macabre as, say, *Hospital*, and at the same time as innocuous as a TV sitcom. It manages to be neither.

Walter Matthau, engaging as a middle-aged lech, is one of four stars in the film, herein a newly-widowed medic out to make up for lost infidelity time; Glenda Jackson, divorced from a philanderer, seeks a faithful new mate; Art Carney is a near-senile hospital chief of staff whose mistakes are supposed to be funny but come off as really nasty; Richard Benjamin is a young doctor whose part is essentially to provide plot exposition.

The film is thus a middle-years comedy-romance vehicle for Matthau and Jackson, latter in her first made-in-Hollywood project and appearing none too comfortable either; the lightness of her *A Touch of Class* Oscar-winning performance is gone.

Carney also huffs and puffs his way uncomfortably through an unsympathetic part. Benjamin relaxes and Matthau seems mellow enough.

....

■ HOUSEKEEPING

1987, 116 MINS, US ◇ Ⓥ

Dir Bill Forsyth   *Prod* Robert I. Colesberry   *Scr* Bill Forsyth   *Ph* Michael Coulter   *Ed* Michael Ellis   *Mus* Michael Gibbs   *Art Dir* Adrienne Atkinson

● Christine Lahti, Sara Walker, Andrea Burchill, Anne Pitoniak (Columbia)

Both enervating and exhilarating, *Housekeeping* is a very composed film about eccentric behavior. It is beautifully observed in many of its details, particularly in its very close examination of the relationship between sisters.

Based upon Marilynne Robinson's well-regarded novel, Forsyth's screenplay is structured around the impulsive arrivals and departures of characters fundamental to the lives of two sisters in Washington State after World War II. Men never enter the picture, as the girls successively live with their mother, grandmother, great-aunts and mother's sister in the splendid isolation of a small mountain town.

Six years after their abandonment, when the girls are on the brink of adolescence, into their lives steps their long-lost aunt Sylvie (Christine Lahti). Tale then becomes that of the proverbial crazy ladies in the old house on the edge of town, but played rigorously without sentimentality or cuteness.

Newcomers Sara Walker and Andrea Burchill are splendid as the girls, as they manage to suggest the lifelong and quite particular bond between the sisters as much through body language and looks as through dialog.

....

■ HOUSE OF BAMBOO

1955, 102 MINS, US ◇

Dir Samuel Fuller   *Prod* Buddy Adler   *Scr* Harry Kleiner, Samuel Fuller   *Ph* Joe MacDonald   *Ed* James B. Clark   *Mus* Leigh Harline   *Art Dir* Lyle Wheeler, Addison Hehr

● Robert Ryan, Robert Stack, Shirley Yamaguchi, Cameron Mitchell, Brad Dexter, Sessue Hayakawa (20th Century-Fox)

House of Bamboo is a regulation gangster story played against a modern-day Tokyo setting.

Novelty of scene and a warm, believable performance by Japanese star Shirley Yamaguchi are two of the better values in the production. Had story treatment and direction been on the same level of excellence, *House* would have been an allround good show.

Pictorially, the film is beautiful to see; the talk's mostly in the terse, tough idiom of yesteryear mob pix. While plot deals with some mighty tough characters who are trying to organize Tokyo along Chicago gangland lines, the violence introduced seems hardly necessary to the melodramatic points being made.

Robert Stack, required to overplay surliness by the direction, is an undercover agent out to get the murderer of a GI and break up the gang of renegade Yanks.

....

■ HOUSE OF CARDS

1968, 105 MINS, US ◇

Dir John Guillermin   *Prod* Dick Berg   *Scr* James P. Bonner   *Ph* Alberto Pizzi   *Ed* Terry Williams   *Mus* Francis Lai   *Art Dir* Aurelio Crugnola

● George Peppard, Inger Stevens, Orson Welles, Keith Michell, William Job, Maxine Audley (Universal)

George Peppard is in breezy vigorous form as rescuer of a lady in distress in a thriller that has quite a measure of excitement and style, though the screenplay, based on Stanley Ellins' novel, has plenty of straggly ends. However, there are elements of a Hitchcockian thriller.

Story has Peppard as a Yank drifter in France who falls into the job of tutor to the young son of the widow of a French general killed in the Algerian war. He's installed in the de Villemont mansion and meets the curious and sinister de Villemont family.

Peppard offers a nice combo of exuberant cheek and muscle and Inger Stevens as the young widow keeps the romantic angle dangling tantalizingly. Orson Welles is not over used, but his flamboyance fits the role of a menacing conspirator effectively, and Keith Michell is suavely sinister.

Director John Guillermin makes the most of highspots but often cannot get the conversational and plot-laying bits off the ground.

....

■ HOUSE OF ROTHSCHILD

1934, 94 MINS, US ◇

Dir Alfred Werker   *Scr* Nunnally Johnson   *Ph* Peverell Marley   *Mus* Alfred Newman

● George Arliss, Boris Karloff, Loretta Young, Robert Young, C. Aubrey Smith, Florence Arliss (Twentieth Century)

A fine picture on all counts in the acting, writing, and directing. It handles the delicate subject of anti-semitism with tact and restraint. The Rothschild family, through its intimate financial connection with the Napoleonic wars, affords a meaty story [based on the play by G.H. Westley].

George Arliss plays the father and founder of the family, Mayer Rothschild, and when the narrative skips 35 years he is also the son, Nathan, head of the London branch of the banking firm. Nathan's daughter is played by Loretta Young, who never looked better. She falls in love with an English gentile officer (Robert Young).

Nathan opposes the marriage, fearing his daughter will suffer indignities because of her race. Ultimately his opposition melts and the pair are last seen in the luxuriant colors of the Technicolor sequence, in which Rothschild is made an English baron at a regal investiture, which brings the picture to an opulent close.

The real Mrs Arliss plays her husband's make-believe wife. Her performance is very able and she is at all times an attractice matron. There are numerous minor performance of merit, including a sentimentalized Duke of Welington handled by the astute C. Aubrey Smith.

□ 1934: Best Picture (Nomination)

....

■ HOUSE OF USHER

1960, 79 MINS, US ◇ Ⓥ

Dir Roger Corman   *Prod* Roger Corman   *Scr* Richard Matheson   *Ph* Floyd Crosby   *Ed* Anthony Carras   *Mus* Les Baxter   *Art Dir* Daniel Haller

● Vincent Price, Mark Damon, Myrna Fahey, Harry Ellerbe (American International)

It's not precisely the Edgar Allan Poe short story that emerges in *House of Usher*, but it's a reasonably diverting and handsomely mounted variation. In patronizingly romanticizing Poe's venerable prose, scenarist Richard Matheson has managed to preserve enough of the original's haunting flavor and spirit. The elaborations change the personalities of the three central characters, but not recklessly so.

In Poe's tale, the first-person hero is a friend of Roderick Usher, not his enemy and the romantic wooer of his doomed sister, the Lady Madeline. Matheson's version, however, accomplishes this alteration without ruining the impact of the chilling climax, in which Madeline (Myrna Fahey), buried alive by her brother (Vincent Price) while under a cataleptic trance, breaks free from her living tomb.

Price is a fine fit as Usher, and Fahey successfully conveys the transition from helpless daintiness to insane vengeance. Hero Mark Damon has his better moments when the going gets gory and frenzied, but lacks the mature command required for the role. Harry Ellerbe is outstanding as an old family retainer.

The cobweb-ridden, fungus-infected, mist-pervaded atmosphere of cadaverous gloom has been photographed with great skill by Floyd Crosby and enhanced further by Ray Mercer's striking photographic effects and the vivid color, most notably during a woozy dream sequence.

■ **HOUSE OF WAX**

1953, 90 MINS, US ◇ ▽

Dir Andre de Toth *Prod* Bryan Foy *Scr* Crane Wilbur *Ph* Bert Glennon, Peverell Marley *Ed* Rudi Fehr *Mus* David Buttolph *Art Dir* Stanley Fleischer
● Vincent Price, Frank Lovejoy, Phyllis Kirk, Carolyn Jones, Charles Bronson, Reggie Rymal (Warner)

This remake of Charles Belden's *Mystery of the Wax Museum* (1933) is given the full 3-D treatment in Crane Wilbur's screenplay. Andre de Toth's direction, while uneven, nonetheless gears it to the medium – chairs flying into the audience, cancan dancers pirouetting full into the camera, the barker's pingpong ball, as a pitchman's prop, likewise shooting out at the audience, the muscular menace springing as if from the theatre into the action. The stereophonic sound further assists in the illusion.

Warners employs the Gunzburg Bros' NaturalVision technique, first introduced in Arch Oboler's *Bwana Devil*. It achieves maximum results with the eerie chases, ghoulish shenanigans in the NY City morgue, the '14th St. Music Hall' (sic!) interior for the cancan, the police headquarters' flashbacks, and the like.

Casting is competent, Vincent Price is capital as the No. 1 menace. Frank Lovejoy is authoritative as the lieutenant. Phyllis Kirk is purty as the ingenue who looks fairly convincingly scared but not so in the scream department – she needs a good, shrill, piercing shrieker as voice standin. Paul Picerni is okay as the juvenile and Carolyn Jones makes her moments count as the flighty kid who gets bumped off. Charles Bronson is the No. 2 menace, as the deaf-mute, and Reggie Rymal, as the barker, is also standout.

■ **HOUSE ON CARROLL STREET, THE**

1988, 100 MINS, US ◇ ▽

Dir Peter Yates *Prod* Peter Yates, Robert F. Colesberry *Scr* Walter Bernstein *Ph* Michael Ballhaus *Ed* Ray Lovejoy *Mus* Georges Delerue *Art Dir* Stuart Wurtzel

● Kelly McGillis, Jeff Daniels, Mandy Patinkin, Christopher Rhode, Jessica Tandy (Orion)

In this story of a sleuth trailing improbable characters involved in a ridiculous conspiracy, Kelly McGillis is the idealistic and hardly convincing political activist who in 1951 refuses to answer questions before a Senate hearing on her involvement in a controversial organization.

She takes a job reading to a crotchety old blind lady (Jessica Tandy) whose row house garden is adjacent to another brownstone where there are mysterious goings-on. It just so happens the same senator (Mandy Patinkin) who grilled her about her political leanings is in the house shouting as an interpreter translates into German.

McGillis is intrigued. She collects about three clues and figures out Patinkin is smuggling Nazis in by having them take the names of dead Jews.

Jeff Daniels is Ned to McGillis' Nancy Drew. He is the FBI agent who manages to come in at exactly the right moments to save her from whatever perilous predicament she is in at the time – no matter how preposterous.

■ **HOUSE ON HAUNTED HILL, THE**

1958, 75 MINS, US ▽

Dir William Castle *Prod* William Castle *Scr* Robb White *Ph* Carl E. Guthrie *Ed* Roy Livingston *Mus* Von Dexter *Art Dir* David Milton
● Vincent Price, Carol Ohmart, Richard Long, Alan Marshal, Carolyn Craig, Elisha Cook Jr (Allied Artists)

The screenplay is the one about the group of people who promise to spend the night in a haunted house. In this case, it's for pure monetary gain. Vincent Price, owner of the house, is offering $10,000 to anyone who lasts out the night. There is a gimmick in the plot which explains the screams, ghosts, bubbling vats of lye and perambulating skeletons.

Haunted Hill is expertly put together. There is some good humor in the dialog which not only pays off well against the ghostly elements, but provides a release for laughter so it does not explode in the suspense sequences. The characters are interesting and not outlandish, so there is some basis of reality. Director William Castle keeps things moving at a healthy clip.

Robb White and Castle have a new gimmick called 'Emergo'. This device is an illuminated skeleton mounted on trolley wires, moving out from the side of the screen over the heads of the audience.

■ **HOUSE ON 92ND ST., THE**

1945, 83 MINS, US

Dir Henry Hathaway *Prod* Louis de Rochemont *Scr* Barre Lyndon, Charles G. Booth, John Monks Jr *Ph* Norbert Brodine *Ed* Harmon Jones *Mus* David Buttolph *Art Dir* Lyle Wheeler, Lewis Creber
● William Eythe, Lloyd Nolan, Signe Hasso, Gene Lockhart, Leo G. Carroll (20th Century-Fox)

Twentieth-Fox, employing somewhat the technique of *The March of Time* has parlayed the latter with facilities and files of the FBI in arriving at *The House on 92nd St*. It doesn't matter much whether it's east or west 92nd – the result is an absorbing documentation that's frequently heavily-steeped melodrama.

House is comprised of prewar and wartime footage taken by the FBI, and it ties together revelations of the vast Nazi spy system in the United States. Woven into this factual data, along with what the foreword reveals is a thorough cooperation of the FBI in making the film, are the dramatic elements inserted by Hollywood in general and 20th-Fox in particular.

Lloyd Nolan is the FBI inspector in charge of ferreting out the espionage on a secret formula sought by the Nazis; William Eythe is the young German-American sent to Germany by US-located Nazis (and the FBI) to learn espionage and sabotage; Signe Hasso plays a key link to the Nazi system in this country.

■ **HOUSE PARTY**

1990, 100 MINS, US ◇ ▽

Dir Reginald Hudlin *Prod* Warrington Hudlin *Scr* Reginald Hudlin *Ph* Peter Deming *Ed* Earl Watson *Mus* Marcus Miller *Art Dir* Bryan Jones
● Christopher Reid, Robin Harris, Christopher Martin, Martin Lawrence, Tisha Campbell, A.J. Johnson (New Line)

House Party captures contemporary black teen culture in a way that's fresh, commercial and very catchy. Filmmaking team of Reggie and Warrington Hudlin make a strikingly assured debut feature blending comedy, hip-hop music and dancing in a pic that moves to a kinetic, nonstop rhythm.

Rap duo Kid 'N' Play (Christopher Reid and Christopher Martin) play colleagues in rhyme, trying to get away with throwing a booming house party the night Play's parents are away and Kid is grounded by his Pop (Robin Harris) for getting in a fight at school.

En route to the party, Kid is pursued by the school thugs (rap trio Full Force), and all of them are pursued by the neighborhood cops. Then unwitting Kid becomes an object of desire for both of the young ladies Play is trying to impress (Tisha Campbell and A.J. Johnson).

Writer-director Reggie Hudlin, who expanded *House Party* from a short he made while a student at Harvard, injects pic with the cartoonish style and captivating rhythm of today's rap scene.

■ **HOWARD THE DUCK**

1986, 111 MINS, US ◇ ▽

Dir Willard Huyck *Prod* Gloria Katz *Scr* Willard Huyck, Gloria Katz *Ph* Richard H. Kline *Ed* Michael Chandler, Sidney Wolinsky *Mus* John Barry *Art Dir* Peter Jamison
● Lea Thompson, Jeffrey Jones, Tim Robbins, Ed Gale, Paul Guilfoyle (Lucasfilm)

Scripters have taken the cigar chompin', beer drinkin' comic book character [created by Steve Gerber] and turned him into a wide-eyed, cutesy, midget-sized extraterrestrial accidentally blown to Cleveland from a misdirected laser beam.

Howard encounters rock singer Beverly Switzler (Lea Thompson) after a few harrowing minutes on Earth and they become instant friends after he defends her from a couple of menacing punkers.

Pic then lapses into formulaic predictability with nearly an hour of frenetic chase scenes and technically perfect explosions from Industrial Light & Magic as Thompson and Tim Robbins try to thwart the authorities' attempts to capture the duck before he gets a chance to be beamed.

■ **HOW GREEN WAS MY VALLEY**

1941, 120 MINS, US

Dir John Ford *Prod* Darryl F. Zanuck *Scr* Philip Dunne *Ph* Arthur Miller *Ed* James B. Clark *Mus* Alfred Newman
● Walter Pidgeon, Maureen O'Hara, Donald Crisp, Roddy McDowall, Barry Fitzgerald, Anna Lee (20th Century-Fox)

Based on a best-selling novel, this saga of Welsh coal-mining life is replete with much human interest, romance, conflict and almost every other human emotion. It's a warm, human story that Richard Llewellyn wrought basically, and the skillful John Ford camera-

H

painting, from a fine scenario by Philip Dunne, needed only expert casting to round out the job.

Donald Crisp and Sara Allgood, as Pa and Ma Morgan, the heads of the Welsh mining family, are an inspired casting. Walter Pidgeon is excellent as the minister; Maureen O'Hara splendid as the object of his unrequited love, who marries the mineowner's son out of pique.

And, above all, there is Roddy McDowell. He's winsome, manly, and histrionically proficient in an upright, two-fisted manner.

The transition from book to screen also utilizes the first person singular narrative form, with graphic delineations of how green, indeed, was young Huw (pronounced Hugh) Morgan's valley as he recounts his life from childhood, unfolding the fullness of the Morgans' honest, God-fearing, industrial life span in the Welsh valley.

□ 1941: Best Picture

....

■ HOW I WON THE WAR

1967, 109 MINS, UK ◇ ⱱ
Dir Richard Lester *Prod* Richard Lester *Scr* Charles Wood *Ph* David Watkin *Ed* John Victor Smith *Mus* Ken Thorne *Art Dir* Philip Harrison, John Stoll
● Michael Crawford, John Lennon, Roy Kinnear, Lee Montague, Jack MacGowran, Michael Hordern (United Artists)

Patrick Ryan's novel has been adapted into a screenplay which, as directed by Richard Lester, substitutes motion for emotion, reeling for feeling, and crude slapstick for telling satire. Film opens at a superficial level of fast comedy, but never develops further.

Michael Crawford is top-featured as a gee-whiz British Army officer whose unthinking ineptitude kills off, one by one, all members of his unit. John Lennon, whose billing far exceeds his part, and contribution, plays one of the crew.

Episodic treatment cross-cuts between plot turns, and actual footage of Second World War battles, latter tinted in different hues.

....

■ HOWLING, THE

1981, 91 MINS, CANADA ◇
Dir Joe Dante *Prod* Daniel H. Blatt *Scr* John Sayles, Terence H. Winkless *Ph* John Hora *Ed* Mark Goldblatt, Joe Dante *Mus* Pino Donaggio *Art Dir* Robert A. Burns
● Dee Wallace, Patrick Macnee, Kevin McCarthy, John Carradine, Slim Pickens (International/Avco Embassy)

Director Joe Dante's work reflects Alfred Hitchcock's insistence that terror and suspense work best when counterbalanced by a chuckle or two.

There are good one-liners throughout, some delivered straight-faced by Kevin McCarthy as an empty-headed TV news producer and Dick Miller as the colorful expert on werewolves. And in a picture like this, John Carradine and Slim Pickens only have to open their mouths to get a laugh from long-time appreciative fans.

But this is supposed to be a horror film, after all. And it definitely is in a good old-fashioned way, complete with a girl venturing out alone with a flashlight to investigate a weird noise. In large part the picture works because of the make-up effects created by Rob Bottin.

Wallace, who was exceptional as the lonely woman at the bar in '10,' turns in another solid performance in a much dumber role. As the anchorlady, she has set herself out as bait for psycho Robert Picardo, meeting him in a porno shop where he winds up shot to death by cops. Back at the TV station, Belinda Balaski and Dennis Dugan are still working on the Picardo story, picking up clues that lead them into a study of werewolves.

If the picture has a major problem, it is that Dante uses up his best effects midway through the picture, leaving him with little for the grand surprise that's supposed to come at the end.

....

■ HOW THE WEST WAS WON

1962, 155 MINS, US ◇ ⱱ
Dir Henry Hathaway, John Ford, George Marshall *Prod* Bernard Smith *Scr* James R. Webb *Ph* William H. Daniels, Milton Krasner, Charles Lang Jr, Joseph LaShelle *Ed* Harold F. Kress *Mus* Alfred Newman *Art Dir* George W. Davis, William Ferrari, Addison Hehr
● James Stewart, Hendry Fonda, Gregory Peck, Debbie Reynolds, Richard Widmark, John Wayne (M-G-M/Cinerama)

It would be hard to imagine a subject which lends itself more strikingly to the wide-screen process than this yarn of the pioneers who opened the American West. It's a story which naturally puts the spotlight on action and adventure, and the three directors between them have turned in some memorable sequences.

George Marshall, for example, has the credit for the buffalo stampede, started by the Indians when the railroad was moving out West. This magnificently directed sequence is as vivid as anything ever put on celluloid. Undoubtedly the highlight of Henry Hathaway's contribution is the chase of outlaws who attempt to hold up a train with a load of bullion. John Ford's directorial stint is limited to the Civil War sequences, and though that part does not contain such standout incident, there is the fullest evidence of his high professional standards.

The storyline is developed around the Prescott family, as they start on their adventurous journey out west. Karl Malden and Agnes Moorehead are the parents, and with them are their two daughters, played by Debbie Reynolds and Carroll Baker. They start their journey out West down the Erie Canal, and when James Stewart, a fur trapper, comes on the scene, it's love at first sight for Baker.

Although they've headed in opposite directions, she eventually gets her man. After her parents lose their lives when their raft capsizes in the rapids – and that's another of the highly vivid sequences directed by Hathaway – Reynolds joins a wagon train to continue her journey and tries, in vain, to resist the charms of Gregory Peck, a professional gambler, who is first attracted to her when she's believed to have inherited a gold mine.

Peck gives a suave and jovial gloss to his role of the gambler, and though it's an undemanding part he gives it notable distinction. Stewart has some fine, if typical, moments in his scenes.

Richard Widmark makes a vital impression as the head man of the construction team building the railroad. John Wayne is another top ranking star with only a minor part as General Sherman in the Civil War episode, but he, too, makes the charactor stand out.

Spencer Tracy is heard but not seen as the narrator. In a clear, well-spoken commentary he provides the introducton to the story, and also the closing comments.

□ 1963: Best Picture (Nomination)

....

■ HOW TO GET AHEAD IN ADVERTISING

1989, 95 MINS, UK ◇ ⱱ
Dir Bruce Robinson *Prod* David Wimbury *Scr* Bruce Robinson *Ph* Peter Hannan *Ed* Alan Strachan *Mus* David Dundas, Rick Wentworth *Art Dir* Michael Pickwood
● Richard E. Grant, Rachel Ward, Richard Wilson, Jacqueline Tong, John Shrapnel (Handmade)

As a hotshot go-getter in the British equivalent of Madison Avenue, Richard E. Grant is having a problem coming up with an origi-

nal campaign for a pimple cream and the pressure is on from the client and his boss (wonderfully droll Richard Wilson).

As dutiful wives do, Rachel Ward tries to assure him that something in his genius will come forward, but he's floundering.

When a small boil breaks out on his own neck, Grant realizes the stress has become too much and it's time to quit the business. It's too late. The boil begins to grow – and starts to talk, giving form to all that's vile and venal in his nature.

The picture would be genuinely hilarious were the subject matter not so overworked.

....

■ HOW TO MARRY A MILLIONAIRE

1953, 95 MINS, US ◇ ⱱ
Dir Jean Negulesco *Prod* Nunnally Johnson *Scr* Nunnally Johnson *Ph* Joe MacDonald *Ed* Louis Loeffler *Mus* Cyril Mockridge *Art Dir* Lyle R. Wheeler, Leland Fuller
● Betty Grable, Marilyn Monroe, Lauren Bacall, David Wayne, Rory Calhoun, Cameron Mitchell (20th Century-Fox)

The script draws for partial source material on two plays, Zoe Akins' *The Greeks Had a Word for It* and *Loco* by Dale Eunson and Katherine Albert. Nunnally Johnson has blended the legiter ingredients with his own material for snappy comedy effect.

The plot has three girls pooling physical and monetary resources for a millionaire man hunt and as the predatory sex game unfolds the chuckles are constant. Each winds up with a man. One is David Wayne, a fugitive from Uncle Sam's Internal Revenue agents whose apartment the girls have leased as a base for the chase. He gets Marilyn Monroe.

Another is Cameron Mitchell, a young tycoon who dresses like a lowly wage slave. He winds up with Lauren Bacall. Third is Rory Calhoun, a poor but honest forest ranger who gains Betty Grable as a fire-watching companion. None is what the femme trio expected to get when the hunt started.

Certain for audience favor is Monroe's blonde with astigmatism who goes through life bumping into things, including men, because she thinks glasses would detract. Also captivating is Grable's Loco, a friendly, cuddly blonde who turns situations to advantage until the great outdoors overwhelms her. As the brains of the trio, Bacall's Schatze is a wise-cracking, hard-shelled gal who gives up millions for love and gets both.

A real standout among the other players is William Powell as the elderly Texas rancher who woos, wins and then gives up Bacall.

....

■ HOW TO MURDER YOUR WIFE

1965, 118 MINS, US ◇ ⱱ
Dir Richard Quine *Prod* Jack Lemmon, George Axelrod, Richard Quine *Scr* George Axelrod *Ph* Harry Stradling *Ed* David Wagner *Mus* Neal Hefti
● Jack Lemmon, Virna Lisi, Terry-Thomas, Eddie Mayehoff, Claire Trevor, Sidney Blackmer (Murder/United Artists)

George Axelrod's plot deals with the antics of a bachelor cartoonist, played by Jack Lemmon, who has a policy of acting out the escapades of his newsprint sleuth hero to test their credibility before actually committing them to paper. So it is that, awakening one morning to find himself married to an Italian dish who had popped out of a cake at a party the night before and after trying to make a go of this unwanted wedlock, he simulates the 'murder' of said spouse one evening by dumping a dummy likeness of her into a building construction site.

When Lemmon's wife, played by Virna Lisi, spots the cartoonist's sketches of his 'crime' on his work table she panics and flees.

The strip appears in the papers and, unable to explain his wife's whereabouts, Lemmon is arrested for murder and brought to trial.

All of this has moments of fine comic style but, overall, emerges as prefabricated as Lemmon's comic strip character. The comedian's efforts are considerable and consistent but finesse and desire aren't enough to overcome the fact that Axelrod's script doesn't make the most of its potentially antic situations.

• •

■ HOW TO SAVE A MARRIAGE AND RUIN YOUR LIFE

1968, 102 MINS, US ◇

Dir Fielder Cook *Prod* Stanley Shapiro *Scr* Stanley Shapiro *Ph* Lee Garmes *Ed* Philip Anderson *Mus* Michel Legrand *Art Dir* Robert Clatworthy
● Dean Martin, Stella Stevens, Eli Wallach, Anne Jackson, Betty Field (Columbia)

How to Save a Marriage and Ruin Your Life is an amusing Stanley Shapiro comedy about divorce and marital infidelity. Made under the title *Band of Gold*, the lush production stars Dean Martin, Stella Stevens, Eli Wallach and Anne Jackson.

Plot complications derive from Wallach's longtime infidelity with Jackson, Katherine Bard demonstrating in her brief footage that Wallach's home life is nothing. Martin confuses Jackson with Stevens, latter assuming his romantic advances are legit, instead of the ruse which Martin intends.

Gag situations include a fake deceased wife, milked for more than it's worth. The situations play better than they can be described; on the other hand, none is especially hard-core hilarity.

• •

■ HOW TO STEAL A MILLION

1966, 127 MINS, US ◇

Dir William Wyler *Prod* Fred Kohlmar, William Wyler *Scr* Harry Kurnitz *Ph* Charles Lang *Ed* Robert Swink *Mus* Johnny Williams *Art Dir* Alexandre Trauner
● Audrey Hepburn, Peter O'Toole, Eli Wallach, Hugh Griffith, Charles Boyer, Marcel Dalio (20th Century-Fox)

How to Steal a Million returns William Wyler to the enchanting province of the *Roman Holiday*. Lensed in Paris, advantageous use is made of the actual story locale to give unusual visual interest.

Plot centers on a fraud in the art world via forging 'masterpieces'. Based on a story by George Bradshaw, the script twirls around Audrey Hepburn, daughter of a distinguished French family whose father, Hugh Griffith, is a faker of genius. She has given up trying to reform him, continuing only to hope he won't get into too much trouble. Peter O'Toole is a private detective who specializes in solving crimes in the world of art, but whom femme thinks is a burglar after she discovers him in the family home in the middle of the night apparently trying to make off with a canvas.

Griffith is a particular standout as the elegant Parisian oddball with a compulsion to forge the greatest impressionistic painters.

• •

■ HOW TO SUCCEED IN BUSINESS WITHOUT REALLY TRYING

1967, 121 MINS, US ◇ ⓥ

Dir David Swift *Prod* David Swift *Scr* David Swift *Ph* Burnett Guffey *Ed* Ralph Winters, Allan Jacobs *Mus* Frank Loesser *Art Dir* Robert Boyle
● Robert Morse, Michele Lee, Rudy Vallee, Anthony Teague, Maureen Arthur (Mirisch)

An entertaining, straightforward filming of the [1961] legituner, featuring many thesps

in their stage roles. David Swift's production is generally fast-moving in tracing the rags-to-riches rise of Robert Morse within Rudy Vallee's biz complex. Colorful production values maintain great eye appeal.

Swift, besides producing-directing (and appearing briefly as an elevator operator), adapted the legit book by Abe Burrows, Jack Weinstock and Willie Gilbert, based on Shepherd Mead's novel.

Most of Frank Loesser's literate melodies have been retained including 'I Believe in You', 'The Company Way', 'Been a Long Day', and 'Brotherhood of Man'.

Plot concerns windowwasher Morse who, by superior instinct for advancement and survival, becomes a top exec in Vallee's company in a matter of days. He becomes so big that former well-wishers plot his downfall.

The pixie-like Morse is excellent, with both voice and facial expressions right on target all the time. Michele Lee shows the same uninhibited freshness and charm that made Doris Day a film star.

• •

■ HUCKLEBERRY FINN

1931, 79 MINS, US

Dir Norman Taurog *Scr* Grover Jones, William Slavens McNutt *Ph* David Abel
● Jackie Coogan, Mitzi Green, Junior Durkin, Jackie Searl, Clara Blandick, Jane Darwell (Paramount)

It's the second Mark Twain story to be done by Paramount, first being *Tom Sawyer*. Same quartet that did *Sawyer* reunite in Jackie Coogan, Junior Durkin, Mitzi Green and Jackie Searl. The latter two only appear in a minor way at the beginning. That's after the first 1,000 feet or so when Searl, Green and the others practically disappear, a young adolescent (looking like sweet 16) taking up from there on. She's attractice, soft-voiced Charlotte V. Henry for whom Huck Finn changes his mind about women.

Durkin is excellent throughout, overshadowing Coogan, who in spots is permitted to appear and talk in a too adult manner. His early love scene assignments with Mitzi Green drag in an unnatural touch. But for Durkin's able and natural characterization all the way, this might have meant serious injury to the picture.

Norman Taurog's direction is balanced and smooth.

• •

■ HUCKLEBERRY FINN

1939, 88 MINS, US ⓥ

Dir Richard Thorpe *Prod* Joseph L. Mankiewicz *Scr* Hugo Butler *Ph* John F. Seitz *Ed* Frank E. Hull *Mus* Jerome Moross *Art Dir* Cedric Gibbons, Randall Duell
● Mickey Rooney, Walter Connolly, William Frawley, Rex Ingram (M-G-M)

Picture is a fairly close adaptation of the original Mark Twain work, but has not been able to catch the rare and sparkling humor and general sincerity of the author's original. Furthermore, young Rooney seems too mature for his years.

Huckleberry Finn is naturally the dominating character in the story. Taken under the wings of Elizabeth Risdon and Clara Blandick for upbringing and an education, Mickey can't stand for school and dressing up. When his father appears to demand money from the sisters, Rooney disappears. Meeting Rex Ingram, an escaping slave, pair start down the river on a raft.

Many opportunities for comedy situations are missed.

Rex Ingram stands out boldly in support. He gives an honest and effective characterization of the runaway slave.

• •

■ HUD

1963, 113 MINS, US ⓥ

Dir Martin Ritt *Prod* Martin Ritt, Irving Ravetch *Scr* Irving Ravetch, Harriet Frank Jr *Ph* James Wong Howe *Ed* Frank Bracht *Mus* Elmer Bernstein *Art Dir* Hal Pereira, Tambi Larsen
● Paul Newman, Melvyn Douglas, Patricia Neal, Brandon de Wilde (Paramount)

Hud is a near miss. Where it falls short of the mark is in its failure to filter its meaning and theme lucidly through its characters and story.

The screenplay, adapted from a novel by Larry McMurty, tells a tale of the modern American West, of its evolution from the land of pioneer ethics, of simple human gratifications unmotivated by greed, to the rangy real estate of shallow, mercenary creatures who have inherited the rugged individualism of the early settlers, but not their souls, their morals or their principles.

The new westerner is Hud (Paul Newman), noxious son of old Homer Bannon (Melvyn Douglas), pioneer Texas Panhandler who detests his offspring with a passion that persists to his bitter end, after he has just witnessed the liquidation of his entire herd of cattle (hoof and mouth disease) and the attempt of his son to have him declared incompetent to run his ranch.

It is in the relationship of father and son that the film slips. It is never clear exactly why the old man harbors such a deep-rooted, irrevocable grudge against his lad.

But the picture has a number of elements of distinction and reward. The four leading performances are excellent. Newman creates a virile, pernicious figure as that ornery title critter. The characteristics of old age are marvelously captured and employed by Douglas. Another fine performance is by Brandon de Wilde as Newman's nephew. Patricia Neal comes through with a rich and powerful performance as the housekeeper assaulted by Newman.

• •

■ HUDSON HAWK

1991, 95 MINS, US ◇ ⓥ

Dir Michael Lehmann *Prod* Joel Silver *Scr* Steven E. de Souza, Daniel Waters *Ph* Dante Spinotti *Ed* Chris Lebenzon, Michael Tronick *Mus* Michael Kamen, Robert Kraft *Art Dir* Jack DeGovia
● Bruce Willis, Danny Aiello, Andie MacDowell, James Coburn, Richard E. Grant, Sandra Bernhard (Tri-Star/Silver/ABC Bone)

Ever wondered what a Three Stooges short would look like with a $40 million budget? Then meet *Hudson Hawk*, a relentlessly annoying clay duck that crash-lands in a sea of wretched excess and silliness. Those willing to check their brains at the door may find sparse amusement in pic's frenzied pace.

Bruce Willis plays just-released-from-prison cat burglar Hudson Hawk, who's immediately drawn into a plot to steal a bunch of Leonardo Da Vinci artifacts by, among others, a twisted billionaire couple (Richard E. Grant, Sandra Bernhard), a twisted CIA agent (James Coburn) and an agent for the Vatican (Andie MacDowell). Mostly, though, Hawk hangs with his pal Tommy (Danny Aiello), as the two croon old tunes to time their escapades.

Director Michael Lehmann, who made his feature debut with the deliciously subversive *Heathers*, simply seems overwhelmed by the scale and banality of the screenplay [from a story by Willis]. Very few of the scenes actually seem connected.

The film primarily gives Willis a chance to toss off poor man's *Moonlighting* one-liners in the midst of utter chaos. Grant, Bernhard and Coburn do produce a few bursts of scatological humor based on the sheer energy of their over-the-top performances.

• •

H

■ **HUE AND CRY**

1947, 82 MINS, UK ⓥ

Dir Charles Crichton *Prod* Michael Balcon
Scr T.E.B. Clarke *Ph* Douglas Slocombe *Ed* Charles
Hasse *Mus* Georges Auric *Art Dir* Norman Arnold
● Alastair Sim, Valerie White, Jack Warner, Harry
Fowler (Ealing)

Principal actor is ex-news vendor Harry Fowler, who has played various cockney parts on
the screen, but who fails to make the main
character credible. And everything depends
on believing in him.

Story revolves around a gang of crooks who
use a serial story in *The Trump*, a kids' weekly,
as a means of communication. Joe Kirby, an
imaginative youngster, spots this, and in
spite of discouragement from his boss and an
alleged detective, he perseveres, interests his
pals, and brings off a great coup when boys of
all ages flock to the bomb-ravaged wastes of
dockland for a roundup of the criminals.

Director Charles Crichton has been conscientious, but queer camera angles and
shadows can add little thrill when the original material lacks it.

■ **HUMAN DESIRE**

1954, 90 MINS, US

Dir Fritz Lang *Prod* Lewis J. Rachmil *Scr* Alfred
Hayes *Ph* Burnett Guffey *Ed* Robert Peterson
Mus Daniele Amfitheatrof
● Glenn Ford, Gloria Grahame, Broderick Crawford,
Edgar Buchanan, Kathleen Case, Peggy Maley
(Columbia)

The audience meets some wretched characters on the railroad in this adaptation of the
Emile Zola novel, *The Human Beast*. A French
picturization of the work was done earlier
with heavy accent on psychological study of
an alcohol-crazed killer.

Fritz Lang, director, goes overboard in his
effort to create mood. Long focusing on locomotive speeding and twisting on the rails is
neither entertaining nor essential to the plot.

At the outset the screenplay provides much
conversation about the fact that Glenn Ford,
who's back on the job as an engineer, had
been fighting the war in Korea. There's not
much point to this, considering that Ford's
background has little bearing on the yarn.

Broderick Crawford, Gloria Grahame and
Ford make a brooding, sordid triangle, hopelessly involved. Crawford is utterly frustrated
in his effort to please his wife (Grahame) and
stay on an even keel with his heartless boss.
Grahame is a miserable character, alternately denying and admitting she has given
herself to other men. Ford dates Grahame
and toys with the idea of murdering her
husband.

■ **HUMAN FACTOR, THE**

1979, 115 MINS, UK ◇

Dir Otto Preminger *Prod* Otto Preminger *Scr* Tom
Stoppard *Ph* Mike Molloy *Ed* Richard Trevor
Mus Richard Logan, Gary Logan *Art Dir* Ken Ryan
● Richard Attenborough, John Gielgud, Derek Jacobi,
Robert Morley, Ann Todd, Nicol Williamson
(M-G-M/Preminger)

Graham Greene's low-keyed, highly absorbing 1978 novel of an aging English double
agent finding himself trapped into defecting
to Moscow and leaving his family behind
may have seemed like ideal material for Otto
Preminger's style of dispassionate ambiguity,
but helmer doesn't seem up to the occasion,
bringing little atmosphere or feeling to the
delicate ticks of the story.

Nicol Williamson limns the lead role of a
Secret Service desk man who, due not to
political commitment but loyalty to a friend
from his days in Africa, discreetly passes
occasional information to the East.

When a leak in his department is
discovered and office partner Derek Jacobi,
mistakenly identified as the culprit, is eliminated, Williamson feels the walls closing in
on him.

■ **HUMAN JUNGLE, THE**

1954, 82 MINS, US

Dir Joseph M. Newman *Prod* Hayes Goetz
Scr William Sackheim, Daniel Fuchs *Ph* Ellis Carter
Ed Lester Sansom, Samuel Fields *Mus* Hans Salter
Art Dir David Milton
● Gary Merrill, Jan Sterling, Paula Raymond, Emile
Meyer, Regis Toomey, Chuck Connors (Allied Artists)

The Human Jungle is a sock big-city police
story packed with sex as well as violence and
excitement. The politics of a metropolitan
police department backdrop an almost documentary narrative which has been imaginatively directed by Joseph M. Newman
with punchy overtones.

Feature is marked by standout portrayals of
a hand-picked cast who insert forceful realism into natural characterizations. Gary
Merrill, a police captain who had passed his
bar exams and is about to leave the force, is
prevailed upon to head the notorious Heights
district of the city, where conditions have
reached the point that no one is safe. In his
revitalization of his department and attempts
to solve a murder he meets with opposition
both from some of his own men and those
above him, but finally cracks the case and
whips the district into shape.

Merrill gives true meaning to his part and
Jan Sterling belts over the role of a tough
blonde who is used as an alibi by Chuck Connors, excellent in his characterizing of the
murderer.

■ **HUMANOIDS FROM THE DEEP**

1980, 80 MINS, US ◇ ⓥ

Dir Barbara Peeters *Prod* Martin B. Cohen, Hunt
Lowry *Scr* Frederick James *Ph* Daniele Lacambre
Ed Mark Goldblatt *Mus* James Horner
Art Dir Michael Erler
● Doug McClure, Ann Turkel, Vic Morrow, Cindy
Weintraub (New World)

With *Humanoids from the Deep*, Roger Corman
comes full circle back to his very first film as a
producer, *Monster from the Ocean Floor* [1954]
Despite costing 100 times as much, new pic
has similar premise and same raison d'etre,
that of pocketing a profit from drive-in dates.

Tried-and-true formula of countless
sci-fiers of the 1950s is revived as gruesome,
amphibious creatures rise from the ocean to
stalk and destroy terrified humans. General
pattern here has monsters systematically
killing the guys and raping the girls.

Given the nonsensical script and fact that
considerable footage was added, editor Mark
Goldblatt did a good job in making disparate
elements at least hang together and play
coherently. James Horner's score makes it
seem that more is happening than actually
takes place.

■ **HUMORESQUE**

1946, 123 MINS, US

Dir Jean Negulesco *Prod* Jerry Wald *Scr* Clifford
Odets, Zachary Gold *Ph* Ernest Haller *Ed* Rudi
Fehr *Mus* Franz Waxman *Art Dir* Hugh Reticker
● Joan Crawford, John Garfield (Warner)

Humoresque combines classical music and
drama into a top quality motion picture. A
score of unusual excellence gives freshness to
standard classics and plays as important a
part as Fannie Hurst's familiar story of a
young violinist who rises to concert heights
from the lower East Side of New York. Technically a remake (it was first produced in

1920) this version is virtually a new story,
stripped of any racial connotations as was the
case originally. Footage is long, running more
than two hours, but does not drag because of
the score potency and performance quality.

Integration of music and drama ties the two
together so tightly there is never a separation.
Some 23 classical numbers are included, plus
a number of pop pieces used as background
for cafe sequences.

Principal footage goes to John Garfield as
the young violinist who, encouraged by his
mother's interest, devotes his life to music.
He turns in a distinguished, thoroughly
believable performance. Adding to the effectiveness is the nigh-flawless fingering and
bowing during the violin shots. Joan Crawford's role is an acting part, rather than a typical femme star assignment, and she makes
the most of it.

■ **HUNCHBACK OF NOTRE DAME, THE**

1923, 135 MINS, US ⊗ ⓥ

Dir Wallace Worsley *Scr* Edward T. Lowe, Perley
Poore Sheehan *Ph* Robert Newhard, Tony Kornman
Art Dir E.E. Sheeley, Sydney Ullman, Stephen Goosson
● Lon Chaney, Ernest Torrence, Patsy Ruth Miller,
Norman Kerry, Kate Lester, Brandon Hurst (Universal
Super-Jewel)

The programmed statistical recordings say
this picture cost U over a million; that it
called for tons of materials and hundreds of
people, all sounding truthful enough (except
the cost) after seeing it and the total achieved
seems to have been a huge – mistake. *The
Hunchback of Notre Dame* [from the novel by
Victor Hugo] is a two-hour nightmare. It's
murderous, hideous and repulsive.

Lon Chaney's performance as a performance entitles him to starring honors. His mis-
shapened figure from the hump on his back to
the deadeyed eye on his face cannot stand off
his acting nor his acrobatics, nor his general
work of excellence throughout this film. And,
when the hunchbank dies, you see Jehan
(Brandon Hurst) stab him not once, but
twice, and in the back or in the hump.

Knives were plentiful in the reign of Louis
XI, 1482, in France. So were the tramps,
with Clopin (Ernest Torrence) as King of the
Bums making the misery stand out.

Patsy Ruth Miller is Esmeralda, a sweetly
pretty girl carrying her troubles nicely
enough for the heavy work thrust upon her
and with the absence of heavy emoting. Norman Kerry is the gallant Phoebus and a luke-
warm lover at times.

■ **HUNCHBACK OF NOTRE DAME, THE**

1939, 115 MINS, US ⓥ

Dir William Dieterle *Prod* Pandro S. Berman
Scr Sonya Levien *Ph* Joseph H. August *Ed* William
Hamilton, Robert Wise *Mus* Alfred Newman *Art
Dir* Van Nest Polglase, Al Herman
● Charles Laughton, Cedric Hardwicke, Maureen
O'Hara, Thomas Mitchell, Edmond O'Brien (RKO)

Parading vivid and gruesome horror, with
background of elaborate medieval pageantry
and mob scenes, *Hunchback of Notre Dame* is a
super thriller-chiller.

From a strictly critical viewpoint, picture
has its shortcomings. The elaborate sets and
wide production sweep overshadows to a
great extent the detailed dramatic motivation
of the Victor Hugo tale. While the background is impressive and eye-filling, it
detracts many times from the story, especially in the first half.

Supporting cast is studded with topnotch
performers for each role. Cedric Hardwicke is
the villainous King's High Justice; Thomas
Mitchell is the king of the beggars; Maureen
O'Hara (excellent) is the gypsy girl who befriends the hunchback on the pillory and is
saved by him later.

Production displays lavish outlay in costs for elaborate sets and thousands of extras for the mob scenes.

••••••••••••••••••••••••••••••••••••••

■ HUNCHBACK OF NOTRE DAME, THE

1957, 103 MINS, US ◇ Ⓥ

Dir Jean Delannoy   *Prod* Robert Hakim, Raymond Hakim   *Scr* Jean Aurenche, Jacques Prevert   *Ph* Michel Kelber   *Ed* Henri Taverna   *Mus* Georges Auric   *Art Dir* Rene Renoux

● Gina Lollobrigida, Anthony Quinn, Jean Danet, Alain Cuny, Maurice Sarfati, Danielle Dumont (Allied Artists)

This version of the Victor Hugo classic, although beautifully photographed and extravagantly produced, is ponderous, often dull and far overlength.

Gina Lollobrigida is co-starred with Anthony Quinn, who plays the Quasimodo role previously enacted by Lon Chaney and Charles Laughton. Producers seem more inclined to offer spectacle than concentrate on pointing up story line with any degree of freshness.

Lollobrigida appears to be somewhat miscast as a naive gypsy girl of 15th-century Paris, but occasionally displays flashes of spirit. Quinn, as the hunchbacked bellringer of Notre Dame who saves the gypsy girl from hanging and hides her within the sanctuary of the cathedral, where he becomes her devoted slave, gives a well-etched impression of the difficult role. His makeup is not as extreme as either of the two previous characterizations.

••••••••••••••••••••••••••••••••••••••

■ HUNGER, THE

1983, 97 MINS, US ◇ Ⓥ

Dir Tony Scott   *Prod* Richard Shepherd   *Scr* Ivan Davis, Michael Thomas   *Ph* Stephen Goldblatt   *Ed* Pamela Power   *Mus* Michel Rubini, Denny Jaeger   *Art Dir* Brian Morris

● Catherine Deneuve, David Bowie, Susan Sarandon, Cliff De Young, Beth Ehlers, Dan Hedaya (Richard Shepherd/M-G-M/United Artists)

Like so many other films from British commercials directors, *The Hunger* is all visual and aural flash, although this modern vampire story looks so great, as do its three principal performers, and is so bizarre that it possesses a certain perverse appeal.

Opening sequence provides viewers with a pretty good idea of what's in store. Catherine Deneuve and David Bowie pick up a couple of punky rock 'n' rollers. Deneuve and Bowie commit a double murder in their elegantly appointed New York apartment, and the prevailing motif of sex mixed with bloody death is established.

Although Deneuve and Bowie privately vow to stay with one another forever, Bowie soon notices himself growing rapidly older and visits author-doctor Susan Sarandon, who is preoccupied with the problem of accelerated aging. Shunned by her, Bowie deteriorates quickly and Deneuve buries him in a box in her attic next to her previous lovers.

Distraught over her mistreatment of Bowie, Sarandon begins visiting Deneuve, and a provative highlight is their seduction and lovemaking scene.

In his feature debut, director Tony Scott, brother of Ridley, exhibits the same penchant for elaborate art direction, minimal, humorless dialog and shooting in smoky rooms.

••••••••••••••••••••••••••••••••••••••

■ HUNTER, THE

1980, 117 MINS, US ◇ Ⓥ

Dir Buzz Kulik   *Prod* Mort Engelberg   *Scr* Ted Leighton, Peter Hyams   *Ph* Fred J. Koenekamp   *Ed* Robert Wolfe   *Mus* Michel Legrand   *Art Dir* Ron Hobbs

● Steve McQueen, Eli Wallach, Kathryn Harrold, Ben Johnson (Paramount/Rastar/Mort Engelberg)

Fact that the overlong pic is based on adventures of a modern-day bounty hunter may have hampered filmmakers' imagination, as attempt to render contradictions of real-life Ralph 'Papa' Thorson, who's into classical music and astrology as well as hauling in fugitives from justice, has made for an annoyingly unrealized and childish onscreen character.

Steve McQueen may have felt that the time had come to revise his persona a bit, but what's involved here is desecration. Given star's rep since *Bullitt* as a terrific driver, someone thought it might be cute to make him a lousy one here, but seeing him crash stupidly into car after car runs the gag into the ground. *The Hunter* [based on the book by Christopher Keane] is a western in disguise.

Only sequence which remotely delivers the goods has McQueen chasing a gun-toting maniac in Chicago. Pic's finale, which has star fainting when pregnant g.f. Kathryn Harrold gives birth, merely puts capper on overall misconception.

••••••••••••••••••••••••••••••••••••••

■ HUNT FOR RED OCTOBER, THE

1990, 137 MINS, US ◇ Ⓥ

Dir John McTiernan   *Prod* Mace Neufeld   *Scr* Larry Ferguson, Donald Stewart   *Ph* Jan De Bont   *Ed* Dennis Virkler, John Wright   *Mus* Basil Poledouris   *Art Dir* Terence Marsh

● Sean Connery, Alec Baldwin, Scott Glenn, Sam Neill, James Earl Jones, Joss Ackland (Paramount)

The Hunt for Red October is a terrific adventure yarn. Tom Clancy's 1984 Cold War thriller has been thoughtfully adapted to reflect the mellowing in the US-Soviet relationship.

Sean Connery is splendid as the renegade Soviet nuclear sub captain pursued by CIA analyst Alec Baldwin and the fleets of both superpowers as he heads for the coast of Maine. The filmmakers have wisely opted to keep the story set in 1984 – 'shortly before Gorbachev came to power', as the opening title puts it.

Looking magnificent in his captain's uniform and white beard, Connery scores as the Lithuanian Marko Ramius, a coldblooded killer and a meditator on Hindu scripture.

Baldwin's intelligent and likable performance makes his Walter Mittyish character come alive. He's combating not only the bulk of the Soviet fleet but also the reflexive anti-Communist mentality of most pursuing on the US side – not including his wise and avuncular CIA superior James Earl Jones.

The Industrial Light & Magic special visual effects unit does yeoman work in staging the action with cliffhanger intensity.

••••••••••••••••••••••••••••••••••••••

■ HUNTING PARTY, THE

1971, 108 MINS, UK ◇

Dir Don Medford   *Prod* Lou Morheim   *Scr* William Norton, Gilbert Alexander, Lou Morheim   *Ph* Cecilio Paniagua   *Ed* Tom Rolf   *Mus* Riz Ortolani   *Art Dir* Enrique Alarcon

● Oliver Reed, Candice Bergen, Gene Hackman, Simon Oakland, G.D. Spradling, Bernard Kay (United Artists)

It isn't as hard to believe that excellent actors Oliver Reed and Gene Hackman would accept roles like those they are given in *The Hunting Party* because they were undoubtedly well paid (indeed, overpaid, considering the performances they give). But to find such fine supporting players as Mitchell Ryan, Simon Oakland and Dean Selmier in this minor effort is really surprising.

Basically, Reed (who's illiterate) and his gang, kidnap a teacher (Candice Bergen) who turns out to be the wife of the local cattlebaron (Gene Hackman), who is out on

a hunting party with some other millionaire friends. When he hears the news, Hackman starts a search for the gang, armed with new high-power rifles capable of killing from 800 yards. One by one the gang is picked off from a safe distance until the eventual showdown with only Hackman trailing Reed and Bergen (by now in love with the outlaw, of course) onto a desert.

Seldom has so much fake blood been splattered for so little reason.

••••••••••••••••••••••••••••••••••••••

■ HURRICANE

1979, 119 MINS, US ◇ Ⓥ

Dir Jan Troell   *Prod* Dino De Laurentiis   *Scr* Lorenzo Semple Jr   *Ph* Sven Nykvist   *Ed* Sam O'Steen   *Mus* Nino Rota   *Art Dir* Danilo Donati

● Jason Robards, Mia Farrow, Max Von Sydow, Trevor Howard, Dayton Ka'ne, Timothy Bottoms (Paramount/De Laurentiis)

The storm blows fiercely but the love story doesn't match its power in *Hurricane*. Dino De Laurentiis' epic reportedly delivered with a $22 million negative cost.

Charles Nordhoff and James Norman Hall's novel, *The Hurricane*, was filmed relatively faithfully in 1937 by John Ford.

The context and conflicts in the new production have been altered significantly. Script sets the tale in Eastern Samoa, circa 1920, with Jason Robards lording it over the natives on behalf of the US navy. The female love interest is now a white woman, with Mia Farrow sailing in from Boston to see her commander father, but gradually becoming involved with the young chieftain of a nearby island (Dayton Ka'ne).

The hurricane itself, which runs 25 minutes and was created entirely on location in Bora Bora by a special effects team led by Glen Robinson, who performed the same function on the 1937 production, Aldo Puccini and Joe Day, is impressive enough.

••••••••••••••••••••••••••••••••••••••

■ HURRICANE, THE

1937, 110 MINS, US Ⓥ

Dir John Ford   *Prod* Samuel Goldwyn   *Scr* Dudley Nichols, Oliver H.P. Garrett   *Ph* Bert Glennon   *Ed* Lloyd Nosler   *Mus* Alfred Newman   *Art Dir* Richard Dan, Alexander Golitzen

● Dorothy Lamour, Jon Hall, Mary Astor, C. Aubrey Smith, Thomas Mitchell, Raymond Massey (Goldwyn/United Artists)

Turned out on a broad canvas, *The Hurricane* is a scenically pretentious and colorful spectacle which has as its climax a hurricane sequence that is compellingly realistic. The authors of the novel, Charles Nordhoff and James Norman Hall, also wrote the story of *Mutiny on the Bounty*.

The force of the story does not stop with the hurricane triumph nor the brutality of prison officers, pictured as worse than ever accredited to Devil's Island. neither does it stop with the successful dramatic escape of the romantic lead (Jon Hall) amidst frightful odds. There is also a highly emotional love story woven around Hall and Dorothy Lamour, latter playing the native girl who marries him as the picture opens.

The big blow is reputed to cost $300,000. That's not unbelievable. It is understood the total cost of the picture ran to $1.75 million.

Performances are specially good from Hall down. A finely turned character is that of the governor, another Javert (*Les Miserables*), done capitally and forcefully by Raymond Massey.

••••••••••••••••••••••••••••••••••••••

■ HURRY SUNDOWN

1967, 146 MINS, US ◇

Dir Otto Preminger   *Prod* Otto Preminger   *Scr* Thomas C. Ryan, Horton Foote   *Ph* Milton Krasner, Loyal Griggs   *Ed* Louis Loeffler, James D. Wells

Mus Hugo Montenegro   *Art Dir* Gene Callahan
● Michael Caine, Jane Fonda, John Phillip Law, Diahann Carroll, Faye Dunaway, Burgess Meredith (Paramount/Sigma)

In *Hurry Sundown*, based on the novel [by K.B. Gilden], producer-director Otto Preminger has created an outstanding, tasteful but hard-hitting, and handsomely-produced film about racial conflict in Georgia circa 1945. Told with a depth and frankness, the story develops its theme in a welcome, straightforward way that is neither propaganda nor mere exploitation material. Cast with many younger players, all of whom deliver fine performances.

Michael Caine leads the stars, and delivers an excellent performance as the white social climber managing the Georgia land holdings of wife Jane Fonda.

Two tracts block Caine's plans, those of distant relative John Phillip Law and Negro Robert Hooks, both just-returned war vets.

....

■ HUSBANDS

1970, 154 MINS, US ◇
Dir John Cassavetes   *Prod* Al Ruban, Sam Shaw   *Scr* John Cassavetes   *Ph* Victor Kemper   *Ed* Peter Tanner
● Ben Gazzara, Peter Falk, John Cassavetes, Jenny Runacre, Jenny Lee Wright, Noelle Kao (Columbia)

Appalled and horrified by the death of their best friend, three middleclass, not-quite-middleaged family men explode and ricochet off on a marathon New York-to-London binge.

Director-writer-actor John Cassavetes, Ben Gazzara and Peter Falk are the 'husbands', who, in the face of death, revert to drunken, giggling, horseplaying adolescence, and, with a stunningly-talented supporting cast, create and improvise a memorably touching, human and very funny film.

Fleeing from the beer foam and grime of a lower New York bar in a sudden panicked flight to London, Cassavetes, Falk and Gazzara are three of the uncoolest married men to ever go on the make.

In a superb cast, Jenny Runacre, a tall lovely blonde English girl gives a touching performance as Cassavetes' neurotic pick-up.

....

■ HUSH ... HUSH, SWEET CHARLOTTE

1964, 134 MINS, US ▼
Dir Robert Aldrich   *Prod* Robert Aldrich   *Scr* Henry Farrell, Lukas Heller   *Ph* Joseph Biroc   *Ed* Michael Luciano   *Mus* Frank DeVol   *Art Dir* William Glasgow
● Bette Davis, Olivia de Havilland, Joseph Cotten, Agnes Moorehead, Cecil Kellaway, Mary Astor (20th Century-Fox)

Robert Aldrich's followup (but no relation) to *What Ever Happened to Baby Jane?* is a shocker. Bette Davis again stars, with Olivia de Havilland returning to the screen in the role which Joan Crawford started but due to continued illness had to abandon.

Davis lives in the reflection of a dreadful past, the macabre murder and mutilation of her married lover hanging over her as she frequently confuses the past with the present as her mental balance is threatened. De Havilland, as her cousin, lives very much for the present – and future – as she attempts to soothe and rationalize with the deeply emotional mistress of the house.

Based upon a story by Henry Farrell, who also authored *Baby Jane*, screenplay by Farrell and Lukas Heller (latter scripted *Jane*) opens in 1927 in the Louisiana plantation house of Davis' father, who warns a neighboring married man to break off all romantic relations with his daughter. The main story swings to the present, again in the mansion where Davis lives alone with her memories which threaten to destroy her.

Davis' portrayal is reminiscent of *Jane* in its emotional overtones, in her style of characterization of the near-crazed former Southern belle, aided by haggard makeup and outlandish attire. It is an outgoing performance, and she plays it to the limit. De Havilland, on the other hand, is far more restrained but none the less effective dramatically in her offbeat role.

....

■ HUSSY

1980, 95 MINS, UK ◇ ▼
Dir Matthew Chapman   *Prod* Jeremy Watt   *Scr* Matthew Chapman   *Ph* Keith Goddard   *Ed* Bill Blunden   *Mus* George Fenton   *Art Dir* Hazel Peiser
● Helen Mirren, John Shea, Jenny Runacre, Murray Salem, Paul Angelis (Kendon)

Somewhere in scripter-director Matthew Chapman's first feature there's a valid love story trying to get out. It stays buried for lack of an objective eye – that of an experienced producer, perhaps – to see the pitfalls of an acceptably lightweight project that strives for serious significance.

John Shea's performance as Helen Mirren's lover, a transient American working as spotlight operator at the London stripjoint where she hosts and hooks is mostly bland, but occasionally effective in hinting at a murkier past than his guileless looks suggest. Mirren would have come off better had she been directed towards a less ponderous conception of the role.

Neither lead is helped by dialog which badly needed that ruthless impartial eye; as it is, there are some leaden, even laughable, moments.

....

■ HUSTLE

1975, 120 MINS, US ◇
Dir Robert Aldrich   *Prod* Robert Aldrich   *Scr* Steve Shagan   *Ph* Joseph Biroc   *Ed* Michael Luciano   *Mus* Frank DeVol   *Art Dir* Hilyard Brown
● Burt Reynolds, Catherine Deneuve, Ben Johnson, Paul Winfield, Eileen Brennan, Eddie Albert (Paramount)

Rober Aldrich's sharp-looking film reunites him with Burt Reynolds, starring here as a hardening detective trying to short circuit the solution of a femme teenager's dope suicide because the trail may lead to Eddie Albert, a noted lawyer with many uptown and downtown connections.

Reynolds is torn between his duty and his personal attraction-resistance to mistress Catherine Deneuve.

Ben Johnson and Eileen Brennan are the parents of the dead girl, and Johnson on his own doggedly tracks down clues which explode some darker family secrets while goading Reynolds into frantic coverup action.

The film's drawbacks are simply a lack of some restraint, since otherwise all the elements are present for a sensational, hard-hitting human story.

....

■ HUSTLER, THE

1961, 134 MINS, US ▼
Dir Robert Rossen   *Prod* Robert Rossen   *Scr* Robert Rossen, Sidney Carroll   *Ph* Gene Shufton   *Ed* Dede Allen   *Mus* Kenyon Hopkins   *Art Dir* Harry Horner, Albert Brenner
● Paul Newman, Jackie Gleason, Piper Laurie, George C. Scott, Myron McCormick, Murray Hamilton (20th Century-Fox)

The Hustler belongs to that school of screen realism that allows impressive performances but defeats the basic goal of pure entertainment.

Film is peopled by a set of unpleasant characters set down against a backdrop of cheap pool halls and otherwise dingy surroundings. Chief protagonist is Paul Newman, a pool

shark with a compulsion to be the best of the lot – not in tournament play but in beating Chicago's bigtime player (Jackie Gleason). Unfoldment of the screenplay, based on novel by Walter S. Tevis, is far overlength, and despite the excellence of Newman's portrayal of the boozing pool hustler the sordid aspects of overall picture are strictly downbeat.

Newman is entirely believable in the means he takes to defeat Gleason, and latter socks over a dramatic role, which, though comparatively brief, generates potency. In some respects, the quiet strength of his characterization overshadows Newman in their scenes together. Piper Laurie establishes herself solidly as a hard-drinking floosie who lives with Newman, and George C. Scott scores as a gambler who promotes Newman and teaches him the psychology of being a winner.

□ 1961: Best Picture (Nomination)

....

■ I ACCUSE!

1958, 99 MINS, UK
Dir Jose Ferrer   *Prod* Sam Zimbalist   *Scr* Gore Vidal   *Ph* Freddie A. Young   *Ed* Frank Clarke   *Mus* William Alwyn   *Art Dir* Elliot Scott
● Jose Ferrer, Anton Walbrook, Viveca Lindfors, Leo Genn, Emlyn Williams, David Farrar (M-G-M)

This version of the drama of the Dreyfus case, one of the greatest miscarriages of justice in history, makes strong, if plodding, entertainment.

The story concerns the plight of a Jewish staff officer of the French army who is unjustly accused of treason, found guilty through being framed to save the army's face, and condemned to life imprisonment on Devil's Island. Friends fighting to restore his tarnished honor force a re-trial.

Jose Ferrer takes on the heavy task of playing Dreyfus and of directing. His performance is a wily, impeccable one, but it comes from the intellect rather than the heart and rarely causes pity. He makes Dreyfus a staid, almost fanatical patriot. The action is throughout rather static, but the court scenes are pregnant with drama, thanks to a literate screenplay by Gore Vidal [from a book by Nicholas Halasz].

Anton Walbrook, the real culprit, gives a splendid performance – suave, debonair and fascinating. And equally impressive is Donald Wolfit as the army's top guy who claims that the honor of the French army is more important than the fate of one man.

....

■ I AM A FUGITIVE FROM A CHAIN GANG

1932, 93 MINS, US ▼
Dir Mervyn LeRoy   *Prod* Hal B. Wallis   *Scr* Sheridan Gibney, Brown Holmes   *Ph* Sol Polito   *Ed* William Holmes   *Mus* Leo Forbstein (dir.)   *Art Dir* Jack Okey
● Paul Muni, Glenda Farrell, Helen Vinson, Preston Foster, Edward J. McNamara (Warner)

I Am a Fugitive from a Chain Gang is a picture with guts. It grips with its stark realism and packs lots of punch.

It's a sympathetic, unbiased cinematic transposition of the Robert E. Burns autobiography.

Paul Muni breaks away from the chain gang twice. In between he achieves success in his preferred field of engineering until a romantic angle prompts him voluntarily to surrender as the wanted fugitive, on the promise and belief he will be pardoned in 90 days. The prison board stalls that, despite influential appeals, leading into the second break away from the chain gang. The finale is stark in its realism.

Muni turns in a pip performance. Glenda Farrell and Helen Vinson, the only two femmes of any prominence, are oke in their parts. Hale Hamilton as an overly benign and saccharine rev, the brother of the escaped convict, is an especial click in the characterization.

□ 1932/33: Best Picture (Nomination)

························

■ **ICE CASTLES**

1978, 113 MINS, US ◇ ▽

Dir Donald Wrye *Prod* John Kemeny *Scr* Donald Wrye, Gary L. Bain *Ph* Bill Butler *Ed* Michael Kahn, Maury Winetrobe, Melvin Shapiro *Mus* Marvin Hamlisch *Art Dir* Joel Schiller

● Lynn-Holly Johnson, Robby Benson, Colleen Dewhurst, Tom Skerritt, Jennifer Warren, David Huffman (Columbia)

Ice Castles combines a touching love story with the excitement and intense pressure of Olympic competition skating.

Lynn-Holly Johnson portrays a farm girl from upstate Iowa who has the raw talent to be a great skater. Under the training and encouragement of local ice rink operator Colleen Dewhurst, she wins a regional competition, where she is spotted by Olympic coach Jennifer Warren.

Warren propels Johnson to instant stardom as a Cinderella figure who comes out of nowhere to win the hearts of the American people. All is progressing smoothly until Johnson has a freak accident, and is partially blinded. Robby Benson, who plays Johnson's boyfriend, and Tom Skerritt, her father, bring the teenager out of her shell, leading up to the inspiring ending.

Dewhurst, who appears all too infrequently in pix, excels in her role as the hard-bitten ex-skater trying not to live out her failed dreams through Johnson. Skerritt gives another outstanding perf as the overly-protective father who also realizes his failings. Johnson shows the potential of being an excellent actress, in addition to a top skater. She is consistently believable, even in the more maudlin moments.

························

■ **ICE COLD IN ALEX**

1958, 132 MINS, UK ▽

Dir J. Lee Thompson *Prod* W.A. Whittaker *Scr* T.J. Morrison, Christopher Landon *Ph* Gilbert Taylor *Ed* Richard Best *Mus* Leighton Lucas *Art Dir* Robert Jones

● John Mills, Sylvia Syms, Anthony Quayle, Harry Andrews, Diane Clare, Peter Arne (Associated British)

Based on a slight, real-life anecdote, pic [from Christopher Landon's novel] is the story of a handful of people who drive an ambulance through the mine-ridden, enemy-occupied desert after the collapse of Tobruk in 1942.

There are a nerve-strained officer who has taken to the bottle, his tough, reliable sergeant-major, a couple of nurses and a South African officer. Director J. Lee Thompson captures the stark, pitiless atmosphere of the desert superbly. The screenplay skillfully blends excitement, a hint of romance and a fearful sense of danger.

John Mills is the skipper, strained to the limit, who seeks solace in a few swift swigs. This is a credible, edgy performance. Anthony Quayle, as the South African, has a suspect accent but brings a plausible charm to the role. Harry Andrews is first-rate as the sergeant-major. Stripped of any glamor, Sylvia Syms fits snugly into the plot. Diane Clare, a newcomer, plays a frightened nurse who gets bumped off half way through the film.

■ **ICE STATION ZEBRA**

1968, 152 MINS, US ◇ ▽

Dir John Sturges *Prod* Martin Ransohoff *Scr* Douglas Heyes *Ph* Daniel L. Fapp *Ed* Ferris Webster *Mus* Michel Legrand *Art Dir* George W. Davis, Addison Hehr

● Rock Hudson, Ernest Borgnine, Patrick McGoohan, Jim Brown, Tony Bill (M-G-M/Filmways)

Action adventure film, in which US and Russian forces race to recover some compromising satellite photography from a remote Polar outpost. Alistair MacLean's novel adapted into a screen story is seeded with elements of intrigue, as Rock Hudson takes aboard a British secret agent, Patrick McGoohan; an expatriate, professional anti-Communist Russian, Ernest Borgnine; and an enigmatic Marine Corps captain, Jim Brown.

Action develops slowly, alternating with some excellent submarine interior footage, and good shots – of diving, surfacing and maneuvering under an ice field.

Film's biggest acting asset is McGoohan, who gives his scenes that elusive 'star' magnetism. He is a most accomplished actor with a three-dimensional presence all his own.

Hudson comes across quite well as a man of muted strength. Borgnine's characterization is a nicely restrained one. Brown, isolated by script to a suspicious personality, makes the most of it.

························

■ **I CONFESS**

1953, 95 MINS, US ▽

Dir Alfred Hitchcock *Prod* Alfred Hitchcock *Scr* George Tabori, William Archibald *Ph* Robert Burks *Ed* Rudi Fehr *Mus* Dimitri Tiomkin *Art Dir* Edward S. Haworth

● Montgomery Clift, Anne Baxter, Karl Malden, Brian Aherne, O.E. Hasse, Roger Dann (Warner)

An interesting plot premise holds out considerable promise for this Alfred Hitchcock production, but *I Confess* is short of the suspense one would expect. Hitchcock used the actual streets and buildings of picturesque Quebec to film the Paul Anthelme play on which the screenplay is based.

Intriguing story idea finds a priest facing trial for a murder he didn't commit, and refusing to clear himself even though the killer had confessed to him in the sanctity of the church. Quite a moral question is posed in the problem of just how sacred is a church confessional, particularly when it leaves a killer to roam free to kill again.

Chief exponents of the melodrama are Montgomery Clift, the priest, and Anne Baxter, a married woman who still believes she is in love with him, even though he ended their youthful romance and entered the church.

While Hitchcock short-changes on the expected round of suspense for which he is noted, he does bring out a number of top-flight performances and gives the picture an interesting polish that is documentary at times. Clift's ability to project mood with restrained strength is a high spot of the film, and he is believable as the young priest. Physically, he doesn't have as mature an appearance as the role opposite Baxter calls for, but otherwise, his work is flawless.

························

■ **I COVER THE WATERFRONT**

1933, 72 MINS, US

Dir James Cruze *Scr* Wells Root, Jack Jevne *Ph* Ray June *Ed* Grant Whytock

● Claudette Colbert, Ben Lyon, Ernest Torrence, Hobart Cavanaugh, Maurice Black (United Artists)

Rather than an adaption of the Max Miller book, this is a homemade studio yarn carrying the original's title.

Around Ernest Torrence's Eli Kirk, a deep-sea skipper and smuggler who has few scru-

ples, except those concerning his daughter, the scenarist has built a fable that manages to keep some of Miller's waterfront-reporting color alive, but much of it accomplished by the exaggeration route. Ben Lyon, as the reporter, is still another legman who calls his editor names on the phone and in the office, but holds his job anyway. For years he's been promising a sensational expose on Kirk's activities and finally he delivers. Kirk is caught while landing Chinamen inside shark skins.

Meanwhile Lyon and Claudette Colbert, Kirk's unsuspecting daughter, carry on a hot love affair, including a night at Lyon's apartment, with the customary breakfast in the a.m. Lyon originally intended to get Kirk through his daughter, but he falls in love, which is a cinch to see in advance, as is the finish.

························

■ **IDEAL HUSBAND, AN**

1947, 96 MINS, UK ◇ ▽

Dir Alexander Karda *Prod* Alexander Karda *Scr* Lajos Biro *Ph* Georges Perinal *Ed* Oscar Hafenrichter *Mus* Arthur Benjamin *Art Dir* Vincent Korda

● Paulette Goddard, Michael Wilding, Hugh Williams, Diana Wynyard, C. Aubrey Smith, Glynis Johns (British Lion)

This version of the Oscar Wilde 1895 play is given handsome mounting by Alexander Korda. Yet he could do little more than put the play on the screen, stage asides and all.

Story relates how Hugh Williams, under-secretary of the foreign office and marked for a Cabinet post, in his youth profited by selling a Cabinet secret about the Suez Canal, thereby founding his fortune and his political career. Arrival of Paulette Goddard, an adventuress and old school friend of his wife complicates matters. She knows about Williams' misdeed and threatens him with exposure if he doesn't support a phony Argentine canal scheme in parliament.

At first he agrees, but his wife, Diana Wynyard, persuades him to refuse. It looks like the end of his career and marriage, until his best friend, Michael Wilding, takes a hand.

It seems a brave experiment to cast Goddard as the adventuress. But it doesn't quite come off. Not a solitary epigram is thrown off with spontaneity, and her loveliness in gorgeous costumes is inadequate compensation.

························

■ **IDOLMAKER, THE**

1980, 107 MINS, US ◇ ▽

Dir Taylor Hackford *Prod* Gene Kirkwood, Howard W. Koch Jr *Scr* Edward Di Lorenzo *Ph* Adam Holender *Ed* Neil Travis *Mus* Jeff Barry *Art Dir* David L. Snyder

● Ray Sharkey, Paul Land, Olympia Dukakis, Peter Gallagher (United Artists)

Though it's marred by an overly melodramatic and dubious finale, *The Idolmaker* is an unusually compelling film about the music business in the late 1950s and early 1960s. It shows how teen idols were created, promoted, and discarded by entrepreneurs cynically manipulating the adolescent audience. Ray Sharkey is superb in the title role.

Script is a roman-a-clef of the career of Bob Marcucci who, along with Dick Clark, guided Frankie Avalon to stardom and then created Fabian as Avalon's successor.

Viewers will have no trouble recognizing Paul Land as the Avalon figure or Peter Gallagher as Fabian.

All of the elements are shown in believable detail, though the payola and organized crime elements of the record industry are not indicated on the higher levels, an unfortunate omission.

························

■ I DON'T WANT TO BE BORN

1975, 90 MINS, UK ◇ ⓥ
Dir Peter Sasdy *Scr* Stanley Price *Ph* Kenneth
Talbot *Ed* Keith Palmer *Mus* Ron Grainer
Art Dir Roy Stannard
● Joan Collins, Eileen Atkins, Donald Pleasence, Ralph
Bates, Caroline Munro, Hilary Mason (Unicapital)

This is an exceedingly stylish thriller about
a satanically possessed infant, Joan Collins'
abnormally strong newborn son, who inflicts
scratches on cribside visitors, and wreaks
havoc on his room when no one is around.

After a succession of bizarre occurrences,
including the mysterious death of the baby's
nursemaid, a frantic Collins (looking and acting splendidly as the begrieved mother) and
her Italian husband, nicely played by horror
vet Ralph Bates, turn to doctor Donald Pleasence for the answers, then to Bates' nun sister (Eileen Atkins, in a striking performance).

Director Peter Sasdy, works as much below
the surface as above it with great effect.
There are plenty of shots of the sweetest baby
imaginable, followed with shots of the
violence it apparently perpetrated, showing
only the terrified victims.

■ I DREAM OF JEANIE

1952, 90 MINS, US ◇
Dir Allan Dwan *Prod* Allan Dwan *Scr* Alan Le May
Ph Reggie Lanning *Ed* Fred Allen *Mus* Robert
Armbruster (adapt.) *Art Dir* Frank Hotaling
● Ray Middleton, Bill Shirley, Muriel Lawrence, Eileen
Christy, Richard Simmons, Rex Allen (Republic)

A pseudo-biopic around the life and songs of
Stephen Foster gets a pretentious treatment.

Foster's folksy tune-smithing is featured in
21 of his cleffings that are used for the musical portions. Picture could have used a script
and performances to match the singing.

The formula plot shows young Foster as a
dreamer who makes nothing from his music
until his business-like brother takes over. An
unrequited love affair finally causes Foster to
run away but he is pursued by another
femme named Jeanie and when she catches
up with him he realizes she's the girl, and
thus the title tune is born.

Bill Shirley plays Foster, tenoring 'Oh Susanna', 'Old Dog Tray', 'Camptown Races'
and others. Eileen Christy is the vivacious
Jeanie who gets Foster. Among her songs is 'I
See Her Still in My Dreams' with Shirley.

■ IF....

1968, 110 MINS, UK ◇ ⓥ
Dir Lindsay Anderson *Prod* Michael Medwin, Lindsay
Anderson *Scr* David Sherwin *Ph* Miroslav
Ondricek *Ed* David Gladwell *Mus* Marc Wilkinson
Art Dir Jocelyn Herbert
● Malcolm McDowell, David Wood, Richard Warwick,
Christine Noonan, Robert Swann, Peter Jeffrey
(Memorial)

Punchy, poetic pic that delves into the epic
theme of youthful revolt.

if.... is ostensibly about a rigid tradition-
ridden British private boarding school for
boys from 11 to 18. The film blocks out a
series of incidents that lead to a small group
rebelling with mortars, machine guns, gas
bombs and pistols.

Film is divided into chapter headings as the
boys arrive for a new term.

The teachers, nurses, housemasters, etc.,
are all fairly typed characters but never descend to caricatures, which is true of the many
students.

There is a romantic dash during the early
part of the film in the growing insistence of
three rebel friends that all is not right in this
caste-ridden school. But there is never any
sentimentality, which makes the film's veering to a bloody revolt acceptable.

Film is a generalized tale of revolt. The
violence is symbolical and reflects and comments on it rather than sentimentalizing it or
trying to make it realistic.

■ IF I HAD A MILLION

1932, 85 MINS, US
Dir Ernst Lubitsch, Norman Taurog, Stephen Roberts,
Norman McLeod, James Cruze, William A. Seiter, H.
Bruce Humberstone *Scr* Claude Binyon, Whitney
Bolton, Malcolm Stuart Boylan, John Bright, Sidney
Buchman, Lester Cole, Isabel Dawn, Boyce DeGaw,
Walter De Leon, Oliver H. P. Garrett, Harvey Gates,
Grover Jones, Ernst Lubitsch, Lawton Mackall, Joseph L.
Mankiewicz, William Slavens McNutt, Seton I. Miller,
Tiffany Thayer
● Charles Laughton, W. C. Fields, Charlie Ruggles,
George Raft, Wynne Gibson, Richard Bennett
(Paramount)

The episodes depicting what certain individuals would do if they had $1 million are not
without their moments, some, of course, more
effective than others. With so many cooks
concerned, this cinematic porridge is naturally replete with a diversity of seasonings.
Just who's responsible for which sequence
isn't disclosed, although the scene with
Charles Laughton giving his boss a lusty
Bronx cheer, upon becoming one of the
beneficiaries, is said to be 100% Ernst
Lubitsch in writing and direction.

George Raft's million is worthless because
he is a fourth-time offender for forgery, and
none believes his signature on the certified
check.

Similarly Gary Cooper, Jack Oakie and
Roscoe Karns as the triumvirate of marines
look at the million dollar check received by
Cooper, and also observe that it's 1 April on
the calendar, and that's that.

May Robson converts the old ladies' home
in which she's a 'guest' into a clubhouse,
when her million arrives, and bakes pies for
Richard Bennett, who plays the eccentric
millionaire who had hit upon the telephone
directory potshot idea as a means for
distributing his wealth.

Charlie Ruggles' sequence has about the
longest footage, while Laughton's Bronx
cheerio is the snappiest, and probably most
effective.

W. C. Fields and Alison Skipworth man a
vanguard of used flivvers as the means to
attack the road hogs who endanger the other
motorists, by running them up the sidewalks
and into wrecks themselves.

■ IF IT'S TUESDAY, THIS MUST BE BELGIUM

1969, 99 MINS, US ◇
Dir Mel Stuart *Prod* Stan Margulies *Scr* David
Shaw *Ph* Vilis Lapenieks *Ed* David Saxon
Mus Donovan *Art Dir* Marc Frederix
● Suzanne Pleshette, Ian McShane, Mildred Natwick,
Murray Hamilton, Sandy Baron, Reva Rose (United
Artists)

David Shaw's screenplay manages to cover
many of the European tour cliches. There are
some script anomalies that briefly puzzle, but
not to a degree that they detract from the fun.

Although the touring group is conducted by
a British guide (Ian McShane), supposedly
versed in all languages and emergencies, they
suddenly find themselves with a fluttery
femme type (Patricia Routledge). She's unexplained, unorthodox and delightful.

While Shaw's main storyline is based on
the adventures of a polyglot pack of Yank
tourists, trying to keep up with a hectic
schedule, it is padded with enough sidebar
items to make it a miniature *Grand Hotel* on
wheels.

Besides the friction caused by the inconve-
niences enroute, there's personal friction be-

tween McShane and femme tourist Suzanne
Pleshette.

■ I KNOW WHERE I'M GOING!

1945, 91 MINS, UK
Dir Michael Powell, Emeric Pressburger *Prod* Michael
Powell, Emeric Pressburger *Scr* Michael Powell,
Emeric Pressburger *Ph* Erwin Hillier *Ed* John
Seabourne *Mus* Allan Gray *Art Dir* Alfred Junge
● Wendy Hiller, Roger Livesey, Pamela Brown, Petula
Clark, Nancy Price, Finlay Currie (Archers)

I Know Where I'm Going! has all the values of a
documentary as a foundation for the tale of a
girl who is sure she knows where she is going
until she gets sidetracked – and likes it.

As the girl Wendy Hiller repeats her convincing portrayal of character development
which made *Pygmalion* a personal triumph for
her. Hard as nails in the opening sequences,
when she tells her father, a bank manager,
she is off to the Island of Mull to marry the
multi-millionaire boss of a great chemical
combine, she dismisses his objections to the
May-December misalliance by insisting her
fiance is no older than her father – 'and
you're rather nice, daddy.'

It is only when a gale prevents her from
reaching the island and her waiting bride-
groom-to-be she finds heartless ambition to
marry money becoming less attractive, the
process of disillusionment aided and abetted
by her proximity to a young navy officer
(Roger Livesey) who begins by telling her
what he thinks of gold diggers generally, and
winds up by walloping her in the best-ap-
proved Cagney fashion.

■ I LIVE IN GROSVENOR SQUARE

1945, 114 MINS, UK
Dir Herbert Wilcox *Prod* Herbert Wilcox
Scr Nicholas Phipps, William D. Bayles *Ph* Otto
Heller *Ed* Vera Campbell *Mus* Anthony Collins *Art
Dir* William C. Andrews
● Anna Neagle, Dean Jagger, Rex Harrison, Robert
Morley (Associated British)

Story by British newspaperman Maurice
Cowan is based on the real-life events – that
of the Air Corps crew sacrificing themselves
to save inhabitants of an English village.

Anna Neagle gives a most convincing performance. Dean Jagger's love scenes, though
a trifle long, are played with the subtlety one
would expect in an American sergeant's diffidence towards a duke's grand-daughter. Rex
Harrison as the major looks sure to impress
American femmes in the service, even though
the heroine jilts him.

Of the other players, Jane Darwell gives a
lesson in how to play a bit part so it won't be
forgotten. Herbert Wilcox's direction is
perfect.

■ I'LL CRY TOMORROW

1955, 117 MINS, US ⓥ
Dir Daniel Mann *Prod* Lawrence Weingarten
Scr Helen Deutsch, Jay Richard Kennedy *Ph* Arthur E.
Arling *Ed* Harold F. Kress *Mus* Alex North
Art Dir Cedric Gibbons, Malcolm Brown
● Susan Hayward, Richard Conte, Eddie Albert, Jo
Van Fleet, Don Taylor, Margo (M-G-M)

This pulls no punches in showing a rising
star's fall into alcoholic degradation that
plumbs Skid Row sewers before Alcoholics
Anonymous provides the faith and guidance
to help her up again. [The biopic is based on
Lillian Roth's own book.]

No particular person or circumstance is
blamed for Roth's downfall, but the viewers
will be able to fasten on any one of several
possible causes. The first is the stingingly
cruel portrayal of the stage mother, played
with great trouping skill by Jo Van Fleet, as

287

she pushes her daughter towards the career she never had. The death of Roth's first love, effectively realized by Ray Danton, is a blow of fate and the start of the crackup.

Susan Hayward, along with the sock of her sustained character creation, reveals pleasant pipes and song-belting ability.

●●●●●●●●●●●●●●●●●●●●●●●●●●●●●

■ ILLEGALLY YOURS

1988, 102 MINS, US ◇

Dir Peter Bogdanovich   *Prod* Peter Bogdanovich   *Scr* M.A. Stewart, Max Dickens   *Ph* Dante Spinotti   *Ed* Richard Fields   *Mus* Phil Marshall   *Art Dir* Jane Musky

● Rob Lowe, Colleen Camp, Kenneth Mars, Harry Carey Jr, Kim Myers (De Laurentiis/Crescent Moon)

Illegally Yours is an embarrassingly unfunny attempt at screwball comedy, marking a career nadir for producer-director Peter Bogdanovich and his miscast star Rob Lowe.

Hectic pre-credits sequence, loaded with telltale, expository voiceover by Lowe, crudely sets up an uninteresting story of a blackmailer's murder, witnessed by young Kim Myers and her friend L.B. Straten, in which innocent Colleen Camp is arrested as the fall guy. An audiotape recording of the murder is the item everyone is trying to get their hands on.

Lowe is cast, with unbecoming glasses throughout, as a college dropout trying to get his life in order back home in St Augustine, Fla. Between endless pratfalls Lowe finds himself on jury duty in Camp's case.

En route to sorting out the boring mystery of what became of the kidnaper's corpse, Lowe is thoroughly out of his element, even adopting a silly voice for a dumb drag scene. Camp is given little to do and no chemistry develops between the mismatched stars.

●●●●●●●●●●●●●●●●●●●●●●●●●●●●●

■ ILL MET BY MOONLIGHT

1957, 104 MINS, UK

Dir Michael Powell, Emeric Pressburger   *Prod* Michael Powell, Emeric Pressburger   *Scr* Michael Powell, Emeric Pressburger   *Ph* Christopher Challis   *Ed* Arthur Stevens   *Mus* Mikis Theodorakis   *Art Dir* Alex Vetchinsky

● Dirk Bogarde, Marius Goring, David Oxley, Cyril Cusack, Laurence Payne, Michael Gough (Rank/Archers)

Michael Powell and Emeric Pressburger take as their subject an operation in occupied Crete [from the book by W. Stanley Moss]. Two British officers, with the aid of local patriots, are given the job of kidnapping the German commander-in-chief and transporting him to Cairo.

The job of hijacking the general is accomplished with remarkable ease and luck. His car is ambushed and he's driven through endless road blocks to a mountain hideout. Then comes the tricky part. The general has to be led to the beachhead selected by the British navy for transportation to Egypt.

Dirk Bogarde turns in a smooth and satisfying performance as a British major, with David Oxley giving valuable aid as his No. 2 man. Marius Goring, as the general, is smugly confident that he'll be rescued by his own men and gallantly accepts the fact that he's been outwitted by a bunch of amateurs.

●●●●●●●●●●●●●●●●●●●●●●●●●●●●●

■ I'LL NEVER FORGET WHAT'S 'IS NAME

1967, 97 MINS, UK ◇

Dir Michael Winner   *Prod* Michael Winner   *Scr* Peter Draper   *Ph* Otto Heller   *Ed* Bernard Gribble   *Mus* Francis Lai   *Art Dir* Seamus Flannery

● Orson Welles, Oliver Reed, Carol White, Harry Andrews, Michael Hordern, Wendy Craig (Universal/Scimitar)

Story concerns a successful and resentful

whizkid of the advertising game (Oliver Reed), who opts out to join a pal in running an esoteric literary magazine. Separated from his wife, he is a womanizer of perpetual appetite, taking one off to a lonely and disused railroad station and establishing a flightly relationship with a secretary (Carol White), who is prim at heart and takes it all seriously.

Thus the theme is the aridity of fashionable achievement, and the sour smell of success is hammered home by director Michael Winner with an insistence that destroys its own claims and closes with a final scene of stunning vulgarity.

Oliver Reed looks grim and disenchanted throughout, but hasn't the power to suggest that there's much talent going to waste.

In addition to Orson Welles, White registers as the girl torn between her virginal upbringing and her beckoning by Reed. The role is inconclusive, but she gives it the stamp of charm and unforced sweetness.

●●●●●●●●●●●●●●●●●●●●●●●●●●●●●

■ ILLUSTRATED MAN, THE

1969, 103 MINS, US ◇ 🟤

Dir Jack Smight   *Prod* Howard B. Kreitsek, Ted Mann   *Scr* Howard B. Kreitsek   *Ph* Philip Lathrop   *Ed* Archie Marshek   *Mus* Jerry Goldsmith   *Art Dir* Joel Schiller

● Rod Steiger, Claire Bloom, Robert Drivas, Don Dubbins, Jason Evans (Warner/Seven Arts)

The Illustrated Man has going for it two major aspects: a derivative Ray Bradbury story and an obtuse, time-fragmented, humanistic, allegorical morality play.

Rod Steiger and Claire Bloom star in a story told in flashback and flash-forward, from a rural lakeside camp occupied for an afternoon and a night around Labor Day 1933 by wandering drifter Steiger and neighborhood boy Robert Drivas.

Steiger is gradually revealed to be almost totally covered with tattoos – he prefers the phrase 'skin illustrations' – each representing some sort of adventure. Plot selects three of those adventures.

The interpretations of the story are manifold. Steiger's character is apparently an eternal Adam, wandering through the ages and encountering challenges, the marks and memories of which are the tattoos.

●●●●●●●●●●●●●●●●●●●●●●●●●●●●●

■ I LOVE MELVIN

1953, 76 MINS, US ◇

Dir Don Weis   *Prod* George Wells   *Scr* George Wells, Ruth Brooks Flippen   *Ph* Harold Rosson   *Ed* Adrienne Fazan   *Mus* George Stoll (dir.)   *Art Dir* Cedric Gibbons, Jack Martin Smith, Eddie Imazu

● Donald O'Connor, Debbie Reynolds, Una Merkel, Richard Anderson, Jim Backus, Robert Taylor (M-G-M)

This is a lively, youthful musical comedy with a script, taken from a story by Laslo Vadney, that provides interesting substance to a fluffy affair.

Donald O'Connor and Debbie Reynolds are the youthful sparkplugs and both perform to advantage under Don Weis' direction. Bounciest number they do together is 'Where Did You Learn to Dance', an informal affair of charm. O'Connor does some skating terps to 'Life Has Its Funny Little Ups and Downs', with little Noreen Corcoran supplying the appealing vocal. The big production number is 'Saturday Afternoon before the Game', in which Reynolds plays the football and reveals every curve in a pigskin costume. The songs are by Josef Myrow and Mack Gordon.

Plot finds O'Connor a bulb-carrier for Jim Backus, *Look* photog. He falls in love with Reynolds, a chorus cutie, and gives her the impression he is a photographer. He launches a campaign of picture-taking with her as model and she, and her family, believe the gal will make the *Look* cover. O'Connor fakes a cover but the stunt backfires.

Una Merkel and Allyn Joslyn are very good as Reynolds' parents, as is little Corcoran as her kid sister. Richard Anderson is delightful as Reynolds' stuffed-shirt suitor, favored by Joslyn. Backus plays his photog role for sure chuckles. Robert Taylor makes a brief guest appearance. Robert Alton staged and directed the dances.

●●●●●●●●●●●●●●●●●●●●●●●●●●●●●

■ I LOVE YOU, ALICE B. TOKLAS

1968, 92 MINS, US 🟤

Dir Hy Averback   *Prod* Charles Maguire   *Scr* Paul Mazursky, Larry Tucker   *Ph* Philip Lathrop   *Ed* Robert C. Jones   *Mus* Elmer Bernstein   *Art Dir* Pato Guzman

● Peter Sellers, Jo Van Fleet, Leigh Taylor-Young, Joyce Van Patten, David Arkin, Herb Edelman (Warner/Seven Arts)

Film is not heavyhanded in its approach either to hippie life, or to what is considered 'normal' modes of behavior. Instead, there is a sympathetic look at the advantages and disadvantages of each.

Pic derives its prime value from an excellent screenplay. Story is relatively simple: Peter Sellers, an LA lawyer, turns on to hippie life as an escape from conformity and hypocrisy. Later, he finds out that human nature is independent of superficial environment, returns briefly to his former life, but winds up running away again.

Film blasts off into orbit via top-notch acting and direction. Sellers' performance – both in scenes which spotlight his character as well as ensemble sequences in which everyone is balanced nicely – is an outstanding blend of warmth, sensitivity, disillusion and optimism.

Jo Van Feet is simply brilliant as Sellers' mother, with Salem Ludwig also on target as his dad. Joyce Van Patten's performance as Sellers' pushy fiancee is delightful.

●●●●●●●●●●●●●●●●●●●●●●●●●●●●●

■ I LOVE YOU TO DEATH

1990, 96 MINS, US ◇ 🟤

Dir Lawrence Kasden   *Prod* Jeffrey Lurie, Ron Moler, Patrick Wells, Lauren Weissman   *Scr* John Kostmayer   *Ph* Owen Roisman   *Ed* Anne V. Coates   *Mus* James Horner   *Art Dir* Lilly Kilvert

● Kevin Kline, Tratey Ullman, Joan Plowright, River Phoenix, William Hurt, Keanu Reeves (Chestnut Hill)

I Love You to Death is a stillborn attempt at black comedy.

Opening credits stress tale is based on a true story, but John Kostmayer's screenplay never makes events remotely interesting. Kevin Kline creates a stereotypical Italian restaurant owner who can't help cheating with scores of women on his frumpish wife, Tracey Ullman. Awkward script has Ullman discovering Kline in a tryst at a library and, after brief consultation with her Yugoslav mom Joan Plowright, resolving to kill him.

Harold and Maude it ain't. Film founders because the cast is out of control. Chief culprit is Hurt, as a hired space cadet hitman, who pulls faces embarrassingly here as a retarded hippie.

At the other extreme, the three British actresses are models of professionalism. Ullman unfortunately fades into the woodwork by steadfastly adopting a bland speech pattern and looking as homely as possible. Plowright is solid as her mom.

●●●●●●●●●●●●●●●●●●●●●●●●●●●●●

■ IMAGES

1972, 100 MINS, UK ◇

Dir Robert Altman   *Prod* Tommy Thompson   *Scr* Robert Altman   *Ph* Vilmos Zsigmond   *Ed* Graeme Clifford   *Mus* John Williams   *Art Dir* Leon Ericksen

● Susannah York, Rene Auberjonois, Marcel Bozzuffi, Hugh Millais, Cathryn Harrison (Lion's Gate/Hemdale)

Robert Altman made this interior drama about a woman going through hallucination and nearing madness in Ireland. Delving into effects of permissiveness on a hidebound, repressed nature, it also shows a probing insight into mental disorder.

Susannah York, writing a fairy tale for children about mysterious woods and a unicorn that acts as a counterpoint to her real life losing of touch with reality, imagines phone calls saying her husband is with another woman and when they go to their country house for the weekend two men in her life intrude as imaginary, or, in one case, real.

York has the intensity and innocence marked by strain as well as sensual underpinnings, and brings off the final denouement with restraint and potency.

■ I'M ALL RIGHT, JACK

1959, 105 MINS, UK Ⓥ
Dir John Boulting *Prod* Roy Boulting *Scr* Frank Harvey, John Boulting *Ph* Max Greene *Ed* Anthony Harvey *Mus* Ken Hare
● Ian Carmichael, Peter Sellers, Terry-Thomas, Richard Attenborough, Dennis Price, Margaret Rutherford (British Lion/Boulting Brothers)

The Boulting Brothers' target [from the novel by Alan Hackney] is British factory life, trade unionism and the general possibility that everybody is working for one person – himself.

Ian Carmichael plays an ex-university type who wants to get an executive job in industry. Instead, he is given a job as a factory worker by his uncle who wants him in as a stooge for a secret, dirty financial deal. Carmichael becomes the unwitting cause of a factory strike that swells to nationwide proportions. Gradually he begins to realize that he has been taken for a ride.

Carmichael slides smoothly through his performance, but it is Peter Sellers, as the chairman of the factory's union works committee, who makes the film. With a makeup that subtly suggests Hitler, he brings rare humor and an occasional touch of pathos to the role. Sellers' strength is that he does not deliberately play for laughs. He produces them from the situations and sharp dialog.

Dennis Price and Richard Attenborough as shady employers and Terry-Thomas as a bewildered personnel manager also provide rich roles.

■ I MARRIED A COMMUNIST

1949, 72 MINS, US
Dir Robert Stevenson *Prod* Sid Rogell *Scr* Charles Grayson, Robert Hardy Andrews *Ph* Nicholas Musuraca *Ed* Roland Gross *Mus* Leigh Harline
● Laraine Day, Robert Ryan, John Agar, Thomas Gomez, Janis Carter (RKO)

As a straight action fare, *I Married a Communist* generates enough tension to satisfy the average customer. Despite its heavy sounding title, pic hews strictly to tried and true meller formula.

Screenplay uses the simple and slightly naive device of substituting Communist for gangsters in a typical underworld yarn.

Pic is so wary of introducing any political gab that at one point when Commie trade union tactics are touched upon, the soundtrack is dropped.

Robert Ryan plays an ex-comrade who turns up in San Francisco as vice-prexy of a shipping company and bigtime labor relations expert. In the midst of waterfront union negotiations, the Commie chieftain (Thomas Gomez) enters to remind Ryan that he can't quit the mob and had better follow the Party's directive to stir up labor trouble.

■ I MARRIED A MONSTER FROM OUTER SPACE

1958, 78 MINS, US Ⓥ
Dir Gene Fowler Jr *Prod* Gene Fowler Jr *Scr* Louis Vittes *Ph* Haskell Boggs *Ed* George Tomasini *Art Dir* Hal Pereira, Henry Bumstead
● Tom Tryon, Gloria Talbott, Ken Lynch, John Eldridge, Alan Dexter, Jean Carson (Paramount)

Premise of the screenplay deals with a race of monsters from another galaxy who invade the earth and secretly take over the form of some of the male townspeople. Film opens with Gloria Talbott marrying Tom Tryon, unaware the man she loves is now one of these monsters.

After a year of tension she follows him one night and watches him change into his original form and enter a spaceship. Through her doctor, to whom she goes in her terror, enough normal people are recruited to successfully break up the invasion by an attack on spaceship.

Gene Fowler Jr's direction, while sometimes slow, latches onto mounting suspense as action moves to a climax. He gets the benefit of outstanding special photographic effects from John P. Fulton, which aid in maintaining interest.

■ I'M DANCING AS FAST AS I CAN

1982, 106 MINS, US ◇ Ⓥ
Dir Jack Hofsiss *Prod* Edgar J. Scherick, Scott Rudin *Scr* David Rabe *Ph* Jan de Bont *Ed* Michael Bradsell *Mus* Stanley Silverman *Art Dir* David Jenkins
● Jill Clayburgh, Nicol Williamson, Dianne Wiest, Joe Pesci, Geraldine Page, James Sutorius (Paramount)

Crucial inability of a film to get inside a character's head spells big trouble for *I'm Dancing As Fast As I Can*. Result here is that Jill Clayburgh's constantly center-stage character comes off as the 'pill-popping dingbat' she's called at one point, rather than as a fascinating lady with a major problem.

Based on Barbara Gordon's popular autobiographical tome, screenplay minutely charts Clayburgh's compulsive reliance on Valium, her disastrous effort to go cold turkey and her subsequent rehabilitation in an institution.

At the outset, Clayburgh is presented as a successful docu filmmaker for television. A little professional crisis presents itself. Pop goes a pill or two. A teeny tiff with b.f. Nicol Williamson. Down with another couple of blue tablets.

Only two members of the large supporting cast, Dianne Wiest and Geraldine Page, have any chance to develop their characters, and both do well.

■ I'M NO ANGEL

1933, 87 MINS, US
Dir Wesley Ruggles *Scr* Mae West *Ph* Leo Tover *Mus* Harvey Brooks
● Mae West, Cary Grant, Edward Arnold, Ralf Harolde, Russell Hopton, Gregory Ratoff (Paramount)

It's fairly obvious that the same plot mechanics and situations [from suggestions by Lowell Brentano and a treatment by Harlan Thompson] without Mae West wouldn't be a motion picture at all. But that's no criticism. It's all West, plus a good directing job by Wesley Ruggles and first-rate studio production quality in all departments.

Laughs are all derived from the West innuendos and the general good-natured bawdiness of the heroine, whose progress from a carnival mugg-taker to a deluxe millionaire-annexer is marked by a succession of gentlemen friends, mostly temporary and usually suckers.

When reaching affluence the carnival gal is serviced by four colored maids in an ultra-

penthouse and garbed in the flashy manner of an Oriental potentate's pampered pet.

Every now and again West bursts into a song, generally just a chorus or a strain. They're of the Frankie and Johnny genre, but primarily she plays a lion tamer, not a songstress.

■ IMITATION OF LIFE

1934, 116 MINS, US
Dir John M. Stahl *Prod* Carl Laemmle Jr *Scr* William Hurlburt *Ph* Merritt Gerstad *Ed* Philip Cahn, Maurice Wright *Mus* Heinz Roemheld (dir.) *Art Dir* Charles D. Hall
● Claudette Colbert, Warren William, Louise Beavers, Fredi Washington, Rochelle Hudson (Universal)

Imitation of Life is a strong picture with an unusual plot. A young white widow (Claudette Colbert) with a baby girl goes into a business partnership with her colored maid (Louise Beavers) who also has a baby girl. In the passage of years a small business becomes a factory and they are wealthy. But neither the white woman nor the negress derive much joy. And because of their daughters.

Most arresting part of the picture and overshadowing the conventional romance between the late thirtyish white widow and Warren William is the tragedy of Aunt Delilah's girl born to a white skin and Negro blood. This subject is treated on the screen for the first time here. Girl is miserable being unable to adjust herself to the lot of her race and unable to take her place among the whites.

John M. Stahl directs this kind of thing very well. He keeps the Fannie Hurst 'success story' brand of snobbishness under control and the film flows with mounting interest, if at moments a trifle slowly.

Picture is stolen by the Negress, Beavers, whose performance is masterly. This lady can troupe. She takes the whole scale of human emotions from joy to anguish and never sounds a false note.
□ 1934: Best Picture (Nomination)

■ IMITATION OF LIFE

1959, 125 MINS, US ◇ Ⓥ
Dir Douglas Sirk *Prod* Ross Hunter *Scr* Eleanore Griffin, Allan Scott *Ph* Russell Metty *Ed* Milton Carruth *Mus* Frank Skinner *Art Dir* Alexander Golitzen, Richard H. Riedel
● Lana Turner, John Gavin, Sandra Dee, Dan O'Herlihy, Robert Alda, Susan Kohner (Universal)

Imitation of Life is a remake of Fannie Hurst's novel of the early 1930s. Lana Turner is outstanding in the pivotal role played in Universal's 1934 version by Claudette Colbert. Scripters Eleanore Griffin and Allan Scott have transplanted her from the original pancake-and-flour business to the American stage.

While this device lends more scope, it also results in the overdone busy actress/neglected daughter conflict, and thus the secondary plot of a fair-skinned Negress passing as white becomes the film's primary force. The relationship of the young colored girl and her mother – played memorably by Susan Kohner and Juanita Moore – is sometimes overpowering, while the relationship of Turner and her daughter, Sandra Dee, comes to life only briefly when both are in love with same man, John Gavin.

Turner plays a character of changing moods, and her changes are remarkably effective, as she blends love and understanding, sincerity and ambition. The growth of maturity is reflected neatly in her distinguished portrayal. In smaller roles, both Robert Alda, as an opportunist agent, and Dan O'Herlihy, as a playwright, are excellent.

■ IMMEDIATE FAMILY

1989, 95 MINS, US ◇ Ⓥ

Dir Jonathan Kaplan   *Prod* Sarah Pillsbury, Midge Sanford   *Scr* Barbara Benedek   *Ph* John W. Lindley   *Ed* Jane Kurson   *Mus* Brad Fiedel   *Art Dir* Mark Freeborn

● Glenn Close, James Woods, Mary Stuart Masterson, Kevin Dillon, Linda Darlow, Jane Greer (Columbia/Sanford-Pillsbury)

Definitely no comedy, *Immediate Family* nonetheless explodes with bursts of laughter that lighten the heartbreak of a lot of nice people tormented by their own best intentions.

For Solomon and generations of juvenile judges since, there's no tougher case to call than competing claims for a baby. But Solomon's solution wouldn't work for *Family*, in which Glenn Close and Mary Stuart Masterson are each so deserving.

Granted, the plot requires no elaborate examination: after 11 years of marriage, James Woods and Glenn Close are still achingly childless. After no years of marriage, young Mary Stuart Masterson and boyfriend Kevin Dillon face impending parenthood under circumstances that could wreck their chances for a happier life later.

The solution, so obviously simple in a lawyer's office, is that Woods and Close will adopt Masterson's baby. But first the lawyer thinks everybody should get better acquainted.

Clever as she is, Close keeps her potentially cloying part understated; there's no need to hang a sign on her suffering. Young Masterson is simply superb, managing to first earn the audience's sympathy and then keep hold when some might be tempted to turn away.

■ IMPORTANCE OF BEING EARNEST, THE

1952, 95 MINS, UK ◇ Ⓥ

Dir Anthony Asquith   *Prod* Teddy Baird   *Scr* Anthony Asquith   *Ph* Desmond Dickinson   *Ed* John D. Guthridge   *Mus* Benjamin Frankel   *Art Dir* Carmen Dillon

● Michael Redgrave, Edith Evans, Michael Denison, Dorothy Tutin, Margaret Rutherford, Joan Greenwood (Javelin/Two Cities)

All the charm and glossy humor of Oscar Wilde's classic comedy emerges faithfully in this British production. Apart from a few minor cuts, director Anthony Asquith has taken few liberties with the original. His skilful direction extracts all the polish of Wilde's brilliant dialog.

Michael Redgrave brings a wealth of sincerity to the role of the earnest young man, without knowledge of his origin, whose invention of a fictitious brother leads to romantic complications. Michael Denison plays the debonair Algernon Moncrieff in a gay lighthearted style, and makes his characterization the pivot for much of the comedy.

The two romantic femme roles are adroitly played by Joan Greenwood and Dorothy Tutin.

■ IMPOSSIBLE OBJECT

1973, 110 MINS, FRANCE ◇

Dir John Frankenheimer   *Scr* Nicolas Mosley   *Ph* Claude Renoir   *Ed* Albert Jurgenson   *Mus* Michel Legrand   *Art Dir* Alexandre Trauner

● Alan Bates, Dominique Sanda, Evans Evans, Lea Massari, Michel Auclair, Laurence de Monaghan (Franco-Londen/Euro International)

John Frankenheimer spent over a year in Paris and then made this film for a local company, albeit mainly in English with passages between French people in French. It is a many-pronged affair in a tale of a writer whose inventions and real life may not always be extricable. It mixes romantic drama, situation comedy and insights into Americans or British abroad.

Alan Bates is a writer, living in a country home in France, outside Paris, with three sons and an American wife. He meets brooding but delicately sensual Dominique Sanda, who is married, in a museum and love blossoms. Film flits lightly over the affair, the writer's embroidery on it and sideline events that reflect on it until sudden swerve to tragedy.

Though pic segues from fantasy to implied realism, pic has an airy grace, fine playing down the line.

■ IMPOSTOR, THE

1944, 93 MINS, US

Dir Julien Duvivier   *Prod* Julien Duvivier   *Scr* Julien Duvivier, Stephen Longstreet, Marc Connelly, Lynn Starling   *Ph* Paul Ivano   *Ed* Paul Landres   *Mus* Dimitri Tiomkin   *Art Dir* John B. Goodman, Eugene Lourie

● Jean Gabin, Richard Whorf, Ellen Drew, Peter Van Eyck (Universal)

Fall of France in 1940, and subsequent formation of Free French units in Africa, forms basis for this adventure drama, which unfolds tale of regeneration of a confirmed criminal through comradeship in arms. Julien Duvivier fails to generate pace fast enough to carry picture along for more than moderate attention.

Story tells of how Jean Gabin is saved from the guillotine, for murder, at Tours by Nazi air bombing, heads south and assumes the identity, papers and uniform of a dead French soldier along the road. Joining group of refugee soldiers who enlist in the Free French forces, Gabin's army association gradually transforms the criminal; he leads a small unit overland for attack on Italian desert base and is decorated for gallantry, under the name of the dead man whose identity he assumed.

■ IMPROPER CHANNELS

1981, 91 MINS, CANADA ◇

Dir Eric Till   *Prod* Morrie Ruvinsky, Alfred Pariser   *Scr* Morrie Ruvinsky, Ian Sutherland, Adam Arkin   *Ph* Tony Richmond   *Mus* Mickey Erbe, Maribeth Solomon   *Art Dir* Minkey Dalton, Charles Dunlop

● Alan Arkin, Mariette Hartley, Sarah Stevens, Monica Parker (Paragon)

Alan Arkin puts his hapless schnook characterization to good use in *Improper Channels*. It's a screwball comedy that starts slowly, shifts into overdrive, peters out a bit halfway through and then gets its second wind for a fast-paced, down-with-the-computer finish.

He's an architect, separated from his writer spouse (Mariette Hartley) and precocious five-year-old daughter (Sarah Stevens). And one thing leads to another; the daughter is injured slightly in his camper and when taken to hospital she is thought to have been beaten by her father.

A domineering social worker (Monica Parker) has a computer expert call up all available information on Arkin and the daughter is bundled off by court order to an orphanage. Arkin and Hartley attempt to get her back.

Eric Till's direction is surefire most of the time, though he's let down by a script that wants to do too much. Pic was shot under the title of '*Proper Channels*' and was changed for reasons not explained.

■ IMPULSE

1990, 108 MINS, US ◇ Ⓥ

Dir Sondra Locke   *Prod* Albert S. Ruddy, Andre Morgan   *Scr* John De Marco, Leigh Chapman   *Ph* Dean Semler   *Ed* John W. Wheeler   *Mus* Michel Colombier   *Art Dir* William A. Elliott

● Theresa Russell, Jeff Fahey, George Dzundza, Alan Rosenberg, Shawn Elliott, Nicholas Mele (Ruddy-Morgan/Warner)

Theresa Russell gives a solid performance in Sondre Locke's well-directed film noir. Russell is a beautiful undercover cop whose life is going nowhere, hence the title: she would like to break out of her rut and act on impulse like one of the prostitute or druggie personas she routinely adopts in her work.

Along with her sexist boss George Dzundza, she's assigned to work with young assistant d.a. Jeff Fahey to find missing witness Shawn Elliott in an important gangster case. Elliott has $900,000 stolen in a Colombian drug deal, and there's only three weeks to find him before Fahey begins the trial.

Russell and Fahey have some interesting exchanges that expose their characters. Sharpest writing comes in a scene of Fahey and his partner Alan Rosenberg talking about women and relationships in terms from real estate.

Director Locke, in her second feature after *Ratboy*, gets high marks for the visceral, swift nature of her violent stagings. She also manages an impressively tactile sex scene that involves Russell and Fahey.

■ IN A LONELY PLACE

1950, 92 MINS, US Ⓥ

Dir Nicholas Ray   *Prod* Henry S. Kesler   *Scr* Andrew Solt   *Ph* Burnett Guffey   *Ed* Viola Lawrence   *Mus* George Antheil

● Humphrey Bogart, Gloria Grahame, Frank Lovejoy, Robert Warwick, Jeff Donnell, Martha Stewart (Columbia/Santana)

In *Lonely Place* Humphrey Bogart has a sympathetic role though cast as one always ready to mix it with his dukes. He favors the underdog; in one instance he virtually has a veteran, brandy-soaking character actor (out of work) on his very limited payroll.

As the screenplay scrivener who detests the potboilers, Bogart finds himself innocently suspected of a girl's slaying. Although continually kept under suspicion, he ignores the police attempt to trap him into a confession, at the same time falling for a gal neighbor.

Director Nicholas Ray maintains nice suspense. Bogart is excellent. Gloria Grahame, as his romance, also rates kudos. [Screenplay is from a story by Dorothy B. Hughes, adapted by Edmund H. North.]

■ IN COLD BLOOD

1967, 133 MINS, US Ⓥ

Dir Richard Brooks   *Prod* Richard Brooks   *Scr* Richard Brooks   *Ph* Conrad Hall   *Ed* Peter Zinner   *Mus* Quincy Jones   *Art Dir* Robert Boyle

● Robert Blake, Scott Wilson, John Forsythe, Paul Stewart, Gerald S. O'Loughlin, Jeff Corey (Columbia)

In the skillful hands of adapter-director-producer Richard Brooks, Truman Capote's *In Cold Blood*, the non-fiction novel-like account about two Kansas killers, becomes on screen a probing, sensitive, tasteful, balanced and suspenseful documentary-drama.

Film has the look and sound of reality, in part from use of actual locales in six states and non-pros as atmosphere players, the rest from Brooks' own filmmaking professionalism. Planned as a $3 million, 124-day pic, it came in for $2.2 million in 80 days.

Heading the competent cast are Robert Blake and Scott Wilson, bearing a striking resemblance to the now-dead Kansas drifters who, in the course of a burglary on 15 November, 1959, murdered four of a family. Almost six years later, after an exhausted appeal route, they were hanged. John Forsythe plays the chief investigator who broke the case.

Brooks' screenplay and direction are remarkable in that pic avoids so many pitfalls: it is not a crime meller, told either from the police or criminal viewpoint; it is not social tract against capital punishment; it is not cheap exploitation material; and it is not amateurish in technical execution, despite its realistic flavor.

．．．．．．．．．．．．．．．．．．．．．．．．．．

■ IN COUNTRY

1989, 120 MINS, US ◇ ▽

Dir Norman Jewison   *Prod* Norman Jewison, Richard Roth   *Scr* Frank Pierson, Cynthia Cidre   *Ph* Russell Boyd   *Ed* Anthony Gibbs, Lou Lombardo   *Mus* James Horner   *Art Dir* Jackson DeGovia
● Bruce Willis, Emily Lloyd, Joan Allen, Kevin Anderson, John Terry (Warner)

Norman Jewison usually is a commanding storyteller, but *In Country* is a film with two stories that fail to add up to something greater: a country girl's coming of age, and a troubled Vietnam veteran's coming to terms with his haunting memories of war [from the novel by Bobbie Ann Mason].

Emily Lloyd, in a sparky performance that seizes control of the movie, plays Samantha Hughes, a spirited, just-minted high school graduate from the small town of Hopewell, Ky. She lives in a ramshackle house with Bruce Willis, who turns in a likable but unremarkable interpretation of her moody uncle Emmett, a veteran who has suffered lasting emotional damage from his nightmarish tour of duty in 'Nam.

Lloyd's father, who also served 'in country,' was killed in combat before she was born. She likes the freedom of living with Willis, who permits Lloyd unsupervised liaisons with her callow basketball star boyfriend (Kevin Anderson). She's not especially close to her mother, Willis' sister, played deftly by Joan Allen.

Willis generates sympathy for his tormented character, but the one-dimensional script and his still limited range conspire to make Emmett a stolid caricature of the spirtually wounded veteran.

．．．．．．．．．．．．．．．．．．．．．．．．．．

■ I NEVER PROMISED YOU A ROSE GARDEN

1977, 96 MINS, US ◇ ▽

Dir Anthony Page   *Prod* Terence F. Deane, Daniel H. Blatt, Michael Hausman   *Scr* Lewis John Carlino, Gavin Lambert   *Ph* Bruce Logan   *Ed* Garth Craven   *Mus* Paul Chihara   *Art Dir* Toby Rafelson
● Kathleen Quinlan, Bibi Andersson, Ben Piazza, Lorraine Gary, Darlene Craviotto, Reni Santoni (Imorh/New World)

Good intentions and sensationalism compete for viewer interest in this filmization of Joanne Greenberg's novel about the tentative recovery of a psychotic young woman. Unfortunately, both lose. Good intentions resolve into highminded tedium.

The pic's central problem is its structure. The girl (Kathleen Quinlan) is presented at the outset as a certifiable nutto teenager, being escorted by her parents (Lorraine Gary and Ben Piazza) to what appears to be a tastefully landscaped institution. An improved mental state is a certainty, otherwise there's no film.

Quinlan is an untypical young actress, who lends freshness and admirable reserve to a role that could have lapsed entirely into histrionic hysterics.

．．．．．．．．．．．．．．．．．．．．．．．．．．

■ I NEVER SANG FOR MY FATHER

1970, 92 MINS, US ◇ ▽

Dir Gilbert Cates   *Prod* Gilbert Cates   *Scr* Robert Anderson   *Ph* Morris Hartzband   *Ed* Angelo Ross   *Mus* Al Gorgoni, Barry Mann   *Art Dir* Hank Aldrich

● Melvyn Douglas, Gene Hackman, Dorothy Stickney, Estelle Parsons, Elizabeth Hubbard, Lovelady Powell (Columbia/Jamel)

Film version of Robert Anderson's 1968 play is distended and lacking clear point of view. Mostly the story of a middle-aged man still strung up by a family umbilical cord, the film veers awkwardly into problems of the aged. However, the performances of father Melvyn Douglas, mother Dorothy Stickney, son Gene Hackman and daughter Estelle Parsons are superb.

Anderson's basic plot line involves the widower Hackman, still lashed to his parents through the verbal bonds of Douglas' coldhearted feelings. Parsons as the daughter was luckier: she was banished for marrying a Jew, and was forced to make a new life.

Trouble is, given all this acting talent, the direction, writing and pacing are dreary.

．．．．．．．．．．．．．．．．．．．．．．．．．．

■ IN HARM'S WAY

1965, 165 MINS, US ▽

Dir Otto Preminger   *Prod* Otto Preminger   *Scr* Wendell Mayes   *Ph* Loyal Griggs   *Ed* George Tomasini, Hugh S. Fowler   *Mus* Jerry Goldsmith   *Art Dir* Lyle Wheeler
● John Wayne, Kirk Douglas, Patricia Neal, Tom Tryon, Paula Prentiss, Henry Fonda (Paramount)

John Wayne is in every sense the big gun of *In Harm's Way*. Without his commanding presence, chances are director-producer Otto Preminger probably could not have built the head of steam this film generates and sustains for two hours and 45 minutes.

Although the personal drama that unites and divides the lives of navy people caught up in this dramatization of US efforts to strike back within the year after the Pearl Harbor disaster doesn't win any prizes for creativity, Preminger uses it effectively to establish a bond between the characters and the audience. It's a full, lusty slice of life in a time of extreme stress that Wendell Mayes has fashioned from the novel by James Bassett.

Romantic coupling of Wayne and Patricia Neal, as a navy nurse, is the most natural stroke of man and woman casting in many a year.

Neal brings to her role a beautifully proportioned, gutsy strength and sensitivity.

Through skillful blending of fact and fiction, Preminger provides, in the picture's action stretches, a highly suspenseful and, at times, shatteringly realistic account of an underdog US navy task force boldly seeking out a Japanese group of ships. The sea battle sequences are filmmaking at its best.

There are some heroics that come out of a traditional mold and fall to Kirk Douglas to carry off as a hard-drinking exec officer, and buddy of Wayne, brooding the loss at Pearl Harbor of his double-timing wife. Henry Fonda, as the four-star boss of this navy show, moves in and out of the story, hitting the mark every time.

．．．．．．．．．．．．．．．．．．．．．．．．．．

■ IN LIKE FLINT

1967, 115 MINS, US ◇ ▽

Dir Gordon M. Douglas   *Prod* Saul David   *Scr* Hal Fimberg   *Ph* William C. Daniels   *Ed* Hugh S. Fowler   *Mus* Jerry Goldsmith   *Art Dir* Jack Martin Smith, Dale Hennesy
● James Coburn, Lee J. Cobb, Jean Hale, Andrew Duggan, Anna Lee, Yvonne Craig (20th Century-Fox)

Girls, gimmicks, girls, gags, and more girls are the essential parameters of *In Like Flint*. With James Coburn encoring as the urbane master sleuth, also harried boss Lee J. Cobb, this pic turns on a femme plot to take over the world.

As for the story, the tongue is best put way out in the cheek. Anne Lee, ever a charming

and gracious screen personality, is part of a triumvirate bent on seizing world power.

Lee's plot in this film comes a cropper when her male allies – corrupt General Steve Ihnat and cohorts, who have substituted an actor, Andrew Duggan, for the real US President, also played by Duggan – move in to snatch the ultimate prize.

While the dialog scenes tend to be a mite sluggish, pace picks up regularly with slam-bang action sequences.

．．．．．．．．．．．．．．．．．．．．．．．．．．

■ IN LOVE AND WAR

1958, 107 MINS, US ◇

Dir Philip Dunne   *Prod* Jerry Wald   *Scr* Edward Anhalt   *Ph* Leo Tover   *Ed* William Reynolds   *Mus* Hugo Friedhofer   *Art Dir* Lyle R. Wheeler, George W. Davis
● Robert Wagner, Dana Wynter, Jeffrey Hunter, Hope Lange, Bradford Dillman, Sheree North (20th Century-Fox)

In Love and War is a keen appraisal of the utility of love and the futility of war. Based on Anton Myrer's novel, *The Big War*, it is hardhitting, both in action and dialog. The characterizations are built in San Francisco and the Monterey Peninsula, and the sequences are particularly effective. The Pacific war footage, however, tends to ramble and with little or no forward movement.

Story is of the changing ideals and growing maturity of three marines entrenched in the Second World War. At the start, Jeffrey Hunter is the patriot, Robert Wagner the coward and Bradford Dillman the intellectual who fights because he must. More than one of war, the tale is one of love, Wagner for Sheree North, Hunter for Hope Lange and Dillman, having discarded Dana Wynter, for France Nuyen.

High spots are numerous, and the seven stars – plus comic Mort Sahl in his first film role – are excellent. Sahl's Jewish marine role was written especially for him, and, from the sound of it, by him.

．．．．．．．．．．．．．．．．．．．．．．．．．．

■ IN OLD ARIZONA

1929, 94 MINS, US

Dir Irving Cummings, Raoul Walsh   *Scr* Tom Barry   *Ph* Arthur Edeson
● Warner Baxter, Edmund Lowe, Dorothy Burgess, J. Farrell McDonald, Fred Warren (Fox)

A long time ago Winnie Sheehan said Fox would never turn loose a full length talker until the studio was convinced the picture was right. *In Old Arizona* that it's right is unquestioned at this time. It's the first outdoor talker and a western, with a climax twist to make the story stand out from the usual hill and dale thesis. It's outdoors, it talks and it has a great screen performance by Warner Baxter. That it's long and that it moves slowly is also true, but the exterior sound revives the novelty angle again.

Dorothy Burgess is cast as Tonia, a Mexican vixen who plays the boys across the boards and finally gets in a jam between the Cisco Kid (Warner Baxter) and the army sergeant who is pursuing the bandit.

Raoul Walsh is given screen and program credit for having co-directed this film, as he actually started it and was intent on finishing and playing the Cisco Kid in it. An unfortunate accident made this impossible, hence Irving Cummings' assignment.
□ 1928/29: Best Picture (Nomination)

．．．．．．．．．．．．．．．．．．．．．．．．．．

■ IN OLD CHICAGO

1938, 110 MINS, US ▽

Dir Henry King   *Prod* Darryl Zanuck   *Scr* Lamar Trotti, Sonya Levien   *Ph* Peverell Marley   *Ed* Barbara McLean   *Mus* Louis Silvers (dir.)   *Art Dir* William

Darling, Rudolph Sternad
● Tyrone Power, Alice Faye, Don Ameche, Alice Brady, Andy Devine, Brian Donlevy (20th Century-Fox)

An elaborate and liberally budgeted entertainment, the pictorial climax is the Chicago fire of 1871. This portion envisaging mob panic, desperate efforts to stop the fire by dynamiting, etc, is highly effective.

It is historically cockeyed in the placement of its main characters, and its story [by Niven Busch] is mere rehash of corrupt political mismanagement of a growing American city. But as a film entertainment it is socko.

The O'Leary family plays the most important part in the story, even to the point where one of the sons is projected as mayor of the city at the time of the fire, and another is pictured as the dishonest political boss, saloonkeeper and villain.

First portion (80 minutes) carries the characters to the eve of the great fire. Scores of elaborate scenes establish the primitive type of architecture of the frame-built, rambling town with its unpaved, muddy streets. Most of the action is laid in gaudy saloons and beer halls. Chicago is pictured as a dirty and corrupt city, a Sodom on the brink, ready for the torch of annihilation. Second part contains views of the holocaust, and a devastating series of actual and processed shots.

Alice Brady and Alice Faye give the outstanding performances. Brady is Mrs O'Leary, an honest, hardworking laundress with a pleasing Irish brogue. Tyrone Power as the film's heavy is good in his romantic scenes with Faye, who appears as a musical hall singer. Latter is especially effective when singing several musical numbers, tuned by Mack Gordon and Harry Revel, of which 'In Old Chicago' is the best. Don Ameche is a vehement political reformer and Brian Donlevy plays a dive keeper and crooked politician.
□ 1937: Best Picture (Nomination)

■ I OUGHT TO BE IN PICTURES

1982, 107 MINS, US ◇ ⊕
Dir Herbert Ross *Prod* Herbert Ross, Neil Simon
Scr Neil Simon *Ph* David M. Walsh *Ed* Sidney Levin *Mus* Marvin Hamlisch *Art Dir* Albert Brenner
● Walter Matthau, Ann-Margret, Dinah Manoff, Lance Guest, Lewis Smith, Martin Ferrero (20th Century-Fox)

Neil Simon's *I Ought to Be in Pictures* is a moving family drama, peppered with the author's patented gag lines and notable for sock performances by Dinah Manoff and Walter Matthau.

Nimbly opened-out from the 1980 stage version by helmer Herbert Ross, film concerns a 19-year-old, spunky Brooklyn girl Libby (Dinah Manoff reprising her stage role), who hitchhikes to Los Angeles to break into films as an actress but more importantly see her dad who left her, a brother and mom for good 16 years earlier.

Dad is Herb Tucker (Walter Matthau), a once-successful feature and TV scripter now given over to gambling and drinking. Tucker's loyal g.f. Steffie (Ann-Margret) is supportive but has her own children to take care of.

Key factor in making this work is apt casting, with Manoff outstanding in avoiding direct sentimentality in the showy central role. For his part, Matthau makes a ne'er-do-well character immensely sympathetic in spite of his shortcomings.

■ IN SEARCH OF GREGORY

1970, 90 MINS, UK/ITALY ◇
Dir Peter Wood *Prod* Joseph Janni, Daniele Senatore *Scr* Tonnio Guerra, Lucille Laks *Ph* Otto Heller, Giorgio Tonti *Ed* John Bloom *Mus* Ron Grainer *Art Dir* Piero Poletto

● Julie Christie, Michael Sarrazin, John Hurt, Paola Pitagora, Roland Culver, Tony Selby (Vic/Vera)

A superbly-wrought gem about the romantic illusions people, especially would-be lovers, search for in one another, with Julie Christie ideally cast as the seeker and Michael Sarrazin as her fantasy.

Christie, the daughter of an incurably romantic and frequently married Swiss financier, played with charming elan by Adolfo Celi, is living a life of quiet domesticity in Rome when she is invited by papa to attend his latest nuptial.

Her real attraction in Geneva is Celi's calculating description of his house guest from San Francisco, a tall, handsome 'likeable maniac'. At the airport, she spots a giant poster of Sarrazin, an auto-ball champion, and in her imagination he becomes the physical embodiment of her romantic fantasies about Gregory.

■ IN SEARCH OF THE CASTAWAYS

1962, 100 MINS, UK ◇ ⊛
Dir Robert Stevenson *Prod* Walt Disney *Scr* Lowell S. Hawley *Ph* Paul Beeson *Ed* Gordon Stone *Mus* William Alwyn *Art Dir* Michael Stringer
● Maurice Chevalier, Hayley Mills, George Sanders, Wilfrid Hyde White, Michael Anderson Jr, Wilfrid Brambell (Walt Disney)

Castaways is a blend of every Disney trick, combining adventure and humor. Jules Verne's yarn concerns a French scientist who finds a bottle containing a note which reveals the whereabouts of Captain Grant who mysteriously disappeared two years before. The Frenchman and the sea captain's two children persuade a wealthy shipping owner and his son to set off for South America in search of the missing man. The trail eventually leads successfully to Australia and New Zealand.

The party survives giant condors, jaguars, flood, lightning, crocodiles, an avalanche, an earthquake, a huge waterspout, mutiny by Grant's former quartermaster, imprisonment by unfriendly Maoris and an erupting volcano.

Thesping is done throughout with a tongue in the cheek exuberance which suggests that Disney and director Robert Stevenson have given the actors the go ahead to have fun. At times it almost looks as if they are making up the situations and dialog as they go along.

■ IN SOCIETY

1944, 73 MINS, US
Dir Jean Yarbrough *Prod* Edmund L. Hartmann *Scr* John Grant, Edmund L. Hartmann, Hal Fimberg *Ph* Jerome Ash *Ed* Philip Cahn *Mus* Edgar Fairchild (dir) *Art Dir* John B.Goodman, Eugene Lourie
● Bud Abbott, Lou Costello, Marion Hutton (Universal)

Basic idea of story spots Abbott and Costello as two struggling, extra-dumb plumbers being accidentally invited to a high society weekend soiree. Their exertions and blundering efforts to adjust themselves to new surroundings furnish the pegs on which many gags are strung. But even before reaching Hollywood's idea of effete society, a bunch of new and old comedy routines are dusted off and whipped across deftly.

Costello works in his old stride, while Abbott is more efficient, smooth-working than ever as straight in the laugh combo. Marion Hutton, a femme taxi dancer, provides the slight romantic twist opposite the wealthy Kirby Grant. She's supposed to be Costello's sweetie, but that's strictly for laughs, Hutton being Betty Hutton's sis.

■ IN THE COOL OF THE DAY

1963, 91 MINS, US ◇
Dir Robert Stevens *Prod* John Houseman *Scr* Meade Roberts *Ph* Peter Newbrook *Ed* Thomas Stanford *Mus* Francis Chagrin
● Peter Finch, Jane Fonda, Angela Lansbury, Constance Cummings, Arthur Hill, Alexander Knox (M-G-M)

John Houseman production was written for the screen from the novel by Susan Ertz. It concerns the romantic encounter that is briefly consummated during a mutual visit to Greece by an English book publisher (Peter Finch) who is taunted and tormented by a grudging, embittered, anti-social wife (Angela Lansbury), and a fragile American girl (Jane Fonda) who has been sheltered and protected to the point of absurdity by her adoring, but overly-finicky husband (Arthur Hill).

Most of this romantic schmaltz is set against some interesting Greek scenery such as the Parthenon and the Acropolis.

Peter Newbrook photographs ruins well, but is less effective with people. For example, he manages to disregard the dancers' legs in the course of a Grecian folk dance scene.

Lansbury gets off the best acting in the film as Finch's sour, scarfaced wife. She stirs up the only fun in the generally sour proceedings. Fonda, sporting a Cleopatra haircut, is all passion and intensity. When she loves, boy, she really loves. Finch wears one expression. It appears to be boredom, which is understandable.

■ IN THE FRENCH STYLE

1963, 104 MINS, US
Dir Robert Parrish *Prod* Irwin Shaw, Robert Parrish *Scr* Irwin Shaw *Ph* Michel Kelber *Ed* Renee Lichtig *Mus* Joseph Kosma *Art Dir* Rino Mondellini
● Jean Seberg, Stanley Baker, Addison Powell, James Leo Herlihy, Philippe Forquet (Shaw-Parrish)

Irwin Shaw and Robert Parrish have fashioned a sophisticated love story of Paris, of an American girl in love with the life not quite for her, in their indie based upon two of Shaw's stories, *In the French Style* and *A Year to Learn the Language.*

Jean Seberg stars as the 19-year-old Chicago girl, a would-be painter who dreams of conquering the capital of art, naive, ambitious, impressionable, who has her father's financial backing for one year to prove herself. She meets early romantic disillusionment, when she becomes involved with a young French engineering student whom she believes older than she.

Seberg brings life and brilliance to her portrayal, registering strongly both in the more dramatic and lighter moments. In Stanley Baker, the correspondent with whom she has a lingering affair, she has a firstrate costar who makes a good impression. Philippe Forquet, the youth, is brash and talented.

■ IN THE HEAT OF THE NIGHT

1967, 109 MINS, US ◇ ⊛
Dir Norman Jewison *Prod* Walter Mirisch *Scr* Stirling Silliphant *Ph* Haskell Wexler *Ed* Hal Ashby *Mus* Quincy Jones *Art Dir* Paul Groesse
● Sidney Poitier, Rod Steiger, Warren Oates, Lee Grant, Scott Wilson, Larry Gates (United Artists)

An excellent Sidney Poitier performance, and an outstanding one by Rod Steiger, overcome some noteworthy flaws to make *In the Heat of the Night*, an absorbing contemporary murder drama, set in the deep, red-necked South. Norman Jewison directs, sometimes in pretentious fashion, an uneven script.

Stirling Silliphant's script, adapted from John Ball's novel *Heat*, is erratic, indulging in heavy-handed, sometimes needless plot diversion, uncertain character development, and a rapid-fire denouement.

Intriguing plot basis has Poitier as the detective, accidentally on a visit to his Mississippi hometown where a prominent industrialist is found murdered. Arrested initially on the assumption that a Negro, out late at night, must have done the deed, Poitier later is thrust, by his boss in Philadelphia, his own conscience, and a temporary anti-white emotional outburst, into uneasy collaboration with local sheriff Steiger.

Steiger's transformation from a diehard Dixie bigot to a man who learns to respect Poitier stands out in smooth comparison to the wandering solution of the murder.
□ 1967: Best Picture

....

■ IN THE SPIRIT

1990, 93 MINS, US ◇ ▽
Dir Sandra Seacot   *Prod* Julian Schlossberg
Scr Jeannie Berlin, Laurie Jones   *Ph* Dick Quinlan
Ed Brad Fuller   *Mus* Patrick Williams   *Art Dir* Michael C. Smith
● Elaine May, Marlo Thomas, Jeannie Berlin, Peter Falk, Melanie Griffith, Olympia Dukakis (Running River/Castle Hill)

Elaine May and Marlo Thomas make a memorable screen odd couple in *In the Spirit*. Kooky black comedy is an unusual case of big-name talent gathering with friends to make a low-budget pic freed of mainstream good taste and gloss.

Like Jules Feiffer's *Little Murders* (1971) New York is a nightmare, with May moving back to Gotham from Beverley Hills with her just-fired hubby Peter Falk. She's thrown together with ditzy mystic Thomas after hiring her to redecorate an apartment.

Almost as goofy as Thomas is Jeannie Berlin, a prostie neighbor (and real life daughter of May). Coscripter Berlin writes herself out of the picture after the second reel and *Spirit* spins off in a different direction. Thomas and May flee the city to hole up at Michael Emil's new age retreat in upstate NY, pursued by a murderer.

First-time director Sandra Seacat emphasizes slapstick but also female bonding as the gals on the lam reach beyond their wacky survivalist tactics to address feminist issues.

May is very funny, giving a lesson in rat-a-tat-tat delivery. Thomas proves a perfect foil.

....

■ IN TOO DEEP

1990, 106 MINS, AUSTRALIA ◇
Dir Colin South, John Tatoulis   *Prod* Colin South, John Tatoulis   *Scr* Deborah Parsons   *Ph* Mark Gilfedder, Peter Zakharov   *Ed* Michael Collins, Nicolas Lee
Mus Tassos Ioannides   *Art Dir* Phil Chambers
● Hugo Race, Santha Press, Rebekah Elmaloglou, John Flaus (Media World)

This moody, erotic thriller from two first-time directors overcomes its slight narrative with its confident, bravura direction and cinematography.

Pic has the look and feel of a French film, in that atmosphere and sexual tension take pride of place over a slender plotline involving an affair between a femme jazz singer, Wendy (Santha Press), and Mack (Hugo Race) a knife-wielding young hood. Also involved is Wendy's young sister, JoJo (Rebekah Elmaloglou), a 15-year-old who gets turned on by her sister's sexual activities.

Tale takes place in an Australian city (Melbourne) in the middle of summer; heat is a factor in every sense of the word. Characters perspire a lot, and no wonder, given the energy of the numerous sex scenes.

Race, an Aussie rock singer, gives Mark a sinister persona. Newcomer Press is a knock-out. Elmaloglou is touching as the aroused

teen whose attraction for her sister's dangerous boyfriend nearly ends in tragedy.

....

■ IN WHICH WE SERVE

1942, 113 MINS, UK ▽
Dir Noel Coward, David Lean   *Prod* Noel Coward
Scr Noel Coward   *Ph* Ronald Neame   *Mus* Noel Coward   *Art Dir* David Rawnsley
● Noel Coward, John Mills, Bernard Miles, Celia Johnson, Michael Wilding, Richard Attenborough (Two Cities)

No less than half a dozen credits for this film go to Noel Coward. And they're well earned. It is the story of a British destroyer, from its completion to its destruction at sea by the Germans. She is dive-bombed in the Battle of Crete, but the survivors carry on the fight. It is a grim tale sincerely picturized and splendidly acted throughout. Only one important factor calls for criticism. It is that all the details are too prolonged.

The author-producer-scriptwriter-composer and co-director gives a fine performance as the captain of the vessel, but acting honors also go to the entire company.

Stark realism is the keynote of the writing and depiction, with no glossing of the sacrifices constantly being made by the sailors. They are seen clinging to a rubber raft, with cut-ins of several of them thinking of their wives and families at home and then flashing back to them in the water. This effect is impressive to a degree.
□ Best Picture (Nomination)

....

■ INADMISSIBLE EVIDENCE

1968, 94 MINS, UK
Dir Anthony Page   *Prod* Ronald Kinnoch   *Scr* John Osborne   *Ph* Kenneth Hodges   *Ed* Derek York   *Art Dir* Seamus Flannery
● Nicol Williamson, Eleanor Fazan, Jill Bennett, Peter Sallis, David Valla, Eileen Atkins (Woodfall)

As a play, the best thing about *Inadmissible Evidence* was Nicol Williamson, who brought to life the tormented, mediocre, bullying coward that John Osborne had conceived on paper. Same holds true for the screen version in which same actor appears. There is value and insight to the film. Yet much of it is opaque and confusing.

Evidence remains primarily a play. It is Osborne talking about a certain stage of civilization and various kinds of people it produces.

Williamson, as the lawyer who has achieved a certain measure of material success, is flagrantly promiscuous, professionally mediocre and personally a boor.

Williamson achieves the feat of making a big man look fragile, of gaining sympathy for boorish behavior and pitying insights of a coward and scoundrel.

Picture is in black-and-white and it adds to the bleakness of the portrait being presented. Yet the same effect could have been achieved had film been done in color.

....

■ INCHON

1981, 140 MINS, S. KOREA/US ◇
Dir Terence Young   *Prod* Mitsuharu Ishii   *Scr* Robin Moore/Laird Koenig   *Ph* Bruce Surtees   *Mus* Jerry Goldsmith
● Laurence Olivier, Jacqueline Bisset, Ben Gazzara, Toshiro Mifune, Richard Roundtree (One Way)

A major battle of the Korean war is given a decidedly religious viewpoint via *Inchon*,' a $46 million pic from One Way Prods, an org affiliated with the Rev Sun Myung Moon (who gets screen credit as special advisor on Korean matters).

Laurence Olivier plays Gen Douglas MacArthur in this film that was four years in the making and bills 50,000 extras.

Plot involves the general's orchestration of the 1950 landing at the South Korean port of Inchon by United Nations forces, with heavy emphasis on divine guidance. Olivier is convincing in his role throughout most of the saga, the only member of the cast to achieve that status.

Screenplay [from a story by Robin Moore and Paul Savage] generally treats all others as one-dimensional buffoons, giving them lines that are unintentionally laughable. One reason is that all plot digressions are simply window dressing to the film's focus on the brutally invading North Koreans and the big-scale counterattack by the good guys. No speaking roles are given the Communists, for example.

....

■ INCIDENT, THE

1967, 99 MINS, US ◇ ▽
Dir Larry Peerce   *Prod* Monroe Sachson, Edward Meadow   *Scr* Nicholas E. Baehr   *Ph* Gerald Hirschfeld   *Ed* Armand Lebowitz   *Mus* Terry Knight   *Art Dir* Manny Gerard
● Tony Musante, Martin Sheen, Beau Bridges, Bob Bannard, Ed McMahon, Diana Van der Vlis (20th Century-Fox/Moned)

Strong casting, impressive direction and generally sharp writing (from an old TV script) make *The Incident* a very fine episodic drama about two toughs who intimidate passengers on a NY subway train.

Some overexposure and relaxed editing flag the pace, but, overall, the production is a candid indictment, in situation and in dialog, of alienation.

Baehr's screenplay spotlights Tony Musante and Martin Sheen, out-for-kicks pair, who terrorize 16 train riders. Latter include soldiers Beau Bridges and Bob Bannard, middle-class couple Ed McMahon and Diana Van der Vlis (with child), elderly marrieds Jack Gilford and Thelma Ritter. The two toughs lay bare the weaknesses in all characters.

....

■ INCREDIBLE JOURNEY, THE

1963, 86 MINS, US ◇ ▽
Dir Fletcher Markle   *Prod* James Algar   *Scr* James Algar   *Ph* Kenneth Peach, Jack Couffer, Lloyd Beebe   *Ed* Norman Palmer   *Mus* Oliver Wallace
● Emile Genest, John Finlayson, Ronald Cohoon (Walt Disney)

Sheila Burnford's book of the same title is given a vivid translation in *The Incredible Journey*. The Walt Disney presentation is an exceptionally good, colorful adventure tale.

A bull terrier, Siamese cat and Labrador retriever comprise the unlikely trio of pals who, farmed out to a friend of their owners, embark on the journey – over 200 miles of treacherous Canadian terrain. They encounter crisis after crisis in what is a remarkable, nay incredible, fight to survive all sorts of adversities in their trip all the way home.

Director Fletcher Markle, with the assist of an animal trainer, has gotten an abundance of child-appealing excitement on the screen. And he sees to it that the story is told simply and directly, what with the humans on view exchanging dialog in honest fashion and an offscreen commentary by Rex Allen.

....

■ INCREDIBLE SARAH, THE

1976, 105 MINS, UK ◇ ▽
Dir Richard Fleischer   *Prod* Helen M. Strauss   *Scr* Ruth Wolff   *Ph* Christopher Challis   *Ed* John Jympson
Mus Elmer Bernstein   *Art Dir* Elliot Scott
● Glenda Jackson, Daniel Massey, Yvonne Mitchell, Douglas Wilmer, David Langton, Simon Williams (Readers Digest)

Ruth Wolff's script, conceded in opening titles to be a 'free' interpretation of Sarah

293

Bernhardt's early years, follows the famed actress from her early halting years on the French stage, then through an initial period of fame, notoriety and finally a youthful comeback of sorts at age 35. Glenda Jackson's versatile performance ranges from backstage, intimate situations to several lengthy excerpts from Bernhardt vehicles.

This is the story of a theatrical personality, not your average housewife. The achievement here is that Jackson makes the character comprehensible and, in a qualified way, admirable, notwithstanding the clear evidence of a totally selfcentered nature.

Strong supporting cast includes Daniel Massey as a playwright friend, and Simon Williams as an early lover and father of Bernhardt's son.

■ INCREDIBLE SHRINKING MAN, THE

1957, 81 MINS, US ⓥ

Dir Jack Arnold   *Prod* Albert Zugsmith   *Scr* Richard Matheson   *Ph* Ellis W. Carter   *Ed* Al Joseph   *Mus* Joseph Gershenson   *Art Dir* Alexander Golitzen, Robert Clatworthy

● Grant Williams, Randy Stuart, April Kent, Paul Langton, Raymond Bailey, William Schallert (Universal)

Richard Matheson scripted from his novel and, while most science-fiction thrillers usually contrive a happy ending, there's no compromise here. Six-footer Grant Williams and his wife (Randy Stuart) run into a fog while boating. She's below, so is untouched, but Williams gets the full force. Soon after, he finds himself shrinking and doctors decide the radioactivity in the fog has reversed his growth processes.

Director Jack Arnold works up the chills for maximum effect by the time Williams is down to two inches and the family cat takes after him. Also harrowing are his adventures in the cellar with, to him, a giant spider, which he manages to kill using a straight pin as a lance.

The technical staff has done an outstanding job of the trick stuff. Optical effects by Roswell A. Hoffmann and Everett H. Broussard make the shrinking visually effective.

■ INCREDIBLE SHRINKING WOMAN, THE

1981, 88 MINS, US ◇

Dir Joel Schumaker   *Prod* Hank Moonjean   *Scr* Jane Wagner   *Ph* Bruce Logan   *Ed* Jeff Gourson   *Mus* Suzanne Ciani   *Art Dir* Raymond A. Brandt

● Lily Tomlin, Charles Grodin, Ned Beatty, Henry Gibson, Maria Smith, Mark Blankfield (Universal)

Story of a contemporary housewife whose consistent use of chemically injected brand name foods, soap powders and aerosol-propelled products causes her to shrink to miniscule proportions is often strangely humorous with an underlying note of scathing social satire.

Director Joel Schumacher and writer-exec producer Jane Wagner have done a commendable job of creating a portrait of life in Anywhere USA where the tireless wife-mother (Lily Tomlin) must run a household, referee screaming kids and spruce up for her hard-working husband by the time evening rolls around.

Unfortunately, even Tomlin's talents begin to wear thin two-thirds into the film when she's kidnapped by baddies who want to use her to formulate a serum that will reduce the size of anyone in their way.

In supporting roles, ad exec hubby Charles Grodin (who perpetuates the very products that brought Tomlin to her unfortunate circumstance) and his boss Ned Beatty are first-rate. Problem is the premise just tires prematurely.

■ INDEPENDENCE DAY

1983, 110 MINS, US ◇ ⓥ

Dir Robert Mandel   *Prod* Daniel H. Blatt, Robert Singer   *Scr* Alice Hoffman   *Ph* Chuck Rosher   *Ed* Dennis Virkler, Tina Hirsch   *Mus* Charles Bernstein   *Art Dir* Stewart Campbell

● Kathleen Quinlan, David Keith, Frances Sternhagen, Cliff DeYoung, Dianne Wiest, Josef Sommer (Warner)

Independence Day is an unpleasant dramatic study of young people in a small southwestern town facing family problems and the perennial career decision: to stay home or trek to the big city. Despite some yeoman acting by a talented cast of character actors, the predictable and contrived storyline proves intractable.

Alice Hoffman's unfocused screenplay centers upon two people in their 20s: Mary Ann Taylor (Kathleen Quinlan), a waitress in her dad's diner in the tiny south-western town and Jack Parker (David Keith), a gas station mechanic just home after an unsuccessful stay at engineering school.

While the duo's romance blossoms, Parker is coping with his suicidal sister Nancy (Dianne Wiest), her philandering, wife-beating husband Les (Cliff DeYoung) and his own brutish father (Noble Willingham).

Keith reinforces his image as a likable and forceful young performer while Quinlan demonstrates the ambivalence of love vs a career quite skillfully.

■ INDIANA JONES AND THE LAST CRUSADE

1989, 127 MINS, US ◇ ⓥ

Dir Steven Spielberg   *Prod* Robert Watts   *Scr* Jeffrey Boam   *Ph* Douglas Slocombe   *Ed* Michael Kahn   *Mus* John Williams   *Art Dir* Elliot Scott

● Harrison Ford, Sean Connery, Denholm Elliott, Alison Doody, John Rhys-Davies, River Phoenix (Lucasfilm)

More cerebral than the first two Indiana Jones films, and less schmaltzy than the second, this literate adventure should entertain and enlighten kids and adults alike.

The Harrison Ford-Sean Connery father-and-son team gives *Last Crusade* unexpected emotional depth, reminding us that real film magic is not in special effects.

Witty and laconic screenplay, based on a story by George Lucas and Menno Meyjes, takes Ford and Connery on a quest for a prize bigger than the Lost Ark of the Covenant – the Holy Grail.

Connery is a medieval lit prof with strong religious convictions who has spent his life assembling clues to the grail's whereabouts. Father and more intrepid archaeologist son piece them together in an around-the-world adventure, leading to a touching and mystical finale. The love between father and son transcends even the quest for the Grail, which is guarded by a spectral 700-year-old knight beautifully played by Robert Eddison. This film minimizes the formulaic love interest, giving newcomer Alison Doody an effectively sinuous but decidedly secondary role.

■ INDIANA JONES AND THE TEMPLE OF DOOM

1984, 118 MINS, US ◇ ⓥ

Dir Steven Spielberg   *Prod* Robert Watts   *Scr* Willard Huyck, Gloria Katz   *Ph* Douglas Slocombe   *Ed* Michael Kahn   *Mus* John Williams   *Art Dir* Elliot Scott

● Harrison Ford, Kate Capshaw, Ke Huy Quan, Amrish Puri, Roshan Seth, Philip Stone (Lucasfilm)

Steven Spielberg has packed even more thrills and chills into this followup than he did into the earlier pic, but to exhausting and numbing effect.

Prequel finds dapper Harrison Ford as

Indiana Jones in a Shanghai nightclub in 1935, and title sequence, which features Kate Capshaw chirping Cole Porter's 'Anything Goes' looks like something out of Spielberg's *1941*.

Ford escapes from an enormous melee with the chanteuse and Oriental moppet Ke Huy Quan and they head by plane to the mountains of Asia where they are forced to jump out in an inflatable raft coming to rest in an impoverished Indian village.

Community's leader implores the ace archaeologist to retrieve a sacred, magical stone which has been stolen by malevolent neighbors.

Remainder of the yarn is set in labyrinth of horrors lorded over by a prepubescent maharajah, where untold dangers await the heroes.

What with John Williams' incessant score and the library full of sound effects, there isn't a quiet moment in the entire picture.

Ford seems effortlessly to have picked up where he left off when Indiana Jones was last heard from, although Capshaw, who looks fetching in native attire, has unfortunately been asked to react hysterically to everything that happens to her.

■ INDISCREET

1931, 93 MINS, US ⓥ

Dir Leo McCarey   *Scr* DeSylva, Brown and Henderson   *Ph* Ray June, Gregg Toland   *Ed* Hal C. Kern   *Art Dir* Alfred Newman

● Gloria Swanson, Ben Lyon, Monroe Owsley, Barbara Kent, Arthur Lake, Maude Eburne (United Artists)

An original story of the musical comedy writing trio of DeSylva, Brown and Henderson, it is without music of moment or quantity. The three boys have fashioned a composite of a lot of other stories, giving it all an original slant. Direction, production and playing fit. As a comedy-drama it is more comedy than drama.

Story starts with s.a. and never stops. The menace is ever on the make, becoming engaged to a younger sister after being thrown down by the sister she had lived with.

Gloria Swanson has most of the laughs, through dialog mostly, but Arthur Lake, as a lovesick kid, gets his points over punchily. They are not as plentiful as Swanson's but they are more bangy and longer remembered.

Ben Lyon plays the light minded but sincere author who falls for Jerry (Swanson) but won't listen about her past when she gets to the point of should a woman tell.

■ INDISCREET

1958, 100 MINS, US ◇ ⓥ

Dir Stanley Donen   *Prod* Stanley Donen   *Scr* Norman Krasna   *Ph* Frederick A. Young   *Ed* Jack Harris   *Mus* Richard Rodney Bennett, Ken Jones   *Art Dir* Don Ashton

● Cary Grant, Ingrid Bergman, Cecil Parker, Phyllis Calvert, David Kossoff, Megs Jenkins (Grandon/Warner)

A beguiling love story delicately deranged by the complications of sophisticated comedy, *Indiscreet* is an expert film version of Norman Krasna's 1953 stage play, *Kind Sir*. Though tedious in its opening reels, the production warms up in direct relation to the heat of the love affair and, in the end, manages to fade out in a blaze of playful merriment.

As the successful actress who has yet to find love, Ingrid Bergman is alluring, most affectionate and highly amusing. Cary Grant makes a ripping gadabout, conniving and gracious, his performance sometimes hilarious and always smooth.

Moving from the New York of *Kind Sir*, the locale has been shipped to London where Bergman lives and wants to love. Grant, a rich American who holds a NATO post, lives there too (at least on weekends, commuting as he does from Paris) and he too wants to love. But the difference is he wants nothing of marriage and, to protect all concerned, advises Bergman on first meeting that he is a married man, separated and unable to obtain a divorce. Still she invites him to the ballet.

Cecil Parker, as the brother-in-law, becomes funnier as he becomes more unnerved, and Phyllis Calvert is excellent as the sister. Megs Jenkins turns in a fine performance as the maid, and David Kossoff, as the chauffeur, admirably grabs the high spot of hilarity with his pseudo-lover stroll-on.

● ●

■ **INDISCRETION OF AN AMERICAN WIFE**

1954, 63 MINS, ITALY/US ▼

Dir Vittorio De Sica   *Prod* Vittorio De Sica   *Scr* Cesare Zavattini, Luigi Chiarini, Giorgio Prosperi, Truman Capote   *Ph* G.R. Aldo   *Ed* Eraldo Da Rema, Jean Barker   *Mus* Alessandro Cicognini

● Jennifer Jones, Montgomery Clift, Gino Cervi, Richard Beymer (Columbia)

The plot of *Indiscretion of an American Wife* is told rather precisely in the title. It is an Italian-filmed feature, very consciously arty and foreign, but with the American star names of Jennifer Jones and Montgomery Clift.

The picture was directed by Vittorio De Sica from Cesare Zavattini's story, *Terminal Station.* The lensing was done in its entirety in the Stazione Termini in Rome, where the story of an American housewife saying farewell to her holiday lover takes place.

US distribution rights to the picture, held by Selznick Releasing Organization, were turned over to Columbia and the footage edited down considerably from its foreign release length [87 minutes]. In fact the trimming was so drastic Columbia ordered a musical prolog from SRO to pad out the footage, so *Indiscretion* got an eight-minute hitchhiker riding along.

As typical of foreign film pretentions, much use is made of bits and types flowing through the busy railway terminal to color and add movement to the picture. Outside of the agonizing moments of farewells between Jones, Philadelphia housewife returning to her safe hearth, and her younger holiday lover, Clift, the story's dramatic suspense pull is developed around the couple's arrest after being discovered in an extremely compromising embrace in a secluded spot.

The stars give the drama a real pro try and the professional standards of delivery are high, even though the character interpretations will not be liked by all.

● ●

■ **INFORMER, THE**

1935, 91 MINS, US ▼

Dir John Ford   *Prod* Cliff Reid   *Scr* Dudley Nichols   *Ph* Joseph H. August   *Ed* George Hively   *Mus* Max Steiner   *Art Dir* Van Nest Polglase, Charles Kirk

● Victor McLaglen, Heather Angel, Preston Foster, Margot Grahame, Wallace Ford, Una O'Connor (RKO)

The Informer is forcefully and intelligently written, directed and acted. Story [by Liam O'Flaherty] deals with the Irish rebellion against British authority prior to 1922, when the Irish Free State's creation finally removed the hated symbols of British domination.

Amidst the rebellion-rife slums of Dublin a huge ox of a peasant, named Gypo Nolan (Victor McLaglen) loves Katie Fox (Margot Grahame) who picks up her room rent on the streets. Gypo reproaches her and is in turn taunted for his miserable poverty and inability to provide money. Stung by the girl's bitterness, Gypo, in fascinated horror at his own wickedness, deliberately turns informer on his best friend to obtain $100 reward. Irony of this deed is that Gypo is really a softie,

having been court martialed and expelled from the Republican army for failing to carry out a political assassination.

What makes the picture powerful is the faithful characterization of McLaglen as guided and developed by the direction of John Ford. Gypo is a blundering, pathetic fool who is not basically vicious yet is guilty of a truly foul betrayal.

Wallace Ford, as the boy who is turned in, is smartly cast. Margot Grahame grabs some attention as the harlot. Preston Foster, a good actor, is the head of the Republican underground battalion.

☐ 1935: Best Picture (Nomination)

● ●

■ **INFORMERS, THE**

1963, 105 MINS, UK

Dir Ken Annakin   *Prod* William McQuitty   *Scr* Alun Falconer   *Ph* Reginald Wyer   *Ed* Alfred Roome   *Mus* Clifton Parker

● Nigel Patrick, Frank Finlay, Derren Nesbitt, Colin Blakely, Catharine Woodville, Maggie Whiting (Rank)

Here's a tough, hard-hitting, cops-and-robbers thriller set in London's underworld which, despite the story line, situations and characters occasionally tripping themselves up, crackles along at a brisk pace and has the smell of authenticity.

Douglas Warner's novel, *Death of a Snout,* has been turned into a slick screenplay. Central character is Chief Inspector Johnno (Nigel Patrick) a dedicated cop at Scotland Yard. He has many contacts in the underworld and the snouts, or informers, feed him with many a juicy lead to solving a crime. But Johnno's chief insists that personal contact with informers should be out. From now on, scientific methods must be used. But Johnno believes he is close to cracking the gang that has been pulling off some audacious banknote robberies and is sure that one of his most wily informants can put him on the trail. So he disobeys orders.

Patrick gives a suave, dominating performance in which, till the finale, he uses brain rather than brawn. Of the assorted villains, outstanding are Frank Finlay as the bossman and Derren Nesbitt, with an insidious study in oily menace, as the pimp who organizes the robberies.

● ●

■ **INHERIT THE WIND**

1960, 126 MINS, US ▼

Dir Stanley Kramer   *Prod* Stanley Kramer   *Scr* Nathan E. Douglas, Harold Jacob Smith   *Ph* Ernest Laszlo   *Ed* Fredric Knudtson   *Mus* Ernest Gold   *Art Dir* Rudolph Sternad

● Spencer Tracy, Fredric March, Gene Kelly, Florence Eldridge, Harry Morgan, Philip Coolidge (United Artists)

This is a rousing and fascinating motion picture. Producer-director Stanley Kramer has held the action in tight check, whether in a stifling country court or recording the swelling emotion of mob religious fervor, indignation and fury.

One suspects it needed a strong hand to restrain the forensics of Spencer Tracy and Fredric March as defense and prosecution attorneys in this drama inspired by the 1925 trial in Dayton, Tennessee, of a young high school teacher, John T. Scopes, for daring to teach Darwin's theory of evolution. Roles of Tracy and March equal Clarence Darrow and William Jennings Bryan who collided on evolution.

Tracy and March go at each other on the thespic plane as one might imagine Dempsey and Louis. March actually has the more colorful role as Matthew Harrison Brady (Bryan) because, with the aid of face-changing makeup, he creates a completely different character, whereas Tracy is not so benefited and has to rely solely upon his power of

illusion. That is a most persuasive power indeed.

The scenario, which broadens the scope of the play by Jerome Lawrence and Robert E. Lee, is a most commendable job. It is shot through with dialog that it florid, witty, penetrating, compassionate and sardonic. A good measure of the film's surface bite is contributed by Gene Kelly as a cynical Baltimore reporter (patterned after Henry L. Menken) whose paper comes to the aid of the younger teacher played by Dick York. Kelly demonstrates again that even without dancing shoes he knows his way on the screen.

● ●

■ **IN-LAWS, THE**

1979, 103 MINS, US ◇ ▼

Dir Arthur Hiller   *Prod* Arthur Hiller   *Scr* Andrew Bergman   *Ph* David M. Walsh   *Ed* Robert E. Swink   *Mus* John Morris   *Art* Pato Guzman

● Peter Falk, Alan Arkin, Richard Libertini, Nancy Dussault, Arlene Golonka (Warner)

Peter Falk and Alan Arkin were the perfect choices to play an addled CIA agent and a Gotham dentist, respectively. Brought together by the impending marriage of their individual offspring (Michael Lembeck and Penny Peyser), they're quickly at one another's throats, as Falk lures Arkin into a never-ending series of improbable adventures.

Script elements include stolen US treasury plates, underworld thugs, and a South American banana republic and its deranged leader.

Under Arthur Hiller's fast-paced and engaging direction, everything keeps moving quickly enough to stymie audience qualms about plotting, character developments and a rapidly-compressed time frame.

● ●

■ **INN OF THE SIXTH HAPPINESS, THE**

1958, 160 MINS, UK ◇

Dir Mark Robson   *Prod* Buddy Adler   *Scr* Isobel Lennart   *Ph* Freddie A. Young   *Ed* Ernest Walter   *Mus* Malcolm Arnold   *Art Dir* John Box, Geoffrey Drake

● Ingrid Bergman, Curt Jurgens, Robert Donat, Ronald Squire, Athene Seyler, Peter Chong (20th Century-Fox)

Based on Alan Burgess' novel *The Small Woman* which, in turn, was based on the adventures of a real person, the film has Ingrid Bergman as a rejected missionary in China, who gets there determinedly under her own steam. First met with hostility by the natives, she gradually wins their love and esteem. She falls in love with a Eurasian colonel, converts a powerful mandarin to Christianity and becomes involved in the Chino-Japanese war. Finally she guides 100 children to the safety of a northern mission by leading them on an arduous journey across the rugged mountains and through enemy territory.

The inn in the film is run by Bergman and an elderly missionary (Athene Seyler). Here they dispense hospitality and Bible stories to the muleteers in transit. Bergman's early scenes as she strives to get to China and those in which she gradually settles down in her environment and begins the urgent task of winning the confidence of the Chinese are brilliantly done with humor and a sense of urgent dedication.

Curt Jurgens is less happily served as the Eurasian colonel. The slender love theme seems to have been dropped into the main story and Jurgens has less command of the awkward role than usual.

A standout performance comes from Robert Donat as an astute yet benign mandarin. It was Donat's swansong before his untimely death and only rarely can signs of his physical collapse be detected.

The film was shot in Wales and in the Elstree studio, converted expertly into a

Chinese village. Mark Robson's direction slickly catches both the sweep of the crowd sequences and the more intimate ones.

■ **INNERSPACE**

1987, 120 MINS, US ◇ Ⓥ
Dir Joe Dante   *Prod* Michael Finnell   *Scr* Jeffrey Boam, Chip Proser   *Ph* Andrew Laszlo   *Ed* Kent Beyda   *Mus* Jerry Goldsmith   *Art Dir* James H. Spencer
● Dennis Quaid, Martin Short, Meg Ryan, Kevin McCarthy, Fiona Lewis, Vernon Wells (Spielberg/Amblin)

Hot Dog Air Force flyer Dennis Quaid is prepared at the outset to be shrunken and pilot a tiny craft through the bloodstream of a laboratory rabbit. Evildoers are on to the unprecedented experiment and the syringe bearing the fearless voyager finally implants itself in the behind of Martin Short, a hapless grocery clerk.

Filmmakers' ingenuity quickly begins asserting itself. As Quaid travels through different parts of the unsuspecting shnook's body and speaks to him over his radio, Short believes he's going crazy before finally accepting what's happened to him.

Quaid is engagingly reckless and gung-ho as the pioneer into a new dimension, although he is physically constrained in his little capsule for most of the running time. Short has infinitely more possibilities and makes the most of them, coming into his own as a screen personality as a mild-mannered little guy who rises to an extraordinary situation. Meg Ryan is game as the spirited doll both men hanker for, and supporting cast is filled out with a good assortment of familiar faces.

■ **INNOCENT BYSTANDERS**

1972, 111 MINS, UK ◇
Dir Peter Collinson   *Prod* George H. Brown   *Scr* James Mitchell   *Ph* Brian Probyn   *Ed* Alan Pattillo   *Mus* John Keating   *Art Dir* Maurice Carter
● Stanley Baker, Geraldine Chaplin, Donald Pleasence, Dana Andrews, Sue Lloyd, Warren Mitchell (Sagittarius)

Innocent Bystanders is a violence-packed, often-confusing but usually-interesting meller of secret agents on the prowl to track down and capture a Russian scientist escaped from a Siberian prison. Scene shifts from London to N.Y., thence to Turkey, where major portion of action unfolds against colorful location backgrounds.

Stanley Baker is chief protagonist, once top agent of Britain's hush-hush spy organization but now regarded as slipped by his chief (Donald Pleasence), who in a final assignment gives him a chance to redeem himself on the scientist caper.

Never exactly explained is the reason for the desperate hunt of the scientist. Script by James Mitchell [from a novel by James Munro] is sufficiently exciting, however, and direction by Peter Collinson so realistic, that interest never lags.

■ **INNOCENT MAN, AN**

1989, 113 MINS, US ◇ Ⓥ
Dir Peter Yates   *Prod* Ted Field, Robert W. Cort   *Scr* Larry Brothers   *Ph* William A. Fraker   *Ed* Stephen A. Rotter, William S. Scharf   *Mus* Howard Shore   *Art Dir* Stuart Wurtzel
● Tom Selleck, F. Murray Abraham, Laila Robins, David Rasche, Richard Young (Touchstone/Silver Screen Partners IV)

This collection of cliches accomplishes the almost unthinkable by bringing the prison genre to a new low.

Nightmarishly structured, the film takes half-hour before Tom Selleck's everyman,

Jimmie Rainwood, gets wrongfully framed by two corrupt vice cops (David Rasche and Richard Young). Then he spends more than an hour in stir before he gets released to seek vengeance on the duo in one of the more absurd finales in memory.

In between, Jimmie gets a lesson in prison survival from the cell-wise Virgil (F. Murray Abraham), learning to do the previously unthinkable to survive the hellish conditions.

■ **INNOCENTS, THE**

1961, 99 MINS, UK
Dir Jack Clayton   *Prod* Jack Clayton   *Scr* William Archibald, Truman Capote   *Ph* Freddie Francis   *Ed* James Clark   *Mus* Georges Auric   *Art Dir* Wilfred Shingleton
● Deborah Kerr, Michael Redgrave, Peter Wyngarde, Megs Jenkins, Martin Stephens, Pamela Franklin (20th Century-Fox)

Based on Henry James' story *Turn of the Screw* this catches an eerie, spine-chilling mood right at the start and never lets up on its grim, evil theme. Director Jack Clayton makes full use of camera angles, sharp cutting, shadows, ghost effects and a sinister soundtrack.

Deborah Kerr has a long, arduous role as a governess in charge of two apparently angelic little children in a huge country house. Gradually she finds that they are not all that they seem on the surface. Her determination to save the two moppets' corrupted souls leads up to a tragic, powerful climax.

Clayton's small but expert cast do full justice to their tasks, Kerr runs a wide gamut of emotions in a difficult role in which she has to start with an uncomplicated portrayal and gradually find herself involved in strange, unnatural goings-on, during which she sometimes doubts her own sanity. Clayton has also coaxed a couple of remarkable pieces of playing from the two youngsters, Martin Stephens and Pamela Franklin, extraordinary blends of innocence and sophistry.

■ **INSERTS**

1975, 117 MINS, UK ◇
Dir John Byrum   *Prod* Davina Belling, Clive Parsons   *Scr* John Byrum   *Ph* Denys Cooper   *Ed* Mike Bradsell   *Art Dir* John Clark
● Richard Dreyfuss, Jessica Harper, Stephen Davis, Veronica Cartwright, Bob Hoskins (United Artists)

Despite its British label, this is a thoroughly Yank pic that dips into nostalgia and Hollywood 1930s themes.

Richard Dreyfuss is all coiled disdain as a once-great director reduced to stag pix.

Dreyfuss manages to add some unusual touches to them as the moneyman walks in with a lissome girl he is planning to marry but whom he treats as a child.

The boss leaves the girl with Dreyfuss; the girl wants to be in pictures and finally decides to pose for inserts; they are caught by the boss, who is not sure what happened but takes off with the camera and material.

Jessica Harper scores as the shrewd innocent and Stephen Davies and Bob Hoskins are right as the actor and boss respectively. But it is all somewhat too surface despite allusions to Hollywood 1930s types.

■ **INSIDE DAISY CLOVER**

1965, 128 MINS, US ◇
Dir Robert Mulligan   *Prod* Alan J. Pakula   *Scr* Gavin Lambert   *Ph* Charles Lang   *Ed* Aaron Stell   *Mus* Andre Previn   *Art Dir* Robert Clatworthy
● Natalie Wood, Christopher Plummer, Robert Redford, Roddy McDowall, Ruth Gordon, Katharine Bard (Warner)

There will be those who may claim *Inside Daisy Clover* is based upon the true-life story

of an actress who rose to shining blonde stardom. Alan J. Pakula and Robert Mulligan focus their sights upon a teenage beach gamin who becomes a Hollywood star of the 1930s. Covering a two-year period, the outcome is at times disjointed and episodic as the title character played by Natalie Wood emerges more nebulous than definitive.

Femme star seems to be eternally searching for the meaning of her role; she is almost inarticulate for long intervals and whoever is in a scene with her generally engages in a monolog since there is seldom dialog between them. The Gavin Lambert screenplay, based on his own novel, hop-skips through a brief romance with a screen idol, her one-day marriage, desertion and divorce; a nervous breakdown after the death of her mother.

Probably the outstanding parts of pic are two novel musical numbers, one in which the studio boss introduces his new star in a specially-made film shown at a party and second featuring her after she's reached stardom.

Wood is better than her part. Her co-star is Christopher Plummer, who gives polish and some stiffness to the sadistic studio head bound to build himself a star.

■ **INSIDE MOVES**
THE GUYS FROM MAX'S BAR

1980, 113 MINS, US ◇ Ⓥ
Dir Richard Donner   *Prod* Mark M. Tanz, R.W. Goodwin   *Scr* Valerie Curtin, Barry Levinson   *Ph* Laszlo Kovacs   *Ed* Frank Morriss   *Mus* John Barry   *Art Dir* Charles Rosen
● John Savage, David Morse, Diana Scarwid, Harold Russell, Amy Wright, Tony Burton (AFD/Goodmark)

Inoffensive and essentially compassionate, *Inside Moves* is also a highly conventional and predictable look at handicapped citizens trying to make it in everyday life.

Director Richard Donner focuses on the intermittently tense relationship between insecure, failed suicide John Savage and volatile David Morse.

Basic plot movement [from the novel by Todd Walton] has Savage, permanently hobbled after jumping off a building, gradually regaining confidence.

Performances can't be faulted, with Savage seeming truly disturbed at the start, only to slowly come to terms with himself. In his feature debut, Morse puts across the called-for ambition and later shallowness, and Diana Scarwid hits the right notes as a 'normal' young woman forced to confront her own limitations via the outwardly afflicted.

■ **INSIGNIFICANCE**

1985, 108 MINS, UK ◇ Ⓥ
Dir Nicolas Roeg   *Prod* Jeremy Thomas   *Scr* Terry Johnson   *Ph* Peter Hannan   *Ed* Tony Lawson   *Mus* Stanley Myers   *Art Dir* David Brockhurst
● Gary Busey, Tony Curtis, Michael Emil, Theresa Russell, Will Sampson (Zenith/Recorded Picture)

A comedy set in a New York hotel room over a sweaty night in 1953 might seem an odd assignment for such a serious and innovative director as Nicolas Roeg.

Story concerns four celebrated American figures of the 1950s who, for legal reasons are not specifically named. That's all to the good since pic dispenses with biographical detail to focus on the nature of celebrity in Cold War America.

Film was scripted by Terry Johnson from his stage play. Although legit text is not opened out in a traditional way, beautifully lensed views of the NY landscape and flashbacks give the film a sense of scale. When, towards the end of the film, the Elevator Attendant greets the dawn Cherokee-style, the hotel room has become a microcosm of the world outside.

Those on the lookout for philosophical

reflections will find plenty to think about in the pic's meditations upon relativity and the coming together of time. *Insignificance* also works on a simpler level as a depiction of four people struggling against despair.

■ **INSPECTOR CLOUSEAU**

1968, 105 MINS, UK ◇

Dir Bud Yorkin   *Prod* Lewis J. Rachmil   *Scr* Tom Waldman, Frank Waldman   *Ph* Arthur Ibbetson   *Ed* John Victor Smith   *Mus* Ken Thorne   *Art Dir* Michael Stringer

● Alan Arkin, Frank Finlay, Delia Boccardo, Patrick Cargill, Beryl Reid, Barry Foster (United Artists/Mirisch)

Inspector Clouseau, the gauche and Gallic gumshoe, gets a healthy revitalization via Alan Arkin in the title role and director Bud Yorkin.

Film is a lively, entertaining and episodic story of bank robbers. Good scripting, better acting and topnotch direction get the most out of the material.

Clouseau is assigned to Scotland Yard to help solve a major bank heist. Story develops to a simultaneous robbery of about a dozen Swiss banks, by a ring whose members wear face masks patterned after Clouseau.

Story develops in leisurely fashion, which could have worked to overall disadvantage were it not for the excellent work of Arkin and Yorkin which keeps plot adrenalin flowing. Instead, enough momentum is sustained to hold amused interest.

■ **INTERIORS**

1978, 93 MINS, US ◇ Ⓥ

Dir Woody Allen   *Prod* Charles H. Joffe   *Scr* Woody Allen   *Ph* Gordon Willis   *Ed* Ralph Rosenblum   *Art Dir* Mel Bourne

● Kristin Griffith, Mary Beth Hurt, Richard Jordan, Diane Keaton, E.G. Marshall, Geraldine Page (United Artists)

Watching this picture a question keeps recurring: what would Woody Allen think of all this? Then you remember he wrote and directed it.

The film is populated by characters reacting to situations Allen has satirized so brilliantly in other pictures. Diane Keaton is a suffering poet married to Richard Jordan, a novelist overshadowed by Keaton's accomplishments and talents. Keaton has two sisters – Kristin Griffith, a television actress, and Mary Beth Hurt, the most gifted of the three, but the least directed.

What would be called the film's action – like Ingmar Bergman's pictures, the movement is interior, in the mind – revolves around the relationship among the sisters and their parents, E.G. Marshall and Geraldine Page.

Interiors also looks like a Bergman film. Characters are photographed against blank walls, Keaton's discussions with her analyst appear almost to be a confession into the camera. And the final third of *Interiors* was shot near the ocean in Long Island and looks like the Swedish island on which Bergman has photographed so many of his films.

Keaton's role is the most difficult, but her performance the least believable of the eight principals. Maureen Stapleton as the woman Marshall marries after divorcing Page, is the only character who reacts more from the heart than the head.

■ **INTERLUDE**

1968, 113 MINS, UK Ⓥ

Dir Kevin Billington   *Prod* David Deutsch   *Scr* Lee Langley, Hugh Leonard   *Ph* Gerry Fisher   *Ed* Bert Bates   *Mus* Georges Delerue   *Art Dir* Tony Woollard

● Oskar Werner, Barbara Ferris, Virginia Maskell, Donald Sutherland, Nora Swinburne (Columbia/Domino)

Interlude is not just another *Brief Encounter* type of romantic drama; it is one of the best of its class. Oskar Werner and Barbara Ferris are the star-crossed, and star-billed, lovers in this handsome production, filmed in England.

All the excitement and ecstacy, as well as the bittersweet, foredoomed disenchantment of extra-marital romance are contained in the original screenplay. Strong writing, superior acting and firstrate direction make this a powerful, personal drama.

Werner plays a temperamental symphonic conductor who is interviewed by Ferris, a newspaper reporter, the story unfolding in flashback format.

A tender, fragile atmosphere is established early, and sustained quite well.

Werner's performance is excellent, despite some wardrobe and makeup which occasionally fights the credibility of his character. Ferris is outstanding; to her goes the burden of commingling the love-hate, up-down, sweet-sour aspects of the affair, and she carries it superbly. Virginia Maskell's character, unlike the stock 'wife,' comes to life.

■ **INTERMEZZO**

1939, 70 MINS, US Ⓥ

Dir Gregory Ratoff   *Prod* David O. Selznick   *Scr* George O'Neil   *Ph* Gregg Toland   *Ed* Hal C. Kern, Francis D. Lyon   *Mus* Lou Forbes (dir.)   *Art Dir* Lyle R. Wheeler

● Leslie Howard, Ingrid Bergman, Edna Best, John Halliday (United Artists/Selznick)

Intermezzo is an American remake of a picture turned out three years earlier in Sweden which Gustav Molander directed, with Ingrid Bergman in the femme lead.

Story structure [based on original by Molander and Gosta Stevens] is a love triangle involving a famed concert violinist and a young girl pianist, but the romance lacks persuasiveness.

Leslie Howard, who functions as star and associate producer, is eclipsed by Bergman. Latter is beautiful, talented and convincing, providing an arresting performance and a warm personality that introduces a new stellar asset to Hollywood. She has charm, sincerity and an infectious vivaciousness.

Picture unwinds at a leisurely pace, without theatrics of too great intensity in the romantic passages.

■ **INTERNAL AFFAIRS**

1990, 117 MINS, US ◇ Ⓥ

Dir Mike Figgis   *Prod* Frank Mancuso Jr   *Scr* Henry Bean   *Ph* John A. Alonzo   *Ed* Robert Estrin   *Mus* Mike Figgis, Anthony Marinelli, Brian Banks   *Art Dir* Waldemar Kalinowski

● Richard Gere, Andy Garcia, Nancy Travis, Laurie Metcalf, William Baldwin (Paramount)

The title is a clever double entendre, as Andy Garcia plays LAPD internal affairs division investigator Raymond Avila, pulled into a psychological game of chicken with quarry Dennis Peck (Richard Gere), a much-honored street cop who manipulates his position as easily as he does the people around him.

Played by Gere with a constant sense of menace, Peck preys on Raymond's insecurities by insinuating that he's bedded his wife (Nancy Travis) – increasingly neglected, ironically, as Raymond thrusts his all into the case.

While hardly new territory, director Mike Figgis wrings every ounce of tension from tyro writer Henry Bean's screenplay and, most impressively, elicits firstrate performances from top to bottom.

The look, too, immeasurably helps in creating a foreboding atmosphere. Figgis never lets the pace slow long enough to expose the story's thinness despite, in retrospect, a moderate amount of action.

■ **INTERNATIONAL VELVET**

1978, 125 MINS, UK ◇ Ⓥ

Dir Bryan Forbes   *Prod* Bryan Forbes   *Scr* Bryan Forbes   *Ph* Tony Imi   *Ed* Timothy Gee   *Mus* Francis Lai   *Art Dir* Keith Wilson

● Tatum O'Neal, Christopher Plummer, Anthony Hopkins, Nanette Newman, Peter Barkworth, Dinsdale Landen (M-G-M)

International Velvet is an extremely fine film for (in the best sense) family audiences. Bryan Forbes wrote, produced and directed the sequel to *National Velvet* [1944] in such a way as to provide sentiment, excitement and dual-level drama that should ring true with its target audience. Tatum O'Neal heads a strong cast as an orphaned teenager whose attachment to a horse leads to her own adjustment and maturity.

In the new script, the original Velvet Brown is now nearing middle age as a childless divorcee though happy in a relationship with Christopher Plummer, an author who provides her much emotional support. It's Nanette Newman's good fortune to play the role, and she does so excellently.

All this is to the good while O'Neal evolves from a hostile alien orphan to a high degree of adolescent maturity. Anthony Hopkins is excellent as the equestrian team trainer whose dedication to the sport will give contemporary audiences a graceful exposition of what is going on.

■ **INTERNS, THE**

1962, 130 MINS, US Ⓥ

Dir David Swift   *Prod* Robert Cohn   *Scr* Walter Newman, David Swift   *Ph* Russell L. Metty   *Ed* Al Clark, Jerome Thoms   *Mus* Leith Stevens   *Art Dir* Don Ament

● Michael Callan, Cliff Robertson, James MacArthur, Nick Adams, Telly Savalas, Stefanie Powers (Columbia)

In its apparent attempt to dramatize candidly and irreverently the process by which school-finished candidate medics manage to turn into regular doctors, the film somehow succeeds in depicting the average intern as some kind of a Hippocratic oaf. At times it comes perilously close to earning the nickname, *Carry On, Intern*.

The separate stories of five interns, four male and one female, are traced alternately in a sort of razzle-dazzle style by the screenplay from Richard Frede's novel. Three of the stories are predictable from the word go and the other two are thoroughly unbelievable.

As these personal stories unfold, a kind of cross-section of hospital life is transpiring in the background. Chief features are a rather gory childbirth sequence, a mercy killing incident and a wild party passage imitative of the one in *Breakfast at Tiffany's*, but hardly as appropriate or amusing. Support characters run to stereotype, i.e. the ugly, prim nurse who removes her spex, lets her hair down, gets stinko and becomes the hit of the party.

■ **INTO THE NIGHT**

1985, 115 MINS, US ◇ Ⓥ

Dir John Landis   *Prod* George Folsey Jr, Ron Koslow   *Scr* Ron Koslow   *Ph* Robert Paynter   *Ed* Malcolm Campbell   *Mus* Ira Newborn   *Art Dir* John Lloyd

● Jeff Goldblum, Michelle Pfeiffer, Richard Farnsworth, Irene Papas, Kathryn Harrold, Paul Mazursky (Universal)

Over in the suburbs dwells quiet aerospace engineer Jeff Goldblum whose job is going nowhere while his wife goes too far with another man. Mulling all this over in the middle of the night, Goldblum ambles aimlessly out to the airport where Michelle

Pfeiffer has just arrived with six smuggled emeralds.

Apparently, Pfeiffer has performed this chore for one or more boyfriends and the promise of some cash, but she is hardly prepared for the four killers awaiting her arrival. Fleeing them, she leaps into Goldblum's car and from then on, it's just one misadventure and murder after another.

In pursuit of the jewels are a series of cameo-plus parts handled by Irene Papas, Roger Vadim, David Bowie and a band of Iranian zanies that includes director John Landis himself.

The film itself tries sometimes too hard for laughs and at other times strains for shock. Goldblum is nonetheless enjoyable as he constantly tries to figure out just what he's doing in all of this.

■ INTOLERANCE

1916, 209 MINS, US ⊗ ⊤
Dir D.W. Griffith   *Prod* D.W. Griffith   *Scr* D.W. Griffith   *Ph* Billy Bitzer, Karl Brown   *Ed* James E. Smith, Rose Smith   *Mus* Joseph Carl Breil
● Lillian Gish, Mae Marsh, Robert Harron, Miriam Cooper, Walter Long, Tully Marshall   (Wark)

Intolerance reflects much credit to the wizard director, for it required no small amount of genuine art to consistently blend actors, horses, monkeys, geese, doves, acrobats and ballets into a composite presentation of a film classic.

It attempts to tell four distinct stories at the same time – more or less sucessfully accomplished by the aid of flashbacks, fade-outs and fade-ins. The four tales are designed to show that intolerance in various forms existed in all ages.

Three of the exemplifications are based upon historical fact, the fourth visualized by a modern melodrama that hits a powerful blow at the hypocrisy of certain forms of up-to-date philanthropy. The ancient periods depict mediaeval France in the reign of Charles IX, with the horrors of massacre perpetrated by Catherine de Medici; Jersualem at the birth of the Christian era, with one or two historical episodes in the life of Christ, and a shadow suggestion of the Crucifixion.

The martial visualizations confined principally to the Babylonian period (about 500 B.C.), when Belshazzar's army was defeated by the Persians under the military direction of Cyrus. Words cannot do justice to the stupendousness of these battle scenes or feasts.

■ INVASION OF THE BODY SNATCHERS

1956, 80 MINS, US ⊤
Dir Don Siegel   *Prod* Walter Wanger   *Scr* Daniel Mainwaring   *Ph* Ellsworth Fredricks   *Ed* Robert S. Eisen   *Mus* Carmen Dragon   *Art Dir* Ted Haworth
● Kevin McCarthy, Dana Wynter, Larry Gates, King Donovan, Carolyn Jones, Whit Bissell   (Allied Artists)

This tense, offbeat piece of science-fiction is occasionally difficult to follow due to the strangeness of its scientific premise. Action nevertheless is increasingly exciting.

Plotwise, narrative opens on a strange hysteria that is spreading among the populace of a small California town. Townspeople appear as strangers to their relatives and friends, while retaining their outward appearances. Kevin McCarthy, a doctor, is confronted with solving these mysterious happenings, and helping him is Dana Wynter, with whom he's in love.

A weird form of plantlife has descended upon the town from the skies. Tiny, this ripens into great pods and opens, from each of which emerges a 'blank', the form of each man, woman and child in the town. During their sleep, the blank drains them of all but their impulse to survive.

Adapted from Jack Finney's *Collier's* serial,

characterizations and situations are sharp. Don Siegel's taut direction is fast-paced generally, although in his efforts to spark the climax he permits McCarthy to overact in several sequences.

■ INVASION OF THE BODY SNATCHERS

1978, 115 MINS, US ◇ ⊤
Dir Philip Kaufman   *Prod* Robert H. Solo   *Scr* W.D. Richter   *Ph* Michael Chapman   *Ed* Douglas Stewart   *Mus* Denny Zeitlin   *Art Dir* Charles Rosen
● Donald Sutherland, Brooke Adams, Leonard Nimoy, Veronica Cartwright, Jeff Goldblum, Kevin McCarthy   (United Artists)

Invasion of the Body Snatchers validates the entire concept of remakes. This new version of Don Siegel's 1956 cult classic not only matches the original in horrific tone and effect, but exceeds it in both conception and execution.

W.D. Richter has updated and changed the locale of Jack Finney's serial story to contemporary San Francisco, where Donald Sutherland is a public health inspector, assisted by Brooke Adams. Following the blanketing of the city by spidery webs, Adams notices unusual and sudden changes in b.f. Art Hindle, who becomes emotionless and distant.

Similar transformations are happening all over the city, and while at first Sutherland doubts Adams' sanity, he is soon won over to her paranoia. He invokes the help of an est-type of psychiatrist played with wonderful shading by Leonard Nimoy.

Jeff Goldblum and Veronica Cartwright portray a couple who stumble on one of the blank pod bodies before Goldblum succumbs. As the legions of zombies grows, these four remain about the only humans left, and the latter part of *Body Snatchers* details with methodical ominousness their pursuit.

Sutherland has his best role since *Klute*. He gets excellent support from Adams, who projects a touching vulnerability.

Film buffs will have a delight in spotting Kevin McCarthy, who starred in the original version, picking up exactly where he left off at the first pic's finale.

■ INVISIBLE MAN, THE

1933, 70 MINS, US
Dir James Whale   *Prod* Carl Laemmle Jr   *Scr* R. C. Sherriff   *Ph* Arthur Edeson, John Mescall   *Ed* Maurice Pivar, Ted J. Kent   *Art Dir* Charles D. Hall
● Claude Rains, Gloria Stuart, Henry Travers, William Harrigan, Una O'Connor, Holmes Herbert   (Universal)

The strangest character yet created by the screen [from the novel by H.G. Wells] roams through *The Invisible Man*. Sometimes he is seen, dressed and bandaged up into a fantastic, eerie-looking figure, at other times he is moving through the action unseen.

As the invisible madman (Claude Rains) is moving around, the negative reflects the things he does, such as rocking in a chair, smoking a cigarette, carrying something, opening doors, or socking someone in the jaw with the impact felt rather than seen.

First reel evokes considerable comedy in sequences at a small country inn where the invisible one secures lodging and indulges in his first murder. The innkeeper and his wife (Forrester Harvey and Una O'Connor, respectively) are swell comedy types and make the most of the opportunity. O'Connor relies a lot on a very shrill scream.

At the outset it is learned that a young chemist has discovered a terrible formula, including a very dangerous drug, that makes human flesh invisible. His interest had been strictly scientific but the drug had the effect, after use, of turning him into a maniac. At about the time he starts the murders he is

looking for the antidote to bring him back to a normal condition.

■ INVITATION TO THE DANCE

1956, 93 MINS, US ◇ ⊤
Dir Gene Kelly   *Prod* Arthur Freed   *Scr* Gene Kelly   *Ph* Freddie Young, Joseph Ruttenberg   *Ed* Raymond Poulton, Robert Watts, Adrienne Fazan   *Mus* Andre Previn, Ibert, Rimsky-Korsakov
● Gene Kelly, Igor Youskevitch, Claire Sombert, Carol Haney, David Kasday   (M-G-M)

Invitation to the Dance, a full-length dance feature, is a bold and imaginative experiment in film-making. Through the medium of the dance alone, producer Arthur Freed and director-choreographer-performer Gene Kelly tell three separate stories. There is no dialog. Just ballet music, colorful costumes, and skillful photography.

Kelly has assembled a crew of outstanding hoofers, including such experts as Tamara Toumanova, Claire Sombert, Carol Haney, Diana Adams, Igor Youskevitch, and Belita. Standout sequence is the middle entry, *Ring around the Rosy*. Using the children's song and game as the teeoff, the dance story to Andre Previn's music follows the career of a bracelet as it changes hands in the perennial game of love.

The opening number is similar to the Pagliacci theme as the clown (Kelly) is frustrated in his unrequited love for the beautiful ballerina (Sombert).

The final sequence is a combination of live action and animations, the cartoon sequences being provided by Fred Quimby, William Hanna and Joseph Barbera.

■ IPCRESS FILE, THE

1965, 109 MINS, UK ◇ ⊤
Dir Sidney J. Furie   *Prod* Harry Saltzman   *Scr* Bill Canaway, James Doran   *Ph* Otto Heller   *Ed* Peter Hunt   *Mus* John Barry   *Art Dir* Ken Adam
● Michael Caine, Nigel Green, Guy Doleman, Sue Lloyd, Gordon Jackson, Aubrey Richards   (Rank)

Harry Saltzman and Albert R. Broccoli, who produce the Bond razamatazz, diversify by bringing to the screen a kind of 'anti-Bond' spy in the character of Harry Palmer, based on Len Deighton's novel. The result is probably rather more true to the facts of intelligence life than the Bond world of fantasy.

Intelligence man Harry Palmer (Michael Caine) is an undisciplined sergeant who is seconded to intelligence work and finds that it is more legwork and filling in forms than inspired hunches and glamorous adventure.

Present adventure concerns the steps taken to retrieve a missing boffin and involves the agent being captured by the enemy and subjected to acute brainwashing. Pic does not build up to the type of suspense usually demanded of such thrillers.

Sidney J. Furie's direction, allied with Otto Heller's camera, provides some striking effects. But sometimes he gets carried away into arty-crafty fields with low-angle shots and symbolism adding to the confusion of the screenplay.

Caine skillfully resists any temptation he may have had to pep up the proceedings. In fact, his consistent underplaying adds considerably to the pull of the picture.

■ IRENE

1940, 104 MINS, US ◇
Dir Herbert Wilcox   *Prod* Herbert Wilcox   *Scr* Alice Duer Miller   *Ph* Russell Metty   *Ed* Elmo Williams   *Mus* Harry Tierney, Joseph McCarthy   *Art Dir* L.P. Williams
● Anna Neagle, Ray Milland, Roland Young, Alan Marshal, May Robson, Billie Burke   (Imperadio/RKO)

Back in 1919–20 a smash musical comedy

and then in 1926 a hit First National film starring Colleen Moore, *Irene* emerges this time as dated celluloidia. It's old-fashioned from several angles, further handicapped by familiar story pattern.

Starring combination of Anna Neagle and Ray Milland cannot wholly carry this film over the hurdles. The negative factors are not so much in the acting as they are in Alice Duer Miller's screenplay and Herbert Wilcox's direction, neither of which is ultra-1940. The screenplay and direction, too, closely follow the original film. In the Colleen Moore starrer a 1,000-foot segment of a grand ball was given over to a color sequence, quite revolutionary in those days, but reprised now it just makes the fore and afterparts in black and white look all the more ordinary in comparison.

Neagle, as the girl who steps from the tenements to a modeling job and then into society, gives a rather spotty performance. She's too broadly Irish, for one thing, and not flattered by the camera in the first 50 minutes for another. In the color sequences she shows up much better, her red hair being especially noticeable, and is okay in one feathery dance routine, and when singing 'Alice Blue Gown'. However, she doesn't give the part the comedy content Moore did, which makes the Hibernian dialect all the more unnecessary.

'Castle In Your Dreams', 'Gown' and the title song are still very worthy tunes, from the original score.

Roland Young, noted for his dry comedy, is merely dry in this picture as manager of Mme Lucy's. Two other performers wasted are Isabel Jewell and Doris Noland, Neagle's tenement house pals. Marsha Hunt hasn't much to do as the almost-jilted sweetie of Alan Marshal, while May Robson's role as the motherly but straitlaced Irish grandmother is overdone and unbelievable.

● ●

■ **IRISHMAN, THE**

1978, 108 MINS, AUSTRALIA ◇ ⊛

Dir Donald Crombie *Prod* Anthony Buckley
Scr Donald Crombie *Ph* Peter James *Ed* Tim Wellburn *Mus* Charles Marawood *Art Dir* Owen Williams
● Michael Craig, Simon Burke, Robin Nevin, Lou Brown, Vincent Ball, Bryan Brown (Forest Home)

The north of Queensland in the 1920s must have been much like west Texas at the turn of the century if we can believe the movies. A hard land populated by hard men and women working hard in hard conditions. But times are a-changing, and whenever that happens there's usually a rugged but dogged individual who praises the candle and cries out against the light of progress. One such is Paddy Doolan, the eponymous migrated Celt.

Paddy the teamster, with his team of 20 giant Clydesdale draught horses crossing the great wide river, open the film and immediately create awe and admiration. They are such superb beasts that it is made that much easier to accept Paddy's stubbornness later when he refuses to see that his team is being superseded by the internal combustion engine.

His wife is sensible, yet acquiescent; his older son, Will, defiant; the youngest, and most sensitive – and ultimately therefore the most affected – is bewildered, but devotedly and hopelessly goes with Paddy. And his 'My father, right or wrong' feelings are inevitably eroded. In any event Paddy's recalcitrance demolishes the family, eventually destroys his self-esteem and ultimately himself.

The film has great moments of emotional triumph, and at times is unabashedly sentimental, but it never descends to mawkishness.

● ●

■ **IRMA LA DOUCE**

1963, 147 MINS, US ◇ ⊛

Dir Billy Wilder *Prod* Billy Wilder *Scr* Billy Wilder, I.A.L. Diamond *Ph* Joseph LaShelle *Ed* Daniel Mandell *Mus* Andre Previn *Art Dir* Alexander Trauner
● Jack Lemmon, Shirley MacLaine, Lou Jacobi, Bruce Yarnell, Herschel Bernardi, Hope Holiday (United Artists)

On the plus side of the *Irma* ledger, there are scintillating performances by Jack Lemmon and Shirley MacLaine, a batch of jovial supporting portrayals, a striking physical production and a number of infectious comedy scenes.

But *Irma* also misses on several important counts, and the fact that it does illustrates the sizable problems inherent in an attempt to convert a legit musical into a tuneless motion picture farce. But what hurts the film the most is its length. Two hours and 27 minutes is an awfully long haul for a frivolous farce.

The hot-and-cold scenario, based on the play by Alexandre Breffort, traces the love affair of Irma (MacLaine), a proud and profitable practitioner of the oldest profession, and a young gendarme (Lemmon) who gets bounced off the force when he makes the mistake of taking his job seriously. Lemmon becomes number one mec, or pimp, on the block when he knocks his predecessor's block off, thereby inheriting Irma and the rights to her estate.

Lemmon plays his juicy role to the hilt, and there are moments when his performance brings to mind some of the great visual comedy of the classic silent film clowns. His portrayal of his British alter ego is a kind of cross between Jose Ferrer's characterization of Toulouse-Lautrec and Richard Haydn's caricature of an Englishman. MacLaine delivers a winning performance in the title role, and has never looked better. There's a whale of a comedy portrayal by Lou Jacobi as the versatile bistro boss-barkeep, Moustache.

● ●

■ **IRONWEED**

1987, 144 MINS, US ◇ ⊛

Dir Hector Babenco *Prod* Keith Barish, Marcia Nasatir *Scr* William Kennedy *Ph* Lauro Escorel *Ed* Anne Goursand *Mus* John Morris *Art Dir* Jeannine C. Oppewall
● Jack Nicholson, Meryl Streep, Carroll Baker, Michael O'Keefe (Taft/Barish/Tri-Star)

Unrelentingly bleak, *Ironweed* is a film without an audience and no reason for being except its own self-importance. It's an event picture without the event. Whatever joy or redemption William Kennedy offered in his Pulitzer prize-winning novel is nowhere to be found, surprising since he wrote the screenplay.

The story of Francis Phelan (Jack Nicholson) who returns to his native Albany in 1938 literally carrying a lifetime of ghosts with him is loaded with elaborate expository passages trying to account for why an obviously intelligent individual has abandoned his family for a bum's life.

Phelan's movement around Albany is like a passage through the rings of hell, but instead of coming out at paradise, he's still the same old bum at the end.

Nicholson and Meryl Streep have approximately three scenes together and though they clearly have a great deal of affection for each other, they are beyond passion.

● ●

■ **IRRECONCILABLE DIFFERENCES**

1984, 114 MINS, US ◇ ⊛

Dir Charles Shyer *Prod* Alex Winitsky, Arlene Sellers *Scr* Nancy Meyers, Charles Shyer *Ph* William Fraker *Ed* John Burnett *Mus* Paul de Senneville *Art Dir* Ida Random

● Ryan O'Neal, Shelley Long, Drew Barrymore, Sam Wanamaker, Allen Garfield, Sharon Stone (Hemdale)

Irreconcilable Differences begins strongly as a human comedy about a nine-year-old who decides to take legal action to divorce her parents. Unfortunately, this premise is soon jettisoned for a rather familiar tale of a marriage turned sour as shown step-by-step. Set in the world of Hollywood writers and filmmakers, the story is also more fun for the cognoscenti than the average filmgoer.

On the witness stand the seeds of their dissatisfaction emerge in the three principals' testimony. It is regrettably an uninspired and improbable device to tell the yarn. Not a great deal of perception emerges.

Ryan O'Neal and Shelley Long spark off a nice romantic chemistry but really need a better vehicle to show off their craft.

● ●

■ **IS PARIS BURNING?**

1966, 185 MINS, US/FRANCE ◇

Dir Rene Clement *Prod* Paul Graetz *Scr* Gore Vidal, Francis Coppola, Marcel Moussy *Ph* Marcel Grignon *Ed* Robert Lawrence *Mus* Maurice Jarre *Art Dir* Willy Holt
● Jean-Paul Belmondo, Charles Boyer, Gert Frobe, Anthony Perkins, Simone Signoret, Orson Welles (Paramount/Seven Arts/Transcontinental/Marianne)

This French-made Yank-backed spectacle traces the uprising in Paris leading to the oncoming Allies changing their plans to invade the city rather than bypass it, as intended. Underlying dilemma faces the German commander, General Von Choltitz, who has been ordered to destroy Paris, if necessary or if it could not be held. The title is from Hitler's maniacal telephone demands to know if Paris was burning.

It is built on the premature uprising within the French resistance groups, and then the tensions as Paris is undermined with explosives and Von Choltitz hesitates as he realizes that Hitler is mad and that destruction of Paris will not help the German cause or the now hopeless Nazi war effort.

Gert Frobe has the pivotal part as Von Choltitz who is a career soldier and not above destroying Paris if a necessity. He plays it with proper despair and does not overdo the sentimental aspect of the man.

The street fighting is done with fervor and dynamism and little cameos gives an ironic, tender, dramatic, pathetic feel to the overall happening.

● ●

■ **ISADORA**

1969, 141 MINS, UK ◇ ⊛

Dir Karel Reisz *Prod* Robert Hakim, Raymond Hakim *Scr* Melvyn Bragg, Clive Exton, Margaret Drabble *Ph* Larry Pizer *Ed* Tom Priestley *Mus* Maurice Jarre *Art Dir* Jocelyn Herbert
● Vanessa Redgrave, John Fraser, James Fox, Jason Robards, Ivan Tchenko, Bessie Love (Universal)

The tragic lifelong odyssey of Isadora Duncan, whose consistent non-conformity brought her as much public success as it did personal failure, is told with a remarkable degree of excellence.

The free-thinking aspects of Duncan's life (unabashed out-of-wedlock affairs and births, hedonism, political idealism, naivete, etc.), are emphasized in this sensitive, lucid, beautifully-fashioned and masterfully executed personal tragedy.

Story unfolds as Duncan (Vanessa Redgrave) dictates memoirs to her secretary. Redgrave's performance in these scenes, with hollow eyes and a weathered face suggesting the inevitable ends of dissipation, plus her perfect projection of aging flamboyance, demands equality with Gloria Swanson's classic performance in *Sunset Boulevard*. Where the film falters is its length and pacing.

●●●●●●●●●●●●●●●●●●●●●●●●●●●●

■ I SHOT JESSE JAMES

1949, 81 MINS, US

Dir Samuel Fuller   *Prod* Charles K. Hittleman
Scr Samuel Fuller   *Ph* Ernest Miller   *Ed* Paul Landres
Mus Albert Glasser
● Preston Foster, Barbara Britton, John Ireland, Reed Hadley, J. Edward Bromberg (Screen Guild)

I Shot Jesse James is a character study of the man who felled the west's most famous outlaw with a coward's bullet. It's an interesting treatment that doesn't overlook necessary plot and action.

While Preston Foster and Barbara Britton carry star roles, it's John Ireland, as the notorious Bob Ford, who dominates the story.

Spiced in the plot footage are any number of forthright physical clashes, capably staged by Samuel Fuller's direction. Latter is not quite as adept in handling the character study motivation but the players carry off these angles with considerable ability.

Ireland's performance is clearly drawn and even manages a trace of sympathy. Britton fits well into the role of his beloved, who turns to Foster in the end. Foster is good as the prospector who turns marshal.

●●●●●●●●●●●●●●●●●●●●●●●●●●●●

■ I START COUNTING

1970, 105 MINS, UK ◇ Ⓥ

Dir David Greene   *Prod* David Greene   *Scr* Richard Harris   *Ph* Alex Thomson   *Ed* Kwith Palmer
Mus Basil Kirchin   *Art Dir* Arnold Chapkis
● Jenny Agutter, Bryan Marshall, Clare Sutcliffe, Simon Ward, Gregory Phillips, Lana Morris (United Artists)

Jenny Agutter plays a schoolgirl, adopted, who worships her elder 'brother' who, unwittingly, has become a father-figure in the household. A series of local sex crimes strikes a sinister note and from slender clues (neatly produced as red herrings) the girl suspects that her worshipped brother is the perpetrator.

Her friend (Clare Sutcliffe) is an extroverted little chippie, pert, provocative and pathetic in the way that she tries to kid everybody that she's sexually experienced. Agutter, who tries to keep up with the fantasy, is the more believable but perhaps the less amusing character.

The two kids spend much time in the condemned house in which Agutter used to live. It's bang in the middle of woods which is the danger area operated by the sex-maniac.

●●●●●●●●●●●●●●●●●●●●●●●●●●●●

■ ISHTAR

1987, 107 MINS, US ◇ Ⓥ

Dir Elaine May   *Prod* Warren Beatty   *Scr* Elaine May   *Ph* Vittorio Storaro   *Ed* Stephen A. Rotter, William Reynolds, Richard Cirincione   *Mus* John Strauss (co-ord.)   *Art Dir* Paul Sylbert
● Warren Beatty, Dustin Hoffman, Isabelle Adjani, Charles Grodin, Jack Weston, Tess Harper (Columbia)

Here's how the story goes: Warren Beatty and Dustin Hoffman are struggling and mightily untalented songwriters-singers in New York. They hook up with talent agent Jack Weston (who delivers a fine character performance) and wind up getting booked into the Chez Casablanca in Morocco. Yes, there's the obvious parallels to the Hope-Crosby *Road* films.

Arrival in Africa finds Beatty-Hoffman stopping in the mythical kingdom of Ishtar, where swirl of events leads them into vortex of Middle East political turmoil, with Isabelle Adjani functioning as a left-wing rebel trying to overthrow the US-backed Emir of Ishtar.

Enter Charles Grodin, who upstages all involved via his savagely comical portrayal of a CIA agent. He provides the connecting link as a series of zigzag plot points unfold because of an important map.

Desert sequences provide some of the film's high points as Beatty and Hoffman finally develop some genuine rapport under adverse conditions. There are also a few hilarious scenes as vultures circle an exhausted Hoffman and later as he's thrust into role as a translator for gunrunners and their Arab buyers.

●●●●●●●●●●●●●●●●●●●●●●●●●●●●

■ ISLAND, THE

1980, 114 MINS, US ◇ Ⓥ

Dir Michael Ritchie   *Prod* Richard D. Zanuck, David Brown   *Scr* Peter Benchley   *Ph* Henri Decae
Ed Richard A. Harris   *Mus* Ennio Morricone
Art Dir Dale Hennesy
● Michael Caine, David Warner, Angela Punch McGregor, Frank Middlemass (Universal/Zanuck-Brown)

This latest summertime tale from the water-obsessed pen of Peter Benchley gets off to a bristling start as a charter boat-load of boozy business types is ambushed by something or someone that leaves hatchets planted in their skulls and severed limbs scattered aboard.

Cut to British journalist Michael Caine, who persuades his editor that his latest Bermuda Triangle-type ship disappearance justifies his personal research.

But once the mystery is banally resolved – the island is inhabited by a tribe of buccaneers who've been inbreeding for 300 years and prey on pleasure ships – the film degenerates into a violent chase melodrama.

Michael Ritchie's witty direction is abandoned in the violence, and periodic efforts to revive the built-in comedy fall flat.

●●●●●●●●●●●●●●●●●●●●●●●●●●●●

■ ISLAND AT THE TOP OF THE WORLD, THE

1974, 95 MINS, US ◇ Ⓥ

Dir Robert Stevenson   *Prod* Winston Hibler   *Scr* John Whedon   *Ph* Frank Phillips   *Ed* Robert Stafford
Mus Maurice Jarre   *Art Dir* Peter Ellenshaw
● David Hartman, Donald Sinden, Jacques Marin, David Gwillim, Agneta Eckemyr (Walt Disney)

Title pretty much describes pic's theme, carrying the story of four Polar explorers discovering a lost land inhabited by Vikings. Based on the novel [*The Lost Ones*] by Ian Cameron, script limns a rich Englishman in 1907 flying into the Arctic wilderness in search of his missing son.

Pic occasionally takes on the aspect of old-fashioned adventure, as the explorers find a mysterious valley warmed by volcanic heat in the midst of the Arctic wastes and a settlement of Norsemen who might be the descendants of Eric the Red's second expedition to Greenland in the 10th century.

Donald Sinden portrays the titled Englishman and Jacques Marin plays the French designer and captain of the balloon which figures so prominently in suspenseful action. All deliver realistic performances. An interesting newcomer is Agneta Eckemyr, cast as a Viking maid.

●●●●●●●●●●●●●●●●●●●●●●●●●●●●

■ ISLAND IN THE SKY

1953, 108 MINS, US

Dir William A. Wellman   *Prod* Robert Fellows
Scr Ernest K. Gann   *Ph* Archie Stout   *Ed* Ralph Dawson   *Mus* Emil Newman   *Art Dir* James Basen
● John Wayne, Lloyd Nolan, Walter Abel, James Arness, Andy Devine (Warner/Wayne-Fellows)

An articulate drama of men and planes has been fashioned from Ernest K. Gann's novel. The Wayne-Fellows production was scripted with care by Gann for aviation aficionado William A. Wellman who gives it sock handling to make it a solid piece of drama revolv-

ing around an ATC plane crash in Arctic wastes.

The film moves back and forth very smoothly from the tight action at the crash site to the planning and execution of the search. It's a slick job by all concerned.

John Wayne is the ATC pilot downed with his crew, James Lydon, Hal Baylor, Sean McClory and Wally Cassell, in an uncharted section of Labrador. How he holds them together during five harrowing days before rescue comes on the sixth is grippingly told. Each of the players has a chance at a big scene and delivers strongly.

The snow-covered Donner Lake area near Truckee, Calif, subbed for the story's Labrador locale and provides a frosty, shivery dressing to the picture. Both the lensing by Archie Stout and the aerial photography by William Clothier are important factors in the drama and thrills. Title derives from the fancy that pilots are men apart, their spirits dwelling on islands in the sky.

●●●●●●●●●●●●●●●●●●●●●●●●●●●●

■ ISLAND OF DR MOREAU, THE

1977, 98 MINS, US ◇ Ⓥ

Dir Don Taylor   *Prod* John Temple-Smith, Skip Steloff   *Scr* John Herman Shaner, Al Ramrus   *Ph* Gerry Fisher
Ed Marion Rothman   *Mus* Laurence Rosenthal
Art Dir Philip Jefferies
● Burt Lancaster, Michael York, Nigel Davenport, Barbara Carrera, Richard Basehart, Nick Cravat (American International)

This $6 million adaptation of the H.G. Wells horror-fantasy tale, previously filmed in 1932 by Paramount as *Island of Lost Souls*, is a handsome, well-acted, and involving piece of cinematic storytelling, made in the Virgin Islands.

Burt Lancaster has the lead role of the renegade scientist who dabbles in forbidden eugenic experiments on a remote Pacific island, where Michael York is washed up in a shipwreck in the early days of the 20th century.

Wells showed an uncanny gift for prophecy in his imaginative tales, and the doctor's experiments on beasts and humans eerily foreshadowed the Nazis' use of humans as guinea pigs.

Lancaster, despite his ungodly ideas, is given some resonance as a man who thinks his demented work is for the betterment of the human race.

York gives one of his best performances, and Barbara Carrera's enigmatic beauty is evocatively treated.

●●●●●●●●●●●●●●●●●●●●●●●●●●●●

■ ISLAND OF LOST SOULS

1933, 72 MINS, US

Dir Erle C. Kenton   *Scr* Waldemar Young, Philip Wylie   *Ph* Karl Struss
● Charles Laughton, Bela Lugosi, Richard Arlen, Leila Hyams, Kathleen Burke, Arthur Hohl (Paramount)

With such actors as Charles Laughton, Richard Arlen and Bela Lugosi in the cast, *Souls* is provided with a mainstay.

While the action is not designed to appeal to other than the credulous, there are undoubtedly some horror sequences which are unrivaled. Those studies of a galaxy of Dr Moreau's 50-50 man and beast creations, as an example, will pique any type of mentality.

The tramp steamer in a fog, its decks laden with crates of wild animals consigned to Moreau's mysterious island, is good picturization.

Romance is essentially light, and with a story of this kind [by H. G. Wells] it should be. The extra billing given Kathleen Burke as Lota, the Panther Woman, is strictly for the marquee. Girl is too much like a girl to even suggest transformation from a beast.

●●●●●●●●●●●●●●●●●●●●●●●●●●●●

ISLANDS IN THE STREAM

1977, 105 MINS, US ◇ ▼

Dir Franklin J. Schaffner *Prod* Peter Bart, Max
Palevsky *Scr* Denne Bart Petitclerc *Ph* Fred
Koenekamp *Ed* Robert Swink *Mus* Jerry Goldsmith
Art Dir William J. Creber

● George C. Scott, David Hemmings, Gilbert Roland,
Susan Tyrrell, Richard Evans, Claire Bloom (Paramount)

While too introspective a story to be really
compelling screen drama, Franklin J.
Schaffner's film of *Islands in the Stream* is at
least a proper valedictory to the era
epitomized by author Ernest Hemingway.
Hawaiian locations provide a superb
physical backdrop (simulating The Bahamas,
circa 1940) for the production.

George C. Scott's semi-Hemingway pivotal
character lives on a remote island, to which
travel his three sons by broken marriages, as
the world moves into the globe-shrinking
holocaust of World War II.

One can admire and follow the film without
ever really getting enthusiastic about it,
because of the way in which it has been written, acted and directed. There's a pervading
sensitivity and restrained respect for the
moral antiquity which is herein respresented.

I, THE JURY

1953, 87 MINS, US

Dir Harry Essex *Prod* Victor Saville *Scr* Harry Essex
Ph John Alton *Ed* Frederick Y. Smith *Mus* Franz
Waxman *Art Dir* Wiard Ihnen

● Biff Elliot, Preston Foster, Peggie Castle, Margaret
Sheridan, Alan Reed, Elisha Cook Jr (United Artists/
Parklane)

Harry Essex both directed and wrote from
Mickey Spillane's novel of the same title. The
suspense element is not too strong, but such
ingredients as brutal mob strong boys, effete
art collectors with criminal tendencies, sexy
femmes with more basic tendencies, and a
series of unsolved killings, are mixed together
in satisfactory quantities. The raw sex that is
a prime feature of Spillane's book characters
is less forthright on film.

Hardboiled private eye Mike Hammer
traces the killer of a friend, uncovers some
unsavory rackets while doing so and then
shoots down the killer at the finale. The stereo lensing by John Alton is good, and without obvious 3-D trickery. Depth treatment
and the Franz Waxman score are good assists
for meller mood.

Picture introduces Biff Elliot as the sadistic
Hammer, a character with a big chip on his
shoulder. Elliot does okay by the assignment,
although seemingly a bit less mature than
readers may picture the book private eye.
Peggie Castle, a psychiatrist, is the chief sex
lure and is excellent. Preston Foster is competent as the police captain. Margaret Sheridan
shows up in firstrate style as Hammer's
secretary.

IT

1927, 64 MINS, US ⊗

Dir Clarence Badger *Prod* B.P. Schulberg *Scr* Hope
Loring, Louis D. Lighton, George Marion Jr., Elinor
Glyn *Ph* H. Kinley Martin *Ed* E. Lloyd Sheldon
● Clara Bow, Antonio Moreno, William Austin,
Jacqueline Gadsdon, Julia Swayne Gordon, Gary
Cooper (Paramount)

It is one of those pretty little Cinderella stories where the poor shop girl marries the
wealthy owner of the big department store in
which she works. Elinor Glyn makes her
debut as a picture actress.

But you can't get away from this Clara Bow
girl. She certainly has that certain 'It' for
which the picture is named, and she just runs
away with the film.

Antonio Moreno looks just about old

enough to fall for the Bow type of flapper, in
fact, just a little too old and ready to fall. William Austin is immense and furnishes the
greater part of the laughs.

It starts in a department store, where the
father has just turned the business over to the
son. His pal comes in to congratulate him
and makes a tour of inspection with him. He
is all het up over the Glyn story of 'It' in a
magazine and starts looking for 'It' among
the shop girls, ending up with being sure that
he has found 'It' in Betty Lou (Bow).

IT CAME FROM OUTER SPACE

1953, 80 MINS, US ▼

Dir Jack Arnold *Prod* William Alland *Scr* Harry
Essex *Ph* Clifford Stine *Ed* Paul Weatherwax
Mus Joseph Gershenson (dir.) *Art Dir* Bernard
Herzbrun, Robert Boyle

● Richard Carlson, Barbara Rush, Charles Drake,
Russell Johnson, Kathleen Hughes, Joseph Sawyer
(Universal)

Picture has been smartly fashioned to take
advantage of all the tricks of science-fiction
and 3-D. Stereo process is not used as just an
excuse to pelt an audience with flying objects
and, with one exception, when missiles come
out of the screen they are tied in logically
with the story.

Direction by Jack Arnold whips up an air of
suspense and there is considerable atmosphere of reality created, which stands up well
enough if the logic of it all is not examined too
closely. Some of the threat posed by the landing of visitors from space on earth is lessened
when it is established the chance visitors
intend no harm.

Otherwise, the Ray Bradbury story proves
to be good science-fiction. Yarn opens with
Richard Carlson, a scientist, and Barbara
Rush, his school-teacher fiancee, observing
the landing of a fiery object in the Arizona
desert. At first believing it is a meteor, Carlson changes his opinion when he ventures
into the crater. Strange things begin to happen in the community. Townspeople disappear and their likenesses are taken over by
the space visitors.

Carlson is excellent as the scientist, and
Rush makes an attractive partner. Charles
Drake is good as the sheriff, and there are
some excellent supporting performances.

IT HAPPENED HERE

1964, 99 MINS, UK

Dir Kevin Brownlow, Andrew Mollo *Prod* Kevin
Brownlow, Andrew Mollo *Scr* Kevin Brownlow,
Andrew Mollo *Ph* Peter Suschitzky *Ed* Kevin
Brownlow *Mus* Jack Beaver *Art Dir* Andrew Mollo
● Pauline Murray, Sebastian Shaw, Nicolette Bernard,
Bart Allison, Stella Kemball, Fiona Leland (Rath)

It Happened Here tells the story of what might
have happened had England been occupied
by the Germans. The action takes place in
1943. There's also a story line going through.
It centres on the experience of an English
nurse who, in order to help, joins the Fascist-
controlled Immediate Organization. She
soon finds out that her uniform alienates
those around here. She eventually tries to
help a wounded partisan. Her action is discovered and she's punished for associating
with 'the other side'.

The film shows brutality on both sides. Its
message is that Nazism leads to violence everywhere. Film poses the question: can
Nazism only be wiped out by Nazi methods?

But despite all controversy, film reveals a
tremendous task. Compliments galore should
go to the two young men who created it:
Kevin Brownlow and Andrew Mollo, the
former a professional film editor, the latter
assistant director to Tony Richardson who,
incidentally, contributed the money to complete the film.

It Happened Here is a non-professional feature
which began as an amateur project on 16mm
and remained so until financing was secured
six years (!) after production had started. The
early material was then 'blown-up' and rest
of the film was shot on standard 35mm. Most
of the cast is nonprofessional. One is hardly
aware of this. Film cost a mere $20,000.

IT HAPPENED IN BROOKLYN

1947, 102 MINS, US

Dir Richard Whorf *Prod* Jack Cummings *Scr* Isobel
Lennart *Ph* Robert Planck *Ed* Blanche Sewell
Mus Jule Styne *Art Dir* Cedric Gibbons, Leonid Vasian
● Frank Sinatra, Kathryn Grayson, Peter Lawford,
Jimmy Durante, Gloria Grahame (M-G-M)

Much of the lure will result from Frank Sinatra's presence in the cast. Guy's acquired the
Bing Crosby knack of nonchalance, throwing
away his gag lines with fine aplomb. He kids
himself in a couple of hilarious sequences and
does a takeoff on Jimmy Durante, with
Durante aiding him, that's sockeroo.

Other stars also shine, although Durante
has to struggle with some lines that don't do
his particular brand of comedy too much
good. Kathryn Grayson is beauteous and
appealing as the love interest but the sound
recording doesn't do her singing any good.
Peter Lawford also makes out well and pulls
a surprise with a jive rendition of a novelty
tune 'Whose Baby Are You?'

Isobel Lennart's nicely-handled adaptation
of an original story by John McGowan has
Sinatra as a lonesome GI in London, thirst-
ing for the Flatbush camaraderie. Before
heading for home, he meets Lawford, young
British nobleman whose longhair inclinations
have made him a stuffed shirt, and tries to
pull the Britisher out of his rut.

Back in Brooklyn, Sinatra returns to his old
highschool to check with his draft board and
meets Grayson, the music teacher, plus
Durante, the school's oldtime janitor. Unable
to find a room, he moves in with Durante,
and begins falling in love with Grayson. Lawford appears on the scene and also immediately falls in love with Grayson.

Interspersed in the story are a group of six
new tunes from the able pianos of Sammy
Cahn and Jule Styne. Richard Whorf has
directed the film with a light touch that gets
the most out of the comedy situations.

I, THE JURY

1982, 109 MINS, US ◇ ⓥ

Dir Richard T. Heffron *Prod* Robert Solo *Scr* Larry
Cohen *Ph* Andrew Laszlo *Ed* Garth Craven
Mus Bill Conti *Art Dir* Robert Gundlach
● Armand Assante, Barbara Carrera, Laurene Landon,
Alan King, Geoffrey Lewis, Paul Sorvino
(American Cinema/Larco/Solofilm)

Almost 30 years after the first screen edition
of Mickey Spillane's first Mike Hammer
novel, the update of *I, the Jury* has all the
updated violence, nudity, wit and style that
was missing from the puritanical 1953
original.

By comparison, the souped-up remake is
hard as nails, with Armand Assante plausibly
macho and ruggedly sexy as the amoral
private eye who avenges the murder of his
old Vietnam war buddy.

Scripter Larry Cohen's plotting is swift,
suitably enigmatic and well stocked with
well-stacked and well-exposed babes, of
which the prime specimen is Barbara Carrera
in an arousingly arranged seduction scene
with Assante.

Carrera is just one of numerous villains as
the operator of a not-to-be believed sex
therapy clinic. The ultimate heavy in this
tangled tale is proficiently portrayed by
Barry Snider as a former CIA operative
whose computerized exurban fortress is

penetrated by Hammer in a penultimate sequence of rousing action.

. . . .

■ IT HAPPENED ONE NIGHT

1934, 105 MINS, US

Dir Frank Capra   *Prod* Frank Capra   *Scr* Robert Riskin   *Ph* Joseph Walker   *Ed* Gene Havlick   *Mus* Louis Silvers (dir.)   *Art Dir* Stephen Goosson
● Clark Gable, Claudette Colbert, Walter Connolly, Roscoe Karns, Jameson Thomas, Alan Hale (Columbia)

The story [by Samuel Hopkins Adams] has that intangible quality of charm which arises from a smooth blending of the various ingredients. It starts off to be another long-distance bus story, but they get out of the bus before it palls.

Plot is a simple one. The headstrong but very charming daughter of a millionaire marries a suitor of whom her father does not approve. She quarrels with her father on the yacht off Miami, and the girl goes over the rail. She seeks to make her way to New York, with the old man raising the hue and cry. Clark Gable who has just been fired from his Florida correspondent's job, is on the same bus.

But the author would have been nowhere without the deft direction of Frank Capra and the spirited and good-humored acting of the stars and practically most of their support. Walter Connolly is the only other player to get much of a show, but there are a dozen with bit parts well played.

Claudette Colbert makes hers a very delightful assignment and Gable swings along at sustained speed. Both play as though they really liked their characters, and therein lies much of the charm.
□ 1934: Best Picture

. . . .

■ IT HAPPENED TOMORROW

1944, 84 MINS, US

Dir Rene Clair   *Prod* Arnold Pressburger   *Scr* Dudley Nichols, Rene Clair   *Ph* Archie J. Stout   *Ed* Fred Pressburger   *Mus* Robert Stolz   *Art Dir* Erno Metzner
● Dick Powell, Linda Darnell, Jack Oakie, Edgar Kennedy (United Artists)

It Happened Tomorrow poses a novel premise on which to spin a comedy-drama – what happens when a cub reporter gets a copy of tomorrow's newspaper. Results provide diverting escapist entertainment, with many sparkling moments and episodes along the line.

Although there are numerous broadly sketched sequences aimed for laugh reaction, picture carries undercurrent of Continental directing technique of Rene Clair. The welding is more than passably successful, but main credit for picture's status can be handed to script by Clair and Dudley Nichols [based on 'originals' by Lord Dunsany, Hugh Wedlock and Howard Snyder, and ideas of Lewis R. Foster]; it picks up every chance for a chuckle or laugh in both dialog and situation.

Dick Powell, cub on the sheet, is befriended by the rag's veteran librarian who, after death, hands the youth copies of the next day's paper for three successive days.

Interwoven is his meeting and quick romance with Linda Darnell, medium and niece of mindreader Jack Oakie.

. . . .

■ IT LIVES AGAIN

1978, 91 MINS, US ◇ ▼

Dir Larry Cohen   *Prod* Larry Cohen   *Scr* Larry Cohen   *Ph* Fenton Hamilton   *Ed* Curt Burch, Louis Friedman, Carol O'Blath   *Mus* Bernard Herrmann, Laurie Johnson
● Frederic Forrest, Kathleen Lloyd, John P. Ryan, John Marley, Andrew Duggan, Eddie Constantine (Warner

In his sequel to *It's Alive*, Larry Cohen aims squarely at the same audience, which should be attracted back for more of the murderous babies.

As in the original, producer-director-writer Cohen does not show a lot of the demonic infants nor explain what they really are. But whatever got into the blood of the first mom is now rampant through the country and they're aborning everywhere, threatening the survival of humanity.

Though this is all so much silliness, Cohen effectively uses a good cast topped by Frederic Forrest and Kathleen Lloyd to build up suspense for the slashing, growling attacks by the terrible tykes.

Since the babies are fairly defenseless except at close range, Cohen must go to ridiculous lengths to get his well-armed characters into vulnerable positions, wrapping up with a totally absurd police siege. When the kids are about to bite, though, it's good horror-house fun.

. . . .

■ IT SHOULD HAPPEN TO YOU

1954, 86 MINS, US ▼

Dir George Cukor   *Prod* Fred Kohlman   *Scr* Garson Kanin   *Ph* Charles Lang   *Ed* Charles Nelson   *Mus* Frederick Hollander
● Judy Holliday, Peter Lawford, Jack Lemmon, Michael O'Shea, Vaughn Taylor, Connie Gilchrist (Columbia)

Judy Holliday is reunited with director George Cukor and scripter Garson Kanin, a trio that clicked big with *Born Yesterday*, and the laugh range is from soft titters to loud guffaws as Cukor's smartly timed direction sends the players through hilarious situations. Plot is about a small town girl who comes to the big city to make a name for herself. Fresh angles belt the risibilities while dialog is adult, almost racy at times.

As the Gladys Glover of the plot, Holliday has a romp for herself, and she gets major assists in the comedy from Peter Lawford and Jack Lemmon, making his major screen bow.

Gladys has a different angle to flashing her name in the best places. With her meager savings she rents a signboard on Columbus Circle and has her name emblazoned thereon. This quest for fame sets off a lot of repercussions. She becomes a television celebrity and is pursued romantically by Lawford. Also in the amatory chase is Lemmon, who has a hard time keeping his romance with the new celebrity on even keel.

. . . .

■ IT STARTED WITH EVE

1941, 90 MINS, US

Dir Henry Koster   *Prod* Henry Koster, Joe Pasternak   *Scr* Norman Krasna, Leo Townsend   *Ph* Rudolph Mate   *Ed* Bernard W. Burton   *Mus* Hans J. Salter
● Deanna Durbin, Charles Laughton, Robert Cummings, Guy Kibbee (Universal)

Expertly tailored to the combined talents of Deanna Durbin and Charles Laughton. *It Started with Eve* is a neatly-devised romantic comedy drama. Story is one of those typical Cinderella tales, developed at a consistently fast pace, with plenty of spontaneous comedy exploding en route.

Laughton, crusty and cantankerous old millionaire, has the presses stopped, ready to toss his obit across the front pages. His son (Robert Cummings) suddenly arrives from a Mexican trip with his fiancee. Dying man insists on seeing the future wife, and when Cummings fails to locate her quickly, grabs a hatcheck girl (Durbin) as substitute. Miraculous recovery results from Durbin's visit, with Cummings getting into deep complications through necessity of continuing the duplicity – at the same time placating his fiancee.

Henry Koster gets the utmost out of Durbin's unsophisticated youthfulness, contrast-

ing this effectively with the character performance of Laughton as the dictatorial tycoon for a slick piloting job.

. . . .

■ ITALIAN JOB, THE

1969, 100 MINS, UK ◇ ▼

Dir Peter Collinson   *Prod* Michael Deeley   *Scr* Troy Kennedy Martin   *Ph* Douglas Slocombe   *Ed* John Trumper   *Mus* Quincy Jones   *Art Dir* Michael Knight
● Michael Caine, Noel Coward, Benny Hill, Raf Vallone, Tony Beckley, Rossano Brazzi (Paramount/Oakhurst)

Michael Caine plays a minor crook who inherits from a dead pal (Rossano Brazzi) the idea and key plan of a heist for landing a haul of $4 million in gold ingots from a security van in Turin, Italy. Scheme involves an elaborate way of throwing the Turin traffic into a colossal, chaotic tangle on which the robbery and getaway depends.

The crime is bankrolled and masterminded by Noel Coward, a top criminal, from a London jail which he virtually controls with sybaratic authority. Caine's assembled gang of crooks seem a bumbling crowd, unfitted to take on the Mafia, which is naturally taking a menacing interest in the scheme.

The cast does its stuff to good effect. Coward, as the highly patriotic, business-like master crook, brings all his imperturbable sense of irony and comedy to his role.

. . . .

■ IT'S A GIFT

1935, 73 MINS, US ▼

Dir Norman McLeod   *Prod* William LeBaron   *Scr* Jack Cunningham, Charles Bogle [= W.C. Fields], J.P. McEvoy   *Ph* Henry Sharp   *Art Dir* Hans Dreier, John B. Goodman
● W.C. Fields, Jean Rouverol, Julian Madison, Kathleen Howard, Tammany Young, Baby LeRoy (Paramount)

Practically a comedy monolog for W.C. Fields, with little help from a number of others. No plot, no suspense; rather coarse-grained in spots, but packing a load of belly laughs for people who like that sort of humor.

The plot is merely that Fields buys a California orange grove and drives the family out in the car. It's a bit of desert in between the other groves, but Fields is tipped off that it's vital to the building of a racetrack, so he gets $40,000 and a real grove.

Fields holds the screen about 80% of the time, which is just as well since no one else is given anything. Kathleen Howard acts the bossy wife with main strength.

. . . .

■ IT'S A MAD MAD MAD MAD WORLD

1963, 190 MINS, US ◇ ▼

Dir Stanley Kramer   *Prod* Stanley Kramer   *Scr* William Rose, Tania Rose   *Ph* Ernest Laszlo   *Ed* Fred Knudtson   *Mus* Ernest Gold   *Art Dir* Rudolph Sternad
● Spencer Tracy, Milton Berle, Sid Caesar, Mickey Rooney, Ethel Merman, Phil Silvers (United Artists)

It's a mad, mad, mad, mad picture. Being a picture of extravagant proportions, even its few flaws are king-sized, but the plusses outweigh by far the minuses. It is a throwback to the wild, wacky and wondrous time of the silent screen comedy, a kind of Keystone Kop Kaper with modern conveniences.

The plot is disarmingly simple. A group of people are given a clue by a dying man (Jimmy Durante) as to the whereabouts of a huge sum of money he has stolen and buried. Unable to come to a compromise in apportionment of the anticipated loot, each sets out for the roughly specified site of the buried cash, breaking his back to beat the others there. All are unaware that they are under secret surveillance by state police authorities, who are allowing them simply to lead the way to the money.

Nothing is done in moderation in this picture. All the stops are out. Nobody goes around what they can go over, under, through or into. Yet, as noted, the film is not without its flaws and oversights. Too often it tries to throw a wild haymaker where a simple left jab would be more apt to locate the desired target. Certain pratfalls and sequences are unneccessarily overdone to the point where they begin to grow tedious and reduce the impact of the whole.

An array of top-ranking comics has been rounded up by director Stanley Kramer, making this one of the most unorthodox and memorable casts on screen record. The comic competition is so keen that it is impossible to single out any one participant as outstanding.

● ● ● ● ● ● ● ● ● ● ● ● ● ● ● ● ● ●

■ IT'S A WONDERFUL LIFE

1946, 120 MINS, US ⓥ

Dir Frank Capra *Prod* Frank Capra *Scr* Frances Goodrich, Albert Hackett *Ph* Joseph Walker, Joseph Biroc *Ed* William Hornbeck *Mus* Dimitri Tiomkin *Art Dir* Jack Okey
● James Stewart, Donna Reed, Lionel Barrymore, Thomas Mitchell, Gloria Grahame (RKO/Liberty)

The tale, flashbacked, essentially is simple. At 30 a small-town citizen feels he has reached the end of his rope, mentally, morally, financially. All his plans all his life have gone awry. Through no fault of own he faces disgrace. If the world isn't against him, at least it has averted its face. As he contemplates suicide, Heaven speeds a guardian angel, a pixyish fellow of sly humor, to teach the despondent most graphically how worthwhile his life has been and what treasures, largely intangible, he does possess.

The recounting of this life is just about flawless in its tender and natural treatment; only possible thin carping could be that the ending is slightly overlong and a shade too cloying for all tastes.

James Stewart's lead is braced by a full fanspread of shimmering support. In femme lead, Donna Reed reaches full-fledged stardom. As a Scrooge-like banker, Lionel Barrymore lends a lot of lustre. Thomas Mitchell especially is effective as lead's drunken uncle.
□ 1946: Best Picture (Nomination)

● ● ● ● ● ● ● ● ● ● ● ● ● ● ● ● ● ●

■ IT'S A WONDERFUL WORLD

1939, 84 MINS, US

Dir W.S Van Dyke *Prod* Frank Davis *Scr* Ben Hecht *Ph* Oliver T. Marsh *Ed* Harold F. Kress *Mus* Edward Ward *Art Dir* Cedric Gibbons, Paul Groesse
● Claudette Colbert, James Stewart, Guy Kibbee, Frances Drake, Nat Pendleton, Edgar Kennedy (M-G-M)

Metro saturates the screwball comedy type of picture with some pretty broad burlesque in *It's a Wonderful World*.

Claudette Colbert is a zany poetess in continual conflict and love with James Stewart. Story [an original by Ben Hecht and Herman J. Mankiewicz] is thinly laid foundation to provide the wacky and slapsticky situations and rapid-fire laugh dialog.

Stewart, a novice private detective, is assigned to watch millionaire Ernest Truex. Latter goes on a bender, and winds up convicted of a murder. Stewart is implicated, and escapes from the train en route to prison determined to solve the murder mystery and save his client. Kidnapping Colbert and requisitioning her car, Stewart runs through series of disguises – a Boy Scout leader, chauffeur, and actor.

W.S. Van Dyke presents the yarn with good humor and a let's-have-fun attitude.

● ● ● ● ● ● ● ● ● ● ● ● ● ● ● ● ● ●

■ IT'S ALIVE

1974, 90 MINS, US ◇ ⓥ

Dir Larry Cohen *Prod* Larry Cohen *Scr* Larry Cohen *Ph* Fenton Hamilton *Ed* Peter Honess *Mus* Bernard Herrmann
● John Ryan, Sharon Farrell, Andrew Duggan, Guy Stockwell, James Dixon, Michael Ansara (Larco)

This stomach-churning little film is a 'Son of the Exorcist' horror pic about a monstrous newborn baby who goes on a murder rampage through LA before being blown to smithereens in a police ambush.

Bernard Herrmann's score, while not one of his most memorable, is highly effective in creating tension, but one wonders why an artist of his caliber lowered himself into such muck.

Script sidesteps an answer to what caused the aberration in the womb of Sharon Farrell. Hubby John Ryan feels vaguely guilty, and his earlier contemplation of an abortion is thrown back in his face.

The far-fetched rampage by the fleetingly-glimpsed infant gives director Larry Cohen the chance to shoot a few technically interesting scenes.

● ● ● ● ● ● ● ● ● ● ● ● ● ● ● ● ● ●

■ IT'S ALWAYS FAIR WEATHER

1955, 102 MINS, US ◇ ⓥ

Dir Gene Kelly, Stanley Donen *Prod* Arthur Freed *Scr* Betty Comden, Adolph Green *Ph* Robert Bronner *Ed* Adrienne Fazan *Mus* Andre Previn *Art Dir* Cedric Gibbons, Arthur Lonergan
● Gene Kelly, Dan Dailey, Cyd Charisse, Dolores Gray, Michael Kidd (M-G-M)

As well as spoofing television, *It's Always Fair Weather* also takes on advertising agencies and TV commercials, and what emerges is a delightful musical satire.

Betty Comden and Adolph Green, vet scripters of both Broadway and film tuners, present Gene Kelly, Dan Dailey, and Michael Kidd as a trio of former GI buddies who meet 10 years after World War II. Somehow the warm friendship that existed during the war years has deteriorated into a sour reunion as different interests have driven the buddies apart.

Dolores Gray, as the temperamental, syrupy hostess, registers excellently in appearance, emoting and warbling. Kidd, better known as a choreographer, emerges as a seasoned musicomedy performer.

Kelly, Dailey and Kidd score in group routines and Kelly and Dailey have a field day in solo outings. Kelly's roller skating routine and Dailey's drunk act at a chi-chi party are standouts. Cyd Charisse has only one terp routine, but she carries it off to perfection.

● ● ● ● ● ● ● ● ● ● ● ● ● ● ● ● ● ●

■ IT'S MY TURN

1980, 91 MINS, US ◇ ⓥ

Dir Claudia Weill *Prod* Martin Elfand *Scr* Eleanor Bergstein *Ph* Bill Butler *Ed* Byron Brandt, Marjorie Fowler, James Coblenz *Mus* Patrick Williams *Art Dir* Jack Delovia
● Jill Clayburgh, Michael Douglas, Charles Grodin, Beverly Garland, Steven Hill (Columbia/Rastar)

In her second feature, director Claudia Weill has managed to zero in on both the funny and tragic sides of falling in love while keeping the action moving and the story intact. If there is a tendency for the editing to be a bit choppy and the camera shots a tinge forced or unimaginative, Weill is a pro with actors.

Jill Clayburgh limns an offbeat but intellectually over-achieving mathematics professor residing with perpetually humorous building developer Charles Grodin in Chicago. She quickly finds herself in the arms of Michael Douglas during a trip to New York.

Probably the most endearing aspect here is the way action so easily moves from screwball

to intellectual humour and then on to numerous emotionally touching moments.

● ● ● ● ● ● ● ● ● ● ● ● ● ● ● ● ● ●

■ IT!
THE TERROR FROM BEYOND SPACE

1958, 68 MINS, US

Dir Edward L. Cahn *Prod* Robert E. Kent *Scr* Jerome Bixby *Ph* Kenneth Peach Sr *Ed* Grant Whytock *Mus* Paul Sawtell, Bert Shefter *Art Dir* William Glasgow
● Marshall Thompson, Shawn Smith, Kim Spalding, Ann Doran, Richard Benedict, Ray Corrigan (Vogue)

'It' is a Martian by birth, a Frankenstein by instinct, and a copycat. The monster dies hard, brushing aside grenades, bullets, gas and an atomic pile, before snorting its last snort. It's old stuff, with only a slight twist.

Film starts some dozen years in the future [from 1958] with a disabled US rocketship on Mars. Only one of the 10 space travellers has survived, and a second rocketship has landed to drag him back to Earth where he is to face a courtmartial. The government is of the opinion the spaceman murdered his companions so he could hoard the food and stay alive until help arrived. But the accused swears the nine deaths came at the hands of a strange 'It'-type monster.

Most of the film is spent aboard the second rocketship on its way to Earth, and, to spice up the trip, the monster has stowed away. It kills with a swat of its grisly hand, then sucks all available liquids from its victims.

None of the performances is outstanding. Ray 'Crash' Corrigan makes a fetching monster. Technical credits are capable.

● ● ● ● ● ● ● ● ● ● ● ● ● ● ● ● ● ●

■ IVANHOE

1952, 107 MINS, UK ◇ ⓥ

Dir Richard Thorpe *Prod* Pandro S. Berman *Scr* Noel Langley, Aeneas MacKenzie *Ph* F.A. Young *Ed* Frank Clarke *Mus* Miklos Rozsa *Art Dir* Alfred Junge, Roger Furse
● Robert Taylor, Elizabeth Taylor, Joan Fontaine, George Sanders, Emlyn Williams, Robert Douglas (M-G-M)

Ivanhoe is a great romantic adventure, mounted extravagantly, crammed with action, and emerges as a spectacular feast.

Both the romance and the action are concentrated around Robert Taylor who, as Ivanhoe, is the courageous Saxon leader fighting for the liberation of King Richard from an Austrian prison and his restoration to the throne. Two women play an important part in his life. There is Rowena (Joan Fontaine), his father's ward, with whom he is in love; and Rebecca (Elizabeth Taylor), daughter of the Jew who raises the ransom money. She is in love with him.

Taylor sets the pace with a virile contribution which is matched by George Sanders as his principal adversary. Fontaine contributes to all the requisite charm and understanding as Rowena.
□ 1952: Best Picture (Nomination)

● ● ● ● ● ● ● ● ● ● ● ● ● ● ● ● ● ●

■ I'VE HEARD THE MERMAIDS SINGING

1987, 81 MINS, CANADA ◇ ⓥ

Dir Patricia Rozema *Prod* Patricia Rozema, Alexandra Raffe *Scr* Patricia Rozema *Ph* Douglas Koch *Ed* Patricia Rozema *Mus* Mark Korven *Art Dir* Valanne Ridgeway
● Sheila McCarthy, Paule Baillargeon, Ann-Marie McDonald, John Evans (Vos)

I've Heard The Mermaids Singing neatly blends film and video and comedy with serious undertones.

Plot centers on a klutzy and innocent temporary secretary (Sheila McCarthy) who is jobbed in at an art gallery run by an older femme, whom it is established quickly on takes a flagged fancy to her without the secretary cottoning on.

Living alone in cramped quarters, the secretary lives a fantasy life via deliberately grainy black-&-white scenes in which she flies through the air, walks on water and actually hears mermaids singing. Those sequences are soaringly portrayed with accompanying classical music [from Delibes' *Lakme*]. In other off-times, she observes daily life by taking photographs.

The secretary later discovers what appears to be the owner's own thrill-making canvases. Taking one of them, cleverly just a blaze of framed white light, the secretary hangs it in the gallery; it's heralded by the press, and the gallery owner attains fame. But the secretary is dejected because of the growing love affair between the two other women and rejection of her photos.

McCarthy, a waif-faced Canadian stage thesp in her first lead film role, gives a dynamic, strongly believable and constantly assured performance. She is ably assisted by Paule Baillargeon (the gallery owner).

· ·

■ I WALK ALONE

1947, 97 MINS, US

Dir Byron Haskin   *Prod* Hal. B. Wallis   *Scr* Charles Schnee   *Ph* Leo Tover   *Ed* Arthur Schmidt   *Mus* Victor Young   *Art Dir* Hans Dreier, Franz Bachelin
● Burt Lancaster, Lizabeth Scott, Kirk Douglas, Wendell Corey (Paramount)

I Walk Alone is tight, hard-boiled melodrama. A number of unusually tough sequences are spotted. One, in particular, is bloody beating handed out to Burt Lancaster by a trio of bruisers who spare no punches. Another is the dark-street stalking and gore-tinged death meted out to Wendell Corey.

There's a Rip Van Winkle angle to the plot wherein a gangster returns from 14 years in prison to find that his former cronies now wear the garb of respectability and are in such pseudo-legit rackets as used cars, night clubs, etc. Charles Schnee's screenplay, from the play *Beggars Are Coming to Town* by Theodore Reeves, makes much of the basic story's flavor, although letting dialog run away with a few scenes.

Lancaster belts over his assignment as the former jailbird who returns from prison to find the parade has passed him by and that old friends have given him the double-cross. Melodrama develops as Lancaster plots to muscle in on Kirk Douglas' nitery.

Lizabeth Scott holds up her end capably as co-star, making role of nitery singer who falls for Lancaster after a cross from Douglas, believable. Douglas is a standout as the hood turned respectable and fighting a losing battle to hold his kingdom together against Lancaster's assault.

· ·

■ I WALK THE LINE

1970, 96 MINS, US ◇ ▽

Dir John Frankenheimer   *Prod* Harold D. Cohen   *Scr* Alvin Sargent   *Ph* David M. Walsh   *Ed* Henry Berman   *Mus* Johnny Cash   *Art Dir* Albert Brenner
● Gregory Peck, Tuesday Weld, Estelle Parsons, Ralph Meeker, Lonny Chapman, Charles Durning (Columbia)

Like the Johnny Cash ballads that comprise its background scores and make an intangible emotional commentary on the story, *I Walk the Line* has an authentic, somber and gritty feel of life in the Tennessee back hills, Gregory Peck is the sheriff compromised by Tuesday Weld, moonshiner Ralph Meeker's nubile and sexually precocious daughter, and Estelle Parsons is Peck's desperate wife.

Each create thoroughly believable characters whose passions and individual codes are on a course of inevitable tragedy. Aesthetically, director John Frankenheimer has made a downbeat folk ballad that

rings true to its people and setting.

Weld is striking as the moonshiner's daughter, capturing just the right accent and qualities of late teenage sensuality, amorality and dumb innocence to make her a fatal attraction for an older married man.

· ·

■ I WANT TO GO HOME

1989, 105 MINS, FRANCE ◇ ▼

Dir Alain Resnais   *Prod* Marin Karmitz   *Scr* Jules Feiffer   *Ph* Charlie Van Damme   *Ed* Albert Jurgenson   *Mus* John Kander   *Art Dir* Jacques Saulnier
● Adolph Green, Gerard Depardieu, Linda Lavin, Laura Benson, Micheline Presle, Geraldine Chaplin (MK2/Films A2/La Sept)

Jules Feiffer and Alain Resnais make strange bedfellows – the product of their union is this stillborn satiric comedy about an American cartoonist in Paris.

Central character is a cantankerous American cartoonist, played as a likable kvetch by songwriter and musical comedy veteran Adolph Green. He is making his first trip abroad, accompanied by Linda Lavin, to attend an exhibition of comic strip art in which his work figures.

Green's real reason is to see his neurotic daughter (Laura Benson), who's fled uncivilized Cleveland to enroll as a literature student at the Sorbonne. Mad about Flaubert, she has become starryeyed before her evasive professor Gerard Depardieu, who happens to be a comic book fan and one of Green's most ardent admirers.

Departieu drags the flattered Green and Lavin to the posh country manor of his mother Micheline Presle, who indulges her son's obsessive Yank-collecting.

The performances are broad Broadway. Depardieu, in his first English-speaking part, knows how to charm with blithe timing but the role never grows beyond the cultural stereotype of the philandering Paris intellectual.

· ·

■ I WANT TO LIVE

1958, 120 MINS, US ▽

Dir Robert Wise   *Prod* Walter Wanger   *Scr* Nelson Gidding, Don M. Mankiewicz   *Ph* Lionel Lindon   *Ed* William Hornbeck   *Mus* Johnny Mandel   *Art Dir* Edward Haworth
● Susan Hayward, Simon Oakland, Virginia Vincent, Theodore Bikel, Wesley Lau, Philip Coolidge (United Artists/Figaro)

I Want to Live is a drama dealing with the last years and the execution of Barbara Graham (Susan Hayward), who was convicted at one time or another of prostitution, perjury, forgery and murder. It is a damning indictment of capital punishment.

There is no attempt to gloss the character of Barbara Graham, only an effort to understand it through some fine irony and pathos. She had no hesitation about indulging in any form of crime or vice that promised excitement on her own, rather mean, terms. The screenplay is based on newspaper and magazine articles by San Francisco reporter Ed Montgomery, and on letters written by the woman herself. Its premise is that she was likely innocent of the vicious murder for which she was executed in the California gas chamber.

The final 30-40 minutes of the film are a purposely understated account of the mechanics involved in the state's legal destruction of life. The execution sequence is almost unbearable, mounting unswervingly in its intensity.

Hayward brings off this complex characterization. Simon Oakland, as Montgomery, who first crucified Barbara Graham in print and then attempted to undo what he had done, underplays his role with assurance.

· ·

■ I WAS A COMMUNIST FOR THE F.B.I.

1951, 82 MINS, US

Dir Gordon Douglas   *Prod* Bryan Foy   *Scr* Crane Wilbur   *Ph* Edwin B. DuPar   *Ed* Folmar Blangsted   *Art Dir* Leo K. Kuter
● Frank Lovejoy, Dorothy Hart, Philip Carey, James Millican, Richard Webb, Konstantin Shayne (Warner)

From the real life experiences of Matt Cvetic, scripter Crane Wilbur has fashioned an exciting film. Direction of Gordon Douglas plays up suspense and pace strongly, and the cast, headed by Frank Lovejoy in the title role, punches over the expose of the Communist menace.

Cvetic's story is that of a man who, for nine years, was a member of the Commie party so he could gather information for the FBI. His informer role was made all the harder because his patriotic brothers and young son hated him for the Red taint. Picture picks up the double life as Gerhardt Eisler comes to Pittsburgh to ready the Red cell for strike violence and racial hatred.

Excitement and suspense are set up in the many near-escapes from exposure that Lovejoy goes through before he completes his job by revealing Commies and their activities before the UnAmerican Activities Committee. There's a brief touch of romance, too, in the person of Dorothy Hart, a card-carrying schoolteacher who finally sees the light and is saved from Commie reprisal by Lovejoy.

· ·

■ I WAS A MALE WAR BRIDE

1949, 105 MINS, US

Dir Howard Hawks   *Prod* Sol C. Siegel   *Scr* Charles Lederer, Leonard Spigelgass, Hagar Wilde   *Ph* Norbert Brodine, Osmond Borrodaile   *Ed* James B. Clark   *Mus* Cyril J. Mockridge
● Cary Grant, Ann Sheridan, Marion Marshall, Randy Stuart (20th Century-Fox)

Title describes the story perfectly. Cary Grant is a French army officer who, after the war, marries Ann Sheridan, playing a WAC officer. From then on it's a tale of Grant's attempts to get back to the US with his wife by joining a contingent of war brides.

Picture's chief failing, if it can be called that in view of the frothy components, is that the entire production crew, from scripters to director Howard Hawks and the cast, were apparently so intent on getting the maximum in yocks that they overlooked the necessary characterizations.

Story was filmed for the most part in Germany, until illness of the stars and several of the supporting players forced their return to Hollywood, where the remaining interiors were lensed. Illness, however, did not hamper the cast's cavortings.

· ·

■ I WAS HAPPY HERE

1966, 91 MINS, UK ◇

Dir Desmond Davis   *Prod* Roy Millichip   *Scr* Edna O'Brien, Desmond Davis   *Ph* Manny Wynn   *Ed* Brian Smedley-Aston   *Mus* John Addison   *Art Dir* Tony Woollard
● Sarah Miles, Cyril Cusack, Julian Glover, Sean Caffrey, Marie Kean, Cardew Robinson (Partisan)

Sarah Miles plays a girl who escapes from an Irish village to London, believing that her fisherboy sweetheart will follow her. He doesn't and Miles, lonely and unhappy in the big city, falls into a disastrous marriage with a pompous, boorish young doctor. After a Christmas Eve row, she rushes back to the Irish village, but is disillusioned when she finds that though the village has not changed, she has.

The story is told largely in flashback but Davis has skillfully woven the girl's thoughts and the present happenings by swift switching which, occasionally, is confusing but mostly is sharp and pertinent.

J

Miles gives a most convincing performance, a slick combo of wistful charm but with the femme guile never far below the surface. But Julian Glover makes heavy weather of his role as the girl's insufferable husband.

Filmed entirely on location in County Clare, Ireland, and London, the contrast between the peaceful, lonely sea-coast village and the less peaceful but equally lonely bustling London is artfully wed.

....

■ I WAS MONTY'S DOUBLE

1958, 100 MINS, UK
Dir John Guillermin   *Prod* Maxwell Setton   *Scr* Bryan Forbes   *Ph* Basil Emmott   *Ed* Max Benedict   *Mus* John Addison   *Art Dir* W.E. Hutchinson
● John Mills, Cecil Parker, M.E. Clifton James, Michael Hordern, Marius Goring, Sidney James (Associated British)

I Was Monty's Double tells about a great and important wartime hoax, almost incredible in its audacity. Clifton James, a smalltime stock actor serving as a junior officer in the Royal Army Pays Corps, bore a startling resemblance to General Montgomery. This was used in a daring scheme devised by Army Intelligence to persuade the Germans that the forthcoming Allies' invasion might well take place on the North African coast.

The deception proved so successful that the enemy moved several divisions to the North African coast, a move which helped the actual invasion tremendously. The film has several moments of real tension.

Plenty of news footage has been woven into the pic and it has been done with commendable ingenuity. Bryan Forbes' taut screenplay [based on James' book] is liberally spiced with humor. James plays both himself and Montgomery. Apart from his uncanny resemblance to Monty, James shows himself to be a resourceful actor in his own right.

....

■ I WILL . . . I WILL . . . FOR NOW

1976, 107 MINS, US ◇ ⓥ
Dir Norman Panama   *Prod* George Barrie   *Scr* Norman Panama, Albert E. Lewin   *Ph* John A. Alonzo   *Ed* Robert Lawrence   *Mus* John Cameron   *Art Dir* Fernando Carrere
● Elliott Gould, Diane Keaton, Paul Sorvino, Victoria Principal, Robert Alda, Madge Sinclair (Brut)

I Will . . . I Will . . . For Now is passable fluff. Elliott Gould and Diane Keaton (as unhappy marriage/divorce partners), their less-than-disinterested lawyer Paul Sorvino, and condominium sexpot Victoria Principal, star.

Story finds horny Gould jealous that divorced wife Keaton has a lover, but he doesn't know it's Sorvino. When Keaton's sister Candy Clark has a modern contract-type marriage, pair decide to try life again under that new form, drafted with an eye to self-destruction by Sorvino.

Principal and her distant husband Warren Berlinger supply the formula comedy when couples get rooms mixed up in chic sex clinic run by Robert Alda and Madge Sinclair.

....

■ JABBERWOCKY

1977, 100 MINS, UK ◇ ⓥ
Dir Terry Gilliam   *Prod* Sandy Lieberson   *Scr* Terry Gilliam, Charles Alverson   *Ph* Terry Bedford   *Ed* Michael Bradsell   *Mus* De Wolfe   *Art Dir* Millie Burns

● Michael Palin, Max Wall, Deborah Fallender, John Le Mesurier, Annette Badland, Warren Mitchell (Columbia/White)

A Monty Python splinter faction bears responsibility for *Jabberwocky*, a medieval farce based on a Lewis Carroll poem. Film is long on jabber but short on yocks.

Ex-Pythonite Terry Gilliam directed and coscripted. Michael Palin is well-cast as a bumpkin who threads his way through jousting knights, grubby peasants, 'drag' nuns, and damsels both fair and plump to become the inadvertent hero who slays the vile monster menacing Max Wall's cartoon kingdom. The monster, who doesn't appear till the final minutes, is a work of inspired dark imagination.

Film goes for gags instead of sustained satire, including several typically English lavatorial jokes also some repulsively bloody ones.

Some of the slapstick works okay but at a very intermittent pace in a mish-mash scenario.

....

■ JACARE

1942, 65 MINS, US
Dir Charles E. Ford   *Prod* Jules Levey   *Scr* Thomas Lennon   *Mus* Miklos Rozsa
● Frank Buck, James M. Dannaldson, Miguel Rojinsky (Mayfair)

Produced in Brazil, excepting for studio scenes introducing Frank Buck, this typical 'bring-'em-back-alive' jungle thriller stacks up strongly in the Buck string of wild animal screen epics.

This Buck jungler is outstanding for the smooth way in which it unfolds an intelligent story, minus dull spots. Aside from the introductory trimmings, the picture is a series of adventures and struggles to capture denizens of the jungle.

Recital builds suspense as to what the Jacare really is, with climax sharply pointed up as a whole river-bank filled with them is revealed.

Charles E. Ford, former Universal newsreel editor, is credited on the film with directing Ford died on the Coast after returning from the trip. Production is a credit to his skill at maintaining maximum interest. Buck employs his familiar clipped phrases in narrating the whole picture, and is okay in his brief initial appearance.

....

■ JACK LONDON

1943, 92 MINS, US ⓥ
Dir Alfred Santell   *Prod* Samuel Bronston   *Scr* Ernest Pascal   *Ph* John W. Boyle   *Ed* William Ziegler   *Mus* Fred Rich
● Michael O'Shea, Susan Hayward, Osa Massen, Virginia Mayo (United Artists)

Samuel Bronston has brought to the screen one of the great men of American letters, Jack London, and if ever there was a blood-and-guts subject for Hollywood treatment, London has long seemed a natural. But the play's still the thing. *Jack London*, an adaptation of a book written by the author's wife, Charmian, has much of the writer-adventurer's life crammed into its 92 minutes, but somewhere along the line it has missed fire.

One of the main snags to *London* is the fact that one of the film's two most important characters – Charmian London, the author's wife – fails to appear until the film has consumed half its running time. Susan Hayward is starred in the role, as is Michael O'Shea in the title part, and for a starred performer to be absent for that length of time is dangerous scripting and directing, let alone producing.

O'Shea, comparative newcomer to Hollywood from the Broadway stage, is miscast in

the title role. His physique, for one, is not what one might expect of a two-fisted Jack London, and a couple of the scenes in which he delivers kayo blows are too obviously staged. His performance generally is uncertain.

....

■ JACKSON COUNTY JAIL

1976, 89 MINS, US ◇ ⓥ
Dir Michael Miller   *Prod* Jeff Begun   *Scr* Donald Stewart   *Ph* Bruce Logan   *Ed* Caroline Ferriol   *Mus* Loren Newkirk   *Art Dir* Michael McCloskey
● Yvette Mimieux, Tommy Lee Jones, Robert Carradine, Frederic Cook, Severn Darden, Howard Hesseman (New World)

Pic has a predictable, uncomplicated plot. A fashionable ad woman (Yvette Mimieux) leaves her career and her cheating lover behind in LA, destination New York. Along the way, she gets beaten up by juvenile hitch-hikers (Robert Carradine is one of them) who steal her car, leaving her stranded in some ambiguous western town where she's promptly thrown in jail on phony charges and raped by a psychotic jailkeeper.

She kills the jailkeeper and is forced to go on the lam with a rowdy but caring inmate (Tommy Lee Jones), a radical country boy who steals 'because everyone is dishonest'.

The after-effects of the rape are handled with more care than usual, and Mimieux turns in a convincing, well-controlled performance.

....

■ JACOB'S LADDER

1990, 113 MINS, US ◇ ⓥ
Dir Adrian Lyne   *Prod* Alan Marshall   *Scr* Bruce Joel Rubin   *Ph* Jeffrey L. Kimball   *Ed* Tom Rolf, Peter Amundsun, B.J. Sears   *Mus* Maurice Jarre   *Art Dir* Brian Morris
● Tim Robbins, Elizabeth Pena, Danny Aiello, Matt Craven, Ving Rhames, Macaulay Culkin (Carolco)

Jacob's Ladder means to be a harrowing thriller about a Vietnam vet (Tim Robbins) bedeviled by strange visions, but the $40 million production is dull, unimaginative and pretentious.

Writer Bruce Joel Rubin (*Ghost*) telegraphs his plot developments and can't resist throwing in supernatural elements that prompt giggles at the most unfortunate moments. Right from the battlefield prolog in Vietnam, where members of Robbins' battalion act strangely and throw fits, it's clear that somebody messed with their brains.

Robbins, whose earnest and touching performance belongs in a better film, spends most of the story struggling to understand the 'demons' pursuing him back home in NY.

Director Adrian Lyne adds nothing fresh visually or dramatically to previous film and TV depictions of troubled Viet vets' psyches.

Living in a dim, dingy apartment and working in a dronelike postal service job, Robbins was wrongly told by the army that he was discharged on psychological grounds. His very existence denied by the Veterans Administration, he thinks he's possessed, but eventually pieces together the truth with the help of his battalion buddies.

....

■ JAGGED EDGE

1985, 108 MINS, US ◇ ⓥ
Dir Richard Marquand   *Prod* Martin Ransohoff   *Scr* Joe Eszterhas   *Ph* Matthew F. Leonetti   *Ed* Sean Barton, Conrad Buff   *Mus* John Barry   *Art Dir* Gene Callahan
● Jeff Bridges, Glenn Close, Peter Coyote, Robert Loggia, Leigh Taylor-Young, John Dehner (Columbia)

A well-crafted, hardboiled mystery by Joe Eszterhas, with sharp performances by murder suspect Jeff Bridges and tough-but-smitten defense attorney Glenn Close.

The murder victim was a socialite and heiress. Her husband (Bridges), a very upwardly mobile San Francisco newspaper publisher, now owns his wife's fortune. Embittered by past experiences in criminal law, Close is pressed to defend Bridge, once he convinces her of his innocence. Then she falls in love with him. Triple-Oscar nominees Bridges and Close play a balancing act that is both glossy and psychologically interesting.

Courtroom drama, which is becoming increasingly hard to make on the big screen, consumes perhaps 30% of this film and, for the most part, the benchmarks are compelling.

Pic, in quick strokes, raises jagged questions about an imperfect justice system. Although the conflicting parameters of mother-lover-professional woman are becoming naggingly repetitive, the Close persona is a fully realized and dimensional one.

....

■ JAILHOUSE ROCK

1957, 96 MINS, US Ⓥ

Dir Richard Thorpe   *Prod* Pandro S. Berman   *Scr* Guy Trosper   *Ph* Robert Bronner   *Ed* Ralph E. Winters   *Mus* Jeff Alexander (sup.)   *Art Dir* William A. Horning, Randall Duell
● Elvis Presley, Judy Tyler, Mickey Shaughnessy, Vaughn Taylor, Jennifer Holden, Dean Jones (M-G-M/Avon)

The production carries a contrived plot but under Richard Thorpe's deft direction unfolds smoothly. Director has been wise enough to allow Elvis Presley (in his third starrer) his own style, and build around him.

Narrative [from a story by Ned Young] intros Presley as a hot-tempered but affable youngster who goes to prison on a manslaughter rap after being involved in a barroom fight. In stir he's cell-mated with Mickey Shaughnessy, who teaches him his dog-eat-dog philosophy, and also some singing tricks. Released, but now embittered and cynical, he claws his way to fame in the music world, riding alike over friend and foe, even Judy Tyler, a music exploitation agent who has helped in his discovery and is partnered with him in their own record company.

Singer is on for six songs, top being the title production number in a prison setting. Star receives good support, Tyler – killed in an auto accident [soon after film completed] – coming through nicely and Shaughnessy hard-hitting as the tough ex-con who becomes Presley's flunky after following youngster in release from prison.

....

■ JAKE SPEED

1986, 100 MINS, US ◇ Ⓥ

Dir Andrew Lane   *Prod* Andrew Lane, Wayne Crawford, William Ivey   *Scr* Wayne Crawford, Andrew Lane   *Ph* Bryan Loftus   *Ed* Fred Stafford   *Mus* Mark Snow   *Art Dir* Norman Baron
● Wayne Crawford, Dennis Christopher, Karen Kopins, John Hurt, Leon Ames (Crawford-Lane/Foster/Balcor)

Jake Speed is fun – a deliberately mindless adventure that keeps tongue firmly in cheek.

A family is worried about their daughter's disappearance in Paris. Pop wanders in, saying they ought to hire Jake Speed, a hero of paperback thrillers to find her. Pop gets sent to bed because he's obviously senile.

But daughter number two gets a note to meet Jake Speed at a seedy bar. She goes, meets Speed and his sidekick author Remo.

After a hilarious false start once in Africa (where the daughter has been sent to), the trio crashes the den of the international white slavers lorded over by a malicious and deliciously evil John Hurt.

Speed is well played by a heavy-lidded and laconic Wayne Crawford who talks as an old-fashioned paperback hero would – in cliches.

....

■ JAMAICA INN

1939, 99 MINS, UK Ⓥ

Dir Alfred Hitchcock   *Prod* Erich Pommer, Charles Laughton   *Scr* Sidney Gilliat, Joan Harrison, J.B. Priestley   *Ph* Harry Stradling, Bernard Knowles   *Ed* Robert Hamer   *Mus* Eric Fenby   *Art Dir* Tom Morahan
● Charles Laughton, Maureen O'Hara, Emlyn Williams, Robert Newton, Basil Radford (Mayflower)

Superb direction, excellent casting, expressive playing and fine production offset an uneven screenplay to make *Jamaica Inn* a gripping version of the Daphne du Maurier novel. Since it's frankly a blood-'n'-thunder melodrama, the story makes no pretense at complete plausibility.

Yarn concerns a gang of smugglers and shipwreckers on the Cornish coast in the early 19th century and the district squire who is their undercover brains. Young naval officer joins the band to secure evidence against them and a young girl who comes from Ireland to stay with her aunt saves him from being hanged by the desperadoes.

Balance of the story is a development of the chase technique. Atmosphere of the seacoast and the moors is strikingly recreated and the action scenes have a headlong rush. Withal, there are frequent bits of brilliant camera treatment and injections of salty humor. It's a typical Alfred Hitchcock direction job.

Charles Laughton has a colorful, sinister part in the villainous squire with a strain of insanity. Maureen O'Hara is a looker and plays satisfactorily in the limited confines of the ingenue part.

....

■ JANE EYRE

1944, 97 MINS, US

Dir Robert Stevenson   *Prod* William Goetz   *Scr* Aldous Huxley, Robert Stevenson, John Houseman   *Ph* George Barnes   *Ed* Walter Thompson   *Mus* Bernard Herrmann   *Art Dir* William Pereira
● Orson Welles, Joan Fontaine, Margaret O'Brien, Peggy Ann Garner, Agnes Moorehead (20th Century-Fox)

Charlotte Bronte's Victorian novel, *Jane Eyre*, reaches the screen in a drama that is as intense on celluloid as it is on the printed page. This picture has taken liberties with the novel that may be chalked off to cinematic expediency, but there is, nonetheless, a certain script articulation that closer heed to the book could possibly not have achieved.

Jane Eyre is the story of a girl who, after a childhood during which she was buffeted about in an orphanage, secures a position as governess to the ward of one Edward Rochester, sire of an English manor house called Thornfield. Jane Eyre eventually falls in love with him, and he with her. When their wedding is interrupted by a man who accuses Rochester of already being married, there is divulged the secret that Rochester has kept for many years.

Joan Fontaine and Orson Welles are excellent, though the latter is frequently inaudible in the slur of his lines. It is a large cast and one that acquits itself well. Notable in the support are Henry Daniell, as Brocklehurst, the cruel overseer of the orphanage; Margaret O'Brien, the ward of Rochester.

....

■ JANE EYRE

1971, 110 MINS, UK ◇ Ⓥ

Dir Delbert Mann   *Prod* Frederick Brogger   *Scr* Jack Pulman   *Ph* Paul Beeson   *Ed* Peter Boita   *Mus* John Williams   *Art Dir* Alex Vetchinsky

● George C. Scott, Susannah York, Ian Bannen, Jack Hawkins , Nyree Dawn Porter, Rachel Kempson (Omnibus/Sagittarius)

Charlotte Bronte's tearjerker is put over stolidly and fails to touch and move the emotions as fluently as the 1943 version with Joan Fontaine and Orson Welles.

Delbert Mann's direction and Jack Pulman's screenplay both tend to play up incident rather than characters underlining that, despite its fame, Bronte's story is pretty much a novelletish theme.

Casting is by no means right. George C. Scott as Rochester tends to play the role rather like Patton on a well-deserved leave, and fails to bring out the smouldering romanticism, mixed with tyranny and selfishness, which characterized Rochester, though his first scene with Jane has a sharp, sardonic tang. Since Jane Eyre is constantly described as plain, and as Susannah York who plays the heroine, patently isn't plain, credibility is strained. York gives a pleasant but not wholly convincing portrayal.

....

■ JANUARY MAN, THE

1989, 97 MINS, US ◇ Ⓥ

Dir Pat O'Connor   *Prod* Norman Jewison   *Scr* John Patrick Shanley   *Ph* Jerzy Zielinski   *Ed* Lou Lombardo   *Mus* Marvin Hamlisch   *Art Dir* Philip Rosenberg
● Kevin Kline, Susan Sarandon, Mary Elizabeth Mastrantonio, Harvey Keitel, Danny Aiello, Rod Steiger (M-G-M)

Kevin Kline as an unorthodox but indispensable detective tracking a serial strangler infuses this improbable Gotham-set romantic policier with personality.

Kline is Nick Starkey, a disgraced cop who can't get along with the establishment but is summoned from exile to crack an unsolvable crime.

Kline has been hung out to dry on dubious allegations of graft by his mean-spirited brother, Police Commissioner Frank Starkey (Harvey Keitel), and brutish Mayor Eamon Flynn (Rod Steiger).

Apparently he's also the only investigative genius in the entire NYPD, which Kline agrees to rejoin if he's allowed to cook dinner for Keitel's haughty, social climbing wife Christine (Susan Sarandon). Kline also strikes sexual sparks with the mayor's daughter Bernadette (Mary Elizabeth Mastrantonio) whose friend was murdered by the break-and-enter strangler.

There's a false ending that does little to make up for the picture's dearth of dry-throat suspense. Steiger has some volcanic moments in this comeback turn, while the other supporting actors provide serviceable foils for Kline's quirky cop.

New York so bereft of grit and character that it could be Toronto – which it often is, with the exception of the Times Square opening and pick-up shots.

....

■ JAPANESE WAR BRIDE

1952, 91 MINS, US

Dir King Vidor   *Prod* Joseph Bernhard, Anson Hall   *Scr* Catherine Turney   *Ph* Lionel Lindon   *Ed* Terry Morse   *Mus* Emil Newman, Arthur Lange   *Art Dir* Danny Hall
● Shirley Yamaguchi, Don Taylor, Cameron Mitchell, Marie Windsor, James Bell (Bernhard/20th Century-Fox)

Shirley Yamaguchi, Japanese film star, plays the title role and fits naturally into the story. Her restrained personality is ingratiating. Don Taylor is good as the Korean War veteran who marries her and brings her to Salinas, Cal, for a new life in an American farming community where public opinion is prejudiced.

J

The Catherine Turney script, based on a story by Anson Bond, brings the bride up against such pitfalls as reluctant acceptance by the groom's family, a jealous sister-in-law, anti-Jap feeling among some of the farmers and similar standard dramatic angles that go with plot. Story comes to its head when the sister-in-law spreads rumor that the child born to the couple was actually fathered by a neighboring Japanese farmer.

JASON AND THE ARGONAUTS

1963, 104 MINS, UK ◇ ⓥ

Dir Don Chaffey *Prod* Charles H. Schneer *Scr* Jan Read, Beverley Cross *Ph* Wilkie Cooper *Ed* Maurice Rootes *Mus* Bernard Herrmann *Art Dir* Geoffrey Drake
● Todd Armstrong, Nancy Kovack, Gary Raymond, Laurence Naismith, Niall MacGinnis, Douglas Wilmer (Columbia)

Jason and the Argonauts stems from the Greek mythological legend of Jason and his voyage at the helm of the Argo in search of the Golden Fleece. The $3 million film has a workable scenario and has been directed resourcefully and spiritedly by Don Chaffey, under whose leadership a colorful cast performs with zeal.

Among the spectacular mythological landscape and characters brought to life through the ingenuity of illusionist Ray Harryhausen are a remarkably lifelike mobile version of the colossal bronze god, Talos; fluttery personifications of the bat-winged Harpies; a miniature representation of the 'crashing rocks' through which Jason's vessel must cruise; a menacing version of the seven-headed Hydra; a batch of some astonishingly active skeletons who materialize out of the teeth of Hydra; and a yare replica of the Argo itself.

Handsome Todd Armstrong does a commendable job as Jason and Nancy Kovak is beautiful as his Medea.

JAWS

1975, 124 MINS, US ◇

Dir Steven Spielberg *Prod* Richard D. Zanuck, David Brown *Scr* Peter Benchley, Carl Gottlieb *Ph* Bill Butler, Rexford Metz *Ed* Verna Fields *Mus* John Williams *Art Dir* Joseph Alves Jr
● Roy Scheider, Robert Shaw, Richard Dreyfuss, Lorraine Gary, Murray Hamilton, Carl Gottlieb (Universal)

Jaws, Peter Benchley's bestseller about a killer shark and a tourist beach town, is an $8 million film of consummate suspense, tension and terror. It stars Roy Scheider as the town's police chief torn between civic duty and the mercantile politics of resort tourism; Robert Shaw, absolutely magnificent as a coarse fisherman finally hired to locate the Great White Shark; and Richard Dreyfuss, in another excellent characterization as a likeable young scientist.

The fast-moving film engenders enormous suspense as the shark attacks a succession of people; the creature is not even seen for about 82 minutes, and a subjective camera technique makes his earlier forays excruciatingly terrifying all the more for the invisibility.

John Williams' haunting score adds to the mood of impending horror. All other production credits are superior.

JAWS 2

1978, 117 MINS, US ⓥ

Dir Jeannot Szwarc *Prod* Richard D. Zanuck, David Brown *Scr* Carl Gottlieb, Howard Sackler *Ph* Michael Butler *Ed* Neil Travis *Mus* John Williams *Art Dir* Joe Alves
● Roy Scheider, Lorraine Gary, Murray Hamilton, Joseph Mascolo, Jeffrey Kramer, Collin Wilcox (Universal

Despite a notable but effective change in story emphasis, *Jaws 2* is a worthy successor in horror, suspense and terror to its 1975 smash progenitor.

The Peter Benchley characters of offshore island police chief Roy Scheider, loyal spouse Lorraine Gary, temporizing mayor Murray Hamilton and Gee-whiz deputy Jeffrey Kramer are used as the adult pegs for the very good screenplay. The targets of terror, and the principal focus of audience empathy, are scores of happy teenagers.

So strong is the emphasis on adolescent adrenalin that *Jaws 2* might well be described as the most expensive film ($20 million) that American International Pictures never made.

Suffice to say that the story again pits Scheider's concern for safety against the indifference of the town elders as evidence mounts that there's another great white shark out there in the shallow waters. Ever-more complicated teenage jeopardy leads to the climactic showdown with a buried cable.

JAWS 3-D

1983, 97 MINS, US ◇ ⓥ

Dir Joe Alves *Prod* Robert Hitzig *Scr* Richard Matheson, Carl Gottlieb *Ph* James A. Contner *Ed* Randy Roberts *Mus* Alan Parker, John Williams *Art Dir* Woods Mackintosh
● Dennis Quaid, Bess Armstrong, Simon MacCorkindale, Louis Gossett Jr, John Putch, Lea Thompson (Universal/Landsburg)

The *Jaws* cycle has reached its nadir with this surprisingly tepid 3-D version.

Gone are Roy Scheider, the summer resort of Amity, and even the ocean. They have been replaced by Florida's Sea World, a lagoon and an Undersea Kingdom that entraps a 35-foot Great White, and a group of young people who run the tourist sea park.

The picture includes two carry-over characters from the first two *Jaws*, Scheider's now-grown sons, who are played by nominal star Dennis Quaid as the older brother turned machine engineer and kid brother John Putch.

Femme cast is headed by Bess Armstrong as an intrepid marine biologist who lives with Quaid.

Director Joe Alves, who was instrumental in the design of the first *Jaws* shark and was the unsung production hero in both the first two pictures, fails to linger long enough on the Great White.

JAZZ ON A SUMMER'S DAY

1959, 78 MINS, US ◇ ⓥ

Dir Bert Stern *Ph* Bert Stern, Ray Phelan, Courtney Hafela *Ed* Aram Avakian *Mus* Hoagy Carmichael, Duke Ellington, Count Basie, Seymour Simons, Gerald Marks, Thelonious Monk, Chuck Berry
● (Raven)

Outstanding feature-length documentary centered around the Newport Jazz Festival. It's a document of the medium, spanning most of the jazz styles and including a rich selection of top performers and material. It's Americana, and a document of its time as well via observation of audiences and the life surrounding the Newport event, not least the neatly-integrated footage concerning the America Cup Yacht Races.

Structure of the film basically follows that of the two-day event around which it centers, with occasional digressions, over the jazz soundtrack, to other nearby scenes such as the cup races, children playing, wave and water effects, reflections, all neatly matched to mood of motif being played. Juxtaposition is sometimes humorous, sometimes ironic, at others merely illustrative, but always deft.

On-the-spot lensing under difficult lighting conditions, both daytime and night-time, is often incredibly good. Some unprecedented effects are achieved by cameramen Bert Stern, Ray Phelan, and Courtney Hafela (under Stern's imaginative and stylish guidance). Similar plaudits also for an oustanding (magnetic) sound recording job, all part of near-perfect teamwork on pic.

JAZZ SINGER, THE

1927, 88 MINS, US ⓥ

Dir Alan Crosland *Scr* Al Cohn, Jack Jarmuth *Ph* Hal Mohr *Ed* Harold McCord
● Al Jolson, May McAvoy, Warner Oland, Eugenie Besserer, William Demarest, Otto Lederer (Warner Bros.)

Undoubtedly the best thing Vitaphone has ever put on the screen. The combination of the religious heart interest story [based on the play by Samson Raphaelson] and Jolson's singing 'Kol Nidre' in a synagog while his father is dying and two 'Mammy' lyrics as his mother stands in the wings of the theatre, and later as she sits in the first row, carries abundant power and appeal.

But *The Jazz Singer* minus Vitaphone [synchronized sound system] is something else again. There's really no love interest in the script, except between mother and son.

Al Jolson, when singing, is Jolson. There are six instances of this, each running from two to three minutes. When he's without that instrumental spur Jolson is camera-conscious. But as soon as he gets under cork the lens picks up that spark of individual personality solely identified with him. That much goes with or without Vitaphone.

The picture is all Jolson, although Alan Crosland, directing, has creditably dodged the hazard of over-emphasizing the star as well as refraining from laying it on too thick in the scenes between the mother and boy. The film dovetails splendidly, which speaks well for those component parts of the technical staff. Cast support stands out in the persons of Eugenie Besserer, as the mother; Otto Lederer, as a friend of the family; and Warner Oland as the father.

JAZZ SINGER, THE

1952, 106 MINS, US ◇

Dir Michael Curtiz *Prod* Louis F. Edelman *Scr* Frank Davis, Leonard Stern, Lewis Meltzer *Ph* Carl Guthrie *Ed* Alan Crosland Jr *Mus* Ray Heindorf (dir.) *Art Dir* Leo K. Kuter
● Danny Thomas, Peggy Lee, Mildred Dunnock, Eduard Franz, Tom Tully, Allyn Joslyn (Warner)

Warners' remake of Al Jolson's 1927 Vitaphone film hit is still sentimental, sometimes overly so. A drama with songs importantly spotted with beautiful Technicolor cloaking.

Lee, in her first feature film lead, sparks the song offerings in sock style, and is okay in the acting demands as a musical comedy-record star who loves and promotes the career of a cantor's son (Danny Thomas). Latter is excellent in a sentimental part, making the most of several genuine tearjerker sequences.

Eduard Franz is the cantor expecting his son to follow in his footsteps, but the updated plot has Thomas returning from two years in Korea with showbiz in mind. He breaks with his father, and goes to New York for a precarious career-launching with the help of Lee, already established.

JAZZ SINGER, THE

1980, 115 MINS, US ◇ ⓥ

Dir Richard Fleischer, [Sidney J. Furie] *Prod* Jerry Leider *Scr* Herbert Baker *Ph* Isidore Mankofsky *Ed* Frank J. Urioste, Maury Winetrobe *Mus* Neil

Diamond, Leonard Rosenman   *Art Dir* Harry Horner
● Neil Diamond, Laurence Olivier, Lucie Arnaz, Catlin Adams (AFD/Leider)

This third screen version of *The Jazz Singer* asks the same question as the 1927 Al Jolson history maker and the 1952 Danny Thomas update – can a nice cantor's son break with family and tradition to make it as a popular entertainer? No one's going to get sweaty palms waiting for the answer, as Samson Raphaelson's venerable chestnut lacks urgency and plausible incidental detail.

Screenplay, credited to Herbert Baker, with adaptation by Stephen H. Foreman, follows general line of earlier incarnations. However, elimination of the mother character in favor of a traditional wife k.o.'s any attempt at a reprise of 'Mammy'.

Richard Fleischer took over midway through shooting, and the best that can be said for the direction is that there's no disruption of the by-the-numbers style.

．．．．．．．．．．．．．．．．．．．．．．．．．．．

■ **JENNIFER ON MY MIND**

1971, 90 MINS, US ◇

Dir Noel Black   *Prod* Bernard Schwartz   *Scr* Erich Segal   *Ph* Andrew Laszlo   *Ed* Jack Wheeler   *Mus* Stephen J. Lawrence   *Art Dir* Ben Edwards
● Michael Brandon, Tippy Walker, Lou Gilbert, Steve Vinovich, Peter Bonerz, Renee Taylor (United Artists)

Jennifer on My Mind is a black comedy about an aimless wealthy Jewish youth who falls in love with a bored and impulsive upperclass suburban girl whom he meets in Venice. Story unravels through a series of flashbacks narrated by the youth, Marcus, speaking into a tape recorder as he attempts to cope with the fact that he has killed his love, Jennifer, when in response to her painful pleading, he reluctantly injected her with heroin.

Film, written by Erich Segal and directed by Noel Black, is sort of a cross between their respective previous features, *Love Story* and *Pretty Poison* with an added sprinkling of 'relevant' social commentary.

The delightfully ridiculous plot, mock-sentimental narration, absurd dialog, infectious syrupy music and intermittent idyllic interludes all parody *Love Story*. And yet, like *Pretty Poison*, this is a potpourri of disarming satire, black comedy and poignancy that creates a strangely haunting aura.

Michael Brandon, as Marcus, is charmingly boyish and natural. Tippy Walker, as Jennifer, comes across with a bitchy ethereal allure.

．．．．．．．．．．．．．．．．．．．．．．．．．．．

■ **JEOPARDY**

1953, 68 MINS, US

Dir John Sturges   *Prod* Sol Baer Fielding   *Scr* Mel Dinelli   *Ph* Victor Milner   *Ed* Newell P. Kimlin   *Mus* Dimitri Tiomkin   *Art Dir* Cedric Gibbons, William Ferran
● Barbara Stanwyck, Barry Sullivan, Ralph Meeker, Lee Aaker (M-G-M)

The misadventures that befall a family of three vacationing at an isolated coast section of Lower California have been put together in an unpretentious, tightly-drawn suspense melodrama.

There's no waste motion or budget dollars in the presentation. Plot has a tendency to play itself out near the finale, but otherwise is expertly shaped in the screenplay from a story by Maurice Zimm.

Barbara Stanwyck, Barry Sullivan and their small son (Lee Asker) are vacationing at a deserted Mexican beach. An accident pins Sullivan's leg under a heavy piling that falls from a rotten jetty. Knowing the rising tide will cover him within four hours Stanwyck takes off in the family car to find either help or a rope strong enough to raise the piling. The mission is sidetracked when she comes

across Ralph Meeker, a desperate escaped convict. He takes her prisoner and commandeers the car.

The performances by the four-member cast are very good, being expertly fitted to the change of mood from the happy, carefree start to the danger of the accident and the menace of the criminal. Scenes of Sullivan and young Aaker together bravely facing the peril of the tide while Stanwyck frantically seeks help are movingly done.

．．．．．．．．．．．．．．．．．．．．．．．．．．．

■ **JEREMIAH JOHNSON**

1972, 110 MINS, US ◇ Ⓥ

Dir Sydney Pollack   *Prod* Joe Wizan   *Scr* John Milius, Edward Anhalt   *Ph* Duke Callaghan   *Ed* Thomas Stanford   *Mus* John Rubinstein, Tim McIntire   *Art Dir* Edward S. Haworth
● Robert Redford, Will Geer, Stefan Gierasch, Delle Bolton, Josh Albee, Joaquin Martinez (Warner)

Jeremiah Johnson based on Vardis Fisher's novel. *Mountain Man* and a story, *Crow Killer*, by Raymond W. Thorp and Robert Bunter is a sort of man of whom legends or sagas are made. Pic leans towards the latter as it meticulously, sans grandiloquence, lays out the life of a male dropout, circa 1825, who decides to live in the Rocky Mountains as a trapper.

Director Sydney Pollack has given a skilled, observant mounting as he carefully allows the man to grow in experience and knowhow.

Robert Redford, as Johnson, has a solid stamina, a fine feel for the speech of the time, giving an auto-didactic flair as he sometimes comments the actions. He begins to trade with the Indians and wins the esteem of a Crow nation chief to whom he gives a present, to find he must accept the chief's daughter in return.

The film has its own force and beauty and the only carp might lie in its not always clear exegesis of the humanistic spirit and freedom most of its characters are striving for.

．．．．．．．．．．．．．．．．．．．．．．．．．．．

■ **JEREMY**

1973, 90 MINS, US

Dir Arthur Barron   *Prod* Elliott Kastner   *Scr* Arthur Barron   *Ph* Paul Goldsmith   *Ed* Zina Voynow, Nina Feinberg   *Mus* Lee Holdridge, Joseph Brook   *Art Dir* Peter Bocour
● Robby Benson, Glynnis O'Connor, Len Bari, Leonard Cimino, Ned Wilson, Chris Bohn (Kenasset/United Artists)

Jeremy, played with adolescent rumpled and bumbling charm by Robby Benson, falls for a newcomer to his school, reserved but lovely little child-woman Glynnis O'Connor. Jeremy plays the cello, loves horses. The girl, Susan, studies classical dancing. Their idyll is shattered by her father deciding to leave New York and go back to Detroit.

Arthur Barron does not force things and handles this slight but glowing pic with insight. Jeremy's waiting outside her house in the morning and faking running into her and admitting it, their visit to horses' training, their first love, done with modesty and the right flair, and their final disarray and her leaving are executed touchingly.

．．．．．．．．．．．．．．．．．．．．．．．．．．．

■ **JERK, THE**

1979, 104 MINS, US ◇

Dir Carl Reiner   *Prod* David V. Picker, William E. McEuen   *Scr* Steve Martin, Carl Gottlieb, Michael Elias   *Ph* Victor J. Kemper   *Ed* Bud Molin   *Mus* Jack Elliott   *Art Dir* Jack Collis
● Steve Martin, Bernadette Peters, Catlin Adams, Mabel King, Richard Ward (Universal/Aspen)

Pic is an artless, non-stop barrage of off-the-wall situations, funny and unfunny jokes, generally effective and sometimes hilarious sight gags and bawdy non sequiturs.

The premise of *The Jerk* can be found in one of Steve Martin's more famous routines. Upon receiving the stunning news that he's the adopted, not natural, son of black parents Martin leaves home with his dog to make his way in the world. Opening sequences with the family are among the best.

Martin's odyssey through contemporary America sees him taking odd jobs, such as a gas station attendant for proprietor Jackie Mason and as the driver of an amusement park train, and taking up with women.

But lunacy is never strayed from very far, as Martin strikes it rich as the inventor of a ridiculous nose support device for eyeglasses. Hilarity ebbs during his decline and fall.

．．．．．．．．．．．．．．．．．．．．．．．．．．．

■ **JERUSALEM FILE, THE**

1972, 95 MINS, US ◇ Ⓥ

Dir John Flynn   *Prod* Ram Ben Efraim   *Scr* Troy Kennedy Martin   *Ph* Raoul Coutard, Brian Probyn   *Ed* Norman Wanstall   *Mus* John Scott   *Art Dir* Peter Williams
● Bruce Davison, Nicol Williamson, Daria Halprin, Donald Pleasence, Ian Hendry, Koya Yair Rubin (Sparta/Leisure)

This minor effort, shot entirely on location in Israel, particularly Jerusalem and Tel Aviv University, is almost as confused in its production as it is in its political message. The latter, presumably, is meant to be an example of university student idealists combating Establishment rules and regulations. What it comes off as, instead, is making an American student (albeit, a pretty stupid one) the deus ex machina for some wholesale slaughter of both Israeli students and their Arabian counterparts.

For students, indeed, this is a most inviting school where a girl student (Daria Halprin) can live openly with one of her instructors (Nicol Williamson). There's little academic work shown. Purportedly archaeology students, there are some fast shots of a small excavation and an even faster remark by Williamson to some 'interesting shards on the table'.

．．．．．．．．．．．．．．．．．．．．．．．．．．．

■ **JESSE JAMES**

1939, 103 MINS, US ◇ Ⓥ

Dir Henry King   *Prod* Nunnally Johnson   *Scr* Nunnally Johnson   *Ph* W. Howard Greene, George Barnes   *Ed* Barbara McLean   *Mus* Louis Silvers
● Tyrone Power, Henry Fonda, Nancy Kelly, Randolph Scott, Brian Donlevy (20th Century-Fox)

Jesse James, notorious train and bank bandit of the late 19th century, and an important figure in the history of the midwest frontier, gets a drastic bleaching. Script by Nunnally Johnson is an excellent chore, nicely mixing human interest, dramatic suspense, romance and fine characterizations for swell entertainment.

Tyrone Power capably carries the title spot, but is pressed by Henry Fonda as his brother.

Story follows historical fact [assembled by Rosalind Shaffer and Jo Frances James] close enough with allowance for dramatic license, hitting sidelights of James in his brushes with the law. Initial train holdup is vividly presented, with all other robberies left to imagination.

Picture starts with foreword on the ruthless manner in which railroads acquired farms for right-of-way through midwest.

．．．．．．．．．．．．．．．．．．．．．．．．．．．

■ **JESUS CHRIST SUPERSTAR**

1973, 107 MINS, US ◇ Ⓥ

Dir Norman Jewison   *Prod* Norman Jewison, Robert Stigwood   *Scr* Melvyn Bragg, Norman Jewison   *Ph* Douglas Slocombe   *Ed* Anthony Gibbs   *Mus* Andrew Lloyd Webber   *Art Dir* Richard MacDonald

J

● Ted Neeley, Carl Anderson, Yvonne Elliman, Barry Dennen, Bob Bingham, Joshua Mostel (Universal)

Norman Jewison's film version of the 1969 legit stage project in a paradoxical way is both very good and very disappointing at the same time. The abstract film concept veers from elegantly simple through forced metaphor to outright synthetic in dramatic impact.

The filming concept is that of a contemporary group of young players performing sequential production numbers in the barren desert, utilizing sketchy props and costumes. No mob scenes a la DeMille, no heavy production spectaculars, no familiar screen names in cameos. So far, so good.

But then something happens as Carl Anderson (outstanding as Judas in the film's best performance) finds himself, in the midst of 'Damned for All Time' running away from contemporary tanks and ducking modern jet fighters. Suddenly it's Catch-22 time, which the very moving 'Last Supper' sequence can only counteract instead of contributing to a mounting dramatic impact.

Barry Dennen's Pontius Pilate is intrusively effective far beyond the pragmatic urbanity called for, Joshua Mostel's King Herod is less a dissolute sybarite than a swishy, roly-poly cherub. Finally 'Superstar' blares forth with the shallow impact of an inferior imitation of Isaac Hayes.

．．．．．．．．．．．．．．．．．．．．．．．．．．

■ JET PILOT

1957, 112 MINS, US ◇

Dir Josef von Sternberg   Prod Jules Furthman
Scr Jules Furthman   Ph Winton C. Hoch   Ed Michael R. McAdam, Harry Marker, William M. Moore
Mus Bronislau Kaper   Art Dir Albert
S.D'Agostino, Field Gray
● John Wayne, Janet Leigh, Jay C. Flippen, Paul Fix, Richard Rober, Roland Winters (RKO)

Jet Pilot was made around 1950 and kept under wraps by indie film-maker Howard Hughes for unstated (but much speculated upon) reasons. Its story has a pretty, young girl as a Russian jet pilot who, on a spy mission, wings into a love match with an American airman in the United States.

Questionable is the casting of Janet Leigh. While John Wayne fits the part of a colonel in the Yank Air Force, the slick chick looks more at home in a bathing suit at Palm Springs than she does jockeying a Soviet MIG, and shooting down her own countrymen, in Russia. The incongruity would appear less glaring if Pilot were out to be a takeoff on secret agent stuff. But much of it is played straight.

Film opens at a US airbase in Alaska where Wayne is in charge. Leigh flies in, tells skeptic Wayne that she escaped from Russia, and is taken in tow by the colonel who gets the assignment of seeking information from her. Picture moves to Palmer Field and Palm Springs, love blossoms, marriage follows. Then it's discovered that Leigh is a spy.

．．．．．．．．．．．．．．．．．．．．．．．．．．

■ JEW SUSS

1934, 120 MINS, UK

Dir Lothar Mendes   Prod Michael Balcon
Scr Dorothy Farnum, A. R. Rawlinson   Ph Bernard Knowles   Ed Otto Ludwig   Mus Louis Levy (dir.)
Art Dir Alfred Junge
● Conrad Veidt, Frank Vosper, Cedric Hardwicke, Benita Hume, Gerald du Maurier, Pamela Ostrer (Gaumont-British)

It's a spectacle of no small proportions, the saga of Jew Joseph Suss-Oppenheimer, who ruthlessly achieves the economic power which permits him, a truly sensitive alumnus of the ghetto, to mingle with the Wurttemberg ducal nobility.

In transmuting Lion Feuchtwanger's weighty book to the screen, director Lothar Mendes and his scriptists manifest much ingenuity and skill to paint in celluloid what the German author did in his powerful novel. They just miss in presenting the major story thread. There are too many loose skeins in the plot knitting. (Locale and period is 18th century Duchy of Wurttemberg, Germany.)

Jew Suss is all Conrad Veidt, a consummate screen artist whose histrionic skill pars the best on stage or screen. Frank Vosper as the rapacious duke is excellent. Likewise Cedric Hardwicke and Gerald du Maurier in character assignments, along with Paul Graetz as the homely philosophical Landauer and Pamela Ostrer as Naomi, Suss' daughter.

．．．．．．．．．．．．．．．．．．．．．．．．．．

■ JEWEL OF THE NILE, THE

1985, 104 MINS, US ◇ ⓥ

Dir Lewis Teague   Prod Michael Douglas   Scr Mark Rosenthal, Lawrence Konner   Ph Jan De Bont
Ed Michael Ellis, Beter Boita   Mus Jack Nitzsche
Art Dir Richard Dawking, Gerry Knight
● Michael Douglas, Kathleen Turner, Danny DeVito, Spiros Focas, Avner Eisenberg, Paul David Magid
(20th Century-Fox)

As a sequel to Romancing the Stone, the script of The Jewel of the Nile is missing the deft touch of the late Diane Thomas but Lewis Teague's direction matches the energy of the original.

Michael Douglas and Kathleen Turner again play off each other very well, but the story is much thinner. The main problem is the dialog, which retains some of the old spirit but too often relies on the trite.

Story picks up six months after Stone's happy ending and Douglas and Turner have begun to get on each other's nerves. She accepts an invitation from a sinister potentate (Spiros Focas) to accompany him and write a story about his pending ascendency as desert ruler.

Left behind, Douglas runs into the excitable Danny DeVito and they become unwilling allies, again in pursuit of a jewel.

．．．．．．．．．．．．．．．．．．．．．．．．．．

■ JEZEBEL

1938, 100 MINS, US ⓥ

Dir William Wyler   Prod William Wyler   Scr Clements Ripley, Abem Finkel, John Huston   Ph Ernest Haller
Ed Warren Low   Mus Max Steiner   Art Dir Robert Haas
● Bette Davis, Henry Fonda, George Brent, Margaret Lindsay, Donald Crisp, Fay Bainter (Warner)

This just misses sock proportions. That's due to an anti-climactic development on the one hand, and a somewhat static character study of the Dixie vixen, on the other.

Against an 1852 New Orleans locale, when the dread yellow jack (yellow fever epidemic) broke out, the astute scriveners have fashioned a rather convincing study of the flower of Southern chivalry, honor and hospitality. Detracting is the fact that Bette Davis' 'Jezebel' suddenly metamorphoses into a figure of noble sacrifice and complete contriteness.

However, William Wyler's direction draws an engrossing cross-section of old southern manners and hospitality. It's undoubtedly faithful to a degree, and not without its charm. At times it's even completely captivating.

Henry Fonda and George Brent are the two whom Davis viciously pits against each other; and later, Richard Cromwell must likewise challenge the champ dueling Brent. Latter's conception of the southern gentleman who exaggeratedly arranges pistols-for-two, whether in tavern or drawing room, and with equal eclat and Dixie elan, is in keeping with what is the most virile characterization in the picture.

Particularly noteworthy is Max Steiner's expert musical score, which more than merely sets the moods.
☐ 1938: Best Picture (Nomination)

．．．．．．．．．．．．．．．．．．．．．．．．．．

■ JIM THORPE – ALL-AMERICAN

1951, 107 MINS, US

Dir Michael Curtiz   Prod Everett Freeman
Scr Douglas Morrow, Everett Freeman   Ph Ernest Haller   Ed Folmar Blangsted   Mus Max Steiner
● Burt Lancaster, Charles Bickford, Steve Cochran, Phyllis Thaxter, Dick Wesson, Nestor Paiva (Warner)

One of the great stories in American sports history – the real-life yarn of Jim Thorpe, the Indian athlete – is compellingly told in Jim Thorpe – All-American. Only a few fictional liberties have been taken in telling of how Thorpe came off an Oklahoma reservation to establish himself as the greatest all-round athlete of modern times.

Pic re-creates a number of events from sports history. There is the sensational 13-13 tie between unbeaten gridiron Titans – Penn and Carlisle – in the duel in which Ashenbrunner of Penn stacked up against Thorpe of Carlisle. There are re-creations of the 1912 and 1924 Olympics (with an assist from stock shots). There are neatly directed sequences of Thorpe as a professional grid star, of his Herculean mastery of every track event in the book.

All these Burt Lancaster has helped capture in the spirit of the grim-visaged, moody Indian. Charles Bickford plays 'Pop' Warner, Thorpe's Carlisle mentor and friend, with restraint and credence. Phyllis Thaxter plays the white girl who became Thorpe's wife, only to divorce him when she could no longer tolerate the sullenness and despair that gripped him following the death of their son and his subsequent athletic decline.

．．．．．．．．．．．．．．．．．．．．．．．．．．

■ JINXED!

1982, 103 MINS, US ◇ ⓥ

Dir Don Siegel   Prod Herb Jaffe   Scr Bert Blessing, David Newman   Ph Vilmos Zsigmond   Ed Doug Steward   Mus Bruce Roberts, Miles Goodman
Art Dir Ted Haworth
● Bette Midler, Ken Wahl, Rip Torn, Val Avery, Jack Elam, Benson Fong (M-G-M/United Artists/Jaffe)

They tried and tried to come up with a better title for Jinxed!, but somehow they kept returning to the only one that was fitting. The exclamation point emphasizes the totality of the disaster. Director Don Siegel's w.k. disillusionment with the project is fully understandable.

Idea seems to have been a darkly comic version of The Postman Alway Rings Twice, with perhaps a touch of A Place in the Sun.

Set in Loserville, USA, represented by Reno, tale presents casino dealer Ken Wahl as the hapless victim of seedy gambler Rip Torn. Once Torn sits down at his blackjack table, Wahl knows he'll soon be out of a job, such is the fantastic luck his tormentor enjoys. Torn also gives grief to his smalltime singer g.f. Bette Midler, who is sufficiently taken with Wahl's charms to rope him into a scheme, a la James M. Cain, to bump off her lover.

．．．．．．．．．．．．．．．．．．．．．．．．．．

■ JOAN OF ARC

1948, 150 MINS, US ◇ ⓥ

Dir Victor Fleming   Prod Walter Wanger
Scr Maxwell Anderson, Andrew Solt   Ph Joseph Valentine   Ed Frank Sullivan   Mus Hugo Friedhofer
Art Dir Richard Day
● Ingrid Bergman, Jose Ferrer, Ward Bond, Francis L. Sullivan, Cecil Kellaway (RKO/Sierra)

Joan of Arc [from the play, Joan of Lorraine, by Maxwell Anderson] is a big picture in every respect. It has size, color, pageantry, a bold, historic bas-relief. It has authority, conviction, an appeal to faith and a dedication to a cause that leaves little wanting. And then, of course, *Joan of Arc* has Ingrid Bergman and a dream supporting cast.

Fleming has done an exciting job in blending the symbolism, the medieval warfront heroics, and the basic dramatic elements into a generally well-sustained whole.

There are certain misfires and false keynotes which militate against the desired consistency, such as Jose Ferrer's tiptop impersonation of the Dauphin, later to become the King of France, who makes his characterization so much the complete nitwit that the audience may well wonder at the complete obeisance of Joan to this weakling sovereign, regardless of the fact he is a symbol of the realm. The churchly gradations are also script shortcomings.

The majesty of the earlier sequences is compelling almost all the way. When Joan edicts that 'our strength is in our faith', when she leads her army in the Battle of Orleans, when she is betrayed by the Burgundians in calumny with the English, when in the earlier scenes she wins the grudging alliance of the Governor of Vaucouleurs and the courtiers at Chinon, Bergman makes Joan a vivid albeit spiritual personality.

The color by Technicolor is magnificent. The production is lavish and looks every bit of its $4 million-plus.

························

■ **JOANNA**

1969, 107 MINS, UK ◇
Dir Michael Sarne *Prod* Michael S. Laughlin
Scr Michael Sarne *Ph* Walter Lassally *Ed* Norman Wanstall *Mus* Rod McKuen *Art Dir* Michael Wield
● Genevieve Waite, Christian Doermer, Calvin Lockhart, Donald Sutherland, Glenna Forster-Jones (20th Century-Fox/Laughlin)

White girl loves black boy, black girl loves white boy.

A sometimes funny, often tearful tale of the deflowering of a scatterbrained English girl turned loose in wicked, wanton London. Director Michael Sarne's script contains too few hits and too many misses.

Genevieve Waite moves into London to study art. What she actually studies is male anatomy, mostly out of class.

Waite, with a most irritating voice, is pretty, all wide-eyed innocence even after she's introduced to London's la dolce vita by a Negro girl friend. Having devoted the best years of her life learning to put on eye makeup instead of the facts of life, it figures that Waite winds up pregnant but unwed. The knave who does her in is a Negro nightclub owner-hoodlum played well by Calvin Lockhart.

The film abounds with strange but colorful types, the most impressive being Donald Sutherland as a fatalistic young lord who's dying of leukemia.

The best thing about *Joanna* is the superb color photography of Walter Lassally.

························

■ **JOE**

1970, 107 MINS, US ◇ Ⓥ
Dir John G. Avildsen *Prod* David Gil *Scr* Norman Wexler *Ph* John G. Avildsen *Ed* George T. Norris
● Dennis Patrick, Peter Boyle, Susan Sarandon, Patrick McDermott, Audrey Caire, K. Callan (Cannon)

Joe deals with a NY ad agency exec (Dennis Patrick) who murders his daughter's junkie lover after the girl winds up in Bellevue suffering from an overdose of speed. Through a somewhat implausible coincidence, he is found out by a hardhat factory worker, the Joe of the title (Peter Boyle), who applauds

his action as a blow struck for God and country.

The two begin a class-spanning relationship which brings them nervously together in the realization that the American dream has somehow turned sour for them.

Pretty, it's not. By concentrating on the extremist fringes of the various social elements involved, Norman Wexler's script makes audience identification well-nigh impossible and at the same time abstracts the questions in a way that gives the pic real importance.

························

■ **JOE KIDD**

1972, 87 MINS, US ◇ Ⓥ
Dir John Sturges *Prod* Sidney Beckerman *Scr* Elmore Leonard *Ph* Bruce Surtees *Ed* Ferris Webster *Mus* Lalo Schifrin *Art Dir* Alexander Golitzen, Henry Bumstead
● Clint Eastwood, Robert Duvall, John Saxon, Don Stroud, Stella Garcia, James Wainwright (Malpaso/Universal)

Not enough identity is given Clint Eastwood in a New Mexico land struggle in which no reason is apparent for his involvement, but John Sturges' direction is sufficiently compelling to keep guns popping and bodies falling.

Spectator is never entirely certain of Eastwood's status, apart from his owning a small spread and being hired to lead a party of gunmen to kill a rebellious Spanish-American who heads fight to save original Spanish land grants of his people. Elmore Leonard's script lacks proper motivation as Eastwood throws in with the oldtimers whose land his temporary employer is trying to take over.

Highlight of entire footage is when Eastwood and a few men run a railroad engine through the bar where some of the gunmen are holding forth and mow them down.

························

■ **JOE LOUIS STORY, THE**

1953, 88 MINS, US Ⓥ
Dir Robert Gordon *Prod* Sterling Silliphant
Scr Robert Sylvester *Ph* Joseph Brun *Ed* David Kummins *Mus* George Bassman
● Coley Wallace, Paul Stewart, Hilda Simms, James Edwards, John Marley (United Artists)

The Joe Louis Story is a dramatic recap of the personal and ring history of the respected Negro American fighter. The film, acted out by a predominantly colored cast headed by Coley Wallace (as the champ), rates high on sincerity, is alternately touching, understanding and heartpoundingly exciting.

Coley Wallace is the spitting image of Joe, from his muscular body to the expressionless face that so unexpectedly breaks out into a broad, friendly grin. He carries off the ring scenes and does well against Hilda Simms who plays Mrs Louis.

Integration of real fight shots, from the early bouts to the pummeling Joe took from Schmeling, the triumphant return match and the tragic attempt in 1951 when the aging Louis came out of retirement to be 'murdered' by Rocky Marciano, is excellently handled and accounts for the picture's sock appeal.

Director Robert Gordon deserves kudos for keeping the action tight and dramatic, never losing sight that he is trying to humanize the story of an idol whom most people only knew in the glare of the arena. Sylvester's intelligent script helps a great deal in making Louis come alive as a slugger and as a colored boy with decent instincts but incompletely equipped to live up to everything that being a 'celebrity' implies.

························

■ **JOE VERSUS THE VOLCANO**

1990, 102 MINS, US Ⓥ
Dir John Patrick Shanley *Prod* Teri Schwartz
Scr John Patrick Shanley *Ph* Stephen Goldblatt
Ed Richard Halsey *Mus* Georges Delerue *Art Dir* Bo Welch
● Tom Hanks, Meg Ryan, Lloyd Bridges, Robert Stack, Abe Vigoda, Ossie Davis (Amblin/Warner)

Joe Versus the Volcano is an overproduced, disappointing shaggy dog comedy: A nebbish is bamboozled by unscrupulous types to trade his meaningless existence for a grand adventure that's linked to a suicide pact.

Pic starts promisingly with Tom Hanks going to work in the ad department of the grungy American Panascope surgical supplies factory. Meg Ryan as DeDe (in the first of her three gimmicky roles) sports dark hair in an amusingly ditzy Carol Kane impression as his mousey coworker. As an in-joke, the real Carol Kane pops up also in black wig later in the film, uncredited.

Hanks is a hypochondriac and his doctor, guest star Robert Stack, diagnoses a 'brain cloud', giving the hapless guy only six months to live. Coincidentally, eccentric superconductors tycoon Lloyd Bridges pops in to offer Hanks to 'live like a king' for 20 days before heading for a remote Polynesian island to 'die like a man', i.e. jump into an active volcano to appease the fire god.

Hanks indulges himself in some rather unfunny solo bits. Ryan has fun in her three personas, but they're simply revue sketches.

························

■ **JOEY**

1985, 95 MINS, US ◇ Ⓥ
Dir Joseph Ellison *Prod* Joseph Ellison *Scr* Joseph Ellison *Ph* Oliver Wood *Ed* Christopher Andrews
Mus Jim Roberge
● Neill Barry, James Quinn, Elisa Heinsohn, Linda Thorson, Ellen Hammill, Rickey Ellis (Rock 'n' Roll/Satori)

An intelligent, engaging pic about a youngster who's into the rock 'n' roll music of the 1950s.

Joey (Neill Barry), age 17, likes to play guitar the way his dad, Joe Sr (James Quinn) used to. In fact, Joe Sr was lead singer for a rock group, the Delsonics, before falling on hard times and taking to the bottle. Joey and his high school friends have formed a group of their own, and they win a successful audition to play backup to some of the original 1950s and 1960s groups due to appear in the Royal New York Doo-Wopp Show, to be held at Radio City. Show's creator and producer Frankie Lanz plays himself in the film.

Leads are excellent, with Barry a very personable hero, Elisa Heinsohn a charming heroine and Quinn managing to give Joey's has-been father genuine dimension.

························

■ **JOHN AND MARY**

1969, 92 MINS, US ◇ Ⓥ
Dir Peter Yates *Prod* Ben Kadish *Scr* John Mortimer *Ph* Gayne Rescher *Ed* Frank P. Keller
Mus Quincy Jones *Art Dir* John Robert Lloyd
● Dustin Hoffman, Mia Farrow, Michael Tolan, Sunny Griffin, Stanley Beck, Tyne Daly (20th Century-Fox/Debrod)

John and Mary is a slight, indeed simple story that begins with sex and ends with love. The two title characters, played by Dustin Hoffman and Mia Farrow, do not even learn each other's name until the final frame.

The skeletal plot [from a novel by Mervyn Jones] has John meet Mary in one of those desperate, swinging singles establishments on New York's upper east side. They return to his apartment, have sex and the film opens with their awakening the next morning.

John is selfish and self-satisfied, but Hoffman projects a screen personality which insists that more is present than is getting through the camera's eye. Mary is much more attractive, feminine and alive. And Farrow enlarges the character sufficiently to make her worth caring about.

The entire charade is smoothly contrived.

....

■ JOHN HUSTON & THE DUBLINERS

1987, 60 MINS, US ◇

Dir Lilyan Sievernich   *Prod* Lilyan Sievernich   *Ph* Lisa Rinzler   *Ed* Miroslav Janek   *Mus* Alex North
● John Huston, Anjelica Huston, Tony Huston, Donal McCann, Rom Shaw (Liffen)

John Huston & The Dubliners is a perceptive documentary on legendary director John Huston and his working methods, shot on the set of his film *The Dead* (1987).

Documaker Lilyan Sievernich (whose husband Chris is an executive producer of *The Dead*) succeeds in revealing, by interviews with Huston, his cast and crew members, plus verite footage of scenes being filmed and rehearsed, how Huston gets exactly what he wants by gentle suggestions, cajoling and simply doing things till they come out right.

When Sievernich presses Huston with a leading question or threatens to become overly analytical towards his work, he smoothly scoffs at such notions and sets the discussion back on track in self-effacing fashion. As his film editor Roberto Silvi says: 'He's one of the last gentlemen in this industry.'

Docu give glimpses of some moving scenes from *The Dead*, including 78-year-old actress Cathleen Delany singing a song, coached by Irish tenor Frank Patterson, who's also in the cast.

....

■ JOHN PAUL JONES

1959, 126 MINS, US ◇

Dir John Farrow   *Prod* Samuel Bronston   *Scr* John Farrow, Jesse Lasky Jr   *Ph* Michel Kelber   *Ed* Eda Warren   *Mus* Max Steiner
● Robert Stack, Marisa Pavan, Charles Coburn, Erin O'Brien, Jean-Pierre Aumont, Bette Davis (Warner)

John Paul Jones has some spectacular sea action scenes and achieves some freshness in dealing with the Revolutionary War. But the Samuel Bronston production doesn't get much fire-power into its characters. They end, as they begin, as historical personages rather than human beings.

John Farrow's direction of such scenes as the battle of Jones' *Bon Homme Richard* with the British *Serapis* is fine, colorful and exciting. Perhaps because Jones himself was a man of action, the story gets stiff and awkward when it moves off the quarterdeck and into the drawing room.

The screenplay attempts to give the story contemporary significance by opening and closing with shots of the present US Navy, emphasizing the tradition Jones began almost single-handed. The interim picks up Jones as a Scottish boy who runs away to sea, becomes a sea captain, and winds up in the American colonies as they prepare for the War of Independence.

The historical figures tend to be stiff or unbelievable. Charles Coburn, as Benjamin Franklin, has a fussy charm, and Macdonald Carey, as Patrick Henry, is good. The brief appearance of Bette Davis as Catherine the Great of Russia is the cliche portrait of that vigorous empress, a woman bordering on nymphomania.

Robert Stack in the title role gives a robust portrayal. Marisa Pavan, as a titled Frenchwoman, is sweet but rather lifeless, while Jean-Pierre Aumont, as Louis XVI, seems a stronger monarch than the usual portrait of that doomed king.

....

■ JOHNNY ALLEGRO

1949, 80 MINS, US

Dir Ted Tetzlaff   *Prod* Irving Starr   *Scr* Karen DeWolf, Guy Endore   *Ph* Joseph Biroc   *Ed* Jerome Thomas   *Mus* George Duning
● George Raft, Nina Foch, George Macready, Will Geer, Gloria Henry (Columbia)

Johnny Allegro is a typical George Raft melodrama. Plot rings in a twist or two to dress up the melodrama of an ex-gangster who is trying to go straight and who takes on a dangerous assignment from the government to help prove his good intentions. From the time Raft crosses paths with Nina Foch, wife of a bigtime international agent, his fate is marked with danger.

Foch pleases in her assignment as a gal who is not all bad and only needs Raft to put her on the proper course. George Macready is the villainous husband, working with foreign powers to flood the country with counterfeit and disrupt the national economy.

....

■ JOHNNY BELINDA

1948, 101 MINS, US Ⓥ

Dir Jean Negulesco   *Prod* Jerry Wald   *Scr* Irmgard von Cube, Allen Vincent   *Ph* Ted McCord   *Ed* David Weisbart   *Mus* Max Steiner   *Art Dir* Robert M. Haas
● Jane Wyman, Lew Ayres, Charles Bickford, Agnes Moorehead, Stephen McNally, Jan Sterling (Warner)

Johnny Belinda is a story that easily could have become a display of scenery-chewing theatrics. It has its theatrics but they spring from a rather earnest development of story fundamentals, tastefully handled. Jean Negulesco's direction never overplays the heartstrings, yet keeps them constantly twanging, and evidences a sympathetic instinct that is reflected in the performance.

[In this adaptation of the stage play by Elmer Harris,]: Jane Wyman portrays a mute slattern completely devoid of film glamour. It is a personal success; a socko demonstration that an artist can shape a mood and sway an audience through projected emotions without a spoken word.

Plot essentials cover a deaf-mute girl, dwelling with her father and resentful aunt on a barren farm in Nova Scotia. A village romeo rapes her. She has a baby and events move forward until the deaf-mute kills her ravisher when he tries to take the baby. She is tried for murder.

Charles Bickford walks off with the assignment of Belinda's father. His handling of the part of the dour Scot farmer registers strongly, pulling audience interest all the way.
□ 1948: Best Picture (Nomination)

....

■ JOHNNY COOL

1963, 103 MINS, US

Dir William Asher   *Prod* William Asher, Peter Lawford   *Scr* Joseph Landon   *Ph* Sam Leavitt   *Ed* Otto Ludwig   *Mus* Billy May
● Henry Silva, Elizabeth Montgomery, Marc Lawrence, Telly Savalas, Jim Backus, Sammy Davis Jr (Chrislaw)

Henry Silva, as a Sicilian-born assassin, is at home as the 'delivery boy of death' for deported underworld kingpin Marc Lawrence. While his escapades would probably fall apart if analyzed, he puts such driving force into them that the viewer becomes too involved to dispute his actions.

Elizabeth Montgomery, however, plays the emotionally and morally mixed-up heroine like a high-school drama teacher demonstrating to her class how to play a nymphomaniac – 10% sex, 90% self-consciousness.

Joseph Landon's script [from John McPartland's novel *The Kingdom of Johnny Cool*] has more holes in it than a Swiss cheese but he stuffs most of them with action and director

William Asher cuts the action in thick slices. Plot centers on Silva doing a job for Lawrence which takes him from Sicily to Rome, then to NY, LA and Las Vegas before he's finished. When a doll comes into his life and gets worked over by some hoods, he adds revenge to his baser reasons for wiping out his assorted victims.

....

■ JOHNNY GUITAR

1954, 111 MINS, US ◇ Ⓥ

Dir Nicholas Ray   *Scr* Philip Yordan   *Ph* Harry Stradling   *Ed* Richard L. Van Enger   *Mus* Victor Young
● Joan Crawford, Sterling Hayden, Mercedes McCambridge, Scott Brady, Ward Bond, Ben Cooper (Republic)

Joan Crawford, whose previous western was *Montana Moon* in 1930, has another try at the wide open spaces with *Johnny Guitar*. Like *Moon*, it proves the actress should leave saddles and levis to someone else and stick to city lights for a background.

The Roy Chanslor novel on which Philip Yordan based the screenplay provides this Republic release with a conventional oater basis. Scripter Yordan and director Nicholas Ray became so involved with character nuances and neuroses, that 'Johnny Guitar' never has enough chance to rear up in the saddle and ride at an acceptable outdoor pace.

Crawford plays Vienna, strong-willed owner of a plush gambling saloon standing alone in the wilderness of Arizona. She knows the railroad's coming through and she will build a whole new town and get rich. Opposing her is Mercedes McCambridge, bitter, frustrated leader of a nearby community.

Love, hate and violence, with little sympathy for the characters, is stirred up during the overlong film.

....

■ JOHNNY HANDSOME

1989, 95 MINS, US ◇ Ⓥ

Dir Walter Hill   *Prod* Charles Roven   *Scr* Ken Friedman   *Ph* Matthew F. Leonetti   *Ed* Freeman Davies   *Mus* Ry Cooder   *Art Dir* Gene Rudolf
● Mickey Rourke, Ellen Barkin, Elizabeth McGovern, Morgan Freeman, Forest Whitaker, Scott Wilson (Carolco/Guber-Peters)

A promising idea is gunned down by sickening violence and a downbeat ending in *Johnny Handsome*, a Mickey Rourke vehicle.

At the outset, John Sedley (Rourke) is anything but handsome. Born with a cleft palate and badly disfigured face, he's struggled through life and wound up a petty criminal.

Johnny is sent to the pen where he comes to the attention of kindly Dr Resher (Forest Whitaker), a plastic surgeon who, after a series of painful ops, has Johnny looking like Mickey Rourke. Johnny is allowed out of prison each day to work on the docks, where he meets pretty accountant Elizabeth McGovern and a relationship blossoms.

But Johnny isn't content with his new circumstances: he wants revenge. He plots with his old gang members (who don't recognize him) to rob the dockyard payroll, meaning to double-cross them. It all leads to a grim, violent downer of an ending.

Rourke works hard at his character but fails to make Johnny the least bit sympathetic. Ellen Barkin creates one of the ugliest femme characters seen in recent films, while Lance Henriksen is typecast as yet another seedy hood.

....

■ JOHNNY O'CLOCK

1947, 95 MINS, US

Dir Robert Rossen   *Prod* Edward G. Nealis   *Scr* Robert Rossen   *Ph* Burnett Guffey   *Ed* Warren Low, Al Clark   *Mus* George Duning   *Art Dir* Stephen Goosson, Cary Odell

● Dick Powell, Evelyn Keyes, Lee J. Cobb, Ellen Drew, Nina Foch, Jeff Chandler (Columbia)

This is a smart whodunit, with attention to scripting, casting and camerawork lifting it above the average. Pic has action and suspense, and certain quick touches of humor to add flavor. Ace performances by Dick Powell, as a gambling house overseer, and Lee J. Cobb, as a police inspector, also up the rating.

Plot concerns Powell's operation as a junior partner in Thomas Gomez's gambling joint, and his allure for the ladies, especially Ellen Drew, the boss's wife. A cop tries to cut into the gambling racket and is murdered. The hatcheck girl, sweet on the cop, is also killed. When the checker's dancer sister (Evelyn Keyes) comes to find out what happened to the girl, she steps into a round of mystery centering about Powell.

Although the plot follows a familiar pattern, the characterizations are fresh and the performances good enough to overbalance. Dialog is terse and topical, avoiding the sentimental, phoney touch. Unusual camera angles come along now and then to heighten interest and momentarily arrest the eye. Strong teamplay by Robert Rossen, doubling as director-scripter, and Milton Holmes, original writer and associate producer, also aids in making this a smooth production.

■ JOKERS, THE

1967, 94 MINS, UK ◇
Dir Michael Winner *Prod* Maurice Foster, Ben Arbeid *Scr* Dick Clement, Ian La Frenais *Ph* Kenneth Hodges *Ed* Bernard Gribble *Mus* Johnny Pearson *Art Dir* John Blezard
● Michael Crawford, Oliver Reed, Harry Andrews, James Donald, Daniel Massey, Michael Hordern (Rank Gildor-Scimitar)

Pic has the supreme virtue of portraying young people as they are, without patronizing or exploiting them: restless, somewhat disenchanted, privately aware of their immaturity, and with a tendency to rush needlessly into action with a later psychological hangover in many cases.

Michael Crawford and Oliver Reed are two brothers, the former just expelled from still another college for a practical joke, the latter the author of that scheme. Together, they plan and execute a national outrage – theft of the Crown Jewels, with no intent to keep them, just to carry off the theft.

Sight gags and underplayed British throwaway gags are interleaved neatly with the growing suspense over whether the guys will succeed.

■ JOLSON SINGS AGAIN

1949, 96 MINS, US ◇ ⓥ
Dir Henry Levin *Prod* Sidney Buchman *Scr* Sidney Buchman *Ph* William Snyder *Ed* William Lyon *Mus* George Duning
● Larry Parks, Barbara Hale, William Demarest, Ludwig Donath, Bill Goodwin (Columbia)

It is only natural that the durability of Al Jolson, as the all-time No 1 performing personality in show business, would be matched by an equally rich real-life story. *Jolson Sings Again* proves that.

On a broad canvas is projected Jolson's wartime tours under Special Services, singing from the Aleutians to the Caribbean bases until he finally contracts the serious fever which laid him low in North Africa. Barbara Hale reenacts the nurse technician from Little Rock who is now Mrs Jolson.

Larry Parks, again playing Jolson, remains an uncannily faithful personator of the star.

■ JOLSON STORY, THE

1946, 120 MINS, US ◇ ⓥ
Dir Alfred E. Green *Prod* Sidney Skolsky *Scr* Stephen Longstreet *Ph* Joseph Walker *Ed* William Lyon *Art Dir* Stephen Goosson, Walter Holscher
● Larry Parks, Evelyn Keyes, William Demarest, Bill Goodwin, Ludwig Donath, Tamara Shayne (Columbia)

Jolson's singing proves the big excitement for this Technicolorful film biog of the great mammy-singer's career.

The Jolson Story emerges as an American success story in song. The yearning to sing to give generously of himself, cued by the still famed-in-showbiz catchphrase, 'You ain't heard nothin' yet'; the Sunday nights at the Winter Garden, the birth of the runway as Jolson got closer to his audience, the incidental whistling in between vocalizing – all these are recaptured for the screen.

But there's lots more on and off the screen. As Evelyn Keyes plays Ruby Keeler – only she's called Julie Benson – in meticulous manner, she helps carry the boy-girl saga.

But the real star of the production is that Jolson voice and that Jolson medley. It was good showmanship to cast this film with lesser people, particularly Larry Parks as the mammy kid. It's quite apparent how he must have studied the Jolson mannerisms in black-and-white because the vocal synchronization (with a plenitude of closeups) defies detection.

■ JONATHAN LIVINGSTON SEAGULL

1973, 114 MINS, US ◇ ⓥ
Dir Hall Bartlett *Prod* Hall Bartlett *Scr* Richard Bach, Hall Bartlett *Ph* Jack Couffer *Ed* Frank Keller *Mus* Neil Diamond *Art Dir* Boris Leven
● (Paramount)

Before the fact, nobody could have foretold the success of Richard Bach's book, *Jonathan Livingston Seagull*, and Hall Bartlett's $1.5 million film version poses the same question. The pastoral allegory, filmed with live birds and locations while some well-known players essay the vocal chores, is a combination of teenybopper psychedelics, facile moralizing, Pollyanna polemic, and superb nature photography.

Though not credited, per arrangement, the vocal cast draws on many fine players. James Franciscus dubs the title bird, a non-conformist who wants to dive for fish instead of foraging in garbage like gulls always do. A puzzlement to his early girl friend, essayed by Kelly Harmon, and his parents (Dorothy McGuire and Richard Crenna), Jonathan is banished from the flock by elder Hal Holbrook. After cruising the world, he passes (via saturated color printing) to another level of existence.

Now there's nothing wrong with uplift, except that exhortations customarily are banal. That is, the end is nearly destroyed by the means.

■ JOSEPH ANDREWS

1977, 103 MINS, UK ◇ ⓥ
Dir Tony Richardson *Prod* Neil Hartley *Scr* Allan Scott, Chris Bryant *Ph* David Watkin *Ed* Thom Noble *Mus* John Addison *Art Dir* Michael Annals
● Ann-Margret, Peter Firth, Michael Hordern, Beryl Reid, Jim Dale, Natalie Ogle (Woodfall)

Joseph Andrews is a tired British period piece about leching and wenching amidst the high-and low-life of Henry Fielding's England. Tony Richardson's film is a ludicrous mix of underplayed bawdiness and sporadic vulgarity.

Large cast of otherwise British players is headed by Ann-Margret, sometimes appearing grotesque in her rendition of Lady Booby,

the noblewoman-with-a-past with the hots for servant Peter Firth in title role.

Fielding's story of concealed identities and misplaced birth origins has of course been the inspiration for generations of successively updated farce. Herein, Richardson has attempted to pump up the project via the casting of some famed British thesps – John Gielgud, Peggy Ashcroft, Hugh Griffith among some 14 guest stars in cameos.

■ JOURNEY, THE

1959, 122 MINS, US ◇
Dir Anatole Litvak *Prod* Anatole Litvak *Scr* George Tabori *Ph* Jack Hildyard *Ed* Dorothy Spencer *Mus* Georges Auric
● Yul Brynner, Deborah Kerr, Jason Robards, Robert Morley, E.G. Marshall, Kurt Kasznar (Alby)

The Journey is a relatively short one, geographically speaking. It leads from Budapest to the Austrian frontier, a distance of about 100 miles. A group of passengers, American, British, French, Israeli etc, is trapped at Budapest airport by the 1956 Hungarian uprising. The Red Army grounds the civilian planes, so this particular group has to take a bus to Vienna.

At the last checkpoint on the border the Russian commander is Yul Brynner. He delays the party, ostensibly to verify their passports and exit permits. His reasons are not clear. One seems to be his purely whimsical desire for western company. Another is his suspicion that one member of the party (Jason Robards) is one of the Hungarian rebel leaders.

What it eventually simmers down to is a political-sexual triangle, with Brynner jealous of Deborah Kerr's attachment to Robards. Litvak finds he can tell his story almost entirely through Kerr (the west) and Brynner (the east), so the subsidiary characters and their subplots suffer.

This neglect is justified, however, chiefly by the projection of Brynner's characterization. He is capricious, sentimental, cruel, eager for love and suspicious of attention. Kerr has the difficult assignment of being in love with one man, Robards, and yet unwillingly attracted to another, Brynner, who is the opposite of all she admires and loves. She is brilliant and moving as a woman alone in an unbearable situation. Jason Robards in his film bow, is excellent.

■ JOURNEY OF NATTY GANN, THE

1985, 105 MINS, US ◇ ⓥ
Dir Jeremy Paul Kagan *Prod* Michael Lobell *Scr* Jeanne Rosenberg *Ph* Dick Bush *Ed* David Holden *Mus* James Horner *Art Dir* Paul Sylbert
● Meredith Salenger, John Cusack, Ray Wise, Scatman Crothers, Barry Miller, Lainie Kazan (Walt Disney)

More a period piece of Americana than a rousing adventure, *The Journey of Natty Gann* is a generally diverting variation on a boy and his dog: this time it's a girl and her wolf.

Set in the Depression in Chicago, story has widower Saul Gann desperate to find employment to support himself and daughter Natty. He's offered a job at the lumber camp out in Washington State and reluctantly takes it, promising to send for Natty as soon as he can. He leaves her under the auspices of a floozie hotel manager.

The girl runs away and remainder of pic is her sojourn across America in search of her dad. Along the way she rescues a wolf from its captors, and he becomes her endearing traveling partner.

Director Jeremy Paul Kagan extracts an engaging performance from Meredith Salenger as the heroine. Rest of the cast is fine, with John Cusack as her begrudging but good buddy and Barry Miller as the witty entrepreneurial leader of a hobo brat pack.

● ●

■ JOURNEY TO THE CENTER OF THE EARTH

1959, 132 MINS, US ◇ Ⓥ

Dir Henry Levin   *Prod* Charles Brackett   *Scr* Charles Brackett, Walter Reisch   *Ph* Leo Tover   *Ed* Stuart Gilmore, Jack W. Holmes   *Mus* Bernard Herrmann
● Pat Boone, James Mason, Arlene Dahl, Diane Baker, Peter Ronson, Thayer David (20th Century-Fox)

The Charles Brackett production takes a tongue-in-cheek approach to the Jules Verne story, but there are times when it is difficult to determine whether the film-makers are kidding or playing it straight. The actors neither take themselves nor the picture seriously, which is all on the plus side.

The story concerns an expedition, led by James Mason, who plays a dedicated scientist, to the center of the earth. Among those who descend to the depths with Mason are Pat Boone, one of his students; Arlene Dahl, the widow of a Swedish geologist who steals Mason's information and tries to beat him to the 'underworld'; and Peter Ronson, an Icelandic guide and jack-of-all-trades.

The descent is a treacherous one, filled with all kinds of dangers – underground floods, unusual winds, excessive heat, devious paths. Before reaching their goal, the intrepid explorers confront pre-historic monsters, a forest of mushrooms, a cavern of quartz crystals, and a salt vortex.

Boone is given an opportunity to throw in a couple of songs. Romance is not neglected. Waiting at home in Edinburgh for Boone is Diane Baker, Mason's niece. And it's obvious that Mason and the widow Dahl will end up in a clinch despite their constant bickering during the expedition.

● ●

■ JOY IN THE MORNING

1965, 101 MINS, US ◇

Dir Alex Segal   *Prod* Henry T. Weinstein   *Scr* Sally Benson, Alfred Hayes, Norman Lessing   *Ph* Ellsworth Fredericks   *Ed* Tom McCarthy   *Mus* Bernard Herrmann   *Art Dir* George W. Davis, Carl Anderson
● Richard Chamberlain, Yvette Mimieux, Arthur Kennedy, Oscar Homolka, Joan Tetzel, Sidney Blackmer (M-G-M)

Undoubted appeal of the Betty Smith novel fails to come through in any appreciable measure in its filmic translation, at best a lightweight entry.

Story is of a young couple's first year of marriage at a small mid-western college in late 1920s where groom is working his way through law school. Weakness of picture lies in the treatment. There is an absence of anything unusual happening and nothing is accomplished to overcome this lack through strong buildup of characterization.

Richard Chamberlain seldom appears at ease as the young husband-student who has difficulty in making ends meet as he takes a night watchman job to augment his day jobs, leaving only scarce time for family life and classes. Yvette Mimieux fares a little better, as she babysits to help out, then leaves Chamberlain when she finds she's pregnant so he won't have additional worries. Arthur Kennedy as the husband's father brings them together again in a gruff role.

● ●

■ JUAREZ

1939, 125 MINS, US Ⓥ

Dir William Dieterle   *Prod* Hal B. Wallis   *Scr* John Huston, Wolfgang Reinhardt, Aeneas Mackenzie   *Ph* Tony Gaudio   *Ed* Warren Low   *Mus* Erich Wolfgang Korngold   *Art Dir* Anton Grot
● Paul Muni, Bette Davis, Brian Aherne, Claude Rains, John Garfield, Donald Crisp (Warner)

To the list of distinguished characters whom he has created in films, Paul Muni adds a portrait of Benito Pablo Juarez, Mexican patriot and liberator. With the aid of Bette Davis, co-starring in the tragic role of Carlota, and of Brian Aherne giving an excellent performance as the ill-fated Maximilian, Muni again commands attention.

Muni does not dominate in this film [based on a play by Franz Werfel and novel *The Phantom Crown* by Bertita Harding] emphasis constantly is on the figure of Maximilian, the young Austrian prince who was persuaded by Napoleon III of France to proclaim himself and his wife, Carlota, rulers of the Mexican people.

Juarez, native Indian, was the elected head of the republic when the Hapsburg prince took over under sponsorship of French troops. Defeated by foreign invaders Juarez carried on guerilla warfare for several years.

Aherne seldom has appeared to such advantage as in this picture. His desire for fair play, his hopeless plea for Mexican unity and the manner in which he accepts defeat and court martial provide ample reasons for sympathy.

● ●

■ JUBAL

1956, 100 MINS, US ◇ Ⓥ

Dir Delmer Daves   *Prod* William Fadiman   *Scr* Delmer Daves, Russell S. Hughes   *Ph* Charles Lawton Jr   *Ed* Al Clark   *Mus* David Raksin
● Glenn Ford, Ernest Borgnine, Rod Steiger, Valerie French, Felicia Farr, Basil Ruysdael (Columbia)

The strong point of this gripping dramatic story set in pioneer Wyoming is a constantly mounting suspense.

Delmer Daves' direction and the script from Paul I. Wellman's novel carefully build towards the explosion that's certain to come, taking time along the way to make sure that all characters are well-rounded and understandable. Capping all this emotional suspense is the backdrop of the Grand Teton country in Wyoming.

Glenn Ford, a drifting cowpoke, runs into trouble when he takes a job on the cattle ranch operated by Ernest Borgnine. Valerie French, the rancher's amoral wife, makes an open but abortive play for him and Rod Steiger, who doesn't like to see himself replaced in her extra-marital activities, plots to get even with his possible rival.

Oddly enough, much of the footage is free of actual physical violence, but the nerves are stretched so taut that it's almost a relief when it does come. Ford is effective in his underplaying of the cowpoke who wants to settle down. Borgnine is excellent as the rough but gentle man. Steiger spews evil venom as the cowhand who wants the ranch and the rancher's wife.

● ●

■ JUBILEE

1978, 103 MINS, UK ◇ Ⓥ

Dir Derek Jarman   *Prod* Howard Malin, James Whaley   *Scr* Derek Jarman   *Ph* Peter Middleton   *Ed* Tom Priestley, Nick Barnard   *Mus* Suzi Pinns, Brian Eno, Adam and the Ants and others   *Art Dir* Christopher Hobbs
● Jenny Runacre, Jordan, Little Nell, Linda Spurrier, Toyah Wilcox, Ian Charleson (Megalovision)

Derek Jarman's *Jubilee* is one of the most original, bold, and exciting features to have come out of Britain in the 1970s.

The year is 1578. Queen Elizabeth I is transported by an angel into the future (roughly the present), where she has 'the shadow of the time' revealed to her.

Observing a renegade women's collective (a pyromaniac, a punk star, a nympho, a bent historian, etc), Her Majesty watches as the 'ladies' and their friends go about their picaresque misadventures – disrupting a cafe, a punk audition, a murder spree.

Through this process of disemboweling the present through the memory of the past and the anticipation of the future, Jarman unravels the nation's social history in a way that other features haven't even attempted.

At times, amidst the story's violence (there are two vicious killings), black humor, and loose fire hose energy, the film – like the characters – seems to career out of control.

Toyah Wilcox, as an over-the-edge firebug, gives the film's finest performance; Jenny Runacre, in a demanding dual role as Elizabeth I and the leader of the collective, is marvelous. And Orlando, as the world-owning impresario Borgia Ginz, steals every scene he's in.

● ●

■ JUDGE PRIEST

1934, 80 MINS, US

Dir John Ford   *Prod* Sol M. Wurtzel   *Scr* Dudley Nichols, Lamar Trotti   *Ph* George Schneiderman   *Mus* Cyril J. Mockridge
● Will Rogers, Henry B. Walthall, Tom Brown, Anita Louise, Rochelle Hudson, Berton Churchill (Fox)

Difficult, beforehand, to reconcile the idea of Irvin Cobb's *Judge Priest* with Will Rogers. Cobb's long series of stories have suggested another type; portly, slightly pompous on occasion and somewhat lethargic in movement, and that isn't Will Rogers. But Rogers makes the old judge completely his own.

At best the story is thin: the love of his nephew for the girl whose father is not known. The father is in town, and when he slugs a man for jeering at her the victim later gangs up on him with two of his pals. The father cuts his assailant and is put on trial. He refuses to make the explanation which would be his legal out anywhere in the south.

The judge's political rival demands that he surrender the bench, since his nephew is lawyer for the defense. Heartbroken at this aspersion of his integrity, the judge appoints a substitute. But that night the minister talks with him. By a ruse they persuade the pompous old prosecutor to reopen the case.

It's a play of strange reactions. In the court scenes a bit of comedy relief is the effort of one of the jurors to rid himself of the product of his cud chewing. Several of the scenes are punctured with a laugh when the well-aimed shot lands in the cuspidor. Most of the comedy, however, is contributed by Rogers and Stepin Fetchit, a natural foil to the Rogers character. Other efforts at local color through the use of Negroes are less effective.

● ●

■ JUDGMENT AT NUREMBERG

1961, 190 MINS, US Ⓥ

Dir Stanley Kramer   *Prod* Stanley Kramer   *Scr* Abby Mann   *Ph* Ernest Laszlo   *Ed* Fred Knudtson   *Mus* Ernest Gold   *Art Dir* Rudolph Sternad
● Spencer Tracy, Burt Lancaster, Richard Widmark, Marlene Dietrich, Maximilian Schell, Judy Garland (United Artists)

At 190 minutes *Judgment at Nuremberg* is more than twice the size of the concise, stirring and rewarding production on television's *Playhouse 90* early in 1959. A faster tempo by producer-director Stanley Kramer and more trenchant script editing would have punched up picture.

Abby Mann's drama is set in Nuremberg in 1948, the time of the Nazi war crimes trials. It deals not with the trials of the more well-known Nazi leaders, but with members of the German judiciary who served under the Nazi regime.

The intense courtroom drama centers on two men: the presiding judge (Spencer Tracy) who must render a monumental decision, and the principal defendant (Burt

Lancaster), at first a silent, brooding figure, but ultimately the one who rises to pinpoint the real issue and admit his guilt.

Where the stars enjoy greater latitude and length of characterization, such as in the cases of Tracy, Maximilian Schell and Richard Widmark (latter two as defense counsel and prosecutor, respectively), the element of personal identity does not interfere. But in the cases of those who are playing brief roles, such as Judy Garland and Montgomery Clift, the spectator has insufficient time to divorce actor from character.

Tracy delivers a performance of great intelligence and intuition. He creates a gentle, but towering, figure, compassionate but realistic, warm but objective. Schell repeats the role he originated, with electric effect, on the TV program, and again he brings to it a fierce vigor, sincerity and nationalistic pride. Widmark is effective as the prosecutor ultimately willing to compromise and soft-pedal his passion for stiff justice when the brass gives the political word.

Lancaster as the elderly, respected German scholar-jurist on trail for his however-unwilling participation in the Nazi legal machine never quite attains the cold, superior intensity that Paul Lukas brought to the part on TV. Marlene Dietrich is persuasive as the aristocratic widow of a German general hanged as a war criminal, but the character is really superfluous to the basic issue.

☐ 1961: Best Picture (Nomination)

■ JUDITH

1966, 105 MINS, US ◇

Dir Daniel Mann   *Prod* Kurt Unger   *Scr* John Michael Hayes   *Ph* John Wilcox   *Ed* Peter Taylor   *Mus* Sol Kaplan   *Art Dir* Wilfrid Shingleton

● Sophia Loren, Peter Finch, Jack Hawkins, Hans Verner, Zharira Charifai, Shraga Friedman (Paramount)

Israel in its birth pains back-drops this frequently-tenseful adventure tale realistically produced in its actual locale. The production combines a moving story with interesting, unfamiliar characters.

The screenplay, based on an original by Lawrence Durrell, is two-pronged: the story of Sophia Loren, as the Jewish ex-wife of a Nazi war criminal who betrayed her and sent her to Dachau, intent upon finding him and wreaking her own brand of vengeance, and the efforts of the Haganah, Israel's underground army, to capture him.

Under Daniel Mann's forceful direction, the two points are fused as femme finds herself obliged to throw in with the Israelis, who use her to track down the man they know is in the Middle East but do not know how to identify.

Loren is excellent. It is a colorful role for her, particularly in her recollections of the young son she thought murdered until the Nazi, finally captured, tells her he is still alive.

Peter Finch, as a kibbutz leader and one of the Haganah, registers effectively and creates an indelible impression of what Israeli leaders accomplished in setting up their own state.

Nicolas Roeg is credited with second unit direction and additional photography.

■ JUDITH OF BETHULIA

1914, 62 MINS, US ⊗

Dir D.W. Griffith   *Scr* D.W. Griffith   *Ph* Billy Bitzer   *Ed* James E. Smith

● Blanche Sweet, Henry B. Walthall, Robert Harron, Mae Marsh, Lillian Gish, Lionel Barrymore (Biograph)

Judith of Bethulia is in four-and-a-half reels, founded upon the biblical tale, with the captions probably culled from the poem of Thomas Bailey Aldrich.

In spite of the undoubtedly vast sum expended for architectural and other props to conform to the period in which the story is laid, Lawrence Marsden did not deem it necessary to recruit a cast of star players. He succeeded in utilizing the services of competent ones in the regular Biograph company. For the name part he selected Blanche Sweet; Henry Walthall for Holofernes; Robert Harron for Nathan; J. Jiquel Lanoe for the Chief Eunuch; Harry Carey for the Traitor, and so on.

There are two parts that stand out – Judith far beyond all the others, with Holofernes a safe second. Fine as is the acting of the principals, the chief thing to commend is the totally wonderful handling of the mobs and the seriousness with which each super performs his individual task.

■ JUGGERNAUT

1974, 109 MINS, UK ◇

Dir Richard Lester   *Prod* Richard DeKoker   *Scr* Richard DeKoker, Alan Plater   *Ph* Gerry Fisher   *Ed* Tony Gibbs   *Mus* Ken Thorne   *Art Dir* Terence Marsh

● Richard Harris, Omar Sharif, David Hemmings, Anthony Hopkins, Shirley Knight, Ian Holm (United Artists)

Juggernaut stars Richard Harris as an explosives demolition expert aboard Omar Sharif's luxury liner where several bombs have been planted.

The action aboard the ship, to which Harris, David Hemmings and other demolition team members have been flown, alternates with land drama, where shipline executive Ian Holm, detective Anthony Hopkins (whose wife Caroline Mortimer and children are aboard the vessel), and others, attempt to locate the phantom bomber who calls himself Juggernaut in a series of telephone calls demanding a huge ransom.

At sea, Shirley Knight wanders in and out of scenes as a romantic interest for Sharif, while Roy Kinnear comes off best of the whole cast as a compulsively cheerful social director.

■ JUGGLER, THE

1953, 84 MINS, US

Dir Edward Dmytryk   *Prod* Stanley Kramer   *Scr* Michael Blankfort   *Ph* Roy Hunt   *Ed* Aaron Stell   *Mus* George Antheil   *Prod Des* Rudolph Sternad

● Kirk Douglas, Milly Vitale, Paul Stewart, Joey Walsh, Alf Kjellin (Kramer/Columbia)

The Juggler deals with a man who has become a neurotic from his long imprisonment in Nazi concentration camps, and how he gradually comes to realize his illness and seek help from new-found friends. The story-telling [from the novel by Michael Blankfort] has one serious flaw. It fails to establish early the nature and cause of Kirk Douglas' illness and, as a result, his acts of violence have an adverse reaction, instead of gaining sympathy.

Once a famous European juggler, Douglas arrives with other DPs for refuge in Israel. While in a temporary camp, his strange actions arouse interest of the camp psychiatrist. Douglas denies any illness and runs away. In his flight across the country, he takes up with Joey Walsh, a young orphan, and together they head north for Nazareth where Douglas hopes to lose himself.

Douglas, under Edward Dmytryk's well-coordinated direction, does an excellent job of selling the erratic character of the juggler. Milly Vitale is very appealing as the girl Douglas meets on a kibbutz.

The camerawork of Roy Hunt flows freely over the Israel countryside, giving an authentic, almost documentary flavor to the story.

■ JULIA

1977, 116 MINS, US ◇ Ⓥ

Dir Fred Zinnemann   *Prod* Richard Roth   *Scr* Alvin Sargent   *Ph* Douglas Slocombe   *Ed* Walter Murch   *Mus* Georges Delerue   *Art Dir* Gene Callahan, Willy Holt, Carmen Dillon

● Jane Fonda, Vanessa Redgrave, Jason Robards, Maximilian Schell, Hal Holbrook, Rosemary Murphy (20th Century-Fox)

Fred Zinnemann's superbly sensitive film explores the anti-Nazi awakening in the 1930s of writer Lillian Hellman via persecution of a childhood friend, portrayed in excellent characterization by Vanessa Redgrave in title role. Richard Roth's production is handsome and tasteful.

Hellman's book *Pentimento* was the basis for literate screenplay. The warm and innocently-intimate childhood relationship between two girls serves as the solid foundation for later contrasting tragedy when their lives diverge.

The period environment, brilliantly recreated in production design, costuming and color processing, complements the topflight performances and direction.

Jane Fonda and Redgrave, neither one a shrinking violet in real life, are dynamite together on the screen.

☐ 1977: Best Picture (Nomination)

■ JULIUS CAESAR

1953, 121 MINS, US Ⓥ

Dir Joseph L. Mankiewicz   *Prod* John Houseman   *Scr* Joseph L. Mankiewicz   *Ph* Joseph Ruttenberg   *Ed* John Dunning   *Mus* Miklos Rozsa   *Art Dir* Cedric Gibbons, Edward Carfagno

● Marlon Brando, James Mason, John Gielgud, Louis Calhern, Greer Garson, Deborah Kerr (M-G-M)

To those normally allergic to Shakespeare, this will be a surprise – a tense, melodramatic story, clearly presented, and excellently acted by one of the finest casts assembled for a film. Presented in its traditional, classic form, there is no attempt to build up the spectacle or battle scenes to gain sweep. The black-&-white camera has been used effectively, the stylized settings simulate scope, and the costumes breathe authenticity.

Highlight of the film is the thesping. Every performance is a tour de force. Any fears about Marlon Brando appearing in Shakespeare are dispelled by his compelling portrayal as the revengeful Mark Antony. The entire famous funeral speech takes on a new light.

John Gielgud, as the 'lean and hungry' Cassius is superb. The English actor portrays the chief conspirator with sympathetic understanding. James Mason, as the noble, honorable Brutus, is equally excellent. As the close friend of Caesar, who joined the conspiracy out of noble motives, Mason is determined though ridden by guilt feelings. His falling out with Cassius at the Battle of Philippi and the scene with his wife, portrayed by Deborah Kerr, make for moving drama.

Louis Calhern's Caesar is another triumph. He plays the soldier-hero with proper restraint and feeling. Edmond O'Brien, though better known for his toughguy roles, is an effective Casca. The picture is so big that the two femme stars, Kerr and Greer Garson, are seen in gloried bits. However, both acquit themselves creditably.

☐ 1953: Best Picture (Nomination)

■ JULIUS CAESAR

1970, 117 MINS, UK ◇ Ⓥ

Dir Stuart Burge   *Prod* Peter Snell   *Scr* Robert Furnival   *Ph* Ken Higgins   *Ed* Eric Boyd Perkins   *Mus* Michael Lewis   *Art Dir* Julia Trevelyan Oman

J

● Charlton Heston, Jason Robards, John Gielgud, Richard Johnson, Robert Vaughn, Richard Chamberlain (Commonwealth United)

This stab at Shakespeare's *Julius Caesar*, a drama of political intrigue, corruption, ambition, envy, rhetoric and conspiratorial cunning, is disappointing.

Under Stuart Burge's firm direction the highspots are brought out effectively but the backgrounds and crowd sequences are stagey and lack the passion and abandon needed to project the star scenes.

Biggest disappointment is Jason Robards' Brutus. He rarely suggests 'the noblest Roman of them all' and his delivery of Shakespeare's verse is flat, uninspired and totally dull.

John Gielgud in the significant but smallish title role, is probably the one that comes nearest to true Shakespearian thesping.

Charlton Heston makes a praiseworthy stab at Mark Antony, giving the role a dominating power.

● ●

■ **JUMPIN' JACK FLASH**

1986, 100 MINS, US ◇ Ⓥ

Dir Penny Marshall   *Prod* Lawrence Gordon, Joel Silver   *Scr* David H. Franzoni, J.W. Melville, Patricia Irving, Christopher Thompson   *Ph* Matthew F. Leonetti   *Ed* Mark Goldblatt   *Mus* Thomas Newman   *Art Dir* Robert Boyle
● Whoopi Goldberg, Jonathan Pryce, Jim Belushi, Carol Kane, Annie Potts, Peter Michael Goetz (Gordon/Silver)

Jumpin' Jack Flash is not a gas, it's a bore. A weak idea and muddled plot poorly executed not surprisingly results in a tedious film with only a few brief comic interludes from Whoopi Goldberg to redeem it.

Anyone who has been longing for a film in which an office worker talks dirty to a computer terminal should find *Jumpin' Jack Flash* just what they've been waiting for.

Goldberg is Terry Doolittle. Just when her life is looking most bleak along comes Jack (Jonathan Pryce). He's a British spy trapped somewhere behind the Iron Curtain who somehow, someway, taps into Goldberg's terminal and asks for help to escape.

Goldberg is plunged into a web of intrigue involving a sinister repairman (Jim Belushi) who conveniently disappears, a crippled diplomat (Roscoe Lee Browne) and another spy (Jeroen Krabbe) who winds up floating face down in the East River.

● ●

■ **JUNGLE BOOK, THE**

1942, 108 MINS, US ◇ Ⓥ

Dir Zoltan Korda   *Prod* Alexander Korda   *Scr* Laurence Stallings   *Ph* Lee Garmes, W. Howard Green   *Ed* William Hornbeck   *Mus* Miklos Rozsa   *Art Dir* Vincent Korda
● Sabu, Joseph Calleia, John Qualen, Frank Puglia, Rosemary De Camp, Patricia O'Rourke (United Artists/Korda)

On the same grand scale of pictorial elaborateness which characterized *Thief of Bagdad*, Alexander Korda brings again to the screen the diminutive East Indian player, Sabu, in a film version of Rudyard Kipling's *Jungle Book*.

Kipling's character, Mowgli, who strayed into the jungle as a child and was brought up by a she-wolf, is most likely to be confused by filmgoers with Tarzan. Laurence Stallings wrote the screenplay and some of the human-interest elements are slighted. Mowgli's return to the native village as a grown-up youth and his subsequent adventures in civilization are handled in neither a humorous nor dramatic manner. The saga of the boy who could converse with animals is related very seriously, whereas the theme might have

been better entertainment if treated in a lighter vein.

● ●

■ **JUNGLE BOOK, THE**

1967, 78 MINS, US ◇

Dir Wolfgang Reitherman   *Prod* Walt Disney   *Scr* Larry Clemmons, Ralph Wright, Ken Anderson, Vance Gerry   *Ed* Tom Acosta, Norman Carlisle   *Mus* George Bruns
● (Walt Disney)

The Jungle Book, based on the Mowgli stories by Rudyard Kipling, was the last animated feature under Walt Disney's personal supervision before his death.

It was filmed at a declared cost of $4 million over a 42-month period. Full directorial credit is given to Wolfgang Reitherman, a 35-year Disney vet. Reitherman was one of several *Jungle* hands who worked on Disney's first animated feature, *Snow White and the Seven Dwarfs*.

Friendly panther, vocalized by Sebastian Cabot, discovers a baby boy in the jungle, and deposits him for upbringing with a wolf family, John Abbott and Ben Wright. At aged 10, boy, looped by Clint Howard, is seen in need of shift to the human world, because man-hating tiger (George Sanders) has returned to the jungle.

Encounters along the way include a friendship with a devil-may-care bear, expertly cast with the voice of Phil Harris. The standout song goes to Harris, a rhythmic 'Bare Necessities' extolling the value of a simple life and credited to Terry Gilkyson.

Robert B. and Richard M. Sherman wrote five other songs, best of which is 'Wanna Be Like You', sung in free-wheeling fashion by Louis Prima, vocalizing the king of a monkey tribe.

● ●

■ **JUNGLE FEVER**

1991, 132 MINS, US ◇ Ⓥ

Dir Spike Lee   *Prod* Spike Lee   *Scr* Spike Lee   *Ph* Ernest Dickerson   *Ed* Sam Pollard   *Mus* Stevie Wonder, Terence Clanchard   *Art Dir* Wynn Thomas
● Wesley Snipes, Annabella Sciorra, Spike Lee, Ossie Davis, Ruby Dee, John Turturro (Universal/40 Acres & a Mule)

The jungle is decidedly present but the fever is notably missing in Spike Lee's exploration of racial tensions in urban America. Lee tackles the subject of interracial romance from the unavoidable vantage point that, while things today are more open, they are also considerably more volatile and complex.

Little time is actually spent with the black man and white woman whose relationship is the core of the drama. Steering clear of conventional romantic scenes once the couple gets together, Lee instead uses the affair to detonate dozens of reactive sequences, showing how the blacks and Italians close to the principals deal with the developments.

Given the violent emotions triggered in others, it would have helped to see more of Flipper Purify (Wesley Snipes) and Angie Tucci's (Annabella Sciorra) feelings about each other as the surrounding fireworks go off.

Flipper is unceremoniously kicked out his Harlem apartment and forced to move back in with his father (Ossie Davis), an ultra-righteous ex-preacher, and kindly mother (Ruby Dee). Angie is brutally beaten by her father and sent packing to a girlfriend's.

Performances are all pointed and emotionally edgy. Film feels too long, but it ends powerfully, as the audience exits with the view that both the white and black communities are deeply troubled and have a very long way to go to resolve their differences.

● ●

■ **JUNIOR BONNER**

1972, 100 MINS, US ◇ Ⓥ

Dir Sam Peckinpah   *Prod* Joe Wizan   *Scr* Jeb Rosebrook   *Ph* Lucien Ballard   *Ed* Robert Wolf   *Mus* Jerry Fielding   *Art Dir* Edward S. Halworth
● Steve McQueen, Robert Preston, Ida Lupino, Ben Johnson, Joe Don Baker, Barbara Leigh (ABC)

The latterday film genre of misunderstood-rodeo-drifter gets one of its best expositions in *Junior Bonner*. Steve McQueen stars handily in the title role.

Jeb Rosebrook's original screenplay, combined with uniformly adroit casting and sensitive direction, has the virtues of solid construction and economy of dialog. To be sure, the plot is somewhat biased in favor of the restless wanderings of McQueen, in that the alternatives are nearly caricature conformity; but overall there is a good balance.

Filmed in and around Prescott, Arizona, the film depicts the efforts of McQueen to look good in his hometown rodeo.

Director Sam Peckinpah's reputation for violence is herein exorcised in the rodeo and brawl sequences. Audiences which consider such rough-and-tumble as innocuous, vicarious ventilation will get their fill, though others may perceive a bit more.

● ●

■ **JUNO AND THE PAYCOCK**

1930, 95 MINS, UK

Dir Alfred Hitchcock   *Prod* John Maxwell   *Scr* Alfred Hitchcock, Alma Reville   *Ph* Jack Cox   *Ed* Emile de Ruelle   *Art Dir* Norman Arnold
● Sara Allgood, Edward Chapman, Maire O'Neil, Sydney Morgan, Kathleen O'Regan, John Laurie (British International)

Cast consists almost entirely of Irish players.

Kathleen O'Regan succeeds only in looking awkward. Edward Chapman is by no means the Paycock of Arthur Sinclair's stage interpretation. He loses a lot of the humor and mugs too much. Sara Allgood is a flat Juno and Maire O'Neil introduces some of the gestures she used on the stage when playing Juno.

Three-quarters of the film is just photographed stage play [by Sean O'Casey] – excellently photographed, but slow in action. The rest moves fast, building up a swift climax of drab tragedy with the seduction of Mary (O'Regan), the shooting of Jerry (John Laurie), and the loss of the money due under the will. The end of the play has been dropped.

Irish atmosphere of the tenement life incidental to the country is well caught, director Alfred Hitchcock having a flair for sniping the real feeling of the submerged tenth.

● ●

■ **JUPITER'S DARLING**

1955, 93 MINS, US ◇

Dir George Sidney   *Prod* George Wells   *Scr* Dorothy Kingsley   *Ph* Paul C. Vogel, Charles Rosher   *Ed* Ralph E. Winters   *Mus* David Rose   *Art Dir* Cedric Gibbons, Urie McCleary
● Esther Williams, Howard Keel, Marge Champion, Gower Champion, George Sanders, Richard Haydn (M-G-M)

As a takeoff, with satirical treatment, on costume actioners, *Jupiter's Darling* is a fairly entertaining, although a hit-and-miss affair. It has Esther Williams in some outstanding swim numbers, and Howard Keel's robust singing.

Robert E. Sherwood's stage play, *Road to Rome*, dealing with Hannibal's invasion of Rome, served as the foundation for Dorothy Kingsley's screenplay.

The two water numbers given Williams stack up with her best. One is an imaginatively staged dream ballet. The other carries an essential part of the story, and its chase

315

theme is developed into taut suspense drama as she flees through vast underwater reaches from pursuing barbarians seeking to recapture her for Keel's conquering Hannibal.

■ JUST A GIGOLO

1978, 105 MINS, W. GERMANY ◇ ▽

Dir David Hemmings   *Prod* Rolf Thiele   *Scr* Joshua Sinclair, Ennio De Concini   *Ph* Charly Steinberger   *Ed* Susan Jaeger, Maxine Julius, Fred Srp   *Mus* Gunther Fischer   *Art Dir* Peter Rothe
● David Bowie, Sydne Rome, Kim Novak, David Hemmings, Maria Schell, Marlene Dietrich (Leguan)

Handsomely photographed in Berlin and directed with finesse by David Hemmings, David Bowie is a Prussian war vet back from the dead who drifts from one demeaning job to another and finally into employment as a gigolo.

The fascinating casting includes Marlene Dietrich and the return of Kim Novak. Sydne Rome is an appealing revelation.

Dietrich, so long away from the screen, is perforce hypnotic in what amounts to a cameo (she also touchingly croons the ever-green title song), in which she adds Bowie to her gigolo stable. Novak also makes a strong impression.

The film delivers a lot of bittersweet entertainment and is never less than engrossing. Period mood is a great strength, with an effective visual mixture of sepia and soft color tints, and a music track of period ballads and jolly ragtime tunes.

■ JUST LIKE IN THE MOVIES

1990, 90 MINS, US ◇

Dir Bram Towbin, Mark Halliday   *Prod* Alon Kasha   *Scr* Bram Towbin, Mark Halliday   *Ph* Peter Fernberger   *Ed* Jay Keuper   *Mus* John Hill   *Art Dir* Marek Dobrowolski
● Jay O. Sanders, Alan Ruck, Kathrine Borowitz, Michael Jeter, Alex Vincent (Alon Kasha)

The codirectors drew on their experience as cinematographers for a private investigator to fashion a screenplay that could be described as a seriocomic cross between *The Conversation* and *Kramer vs. Kramer*.

Jay O. Sanders is exceptionally good as Ryan Legrand, a New York investigator who specializes in matrimonial cases. Legrand takes a dead-serious, just-the-facts approach to gathering evidence of adultery, leaving most of the jokes to his free-spirited cinematographer, Dean (Alan Ruck).

Legrand has kept a tight leash on his emotions for far too long. So he joins a video dating service, and gets involved with a struggling actress, Tura (Katherine Borowitz). When Legrand ruins a weekend with her friends with his moody peevishness, she drifts away from him. Heartbroken, Legrand responds the only way he knows how – he begins a surveillance of her.

The biggest laughs come from incidental details and loony supporting characters; *Just Like in the Movies* makes the most of a limited budget.

■ JUST ONE OF THE GUYS

1985, 100 MINS, US ◇ ▽

Dir Lisa Gottlieb   *Prod* Andrew Fogelson   *Scr* Dennis Feldman, Jeff Franklin   *Ph* John McPherson   *Ed* Lou Lombardo   *Mus* Tom Scott   *Art Dir* Paul Peters
● Joyce Hyser, Clayton Rohner, Billy Jacoby, William Zabka, Toni Hudson, Sherilyn Fenn (Summa/Triton)

Popular and tenacious high school girl passing herself off as a boy at a rival campus serves as a deceptive cover for this comedy that's really about what it's like to be an outsider in the rigid teenage caste system.

Joyce Hyser, affecting a lower register, a short haircut, and a subtle swagger, is not totally convincing as a boy because she's too pretty and too chic.

The scenario sets up the motivation for Hyser to act a boy when she becomes convinced that she lost a chance to win a summer intern job on the local daily newspaper because her journalism teacher considered her another pretty face instead of an intelligent writer.

But this feminist point is then abandoned when her new teacher makes it clear she lost the job because her contest entry was boring. You guessed it: she writes about what it's like to be a girl playing a boy in high school locker rooms, etc.

Key male part of quiet outsider whom Hyser brings to life is essayed by another film newcomer, Clayton Rohner, but Rohner looks too old to be a high school kid.

■ JUSTINE

1969, 117 MINS, US ◇ ▽

Dir George Cukor   *Prod* Pandro S. Berman   *Scr* Lawrence B. Marcus   *Ph* Leon Shamroy   *Ed* Rita Rowland   *Mus* Jerry Goldsmith   *Art Dir* Jack Martin Smith, William Crebee, Fred Harpman
● Anouk Aimee, Dirk Bogarde, John Vernon, Anna Karina, Philippe Noiret, Michael York (20th Century-Fox)

Difficulties and hazards involved in compressing four novels into a single film are self-revelatory. Based upon Lawrence Durrell's novel, *Justine* and three other volumes comprising author's *Alexandria Quartet*, the plottage is particularly difficult to follow.

While the story rivets on Anouk Aimee as the Egyptian Jewess, a prostitute wed to one of her country's most powerful financiers, there are such a multiplicity of elements and forms of love as to prove overly-burdensome for the screen.

As a further hurdle to easy comprehension, Aimee, a French actress, frequently cannot be understood.

Aimee is arresting in her delineation and frequently gives an exciting performance. Michael York, as the Englishman, shares male honors with Dirk Bogarde, playing a British diplomat, and John Vernon, the husband, who heads the Coptics' plans to save their own necks in Egypt.

■ J.W. COOP

1971, 112 MINS, US ◇

Dir Cliff Robertson   *Prod* Cliff Robertson   *Scr* Cliff Robertson   *Ph* Frank Stanley   *Ed* Alex Beaton   *Mus* Louie Shelton, Don Randi
● Cliff Robertson, Geraldine Page, Christine Ferrare, R.G. Armstrong, John Crawford (Columbia)

J.W. Coop is an engaging yarn which follows the reorientation of a rodeo rider, who after spending 10 years in jail for passing a bum check and fighting with a sheriff, is released to discover he is in collision with a totally-unexpected present.

Cliff Robertson, who stars, produced, directed and scripted, has fashioned from all angles a strong, believable character study of a professional rider who finds he must not only adjust to radically altered American attitudes, but also to the rodeo circuit, which has taken on a big business air that is alien to him.

There are also startling social changes that Coop must cope with, including adjusting to a free-thinking, on-the-road woman who besides offering him no-strings companionship, attempts to turn him around by educating him to the reality of an altered society, the problems of pollution and humorously trying to turn him on to soybeans and other health foods.

Robertson's sensitive treatment and savvy direction has created a character at once heroic and tragic.

■ K-9

1989, 102 MINS, US ◇ ▽

Dir Rod Daniel   *Prod* Lawrence Gordon, Charles Gordon   *Scr* Steven Siegel, Scott Myers   *Ph* Dean Semler   *Ed* Lois Freeman-Fox   *Mus* Miles Goodman   *Art Dir* George Costello
● James Belushi, Mel Harris, Kevin Tighe, Ed O'Neill, Jerry Lee (Gordon/Universal)

The mismatched-buddy cop picture has literally and perhaps inevitably gone to the dogs, and the only notable thing about *K-9* is that it managed to dig up the idiotic premise first.

Since the black-white pairing in *48HRS.*, there have been numerous cop film teamings. *K-9* has all the trapping of its precedessors: a flimsy plot dealing with the cop (Belushi) trying to break a drug case, an unwanted partner (Jerry Lee, a gifted German shepherd) being foisted on him and a grudging respect that develops between the two during the course of a series of shootouts, brawls and sight gags.

There are a few amazing moments (the dog's rescue of Belushi in a bar). In between lingers lots of standard action-pic fare, plenty of toothless jokes and some down-right mangy dialog.

■ KALEIDOSCOPE

1966, 102 MINS, UK ◇

Dir Jack Smight   *Prod* Elliott Kastner   *Scr* Robert Carrington, Jane-Howard Carrington   *Ph* Christopher Challis   *Ed* John Jympson   *Mus* Stanley Myers   *Art Dir* Maurice Carter
● Warren Beatty, Susannah York, Clive Revill, Eric Porter, Murray Melvin, George Sewell (Winkast/Warner)

Kaleidoscope is an entertaining comedy suspenser about an engaging sharpie who tampers with playing card designs so he can rack up big casino winnings. The production has some eyecatching mod clothing styles, inventive direction and other values which sustain the simple story line.

The original screenplay turns on the exploits of Warren Beatty as he etches hidden markings on cards, wins big at various Continental casinos and, via an affair with Susannah York, comes under ire of her dad, Scotland Yard inspector Clive Revill.

The relaxed progress of the story becomes, under Jack Smight's direction, more dynamic through his use of Christopher Challis' mobile camera. Subsidiary events and characterizations – York's dress shop, her estrangement from Revill, latter's mechanical toy hobby, Eric Porter's deliberate viciousness, climactic card game, chase, etc – keep the pace moving.

■ KANSAS CITY BOMBER

1972, 99 MINS, US ◇ ▽

Dir Jerrold Freedman   *Prod* Marty Elfand   *Scr* Thomas Rickman, Calvin Clements   *Ph* Fred Koenekamp   *Ed* David Berlatsky   *Mus* Don Ellis   *Art Dir* Joseph R. Jennings
● Raquel Welch, Kevin McCarthy, Helena Kallianiotes, Norman Alden, Jeanne Cooper, Jodie Foster (M-G-M)

Kansas City Bomber provides a gutsy, sensitive

and comprehensive look at the barbaric world of the roller derby. Rugged, brawling action will more than satisfy those who enjoy that type of commercial carnage, while the script explores deftly the cynical manipulation of players and audiences.

Barry Sandler's original story, written for a university thesis, has been scripted into a well-structured screenplay, in which most dialog is appropriate to the environment.

Raquel Welch, who did a lot of her own skating, is most credible as the beauteous but tough star for whom teamowner Kevin McCarthy has big plans. A fake grudge fight moves her from KC to Portland, where McCarthy is building his team for a profitable sale. At the same time, Welch is torn between her professional life and her two fatherless children.

■ KANSAS CITY CONFIDENTIAL

1952, 98 MINS, US

Dir Phil Karlson   *Prod* Edward Small   *Scr* George Bruce, Harry Essex   *Ph* George Diskant   *Ed* Buddy Small   *Mus* Paul Sawtell
● John Payne, Coleen Gray, Preston Foster, Lee Van Cleef, Neville Brand, Jack Elam (Edward Small/United Artists)

A fast-moving, suspenseful entry for the action market [from a story by Harold R. Greene and Rowland Brown].

Mastermind of a holdup on a Kansas City bank is former police captain Preston Foster. Wearing a mask to conceal his identity, he rounds up three gunmen to pull the job. Heist is executed successfully but police seize ex-con John Payne as a prime suspect.

Cleared later, Payne hunts down the gang whom he suspects of framing him. It's a dangerous mission that leads to Guatemala.

With exception of the denouement, director Phil Karlson reins his cast in a grim atmosphere that develops momentum through succeeding reels.

Payne delivers an impressive portrayal of an unrelenting outsider who cracks the ring.

■ KARATE KID, THE

1984, 126 MINS, US ◇ Ⓥ

Dir John G. Avildsen   *Prod* Jerry Weintraub
Scr Robert Mark Kamen   *Ph* James Crabe   *Ed* Bud Smith, Walt Mulconery, John G. Avildsen   *Mus* Bill Conti   *Art Dir* William J. Cassidy
● Ralph Macchio, Pat Morita, Elisabeth Shue, Martin Kove, Randee Heller, William Zabka (Columbia/Delphi II)

John G. Avildsen is back in the *Rocky* ring with *The Karate Kid*. More precisely, it is a *Rocky* for kids.

Daniel (Ralph Macchio) and his mother (Randee Heller) move from their home in New Jersey to Southern California.

Daniel encounters the attacks of his schoolmates and he is well established as an underdog.

Enter Mr Miyagi (Pat Morita), the mysterious maintenance man who takes Daniel under-wing. Daniel wants Miyagi to teach him how to defend himself, but the old man resists until Daniel learns that karate is a discipline of the heart and mind, of the spirit, not of vengeance and revenge.

Morita is simply terrific, bringing the appropriate authority and wisdom to the part.

■ KARATE KID PART II, THE

1986, 113 MINS, US ◇ Ⓥ

Dir John G. Avildsen   *Prod* Jerry Weintrab   *Scr* Robert Mark Kamen   *Ph* James Crabe   *Ed* David Garfield, Jane Kurson   *Mus* Bill Conti   *Art Dir* William J. Cassidy
● Ralph Macchio, Pat Morita, Nobu McCarthy, Danny Kamekona, Yuji Okumoto, Tamlyn Tomita (Weintraub/Columbia-Delphi II)

Film literally picks up where the 1984 one left off, with spunky teen Ralph Macchio winning a karate contest against no-good ruffians.

Informed that his father is gravely ill, Pat Morita heads back to his native Okinawa, with Macchio in tow. His father, who soon dies, turns out to be the last of Morita's concerns.

Morita loved a young woman on the island but left in deference to her arranged marriage to Sato. Latter, also a karate expert, has never forgiven Morita for backing out of a fight which would have determined who got the girl. In addition, Sato's nephew takes an instant disliking to Macchio.

Script delivers any number of wise old Eastern homilies. Anyone over the age of 18 is liable to start fidgeting when Macchio dominates the action, but then viewers beyond that advanced age are irrelevant with this film.

■ KARATE KID III, THE

1989, 111 MINS, US ◇ Ⓥ

Dir John G. Avildsen   *Prod* Jerry Weintraub
Scr Robert Mark Kamen   *Ph* Stephen Yaconelli   *Ed* John Carter, John G. Avildsen   *Mus* Bill Conti   *Art Dir* William F. Matthews
● Ralph Macchio, Pat Morita, Robyn Lively, Thomas Ian Griffith, Martin L. Kove (Columbia)

The makers of *The Karate Kid III* – also responsible for its successful predecessors – have either delivered or taken a few too many kicks to the head along the way, resulting in a particularly dimwitted film that will likely spell the death of the series.

The only remarkable things about it are that Ralph Macchio still looks young enough to play a 17-year-old, and that Noriyuki 'Pat' Morita can still milk some charm from his character by mumbling sage Miyagi-isms about things like life and tree roots, despite their utter inanity this time around.

Martin L. Kove reprises his role from the first pic as Kreese, the nasty karate master previously humbled by Miyagi (Morita) and still bitter from the experience.

This time, however, he has a patron – former Vietnam buddy Terry (Thomas Ian Griffith), who apparently has made millions dumping toxic chemicals yet has nothing better to do than devote his time to seeking vengeance against Miyagi and protege Daniel (Macchio) on Kreese's behalf.

■ KEEP SMILING

1938, 91 MINS, UK

Dir Monty Banks   *Prod* Robert T. Kane   *Scr* William Conselman, Val Valentine, Rodney Ackland   *Ph* Mutz Greenbaum   *Ed* James B. Clark
● Gracie Fields, Roger Livesey, Mary Maguire, Peter Coke, Jack Donohue, Hay Petrie (20th Century-Fox)

Keep Smiling was carefully prepared with an eye to establishing the topflight British star Gracie Fields in the US. Results are meritorious, mainly due to preparation of the screenplay by William Conselman, Hollywood veteran, and direction by Monty Banks, which injects more of the American type of humor than has been present in earlier Fields starrers.

Film is good entertainment, a fast-moving filmusical with several songs delivered in crackerjack style by Fields. Story concerns show troupe headed by Fields which gets stranded; beds in at farm of girl's grandfather; luckily acquires a bus for a tour; and winds up for a two-year engagement at a pavilion near Brighton.

Fields delivers three comedy numbers, a torch song, one swing tune that has possibilities of popularity with the bands, 'Swing Your Way to Happiness', and scores decis-

ively in singing the religious choral, 'Jerusalem', in a small church setting.

Mary Maguire is only American player in cast, and is satisfactory as the dancing ingenue who provides the romantic interest. Mr Skip, the wirehair, is the canine who became rather famous as Astra in *The Thin Man*.

■ KEEP, THE

1983, 96 MINS, UK/US ◇ Ⓥ

Dir Michael Mann   *Prod* Gene Kirkwood, Howard W. Koch Jr   *Scr* Michael Mann   *Ph* Alex Thomson   *Ed* Dov Hoenig   *Mus* Tangerine Dream   *Art Dir* John Box
● Scott Glenn, Alberta Watson, Jurgen Prochnow, Robert Prosky, Gabriel Byrne, Ian McKellen (Paramount)

Buried deep within *The Keep's* mysterious exterior lies that chilling Hollywood question: how do these dogs get made?

After his promising debut with *The Thief*, this is writer-director Michael Mann's second feature [from a novel by F. Paul Wilson], testimony again to the one-step-forward, two-steps-back career theory.

Some Germans have arrived at a small Rumanian village, unaware and unafraid that the keep where they will be headquartered has an uneasy history. Their commander (Jurgen Prochnow) is a nice guy despite his job with the Wehrmacht and it's hardly his fault that his troops are gradually being eaten alive and blown apart by an unseen force that moves smokily through the keep.

Professorial Ian McKellen is brought from a concentration camp to help solve the mystery, and brings his imminently assaultable daughter (Alberta Watson). While she's being raped, the monster emerges from his fog and blows those bad guys apart, making a friend of her father.

Somewhere across the dark waters, all this commotion wakes up Scott Glenn, who sets out for the keep to make sure the monster doesn't use the professor to get out.

■ KELLY'S HEROES

1970, 148 MINS, US/YUGOSLAVIA ◇ Ⓥ

Dir Brian G. Hutton   *Prod* Gabriel Katzka, Sidney Beckerman   *Scr* Troy Kennedy Martin   *Ph* Gabriel Figueroa   *Ed* John Jympson   *Mus* Lalo Schifrin   *Art Dir* Jonathan Barry
● Clint Eastwood, Telly Savalas, Don Rickles, Carroll O'Connor, Donald Sutherland, Gavin MacLeod (M-G-M)

Clint Eastwood, Telly Savalas, Don Rickles and Donald Sutherland are among the stars cast as lovable roughnecks who decide to steal $16 million in gold bullion; it belongs to the Germans, so that's okay.

Nearly satirical in its overall effect, plot caroms between cliche dogface antics, detailed and gratuitous violence, caper melodramatics, and outrageous anachronism.

Eastwood stumbles onto knowledge of the gold stash from captured German officer David Hurst. Savalas, senior non-com in the platoon leisurely commanded by Hal Buckley, comes around to participating in the theft during a dull r&r period.

Eastwood's performance remains in his traditional low-key groove, thereby creating an adrenalin vacuum filled to the brim by the screen-dominating presence of Savalas and Sutherland.

■ KENTUCKIAN, THE

1955, 103 MINS, US ◇ Ⓥ

Dir Burt Lancaster   *Prod* Harold Hecht   *Scr* A.B. Guthrie Jr   *Ph* Ernest Laszlo   *Ed* William B. Murphy   *Mus* Bernard Herrmann

● Burt Lancaster, Dianne Foster, Diana Lynn, John McIntire, Walter Matthau, John Carradine (United Artists)

The rather simple story of a pioneer father, his son and their dream of new lands is the basis for this adventure-drama. The footage is long and often slow, with the really high spots of action rather scattered.

Burt Lancaster takes on the added chore of director for the production. He does a fairly competent first-job of handling most every one but himself.

Dianne Foster makes a strong impression as Hannah the bound girl who takes up with Lancaster and his young son (Donald Mac-Donald) after they use their riverboat passage money to pay off her indentures to a mean tavernkeeper. She, more than anyone else in the cast, adds something other than just a surface response to the story situations.

Diana Lynn is competent and attractive but, unfortunately, her role doesn't count for much in the overall drama. There's too much of ten-twent-thirt flamboyance to Walter Matthau's portrayal of the whip-cracking heavy.

■ KENTUCKY FRIED MOVIE, THE

1977, 90 MINS, US ◇ ⓥ
Dir John Landis *Prod* Robert K. Weiss *Scr* David Zucker, Jim Abrahams, Jerry Zuker *Ph* Stephen M. Katz *Ed* George Folsey Jr *Mus* Igo Kantor *Art Dir* Rich Harvel
● Donald Sutherland, George Lazenby, Henry Gibson, Bill Bixby, Tony Dow (Kentucky Fried Theatre)

The Kentucky Fried Movie boasts excellent production values and some genuine wit, though a few of the sketches are tasteless.

Some of the appeal of this kind of material is purely juvenile – the dubious kick of hearing 'TV performers' use foul language and seeing them perform off-color activities – but there is also a more substantial undertone in using satire of TV and films as a means of satirizing American cultural values.

Though each viewer will have his favourites, the standout segs certainly include *Zinc Oxide*, a terrific physical comedy routine spoofing an educational film, *Cleopatra Schwartz*, parody of a Pam Grier action film, but with a black Amazon woman married to a rabbi.

■ KEY LARGO

1948, 100 MINS, US ⓥ
Dir John Huston *Prod* Jerry Wald *Scr* Richard Brooks, John Huston *Ph* Karl Freund *Ed* Rudi Fehr *Mus* Max Steiner *Art Dir* Leo K. Kuter
● Humphrey Bogart, Edward G. Robinson, Lauren Bacall, Lionel Barrymore, Claire Trevor, Thomas Gomez (Warner)

A tense film thriller has been developed from Maxwell Anderson's play, *Key Largo*. Emphasis is on tension in the telling, and effective use of melodramatic mood has been used to point up the suspense.

There are overtones of soapboxing on a better world but this is never permitted to interfere with basic plot. Key West locale is an aid in stressing tension that carries through the plot. Atmosphere of the deadly, still heat of the Keys, the threat of a hurricane and the menace of merciless gangsters make the suspense seem real, and Huston's direction stresses the mood of anticipation.

Humphrey Bogart is seen as a veteran, stopping off at Key Largo to visit the family of a buddy killed in the war. He finds the run-down hotel taken over by a group of gangsters, who are waiting to exchange a load of counterfeit for real cash. Kept prisoners over a long day and night, during which a hurricane strikes, the best and the worst is brought out in the characters.

The excitement generated is quiet, seldom rambunctious or slambang, although there are moments of high action. The performances are of uniform excellence and go a long way towards establishing credibility of the events.

■ KEY TO THE CITY

1950, 100 MINS, US
Dir George Sidney *Prod* Z. Wayne Griffin *Scr* Robert Riley Crutcher *Ph* Harold Rosson *Ed* James E. Newcom *Mus* Bronislau Kaper
● Clark Gable, Loretta Young, Marilyn Maxwell, Frank Morgan, Raymond Burr (M-G-M)

Key to the City is a noisy, wise-cracking comedy. Dialog is flip and pseudo-sophisticated, proper for telling the plot of a quickie romance that is bred at a mayors' convention in San Francisco. Clark Gable is the honest mayor of a northern California city. Story brings Loretta Young, the equally honest mayor from New England, into antagonistic contact.

Together they strike sparks despite character opposites, become involved in unwelcome adventures that keep them in and out of jail, and find love on the fog-shrouded Telegraph Hill.

George Sidney's direction captures the noisy convention atmosphere and keys the entire movement in that vein. Raucousness was the best method of selling the yarn and keeping the laugh punchy.

■ KEY, THE

1934, 82 MINS, US
Dir Michael Curtiz *Scr* Laird Doyle *Ph* Ernest Haller *Ed* William Clemens, Thomas Richards *Art Dir* Robert Haas
● William Powell, Edna Best, Colin Clive, Hobart Cavanaugh, Halliwell Hobbes, Henry O'Neill (Warner)

Setting of *The Key*, adapted from the London stage play [by R. Gore-Browne and J. L. Hardy], is the Irish revolution of 1920. Recalled is that chapter of Anglo-Gaelic relations in which the marauding Black-and-Tan troops, the street-sniping patriots and the phantom-moving Michael Collins combined to make a gory, tumultuous time of it.

Only a minor part of the color and dynamic drama that these pages afford has been captured by the picture. But there is enough pulsing sweep to the background episodes to overcome the vapidity of a formula triangle – husband (Colin Clive), wife (Edna Best) and returned lover (William Powell) – to give the film an above-average rating.

Powell is starred, but the acting honors go to Clive. Fault doesn't lie with Powell. It's a role that's as wooden as the central plot itself. When the characterization calls for a debonair, glib fellow with a flair for getting himself out of femme complications, the Powell personality clicks on all cylinders. Later, when the tale gives way to self-sacrificing, Powell becomes a puppet moving this way and that to the tug of the strings.

For Best it's a debut in American films. Hers is also a puppetlike part, giving her little chance to register anything but anguish. Next to Clive the standout bit of acting is delivered by J. M. Kerrigan who, as a noncombatant Irish, does the contacting between the revolutionists and the invading Black-and-Tans.

■ KEY, THE

1958, 134 MINS, UK ⓥ
Dir Carol Reed *Prod* Carl Foreman *Scr* Carl Foreman *Ph* Oswald Morris *Ed* Bert Bates *Mus* Malcolm Arnold *Prod Des* Wilfrid Shingleton
● William Holden, Sophia Loren, Trevor Howard, Oscar Homolka, Kieron Moore, Bernard Lee (Open Road/Columbia)

Based on Jan De Hartog's novel *Stella*, this is a wartime yarn, with William Holden and Trevor Howard as commanders of tugs engaged on convoy rescue duty in U-Boat Alley – the Western Approaches. This highly hazardous chore provides *The Key* with some standout thrills which alone make the pic great entertainment.

When Holden joins up with his old buddy Howard, he finds him sharing an apartment with a beautiful Swiss refugee, played with dignity and sensitive understanding by Sophia Loren. She identifies both these men with her dead fiance. When Howard is killed, Holden uses the spare key that Howard has given him to keep the apartment among tug men. Holden and Loren fall in love.

There are some outstanding scenes as, for instance, when Holden takes over command of his ship and indulges in crazy maneuvers to test its seaworthiness; a splendidly played tipsy scene between Howard and Holden; a fierce bombing and fire sequence at sea; and a tender moment when Holden and Loren fall in love.

■ KEYS OF THE KINGDOM, THE

1944, 137 MINS, US
Dir John M. Stahl *Prod* Joseph L. Mankiewicz *Scr* Joseph L. Mankiewicz, Nunnally Johnson *Ph* Arthur Miller *Ed* James B. Clark *Mus* Alfred Newman *Art Dir* James Basevi, William Darling
● Gregory Peck, Thomas Mitchell, Vincent Price, Roddy McDowall, Edmund Gwenn, Cedric Hardwicke (20th Century-Fox)

A cavalcade of a priest's life, played excellently by Gregory Peck, what transcends all the cinemaction is the impact of tolerance, service, faith and godliness.

Where the monsignor (Cedric Hardwicke) comes to out the aged, limping and poor father (Peck), he departs with humility and a new respect after he reads the good father's journal, first of unrequited love (in youth) and later in unselfish devotion, self-punishing denials and unswerving fealty to his mission as it covers more than a half century. The action (from A.J. Cronin's bestseller) starts in Scotland, shifts to China and thence back to the land of his birth.

There is a spell of prime-of-life accomplishment as he makes some headway in the far province of Chek Kow, even unto saving the life of the wealthy local mandarin's son and heir through emergency lancing of the boy's blood-poisoned arm. But comes civil war, and his mission on the beautiful Hill of the Green Jade happens to fall in direct line of fire between the authoritative army and the Chinese bandits.

■ KHARTOUM

1966, 134 MINS, UK ◇ ⓥ
Dir Basil Dearden *Prod* Julian Blaustein *Scr* Robert Ardrey *Ph* Edward Scaife *Ed* Fergus McDonell *Mus* Frank Cordell *Art Dir* John Howell
● Charlton Heston, Laurence Olivier, Richard Johnson, Ralph Richardson, Alexander Knox, Johnny Sekka (United Artists)

Khartoum is an action-filled entertainment pic which contrasts personal nobility with political expediency. The colorful production builds into spectacular display, enhanced by Cinerama presentation, while Charlton Heston and Laurence Olivier propel towards inevitable tragedy the drama of two sincere opponents.

Filmed in Egypt and finished at England's Pinewood Studios, the historical drama depicts the events leading up to the savage death of General Charles Gordon, famed British soldier, as he sought to mobilize public opinion against the threat of a religious-political leader who would conquer the Arab world.

Heston delivers an accomplished performance as Gordon, looking like the 50-year-old trim soldier that Gordon was when picked to evacuate Khartoum of its Egyptian inhabitants.

Olivier, playing the Mahdi, is excellent in creating audience terror of a zealot who sincerely believes that a mass slaughter is Divine Will, while projecting respect and compassion for his equally-religious adversary.

Basil Dearden directs with a fine hand, while Yakima Canutt, second unit director given prominent screen credit, works simultaneously to create much big-screen razzle-dazzle action.

．．．．．．．．．．．．．．．．．．．．．．．．．．．．

■ **KICKBOXER**

1989, 105 MINS, US ◇ ⓥ
Dir Mark DiSalle, David Worth *Prod* Mark DiSalle *Scr* Glenn Bruce *Ph* Jon Kranhouse *Ed* Wayne Wahram *Mus* Paul Hertzog *Art Dir* Shay Austin
● Jean-Claude Van Damme, Denis Alexio, Dennis Chan, Tong Po, Haskell Anderson, Rochelle Ashana (Kings Road)

Combine *Karate Kid* and *Rocky* with a bit more blood and gore, dull direction and a smattering of inept actors and you have *Kickboxer*.

Pic opens with Dennis Alexio (Eric Sloane) being crowned world kickboxing champion, watched by his younger brother Jean-Claude Van Damme. The duo head off to Thailand to take on the originators of kickboxing after being asked some inane questions by a journalist.

Alexio fights, and is crippled by top Thai fighter Tong Po, leaving Van Damme to swear revenge. He finds out the only way he can defeat Po is by learning Muay-Thai fighting and sets off to convince eccentric Dennis Chan (Xian Chow) to teach him.

Much of *Kickboxer* is macho nonsense full of cliche characters and risible dialog. There is no denying, though, that the fight scenes – choreographed by Van Damme – are well handled.

．．．．．．．．．．．．．．．．．．．．．．．．．．．．

■ **KID, THE**

1921, 80 MINS, US ⊗ ⓥ
Dir Charles Chaplin, Chuck Reisner *Prod* Charles Chaplin *Scr* Charles Chaplin *Ph* Rollie Totheroh
● Charles Chaplin, Jackie Coogan, Edna Purviance, Carl Miller, Tom Wilson, Chuck Reisner (Chaplin/First National)

In this, Chaplin is less of the buffoon and more of the actor. But his comedy is all there and there is not a dull moment once the comedian comes into the picture, which is along about the middle of the first reel.

Introduced as 'a picture with a smile – perhaps a tear', it proves itself just that. For while it will move people to uproarious laughter and keep them in a state of uneasing delight, it also will touch their hearts and win sympathy, not only for the star, but for his leading woman, and little Jackie Coogan.

There are characteristic 'Chaplin touches'. A fine instance of imagination is where he dreams of Heaven. His slum alley is transformed into a bit of Paradise, with everybody – including his Nemesis, the cop, and a big bully who had wrecked a brick wall and bent a lamppost swinging at Charlie – turned into angels.

．．．．．．．．．．．．．．．．．．．．．．．．．．．．

■ **KID BROTHER, THE**

1927, 83 MINS, US ⊗
Dir Ted Wilde *Prod* Harold Lloyd *Scr* John Grey, Tom Crizer, Ted Wilde *Ph* Walter Lundin
● Harold Lloyd, Jobyna Ralston, Walter James (Lloyd/Paramount)

Harold Lloyd has clicked again with *The Kid Brother*, about as gaggy a gag picture as he has ever done. It is just a series of gags, one following the other, some funny and others funnier.

Lloyd is somewhat different in the picture than he has been heretofore. In this case he is the youngest son of a family of three boys who live with their father, a widower.

His opening scene shows him performing this last task with the aid of a butter churn, an ingenious mechanical arrangement for the wringing out and hanging of the clothes with the aid of a kite which carries the clothes aloft as they come from the wringer.

When dad finds out that a medicine show has made a pitch and that the boy has given them a license, her orders the youngster to go down and close up the show. There are a couple of gags here that get over for howls, especially that of causing the amateur sheriff to disappear and his final hanging up against the back of the stage securely handcuffed.

Jobyna Ralston plays opposite Lloyd as the little medicine show girl and handles herself perfectly. Walter James as the comedian's father acquits himself with honors.

．．．．．．．．．．．．．．．．．．．．．．．．．．．．

■ **KID FOR TWO FARTHINGS, A**

1955, 96 MINS, UK ◇
Dir Carol Reed *Prod* Carol Reed *Scr* Wolf Mankowitz *Ph* Ted Scaife *Ed* A.S. Bates *Mus* Benjamin Frankel *Art Dir* Wilfrid Shingleton
● Celia Johnson, Diana Dors, David Kossoff, Brenda De Banzie, Joe Robinson (London)

Carol Reed has extracted a great deal of charm from Wolf Mankowitz's novel. This is not a conventional story, but a series of cameos set in the Jewish quarter of London and around the famed Petticoat Lane.

Some of the Petticoat Lane scenes were filmed on location, and the characters mainly are real enough.

Reed's direction is bold and authoritative. He uses color for the first time in his career with telling effect and, within the framework of the setting, has achieved all that could have been expected. David Kossoff gives a performance as the trouser-maker (with an unusual bent towards philosophy) that is a model of sincerity. Diana Dors plays her part as a blonde popsie with complete conviction. Celia Johnson is badly miscast as the boy's mother, and hardly ever comes to grips with the role.

．．．．．．．．．．．．．．．．．．．．．．．．．．．．

■ **KID FROM BROOKLYN, THE**

1946, 114 MINS, US ◇ ⓥ
Dir Norman Z. McLeod *Prod* Samuel Goldwyn *Scr* Don Hartman, Melville Shavelson *Ph* Gregg Toland *Ed* Daniel Mandell *Mus* Sylvia Fine, Max Liebman *Art Dir* Perry Ferguson, Stewart Chaney, McClure Capps
● Danny Kaye, Virginia Mayo, Vera-Ellen, Steve Cochran, Eve Arden, Lionel Stander (RKO/Goldwyn)

Based on the old Harold Lloyd starrer, *The Milky Way* (originally legit play by Lynn Root and Harry Clark), the film is aimed straight at the bellylaughs and emerges as a lush mixture of comedy, music and gals, highlighted by beautiful Technicolor and ultra-rich production mountings.

Danny Kaye is spotted in almost three-fourths of the picture's sequences, but the audience will be clamoring for more at the final fadeout. Zany comic clicks with his unique mugging, song stylizing and antics, but still packs in plenty of the wistful appeal.

With a top cast and screenplay to work with, director Norman Z. McLeod gets the most out of each situation. Story has Kaye as a mild-mannered milkman who gets involved with a prizefight gang when he accidentally

knocks out the current middleweight champ. With the champ's publicity shot to pieces, his manager decides to capitalize on the situation by building Kaye into a contender and then cleaning up on the title bout.

Kaye's supporting cast does uniformly fine work, keeping their sights trained on the comedy throughout. Virginia Mayo, as the love interest, serves as a beautiful foil for Kaye's madcap antics and sings two ballads in acceptable fashion. Vera-Ellen gets in ably on the comedy and does some spectacular terpsichore in two equally spectacular production numbers.

．．．．．．．．．．．．．．．．．．．．．．．．．．．．

■ **KID GALAHAD**

1937, 100 MINS, US
Dir Michael Curtiz *Prod* Samuel Bischoff *Scr* Seton I. Miller *Ph* Gaetano Gaudio *Ed* George Amy *Mus* Heinz Roemheld, Max Steiner *Art Dir* Carl Jules Weyl
● Edward G. Robinson, Bette Davis, Humphrey Bogart, Wayne Morris, Jane Bryan, Harry Carey (Warner)

One of the oldest stories in pictures – the grooming of a heavyweight champion – has been done again with good results [from a novel by Francis Wallace].

The treatment is sophisticated and production deluxe. Also more than the usual amount of romance for a slugfest. This allows room for Bette Davis to moon over the clean kid from the farm, and for the fight manager's convent-bred sister to also fall in love with him.

But essentially it's the story of the kid's manager (Edward G. Robinson) who maneuvers to match the bellhop-pugilist (Wayne Morris) in order to pay off the grudge he holds for a felonious fellow-manager (Humphrey Bogart) whose methods are always on the muscle side.

Davis has two or three nice opportunities and as usual handles herself throughout with plenty of noodle work. She's been photographed for glittering results in a couple of the sequences by Tony Gaudio. Script adroitly avoids any line or allusion that could identify her as the mistress of Robinson, who, however, is constantly walking into her apartment with a proprietary air. Davis also sings one song in a night club sequence, voice seemingly being doubled.

Robinson and Bogart, both grim guys, make their rivalry entirely plausible. Both performers know how.

．．．．．．．．．．．．．．．．．．．．．．．．．．．．

■ **KID GALAHAD**

1962, 95 MINS, US ◇ ⓥ
Dir Phil Karlson *Prod* David Weisbart *Scr* William Fay *Ph* Burnett Guffey *Ed* Stuart Gilmore *Mus* Jeff Alexander *Art Dir* Cary Odell
● Elvis Presley, Gig Young, Lola Albright, Joan Blackman, Charles Bronson (United Artists)

Two of the screen's most salable staples are united in *Kid Galahad*. One is Elvis Presley. The other is one of the most hackneyed yarns in the annals of cinema fiction – the one about the wholesome, greenhorn kid who wanders into training camp (be it Stillman's Gym or the Catskills), kayoes with one mighty right the hardest belter on the premises, gets an instant nickname and proceeds to score a string of victories en route to the inevitable big fight in which the fix is on.

Presley's acting resources are limited. It is, however, a surprisingly paunchy Presley in this film, and the added avoirdupois, unaided by camera, is not especially becoming. Elvis sings some half a dozen songs.

Gig Young labors through the trite, confusing part of the mixed-up proprietor of the upstate boxing stable. Pretty Joan Blackman overacts as Presley's girl. But there are two strong principal performers. One is Lola

Albright as Young's unrequited torch-carrier, the other Charles Bronson as an understanding trainer.

Idyllwild, California, does not closely resemble the Catskill Mountain terrain of NY, locale of the story.

•••••••••••••••••••••••••••••••

■ KID MILLIONS

1934, 90 MINS, US ◇

Dir Roy Del Ruth   *Prod* Samuel Goldwyn   *Scr* Arthur Sheekman, Nat Perrin, Nunnally Johnson   *Ph* Ray June   *Ed* Stuart Heisler   *Art Dir* Richard Day
● Eddie Cantor, Ann Sothern, Ethel Merman, George Murphy, Eve Sully, Jesse Block (Goldwyn/United Artists)

Another Samuel Goldwyn-Eddie Cantor musical comedy extravaganza and again strong entertainment. Follows more or less the comedy lines of all Cantor pictures. And with Cantor singing the same kind of songs.

For a final sequence an ice cream factory number in Technicolor is one of the finest jobs of tint-work yet turned out by the Kalmus lab, and the joint Seymour Felix-Willy Pogany handling of the colors, mass movements and girls creates a flaming crescendo for the production.

Cantor gives a lot of punch-lines to Eve Sully. Vaudeville comedienne makes a nice impression on her film debut. Jesse Block, her partner, gets plenty of neglect in the script, and so leaves little behind. Ethel Merman tops all her previous screen appearances. Warren Hymer is a strong asset, also.

Story works up to an Egyptian comedy sequence, with harem, mummy, torture chamber and underground wealth as elements.

•••••••••••••••••••••••••••••••

■ KIDNAPPED

1960, 97 MINS, US ◇ Ⓥ

Dir Robert Stevenson   *Prod* Walt Disney   *Scr* Robert Stevenson   *Ph* Paul Beeson   *Ed* Gordon Stone   *Mus* Cedric Thorpe Davie
● Peter Finch, James MacArthur, Bernard Lee, Niall MacGinnis, John Laurie, Peter O'Toole (Walt Disney)

Walt Disney's live-action feature is a faithful recreation of the Robert Louis Stevenson classic. The film itself is sluggish because its story line is not clear enough and for other reasons does not arouse any great anxiety or excitement in the spectator.

James MacArthur plays the young 18th-century Scottish boy cheated of his inheritance by a conniving uncle. The boy is kidnapped by a cruel shipsmaster for sale as an indentured servant in the Carolinas. He escapes through the aid of a dashing fellow Scotsman (Peter Finch).

From a story point of view, the screenplay is weak. It is never clear what the aim of the principals is, so there is not much for the spectator to pull for. Individual scenes play, but there is no mounting or cumulative effect.

Kidnapped was photographed on location in Scotland and at Pinewood, London. The locations pay off richly, with an authentic flavor. Perhaps too richly, with accents as thick as Scotch oatmeal.

Finch as the swashbuckling follower of the exiled Stuart kings is a tremendous aid to the production. MacArthur gives a sturdy performance, handicapped by little opportunity for flexibility of character.

•••••••••••••••••••••••••••••••

■ KIDNAPPED

1972, 100 MINS, UK ◇ Ⓥ

Dir Delbert Mann   *Prod* Frederick H. Brogger   *Scr* Jack Pulman   *Ph* Paul Beeson   *Ed* Peter Boita   *Mus* Roy Budd   *Art Dir* Alex Vetchinsky
● Michael Caine, Trevor Howard, Jack Hawkins, Donald Pleasence, Gordon Jackson, Vivien Heilbron (Omnibus)

Combination of Robert Louis Stevenson's *Kidnapped* and its lesser-known sequel *Catriona* results in an intriguing adventure piece set against that period in Scottish history when the English were trying to take over that country's rule.

The dying struggle between a few remaining clans who refuse to relinquish their sovereignty, and English King George who sends his redcoats into the Highlands to stamp out rebellion, is graphically depicted through the personalized story of one of the Stuarts. This overshadows the story of David Balfour, hero of *Kidnapped*, the 18th-century Scottish lad cheated of his inheritance by a conniving uncle, but pic loses nothing in the telling.

Michael Caine plays the swashbuckling character of Alan Breck, who embodies the spirit of the bloody but unbowed Highlanders. Delbert Mann's direction catches the proper flavor of the times.

Lawrence Douglas portrays David Balfour, who becomes a follower of Breck, a man with a price on his head, trying to escape to France after the bloodbath of Culloden in 1746.

•••••••••••••••••••••••••••••••

■ KILLER ELITE, THE

1975, 122 MINS, US ◇

Dir Sam Peckinpah   *Prod* Martin Baum, Arthur Lewis   *Scr* Marc Norman, Stirling Silliphant   *Ph* Phil Lathrop   *Ed* Garth Craven, Tony De Zarroga, Monty Hellman   *Mus* Jerry Fielding   *Art Dir* Ted Haworth
● James Caan, Robert Duvall, Arthur Hill, Bo Hopkins, Mako, Burt Young (United Artists)

The Killer Elite is an okay Sam Peckinpah actioner starring James Caan and Robert Duvall as two modern mercenaries who wind up stalking each other in a boringly complex double-cross plot [from the novel by Robert Rostand].

The initial Caan-Duvall camaraderie abruptly ends when Duvall switches sides to kill Helmut Dantine and disable Caan. Latter rehabilitates himself, with the help of nurse Kate Heflin (who could cure many a serious illness).

But CIA exec Tom Clancy's subcontract, to protect Asian political leader Mako and family from some other Asian killers who have also hired Duvall, brings Caan back into action. Street shootouts, car chases and a climactic facedown resolve many of the convoluted plot turns.

•••••••••••••••••••••••••••••••

■ KILLER MCCOY

1947, 103 MINS, US

Dir Roy Rowland   *Prod* Sam Zimbalist   *Scr* Frederick Hazlitt Brennan   *Ph* Joseph Ruttenberg   *Ed* Ralph E. Winters   *Mus* David Snell   *Art Dir* Cedric Gibbons, Eddie Imazu
● Mickey Rooney, Brian Donlevy, Ann Blyth, James Dunn (M-G-M)

Metro has concocted a fast action melodrama in *Killer McCoy* [based on the screenplay for their 1938 film, *The Crowd Roars*], to introduce Mickey Rooney to adult roles. Sentimental hoke is mixed with prize ring action but never gets too far out of hand.

Rooney makes much of his tailormade assignment in the title role. He's a tough kid who comes up to ring prominence after accidentally killing his friend, the ex-champ, who had started him on the road up. There's nothing that's very original with the story but scripting by Frederick Hazlitt Brennan has given it realistic dialog that pays off.

Plot develops from time Rooney and his sot of a father, James Dunn, become a song-and-dance team to pad out vaude tour being made by a lightweight champion. Through this association Rooney moves into the ring.

Highlights are 'Swanee River' soft-shoed by Rooney and Dunn; sweet, sentimental court-

ing of Rooney and Ann Blyth; and the fistic finale that features plenty of rugged action.

Brian Donlevy gives strong touch to the gambler role and Blyth gets the most out of every scene. Dunn hokes up assignment as the drunken actor-father with just the right amount of overplaying to stress 'ham' character.

•••••••••••••••••••••••••••••••

■ KILLER'S KISS

1955, 67 MINS, US

Dir Stanley Kubrick   *Prod* Stanley Kubrick, Morris Bousel   *Scr* Stanley Kubrick   *Ph* Stanley Kubrick   *Ed* Stanley Kubrick   *Mus* Gerald Fried
● Frank Silvera, Jamie Smith, Irene Kane, Jerry Jarret (Minotaur/United Artists)

Ex-*Look* photographer Stanley Kubrick turned out *Killer's Kiss* on the proverbial shoestring. *Kiss* was more than a warm-up for Kubrick's talents, for not only did he co-produce but he directed, photographed and edited the venture from his own screenplay and original story.

Familiar plot of boy-meets-girl finds small-time fighter Jamie Smith striking up a romance with taxi dancer Irene Kane.

Kubrick's low-key lensing occasionally catches the flavor of the seamy side of Gotham life. His scenes of tawdry Broadway, gloomy tenements and grotesque brick-and-stone structures that make up Manhattan's downtown eastside loft district help offset the script's deficiencies.

•••••••••••••••••••••••••••••••

■ KILLERS, THE

1946, 103 MINS, US

Dir Robert Siodmak   *Prod* Mark Hellinger   *Scr* Anthony Veiller   *Ph* Woody Bredell   *Ed* Arthur Hillton   *Mus* Miklos Rozsa   *Art Dir* Jack Otterson, Martin Obana
● Burt Lancaster, Ava Gardner, Edmond O'Brien, Albert Dekker, Sam Levene (Universal/Hellinger)

Taken from Ernest Hemingway's story of the same title, picture is a hard-hitting example of forthright melodrama in the best Hemingway style.

Performances without exception are top quality. It's a handpicked cast that troupes to the hilt to make it all believable. Film introduces Burt Lancaster from legit. He does a strong job, serving as the central character around whom the plot revolves. Edmond O'Brien, insurance investigator who probes Lancaster's murder, is another pivotal character who adds much to the film's acting polish. Ava Gardner is the bad girl of the piece.

Plot opens with Lancaster's murder in a small town. O'Brien takes it from there, trying to piece together events that will prove the murder of smalltown service station attendant has more significance than appears on the surface. Story has many flashbacks, told when O'Brien interviews characters in Lancaster's past, but it is all pieced together neatly for sustained drive and mood, finishing with expose of a colossal double-cross. Every character has its moment to shine and does.

Hellinger assured a music score that would heighten mood of this one by using Miklos Rozsa, and the score is an immeasurable aid in furthering suspense.

•••••••••••••••••••••••••••••••

■ KILLERS, THE

1964, 95 MINS, US ◇ Ⓥ

Dir Don Siegel   *Prod* Don Siegel   *Scr* Gene L. Coon   *Ph* Richard L. Rawlings   *Ed* Richard Belding   *Mus* Johnny Williams   *Art Dir* Frank Arrigo, George Chan
● Lee Marvin, Angie Dickinson, John Cassavetes, Ronald Reagan, Clu Gulager, Claude Akins (Universal)

K

Spawned as the pilot (*Johnny North*) of Revue's projected series of two-hour films for television, but scratched when NBC balked at what was deemed an overdose of sex and brutality, this rehash of *The Killers* was redirected to theatrical exhibition, where it emerges a throwback to the period of crime and violence that monopolized the screen in the late 1930s and early 1940s.

Gene L. Coon's scenario is similar in basic structural respects, but different in character and plot specifics, to Mark Hellinger's 1946 vintage elaboration on Hemingway's concise short story. In this version, the 'hero' (John Cassavetes) is a racing car driver, which provides the background for some flashy track scenes. But Coon's screenplay is burdened with affected dialog and contrived plotwork. Virtually nothing of the original Hemingway remains.

Of the actors, Cassavetes and Clu Gulager come off best, the former arousing interest with his customary histrionic drive and intensity, the latter fashioning a colorful study in evil, a portrait of playful sadism. Lee Marvin has some impact as another distorted menace, approaching his role with the cold-blooded demeanor for which he is celebrated. Ronald Reagan fails to crash convincingly through his goodguy image in his portrayal of a ruthless crook.

· · · · · · · · · · · · · · · · · · · ·

■ KILLING, THE

1956, 84 MINS, US ▽

Dir Stanley Kubrick *Prod* James B. Harris *Scr* Stanley Kubrick *Ph* Lucien Ballard *Ed* Betty Steinberg *Mus* Gerald Fried *Art Dir* Ruth Sobotka

● Sterling Hayden, Coleen Gray, Marie Windsor, Elisha Cook, Vince Edwards, Ted De Corsia (United Artists)

This story of a $2 million race track holdup and steps leading up to the robbery, occasionally told in a documentary style which at first tends to be somewhat confusing, soon settles into a tense and suspenseful vein which carries through to an unexpected and ironic windup.

Sterling Hayden, an ex-con, masterminds the plan which includes five men. Stanley Kubrick's direction of his own script [from the novel *Clean Break* by Lionel White] is tight and fast-paced, a quality Lucien Ballard's top photography matches to lend particular fluidity of movement.

Characters involved in the crime include Elisha Cook, a colorless little cashier at the track who is hopelessly in love with his glamorous, trampish wife, Marie Windsor; Ted De Corsia, a racketeering cop; Jay C. Flippen, a reformed drunk; and Joe Sawyer, track bartender.

Hayden socks over a restrained characterization, and Cook is a particular standout. Windsor is particularly good, as she digs the plan out of her husband and reveals it to her boyfriend.

· · · · · · · · · · · · · · · · · · · ·

■ KILLING DAD

1989, 93 MINS, UK ◇ ▽

Dir Michael Austin *Prod* Iain Smith *Scr* Michael Austin *Ph* Gabriel Beristain *Ed* Edward Marnier *Art Dir* Adrienne Atkinson

● Denholm Elliott, Julie Walters, Richard E. Grant, Anna Massey, Laura del Sol (Scottish TV/British Screen/Applecross)

First-time writer-director Michael Austin here proves he can direct; unfortunately his script is not up to par. The black humor he is trying for does not come off and he has to resort to slapstick to get the odd laugh.

Pic opens when Edith Berg (Anna Massey) receives a letter from her long-lost husband Nathy (Denholm Elliott) who left home 23 years ago claiming he was going to buy some

cigarets. He wants to come home, but the news doesn't please his son Alistair Berg (Richard E. Grant) who enjoys a peaceful existence with his mother.

He travels to Southend, on the coast, checks into the same faded hotel as his father with the plan to kill Elliott. What he finds is an unreformed character who gets drunk, lies and 'borrows' money and lives with Judith (Julie Walters).

The acting is all first-rate. Elliott has his drunk act down to a fine art, and gives his character an added sly and charming edge. Walters as the faded Judith is excellent, but for her the role is not particularly testing. Grant sports a wacky pudding bowl haircut in an attempt to get laughs, but his performance is gently menacing.

· · · · · · · · · · · · · · · · · · · ·

■ KILLING FIELDS, THE

1984, 141 MINS, UK ◇ ▽

Dir Roland Joffe *Prod* David Puttnam *Scr* Bruce Robinson *Ph* Chris Menges *Ed* Jim Clark *Mus* Mike Oldfield *Art Dir* Roy Walker

● Sam Waterston, Haing S. Ngor, John Malkovich, Julian Sands, Craig T. Nelson (Enigma)

A story of perseverance and survival in hell on earth, *The Killing Fields* represents an admirable, if not entirely successful, attempt to bring alive to the world film audience the horror story that is the recent history of Cambodia.

Based on Pulitzer Prize-winning NY *Times* reporter Sydney Schanberg's 1980 article *The Death and Life of Dith Pran*, film is designed as a story of friendship, and it is on this level that it works least well. The intent and outward trappings are all impressively in place, but at its heart there's something missing.

Action begins in 1973, with Schanberg (Sam Waterston) arriving in Cambodia and being assisted in his reporting by Dith Pran (Haing S. Ngor), an educated, exceedingly loyal native.

Through a stupendous effort, and at great risk to his own existence, Dith Pran manages to save the lives of Schanberg and some colleagues after their capture by the victorious Khmer Rouge two years later.

Dith Pran is later transferred to a re-education camp in the Cambodian Year Zero.

It is during the long camp and escape sequences, which are largely silent, that the film reaches its most gripping heights.

Because of the overall aesthetic, which does not go in for nuances of character, performances are basically functional. Fortunately, nonpro Haing S. Ngor is a naturally sympathetic and camera-receptive man and he effectively carries the weight of the film's most important sequences.

□ 1984: Best Picture (Nomination)

· · · · · · · · · · · · · · · · · · · ·

■ KILLING OF A CHINESE BOOKIE, THE

1976, 135 MINS, US ◇

Dir John Cassavetes *Prod* Al Ruban *Scr* John Cassavetes *Ph* [uncredited] *Ed* Tom Cornwell *Mus* Bo Harwood *Art Dir* Sam Shaw

● Ben Gazzara, Timothy Agoglia Carey, Azizi Johari, Meade Roberts, Seymour Cassel, Alice Friedland (Faces)

True to form, John Cassavetes challenges a Hollywood cliche: that technology is so advanced even the worst films usually look good. With ease, he proves that an awful film can look even worse.

As a LA strip-show operator, Ben Gazzara gets into hock to the mob, which asks him to erase the debt by knocking off an elderly Chinese bookie (Soto Joe Hugh) who accepts the bullet as if he's glad to get out of the picture.

In the process, Gazzara picks up a stomach wound of his own, which causes great pain initially, but is soon forgotten in

the thrill of more aimless improvisation with girls and gangsters.

There's no cinematography credit, which suggests Cassavetes either added that hat to his writer-director wardrobe, or the real culprit left town ahead of the posse.

· · · · · · · · · · · · · · · · · · · ·

■ KILLING OF ANGEL STREET, THE

1981, 101 MINS, AUSTRALIA ◇

Dir Donald Crombie *Prod* Anthony Buckley *Scr* Evan Jones, Michael Craig, Cecil Holmes *Ph* Peter James *Ed* Tim Wellburn *Mus* Brian May *Art Dir* Lindsay Hewson

● Liz Alexander, John Hargreaves, Alexander Archdale (Forest Home/AFC/GUO/Endeavour)

Director Donald Crombie's fourth feature, like his best-known works, *Caddie* and *Cathy's Child*, boldly tackles an urban problem – rampant redevelopment by unscrupulous corporate manipulators. It is a powerful, hard-hitting and provocative story about corruption permeating the highest levels of society – the more so because it has a strong basis in fact.

The eponymous Angel Street consists of a row of old but charming terrace houses on the shores of Sydney Harbor, almost within spitting-distance of the famed bridge. An outwardly respectable development company, headed by a Knight of the Realm, wants to buy the homes, raze them, and erect high-rise apartments. Their methods of persuasion are far from subtle.

Then the crusty leader of the residents' action group B.C. Simmonds (Alexander Archdale), dies under suspicious circumstances. His daughter, Jessica (Liz Alexander), takes up the cudgels, aided by Communists union official, Elliot (John Hargreaves), with whom she has a brief, if improbable romantic interlude. Their opponents are not simply the developers. The film depicts an unholy alliance between big business and government.

· · · · · · · · · · · · · · · · · · · ·

■ KILLING OF SISTER GEORGE, THE

1968, 138 MINS, US ◇ ▽

Dir Robert Aldrich *Prod* Robert Aldrich *Scr* Lukas Heller *Ph* Joseph Biroc *Ed* Michael Luciano *Mus* Gerald Fried *Art Dir* William Glasgow

● Beryl Reid, Susannah York, Coral Browne, Ronald Fraser, Patricia Medina, Hugh Paddick (Palomar/Associates & Aldrich)

Frank Marcus' legiter, adapted by Lukas Heller, describes the erosion of a longtime lesbian affair between Beryl Reid – by day, the bleeding-heart heroine of a British TV sudser; by night, gin-guzzling dominant lover – and Susannah York.

Breakup is cued by decision to write Reid out of her key TV role, as executed with relish by Coral Browne, a broadcast exec who catches York's eye.

The basic thrust of the plot is the gradual development of a rapport and sympathy with Reid, in inverse ratio to the loss of respect for York.

Reid, for her part, carries it off superbly, from her pre-title nastiness to the pathetic freeze-frame-out, as she sits alone in a TV studio, contemplating her future career – that of a cartoon voice-over. Browne, with a role pitched at constant level, is excellent.

Director Robert Aldrich has achieved the look and feel of a made-in-Britain pic, although most of it was shot near downtown LA.

· · · · · · · · · · · · · · · · · · · ·

■ KILL-OFF, THE

1989, 95 MINS, US ◇ ▽

Dir Maggie Greenwald *Prod* Lydia Dean Pilcher *Scr* Maggie Greenwald *Ph* Declan Quinn *Ed* James Y. Kwei *Mus* Evan Lurie *Art Dir* Pamela Woodbridge

● Loretta Gross, Andrew Lee Barrett, Jackson Sims, Steve Monroe, Cathy Haase (Filmworld)

The Kill-Off is a rigorous, well-acted adaptation of a hardboiled novel by Jim Thompson, with an unrelentingly grim view of human nature.

Loretta Gross gives a strong performance as Luane DeVore, an acid-tongued gossip-monger hated by almost everyone in her little community. She feigns a bedridden, feeble condition so that her husband (Steve Monroe), 20 years her junior, will take care of her hand and foot.

Things come to a head when folks decide to get rid of her, including Monroe, a slow-witted fellow whose new girlfriend (Cathy Haase) plots against his wife. Gross' death is followed by some bitter confrontations and a nihilistic finish.

Ensemble acting brings out the bitterness and hopelessness of a ragtag group of trapped characters. It's not a pretty picture, but helmer Maggie Greenwald keeps tight control of mood and tone.

●●●●●●●●●●●●●●●●●●●●●●●●●●●●●

■ KIM

1950, 112 MINS, US ◇ ⑦

Dir Victor Saville   *Prod* Leon Gordon   *Scr* Leon Gordon, Helen Deutsch, Richard Schayer   *Ph* William Skall   *Ed* George Boemler   *Mus* Andre Previn
● Errol Flynn, Dean Stockwell, Paul Lukas, Robert Douglas, Thomas Gomez, Cecil Kellaway (M-G-M)

Metro has quite a spectacle, but not much else, in this version of Rudyard Kipling's *Kim*. The story of youthful adventure in India comes to the screen as rambling, overlength, spotty entertainment.

Visual dressing helps somewhat to carry the episodic plot line and story does have its appealing moments, particularly when young Dean Stockwell is on screen – a young orphan who plays at being a native and encounters derrin-do adventures while aiding British intelligence ferret out a dastardly Czarist Russian plot to seize India.

Errol Flynn is the star, playing with flamboyant gusto the wily and amorous horse-trader who aids the government and Kim.

The lama sequences, in which Paul Lukas plays the holy man who advises young Kim, are much too long and slow.

●●●●●●●●●●●●●●●●●●●●●●●●●●●●●

■ KIND HEARTS AND CORONETS

1949, 106 MINS, UK ⑦

Dir Robert Hamer   *Prod* Michael Balcon   *Scr* Robert Hamer, John Dighton   *Ph* Douglas Slocombe, Jeff Seaholme   *Ed* Peter Tanner   *Mus* Mozart   *Art Dir* William Kellner
● Dennis Price, Alec Guinness, Valerie Hobson, Joan Greenwood, Miles Malleson (Ealing)

Story of the far-removed heir to the Dukedom of Chalfont who disposes of all the obstacles to his accession to the title and subsequently finds himself guilty for a murder of which he is innocent may appear to be somewhat banal. But translation to a screen comedy has been effected with a mature wit.

Opening shot shows the arrival of the executioner at the prison announcing that this is his grand finale. Then the story is told in a constant flashback, recounting the methodical manner in which the one-time draper's boy works his way up to the dukedom. In this role Dennis Price is in top form, giving a quiet, dignified and polished portrayal.

Greatest individual acting triumph, however, is scored by Alec Guinness who plays in turn all the members of the ancestral family.

●●●●●●●●●●●●●●●●●●●●●●●●●●●●●

■ KIND OF LOVING, A

1962, 112 MINS, UK ⑦

Dir John Schlesinger   *Prod* Joseph Janni   *Scr* Willis Hall, Keith Waterhouse   *Ph* Denys Coop   *Ed* Roger Cherrill   *Mus* Ron Grainer   *Art Dir* Ray Simm
● Alan Bates, June Ritchie, Thora Hird, James Bolam (Anglo-Amalgamated)

The screenplay by Keith Waterhouse and Willis Hall [based on the novel by Stan Barstow] is set in a Lancashire industrial town and tells the bittersweet yarn of a young draftsman who is attracted by a typist in the same factory. It is a physical attraction which he cannot resist. She, on the other hand, has a deeper feeling for him.

The fumbling romance proceeds, often hurtfully, often poignantly. The inevitable happens. She becomes pregnant and he grudgingly marries her. It is obvious from the start that the union is purely physical and it is not helped by the nagging of her mother.

Schlesinger handles this film with a sharp documentary eye, but does not forget that he is unfolding a piece of fiction. The tremulous moment when the girl first gives in to the boy's physical craving, an opening wedding sequence, the desolate seashore when they go on honeymoon, the girl discussing birth-control hesitantly, a pub crawl, the tender scenes as the young lovers walk in the park. These and many other sequences are all handled with tact, shrewd observation and wit.

Ritchie makes an appealing debut as the bewildered Lancashire lass. Bates is a likeable hero who will hold most audience's sympathy despite his weaknesses. Photographed in many parts of Lancashire to represent a composite town, lenser Coop has skillfully caught the peculiar grey drabness of the area.

●●●●●●●●●●●●●●●●●●●●●●●●●●●●●

■ KINDERGARTEN COP

1990, 110 MINS, US ◇ ⑦

Dir Ivan Reitman   *Prod* Ivan Reitman, Brian Grazer   *Scr* Murray Salem, Herschel Weingrod, Timothy Harris   *Ph* Michael Chapman   *Ed* Sheldon Kahn, Wendy Bricmont   *Mus* Randy Edelman   *Art Dir* Bruno Rubeo
● Arnold Schwarzenegger, Penelope Ann Miller, Pamela Reed, Linda Hunt, Richard Tyson, Carroll Baker (Universal)

The polished comic vision that gave *Twins*, Arnold Schwarzenegger's comedy break-through, a storybook shine completely eludes director Ivan Reitman here. Result is a mish-mash of violence, psycho-drama and luke-warm kiddie comedy [story by Murray Salem].

Schwarzenegger plays a stoic, unfriendly and ultra-dedicated LA cop obsessed with putting away a murderous drug dealer (Richard Tyson). He needs the testimony of Tyson's ex-wife, who's supposedly living in Oregon on piles of drug money she stole from Tyson. Plan is for Schwarzenegger's goofy gal-pal partner (Pamela Reed) to infiltrate the kindergarden as a teacher and figure out which kid is Tyson's, but when Reed gets a bad stomach flu Schwarzenegger has to report for the job.

It's supposed to be wildly funny to have this grim, musclebound control freak confronted with five-year-olds he can't intimidate, but it isn't. Schwarzenegger has to carry the pic alone; he never finds his focus.

Reed takes a good, feisty stab at holding up her corner of the pic, and Penelope Ann Miller is fittingly sweet and vulnerable as the single mother who romances Schwarzenegger.

●●●●●●●●●●●●●●●●●●●●●●●●●●●●●

■ KING AND COUNTRY

1964, 88 MINS, UK

Dir Joseph Losey   *Prod* Joseph Losey, Norman Priggen   *Scr* Evan Jones   *Ph* Denys Coop   *Ed* Reginald Mills   *Mus* Larry Adler   *Art Dir* Peter Mullins
● Dirk Bogarde, Tom Courtenay, Leo McKern, Barry Foster, James Villiers, Peter Copley (Warner-Pathé)

The story of Private Hamp, a deserter from the battle front in World War I, has already been told on radio, television and the stage, but undeterred by this exposure, director Joseph Losey has attacked the subject with confidence and vigor, and the result is a highly sensitive and emotional drama, enlivened by sterling performances and a sincere screenplay.

The action takes place behind the lines at Passchendaele, where Hamp, a volunteer at the outbreak of war, and the sole survivor of his company, decides one day to 'go for a walk'. In fact, he contemplates walking to his home in London, but after more than 24 hours on the road, and near the embarkation port of Calais, he's picked up by the Military Police and sent back to his unit to face court-martial for desertion.

The job of defending the private goes to Dirk Bogarde, a typically arrogant officer who accepts the assignment because it is his duty to do so. But during his preliminary investigation, he responds to Hamp's beguiling simplicity and honesty, coming to the inevitable conclusion that he was not responsible for his actions.

Notwithstanding its technical excellence, the picture [based on a play by John Wilson and a novel by James Lansdale Hodson] is carried by the outstanding performances of its three stars. Tom Courtenay gives a compelling study of a simple minded soldier, unable to accept the fact that he has committed a heinous crime, and unable to believe that he will suffer the maximum penalty. Bogarde's portrayal of the defending officer is also distinguished by its sincerity, and though his courtroom clash with the medico provides a dramatic highlight, it is achieved more through conviction than histrionic outburst. Completing the stellar trio, Leo McKern's study of the medical officer is faultless, and in his big scene he unerringly stands up to Bogarde's cross-examination, insisting that Hamp – like many other privates – was just a malingerer, and that the few moments he spent with him was enough to justify his diagnosis.

●●●●●●●●●●●●●●●●●●●●●●●●●●●●●

■ KING AND I, THE

1956, 133 MINS, US ◇ ⑦

Dir Walter Lang   *Prod* Charles Brackett   *Scr* Ernest Lehman   *Ph* Leon Shamroy   *Ed* Robert Simpson   *Mus* Richard Rodgers   *Art Dir* Lyle R. Wheeler, John De Cuir
● Deborah Kerr, Yul Brynner, Rita Moreno, Martin Benson, Terry Saunders, Rex Thompson (20th Century-Fox)

All the ingredients that made Rodgers & Hammerstein's [1951] *The King and I* a memorable stage experience have been faithfully transferred to the screen. The result is a pictorially exquisite, musically exciting, and dramatically satisfying motion picture.

With Deborah Kerr in the role originally created by Gertrude Lawrence, and Yul Brynner and Terry Saunders repeating their stage performances, the production has the talent to support the opulence of this truly blockbuster presentation. CinemaScope 55, originally introduced with R&H's *Carousel*, attains its full glory with *The King and I*.

As the Victorian Englishwoman who comes to Siam to teach Western manners and English to the royal household, Kerr gives one of her finest performances. She handles the role of Mrs Anna, with charm and understanding and, when necessary, the right sense of comedy.

As the brusque, petulant, awkwardly-kind despot confused by the conflicts of Far Eastern and Western cultures, Yul Brynner gives an effective, many-shaded reading.

Although unbilled, the singing voice of Kerr is Marni Nixon. It is ghosted so well that it is hard to believe that it is not Kerr.

The film suggests a stronger romantic feeling between Mrs Anna and the king than was presented in the legituner, but it is done with the utmost delicacy.

□ 1956: Best Picture (Nomination)

■ KING CREOLE

1958, 116 MINS, US ⑦
Dir Michael Curtiz *Prod* Hal B. Wallis *Scr* Michael V. Gazzo, Herbert Baker *Ph* Russell Harlan *Ed* Warren Low *Mus* Walter Scharf (arr.) *Art Dir* Hal Pereira, J. McMillan Johnson
● Elvis Presley, Carolyn Jones, Walter Matthau, Dolores Hart, Dean Jagger, Vic Morrow (Paramount)

The picture is based on Harold Robbins' novel, *A Stone for Danny Fisher*, but the locale has been switched to New Orleans, to Bourbon Street and to an indigenous cafe called the King Creole. Elvis Presley is a high school youth who is prevented from graduation by his attempts to take care of his weakwilled father and the density of his school teachers. He gets involved in a minor theft but thereafter goes straight when given a chance to perform in Paul Stewart's Vieux Carre saloon. His brief fling at crime returns to haunt him when the local crime boss (Walter Matthau) decrees that Presley shall leave Stewart and come sing for him.

Essentially a musical, since Presley sings 13 new songs, including a title number, film runs a little long and the premise that Matthau would launch a minor crime wave just to get one performer for his club is a little shaky.

Presley shows himself to be a surprisingly sympathetic and believable actor on occasion. He also does some very pleasant, soft and melodious, singing. Carolyn Jones contributes a strong and bitter portrait of a good girl gone wrong, moving and pathetic.

■ KING DAVID

1985, 114 MINS, US ◇ ⑦
Dir Bruce Beresford *Prod* Martin Elfand *Scr* Andrew Birkin, James Costigan *Ph* Donald McAlpine *Ed* William Anderson *Mus* Carl Davis *Art Dir* Ken Adam
● Richard Gere, Edward Woodward, Denis Quilley, Niall Buggy, Jack Klaff, Cherie Lunghi (Paramount)

King David is an intensely literal telling of familiar portions of the saga of Israel's first two rulers, more historical in approach than religious.

David moves from one monumental event to the next, trying to cover as much of the story as possible. The result is to minimize each step and every complex relationship (and doubtlessly confuse many of those who haven't been to Sunday School for awhile).

Though the overall problems may not be of his making, Richard Gere is of little help in the title role. Granted, he could have been truly awful (which he isn't), but he doesn't seem comfortable, either.

Holding back, Gere rarely makes it felt why he loves Absalom so, or lusts after Bathsheba or tolerates Saul's persecution beyond the fact that it says so in the Bible (or in the script).

David really isn't as trifling as quick summary makes it seem. There's a lot of history here, brought to life with good period film work and performances are generally fine.

■ KING IN NEW YORK, A

1957, 105 MINS, UK ⑦
Dir Charles Chaplin *Prod* Charles Chaplin *Scr* Charles Chaplin *Ph* Georges Perinal *Ed* Spencer Reeves *Mus* Charles Chaplin *Art Dir* Allan Harris
● Charles Chaplin, Dawn Addams, Oliver Johnston, Maxine Audley, Harry Green, Michael Chaplin (Archway)

Charles Chaplin's first British offering is a tepid disappointment. Tilting against American TV is fair game and while doing this Chaplin contributes some shrewd, funny observations on a vulnerable theme. But when he sets his sights on the problem of Communism and un-American activities, the jester's mask drops. He loses objectivity and stands revealed as an embittered man.

The story has Chaplin as the amiable, dethroned monarch of Estrovia. He surives a revolution and, with his ambassador, seeks New York sanctuary. He arrives to find that his prime minister has decamped with the treasury and the king is financially flat. His matrimonial status is also rocky.

Dawn Addams is a winning tele personality who charmingly tricks Chaplin into guesting on her show. Overnight, he becomes a TV star. He then befriends a politically-minded 10-year-old whose parents are on the mat for not squealing on friends who are suspect by the Un-American Activities Committee. As a result, Chaplin is himself arraigned before this committee.

The way in which Chaplin poses his political problems through the mouth of a child is both queasy and embarrassing. On the funny side, there are such good moments as when Chaplin is being fingerprinted while being enthusiastically interviewed on US as the land of the free. But, largely, the humor is half-hearted and jaded.

■ KING KONG

1933, 100 MINS, US
Dir Ernest B. Schoedsack, Merian C. Cooper *Prod* Ernest B. Schoedsack, Merian C. Cooper *Scr* James Creelman, Ruth Rose, Merian C. Cooper *Ph* Edward Lindon, Vernon L. Walker, J. O. Taylor *Ed* Ted Cheeseman *Mus* Max Steiner *Art Dir* Carroll Clark, Al Herman
● Fay Wray, Robert Armstrong, Bruce Cabot, Frank Reicher, Sam Hardy, Noble Johnson (RKO)

Highly imaginative and super-goofy yarn is mostly about a 50-foot ape who goes for a five-foot blonde. According to the billing the story is 'from an idea conceived' by Merian C. Cooper and Edgar Wallace. For their 'idea' they will have to take a bend in the direction of the late Conan Doyle and his *Lost World*, which is the only picture to which *Kong* can be compared.

Kong is the better picture. It takes a couple of reels for *Kong* to be believed, and until then it doesn't grip. But after the audience becomes used to the machine-like movements and other mechanical flaws in the gigantic animals on view, and become accustomed to the phoney atmosphere, they may commence to feel the power.

Neither the story nor the cast gains more than secondary importance, and not even close. Technical aspects are always on top. The technicians' two big moments arrive in the island jungle, where Kong and other prehistoric creatures reign, and in New York where Kong goes on a bender.

Fay Wray is the blonde who's chased by Kong, grabbed twice, but finally saved. It's a film-long screaming session for her, too much for any actress and any audience. The light hair is a change for Wray. Robert Armstrong, as the explorer, and Bruce Cabot, as the blonde's other boy friend who doesn't make her scream, are the remaining principal characters and snowed under by the technical end.

A gripping and fitting musical score and some impressive sound effects rate with the scenery and mechanism in providing *Kong* with its technical excellence.

■ KING KONG

1976, 134 MINS, US ◇ ⑦
Dir John Guillermin *Prod* Dino De Laurentiis *Scr* Lorenzo Semple Jr *Ph* Richard H. Kline *Ed* Ralph E. Winters *Mus* John Barry *Art Dir* Archie J. Bacon, David A. Constable, Robert Gundlach
● Jeff Bridges, Charles Grodin, Jessica Lange, John Rudolph, Rene Auberjonois, Julius Harris (Paramount)

Faithful in substantial degree not only to the letter but also the spirit of the 1933 classic for RKO, this $22 million-plus version neatly balances superb special effects with solid dramatic credibility.

In the original, documentary producer-promoter Robert Armstrong took aspiring actress Fay Wray on an expedition to a lost Pacific island. A gigantic humanoid gorilla was found, then brought back to civilization where he wasted part of NY searching for Wray.

In Lorenzo Semple's literate modernization, Charles Grodin is the promoter, this time a scheming oil company explorer.

Rick Baker is acknowledged for his 'special contributions' to the Kong character; this means that Baker did virtually all of the perfectly-matched and expertly-sized closeups, in which the beast's range of emotions emerges with telling effect.

■ KING KONG LIVES

1986, 105 MINS, US ◇ ⑦
Dir John Guillermin *Prod* Martha Schumacher *Scr* Ronald Shusett, Steven Pressfield *Ph* Alec Mills *Ed* Malcolm Cooke *Mus* John Scott *Art Dir* Peter Murton
● Peter Elliot, George Yiasomi, Brian Kerwin, Linda Hamilton, John Ashton (De Laurentiis)

Film leads off with the previous [1976] pic's closing footage. Advancing to the present, the giant ape is stunningly revealed to be breathing via life-support systems, with Linda Hamilton heading a surgical team preparing to give him an artificial heart.

Brian Kerwin enters from far-off Borneo, where he has stumbled on a female Kong. He delivers her to the Hamilton group so her blood can be used for the heart transplant operation.

In portraying an Indiana Jones-type figure Kerwin strains for plausibility and film swiftly begins to lose some early credibility. His tough jungle ways are unconvincingly transformed into sensitive concern for both animals.

Meantime, the proximity of the two Kongs prompts these primates to discover what comes naturally. This would prove to be the moment when director John Guillermin loses all control of the pic. Mindless chase then proceeds pell mell for the rest of the film, with the army in hot pursuit.

■ KING OF COMEDY, THE

1983, 101 MINS, US ◇ ⑦
Dir Martin Scorsese *Prod* Arnon Milchan *Scr* Paul D. Zimmerman *Ph* Fred Schuler *Ed* Thelma Schoonmaker *Mus* Robbie Robertson *Art Dir* Boris Leven
● Robert De Niro, Jerry Lewis, Diahnne Abbott, Sandra Bernhard, Shelley Hack, Tony Randall (20th Century-Fox)

The King of Comedy is a royal disappointment. To be sure, Robert De Niro turns in another virtuoso performance for Martin Scorsese, just as in their four previous efforts. But once again – and even more so – they come up

323

with a character that it's hard to spend time with. Even worse, the characters – in fact, all the characters – stand for nothing.

De Niro plays a would-be stand-up comic, determined to start at the top by getting a gig on Jerry Lewis' popular talk show. Worse still, he has a sidekick, (Sandra Bernhard) who's even nuttier than he is, only slightly more likable because she's slightly more pathetic in her desperate fantasy love for Lewis.

When all else fails, the pair kidnap Lewis to get what they want: He a spot on the show, she a night of amour.

Diahnne Abbott is excellent as a girl embarrassingly drawn into De Niro's fantasy world.

••••••••••••••••••••••••••••••••

■ **KING OF JAZZ, THE**

1930, 98 MINS, US ◇ ⓥ

Dir J. Murray Anderson *Ph* Hal Mohr, Jerome Ash *Ed* Robert Carlisle *Mus* Ferde Grofe (dir.) *Art Dir* Herman Rosse

● Paul Whiteman and His Band, John Boles, Laura La Plante, Jeanette Loff (Universal)

The King of Jazz as directed by J. Murray Anderson on his first talker attempt cost Universal $2 million in his inexperienced hands.

The millions who never heard the great Paul Whiteman band play George Gershwin's *Rhapsody in Blue* won't hear it here, either. Anderson sees fit to scramble it up with 'production'. It's all busted to pieces.

Nothing here counts excepting Whiteman, his band and the finale, 'The Melting Pot'. This is an elaborately produced number, in the same manner that Anderson or Ziegfeld would have put it on in a stage show.

••••••••••••••••••••••••••••••••

■ **KING OF KINGS, THE**

1927, 155 MINS, US ◇ ⊗ ⓥ

Dir Cecil B. DeMille *Prod* Cecil B. DeMille *Scr* Jeanie Macpherson *Ph* Peverell Marley *Ed* Anne Bauchens, Harold McLernon *Art Dir* Mitchell Leisen, Anton Grot

● H.B. Warner, Dorothy Cumming, Ernest Torrence, Joseph Schildkraut, James Neill, Jacqueline Logan (DeMille/PDC)

Tremendous is *The King of Kings* – tremendous in its lesson, in the daring of its picturization for a commercial theatre and tremendous in its biggest scene, the Crucifixion of Christ.

Technicolor is employed in two sections of the 14 reels, at its commencement and near the finish.

In scenes such as the Last Supper, the seduction of Judas by the Romans to betray The Christ, the healing miracles, the driving out of the evil spirits from Mary or the carrying of the Cross by Jesus (one of the most excellent in execution after the Crucifixion of the picture), there is a naturalnes that is entrancing.

And the acting is no less. The Schildkrauts (father and son), after H.B. Warner, come first to attention, the father as Caiaphas, the High Priest of Israel, and the younger as Judas, the traitor. And again no less is Ernest Torrence as Peter, Robert Edeson as Matthew, and perhaps others likewise of the Twelve Disciples, whose desertion of Jesus is brought out pathetically, almost, while His reappearance amidst them after the resurrection is an inner thrill.

••••••••••••••••••••••••••••••••

■ **KING OF KINGS**

1961, 168 MINS, US/SPAIN ◇ ⓥ

Dir Nicholas Ray *Prod* Samuel Bronston *Scr* Philip Yordan *Ph* Franz F. Planer, Milton Krasner, Manuel Berenguer *Ed* Harold Kress *Mus* Miklos Rozsa *Art Dir* Georges Wakhevitch

● Jeffrey Hunter, Hurd Hatfield, Ron Randell, Harry Guardino, Rip Torn, Frank Thring (M-G-M/Bronston)

King of Kings wisely substitutes characterizations for orgies. Director Nicholas Ray has brooded long and wisely upon the meaning of his meanings, has planted plenty of symbols along the path, yet avoided the banalities of religious calendar art.

The sweep of the story presents a panorama of the conquest of Judea and its persistent rebelliousness, against which the implication of Christ's preachments assume, to pagan Roman overlords, the reek of sedition. All of this is rich in melodrama, action, battle and clash. But author Philip Yordan astutely uses the bloodthirsty Jewish patriots, unable to think except in terms of violence, as telling counterpoint to the Messiah's love-one-another creed.

Jeffrey Hunter's blue orbs and auburn bob (wig, of course) are strikingly pictorial. The handling of the Sermon on the Mount which dominates the climax of the first part before intermission is wonderfully skillful in working masses of people into an alternation of faith and skepticism while cross-cutting personal movement among them of the Saviour and his disciples.

Irish actress Siobhan McKenna as the Virgin Mary infuses a sort of strength-through-passivity, infinitely sad yet never surprised. The 16-year-old Chicago schoolgirl, Brigid Bazlen, portrays Salome as a Biblical juvenile delinquent, who bellydances rather than jitterbugs.

The brutish, muscle-bound Barabbas of Harry Guardino makes a pretty good case that sedition frequently hurts only itself.

••••••••••••••••••••••••••••••••

■ **KING OF MARVIN GARDENS, THE**

1972, 103 MINS, US ◇

Dir Bob Rafelson *Prod* Bob Rafelson *Scr* Jacob Brackman *Ph* Laszlo Kovacs *Ed* John F. Link II *Art Dir* Toby Carr Rafelson

● Jack Nicholson, Bruce Dern, Ellen Burstyn, Julia Anne Robinson, Scatman Crothers, Charles Lavine (BBS/Columbia)

Admirers of director Bob Rafelson's previous feature, *Five Easy Pieces*, will be stunned by the tedious pretensions of his newest effort.

Chief culprit is undoubtedly former film critic Jacob Brackman, who drafted the screenplay from a story contrived jointly with Rafelson. Tale centres on the relationship between two brothers – the older (Bruce Dern) a self-deceiving wheeler-dealer, flanked by two chippies (Ellen Burstyn and Julia Anne Robinson); the younger (Jack Nicholson) a self-effacing FM-radio monologist who allows himself to be seduced by his brother's bravura lifestyle.

Yet for all the artistic and intellectual shortcomings, there are sufficient moments of demonstrable talent that suggest what Rafelson could have achieved with better material. Both Dern and Burstyn go far toward filling in the many characterizational holes.

••••••••••••••••••••••••••••••••

■ **KING OF NEW YORK**

1990, 103 MINS, ITALY/US ◇ ⓥ

Dir Abel Ferrara *Prod* Mary Kane *Scr* Nicholas St John *Ph* Bojan Bazelli *Ed* Anthony Redman *Mus* Joe Delia *Art Dir* Alex Tavoularis

● Christopher Walken, David Caruso, Larry Fishburne, Victor Argo, Wesley Snipes, Janet Julian (Reteitalia/Scena/Caminito)

A violence-drenched fable of Gotham druglords, *King of New York* is unusual in being an all-American production fully financed by European sources (Italy in this case). It's the first bit that's unusual.

The screenplay coolly depicts Christopher Walken as a fresh-out-of-prison gangster who vows to take over Gotham's $1 billion-plus drug industry. With his mainly black henchmen he blows away leading Colombian, Ita-

lian and Chinese kingpins and soon sets up shop at the Plaza Hotel (protected by two beautiful femme bodyguards) as the King of New York.

Director Abel Ferrara has an ominous view of New York where deadly violence can erupt instantaneously. Also impressive are large-scale setpieces, including a climax shot in Times Square, as well as a balletic orgy of bloodletting (in which Walken's bodyguards are killed).

Complementing Walken's bravura turn are equally flamboyant performances by David Caruso as the young Irish cop out to destroy Walken, and Larry Fishburne as Walken's slightly crazy aide-de-camp.

••••••••••••••••••••••••••••••••

■ **KING OF THE KHYBER RIFLES**

1953, 100 MINS, US ◇

Dir Henry King *Prod* Frank P. Rosenberg *Scr* Ivan Goff, Ben Roberts *Ph* Leon Shamroy *Ed* Barbara McLean *Mus* Bernard Herrmann *Art Dir* Lyle R. Wheeler, Maurice Ransford

● Tyrone Power, Terry Moore, Michael Rennie, John Justin, Guy Rolfe (20th Century-Fox)

Picture is laid in the India of 1857 when British colonial troops were having trouble with Afridi tribesmen. The plot opens with Tyrone Power, a half-caste English officer, being assigned to the Khyber Rifles, a native troop at a garrison headed by Michael Rennie, English general. For romance, Rennie has a daughter, Terry Moore, who is instantly attracted to Power despite British snobbery over his mixed blood.

From here on, the footage is taken up with developing the romance while the hero protects the heroine from native dangers and kidnap attempts by Guy Rolfe, leader of the Afridis and a foster brother of Power's.

The male heroics are played with a stiff-lipped, stout-fellowish Britishism perfectly appropriate to the characters. Power is a good hero, Moore attractively handles the heroine unabashedly pursuing her man. Rennie is excellent as the commanding general and Rolfe does another of his topnotch villains.

A rousing finale climaxes the story, based on the Talbot Mundy novel, and in between CinemaScope adds sweep and spectacle to the India settings, facsimiled by the terrain around California's Lone Pine area.

••••••••••••••••••••••••••••••••

■ **KING RALPH**

1991, 97 MINS, US ◇ ⓥ

Dir David S. Ward *Prod* Jack Brodsky *Scr* David S. Ward *Ph* Kenneth MacMillan *Ed* John Jympson *Mus* James Newton Howard *Art Dir* Simon Holland

● John Goodman, Peter O'Toole, John Hurt, Camille Coduri, Richard Griffiths, Leslie Phillips (Universal/Mirage/Jbro)

Crowned with John Goodman's lovable loutishness and a regally droll performance by Peter O'Toole, *King Ralph* doesn't carry much weight in the story department, though the wispy premise is handled with a blend of sprightly comedy and sappy romance.

Britain's entire royal family dies in a pre-credit sequence, resulting in a boorish American nightclub entertainer – the product of a dalliance between a prince and the American's paternal grandmother – becoming king.

After that, it's a basic fish-out-of-water tale, with King Ralph (Goodman) adjusting to the perks and constraints of nobility, aided by a group of harried advisers including his mentor Willingham (O'Toole) and officious bureaucratic Phipps (Richard Griffiths).

John Hurt plays a British lord seeking to bring the new king down so his own family can regain the throne. He facilitates a liaison between the king and a buxom lower-class

British girl (Camille Coduri) in order to force his resignation.

Lensing was done on UK locations and at London's Pinewood Studios.

■ KING RAT

1965, 134 MINS, US ⊙

Dir Bryan Forbes *Prod* James Woolf *Scr* Bryan Forbes *Ph* Burnett Guffey *Ed* Walter Thompson *Mus* John Barry *Art Dir* Robert Smith

● George Segal, Tom Courtenay, James Fox, Patrick O'Neal, Denholm Elliott, John Mills (Coleytown/Columbia)

Filmed near Hollywood but having the feel and casting of an overseas pic, *King Rat* is a grim, downbeat and often raw prison camp drama depicting the character destruction wrought by a smalltime sharpie on fellow inmates of a Japanese POW site in the final days of the Second World War pic has some fine characterizations and directions, backed by stark, realistic and therefore solid production values, which offset in part its overlength and some script softness.

George Segal does an excellent job as US Corporal King, the 'Rat', a con artist who manipulates the meagre goods and characters of other prisoners, most of whom have higher military rank. Director Bryan Forbes has sharply etched his main character.

Ditto for Tom Courtenay, the young British officer trying to perform provost-marshal duties in the behind-the-wire hierarchy topped by weary, but worldly and practical John Mills, effective in brief footage.

James Fox, another young British officer, registers solidly as he comes under Segal's influence and develops an affection for him.

■ KING RICHARD AND THE CRUSADERS

1954, 113 MINS, US ◇ ⊙

Dir David Butler *Prod* Henry Blanke *Scr* John Twist *Ph* J. Peverall Marley *Ed* Irene Morra *Mus* Max Steiner

● Rex Harrison, Virginia Mayo, George Sanders, Laurence Harvey, Robert Douglas, Michael Pate (Warner)

The Talisman, Walter Scott's classic about the third crusade, gets the full spectacle treatment in this entry.

The Scott classic details the efforts of Christian nations from Europe, marshalled under the leadership of England's King Richard, to gain the Holy Grail from the Mohammedans. In addition to the fighting wiles of the crafty Moslems, King Richard must contend with the sinister ambitions of some of his entourage and these rivalries almost doom the crusade.

David Butler's direction manages to keep a long show nearly always moving at a fast clip. Especially attractive to the action-minded will be the jousting sequences, either those showing training or those in deadly seriousness, and the bold battling is mostly concerned with combat between the forces of good and evil among the crusaders themselves. The script is especially good in its dialog, particularly that handed to Rex Harrison.

■ KING SOLOMON'S MINES

1937, 80 MINS, UK ⊙

Dir Robert Stevenson *Prod* Geoffrey Barkas *Scr* Michael Hogan, Roland Pertwee, A.R. Rawlinson, Charles Bennett, Ralph Spence *Ph* Glen MacWilliams *Ed* Michael Gordon *Mus* Mischa Spoliansky *Art Dir* Alfred Junge

● Paul Robeson, Cedric Hardwicke, Roland Young, John Loder, Anna Lee, Makubalo Hlubi (Gaumont-British)

With all the dramatic moments of H. Rider Haggard's adventure yarn, and production values reaching high and spectacular standards, here is a slab of genuine adventure decked in finely done, realistic African settings and led off by grand acting from Cedric Hardwicke and Paul Robeson, whose rich voice is not neglected.

Entire action is laid in the African interior, and shifts from the veldt and the desert to a native kraal, where the tale is enlivened by spectacular sequences of native war councils, with a pitched battle between two tribes magnificently and thrillingly staged.

Climax carries the action into the long-lost mines, where untold diamond wealth is hoarded, closing with a terrifying eruption of a volcano.

Robeson is a fine, impressive figure as the native carrier proved to be a king, and puts on a proud dignity that his frequent lapses into rolling song cannot bring down. Hardwicke is excellent as a tough white hunter, and Roland Young puts in his lively vein of comedy to excellent effect. John Loder and Anna Lee are less effective on the romantic side.

■ KING SOLOMON'S MINES

1950, 102 MINS, US ⊙

Dir Compton Bennett, Andrew Marton *Prod* Sam Zimbalist *Scr* Helen Deutsch *Ph* Robert Surtees *Ed* Ralph E. Winters, Conrad A. Nervig *Mus* Mischa Spoliansky

● Stewart Granger, Deborah Kerr, Richard Carlson, Hugo Haas (M-G-M)

King Solomon's Mines has been filmed against an authentic African background, lending an extremely realistic air to the H. Rider Haggard classic novel of a dangerous safari and discovery of a legendary mine full of King Solomon's treasure.

The standout sequence is the animal stampede, minutes long, that roars across the screen to the terrifying noise of panic-driven hoofbeats. It's a boff thriller scene.

Cast-wise, the choice of players is perfect. Stewart Granger scores strongly as the African hunter who takes Deborah Kerr and her brother (Richard Carlson) on the dangerous search for her missing husband. Kerr is an excellent personification of an English lady tossed into the raw jungle life, and Carlson gets across as the third white member of the safari.

□ 1950: Best Picture (Nomination)

■ KING SOLOMON'S MINES

1985, 100 MINS, US ◇ ⊙

Dir J. Lee Thompson *Prod* Menahem Golan, Yoram Globus *Scr* Gene Quintano, James R. Silke *Ph* Alex Phillips *Ed* John Shirley *Mus* Jerry Goldsmith *Art Dir* Luciano Spadoni

● Richard Chamberlain, Sharon Stone, Herbert Lom, John Rhys-Davies, Ken Gampu, June Buthelezi (Cannon)

Cannon's remake of *King Solomon's Mines* treads heavily in the footsteps of that other great modern hero, Indiana Jones – too heavily.

Where Jones was deft and graceful in moving from crisis to crisis, *King Solomon's Mines* is often clumsy with logic, making the action hopelessly cartoonish. Once painted into the corner, scenes don't resolve so much as end before they spill into the next cliff-hanger.

It's an unrelenting pace with no variation that ultimately becomes tedious. Neither the camp humor or the romance between Richard Chamberlain as the African adventurer Allan Quatermain and heroine-in-distress Sharon Stone breaks the monotony of the action.

Script plays something like a child's maze with numerous deadends and detours on the way to the buried treasure.

■ KING, QUEEN, KNAVE

1972, 92 MINS, W. GERMANY/US ◇

Dir Jerzy Skolimowski *Prod* Lutz Hengst *Scr* David Seltzer, David Shaw *Ph* Charly Steinberger *Ed* Mel Shapiro *Mus* Stanley Myers *Art Dir* Rolf Zehetbauer

● David Niven, Gina Lollobrigida, John Moulder Brown, Mario Adorf, Carl Fox-Duering, Christopher Sandford (Maran/Wolper)

Polski director Jerzy Skolimowski, working in Germany, brings off an intermittently funny black comedy on first love, avariciousness and, underneath, a subversive look at economic booms and human relations in the upper classes.

Based on Vladimir Nabokov's pithy novel, its obvious tricky word play, ironic nostalgia and interplay of love, are hard to duplicate on film. Skolimowski wisely concentrates on making it as visual as possible. It does not work, for the characters are not well blocked out and the humor is oblique, but present enough for some yocks.

A gauche young orphan is invited, by an uncle he has never seen, to Germany. The blundering boy likes his easygoing uncle, David Niven, but is smitten by his sexy aunt Gina Lollobrigida who first decides to seduce the boy and then have him kill her husband to inherit the fortune.

■ KINGDOM OF THE SPIDERS

1977, 94 MINS, US ◇ ⊙

Dir John Cardos *Prod* Igo Canter, Jeffrey M. Sneller *Scr* Richard Robinson, Alan Caillou *Ph* John Morrill *Ed* Steve Zaillian, Igo Canter *Art Dir* Rusty Rosene

● William Shatner, Tiffany Bolling, Woody Strode, Lieux Dressler, Altovise Davis, David McLean (Dimension)

Though hardly original, *Kingdom of the Spiders* creates its creeps and scares with care, accomplishing exactly what it sets out to do. The filmmakers have done a job that will satisfy the audience.

On paper, the picture sounds like most of many predecessors: likable scientist William Shatner, helped by beautiful, but capable woman scientist, Tiffany Bolling, find something amiss among the tarantulas of Arizona.

This time it's not nuclear testing, but chemical insecticides that's causing the trouble. Their problem: stop the little beasties before they eat the world.

But Shatner and Bolling work well together on a believable script, adding an amusing mach-feminism clash along the way that's well done.

■ KINGS GO FORTH

1958, 109 MINS, US

Dir Delmer Daves *Prod* Frank Ross *Scr* Merle Miller *Ph* Daniel L. Fapp *Ed* William Murphy *Mus* Elmer Bernstein *Art Dir* Fernando Carrere

● Frank Sinatra, Tony Curtis, Natalie Wood, Leora Dana, Karl Swenson, Ann Codee (United Artists)

Frank Sinatra goes soldiering in this adaptation of Joe David Brown's novel, *Kings Go Forth*. It's a simple, rather straightforward action-romance, laid against the attractive background of the French Riviera and the Maritime Alps.

The race angle is played to the hilt. The girl, played by Natalie Wood – an American living in France – is of mixed blood, her mother being white and the (dead) father having been a Negro. This revelation is the key to Wood's romantic entanglements. It leaves Sinatra stunned for a while and produces a rather cynical attitude in playboy Tony Curtis. Neither reaction rings particularly true.

It's an odd war that is being fought in this picture. The men fight and die in the mountains during the week. On weekends, there are passes for visits to the Riviera. The year is late 1944, and while Allied armies push into and beyond Paris the American Seventh Army has the job of cleaning out pockets of German resistance in the south.

Among the replacements joining Sinatra's platoon is Curtis, a rich man's son, with charm to spare and an eye for all the angles. Sinatra meets Wood and falls in love with her. She in turn falls in love with Curtis.

Sinatra, the rough-tough soldier, creates sympathy by underplaying the role. Wood looks pretty, but that's just all. Curtis has experience acting the heel, and he does a repeat. He's best when acting the charm boy.

●●●●●●●●●●●●●●●●●●●●●●●●●●●●●●●●●●●●●

■ **KINGS OF THE SUN**

1963, 108 MINS, US ◇

Dir J. Lee Thompson   *Prod* Lewis J. Rackmil   *Scr* Elliott Arnold, James R. Webb   *Ph* Joseph MacDonald   *Ed* William Reynolds   *Mus* Elmer Bernstein   *Art Dir* Alfred Ybarra

● Yul Brynner, George Chakiris, Shirley Anne Field, Richard Basehart, Brad Dexter, Barry Morse (Mirisch/United Artists)

The screenplay from a story by Elliott Arnold is a kind of southern western. It describes, in broad, vague, romantic strokes the flight of the Mayan people from their homeland after crushing military defeat, their establishment of a new home, and their successful defense of it against their former conquerors thanks to the aid of a friendly resident tribe that has been willing to share the region in which the Mayans have chosen to relocate.

In more intimate terms, it is the story of the young Mayan king (George Chakiris), the leader (Yul Brynner) of the not-so-savage tribe that comes to the ultimate defense of the Mayans, and a Mayan maiden (Shirley Anne Field).

Brynner easily steals the show with his sinewy authority, masculinity and cat-like grace. Chakiris is adequate, although he lacks the epic, heroic stature with which the role might have been filled. Field is an attractive pivot for the romantic story. Others of importance include Richard Basehart as a high priest and advisor who gives consistently lousy advice.

Direction by J. Lee Thompson has its lags and lapses, but he has mounted his spectacle handsomely and commandeered the all-important battle sequences with vigor and imagination. The picture was filmed entirely in Mexico: interiors in Mexico City and exteriors in the coastal area of Mazatlan and in Chichen Itza near Yucatan.

●●●●●●●●●●●●●●●●●●●●●●●●●●●●●●●●●●●●●

■ **KINGS ROW**

1941, 127 MINS, US ⦿

Dir Sam Wood   *Prod* Hal B. Wallis   *Scr* Casey Robinson   *Ph* James Wong Howe   *Ed* Ralph Dawson   *Mus* Erich Wolfgang Korngold

● Ann Sheridan, Robert Cummings, Ronald Reagan, Betty Field, Charles Coburn, Claude Rains (Warner)

Kings Row, Henry Bellamann's widely-read novel of small-town life at the turn of the century, becomes an impressive and occasionally inspiring, though overlong picture under Sam Wood's eloquent direction. It is an atmospheric story, steadily engrossing and plausible.

In broad outline, it is the story of the town, Kings Row, as well as of several of its people. Yarn is in three distinct parts, opening with the childhood of the five leading characters. Narration then jumps 10 years, picking up the thread as the hero begins studying medicine under the tutelage of the stern, awesome local physician-recluse.

Concluding portion includes the hero's return from studying in Vienna, his begin-

nings as a pioneer psychiatrist, his treatment and saving of his boyhood friend, and his romance with a new resident of the town, a beauteous girl from Vienna.

Ann Sheridan seems too casual in the early sequences as the clear-eyed, wholesome girl from the slums. However, she rises admirably to the emotional demands of the later scenes.

Robert Cummings is not entirely able to redeem a slight stuffiness in the character of the hero.

☐ 1942: Best Picture (Nomination)

●●●●●●●●●●●●●●●●●●●●●●●●●●●●●●●●●●●●●

■ **KISMET**

1944, 100 MINS, US ◇ ⦿

Dir William Dieterle   *Prod* Everett Riskin   *Scr* John Meehan   *Ph* Charles Roeber   *Ed* Ben Lewis   *Mus* Herbert Stothart   *Art Dir* Cedric Gibbons, Daniel B. Cathcart

● Ronald Colman, Marlene Dietrich, James Craig, Edward Arnold (M-G-M)

The sheer mystic fantasy of Baghdad and its royal pomp and splendor [from Edward Knoblock's play] remain acceptable escapism. The fantasy under lavish Culver City and Natalie Kalmus (Technicolor) production auspices is beautifully investitured. Ronald Colman as the beggar-sometimes-prince, Marlene Dietrich as the dancing girl with the gold-painted gams, Edward Arnold as the double-dealing Grand Vizier, James Craig as the Caliph-sometimes-turned-gardener's son, and Joy Ann Page as Colman's sheltered daughter are a convincing casting.

Colman, the king of beggars, is impressive as the phoney prince. He lends conviction to his role, so dominating the proceedings that he makes Legs Dietrich more or less of a stooge. However, she comes through in the highlight opportunity accorded her when she does her stuff for the Vizier and Colman. Dietrich's terp specialty and getup is out of the dream book, but boffo. Thereafter Kismet (fate) follows the beggar-prince's hopes.

●●●●●●●●●●●●●●●●●●●●●●●●●●●●●●●●●●●●●

■ **KISMET**

1955, 112 MINS, US ◇ ⦿

Dir Vincente Minnelli   *Prod* Arthur Freed   *Scr* Charles Lederer, Luther Davis   *Ph* Joseph Ruttenberg   *Ed* Adrienne Fazan   *Mus* Robert Wright, George Forrest   *Art Dir* Cedric Gibbons, Preston Ames

● Howard Keel, Ann Blyth, Dolores Gray, Vic Damone, Monty Woolley, Sebastian Cabot (M-G-M)

Opulent escapism is what *Kismet* has to sell. Howard Keel is the big entertainment factor and, in somewhat lesser degree, so is Dolores Gray. Without these two there would be very few minutes that could be counted as really good fun. Robust in voice and physique, Keel injects just the right amount of tongue-in-cheek into his role of Bagdad rogue.

The other two stars are Ann Blyth and Vic Damone. Vocally, as Keel's daughter, Blyth does the proper thing with 'Baubles, Bangles and Beads', 'And This Is My Beloved' and 'Stranger in Paradise'. So does Damone, as the young caliph who loves the poet's daughter. But otherwise their romantic pairing does not come off.

Founded on Edward Knoblock's *Kismet*, the Bagdad fable tells of how the supposedly magical powers of street poet Keel are commandeered by the scheming wazir to advance his own power.

●●●●●●●●●●●●●●●●●●●●●●●●●●●●●●●●●●●●●

■ **KISS BEFORE DYING, A**

1956, 94 MINS, US ◇

Dir Gerd Oswald   *Prod* Robert L. Jacks   *Scr* Lawrence Roman   *Ph* Lucien Ballard   *Ed* George Gittens   *Mus* Lionel Newman

● Robert Wagner, Jeffrey Hunter, Joanne Woodward, Virginia Leith, Mary Astor, George Macready (Crown/United Artists)

This multiple-murder story is an offbeat sort of film, with Robert Wagner portraying a calculating youth who intends to allow nothing to stand in his way to money. The screenplay is from a novel by Ira Levin. Gerd Oswald's restrained direction suits the mood.

Wagner's troubles start in opening scene, when he learns that his college sweetheart (Joanne Woodward) is expecting a baby, a circumstance that means she'll be disinherited by her wealthy father and his plans to latch onto the family fortune ruined. He pushes her to her death from the top of a building where they've gone to get a wedding license, and since no one knows they've been dating (hard for the spectator to swallow), Wagner is in the clear.

Wagner registers in killer role. Woodward is particularly good as the pregnant girl, and Virginia Leith acceptable as her sister. Jeffrey Hunter is lost as a part-time university professor responsible for the final solution of the crimes. Mary Astor and George Macready are okay as Wagner's mother and the girls' father.

●●●●●●●●●●●●●●●●●●●●●●●●●●●●●●●●●●●●●

■ **KISS ME DEADLY**

1955, 105 MINS, US ⦿

Dir Robert Aldrich   *Prod* Robert Aldrich   *Scr* A.I. Bezzerides   *Ph* Ernest Laszlo   *Ed* Mike Luciano   *Mus* Frank DeVol

● Ralph Meeker, Albert Dekker, Paul Stewart, Wesley Addy, Maxine Cooper, Cloris Leachman (Parklane)

The ingredients that sell Mickey Spillane's novels about Mike Hammer, the hardboiled private eye, are thoroughly worked over in this presentation built around the rock-and-sock character. Ralph Meeker takes on the Hammer character and as the surly, hit first, ask questions later, shamus turns in a job that is acceptable, even if he seems to go soft in a few sequences.

From the time Hammer picks up a half-naked blonde on a lonely highway he's in for trouble. The girl is killed and he nearly so in an arranged accident. This gets his curiosity aroused and he sets about trying to unravel the puzzle.

The trail leads to a series of amorous dames, murder-minded plug-uglies and dangerous adventures that offer excitement but have little clarity to let the viewer know what's going on.

●●●●●●●●●●●●●●●●●●●●●●●●●●●●●●●●●●●●●

■ **KISS ME GOODBYE**

1982, 101 MINS, US ◇ ⦿

Dir Robert Mulligan   *Prod* Robert Mulligan   *Scr* Charlie Peters   *Ph* Donald Peterman   *Ed* Sheldon Kahn   *Mus* Ralph Burns   *Art Dir* Philip M. Jefferies

● Sally Field, James Caan, Jeff Bridges, Paul Dooley, Claire Trevor, Mildred Natwick (Boardwalk/Sugarman/Barish/20th Century-Fox)

Essentially a mild, de-sexed remake of the 1977 Brazilian art house hit *Dona Flor and Her Two Husbands*, tale begins with Sally Field starting her life up again after the death, three years earlier, of her talented theatrical hubby (James Caan).

Field opens up her old apartment again and, to the bewilderment of her snobbish mother (Claire Trevor), has decided to marry Egyptologist Jeff Bridges. Shortly before the wedding, however, Caan's ghost decides to join Field back in the apartment, making possible all sorts of 'zany' scenes such as having Caan talk to his former wife while Bridges tries to make love to her.

Almost all the alleged humor stems from Field relating to Caan, whom no one else can hear or see, while she tries to engage in everyday activities.

K

Supporting performers are simply called upon to register stock reactions to the same joke, over and over again.

....

■ KISS ME KATE

1953, 109 MINS, US ◇ ⓥ

Dir George Sidney   *Prod* Jack Cummings
Scr Dorothy Kingsley   *Ph* Charles Rosher   *Ed* Ralph E. Winters   *Mus* Andre Previn, Saul Chaplin (dir.)   *Art Dir* Cedric Gibbons, Urie McLeary
● Kathryn Grayson, Howard Keel, Ann Miller, Keenan Wynn, Bobby Van, James Whitmore (M-G-M)

Kiss Me Kate is Shakespeare's *Taming of the Shrew* done over in eminently satisfying fasion via a collaboration of superior song, dance and comedy talents. The pictorial effects achieved with the 3-D lensing mean little in added entertainment.

But the play's the thing, of course, and *Kate* has it. Dorothy Kingsley's screenplay, from the [1948] Samuel and Bella Spewack legiter, was hep handling of a tricky assignment. Under George Sidney's skilled direction, *Kate* unfolds smoothly all the way as it goes back and forth from the backstage story to the play within the play and works in the numerous – and brilliant – Cole Porter tunes.

Howard Keel is a dynamic male lead, in complete command of the acting role and registering superbly with the songs. Kathryn Grayson is fiery and thoroughly engaging as Kate, tamed by Keel in *Shrew* (play within play) and succumbing to his charms backstage after much romantic maneuvering.

Only song not from the play prototype is 'From This Moment On' and it's an agreeable newcomer, as delivered by Tommy Rall.

Keenan Wynn and James Whitmore play a couple of hoods bent on collecting an IOU received in a floating crapgame. In a bit of delightful incongruity they segue into a song and dance piece titled 'Brush Up Your Shakespeare' that has hilarious effect.

Choreography (Hermes Pan) and musical direction (Andre Previn and Saul Chaplin) round out the list of important credits.

....

■ KISS ME, STUPID

1964, 126 MINS, US

Dir Billy Wilder   *Prod* Billy Wilder   *Scr* Billy Wilder, I.A.L. Diamond   *Ph* Joseph LaShelle   *Ed* Daniel Mandell   *Mus* Andre Previn   *Art Dir* Alexandre Trauner
● Dean Martin, Kim Novak, Ray Walston, Felicia Farr, Cliff Osmond, Barbara Pepper (Lopert/Phalanx/Mirisch)

Kiss Me, Stupid is not likely to corrupt any sensible audience. But there is a cheapness and more than a fair share of crudeness about the humor of a contrived double adultery situation that a husband-wife combo stumble into. In short, the Billy Wilder-I.A.L. Diamond script – the credits say it was triggered by an Italian play, *L'oradella fantasia* by Anna Bonacci – calls for a generous seasoning of Noel Coward but, unfortunately, it provides a dash of same only now and again.

Wilder, usually a director of considerable flair and inventiveness (if not always impeccable taste), has not been able this time out to rise above a basically vulgar, as well as creatively delinquent, screenplay, and he has got at best only plodding help from two of his principals, Dean Martin and Kim Novak.

The thespic mainstays are Ray Walston and Cliff Osmond, while Felicia Farr registers nicely as the former's attractive and sexually aggressive wife (within matrimonial limits until things get out of hand). Walston plays broadly and with suggestion of farce, never completely realized.

Wilder has directed with frontal assault rather than suggestive finesse the means by which Walston and Osmond, a pair of ama-

teur songwriters in a Nevada waystop – called Climax – on the route from Las Vegas to California, contrive to bag girl-crazy star Martin and sell him on their ditties. Idea is to make Martin stay overnight in Walston's house, to get latter's wife out of the way by creating a domestic crisis and substitute as wife for a night of accommodation with the celebrity a floozy (Novak) from a tavern.

The score, which figures rather prominently as story motivation and is orchestrated appropriately under the baton of Andre Previn, carries the unusual credit of songs by Ira and George Gershwin. Introed are three unpublished melodies by the long deceased composer to which brother Ira has provied special lyrics. Numbers pleasant but not exceptionally impressive are 'Sophia', 'I'm a Poached Egg' and 'All the Livelong Day'.

....

■ KISS OF DEATH

1947, 98 MINS, US

Dir Henry Hathaway   *Prod* Fred Kohlmar   *Scr* Ben Hecht, Charles Lederer   *Ph* Norbert Brodine   *Ed* J. Watson Webb Jr   *Mus* David Buttolph   *Art Dir* Lyle R. Wheeler, Leland Fuller
● Victor Mature, Brian Donlevy, Coleen Gray, Richard Widmark, Karl Malden, Mildred Dunnock (20th Century-Fox)

Kiss of Death [based on the novel by Eleazar Lipsky] is given the same semi-documentary treatment that 20th-Fox used in its three fact dramas, *The House on 92nd Street*, *13 Rue Madeleine* and *Boomerang!*.

Theme is of an ex-convict who sacrifices himself to gangster guns to save his wife and two small daughters. Henry Hathaway's real-life slant on direction brings the picture close to authentic tragedy.

Victor Mature, as the ex-convict, does some of his best work. Brian Donlevy and Coleen Gray also justify their star billing, Donlevy as the assistant district attorney who sends Mature to Sing Sing for a jewelry store robbery, and later makes use of him as a stool pigeon, Gray as the girl Mature marries after being paroled.

The acting sensation of the piece is Richard Widmark, as the dimwit, blood-lusty killer.

Plot hook of the script is the decision of Mature to turn stoolie when he learns that his wife has been driven to suicide by his pals, who had promised to care for her while he was in prison, and that his two children have been put in an orphanage. He fingers Widmark for a murder rap in return for parole, marries Gray and starts a new home for his children, only to live in terror when Widmark is acquitted and set at liberty.

....

■ KISS OF THE SPIDER WOMAN

1985, 119 MINS, US/BRAZIL ◇ ⓥ

Dir Hector Baberico   *Prod* David Weisman   *Scr* Leonard Schrader   *Ph* Radolfo Sanchez   *Ed* Mauro Alice   *Mus* John Neschling   *Art Dir* Clovis Bueno
● William Hurt, Raul Julia, Sonia Braga, Jose Lewgoy, Nuno Leal Maia, Antonio Petrim (SugarLoaf/HB Filmes)

Drama [based on the novel by Manuel Puig] centers upon the relationship between cellmates in a South American prison. Molina, played by William Hurt, is an effeminate gay locked up for having molested a young boy, while Valentin, played by Raul Julia, is a professional journalist in for a long term due to his radical political activities under a fascist regime.

They have literally nothing in common except their societal victimization, but to pass the time Molina periodically entertains Valentin with accounts of old motion pictures.

Puig kicked his book off with a ravishing account of the 1940s horror pic *Cat People*, but

director Hector Babenco and scenarist Leonard Schrader have opted to concentrate on two purely imaginary films to intertwine with the narrative.

Individual reactions to the work overall will depend to a great extent on feelings about Hurt's performance. Some will find him mesmerizing, others artificially lowkeyed. By contrast, Julia delivers a very strong, straight and believable performance as an activist who at first has little patience with Hurt's predilection for escapism, but finally meets him halfway.

After the raw street power of *Pixote*, Babenco has employed a slicker, more choreographed style here. Shot entirely in Sao Paulo, film boasts fine lensing.

□ 1985: Best Picture (Nomination)

....

■ KISS THE BLOOD OFF MY HANDS

1948, 79 MINS, US

Dir Norman Foster   *Prod* Richard Vernon   *Scr* Leonard Bercovici   *Ph* Russell Metty   *Ed* Milton Carruth   *Mus* Miklos Rozsa   *Art Dir* Bernard Herzbrun, Nathan Juran
● Joan Fontaine, Burt Lancaster, Robert Newton (Universal)

Kiss the Blood Off My Hands, adapted from Gerald Butler's novel of postwar violence and demoralization, is an intensely moody melodrama.

The yarn concerns an uprooted vet of the Second World War whose life is shattered after he accidentally kills a man in a London pub. Although based on a formula plot, this film is lifted out of the run-of-the-mill class through Norman Foster's superior direction, first-rate thesping and well-integrated production mountings.

Lancaster delivers a convincing and sympathetic portrayal of a tough hombre who can't beat the bad breaks. Fontaine performs with sensitivity and sincerity in a demanding role. As the heavy, Newton is properly oily and detestable.

....

■ KISS THE BOYS GOODBYE

1941, 83 MINS, US

Dir Victor Schertzinger   *Prod* William LeBaron   *Scr* Harry Tugend, Dwight Taylor   *Ph* Ted Tetzlaff   *Ed* Paul Weatherwax   *Mus* Victor Schertzinger
● Mary Martin, Don Ameche, Oscar Levant, Jerome Cowan (Paramount)

In converting Clare Boothe's satirical comedy to films, Paramount made some major revisions of the original, substituting a group of tuneful songs for the playwright's satirical barbs, and coming up with a light, humorous and breezy piece of entertainment.

Picture effectively showcases the acting and vocal talents of Mary Martin, who ably carries the full burden of the picture with a topnotch performance.

Boothe's play was a satire on the search for the Scarlett to portray the lead in *Gone with the Wind*. For picture purposes, the lead sought is a southern beauty for a Broadway show to be produced by Jerome Cowan, angeled by Raymond Walburn and staged by Don Ameche. Publicity stunt sends Ameche and composer Oscar Levant on tour of the south.

Schertzinger most ably pilots the compact and laugh-studded script. Songs are deftly spotted, and numerous spontaneous Dixie cracks against the 'damn' Yankees catch attention and laughs.

Ameche grooves as the play director and romantic interest in a straight line without much enthusiasm. Levant is Levant – a dour composer without a smile but withal credited with discovering the abilities of Martin about the same time the audience does.

....

■ KISS TOMORROW GOODBYE

1950, 102 MINS, US ⊛
Dir Gordon Douglas   *Prod* William Cagney
Scr Harry Brown   *Ph* Peverell Marley   *Ed* Truman K.
Wood, Walter Hannemann   *Mus* Carmen Dragon
● James Cagney, Barbara Payton, Helena Carter,
Ward Bond, Luther Adler, Barton MacLane (Warner)

Yarn [from Horace McCoy's story of the same name] opens with the trial of an assorted bunch of heavies and then quickly segues into a flashback to tell how circumstances put them in the courtroom. Flashback kicks off with a jailbreak, and the pace doesn't slow down as it takes James Cagney through a series of murders, robberies and romantic episodes.

Character is tough, but Cagney gives it an occasional light touch. He starts displaying his wanton meanness immediately by ruthlessly killing his jailbreak partner, beating the latter's sister into romantic submission and staging a daring daylight robbery of a market.

Cagney has two femme stars to court. Barbara Payton impresses as the girl who first falls victim to his tough fascination. Helena Carter is very good as a bored rich girl.

■ KISSIN' COUSINS

1964, 96 MINS, US ◇ ⊛
Dir Gene Nelson   *Prod* Sam Katzman   *Scr* Gerald
Drayson Adams, Gene Nelson   *Ph* Ellis W. Carter
Ed Ben Lewis   *Mus* Fred Karger   *Art Dir* George W.
Davis, Eddie Imazu
● Elvis Presley, Arthur O'Connell, Glenda Farrell, Jack
Albertson, Pam Austin, Yvonne Craig (M-G-M)

This Elvis Presley concoction is a pretty dreary effort. Gerald Drayson Adams came up with a ripe story premise, but he and Gene Nelson appear to have run dry of creative inspiration in trying to develop it. Yarn is concerned with the problem faced by the US government in attempting to establish an ICBM base on land owned by an obstinate hillbilly clan. To solve the problem, the air force sends in a lieutenant (Presley) who is kin to the stubborn critters, among whom is his lookalike cousin (Elvis in a blond wig, no less).

Histrionically, Presley does as well as possible under the circumstances. He also sings eight songs. Arthur O'Connell is excellent as the patriarch of the mountain clan, but what a mountainous waste of talent.

■ KITCHEN TOTO, THE

1987, 95 MINS, UK ◇ ⊛
Dir Harry Hook   *Prod* Ann Skinner   *Scr* Harry Hook
Ph Roger Deakins   *Ed* Tom Priestley   *Mus* John
Keane   *Art Dir* Jamie Leonard
● Bob Peck, Phyllis Logan, Edwin Mahinda, Kirsten
Hughes, Robert Urquhart (British Screen/Film
Four/Skreba)

Pic unfolds in 1950 when the British were facing attacks from a Kikuyu terrorist group known as Mau Mau. Bob Peck plays a regional police officer in charge of a small force of native Africans who lives with his frustrated wife (Phyllis Logan) and son.

When Mau Mau murder a black priest who's condemned them from his pulpit, Peck agrees to take in the dead man's young son (Edwin Mahinda) as his 'kitchen toto', or houseboy.

Story unfolds from the perspective of this alert, intelligent youngster who's torn between his tribal feelings on the one hand and the loyalties he has both to his murdered father and to the British who, despite their unthinking and ingrained racism, have been kind to him.

Peck is solid as the cop, Logan suitably tight-lipped as his repressed wife, and young

Edwin Mahinda excellent as the troubled, tragic hero, torn between two sides in an ugly conflict.

■ KITTY

1945, 103 MINS, US
Dir Mitchell Leisen   *Prod* Mitchell Leisen   *Scr* Darrell
Ware, Karl Tunberg   *Ph* Daniel L. Fapp   *Ed* Alma
Macrorie   *Mus* Victor Young   *Art Dir* Hans Dreier,
Walter Tyler
● Paulette Goddard, Ray Milland, Patric Knowles,
Reginald Owen, Cecil Kellaway (Paramount)

Plot [from a novel by Rosamond Marshall] tells of an 18th-century easy lady who rose from the London slums to high position in court society – a society that was no better than that from which she rose; it only dressed better.

The Kitty depicted in the film is a petty thief and beggar who gets a start towards a cleaner life after becoming a model for Gainsborough's portrait of a lady. The portrait and Kitty attract the attention of several society fops. One, an impoverished nobleman with few scruples, takes her into his home, gives her a fictional background and plots her marriage to a duke.

Paulette Goddard credibly depicts Kitty in the various phases of the slum girl's rise in station. Ray Milland has the more difficult task of keeping the unpleasant, foppish character of Sir Hugh Marcy, Kitty's beloved, consistent and does well by it. Reginald Owen and Cecil Kellaway deliver character gems. The first is the doddering Duke of Malmunster, who strives to keep his faded youth revived with port wine. The other is Gainsborough, the painter who discovers Kitty.

■ KITTY AND THE BAGMAN

1982, 95 MINS, AUSTRALIA ◇ ⊛
Dir Donald Crombie   *Prod* Anthony Buckley   *Scr* John
Burney, Philip Cornford   *Ph* Dean Semler   *Mus* Brian
May   *Art Dir* Owen Williams
● Liddy Clark, John Stanton, Val Lehman, Gerard
Maguire, Collette Mann, Reg Evans (Forest Home)

Donald Crombie, best known for *Caddie* [1976], scores again with a light, frothy bag of entertainment set in Sydney during the naughty 1920s. Pic veers wildly from serious drama to a zany spoofing of the underworld genre.

Yarn revolves around two waterfront crime queens, their pimps and beaus and 'bagmen'. Latter are not the counterpart of Gotham's bag women, but rather corrupt police go-betweens who hover betwixt the law and the crooks. Kitty, wonderfully and zestfully portrayed by Liddy Clark, rises from an innocent young bride arriving at the end of World War I, to the owner of the 'Top Hat' a no-holds-barred niterie.

Story weaves in and out, punctuated by dockside brawls, hair-pulling fights between Kitty and her Irish competitor Big Lil Delaney, shoot-outs in the streets and car chases, most of them handled whimsically.

■ KITTY FOYLE

1940, 105 MINS, US ⊛
Dir Sam Wood   *Prod* David Hempstead   *Scr* Dalton
Trumbo, Donald Ogden Stewart   *Ph* Robert De
Grasse   *Ed* Henry Berman   *Mus* Roy Webb
Art Dir Van Nest Polglase
● Ginger Rogers, Dennis Morgan, James Craig,
Eduardo Ciannelli, Ernest Cossart, Gladys Cooper
(RKO)

This is a film translation of Christopher Morley's bestseller expounding the romantic life of a white-collar girl – her happiness and heartbreaks and final decision for lifelong happiness. Picture is unfolded in retrospect

from the time the girl is forced to choose between two men – one whom she madly loves, but cannot offer marriage, and the other waiting at church.

This swings the story back to Philadelphia, at time she falls in love with scion of rich family on the other side of the tracks. Romance proceeds apace, with girl followed to New York and married. But boy's straight-laced family provides disillusionment, separation and finally divorce, with Kitty suffering double tragedy of her baby's death and remarriage of husband in his own social set.

Despite its episodic, and at times, vaguely-defined motivation, picture on whole is a poignant and dramatic portraiture of a typical Cinderella girl's love story. Several good comedy sequences interline the footage, deftly written and directed.

Ginger Rogers provides a strong dramatic portrayal in the title role, aided by competent performances by Dennis Morgan and James Craig.

☐ 1940: Best Picture (Nomination)

■ KLANSMAN, THE

1974, 112 MINS, US ◇ ⊛
Dir Terence Young   *Prod* William Alexander
Scr Millard Kaufman, Samuel Fuller   *Ph* Lloyd Ahern
Ed Gene Milford   *Mus* Dale O. Warren, Stu Gardner
Art Dir John S. Poplin
● Lee Marvin, Richard Burton, Cameron Mitchell, Lola
Falana, Luciana Paluzzi, David Huddleston (Paramount)

The Klansman is a perfect example of screen trash that almost invites derision. Terence Young's miserable film stars Lee Marvin, as a Dixie sheriff with lots of unoriginal, cliche racial trouble on his hands, and Richard Burton as an unpopular landowner in a performance as phony as his southern accent. There's not a shred of quality, dignity, relevance or impact in this yahoo-oriented bunk [from a novel by William Bradford Huie].

The small town is a Ku Klux Klan hotbed, headed by mayor David Huddleston. When Linda Evans gets raped, the KKK, including Marvin's deputy (Cameron Mitchell), suspect Spence Wil-Dee, but take out their frustration on a friend of film-debuting O. J. Simpson.

■ KLUTE

1971, 114 MINS, US ◇ ⊛
Dir Alan J. Pakula   *Prod* Alan J. Pakula, David Lange
Scr Andy Lewis, Dave Lewis   *Ph* Gordon Willis
Ed Carl Lerner   *Mus* Michael Small   *Art Dir* George
Jenkins
● Jane Fonda, Donald Sutherland, Charles Cioffi, Roy
Scheider, Dorothy Tristan, Rita Gam (Warner)

Despite a host of terminal flaws, *Klute* is notable for presenting Jane Fonda as a much-matured actress in a role which demands that she make interesting an emotionally-unstable professional prostitute. Produced handsomely in New York, but directed tediously by Alan J. Pakula, the film is a suspenser without much suspense. Donald Sutherland shares above-title billing in a line-throwing, third-banana trifle of a part.

The script concerns a mysterious disappearance in New York of out-of-towner Robert Milli. Sutherland, a family friend who is also a cop named Klute, tries to discover what happened. The only clue is Fonda, known to the police as a hooker.

It becomes obvious too early that Charles Cioffi, a family friend and business associate of the missing man, has a few kinky sex problems. The film's wanderings through the sordid side of urban life come across more as titilation than logical dramatic exposition.

The only rewarding element is Fonda's performance. At last, and by no means not too late, there is something great coming off the screen.

••••••••••••••••••••••••••

■ KNACK, THE ... AND HOW TO GET IT

1965, 84 MINS, UK

Dir Richard Lester   *Prod* Oscar Lewenstein
Scr Charles Wood   *Ph* David Watkin   *Ed* Anthony Gibbs   *Mus* John Barry   *Art Dir* Assheton Gorton
● Rita Tushingham, Ray Brooks, Michael Crawford, Donal Donnelly, John Bluthal, Wensley Pithey (Woodfall)

There is, according to the theory expounded in *The Knack*, quite a knack in the art of making it successfully with girls. And that about sums up the plot [from the play by Ann Jellicoe] of this offbeat production.

The expert exponent of the knack is played by Ray Brooks, and the immediate target is Rita Tushingham, a young girl just up from the country and hopefully setting off in search of the YWCA. The other two characters are both young men being instructed how to acquire the knack from the master. As Michael Crawford plays a schoolteacher, it is a neat trick to cut into schoolroom lessons with the same dialog as that used by Brooks to his two friends.

The four performances are exceptionally good. Tushingham's wide-eyed innocence is just right, and she plays with her familiar charm. Brooks is superbly confident as the glamor boy with the knack, and Crawford and Donal Donnelly both hit the right mixture of eagerness and innocence.

••••••••••••••••••••••••••

■ KNIGHT WITHOUT ARMOUR

1937, 108 MINS, UK

Dir Jacques Feyder   *Prod* Alexander Korda
Scr Frances Marion, Lajos Biro, Arthur Wimperis
Ph Harry Stradling   *Ed* Francis Lyon, William Hornbeck   *Mus* Miklos Rozsa   *Art Dir* Lazare Meerson
● Marlene Dietrich, Robert Donat, Irene Vanbrugh, Herbert Lomas, Austin Trevor, Basil Gill (London Films)

A labored effort to keep this picture neutral on the subject of the Russian Revolution finally completely overshadows the simple love story intertwining Marlene Dietrich and Robert Donat.

Film is not a standout because Frances Marion's screenplay, for one thing, has lost a great deal of James Hilton's characterization in the original novel and dispensed almost entirely with the economic and physical-privation angles leading up to the revolution. Result is that only those familiar with the pre-1917 Russia will understand what the shootin's all about.

Story reveals Donat as a young British secret service agent who becomes a Red to achieve his purpose. He's sent to Siberia just before the outbreak of the World War and returns after the revolution as an assistant commissar. He rescues Dietrich's countess from execution.

Performances on the whole are good, though Dietrich restricts herself to just looking glamorous in any setting or costume. Donat handles himself with restraint and capability. There's only one other important cast assignment, John Clements as a hyper-sensitive commissar.

••••••••••••••••••••••••••

■ KNIGHTRIDERS

1981, 145 MINS, US ◇

Dir George A. Romero   *Prod* Richard P. Rubinstein
Scr George A. Romero   *Ph* Michael Gornick
Ed George A. Romero, Pasquale Buba   *Mus* Donald Rubinstein   *Art Dir* Cletus Anderson
● Ed Harris, Gary Lahti, Tom Savini, Brother Blue, Cynthia Adler (Laurel)

A potentially exciting concept – that of modern-day knights jousting on motorcycles – is all that's good with *Knightriders*. Otherwise, George A. Romero's homage to the Arthurian ideal falls flat in all departments.

Premise is that of an itinerant troupe devoted to ancient principles which pays its way staging Renaissance fairs featuring bloodless jousts. Opening reel or so features one such event in agreeable fashion, even as it plants seeds of dissent within the ranks.

But all Romero can come up with in the way of drama over the next two-plus hours is the spectacle of invidious, greedy big city promoters and agents preying upon the group, with the pure, idealistic King Arthur figure going off to sulk when several of his men are seduced by the notion of becoming media stars.

Both the film's look, with its medieval costumes and bucolic settings, and the long stretches of high-minded talk, most about how pressures to be co-opted into society must be resisted, lend proceedings the air of a stale hippie reverie.

Another liability is the sullen, essentially unsympathetic 'King' of Ed Harris, who is never allowed to project the magnetism or romance expected of such a dreamer.

••••••••••••••••••••••••••

■ KNIGHTS OF THE ROUND TABLE

1953, 115 MINS, US/UK ◇ ▽

Dir Richard Thorpe   *Prod* Pandro S. Berman
Scr Talbot Jennings, Jan Lustig, Noel Langley
Ph Freddie Young, Stephen Dade   *Ed* Frank Clarke
Mus Miklos Rozsa   *Art Dir* Alfred Junge, Hans Peters
● Ava Gardner, Mel Ferrer, Anne Crawford, Stanley Baker, Gabriel Woolf (M-G-M)

Metro's first-time-out via CinemaScope is a dynamic interpretation of Thomas Malory's classic *Morte d'Arthur*. The action is fierce as the gallant Lancelot fights for his king, and armies of lancers are pitted against each other in combat to the death. The story has dramatic movement – it could easily have come off stiltedly under less skillful handling – as the knight's love for his queen nearly causes the death of both.

The carefully developed script plus knowing direction by Richard Thorpe give the legendary tale credibility. It's storybook stuff – and must be accepted as such – but the astute staging results in a walloping package of entertainment for all except, perhaps, the blase.

Robert Taylor handles the Lancelot part with conviction; apparently he's right at home with derring-do heroics. Not apparently at home is Ava Gardner. She gets by fair enough but the role of the lovely Guinevere calls for more projected warmth. Mel Ferrer does an excellent job of portraying the sincere and sympathetic King Arthur. Gabriel Woolf, as the knight in search of the Holy Grail, is standout.

••••••••••••••••••••••••••

■ KOTCH

1971, 113 MINS, US ◇ ▽

Dir Jack Lemmon   *Prod* Richard Carter   *Scr* John Paxton   *Ph* Richard H. Kline   *Ed* Ralph E. Winters
Mus Marvin Hamlisch   *Art Dir* Jock Poplin
● Walter Matthau, Deborah Winters, Felicia Farr, Charles Aidman, Ellen Geer (ABC Pictures)

Kotch is a great film in several ways: Jack Lemmon's outstanding directorial debut; Walter Matthau's terrific performance as an unwanted elderly parent who befriends a pregnant teenager; John Paxton's superior adaptation of Katharine Topkins' novel and a topnotch supporting cast. This heart-warming, human comedy will leave audiences fully nourished, whereas they should be left a bit starved for more.

Paxton's script fully develops many interactions between Matthau and the other players. There's Charles Aidman, smash as his loving son, slightly embarrassed at Dad's apparent dotage; Felicia Farr, Aidman's wife who wants Pop out of the house; and Deborah Winters, as the couple's baby-sitter made pregnant by Darrell Larson, then shipped off in disgrace by her brother.

The film's somewhat too leisurely pace often sacrifices primary plot movement to brilliantly-filmed digression-vignette. Basically the story has Matthau and Winters sharing a desert house together. She learns a lot about life from him, and he has the opportunity to act as a loving father and friend.

••••••••••••••••••••••••••

■ KOYAANISQATSI

1982, 87 MINS, US ◇ ▽

Dir Godfrey Reggio   *Prod* Godfrey Reggio   *Scr* Ron Fricke, Godfrey Reggio, Michael Hoenig, Alton Walpole   *Ph* Ron Fricke   *Ed* Alton Walpole, Ron Fricke   *Mus* Philip Glass, Michael Hoenig
● (IRE)

Koyaanisqatsi is at first awe-inspiring with its sweeping aerial wilderness photography. It becomes depressing when the phone lines, factories, and nuke plants spring up. The pic then runs the risk of boring audiences with shot after glossy shot of man's commercial hack job on the land and his resulting misery.

The viewer is relentlessly bombarded with images reminiscent of the title's Hopi Indian meaning, 'crazy life', while Philip Glass' tantalizing but dirgelike score drones on.

A lion's share of the pic is a cynical display of decadence intending to edify and anger to action, but instead alienating with its one-sidedness. Simple message in Godfrey Reggio's direction seems to state that Americans are not much more than the cars they assemble and the hot dogs and Twinkies they package.

••••••••••••••••••••••••••

■ KRAKATOA, EAST OF JAVA

1969, 135 MINS, US ◇ ▽

Dir Bernard L. Kowalski   *Prod* William R. Forman
Scr Clifford Gould, Bernard Gordon   *Ph* Manuel Berenguer   *Ed* Maurice Rootes   *Mus* Frank DeVol
Art Dir Eugene Lourie
● Maximilian Schell, Diane Baker, Brian Keith, Barbara Werle, John Leyton, Rossano Brazzi (Parafrance/Cinerama)

Krakatoa, East of Java plods through a search for a sunken treasure on a boat that contains a score of one-dimensional characters.

It is the late 19th century and somewhere in the Far East a boat is loading. An amiable captain, Maximilian Schell, is forced to take on convicts. He has a diver and balloonist to help him, his girl, who is searching for her son, and a mixed crew.

In the background is a rumbling and warning that a big volcano near where they are going, Krakatoa, may erupt again but the captain scoffs that it has been quiet for 200 years.

Director Kowalski, for his first pic, steered for simplicity and gives it a standard action feeling if more inventiveness and perhaps a sympathetic tongue-in-cheek approach could have given this the lift and charm that it lacks.

••••••••••••••••••••••••••

■ KRAMER VS. KRAMER

1979, 105 MINS, US ◇ ▽

Dir Robert Benton   *Prod* Stanley R. Jaffe   *Scr* Robert Benton   *Ph* Nestor Almendros   *Ed* Jerry Greenberg
Art Dir Paul Sylbert
● Dustin Hoffman, Meryl Streep, Justin Henry, Jane Alexander, Howard Duff, JoBeth Williams (Columbia)

Kramer vs. Kramer is a perceptive, touching, intelligent film about one of the raw sores of contemporary America, the dissolution of the family unit. In refashioning Avery Corman's novel, director-scripter Robert Benton has used a highly effective technique of short, poignant scenes to bring home the message that no one escapes unscarred from the trauma of separation.

It is in the latter arena that *Kramer* takes place, as Meryl Streep breaks with up-and-coming ad exec Dustin Hoffman and tyke Justin Henry to find her own role in life. Hoffman is thus left with a six-year-old son and begins a process of 'parenting' that is both humorous and affecting. Three-quarters into the film, Streep comes to claim her first-born with the traditional mother's prerogative and a nasty court battle ensues.
□ 1979: Best Picture

■ KRAYS, THE

1990, 119 MINS, UK ◇ ⓥ
Dir Peter Medak *Prod* Dominic Anciano, Ray Burdis
Ph Philip Ridley *Ph* Alex Thomson *Ed* Martin Walsh
Mus Michael Kamen *Art Dir* Michael Pickwoad
● Billie Whitelaw, Gary Kemp, Martin Kemp, Susan Fleetwood, Avis Bunnage, Kate Hardie (Parkfield/Fugitive)

The Krays is a chilling, if somewhat monotonous, biopic charting the rise and fall of two prominent hoods in 1950-60s London, cockney lads whose psychosexual warping leads them into ultraviolence.

Screenwriter Philip Ridley deftly explores the cynical amorality of the us-vs-them lower-class milieu, and the destructive effect of smothering mom Billie Whitelaw (in a superb performance) on her sociopathic twins, while virtually ignoring the standard cops-and-robbers dramaturgy of gangster films.

As the Krays, the brothers Kemp, who both had considerable acting experience before beginning their rock careers in Spandau Ballet, are just right in their deadeyed portrayal of what a rival thug calls 'a pair of movie gangsters'. Indeed, they are among the most repellent gangsters to come along since Richard Widmark pushed an old lady in a wheelchair down the stairs in *Kiss of Death*.

Director Peter Medak, who knew the Krays when he was an a.d. works skilfully to conjure up a cold and eerie atmosphere.

■ KREMLIN LETTER, THE

1970, 118 MINS, US ◇
Dir John Huston *Prod* Carter De Haven, Sam Weisenthal *Scr* John Huston, Gladys Hill *Ph* Ted Scaife *Ed* Russell Lloyd *Mus* Robert Drasnin
● Bibi Andersson, Richard Boone, Nigel Green, Dean Jagger, Max Von Sydow, Orson Welles (20th Century-Fox)

An American official sends a letter about China to the Kremlin and it must be gotten back because of its explosiveness and lack of authorization. This is the nub of Noel Behn's novel.

The story in cinematic form is a conglomerate of scenes, each of which makes for valuable viewing, but with the piecing together another thing. Thus is this nastiness of the spy business graphically described.

It is an engagingly photographed piece of business.

Max Von Sydow is a political strong man within the Russian regime. Ex-US Navy officer Patrick O'Neal has the job of salvaging the Kremlin Letter. But Russia, in the person of Richard Boone, also would like to retrieve the document. Participants include George Sanders, as a homo female impersonator in San Francisco. Orson Welles is a key Soviet man who is in New York to address

the United Nations; Bibi Andersson is a prostitute married to agent Von Sydow.

■ KRULL

1983, 117 MINS, US ◇ ⓥ
Dir Peter Yates *Prod* Ron Silverman *Scr* Stanford Sherman *Ph* Peter Suschitzky *Ed* Ray Lovejoy
Mus James Horner *Art Dir* Stephen Grimes
● Ken Marshall, Lysette Anthony, Freddie Jones, Francesca Annis, Alun Armstrong, David Battley (Columbia)

Although inoffensively designed only to please the senses and appeal to one's whimsical sense of adventure, *Krull* nevertheless comes off as a blatantly derivative hodgepodge of *Excalibur* meets *Star Wars*. Lavishly mounted at a reported cost of $27 million, the collection of action set pieces never jells into an absorbing narrative.

Plot is as old as the art of story-telling itself. Young Prince Colwyn (Ken Marshall) falls heir to a besieged kingdom, but must survive a Ulysses-scaled series of tests on the way to rescuing his beautiful bride from the clutches of the Beast, whose army of slayers imperils his journey every step of the way.

Crucial to Colwyn's quest is his recovery of the glaive, a razor-tipped, spinning boomerang which will enable him to combat the Beast. This fancy piece of magical jewelry holds the same importance as the Excalibur sword did for Arthur.

Professionalism of director Peter Yates, the large array of production and technical talents and, particularly, the mainly British actors keep things from becoming genuinely dull or laughable.

■ LA BAMBA

1987, 108 MINS, US ◇ ⓥ
Dir Luis Valdez *Prod* Taylor Hackford, Bill Borden
Scr Luis Valdez *Ph* Adam Greenberg *Ed* Sheldon Kahn, Don Brochu *Mus* Carlos Santana, Miles Goodman *Art Dir* Vince Cresciman
● Lou Diamond Phillips, Esai Morales, Rosana De Soto, Elizabeth Pena, Danielle von Zerneck (New Visions)

There haven't been too many people who died at age 17 who have warranted the biopic treatment, but 1950s rock 'n' roller Ritchie Valens proves a worthy exception in *La Bamba*.

Known primarily for his three top-10 tunes, *Come On Let's Go, Donna* and the title cut, Valens was killed – just eight months after signing his first recording contract – in the 1959 private plane crash that also took the lives of Buddy Holly and The Big Bopper, and thus attained instant legendhood.

For anyone to achieve his dreams by 17 is close to miraculous. It was even more so for Valens who, less than two years before his death, was a Mexican-American fruitpicker named Ricardo Valenzuela living in a tent with his family in Northern California.

La Bamba is engrossing throughout and boasts numerous fine performances. In Lou Diamond Phillips' sympathetic turn, Valens comes across as a very fine young man, caring for those important to him and not over-awed by his success. Rosana De Soto scores as his tireless mother, and Elizabeth Pena has numerous dramatic moments as Bob's distraught mate.

■ L.A. STORY

1991, 95 MINS, US ◇ ⓥ
Dir Mick Jackson *Prod* Daniel Melnick, Michael Rachmil *Scr* Steve Martin *Ph* Andrew Dunn
Ed Richard A. Harris *Mus* Peter Melnick
Art Dir Lawrence Miller
● Steve Martin, Victoria Tennant, Richard E. Grant, Marilu Henner, Sarah Jessica Parker, Susan Forristal (Carolco/Indieprod/LA Films)

Goofy and sweet, *L.A. Story* constitutes Steve Martin's satiric valentine to his hometown and a pretty funny comedy in the bargain.

Martin is in typically nutty form as an LA TV meteorologist who doesn't hestitate to take the weekends off since the weather isn't bound to change. What he can't predict, however, is the lightning bolt that hits him in the form of Brit journalist Victoria Tennant, who arrives to dish up the latest English assessment of America's new melting pot.

Martin's relationship with his snooty longtime g.f. Marilu Henner is essentially over and, convinced that nothing can ever happen with his dreamgirl, he stumblingly takes up with ditzy shopgirl Sarah Jessica Parker.

Even after Martin and Tennant have gotten together and he has declared the grandest of romantic intentions, the future looks impossible, as she has promised her ex (Richard E. Grant) to attempt a reconciliation.

Despite the frantic style, the feeling behind Martin's view of life and love in LA comes through, helped by the seductively adoring treatment of Tennant (actually Martin's wife).

■ LABYRINTH

1986, 101 MINS, US ◇ ⓥ
Dir Jim Henson *Prod* Eric Rattray *Scr* Terry Jones
Ph Alex Thomson *Ed* John Grover *Mus* Trevor Jones *Art Dir* Elliot Scott
● David Bowie, Jennifer Connelly, Toby Froud, Shelley Thompson, Christopher Malcolm, Natalie Finland (Henson/Lucasfilm)

An array of bizarre creatures and David Bowie can't save *Labyrinth* from being a crashing bore. Characters created by Jim Henson and his team become annoying rather than endearing.

What is even more disappointing is the failure of the film on a story level. Young Sarah (Jennifer Connelly) embarks on an adventure to recover her baby stepbrother from the clutches of the Goblin King (David Bowie) who has taken the child for some unknown reason to his kingdom.

Story soon loses its way and never comes close to archetypal myths and fears of great fairy tales. Instead it's an unconvincing coming of age saga.

As the Goblin King, Bowie seems a fish out of water – too serious to be campy, too dumb to be serious.

■ LADY AND THE TRAMP

1955, 75 MINS, US ◇ ⓥ
Dir Hamilton Luske, Clyde Geronimi, Wilfred Jackson
Prod Walt Disney *Scr* Erdman Penner, Joe Rinaldi, Ralph Wright, Don DaGradi *Ed* Don Halliday
Mus Oliver Wallace
● (Walt Disney)

A delight for the juveniles and lots of fun for adults, *Lady and the Tramp* is the first animated feature in CinemaScope and the wider canvas and extra detail work reportedly meant an additional 30% in negative cost. It was a sound investment.

This time out the producer turned to members of the canine world and each of these hounds of Disneyville reflects astute drawing-board knowhow and richly-humorous invention. The songs by Peggy Lee and Sonny Burke figure importantly, too.

Characters of the title are a cutie-pie faced and ultra-ladylike spaniel and the raffish mutt from the other side of the tracks. In 'featured' roles are Trusty, the bloodhound who's lost his sense of smell, and Jock, a Scottie with a sense of thrift. Both have a crush on Lady but her on-and-off romance with Tramp finally leads to a mating of the minds, etc, and a litter basket.

....

■ **LADY BE GOOD**

1941, 110 MINS, US
Dir Norman Z. McLeod *Prod* Arthur Freed *Scr* Jack McGowan, Kay Van Riper, Jock McClain *Ph* George Folsey, Oliver Marsh *Ed* Frederick J. Smith *Mus* George Stoll (dir.)
● Eleanor Powell, Ann Sothern, Robert Young, Lionel Barrymore, John Carroll, Red Skelton (M-G-M)

The plot bears no resemblance to the Guy Bolton book of the original 1924 stage musical, which was one of the major springboards for Fred and Adele Astaire. The songs in this picture are likewise no relation to the click Gershwin score.

There are flagrant examples in the film of poor direction, unimaginative story-telling and slipshod photography. The picture looks as though director Norman Z. McLeod was given a time allotment to fill, no matter how, and he did.

While confused, the story pattern is familiar – that of a crack songwriting team splitting up and becoming individually unsuccessful until resuming their partnership. In this instance it's the case of ex-waitress Ann Sothern and composer Robert Young, who click, marry and then get divorced when Young goes high-hat and social. Then they click and marry again – and again she goes into the divorce courts, which gives the audience a double-dose of flashbacks out of the stories told Judge Lionel Barrymore. It's a waste of Barrymore.

....

■ **LADY CAROLINE LAMB**

1972, 122 MINS, UK/ITALY ◇ Ⓥ
Dir Robert Bolt *Prod* Fernando Ghia *Scr* Robert Bolt *Ph* Oswald Morris *Ed* Norman Savage *Mus* Richard Rodney Bennett *Art Dir* Carmen Dillon
● Sarah Miles, Jon Finch, Richard Chamberlain, John Mills, Margaret Leighton, Pamela Brown (Anglo-EMI/Pulsar/Vides)

If it's that relative rarity, a lushly, unabashedly romantic – yet tastefully executed – tale that you relish, then *Lady Caroline Lamb* is your likely cup of tea.

For his first stint behind the camera, Robert Bolt comes up with a period piece which rings a number of contemporary bells, both emotional and intellectual. His tragic heroine, a controversial free thinker of the early British 1800s, has obvious parallels in present-day femme emancipation.

Outlined, her story follows her headlong flight into matrimony with the politically promising Lamb, then into an equally breathless and unpondered but this time scandalous affair with Byron, and on to her final climactic sacrifice on behalf of her husband's career.

Sarah Miles shines in a tailored role. Similarly, Jon Finch, as her husband, lends conviction to the film's most difficult part.

....

■ **LADY CHATTERLEY'S LOVER**

1981, 105 MINS, FRANCE/UK ◇
Dir Just Jaeckin *Prod* Andre Djaoui, Christopher Pierce *Scr* Just Jaeckin, Christopher Wicking *Ph* Robert Fraisse *Ed* Eunice Mountjoy *Mus* Stanley Myers *Art Dir* Anton Furst
● Sylvia Kristel, Shane Briant, Nicholas Clay (Producteurs Associes/Cannon)

This Franco-British production of *Lady Chat-*

terley's Lover is a cop-out adaptation of D.H. Lawrence's one time scandalous literary hymn to human sexuality. It's coy and superficial, worth little as erotic fare and not considerably more as sentimental drama.

The sex scenes are all the more unmoving because the surrounding story and characters are inadequately realized. Lady Chatterley (Sylvia Kristel) is the wife of an English aristocrat wounded in the World War I and totally paralyzed from the waist down. Starved for carnal affection, she becomes the lover of Chatterley's gamekeeper and meets him daily for long sessions of passionate lovemaking.

The love scenes are commonplace, summary, tritely lyrical and lacking in sensuality; no more daring than equivalent scenes in any other commercial product with a frank romantic angle.

Kristel is attractive but inexpressive as an actress. Nicholas Clay lacks rawness and definition as her lower-class lover.

....

■ **LADY EVE, THE**

1941, 90 MINS, US Ⓥ
Dir Preston Sturges *Prod* Paul Jones *Scr* Preston Sturges *Ph* Victor Milner *Mus* Leo Shuken, Charles Bradshaw
● Henry Fonda, Barbara Stanwyck, Charles Coburn, Eugene Pallette, William Demarest, Eric Blore (Paramount)

Third writer-director effort of Preston Sturges [from a story by Monckton Hoffe] is laugh entertainment of top proportions with its combo of slick situations, spontaneous dialog and a few slapstick falls tossed in for good measure.

Basically, story is the age-old tale of Eve snagging Adam, but dressed up with continually infectious fun and good humor. Barbara Stanwyck is girl-lure of trio of confidence operators. She's determined, quick-witted, resourceful and personable. Henry Fonda is a serious young millionaire, somewhat sappy, deadpan and slow-thinking, returning from a year's snake-hunting expedition up the Amazon. He's a cinch pushover for girl's advances on the boat – but pair fall in love, while girl flags Charles Coburn's attempts to coldeck the victim at cards.

Sturges provides numerous sparkling situations in his direction and keeps picture moving at a merry pace. Stanwyck is excellent in the comedienne portrayal, while Fonda carries his assignment in good fashion. Coburn is a finished actor as the con man.

....

■ **LADY FROM SHANGHAI, THE**

1948, 86 MINS, US Ⓥ
Dir Orson Welles *Prod* Orson Welles *Scr* Orson Welles *Ph* Charles Lawton Jr *Ed* Viola Lawrence *Mus* Heinz Roemheld *Art Dir* Stephen Goosson, Sturges Carne
● Rita Hayworth, Orson Welles, Everett Sloane, Ted De Corsia, Glenn Anders (Columbia)

Script is wordy and full of holes which need the plug of taut story telling and more forthright action. Rambling style used by Orson Welles has occasional flashes of imagination, particularly in the tricky backgrounds he uses to unfold the yarn, but effects, while good on their own, are distracting to the murder plot. Contributing to the stylized effect stressed by Welles is the photography, which features artful compositions entirely in keeping with the production mood.

Story [from a novel by Sherwood King] tees off in New York where Welles, as a philosophical Irish seaman, joins the crew of a rich man's luxury yacht. Schooner's cruise and stops along the Mexican coast en route to San Francisco furnish varied and interesting backdrops. Welles' tries for effect reach their peak with the staging of climatic chase se-

quences in a Chinese theatre where performers are going through an Oriental drama, and in the mirror room of an amusement park's crazy house.

Welles has called on players for stylized performances. He uses an Irish brogue and others depict erratic characters with little reality. Hayworth isn't called on to do much more than look beautiful. Best break for players goes to Everett Sloane, and he gives a credible interpretation of the crippled criminal attorney.

....

■ **LADY ICE**

1973, 93 MINS, US ◇ Ⓥ
Dir Tom Gries *Prod* Harrison Starr *Scr* Alan Trustman, Harold Clemens *Ph* Lucien Ballard *Ed* Robert Swink, William Sanda *Mus* Perry Botkin Jr *Art Dir* Joel Schiller
● Donald Sutherland, Jennifer O'Neill, Robert Duvall, Patrick Magee (Tomorrow)

Lady Ice comes off as a routine programmer, due for the most part to the listless performance of Donald Sutherland in the male lead. It is due to the superior work by Robert Duvall in a small role as a Dept of Justice officer and Jennifer O'Neill, as the gorgeous lady crook of the title, that the film comes off at all.

Shot on location for the most part, the handsomely-lensed actioner [from a story by Alan Trustman] pits jewel thieves against an insurance company private eye (Sutherland) in recovery of $3 million in ice from a Chicago holdup. O'Neill turns out to be the lady in charge of the caper. The rather thin plot is made up of numerous chases, a bit of violence and long, dull passages of Sutherland trying to make it with the lady criminal.

....

■ **LADY IN A CAGE**

1964, 94 MINS, US Ⓥ
Dir Walter Grauman *Prod* Luther Davis *Scr* Luther Davis *Ph* Lee Garmes *Ed* Leon Barsha *Mus* Paul Glass *Art Dir* Hal Pereira, Rudy Sternad
● Olivia de Havilland, Ann Sothern, Jeff Corey, James Caan, Jennifer Billingsley, Rafael Campos (Paramount)

There's not a single redeeming character or characteristic to producer Luther Davis' sensationalistically vulgar screenplay [based on a novel by Robert Durand]. It is haphazardly constructed, full of holes, sometimes pretentious and in bad taste.

Had the basic premise – of an invalid woman trapped in her private home elevator when the power is cut off – been developed simply, neatly and realistically, gripping dramatic entertainment might have ensued. But Davis has chosen to employ his premise as a means to expose all the negative aspects of the human animal. He has infested the caged woman's house with as scummy an assortment of characters as literary imagination might conceive.

Among those who greedily invade her abode are a delirious wino (Jeff Corey), a plump prostitute (Ann Sothern) and three vicious young hoodlums (James Caan, Jennifer Billingsley and Rafael Campos).

Olivia de Havilland plays the unfortunate woman in the elevator, and gives one of those ranting, raving, wild-eyed performances often thought of as Academy Award oriented. Actually, the role appears to require more emotional stamina than histrionic deftness. Caan, as the sadistic leader of the little rat-pack, appears to have been watching too many early Marlon Brando movies.

....

■ **LADY IN CEMENT**

1968, 93 MINS, US ◇
Dir Gordon Douglas *Prod* Aaron Rosenberg *Scr* Marvin H. Albert, Jack Guss *Ph* Joseph Biroc *Ed* Robert Simpson *Mus* Hugo Montenegro *Art Dir* Leroy Deane

● Frank Sinatra, Raquel Welch, Richard Conte, Martin Gabel, Lainie Kazan (20th Century-Fox)

Lady in Cement, follow-up to *Tony Rome*, stars Frank Sinatra as a Miami private eye on the trail of people in whom there couldn't be less interest. Raquel Welch adds her limited, but beauteous contribution, and Dan Blocker is excellent as a sympathetic heavy.

Episodic script is from Marvin H. Albert's novel, in which Sinatra, while scuba-diving off his beat, discovers a nude looker anchored in cement on the floor of the bay. Blocker hires Sinatra to find his lost sweetie, who turns out to be the dead gal.

Welch, Martin Gabel and Steve Peck come under suspicion. Richard Conte is a local police detective, and Paul Henry appears as a vice squad officer, one of whose jobs involves working the streets in drag.

● ●

■ LADY IN RED, THE

1979, 93 MINS, US ◇ ▼

Dir Lewis Teague   *Prod* Julie Corman   *Scr* John Sayles   *Ph* Daniel Lacambre   *Ed* Larry Bock, Ron Medico, Lewis Teague   *Art Dir* Joe McAnelly
● Pamela Sue Martin, Robert Conrad, Louise Fletcher, Christopher Lloyd, Robert Hogan (New World)

Ostensibly a return to the gangster genre, *The Lady in Red* is in many ways a compendium of variations on the 'woman in jeopardy' format.

The lady of the title gamely struggles through life as a tyrannized daughter, mistreated lover, ill-paid working girl, prisoner in a women's ward, professional hooker and full-fledged gangster, among other roles.

With her sights vaguely set on Hollywood, farm girl Pamela Sue Martin heads first for Chicago, where one mishap after another lands her in prison, then in the employ of classy madam Louise Fletcher.

Lewis Teague, a former second-unit director, guides his large cast reasonably well through John Sayles' craftsmanlike script.

● ●

■ LADY IN THE DARK

1944, 100 MINS, US ◇

Dir Mitchell Leisen   *Prod* Mitchell Leisen   *Scr* Frances Goodrich, Albert Hackett   *Ph* Ray Rennahan   *Ed* Alma Macrorie   *Mus* Robert Emmett Dolan (dir)   *Art Dir* Hans Dreier
● Ginger Rogers, Ray Milland, Jon Hall, Warner Baxter, Barry Sullivan, Mischa Auer (Paramount)

Produced on a lavish scale and in very fine taste against backgrounds of a glittering character with costuming that fills the eye, *Lady in the Dark* is at the outset a technically superior piece of craftsmanship. Paramount spent $185,000, and total negative nick is reported at $2.8 million. It looks it.

Mitchell Leisen produced and also directed from a surefire script based on the [1941] Broadway stage hit by Moss Hart, with music by Kurt Weill and lyrics by Ira Gershwin. An additional song, 'Suddenly It's Spring', was written by Johnny Burke and James Van Heusen.

Ginger Rogers plays the editor of a fashion magazine who, realizing she's on the edge of a nervous breakdown, finally places herself in the hands of a psychoanalyst. She resists his ministrations but ultimately goes through with it all and finally finds herself, the wall she had built around herself and her emotions since childhood ultimately being broken down. The dream sessions are reflections of her disturbed mind.

Playing the ad manager for the society mag and the only man in her life who has sought to set himself up as Rogers' superior, irritating her all along the line, Ray Milland gives an excellent performance.

● ●

■ LADY IN THE LAKE

1946, 103 MINS, US

Dir Robert Montgomery   *Prod* George Haight   *Scr* Steve Fisher   *Ph* Paul C. Vogel   *Ed* Gene Ruggiero   *Mus* David Snell   *Art Dir* Cedric Gibbons, Preston Ames
● Robert Montgomery, Audrey Totter, Lloyd Nolan (M-G-M)

Lady in the Lake institutes a novel method of telling the story, in which the camera itself is the protagonist, playing the lead role from the subjective viewpoint of star Robert Montgomery. Idea comes off excellently, transferring what otherwise would have been a fair whodunit into socko screen fare.

Montgomery starts telling the story in retrospect from a desk in his office, but when the picture dissolves into the action, the camera becomes Montgomery, presenting everything as it would have been through the star's eyes. Only time Montgomery is seen thereafter is when he's looking into a mirror or back at his desk for more bridging of the script.

Camera thus gets bashed by the villains, hits back in turn, smokes cigarettes, makes love and, in one of the most suspenseful sequences, drives a car in a hair-raising race that ends in a crash. Paul C. Vogel does a capital job with the lensing throughout, moving the camera to simulate the action of Montgomery's eyes as he walks up a flight of stairs, etc. Because it would be impossible under the circumstances to cut from Montgomery to another actor to whom he's talking, the rest of the cast was forced to learn much longer takes than usual.

Steve Fisher has wrapped up the Chandler novel into a tightly-knit and rapidly-paced screenplay. Montgomery plays private detective Philip Marlowe, who's dealt into a couple of murders when he tries to sell a story based on his experiences to a horror story mag. Audrey Totter, as the gal responsible for it all, is fine in both her tough-girl lines and as the love interest.

● ●

■ LADY IS WILLING, THE

1942, 93 MINS, US

Dir Mitchell Leisen   *Prod* Charles K. Feldman   *Scr* James Edward Grant, Albert McCleery   *Ph* Ted Tetzlaff   *Ed* Eda Warren   *Mus* W. Frank Harling
● Marlene Dietrich, Fred MacMurray, Aline MacMahon (Columbia/Feldman Group)

The Lady Is Willing is a racy and sophisticated marital comedy that carries a good share of amusement for adult audiences.

Picture carries light and breezy tempo in the first portion, with adoration of cute baby as motivating factor in holding interest. An inconclusive finish, with the oldy situation of an emergency operation necessary to save the child's life, and the pendulum-swinging problem of life-and-death crisis, allows the tale to sluff off with elemental formula convenience.

Familiar banter is apparent throughout. Despite this, strong performances by both principals succeed in holding up interest until the tale swings into heart-tug cliches. The baby's crisis is too extended and not handled in manner to hold audience attention on the dramatic elements attempted.

● ●

■ LADY L

1965, 124 MINS, US/ITALY ◇

Dir Peter Ustinov   *Prod* Carlo Ponti   *Scr* Peter Ustinov   *Ph* Henri Alekan   *Ed* Roger Dwyre   *Mus* Jean Francaix
● Sophia Loren, Paul Newman, David Niven, Claude Dauphin, Philippe Noiret, Michel Piccoli (M-G-M/Ponti)

Experiment of starting and ending this pic with Sophia Loren as an 80-year-old, an alleged aristocrat with a somewhat simpering

tedious voice, doesn't come off. Not till the Italian dish reverts to her own radiant, lush self will her followers settle down comfortably. David Niven is immaculately debonair and wittily amusing, but Paul Newman, though turning in a thoroughly competent performance, is not happily cast – his role calling out for the dependable mixture of solidity and lightness.

Film, from Romain Gary's novel, was originally planned as a straight drama, but things misfired. Ustinov was later brought in to do a doctoring job. But, despite the cost, he took on the chore only on the proviso that he could wipe the slate clean and start afresh. His nimble brain and characteristics have since clearly shaped the entire project.

Story, set in Paris and Switzerland at the turn of the century, has Loren as an aging, allegedly aristocratic mystery woman recounting her life story for the benefit of a biographer (Cecil Parker).

Ustinov weighs in with a choice cameo as the doddering Prince Otto.

● ●

■ LADY OF BURLESQUE

1943, 89 MINS, US ▼

Dir William Wellman   *Prod* Hunt Stromberg   *Scr* James Gunn   *Ph* Robert de Grasse   *Ed* James Newcom   *Mus* Arthur Lange
● Barbara Stanwyck, Michael O'Shea, J. Edward Bromberg (United Artists)

Although *Lady of Burlesque* is based on Gypsy Rose Lee's novel, *G-String Murders*, story plows an obvious straight line in generating the whodunit angles, and two gal burlesque performers are knocked off in succession before the culprit is disclosed. But gallant trouping by Barbara Stanwyck, colorful background provided by Stromberg, and speedy direction by William Wellman, carry picture through for good entertainment for general audiences.

Story centers around a burlesque stock company established in an old opera house. Stanwyck is the striptease star in process of buildup by manager J. Edward Bromberg, with Michael O'Shea the lowdown comedian who's continually making romantic pitches to the girl.

Picture gets off to zestful start, with stage show background in which Stanwyck socks over 'Take off the E String, Play It on the G String', and Frank Fenton deliberately off-keys 'So This Is You'. There's a sudden raid and wagon backup; release on bail and then showdown to generate various motives for the coming murders. After swinging into the strange use of a G string for strangulation of the victims, it's just a matter of time before the windup.

● ●

■ LADY ON A TRAIN

1945, 96 MINS, US

Dir Charles David   *Prod* Felix Jackson   *Scr* Edmund Beloin, Robert O'Brien   *Ph* Woody Bredell   *Ed* Ted Kent   *Mus* Miklos Rozsa   *Art Dir* John B. Goodman, Robert Clatworthy
● Deanna Durbin, Ralph Bellamy, Edward Everett Horton, Dan Duryea, George Coulouris (Universal)

Lady on a Train is a mystery comedy containing plenty of fun for both whodunit and laugh fans. Melodramatic elements in the Leslie Charteris original are flippantly treated without minimizing suspense, and the dialog contains a number of choice quips that are good for hefty laughs.

Deanna Durbin sings three tunes as well as handling herself excellently in the comedy role. Songs are all delivered against a background of menace. Actress is seen as a murder mystery addict who witnesses a murder from her train window while arriving in Grand Central station. Police discount her

L

story and she turns to David Bruce, mystery writer, for help. Her pursuit of the writer to enlist his aid is good funning and accounts for some hilarious sequences.

. . . .

■ **LADY SINGS THE BLUES**

1972, 144 MINS, US ◇ ⊙
Dir Sidney J. Furie   *Prod* Jay Weston, James S. White
Scr Terence McCloy, Chris Clark, Suzanne De Passe
Ph John Alonzo   *Ed* Argyle Nelson   *Mus* Michel Legrand   *Art Dir* Carl Anderson
● Diana Ross, Billy Dee Williams, Richard Pryor, James Callahan, Paul Hampton, Sid Melton (Paramount)

Individual opinions about *Lady Sings The Blues* may vary markedly, depending on a person's age, knowledge of jazz tradition and feeling for it, and how one wishes to regard the late Billie Holiday as both a force and a victim of her times. However, the film serves as a very good screen debut vehicle for Diana Ross, supported strongly by excellent casting, handsome 1930s physical values, and a script which is far better in dialog than structure.

Basis for the script is Holiday's autobiog *Lady Sings the Blues*, written with William Dufty only three years before her death in 1959 at age 44. Given that the script and production emphasis is on Ross as Holiday (and not on Holiday's life as interpreted by Ross), it still requires a severe gritting of teeth to overlook the truncations, telescoping and omissions.

Holiday's personal romantic life herein is restricted to Billy Dee Williams as Louis McKay, her third husband. Williams makes an excellent opposite lead, and Richard Pryor registers strongly as her longtime piano-playing friend who eventually is beaten to death in LA by hoods who want him to pay for the dope he procured for her.

. . . .

■ **LADY VANISHES, THE**

1938, 96 MINS, UK ⊙
Dir Alfred Hitchcock   *Prod* Edward Black   *Scr* Sidney Gilliat, Frank Launder   *Ph* Jack Cox   *Ed* Alfred Roome, R.E. Dearing   *Mus* Louis Levy (dir.)
Art Dir Alex Vetchinsky
● Margaret Lockwood, Michael Redgrave, Paul Lukas, May Whitty, Cecil Parker, Linden Travers (Gainsborough/Gaumont-British)

An elderly English governess, homeward bound, disappears from a transcontinental train, and a young girl, who says she recently received a blow on the head, is confronted by numerous other passengers who say they never saw the governess. This becomes so persistent the girl finally thinks she has gone nuts.

The story [from the novel *The Wheel Spins* by Ethel Lina White] is sometimes eerie and eventually melodramatic, but it's all so well done as to make for intense interest. It flits from one set of characters to another and becomes slightly difficult to follow, but finally all joins up.

This film, minus the deft and artistic handling of the director, Alfred Hitchcock, despite its cast and photography, would not stand up for Grade A candidacy. Margaret Lockwood is the central femme character; Michael Redgrave, as the lead, is a trifle too flippant. Naunton Wayne, Basil Radford, Paul Lukas (as a credibly villainous doctor), May Whitty, (as the governess) and Catherine Lacey (a villainess disguised as a nun are excellent.

. . . .

■ **LADY VANISHES, THE**

1979, 99 MINS, UK ◇ ⊙
Dir Anthony Page   *Prod* Tom Sachs   *Scr* George Axelrod   *Ph* Douglas Slocombe   *Ed* Russell Lloyd
Mus Richard Hartley   *Art Dir* Wilfrid Shingleton

● Elliott Gould, Cybill Shepherd, Angela Lansbury, Herbert Lom, Ian Carmichael, Arthur Lowe (Hammer)

The Lady Vanishes is a midatlantic mish-mash with some moderately amusing moments but no cohesive style.

The production has Cybill Shepherd as a madcap Yank heiress and Elliott Gould as a *Life* mag photographer foiling a political conspiracy aboard a train outbound from prewar Germany. Slapstick suspense and mystery elements that will fool almost no one add up to a heavy-handed affair.

The script from an Ethel Lina White novel is best when dwelling on English eccentricity to make the film's most endearing impression.

Shepherd and Gould stack up as contrived cliches, characters that jar rather than complement.

Alfred Hitchcock's original version, circa 1938, had pretty much everything the remake doesn't.

. . . .

■ **LADYHAWKE**

1985, 124 MINS, US ◇ ⊙
Dir Richard Donner   *Prod* Richard Donner, Lauren Schuler   *Scr* Edward Khmara, Michael Thomas, Tom Mankiewicz   *Ph* Vittorio Storaro   *Ed* Stuart Baird
Mus Andrew Powell   *Art Dir* Wolf Kroeger
● Matthew Broderick, Rutger Hauer, Michelle Pfeiffer, Leo McKern, John Wood, Ken Hutchison (Warner/20th Century-Fox)

LadyHawke is a very likeable, very well-made fairytale that insists on a wish for its lovers to live happily ever after.

Handsome Rutger Hauer is well-cast as the dark and moody knight who travels with a hawk by day. Lovely Michelle Pfeiffer is perfect as the enchanting beauty who appears by night, always in the vicinity of a vicious but protective wolf.

As readers of one or more variations of this legend will instantly recognize, Pfeiffer is the hawk and Hauer the wolf, each changing form as the sun rises and sets, former lovers cursed to never humanly share the clock together.

The spell was cast by an evil bishop (John Wood) when Pfeiffer spurned him for Hauer, who is now bent on revenge, with the help of young Matthew Broderick, the only one to ever escape Wood's deadly dungeon.

Though simple, the saga moves amidst beautiful surroundings (filmed in Italy), and is worthwhile for its extremely authentic look alone.

. . . .

■ **LADYKILLERS, THE**

1955, 96 MINS, UK ◇ ⊙
Dir Alexander Mackendrick   *Prod* Michael Balcon
Scr William Rose   *Ph* Otto Heller   *Ed* Jack Harris
Mus Tristram Cary   *Art Dir* Jim Morahan
● Alec Guinness, Cecil Parker, Herbert Lom, Peter Sellers, Katie Johnson, Danny Green (Ealing)

This is an amusing piece of hokum, being a parody of American gangsterdom interwoven with whimsy and exaggeration that makes it more of a macabre farce. Alec Guinness sinks his personality almost to the level of anonymity. Basic idea of thieves making a frail old lady an unwitting accomplice in their schemes is carried out in ludicrous and often tense situations.

A bunch of crooks planning a currency haul call on their leader, who has temporarily boarded with a genteel widow near a big London rail terminal. They pass as musicians gathering for rehearsals, but wouldn't deceive a baby.

Guinness tends to overact the sinister leader while Cecil Parker strikes just the right note as a conman posing as an army officer. Herbert Lom broods gloomily as the most ruthless of the plotters, with Peter Sellers

contrasting well as the dumb muscle man. Danny Green completes the quintet.

. . . .

■ **LAIR OF THE WHITE WORM, THE**

1989, 93 MINS, UK ◇ ⊙
Dir Ken Russell   *Prod* Ken Russell   *Scr* Ken Russell
Ph Dick Bush   *Ed* Peter Davies   *Mus* Stanislas Syrewicz   *Art Dir* Anne Tilby
● Amanda Donohoe, Hugh Grant, Catherine Oxenberg, Sammi Davis, Peter Capaldi (White Lair/Vestron)

Adapted from a tale by Bram Stoker, creator of Dracula, *Lair*, a rollicking, terrifying, post-psychedlic headtrip, features a fangy vampiress of unmatched erotic allure. Lady Sylvia Marsh (Amanda Donohoe) lives in a sprawling mansion not far from the state-of-the-art castle inhabited by Lord James D'Ampton (Hugh Grant).

On the day of a big party, just before nightfall, archaeology student Angus (Peter Capaldi) finds a bizarre, unclassifiable skull. The castle party is celebrating Lord James' inheritance of the estate as well as a family holiday commemorating a legendary ancestor said to have slain a dragon. In the Lampton clan mythology, the dragon is represented as an overblown, jawsy white worm.

Soon the duke and the digger divine an eerie connection between the mysteriously burgled skull, the white worm legend and cases of snakebite plus more strange disappearances close by the Lady's mansion. Then things start to get scary.

Donohoe as the vampire seductress projects a beguiling sexuality that should suck the resistance out of all but the most cold-blooded critics. She is also hilarious, a virtue shared by everyone and everything in *The Lair of the White Worm*.

. . . .

■ **LAMBADA**

1990, 98 MINS, US ◇ ⊙
Dir Joel Silberg   *Prod* Peter Shepherd   *Scr* Joel Silberg, Sheldon Renan   *Ph* Roberto D'Ettore Piazzoli
Ed Marcus Manton   *Mus* Greg Manton   *Art Dir* Bill Cornford
● J. Eddie Peck, Melora Hardin, Shabba-Doo, Ricky Paull Goldin, Basil Hoffman (Cannon)

Lambada's peripheral dance segs don't add up to $7 worth of lambada. Still, director/cowriter Joel Silberg keeps the story lively on a cartoonish-level.

J. Eddie Peck plays the Beverly Hills teacher by day, East LA lambada dancer by night, his sculpted dancer's physique straining the credibility of this most unlikely of teen fantasy scenarios. He forgoes evenings at home with his wife and son to motorbike over to the lambada club where he teaches math in the back room to a gang of east side dropouts.

His lambada prowess intrigues one of the BH highschoolers, sexually precocious Sandy (Melora Hardin), who stumbles onto the scene and sets out to seduce or blackmail him, unaware of his real, noble reason for leading this double life.

The dancing occupies little screen time compared to the sudsy intrigue Sandy stirs up on the school front, and what lambadaing there is, is photographed mostly in tight titillating shots that lack context.

. . . .

■ **LANCELOT AND GUINEVERE**

1963, 116 MINS, US ◇ ⊙
Dir Cornel Wilde   *Prod* Cornel Wilde, Bernard Luber
Scr Richard Schayer, Jefferson Pascal   *Ph* Harry Waxman   *Ed* Frederick Wilson   *Mus* Ron Goodwin
Art Dir Maurice Carter
● Cornel Wilde, Jean Wallace, Brian Aherne, George Baker, John Longden, Iain Gregory (Emblem/Universal

333

This version of the much-told tale of King Arthur and the Knights of the Round Table is an elaborately mounted production that generates fair amounts of interest and excitement when the fighting's going on but barely rises above the routine in story-telling the legend.

It's Cornel Wilde most of the way, he having coproduced, directed and costarred with his wife, Jean Wallace, latter making a beautiful Guinevere.

This outing smacks of modernization in terms of plot situation. But not filmmaking technique. King Arthur eagerly awaits his Guinevere at the altar in his Camelot and she's escorted by the gallant Lancelot (Wilde). The marriage takes place, but despite the affection Lancelot feels for his king, he shares a bed with the lady whose name he reduces in the dialog to just plain Guin.

The outdoor scenes, which were filmed in Yugoslavia with native cavalrymen, are in some measure pictorially effective but at times director Wilde is just focusing on so much confused action. No telling how much footage was left on the plains of Titoland or the cutting-room floor of Pinewood Studios, London, where the interiors were lensed.

An accomplished job is turned in by Brian Aherne, as King Arthur, who's able to give a good reading even when dialog is stilted. Wilde and Wallace are believable, John Longden is properly sinister as Arthur's rival for the crown and Iain Gregory is appealing as a young knight fighting side by side with Lancelot.

■ **LAND BEFORE TIME, THE**

1988, 66 MINS, US ◇ ⓥ
Dir Don Bluth   *Prod* Don Bluth, Gary Goldman, John Pomeroy   *Scr* Stu Krieger   *Ph* Jim Mann   *Ed* Dan Molina, John K. Carr   *Mus* James Horner   *Art Dir* Don Bluth
● (Sullivan-Bluth/Amblin)

Sure, kids like dinosaurs, but beyond that, premise doesn't find far to go. Story is about Littlefoot (Gabriel Damon), an innocent dinosaur tyke who gets separated from his family and after a perilous journey finds them again in a new land.

In this case it's a journey from a dried-up part of the land to another, known as the Great Valley, where the herds frolic in abundant greenery.

After Littlefoot's mother dies, he has to make the journey alone, dodging hazards like earthquakes, volcanoes and a predatory carnivore named Sharptooth. Along the way, he pulls together a band of other little dinosaurs of different species who've been brought up not to associate with each other.

Idea develops that surviving in a changing environment depends on achieving unity among the species.

For the most part, pic is about as engaging as what's found on Saturday morning TV.

■ **LAND OF THE PHARAOHS**

1955, 103 MINS, US ◇
Dir Howard Hawks   *Prod* Howard Hawks
Scr William Faulkner, Harry Kurnitz, Harold Jack Bloom   *Ph* Lee Garmes, Russell Harlan   *Ed* V. Sagovsky, Rudi Fehr   *Mus* Dimitri Tiomkin   *Art Dir* Alexandre Trauner
● Jack Hawkins, Joan Collins, Dewey Martin, Alexis Minotis, James Robertson Justice (Continental/Warner)

Egypt of 5,000 years ago comes to life in *Land of the Pharaohs*, a tremendous film spectacle. From the opening shot of a great pharaoh and his thousands of soldiers returning from successful battle laden with vast treasure, an audience is constantly overwhelmed with spectacle, either in the use of cast thousands,

tremendously sized settings or the surging background score by Dimitri Tiomkin.

The story tells of a great pharaoh, ably played by Jack Hawkins, who for 30 years drives his people to build a pyramid in which his body and treasure shall rest secure for evermore, and of a woman, portrayed by Joan Collins, a captivating bundle of s.a., who conspires to win his kingdom and riches for herself.

When the viewing senses begin to dull from the tremendous load of spectacle, the script and Hawks' direction wisely switch to sex and intrigue.

Alexis Minotis, Greek actor, lends the picture a fine performance as Hamar, the high priest.

■ **LAND THAT TIME FORGOT, THE**

1975, 91 MINS, UK ◇
Dir Kevin Connor   *Prod* John Dark   *Scr* James Cawthorn, Michael Moorcock   *Ph* Alan Hume   *Ed* John Ireland   *Mus* Douglas Gamley   *Art Dir* Bert Davey
● Doug McClure, John McEnery, Susan Penhaligon, Keith Barron, Anthony Ainley, Godfrey James (American International)

Adapted from Edgar Rice Burroughs' *The Land That Time Forgot* the 'land' in question is an uncharted island, icy on the outside and smoldering within, that's populated with all sorts of big critters.

This island of Caprona is reached by a German submarine which torpedoes an English ship. The survivors, led by Doug McClure, come aboard and capture the sub. But McEnery gets it back. Then McClure takes over again. By this time, it's no wonder the sub is lost in the Antarctic. Luckily, they spot Caprona, easing the sub through an underground tunnel where it's attacked by a Mososaurus.

Somebody identifies the problem immediately. 'This can't be. These creatures have been extinct for millions of years.'

■ **LANDLORD, THE**

1970, 112 MINS, US ◇
Dir Hal Ashby   *Prod* Norman Jewison   *Scr* William Gunn   *Ph* Gordon Willis   *Ed* William Abbott Sawyer, Edward Warschilka   *Mus* Al Kooper   *Art Dir* Robert Boyle
● Beau Bridges, Lee Grant, Diana Sands, Pearl Bailey, Marki Bey, Louis Gossett (United Artists/Mirisch)

Beau Bridges heads the uniformly excellent cast as a bored rich youth who buys a black ghetto apartment building and learns something about life.

A novel by Kristin Hunter has been scripted into what is essentially a two-part story. First, Bridges and his economically secure family are played off and against the black tenants whom he inherits in his ghetto building. Then, Bridges' sexual encounter with married Diana Sands results in a mixed race baby and a confrontation with some hard facts of life.

The film is most successful when people are interacting with people. Pearl Bailey's performance is a terrific showpiece for her talents. Sands makes a powerful impression as a flirtatious but loving wife to Louis Gossett.

■ **LASSITER**

1984, 100 MINS, US ◇ ⓥ
Dir Roger Young   *Prod* Albert S. Ruddy   *Scr* David Taylor   *Ph* Gil Taylor   *Ed* Benjamin Weissman   *Mus* Ken Thorne   *Art Dir* Peter Mullins
● Tom Selleck, Jane Seymour, Lauren Hutton, Bob Hoskins, Joe Regalbuto, Ed Lauter (Golden Harvest/Warner)

Set in London in 1934, *Lassiter* is part caper picture, part intrigue story. Nick Lassiter (Tom Selleck) is an elegant jewel thief who is blackmailed by a coalition of the FBI and English police to liberate $10 million in Nazi diamonds passing through London. Selleck resists, but really isn't given much choice since the alternative is a stay in a British prison.

The diamonds are to be transported out of London by none other than Lauren Hutton, playing German agent Countess Kari von Fursten.

Hutton is totally unbelievable with her Germanic accent and evil habits. As the girlfriend, Jane Seymour is wasted. Her role is basically to stand by as Selleck races about trying to grab the diamonds and run.

■ **LAST AMERICAN HERO, THE**

1973, 95 MINS, US ◇ ⓥ
Dir Lamont Johnson   *Prod* William Roberts, John Cutts   *Scr* William Roberts   *Ph* George Silano   *Ed* Tom Rolf, Robbe Roberts   *Mus* Charles Fox   *Art Dir* Lawrence Paull
● Jeff Bridges, Valerie Perrine, Geraldine Fitzgerald, Ned Beatty, Art Lund, Gary Busey (20th Century-Fox)

After a fumbling start which looks like bad editing for TV, *The Last American Hero* [based on two articles by Tom Wolfe] settles into some good, gritty, family Americana, with Jeff Bridges excellent as a flamboyant auto racer determined to succeed on his own terms and right a wrong to his father, played expertly by Art Lund.

Bridges and Gary Busey are moonshiner Lund's boys, with Geraldine Fitzgerald a concerned wife and mother. Bridges' backroad hot-rodding outrages a revenuer into busting Lund, who gets time for illegal liquor distilling. Bridges takes to the racing circuit to buy Lund some prison privileges.

Between the script, Lamont Johnson's sure direction, and the excellent performances, all but the early choppy scenes add up to a welltold story.

■ **LAST ANGRY MAN, THE**

1959, 100 MINS, US ◇ ⓥ
Dir Daniel Mann   *Prod* Fred Kohlmar   *Scr* Gerald Green, Richard Murphy   *Ph* James Wong Howe   *Ed* Charles Nelson   *Mus* George Duning
● Paul Muni, David Wayne, Betsy Palmer, Luther Adler, Joby Baker, Nancy Pollock (Columbia)

The Last Angry Man is as pungent and indelible as Brooklyn on a hot summer afternoon. It has faults: but it is possible to overlook whatever imperfections stud the production because so much of it is so good and, add, so rare.

The film is taken from Gerald Green's bestselling novel about a Jewish doctor, a character based on Green's own father. Director Daniel Mann had his problems in getting the story on film, shooting much of it on Brooklyn locations, but the finished product is worth the labor.

The conflict in the story arises from the lifetime of selfless service by the doctor (Paul Muni) when placed in conjunction with the commercial demands of contemporary television. Television wants to exploit the Jewish doctor, to associate with him so it can claim some of his virtues. Muni is an immigrant who has absorbed his Americanism from Jefferson, from Emerson and Thoreau, and he believes what they said.

Muni gives a superlative performance. Someone chides him at one point for thinking of himself as an Albert Schweitzer. A Schweitzer he isn't, but in Muni's character delineation it's apparent it's the men like him who keep the world going. David Wayne, as his abrasive agent, is allowed no histrionics, but his conviction must be absolute. Wayne is as persuasive as his narrow lapels and button-down collars.

••••••••••••••••••••••••••••••••

■ **LAST DAYS OF POMPEII, THE**

1935, 96 MINS, US ⑲
Dir Ernest B. Schoedsack   *Prod* Merian C. Cooper
Scr James A. Creelman, Melville Baker, Ruth Rose, Boris Ingster   *Ph* J. Roy Hunt, Eddie Linden Jr   *Ed* Archie Marshek   *Mus* Roy Webb
● Preston Foster, Basil Rathbone, Alan Hale, John Wood, Louis Calhern, Dorothy Wilson (RKO)

Last Days of Pompeii is a spectacle picture, full of action and holds a good tempo throughout.

What is presented is a behind-the-scenes of Roman politics and commerce both of which are shown as smeared with corruption and intrigue.

Basil Rathbone comes very close to stealing the picture with his playing of Pontius Pilate. Jesus crosses the path of Marcus (Preston Foster) one time gladiator who is in Judea on a little business deal (horse stealing) which he carries out as the silent partner of Pilate.

Foster has the central role. He carries through from the boyish blacksmith of the opening sequence to the rich man who in the end sees his beloved son face probable death in the arena (just before the volcano erupts). On the way he is gladiator, slave trader, horse-stealer and general tough guy, but more the victim of a fierce semi-barbaric environment than of any personal cruelty trait.

••••••••••••••••••••••••••••••••

■ **LAST DETAIL, THE**

1973, 103 MINS, US ◇ ⑲
Dir Hal Ashby   *Prod* Gerald Ayres   *Scr* Robert Towne   *Ph* Michael Chapman   *Ed* Robert C. Jones   *Mus* Johnny Mandel   *Art Dir* Michael Haller
● Jack Nicholson, Otis Young, Randy Quaid, Clifton James, Michael Moriarty, Carol Kane (Columbia)

The Last Detail is a salty, bawdy, hilarious and very touching story about two career sailors escorting a naval prison a dumb boot sentenced for petty thievery. Jack Nicholson is outstanding at the head of a superb cast.

Robert Towne's outstanding adaptation of Darryl Ponicsan's novel has caught the flavor of noncombat military life. The dialog vulgarisms are simply part of the eternal environment of men in uniform.

Randy Quaid is cast as a teenage misfit. A bungled ripoff of some charity money has gotten him eight years in Portsmouth. Nicholson and Otis Young, awaiting new assignments at a receiving station, draw escort duty. With several days of transit time allowed, Nicholson decides to set a leisurely pace. The essence of the story is the exchange of compassion between the guards and prisoner, and the latter's effect on his escorts.

••••••••••••••••••••••••••••••••

■ **LAST EMBRACE**

1979, 103 MINS, US ◇ ⑲
Dir Jonathan Demme   *Prod* Michael Taylor, Dan Wigutow   *Scr* David Shaber   *Ph* Tak Fujimoto   *Ed* Barry Malkin   *Mus* Miklos Rozsa   *Art Dir* Charles Rosen
● Roy Scheider, Janet Margolin, Christopher Walken, Sam Levene (United Artists)

Director Jonathan Demme proves conclusively that he can handle a strictly commercial assignment, while embellishing it with the creative touches that mark a firstrate filmmaker.

Last Embrace tells of a government agent being phased out after a nervous breakdown, triggered by his wife's murder. Roy Scheider is the paranoid subject of more attention than he'd prefer, especially when it comes from Janet Margolin, a wigged-out grad student.

Story is from Murray Teigh Bloom's novel, *The Thirteenth Man*.

The Hitchcock references are frequent. Scheider delivers a convincing, nerve-tingling perf that reaffirms he can handle a romantic lead. Margolin is highly appealing as the revenge-minded femme.

Christopher Walken is seen briefly in a cameo performance as Scheider's boss.

••••••••••••••••••••••••••••••••

■ **LAST EMPEROR, THE**

1987, 160 MINS, UK/ITALY ◇ ⑲
Dir Bernardo Bertolucci   *Prod* Jeremy Thomas
Scr Mark Peploe, Bernardo Bertolucci   *Ph* Vittorio Storaro   *Ed* Gabriella Cristiani   *Mus* Ryuichi Sakamoto, David Byrne, Cong Su   *Art Dir* Ferdinando Scarfiotti
● John Lone, Joan Chen, Peter O'Toole, Ying Ruocheng, Victor Wong, Dennis Dun (Thomas)

A film of unique, quite unsurpassed visual splendor, *The Last Emperor* makes for a fascinating trip to another world, but for the most part also proves as remote and untouchable as its subject, the last imperial ruler of China. A prodigious production in every respect, Bernardo Bertolucci's film is an exquisitely painted mural of 20th-century Chinese history as seen from the point of view of a hereditary leader who never knew his people.

In 1908, the three-year-old Pu Yi is installed as Lord of Ten Thousand Years, master of the most populous nation on earth. Shortly, he is forced to abdicate, but is kept on as a symbolic figure, educated by his English tutor and tended to by a court that includes 1,500 eunuchs and countless other manipulative advisers.

Technically considered a god, little Pu Yi can do anything he wishes except leave the great Forbidden City in Peking. He's a prisoner in the most glorious gilded cage ever created.

Finally booted out by the new government, Pu Yi, by now in his late 20s, moves with his two wives to Tientsin and lives like a Western playboy, wearing tuxedos at elegant dances while gradually coming under the influence of the Japanese, who eventually install him as puppet emperor of Manchuria, home of his ancestors.

After World War II, he is imprisoned for 10 years by the communists, during which time he writes his memoirs, and ends his life as a gardener and simple citizen in Mao's China.

At every moment, the extraordinary aspects of both the story and the physical realization of it are astonishing to witness. For virtually the first 90 minutes, Bertolucci makes full use of the red-dominatd splendor of the Forbidden City, which has never before been opened up for use in a Western film.

John Lone, who plays Pu Yi from age 18 to 62, naturally dominates the picture with his carefully judged, unshowy delineation of a sometimes arrogant, often weak man. Joan Chen is exquisite and sad as his principal wife who almost literally fades away, and Peter O'Toole, as Lone's tutor, doesn't really have that much to do but act intelligently concerned for the emperor's well-being.
☐ 1987: Best Picture

••••••••••••••••••••••••••••••••

■ **LAST EXIT TO BROOKLYN**

1989, 102 MINS, W. GERMANY ◇
Dir Uli Edel   *Prod* Bernd Eichinger, Herman Weigel
Scr Desmond Nakano   *Ph* Stefan Czapsky   *Ed* Peter Przygodda   *Mus* Mark Knopfler   *Art Dir* David Chapman
● Stephen Lang, Jennifer Jason Leigh, Burt Young, Peter Dobson, Jerry Orbach, Alexis Arquette (Neue Constantin/Bavaria/Allied)

Last Exit to Brooklyn is a bleak tour of urban hell, a $16 million Stateside-lensed production of Hubert Selby Jr's controversial

1964 novel. But it doesn't hold a scalpel to the lacerating torrential prose that made the book so cringingly urgent.

Director Uli Edel, whose international reputation was made on the 1980 teen drug drama *Christiane F.*, proves himself an accomplished professional. What he lacks is that fundamental gift of empathy that would make these damned souls more than just figures under a cinematic microscope.

Action is set in a working-class section of Brooklyn in 1952, close by the navy yards where young Americans are embarking for the Korean War. Many residents are engaged in a bitter six month strike against a local factory. Film's spectacular centerpiece is a well-staged riot pitting strikers against police when factory management uses scab labour to break the picket lines.

One of the protagonists is Stephen Lang, a venal married shop steward and secretary of the strike office who has been dipping into the union till to subsidize his first homosexual affair. When union boss Jerry Orbach boots him out, Lang is dropped by his mercenary lover. A subhuman band of local goons thrashes Lang to within an inch of his life (and 'crucifies' him on a wooden crossbeam).

Other major character is a tawdry, hard-drinking teen hooker named Tralala (Jennifer Jason Leigh), who lures unsuspecting bar-hopping servicemen to a back lot where they are mugged and robbed by the band. One night she gets drunk and defiantly declares herself open for sexual services to the neighbourhood bar's entire clintele.

The resulting gangbang, one of the most horrific passages in Selby Jr's book, is here sanitized and given a hopeful finish.

••••••••••••••••••••••••••••••••

■ **LAST HARD MEN, THE**

1976, 103 MINS, US ◇ ⑲
Dir Andrew V. McLaglen   *Prod* Walter Seltzer, Russell Thacher   *Scr* Guerdon Trueblood   *Ph* Duke Callaghan   *Ed* Fred Chulack   *Mus* Jerry Goldsmith   *Art Dir* Edward Carfagno
● Charlton Heston, James Coburn, Barbara Hershey, Jorge Rivero, Michael Parks, Larry Wilcox (20th Century-Fox)

The Last Hard Men is a fairly good actioner with handsome production values and some thoughtful overtones. Charlton Heston and James Coburn are both fine as a retired lawman and his half-Indian nemesis matching their wits in 1909 Arizona along the way to one last bloody confrontation.

Coburn escapes from a Yuma prison gang to wreak carefully planned revenge on Heston, who killed his wife years ago in a scatter-shot shootout. Recruiting a motley gang Coburn lures the anxious Heston out of Tucson by kidnapping and molesting his daughter (Barbara Hershey).

The details of life at a crucial transition point in American history are well captured in the script and in the art direction.

••••••••••••••••••••••••••••••••

■ **LAST HURRAH, THE**

1958, 121 MINS, US ⑲
Dir John Ford   *Prod* John Ford   *Scr* Frank Nugent
Ph Charles Lawton Jr   *Ed* Jack Murray   *Art Dir* Robert Peterson
● Spencer Tracy, Jeffrey Hunter, Dianne Foster, Pat O'Brien, Basil Rathbone, James Gleason (Columbia)

Edwin O'Connor's novel has been transmuted to the screen in slick style. Spencer Tracy makes the most of the meaty role of the shrewd politician of the 'dominantly Irish-American' metropolis in New England (unmistakably Boston but not Boston).

Tracy's resourcefulness in besting the stuffy bankers who nixed a loan for a much needed low-rent housing development; his foiling of the profiteering undertaker when a constituent is buried (the wake is transformed into a political rally); the passionate loyalty of his political devotees; the rivalry between the 'respectable' elements in combating the direct-approach tactics of the Irish-American politicos; the pride in defeat when the 'reform' candidate bests Tracy at the polls; and Tracy's own 'last hurrah' as he tells off the fatuous banker (Willis Bouchey) – with a parting 'like hell I would!' – in reviewing his gaudy career, make for a series of memorable scenes.

Jeffrey Hunter is the shrewd mayor's favored nephew who, despite his ties to the opposition sheet, perceives the old codger's humaneness.

● ●

■ LAST MARRIED COUPLE IN AMERICA, THE

1980, 103 MINS, US ◇ ▽
Dir Gilbert Cates   *Prod* Edward S. Feldman, John Herman Shaner   *Scr* John Herman Shaner   *Ph* Ralph Woolsey   *Ed* Peter E. Berger   *Mus* Charles Fox   *Art Dir* Gene Callahan
● George Segal, Natalie Wood, Richard Benjamin, Dom DeLuise (Universal)

The Last Married Couple In America is basically a 1950s comedy with cursing. John Herman Shaner's script offers not a single new idea about divorce in suburbia and doesn't even develop the cliches well.

Gilbert Cates' direction consists largely of letting his stars reenact favorite roles of the past. So Wood plays the nice pretty lady who wants a happy, faithful marriage to George Segal, who plays the nice, handsome husband befuddled by the world around him.

Richard Benjamin is again the neurotic modern male and Dom DeLuise the likable, nutty fat guy, while Valerie Harper is essentially Rhoda running rampant, tresses turned blonde from the sheer excitement of it all.

● ●

■ LAST MOVIE, THE

1971, 110 MINS, US ◇
Dir Dennis Hopper   *Prod* Paul Lewis   *Scr* Stewart Stern   *Ph* Laszlo Kovacs   *Ed* David Berlatsky   *Art Dir* Leon Erickson
● Dennis Hopper, Stella Garcia, Sam Fuller, Daniel Ades, Tomas Milian, Don Gordon (Universal)

The narrative fluidity, using of myths for a statement on youth, so effective in Dennis Hopper's *Easy Rider* are here overdone and film suffers from a multiplicity of themes, ideas and its fragmented style with flash-forwards intertwined.

Film begins with Hopper wandering all bloody among Peruvian Indians playing at filmmaking with cameras, booms, etc., made of rattan. A local priest complains of the violence the film people have left behind among his people whose playing at it leads to a kind of passion play and the hunted and finally crucified figure becomes Hopper.

Then a scene from the film shot there, a gun battle with horses falling and men bloodied. Sam Fuller plays a no-nonsense director with aplomb in these scenes. Hopper has the canteen, plays stuntman and stays on with a native girl, dreaming of building a resort and using the set for other productions. This does not pan out.

Stella Garcia is effective as the native girl who is not moved by the dead she does not know while Hopper has an American innocence tempered with violent rage when things go beyond his ken.

● ●

■ LAST OF ENGLAND, THE

1987, 87 MINS, UK/W. GERMANY ◇ ⑰
Dir Derek Jarman   *Prod* James Mackay, Don Boyd   *Scr* [uncrediited]   *Ph* Derek Jarman, Christopher Hughes, Cerith Wyn Evans, Richard Heslop   *Ed* Peter Cartwright, Angus Cook, Sally Yeadon, John Maybury   *Mus* Simon Turner, Andy Gill, Mayo Thompson, Albert

Oehlen, Barry Adamson, El Tito   *Art Dir* Christopher Hobbs
● Tilda Swinton, Spencer Leigh, Spring, Gay Gaynor, Matthew Hawkins, Gerard McArthur (British Screen/Film Four/ZDF/Anglo-International)

The Last of England has the rare ability to envelop one in its swirling images and bleak comedy one moment, and send a viewer off to sleep the next.

Following the avant-garde helmer's most accessible film to date, the 1986 *Caravaggio*, he returns with a blatantly personal vision which combines documentary-style footage of ruined streets, home movies, and a segment with glimpses of a screen story. All is filmed and linked abstractly, but without the glimmer of plot or narrative line.

The Last of England is a self-indulgent number, opening with an actor (Spring) kicking and abusing a Caravaggio painting, 'Profane Love', and proceeding with a tirade of images of urban destruction and deprived youth. Interspersed are extracts from the Jarman family's home movies, which make an interesting contrast to the abrasive images with their views of colonial and RAF life.

● ●

■ LAST OF MRS CHEYNEY, THE

1929, 94 MINS, US
Dir Sidney Franklin   *Ph* William Daniels
● Norma Shearer, Basil Rathbone, George Barraud, Herbert Bunston, Hedda Hopper, Moon Carroll (M-G-M)

Whole story [from the play by Frederick Lonsdale] is sentimental, a deftly manipulated series of the bunk about the good girl drawn into associations with a band of crooks, getting herself accepted into society so they can prey upon the rich, the girl all the time retaining the chaste and delicate spirit of a nun.

It's bum literature but great theatre, particularly here with a splendid group of players. Norma Shearer does extremely well with the heroine. She most successfully plays the role of elegance and high breeding, the two qualities which are the key to making Mrs Cheyney plausible.

Basil Rathbone falls into a role for his casual, easy stage style, and the character of Lord Elton, composite of stupidity and meanness and the whole trick of the play's sentimental punch, is happily in the hands of Herbert Bunston, to whom it is pie.

The picture's finish could be made brisker.

● ●

■ LAST OF MRS. CHEYNEY, THE

1937, 95 MINS, US
Dir Richard Boleslawki   *Prod* Lawrence Weingarten   *Scr* Leon Gordon, Samson Raphaelson, Monckton Hoffe   *Ph* George Folsey   *Ed* Frank Sullivan   *Mus* William Axt
● Joan Crawford, William Powell, Robert Montgomery, Frank Morgan, Jessie Ralph, Nigel Bruce (M-G-M)

The Last of Mrs Cheyney is a a Metro remake of its own dialog film made in 1929 with Norma Shearer. it's from the [Frederick] Lonsdale play which Ina Claire, Roland Young and A.E. Matthews first did on Broadway in 1925. Present filmization more nearly approximates a picture than the 1929 film which was, then, more a straight transmutation of the play in celluloid form.

This is Richard Boleslawski's post-mortem release. Another director wound up the perfunctory details, but Boleslawski gets, and merits, the sole directorial billing. His hand is evident in a number of fine scenes, pacing this society crook comedy-drama with effective contrasts of suspense and laughs.

Scenes which are outstanding are made so by a rare combination of pace, scripting and direction. The sequence, for example, where

the snooty English household is wondering what will happen to the crooks (Joan Crawford and her accomplice, William Powell) is a double-broadside in deft comedy painting.

In similar vein, the weekenders' truth-game less pointedly, but not too subtly, mirrors the foibles of the same group – the two-timing wife who has had 14 'cousins' (male) for constant companionship; her stupid husband; another lady of easy virtue; the engagingly lecherous male (Robert Montgomery), but frankly so: the duchess-hotesss (capably played by Jessie Ralph), who confesses she came into royalty via the London Gayety chorus-line, etc.

● ●

■ LAST OF SHEILA, THE

1973, 120 MINS, US ◇ ▽
Dir Herbert Ross   *Prod* Herbert Ross   *Scr* Stephen Sondheim, Anthony Perkins   *Ph* Gerry Turpin   *Ed* Edward Warschilka   *Mus* Billy Goldenberg   *Art Dir* Ken Adam
● Richard Benjamin, Dyan Cannon, James Coburn, Joan Hackett, James Mason, Raquel Welch (Warner)

The Last of Sheila is a major disappointment. Result is far from the bloody *All About Eve* predicted and is simply a confused and cluttered demi *Sleuth*, grossly overwritten and underplayed.

Co-scripters Stephen Sondheim and Anthony Perkins are puzzle game fanatics, and the plot constructed for their first feature is self-indulgent camp at its most deadly.

The *Sheila* of the title is the luxury yacht named after the late wife of a Hollywood producer (James Coburn) killed by a hit-and-run driver shortly after exiting a raucous Beverly Hills party. A year later, Coburn asks six of those party guests for a week's Riviera cruise aboard the *Sheila*. Invitees include a glamorous Hollywood star (Raquel Welch), her business agent husband (Ian McShane), a fading director (James Mason), a struggling scriptwriter (Richard Benjamin), his wife (Joan Hackett) and an aggressive femme talent agent (Dyan Cannon).

On board, Coburn initiates a week-long game in which each guest is given a card indicating a secret which is to be discovered by the others. Since one of the cards reads 'I am a hit-and-run driver' the mystery concerns the person responsible for Sheila's demise.

Flashbacks, premature confessions and more murders flesh out the overlong running time. Cast is generally superior to the material with Cannon walking away with the honors as a recognizable femme talent packager with a vulgar, acid tongue.

● ●

■ LAST OF THE FINEST, THE

1990, 106 MINS, US ◇
Dir John Mackenzie   *Prod* John A. Davis   *Scr* Jere Cunningham, Thomas Lee Wright, George Armitage   *Ph* Juan Ruiz-Anchia   *Ed* Graham Walker   *Mus* Jack Nitzsche, Michael Hoenig   *Art Dir* Laurence G. Paull
● Brian Dennehy, Joe Pantoliano, Jeff Fahey, Bill Paxton, Deborra-Lee Furness, Guy Boyd (Davis/Orion)

The Last of the Finest belongs to a rarely attempted brand of pastiche film. The central characters are Brian Dennehy and his band of dedicated cops who tumble upon a bunch of corrupt characters (who parallel the Iran-Contra protagonists) while working on a drug bust.

Despite the deficiencies of a script that unwisely mixes tongue-in-cheek elements with soapbox messages, Scottish director John Mackenzie keeps the pic moving and enjoyable on a strictly thriller level. Its unsubtle references to Iran-Contra are more fun for film historians than action fans.

Dennehy is excellent in delivering a liberal message in the form of a free-thinking independent who's tired of the expediency and greed of a system riddled with phony patriots. Guy Boyd ably leads the group of Machiavellian villains and Aussie thesp Deborra-Lee Furness makes a good impression as Dennehy's wife.

....

■ LAST PICTURE SHOW, THE

1971, 118 MINS, US Ⓥ

Dir Peter Bogdanovich   *Prod* Stephen J. Friedman   *Scr* Larry McMurty, Peter Bogdanovich   *Ph* Robert Surtees   *Ed* Donn Cambern   *Art Dir* Walter Scott Herndon

● Timothy Bottoms, Jeff Bridges, Cybill Shepherd, Ben Johnson, Cloris Leachman, Ellen Burstyn (BBS)

Notre Dame professor Edward Fischer has said that 'the best films, like the best books, tell how it is to be human under certain circumstances'. Larry McMurtry did a beautiful job of this in his small novel (which he transferred to the screen), *The Last Picture Show.*

Timothy Bottoms and Jeff Bridges portray the pair of youths who complement each other's limited potential. Physically, they're much alike – football-playing, lanky, likable products of the Texas plains; mentally, or emotionally, they move on different planes. Bridges is the high school hero, more aggressive; Bottoms is the more sensitive, hence the more lonely, of the pair.

The boys grow a bit, some good people die, a few more secrets are revealed, and another 'nothing' decade has passed. Bridges, spurned by his girl, joins the army; Bottoms matures a bit. Not much else happens.

The best, most solid, most moving performances in the film are given by Ben Johnson, that old John Ford regular, as Sam The Lion, the owner of the picture show and pool room where the town boys spend most of their time; and Cloris Leachman as the football coach's wife, who introduces Bottoms to sex.

Peter Bogdanovich elected to shoot the film in black and white, artistically appropriate for the dust-blown, tired little community, but Robert Surtees (who's a master with color) doesn't bring off the tones of gray. There is excellent use of many pop tunes of the period and only introduced in a natural manner – a nickel in a jukebox, a car radio, or an early television set.

☐ 1971: Best Picture (Nomination)

....

■ LAST REMAKE OF BEAU GESTE, THE

1977, 84 MINS, US ◇ Ⓥ

Dir Marty Feldman   *Prod* William S. Gilmore   *Scr* Marty Feldman   *Ph* Gerry Fisher   *Ed* Jim Clark, Arthur Schmidt   *Mus* John Morris   *Art Dir* Brian Eatwell

● Ann-Margret, Marty Feldman, Michael York, Peter Ustinov, James Earl Jones, Trevor Howard (Universal)

Marty Feldman's directorial debut on *The Last Remake of Beau Geste* emerges as an often hilarious, if uneven, spoof of Foreign Legion adventure films. An excellent cast, top to bottom, gets the most out of the stronger scenes, and carries the weaker ones.

Feldman stars [in a story by him and Sam Bobrick] as the ugly duckling brother of Michael York (as Beau Geste), both adopted sons of Trevor Howard, an aging lech whose marriage to swinger Ann-Margret causes York to join the Foreign Legion and Feldman to serve time for alleged theft of a family gem.

Feldman joins York in the desert, where sadistic Peter Ustinov and bumbling Roy Kinnear run the garrison for urbane Henry Gibson, in the character of the Legion general.

■ LAST RUN, THE

1971, 92 MINS, US ◇ Ⓥ

Dir Richard Fleischer   *Prod* Carter de Haven   *Scr* Alan Sharp   *Ph* Sven Nykvist   *Ed* Russell Lloyd   *Mus* Jerry Goldsmith   *Art Dir* Roy Walker, Jose Maria Tapiador

● George C. Scott, Tony Musante, Trish Van Devere, Colleen Dewhurst (M-G-M)

The Last Run is a suspense melodrama with a set of criminal characters to keep action lively but its story line is so blurred by unexplained elements that it emerges little more than an ordinary actioner. George C. Scott gives certain authority to a hardhitting role.

Produced in Spain by Carter De Haven and directed by Richard Fleischer, taking over from John Huston, who ankled the assignment, film gains in pictorial interest from constant shrewd use of colorful backgrounds. Original screenplay by Alan Sharp is designed as a saga of a man on the run after his escape from a prison van, and an old hand directing this flight. What comes out on screen militates against ready acceptance of this premise due to haphazard writing.

Scott plays a retired American mobster who once drove for criminals in fast getaways. He returns to activity after nine years to aid an escaped con and whisk him across the Spanish border into France. It's all pretty fuzzy and audience is at a loss to understand the whys and wherefores of the action.

....

■ LAST STARFIGHTER, THE

1984, 100 MINS, US ◇ Ⓥ

Dir Nick Castle   *Prod* Gary Adelson, Edward O. Denault   *Scr* Jonathan Betuel   *Ph* King Baggot   *Ed* C. Timothy O'Meara   *Mus* Craig Safan   *Art Dir* Ron Cobb

● Lance Guest, Robert Preston, Dan O'Herlihy, Catherine Mary Stewart, Barbara Bosson, Norman Snow (Universal/Lorimar)

With *The Last Starfighter*, director Nick Castle and writer Jonathan Betuel have done something so simple it's almost awe-inspiring: they've taken a very human story and accented it with sci-fi special effects, rather than the other way around.

Lance Guest is a teenager with a talent for a lone video game that was somehow dropped off at his mother's rundown, remote trailer park when it should have been delivered to Las Vegas. And when he breaks the record for destroying alien invaders, Guest not only excites the whole trailer park, he attracts a visit from Robert Preston.

There is never a moment that all of this doesn't seem quite possible, accompanied by plenty of building questions about what's going to happen next.

....

■ LAST SUMMER

1969, 97 MINS, US ◇ Ⓥ

Dir Frank Perry   *Prod* Frank Perry   *Scr* Eleanor Perry   *Ph* Gerald Hirschfeld   *Ed* Sidney Katz   *Mus* John Simon

● Barbara Hershey, Richard Thomas, Bruce Davison, Cathy Burns (Allied Artists/Alsid)

A solid insight into a quartet during a summer that also has fine acting and sensitive direction and writing.

A pretty, vivacious, headstrong girl finds a dying sea gull on the beach. She beseeches two youths to help her. They remove a hook from its throat and the three become friends.

The boys are expertly played by Bruce Davison and Richard Thomas, and Cathy Burns is engaging and touching as the lonely, homely little girl, drawn to those more emancipated friends, but finally appalled by their cowardice and cruelty, only to be the victim of their pent-up inarticulate needs.

Nicely hued, film has a frankness that is not forced and Eleanor Perry's dialog, if sometimes taking precedence over more visual revelations, is just and makes a statement about fairly-affluent youth.

....

■ LAST TANGO IN PARIS

1972, 130 MINS, ITALY, FRANCE ◇ Ⓥ

Dir Bernardo Bertolucci   *Prod* Alberto Grimaldi   *Scr* Bernardo Bertolucci, Franco Arcalli   *Ph* Vittorio Storaro   *Ed* Franco Arcalli   *Mus* Gato Barbieri   *Art Dir* Ferdinando Scarfiotti

● Marlon Brando, Maria Schneider, Darling Legitmus, Jean-Pierre Leaud, Massimo Girotti, Laura Betti (PEA/Artistes Associes)

Bernardo Bertolucci's *Last Tango in Paris* is an uneven, convoluted, certainly dispute-provoking study of sexual passion in which Marlon Brando gives a truly remarkable performance.

Brando plays an aging Lothario trailing the debris of a failed life who has wound up in Paris married to an unfaithful hotelkeeper. Pic opens on the day of his wife's suicide when the distraught Brando meets a young girl (Maria Schneider) while both are inspecting a vacant apartment. After a sudden, almost savage sexual encounter, Brando proposes that they meet in the apartment on a regular basis. Brando insists that no names or personal information be exchanged, that the affair remain purely carnal.

Plot has all the ingredients of a 1940s meller. Bertolucci uses it to explore the psyche of a man at the end of his emotional and sexual tether and at the same time to investigate on the most primitive level the chemistry of romantic love.

Schneider is standout as the girl, a difficult role played semi-tart, but one whose motivations remain cloudy through the murderous finale.

....

■ LAST TEMPTATION OF CHRIST, THE

1988, 164 MINS, US ◇ Ⓥ

Dir Martin Scorsese   *Prod* Barbara De Fina   *Scr* Paul Schrader   *Ph* Michael Ballhaus   *Ed* Thelma Schoonmaker   *Mus* Peter Gabriel   *Art Dir* John Beard

● Willem Dafoe, Harvey Keitel, Barbara Hershey, Harry Dean Stanton, David Bowie, Verna Bloom (Universal/Cineplex Odeon)

A film of challenging ideas, and not salacious provocations, *The Last Temptation of Christ* is a powerful and very modern reinterpretation of Jesus as a man wracked with anguish and doubt concerning his appointed role in life. Pic was lensed on Moroccan locations for a highly restrictive $6.5 million.

As a written prolog simply states, *Last Temptation* aims to be a 'fictional exploration of the eternal spiritual conflict,' 'the battle between the spirit and the flesh,' as Nikos Kazantzakis summarized the theme of his novel.

After rescuing Mary Magdalene from the stone-throwers, Jesus tentatively launches his career as religious leader. But only after his return from the desert and his hallucinatory exposure to representations of good and evil, is he transformed into a warrior against Satan, finally convinced he is the son of God.

Blondish and blue-eyed in the Anglo-Saxon tradition, Willem Dafoe offers an utterly compelling reading of his character. Harvey Keitel puts across Judas' fierceness and loyalty, and only occasionally lets a New York accent and mannered modernism detract from total believability.

Barbara Hershey, adorned with tattoos, is an extremely physical, impassioned Mary Magdalene. One could have used more of David Bowie's subdued, rational Pontius Pilate.

....

■ LAST TYCOON, THE

1976, 122 MINS, US ◇ Ⓥ

Dir Elia Kazan   *Prod* Sam Spiegel   *Scr* Harold Pinter   *Ph* Victor Kemper   *Ed* Richard Marks   *Mus* Maurice Jarre   *Art Dir* Gene Callahan

● Robert De Niro, Tony Curtis, Robert Mitchum,

Jeanne Moreau, Jack Nicholson, Donald Pleasence (Paramount)

The Last Tycoon is a handsome and lethargic film, based on F. Scott Fitzgerald's unfinished Hollywood novel of the 1930s, as adapted by Harold Pinter. Producer Sam Spiegel's contribution is admirable, but Elia Kazan's direction of the Pinter plot seems unfocussed though craftsmanlike. Robert De Niro's performance as the inscrutable boy-wonder of films is mildly intriguing.

In an apparent attempt to avoid making a nostalgia film, the few choice bits of environmental interest emerge mostly as awkward interruptions in the main plot.

Ingrid Boulting is the elusive charmer who penetrates somewhat into De Niro's interior, but since her own expressions are limited in scope, we don't really know what she finds there. So, too, Theresa Russell, as Robert Mitchum's daughter, tries for De Niro, but at least she emerges as perhaps the only credible principal character in the piece.

■ LAST UNICORN, THE

1982, 84 MINS, US ◇ ▽
Dir Arthur Rankin Jr, Jules Bass *Prod* Arthur Rankin Jr, Jules Bass *Scr* Peter S. Beagle *Ph* Hiroyasu Omoto *Ed* Tomoko Kida *Mus* Jimmy Webb *Art Dir* Arthur Rankin Jr.
● (Rankin-Bass/ITC)

The Last Unicorn represents a rare example of an animated kids' pic in which the script and vocal performances outshine the visuals.

Quest framework provided by Peter S. Beagle's adaptation of his own novel ideally serves an animated musical film's need to introduce an assortment of colorful characters who can deliver specialty numbers. Continuing thread is the search of the fabled last unicorn, in this case a beautiful white mare, for the rest of her breed, which has reportedly been vanquished by the terrible red bull.

However vapid the unicorn may appear to the eye, Mia Farrow's voice brings an almost moving plaintive quality to the character which sees the entire film through. Alan Arkin also scores as the bumbling magician, as do Christopher Lee as the evil king and, in a show-stopping turn, Paul Frees as a peg-legged, eye-patched cat.

■ LAST VALLEY, THE

1971, 125 MINS, UK/US ◇ ▽
Dir James Clavell *Prod* James Clavell *Scr* James Clavell *Ph* John Wilcox *Ed* John Bloom *Mus* John Barry *Art Dir* Peter Mullins
● Michael Caine, Omar Sharif, Florinda Bolkan, Nigel Davenport, Per Oscarsson, Arthur O'Connell (ABC/Season)

The Last Valley is a disappointing 17th-century period melodrama about the fluid and violent loyalties attendant on major civil upheaval. Shot handsomely abroad for about $6 million and top-featuring Michael Caine and Omar Sharif in strong performances, James Clavell's film emerges as heavy cinematic grand opera in tab version format, too literal in historical detail to suggest artfully the allegories intended and, paradoxically, too allegorical to make clear the actual reality of the Thirty Years War.

Clavell adapted a J.B. Pick novel in which Sharif, neither peasant nor nobleman, is fleeing the ravages of war and finds a valley still spared from cross-devastation. Caine, hard-bitten leader of mercenaries, also discovers the locale. At Sharif's urging Caine decides to live in peace for the winter with the residents, headed by Nigel Davenport and an uneasy truce develops.

The fatuous political and religious and social rationalizations of behavior get full exposition. But the whole entity doesn't play

well together as Clavell's script often halts for declamations.

■ LAST WALTZ, THE

1978, 115 MINS, US ◇ ▽
Dir Martin Scorsese *Prod* Robbie Robertson *Ph* Michael Chapman, Laszlo Kovacs, Vilmos Zsigmond, David Myers, Bobby Byrne, Michael Watkins, Hiro Narita *Ed* Yeu-Bun Lee, Jan Roblee *Art Dir* Boris Leven
● Bob Dylan, Joni Mitchell, Neil Diamond, Van Morrison, Eric Clapton, The Band (United Artists)

The Last Waltz is an outstanding rock documentary of the last concert by The Band on Thanksgiving 1976 at Winterland in San Francisco.

By itself The Band performs 12 numbers. The group backs up guest artists on another dozen. They include Ronnie Hawkins, Dr. John, Neil Young, the Staples, Neil Diamond, Joni Mitchell, Paul Butterfield, Muddy Waters, Eric Clapton, Emmylou Harris, Van Morrison, Bob Dylan, Ringo Starr and Ron Wood.

Director Martin Scorsese has succeeded on a number of fronts. First, he recognized that this concert deserved cinematic preservation. The Band was an important and intelligent force in rock music on its own and as a backup group for Bob Dylan and Ronnie Hawkins.

This film is a chronicle of one important group very much a part of the music of the late 1960s and 1970s and it's also a commentary on those times. It's 90% concert film and 10% history. Unlike so many of their colleagues, the members of The Band are competent musicians and spokesmen.

■ LAST WAVE, THE

1977, 106 MINS, AUSTRALIA ◇ ▽
Dir Peter Weir *Scr* Tony Morphett, Petru Popescu, Peter Weir *Ph* Russell Boyd *Ed* Max Lemon *Mus* Charles Wain
● Richard Chamberlain, Olivia Hamnett, David Gulpilil, Frederick Parslow, Nandjiwarra Amagula (Ayer/SAFC/AFC)

Australian director Peter Weir's film about the possibility of a coming tidal wave that may destroy the country or the world. Richard Chamberlain is highly effective as a young lawyer caught up in a case of an aborigine murdered by some others in town.

The lawyer has strange dreams that involve one of the accused men trying to give him some sort of sacred stone. He takes their case and tries to insist it was tribal but the man he has dreamed of, who at first tries to help him, begs off when an old patriarch seems to exert power on him.

Film builds, and though it sometimes falters in narrative, picks up again as Chamberlain turns out to be a sort of psychic member of a mysterious people who supposedly came to Australia long ago and disappeared.

■ LAST WINTER, THE

1990, 103 MINS, CANADA ◇
Dir Aaron Kim Johnston *Prod* Jack Clements, Ken Rodeck, Joe MacDonald, Ches Yetman *Scr* Aaron Kim Johnston *Ph* Ian Elkin *Ed* Lara Mazur *Mus* Victor Davies *Art Dir* Perri Gorrare
● Gerard Parkes, Joshua Murray, David Ferry, Wanda Cannon (Rode/Aaron/NFBC)

This vivid, imaginative tale of a Manitoba farmboy's coming of age captures a uniquely Canadian heartland experience. Writer-director Aaron Kim Johnson has crafted a tribute to his childhood in a tale seen through the eyes of a 10-year-old Will (Joshua Murray) as he resists his family's move to the city.

Beset with growing pains and upset by the prospect of being uprooted, Will creates a

fantasy shield between himself and reality, hallucinating a white horse named Winter who charges across the farmland bearing some mysterious message. His closest ties are to his Grampa Jack (Gerard Parkes) and his cousin Kate, whom he's in love with.

The overwhelming presence of the land and weather are captured in Ian Elkin's clean, crisp photography, and the winter storms and snowdrifts painstakingly evoked by the art department. Johnston draws lovely performances from the children, especially Murray. Parkes forges a convincing link with the young actor as his elderly confidant.

■ LATE SHOW, THE

1977, 94 MINS, US ◇ ▽
Dir Robert Benton *Prod* Robert Altman *Scr* Robert Benton *Ph* Chuck Rosher *Ed* Lou Lombardo *Mus* Kenn Wannberg *Art Dir* Bob Gould
● Art Carney, Lily Tomlin, Bill Macy, Eugene Roche, Joanna Cassidy, John Considine (Warner)

Art Carney and Lily Tomlin make an arresting screen duo in *The Late Show*, a modest meller and a tribute to the private eye yarns of the 1940s.

The process has given Carney and Tomlin the freedom to create two extremely sympathetic characters. Both performances are knockout.

Carney plays an aging private detective trying to maintain his dignity while scratching out a living on the sordid underbelly of Los Angeles. When his onetime partner (Howard Duff in an opening cameo) is murdered, Carney, in the best Sam Spade tradition, vows to get the killer.

The trail begins with Tomlin whose stolen cat Duff had been hired to find. Top-heavy plot unwinds with the usual potboiler ingredients – blackmail, murder, philandering wives and double-cross.

■ LAUGHTER IN PARADISE

1951, 94 MINS, UK
Dir Mario Zampi *Prod* Mario Zampi *Scr* Michael Pertwee, Jack Davies *Ph* William McLeod *Ed* Giulio Zampi *Mus* Stanley Black *Art Dir* Ivan King
● Alastair Sim, Fay Compton, Guy Middleton, George Cole, Hugh Griffith, Ernest Thesiger (Associated British)

Producer-director Mario Zampi very nearly succeeds in bringing off an outstanding comedy with *Laughter in Paradise*. Plot describes what happens after a practical joker leaves $140,000 to each of four relatives provided they fulfill certain stipulated conditions.

His sister (Fay Compton), who has always been tough on housemaids, has to hold a job as a domestic for 28 days. A cousin (Alastair Sim), who secretly writes trashy thrillers, has to get himself sentenced to 28 days in jail. A distant relative (George Cole), a timid bank clerk, has to hold up his bank manager, while another relation (Guy Middleton), who is something of a philanderer, has to marry the first single girl he meets.

The plum comedy part is undoubtedly Sim's, his endeavors to land in jail being loaded with chuckles.

■ LAUGHTER IN THE DARK

1969, 101 MINS, UK/FRANCE ◇
Dir Tony Richardson *Prod* Neil Harley *Scr* Edward Bond *Ph* Dick Bush *Ed* Charles Rees *Art Dir* Julia Oman
● Nicol Williamson, Anna Karina, Jean-Claude Drouot, Sheila Burrell, Sian Phillips, Kate O'Toole (Gershwin-Kastner/Marceau/Woodfall)

Fascinating attempt to transpose the Nabokov novel to the screen. Director Tony Richardson is able to capture the novel's profound human insights, and, as in *Lolita*, the compulsions and perversities that for Nabokov are the very stuff of the psyche.

The intricate story centers on a wealthy, titled young art dealer, Edward (Nicol Williamson) who is attracted to usherette Margot (Anna Karina), continues to return to the theatre and finally arranges to meet her.

Richardson's direction ranges from brilliantly evocative to confusing. During some of the most humorous scenes one suspects Richardson is actually serious.

Williamson, who replaced Richard Burton in the lead role, is the perfect physical type and so good as to be almost difficult to watch. Both Karina and Drouot are also excellent.

• •

■ **LAURA**

1944, 88 MINS, US ⓥ

Dir Otto Preminger *Prod* Otto Preminger *Scr* Jay Dratler, Betty Reinhardt, Samuel Hoffenstein *Ph* Joseph LaShelle *Ed* Louis Loeffler *Mus* David Raksin *Art Dir* Lyle R. Wheeler, Leland Fuller
● Gene Tierney, Dana Andrews, Clifton Webb, Vincent Price, Judith Anderson, Dorothy Adams (20th Century-Fox)

The film's deceptively leisurely pace at the start, and its light, careless air, only heighten the suspense without the audience being conscious of the buildup. What they are aware of as they follow the story [from the novel by Vera Caspary] is the skill in the telling. Situations neatly dovetail and are always credible. Developments, surprising as they come, are logical. The dialog is honest, real and adult.

The yarn concerns an attractive femme art executive who has been brutally murdered in her New York apartment, and the attempts of a police lieutenant to solve the case. Beginning by interviewing the girl's intimates, the sleuth's trail leads him from one friend to another, all becoming suspect in the process.

Clifton Webb makes a debonair critic-columnist. Dana Andrews' intelligent, reticent performance as the lieutenant gives the lie to detectives as caricatures. Gene Tierney makes an appealing figure as the art executive and Vincent Price is convincing as a weak-willed ne'er-do-well.

• •

■ **LAVENDER HILL MOB, THE**

1951, 81 MINS, UK ⓥ

Dir Charles Crichton *Prod* Michael Balcon, Michael Truman *Scr* T.E.B. Clarke *Ph* Douglas Slocombe *Ed* Seth Holt *Mus* Georges Auric *Art Dir* William Kellner
● Alec Guinness, Stanley Holloway, Sidney James, Alfie Bass, Marjorie Fielding, Ronald Adam (Ealing)

With *The Lavender Hill Mob*, Ealing clicks with another comedy winner.

Story is notable for allowing Alec Guinness to play another of his w.k. character roles. This time, he is the timid escort of bullion from the refineries to the vaults. For 20 years he has been within sight of a fortune, but smuggling gold bars out of the country is a tough proposition. Eventually, with three accomplices, he plans the perfect crime. Bullion worth over £1 million is made into souvenir models of the Eiffel Tower and shipped to France.

One of the comedy highspots of the film is a scene at a police exhibition where Guinness and his principal accomplice (Stanley Holloway) first become suspect. They break out of the cordon, steal a police car, and then radio phony messages through headquarters. This sequence and the other action scenes are crisply handled, with a light touch.

Guinness, as usual, shines as the trusted escort, and is at his best as the mastermind plotting the intricate details of the crime. Holloway is an excellent aide, while the two

professional crooks in the gang (Sidney James and Alfie Bass) complete the quartet with an abundance of cockney humor.

• •

■ **LAWLESS BREED, THE**

1952, 83 MINS, US ◇

Dir Raoul Walsh *Prod* William Alland *Scr* Bernard Gordon *Ph* Irving Glassberg *Ed* Frank Gross *Art Dir* Bernard Herzbrun, Richard H. Riedel
● Rock Hudson, Julie Adams, Mary Castle, John McIntire, Hugh O'Brian, Dennis Weaver (Universal)

Early-west gunman, John Wesley Hardin, has his life put on film in *The Lawless Breed*. Presumably based on Hardin's actual story of his career, published when he was released from a Texas prison after serving 16 years for killing a law man, the production has plenty of robust action stirred up by Raoul Walsh's direction.

The plot unfolds episodically and swiftly, telling how Hardin earned his reputation as a killer after getting his first victim in self defense, goes on the lam from the law and vengeance-seeking kinfolks, is forced into more killings, loses his sweetheart (Mary Castle) to a posse's bullets and acquires a new one in Julie Adams, the girl who later becomes his wife.

Rock Hudson does a very good job of the main character, and Adams makes much of her femme lead. John McIntire scores in dual roles, one as Hardin's overly-righteous, preacher father, and the other as the gunman's uncle.

• •

■ **LAWMAN**

1971, 98 MINS, UK ◇

Dir Michael Winner *Prod* Michael Winner *Scr* Gerald Wilson *Ph* Bob Paynter *Ed* Freddie Wilson *Mus* Jerry Fielding *Art Dir* Stan Jolley
● Burt Lancaster, Robert Ryan, Lee J. Cobb, Sheree North, Joseph Wiseman, Robert Duvall (Scimitar)

Michael Winner, an exuberant British director, led with his chin in deciding to go to the States (Mexico) to make a western – his first.

Burt Lancaster, with cold eyes, strong chin, stiff behavior, minimal talk and a swift line on the draw, plays a marshall so dedicated to being a lawman that he is inflexible and even arrogant in his intepretation of it. He rides into a nearby town to pick up a bunch of locals who, on a drunken spree, were responsible for the death of an old man. He finds that they all work for the local bossman, played by Lee J. Cobb. Cobb's a guy who enjoys local power but hates violence. Robert Ryan is the town's weak marshal, who in the end is swayed to action with Lancaster.

Point of the story is just how far a man can compromise with his conscience and whether the end justifies the means.

Lancaster, as usual, is a highly convincing marshal, tough and taciturn. Ryan is also excellent as the faded, weak marshal with only memories. But it's Cobb who quietly steals the film as the local boss who, however, unlike in many such films, is no ruthless villain.

• •

■ **LAWRENCE OF ARABIA**

1962, 222 MINS (1989: 216 MINS), UK ◇ ⓥ

Dir David Lean *Prod* Sam Spiegel *Scr* Robert Bolt *Ph* Frederick A. Young *Ed* Anne V. Coates *Mus* Maurice Jarre *Art Dir* John Box, John Stoll
● Peter O'Toole, Alec Guinness, Anthony Quinn, Jack Hawkins, Omar Sharif, Anthony Quayle (Horizon)

Some $15 million, around three years in time, much hardship, and incredible logistics have been poured into this kingsize adventure yarn. Made in Technicolor and Super Panavision 70 it is a sweepingly produced, directed and lensed job. Authentic desert lo-

cations, a stellar cast and an intriguing subject combine to put this into the blockbuster league.

It had best be regarded as an adventure story rather than a biopic, because Robert Bolt's well written screenplay does not tell the audience anything much new about Lawrence of Arabia, nor does it offer any opinion or theory about the character of this man or the motivation for his actions. So he remains a legendary figure and a shadowy one. Another cavil is that clearly so much footage has had to be tossed away that certain scenes are not developed as well as they might have been, particularly the ending. Storyline concerns Lawrence as a young intelligence officer in Cairo in 1916. British Intelligence is watching the Arab revolt against the Turks with interest as a possible buffer between Turkey and her German allies. Lawrence (Peter O'Toole) is grudgingly seconded to observe the revolt at the request of the civilian head of the Arab bureau. Lawrence sets out to find Prince Feisal, top man of the revolt. From then on his incredible adventures begin.

He persuades Feisal to let him lead his troops as guerrilla warriors. He tackles inter-tribal warfare but still they arduously take the Turkish port of Aqaba. Lawrence is given the task of helping the Arabs to achieve independence and he becomes a kind of desert Scarlet Pimpernel. He reaches Deraa before the British Army is in Jerusalem, he is captured by the Turks, tortured and emerges a shaken, broken and disillusioned man. Yet still he takes on the job of leading a force to Damascus.

Lean and cameraman F.A. Young have brought out the loneliness and pitiless torment of the desert with an artistic use of color and with almost every frame superbly mounted. Maurice Jarre's musical score is always contributory to the mood of the film.

Peter O'Toole, after three or four smallish, but effective, appearances in films, makes a striking job of the complicated and heavy role of Lawrence. His veiled insolence and contempt of high authority, his keen intelligence and insight, his gradual simpatico with the Arabs and their way of life, his independence, courage, flashy vanity, withdrawn moments, pain, loneliness, fanaticism, idealism and occasional foolishness.

Jack Hawkins plays General Allenby with confidence and understanding and Arthur Kennedy provides a sharp portrayal of a cynical, tough American newspaperman. The two top support performances come from Alec Guinness as Prince Feisal and Anthony Quayle as a stereotyped, honest, bewildered staff officer. Only Anthony Quinn, as a larger-than-life, proud, intolerant Arab chief seems to obtrude overmuch and tends to turn the performance into something out of the Arabian Nights.

□ 1962: Best Picture

• •

■ **LE MANS**

1971, 108 MINS, US ◇

Dir Lee H. Katzin, [John Sturges] *Prod* Jack N. Reddish *Scr* Harry Kleiner *Ph* Robert B. Hauser, Rene Guissart Jr *Ed* Donald W. Ernst *Mus* Michel Legrand
● Steve McQueen, Siegfried Rauch, Elga Andersen, Ronald Leigh-Hunt (Solar/Cinema Center)

Marked by some spectacular car-racing footage, *Le Mans* is a successful attempt to escape the pot-boiler of prior films on same subject. The solution was to establish a documentary mood. Steve McQueen stars (and races).

Filmed abroad on actual French locales, the project began under director John Sturges. Creative incompatibilities brought McQueen, his Solar Prods indie, and Cinema Center Films to the mat, and as the dust settled Sturges was out and Lee H. Katzin finished the film and gets solo screen credit.

The spare script finds McQueen returning to compete in the famed car race a year after he has been injured. Elga Andersen, wife of a driver killed in the same accident, also returns, somewhat the worse for emotional wear. Siegfried Rauch is McQueen's continuing rival in racing competition.

The film establishes its mood through some outstanding use of slow motion, multiple-frame printing, freezes, and a most artistic use of sound – including at times no sound. The outstanding racing footage not only enhances the effects, but stands proudly on its own feet in straight continuity.

■ **LEAGUE OF GENTLEMEN, THE**

1960, 116 MINS, UK ⓥ
Dir Basil Dearden *Prod* Michael Relph, Basil Dearden *Scr* Bryan Forbes *Ph* Arthur Ibbetson *Ed* John Guthridge *Mus* Philip Green
● Jack Hawkins, Nigel Patrick, Roger Livesey, Richard Attenborough, Bryan Forbes, Kieron Moore (Allied Film Makers)

The first entry from Allied film Makers – consisting of actors Jack Hawkins, Richard Attenborough and Bryan Forbes, producer Michael Relph and director Basil Dearden – is a smooth piece of teamwork.

Hawkins, disgruntled at being axed from the army which he has faithfully served for many years, decides to have a go at a bank robbery. He picks up the idea from an American thriller and recruits seven broke and shady ex-officers, all experts in their own line in the army. The gang goes into hiding while every phase of the operation is planned down to the last detail. As a military exploit, the entire gang would have earned medals. As it is pulled off they are eventually tripped up by a slight, unforeseen happening.

Forbes has written a strong, witty screenplay from John Boland's novel. It takes time to get under way, but once the gang is formed, the situations pile up to an exciting and funny finale. Dearden's direction is sure and Arthur Ibbetson has turned in some excellent camerawork. The eight members of the gang all give smooth, plausible performances, with Hawkins and Patrick, as his second-in-command, having the meatiest roles.

■ **LEARNING TREE, THE**

1969, 106 MINS, US ◇ ⓥ
Dir Gordon Parks *Prod* Gordon Parks *Scr* Gordon Parks *Ph* Burnett Guffey *Ed* George R. Rohrs *Mus* Gordon Parks *Art Dir* Ed Engoron
● Kyle Johnson, Alex Clarke, Estelle Evans, Dana Eclar, Mira Waters (Warner/Seven Arts)

The Learning Tree is a sentimental, sometimes awkward, but ultimately moving film about the growing-up of a black teenager in rural Kansas during the 1920s. It is, apparently, the first film financed by a major company to be directed by a Negro.

Film recounts, in short, episodic passages, how a talented and perceptive 15-year-old boy learns about life from a variety of characters, situations and personal encounters.

The worst moments occur when director Gordon Parks interpolates small sermonettes. Also, the film cannot quite carry the large helping of melodrama which occurs near the end. But on the whole this is an impressive, strong film. The 1963 novel of his on which it is based is purportedly semi-autobiographical.

■ **LEATHER BOYS, THE**

1964, 108 MINS, UK ⓥ
Dir Sidney J. Furie *Prod* Raymond Stross *Scr* Gillian Freeman *Ph* Gerry Gibbs *Ed* Reginald Beck *Mus* Bill McGuffie *Art Dir* Arthur Lawson

● Rita Tushingham, Colin Campbell, Dudley Sutton, Gladys Henson, Avice Landon, Betty Marsden (British Lion/Garrick)

Main theme is the doomed marriage of a couple of immature kids. Reggie (Colin Campbell), who spends a riotous leisure as a motorcyclist, hitches up with Dot (Rita Tushingham), who sees the union as a release from parental control.

The crackup comes when Dot turns out an incompetent wife, chary of making beds and relying on a daily diet of canned beans. This dampens Reggie's sex urge and he departs to live with grandma and takes up with a 'buddy' called Peter (Dudley Sutton).

Despite Pete's insistent affection, his reluctance to associate with girls, and his housekeeping ability. Reggie does not wise up to the fact that he's a homosexual. As the audience gets the drift early, this somewhat punctures the plot.

Virtues of the pic lie in Sidney Furie's direction and in the two male performances. Furie has a sharp eye for sleazy detail, and he uses the underprivileged backgrounds to telling visual effect. Gillian Freeman's screenplay, culled from a novel by Eliot George, is also capable in its ear for verbal mannerisms, but it doesn't give coherence to the characters. Little sympathy can be stirred up for any of them.

Dudley Sutton, however, registers strongly as the spry, loyal Pete.

■ **LEAVE ALL FAIR**

1985, 88 MINS, NEW ZEALAND ◇
Dir John Reid *Prod* John O'Shea *Scr* Stanley Harper, Maurice Pons, Jean Betts, John Reid *Ph* Bernard Lutic *Ed* Ian John *Mus* Stephen McCurdy *Art Dir* Joe Bleakley
● John Gielgud, Jane Birkin, Feodor Atkine, Simon Ward (Pacific/Goldeneye/Challenge)

Lensed entirely in France, this elegiac story about the husband of New Zealand writer Katherine Mansfield, who died in 1922 while returning to places where they'd lived together to oversee the publishing of a book based on her letters to him, is a sober, affecting experience.

John Gielgud, playing another elderly man of letters, returns to France to meet his publisher (Feodor Atkine). The trip brings back memories of his life with Mansfield (Jane Birkin), memories made more painful when he meets Atkine's mistress, Marie (also played by Birkin), who not only resembles his long-dead wife, but is also a New Zealander.

Lushly photographed pic is as gentle and nuanced as Mansfield's own writings, and the scenes between Gielgud and Birkin play with subtlety and insight.

■ **LEFT HAND OF GOD, THE**

1955, 87 MINS, US ◇ ⓥ
Dir Edward Dmytryk *Prod* Buddy Adler *Scr* Alfred Hayes *Ph* Franz Planer *Ed* Dorothy Spencer *Mus* Victor Young *Art Dir* Lyle Wheeler, Maurice Ransford
● Humphrey Bogart, Gene Tierney, Lee J. Cobb, Agnes Moorehead, E.G. Marshall, Carl Benton Reid (20th Century-Fox)

Based on the novel by William E. Barrett, the film is somewhat provocative, in that its central character is a man who masquerades as a priest. Carrying on this deception is Yank flier Humphrey Bogart, who believes it to be the sole way he can escape as prisoner of Chinese warlord Lee J. Cobb.

What transpires in a remote Chinese province after Bogart dons the ecclesiastical robes in 1947 largely adds up to character studies of the fake priest and his immediate

colleagues at a Catholic mission, where all are stationed. For the drama and suspense aren't to be found in whether the flier escapes from China but in the soul-searching he subjects himself in continuing the masquerade.

Besides Bogart, others who have their own mental conflicts are Gene Tierney, E.G. Marshall, and Agnes Moorehead.

■ **LEFT-HANDED GUN, THE**

1958, 105 MINS, US
Dir Arthur Penn *Prod* Fred Coe *Scr* Leslie Stevens *Ph* J. Peverell Marley *Ed* Folmar Blangsted *Mus* Alexander Courage *Art Dir* Art Loel
● Paul Newman, Lita Milan, Hurd Hatfield, James Congdon, James Best, John Dehner (Warner)

The Left-Handed Gun is another look at Billy the Kid, probably America's most constantly celebrated juvenile delinquent. In this version he's Billy, the crazy, mixed-up Kid. The picture is a smart and exciting western paced by Paul Newman's intense portrayal.

The screenplay is based on a [1955] teleplay by Gore Vidal called *The Death of Billy the Kid*. The action is concerned with the few events that led up to the slaying of the Brooklyn boy by lawman Pat Garrett. Stevens emphasizes the youthful nature of the desperado by giving him two equally young companions, James Best and James Congdon. The three team after Newman's mentor, cattleman Colin Keith-Johnston, is shot by a crooked officer of the law. Newman is determined to avenge the cattleman's death, and the plot becomes a crazed crusade in which Newman, Best and Congdon are all killed, the death of a badman and the birth of a legend.

The best parts of the film are the moments of hysterical excitement as the three young desperados rough-house with each other as feckless as any innocent boys and in the next instant turn to deadly killing without flicking a curly eyelash.

In his first picture, director Arthur Penn shows himself in command of the medium. Newman dominates but there are excellent performances from others, including Lita Milan in a dimly-seen role as his Mexican girl friend, John Dehner as the remorseless Pat Garrett, and Hurd Hatfield, a mysterious commentator on events.

■ **LEGACY, THE**

1979, 100 MINS, US ◇ ⓥ
Dir Richard Marquand *Prod* David Foster *Scr* Jimmy Sangster, Patric Tilley, Paul Wheeler *Ph* Dick Bush, Alan Hume *Ed* Anne V. Coates *Mus* Michael J. Lewis *Art Dir* Disley Jones
● Katharine Ross, Sam Elliott, Hildegarde Neill, Roger Daltrey, John Standing, Charles Gray (Universal/Turman-Foster)

Using the hoary convention of stranding a young couple in the mansion of a reclusive millionaire whose guests are progressively bumped off in an assortment of gruesome ways, *The Legacy* tries for an added dimension of satanic possession, but winds up a tame, suspenseless victim of its own lack of imagination.

Katharine Ross and Sam Elliott play the Yank couple, a pair of architects mysteriously summoned for an assignment in England. When they're accidentally forced off a country road by a chauffeured Rolls, owner John Standing invites them back for 'tea'. They find themselves trapped in the house for the weekend.

The film, directed with no tension or suspenseful pacing by former TV director Richard Marquand, takes an eternity to get down to business.

■ LEGAL EAGLES

1986, 114 MINS, US ◇ Ⓥ

Dir Ivan Reitman *Prod* Ivan Reitman *Scr* Jim Cash,
Jack Epps Jr. *Ph* Laszlo Kovacs *Ed* Sheldon Kahn,
Pem Herring, William Gordean *Mus* Elmer Bernstein
Art Dir John DeCuir

● Robert Redford, Debra Winger, Daryl Hannah, Brian
Dennehy, Terence Stamp, Steven Hill (Northern Lights)

Loss of intrigue with a scattered plot involving art fraud and murder is made up for by
an often witty, albeit lightweight dialog led
by the ever-boyish star Robert Redford.

Lavish production opens with charmer
Redford as one of the d.a.'s office's winnin-
gest attorneys, Tom Logan, assigned to prosecute the daughter of a famous artist for
trying to steal one of her dead father's
paintings.

He faces the opposing counsel of Laura
Kelly (Debra Winger), a court-appointed
defense attorney known for daffy courtroom
antics to get her clients off.

It's when the burglary charges are suddenly dropped against the unbalanced defendant Chelsea Deardon (Daryl Hannah) that
he decides to go over to Winger's side to discover why.

Winger and Redford work well as an attorney team, but in true yuppie form become
more friends attracted by each others' professional acumen than by each other's bodies.

■ LEGEND

1985, 94 MINS, US ◇ Ⓥ

Dir Ridley Scott *Prod* Arnon Milchan *Scr* William
Hjortsberg *Ph* Alex Thomson *Ed* Terry Rawlings
Mus Jerry Goldsmith [US version: Tangerine Dream]
Art Dir Assheton Gorton

● Tom Cruise, Mia Sara, Tim Curry, David Bennent,
Alice Playten, Billy Barty (Legend/20th Century-Fox)

Legend is a fairytale produced on a grand
scale, set in some timeless world and peopled
with fairies, elves and goblins, plus a spectacularly satisfying Satan. At the same time, the
basic premise is alarmingly thin, a compendium of any number of ancient fairytales.

Plot concerns a heroic young peasant, Jack,
who takes his sweetheart, Princess Lili, to see
the most powerful creatures on earth, the last
surviving unicorns. Unknown to the young
lovers, Darkness (i.e. The Devil) is using the
innocence of Lili as a bait to trap and emas-
culate the unicorns.

Kids of all ages should be entranced by the
magnificent make-up effects of Rob Bottin
and his crew, from the smallest elves to the
giant Darkness. The latter is unquestionably
the most impressive depiction of Satan ever
brought to the screen. Tim Curry plays him
majestically with huge horns, cloved feet, red
leathery flesh and yellow eyes, plus a res-
onantly booming voice.

Also registering strongly is David Bennent
as a knowing pixie with large, pointed ears.

Ironically, for a film that celebrates nature,
Legend was almost entirely lensed on the large
Bond set at Pinewood (production was inter-
rupted by a fire which destroyed the set).

■ LEGEND OF HELL HOUSE, THE

1973, 94 MINS, UK ◇ Ⓥ

Dir John Hough *Prod* Albert Fennell, Norman T.
Herman *Scr* Richard Matheson *Ph* Alan Hume
Ed Geoffrey Foot *Mus* Brian Hodgson, Delia
Derbyshire *Art Dir* Robert Jones

● Pamela Franklin, Roddy McDowall, Clive Revill,
Gayle Hunnicutt, Roland Culver, Peter Bowles
(Academy)

Richard Matheson's scripting of his novel
Hell House builds into an exceptionally
realistic and suspenseful tale of psychic
phenomena. John Hough's direction maintains this spirit as his cast of characters arrive

at the deserted Hell House with an assignment from its present tycoon owner to learn
the truth about survival after death, a secret
he believes the house with its terrifying history may hold.

Sent on the mission are a physicist, a
femme mental medium and a physical
medium. Latter is the only survivor of a similar investigation 20 years before when eight
scientists were either killed or driven to
insanity. Wife of the physicist also is a member of the party. Shock value is an important
element as audience literally feels the unseen
power that exists in the house.

Clive Revill, the physicist, who attempts to
clear the house of its evil, Pamela Franklin,
the mental medium and Roddy McDowall
the survivor of the previous incursion, are all
first-rate.

■ LEGEND OF LYLAH CLARE, THE

1968, 127 MINS, US ◇

Dir Robert Aldrich *Prod* Robert Aldrich *Scr* Hugo
Butler, Jean Rouverol *Ph* Joseph Biroc *Ed* Michael
Luciano *Mus* Frank DeVol *Art Dir* George W. Davis,
William Glasgow

● Kim Novak, Peter Finch, Ernest Borgnine, Milton
Selzer, Rossella Falk, Gabriele Tinti (M-G-M)

Script spotlights the making of a film about
Lylah Clare, a world famous pic star who
died some time before under mysterious
circumstances.

Her onetime producer-discoverer, who is
'fighting the big C' after a visit to the Mayo
clinic, wants as his swan song to revive the
Clare legend via a biopic, and succeeds in
convincing Lewis Zarkan, the director who
made her and was briefly in love with her, to
coach look-alike Elsa Brinkman into capturing the departed star's mannerisms.

Pic is at its best when it spotlights the
dilemma of the girl reincarnating the defunct
star, especially when Elsa grotesquely
switches to Lylah's vulgar German accented
tones and phrases or when she imagines the
scenes of her predecessor's violent death.

Though only intermittently given a challenging scene or two, Kim Novak brings off
her dual role as Elsa-Lylah well. Peter Finch
is very good as the director who's her doing
and undoing, and there's a very amusing and
talented performance by Ernest Borgnine as
a studio boss.

■ LEMON DROP KID, THE

1951, 91 MINS, US Ⓥ

Dir Sidney Lanfield *Prod* Robert L. Welch
Scr Edmund Hartmann, Robert O'Brien *Ph* Daniel L.
Fapp *Ed* Archie Marshek *Mus* Jay Livingston, Ray
Evans *Art Dir* Hal Pereira, Franz Bachelin

● Bob Hope, Marilyn Maxwell, Lloyd Nolan, Jane
Darwell, Andrea King, Fred Clark (Paramount)

The Lemon Drop Kid is neither true Damon
Runyon, from whose short story of the same
title it was adapted, nor is it very funny Bob
Hope.

Although Hope is the principal interest and
gets most of the laughs, his comedy style, and
particularly his wise-cracking lines, are at the
root of the picture's failure. It not only
destroys the Runyonesque sentimental flavor
but actually pulls the props from under the
inherent humor of the story.

Marilyn Maxwell is decorative as the
sophisticated and therefore un-Runyon love
interest, and she teams neatly with the star in
the catchy incidental songs. Other members
of the cast are generally excellent, primarily
because they conform to the Runyon requirements. Thus, Lloyd Nolan is passable though
a trifle over-suave as a racketeer, while Jane
Darwell, Fred Clark, Jay C. Flippen, William
Frawley, Harry Bellaver, Sid Melton and
various others are properly intense and

therefore genuinely comic as assorted minor
hoodlums.

■ LEMON POPSICLE

1978, 100 MINS, ISRAEL ◇

Dir Boaz Davidson *Prod* Menahem Golan, Yoram
Globus *Scr* Boaz Davidson, Eli Tabor *Ph* Adam
Greenberg *Ed* Alain Jakubowicz

● Yiftach Katzur, Anat Atzmon, Jonathan Segal, Zachi
Noy (Noah)

Lemon Popsicle takes place in Tel Aviv in the
late 1950s. Three youths – Benz, Momo, and
Yudaleh – have only girls on their mind,
while the hit-parade on the radio
(Elvis Presley) reflects their own emotional
engagement in the world.

Benz, a shy, sensitive lad, falls in love with
Nili, who prefers his best chum, Momo.
Momo gets Nili pregnant, then drops her as
the summer vacation starts; Benz stays
behind to arrange the necessary abortion. He
confesses his love and things appear running
his way, when the school term starts and Nili
is back again in the arms of Momo.

The schoolboy romance also has a funnier
side to it. It's in the search for an initial
sexual experience – first with a middle-age
nympho where Benz delivers ice, then with a
prostitute who gives them the crabs – both
handled with appropriate gags to put the
scenes over.

■ LENNY

1974, 111 MINS, US Ⓥ

Dir Bob Fosse *Prod* Marvin Worth *Scr* Julian Barry
Ph Bruce Surtees *Ed* Alan Heim *Mus* Ralph Burns
Art Dir Joel Schiller

● Dustin Hoffman, Valerie Perrine, Jan Miner, Stanley
Beck, Gary Morton, Rashel Novikoff (United Artists)

Lenny Bruce was one of the precursors of
social upheaval, and like most pioneers, he
got clobbered for his foresight. Bob Fosse's
remarkable film version of Julian Barry's
legit play, *Lenny*, stars Dustin Hoffman in an
outstanding performance.

Production was photographed in black and
white, lending not only a slight period
influence but also capturing the grit and
the sweat, as well as the private and
public tortures of its principal character in
uncompromising terms.

Barry's excellent script takes the form of
flashback, but with some partial flashforward
scenes. Three key figures in Bruce's life – wife
Valerie Perrine in a sensational performance,
hardcharger mother Jan Miner in a beautiful
characterization, and Stanley Beck in top
form as Bruce's agent – are being tape-inter-
viewed after his death by an unseen party,
whose motives are never clear.

□ 1974: Best Picture (Nomination)

■ LEO THE LAST

1970, 103 MINS, UK ◇

Dir John Boorman *Prod* Robert Chartoff, Irwin
Winkler *Scr* William Stair, John Boorman *Ph* Peter
Suschitzley *Ed* Tom Priestly *Mus* Fred Myrow
Art Dir Tony Wollard

● Marcello Mastroianni, Billie Whitelaw, Calvin
Lockhart, Glenna Forster Jones, Vladek Sheybal, Gwen
Ffrangcon-Davis (United Artists)

An absurd satire on dethroned European
royalty with a neo-realistic view of the
London ghetto.

Marcello Mastroianni, the last of his line,
lives in exile in a magnificent London town-
house at the end of a cul-de-sac in a black
ghetto area. He is a totally ineffectual, sheltered sickly man, whose only human contacts
are a flock of parasitic social magpies.

Footage on the ghetto comings and goings,
as orchestrated by Director John Boorman,
has a gritty documentary feel.

There is a grotesquely hilarious scene of a mass nude water therapy of Mastroianni's entourage led by society doctor David de Keyser.

But the two sequences are all that work in *Leo*. The rest is at best silly, at worst pretentious allegory and unsuccessful social comment.

● ●

■ LEOPARD MAN, THE

1943, 63 MINS, US ⊤

Dir Jacques Tourneur   *Prod* Val Lewton   *Scr* Ardel Wray   *Ph* Robert de Grasse   *Ed* Mark Robson   *Mus* Roy Webb

● Dennis O'Keefe, Margo, Jean Brooks, Isabel Jewell (RKO)

Both script [from the novel *Black Alibi* by Cornell Woolrich] and direction noticeably strain to achieve effects of *Cat People* but fall far short of latter standard and follow too many confusing paths. After brief introduction, it's a series of chases and murders, with a tame leopard blamed for the latter until strange happenings are pinned on one of the players. It's all confusion, in fact too much for an audience to follow.

Dennis O'Keefe is press agent for a New Mexican nitery and rents a tame black leopard for a publicity stunt which backfires when the cat escapes and a girl is presumably killed by the fugitive. Yarn then spins through regulation eerie channels with two other strange murders enacted – one being in the timeworn setting of a cemetery and windstorm combined. O'Keefe and Margo stick around long enough to trip the real culprit by time for the fadeout to come along.

● ●

■ LES GIRLS

1957, 114 MINS, US ◇ ⊤

Dir George Cukor   *Prod* Sol C. Siegel   *Scr* John Patrick   *Ph* Robert Surtees   *Ed* Ferris Webster   *Mus* Cole Porter   *Art Dir* William A. Horning, Gene Allen

● Gene Kelly, Mitzi Gaynor, Kay Kendall, Taina Elg, Jacques Bergerac, Leslie Phillips (M-G-M)

Les Girls is an exceptionally tasty musical morsel that is in the best tradition of the Metro studio. It's an original and zestful entry that would have been greeted with critical handsprings if it had been originally presented on the Broadway stage.

The musical is set in London, Paris and Granada, Spain. It's the story of a song-and-dance team made up of Gene Kelly and Mitzi Gaynor, Kay Kendall and Taina Elg. Known as 'Barry Nichols and Les Girls', they are a popular Continental act. Many years after the act has broken up, Kendall, now the wife of an English peer, has written a book of reminiscences that lands her in a London court, the defendant in a libel suit brought by Elg, now married to a French industrialist. The court trial provides the setting for a series of flashbacks. Each gives a different version of what happened.

The excursion into the past provides the setting for a number of Cole Porter tunes and dances brightly staged by Jack Cole as 'Les Girls' appear in niteries in France and Spain. Porter created seven new songs for the picture.

Kendall emerges as a delightful comedienne in her first American picture. Elg, a Finnish actress-ballerina who portrays a French girl, has a quality that is exceedingly appealing. Gaynor is the wholesome, uncomplicated member of the troupe.

● ●

■ LES MISERABLES

1935, 109 MINS, US ⊤

Dir Richard Boleslavski   *Scr* W.P. Lipscomb   *Ph* Gregg Toland   *Ed* Barbara McLean   *Mus* Alfred Newman (dir.)

● Fredric March, Charles Laughton, Cedric Hardwicke,

Rochelle Hudson, Marilynne Knowlden, Frances Drake (20th Century/United Artists)

Les Miserables will satisfy the most exacting Victor Hugo followers, and at the same time please those looking only for entertainment, regardless of literary backgrounds. The task of boiling down the lengthy Hugo novel is accomplished by W.P. Lipscomb with no loss of flavor. The essence of the original is faithfully retained.

Fredric March makes the screen Jean Valjean a living version of the panegyrical character. He is the same persecuted, pursued, pitiable, but always admirale man that all readers of the book must visualize. Side by side with March, throughout the picture, is Charles Laughton, as Javert, the cop. His performance is much more on the quiet side, but equally powerful and always believable.

Valjean's service in the galley, to which he is sentenced for stealing a loaf of bread; Javert's pursuit of Valjean and his foster-daughter; the revolt of the French students; the race of Valjean, with the injured Marius on his shoulders, through the stinking sewers of Paris, all breath-taking action passages, are brilliantly managed.

□ 1935: Best Picture (Nomination)

● ●

■ LES MISERABLES

1952, 105 MINS, US

Dir Lewis Milestone   *Prod* Fred Kohlmar   *Scr* Richard Murphy   *Ph* Joseph La Shelle   *Ed* Hugh Fowler   *Mus* Alex North   *Art Dir* Lyle Wheeler, J. Russell Spencer

● Michael Rennie, Debra Paget, Robert Newton, Edmund Gwenn, Sylvia Sidney, Cameron Mitchell (20th Century-Fox)

Victor Hugo's somber classic was previously lensed by the Fox Film Co in 1919, again by Universal in 1927, United Artists had a release out in 1935 and there was a French production in 1936.

In the first episode, when Valjean is sentenced to 10 years as a galley slave for stealing a loaf of bread, director Lewis Milestone permits the players and scenes to cry out flamboyantly against such injustice and the stark miseries of a prison ship existence.

The film actually gets going when Valjean, released under parole, becomes a successful pottery owner after getting his first lesson in humanity from a kindly bishop, beautifully played by Edmond Gwenn. It is during this time that he aids Sylvia Sidney, a poor, dying woman, and takes in her daughter (Debra Paget).

Rennie does exceptionally well with his role, particularly after the convict ship episode.

● ●

■ LETHAL WEAPON

1987, 110 MINS, US ◇ ⊤

Dir Richard Donner   *Prod* Richard Donner, Joel Silver   *Scr* Shane Black   *Ph* Stephen Goldblatt   *Ed* Stuart Baird   *Mus* Michael Kamen, Eric Clapton   *Art Dir* J. Michael Riva

● Mel Gibson, Danny Glover, Gary Busey, Mitchell Ryan, Tom Atkins (Warner)

Lethal Weapon is a film teetering on the brink of absurdity when it gets serious, but thanks to its unrelenting energy and insistent drive, it never quite falls.

Danny Glover is a family-man detective who gets an unwanted partner in the possibly psychotic Mel Gibson. Story is on the back burner as the two men square off against each other, more as adversaries than partners.

Gibson is all live wires and still carries Vietnam with him 20 years after the fact. Though he's 15 years his senior and also a Nam vet, Glover is meant to be a sensitive man of the 1980s. Gibson simmers while Glover worries about his pension.

While the film is trying to establish its emotional underpinnings, a plot slowly unfolds involving a massive drug smuggling operation headed by the lethal Vietnam vet Joshua (Gary Busey).

Ultimately the common-ground for Glover and Gibson is staying alive as the film attempts to shift its buddy story to the battlefields of LA.

Gibson, in one of his better performances, holds the fascination of someone who may truly be dangerous. Glover, too, is likable and so is Darlene Love as his wife, but he and Gibson come from two different worlds the film never really reconciles.

● ●

■ LETHAL WEAPON 2

1989, 113 MINS, US ◇ ⊤

Dir Richard Donner   *Prod* Richard Donner, Joel Silver   *Scr* Jeffrey Boam   *Ph* Stephen Goldblatt   *Ed* Stuart Baird   *Mus* Michael Kamen, Eric Clapton, David Sanborn   *Art Dir* J. Michael Riva

● Mel Gibson, Danny Glover, Joe Pesci, Joss Ackland, Derrick O'Connor (Silver/Warner)

Loaded with the usual elements, *Lethal Weapon 2* benefits from a consistency of tone that was lacking in the first film. This time, screenwriter Jeffrey Boam [working from a story by Shane Black and Warren Murphy] and director Richard Donner have wisely trained their sights on humor and the considerable charm of Mel Gibson and Danny Glover's onscreen rapport.

They've also dreamed up particularly nasty villains and incorporated enough chases and shootouts to hold the attention of a hyperactive nine-year-old.

Plot sets the duo after South African diplomats using their shield of immunity to smuggle drugs. Tagging along for the ride in a hilarious comic turn is Joe Pesci as an unctuous accountant who laundered the baddies' money and now needs witness protection to stay out of the washing machine himself.

There's also a fleeting entanglement between Riggs (Mel Gibson) and the lead villain's secretary (the sparkling Patsy Kensit) that adds some welcome sex appeal.

● ●

■ LET'S DO IT AGAIN

1975, 112 MINS, US ◇

Dir Sidney Poitier   *Prod* Melville Tucker   *Scr* Richard Wesley   *Ph* Donald M. Morgan   *Ed* Pembroke J. Herring   *Mus* Curtis Mayfield   *Art Dir* Alfred Sweeney

● Sidney Poitier, Bill Cosby, Calvin Lockhart, John Amos, Jimmie Walker, Ossie Davis (Warner)

A Timothy March story has been scripted into a loosely-strung series of sketches which amiably advance the story. Sidney Poitier, who has a mysterious hex power, and Bill Cosby, whose versatility herein seems as great as that of Peter Sellers, hie to New Orleans to parlay a bankroll into big winnings for their lodge, presided over by a patriarchal Ossie Davis.

With wives Lee Chamberlin and Denise Nicholas in tow, the pair confound oldtime gangster John Amos and new-wave hood Calvin Lockhart.

The secret weapon Poitier uses is his hypnotic transformation of puny Jimmie Walker from a 'before' gymnasium advertisement into a pugilistic dynamo. The film could have been a nightmare of lethargy, but it's a good mixture of broad comedy.

● ●

■ LET'S MAKE LOVE

1960, 118 MINS, US ◇ ⊤

Dir George Cukor   *Prod* Jerry Wald   *Scr* Norman Krasna, Hal Kanter   *Ph* Daniel L. Fapp   *Ed* David Bretherton   *Mus* Lionel Newman (dir.)   *Art Dir* Lyle R. Wheeler, Gene Allen

● Marilyn Monroe, Yves Montand, Tony Randall, Frankie Vaughan, Wilfrid Hyde White (20th Century-Fox)

After the film has been underway about 12 minutes, the screen goes suddenly dark (the scene is rehearsal of an off-Broadway show) and a lone spotlight picks up Marilyn Monroe wearing black tights and a sloppy wool sweater. She announces, with appropriate musical orchestration, that her name is Lolita and that she isn't allowed to play (pause) with boys (pause) because her heart belongs to daddy (words and music by Cole Porter).

This not only launches the first of a series of elegantly designed (by Jack Cole) production numbers and marks one of the great star entrances ever made on the screen, but is typical of the entire film – which has taken something not too original (the Cinderella theme) and dressed it up like new.

Monroe, of course, is a sheer delight in the tailor-made role of an off-Broadway actress who wants to better herself intellectually (she is going to night school to study geography), but she also has a uniquely talented co-star in Yves Montand. Latter gives a sock performance, full of both heart and humour, as the richest man in the world who wants to find a woman who'll love him for himself alone.

Whenever the story threatens to intrude with tedium, there's a knockout Cole Porter musical number. In addition to 'My Heart Belongs to Daddy,' film introduces four new songs by Sammy Cahn and Jimmy Van Heusen, the best of which are the title song and something called 'Specialization', which Monroe and Frankie Vaughan tear off with gusto. Another highlight is a comedy sequence in which Montand brings on Milton Berle, Bing Crosby and Gene Kelly (playing themselves) to coach him in the musical comedy arts.

Aside from these gimmicks, picture gets solid support from Tony Randall, cast as Montand's worried p.r. man. It's not an exceptionally funny part, but because he plays it so straight, Randall gets a boff comedy reaction.

. . . .

■ LETTER, THE

1940, 95 MINS, US ⓥ

Dir William Wyler   *Prod* Hal B. Wallis, Robert Lord   *Scr* Howard Koch   *Ph* Tony Gaudio   *Ed* George Amy, Warren Low   *Mus* Max Steiner   *Art Dir* Carl Jules Weyl

● Bette Davis, Herbert Marshall, James Stephenson, Gale Sondergaard, Sen Yung (Warner)

The Letter has a history running back to 1927. Twice before it has been seen in legit and once before (1929) in films, each time with a top femme star in the principal role. Yet never has [the W. Somerset Maugham play] been done with greater production values, a better all-around cast or finer direction. Its defect is its grimness. The continued seriousness tends to make the film at times seem drawn out. Director William Wyler, however, sets himself a tempo which is in rhythm with the Malay locale. As a whole, it's very effective.

Story is essentially a mystery. It opens with Bette Davis shooting a man dead as he runs from her plantation house. The question mark from there to the climax is why? She explains to her planter-husband (Herbert Marshall) and an attorney friend (James Stephenson) that the mudered man, an old family intimate, had made advances to her and in her angry resentment she picked up a revolver. It's evident from the coolness of her recital that she's not telling the truth.

Stephenson's smart native assistant, excellently played by Sen Yung, brings him word of a letter she has written. It was to the man she killed and was in the hands of his wife, a Malay gal (Gale Sondergaard). Through it, it is revealed that for 10 years the murderess has been having an affair with her victim and the fatal triggerwork resulted when she discovered he had thrown her over for the beauteous native.

Davis' frigidity at times seems to go even beyond the characterization. It seems often to lack spontaneity, although it is difficult and deserves no belittling. On the other hand, Marshall never falters. Virtually stealing thesp honors in the pic, however, is Stephenson as the attorney, while Sondergaard is the perfect mask-like threat.

Set is of tremendous proportions and the music by Max Steiner is particularly noteworthy in creating and holding a mood, as well as in pointing up the drama.

☐ 1940: Best Picture (Nomination)

. . . .

■ LETTER FROM AN UNKNOWN WOMAN

1948, 84 MINS, US ⓥ

Dir Max Ophuls   *Prod* John Houseman   *Scr* Howard Koch   *Ph* Franz Planer   *Ed* Ted J. Kent   *Mus* Daniele Amfitheatrof   *Art Dir* Alexander Golitzer

● Joan Fontaine, Louis Jourdan, Mady Christians (Rampart/Universal)

Picture teams Joan Fontaine and Louis Jourdan as co-stars and they prove to be a solid combination. Both turn in splendid performances in difficult parts that could easily have been overplayed.

Story [based on a novel by Stefan Zweig] follows a familiar patttern but the taste with which the film has been put together in all departments under John Houseman's production supervision makes it a valid and interest-holding drama. The mounting has an artistic flavor that captures the atmosphere of early-day Vienna and has been beautifully photographed.

Story unfolds in flashback, a device that makes plot a bit difficult to follow at times, but Max Ophuls' direction holds it together. He doesn't rush his direction, adopting a leisurely pace that permits best use of the story. Film is endowed with little touches that give it warmth and heart while the tragic tale is being unfolded.

It concerns a young girl who falls in love with a neighbor, a concert pianist. Years later she again meets her only love but he fails to remember. Story is told as he reads a letter from the girl, written after the second meeting.

. . . .

■ LETTER TO BREZHNEV

1985, 95 MINS, UK ◇ ⓥ

Dir Chris Bernard   *Prod* Janet Goddard   *Scr* Frank Clark   *Ph* Bruce McGowan   *Ed* Lesley Walker   *Mus* Alan Gill   *Art Dir* Lez Brotherston, Nick Englefield, Jonathan Swain

● Alexandra Pigg, Alfred Molina, Peter Firth, Margi Clarke, Tracy Lea, Ted Wood (Yeardream/Film Four/Palace)

This is a farce, penned with wit and acted with appropriate deadpan honesty by all the principals. Picture a Russian ship docking in Liverpool. Two sailors go ashore for a night on the town, both primed with Beatles folklore and one speaking enough English to get them both by with the lasses in a dancehall.

As for the girls, one works in a chicken-factory and does little else than look forward to the weekend conquests. The other is on the dole, but has a romantic view in regard to her bed partners.

Elaine, the Liverpool innocent, meets Peter, the Russian romantic from the Black Sea. They fall in love at first sight.

When they part, the naive Elaine finds it unfair that the world's political stage should prove a hindrance to their ever seeing each other again. So she writes a letter to Brezhnev – and gets an answer. To wit: if you really love your Russian sailor, come to the Soviet Union to marry him and settle down as an adopted citizen.

Alexandra Pigg (Elaine) and Margi Clarke (Teresa) are a tickling pair of working girl types right out of that British tradition going back to 'Free Cinema' days.

. . . .

■ LETTER TO THREE WIVES, A

1948, 108 MINS, US

Dir Joseph L. Mankiewicz   *Prod* Sol C. Siegel   *Scr* Joseph L. Mankiewicz   *Ph* Arthur Miller   *Ed* J. Watson Webb Jr   *Mus* Alfred Newman   *Art Dir* Lyle R. Wheeler, J. Russell Spencer

● Jeanne Crain, Linda Darnell, Ann Sothern, Kirk Douglas, Paul Douglas, Thelma Ritter (20th Century-Fox)

While the picture is standout in every aspect, there are two factors mainly responsible for its overall quality. One is the unique story, adapted from a John Klempner novel by Vera Caspary and given a nifty screenplay by Joseph L Mankiewicz.

Idea has three young housewives in Westchester, NY (much of the film was shot on location in the east), all jealous of the same she-wolf who grew up with their husbands. The 'other woman' addresses a letter to all three wives explaining that she has run away with one of their spouses but without identifying which one. The audience is then given a chance to figure out which one it is, before a surprise denouement explains all.

Other standout aspect is the fine film debut of legit actor Paul Douglas. His role in *Wives* is that of a big, blustering but slightly dumb tycoon and he really gives it a ride with some neat character shading. He's equally good in the more serious romantic moments with Linda Darnell.

Rest of the cast is equally good. Jeanne Crain, Darnell and Ann Sothern, as the three fraus, each turns in a job as good as anything they've done. Kirk Douglas, playing Sothern's husband, is fine as the serious-minded literature prof who can't take his wife's soap-opera writing.

Story is bridged by the off-screen voice of the she-wolf, who is built into a character resembling every man's dream gal by the dialog. Mankiewicz, wisely, never shows her.

☐ 1949: Best Picture (Nomination)

. . . .

■ LEVIATHAN

1989, 98 MINS, US ◇ ⓥ

Dir George Pan Cosmates   *Prod* Luigi De Laurentiis, Aurelio De Laurentiis   *Scr* David Peoples, Jeb Stuart   *Ph* Alex Thomson   *Ed* Roberto Silvi, John F. Burnett   *Mus* Jerry Goldsmith   *Art Dir* Ron Cobb

● Peter Weller, Richard Crenna, Amanda Pays, Daniel Stern, Ernie Hudson (De Laurentiis/Gordon/M-G-M)

Breed an *Alien* with a *Thing*, marinate in salt water, and you get a *Leviathan*. It's a soggy recycling [story by David Peoples] of gruesome monster attacks unleashed upon a crew of macho men and women confined within a far-flung scientific outpost.

A stock team of six ethnically mixed men and two alluring women is working out of a mining camp 16,000 feet down on the Atlantic floor, and only has a short time to go until heading back to the surface.

In the meantime, one of the crew, the randy Daniel Stern takes ill after investigating the sunken remains of a Russian ship named Leviathan, dies, and begins transforming into a grotesque, eel-like creature.

The same fate awaits Lisa Eilbacher, and medic Richard Crenna quickly deduces that some genetic transferal is going on. Remainder of the action sees crew members doing fierce battle with the ever-growing creature and being horrifically eliminated one by one.

343

Shot on elaborate sets in Rome, pic boasts impressive production design by Ron Cobb.

●●●●●●●●●●●●●●●●●●●●●●●●●●●●●●

■ LIANNA

1983, 110 MINS, US ◇ ⊤

Dir John Sayles   *Prod* Jeffrey Nelson   *Scr* John Sayles   *Ph* Austin de Besche   *Ed* John Sayles   *Mus* Mason Daring   *Art Dir* Jeanne McDonnell
● Linda Griffiths, Jane Hallaren, Jon DeVries, Jo Henderson, Jesse Solomon, John Sayles (Winwood)

John Sayles again uses a keen intelligence and finely tuned ear to tackle the nature of friendship and loving in *Lianna*.

Story of a 33-year-old woman (Linda Griffiths), saddled with an arrogant and unsupportive professor-husband (John DeVries) who constricts her life until she finds herself falling in love, for the first time, with a woman teacher (Jane Hallaren).

Particularly well-drawn are her husband's doubly-hurt sense of sexual betrayal, the half-formed understandings of her children, who've only just become aware of conventional sexual realities, and the ambivalence of once-close women friends.

Paced by Griffiths' excellent pivotal performance, the film is marked by fine acting overall, particularly Hallaren as the catalytic lover scared off by the intensity of Griffiths' feelings; DeVries as the acerbic, insecure academic mate; Jo Henderson as the retroactively frightened best girlfriend; and Jesse Solomon as the wise-beyond-years pubescent son. Sayles himself appears to good effect as a supportive friend.

●●●●●●●●●●●●●●●●●●●●●●●●●●●●

■ LIBEL

1959, 100 MINS, UK ◇

Dir Anthony Asquith   *Prod* Anatole De Grunwald   *Scr* Anatole De Grunwald, Karl Tunberg   *Ph* Robert Krasker   *Ed* Frank Clarke   *Mus* Benjamin Frankel
● Dirk Bogarde, Olivia de Havilland, Paul Massie, Robert Morley, Wilfrid Hyde White, Richard Wattis (M-G-M)

Based on a 25-year-old play by Edward Wooll, *Libel* has been turned into a stylish and holding film. The idea is simple enough. Is Sir Mark Loddon (Dirk Bogarde), owner of one of the stately homes of England, really Loddon or an unscrupulous imposter, as alleged by a wartime comrade?

The case is sparked off when a young Canadian airman sees a TV program introducing Loddon. He is convinced that he is really Frank Welney, a small part actor. The three were in prison camp together and he is confident that Loddon was killed during a prison break. He exposes the alleged phoney in a newspaper and Loddon is persuaded by his wife to sue.

Bogarde carries much of the onus since he plays both Loddon (during the war and at the time of the trial) and Welney. He does a standout job, suggesting the difference in the two characters remarkably well with the aid of only a slight difference in hair style. Paul Massie gives a likeable, though somewhat even-key, performance as the young man whose suspicions trigger the drama. Olivia de Havilland, as Bogarde's wife, has two or three very good scenes which she handles well.

Because much of the off-court scenes were actually shot at Woburn Abbey, stately home of the Duke of Bedford, the production is given much budget-value.

●●●●●●●●●●●●●●●●●●●●●●●●●●●

■ LIBELED LADY

1936, 85 MINS, US

Dir Jack Conway   *Prod* Lawrence Weingarten   *Scr* Maurine Watkins, Howard Emmett Rogers, George Oppenheimer   *Ph* Robert Brodine   *Ed* Frederick Y. Smith   *Mus* William Axt

● Jean Harlow, William Powell, Myrna Loy, Spencer Tracy, Walter Connolly, Charley Grapewin (M-G-M)

Even though *Libeled Lady* goes overboard on plot and its pace snags badly in several spots, Metro has brought in a sockeroo of a comedy. It's broad farce for the most part, and the threesome consisting of William Powell, Spencer Tracy and Jean Harlow lend themselves perfectly to the task.

Of the starring foursome Myrna Loy's is the only behavior which is kept pretty much on a serious plane. As the much misunderstood poor little rich girl, she projects an effective performance and, with Powell in the later reels, accounts for plenty romantic arias.

Story [by Wallace Sullivan] takes for itself a Park Avenue plus newspaper row theme. Picture seeks to tell of what befalls Powell when, as the trouble-shooter for a newspaper, he undertakes to frame a young millionairess and thereby compel her to drop a $5 million libel suit. The expected occurs; he falls in love with her.

Concerned with Powell in the frame are Tracy, managing editor of the sheet, and the latter's fiancee (Harlow). Latter turns out a corking straight for the sophisticated, suave manner of Powell and she frequently steals the picture when the opportunities for cutting loose fall her way.

Tracy has the least juicy assignment, but the characterization is right up his alley. Walter Connolly registers in crack fashion, as usual, in the part of Loy's father.

☐ 1936: Best Picture (Nomination)

●●●●●●●●●●●●●●●●●●●●●●●●●●●

■ LIBERATION OF L.B. JONES, THE

1970, 102 MINS, US ◇ ⊤

Dir William Wyler   *Prod* Ronald Lubin   *Scr* Sterling Silliphant, Jesse Hill Ford   *Ph* Robert Surtees   *Ed* Robert Swink, Carl Kress   *Mus* Elmer Bernstein   *Art Dir* Kenneth A. Reid
● Lee J. Cobb, Anthony Zerbe, Roscoe Lee Browne, Lola Falana, Lee Majors, Barbara Hershey (Columbia)

This story of a glossed-over Negro's murder by a Dixie policeman is, unfortunately, not much more than an interracial sexploitation film.

Story kicks off as Lee Majors and bride Barbara Hershey come to live with Majors' uncle Lee J. Cobb, while Yaphet Kotto comes home to murder bestial cop Arch Johnson. Roscoe Lee Browne is town's Negro funeral director, the title character who seeks a divorce (the liberation) from unfaithful wife Lola Falana. Her lover is Anthony Zerbe, Johnson's police buddy.

The well-structured plot [from the novel *The Liberation of Lord Byron Jones* by Jesse Hill Ford] finds lawyer Cobb trying to avoid an open-court revelation that a white married cop is a Negro woman's lover.

●●●●●●●●●●●●●●●●●●●●●●●●●●●

■ LICENCE TO KILL

1989, 133 MINS, UK ◇ ⊤

Dir John Glen   *Prod* Albert R. Broccoli, Michael G. Wilson   *Scr* Richard Maibaum, Michael G. Wilson   *Ph* Alec Mills   *Ed* John Grover   *Mus* Michael Kamen   *Art Dir* Peter Lamont
● Timothy Dalton, Carey Lowell, Robert Davi, Talisa Soto, Anthony Zerbe (United Artists/Eon)

The James Bond production team has found its second wind with *Licence to Kill*, a cocktail of high-octane action, spectacle and drama.

Presence for the second time of Timothy Dalton as the sauve British agent clearly has juiced up scripters, and director John Glen.

Out go the self-parodying witticisms and over-elaborate high-tech gizmos that showed pre-Dalton pics to a walking pace. Dalton

plays 007 with a vigor and physicality that harks back to the earliest Bond pics, letting full-bloodied actions speak louder than words.

The thrills-and-spills chases are superbly orchestrated as pic spins at breakneck speed through its South Florida and Central American locations. Bond survives a series of underwater and mid-air stunt sequences that are above par for the series.

He's also pitted against a crew of sinister baddies (led by Robert Davi and Frank McRae) who give the British agent the chance to use all his wit and wiles. Femme elements in the guise of Carey Lowell and Talisa Soto add gloss but play second fiddle to the action.

●●●●●●●●●●●●●●●●●●●●●●●●●●

■ LIES MY FATHER TOLD ME

1975, 103 MINS, CANADA ◇

Dir Jan Kadar   *Prod* Anthony Bedrich, Harry Gulkin   *Scr* Ted Allan   *Ph* Paul Van Der Linden   *Ed* Edward Beyer, Richard Marks   *Mus* Sol Kaplan   *Art Dir* Francois Barbeau
● Yossi Yadin, Len Birman, Marilyn Lightstone, Jeffrey Lynas, Ted Allan, Barbara Chilcott (Pentimento/Pentacle VIII)

Set in Montreal in the 1920s, this centres on an emotional relationship between a young boy, portrayed by newcomer Jeffrey Lynas, and his aged, peddler grandfather, played by Israeli actor Yossi Yadin. Threatening this relationship at all times is the boy's hard luck, no talent father, etched by a ruggedly vigorous Len Birman, and his long-suffering mother, a dramatic leavening force played by Marilyn Lightstone.

The grandfather spins fanciful tales for the boy, and takes him on his peddling rounds, while the father tries to wheedle money from him for various unsuccessful invention schemes.

Czech director Jan Kadar has assembled a topnotch, uniformly handsome cast and his lingering over certain moments is a decided virtue. *Lies My Father Told Me* is an absorbing nostalgic trip for anyone who has ever felt close to a grandparent, and it is a powerful but never pushy statement.

●●●●●●●●●●●●●●●●●●●●●●●●●●●

■ LIFE AND DEATH OF COLONEL BLIMP, THE

1943, 163 MINS, UK ◇ ⊤

Dir Michael Powell, Emeric Pressburger   *Prod* Michael Powell, Emeric Pressburger   *Scr* Michael Powell, Emeric Pressburger   *Ph* Georges Perinal   *Ed* John Seabourne   *Mus* Allan Gray   *Art Dir* Alfred Junge
● Roger Livesey, Deborah Kerr, Anton Walbrook, Roland Culver, Albert Lieven, James McKechnie (Archers/Independent)

Here is an excellent film whose basic story could have been told within normal feature limits, but which, instead, is extended close to three hours. Longer or shorter, this panorama of British army life is depicted with a technical skill and artistry that marks it as one of the really fine pix to come out of a British studio.

It's a clear, continuous unreeling of events in the life of an English military man, from the Boer War, through World War I and up to the completion of the training and equipment of England's Home Guard. Story revolves around an officer (Clive Candy) who has spent all his life in the army and still feels the German people as a whole are decent human beings, and that they're only tools of their war lords.

The role of Candy is spasmodically well enacted by Roger Livesey, who looks a little too mature in the scenes of his younger days and a bit too virile at the finish. More generous praise should go to Anton Walbrook as an Uhlan officer. This is an excellent characterization depicted with delicacy and sensitiveness. Deborah Kerr contributes attractively as the feminine lead in three separate characters through the generations, and a score of other artists leave little to criticize from the histrionic side.

Title is based on the symbolic figure of the old-time English officers who have been axed, not only due to age but because of their contempt for present methods of warfare as compared with 'the good old days'. Cartoonist Low, in the *Evening Standard*, christened them 'Colonel Blimps'.

．．．．．．．．．．．．．．．．．．．．．．．．．．．．．．

■ **LIFE AND TIMES OF JUDGE ROY BEAN, THE**

1972, 120 MINS, US ◇ ⓥ
Dir John Huston   *Prod* John Foreman   *Scr* John Milius   *Ph* Richard Moore   *Ed* Hugh S. Fowler   *Mus* Maurice Jarre   *Art Dir* Tambi Larsen
● Paul Newman, Victoria Principal, Anthony Perkins, Ned Beatty, John Huston, Ava Gardner (First Artists)

The Life and Times of Judge Roy Bean has a title card to the effect: 'Maybe this isn't the way it was – it's the way it should have been'. For some, perhaps, that will set up this $4 million freedom freeway spoof.

The two-hour running time is not fleshed out with anything more than scenic vignettes, sometimes attempting to recreate the success of *Butch Cassidy and the Sundance Kid*, with an Alan and Marilyn Bergman-lyricked tune and Maurice Jarre's music sometimes attempting honest spoofing of westerns, and sometimes trying to play the story historically straight. The overkill and the underdone do it in.

Newman (Bean) arrives in Texas badlands, draws a moustache on his wanted poster and announces himself at the saloon. He is promptly beaten, robbed, tied to a horse and run out over the prairie to die. Mexican towngirl Victoria Principal saves him. He returns to the saloon, massacres everyone there and then sits down to wait to 'kill all of your kind'.

Newman is good as Bean, injecting charm into the character along with the rough exterior. Principal is impressive in her first major role.

．．．．．．．．．．．．．．．．．．．．．．．．．．．．．．

■ **LIFE AT THE TOP**

1965, 118 MINS, UK
Dir Ted Kotcheff   *Prod* James Woolf   *Scr* Mordecai Richler   *Ph* Oswald Morris   *Ed* Derek York   *Mus* Richard Addinsell   *Art Dir* Ted Marshall
● Laurence Harvey, Jean Simmons, Honor Blackman, Michael Craig, Donald Wolfit, Robert Morley (Romulus)

Some of the gloss of *Room at the Top* rubs off on this follow-up, but the film lacks both the motivation and rare subtlety which elevated its predecessor.

Based upon a second novel by John Braine, the sombre, sometimes dreary but usually honest drama picks up its narrative 10 years later. The Mordecai Richler screenplay continues the story of the young, designing opportunist who rose to the top in social and business standing, but at loss of his self-respect, as limned in *Room*. Now, however, after having enjoyed the position he sought for a decade, he is even more aware of the necessity of clinging to his ideals and tries to do something about a life he has found empty.

Laurence Harvey continues in the mood of his character in *Room*, now sales chief of his millionaire father-in-law's woolen mills in a sooty Yorkshire town. Jean Simmons as his wife (replacing Heather Sears in original role) has a rather unsympathetic character which she nonetheless enacts persuasively.

．．．．．．．．．．．．．．．．．．．．．．．．．．．．．．

■ **LIFE FOR RUTH**

1962, 91 MINS, UK
Dir Basil Dearden   *Prod* Michael Relph   *Scr* Janet Green, John McCormick   *Ph* Otto Heller   *Ed* John Guthridge   *Mus* William Alwyn   *Art Dir* Alex Vetchinsky
● Michael Craig, Patrick McGoohan, Janet Munro, Paul Rogers, Megs Jenkins, Frank Finlay (Rank/Allied Film Makers)

First problem that confronts an honest working man (Michael Craig) occurs when his eight-year-old daughter and her next door playmate are involved in a boating accident. His daughter is clinging to the boat and is not in such immediate danger as the drowning boy. Which should he try first to save?

He rescues both, but by then his daughter is gravely ill. Only a blood transfusion can save her. Because of his strict religious principles (he is a member of the Jehovah's witness sect, though it is not stated in the film) he adamantly refuses, and the child dies. That was his second distressing problem.

The doctor who urged the transfusion is so irate that he gets the father tried for manslaughter. This is good telling stuff for drama and it brings up issues about religion, the law, conscience, marital relationship all posed with intelligence and conviction.

Thesping is crisp all around, with Craig surmounting a gloomy type of role as the dogged religionist, and Janet Munro as his baffled dismayed young wife. Patrick McGoohan is excellent in a tricky role [the doctor] which is not so clearly defined as the other top jobs.

Otto Heller's bleak photography of the North of England setting and William Alwyn's unobtrusive musical score all lend aid to Dearden's adroit direction.

．．．．．．．．．．．．．．．．．．．．．．．．．．．．．．

■ **LIFE IS CHEAP...**
...BUT TOILET PAPER IS EXPENSIVE

1990, 90 MINS, US ◇ ⓥ
Dir Wayne Wang   *Prod* Winnie Fredriksz   *Scr* Spencer Nakasako   *Ph* Amir M. Mokri   *Ed* Chris Sanderson, Sandy Nervig   *Mus* Mark Alder   *Art Dir* Collete Koo
● Spencer Nakasako, Cora Miao, Victor Wong, John K. Chan, Chan Kim Wan (Far East Stars)

Audaciously stylish and visually mesmerizing, *Life Is Cheap* aims to evoke the uncertain mood of present-day Hong Kong as viewed from the perspective of an Asian-American naif. Director Wayne Wang's tart take on the conundrum of Chinese identity has all the narrative logic of a tilted pinball machine.

Screenwriter-star Spencer Nakasako is a half-Chinese, half-Japanese, all-American stablehand from San Francisco who has agreed to act as a courier for a San Francisco Triad, the Chinese mafia, in return for an all-expenses-paid sojourn in Hong Kong. The black-Stetsoned, cowboy-booted hero wants to see the legendary port before its takeover by China. In the wake of Tiananmen Square, it's a city of '5½ million sitting ducks'.

Handcuffed to an attache case destined for the 'Big Boss' in Hong Kong, the hero seeks to unlock the enigma of '5,000 years of Chinese culture'. Wang skewers the lofty notion of Chinese self-superiority by populating his film with a widely variegated gallery of funny and flawed characters.

．．．．．．．．．．．．．．．．．．．．．．．．．．．．．．

■ **LIFE OF BRIAN**

1979, 93 MINS, UK ◇ ⓥ
Dir Terry Jones   *Prod* John Goldstone   *Scr* Graham Chapman, John Cleese, Terry Gilliam, Eric Idle, Terry Jones, Michael Palin   *Ph* Peter Biziou   *Ed* Julian Doyle   *Mus* Geoffrey Burgon   *Art Dir* Terry Gilliam
● Terry Jones, Michael Palin, John Cleese, Eric Idle, Spike Milligan, George Harrison (Warner/Orion)

Monty Python's *Life Of Brian*, utterly

irreverent tale of a reluctant messiah whose impact proved somewhat less pervasive than that of his contemporary Jesus Christ, is just as wacky and imaginative as their earlier film outings. Film was shot using stunning Tunisian locales.

As an adult in Roman-occupied Palestine, Brian's life parallels that of Jesus, as he becomes involved in the terrorist Peoples Front of Judea, works as a vendor at the Colosseum, paints anti-Roman graffiti on palace walls, unwittingly wins a following as a messiah and is ultimately condemned to the cross by a foppish Pontius Pilate.

Tone of the film is set by such scenes as a version of the sermon on the mount in which spectators shout out that they can't hear what's being said and start fighting amongst themselves.

．．．．．．．．．．．．．．．．．．．．．．．．．．．．．．

■ **LIFE OF EMILE ZOLA, THE**

1937, 123 MINS, US ⓥ
Dir William Dieterle   *Prod* Henry Blanke   *Scr* Heinz Herald, Geza Herczeg, Norman Reilly Raine   *Ph* Tony Gaudio   *Ed* Warren Low   *Mus* Max Steiner   *Art Dir* Anton Grot
● Paul Muni, Gloria Holden, Gale Sondergaard, Joseph Schildkraut, Robert Warwick, Robert Barrat (Warner Bros.)

The Life of Emile Zola is a vibrant, tense and emotional story about the man who fought a nation with his pen and successfully championed the cause of the exiled Capt Alfred Dreyfus. With Paul Muni in the title role, supported by distinguished players, the film is finely made.

The picture is Muni's all the way, even when he is off screen. Covering a period of the last half of the past century, action is laid in Paris, except for short interludes in England and on Devil's Island, whither Dreyfus was banished by court-martial after conspiracy charges that he betrayed military secrets to Germany. Although the release of Dreyfus is made the principal dramatic incident of the picture, the development of the character and career of Zola remains dominant.

Thus, the audience is informed of the derivation of his earlier novels of *Nana*, in which he stripped the Paris underworld of its glitter and laid it bare, and his other crusading works. In his late years he takes up the fight to free Dreyfus and purge the French army general staff of deceit and conspiracy.

Joseph Schildkraut as Dreyfus, Gale Sondergaard as his wife, and Erin O'Brien-Moore in a lesser role, as the inspiration for the conception of *Nana*, leave deep impressions. Racial theme is lightly touched upon, but impressive notwithstanding.
□ 1937: Best Picture

．．．．．．．．．．．．．．．．．．．．．．．．．．．．．．

■ **LIFE STINKS**

1991, 95 MINS, US ◇ ⓥ
Dir Mel Brooks   *Prod* Mel Brooks   *Scr* Mel Brooks, Rudy De Luca, Steve Haberman   *Ph* Steven Poster   *Ed* David Rawlins, Anthony Redman, Michael Mulconery   *Mus* John Morris   *Art Dir* Peter Larkin
● Mel Brooks, Lesley Ann Warren, Jeffrey Tambor, Stuart Pankin, Howard Morris, Rudy De Luca (Brooksfilms)

Mel Brooks' *Life Stinks* is a fitfully funny vaudeville caricature about life on Skid Row. Premise of a rich man who chooses to live among the poor for a spell feels sorely undeveloped, and suffers from the usual gross effects and exaggerations.

Pic gets off to a good start with Brooks' callous billionaire Goddard Bolt informing his circle of yes-men of his plans to build a colossal futuristic development on the site of Los Angeles' worst slums, the plight of its residents be damned.

345

Tycoon Jeffrey Tambor bets his rival that he can't last a month living out in the neighborhood he intends to buy.

In a series of vignettes that play like blackout routines, Bolt, renamed Pepto by a local denizen, tries various survival tactics, such as dancing for donations. After being robbed of his shoes, he encounters baglady Lesley Ann Warren, a wildly gesticulating man-hater who slowly comes to admit Pepto is the only person she can stand.

Some effective bug-eyed, free-wheeling comedy is scattered throughout, much of it descending to the Three Stooges level of sophistication. But distressingly little is done with the vast possibilities offered by the setting and the characters populating it.

••••••••••••••••••••••••

■ **LIFEBOAT**

1944, 86 MINS, US ⓥ

Dir Alfred Hitchcock   *Prod* Kenneth Macgowan
Scr Jo Swerling   *Ph* Glen MacWilliams   *Ed* Dorothy Spencer   *Mus* Hugo Friedhofer   *Art Dir* James Basevi, Maurice Ransford
● Tallulah Bankhead, William Bendix, Walter Slezak, John Hodiak, Hume Cronyn, Canada Lee
(20th Century-Fox)

John Steinbeck's devastating indictment of the nature of Nazi bestiality, at times an almost clinical, dissecting room analysis, emerges as powerful adult motion picture fare.

The picture is based on an original idea of director Alfred Hitchcock's. Hitchcock, from accounts, first asked Steinbeck to write the piece for book publication, figuring that if it turned out a big seller the exploitation value for film purposes would be greatly enhanced. The author, however, would not undertake the more ambitious assignment and wrote the story for screen purposes only, with Jo Swerling handling the adaptation.

Patterned along one of the simplest, most elementary forms of dramatic narration, the action opens and closes on a lifeboat. It's a lusty, robust story about a group of survivors from a ship sunk by a U-boat. One by one the survivors find precarious refuge on the lifeboat. Finally they pick up a survivor from the German U-boat. He is first tolerated and then welcomed into their midst. And he repays their trust and confidence with murderous treachery.

Walter Slezak, as the German, comes through with a terrific delineation. Henry Hull as the millionaire, William Bendix as the mariner with a jitterbug complex who loses a leg, John Hodiak as the tough, bitter, Nazi-hater, and Canada Lee as the colored steward, deliver excellent characterizations.

Hitchcock pilots the piece skillfully, ingeniously developing suspense and action. Despite that it's a slow starter, the picture, from the beginning, leaves a strong impact and, before too long, develops into the type of suspenseful product with which Hitchcock has always been identified.

••••••••••••••••••••••••

■ **LIFEFORCE**

1985, 101 MINS, US ◊ ⓥ

Dir Tobe Hooper   *Prod* Menahem Golan, Yoram Globus   *Scr* Dan O'Bannon, Don Jakoby   *Ph* Alan Hume   *Ed* John Grover   *Mus* Henry Mancini
Art Dir John Graysmark
● Steve Railsback, Peter Firth, Frank Finlay, Mathilda May, Patrick Stewart, Michael Gothard (Cannon)

For about the first 10 minutes, this $22.5 million pic indicates it could be a scary sci-fier as Yank and British space travelers discover seemingly human remains in the vicinity of Halley's Comet and attempt to bring home three perfectly preserved specimens.

The astronauts don't make it back but the humanoids do, and one of them, Space Girl

(Mathilda May), is possessed of such a spectacularly statuesque physique that she could probably have conquered all of mankind even without her special talents, which include a form of electroshock vampirism and the ability to inhabit other bodies.

Pic [from the novel *The Space Vampires* by Colin Wilson] descends into subpar Agatha Christie territory, as fanatical inspector Peter Firth and surviving astronaut Steve Railsback scour the countryside for the deadly Space Girl and make a pit stop at an insane asylum to provide for further hysteria.

Even though she turns millions of Londoners into fruitcakes and threatens the entire world, Railsback just can't get the naked Space Girl out of his mind.

In the meantime, Firth makes his way through scores of zombies in a burning London in hopes of nailing Space Girl.

••••••••••••••••••••••••

■ **LIFEGUARD**

1976, 96 MINS, US ◊ ⓥ

Dir Daniel Petrie   *Prod* Ron Silverman   *Scr* Ron Koslow   *Ph* Ralph Woolsey   *Ed* Argyle Nelson Jr   *Mus* Dale Menten
● Sam Elliott, Anne Archer, Stephen Young, Parker Stevenson, Kathleen Quinlan Steve Burns (Paramount)

Lifeguard is an unsatisfying film, of uncertain focus on a 30-ish guy who doesn't yet seem to know what he wants. Script takes Sam Elliott through another Southern California beach summer as a career lifeguard, encountering the usual string of offbeat characters found in the type of made-for-TV feature which this project resembles.

There are, of course, some advantages – like periodic playmate Sharon Weber; Kathleen Quinlan, supposedly underage (but looking far more mature) teenager who has a crush on him; and Anne Archer, long-ago high-school sweetheart now divorced.

Elliott, who has some beefcake value, projects a character who is mostly a passive reactor rather than a person in sure command of his fate.

••••••••••••••••••••••••

■ **LIGHT AT THE EDGE OF THE WORLD, THE**

1971, 120 MINS, US ◊ ⓥ

Dir Kevin Billington   *Prod* Kirk Douglas   *Scr* Tom Rowe, Rachel Billington, Paquita Villanova, Bertha Dominguez   *Ph* Henri Decae   *Ed* Bert Bates   *Mus* Piero Piccioni   *Art Dir* Enrique Alarcon
● Kirk Douglas, Yul Brynner, Samantha Eggar, Jean Claude Drouot, Fernando Rey, Renato Salvatori
(National General)

Jules Verne's *The Light at the Edge of the World* shapes up as good action-adventure escapism. The stars are Kirk Douglas, who produced on Spanish locations, as the sole survivor on an island captured by pirate Yul Brynner, with Samantha Eggar as a shipwrecked hostage.

Douglas is a bored assistant to lighthouse-keeper Fernando Rey on a rock off the tip of South America in 1865. Massimo Ranieri, a young man rounding out the group, is brutally killed with Rey when Brynner's pirate ship takes over the island. Douglas escapes and ekes out a passive survival. When Brynner's men darken the regular beacon and erect a false light to snare Cape Horn vessels, Douglas rescues Renato Salvatori from slaughter and begins to fight back.

Eggar, saved from the shipwreck, is used by Brynner as a look-alike of Douglas' old secret love. From this point on, it's all downhill until the exciting confrontation between Douglas and Brynner atop the burning lighthouse.

••••••••••••••••••••••••

■ **LIGHT IN THE PIAZZA**

1962, 102 MINS, US ◊

Dir Guy Green   *Prod* Arthur Freed   *Scr* Julius J. Epstein   *Ph* Otto Heller   *Ed* Frank Clarke   *Mus* Mario Nascimbene   *Art Dir* Frank White
● Olivia de Havilland, Rossano Brazzi, Yvette Mimieux, George Hamilton, Barry Sullivan (M-G-M)

Discerningly cast and deftly executed under the imaginative guidance of director Guy Green, the Arthur Freed production, filmed in the intoxicatingly visual environments of Rome and Florence, is an interesting touching drama based on a highly unusual romantic circumstance created in prose by Elizabeth Spencer. The film has its flaws, but they are minor kinks in a satisfying whole.

Epstein's concise and graceful screenplay examines with reasonable depth and sensible restraint the odd plight of a beautiful, wealthy 26-year-old American girl (Yvette Mimieux) who, as a result of a severe blow on the head in her youth, has been left with a permanent 10-year-old mentality.

It is, too, the story of her mother's (Olivia de Havilland) dilemma – whether to commit the girl to an institution, as is the wish of her husband (Barry Sullivan), who superficially sees in the measure a solution to his marital instability, or pave the way for the girl's marriage to a well-to-do young Florentine fellow (George Hamilton) by concealing knowledge of the child's retarded intelligence.

It's Mimieux's picture. The role requires an aura of luminous naivete mixed with childish vacancy and a passion for furry things and kind, attractive people. That's precisely what it gets. Hamilton acceptably manages the Italian flavor and displays more animation than he normally has. De Havilland's performance is one of great consistency and subtle projection.

••••••••••••••••••••••••

■ **LIGHTHORSEMEN, THE**

1987, 128 MINS, AUSTRALIA ◊ ⓥ

Dir Simon Wincer   *Prod* Ian Jones, Simon Wincer   *Scr* Ian Jones   *Ph* Dean Semler   *Ed* Adrian Carr   *Mus* Mario Millo   *Art Dir* Bernard Hides
● Jon Blake, Peter Phelps, Tony Bonner, Bill Kerr, John Walton (RKO/Picture Show)

Toward the end of this epic about Aussie cavalry fighting in the Middle East in 1917, there's a tremendously exciting and spectacular 14-minute sequence in which soldiers of the Light Horse charge on German/Turkish-occupied Beersheba. It's a pity writer and coproducer Ian Jones couldn't come up with a more substantial storyline to build around his terrific climax.

Focus of attention is on Dave Mitchell, very well played by Peter Phelps. Opening sequence, which is breathtakingly beautiful, is set in Australia and involves young Dave deciding to enlist in the Light Horse after seeing wild horses being mustered for shipment to the Middle East.

Main story involves four friends (Jon Blake, John Walton, Tim McKenzie, Gary Sweet) who are members of the Australian cavalry, chaffing because the British, who have overall command of allied troops in the area, misuse the cavalry time and again, forcing the Australians to dismount before going into battle.

The principal leads are very well played, with Phelps a standout as the most interesting of the young soldiers. Walton scores as the quick-tempered leader of the group, while McKenzie creates a character out of very little material. Topbilled Blake is thoroughly charming as Scotty.

••••••••••••••••••••••••

L

■ LIGHTS OF NEW YORK

1928, 57 MINS, US
Dir Bryan Foy *Scr* Hugh Herbert, Murray Roth
Ph E.H. Dupar
● Helene Costello, Cullen Landis, Gladys Brockwell, Mary Carr, Wheeler Oakman, Eugene Pallette (Warner)

This picture got pretty billing in Warners describing it as 'The first 100 per cent all-talking picture'. Every character speaks, more or less. But it's not an expensively made picture in appearance, either in sets or cast.

This is an open-face story with roll-your-own dialog. It's underworld, starting in a small town and moving to a nite club on the Giddy Wild Way. There are bootleggers and gunmen, cops and mugs, the latter a couple of simps falling for con men back home in a hotel about twice the size of the town – from the looks of the set.

The cast of nearly all vaudeville actors talks the best they may, in lieu of legits or picture actors who can't talk. Gladys Brockwell, as the mistress, runs ahead and far, with Robert Elliott as the detective second. Bryan Foy directed – his first full-length talker. And there's some credit in that for him, considering there's no class to story or picture.

Helene Costello, in the fem lead, is a total loss. For talkers she had better go to school right away. Cullen Landis, opposite, seems to talk with much effort. Wheeler Oakman as the legger gets through fairly, burdened with much of the bad dialog. Mary Carr in a bit as the mother gives an illustration of what may be accomplished from experience. Tom McGuire nicely plays and looks a police chief, with hardly anything to say.

■ LIGHTSHIP, THE

1985, 89 MINS, US ◇ ▽
Dir Jerzy Skolimowski *Prod* Bill Benenson, Moritz Borman *Scr* William Mai, David Taylor *Ph* Charly Steinberger *Ed* Barry Vince *Mus* Stanley Myers
Art Dir Holger Gross
● Robert Duvall, Klaus Maria Brandauer, Tom Bower, Robert Costanzo, Badja Djola, William Forsythe (CBS)

Jerzy Skolimowski's *The Lightship* is based on a novella by the highly regarded German writer Siegfried Lenz. It was filmed in West Germany on the island of Sylt with an all English-speaking cast, the story transferred from its North Sea setting to the coastal waters off Norfolk.

The setting is the only seaworthy lightship left, and it's on this precarious wreck that everything takes place. The other major plus is the acting duel between Robert Duvall and Klaus Maria Brandauer, both with thespian styles of their own and in direct contrast to each other. Since the roles of the hijacker Caspary and the Coast Guard captain Miller had to be switched before shooting began, one senses a battle of wits all the way down the line.

Further, Skolimowski is notorious for improvisation himself, so the script reportedly went through three changes – in addition to adding a saving narrative commentary on the editing table.

As a psychological thriller, *The Lightship* has its tense entertainment moments, but the narrative line takes so many detours that the problem is trying to figure out the non sequiturs as they surface out of nowhere.

■ LI'L ABNER

1959, 113 MINS, US ◇ ▽
Dir Melvin Frank *Prod* Norman Panama, Melvin Frank *Scr* Norman Panama, Melvin Frank *Ph* Daniel L. Fapp *Ed* Arthur P. Schmidt *Mus* Gene De Paul
Art Dir Hal Pereira, J. McMillan Johnson
● Peter Palmer, Leslie Parrish, Stubby Kaye, Howard St John, Julie Newmar, Stella Stevens (Paramount)

The Norman Panama-Melvin Frank filmiza-

tion of their Broadway hit is lively, colorful and tuneful, done with smart showmanship in every department.

Congress plans to use L'il Abner's hometown of Dogpatch for an atom bomb testing ground, it being the most worthless locale in the US. Dogpatchers must prove the town has some value so it will be spared. The item found is Mammy Yokum's Yokumberry Tonic, a stimulant to health and wealth and romance. The plot then thickens as private enterprise and the US government compete for the celebrated syrup.

The plimsoll mark on Alvin Colt's costumes for the female members of the cast is notably low throughout, and some of the humor is strongly Chic Sale. The songs, by Gene De Paul and Johnny Mercer, are breezy and amusing.

DeeDee Wood's dances, based on Michael Kidd's stage choreography, move more freely than usual, unconfined by conventional limits, and have considerable dazzle. The vocal numbers tend to get bunched up, as if the missing stage footlights were still imposing their limitations.

Characterizations are as deliberately unreal as the costumes and settings. Because of this, the principals don't have much chance to display anything but the broadest sort of caricature. Peter Palmer, who created the role on Broadway of Li'l Abner, repeats his assignment here. Leslie Parrish, a delectable dish, essays Daisy Mae, and although delectable, the dish could do with a dash of spice. Stubby Kaye, another Gotham original, creates the most fun with a brisk portrayal of Marryin' Sam. Howard St John, still another of the originals, has the best scene in the film as General Bullmoose. Julie Newmar and Stella Stevens are handsome and amusing as sexy sirens.

■ LILI

1953, 80 MINS, US ◇ ▽
Dir Charles Walters *Prod* Edwin H. Knopf
Scr Helen Deutsch *Ph* Robert Planck *Ed* Ferris Webster *Mus* Bronislau Kaper *Art Dir* Cedric Gibbons, Paul Groesse
● Leslie Caron, Mel Ferrer, Jean Pierre Aumont, Zsa Zsa Gabor, Kurt Kasznar, Amanda Blake (M-G-M)

Leslie Caron is a young French orphan who turns to a fascinating carnival magician, Jean Pierre Aumont, for help [in this version of a story by Paul Gallico]. He's a Gallic wolf, but Lili's naive, 16-year-old innocence is too much for him, so he brushes her off with a waitress job with the show. Mel Ferrer, a puppeteer, uses his little friends to woo her from her sorrow.

The impromptu performance is so successful, Ferrer makes it part of the act he does with Kurt Kasznar and four puppets. Gruff and moody in his dealings with the girl, the puppet master actually loves her and is jealous over her continuing infatuation for Aumont. This jealousy leads him to slap her just at the time she is again desperate, after having discovered that Aumont is married to his assistant, Zsa Zsa Gabor. The girl packs her things and leaves.

Caron's metamorphosis from the forlorn little ugly duckling to a pixie-faced, attractive young lady is well-handled. Ferrer goes through most of the film in a pout, both from jealousy and because his dancing career was halted by a war injury. Aumont is delightful as the magician and his act with Gabor, staged almost as a production piece, is a high-light.

■ LILIES OF THE FIELD

1963, 94 MINS, US ▽
Dir Ralph Nelson *Prod* Ralph Nelson *Scr* James Poe *Ph* Ernest Heller *Ed* John McCafferty
Mus Jerry Goldsmith

● Sidney Poitier, Lilia Skala, Lisa Mann, Stanley Adams, Dan Frazer (Rainbow/United Artists)

Made on a modest budget and filmed entirely on location in Arizona, *Lilies* reveals Sidney Poitier as an actor with a sharp sense of humor. He is a journeyman laborer, touring the countryside in his station wagon, working when the fancy moves him, and traveling on when he feels the need for a change. That is his philosophy until he stops one day at a lonely farm to refill his radiator, but he meets his match in the five women who run the place.

They are all members of a holy order from East Germany, and are working arid land that has been bequeathed them. As the Mother Superior sets eyes on Poitier she is convinced that God has answered her prayers and sent a strong healthy man, to fix the roof of their farmhouse.

Many factors combine in the overall success of the film, notably the restrained direction by Ralph Nelson, a thoroughly competent screenplay by James Poe, and, of course, Poitier's own standout performance. There are a number of diverting scenes that remain in the memory, such as Poitier giving the Sisters an English lesson, with gestures to demonstrate the meaning of the phrases, and later leading them in the singing of 'Aymen'.
□ 1963: Best Picture (Nomination)

■ LILITH

1964, 110 MINS, US ▽
Dir Robert Rossen *Prod* Robert Rossen *Scr* Robert Rossen *Ph* Eugen Shuftan *Ed* Aram Avakian
Mus Kenyon Hopkins *Art Dir* Richard Sylbert
● Warren Beatty, Jean Seberg, Peter Fonda, Kim Hunter, Jessica Walter, Gene Hackman (Columbia)

Lilith is the story of a young man who becomes an occupational therapist in a private mental institution where patients share three conditions – schizophrenia, wealth and uncommon intelligence. Untrained in medicine, he nevertheless takes the job because he feels he can help suffering humanity.

Whatever clarity the narrative has in its early reels is shrouded in mist as his relations with a beautiful young patient begin to develop. Unfoldment is complex and often confusing. Robert Rossen as producer-scripter-director frequently fails to communicate to the spectator. Audience is left in as much of a daze as the hero is throughout most of the film.

Warren Beatty undertakes lead role with a hesitation jarring to the watcher. His dialog generally is restricted to no more than a single, or at most two sentences, and often the audience waits uncomfortably for words which never come while Beatty merely hangs his head or stares into space. As he finds himself falling in love with Jean Seberg, a fragile girl who lives in her own dream-world and wants love, the change of character from one fairly definitive in the beginning to the gropings of a sexually-obsessed mind never carries conviction.

In adapting the J.R. Salamanca novel, Rossen approaches his task with obvious attempt to shock.

■ LIMELIGHT

1952, 135 MINS, US ▽
Dir Charles Chaplin *Prod* Charles Chaplin
Scr Charles Chaplin *Ph* Karl Struss *Ed* Joe Inge
Mus Charles Chaplin *Art Dir* Eugene Lourie
● Charles Chaplin, Claire Bloom, Sydney Chaplin, Nigel Bruce, Norman Lloyd, Buster Keaton (Celebrated/United Artists)

Charlie Chaplin's production is probably derivative of his personal career over the years. Its backdrop is the British Stage. Departing from most forms of Hollywood

347

stereotype, the film has a flavor all its own in the sincere quality of the story anent the one-time great vaudemime and his rescue of a femme ballet student from a suicide attempt and subsequently from great mental depression.

Production-wise, *Limelight* is a one-man show since Chaplin does almost everything but grow his own rawstock. The British music hall milieu of 1917 and the third-rate rooming house, where a good deal of the story unfolds, come through as honest reproductions.

While Chaplin is the star, he must surrender some spotlight to Claire Bloom, recruited from the British stage, for the second lead. As the frustrated terper, the delicately beautiful young actress gives a sensitive and memorable performance.

Chaplin's real-life son, Sydney, is gentle and shy as the composer in love with Bloom.

....

■ LINEUP, THE

1958, 85 MINS, US

Dir Don Siegel *Prod* Jaime Del Valle *Scr* Stirling Silliphant *Ph* Hal Mohr *Ed* Al Clark *Mus* Mischa Bakaleinikoff *Art Dir* Ross Belleh
● Eli Wallach, Robert Keith, Warner Anderson, Richard Jaeckel, Mary LaRoche, William Leslie (Columbia)

The Lineup is based on a popular teleseries [1954–60] and has some of the same characters. But the screenplay is original material. The production is a moderately exciting melodrama based on dope smuggling in San Francisco, but short on action until the final, well-plotted and photographed, climax.

The action centers around the attempt by a narcotics gang to get the heroin it has planted abroad in the possession of travelers debarking in San Francisco. Eli Wallach heads the gang's pickup squad, aided by brains Robert Keith and driver Richard Jaeckel.

The best part of the action is its background, the Mark Hopkins motel, a Nob Hill mansion, Sutro's museum, the Opera House. There is also a good chase sequence at the end on an unfinished freeway. But the early parts of the film waste too much time on police procedure and lingo.

Wallach is wasted in the leading role. He seems an ordinary heavy, competent but not particularly interesting.

....

■ LINK

1986, 103 MINS, UK ◇ Ⓥ

Dir Richard Franklin *Prod* Richard Franklin *Scr* Everett DeRoche *Ph* Mike Molloy *Ed* Andrew London *Mus* Jerry Goldsmith *Art Dir* Norman Garwood
● Terence Stamp, Elizabeth Shue, Steven Pinner, Richard Garnett (Thorn EMI)

You know right off the film is in trouble when the chimpanzees outperform their human counterparts.

Credit here goes to animal trainer Ray Berwick for getting a full range of expressions out of the primates that director Richard Franklin couldn't get out of the actors.

Film plods along for almost an hour at an isolated English coastal manor house where pre-eminent primatologist Dr Steven Phillip (Terence Stamp) conducts rudimentary experiments on a handful of chimps.

The chimps' malevolent ringleader, Link, takes over the lead from the first time he is seen as the tuxedoed butler – even though he never utters a word.

Presumably, it's when we find out that Link, is not the duitful cigar-smoking house servant that things are supposed to get scary.

....

■ LION IN WINTER, THE

1968, 135 MINS, UK ◇ Ⓥ

Dir Anthony Harvey *Prod* Martin H. Poll *Scr* James Goldman *Ph* Douglas Slocombe *Ed* John Bloom *Mus* John Barry *Art Dir* Peter Murton
● Peter O'Toole, Katharine Hepburn, Jane Merrow, John Castle, Timothy Dalton, Anthony Hopkins (Avco Embassy)

The Lion in Winter, based on James Goldman's play (1966) about treachery in the family of England's King Henry II, is an intense, fierce, personal drama put across by outstanding performances of Peter O'Toole and Katherine Hepburn. Director Anthony Harvey has done excellent work with a generally strong cast and a literate adaptation.

Title refers to the late period in the life of Henry II, when a decision on succession is deemed advisable. His exiled, embittered and imprisoned wife, Eleanor of Aquitaine, and three legitimate male offspring, are gathered, along with his mistress and her brother, youthful king Philip of France.

In one day, the seven characters are stripped bare of all inner torments, outward pretensions and governing personality traits. Goldman has blended in his absorbing screenplay elements of love, hate, frustration, fulfillment, ambition and greed. O'Toole scores a bullseye as the king, while Hepburn's performance is amazing.

□ 1968: Best Picture (Nomination)

....

■ LION IS IN THE STREETS, A

1953, 87 MINS, US ◇

Dir Raoul Walsh *Prod* William Cagney *Scr* Luther Davis *Ph* Harry Stradling *Ed* George Amy *Mus* Franz Waxman *Art Dir* Wiard Ihnen
● James Cagney, Barbara Hale, Anne Francis, Warner Anderson, John McIntire, Jeanne Cagney (Warner)

The Adria Locke Langley novel was a long time coming to the screen since first purchased by the Cagneys for filming. Along the way it lost a lot of the shocker quality and emerges as just an average drama of a man's political ambitions.

The production deals with a backwoods politician who nearly forces his ambitions on a cotton-growing state. The novel had him succeeding in doing so for a long time, but the film thwarts his drive for power before he can be elected governor.

The development of the principal character and the story have a sketchy feel against which Raoul Walsh's direction has its problems.

James Cagney plays the swamp peddler who tries to ride into the governor's mansion by making a crusade of the plight of poor sharecroppers. The portrayal has an occasional strength, but mostly is a stylized performance done with an inconsistent southern dialect that rarely holds through a complete line of dialog.

Barbara Hale is sweet and charming as the schoolteacher who marries him. The fiery Flamingo of the book has been watered down considerably and doesn't give Anne Francis much opportunity.

....

■ LION OF THE DESERT

1981, 162 MINS, LIBYA/UK ◇

Dir Moustapha Akkad *Prod* Moustapha Akkad *Scr* H.A.L. Craig *Ph* Jack Hildyard *Ed* John Shirley *Mus* Maurice Jarre *Art Dir* Mario Garbuglia
● Anthony Quinn, Oliver Reed, Rod Steiger, John Gielgud, Irene Papas (Rat Vallone/Falcon)

Filmed as 'Omar Mukhtar' in 1979 at a cost reportedly exceeding $30 million, 'Lion of the Desert' is a very well-produced, frequently-stirring war film about a Libyan anti-colonial hero.

Functional script by H.A.L. Craig concentrates on the Italians' efforts in 1929–31 to conquer Libya. Mussolini (Rod Steiger in two effective scenes as the strutting fascist leader) sends his general Graziani (Oliver Reed) to put down the Bedouins led by Omar Mukhtar (Anthony Quinn). Quinn is a white-bearded old teacher and freedom fighter who has been battling the Italians for 20 years.

Film's many large-scale battle scenes include two ingenious ambushes where Mukhtar succeeds in beating the better-equipped Italian forces. Producer-director Moustapha Akkad stages such action with laudable scope, but much of the battle footage is impersonal.

While never explicit, the overtones of the Bedouins' desire for international recognition, Mukhtar's insistence that confiscated lands must be returned (with new Italian settlements on them not to be tolerated) and other militant dialog emphasize parallels with today's Palestinians.

Quinn is well cast as Omar Mukhtar and brings warmth and dimension to a stock national hero assignment.

....

■ LIONHEART

1987, 104 MINS, US ◇

Dir Franklin J. Schaffner *Prod* Stanley O'Toole, Talia Shire *Scr* Menno Meyjes, Richard Outten *Ph* Alec Mills *Ed* David Bretherton, Richard Haines *Mus* Jerry Goldsmith *Art Dir* Gil Parrondo
● Eric Stoltz, Gabriel Byrne, Nicola Cowper, Dexter Fletcher, Deborah Barrymore (Talia film II/Orion)

The Children's Crusade of the 12th century is the subject of Franklin J. Schaffner's *Lionheart*, a flaccid, limp kiddie adventure yarn with little of its intended grand epic sweep realized. Based partly on myth, partly on historical accounts, the story concerns bands of medieval tykes who set out to search for the elusive King Richard II on his quest to recapture the Holy Land from the Moslems.

Young knight Robert Nerra (Eric Stoltz) rides off disillusioned from his first battle and meets up with mystical Blanche (pretty Nicola Cowper) and her brother Michael (Dexter Fletcher), two teen circus performers who convince him to travel to Paris and join King Richard's crusade.

The dark threat of the Black Prince looms overhead in all corners of the misty forest. Gabriel Byrne plays him like an ennui-stricken Darth Vader. His goal is to recruit all the kids and sell them into slavery.

....

■ LIONS LOVE

1969, 115 MINS, US ◇

Dir Agnes Varda *Prod* Agnes Varda *Scr* Agnes Varda *Ph* Stefan Larner *Ed* Robert Dalva *Mus* Joseph Byrd *Art Dir* Jack Wright III
● Viva, Jerome Ragni, James Rado, Shirley Clarke, Carlos Clarens (Raab)

Actors in Hollywood were once called lions. Occupying a Hollywood house Viva, Jerome Ragni and James Rado are actors in love. Hence the title.

Into this menage a trois comes filmmaker Shirley Clarke come to Hollywood to make a movie. During a period of about a week, these four plus assorted producers, actors, children and film buffs play themselves in facsimiles of their real lives. Director Agnes Varda presents her fascination with the banal myth and mania that is Southern California.

The result is a pleasant, sometimes humorous blend of style and technique that ultimately is unsuccessful.

Viva playing Viva in one of the Andy Warhol exercises can be hugely revealing of her humor and personality. But Viva playing an actress called Viva as written by Agnes Varda loses much of her meaning. Similarly with Shirley Clarke.

....

L

■ LIPSTICK

1976, 89 MINS, US ◇ ⓥ

Dir Lamont Johnson *Prod* Freddie Fields *Scr* David Rayfiel *Ph* Bill Butler, William A. Fraker *Ed* Marion Rothman *Mus* Michel Polnareff, Jimmie Haskell *Art Dir* Robert Luthardt

● Margaux Hemingway, Chris Sarandon, Perry King, Anne Bancroft, Robin Gammell, Mariel Hemingway (Paramount/De Laurentiis)

Lipstick has pretensions of being an intelligent treatment of the tragedy of female rape. But by the time it's over, the film has shown its true colors as just another cynical violence exploitationer.

David Rayfiel's script tells how high-fashion model Margaux Hemingway is brutally assaulted by mild-mannered music teacher Chris Sarandon.

The early-on rape sequence (coming less than 20 minutes into the film) is really the dramatic highlight. Somehow one just knows that society's procedures will degrade the rape victim and that the ending of the film will contrive some opportunity for partially justified violence.

Margaux Hemingway's dramatic limitations lend more believability to the role. Sarandon's performance is powerful in its quiet menace.

■ LIQUID SKY

1982, 118 MINS, US ◇ ⓥ

Dir Slava Tsukerman *Prod* Slava Tsukerman *Scr* Slava Tsukerman, Nina Kerova, Anne Carlisle *Ph* Yuri Neyman *Ed* Sharyn Leslie Ross *Mus* Slava Tsukerman, Brenda Hutchinson, Clive Smith *Art Dir* Marina Levikova

● Anne Carlisle, Paula Sheppard, Susan Doukas, Otto Von Wernherr, Bob Brady, Elaine Grove (Z Films)

Liquid Sky is an odd, yet generally pleasing mixture of punk rock, science fiction, and black humor. Story centers on Anne Carlisle, a new wave fashion model who inhabits a world of high-decibel noise, drug addicts (title is slang expression for heroin) and casual sex. Although Carlisle is part of the scene, she doesn't embrace any of its vices.

Unbeknownst to the crowd, a pie-plate sized flying saucer takes up residence in the neighborhood. The creature proceeds to eliminate Carlisle's lovers as they reach orgasm. Carlisle assumes she's developed some strange curse. At first she uses this power for revenge but later attempts to warn her skeptical friends.

Created by Russian emigrees living in New York City, *Liquid Sky* possesses a sophisticated sense of humor. It's view of a changing society is offered up in fiercely black comic tones. Neither the new guard nor the old escapes the filmmakers' barbed observations.

■ LIQUIDATOR, THE

1966, 104 MINS, UK ◇

Dir Jack Cardiff *Prod* Jon Pennington *Scr* Peter Yeldham *Ph* Ted Scaife *Ed* Ernest Walter *Mus* Lalo Schifrin *Art Dir* John Blezard

● Rod Taylor, Trevor Howard, Jill St. John, Wilfrid Hyde White, David Tomlinson, Akim Tamiroff (M-G-M)

This spy yarn features Boysie Oakes, a creation of John Gardner. Peter Yeldham's screenplay and Jack Cardiff's direction combine plenty of action and some crisp wisecracking.

Where Boysie Oakes (Rod Taylor) is different from his [1960s] counterparts is that he is neither a pro undercover agent nor an enthusiastic amateur with a flair. In fact, he is a vulnerable sort of guy who hates killing. An ex-sergeant who accidentally saves Trevor Howard's life, he is conned into joining the service by Howard (Security's No 2).

He compromises by hiring a professional killer to do the dirty work for him, an angle which has promise as a film plot. But this fairly quickly gets sidetracked when Oakes takes 'No 2's' lush secretary for a dirty weekend on the Riviera.

There are plenty of holes in the plot, but no matter. The vulnerable Oakes is played with plenty of charm and guts by Taylor, though he hardly suggests a character with such fundamental failings and frailties as Boysie.

■ LIST OF ADRIAN MESSENGER, THE

1963, 98 MINS, US ⓥ

Dir John Huston *Prod* Edward Lewis *Scr* Anthony Veiller *Ph* Joe MacDonald, Ted Scaife *Ed* Terry O. Morse *Mus* Jerry Goldsmith *Art Dir* Alexander Golitzen, Stephen Grimes, George Webb

● George C. Scott, Dana Wynter, Clive Brook, Gladys Cooper, Herbert Marshall, Jacques Roux (Universal)

Anthony Veiller's screenplay, based on a story by Philip MacDonald, is a kind of straight-laced version of *Kind Hearts and Coronets*. It is the story of a retired British Intelligence officer's efforts to nab a killer who has ingeniously murdered 11 men who represent obstacles to his goal – the acquisition of a huge fortune to which he will become heir as soon as he eliminates the 12th obstacle, the 12-year-old grandson of his aged uncle, the wealthy Marquis of Gleneyre.

The film hums along smoothly and captivatingly until the killer, having disposed of number 11, shows up at the estate of the Marquis, where he plans to dispose of the lad from the inside. Here the story begins to fall apart. Since both Scotland Yard and our principal investigator (George C. Scott) are at this time fully aware of who and where their man is, and what he is up to, it is an incredibly contrived story distortion to suppose that they would let him roam about freely for several days.

An even more damaging miscue is the utilization of stars who are hidden behind facial disguises in fundamentally inconsequential roles. All the putty peeling begins to get downright monotonous towards the end. Of the five stars who 'guest,' Kirk Douglas has the major assignment and carries it off colorfully and credibly. The others are Tony Curtis, Burt Lancaster, Robert Mitchum and Frank Sinatra. Only Mitchum is easily recognizable beneath the facial stickum.

Huston directs the film with style and flair. Credit is due makeup man Bud Westmore for his concealment of several of the most familiar faces of the 20th century.

■ LISZTOMANIA

1975, 104 MINS, UK ◇

Dir Ken Russell *Prod* Roy Baird, David Puttnam *Scr* Ken Russell *Ph* Peter Suchitzky *Ed* Stuart Baird *Mus* Rick Wakeman (arr.) *Art Dir* Philip Harrison

● Roger Daltrey, Sara Kestelman, Paul Nicholas, Fiona Lewis, Veronica Quilligan, Ringo Starr (Warner)

Ken Russell's *Lisztomania*, combines his customary zany and bawdy artfulness with a style close to *Tommy*.

Liszt is depicted as somewhat of a self-indulgent professional hustler, outdone only by Wagner, whose added ambition of unifying Germany lends the kind of 'meaningful commitment' so often necessary to put over otherwise mediocre pop music. Daltrey and Paul Nicholas handle their parts with flair.

■ LITTLE BIG MAN

1970, 147 MINS, US ◇ ⓥ

Dir Arthur Penn *Prod* Stuart Millar, Arthur Penn *Scr* Calder Willingham *Ph* Harry Stradling Jr *Ed* Dede Allen *Mus* John Hammond *Art Dir* Angelo Graham

● Dustin Hoffman, Faye Dunaway, Martin Balsam, Richard Mulligan, Chief Dan George, Jeff Corey (Cinema Center)

Little Big Man is a sort of vaudeville show, framed in fictional biography, loaded with sketches of varying degrees of serious and burlesque humor, and climaxed by the Indian victory over Gen George A. Custer at Little Big Horn in 1876.

The story strand [from the novel by Thomas Berger] is Dustin Hoffman's long life (he is over 120 at prolog and epilog brackets), especially his years as an adopted Indian who witnessed Custer's megalomaniacal massacre attempt that backfired.

Might it be a serious attempt to right some unretrievable wrong via gallows humor which avoids the polemics? This seems to be the course taken; the attempt at least can be respected in theory.

Chief Dan George, is outstanding as an Indian chief who provides periodic inputs of philosophy. Faye Dunaway is first the preacher's over-sexed wife, later a prostitute admired by Wild Bill Hickok, played well by Jeff Corey; and Martin Balsam is a swindling traveling beggar.

■ LITTLE CAESAR

1931, 77 MINS, US ⓥ

Dir Mervyn LeRoy *Scr* Francis E. Faragoh, Robert W. Lee *Ph* Tony Gaudio *Ed* Ray Curtiss *Mus* Erno Rapee (dir.) *Art Dir* Anton Grot

● Edward G. Robinson, Douglas Fairbanks Jr., Glenda Farrell, Sidney Blackmer, Thomas Jackson, Ralph Ince (First National)

There are enough killings herein to fill the quota for an old time cowboy-Indian thriller. And one tough mugg, in the title part, who is tough all the way from the start, when he's a bum with ambition, to the finish, when he's a bum again, but a dead one.

For a performance as 'Little Caesar' no director could ask for more than Edward G. Robinson's contribution. Here, no matter what he has to say, he's entirely convincing.

Young Douglas Fairbanks is splendid as the gunman's friend. Another junior, William Collier Jr. contributes real trouping to a part that seemed out of his line. There are no off-key performances in the picture.

No new twists to the gunman stuff [from the novel by W.R. Burnett] same formula and all the standard tricks, but Mervyn LeRoy, directing, had a good yarn to start with and gives it plenty of pace besides astute handling.

■ LITTLE DARLINGS

1980, 92 MINS, US ◇ ⓥ

Dir Ronald F. Maxwell *Prod* Stephen J. Friedman *Scr* Kimi Peck, Dalene Young *Ph* Fred Batka *Ed* Pembroke J. Herring *Mus* Charles Fox *Art Dir* William Hiney

● Tatum O'Neal, Kristy McNichol, Matt Dillon, Armande Assante, Krista Errickson (Paramount)

Little Darlings makes an honest effort to deal with the sexual stirrings of two teenage girls, but many adults are likely to dismiss the effort as puppy love with appeal to prurient interests.

Tatum O'Neal and Kristy McNichol are both excellent as virgins of widely different social backgrounds who meet at summer camp. O'Neal is a sheltered rich girl and McNichol the poor, streetwise urchin but their different upbringings do not release their shared hesitancy about making love for the first time.

In his feature debut, director Ronald F. Maxwell isn't perfect. But he gets several fine scenes from his performers, especially when O'Neal deals with her love interest, when NcNichol deals with her love interest, and best of all, when O'Neal and McNichol finally level with each other.

■ LITTLE DORRIT

1987, 360 MINS, UK ◇ ⊽

Dir Christine Edzard *Prod* Richard Goodwin, John Brabourne *Scr* Christine Edzard *Ph* Bruno de Keyzer *Ed* Oliver Stockman, Fraser Maclean *Mus* Michel Sanvoisin (arr.)

● Alec Guinness, Derek Jacobi, Cyril Cusack, Sarah Pickering, Joan Greenwood, Max Wall (Sands/Cannon)

Little Dorrit is a remarkable achievement. For writer/director Christine Edzard the epic project [from the novel by Charles Dickens] was obviously a labor of love, and what she has accomplished on a small budget is astounding.

The project is in fact two films, each three hours long [I: *Nobody's Fault*, 177 mins; II: *Little Dorrit's Story*, 183 mins], with the latter being virtually a remake of the former. A large cast of uniformly excellent British actors is topped off by quite brilliant portrayals by Alec Guinness as William Dorrit, and Derek Jacobi as Arthur Clennam.

In the second part you see from a different angle the story of the family's plight, and why they are in prison. Sarah Pickering bestows Amy Dorrit with the gentle firmness to look after her father, brother and sister, and when Jacobi appears on the scene slowly falls in love with him.

The family travels abroad and during a plush dinner in Rome to celebrate the marriage of Fanny Dorrit (Amelda Brown) and Sparkler (Simon Dormandy), Guinness finally goes mad, and delivers a speech as if he were still in the Marshalsea.

Pic then follows Pickering discovering Jacobi is in prison and her efforts to raise the money to free him.

Six hours of viewing obviously allows full characterization and depth of story – though some characters from the novel are still missing – but the style of showing virtually the same story through two people [Clennam and Amy] allows charming reinterpretations of certain scenes, and presents a fully rounded piece as never usually found in the cinema.

The pic, which is set in the 1820s, was shot entirely in a studio owned by Sands Films in the middle of Dickens territory, in Rotherhithe close to the Thames, and the painted sets give the film a rich theatrical texture while not deflecting from the story.

■ LITTLE DRUMMER GIRL, THE

1984, 130 MINS, US ◇ ⊽

Dir George Roy Hill *Prod* Robert L. Crawford *Scr* Loring Mandel *Ph* Wolfgang Treu *Ed* William Reynolds *Mus* Dave Grusin *Art Dir* Henry Bumstead

● Diane Keaton, Yorgo Voyagis, Klaus Kinski, Sami Frey, Michael Cristofer, David Suchet (Pan Arts)

George Roy Hill has made a disappointingly flat film adaptation of one of John Le Carre's top novels, *The Little Drummer Girl*. Overlong and, for the most part, indifferently staged on a multitude of foreign locales, pic can't help but intrigue due to the intense subject matter, that of complex Israeli and Palestinian espionage and terrorism.

Diane Keaton plays the role of Charlie, in the book a virulently pro-Palestinian British actress generally agreed to have been inspired by Vanessa Redgrave.

No matter, though, for events quickly take Keaton out of the UK. A team of Israeli operatives, led by the supremely self-confident Klaus Kinski, recruits her in Greece, breaks down her Arab sympathies and eventually puts her in place as an ideal agent.

Keaton's loud, pushy, erratic showbiz character isn't all that easy to warm up to.

■ LITTLE FAUSS AND BIG HALSY

1970, 98 MINS, US ◇

Dir Sidney J. Furie *Prod* Albert S. Ruddy *Scr* Charles Eastman *Ph* Ralph Woolsey *Ed* Argyle Neson Jr *Mus* Johnny Cash, Bob Dylan, Carl Perkins *Art Dir* Lawrence G. Paul

● Robert Redford, Michael J. Pollard, Lauren Hutton, Noah Beery, Lucille Benson, Ray Ballard (Paramount)

Little Fauss and Big Halsy is an uneven, sluggish story of two motorcycle racers – Robert Redford playing a callous heel and Michael J. Pollard as a put-upon sidekick who eventually (in modified finale) surpasses his fallen idol.

Hampered by a thin screenplay, film is padded further by often-pretentious direction by Sidney J. Furie against expansive physical values.

What is very disappointing is the lack of strong dramatic development. Redford's character is apparent in his very first scene; it never changes. It is in effect the carrier frequency on which Pollard and others must beat, the end result is erratic.

Pollard is very good in lending depth to his character, though his dialect often obscures his dialog.

■ LITTLE FOXES, THE

1941, 115 MINS, US

Dir William Wyler *Prod* Samuel Goldwyn *Scr* Lillian Hellman, Dorothy Parker, Arthur Kober, Alan Campbell *Ph* Gregg Toland *Ed* Daniel Mandell *Mus* Meredith Wilson

● Bette Davis, Herbert Marshall, Teresa Wright, Richard Carlson, Patricia Collinge, Dan Duryea (RKO/Goldwyn)

From starring Bette Davis down the line to the bit roles portrayed by minor Negroes the acting is well nigh flawless. And standing out sharply in Lillian Hellman's searing play about rapacious people are several performers who appeared in the 1939 Broadway stage version, i.e. Patricia Collinge, Carl Benton Reid, Dan Duryea and Charles Dingle.

In the natural padding out of the story permitted by a screenplay permits the injection of romance between Teresa Wright, as Davis' daughter, and Richard Carlson, playing a young newspaperman.

The story is about the Hubbard family of the deep south – as mercenary a foursome as has never emerged from fact or fiction. In this picture Davis also murders her husband, played by Herbert Marshall, but with the unique weapon of disinterest. When Marshall, in the throes of a heart attack, crashes a bottle of medicine that can save his life, Davis sits by and watches him do a dying swan. That's her way of killing the man who had refused to help finance the get-rich scheme of her brothers.

Marshall turns in one of his top performances in the exacting portrayal of a suffering, dying man.

On top of the smooth pace, Wyler has handled every detail with an acutely dramatic touch.

□ 1941: Best Picture (Nomination)

■ LITTLE LORD FAUNTLEROY

1921, 120 MINS, US ⊗

Dir Alfred E. Green, Jack Pickford *Scr* Bernard McConville *Ph* Charles Rosher *Mus* Louis F. Gottschalk

● Mary Pickford, Claude Gillingwater, Joseph Dowling, James Marcus, Kate Price, Rose Dione (Pickford/United Artists)

Little Lord Fauntleroy is a perfect Pickford picture. It exploits the star in dual roles, one of them one of the immortal and classic boy parts of all times. Mary Pickford shows a range of versatility, between the blue-blooded sombre mother and the blue-blooded but mischievous kid, that is almost startling. She meets herself many times in double exposures, and she is taller than herself and different from herself, and incredibly true to each.

Only director Jack Pickford could have introduced the whimsical and always amusing touches of raw boyishness in the fighting, grimacing, scheming, lovable kid that Pickford again turns out to be. She jumps off high perches onto other boys' backs, she wrestles and does trick ju-jitsus, she dodges and climbs and leans and tumbles and hand-stands.

While *Fauntleroy* is not sensational, it is a human and appealing story.

■ LITTLE LORD FAUNTLEROY

1936, 98 MINS, US ⊽

Dir John Cromwell *Prod* David O. Selznick *Scr* Hugh Walpole *Ph* Charles Rosher *Mus* Max Steiner *Art Dir* Sturges Carne

● C. Aubrey Smith, Freddie Bartholomew, Dolores Costello Barrymore, Henry Stephenson, Guy Kibbee, Mickey Rooney (Selznick/United Artists)

As his first for Selznick International after leaving Metro, David O. Selznick turns in a fine, sensitive picture in *Little Lord Fauntleroy*, which may well rank with his *David Copperfield* and *A Tale of Two Cities*. It's a transmutation of Frances Hodgson Burnett's mid-Victorian saga.

A theme as prissy as *Fauntleroy*, where the earl-to-be calls his mother 'Dearest', might have proved quite hazardous in anything but the most expert hands. As Hugh Walpole adapts it. John Cromwell directs it and a sterling cast troups it – all under Selznick's keen aegis – it's very palatable cinematic. fare.

Young Freddie Bartholomew is capital in the title role and Dolores Costello Barrymore, marking her film comeback, as 'Dearest', his young and widowed mother, are an ideal coupling in the two principal roles. C. Aubrey Smith as the gruff and grumpy earl who blindly hates his daughter-in-law just because she's American, well-nigh steals the picture in a characterization setup that's a match for this vet thespian. Henry Stephenson as the English barrister is on a par in a role that calls for much restraint.

■ LITTLE MALCOLM AND HIS STRUGGLE AGAINST THE EUNUCHS

1974, 112 MINS, UK ◇

Dir Stuart Cooper *Prod* Gavrik Losey *Scr* Derek Woodward *Ph* John Alcott *Ed* Ray Lovejoy *Mus* Stanley Myers

● John Hurt, John McEnery, Raymond Platt, Rosalind Ayres, David Warner (Apple)

Adapted by Derek Woodward from a mid-1960s play by David Halliwell, item emerges as a frequently hilarious, generally thought-provoking and sobering, beautifully acted, but a trifle overlong and repetitious film of uncertain destination.

On one level, story dealing with a carefully-plotted sham uprising by a trio of students draws laughs in its Mitty-ish mock evocations of socio-political tirades, while subsurface the conclusions drawn are frightening as evidenced in the climactic scene of useless violence against a girl.

There's a trace of *Clockwork Orange* here and there (and not only because pix shares same lenser, John Alcott), and it's grimly amusing in a similar way, but there the resemblance ends.

Performances are all tops.

■ LITTLE MISS BROADWAY

1938, 70 MINS, US Ⓥ
Dir Irving Cummings   *Prod* David Hempstead
Scr Harry Tugent, Jack Yellen   *Ph* Arthur Miller
Ed Walter Thompson   *Mus* Louis Silvers (dir.)
● Shirley Temple, George Murphy, Jimmy Durante,
Phyllis Brooks, Edna May Oliver, George Barbier
(20th Century-Fox)

In *Little Miss Broadway*, Shirley Temple shows an improvement in her tap dancing, her singing and her ability to turn on at will whatever emotional faucet is demanded by the script.

With Jimmy Durante, George Murphy, Edna Mae Oliver, George Barbier, Donald Meek and El Brendel in featured roles, something approaching hilarity is expected. The result is far short of the promise. Shirley is a standout, but the others through faulty cutting of the film and undeveloped opportunities in the script never quite get their openings to score.

Shirley is introduced as a ward in an orphan asylum. She is discharged into the care of an uncle (Edward Ellis) who manages a theatrical hotel near Broadway called Variety. Edna May Oliver, who owns the building and lives close by, is annoyed by the constant rehearsing of the acts and decides to close the place by demanding immediate payment of past due rent.

Her nephew (George Murphy) intercedes at the behest of Shirley Temple, but the issue finds its way to court where the acts give a dress rehearsal of a musical revue, which they hope will earn enough money to meet the financial obligation.

Walter Bullock and Harold Spina have written six songs which Shirley sings, some solo, others with chorus.

■ LITTLE MISS MARKER

1980, 103 MINS, US ◇ Ⓥ
Dir Walter Bernstein   *Prod* Jennings Lang   *Scr* Walter
Bernstein   *Ph* Philip Lathrop   *Ed* Eve Newman
Mus Henry Mancini   *Art Dir* Edward C. Carfagno
● Walter Matthau, Julie Andrews, Tony Curtis, Sara
Stimson, Bob Newhart (Universal)

There is something irresistible about the story of a darling little girl left in the care of colorfully kind gamblers, which explains why this is the fourth attempt to bring Damon Runyon's story to the screen. But writer-director Walter Bernstein blows his directorial debut completely.

It's a shame, because seemingly if ever there was an actor who should play 'Sorrowful Jones' it's Walter Matthau and Bob Newhart should have been a wonderful 'Regret', while Tony Curtis could have been a respectable antagonist.

But they are all flat in their parts and that has to be Bernstein's fault. Even worse, Julie Andrews is woefully miscast with her British accent and Lee Grant gets no more than a bit part as a judge. The only really decent thing about the picture is little Sara Stimson.

■ LITTLE MURDERS

1971, 110 MINS, US ◇ Ⓥ
Dir Alan Arkin   *Prod* Jack Brodsky, Elliott Gould
Scr Jules Feiffer   *Ph* Gordon Willis   *Ed* Howard
Kuperman   *Mus* Fred Kaz
● Elliott Gould, Marcia Rodd, Vincent Gardenia,
Elizabeth Wilson, Donald Sutherland, Alan Arkin
(20th Century-Fox)

Alan Arkin, making a most impressive directorial debut, has made a film that is not only funny but devastating in its emotional impact.

Arkin's actors play very broadly, just at the edge of the caricatures they are in Jules Feiff-

er's screenplay. But they fill in the outlines with such a wealth of human detail that it's impossible not to identify with them. Both comedy and horror, therefore, hit closer to home.

Coproducer Elliott Gould plays a photographer who was successful until he began to 'lose the people' in his pictures, and found it unnecessary or impossible either to fight or really 'feel'. Into his life comes Marcia Rodd, a girl who would like to mold him into 'a strong, vital, self-assured man, that I can protect and take care of'.

Then the world gets in the way, and Feiffer once and for all stops being the amiably satiric cartoonist, and hurtles towards a painful conclusion: that the only way for the 'mad' and the 'alienated' to get back into the world is to adopt its insanity.

Vincent Gardenia, Elizabeth Wilson and Jon Korkes are excellent as Rodd's extraordinary family. Juicy 'bits' are played by Arkin as a paranoid detective, Lou Jacobi, as a judge who remembers his days on the Lower East Side; and Donald Sutherland, as a hip minister.

■ LITTLE NIGHT MUSIC, A

1977, 124 MINS, AUSTRIA/US/W. GERMANY ◇ Ⓥ
Dir Hal Prince   *Prod* Elliott Kastner   *Scr* Hugh
Wheeler   *Ph* Arthur Ibbetson   *Ed* John Jumpson
Mus Stephen Sondheim
● Elizabeth Taylor, Diana Rigg, Len Cariou, Hermione
Gingold, Lesley-Ann Down, Laurence Guittard
(Sascha-Wien/Kastner)

A Little Night Music is based on an earlier film by Ingmar Bergman [*Smiles of a Summer Night*, 1955] that was turned into a [1973] hit Broadway musical with music and lyrics by Stephen Sondheim. In this refilming Hal Prince repeats as director.

All this fuses into an elegant looking, period romantic charade.

There is one sprightly number as the assorted characters set out for a country dinner that will resolve their complicated love problems. There is a noted promiscuous actress ready to settle down with a steady man and her teenage daughter, a staid lawyer with a young wife of 18 whose marriage has yet to be consummated, plus his son and a fiery army lieutenant, lover of the actress, and his jealous but submissive wife.

Uneven and sometimes slow, pic has good looks.

■ LITTLE NIKITA

1988, 98 MINS, US ◇ Ⓥ
Dir Richard Benjamin   *Prod* Harry Gittes   *Scr* John
Hill, B. Goldman   *Ph* Laszlo Kovacs   *Ed* Jacqueline
Cambas   *Mus* Marvin Hamlisch   *Art Dir* Gene
Callahan
● Sidney Poitier, River Phoenix, Richard Jenkins,
Caroline Kava (Columbia)

Little Nikita never really materializes as a taut espionage thriller and winds up as an unsatisfying execution of a clever premise – a teen's traumatic discovery that his parents are Soviet spies.

Film opens strongly as parallel storylines unfold and audience is drawn in by the need to decipher the link between the mission of a Soviet agent and an all-American family in the mythical San Diego suburb of Fountain Grove.

Poised at the juncture of these developments is FBI agent Sidney Poitier, whose natural intensity seems just right for the role.

Poitier encounters River Phoenix, a youngster who decides to apply for the Air Force Academy, on a routine FBI check. When some peculiar data turns up on Phoenix' parents – convincingly portrayed by Richard Jenkins and Caroline Kava – Poitier begins

an investigation that leads to an almost avuncular bonding with Phoenix.

■ LITTLE PRINCE, THE

1974, 88 MINS, UK ◇ Ⓥ
Dir Stanley Donen   *Prod* Stanley Donen   *Scr* Alan Jay
Lerner   *Ph* Christopher Challis   *Ed* Peter Boita, John
Guthridge   *Mus* Frederick Loewe   *Art Dir* John Barry
● Richard Kiley, Steven Warner, Bob Fosse, Gene
Wilder, Joss Ackland, Clive Revill (Paramount)

Handsome production plus excellent photography and effects cannot obscure the limited artistic achievement of *The Little Prince*. Alan Jay Lerner's adaptation of the book by Antoine De Saint-Exupery is flat and his lyrics are unmemorable, as are Frederick Loewe's melodies. Richard Kiley is cast as the childman, and Steven Warner is the manchild, who ruminate on the meaning of a good life. Some okay cameo appearances by Bob Fosse, Gene Wilder, and others lend transient sparkle.

Kiley, who never forgot his youthful fantasies, makes a forced landing in a desert, where Warner, an interspace traveler, comes upon him and his grounded airplane. A series of vignettes, delicate in their import and rendered opaque by the script, supposedly make Kiley a better man for the experience.

■ LITTLE ROMANCE, A

1979, 108 MINS, US/FRANCE ◇ Ⓥ
Dir George Roy Hill   *Prod* Yves Rousset-Rouard,
Robert L. Crawford   *Scr* Allan Burns   *Ph* Pierre-
William Glenn   *Ed* William Reynolds   *Mus* Georges
Delerue   *Art Dir* Henry Bumstead
● Laurence Olivier, Arthur Hill, Sally Kellerman, Diane
Lane, Thelonious Bernard, Broderick Crawford
(Orion/Pan Arts/Trinacra)

Scripter Allan Burns has craftily kept the point of view of the youngsters, Diane Lane and Thelonious Bernard, while the adults, with certain exceptions, are seen as suitably grotesque and ridiculous, giving *Romance* a crest of humor on which to ride.

Lane is the offspring of flighty jet-setter Sally Kellerman, who spends the film mooning over auteur director David Dukes, rather than hubby Arthur Hill. The teenagers are drawn to one another, persevere in the face of family pressure, and eventually take off in pursuit of a romantic ideal.

Fulcrum in script is the beneficent boulevardier, limned by Laurence Olivier in a modern refashioning of the old Maurice Chevalier role. The prototypical lovable scoundrel, Olivier hams it up unmercifully.

■ LITTLE SHOP OF HORRORS

1986, 88 MINS, US ◇ Ⓥ
Dir Frank Oz   *Prod* David Geffen   *Scr* Howard
Ashman   *Ph* Robert Paynter   *Ed* John Jympson
Mus Alan Menken   *Art Dir* Roy Walker
● Rick Moranis, Ellen Greene, Vincent Gardenia, Steve
Martin, Jim Belushi, John Candy (Warner/Geffen)

Little Shop of Horrors is a fractured, funny production transported rather reluctantly from the stage to the screen. Almost nothing is left besides the setting and story outline from the 1961 Roger Corman film that inspired the 1982 stage musical. Tone, intent and execution are miles apart.

Living a rather mundane life, working in Mushnik's flower shop are Seymour (Rick Moranis) and Audrey (Ellen Greene), that is until lightning strikes and the natural order of things is turned upside down. Through a chain of events just silly enough to be fun, Seymour becomes the proud owner of Audrey II, a rare breed of plant that makes him famous and his boss (Vincent Gardenia) prosperous. Audrey II develops an insatiable appetite for human flesh.

. . . .

■ LITTLE SHOP OF HORRORS, THE

1961, 70 MINS, US Ⓥ

Dir Roger Corman   *Prod* Roger Corman   *Scr* Charles B. Griffiths   *Ph* Archie Dalzell   *Ed* Marshall Neilan Jr.   *Mus* Fred Katz   *Art Dir* Daniel Haller
● Jonathan Haze, Jackie Joseph, Mel Welles, Myrtle Vail, Leola Wendorff, Jack Nicholson (Filmgroup)

Reportedly only two shooting days and $22,500 went into the making of this picture, but limited fiscal resources didn't deter Roger Corman and his game, resourceful little Filmgroup from whipping up a serviceable parody of a typical screen horror number.

Little Shop of Horrors is kind of one big sick joke, but it's essentially harmless and good-natured. The plot concerns a young, goofy florist's assistant who creates a talking, blood-sucking, man-eating plant, then feeds it several customers from skid row before sacrificing himself to the horticultural gods.

There is a fellow who visits the Skid Row flower shop to munch on purchased bouquets ('I like to eat in these little out-of-the-way places'). There is also the Yiddish proprietor, distressed by his botanical attraction ('we not only got a talking plant, we got one dot makes smart cracks'), but content to let it devour as the shop flourishes. And there are assorted quacks, alcoholics, masochists [Jack Nicholson, as a dental patient], sadists and even a pair of private-eyes who couldn't solve the case of the disappearing fly in a hothouse for Venus Fly-Traps.

The acting is pleasantly preposterous. Mel Welles, as the proprietor, and Jonathan Haze, as the budding Luther Burbank, are particularly capable, and Jackie Joseph is decorative as the latter's girl. Horticulturalists and vegetarians will love it.

. . . .

■ LITTLE WOMEN

1933, 117 MINS, US

Dir George Cukor   *Prod* Merian C. Cooper   *Scr* Sarah Y. Mason, Victor Heerman   *Ph* Henry Gerrard   *Ed* Jack Kitchin
● Katharine Hepburn, Joan Bennett, Paul Lukas, Frances Dee, Jean Parker, Edna May Oliver (Radio)

Little Women is a profoundly moving history of youth and in this celluloid transcription [of the novel by Louisa M. Alcott] its deeply spiritual values are revealed with a simple earnestness.

Katharine Hepburn as Jo creates a new and stunningly vivid character; strips the Victorian hoyden of her too syrupy goody-goodiness; and endows the role with awkwardly engaging youth energy that makes it the essence of flesh and blood reality.

Story is full of tearfully sentimental passages, but they are managed with beautiful restraint. There is the heavily tearful episode of Beth's sickroom scene, in which the pathetic possibilities are realized to the last extreme by the rigid restriction of obvious acting.

A notable company of standard screen names supports the star. Joan Bennett, Frances Dee and Jean Parker (as Beth) complete the feminine quartet, all playing with a persuasive charm. Paul Lukas contributes a characteristic portrait as Prof Bhaer and Spring Byington is a conspicuous point of casting strength.

☐ 1932/33: Best Picture (Nomination)

. . . .

■ LITTLE WOMEN

1949, 121 MINS, US ◇ Ⓥ

Dir Mervyn LeRoy   *Prod* Mervyn LeRoy   *Scr* Andrew Solt, Sarah Y. Mason, Victor Heeman   *Ph* Robert Planck, Charles Schoenbaum   *Ed* Ralph E. Winters   *Mus* Adolph Deutsch

● June Allyson, Peter Lawford, Margaret O'Brien, Elizabeth Taylor, Janet Leigh, Rossano Brazzi (M-G-M)

Metro has combined a star constellation for its unstinting re-make of Louisa May Alcott's *Little Women*, the old-lace classic of a quartet of daughters and their strivings in Civil War years.

The tender story, with its frank and unashamed assault on the emotions, still has its effective moments at times when the sentiment doesn't grow a little too thick.

Playing Jo, the part which won critical plaudits for Katharine Hepburn in 1933, June Allyson's thesping dominates the film.

As Beth, the youngest of the group, Margaret O'Brien is peculiarly subdued except for one touching scene in which she speaks of her nearing death. In the two other most important parts, Elizabeth Taylor and Janet Leigh neatly counterfoil Allyson's irrepressible cavortings.

. . . .

■ LITTLEST REBEL, THE

1935, 70 MINS, US Ⓥ

Dir David Butler   *Prod* Darryl Zanuck, B.G. DeSylva   *Scr* Edwin Burke   *Ph* John Seitz   *Ed* Irene Morra   *Mus* Cyril Mockridge (dir.)   *Art Dir* William Darling
● Shirley Temple, John Boles, Jack Holt, Karen Morley, Bill Robinson, Guinn Williams (20th Century-Fox)

The Littlest Rebel is a good Shirley Temple picture. It happens to be very similar in title, plantation locale, Negro comedy, and in general mechanics to *The Little Colonel* (1935).

Shrewdly playing both sides, as between the north and the south, script [from the play by Edward Peble] throws a lot of dialog to the Confederacy. All bitterness and cruelty has been rigorously cut out and the Civil War emerges as a misunderstanding among kindly gentlemen with eminently happy slaves and a cute little girl who sings and dances through the story.

Picture opens just before war is declared. The tot is giving a party to all the well-mannered children of the Virginia aristocracy and a good deal of sly comedy is slipped in at the table, and later when the children skip the minuet with genteel dignity. War brings successive losses culminating in the death of the mother (Karen Morley).

Bill Robinson and the child again dance. Robinson is once more the trusty family butler who guards little missy. John Boles, Jack Holt and Karen Morley are just routine adults who react to the charm of a little girl.

. . . .

■ LIVE AND LET DIE

1973, 121 MINS, UK ◇ Ⓥ

Dir Guy Hamilton   *Prod* Albert R. Broccoli, Harry Saltzman   *Scr* Tom Mankiewicz   *Ph* Ted Moore   *Ed* Bert Bates, Raymond Poulton, John Shirley   *Mus* George Martin   *Art Dir* Syd Cain, Stephen Hendrick
● Roger Moore, Yaphet Kotto, Jane Seymour, Clifton James, Julius W. Harris, Geoffrey Holder (United Artists/Eon)

Live and Let Die, the eighth Cubby Broccoli-Harry Saltzman film based on Ian Fleming's James Bond, introduces Roger Moore as an okay replacement for Sean Connery. The script reveals that plot lines have descended further to the level of the old Saturday afternoon serial.

Here Bond's assigned to ferret out mysterious goings on involving Yaphet Kotto, diplomat from a Caribbean island nation who in disguise also is a bigtime criminal. The nefarious scheme in his mind: give away tons of free heroin to create more American dopers and then he and the telephone company will be the largest monopolies. Jane Seymour, Kotto's tarot-reading forecaster, loses her skill after turning on to Bond-age.

The comic book plot meanders through a series of hardware production numbers. These include some voodoo ceremonies; a hilarious airplane-vs-auto pursuit scene; a double-decker bus escape from motorcycles and police cars; and a climactic inland waterway powerboat chase. Killer sharks, poisonous snakes and man-eating crocodiles also fail to deter Bond from his mission.

. . . .

■ LIVE NOW – PAY LATER

1962, 104 MINS, UK

Dir Jay Lewis   *Prod* Jack Hanbury   *Scr* Jack Trevor Story   *Ph* Jack Hildyard   *Ed* Roger Cherrill   *Mus* Ron Grainer   *Art Dir* Lionel Couch
● Ian Hendry, June Ritchie, John Gregson, Liz Frazer, Geoffrey Keen, Peter Butterworth (Regal International/Woodlands)

Jack Trevor Story's screenplay [from Jack Lindsay's novel, *All on the Never-Never*] has many amusing moments, but overall it is untidy and does not develop the personalities of some of the main characters sufficiently. Extraneous situations are dragged in without helping the plot development overmuch.

Ian Hendry plays a smart aleck, philandering, doublecrossing tallyman who, with two illegitimate babies to his discredit, still finds that the easiest way to bluff his femme patrons into getting hocked up to their eyebrows in installment buying is via the boudoir. The character has a certain brash, breezy assurance, but no charm. And that's the way Hendry plays it, to the point of irritation.

In most of the film he is trying to patch up a row that he has had with his steady girl friend. For the remainder, he is cheating his employer (John Gregson), a real estate agent and a string of creditors.

June Ritchie, as the main girl in the case, confirms the promising impression she made in her debut in *A Kind of Loving*, but she can do little in this cardboard role of wronged young mistress.

. . . .

■ LIVES OF A BENGAL LANCER, THE

1935, 110 MINS, US Ⓥ

Dir Henry Hathaway   *Prod* Louis D. Lighton   *Scr* Waldemar Young, John L. Balderston, Achmed Abdullah, Grover Jones, W.S. McNutt   *Ph* Charles Lang, Ernest Schoedsack   *Ed* Ellsworth Hoagland   *Mus* Milan Roder   *Art Dir* Hans Dreier, Roland Anderson
● Gary Cooper, Franchot Tone, Richard Cromwell, Guy Standing, C. Aubrey Smith (Paramount)

Work on *Lancer* commenced four years earlier when Ernest Schoedsack went to India for exteriors and atmosphere. Some of the Schoedsack stuff is still in, but in those four years the original plans were kicked around until lost. Included in the scrapping was the Francis Yeats-Brown novel.

From the book only the locale and title have been retained. With these slim leads five studio writers went to work on a story, and they turned in a pip. In theme and locale *Lancer* is of the *Beau Geste* school. A sweeping, thrilling military narrative in Britain's desert badlands.

There is a stirring emotional conflict between father and son, the former a traditional British commander with whom discipline and loyalty to the service come first, and the boy rebelling at his father's cold-blooded attitude.

Gary Cooper and Franchot Tone, as a pair of experienced officers, are not directly involved in the main theme beyond being actuated by it, but they are the picture's two most important characters and provide the story with its dynamite.

Story concerns their rescue of the colonel's son after the latter's disillusionment over his father's reception of him makes him a setup for capture by a warring native chieftain.

Tone establishes himself as a first-rate light comedian. But in their own way Cooper, Sir Guy Standing, Richard Cromwell, C. Aubrey Smith and Douglas Dumbrille also turn in some first-rate trouping.

□ 1935: Best Picture (Nomination)

■ LIVING DAYLIGHTS, THE

1987, 130 MINS, UK ◇ ▼
Dir John Glen   *Prod* Albert R. Broccoli, Michael G. Wilson   *Scr* Richard Maibaum, Michael G. Wilson   *Ph* Alec Mills   *Ed* John Grover, Peter Davies   *Mus* John Barry   *Art Dir* Peter Lamont
● Timothy Dalton, Maryam d'Abo, Jeroen Krabbe, Joe Don Baker, John Rhys-Davies, Art Malik (UA/Eon)

Timothy Dalton, the fourth Bond, registers beautifully on all key counts of charm, machismo, sensitivity and technique. In *The Living Daylights* he's abetted by material that's a healthy cut above the series norm of super-hero fantasy.

There's a more mature story of its kind, too, this one about a phony KGB defector involved in gunrunning and a fraternal assassination plot.

There are even some relatively touching moments of romantic contact between Dalton and lead femme Maryam d'Abo as Czech concert cellist. Belatedly, the Bond characterization has achieved appealing maturity.

D'Abo, in a part meant to be something more than that of window-dressed mannikin, handles her chores acceptably. Able support is turned in by Joe Don Baker as a nutcase arms seller, Jeroen Krabbe and John Rhys-Davies as respective KGB bad and good types (a little less arch than the usual types), and Art Malik as an Oxford-educated Afghan freedom fighter.

■ LIVING FREE

1972, 90 MINS, UK ◇ ▼
Dir Jack Couffer   *Prod* Paul Radin   *Scr* Millard Kaufman   *Ph* Wolfgang Suschitsky   *Ed* Don Deacon   *Mus* Sol Kaplan   *Art Dir* John Stoll
● Nigel Davenport, Susan Hampshire, Geoffrey Keen, Edward Judd (Open Road/Highroad)

The same loving care that characterized *Born Free*, based on the true-life experiences of a British couple in Kenya and their pet lioness Elsa, is evident in the sequel.

Sensitive screenplay, based on the Joy Adamson book of her and her gamewarden-husband's efforts to assure that the cubs, following the death of their mother, shall live free and not be sent to a zoo, often carries a dramatic pitch. Possibly the most remarkable facet of picture is the animal photography of the cubs and other beasts that they encounter.

Some slight confusion exists in opening reels as the past of Elsa is reviewed briefly, but script develops logically as Nigel Davenport and Susan Hampshire, as the couple, are faced with the problem of the cubs' future after they turn to raiding natives' goat herds. Davenport resigns as a warden to devote himself entirely to capturing cubs and transporting them to a game preserve 700 miles distant.

■ LOCAL HERO

1983, 111 MINS, UK ◇ ▼
Dir Bill Forsyth   *Prod* David Puttnam   *Scr* Bill Forsyth   *Ph* Chris Menges   *Ed* Michael Bradsell   *Mus* Mark Knopfler   *Art Dir* Roger Murray-Leach
● Burt Lancaster, Peter Riegert, Fulton MacKay, Denis Lawson, Norman Chancer, Peter Capaldi (Enigma/Goldcrest)

While modest in intent and gentle in feel, *Local Hero* is loaded with wry, offbeat humor.

Basic story has Peter Riegert, rising young executive in an enormous Houston oil firm, sent to Scotland to clinch a deal to buy up an entire village, where the company intends to construct a new oil refinery. Far from being resistant to the idea of having their surroundings ruined by rapacious, profit-minded Yankees, local Scots can hardly wait to sign away their town, so strong is the smell of money in the air.

Back in Houston, oil magnate Burt Lancaster keeps up to date on the deal's progress with occasional phone calls to Riegert, but is more concerned with his prodding, sadistic psychiatrist and his obsessive hobby of astronomy, which seems to dictate everything he does.

Riegert's underplaying initially seems a bit inexpensive, but ultimately pays off in a droll performance. As his Scottish buddy, the gangling Peter Capaldi is vastly amusing, and Denis Lawson is very good as the community's chief spokesman.

■ LOCK UP

1989, 105 MINS, US ◇ ▼
Dir John Flynn   *Prod* Lawrence Gordon, Charles Gordon   *Scr* Richard Smith, Jeb Stuart, Henry Rosenbaum   *Ph* Donald E. Thorin   *Ed* Michael N. Knue, Donald Brochu   *Mus* Bill Conti   *Art Dir* Bill Kenney
● Sylvester Stallone, Donald Sutherland, John Amos, Sonny Landham, Tom Sizemore (White Eagle/Carolco)

Lock Up is made in the same, simplistic vein as most other Sylvester Stallone pics – putting him, the blue-collar protagonist, against the odds over which he ultimately prevails.

Emotional guy that he is, Stallone couldn't wait for his six-month prison term to be up because in the meantime his foster father may die, so he escapes to see him one last time. It seems his cold-hearted warden (Donald Sutherland) wouldn't allow him a supervised furlough to make the trip.

As revealed through the monosyllabic posturing, Sutherland is the vengeful, sadistic type.

The rest of the film is Stallone trying to survive 'hell' that Sutherland, as the Devil, has diabolically allowed to run amok.

Short of ordering, 'kill, kill,' Sutherland allows certain of his uniformed henchmen backed up by lifer prisoner/ringleader Chink (Sonny Landham) to bring Stallone down.

Darlanne Fluegel, as his faithful girlfriend, shows up occasionally to present the soft side of things but her character's only interesting attribute is that she's not a man.

■ LOCK UP YOUR DAUGHTERS!

1969, 102 MINS, UK ◇
Dir Peter Coe   *Prod* David Deutsch   *Scr* Keith Waterhouse, Willis Hall   *Ph* Peter Suschitzky   *Mus* Ron Grainer   *Art Dir* Tony Woollard
● Christopher Plummer, Susannah York, Glynis Johns, Ian Bannen, Tom Bell, Elaine Taylor (Columbia/Domino)

Much of the wit and satire in this portrait of the permissive morals and the corruptive decay of the 18th century is blunted, making it a noisy, bawdy, slapstick yarn about three sex-starved sailors on the rampage.

The scrappy storyline, drawn from Henry Fielding's *Rape Upon Rape* and John Vanbrugh's Restoration comedy *The Relapse*, plus the Mermaid Theatre musical written by Bernard Miles, can hardly be defined. It centers around the romantic entanglements of three wenches and their sailors which, after many misfortunes, complications and misunderstandings, land practically everybody in court.

Christopher Plummer as Lord Foppington hardly does his screen reputation much good. He plays the effete aristocrat in a mannered

way but extracts only exaggerated humor from it.

■ LOCKET, THE

1946, 83 MINS, US
Dir John Brahm   *Prod* Bert Granet   *Scr* Sheridan Gibney   *Ph* Nicholas Musuraca   *Ed* J.R. Whittredge   *Mus* Roy Webb   *Art Dir* Albert S. D'Agostino, Alfred Herman
● Laraine Day, Brian Aherne, Robert Mitchum, Gene Raymond (RKO)

The Locket is a case history of a warped mind and its effect on the lives of those it touches intimately. Vehicle is a strong one for Laraine Day and she does much with the role of Nancy, a girl with an abnormal obsession that wrecks the lives of four men who love her.

Nancy is a young woman, marked in childhood by the cruel misunderstanding of a rich lady in whose home her mother is housekeeper. The misunderstanding, over a missing locket, influence Nancy to strange acts in her adult life.

Story carries the flashback technique to greater lengths than generally employed. The writing by Sheridan Gibney displays an understanding of the subject matter and proves a solid basis for the able performances achieved by John Brahm's direction. Latter gears his scenes for full interest and carefully carries forward the doubt – and audience hope – that Nancy is not the villainess.

■ LODGER, THE

1932, 85 MINS, UK
Dir Maurice Elvey   *Prod* Julius Hagen   *Scr* Ivor Novello, Miles Mander, Paul Rotha, H. Fowler Mear   *Ph* Basil Emmott, Sydney Blythe
● Ivor Novello, Elizabeth Allan, Jack Hawkins, A. W. Baskcomb, Barbara Everest, Peter Gawthorne (Twickenham)

The Lodger, from the novel by Mrs Belloc Lowndes, was made as a silent some years previously. Despite its subject of Jack the Ripper, this is an eerie, absorbing story without being morbid.

Running parallel with the narration of the frightful murders is a sweet love story, gentle and poetic. Ivor Novello plays a sensitive musician with a sorrow so great he is unable to confide in anyone, not even the girl he loves, and who tells him she would believe anything he told her. Novello has an arresting personality, which photographs romantically.

Love scenes are ably supported by Elizabeth Allan, whose depiction of a working girl carried off her feet by a romantic, soulful musician is a fine piece of acting.

■ LODGER, THE

1944, 84 MINS, US ▼
Dir John Brahm   *Prod* Robert Bassler   *Scr* Barre Lyndon   *Ph* Lucien Ballard   *Ed* J. Watson Webb   *Mus* Hugo Friedhofer   *Art Dir* James Baseri, John Ewing
● Merle Oberon, George Sanders, Laird Cregar, Cedric Hardwicke (20th Century-Fox)

With a pat cast, keen direction and tight scripting, 20th-Fox has an absorbing and, at times, spine-tingling drama concocted from Marie Belloc Lowndes' novel *The Lodger*. It's a super chiller-diller in its picturization of a Scotland Yard manhunt for London's Jack the Ripper.

Director John Brahm and scripter Barre Lyndon make it as much a psychological study of the halfcrazed 'Lodger' (Laird Cregar), as if in a deftly-paced horrific whodunit in trying to outline some explanation for the repeated throatslashings of London stage women, neither has even slightly deviated from the swift weaving of events. Aside from preliminary steps, sequence of events mounts in rapid succession with suspense injected time after time with telling effect.

It is Laird Cregar's picture. As 'The Ripper' he gives an impressive performance. It is a relentless, at times pathetic character as he pursues his self-appointed task of avenging his brother. His precise diction and almost studied poise make his characterization all the more impressive.

Merle Oberon is highly effective as Kitty, the dancer, of respectable family whose stardom is nearly abruptly ended. Stage sequences show her a graceful dancer in abbreviated skirt and provide the bright contrast to somber and melodramatic passages. Kept more or less in the background initially, her scene in the dressing room, when she pleads for her life, is the high dramatic spot of the production. George Sanders, cast as a sleuth, is strong.

■ LOGAN'S RUN

1976, 118 MINS, US ◇ Ⓥ
Dir Michael Anderson *Prod* Saul David *Scr* David Zelag Goodman *Ph* Ernest Laszlo *Ed* Bob Wyman *Mus* Jerry Goldsmith *Art Dir* Dale Hennesy
● Michael York, Richard Jordan, Jenny Agutter, Roscoe Lee Browne, Farrah Fawcett, Michael Anderson Jr (M-G-M)

Logan's Run is a rewarding futuristic film that appeals both as spectacular-looking escapist adventure as well as intelligent drama.

Heading the cast are Michael York and Richard Jordan, two members of a security guard force which supervises the life of a domed-in hedonistic civilization all comprised of persons under the age of 30; after that, the civilization's tribal rules call for a ceremony called 'renewal', though nobody's quite sure what that entails.

York, intrigued and abetted by Jenny Agutter, decides to flee, with Jordan. Peter Ustinov is featured as a withered old man living alone on the outside, in the ruins of Washington, DC.

The three young principals and Ustinov come off very well.

■ LOLITA

1962, 152 MINS, US Ⓥ
Dir Stanley Kubrick *Prod* James B. Harris *Scr* Vladimir Nabokov *Ph* Oswald Morris *Ed* Anthony Harvey *Mus* Nelson Riddle *Art Dir* William Andrews
● James Mason, Shelley Winters, Peter Sellers, Sue Lyon, Marianne Stone (M-G-M/Seven Arts)

Vladimir Nabokov's witty, grotesque novel is, in its film version, like a bee from which the stinger has been removed. It still buzzes with a sort of promising irreverence, but it lacks the power to shock and, eventually, makes very little point either as comedy or satire. The novel has been stripped of its pubescent heroine and most of its lively syntax, graphic honesty and sharp observations on people and places in a land abundant with cliches.

The result is an occasionally amusing but shapeless film about a middleaged professor who comes to no good end through his involvement with a well-developed teenager. The fact that the first third of the picture is so good, bristling with Nabokovisms – a gun, for example, referred to as a tragic treasure – underscores the final disappointment.

There is much about the film that is excellent. James Mason has never been better than he is as erudite Humbert Humbert, driven by a furious passion for a rather slovenly, perverse 'nymphet' (a term, incidentally, which is used only once in the entire film). He

is especially good in the early sequences as he pursues Lolita to the point where he even marries her mother, whom Shelley Winters plays to bumptious perfection.

Matching these two performances is that of Peter Sellers who, as a preposterously smug American playwright (Mason's rival for Lolita's affections), gets a chance to run through several hilarious changes of character.

Sue Lyon makes an auspicious film debut as the deceitful child-woman who'd just as soon go to a movie as romp in the hay. It's a difficult assignment and if she never quite registers as either wanton or pathetic it may be due as much to the compromises of the script as to her inexperience.

■ LOLLY-MADONNA XXX

1973, 105 MINS, US ◇
Dir Richard C. Sarafian *Prod* Rodney Carr-Smith *Scr* Rodney Carr-Smith, Sue Grafton *Ph* Philip Lathrop *Ed* Tom Rolf *Mus* Fred Myrow *Art Dir* Herman Blumenthal
● Rod Steiger, Robert Ryan, Jeff Bridges, Scott Wilson, Katherine Squire, Tresa Hughes (M-G-M)

Sue Grafton's novel, *The Lolly-Madonna War*, has been handsomely and sensitively filmed. Excellent performances abound by older and younger players in a mountain-country clan feud story which mixes extraordinary human compassion with raw but discreet violence.

It doesn't take much extrapolation effort to lift the story from its down-home setting and transpose it to the level of national and international politics.

Rod Steiger heads one clan, which also includes Katherine Squire in outstanding performance as his wife, plus Scott Wilson, Timothy Scott, Ed Lauter, Randy Quaid and Jeff Bridges as the sons. The opposition clan is headed by Robert Ryan, with Tresa Hughes' also outstanding as his wife. A land dispute has brought the families to the edge of violence.

Trigger for the explosion is a fake postcard sent by Kiel Martin, signed by a non-existent, apparent bride-to-be named Lolly-Madonna with three X's appended in the childish manner. Wilson and Lauter, having glommed the postcard as Martin knew they would, kidnap Season Hubley, a traveler who arrives at the moment when the fake bride was to have met her husband-to-be.

Steiger and Ryan dominate the film through their children's actions, and director Richard C. Sarafian has endowed the picture with a moody, menacing atmosphere.

■ LONE WOLF McQUADE

1983, 107 MINS, US ◇ Ⓥ
Dir Steve Carver *Prod* Yoram Ben-Ami, Steve Carver *Scr* B.J. Nelson *Ph* Roger Shearman *Ed* Anthony Redman *Mus* Francesco De Masi *Art Dir* Norm Baron
● Chuck Norris, David Carradine, Barbara Carrera, Leon Isaac Kennedy, Robert Beltran, L.Q. Jones (1818 Production/Top Kick)

Fans of *Soldier of Fortune* magazine will think they've been ambushed and blown away to heaven by *Lone Wolf McQuade*. Every conceivable type of portable weapon on the world market is tried out by the macho warriors on both sides of the law in this modern western, which pits Texas Ranger Chuck Norris and his cohorts against multifarious baddies who like to play rough.

Opening sequence, showing the grizzled Norris busting up a gang of Mexican horse rustlers, makes it clear that film's primary source of inspiration is Sergio Leone.

Vile David Carradine is in the business of hijacking US Army weapons shipments and selling them to Central American terrorist groups. Norris and FBI agent Leon Isaac

Kennedy finally locate Carradine's secret airstrip, and after a setback there, track him down at a compound loaded with all manner of armaments.

■ LONELINESS OF THE LONG DISTANCE RUNNER, THE

1962, 104 MINS, UK
Dir Tony Richardson *Prod* Tony Richardson *Scr* Alan Sillitoe *Ph* Walter Lassally *Ed* Antony Gibbs *Mus* John Addison *Prod Des* Ralph Brinton
● Tom Courtenay, Michael Redgrave, James Bolam, Avis Bunnage, Alec McCowen, Julia Foster (British Lion/Woodfall)

It is difficult to conjure up much sympathy for the young 'hero' who comes out as a disturbed young layabout (he seems thoroughly to deserve his fate of landing in Borstal, the corrective establishment for British juve delinquents). Yet the performance of Tom Courtenay and the imaginative, if sometimes overfussy, direction of Tony Richardson, plus some standout lensing by Walter Lassally makes this a worthwhile pic.

Alan Sillitoe has written a sound screenplay for his own short story. Though there are obvious signs of padding, it remains a thoroughly professional job. The flashback technique is used ingeniously, though perhaps overmuch.

Courtenay plays a young man from an unhappy home in the Midlands. Apparently on the ground that the world owes him a living, he seems not interested in work and, inevitably drifts into petty crime and gets sent to Borstal.

He is resentful about 'the system' and takes a strange way of getting back at it. A natural born runner ('we had plenty of practice in running away from the police in our family,' he says bitterly), he is selected to represent Borstal in a long distance race against a public school team. It is the ambition of the governor (Michael Redgrave) to win the cup for Borstal.

Michael Redgrave as the rather pompous, stuffy governor who, to Courtenay's jaundiced eye, represents the system, brings his polished touch to a role that could have become irritating.

■ LONELY ARE THE BRAVE

1962, 107 MINS, US Ⓥ
Dir David Miller *Prod* Edward Lewis *Scr* Dalton Trumbo *Ph* Philip Lathrop *Ed* Leon Barsha *Mus* Jerry Goldsmith *Art Dir* Alexander Golitzen, Robert E. Smith
● Kirk Douglas, Gena Rowlands, Walter Matthau, Michael Kane, Carroll O'Connor (Universal)

Often touching, and well served by its performances and photography, *Lonely Are the Brave* ultimately blurs its focus on the loner fenced in and bemused by the encroachments and paradoxes of civilization. Its makers have approached the misfit theme with a skittishness not unlike that exhibited by cowboy Kirk Douglas's horse. They have settled for surface instead of substance.

The failure of the Dalton Trumbo screenplay from an Edward Abbey novel [Brave Cowboy] is that it does not provide viewers with a sustained probing of the hero's perplexity.

The plot is sparing enough. Douglas, the footloose, arrives back at the New Mexico homestead of old friends Michael Kane and Gena Rowlands. Kane is in the Albuquerque jail on an aid-and-comfort to wetbacks rap, and good guy Douglas contrives to get himself tossed into the same pokey from where he plans to bust out with Kane. The buddy opts to stay, however – his ways are changed, and there is the wife and a son to consider – but Douglas, not one for the year's confinement he faces, makes off and takes to the hills ringing town.

As the loner, Douglas is extremely likable and understands his part within its limitations, as written. Most beguiling performance, however, is turned in by Walter Matthau as the laconic and harassed sheriff, who has never faced his quarry but develops an intuitive sympathy for him.

■ **LONELY GUY, THE**

1984, 90 MINS, US ◇ ▼
Dir Arthur Hiller *Prod* Arthur Hiller *Scr* Ed Weinberger, Stan Daniels *Ph* Victor J. Kemper *Ed* William Reynolds, Raja Gosnell *Mus* Jerry Goldsmith *Art Dir* James D. Vance
● Steve Martin, Charles Grodin, Judith Ivey, Steven Lawrence, Robyn Douglass, Merv Griffin (Universal)

Derived from a comic tome by Bruce Jay Friedman, premise has Steve Martin bounced by sexpot girlfriend Robyn Douglass and thereby banished to the world of Lonely Guys. He meets and commiserates with fellow LG Charles Grodin, who gets Martin to buy a fern with him and throws a party attended only by Martin and a bunch of lifesized cardboard cutouts of celebs like Dolly Parton and Tom Selleck.

Finally, Martin meets cute blonde Judith Ivey, who, having been previously married to six Lonely Guys, instantly falls for him.

Martin's trademark wacky humor is fitfully in evidence, but seems much more repressed than usual in order to fit into the relatively realistic world of single working people.

■ **LONELY HEARTS**

1982, 95 MINS, AUSTRALIA ◇ ▼
Dir Paul Cox *Prod* John B. Murray *Scr* Paul Cox, John Clarke *Ph* Yuri Sokol *Ed* Tim Lewis *Mus* Norman Kaye *Art Dir* Neil Angwin
● Wendy Hughes, Norman Kaye, Jon Finlayson, Julia Blake, Jonathan Hardy (Adams-Packer)

A slowly-developing romance between a 50-ish bachelor piano tuner and a 30-ish spinsterly bank clerk hardly seems the stuff from which viable motion pictures are made. Director Paul Cox's treatment of his own story is dull, plodding and uninspiring fare.

Norman Kaye plays Peter, a nervous, vapid character who is so weak he nearly recedes into the woodwork. Wendy Hughes is Patricia, dowdy, sexually repressed, and, smothered by her parents. They meet through a dating service after his mother dies, and embark on possibly the world's longest and dreariest courtship.

Both Kaye and Hughes struggle to make their characters interesting or engaging. A few all-too-rare lively moments are provided by Julia Blake as Peter's overbearing sister, Jon Finlayson as a camp theatre director, and Ronald Falk as a twee wig salesman.

■ **LONELY PASSION OF JUDITH HEARNE, THE**

1987, 110 MINS, UK ◇ ▼
Dir Jack Clayton *Prod* Peter Nelson, Richard Johnson *Scr* Peter Nelson *Ph* Peter Hannan *Ed* Terry Rawlings *Mus* Georges Delerue *Art Dir* Michael Pickwood
● Maggie Smith, Bob Hoskins, Wendy Hiller, Marie Kean, Ian McNeice (Handmade/United British Artists)

An ensemble of sterling performances highlights *The Lonely Passion of Judith Hearne*, an intelligent, carefully crafted adaptation of Brian Moore's well-regarded first novel. Film's centerpiece is Maggie Smith's exceptionally detailed portrait of the title character, a middle-aged Irish spinster who tragically deludes herself into imagining herself involved in a great romance.

Judith is a fragile bird, a part-time piano teacher in 1950s Dublin who has every reason to be desperate about life but still manages to look on the bright side. Moving into a new boarding house, she takes a liking to her landlady's brother James (Bob Hoskins), a widower recently returned from 30 years in New York, and begins stepping out with him.

Once James takes her to a fancy dinner at the Shelbourne Hotel, Judith is sure his intentions are serious. Unfortunately, she allows a misunderstanding between them to assume traumatic proportions, and her heartbreak and disappointment lead her down a spiraling road of despair, alcoholism, ostracism and religious rejection.

Hoskins, laying a brash New York accent over a hint of the Irish, brings great energy and creative bluster to the irrepressible dreamer who has been instilled with Yankee get-up-and-go.

■ **LONG AND THE SHORT AND THE TALL, THE**

1961, 105 MINS, UK
Dir Leslie Norman *Prod* Michael Balcon *Scr* Wolf Mankowitz *Ph* Erwin Hillier *Ed* Gordon Stone *Mus* Stanley Black *Art Dir* Terence Verity, Jim Morahan
● Richard Todd, Laurence Harvey, Richard Harris, Ronald Fraser, David McCallum, John Meillon (Associated British)

Director and scriptwriter have not been able to resist the temptation to take a great deal of Willis Hall's war play into the open air of the jungle. This is a pity. It loses the sense of pent-in suspense that marked the play so effectively and it also shows up the fact that the Elstree 'jungle' is rather phoney.

Film depends on characterization rather than on the thinnish plot. It's set in the Far East jungle during the Japanese campaign. A small patrol led by a sergeant (Richard Todd) is cut off. Suddenly 'sparks' makes radio contact and jabbering Japanese voices nearby cause them to realize that they're in a spot.

A lone Japanese scout moves into their position and Todd insists that they must get him back to base alive as a source of information. The remainder want to bump him off with the solitary, surprise exception of a loudmouthed and brash private (Laurence Harvey).

Standout performance comes from Harvey. It is dramatic license that enables him to behave in a way that would undoubtedly have had him up on a charge in a real situation.

The bewildered Jap, subtly played by Kenji Takaki, is another very sound performance. In fact there is no weak link in the cast. Todd is a dogged, worried sergeant; Richard Harris shapes very good as his righthand man, and Ronald Fraser is fine as a dour Scot.

■ **LONG DAY'S DYING, THE**

1968, 93 MINS, UK ◇
Dir Peter Collinson *Prod* Harry Fine, Peter Collinson *Scr* Charles Wood *Ph* Brian Probyn *Ed* John Trumper *Art Dir* Disley Jones
● David Hemmings, Tom Bell, Tony Beckley, Alan Dobie (Paramount)

The Long Day's Dying is a bore. In tracing the steps of three British soldiers and their German captive during a single day of weary trekking through the European countryside, it adds nothing in the way of insight or impact to the dreary platitudes of countless previous anti-war pix.

Charles Wood's script is lacking in dramatic momentum and fails to clarify the four protagonists' characters. Even worse, no sympathy or interest is developed for any of the men.

Script's use of interior monologs is clumsy, frequently counterpointing the various men's thoughts in an archly poetic way and never helping to define their inner natures.

Direction by Peter Collinson is lackluster. When not relying on established tricks of documentary filmmaking or more up-to-date visual affectations, he holds on closeups of his 'thinking' actors. Fact that all four players register little beyond grim impassivity hardly lightens the pace of this lethargic film.

■ **LONG DAY'S JOURNEY INTO NIGHT**

1962, 176 MINS, US ▼
Dir Sidney Lumet *Prod* Ely Landau *Ph* Boris Kaufman *Ed* Ralph Rosenbaum *Mus* Andre Previn *Art Dir* Richard Sylbert
● Katharine Hepburn, Ralph Richardson, Jason Robards, Dean Stockwell, Jeanne Barr (Landau)

This is an excellent film adaption of the late Eugene O'Neill's lengthy stage work. It has power in its characters and their tortured introspective lives. There have been a few cuts but otherwise it is as O'Neill wrote it. And his powerful language manages to overcome the limited sets and dependence on the spoken word.

It takes a family through the probing of themselves, their relations and their relative reasons for acting as they do. It all develops when the mother one day begins to sink back to drug addiction.

Katherine Hepburn's beautifully boned face mirrors her anguish and needs. She makes the role of the mother breathtaking and intensely moving. There is balance, depth and breadth in her acting. Ralph Richardson brings his authority to the part of the miserly father who had made money as a theatrical matinee idol but can't shake his skinflint habits because of a childhood of poverty. Jason Robards has flair and insight as the tortured older brother while Dean Stockwell is effective as the younger brother.

Made reportedly for $400,000, since the principals took minimum pay because of their desire to do the property.

■ **LONG DUEL, THE**

1967, 115 MINS, UK ◇
Dir Ken Annakin *Prod* Ken Annakin *Scr* Peter Yeldham *Ph* Jack Hildyard *Ed* Bert Bates *Mus* John Scott *Art Dir* Alex Vetchinsky
● Yul Brynner, Trevor Howard, Harry Andrews, Andrew Keir, Charlotte Rampling, Virginia North (Rank)

Produced and directed by Ken Annakin at Pinewood and on location in Granada, Spain, this is an ambitious actioner which has plenty of punch.

But the yarn, though based on fact, unfolds with little conviction and is repeatedly bogged down by labored dialog and characterization in Peter Yeldham's screenplay [based on a story by Ranveer Singh]. Story is set on the Indian Northwest Frontier during the 1920s and basically hinges on the uneasy relationship and lack of understanding between most of the British top brass and the native tribes. Trevor Howard, an idealistic police officer, is very conscious of the need for tact and diplomacy when handling the touchy natives.

When he is ordered to track down the Bhanta tribe leader (Yul Brynner), who is trying to lead his people from the bondage of the British, Howard recognizes Brynner as a fellow idealist and an enemy to respect.

■ **LONG GOOD FRIDAY, THE**

1981, 114 MINS, UK ◇ ▼
Dir John Mackenzie *Prod* Barry Hanson *Scr* Barrie Keeffe *Ph* Phil Meheux *Ed* Mike Taylor *Mus* Francis Monkman *Art Dir* Vic Symonds

● Bob Hoskins, Helen Mirren, Eddie Constantine, Dave King, Brian Hall (Calendar/Black Lion)

In many respects a conventional thriller set in London's underworld, *The Long Good Friday* is much more densely plotted and intelligently scripted than most such yarns.

Bob Hoskins displays natural, and sizable, big-screen presence, and works out first-rate in the anchor role of a gangland boss faced with a series of seemingly gratuitous reprisals by unknown ill-wishers against his waterfront empire.

He starts as a larger-than-life figure, confidently negotiating American finance for a massive land development project. But Hoskins' overweening exterior crumbles as some of his best men are murdered.

When it becomes clear that his adversary is the provisional Irish Republican Army, he pits his Mafia-style muscle against the IRA's professional terrorism.

The narrative is steered competently, but visual style is too stolid to lend due gut-impact.

■ LONG GOODBYE, THE

1973, 112 MINS, US ◇ Ⓥ

Dir Robert Altman *Prod* Jerry Bick *Scr* Leigh Brackett *Ph* Vilmos Zsigmond *Ed* Lou Lombardo *Mus* John Williams
● Elliott Gould, Nina van Pallandt, Sterling Hayden, Henry Gibson, Mark Rydell, Jim Bouton (United Artists)

Robert Altman's film version of Raymond Chandler's novel is an uneven mixture of insider satire on the gumshow film genre, gratuitous brutality, and sledgehammer whimsy.

Leigh Brackett adapted the Chandler book; she, Jules Furthman and William Faulkner scripted Chandler's *The Big Sleep* [1946]. Herein, the Philip Marlowe character becomes embroiled in a Malibu murder, stolen money, the apparent death of his best friend, and compounded double-cross.

No longer the sardonic idealist, Marlowe has become part Walter Mitty. Elliott Gould keeps a low dramatic profile throughout as a passive catalyst. Nina van Pallandt makes an American film bow as the wife of dried-up author Sterling Hayden (Dan Blocker was to have been cast, and his passing is tributed in an end title card 'with special remembrance'), whose periodic disappearances include a visit to Henry Gibson's high-priced sanatorium.

Mark Rydell returns to acting after a decade of directing to play a kooky criminal, whose twisted mind runs to bashing in the face of Jo Ann Brody with a soft drink bottle.

■ LONG GRAY LINE, THE

1955, 135 MINS, US ◇

Dir John Ford *Prod* Robert Arthur *Scr* Edward Hope *Ph* Charles Lawton Jr *Ed* William Lyon *Mus* George Duning *Art Dir* Robert Peterson
● Tyrone Power, Maureen O'Hara, Robert Francis, Ward Bond, Donald Crisp (Columbia)

The Long Gray Line is a standout drama on West Point.

For Tyrone Power the role of Marty Maher, Irishman through whose eyes the story is told, is a memorable one. Maureen O'Hara brings to the role of Maher's wife her Irish beauty and seldom displayed acting ability. Both are very fine.

Robert Arthur's exceptionally well-fashioned production is based on *Bringing Up the Brass*, the autobiography of Maher's 50 years at the Point which he wrote with Nardi Reeder Campion. A screenplay that is full of wonderfully human touches gives just the right foundation for John Ford to show his love for country (and the Irish) with his direction. Story oscillates between unash-

amed sniffles and warm chuckles, Ford not being afraid to bring a tear or stick in a laugh.

■ LONG RIDERS, THE

1980, 100 MINS, US ◇ Ⓥ

Dir Walter Hill *Prod* Tim Zinnemann *Scr* Bill Bryden, Steven Phillip Smith, Stacy Keach, James Keach *Ph* Ric Waite *Ed* David Holden, Freeman Davies *Mus* Ry Cooder *Art Dir* Jack T. Collis
● David Carradine, Keith Carradine, Stacy Keach, James Keach, Dennis Quaid, Randy Quaid (United Artists)

The Long Riders is striking in several ways, not the least of which being the casting of actor brothers as historical outlaw kin, but narrative is episodic in the extreme.

Yarn opens in bang-up fashion with a bank robbery, after which trigger-happy Dennis Quaid is kicked out of the Younger-James-Miller gang for needlessly murdering a man during stick-up. With no time frame provided, pic proceeds by alternating scenes of further crimes, the men at play in whorehouses and courting women, and the law bungling initial attempts to capture the troublemakers.

Director Walter Hill resolutely refuses to investigate the psychology or motivations of his characters, explaining away men's life of banditry as a 'habit' acquired in wake of the Civil War.

What's ultimately missing is a definable point of view which would tie together the myriad events on display and fill in the blanks which Hill has imposed on the action by sapping it of emotional or historical meaning.

■ LONG SHIPS, THE

1964, 124 MINS, UK/YUGOSLAVIA ◇

Dir Jack Cardiff *Prod* Irving Allen *Scr* Berkely Mather, Beverley Cross *Ph* Christopher Challis *Ed* Geoff Foot *Mus* Dusan Radic *Art Dir* John Hoesli
● Richard Widmark, Sidney Poitier, Russ Tamblyn, Rosanna Schiaffino, Beba Loncar, Oscar Homolka (Columbia/Warwick/Avala)

Any attempt to put this into the epic class falls down because of a hodge-podge of a storyline, a mixture of styles and insufficient development of characterization.

The plot, which has obviously suffered in both editing and censorial slaps, is a conglomeration of battles, double-crossing, sea-storms, floggings, unarmed combat with occasional halfhearted peeks at sex. Throughout there's a great deal of noise and the entire experience is a very long drag.

Film [based on the novel by Frans G. Bengtsson] concerns the rivalry of the Vikings and the Moors in search of a legendary Golden Bell, the size of three men and containing 'half the gold in the world'. Leaders of the rival factors are Richard Widmark, an adventurous Viking con man, who plays strictly tongue in cheek, and Sidney Poitier, dignified, ruthless top man of the Moors. In contrast to Widmark, he seeks to take the film seriously. The clash in styles between these two is a minor disaster.

■ LONG WALK HOME, THE

1990, 97 MINS, US ◇ Ⓥ

Dir Richard Pearce *Prod* Howard W. Koch Jr *Scr* John Cork *Ph* Roger Deakins *Ed* Bill Yahraus *Mus* George Fenton *Art Dir* Blake Russell
● Sissy Spacek, Whoopi Goldberg, Dwight Schultz, Ving Rhames, Dylan Baker, Erika Alexander (New Visions)

Set in Montgomery, Alabama, during the 1955 civil rights bus boycott, *The Long Walk Home* is an effectively mounted drama about the human impact of changing times on two

families, with sturdy performances by Sissy Spacek as an uppercrust white housewife and Whoopi Goldberg as her maid.

Spacek's Miriam Thompson is a prim model of upper-middle-class Southern womanhood who cannot run her household without her indispensable maid Odessa.

Racist jokes are commonplace during cocktail parties and family dinners, where Spacek's brother-in-law (Dylan Baker) espouses hard-line segregationist attitudes.

Goldberg's hard-working husband (Ving Rhames) and three well-mannered kids make a loving family, but the household's mood is tense because of external events. Local black leaders call for a bus boycott to end segregated seating. As the black boycott stiffens, so does white resistance, which turns ugly with the bombing of Martin Luther King's house. Afraid of change, the town establishment refuses to compromise.

The film resists the temptation to succumb to sentimentality and offers believable characterizations in the context of its time and place.

■ LONGEST DAY, THE

1962, 180 MINS, US ◇

Dir Ken Annakin, Andrew Marton, Bernhard Wicki *Prod* Darryl F. Zanuck *Scr* Cornelius Ryan, Romain Gary, James Jones, David Pursall, Jack Seddon *Ph* Jean Bourgoin, Henri Persin, Walter Wottitz, Guy Tabary *Ed* Samuel E. Beetley *Mus* Maurice Jarre, Paul Anka *Art Dir* Ted Haworth, Leon Barsacq, Vincent Korda
● John Wayne, Robert Mitchum, Henry Fonda, Robert Ryan, Richard Todd, Richard Burton (20th Century-Fox)

Darryl F. Zanuck achieves a solid and stunning war epic. From personal vignettes to big battles, it details the first day of the D-Day Landings by the Allies on 6 June 1944.

The savage fury and sound of war are ably caught on film. It emerges as a sort of grand scale semi-fictionalized documentary concerning the overall logistics needed for this incredible invasion. It carries its three hour length by the sheer tingle of the masses of manpower in action, peppered with little ironic, sad, silly actions that all add up to war.

The use of over 43 actual star names in bit and pivotal spots helps keep up the aura of fictionalized documentary. But it is the action, time and place, and the actual machinery of war, that are the things.

The battles ably take their places among some of the best ever put on the screen. A German strafing the beach, Yanks scaling a treacherous cliff only to find that there was no big gun there, British commandos taking a bridge, Yanks blowing up a big bunker, the French taking a town, all are done with massive pungent action. The black and white and CinemaScope screen help keep the focus on surge and movement.
□ 1962: Best Picture (Nomination)

■ LONGEST YARD, THE

1974, 121 MINS, US ◇ Ⓥ

Dir Robert Aldrich *Prod* Albert S. Ruddy *Scr* Tracy Keenan Wynn *Ph* Joseph Biroc *Ed* Michael Luciano *Mus* Frank DeVol *Art Dir* James S. Vance
● Burt Reynolds, Eddie Albert, Ed Lauter, Michael Conrad, Jim Hampton, Harry Caesar (Paramount)

The Longest Yard is an outstanding action drama, combining the brutish excitement of football competition with the brutalities of contemporary prison life. Burt Reynolds asserts his genuine star power, here as a former football pro forced to field a team under blackmail of warden Eddie Albert.

In contrast to most hard-action films, this is quality action drama, in which brute force is fully motivated and therefore totally acceptable. At the same time, the metaphysics of

L

football are neatly interwoven with the politics and bestialities of totalitarian authority.

Script, from a story credited to producer Albert S. Ruddy, finds Reynolds arriving at Albert's prison. Ed Lauter, his chief guard, also coaches the guards' clumsy football team. Reynolds is forced to form an inmates' team from a ragtag bunch of cons, with a no-win payoff: if he loses, Lauter's guards will rub it in; if he wins, Albert's vengeance is certain.

■ LONGTIME COMPANION

1990, 96 MINS, US ◇ Ⓥ

Dir Norman Rene *Prod* Stan Wlodkowski *Scr* Craig Lucas *Ph* Tony Jennelli *Ed* Katherine Wenning *Mus* Liz Vollack (sup.) *Art Dir* Andrew Jauknoss
● Bruce Davison, Campbell Scott, Stephen Caffrey, Mark Lamos, Patrick Cassidy, Mary-Louise Parker (American Playhouse)

The first feature film to tell the story of how AIDS devastated and transformed the gay community, *Longtime Companion* is simply an excellent film, with a graceful, often humorous script and affecting performances.

Story begins during the carefree pre-AIDS party days on Fire Island, where Willy (Campbell Scott) and Fuzzy (Stephen Caffrey) meet and begin a relationship that brings together an extended circle of friends. It's the same day a *New York Times* article announces a rare disease spreading among gay men. A year later, Willy's best friend John (Dermont Mulroney) becomes violently ill and dies. It's only the beginning. One by one, this community of actors, writers and lawyers is affected.

Among the most piercing events is the deterioration of a TV scripter, Sean (Mark Lamos), who is cared for by his lover, David (Bruce Davison), who owns the beach house where the friends always have gathered.

Strength of Craig Lucas' script is the way it weaves emotional and informational material together.

■ LOOK BACK IN ANGER

1959, 115 MINS, UK Ⓥ

Dir Tony Richardson *Prod* Gordon L.T. Scott *Scr* Nigel Kneale *Ph* Oswald Morris *Ed* Richard Rest *Mus* John Addison (sup.), Chris Best
● Richard Burton, Claire Bloom, Mary Ure, Edith Evans, Gary Raymond, Donald Pleasence (Woodfall)

Tony Richardson, who staged the play, *Look Back in Anger*, which helped to hoist John Osborne into the bigtime, tackles the same subject as his first directorial chore. Richardson's is a technical triumph, but somewhere along the line he has lost the heart and the throb that made the play an adventure. The film simultaneously impresses and depresses.

In the play, Jimmy Porter was a rebel – but a mixed-up weakling of a rebel. In the film, as played by Richard Burton, he is an arrogant young man who thinks the world owes him something but cannot make up his mind what it is – and certainly doesn't deserve the handout.

Burton glowers sullenly, violently and well as Porter and it is not his fault that the role gives him little opportunity for variety. Mary Ure (repeating her London & Broadway stage role) as the downtrodden, degraded young wife is first-class. Claire Bloom plays the 'other woman' with a neat variation of bite and comehitherness. Gary Raymond makes an instant impact as the cosy, kindly friend of the unhappy couple.

■ LOOK WHO'S TALKING TOO

1990, 81 MINS, US ◇ Ⓥ

Dir Amy Heckerling *Prod* Jonathan D. Krane *Scr* Amy Heckerling, Neal Israel *Ph* Thoms Del Ruth *Ed* Debra Chiate *Mus* David Kitay, Maureen Crowe *Art Dir* Reuben Freed

● John Travolta, Kirstie Alley, Olympia Dukakis, Elias Koteas, Twink Caplan, Neal Israel (Tri-Star)

This vulgar sequel to 1989's longest-running sleeper hit looks like a rush job. Joined by her husband Neal Israel (who also appears as star Kirstie Alley's mean boss) in the scripting, filmmaker Amy Heckerling overemphasizes toilet humor and expletives to make the film appealing mainly to adolescents rather than an across-the-board family audience.

Unwed mom Alley and cabbie John Travolta are married for the sequel, with her cute son Mikey metamorphosed into Lorne Sussman, still voiceovered as precocious by Bruce Willis. First mutual arrival is undeniably cute Megan Milner, unfortunately voiced-over by Roseanne Barr. Comedienne gets a couple of laughs but is generally dull, leaving Willis to again carry the load in the gag department with well-read quips.

Plotline revolves around the bickering of Alley and Travolta whose jobs (accountant and would-be airline pilot) and personalities clash, as well as the rites of passage of the two kids. New characters, notably Alley's obnoxious brother Elias Koteas, are added to ill effect. Mel Brooks is enlisted to voice-over Mr Toilet Man, a fantasy bathroom bowl come to life, spitting blue water and anxious to bite off Mikey's privates.

■ LOOKER

1981, 94 MINS, US ◇

Dir Michael Crichton *Prod* Howard Jeffrey *Scr* Michael Crichton *Ph* Paul Lohmann *Ed* Carl Kress *Mus* Barry De Vorzon *Art Dir* Dean Edward Mitzner
● Albert Finney, James Coburn, Susan Dey, Leigh Taylor-Young (Ladd/Warner)

Writer-director Michael Crichton has used interesting material, public manipulation by computer-generated TV commercials, to create *Looker*, a silly and unconvincing contempo sci-fi thriller.

Albert Finney, sporting a neutral American accent, heads the cast as Dr Larry Roberts, a leading Los Angeles plastic surgeon being set up as the fall guy in a string of murders of beautiful models who happen to be his patients. Bypassing the police detective (Dorian Harewood) on the case, Roberts teams with model Cindy (Susan Dey) to track down the real killers, with Cindy infiltrating a suspicious research institute run by Jennifer Long (Leigh Taylor-Young) as part of the conglomerate Reston Industries headed by John Reston (James Coburn).

Long has been developing the perfect TV commercials, using plastic surgery-augmented beautiful women as models and expanding into computer-generated simulation techniques. Reston has used these experiments to go beyond subliminal advertising to create hypnotic messages that can sell products or even political candidates.

With numerous lapses in credibility, Crichton falls back upon motifs better used in his *Westworld* picture: computer simulations (for robots), TV blurb soundstages (for film backlots) and assorted fancy chases.

■ LOOKIN' TO GET OUT

1982, 104 MINS, US ◇ Ⓥ

Dir Hal Ashby *Prod* Robert Schaffel *Scr* Al Schwartz, Jon Voight *Ph* Haskell Wexler *Ed* Robert C. Jones *Mus* Johnny Mandel *Art Dir* Robert Boyle
● Jon Voight, Ann-Margret, Burt Young, Bert Remsen, Jude Farese, Allen Keller (Northstar International/Lorimar)

Hal Ashby's *Lookin' to Get Out* is an ill-conceived vehicle for actor (and co-writer) Jon Voight to showcase his character comedy

talents in a loose, semi-improvised environment.

Alex (Jon Voight) and Jerry (Burt Young) are the central figures, who flee New York to Las Vegas to escape thugs Harry (Jude Farese) and Joey (Allen Keller) whose $10,000 Alex has dropped in a poker game. In an increasingly contrived and unconvincing series of coincidences and turns of luck, duo set up shop in the *Doctor Zhivago* suite of the M-G-M Grand Hotel and use a false identity to obtain unlimited credit from the casino.

Occasionally amusing, picture often has the feel of being improvised, with director Ashby giving Voight a loose rein to inject physical business and odd dialog into a scene. Interplay between Voight and Young is the film's raison d'etre.

■ LOOKING FOR MR GOODBAR

1977, 135 MINS, US ◇ Ⓥ

Dir Richard Brooks *Prod* Freddie Fields *Scr* Richard Brooks *Ph* William A. Fraker *Ed* George Grenville *Mus* Artie Kane *Art Dir* Edward Carfagno
● Diane Keaton, Tuesday Weld, William Atherton, Richard Kiley, Richard Gere, Tom Berenger (Paramount)

In *Looking for Mr Goodbar*, writer-director Richard Brooks manifests his ability to catch accurately both the tone and subtlety of characters in the most repellant environments – in this case the desperate search for personal identity in the dreary and self-defeating world of compulsive sex and dope. Diane Keaton's performance as the good/bad girl is excellent.

Judith Rossner's novel was the basis for Brooks' fine screenplay about a girl who flees from a depressing home environment into the frantic world of singles bars and one-night physical gropings. The Jekyll-Hyde character caroms from sincere concern for teaching children to night-crawling of the seamiest sort.

At its best, the film, through Tuesday Weld's great performance as Keaton's sister who wanders from trend to trend, suggests dimly some alternatives.

■ LOOKING GLASS WAR, THE

1970, 106 MINS, UK ◇ Ⓥ

Dir Frank R. Pierson *Prod* John Box *Scr* Frank R. Pierson *Ph* Austin Dempster *Ed* Willy Kemplen *Mus* Wally Stott *Art Dir* Terence Marsh
● Christopher Jones, Pia Degermark, Ralph Richardson, Paul Rogers, Anthony Hopkins, Susan George (Columbia/Frankovich)

Based on the John Le Carre novel about Cold War espionage, *The Looking Glass War* is most notable as the feature directorial debut of writer Frank R. Pierson.

Christopher Jones and Pia Degermark head a featured cast which also includes excellent performances by Ralph Richardson and Paul Rogers.

Jones, a ship-jumping Polish seaman, is recruited by Richardson and Rogers, two old hands in British espionage, to enter East Germany to verify some missile sites.

Anthony Hopkins, a younger undercover agent, is a key character as he shares many youthful reservations in an atmosphere charged with memories of an earlier, simpler spy game.

Pierson's adaptation has some superior dialog and structuring.

■ LOOPHOLE

1981, 105 MINS, UK ◇

Dir John Quested *Prod* David Korda, Julian Holloway *Scr* Jonathan Hales *Ph* Michael Reed *Ed* Ralph Sheldon *Mus* Lalo Schifrin *Art Dir* Syd Cain

● Albert Finney, Martin Sheen, Susannah York, Colin Blakely, Jonathan Pryce (Brent Walker)

A clever plan to knock off a rich London bank is about the only thing that works in 'Loophole.' The caper, filmed in and around the British capital, squanders some fine talent on a trite, low-voltage script.

Albert Finney as the mastermind of the heist, and Martin Sheen as an honest architect who lends the gang his talents in order to bail himself out of hock to his own bank, perform okay with little room to flex their histrionic skills.

As scripted from a Robert Pollock novel, the plot isn't exactly mint new, with Finney & Co utilizing the rat infested sewer tunnels under mid-town London for access to and getaway from the bank's vault. A downpour almost wreaks its own brand of providential justice in the only sequence with any kind of charge for action or suspense fans.

- -

■ LOOSE CANNONS

1990, 93 MINS, US ◇ ⊛
Dir Bob Clark   *Prod* Aaron Spelling, Alan Greisman
Scr Richard Christian Matheson, Richard Matheson, Bob Clark   *Ph* Reginald H. Morris   *Ed* Stan Cole
Mus Paul Zaza   *Art Dir* Harry Pottle
● Gene Hackman, Dan Aykroyd, Dom DeLuise, Ronny Cox, Nancy Travis (Tri-Star)

Dan Aykroyd's dexterous multipersonality schtick is the only redeeming feature of this chase-heavy comedy, up on the homevid heap.

Director Bob Clark manages to make his low-brow comedy *Porky's* look like *Amadeus* with this latest salvo into the police-buddy genre, while Gene Hackman continues his befuddling penchant for sprinkling his overflowing resume with shameful losers.

Loose Cannons may be best remembered for its unbelievably convoluted screenplay – a concoction of elements from *Lethal Weapon 2*, *Midnight Run* and *Beverly Hills Cop*, all played at the speed of Warner Bros cartoon.

Plot involves gruesome murders, a secret 45-year-old porno film, a candidate for the chancellorship of West Germany and a horde of Uzi-brandishing neo-Nazis. All of that is irrelevant to the main plot, which pairs the gruff Mac (Hackman) with the Sybil-like Ellis (Aykroyd) – recently (and apparently prematurely) reactivated by his police-captain uncle after suffering a nervous breakdown that causes him to lapse into multiple personalities.

- -

■ LOOSE CONNECTIONS

1983, 99 MINS, UK ◇ ⊛
Dir Richard Eyre   *Prod* Simon Perry   *Scr* Maggie Brooks   *Ph* Clive Tickner   *Ed* David Martin
Mus Dominic Muldowney, Andy Roberts
● Stephen Rea, Lindsay Duncan, Jan Niklas, Carole Harrison, Gary Olsen, Frances Low (Umbrella/Greenpoint)

Richard Eyre's second theatrical feature is an exceedingly amiable comic battle of the sexes.

Sally (Lindsay Duncan), together with two girlfriends, has built a jeep in which to drive from London to a feminist conference in Munich, but at the last moment she is left on her own. She takes a newspaper ad for a fellow driver, seeking a female non-smoking vegetarian, who speaks German and knows something about car engines. The only applicant is Harry (Stephen Rea), who claims to fill all the requirements except sex, and furthermore claims he's gay. Needless to say, Harry's a liar.

The trip to Munich is one comic disaster after another. But the odd couple are drawn to each other, and the inevitable happens. Both roles are played to perfection. It's not a film of hearty laughs, but of continual quiet chuckles.

- -

■ LOOT

1970, 101 MINS, UK ◇ ⊛
Dir Silvio Narizzano   *Prod* Arthur Lewis   *Scr* Ray Galton, Alan Simpson   *Ph* Austin Dempster   *Ed* Martin Charles   *Mus* Keith Mansfield, Richard Willing-Denton   *Art Dir* Anthony Pratt
● Richard Attenborough, Lee Remick, Hywel Bennett, Roy Holder, Milo O'Shea, Dick Emery (British Lion)

Joe Orton's macabre black comedy has transferred uneasily to the screen, the opening-out in the script having robbed the yarn of much of its comic tension. Nevertheless, it has enough speed, inventiveness and sharp, acid, irreverent comedy to satisfy many.

Story has Hywel Bennett and Roy Holder as two shiftless chums who, anxious to get rich quick, decide to blow a bank. They pull off the raid and elect to hide the loot in the coffin of Holder's mother, who has conveniently died. But there's no room for the cash and the corpse, so the poor woman's hidden in the lavatory.

The hotel belonging to Holder's father (Milo O'Shea) becomes a bedlam of frenzied rushing around, complicated by the arrival of an eccentric, pompous and venal inspector (Richard Attenborough) and Lee Remick, as a gold-digging sexpot of a private nurse.

Attenborough appears to be trying far too hard to get his effects. O'Shea is amiably amusing and bewildered. Remick is coolly efficient as the femme fatale, and Bennett and Holder keep their body- and loot-snatching roles to a high pitch of energetic activity.

- -

■ LORD JIM

1965, 154 MINS, UK/US ◇ ⊛
Dir Richard Brooks   *Prod* Richard Brooks   *Scr* Richard Brooks   *Ph* Frederick A. Young   *Ed* Alan Osbiston
Mus Bronislau Kaper   *Art Dir* Geoffrey Drake
● Peter O'Toole, James Mason, Curt Jurgens, Jack Hawkins, Eli Wallach, Dahlia Levi (Columbia/Keep)

Many may be disappointed with Richard Brooks' handling of the Joseph Conrad novel. The storyline is often confused, some of the more interesting characters emerge merely as shadowy sketches. Brooks, while capturing the spirit of adventure of the novel, only superficially catches the inner emotional and spiritual conflict of its hero. In this he is not overly helped by Peter O'Toole whose performance is self-indulgent and lacking in real depth.

The story concerns a young merchant seaman. In a moment of cowardice he deserts his ship during a storm and his life is dogged throughout by remorse and an urge to redeem himself. His search for a second chance takes him to South Asia. There he becomes the conquering hero of natives oppressed by a fanatical war lord.

Brooks has teetered between making it a fullblooded, no-holds-barred adventure yarn and the fascinating psychological study that Conrad wrote. O'Toole, though a fine, handsome figure of a man, goes through the film practically expressionless and the audience sees little of the character's introspection and soul searching.

Of the rest of the cast the two who stand out, mainly because they are provided with the best opportunities, are Eli Wallach and Paul Lukas.

- -

■ LORD LOVE A DUCK

1966, 105 MINS, US
Dir George Axelrod   *Prod* George Axelrod   *Scr* Larry H. Johnson, George Axelrod   *Ph* Daniel L. Fapp
Ed William A. Lyon   *Mus* Neal Hefti   *Art Dir* Malcolm Brown

● Roddy McDowall, Tuesday Weld, Lola Albright, Martin West, Ruth Gordon, Harvey Korman (Charleston/United Artists)

Some may call George Axelrod's *Lord Love a Duck* satire, others way-out comedy, still others brilliant, while there may be some who ask, what's it all about?

Whatever the reaction, there is no question that the film [based on Al Hire's novel] is packed with laughs, often of the truest anatomical kind, and there is a veneer of sophistication which keeps showing despite the most outlandish goings-on. Some of the comedy is inspirational, a gagman's dream come true, and there is bite in some of Axelrod's social commentary beneath the wonderful nonsense.

The characters are everything here, each developed brightly along zany lines, topped by Roddy McDowall as a Svengali-type high school student leader who pulls the strings on the destiny of Tuesday Weld, an ingenuish-type sexpot whose philosophy is wrapped up in her words 'Everybody's got to love me'.

McDowall is in good form as the mastermind of the school, and he has a strong contender for interest in blonde Weld in a characterization warm and appealing. Scoring almost spectacularly is Lola Albright as Weld's mother, a cocktail bar 'bunny' who commits suicide when she thinks she's ruined her daughter's chances for marriage.

- -

■ LORD OF THE FLIES

1963, 90 MINS, UK
Dir Peter Brook   *Prod* Lewis Allen, Dana Hodgdon
Scr Peter Brook   *Ph* Tom Hollyman   *Ed* Peter Brook, J.C. Griel, M. Lubtchansky   *Mus* Raymond Leppard
● James Aubrey, Tom Chapin, Hugh Emwards, Roger Elwin, Tom Gaman (Two Arts)

The theme of young boys reverting to savagery when marooned on a deserted island has its moments of truth, but this pic rates as a near-miss on many counts.

Titles adequately indicate that evacuation in some future war has a group of youngsters surviving an air crash on a tropical island. They meet, and one boy is elected chief, but with dissent from another. Latter says his group will become hunters and they are soon drawing blood from some wild pigs and evolving tales of a monster on the island. The last-named is a dead paratrooper swaying on a ledge. But soon the hunting group goes completely native and persecutes and even exterminates those of the other group.

Peter Brook has coaxed fairly natural performances from his group of English youths. But he has drawn out his tale on a seemingly too schematic level to emerge more than illustration of the William Golding best-selling book than a film version standing on its own.

Lensing is curiously metallic but the on-the-spot shooting in the Puerto Rican jungles and beaches helps. Pic was made with US and Puerto Rican funds but with a British director and thesps.

- -

■ LORD OF THE FLIES

1990, 90 MINS, US ◇ ⊛
Dir Harry Hook   *Prod* Ross Milloy, David V. Lester
Scr Sara Schiff   *Ph* Martin Fuhrer   *Ed* Tom Priestley
Mus Philippe Sarde   *Art Dir* Jamie Leonard
● Balthazar Getty, Chris Furth, Danuel Pipoly, Badgett Dale, Edward Taft, Andrew Taft (Jack's Camp/Signal Hill)

The notion that the story of civilized boys reverting to savagery on a desert isle would be improved by shooting in color and substituting American actors for British child thesps is an odd one indeed.

Peter Brook's black and white version of William Goldings's *Lord of the Flies* is no classic, but it stands miles above this thoroughly undistinguished and unnecessary remake. Lewis Allen, one of the producers of the earlier version and exec producer of the remake with Peter Newman, made this film 'to protect the first film and to prevent television movie-of-the-week imitations after Golding received the Nobel Prize for literature.'

Here, director Harry Hook's literal, unimaginative visual approach makes the tale seem mundane and tedious.

The flat screenplay makes all the boys seem like dullards and does little to help differentiate the cast members, most of whom seem cut from the same mold, of bland cuteness. Nor do these boys seem to be living through the kind of gritty physical experience that would make the allegory spring to life.

. . . .

■ LORD OF THE RINGS, THE

1978, 131 MINS, US ◇ ⓥ
Dir Ralph Bakshi   *Prod* Saul Zaentz   *Scr* Chris Conkling, Peter S. Beagle   *Mus* Leonard Rosenman
● (Fantasy)

Students of animated technique and Tolkien story-telling will find a lot to like in what Ralph Bakshi has done with *Lord of the Rings*. Unquestionably, Bakshi has perfected some outstanding pen-and-ink effects while translating faithfully a portion of J.R.R. Tolkien's trilogy. But in his concentration on craft and duty to the original story – both admirable in themselves – Bakshi overlooks the uninitiated completely.

Quite simply, those who do not know the characters of Middle Earth going in will not know them coming out. The introductory narration explaining the Rings is confusing, making the rest of the quest seem pointless in many places. Boring is an equally good word, especially toward the end of two hours.

. . . .

■ LORDS OF DISCIPLINE, THE

1983, 102 MINS, US ◇ ⓥ
Dir Franc Roddam   *Prod* Herb Jaffe, Gabriel Katzka   *Scr* Thomas Pope, Lloyd Fonvielle   *Ph* Brian Tufano   *Ed* Michael Ellis   *Mus* Howard Blake   *Art Dir* John Graysmark
● David Keith, Robert Prosky, G.D. Spradlin, Barbara Babcock, Michael Biehn, Rick Rossovich (Paramount)

The Lords of Discipline laces a military school Watergate saga with heavy doses of sadism, racism and macho bullying. Designed as an expose of the corruption to be found within the hallowed walls of a venerable American institution, pic wants to have it both ways.

Set around 1964, drama follows cadet David Keith through his senior year at the Carolina Military Institute. Year in question is a notable one for the school because the first black cadet in its history has been enrolled.

As far as the new recruits are concerned, the poop hits the fan on 'hell night', which is just as bad as it sounds. With the full sanction of the faculty, upper classmen are permitted, even encouraged, to turn strong young men into oatmeal, running them through an evening of physical horrors under the guise of building character. One boy dies as a result, which leads outsider type Keith onto the existence of The Ten, a secret society to ferret out undesirables.

British director Franc Roddam had to wait over three years to make his American directorial debut and, ironically, ended up doing most of this film in Britain when no US school would allow lensing on its grounds.

. . . .

■ LORDS OF FLATBUSH

1974, 86 MINS, US ◇ ⓥ
Dir Stephen F. Verona, Martin Davidson   *Prod* Stephen F. Verona   *Scr* Stephen F. Verona, Gayle Gleckler, Martin Davidson   *Ph* Joseph Mangine, Edward Lachman   *Ed* Stan Siegel, Muffie Meyer   *Mus* Joe Brooks   *Art Dir* Glenda Miller
● Perry King, Sylvester Stallone, Henry Winkler, Paul Mace, Susan Blakely, Maria Smith (Columbia)

Life among the leather-jacket high school set of Flatbush is the subject of this indie filmed in Brooklyn, NY, locale. Pic is episodic in narrative, particularly in first few reels burdened mostly by irrelevant action, but when actual story line is reached focuses on two of the members of a social club called Lords of Flatbush.

Perry King and Sylvester Stallone play a couple of would-be toughies who occasionally leave their pals for some dating. Stallone's romancing leads to getting his pal (Maria Smith) pregnant, and King to getting the final brushoff from femme (Susan Blakely) he pursues. Not too much finesse distinguishes the script, which carries neither warmth nor particular interest for the various characters.

Both actors do well enough by their roles.

. . . .

■ LORNA

1965, 78 MINS, US
Dir Russ Meyer   *Prod* Russ Meyer   *Scr* James Griffith   *Ph* Russ Meyer   *Ed* Russ Meyer   *Mus* Hal Hooper, James Griffith
● Lorna Maitland, Mark Bradley, James Rucker, Hal Hooper, Doc Scortt, James Griffith (Eve)

A sort of sex morality play, *Lorna* is Russ Meyer's first serious effort after six nudie pix.

Meyer's story concerns Lorna Maitland as the buxom wife of James Rucker, a handsome young clod who each day joins Hal Hopper and Doc Scortt in commuting to work at a salt mine. (Latter is not the first Biblical overtone, since Griffith portrays a firebrand preacher-Greek chorus who greets audience via clever subjective camera intro with ominous foreboding of sin and payment therefor.)

Mark Bradley, escaped con and vicious killer, encounters Maitland in the fields with predictable results, after which she takes him home for encores.

Maitland has a sensual voice although vocal projection is her least asset. Bradley has rugged looks, a voice to match, and a bigger future in films. His role requires expressions of fear, boredom, tenderness and amoral viciousness, and he is up to them all. Griffith is a two-time loser, having overacted a trite part which he himself wrote.

. . . .

■ LOSERS, THE

1970, 95 MINS, US ◇ ⓥ
Dir Jack Starrett   *Prod* Joe Solomon   *Scr* Alan Caillou   *Ph* Nonong Rasca   *Ed* James Moore   *Mus* Stu Phillips
● William Smith, Bernie Hamilton, Adam Roarke, Daniel Kemp, Houston Savage, Gene Cornelius (Fanfare)

Director Jack Starrett took his motley crew of actors to the Philippines which is supposed to pass, on the screen, as Vietnam. The viewer is asked to believe that a contingent of motor cycle bums would be hired by the US to rescue a CIA agent, held prisoner in Cambodia by the North Vietnamese or Red Chinese, it's never really made clear.

The script is so inane, with not even a feeble attempt at logic, that what are intended as serious moments come off as funny.

Some of the acting is excellent – Bernie Hamilton makes his army captain a human being; Adam Roarke's Duke is better than the part deserves; Paul Koslo, as one of the cycle riders who falls for a native girl (Ana Korita) he meets in a brothel is very effective.

. . . .

■ LOSIN' IT

1983, 104 MINS, US ◇ ⓥ
Dir Curtis Hanson   *Prod* Bryan Gindoff, Hannah Hempstead   *Scr* B.W.L. Norton   *Ph* Gil Taylor   *Ed* Richard Halsey   *Mus* Ken Wannberg   *Art Dir* Robb Wilson King
● Tom Cruise, Jackie Earle Haley, John Stockwell, Shelley Long, John P. Navin Jr, Hector Elias (Embassy)

As often noted, the problem with porno is that there are only so many ways to show people having sex; the problem with films like *Losin'* is that there are only so many ways to show teenagers not having sex.

But director Curtis Hanson makes a commendable effort with a rather obvious story about three teenage boys who head for a wild weekend in Tijuana, hoping to trade hard cash for manly experience.

Though none is really very experienced, each is sophisticated to a stereotyped degree. There's the high-school hunk (John Stockwell) who's actually had a girl; the blustering faker (Jackie Earle Haley), whose experience is limited to his own imagination; and the sensitive innocent, (Tom Cruise) – who isn't sure he wants it, but is destined for the best time to be had by all.

Naturally, they are accompanied by wimpy John P. Navin Jr, brought along only because he has the necessary cash to make the trip possible. And along the way they pick up crazy – but nice – Shelley Long, on the lam from her husband.

This doesn't sound like much and it isn't, but the picture is a solid credit for all involved.

. . . .

■ LOST ANGELS

1989, 116 MINS, US ◇ ⓥ
Dir Hugh Hudson   *Prod* Howard Rosenman, Thomas Baer   *Scr* Michael Weller   *Ph* Juan Ruiz-Anchia   *Ed* David Gladwell   *Mus* Philippe Sarde   *Art Dir* Assheton Gorton
● Donald Sutherland, Adam Horovitz, Amy Locane, Don Bloomfield, Celia Weston (Orion)

Lost Angels suffers from some of the communication problems which bedevil its young, inarticulate hero. Hugh Hudson's wannabe *Rebel without a Cause* update tries to be a serious exploration of throwaway middle-class teens in the San Fernando Valley, but despite some gripping moments it's often cliched and incoherent.

Adam Horovitz of the Beastie Boys rap band has a sympathetic presence but not enough to do as the troubled lead.

It's another of those films about mental illness that tries to have it both ways, perhaps for fear of turning off the audience by presenting a lead who is truly disturbed.

The film powerfully conveys the latent violence just below the brooding surface of Horovitz' quiet demeanor. Whether it's the prelude to a freakout as he learns he's being locked up, or a fistfight with shrink Donald Sutherland, or a nightmarish violence-seeking trip to a Latino area, Horovitz has the ability to impersonate a stick of dynamite.

Sutherland brings subtlety to his occasional scenes as a scruffy shrink who has enough emotional problems to be empathetic.

. . . .

■ LOST COMMAND

1966, 129 MINS, US ◇ ⓥ
Dir Mark Robson   *Prod* Mark Robson   *Scr* Nelson Gidding   *Ph* Robert Surtees   *Ed* Dorothy Spencer   *Mus* Franz Waxman   *Art Dir* John Stoll
● Anthony Quinn, Alain Delon, George Segal, Michele Morgan, Maurice Ronet, Claudia Cardinale (Columbia)

Lost Command is a good contemporary action-melodrama about some French paratroopers who survive France's humiliation and defeat

359

in Southeast Asia, only to be sent to rebellious Algeria. Filmed in Spain, the Mark Robson production [based on a novel by Jean Larteguy] has enough pace, action and exterior eye appeal to overcome a sometimes routine script.

Anthony Quinn heads the players as the gruff, low-born soldier who has risen to field grade rank because of the attrition of Indo-Chinese guerrilla warfare which decimated the ranks of the French army.

Providing a two-way contrast, and exemplifying the extremes to which the Quinn character never extends, are Alain Delon and Maurice Ronet. Delon is the sensitive, quiet but effective assistant who, at fadeout, leaves military service, since fighting in itself has become meaningless. Ronet is brutal, sadistic and callous, yet with enough fighting effectiveness to be needed in battle.

This very meaty and pathetic plot irony will strike some as underdeveloped, in that Quinn and Segal never effect a personal confrontation until latter is needlessly killed by Ronet, but by then it is too late.

■ LOST HORIZON

1937, 125 MINS, ▼

Dir Frank Capra   *Prod* Frank Capra   *Scr* Robert Riskin   *Ph* Joseph Walker   *Ed* Gene Havlick   *Mus* Dimitri Tiomkin   *Art Dir* Stephen Goosson
● Ronald Colman, Edward Everett Horton, H.B. Warner, Jane Wyatt, Sam Jaffe, Margo (Columbia)

So canny are the ingredients that where credulity perhaps rears its practical head, audiences will be carried away by the histrionic illusion, skill and general Hollywood ledgerdemain which so effectively capture the best elements in this $2.5 million saga of Shangri-La.

Ronald Colman, with fine restraint, conveys the metamorphosis of the foreign diplomat falling in with the Arcadian idyll that he beholds in the Valley of the Blue Moon.

Sam Jaffe is capital as the ancient Belgian priest who first founded Shangri-La some 300 years ago – a Methuselah who is still alive, thanks to the Utopian philosophy of the community he has nurtured.

As H.B. Warner (the venerable Chang and oldest disciple of the High Lama) expounds it, the peaceful valley's philosophy of moderation in work, food, drink, pleasure, acquisition and all other earthly wants, is cannily scripted for audience appeal. Whether it's James Hilton's original novel or Robert Riskin's celluloid transmutation, the scripting contribution is one of the picture's strongest assets.

It opens vigorously in Baskul, showing the English community evacuating under the onslaught of Chinese bandits. The last plane out throws Colman together with the fussbudget archaeologist (Edward Everett Horton), the Ponzi plumber (Thomas Mitchell), the ailing waif of the world (Isabel Jewell), and Colman's screen brother (well played by John Howard). It's in Shangri-La that Jane Wyatt so vigorously establishes herself as Colman's vis-a-vis, looking decidedly comely and handling her romance opportunities with definite understanding.
□ 1937: Best Picture (Nomination)

■ LOST HORIZON

1973, 150 MINS, US ◇

Dir Charles Jarrott   *Prod* Ross Hunter   *Scr* Larry Kramer   *Ph* Robert Surtees   *Ed* Maury Winetrobe   *Mus* Burt Bacharach   *Art Dir* Preston Ames
● Peter Finch, Liv Ullmann, Sally Kellerman, George Kennedy, Michael York, Olivia Hussey (Columbia)

Some 36 years after Frank Capra's filmization of James Hilton's *Lost Horizon* novel premiered comes producer Ross Hunter's

lavish updated and musical adaptation. The form is that of filmed operetta in three acts, superbly mounted, and cast with an eye to international markets.

The script structure parallels that of the Capra film – opening after the majestic main title landscape of snowy mountains with the tumultous escape from rioting Asians in a kidnapped plane; the crash in the uncharted Himalayas rescued by an inscrutable major domo who takes the disparate survivors to the nestled Utopia of Shangri-La, where the outsiders resolve their personal destinies.

Peter Finch heads the cast as Conway, an international statesman selected by high lama Charles Boyer to succeed to rule of Shangri-La, where the world's wisdom is being preserved against the foreseen Apocalypse. Sir John Gielgud is the high lama's chief aide who reveals the mystery of the place to Finch.

Only Michael York, in a dramatically-crippled supporting banana role, and Olivia Hussey, an awkwardly exotic soubrette, fail to get off the ground.

■ LOST IN AMERICA

1985, 91 MINS, US ◇ ▼

Dir Albert Brooks   *Prod* Marty Katz   *Scr* Albert Brooks, Monica Johnson   *Ph* Eric Saarinen   *Ed* David Finfer   *Mus* Arthur B. Rubinstein   *Art Dir* Richard Sawyer
● Albert Brooks, Julie Hagerty, Garry Marshall, Art Frankel, Michael Greene, Tom Tarpey (Geffen)

Film opens on Albert Brooks and wife Julie Hagerty in bed on eve of their move to a $450,000 house and also what Brooks presumes will be his promotion to a senior exec slot in a big ad agency. Brooks is a nervous mess, made worse when vaguely bored Hagerty tells him their life has become 'too responsible, too controlled.'

Her suppressed wish for a more dashing life comes startlingly true the next day when a confident Brooks glides into his boss' LA office only to hear that his expected senior v.p. stripes are going to someone else and he's being transferred to New York.

Brooks quits his job and convinces his wife to quit her personnel job. The pair will liquidate their assets, buy a Winnebago, and head across America.

Brooks, who directed and cowrote with Monica Johnson, is irrepressible but always very human.

■ LOST PATROL, THE

1934, 74 MINS, US

Dir John Ford   *Prod* Cliff Reid   *Scr* Dudley Nichols, Garrett Fort   *Ph* Harold Wenstrom   *Ed* Paul Weatherwax   *Mus* Max Steiner   *Art Dir* Van Nest Polglase, Sidney Ullman
● Victor McLaglen, Boris Karloff, Wallace Ford, Reginald Denny, J. M. Kerrigan (RKO)

Not a woman in the cast and substantially little as to story, but under the weight of suspense, dialog and competency of direction *Lost Patrol* tips the scales favorably as entertainment.

All of the action [from the story *Patrol* by Philip MacDonald] takes place in the Mesopotamian desert during the campaign of the English against militant Arabs in 1917. Outside of the bleak desert, the only other change of scene throughout the picture's length is the oasis which a patrol, lost after the commanding officer has been killed, discovers. It is here where one by one the men either die or are bumped off by Arabs, until Victor McLaglen is the last.

McLaglen, the sergeant who inherits command of the patrol, turns in a good job in the kind of a part that's particularly suited to this actor. As a Bible nut, Boris Karloff is on a

somewhat different assignment. He gives a fine account of himself.

■ LOST SQUADRON, THE

1932, 80 MINS, US ▼

Dir George Archainbaud   *Prod* David O. Selznick   *Scr* Wallace Smith, Herman J. Mankiewicz, Robert Presnell   *Ph* Edward Cronjager   *Art Dir* Max Ree
● Richard Dix, Mary Astor, Erich von Stroheim, Dorothy Jordan, Joel McCrea, Robert Armstrong (RKO)

Squadron glorifies the cinematic stunt flyer. [From the *Liberty* magazine story] by Dick Grace, the most illustrious of the Hollywood aerial daredevils, it is not without authority, even though the dramatics are a bit strained.

The 'behind the scenes' of an aerial film production is the best appeal *Squadron* has. It's a story-within-a-story. Although the basic premise might be regarded as trite and familiar, the detail of the skullduggery of a jealous husband-director, along with his fanatical zeal in injecting realism into the aerial crash stuff, is 100% new for the screen.

Erich von Stroheim plays the director (alias Arnold von Furst in the picture) to the hilt, i.e. the role of a domineering, militaristic Prussian film director who is a martinet on location, callous to all else but the box-office effect of his celluloid production.

Action takes Richard Dix, Joel McCrea, Robert Armstrong and Hugh Herbert from an aviation corps right after the war to Hollywood, where Armstrong has preceded them and won some standing as an aerial stuntist.

With the quartet reunited as Hollywoodian stunt flyers (Dick Grace, Art Gobel, Leo Nomis and Frank Clark get the billing for the actual aerial stunting), von Stroheim as the jealous director motivates the action toward a realistic crack-up by putting acid on the control wires of the ship which Dix has screen antagonist, was supposed to have piloted.

Mary Astor is unhappily cast as an ambitious actress who first throws over Dix while he's on the other side for a sinecure under a masculine protector, and who later marries von Furst to further her career on the screen.

■ LOST WEEKEND, THE

1945, 104 MINS, US ▼

Dir Billy Wilder   *Prod* Charles Brackett   *Scr* Charles Brackett, Billy Wilder   *Ph* John F. Seitz   *Ed* Doane Harrison   *Mus* Miklos Rozsa   *Art Dir* Hans Dreier, Earl Hedrick
● Ray Milland, Jane Wyman, Howard da Silva, Philip Terry (Paramount)

The filming by Paramount of *The Lost Weekend* marks a particularly outstanding achievement in the Hollywood setting. The psychiatric study of an alcoholic, it is an unusual picture. It is intense, morbid – and thrilling.

Weekend is the specific story [from the novel by Charles R. Jackson] of a quondam writer who has yet to put down his first novel on paper. He talks about it continuously but something always seems to send him awry just when he has a mind to work. Booze. Two quarts at a time. He goes on drunks for days. And his typewriter invariably winds up in the pawnshop.

Ray Milland has certainly given no better performance in his career. Drunks may frequently excite laughter, but at no time can there be even a suggestion of levity to the part Milland plays. Only at the film's end is the character out of focus, but that is the fault of the script. The suggestion of rehabilitation should have been more carefully developed.

Jane Wyman is the girl, Philip Terry the brother. They help make the story overshadow the characters. The entire cast, in fact, contributes notably. And that goes especially for Howard da Silva as the barten-

der. Billy Wilder's direction is always certain, always conscious that the characters were never to over-state the situations.
□ 1945: Best Picture

. . . .

■ LOST WORLD, THE

1960, 97 MINS, US ◇ ⓥ
Dir Irwin Allen   *Prod* Irwin Allen   *Scr* Charles Bennett, Irwin Allen   *Ph* Winton Hoch   *Ed* Hugh S. Fowler   *Mus* Paul Sawtell, Bert Shefter   *Art Dir* Duncan Cramer, Walter M. Simonds
● Michael Rennie, Jill St John, David Hedison, Claude Rains, Fernando Lamas, Richard Haydn (20th Century-Fox)

Watching *The Lost World* is tantamount to taking a trip through a Coney Island fun house. The picture's chief attraction is its production gusto. Emphasis on physical and pictorial values makes up, to some extent, for its lack of finesse in the literary and thespic departments.

In translating the Arthur Conan Doyle story to the screen for the second time (after a lapse of 36 years since the first, silent version), Irwin Allen and Charles Bennett have constructed a choppy, topheavy, deliberately-paced screenplay that labors too long with exposition and leaves several loose ends dangling. Allen's direction is not only sluggish but has somehow gotten more personality into his dinosaurs than into his people.

Among the curious individuals who venture into this treacherous hidden area at the headwaters of the Amazon are Claude Rains, overly affected as Professor George Edward Challenger; Michael Rennie, a bit wooden as a titled playboy with a notorious reputation; Jill St John, ill-at-ease as an adventuress who chooses tight pink capri pants as suitable garb for an Amazonian exploration; David Hedison, bland as a newsman-photog; and Fernando Lamas, unconvincing as a Latin guitar-player and helicopter-operator.

With the exception of one or two mighty ineffectual prehistoric spiders and a general absence of genuine shock or tension, the production is something to behold. The dinosaurs are exceptionally lifelike (although they resemble horned toads and alligators more than dinosaurs) and the violent volcanic scenery (like hot, bubbling chili sauce) and lush vegetation form backdrops that are more interesting and impressive than the action taking place in front of them.

. . . .

■ LOUISIANA STORY

1948, 77 MINS, US
Dir Robert Flaherty   *Prod* Robert Flaherty   *Scr* Robert Flaherty, Frances Flaherty   *Ph* Richard Leacock   *Ed* Helen Van Dongen   *Mus* Virgil Thomson
● Joseph Boudreaux, Lionel Le Blanc, Mrs. E. Bienvenu, Frank Hardy, C.T. Guedry (Lopert Films)

Louisiana Story is a documentary-type story told almost purely in camera terms. It has a slender, appealing story, moments of agonizing suspense, vivid atmosphere and superlative photography.

Filmed entirely in the bayou country of Louisiana, the picture tells of the Cajun (Acadian) boy and his parents, who live by hunting and fishing in the alligator-infested swamps and streams, and of the oil-drilling crew that brings its huge derrick to sink a well.

There probably aren't more than 100 lines of dialog in the entire picture – long sequences being told by the camera, with eloquent sound effects and Virgil Thomson's expressive music as background. There are no real heroes or villains (unless the terrifying alligators could be considered the latter). The simple Cajun family is friendly, and the oil-drilling crew is pleasant and likable.

Standard Oil of NJ contributed the necessary $200,000 production coin to Flaherty.

. . . .

■ LOVE

1927, 84 MINS, US ⊗
Dir Edmund Goulding   *Prod* Edmund Goulding   *Scr* Frances Marion, Marian Ainslee, Ruth Cummings, Lorna Moon   *Ph* William Daniels   *Ed* Hugh Wynn   *Mus* Ernst Luz   *Art Dir* Cedric Gibbons, Alexander Toluboff
● Greta Garbo, John Gilbert, George Fawcett, Emily Fitzroy, Brandon Hurst, Philippe De Lacy (M-G-M)

What is there to tell about the Tolstoy story *Anna Karenina*? Its locale is Russia in the time of the Czars. Anna (Greta Garbo) has a husband and a young son; Vronsky (John Gilbert), a military heritage and a desire for Anna. For screen purposes it's enough that both are of the aristocracy, which permits Garbo long, stately gowns and Gilbert a series of uniforms that would make a buck private out of the student prince.

There are rich interiors, appropriate exteriors and an excellent officers' steeplechase to get the action figuratively off of a couch for a while. Besides which Garbo and Gilbert supposedly care for each other in the script.

Anyway, director Edmund Goulding hasn't let the title run away with his sense of discretion. Possibly has leaned over backwards to the extent of keeping this picture from becoming a rave. When all is said and done, *Love* is a cinch because it has Gilbert and Garbo.

. . . .

■ LOVE AFFAIR

1939, 87 MINS, US ⓥ
Dir Leo McCarey   *Prod* Leo McCarey   *Scr* Delmer Daves, Donald Ogden Stewart   *Ph* Rudolph Mate   *Ed* Edward Dmytryk, George Hively
● Irene Dunne, Charles Boyer, Maria Ouspenskaya, Lee Bowman, Astrid Allwyn, Maurice Moscovich (RKO)

Leo McCarey's initial production for RKO as a producer-director offers an entirely new approach to accepted technique. Basically, it's the regulation formula of boy-meets-girl [story by McCarey and Mildred Cram]. But first half is best described as romantic comedy, while second portion switches to drama with comedy.

Aboard boat sailing from Naples to New York, Charles Boyer starts a flirtation with Irene Dunne. He is engaged to heiress Astrid Allwyn, and she to Lee Bowman. They separate on docking with pact to meet six months later atop the Empire State building.

Dunne slips to Philadelphia to sing in a night club, while Boyer applies himself to painting. While on her way to keep tryst on appointed day, Dunne is injured in a traffic accident. Faced with life of a cripple, girl refuses to contact Boyer to explain.

Dunne is excellent in a role that requires both comedy and dramatic ability. Boyer is particularly effective as the modern Casanova. Maria Ouspenskaya provides a warmly sympathetic portrayal as Boyer's grandmother in Madeira.
□ 1939: Best Picture (Nomination)

. . . .

■ LOVE AND BULLETS

1979, 95 MINS, UK ◇ ⓥ
Dir Stuart Rosenberg   *Prod* Pancho Kohner   *Scr* Wendell Mayes, John Melson   *Ph* Fred Koenekamp, Anthony Richmond   *Ed* Michael Anderson   *Mus* Lalo Schifrin   *Art Dir* John DeCuir
● Charles Bronson, Rod Steiger, Jill Ireland, Strother Martin, Bradford Dillman, Michael Gazzo (ITC/Grade)

Slowly and predictably, script plots Charles Bronson's mission, on behalf of the FBI, to pick up a mobster's moll (Jill Ireland) who's got separated from her paramour and is

presumed to be a mine of incriminating information.

Bronson's personal obsession with bringing down the gangland king is accentuated when he discovers the girl knows nothing after all, and then falls for her. When the mob, equally convinced she'll shop them, have her killed, he takes private revenge.

Rod Steiger's performance as the effete Mafia boss is tantalizing. So too is the emergent love affair between Bronson and Ireland, her comic talent largely starved for lack of material.

Director Stuart Rosenberg could have glossed over the plot's less believable twists with a brisker style and a lot more attack.

. . . .

■ LOVE AND DEATH

1975, 85 MINS, US ◇
Dir Woody Allen   *Prod* Charles H. Joffe   *Scr* Woody Allen   *Ph* Ghislain Cloquet   *Ed* Ralph Rosenblum, Ron Kalish   *Art Dir* Willy Holt
● Woody Allen, Diane Keaton (United Artists)

Woody Allen and Diane Keaton invade the land and spirit of Anton Chekhov. *Love and Death* is another mile-a-minute visual-verbal whirl by the two comedy talents, this time through Czarist Russia in the days of the Napoleonic Wars.

Allen's script traces his bumbling adventures with distant cousin Keaton, latter outstanding as a prim lady of both philosophical and sexual bent. Between malaprop battlefield heroics and metaphysical deliberations, Allen eventually combines with Keaton in an assassination attempt on Napoleon himself. It is impossible to catalog the comedic blueprint; suffice to say it is another zany product of the terrific synergism of the two stars.

About 54 supporting players have roles which range from a few feet to a few frames. Joffe's location production was shot in France and Hungary, where some gorgeous physical values serve as backdrop to the kooky antics.

. . . .

■ LOVE AND MONEY

1982, 90 MINS, US ◇
Dir James Toback   *Prod* James Toback   *Scr* James Toback   *Ph* Fred Schuler   *Ed* Dennis Hill   *Mus* Aaron Copland   *Art Dir* Lee Fischer
● Ray Sharkey, Ornella Muti, Klaus Kinski, Armand Assante, King Vidor, Susan Heldfond (Lorimar/Paramount)

Love and Money is an arresting romantic suspense film which, in spite of several good performances and well-crafted individual scenes, fails to ignite.

Ray Sharkey toplines as Byron Levin, a case of arrested development who works in an LA bank and lives with his senile grandpa (King Vidor) and librarian girl friend Vicky (Susan Heldfond). He comes out of his robot-like shell upon meeting the beautiful Catherine (Ornella Muti), young wife of multinational business magnate Stockheinz (Klaus Kinski).

Following an intense romance with Catherine, Levin becomes involved in an international plot masterminded by Stockheinz to help him deal with Latin American dictator Lorenzo Prado (Armand Assante), not coincidentally Levin's former college roommate.

Muti makes a strong US picture debut, augmenting her famous exotic beauty with some powerful thesping.

. . . .

■ LOVE AND PAIN AND THE WHOLE DAMN THING

1973, 110 MINS, US ◇
Dir Alan J. Pakula   *Prod* Alan J. Pakula   *Scr* Alvin Sargent   *Ph* Geoffrey Unsworth   *Ed* Russell Lloyd   *Mus* Michael Small   *Art Dir* Enrique Alarcon

● Maggie Smith, Timothy Bottoms, Don Jaime de Mora y Aragon, Emiliano Redondo, Charles Baxter, Margaret Modlin (Columbia)

For almost three-quarters of its overlong running time, *Love and Pain . . . etc* works as a modest, affecting romantic comedy about two mismatched neurotics stumbling into love during a Spanish tour. But pic succumbs to a fatal attack of *Love Story*itis, and goes down for the count.

Timothy Bottoms plays the shy, asthmatic son of a professor packed off to Spain for the summer. Bottoms joins a tourist bus where he is seated next to Maggie Smith, a jumpy lady of middle age who frequently bumps into her own shadow. For most of the film they trip over each other, explore the countryside and gradually accept a warmth and companionship that leads to a believable affair. Then Smith reveals she's dying.

Smith, as ever, is luminous, and Bottoms tackles a difficult role with ease. One only wishes the scripter had left well enough alone.

■ LOVE AT FIRST BITE

1979, 96 MINS, US ◇ ▼
Dir Stan Dragoti   *Prod* Joel Freeman   *Scr* Robert Kaufman   *Ph* Edward Rosson   *Ed* Mort Fallick, Allan Jacobs   *Mus* Charles Bernstein   *Art Dir* Serge Krizman
● George Hamilton, Susan Saint James, Richard Benjamin, Dick Shawn, Arte Johnson (American International)

'What would happen if Dracula was victimized by life in modern New York City?

It's a fun notion and George Hamilton makes it work. In the first place, he's funny just to watch. Veteran make-up artist William Tuttle, who created Lugosi's Dracula look in 1934, retains the grey, drained visage while adding a nutty quality that Hamilton accents with the arch of an eyebrow.

Story evicts Dracula from his Transylvania castle and takes him in pursuit of Susan Saint James, a fashion model he loves from an old photo. In the care of his bumbling manservant, slightly overplayed by Arte Johnson, Hamilton's coffin is naturally misrouted by the airline, winding up in a black funeral home.

Director Stan Dragoti keeps the chuckles coming, spaced by a few good guffaws.

■ LOVE AT LARGE

1990, 97 MINS, US ◇
Dir Alan Rudolph   *Prod* David Blocker   *Scr* Alan Rudolph   *Ph* Elliot Davis   *Ed* Lisa Churgin   *Mus* Mark Isham   *Art Dir* Steven Legler
● Tom Berenger, Elizabeth Perkins, Anne Archer, Ted Levine, Annette O'Toole, Kate Capshaw (Orion)

Alan Rudolph's film is a tongue-in-cheek take on the gumshoe genre that mostly seeks to explore the perplexing possibilities of love.

Wealthy and idle Dolan (Anne Archer) hires rumpled cheap detective Harry Dobbs (Tom Berenger) to trail a lover she underdescribes. Berenger picks the wrong guy and ends up pursuing a quarry far more interesting than the intended – this one's not only married, he's got two separate families. Meanwhile, he's being followed by novice detective Stella (Elizabeth Perkins), who's been hired by his unreasonably jealous, crockery-throwing girlfriend, Doris (Ann Magnuson).

It's the endless round of illogical but irresistible liaisons and the characters' own unfathomable peculiarities that form the basis of this dizzy sendup of romance. Berenger, with his squashed hat and growling delivery, is slyly amusing as Dobbs, while Perkins exudes a flinty, provocative chemistry.

■ LOVE BUG, THE

1969, 108 MINS, US ◇
Dir Robert Stevenson   *Prod* Bill Walsh   *Scr* Bill Walsh, Don DaGradi   *Ph* Edward Colman   *Ed* Cotton Warburton   *Mus* George Bruns   *Art Dir* Carroll Clark, John B. Mansbridge
● Dean Jones, Michele Lee, David Tomlinson, Buddy Hackett, Joe Flynn (Walt Disney)

This is a cutie, the story of a little foreign car whose philosophy is 'be nice to me and I'll be nice to you'. Because Dean Jones, a second-rate racing driver, objects to David Tomlinson, a wealthy, but stuffy, racer, kicking it, the little car – a Volkswagen – adopts Jones and wins a flock of races for him.

For sheer inventiveness of situation and the charm that such an idea projects, *The Love Bug* rates as one of the better entries of the Disney organization.

Treatment is light and imaginative, and Herbie gradually takes on all the attributes of a human. Herbie is all heart, while having a will of iron, muscles of steel, the strength of 10 and a stubborn streak.

Direction by Robert Stevenson, who also helmed the classic *Mary Poppins*, is fast and fanciful, warmly attuned to the demands of the premise and getting the most from his cast.

Jones delivers well as the driver who thinks it's his driving which wins him all those races.

■ LOVE CHILD

1982, 97 MINS, US ◇ ▼
Dir Larry Peerce   *Prod* Paul Maslansky   *Scr* Anne Gerard, Katherine Specktor   *Ph* James Pergola   *Ed* Bob Wyman   *Mus* Charles Fox   *Art Dir* Don Ivey
● Amy Madigan, Beau Bridges, Mackenzie Phillips, Albert Salmi, Joanna Merlin, Margaret Whitton (Ladd/Warner)

Love Child, subtitled 'a true story' is a tasteful and sincere filmization of young Ohioan Terry Jean Moore's battle to have and keep her baby (fathered by a guard) while serving a 20-year robbery term in Broward Correctional Institution in Florida.

In a strong screen debut, freckled Amy Madigan toplines as Moore, who while hitchhiking with her wild cousin Jesse (Lewis Smith), takes the rap when Jesse robs their driver of $5 while trying to steal the car.

Possessing a wild temper and perennial chip on her shoulder, Moore looks headed for doom in stir. Befriended by a personable, guard, Jack Hansen (Beau Bridges) and a sympathetic young lesbian, J.J. (Mackenzie Phillips), she adjusts and even seems en route to legal freedom.

Targeting the picture squarely at a femme audience, script [from a story by Anne Gerard] emphasizes Moore's self-reform as catalyzed by her awareness of the baby growing inside her and the new responsibility it represents. Madigan is excellent in the physically demanding central role.

■ LOVE HAS MANY FACES

1965, 104 MINS, US ◇
Dir Alexander Singer   *Prod* Jerry Bresler   *Scr* Marguerite Roberts   *Ph* Joseph Ruttenberg   *Ed* Alma Macrorie   *Mus* David Raksin   *Art Dir* Alfred Sweeney
● Lana Turner, Cliff Robertson, Hugh O'Brian, Ruth Roman, Stefanie Powers, Virginia Grey (Columbia)

High life among American beach bums in Acapulco is lavishly dramatized in this Jerry Bresler production starring Lana Turner, Cliff Robertson and Hugh O'Brian.

Turner portrays a millionairess surrounded by moochers – including her husband, Robertson – and desperately striving for unfound happiness in her own particular brandy-swilling world. Narrative concerns the love affairs – the many faces of love – at the glamorous resort.

Alexander Singer's direction gets the utmost in values from his story and cast, although none of latter is particularly sympathetic. O'Brian is an expert in the art of sharing his company for money and as a sideline indulges in friendly blackmail, in this case Ruth Roman, a wealthy divorcee.

Turner lends conviction in a demanding part and Robertson is forceful as her husband who married her for her money but finds his life distasteful. O'Brian turns in a good job as a beach parasite who sells his wares to avid young touristas.

■ LOVE IN THE AFTERNOON

1957, 126 MINS, US ▼
Dir Billy Wilder   *Prod* Billy Wilder   *Scr* Billy Wilder, I.A.L. Diamond   *Ph* William Mellor   *Ed* Leonid Azar   *Mus* Franz Waxman (adapt.)   *Art Dir* Alexandre Trauner
● Gary Cooper, Audrey Hepburn, Maurice Chevalier, John McGiver, Van Doude, Lise Bourdin (Allied Artists)

Title-wise, *Love in the Afternoon* is fitting, being far more communicative of the film's content than the original [Claude Anet novel] *Ariane*. It is all about romance before nightfall, in Paris, with Audrey Hepburn and Gary Cooper as the participants. Under Billy Wilder's alternately sensitive, mirthful and loving-care direction, and with Maurice Chevalier turning in a captivating performance as a private detective specializing in cases of amour, the production holds enchantment and delight in substantial quantity.

Love in the Afternoon, though, is long and the casting of Cooper as the eager beaver Romeo is curious. Consider this wealthy American businessman (Cooper) constantly as the woo merchant in his lavish Parisian hotel suite, first with Madame X and then Ariane (Hepburn). Several scenes spill out before Cooper comes on camera, and then on it's love in the afternoon.

It's in Chevalier's files that his daughter, the lovely, wistful Hepburn, as a cello student, comes upon knowledge of Cooper's international conquests, runs to him with the warning that his current passion (Madame X) has a husband (Mr X) bent on murder, and finds herself soon to become a candidate for one of her own father's file cards.

Mr X is John McGiver, suitably frenzied as the husband suspecting his mate has taken to play with another. It's a floating-in-air kind of story. And being innocent of earthiness there is no offensiveness in the content.

■ LOVE IS A MANY-SPLENDORED THING

1955, 102 MINS, US ◇ ▼
Dir Henry King   *Prod* Buddy Adler   *Scr* John Patrick   *Ph* Leon Shamroy   *Ed* William Reynolds   *Mus* Alfred Newman   *Art Dir* Lyle R. Wheeler, George W. Davis
● William Holden, Jennifer Jones, Torin Thatcher, Isobel Elsom, Virginia Gregg, Candace Lee (20th Century-Fox)

Love, as portrayed and dramatized in this fine and sensitive production based on the Han Suyin bestseller, is indeed a many-splendored thing. It's an unusual picture in many ways, shot against authentic Hong Kong backgrounds and offbeat in its treatment, yet a simple and moving love story.

William Holden as the American correspondent, and Jennifer Jones as the Eurasian doctor, make a romantic team of great appeal.

But it must also be said that, up to the middle of the film, things go rather slowly. Director Henry King makes this into a love story that allows little else to intrude. Both he and writer John Patrick apparently thought a romantic theme should be enough.

King and lenser Leon Shamroy do a magnificent job in utilizing the Hong Kong backgrounds.
□ 1955: Best Picture (Nomination)

....

■ LOVE LETTERS

1983, 98 MINS, US ◇ ⓥ

Dir Amy Jones *Prod* Roger Corman *Scr* Amy Jones *Ph* Alec Hirschfeld *Ed* Wendy Greene *Mus* Ralph Jones *Art Dir* Jeannine Oppewall
● Jamie Lee Curtis, James Keach, Amy Madigan, Bud Cort, Matt Clark, Bonnie Bartlett (New World)

Love Letters is a fine intimate drama from writer-director (and former editor) Amy Jones. Although overly schematic and lacking a certain humor that might have been welcome, film is much closer to the tradition of personal European filmmaking.

Although in no way intended to seem typical, Jamie Lee Curtis is seen living a life that is certainly shared by many young contempo women.

Suddenly, barely past ago 40, Curtis' mother dies, and the daughter discovers a collection of old letters which reveal the secret love of her mother's life, a love which can stand as a pure ideal to Curtis.

While pouring over the missives, Curtis meets prosperous photographer James Keach, a 40-ish married man with two kids.

Also believable are the intense and sweaty sex scenes, into which Curtis throws herself with increasing abandon, and the exchanges with her best friend (Amy Madigan) who delivers conventional put-downs of modern men by way of rationalizing a vow of celibacy.

....

■ LOVE ME TENDER

1956, 94 MINS, US ⓥ

Dir Robert D. Webb *Prod* David Weisbart *Scr* Robert Buckner *Ph* Leo Tover *Mus* Lionel Newman *Art Dir* Lyle R. Wheeler, Maurice Ransford
● Richard Egan, Debra Paget, Elvis Presley, Robert Middleton, William Campbell, Neville Brand (20th Century-Fox)

Appraising Presley as an actor, he ain't. Not that it makes much difference. There are four songs, and lotsa Presley wriggles thrown in for good measure.

Screenplay from a story by Maurice Geraghty is synthetic. Story line centers on Presley, the youngest of four brothers, who stayed on their Texas farm while the older three are away fighting the Yankees. The older brother (Richard Egan) left a gal (Debra Paget) and, when word comes that he's been killed in battle, she weds Presley. When the three boys come home to resume their civvy ways, it's hard to keep Egan down on the farm because he's still in love with Paget, now his brother's wife.

Egan is properly stoic as the older brother while Paget does nothing more than look pretty and wistful throughout. Mildred Dunnock gets sincerity into the part of mother of the brood, an achievement. Nobody, however, seems to be having as much fun as Presley especially when he's singing the title song, 'Poor Boy', 'We're Gonna Move' and 'Let Me'. Tunes were written by Presley and Vera Matson.

....

■ LOVE PARADE, THE

1929, 107 MINS, US

Dir Ernst Lubitsch *Scr* Guy Bolton, Ernst Vajda *Ph* Victor Milner *Mus* Victor Schertzinger *Art Dir* Hans Dreier
● Maurice Chevalier, Jeanette MacDonald, Lupino Lane, Lillian Roth, Eugene Pallette, Edgar Norton (Paramount)

In *The Love Parade*, second starring talker for Maurice Chevalier, Paramount has its first original screen operetta production whose story is more than made up in magnificence of sets and costumes, tuneful music, subtlety of direction, comedy and general appeal. It's a fine, near-grand entertainment.

At the outset the Chevalier personality is put to the fore in the manner the Parisian music-hall star knows best.

In Jeanette MacDonald, ingenue prima donna from Broadway, Chevalier has an actress opposite who all but steals the picture.

The story says that the philandering Parisian, brought back to Sylvania, ruled by MacDonald, because of his scandalous affairs as a military attache in France's capital, must, in accepting marriage to the queen, keep his fingers out of all matters of state and be subject to her own commands.

The wedding is an extravaganza, with one of the largest sets ever built, but musically lacks the punch of other scenes.

Guy Bolton wrote the libretto for *Love Parade* [from the play *The Prince Consort* by Leon Xanrof and Jules Chancel].

It can be said that this is the first true screen musical.
□ 1929/30: Best Picture (Nomination)

....

■ LOVE STORY

1970, 99 MINS, US ◇ ⓥ

Dir Arthur Hiller *Prod* Howard G. Minsky, David Golden *Scr* Erich Segal *Ph* Dick Kratina *Ed* Robert C. Jones *Mus* Francis Lai *Art Dir* Robert Gundlach
● Ali MacGraw, Ryan O'Neal, John Marley, Ray Milland, Russell Nype, Katherine Balfour (Paramount)

Love Story is an excellent film. Made for about $2.2 million the Paramount release is generally successful on all artistic levels, propelled by the best-selling Erich Segal novel written from the original screenplay.

Ali MacGraw is a girl of poor origins who has worked her way to high academic status; Ryan O'Neal, restive in his identity, but at the outset just another rich man's athletic-oriented son at the old family college, develops true manliness from his love for her, through their marriage and the severe challenge of her terminal illness.

John Marley is excellent as MacGraw's father and Ray Milland is outstanding as O'Neal's cold father. Both men go way beyond the superficial trappings of their roles and make the characters vital.

It's O'Neal's picture by a good margin.
□ 1970: Best Picture (Nomination)

....

■ LOVE STREAMS

1984, 136 MINS, US ◇ ⓥ

Dir John Cassavetes *Prod* Menahem Golan, Yoram Globus *Scr* John Cassavetes, Ted Allan *Ph* Al Ruban *Ed* George Villasenor *Mus* Bo Harwood
● Gena Rowlands, John Cassavetes, Diahnne Abbott, Seymour Cassel, Margaret Abbott, Jakob Shaw (Cannon)

John Cassavetes' *Love Streams* shapes up as one of the filmmaker's best, both artistically and commercially, in some time, emotionally potent, technically assured and often brilliantly insightful.

Reflecting the title, the plot begins with two separate flows. Robert Harmon (Cassavetes) is a successful writer from the Gay Talese school currently researching the subject of love for sale on a first-hand basis. Inter-cut is Sarah Lawson's (Gena Rowlands) story – an emotionally erratic woman proceeding through a divorce and custody case.

One can nit-pick about the picture's length and use of repetition but these are minor points in the overall strength of the production. The dramatic rollercoaster ride of frightening and funny moments leave little room for indifference.

....

■ LOVE WALTZ, THE

1930, 70 MINS, GERMANY

Dir Wilhelm Thiele *Prod* Erich Pommer *Scr* Hans Muller, Robert Liebmann *Ph* Werner Brandes, Konstantin Tschet *Mus* Werner Heymann
● Lilian Harvey, John Batten, Georg Alexander (UFA)

The all-English dialog version of this UFA talker is a presentable piece of work, even allowing for blemishes. Film errs somewhat in starting off as snappy comedy and ending up as the usual Ruritanian romance, being much more entertaining first half than in the final reels. Production is a mixture of imitation American slickness and Germanic artistry, with the result much of the footage is very easy to the eye.

Story is the usual sugary mixture expected of the species, telling how a bored youngster rivets himself on an equally bored archduke, who is due to get engaged to an even more bored princess.

Usual Erich Pommer touches noticeable.

Lilian Harvey isn't photographed to the best advantage and John Batten hasn't much difficulty in getting honors among the leads, although Georg Alexander's work as the duke is a smooth job, nicely rounded off.

The English version was done under the supervision of Carl Winston, who went to Berlin. Harvey, being of English extraction, plays her role in both versions, and young Englishman Batten handles the Willi Fritsch character.

....

■ LOVE WITH THE PROPER STRANGER

1963, 102 MINS, US ⓥ

Dir Robert Mulligan *Prod* Alan J. Pakula *Scr* Arnold Schulman *Ph* Milton Krasner *Ed* Aaron Stell *Mus* Elmer Bernstein *Art Dir* Hal Pereira, Roland Anderson
● Natalie Wood, Steve McQueen, Edie Adams, Herschel Bernardi, Tom Bosley (Paramount)·

Proper Stranger is a somewhat unstable picture, fluctuating between scenes of a substantial, lifelike disposition and others where reality is suspended in favor of deliberately exaggerated hokum. Fortunately the film survives these shortcomings through its sheer breezy good nature and the animal magnetism of its two stars.

Arnold Schulman's scenario describes the curious love affair that evolves between two young New York Italians – a freedom-loving freelance musician (Steve McQueen) and a sheltered girl (Natalie Wood) – when she becomes pregnant following their one-night stand at a summer resort.

Wood plays her role with a convincing mixture of feminine sweetness and emotional turbulence. McQueen displays an especially keen sense of timing. Although he's probably the most unlikely Italian around (the character could and should obviously have been altered to Irish Catholic), he is an appealing figure nevertheless.

Fine supporting work is contributed by Edie Adams as an accommodating stripper, Herschel Bernardi asWood's overly protective older brother and Tom Bosley as a jittery suitor.

Robert Mulligan's direction runs hot and cold, like the screenplay and the film itself.

....

■ LOVED ONE, THE

1965, 119 MINS, US

Dir Tony Richardson *Prod* Martin Ransohoff, John Calley, Haskell Wexler *Scr* Christopher Isherwood, Terry Southern *Ph* Haskell Wexler *Ed* Antony Gibbs, Hal Ashby, Brian Smedley-Aston *Mus* John Addison *Art Dir* Rouben Ter-Arutunian
● Robert Morse, Anjanette Comer, Jonathan Winters, Rod Steiger, James Coburn, John Gielgud (M-G-M)

Poor taste is prominent in the Terry Southern-Christopher Isherwood script, based on Evelyn Waugh's scathing 1948 satire of the mortuary business in California.

Most of the subtlety of Waugh's approach is lost in an episodic screenplay bearing only a wavering story line and given often to sight gags.

Story centers around the pomp and ceremony attendant upon the daily operation of a posh mortuary and a climaxing idea (not in the book) by a sanctimonious owner of a Southern California cemetery of orbiting cadavers into space so he can convert to a senior citizens' paradise for additional profit.

Robert Morse as the poet who falls in love with the lady cosmetician (later promoted to embalmer) while making arrangements for his uncle's interment, plays it light and airy, like a soul apart. Anjanette Comer, whose life is dedicated to her work and Whispering Glades Memorial Park gives almost ethereal portraiture to her embalmer character.

Jonathan Winters appears in a dual role, shining both as the owner of Whispering Glades and his twin brother, who operates the nearby pet graveyard and is patron of a 13-year-old scientific whiz who invents a rocket capable of projecting bodies into orbit.

．．．．．．．．．．．．．．．．．．．．．．．．．．．．．

■ LOVELY WAY TO DIE, A

1968, 103 MINS, US ◇

Dir David Lowell Rich *Prod* Richard Lewis *Scr* A.J. Russell *Ph* Moe Hartzband *Ed* Sidney Katz *Mus* Kenyon Hopkins *Art Dir* Willard Levitas
● Kirk Douglas, Sylva Koscina, Eli Wallach, Kenneth Haigh, Gordon Peters, Martyn Green (Universal)

This is the kind of hard-hitting polished murder-mystery meller that Kirk Douglas can play in his sleep. Cast with the cool, aloof Sylva Koscina and Eli Wallach, the screenplay is crisp and tangy, though the plotline wavers at a few spots.

Douglas is a cop whose belief is that hands are made for shooting, punching, holding drinks and caressing dames. As a protest at the mollycoddling of hoods by the police he turns in his badge, to be hired by Wallach, a shrewd homespun attorney, to protect Koscina, being defended by Wallach on a rap of murdering her husband.

As a male bodyguard Douglas is intrigued by the girl. As an ex-cop he's intrigued by the murder mystery.

Douglas plays the confident, flip, resourceful he-man with a suave winning way with the femmes, in his customary easy-going fashion and Koscina's hot-and-cold attitude to his boudoir advances are both amusing and helpful to the atmosphere of the mystery yarn.

．．．．．．．．．．．．．．．．．．．．．．．．．．．．．

■ LOVER COME BACK

1961, 107 MINS, US ◇ Ⓥ

Dir Delbert Mann *Prod* Stanley Shapiro, Martin Melcher *Scr* Stanley Shapiro, Paul Henning *Ph* Arthur E. Arling *Ed* Marjorie Fowler *Mus* Frank DeVol *Art Dir* Alexander Golitzen, Robert Clatworthy
● Rock Hudson, Doris Day, Tony Randall, Edie Adams, Jack Oakie, Jack Kruschen
(Universal)

This is a funny, most-of-the-time engaging, smartly produced show. Farce has Rock Hudson as would-be conqueror of Doris Day, who as the victim of a who's-who deception plays brinkmanship with surrender. There's a bed scene but this is all right because the two, while not remembering the Maryland ceremony (due to being stoned under preposterous circumstances), were legally hitched.

Hudson and Day are rival Madison Avenue ad account people. He deceives her into thinking he's a scientist working on an actually non-existent product called VIP. She

undertakes to wrest the VIP account from the masquerading Hudson. He meanwhile is trying to maneuver her into romantic conquest.

Tony Randall draws yocks consistently as head of an agency he inherited but doesn't really helm because he can't make decisions. Jack Oakie plays broadly and humorously the part of a floor-wax maker who goes to the agency offering him the best girls and bourbon. Edie Adams clicks as a chorus girl trying to get ahead, and Jack Kruschen, as a partly screwball scientist, also wins laughs.

．．．．．．．．．．．．．．．．．．．．．．．．．．．．．

■ LOVERS AND OTHER STRANGERS

1970, 104 MINS, US ◇ Ⓥ

Dir Cy Howard *Prod* David Susskind *Scr* Renee Taylor, Joseph Bologna, David Zelag *Ph* Andy Laszlo *Ed* David Bretherton, Sidney Katz *Mus* Fred Karlin *Art Dir* Ben Edwards
● Bea Arthur, Bonnie Bedelia, Michael Brandon, Richard Castellano, Robert Dishy, Harry Guardino (ABC)

Lovers And Other Strangers tells in a delightful way of the marriage of a young couple who have been making it on the sly for over a year. Comedy vignettes reveal in amusing and compassionate fashion the assorted marital foibles of members of both families.

Bonnie Bedelia and Michael Brandon, the couple in question, have their own life style which rubs against but does not destroy relations with their respective parents. Gig Young and Cloris Leachman are her folks, while Richard Castellano and Bea Arthur are his.

Screenplay [from the play by Joseph Bologna and Renee Taylor] is essentially a string of intercut vignettes about the young couple's relatives. On the girl's side of things, Young has been having a side affair with Anne Jackson for some years; she is perfect.

．．．．．．．．．．．．．．．．．．．．．．．．．．．．．

■ LOVES OF JOANNA GODDEN, THE

1947, 91 MINS, UK

Dir Charles Frend *Prod* Michael Balcon *Scr* H.E. Bates, Angus MacPhail *Ph* Douglas Slocombe *Ed* Michael Truman *Mus* Ralph Vaughan Williams *Art Dir* Duncan Sutherland
● Googie Withers, Jean Kent, John McCallum, Derek Bond, Chips Rafferty (Ealing)

As a record of sheep farming in a corner of England in 1905, this picture [based on the novel by Sheila Kaye-Smith] may have its points. But as a story of a high-spirited, lovely young woman who inherits a farm and is expected to marry and let her husband do the job, the picture falls short of its intentions. So enamored did producer and director become with their location, that they were determined to teach audiences all they had learned about sheep breeding.

Set against the background of the Romney Marshes in Kent, Joanna (Googie Withers), impetuous and self-willed, is bequeathed one of the leading farms on the Marsh. A codicil in her father's will expresses the hope that she will marry neighbor-farmer Arthur Alce (John McCallum). Determined to defy the conventions of the time, she outrages the countryside by running the farm herself and by her experiments in cross-breeding and ploughing. Stinting herself and luxury, she sends her young sister, Ellen (Jean Kent), to a finishing school, from which the girl returns an accomplished golddigger.

Joanna has a mild affair with Collard (Chips Rafferty), the man engaged to look after her sheep, before she falls for a local aristocrat, Martin Trevor (Derek Bond). The banns are put up, but Martin is drowned. Meanwhile Ellen has bewitched Arthur Alce, Joanna's 'old faithful,' marries him, and deserts him for an old man with money.

Withers looks as attractive as she has ever done, but her characterization of the name part has a soporific monotony.

The men fare somewhat better, although McCallum is given little to lighten his dourness. Bond gives a natural and pleasant performance as Martin, and Rafferty disappears far too early.

．．．．．．．．．．．．．．．．．．．．．．．．．．．．．

■ LOVESICK

1983, 95 MINS, US ◇ Ⓥ

Dir Marshall Brickman *Prod* Charles Okun *Scr* Marshall Brickman *Ph* Gerry Fisher *Ed* Nina Feinberg *Mus* Philippe Sarde *Art Dir* Philip Rosenberg
● Dudley Moore, Elizabeth McGovern, Alec Guinness, John Huston, William Shawn, Alan King (Ladd/Warner)

An engaging idea – Dudley Moore as a successful, married shrink who becomes obsessed with a beautiful patient (Elizabeth McGovern) – is rendered inoperable by Marshall Brickman's witless script and uninspired direction.

Perhaps most descriptive of the script's desperation is the gimmicky inclusion of Sigmund Freud, who mystically materializes in the person of Alec Guinness whenever Moore seeks professional help. Guinness properly plays it straight and slightly aloof, telling Moore that his obsession with McGovern 'reminds us what we really are – animals – take it or leave it.' Pure Freud.

Ron Silver is fine as an arrogant actor but Gene Sacks as a suicidal patient, John Huston and Alan King as stuffy doctors, and Renee Taylor, as a patient, are all embarrassing.

．．．．．．．．．．．．．．．．．．．．．．．．．．．．．

■ LOVIN' MOLLY

1974, 98 MINS, US ◇

Dir Sidney Lumet *Prod* Stephen Friedman *Scr* Stephen Friedman *Ph* Edward Brown *Ed* Joanne Burke *Mus* Fred Hellerman *Art Dir* Gene Coffin
● Anthony Perkins, Beau Bridges, Blythe Danner, Edward Binns, Susan Sarandon, Conrad Fowkes (Columbia)

The film version of Larry McMurtry's novel, *Leaving Cheyenne* emerges as a misguided, heavy-handed attempt to span 40 years in the lives of three Texas rustics and their bizarre but homey menage a trois.

Divided into three main sections, *Lovin' Molly* opens in 1925 and sets up the situation in which two farmboy friends (Anthony Perkins, Beau Bridges) wage amicable war for the affections of a liberated earth mother (Blythe Danner) who loves them both in her fashion. Jumping to 1945 with a voiceover bridge, Danner has been married and widowed to a third young man (Conrad Fowkes) while continuing her sidebar relationships and bearing two children by a married Perkins and still-bachelor Bridges.

Pic's final section takes place in 1964 as the three find their time running out. Perkins dies of a heart attack and the ever-ready Bridges beds down with the accommodating Danner for what must be the 4,160th time.

．．．．．．．．．．．．．．．．．．．．．．．．．．．．．

■ LOVING

1970, 89 MINS, US ◇ Ⓥ

Dir Irvin Kershner *Prod* Don Devlin, Raymond Wagner *Scr* Don Devlin *Ph* Gordon Willis *Ed* Robert Lawrence *Mus* Bernardo Segall *Art Dir* Walter Scott Herndon
● George Segal, Eva Marie Saint, Sterling Hayden, Keenan Wynn, Nancie Phillips, Janis Young (Columbia)

A good story about marriage crackups among the fortyish set in suburbia.

A novel by J. M. Ryan was basis for the script, which is handicapped by a protagonist who, while not supposed to be sympathetic, isn't even interesting in his selfishness and immaturity.

George Segal is the character, an aging commercial artist who would seem in reality to have been long-since crushed by the forces against which he continually rails. Eva Marie Saint is quite outstanding as the slightly-nagging but steadfast wife. Her character is also hampered by some incredulity of premise, but she more than overcomes the liability.

Within script limitations, cast delivers well, Saint in the extreme, Segal however never quite believable.

■ **LOVING COUPLES**

1980, 97 MINS, US ◇ ⓥ
Dir Jack Smight *Prod* Renee Valente *Scr* Martin Donovan *Ph* Philip Lathrop *Ed* Grey Fox, Frank Urioste *Mus* Fred Karlin *Art Dir* Jan Scott
● Shirley MacLaine, James Coburn, Susan Sarandon, Sally Kellerman, Stephen Collins (20th Century-Fox)

Loving Couples opens with a snappy cute meet. Shirley MacLaine is riding a horse and Stephen Collins, driving along in a sports car, stares at her, misses a turn in the road and crashes. She rides over to the prone Collins and rips open his pants. Well, she's a doctor.

Young stud Collins tries to put the make on her. Not too long after he gets it. She's not getting much attention from her work-obsessed doctor husband (James Coburn) who learns of her affair from Collins' live-in friend (Susan Sarandon). And they, in turn, fall into a motel bed.

It's all fun and sexual games. Direction by Jack Smight is assured and never lags. MacLaine is in top form, sassy and sweet in turn. Coburn delivers a casually effective light comedy performance. Sarandon is topnotch.

■ **LOVING YOU**

1957, 101 MINS, US ◇ ⓥ
Dir Hal Kanter *Prod* Hal B. Wallis *Scr* Herbert Baker, Hal Kanter *Ph* Charles Lang *Ed* Howard Smith *Mus* Walter Scharff (arr.) *Art Dir* Hal Pereira, Albert Nozaki
● Elvis Presley, Lizabeth Scott, Wendell Corey, Dolores Hart, James Gleason (Paramount)

Elvis Presley's second screen appearance is a simple story, in which he can be believed, which has romantic overtones and exposes the singer to the kind of thing he does best, i.e. shout out his rhythms, bang away at his guitar and perform the strange, knee-bending, hip-swinging contortions that are his trademark.

Apart from this, Presley shows improvement as an actor. It's not a demanding part and, being surrounded by a capable crew of performers, he comes across as a simple but pleasant sort. Film introes Dolores Hart, in an undemanding role as Presley's girl.

Story has Presley picked up by Lizabeth Scott, a publicity girl touring with a hillbilly band on a whistlestop tour. She gets Wendell Corey, the leader of the outfit, to take on Presley, and they stunt him into a rock 'n' roll personality. Of course, there are complications and Presley takes himself off just as he's supposed to go on a national TV show.

■ **L-SHAPED ROOM, THE**

1962, 142 MINS, UK ⓥ
Dir Bryan Forbes *Prod* James Woolf, Richard Attenborough *Scr* Bryan Forbes *Ph* Douglas Slocombe *Ed* Anthony Harvey *Mus* John Barry *Art Dir* Ray Simm
● Leslie Caron, Tom Bell, Brock Peters, Cicely Courtneidge, Avis Bunnage, Bernard Lee (Romulus)

Lynne Reid Banks' bestseller novel seemed, on the surface, to be unlikely material for a film. Largely set in the restricted area of a faded lodging house the novel had little enough glamour or strength of plot to recommended it, excellently written though it was. But Bryan Forbes' screenplay and his tactful, sensitive direction create a tender study in loneliness and frustrated love.

Yarn concerns a girl (Leslie Caron) with a background of provincial France who, in London, has a brief affair resulting in pregnancy. Rejecting the idea of an abortion she decides to live it out on her own. And, in the loneliness of her L-shaped room in a seedy tenement, she finds a new hope and purpose in life through meeting others who, in various ways, suffer their own loneliness and frustration.

This brief outline gives no credit to the film's many subtle undertones. Not a great deal happens but it is a thoroughly holding and intelligent film having the quality of a film like *Marty*.

Caron and Tom Bell make a strong team. Though they, plus Brock Peters, as Negro lad, bear the brunt of such action as there is, the trio are well supported by a number of others.

Vet Cicely Courtneidge make a sharp comeback as a retired vaude artist, living with her cat and her faded press clippings. Other notable jobs are done by Avis Bunnage (a landlady who prides herself on the respectability of her house, despite two of her lodgers being prosties) and Bernard Lee, as her boozey, hearty gentleman friend.

■ **LUCK OF GINGER COFFEY, THE**

1964, 100 MINS, US/CANADA
Dir Irvin Kershner *Prod* Leon Roth *Scr* Brian Moore *Ph* Manny Wynn *Ed* Anthony Gibbs *Mus* Bernardo Segall *Art Dir* Harry Horner
● Robert Shaw, Mary Ure, Liam Redmond, Tom Harvey, Libby McClintock, Leo Leyden (Roth)

The Luck of Ginger Coffey is a well-turned-out drama based on a Brian Moore novel.

Robert Shaw and Mary Ure are a married couple who have found the going in Montreal rough since they arrived from Dublin six months before to make their new home in Canada. The husband, who cannot keep a job, has spent the passage money on which the wife was depending to return them to Ireland should they not make the grade. A marital crisis therefore arises, since the wife believes that with her husband's superior attitude he will always be unable to hold a job in Canada.

Shaw plays his brash Irishman with sincerity and Ure lends credence to the wife, both scoring strongly.

■ **LUCKY JIM**

1957, 95 MINS, UK ⓥ
Dir John Boulting *Prod* Roy Boulting *Scr* Patrick Campbell, Jeffrey Dell *Ph* Max Greene *Ed* Max Benedict *Mus* John Addison *Art Dir* Elliott Scott
● Ian Carmichael, Terry-Thomas, Hugh Griffith, Sharon Acker, Clive Morton, Kenneth Griffith (Charter/British Lion)

Kingsley Amis's novel has been built up into a farcical comedy which, though slim enough in idea, provides plenty of opportunity for smiles, giggles and belly laughs. John Boulting directs with a lively tempo and even though the comedy situations loom up with inevitable precision, they are still irresistible.

The lightweight story spotlights Ian Carmichael as a junior history lecturer at a British university in the sticks who becomes disastrously involved in such serious college goings-on as a ceremonial lecture on 'Merrie England' and a procession to honor the new university chancellor. There are also some minor shenanigans such as a riotous car chase, a slaphappy fist fight, a tipsy entry into a wrong bedroom containing a girl he is trying to shake off and a number of other happy-go-lucky situations.

The screenplay veers from facetiousness to downright slapstick but never lets up on its irresistible attack on the funnybone. Carmichael is a deft light-comedy performer who proves that he also can take hold of a character and make him believable.

■ **LUCKY LADY**

1975, 177 MINS, US ◇
Dir Stanley Donen *Prod* Michael Gruskoff *Scr* Willard Huyck, Gloria Katz *Ph* Geoffrey Unsworth *Ed* Peter Boita, George Hively, Tom Rolf *Mus* Ralph Burns *Art Dir* John Barry
● Gene Hackman, Liza Minnelli, Burt Reynolds, Geoffrey Lewis, John Hillerman, Bobby Benson (20th Century-Fox)

What appears to have been conceived as a madcap Prohibition-era action comedy, combined with an amusing romantic menage, emerges as forced hokum.

Successive vignettes take the stars through a series of expansive smuggling routines. Burt Reynolds, a gringo on the lam in Mexico, figures he can assume the dual role of major smuggler and lover of Liza Minnelli when her husband dies. Gene Hackman, also on the run, assumes a leadership role and the trio begin running hooch.

They encounter the likes of Michael Hordern, an urbane ship captain; John Hillerman, a feisty hood and Geoffrey Lewis, trigger-happy Coast Guard.

Some smart-looking production work survives the plot (admitted budget was $12.6 million).

■ **LUCKY LUCIANO**

1973, 113 MINS, ITALY/FRANCE ◇ ⓥ
Dir Francesco Rosi *Prod* Franco Cristaldi *Scr* Francesco Rosi, Lino Jannuzzi, Tonino Guerra *Ph* Pasqualino De Santis *Ed* Ruggero Mastroianni *Mus* Piero Piccioni *Art Dir* Andrea Crisanti
● Gian Maria Volonte, Rod Steiger, Charles Siragusa, Edmond O'Brien, Vincent Gardenia (Vides/La Boetie)

Most films by Francesco Rosi probe well under the surface of people and events to establish a constant link between the legal and illegal exercise of power. In *Lucky Luciano* the search is expanded to embrace an interdependent crime empire operating in America and Italy, with roots in many other points on the map. But Rosi takes crime kingpin Lucky Luciano as his main clinical study, objective enough throughout to question his own facts, legendary accusations and hearsay.

Crime action is condensed in first few reels in sharply-paced scenes and montage escalating Luciano to the Mafia throne, his arrest and conviction in the mid-1930s, with his deportation to Italy after serving nine years of a 30-50-year prison term.

■ **LUDWIG**

1973, 186 MINS, ITALY/FRANCE/W. GERMANY ◇
Dir Luchino Visconti *Prod* Ugo Santalucia *Scr* Luchino Visconti, Enrico Medioli, Suso Cecchi D'Amico *Ph* Armando Nannuzzi *Ed* Ruggero Mastroianni *Mus* Franco Mannino (sup.) *Art Dir* Mario Chiari, Mario Scisci
● Helmut Berger, Romy Schneider, Trevor Howard, Silvana Mangano, Gert Frobe, Helmut Griem (Mega/Cinetel/Divina)

As his 12th feature film, and third project based on German history and personages, Luchino Visconti chose King Ludwig II (Helmut Berger), the so-called 'mad' monarch of Bavaria. *Ludwig* bears the Visconti stamp of dazzling, tasteful opulence and an operatic style. However, story construction is at first confusing.

To its credit the English version [translated by William Weaver] is literate, free of arch transliteration, and dotted with occasional brilliant aphorism. But it barely helps the limitations of the overall structure.

Major phases of Ludwig's life include his patronage of composer Richard Wagner, portrayed effectively by Trevor Howard; the spendthrift erection of castles; the introverted indifference to his responsibilities as king; a long platonic love affair with Empress Elisabeth of Austria, played with great compassion by the spectacularly beautiful Romy Schneider; and a pervading atmosphere of latent, then overt homosexuality.

The score utilizes themes of Wagner, Schumann and Offenbach, with piano solos and orchestra conducting by Franco Mannino. Wagner's last original piano composition is performed publicly for first time herein.

■ LULLABY OF BROADWAY

1951, 91 MINS, US ◇

Dir David Butler   *Prod* William Jacobs   *Scr* Earl Baldwin   *Ph* Wilfrid M. Cline   *Ed* Irene Morra   *Mus* Ray Heindorf (dir.)   *Art Dir* Douglas Bacon
● Doris Day, Gene Nelson, S.Z. Sakall, Billy De Wolfe, Gladys George, Florence Bates (Warner)

Mounted in gorgeous Technicolor, and displaying the song-and-dance talents of co-stars Doris Day and Gene Nelson, *Lullaby of Broadway* has a solid comedy story line, deft direction and a capable cast.

Film gets away from the regular practice of injecting too many elaborate production numbers. Most of the tunes are hits of the previous two decades. Day scores with her solo song-and-dance routines, including 'Just One of Those Things' and 'You're Getting to Be a Habit with Me'. She teams with Nelson for tune-and-terping of 'Somebody Loves Me', 'I Love the Way You Say Goodnight' and 'Lullaby of Broadway'.

Story has Day returning from several years in England to meet her mother (Gladys George) former stage headliner who hit the skids due to drink. Girl arrives at supposed mansion of her mother, and is taken in tow by Billy De Wolfe and Anne Triola, two at-liberty vaudevillians working as butler and maid. Sakall, elderly owner of the house, takes an interest in the girl and gets involved in ensuing complications when his wife suspects an affair.

■ LUNA, LA

1979, 145 MINS, ITALY ◇

Dir Bernardo Bertolucci   *Prod* Giovanni Bertolucci   *Scr* Giuseppe Bertolucci, Bernardo Bertolucci, Clare Peploe   *Ph* Vittorio Storaro   *Ed* Gabriella Cristiani   *Art Dir* Gianni Silvestri, Maria Paula Maiano
● Jill Clayburgh, Matthew Barry, Renato Salvatori, Tomas Milian, Fred Gwynne, Veronica Lazar (20th Century-Fox/Fiction)

La Luna is a spectacle-sized melodrama filled with a variety of themes – plots and subplots that merge asymmetrically into a melodramatic mold.

The saga is of Jill Clayburgh as Yank lyric star afflicted with professional neuroses, fading pipes, a son on drugs and a close-to-incest mother-son development.

Sudden death of singer's spouse and decision to resume singing in Italy with son Joe accompanying, moves the scene from Brooklyn Heights to Rome where the mother-son cleft takes over from Verdi appearances. Her battle to break down his detachment and drug habit is the core of the film – with her own career at stake as the voice gives under stress.

Clayburgh is hard pressed to sustain the melodramatics of *Luna*.

■ LUST FOR LIFE

1956, 122 MINS, US ◇ ▼

Dir Vincente Minnelli   *Prod* John Houseman   *Scr* Norman Corwin   *Ph* F.A. Young, Russell Harlan   *Ed* Adrienne Fazan   *Mus* Miklos Rozsa   *Art Dir* Cedric Gibbons, Hans Peters, Preston Ames
● Kirk Douglas, Anthony Quinn, James Donald, Pamela Brown, Everett Sloane, Niall MacGinnis (M-G-M)

This is a slow-moving picture whose only action is in the dialog itself. Basically a faithful portrait of Van Gogh, *Lust for Life* is nonetheless unexciting. It misses out in conveying the color and entertainment of the original Irving Stone novel. It's a tragic recap that Stone penned, but still there was no absence of amusing incidents.

Lensed in Holland and France, *Lust for Life* is largely conversation plus expert tint photography, and both on a high level.

Kirk Douglas plays the title role with undeniable understanding of the artist. He's a competent performer all the way, conveying the frustrations which beset Van Gogh in his quest for knowledge of life and the approach to putting this on canvas.

But somehow the measure of sympathy that should be engendered for the genius who was to turn insane is not realized. To draw a comparison, Jose Ferrer in *Moulin Rouge* made Toulouse-Lautrec 'closer' to the audience.

■ LUST IN THE DUST

1984, 87 MINS, US ▼

Dir Paul Bartel   *Prod* Allan Glaser, Tab Hunter   *Scr* Philip Taylor   *Ph* Paul Lohmann   *Ed* Alan Toomayan   *Mus* Peter Matz, Karen Hart   *Art Dir* Walter Pickette
● Tab Hunter, Divine, Lainie Kazan, Geoffrey Lewis, Henry Silva, Cesar Romero (Fox Run)

Lust In The Dust is a saucy, irreverent, quite funny send-up of the Western. Film takes some of the old-time conventions – the silent stranger, the saloon singer with a past, the motley crew of crazed gunslingers, the missing stash of gold – and stands them on their head with outrageous comedy and imaginative casting.

Prevailing attitude is established immediately via some florid narration and the sight of the outsized Divine making his way across the desert in full drag on a donkey. Upon meeting Tab Hunter, the epitome of the straight-arrow hero of few words, Divine's character, Rosie, explains to him, in flashback, she's just been gang-raped by Geoffrey Lewis' bunch of Third World outlaws (and outlasted them all).

Duo arrives in the squalid little town of Chili Verde, where the entire populace seems to hang out at the cantina of Lainie Kazan.

Outrageous tale is handled with fine high humor by director Paul Bartel. Picture is Divine's for the taking, and take it he does with a vibrant, inventive comic performance.

■ LUSTY MEN, THE

1952, 112 MINS, US ▼

Dir Nicholas Ray   *Prod* Jerry Wald   *Scr* Horace McCoy, David Dortort   *Ph* Lee Garmes   *Ed* Ralph Dawson   *Mus* Roy Webb   *Art Dir* Albert S. D'Agostino, Alfred Herman
● Susan Hayward, Robert Mitchum, Arthur Kennedy, Arthur Hunnicutt, Frank Faylen, Walter Coy (Wald-Krasna/RKO)

Robert Mitchum is a faded rodeo champion who has fallen on bad days after an accident. Returning broke to the tumbledown ranch where he spent his boyhood, he finds the property desired by Arthur Kennedy, poor cowpoke, and his wife (Susan Hayward). Tales of Mitchum's past glory light a fire under Kennedy, who sees a chance at quick realization of his ranch-owning yen via rodeoing prizes.

As the days pass, Kennedy wins money and develops a taste for the glory that goes with success but Mitchum has a growing interest in Hayward.

A lot of actual rodeo footage is used to backstop the story [suggested by one by Claude Stanush]. A somewhat slow starter, once underway it is kept playing with growing interest under Nicholas Ray's firm direction.

■ LUV

1967, 93 MINS, US ◇ ▼

Dir Clive Donner   *Prod* Martin Manulis   *Scr* Elliott Baker   *Ph* Ernest Laszlo   *Ed* Harold F. Kress   *Mus* Gerry Mulligan   *Art Dir* Al Brenner
● Jack Lemmon, Peter Falk, Elaine May, Nina Wayne, Eddie Mayehoff, Paul Hartman (Columbia)

As a play, Murray Schisgal's *Luv* was a hit comedy which ran more than two years on Broadway. Many of the beguiling qualities are lost in its transference to the screen. Where the legiter was wildly absurd and deliciously outlandish much of the humor of the picture is forced, proving that a sophisticated stage comedy isn't always ideal fare for the screen.

Opening on Manhattan Bridge, where Jack Lemmon, a self-proclaimed failure, is about to commit suicide, story takes form as Peter Falk, a self-proclaimed success, comes along and saves him. Falk recognizes in Lemmon an old school friend and takes him home to meet his wife, whom he immediately tries to palm off on Lemmon so he can get a divorce and marry the girl of his dreams, a gymnasium instructor named Linda.

Clive Donner's direction fits the frantic overtones of unfoldment, but in this buildup occasionally goes overboard for effect. Lemmon appears to over-characterize his role, a difficult one for exact shading. Falk as a bright-eyed schemer scores decisively in a restrained comedy enactment for what may be regarded as pic's top performance.

■ LYDIA

1941, 103 MINS, US

Dir Julien Duvivier   *Prod* Alexander Korda   *Scr* Ben Hecht, Sam Hoffenstein   *Ph* Lee Garmes   *Ed* William Hornbeck   *Mus* Miklos Rozsa   *Art Dir* Vincent Korda
● Merle Oberon, Edna May Oliver, Alan Marshal, Joseph Cotten (United Artists)

A man loves 'em and leaves 'em but a woman carries the torch for an early romance down through the years. Proceeding on this premise *Lydia* displays the life span of a woman from 20 to 60, and her torching for a lover whose promises and memories are forgotten 35 years later.

Original story, by Julien Duvivier and Ladislas Bush-Fekete, carries on romantic frustration in a minor key. It's strictly a character study of a gal pursued and loved by three men of various standings – football hero, famous doctor, and blind musical genius – but who holds in her heart through the years the brief, but hot, romance with a seafarer-lover.

Dialog and narrative, with frequent use of cutbacks for the story telling, does not add to the speed of the unreeling under the leisurely direction by Duvivier.

Merle Oberon takes full advantage of her prominent role to turn in an excellent performance. Makeup for the span of years is particularly excellent.

M

M

M

1951, 88 MINS, US

Dir Joseph Losey   *Prod* Seymour Nebenzal   *Scr* Leo Katcher, Norman Reilly Raine, Waldo Salt   *Ph* Ernest Laszlo   *Ed* Edward Mann   *Mus* Michel Michelet   *Art Dir* Martin Obzina

● David Wayne, Luther Adler, Howard Da Silva, Martin Gabel, Raymond Burr, Glenn Anders (Columbia)

M is a remake of picture produced in Germany by Seymour Nebenzal in 1933. Principal change is its shift in locale, presumably to California.

David Wayne, as the killer of small children, is effective and convincing. Luther Adler, as a drunken lawyer member of a gangster mob, turns in an outstanding performance, as do Martin Gabel, the gangleader, and Howard da Silva and Steve Brodie as police officials.

Story is that of a killer (Wayne), whose only victims are children. The city is up in arms over failure of the police to nab the murderer. A series of raids by police is hampering the activities of a crime syndicate headed by Gabel. Mob knows it cannot continue with its floating dice games, bookie joints and other enterprises until the killer is caught. To protect his rackets, Gabel orders his gang to catch the killer.

Joseph Losey's direction has captured the gruesome theme skilfully.

MACAO

1952, 81 MINS, US ⓥ

Dir Josef von Sternberg   *Prod* Alex Gottlieb   *Scr* Bernard C. Schoenfeld, Stanley Rubin   *Ph* Harry J. Wild   *Ed* Samuel E. Beetley, Robert Golden   *Mus* Anthony Collins   *Art Dir* Albert S. D'Agostino, Ralph Berger

● Robert Mitchum, Jane Russell, William Bendix, Thomas Gomez, Gloria Grahame, Brad Dexter (RKO)

Macao pairs Jane Russell and Robert Mitchum; contains the cliche elements of adventure, romance and intrigue; and is set in the mysterious Orient.

Story is set in the Portuguese colony south of Hong Kong. It opens with the arrival of three Americans – Russell, a cynical, wisecracking chirper; Mitchum, an ex-GI running away from a minor shooting scrape; and William Bendix, disguised as a salesman but in reality a New York detective entrusted with the job of bringing back to the States Brad Dexter, local gambling kingpin.

Dexter engages Russell to sing at his club and makes a play for her, to the displeasure of his girl friend (Gloria Grahame). Believing Mitchum to be the New York cop, Dexter fails in an attempt to bribe him to leave the island and resorts to more drastic means.

MacARTHUR

1977, 128 MINS, US ◇ ⓥ

Dir Joseph Sargent   *Prod* Frank McCarthy   *Scr* Hal Barwood, Matthew Robbins   *Ph* Mario Tosi   *Ed* George Jay Nicholson   *Mus* Jerry Goldsmith   *Art Dir* John J. Lloyd

● Gregory Peck, Ed Flanders, Dan O'Herlihy, Marj Dusay, Sandy Kenyon, Nicolas Coster (Universal/Zanuck-Brown)

MacArthur is as good a film as could be made, considering the truly appalling egomania of its subject. Film stars Gregory Peck in an

excellent and remarkable characterization.

Screenplay depicts the public aspects of Douglas MacArthur's life from Corregidor in 1942 to dismissal a decade later in the midst of the Korean War, all framed between segments of his farewell address to West Point cadets.

Unlike *Patton*, which was loaded with emotional and physical action highlights, *MacArthur* is a far more introspective and introverted story. There are moments when, despite all evidence to the contrary, one actually can believe that MacArthur thought he possessed the only true vision of battle strategy; yet a second later, the vibrations of a brassbound poseur come across all too clearly.

MACBETH

1948, 106 MINS, US ⓥ

Dir Orson Welles   *Prod* Orson Welles   *Scr* Orson Welles   *Ph* John L. Russell   *Ed* Louis Lindsay   *Mus* Jacques Ibert   *Art Dir* Fred Ritter

● Orson Welles, Jeanette Nolan, Dan O'Herlihy, Roddy McDowall, John Dierkes (Republic/Mercury)

Welles' idea of Shakespeare is such a personalized version. Production was comparatively inexpensive – and looks it. Mood is as dour as the Scottish moors and crags that background the plot. Film is crammed with scenery-chewing theatrics in the best Shakespearean manner with Welles dominating practically every bit of footage.

Only a few of the Bard's best lines are audible. The rest are lost in strained, dialectic gibbering that is only sound, not prose. At best, Shakespeare dialog requires close attention; but even intense concentration can't make intelligible the reading by Welles and others in the cast.

Macbeth, the play, devotes considerable time to depicting femme influence on the male to needle his vanity and ambition into murder for a kingdom. *Macbeth*, the film, devotes that footage to the male's reaction to the femme needling. Several Shakespeare characters have been turned into a Welles-introduced one, a Holy Father.

Welles introduces Jeanette Nolan as Lady Macbeth. Her reading is best in the 'out, damned spot' scene. Dan O'Herlihy fares best as Macduff, his reading having the clearest enunciation.

MACHINE GUN KELLY

1958, 84 MINS, US

Dir Roger Corman   *Prod* Roger Corman   *Scr* R. Wright Campbell   *Ph* Floyd Crosby   *Ed* Ronald Sinclair   *Mus* Gerald Fried   *Art Dir* Daniel Haller

● Charles Bronson, Susan Cabot, Morey Amsterdam, Jack Lambert, Connie Gilchrist (American-International)

Machine Gun Kelly beats out a tattoo of the 1930s in its account of the criminal career of one of that decade's most notorious outlaws. Roger Corman has taken a good screenplay and made a first-rate little picture out of the depressing but intriguing account of a badman's downfall.

Charles Bronson plays Kelly, shown as an undersized sadist who grows an extra foot or so as soon as he gets a submachine gun tucked under his arm. His exploits, proceeding from penny ante robbery to bigtime kidnapping, are adroitly and swiftly shown.

Bronson gives a brooding, taut performance. Susan Cabot is good as the woman behind his deeds, and Morey Amsterdam contributes an offbeat portrayal of a squealer who has the final revenge of turning Kelly in. Gerald Fried, using piano and taps for an unusual and striking combination, has done a fine progressive jazz score.

MACKENNA'S GOLD

1969, 128 MINS, US ◇ ⓥ

Dir J. Lee Thompson   *Prod* Carl Foreman   *Scr* Carl Foreman   *Ph* Joseph MacDonald   *Ed* Bill Lenny   *Mus* Quincy Jones   *Art Dir* Geoffrey Drake

● Gregory Peck, Omar Sharif, Telly Savalas, Julie Newmar, Camilla Sparv, Keenan Wynn (Columbia)

Mackenna's Gold is a standard western. The plot is good, the acting adequate. But it's the scenery – the vastness of the west – the use of cameras, and of horses, and the special effects which keep the viewer involved and entertained.

There are a few plot twists, but for the most part the story is predictable. Mackenna (Gregory Peck) has memorized a map, now destroyed, which will lead to a canyon of gold. The gold belongs to the Apaches, and it has been decreed by the Apache Gods that the gold remain untouched.

But now the young Apache warriors want the gold to support them in their fight against the white men. The Mexican bandit Colorado (Omar Sharif) wants the gold so he can emigrate to Paris and become a gentleman.

Sharif captures Peck and forces him to lead them to the gold.

MACKINTOSH MAN, THE

1973, 98 MINS, UK ◇ ⓥ

Dir John Huston   *Prod* John Foreman   *Scr* Walter Hill   *Ph* Oswald Morris   *Ed* Russell Lloyd   *Mus* Maurice Jarre   *Art Dir* Terry Marsh

● Paul Newman, Dominique Sanda, James Mason, Harry Andrews, Ian Bannen, Michael Hordern (Warner)

The Mackintosh Man is a tame tale of British espionage and counter-espionage, starring Paul Newman as a planted assassin, James Mason as a cynical right-wing politician in reality a spy, and Dominique Sanda as a combo semi-romantic interest and foreign-market star bait.

Walter Hill has adapted Desmond Bagley's novel, *The Freedom Trap*, into a serviceable meller form. Harry Andrews, a British secret agent, recruits Newman to pull a jewel heist by mail, in order to establish his criminal credentials, so that he may escape with Ian Bannen, a state secrets betrayor, and thereby ferret out Mason, who has carried on a 25-year career as a politician but has been a foreign agent.

There's a whole lot of nothing going on here.

MACOMBER AFFAIR, THE

1947, 89 MINS, US

Dir Zoltan Korda   *Prod* Benedict Bogeaus   *Scr* Casey Robinson, Seymour Bennett   *Ph* Karl Struss   *Ed* George Feld, Jack Wheeler   *Mus* Miklos Rozsa   *Art Dir* Erno Metzner

● Gregory Peck, Robert Preston, Joan Bennett (United Artists)

The Macomber Affair, with an African hunt background, isn't particularly pleasant in content, even though action often is exciting and elements of suspense frequently hop up the spectator. Certain artificialities of presentation, too, and unreal dialog are further strikes against picture, [based on a short story by Ernest Hemingway], although portion of footage filmed in Africa is interesting.

Robert Preston enacts role of Francis Macomber, a rich American with an unhappy wife (Joan Bennett), who arrives at Nairobi and hires Gregory Peck, a white hunter, to take him lion hunting. On the safari, this time in cars, Macomber can't stand up under a lion charge and his wife sees him turn coward. The white hunter kills the lion. Thereafter, Macomber broods over his shame and his wife falls for the hunter.

African footage is cut into the story with showmanship effect, and these sequences build up suspense satisfactorily. There are closeups of lions and other denizens of the veldt, and scenes in which lion and water buffalo charge, caught with telescopic lenses by camera crew sent to Africa from England, will stir any audience. These focal points of the story out-interest the human drama as developed in scripters' enmeshing trio of stars.

■ MAD ABOUT MUSIC

1936, 98 MINS, US

Dir Norman Taurog *Prod* Joe Pasternak *Scr* Bruce Manning, Felix Jackson *Ph* Joseph Valentine *Ed* Philip Kahn
● Deanna Durbin, Herbert Marshall, Arthur Treacher, Gail Patrick, William Frawley, Jackie Moran (Universal)

Mad about Music has a genuine and enthralling, if somewhat obvious story [by Marcella Burke and Frederick Kohner]. Idea is a simple one. So as not to risk her popularity as a glamour girl, a beauteous widowed film star unwillingly hides her 14-year-old daughter away in a Swiss boarding school. Although the youngster is inordinately proud of her illustrious mother, she must cherish her affection in secret.

When the other girls talk about their parents, the youngster takes refuge in telling of the fabulous exploits of her imaginary father, whom she describes as an explorer and big game hunter. When circumstances force her to make good the yarns, she imposes on a vacationing British composer to pretend to be her legendary father.

As evidence that Deanna Durbin is growing up, in this film she is given a beau for the first time. It's still purely in the puppy-love status. She has acquired more varied technique before the camera, without losing her ingenuous charm nor her luminous screen personality.

As the adopted-by-surprise father, Herbert Marshall plays with unaccustomed warmth. Although her part is important to the story, Gail Patrick gets comparatively little footage as the actress-mother.

■ MAD MAX

1979, 90 MINS, AUSTRALIA ◇ Ⓥ

Dir George Miller *Prod* Byron Kennedy *Scr* George Miller, James McCausland *Ph* David Eggby *Ed* Tony Paterson, Cliff Hayes *Mus* Brian May *Art Dir* Jon Dowding
● Mel Gibson, Joanne Samuel, Hugh Keays-Byrne, Steve Bisley, Roger Ward, Vince Gil (Roadshow)

Mad Max is an all-stops-out, fast-moving exploitation pic in the tradition of New World/American International productions. The plot is extremely simple. A few years from now (opening title), the Australian countryside is terrorized by marauders who create mayhem on the roads. A crack police force opposes the villains.

Mad Max is one of the fastest and most ruthless of these cops of the future. Max quits the force to take a vacation with his wife and baby. But when The Toecutter's gang kills his wife and child, he dons his leather uniform again to hunt them down.

Stunts themselves would be nothing without a filmmaker behind the camera and George Miller, a lawyer and film buff making his first feature, shows he knows what cinema is all about.

The film belongs to the director, cameraman and stunt artists: it's not an actor's piece, though the leads are all effective.

■ MAD MAX 2

1981, 94 MINS, AUSTRALIA ◇

Dir George Miller *Prod* Byron Kennedy *Scr* George Miller, Terry Hayes, Brian Hannant *Ph* Dean Semler *Ed* David Stiven, Tim Wellburn, Michael Chigwin *Mus* Brian May

● Mel Gibson, Bruce Spence, Kjell Nilsson, Emil Minty, Virginia Hey, Vernon Wells (Roadshow)

Uncomplicated plot has Max (Mel Gibson), a futuristic version of the western gunslinger, reluctantly throwing in his lot with a communal group whose lifesupport system is a rudimentary refinery in the desert (he needs the gas).

Western parallel continues as the compound is under continual attack from a bunch of marauders led by the gravel-voiced, metal-visored villain Humungus (Kjell Nilsson).

Ever-the-loner Max decides to strike out on his own again, and is saved by his friend the Gyro Captain (Bruce Spence) who swoops down from the clouds, and takes him back to the safety of the compound

The climactic chase has Max at the wheel of a super-tanker in a desperate flight to Paradise 2,000 miles away (the promised land is the tourist resort on the Queensland Gold Coast, an unexpected touch of black humour).

It's a dazzling demolition derby, as men and machines collide and disintegrate, featuring very fine stunt work and special effects.

Director Miller keeps the pic moving with cyclonic force, photography by Dean Semler is first class, editing is supertight, and Brian May's music is stirring.

■ MAD MAX BEYOND THUNDERDOME

1985, 106 MINS, AUSTRALIA ◇ Ⓥ

Dir George Miller, George Ogilvie *Prod* George Miller *Scr* Terry Hayes, George Miller *Ph* Dean Semler *Ed* Richard Francis-Bruce *Mus* Maurice Jarre *Art Dir* Graham Walker
● Mel Gibson, Tina Turner, Angelo Rossitto, Helen Buday, Rod Zuanic, Frank Thring (Kennedy-Miller)

The third in the series opens strong with Mel Gibson being dislodged from his camel train by low-flying Bruce Spence in an airborne jalopy (providing as much fun here as he did as the gyro Captain in the earlier *Max* films, this time accompanied by Adam Cockburn as his daredevil son).

To retrieve his possessions, Gibson has to confront Tina Turner, the improbably named Aunty, mistress of Bartertown, a bizarre bazaar where anything – up to and including human lives – is traded as the only form of commerce in the post-apocalyptic world.

Turner throws him a challenge: engage in a fight to the death with a giant known as The Blaster (Paul Larsson) in the Thunderdome, a geometric arena which serves as a kind of futuristic Roman Colosseum for the delectation of the locals.

Gibson impressively fleshes out Max, Tina Turner is striking in her role as Aunty (as well as contributing two topnotch songs, which open and close the picture) and the juves are uniformly good.

■ MAD ROOM, THE

1969, 93 MINS, US ◇

Dir Bernard Girard *Prod* Norman Maurer *Scr* Bernard Girard, A.Z. Martin *Ph* Harry Stradling Jr. *Ed* Pat Somerset *Mus* Dave Grusin *Art Dir* Sidney Litwack
● Shelley Winters, Stella Stevens, Barbara Sammeth, Michael Burns, Skip Ward (Columbia)

Weak story which pretends to be a psycho-suspense yarn. Screenplay is based on the 1940 play, *Ladies in Retirement*, filmed in 1941 by Columbia, with Ida Lupino, Elsa Lanchester, Edith Barrett.

Shelley Winters, surrounded by an able cast, thin plot, good color and some magnificent scenery on and near Vancouver Island, is the better part of the pic.

Barbara Sammeth and Michael Burns, playing brother and sister recently released from a mental institution, are the focus of the story which is long on melodramatics. Script has a patent mystery plot in which the real murderer isn't exposed until the film's end but any astute filmgoer will perceive the twist long before it comes on the screen.

Winters plays a wealthy widow living with young companion Stella Stevens. The young brother and sister of Stevens have been released from a mental institution where they were confined, supposedly for the murder of their parents.

■ MADAME BOVARY

1949, 114 MINS, US Ⓥ

Dir Vincente Minnelli *Prod* Pandro S. Berman *Scr* Robert Ardrey *Ph* Robert Planck *Ed* Ferris Webster *Mus* Miklos Rozsa
● Jennifer Jones, James Mason, Van Heflin, Louis Jourdan, Christopher Kent, Gene Lockhart (M-G-M)

As a character study, *Madame Bovary* is interesting to watch, but hard to feel. It is a curiously unemotional account of some rather basic emotions. However, the surface treatment of Vincente Minnelli's direction is slick and attractively presented.

Jennifer Jones is the daring Madame Bovary. The character is short on sympathy, being a greedy woman so anxious to better her position in life that sin and crime do not shock her moral values. Jones answers to every demand of direction and script.

Van Heflin portrays her doctor husband, an essentially weak man whose evident flaws in abiding with a greedy wife are not too satisfactorily explained away by his love for her.

The Bovary quest for something better than she has is brought to light at the trial of Gustave Flaubert, author of the realistically treated novel that brought about his arrest. James Mason is excellent as the author.

■ MADAME CURIE

1943, 125 MINS, US

Dir Mervyn LeRoy *Prod* Sidney Franklin *Scr* Paul Osborn, Paul Rameau *Ph* Joseph Ruttenberg *Ed* Harold F. Kress *Mus* Herbert Stothart *Art Dir* Cedric Gibbons, Paul Groesse
● Greer Garson, Walter Pidgeon, Robert Walker, Van Johnson, Margaret O'Brien (M-G-M)

Every inch a great picture. *Madame Curie* absorbingly tells of the struggle and heartaches that ultimately resulted in the discovery of radium.

Sidney Franklin, producer, and Mervyn LeRoy, director, have instilled into the story of Madame Curie and her scientist-husband a particularly high degree of entertainment value where in less-skilled hands the romance of radium and its discovery may have struck out.

While the events leading up to the discovery of radium and the fame it brought Madame Curie are of the greatest underlying importance to the picture as entertainment, it's the love story that dominates all the way. Thus, this is not just the saga of a great scientist nor just a story of test tubes and laboratories.

Film is based on the book *Madame Curie*, written by Eve Curie, daughter of the Polish teacher-scientist who quite by accident came upon the source of the element. It is adapted with great skill by Paul Osborn and Paul H. Rameau, with a few stretches of narration by James Hilton. It throws Greer Garson and Walter Pidgeon together immediately after the opening and, as the romance between them ripens, it gathers terrific momentum.
☐ 1943: Best Picture (Nomination)

M

■ MADAME DUBARRY

1934, 75 MINS, US

Dir William Dieterle   *Scr* Edward Chodorov   *Ph* Sol Polito

● Dolores Del Rio, Reginald Owen, Victor Jory, Osgood Perkins, Verree Teasdale, Anita Louise (Warner)

Madame Dubarry is a Hollywood idea of Versailles. Under William Dieterle's directorial aegis, the decadent court of Louis XV becomes even more so in its broad well-nigh travesty version of the comtesse's influence on the doddering Louie.

Script is a chameleon affair. It emphasizes the stupid extravagances of a former street waif who wants to go sleighing in the midst of summer; and in another moment seeks to suggest that perhaps some of her devious ways achieved some good. Such as when the English ambassador opines that getting rid of the French prime minister (caught in Dubarry's boudoir) has achieved something which his Brittanic majesty and other diplomats in the French court long tried but heretofore couldn't accomplish.

Dolores Del Rio's Dubarry is rarely believable. It's a theatrical conception eclipsed by the performances of Reginald Owen, who is capital as the senile Louie, and Victory Jory as d'Aiguillon. Osgood Perkins' Richelieu doesn't register.

Dubarry as a production is very Busby Berkeley. In its tinsel, costuming, and general pretentiousness it's more musical comedy than history.

■ MADAME SOUSATZKA

1988, 122 MINS, UK/US ◇ ⊛

Dir John Schlesinger   *Prod* Robin Dalton   *Scr* Ruth Prawer Jhabvala   *Ph* Nat Crosby   *Ed* Peter Honess   *Mus* Gerald Gouriet   *Art Dir* Luciana Arrighi

● Shirley MacLaine, Navin Chowdhry, Peggy Ashcroft, Twiggy, Shabana Azmi, Leigh Lawson (Sousatzka/Cineplex Odeon)

Although essentially a rather old-fashioned British pic, *Madame Sousatzka* is filled with pleasures, not the least of them being Shirley MacLaine's effervescent performance.

Setting is London where middle-aged Mme Sousatzka, of Russian parentage but raised in New York, teaches piano to only the most gifted students. She insists her pupils not only learn to play, but also to live the kind of traditional cultured lifestyle which she herself does.

Her latest protege is a 15-year-old Indian youth, Manek (Navin Chowdhry) whose mother (Shabana Azmi) left Calcutta years before to get away from her husband.

Sousatzka lives in a crumbling house owned by old Lady Emily (Peggy Ashcroft). Besides Sousatzka, her tenants include a model and would-be pop singer (delightfully played by Twiggy) who looks much younger than she is; and a middle-aged gay osteopath (Geoffrey Bayldon).

Crucial, though, is the central relationship between MacLaine, who's seldom been better than she is here, and the youngster, warmly played by Chowdry. All their scenes have great charm, with the piano playing effectively handled.

■ MADAME X

1929, 95 MINS, US

Dir Lionel Barrymore   *Scr* Willard Mack   *Ph* Arthur Reed   *Art Dir* Cedric Gibbons

● Ruth Chatterton, Lewis Stone, Raymond Hackett, John P. Edington, Ullric Haupt, Sidney Toler (M-G-M)

This is Lionel Barrymore's first full-length directorial effort on a talker. Taking *X* as an actor-proof meller and conceding its author, the Frenchman Alexandre Bisson, knew emotion well enough to make it do somersaults in this tale, Barrymore had no difficult job with the story and cast.

But Barrymore excels in the minor bits and roles: the above-par park scene; the immensely human bit in the hotel's corridor with the landlord wanting his room rent from the besotted Jacqueline (Ruth Chatterton); or the superb scene wholly dominated by the doctor (John P. Edington).

The two big moments are Jacqueline killing her small-time blackmailing companion to prevent her son discovering what a horror his mother has become; the other the famous trial scene, the grand finale which made *Madame X* on the stage.

Chatterton has not a flaw in her performance or make up. Next to Chatterton and Edington comes Raymond Hackett as the son.

■ MADAME X

1937, 75 MINS, US

Dir Sam Wood   *Prod* James Kevin McGuinness   *Scr* John Meehan   *Ph* John Seitz   *Ed* Frank E. Hull   *Mus* David Snell

● Gladys George, John Beal, Warren William, Reginald Owen, William Henry, Henry Daniell (M-G-M)

This is a reverent handling of the Alexandre Bisson play, chosen by M-G-M as a vehicle to demonstrate the dramatic and emotional talent of Gladys George. It's a quiet, comforting sniffle.

Script follows with devotion the familiar developments, and the dialog is as modern as the action permits. Sam Wood's direction is conventionally sound and the production is of the best.

George's performance is effective, and her characterization of the tipsy, defeated and maudlin old woman is faithful and moving. Warren William plays the hard-hearted husband who refuses to forgive his wife's indiscretions; Reginald Owen is the friend, Douvel; Henry Daniell is the villain, Lerocle.

John Beal has the prize spot of Raymond, youthful public defender of his mother, whose identity is unknown to him. His address to the court is recited with conviction and emotion.

■ MADAME X

1966, 99 MINS, US ◇ ⊛

Dir David Lowell Rich   *Prod* Ross Hunter   *Scr* Jean Holloway   *Ph* Russell Metty   *Ed* Milton Carruth   *Mus* Frank Skinner   *Art Dir* Alexander Golitzen, George Webb

● Lana Turner, John Forsythe, Ricardo Montalban, Burgess Meredith, Constance Bennett, Keir Dullea (Universal)

Latest time out for Alexandre Bisson's now-classic 1909 drama of mother love is an emotional, sometimes exhausting and occasionally corny picture. Lana Turner takes on the difficult assignment of the frustrated mother, turning in what many will regard as her most rewarding portrayal. Producer Ross Hunter draws generally on the original plot but has changed the locale from Paris to the US for pic's opening and climax.

Screenplay now has femme star very much in love with her husband, instead of running away from her spouse, as in the original, to join her lover. However, following an affair with a rich playboy, who is accidentally killed while she is in his apartment, she is talked by her mother-in-law into disappearing in a phony drowning episode to save her politically-minded husband and young son from scandal.

John Forsythe excels as the husband, whose political career forces him to absent himself from home for long periods of time and thus lays the ground for his lonely wife's indiscretion. Ricardo Montalban is persuasive as the playboy who falls to his death, and Constance Bennett – in her last film appearance before her death – endows the mother-in-law role with quiet dignity and strength.

■ MADE IN PARIS

1966, 103 MINS, US ◇

Dir Boris Sagal   *Prod* Joe Pasternak   *Scr* Stanley Roberts   *Ph* Milton Krasner   *Ed* William McMillin   *Mus* George Stoll   *Art Dir* George W. Davis, Preston Ames

● Ann-Margret, Louis Jourdan, Richard Crenna, Edie Adams, Chad Everett, John McGiver (Euterpe/M-G-M)

A Parisian setting and some snazzy femme costumes provide the major props for this otherwise weak and formula comedy programmer. Sexy plot overtones are too protracted in scripting, and become boring via heavy-handed direction. Ann-Margret and Louis Jourdan top the list of adequate players.

Stanley Roberts' dull script, strongly reminiscent of yesteryear Doris Day-Rock Hudson-Cary Grant plots (but less effective), finds fashion buyer Ann-Margret rushed to Paris from the lecherous arms of her employer's son (Chad Everett). Jourdan is the French designer, who, it appears, has had what is usually called an adult arrangement with Edie Adams, whom Ann-Margret has replaced. Richard Crenna is a foreign correspondent who bobs from time to time.

Plotting permits Ann-Margret to essay some wild terpery, which David Winters choreographed to the desired effect. Mongo Santamaria and band provide a solid beat for the bumps.

■ MADEMOISELLE

1967, 100 MINS, UK/FRANCE

Dir Tony Richardson   *Prod* Oscar Lewenstein   *Scr* Jean Genet   *Ph* David Watkin   *Ed* Anthony Gibbs   *Art Dir* Jacques Saulnier

● Jeanne Moreau, Ettore Manni, Keith Skinner, Jeanne Beretta, Mony Rey (United Artists/Woodfall/Procinex)

French-British coproduction mixes Tony Richardson's free-wheeling style and the script of the controversial French writer-playwright Jean Genet. It has two versions, one English and one French, since French star Jeanne Moreau is bilingual.

A small French farming town is the locale. Story is about an arsonist who is terrorizing the people. A poisoned drinking well, and opened irrigation ditches which flood the farms, finally lead the populace to form a lynching mob.

The ingrained suspicion regarding a foreigner makes an Italian woodcutter (Ettore Manni), living in the town, the scapegoat.

Moreau's presence manages to make her schoolmarm character quite plausible in revealing her lurking lusts. But the remainder is somewhat sketchy, even though Manni has the virility to bring on hatreds from the other men and finally his own demise. The script seemingly needed more depth and background to the characters. Either that or almost surrealistic playing and treatment.

■ MADIGAN

1968, 101 MINS, US ◇ ⊛

Dir Don Siegel   *Prod* Frank P. Rosenberg   *Scr* Henri Simoun, Abraham Polonsky   *Ph* Russell Metty   *Ed* Milton Shifman   *Mus* Don Costa   *Art Dir* Alexander Golitzen, John Austin

● Richard Widmark, Henry Fonda, Inger Stevens, Harry Guardino, James Whitmore, Susan Clark (Rank/Universal)

Abraham Polonsky's screenplay adaptation of Richard Dougherty's *The Commissioner* is tough and to the point, bringing out the side issue problems but without dallying with them overmuch.

Pic gets away to a flying start, with Richard Widmark as a dedicated cop who isn't above using his badge for some fringe benefits, and sidekick Harry Guardino bursting into a sleazy bedroom to pick up a wanted killer for questioning.

Momentarily distracted by the nude broad in the room Widmark and Guardino are taken off guard and the psychopathic killer, played with menacing hysteria by Steve Ihnat, goes on the lam. Cops are given 72 hours to pick him up.

This is a good solid big-city adventure yarn with Widmark at his best. Guardino tags along satisfactorily as his buddy. Henry Fonda plays the commissioner with the cool austerity and deceptive slowness that he made peculiarly his own and James Whitmore is a tower of strength as the chief inspector.

....

■ MADWOMAN OF CHAILLOT, THE

1969, 142 MINS, US ◇ ⒱
Dir Bryan Forbes *Prod* Ely Landau *Scr* Edward Anhalt *Ph* Claude Renoir, Burnett Guffey *Ed* Roger Dwyre *Mus* Michael J. Lewis *Art Dir* Georges Petitot
● Katharine Hepburn, Richard Chamberlain, Yul Brynner, Margaret Leighton, John Gavin, Giulietta Masina (Warner/Seven Arts)

Story of struggle between good and evil becomes audience's struggle against tedium. Margaret Leighton with her imaginary dog and Giulietta Masina with her imaginary amours ricochet around the Chaillot district of Paris sharing a phantom world of the past with Katharine Hepburn.

Hepburn, as equally disturbed Countess Aurelia, the madwoman of Chaillot, measures life somewhere between a lover lost years ago and a missing feathered boa. Richard Chamberlain, an active pacifist, and Danny Kaye, a local ragpicker, rattle the countess into the present with the news that there's a plot afoot – or underfoot – to destroy Paris.

Film doesn't come off. Hepburn fails to capture the fantasy-spirit of the countess. Her performance suffers because of indecision.

....

■ 'MAGGIE', THE

1954, 93 MINS, UK
Dir Alexander Mackendrick *Prod* Michael Balcon *Scr* William Rose *Ph* Gordon Dines *Ed* Peter Tanner *Mus* John Addison
● Paul Douglas, Alex Mackenzie, James Copeland, Abe Barker, Tommy Kearins, Hubert Gregg (Ealing)

One of the small coastal colliers which ply in Scottish waters provides the main setting for this Ealing comedy. The story of a hustling American businessman who gets involved with a leisurely-minded but crafty skipper gives the film an Anglo-US flavor.

The yarn has been subtly written as a piece of gentle and casual humor. The pace is always leisurely, and the background of Scottish lakes and mountains provides an appropriate backcloth to the story.

The skipper of the *Maggie* is a crafty old sailor, short of cash to make his little coaster seaworthy. By a little smart practice he gets a contract to transport a valuable cargo but when a hustling American executive realizes what has happened, he planes from London to Scotland to get his goods transferred to another vessel.

There is virtually an all-male cast with only minor bits for a few femme players. Paul Douglas, playing the American executive,

provides the perfect contrast between the old world and the new. His is a reliable performance which avoids the pitfall of overacting.

....

■ MAGIC

1978, 106 MINS, US ◇ ⒱
Dir Richard Attenborough *Prod* Joseph E. Levine, Richard P. Levine *Scr* William Goldman *Ph* Victor J. Kemper *Ed* John Bloom *Mus* Jerry Goldsmith *Art Dir* Terence Marsh
● Anthony Hopkins, Ann-Margret, Burgess Meredith, Ed Lauter, E.J. Andre, Jerry Houser (20th Century-Fox)

The premise is that of a dummy slowly taking over the personality of its ventriloquist-master. In adapting his own best-seller, William Goldman has opted for an atmospheric thriller, a mood director Richard Attenborough fleshes out to its fullest.

The dilemma of *Magic* is that the results never live up to the standards established in the film's opening half-hour. Through flashbacks and claustrophic editing, the relationship between Anthony Hopkins and his eerily-realistic dummy, Fats, is well-documented. So is the introduction of Burgess Meredith, well cast as a Swifty Lazar-type of superagent.

When Hopkins declines a lucrative TV contract because of insecurity, and flees to his boyhood Catskills home, where a high school girl on whom he had a crush (Ann-Margret) is enmeshed in a disastrous marriage to redneck Ed Lauter, *Magic* becomes disappointingly transparent. Goldman has Hopkins becoming involved in the standard love triangle that inevitably leads to disaster for all parties concerned.

The ventriloquism and magic stunts are expertly done by Hopkins, with the aid of tech advisor Dennis Alwood.

But as the Meredith character notes early on, 'Magic is misdirection'. That sentiment applies equally to the film.

....

■ MAGIC BOX, THE

1951, 118 MINS, UK ◇
Dir John Boulting *Prod* Ronald Neame *Scr* Eric Ambler *Ph* Jack Cardiff *Ed* Richard Best *Mus* William Alwyn *Art Dir* T. Hopewell Ash
● Robert Donat, Margaret Johnston, Maria Schell, Robert Beatty, James Kenney, Bernard Miles (Festival/British Lion)

The Magic Box is a picture of great sincerity and integrity, superbly acted and intelligently directed. Biopic of William Friese-Greene, the British motion picture pioneer, is charged with real life drama.

Eric Ambler's screenplay is taken from Ray Allister's biography, *Friese-Greene: Close-up of an Inventor*. And the script pinpoints all the major triumphs and tragedies in the life of this pioneer, from his youthful beginnings as a photographer's assistant, to his death in 1921 at a film industry meeting with only the price of a cinema ticket in his pocket.

The selection of Robert Donat as Friese-Greene is an excellent one. Always a polished performer, he brings a new depth of sincerity and understanding to the role. His two wives are portrayed with infinite charm by Maria Schell and Margaret Johnston. Schell, as the ailing girl from Switzerland, shares the inventor's first and greatest triumph. Johnston shares only his failures.

Many front ranking stars have little more than walk-on bits, and quite a few just make a brief appearance without even dialog. Mention must be made of a fine cameo from Laurence Olivier as a policeman who is the first to see the inventor's moving picture.

....

■ MAGIC CHRISTIAN, THE

1969, 95 MINS, UK ◇ ⒱
Dir Joseph McGrath *Prod* Denis O'Dell *Scr* Terry Southern, Joseph McGrath, Peter Sellers *Ph* Geoffrey Unsworth *Ed* Kevin O'Connor *Mus* Ken Thorne *Art Dir* Assheton Gorton
● Peter Sellers, Ringo Starr, Richard Attenborough, Christopher Lee, Raquel Welch, Laurence Harvey (Commonwealth United/Grand)

A spotty, uneven satire [from the novel by Terry Southern] with a number of good yocks, but insufficient sustained wit or related action. As Peter Sellers and Co swipe at the Establishment, authority, blimpishness and sacred cows, there's a great dismal feeling of self-indulgence as of a pic created merely to please an assorted bunch of chums. Much of it is too 'clever' by half.

Sellers gives a very bright and stylish performance as the posh Sir Guy Grand, richest man in the world, who adopts a young fallout hobo (Ringo Starr) and then sets out to prove to him man's venality.

Though Sellers gives one of his brightest and best-observed appearances, Ringo Starr's effort to project himself as a non-Beatle actor is a distinct non-event.

....

■ MAGNIFICENT AMBERSONS, THE

1942, 88 MINS, US ⒱
Dir Orson Welles *Prod* Orson Welles *Scr* Orson Welles *Ph* Stanley Cortez *Ed* Robert Wise, Mark Robson *Mus* Bernard Herrmann, Roy Webb *Art Dir* Mark Lee Kirk
● Joseph Cotten, Dolores Costello, Anne Baxter, Tim Holt, Agnes Moorehead, Ray Collins (RKO/Mercury)

In *The Magnificent Ambersons*, Orson Welles devotes 9,000 feet of film to a spoiled brat who grows up as a spoiled, spiteful young man. This film hasn't a single moment of contrast; it piles on and on a tale of woe, but without once striking at least a true chord of sentimentality.

The central character is Tim Holt, who is portrayed first as the spoiled, curly-haired darling of the town's richest family, and then for the major portion as a conceited, power-conscious, insufferable youth.

Welles comes up with a few more tricks in the direction of the dialog. He plays heavily on the dramatic impact of a whisper, and on the threatened or actual hysterics of a frustrated woman as played by Agnes Moorehead.
□ 1942: Best Picture (Nomination)

....

■ MAGNIFICENT DOLL

1946, 93 MINS, US
Dir Frank Borzage *Scr* Irving Stone *Ph* Joseph Valentine *Ed* Ted J. Kent *Mus* H. J. Salter *Art Dir* Alexander Golitzen
● Ginger Rogers, David Niven, Burgess Meredith (Universal/Hallmark)

Dolly Madison has always been considered one of the most colorful figures in this country's early history and her true life story would probably have been a natural for films. It's difficult to understand, therefore, why Irving Stone, who's credited with both the original story and screenplay, went out of his way to slough off facts in favor of fiction. Incident in which Dolly salvaged important government documents from under the noses of the British in the War of 1812, for example, is given a quick brushoff. In its place, Stone has substituted such obvious fiction as having Aaron Burr, with a crush on Dolly, give up his claims to the presidency just because Dolly talked him out of it.

Picture's chief graces result from the fine work of the cast under Frank Borzage's competent direction. Ginger Rogers gives expert handling to the title role, making the transition from one emotion to another in good fashion.

David Niven plays the scoundrelly Burr, sneering when he has to and being tender in his love scenes with Rogers. He hams up several sequences but he couldn't do otherwise with the script. Burgess Meredith shines as James Madison, making the idealistic president convincing enough.

Story is told by Dolly in retrospect, with her monolog bridging the gaps. It picks her up as a young girl on her father's plantation in Virginia, carries through her first unhappy marriage, then her love affair with Burr and eventual marriage to Madison.

. . . .

■ MAGNIFICENT OBSESSION

1935, 110 MINS, US

Dir John M. Stahl   *Prod* John M. Stahl   *Scr* George O'Neil, Sarah Y. Mason, Victor Heerman   *Ph* John Mescall   *Ed* Milton Carruth   *Mus* Franz Waxman
● Irene Dunne, Robert Taylor, Charles Butterworth, Betty Furness, Sara Haden, Ralph Morgan (Universal)

If its 110 minutes' running time makes it appear a bit sluggish, the sensitive and intelligent development [from the novel by Lloyd C. Douglas] ultimately makes the initial lethargic progression appear justified. With its metaphysical theme of godliness and faith, the spiritual background of *Magnificent* is magnificent.

It's patent that Irene Dunne and Robert Taylor, co-starred, must clinch for the finale, even though it was a drunken mishap by the wastrel (Taylor) which had something to do with the death of the venerable Dr Hudson. Dunne is the widow of Dr Hudson, and Taylor's ultimate reformation is achieved because of the romantic attachment for her.

That he becomes a Nobel prize-winner and a surgical marvel in six or seven years, finally achieving the restoration of her sight (after a high-powered battery of medical savants had previously failed to accomplish anything) is rather deftly skirted, for all the theatricalism of the basic elements.

Besides the stellar pair, Charles Butterworth and Betty Furness in secondary prominence scintillate.

. . . .

■ MAGNIFICENT OBSESSION

1954, 107 MINS, US ◇ Ⓥ

Dir Douglas Sirk   *Prod* Ross Hunter   *Scr* Robert Blees   *Ph* Russell Metty   *Ed* Milton Carruth   *Mus* Frank Skinner   *Art Dir* Bernard Herzbrun, Emrich Nicholson
● Jane Wyman, Rock Hudson, Barbara Rush, Agnes Moorehead, Otto Kruger, Gregg Palmer (Universal)

The same inspirational appeal which marked the 1935 making of Lloyd C. Douglas' bestseller is again caught in this version of *Magnificent Obsession*, with Jane Wyman and Rock Hudson undertaking the roles previously enacted by Irene Dunne and Robert Taylor. It is a sensitive treatment of faith told in terms of moving, human drama which packs emotional impact.

As megged by Douglas Sirk from Robert Blees' moving and understanding screenplay, the Ross Hunter production, impressively mounted, commands dramatic attention. Characters become alive and vital and infuse spiritual theme with a rare sort of beauty.

Hudson is the rich playboy responsible for Wyman's blindness who renounces his past existence to devote himself to study and work, hoping as a surgeon to cure her.

Film takes its title from the 'magnificent obsession' which possessed a doctor for whose death Hudson is indirectly responsible.

. . . .

■ MAGNIFICENT SEVEN, THE

1960, 128 MINS, US ◇ Ⓥ

Dir John Sturges   *Prod* John Sturges   *Scr* William Roberts   *Ph* Charles Lang Jr   *Ed* Ferris Webster   *Mus* Elmer Bernstein   *Art Dir* Edward FitzGerald
● Yul Brynner, Eli Wallach, Steve McQueen, Horst Buchholz, Charles Bronson, Robert Vaughan (United Artists)

Until the women and children arrive on the scene about two-thirds of the way through, *The Magnificent Seven* is a rip-roaring rootin' tootin' western with lots of bite and tang and old-fashioned abandon. The last third is downhill, a long and cluttered anti-climax in which 'The Magnificent Seven' grow slightly too magnificent for comfort.

Odd foundation for the able screenplay is the Japanese film, *Seven Samurai*. The plot, as adapted, is simple and compelling. A Mexican village is at the mercy of a bandit (Eli Wallach), whose recurrent 'visits' with his huge band of outlaws strip the meek peasant people of the fruits of their labors. Finally, in desperation, they hire seven American gunslingers for the obvious purpose.

There is a heap of fine acting and some crackling good direction by John Sturges mostly in the early stages, during formation of the central septet. Wallach creates an extremely colorful and arresting figure as the chief antagonist. Of the big 'Seven', Charles Bronson, James Coburn and Steve McQueen share top thespic honors, although the others don't lag by much, notably Horst Buchholz and Brad Dexter. Bronson fashions the most sympathetic character of the group. Coburn, particularly in an introductory sequence during which he reluctantly pits his prowess with a knife against a fast gun in an electrifying showdown, is a powerful study in commanding concentration.

Elmer Bernstein's lively pulsating score, emphasizing conscious percussion, strongly resembles the work of Jerome Moross for *The Big Country*.

. . . .

■ MAGNUM FORCE

1973, 122 MINS, US ◇ Ⓥ

Dir Ted Post   *Prod* Robert Daley   *Scr* John Milius, Michael Cimino   *Ph* Frank Stanley   *Ed* Ferris Webster   *Mus* Lalo Schifrin   *Art Dir* Jack Collis
● Clint Eastwood, Hal Holbrook, Mitchell Ryan, Felton Perry, David Soul, Robert Urich (Malpaso/Warner)

Magnum Force is an intriguing followup to *Dirty Harry* [1971] in that nonconformist Frisco detective Clint Eastwood is faced with tracking down a band of vigilante cops headed by Hal Holbrook, his nominal superior and career nemesis. The story contains the usual surfeit of human massacre for the yahoo trade, as well as a few actual thoughts.

In *Harry* there was a script loaded in favor of the end justifying the means by those pledged to law enforcement. The interesting twist in *Magnum Force* is that Eastwood stumbles on a group of bandit cop avengers. The plot [based on a story by John Milius] thus forces Eastwood to render a judgement in favor of the present system.

Eastwood and new partner Felton Perry are helping investigate a number of bloody murders of local crime leaders, but the evidence finally begins to point at four rookie cops – David Soul, Tim Matheson, Robert Urich and Kip Niven – who eventually tip their hand to Eastwood.

. . . .

■ MAGUS, THE

1969, 117 MINS, UK ◇

Dir Guy Green   *Prod* Jud Kinberg, John Kohn   *Scr* John Fowles   *Ph* Billy Williams   *Ed* Max Benedict   *Mus* John Dankworth   *Art Dir* Don Ashton
● Michael Caine, Anthony Quinn, Candice Bergen, Anna Karina, Paul Strassino, Julian Glover (20th Century-Fox/Blazer

The Magus is an esoteric, talky, slowly-developing, sensitively-executed, and somewhat dull film. Adapted by John Fowles from his novel, the production, filmed largely on Majorca (although setting is Greece), is a black fantasy-drama of self-realization. Michael Caine stars, in one of his better performances, along with Anthony Quinn, Candice Bergen and Anna Karina.

This near-miss is not without many notable virtues. Fowles' script sustains interest in its convolutions; direction is resourceful and sensitive; Caine is far more dynamic than usual and Quinn and the two femme stars register strongly.

Caine is an English teacher dispatched to a Greek island as replacement for a suicide. On the island, he meets Quinn, who is a mystic, or a wealthy spiritual hedonist playing God, or a film producer, or a recluse.

Those eager to shift intellectual planes for sheer enjoyment may find the pacing too expository and pedantic: those willing enough to be drawn along might crave more optical effects.

. . . .

■ MAHLER

1974, 115 MINS, UK ◇ Ⓥ

Dir Ken Russell   *Prod* Roy Baird   *Scr* Ken Russell   *Ph* Dick Bush   *Ed* Michael Bradsell   *Mus* John Forsythe (co-ord.)   *Art Dir* Ian Whittaker
● Robert Powell, Georgina Hale, Richard Morant, Lee Montague, Rosalie Crutchley, Antonia Ellis (Goodtime)

Mahler is another maddening meeting of Russellian extremes, brilliant and irritating, inventive and banal, tasteful and tasteless, exciting and disappointing.

Flashbacks during composer Gustav Mahler's 1911 train ride to a Vienna deathbed give us glimpses of oppressed youth, childhood memories mirrored in his work, early frustrations as he is forced to conduct so that he can buy time in which to compose, a love-hate relationship with his young wife, a conversion from Judaism to ease his nomination to an important musical post, his constant obsession with death, and so on.

At its frequent best, it mirrors admirably, movingly and even excitingly, the moments of (musical) creation and inspiration, and the torment and basic loneliness of the artist.

. . . .

■ MAIN EVENT, THE

1979, 112 MINS, US ◇ Ⓥ

Dir Howard Zieff   *Prod* Jon Peters   *Scr* Gail Parent, Andrew Smith   *Ph* Mario Tosi   *Ed* Edward Warschika   *Mus* Gary Le Mel   *Art Dir* Charles Rosen
● Barbra Streisand, Ryan O'Neal, Paul Sand, Patti D'Arbanville (Warner/First Artists/Barwood)

Instead of a comic knockout, this is more of a cream puff.

Situation of a bankrupt perfume queen left with a sore-handed fighter as her only asset has comic potential, but producers Barbra Streisand and Jon Peters, and director Howard Zieff, pad the story unmercifully.

Streisand is the garrulous yenta, after the passive and resistant Ryan O'Neal to resume his championship form and win her back the $60,000 she unknowingly wasted on him in her plush days.

Zieff has chosen to emphasize sexual innuendo and result is a low-blow effort that evokes more titters than guffaws. Romantic aspects, which should be chief draw of *Main Event*, are also blunted, until a final seduction scene instigated by Streisand that gives the pic its only resonance.

. . . .

M

■ MAJOR AND THE MINOR, THE

1942, 100 MINS, US

Dir Billy Wilder   *Prod* Arthur Hornblow Jr   *Scr* Charles Brackett, Billy Wilder   *Ph* Leo Tover   *Ed* Doane Harrison   *Mus* Robert Emmett Dolan
● Ginger Rogers, Ray Milland, Diana Lynn, Robert Benchley, Rita Johnson (Paramount)

The Major and the Minor is a sparkling and effervescing piece of farce-comedy. Story [suggested by a play by Edward Childs Carpenter and story by Fanny Kilbourne] is light, fluffy, and frolicsome. Ginger Rogers, disillusioned by New York, decides to head back home to Iowa. Her savings are not sufficient for ticket, she dolls up as a youngster under 12 to ride on half rate. But complications arise that throw her into compartment of Ray Milland, major at a boys' military academy, and into the school for a three-day layover.

During the interim, there's a Cinderella-esque romance developed while Rogers, in the moppet getup, is pursued by the adolescent cadet officers for some rousing laugh episodes.

Both script and direction swing the yarn along at a consistent pace, with the laughs developing naturally and without strain.

■ MAJOR BARBARA

1941, 113 MINS, UK ⊙

Dir Gabriel Pascal   *Prod* Gabriel Pascal   *Scr* George Bernard Shaw, Harold French   *Ph* Ronald Neame   *Ed* Charles Frend   *Mus* William Walton   *Art Dir* Vincent Korda, John Bryan
● Wendy Hiller, Rex Harrison, Robert Morley, Robert Newton, Emlyn Williams, Deborah Kerr (Pascal)

Major Barbara is the second film from the partnership of George Bernard Shaw and Gabriel Pascal. Adapted from an old Shaw play, circa 1905, it still carries the lightning thrusts of Shavian
caustic satire at any and all levels of society.

The script, prepared by Shaw, closely follows his original. Wendy Hiller, daughter of a multi-millionaire sincerely works to save souls as the Salvation Army major in the Limehouse slums. Pecunious Rex Harrison, Greek scholar,
falls in love at first sight.

Hiller is suddenly disillusioned in the Army soul-saving when heavy financial aid is gladly accepted from her munitions-making father and a rich distiller. It's then that the father takes his odd family and stranger menage through his factories, demonstrating he is doing more to improve conditions of his workers than could be accomplished in Limehouse.

Hiller, lead in *Pygmalion*, delivers an excellent and personable performance throughout, and does much to carry the story along through some rather dull and weighty passages. Harrison does well as the Greek scholar but secondary acting honors are shared by Robert Morley, as the father, and Robert Newton, a tough limey whose soul is finally saved.

■ MAJOR DUNDEE

1965, 134 MINS, US ◇ ⊙

Dir Sam Peckinpah   *Prod* Jerry Bresler   *Scr* Harry Julian Fink, Oscar Saul, Sam Peckinpah   *Ph* Sam Leavitt   *Ed* William A. Lyon, Don Starling, Howard Kunin   *Mus* Daniel Amfitheatrof
● Charlton Heston, Richard Harris, Jim Hutton, James Coburn, Michael Anderson Jr, Senta Berger (Columbia)

Somewhere in the development of this Jerry Bresler production the central premise was sidetracked and a maze of little-meaning action substituted. What started out as a straight story-line (or, at least, idea) – a troop of US Cavalry chasing a murderous Apache

and his band into Mexico to rescue three kidnapped white children and avenge an Indian massacre – devolves into a series of sub-plots and tedious, poorly edited footage in which much of the continuity is lost.

Sam Peckinpah's direction of individual scenes is mostly vigorous but he cannot overcome the weakness of screenplay of whose responsibility he bears a share with Harry Julian Fink and Oscar Saul. Use of offscreen narration, ostensibly from the diary of one of the troopers on the march, reduces impact and is a further deterrent to fast unfoldment.

Charlton Heston delivers one of his regulation hefty portrayals and gets solid backing from a cast headed by Richard Harris as the rebel captain, who presents a dashing figure. Jim Hutton as an energetic young lieutenant and James Coburn an Indian scout likewise stand out.

■ MAKE WAY FOR TOMORROW

1937, 91 MINS, US

Dir Leo McCarey   *Prod* Leo McCarey   *Scr* Vina Delmar   *Ph* William Mellor   *Ed* LeRoy Stone   *Mus* Boris Morros (dir.)   *Art Dir* Hans Dreier, Bernard Herzbrun
● Victor Moore, Beulah Bondi, Fay Bainter, Thomas Mitchell, Ray Mayer, Barbara Read (Paramount)

Rugged simplicity marks this Leo McCarey production [from a novel by Josephine Laurence and a play by Helen and Nolan Leary]. It is a tear-jerker, obviously grooved for femme fans.

McCarey, who also directed, has firmly etched the dilemma in which an elderly married couple find themselves when they lose their old dwelling place and their five grown-up children are non-receptive. He keeps audience interest focused on old Lucy Cooper and Pa Cooper as they are separated, each finding themselves in the way and not fitting in with the two households (one with a son and the other with a daughter).

Victor Moore essays a serious role as Pa Cooper without firmly establishing himself in the new field. He continues to be more Victor Moore than an old grandfather, and he makes the biggest impression in the lighter, more whimsical moments. Beulah Bondi, as the aged Lucy is standout from the viewpoint of clever character work and make-up. She has some of the meaty scenes and makes them real.

Fay Bainter does splendidly as the wife of George Cooper, one of the sons to whose house the mother goes to live. Maurice Moscovitch, as the ardent listener to the old man's woes and who understands him better than his own children, contributes a neat portrayal.

■ MAKING LOVE

1982, 111 MINS, US ◇ ⓥ

Dir Arthur Hiller   *Prod* Allen Adler, Daniel Melnick   *Scr* Barry Sandler   *Ph* David M. Walsh   *Ed* William H. Reynolds   *Mus* Leonard Rosenman   *Art Dir* James D. Vance
● Michael Ontkean, Kate Jackson, Harry Hamlin, Wendy Hiller, Arthur Hill, Nancy Olson (20th Century-Fox/Indie)

This homosexual-themed domestic drama of a married man's 'coming out' stands up well on all counts, emerging as an absorbing tale.

First half-hour presents Michael Ontkean and Kate Jackson as a successful young LA couple, he a medic and she a fast-rising TV exec. Then Ontkean meets Harry Hamlin, a gay writer whose good looks provide him with enough easy one-night stands to do without any emotional commitment. Ontkean takes the plunge with Hamlin and finds he likes it, so much so that he quickly knows his marriage is finished.

Working from a story by A. Scott Berg, Barry Sandler has penned a fine, aware screenplay.

Director Arthur Hiller has elicited strong performances from his three principals, and he also carries off the device of having the trio directly address the audience with their thoughts from time to time.

■ MALTA STORY

1953, 103 MINS, UK ⓥ

Dir Brian Desmond Hurst   *Prod* Peter de Sarigny   *Scr* William Fairchild, Nigel Balchin   *Ph* Robert Krasker   *Ed* Michael Gordon   *Mus* William Alwyn   *Art Dir* John Howell
● Alec Guinness, Jack Hawkins, Anthony Steel, Muriel Pavlow, Flora Robson, Renee Asherson (Rank)

This is an epic story of the courage and endurance of the people and defenders of the island of Malta. It is handled in grimly realistic but not over-dramatic style. Camerawork is excellent, and some vivid war scenes of attacks on convoys are genuine newsreel shots.

Alec Guinness plays a camera reconnaissance pilot enroute to Egypt. His plane is blown up, leaving him stranded in Malta. He is roped in to continue his activities during the siege of 1942 since his pictures disclose freight trains in Italy packed with gliders obviously intended for an invasion of the island. Jack Hawkins is the air officer in command who stands helplessly by while his airfields are blasted night and day.

A dual love interest impinges rather apologetically upon this war scarred scene, with Muriel Pavlow giving an endearing performance as a Maltese girl in love with her chief, played in a forthright manner by Anthony Steel. Flora Robson gives a distinguished characterization of a steadfast, sorrowing Maltese mother stoically facing the prospect of her son's execution for treason.

Bulk of the acting laurels go to Guinness, who here forsakes his chameleon-like whimsicality for the shy diffident charm of an inexperienced lover.

■ MALTESE FALCON, THE

1931, 80 MINS, US ⓥ

Dir Roy Del Ruth   *Scr* Maude Fulton, Lucien Hubbard, Brown Holmes   *Ph* William Rees
● Bebe Daniels, Ricardo Cortez, Dudley Digges, Una Merkel, Robert Elliot, Thelma Todd (Warner)

Bringing *The Maltese Falcon* to the screen as Warners have done was no easy job. But director Roy Del Ruth lets things take their course and, with a naturally nonchalant although extremely odd private detective in Ricardo Cortez, takes his audience out of the screen story rut for a series of surprise incidents and a totally different finis.

Although four men are murdered and two corpses revealed to the audience, the story treatment [from Dashiell Hammett's novel] and the Cortez smile are such that a quick thrill is permitted, a laugh, and then, through the first 75% of the footage, additionally interest to well-sustained curiosity.

It can't be called naughty, even though Bebe Daniels as Ruth Wonderly spends the second night in the elaborate apartment of this unusual private detective.

The mystery element is so flung about that not until the last reel or so does the most studious follower know who did any of the killings. Meantime a number of clever gags happen through Sam Spade in disarming people, then apologizing; taking money and then having it taken from him; making love one minute and turning the girl over to the police the next.

■ MALTESE FALCON, THE

1941, 100 MINS, US ⓥ
Dir John Huston   *Prod* Hal B. Wallis   *Scr* John
Huston   *Ph* Arthur Edeson   *Ed* Thomas Richards
Mus Adolph Deutsch   *Art Dir* Robert Haas
● Humphrey Bogart, Mary Astor, Peter Lorre, Sydney
Greenstreet, Elisha Cook Jr, Gladys George (Warner)

This is one of the best examples of actionful
and suspenseful melodramatic story telling in
cinematic form. Unfolding a most intriguing
and entertaining murder mystery, picture
displays outstanding excellence in writing,
direction, acting and editing.

John Huston, makes his debut as a film
director. He also wrote the script solo,
endowing it with well-rounded episodes of
suspense and surprise and carrying along
with consistently pithy dialog.

Humphrey Bogart gives an attention-
arresting portrayal that not only dominates
the proceedings throughout but is the major
motivation in all but a few minor scenes.
Mary Astor skillfully etches the role of an adventuress. Sydney Greenstreet, prominent
member of the Lunt-Fontaine stage troupe,
scores heavily in his first screen appearance.

Story in Dashiell Hammett's best style
details the experiences of private detective
Bogart when called in to handle a case for
Astor – shortly finding himself in the middle
of double-crossing intrigue and several murders perpetrated by strange characters bent
on obtaining possession of the famed beje-
weled Maltese Falcon. Keeping just within
bounds of the law, and utilizing sparkling
ingenuity in gathering up the loose ends and
finally piecing them together, Bogart is able
to solve the series of crimes for the benefit of
the police.

☐ 1942: Best Picture (Nomination)

■ MAME

1974, 132 MINS, US ◇ ⓥ
Dir Gene Saks   *Prod* Robert Fryer, James Cresson
Scr Paul Zindel   *Ph* Philip Lathrop   *Ed* Maury
Winetrobe   *Mus* Jerry Herman
● Lucille Ball, Robert Preston, Beatrice Arthur, Kirby
Furlong, Bruce Davison, Joyce Van Patten
(Warner/ABC)

The Lucille Ball version, or reincarnation, of
Mame, lavishly costumed by Theadora van
Runkle, with Jerry Herman's [1966] musical
numbers smartly choreographed by Onna
White is a fantasy of the good old days of
prohibition, the depression and the world
travel folders.

The narrative pretty much follows the
familiar sequence of events. Mame is first
discovered in the midst of prohibition, the
Charleston and progressive education. She
goes down with the market in 1929, tackles
show business, then clerking, is rescued by
the romantic Beauregard and spends the rest
of her life travelling.

A comedy with songs, not a musical
comedy, per se, this *Mame* climaxes with its
foxhunting number in Georgia.

■ MAMMY

1930, 83 MINS, US ◇
Dir Michael Curtiz   *Scr* L.G. Rigby, Joseph Jackson
Ph Barney McGill   *Mus* Irving Berlin
● Al Jolson, Lois Moran, Louise Dresser, Lowell
Sherman, Hobart Bosworth, Mitchell Lewis (Warner)

A lively picture [from the musical *Mr Bones*],
with Al Jolson singing new and old songs,
including among the Irving Berlin new numbers a couple of melodious hits.

Here is a minstrel show on the stage and on
the street – the parade, the blacking up in the
dressing room, and the semi-circle with its
white face interlocutor, songs by the quartet,
jokes by the end men, and dancing. The one

section where Technicolor is employed is on
the extended semi-circle minstrel scene.

Jolson is one of the ends and Mitchell Lewis
the other. Lowell Sherman is the interlocutor,
William West. It's Sherman who starts and
bawls up the works. The show owner's
daughter (Lois Moran) is in love with him,
but he's just fooling around. Sherman does
not resent it even when Jolson makes a jealous play to help along Moran, leaving the
impression he wants the girl himself.

[When Sherman is accidentally shot during
a performance,] Jolson runs away, going
home to see mammy. When mammy tells her
boy to always hold his head up, he rides the
next freight back.

■ MAN, THE

1972, 93 MINS, US ◇
Dir Joseph Sargent   *Prod* Lee Rich   *Scr* Rod Serling
Ph Edward C. Rosson   *Ed* George Nicholson
Mus Jerry Goldsmith   *Art Dir* James G. Hulsey
● James Earl Jones, Martin Balsam, Burgess Meredith,
Lew Ayres, William Windom, Barbara Rush (ABC Circle)

The Man is a compelling and somtimes explosive adaptation of the Irving Wallace bestseller. James Earl Jones portrays the black
man who ascends so unexpectedly and without precedent to the presidency of the United
States.

He gains his top position through the rules
of succession. As president pro tem of the
Senate, he automatically is elevated when the
president and speaker of the House are killed
in the collapse of a building in Germany and
the vice-president, incapacitated by a stroke,
announces he cannot take over the office of
the president.

Jones delivers an honest, forceful characterization of the president who accepts his fate
with humility but discovers his own strength
as a man through learning his own powers to
cope.

■ MAN BETWEEN, THE

1953, 101 MINS, UK
Dir Carol Reed   *Scr* Harry Kurnitz   *Ph* Desmond
Dickinson   *Ed* A.S. Bates   *Mus* John Addison   *Art
Dir* Andre Andrejew
● James Mason, Claire Bloom, Hildegarde Neff,
Geoffrey Toone, Dieter Krause (London)

Carol Reed picks war-torn Berlin for a story
of political intrigue, capitalizing on the
obvious potentialities of the divided capital.

From an original story by Walter Ebert,
Harry Kurnitz fashions a script crammed
with lively suspense values. Atmosphere is
created almost from the opening shot although it takes some time for the plot of sinister
intrigue to emerge clearly.

It is virtually a battle of wits between east
and west, with the Red Zone police striving
to end the trafficking of human bodies into
the Western Zone. The plot is woven around
Claire Bloom, an English girl, who comes to
spend a holiday with her brother, an army
major, and her sister-in-law, a German girl,
and James Mason, an East Berliner who rescues her after she is mistakenly picked up by
Red police.

Best suspense derives from the plot by
Mason to get the girl back to her brother.
The familiar screen chase is heightened by
the contrasting locales.

■ MAN CALLED HORSE, A

1970, 114 MINS, US ◇ ⓥ
Dir Elliot Silverstein   *Prod* Sandy Howard   *Scr* Jack
DeWitt   *Ph* Robert Hauser   *Ed* Philip Anderson
Mus Leonard Rosenman   *Art Dir* Dennis Lynton Clark
● Richard Harris, Judith Anderson, Jean Gascon,
Manu Tupou, Corinna Tsopei, Dub Taylor (Cinema
Center

A Man Called Horse is said to be an authentic
depiction of American Indian life in the
Dakota territory of about 1820. Authentic it
may be, but an absorbing film drama it is
not. Sandy Howard's Durango-lensed production stars Richard Harris as an English
nobleman captured by the Sioux. Captivity
segues to understanding and finally to tribal
membership.

Jack DeWitt's spare-dialog adaptation of a
1950 Dorothy M. Johnson story, features a
lot of non-subtitled Sioux lingo, broken up by
Harris' expository passages with half-breed
Jean Gascon.

Performances are generally good, especially
that of Gascon, while Judith Anderson lends
both pathos and broad comedy in her rendition. Harris is unevenly stiff.

■ MAN FOR ALL SEASONS, A

1966, 120 MINS, UK ◇ ⓥ
Dir Fred Zinnemann   *Prod* Fred Zinnemann
Scr Robert Bolt   *Ph* Ted Moore   *Ed* Ralph Kemplin
Mus Georges Delerne   *Art Dir* John Box
● Paul Scofield, Wendy Hiller, Leo McKern, Robert
Shaw, Orson Welles, Susannah York (Highland/
Columbia)

Producer-director Fred Zinnemann has
blended all filmmaking elements into an
excellent, handsome and stirring film version
of *A Man for All Seasons*. Robert Bolt adapted
his 1960 play, a timeless, personal conflict
based on the 16th century politico-religious
situation between adulterous King Henry
VIII and Catholic Sir Thomas More.

Basic dramatic situation is that of a minister of the crown and his conscience being
challenged by the imperious point of view
which maintains that the lack of explicit support to an erring king is equivalent to disloyalty. This is the usual human dilemma
whenever expediency confronts integrity.

Paul Scofield delivers an excellent performance as More, respected barrister, judge and
chancellor who combined an urbane polish
with inner mysticism. Faced with mounting
pressure to endorse publicly the royal marriage of Henry VIII to Anne Boleyn, More
armed with legalistic knowhow, More out-
foxed his adversaries until 'perjury' was used
to justify a sentence of death.

Robert Shaw is also excellent as the king,
giving full exposition in limited footage to the
character: volatile, educated, virile, arrogant,
yet sensitive (and sensible) enough to put the
squeeze on More via subordinates, mainly
Thomas Cromwell, played by Leo McKern.

Orson Welles in five minutes (here an early
confrontation, as Cardinal Wolsey, with
More), achieves outstanding economy of
expression.

☐ 1966: Best Picture

■ MAN FRIDAY

1975, 115 MINS, UK ◇
Dir Jack Gold   *Prod* David Korda   *Scr* Adrian
Mitchell   *Ph* Alex Phillips   *Ed* Anne V. Coates
Mus Carl Davis   *Art Dir* Peter Murton
● Peter O'Toole, Richard Roundtree, Peter Cellier,
Christopher Cabot, Joel Fluellen, Sam Sebroke
(Keep/ABC/ITC)

Another variation of Daniel Defoe's classic
has Crusoe (Peter O'Toole) discovering his
Friday (Richard Roundtree) after the shipwrecked mariner has brutally shot and killed
the black's companions, washed up on 'his'
island after a storm.

O'Toole's Crusoe proceeds to subdue and
then teach and indoctrinate the 'savage', with
missionary zeal, into the manners and mores
of western society, not forgetting the master-
slave relationship.

Slowly, however, Friday begins to question him, his theories and teachings, soon in effect himself becoming the teacher of newer, freer, more open-minded ideas and ideals.

O'Toole speaks his lighter lines with panache and humor, but becoming very moving indeed when seized by loneliness and despair.

••••••••••••••••••••••••••••

■ MAN FROM HONG KONG, THE

1975, 99 MINS, HONG KONG/AUSTRALIA ◇
Dir Brian Trenchard-Smith *Prod* Raymond Chow, John Fraser *Scr* Brian Trenchard-Smith *Ph* Russell Boyd *Ed* Ron Williams *Mus* Noel Quinlan *Art Dir* David Copping, Chien Sun
● Jimmy Wang Yu, George Lazenby, Ros Spiers, Hugh Keays-Byrne, Roger Ward, Rebecca Gilling (Golden Harvest/Movie)

A Hong Kong policeman (Wang Yu) is sent to Australia to extradite a Chinese courier who works for an international drug syndicate. He gets involved with the syndicate, and, as per usual wipes it out in a final battle that ends with Wang escaping from a towering inferno.

Wang, though lacking the charisma of the late Bruce Lee, does have an aura of realism about him. George Lazenby does little for his image as an actor by appearing as a heavy Mr Big, called Wilton.

The Hong Kong-Australian James Bond hybrid, the first coproduction of its kind, comes off well for a kung-fu pic. There are the usual chases around Sydney, with an unusual kite chase sequence. There is also some excellent aerial photography of both Hong Kong and Sydney.

••••••••••••••••••••••••••••

■ MAN FROM LARAMIE, THE

1955, 102 MINS, US ◇ Ⓥ
Dir Anthony Mann *Prod* William Goetz *Scr* Philip Yordan, Frank Burt *Ph* Charles Lang *Ed* William Lyon *Mus* George Duning *Art Dir* Cary Odell
● James Stewart, Arthur Kennedy, Donald Crisp, Cathy O'Donnell, Alex Nicol, Aline MacMahon (Columbia)

Basically, the plot concerns the search by James Stewart, army captain on leave, for the man guilty of selling repeating rifles to an Apache tribe. The rifles had been used to wipe out a small cavalry patrol to which Stewart's younger brother had been attached so there is a motive of personal vengeance.

Violence gets into the act early and repeats with regularity as Stewart's trail crosses with a number of warped, sadistic characters.

Stewart goes about his characterization with an easy assurance. Arthur Kennedy, Donald Crisp and Alex Nicol are firstrate in their delineations of the twisted people on the ranch. Distaff characters are done by Cathy O'Donnell, good as the girl who wants to escape from the influence of the ranch, and Aline MacMahon, who gives a socko portrayal of a tough old rancher.

••••••••••••••••••••••••••••

■ MAN FROM SNOWY RIVER, THE

1982, 102 MINS, AUSTRALIA ◇ Ⓥ
Dir George Miller *Scr* John Dixon, Fred Cullen *Ph* Keith Wagstaff *Ed* Adrian Carr *Mus* Bruce Rowland *Art Dir* Leslie Binns
● Kirk Douglas, Jack Thompson, Tom Burlinson, Sigrid Thornton, Lorraine Bayly (Edgley/Cambridge)

Here is a rattling good adventure story, inspired by a legendary poem [by A.B. 'Banjo' Paterson] which nearly every Australian had drummed into him as a child, filmed in spectacularly rugged terrain in the Great Dividing Ranges in Victoria.

Kirk Douglas plays two brothers who have had a terrible falling-out for reasons explained late in the narrative. While one brother, the wealthy autocratic landowner

Harrison fits him like a glove, the actor is less believable as Spur, a gruff, grizzled, out-of-luck prospector.

Apparently, Douglas wrote or rewrote some of the dialog; hopefully not some of Spur's groaners like 'It's a hard country, made for hard men'.

Tom Burlinson shines in his first feature film role as Jim, well matched by Sigrid Thornton as Harrison's high-spirited daughter. Jack Thompson shares top billing with Douglas as Clancy, the crack horseman who becomes Jim's mentor.

••••••••••••••••••••••••••••

■ MAN IN THE GRAY FLANNEL SUIT, THE

1956, 152 MINS, US ◇
Dir Nunnally Johnson *Prod* Darryl F. Zanuck *Scr* Nunnally Johnson *Ph* Charles G. Clarke *Ed* Dorothy Spencer *Mus* Bernard Herrmann
● Gregory Peck, Jennifer Jones, Fredric March, Marisa Pavan, Lee J. Cobb, Ann Harding (20th Century-Fox)

This is the story of a young American suburbanite who gets a chance to become a big shot and turns it down because he realizes that he's a nine-to-five man to whom family means more than success.

It's also the story of a man with a conscience, who had a love affair in Rome which resulted in a child. When he tells his wife about it, their marriage almost breaks up.

As the 'Man in the Gray Flannel Suit', Gregory Peck is handsome and appealing, if not always convincing. It is only really in the romantic sequences with Marisa Pavan, who plays his Italian love, that he takes on warmth and becomes believable. Pavan is human and delightful.

Playing opposite Peck as his wife is Jennifer Jones, and her concept of the role is faulty to a serious degree. Jones allows almost no feeling of any real relationship between her and Peck. They never come alive as people.

As the broadcasting tycoon, Fredric March is excellent, and the scenes between him and Peck lift the picture high above the ordinary.

••••••••••••••••••••••••••••

■ MAN IN THE IRON MASK, THE

1939, 110 MINS, US
Dir James Whale *Prod* Edward Small *Scr* George Bruce *Ph* Robert Planck *Ed* Grant Whytock *Mus* Lucien Moraweck *Art Dir* John Du Casse Schulze
● Louis Hayward, Joan Bennett, Joseph Schildkraut, Alan Hale, Warren William (United Artists)

Alexander Dumas' classic, presented for the first time in film form, is a highly entertaining adventure melodrama. Story has a verve in its tale of dual heirship to the throne of France, used by Dumas as basis of his novel. D'Artagnan and the Three Musketeers reappear as stalwart supporters of Philippe, twin brother of Louis XIV, who is tossed into the Bastille with a fiendishly designed locked iron mask.

Louis Hayward, carrying the dual role of the arrogant Louis XIV and the vigorously self-assured Philippe, gives one of the finest dual characterizations of the screen. He vividly contrasts the king's personality, with its slight swish, with the manly and romantic attitude of twin brother Philippe.

Joan Bennett, is capably romantic. Warren William is carefree and colorful.

••••••••••••••••••••••••••••

■ MAN IN THE WHITE SUIT, THE

1951, 97 MINS, UK Ⓥ
Dir Alexander Mackendrick *Prod* Michael Balcon, Sidney Cole *Scr* Roger MacDougall, John Dighton, Alexander Mackendrick *Ph* Douglas Slocombe *Ed* Bernard Gribble *Mus* Benjamin Frankel *Art Dir* Jim Morahan
● Alec Guinness, Joan Greenwood, Cecil Parker, Michael Gough, Ernest Thesiger, Vida Hope (Ealing)

The plot is a variation of an old theme, but it comes out with a nice fresh coat of paint. A young research scientist invents a cloth that is everlasting and dirt resisting. The textile industry sees the danger signal and tries to buy him out, but he outwits them.

Particular tribute must be paid to the sound effects department. The bubbly sound of liquids passing through specially prepared contraptions in the lab is one of the most effective running gags seen in a British film.

Alec Guinness, as usual, turns in a polished performance. His interpretation of the little research worker is warm, understanding and always sympathetic. Joan Greenwood is nicely provocative as the mill-owner's daughter who encourages him with his work, while Cecil Parker contributes another effective character study as her father. Michael Gough and Ernest Thesiger represent the textile bosses who see disaster. Vida Hope makes a fine showing as one of the strike leaders who fears unemployment returning to the mills.

••••••••••••••••••••••••••••

■ MAN OF A THOUSAND FACES

1957, 122 MINS, US
Dir Joseph Pevney *Prod* Robert Arthur *Scr* R. Wright Campbell, Ivan Goff, Ben Roberts *Ph* Russell Metty *Ed* Ted J. Kent *Mus* Frank Skinner *Art Dir* Alexander Golitzen, Eric Orbom
● James Cagney, Dorothy Malone, Jane Greer, Jim Backus, Robert J. Evans, Marjorie Rambeau (Universal)

The title stems from the billing given the late Universal, later Metro, star, Lon Chaney by an alert publicity man. The screenplay, based on a story by Ralph Wheelwright, is mainly concerned with Chaney's complicated domestic problems. His achievements as a consummate artist, while woven into the story, are secondary to his mixed-up private life.

The story, in swift sequences, takes Chaney from his early boyhood to his death of throat cancer. Born of deaf and dumb parents, this is an important emotional factor in Chaney's motivations. Screenplay ranges song-and-dance vaudeville days, two marriages, the birth of his son, early struggles as a Hollywood extra, eventual rise to stardom, and tragic death.

As Chaney, James Cagney has immersed himself so completely in the role that it is difficult to spot any Cagney mannerisms. Jane Greer, as his second wife, is particularly appealing in her devotion to her 'difficult' spouse. Dorothy Malone is fine as the wife who deems her career as a singer more important than raising children. A real heart-tug is provided by Celia Lovsky as Chaney's deaf and dumb mother. Bud Westmore deserves special mention for the excellent make-up jobs on the various characters portrayed by Chaney.

••••••••••••••••••••••••••••

■ MAN OF AFRICA

1954, 73 MINS, UK ◇
Dir Cyril Frankel *Prod* John Grierson *Scr* Montagu Slater *Ph* Denny Densham *Ed* Alvin Bailey *Mus* Malcolm Arnold
● Violet Mukabureza, Frederick Bijurenda, Mattayo Bukwirwa, Butensa, Seperiera Mpambara, Blaseo Mbalinda (Group Three)

Struggle for existence insofar as a native tribe is concerned is leisurely told in *Man of Africa*, a semi-documentary filmed in the more remote parts of Uganda. To the picture's credit it eschews the hoky aspects found in most films lensed in 'darkest Africa', but this British import is often languorous to the point of becoming dull.

Producer of the Group Three picture was noted documentarian John Grierson. It's an interesting phase of African life that he chose to focus upon. But one suspects that a sketchy story contributed by director Cyril Frankel detracts more than adds to the realism.

For, in depicting the migration of a tribe to virgin country after the fertility of their homeland has been exhausted, Grierson has seen fit to include a romance between a clerk-turned-farmer and a native belle.

On the brighter side of the ledger are scenes which show the basic kindness of pygmies who are native to the Kigezi territory. They aid an injured settler and later save his child when malaria strikes the pioneers. If anything this unassuming import shows that even among African natives prejudice thrives upon misunderstanding.

Dialog of the players is in English. Cast is headed by Violet Mukabureza and Frederick Bijurenda who do as best they can in portraying the romantic couple.

●●●●●●●●●●●●●●●●●●●●●●●●●●●●●●●●

■ MAN OF ARAN

1934, 75 MINS, UK

Dir Robert J. Flaherty   *Prod* Michael Balcon
Scr Robert J. Flaherty, Frances Flaherty, John Goldman   *Ph* Robert J. Flaherty   *Ed* John Goldman
Mus John Greenwood
● Colman 'Tiger' King, Maggie Dirrane, Michael Dillane, Pat Mullen (Gainsborough/Gaumont-British)

Colman King, Maggie Dirrane, and Michael Dillane are the central characters. They are not actors, but natives of the barren, sea-beaten islands off the western coast of Ireland, where this picture takes place. They play themselves. The sea is the villain and the quest for food the plot of this peasants-among-peasants picture, which rates high artistically.

Naturally the big item in such a picture is the camerawork. This is splendid. With only drab grays and speckled whites to deal with, the lens has done right by the cause of sheer beauty and rugged grandeur. The Aran natives are pictured as brave and indomitable, unembittered by the rigors of their lot.

Said to have been two years in the making, the film bespeaks a canny technique and an inspirational sympathy on the part of Flaherty and his co-workers. There is practically no dialog except short sentences of warning, advice, comment on the hazards of shark-hunting.

●●●●●●●●●●●●●●●●●●●●●●●●●●●●●●●●

■ MAN OF FLOWERS

1983, 93 MINS, AUSTRALIA ◇ ▼

Dir Paul Cox   *Prod* Jane Ballantyne, Paul Cox
Scr Paul Cox, Bob Ellis   *Ph* Yuri Sokol   *Ed* Tim Lewis
Art Dir Asher Bilu
● Norman Kaye, Alyson Best, Chris Haywood, Sarah Walker, Julia Blake, Bob Ellis (Flowers)

Paul Cox's film, flickering between realism and fantasy, follows the progress of Bremer, a rich naive eccentric (Norman Kaye), whose inherited wealth both protects him from the coldness of the outside world and isolates him from its warmth. He is cocooned in a childlike innocence, dwelling on the sexual exploration of his boyhood.

Man of Flowers opens with an astonishingly erotic strip by Lisa, the model. She strips, nothing more, nothing less. Is her stated affection for him genuine, or is she attracted by his money? Cox keeps the bond teasingly ambiguous.

At times *Man of Flowers* creates Hitchcock-like tension, but when the suspense becomes uncomfortable Cox lets his audience off the hook with a little wry humor. The expected black climax is never allowed to occur.

Kaye delivers a wonderful, understated performance as Bremer and Alyson Best is a delightfully enigmatic Lisa.

●●●●●●●●●●●●●●●●●●●●●●●●●●●●●●●●

■ MAN OF LA MANCHA

1972, 130 MINS, US ◇ ▼

Dir Arthur Hiller   *Prod* Arthur Hiller   *Scr* Dale Wasserman   *Ph* Giuseppe Rotunno   *Ed* Robert C. Jones   *Mus* Mitch Leigh   *Art Dir* Luciano Damiani
● Peter O'Toole, Sophia Loren, James Coco, Harry Andrews, John Castle, Brian Blessed (United Artists/Pea/Europee Associate)

Man of La Mancha, produced in the style of the [1965 Mitch Leigh-Joe Darion] musical play from which it was adapted, is the fanciful tale of Don Quixote, that fictional Middle Ages lunatic living in a personal world of chivalry long-since past. The Arthur Hiller production of Dale Wasserman's book is more a vehicle for music than the narrative.

Peter O'Toole enacts the dual role of Miguel de Cervantes and his classic character, a difficult assignment which the actor undertakes with heroic overtones. Sophia Loren appears in the dual Dulcinea-Aldonza role, and James Coco is Sancho Panza, the ever-faithful squire.

O'Toole persuasively brings to life the demented would-be knight.

Loren, no songbird she, does her own warbling, as does Coco, but O'Toole's numbers actually are sung by Simon Gilbert, a London actor-singer of fine voice.

●●●●●●●●●●●●●●●●●●●●●●●●●●●●●●●●

■ MAN OF THE WEST

1958, 100 MINS, US ◇

Dir Anthony Mann   *Prod* Walter M. Mirisch
Scr Reginald Rose   *Ph* Ernest Haller   *Ed* Richard Heermance   *Mus* Leigh Harline   *Art Dir* Hilyard Brown
● Gary Cooper, Julie London, Lee J. Cobb, Arthur O'Connell, Jack Lord, Royal Dano (United Artists/Mirisch Artists)

The screenplay, from a novel by Will C. Brown, has Gary Cooper as a reformed gunman, now a respected citizen entrusted with the savings of his community. He is on a mission to get the town a schoolteacher when he is robbed of the money by members of his old gang. It is also somewhat by accident that he, and two other victims (Julie London and Arthur O'Connell), wind up taking refuge in the bandits' hideout, which had once been Cooper's, too.

Superficially, the story is simply the account of Cooper's efforts to free himself, London and O'Connell of the outlaws. It is given dimension by the fact that to do this he must revert to the savagery he has foresworn.

Cooper gives a characteristically virile performance, his dominance of the outlaws quietly believable, while London achieves some touching and convincing moments in a difficult role. Lee J. Cobb, a frontier Fagan of demoniac violence and destruction, and Arthur O'Connell, with whimsical grace and gaiety, add considerably to the picture's interest.

●●●●●●●●●●●●●●●●●●●●●●●●●●●●●●●●

■ MAN WHO FELL TO EARTH, THE

1976, 140 MINS, UK ◇ ▼

Dir Nicolas Roeg   *Prod* Michael Deeley, Barry Spikings   *Scr* Paul Mayersberg   *Ph* Anthony Richmond   *Ed* Graeme Clifford   *Mus* John Phillips (dir.)
● David Bowie, Candy Clark, Rip Torn, Buck Henry, Bernie Casey, Jackson D. Kane (British Lion)

Basic plot has David Bowie descend to Earth from another planet to secure water supply for the folks at home. To help achieve this end, he soon uses his superior intelligence to accumulate vast earthbound wealth and power.

It's a story that must be seen and not told, so rich is it in subplots mirroring the 'pure' spaceman's reaction to a corrupt environment. In fact, pic is perhaps too rich a morsel, too cluttered with themes.

Visually and aurally, it's stunning stuff throughout, and Bowie's choice as the ethereal visitor is inspired.

Candy Clark, as his naive but loving mate, performs well in intimate scenes with Bowie, especially the introductory ones, which are among pic highlights.

●●●●●●●●●●●●●●●●●●●●●●●●●●●●●●●●

■ MAN WHO HAUNTED HIMSELF, THE

1970, 94 MINS, UK ◇ ▼

Dir Basil Dearden   *Prod* Michael Relph   *Scr* Basil Dearden, Michael Relph   *Ph* Tony Spratling
Ed Teddy Darvas   *Mus* Michael J. Lewis   *Art Dir* Albert Witherick
● Roger Moore, Hildegard Neil, Alastair Mackenzie, Hugh Mackenzie, Kevork Malikyan, Thorley Walters (Associated British)

Roger Moore plays a conservative, ambitious City business man who is involved in a car smash in which he was guilty of reckless, out-of-character driving. From the moment of his recovery strange things begin to happen. He is apparently in two places at once. He apparently indulges in sharp business practice. He is apparently having an affair with a girl who he has only once met, and casually.

The uncanny situation begins to prey on Moore's mind. Has he an unscrupulous double? Or is it all a figment of his imagination? These are the headaches that prey on Moore and add up to a tense riddle.

Hildegard Neil as Moore's wife has only a cardboard role, but handles the disintegration of her marriage competently.

●●●●●●●●●●●●●●●●●●●●●●●●●●●●●●●●

■ MAN WHO KNEW TOO MUCH, THE

1935, 74 MINS, UK ▼

Dir Alfred Hitchcock   *Prod* Michael Balcon
Scr A.R. Rawlinson, Edwin Greenwood, Charles Bennett, D.B. Wyndham-Lewis, Emlyn Williams   *Ph* Curt Courant   *Ed* H. St. C. Stewart   *Mus* Arthur Benjamin   *Art Dir* Alfred Junge, Peter Proud
● Leslie Banks, Edna Best, Peter Lorre, Frank Vosper, Hugh Wakefield, Nova Pilbeam (Gaumont-British)

An unusually fine dramatic story handled excellently from a production standpoint. Built along gangster lines, but from an international crook standpoint, with a lot of melodramatic suspense added.

Starts at a party in St Moritz. A man is shot during a dance. He whispers to a friend that there's a message in a brush in his bathroom. Friend realizes the dying man was in the secret service and gets the message. Before he can communicate with the police he is handed a note saying his daughter has been kidnapped and will be killed if he talks.

Back to London and the cops can't make the man or his wife say anything. Finally the man locates the gang's meeting place. He discovers that an attempt will be made to kill a famous international statesman at the Albert Hall that night and manages to communicate that news to his wife, although he is held prisoner.

Scene at Albert Hall is highly exciting and beautifully handled. Acting is splendid most all of the way. Leslie Banks is a fine actor, although the assignment is a bit heavy for him. Edna Best looks well but is not convincing in some of the toughest passages. Peter Lorre's work stands out again. He's the gang chief.

●●●●●●●●●●●●●●●●●●●●●●●●●●●●●●●●

■ MAN WHO KNEW TOO MUCH, THE

1956, 119 MINS, US ◇ ▼

Dir Alfred Hitchcock   *Prod* Alfred Hitchcock   *Scr* John Michael Hayes, Angus McPhail   *Ph* Robert Burke
Ed George Tomasini   *Mus* Bernard Herrmann   *Art Dir* Hal Pereira, Henry Bumstead
● James Stewart, Doris Day, Brenda de Banzie, Bernard Miles, Daniel Gelin, Ralph Truman (Paramount)

With Alfred Hitchcock pulling the suspense strings, *The Man Who Knew Too Much* is a good thriller. Hitchcock backstops his mystery in the colorful locales of Marrakesh in French Morocco and in London. While drawing the footage out a bit long, he still keeps suspense working at all times and gets strong performances from the two stars and other cast members. Hitchcock did the same pic under the same title for Gaumont-British back in 1935.

James Stewart ably carries out his title duties – he is a doctor vacationing in Marrakesh with his wife and young son. When he witnesses a murder and learns of an assassination scheduled to take place in London, the boy is kidnapped by the plotters to keep the medico's mouth shut.

Stewart's characterization is matched by the dramatic work contributed by Doris Day as his wife. Both draw vivid portraits of tortured parents when their son is kidnapped. Additionally, Day has two Jay Livingston-Ray Evans tunes to sing: 'Whatever Will Be' and 'We'll Love Again', which are used storywise and not just dropped into the plot.

Young Christopher Olsen plays the son naturally and appealingly.

■ **MAN WHO LOVED CAT DANCING, THE**

1973, 114 MINS, US ◇ ⓥ

Dir Richard C. Sarafian *Prod* Martin Poll, Eleanor Perry *Scr* Eleanor Perry *Ph* Harry Stradling Jr *Ed* Tom Rolf *Mus* John Williams *Art Dir* Edward C. Carfagno

● Burt Reynolds, Sarah Miles, Lee J. Cobb, Jack Warden, George Hamilton, Bo Hopkins (M-G-M)

The Man Who Loved Cat Dancing, supposedly a period western told from a woman's viewpoint, emerges as a steamy, turgid meller, uneven in dramatic focus and development. Crucial flaw is the adaptation by Eleanor Perry.

Marilyn Durham's novel, which gets its offbeat title from the fact that 'Cat Dancing' is the name of Burt Reynold's dead Indian wife, tells how Sarah Miles, fleeing from husband George Hamilton, accidentally witnesses a train robbery and is virtually kidnapped by the gang. Reynolds has his hands full, for about two-thirds of the film, keeping brutish Jack Warden and Bo Hopkins (the latter outstanding) from raping Miles; for the last third, his hands are full of her.

The femme lead role calls less for acting ability than a willingness to be dragged, beaten, stomped on, and abused in a variety of ways.

Lee J. Cobb is the stoic Wells Fargo detective who, with Hamilton in tow, tracks down the surviving bandits to an Indian village.

■ **MAN WHO LOVED WOMEN, THE**

1983, 110 MINS, US ◇ ⓥ

Dir Blake Edwards *Prod* Blake Edwards, Tony Adams *Scr* Blake Edwards, Milton Wexler, Geoffrey Edwards *Ph* Haskell Wexler *Ed* Ralph E. Winters *Mus* Henry Mancini *Art Dir* Roger Maus

● Burt Reynolds, Julie Andrews, Kim Basinger, Marilu Henner, Barry Corbin, Cynthia Sikes (Columbia)

The Man Who Loved Women is truly woeful, reeking of production-line, big star filmmaking and nothing else.

Once again, Burt Reynolds appears as the irresistible, yet sensitive, modern man in search of something fulfilling in his life. This time, Reynolds' angst is examined in flashback from his funeral in the words of his psychiatrist (Julie Andrews). And they are terrible words, to be sure. From the start, the psychobabble she spouts is so stilted and stupid that it raises false hopes that *Women* must surely be a satire, and perhaps a promising one.

Had not director Blake Edwards been fooling around with an 'American extension' of Francois Truffaut's 1977 film of the same title, there probably was a better picture contained here in Reynolds' one really amusing sojourn into a bemused, adulterous affair with Kim Basinger.

She's great as Houston millionaire Barry Corbin's kinky wife, given to stopwatch dalliances in dangerous places.

■ **MAN WHO NEVER WAS, THE**

1956, 103 MINS, UK ◇

Dir Ronald Neame *Prod* Andre Hakim *Scr* Nigel Balchin *Ph* Oswald Morris *Mus* Alan Rawsthorne

● Clifton Webb, Gloria Grahame, Robert Flemyng, Josephine Griffin, Stephen Boyd, Andre Morell (20th Century-Fox)

Of all the fantastic stories to come out of World War II the use by British Naval Intelligence of a corpse to deceive the Germans about the planned invasion of Sicily undoubtedly out-fictions fiction.

The role of Montagu, the 'master planner', is distinctly offbeat for Clifton Webb and, on the whole, he handles it competently.

The star of this show is the corpse which, dressed up as a British marine major, is allowed to float ashore on the coast of Spain. It carries confidential letters with references to the forthcoming invasion of Greece, a ruse which actually fooled the Germans and saved many Allied lives.

Wisely realizing that this painstaking process, however unusual, lacks action and is bound to become tedious after a while, scripter Nigel Balchin [adapting the novel by Ewen Montagu] has introduced the figure of a young Irishman sent to London by the Germans to check on the identity of Major Martin. Gloria Grahame, assigned to be the girlfriend of 'Major Martin', seems an unhappy choice for the part, and she overplays it badly. By contrast, Josephine Griffin, a British newcomer, is completely believable.

■ **MAN WHO SHOT LIBERTY VALANCE, THE**

1962, 123 MINS, US ⓥ

Dir John Ford *Prod* Willis Goldbeck *Scr* James Warner Bellah, Willis Goldbeck *Ph* William H. Clothier *Ed* Otho Lovering *Mus* Cyril J. Mockridge *Art Dir* Hal Pereira, Eddie Imazu

● James Stewart, John Wayne, Vera Miles, Lee Marvin, Edmond O'Brien, John Carradine (Paramount)

The Man Who Shot Liberty Valance is an entertaining and emotionally involving western. Yet, while it is an enjoyable film it falls distinctly shy of its innate story potential.

Director John Ford and the writers have somewhat overplayed their hands. They have taken a disarmingly simple and affecting premise, developed it with craft and skill to a natural point of conclusion, and then have proceeded to run it into the ground, destroying the simplicity and intimacy for which they have striven. The long screenplay from a short story by Dorothy M. Johnson has Stewart as a dude eastern attorney forging idealistically into lawless western territory, where he is promptly greeted by the sadistic, though sponsored, brutality of Valance (Lee Marvin), a killer who owes his allegiance to the vested interests of wealthy cattlemen opposed to statehood, law and order.

The audience instantly senses that Stewart did not fire the fatal shot that gives him his reputation and destines him for political fame. Because the audience knows that: (1) Stewart can't hit a paint can at 15 paces, (2) Stewart has won the heart of the sweetheart of John Wayne, best shot in the territory and a man of few words but heroically alert and forthright. Had the body of the film (it is told in flashback) ended at this maximum point, it

would have been a taut, cumulative study of the irony of heroic destiny.

Stewart and Wayne do what comes naturally in an engagingly effortless manner. Vera Miles is consistently effective. Marvin is evil as they come. There is a portrayal of great strength and dignity by Woody Strode. But the most memorable characterization in the film is that of Edmond O'Brien as a tippling newspaper editor deeply proud of his profession.

■ **MAN WHO WATCHED THE TRAINS GO BY, THE**

1952, 80 MINS, UK ◇ ⓥ

Dir Harold French *Prod* Raymond Stross *Scr* Harold French *Ph* Otto Heller *Mus* Benjamin Frankel

● Claude Rains, Marta Toren, Herbert Lom, Marius Goring, Anouk Aimee, Ferdy Mayne (Stross/Shaftel)

While it varies from the original Georges Simenon novel, this keeps to essentially the same main character about whom the entire plot revolves.

Main figure is Claude Rains, loyal chief clerk to a firm of Dutch merchants, whose world of honesty and integrity is shattered when he discovers that his boss has been misappropriating the company's money to keep a French woman in luxury. But this meek, dutiful servant, who all his life has watched the trains go by to alluring capitals like Brussels and Paris, turns when he discovers his boss is running off with the firm's money. He takes the cash himself and goes to Paris, where he is involved in a series of implausible but exciting adventures with the girl who was at the root of the trouble.

Rains plays the main role of the chief clerk with quiet, dignified restraint. Toren, as the unscrupulous woman, fills the part with a vivid and believable characterization. Marius Goring gives a polished performance as the French detective while Anouk Aimee has a bit as a Paris streetwalker.

■ **MAN WHO WOULD BE KING, THE**

1975, 129 MINS, UK ◇

Dir John Huston *Prod* John Foreman *Scr* John Huston *Ph* Oswald Morris *Mus* Maurice Jarre

● Sean Connery, Michael Caine, Christopher Plummer, Saeed Jaffrey, Shakira Caine (Columbia/Allied Artists)

Whether it was the intention of John Huston or not, the tale of action and adventure is a too-broad comedy, mostly due to the poor performance of Michael Caine.

As Peachy Carnehan, a loudmouth braggart and former soldier in the Indian army, Caine joins forces with another veteran, Daniel Dravot (Sean Connery), to make their fortunes in a mountain land beyond Afghanistan. Connery, in the title role, gives a generally credible, but not very sympathetic, portrayal of the man thrust into potential greatness.

The most redeeming aspect of the film is the performance of Christopher Plummer as Rudyard Kipling, from whose classic story pic is a variation. Despite the small amount of footage he well deserves his star billing.

■ **MAN WITH BOGART'S FACE, THE**

1980, 106 MINS, US ◇ ⓥ

Dir Robert Day *Prod* Andrew J. Fenady *Scr* Andrew J. Fenady *Ph* Richard C. Glouner *Ed* Eddie Saeta *Mus* George Duning *Art Dir* Richard McKenzie

● Robert Sacchi, Franco Nero, Michelle Phillips, Olivia Hussey, Herbert Lom, Misty Rowe (20th Century-Fox)

Clearly and intentionally the picture is a gimmick. Bogart look-alike Robert Sacchi plays Bogart as Bogart himself might have portrayed private eye Sam Marlow, always relating incidents and personalities to stars

M

and films of yesteryear. Producer Andrew J. Fenady, whose script is based on his own novel, has sprinkled his involved plot with a continuous flow of laugh lines. It adds up to a lot of fun.

As the film opens, the star has just undergone facial surgery, and immediately sets up shop as a private eye, hiring Misty Rowe as his luscious but scatterbrained secretary.

The action – and there is plenty of it – is played against some handsome backgrounds, including expensive yachts and the palace-like home of Turkish magnate Franco Nero, with his bevy of belly dancers.

．．．．．．．．．．．．．．．．．．．．．．．．．．．．．

■ MAN WITH THE GOLDEN ARM, THE

1955, 119 MINS, US ▼

Dir Otto Preminger *Prod* Otto Preminger *Scr* Walter Newman, Lewis Meltzer *Ph* Sam Leavitt *Ed* Louis Loeffler *Mus* Elmer Bernstein *Art Dir* Joseph Wright
● Frank Sinatra, Eleanor Parker, Kim Novak, Arnold Stang, Darren McGavin, Robert Strauss
(Carlyle/United Artists)

Otto Preminger's *The Man with the Golden Arm* is a feature that focuses on addiction to narcotics. Clinical in its probing of the agonies, this is a gripping, fascinating film, expertly produced and directed and performed with marked conviction by Frank Sinatra as the drug slave.

Sinatra returns to squalid Chicago haunts after six months in hospital where he was 'cured' of his addiction. Thwarted in his attempt to land a job as a musician, he resumes as the dealer in a smalltime professional poker game.

Eleanor Parker is a pathetic figure as his wife, pretending to be chair-ridden for the sole purpose of making Sinatra stay by her side. A downstairs neighbor is Kim Novak, and the s.a. angles are not overlooked by the camera. Arnold Stang is Sparrow, Sinatra's subservient sidekick with the larcenous inclinations.

It's the story that counts most, however. Screenplay from the Nelson Algren novel, analyzes the drug addict with strong conviction. What goes on looks for real.

Novel titles are by Saul Bass, and the music by Elmer Bernstein deftly sets the mood.

．．．．．．．．．．．．．．．．．．．．．．．．．．．．．

■ MAN WITH THE GOLDEN GUN, THE

1974, 123 MINS, UK ◇ ▼

Dir Guy Hamilton *Prod* Albert R. Broccoli, Harry Saltzman *Scr* Richard Maibaum, Tom Mankiewicz *Ph* Ted Moore, Oswald Morris *Ed* John Shirley, Raymond Poulton *Mus* John Barry *Art Dir* Peter Murton
● Roger Moore, Christopher Lee, Britt Ekland, Maud Adams, Herve Villechaize, Clifton James (U.A./Eon)

Screenwriters' mission this ninth time around was to give the James Bond character more maturity, fewer gadgetry gimmicks, and more humor. On the last item they fumbled badly; and the comparatively spare arrays of mechanical devices seem more a cost-cutting factor.

Story diverts Bond from tracking down a missing solar energy scientist towards the mission of locating mysterious international hit man (Christopher Lee) who uses tailor-made gold bullets on his contract victims. To nobody's surprise, Lee has the solar energy apparatus installed on his Hong Kong area island hideaway. Bond naturally conquers all obstacles, and finds some fadeout sack time for Britt Ekland, the local British intelligence charmer.

．．．．．．．．．．．．．．．．．．．．．．．．．．．．．

■ MAN WITH TWO BRAINS, THE

1983, 93 MINS, US ◇ ▼

Dir Carl Reiner *Prod* David V. Picker, William E. McEuen *Scr* Carl Reiner, Steve Martin, George Gipe *Ph* Michael Chapman *Ed* Bud Molin *Mus* Joel Goldsmith *Art Dir* Polly Platt

● Steven Martin, Kathleen Turner, David Warner, Paul Benedict, Richard Brestoff, James Cromwell (Aspen/Warner)

The Man with Two Brians is a fitfully amusing return by Steve Martin to the broad brand of lunacy that made his first feature, *The Jerk* [1979], so successful.

Plot is a frayed crazy quilt barely held together as if by clothespins. Ace neurosurgeon Martin almost kills beauteous Kathleen Turner in an auto accident, only to save her via his patented screwtop brain surgery technique. Turner proves to be a master at withholding her sexual favors from her frustrated husband, who decides to take her on a honeymoon to Vienna in an attempt to thaw her out.

While there, Martin visits the lab of colleague David Warner and meets the love of his life, a charming woman and marvelous conversationalist who also happens to be a disembodied brain suspended in a jar, her body having been the victim of a crazed elevator killer.

Much humor, of course, stems from the befuddled Martin groveling at the feet of the knockout Turner he comes to call a 'scum queen', but too much of the film seems devoted to frantic overkill to compensate for general lack of bellylaughs and topnotch inspiration.

Martin delivers all that's expected of him as a performer, and Turner is a sizzling foil for his comic and pent-up sexual energy.

．．．．．．．．．．．．．．．．．．．．．．．．．．．．．

■ MAN WITHIN, THE

1947, 86 MINS, UK ◇

Dir Bernard Knowles *Prod* Sydney Box *Scr* Muriel Box, Sydney Box *Ph* Geoffrey Unsworth *Ed* Alfred Roome *Mus* Clifton Parker *Art Dir* Andrew Mazzei
● Michael Redgrave, Jean Kent, Joan Greenwood, Richard Attenborough, Francis L. Sullivan, Ronald Shiner (Gainsborough)

This adaptation of Graham Greene's novel has much to commend it. Most glaring fault is amount of talk used.

Story is told in flashback while Richard Attenborough is undergoing torture in prison. He relates how, as an orphan, he becomes the ward of Michael Redgrave, goes to sea with him and his crew of smugglers and is sharply disciplined because he is a poor sailor. He loathes the life and when he is flogged for an offense he did not commit, his love and admiration for his guardian turn to hate. He takes vengeance by giving him away to the customs men. In the ensuing fight one of the customs men is killed and several smugglers are arrested.

Attenborough flees, taking refuge in a lonely cottage the boy meets the step-daughter of the murdered man who approves his treachery and incites him to give evidence against his former shipmates.

Most mature performance comes from Redgrave who plays the gentleman-smuggler with a sure touch. Attenborough, as the coward, who finds courage, has his moments, but Joan Greenwood is somewhat handicapped by a slow genuine Sussex dialect as Attenborough's real love. Jean Kent is alarmingly modern as an 1820 vamp.

．．．．．．．．．．．．．．．．．．．．．．．．．．．．．

■ MAN WITHOUT A STAR

1955, 89 MINS, US ◇ ▼

Dir King Vidor *Prod* Aaron Rosenberg *Scr* Borden Chase, D.D. Beauchamp *Ph* Russell Metty *Ed* Virgil Vogel *Mus* Joseph Gershenson *Art Dir* Alexander Golitzen, Richard H. Riedel
● Kirk Douglas, Jeanne Crain, William Campbell, Claire Trevor, Richard Boone, Jay C. Flippen (Universal)

Kirk Douglas, in the title role, takes easily to the saddle as a tumbleweed cowpoke who has

a way with a sixgun or the ladies. William Campbell scores as the young greenhorn who learns his cowboying from Douglas and about the wrong kind of women from Jeanne Crain.

The latter is technically skilled in her delineation of a ruthless owner of a big ranch, not above using sex in her determination to keep the range unfenced, but is not quite believable as a sexpot. Claire Trevor is in a character she does well, playing what is, by implication, the town madam with a heart of gold, and with a soft spot in it for the wandering Douglas.

The plot is basic western in this setup of open versus fenced land, but writing variations keep it fresh and the action high as things move towards the climax.

．．．．．．．．．．．．．．．．．．．．．．．．．．．．．

■ MAN, WOMAN AND CHILD

1983, 99 MINS, US ◇ ▼

Dir Dick Richards *Prod* Elmo Williams, Elliott Kastner *Scr* Erich Segal, David, Z. Goodman *Ph* Richard H. Kline *Ed* David Bretherton *Mus* Georges Delerue *Art Dir* Dean-Edward Mitzner
● Martin Sheen, Blythe Danner, Sebastian Dungan, Arlene McIntyre, Missy Francis, David Hemmings (Paramount)

Man, Woman and Child is a sweetly dramatic picture which, unfortunately, reaches so hard for sobs at the end that all logic is suspended.

Despite the problems in the screenplay adaptation of Erich's Segal's novel by Segal and David Z. Goodman, there are still some fine performances here, tautly directed.

Martin Sheen is superb as a happily married husband of Blythe Danner and father of Arlene McIntyre and Missy Francis. But trouble arrives with news that a brief fling of the past in France (seen in flashback with Nathalie Nell) has caused a problem for the present.

Nell has been killed in an accident, leaving a son by Sheen that he never knew about. For Sheen, the only decent thing to do is confess all to Danner and invite the boy to the US for a get-acquainted visit.

Danner is also excellent in her hurt reaction, torn between love for her husband and resentment of the young intruder – young Sebastian Dungan is a real discovery.

But *Man, Woman* concludes with one of those annoying film situations where the characters have several choices of what to do – and select the one that makes the least sense.

．．．．．．．．．．．．．．．．．．．．．．．．．．．．．

■ MANCHURIAN CANDIDATE, THE

1962, 126 MINS, US ▼

Dir John Frankenheimer *Prod* George Axelrod, John Frankenheimer *Scr* George Axelrod *Ph* Lionel Lindon *Ed* Ferris Webster *Mus* David Amram *Prod Des* Richard Sylbert
● Frank Sinatra, Laurence Harvey, Janet Leigh, Angela Lansbury, Henry Silva, Leslie Parrish (United Artists)

George Axelrod and John Frankenheimer's jazzy, hip screen translation of Richard Condon's bestselling novel works in all departments.

Its story of the tracking down of a brainwashed Korean war 'hero' being used as the key figure in an elaborate Communist plot to take over the US government is, on the surface, one of the wildest fabrications any author has ever tried to palm off on a gullible public. But the fascinating thing is that, from uncertain premise to shattering conclusion, one does not question plausibility – the events being rooted in their own cinematic reality.

Manchurian Candidate gets off to an early start (before the credits) as a dilemma wrapped in an enigma: a small American patrol in Korea is captured by the Chinese Communists. Shortly thereafter, the sergeant of the group, Laurence Harvey, is seen being welcomed home in Washington as a Congressional Medal of Honor winner, having been recommended for that award by his captain, Frank Sinatra, who led the illfated patrol.

But something is obviously wrong. Harvey himself admits to being the least likely of heroes, and Sinatra, though he testifies that the sergeant is 'the bravest, most honorable, most loyal' man he knows, realizes this is completely untrue. But why?

The captain's subsequent pursuit of the truth comprises the bizarre plot which ranges from the halls of Congress, New York publishing circles and an extremely unlikely Communist hideout in mid-Manhattan, to a literally stunning climax at a Madison Square Garden political convention.

■ **MANDALAY**

1934, 65 MINS, US
Dir Michael Curtiz   *Prod* Robert Presnell   *Scr* Austin Parker, Charles Kenyon   *Ph* Tony Gaudio   *Ed* Thomas Pratt   *Art Dir* Anton Grot
● Kay Francis, Lyle Talbot, Ricardo Cortez, Warner Oland, Lucien Littlefield, Ruth Donnelly (Warner)

Kay Francis is a girl of doubtful past, present and future who eventually casts her lot with an outcast doctor in what an extra reel may have developed as possible reformation for both.

Picture trips along at a nice pace and except for one spot, toward the end, invites no adverse reaction. This is in connection with the faked suicide of Ricardo Cortez, a gun-runner who leaves an empty poison bottle and an open window in his ship's cabin as evidence of his act.

The audience is let in on the phony suicide, whereas it would have been more effective to spring the surprise and the explanation on the audience the same as on people in the cast, notably Francis.

Much of the action [from a story by Paul Hervey Fox] occurs on a boat bound from Rangoon for Mandalay. Earlier sequences are in the former seaport, where the heroine has been forced into a life of doubtful purity when her gun-runner boyfriend takes a run-out powder. This portion of the story isn't as convincing as it might be. Manner in which Warner Oland browbeats her into working for his joint is anything but convincing, either.

■ **MANDINGO**

1975, 126 MINS, US ◇
Dir Richard Fleischer   *Prod* Dino De Laurentiis   *Scr* Norman Wexler   *Ph* Richard H. Kline   *Ed* Frank Bracht   *Mus* Maurice Jarre   *Art Dir* Boris Leven
● James Mason, Susan George, Percy King, Richard Ward, Branda Sykes, Ken Norton (Paramount)

Based on Kyle Onstott's novel of sexploitation sociology, *Mandingo* is an embarrassing and crude film which wallows in every cliche of the slave-based white society in the pre-Civil War South.

The cornball adaptation is exceeded in banality only by the performances of James Mason, slave-breeder father of son Percy King, who in turn develops what passes for genuine effection for Brenda Sykes, while wife Susan George descends into revenge with Ken Norton, stud slave whom King also has befriended for purposes of pugilistic gambling. Lots of cardboard tragedy ensues.

■ **MANDY**

1952, 92 MINS, UK
Dir Alexander Mackendrick   *Prod* Michael Balcon   *Scr* Nigel Balchin, Jack Whittingham   *Ph* Douglas Slocombe   *Ed* Seth Holt   *Mus* William Alwyn   *Art Dir* Jim Morahan

● Phyllis Calvert, Jack Hawkins, Terence Morgan, Mandy Miller, Godfrey Tearle, Marjorie Fielding (Ealing)

This story of a deaf-and-dumb child has obvious tear-jerking angles which have been freely exploited.

Central character in the yarn, which is based on a novel by Hilda Lewis, *This Day Is Ours*, is a young child who was born deaf and is, inevitably, dumb. Against a background of parental disagreement, the plot traces the methods used in teaching youngsters the art of lip-reading and expression.

The dominating performance comes from little Mandy Miller in the title role. The best adult performance comes from Jack Hawkins who makes the headmaster a vital and sincere character. Godfrey Tearle and Marjorie Fielding as the child's grandparents top a sound supporting cast.

■ **MANHATTAN**

1979, 96 MINS, US Ⓥ
Dir Woody Allen   *Prod* Charles H. Joffe   *Scr* Woody Allen, Marshall Brickman   *Ph* Gordon Willis   *Ed* Susan E. Morse   *Mus* Tom Pierson (arr.)   *Art Dir* Mel Bourne
● Woody Allen, Diane Keaton, Michael Murphy, Mariel Hemingway, Meryl Streep (United Artists)

Woody Allen uses New York City as a backdrop for the familiar story of the successful but neurotic urban over-achievers whose relationships always seem to end prematurely. The film is just as much about how wonderful a place the city is to live in as it is about the elusive search for love.

Allen has, in black and white, captured the inner beauty that lurks behind the outer layer of dirt and grime in Manhattan.

The core of the story revolves around Allen as Isaac Davis, an unfulfilled television writer and his best friends, Yale and Emily, an upper-middle class, educated Manhattan couple. Isaac has lately taken up with Tracy (Mariel Hemingway) a gorgeous 17-year-old, but the age difference is becoming too much of an obstacle for him.

That's especially the case when he meets Yale's girlfriend, Mary, a fast-talking, pseudo-intellectual, expertly played by Diane Keaton, to whom Isaac is instantly attracted.

■ **MANHATTAN PROJECT, THE**

1986, 117 MINS, US ◇ Ⓥ
Dir Marshall Brickman   *Prod* Jennifer Ogden, Marshall Brickman   *Scr* Marshall Brickman, Thomas Baum   *Ph* Billy Williams   *Ed* Nina Feinberg   *Mus* Philippe Sarde   *Art Dir* Philip Rosenberg
● John Lithgow, Christopher Collet, Cynthia Nixon, Jill Eikenberry, John Mahoney, Sully Boyar (Gladden)

Marshall Brickman's *The Manhattan Project* is a warm, comedy-laced doomsday story.

Premise has 16-year-old student Paul Stevens (Christopher Collet) tumbling to the fact that the new scientist in town, Dr Mathewson (John Lithgow), is working with plutonium in what fronts as a pharmaceutical research installation. While Mathewson is romancing Stevens' mom (Jilly Eikenberry), the genius kid is plotting with his helpful girlfriend Jenny (Cynthia Nixon) to steal a canister of plutonium and build an atomic bomb. Their goal: to expose the danger of the secret nuclear plant placed in their community.

Using clever one-liners and many humorous situations, Brickman manages successfully to sugarcoat the story's serious message.

■ **MANHUNTER**

1986, 119 MINS, US ◇ Ⓥ
Dir Michael Mann   *Prod* Richard Roth   *Scr* Michael Mann   *Ph* Dante Spinotti   *Ed* Dov Hoenig   *Mus* The Reds, Michel Rubini   *Art Dir* Mel Bourne

● William L. Petersen, Kim Greist, Joan Allen, Brian Cox, Dennis Farina, Tom Noonan (De Laurentiis/Roth)

Manhunter is an unpleasantly gripping thriller that rubs one's nose in a sick criminal mentality for two hours.

Pic is based upon Thomas Harris' well-received novel *Red Dragon* and deals with a southern former FBI agent (William L. Petersen) who is summoned from retirement to work on a particularly perplexing case, that of a mass murderer who appears to stalk and select his victims with particular care.

Petersen's excellent deductive talents are due, in large measure, to his tendency to deeply enter the minds of killers, to begin thinking like them.

This trick takes the film into interesting Hitchcockian guilt transference territory and Mann's grip on his material is tight and sure. Director is at all times preoccupied by visual chic.

Tom Noonan cuts a massive swath as the killer, who late in the game is surprisingly humanized by a blind girl, played in enormously touching fashion by Joan Allen.

■ **MANITOU, THE**

1978, 104 MINS, US ◇
Dir William Girdler   *Prod* William Girdler   *Scr* William Girdler, Jon Cedar, Tom Pope   *Ph* Michel Hugo   *Ed* Bub Asman   *Mus* Lalo Schifrin   *Art Dir* Walter Scott Herndon
● Tony Curtis, Michael Ansara, Susan Strasberg, Stella Stevens, Jon Cedar, Burgess Meredith (Avco Embassy/Weist-Simon)

This bout between good and Satan includes some scares, camp and better than average credits.

This time the demon is a 400-year-old American Indian medicine man. He's a little devil in the literal sense, thanks to over-exposure to x-rays which has shriveled him into a three-foot tall redskin monster. Until he can make a rather dramatic entrance onto the floor of a hospital bedroom, he can be found – growing as a fetus – on Susan Strasberg's upper back.

Michael Ansara, a modern-day medicine man, is imported from South Dakota to deliver the evil spirit and return him to the place where 400-year-old medicine men hibernate.

Tony Curtis plays a charlatan of the supernatural, reading tarot cards for rich old ladies. He's romantically involved with Strasberg and does most of the coordinating for the exorcism – booking the medicine man, arranging for cooperation from the hospital, etc.

His character is a nice twist – bogus genie in a situation where the unseen powers really are controlling things. But in general Curtis is too serious about it all. Only Burgess Meredith as a befuddled professor of anthropology has any fun with his part.

■ **MANNEQUIN**

1987, 89 MINS, US ◇ Ⓥ
Dir Michael Gottlieb   *Prod* Art Levinson   *Scr* Michael Gottlieb, Edward Rugoff   *Ph* Tim Suhrstedt   *Ed* Richard Halsey   *Mus* Sylvester Levay   *Art Dir* Richard Amend
● Andrew McCarthy, Kim Cattrall, Estelle Getty, G.W. Bailey, Carole Davis, Meshach Taylor (Gladden)

Mannequin is as stiff and spiritless as its title suggests.

A mannequin (Kim Cattrall) is the latest reincarnation of an Egyptian princess who has known Christopher Colombus and Michelangelo in her journey through time. He's an aspiring artist working as a model maker (Andrew McCarthy) and creator of a mannequin which has the likeness of a woman he could easily love – if only she were real.

Night work makes strange bedfellows of McCarthy and Hollywood (Meshach Taylor), the flamboyant near-transvestite who dresses the store windows, and of McCarthy and Emmy (Cattrall), his mannequin. She comes alive when they're alone together, but reverts back to her cold self if anyone else appears.

McCarthy and Cattrall certainly are an attractive couple – when she's alive – but they don't get to do much more than kiss and dance around the store after hours. Comic development is given over to the secondary characters (Taylor, James Spader and the night watchman, G.W. Bailey).

· ·

■ MANPOWER

1941, 100 MINS, US
Dir Raoul Walsh   *Prod* Mark Hellinger   *Scr* Richard Macauley, Jerry Wald   *Ph* Ernest Haller   *Ed* Ralph Dawson   *Mus* Adolph Deutsch
● Edward G. Robinson, Marlene Dietrich, George Raft, Alan Hale, Frank McHugh, Eve Arden (Warner)

There's plenty of rough and rowdy action and dialog in this melodrama, premised on the triangle formula.

Zestful direction of Raoul Walsh cannot be discounted here. He keeps things moving at a fast clip and displays the individual talents of Edward G. Robinson, Marlene Dietrich and George Raft to utmost advantage.

Story tells of the adventures of a construction and maintenance crew for power lines. Raft and Robinson are buddies in the outfit, and when Robinson is burned by a high tension wire he's made foreman of the gang. Dietrich is the daughter of crew-member Egon Brecher, getting parole from a year's stretch in prison. She works in a clip joint, and enacts the role to perfection. Raft tabs her immediately, but Robinson falls in love with her for quick marriage.

First third of the picture displays racy action and spicy dialog for maximum attention, and then drifts into formula triangle dramatics. Robinson delivers a vivid portrayal as the foreman-lineman who manhandles the gals too fast until he meets Dietrich. Latter provides a stereotyped performance as the clip-joint inmate, and sings one song chorus throatily.

· ·

■ MAN'S FAVORITE SPORT?

1964, 120 MINS, US ◇ ⓥ
Dir Howard Hawks   *Prod* Howard Hawks   *Scr* John Fenton Murray, Steve McNeil   *Ph* Russell Harlan   *Ed* Stuart Gilmore   *Mus* Henry Mancini   *Art Dir* Alexander Golitzen, Tambi Larsen
● Rock Hudson, Paula Prentiss, Maria Perschy, John McGiver, Charlene Holt, Roscoe Karns (Universal)

The comically ripe premise from the story *The Girl Who Almost Got Away* by Pat Frank, is what happens when a celebrated but fraudulent piscatorial authority and fishing equipment salesman for Abercrombie & Fitch who doesn't know how to fish is suddenly ordered by his unaware boss to compete in a fishing tournament?

For a while, the adventures of this angler (Rock Hudson) romp along with a kind of breezy *Field & Stream* charm, bolstered by some inventive slapstick ideas, cleverly devised characters and occasionally sharp dialog. But then, poof, the fish story begins to sag under the weight of its bulky romantic midsection and lumbers along tediously and repetitiously to a long overdue conclusion.

Matters are helped along somewhat by an attractive and spirited cast, but not enough to keep the film consistently amusing.

Hawks purportedly utilized unorthodox directorial techniques, such as filming in sequence a day at a time in order to capture an air of comic spontaneity. Since some of the sight gag passages are uproarious, there is a lot to be said for this technique. But it appears that the main trouble with Hawks' day-at-a-time approach to comedy is that there were too many days or not enough comedy or a combination of both.

· ·

■ MANSLAUGHTER

1930, 82 MINS, US
Dir George Abbott   *Scr* George Abbott   *Ph* Archie J. Stout   *Art Dir* Otto Lovering
● Claudette Colbert, Fredric March, Emma Dunn, Natalie Moorhead, Richard Tucker (Paramount Publix)

This is a remake of a 1922 silent with Thomas Meighan doing the d.a. role which Fredric March now has. Leatrice Joy in the silent version of the Alice Duer Miller *SatEvePost* story gives way to Claudette Colbert.

George Abbott, in adapting and directing, has endeavored to overcome some of the banalities which, in 1922, were standard. Instead of following the original hoke situation of the candidate-for-governor-hero previously re-encountering, on a breadline, the girl he sent to prison, March is shown doing a mild stooge bum, but coming back into private law practice without the old hokum bucket trimmings.

The aftermath of maid and mistress meeting on equal terms in jail is retained and rather convincingly carried through, but in between there's much that's boloney.

Colbert follows through the original idea of a snobbish characterization, remade by her prison experience, although it's still a grand excuse for a fashion-parade.

· ·

■ MARATHON MAN

1976, 125 MINS, US ◇ ⓥ
Dir John Schlesinger   *Prod* Robert Evans, Sidney Beckerman   *Scr* William Goldman   *Ph* Conrad Hall   *Ed* Jim Clark   *Mus* Michael Small   *Art Dir* Richard MacDonald
● Dustin Hoffman, Laurence Olivier, Roy Scheider, William DeVane, Marthe Keller, Fritz Weaver (Paramount)

Film spends literally half of its length getting some basic plot pieces [from the novel by William Goldman] fitted and moving. By which time it's asking a lot if anybody still cares why Dustin Hoffman's brother Roy Scheider is a mysterious globetrotter; why Laurence Olivier as an ex-Nazi disguises his appearance to leave a jungle hideaway to go to NY; why US secret agent William DeVane seems in league with Olivier and his goons, Richard Bright and Marc Lawrence; why Marthe Keller throws herself at Hoffman; why the memory of Hoffman's dishonored professor-father, a victim of the McCarthy era, relates to anything.

Hoffman, you see, is stuck in the role of a bewildered man-in-the-middle about whom bodies fall like flies; eventually he gets into the swing of things and kills a few on his own.

· ·

■ MARCH OR DIE

1977, 106 MINS, US ◇
Dir Dick Richards   *Prod* Dick Richards, Jerry Bruckheimer   *Scr* David Zelag Goodman   *Ph* John Alcott   *Ed* O. Nicholas Brown   *Mus* Maurice Jarre   *Art Dir* Gil Parrondo
● Gene Hackman, Terence Hill [= Mario Girotti], Max Von Sydow, Catherine Deneuve, Ian Holm, Jack O'Halloran (ITC-Associated General)

This Foreign Legion adventure caper, replete with international cast and crew, has lots of actionful battle scenes, a few squeamish torture scenes, and beautiful photography on actual locations.

Terence Hill, the Italian actor with the Yankee name, shows a tongue-in-cheek approach to his role that allows him to dominate every scene he's in. Also first rate is Britisher Ian Holm, as El Krim, the fanatic Arab chieftain.

Biggest disappointment is the 'acting' of Gene Hackman who walks listlessly through the major role of a washed-out West Pointer who has given 16 years of his life to the Legion.

This is the film in which Hackman suffered a back injury but there's no indication of it. The most physical activity he undergoes is riding a horse.

· ·

■ MARIA'S LOVERS

1984, 100 MINS, US ◇ ⓥ
Dir Andrei Konchalovsky   *Prod* Bosko Djordjevic, Lawrence Taylor-Mortorff   *Scr* Gerard Brach, Andrei Konchalovsky, Paul Zindel, Marjorie David   *Ph* Juan Ruiz-Anchia   *Ed* Jeanine Opewall   *Mus* Gary S. Renal   *Art Dir* David Brisbin
● Nastassja Kinski, John Savage, Robert Mitchum, Keith Carradine, Anita Morris, Bud Cort (Cannon)

The first American feature film by Russian director Andrei Konchalovsky, *Maria's Lovers* is a turbulent, quite particularized period romance about the sometime lack of synchronization of love and sex.

Opening sequence makes use of excerpts from John Huston's great postwar US Army documentary *Let There Be Light* to introduce the phenomenon of returning soldiers with psychological disabilities. Climaxing this is a mock verite interview with vet John Savage, who survived a Japanese prison camp and is terribly glad to be home in smalltown Pennsylvania.

His grizzled father Robert Mitchum gives Savage an understated welcome, and latter then has the misfortune of dropping by the home of his great love, Nastassja Kinski, just as she turns up in the grasp of another soldier, Vincent Spano.

Spano finally backs off, leaving the childhood sweethearts free to marry in a Russian Orthodox service.

Konchalovsky's storytelling proceeds at a smooth pace and contains certain interesting wrinkles, such as Mitchum's discouraging his son from pursuing Kinski because he himself is secretly interested in her.

· ·

■ MARIE

1985, 112 MINS, US ◇ ⓥ
Dir Roger Donaldson   *Prod* Frank Capra Jr   *Scr* John Briley   *Ph* Chris Menges   *Ed* Neil Travis   *Mus* Francis Lai   *Art Dir* Ron Foreman
● Sissy Spacek, Jeff Daniels, Keith Szarabajka, Morgan Freeman, Fred Thompson, Lisa Banes (De Laurentiis)

Marie is a powerfully-made political melodrama, the many strengths of which are vitiated only by the relative familiarity of the expose, little person-vs.-the establishment framework. Sissy Spacek adds another excellent characterization to her credits.

Based on a book [*Marie: A True Story*] by Peter Maas, tale opens in 1968 with a rough scene in which Spacek and her small kids leave home after she is brutalized by her husband. Five years later, after educating herself further, she gets a job as extradition director and, before long, is appointed chairman of the parole board for the State of Tennessee.

Helping guide her up the twisting stairway of the political system is ostensible friend Jeff Daniels, a close aide of Governor Blanton who frequently comes to Spacek with overt suggestions that she speed through the parole of certain individuals.

John Briley has set the story down in cogent fashion, and director Donaldson has brought tremendous freshness to its telling.

Spacek is right at home with her role while Jeff Daniels is outstanding as her duplicitous associate.

● ●

■ MARIE ANTOINETTE

1938, 160 MINS, US

Dir W.S. Van Dyke *Prod* Hunt Stromberg
Scr Claudine West, Donald Ogden Stewart, Ernest Vajda *Ph* William Daniels *Ed* Robert J. Kern
Mus Herbert Stothart *Art Dir* Cedric Gibbons, William A. Horning
● Norma Shearer, Tyrone Power, John Barrymore, Robert Morley, Anita Louise, Joseph Schildkraut (M-G-M)

Produced on a scale of incomparable splendor and extravagance, *Marie Antoinette* approaches real greatness as cinematic historical literature.

What is related on the screen is a brilliant, historic tragedy – the crushing of the French monarchy by revolution and terror. Stefan Zweig's biography of Marie Antoinette is the source from which the screenwriters have drawn most of their material.

First part is concerned with the vicious intrigues of the Versailles court and the power exerted by Mme du Barry and the traitorous Orleans. The ensembles, arranged by Albertina Rasch, suggest beautiful paintings. Second portion opens with the expose of the fraudulent sale of a diamond necklace, which precipitated the enmity of the nobility. With an aroused nation and the queen as the point of attack, the action moves swiftly to the pillage of the castle, the royal arrest, the unsuccessful escape to the border, the trials and execution of the rulers.

Norma Shearer's performance is lifted by skillful portrayal of physical and mental transitions through the period of a score of years. Her moments of ardor with Ferson (Tyrone Power) are tender and believable.

Outstanding in the acting, however, is Robert Morley, who plays the vacillating King Louis XVI. He creates sympathy and understanding for the kingly character, a dullard and human misfit.

John Barrymore as the aged Louis XV leaves a deep impress. Joseph Schildkraut is the conniving Duc d'Orleans and scores as a fastidious and scheming menace. Gladys George makes much from a few opportunities as Mme du Barry.

When illness prevented Sidney Franklin from assuming the direction of the film after arduous preparation, W.S. Van Dyke was assigned the task.

● ●

■ MARJORIE MORNINGSTAR

1958, 125 MINS, US ◇ ▼

Dir Irving Rapper *Prod* Milton Sperling *Scr* Everett Freeman *Ph* Harry Stradling *Ed* Folmar Blangsted
Mus Max Steiner *Art Dir* Malcolm Bert
● Gene Kelly, Natalie Wood, Claire Trevor, Everett Sloane, Martin Milner, Ed Wynn (Warner/Beachwold)

There was in the original bestseller of Herman Wouk an attempt to isolate and examine a particular segment of American life, the upper middle class Jewish stratum of Manhattan. Producer Milton Sperling has kept some aspects of the original idea, the characters are still part of their racial and religious background, but the Jewish flavor has been watered down.

Natalie Wood gives a glowing and touching performance as the title heroine. Gene Kelly is moving as her romantic vis-a-vis, Claire Trevor and Everett Sloane are strong in support and Martin Milner is an important younger leading man. Ed Wynn is the stand-out as Marjorie's Uncle Samson.

The title is the clue to story. When Marjorie changes her name from Morgenstern to Morningstar, she unwittingly cuts herself off from the Jewish background and plunges without support into a world of no visible connections and even less stability. She falls in love with Kelly, one of those fascinating men of small talent who flourish in the theatrical fringe of Broadway. He has changed his name, too, from Ehreman to Airman and the resulting rootlessness has left him uneasy and unsatisfied – although he never truly understands why. Marjorie caroms from his rejection to a doctor (Balsam). Always standing by is hard-working playwright Milner.

● ●

■ MARK OF ZORRO, THE

1940, 93 MINS, US

Dir Rouben Mamoulian *Prod* Raymond Griffith
Scr John Tainter Foote, Garrett Fort, Bess Meredyth
Ph Arthur Miller *Ed* Robert Bischoff *Mus* Alfred Newman *Art Dir* Richard Day, Joseph C. Wright
● Tyrone Power, Linda Darnell, Basil Rathbone, Gale Sondergaard, Eugene Pallette, J. Edward Bromberg (20th Century-Fox)

In the 1920s Douglas Fairbanks started his series of historical super-spectacles with *The Mark of Zorro*, a tale of early California under Spanish rule, adapted from Johnston McCulley's story, *The Curse of Capistrano*. In the remake 20th-Fox inducts Tyrone Power into the lead spot.

The colorful background, detailing Los Angeles as little more than a pueblo settlement under the Spanish flag, is utilized for some thrilling melodramatics unfolded at a consistently rapid pace. Picture consumes a third of its footage in setting the characters and period, and in the early portion drags considerably. But once it gets up steam, it rolls along with plenty of action and, despite its obvious formula of hooded Robin Hood who terrorizes the tax-biting officials of the district to finally triumph for the peons and caballeros, picture holds plenty of entertainment.

Power is not Fairbanks (the original screen Hood) but, fortunately, neither the script nor direction forces him to any close comparison. He's plenty heroic and sincere in his mission, and delays long enough en route for some romantic interludes with the beauteous Linda Darnell.

After an extensive education in the Spanish army in Madrid, Power returns to California to find his father displaced as Alcalde of Los Angeles by thieving J. Edward Bromberg. Latter, with aid of post captain Basil Rathbone and his command, terrorizes the district and piles on burdensome taxes. Power embarks on a one-man Robinhoodian campaign of wild riding and rapier-wielding to clean up the situation and restore his father to his rightful position. And there's a sweet romance with Darnell, niece of Bromberg, who is unsympathetic to his policies.

Sword duel between Power and Rathbone, running about two minutes, is a dramatic highlight.

● ●

■ MARLOWE

1969, 95 MINS, US ◇

Dir Paul Bogart *Prod* Gabriel Katzka, Sidney Beckerman *Scr* Stirling Silliphant *Ph* William H. Daniels *Ed* Gene Ruggiero *Mus* Peter Matz *Art Dir* George W. Davis, Addison Hehr
● James Garner, Gayle Hunnicutt, Carroll O'Connor, Rita Moreno, Sharon Farrell, Bruce Lee (Katzka-Berne/Cherokee/Beckerman)

Raymond Chandler's private eye character, Philip Marlowe, is in need of better handling if he is to survive as a screen hero. *Marlowe*, is a plodding, unsure piece of socalled sleuthing in which James Garner can never make up his mind whether to play it for comedy or hardboil.

Stirling Silliphant's adaptation of *The Little Sister* comes out on the confused side, with too much unexplained action. Garner as the private eye is hired by a girl from Kansas to find her missing brother, then finds himself involved in a maze in which he's as mystified as the spectator.

Garner walks through the picture mostly with knotted brow, but Gayle Hunnicutt as the actress is nice to look at toward the end. Rita Moreno as a strip dancer delivers soundly, but a peeler does not a picture make.

● ●

■ MARNIE

1964, 130 MINS, US ◇ ▼

Dir Alfred Hitchcock *Prod* Alfred Hitchcock *Scr* Jay Presson Allen *Ph* Robert Burks *Ed* George Tomasini *Mus* Bernard Herrmann *Art Dir* Robert Boyle
● Tippi Hedren, Sean Connery, Diane Baker, Martin Gabel, Louise Latham, Bruce Dern (Universal)

Marnie is the character study of a thief and a liar, but what makes her tick remains clouded even after a climax reckoned to be shocking but somewhat missing its point.

Tippi Hedren, whom Hitchcock intro'd in *The Birds* returns in a particularly demanding role and Sean Connery makes his American film bow, as the two principal protagonists in this adaptation of Winston Graham's best-seller. Complicated story line offers Hedren as a sexy femme who takes office jobs, then absconds with as much cash as she can find in the safe, changing color of her tresses and obtaining new employment for similar purposes. Plot becomes objective when she is recognized by her new employer, book publisher Connery, as the girl who stole $10,000 from a business associate, and rather than turn her in marries her.

That's merely the beginning, and balance of unfoldment dwells on husband's efforts to ferret mystery on why she recoils from the touch of any man – himself included – and why other terrors seem to overcome her.

Hedren, undertaking role originally offered Grace Kelly for a resumption of her screen career, lends credence to a part never sympathetic. It's a difficult assignment which she fulfills satisfactorily, although Hitchcock seldom permits her a change of pace which would have made her character more interesting. Connery handles himself convincingly, but here, again, greater interest would have resulted from greater facets of character as he attempts to explore femme's unexplained past.

● ●

■ MAROC 7

1967, 91 MINS, UK

Dir Gerry O'Hara *Prod* John Gale, Leslie Phillips
Scr David Osborn *Ph* Kenneth Talbot *Ed* John Jympson *Mus* Kenneth V. Jones, Paul Ferris *Art Dir* Seamus Flannery
● Gene Barry, Cyd Charisse, Elsa Martinelli, Leslie Phillips, Denholm Elliott, Alexandra Stewart (Cyclone/Rank)

The cops-and-robbers thriller lacks the necessary for such a subject. Writer David Osborn's main ace is to make most of his leading characters suspect, although cinemagoers will often be in doubt as to whether the characters are goodies or baddies and the answer never offers much of a kick. Performances are mainly smooth but do not engineer much excitement. On the other hand, the genuine Moroccan backgrounds give a colorful zest to the action.

Story has Cyd Charisse as a sophisticated editress of a fashionable magazine. Her frequent trips abroad with a photographic team and a bunch of leggy, photogenic models are ostensibly for magazine layouts, but actually

M

are a front for daring jewel robberies. Her chief model (Elsa Martinelli) and her cameraman-partner (Leslie Phillips) are both in on the murky deals.

Suspecting this, special cop Gene Barry poses as a thief, uses a blackmailing technique and forces Charisse to let him tag along on her latest trip to Morocco, where she's got her predatory eye on a priceless medallion.

● ●

■ MAROONED

1969, 134 MINS, US ◇ ⓣ

Dir John Sturges *Prod* Mike Frankovich *Scr* Mayo Simon *Ph* Daniel Fapp *Ed* Walter Thompson *Mus* [none] *Art Dir* Lyle R. Wheeler
● Gregory Peck, Richard Crenna, David Janssen, James Franciscus, Gene Hackman, Lee Grant (Columbia)

What happens when a lunar rocket fails to fire for reentry to earth's gravity? The men on such a capsule become lost in space. Such is the situation presented in the gripping drama, *Marooned*, a film, [based on a novel by Martin Cardin] which is part documentary, part science fiction. The film is superbly crafted, taut and a technological cliff-hanger.

The production's major flaw is a hokey old fashioned Hollywood Renfrew-to-the-rescue climax that is dramatically, logically and technologically unconvincing.

For the first four-fifths of his mission, director John Sturges fashions spectacular documentary footage of launchings, on location work at Cape Kennedy, special effects, studio set ups and scenes on close-circuit TV into an edge-of-the-seat drama in which personalities and human conflicts are never subordinated to the hardware.

● ●

■ MARRIAGE OF A YOUNG STOCKBROKER, THE

1971, 95 MINS, US ◇

Dir Lawrence Turman *Prod* Lawrence Turman *Scr* Lorenzo Semple Jr *Ph* Laszlo Kovacs *Ed* Frederic Steinkamp *Mus* Fred Karlin *Art Dir* Pato Guzman
● Richard Benjamin, Joanna Shimkus, Elizabeth Ashley, Adam West, Patricia Barry, Tiffany Bolling (20th Century-Fox)

Based on a Charles Webb novel, the Lorenzo Semple Jr adaptation features Richard Benjamin as a dull husband given to casual voyeurism, and Joanna Shimkus as his equally confused wife. The bittersweet emotional drama unfolds in parallel with some superb high and low comedy.

Benjamin and Shimkus have an all-too-true marital blandness, disrupted by his predilection for eyeing girls. The hang-up is nowhere near criminal; in fact it's rather innocent. But Shimkus has had it, and packs off to Pasadena where barracuda sister Elizabeth Ashley, who already has emasculated hubby Adam West, begins stage-managing a divorce.

Semple's script is well structured and the dialog is superb. The varying elements of farce and satire are neatly interwoven on the genuine marital tragedy in progress. No element overpowers another nor the overall feel. Lawrence Turman's direction is incisive.

● ●

■ MARRIAGE-GO-ROUND, THE

1960, 98 MINS, US ◇

Dir Walter Lang *Prod* Leslie Stevens *Scr* Leslie Stevens *Ph* Leo Tover *Ed* Jack W. Holmes *Mus* Dominic Frontiere *Art Dir* Duncan Cramer, Maurice Ransford
● Susan Hayward, James Mason, Julie Newman, Robert Paige (20th Century-Fox)

Something appears to have gone wrong somewhere between Broadway, where The *Marriage-Go-Round* sustained itself as a hit

play from October 1958 to February 1960, and Hollywood, where it is just a rather tame and tedious film. There isn't a great deal of novelty or merriment in the Leslie production, which Stevens adapted from his own play.

It rotates laboriously around one joke – the idea that an amorous Amazonian doll from Sweden would match endowments, gene for gene, with a brilliant cultural anthropology professor from the US. Since the prof is a happily-married monogamist, Miss Sweden's forward pass is intercepted right in the shadow of the goal (of bed) posts.

In the role of the professor, James Mason is competent, managing to stay reasonably appealing in a perpetual state of mild flabbergastedness. Susan Hayward does exceptionally well in the role of the wife. Julie Newmar, who won the Antoinette Perry Award as best supporting actress for her Broadway performance as the gregarious glamorpuss from Scandinavia, appears to have misplaced her award-winning attributes. The intimacy of larger-than-life celluloid reveals a queen-sized heap of overacting from the blonde bombshell.

● ●

■ MARRIED TO THE MOB

1988, 103 MINS, US ◇ ⓣ

Dir Jonathan Demme *Prod* Kenneth Utt, Edward Saxon *Scr* Barry Strugatz, Mark R. Burns *Ph* Tak Fujimoto *Ed* Craig McKay *Mus* David Byrne *Art Dir* Kristi Zea
● Michelle Pfeiffer, Matthew Modine, Dean Stockwell, Mercedes Ruehl, Alec Baldwin (Mysterious Arts/Demme/Orion)

Fresh, colorful and inventive, *Married to the Mob* is another offbeat entertainment from director Jonathan Demme.

Storyline's basic trajectory has unhappy suburban housewife Michelle Pfeiffer taking the opportunity presented by the sudden death of her husband, who happens to have been a middle-level gangster, to escape the limitations of her past and forge a new life for herself and her son in New York City.

Opening with a hit on a commuter train and following with some murderous bedroom shenanigans, film establishes itself as a suburban gangster comedy. Demme and his enthusiastic troupe of actors take evident delight in sending up the gauche excesses of these particular nouveau riches, as the men strut about in their pinstripes and polyester and the women spend their time at the salon getting their hair teased.

The enormous cast is a total delight, starting with Pfeiffer, with hair dyed dark, a New York accent and a continuously nervous edge. Matthew Modine proves winning as the seemingly inept FBI functionary who grows into his job, and Dean Stockwell is a hoot as the unflappable gangland boss, slime under silk and a fedora.

● ●

■ MARRYING MAN, THE

1991, 115 MINS, US ◇ ⓣ

Dir Jerry Rees *Prod* David Permut *Scr* Neil Simon *Ph* Donald E. Thorin *Ed* Michael Jablow *Mus* David Newman *Art Dir* William F. Matthews
● Kim Basinger, Alec Baldwin, Robert Loggia, Elisabeth Shue, Armand Assante, Paul Reiser (Hollywood/Silver Screen Partners IV)

The Marrying Man is a stillborn romantic comedy of staggering ineptitude. Author Neil Simon reportedly disowned this film. An awkward flashback structure tells of egotistical toothpaste heir Alec Baldwin falling in love with chanteuse Kim Basinger on an outing in 1948 with his buddies to Las Vegas.

Instead of marrying his beautiful g.f. back in LA (Elisabeth Shue), Baldwin is forced into a shotgun wedding with Basinger by

Armand Assante as Bugsy Siegel, Basinger's main man. Key plot point is that this is Bugsy's 'revenge' for catching Baldwin in the sack with his g.f. Also unbelievable are the duo's several breakups and remarriages.

Lack of chemistry between the two principals is only the first problem with *Marrying Man*. Obvious re-shoots result in an unwieldy package that has the film climaxing with perhaps 30 minutes to go, making it play like an original and a sequel spliced together.

● ●

■ MARTIN

1978, 95 MINS, US ◇ ⓣ

Dir George A. Romero *Prod* Richard Rubinstein *Scr* George A. Romero *Ph* Michael Gornick *Ed* George A. Romero *Mus* Donald Rubinstein
● John Amplas, Lincoln Maazel, Christine Forrest, Elayne Nadeau (Laurel)

Title character in *Martin* is a supposed 84-year-old vampire whose youthful visage has survived his escape from Rumania through his contemporary journey to Braddock, Pa, where grandfather Lincoln Maazel is determined to drive out 'Nosferatu', with Martin as the last remaining relative afflicted with the family curse.

This urban vampire kills not with his teeth, but with prepackaged razor blades, neatly slicing veins and arteries for his mealtime pleasure.

Pittsburgh-based auteur George A. Romero is still limited by apparently low budgets. But he has inserted some sepia-toned flashback scenes of Martin in Rumania that are extraordinarily evocative, and his direction of the victimization scenes shows a definite flair for suspense.

● ●

■ MARTY

1955, 93 MINS, US ⓣ

Dir Delbert Mann *Prod* Harold Hecht *Scr* Paddy Chayefsky *Ph* Joseph LaShelle *Ed* Alan Crosland Jr *Mus* Roy Webb
● Ernest Borgnine, Betsy Blair, Esther Minciotti, Augusta Ciolli, Joe Mantell, Karen Steele (United Artists)

Based on Paddy Chayefsky's teleplay, and screenplayed by the author, *Marty* has been fashioned into a sock picture. It's a warm, human, sometimes sentimental and an enjoyable experience. Although filmed on a modest budget (reportedly about $300,000), there is no evidence of any stinting in the production values.

Basically, it's the story of a boy and girl, both of whom consider themselves misfits in that they are unable to attract members of the opposite sex. The boy is sensitively played by Ernest Borgnine and the girl is beautifully played by Betsy Blair.

Chayefsky has caught the full flavor of bachelor existence in a Bronx Italian neighborhood. The meetings at a bar and grill, the stag-attended dances, the discussions about girls and 'what do we do tonight?' poser ring with authenticity.
□ 1955: Best Picture

● ●

■ MARY OF SCOTLAND

1936, 123 MINS, US ⓣ

Dir John Ford *Prod* Pandro S. Berman *Scr* Dudley Nichols *Ph* Joseph H. August *Mus* Maurice de Packh *Art Dir* Van Nest Polglase, Carroll Clark
● Katherine Hepburn, Frederic March, Florence Eldridge, Douglas Walton, John Carradine (RKO)

When RKO set about the task of transmuting this Maxwell Anderson-Theatre Guild play to the screen, it had two possibilities. Could have softened the story and played up the business of a woman who threw away her kingdom for love and thus sold the picture as sheer entertainment; or it could have taken the hard way, telling the story beautifully, artistically, delicately, with meticulous attention to detail and portrayal. Having decided to do it the latter way, there can be nothing but credit to the production.

The really curious point about the film is its casting. On the face of it, Katharine Hepburn would seem to be the wrong choice for the character of the Scots queen. She is nowhere as hard as she should be, she nowhere shows the strength of courage and decision that the school-books talk of. And that is all in the film's favor because it humanizes it all.

Frederic March as Hepburn's vis-a-vis in the role of the swashbuckling Bothwell is a natural and excellent choice, playing the slap-dash earl to the hilt. Florence Eldridge as Elizabeth is again a questionable choice from a strict historical standpoint. She, too, turns in such a fine acting job as to convince quite definitely of the wisdom of it.

In handling the photography and physical production, Ford put emphasis on shadows, several times achieving surprisingly strong effects.

· ·

■ **MARY POPPINS**

1964, 140 MINS, US ◇ Ⓥ

Dir Robert Stevenson   *Prod* Walt Disney, Bill Walsh
Scr Bill Walsh, Don DaGradi   *Ph* Edward Colman
Ed Cotton Warburton   *Mus* Richard M. Sherman,
Robert B. Sherman   *Art Dir* Carroll Clark, William H.
Tuntke
● Julie Andrews, Dick Van Dyke, David Tomlinson,
Glynis Johns, Karen Dotrice, Elsa Lanchester (Walt
Disney)

Disney has gone all-out in his dream-world rendition [from the books by P.L. Travers] of a magical Engish nanny who one day arrives on the East Wind and takes over the household of a very proper London banker. Besides changing the lives of everyone therein, she introduces his two younger children to wonders imagined and possible only in fantasy.

Among a spread of outstanding songs perhaps the most unusual is 'Chim-Chim-Cheree', sung by Dick Van Dyke, which carries a haunting quality. Dancing also plays an important part in unfolding the story and one number, the Chimney-Sweep Ballet, performed on the roofs of London and with Van Dyke starring, is a particular standout. For sheer entertainment, a sequence mingling live-action and animation in which Van Dyke dances with four little penguin-waiters is immense.

Julie Andrews' first appearance on the screen is a signal triumph and she performs as easily as she sings, displaying a fresh type of beauty nicely adaptable to the color cameras. Van Dyke, as the happy-go-lucky jack-of-all-trades, scores heavily, the part permitting him to showcase his wide range of talents.

☐ 1964: Best Picture (Nomination)

· ·

■ **MARY, QUEEN OF SCOTS**

1972, 128 MINS, UK ◇

Dir Charles Jarrott   *Prod* Hal B. Wallis   *Scr* John
Hale   *Ph* Christopher Challis   *Ed* Richard Marden
Mus John Barry   *Art Dir* Terry Marsh
● Vanessa Redgrave, Glenda Jackson, Patrick
McGoohan, Timothy Dalton, Nigel Davenport, Trevor
Howard (Universal)

A large cast of excellent players appears to good advantage under the direction of Charles Jarrott. Superior production details and the cast help overcome an episodic, rambling story.

Mary Stuart (Vanessa Redgrave) emerges as a romantic, immature but idealistic young woman. Her perilous position was repeatedly confounded by the machinations of half-brother (later King) James Stuart (played by

Patrick McGoohan), the blunt but well-meant efforts of eventual husband and lover Lord Bothwell (Nigel Davenport), the paranoid homosexual, and bisexual inclinations of second husband Henry Darnley (Timothy Dalton), and the low-key, amiable clerical advisor, David Riccio (Ian Holm).

Elizabeth (Glenda Jackson) in contrast had a well-oiled machine of intrigue: advisor William Cecil (Trevor Howard), a power-hungry, lover Robert Dudley (Daniel Massey), and the corrupt cooperation of McGoohan and other Scottish factions.

The result of such a dramatic imbalance renders Redgrave's character that of a storm-tossed waif, while Jackson benefits from a far more well-defined character.

The face-to-face confrontations between the two women are said to be historically inaccurate. The script almost has to have one, and these brief climactic encounters are electric.

· ·

■ **M*A*S*H**

1970, 116 MINS, US ◇ Ⓥ

Dir Robert Altman   *Prod* Ingo Preminger   *Scr* Ring
Lardner Jr   *Ph* Harold E. Stone   *Ed* Danford B.
Greene   *Mus* Johnny Mandel   *Art Dir* Jack Martin
Smith
● Elliott Gould, Donald Sutherland, Tom Skerritt, Sally
Kellerman, Jo Ann Pflug, Rene Auberjonois
(20th Century-Fox/Aspen)

A Mobile Army Surgical Hospital (M*A*S*H) two minutes from bloody battles on the 38th Parallel of Korea, is an improbable setting for a comedy, even a stomach-churning, gory, often tasteless, but frequently funny black comedy.

Elliott Gould, Donald Sutherland and Tom Skerritt head an extremely effective, low-keyed cast of players whose skillful subtlety eventually rescue an indecisive union of script and technique.

Gould is the totally unmilitary but arrogantly competent, supercool young battlefield surgeon, a reluctant draftee whose credo is let's get the job done and knock off all this Army muck.

The sardonic, cynical comments of the doctors and nurses patching and stitching battle-mangled bodies and casually amputating limbs before sending their anonymous patients out may be distasteful to some. It has the sharp look of reality when professionals become calloused from working 12 hours at a stretch to keep up with the stream of casualties from the battlefield.

☐ 1970: Best Picture (Nomination)

· ·

■ **MASK**

1985, 120 MINS, US ◇ Ⓥ

Dir Peter Bogdanovich   *Prod* Martin Starger
Scr Anna Hamilton Phelan   *Ph* Laszlo Kovacs
Ed Barbara Ford   *Art Dir* Norman Newberry
● Cher, Sam Elliott, Eric Stoltz, Estelle Getty, Richard
Dysart, Laura Dern (Universal)

Based on a true story, *Mask* is alive with the rhythms and textures of a unique life. Rocky Dennis (Eric Stoltz) is a 16-year-old afflicted with a rare bone disease which has ballooned his head to twice its normal size and cast the shadow of an early death over him.

Rocky is one of those rare individuals who has a vitality and gift for life and the emphasis here is not on dying, but living. The irony of the title is that his feelings are exposed far more than is customary and his experiences are intensified rather than dulled.

One of the accomplishments of *Mask* is the fullness of the environment it creates. Foremost in that portrait is Rocky's mother Rusty (Cher) and her motorcycle-gang friends.

Both in the background and foreground, *Mask* draws a vivid picture of life among a particular type of lower middle class Southern California whites.

Much of the credit for keeping the film from tripping over itself must go to the cast, especially Stoltz, who, with only his eyes visible behind an elaborate makeup job, brings a lively, life-affirming personality to his role without a trace of self-pity. Equally fine is Cher, who perfectly suggests a hard exterior covering a wealth of conflicting and confused feelings.

· ·

■ **MASK OF DIMITRIOS, THE**

1944, 96 MINS, US

Dir Jean Negulesco   *Prod* Henry Blanke   *Scr* Frank
Gruber   *Ph* Arthur Edeson   *Ed* Frederick Richards
Mus Adolph Deutsch   *Art Dir* Ted Smith
● Sydney Greenstreet, Zachary Scott, Faye Emerson,
Peter Lorre, Victor Francen (Warner)

Backgrounded with international intrigues, *The Mask of Dimitrios* has an occasional element of suspense, but those moments are comparatively few.

Dimitrios, which traces the year-long international criminal career of one Dimitrios Makropoulos (played by Zachary Scott), has the benefit of a good cast headed by Sydney Greenstreet and Peter Lorre, but it is mostly a conversational piece that too frequently suggests action in the dialog where, actually, the film itself practically has none.

Talky script [from the novel by Eric Ambler] slows the pace to a walk. Greenstreet and Lorre are capital as a criminal and mystery writer, respectively, while Scott gives a plausible performance as the titular character. The rest are mainly bits.

· ·

■ **MASK OF FU MANCHU, THE**

1932, 66 MINS, US

Dir Charles Brabin   *Scr* Irene Kuhn, Edgar Allan Woolf,
John Willard   *Ph* Tony Gaudio   *Ed* Ben Lewis
● Boris Karloff, Lewis Stone, Karen Morley, Charles
Starrett, Myrna Loy, Jean Hersholt (M-G-M)

Fu Manchu's latest mission is discovery of the tomb of Genghis Khan. Possession of the mask and sword of Genghis would give Fu the leadership of the East. Then he could lead his subjects on to victory in the western world, with ultimate extermination of the white race which he fanatically despises.

Fu (Boris Karloff) has a daughter (Myrna Loy) who's not so pleasant herself. After pop is through torturing the best looking white men for his own purpose, daughter gets 'em for hers. She has the biggest boudoir couch this side of Peking, and pop doesn't object.

So that Fu doesn't get to the late Genghis' paraphernalia first, Scotland Yard dispatches a museum expedition to the spot. After that it's a contest over the tomb's contents. Just as Lewis Stone, as Inspector Nayland Smith of Scotland Yard, is about to be lowered into the cavernous mouths of a troupe of starving crocodiles he manages to escape.

Everybody is handicapped by the story and situations [from the story by Sax Rohmer]. It's strange how bad such troupers as Stone and Jean Hersholt can look when up against such an assignment as this.

· ·

■ **MASQUE OF THE RED DEATH, THE**

1964, 86 MINS, US ◇ Ⓥ

Dir Roger Corman   *Prod* Roger Corman   *Scr* Charles
Beaumont, R. Wright Campbell   *Ph* Nicolas Roeg
Ed Ann Chegwidden   *Mus* David Lee   *Art Dir* Robert
Jones
● Vincent Price, Hazel Court, Jane Asher, David
Weston, Patrick Magee, Nigel Green (American
International)

Roger Corman has garmented his film, lensed in England, with prodution values. His color camera work, his sets, music and plot unfoldment itself – if the latter is vague and a bit involved it still fits into the pattern

M

intended – establish an appropriate mood for pic's tale of terror and in addition it's evident Corman doesn't take his subject [based on stories by Edgar Allan Poe] too seriously.

Vincent Price is the very essence of evil, albeit charming when need be, and as film progresses the dark workings of his mind are stressed, tortuously intent on evil as a follower of the Devil. He plays Prince Prospero, a tyrannical power in Spain in the Middle Ages, who seizes a young girl and tries to make her choose between his saving the life of her beloved or her father, even as the Red Death is killing off most of his impoverished serfs. A strange and uninvited guest to the Bacchanalian orgy he is staging for his noble guests stalks through the festivities to transform the Masque Ball into a Dance of Death.

• •

■ MASQUERADE

1965, 102 MINS, UK ◇

Dir Basil Dearden   *Prod* Michael Relph   *Scr* William Goldman, Michael Relph   *Ph* Otto Heller   *Ed* John Gutheridge   *Mus* Philip Green
● Cliff Robertson, Jack Hawkins, Marisa Mell, Christopher Witty, Bill Fraser, Michel Piccoli (United Artists)

Michael Relph and Basil Dearden have had themselves a ball with *Masquerade*, for once forgetting the sociological themes which they often blend with their dramas, and turning out a clever, tongue-in-cheek spoof of the cloak-and-dagger yarns.

Relph and William Goldman have jettisoned much of the earnestness of the Victor Canning novel, *Castle Minerva*, retaining mainly the plotline and characters.

The story involves kidnapping, disguised identity, macabre doings in a travelling circus, a mysterious Spanish girl and escape from an eerie castle.

The British Foreign Office hires Jack Hawkins and Cliff Robertson for a daring mission. Hawkins is an ex-war colonel and hero. In this film, he obviously relishes being able to spoof the sort of stiff upper lip roles that so often he has to play seriously. Robertson is an American soldier of fortune who is down on his luck. Their job is to abduct the young heir to the throne of a Near East state and keep him under wraps for a few weeks until he comes of age and is able to sign a favourable oil concession to Britain.

• •

■ MASQUERADE

1988, 91 MINS, US ◇ Ⓥ

Dir Bob Swaim   *Prod* Michael I. Levy   *Scr* Dick Wolf   *Ph* David Watkin   *Ed* Scott Conrad   *Mus* John Barry   *Art Dir* John Kasarda
● Rob Lowe, Meg Tilly, Doug Savant, Kim Cattrall, John Glover (M-G-M/Levy)

Masquerade, set in the Hamptons among the genteel with their weathered mansions and racing yachts, is like many poor-little-rich-girl stories; a beautiful backdrop and dreamy settings aren't enough to compensate for uninvolving characters caught in an unsuspenseful scheme.

Meg Tilly's womanizing, drunkard stepfather (John Glover) is in on a plot with Rob Lowe who, unbeknownst to her, is intent upon securing her hand in marriage so that he and his buddy will be set for life.

In the beginning, Lowe is a rake, the cocky captain of the racing boat *Obsession* while at the same time making it with the boat owner's much younger wife (Kim Cattrall). Tilly's just out of a Catholic women's college, innocent and apparently chaste.

It seems the Hamptons is not the bucolic haven it's cracked up to be. The police take their oath as peace officers to hearts – that is, not upsetting the influential and wealthy community that pads the wallets for off-duty cops moonlighting at ritzy parties.

That leaves the snooping to an eager rookie (Doug Savant), seemingly wanting to protect the interests of Tilly, the girl he's always loved, as she takes the fall for a murder she didn't commit.

• •

■ MASSACRE IN ROME

1973, 103 MINS, ITALY ◇ Ⓥ

Dir George Pan Cosmatos   *Prod* Carlo Ponti   *Scr* Robert Katz, George Pan Cosmatos   *Ph* Marcello Gatti   *Ed* Francoise Bonnot, Roberto Silvi   *Mus* Ennio Morricone   *Art Dir* Arrigo Berschi
● Richard Burton, Marcello Mastroianni, Leo McKern, John Steiner, Delia Boccardo (Champion)

Massacre in Rome depends on its dramatic documentary flavor for a number of spell-binding sequences and its polemical shafts at Vatican reticence in resisting the massacre of 300 Italian hostages in reprisal for a partisan assault on a German storm troop detachment in Rome.

The film generally hews close to the controversial book, *Death in Rome*, by Robert Katz. Screenplay veers from the facts as Katz originally researched and presented them, with minor fictional treatment in a few characters, but does not detract from the over-riding moral treatment involved in the wholesale slaughter of innocents, many of them Jews, in the Ardeatine Caves on the outskirts of Rome.

Richard Burton as Germany security forces commander Col Kappler gets a richer portrait than his superiors and subordinates.

• •

■ MASTER GUNFIGHTER, THE

1975, 121 MINS, US ◇

Dir Frank Laughlin [= Tom Laughlin]   *Prod* Philip L. Parslow   *Scr* Harold Lapland   *Ph* Jack A. Marta   *Ed* William Reynolds, Danford Greene   *Mus* Lalo Schifrin   *Art Dir* Albert Brenner
● Tom Laughlin, Ron O'Neal, Lincoln Kilpatrick, GeoAnn Sosa, Barbara Carrera, Victor Campos (Billy Jack)

A curious blend of amateurish plotting and slick production values, Tom Laughlin's *The Master Gunfighter* also presents an ambiguous moral attitude toward the old West. The oater, attractively lensed on northern California locations, alternates sermonizing with gunfights and sword fights.

The Laughlin character talks like a liberal but behaves like a reactionary, and therein lies the confusion. It's a throwback to an earlier age of swashbuckling, but the blend with contemporary bleeding heart attitudes makes the film seem hypocritical.

Action fans will find a good quota of kicks if they can sit through the turgid passages.

Ron O'Neal is Laughlin's chief antagonist, but doesn't arouse much interest as a character. In the lead femme roles, GeoAnn Sosa is spunky and charming, but Barbara Carrera betrays her fashion model background with her blank beauty.

Laughlin's wife Delores Taylor, gets exec producer credit, and their nine-year-old son Frank Laughlin is billed as director.

• •

■ MASTER RACE, THE

1944, 94 MINS, US Ⓥ

Dir Herbert J. Biberman   *Prod* Robert S. Golden   *Scr* Herbert J. Biberman, Anne Froelick, Rowland Leigh   *Ph* Russell Metty   *Ed* Ernie Leadlay   *Mus* Roy Webb   *Art Dir* Albert S. D'Agostino, Jack Okey
● George Coulouris, Osa Massen, Stanley Ridges, Lloyd Bridges, Nancy Gates, Morris Carnovsky (RKO)

Eddie Golden originally selected the title as a likely one for a picture, and then searched for a yarn to pin it to in order to dramatically show the arrogance and synthetic character of the barbaric Nazis. He selected a period

when the German armies were fleeing in disorder, and the final unconditional surrender of the Nazi minions.

Picture opens with clips of the D-Day invasion of 6 June for brief footage, and then swings to headquarters of George Coulouris, member of the German general staff, where he tells assemblage of German officers that the war is lost and they are to proceed according to individual instructions to points designated to create dissension among the peoples of the liberated countries to further destroy Europe so that the self-styled master race can again rise to rule the continent.

• •

■ MATA HARI

1931, 90 MINS, US

Dir George Fitzmaurice   *Scr* Benjamin Glazer, Leo Birinski, Doris Anderson, Gilbert Emery   *Ph* William Daniels   *Ed* Frank Sullivan
● Greta Garbo, Ramon Novarro, Lionel Barrymore, Lewis Stone, C. Henry Gordon, Karen Morley (M-G-M)

Greta Garbo, Ramon Novarro, Lionel Barrymore and Lewis Stone – the Metro Tragedy Four – dominate the whole affair, making the picture, as a picture, very secondary.

It needs its cast names at all times, being a yarn which can't stand up for long on its own gams. Though Garbo is sexy and hot in a less subtle way this time, and though the plot goes about as far as it can in situation warmth, the story presents nothing sensational. Its few attempts at power are old style and all have been used before in similar trite spy stories.

Garbo does a polite cooch to Oriental music as a starter and in the same number makes a symbolic play for a huge idol, with the hips in motion all the while. The finish is a neatly masked strip with Greta's back to the lens.

Two other torrid moments later in the running are given to Garbo and Novarro. Both times they turn out the lights.

Mata Hari's method for grabbing enemy info, if this scenario is authentic, was to get 'em in the bedroom and keep 'em interested, while an assistant operative snatches the papers.

Barrymore and Stone are playing what, for them, are minor parts. Barrymore, as a broken general who loses his honor and finally his life through the glamorous Mata Hari, succeeds in inserting a punch in his moments of despair. But Stone is under wraps with a semi-villainous assignment that doesn't warrant his ability.

• •

■ MATCHMAKER, THE

1958, 100 MINS, US

Dir Joseph Anthony   *Prod* Don Hartman   *Scr* John Michael Hayes   *Ph* Charles Lang   *Ed* Howard Smith   *Mus* Adolph Deutsch   *Art Dir* Hal Pereira, Roland Anderson
● Shirley Booth, Anthony Perkins, Shirley MacLaine, Paul Ford, Robert Morse, Wallace Ford (Paramount)

Based on the Thornton Wilder Broadway hit, Shirley Booth takes the Ruth Gordon stage role of 'marriage counsellor', dominating character in this yarn of 1884. Its period unfoldment permits added opportunity for laughs, some of the belly genre. The Yonkers screenplay catches every nuance of the situation of the widowed Booth ostensibly seeking a wife for the grasping Yonkers merchant (Paul Ford) while adroitly plotting to capture him for her own. Use of 'asides' by various principals, speaking directly into the camera, peppers the action.

Most of the story unreels in New York, where Ford goes from nearby Yonkers to propose to Shirley MacLaine, a man-hungry milliner, and to meet a sexpot promised by Booth, who against his will has taken over

Ford's romantic interests. Following Ford are the two over-worked clerks in his general store (Anthony Perkins and Robert Morse) who pool their resources and determine to live it up in the big city, with 10 bucks between them.

Booth is no less than superb in her role, draining part of comedic possibilities. Perkins' switch to farce is also a bright experience. Ford is immense as the romantically-inclined but tight small-towner, and MacLaine is pert and lovely. Morse, from the original Broadway cast, amusingly enacts Perkins' pardner.

••••••••••••••••••••••••••••••••••

■ MATEWAN

1987, 130 MINS, US ◇ ⊛

Dir John Sayles   *Prod* Peggy Rajski, Maggie Renzi   *Scr* John Sayles   *Ph* Haskell Wexler   *Ed* Sonya Polonsky   *Mus* Mason Daring   *Art Dir* Nora Chavooshian

● Chris Cooper, Will Oldham, Mary McDonnell, Bob Gunton, James Earl Jones, Kevin Tighe (Cinecom)

Matewan is a heartfelt, straight-ahead tale of labor organizing in the coal mines of West Virginia in 1920 that runs its course like a train coming down the track.

Among the memorable characters is Joe Kenehan (Chris Cooper), a young union organizer who comes to Matewan to buck the bosses. With his strong face and Harrison Ford good-looks, Cooper gives the film its heartbeat.

Of the townfolk, 16-year-old Danny (Will Oldham) is already a righteous preacher and a seasoned union man who passionately takes up the working man's struggle. Director John Sayles adds some texture to the mix by throwing in Italian immigrants and black migrant workers who become converted to the union side.

Most notable of the black workers is 'Few Clothes' Johnson (James Earl Jones), a burly good-natured man with a powerful presence and a quick smile. Jones' performance practically glows in the dark. Also a standout is Sayles veteran David Strathairn as the sheriff with quiet integrity who puts his life on the line.

••••••••••••••••••••••••••••••••••

■ MATTER OF LIFE AND DEATH, A

1946, 104 MINS, UK ◇

Dir Michael Powell, Emeric Pressburger   *Prod* Michael Powell, Emeric Pressburger   *Scr* Michael Powell, Emeric Pressburger   *Ph* Jack Cardiff   *Ed* Reginald Mills   *Mus* Allan Gray   *Art Dir* Alfred Junge

● David Niven, Kim Hunter, Marius Goring, Roger Livesey, Raymond Massey, Richard Attenborough (Archers)

Like other Powell-Pressburger pictures, the striving to appear intellectual is much too apparent. Less desire to exhibit alleged learning, and more humanity would have resulted in a more popular offering.

For the first 10 minutes, apart from some pretentious poppycock, the picture looks like living up to its boosting. This is real cinema, then action gives way to talk, some of it flat and dreary. Story is set in this world (graced with Technicolor), and the Other World (relegated to dye monochrome) as it exists in the mind of an airman whose imagination has been affected by concussion.

Returning from a bomber expedition, Squadron-Leader David Niven is shot up. Last of the crew, minus a parachute, and believing the end is inevitable, before bailing out talks poetry and love over the radio to Kim Hunter, American WAC on nearby air station. Miraculously Niven falls into the sea, is washed ashore apparently unhurt, and by strange coincidence meets Kim. They fall desperately in love.

Meanwhile in the Other World there's much bother. Owing to delinquency of Heavenly Conductor Marius Goring, Niven has failed to check in, and Goring is despatched to this world to persuade Niven to take his rightful place and balance the heavenly books.

Obviously experimental in many respects, the designs for the Other World are a matter of taste, but with all their ingenuity Powell, Pressburger, and Alfred Junge could only invent a heaven reminiscent of the Hollywood Bowl and an exclusive celestial night club where hostesses dish out wings to dead pilots.

••••••••••••••••••••••••••••••••••

■ MAURICE

1987, 140 MINS, UK ◇ ⊛

Dir James Ivory   *Prod* Ismail Merchant   *Scr* Kit Hesketh-Harvey, James Ivory   *Ph* Pierre Lhomme   *Ed* Katherine Wenning   *Mus* Richard Robbins   *Art Dir* Brian Ackland-Snow

● James Wilby, Hugh Grant, Rupert Graves, Denholm Elliott, Simon Callow, Billie Whitelaw (Merchant-Ivory)

Maurice, based on a posthumously published novel by E.M. Forster, is a well-crafted pic on the theme of homosexuality. Penned in 1914 but not allowed to be published until 1971 (a year after Forster's death) because of its subject matter, *Maurice* is not ranked among Forster's best work. Key opening scene has Maurice as a schoolboy on a beach-side outing being lectured by his teacher (Simon Callow), in comically fastidious fashion, on the changes that will soon occur in his body with the onset of puberty.

Maurice Hall (James Wilby) is next seen grown up and attending Cambridge where, he meets handsome Clive Durham (Hugh Grant). Durham falls in love with him and though resisting at first Maurice later reciprocates, all on a platonic level.

Durham, under pressure from his mother (Judy Parfitt), gets married to a naive girl (Phoebe Nicholls) while Maurice finally physically consummates his homosexual inclination with Durham's young gamekeeper Alec Scudder (Rupert Graves).

Wilby as Maurice gives a workmanlike performance, adequate to the role but never soaring. He is far outshadowed by a superlative supporting cast.

••••••••••••••••••••••••••••••••••

■ MAUSOLEUM

1983, 96 MINS, US ◇ ⊛

Dir Michael Dugan   *Prod* Robert Madero, Robert Barich   *Scr* Robert Barich, Robert Madero   *Ph* Robert Barich   *Ed* Richard C. Bock   *Mus* Jaime Mendoza-Nava   *Art Dir* Robert Burns

● Marjoe Gortner, Bobbie Bresee, Norman Burton, Maurice Sherbanee, La Wanda Page, Laura Hippe (Western International)

Mausoleum is an engaging minor film concerning demonic possession, presenting variations on *The Exorcist* format. Not the stab 'n' slab genre picture one might infer from its title, film should please aficionados of old-fashioned B-horror films.

Bobbie Bresee toplines as Susan Farrell, a 30-year-old woman who has been possessed by a demon at age 10 after strolling into the family mausoleum, carrying on a centuries-old family curse affecting the first-born. Twenty years after, the demon has finally taken over, going on a killing spree that arouses the suspicions of her husband Oliver (Marjoe Gortner). Friend and psychiatrist Dr Andrews (Norman Burton) is enlisted to help Susan and ultimately bests the demon.

Bresee is extremely seductive here in the femme fatale role, complete with stock victims such as the shady gardener, unwary delivery boy, etc.

••••••••••••••••••••••••••••••••••

■ MAX DUGAN RETURNS

1983, 98 MINS, US ◇ ⊛

Dir Herbert Ross   *Prod* Herbert Ross, Neil Simon   *Scr* Neil Simon   *Ph* David M. Walsh   *Ed* Richard Marks   *Mus* David Shire   *Art Dir* Albert Brenner

● Marsha Mason, Jason Robards, Donald Sutherland, Matthew Broderick, Dody Goodman, Sal Vicuso (20th Century-Fox)

Max Dugan Returns is a consistently happy comedic fable which should please romanticists drawn to a teaming of Neil Simon, Marsha Mason and Herbert Ross. Once more, Simon's pen turns to the problems of parental relationships – especially reunion after long estrangement – but largely leaves aside any heavy emotional involvement or rapid fire comedy.

Struggling to raise a 15-year-old son (Matthew Broderick) on a meagre teacher's salary, widow Mason maintains a wonderful attitude as her refrigerator breaks, her old car barely runs but gets stolen to boot, and life generally never quite works. Broderick is a good kid who accepts her poor-but-honest morality very well. In addition, there's a budding romance with Donald Sutherland, an exceptionally intelligent detective who's investigating the theft of her car.

Out of a dark night, however, returns Max Dugan (Jason Robards), the father who abandoned Mason when she was nine years old. Dying of a heart ailment, Robards is carrying a satchel full of remorse and a suitcase crammed with cash left over from a checkered career in Las Vegas.

••••••••••••••••••••••••••••••••••

■ MAXIE

1985, 90 MINS, US ◇ ⊛

Dir Paul Aaron   *Prod* Carter De Haven   *Scr* Patricia Resnick   *Ph* Fred Schuler   *Ed* Lynzee Klingman   *Mus* Georges Delerue   *Art Dir* John Lloyd

● Glenn Close, Mandy Patinkin, Ruth Gordon, Barnard Hughes, Valerie Curtin, Googy Gress (Orion/Aurora/Elsboy)

As forgettable as it is well-meaning, *Maxie* represents a stab at an old-fashioned sort of romantic fantasy, as well as first chance at a full-blown starring role for Glenn Close. A concoction like this needs lots of fizz, but the bubbly here has gone mostly flat, and what's left evaporates quickly.

Much of the credit for keeping it alive at all must go to Mandy Patinkin, who shows himself to be a good-looking leading man with a rare light touch for romantic comedy.

Based on the novel *Marion's Wall* by Jack Finney, *Maxie* tells the story of a dead person returning to inhabit the body of a living soul. Such is what happens to Close, the normal, cheerful wife of book specialist Patinkin. When he uncovers a message on the wall from a certain 'Maxie' who lived in the 1920s, Patinkin becomes quite taken with the jazz age flapper who bore a striking resemblance to his wife.

She has some very good comic moments, but Close may be too down-to-earth an actress for foolishness of this kind. The late Ruth Gordon, in her last film role, contributes another of her patented nutty neighbor turns.

••••••••••••••••••••••••••••••••••

■ MAXIMUM OVERDRIVE

1986, 97 MINS, US ◇ ⊛

Dir Stephen King   *Prod* Martha Schumacher   *Scr* Stephen King   *Ph* Armando Nannuzzi   *Ed* Evan Lottman   *Mus* AC/DC   *Art Dir* Giorgio Postiglione

● Emilio Estevez, Pat Hingle, Laura Harrington, Yeardley Smith, John Short, Ellen McElduff (De Laurentiis)

Master manipulator Stephen King, making his directoral debut from his own script, fails to create a convincing enough environment to make the kind of nonsense he's offering here believable or fun.

King starts out with a small-town idyll soon disrupted by a mindless revolt of trucks. He collects a typical mix of rednecks, good old boys, restless youth, drifters and the decent folk in a small corner of North Carolina where they hole up at a truck stop as the trucks stampede.

Truck stop is run as if it were a feudal fiefdom, complete with arsenal, by redneck despot Pat Hingle who gives an amusing performance as a true screen swine. Also on hand is Emilio Estevez as a cook in bondage to Hingle by virtue of his probation from the pen, but he's gone to college and is really a good kid.

■ **MAYERLING**

1968, 140 MINS, UK/FRANCE ◇ Ⓥ
Dir Terence Young *Prod* Robert Dorfman
Scr Terence Young, Denis Cannan *Ph* Henri Alekan *Ed* Benedik Rayner *Mus* Francis Lai *Art Dir* Georges Wakhevitch
● Omar Sharif, Catherine Deneuve, James Mason, Ava Gardner, James Robertson Justice, Genevieve Page (Winchester/Corona)

Film misfires through a flattish script and uninspired performances by two leads, Omar Sharif and Catherine Deneuve. Director Terence Young has used two novels [*Mayerling* and *The Archduke* by Michael Arnold] and much historical background research as the basis for his theory on how Crown Prince Rudolf of Austria and his young baroness mistress met their deaths in the Royal Hunting Lodge at Mayerling in the late 19th century.

The screenplay rarely touches any heights of romantic ecstasy. The political background – the always shaky Austrian throne, the students' violent protests, court intrigue – is introduced promisingly at the beginning, but later gets swamped in the romantic story which is protracted, humorless, often hesitant and plodding.

Sharif shows fire as the arrogant, ambitious son of Emperor Franz-Josef, torn between a desire to get things moving on a new progressive scale, and his loyalty to Habsburg tradition.

His romance with Catherine Deneuve is a singularly flat and prosaic affair. Deneuve's performance is too demure.

Ava Gardner makes an impact throughout.

■ **McCABE AND MRS. MILLER**

1971, 121 MINS, US ◇ Ⓥ
Dir Robert Altman *Prod* David Foster, Mitchell Brower *Scr* Robert Altman, Brian McKay *Ph* Vilmos Zsigmond *Ed* Louis Lombardo *Mus* Leonard Cohen *Art Dir* Leon Ericksen
● Warren Beatty, Julie Christie, Rene Auberjonois, William Devane, Shelley Duvall, Keith Carradine (Warner)

Robert Altman's *McCabe and Mrs Miller* is a disappointing mixture. A period story about a small northwest mountain village where stars Warren Beatty and Julie Christie run the bordello, the production suffers from overlength; also a serious effort at moody photography which backfires into pretentiousness; plus a diffused comedy-drama plot line which is repeatedly shoved aside in favor of bawdiness.

Edmund Naughton's novel, *McCabe*, was shot around Vancouver under the title, *The Presbyterian Church Wager*, named for a fictional town. Rene Auberjonois is top-featured as a saloon-bordello owner whose monopoly on fun and games is broken by roving gambler Beatty. Christie becomes Beatty's partner in the flourishing enterprise.

Beatty seems either miscast or misdirected. His own youthful looks cannot be

concealed by a beard, make-up, a grunting voice and jerky physical movements; the effect resembles a high-school thesp playing Rip Van Winkle. Christie on the other hand is excellent.

■ **McKENZIE BREAK, THE**

1970, 106 MINS, US ◇
Dir Lamont Johnson *Prod* Jules Levy, Arthur Gardner, Arnold Laven *Scr* William Norton *Ph* Michael Reed *Ed* Tom Rolf *Mus* Riz Ortolani
● Brian Keith, Helmut Griem, Ian Hendry, Patrick O'Connell, Caroline Mortimer, Horst Janson (United Artists)

The McKenzie Break is a taut, classically crafted World War II POW escape drama with an original twist. This time it is the Germans, a corps of crack U-boat officers, led by Helmut Griem, breaking out of a camp in Scotland.

An imaginative, intelligent script [from a novel by Sidney Shelley], crackling direction by Lamont Johnson, and strong, three-dimension portrayals by Griem and Brian Keith, as a British intelligence officer trying to outguess and out-maneuver the Nazi, transform the film into a tense personal duel that maintains its suspense until the final frames.

Griem is hardly the stereotype brutal Nazi, but nevertheless he is a model Hitler youth risen to young U-boat captain. He runs the prison like a youth camp, keeping his British captors at bay with riots and demonstrations planned to the split second. It is all a coverup, and training, for the escape.

■ **McLINTOCK!**

1963, 127 MINS, US ◇
Dir Andrew V. McLaglen *Prod* Michael Wayne
Scr James Edward Grant *Ph* William H. Clothier *Ed* Otho Lovering *Mus* Frank DeVol *Art Dir* Hal Pereira, Eddie Imazu
● John Wayne, Maureen O'Hara, Yvonne De Carlo, Patrick Wayne, Stefanie Powers (Batjac/United Artists)

McLintock!, most of all, is a John Wayne western. The style of the production is forked-tongue-in-cheek. Nucleus of yarn is the marital duel between Wayne, straight-shooting, rough-and-tumble, high-living, hard-drinking cattle baron whose town has been named after him, and Maureen O'Hara, who has more reservations than a Comanche real estate agent.

Wayne is in his element, or home, home on the Waynge. O'Hara gives her customary high-spirited performance, although it's never quite clear what she's so darned sore about. Yvonne De Carlo is attractive as Wayne's cook, Stefanie Powers likewise as his college educated daughter. Vying for the latter's affection are Patrick Wayne, who etches a likable characterization, and Jerry Van Dyke, who gives a skillfully oafish performance.

■ **McQ**

1974, 115 MINS, US ◇ Ⓥ
Dir John Sturges *Prod* Jules Levy, Arthur Gardner, Lawrence Roman *Scr* Lawrence Roman *Ph* Harry Stradling *Ed* William Ziegler *Mus* Elmer Bernstein *Art Dir* Walter Simonds
● John Wayne, Eddie Albert, Diana Muldaur, Colleen Dewhurst, Clu Gulager, Julie Adams (Batjac/Levy-Gardner)

McQ is a good contemporary crime actioner filmed entirely in Seattle, with John Wayne discovering that his slain buddy was a member of a crooked police ring stealing dope evidence.

Featured as an aging bar waitress from whom Wayne obtains evidence, Colleen Dewhurst is outstanding in her two scenes.

McQ attracts and sustains continued interest from the opening frames, where William Bryant, after shooting two policemen, is himself revealed as one, just before being killed. Eddie Albert, as Wayne's superior, makes the usual knee-jerk response (arrest radical hippies) while Wayne suspects big time dope dealer Al Lettieri.

■ **McVICAR**

1980, 111 MINS, UK ◇ Ⓥ
Dir Tom Clegg *Prod* David Gideon Thomson, Jackie Curbishley *Scr* John McVicar, Tom Clegg *Ph* Vernon Layton *Ed* Peter Boyle *Mus* Jeff Wayne *Art Dir* Brian Ackland-Snow
● Roger Daltrey, Adam Faith, Cheryl Campbell, Steven Berkoff (Curbishley-Baird/The Who/Polydor)

Feature is a conscientious reconstruction of several crucial months in the life of John McVicar, who escaped from the high-security wing of an English prison where he was serving eight years for robbery with violence.

McVicar is the author of the book *McVicar by Himself*, which was used as the basis of the film.

Roger Daltrey projects a disquieting mix of danger and vulnerability. Moreover, his characterization goes a long way towards supplying the sense of a mind at work behind the uncompromising, bony face and the thuggish look in the eyes.

Tom Clegg's firm direction is unflamboyant. Although much of the drama certainly doesn't call for obtrusive style, there are moments when more panache would not have come amiss.

There's an excellent, humorous performance by Adam Faith as Probyn, and a chillingly manic one by Steven Berkoff, in a role modelled on an actual inmate.

■ **ME, NATALIE**

1969, 110 MINS, US ◇
Dir Fred Coe *Prod* Stanley Shapiro *Scr* A. Martin Zweiback *Ph* Arthur J. Ornitz *Ed* Sheila Bakerman *Mus* Henry Mancini *Art Dir* George Jenkins
● Patty Duke, James Farentino, Martin Balsam, Elsa Lanchester, Salome Jens, Nancy Marchand (Cinema Center)

Me, Natalie is the type of picture which might have gone overboard in contrivance and oversentimentality, in monotonous rendition of personal feelings of its title character. Instead, it is sensitive, often-poignant drama painted with a light touch of an ugly duckling trying to find her place in the scheme of things.

Patty Duke, in title role, delivers a warm, roundly-developed characterization of a girl who all her life has tried to be pretty, and is keenly aware she isn't nor ever will be.

The title character engages in a great deal of offscreen running commentary throughout the film, explaining her feelings and her philosophy, which gives audience an insight into her feelings without slowing the pace, generally held to an interesting temp.

As the mother, Nancy Marchand delivers a tremendous performance.

■ **MEAN SEASON, THE**

1985, 103 MINS, US ◇ Ⓥ
Dir Phillip Borsos *Prod* David Foster, Larry Turman *Scr* Leon Piedmont *Ph* Frank Tidy *Ed* Duwayne Dunham *Mus* Lalo Schifrin *Art Dir* Philip Jefferies
● Kurt Russell, Mariel Hemingway, Richard Jordan, Richard Masur, Joe Pantoliano, Richard Bradford (Orion)

Based on the novel, *In the Heat of the Summer*, by former *Miami Herald* crime reporter John Katzenbach, pic establishes solid Florida

385

heat and humidity as the 'mean' background to a series of murders that perversely link together the killer (Richard Jordan), and a Miami police reporter (Kurt Russell) who becomes the psychopath's personal spokesman.

Jordan is at his shrewdly crazed best, anchoring the movie with a felt terror, initially just through his off-screen voice as he manipulates the reporter over the phone and ultimately through his cunning.

Russell plays a reporter (production used the city room of the *Miami Herald*) who, credibly enough, gets swept away with all the national hype he's getting as the only man who can talk to the killer.

His live-in elementary school teacher, g.f., essayed rather uneventfully by Mariel Hemingway, grows outraged as the reporter succumbs to his own ego, to the killer's tantalizing calls, and to his increased stature as newsmaker.

···

■ **MEAN STREETS**

1973, 110 MINS, US ◇ ⱱ
Dir Martin Scorsese   *Prod* Jonathan T. Taplin
Scr Martin Scorsese, Mardik Martin   *Ph* Kent Wakeford   *Ed* Sid Levin
● Robert De Niro, Harvey Keitel, David Proval, Amy Robinson, Richard Romanus, Cesare Danova (TPS/Warner)

In essence *Mean Streets* is an updated, downtown version of *Marty* (1955), with small-time criminality replacing those long stretches of beer-drinking in a Bronx bar. Four aging adolescents, all in their mid-20s but still inclined toward prankish irresponsibility, float among the lower-class denizens of Manhattan's Little Italy, struggling to make a living out of loan-sharking, the numbers game and bartending.

The hero, competently played by Harvey Keitel, is on the verge of taking over a restaurant for his vaguely Mafioso uncle (Cesar Danova in a compelling, deglamorized interpretation), but his climb to respectability is obstructed by his kinship with the trouble-making Robert De Niro and his budding love for De Niro's epileptic cousin, played rather confusingly by Amy Robinson.

Screenplay, instead of developing these characters and their complex interactions, remains content to sketch in their day-to-day happenings. But Scorsese is exceptionally good at guiding his largely unknown cast to near-flawless recreations of types. Outstanding in this regard is De Niro.

···

■ **MEATBALLS**

1979, 92 MINS, CANADA ◇ ⱱ
Dir Ivan Reitman   *Prod* Dan Goldberg   *Scr* Len Blum, Dan Goldberg, Janis Allen, Harold Ramis   *Ph* Don Wilder   *Ed* Debra Karen   *Mus* Elmer Bernstein
Art Dir David Charles
● Bill Murray, Harvey Atkin, Kate Lynch, Russ Banham, Kristine DeBell (Paramount)

It's difficult to come up with a more cliche situation for a summer pic than a summer camp, where all the characters and plot turns are readily imaginable. That makes director Ivan Reitman's accomplishment all the more noteworthy.

Bill Murray limns a head counselor in charge of a group of misfit counselors-in-training. The usual types predominate: the myopic klutz, the obese kid who wins the pig-out contest, the smooth-talking lothario, and a bevy of comely lasses.

Scripters have managed to gloss over the stereotypes and come up with a smooth-running narrative that makes the camp hijinks part of an overall human mosaic. No one is unduly belittled or mocked, and

Meatballs is without the usual grossness and cynicism of many contempo comedy pix.

···

■ **MECHANIC, THE**

1972, 100 MINS, US ⱱ
Dir Michael Winner   *Prod* Robert Chartoff, Irwin Winkler, Lewis John Carlino   *Scr* Lewis John Carlino
Ph Richard Kline   *Ed* Frederick Wilson   *Mus* Jerry Fielding   *Art Dir* Rodger Maus
● Charles Bronson, Keenan Wynn, Jan-Michael Vincent, Jill Ireland, Linda Ridgeway, Frank deKova (United Artists)

A mechanic, in underworld parlance, is a highly-skilled contract killer. Possibilities of limning such a character are realistically pointed up in this action-drenched gangster yarn burdened with an overly-contrived plot development.

For the first few reels, footage is more a series of episodes – not always clear, at that – than carrying a sustained story line. Credibility is sometimes further strained during first half of film when Bronson oscillates between a typical hood at work and lolling in a luxurious apartment far removed from world of crime.

Michael Winner keeps the tempo at fever-pitch despite deficiencies of feature's opening sequences.

Bronson plays the son of a former gang leader cut down in his prime, left a fortune but still associated with crime as a hired executioner.

···

■ **MEDIUM, THE**

1951, 85 MINS, US ⱱ
Dir Gian-Carlo Menotti   *Prod* Walter Lowendahl
Scr Gian-Carlo Menotti   *Ph* Enzo Serafin
Ed Alexander Hammid   *Mus* Gian-Carlo Menotti
● Marie Powers, Anna Maria Alberghetti, Leo Coleman, Belva Kibler, Beverly Dame, Donald Morgan (Transfilm)

Composer-librettist Gian-Carlo Menotti, who surprised Broadway by turning out two successive operas, *The Medium* and *The Consul*, that became legit hits, turns film director and makes *The Medium* into an impressive pic. The work is limited by the fact that it is stark modern opera, all in song or recitative.

Menotti filmed the opus in Rome, utilizing Marie Powers and Leo Coleman from the original legit cast, and the 15-year-old Italian coloratura find, Anna Maria Alberghetti, in her film debut, for the third principal. Menotti is too fond of the camera, and too intent on trick angles and effects. He overworks the close-ups. But he comes up with some nifty shots that dovetail with the bizarre opus.

Story is that of a shabby medium, Madame Flora (Powers), living with her daughter Monica (Alberghetti), and Toby, a mute gypsy waif they adopted (Coleman), and the seances they hold for gullible clients.

Mme Flora, who is given to drink, disrupts one seance suddenly when she fancies someone's hand at her throat trying to choke her. She accuses her customers and then Toby of the deed, and when they deny it, is distraught. Fear of some supernatural power turning on her for her shams drives her further towards the bottle.

Although the picture was filmed in Italy, it has no particular locale, and is sung entirely in English. Sets are simple and costumes and makeup properly drab. Film shows a tightened budget without cheapness of quality.

···

■ **MEDIUM COOL**

1969, 110 MINS, US ◇ ⱱ
Dir Haskell Wexler   *Prod* Tully Friedman, Haskell Wexler   *Scr* Haskell Wexler   *Ph* Haskell Wexler
Ed Verna Fields   *Mus* Mike Bloomfield   *Art Dir* Leon Ericksen

● Robert Forster, Verna Bloom, Peter Bonerz, Marianna Hill, Harold Blankenship, Charles Geary (Paramount/H&J)

Photographed in Chicago against the clamor and violence of the 1968 Democratic National Convention, where cast principals were on their own as they made their way through the crowds and police lines. Buildup to these later sequences frequently is confusing and motives difficult to fathom.

Director Haskell Wexler, in his first indie production, mixes 'reality' with the 'theatrical', his two chief protagonists a realistic TV newsreel cameraman and a young hillbilly mother come to Chicago with her young son.

Wexler adopts a documentary approach which helps sustain the mood and his cast fits into this pattern.

Robert Forster is strongly cast as the lenser who refuses to become emotionally involved with any of his assignments until caught up in the injustice done to a Negro and while on TV assignment, falls in love with a young mother.

···

■ **MEDUSA TOUCH, THE**

1978, 110 MINS, UK ◇ ⱱ
Dir Jack Gold   *Prod* Lew Grade, Arnon Milchan, Elliot Kastner   *Scr* John Briley, Jack Gold   *Ph* Arthur Ibbetson   *Ed* Anne V. Coates   *Art Dir* Peter Mullins
● Richard Burton, Lino Ventura, Lee Remick, Harry Andrews, Marie-Christine Barrault, Michael Hordern (ITC)

Another disaster film? Not exactly, even if at the end a London cathedral caves in, with many victims trapped underneath the rubble but with the Queen of England saved in the nick of time. These scenes, realistically treated and technically good, are among the highlights of this lavishly-produced film.

John Morlar (Richard Burton) is attacked by an unknown intruder who bashes in his skull. Why? The man didn't seem to have a single enemy. Inspector Brunel is puzzled. Why a French detective instead of British? Apparently due to French financial participation in this film. In any case, it allows Lino Ventura to make his British film debut and very good he is.

Brunel finally discovers a clue leading to a psychiatrist played by Lee Remick. She had treated Morlar for reasons not stated at once.

It turns out that Morlar is not dead at all. His mind is fighting a desperate battle to survive. Even as a child, Morlar proved a very odd number indeed. His files relate to a vast series of disasters and apparently unsolved mysteries.

Director Jack Gold controls all the angles of this improbable story. Burton has some very effective moments too as does Remick.

···

■ **MEET JOHN DOE**

1941, 129 MINS, US ⱱ
Dir Frank Capra   *Prod* Frank Capra   *Scr* Robert Riskin   *Ph* George Barnes   *Ed* Daniel Mandell
Mus Dimitri Tiomkin
● Gary Cooper, Barbara Stanwyck, Edward Arnold, Walter Brennan (Warner)

Pict tells the story of the rehabilitation of a tramp ex-baseball player who assents to the role of a puppet social
reformer in the hands of a young woman columnist on a metropolitan newspaper.

The heroine, having been fired from her job through a change in the sheet's ownership, regains her place by inventing a fictitious John Doe as author of a letter of protest against the prevailing injustices of a political and social system which permits hunger in a land of plenty and idleness in a world where much remains to be accomplished. As earnest of his appeal he declares he will commit suicide on Christmas Eve in expiation for the sins of society.

The synthetic fabric of the story is the weakness of the production, despite the magnificence of the Frank Capra-directed superstructure. But Robert Riskin, who wrote the screenplay from an original story by Richard Connell and Robert Presnell, leaves the audience at the finale with scarcely more than the hope that some day selfishness, fraud and deceit will be expunged from human affairs.

■ MEET ME AT THE FAIR

1952, 87 MINS, US ◇

Dir Douglas Sirk   *Prod* Albert J. Cohen   *Scr* Irving Wallace   *Ph* Maury Gertsman   *Ed* Russell Schoengarth   *Mus* Joseph Gershenson (dir.)   *Art Dir* Bernard Herzbrun, Eric Orborn
● Dan Dailey, Diana Lynn, Chet Allen, Scatman Crothers, Hugh O'Brian, Carole Mathews (Universal)

The production has a period flavor featuring nostalgia and schmaltz against a 1904 setting. The old-fashioned drama [from the novel *The Great Companions* by Gene Markey, adapted by Martin Berkeley] revolves around an orphan kid who runs away from a grim institution, takes up with a medicine man, with his new friend charged with kidnapping. Before it's all over, the medicine man and the kid are mixed up in a political fight and eventually bring about reforms at the orphanage.

Best in the musical department is Carole Mathews doing 'Bill Bailey' and the title number. She also works with Dan Dailey on 'Remember the Time' and generally impresses.

Dailey is very likeable as the medicine man, giving the character a good-natured flavor that helps the film.

■ MEET ME IN ST LOUIS

1944, 118 MINS, US ◇ ▼

Dir Vincente Minnelli   *Prod* Arthur Freed   *Scr* Irving Brecher, Fred F. Finklehoffe   *Ph* George Folsey   *Ed* Albert Akst   *Art Dir* Cedric Gibbons, Lemuel Ayers, Jack Martin Smith
● Judy Garland, Margaret O'Brien, Mary Astor, Lucille Bremer, Tom Drake, Marjorie Main (M-G-M)

Meet Me in St Louis is wholesome in story [from the book by Sally Benson] colorful both in background and its literal Technicolor, and as American as the World's Series.

As Leon Ames plays the head of the Alonzo Smith clan it's a 1903 life-with-father. Mary Astor is the understanding and, incidentally, quite handsome mother as they worry about Judy Garland and Lucille Bremer, playing their daughters. Henry H. Daniels Jr is the self-sufficient brother, off to Princeton, but the romantic travail of the two older girls is the fundamental. Backgrounded are Marjorie Main, capital as the maid who almost bosses the household, and the still-gallant Harry Davenport, now 80-ish, who is grandpa.

It's the time of the St Louis Fair, hence the title song, and everything that makes for the happy existence of a typical American family is skillfully panoramaed.

Seasonal pastorals, from summer into the next spring, take the Smith clan through their appealing little problems. Judy Garland's plaint about 'The Boy Next Door' (played by Tom Drake); the Paul Jones dance routine to the tune of 'Skip to My Lou'; the Yuletide thematic, 'Have Yourself a Merry Christmas'; and the 'Trolley Song', en route to the Fairgrounds, are four socko musical highlights. They have been intelligently highlighted and well-paced by director Vincente Minnelli.

Garland achieves true stature with her deeply understanding performance, while her sisterly running-mate, Lucille Bremer,

likewise makes excellent impact with a well-balanced performance.

■ MELVIN AND HOWARD

1980, 93 MINS, US ◇ ▼

Dir Jonathan Demme   *Prod* Art Linson, Don Phillips   *Scr* Bo Goldman   *Ph* Tak Fujimoto   *Ed* Craig McKay   *Mus* Bruce Langhorne   *Art Dir* Toby Rafelson
● Paul Le Mat, Jason Robards, Mary Steenburgen, Michael J. Pollard, Dabney Coleman, Gloria Grahame (Universal)

A pungent fable about the elusiveness of the American Dream, *Melvin and Howard* is a richly textured, highly individualistic look at Melvin Dummar, a man in over his head both before and after becoming the beneficiary of $156 million via Howard Hughes' so-called Mormon will. Jonathan Demme's tour-de-force direction, the imaginative screenplay and top-drawer performances from a huge cast fuse in an unusual, original creation.

Dummar's chance encounter with a man representing himself as the reclusive tycoon occupies first reel or so and, despite Jason Robards' amusing portrait of Hughes as a grizzled old coot, pic takes awhile generating a full head of steam. As his two-time bride and divorcee Mary Steenburgen says, Melvin is a loser, and early footage focusing upon his inability to cope with family or jobs makes for somewhat uncertain p.o.v.

Film is exemplary for its rare concentration on the quality, and lack of it, in Middle American life, and incisive, if indirect, examination of the no-win syndrome for contemporary proletariat.

■ MEMOIRS OF A SURVIVOR

1981, 117 MINS, UK ◇

Dir David Gladwell   *Prod* Michael Medwin, Penny Clark   *Scr* Kerry Crabbe, David Gladwell   *Ph* Walter Lassally   *Ed* William Shapter   *Mus* Mike Thorn
● Julie Christie, Christopher Guard, Leonie Mellinger, Debbie Hutchins, Pat Keen, Nigel Hawthorne (EMI/Memorial/NFFC)

The film [from the novel by Doris Lessing] depicts Julie Christie as D, an attractive middle-aged woman living alone in the midst of the chaos occurring around her. She dreams of a Victorian time and can go through a wall to witness events.

A little girl, maybe her, is seen in the rich, gilded interiors adroitly given a candlelight feeling by lenser Walter Lassally. The mother is annoyed at not being able to read, work and find herself while the little girl is somewhat neglected by mom and her austere father who at one time contemplates her undraped body while she is asleep.

But reality is grim. A teenage girl is moved in with D and she takes care of her. The girl becomes involved with a young man trying to help vagrant children, living in an abandoned subway station. They have already killed one of his helpers and cannibalized others.

People are leaving the stricken city with some indications of an outside government that gives orders. Strife is not due to any atomic war but just communal life running down.

Christie emerges as a fine character player despite her still potent attractiveness. Director David Gladwell apparently did not have the budget to give a more solid look to the degenerating city.

■ MEMPHIS BELLE

1990, 106 MINS, UK ◇ ▼

Dir Michael Caton-Jones   *Prod* David Puttnam, Catherine Wyler   *Scr* Monte Merrick   *Ph* David Watkin   *Ed* Jim Clark   *Mus* George Fenton   *Art Dir* Stuart Craig

● Matthew Modine, Eric Stoltz, Tate Donovan, D.B. Sweeney, David Strathairn, John Lithgow (Enigma)

Offering a romanticized view of heroism drawn from the Hollywood war epic, *Memphis Belle* is unashamedly commercial. Its moral fabric is thinner than that of other David Puttnam productions.

Pic's subject is the 25th and final mission of the Memphis Belle, the most celebrated of the US Air Force B-17 bombers. The plane flew 24 perfect missions, and its 25th became part of a massive p.r. drive to boost war-bond sales and morale.

The plane and its team are sent to Germany to drop one last load, setting the scene for suspense, tension, terror and a fitting celebration when all return safe and (almost) sound.

Large chunk of the film is set on the ground, providing adequate exposition of events and character to involve the audience in the mission. Played up is the fact that these 10 guys are barely out of their teens and don't see themselves as heroes.

Original footage from the 1944 documentary *Memphis Belle* by William Wyler, father of coproducer Catherine Wyler, is used for the guaranteed tearjerking scene, with letters from parents of dead soldiers read over it by the commanding officer, thoughtfully played by David Strathairn.

■ MEN, THE

1950, 85 MINS, US ▼

Dir Fred Zinnemann   *Prod* Stanley Kramer   *Scr* Carl Foreman   *Ph* Robert De Grasse   *Ed* Harry Gerstad   *Mus* Dimitri Tiomkin
● Marlon Brando, Teresa Wright, Everett Sloane, Jack Webb, Richard Erdman (United Artists)

In *The Men* producer Stanley Kramer turns to the difficult cinematic subject of paraplegics, so expertly treated as to be sensitive, moving and yet, withal, entertaining and earthy-humored.

From the opening shot, a tensely-played battle scene where Lieutenant Wilozek (Marlon Brando) suffers his crushing wound, *The Men* maintains its pace and interest. Thereafter, the film centers on the overwhelming problems of paralyzed vets who must be convinced that their wounds are incurable and that they must yet fight their way to a useful existence.

While the film personalizes the story of Wilozek and his fiancee (Teresa Wright), the camera's scope is broader.

Brando, who film-debuts as Wilozek, fails to deliver the necessary sensitivity and inner warmth.

■ MEN DON'T LEAVE

1990, 113 MINS, US ◇ ▼

Dir Paul Brickman   *Prod* John Avnet   *Scr* Barbara Benedek, Paul Brickman   *Ph* Bruce Surtees   *Ed* Richard Chew   *Mus* Thomas Newman   *Art Dir* Barbara Ling
● Jessica Lange, Chris O'Donnell, Charlie Corsmo, Arliss Howard, Tom Mason, Joan Cusack (Geffen/Warner)

Men Don't Leave is a quietly moving tale of a widow (Jessica Lange) and her struggle to support her two sons in shabby Baltimore surroundings.

Suggested by Moshe Mizrahi's 1981 French film *La via continue* with Annie Girardot, *Men Don't Leave* is directed by Paul Brickman.

The title misleadingly suggests a feminist tract, not the warm-hearted comedy-drama this pic becomes after getting past the disjointed kitchen-sink melodrama of debt-ridden husband Tom Mason's death and Lange's selling of the family's suburban home. The move to Baltimore revives what seemed a terminally ill film and brings it compellingly to life.

Playing the role at first with an unmodulated emotional glaze, the taciturn Lange is pulled back to life by the spirited behaviour of her boys, superbly played by newcomers Chris O'Donnell and Charlie Korsmo; by O'Donnell's sweet but loopy g.f. Joan Cusack, and by the engagingly offbeat b.f. Arliss Howard.

The film's dramatic heart is a sequence showing Lange, after losing her job in a blowup against restaurant boss Kathy Bates, descending into a catatonic state and refusing to leave her bed for days as the apartment turns into a quiet vision of hell. It's a scary piece of acting by Lange, beautifully directed by Brickman, and it turns a somewhat meandering film into a memorable emotional experience.

● ●

■ MEN IN HER LIFE, THE

1941, 89 MINS, US

Dir Gregory Ratoff   *Prod* Gregory Ratoff
Scr Frederick Kohner, Michael Wilson, Paul Trivers
Ph Harry Stradling, Arthur Miller   *Ed* Francis D. Lyon
Mus David Raksin
● Loretta Young, Conrad Veidt, Dean Jagger, Otto Kruger, Ann Todd, John Shepperd (Columbia)

Eleanor Smith's novel of the 1860s, *Ballerina*, in providing basis for the tale, details the intensive training required to bring a ballet dancer to stardom – and her love life along the way. Loretta Young comes under the stern hand of elderly ballet master Conrad Veidt, marrying him in appreciation after a sensational debut, although in love with young John Shepperd. After Veidt's death, she marries shipping magnate Dean Jagger, and honeymoon tour of Europe finds her forgetting the stage life. But she returns to dancing for separation, and bears a daughter (Ann Todd), whom Jagger eventually finds and takes back to New York for proper rearing.

Gregory Ratoff overcomes much of the story immobility through carrying various dramatic episodes to dramatic peaks, and then veering away to the next sequence without holding on the climax. Ratoff also generates strong sympathy in the latter reels with the mother-love hearttugs for the absent child.

● ●

■ MEN OF TWO WORLDS

1946, 109 MINS, UK ◇

Dir Thorold Dickinson   *Scr* Thorold Dickinson, Herbert W. Victor   *Ph* Desmond Dickinson   *Ed* Aben Jaggs
Mus Arthur Bliss   *Art Dir* Tom Morahan
● Eric Portman, Phyllis Calvert, Orlando Martins, Robert Adams (Two Cities)

This ambitious Two Cities production, which enters the $4 million class, is honest, dull and in Technicolor. With the best intentions, it states the case for a scientific treatment of sleeping sickness among the African tribes as opposed to witchcraft and superstition. But it is a statement of the obvious.

Film was three years in production with delays that appear to have badly dented the screenplay. It began in 1943. Eight months were spent in Tanganyika choosing locations. On the way out a U-boat sank cameras and stock. Film unit was put ashore 1,000 miles from Lagos, where its only still camera was impounded. Slow convoys, bad weather, a strike of lab men in Hollywood, delays waiting for Technicolor equipment, all brought costly handicaps to the enterprise. Director Thorold Dickinson has done his best, but the result is a long stretch of mumbo-jumbo, unrelieved by imaginative treatment or pictorial thrills.

Randall, the district commissioner, plans to evacuate an African village to save the inhabitants from the man-killing tse-tse fly. His assistant is Kisenga, a noble savage who has risen from ancestral swamps, found culture in England and gone back to his tribe as a musician and composer. He takes Randall's side in the fight against sleeping sickness, but the power of black magic in the hands of the local witch doctor, Magole (played with remarkable force by Orlando Martins), is too much for him.

● ●

■ MEN WITHOUT WOMEN

1930, 76 MINS, US

Dir John Ford   *Scr* John Ford, James Kevin McGuinness, Dudley Nichols   *Ph* Joseph H. August
Ed Paul Weatherwax   *Mus* Peter Brunellin, Glen Knight   *Art Dir* William S. Darling
● Kenneth MacKenna, Frank Albertson, Paul Page, Warren Hymer, Walter McGrail (Fox)

Story and characters are built up with uncanny shrewdness. It opens in Shanghai with a shore party of American gobs going whoopee in an enormous establishment of entertainment of various kinds, mostly a vast bar and many fluttering petticoats and kimonos.

Back to the ship some great views of a sub streaking out to sea at night in clouds of black smoke and weird light and water reflections. Sub is run down in a collision and goes to the bottom in 90 feet of water with all escape cut off, and here begins the sledge hammer situation that lasts to the finish. Finale is a whooping bit of flagwaving.

Kenneth MacKenna, as Chief Torpedoman Burke, does nicely with a heroic lead, but the punch of the acting is the surprise comedy bits of a number of minor characters. It is these touches and the grim comedy of the lines that lift the picture out of melodrama to an illusion of reality.

● ●

■ MEN'S CLUB, THE

1986, 100 MINS, US ◇ Ⓥ

Dir Peter Medak   *Prod* Howard Gottfried
Scr Leonard Michaels   *Ph* John Fleckenstein
Ed Cynthia Scheider, David Dresher, Bill Butler
Mus Lee Holdridge   *Art Dir* Ken Davis
● Roy Scheider, Frank Langella, Harvey Keitel, Treat Williams, Richard Jordan, David Dukes (Atlantic)

Those who think men are immature, destructive, insensitive and basically animals may find *The Men's Club* great fun. Others are likely to balk at the film's contrived and dated treatment of the battle between the sexes.

Film is a distasteful piece of work that displays the worst in men. Leonard Michaels' screenplay [from his novel] is all warts and no insight, full of self-loathing for the gender. In addition, film making is as tired as the material. Pic plays like a stageplay, so static is Peter Medak's direction.

A group of friends nearing age 40 get together and for most of the film's 100 minutes the camera is on their heads talking. Leader of the group is Cavanaugh (Roy Scheider), supposedly a retired baseball star who looks too unhealthy to have ever played anything more strenuous than cards.

● ●

■ MEPHISTO WALTZ, THE

1971, 115 MINS, US ◇ Ⓥ

Dir Paul Wendkos   *Prod* Quinn Martin   *Scr* Ben Maddow   *Ph* William W. Spencer   *Ed* Richard Brockway   *Mus* Jerry Goldsmith   *Art Dir* Richard Y. Hamen
● Alan Alda, Jacqueline Bisset, Barbara Parkins, Bradford Dillman, William Windom, Curt Jurgens (20th Century-Fox)

Based on the novel by Fred Mustard Stewart, pic follows in deadpan style the antics of a deranged concert pianist (Curt Jurgens), dying of leukemia whose lust for his daughter (Barbara Parkins) and devotion to devil-worship destroy the marriage of writer Alan Alda and Jacqueline Bisset.

To revive his sexual prowess, Jurgens has Alda killed, then assumes his body. A trifle slow on the uptake, Bisset finally realizes something is amiss after her daughter dies under mysterious conditions. Alda-cum-Jurgens starts getting ruthless in bed, and the ex-husband of Parkins (Bradford Dillman) tells her (before being killed) of a monster child miscarried by Parkins and sired by her father.

Main fault is a tired script with more than a full quota of arch, laughable dialog, spouted with relish by performers struggling to keep their heads above water.

● ●

■ MERCENARIES, THE

1968, 106 MINS, UK ◇

Dir Jack Cardiff   *Prod* George Englund   *Scr* Quentin Werty, Adrian Spies   *Ph* Edward Scaife   *Ed* Ernest Walter   *Mus* Jacques Loussier
● Rod Taylor, Yvette Mimieux, Peter Garsten, Jim Brown, Kenneth More, Andre Morell (M-G-M)

Based on the Congo uprising, this is a raw adventure yarn [from a novel by Wilbur Smith] with some glib philosophizing which skates superficially over the points of view of the cynical mercenaries and the patriotic Congolese.

Rod Taylor plays a hardbitten mercenary major who's prepared to sweat through any task, however dirty, providing his fee is okay. He's assigned by Congo's president to take a train through rebel Simba-held country and bring back fugitives and a load of uncut diamonds stashed away in a beleaguered town.

The action is taken care of effectively but the rapport between some of the characters is rarely smooth nor convincing enough. Pic was filmed in Africa and at Metro's British studios.

Acting is mostly of a straightforward nature for the script does not lend itself to a subtlety of characterization. Taylor makes a robust hero while Jim Brown brings some dignity and interest to the role of the Congolese native.

● ●

■ MERMAIDS

1990, 111 MINS, US ◇ Ⓥ

Dir Richard Benjamin   *Prod* Lauren Lloyd, Wallis Nicita, Patrick Palmer   *Scr* June Roberts   *Ph* Howard Atherton   *Ed* Jacqueline Cambas   *Mus* Jack Nitzsche   *Art Dir* Stuart Wurtzel
● Cher, Bob Hoskins, Winona Ryder, Michael Schoeffling, Christina Ricci, Caroline McWilliams (Orion)

As eccentric mother-daughter films go, this one [from the novel by Patty Dann] falls into the same category as *Terms of Endearment*, with many of the same comedic pleasures and dramatic pitfalls.

Set in the early 1960s, *Mermaids* begins rousingly, introducing flamboyant Mrs Flax (Cher) and her two daughters: confused Charlotte (Winona Ryder), 15, who is obsessed with Catholicism, and Kate (Christina Ricci), nine, who's obsessed with swimming.

Constantly on the move due to mother's vagabond ways, they soon relocate to a small New England town that brings with it new romantic entanglements. Mrs Flax takes up with a lovelorn shoe salesman (Bob Hoskins), while Charlotte becomes enamored with a dreamy groundskeeper (Michael Schoeffling) from the local nunnery, conveniently situated just down the road.

M

Since she's unable to communicate with her wanton mother, Ryder's dialog is largely limited to voiceover confessions and pleas to God, often while staring intently, wordless and wide-eyed, at her mother or Joe (Schoeffling), the unsuspecting object of her near-crazed lust.

The delightful Ryder, billing notwithstanding, is really the star. Cher is also fine as the cavalier, self-centered mom, an equally amusing if less sympathetic character.

. . . .

■ MERRILL'S MARAUDERS

1962, 98 MINS, US ◇ ⒱
Dir Samuel Fuller   *Prod* Milton Sperling   *Scr* Milton Sperling, Samuel Fuller   *Ph* William Clothier   *Ed* Folmar Blangsted   *Mus* Howard Jackson
● Jeff Chandler, Ty Hardin, Peter Brown, Andrew Duggan, Luz Valdez (United States)

Jeff Chandler's last role, as Brigadier General Frank Merrill, is one of his best. The rugged, gray-thatched Chandler fits this role naturally and portrays one of World War II's most colorful personalities with a proper blend of military doggedness and personal humanity.

When Samuel Fuller – he was a GI in Europe – took his small cast and crew to the Philippines to shoot *Merrill's Marauders*, he did plenty of preliminary screening and, down the line, he got the results he wanted. After Chandler, this film owes much of its excellence to William Clothier's Technicolor photography, both in his feeling for cinematic design and his superb use of color.

Charlton Ogburn's book was a springboard only for the scenarists. They elaborated it into a screenplay that balances battle scenes with character-establishing vignettes and gives the subject-hero a closer contact with his men through playing his story against the background of their daily activities, their fixture of personalities.

Ty Hardin's Lieutenant Stockton is a stock character – the young, still over-sensitive officer – but he conveys a tenderness, a sense of truth that keeps the role from seeming stereotyped.

. . . .

■ MERRILY WE LIVE

1938, 90 MINS, US
Dir Norman Z. McLeod   *Prod* Hal Roach, Milton H. Bren   *Scr* Eddie Moran, Jacke Jevne   *Ph* Norbert Brodine   *Ed* William Terhune   *Mus* Marvin Hatley (dir.)
● Constance Bennett, Brian Aherne, Billie Burke, Alan Mowbray, Patsy Kelly, Ann Dvorak (Roach/M-G-M)

It's all in the acting and directing. Director Norman Z. McLeod has the knack of building up gags until he has three or four racing each other to the big laugh. Most of the fun comes from a fine performance by Billie Burke, who plays a scatterbrain wife and mother in a family of irresponsibles.

Burke has a weakness for helping worthless humanity. Brian Aherne is welcomed to the fold. It happens he isn't a tramp at all, but a writer who forgot to shave on the morning his flivver broke down when he stops by to use the telephone. Once inside, he decides to stay.

In his calm and self-possessed manner he begins to bring some order out of the confusion in which the Kilbourne family lives. This leads to a romance with the elder daughter (Constance Bennett), and a timely word which clinches an important business deal for the head of the house.

Bennett gives a good performance and appears in some striking costumes. Alan Mowbray, as the family butler, contributes to the hilarity, as do Patsy Kelly, in a small part, and Bonita Granville and Tom Brown.

. . . .

■ MERRY CHRISTMAS, MR. LAWRENCE

1983, 122 MINS, NEW ZEALAND/JAPAN/UK ◇ ⒱
Dir Nagisa Oshima   *Prod* Jeremy Thomas   *Scr* Nagisa Oshima, Paul Mayersberg   *Ph* Toichiro Narushima   *Ed* Tomoyo Oshima   *Mus* Ryuichi Sakamoto   *Art Dir* Shigemasa Toda
● David Bowie, Tom Conti, Ryuichi Sakamoto, Takeshi, Jack Thompson (Recorded Picture)

By no means an easy picture to deal with, this thinking man's version of *The Bridge on the River Kwai* makes no concessions to the more obvious commercial requirements, unless it is the selection of David Bowie, the pop star, for the leading dramatic role.

The strongest points of the script, penned by Nagisa Oshima and Paul Mayersberg from a novel [*The Seed and the Sower*] by South African author Laurens van der Post, are the philosophical and emotional implications, brought up in a careful and intricate comparison between Orient and Occident on every possible level. The weakest point is its construction, sturdy and compact up to the point when it has to use flashbacks in order to explain the British side of the allegory.

Set in a Japanese prisoner-of-war camp in Java, the plot has a Japanese captain, Yonoi (Ryuichi Sakamoto), trying to impose his own ideas of discipline, honor, order and obedience, in a clash with a British major, Celliers (Bowie), who represents the diametrically opposed train of thought.

The conflict between the two leading figures is better verbalized by Colonel Lawrence (Tom Conti), who lends his name to the film's title, and Hara (Takeshi), the Japanese sergeant whose popular origins allow him much more freedom of emotions.

. . . .

■ MERRY WIDOW, THE

1934, 110 MINS, US
Dir Ernst Lubitsch   *Prod* Ernst Lubitsch   *Scr* Ernest Vajda, Samson Raphaelson   *Ph* Oliver T. Marsh   *Ed* Frances Marsh   *Mus* Herbert Stothart (adapt.)   *Art Dir* Cedric Gibbons, Gabriel Scognamillo, Frederic Hope
● Maurice Chevalier, Jeanette MacDonald, Edward Everett Horton, Una Merkel, George Barbier, Minna Gombell (M-G-M)

Ernst Lubitsch has here brought the field of operetta to the level of popular taste. Besides Lubitsch, the many involved include Ernest Vajda and Samson Raphaelson on the book; Herbert Stothart on the music; Richard Rodgers, Lorenz Hart and Gus Kahn on the 1934 lyrics. They are, 26 years after, the collaborators on the original *Widow* by Franz Lehar, Victor Leon and Leo Stein. Two or three new airs have been added, but the music still stands pat on Lehar – smartly so.

In his leads, Lubitsch picked a double plum out of the talent grab bag. Maurice Chevalier and Jeanette MacDonald both are aces as Danilo and Sonia. The former Paramount pair once again works beautifully in harness. Supporting players are in chiefly for comedy purposes, and include such expert vets as Edward Everett Horton, George Barbier, Una Merkel, Sterling Holloway and Herman Bing.

. . . .

■ MESSAGE, THE

1976, 179 MINS, UK ◇ ⒱
Dir Moustapha Akkad   *Prod* Moustapha Akkad   *Scr* H.A.L. Craig   *Ph* Jack Hildyard   *Ed* John Bloom   *Mus* Maurice Jarre   *Art Dir* Norman Dorme, Abdel Mouneim Chukri
● Anthony Quinn, Irene Papas, Michael Ansara, Johnny Sekka, Michael Forest, Damien Thomas (Filmco)

The Message, Moustapha Akkad's $17 million saga of the birth of the Islamic religion, bears favorable comparison as a religious epic. H.A.L. Craig's screenplay is remarkably literate, sometimes witty and ironic, but ultimately and perhaps inevitably simplistic.

The action snowballs from underground cell meetings by followers of Mohammad, through brutal harassment, expulsion from Mecca, pitched battles in the desert, and the final conquering pilgrimage back to Mecca. Throughout the narrative there is uncommon respect for the mind and the eye.

Ultimately it's a triumph for Akkad who welded a logistically sprawling epic into coherence. His crowd scenes are credible and the battle scenes superbly rendered.

. . . .

■ METEOR

1979, 103 MINS, US ◇ ⒱
Dir Ronald Neame   *Prod* Arnold Orgolini, Theodore Parvin   *Scr* Stanley Mann, Edmund H. North   *Ph* Paul Lohmann   *Ed* Carl Kress   *Mus* Laurence Rosenthal   *Art Dir* Edward Carfagno
● Sean Connery, Natalie Wood, Karl Malden, Brian Keith, Martin Landau, Trevor Howard (American International)

Meteor really combines several disasters in one continuous cinematic bummer. Along with the threat of a five-mile-wide asteroid speeding towards earth, with smaller splinters preceding it, there's an avalanche, an earthquake, a tidal wave and a giant mud bath. All in all, special effects wizards Glen Robinson and Robert Staples, along with stunt coordinator Roger Greed, got a good workout.

Inevitably, topliners Sean Connery as an American scientist, Brian Keith as his Soviet counterpart, and Natalie Wood as the translator in between them, take a back seat to the effects.

Avalanche sequence is one of the best in memory, aided by the fact that producers were allowed to blow up a mountain in the Swiss Alps.

. . . .

■ METROPOLITAN

1990, 98 MINS, US ◇ ⒱
Dir Whit Stillman   *Prod* Whit Stillman   *Scr* Whit Stillman   *Ph* John Thomas   *Ed* Chris Tellefsen   *Mus* Mark Suozzo, Tom Judson
● Carolyn Farina, Edward Clements, Christopher Eigeman, Taylor Nichols (Westerley Film-Video)

Filmmaker Whit Stillman makes a strikingly original debut with *Metropolitan*, a glib, ironic portrait of the vulnerable young heirs to Manhattan's disappearing debutante scene. Story centers on a set of East Side friends who dub themselves the SFRP (or 'Sally Fowler Rat Pack', after the girl whose Park Avenue apartment they gather in) and, more amusingly, UHBs, for Urban Haute Bourgeoisie.

They drag into their number a newcomer, Tom (Edward Clements), who openly disapproves of them but nonetheless shows up every night for private gatherings after black-tie parties and dances. A self-serious but insensitive young man, Tom inspires the first-time love of Audrey (Carolyn Favina). Tom repeatedly humiliates her as he continues to pursue an old flame, Serena (Elizabeth Thompson).

Among the fine cast, Christopher Eigeman stands out as Nick, the funny, arrogant group leader who's as jovially self-aware and self-mocking as his new friend, Tom, is stilted and blind to himself.

Pic is a true independent production, financed by Stillman (who sold his Manhattan apartment) and several friends.

. . . .

■ MIAMI BLUES

1990, 99 MINS, US ◇ ⒱
Dir George Armitage   *Prod* Jonathan Demme, Gary Goetzman   *Scr* George Armitage   *Ph* Tak Fujimoto   *Ed* Craig McKay   *Mus* Gary Chang   *Art Dir* Maher Ahmad

● Alec Baldwin, Fred Ward, Jennifer Jason Leigh, Nora Dunn, Charles Napier (Tristes Tropiques)

Based on Charles Willeford's novel, this quirky and sometimes brutally funny film strings together terrific moments but never takes a point of view.

Junior (Alec Baldwin) blows into town, initiates a crime spree with a homicide detective's stolen badge and settles down with a simple-minded hooker named Susie (Jennifer Jason Leigh). The sense that Junior can go off at any time, and the explosive and graphic bursts of violence create tension throughout.

Baldwin is more than equal to the task, and his intense machismo and make-believe posturing bring to mind some of Robert De Niro's menace in *Taxi Driver*. Leigh also is wondrously odd, her eyebrows knitting in frustration at the simplest of questions, her drawl filled with rapture at the recipes she can concoct for her new beau.

Pic, however, is missing a key ingredient: a discernible plot. If it's the detective (Fred Ward) seeking to reclaim his badge, false teeth and gun, it's a wispy one at best.

■ **MICKEY ONE**

1965, 90 MINS, US

Dir Arthur Penn   *Prod* Arthur Penn   *Scr* Alan M. Surgal   *Ph* Ghislain Cloquet   *Ed* Aram Avakian   *Mus* Jack Shaindlin

● Warren Beatty, Hurd Hatfield, Alexandra Stewart, Teddy Hart, Jeff Corey, Franchot Tone (Florin/Tatira)

Mickey One could be described as a study in regeneration, but screenplay is overloaded with symbolic gestures which obscure the main objectives of the plot.

Title character is a one-time top nitery comic who has been leading an extravagant life, getting mixed up with dames and gamblers. In a bid to get away from his past and start afresh, he assumes the identity of a Pole whose name is conveniently abbreviated to Mickey One. He gradually drifts back to the world of night clubs, and in a sleazy West Chicago joint rediscovers the art of wowing an audience.

To this point, the plot develops reasonably smoothly and the few touches of symbolism are not entirely unacceptable. Thereafter, however, symbolism runs riot, occasionally to the point of pretentiousness.

Arthur Penn must accept his share of responsibility for the confused style and bewildering nature of the more obscure sequences. But in his main intention he is powerfully backed by Warren Beatty, who gives a commanding, though highly mannered, performance – a consistently dominating study of a man who lives in fear of his past.

■ **MICKI & MAUDE**

1984, 118 MINS, US ◇ ▼

Dir Blake Edwards   *Prod* Tony Adams   *Scr* Jonathan Reynolds   *Ph* Harry Stradling   *Ed* Ralph E. Winters   *Mus* Lee Holdridge, Michael Legrand   *Art Dir* Rodger Maus

● Dudley Moore, Amy Irving, Ann Reinking, Richard Mulligan, George Gaynes, Wallace Shawn (Columbia-Delphi III/BEE)

Micki & Maude is a hilarious farce. For his part, Dudley Moore is in top antic form, and Amy Irving has never been better.

Debuting screenwriter Jonathan Reynolds has constructed a farce of simple, classical proportions about a man who accidentally gets his wife and new girlfriend pregnant at virtually the same time.

The host of a silly TV show which does features on things like the food at an election night celebration, Moore rarely gets to see his attorney wife (Ann Reinking) due to her hectic schedule, finding time only for a quickie in the back of a limousine.

On the job for his show, Moore meets comely Amy Irving, who easily seduces him on their next encounter. Premise is set up shortly thereafter, when both women announce that they are pregnant.

■ **MIDDLE AGE CRAZY**

1980, 89 MINS, CANADA ◇ ▼

Dir John Trent   *Prod* Robert Cooper   *Scr* Carl Kleinschmidt   *Ph* Reginald Morris   *Ed* John Kelly   *Mus* Matthew McCauley   *Art Dir* Karen Bromley

● Bruce Dern, Ann-Margret, Graham Jarvis, Helen Hughes, Deborah Wakeham (20th Century-Fox/Tormont)

Bobby Lee (Bruce Dern) is a successful building contractor on the verge of his 40th birthday. He is getting hung up on his milestone date as a result of his wife's persistence that he's still the old stud she married.

Constant reminders from friends and family on his dependability eventually drive him to change his style. He buys a Porsche, dresses up like a drugstore cowboy, and has a brief fling with a Dallas Cowgirl (Deborah Wakeham).

He finally decides family and responsibility aren't so bad after all. The revelation is pat and steeped in sentimentality. A quick resolution would have been more in keeping with the movie's acerbic wit.

Dern emerges a likable family man with deep reservations about his lot in life. The actor is equally convincing dressed in three-piece suits or denim and boots. Ann-Margret as his wife is also outstanding.

■ **MIDDLE AGE SPREAD**

1979, 94 MINS, NEW ZEALAND ◇

Dir John Reid   *Prod* John Barnett   *Scr* Keith Aberdein   *Ph* Alun Bollinger   *Ed* Michael Horton   *Mus* Stephen McCurdy

● Grant Tilly, Donna Akersten, Dorothy McKegg, Bridget Armstrong, Bevan Wilson, Peter Sumner (Endeavour/NZ Film Commission)

Middle Age Spread centres on Colin (Grant Tilly), a college teacher whose promotion to principal coincides with a number of personal crises.

Not least are a widening girth, which has him jogging round the streets at night, and a tentative first-and-last affair with a much younger teaching colleague, Judy (Donna Akersten).

At a dinner party he hosts, with his increasingly sexually-disinterested wife, Elizabeth (Dorothy McKegg), the morality and values of their tight-knit circle of friends are played out with deadly accuracy.

To his credit, director John Reid, one of the actors in the original stage presentation, has created a film that is not just a pale adaptation of the play.

■ **MIDNIGHT**

1939, 92 MINS, US

Dir Mitchell Leisen   *Prod* Arthur Hornblow Jr   *Scr* Charles Brackett, Billy Wilder   *Ph* Charles Lang Jr   *Ed* Doane Harrison   *Mus* Frederick Hollander   *Art Dir* Hans Dreier, Robert Usher

● Claudette Colbert, Don Ameche, John Barrymore, Francis Lederer, Mary Astor, Hedda Hopper (Paramount)

Story [from one by Edwin Justus Mayer and Franz Schulz] is light, but with a good share of humorous moments, many of them of the screwball variety. It's a slender thread, however, on which to tie series of incidents in adventures of a stranded showgirl in Paris.

After a flirtation with Don Ameche, Claudette Colbert crashes a musicale and poses as a countess. This leads to job for John Barrymore, in which she is to attract the amorous attentions of Francis Lederer away from Barrymore's wife, Mary Astor. For her assignment, Colbert is provided with elaborate wardrobe and a hotel suite.

Direction by Mitchell Leisen is generally satisfactory, although picture is slow in getting under way and has several spots that could be tightened. Editing shows sketchiness in several instances.

■ **MIDNIGHT COWBOY**

1969, 119 MINS, US ◇ ▼

Dir John Schlesinger   *Prod* Jerome Hellman, John Schlesinger   *Scr* Waldo Salt   *Ph* Adam Holender   *Ed* Hugh A. Robertson   *Mus* John Barry (sup.)

● Dustin Hoffman, John Voight, Sylvia Miles, John McGiver, Brenda Vaccaro, Bernard Hughes (United Artists)

Midnight Cowboy, is the sometimes amusing but essentially sordid saga of a male prostitute in Manhattan. Dustin Hoffman is cast as gimp-legged, always unshaven, a cough-wracked petty chiseler who at first exploits and then befriends the stupid boy hustler from Texas. The title role is played by Jon Voight.

The film [from a novel by James Leo Herlihy] is full of unnice people from bad environments. It is obsessed with mercenary sex and haunted by memories of cruel group ravishments. Indignity is endemic.

Voight travels north by bus through an America that is mocked in every sign along the road.

It is never easy to work up a liking for either of the two main bums in this pantheon of lost souls.

Midnight Cowboy has a miscellany of competent bit players and a good deal of both sly and broad humor.

□ 1969: Best Picture

■ **MIDNIGHT EXPRESS**

1978, 120 MINS, UK ◇ ▼

Dir Alan Parker   *Prod* David Puttnam   *Scr* Oliver Stone   *Ph* Michael Seresin   *Ed* Gerry Hambling   *Mus* Giorgio Moroder   *Art Dir* Geoffrey Kirkland

● Brad Davis, Randy Quaid, John Hurt, Bo Hopkins, Paul Smith, Mike Kellin (Casablanca)

Midnight Express is a sordid and ostensibly true story about a young American busted for smuggling hash in Turkey and his subsequent harsh imprisonment and later escape. Cast, direction and production are all very good, but it's difficult to sort out the proper empathies from the muddled and moralizing screenplay which, in true Anglo-American fashion, wrings hands over alien cultures as though our civilization is absolutely perfect.

Oliver Stone is credited for adapting the book by Billy Hayes, young tourist who, in the midst of airline terrorism and world pressure on Turkey over drug farming, is discovered wearing a not-insignificant amount of hash strapped to his body. Brad Davis plays Hayes in a strong performance.

Acceptance of the film depends a lot on forgetting several things: he was smuggling hash; Turkey is entitled to its laws, and is no more guilty of penal corruption and brutality than, say, the US, UK, France, Germany, etc; a world tourist can't assume that a helpful father (played well by Mike Kellin) is going to have the same clout with some midwestern politicians; nor can an American expect to be treated with kid gloves everywhere.

However, the script loads up sympathy for Davis, also fellow convicts Randy Quaid (a psycho character), John Hurt (a hard doper) and Norbert Weisser (playing the obligatory

gay inmate), by making the prison
authorities even worse.
□ 1978: Best Picture (Nomination)

....

■ MIDNIGHT MAN, THE

1974, 117 MINS, US ◇

Dir Roland Kibbee, Burt Lancaster   *Prod* Roland
Kibbee, Burt Lancaster   *Scr* Roland Kibbee, Burt
Lancaster   *Ph* Jack Priestley   *Ed* Frank Morriss
Mus Dave Grusin   *Art Dir* James D. Vance
● Burt Lancaster, Susan Clark, Cameron Mitchell,
Morgan Woodward, Harris Yulin, Joan Lorring
(Universal)

The Midnight Man stars Burt Lancaster as a
paroled ex-cop stumbling into a series of
small-town murders. With Roland Kibbee,
Lancaster adapted, produced and directed on
some refreshingly different locations in South
Carolina. The cluttered plot's twists and
turns get tiring after 117 minutes, but the
violence highlights are well motivated and
discreetly executed.

Script derives from a David Anthony novel,
The Midnight Lady and the Mourning Man.
Lancaster, out on parole after killing his
wife's lover, is reduced to a campus security
job under the auspices of his longtime pal
(Cameron Mitchell). Susan Clark is
Lancaster's sexy parole officer.

The murder of Catherine Bach, whose
personal trauma was committed to a tape
stolen from psychologist Robert Quarry,
triggers an awful lot of storytelling.

....

■ MIDNIGHT RUN

1988, 122 MINS, US ◇ ⒯

Dir Martin Brest   *Prod* Martin Brest   *Scr* George
Gallo   *Ph* Donald Thorin   *Ed* Billy Weber, Chris
Lebenzon, Michael Tronick   *Mus* Danny Elfman
Art Dir Angelo Graham
● Robert De Niro, Charles Grodin, Yaphet Kotto, John
Ashton, Dennis Farina (City Lights)

Midnight Run shows that Robert De Niro can
be as wonderful in a comic role as he is in a
serious one. Pair him, a gruff ex-cop and
bounty hunter, with straight man Charles
Grodin, his captive, and the result is one of
the most entertaining, best executed, original
road pictures *ever*.

It's De Niro's boyish charm that works for
him every time and here especially as the
scruffy bounty hunter ready to do his last job
in a low-life occupation. He's to nab a philan-
thropically minded accountant hiding out in
Gotham (Grodin) who embezzled $15 million
from a heroin dealer/Las Vegas mobster and
return him to Los Angeles in time to collect a
$100,000 fee by midnight Friday.

Kidnapping Grodin is the easy part; getting
him back to the west coast turns out to be
anything but easy. The two guys, who can't
stand each other, are stuck together for the
duration of a journey neither particularly
wants to be on.

Midnight Run is more than a string of well-
done gags peppered by verbal sparring between a reluctant twosome; it is a terrifically
developed script full of inventive, humorous
twists made even funnier by wonderfully realized secondary characters.

....

■ MIDSUMMER NIGHT'S DREAM, A

1935, 132 MINS, US ⒱

Dir Max Reinhardt, William Dieterle   *Prod* Henry
Blanke   *Scr* Charles Kenyon, Mary C. McCall Jr
Ph Hal Mohr   *Ed* Ralph Dawson   *Mus* Erich Wolfgang
Korngold (adapt.)   *Art Dir* Anton Grot
● James Cagney, Olivia de Havilland, Ian Hunter,
Verree Teasdale, Joe E. Brown, Dick Powell (Warner)

Question of whether a Shakespearean play
can be successfully produced on a lavish scale
for the films is affirmatively answered by this

commendable effort. The familiar story of *A
Midsummer Night's Dream*, half of which is laid
in a make-believe land of elves and fairies, is
right up the film alley technically.

The fantasy, the ballets of the Oberon and
Titania cohorts, and the characters in the
eerie sequences are convincing and illusion
compelling. Film is replete with enchanting
scenes, beautifully photographed and charmingly presented. All Shakespearian devotees
will be pleased at the soothing treatment
given to the Mendelssohn score.

The women are uniformly better than the
men. They get more from their lines. The
selection of Dick Powell to play Lysander was
unfortunate. He never seems to catch the spirit of the play or role. And Mickey
Rooney, as Puck, is so intent on being cute
that he becomes almost annoying.

There are some outstanding performances,
however, notably Victor Jory as Oberon. His
clear, distinct diction indicates what can be
done by careful recitation and good recording; Olivia de Havilland, as Hermia, is a fine
artist here; others are Jean Muir, Verree
Teasdale and Anita Louise, the latter beautiful as Titania but occasionally indistinct in
her lines.

Jimmy Cagney, as Bottom, registers effectively mainly in the romantic passages with
Anita Louise.
□ 1935: Best Picture (Nomination)

....

■ MIDSUMMER NIGHT'S SEX COMEDY, A

1982, 88 MINS, US ◇ ⒱

Dir Woody Allen   *Prod* Robert Greenhut   *Scr* Woody
Allen   *Ph* Gordon Willis   *Ed* Susan E. Morse
Art Dir Mel Bourne
● Woody Allen, Mia Farrow, Jose Ferrer, Julie
Hagerty, Tony Roberts, Mary Steenburgen (Orion)

Woody Allen's *A Midsummer Night's Sex
Comedy* is a pleasant disappointment,
pleasant because he gets all the laughs he
goes for in a visually charming, sweetly paced
picture, a disappointment because he doesn't
go for more.

The time is the turn of the century, the
place a lovely old farmhouse in upstate New
York. Here, Wall St stockbroker Allen spends
his spare time inventing odd devices and trying to bed his own wife (Mary Steenburgen)
who has turned cold.

Arriving for a visit – and also a wedding –
are Steenburgen's cousin Jose Ferrer, a
stuffy, pedantic scholar, and his bride to be
(Mia Farrow), a former near-nympho who's
decided to settle down with Ferrer's intellect.

Also arriving are Allen's best friend, who
else but Tony Roberts, an amorous physician
and his current short-term fling (Julie
Hagerty), a nurse dedicated to the study of
anatomy and all its possibilities.

With this daffy assortment and Allen's gift
for laugh-lines, the picture can't avoid being
fun, even at a rather leisurely pace in keeping
with its times.

....

■ MIDWAY

1976, 132 MINS, US ◇ ⒱

Dir Jack Smight   *Prod* Walter Mirisch   *Scr* Donald S.
Sanford   *Ph* Harry Stradling Jr   *Ed* Robert Swink,
Frank J. Urioste   *Mus* John Williams   *Art Dir* Walter
Tyler
● Charlton Heston, Henry Fonda, James Coburn,
Glenn Ford, Hal Holbrook, Toshiro Mifune (Universal)

The June 1942 sea-air battle off Midway
Island was a turning point in World War II.
However, the melee of combat was the usual
hysterical jumble of noise, explosion and violent death. *Midway* tries to combine both
aspects but succumbs to the confusion.

Henry Fonda's performance as Pacific Fleet
Commander Chester W. Nimitz towers over
everything else.

The Midway battle followed the Mames
Doolittle air raid on Tokyo in April 1942.
The turnback of the Japanese Navy effectively cleared the West Coast from attack,
and gave the US time enough to mobilize for
the long road back across the Pacific.

....

■ MIGHTY JOE YOUNG

1949, 88 MINS, US ⒱

Dir Ernest B. Schoedsack   *Prod* John Ford, Merian C.
Cooper   *Scr* Ruth Rose   *Ph* J. Roy Hunt   *Ed* Ted
Cheeseman   *Mus* Roy Webb
● Terry Moore, Ben Johnson, Robert Armstrong (RKO)

Mighty Joe Young is fun to laugh at and with,
loaded with incredible corn, plenty of humor,
and a robot gorilla who becomes a genuine
hero. The technical skill of the large staff of
experts gives the robot life.

Plot deals with a gorilla, raised in the African jungle by a young girl. Both the girl and
the giant ape are happy with their rusticating
until a safari headed by Broadway producer
Robert Armstrong arrives in the jungle. Armstrong immediately sees the possibilities of
the ape and the girl.

The presentation by John Ford and Cooper
pulls all stops in slugging away at audience
risibilities while pointing up the melodramatic phases. It's this general air of tongue-in-
cheek treatment that makes the corn
palatable.

....

■ MIKEY AND NICKY

1976, 119 MINS, US ◇ ⒱

Dir Elaine May   *Prod* Michael Hausman   *Scr* Elaine
May   *Ph* Victor J. Kemper, Lucien Ballard, Jerry File,
Jack Cooperman   *Ed* John Carter   *Mus* John Strauss
Art Dir Paul Sylbert
● Peter Falk, John Cassavetes, Ned Beatty, Rose Arrick,
Carol Grace, William Hickey (Paramount)

Peter Falk and John Cassavetes star as two
old friends whose relationship is falling apart;
two hours later, it is apparent there never was
a friendship to begin with.

Cassavetes is a low-level criminal marked
for extinction by ganglord Sanford Meisner,
who employs Ned Beatty as hit man. Cassavetes calls Falk to help him, though neither
Cassavetes nor the audience is certain that
Falk isn't part of the rubout strategy. That's
the superficial hook on which hangs the real
story of human relationships and mutual
abuse.

The interplay between the stars is excellent,
Cassavetes slowly but steadily digging his
own grave as he reveals his shallowness in
dealings with Falk, girl friend Carol Grace
(a beautiful performance) and estranged wife
Joyce Van Patten (a brief but excellent
characterization).

....

■ MILAGRO BEANFIELD WAR, THE

1988, 117 MINS, US ◇ ⒱

Dir Robert Redford   *Prod* Robert Redford, Moctesuma
Esparza   *Scr* David Ward, John Nichols   *Ph* Robbie
Greenberg   *Ed* Dede Allen, Jim Miller   *Mus* Dave
Grusin   *Art Dir* Joe Aubel
● Ruben Blades, Richard Bradford, Sonia Braga, Julie
Carmen, John Heard, Melanie Griffith (Universal)

The Milagro Beanfield War is a charming, fanciful little fable built around weighty issues
concerning the environment, the preservation
of a cultural heritage and the rights of citizens
versus the might of the dollar.

The director and his screenwriters, who
adapted John Nichols' 1974 novel, adeptly
juggle at least a dozen major characters in
telling the story of how one man's decision to
cultivate his land, which is coveted by outside
developers intent upon building a resort,
leads to a standoff between natives of the area
and the big boys.

Redford and company have put a quirky twist on the material, investing it with a quasi-mystical aspect as well as some raw comedy.

Set in modern-day New Mexico, tale is set in motion when improverished farmer Joe Mondrago (Chick Vennera) improperly diverts some water from a main irrigation channel onto his own modest plot of land in order to start up a beanfield. This little act of defiance stirs up the handful of activists in the affected village, notably garage owner Ruby Archuleta (Sonia Braga), who recruits dropped out radical attorney and newspaperman Charley Bloom (John Heard) to rally 'round the cause.

■ MILDRED PIERCE

1945, 109 MINS, US ⓥ
Dir Michael Curtiz *Prod* Jerry Wald *Scr* Ranald MacDougall *Ph* Ernest Haller *Ed* David Weisbart *Mus* Max Steiner *Art Dir* Anton Grot
● Joan Crawford, Jack Carson, Zachary Scott, Eve Arden, Ann Blyth, Bruce Bennett (Warner)

At first reading James M. Cain's novel of the same title might not suggest screenable material, but the cleanup job has resulted in a class feature, showmanly produced by Jerry Wald and tellingly directed by Michael Curtiz.

It skirts the censorable deftly, but keeps the development adult in dealing with the story of a woman's sacrifices for a no-good daughter. High credit goes to Ranald MacDougall's scripting for his realistic dialog and method of retaining the frank sex play that dots the narrative while making the necessary compromises with the blue-pencillers.

Story is told in flashback as Mildred Pierce is being questioned by police about the murder of her second husband. Character goes back to the time she separated from her first husband and how she struggled to fulfill her ambitions for her children.

The dramatics are heavy but so skillfully handled that they never cloy. Joan Crawford reaches a peak of her acting career in this pic. Ann Blyth, as the daughter, scores dramatically in her first genuine acting assignment. Zachary Scott makes the most of his character as the Pasadena heel, a talented performance.
□ 1945: Best Picture (Nomination)

■ MILLER'S CROSSING

1990, 114 MINS, US ◇ ⓥ
Dir Joel Coen *Prod* Ethan Coen, Mark Silverman *Scr* Joel Coen, Ethan Coen *Ph* Barry Sonnenfeld *Ed* Michael Miller *Mus* Carter Burwell *Art Dir* Dennis Gassner
● Gabriel Byrne, Albert Finney, Marcia Gay Harden, Jon Polito, John Turturro, J.E. Freeman (Circle/Pedas-Barenhotz-Durkin)

Substance is here in spades, along with the twisted, brilliantly controlled style on which filmmakers Joel and Ethan Coen made a name.

Story unspools in an unnamed Eastern city in the 1930s where dim but ambitious Italian gangster Johnny Caspar (Jon Polito) has a problem named Bernie Bernbaum (John Turturro). Caspar wants approval from the city's Irish political boss, Leo (Albert Finney), to rub out the cause of his complaint, but Leo's not giving in. He's fallen in love with Bernie's sister, Verna (Marcia Gay Harden), who wants Bernie protected.

Leo's cool, brainy aide-de-camp Tom (Gabriel Byrne) sees that Leo is making a big mistake, and it's up to Tom to save him as his empire begins to crumble. The complication is that Tom also is in love with Verna, though he's loath to admit it.

Rarely does a screen hero of Tom's gritty dimensions come along, and Irishman Byrne

brings him gracefully and profoundly to life. As portrayed by screen newcomer Harden, Verna has the verve and flintiness of a glory-days Bette Davis or Barbara Stanwyck.

Also outstanding is Finney as the big-hearted political fixer who usually has the mayor and the police chief seated happily across his desk. He's as cool in a spray of bullets as he is vulnerable in affairs of the heart.

Buffs will note cameos by director Sam Raimi, with whom the Coens collaborated on his *Evil Dead*, and Frances McDormand, who made her indelible debut in *Blood Simple*.

■ MILLION POUND NOTE, THE

1954, 92 MINS, US ◇ ⑦
Dir Ronald Neame *Prod* John Bryan *Scr* Jill Craigie *Ph* Geoffrey Unsworth *Ed* Clive Donner *Mus* Jack Maxsted
● Gregory Peck, Jane Griffiths, Ronald Squire, Joyce Grenfell, Reginald Beckwith, Hartley Power (Group)

Mark Twain's classic story of the penniless American who is given a million pound bank note in a wager and succeeds in keeping it intact for a month, makes gentle screen satire.

With Edwardian settings providing a fascinating background, the yarn suffers from the protracted exploitation of one basic joke. It is sustaining and amusing for a time, but there are very few single gags that can successfully hold up for 92 minutes. *Note* is not an exception.

The plot is based on a bet between two brothers (Ronald Squire and Wilfrid Hyde White) that a man with a million pound bank note in his possession could live on the fat of the land for a month without having to break into it. The guinea pig for their wager is Gregory Peck, a penniless American stranded in London. And, sure enough, he finds this an open sesame to food, clothes, hotels and, naturally, society.

■ MILLIONAIRESS, THE

1960, 90 MINS, UK ◇
Dir Anthony Asquith *Prod* Dimitri De Grunwald *Scr* Wolf Mankowitz *Ph* Jack Hildyard *Ed* Anthony Harvey *Mus* George van Parys
● Sophia Loren, Peter Sellers, Alastair Sim, Vittorio De Sica, Dennis Price, Alfie Bass (20th Century-Fox)

This stylized pic has Sophia Loren at her most radiant, wearing a series of stunning Balmain gowns. George Bernard Shaw's Shavianisms on morality, riches and human relationship retain much of their edge, though nudged into a practical screenplay by Wolf Mankowitz.

Anthony Asquith's direction often is slow, but he breaks up the pic with enough hilarious situation to keep the film from getting tedious. A major fault is that the cutting of the film, which is mainly episodic, is often needlessly jerky and indecisive. But against this, there is handsome artwork and the relish with which Jack Hildyard has brought his camera to work on them.

Briefly, the yarn concerns a beautiful, spoiled young heiress who has all the money in the world but can't find love. Her eccentric deceased old man has stipulated that she mustn't marry unless the man of her choice can turn $1,400 into $42,000 within three months. She cheats. Her first marriage flops, she contemplates suicide and then sets her cap for a dedicated, destitute Indian doctor runing a poor man's clinic. He's attracted to her, but scared of her money and power.

Loren is a constant stimulation. She catches many moods. Whether she's wooing the doctor brazenly, confiding in a psychiatrist, trying to commit suicide, upbraiding her lawyer or just pouting she is

fascinating. Sellers plays the doctor straight, apart from an offbeat accent, but he still manages to bring in some typical Sellers comedy touches which help to make it a fascinating character study. He even injects a few emotional throwaways which are fine.

■ MILLIONS LIKE US

1943, 103 MINS, UK
Dir Frank Launder, Sidney Gilliat *Scr* Frank Launder, Sidney Gilliat *Ph* Jack Cox, Roy Frogwell *Mus* Louis Levy
● Eric Portman, Patricia Roc, Gordon Jackson, Anne Crawford, Basil Radford, Naunton Wayne (Gainsborough)

Film is designed as patriotic propaganda on the UK front, minus flag waving and suchlike. Acting throughout is superior to the story, and is of such a high quality it ought to make almost any film script interesting. It would not be at all surprising if the creation of this abundance of histrionic talent was due to slickness of direction.

The main star (in point of reputation) is Eric Portman, who has a relatively small part, but gives to it a dignified and intelligent portrayal. The outstanding roles are Patricia Roc and Gordon Jackson – she a factory worker, and he a young airman. Their lovemaking is crudely simple, but so sincere as to lift it out of the commonplace.

The list of players includes a pair of prominent artists who appeared in the writers' successful *The Lady Vanishes*, when they scored smartly as a couple of silly Englishmen. An attempt is made to reproduce them in this picture, but without the same success. It really is unfair to Basil Radford and Naunton Wayne.

■ MIND BENDERS, THE

1963, 101 MINS, UK
Dir Basil Dearden *Prod* Michael Relph *Scr* James Kennaway *Ph* Denys Coop *Ed* John D. Guthridge *Mus* Georges Auric *Art Dir* James Morahan
● Dirk Bogarde, Mary Ure, John Clements, Michael Bryant, Wendy Craig (Anglo-Amalgamated)

James Kennaway's original screenplay finds the peg for its bizarre plot in 'reduction of sensation' experiments reportedly done both in the US and Britain. By eliminating a subject's various senses by submerging him in an isolation tank a shortcut to brainwashing is achieved. Once the basic story pattern has been established, it moves into a fascinating study of how a man's mind can be twisted by a laboratory technique.

Suicide of elderly scientist Harold Goldblatt prompts an investigation by secret agent John Clements to determine whether military security has been violated. Clements suspects Goldblatt has turned traitor. But the scientist's associate, Dirk Bogarde, denies any treason has been committed and blames Goldblatt's death as a result of the experiments. Bogarde voluntarily submits to isolation to prove his theory.

Under Basil Dearden's firm direction, the cast absorbingly captures suspense and gruesome space age qualities frequently generated by Kennaway's script. Bogarde emerges as a dedicated scientist who shades his role with lotsa realism. Mary Ure's portrayal of the spurned wife is a touching piece of thesping.

■ MINISTRY OF FEAR

1944, 84 MINS, US
Dir Fritz Lang *Prod* Seton I. Miller *Scr* Seton I. Miller *Ph* Henry Sharp *Ed* Archie Marshek *Mus* Victor Young *Art Dir* Hans Dreier, Hal Pereira

● Ray Milland, Marjorie Reynolds, Dan Duryea, Carl Esmond, Hillary Brooke, Alan Napier (Paramount)

Fritz Lang, a master at getting the most out of mystery, intrigue and melodrama, in his direction apparently didn't have his way from beginning to end on *Ministry of Fear*. Pic [from the novel by Graham Greene] starts out to be a humdinger, and continues that way for the most part, but when the roundup of the spy gang gets underway the situation becomes drawn out and elementary, marring the footage that preceded.

Ray Milland, in the role of an ex-asylum inmate, who is released after serving two years for the 'mercy' killing of his incurable wife, gives a forthright performance. He is tossed into the midst of a spy chase when, in purchasing a ticket to London upon leaving the asylum, he is drawn to the crowds at a British fair and wins a cake by guessing its weight. The cake contains a capsule which one of the spies is to have delivered to other enemy agents.

■ MINIVER STORY, THE

1950, 104 MINS, UK/US

Dir H.C. Potter   *Prod* Sidney Franklin   *Scr* Ronald Millar, George Froeschel   *Ph* Joseph Ruttenberg   *Ed* Frank Clarke   *Mus* Miklos Rozsa
● Greer Garson, Walter Pidgeon, John Hodiak, Leo Genn, Cathy O'Donnell, Peter Finch (M-G-M)

No one seriously expected a second *Mrs Miniver* when *The Miniver Story* was in the making. It is difficult to capture the magical quality of the original, and this trades on its predecessor's name and the drawing power of Greer Garson and Walter Pidgeon.

Opening with a strangely pallid reproduction of London on VE day, Mrs Miniver finds herself caught in the exuberant melee following the news that the war is over. She has just come from a doctor, realizes she has not long to live and bravely determines to keep the news from her family.

Chief laurels go to Greer Garson who, even with the unmistakable signs of illness and mental stress, makes feasible the husband's claim that she looks as lovely as ever.

John Hodiak gives a fine clear-cut performance.

■ MINNIE AND MOSKOWITZ

1971, 114 MINS, US ◇

Dir John Cassavetes   *Prod* Al Ruban   *Scr* John Cassavetes   *Ph* Arthur J. Ornitz, Alric Edens, Michael Margulies   *Ed* Fred Knudtson   *Mus* Bo Harwood
● Gena Rowlands, Seymour Cassel, Val Avery, Tim Carey, Katherine Cassavetes, John Cassavetes (Universal)

Gena Rowlands and Seymour Cassel play the title roles in *Minnie And Moskowitz*, an oppressive and irritating film in which a shrill and numbing hysteria of acting and direction soon kills any empathy for the loneliness of the main characters. John Cassavetes wrote and directed in his now-familiar home-movie improvisational and indulgent style.

The characters in Cassavetes' script are the 'little people' who inhabit kitchen-sink dramas. When such people exist in reality, they are leasebreakers, who lower property values, create Saturday night brawls and otherwise earn the total contempt of neighbors.

Cassavetes has laid on with a trowel the silicones of borderline personal psychosis. The principals live on the knife-edge of breakdown.

Rowlands, fed up with a back-street affair with Cassavetes, unbilled as a married man whose wife Judith Roberts tries suicide, has a friend in co-worker Elsie Ames but little more. Rescuing her from a tight situation

with pushy blind date Val Avery, Seymour Cassel outdoes in boorishness anything Avery might have tried. Cassel makes King Kong look like Cary Grant.

■ MIRACLE, THE

1959, 121 MINS, US ◇

Dir Irving Rapper   *Prod* Henry Blanke   *Scr* Frank Butler   *Ph* Ernest Haller   *Ed* Frank Bracht   *Mus* Elmer Bernstein
● Carroll Baker, Roger Moore, Walter Slezak, Vittorio Gassman, Katina Paxinou, Gustavo Rojo (Warner)

Warner Bros.' multi-million dollar spectacle, though laid in the 19th century is a 'biblical' subject with elements and approach of such films. The production has bullfights, military battles, lavish ballroom parties, music, dancing, gypsies and vaulted cathedrals echoing to choirs of nuns. It has about everything, in fact, except a genuinely spiritual story.

The Miracle was a costume special of the German stager Max Reinhardt. Its theme is the recurrent one in religious legend, of the god, goddess or angel who assumes human shape to intervene directly in the affairs of men.

According to the screenplay, based on Karl Vollmoeller's old play, Carroll Baker is a postulant at a Spanish convent when she falls in love with Roger Moore, a soldier in the future Duke of Wellington's army, then battling Napoleon in Spain. When she leaves the convent to follow Moore, the statue of the Virgin in the chapel comes down from its pedestal and assumes the form of the postulant. And Baker is off on various adventures.

Irving Rapper's direction is effective in the spacious exteriors, moving massed groupings with force and interest. It is less perceptive in the handling of individuals and their interaction. As for the theme itself, it is not exactly clear what 'The Miracle' is supposed to do, other than give Baker a chance to gallivant about Europe in a variety of costumes.

■ MIRACLE CAN HAPPEN, A (ON OUR MERRY WAY)

1948, 107 MINS, US

Dir King Vidor, Leslie Fenton   *Prod* Benedict Bogeaus, Burgess Meredith   *Scr* Laurence Stallings, Lou Breslow   *Ph* Edward Cronjager, Joseph Biroc, Gordon Avil, John Seitz, Ernest Laszlo   *Ed* James Smith   *Mus* Heinz Roemheld   *Art Dir* Ernst Fegte, Duncan Cramer
● Burgess Meredith, Paulette Goddard, Fred MacMurray, James Stewart, Dorothy Lamour, Henry Fonda (United Artists)

The fact that this attempt at whimsy doesn't always come off is incidental; just look at the names! The pic opens with a pair of surefire names like Goddard and Meredith – and in bed, too.

Then Stewart, Fonda, and Harry James. Plus Lamour and Victor Moore, in a Hollywood satire, or how the sarong became famous. Followed by Fred MacMurray and William Demarest. All in episodic sequences detailing what an inquiring reporter encounters when he seeks to have answered the question of how a child influenced the lives of a group of selected adults.

Meredith is the reporter, so-called. Actually he's only a classified-ad solicitor for a newspaper. But he's lied to his recent bride; he's told her he's the inquiring reporter. Through a subterfuge, however, he assumes the mantle of the paper's actual I.R., a long-time ambition, for just this one question.

The cast couldn't have been better. The story's execution falters because a scene here and there is inclined to strive too much for its whimsical effect. But Meredith responds capitally to the mood of the character he plays,

being given more of a chance to do so than any of the other stars.

■ MIRACLE OF MORGAN'S CREEK, THE

1944, 101 MINS, US

Dir Preston Sturges   *Prod* Preston Sturges   *Scr* Preston Sturges   *Ph* John F. Seitz   *Ed* Stuart Gilmore   *Mus* Leo Shuken, Charles Bradshaw   *Art Dir* Hans Dreier, Ernst Fegte
● Eddie Bracken, Betty Hutton, Diana Lynn, William Demarest (Paramount)

Morgan's Creek is the name of the town where the action takes place and the miracle, as director Preston Sturges terms it, is the birth to Eddie Bracken and Betty Hutton of a set of sextuplets.

Done in the satirical Sturges vein, and directed with that same touch, the story makes much of characterization and somewhat wacky comedy, plus some slapstick, with excellent photography figuring throughout. The Sturges manner of handling crowds and various miscellaneous characters who are almost nothing more than flashes in the picture, such as the smalltown attorney and the justice of the peace, contribute enormously to the enjoyment derived.

However, some of the comedy situations lack punch, and the picture is slow to get rolling, but ultimately picks up smart pace and winds up quite strongly on the birth of the sextuplets with the retiring Bracken and Hutton as national heroes.

Bracken is a smalltown bank clerk who yearns to get into uniform and is madly in love with Hutton. Getting out on an all-night party with soldiers, the latter wakes up to remember that she married a serviceman, but can't remember the name, what the spouse looked like, or anything except that they didn't give their right names.

Bracken does a nice job. Hutton and he make a desirable team. Among the supporting cast, largest assignment is that given William Demarest, smalltown cop father of Hutton, who has his troubles with his daughters, the other being attractive Diana Lynn.

■ MIRACLE ON 34TH STREET

1947, 95 MINS, US ♥

Dir George Seaton   *Prod* William Perlberg   *Scr* George Seaton   *Ph* Charles Clarke, Lloyd Ahern   *Ed* Robert Simpson   *Mus* Cyril J. Mockridge   *Art Dir* Richard Day, Richard Irvine
● Maureen O'Hara, John Payne, Edmund Gwenn, Natalie Wood, Thelma Ritter (20th Century-Fox)

So you don't believe in Santa Claus? If you want to stay a non-believer don't see *Miracle*.

Film is an actor's holiday, providing any number of choice roles that are played to the hilt. Edmund Gwenn's Santa Claus performance proves the best in his career, one that will be thoroughly enjoyed by all filmgoers. Straight romantic roles handed Maureen O'Hara and John Payne as co-stars also display pair to advantage.

Valentine Davies' story poses question of just how valid is the belief in Santa Claus. Gwenn, old man's home inmate, becomes Santy at Macy's Department Store, events pile up that make it necessary to actually prove he is the McCoy and not a slightly touched old gent. Gwenn is a little amazed at all the excitement because he has no doubt that he's the real article.

Gene Lockhart's performance as judge is a gem, as is Porter Hall's portrayal of a neurotic personnel director for Macy's. Surprise moppet performance is turned in by little Natalie Wood as O'Hara's non-believing daughter who finally accepts Santy. It's a standout, natural portrayal.

□ 1947: Best Picture (Nomination)

■ MIRACLE WORKER, THE

1962, 106 MINS, US ▽

Dir Arthur Penn *Prod* Fred Coe *Scr* William Gibson
Ph Ernest Caparros *Ed* Aram Avakian *Mus* Laurence
Rosenthal *Art Dir* George Jenkins
● Anne Bancroft, Patty Duke, Victor Jory, Inga
Swenson, Andrew Prine (United Artists)

A celebrated television show, later a critical,
artistic and popular hit on the stage, the Fred
Coe production was directed by Arthur Penn,
who staged the legit version, and stars Anne
Bancroft and Patty Duke in the roles they
introduced to Broadway.

Gibson's screenplay relates the story of the
young Helen Keller and how, through the
dedication, perseverance and courage of her
teacher, Annie Sullivan, she establishes a
means of communication with the world she
cannot see or hear.

Where the picture really excels, outside of
its inherent story values, is in the realm of
photographic technique. It is here that director Penn and cameraman Ernest Caparros
have teamed to create artful, indelible strokes
of visual storytelling and mood-molding. The
measured dissolves, focal shifts and lighting
and filtering enrich the production considerably. Add to these attributes the haunting,
often chilling, score by Laurence Rosenthal.

■ MIRAGE

1965, 108 MINS, US ▽

Dir Edward Dmytryk *Prod* Harry Keller *Scr* Peter
Stone *Ph* Joseph MacDonald *Ed* Ted J. Kent
Mus Quincy Jones
● Gregory Peck, Diane Baker, Walter Matthau, Kevin
McCarthy, Jack Weston, Leif Erickson (Universal)

Mirage starts as a mystery, unfolds as a mystery, ends as a mystery. There are moments
of stiff action and suspense but plot is as confusing as it is overly-contrived.

Gregory Peck stars as an amnesiac trying to
learn why he is the target for assassins. Story
is about a man in NY who suddenly discovers
he cannot remember any part of his past life.
Returning to his apartment from a big office
building which was suddenly without lights
and where a prominent man plunged to his
death from the 27th floor, he is confronted by
a stranger holding a gun who informs him
he's taking Peck to a man he has never heard
of. Knocking the gunman out, he goes to the
police to demand protection, only to discover
he's a thoroughly confused man.

Edward Dmytryk in his taut direction
keeps a tight rein on pace and manages vigorous movement in individual sequences, but
cannot overcome script deficiencies. Peck's
character is not clearly drawn but actor
makes the most of what's offered him as a
brooding man trying to save his life. Diane
Baker flits in and out of plot as a mysterious
figure whose true identity is never
established.

■ MIRROR CRACK'D, THE

1981, 105 MINS, UK ◇ ▽

Dir Guy Hamilton *Prod* John Brabourne, Richard
Goodwin *Scr* Jonathan Hales, Barry Sandler
Ph Christopher Challis *Ed* Richard Mardon *Mus* John
Cameron *Art Dir* Michael Stringer
● Angela Lansbury, Elizabeth Taylor, Kim Novak, Rock
Hudson, Geraldine Chaplin, Tony Curtis (EMI)

EMI's third Agatha Christie mystery [from
her novel *The Mirror Crack'd from Side to Side*]
is a nostalgic throwback to the genteel British
murder mystery pix of the 1950s.

Though Angela Lansbury is top-billed in
the role of Christie's famed sleuth Jane
Marple, the central part really is Elizabeth
Taylor's. Taylor comes away with her most
genuinely affecting dramatic performance in
years as a film star attempting a comeback
following an extended nervous breakdown.

The Taylor character and those close to her
have been haunted by the memory of an
apparently accidental catastrophe which
proves to have been caused by one of the
minor characters.

Taylor has an uproarious good time as she
trades bitchy insults with Kim Novak.

Adroit supporting performances are given
by Tony Curtis, Rock Hudson as Taylor's
husband and director, and Geraldine
Chaplin.

■ MISERY

1990, 107 MINS, US ◇ ▽

Dir Rob Reiner *Prod* Andrew Scheinman, Rob Reiner
Scr William Goldman *Ph* Barry Sonnenfeld
Ed Robert Leighton *Mus* Marc Shaiman
Art Dir Norman Garwood
● James Caan, Kathy Bates, Frances Sternhagen,
Richard Farnsworth, Lauren Bacall, Graham Jarvis
(Castle Rock/Nelson)

Misery is a very obvious and very commercial
gothic thriller, a functional adaptation of the
Stephen King bestseller.

Basically a two-hander, *Misery* is the name
of the 19th-century heroine of a series of
gothic romances penned by James Caan.
During the opening credits his car crashes on
slippery Colorado roads and Kathy Bates
digs him out of the snow and wreckage.

A plump former nurse, she fixes up his severely injured legs and virtually holds him prisoner, incommunicado, for the rest of the
film. As in the classic Robert Aldrich gothics
like *What Ever Happened to Baby Jane?*, the fun
comes from the ebb and flow nastiness of the
two characters in a love/hate (often hate/
hate) relationship.

Key plot gimmick is that Caan's killed off
the profitable but hack-work Misery character, an act that turns adoring fan Bates
against him and sets in motion her obsession
that he resurrect the fictional character.

Casting of Caan is effective, as his snide
remarks and grumpy attitude are backed up
by a physical dimension that makes believable his inevitable fighting back. Bates has a
field day with her role, creating a quirky,
memorable object of hate.

Tech credits on this $21 million pic are very
good, including Reno-area location shots.

■ MISFITS, THE

1961, 124 MINS, US ▽

Dir John Huston *Prod* Frank E. Taylor *Scr* Arthur
Miller *Ph* Russell Metty *Ed* George Tomasini
Mus Alex North *Art Dir* Stephen Grimes, William
Newberry
● Clark Gable, Marilyn Monroe, Montgomery Clift,
Thelma Ritter, Eli Wallach (United Artists)

At face value, *The Misfits*, is a robust, high-
voltage adventure drama, vibrating with
explosively emotional histrionics, conceived
and executed with a refreshing disdain for
superficial technical and photographic slickness in favor of an uncommonly honest and
direct cinematic approach. Within this
framework, however, lurks a complex mass of
introspective conflicts, symbolic parallels and
motivational contradictions, the nuances of
which may seriously confound general
audiences.

Clark Gable essays the role of a self-sufficient Nevada cowboy, a kind of last of the
great rugged individualists – a noble misfit.
Into his life ambles a woman (Marilyn Monroe) possessed of an almost uncanny degree
of humanitarian compassion. Their relationship matures smoothly enough until Gable
goes 'mustanging', a ritual in which wild,
'misfit' mustangs are rudely roped into captivity. Revolted by what she regards as cruel
and mercenary, Monroe, with the aid of yet
another misfit, itinerant, disillusioned rodeo

performer Montgomery Clift, strives to free
the captive horses.

The film is somewhat uneven in pace and
not entirely sound in dramatic structure.
Character development is choppy in several
instances. The one essayed by Thelma Ritter
is essentially superfluous and, in fact, abruptly abandoned in the course of the story.
Eli Wallach's character undergoes a severely
sudden and faintly inconsistent transition.
Even Monroe's never comes fully into focus.

■ MISHIMA
A LIFE IN FOUR CHAPTERS

1985, 120 MINS, US ◇ ▽

Dir Paul Schrader *Prod* Mata Yamamoto, Tom
Luddy *Scr* Paul Schrader, Leonard Schrader, Chieko
Schrader *Ph* John Bailey *Ed* Michael Chandler,
Tomoyo Oshima *Mus* Philip Glass *Art Dir* Eiko
Ishioka
● Ken Ogata, Kenji Sawada, Yasosuke Bando,
Toshiyuki Nagashima (Zoetrope/Filmlink/Lucasfilm)

Paul Schrader's film *Mishima* is a boldly conceived, intelligent and consistently absorbing
study of the Japanese writer and political iconoclast's life, work and death.

The most famous of contemporary Japanese novelists to Westerners, Yukio Mishima
was also a film actor and director and leader
of a militant right-wing cult bent upon restoring the glory of the emperor. He became forever notorious in 1970 when, accompanied by
a few followers, he entered a military garrison
in Tokyo, 'captured' a general, delivered an
impassioned speech to an assembly and then
committed *seppuku* (ritual suicide).

Instead of pretending to deliver a fully factual, detailed biopic, director Paul Schrader,
his coscreenwriter and brother Leonard and
other collaborators have opted to combine
relatively realistic treatment of some aspects
of Mishima's life, particularly his final day,
with highly stylized renditions of assorted
semi-autobiographical literary works (*Temple
of the Golden Pavilion*, *Kyoko's House* and *Runaway Horses*) in an effort to convey key points
about the man's personality and credos.

Pacing sometimes lags, particularly in the
fictional interludes, and uninitiated audiences may be confused at times. Production
itself, however, is stunning, and performances, led by that of Ken Ogata as the adult
Mishima, are authoritative and convincing.
[Pic is in Japanese with English subtitles, and
narration read by Roy Scheider.]

■ MISS FIRECRACKER

1989, 102 MINS, US ◇ ▽

Dir Thomas Schlamme *Prod* Fred Berner *Scr* Beth
Henley *Ph* Arthur Albert *Ed* Peter C. Frank
Mus David Mansfield *Art Dir* Kristi Zea
● Holly Hunter, Mary Steenburgen, Tim Robbins, Alfre
Woodard, Scott Glenn (Corsair)

Holly Hunter reprises her stage role [in Beth
Henley's play *The Miss Firecracker Contest*] as
Carnelle, a former goodtime girl whose
dream is to win the local Miss Firecracker
contest in her hometown of Yazoo City, Miss.
Her cousin (Mary Steenburgen) won the
crown over a decade earlier, and against all
odds Carnelle makes it to the finals as an
alternate.

Miss Firecracker is peopled with oddball characters, notably Tim Robbins as Steenburgen's free spirit brother and Alfre Woodard
as the black seamstress assigned to fabricate
Carnelle's contest costume.

Putting the show over with a bang is Hunter, the epitome of energy in a tailormade
feisty role. She very accurately judges the line
between high and low camp in her climactic
tapdance for the talent contest, entertaining
but just klutzy enough to be authentic.

Steenburgen and Woodard are consistent
scene-stealers here, former dead-on as a

Southern belle putting on airs and latter revivifying ethnic stereotypes such as bugged-out eyes into a hilarious, original character.

● ●

■ **MISS SADIE THOMPSON**

1953, 90 MINS, US ◇ ⓥ

Dir Curtis Bernhardt   *Prod* Jerry Wald   *Scr* Harry Kleiner   *Ph* Charles Lawton Jr   *Ed* Viola Lawrence   *Mus* George Duning   *Art Dir* Carl Anderson
● Rita Hayworth, Jose Ferrer, Aldo Ray, Russell Collins, Peggy Converse, Charles Bronson (Columbia/Beckworth)

Rain, the stage play which John Colton made from W. Somerset Maugham's story about sex, sin and salvation in the tropics, is back for a third try as a motion picture. This time it's a modernized version fancied up with 3-D and Technicolor.

The production uses an authentic island background for the story, the lensing having been done in Hawaii, so the presentation has a lush tropical look.

In this treatment, Sadie is a shady lady chased out of a Honolulu bawdy house by Davidson, a man determined to keep sin out of the islands. She dodges deportation to San Francisco, where she's wanted for another rap, by taking a ship for New Caledonia. Enroute, the ship is quarrantined at an island occupied mostly by Marines.

The dramatic pacing of Curtis Bernhardt's direction achieves a frenzied jazz tempo, quite in keeping with the modernization, and most of the performances respond in kind, especially that of Rita Hayworth. She catches the feel of the title character well, even to braving completely deglamorizing makeup, costuming and photography to fit her physical appearance to that of the bawdy, shady lady that was Sadie Thompson. Less effective is Jose Ferrer's Alfred Davidson, no longer a missionary bigot but a straight layman bigot. Missing under the change is the religious fanaticism that motivated and made understandable the original Freudian character.

Aldo Ray, playing Sergeant O'Hara, the Marine who makes an honest woman of Sadie, is good.

● ●

■ **MISSING**

1982, 122 MINS, US ◇ ⓥ

Dir Constantine Costa-Gavras   *Prod* Edward Lewis, Mildred Lewis   *Scr* Constantine Costa-Gavras, Donald Stewart   *Ph* Ricardo Aronovich   *Ed* Francoise Bonnot   *Mus* Vangelis   *Art Dir* Peter Jamison
● Jack Lemmon, Sissy Spacek, Melanie Mayron, John Shea, Charles Cioffi, David Clennon (Universal)

Although the country in question is never named, the subject here is unequivocally that of US involvement in the 1973 military coup in Allende's Chile.

Based on the true story of a young American, Charles Horman, who disappeared during the Chile coup, drama [from a book by Thomas Hauser], presents John Shea and Sissy Spacek as a vaguely counter-culturish couple living in Santiago.

When Shea inexplicably disappears and Spacek can get nowhere in locating him, his father (Jack Lemmon) flies down to get heavy with US government officials.

Real jolt of the picture, which comes across on an effective personal level due to its impact on Lemmon derives from the premise that, when pressed, the US government places the interests of business above those of individual citizens.

Lemmon is superior as a man facing up to issues he never wanted to confront personally. Edgy and belligerent most of the time, Spacek is more constrained but she's fully believable.

□ 1982: Best Picture (Nomination)

● ●

■ **MISSING IN ACTION**

1984, 101 MINS, US ◇ ⓥ

Dir Joseph Zito   *Prod* Menahem Golan, Yoram Globus   *Scr* James Bruner   *Ph* Joao Fernandes   *Ed* Joel Goodman   *Mus* Jay Chattaway   *Art Dir* Ladi Wilheim
● Chuck Norris, M. Emmet Walsh, Lenore Kasdorf, James Hong, Pierrino Mascarino, Ernie Ortega (Cannon)

With the Philippines filling in for Vietnam jungles, with Chuck Norris kicking and firing away, with a likable sidekick in the black marketeering figure of M. Emmet Walsh, and with a touch of nudity in sordid Bangkok bars, writer James Bruner and director Joseph Zito have marshalled a formula pic with a particularly jingoistic slant: even though the war is long over, the Commies in Vietnam still deserve the smack of a bullet.

Norris plays a former North Vietnamese prisoner, an American colonel missing in action for seven years, who escapes to the US and then returns to Vietnam determined to find MIAs and convince the world that Yanks are still imprisoned in Vietnam.

● ●

■ **MISSION, THE**

1986, 128 MINS, UK ◇ ⓥ

Dir Roland Joffe   *Prod* Fernando Ghia, David Puttnam   *Scr* Robert Bolt   *Ph* Chris Menges   *Ed* Jim Clark   *Mus* Ennio Morricone   *Art Dir* Norma Dorme
● Robert De Niro, Jeremy Irons, Ray McAnally, Liam Neeson, Aidan Quinn, Ronald Pickup (Goldcrest/Kingsmere/Enigma)

The script of this $23 million pic is based on a little-known but nonetheless intriguing historical incident in mid-18th-century South America, pitting avaricious colonialists against the Jesuit order of priests.

The fillip is the presence in the leads of Robert De Niro and Jeremy Irons, a nifty combo of British classicism with American box-office appeal. The two principal actors work hard to animate their parts. But there is little to do. *The Mission* is probably the first film in which De Niro gives a bland, uninteresting performance.

The fundamental problem is that the script is cardboard thin, pinning labels on its characters and arbitrarily shoving them into various stances to make plot points.

□ 1986: Best Picture (Nomination)

● ●

■ **MISSION TO MOSCOW**

1943, 123 MINS, US

Dir Michael Curtiz   *Prod* Robert Buckner   *Scr* Howard Koch   *Ph* Bert Glennon   *Ed* Owen Marks   *Mus* Max Steiner
● Walter Huston, Ann Harding, Oscar Homolka, Gene Lockhart, Eleanor Parker, Helmut Dantine (Warner)

Film is of a highly intellectual nature, requiring constant attention and thought if it is to be fully appreciated. It is pretty much in the nature of a lengthy monolog, with little action.

It is truly a documentary; Hollywood's initial effort at living history. Every character is the counterpart of an actual person. Real names are used throughout – Roosevelt, Churchill, Stalin, Davies, Litvinov, et al and the casting is aimed for physical likeness to the person portrayed. The jolting realism of the likenesses is far from the least of the picture's interesting aspects.

Outstanding in the tremendous cast are Walter Huston as Davies, Ann Harding as Mrs Davies, Oscar Homolka as Litvinov, Gene Lockhart as Molotov, Barbara Everest as Mrs Litvinov, Vladimir Sokoloff as Kalinin, and Dudley Field Malone as Churchill.

Film follows pretty much in chronological order from the time of Roosevelt's appointment of the progressively-minded, capitalist-

corporation lawyer Joseph E. Davies to the post of ambassador to Russia.

Manner of presentation of the film is the use of Huston's voice off-screen, employing the first person, to describe his tours and many of the events. Then, where the action permits, the film lapses into regular direct dialog among the characters on the screen.

● ●

■ **MISSIONARY, THE**

1983, 90 MINS, UK ◇ ⓥ

Dir Richard Loncraine   *Prod* Neville C. Thompson, Michael Palin   *Scr* Michael Palin   *Ph* Peter Hannan   *Ed* Paul Green   *Mus* Mike Moran   *Art Dir* Norman Garwood
● Michael Palin, Maggie Smith, Trevor Howard, Denholm Elliott, Michael Hordern, Graham Crowden (HandMade)

Turn-of-the-century English gentry targeted in *The Missionary* remains good for laughs, especially in the hands of the talented Michael Palin. But Palin's script meanders wastefully across three separate story possibilities, never making full use of any of them.

As the Anglican title character called home to England, Palin has a brief encounter on the boat with Her Ladyship Maggie Smith who exhibits a keen interest in pagan fertility symbols. But the reverend's mind is on marriage to his childhood sweetheart (Phoebe Nicholls), whose most romantic thoughts center on how well she has managed to file and crossfile his letters for 10 years.

Once in London, Palin is assigned by Bishop Denholm Elliott to start a slum mission for 'fallen women'. And here comes Smith with the seed money Palin needs, provided he's friendly in return since her married life with stuffy Trevor Howard is a bit empty.

● ●

■ **MISSOURI BREAKS, THE**

1976, 126 MINS, US ◇ ⓥ

Dir Arthur Penn   *Prod* Elliott Kastner, Robert M. Sherman   *Scr* Thomas McGuane   *Ph* Michael Butler   *Ed* Jerry Greenberg, Stephen Rotter, Dede Allen   *Mus* John Williams   *Art Dir* Albert Brenner
● Marlon Brando, Jack Nicholson, Kathleen Lloyd, Randy Quaid, Frederic Forrest, Harry Dean Stanton (United Artists)

The environment is the Montana headlands of the Missouri River, where pioneer John McLiam is range boss, local political muscle and pretty well master of the territory. Enter Jack Nicholson, leader of the area's horse thieves, out to avenge a colleague's death while facilitating his work by buying a ranch near the McLiam property as a rest stop for stolen horses.

Finally comes Marlon Brando, vicious frontier hired gun, engaged by McLiam to ferret out the Nicholson gang.

The trouble with *The Missouri Breaks* is that one is seriously drawn to it on its upfront elements, but leaves with a depressing sense of waste. As a film achievement it's corned beef and ham hash.

● ●

■ **MISTER FROST**

1990, 104 MINS, FRANCE/UK ◇ ⓥ

Dir Philippe Setbon   *Prod* Xavier Gelin   *Scr* Philippe Setbon, Brad Lynch   *Ph* Dominique Brenguier   *Ed* Ray Lovejoy   *Art Dir* Max Berto
● Jeff Goldblum, Alan Bates, Kathy Baker, Roland Girand, Jean-Pierre Cassel, Daniel Gelin (Hugo/AAA/OMM)

Mister Frost is a tepid thriller about a mass murderer who claims to be the devil himself. Jeff Goldblum is a seemingly cordial country gentleman (in England, apparently) who casually confesses to police to having tortured and murdered no less than 24 men, women and children, buried on his property.

Most of the story is set in a clinic 'somewere in Europe' where Goldblum breaks his silence to communicate with lady psychiatrist Kathy Baker. Yes, he's Satan in person, he tells her, and he's fuming mad because modern psychiatry has cheated him out of authorship in 20th century evil. Now he wants to make a comeback and has chosen Baker as his agent.

None of this is particularly terrifying or gripping, especially since Gallic writer-helmer Philippe Setbon is incapable of creating any suspenseful doubt about whether Goldblum is indeed Satan, or merely a dangerous schizophrenic with psychic and hypnotic powers.

● ●

■ MISTER MOSES

1965, 115 MINS, US ◇

Dir Ronald Neame   *Prod* Frank Ross   *Scr* Charles Beaumont, Monja Danischewsky   *Ph* Oswald Morris   *Ed* Phil Anderson, Peter Wetherley   *Mus* John Barry
● Robert Mitchum, Carroll Baker, Ian Bannen, Alexander Knox, Raymond St Jacques, Orlando Martins (United Artists)

The Biblical Moses, in a manner, has been updated for this Frank Ross production, switching the plot to an American diamond smuggler leading an African tribe to a promised land. Director Ronald Neame has taken every advantage of fascinating African terrain for his unusual adventure yarn from Max Catto's novel.

Film takes its motivation from orders by the district commissioner for a village, threatened by flood waters of a new dam being constructed, to evacuate. The religious-minded chief, who has heard the story of Moses from a missionary and his daughter who live with the tribe, refuses to take his people in helicopters to be provided for purpose, because the Bible says the children of Israel, when they went to their promised land, took their animals with them. No animals, no go.

Robert Mitchum, a medicine-man who smuggles diamonds, is set down in this ticklish situation, a guy known as Dr Moses. The chief hails him as the true Moses who will lead them to a special government preserve.

● ●

■ MISTER QUILP

1975, 117 MINS, UK ◇

Dir Michael Tuchner   *Prod* Helen M. Strauss   *Scr* Louis Kamp, Irene Kamp   *Ph* Christopher Challis   *Ed* John Jympson   *Mus* Anthony Newley   *Art Dir* Elliot Scott
● Anthony Newley, David Hemmings, David Warner, Michael Hordern, Paul Rogers, Jill Bennett (Avco Embassy)

Mister Quilp is a sprightly musical version of Charles Dickens' *The Old Curiosity Shop*.

Anthony Newley, a corrupt lender in league with fringe lawyer David Warner and latter's sister Jill Bennett, harasses shopowner Michael Hordern and granddaughter Sarah Jane Varley, both rescued in time by arrival of Paul Rogers, Hordern's wealthy long-lost brother.

Peter Duncan, as Varley's admirer, David Hemmings as a likable boulevardier, Mona Washbourne as a delightful traveling show operator who befriends the fleeing Varley and Hordern, Sarah Webb as a plaintive street urchin, Philip Davis as Newley's whipping boy and Yvonne Antrobus as Newley's long-suffering wife all complement the main plot line. Casting is uniformly excellent.

● ●

■ MISTER ROBERTS

1955, 120 MINS, US ◇ Ⓥ

Dir John Ford, Mervyn LeRoy   *Prod* Leland Hayward   *Scr* Frank Nugent, Joshua Logan   *Ph* Winton Hoch   *Ed* Jack Murray   *Mus* Franz Waxman   *Art Dir* Art Loel

● Henry Fonda, James Cagney, William Powell, Jack Lemmon, Betsy Palmer, Ward Bond (Orange/Warner)

Thomas Heggen's salty comedy about life aboard a Navy cargo ship had no trouble moving from the printed page to the stage [in a play by Heggen and Joshua Logan]. Figuring importantly in the sock manner with which it all comes off on the screen is the directorial credit shared by John Ford and Mervyn LeRoy, the former having had to bow out because of illness midway in production.

Henry Fonda, who scored on the stage in the title role, repeats in the picture as the cargo officer who resented not being in the thick of the fighting in the Pacific during World War II.

James Cagney is simply great as the captain of the ship. William Powell tackles the role of ship's doctor with an easy assurance that makes it stand out and Jack Lemmon is a big hit as Ensign Pulver.

□ 1955: Best Picture (Nomination)

● ●

■ MISUNDERSTOOD

1984, 91 MINS, US ◇ Ⓥ

Dir Jerry Schatzberg   *Prod* Tarak Ben Ammar   *Scr* Barra Grant   *Ph* Pasqualino De Santis   *Ed* Marc Laub   *Mus* Michael Hoppe   *Art Dir* Joel Schiller
● Gene Hackman, Henry Thomas, Rip Torn, Huckleberry Fox, Maureen Kerwin, Susan Anspach (Accent/Keith Barish/Vides)

Misunderstood, a somber and largely unsentimental study of a rift and ultimate reconciliation between father and son, is a 'remake and adaptation' of Luigi Comencini's 1967 Italian pic *Incompreso*.

New version places former post-war black marketeer and now shipping magnate Gene Hackman in a palatial home in Tunisia. His wife has just died, and Hackman has a tough time breaking the news to his seven-or-eight-year-old son, Henry Thomas. In his opinion, his other son, Huckleberry Fox, is simply too young to comprehend what's happened.

When his relative Rip Torn suggests Hackman is too stern with the boys, that he expects too much of them, the latter protests he's trying to treat Thomas like a grownup.

Ultimately, Thomas is seriously injured in a fall, and he and Hackman finally break through to each other.

● ●

■ MIXED BLOOD

1984, 97 MINS, US ◇ Ⓥ

Dir Paul Morrissey   *Prod* Antoine Gannage, Teven Fierberg   *Scr* Paul Morrissey   *Ph* Stefan Zapasnik   *Ed* Scott Vickrey   *Mus* Andy Hernandez   *Art Dir* Stephen McCabe
● Marilia Pera, Richard Ulacia, Linda Kerridge, Geraldine Smith, Angel David, Ulrich Berr (Sef Saellite)

A tale of rival youth gangs tied into the city's drug scene, *Mixed Blood* paints a colorful story of kingdom building, corruption and revenge. Adopting an overblown style of performance, the picture maintains an edgy quality where one is often wondering whether to laugh or shudder at the proceedings.

Brazilian actress Marilia Pera arrives on the scene like some loud, conquering hero and with her son, Thiago (Richard Ulacia), fashions a Hispanic ring of young teenagers to challenge an established gang. After stealing a shipment intended for the reigning Puerto Rican Group, Rita la Punta (Pera) sets up her own operation.

The offbeat nature of the piece is further reinforced by the mixture of pro and amateur talent and a variety of acting styles.

● ●

■ MO' BETTER BLUES

1990, 127 MINS, US ◇ Ⓥ

Dir Spike Lee   *Prod* Spike Lee   *Scr* Spike Lee   *Ph* Ernest Dickerson   *Ed* Sam Pollard   *Mus* Bill Lee   *Art Dir* Wynn Thomas
● Denzel Washington, Spike Lee, Wesley Snipes, Joie Lee, Cynda Williams, Giancarlo Esposito (40 Acres & a Mule/Universal)

Personal rather than social issues come to the fore in *Mo' Better Blues*, a Spike Lee personality piece dressed in jazz trappings that puffs itself up like *Bird* but doesn't really fly. More focused on the sexual dilemmas of its main character than on musical themes, pic might well be subtitled *He's Gotta Have It*.

Pic's fabulous opening sequence, in which the camera does a sensual pan of jazz images – a horn, a man's ear, his mouth – raises expectations for a definitive film on jazz and an ambitious step forward for Lee. But the script unfolds to notes from a different scale: basically the same unique but limited range Lee has drawn on before.

Contemp tale stars Denzel Washington as Bleek Gilliam, a self-absorbed New York horn player who leads a jazz quintet on a roll at a trendy Manhattan club called Beneath the Underdog. The diminutive Lee plays Giant (as in 'giant pain in the ass', one character observes), Bleek's ne'er-do-well friend who's found a precarious niche as the band's manager. Joie Lee (Lee's sister) and Cynda Williams play the women who compete for Bleek's attention. Also overlooked by the self-centered trumpeter is his sax player, Shadow (Wesley Snipes, in a standout perf).

But if *Mo' Better* is soft in the center, the characters in and around the band and the nightclub provide winning entertainment.

● ●

■ MOANA

1926, 69 MINS, US ⊗

Dir Robert Flaherty   *Prod* R.J. Flaherty, F.H. Flaherty   *Scr* Robert Flaherty, Julian Johnson   *Ph* Robert Flaherty
● (Paramount)

A magnified travel film, it's interesting and has been well done, but there's no story, and a travelog is a travelog.

The Flahertys were responsible for *Nanook of the North*. Here they have delved into the southern climes for their subject matter. A subtitle states that the men lingered with the Samoans for two years in order to win the confidence of the tribe and get the inside native stuff.

The action contains a couple of modified laughs and holds some exceptionally eye-filling rugged shorelines, with the surf pounding. The spearing of fish, the capture of a giant turtle in the water by two swimmers and the riding of the breakers by a homemade skiff provide the major 'action' scenes.

● ●

■ MOB, THE

1951, 87 MINS, US

Dir Robert Parrish   *Prod* Jerry Bresler   *Scr* William Bowers   *Ph* Joseph Walker   *Ed* Charles Nelson   *Mus* George Duning
● Broderick Crawford, Betty Buehler, Richard Kiley, Neville Brand, Ernest Borgnine, Carleton Young (Columbia)

Broderick Crawford is fine as a cop who poses as a hood to overthrow racketeers who've been shaking down dock workers on the waterfront. Fist fights, gunfire and some salty dialog and sexy interludes involving Crawford with Lynne Baggett enliven the proceedings considerably.

Crawford, altar-bound, gets called back to track the responsible party down, the victim being a brother cop. Difficult-to-find trail leads him to New Orleans and back to his starting point, California, right into the police department itself.

Scripter William Bowers has studded the Ferguson Findley original with some logically developed clues designed to throw the customers off the track. It's definitely a surprise when the true culprit is exposed.

Betty Buehler is thoroughly sympathetic as Crawford's girl friend, and Baggett and Jean Alexander as manbait planted to distract Crawford from his pursuits spark the distaff end expertly.

· ·

■ MOBY DICK

1930, 70 MINS, US

Dir Lloyd Bacon   *Scr* J. Grubb Alexander   *Ph* Robert Kurrle

● John Barrymore, Joan Bennett, Lloyd Hughes, May Boley, Walter Long (Warner)

The Sea Beast was a money picture for Warners in 1926. [This sound remake, using the title of Herman Melville's original novel,] again stars John Barrymore.

Moby Dick is just as smart as ever, but Barrymore is smarter. He's got a better whale to work with this time. And Moby Dick deserves his finish, after Barrymore has chased him over seven seas for seven years because of that leg bite.

Back home the demure Joan Bennett, who could never grow old out in New Bedford, waits for her whaling boy friend to return. *Moby Dick* is stirring, even if you don't believe in whales. And this one's said to have cost Warners $120,000, with or without teeth.

· ·

■ MOBY DICK

1956, 116 MINS, UK ◇ Ⓥ

Dir John Huston   *Prod* John Huston   *Scr* Ray Bradbury, John Huston   *Ph* Oswald Morris, Freddie Francis   *Ed* Russell Lloyd   *Mus* Philip Stainton   *Art Dir* Ralph Brinton

● Gregory Peck, Richard Basehart, Leo Genn, Harry Andrews, Orson Welles, Bernard Miles (Moulin/Warner)

Costly weather and production delays on location in Ireland and elsewhere enlarged the bring-home price on John Huston's *Moby Dick* to as high as $5 million.

Moby Dick is interesting more often than exciting, faithful to the time and text [of the Herman Melville novel] more than great theatrical entertainment. Essentially it is a chase picture and yet not escaping the sameness and repetitiousness which often dulls the chase formula.

It was astute of Huston to work out a print combining color and black-and-white calculated to capture the sombre beauties of New Bedford, circa 1840, and its whaling ways.

Orson Welles appears early and briefly as a local New Bedford preacher who delivers a God-fearing sermon on Jonah and the whale. Welles turns in an effective bit of brimstone exhortation, appropriate to time and place.

Gregory Peck hovers above the crew, grim-faced and hate-obsessed. He wears a stump leg made of the jaw of a whale and he lives only to kill the greatest whale of all, the white-hided super-monster, Moby Dick, the one which had chewed off his leg. Peck's Ahab is not very 'elemental'. It is not that he fails in handling the rhetoric. Actually he does quite well with the stylized speech in which Melville wrote and which Ray Bradbury and Huston have preserved in their screenplay. It's just that Peck often seems understated and much too gentlemanly for a man supposedly consumed by insane fury.

· ·

■ MODEL SHOP

1969, 90 MINS, US ◇

Dir Jacques Demy   *Prod* Jacques Demy   *Scr* Jacques Demy, Adrien Joyce   *Ph* Michel Hugo   *Ed* Walter Thompson   *Mus* Spirit   *Art Dir* Kenneth A. Reid

● Anouk Aimee, Gary Lockwood, Alexandra Hay, Carol Cole, Severn Darden, Tom Fielding (Columbia)

French filmmaker Jacques Demy brings a fresh look at LA and American youth, plus a revealing eye for the character and feel of the sprawling California city.

And it is a work of love in its attitude towards the city and its characters. Demy can be sentimental, sans bathos or mawkishness, and comes up with a day in the life of a 26-year-old youthful drifter whose one romantic interlude is a step in coping with his life.

There is not much story here, but rather a revealing series of incidents that serve as a backdrop for a poetic tale of human disarray, fleeting comprehension and a surface gentleness that belies an underlying discontent and groping for meaning, love and aim by its disparate but well mimed characters.

· ·

■ MODERN LOVE

1990, 109 MINS, US ◇

Dir Robby Benson   *Prod* Robby Benson   *Scr* Robby Benson   *Ph* Christopher G. Tufty   *Ed* Gib Jaffe   *Mus* Don Peake   *Art Dir* Carl E. Copeland

● Robby Benson, Karla De Vito, Rue McClanahan, Burt Reynolds, Frankie Valli, Louise Lasser (Lyric/Soisson-Murphy)

Written, produced and directed by Robby Benson, shot in South Carolina and starring Benson and his family and friends, *Modern Love* was actually put together as part of a state university media class he was teaching in Columbia, SC, where some scenes were lensed.

It follows the adventures of Greg and a ditzy urologist named Billie (Benson and wife Karla DeVito) who 'meet cute' when she examines him in her office. Their whirlwind courtship consists of dozens of shots of them kissing against pretty backdrops, followed by telling each other lame jokes and then giggling and saying 'I'm sorry.'

Pic improves as it moves into their family years, with Benson's frustrated attempts to be a handson father giving things an interesting twist and DeVito getting a more substantial role as a capable mom, peacemaker and would-be nightclub comic.

Benson, a fairly capable director, works hard at pumping energy and humor into a flat script.

· ·

■ MODERN TIMES

1936, 85 MINS, US Ⓥ

Dir Charles Chaplin   *Prod* Charles Chaplin   *Scr* Charles Chaplin   *Ph* Rollie Totheroh, Henry Bergman   *Mus* Charles Chaplin

● Charles Chaplin, Paulette Goddard, Henry Bergman, Chester Conklin (United Artists)

Whatever sociological meanings some will elect to read into *Modern Times*, there's no denying that as a cinematic entertainment Chaplin's first picture since *City Lights* (1931) is wholesomely funny.

The pathos of the machine worker who suffers temporary derangement, as he tightens the bolts on a factory treadmill to a clocklike tempo, gives way to a series of similarly winning situations. In each the victim of circumstance meets temporary frustration, almost inevitably resulting in a ride in Black Maria. When finally achieving what promises to be a semblance of economic security the menace, in the form of the law, enters to arrest Paulette Goddard as a refugee vagrant.

Modern Times is as 100% a one-man picture as probably is possible. Chaplin the pantomimist stands or falls by his two years' work. Dialogue is almost negligible. And when the music is inadequate Chaplin frankly recourses to plain titles.

Goddard, a winsome waif attired almost throughout in short, ragged dress, registers handily. Chaplin's old standbys, notably Henry Bergman (also an assistant director), Chester Conklin, Hank Mann and Allen Garcia, contribute nicely.

· ·

■ MODERNS, THE

1988, 126 MINS, US ◇ Ⓥ

Dir Alan Rudolph   *Prod* Carolyn Pfeiffer, David Blocker   *Scr* Alan Rudolph, John Bradshaw   *Ph* Toyomichi Kurita   *Ed* Debra T. Smith, Scott Brock   *Mus* Mark Isham   *Art Dir* Steven Legler

● Keith Carradine, Linda Fiorentino, John Lone, Wallace Shawn, Genevieve Bujold, Geraldine Chaplin (Alive/Nelson)

The artistic world of Paris in the 1920s comes to life as if in a lustrous dream in *The Moderns*, a romantic's lush vision of a group of expatriate Americans at a time and place of some of the century's most tumultuous creative activity.

There is Nick Hart (Keith Carradine) who, at 33, is viewed suspiciously for not having made it yet as an artist. Oiseau (Wallace Shawn), a gossip columnist for the *Tribune*, who dreams only of going to Hollywood; Bertram Stone (John Lone), an elegant, rich, philistine art dealer with a disturbing violent streak; his wife, Rachel (Linda Fiorentino), with whom Nick has a past and, he hopes, a future; and Hemingway himself (Kevin J. O'Connor) who amusingly careens through the action in varying states of inebriation, trying out titles for a new book.

Also critical to the assorted personal equations are Libby (Genevieve Bujold), an impoverished gallery owner with values diametrically opposed to those of Stone, and Nathalie (Geraldine Chaplin), a patroness of the arts who convinces Nick to execute some spectacular forgeries.

Carradine has never been better, as he conveys the strong feelings he has for art and his estranged wife as well as the diffidence that has set in due to years of frustration and lack of recognition. Lone is the picture of disciplined decadence, a magnetic figure who commands fascination, and Fiorentino is ideal as the gorgeous American of a prosaic background over whom men may lose their hearts, mind and lives.

· ·

■ MODESTY BLAISE

1966, 118 MINS, UK ◇

Dir Joseph Losey   *Prod* Joseph Janni   *Scr* Evan Jones   *Ph* Jack Hildyard   *Ed* Reginald Beck   *Mus* John Dankworth   *Art Dir* Richard Macdonald

● Monica Vitti, Terence Stamp, Dirk Bogarde, Harry Andrews, Michael Craig, Alexander Knox (20th Century-Fox)

Modesty Blaise is one of the nuttiest, screwiest pictures ever made. Not merely a spy spoof, based on a book and a comic strip about a femme James Bond type, the colorful production gives the horse laugh to many different film plots and styles. Fine direction and many solid performances are evident.

Evan Jones has concocted a wacky screenplay, most immediately derived from the English comic strip by Peter O'Donnell and Jim Holdaway, which propels Blaise, played by Monica Vitti, into a British government espionage scheme. Heading the opposition is Dirk Bogarde, an effete international criminal, while Vitti is aided by longtime sidekick, bedhopping Terence Stamp.

Vitti's English is adequate for her part; her body English, however, transcends all language barriers. Stamp is good, and appropriately animated. Bogarde's jaded urbanity is very good, and all other players register in solid support.

· ·

MOGAMBO

1953, 115 MINS, US ◇ ▼

Dir John Ford   *Prod* Sam Zimbalist   *Scr* John Lee Mahin   *Ph* Robert Surtees, F.A. Young   *Ed* Frank Clarke   *Mus* [none]   *Art Dir* Alfred Junge
● Clark Gable, Ava Gardner, Grace Kelly, Donald Sinden, Eric Pohlmann, Laurence Naismith (M-G-M)

The lure of the jungle and romance get a sizzling workout in *Mogambo* and it's a socko package of entertainment, crammed with sexy two-fisted adventure.

While having its origin in the Wilson Collison play [*Red Dust*], this remake is fresh in locale and characterizations switching from the rubber plantations of Indo-China to the African veldt and updating the period.

John Lee Mahin's dialog and situations are unusually zippy and adult. Ava Gardner feeding a baby rhino and elephant, and her petulant storming at a pet boa constrictor to stay out of her ber, are good touches.

The romantic conflict boils up between the principals during a safari into gorilla country, where an anthropologist and his wife plan to do research. Clark Gable is the great white hunter leading the party. Gardner is the girl on the prowl for a man, and who has now settled on Gable. To get him she has to offset the sweeter charms of Grace Kelly, the wife, who also has become smitten with the Gable masculinity and is ready to walk out on Donald Sinden, the unexciting anthropologist. For the second time in Metro history, a picture has been made without a music score (*King Solomon's Mines* was the first) and none is needed as the sounds of the jungle and native rhythms are all that are required.

MOLLY MAGUIRES, THE

1970, 124 MINS, US ◇ ▼

Dir Martin Ritt   *Prod* Martin Ritt, Walter Bernstein   *Scr* Walter Bernstein   *Ph* James Wong Howe   *Ed* Frank Bracht   *Mus* Henry Mancini   *Art Dir* Tambi Larsen
● Sean Connery, Richard Harris, Samantha Eggar, Frank Finlay, Anthony Zerbe, Bethel Leslie (Paramount/Tamm)

The Molly Maguires, based on a Pennsylvania coal miners' rebellion of the late 19th century, is occasionally brilliant. Sean Connery, Richard Harris and Samantha Eggar head a competent cast.

Story background ('suggested' by an Arthur H. Lewis book) depicts Irish immigrants existing in the sort of company-captivity common to other American industries of the period. Employer abuses had led to unsuccessful strikes, after which the workers spawned an underground militant group.

Story is primarily that of Harris, hired by the mineowners to infiltrate the workers' ranks. Connery is a rebel leader. Eggar appears occasionally for some light romantic interludes with Harris.

MOMENT BY MOMENT

1978, 105 MINS, US ◇

Dir Jane Wagner   *Prod* Robert Stigwood   *Scr* Jane Wagner   *Ph* Philip Lathrop   *Ed* John F. Burnett   *Mus* Lee Holdridge   *Art Dir* Harry Horner
● Lily Tomlin, John Travolta, Andra Akers, Bert Kramer, Shelley R. Bonus, Debra Feuer (Universal)

What seemed like inspired casting on paper, the teaming of John Travolta and Lily Tomlin, fails badly in execution.

The lion's share of the blame must go to writer-director (and long-time Tomlin collaborator) Jane Wagner, who concocted this improbable story of a Beverly Hills chic housewife whose marriage has gone sour, and who meets up with an insecure young drifter, with whom she has an affair.

Insouciant and likable from the outset, Travolta pursues the distant Tomlin like a determined puppy dog – once he latches on, she can't shake him loose. The first half hour of the pic, with this unusual courtship, is appealing, and only makes what follows more of a letdown.

Approaching Trisha as if she was one of her stable theatrical creations, Tomlin never varies her nasal monotone, nor her imperturbable exterior. It's a one-note performance that frustrates the entire picture.

Not helping matters is Wagner's banal script, which has cliche piled atop cliche, and dialog that evokes embarrassing laughter.

MOMENT TO MOMENT

1966, 108 MINS, US ◇

Dir Mervyn LeRoy   *Prod* Mervyn LeRoy   *Scr* John Lee Mahin, Alec Coppel   *Ph* Harry Stradling   *Ed* Philip W. Anderson   *Mus* Henry Mancini   *Art Dir* Alexander Golitzen, Alfred Sweeney
● Jean Seberg, Honor Blackman, Sean Garrison, Arthur Hill, Gregoire Aslan, Peter Robbins (Universal)

Mervyn LeRoy, who has tackled just about every type of film, returns to romantic melodrama in *Moment to Moment*, an unabashed sudser. A mild suspense story blending a wife's infidelity and amnesia, the film doesn't entirely jell for several reasons, mainly thin scripting, weak acting and LeRoy's own too-leisurely pace.

John Lee Mahin joined Alec Coppel in adapting latter's story about a happily-married Yank wife, increasingly neglected by headshrinker hubby who is on the lecture circuit all over Europe while she and the kid remain on the Riviera. A US naval officer has an affair with her, provoking a physical argument and a shooting.

Jean Seberg lacks dimension as the wife, even allowing for the script. In early scenes, an overly passive limning – which suggests jaded boredom instead of a well-adjusted spouse in a single fall from grace – robs the role of most sympathy.

MOMENTS

1975, 92 MINS, UK ◇

Dir Peter Crane   *Prod* Peter Crane, Michael Sloane, David M. Jackson   *Scr* Michael Sloane   *Ph* Wolfgang Suschitzky   *Ed* Roy Watts   *Mus* John Cameron   *Art Dir* Bruce Atkins
● Keith Michell, Angharad Rees, Bill Fraser, Jeanette Sterke, Donald Hewlett, Keith Bell (Pemini)

Despite technical flaws, this item comes across as a sincere and often moving film. Yarn probes into man's loneliness and the dead-end meaninglessness of a middle-aged accountant (Keith Michell) who, after 20 years at his job and after the death of his wife and children in a car crash, decides to return to a resort hotel in the off-season where he had once lived happy moments, and put an end to his life.

Relationship between him and a young, flighty and vivacious girl (Angharad Rees) who temporarily prevents him from carrying out his project is touchingly told as director Peter Crane plays off each of the antipodic characters. At times characterization of the man, though always believable, is too turgid and self-conscious; his poses of internal suffering are a trifle too histrionic and become wearisome.

MOMMIE DEAREST

1981, 129 MINS, US ◇

Dir Frank Perry   *Prod* Frank Yablans   *Scr* Frank Yablans, Frank Perry, Tracy Hotchner, Robert Getchell   *Ph* Paul Lohmann   *Ed* Peter E. Berger   *Mus* Henry Mancini   *Art Dir* Bill Malley
● Faye Dunaway, Diana Scarwid, Steve Forrest, Howard Da Silva, Jocelyn Brando (Paramount)

This is Faye Dunaway as Joan Crawford and the results are, well, screen history. Dunaway does not chew scenery. Dunaway starts neatly at each corner of the set in every scene and swallows it whole, costars and all.

Prior to her death, Crawford once commented that Dunaway was among the best of up-and-coming young actresses. Too bad Crawford isn't around to comment now. Too bad, Crawford isn't around to comment on the whole endeavor.

Much has been written and said pro-and-con about Crawford since daughter Christina wrote the book on which this film is based. Whatever the truth, director Frank Perry's portrait here is sorry indeed, 129 minutes with a very pathetic and unpleasant individual.

The story is familiar: self-centred, insecure and pressured movie queen adopts two babies for both love and personal aggrandizement. Growing up, the kids are battered between luxurious pampering and abuse, never finding real affection with mother, who finally dies and cuts them out of the will, reaching beyond the grave for final revenge.

As Christina, Diana Scarwid is okay, but unexceptional. Much better is little Mara Hobel as Christina the child, genuinely touching at times. Rutanya Alda is also fine as Crawford's long-suffering but loving assistant.

MONEY PIT, THE

1986, 91 MINS, US ◇ ▼

Dir Richard Benjamin   *Prod* Frank Marshall, Kathleen Kennedy, Art Levinson   *Scr* David Giler   *Ph* Gordon Willis   *Ed* Jacqueline Cambas   *Mus* Michel Colombier   *Art Dir* Patrizia Von Brandenstein
● Shelley Long, Tom Hanks, Alexander Godunov, Maureen Stapleton, Joe Mantegna (Amblin)

The Money Pit is simply the pits. Shortly after the starring couple has bought a beautiful old house which quickly shows itself to be at the point of total disrepair, Tom Hanks says to Shelley Long, 'It's a lemon, honey, let's face it'. There is really very little else to be said about this gruesomely unfunny comedy.

Unofficial remake of the 1948 Cary Grant-Myrna Loy starrer *Mr Blandings Builds His Dream House* begins unpromisingly and slides irrevocably downward from there.

Most of the scenes in this demolition derby begin with something or other caving in or falling apart, an event which is invariably followed by the two leads yelling and screaming at each other for minutes on end.

MONEY TRAP, THE

1966, 91 MINS, US

Dir Burt Kennedy   *Prod* Max E. Youngstein, David Karr   *Scr* Walter Bernstein   *Ph* Paul C. Vogel   *Ed* John McSweeney   *Mus* Hal Schaefer   *Art Dir* George W. Davis, Carl Anderson
● Glenn Ford, Elke Sommer, Rita Hayworth, Ricardo Montalban, Joseph Cotten, Tom Reese (M-G-M)

A story of a policeman-turned-thief, *The Money Trap* is aptly named – but only as far as production coin is concerned. A cliche-plotted, tritely written script that is not to be believed could not be salvaged even by far better direction and performances.

Walter Bernstein's adaptation of a Lionel White novel has the kernel of a good drama about a contemporary problem, that of an underpaid gumshoe dazzled into dishonesty by the riches of the criminals whom he encounters. Nearly all interest in this angle is snuffed out by extraneous, unbelievable subplots.

M

Specifically, Glenn Ford is the cop, husband of Elke Sommer. They live in a splashy pad made possible by her father's will and stocks. When the latter pass a divvy, hard times loom. Wife's idea to economize: fire the servants.

Add Joseph Cotten, a medic who supposedly works for the Syndicate. When he kills a junkie accomplice and reports it as self-defense from a supposed burglary, Ford gets the theft idea, keeps it from Ricardo Montalban (his partner, who later finds out and wants in).

. . . .

■ MONKEY BUSINESS

1952, 97 MINS, US Ⓥ

Dir Howard Hawks   *Prod* Sol C. Siegel   *Scr* Ben Hecht, Charles Lederer, I.A.L. Diamond   *Ph* Milton Krasner   *Ed* William B. Murphy   *Mus* Leigh Harline   *Art Dir* Lyle Wheeler, George Patrick
● Cary Grant, Ginger Rogers, Charles Coburn, Marilyn Monroe, Hugh Marlowe, Larry Keating (20th Century-Fox)

Attempt to draw out a thin, familiar slapstick idea isn't carried off.

Story has Cary Grant as a matured research chemist, working on a formula to regenerate human tissue and using monkeys in his lab as guinea pigs for his elixir-of-youth experiments. Ginger Rogers is his amiable wife, still madly enough in love with him to forgive his absentmindedness.

One of the lab monkeys breaks loose, mixes up an assortment of chemical ingredients lying about, dumps the concoction into the water-cooler. First Grant, then Rogers, drink from the cooler, and immediately get teenage notions, emotions and symptoms.

Grant plays the role sometimes as if his heart isn't completely in it. Rogers, looking beautiful, makes as gay a romp of it as she can. Marilyn Monroe's sex appeal is played up for all it's worth (and that's not inconsiderable), as she appears as a nitwit secretary.

. . . .

■ MONKEY SHINES

1988, 115 MINS, US ◇ Ⓥ

Dir George A. Romero   *Prod* Charles Evans   *Scr* George A. Romero   *Ph* James A. Contner   *Ed* Pasquale Buba   *Mus* David Shire   *Art Dir* Cletus Anderson
● Jason Beghe, John Pankow, Melanie Parker, Joyce Van Patten (Orion)

Monkey Shines is a befuddled story about a man constrained from the neck down told by a director confused from the neck up.

Jason Beghe starts out as a very virile, able-bodied young man with everything going for him, an up-and-coming physical specimen much desired by girlfriend Janine Turner and fawned over by mother Joyce Van Patten.

An accident robs Beghe of all physical ability below his jawline, leaving him despondently dependent on an array of technology.

As melodrama, this is all pretty good stuff and could have continued to a convincing conclusion. But by contract, inclination and reputation (not to mention the book [by Michael Stewart] the film's based on), Romero is a horror-film director.

So here comes Beghe's best friend John Pankow, a yuppie mad scientist busy at the nearby university slicing up the brain of a dead Jane Doe and injecting the hormones into monkeys to make them smarter.

To help his friend, Pankow volunteers one of his highly intelligent, chemically dependent capuchins to be trained by Melanie Parker to serve as Beghe's companion and helper. For a while, this all works beautifully. Until something dreadful happens.

. . . .

■ MONSIEUR VERDOUX

1947, 122 MINS, US Ⓥ

Dir Charles Chaplin   *Prod* Charles Chaplin   *Scr* Charles Chaplin   *Ph* Roland Totheroh   *Ed* Willard Nico   *Mus* Charles Chaplin   *Art Dir* John Beckman
● Charles Chaplin, Martha Raye, Isobel Elsom, Marilyn Nash (United Artists)

Comedy based on the characterization of a modern Parisian Bluebeard treads danger shoals indeed. Even if the accent were more effective, the fundamentals are unsound when it's revealed that Chaplin has been driven to marrying and murdering middling mesdames in order to provide for his ailing wife and their son of 10 years' marriage.

Chaplin generates little sympathy. His broad-mannered antics, as a many-aliased fop on the make for impressionable matrons; the telltale technique, a hangover from his bankteller's days, of counting the bundles of francs in the traditional nervous manner of rapid finger movement; the business of avoiding Martha Raye at that garden party, when he finally woos and wins Isobel Elsom; the neo-*American Tragedy* hokum in the rowboat-on-the-lake scene with Raye; the mixed bottles of poisoned wine [again Raye, with oldtime musicomedy star Ada-May (Weeks) as the blowsy buxom blonde of a maid in support]; and all the rest of it is only spotty.

Chaplin's endeavor to get his 'common man' ideology into the film militates against its comedy values. Point is that depressions in the economy force us into being ruthless villains and murderers, despite the fact we are actually kind and sympathetic.

Chaplin also rings in another of his favorite themes, his strong feelings against war.

Chaplin's direction is disjointed on occasion, although perhaps the natural enough result of a leisurely production schedule which ranged up to five years. Chaplin's score, however, is above par, fortifying the progression in no small measure.

. . . .

■ MONSIGNOR

1982, 122 MINS, US ◇ Ⓥ

Dir Frank Perry   *Prod* Frank Yablans, David Niven Jr.   *Scr* Abraham Polonsky, Wendell Mayes   *Ph* Billy Williams   *Ed* Peter E. Berger   *Mus* John Williams   *Art Dir* John DeCuir
● Christopher Reeve, Genevieve Bujold, Fernando Rey, Jason Miller, Joe Cortese, Adolfo Celi (20th Century-Fox)

Lots of potential for a rare, absorbing, behind-the-scenes look at the Vatican is totally blown in *Monsignor*. Constructed as a scene-by-scene 'expose' of all sorts of nefarious goings-on in post-Second World War Rome, the self-serious $12 million pic [from the novel by Jack Alain Leger] teeters on the brink of being an all-out-hoot through much of its running time.

Introductory sequences briefly limn Brooklyn boy Christopher Reeve's ordination and subsequent service as a military chaplain on the European front, where he commits his first major priestly sin by gunning down a bunch of Nazis.

Upon reaching Rome, brash kid makes a big impression on Papal assistant Fernando Rey and is given control over the financially ailing church's commissary. Reeve makes use of his position to strike a deal with Sicilian mafioso Jason Miller to share in black market profits.

The rising opportunist meets novice nun Genevieve Bujold, and it isn't long before the two bed down.

It's amazing that neither Abraham Polonsky nor Wendell Mayes, both outstanding screenwriters, didn't spot the most gaping fundamental flaw here, namely the lack of any convincing explanation why Reeve's character became a priest in the first place.

. . . .

■ MONTE WALSH

1970, 99 MINS, US ◇ Ⓥ

Dir William A. Fraker   *Prod* Hal Landers, Bobby Roberts   *Scr* Lukas Heller, David Zelag Goodman   *Ph* David M. Walsh   *Ed* Dick Brockway   *Mus* John Barry   *Art Dir* Al Brenner
● Lee Marvin, Jeanne Moreau, Jack Palance, Mitch Ryan, Jim Davis, John 'Bear' Hudkins (Cinema Center)

Monte Walsh is a listless, wandering story of the old American West, which takes too long to get moving. Lee Marvin stars as a taciturn roughneck whose tragic romance with Jeanne Moreau comes across as irrelevant digression in a confused story.

This film [from a novel by Jack Schaefer] attempts meaningful exposition of the reality of an aging cowboy. Unfortunately, it appears that Marvin was simply playing his image, while other thesps were going through uncertain motions, and nobody had an eye out for exactly what direction the film was supposed to be taking.

Moreau's scenes are more like padded inserts than vital plot turns. The basic feeble theme is what happened to prototype pioneers when Eastern money bought up ranches and began operating long-distance.

. . . .

■ MONTH IN THE COUNTRY, A

1987, 96 MINS, UK ◇ Ⓥ

Dir Pat O'Connor   *Prod* Kenith Trodd   *Scr* Simon Gray   *Ph* Kenneth Macmillan   *Ed* John Victor Smith   *Mus* Howard Blake   *Art Dir* Leo Austin
● Colin Firth, Kenneth Branagh, Natasha Richardson, Patrick Malahide, Richard Vernon (Euston)

A Month in the Country is a gentle but moving pic about two men recovering from the horrors of World War I during an idyllic summer in remote rolling English countryside.

Pic opens with Birkin (Colin Firth) arriving at the remote Yorkshire village of Oxgodby to uncover a medieval wall painting in the local church. There he meets Moon (Kenneth Branagh), who is excavating a grave outside the churchyard.

Both are tormented by their war experiences, but during a beautiful summer month they experience the tranquility of the idyllic community that gradually helps them come to terms with their problems.

Birkin falls in love with the wife (Natasha Richardson) of an unfriendly local vicar, but never lets on to her about his passion, while the Branagh character turns out to be a homosexual.

Firth and Branagh are talented young actors – especially Branagh who has great screen presence. Richardson looks slightly uncomfortable in a very understated role.

. . . .

■ MONTY PYTHON AND THE HOLY GRAIL

1975, 89 MINS, UK ◇

Dir Terry Gilliam, Terry Jones   *Prod* Mark Forstater   *Scr* Graham Chapman, John Cleese, Gilliam, Eric Idle, Jones, Michael Palin   *Ph* Terry Bedford   *Ed* John Hackney   *Mus* DeWolfe   *Art Dir* Roy Smith
● Graham Chapman, John Cleese, Terry Gilliam, Eric Idle, Terry Jones, Michael Palin (Python)

Monty Python's Flying Circus, the British comedy group which gained fame via BBC-TV, send-up Arthurian legend, performed in whimsical fashion with Graham Chapman an effective straight man as King Arthur.

Story deals with Arthur's quest for the Holy Grail and his battles along the way with various villains and is basically an excuse for set pieces, some amusing, others overdone.

Running gags include lack of horses for Arthur and his men, and a lackey clicking cocoanuts together to make suitable hoof noises as the men trot along. The extravagantly gruesome fight scenes, including one which ends with a man having all four limbs severed, will get laughs from some and make others squirm.

● ●

■ MONTY PYTHON'S THE MEANING OF LIFE

1983, 103 MINS, UK ◇ ⓥ

Dir Terry Jones   *Prod* John Goldstone   *Scr* Graham Chapman, John Cleese, Terry Gilliam, Eric Idle, Terry Jones, Michael Palin   *Ph* Peter Hannan   *Ed* Julian Doyle   *Mus* Eric Idle, Terry Jones, Michael Palin, Graham Chapman, John Cleese, John du Prez, Dave Howman, Andre Jacquemin   *Art Dir* Harry Lange
● Graham Chapman, John Cleese, Terry Gilliam, Eric Idle, Terry Jones, Michael Palin (HandMade)

Gross, silly, caustic, tasteless and obnoxious are all adjectives that alternately apply to *Monty Python's The Meaning of Life* though probably the most appropriate description would simply be funny.

Pic opens with an amusing short film of its own where elderly workers unite against their younger bosses and then segues to the real task – finding the meaning of life. Tracing the human existence from birth through death, the group touches on such areas as religion, education, marriage, sex and war in a way it was no doubt never taught in school or in the home. Though there are some rough spots along the way (some of the passages on war don't register) most of the sections get their maximum comedic punch by not being allowed to linger for too long.

The writing truly offers bits of comedic brilliance though, like any film of this nature, has a few duds mixed in.

● ●

■ MOON AND SIXPENCE, THE

1942, 89 MINS, US ◇ ⓥ

Dir Albert Lewin   *Prod* David L. Loew, Albert Lewin   *Scr* Albert Lewin   *Ph* John F. Seitz   *Ed* Richard L. Van Enger   *Mus* Dimitri Tiomkin   *Art Dir* Gordon Wiles
● George Sanders, Herbert Marshall, Doris Dudley, Steve Geray, Eric Blore, Elena Verdugo (United Artists)

Somerset Maugham's widely read novel has been made into an intriguing, distinctive screen vehicle. The story of an English stockbroker who reached for the moon and ultimately won fame as a painter, only just before his death, at times is reminiscent of *Citizen Kane*.

While Herbert Marshall figures importantly, as he retraces the story of the painter, it is really George Sanders' picture. He makes the strange life of the struggling artist live, and it's his outstanding screen role to date.

The episodes in the distant island of Tahiti are rich in tropical flavor. The Tahitian portion of the story offers startling contrast in humorous moments and in most impressive scenes of film.

Albert Lewin's direction is keenly intelligent, shifting readily from lighter, funny moments to the harshly dramatic. Camerawork of John F. Seitz is on the same high plane.

● ●

■ MOON OVER PARADOR

1988, 105 MINS, US ◇ ⓥ

Dir Paul Mazursky   *Prod* Paul Mazursky   *Scr* Leon Capetanos, Paul Mazursky   *Ph* Donald McAlpine   *Ed* Stuart Pappe   *Mus* Maurice Jarre   *Art Dir* Pato Guzman
● Richard Dreyfuss, Raul Julia, Sonia Braga, Jonathan Winters, Fernando Rey, Sammy Davis Jr (Universal)

Paul Mazursky's elaborate farce about the actor as imposter (here posing as dictator of the mythical Latin nation Parador) has moments of true hilarity emerging only fitfully from a ponderous production.

Pic has Richard Dreyfuss well-cast as a fairly successful stage and film actor on a lo-cation shoot in the English-speaking Parador. He's given an offer he can't refuse by police chief Raul Julia to impersonate the just-deceased dictator.

Dreyfuss reluctantly adopts the role, but soon takes on the new persona in earnest after being coached by the dictator's sexy mistress Madonna (Sonia Braga in a flamboyant, delicious turn).

Ruse comes to a climax when Dreyfuss starts instituting reforms inimical to Julia and other powerful interests.

Dreyfuss' panache carries the film most of the way, ably played off Braga's lusty and glamourous character. Julia is very convincing as the stern local despot and Jonathan Winters makes the most of his transparent Ugly American role as a CIA man in Parador.

● ●

■ MOON ZERO TWO

1969, 100 MINS, UK ◇

Dir Roy Ward Baker   *Prod* Michael Carreras   *Scr* Michael Carreras   *Ph* Paul Besson   *Ed* Spencer Reeve   *Mus* Don Ellis   *Art Dir* Scott MacGregor
● James Olson, Catherine Schell, Warren Mitchell, Adrienne Corri, Bernard Bresslaw, Dudley Foster (Hammer)

Moon Zero Two [from an original story by Gavin Lyall, Frank Hardman and Martin Davison] never makes up its mind whether it is a spoof or a straightforward space-adventure yarn. Overall it's a fairly dull experience, despite some capable artwork and special effects.

Space travel has progressed by 2021, and the moon's virtually oldhat. First man to set foot on Mars (James Olson) declines to work as a regular passenger pilot.

Final sequence offers a spot of excitement, but the whole film tends to limp. Moon City's airport, its Wild West saloon and other amenities are presumably meant to be satire but it doesn't come off.

Olson is a melancholy hero. Mitchell plays with tongue in cheek, Bernard Bresslaw as one of his thugs seems bewildered by the entire proceedings.

● ●

■ MOONFLEET

1955, 86 MINS, US ◇ ⓥ

Dir Fritz Lang   *Prod* John Houseman   *Scr* Jan Lustig, Margaret Fitts   *Ph* Robert Planck   *Ed* Albert Akst   *Mus* Miklos Rozsa, Vicente Gomez   *Art Dir* Cedric Gibbons, Hans Peters
● Stewart Granger, George Sanders, Joan Greenwood, Viveca Lindfors, Jon Whiteley, Liliane Montevecchi (M-G-M)

Costumed action, well-spiced with loose ladies and dashing rakehellies, is offered in *Moonfleet*. With mood and action the keynote of the John Houseman production, the direction by Fritz Lang plays both hard, developing considerable movement in several rugged action sequences without neglecting suspense. Period of the J. Meade Falkner novel is the 1750s.

Stewart Granger was a good choice for the dubious hero of the story, a high-living dandy who heads a gang of murderous smugglers headquartering in the English coastal village of Moonfleet. Yarn opens on a Macbeth note of cold, wild-swept moors, and scary, dark shadows, establishing an eerie flavor for the kickoff.

Later, it reminds of *Treasure Island* a bit when Granger and a small boy go through some highly imaginative adventures.

● ●

■ MOONLIGHT SONATA

1937, 90 MINS, UK ⓥ

Dir Lothar Mendes   *Scr* Edward Knoblock, E.M. Delafield   *Ph* Jan Stallich
● Ignace Jan Paderewski, Charles Farrell, Marie Tempest, Barbara Green, Eric Portman, Graham Browne (Pall Mall)

Charming love story woven round the central personality of the world-famous pianist, Paderewski. For the highbrows there will probably not be enough of the maestro's genius – for the lowbrows, there will certainly be too much.

Locale is Sweden, where Charles Farrell, agent for a country estate, declares his love for Ingrid, granddaughter of the baroness, by whom he is employed. Forced landing by a passenger plane bound for Paris brings into the household for temporary hospitality three men, one of them Paderewski; another, a plausible, much-traveled gent of doubtful antecedents.

Baroness is honoured by the presence of the famous musician but soon distrusts the boastful young man-about-town. He makes a play for the young girl, who, having led a hermit-like existence, gets carried away by his worldliness and is hopelessly infatuated.

Charles Farrell has little to do but look on wistfully while his lady is alienated from him; Eric Portman gives a polished, scoundrelly performance; Barbara Greene is attractive and sincere as Ingrid: Marie Tempest, in her first screen role, is her usual delightful self. Of the aged maestro there can be no criticism; they wished to weave a story around him, and artistically and unpretentiously they have succeeded.

● ●

■ MOONRAKER

1979, 126 MINS, UK ◇ ⓥ

Dir Lewis Gilbert   *Prod* Albert R. Broccoli   *Scr* Christopher Wood   *Ph* Jean Tournier   *Ed* John Glen   *Mus* John Barry   *Art Dir* Ken Adam
● Roger Moore, Lois Chiles, Michael Lonsdale, Richard Kiel, Bernard Lee, Corinne Clery (United Artists/Eon)

Christopher Wood's script takes the characters exactly where they always go in a James Bond pic and the only question is whether the stunts and gadgets will live up to expectations. They do.

The main problem this time is the outer-space setting which somehow dilutes the mammoth monstrosity that 007 must save the world from. One more big mothership hovering over earth becomes just another model intercut with elaborate interiors.

The visual effects, stuntwork and other technical contributions all work together expertly to make the most preposterous notions believable. And Roger Moore, though still compared to Sean Connery, clearly has adapted the James Bond character to himself and serves well as the wise-cracking, incredibly daring and irresistible hero.

● ●

■ MOON-SPINNERS, THE

1964, 118 MINS, UK ◇ ⓥ

Dir James Neilson   *Prod* Bill Anderson   *Scr* Michael Dyne   *Ph* Paul Beeson, John Wilcox, Michael Reed   *Ed* Gordon Stone   *Mus* Ron Grainer   *Art Dir* Tony Masters
● Hayley Mills, Eli Wallach, Peter McEnery, Joan Greenwood, Irene Papas, Pola Negri (Walt Disney)

With a mixture of American, English and Greek talents, engaged in a silly but zestful tale of villainy undone, told against some photogenic landscapes, *Moon-Spinners* naturally concentrates on Hayley Mills. With action the keyword in the loosely-knit script [from Mary Stewart's novel] this keeps the young lady perpetually on the move. Her adventures into first-puppy-love and feats of derring-do are accomplished with equal amounts of energy. She's never still long enough for her virtue or her life to be in danger.

Tale chiefly concerns two English females (Mills and Joan Greenwood) becoming involved in a jewel-theft adventure that concerns the Moon-Spinners, the Cretan inn where they're staying. The intrigue includes an odd but colorful assortment of local types headed by Eli Walach, a most hissable villain, his sister (Irene Papas) and a young, mysterious Englishman (Peter McEnery).

Wallach comes off best by playing his villainy straight – vicious, unfeeling and rotten to the core. He'd willingly shoot his nephew to keep the boy's mother from ratting on him. Irene Papas, a superb Greek actress with a wonderfully expressive face, gives more dignity and feeling to her tiny role than it deserves.

■ MOONSTRUCK

1987, 102 MINS, US ◇ ⓥ
Dir Norman Jewison *Prod* Patrick Palmer *Scr* John Patrick Shanley *Ph* David Watkin *Ed* Lou Lombardo *Mus* Dick Hyman *Art Dir* Philip Rosenberg
● Cher, Nicholas Cage, Vincent Gardenia, Olympia Dukakis, Danny Aiello, Julie Bovasso (M-G-M)

Norman Jewison's film is a mostly appetizing blend of comedy and drama carried by snappy dialog and a wonderful ensemble full of familiar faces. Leads Cher and Nicolas Cage are both solid and appealing, but it's the pic's older lovers – especially the splendidly controlled Olympia Dukakis – who give *Moonstruck* its endearing spirit.

Cher is Loretta Castorini, a vaguely dour, superstitious widow who believes her previous marriage – she was wed at City Hall, her father didn't give her away, her husband was killed when he was hit by a bus – was felled by bad luck.

Film begins with her accepting a wedding proposal, on bended knee, from the altogether unprepossessing Johnny Cammareri (Tony Aiello), who shortly thereafter heads off to Sicily to be at the bedside of his dying mother.

Loretta, resigned to accepting mediocrity (she admits to her mother that she doesn't love Johnny) for the sake of security, receives a shock upon meeting his kid brother. Cage's Ronny is a brooding, vital, angry, barely contained force haunted by his past.

In Rose Castorini (Loretta's mother), Dukakis fleshes out a good, tired woman who is nothing less than mystified by the actions of her husband, and what her response should be. It's a warm, lyrical performance, that provides the finest moments in the film.
□ 1987: Best Picture (Nomination)

■ MOONTIDE

1942, 94 MINS, US
Dir Archie Mayo *Prod* Mark Hellinger *Scr* John O'Hara *Ph* Charles Clarke *Ed* William Reynolds *Mus* Cyril Mockridge, David Buttolph
● Jean Gabin, Ida Lupino, Thomas Mitchell, Claude Rains, Jerome Cowan (20th Century-Fox)

Much of the success of the film [from the 1940 bestseller by Willard Robertson] may hinge on reaction to Jean Gabin. He's a pleasing and able player, but fails to project warmth and personal feeling.

Gabin, known as an earthy player in France, is given just that type of role in *Moontide*. He's an itinerant dock-worker who for years hasn't had a home and is chiefly interested in getting drunk. Until, that is, he rescues from the surf a hash-house waitress (Ida Lupino) intent on killing herself.

Moontide is a series of incidents, although the overall impression is of a single important event in a man's life. Despite the speed with which director Archie Mayo paints each incident, the total effect is one of slowness and lacking suspense. Mayo's artistic direction is

too even-paced to provide the occasional kick that any story requires.

■ MORE

1969, 115 MINS, LUXEMBOURG ◇
Dir Barbet Schroeder *Prod* Dave Lewis, Charles Lachman *Scr* Barbet Schroeder, Paul Gegauff *Ph* Nestor Almendros *Ed* Denise De Casabianca *Mus* The Pink Floyd
● Mimsy Farmer, Klaus Grunberg, Heinz Engelmann, Michel Chanderli (Jet/Two World)

In his first pic director Barbet Schroeder shows an insight into [late 1960s] youths, be they American or Europeans, who have been labeled everything from beatnik to yippie. There is no attempt to go in for forced erotics, violence, nudity or titillating amoralism. He gives a feeling of how it is sans didactics or obviousness. Drug-taking is a part of it in this tale of a youth from Germany destroyed by it.

The German boy meets a pretty, independent American girl. They soon become lovers and he follows her to Ibiza, a Spanish island, where they have an idyll in a beach house.

Brilliantly shot in arresting hues, it escapes picturesqueness and delves into its characters with sympathy and ease, sans indulgence. Mimsy Farmer reveals a potent personality and gives her role of the girl a tension, inner hurt and alienation.

■ MORE AMERICAN GRAFFITI

1979, 111 MINS, US ◇ ⓥ
Dir B.W.L. Norton *Prod* Howard Kazanjian *Scr* B.W.L. Norton *Ph* Caleb Deschanel *Ed* Tina Hirsch *Art Dir* Ray Storey
● Candy Clark, Bo Hopkins, Ron Howard, Scott Glenn, Paul Le Mat, Charles Martin Smith (Universal/Lucasfilm)

More American Graffiti may be one of the most innovative and ambitious films of the last five years, but by no means is it one of the most successful. In trying to follow the success of George Lucas' immensely popular 1973 hit, writer-director B.W.L. Norton overloads the sequel with four wholly different cinematic styles to carry forward the lives of *American Graffiti*'s original cast.

While dazzling to the eye, the flirtation with split-screen, anamorphic, 16mm and 1:85 screen sizes does not justify itself in terms of the film's content.

Part of Norton's presumed goal, of course, is to show how the 1960s fractured and split apart. But without a dramatic glue to hold the disparate story elements together, *Graffiti* is too disorganized for its own good.

■ MORE THE MERRIER, THE

1943, 101 MINS, US ⓥ
Dir George Stevens *Prod* George Stevens *Scr* Robert Russell, Frank Ross, Richard Flourney, Lewis R. Foster *Ph* Ted Tetzlaff *Ed* Otto Meyer
● Jean Arthur, Joel McCrea, Charles Coburn, Richard Gaines, Bruce Bennett, Frank Sully (Columbia)

A sparkling and effervescing piece of entertainment, *The More the Merrier*, is one of the most spontaneous farce-comedies of the wartime era. Although Jean Arthur and Joel McCrea carry the romantic interest, Charles Coburn walks off with the honors.

Story is premised on the housing conditions existing in wartime Washington. Coburn arrives in town and sublets half interest in Miss Arthur's minute apartment, and when he finds the girl without a boy friend, conveniently picks up McCrea – Air Force sergeant in town to get orders for secret mission – to become partner in his share of the housing layout. Naturally complications ensue in hilarious fashion until Coburn backs out to watch the culmination of the romance he very effectively cooks up.
□ 1943: Best Picture (Nomination)

■ MORE THINGS CHANGE, THE

1986, 95 MINS, AUSTRALIA ◇
Dir Robyn Nevin *Prod* Jill C. Robb *Scr* Moya Wood *Ph* Dan Burstall *Ed* Jill Bilcock *Mus* Peter Best *Art Dir* Josephine Ford
● Judy Morris, Barry Otto, Victoria Longley, Lewis Fitz-Gerald, Peter Carroll (Syme)

The More Things Change is a universally topical film about a modern marriage, told with humor and insight. It's also splendidly acted.

Connie (Judy Morris) and Lex (Barry Otto) are happily married with a small son. They've decided to opt out of the rat race, and have purchased a small but spectacularly beautiful farm two hours' drive from the city, but until the farm is self-sufficient one of them has to keep working. A live-in babysitter is the answer, and Connie engages Geraldine (Victoria Longley).

The viewer's expectations are, naturally, that Lex and Geraldine will have an affair, but Moya Wood's sharp screenplay is much more subtle than that, making this a film where all the characters are a pleasure.

■ MORGAN (A SUITABLE CASE FOR TREATMENT)

1966, 97 MINS, UK ⓥ
Dir Karel Reisz *Prod* Leon Clore *Scr* David Mercer *Ph* Larry Pizer *Ed* Tom Priestley *Mus* Johnny Dankworth *Art Dir* Philip Harrison
● Vanessa Redgrave, David Warner, Robert Stephens, Irene Handl, Newton Blick, Nan Munro (British Lion/Quintra)

Morgan follows the frequently funny, sometimes pathetic but relentlessly lunatic exploits of an eccentric artist to his eventual, though not inevitable, incarceration in an insane asylum. Although it is established that the title character, played with zest and skill by David Warner, was always engagingly dotty, his latest bizarre binge is triggered by his opposition to ex-wife's (Vanessa Redgrave) impending marriage to a sympathetic and likeable suitor.

Spare, straight-line plot follows Morgan's misguided but amusingly slapstick attempts to win back his mate, Leonie, who, though displaying a tolerance and protectiveness bordering on the saintly, longs for a less frenetic and wearying life with a 'normal' husband. To director Karel Reisz's credit, the suitor, well played by Robert Stephens, is never cast as a villain.

Schizophrenia seems to have infected Reisz's direction. Instead of providing the subtle, gradually disintegrating character of Morgan, Reisz dwells on the comedic aspects of each prank, cunningly milked for maximum yaks, in the process ceding any hope of the observer taking Morgan seriously.

■ MORITURI

1965, 118 MINS, US ⓥ
Dir Bernhard Wicki *Prod* Aaron Rosenberg *Scr* Daniel Taradash *Ph* Conrad Hall *Ed* Joseph Silver *Mus* Jerry Goldsmith *Art Dir* Jack Martin Smith, Herman A. Blumenthal
● Marlon Brando, Yul Brynner, Janet Margolin, Trevor Howard, Martin Benrath, Hans Christian Blech (20th Century-Fox)

Morituri is a Second World War sea drama of sometimes battering impact. Starring Marlon Brando and Yul Brynner, the production carries strong suspense at times and a brooding menace that communicates to the spectator.

Action takes place aboard a German blockade runner in 1942 en route from Yokohama to Bordeaux with a cargo of 7,000 tons of indispensable crude rubber for the Nazis, which the Allies also want. British put a man on the freighter with orders to disarm explosive charges by which the captain would scuttle his ship rather than allow capture.

Both Brando and Brynner contribute hard-hitting performances, Brando as the saboteur and Brynner as captain. Former, a German deserter threatened with return to Germany and certain death if he doesn't acquiesce to British demand, gives his impersonation almost tongue-in-cheek handling.

In top support, Trevor Howard is in briefly as a British Intelligence officer, and Martin Benrath makes the most of his role as exec officer, a Nazi who takes over the ship when Brynner becomes raging drunk.

■ **MORNING AFTER, THE**

1986, 103 MINS, US ◇ ⑦
Dir Sidney Lumet   *Prod* Bruce Gilbert   *Scr* James
Hicks   *Ph* Andrzej Barthowiak   *Ed* Joel Goodman
Mus Paul Chihara   *Art Dir* Albert Brenner
● Jane Fonda, Jeff Bridges, Raul Julia, Diane Salinger,
Richard Foronjy (Lorimar/American Filmworks)

Overwrought and implausible, *The Morning After* is a dramatic situation in search of a thriller plot. Jane Fonda stars as a boozy, washed-up actress who wakes up one morning next to a man with a dagger in his heart, and her efforts to cope with the dilemma are neither terribly suspenseful nor entertaining.

She removes any trace that she was ever present at the fellow's place, doesn't call the cops and heads for the airport, where she hooks up with friendly redneck Jeff Bridges, who gradually insinuates himself into her life.

Along the way, Fonda battles the bottle, succumbs to Bridges' charms and is forced into a divorce by estranged hubby but good chum Raul Julia, an outrageously successful Beverly Hills hairdresser who now wants to marry a Bel-Air heiress.

While attempting to build up tension, Fonda and director Sidney Lumet more often succeed in creating hysteria.

■ **MORNING GLORY**

1933, 70 MINS, US ⑦
Dir Lowell Sherman   *Prod* Pandro S. Berman
Scr Howard J. Green   *Ph* Bert Glennon   *Ed* George
Nicholls   *Mus* Max Steiner
● Katharine Hepburn, Douglas Fairbanks Jr, Adolphe
Menjou, Mary Duncan, C. Aubrey Smith (Radio)

Morning Glory isn't an entirely happy choice for Katharine Hepburn but the star provides a strong performance. This one is heavy on legit class and lacks action and sustained conflict.

Story [from the stage play by Zoe Akins] is at great pains to build up the charming character of a well-bred, utterly innocent country girl who comes to Broadway seeking footlight fame. No sooner is the thoroughly lovable figure built to completeness than the hapless little Cinderella is dragged through the mud of backstage casual amours. This happens less than midway of the footage, and thereafter the grip of an engaging story relaxes fatally. The fate of this bedraggled Cinderella becomes a matter of indifference.

Aside from its story defects, the picture is excellent in technique. Dialog is pointed and terse, and the photography is magnificent. A first-rate supporting cast gives Hepburn invaluable co-operation, notably a fine, intelligent handling of the male lead by Douglas Fairbanks Jr and a characteristically suave performance by Adolphe Menjou.

■ **MOROCCO**

1930, 90 MINS, US ⑦
Dir Josef von Sternberg   *Prod* Hector Turnbull
Scr Jules Furthman   *Ph* Lee Garmes, Lucien Ballard
Ed Sam Winston   *Mus* Karl Hajer   *Art Dir* Hans Dreier

● Gary Cooper, Marlene Dietrich, Adolphe Menjou,
Ulrich Haupt, Juliette Compton, Francis McDonald
(Paramount)

Morocco is too lightweight a story to be counterbalanced by the big-time direction given it. Marlene Dietrich has little opportunities in her first American talker. There's nothing to the picture, except what Josef von Sternberg gives it in direction, and that's giving it more than it's got.

The story [from the novel *Amy Jolly* by Benno Vigny] is given a terrific kick early, when Dietrich arrives in Morocco to star in the concert hall. The first evening of her appearance she gives the key to her home to a legionnaire, Cooper. After that the rest is apple sauce, even to her joining the female followers of the troops to keep near her soldier.

Adolphe Menjou has a walkthrough role, done with his acknowledged suavity. Ulrich Haupt handles a minor role very nicely. Cooper plays excellently. He gets the precise spirit of his role.

■ **MOSCOW NIGHTS**

1935, 77 MINS, UK ⑦
Dir Anthony Asquith   *Prod* Alexis Granowski, Max
Schach   *Scr* Eric Seipmann, Anthony Asquith
Ph Philip Tannura   *Ed* William Hornbeck, Francis
Lyon   *Art Dir* Vincent Korda
● Harry Baur, Laurence Olivier, Penelope Dudley-
Ward, Athene Seyler, Hay Petrie (Denham/London/
Capitol)

Moscow Nights is a triumph for director Anthony Asquith in that you are actually transported to Russia in 1916, and no book could give you a more vivid spectacle of things as they existed at that time. Not once is it deemed necessary to resort to comedy relief. It is really and truly a triumph of film direction.

Plot is conventional enough, but it is the atmosphere in which it is disclosed. A handsome young Russian officer (Laurence Olivier) is carried into a hospital in a delirious condition from war wounds. Upon regaining consciousness he discovers a celestial-looking Red Cross nurse in the person of Penelope Dudley-Ward, and falls hard. She is, however, engaged to a middle-aged war profiteer who pays off the mortgage on her parents' home. The profiteer boasts he was born a peasant and is still a peasant. Part is played by Harry Baur, a Continental actor, who brings to the role a dominance that always falls short of being repellent.

Laurence Olivier has looks, charm and acting ability. This is his first big opportunity, and he takes advantage of it to the full. The supporting cast is of a very high order, notably Athene Seyler, Kate Cutler, Morton Selten and Hay Petrie.

■ **MOSCOW ON THE HUDSON**

1984, 115 MINS, US ◇ ⑦
Dir Paul Mazursky   *Prod* Paul Mazursky   *Scr* Paul
Mazursky, Leon Capetanos   *Ph* Donald McAlpine
Ed Richard Halsey   *Mus* David McHugh   *Art Dir* Pato
Guzman
● Robin Williams, Maria Conchita Alonso, Cleavant
Derricks, Alejandro Rey, Savely Kramarov, Elya Baskin
(Columbia)

Moscow on the Hudson is a sweet, beautifully performed picture that unfortunately wanders around several patriotic themes.

Directed by Paul Mazursky with his usual unusual touches, *Moscow* would be in a lot of trouble without a superbly sensitive portrayal by Robin Williams of a gentle Russian circus musician who makes a sudden decision to defect while visiting the US.

As Mazursky sees it, Williams thus becomes one more in a flood of immigrants who

still are coming to this country and discovering virtues that those already here many times forget. Of course, they also encounter the faults, as well.

The entire film is full of performers working way beyond the material. Cleavant Derricks is especially good. Maria Conchita Alonso is also spirited as Williams' Italian girlfriend.

■ **MOSES**

1975, 140 MINS, UK/ITALY ◇ ⑦
Dir Gianfranco de Bosio   *Prod* Vincenzo Labella
Scr Anthony Burgess, Vittorio Bonicelli, Gianfranco de
Bosio   *Ph* Marcello Gatti   *Ed* Gerry Hambling et al
Mus Ennio Morricone
● Burt Lancaster, Anthony Quayle, Ingrid Thulin, Irene
Papas, Mariangela Melato, William Lancaster (ITC/RAI)

Moses is another attempt at compressing a big slice of Biblical drama, and the inevitable result is superficial story telling. The film was impressively photographed in Israel and has Burt Lancaster in a restrained portrayal as the patriarch of the ancient Hebrews who leads them from Egyptian bondage to the promised land.

Pic strikes a reasonable balance between spectacle and narrative. But the net effect is one of flat earnestness, a tale more of tribute than of dimensional human saga.

Feature was 'inspired' by the TV mini-series, *Moses, the Lawgiver*. Besides recutting, the theatrical edition assertedly contains much footage not included in the TV version.

Lancaster delivers his usual polished professionalism, arrayed in seasoned if undistinguished support are Anthony Quayle and Ingrid Thulin as his brother and sister, Irene Papas as his wife, and Laurent Terzieff as the young Egyptian monarch loathe to free his Jewish serfs.

■ **MOSQUITO COAST, THE**

1986, 117 MINS, US ◇ ⑦
Dir Peter Weir   *Prod* Jerome Hellman   *Scr* Paul
Schrader   *Ph* John Seale   *Ed* Thom Noble
Mus Maurice Jarre   *Art Dir* John Stoddart
● Harrison Ford, Helen Mirren, River Pheonix, Jadrien
Steele, Hilary Gordon, Rebecca Gordon (Warner)

It is hard to believe that a film as beautiful as *The Mosquito Coast* [adapted from the novel by Paul Theroux] can also be so bleak, but therein lies its power and undoing. A modern variation of *Swiss Family Robinson*, it starts out as a film about idealism and possibilities, but takes a dark turn and winds up questioning the very values it so powerfully presents. There's a stunning performance by Harrison Ford with firstrate film-making by Peter Weir.

Ford's Allie Fox is a world-class visionary with the power to realize his vision. He rants and raves against pre-packaged, mass consumed American culture and packs up his wife and four kids and moves them to a remote Caribbean island – the Mosquito Coast.

Fox transforms a remote outpost on the island into a thriving community equipped with numerous Rube Goldberg-like gadgets to harness the forces of nature and make life better for the inhabitants. For a while it's an idyllic little utopian community, but the seeds of its downfall are present even as it thrives.

As Fox starts to unravel so does the film. None of the outside antagonists supplied by Paul Schrader's screenplay are fitting adversaries for Fox' genius.

■ **MOTHER LODE**

1982, 101 MINS, US ◇ ⑦
Dir Charlton Heston   *Prod* Fraser Clarke Heston
Scr Fraser Clarke Heston   *Ph* Richard Leiterman
Ed Eric Boyd Perkins   *Mus* Ken Wannberg
Art Dir Douglas Higgins

● Charlton Heston, Nick Mancuso, Kim Basinger, John Marley, Dale Wilson (Agamemnon)

As the title indicates, the consuming issue in *Mother Lode* is a search for gold. The picture is not without shortcomings, but is long on good performances, charismatic people in the three principal roles, compelling outdoor aerial sequences in the Cassiar Mountains of British Columbia and high-level suspense throughout.

The role of Silas McGee, the disreputable Scottish miner trying to protect his great secret find, is a switch to villainy for Charlton Heston, but he relishes the role and even makes a creditable pass at a thick Scottish brogue. Nick Mancuso, as the bush-pilot protagonist who would delve the secret location of the lode at any cost, is the character around which the suspense must swirl, and he manages to keep matters tense to the very end.

Kim Basinger, the only femme in the picture, provides the reason for some unusual plot twists, and comes across as a beauteous screen personality.

■ MOTHER WORE TIGHTS

1947, 107 MINS, US ◇
Dir Walter Lang *Prod* Lamar Trotti *Scr* Lamar Trotti
Ph Harry Jackson *Ed* J. Watson Webb Jr *Mus* Mack Gordon, Josef Myrow *Art Dir* Richard Day, Joseph C. Wright
● Betty Grable, Dan Dailey, Mona Freeman, Connie Marshall (20th Century-Fox)

Mother Wore Tights [based on the book by Miriam Young] is a familiarly styled Technicolor musical opus on the life and times of a song-and-dance team that knocked around the vaude circuits about the century's turn. Leisurely paced and loosely constructed as a series of undramatic vignettes, picture will appeal to patrons who prefer their nostalgia trowelled on thickly and sweetly.

Musical is severely limited by its long and mediocre score of tunes, which are presented without any visual imaginative touches. Numerous hoofing sequences featuring Betty Grable and vis-a-vis Dan Dailey also fail to rate the heavy accent put on them by the footage. Chief drawback, however, is the rambling story, whose lack of both major and minor climaxes is made glaring by Walter Lang's deadpan direction and a script which pulls out all the stops in its use of cliches and sentimentalism.

Yarn, unfolding via simple flashbacks to the commentary of the hoofers' younger daughter, progresses through the various stages of the vaude team's career.

■ MOTHER, JUGS & SPEED

1976, 95 MINS, US ◇ Ⓥ
Dir Peter Yates *Prod* Peter Yates, Tom Mankiewicz
Scr Tom Mankiewicz *Ph* Ralph Woolsey *Ed* Frank P. Keller *Art Dir* Walter Scott Herndon
● Raquel Welch, Bill Cosby, Harvey Keitel, Allen Garfield, Larry Hagman, L.Q. Jones (20th Century-Fox)

The three titular characters are Bill Cosby, Raquel Welch, Harvey Keitel, all very pleasant in their roles as ambulance drivers for company owner Allen Garfield. Their easy-going camaraderie, which provides a strong role for Welch, allows for many good behavioral moments.

The film starts off as pure farce but veers into tragedy when young driver Bruce Davison is killed by a junkie's shotgun.

Other supporting characters also suffer from the film's opportunistic grab-bag tendencies.

The film, based on a story by Stephen Manes and Tom Mankiewicz, remains oddly appealing despite its serious flaws – in many

ways it's an accurate reflection of what really goes on in hustling ambulance outfits.

■ MOTOR PSYCHO

1965, 73 MINS, US
Dir Russ Meyer *Prod* Russ Meyer *Scr* Russ Meyer, W. E. Sprague *Ph* Russ Meyer *Ed* Charles G. Schelling *Mus* Igo Kantor
● Stephen Oliver, Haji, Alex Rocco, Holle K. Winters, Joseph Cellini, Thomas Scott (Eve)

Motor Psycho is a violent Russ Meyer production concerning three young bums on a rape-murder spree in a California desert town. Slick, well-made and initially absorbing, it features sex angles which kill the credibility of a script which itself is long on loose ends and short on moral compensation.

Stephen Oliver, Joseph Cellini and Thomas Scott are the vagrants who, within the first five minutes, have viciously beaten Steve Masters and raped his wife Arshalouis Aivasian. Holle K. Winters is then assaulted while hubby Alex Rocco is down the road resisting the advances of busty Sharon Lee.

At length, Coleman Francis is beaten and accidently killed when the gang moves in on his younger wife, played by a gal named Haji. Rest of pic concerns Rocco's trackdown of the trio, in which he is joined by Haji, left for dead after Oliver shoots her.

Meyer's direction is good, while his interesting and crisp camera work is excellent.

■ MOULIN ROUGE

1952, 118 MINS, UK ◇ Ⓥ
Dir John Huston *Scr* John Huston, Anthony Veiller
Ph Oswald Morris *Ed* Ralph Kemplen *Mus* Georges Auric *Art Dir* Paul Sheriff
● Jose Ferrer, Colette Marchand, Suzanne Flon, Zsa Zsa Gabor, Katherine Kath (Romulus)

Jose Ferrer endows with conviction the part of Toulouse-Lautrec, the cultured, gifted artist of Paris in the 1880s whose glaring deformity – a childhood accident impeded growth of his legs – repulses the women whom he constantly seeks.

John Huston's direction is superb in the handling of individual scenes. The can-can ribaldry, the frank depiction of streetwalkers, the smokey atmosphere of Parisian bistro life – they come through in exciting pictorial terms. Each scene has a framed appearance which richly sets off the action. And the Technicolor tinting captures the flamboyant aura of Montmartre.

But overall, the production, while of great scenic merit, requires some dramatic explosiveness. The story unfolds in a constantly minor-key tone.

Filmed in France and England, the pic is an adaptation of the best-selling novel by Pierre La Mure.
□ 1952: Best Picture (Nomination)

■ MOUNTAIN MEN, THE

1980, 102 MINS, US ◇ Ⓥ
Dir Richard Lang *Prod* Martin Shafer, Andrew Scheinman *Scr* Fraser Clarke Heston *Ph* Michael Hugo *Ed* Eva Ruggiero *Mus* Michel Legrand *Art Dir* Bill Kenney
● Charlton Heston, Brian Keith, Victoria Racimo, Seymour Cassel, John Glover (Columbia)

Does anyone want to see Charlton Heston as Grizzly Adams? That's the question arising from Columbia's lethargic wilderness pic *The Mountain Men*.

Screenplay by star's son Fraser Clarke Heston is loaded with vulgarities that seem excessive for the genre, and scene after scene dwells on bloody hand-to-hand battles between Indians and the grizzled trappers played by Heston and sidekick Brian Keith.

Film takes ages to drag from one plot development to another, though the Indian battles are with sufficient regularity to keep the audience from snoozing. Basic storyline is Heston's courtly protection of runaway Indian squaw Victoria Racimo and the violent attempts by her former Indian mate Stephen Macht to win her back. It's a limp feature debut for director Richard Lang.

■ MOUNTAINS OF THE MOON

1990, 135 MINS, US ◇ Ⓥ
Dir Bob Rafelson *Prod* Daniel Melnick *Scr* William Harrison, Bob Rafelson *Ph* Roger Deakins *Ed* Thom Noble *Mus* Michael Small *Art Dir* Norman Reynolds
● Patrick Bergin, Iain Glen, Fiona Shaw, Richard E. Grant, Peter Vaughan, Anna Massey (Carolco/Indieprod)

Bob Rafelson's *Mountains of the Moon* is an outstanding adventure film, adapted from William Harrison's book *Burton and Speke* and the journals of 19th-century explorers Richard Burton and John Hanning Speke. Without sacrificing the historical context this pic provides deeply felt performances and refreshing, offbeat humour.

Starting in 1854, pic documents duo's ill-fated first two expeditions to Africa, climaxing with Speke's discovery of what became named Lake Victoria, the true source of the Nile (though Speke could not prove same). Roger Deakins' gritty, realistic photography of rugged Kenyan locations contrasts with segments of cheery beauty back home in England between treks.

Rafelson brings expert detailing to the saga. The male bonding theme of the two explorers is forcefully and tastefully told. Besides its vivid presentation of the dangers posed by brutal, hostile African tribes, pic strongly develops its major themes of self-realization and self-aggrandizement.

As Speke, Scots actor Iain Glen creates sympathy for a wayward character. He resembles David Bowie on screen, a reminder that project originally was planned as a vehicle for British rock stars including Bowie until wiser heads prevailed.

■ MOURNING BECOMES ELECTRA

1947, 173 MINS, US
Dir Dudley Nichols *Prod* Dudley Nichols *Scr* Dudley Nichols *Ph* George Barnes *Ed* Roland Gross, Chandler House *Mus* Richard Hageman *Art Dir* Albert S. D'Agostino
● Rosalind Russell, Michael Redgrave, Raymond Massey, Katina Paxinou, Leo Genn, Kirk Douglas (RKO)

Eugene O'Neill's post-Civil War version of the ancient Greek classic was at best 'good for those who like that sort of thing'. The success of the 1931 play proved that there were plenty who did – or who were drawn by the O'Neill name and/or a sense that they owed it to themselves aesthetically to see *Electra*.

Unfortunately, the picture – although still laden with tense drama – lacks much of the impact of the play. The five-hour play (plus an hour's intermission for dinner) seemed less long than the 2 hours and 53 minutes of picture, which is run without intermission.

Nichols, who produced, directed and wrote the adaptation for the screen, will rate a bow from the O'Neill lovers in that he has made no compromises. The picture is every bit as unrelenting in its detailing of family tragedy, brought on by the warping effect of Puritan conscience in conflict with human emotion, as was the play. Even the distorted Oedipus relationships are unflaggingly handled. Never is there concession to a smile or other relaxation from the hammering tragedy of murder, self-destruction and twisted, dramatic emotionalism. The legend has been set down in almost modern surroundings and given the locale and speech, the morals and manners of Civil War New England.

Performances are uniformly good, although they never rise beyond the drama that is inherent in the situations themselves. Too often the emoting consists of Rosalind Russell, and Michael Redgrave popping their eyes. Outstanding are Raymond Massey and Henry Hull, the latter in the secondary role of an aged retainer.

....

■ MOUSE THAT ROARED, THE

1959, 83 MINS, UK ◇ ⓥ

Dir Jack Arnold *Prod* Walter Shenson *Scr* Roger MacDougall, Stanley Mann *Ph* John Wilcox *Ed* Raymond Poulton *Mus* Edwin Astley
● Peter Sellers, Jean Seberg, David Kossoff, William Hartnell, Leo McKern, Macdonald Parke (Open Road/Columbia)

Screen satire can be as risky as a banana-skin on a sidewalk. There are a few occasions when *The Mouse That Roared* gets oversmart, but on the whole it keeps its slight amusing idea bubbling happily in the realms of straightforward comedy. It's a comedy in the old Ealing tradition.

The yarn [from the novel by Leonard Wibberly] concerns the Grand Duchy of Grand Fenwick, the world's smallest country, which relies for its existence on the export of a local wine to the US. When California bottles a cheaper, inferior imitation, Grand Fenwick is on verge of going broke. So the prime minister hits on the wily scheme of going to war against America, on the grounds that the loser in any war is invariably on the receiving end of hefty financial handouts from the winners.

But the invasion of NY by an army of 20 men with mail uniforms and bows and arrows goes awry.

Peter Sellers plays three roles in the film. He is the Grand Duchess Gloriana, the prime minister and also the hapless field marshal who upsets the prime minister's plans. Jean Seberg is pretty, but makes little impact, as the heroine. But there is useful work from William Hartnell, David Kossoff, Leo McKern and Macdonald Parke as a pompous American general. The sight of the completely deserted city is an awesome one and owes considerably to Jack Arnold's direction, and remarkable artwork and lensing.

....

■ MOVE OVER, DARLING

1963, 103 MINS, US ◇

Dir Michael Gordon *Prod* Aaron Rosenberg, Martin Melcher *Scr* Hal Kanter, Jack Sher *Ph* Daniel L. Fapp *Ed* Robert Simpson *Mus* Lionel Newman *Art Dir* Jack Martin Smith, Hilyard Brown
● Doris Day, James Garner, Polly Bergen, Chuck Connors, Thelma Ritter, Fred Clark (20th Century-Fox)

Something old, something new, something borrowed, something blue is the nature of *Move Over, Darling*, a reproduction of the 1940 romantic comedy *My Favorite Wife*, which costarred Cary Grant and Irene Dunne.

Its complicated history is revealed in the writing credit: screenplay by Hal Kanter and Jack Sher based on a screenplay by Bella Spewack and Samuel Spewack from a story by Bella Spewack. Samuel Spewack and Leo McCarey.

The 'old' is the basic yarn about the guy who remarries five years after his first wife is thought to have perished only to have his first wife turn up alive and kicking at the outset of his honeymoon. The 'new' are the chiefly lacklustre embellishments tagged on. The 'borrowed', to cite one example, is a telephone sequence that owes more than a little something to Shelley Berman. The 'blue' isn't of a really offensive nature.

Doris Day and James Garner play it to the hilt, comically, dramatically and last, but not least (particularly in the case of the former), athletically. What is missing in their portrayals is a light touch – the ability to humorously convey with a subtle eyelash-bat or eyebrow-arch what it tends to take them a kick in the shins to accomplish.

Others of prominence in the cast are Polly Bergen as the sexually-obsessed second wife (it's never really much of a contest between her and Day), Thelma Ritter as the understanding mother-in-law, and Chuck Connors as the male animal who shared the small island hunk of real estate alone with Day for five years.

....

■ MOVIE MOVIE

1978, 105 MINS, US ◇ ⓥ

Dir Stanley Donen *Prod* Stanley Donen *Scr* Larry Gelbart, Sheldon Keller *Ph* Charles Rosher Jr, Bruce Surtees *Ed* George Hively *Mus* Ralph Burns *Art Dir* Jack Fisk
● George C. Scott, Barbara Harris, Eli Wallach, Trish Van Devere, Red Buttons, Barry Bostwick (Warner)

Stanley Donen's *Movie Movie* is a clumsy attempt to spoof the kind of film fare encountered in pic houses of the 1930s and 1940s. The idea was patronizing in its conception, is a flatout embarrassment in its execution, and weak vehicle for George C. Scott and other principal talents involved.

The overlong, 105-minute feature is split into three parts: a black-and-white sendup of those boxing sagas where the slum youth fueled by earnest ambition gets catapulted to fame and riches (*Dynamite Hands*); a satire of a coming attractions trailer featuring a saga of World War I pilots; and finally, a shot-in-color takeoff of the making of a Flo Ziegfeld-type Broadway musical (*Baxter's Beauties of 1933*).

But instead of gently twitting the conventions of old Hollywood pot-boilers, *Movie Movie* tries to milk the cliches by observing and scorning them simultaneously. The conception is a mess, and it shows.

Things are so muddied that Donen tacked on, after the pic was shot, a prolog by George Burns telling the audience that yes, *Movie Movie* is intended as fun. Too bad Burns didn't stick around for the rest of the film.

....

■ MR ARKADIN

1955, 99 MINS, FRANCE/SPAIN

Dir Orson Welles *Prod* Louis Dolivet *Scr* Orson Welles *Ph* Jean Bourgoin *Ed* Renzo Lucidi *Mus* Paul Misraki *Art Dir* Orson Welles
● Orson Welles, Michael Redgrave, Patricia Medina, Akim Tamiroff, Robert Arden, Paola Mori (Filmorsa)

Arkadin is at once a fascinating (inevitably) and dismaying effort, frequently suggestive of self-parody; and indeed, in scenario and technique, it is an echo of *Kane* and that film's bravura style.

Instead of newspaper tycoon Charles Foster Kane, here is Gregory Arkadin, shadow figure, arch-capitalist, graduate of a Polish 'white slave' ring, but whose laterday power and riches are shrouded. Instead of Kane's Xanadu, Arkadin has a castle in Spain. Instead of inanimate 'Rosebud,' there is a daughter (Welles' wife, Paola Mori), pretty, vital and overprotected.

The visual trickery in *Arkadin*, albeit often irrelevant, is almost always fascinating – just because it's a Welles orchestration, filling the screen with arresting oddment, with delicious detail – with, in short, excitement.

Welles' story is a parable, and verbalized as such by Arkadin at one point. It concerns a scorpion and a frog, and the moral is that character is immutable and thus logical even when seemingly illogical.

Told in flashback, Arkadin is an amnesiac and hires a smalltime Yank smuggler to trace his past. His ulterior purpose is to turn up, and eradicate, old nefarious associates who conceivably might disclose the truth about him to his daughter. The American goes to work, and the murders follow.

Engaging meller it may be, but missing the incisive delineation that marked *Kane*. The melange of darting narrative simply gets the upper hand – a case of visual virtuosity overwhelming the Arkadin parable.

....

■ MR. BILLION

1977, 91 MINS, US ◇ ⓥ

Dir Jonathan Kaplan *Prod* Steven Bach, Ken Friedman *Scr* Ken Friedman, Jonathan Kaplan *Ph* Matthew F. Leonetti *Ed* O. Nicholas Brown *Mus* Dave Grusin *Art Dir* Richard Berger
● Terence Hill [= Mario Girotti], Valerie Perrine, Jackie Gleason, Slim Pickens, William Redfield, Chill Wills (Pantheon)

Terence Hill is charming as an Italian mechanic who inherits a fortune and has a hell of a time getting to Frisco in time to claim it. Valerie Perrine and Jackie Gleason are among those who try to fleece the innocent of his loot. There are many loose ends in the plot, and some choppy sequences, but the pic is brisk enjoyment.

The obvious inspiration for the film was Frank Capra's classic 1936 populist comedy-fantasy, *Mr Deeds Goes to Town*, in which Gary Cooper inherited a fortune only to find himself besieged by greedy city slickers.

Director Jonathan Kaplan also borrows heavily from Alfred Hitchcock. The blend of Capra and Hitchcock doesn't always work,and the film often seems too much of an artificial film buff homage.

....

■ MR BLANDINGS BUILDS HIS DREAM HOUSE

1948, 93 MINS, US ⓥ

Dir H.C. Potter *Prod* Norman Panama, Melvin Frank *Scr* Norman Panama, Melvin Frank *Ph* James Wong Howe *Ed* Harry Marker *Mus* Leigh Harline *Art Dir* Albert S. D'Agostino, Carroll Clark
● Cary Grant, Myrna Loy, Melvyn Douglas, Reginald Denny, Jason Robards, Lex Barker (Selznick/RKO)

Eric Hodgins' novel of the trials and tribulations of the Blandings, while building their dream house, read a lot funnier than they filmed. Norman Panama and Melvin Frank come through with a glossy lustre in handling physical production, but fail to jell the story into solid film fare in their dual scripting.

Film's opening pulls some standard sight gags that register strongly, helped by the business injected through H.C. Potter's direction.

Script gets completely out of hand when unnecessary jealousy twist is introduced, neither advancing the story nor adding laughs.

Grant is up to his usual performance standard as Blandings, getting the best from the material, and Myrna Loy comes through with another of her screen wife assignments nicely. Melvyn Douglas, the lawyer friend of the family, gives it a tongue-in-cheek treatment. Trio's finesse and Potter's light directorial touch do much to give proceedings a lift.

....

■ MR DEEDS GOES TO TOWN

1936, 115 MINS, US ⓥ

Dir Frank Capra *Prod* Frank Capra *Scr* Robert Riskin *Ph* Joseph Walker *Ed* Gene Havlick *Mus* Howard Jackson *Art Dir* Stephen Goosson

M

● Gary Cooper, Jean Arthur, George Bancroft, Lionel Stander, Douglass Dumbrille, Raymond Walburn (Columbia)

Mr Deeds Goes to Town needs the marquee draught of Gary Cooper, Jean Arthur and George Bancroft to make it really go to town. With a sometimes too thin structure [from a story by Clarence Buddington Kelland], the players and director Frank Capra have contrived to convert *Deeds* into fairly sturdy substance. The farce is good-humored and the trouping and production workmanlike, but there are some lapses in midriff that cause considerable uncertainty.

The native Yankee shrewdness endowed Longfellow Deeds takes a male Pollyanna tack that skirts some dangerous shoals. A mug with a $20 million heritage should know how to be more practical about things and while scriptwriter Robert Riskin and Capra have managed to have him turn the tables more or less effectively in the trial before a lunacy commission, there are times when Cooper's impression is just a bit too scatter-brained for sympathetic comfort.

Capra's direction is more mundane than flighty. With machinating attorneys, false claimants to the estate, down-to-earth 'jest folks,' etc, it's to be expected that the general structure will be in like tune.

Deeds is a guy who plays a tuba in bed, slides down bannisters, decides to give away his $20 million just like that, after John Wray in a theatrical hokum bit waves a gun at him, fortified with a quasi-comunistic plea. Combined with some of the other lines and business accorded the male topper, audience credulity, despite the general lightness of the theme, becomes strained.
□ 1936: Best Picture (Nomination)

■ **MR. DESTINY**

1990, 105 MINS, US ◇ ⓥ
Dir James Orr   *Prod* James Orr, Jim Cruickshank, Susan B. Landau   *Scr* James Orr, Jim Cruickshank   *Ph* Alex Thomson   *Ed* Michael R. Miller   *Mus* David Newman   *Art Dir* Michael Seymour
● James Belushi, Linda Hamilton, Michael Caine, Jon Lovitz, Hart Bochner, Rene Russo (Touchstone/Silver Screen Partners IV)

A heavy-handed, by-the-numbers fantasy about an ordinary Joe who thinks his life would have been different if he'd connected with that all-important pitch in a high school baseball game.

James Belushi plays smalltown white-collar working stiff Larry Burrows, who on his depressing 35th birthday stumbles into a bar where a mysterious, twinkly-eyed barman (Michael Caine) serves him up a 'spilt milk' elixir that sends him spinning back in time to take another swat at that baseball.

He hits a home run, and his whole life turns out differently, just as he expected. But guess what? He's not any happier than he was before.

So what if he's married to the dishy prom queen (Rene Russo) and has become the absurdly wealthy president of a sports equipment company – the same one he slaved for in his other life. He misses his original wife (Linda Hamilton) and their unpretentious lifestyle, and whether it makes sense or not, he sets out to win her back.

■ **MR HOBBS TAKES A VACATION**

1962, 115 MINS, US ◇
Dir Henry Koster   *Prod* Jerry Wald   *Scr* Nunnally Johnson   *Ph* William C. Mellor   *Ed* Marjorie Fowler   *Mus* Henry Mancini   *Art Dir* Jack Martin Smith, Malcolm Brown
● James Stewart, Maureen O'Hara, Fabian, John Saxon, Reginald Gardiner, Marie Wilson (20th Century-Fox

Togetherness, all-American family style, is given a gently irreverent poke in the ribs in *Mr Hobbs Takes a Vacation*. This is a fun picture, although it misfires, chiefly in the situation development department.

Nunnally Johnson's screenplay, based on the novel, *Hobbs' Vacation*, by Edward Streeter, is especially strong in the dialog area. The film is peppered with refreshingly sharp, sophisticated references and quips. But Johnson's screenplay falls down in development of its timely premise, leaving the cast and director Henry Koster heavily dependent on their own comedy resources in generating fun.

Hobbs (James Stewart) is a St. Louis banker who has the misfortune to spend his vacation at the seashore with 10 other members of his immediate family, setting up a series of situations roughly designed to illustrate the pitfalls of that grand old Yankee institution, the family reunion.

The picture has its staunchest ally in Stewart, whose acting instincts are so remarkably keen that he can instill amusement into scenes that otherwise threaten to fall flat. Some of the others in the cast, endowed with less intuitive gifts for light comedy, do not fare as well.

Maureen O'Hara is decorative as Mrs Hobbs. Fabian struggles along in an undernourished romantic role, and warbles, with considerable uncertainty, an uninspired ditty, tagged *Cream Puff*, by Johnny Mercer and Henry Mancini, who has composed a satisfactory score for the film. John Saxon is mired in a stereotypical role of a pompously dense intellect.

■ **MR. JOHNSON**

1990, 103 MINS, US ◇ ⓥ
Dir Bruce Beresford   *Prod* Michael Fitzgerald   *Scr* William Boyd   *Ph* Peter James   *Ed* Humphrey Dixon   *Mus* Georges Delerue   *Art Dir* Herbert Pinter
● Maynard Eziashi, Pierce Brosnan, Edward Woodward, Beatie Edney, Denis Quilley (Fitzgerald)

Capitalism and colonialism intertwine like a two-headed snake in this ponderous but well-made film. Director Bruce Beresford's modestly scaled followup to Oscar winner *Driving Miss Daisy* suffers from a slow, marginally involving storyline.

Pic's foremost discovery is Nigerian actor Maynard Eziashi in the title role as a young African obsessed with British mores, resourcefully working outside the rigid limits of his colonial clerkship.

Johnson uses that knack to help his boss Rudbeck (Pierce Brosnan) build a road connecting their small outpost to the outside world, though his consistent circumvention of proper channels eventually catches up with him and proves his downfall.

Working from a 1939 novel by Joyce Carey set in the 1920s, Beresford and writer William Boyd have delivered a film strangely devoid of emotion and lacking a clear point of view.

Brosnan's straight-legged bureaucrat proves so stiff and lifeless there's no sense of caring in any direction, toward either his wife (Beatie Edney) or Johnson. Edward Woodward injects much-needed life into the staid proceedings as a vulgar expatriate English shop owner, a boozy bigot.

■ **MR. LUCKY**

1943, 94 MINS, US ⓥ
Dir H.C. Potter   *Prod* David Hempstead   *Scr* Milton Holmes, Adrian Scott   *Ph* George Barnes   *Ed* Theron Warth   *Mus* Roy Webb   *Art Dir* William Cameron Menzies
● Cary Grant, Laraine Day, Charles Bickford, Gladys Cooper (RKO)

Cary Grant is a resourceful and opportunist gambling operator, figuring on outfitting his outlawed gaming ship for trip to Havana. But coin and draft registration balk his departure. Assuming name and a draft card of a dying 4-F, he launches drive to raise the moola and runs into society heiress Laraine Day. Pursuing her for romantic pitches, he lands as member of the war relief agency and proceeds to ply his con to help the outfit with supplies and boat charters.

Picture carries an authentic ring to operations of bigtime gamblers, and it faithfully follows the professional premise of 'never give the sucker a break, but never cheat a friend'. Writer Milton Holmes, in selling his first screen original, hews closely to the lines of actual incidents rather than depending on synthetic dramatics to drop it into the groove of obvious cinematic dramatics.

■ **MR MAJESTYK**

1974, 104 MINS, US ◇ ⓥ
Dir Richard Fleischer   *Prod* Walter Mirisch   *Scr* Elmore Leonard   *Ph* Richard H. Kline   *Ed* Ralph E. Winters   *Mus* Charles Bernstein
● Charles Bronson, Al Lettieri, Linda Cristal, Lee Purcell, Paul Koslo, Taylor Lacher (Mirisch)

Mr Majestyk makes a first-reel pretense of dealing with the thorny subject of migrant Chicano farm laborers, but social relevance is soon clobbered by the usual Charles Bronson heroics, here mechanically navigated by director Richard Fleischer.

Bronson, in a boringly stoic performance, plays a melon-grower whose fair labor practices are rewarded with a trumped-up assault charge that lands him in jail. During a shootout engineered by Mafia gangsters to free underworld killer Al Lettieri as prisoners are being moved from one jail to another, Bronson captures the hitman and offers to return Lettieri in exchange for his own freedom. Lettieri eventually escapes and vows revenge on Bronson.

The narrative makes little sense unless viewed as a study in pathology.

■ **MR. MOM**

1983, 91 MINS, US ◇ ⓥ
Dir Stan Dragoti   *Prod* Lynn Loring, Lauren Shuler, Harry Colomby   *Scr* John Hughes   *Ph* Victor J. Kemper   *Ed* Patrick Kennedy   *Mus* Lee Holdridge   *Art Dir* Alfred Sweeney
● Michael Keaton, Teri Garr, Frederick Koehler, Taliesin Jaffe, Courtney & Brittany White, Christopher Lloyd (Sherwood/20th Century-Fox)

The comic talents of Michael Keaton and Teri Garr are largely wasted in *Mr Mom*, an unoriginal romantic comedy where breadwinner-husband and homemaker wife switch roles.

Though Keaton and Garr occasionally manage to evoke some pathos and laughs, it's an uphill battle that is won solely on the strength of their individual personalities.

Keaton, close to perfection as the husband and father depressed by unemployment but always a sport with his family, is already a known bundle of comic energy. But he especially shines here in some more dramatic moments with his children.

Garr, as always, is a delight to watch though it would be nice to see her in a role where she wasn't someone's wife or mother. Still, her inspired double takes continue to say more than pages of dialog while her keen timing helps somewhat in the more beleaguered scenes.

■ **MR. NORTH**

1988, 92 MINS, US ◇ ⓥ
Dir Danny Huston   *Prod* Steven Haft, Skip Steloff, Tom Shaw   *Scr* Janet Roach, John Huston, James Costigan   *Ph* Robin Vidgeon   *Ed* Roberto Silvi   *Mus* David McHugh   *Art Dir* Eugene Lee

● Anthony Edwards, Robert Mitchum, Lauren Bacall, Harry Dean Stanton, Anjelica Huston, Mary Stuart Masterson (Heritage/Goldwyn)

By cowriting and serving as executive producer, the late John Huston could be said to have passed the baton to son Danny Huston on *Mr North*. Unfortunately, Danny has not only dropped the stick but tripped over his own feet in his feature film debut, a woefully flat affair which even a stellar cast cannot bring to life.

The 1973 novel by Thornton Wilder is a resolutely old-fashioned tale about an unusually gifted young man who stirs things up among the rich folk in Newport, RI, circa 1926.

Wilder's fanciful yarn has Theophilus North, a bright Yale graduate, arriving in the seaside bastion of old money and extravagance and making his way in society by magically curing the rich of what ails them, and charming them to boot.

All of this gains North a reputation as something of a savior, but doesn't go down too well with the pillar of the local medical community, who drags the shining fellow into court.

Anthony Edwards gives it a reasonable try in the leading role, his matter-of-factness in the face of extraordinary accomplishments proving rather appealing, but he can't single-handedly rescue this waterlogged vessel.

● ●

■ MR SKEFFINGTON

1944, 126 MINS, US ⓥ

Dir Vincent Sherman   *Prod* Philip G. Epstein, Julius J. Epstein   *Scr* Philip G. Epstein, Julius J. Epstein   *Ph* Ernest Haller   *Ed* Ralph Dawson   *Mus* Franz Waxman   *Art Dir* Robert M. Haas
● Bette Davis, Claude Rains, Walter Abel, Richard Waring, George Coulouris (Warner)

Fitting Bette Davis like a silk glove, the same as the gowns which she wears to intrigue the male of the species in defiance of all the laws of good womanhood, in the part of the vainglorious, selfish wife and mother, *Mr Skeffington*, is not only another triumph for the Warner star but also a picture of terrific strength.

Philip G. and Julius J. Epstein, who have given the story fine production and backgrounds, also adapted the book [by 'Elizabeth'] but locale it in America rather than in England. The story moves steadily and smoothly, gathering much impact as it goes along, while also the dialog ranges from the smart to the trenchantly dramatic in liming the life of the woman who lived for her beauty but found that it wasn't of a lasting character.

Davis, playing the coquettish daughter of a once-wealthy family, progresses through the years from 1914 before World War I to the present, going with gradual changes from early girlhood to around 50 years when suddenly aging badly as result of illness.

Opposite Davis is the able Claude Rains, the successful Wall Street tycoon who goes blind and also prematurely ages as result of several years spent in a Nazi concentration camp following the beginning of the Second World War.

● ●

■ MR. SMITH GOES TO WASHINGTON

1939, 126 MINS, US ⓥ

Dir Frank Capra   *Prod* Frank Capra   *Scr* Sidney Buchman   *Ph* Joseph Walker   *Ed* Gene Havlick, Al Clark   *Mus* Dmitri Tiomkin   *Art Dir* Lionel Banks
● Jean Arthur, James Stewart, Claude Rains, Edward Arnold, Thomas Mitchell (Columbia)

Frank Capra goes to Washington in unwinding the story [by Lewis R. Foster], and in so doing provides a graphic picture of just how the national lawmakers operate. Capra never

attempts to expose political skullduggery on a wide scale. He selects one state political machine and after displaying its power and ruthlessness, proceeds to tear it to pieces.

Stewart is a most happy choice for the title role, delivering sincerity to a difficult part that introduces him as a self-conscious idealist, but a stalwart fighter when faced with a battle to overcome the ruthless political machine of his own state. Jean Arthur is excellent as the wisely cynical senatorial secretary who knows the political ropes of Washington.

Replica of the Senate chamber provides a fine set for the filibustering episode.

□ 1939: Best Picture (Nomination)

● ●

■ MR TOPAZE

1961, 95 MINS, UK ◇

Dir Peter Sellers   *Prod* Pierre Rouve   *Scr* Pierre Rouve   *Ph* John Wilcox   *Ed* Geoffrey Foot   *Mus* Georges Van Parys   *Art Dir* Don Ashton
● Peter Sellers, Nadia Gray, Herbert Lom, Leo McKern, Martita Hunt, Billie Whitelaw (20th Century-Fox/De Grunwald)

Peter Sellers plays a kindly, dedicated and very poor schoolmaster in a little French town. His integrity is such that when he refuses to compromise over a pupil's report to satisfy the child's rich, influential grandmother he is fired by the arrogant headmaster. The gullible Sellers is soft-talked into becoming the front for a swindling business man, finds that he has been a pawn but by then has discovered the wicked ways of the world.

The film [from the play by Marcel Pagnol] falls into sharply contrasting moods. The early stages, with Sellers as the gentle, honest schoolmaster is crammed with sly humor.

As a director Sellers brings out some slick performances from his colleagues. Leo McKern tends to overplay the headmaster, yet his scenes with Sellers are lively exchanges. Billie Whitelaw, as the daughter, who Sellers shyly woos, has limited opportunities but does well with them. Michael Gough is splendid as a seedy schoolmaster who is devoted to Sellers. Herbert Lom plays the con man flashily and effectively.

● ●

■ MR. & MRS. BRIDGE

1990, 124 MINS, US ◇ ⓥ

Dir James Ivory   *Prod* Ismail Merchant   *Scr* Ruth Prawer Jhabvala   *Ph* Tony Pierce-Roberts   *Ed* Humphrey Dixon   *Mus* Richard Robbins   *Art Dir* David Gropman
● Paul Newman, Joanne Woodward, Robert Sean Leonard, Margaret Welsh, Kyra Sedgwick, Blythe Danner (Cineplex Odeon/Merchant Ivory/Halmi)

Mr. & Mrs. Bridge is an affecting study of an uppercrust Midwestern family in the late 1930s. Ruth Prawer Jhabvala has adapted two Evan S. Connell novels into a taut script. Books *Mrs. Bridge* (1959) and *Mr. Bridge* (1969) painted (from each spouse's point of view) a portrait of stuffy Kansas City lawyer Walter Bridge and his stifled wife, India, by a steady accretion of anecdotal detail. The screenplay presents a series of highly dramatic scenes in their lives, the payoffs among the novels' hundreds of brief chapters.

Central theme of India Bridge's gradual realization that her life has been crushed in her husband's shadow is strongly conveyed by Woodward in the role.

Casting of hubby Newman as her husband resonates in their intimate scenes, particularly a 1939 vacation to Paris when the Bridges briefly rekindle their romance, only to have it cut short by World War II.

Kyra Sedgwick is smashing as the Bridges'

bohemian daughter who takes off for New York and an arts career.

● ●

■ MR. AND MRS. SMITH

1941, 90 MINS, US ⓥ

Dir Alfred Hitchcock   *Prod* Harry E. Edington   *Scr* Norman Krasna   *Ph* Harry Stradling   *Ed* William Hamilton   *Mus* Roy Webb   *Art Dir* Van Nest Polglase, L.P. Williams
● Carole Lombard, Robert Montgomery, Gene Raymond, Jack Carson, Philip Merivale, Lucile Watson (RKO)

Carole Lombard and Robert Montgomery are teamed successfully here in a light and gay marital farce, with accent on the laugh side through generation of continual bickering of the pair.

The Smiths (Lombard and Montgomery) are happily – though battlingly – married. A bantering question, 'If you had to do it all over would you marry me' and the obvious husbandly reply of 'No', starts things going. Advised that the three-year-old marriage is void because of legal technicalities, Mrs Smith tosses Mr Smith out of the house. Then the yarn develops into a run-around – with Mr making continual stabs to recapture his wife, while his law partner, (Gene Raymond) is a ready victim of her advances aimed at inspiring jealousy.

Alfred Hitchcock, pilots the story in a straight farcical groove – with resort to slapstick interludes or overplaying by the characters. Pacing his assignment at a steady gait, Hitchcock catches all of the laugh values from the above par script of Norman Krasna.

● ●

■ MRS MINIVER

1942, 133 MINS, US ⓥ

Dir William Wyler   *Prod* Sidney Franklin   *Scr* Arthur Wimperis, George Froeschel, James Hilton, Claudine West   *Ph* Joseph Ruttenberg   *Ed* Harold F. Kress   *Mus* Herbert Stothart
● Greer Garson, Walter Pidgeon, Teresa Wright, May Whitty, Reginald Owen, Henry Wilcoxon (M-G-M)

Superbly catching the warmth and feeling of Jan Struther's characters in her best-selling book of sketches, *Mrs Miniver*, Metro has created out of it a poignant story of the joys and sorrows, the humor and pathos of middle-class family life in war-time England.

Its one defect, not uncommon with Metro's prestige product, is its length. It gets about three-quarters of the way through and begins floundering, like a vaude act that doesn't know how to get off the stage.

In addition, the film, in its quiet yet actionful way, is, probably entirely unintentionally, one of the strongest pieces of propaganda against complacency to come out of the war.

When Mrs Miniver's husband is summoned from his bed at 2 a.m. to help rescue the legions of Dunkirk, when her son flies out across the Channel each night, when she frightenedly captures a sick and starving German pilot who bears resemblance to her own boy, *Mrs Miniver* truly brings the war into one's own family.

Greer Garson, with her knee-weakening smile, and Walter Pidgeon, almost equally personable, are the Minivers. Scarcely less engaging or capable are young Teresa Wright as their daughter-in-law and Richard Ney in the difficult role of their son.

It's impossible to praise too highly William Wyler's direction, which hits only one or two false notes throughout the lengthy presentation. His is clearly the understanding heart to whom these are not actors, but people living genuine joy and sorrow and fear and doubt.

□ 1942: Best Picture

● ●

■ MRS SOFFEL

1984, 110 MINS, US ◇ ⑨
Dir Gillian Armstrong   *Prod* Edgar J. Scherick, Scott
Rudin   *Scr* Ron Nyswaner   *Ph* Russell Boyd
Ed Nicholas Beauman   *Mus* Mark Isham
Art Dir Luciana Arrighi
● Diane Keaton, Mel Gibson, Matthew Modine,
Edward Herrmann, Trini Alvarado, Jennie Dundas
(M-G-M)

The potential for a moving, tragic love story
is clearly there, but *Mrs Soffel* proves distressingly dull for most of its running time.

True story is set in Pittsburgh in 1901, and
has Diane Keaton, as the wife of Allegheny
County Prison warden, Edward Herrmann,
recovering from a long illness and resuming
her rounds of quoting scripture to prisoners.
She quickly takes a special interest in two
cons on Death Row, brothers Mel Gibson
and Matthew Modine, who are waiting to be
hung for a murder they were convicted of
committing during a burglary.

Defying all reason, Keaton helps the
brothers escape and thereby undergoes an
instant transformation from respectable
woman to fugitive outlaw.

Final act does carry something of a charge,
but it's too long a ride getting there.

■ MS. 45

1981, 84 MINS, US ◇
Dir Abel Ferrara   *Prod* Rochelle Weisberg
Scr Nicholas St John   *Ph* James Momel
Ed Christopher Andrews   *Mus* Joe Delia
● Zoe Tamerlis, Steve Singer, Darlene Stuto, Jack
Thibeau, Peter Yellen (Rochelle/Navaron)

Crisply-told tale deals with a mute, stunningly attractive young woman worker (Zoe
Tamerlis) in New York's garment district
who is traumatized one night by (1) being
raped in an alley on the way home and then
(2) raped a second time by a burglar waiting
in her apartment.

Killing the burglar in self-defense, she takes
his gun and embarks on a vendetta of shooting down lecherous males. Ultimately her
killing spree becomes undiscriminating in its
victims.

By keeping the picture short and busy, Ferrara makes its far-fetched elements play. His
shock material works mainly by suggestion
but there are enough 'gross' elements to separate thrill-seeking viewers from
traditionalists.

■ MUMMY, THE

1933, 63 MINS, US
Dir Karl Freund   *Prod* Stanley Bergerman   *Scr* John L.
Balderston   *Ph* Charles Stumar   *Art Dir* Willy Pogany
● Boris Karloff, Zita Johann, David Manners, Edward
Van Sloan, Arthur Byron, Bramwell Fletcher (Universal)

The Mummy [from a story by Nina Wilcox
Putnam and Richard Schayer] has some
weird sequences and it is the first starring
film for Boris Karloff.

Revival of the mummy comes
comparatively early in the running time.
The transformation of Karloff's Im-Ho-Tep
from a clay-like figure in a coffin to a living
thing is the highlight.

The sequence in the museum with Im-Ho
planning to kill Helen Grosvenor, of Egyptian heritage, to revive her ancient state, is
too stagey. The mustiness of the tombs
excavated is also over-suggestive of the
Hollywood set.

Other members of the cast are made to
figure as the puppets of Im-Ho and to carry
over the dialog during the few times Karloff
takes intermissions from the camera.
Zita Johann is attractive, but always
role-conscious, as Grosvenor.

■ MUMSY, NANNY, SONNY & GIRLY

1970, 101 MINS, UK ◇ ⑨
Dir Freddie Francis   *Prod* Ronald J. Kahn   *Scr* Brian
Comport   *Ph* David Muir   *Ed* Tristam Cones
Mus Bernard Ebbinghouse   *Art Dir* Maggie Pinhorn
● Michael Bryant, Ursula Howells, Pat Heywood,
Howard Trevor, Vanessa Howard, Robert Swann
(Fitsroy)

An offbeat, low-key horror melodrama – a
macabre combo of Disney and Hammer
films, in which a lady, her maid and two kids
kidnap and murder unsuspecting males.

Story is set in a country estate populated
by mumsy Ursula Howells, nanny Pat
Heywood, sonny Howard Trevor and girly
Vanessa Howard. It's a quaint family, mannered in the niceties of civilized living, except
that they get their kicks from kidnapping
stray males.

The domestic status quo begins to fall apart
after kidnapping playboy Michael Bryant,
blackmailed into coming to the house on
threats of accusing him of the murder of
girlfriend Imogen Hassall.

Players acquit themselves admirably.
Howells, Heywood and Howard are
excellent, Bryant a bit less dynamic than
he should have been.

■ MUPPET MOVIE, THE

1979, 98 MINS, US ◇ ⑨
Dir James Frawley   *Prod* Jim Henson   *Scr* Jerry Juhl,
Jack Burns   *Ph* Isidore Mankofsky   *Ed* Chris
Greenbury   *Mus* Paul Williams   *Art Dir* Joel Schiller
● Charles Durning, Austin Pendleton, Scott Walker
(ITC/Henson)

Jim Henson, Muppet originator, and Frank
Oz, creative consultant, have abandoned the
successful format of their vidshow, and
inserted their creations into a well-crafted
combo of musical comedy and fantasy
adventure.

Result is a muppet update of *The Wizard of
Oz*, with Kermit the Frog leading a motley
Muppet troupe on the asphalt road to
Hollywood. Script incorporates the zingy
one-liners and bad puns that have
become the teleseries' trade mark.

Director James Frawley has a lot of fun
with cinematic sleight-of-hand, including
shots of Kermit pedalling a bicycle, the
Muppets driving cars and trucks, and
additional full-body camerawork.

The cogent storyline runs Kermit through a
gamut of emotions, from self-doubt and
bashful love to a moral showdown on the old
High Noon set.

■ MURDER

1930, 110 MINS, UK ⑨
Dir Alfred Hitchcock   *Prod* John Maxwell   *Scr* Alfred
Hitchcock, Alma Reville   *Ph* Jack Cox   *Ed* Emile de
Ruelle, Rene Harrison   *Art Dir* John Mead
● Herbert Marshall, Norah Baring, Phyllis Konstam,
Edward Chapman, Miles Mander (British International)

Original title of this one was *Enter Sir John*.
Based on the rather highbrow mystery yarn
[by Clemence Dane], it tells how a girl is convicted of murder on circumstantial evidence
and sentenced to death. One of the jurymen,
an actor, sets to work to solve the crime.

Drawback of this type of development is
that the biggest kick in the picture occurs in
the earlier reels.

Well photographed and mounted, it contains all the gadgets of the pet Alfred Hitchcock technique, from quick cutting to skillful
dialog blending.

The dialog is very well written. Long episodes have clever satirical values as attacks
on the conventional and lower-class English.

Acting is very good. Herbert Marshall
beats the cast to it as the knighted actor who

turns amateur detective. Norah Baring is
sympathetic as the suspected girl.

■ MURDER AT THE VANITIES

1934, 95 MINS, US
Dir Mitchell Leisen   *Prod* E. Lloyd Sheldon   *Scr* Carey
Wilson, Joseph Gollomb, Carey Wilson   *Ph* Leo Tover
● Carl Brisson, Victor McLaglen, Jack Oakie, Kitty
Carlisle, Gertrude Michael, Gail Patrick (Paramount)

Herein they mix up the elements of a musical
show and a murder mystery, with effective
comedy to flavor, and come out with
95 minutes of entertainment that should
genuinely satisfy.

Victor McLaglen is in charge of the
investigation of a couple murders that tax his
limited detective prescience. McLaglen
shares with Jack Oakie the comedy burden
and for each it's a strike.

Picture serves to bring out Carl Brisson,
Danish actor who was brought over by
Paramount to get his baptism in this quasi-
musical. In addition to having an ingratiating personality and photographing well, the
foreign import sells his songs for good results.

Brisson has Kitty Carlisle opposite him,
but she's not one-half as important, more attention being directed to Brisson than anyone
else. Together they do several numbers, the
most effective being a seashore interlude in
which the Earl Carroll girls as mermaids
manipulate fans that simulate rolling waves.

Murders are well planted and cast logical
suspicion in several directions. All of the
action occurs backstage at what is represented as the Earl Carroll theatre (now the
Casino), on opening night of a Carroll show.
It's a backstage musical but different.

■ MURDER BY DEATH

1976, 94 MINS, US ◇ ⑨
Dir Robert Moore   *Prod* Ray Stark   *Scr* Neil Simon
Ph David M. Walsh   *Ed* Margaret Booth, John F.
Burnett   *Mus* Dave Grusin   *Art Dir* Stephen Grimes
● Eileen Brennan, Truman Capote, James Coco, Peter
Falk, Alec Guinness, Elsa Lanchester (Columbia)

Murder by Death is a very good silly-funny Neil
Simon satirical comedy, with a super all-star
cast cavorting as recognizable pulp fiction
detectives gathered at the home of Truman
Capote, wealthy hedonist fed up with
contrived gumshoe plots.

Capote makes a good theatrical feature
debut as an impish Sheridan Whiteside,
deploying his guests in a confusing series of
sketches in which separate player teams, then
the ensemble display their flair for low-key
screwball nuttiness.

The cast list reveals the adroit mating of
performer to send-up prototype, plus Alec
Guinness as Capote's butler, Nancy Walker
as mute maid. Every single player conveys a
casualness and off-handedness which, of
course, is the mark of comedic excellence.

■ MURDER BY DECREE

1980, 120 MINS, UK/CANADA ◇ ⑨
Dir Bob Clark   *Prod* Len Herberman   *Scr* John
Hopkins   *Ph* Reg Morris   *Ed* Stan Cole   *Mus* Carl
Zittrer, Paul Zaza   *Art Dir* Harry Pottle
● Christopher Plummer, James Mason, Donald
Sutherland, Genevieve Bujold, David Hemmings, Susan
Clark (Ambassador/CFDC/Famous Players)

Murder by Decree is probably the best Sherlock
Holmes film since the inimitable pairing of
Basil Rathbone and Nigel Bruce in the 1940s
series at Universal.

The film's charm derives mainly from John
Hopkins' literal, deadpan script that makes
no attempt either to mock or contemporize
Sir Arthur Conan Doyle's literary creation.

Ironically, Christopher Plummer works
against this re-creation by presenting a

Holmes who looks as if he's just returned from a Caribbean vacation. Next to James Mason, who may be the most delightful Watson ever to appear on celluloid, Plummer's blonde handsomeness seems especially foreign.

Holmes and Watson are not called in to help solve a series of murders linked to Jack The Ripper. Anthony Quayle, as the new topper at Scotland Yard, has his reasons for excluding them, as does Inspector David Hemmings.

....

■ MURDER, INC.

1960, 103 MINS, US

Dir Burt Balaban, Stuart Rosenberg   *Prod* Burt Balaban   *Scr* Irve Tunick, Mel Barr   *Ph* Gaine Rescher   *Ed* Ralph Rosenblum   *Mus* Frank DeVol   *Art Dir* Dick Sylbert
● Stuart Whitman, May Britt, Henry Morgan, Peter Falk, Sarah Vaughan, David J. Stewart (20th Century-Fox)

Professional killers of the crime syndicate headed by Albert Anastasia and Louis 'Lepke' Buchalter were a scourge in the Depression era. They later became known as Murder, Inc. The screenplay [from the book by Burton Turkus and Sid Feder] takes a leisurely approach to its subject. The pace is too slow, the suspense only occasionally gripping. Moreover, the overall production lacks zing and tension.

Amidst the tawdry backgrounds of Brooklyn's Brownsville section, the script recounts how Lepke and the syndicate shook down the garment district, trucking business and sundry other legitimate enterprises through goon squads and hired killers. Caught in this vicious crime ring through little fault of their own are a young couple – dancer May Britt and singer Stuart Whitman.

With the possible exception of Peter Falk's portrayal of killer Abe Reles, scarcely any of the cast's performances could be rated as dynamic. His delineation sharply defines the brutal nature of the thug who was killed in a 'fall' from Brooklyn's Half Moon Hotel while in 'protective' custody of the NY police.

Whitman appropriately cringes as helpless man dominated by the killers. His role excites little sympathy. Britt has a few sexy scenes but for the most part seems curiously inanimate.

....

■ MURDER IN THE CATHEDRAL

1952, 140 MINS, UK

Dir George Hoellering   *Prod* George Hoellering   *Scr* T.S. Eliot   *Ph* David Kosky   *Ed* Anne Allnatt   *Mus* Laszlo Lajtha   *Art Dir* Peter Pendrey
● Father John Groser, Alexander Gauge, David Ward, George Woodbridge, Basil Burton, T.S. Eliot (Hoellering)

T.S. Eliot's legit play, *Murder in the Cathedral*, has been turned into a moving but very ponderous film.

Story of the life of Thomas Becket, the martyred Archbishop of Canterbury, unfolds too statically in the picture form. Eliot scripted this from his own play, but failed to add sufficient movement.

Plot details how the Archbishop courageously returns to England after seven years of voluntary exile rather than submit to the king's ambition to dominate the church.

Father John Groser, as Archbishop Becket, is impressive amidst the welter of wordage. Mark Dignam, Michael Aldridge, Leo McKern and Paul Rogers, as the four knights sent to destroy Becket, measure up to the high standard of the Old Vic, from which they were borrowed for this film.

....

■ MURDER MOST FOUL

1964, 90 MINS, UK

Dir George Pollock   *Prod* Ben Arbeid   *Scr* David Pursall, Jack Seddon   *Ph* Desmond Dickinson   *Ed* Ernest Walter   *Mus* Ron Goodwin   *Art Dir* Frank White
● Margaret Rutherford, Ron Moody, Charles Tingwell, Andrew Cruickshank, Dennis Price, Francesca Annis (M-G-M)

Margaret Rutherford brings considerable assurance to the third Agatha Christie thriller to cast the doughty oldtimer in the role of Miss Marple, the eccentric amateur sleuth.

Miss Marple is the lone member of a murder jury who holds out for acquittal. Armed only with her experience in amateur mystery theatricals, she proceeds to unsnarl the case and prove herself far more professional than the investigating police.

The picture [from the novel *Mrs McGinty's Dead*] for all its comedy delight and charm does not quite hold up to its predecessors. Miss Marple begins to wear a little thin as she retraces many of the same comedy situations and even some similar dialog.

Stringer Davis again plays the confused partner with a charming personality performance and Charles Tingwell completes the trio as the young inspector who ends up with the credit for solving the crime even though he flails Miss Marple all the way.

....

■ MURDER, MY SWEET

1945, 92 MINS, US ⊙

Dir Edward Dmytryk   *Prod* Adrian Scott   *Scr* John Paxton   *Ph* Harry J. Wild   *Ed* Joseph Noriega   *Mus* Roy Webb   *Art Dir* Albert S. D'Agostino, Carroll Clark
● Dick Powell, Claire Trevor, Anne Shirley, Otto Kruger, Mike Mazurki (RKO)

Murder, My Sweet, a taut thriller about a private detective enmeshed with a gang of black-mailers, is as smart as it is gripping.

Plot ramifications may not stand up under clinical study, but suspense is built up sharply and quickly. In fact, the film gets off to so jet-pulsed a start that it necessarily hits a couple of slow stretches midway as it settles into uniform groove. But interest never flags, and the mystery is never really cleared up until the punchy closing.

Director Edward Dmytryk has made few concessions to the social amenities and has kept his yarn stark and unyielding. Story [from the novel *Farewell, My Lovely* by Raymond Chandler] begins with a private dick hired by an ex-convict to find his one-time girlfriend.

Performances are on a par with the production. Dick Powell is a surprise as the hard-boiled copper. The portrayal is potent and convincing. Claire Trevor is as dramatic as the predatory femme, with Anne Shirley in sharp contrast as the soft kid caught in the crossfire.

....

■ MURDER ON THE ORIENT EXPRESS

1974, 127 MINS, UK ◇ ⊙

Dir Sidney Lumet   *Prod* John Brabourne, Richard Goodwin   *Scr* Paul Dehn   *Ph* Geoffrey Unsworth   *Ed* Anne V. Coates   *Mus* Richard Rodney Bennett   *Art Dir* Tony Walton
● Albert Finney, Lauren Bacall, Ingrid Bergman, Sean Connery, Vanessa Redgrave, Richard Widmark (Paramount)

Murder on the Orient Express is an old-fashioned film. Agatha Christie's 1934 Hercule Poirot novel has been filmed for the first time in a bygone film style as it seems to be some treasure out of a time capsule. Albert Finney and a monstrously large cast of names give the show a lot of class and charm.

Finney is outstanding as Poirot, his makeup, wardrobe and performance a blend of topflight theatre. The mysterious death of Richard Widmark, triggers Finney's investigation at the behest of Martin Balsam, a railroad executive who hopes the crime can be solved before the snowbound train is reached by rescuers.

Amidst fades, repeated cuts to exterior train shots and all those other wonderful film punctuation devices Finney interrogates the passengers.

....

■ MURDER SHE SAID

1961, 86 MINS, UK

Dir George Pollock   *Prod* George H. Brown   *Scr* David Pursall, Jack Seddon   *Ph* Geoffrey Faithfull   *Ed* Ernest Walter   *Mus* Ron Goodwin   *Art Dir* Harry White
● Margaret Rutherford, Arthur Kennedy, Muriel Pavlow, James Robertson Justice, Charles Tingwell, Thorley Walters (M-G-M)

Scripters have made a reasonable job of condensing one of Agatha Christie's complicated mysteries, *4.50 from Paddington*, introducing enough suspects to satisfy most followers of the whodunit.

Miss Marple is returning from London on a train and is amusing herself by looking in at the carriages of another train going the same way on an adjacent track. A blind is suddenly jerked up and she sees a man throttling a girl as the train moves away. She reports it to the railway authority and the local police inspector but neither believes her. She suspects that the body is in the grounds of nearby Ackenthorpe Hall, gets herself a job there, and sets about unravelling the mystery.

Apart from Margaret Rutherford's important contribution, there are several other useful characterizations. James Robertson Justice, as a bad-tempered hypochondriac; Arthur Kennedy, as the local doctor; Thorley Walters, Conrad Phillips and Gerald Cross as Justice's no-good sons and Campbell Stringer, as the librarian, are standout.

....

■ MURDER, SHE SAID

1962, 87 MINS, UK

Dir George Pollock   *Prod* George H. Brown   *Scr* David Pursall, Jack Seddon   *Ph* Geoffrey Faithfull   *Ed* Ernest Walter   *Mus* Ron Goodwin   *Art Dir* Harry White
● Margaret Rutherford, Arthur Kennedy, Muriel Pavlow, James Robertson Justice, Charles Tingwell (M-G-M)

The spectacle of a grand-motherly amateur criminologist outsleuthing the skeptical, methodical professionals provides most of the fun in this somewhat unconvincing, but nonetheless engaging murder mystery manufactured at Metro's British Studios in Borehamwood.

According to the screenplay, from an adaptation by David Osborn of the Agatha Christie novel, *4.50 from Paddington*, Rutherford witnesses a murder transpiring in the compartment of a passing train. Since the police do not believe her story, and being an avid reader of mystery fiction, she takes it upon herself to solve the case, planting herself as maid within the household of the chief suspects.

The George H. Brown production is weak in the motivation area, and there's a sticky and unnecessary parting shot in which Rutherford nixes an absurd marriage proposal from the stingy, irascible patriarch of the house (James Robertson Justice), but otherwise matters purr along at a pleasant clip.

....

M

■ MURDERERS' ROW

1966, 108 MINS, US ◇ Ⓥ

Dir Henry Levin   *Prod* Irving Allen   *Scr* Herbert Baker   *Ph* Sam Leavitt   *Ed* Walter Thompson   *Mus* Lalo Schifrin   *Art Dir* Joe Wright

● Dean Martin, Ann-Margret, Karl Malden, Camilla Sparv, James Gregory, Beverly Adams (Meadway-Claude/Columbia)

It's a wise film producer who knows his own success formula. About the only changes made by Irving Allen in his sequel [also from a novel by Donald Hamilton] to the successful *The Silencers* are in scenery, girls and costumes. The addition of Ann-Margret is notable for some abandoned choreography and a chance to use both of her expressions – the open-mouthed Monroe imitation and the slinky Theda Bara bit.

This time out, Dean Martin's secret agent has to trek to the Riviera to catch that bad old Karl Malden who's about to blow up Washington with a secret beam.

Director Henry Levin's stress on action takes the film out of the comedy range at times. Helm is, of course, given some ridiculous special weapons – this time, a delayed-reaction gun is worked to death (no pun intended). But whenever the viewer begins to take things seriously, Levin cuts back to a laugh bit (Martin ripping off Ann-Margret's miniskirt, which contains an explosive, and hurling it at a wall decorated with Frank Sinatra's picture).

···

■ MURDERS IN THE RUE MORGUE

1932, 60 MINS, US Ⓥ

Dir Robert Florey   *Scr* Tom Reed, Dale Van Every, John Huston   *Ph* Karl Freund

● Bela Lugosi, Sidney Fox, Leon Ames, Bert Roach, Brandon Hurst, Noble Johnson (Universal)

Edgar Allan Poe wouldn't recognize his story, which drops everything but the gorilla killer and the title, completely changes the characters, motives and developments, and is sexed up to the limit. In place of the cool detective whose calculating method was the model for the Sherlock Holmeses and Arsene Lupins that followed, this version's hero is a young medical student who mixes romance with science.

The cast's other scientist, a loony Dr Mirakle played in Bela Lugosi's customary fantastic manner, is an evolution bug who seeks to prove a vague fact by mixing the blood of his captive gorilla with that of Parisian women. The murders – three real and one almost – are results of his fiendish transfusions.

First meeting of the young medico and his sweetheart with Dr Mirakle and his caged gorilla occurs at the doc's side show. The brute snatches the girl's bonnet and from then on by intimation it's shown that the gorilla desires her.

The real threat is the constant possiblity of the gorilla capturing the girl. Sidney Fox overdraws the sweet ingenue to the point of nearly distracting an audience from any fear it might have for her.

···

■ MURPHY'S LAW

1986, 100 MINS, US ◇ Ⓥ

Dir J. Lee Thompson   *Prod* Pancho Kohner   *Scr* Gail Morgan Hickman   *Ph* Alex Phillips   *Ed* Peter Lee Thompson, Charles Simmons   *Mus* Marc Donahue, Valentine McCallum   *Art Dir* William Cruise

● Charles Bronson, Kathleen Wilhoite, Carrie Snodgress, Robert F. Lyons, Angel Tompkins, Richard Romanus (Cannon)

Murphy's Law, a very violent urban crime meller, is tiresome but too filled with extreme incident to be boring.

Title refers not only to the w.k. axiom that, 'Whatever can go wrong will go wrong,' but

to Bronson's personal version of it: 'Don't **** with Jack Murphy.' Title character (played by Charles Bronson) is an LA cop who's down but not quite out, a tough loner whose main companion in life is his flask now that his wife has left him.

Murphy's life is shaken up even more when the ex-wife and numerous others around him are mowed down. Booked for the crimes, he escapes handcuffed to a foul-mouthed female street urchin (Kathleen Wilhoite), and after many more bodies hit the deck, he clears his name by tracking down killer Carrie Snodgress.

···

■ MURPHY'S ROMANCE

1985, 107 MINS, US ◇ Ⓥ

Dir Martin Ritt   *Prod* Laura Ziskin   *Scr* Harriet Frank Jr, Irving Ravetch   *Ph* William A. Fraker   *Ed* Sidney Levin   *Mus* Carole King   *Art Dir* Joel Schiller

● Sally Field, James Garner, Brian Kerwin, Corey Haim, Dennis Burkley, Georgann Johnson (Columbia)

Director Martin Ritt has just the right touch to keep *Murphy's Romance*, a fairly predictable love story, from lapsing into gushy sentimentality of clichés. Unfortunately, this sweet and homey picture which casts two very decent actors (Sally Field and James Garner) in two very decent roles, falls far short of compelling filmmaking.

Field plays a divorced mother who is determined to make a living as a horse trainer on a desolate piece of property on the outskirts of a one-street town in rural Arizona. On practically her first day in the area, she meets Murphy, a widower who is the town's pharmacist and local good guy. He takes a liking to her almost immediately, but it isn't much later until her n'er-do-well former husband, Brian Kerwin, rides back into her life.

What unfolds is how the Field, Garner and Kerwin triangle is resolved with Field leaning toward Garner the whole time.

···

■ MURPHY'S WAR

1971, 108 MINS, UK ◇ Ⓥ

Dir Peter Yates   *Prod* Michael Deeley   *Scr* Stirling Silliphant   *Ph* Douglas Slocombe   *Ed* Frank P. Keller, John Glen   *Mus* John Barry   *Art Dir* Disley Jones

● Peter O'Toole, Sian Phillips, Philippe Noiret, Horst Janson, John Hallam, Ingo Mogendorf (Dimitri de Grunwald)

Peter O'Toole, playing an Irishman for the first time does so with a gleaming zest that brings nerve and style to this wartime anecdote. It was shot mainly in a remote uncomfortable part of Venezuela's Orinoco River and director Peter Yates has brought out every ounce of the discomfort of the location.

Film opens with World War II drawing to a sluggish close. A German U-Boat torpedoes an armed merchantman and all survivors are bumped off, except, apparently, O'Toole, one of the ship's aviation mechanics.

He is rescued by a French oil engineer (Philippe Noiret) who wants nothing more than to lie doggo till the war's over, but he takes O'Toole to a nearby Quaker mission where he's nursed by the missionary-nurse, played by Sian Phillips.

Another survivor is brought to the mission but is killed by the Germans. Before his death he pleads with O'Toole to find his wrecked plane and keep it out of enemy hands. The Mad Murphy has a better idea. He decides to patch it up and blow the submarine to the high heavens.

···

■ MUSIC BOX

1989, 123 MINS, US ◇ Ⓥ

Dir Constantin Costa-Gavras   *Prod* Irwin Winkler   *Scr* Joe Eszterhas   *Ph* Patrick Blossier   *Ed* Joele Van Effenterre   *Mus* Philippe Sarde   *Art Dir* Jeannine Claudia Oppewall

● Jessica Lange, Armin Mueller-Stahl, Frederic Forrest, Donald Moffat, Lukas Haas, Cheryl Lynn Bruce (Carolco)

Jessica Lange plays an accomplished Chicago defense attorney, Ann Talbot, who must defend her own father (Armin Mueller-Stahl) in extradition proceedings when he's accused of having committed war crimes in Hungary during World War II.

Slowly losing her conviction as to her father's innocence, Lange's character pulls out all the stops, including the political connections of her former father-in-law, to try to exonerate her dad.

Even the film's accounts of Holocaust atrocities prove for the most part strangely unaffecting under Joe Eszterhas' limp dialog and Constantin Costa-Gavras' stodgy direction, which relies on a concussive score to try to create tension where there is none.

···

■ MUSIC LOVERS, THE

1971, 122 MINS, UK ◇

Dir Ken Russell   *Prod* Ken Russell   *Scr* Melvyn Bragg   *Ph* Douglas Slocombe   *Ed* Michael Bradsell   *Mus* Andre Previn (dir.)   *Art Dir* Natasha Kroll

● Richard Chamberlain, Glenda Jackson, Max Adrian, Christopher Gable, Izabella Telezynska, Kenneth Colley (United Artists)

There is frequently, but not always, a thin line between genius and madness. By going over that line and unduly emphasizing the mad and the perverse in their biopic of the 19th-century Russian composer Peter Ilyich Tchaikovsky, producer-director Ken Russell and scripter Melvyn Bragg lose their audience. The result is a motion picture that is frequently dramatically and visually stunning but more often tedious and grotesque.

Richard Chamberlain, bushy-bearded and eyes constantly brimming with tears, plays the homosexual, irrationally romantic composer, and Glenda Jackson the neurotic trollop he tragically marries. Their performances are more dramatically bombastic than sympathetic, or sometimes even believable.

Instead of a Russian tragedy, Russell seems more concerned with haunting the viewers' memory with shocking scenes and images. The opportunity to create a memorable and fluid portrait of the composer has been sacrificed for a musical Grand Guignol.

Christopher Gable plays Count Anton Chiluvsky, presumably Chamberlain's true love, as a faun-eyed social butterfly; Izabella Telezynska is the composer's patroness, a wealthy middle-aged widow who loves him but whose own romantic fantasies demand that they never meet but merely correspond by letter, although he lives in luxury on her estate.

···

■ MUSIC MAN, THE

1962, 151 MINS, US ◇ Ⓥ

Dir Morton DaCosta   *Prod* Morton DaCosta   *Scr* Marion Hargrove   *Ph* Robert Burks   *Ed* William Ziegler   *Mus* Meredith Willson   *Art Dir* Paul Groesse

● Robert Preston, Shirley Jones, Buddy Hackett, Hermione Gingold, Paul Ford (Warner)

Allowing something of slowness at the very start and the necessities of establishing the musical way of telling a story, plus the atmosphere of Iowa in 1912, that's about the only criticism of an otherwise building, punching, handsomely dressed and ultimately endearing super-musical.

Call this a triumph, perhaps a classic, of corn, smalltown nostalgia and American love of a parade. Dreamed up in the first instance out of the Iowa memories of Meredith Willson, fashioned into his first legit offering with his long radio musicianship fully manifest therein, the transfer to the screen has been accomplished by Morton DaCosta, as producer-director.

DaCosta's use of several of the original Broadway cast players is thoroughly vindicated. Paul Ford is wonderfully fatuous as the bumptious mayor of River City. Pert Kelton shines with warmth and humanity as the heroine's earthy mother.

But the only choice for the title role, Robert Preston, is the big proof of showmanship in the casting. Warners might have secured bigger screen names but it is impossible to imagine any of them matching Preston's authority, backed by 883 stage performances.
□ 1962: Best Picture (Nomination)

■ MUTINY ON THE BOUNTY

1935, 132 MINS, US ⓥ
Dir Frank Lloyd   *Prod* Irving G. Thalberg   *Scr* Talbot Jennings, Jules Furthman, Carey Wilson   *Ph* Arthur Edeson   *Ed* Margaret Booth   *Mus* Herbert Stothart
● Clark Gable, Charles Laughton, Franchot Tone, Dudley Digges, Donald Crisp, Movita (M-G-M)

This one is Hollywood at its very best. For plot the scenarists have used, with some variations, the first two books of the Charles Nordhoff – James Hall Norman trilogy on the mutiny of Fletcher Christian. Beginnings of the first book and the picture are pretty much the same, as are the details up to the arrival of the hunted mutineers on Pitcairn's Island. Picture ends there, omitting the third book almost entirely.

First hour or so of the film leads up, step by step, to the mutiny, with a flexible 'story' backgrounding some thrilling views of seamanship on a British man-o'-war in the early 18th century, and the cruel Capt Bligh's inhuman treatment of his sailors.

Bligh, through the cruelties he performs and due to the faithful portrait drawn by Charles Laughton, is as despicable a character as has ever heavied across a screen.

Laughton, Clark Gable and Franchot Tone are all that producer Al Lewin and director Frank Lloyd could have wished for in the three key roles. Laughton is magnificent. Gable, as brave Fletcher Christian, fills the doc's prescription to the letter. Tone, likeable throughout, gets his big moment with a morality speech at the finish, and makes the most of it.
□ 1935: Best Picture

■ MY BEAUTIFUL LAUNDRETTE

1985, 97 MINS, UK ◇ ⓥ
Dir Stephen Frears   *Prod* Sarah Radclyffe, Tim Bevan   *Scr* Hanif Kureishi   *Ph* Oliver Stapleton   *Ed* Mick Audsley   *Mus* Stanley Myers   *Art Dir* Hugo Luczyc Wyhowski
● Daniel Day Lewis, Gordon Warnecke, Saeed Jaffrey, Roshan Seth, Shirley Anne Field, Rita Wolf (Working Title/SAF/Channel Four)

Tale of profiteering middle-class Pakistani capitalists making a fortune out of unscrupulous wheeling and dealing in an impoverished London.

Focus is on two youths, friends from schooldays. Johnny is a working-class white whose punkish mates are members of the National Front. Omar lives with his left-leaning widower father in a rundown house by the railway line.

When the film begins, Omar is given a menial job by his wealthy uncle, Nasser. He likes young Omar and gives him a rundown laundrette which he and Johnny convert into a veritable palace of a place, complete with video screens. Meanwhile, a repressed love blossoms between Omar and Johnny, adding tension to the already volatile racial situation.

As always, director Stephen Frears does a superb job of work when given a good script,

and this is a very good script. It's peopled with interesting characters, allowing for a gallery of fine performances and situations.

■ MY BLUE HEAVEN

1950, 96 MINS, US ◇
Dir Henry Koster   *Prod* Sol C. Siegel   *Scr* Lamar Trotti, Claude Binyon   *Ph* Arthur E. Arling   *Ed* James B. Clarke   *Mus* Alfred Newman
● Betty Grable, Dan Dailey, David Wayne, Jane Wyatt, Mitzi Gaynor (20th Century-Fox)

In *My Blue Heaven* the tele theatre stage and the face of the video tube provide the locale for some highly-entertaining goings-on by Betty Grable and Dan Dailey. They're unfortunately involved with an overly-sticky plot.

Yarn has the two stars just moving over from their niche on radio to TV. They're anxious for a baby.

Moved by the happy Pringle family (David Wayne-Jane Wyatt), they try to adopt a baby. This gives the scripters an opportunity to get into considerable detail on both the legal and illegal sides of the adoption business.

While Grable and Dailey offer their capable standard brands of song-and-dance, the real eye-catcher of the pic is a lush, brunet youngster making her initial screen appearance. She's Mitzi Gaynor. She's long on terping and vocalizing.

■ MY BLUE HEAVEN

1990, 95 MINS, US ◇ ⓥ
Dir Herbert Ross   *Prod* Herbert Ross, Anthea Sylbert   *Scr* Nora Ephron   *Ph* John Bailey   *Ed* Stephen A. Rotter   *Mus* Ira Newborn   *Art Dir* Charles Rosen
● Steve Martin, Rick Moranis, Joan Cusack, Melanie Mayron, Carol Kane, Bill Irwin (Hawn-Sylbert/Warner)

Steve Martin and Rick Moranis do the mismatched pair o' guys shtick in *My Blue Heaven*, a lighthearted fairy tale. But scripter Nora Ephron's fish-out-of-water premise isn't funny enough to sustain a whole picture.

Martin plays Vinnie, an incorrigible Italian-American criminal who teaches the white-bread citizens of a suburban town how to loose up and have fun. Moranis plays Barney Coopersmith, a stiff-necked FBI agent who's assigned to settle mobster Martin into a new life 'somewhere in America' as part of a government witness-protection program.

Life in a brand-new subdivision is too placid for Vinnie, who immediately starts getting involved in illegal mischief that brings him into the jurisdiction of the ultra-straight district attorney Hannah Stubbs (Joan Cusack). It's a mess for Moranis, who has to keep getting Vinnie out of the d.a.'s clutches so that he can testify in a New York mob murder trial.

Pic takes some satirical pot-shots at life in the have-a-nice-day suburban bubble, but beyond that it twiddles its thumbs waiting for the mob trial.

■ MY BODYGUARD

1980, 97 MINS, US ◇ ⓥ
Dir Tony Bill   *Prod* Don Devlin   *Scr* Alan Ormsby   *Ph* Michael D. Margulies   *Ed* Stu Linder   *Mus* Dave Grusin   *Art Dir* Jackson de Govia
● Chris Makepeace, Adam Baldwin, Matt Dillon, Ruth Gordon, Joan Cusack (20th Century-Fox)

In his directorial debut, Tony Bill assembles a truly remarkable cast of youngsters with little or no previous acting experience.

Chris Makepeace is superb as the slightly built kid coming anew to a Chicago high school dominated by extortionist gang leader Matt Dillon, also terrific in his part.

Adam Baldwin is a standoffish, uncommunicative brute rumored throughout the

school to be a psychotic weirdo who has killed cops and other kids. Dillon and gang use the rumors to demand payment from smaller fellows for 'protection' from Baldwin.

But Makepeace will not pay up and takes his lumps until befriended by Baldwin, thereby beginning a warm friendship that leads to surprising turns in the plot.

Technically, picture sometimes shows the threads of low-budget shooting, but the distractions are minor.

■ MY BRILLIANT CAREER

1979, 98 MINS, AUSTRALIA ◇ ⓥ
Dir Gillian Armstrong   *Prod* Margaret Fink   *Scr* Eleanor Witcombe   *Ph* Don McAlpine   *Ed* Nick Beauman   *Mus* Nathan Waks
● Judy Davis, Sam Neill, Wendy Hughes, Robert Grubb, Pat Kennedy, Max Cullen (New South Wales/GUO)

This Australian film is a charming look [from the book by Miles Franklin] at 19th-century rural days in general and the stirrings of self-realization and feminine liberation in the persona of a headstrong young girl who wants to go her own way.

Judy Davis is fine as an ugly duckling who blossoms into an independent writer and refuses to give into the ritual and place reserved for women at the time which was, namely, marriage.

She resists marriage to write her book and go on with her own life. Perhaps the last part of her servitude with the farmer and his family is forced. But there is a rightness in tone in delving into the hidebound society and early flaunting of its taboos by an engaging girl.

■ MY CHAUFFEUR

1986, 97 MINS, US ◇ ⓥ
Dir David Beaird   *Prod* Marilyn J. Tenser   *Scr* David Beaird   *Ph* Harry Mathias   *Ed* Richard E. Westover   *Mus* Paul Hertzog   *Art Dir* C.J. Strawn
● Deborah Foreman, Sam J. Jones, Sean McClory, Howard Hesseman, E.G. Marshall (Crown)

David Beaird avowedly set out to imitate the screwball comedies of the 1930s and 1940s and has succeeded admirably, thanks to adorably spunky Deborah Foreman and her stuffy foil, Sam J. Jones. They make quite a pair.

Foreman is a real find, fitting into the mold of Goldie Hawn, Carole Lombard and Claudette Colbert. She not only can say a lot when saying nothing, she's a real pro when it comes to combining high tuned dialog with physical action.

Summoned mysteriously by a millionaire limo company owner (E.G. Marshall), Foreman takes a job as a driver, much to the objections of a wonderful assortment of chauvinistic chauffeurs who want to maintain their male-dominated domain.

She gets the impossible assignments including Jones, a spoiled, domineering industrialist who is, unknown to her, Marshall's son. Romance gradually blossoms.

■ MY COUSIN RACHEL

1952, 98 MINS, US
Dir Henry Koster   *Prod* Nunnally Johnson   *Scr* Nunnally Johnson   *Ph* Joseph La Shelle   *Ed* Louis Loeffler   *Mus* Franz Waxman
● Olivia de Havilland, Richard Burton, Audrey Dalton, Ronald Squire, George Dolenz, John Sutton (20th Century-Fox)

A dark, moody melodrama, with emphasis on tragedy, has been fashioned from Daphne du Maurier's bestseller, *My Cousin Rachel*.

Olivia de Havilland endows the title role with commanding histrionics. Opposite her is

M

Richard Burton, debuting in Hollywood pictures. He creates a strong impression in the role of a love-torn, suspicious man.

The story, set in early 19th-century England, tells of a young man with a deep affection for the foster father who had raised him. When the foster father marries a distant cousin he has met while touring Italy to escape the rigors of winter in Cornwall, the young man is beset with jealousy. This later turns to suspicion and hate when he receives letters that indicate his beloved relative is being poisoned by the bride.

• •

■ MY DARLING CLEMENTINE

1946, 97 MINS, US ▼
Dir John Ford   *Prod* Samuel G. Engel   *Scr* Samuel G. Engel, Winston Miller   *Ph* Joe MacDonald   *Ed* Dorothy Spencer   *Mus* Alfred Newman   *Art Dir* James Basevi, Lyle R. Wheeler
● Henry Fonda, Linda Darnell, Victor Mature, Walter Brennan, Cathy Downs, Ward Bond (20th Century-Fox)

Trademark of John Ford's direction is clearly stamped on the film with its shadowy lights, softly contrasted moods and measured pace, but a tendency is discernible towards stylization for stylization's sake. At several points, the pic comes to a dead stop to let Ford go gunning for some arty effect.

Major boost to the film is given by the simple, sincere performance of Henry Fonda. Script doesn't afford him many chances for dramatic action, but Fonda, as a boomtown marshal, pulls the reins taut on his part charging the role and the pic with more excitement than it really has. Playing counterpoint to Fonda, Victor Mature registers nicely as a Boston aristocrat turned gambler and killer.

Femme lead is held down by Linda Darnell although Cathy Downs plays the title role. As a Mexican firebrand and dancehall belle, Darnell handles herself creditably while the camera work does the rest in highlighting her looks. Downs, in the relatively minor role of Clementine, a cultured Bostonian gal who is in love with Mature, is sweet and winning.

Story opens with the killing of Fonda's brother while they are en route to California on a cattle-herding job. Fonda is offered, and takes, the post of sheriff in a bad man's town in an effort to track down the killers. Crossing paths with Mature in a saloon, Fonda suspects him at first but both become very chummy as Mature is revealed to be a talented surgeon who escaped to a dangerous life because he suffered from consumption.

• •

■ MY DINNER WITH ANDRE

1981, 110 MINS, US ◇
Dir Louis Malle   *Prod* George W. George, Beverly Karp   *Scr* Wallace Shawn, Andre Gregory   *Ph* Jeri Sopanen   *Ed* Suzanne Baron   *Mus* Allen Shawn
● Wallace Shawn, Andre Gregory (Andre)

My Dinner with Andre is something of a film stunt, consisting almost entirely of a conversation over dinner between two theatrical acquaintances. Though conforming to the aloof, cooly observant mode of director Louis Malle's previous pics, *Andre* is really authored by its two players, Wallace Shawn and Andre Gregory, doubling as screenwriters.

Shawn, a cherubic figure roughly playing himself as a sometime playwright and actor, is the audience surrogate, even bookending the film with his voiceover narration accompanying tracking shots of him on the streets of New York City. Somewhat apprehensive, he has dinner at a posh restaurant with Andre, portrayed also semi-autobiographically by theatre director Andre Gregory.

What ensues is an overlong but mainly captivating conversation, consisting largely of stream of consciousness monologs by Gregory.

Where the picture fails is in its lack of balance between the two protagonists. For the first half, Shawn is acceptable in closeup inserts, reacting or just listening to Gregory. However, in the second half Gregory begins making philosophical conclusions which require response or rebuttal and Shawn's haltingly expressed 'little guy' comebacks are inadequate and type his entire performance as comedy relief.

• •

■ MY FAIR LADY

1964, 170 MINS, US ◇ ▼
Dir George Cukor   *Prod* Jack L. Warner   *Scr* Alan Jay Lerner   *Ph* Harry Stradling   *Ed* William Ziegler   *Mus* Frederick Loewe   *Art Dir* Cecil Beaton, Gene Allen
● Audrey Hepburn, Rex Harrison, Stanley Holloway, Wilfrid Hyde White, Gladys Cooper, Jeremy Brett (Warner)

The great longrun stage musical made by Lerner & Loewe (and Herman Levin) out of the wit of Bernard Shaw's play *Pygmalion* has been transformed into a stunningly effective screen entertainment. *My Fair Lady* has riches of story, humor, acting and production values far beyond the average big picture. Warner paid $5.5 million for the rights alone.

Care and planning shine in every detail and thus cast a glow around the name of director George Cukor. The original staging genius of Moss Hart cannot be overlooked as a blueprint for success. But like all great films *My Fair Lady* represents a team of talents. Rex Harrison's performance and Cecil Beaton's design of costumes, scenery and production are the two powerhouse contributions.

This is a man-bullies-girl plot with story novelty. An unorthodox musical without a kiss, the audience travels to total involvement with characters and situation on the rails of sharp dialog and business. The deft segues of dialog into lyric are superb, especially in the case of Harrison.

Only incurably disputatious persons will consider it a defect of *Lady* on screen that Julie Andrews has been replaced by the better known Miss H. She is thoroughly beguiling as Eliza though her singing is dubbed by Marni Nixon.

Stanley Holloway repeats from the Broadway stage version. Again and again his theatrical authority clicks. How this great English trouper takes the basically 'thin' and repetitious, 'With a Little Bit O' Luck' and makes it stand up as gaiety incarnate.

Every one in the small cast is excellent. Mona Washbourne is especially fine as the prim but compassionate housekeeper. Wilfrid Hyde White has the necessary proper gentleman quality as Pickering and makes a good foil for Harrison. Gladys Cooper brings aristocratic common sense to the mother of the phonetics wizard.

A certain amount of new music by Frederick Loewe and added lyrics by Lerner are part of the adjustment to the cinematic medium. But it is the original stage score which stands out.
□ 1964: Best Picture

• •

■ MY FAVORITE BLONDE

1942, 78 MINS, US
Dir Sidney Lanfield   *Prod* Paul Jones   *Scr* Don Hartman, Frank Butler   *Ph* William Mellor   *Ed* William O'Shea   *Mus* David Buttolph
● Bob Hope, Madeleine Carroll, Gale Sondergaard (Paramount)

Madeleine Carroll is ideally cast as a British agent who involves vaudevillian Bob Hope into a helter-skelter coast-to-coast hop from Broadway to Hollywood.

The blend of a secret scorpion (containing the revised flying orders for a convoy of Lock-heed bombers headed for Britain) with the wacky semi-backstage atmosphere, an al fresco plumbers' picnic, Nazi spies etc., has been well kneaded by the authors [from a story by Melvin Frank and Norman Panama] and director Sidney Lanfield himself.

Producer Paul Jones and director Lanfield permit themselves a conceit when Bing Crosby is seen idling at a picnic bus station. Crosby directs the lammister Hope and Carroll toward the picnic grounds. As Hope gives Crosby one of those takes, he muses, 'No, it can't be.' That's all, and it's one of the best laughs in a progressively funny film.

• •

■ MY FAVORITE BRUNETTE

1947, 87 MINS, US ▼
Dir Elliott Nugent   *Prod* Daniel Dare   *Scr* Edmund Beloin, Jack Rose   *Ph* Lionel Lindon   *Ed* Ellsworth Hoagland   *Mus* Robert Emmett Dolan   *Art Dir* Hans Dreier, Earl Hedrick
● Bob Hope, Dorothy Lamour, Peter Lorre, Lon Chaney (Paramount)

Bob Hope, the sad sack would-be sleuth; Hope, the condemned prisoner, nerving out his imminent quietus with unhappy bravado; and Hope, the pushover, squirming uneasily under a chemical yen for the potent Dorothy Lamour charms – it's familiar stuff but still grist for the yock mills.

One long flashback is the device employed. Credits segue into a scene depicting Hope as a condemned murderer being groomed for the gas chamber. To reporters gathered to record his early demise, Hope relates his tale of woe – which at the outset has him as a baby photographer whose frustrated urge towards gumshoeing has inspired the invention of a special keyhole camera.

When Hope's nextdoor neighbor, a private eye, leaves town requesting Hope to tend his office, the comic's usual pot of trouble rises to a simmer. He tangles with Lamour in a fantastic snarl involving a mysterious map (concealed by Hope in a drinking cup container) and Lamour's missing uncle who's been snatched by a gang of international criminals headed by that familiar lawbreaker, Peter Lorre.

Curtain rings down on a solid rib. Hope's impatient executioner turns out to be – you guessed it – Bing Crosby. To which Hope cracks: 'That guy will take any part.' Another pretty conceit that comes off is the use of Alan Ladd in a bit part as the nextdoor detective.

• •

■ MY FAVORITE SPY

1951, 93 MINS, US
Dir Norman Z. McLeod   *Prod* Paul Jones   *Scr* Edmund Hartmann, Jack Sher   *Ph* Victor Milner   *Ed* Frank Bracht   *Mus* Victor Young   *Art Dir* Hal Pereira, Roland Anderson
● Bob Hope, Hedy Lamarr, Francis L. Sullivan, Arnold Moss, John Archer, Iris Adrian (Paramount)

My Favorite Spy is in the same general pattern of other Bob Hope *My Favorite* films, scattering chuckles through the footage, with an occasional howler. Ably partnering is Hedy Lamarr, lending herself to the knockabout pace with a likeable loss of dignity.

Norman Z. McLeod guides the breezy plot with a reasonably consistent speed and manages to make the zany doings fairly easy to follow. Hope, as a burley comic, is talked into doubling for an international spy so the US government can get hold of plans for a pilotless plane. Dispatched to Tangiers with $1 million in a money belt, the masquerading Hope is met by Lamarr, another spy employed by a rival government agent (Francis L. Sullivan).

From here on, the script involves the comic in a wild and woolly free-for-all of danger,

escape, lovely girls and chase that help fill out
the film's 93 minutes.

■ **MY FAVORITE WIFE**

1940, 88 MINS, US ⊙

Dir Garson Kanin   *Prod* Leo McCarey   *Scr* Sam
Spewack, Bella Spewack, Leo McCarey   *Ph* Rudolph
Mate   *Ed* Robert Wise   *Mus* Roy Webb   *Art Dir* Van
Nest Polglase, Mark-Lee Kirk
● Irene Dunne, Cary Grant, Randolph Scott, Gail
Patrick, Ann Shoemaker (RKO)

Irene Dunne and Cary Grant pick up the
thread of marital comedy at about the point
where they left off in *The Awful Truth*. With
these two stars working again with Leo
McCarey, a surefire laughing film is guaranteed. McCarey is the producer of the new picture, which is directed by Garson Kanin, who
filled in for McCarey when the latter was on
the hospital list after an auto smashup.

Plot of the new film is pretty thin in spots
and it is distinctly to the credit of the players
and Kanin that they can keep the laughs
bouncing along. In this connection they have
able assistance from Randolph Scott and Gail
Patrick.

It's a pretty hard yarn to believe at the
beginning when Dunne turns up at home after seven years' absence from her husband
and two small children, who were infants
when she left on a South Sea exploration. She
was shipwrecked and tossed up on one of
those invisible Pacific islands.

She returns, therefore, as a female Enoch
Arden, arriving on the day her husband has
remarried. Of course, if anyone had mentioned the truth to the new wife (Patrick) the
story would have been over right then and
there before it gets underway. Nor does
Dunne mention that Scott was the sole other
survivor of the monsoon, and that he had
come back to civilization with her.

■ **MY FAVORITE YEAR**

1982, 92 MINS, US ◇ ⊙

Dir Richard Benjamin   *Prod* Michael Gruskoff
Scr Norman Steinberg, Dennis Palumbo   *Ph* Gerald
Hirschfeld   *Ed* Richard Chew   *Mus* Ralph Burns
Art Dir Charles Rosen
● Peter O'Toole, Mark Linn-Baker, Jessica Harper,
Joseph Bologna, Bill Macy, Lainie Kazan (Brooksfilms)

An enjoyable romp through the early days of
television, *My Favorite Year* provides a field
day for a wonderful bunch of actors headed
by Peter O'Toole in another rambunctious,
stylish starring turn.

Looking exquisitely ravaged, O'Toole portrays a legendary Hollywood star in the Errol
Flynn mold who, in 1954, the year of the title,
agrees to make his TV debut on *The Comedy
Cavalcade*. O'Toole is put in the hands of
young comedy writer Mark Linn-Baker for
safekeeping, latter's sole responsibility being
to keep his idol sober enough to make it
through the performance a few days later.

Fully cognizant of the kid's mission,
flamboyant star behaves himself for
awhile, but finally falls way off the wagon
after enduring a dinner party at the Brooklyn
home of Linn-Baker's mother. It's madcap
farce from then on.

Linn-Baker is quite appealing and engagingly energetic in an excellent screen debut.
Jessica Harper is fine as a spunky staffer,
Joseph Bologna is wonderfully tyrannical as
the show's star, Bill Macy is particularly
funny as an agonized writer and Lainie
Kazan hilariously overdoes the Jewish
mother bit.

■ **MY FIRST WIFE**

1984, 95 MINS, AUSTRALIA ◇ ⊙

Dir Paul Cox   *Prod* Jane Ballantyne, Paul Cox
Scr Paul Cox, Bob Ellis   *Ph* Yuri Sokol   *Ed* Tim Lewis
Art Dir Asher Bilu
● John Hargreaves, Wendy Hughes, Lucy Angwin,
Anna Jemison, David Cameron, Charles Tingwell
(Dofine)

A lacerating, emotionally exhausting drama
about a marriage breakup, *My First Wife*
manages to breathe new life into familiar
material.

Director Paul Cox and coscripter Bob Ellis
ring a few changes. This 10-year marriage is
collapsing because the wife (Wendy Hughes)
not the husband (John Hargreaves) is having
an affair, and it's the husband who desperately wants her back, willing to forgive and
forget everything if only she'll return to him.

At the same time, Helen, who is obviously
still very fond of him but no longer wants to
live with him, can only stand by helplessly as
he gradually loses his grip. Also at stake is
their young daughter, Lucy, whom Helen
unquestioningly believes should live with her.

Pic rings utterly true, with no false
sentimentality, no firm ending.

■ **MY FOOLISH HEART**

1949, 98 MINS, US

Dir Mark Robson   *Prod* Samuel Goldwyn   *Scr* Julius J.
Epstein, Philip G. Epstein   *Ph* Lee Garmes   *Ed* Daniel
Mandell   *Mus* Victor Young
● Dana Andrews, Susan Hayward, Kent Smith, Lois
Wheeler, Jessie Royce Landis (RKO/Goldwyn)

My Foolish Heart ranks among the better
romantic films.

Picture gets off on the right foot with a
script that is honest and loaded with dialog
that is alive. The screenplay [based on a story
by J. D. Salinger] progresses through several
different stages of emotion.

Plotting opens in 1949, and finds Susan
Hayward at the tailend of an unhappy, wartime marriage with Kent Smith. Before she
has a chance to pass on a part of her unhappiness to Smith, the sight of an old gown
arouses memories and takes her back to 1941
when she was enfolded in romance with Dana
Andrews.

Hayward's performance is a gem, displaying a positive talent for capturing reality.
Opposite her, Andrews' slightly cynical
character of a young man at loose ends comes
to life and earns him a strong credit.

■ **MY FRIEND FLICKA**

1943, 89 MINS, US ◇

Dir Harold Schuster   *Prod* Ralph Dietrich   *Scr* Lillie
Hayward   *Ph* Dewey Wrigley   *Ed* Robert Fritch
Mus Alfred Newman
● Roddy McDowall, Preston Foster, Rita Johnson (20th
Century-Fox)

Basic theme, necessarily limited in appeal
since it's the story of the influence of a wild
pony (Flicka) on the lives and philosophy of a
small family group, required all the topnotch
production values which the producer
provided.

Fine color photography, capable performances by Roddy McDowall, Preston Foster,
Rita Johnson and, of course, the magnificent
horses, are assets.

Essentially it's the story of a daydreaming
youngster's longing for a colt of his own, the
boy's complete transformation once his
rancher-father fulfills his desire, and the trials
and tribulations in taming and nursing the
filly back to health.

■ **MY GAL SAL**

1942, 101 MINS, US ◇

Dir Irving Cummings   *Prod* Robert Masler   *Scr* Seton I.
Miller, Darrell Ware, Karl Tunberg   *Ph* Ernest Palmer
Ed Robert Simpson   *Mus* Alfred Newman (dir)
● Rita Hayworth, Victor Mature, Carole Landis, Phil
Silvers, James Gleason, John Sutton (20th Century-Fox)

Theodore Dreiser's biography of his songwriting brother, Paul Dreiser, parades a
number of popular tunes of the 1890s – several with specially-staged production numbers – to round out a fairly entertaining piece
of filmusical entertainment.

Dreiser's life is far from sugar-coated in its
cinematic unreeling. Young Paul (Victor
Mature) is picked up as the youth who runs
away from home to pursue a musical career
rather than study for the ministry. After a
short stretch as entertainer with a cheap
medicine show, and an intimate association
with Carole Landis, he finally tosses over the
small time for a whirl at the big town of New
York.

There's too much footage consumed in
unnecessary episodes and incidents that
might have been historically correct for the
times, but not important to a straight line
presentation of a musical drama.

Although Mature gives a solid performance
as the songwriter, it's Rita Hayworth who
catches major attention from her first
entrance.

■ **MY GEISHA**

1962, 119 MINS, US ◇

Dir Jack Cardiff   *Prod* Steve Parker   *Scr* Norman
Krasna   *Ph* Shunichiro Nakao   *Ed* Archie Marshek
Mus Franz Waxman   *Art Dir* Hal Pereira, Arthur
Lonergan
● Shirley MacLaine, Yves Montand, Edward G.
Robinson, Robert Cummings, Yoko Tani (Paramount)

Although hampered by a transparent plot, a
lean and implausible one-joke premise and a
tendency to fluctuate uneasily between
comedy and drama, the picture has been
richly and elaborately produced on location
in Japan, cast with perception and a sharp
eye for marquee juxtaposition.

A certain amount of elementary but traditionally evasive information on the Japanese geisha girl weaves helpfully through
Norman Krasna's brittle screenplay about an
American film actress (Shirley MacLaine)
who blithely and vainly executes a monumental practical joke on her insecure direc-
tor-husband (Yves Montand) by
masquerading as a Geisha to win the part of
'Madame Butterfly' in his arty production of
same in Japan.

Just as the comedy is about to peter out,
there is a radical swerve into sentiment and
moral significance. Montand, abruptly (and
at long last) cognizant of what is transpiring,
and deeply hurt, proposes B-girl monkey-
shines, to his bewildered G-girl wife, and the
marriage seems about to go to H.

MacLaine gives her customary spirited
portrayal in the title role, yet skillfully sub-
merges her unpredictably gregarious personality into that of the dainty, tranquil
geisha for the bulk of the proceedings. Montand has his moments.

■ **MY HUSTLER**

1967, 79 MINS, US ◇

Dir Andy Warhol   *Prod* Andy Warhol   *Ph* Andy
Warhol
● Paul America, Ed Wiener, S.P. Farry, Jeanne Vieve
(Warhol)

For all the technical blunders, *My Hustler* possesses some narrative fascination for those
with sufficiently strong stomachs and/or
psyches. A young boy, hired for the weekend

by a wealthy Fire Island homo through the 'Dial-a-Hustler Service,' is fought over by the aging deviate, a girl from next door, and another hustler well past his prime.

What makes the film morbidly absorbing is not the tenuous storyline – which, in the best NY Underground tradition, is never resolved – but the considerable detail with which gay life is documented.

The camera remains stationary for long stretches (one static take lasts a full 30 minutes), and what motion Warhol does employ consists of headache-inducing zooms and wobbly pans. The sound reproduction is so poor as not to deserve the epithet 'amateur'; volume level suggests an aural rollercoaster, about a third of the dialog is muffled, and lip sync is off for most of the film.

■ MY LEFT FOOT

1989, 98 MINS, UK ◇ ⑰

Dir Jim Sheridan *Prod* Noel Pearson *Scr* Shane Connaughton, Jim Sheridan *Ph* Jack Conroy *Ed* J. Patrick Duffner *Mus* Elmer Bernstein *Art Dir* Austen Spriggs

● Daniel Day-Lewis, Ray McAnally, Brenda Fricker, Ruth McCabe, Fiona Shaw (Granada)

First and foremost, *My Left Foot* is the warm, romantic and moving true story of a remarkable man: the Irish writer and painter Christy Brown born with cerebral palsy into an impoverished family. That it features a brilliant performance by Daniel Day-Lewis and a fine supporting cast lifts it from mildly sentimental to excellent.

At his birth, Christy's parents are told their child would be little more than a vegetable, but through his mother's insistence that he fit in with family life, he shows intelligence and strength inside his paralyzed body.

The older Christy amazes his family by writing the word 'mother' on the floor with a piece of chalk gripped in his left foot. He goes on to become an artist – still using that left foot – and is helped by therapist Fiona Shaw, with whom he falls in love.

All performances are on the mark in this perfect little film. Brenda Fricker, as his loving and resilient mother, is excellent, as is the late Ray McAnally as his bricklayer father. *My Left Foot* is not a sad film. In fact, there is a great deal of humor in Day-Lewis's Brown.
□ 1989: Best Picture (Nomination)

■ MY MAN GODFREY

1936, 93 MINS, US ⑰

Dir Gregory LaCava *Prod* Charles R. Rogers *Scr* Morrie Ryskind, Eric Hatch *Ph* Ted Tetzlaff *Ed* Ted Kent *Art Dir* Charles D. Hall

● William Powell, Carole Lombard, Alice Brady, Gail Patrick, Jean Dixon, Alan Mowbray (Universal)

William Powell and Carole Lombard are pleasantly teamed in this splendidly produced comedy. Story is balmy, but not too much so, and lends itself to the sophisticated screen treatment of Eric Hatch's novel.

Lombard has played screwball dames before, but none so screwy as this one. Her whole family, with the exception of the old man, seem to have been dropped on their respective heads when young. Into this punchy society tribe walks Powell, a former social light himself who had gone on the bum over a woman and is trying to become a man once more in butler's livery. He straightens out the family, as well as himself.

Alice Brady, as the social mother in whom the family's psychopathic ward tendencies seemingly originate, does a bangup job with another tough part. Gail Patrick, as Lombard's sparring partner-sister, is excellent. Eugene Pallette, as the harassed father, and Mischa Auer, in a gigolo role, a beautiful

piece of sustained comedy playing and writing, are both fine.

■ MY MAN GODFREY

1957, 92 MINS, US ◇

Dir Henry Koster *Prod* Ross Hunter *Scr* Everett Freeman, Peter Bermeis, William Bowers *Ph* William Daniels *Ed* Milton Carruth *Mus* Frank Skinner *Art Dir* Alexander Golitzen, Richard H. Riedel

● June Allyson, David Niven, Jessie Royce Landis, Robert Keith, Eva Gabor, Martha Hyer (Universal)

Updated version of *My Man Godfrey* is a pretty well turned out comedy with June Allyson and David Niven recreating the original Carole Lombard-William Powell star roles. Ross Hunter's production of the butler to an eccentric New York family of wealth who helps straighten them out, meanwhile recipient of the affections of the younger daughter, manages to pack plenty of lusty humor in the fast 92 minutes.

Where film misses is in the Niven character of butler. The screenplay drags him in by the heels in too fabricated a character – a former Austrian diplomat in the US via illegal entry. Again, the scripters hit upon too ready a solution of the Allyson-Niven romance after Niven has been deported.

Director Henry Koster deftly handles his characters in their comedic paces and succeeds in establishing an aura of screwiness in keeping with the 1936 version. Niven is a particular standout in his helping the family back on their feet after bankruptcy faces them.

Jessie Royce Landis as the wacky society mother registers a definite hit, Martha Hyer as the arrogant elder sister is stunning and Robert Keith ably portrays the father faced with ruin.

■ MY NAME IS JULIA ROSS

1945, 64 MINS, US

Dir Joseph H. Lewis *Prod* Wallace MacDonald *Scr* Muriel Roy Bolton *Ph* Burnett Guffey *Ed* James Sweeney, Henry Batista *Mus* Mischa Bakaleinikoff *Art Dir* Jerome Pycha Jr

● Nina Foch, May Whitty, George Macready, Roland Varno (Columbia)

Mystery melodrama with a psychological twist runs only 64 minutes but it's fast and packed with tense action throughout. Acting and production (though apparently modestly budgeted) are excellent.

New face is Nina Foch, who has looks and talent, while rest of cast is backed notably by May Whitty, George Macready and Roland Varno.

Story [from the novel *The Woman in Red* by Anthony Gilbert] is of gal hired fraudulently as secretary to wealthy English dowager. Purpose of hiring is to impose a murder scheme in which the dowager's son is implicated. The story has its implausibilities, but general conduct of pic negates those factors for overall click results.

Whitty gives creditable performance, so does Macready as her psychiatric son. Others in support acquit themselves well. Joseph H. Lewis directed for pace, and he achieves it all the way.

■ MY PAL GUS

1952, 83 MINS, US

Dir Robert Parrish *Prod* Stanley Rubin *Scr* Fay Kanin, Michael Kanin *Ph* Leo Tover *Ed* Robert Fritch *Mus* Leigh Harline

● Richard Widmark, Joanne Dru, Audrey Totter, George Winslow, Regis Toomey, Joan Banks (20th Century-Fox)

Richard Widmark is a bon-bon manufacturer too busy to devote much time to his small

son. As a result, the kid is a problem child who eventually lands in the progressive school operated by Joanne Dru. Little Winslow takes to the teacher, so does dad, and things are well on their way towards the schoolmarm becoming his new mother when Audrey Totter, Widmark's ex-wife, appears on the scene.

Totter reveals her Mexican divorce is invalid and demands Widmark give up his community property half of his wealth for a valid divorce.

Widmark is very good as the tough, rags-to-riches father, showing both good comedy feeling as well as the more touchingly dramatic flavor required in the final scenes when he tries to take his kid to a mother who doesn't want him.

■ MY SISTER EILEEN

1942, 97 MINS, US

Dir Alexander Hall *Prod* Max Gordon *Scr* Joseph Fields, Jerome Chodorov *Ph* Joseph Walker *Ed* Viola Lawrence *Mus* Morris Stoloff

● Rosalind Russell, Brian Aherne, Janet Blair, Richard Quine, June Havoc, Jeff Donnell (Columbia)

Adaptors Joseph Fields and Jerome Chodorov obviously liked their stage play [adapted from *New Yorker* stories by Ruth McKenney], for in translating it to the screen they've retained virtually the entire format, including all the key dialog. About all they've done has been to fill out the various chinks in the story which had been excluded by the limitations of the single-set play.

In Alexander Hall's direction, the pacing is fast and smooth, with constant use of sight gags and comedy situations. Most of the action still takes place in the Greenwich Village basement studio-apartment, with a crescendo of exaggerated events breaking out near and in the place.

Rosalind Russell's performance as authoress Ruth is an effective blend of curtness and warmth.

■ MY STEPMOTHER IS AN ALIEN

1988, 108 MINS, US ◇ ⑰

Dir Richard Benjamin *Prod* Ronald Parker *Scr* Jerico Weingrod, Herschel Weingrod, Timothy Harris, Jonathan Reynolds *Ph* Richard H. Kline *Ed* Jacqueline Cambas *Mus* Alan Silvestri *Art Dir* Charles Rosen

● Dan Aykroyd, Kim Basinger, Jon Lovitz, Alyson Hannigan, Joseph Maher (Weintraub)

My Stepmother Is an Alien is a failed attempt to mix many of the film genres associated with the 'alien' idea into a sprightly romp.

Dan Aykroyd, as a rumpled, overweight, widower scientist, foils one of his own experiments using lightning and a high-powered satellite dish which results in a signal reaching beyond our galaxy to a planet in peril.

Soon afterwards, a flying saucer lands on a Southern California beach and two aliens alight. They come in the form of quintessential American beauty Kim Basinger in a slinky red sheath dress with an alien-buddy-mentor (the snake, voice courtesy of Ann Prentiss) hiding in her purse.

Their mission is to get Aykroyd to repeat his experiment, which will save their planet.

It is the lengths to which Basinger is expected to go wending her way into Aykroyd's otherwise nerdy suburban lifestyle that is supposed to levitate this fish-out-of-water story to comedic heights.

■ MYRA BRECKINRIDGE

1970, 94 MINS, US ⑰

Dir Michael Sarne *Prod* Robert Fryer *Scr* Michael Sarne, David Giler *Ph* Richard Moore *Ed* Danford B. Greene *Mus* Lionel Newman (sup.) *Art Dir* Jack Martin Smith, Fred Harpman

● Mae West, John Huston, Raquel Welch, Rex Reed, Farrah Fawcett, Roger C. Carmel (20th Century-Fox)

The film version of Gore Vidal's Hollywood-themed transsexual satire starts off promisingly, but after a couple of reels plunges straight downhill under the weight of artless direction.

As a lecherous female agent, Mae West after an absence from the screen of over 26 years provides some funny moments though her part is very short. John Huston, as drama school promoter Buck Loner, is good, while title-roled Raquel Welch – like the film, good at the beginning – has been let down as story progresses to the point where she alone must (but cannot) keep it going.

With David Giler, director Michael Sarne adapted Vidal's novel in such a way as to (1) create some expository interest, (2) abandon the players to carry the ball, and (3) hype the pacing by clip inserts, motivated and otherwise, as unreal and artificial as silicone injections.

. . . .

■ MYSTERIOUS ISLAND

1962, 100 MINS, UK ◇ Ⓥ

Dir Cy Endfield   *Prod* Charles H. Schneer   *Scr* John Prebble, Daniel Ullman, Crane Wilbur   *Ph* Wilkie Cooper   *Ed* Frederick Wilson   *Mus* Bernard Herrmann   *Art Dir* Bill Andrews

● Michael Craig, Joan Greenwood, Michael Callan, Gary Merrill, Herbert Lom, Percy Herbert (Columbia)

Produced in England under Cy Endfield's vigorous direction, the film illustrates the strange plight that befalls three Union soldiers, a newspaperman and a Rebel who, in 1865, escape the siege of Richmond in the inevitable Jules Verne balloon and return to land on an island in the remote South Seas, where they encounter, in chronological order: (1) a giant crab, (2) a giant bird, (3) two lovely shipwrecked British ladies of average proportions, (4) a giant bee, (5) a band of cutthroat pirates, (6) Captain Nemo's inoperative sub, (7) Captain Nemo.

The screenplay, from Verne's novel, winds with a staple of the science-fantasy melodrama – an entire volcanic isle sinking into the sea as the heroes and heroines beat a hasty retreat.

Dramatically the film is awkward, burdened with unanswered questions and some awfully ineffectual giant animals, but photographically it is noteworthy for the Super-dynamation process and special visual effects by Ray Harryhausen.

. . . .

■ MYSTERY OF THE WAX MUSEUM, THE

1933, 78 MINS, US ◇

Dir Michael Curtiz   *Scr* Don Mullaly, Carl Erickson   *Ph* Ray Rennahan   *Ed* George Amy   *Art Dir* Anton Grot

● Lionel Atwill, Fay Wray, Glenda Farrell, Frank McHugh (Warner)

Technicolor horror-mystery production co-featuring Lionel Atwill, Fay Wray, Glenda Farrell and Frank McHugh who struggle about as effectively as Michael Curtiz, the director, with a loose and unconvincing story, to manage a fairly decent job along *Frankenstein* and *Dracula* lines. Loose ends never quite jell but it's one of those artificial things.

Atwill is the maniacal custodian of the London wax museum whose fanatic enterprise with his transplanted museum on American soil leads Farrell, as the sob sister, to unearth this weird yarn, McHugh this time is the city ed. Wray and Allen Vincent are almost negligible in minor romantic background.

■ MYSTERY TRAIN

1989, 113 MINS, US ◇ Ⓥ

Dir Jim Jarmusch   *Prod* Jim Stark   *Scr* Jim Jarmusch   *Ph* Robby Muller   *Ed* Melody London   *Mus* John Lurie   *Art Dir* Dan Bishop

● Masatoshi Nagase, Youki Kudoh, Nicoletta Braschi, Elizabeth Bracco, Joe Strummer, Rick Aviles (JVC/MTI)

Wholly financed by Japanese electronics giant JVC, a first for an American production, *Mystery Train* is a three-episode pic handled by indie writer-director Jim Jarmusch in his usual playful, minimalist style.

It could be almost dubbed 'Memphis Stories', as this is Jarmusch's tribute to the city of Elvis and other musical greats. Characteristically, the director explores the crumbling, decaying edges of the city through the eyes of foreigners: Japanese teenagers, an Italian widow and a British punk.

Story one, *Far from Yokohama*, intros teenagers Jun (Masatoshi Nagase) and Mitzuko (Youki Kudoh), who arrive by train, do a puzzling guided tour of Sun Studio (they can't understand a word the guide says), sit awed in front of a statue of Presley and check into the Arcade Hotel.

Story two, *A Ghost*, features Nicolette Braschi as Luisa, in Memphis to take her deceased husband's body back to Rome. She checks into the Arcade and meets talkative DeeDee (Elizabeth Bracco) in the lobby.

Final segment, *Lost in Space*, picks up the story of abandoned Brit Johnny (Joe Strummer), who goes on a drunken binge with Dee-Dee's brother (Steve Buscemi) and a black friend (Rick Aviles). Johnny shoots a liquor store clerk, and the trio hides out in the Arcade; next morning, trying to stop Johnny from shooting herself, Buscemi gets shot in the leg.

. . . .

■ MYSTIC PIZZA

1988, 104 MINS, US ◇ Ⓥ

Dir Donald Petrie   *Prod* Mark Levinson, Scott Rosenfelt   *Scr* Amy Jones, Perry Howze, Randy Howze, Alfred Uhry   *Ph* Tim Suhrstedt   *Ed* Marion Rothman, Don Brochu   *Mus* David McHugh   *Art Dir* David Chapman

● Julia Roberts, Annabeth Gish, Lili Taylor, Vincent D'Onofrio, William R. Moses (Goldwyn)

Mystic Pizza is a deftly told coming-of-age story [by Amy Jones] about three young femmes as they explore their different destinies, mostly through romance; it's genuine and moving.

Title refers to a pizza parlor in the heavily Portuguese fishing town of Mystic, Conn, where three best friends, two of them sisters, are working the summer after high-school graduation, all on the verge of pursuing different directions in life.

Jojo (Lili Taylor) apparently is headed for marriage to high school sweetheart Bill (Vincent D'Onofrio), but the idea terrifies her, while he's all for it.

Of the two sisters, Daisy (Julia Roberts) is a vamp who's after the good life and knows how to use her looks, while Kat (Annabeth Gish) is the 'perfect' one – headed for college on an astronomy scholarship. Unlike her sister, she's not too savvy about men, and falls for the married man (William Moses) she babysits for, with painful results.

Script is remarkably mature in its dealings with teens. Characters are funny and vulnerable but capable of shaping their lives, and script artfully weaves in themes of class, destiny and friendship.

. . . .

N*n*

■ NAKED AND THE DEAD, THE

1958, 131 MINS, US ◇ Ⓥ

Dir Raoul Walsh   *Prod* Paul Gregory   *Scr* Denis Sanders, Terry Sanders   *Ph* Joseph LaShelle   *Ed* Arthur P. Schmidt   *Mus* Bernard Herrmann   *Art Dir* Ted Haworth

● Aldo Ray, Cliff Robertson, Raymond Massey, Lili St Cyr, Barbara Nichols, Richard Jaeckel (RKO)

The film bears little more than surface resemblance to the hard hitting Norman Mailer novel of the same title. It catches neither the spirit nor the intent of the original yarn and thus becomes just another war picture, weighed with some tedious dialog sporadically lifted from the book.

The characters go through the motions, hating themselves, hating each other, hating the jungle war that flares around them.

The action sequences come in spurts, but when they do, lenser Joseph LaShelle sees to it that they impress and the dangers of the jungle warfare become vividly real. Unfortunately, a good deal of the footage is taken up with the platoon moving up a mountain or down a mountain, crossing rivers, etc and, after a while, these scenes begin to wear thin.

Aldo Ray plays the frustrated, bitter and sadistic Sergeant Croft. It's not a very plausible part in the first place, and the strenuous efforts to 'explain' him (his wife, Barbara Nichols, has been unfaithful) don't help. Ray plays this beefy character with gusto and certain raw power.

As the playboy whom the general picks as his aide, Cliff Robertson turns in a slick performance. He's good in his verbal encounters with the general, whom he eventually defies, but lacks conviction once he's assigned to lead the Croft platoon on its final sortie.

. . . .

■ NAKED CITY, THE

1948, 94 MINS, US

Dir Jules Dassin   *Prod* Mark Hellinger   *Scr* Albert Maltz, Malvin Wald   *Ph* William Daniels   *Ed* Paul Weatherwax   *Mus* Miklos Rozsa, Frank Skinner   *Art Dir* John F. DeCuir

● Barry Fitzgerald, Howard Duff, Dorothy Hart, Don Taylor, Ted De Corsia (Universal)

Naked City is a boldly fashioned yarn about eastside, westside; about Broadway, the elevated, Fifth Avenue; about kids playing hop-skip-and-jump; about a populace of 8 million – about a blond beaut's mysterious murder in an upper-westside apartment house.

Hellinger's off-screen voice carries the narrative. At the very opening he describes New York, with the aid of a mobile camera, and its teeming humanity. Kids at play, subway straphangers, street vendors on Orchard Street. Then that blonde with a questionable background who is mysteriously murdered. The kind of a story that Hellinger, one of the great tabloid crime reporters of the bathtub-gin era, used to write.

In this pic there are no props. A Manhattan police station scene was photographed in the police station; a lower eastside cops-and-robbers chase was actually filmed in the locale; the ghetto and its pushcarts were caught in all their realism.

Throughout, despite its omniscient, stark melodrama, there has been no sight lost of an element of humor. Barry Fitzgerald, as the film's focal point, in playing the police lieutenant of the homicide squad, strides through the role with tongue in cheek, with Don Taylor as his young detective aide.

NAKED EDGE, THE

1961, 99 MINS, US

Dir Michael Anderson   *Prod* Walter Seltzer, George Glass   *Scr* Joseph Stefano   *Ph* Erwin Hillier   *Ed* Gordon Pilkington   *Mus* William Alwyn   *Art Dir* Carmen Dillon

● Gary Cooper, Deborah Kerr, Eric Portman, Diane Cilento, Hermione Gingold, Peter Cushing (United Artists/Pennebaker-Baroda)

The picture that winds up Gary Cooper's long list of credits is a neatly constructed, thoroughly professional little suspense meller.

Based on Max Ehrlich's novel, *First Train to Babylon*, Joseph Stefano's screenplay casts Cooper as an American businessman living in London who, coincidentally to the murder of his business partner (and the disappearance of a couple of hundred thousand dollars), happens to make a killing on the stockmarket, which funds he uses to make an even bigger fortune.

When, five years later, a blackmailer in the form of Eric Portman turns up to accuse her husband of the murder, Deborah Kerr remembers that Cooper, after all, had been the key prosecution witness at the murder trial and had come into a lot of money quite suddenly. The lady's further investigations confirm her suspicions.

Kerr suffers very prettily in a highly emotional role. Cooper, perhaps because he must appear to be enigmatic most of the time, gives a less successful performance. The picture, filmed entirely in London, utilizes some fine British supporting people.

NAKED GUN, THE

1988, 85 MINS, US ◇ ▽

Dir David Zucker   *Prod* Robert K. Weiss   *Scr* Jerry Zucker, Jim Abrahams, David Zucker, Pat Proft   *Ph* Robert Stevens   *Ed* Michael Jablow   *Mus* Ira Newborn   *Art Dir* John J. Lloyd

● Leslie Nielsen, George Kennedy, Priscilla Presley, Ricardo Montalban, O.J. Simpson (Paramount)

Naked Gun is crass, broad, irreverent, wacky fun – and absolutely hilarious from beginning to end.

Subtitled *From the Files of Police Squad!*, based on illfated too-hip-for-TV series a few seasons earlier, comedy from the crazed Jerry Zucker, Jim Abrahams, David Zucker yock factory is chockablock with sight gags.

Leslie Nielsen is the clumsy detective reprising his TV role and George Kennedy his straight sidekick who wreaks havoc in the streets of LA trying to connect shipping magnate and socialite Ricardo Montalban with heroin smuggling.

Scintilla of a plot weaves in an inspired bit of nonsense with Queen Elizabeth II lookalike Jeannette Charles as the target for assassination at a California Angels' baseball games, where she stands up and does the wave like any other foolish-looking fan, plus a May-December romance between Nielsen and vapid-acting Priscilla Presley whose exchanges of alternatingly drippy or suggestive dialog would make great material for a soap parody.

NAKED PREY, THE

1966, 86 MINS, US ◇ ▽

Dir Cornel Wilde   *Prod* Cornel Wilde, Sven Persson   *Scr* Clint Johnson, Don Peters   *Ph* H.A.R. Thomson   *Ed* Roger Cherrill   *Mus* Andrew Tracey

● Cornel Wilde, Gert Van Der Bergh, Ken Gampu, Patrick Mynhardt, Bella Randels, Morrison Gampu (Theodora/Persson/Paramount)

Filmed entirely in South Africa, *The Naked Prey* is a story of a white man's survival under relentless pursuit by primitive tribesman. Told with virtually no dialog, the story embodies a wide range of human emotion, depicted in actual on-scene photography which effects realism via semi-documentary feel.

The basic story is set in the bush country of a century ago, where safari manager Cornel Wilde and party are captured by natives offended by white hunter Gert Van Der Bergh. All save Wilde are tortured in some explicit footage that is not for the squeamish, while he is given a chance to survive – providing he can exist while eluding some dedicated pursuers.

Action then roves between the macroscopic and the microscopic; that is, from long shots of the varying bush country, caught in beautiful soft tones by H.A.R. Thomson's camera, where man is a spot on the landscape, all the way down to minute animal life, in which the pattern of repose, pursuit, sudden death and then repose matches that of Wilde and the natives.

Ken Gampu, film and legit actor in South Africa, is excellent as the leader of the pursuing warriors.

NAKED RUNNER, THE

1967, 104 MINS, UK ◇ ▽

Dir Sidney J. Furie   *Prod* Brad Dexter   *Scr* Stanley Mann   *Ph* Otto Heller   *Ed* Barry Vince   *Mus* Harry Sukman   *Art Dir* Peter Proud

● Frank Sinatra, Peter Vaughan, Derren Nesbitt, Nadia Gray, Toby Robins, Inger Stratton (Warner/Sinatra)

From a Francis Clifford novel, writer Stanley Mann has fashioned a dullsville script, based on premise that British Intelligence cannot assign one of its own to murder a defector to Russia.

Instead, Frank Sinatra, a Second World War spy now a businessman-widower, is dragooned into service, and by events, deliberately staged, is goaded into killing the defector. Not only British Intelligence, but anybody's intelligence, is likely to be affronted by this potboiler.

Sinatra, whose personal magnetism and acting ability are unquestioned, is shot down by script. Peter Vaughan overacts part as the British agent.

NAME OF THE ROSE, THE

1986, 130 MINS, W. GERMANY/ITALY/FRANCE ◇ ▽

Dir Jean-Jacques Annaud   *Prod* Bernd Eichinger   *Scr* Andrew Birkin, Gerard Brach, Howard Franklin, Alain Godard   *Ph* Tonino Delli Colli   *Ed* Jane Seitz   *Mus* James Horner   *Art Dir* Dante Ferretti

● Sean Connery, F. Murray Abraham, Christian Slater, Michel Lonsdale, Ron Perlman, Valentina Vargas (Neue Constantin/Cristaldifilm/Ariane ZDF)

The Name of the Rose is a sorrowfully mediocre screen version of Umberto Eco's surprise international bestselling novel.

Confusingly written and sluggishly staged, this telling of a murder mystery in a 14th-century abbey has been completely flubbed by director Jean-Jacques Annaud and his team of four (credited) screenwriters, as they struggle even to get the basics of the story up on the screen.

Tale has English Franciscan monk Sean Connery and his novice Christian Slater arriving at an Italian abbey in preparation for a conclave. After a series of murders at the massive edifice Connery, in the style of an aspiring Sherlock Holmes, undertakes an investigation of the deaths while more delegates continue to arrive.

One of the latecomers if F. Murray Abraham, an inquisitor who sees Satan behind every foul deed and who threatens to condemn his old rival Connery due to the latter's insistence on seeking a rational solution to the crimes.

Connery lends dignity, intelligence and his lovely voice to the proceedings. His performance, however, along with some tantalizing E.M. Escher-style labyrinths in the interior of the abbey, are about the only blessings.

NANA

1934, 87 MINS, US

Dir Dorothy Arzner   *Prod* Samuel Goldwyn   *Scr* Willard Mack, Harry Wagstaff Gribble   *Ph* Gregg Toland   *Ed* Frank Lawrence   *Mus* Alfred Newman   *Art Dir* Richard Day (dir.)

● Anna Sten, Phillips Holmes, Lionel Atwill, Richard Bennett, Mae Clarke, Muriel Kirkland (Goldwyn/United Artists)

Sam Goldwyn brilliantly launches a new star in a not so brilliant vehicle. Anna Sten has beauty, glamour, charm, histrionic ability (although there are a couple of moments which seemed a bit beyond her), and s.a.

The script is a very free adaptation of Emile Zola's famous novel. Much care is evident to make it as circumspect as possible and yet maintain its color and allure which is the basis of this transition of a Parisian gamine to music hall heights.

It ends on a tragic note with a suicide by the glorified gamine who takes this way out to reunite the two brothers, Phillips Holmes whom she loves, and Lionel Atwill, his maturer kin, who has coveted her and who subsequently patronizes her when the younger brother is transferred with his regiment to Algiers.

In between there is Richard Bennett as the great Greiner, the master showman, who decides to clay this new unglorified model into the toast of the revue halls.

Sten's likening to Marlene Dietrich becomes inevitable. Her throaty manner of singing 'That's Love' (the sole Rodgers-Hart song in the film) brings that home even more forcibly, apart from her light dialectic Teutonic brogue and the same general aura in personality. The Dorothy Arzner style of direction likewise recalls the Sternberg-Mamoulian technique employed in Dietrich's behalf.

NANNY, THE

1965, 93 MINS, UK

Dir Seth Holt   *Prod* Jimmy Sangster   *Scr* Jimmy Sangster   *Ph* Harry Waxman   *Ed* Tom Simpson   *Mus* Richard Rodney Bennett   *Art Dir* Edward Carrick

● Bette Davis, Wendy Craig, Jill Bennett, James Villiers, William Dix, Pamela Franklin (Hammer/Seven Arts)

It's not necessary to be an astute student to guess that Bette Davis as a middle-aged Mary Poppins in a fairly fraught household will eventually be up to no good. Which immediately sets the odds against screenwriter Jimmy Sangster and director Seth Holt. But, in fairness, the balance of power between Davis, posing as a devoted nanny, and William Dix as a knowing youngster who hates Davis's innards, is so skillfully portrayed to make *The Nanny* a superior psycho-thriller.

It's an added plus to the pic that neither writer nor director teeters over the edge into hysterics, and the cast has cottoned on and helped to build up the suspense gently but with a steely pricking of the nerve ends.

Yarn, briefly, concerns the relationship between nanny Davis and Master Joey (Dix) which is less than cordial. He comes out of a school for the unstable to which he has been sent when his baby sister is found drowned in the bath. He insists it was nanny's fault, but, of course, the adults don't believe him.

Davis handles her assignment with marked professionalism, and copes with plenty of

415

knowhow competition. Wendy Craig is fine as a weak, fond young mama whose nerves are shot to pieces by the household happenings.

● ●

■ NANOOK OF THE NORTH

1922, 55 MINS (1947 SOUND VERSION), US
Dir Robert J. Flaherty   *Scr* Robert J. Flaherty, Carl Stearns Clancy   *Ph* Robert J. Flaherty   *Ed* Herbert Edwards (1947)   *Mus* Rudolf Schramm (1947)
● (Revillon Freres)

Nanook of the North is the granddaddy (or the Eskimo equivalent) of all documentaries and widely extolled as the classic in its field. Despite the comparatively primitive technique and the natural difficulties of shooting a film in the frozen Hudson Bay wastelands, every minute of *Nanook* lives up to its reputation.

Yarn holds tremendous interest in detailing the life of an Eskimo family through the seasons of the year.

Ralph Schoolman's narrative hits the proper note. It treats the Eskimos with dignity, yet with a sense of humor, and it never gets pompous. Berry Kroeger likewise sticks to a simple, friendly, yet thoroughly dignified style in speaking the narration.

● ●

■ NARROW MARGIN

1990, 97 MINS, US ◇ ⓥ
Dir Peter Hyams   *Prod* Jonathan A. Zimbert   *Scr* Peter Hyams   *Ph* Peter Hyams   *Ed* James Mitchell   *Mus* Bruce Broughton   *Art Dir* Joel Schiller
● Gene Hackman, Anne Archer, James B. Sikking, J.T. Walsh, M. Emmet Walsh, Susan Hogan (Carolco)

Spectacular stunt work and Canadian locations punch up the train thriller *Narrow Margin*, but feature remake is too cool and remote to grab the viewer. Richard Fleischer's trim 1952 classic for RKO had a negative cost of only $230,000, while the remake logs in at $21 million. That extra bread shows up on screen in impressive production values but filmmaker Peter Hyams fails to make his story involving.

Basic plotline is retained in the new version. In the Charles McGraw role, Gene Hackman plays a deputy d.a. delivering key witness Anne Archer to testify against gangster Harris Yulin. Hackman's teammate, cop M. Emmet Walsh, is killed leaving Hackman and Archer to escape from a helicopter of armed heavies. They flee to a train headed across remote stretches of Canada and have to play cat and mouse with the thugs (led by evil James B. Sikking) who've boarded the train to eliminate them.

Hackman adds panache to a one-dimensional role. Archer is stuck with a nothing part, given barely one monolog to express her character's feelings. Curiously there is no sex or suggestion of romance in the film.

● ●

■ NARROW MARGIN, THE

1952, 71 MINS, US
Dir Richard Fleischer   *Prod* Stanley Rubin   *Scr* Earl Felton   *Ph* George E. Diskant   *Ed* Robert Swink
● Charles McGraw, Marie Windsor, Jacqueline White, Gordon Gebert, Queenie Leonard, Don Beddoe (RKO)

A standard amount of cops-and-robber melodramatics are stirred up most of the time in *The Narrow Margin*. Plot falls apart at the climax, but regulation thriller tricks, tersely played, carry the story [by Martin Goldsmith and Jack Leonard] along sufficiently.

Two Los Angeles detectives (Charles McGraw and Don Beddoe) are sent to Chicago to escort the widow of a racketeer to the Coast for testimony before the grand jury. Beddoe is killed and McGraw starts back with Marie Windsor, closely pursued by gangsters who want to keep the widow from

testifying. Chase makes for some excitement aboard the train as McGraw keeps outwitting the crooks.

Trouping is competent, with McGraw showing up excellently in his tight-lipped, terse cop portrayal. Windsor impresses the most among the femmes.

● ●

■ NASHVILLE

1975, 157 MINS, US ◇
Dir Robert Altman   *Prod* Robert Altman   *Scr* Joan Tewkesbury   *Ph* Paul Lohmann   *Ed* Sidney Levin, Dennis Hill   *Mus* Richard Baskin
● Ned Beatty, Karen Black, Keith Carradine, Geraldine Chaplin, Shelley Duvall, Henry Gibson (Paramount/ABC)

One of the most ambitious, and more artistically, successful, 'backstage' musical dramas, Robert Altman's *Nashville* is strung on the plot thread of a George Wallace-type pre-Presidential campaign in which the interactions of 24 principal characters are followed over the period of a few days in the country music capitol of America.

Outstanding among the players are Henry Gibson, as a respected music vet with an eye on public office; Ronee Blakely, in a great film debut as a c&w femme star on the brink of nervous collapse; Gwen Welles, drawing tears from stone as a pitiably untalented waitress who undergoes the humiliation of stripping at a stag party for a chance to sing.

Among some real life cameos are Elliott Gould and Julie Christie, both as themselves on p.a. tours.

Nashville is one of Altman's best films, free of the rambling insider fooling around that sometimes mars entire chunks of every second or third picture. When he navigates rigorously to defined goals, however, the results are superb.

● ●

■ NASTY HABITS

1976, 98 MINS, UK ◇ ⓥ
Dir Michael Lindsay-Hogg   *Prod* Robert Enders   *Scr* Robert Enders   *Ph* Douglas Slocombe   *Ed* Peter Tanner   *Mus* John Cameron   *Art Dir* Robert Jones
● Glenda Jackson, Melina Mercouri, Geraldine Page, Sandy Dennis, Anne Jackson, Anne Meara (Bowden)

A witty, intelligent screenplay [from Muriel Spark's novella *The Abbess of Crewe*] leaves no doubts that this is the Watergate circus transposed to a convent, complete with Machiavellian intrigues and power plays, sexual hanky panky, visiting plumbers, hypocritical television chats, national and international political play, roving ambassadors, and so on.

Told straight, it's all about the battle for power in a Philly convent once the aged abbess dies, an all-stops-out dirty scrap which pits establishment against young lib 'outsiders' who want a change.

Glenda Jackson is superb, making her role as the scheming climber unerringly her own. Only one actress nearly bests her: Edith Evans in a memorable cameo, the actress' last stint in a distinguished legit/pic career.

● ●

■ NATIONAL LAMPOON'S ANIMAL HOUSE

1978, 109 MINS, US ◇ ⓥ
Dir John Landis   *Prod* Matty Simmons, Ivan Reitman   *Scr* Harold Ramis, Douglas Kenney, Chris Miller   *Ph* Charles Correll   *Ed* George Folsey Jr   *Mus* Elmer Bernstein   *Art Dir* John J. Lloyd
● John Belushi, Tom Matheson, John Vernon, Verna Bloom, Thomas Hulce, Donald Sutherland (Universal)

Steady readers of the *National Lampoon* may find *National Lampoon's Animal House* a somewhat soft-pedalled, punches-pulled parody of college campus life circa 1962. However, there's enough bite and bawdiness to provide lots of smiles and several broad guffaws.

Writers have concocted a pre-Vietnam college confrontation between a scruffy fraternity and high-elegant campus society. Interspersed in the new faces are the more familiar John Vernon, projecting well his meany charisma here as a corrupt dean; Verna Bloom, Vernon's swinging wife; Cesare Danova, the Mafioso-type mayor of the college town; Donald Sutherland as the super-hip young professor in the days when squares were still saying 'hep'.

Of no small and subtle artistic help is the score by Elmer Bernstein which blithely wafts 'Gaudeamus Igitur' themes amidst the tumult of beer 'orgies', neo-Nazi ROTC drills, cafeteria food fights and a climactic disruption of a traditional Homecoming street parade.

Among the younger players, John Belushi and Tim Matheson are very good as leaders of the unruly fraternity, while James Daughton and Mark Metcalf are prominent as the snotty fratmen, all of whom, quite deliberately, look like Nixon White House aides.

● ●

■ NATIONAL LAMPOON'S EUROPEAN VACATION

1985, 94 MINS, US ◇ ⓥ
Dir Amy Heckerling   *Prod* Matty Simmons, Stuart Cornfeld   *Scr* John Hughes, Robert Klane   *Ph* Bob Paynter   *Ed* Pembroke Herring   *Mus* Charles Fox   *Art Dir* Bob Cartwright
● Chevy Chase, Beverly D'Angelo, Jason Lively, Dana Hill, Eric Idle, Victor Lanoux (Warner)

Most imaginative stroke is the passport-stamped credit sequence that opens this sequel to the 1983 *National Lampoon's Vacation*. Story of a frenetic, chaotic tour of the Old World, with Chevy Chase and Beverley D'Angelo reprising their role as determined vacationers, is graceless and only intermittently lit up by lunacy and satire.

As the family of characters cartwheel through London, Paris, Italy and Germany – with the French deliciously taking it on the chin for their arrogance and rudeness – director Amy Heckerling gets carried away with physical humor while letting her American tourists grow tiresome and predictable. Structurally, the film unfolds like a series of travel brochures.

Uneven screenplay never sails, and it's left to Chase to fire up the film. His character is actually rather sympathetic – if boorish – in his insistence on turning every Continental moment into a delight (scanning Paris, he shouts 'I want to write, I want to paint, I got a romantic urge!').

● ●

■ NATIONAL LAMPOON'S VACATION

1983, 96 MINS, US ◇ ⓥ
Dir Harold Ramis   *Prod* Matty Simmons   *Scr* John Hughes   *Ph* Victor J. Kemper   *Ed* Pem Herring   *Mus* Ralph Burns   *Art Dir* Jack Collis
● Chevy Chase, Beverly D'Angelo, Anthony Michael Hall, Imogene Coca, Randy Quaid, John Candy (Warner)

National Lampoon's Vacation is an enjoyable trip through familiar comedy landscapes.

Chevy Chase is perfectly mated with Beverly D'Angelo as an average Chicago suburban couple setting out to spend their annual two-week furlough. Determined to drive, Chase wants to take the two kids to 'Walley World' in California. She would rather fly.

Despite home-computer planning, this trip is naturally going to be a disaster from the moment Chase goes to pick up the new car. No matter how bad this journey gets – and it gets pretty disastrous – Chases perseveres in treating each day as a delight, with D'Angelo's patient cooperation. His son, beautifully played by Anthony Michael Hall, is a help, too.

Vacation peaks early with the family's visit to Cousin Eddie's rundown farm, rundown by the relatives residing there. As the uncouth cousin, Randy Quaid almost steals the picture.

Credit director Harold Ramis for populating the film with a host of well-known comedic performers in passing parts.

■ NATIONAL VELVET

1944, 125 MINS, US ◇ ▼

Dir Clarence Brown *Prod* Pandro S. Berman *Scr* Theodore Reeves, Helen Deutsch *Ph* Leonard Smith *Ed* Robert J. Kern *Mus* Herbert Stothart *Art Dir* Cedric Gibbons, Urie McCleary
● Mickey Rooney, Donald Crisp, Elizabeth Taylor, Anne Revere, Angela Lansbury (M-G-M)

National Velvet is a horse picture with wide general appeal. The production also focuses attention on a new dramatic find – moppet Elizabeth Taylor.

Backgrounded in England, it tells of a former jockey (Mickey Rooney) who's become embittered through circumstances and plans to steal from a family that befriends him. But the family's 11-year-old daughter, Velvet softens him.

From this point on, early in the film, Velvet becomes the dominant character in the story [from the novel by Enid Bagnold]. The kid is nuts about horses. When a neighbor raffles off an unmanageable brute he's unable to handle she wins it on tickets paid for by Rooney. Over the objections of both Rooney and her father, nag is entered in the greatest race in England, the Grand National Sweepstakes.

Story is told with warmth and understanding. There is much detail, in this direction, between husband and wife; between Velvet and her mother and between the two kids, especially when Rooney confesses to an abiding fear of horses ever since he rode in a sweepstakes which ended in another jockey's death.

■ NATURAL, THE

1984, 134 MINS, US ◇ ▼

Dir Barry Levinson *Prod* Mark Johnson *Scr* Robert Towne, Phil Dusenberry *Ph* Caleb Deschanel *Ed* Stu Linder *Mus* Randy Newman *Art Dir* Angelo Graham, Mel Bourne
● Robert Redford, Robert Duvall, Glenn Close, Kim Basinger, Wilford Brimley, Barbara Hershey (Tri-Star)

The Natural is an impeccably made, but quite strange, fable about success and failure in America. Robert Redford plays an aging rookie who takes the baseball world by storm in one season while dealing with demons from his past and present.

While remaining faithful to Bernard Malamud's 1952 novel in many regards, scenarists have drastically altered some major elements. Film thereby has become the story of the redemption of a born athlete whose life didn't unfold as anticipated.

Opening sequences present farmboy Roy Hobbs showing natural skill as a ballplayer and, upon the death of his father, carving his own magical bat, dubbed 'Wonderboy' from the wood of a lightning-struck tree.

Some years later, Hobbs, now in the person of Redford, leaves for Chicago, and raises the eyebrows of ace sports-writer and cartoonist Robert Duvall when he strikes out the majors' greatest hitter (Joe Don Baker) in an impromptu exhibition.

Redford is perfectly cast as the wary, guarded Hobbs. The female characters leave behind a bad taste, however, since they schematically and simplistically stand for the archaic angel-whore syndrome. Whenever he goes for harlots like Barbara Hershey or Kim Basinger, Redford is in big trouble, from which he must be rescued by Glenn Close.

■ NAUGHTY MARIETTA

1935, 105 MINS, US ▼

Dir W.S. Van Dyke *Prod* Hunt Stromberg *Scr* J.L. Mahin, Frances Goodrich, Albert Hackett *Ph* William Daniels *Ed* Blanche Sewell *Mus* Herbert Stothart (adapt.)
● Jeanette MacDonald, Nelson Eddy, Frank Morgan, Elsa Lanchester, Douglas Dumbrille, Joseph Cawthorne (M-G-M)

An adaptation of the Victor Herbert operetta [book and lyrics by Rida Johnson Young] which the singing of Jeanette MacDonald and Nelson Eddy must carry. Much of the original score, plus a couple of added tunes [lyrics by Gus Kahn], is included. There are nine songs, but only one reprise, a martial tune from Eddy and his warriors.

This operetta tells of a group of girls the French government has endowed before they sail to Louisiana, there to find husbands and build up that colony. The princess (MacDonald) escapes with this group from her tyrannical uncle and the aged suitor he has selected. In New Orleans she falls in love with the captain of the mercenaries (Eddy) and again escapes for a happy finish.

The comedy being insufficient to sustain this much footage, with no especially exciting action, provides serious handicaps. Although Marietta may have been naughty in 1910, if she's still naughty it's her secret.

MacDonald sings particularly well and is favored with fine recording and exceptional photography. She also carries her share of the story capably and in her lighter moments gives a hint of what might be.

Picture marks the full-length debut of Eddy who reveals a splendid and powerful baritone with the distinct asset for the camera of not being breathy. Eddy is a tall, nice-looking boy who previously, briefly, appeared in a couple of Metro films. In this picture he sings so often that the script calls for his kidding himself about it.

Frank Morgan does a routine governor, with an eye for an ankle, dominated by his wife. Elsa Lanchester is the wife with an unattractive tendency to mugg her points.
□ 1935: Best Picture (Nomination)

■ NAVIGATOR, THE

1924, 60 MINS, US ⊗

Dir Donald Crisp, Buster Keaton *Scr* Jean Havez, Clyde Bruckman, Joe Mitchell *Ph* Elgin Lessley, Byron Houck *Art Dir* Fred Gabourie
● Buster Keaton, Kathryn McGuire, Frederick Vroom (Metro-Goldwyn)

Keaton's comedy is spotty. That is to say it's both commonplace and novel, with the latter sufficient to make the picture a laugh getter.

The film is novel in that it has Keaton in a deep-sea diving outfit with the camera catching him under water for comedy insertions. There's a possibility of doubling during some of the action, but close-ups are registered under water that reveal Keaton, personally, behind the glass within the helmet.

There's an abundance of funny business in connection with Keaton's going overboard to fix a propeller shaft and a thrill has been inserted through the comedian getting mixed up with a devil fish.

The actual story carries little weight. It has Keaton as a wealthy young man being matrimonially rejected by the girl. Having secured passage to Hawaii, he unknowingly boards a deserted steamship selected to be destroyed by foreign and warring factions. The girl's father, owner of the vessel, visits the dock, is set upon by the rogues who are bent on casting the liner adrift, and when the girl goes to her parent's rescue she is also caught on board with no chance of a return to land. The entire action practically takes place on the deserted ship, with the girl (Kathryn McGuire) and Keaton the only figures.

■ NAVIGATOR, THE

1988, 93 MINS, NEW ZEALAND ◇ ▼

Dir Vincent Ward *Prod* John Maynard *Scr* Vincent Ward, Kelly Lyons, Geoff Chapple *Ph* Geoffrey Simpson *Ed* John Scott *Mus* Davood A. Tabrizi *Art Dir* Sally Campbell
● Bruce Lyons, Chris Haywood, Hamish McFarlane, Marshall Napier, Noel Appleby (Arena film/NZ Film Investment Corp)

The Navigator is remarkable because of its absorbing story that links medieval fears and fortunes to our times, while confirming director Vincent Ward as an original talent.

The story begins in Cumbria in 1348, the year of the Black Death. Young Griffin (Hamish McFarlane) is anxious for the return of his beloved, much-older brother Connor (Bruce Lyons) from the outside world. He is haunted by a dream about a journey, a quest to a great cathedral in a celestial city, and a figure about to fall from a steeple.

When his brother returns to the village with tales of impending doom, the two brothers, with four comrades, set out on the journey fired by Griffin's prophetic dream. It takes them to a city of the late 1980s and on a mission against time if their village is to be saved.

The formidable skills of Ward are shown in the way his story works, not only as adventure, but as the love story of two brothers and a parable of faith and religion.

Geoffrey Simpson's photography – stark black and white for the Cumbrian sequences, color for the enactment of Griffin's dream and visions – is of the highest order, with score by Iranian composer Davood Tabrizi (domiciled in Sydney) empathetic with the whole.

■ NEAR DARK

1987, 95 MINS, US ◇ ▼

Dir Kathryn Bigelow *Prod* Steven-Charles Jaffe *Scr* Eric Red, Kathryn Bigelow *Ph* Adam Greenberg *Ed* Howard Smith *Mus* Tangerine Dream *Art Dir* Stephen Altman
● Adrian Pasdar, Jenny Wright, Lance Henriksen, Bill Paxton, Jenette Goldstein (De Laurentiis)

Near Dark achieves a new look in vampire films. High-powered but pared down, slick but spare, this is a tale that introduces the unearthly into the banality of rural American existence.

Nervous, edgy opening has sharp young cowboy Adrian Pasdar hooking up with Jenny Wright, a good-looking new girl in town not averse to some nocturnal roistering as long as she gets home by dawn.

Wright soon welcomes Pasdar into her 'family', a bunch of real low-down boys and girls that would have done Charles Manson proud. Led by the spidery Lance Henriksen, the gang hibernates by day, but at night scours the vacant landscapes in search of prey.

Script by Kathryn Bigelow and Eric Red is cool and laconic, and the evildoers essentially come off as some very nasty bikers who kill for sport as well as necessity.

Main point of interest will be the work of Bigelow, who has undoubtedly created the most hard-edged, violent actioner ever directed by an American woman.

■ NED KELLY

1970, 101 MINS, UK ◇

Dir Tony Richardson *Prod* Neil Hartley *Scr* Tony Richardson, Ian Jones *Ph* Gerry Fisher *Ed* Charles Rees *Mus* Shel Silverstein *Art Dir* Jocelyn Herbert

● Mick Jagger, Diane Craig, Clarissa Kaye, Frank Thring, Mark McManus, Allen Bickford (Woodfall)

Ned Kelly is basically an outback western in which director and coscripter Tony Richardson's simplicity becomes a pretension of its own. It is a film to which one applies the damning word 'interesting'.

In the 1870s Australia was a brutal frontier, settled by Irish, English and Scots convicts and their descendants.

In the film, the convict stock are continually harassed by the English police troopers and the settlers' ranging cattle and horses impounded by the authorities on the slightest pretext. Unable to exist otherwise, Kelly and the other Irishmen turn to rustling.

Mick Jagger is a natural actor and performer with a wide range of expressions and postures at his instinctive command. Given whiskers, that gaunt, tough pop hero face takes on a classic hard bitten frontier look that is totally believable for the role. However he has no one to play to. Jagger's Clyde has no Bonnie, his Sundance Kid has no Butch Cassidy.

● ●

■ NEIGHBORS

1981, 94 MINS, US ◇
Dir John G. Avildsen   *Prod* Richard D. Zanuck, David Brown   *Scr* Larry Gelbart   *Ph* Gerald Hirschfield   *Ed* Jane Kurson   *Mus* Bill Conti   *Art Dir* Peter Larkin
● John Belushi, Kathryn Walker, Cathy Moriarty, Dan Aykroyd (Columbia)

Essentially the story of *Neighbors* focuses on staid suburbanite John Belushi who is slowly being driven crazy by his new, nutsy neighbors – a dyed blonde, goon Dan Aykroyd and his smooth, sexually scintillating wife Cathy Moriarty. The new couple take over his car, his bank account, his house and even his family while at the same time making it seem like Belushi is a stick-in-the mud poor sport for not going along with it.

Larry Gelbart's script [from the novel by Thomas Berger] seems content to leave it at that, yet both he and director John G. Avildsen take great pains to throw in some serious reminders of just how pathetic the lives of each of these characters are including the fun-loving neighbors. Consequently, other than a few laughs the reason for the film is a little puzzling.

Ultimately it is Belushi and Aykroyd that make the picture work. When they hit the comedic mark, as they more often than not do here, nothing else seems to matter.

● ●

■ NEPTUNE'S DAUGHTER

1949, 92 MINS, US ◇ Ⓥ
Dir Edward Buzzell   *Prod* Jack Cummings   *Scr* Dorothy Kingsley   *Ph* Charles Rosher   *Ed* Irvine Warburton   *Mus* Frank Loesser
● Esther Williams, Red Skelton, Ricardo Montalban, Betty Garrett, Keenan Wynn, Xavier Cugat (M-G-M)

Neptune's Daughter is a neat concoction of breezy, light entertainment. It combines comedy, songs and dances into an amusing froth.

Star sparkplugs are Esther Williams and Red Skelton. Williams' bathing beauty and Skelton's comedy make for a pleasing combination that does much to get over the pleasant, but fluffy, story.

Top tune of the Frank Loesser score is 'Baby, It's Cold Outside', dueted by Williams and Ricardo Montalban, and, for comedy, by Skelton and Garrett.

Story thread holding the antics together concerns itself with a bathing suit designer-manufacturer-model, Williams; her business partner, Keenan Wynn; her dumbdora sister, Betty Garrett; and Skelton, a masseur for a polo club.

Film includes a number of beautifully staged water sequences.

● ●

■ NETWORK

1976, 121 MINS, US ◇ Ⓥ
Dir Sidney Lumet   *Prod* Howard Gottfried   *Scr* Paddy Chayefsky   *Ph* Owen Roizman   *Ed* Alan Heim   *Mus* Elliot Lawrence   *Art Dir* Philip Rosenberg
● Faye Dunaway, William Holden, Peter Finch, Robert Duvall, Wesley Addy, Ned Beatty (M-G-M)

Paddy Chayefsky's absurdly plausible and outrageously provocative original script concerns media running amok.

Sidney Lumet's direction is outstanding.

This is a bawdy, stops-out, no-holds-barred story of a TV network that will, quite literally, do anything to get an audience.

The fictional TV network, United Broadcasting System, has been acquired by a conglomerate headed by Ned Beatty, whose hatchet man, Robert Duvall, succeeds to operating control. Peter Finch, the passe evening news anchorman is about to get the heave. To the dismay of all, Finch announces his own axing, becoming an instant character.

Finch's on-the-air freakout suggests to Faye Dunaway that she turn the news into a gross entertainment package. It works, of course.

□ 1976: Best Picture (Nomination)

● ●

■ NEVADA SMITH

1966, 131 MINS, US ◇ Ⓥ
Dir Henry Hathaway   *Prod* Henry Hathaway   *Scr* John Michael Hayes   *Ph* Lucien Ballard   *Ed* Frank Bracht   *Mus* Alfred Newman   *Art Dir* Hal Pereira, Tambi Larsen, Al Roelofs
● Steve McQueen, Karl Malden, Brian Keith, Arthur Kennedy, Suzanne Pleshette, Raf Vallone (Paramount/Embassy/Solar)

A good story idea – boy avenging his murdered parents and maturing in the process – is stifled by uneven acting, often lethargic direction, and awkward sensation-shock values. Overlength serves to dull the often spectacular production values.

John Michael Hayes scripted in routine fashion a story and screenplay based on a character from Harold Robbins' *The Carpetbaggers*. Hayes' yarn is not a sequel, but a precedessor work, in that it is centered on the Nevada Smith character who acted as guardian to Jonas Cord Jr, the youthful antihero of *Carpetbaggers*.

Steve McQueen is the young half-Indian boy whose parents are brutally murdered by Karl Malden, Arthur Kennedy and Martin Landau. Vowing revenge, McQueen sets off to kill them all. Brian Keith plays the elder Jonas Cord, then an itinerant gunsmith, who befriends the greenhorn and teaches him armed self-defense.

Henry Hathaway's uneven direction alternates jarring, overbearing fisticuffs with exterior footage as spectacular in some cases as it is dull in others.

● ●

■ NEVER GIVE A SUCKER AN EVEN BREAK

1941, 70 MINS, US Ⓥ
Dir Edward Cline   *Scr* John T. Noville, Prescott Chaplin   *Ph* Charles Van Enger   *Ed* Arthur Hilton   *Mus* Frank Skinner
● W.C. Fields, Gloria Jean, Margaret Dumont (Universal)

W.C. Fields parades his droll satire and broad comedy in this takeoff on eccentricities of film making – from personal writings of the original story by Fields under nom de plume of Otis Criblecoblis. It's a hodge-podge of razzle-dazzle episodes, tied together in disjointed fashion but with sufficient laugh content for the comedian's fans.

Story focuses attention on Fields and his presentation of an imaginative script for his next picture at Esoteric Studios. In series of cutbacks depicting wild-eyed action as read by producer Franklin Pangborn, Fields horse-plays in a plane, dives out to land on a mountain plateau safely, and finally leaves the studio to embark on a crashing auto chase.

Fields is Fields throughout. He wrote the yarn for himself, and knew how to handle the assignment. Picture is studded with Fieldsian satire and cracks – many funny and several that slipped by the blue-pencil squad. Byplay and reference to hard liquor is prominent throughout.

● ●

■ NEVER LOVE A STRANGER

1958, 91 MINS, US Ⓥ
Dir Robert Stevens   *Prod* Harold Robbins, Richard Day   *Scr* Harold Robbins, Richard Day   *Ph* Lee Garmes   *Ed* Sidney Katz   *Mus* Raymond Scott   *Art Dir* Leo Kerz
● John Drew Barrymore, Lita Milan, Robert Bray, Steve McQueen, R.G. Armstrong (Allied Artists)

This New York locationed melodrama is so ineptly, unprofessionally done, especially in its handling of such volatile subjects as race and religion, that it has nothing else to recommend it.

John Drew Barrymore plays a young man raised in a Catholic orphanage who discovers when he is almost grown that his parents were Jewish. Under the law, he must be removed to the jurisdiction of an orphanage of his own faith. Young Barrymore is already involved with hoodlum elements and, feeling rejection by the orphanage that has been his home and parents, takes the final plunge into the gangster world.

Barrymore does an able job with his role although he is repeatedly sabotaged by a story that is persistently old hat in its approach to religion, gangsterism and unwed mothers, the three chief plot threads.

● ●

■ NEVER SAY NEVER AGAIN

1983, 137 MINS, US ◇ Ⓥ
Dir Irvin Kershner   *Prod* Jack Schwartzman   *Scr* Lorenzo Semple Jr.   *Ph* Douglas Slocombe   *Ed* Robert Lawrence, Ian Crafford   *Mus* Michel Legrand   *Art Dir* Philip Harrison, Stephen Grimes
● Sean Connery, Klaus Maria Brandauer, Max Von Sydow, Barbara Carrera, Kim Basinger, Alec McCowen (Taliafilm)

After a 12-year hiatus, Sean Connery is back in action as James Bond. The new entry marks something of a retreat from the far-fetched technology of many of the later Bonds in favor of intrigue and romance.

Although it is not acknowledged as such, pic is roughly a remake of the 1965 *Thunderball*. World-threatening organization SPECTRE manages to steal two US cruise missiles and announces it will detonate their nuclear warheads in strategic areas unless their outrageous ransom demands are met.

In short order, Bond hooks up with dangerous SPECTRE agent Fatima Blush (Barbara Carrera), who makes several interesting attempts to kill her prey, and later makes the acquaintance of Domino (Kim Basinger), g.f. of SPECTRE kingpin Largo (Klaus Maria Brandauer), who enjoys the challenge presented by the secret agent as long as he thinks he holds the trump card.

What clicks best in the film is the casting. Klaus Maria Brandauer makes one of the best Bond opponents since very early in the series. Carrera lets out all the stops, while Basinger is luscious as the pivotal romantic and dramatic figure.

N

And then, of course, there's Connery, in fine form and still very much looking the part.

. . . .

■ NEVER SO FEW

1959, 126 MINS, US ◇ ▼

Dir John Sturges   *Prod* Edmund Grainger   *Scr* Millard Kaufman   *Ph* William C. Daniels   *Ed* Ferris Webster   *Mus* Hugo Friedhofer

● Frank Sinatra, Gina Lollobrigida, Peter Lawford, Steve McQueen, Richard Johnson, Paul Henreid (Canterbury/M-G-M)

Never So Few is one of those films in which in-dividual scenes and sequences play with verve and excitement. It is only when the relation of the scenes is evaluated, and their cumulative effect considered, that the threads begin to unravel like an old, worn sock.

The locale of the screenplay, based on Tom T. Chamales' book, is Burma during World War II. Frank Sinatra is the iconoclastic, ruggedly individualistic commander of a small British-American task force. The bulk of his force is made up of native Kachin troops. He is idolized by them and his Occi-dental troops. Chief action of the film has Sinatra leading a foray against a Japanese position near the Chinese border in which some of his men are ambushed by a National-ist Chinese group out for plunder.

Sinatra's romantic interest is Gina Lol-lobrigida, looking like about $15 million, who has been the pampered mistress of mystery man Paul Henreid. She will abandon her plush life with Henreid and go back to India-napolis with Sinatra, she says.

Steve McQueen has a good part, and he delivers with impressive style. Richard John-son, a British actor, is also a standout.

Never So Few did its principal photography on the Metro lot and on domestic locations, but it has some effective Ceylon photography that is neatly blended.

. . . .

■ NEVER TAKE SWEETS FROM A STRANGER

1960, 81 MINS, UK

Dir Cyril Frankel   *Prod* Anthony Hinds   *Scr* John Hunter   *Ph* Freddie Francis   *Ed* Jim Neels   *Mus* Elizabeth Lutyens

● Gwen Watford, Patrick Allen, Felix Aylmer, Niall MacGinnis, Alison Leggatt, Bill Nagy (Hammer)

The yarn is set in Canada. Though filmed in Britain, the Canadian atmosphere is remark-ably well conveyed. It deals with a senile, psychopathic pervert (Felix Aylmer) with a yen for little girls. When he persuades two innocent little girls to dance naked in front of him in exchange for candy, the English parents of one of them decide to take him to court. Unfortunately, they do not realize that he is the local big shot, the man who has helped to build the Canadian town to its prosperity and power.

Gwen Watford and Patrick Allen, as the distraught parents, and Alison Leggatt, as a wise, understanding grandmother, lead a cast which is directed with complete sensitivity by Cyril Frankel. Both Watford and Allen are completely credible while Leggatt, well-served by John Hunter's script, is outstanding.

Aylmer, who doesn't utter a word through-out the film, gives a terrifying acute study of crumbling evil, while Bill Nagy, as his son, is equally effective.

. . . .

■ NEVER TOO LATE

1965, 104 MINS, US ◇

Dir Bud Yorkin   *Prod* Norman Lear   *Scr* Sumner Long   *Ph* Philip Lathrop   *Ed* William Ziegler   *Mus* David Rose   *Art Dir* Edward Carrere

● Paul Ford, Connie Stevens, Maureen O'Sullivan, Tim Hutton, Jane Wyatt, Lloyd Nolan (Tandem/Warner)

Outstanding direction and acting give full life to this well-expanded legiter about an approaching-menopause wife who becomes pregnant to the chagrin of hubby, spoiled-brat daughter, and free-loading son-in-law. Comedy ranges from sophisticated to near-slapstick, all handled in top form.

Sumner Arthur Long adapted his play which though essentially a one-joke affair he has filled out with exterior sequences which enhance, rather than pad. While the result is a family pic, it's not a pollyanna pot pourri of fluff.

Paul Ford and Maureen O'Sullivan are smartly re-teamed in their Broadway roles of small town Massachusetts parents, settled in middle-age habits until wife's increasing fatigue is diagnosed as pregnancy. O'Sullivan looks great and handles light comedy with a warm, gracious flair.

Ford carries the pic as the flustered father-to-be, saddled with the sly grins of neighbors, the incompetency of son-in-law Jim Hutton, and the domestic bumblings of daughter Connie Stevens.

. . . .

■ NEVERENDING STORY, THE

1984, 94 MINS, W. GERMANY ◇ ▼

Dir Wolfgang Petersen   *Prod* Bernd Eichinger, Dieter Geissler   *Scr* Wolfgang Petersen, Herman Weigel   *Ph* Jost Vacano   *Ed* Jane Seitz   *Mus* Klaus Doldinger, Giorgio Moroder   *Art Dir* Rolf Zehetbauer

● Noah Hathaway, Barret Oliver, Tami Stronach, Moses Gunn, Patricia Hayes, Sydney Bromley (Neue Constantin)

Wolfgang Petersen's *The Neverending Story* is a marvelously realized flight of pure fantasy.

With the support of top German, British and US technicians and artists plus a hefty $27 million budget (highest for any film made outside US or USSR), helmer Petersen has improved on pic's immediate forebear, Jim Henson/Frank Oz' 1982 *The Dark Crystal*, by avoiding too much unrelieved strangeness.

Film opens with a little boy, Bastian (Barret Oliver), borrowing a strange-looking book at a local bookstore and holes up in the school attic to read.

Book, titled *The Neverending Story*, depicts a world known as Fantasia, threatened by an advancing force called The Nothing (repre-sented by storms) which is gradually destroy-ing all. To save Fantasia, an ailing empress (Tami Stronach) sends for a young warrior from among the plains people, Atreyu (Noah Hathaway) to go on a quest to find a cure for her illness.

Filming at and backed by Munich's Bavaria Studios, *Story* benefits from special effects technicians working overtime to create a new-look world.

. . . .

■ NEVERENDING STORY II, THE THE NEXT CHAPTER

1990, 89 MINS, GERMANY ◇ ▼

Dir George Miller   *Prod* Dieter Geissler   *Scr* Karin Howard   *Ph* Dave Connell   *Ed* Peter Hollywood, Chris Blunden   *Mus* Robert Folk   *Art Dir* Bob Laing, Gotz Weidner

● Jonathan Brandis, Kenny Morrison, Clarissa Burt, Alexandra Johnes, Martin Umbach, John Wesley Shiff (Geissler)

Follow-up, produced by Germans based in Munich with location filming in Canada, Argentina, Australia, France and Italy, is a natural, since first film directed by Wolfgang Petersen only covered half of Michael Ende's classic novel.

Part II utilizes a whole new cast (except for Thomas Hill, reprising as Koreander the book-seller) to depict adventures in the im-aginary world of Fantasia. Main innovation is that young hero Bastian joins his fantasy counterpart Atreyu in a heroic trek in search of the childlike empress locked in her Ivory Tower in Fantasia, rather than just reading about him.

Another improvement is the inclusion of a delicious villainess, dark beauty Clarissa Burt as Xayide, who suckers Bastian into making numerous wishes, each time losing a bit of his memory in return.

Film is effective in its own right, but as with most sequels, it lacks freshness. American actress Burt is any adolescent boy's fantasy seductress. Rest of the cast is adequate, but a letdown compared with the original's.

. . . .

■ NEW CENTURIONS, THE

1972, 103 MINS, US ◇ ▼

Dir Richard Fleischer   *Prod* Irwin Winkler, Robert Chartoff   *Scr* Stirling Silliphant   *Ph* Ralph Woolsey   *Ed* Robert C. Jones   *Mus* Quincy Jones   *Art Dir* Boris Leven

● George C. Scott, Stacy Keach, Jane Alexander, Scott Wilson, Rosalind Cash, Erik Estrada (Columbia)

The New Centurions is a somewhat unsatisfying film. Story [from Joseph Wambaugh's novel] largely avoids like the plague any real con-frontation with the gray areas of modern-day citizen-police interactions which are at the seat of unrest.

George C. Scott domintes the first 76 min-utes, starring as the oldtime cop with a para-doxical philosophy. He sees nothing wrong in applying some pragmatic justice at the street level (there are several good, sometimes amusing episodes in this regard); at the same time, he is obviously blind to the realization that laws are contemporary reflections of transient attitudes which every few gener-ations undergo a major flushing out.

Also starring is Stacy Keach. The nature of the plot necessarily makes Keach second banana to Scott. After Scott retires from the force the film falls off in impact.

. . . .

■ NEW LEAF, A

1971, 102 MINS, US ◇ ▼

Dir Elaine May   *Prod* Joe Manduke   *Scr* Elaine May   *Ph* Gayne Rescher   *Ed* Fredric Steinkamp, Donald Guidice

● Walter Matthau, Elaine May, Jack Weston, George Rose, William Redfield, James Coco (Koch-Elkins/Paramount)

Walter Matthau is both broad and satirically sensitive and Elaine May has gotten off some sharp and amusing dialog in her screenplay. It's sophisticated and funny, adroitly put together for the most part. May complained in a court action that final cuts were not hers and she would prefer not to have identity as the director.

Matthau is the marriage-aloof middle-ager who's running out of his inheritance because of high living and who has to come upon a rich wife to sustain himself. Rich wife turns out to be unglamorous May. The director and cosmetician have made May about as sexy as an Alsophiplia Grahamicus, which is a new leaf she has cultivated in her role as botanist. A new leaf is also something that Matthau turns over because after he weds May he decides, rather than kill her, to take care of her like the fine character he hadn't been in the past.

William Redfield fits in as the exasperated lawyer who has difficulty in conveying to Matthau that one doesn't drive a Ferrari and live in a luxurious town house when one is broke. James Coco is Uncle Harry, to whom Henry goes for a loan, which is provided on condition that Henry pay it back in six weeks or pay 10 times the principal.

■ NEW LIFE, A

1988, 104 MINS, US ◇ ⓥ

Dir Alan Alda   *Prod* Martin Bregman   *Scr* Alan Alda
Ph Kelvin Pike   *Ed* William Reynolds   *Mus* Joseph
Turrin   *Art Dir* Barbara Dunphy
● Alan Alda, Ann-Margret, Ital Linden, Veronica
Hamel, John Shea (Paramount)

Perhaps trying to break his image as the most conscientiously nice guy of the latter half of the 20th century, Alan Alda has tried to give himself an edge in *A New Life*. As the newly divorced Steve Giardino, he is loud, obnoxious, neurotic, argumentative and manic; he also has permed hair and a beard, smokes, drinks hard liquor rather than wine, and eats red meat instead of chicken and fish.

After some 20 years of marriage, New Yorkers Alda and Ann-Margret decide to call it quits. Alda's screenplay follows the two equally as each endures the predictably excruciating blind dates, singles parties and matchups.

They are tenacious and game, and some months later each meets an attractive new prospect, she a dreamy, younger TriBeCa sculptor (John Shea), he a sharp and similarly younger doctor (Veronica Hamel).

All the actors have the upper-middle-class mannerisms down pat, and make for perfectly agreeable company despite the familiarity of the terrain. Shot mainly in Toronto, pic looks and sounds good.

■ NEW YEAR'S DAY

1989, 89 MINS, US ◇

Dir Henry Jaglom   *Prod* Judith Wolinsky   *Scr* Henry
Jaglom   *Ph* Joey Forsyte
● Maggie Jakobson, Gwen Welles, Melanie Winter,
Henry Jaglom, Milos Forman, Michael Emil
(International Rainbow)

An undifferentiated extension of the same themes, concerns and artistic strategies featured in Henry Jaglom's previous films, *New Year's Day* is nonetheless notable for introducing a luminous new actress, Maggie Jakobson.

Jaglom again stars as a depressed Me Generation obsessive who returns to New York from Los Angeles in the midst of a mid-life crisis.

Arriving on New Year's morning, Jaglom finds his apartment still occupied by three young ladies who thought they had unfil the end of the day to vacate the premises. Instead of booting them out, Jaglom immediately imposes himself upon their most personal concerns, especially those of Jakobson, whose boyfriend continues to fool around with other women throughout the open house the trio holds on their last day as roommates.

Lots of people show up for a drink or two in the course of the day, including Jakobson's parents and shrink, helmer's brother Michael Emil as a randy 'psychosexologist,' and director Milos Forman.

■ NEW YORK STORIES

1989, 123 MINS, US ◇ ⓥ

Dir Martin Scorsese, Francis Coppola, Woody Allen
Prod Robert Greenhut   *Scr* Richard Price, Francis
Coppola, Sofia Coppola, Woody Allen   *Ph* Nestor
Almendros, Vittorio Storaro, Sven Nykvist   *Ed* Thelma
Schoonmaker, Barry Malkin, Susan E. Morse
Mus Carmine Coppola, Kid Creole and the Coconuts
Art Dir Kristi Zea, Dean Tavoularis, Santo Loquasto
● Nick Nolte, Rosanna Arquette, Heather McComb,
Talia Shire, Woody Allen, Mia Farrow (Touchstone)

New York Stories showcases the talents of three of the modern American cinema's foremost auteurs, Martin Scorsese, Francis Coppola and Woody Allen. Scorsese's is aimed at serious-minded adults, Coppola's to children, and Allen's to a more general public looking for laughs.

Scorsese's *Life Lessons* gets things off to a pulsating start, as Nestor Almendros' camera darts, swoops and circles around Nick Nolte and Rosanna Arquette as they face the end of an intense romantic entanglement. The leonine Nolte plays a an abstract painter unprepared for a major gallery opening three weeks away. Announcing that she's had a fling, Arquette, Nolte's lover and artistic protege, agrees to stay on in his loft as long as she no longer has to sleep with him.

At 33 minutes, Coppola's *Life without Zoe* is the shortest of the three, but that is still not nearly short enough. Vignette is a wispy urban fairy tale about a 12-year-old girl who, because her parents are on the road most of the time, basically lives alone at the ritzy Sherry Netherland Hotel.

Happily, Woody Allen salvages matters rather nicely with *Oedipus Wrecks*, about the Jewish mother syndrome. When Allen takes shiksa girlfriend Mia Farrow home for dinner, he winces as mama assails him for choosing a blonde with three kids. Allen's fondest wish – that his mother just disappear – comes true when a magician literally loses her in the course of a trick.

■ NEW YORK, NEW YORK

1977, 153 MINS, US ◇ ⓥ

Dir Martin Scorsese   *Prod* Irwin Winkler, Robert
Chartoff   *Scr* Earl Mac Rauch, Mardik Martin
Ph Laszlo Kovacs   *Ed* Irving Lerner, Marcia Lucas
Mus Ralph Burns (sup.)   *Art Dir* Boris Leven
● Liza Minnelli, Robert De Niro, Barry Primus, Mary
Kay Place, Georgie Auld, George Memmoli
(United Artists)

Taking Liza Minnelli and Robert De Niro from their first meeting after VJ Day, film proceeds slowly and deliberately through their struggle to make it as a band singer and saxophonist and as a marriage in which her voice is early acclaimed while his music is ahead of its time. The two are making it pretty good unitl her pregnancy sidelines her.

Though still professing enduring love, the couple breaks up with the birth of the baby and the film lurches forward several years. Now she's a big film star, banging out the new numbers by John Kander and Fred Ebb, and the 1950s have brought his style into vogue and he's a big name, too, if not as big as she.

In a final burst from Old Hollywood, Minnelli tears into the title song and it's a wowser.

■ NEWSFRONT

1978, 110 MINS, AUSTRALIA ◇ ⓥ

Dir Phillip Noyce   *Prod* David Elfick   *Scr* Phillip
Noyce   *Ph* Vince Monton   *Ed* John Scott
Mus William Motzing   *Art Dir* Lissa Coote
● Bill Hunter, Gerard Kennedy, Angela Punch, Wendy
Hughes, Chris Hayward, John Ewart (Palm Beach)

Set in an historically turbulent period for Australia (1949-56), *Newsfront* deals with the lives of movie newsreel cameramen and uses the events in which they are involved as a sort of microcosmic view of how, in a very short period of time, the country underwent remarkable socio-political change.

The approach is interesting and the film benefits greatly from two central strengths: history and Bill Hunter (as Len Maguire). In his feature film debut, director Phillip Noyce demonstrates his ability to deal with actors, narrative, and choreograph background activity.

By clever merging of b&w newsreel footage and scenario-inspired monochromatic sequences, he moves his film into and out of actuality and fiction in such a way as often to blur the edges so well that it frequently takes a conscious effort to detect the blend-point.

This is especially true in one of his major set-pieces, re-creating the disastrous floods in the Maitland area in the early 1950s.

Plot concerns the rivalry between two competing newsreel companies: Len works for the plodding, traditionally-valued, Aussie-owned Cinetone, and ambitious brother Frank (Gerard Kennedy) has left them to run the go-ahead, pushy, Yank-owned Newsco.

Acting performances are all fine, particularly Angela Punch as the embittered wife, John Dease as the voice-over man, and Chris Hayward as the brash Britisher who gets a job as a camera assistant.

■ NEXT MAN, THE

1976, 108 MINS, US ◇ ⓥ

Dir Richard C. Sarafian   *Prod* Martin Bregman
Scr Mort Fine, Alan Trustman, David M. Wolf, Richard C.
Sarafian   *Ph* Michael Chapman   *Ed* Aram Avakian,
Robert Lovett   *Mus* Michael Kamen   *Art Dir* Gene
Callahan
● Sean Connery, Cornelia Sharpe, Albert Paulsen,
Adolfo Celi, Marco St John, Ted Beniades
(Artists Entertainment)

The Next Man emerges more a slick travesty with political overtones than the cynical suspense meller it was designed to be.

The project apparently grew out of an interesting proposition – a major oil-producing nation breaks with the Middle Eastern oil cartel to join forces with Israel to assure technological development and peace.

Pic is based on an original story by Alan Trustman and producer Martin Bregman. No less than four writers compiled the screenplay and it shows.

Briefly, Sean Connery plays a peace-mongering Saudi Arabian diplomat, dispatched to the UN to plead a case for Israel cooperation. For such arrant revisionism he is plagued by a network of Arab terrorists in whose employ is a beautiful, wealthy playgirl, friskily portrayed by Cornelia Sharpe.

■ NEXT OF KIN

1989, 108 MINS, US ◇ ⓥ

Dir John Irvin   *Prod* Les Alexander, Don Enright
Scr Michael Jenning   *Ph* Steven Poster   *Ed* Peter
Honess   *Mus* Jack Nitzsche   *Art Dir* Jack T. Collis
● Patrick Swayze, Liam Neeson, Adam Baldwin, Helen
Hunt, Andreas Katsulas (Lorimar/Warner)

Interesting wrinkle in Michael Jenning's screenplay, uncredited, (based on a script by Jenning and pic's associate producer, Jeb Stuart) is a mixing and matching of two ethnic strains of the vendetta: backwoods Appalachian version and revenge Sicilian-style.

These plot threads are set in motion when Bill Paxton, a Kentucky boy from the hills now working in Chicago, is ruthlessly murdered by mafia enforcer Adam Baldwin as part of a strong-arm move in the vending machines racket. Paxton's older brother, Patrick Swayze, is a Chicago cop determined to find the killer.

Inferfering with Swayze's efforts is the old-fashioned 'eye for an eye' vengeance demanded by eldest brother Liam Neeson. Picture climaxes with an elaborate war in a Chicago cemetery between Baldwin's mafioso and Neeson's Kentucky kin, matching automatic weaponry with primitive (but reliable) crossbows, hatchets, snakes and knives.

■ NEXT STOP, GREENWICH VILLAGE

1976, 111 MINS, US ◇ ⓥ

Dir Paul Mazursky   *Prod* Paul Mazursky   *Scr* Paul
Mazursky   *Ph* Arthur Ornitz   *Ed* Richard Halsey
Mus Bill Conti   *Art Dir* Phil Rosenberg
● Lenny Baker, Shelley Winters, Ellen Greene, Lois

N

Smith, Christopher Walken, Dori Brenner
(20th Century-Fox)

Next Stop, Greenwich Village is a very beautiful motion picture. Writer-director Paul Mazursky's gentle and touching film is a sort of young adult's *American Graffiti*.

An outstanding cast of New York players, plus Shelley Winters in one of the most superb characterizations of her career, gives the film a wonderful humanity and credibility.

Lenny Baker heads the cast in an excellent depiction of a young Brooklyn boy aiming for an acting career; quite naturally, pop Mike Kellin and mom Winters have their doubts – she being more than willing to articulate them. But Baker, like Don Quixote, sets forth on his quest.

Baker's new life centers around a group of arresting people: Ellen Greene, his girl; Christopher Walken, lothario-playwright; Dori Brenner, the type girl who hides her sensitivities in kookiness; Antonio Fargas, the gay equivalent of Brenner's character and so on.

In dark hair, Winters has managed to escape her near-formula mother role into new creative territory.

● ●

■ NIAGARA

1953, 89 MINS, US ◇ Ⓥ
Dir Henry Hathaway *Prod* Charles Brackett
Scr Charles Brackett, Walter Reisch, Richard Breen
Ph Joe MacDonald *Ed* Barbara McLean *Mus* Sol Kaplan *Art Dir* Lyle R. Wheeler, Maurice Ransford
● Marilyn Monroe, Joseph Cotten, Jean Peters, Casey Adams, Denis O'Dea, Richard Allan (20th Century-Fox)

Niagara is a morbid, clichéd expedition into lust and murder. The atmosphere throughout is strained and taxes the nerves with a feeling of impending disaster. Focal point of all this is Marilyn Monroe, who's vacationing at the Falls with hubby Joseph Cotten.

A Korean War vet, Cotten is emotionally disturbed and his eye-filling blonde wife deliberately goes out of her way to irritate him. She flaunts her physical charms upon mere strangers, taunts him with disparaging remarks and has a clandestine affair in progress with Richard Allan.

These incidents are noticed by Jean Peters and Casey Adams. A honeymooning couple, they're stopping at the same cabins, and it's only too obvious that they'll be involved in the events to come. First, a plot of Monroe and Allan to kill Cotten backfires when the latter shoves his attacker over the Falls. Cotten then hunts down Monroe and strangles her. Now, pure theatrics takes over.

The camera lingers on Monroe's sensuous lips, roves over her slip-clad figure and accurately etches the outlines of her derriere as she weaves down a street to a rendezvous with her lover. As a contrast to the beauty of the female form is another kind of nature's beauty – that of the Falls. The natural phenomena have been magnificently photographed on location.

● ●

■ NICE GIRL LIKE ME, A

1969, 90 MINS, UK ◇ Ⓥ
Dir Desmond Davis *Prod* Roy Millichip *Scr* Anne Piper, Desmond Davis *Ph* Gil Taylor, Manny Wynn
Ed Ralph Sheldon *Mus* Pat Williams *Art Dir* Ken Bridgeman
● Barbara Ferris, Harry Andrews, Gladys Cooper, Bill Hinnant, James Villiers, Fabia Drake (Partisan/Levine)

On the death of her father, Candida (Barbara Ferris) goes to live with two gorgon aunts and escapes them to go to Paris to study languages. Her first tutor is a young student who picks her up and, after a brief idyllic affair, she is pregnant. Back home she confides in Savage (Harry Andrews), a gruff, kindly man who was caretaker to her late father.

She kids her aunts that she is minding the babe for a friend and nips off to Venice to continue her linguistic 'studies'. There, a hip young American picks her up and, pronto, she's carrying a second child.

Screenplay is light and gently amusing but not too cynically flip or gooey and director Davis keeps the film on a non-serious, yet perceptive level.

Ferris is a pleasantly attractive combo of intelligent approach and charm, Andrews is dependable as ever.

● ●

■ NICHOLAS AND ALEXANDRA

1971, 185 MINS, UK ◇ Ⓥ
Dir Franklin J. Schaffner *Prod* Sam Spiegel
Scr James Goldman, Edward Bond *Ph* Freddie Young *Ed* Ernest Walter *Mus* Richard Rodney Bennett *Art Dir* John Box
● Michael Jayston, Janet Suzman, Harry Andrews, Irene Worth, Jack Hawkins, Laurence Olivier (Columbia)

Sam Spiegel comes up with a rarity: the intimate epic, in telling the fascinating story of the downfall of the Romanovs.

The tone is set from the opening sequences depicting the birth of the Russian Emperor and Empress' first boy and heir to the Romanov throne, followed closely by the tragic discovery that the child is haemophilic. Slowly, intrusively, the viewers get to know more about the dominant Alexandra and the frequently vacillating Nicholas, whom she influences in misguided political decisions.

Complicating factors, of course, are the growing unrest of the Russian people culminating in its confused revolution, the constant, distracting worry about the 'bleeding' Czarevitch and, most of all, the dominant influence on the Empress of Rasputin, without whose occult, hypnotic presence she feels the heir will die.

Scripter James Goldman (with an assist from Edward Bond) has provided literate, sparse dialog in fashioning a crystal-clear picture of a confused and confusing period. Certainly, as in the Robert K. Massie book, there's a feel here for tragically opposed worlds both heading blindly on a collision course towards the inevitable bloody clash.

Michael Jayston makes a most believable Nicholas, while Janet Suzman is also just right in the perhaps more difficult role of the Empress.
□ 1971: Best Picture (Nomination)

● ●

■ NICHOLAS NICKLEBY

1947, 108 MINS, UK Ⓥ
Dir Alberto Cavalcanti *Prod* Michael Balcon
Scr John Dighton *Ph* Gordon Dines *Ed* Leslie Norman *Mus* Lord Berners *Art Dir* Michael Relph
● Derek Bond, Cedric Hardwicke, Sally Ann Howes, Sybil Thorndike, Cyril Fletcher, Stanley Holloway (Ealing)

To make an entertaining film of this Dickens classic needed more courage than producer Michael Balcon shows. He should have thought first of the others who care little or nothing whether any particular character or episode is missing as long as the picture does no violence to the author and is entertaining.

The 52 characters of the original prove too much for the scriptwriter. Some minor characters have been left out, and Gride has become amalgamated with Ralph at the end, but the screenplay is more in the nature of a condensation into a series of scenes. And that's the way it appears on the screen.

Nicholas' adventures with the Crummies family has an old ham actor grandly played by Stanley Holloway. The stage scenes are amusing, but they do little to further the main story and, as an interlude, they slow up what action there might be. Scenes in Dothe-

boys Hall, which should have been among the most memorable, are slovenly, untidy and cramped. For some reason, Alfred Drayton, who otherwise gives a fine performance, makes Wackford Squeers a brutish Cockney thug. His forbiding consort, played by Sybil Thorndike, obviously comes from a slightly better family.

Casting any Dickens film is an unenviable chore and Balcon has made as good a job as most producers. Derek Bond brings manly grace to the title role, but betrays inexperience. Nor does Sally Ann Howes, sweet and simple as Kate, rise to her big occasion when her wicked uncle uses her as a decoy to attract his unmoral clients.

● ●

■ NICKELODEON

1976, 121 MINS, US ◇ Ⓥ
Dir Peter Bogdanovich *Prod* Irwin Winkler, Robert Chartoff *Scr* W.D. Richter, Peter Bogdanovich
Ph Laszlo Kovacs *Ed* William Carruth *Mus* Richard Hazard *Art Dir* Richard Berger
● Ryan O'Neal, Burt Reynolds, Tatum O'Neal, Brian Keith, Stella Stevens, John Ritter (Columbia)

Peter Bogdanovich's film is an okay comedy-drama about the early days of motion pictures. Story begins with a group of barnstorming filmmakers in the pre-feature film era, later segues to the adolescence of the industry.

Stars include Ryan O'Neal, struggling lawyer who literally stumbles into directing; Burt Reynolds, roustabout who becomes a leading man; Tatum O'Neal, enterprising California country girl who makes money renting things to the fledgling production units sent here to escape the goon squads of the Motion Picture Patents Co trust; Brian Keith, composite pioneer mogul; and Stella Stevens as an early leading lady.

The O'Neals, Reynolds, Keith and Stevens all engage interest, attention and affection.

● ●

■ NIGHT AND DAY

1946, 120 MINS, US ◇ Ⓥ
Dir Michael Curtiz *Prod* Arthur Schwartz *Scr* Charles Hoffman, Leo Townsend, William Bowers *Ph* Peverell Marley, William V. Skall *Ed* David Weisbart
Mus Cole Porter *Art Dir* John Hughes
● Cary Grant, Alexis Smith, Monty Woolley, Jane Wyman, Dorothy Malone (Warner)

Night and Day is a filmusical, based on the career of Cole Porter. It's to the credit of director Mike Curtiz and the combined scripters that they weighed the fruitful elements so intelligently, and kept it all down as much as they did. Wisely all steered clear of making this a blend of 'and then I wrote' and a Technicolored songplug unspooling.

Here's a guy to whom nothing more exciting happens than that he's born to millions and stays in a 'rut' for the rest of his career by making more money. The plot, per se, therefore is static on analysis but paradoxically it emerges into a surprisingly interesting unfolding. A real-life ambulance driver in World War I, Porter is shown with the French army. Alexis Smith plays the nurse whom he marries; she's previously introduced as of an aristocratic family. And thereafter, save for a fall off a spirited steed which caused Porter much real-life suffering because of broken legs which never set properly, the footage of *Night and Day* is a succession of hit shows and hit songs.

The tunes are chronologically mixed up a bit – a cinematic license with which none can be captious – and the romantic story line takes the accent principally in that Smith seeks to get her husband away from the mad show biz whirl of London and Broadway.

● ●

N

■ NIGHT AND THE CITY

1950, 96 MINS, US

Dir Jules Dassin   *Prod* Samuel G. Engel   *Scr* Jo
Eisinger   *Ph* Max Greene   *Ed* Nick De Maggio,
Sidney Stone   *Mus* Franz Waxman
● Richard Widmark, Gene Tierney, Googie Withers,
Hugh Marlowe, Francis L. Sullivan, Herbert Lom (20th
Century-Fox)

Night and the City is an exciting, suspenseful
melodrama, produced in London [from a
story by Gerald Kersh], which is the story of
a double-crossing heel who finally gets his
just desserts. In this role, Richard Widmark
scores a definite hit. And he has excellent
support right down the line. Gene Tierney
was cast for name value only.

Jules Dassin, in his direction, manages
extraordinarily interesting backgrounds, realistically filmed to create a feeling both of
suspense and mounting menace.

Widmark plays a London hustler willing to
do anything to be somebody. He finally sees
an opportunity in going into partnership with
the father of London's top wrestling promoter
– and setting up his own wrestling enterprise,
depending upon promoter's love for his father
to make a go of it. Idea backfires.

■ NIGHT AT THE OPERA, A

1935, 93 MINS, US Ⓥ

Dir Sam Wood   *Prod* Irving G. Thalberg   *Scr* George
S. Kaufman, Morrie Ryskind   *Ph* Merritt B. Gerstad
Ed William Levanway   *Mus* Herbert Stothart
Art Dir Cedric Gibbons, Ben Carre, Edwin B. Willis
● Groucho Marx, Harpo Marx, Chico Marx, Margaret
Dumont, Siegfried Rumann, Allan Jones (M-G-M)

Story [by James K. McGuinness] is a rather
serious grand opera satire in which the comics conspire to get a pair of Italian singers a
break over here. For their foils the Marxes
have Walter King and Siegfried Rumann as
heavies, Robert Emmett O'Connor as a pursuing flatfoot, and Margaret Dumont to absorb the regulation brand of Groucho insults.

Although King also doubles on the vocals,
Kitty Carlisle and Allan Jones do most of the
singing as the love interest.

Groucho and Chico in a contract-tearing
bit, the Marxes with O'Connor in a bed-
switching idea, and a chase finale in the
opera house are other dynamite comedy
sequences, along with a corking build-up by
Groucho while riding to his room on a trunk.
The backstage finish, with Harpo doing a
Tarzan on the fly ropes, contains more action
than the Marxes usually go in for, but it
relieves the strictly verbal comedy and provides a sock exit.

■ NIGHT CROSSING

1981, 106 MINS, UK ◇

Dir Delbert Mann   *Prod* Tom Loetch   *Scr* John
McGreevey   *Ph* Tony Imi   *Ed* Gordon D. Denner
Mus Jerry Goldsmith   *Art Dir* Rolf Zehetbauer
● John Hurt, Jean Alexander, Glynnis O'Connor, Beau
Bridges, Ian Bannen, Kay Walsh (Walt Disney)

There's plenty of drama hiding in this tale of
two families' daring escape from East to West
Germany by homemade hot-air balloon, but
this Disney production can't find much of it.
Unbelievable mix of actors from different
nations is forced to deliver one bad line after
another.

Story is a dramatic natural, as two construction workers, fed up with life behind the
Iron Curtain, conspire to fashion a giant balloon out of household fabric and pilot it over
the forbidding, heavily guarded half-mile
zone between the two Germanys. First
attempt doesn't quite make it but, despite
fact that the secret police begin sniffing their
trail, they try again, with suspenseful, successful results.

It all happened in 1978–79 and everything
about it would indicate the potential for a
grippingly serious family adventure pic. But
script so seriously stumbles in the exposition
stage that recovery is difficult even in the
close-call climax.

■ NIGHT HAS A THOUSAND EYES

1948, 80 MINS, US

Dir John Farrow   *Prod* Endre Bohem   *Scr* Barre
Lyndon, Jonathan Latimer   *Ph* John F. Seitz   *Ed* Eda
Warren   *Mus* Victor Young   *Art Dir* Hans Dreier,
Franz Bachelin
● Edward G. Robinson, Gail Russell, John Lund,
Virginia Bruce, William Demarest (Paramount)

Suspense is the dominating element in this
thriller which follows a man who can foresee
the future. Told in flashback form, story
starts with Gail Russell about to commit
suicide by jumping from a trestle onto a track
in front of onrushing train, in terror after having been told by Edward G. Robinson, the
diviner, that she will meet a violent death
within a few days.

Events in natural order then are narrated
by Robinson, from time he learned he was
gifted – or damned – with his inner sight to
opening events, and occurrences that follow
leading up to strong climax.

John Farrow's sure directorial hand is seen
throughout unfolding of picture, scripted
melodramatically by Barre Lyndon and
Jonathan Latimer [from a novel by Cornell
Woolrich].

■ NIGHT IN CASABLANCA, A

1946, 85 MINS, US Ⓥ

Dir Archie Mayo   *Prod* David L. Loew   *Scr* Joseph
Fields, Roland Kibbee   *Ph* James Van Trees   *Ed* Gregg
C. Tallas   *Mus* Werner Janssen   *Prod Des* Duncan
Cramer
● Groucho Marx, Harpo Marx, Chico Marx, Lisette
Verea, Charles Drake (United Artists)

This isn't the best the Marx Bros have made
but it's a pretty funny farce.

Postwar Nazi intrigue in Casablanca is the
theme, having to do with the handsome
French flyer who is under a cloud because of
Nazi skullduggery dealing with European
loot cached in the Hotel Casablanca. When
three of the hotel's managers get bumped off
in rapid succession, Groucho gets the nod.
Chico runs the Yellow Camel Co. and Harpo
is his mute pal who later breaks the bank in
the hotel's casino and stumbles on the Nazi
gold through a mishap with the lift.

Against the desert background of French
provincial political bungling and Nazi chicanery the Marxes get off some effective
comedy, and some of it not so. The brighter
spots are the clown fencing duel; the frustrated tryst between Groucho and Lisette
Verea, running from suite to suite, with portable phonograph, champagne cooler, etc;
the sequence with the packing cases and
clothes closet, prior to the getaway; and
finally the air-autotruck chase, winding up
back in the same jail from whence all
escaped.

■ NIGHT MOVES

1975, 99 MINS, US ◇

Dir Arthur Penn   *Prod* Robert M. Sherman   *Scr* Alan
Sharp   *Ph* Bruce Surtees   *Ed* Dede Allen, Stephen A.
Rotter   *Mus* Michael Small   *Art Dir* George Jenkins
● Gene Hackman, Jennifer Warren, Edward Binns,
Harris Yulin, Susan Clark, James Woods (Warner)

Night Moves is a paradox: a suspenseless suspenser, very well cast with players who lend
sustained interest to largely synthetic theatrical characters.

Minor LA detective Hackman, hired by
faded actress Janet Ward to find runaway

teenage daughter Melanie Griffith, becomes
enmeshed in the Florida smuggling operations of John Crawford (Griffith's stepfather), whose classy mistress Jennifer
Warren indirectly helps Hackman's own reconciliation with wife Clark, herself dallying
out of loneliness with Harris Yulin. Stuntmen
Edward Binns and Anthony Costello, and
mechanic Woods, provide a link between the
Hollywood and Florida environments.

Far more meritorious than the play are the
players. Hackman works well with everyone.

■ NIGHT MUST FALL

1964, 99 MINS, UK

Dir Karel Reisz   *Prod* Karel Reisz, Albert Finney
Scr Clive Exton   *Ph* Freddie Francis   *Ed* Philip
Barnikel   *Mus* Ron Grainer   *Prod Des* Timothy O'Brien
● Albert Finney, Susan Hampshire, Mona
Washbourne, Sheila Hancock, Michael Medwin
(M-G-M)

Artfully composed and strikingly photographed, this British-manufactured reproduction of Metro's 1937 shock-suspense
thriller lacks the restraint, clarity and subtlety of its forerunner but makes up, to some
degree, in cinematic flamboyance what it
lacks in dramatic tidiness and conviction.

Albert Finney's performance as the cunning madman is vivid and explosive, and it
might not be too far from wrong to suppose
that the entire project may have germinated
out of his desire to tackle the character.

Vagueness in key dramatic junctures hampers the new version, constructed around the
skeleton of Emlyn Williams' stage play.

That story lapses and irregularities seem
less than drastic is a tribute to the dazzling
execution and a batch of tangy performances.
Finney, in the role first played so well by
Robert Montgomery, is fascinating to watch
as his dispositions shift with maniacal rootlessness. It's an inventive, stimulating portrayal by a gifted actor. Yet Finney's thespic
thunder is often stolen by Mona Washbourne's masterful delineation of the lonely
'invalid' who becomes his victim.

■ NIGHT OF THE FOLLOWING DAY, THE

1969, 93 MINS, UK ◇

Dir Hubert Cornfield   *Prod* Hubert Cornfield
Scr Hubert Cornfield, Robert Phippeny   *Ph* Willi
Kurout   *Ed* Gordon Pilkington   *Mus* Stanley Myers
Art Dir Jean Boulet
● Marlon Brando, Richard Boone, Rita Moreno,
Pamela Franklin, Jess Hahn (Universal/Gina)

The Night of the Following Day begins as an
intriguing, offbeat kidnap drama, but soon
shifts emphasis to delineating the freaked-out
characters of its principals, and ends abruptly on a cop-out note.

Lionel White's book, *The Snatchers*, has been
adapted into a rambling stew of deliberate
and accidental black comedy and melodrama. Pamela Franklin is the prop focal
character, a young woman kidnapped for
ransom by Marlon Brando, Richard Boone,
Rita Moreno and Jess Hahn.

A lot of effective and moody camerawork by
Willi Kurout, combined with the good promise of the first reel and Brando's excellent
physical appearance and dynamism, wash
out as each character loses sympathy and interest. Even Franklin, ostensibly the victim of
the piece, is forgotten for long periods.

■ NIGHT OF THE GENERALS

1967, 148 MINS, UK/FRANCE ◇ Ⓥ

Dir Anatole Litvak   *Prod* Sam Spiegel   *Scr* Joseph
Kessel, Paul Dehn   *Ph* Henri Decae   *Ed* Alan
Osbiston   *Mus* Maurice Jarre   *Art Dir* Alexandre
Trauner

● Peter O'Toole, Omar Sharif, Tom Courtenay, Donald Pleasance, Charles Gray, Joanna Pettet (Columbia/Horizon/Filmsonor)

With an important theme about the nature of guilt and the promise of a teasing battle of wits, this is an interesting feature that lets the tension run slack, being afflicted with galloping inflation of its running-time.

Plot opens in Nazi-occupied Warsaw in 1942, with a prostie being brutally murdered and the killer being recognized as wearing the uniform of a German general. But that's the only clue for Major Grau (Omar Sharif), the Military Intelligence man in charge of the hunt, and he establishes that only three brasshats could have committed the crime, having insufficient alibis.

One is Tanz (Peter O'Toole), a ruthless and devoted Nazi who destroys a quarter of Warsaw as an exercise in discipline. Another is Kahlenberge (Donald Pleasance), a cynical opportunist who has few scruples, but plenty ingenuity. And the third suspect is the pompous Galber (Charles Gray).

Adapted from Hans Helmut Kirst's bitter novel, the story is told in flashback and the technique adds to the somewhat languid effect. But the chief factor militating against conviction is the central performance by O'Toole, which lacks the firm savagery Tanz seems to require.

....

■ NIGHT OF THE HUNTER, THE

1955, 93 MINS, US Ⓥ

Dir Charles Laughton Prod Paul Gregory Scr James Agee Ph Stanley Cortez Ed Robert Golden Mus Walter Schumann
● Robert Mitchum, Shelley Winters, Lillian Gish, Billy Chapin, Peter Graves, James Gleason (Gregory/United Artists)

The relentless terror of Davis Grubb's novel got away from Paul Gregory and Charles Laughton in their translation of Night of the Hunter. This start for Gregory as producer and Laughton as director is rich in promise but the completed product, bewitching at times, loses sustained drive via too many off-beat touches that have a misty effect.

Straight story telling without the embellishments, it would seem, might have rammed home with frightening force the horror of this man's diabolical quest of a hanged murderer's $10,000 which he wants to use in serving his fancied Lord. It builds fine with suspense ingredients to a fitting climax.

Robert Mitchum intermittently shows some depth in his interpretation of the preacher but in instances where he's crazed with lust for the money, there's barely adequate conviction.

....

■ NIGHT OF THE IGUANA

1964, 117 MINS, US Ⓥ

Dir John Huston Prod Ray Stark Scr Anthony Veiller, John Huston Ph Gabriel Figueroa Ed Ralph Kemplen Mus Benjamin Frankel Art Dir Stephen Grimes
● Richard Burton, Ava Gardner, Deborah Kerr, Sue Lyon, James Ward, Grayson Hall (Seven Arts/M-G-M)

This Ray Stark production, is rich in talents. Performances by Richard Burton, Ava Gardner and Deborah Kerr are superlative in demanding roles. Direction by John Huston is resourceful and dynamic as he sympathetically weaves together the often-vague and philosophical threads that mark Tennessee Williams' writing.

Unfoldment takes place mainly in a ramshackle Mexican seacoast hotel where Burton, an unfrocked minister and now guide of a cheap bus tour, takes refuge from his latest flock, a group of complaining American schoolteachers who refuse to believe he actually is a preacher who lost his church. Frank-

ness in dealing with his emotional problems as first he is pursued by a young sexpot in the party, then his involvement with the aggressive, man-hungry hotel owner and a sensitive, itinerant artist travelling with her 97-year-old grandfather, produces compassionate undertones finely realized in situations evoking particular interest.

Burton has stature in the difficult portrayal of the Reverend T. Lawrence Shannon, a part without glamour yet touched with magical significant force as he progresses to the point of a near-mental crackup. Gardner, in the earthy role of Maxine Faulk, the proprietress, is a gutsy figure as she makes her play for the depraved ex-minister, turning in a colorful delineation. Kerr lends warm conviction as the spinster who lives by idealism and her selling of quick sketches, a helpless creature yet endowed with certain innate strength.

....

■ NIGHT OF THE JUGGLER

1980, 100 MINS, US ◇ Ⓥ

Dir Robert Butler Prod Jay Weston Scr Bill Norton Sr, Rick Natkin Ph Victor J. Kemper Ed Argyle Nelson Mus Artie Kane Art Dir Stuart Wurtzel
● James Brolin, Cliff Gorman, Richard Castellano, Abby Bluestone, Dan Hedaya, Julie Carmen (Columbia)

Night Of The Juggler is a relentlessly preposterous picture which never gives its cast a chance to overcome director Robert Butler's passion for mindless action.

This is supposed to be the story [from a novel by William P. McGivern] of James Brolin's frantic pursuit of a kidnapper who grabs his daughter and takes off with her in a car.

But who cares if the performers are never allowed to make the characters come true?

As a frustrated, racist psychotic seeking revenge for the deterioration of his Bronx neighborhood, Cliff Gorman is trapped by the script's needs for him to be so loony you might actually believe in him.

Technically each individual shot was approached with intense concentration on the craft of filmmaking. Which is exactly what's wrong with the picture.

....

■ NIGHT OF THE LIVING DEAD

1968, 90 MINS, US Ⓥ

Dir George A. Romero Prod Russell Streiner, Karl Hardman Scr John A. Russo Ph George A. Romero
● Judith O'Dea, Russell Streiner, Duane Jones, Karl Hardman, Keith Wayne (Image Ten)

Although pic's basic premise is repellent – recently dead bodies are resurrected and begin killing human beings in order to eat their flesh – it is in execution that the film distastefully excels.

No brutalizing stone is left unturned: crowbars gash holes in the heads of the living dead, monsters are shown eating entrails, and – in a climax of unparalleled nausea – a little girl kills her mother by stabbing her a dozen times in the chest with a trowel.

The rest of the pic is amateurism of the first order. Pittsburgh-based director George A. Romero appears incapable of contriving a single graceful set-up, and his cast is uniformly poor.

Both Judith O'Dea and Duane Jones are sufficiently talented to warrant supporting roles in a backwoods community theatre, but Russell Streiner, Karl Hardman, Keith Wayne and Judith Ridley do not suggest that Pittsburgh is a haven for undiscovered thespians.

John A. Russo's screenplay is a model of verbal banality and suggests a total antipathy for his characters.

....

■ NIGHT OF THE LIVING DEAD

1990, 89 MINS, US ◇ Ⓥ

Dir Tom Savani Prod John A. Russo, Russ Steiner Scr George A. Romero Ph Frank Prinzi Ed Tom Dubensky Mus Paul McCollough Art Dir James Feng
● Tony Wood, Patricia Tallman, Tom Towles, McKee Anderson, William Butler, Katie Finnerman (21st Century)

The original producers of Night of the Living Dead have remade their own cult classic in a crass bit of cinematic grave-robbing. The only legitimate reason to remake the 1968 film would have been to improve its effects and sub-$200,000 budget, although the dimly shot black-&-white images were far creepier than any of its color progeny.

The story faithfully follows the original except for the bonehead decision to replace the ending with a 'meaningful' twist that reeks of pretentiousness.

The plot still involves seven people trapped in a farmhouse fending off hordes of walking corpses intent on devouring them. Never explained is what animated the bodies in the first place, although a solid bash to the brain deanimates them.

The hero still is Ben (Tony Wood), and the bad guy still is a middle-aged businessman named Harry (Tom Towles) who holes up in the basement with his wife and daughter. The one beefed-up role is that of the female lead (Patricia Tallman), who reveals a Rambo-esque bent.

....

■ NIGHT PASSAGE

1957, 90 MINS, US ◇

Dir James Neilson Prod Aaron Rosenberg Scr Borden Chase Ph William Daniels Ed Sherman Todd Mus Dimitri Tiomkin Art Dir Alexander Golitzen, Robert Clatworthy
● James Stewart, Audie Murphy, Dan Duryea, Dianne Foster, Elaine Stewart, Brandon deWilde (Universal)

This taut, well-made and sometimes fascinating western is the first use of Technicolor's new widescreen, anamorphic process, Technirama. Borden Chase has fashioned a script around two brothers – James Stewart, decent, upright; Audie Murphy, wild, a deadly gunman. The Technirama process gives new depth and definition, said to combine the principles of both VistaVision and CinemaScope. Pic was lensed in the Durango-Silverton region of Colorado.

Plot carries a railroad-building backdrop. Stewart is a former railroad employee recalled to help transport the payroll to rail's-end, previous attempts to take the money through to rebelling workers having been stymied when outlaw gang conducts series of raids. He becomes involved with gang during a train holdup.

Both stars deliver sound portrayals, Murphy making up in color Stewart's greater footage. Dan Duryea is immense as outlaw chief who isn't quite certain whether he can outdraw Murphy, a wizard with a gun.

....

■ NIGHT PORTER, THE

1974, 115 MINS, US/ITALY ◇ Ⓥ

Dir Liliana Cavani Prod Robert Gordon Edwards, Esae De Simone Scr Liliana Cavani, Italo Moscati Ph Alfio Contin Ed Franco Arcalli Mus Daniele Paris
● Dirk Bogarde, Charlotte Rampling, Philippe Leroy, Gabriele Ferzetti, Isa Miranda, Amedeo Amadio (United Artists)

Liliana Cavani deals with the ambivalent relationship between a concentration camp victim (Charlotte Rampling) and her torturer-lover (Dirk Bogarde) in a strange, brooding tale. There is a touch of Last Tango in Paris in this love affair that does not take society or other people into much account.

It has an apartment, albeit furnished and the couple trapped there, serving for their trysts in Vienna of 1957. They meet accidentally, but the past and a group of still ardent Nazis force them to revert to their camp relationship.

Bogarde is an ex-Storm Trooper who now works as a night porter. He belongs to a group who have managed to be acquitted by doing away with witnesses and destroying evidence.

It's a gritty look at concentration camp quirks, but transposed to a strange drama. Bogarde treads intelligently through his role of an unbalanced man.

••••••••••••••••••••••••••••

■ NIGHT SHIFT

1982, 105 MINS, US ◇ ⓥ

Dir Ron Howard   *Prod* Brian Grazer   *Scr* Lowell Ganz, Babaloo Mandel   *Ph* James Crabe   *Ed* Robert J. Kern, Daniel P. Hanley, Mike Hill   *Mus* Burt Bacharach   *Art Dir* Jack Collis

● Henry Winkler, Michael Keaton, Shelley Long, Gina Hecht, Pat Corley, Bobby DiCicco (Ladd)

Nerdy Henry Winkler is a meek attendant at the city morgue who is the kind of person who'd rather eat a plate of poisonous mushrooms than offend the chef who served them. His life is a mess. To compound matters, he must work the night shift with Looney Tune Michael Keaton – the type of guy who talks non-stop as he blasts rock songs on the radio while dancing up and down the aisles.

At the same time, Winkler befriends Shelley Long, the perennial 'nice girl hooker' who just happens to live next door and happens to have just lost her pimp. It's not long before Winkler and Keaton devise a scheme to act as pimps for Long using the morgue as a base of operation.

Though the plot line hardly sounds like a family film, this is probably the most sanitized treatment of pimps and prostitution audiences will ever see.

None of this much matters, because director Ron Howard and screenwriters Lowell Ganz and Babaloo Mandel, all TV veterans, are only bent on giving the audience a good time.

••••••••••••••••••••••••••••

■ NIGHT THE PROWLER, THE

1978, 90 MINS, AUSTRALIA ◇

Dir Jim Sharman   *Prod* Anthony Buckley   *Scr* Patrick White   *Ph* David Sanderson   *Mus* Cameron Alan

● Ruth Cracknell, John Frawley, Kerry Walker, John Derum, Maggie Kirkpatrick, Terry Camilleri (Chariot)

A hodge-podge of flash forwards, flashbacks, and even some flash sideways, *The Night the Prowler* tells the story, as one pundit put it, of a female slob's search for self-identification.

A young woman (Kerry Walker) moves into adulthood as an overweight, sullen, neurotic and ill-mannered daughter of a couple of middleclass stereotypes. The mother is attractive and dimwitted; the father is dull.

With flashbacks to the various stages of her youth, including the usual father fixation and an engagement to a rather boring young diplomat with a promising future, she fakes (or misinterprets) a visit from a prowler – in her version, with rape in mind.

This event, of course, lessens her chances at a marriage which she wasn't too eager about anyhow and she goes through a series of increasingly demoralizing changes, finally emerging as a leather-clad night prowler on her own.

••••••••••••••••••••••••••••

■ NIGHT TIDE

1961, 85 MINS, US ⓥ

Dir Curtis Harrington   *Prod* Aram Kantarian   *Scr* Curtis Harrington   *Ph* Vilis Lapenieks   *Ed* Jodie Copelan   *Mus* David Raksin   *Art Dir* Paul Mathison

● Dennis Hopper, Linda Lawson, Gavin Muir, Luana Anders (American International/Filmgroup-Virgo

Curtis Harrington, onetime avant-garde filmmaker and assistant to Jerry Wald, made this first feature on an indie basis. Film mixes a love affair with the supernatural. If Harrington displays a good flair for narration and mounting, his feel for mood, suspense and atmospherics is not too highly developed.

A sailor on leave meets a girl who works as a mermaid in a side show on the amusement pier in Venice, California. It develops into love but there is a strangeness in her comportment. Her guardian tells the sailor that he had found her on a Greek island and brought her to the US and that she is really a mermaid. It also develops that two men she had been with were found drowned. The sailor is bewildered but when she almost kills him during skin diving he manages to escape while she disappears.

Dennis Hopper is acceptably bewildered by his plight while Linda Lawson has the exotic looks for the psychotic siren.

••••••••••••••••••••••••••••

■ NIGHT TO REMEMBER, A

1958, 123 MINS, UK ⓥ

Dir Roy Ward Baker   *Prod* William MacQuitty   *Scr* Eric Ambler   *Ph* Geoffrey Unsworth   *Ed* Sidney Hayers   *Mus* William Alwyn   *Art Dir* Alex Vetchinsky

● Kenneth More, Honor Blackman, Anthony Bushell, Laurence Naismith, Kenneth Griffith, David McCallum (Rank)

Producer and director have done an honest job in putting the tragic sinking of the *Titanic* in 1912 on the screen with an impressive, almost documentary flavor. With around 200 speaking roles in the pic, few of the actors are given much chance to develop as characters. Even Kenneth More, in the star role, is only part of a team. The ship itself is the star.

The story tells how the 'unsinkable' new ship set out for the US on the night of 14 April 1912, how it struck an iceberg and sank in less than three hours with 1,302 people drowned and only 705 survivors. The film takes only 37 minutes less than the time of the actual disaster.

The errors and confusion which played a part in the drama are brought out with no whitewashing. Although many of the passengers and crew come vividly to life, there is no attempt to hang a fictional story on any of them. Technically, director Roy Baker does a superb job in difficult circumstances. His direction of some of the panic scenes during the manning of the lifeboats – of which there were not nearly enough to accommodate all on board – is masterly. Eric Ambler's screenplay [from Walter Lord's book], without skimping the nautical side of the job, brings out how some people kept their heads and others became cowards.

Others who manage to make impact are Laurence Naismith as the skipper; Anthony Bushell, captain of the rescue ship; Kenneth Griffith and David McCallum, as a couple of radio operators; Tucker McGuire, as a hearty American woman; George Rose, as a bibulous ship's baker; Michael Goodliffe, as the designer of the ship; and Frank Lawton, as the chairman of the White Star Line.

••••••••••••••••••••••••••••

■ NIGHT TRAIN TO MUNICH

1940, 95 MINS, UK

Dir Carol Reed   *Prod* Edward Black   *Scr* Sidney Gilliat, Frank Launder   *Ph* Otto Kanturek   *Ed* R.E. Dearing, Michael Gordon   *Mus* Louis Levy   *Art Dir* Vetchinsky

● Margaret Lockwood, Rex Harrison, Paul Henreid, Basil Radford, Naunton Wayne, Felix Aylmer (Gaumont-British)

Made by the same British studio that turned out *Lady Vanishes*, the film also has the same general subject matter, the same screenplay

writers, Margaret Lockwood in the femme lead, and even makes similar use of Basil Radford and Naunton Wayne as two tourist Englishmen with a ludicrous interest in cricket.

Much of the film's merit obviously stems from the compact, propulsive screenplay by Sydney Gilliat and Frank Launder, and the razor-edge direction of Carol Reed. Story by Gordon Wellesley opens in the tense days of August 1939 with a Nazi espionage agent in London recapturing two Czechs who have escaped from a concentration camp, an aged armor-plate inventor and his pretty daughter. A British Secret Service operative follows them to Berlin and, after an exciting sequence of events during which war is declared, escapes with them into Switzerland.

Yarn is not only told without a single letdown, but it actually continues to pile up suspense to a nerve-clutching pitch. The headlong chase and escape at the end is a time-tested melodramatic device superbly handled.

Carol Reed's direction is worthy of the best thrillers of Edgar Wallace, for whom he was for many years stage manager. Lockwood is an appealing heroine and her performance is direct and persuasive. Rex Harrison is properly suave as the ubiquitous British operative, while Paul Henreid is rightly cold as the treacherous Gestapo agent. Radford and Wayne repeat their goofy Britisher performances of *Lady Vanishes* and again click. There are countless touches of atmosphere and comedy that add immeasurable flavor and zest to the picture.

••••••••••••••••••••••••••••

■ NIGHT WARNING

1983, 94 MINS, US ◇ ⓥ

Dir William Asher   *Prod* Stephen Breimer, Eugene Mazzola   *Scr* Stephen Breimer, Alan Jay Glueckman, Boon Collins   *Ph* Robbie Greenberg   *Ed* Ted Nicolaou   *Mus* Bruce Langhorne

● Jimmy McNichol, Susan Tyrrell, Bo Svenson, Marcia Lewis, Julia Duffy, Britt Leach (S2D Associates/Royal American)

Night Warning is a fine psychological horror film. As the maniacally possessive aunt and guardian of a 17-year-old boy, Susan Tyrrell gives a tour-de-force performance.

Billy (Jimmy McNichol) is a basketball player at high school who has been brought up by his aunt Cheryl (Tyrrell) after his parents died in a car crash (great stunt footage) 14 years ago. An old maid, Cheryl is over-protective, opposing Billy's desire to go to college in Denver on a hoped-for athletic scholarship to be with his girlfriend.

Cheryl maintains a candlelit memorial to an old boyfriend in the basement. The film's horror content begins (replete with slow-motion violence and plenty of blood) when she kills a young TV repairman after failing to seduce him. Cop on the case Detective Carlson (Bo Svenson). is very closed-minded, ignoring the facts and insisting on linking the crime to a homosexual basketball coach, making Billy the prime suspect instead of his aunt.

••••••••••••••••••••••••••••

■ NIGHTBREED

1990, 99 MINS, US ◇ ⓥ

Dir Clive Barker   *Prod* Gabriella Martinelli   *Scr* Clive Barker   *Ph* Robin Vidgeon   *Ed* Richard Marden, Mark Goldblatt   *Mus* Danny Elfman   *Art Dir* Steve Hardie

● Craig Sheffer, Anne Bobby, David Cronenberg, Charles Haid, Hugh Ross (Morgan Creek)

Writer-director Clive Barker's *Nightbreed* is a mess. Self-indulgent horror pic [from his novel *Cabal*] could be the *Heavens Gate* of its genre, of obvious interest to diehard monster fans but a turnoff for mainstream audiences.

N

Barker's inverted story premise is not explained until halfway through the picture: the last survivors of shapeshifters (legendary monsters including vampires and werewolves) are huddled below ground in a tiny Canadian cemetery near Calgary called Midian, trying to avoid final extinction.

Hero Craig Sheffer is plagued by nightmares and heads there in hopes of becoming a monster, while his nutty shrink (David Cronenberg) is on a messianic mission to destroy the undead critters. Sheffer's normal girlfriend (Anne Bobby) tags along.

Pic presents unrelated sequences of gore and slashing until the ridiculously overproduced finale.

Chief casting gimmick is giving the lead baddie role to revered Canadian director Cronenberg. Horror cultists might enjoy his soft-spoken, monotone performance and in-jokes, but others will merely wonder why a professional actor was cheated out of a salary.

● ●

■ NIGHTCOMERS, THE

1972, 96 MINS, UK ◇ Ⓥ

Dir Michael Winner   *Prod* Michael Winner
Scr Michael Hastings   *Ph* Robert Paynter
Ed Frederick Wilson   *Mus* Jerry Fielding
● Marlon Brando, Stephanie Beacham, Thora Hird, Verna Harvey, Christopher Ellis, Harry Andrews (Scimitar)

The Nightcomers is one of those atmosphere-drenched thrillers in which a semblance of surface decorum and respectability hides a multitude of aberrations beneath. This one, penned by Michael Hastings and inspired by the characters in Henry James' *The Turn of the Screw*, has a hand-tailored starring appearance by Marlon Brando.

Two recently-orphaned children live alone on a British country estate with their nurse, a housekeeper and a gardener, Quint. It's the last-named (played by Brando) who fascinates the boy and girl to such a degree that his instinctive actions, mysterious manners, home-spun philosophising becomes their (only) guide and lifeline.

His sado-carnal affair with the otherwise prim and bourgeois nurse, glimpsed in fleshly violent action by the fascinated boy, is similarly aped by youngsters, as are other aspects of couple's love-hate relationship which, in their unknowing innocence, they adopt and idealize. When the housekeeper decides to fire both nurse and gardener, the children plot to keep them together – forever – by killing them both.

● ●

■ NIGHTHAWKS

1981, 99 MINS, US ◇

Dir Bruce Malmuth   *Prod* Martin Poll   *Scr* David Shaber   *Ph* James A. Contner   *Ed* Christopher Holmes   *Mus* Keith Emerson   *Art Dir* Peter Larkin
● Sylvester Stallone, Billy Dee Williams, Rutger Hauer, Lyndsay Wagner (Universal)

'*Nighthawks*' is an exciting cops and killers yarn with Sylvester Stallone to root for and cold-blooded Rutger Hauer to hate.

Off and running right from the beginning, director Bruce Malmuth presents a vulnerable woman on a dark NY street about to be mugged. Suddenly the guys with the knives discover the woman is Stallone, on decoy duty and backed up by partner Billy Dee Williams.

While Stallone is doing his best to rid Gotham's streets of riff-raff, Hauer is introduced in London as one of the most wanted and most murderous terrorists in the world, a crafty, intelligent killer who has fully rationalized his cause to justify blowing up department stores full of innocent victims, including children. This is an American film debut for Holland's top actor and he plays the part expertly, matching Stallone scene for scene.

Hauer comes to NY accompanied by equally evil Persis Khambatta and pursued by Nigel Davenport, a terrorist expert from Interpol who recruits the assistance of Stallone and Williams.

Though there's never much doubt how the duel will end, the climax is nonetheless surprising and totally satisfying, topping the energy of the previous pursuit.

● ●

■ NIGHTMARE

1964, 83 MINS, UK

Dir Freddie Francis   *Prod* Jimmy Sangster   *Scr* Jimmy Sangster   *Ph* John Wilcox   *Ed* James Needs
Mus Don Banks   *Art Dir* Bernard Robinson, Don Mingaye
● David Knight, Moira Redmond, Brenda Bruce, Jennie Linden (Hammer)

Best features of this highly contrived chiller is the direction and lensing (by Freddie Francis and John Wilcox respectively) of the atmosphere of a house where eerie things happen in this way of shadows, significant noises and the fleeting appearances of a phantom-like woman in white.

Jennie Linden's mother was committed to an asylum when the child was 14, after stabbing her husband. This preys on the child's mind and she is convinced that she may have inherited a streak of madness. She certainly is the victim of bad dreams.

She is taken from school to her home where she is apparently safely guarded by the attention of an adoring housekeeper (Irene Richmond), her school mistress (Brenda Bruce), her young guardian (David Knight) and a nurse (Moira Redmond), posing as a companion. But Knight and Redmond are clandestine lovers. Their attempts to prey on the mind of the girl are elaborately worked out and, though highly incredible, serve as a workmanlike plot for such a modest thriller.

● ●

■ NIGHTMARE ALLEY

1947, 110 MINS, US

Dir Edmund Goulding   *Prod* George Jessel   *Scr* Jules Furthman   *Ph* Lee Garmes   *Ed* Barbara McLean   *Mus* Cyril J. Mockridge   *Art Dir* R. Wheeler, J. Russell Spencer
● Tyrone Power, Joan Blondell, Coleen Gray, Helen Walker, Ian Keith, Mike Mazurki (20th Century-Fox)

Nightmare Alley is a harsh, brutal story [based on the novel by William Lindsay Gresham] told with the sharp clarity of an etching.

The film deals with the roughest phases of carnival life and showmanship. Tyrone Power is Stan Carlisle, reform school graduate, who works his way from carney roustabout to bigtime mentalist and finally to important swindling in the spook racket. Ruthless and unscrupulous, he uses the women in his life to further his advancement, stepping on them as he climbs.

Most vivid of these is Joan Blondell as the girl he works for the secrets of the mind-reading act. Coleen Gray is sympathetic and convincing as his steadfast wife and partner in his act and Helen Walker comes through successfully as the calculating femme who topples Power from the heights of fortune back to degradation as the geek in the carney. Ian Keith is outstanding as Blondell's drunken husband.

● ●

■ NIGHTMARE ON ELM STREET, A

1984, 91 MINS, US ◇ Ⓥ

Dir Wes Craven   *Prod* Robert Shaye   *Scr* Wes Craven   *Ph* Jacques Haitkin   *Ed* Rick Shaine   *Mus* Charles Bernstein   *Art Dir* Greg Fonseca
● John Saxon, Ronee Blakely, Heather Langenkamp, Amanda Wyss, Johnny Depp, Robert Englund (New Line/Media Home/Smart Egg)

A Nightmare on Elm Street is a highly imaginative horror film that provides the requisite shocks to keep fans of the genre happy.

Young teenagers in a Los Angeles neighborhood are sharing common nightmares about being chased and killed by a disfigured bum in a slouch hat who has knives for fingernails. It turns out that years ago, the neighborhood's parents took deadly vigilante action against a child murderer, who apparently is vengefully haunting their kids.

With original special effects, the nightmares are merging into reality, as teens are killed under inexplicable circumstances.

Writer-director Wes Craven tantalizingly merges dreams with the ensuing wakeup reality but fails to tie up his thematic threads satisfyingly at the conclusion.

● ●

■ NIGHTMARE ON ELM STREET 4, A THE DREAM MASTER

1988, 93 MINS, US ◇ Ⓥ

Dir Renny Harlin   *Prod* Robert Shaye, Rachel Talalay   *Scr* Brian Helgeland, Scott Pierce   *Ph* Steven Fierberg   *Ed* Michael N. Knue, Chuck Weiss   *Mus* Craig Safan   *Art Dir* Mick Strawn, C.J. Strawn
● Robert Englund, Lisa Wilcox, Rodney Eastman, Danny Hassal, Andras Jones (New Line/Heron/Smart Egg/Shaye)

Imaginative special effects highlight the fourth entry in the series. As before, Freddy's out for revenge on the kids of Elm Street for their parents' having murdered him after he killed several children in the first place. Freddy's conjured up in the kids' nightmares and a clever plot has him rapidly (and unexpectedly) dispensing with the surviving kids, only to extend his mayhem to their friends, starting with Alice (Lisa Wilcox).

Wilcox in the lead role gives a solid performance ranging from vulnerable to resourceful, as she gains strength from her departed friends to do battle with Freddy.

Robert Englund, receiving star billing for the first time, is delightful in his frequent incarnations as Freddy, delivering his gag lines with relish and making the grisly proceedings funny.

● ●

■ NIGHTMARE ON ELM STREET, PART 2, A FREDDY'S REVENGE

1985, 84 MINS, US ◇ Ⓥ

Dir Jack Sholder   *Prod* Robert Shaye, Sara Risher   *Scr* David Chaskin   *Ph* Jacques Haitkin   *Ed* Arline Garson, Bob Brady   *Mus* Christopher Young
● Mark Patton, Kim Myers, Robert Rusler, Clu Gulager, Hope Lange, Robert Englund (New Line/Heron/Smart Egg)

Beneath its verbose, title, Jack Sholder's follow-up to Wes Craven's 1984 hit is a well-made though familiar reworking of demonic horror material.

Screenplay basically makes a sex change on Craven's original: a teenage boy Jesse Walsh (Mark Patton) is experiencing the traumatic nightmares previously suffered by a young girl, Nancy Thompson. Walsh's family has moved into Thompson's house, five years after the events outlined in the first film.

The slouch-hatted, long, steel fingernails-affixed, disfigured monster Freddy (Robert Englund) is attempting to possess Walsh's body in order to kill the local kids once more and, judging from the film's body count, is quite successful.

Episodic treatment is punched up by an imaginative series of special effects. The standout is a grisly chest-burster setpiece.

Mark Patton carries the show in the central role as not quite a nerd, but strange enough to constitute an outsider presence. Kim Myers scores as his sympathetic girl friend, surmounting her obvious teen lookalike for Meryl Streep image.

．．．．．．．．．．．．．．．．．．．．．．．．．．．．．

■ **NIGHTMARE ON ELM STREET 3 DREAM WARRIORS**

1987, 96 MINS, US ◇ Ⓥ

Dir Chuck Russell *Prod* Robert Shaye, Sara Risher *Scr* Wes Craven, Bruce Wagner, Chuck Russell, Frank Darabont *Ph* Roy H. Wagner *Ed* Terry Stokes, Chuck Weiss *Mus* Angelo Badalamenti *Art Dir* Mick Strawn
● Heather Langenkamp, Patricia Arquette, Larry Fishburne, Priscilla Pointer, Craig Wasson, Robert Englund (New Line/Heron/Smart Egg)

With input from the original's creator, Wes Craven, *3* shifts its focus away from the homely neighborhood horror to a setting of seven nightmare-plagued teens under the care of medicos Priscilla Pointer (instantly hissable) and Craig Wasson (decidedly miscast).

Heather Langenkamp, young heroine of the first film in the series, returns as an intern assigned to the ward. She's been using an experimental dream-inhibiting drug to keep her wits about her and proposes using it on the kids.

While everyone is stewing in their juices, pic is mainly focused on the violent special effects outbursts of Freddy Krueger (ably limned under heavy makeup by Robert Englund), the child murderer's demon spirit who seeks revenge on Langenkamp and the other Elm St kids for the sins of their parents.

Debuting director Chuck Russell elicits poor performances from most of his thesps, making it difficult to differentiate between pic's comic relief and unintended howlers.

．．．．．．．．．．．．．．．．．．．．．．．．．．．．．

■ **NIJINSKY**

1980, 125 MINS, UK ◇ Ⓥ

Dir Herbert Ross *Prod* Nora Kaye, Stanley O'Toole *Scr* Hugh Wheeler *Ph* Douglas Slocombe *Ed* William Reynolds *Mus* John Lanchberry *Art Dir* John Blezard
● Alan Bates, George De La Pena, Leslie Browne, Alan Badel, Janet Suzman (Hera)

In *Nijinsky*, Herbert Ross and scripter Hugh Wheeler have constructed nothing less than a male-to-male romantic tragedy. The film takes the form of a broad flashback covering only two critical years (1912–13) in the young dancer's early 20s.

Beginning with his mentor-lover Sergei Diaghilev (Alan Bates), the period charts Nijinsky's gradual allegiance to a wealthy homosexual patron – brilliantly etched by Alan Badel; and the successful attempt of Hungarian aristocrat Romola de Pulsky (Leslie Browne) to catch Nijinsky on his briefly heterosexual rebound from Diaghilev.

Central theme of Wheeler's script is that Diaghilev's obsessive love for Nijinsky clouded his otherwise shrewd taste, showmanship and business sense.

George De La Pena has the intensity and ambiguous sexual aura to make him a credible Nijinsky.

．．．．．．．．．．．．．．．．．．．．．．．．．．．．．

■ **NINE½ WEEKS**

1986, 113 MINS, US ◇ Ⓥ

Dir Adrian Lyne *Prod* Antony Rufus Isaacs, Zalman King *Scr* Patricia Knop, Zalman King, Sarah Kernochan *Ph* Peter Biziou *Ed* Tom Rolf, Caroline Biggerstaff *Mus* Jack Nitzsche *Art Dir* Ken Davis
● Mickey Rourke, Kim Basinger, Margaret Whitton, David Margulies, Christine Baranski, Karen Young (PSO/Kimmel/Barish/Jonesfilm/Galactic/Triple Ajaxxx)

Only and entire raison d'etre for this screen adaptation of Elizabeth McNeill's novel would be to vividly present the obsessive, all-

consuming passion between a successful Wall Street type and a beautiful art gallery employee, who embark upon an intense love affair that lasts as long as the title indicates.

The film is about the crazy, overwhelming attachment they have with one another, and nothing else. Therefore, the virtual absence of anything interesting happening between them – like plausible attraction, exotic, amazing sex, or, God forbid, good dialog – leaves one great big hole on the screen for two hours.

Mickey Rourke is less than totally convincing as a big businessman, but Kim Basinger is the film's one saving grace, as she manages to retain a certain dignity.

．．．．．．．．．．．．．．．．．．．．．．．．．．．．．

■ **NINE HOURS TO RAMA**

1963, 125 MINS, US ◇

Dir Mark Robson *Prod* Mark Robson *Scr* Nelson Gidding *Ph* Arthur Ibbetson *Ed* Ernest Walker *Mus* Malcolm Arnold *Art Dir* Elliot Scott
● Horst Buchholz, Jose Ferrer, Valerie Gearon, Don Borisenko, Robert Morley, Dione Baker (20th Century-Fox)

At the core, this dramatization of circumstances surrounding the assassination of Mahatma Gandhi is an achievement of insight and impact. The success of a drama focusing its attention on the assassinator of a great man is to make the character of the killer dimensional and clearly motivated. This is achieved in the screenplay from Stanley Wolpert's novel and bolstered by Horst Buchholz's virile portrayal of the perpetrator.

Gandhi's assassination was devised and executed by a fanatic secret faction of his own Hindu followers who blamed his doctrine of passive resistance for their misfortunes in the internal struggle against the Moslems. The complex passions that motivated this misguided faction have been expertly synthesized into one character.

Action of the drama takes place in the nine-hour span culminating with the fatal measure, with several flashback passages to illustrate the incidents of the past that contributed to the unstable frame of mind of the young man.

The story falls down in its development and clarification of certain key secondary characters. A married woman (Valerie Gearon) for whom the killer-to-be has fallen does not make very much sense. And her abrupt metamorphosis from sophisticated lady of the world to devout woman of India in the final scene is both superfluous and dramatically awkward.

Several other important characters, too, are poorly defined, among them the assassin's unwilling accomplice (Don Borisenko), a baffling Indian politico (Robert Morley) and an impulsive prostitute (Diane Baker). But, stacked up against the force of the heart of the matter, these are relatively minor capillary breaks in a fundamentally healthy specimen.

Buchholz delivers a performance of intensity and conviction. Jose Ferrer is excellent as a desperately concerned and conscientious police superintendent guarding Gandhi against disheartening odds. An astonishingly accurate personification of the latter is etched by J. S. Casshyap.

．．．．．．．．．．．．．．．．．．．．．．．．．．．．．

■ **NINE LIVES OF FRITZ THE CAT, THE**

1974, 76 MINS, US ◇ Ⓥ

Dir Robert Taylor *Prod* Steve Krantz *Scr* Fred Halliday, Eric Monte, Robert Taylor *Ph* Ted C. Bemiller, Greg Heschong *Ed* Marshall M. Borden *Mus* Tom Scott and the LA Express
● (American International)

Fritz the Cat is back again. The synthetic troublemaker and dilettante revolutionary

was a trifle anachronistic when he first hit the screens in 1972. He is even more so in *The Nine Lives of Fritz the Cat*. The animated production utilizes several random flashback and flash-forward sequences within the framework of Fritz being chewed out by his wife and lapsing into reveries.

Somewhat forced and dated humor, not too well fluffed up by a frenzied and compulsive hip storytelling style, cartoon feature will please teenage mentalities.

Fact that period flashbacks – to Hitler's last days, to the Depression 1930s – and to a futuristic separate black state, among other segments, are the body of the plot, seems to suggest a lack of current timeliness.

．．．．．．．．．．．．．．．．．．．．．．．．．．．．．

■ **9 TO 5**

1980, 110 MINS, US ◇ Ⓥ

Dir Colin Higgins *Prod* Bruce Gilbert *Scr* Colin Higgins, Patricia Resnick *Ph* Reynaldo Villalobos *Ed* Pembroke J. Herring *Mus* Charles Fox *Art Dir* Dean Mitzner
● Jane Fonda, Lily Tomlin, Dolly Parton, Dabney Coleman, Sterling Hayden (IPC)

Anyone who has ever worked in an office will be able to identify with the antics in *9 to 5*. Although it can probably be argued that Patricia Resnick and director Colin Higgins' script [from a story by Resnick] at times borders on the inane, the bottom line is that this picture is a lot of fun.

Story concerns a group of office workers (Lily Tomlin the all-knowing manager who trained the boss but can't get promoted, Jane Fonda the befuddled newcomer and Dolly Parton the alluring personal secretary) who band together to seek revenge on the man who is making their professional lives miserable.

Tomlin comes off best in the most appealing role as the smart yet under-appreciated glue in the office cement.

Parton makes a delightful screen debut in a role tailored to her already well-defined country girl personality. Surprisingly, Fonda, initiator of the project, emerges as the weakest.

．．．．．．．．．．．．．．．．．．．．．．．．．．．．．

■ **1984**

1956, 90 MINS, UK

Dir Michael Anderson *Prod* N. Peter Rathvon *Scr* William P. Templeton, Ralph Bettinson *Ph* C. Pennington Richards *Ed* Bill Lewthwaite *Mus* Malcolm Arnold *Art Dir* Terence Verity
● Michael Redgrave, Edmond O'Brien, Jan Sterling, David Kossoff, Mervyn Johns, Donald Pleasence (Holiday/Associated British)

A sinister glimpse of the future as envisaged by George Orwell, *1984* is a grim, depressing picture. The action takes place after the first atomic war, with the world divided into three major powers.

London, the setting for the story, is the capital of Oceania and is run by a ruthless regime, the heads of which are members of the inner party while their supporters are in the outer party. There are ministries of Love and Thought, anti-sex leagues and record divisions where the speeches of the great are rewritten from time to time to suit the needs of contemporary events.

The story is built around the illegal romance of two members of the outer party, Edmond O'Brien and Jan Sterling.

Orwell's picture of the ultimate in totalitarian ruthlessness is faithfully presented. Television 'eyes' keep a day-and-night watch on party members in their homes and TV screens are to be found everywhere, blurting out the latest reports on the endless wars with rival powers.

．．．．．．．．．．．．．．．．．．．．．．．．．．．．．

N

NINETEEN EIGHTY-FOUR

1984, 120 MINS, UK ◇ Ⓥ

Dir Michael Radford   *Prod* Simon Perry   *Scr* Michael Radford   *Ph* Roger Deakins   *Ed* Tom Priestley   *Mus* Dominic Muldowney [later replaced by Eurythmics]   *Art Dir* Allan Cameron
● John Hurt, Richard Burton, Suzanna Hamilton, Cyril Cusack, Gregor Fisher, James Walker (Virgin/Umbrella)

In this unremitting downer, writer-director Michael Radford introduces no touches of comedy or facile sensationalism to soften a harsh depiction of life under a totalitarian system as imagined by George Orwell in 1948.

Richard Burton is splendid as inner-party official O'Brien. Ironically, his swansong performance as the deceptively gentle spur to Winston Smith's 'thought-crimes', and then as the all-knowing interrogator who takes on the attributes of a father-figure to the helpless man whom he is intent on destroying, is something new in Burton's repertoire.

Also strong is Suzanna Hamilton as Julia who is the other agent of Smith's downfall. John Hurt as Winston Smith holds center stage throughout.

1941

1979, 118 MINS, US ◇ Ⓥ

Dir Steven Spielberg   *Prod* Buzz Feitshans   *Scr* Robert Zemeckis, Bob Gale   *Ph* William A. Fraker   *Ed* Michael Kahn   *Mus* John Williams   *Art Dir* Dean Edward Mitzner
● Dan Aykroyd, Ned Beatty, John Belushi, Toshiro Mifune, Nancy Allen, Robert Stack (Universal/Columbia/A-Team)

Billed as a comedy spectacle, Steven Spielberg's *1941* is long on spectacle, but short on comedy. The Universal-Columbia Pictures co-production is an exceedingly entertaining, fast-moving revision of 1940s war hysteria in Los Angeles.

Pic [from a story by Robert Zemeckis, Bob Gale and John Milius] is so overloaded with visual humor of a rather monstrous nature that feeling emerges, once you've seen 10 explosions, you've seen them all.

Main comic appeal resides in whatever audience enjoyment will result from seeing Hollywood Boulevard trashed (in miniature scale), paint factories bulldozed, houses toppled into the sea, and a giant ferris wheel rolling to a watery demise.

9/30/55

1977, 101 MINS, US ◇

Dir James Bridges   *Prod* Jerry Weintraub   *Scr* James Bridges   *Ph* Gordon Willis   *Ed* Jeff Gourson   *Mus* Leonard Rosenman   *Art Dir* Robert Luthardt
● Richard Thomas, Susan Tyrrell, Deborah Benson, Lisa Blount, Thomas Hulce, Dennis Quaid (Universal)

Title is the date of the car-crash death of James Dean, and James Bridges' original script tells of the impact on Richard Thomas, starring in an excellent performance as a smalltown Arkansas college kid whose life is permanently transformed by the incident.

Thomas is superb as the kid whose entire attitudes undergo change when news of Dean's death is heard on the radio. Girlfriend Deborah Benson partially shares the grief, but not as much as Lisa Blount, a freakier chick.

Together with chums Thomas Hulce, Dennis Christopher, Dennis Quaid and Mary Kai Clark, Thomas helps commemorate Dean's demise with booze and mock-occult mysticism, leading to a prank on other students.

Susan Tyrrell is outstanding as Blount's flamboyant mother.

99 AND 44/100% DEAD

1974, 97 MINS, US ◇ Ⓥ

Dir John Frankenheimer   *Prod* Joe Wizan   *Scr* Robert Dillon   *Ph* Ralph Woolsey   *Ed* Harold F. Kress   *Mus* Henry Mancini   *Art Dir* Herman Blumenthal
● Richard Harris, Edmond O'Brien, Bradford Dillman, Ann Turkel, Constance Ford, Chuck Connors (20th Century-Fox)

99 and 44/100% Dead starts like a house on fire, with directorial style to burn, but self-incinerates within its first half-hour. Thereafter, audience endures a pointless hour of 'bitter ashes,' which the offended taste with spattering noise rejected' to use Milton's famous line.

Director John Frankenheimer struggles with Robert Dillon's sophomoric, repulsive screenplay about gang warfare, but pyrrhic victory eludes him.

Hired killer Richard Harris enters a mythical, futuristic city 'on the beginning of the third day of the War' and hunts down mob kingpin Bradford Dillman for rival gangster Edmond O'Brien's peace of mind.

For a short while Dillon seems to have parody on his mind. Unfortunately, Dillon has neither the wit nor the invention to sustain this tone for more than a few reels.

NINJA III
THE DOMINATION

1984, 95 MINS, US ◇ Ⓥ

Dir Sam Firstenberg   *Prod* Menahem Golan, Yoram Globus   *Scr* James R. Silke   *Ph* Hanania Baer   *Ed* Michael Duthie   *Mus* Udi Haroaz   *Art Dir* Elliot Ellentuck
● Lucinda Dickey, Jordan Bennett, Sho Kosugi, David Chung, T.J. Castronova (Cannon)

With *Ninja III* producers reunite members of the team that made their second entry in the martial arts series about the more deadly cousins of the Samurai. The new outing into the never-never land of the world's trickiest controlled violence is done with quite a twist.

The twist has several quite humorous aspects, the least of which being that most of the Ninja action is performed by a woman (Lucinda Dickey).

From time to time she bewilders her police officer boyfriend by unconsciously taking over the spirit of an evil Ninja on a visit to Arizona to carry on his wholesale killing of the police force.

Sho Kosugi is the Good Ninja who finally helps the American girl out of her predicament so she can return to her regular pastime.

NINOTCHKA

1939, 111 MINS, US Ⓥ

Dir Ernst Lubitsch   *Prod* Ernst Lubitsch   *Scr* Charles Brackett, Billy Wilder, Walter Reisch   *Ph* William Daniels   *Ed* Gene Ruggiero   *Mus* Werner Heymann   *Art Dir* Cedric Gibbons, Randall Duell
● Greta Garbo, Melvyn Douglas, Bela Lugosi, Sig Rumann, Felix Bressart, Ina Claire (M-G-M)

Selection of Ernst Lubitsch to pilot Garbo in her first light performance in pictures proves a bull's-eye.

The punchy and humorous jabs directed at the Russian political system and representatives, and the contrast of bolshevik receptiveness to capitalistic luxuries and customs, are displayed in farcical vein, but there still remains the serious intent of comparisons between the political systems in the background.

Three Russian trade representatives arrive in Paris to dispose of royal jewels 'legally confiscated'. Playboy Melvyn Douglas is intent on cutting himself in for part of the jewel sale.

Tying up the gems in lawsuit for former owner, Ina Claire, Douglas is confronted by special envoy Garbo who arrives to speed the transactions. Douglas gets romantic, while Garbo treats love as a biological problem.
□ 1939: Best Picture (Nomination)

NINTH CONFIGURATION, THE

1980, 105 MINS, US ◇ Ⓥ

Dir William Peter Blatty   *Prod* William Peter Blatty   *Scr* William Peter Blatty   *Ph* Gerry Fisher   *Ed* T. Battle Davis, Peter Lee-Thompson, Roberto Silvi   *Mus* Barry DeVorzon   *Art Dir* Bill Malley, J. Dennis Washington
● Stacy Keach, Scott Wilson, Jason Miller, Neville Brand (Warner)

The Ninth Configuration is an often confusing story concerning the effects of a new 'doctor' on an institution for crazed military men which manages to effectively tie itself together in the end. Problem is the William Peter Blatty film takes entirely too long to explain itself.

Blatty makes his directorial debut here in addition to performing, producing and writing from his own novel.

Stacy Keach limns an army colonel who has been brought Stateside to play psychiatrist to a compound of disturbed military men. From the beginning it's apparent Keach is infinitely more disturbed than any of the men he is supposed to be treating, making the actor's monotone, robot-like state unbearably grating on the nerves only minutes after his appearance.

NO MERCY

1986, 105 MINS, US ◇ Ⓥ

Dir Richard Pearce   *Prod* D. Constantine Conte   *Scr* Jim Carabatsos   *Ph* Michael Brault   *Ed* Jerry Greenberg, Bill Yahraus   *Mus* Alan Silvestri   *Art Dir* Doug Kraner
● Richard Gere, Kim Basinger, Jeroen Krabbe, George Dzundza, Gary Basaraba, William Atherton (Tri-Star Delphi IV & V)

Despite some graphically brutal violence and a fair bit of 'too-cool' police jargon, *No Mercy* turns out to be a step above most other films in this blooming genre of lone-cop-turned-vigilante stories.

Eddie Jillette (Richard Gere) and his partner, Joe Collins (Gary Basaraba) get wind of a contract to kill a Louisiana crime overlord. They go undercover as the hit men, but find they are dealing with a much bigger, much deadlier fish as Collins is murdered brutally. Jillette has only one lead in tracking his partner's murder, a mysterious blond (Kim Basinger).

From the native, wild beauty of the Louisiana swamplands to the steamy, colourful French quarter of New Orleans, the film is a tightly woven piece.

Credit also goes to Gere, now sporting a noticeably older, grayer look, who manages to bring that maturity to his often typecast roles of the angry young man.

NO SMALL AFFAIR

1984, 102 MINS, US ◇ Ⓥ

Dir Jerry Schatzberg   *Prod* William Sackheim   *Scr* Charles Bolt, Terence Mulcahy   *Ph* Vilmos Zsigmond   *Ed* Priscilla Nedd, Eve Newman, Melvin Shapiro   *Mus* Rupert Holmes   *Art Dir* Robert Boyle
● Jon Cryer, Demi Moore, George Wendt, Peter Frechette, Elizabeth Daily, Ann Wedgeworth (Columbia-Delphi II)

No Small Affair is an okay coming-of-age romance in which the believability of the leading characters far outweighs that of many of the situations in which the script places them.

Film is set in San Francisco and has Jon Cryer as a 16-year-old who's precocious in still photography but not much else, being difficult socially and unresponsive to girls his own age.

By chance, he snaps a shot of a sharp looking gal by the waterfront and, by chance again, he finds her singing in a seedy North Beach nightspot. In a selfless effort to give her sluggish career a boost, he spends his entire life savings and gets her photo placed on top of 175 SF taxicabs.

Ultimately, she is invited to LA by a record company and, before she leaves, the inevitable occurs.

....

■ NO WAY OUT

1987, 116 MINS, US ◇ ⓥ

Dir Roger Donaldson   *Prod* Laura Ziskin, Robert Garland   *Scr* Robert Garland   *Ph* John Alcott   *Ed* Neil Travis   *Mus* Maurice Jarre   *Art Dir* Dennis Washington

● Kevin Costner, Gene Hackman, Sean Young, Will Patton, Howard Duff (Orion)

No Way Out is an effective updating and revamping of the 1948 film noir classic *The Big Clock*, also based on Kenneth Fearing's novel of that name.

Film is set primarily in the Pentagon, with heroic Kevin Costner cast as a Lt Commander assigned to the Secretary of Defense (Gene Hackman), acting as liaison to the CIA under Hackman's righthand man Will Patton.

Costner has a torrid love affair with goodtime girl Sean Young ended when she is murdered by her other lover, Hackman. Costner recognizes his boss in the shadows but Hackman sees only an unidentified figure. Hackman starts a cover-up to find the unidentified man he saw leaving the apartment. Costner is put in charge of the top-security investigation to catch himself.

Costner is extremely low key while Hackman glides through his role and Patton dominates his scenes overplaying his villainous hand. Young is extremely alluring as the heroine.

....

■ NO WAY TO TREAT A LADY

1968, 108 MINS, US ◇ ⓥ

Dir Jack Smight   *Prod* Sol C. Siegel   *Scr* John Gay   *Ph* Jack Priestley   *Ed* Archie Marshek   *Mus* Stanley Myers   *Art Dir* Hal Pereira, George Jenkins

● Rod Steiger, Lee Remick, George Segal, Eileen Heckart, Murray Hamilton, Michael Dunn (Paramount)

Entertaining suspense film neatly laced with mordant humor. Stronger, more appropriate direction could have pushed the film into the category of minor classic.

Plotline casts Rod Steiger as a psychotic theatrical entrepreneur who takes to strangling drab middle-aged women as a means of working out his hangups over his dead mother. He employs a variety of disguises, accents and mannerisms for each murder.

Steiger relishes the multiple aspect of his part, and audiences should equally relish his droll impersonations of an Irish priest, German handyman, Jewish cop, middle-aged woman, Italian waiter and homosexual hairdresser.

Assigned to capture the lunatic ladykiller is a mother-smothered cop, played to perfection by George Segal.

With an excellent cast and a very good screenplay, *No Way to Treat a Lady* comes close to the quality of the best British films of the 1950s.

....

■ NOAH'S ARK
THE STORY OF THE DELUGE

1928, 135 MINS, US

Dir Michael Curtiz   *Prod* Darryl F. Zanuck   *Scr* Darryl F. Zanuck, Anthony Goldeway, De Leon Anthony   *Ph* Hal Mohr, Barney McGill   *Mus* Louis Silvers

● Dolores Costello, George O'Brien, Noah Beery, Guinn Williams, Paul McAllister, Myrna Loy (Warner)

Noah's Ark has touches reminiscent of *Ten Commandments*, *King of Kings*, *Wings*, *The Big Parade* and quite a few other [1920s] screen epics. Better than $1.5 was reported to have been spent on this film.

The Warner staff show everything conceivable under the sun – mobs, mobs and mobs; Niagaras of water; train wreck; war aplenty; crashes; deluges and everything. Nothing is missed from 'way back when folks thought that praying to the real God instead of Jehovah was the right thing until Noah got the message from above that it was not.

The story opens with scenes showing what is left of the world after the big deluge. It then drifts into the age where folks worshipped the Golden Calf and their lust for gold. It flashes modern to the extent of bringing to the fore the selfish motive of man. A flash is shown of the stock exchange in New York on a panicky day. A guy gets bumped off.

Then they hop to Europe. The scene is the Orient Express from Constantinople to Paris just as the First World War is in the air. There are folks of every nationality on the train. War is the topic.

Talk does not enter into the picture until after the first 35 minutes. It starts with love scene between George O'Brien and Dolores Costello and then brings in talk by Wallace Beery, Paul McAllister and Guinn Williams. The Costello voice hurts the impression made by her silent acting.

Beery is great as the Russian spy and as the King. McAllister, an old stage trouper, has a hard job with biblical quotations which are overdone. Voice okay but talk just a bit too much.

....

■ NOBODY WAVED GOODBYE

1964, 80 MINS, CANADA

Dir Don Owen   *Prod* Roman Kroitor, Don Owen   *Scr* Don Owen   *Ph* John Spotton   *Ed* John Spotton, Donald Ginsberg   *Mus* Eldon Rathburn

● Peter Kastner, Julie Biggs, Claude Rae, Toby Tarnow, Charmion King, Ron Taylor (National Film Board of Canada)

This is a simple story, simply told, about a couple of Toronto juves, the boy typically smartalecky, the girl attractive, decent and naive. From truancy and petty offenses, the road is downhill until by fadeout the young couple is split, the girl pregnant, and the boy having to decide whether to go back and face the music for theft, while there's still time to rehabilitate himself.

It's not a flawless film by any means. Some of the dialogue is dull. The acting in instances is bordering on bush league. The camera work veers to the pretentious. By and large, however, even if the story line becomes hokey and a little bush-operaish in content, the film could be a winner.

Peter Kastner and Julie Biggs have high and low points in the leads, but they're naturally charming enough to get away with momentary lapses in their performance.

....

■ NOBODY'S FOOL

1986, 107 MINS, US ◇ ⓥ

Dir Evelyn Purcell   *Prod* James C. Katz, Jon S. Denny   *Scr* Beth Henley   *Ph* Mikhail Suslov   *Ed* Dennis Virkler   *Mus* James Newton Howard   *Art Dir* Jackson DeGovia

● Rosanna Arquette, Eric Roberts, Mare Winningham, Jim Youngs, Louise Fletcher (Island/Katz-Denny)

Nobody's Fool features kookiness without real comedy, romance without magic.

Rosanna Arquette, a smalltown western girl, attends dutifully to her burned-out mother and bratty younger brother as she tries to forget the public shame and ridicule she endured when she impulsively stabbed her old beau in a restaurant. She is as insecure as can be when Eric Roberts, the lighting technician with a visiting theatrical troupe, begins quietly noticing her.

Arquette's performance, like the film, features hits and misses, yet there is something frequently moving about the character's scattershot approach to emotional salvation. Roberts, more subdued than usual, effectively registers the impulses of a young man who thinks he can save Arquette from her prospective dismal fate.

....

■ NOMADS

1985, 100 MINS, US ◇ ⓥ

Dir John McTiernan   *Prod* Elliott Kastner   *Scr* John McTiernan   *Ph* Stephen Ramsey   *Ed* Michael John Bateman   *Mus* Bill Conti   *Art Dir* Marcia Hinds

● Pierce Brosnan, Lesley-Anne Down, Anna-Maria Montecelli, Adam Ant, Hector Mercado, Josie Cotton (PSO/Kastner/Cinema 7)

Nomads avoids the more obvious ripped-guts devices in favor of dramatic visual scares. Director John McTiernan even has some kind of a love interest in his story without cluttering up the plot with sticky romance or strained eroticism. In fact, everything seems to come naturally in a tale that even has the supernatural ring true.

Pierce Brosnan plays French anthropologist Pommier who intends to settle in LA with his wife Niki (Anna-Maria Montecelli), when flesh-and-blood (seemingly) Evil Spirits of nomads he once studied in arctic and desert regions materialize to haunt him. They now look like death-pale punkers.

The acting of Brosnan and Lesley-Anne Down (as a doctor) is the more effective for being restrained. Singer Adam Ant is seen as one of the Nomads.

....

■ NORMA RAE

1979, 113 MINS, US ◇ ⓥ

Dir Martin Ritt   *Prod* Tamara Asseyev, Alex Rose   *Scr* Irving Ravetch, Harriet Frank   *Ph* John A. Alonzo   *Ed* Sidney Levin   *Mus* David Shire   *Art Dir* Walter Scott Herndon

● Sally Field, Beau Bridges, Ron Leibman, Pat Hingle, Gail Strickland (20th Century-Fox)

Norma Rae is that rare entity, an intelligent film with heart.

Films about unions haven't always fared well at the boxoffice, but that didn't deter director Martin Ritt and screenwriters from updating the traditional management-labor struggles to a sharp contemporary setting. Now the battle is being waged in Southern textile mills, where the din of the machinery is virtually unbearable, and workers either go deaf or suffer the consumptive effects of 'brown lung' disease.

Ron Leibman arrives on the scene as a New York-based labor organizer, who picks Sally Field as his most likely convert. This unlikely pairing of Jewish radicalism and Southern miasma is the core of *Norma Rae*, and is made real and touching by the individual performances of Leibman and Field.

The pacing is fresh and never laggard, and *Norma Rae* virtually hums right along.

☐ 1979: Best Picture (Nomination)

....

N

■ NORTH BY NORTHWEST

1959, 136 MINS, UK ◇ ▽

Dir Alfred Hitchcock   *Prod* Alfred Hitchcock
Scr Ernest Lehman   *Ph* Robert Burks   *Ed* George
Tomasini   *Mus* Bernard Herrmann   *Art Dir* Robert
Boyle, William A. Horning
● Cary Grant, Eva Marie Saint, James Mason, Jessie
Royce Landis, Leo G. Carroll, Martin Landau (M-G-M)

North by Northwest is the Alfred Hitchcock
mixture – suspense, intrigue, comedy,
humor. Seldom has the concoction been
served up so delectably. Hitchcock uses
actual locations – the Plaza in New York, the
Ambassador East in Chicago, Grand Central
Station, the 20th Century, Limited, United
Nations headquarters in Manhattan, Mount
Rushmore National Monument, the plains of
Indiana. One scene, where the hero is ambushed by an airplane on the flat, sun-baked
prairie, is a brilliant use of location.

Cary Grant brings technique and charm to
the central character. He is a Madison Avenue man-about-Manhattan, sleekly handsome, carelessly twice-divorced, debonair as
a cigaret ad. The story gets underway when
he's mistaken for a US intelligence agent by a
pack of foreign agents headed by James
Mason. The complications are staggering but
they play like an Olympic version of a three-
legged race.

Grant's problem is to avoid getting knocked
off by Mason's gang without tipping them
that he is a classic case of the innocent bystander. The case is serious, but Hitchcock's
macabre sense of humor and instinct for
romantic byplay never allows it to stay grim
for too long. Suspense is deliberately broken
for relief and then skillfully re-established.

Eva Marie Saint dives headfirst into Mata
Hari and shows she can be unexpectedly and
thoroughly glamorous. She also manages the
difficult impression of seeming basically innocent while explaining how she becomes
Mason's mistress. Mason, in a rather stock
role, is properly forbidding.

Robert Burks' photography, whether in the
hot yellows of the prairie plain, or the soft
green of South Dakota forests, is lucid and
imaginatively composed. It is the first Metro
release in VistaVision. Bernard Herrmann's
score is a tingling one, particularly in the
Mount Rushmore sequences, but light where
mood requires.

■ NORTH DALLAS FORTY

1979, 119 MINS, US ◇ ▽

Dir Ted Kotcheff   *Prod* Frank Yablans   *Scr* Frank
Yablans, Ted Kotcheff, Peter Gent   *Ph* Paul Lohmann
Ed Jay Kamen   *Mus* John Scott   *Art Dir* Alfred
Sweeney
● Nick Nolte, Mac Davis, Charles Durning, Dabney
Coleman, Dayle Haddon, Bo Svenson (Paramount)

It's no surprise that the National Football
League refused to cooperate in the making of
North Dallas Forty. The production is a most
realistic, hard-hitting and perceptive look at
the seamy side of pro football.

What distinguishes this screen adaptation
of Peter Gent's bestseller is the exploration of
a human dimension almost never seen in
sports pix. Most people understand that
modern-day athletes are just cogs in a big
business wheel, but getting that across on the
screen is a whole different matter. And in
large measure, that success is due to a
bravura performance in the lead role by
Nick Nolte.

Ted Kotcheff keeps the action flowing
smoothly, and has perfectly captured the
locker-room intensity and post-game letdown
that never shows up on the tube.

■ NORTH SEA HIJACK

1980, 99 MINS, UK ◇ ▽

Dir Andrew V. McLaglen   *Prod* Elliott Kastner
Scr Jack Davies   *Ph* Tony Imi   *Ed* Alan Strachan
Mus Michael J. Lewis   *Art Dir* Bert Davey
● Roger Moore, James Mason, Anthony Perkins,
Michael Parks, Jack Watson (Universal)

The biggest attraction is the banter between
Roger Moore and the various types with
whom he comes in conflict during his preparations to save a hijacked supply ship.

A misogynistic but dedicated frogman,
whose private crew of frogmen are the only
seeming rescuers of the ship, Moore is today's
ideal male chauvinistic pig. And delights in
it. He doesn't even mind telling the British
Prime Minister (a lady, of course) what he
thinks of the situation.

He's ably supported by James Mason as a
by-the-book admiral. Mason is also given
star billing and almost builds his role into
deserving it but Anthony Perkins and especially Michael Parks certainly belong
below the title.

■ NORTH STAR, THE

1943, 105 MINS, US ▽

Dir Lewis Milestone   *Prod* Samuel Goldwyn
Scr Lillian Hellman   *Ph* James Wong Howe   *Ed* Daniel
Mandell   *Mus* Aaron Copland
● Anne Baxter, Dana Andrews, Walter Huston, Walter
Brennan, Farley Granger, Erich von Stroheim (RKO)

Samuel Goldwyn as the producer and Lillian
Hellman, the writer, team to tell of the Nazi
invasion of the Soviet. As entertainment,
however, there's too much running time consumed before the film actually gets into its
story and, in parts, it is seemingly a too-
obviously contrived narrative detailing the
virtues of the Soviet regime.

Setting the background for the actual climax is a long and sometimes tedious one.
The early parts of the film are almost always
colorful in depicting the simple life of the villagers around whom this story revolves, but
it's a question of too premeditatedly setting, a
stage of a simple, peace-loving people who,
through the bestiality of the enemy, are driven to an heroic defense that must, in time,
become legendary. For this is the story of the
Soviet people as seen through the eyes of a
small village.

Hellman's story, when she finally gets
around to it, is a parallel one, dealing with a
picnic group that's suddenly called on to rush
arms through the German lines to their guerrilla comrades when the sudden invasion
catches them unawares while on a walking
trip. It is an exciting tale from here on in.

■ NORTH WEST FRONTIER

1959, 129 MINS, UK ◇ ▽

Dir J. Lee Thompson   *Prod* Marcel Hellman   *Scr* Robin
Estridge   *Ph* Geoffrey Unsworth   *Ed* Frederick
Wilson   *Mus* Mischa Spoliansky
● Kenneth More, Lauren Bacall, Herbert Lom, Wilfrid
Hyde White, I.S. Johar, Ursula Jeans (Rank)

From a smash opening to quietly confident
fade, *North West Frontier* is basically the ageless chase yarn, transferred from the prairie
to the sun-baked plains of India and done
with a spectacular flourish.

Handled with tremendous assurance by J.
Lee Thompson, the film is reminiscent of the
same director's *Ice Cold in Alex*, with an
ancient locomotive replacing the ambulance
in that desert war story and with hordes of
be-turbaned tribesmen substituting for the
Nazi patrols.

Time is the turn of the century when the
English still held sway in India. Kenneth
More plays an officer ordered to take a boy
prince, sacred figurehead to the Hindus, to

safety in the teeth of Moslems. In company
with an assorted group, More makes his getaway from a besieged citadel in a makeshift
coach drawn by a worn-out locomotive.

Throughout, the cast serves the job
expertly, More coming through as solid and
dependable if a shade too unemotional. Lauren Bacall scores with a keen delineation of
the prince's outspoken nurse. Herbert Lom is
first-rate as a journalist. I.S. Johar is the hit
of the picture as the Indian railroad man.

■ NORTH WEST MOUNTED POLICE

1940, 125 MINS, US ◇

Dir Cecil B. DeMille, Arthur Rosson, Eric Stacey
Prod Cecil B. DeMille   *Scr* Alan LeMay, Jesse Lasky Jr,
C. Gardner Sullivan   *Ph* Victor Milner, W. Howard
Greene   *Ed* Anne Bauchens   *Mus* Victor Young   *Art
Dir* Hans Dreier, Roland Anderson
● Gary Cooper, Madeleine Carroll, Preston Foster,
Paulette Goddard, Robert Preston, George Bancroft
(Paramount)

The story is founded upon an incident of
insurrection and bloodshed which took place
in and around Regina in 1885, when Canadian troops finally subdued a settlers' discontent and revolt.

With that much fact to start from, scripters
weave a story which has its exciting
moments, a reasonable and convincing
romance and a hero who is a pure Texan
from down near the Rio Grande. Gary
Cooper is the man from the South, and although Canadian uprisings are none of his
business (he is one of the Texan Rangers on
search for a murderer) he finds himself in the
middle of gunplay before the end of the
second reel.

Preston Foster as the sergeant-leader of the
redcoats gets the better of Cooper in the contest for Madeleine Carroll. Foster has the girl
and Cooper has George Bancroft, the heavy,
tied up with his lariat and on his way back
home. Before that takes place there are
innumerable plot complications involving
Paulette Goddard, a half-breed vixen; Robert
Preston, one of the mounted who faltered in
outpost duty; Walter Hampden, a big Indian
chief; and Akim Tamiroff and Lynne Overman, who stage their own private duel of
marksmanship, which is hilarious.

Interesting novelty is an introductory
soundtrack talk by DeMille in which he
recounts the historical basis for the film.

■ NORTHWEST PASSAGE

1940, 125 MINS, US ◇ ▽

Dir King Vidor   *Prod* Hunt Stromberg   *Scr* Laurence
Stallings, Talbot Jennings   *Ph* Sidney Wagner, William
V. Skall   *Ed* Conrad A. Nervig   *Mus* Herbert
Stothart   *Art Dir* Cedric Gibbons, Malcolm Brown
● Spencer Tracy, Robert Young, Walter Brennan, Ruth
Hussey, Nat Pendleton, Donald McBride (M-G-M)

Northwest Passage, which hit a negative cost of
nearly $2 million, is a fine epic adventure.
The picture carries through only the first half
of the novel [by Kenneth Roberts] and is so
designated in the main title. The title is misleading from an historical standpoint as it
only covers the one expedition through upper
New York state to the St Lawrence territory
where the village of a hostile tribe is wiped
out.

Spencer Tracy is brilliantly impressive as
the dominating and driving leader of Rogers'
Rangers, a band of 160 trained settlers
inducted into service to clean up the hostile
tribes to make homes and families safe. Robert Young, as the Harvardian who joins the
Rangers to sketch Indians, has a more virile
role than others assigned him and turns in a
fine performance. Walter Brennan provides a
typically fine characterization as the friend of
Young.

There's a peculiar fascination in the unfolding of the historical narrative and adventure of the inspired band on the march to and from the Indian village. It's a continual battle against natural hazards, possible sudden attacks by ambushing enemies, and a display of indomitable courage to drive through swamps and over mountains for days at a time without food. It's grim and stark drama of those pioneers who blazed trails through the wilderness to make living in this country safe for their families and descendants.

- -

■ NOT AS A STRANGER

1955, 135 MINS, US

Dir Stanley Kramer   *Prod* Stanley Kramer   *Scr* Edna Anhalt, Edward Anhalt   *Ph* Franz Planer   *Ed* Fred Knudtson   *Mus* George Antheil   *Art Dir* Rudolph Sternad, Howard Richmond
● Olivia de Havilland, Robert Mitchum, Frank Sinatra, Gloria Grahame, Broderick Crawford, Charles Bickford (United Artists)

Producer Stanley Kramer, a man with a penchant for offbeat choices, took Morton Thompson's best-selling novel of a young doctor as the occasion of his own directorial debut.

Some of the most interesting characterizations appear only in the second story (out of three). Charles Bickford comes near to stealing the picture. Gloria Grahame, as a neurotic widow with lots of money, also stands out, though the part is much changed from the novel and never too clear in her motivations.

Frank Sinatra is another of the players who comes close to doing a little picture stealing. And what about the hero of the story? He's Robert Mitchum and he's considerably over his acting depth. Though some scenes come off fairly well, Mitchum is poker-faced from start to finish.

- -

■ NOT WITH MY WIFE, YOU DON'T!

1966, 118 MINS, US ◇

Dir Norman Panama   *Prod* Norman Panama   *Scr* Norman Panama, Larry Gelbert, Peter Barnes   *Ph* Charles Lang Jr   *Ed* Aaron Stell   *Mus* John Williams   *Art Dir* Edward Carrere
● Tony Curtis, Virna Lisi, George C. Scott, Carroll O'Connor, Richard Eastham, Eddie Ryder (Warner)

Not With My Wife, You Don't! is an outstanding romantic comedy about a US Air Force marriage threatened by jealousy as an old beau of the wife returns to the scene. Zesty scripting, fine performances, solid direction and strong production values sustain hilarity throughout.

Story sets up Tony Curtis and George C. Scott as old Korean conflict buddies whose rivalry for Virna Lisi is renewed when Scott discovers that Curtis won her by subterfuge. The amusing premise is thoroughly held together via an unending string of top comedy situations, including domestic squabbles, flashback, and an outstanding takeoff on foreign pix.

Curtis is excellent as the husband whose duties as aide to Air Force General Carroll O'Connor create the domestic vacuum into which Scott moves with the time-tested instincts of a proven, and non-marrying, satyr.

- -

■ NOTHING BUT THE BEST

1964, 99 MINS, UK ◇

Dir Clive Donner   *Prod* David Deutsch   *Scr* Frederic Raphael   *Ph* Nicholas Roeg   *Ed* Fergus McDonell   *Mus* Ron Grainer   *Art Dir* Reece Pemberton
● Alan Bates, Denholm Elliott, Harry Andrews, Millicent Martin (Domino/Angelo Amalgamated)

This stylish British comedy takes a sly, pen-etrating peek at the social climbing upper classes that use the Old School tie, social connections, well padded bank balances and the Smart Set background to further their material ambitions.

It is ruthless in its unpeeling of the dubious foibles and mannerisms of its characters, none of whom fails to have an axe to gind. It's the story of an ambitious young man of humble background who, excited by the glitter of money, business power and an entry into the fascinating world of Hunt Balls, Ascot, smart restaurants, shooting, hunting, fishin' and the rest of the trappings, lies, bluffs, smiles, cheats, loves, and smoothtalks his way to marrying the boss' daughter, and doesn't stop at murder en route.

Alan Bates, showing a previously unexplored vein of comedy, is firstclass as the dubious hero. This is a measured, confident performance that appeals even when he is behaving at his worst. Many of the top scenes are those with Denholm Elliott who, in fact, turns in the best acting of the lot.

- -

■ NOTHING BUT TROUBLE

1991, 94 MINS, US ◇ ⑰

Dir Dan Aykroyd   *Prod* Robert K. Weiss   *Scr* Dan Aykroyd   *Ph* Dean Cundey   *Ed* Malcolm Campbell, James Symons   *Mus* Michael Kamen   *Art Dir* William Sandell
● Chevy Chase, Dan Aykroyd, John Candy, Demi Moore (Warner/Applied Action)

First-time director Dan Aykroyd might have once parodied this sort of wretched excess in his 'bad-cinema' sketches on *Saturday Night Live*. Premise, stripped to the bone, had potential: a faceless drive-through town seems to have no resident except the cop who miraculously appears to pinch unsuspecting drivers.

The one-joke starter is then taken to absurd extremes as four Manhattan yuppies get shanghaied to the village of Valkenvania, where a demented old judge (Aykroyd, in heavy makeup) metes out executioner-style justice over moving violations.

The story [by Peter Aykroyd] turns into an extended maze with Chevy Chase and Demi Moore as the principal Nintendo-ized targets running through one tepid peril after another, while mouthing banal wisecracks.

It's a good bet a film is in trouble when the highlight comes from seeing John Candy in drag.

- -

■ NOTHING SACRED

1937, 75 MINS, US ◇ ⑰

Dir William A. Wellman   *Prod* David O. Selznick   *Scr* Ben Hecht   *Ph* W. Howard Greene   *Ed* James E. Newcom, Hal Kern   *Mus* Oscar Levant   *Art Dir* Lyle Wheeler
● Carole Lombard, Fredric March, Charles Winninger, Walter Connolly, Sig Rumann, Frank Fay (Selznick/United Artists)

Ben Hecht wrote the adaptation for *Sacred* from the William Street magazine story detailing the experiences of a village beauty who becomes the center of a fantastic newspaper circulation stunt which justifies itself in the belief, unfounded, that the girl has only a short time to live. Hecht handles the material breezily and pungently, poking fun in typical manner of half-scorn at the newspaper publisher, his reporter, doctors, the newspaper business, phonies, suckers, and whatnot.

For added value there is tinting by Technicolor which greatly enhances its pictorial charm. The running time is only 75 minutes, making this a meaty and well-edited piece of entertainment from start to finish. There are no lagging moments.

Fredric March does the reporter behind the dizzy ride given Carole Lombard by a sucker-victimized New York which thinks she already has one foot in the grave. Walter Connolly bristles with importance from a comedy viewpoint as March's publisher-boss. Charles Winninger does the rural medico who hates newspapers but not booze.

- -

■ NOTORIOUS

1946, 101 MINS, US ⑰

Dir Alfred Hitchcock   *Prod* Alfred Hitchcock   *Scr* Ben Hecht   *Ph* Ted Tetzlaff   *Ed* Theron Warth   *Mus* Roy Webb   *Art Dir* Albert S. D'Agostino, Carroll Clark
● Cary Grant, Ingrid Bergman, Claude Rains, Louis Calhern (RKO)

Production and directorial skill of Alfred Hitchcock combine with a suspenseful story and excellent performances to make *Notorious* force entertainment.

The Ben Hecht scenario carries punchy dialog but it's much more the action and manner in which Hitchcock projects it on the screen that counts heaviest. Of course the fine performances by Cary Grant, Ingrid Bergman and Claude Rains also figure. The terrific suspense maintained to the very last is also an important asset.

Story deals with espionage, the picture opening in Miami in the spring of 1946. Bergman's father has been convicted as a German spy. Yarn shifts quickly to Rio de Janeiro, where Bergman, known to be a loyal American, unlike her father, is pressed into the American intelligence service with a view to getting the goods on a local group of German exiles under suspicion.

Inducted into espionage through Cary Grant, an American agent with whom she is assigned to work. Bergman, because she loves Grant, doesn't want to go through with an assignment to feign love for Claude Rains, head of the Brazilian Nazi group.

- -

■ NOW, VOYAGER

1942, 117 MINS, US ⑰

Dir Irving Rapper   *Prod* Hal B. Wallis   *Scr* Casey Robinson   *Ph* Sol Polito   *Ed* Warren Low   *Mus* Max Steiner
● Bette Davis, Paul Henreid, Claude Rains, Bonita Granville, Gladys Cooper, Ilka Chase (Warner)

Voyager, an excursion into psychiatry, is almost episodic in its writing. It affords Bette Davis one of her superlative acting roles, that of a neurotic spinster fighting to free herself from the shackles of a tyrannical mother. A spinster still recalling the frustration of a girlhood love.

The first scenes show Davis as dowdy, plump and possessed of a phobia that fairly cries for the ministrations of a psychiatrist. Treatment by the doctor, played by Claude Rains, transforms the patient into a glamorous, modish, attractive woman who soon finds herself, after long being starved for love.

The yarn's major love crisis focuses on Davis and Paul Henreid, the latter unable to upset the conventions of a complicated marital life. The remote satisfaction of their love, via the emotionally unstable daughter of Henreid, upon whom Davis lavishes a mother's attention, is, perhaps, a rather questionable conclusion, but it's the kind of drama [from a novel by Oliver Higgins Pronty] that demands little credibility.

Henried neatly dovetails and makes believable the sometimes-underplayed character of the man who finds love too late. As the curer of Davis' mental ills, Rains gives his usual restrained, above-par performance. Gladys Cooper is the domineering mother, weighted by Boston's Back Bay traditions and she's also within her metier.

- -

NUNS ON THE RUN

1990, 90 MINS, UK ◇ Ⓥ

Dir Jonathan Lynn   *Prod* Michael White   *Scr* Jonathan
Lynn   *Ph* Michael Garfath   *Ed* David Martin
Mus Yello, Hidden Faces   *Art Dir* Simon Holland
● Eric Idle, Robbie Coltrane, Camille Coduri, Janet
Suzman, Doris Hare, Tom Hickey (HandMade)

Like Jack Lemmon and Tony Curtis in the
Billy Wilder classic *Some Like It Hot*, Eric Idle
and Robbie Coltrane are motivated by fear
for their lives to dress in women's garb. New
pic has rival British and Chinese gangs trying
to recover two suitcases full of illicit cash.

Idle and Coltrane make a wonderful pair of
dumbbells, both in and out of their habits.
Both are oddly believable as nuns, even while
writer/director Jonathan Lynn mines all the
expected comic benefits of drag humor.

Idle and Coltrane are a lookout and a getaway driver for believable nasty London
crime lord Robert Patterson. Their desire to
escape their surroundings and the lure of easy
cash backfire ominously, and they take refuge
in a convent school run by Janet Suzman.

The constant double entendres are done
with wit and the slapstick is mostly agreeable
and efficiently directed, although the sight
gags about Camille Coduri's extreme myopia
are pushed a little far on occasion. Coduri
otherwise is sweet and endearing in the Marilyn Monroe part.

NUN'S STORY, THE

1959, 149 MINS, US ◇ Ⓥ

Dir Fred Zinnemann   *Prod* Fred Zinnemann
Scr Robert Anderson   *Ph* Franz Planer   *Ed* Walter
Thompson   *Mus* Franz Waxman   *Art Dir* Alexander
Trauner
● Audrey Hepburn, Peter Finch, Edith Evans, Peggy
Ashcroft, Dean Jagger, Mildred Dunnock (Warner)

Fred Zinnemann's production is a soaring
and luminous film. Audrey Hepburn has her
most demanding film role, and she gives her
finest performance. Despite the seriousness of
the underlying theme, *The Nun's Story* [from
the book by Kathryn C. Hulme] has the elements of absorbing drama, pathos, humor,
and a gallery of memorable scenes and
characters.

The struggle is that of a young Belgian
woman (Hepburn), to be a successful member of an order of cloistered nuns. The order
(not specified) is as different from the ordinary 'regular guy' motion picture conception
of nuns as the army is from the Boy Scouts.
Its aim is total merging of self.

Although the story is confined chiefly to
three convents, in Belgium and the Congo,
the struggle is fierce. Hepburn, attempting to
be something she is not, is burned fine in the
process.

One of the consistent gratifications is the
cast. In addition to Edith Evans as the
Mother Superior, who might have been a
Renaissance prelate, there is Peggy Ashcroft,
another convent superior, but less the dignitary, more the anchorite. Mildred Dunnock is
a gentle, maiden aunt of a nun; Patricia Collinge, a gossipy cousin.

Peter Finch and Dean Jagger are the only
males in the cast of any stature. Finch, as an
intelligent, attractive agnostic, conveys a
romantic attachment for Hepburn, but in
terms that can give no offense. Dagger is
Hepburn's perturbed loving father but contributes a valuable facet on the story.

Despite the seeming austerity of the story,
Zinnemann has achieved a pictorial sweep
and majesty. Franz Planer's Technicolor
photography has a Gothic grace and muted
splendor, Franz Waxman's score is a great
one, giving proper place to cathedral organs
and Congo drums.

□ 1959: Best Picture (Nomination)

NUTCRACKER

1986, 84 MINS, US

Dir Carroll Ballard   *Prod* Willard Carroll, Donald
Kushner, Peter Locke, Thomas L. Wilhite   *Scr* Kent
Stowell, Maurice Sendak   *Ph* Stephen M. Burum
Ed John Mutt, Michael Silvers   *Mus* Tchaikovsky   *Art
Dir* Maurice Sendak
● Hugh Bigney, Vanessa Sharp, Patricia Barker, Wade
Walthall (Hyperion)

Despite some moments of disarray, *Nutcracker*
is a wonderfully expressive and fanciful film.

This production of the timeless ballet is not
only a beautiful version of the dance, but also
incorporates much of the dark-natured story
of E.T.A. Hoffman's original fairytale, *The
Nutcracker and the Mouse King* – that of a young
girl on the threshold of maturity who confronts many of her fears and hopes through a
dream about sinister controller of the universe, Pasha, and her nutcracker prince.

Whereas live performances have often
underplayed the sensitive storyline in preference to the dance, the film intricately and
subtly delves into the story.

This version of the ballet was presented
first by the Pacific Northwest Ballet in 1983.
The company veers from the often-pat sugar-
plum ballets to a more darkly intense version.

NUTS

1987, 116 MINS, US ◇ Ⓥ

Dir Martin Ritt   *Prod* Barbra Streisand   *Scr* Tom
Topor   *Ph* Andrzej Bartowiak   *Ed* Sidney Levin
Mus Barbra Streisand   *Art Dir* Joel Schiller
● Barbra Streisand, Richard Dreyfuss, Maureen
Stapleton, Karl Malden, Eli Wallach, Robert Webber
(Barwood/Ritt)

Based on the stageplay by Tom Topor, *Nuts*
presents a premise weighted down by porten-
tous performances. Issue of society's right to
judge someone's sanity and the subjectivity of
mental health is not only trite, but dated.
While film ignites sporadically, it succumbs
to the burden of its own earnestness.

As Claudia Draper, an uppercrust New
York kid who has gone off the deep end into
prostitution, Barbra Streisand is good, but
it's too much of a good thing. For the most
part it's a heroic performance, abandoning
many of the characteristic Streisand mannerisms while she allows herself to look seedy.
Streisand is flamboyantly, eccentrically crazy
in a way that implies she is just a spirited
woman society is trying to crush.

Richard Dreyfuss as Streisand's reluctant
public defender is by far the film's most textured character, giving a performance that
suggests a world of feeling and experience not
rushing to gush out at the seams.

Arrested for killing her high-priced trick, it
is Dreyfuss' job to convince a preliminary
hearing that Streisand is mentally competent
enough to stand trial with little help from her
and against her parents' wishes.

NUTTY PROFESSOR, THE

1963, 107 MINS, US Ⓥ

Dir Jerry Lewis   *Prod* Ernest D. Gluckman   *Scr* Jerry
Lewis, Bill Richmond   *Ph* W. Wallace Kelley   *Ed* John
Woodcock   *Mus* Walter Scharf   *Art Dir* Hal Pereira,
Walter Tyler
● Jerry Lewis, Stella Stevens, Del Moore, Kathleen
Freeman, Howard Morris (Paramount)

The Nutty Professor is not one of Jerry Lewis'
better films. Although attractively mounted
and performed with flair by a talented cast,
the production is only fitfully funny. Too
often the film bogs down in pointless, irrelevant or repetitious business, nullifying the
flavor of the occasionally choice comic capers
and palsying the tempo and continuity of the
story.

The star is cast as a meek, homely, acci-
dent-prone chemistry prof who concocts a

potion that transforms him into a handsome,
cocky, obnoxiously vain 'cool cat' type. But
the transfiguration is of the Jekyll-Hyde variety in that it wears off, restoring Lewis to the
original mold, invariably at critical, embarrassing moments.

Another standard characteristic of the
Lewis film is its similarity to an animated
cartoon, especially noticeable on this
occasion in that the professor played by
Lewis is a kind of live-action version of the
nearsighted Mr Magoo.

Musical theme of the picture is the beautiful refrain 'Stella by Starlight'. By starlight or
any other light, Stella is beautiful – Stella Stevens, that is, who portrays the professor's student admirer. Stevens is not only gorgeous,
she is a very gifted actress. This was an
exceptionally tough assignment, requiring of
her almost exclusively silent reaction takes,
and Stevens has managed almost invariably
to produce the correct responsive expression.
On her, even the incorrect one would look
good.

O LUCKY MAN!

1973, 186 MINS, UK ◇ Ⓥ

Dir Lindsay Anderson   *Prod* Michael Medwin, Lindsay
Anderson   *Scr* David Sherwin   *Ph* Miroslav
Ondricek   *Ed* David Gladwell, Tom Priestly   *Mus* Alan
Price   *Art Dir* Jocelyn Herbert
● Malcolm McDowell, Ralph Richardson, Rachel
Roberts, Arthur Lowe, Helen Mirren, Dandy Nichols
(Memorial/SAM)

No less than an epic look at society is created
in Lindsay Anderson's third and most provocative film. It is in the form of a human
comedy on a perky, ambitious but conformist
young man using society's ways to get to the
top.

Malcolm McDowell, though practically on
screen throughout, displays a solid grasp of
character and nuances. He is first a salesman,
then guinea pig to science, assistant to a great
business tycoon, railroaded to prison as a fall
guy, converted to near saintliness, almost
martyred and then returned to conformism
by an almost mystical reaching of understanding through a Zen-Buddhist-like
happening.

The film bows to various film greats but
always assimilated to Anderson's own brand
of epic comedy. The music and songs of Alan-
Price also add by underlining and counterpointing the action.

Ralph Richardson gives his pointed aplomb
to the rich man and as a wise old tailor who
gives the hero a golden suit; Rachel Roberts
is a sexy personnel chief, rich society mistress
and a poverty row housefrau who commits
suicide with expert balance in all. In fact, all
are good, especially Helen Mirren as the
way-out rich girl and Arthur Lowe as an unc-
tous African potentate.

O. HENRY'S FULL HOUSE

1952, 116 MINS, US

Dir Henry Hathaway, Howard Hawks, Henry King,
Henry Koster, Jean Negulesco   *Prod* Andre Hakim
Scr Richard Breen, Walter Bullock, Ivan Goff, Ben
Roberts, Lamar Trotti   *Ph* Lloyd Ahern, Lucien Ballard,
Milton Krasner, Joe MacDonald   *Ed* Nick De Maggio,
Barbara McLean, William B. Murphy   *Mus* Alfred
Newman
● Charles Laughton, Marilyn Monroe, Richard
Widmark, Anne Baxter, Fred Allen, Jeanne Crain (20th
Century-Fox)

This ties together five of O. Henry's classics into a full house of entertainment that has something for all tastes. The five classics are tied together by John Steinbeck's narration.

The Cop and the Anthem gets the quintet off to an enjoyable 19-minute start as Charles Laughton milks the fat part of Soapy, the gentleman bum who tries unsuccessfully to get arrested so he can spend the winter months in a warm jail.

The Clarion Call is a 22-minute excursion into melodrama with a twist. Dale Robertson plays the cop with a conscience who must arrest Richard Widmark, an old pal gone wrong and to whom he owes a debt.

The Last Leaf plunges into dramatics for 23 minutes, with Anne Baxter, Jean Peters and Gregory Ratoff keeping it emotionally sure. It's the tale of a girl, without the will to live because of an unhappy love affair, who believes she will die when the last leaf falls from a vine outside her window.

Fred Allen, Oscar Levant and young Lee Aaker keep amusing a highly burlesqued takeoff on *The Ransom of Red Chief*, the comedy saga of two city slickers who make the mistake of kidnapping for ransom the hellion son of a backwoods Alabama rich farmer. It's broad fun as directed by Howard Hawks.

Picture closes with a choice little account of that tender story of young love, *The Gift of the Magi*, splendidly trouped by Jeanne Crain and Farley Granger.

■ OBJECT OF BEAUTY, THE

1991, 101 MINS, US/UK ◇ ▽
Dir Michael Lindsay-Hogg   *Prod* Jon S. Denny
Scr Michael Lindsay-Hogg   *Ph* David Watkin   *Ed* Ruth Foster   *Mus* Tom Bahler   *Art Dir* Derek Dodd
● John Malkovich, Andie MacDowell, Lolita Davidovich, Rudi Davies, Joss Ackland, Bill Paterson (Avenue/BBC)

The Object of Beauty is a throwback to the romantic comedies of Swinging London cinema, but lacks the punch of the best of that late 1960s genre.

John Malkovich toplines as a ne'er-do-well holed up in a swank London hotel with mate Andie MacDowell. Everyone assumes the two of them are married, but MacDowell is still hitched to estranged hubbie Peter Riegert.

Plot concerns the title object, a small Henry Moore figurine that MacDowell received from Riegert as a present and which Malkovich desperately wants to sell or use for an insurance scam to cover his hotel tab and ongoing business reverses.

Key script contrivance has a deaf-mute maid (Rudi Davies), newly hired at the hotel, becoming obsessed with the Moore sculpture and stealing it for a keepsake.

Malkovich ably brings out the unsympathetic nature of his antihero, but the script doesn't help him much. The viewer will instantly side with MacDowell, whose natural beauty is augmented here by a feisty violent streak whenever Malkovich steps over the line (which is frequent). Result is a mildly diverting but empty picture.

■ OBJECTIVE, BURMA!

1945, 142 MINS, US ▽
Dir Raoul Walsh   *Prod* Jerry Wald   *Scr* Ranald MacDougall, Lester Cole   *Ph* James Wong Howe
Ed George Amy   *Mus* Franz Waxman   *Art Dir* Ted Smith
● Errol Flynn, Henry Hull, William Prince, James Brown, George Tobias (Warner)

Yarn [from an original story by Alvah Bessie] deals with a paratroop contingent dropped behind the Japanese lines in Burma to destroy a radar station. The chutists achieve their objective but while returning to a desig-

nated spot to be picked up by planes and flown back to the base they're overtaken by Japs. Then follows a series of exciting experiences by the troopers against overwhelming odds.

The film has considerable movement, particularly in the early reels, and the tactics of the paratroopers are authentic in their painstaking detail. However, while the scripters have in the main achieved their purpose of heightening the action, there are scenes in the final reels that could have been edited more closely.

Flynn gives a quietly restrained performance as the contingent's leader, while supporting players who also perform capably are Henry Hull, as a war correspondent; William Prince, James Brown, George Tobias, Dick Erdman and Warner Anderson.

■ OBSESSION

1949, 96 MINS, UK
Dir Edward Dmytryk   *Prod* N.A. Bronsten   *Scr* Alec Coppel   *Ph* C. Pennington Richards, Robert Day
Ed Lilo Carruthers   *Mus* Nino Rota
● Robert Newton, Sally Gray, Naunton Wayne, Phil Brown (Rank/Independent Sovereign)

Powerful suspense is the keynote of Edward Dymtryk's first British directional effort and a strong dramatic situation has been developed from Alec Coppel's ill-fated stage play *A Man about a Dog*, which ran for only a few nights.

A straightforward situation is presented in which a doctor plans the 'perfect' murder of his wife's American lover. Firstly the victim is confined in chains and the intention is to keep him alive while the hue and cry is on. If suspicion should fall on the doctor he could always produce the missing person.

In the early stages the pace could be quickened but the whole atmosphere becomes tense when the official Scotland Yard inquiries begin. Naunton Wayne as the Yard superintendent is an example of perfect casting and his nonchalant manner deserves particular praise.

■ OBSESSION

1976, 98 MINS, US ◇ ▽
Dir Brian De Palma   *Prod* George Litto, Harry N. Blum   *Scr* Paul Schrader   *Ph* Vilmos Zsigmond
Ed Paul Hirsch   *Mus* Bernard Herrmann   *Art Dir* Jack Senter
● Cliff Robertson, Genevieve Bujold, John Lithgow, Sylvia Kuumba Williams, Wanda Blackman (Columbia)

Obsession is an excellent romantic and nonviolent suspense drama starring Cliff Robertson and Genevieve Bujold, shot in Italy and New Orleans.

Paul Schrader's script [from a story by Brian De Palma] is a complex but comprehensible mix of treachery, torment and selfishness. Robertson is haunted with guilt for the death of wife Bujold and child Wanda Blackman, both kidnapped in 1959.

Sixteen years later, on a trip abroad, he sees a lookalike to Bujold, and gets swept away with this new girl. John Lithgow, as Robertson's business partner, is not happy with these events.

Robertson's low-key performance is as crucial to the manifold surprise impact as Bujold's versatile, sensual and effervescent charisma.

■ OCEAN'S ELEVEN

1960, 127 MINS, US ◇ ▽
Dir Lewis Milestone   *Prod* Lewis Milestone   *Scr* Harry Brown, Charles Lederer   *Ph* William H. Daniels
Ed Philip W. Anderson   *Mus* Nelson Riddle   *Art Dir* Nicolai Remisoff

● Frank Sinatra, Dean Martin, Sammy Davis Jr, Peter Lawford, Richard Conte, Cesar Romero (Warner)

Although basically a no-nonsense piece about the efforts of 11 ex-war buddies to make off with a multi-million dollar loot from five Vegas hotels, the film is frequently one resonant wisecrack away from turning into a musical comedy. Laboring under the handicaps of a contrived script, an uncertain approach and personalities in essence playing themselves, the production never quite makes its point, but romps along merrily unconcerned that it doesn't.

Coincidence runs rampant in the screenplay, based on a story by George Clayton Johnson and Jack Golden Russell. Set in motion on the doubtful premise that 11 playful, but essentially law-abiding wartime acquaintances from all walks of life would undertake a job that makes the Brink's hoist pale by comparison, it proceeds to sputter and stammer through an interminable initial series of scrambled expository sequences.

Acting under the stigma of their own flashy, breezy identities, players such as Frank Sinatra, Dean Martin, Sammy Davis Jr and Peter Lawford never quite submerge themselves in their roles, nor try very hard to do so. At any rate, the pace finally picks up when the daring scheme is set in motion.

The dialog is sharp, but not always pertinent to the story being told. And director Lewis Milestone has failed to curb a tendency toward flamboyant but basically unrealistic behaviour, as if unable to decide whether to approach the yarn straight or with tongue-in-cheek.

■ OCTAGON, THE

1980, 103 MINS, US ◇ ▽
Dir Eric Karson   *Prod* Joel Freeman   *Scr* Leigh Chapman   *Ph* Michel Hugo   *Ed* Dann Cahn
Mus Dick Halligan   *Art Dir* James Schoppe
● Chuck Norris, Karen Carlson, Lee Van Cleef, Tadashi Yamashita, Carol Bagdasarian, Art Hindle (American Cinema)

A bizarre plot involving the Ninja cult of Oriental assassins with international terrorism provides plenty of chances for Chuck Norris and other martial arts experts to do their stuff, and pic has a nicely stylized look with excellent lensing and music.

Screenwriter Leigh Chapman, working from a story she wrote with Paul Aaron, weaves a wildly incredible but entertaining tale of retired martial arts champ Norris being recruited by wealthy Karen Carlson to rub out the terrorists who have earmarked her for death. Norris gets involved when he realizes his nemesis is Tadashi Yamashita, his sworn enemy from their youthful days as chopsocky pupils.

The vendetta culminates in a pitched battle at the octagonal training compound of the Ninja cult, a school for terrorists of all types.

■ OCTOBER MAN, THE

1947, 93 MINS, UK ▽
Dir Roy Ward Baker   *Prod* Eric Ambler   *Scr* Eric Ambler   *Ph* Erwin Hillier, Russell Thomson   *Ed* Alan Jaggs   *Mus* William Alwyn   *Art Dir* Alex Vetchinsky
● John Mills, Joan Greenwood, Edward Chapman, Kay Walsh (Two Cities)

Author of many thrillers, Eric Ambler makes his debut as producer of his own script, and a fine beginning it is, with John Mills in top form and a grand all-round cast.

Unlike the usual Ambler story, this is not a whodunit or spy story. It's a study of the conflict in the mind of a mentally sick man, not absolutely certain that he hasn't committed murder.

John Mills plays Jim Ackland, an industrial chemist who suffers from a brain injury following an accident in which the child of a friend is killed. He blames himself for the child's death, and develops suicidal tendencies. Released from hospital, he is warned of a possible relapse unless he takes things easy. He returns to work and lives in a suburban hotel inhabited by a small cross-section of the community.

Molly, a fashion model (Kay Walsh), is found murdered and Jim is suspected. From then on it is the police versus Jim until, finally escaping arrest, he tracks down the murderer.

The dialog is taut and adult, and the direction by Roy Ward Baker, onetime assistant to Hitchcock, is imaginative. Only defect is the tempo. For a suspense pic it sometimes lacks pace.

• •

■ OCTOPUSSY

1983, 130 MINS, UK ◇ Ⓥ

Dir John Glen   *Prod* Albert R. Broccoli   *Scr* George MacDonald Fraser, Richard Maibaum, Michael G. Wilson   *Ph* Alan Hume   *Ed* John Grover, Peter Davies, Henry Richardson   *Mus* John Barry   *Art Dir* Peter Lamont
● Roger Moore, Maud Adams, Louis Jourdan, Kristina Wayborn, Kabir Bedi, Steven Berkoff (Eon/United Artists)

Storyline concerns a scheme by hawkish Russian General Orlov (Steven Berkoff) to launch a first-strike attack with conventional forces against the NATO countries in Europe, relying upon no nuclear retaliation by the West due to weakness brought about by peace movement in Europe.

Orlov is aided in his plan by a beautiful smuggler Octopussy (Maud Adams), her trader-in-art-forgeries underling Kamal (Louis Jourdan) and exquisite assistant Magda (Kristina Wayborn). James Bond (Roger Moore, in his sixth entry) is set on their trail when fellow agent 009 (Andy Bradford) is killed at a circus in East Berlin.

Trail takes Bond to India (lensed in sumptuous travelog shots) where he is assisted by local contact Vijay (tennis star Vijay Amritraj in a pleasant acting debut). Surviving an impromptu *Hounds of Zaroff* tiger hunt turned manhunt and other perils, Bond pursues Kamal to Germany for the hair-raising race against time conclusion.

Film's high points are the spectacular aerial stuntwork marking both the pre-credits teaser and extremely dangerous-looking climax.

• •

■ ODD ANGRY SHOT, THE

1979, 90 MINS, AUSTRALIA ◇ Ⓥ

Dir Tom Jeffrey   *Prod* Tom Jeffrey, Sue Milliken   *Scr* Tom Jeffrey   *Ph* Don McAlpine   *Ed* Brian Kavanagh   *Mus* Michael Carlos   *Art Dir* Bernard Hides
● Graham Kennedy, John Hargreaves, John Jarratt, Bryan Brown, Graeme Blundell (Samson)

Australia's involvement in the Vietnamese war created a political and moral dichotomy in the country such as hadn't been seen since the question of conscription at the time of World War I. If anything, Tom Jeffrey's *The Odd Angry Shot* could be said to be cathartic.

The film concentrates on a group of Aussie volunteers. Special Air Service troops, militarily as elite as the Yanks' Special Forces, but in this view, at least, rather more bawdy than the Americans as depicted in *The Deer Hunter*. It is the same futile war, but what Jeffrey has expressed faithfully is the pragmatism and essential hope-of-survival of the troops on the ground.

Jeffrey has been helped immeasurably by his cameraman, Don McAlpine, who worked as a news cameraman in Vietnam.

There is no agonising political or moral message, and Jeffrey maintains the basic good humor of the guys at a very believable pitch.

• •

■ ODD COUPLE, THE

1968, 105 MINS, US ◇ Ⓥ

Dir Gene Saks   *Prod* Howard W. Koch   *Scr* Neil Simon   *Ph* Robert B. Hauser   *Ed* Frank Bracht   *Mus* Neal Hefti   *Art Dir* Hal Pereira, Walter Tyler
● Jack Lemmon, Walter Matthau, John Fiedler, Herbert Edelman, David Sheiner, Larry Haines (Paramount)

The Odd Couple, Neil Simon's smash legit comedy, has been turned into an excellent film starring Jack Lemmon and Walter Matthau. Simon's somewhat expanded screenplay retains the broad, as well as the poignant, laughs inherent in the rooming together of two men whose marriages are on the rocks.

Teaming of Lemmon and Matthau has provided each with an outstanding comedy partner. As the hypochondriac, domesticated and about-to-be-divorced Felix, Lemmon is excellent. Matthau also hits the bullseye in a superior characterization.

Carrying over from the legit version with Matthau are Monica Evans and Carole Shelley, the two English girls from upstairs, and John Fiedler, one of the poker game group which, until Lemmon moved in, revelled in cigarette butts, clumsy sandwiches, and other signs of disarray.

New to the plot is opening scene of Lemmon bumbling in suicide attempts in a Times Square flophouse. By the time he arrives at Matthau's apartment, his amusing misadventures have caused a wrenched beak and neck. Staggered main titles help prolong this good intro.

• •

■ ODD MAN OUT

1947, 116 MINS, UK Ⓥ

Dir Carol Reed   *Scr* F.L. Green, R.C. Sherriff   *Ph* Robert Krasker   *Ed* Fergus McDonnett   *Mus* William Alwyn   *Art Dir* Ralph Brinton
● James Mason, Robert Newton, Robert Beatty, Kathleen Ryan, F.J. McCormick, Cyril Cusack (Two Cities)

Accent in this film [based on the novel by F.L. Green] is on art with a capital A. Carol Reed has made his film with deliberation and care, and has achieved splendid teamwork from every member of the cast. Occasionally too intent on pointing his moral and adorning his tale, he has missed little in its telling.

Story is set in a city in Northern Ireland and takes place between 4 pm and midnight on a winter's day. Johnnie, leader of an organization, sentenced for gun running, has broken gaol and is hiding with his girl Kathleen. He plans a holdup on a mill to obtain funds, and although deprecating violence, he takes a gun. During the holdup he accidentally kills a man, is badly wounded himself, and the driver of the car panics, leaving Johnnie to fend for himself. Bleeding, he stumbles through the city trying to hide from the police.

For Mason two-thirds of the film is silent. From the moment he is wounded he has few lines and has to drag himself along, a hunted man with a fatal wound. It is hardly his fault that, in this passive character that expresses little more than various phases of pain and occasional delirium, he is less effective than he could be.

Making her screen debut, Kathleen Ryan reveals undoubted ability and much promise. Graduate of the Abbey and Gate theatres, this 24-year-old redhead was 'discovered' in Ireland by Reed, who coached and trained her for this part.

• •

■ ODDS AGAINST TOMORROW

1959, 96 MINS, US

Dir Robert Wise   *Prod* Robert Wise   *Scr* John O. Killens   *Ph* Joseph Brun   *Ed* Dede Allen   *Mus* John Lewis
● Harry Belafonte, Robert Ryan, Shelley Winters, Ed Begley, Gloria Grahame (HarBel/United Artists)

On one level, *Odds against Tomorrow* is a taut crime melodrama. On another, it is an allegory about racism, greed and man's propensity for self-destruction. Not altogether successful in the second category, it still succeeds on its first.

The point of the screenplay, based on a novel of the same name by William P. McGivern, is that the odds against tomorrow coming at all are very long unless there is some understanding and tolerance today. The point is made by means of a crime anecdote, a framework not completely satisfactory for cleanest impact.

Harry Belafonte, Robert Ryan and Ed Begley form a partnership with plans to rob a bank with a haul estimated to total $150,000. An ill-matched trio, their optimistic plans are dependent on the closest teamwork. Belafonte, a horse-playing night club entertainer, is something of an adolescent. Ryan is a psychotic. Begley, as ex-cop fired for crookedness, has learned from this experience only not to get caught.

Director Robert Wise has drawn fine performances from his players. It is the most sustained acting Belafonte has done. Ryan makes the flesh crawl as the fanatical bigot. Begley turns in a superb study of a foolish, befuddled man who dies, as he has lived, without knowing quite what he has been involved in.

Shelley Winters etches a memorable portrait, and Gloria Grahame is poignant in a brief appearance. Joseph Brun's black and white photography catches the grim spirit of the story and accents it with some glinting mood shots. John Lewis' music backs it with a neurotic, edgy, progressive jazz score.

• •

■ ODE TO BILLY JOE

1976, 105 MINS, US ◇ Ⓥ

Dir Max Baer   *Prod* Max Baer, Roger Camras   *Scr* Herman Raucher   *Ph* Michel Hugo   *Ed* Frank E. Morriss   *Mus* Michel Legrand   *Art Dir* Philip Jefferies
● Robby Benson, Glynnis O'Connor, Joan Hotchkis, Sandy McPeak, James Best, Terence Goodman (Warner)

Ode to Billy Joe is a superbly sensitive period romantic tragedy, based on Bobbie Gentry's 1967 hit song lyric. Robby Benson is excellent as Billy Joe McAllister, and Glynnis O'Connor is outstanding as his Juliet.

The time is 1953. O'Connor and Benson are both emerging into fumbling sexual awareness, written and acted in a way to bring out all of the humor, heart and horniness that attends on such matters. O'Connor's parents, sensationally played by Sandy McPeak and Joan Hotchkis, have a wary but loving eye out for her.

The puppy love affair unfolds smoothly as it is interwoven with family, church, work and community functions, all of which establish the people as real, loving folk and create a magnificent dramatic environment.

• •

■ ODESSA FILE, THE

1974, 128 MINS, UK/W. GERMANY ◇ Ⓥ

Dir Ronald Neame   *Prod* John Woolf, John R. Sloan   *Scr* Kenneth Ross, George Markstein   *Ph* Oswald Morris   *Ed* Ralph Kemplen   *Mus* Andrew Lloyd Webber   *Art Dir* Rolf Zehetbauer
● Jon Voight, Maximilian Schell, Maria Schell, Mary Tamm, Derek Jacobi, Shmuel Rodensky (Columbia)

The Odessa File is an excellent filmization of

Frederick Forsyth's novel of a reporter who tracks down former Nazi SS officers still undetected in 1960s Germany.

Jon Voight's accidental reading of the diary of a suicide (a Jewish survivor of Nazi prison camps) leads to his attempted infiltration of Odessa, a secret network of SS veterans who have maintained their cover in diverse positions in postwar commerce and government.

Voight's immediate search is for Maximilian Schell, a quest inhibited by secret Odessa officials, but facilitated by Israeli intelligence agents who also get on his tail.

As Voight establishes his credentials in a superb grilling by Noel Willman, his girl (Mary Tamm) is under close surveillance by Odessa-affiliated police, and Klaus Lowitsch is dispatched to kill him.

● ●

■ **OEDIPUS THE KING**

1968, 97 MINS, UK ◇
Dir Philip Saville   *Prod* Michael Luke   *Scr* Michael Luke, Philip Saville   *Ph* Walter Lassally   *Ed* Paul Davies   *Mus* Janni Christou   *Art Dir* Yanni Migadis
● Christopher Plummer, Orson Welles, Lilli Palmer, Richard Johnson, Cyril Cusack (Rank/Crossroads)

This version of Sophocles' play deals fairly superficially with the bare bones of the tragic story of the king, dragged down to degradation after having discovered that, unwittingly, he has murdered his father and married and had children by his mother.

It is filmed with dignity, extremely well directed and excellently acted by a small cast of fine thesps.

Director Philip Saville and, indeed, the translation do not harp so melodramatically on the tragic sequences. Done with restraint, physical action is confined mainly to the assassination of Laius and a recap. Nor is the translation sonorously heavy but retains a dignified poetry.

Christopher Plummer as Oedipus gives a sterling performance. His early clashes with his brother-in-law (Richard Johnson) are striking and the latter's performance is a useful foil to Plummer's.

Lilli Palmer, as the ill-fated Jocasta, does not fully bring out the tragic personality until the final bitter scene, and Orson Welles is unusually subdued, but all the more effective, as Tiresias, the blind prophet of doom.

The film is superbly lensed with the greens and browns making a soft, yet bleak backdrop to the sombre action.

● ●

■ **OF HUMAN BONDAGE**

1934, 83 MINS, US
Dir John Cromwell   *Prod* Pandro S. Berman
Scr Lester Cohen   *Ph* Henry W. Gerrard   *Ed* William Morgan   *Mus* Max Steiner   *Art Dir* Van Nest Polglase, Carroll Clark
● Leslie Howard, Bette Davis, Frances Dee, Kay Johnson, Reginald Denny, Alan Hale (Radio)

Basically, it's an obvious and familiar theme [from the novel by W. Somerset Maugham]. The unrequited love of the art-medical student, inhibited and club-footed to the degree that he stumbles physically, mentally and spiritually, commands respect and sympathy. But as the footage unreels, the feeling grows that he's pretty much of a clunk to go the hard way he does for the strumpet who treats him so shabbily.

Leslie Howard tries hard to mellow his assignment. But somehow he misses at times because the script is too much against him. Perhaps Bette Davis is to blame. She plays her free 'n' easy vamp too well, so that it negates any audience sympathy for the gentle Howard.

Reginald Denny and Alan Hale get over a couple of lusty innings as males on the hunt

who know how to handle gals of her type. Reginald Owen, too, milks his assignment.

Locales are Paris and London, chiefly London, with Davis in Cockney dialect throughout.

● ●

■ **OF HUMAN BONDAGE**

1946, 100 MINS, US
Dir Edmund Goulding   *Prod* Henry Blanke
Scr Catherine Turney   *Ph* Peverell Marley
Ed Clarence Kolster   *Mus* Erich Wolfgang Korngold
Art Dir Hugh Reticker, Harry Kelso
● Eleanor Parker, Paul Henreid, Alexis Smith, Edmund Gwenn, Janis Paige, Patric Knowles (Warner)

Somerset Maugham story has been given excellent period mounting to fit early London background, is well-played and directed in individual sequences, but lacks overall smoothness.

Top roles go to Eleanor Parker, as the tart; Paul Henreid, the sensitive artist-doctor, and Alexis Smith, novelist. A third femme love interest is Janis Paige. Three femmes represent various loves that enter the life of Henreid, frustrated artist, but major interest is concentrated on character played by Parker and how she affects Henreid's happiness.

Edmund Goulding's direction gets good work out of the cast generally and helps interest although most of major characters carry little sympathy, Parker's work is excellent, as is Henreid's depiction of the self-pitying cripple. Smith's role has been edited to a comparatively small part.

● ●

■ **OF HUMAN BONDAGE**

1964, 98 MINS, UK ◉
Dir Ken Hughes, Henry Hathaway   *Prod* James Woolf   *Scr* Bryan Forbes   *Ph* Oswald Morris
Ed Russell Lloyd   *Mus* Ron Goodwin   *Art Dir* John Box
● Kim Novak, Laurence Harvey, Robert Morley, Siobhan McKenna, Roger Livesey, Jack Hedley (Seven Arts/M-G-M)

There was the Leslie Howard/Bette Davis 1934 version of this story and the 1946 entry starring Paul Henried and Eleanor Parker. This stab, with Laurence Harvey and Kim Novak, will not erase the memories. For those who come fresh to *Of Human Bondage*, this perceptive but highly introspective yarn by Somerset Maugham may seem a hard-to-take slab of period meller.

The pic had a ruffled nascency, due primarily to clashes of opinion among top brass. Henry Hathaway quit to let in Ken Hughes as director and it's bruited that the star duo did not always see eye-to-eye on the chore in hand.

Story concerns a withdrawn, young medical student very conscious of his clubfoot who manages to become a doctor in London's East End despite being totally besotted with the tawdry charms of a promiscuous waitress.

Allowing for the fact that Bryan Forbes' screenplay is light on humor, Harvey nevertheless plays the role in such a stiff, martyred manner as to forfeit any sympathy or liking in the audience.

The role that made Davis doesn't serve the same purpose for Novak. Yet she gamely tackles a wide range of emotions and seems to be far more aware of the demands of her role than is her co-star.

Collectors of cinema trivia will notice, with interest, the fleeting appearances by highly-paid scriptwriter Forbes as a student-extra without any lines, an inexplicable throwback to his earlier business of being an actor.

● ●

■ **OF HUMAN HEARTS**

1938, 100 MINS, US
Dir Clarence Brown   *Prod* John W. Considine Jr
Scr Bradbury Foote   *Ph* Clyde DeVinna   *Ed* Frank E. Hull   *Mus* Herbert Stothart   *Art Dir* Cedric Gibbons, Harry Oliver

● Walter Huston, James Stewart, Beulah Bondi, Guy Kibbee, Charles Coburn, John Carradine (M-G-M)

Frontier life in a village on the banks of the Ohio river in the days preceding the Civil War is the background against which Clarence Brown tells the story of a mother's sacrifice for the career of an ungrateful son.

Brown is said to have cherished the idea of producing this story for some time. Screenplay is based on Honore Morrow's story *Benefits Forgot*, published nearly a score of years earlier.

A meaner, more selfish, bigoted and ornery group never existed than these villagers, into whose midst comes a preacher of the Gospel with his wife and 12-year-old son. They had promised him $400 a year to be custodian of their souls, then cut the allowance to $250 and some cast-off clothing for his dependents.

The preacher accepts these terms with humility. The son, however, rebels against the petty tyranny and selfishness of the neighbors.

Latter part of the film relates the boy's brilliant success as a surgeon in the Union army, and his neglect for his mother, now widowed.

Walter Huston is the zealous circuit riding preacher, a man of uncompromising principle. Beulah Bondi is the wife and mother and she shades the transitions of age with convincing acting. Gene Reynolds first appears as the son, a role played by James Stewart in the later scenes.

Chief cause for disappointment with the film is its slow pace, and the defeatist mood of the story.

● ●

■ **OF MICE AND MEN**

1939, 104 MINS, US ◉
Dir Lewis Milestone   *Prod* Hal Roach   *Scr* Eugene Solow   *Ph* Norbert Brodine   *Ed* Bert Jordan
Mus Aaron Copland
● Burgess Meredith, Lon Chaney Jr, Betty Field, Charles Bickford, Roman Bohnen, Bob Steele (Roach/United Artists)

Under skillful directorial guidance of Lewis Milestone, the picture retains all of the forceful and poignant drama of John Steinbeck's original play and novel, in presenting the strange palship and eventual tragedy of the two California ranch itinerants. In transferring the story to the screen, scripter Eugene Solow eliminated the strong language and forthright profanity. Despite this requirement for the Hays whitewash squad, Solow and Milestone retain all of the virility of the piece in its original form.

As in the play, all of the action takes place on the San Joaquin valley barley ranch. George and Lennie catch on as hands. Former's strange wardship of the half-wit possessed of Herculean strength is never quite explained – in fact he wonders himself just why: George keeps Lennie close to him always – continually fearful that the simpleton will kill someone with his brute power. The pair plan to buy a small ranch of their own, where Lennie can raise rabbits, when disaster strikes.

Despite the lack of box-office names in the cast set-up, the players have been excellently selected. Burgess Meredith is capital as George, and Lon Chaney Jr dominates throughout with a fine portrayal of the childlike giant. Betty Field is the sexy wife who encourages approaches from the ranch workers; Bob Steele is her jealous and hard hitting husband.

☐ 1939: Best Picture (Nomination)

● ●

OFFENCE, THE

1973, 112 MINS, UK ◇ ▽

Dir Sidney Lumet   *Prod* Denis O'Dell   *Scr* John Hopkins   *Ph* Gerry Fisher   *Ed* John Victor Smith   *Art Dir* John Clark

● Sean Connery, Trevor Howard, Vivien Merchant, Ian Bannen, Derek Newark, Peter Bowles (United Artists)

There's a powerful confrontation of authority and accused between police sergeant Sean Connery and suspected child molester Ian Bannen in Sidney Lumet's *The Offence*. A brilliant scene, however, does not in itself make for a brilliant overall feature.

This often cold and dreary tale is about the self realization of a veteran police officer that his own mind contains much of the evil with which he is confronted daily. Indeed, his willing accumulation of brutality and violence-packed incidents is recognized almost immediately by Bannen and it is not long before accuser becomes the accused.

However, the lengthy lead-up to this important scene is played against dreary backgrounds and with colorless people.

OFFICER AND A GENTLEMAN, AN

1982, 126 MINS, US ◇ ▽

Dir Taylor Hackford   *Prod* Martin Elfand   *Scr* Douglas Day Stewart   *Ph* Donald Thorin   *Ed* Peter Zinner   *Mus* Jack Nitzsche   *Art Dir* Philip M. Jefferies

● Richard Gere, Debra Winger, Louis Gossett Jr, David Keith, Lisa Blount, Lisa Eilbacher (Lorimar)

An Officer and a Gentleman deserves a 21-gun salute, maybe 42. Rarely does a film come along with so many finely-drawn characters to care about.

Officer belongs to Louis Gossett Jr, who takes a near-cliche role of the tough, unrelenting drill instructor and makes him a sympathetic hero without ever softening a whit.

The title refers to the official reward awaiting those willing to endure 13 weeks of agony in Naval Aviation Officer Candidate School, whose initial aim – via Gossett – is to wash out as many hopefuls as possible before letting the best move on to flight training.

Pic is a bit muddled, via flashback, in setting up Richard Gere's motives for going into the training. Suffice to say he did not enjoy a model childhood. On leave, Gere meets Debra Winger, one of the local girls laboring at a paper mill and hoping for a knight in naval officer's uniform to rescue her from a life of drudgery. It's another fetching little slut role for Winger and she makes the most of it.

A secondary romance involves Gere's friend and fellow candidate, (David Keith) who takes a tumble for Winger's friend (Lisa Blount), another slut but not so fetching.

OH DAD, POOR DAD, MAMMA'S HUNG YOU IN THE CLOSET, AND I'M FEELIN' SO SAD

1967, 86 MINS, US ◇ ▽

Dir Richard Quine   *Prod* Ray Stark, Stanley Rubin   *Scr* Ian Bernard   *Ph* Geoffrey Unsworth   *Ed* Warren Low, David Wages   *Mus* Neal Hefti   *Art Dir* Phil Jeffries

● Rosalind Russell, Robert Morse, Barbara Harris, Hugh Griffith, Jonathan Winters, Lionel Jeffries (Paramount)

Producers have labored mightily to bring forth a mouse. Rosalind Russell is the emasculating mother of Robert Morse, sired by Jonathan Winters who is dead, but stuffed and carried around by his widow as she and son travel about. Barbara Harris is the nymphet chippie who puts the make on Morse so successfully that he kills her in a psycho-substitution for his ma. Hugh Griffith is an ageing lecher eyed by Russell as her next victim.

Despite multi-colored wigs and a game attempt, Russell falls flat. Morse has an appealing, winsome quality which certain film roles will fit, but not this one. Harris does rather well, however, and Griffith is up to the demands of his role. Winters gets the best comedy material, but it clashes with the rest. Film was shot on Jamaica locations, which adds color, but to no avail.

OH, GOD!

1977, 97 MINS, US ◇ ▽

Dir Carl Reiner   *Prod* Jerry Weintraub   *Scr* Larry Gelbert   *Ph* Victor Kemper   *Ed* Bud Molin   *Mus* Jack Elliott   *Art Dir* Jack Senter

● George Burns, John Denver, Teri Garr, Donald Pleasence, Ralph Bellamy, William Daniels (Warner)

Oh, God! is a hilarious film which benefits from the brilliant teaming of George Burns, as the Almighty in human form, and John Denver, sensational in his screen debut as a supermarket assistant manager who finds himself a suburban Moses.

Carl Reiner's controlled and easy direction of a superb screenplay and a strong cast makes the Jerry Weintraub production a warm and human comedy.

An Avery Corman novel is the basis for Larry Gelbart's adaptation which makes its humanistic points while taking gentle pokes at organized Establishment religions, in particular the kind of fund-raising fundamentalism epitomized by Paul Sorvino. Teri Garr is excellent as Denver's perplexed but loyal wife.

OH, MR. PORTER!

1937, 84 MINS, UK

Dir Marcel Varnel   *Prod* Edward Black   *Scr* J.O.C. Orton, Val Guest, Marriott Edgar   *Ph* Arthur Crabtree   *Ed* R.E. Dearing, Alfred Roome   *Mus* Louis Levy (dir.)   *Art Dir* Alex Vetchinsky

● Will Hay, Moore Marriott, Graham Moffatt, Sebastian Smith, Percy Walsh, Dennis Wyndham (Gainsborough)

A railway comedy [story by Frank Launder], reminiscent of *The Ghost Train* (1931), written around the comic personality of Will Hay, supported by his very 'aged' and very 'young' foils.

An amiable misfit, with a brother-in-law in the railway company, is sent as a last resort to a tiny, obscure village in Ireland as stationmaster, where his family hope to be rid of him. Finding a decrepit clerk and fat-boy porter the only occupants of the station, where no train ever stops, the newcomer tries to convert the ramshackle dump into something worthy of his dignity.

He senses a sinister atmosphere, in that his predecessors have either disappeared mysteriously, or gone nutty. Tracking a lost excursion to a disused tunnel and derelict line, the dauntless stationmaster discovers the supposedly ghostly crew are gun-runners about to get over the border.

No love interest to mar the comedy, as far as the juvenile mind is concerned, and the whole thing is amusing, if over-long.

O.H.M.S.

1937, 87 MINS, UK

Dir Raoul Walsh   *Scr* Lesser Samuels, Ralph Bettinson, Austin Melford, Bryan Wallace   *Ph* Roy Kellino   *Ed* Charles Saunders   *Mus* Louis Levy   *Art Dir* Edward Carrick

● Wallace Ford, John Mills, Anna Lee, Grace Bradley, Frank Cellier, Arthur Chesney (Gaumont-British)

Not much to get excited about. Takes off from a fetching theme, but that nothing much eventuates can largely be blamed on a dour and flabby script.

Wallace Ford is a lively enough personality in the central role. Narrative poses him as a petty American racketeer who flees to England from a threatened rap for murder. There he turns to the army as a hideout, enlisting as from Canada. With occasional touches of humor, picture relates his doings as a recruit, adding romance to the proceedings by making Ford the third corner in a play for the sergeant-major's daughter (Anna Lee). His rival, and a good natured one, is his barracks sidekick (John Mills).

Complications develop when Ford's former showgirl flame from the States pops up. Ford stows away on a ship and finds himself occupying the same vessel as his regiment bound for China. The girl is also aboard. Picture goes melodramatic for the final reel.

OH! WHAT A LOVELY WAR

1969, 144 MINS, UK ◇ ▽

Dir Richard Attenborough   *Prod* Brian Duffy, Richard Attenborough   *Scr* Charles Chilton, [Len Deighton]   *Ph* Gerry Turpin   *Ed* Kevin Connor   *Mus* Alfred Ralston   *Art Dir* Don Ashton

● Ralph Richardson, Laurence Olivier, John Gielgud, John Mills, Michael Redgrave, Vanessa Redgrave (Paramount/Accord)

Richard Attenborough's debut as a film director can be labelled with such debased showbiz verbal coinage as fabulous, sensational, stupendous, etc. It also happens to be dedicated, exhilarating, shrewd, mocking, funny, emotional, witty, poignant and technically brilliant.

A satire on war in which the songs are an integral part of the message, it was shot entirely on location, in and around Brighton.

Oh, What a Lovely War is an indictment of war which never relies on violence. Sudden, brutal death in combat is omitted and far more effectively, is rammed home by the symbol of poppies for each death.

The film is a kick in the pants for jingoism, false heroics, vanity and stupidity in high places. It never lessens or denigrates the bravery of those who took part, but brilliantly pinpoints the collective stupidity that made such a holocaust possible. The familiar wartime songs, sentiment, humor and satire are all incorporated, but Attenborough has never allowed any to stretch a mood beyond its capacity.

The film is seen through the eyes and family life of the humble Smith family, whose sons all go to war and are senselessly killed.

OIL FOR THE LAMPS OF CHINA

1935, 110 MINS, US

Dir Mervyn LeRoy   *Prod* Robert Lord   *Scr* Laird Doyle   *Ph* Tony Gaudio   *Ed* William Clemens   *Mus* Leo F. Forbstein (dir.)   *Art Dir* Robert Haas

● Pat O'Brien, Josephine Hutchinson, Jean Muir, Lyle Talbot, John Eldredge, Donald Crisp (Cosmopolitan/Warner)

This story, in book form, was a bestseller for over a year and caused a lot of talk. In transferring it to screen the filmers have taken many liberties, so that it evolves as a choppy, long, and sometimes confused yarn.

Alice Tisdale Hobart's original was an indictment of a great oil company for its subjugation of its employees. Film switches that around to a man's blind struggle against mistreatment, dishonesty in officials, personal misfortune, and rank deception on the part of his officers, with nothing more than faith in 'the company' as his wand.

Story is laid practically entirely in China. The Atlantis Oil Company has sent Pat O'Brien over there to sell oil to the Chinese. Because he's saving the company some money, his first baby dies in childbirth. Because his best friend has lost a minor sales contract, he fires him, etc. Comes the revolution. The rebels try to take a few thousand dollars of the company's money so he risks his life, sees his assistant shot, is badly wounded himself, and is in a hospital for months. But he saves the $15,000. When he's out of the hospital he's rewarded by being demoted.

....

■ OKLAHOMA!

1955, 145 MINS, US ◇ ⓥ

Dir Fred Zinnemann   *Prod* Arthur Hornblow Jr
Scr Sonya Levien, William Ludwig   *Ph* Robert Surtees
Ed Gene Ruggiero   *Mus* Richard Rodgers
Art Dir Oliver Smith
● Gordon MacRae, Shirley Jones, Gloria Grahame, Gene Nelson, Charlotte Greenwood, Rod Steiger (Magna)

The innovating musical comedy magic that Richard Rodgers and Oscar Hammerstein II first created when The Theatre Guild produced their *Oklahoma!* [in 1943] has been captured and, in some details, expanded in the film version. The tunes ring out with undiminished delight. The characters pulsate with spirit. The Agnes De Mille choreography makes the play literally leap.

The wide screen used for the Todd-AO process adds production scope and visual grandeur, capturing a vista of blue sky and green prairie that can be breathtaking.

Heading the cast, Gordon MacRae as Curly, and Shirley Jones as Laurey make a bright, romantic pair. The entire cast goes through its paces with verve and spirit. If the singing is good, the acting just fine, top honors go to De Mille and her dancers.

After all's said and done, the main burden still falls on MacRae and Jones. MacRae not only looks the part of Curly, he acts it out with a modicum of theatrics. He cuts a cleancut figure and he delivers his songs in grand style.

....

■ OKLAHOMA CRUDE

1973, 108 MINS, US ◇ ⓥ

Dir Stanley Kramer   *Prod* Stanley Kramer   *Scr* Marc Norman   *Ph* Robert Surtees   *Ed* Folmar Blangsted
Mus Henry Mancini   *Art Dir* Alfred Sweeney
● George C. Scott, Faye Dunaway, John Mills, Jack Palance, William Lucking, Harvey Jason (Columbia)

Oklahoma Crude is a dramatically choppy potboiler about oil wildcatting in 1913.

Faye Dunaway plays a bitter woman determined to bring in an oil well on her own, aided by Rafael Campos, an Indian laborer. John Mills aiming to help her out after years of parental abandonment, recruits George C. Scott from the hobo jungles. The three of them (Campos is killed off early) joust with Jack Palance, snarling provocateur of the oil trust which wants Dunaway's property.

Since Oklahoma today does not resemble 1913, director Stanley Kramer found a great location in Stockton, California, but the solid impact of that choice is often negated by erratic special effects work.

Scott hunkers around chewing the scenery, but occasionally the interplay with Dunaway is momentarily touching. Mills does well, but Palance's caricature destroys the chance for a good, tough characterization.

....

■ OLD BOYFRIENDS

1979, 103 MINS, US ◇ ⓥ

Dir Joan Tewkesbury   *Prod* Edward R. Pressman, Michele Rappaport   *Scr* Paul Schrader, Leonard Schrader   *Ph* William A. Fraker   *Ed* Bill Reynolds
Mus David Shire   *Art Dir* Peter Jamison
● Talia Shire, Richard Jordan, Keith Carradine, John Belushi, John Houseman, Buck Henry (Avco Embassy)

The premise of *Old Boyfriends* is an intriguing

and universal one, the fantasy of revisiting lovers out of an individual's past.

Script is contemporary and grounded in realism, right down to the shifting morals which have marked male-female relationships in the past. In this case, the femme (Talia Shire) is a clinical psychologist who roots into her past after a failed suicide attempt.

Shire's odyssey takes her across America to old beaux including her college sweetheart (Richard Jordan), high school romance (John Belushi) and first adolescent love (Keith Carradine). The experience proves to be disquieting.

A protege of Robert Altman, novice director Joan Tewkesbury, who scripted his *Nashville*, employs similar loosely narrative techniques, with the Shire character holding together the series of set pieces.

....

■ OLD DARK HOUSE, THE

1932, 74 MINS, US

Dir James Whale   *Prod* Carl Laemmle Jr   *Scr* Benn Levy, R. C. Sherriff   *Ph* Arthur Edeson   *Ed* Clarence Kolster   *Art Dir* Charles D. Hall
● Boris Karloff, Melvyn Douglas, Charles Laughton, Gloria Stuart, Lilian Bond, Ernest Thesiger (Universal)

The [original J.B.] Priestley novel must have been a bit more plausible than as evidenced in the cinematic transition. But regardless, it has all the elements for horror and thriller exploitation, including as it does a mad brute butler (Boris Karloff), insanity, ghosts in the family closets, sex, romance, not to mention the titular setting in a storm-torn Welsh mountain retreat.

Let one stop and think but a few seconds about what's happened on the screen and there'd be no picture; hence, it's been the somewhat too difficult task of the Laemmle studio to pile on trick after trick. For it's a certainty that the average mortal, despite the raging elements without, would have carried on in the storm at any price, or camped out in their motor, rather than sit in for an evening with the eccentric Femm family or their insane butler, Morgan.

Among the performances, Karloff with a characteristically un-drawing-room physical getup, by no means impresses as a sissy by stature, demeanor and surliness. Gloria Stuart gives excellent account of herself, although that extreme decolletage is rather uncalled for considering the locale. Charles Laughton turns in one of his usually tophole performances as the Lancashire knight. Melvyn Douglas is rather hit and miss under the circumstances, and that stable tete-a-tete with Lilian Bond, who is satisfactory up until that point, makes it a bit worse.

....

■ OLD ENOUGH

1984, 91 MINS, US ◇ ⓥ

Dir Marisa Silver   *Prod* Dina Silver   *Scr* Marisa Silver   *Ph* Michael Ballhaus   *Ed* Mark Burns
Mus Julian Marshall   *Art Dir* Jeffrey Townsend
● Sarah Boyd, Rainbow Harvest, Neill Barry, Danny Aiello, Susan Kingsley, Roxanne Hart (Silverfilm)

The tale of friendship between two young girls of widely different social backgrounds, *Old Enough* has just the right balance of humor and insight to connect with audiences.

Produced and directed by sisters Dina and Marisa Silver, the project evolved from Utah's Sundance Institute for Independent Filmmakers. Nonetheless, the simple story and modest budgeted effort need make no excuses for finished product.

Story centers on 12-year-old Lonnie Sloan (Sarah Boyd) from an upper-class New York City family and slightly older Karen Bruckner (Rainbow Harvest) from blue-collar background. Both are at important

emotional turning points when they meet on the street of the widely divergent economic neighborhood. It is an easily understandable attraction of opposites.

The mix of fresh faces and a few seasoned pros in cast all register indelibly. Both Boyd and Harvest have burden of carrying the film, which they accomplish with ease.

....

■ OLD FASHIONED WAY, THE

1934, 69 MINS, US

Dir William Beaudine   *Prod* William LeBaron
Scr Garnett Weston, Jack Cunningham, Charles Bogle [W. C. Fields]   *Ph* Benjamin Reynolds   *Mus* Harry Revel   *Art Dir* John Goodman
● W. C. Fields, Joe Morrison, Judith Allen, Jan Duggan, Nora Cecil, Baby LeRoy (Paramount)

Made to order for W. C. Fields and permitting him to do his old cigar-box juggling among other things, *The Old Fashioned Way* is light comedy material that will please the Fields followers.

A repertoire troupe of the days when *The Drunkard* and *East Lynne* were big draws serves as the background and the small town of Bellefontaine, O, is the locale. It is here that the Great McGonigle, who heads the rep company, runs into all kinds of difficulties, most of them of a financial origin.

At the outset the troupe is on the way to the next stand, Bellefontaine. Train sequences provide some pretty good laughs from the beginning as McGonigle skips a summons and accidentally falls heir to an upper berth, not to mention the reception at Bellefontaine he mistakingly believes to be in his honor.

Joe Morrison is worked in for songs with suitable spots provided for him during the *Drunkard* sequence. Morrison's voice registers well and on the love interest he carries himself through satisfactorily. Romantic side of the story treated lightly but has its place as fitted in, Judith Allen holding up the other end adequately.

....

■ OLD GRINGO

1989, 119 MINS, US ◇ ⓥ

Dir Luis Puenzo   *Prod* Lois Bonfiglio   *Scr* Aida Bortnik, Luis Puenzo   *Ph* Felix Monti   *Ed* Juan Carlos Macias, William Anderson, Glen Farr   *Mus* Lee Holdridge
Art Dir Stuart Wurtzel
● Jane Fonda, Gregory Peck, Jimmy Smits, Patricio Contreras, Jenny Gago (Fonda/Columbia)

Based on Carlos Fuentes' novel *Gringo Viejo*, the complex psychological tableau makes it easy to see why Jane Fonda plopped herself in the plum role of 40-ish spinster on the run Harriet Winslow. She is swept up by accident in the Mexican Revolution and swept off her feet by a charismatic general in Pancho Villa's popular front.

A rakish Jimmy Smits as Gen. Arroyo is superbly cast. He conveys the cocksure yet sensitive machismo and motivations of his character's torment between the revolution he lives and the woman he loves.

As the embittered, sardonic journalist Ambrose Bierce, Gregory Peck has found a role that suits him to a T. He portrays the world-weary Bierce with relish and wit.

The paternalistic figure in a nebulous love triangle with Fonda and Smits, Peck exudes a sympathetic mien despite his crusty exterior. His best moments come long before the denouement, and the film's wittiest lines are his alone.

....

■ OLD MAN AND THE SEA, THE

1958, 86 MINS, US ◇

Dir John Sturges   *Prod* Leland Hayward   *Scr* Peter Viertel   *Ph* James Wong Howe, Floyd Crosby, Tom Tutwiler   *Ed* Arthur P. Schmidt   *Mus* Dimitri Tiomkin
Art Dir Art Loel, Edward Carrere

● Spencer Tracy, Felipe Pazos, Harry Bellaver (Warner)

Ernest Hemingway's introspective one-episode novelette, *The Old Man and the Sea*, is virtually a one-character film, the spotlight being almost continuously on Spencer Tracy as the old Cuban fisherman who meets his final test in his tremendous struggle with the huge marlin.

The picture has power, vitality and sharp excitement as it depicts the gruelling contest between man and fish. It is exquisitely photographed and skillfully directed. It captures the dignity and the stubborness of the old man, and it is tender in his final defeat.

And yet it isn't a completely satisfying picture. There are long and arid stretches, when it seems as if producer and director were merely trying to fill time.

It is Tracy's picture from beginning to end. One could quarrel with his interpretation of the old man. There are moments when he is magnificent and moving, and others when he seems to move in a stupor. It is, on the whole, a distinguished and impressive performance, ranging from the old man's pursuit of the fish, to hooking him, to the long chase and the final slashing battle.

In a supporting part, Felipe Pazos plays the boy who loves the old man and understands him. It is a very appealing and tender performance. Harry Bellaver has a small role as the tavern owner who sympathizes with the old man and, with the rest of the village, learns to admire him for his catch.

John Sturges directs with a view to keeping the essential values intact. It's not his fault that the basic material simply doesn't sustain interest throughout 86 minutes.

. . . .

■ OLD YELLER

1957, 83 MINS, US ◇ Ⓥ

Dir Robert Stevenson   *Prod* Walt Disney   *Scr* Fred Gipson, William Tunberg   *Ph* Charles P. Boyle   *Ed* Stanley Johnson   *Mus* Oliver Wallace   *Art Dir* Carroll Clark
● Dorothy McGuire, Fess Parker, Tommy Kirk, Kevin Corcoran, Chuck Connors (Walt Disney)

Disney organization's flair for taking a homely subject and building a heartwarming film is again aptly demonstrated in this moving story set in 1869 of a Texas frontier family and an old yeller dog. Based on Fred Gipson's novel of same tag, this is a careful blending of fun, laughter, love, adventure and tragedy.

Emphasis is laid upon animal action, including squirrels, jackrabbits, buzzards and newborn calves as well as more rugged depictions. Packed into film's tight footage is the 115-pound dog's fight with a huge bear, its struggle with a marauding wolf and battle with a pack of wild hogs.

. . . .

■ OLIVER!

1968, 146 MINS, UK ◇ Ⓥ

Dir Carol Reed   *Prod* John Woolf   *Scr* Vernon Harris   *Ph* Oswald Morris   *Ed* Ralph Kemplen   *Mus* Lionel Bart   *Art Dir* John Box
● Ron Moody, Shani Wallis, Oliver Reed, Harry Secombe, Hugh Griffith, Jack Wild (Columbia/Romulus)

This $10 million pic is a bright, shiny, heartwarming musical, packed with songs and lively production highspots. Lionel Bart's [1960] stage musical hit is adroitly opened out by director Carol Reed.

Oliver! goes with a cheerful swing, leading up to a strong dramatic climax when Bill Sikes gets his comeuppance. Mark Lester, as the workhouse waif who finds happiness after a basinful of scary adventures, is a frail Oliver, with a tremulous, piping singing voice, but he's vigorous and mischievous

enough, and is sufficiently dewy-eyed and angelic to captivate the audience.

The youngsters are natural scene-stealers but major honors go to a diminutive 15-year-old, Jack Wild, who plays the Artful Dodger with knowing cunning and impudent self-confidence.

Ron Moody's Fagin lacks some of the malignance usually associated with the role of the wily old rascal though he shows sudden flashes of evil temper. He riotously squeezes every morsel of fun out of his tuition scenes with the little pickpockets.

Bart's familiar songs, such as 'Food, Glorious Food,' 'Consider Yourself,' 'I'd Do Anything' and 'Oom-Pah-Pah' are as fresh as ever.

□ 1968: Best Picture

. . . .

■ OLIVER TWIST

1948, 116 MINS, UK Ⓥ

Dir David Lean   *Prod* Ronald Neame   *Scr* David Lean, Stanley Haynes   *Ph* Guy Green   *Ed* Jack Harris   *Mus* Arnold Bax   *Art Dir* John Bryan
● John Howard Davies, Robert Newton, Alec Guinness, Kay Walsh, Francis L. Sullivan, Anthony Newley (Rank/Cineguild)

From every angle this is a superb achievement. Dickens' devotees may object to condensing of the story and omission of some of the minor characters. But what is left still runs close to two hours.

One of its merits is the absence of considerable unnecessary dialog, the child Oliver having the fewest lines ever allotted to so prominent a character. He has the wistful air of the typical Dickens waif and heads almost faultless casting.

Camerawork is on an exceptionally high level. Opening shots of a storm-swept sky and heavy clouds give an eerie quality that immediately grips the imagination. Josephine Stuart's delineation of a woman in labor pains, dragging herself across rain-sodden fields to a distant light that spells sanctuary, is unparalleled in its poignant realism.

Alec Guinness gives a revoltingly faithful portrait of Fagin and Kay Walsh extracts just the right amount of viciousness overcome by pity in her delineation of Nancy. Robert Newton is a natural for the brutish Sikes and gets every ounce out of his opportunities.

. . . .

■ OLIVER'S STORY

1978, 92 MINS, US ◇ Ⓥ

Dir John Korty   *Prod* David V. Picker   *Scr* Erich Segal, John Korty   *Ph* Arthur Ornitz   *Ed* Stuart H. Pappe   *Mus* Francis Lai   *Art Dir* Robert Gundlach
● Ryan O'Neal, Candice Bergen, Nicola Pagett, Edward Binns, Benson Fong, Ray Milland (Paramount)

Love Story is a tough act to follow, but *Oliver's Story* manages to hold its own. The continuation of Erich Segal's tale of fated lovers gets a sensitive and moving treatment from director and coscripter (with Segal) John Korty.

Oliver's Story begins with the burial of Jenny Cavalleri Barrett, whose death closed out the first pic. Ryan O'Neal, working as a lawyer in a prestigious New York firm, is burdened by a sense of despair and loneliness, along with a liberal dose of self-pity.

Enter Candice Bergen as the Bonwit heir in Bonwit Teller, the flip side in looks and disposition to the Jenny character created by Ali MacGraw. Their meeting is one of those coincidences that only occur in films, but Korty and Segal plot the relationship with a sureness that proves to be highly endearing.

The most moving segments come, ironically, not out of the O'Neal-Bergen encounters, but from a few brief scenes between O'Neal and Ray Milland, who encores as his wealthy banker father. It's a tribute to

both performances and Korty's direction that this most basic of conflicts is resolved here in a genuinely satisfying manner.

. . . .

■ OMEGA MAN, THE

1971, 98 MINS, US ◇ Ⓥ

Dir Boris Sagal   *Prod* Walter Seltzer   *Scr* John William Corrington, Joyce H. Corrington   *Ph* Russell Metty   *Ed* William Ziegler   *Mus* Ron Grainer   *Art Dir* Arthur Loel, Walter M. Simonds
● Charlton Heston, Anthony Zerbe, Rosalind Cash, Paul Koslo, Lincoln Kilpatrick, Eric Laneuville (Warner)

The Omega Man is an extremely literate science-fiction drama starring Charlton Heston as the only survivor of a worldwide bacteriological war, circa 1975. Thrust of the well-written story [adapted from Richard Matheson's novel] is Heston's running battle with deranged survivors headed by Anthony Zerbe.

The deserted streets of LA through which Heston drives by day while Zerbe's eye-sensitive mutations hide until nightfall, provide low-key but powerful emphasis on what can and does happen when the machinery of civilized society grinds to a halt.

An Oriental missile war has caused a worldwide plague. Zerbe, formerly a TV newscaster, has become the leader of the mutations, whose extreme reaction to the science which caused the disaster has led to wanton destruction of cultural and scientific objects. Rosalind Cash provides romantic interest for Heston as a member of another band of rural survivors not yet under Zerbe's control.

. . . .

■ OMEN, THE

1976, 111 MINS, US ◇ Ⓥ

Dir Richard Donner   *Prod* Harvey Bernhard   *Scr* David Seltzer   *Ph* Gilbert Taylor   *Ed* Stuart Baird   *Mus* Jerry Goldsmith   *Art Dir* Carmen Dillon
● Gregory Peck, Lee Remick, David Warner, Billie Whitelaw, Leo McKern, Harvey Stevens (20th Century-Fox)

Suspenser starring Gregory Peck and Lee Remick as the unwitting parents of the anti-Christ. Richard Donner's direction is taut. Players all are strong.

There's enough exposition of the Book of Revelation to educate on the spot a person from another civilization. As for any religious commitment needed, that problem is minimal; the only premise one must accept is that the fallen Lucifer remains a very strong supernatural being.

Peck, well cast as a career American ambassador, is convinced by Italian priest Martin Benson to substitute another hospital baby for the one wife Remick lost in childbirth. Five years later, strange things begin to happen.

At various points, portents of Satanism emerge, underscored (or, rather, overscored) by Jerry Goldsmith's heavy music.

. . . .

■ OMEN II, DAMIEN

1978, 109 MINS, US ◇ Ⓥ

Dir Don Taylor   *Prod* Harvey Bernhard, Charles Orme   *Scr* Stanley Mann, Michael Hodges   *Ph* Bill Butler   *Ed* Robert Brown   *Mus* Jerry Goldsmith   *Art Dir* Philip M. Jefferies
● William Holden, Lee Grant, Jonathan Scott-Taylor, Robert Foxworth, Lew Ayres, Sylvia Sidney (20th Century-Fox)

Alas, Little Orphan Damien, lucky enough to be taken in by a rich uncle after bumping off his first pair of foster parents, can't resist killing the second set, too, along with assorted friends of the family. Damien is obviously wearing out his welcome.

Damien is 13 and has a double personality problem, being both an anti-Christ and a rather obnoxious teenager. Stoically played by Jonathan Scott-Taylor, Damien has apparently been behaving himself for the past seven years, since his uncle (William Holden) and aunt (Lee Grant) suspect nothing and love him very much as does his cousin (Lucas Donat).

Only cranky old Aunt Marion (Sylvia Sidney) knows something is wrong with the boy, but a raven gets rid of her. Then a pesky reporter (Elizabeth Shepherd) shows up. So the raven pecks her eyes out and she stumbles in front of a truck.

One day, Damien's platoon sergeant at the military school suggests he reads the *Book of Revelations* and find out why he's special. He soon gets the knack of killing people himself, with spectacular touches that top the decapitations of his tender years.

••••••••••••••••••••••••••••••••••

■ ON A CLEAR DAY YOU CAN SEE FOREVER

1970, 129 MINS, US ◇ ⊛
Dir Vincente Minnelli   *Prod* Howard W. Koch, Alan Jay Lerner   *Scr* Alan Jay Lerner   *Ph* Harry Stradling   *Ed* David Bretherton   *Mus* Burton Lane   *Art Dir* John DeCuir
● Barbra Streisand, Yves Montand, Bob Newhart, Larry Blyden, Simon Oakland, Jack Nicholson (Paramount)

[Based on the Lerner-Lane 1965 Broadway musical], the story line, without the gimmick of reincarnation, is pure soap suds. Barbra Streisand is a chain-smoker so addicted that she doesn't fly because 'I'm afraid of the No Smoking sign'. She is engaged to Larry Blyden, a business school student in the upper 2% of his class who is so square that he is selecting a future employer on the basis of the pension plan.

To stop smoking before an important dinner with the personnel recruiter from Chemical Foods Inc, Streisand crashes a medical school class in hypnotism taught by Yves Montand. He accidentally discovers that she has extra-sensory perception. Under hypnosis, she becomes an aristocratic femme fatale with whom Montand falls in love.

••••••••••••••••••••••••••••••••••

■ ON DANGEROUS GROUND

1951, 82 MINS, US
Dir Nicholas Ray   *Prod* John Houseman   *Scr* A.I. Bezzerides   *Ph* George E. Diskant   *Ed* Roland Gross   *Mus* Bernard Herrmann   *Art Dir* Albert D'Agostino, Ralph Berger
● Ida Lupino, Robert Ryan, Ward Bond, Charles Kemper, Anthony Ross, Sumner Williams (RKO)

Lack of definition in characters is chief flaw in writing, with Nicholas Ray, who also directed, and A.I. Bezzerides sharing the blame for their adaptation of the Gerald Butler novel, *Mad with Much Heart*. There's not much Robert Ryan can do with the character of a cop made tough by the types with whom he is brought into contact, nor does Ida Lupino have much opportunity as a blind girl who presumably softens Ryan's character.

First half of the footage is given over to Ryan's mental travail as a city prowl car cop who favors plenty of roughness for those he arrests. In fact, this ready use of fists eventually gets him assigned out of town to aid a county sheriff hunt down a madman who has killed a little girl. Trail leads to a lonely farmhouse where Ryan and Ward Bond, playing the father of the murder victim, encounter Lupino. The killer is her mentally deficient kid brother (Sumner Williams) whom she has hidden out.

Ray manages to inject an occasional bit of excitement into the yarn, and had the psychotic touches been elimated in the script, film could have qualified as okay, even if grim, melodrama.

••••••••••••••••••••••••••••••••••

■ ON GOLDEN POND

1981, 109 MINS, US ◇
Dir Mark Rydell   *Prod* Bruce Gilbert   *Scr* Ernest Thompson   *Ph* Billy Williams   *Ed* Robert L. Wolfe   *Mus* Dave Grusin   *Art Dir* Stephen Grimes
● Katharine Hepburn, Henry Fonda, Jane Fonda, Dabney Coleman (Universal/ITC/IPC)

Without question, these are major, meaty roles for Katharine Hepburn and Henry Fonda, and there could have been little doubt that the two would work superbly together. Fact that Ernest Thompson's 1978 play backs away from the dramatic fireworks that might have been mutes overall impact of the piece, but sufficient pleasures remain.

Fonda, a retired professor, and Hepburn arrive at their New England cottage to spend their 48th summer together. He's approaching his 80th birthday and, while it's clear that his wife is thoroughly familiar with his crotchety act, his mostly intentional rudeness and irascibility make life difficult for others in his vicinity.

At the half-hour point, along come daughter Jane Fonda, future son-in-law Dabney Coleman and latter's son Doug McKeon. Coleman manages a stand-off with the elder Fonda, but Jane is clearly still terrified of her dad, suffering from lingering feelings of neglect and inferiority.

The film's most moving interlude, a near-death scene, is saved for the end, and both Fonda (pere) and Hepburn are miraculous together here, conveying heartrending intimations of mortality which are doubly powerful due to the stars' venerable status.

••••••••••••••••••••••••••••••••••

■ ON HER MAJESTY'S SECRET SERVICE

1969, 139 MINS, UK ◇ ⊛
Dir Peter Hunt   *Prod* Harry Saltzman, Albert R. Broccoli   *Scr* Richard Maibaum, Simon Raven   *Ph* Michael Reed   *Ed* John Glen   *Mus* John Barry   *Art Dir* Syd Cain
● George Lazenby, Diana Rigg, Telly Savalas, Ilse Steppat, Gabriele Ferzetti, Bernard Lee (United Artists)

Film of break-neck physical excitement and stunning visual attractions in which George Lazenby replaced Sean Connery as James Bond.

Lazenby is pleasant, capable and attractive in the role, but he suffers in the inevitable comparison with Connery. He doesn't have the latter's physique, voice and saturnine, virile looks.

The baddie's hideout is perched on the peak of a Swiss alp, part Playboy Penthouse, part Frankenstein's laboratory, and part cave of the mountain troll. There Telly Savalas is experimenting with biological warfare to take over the world, under the guise of being a research institute for treating allergies.

In *Service* Bond finds his true love, Diana Rigg, coolly beautiful, intelligent, sardonic, and his equal in bed, on skis, driving hellbent on icy mountain roads, and with a few karate chops of her own.

••••••••••••••••••••••••••••••••••

■ ON MY WAY TO THE CRUSADES, I MET A GIRL WHO...

1968, 93 MINS, ITALY/US ◇
Dir Pasquale Festa Campanile   *Prod* Francesco Mazzei   *Scr* Luigi Magni, Larry Gelbart   *Ph* Carlo Di Palma   *Ed* Chas Nelson   *Mus* Riz Ortolami   *Art Dir* Piero Poletto
● Tony Curtis, Monica Vitti, Nino Castelnuovo, Hugh Griffith, John Richardson, Ivo Garrani (Julia/Warner/Seven Arts)

It's a mystery why Warner-Seven Arts abandoned the Italian title, *The Chastity Belt*, even briefly, for the long tongue-twisting title used outside of Italy but there's plenty of entertainment in this release.

Set in the Middle Ages, Larry Gelbart provides an extra measure of modern, romantic candor.

When bumpkin-type provincial noble Guerrando (Tony Curtis) is knighted to become a crusade draftee, he gets a castle, the tax-collecting concession and the right to have affairs with all eligible soft-bosomed femininity in his fief. Only holdout is Boccadoro (Golden Lips) played by Monica Vitti, an emancipated forest wench.

To safeguard his prize, Guerrando locks his chaste spouse into a chastity belt, puts the key into his pocket and heads out across the drawbridge. The indignant medieval feminist is determined to get even.

Director Pasquale Festa Campanile fluctuates between classy ribald satire and stock burlesque.

It is safe to assume that the original English version will further lighten some of the medieval clinkers that show here and there and tighten slack moments.

Curtis and Vitti are not at their best but the latter is much more at home in her role.

••••••••••••••••••••••••••••••••••

■ ON THE BEACH

1959, 134 MINS, US ◇ ⊛
Dir Stanley Kramer   *Prod* Stanley Kramer   *Scr* John Paxton   *Ph* Giuseppe Rotunno   *Ed* Frederic Knudtson   *Mus* Ernest Gold
● Gregory Peck, Ava Gardner, Fred Astaire, Anthony Perkins, Donna Anderson, John Tate (United Artists)

On the Beach is a solid film of considerable emotional, as well as cerebral, content. But the fact remains that the final impact is as heavy as a leaden shroud. The spectator is left with the sick feeling that he's had a preview of Armageddon, in which all contestants lost.

John Paxton, who did the screenplay from Nevil Shute's novel, avoids the usual cliches. There is no sergeant from Brooklyn, no handy racial spokesmen. Gregory Peck is a US submarine commander. He and his men have been spared the atomic destruction because their vessel was submerged when the bombs went off.

The locale is Australia and the time is 1964. Nobody remembers how or why the conflict started. 'Somebody pushed a button,' says nuclear scientist Fred Astaire. Australia, for ill-explained reasons, is the last safe spot on earth. It is only a matter of time before the radiation hits the continent and its people die as the rest of the world has died.

In addition to Peck and Astaire, the other chief characters include Ava Gardner, a pleasure-bent Australian; and a young Australian naval officer and his wife, Anthony Perkins and Donna Anderson. All the personal stories are well-presented. The trouble is it is almost impossible to care with the implicit question ever-present – do they live?

The cast is almost uniformly excellent. Peck and Gardner make a good romantic team in the last days of the planet. Perkins and Anderson evoke sympathy as the young couple. Fred Astaire, in his first straight dramatic role, attracts considerable attention.

••••••••••••••••••••••••••••••••••

■ ON THE BLACK HILL

1988, 116 MINS, UK ◇
Dir Andrew Grieve   *Prod* Jennifer Howarth   *Scr* Andrew Grieve   *Ph* Thaddeus O'Sullivan   *Ed* Scott Thomas   *Mus* Robert Lockhart   *Art Dir* Jocelyn James
● Mike Gwilym, Robert Gwilym, Bob Peck, Gemma Jones, Nesta Harris (BFI/Film Four/British Screen)

A low-budget drama about Welsh hill farmers may not sound broadly appealing, but Andrew Grieve's *On the Black Hill* is a remarkably moving and entertaining film [from the novel by Bruce Chatwin] offering a fascinating view of life in the border country between Wales and England.

Pic follows the Jones family from 1895–1980, but mainly centers around twin brothers Benjamin and Lewis Jones (played by brothers Mike and Robert Gwilym). It is through their inseparability, and the traumas and humor that inspires, that the story is told.

Bob Peck and Gemma Jones are excellent as the Welsh farming couple, and the pic ably displays the hardship of their life. The Gwilyms perform well and are especially good in the twins' later years.

● ●

■ ON THE TOWN

1949, 97 MINS, US ◇ ▽

Dir Gene Kelly, Stanley Donen *Prod* Arthur Freed *Scr* Betty Comden, Adolph Green *Ph* Harold Rosson *Ed* Ralph E. Winters *Mus* Roger Edens, Leonard Bernstein

● Gene Kelly, Frank Sinatra, Betty Garrett, Ann Miller, Jules Munshin, Vera-Ellen (M-G-M)

The pep, enthusiasm and apparent fun the makers of *On the Town* had in putting it together comes through to the audience and gives the picture its best asset.

Gene Kelly, Frank Sinatra and Jules Munshin are the three sailors on a 24-hour leave in New York. Betty Garrett, Ann Miller and Vera-Ellen are the three femmes who wind up with the navy.

Picture is crammed with songs and dance numbers. Picture kicks off and ends with 'New York, New York'. Tune is used in the beginning as a musical backing for a montage of three curious sailors prowling the city's points of interest. It gets the film off to a fascinating start and the style and pacing is continued.

Based on their musical play, the Adolph Green-Betty Comden script puts the players through light story paces as a setup for 10 tunes and dances.

Roger Edens, associate producer, did the music for the six new tunes and lyrics are by Green and Comden. Latter team, with Leonard Bernstein, did the four original numbers.

● ●

■ ON THE WATERFRONT

1954, 108 MINS, US ▽

Dir Elia Kazan *Prod* Sam Spiegel *Scr* Budd Schulberg *Ph* Boris Kaufman *Ed* Gene Milford *Mus* Leonard Bernstein

● Marlon Brando, Karl Malden, Lee J. Cobb, Rod Steiger, Pat Henning, Eva Marie Saint (Columbia)

Longshore labor scandals serve as the takeoff point for a flight into fictionalized violence concerning the terroristic rule of a dock union over its coarse and rough, but subdued, members.

Budd Schulberg's script was based on his own original which in turn was 'suggested' by the Malcolm Johnson newspaper articles. Schulberg greatly enhanced the basic story line with expertly-turned, colorful and incisive dialog.

Under Elia Kazan's direction, Marlon Brando puts on a spectacular show, giving a fascinating, multi-faceted performance as the uneducated dock walloper and former pug, who is basically a softie with a special affection for his rooftop covey of pigeons and a neighborhood girl back from school. Eva Marie Saint has enough spirit to escape listlessness in her characterization.

Story opens with Brando unwittingly setting the trap for the murder of a longshoreman who refuses to abide by the 'deaf and dumb' code of the waterfront.

Lee J. Cobb is all-powerful as the one-man boss of the docks. He looks and plays the part harshly, arrogantly and with authority. Another fine job is executed by Karl Malden as the local Catholic priest who is outraged to

the point that he spurs the revolt against Cobb's dictatorship.

Rod Steiger is a good choice as Brando's brother for both incline toward the hesitant manner of speech that has been especially identified with Brando. Steiger is Cobb's 'educated' lieutenant who is murdered when he fails to prevent Brando from blabbing to the crime probers.

□ 1954: Best Picture

● ●

■ ONCE A THIEF

1965, 106 MINS, US

Dir Ralph Nelson *Prod* Jacques Bar *Scr* Zekial Marko *Ph* Robert Burks *Ed* Fredric Steinkamp *Mus* Lalo Schifrin *Art Dir* George W. Davis, Paul Groesse

● Alain Delon, Ann-Margret, Van Heflin, Jack Palance, John Davis Chandler, Jeff Corey (M-G-M)

Once a Thief packs both violence and young married love in unfoldment of its theme, aptly titled, about an ex-con trying to go straight, but constantly harassed by a vengeful cop.

Once a Thief has a San Francisco setting, where lenser Robert Burks makes interesting use of Chinatown and North Beach locations to backdrop story of $1 million platinum robbery and ultimate violent demise of each member of the five-man gang that pulled the job. Alain Delon not too unwillingly is pulled into the plot when he finds his wife, Ann-Margret working in a cheap nightclub so they may live.

Delon delivers strongly. He's the romantic type who excels also in rugged action. Ann-Margret, too, is firstrate in her role. Van Heflin, as a police inspector who thinks Delon once shot him, and Jack Palance, as Delon's gangster brother, also star.

Heflin, as Delon's nemesis effectively plays the relentless police officer, and Palance, with less footage, similarly scores.

● ●

■ ONCE AROUND

1991, 114 MINS, US ◇ ▽

Dir Lasse Hallstrom *Prod* Amy Robinson, Griffin Dunne *Scr* Malia Scotch Marmo *Ph* Theo Van De Sande *Ed* Andrew Mondshein *Mus* James Horner *Art Dir* David Gropman

● Richard Dreyfuss, Holly Hunter, Danny Aiello, Laura San Giacomo, Gena Rowlands, Roxanne Hart (Universal/Cinecom)

Vast opportunities for unbearable quantities of sentimentality are fortunately squelched in *Once Around*, an intelligently engaging domestic comedy-drama. US debut by Lasse Hallstrom, director of the widely loved 1985 Swedish hit *My Life As a Dog*, keenly delineates how a woman finding happiness with a man for the first time paradoxically involves the serious deterioration of relations within her close-knit family.

Story is hung upon numerous family rituals – weddings, dinners, birthdays, baptisms, funerals – and opening sees thirty-something Holly Hunter being badgered about her marital prospects at the wedding of sister Laura San Giacomo.

Rebuffed by her b.f. (coproducer Griffin Dunne in a neat cameo), Hunter flees chilly Boston for the Caribbean, where she instantly is swept off her feet by irrepressible, vulgar, tireless, wealthy condominium salesman Richard Dreyfuss.

Brightest strategy is forcing the viewer to experience Hunter's family's acceptance of Dreyfuss. His sheer relentlessness darkens the mood and thickens the complexity of the situation, removing the film from the real of the feel-good Hollywood formula.

Danny Aiello (as the father), brightest in an excellent cast, invests all his scenes with evident emotional and mental deliberation.

Hunter has many nice moments. San Giacomo and Gena Rowlands (as the mother) are very much on the money.

● ●

■ ONCE IN PARIS

1978, 100 MINS, US ◇ ▽

Dir Frank D. Gilroy *Prod* Frank D. Gilroy, Manny Fuchs, Gerard Croce *Scr* Frank D. Gilroy *Ph* Claude Saunier *Ed* Robert Q. Lovett *Mus* Mitch Leigh

● Wayne Rogers, Gayle Hunnicutt, Jack Lenoir, Phillippe March, Clement Harari, Tanya Lopert (Gilroy)

Writer-director Frank Gilroy has come up with a highly personalized tale of a rough around-the-edges Yank screenwriter's relationship with a worldly chauffeur and a beauteous British aristocrat. Gilroy's developed the triad in subtle, believable, intelligent and often humorous fashion making *Once in Paris* a super film.

Shot entirely in Paris, with a French crew, the pic gets maximum mileage from its three principals: Wayne Rogers, Gayle Hunnicutt, and Jack Lenoir.

Michael Moore (Rogers) is a scenarist travelling to Paris for the first time to salvage a film script. He is met at the airport and immediately informed that the chauffeur (Lenoir) is a bad egg (he has served time for manslaughter) and will be replaced tout de suite.

The driver stays, of course, and develops a strong friendship with the writer. The writer eventually has an affair with the British aristocrat (Hunnicutt) in Paris on business – she just happens to occupy the hotel suite adjoining the scripter's.

● ●

■ ONCE IS NOT ENOUGH

1975, 121 MINS, US ◇

Dir Guy Green *Prod* Howard W. Koch *Scr* Julius J. Epstein *Ph* John A. Alonzo *Ed* Rita Roland *Mus* Henry Mancini *Art Dir* John DeCuir

● Kirk Douglas, Alexis Smith, David Janssen, George Hamilton, Melina Mercouri, Gary Conway (Paramount)

Jacqueline Susann's final novel, *Once Is Not Enough*, gallumphs to the screen as a tame potboiler. Kirk Douglas heads as a fading film producer devoted to daughter Deborah Raffin, so much so that he marries wealthy Alexis Smith to pay for the daughter's lifestyle.

Raffin resists the casual sexuality epitomized by George Hamilton, wealthy young man-about-town, and stumbles into a genuine love for David Janssen, a fading author who can't get it on in many areas of life anymore. Brenda Vaccaro plays a kooky magazine editor who tries to help Raffin.

Opulent production credits put the shallow dramaturgy even more to shame. Henry Mancini's lush romantic score is appropriate.

● ●

■ ONCE UPON A TIME IN AMERICA

1984, 227 MINS, US ◇ ▽

Dir Sergio Leone *Prod* Arnon Milchan *Scr* Leonardo Benvenuti, Piero De Bernardi, Enrico Medioli, Franco Arcalli, Franco Ferrini, Sergio Leone, Stuart Kaminsky *Ph* Tonino Delli Colli *Ed* Nino Baragli *Mus* Ennio Morricone *Art Dir* Carlo Simi, James Singelis

● Robert De Niro, James Woods, Elizabeth McGovern, Treat Williams, Tuesday Weld, Burt Young (Ladd)

Once upon A Time in America arrives as a disappointment of considerable proportions. Sprawling $32 million saga of Jewish gangsters over the decades is surprisingly deficient in clarity and purpose, as well as excitement and narrative involvement.

Pic opens with a series of extraordinary violent episodes. It's 1933 and some hoods knock off a girlfriend and some cohorts of 'Noodles' (Robert De Niro), while trying to track down the man himself.

Then, action shifts to 1968, when the aging De Niro (superior makeup job) returns to New York after a 35-year absence and reunites with a childhood pal, Fat Moe (Larry Rapp). De Niro is clearly on a mission relating to his past, and his later discovery of a briefcase filled with loot for a contract is obviously a portent of something big to come.

Leone's pattern of jumping between time periods isn't at all confusing and does create some effective poetic echoes, but also seems arbitrary at times and, because of the long childhood section, forestalls the beginning of involvement.

Quiet and subtle throughout, De Niro and his charisma rep the backbone of the picture but, despite frequent threats to become engaging, Noodles remains essentially unpalatable.

ONCE UPON A TIME IN THE WEST

1969, 165 MINS, US/ITALY ◇ ⓥ

Dir Sergio Leone *Scr* Sergio Leone, Sergio Donati *Ph* Tonino Delli Colli *Mus* Ennio Morricone *Art Dir* Carlo Simi

● Henry Fonda, Claudia Cardinale, Jason Robards, Charles Bronson, Gabriele Ferzetti, Lionel Stander (Paramount/Rafran/San Marco)

Henry Fonda and Jason Robards relish each screen minute as the heavies, and Charles Bronson plays Clint Eastwood's 'man with no name' role.

Leone's story here [from one by Dario Argento, Bernardo Bertolucci and himself], presented in broad strokes through careful interconnection of set-piece action, focuses on the various reactions of four people – the three male leads, plus Claudia Cardinale, extremely effective as a fancy lady from New Orleans – to the idea of garnering extreme wealth via ownership of a crucial watertown on the route of the transcontinental railroad.

The paradoxical, but honest 'fun' aspect of Leone's previous preoccupation with elaborately-stylized violence is here unconvincingly asking for consideration in a new 'moral' light. This means that Leone's own special talent for playing with film ideas gets lost in a no man's land of the merely initiative.

ONE DAY IN THE LIFE OF IVAN DENISOVICH

1971, 100 MINS, UK/NORWAY ◇ ⓥ

Dir Caspar Wrede *Prod* Caspar Wrede *Scr* Ronald Harwood *Ph* Sven Nykvist *Ed* Thelma Connell *Mus* Arne Nordheim *Art Dir* Per Schwab

● Tom Courtenay, Espen Skjonberg, James Maxwell, Alfred Burke, Eric Thompson, John Cording (Group W/Norsk/Leontes)

Based on the novel by Alexander Solzhenitsyn, *One Day in the Life of Ivan Denisovich* is a tribute to the inherent dignity of man and his ability to maintain his humanity under seemingly impossible conditions. Though faithful to the novel, the film emerges as strangely unmoving.

Life chronicles a 'good' day for Ivan Denisovich, a prisoner in the eighth year of a 10-year sentence at a Siberian labor camp. The day is filled with small victories over the system. He does not fall ill, he manages to cop some extra food and tobacco, finds a hacksaw blade, builds a cinderblock wall and retires without incurring the wrath of his keepers.

Sincerity (and austerity) of the production, lensed expertly under fierce conditions in Norway by Sven Nykvist, cannot compensate for Caspar Wrede's lackluster direction and a script so sparse it almost seems nonexistent. Considering what they have to work with, the performers are fine, especially Courtenay who captures a mix of wiliness and childlike enthusiasm that is consistently convincing.

ONE FLEW OVER THE CUCKOO'S NEST

1975, 133 MINS, US ◇

Dir Milos Forman *Prod* Saul Zaentz *Scr* Lawrence Hauben, Bo Goldman *Ph* Haskell Wexler, Bill Butler, William Fraker *Ed* Richard Chew, Lynzee Klingman, Sheldon Kahn *Mus* Jack Nitzsche *Art Dir* Paul Sylbert

● Jack Nicholson, Louise Fletcher, William Redfield, Dean Brooks, Seatman Crothers, Danny DeVito (Fantasy)

One Flew over the Cuckoo's Nest is brilliant cinema theatre. Jack Nicholson in an outstanding characterization of asylum anti-hero McMurphy, and Milos Forman's direction of a superbly-cast film is equally meritorious.

The film is adapted from Ken Kesey's novel, the 1963 Broadway legit version of which, by Dale Wasserman, starred Kirk Douglas.

The $3 million film traces the havoc wrecked in Louis Fletcher's zombie-run mental ward when Nicholson (either an illness faker or a free spirit) displays a kind of leadership which neither Fletcher nor the system can handle.

The major supporting players emerge with authority: Brad Dourif (in a part played on Broadway by Gene Wilder), the acne-marked stutterer whose immature sexual fantasies are clarified on the night of Nicholson's aborted escape; Sidney Lassick, a petulant auntie; Will Sampson, the not-so-dumb Indian with whom Nicholson effects a strong rapport; and William Redfield, the over-intelligent inmate.

The film's pacing is relieved by a group escape and fishing boat heist, right out of Mack Sennett, and some stabs at basketball in which Nicholson stations the tall Indian for telling effect. This in turn make the shock therapy sequences awesomely potent.

ONE FOOT IN HEAVEN

1941, 106 MINS, US

Dir Irving Rapper *Prod* Hal B. Wallis *Scr* Casey Robinson *Ph* Charles Rosher *Ed* Warren Low *Mus* Max Steiner

● Fredric March, Martha Scott, Beulah Bondi, Gene Lockhart, Elisabeth Fraser, Harry Davenport (Warner)

A warm and human preachment for godliness, this biography of a Methodist minister is from the best-seller by Hartzell Spence. About the only faults with the picture are its slowness in the first half and the tendency of director Irving Rapper to skip over the hectic postwar depression years. Most of the dramatic wallop is contained in the last 40 minutes, or when the Rev. Spence (Fredric March) is in conflict with the wealthy element in his Denver congregation.

Spence, originally a medical student, comes to religion through listening to an evangelist. He takes his fiancee (Martha Scott) from her opulent Canadian home to his first parish in an Iowa mud-road town. This is the beginning of a trek through similar parishes with the Spences undergoing various privations. They raise three children, likably played by Frankie Thomas, Elisabeth Fraser and Casey Johnson.

March and Scott are both splendid in their roles. The stars carry the brunt of the story, although the cast is both populous and excellent.

□ 1941: Best Picture (Nomination)

ONE FROM THE HEART

1982, 101 MINS, US ◇ ⓥ

Dir Francis Coppola *Prod* Gray Frederickson, Fred Roos, Armyan Bernstein *Scr* Armyan Bernstein, Francis Coppola *Ph* Vittorio Storaro *Ed* Arne Goursaud, Rudi Fehr, Randy Roberts *Mus* Tom Waits *Art Dir* Dean Tavoularis

● Frederic Forrest, Teri Garr, Nastassja Kinski, Raul Julia, Lainie Kazan, Harry Dean Stanton (Zoetrope)

Francis Coppola's *One from the Heart* is a hybrid musical romantic fantasy, lavishing giddy heights of visual imagination and technical brilliance onto a wafer-thin story of true love turned sour, then sweet.

Set against an intentionally artificial fantasy version of Las Vegas – with production designer Dean Tavoularis' studio-recreated casino strip, desert outposts and even the Vegas airport easily the film's best-paid and most dazzling stars – the film quite simply plots the break-up, separate dalliances and eventual happy ending of a pair of five-year lovers (Frederic Forrest and Teri Garr) over the course of a single Independence Day.

He meets a sultry, exotic circus girl (Nastassja Kinski); she's swept away by a suave Latino singing waiter (Raul Julia).

With cheerful intermittent turns by Harry Dean Stanton as Forrest's best friend and partner, and Lainie Kazan as Garr's blowsy, sentimental barmaid buddy, the film's focus turns almost exclusively on Forrest's mounting efforts to win back Garr.

ONE GOOD COP

1991, 105 MINS, US ◇ ⓥ

Dir Heywood Gould *Prod* Laurence Mark *Scr* Heywood Gould *Ph* Ralf Bode *Ed* Richard Marks *Mus* David Foster, William Ross *Art Dir* Sandy Veneziano

● Michael Keaton, Rene Russo, Anthony LaPaglia, Kevin Conway, Rachel Ticotin (Hollywood/Silver Screen Partners IV)

Michael Keaton plays a staunchly decent cop who's as close to his longtime partner (Anthony LaPaglia) as he is to his fashion designer wife (Rene Russo). When widowed LaPaglia is killed in an heroic attempt to save a woman's life, Keaton and Russo take in his three orphaned little girls and decide they want to keep them.

But the authorities seem rather eager to take them away and Keaton's crowded digs can't accommodate a family, so he winds up on a wrong-side-of-the-law stunt to come up with enough money to be a hero at home.

The drug-dealer villains and inner-city skirmishes here are standard issue, and pic's basic parameters are only a cut above telefilm fare. Still, it's the skill with which the writer-director works the audience into the palm of his hand that makes this a crowd-pleaser.

Keaton demonstrates remarkable range and dexterity, giving his best performance since *Clean and Sober* [1988], and soulful LaPaglia, projects a toned-down version of the same true-hearted qualities that made him so winning in *Betsy's Wedding* [1990].

ONE HOUR WITH YOU

1932, 75 MINS, US

Dir Ernst Lubitsch *Prod* Ernst Lubitsch *Scr* Samson Raphaelson *Ph* Victor Milner *Mus* Oscar Strauss, Richard A. Whiting

● Maurice Chevalier, Jeanette MacDonald, Genevieve Tobin, Charlie Ruggles, Roland Young, George Barbier (Paramount)

It's a 100% credit to all concerned, principally Ernst Lubitsch on his production and direction, which required no little courage to carry out the continuity idea. The unorthodoxy concerns Maurice Chevalier's interpolated, confidential asides to his audience, in the *Strange Interlude* manner, although in an altogether gay spirit. Chevalier periodically interrupts the romantic sequence to come downscreen for a close-up to intimately address the 'ladies and gentlemen' as to his amorous problems.

It starts first with the opening scene in the Bois de Boulogne of Paris where Chevalier and his bride (Jeanette MacDonald) of three years are caught necking. The gendarme won't believe it's legal so they retire to their home where, in a boudoir scene, Chevalier interrupts just in time for that first aside to tell the audience that they really are married.

From then on Genevieve Tobin in an obvious 'make' role completes the triangle, with Chevalier periodically soliloquizing in a chatty, intimate manner (taking the audience into his marital confidence, so to speak) on what is he to do under the circumstances.

The excellent script [from the play by Lothar Schmidt] is replete with many niceties and touches which Lubitsch has skillfully dovetailed, without overdoing the detail. On top of that, Jeanette MacDonald is a superb vis-a-vis for the star, intelligently getting her song lyrics over in a quiet, chatty manner.
□ 1931/32: Best Picture (Nomination)

. . . .

■ ONE HUNDRED AND ONE DALMATIANS

1961, 79 MINS, US ◇

Dir Wolfgang Reitherman, Hamilton S. Luske, Clyde Geronimi   *Prod* Walt Disney   *Scr* Bill Peet
Ed Donald Halliday, Roy M. Brewer Jr   *Mus* George Bruns   *Art Dir* Ken Anderson
● (Walt Disney)

While not as indelibly enchanting or inspired as some of the studio's most unforgettable animated endeavors, this is nonetheless a painstaking creative effort. There are some adults for whom 101 – count 'em – dalmatians is about 101 dalmatians too many, but even the most hardened, dogmatic pooch-detester is likely to be amused by several passages in this story.

Bill Peet's screen yarn, based on the book by Dodie Smith, is set in London and concerned with the efforts of Blighty's four-legged population to rescue 99 dognapped pups from the clutches of one Cruella De Ville, a chic up-to-date personification of the classic witch. The concerted effort is successful thanks to a canine sleuthing network ('Twilight Bark') that makes Scotland Yard an amateur outfit by comparison.

Film purportedly is the $4 million end product of three years of work by some 300 artists. It benefits from the vocal versatility of a huge roster of 'voice' talents, including Rod Taylor, J. Pat O'Malley and Betty Lou Gerson. There are three songs by Mel Leven, best and most prominent of which is 'Cruella De Ville'.

. . . .

■ ONE HUNDRED MEN AND A GIRL

1937, 85 MINS, US

Dir Henry Koster   *Prod* Joe Pasternak   *Scr* Bruce Manning, Charles Kenyon, James Mulhauser
Ph Joseph Valentine   *Ed* Bernard W. Burton
Mus Charles Previn (dir.)   *Art Dir* John Harkrider
● Deanna Durbin, Adolphe Menjou, Alice Brady, Eugene Pallette, Mischa Auer, Leopold Stokowski (Universal)

Deanna Durbin is a bright, luminous star in her second picture, *One Hundred Men and a Girl*. Its originality rests on a firm and strong foundation, craftsmanship which has captured popular values from Wagner, Tchaikovsky, Liszt, Mozart and Verdi.

Universal wisely gives her excellent support in Leopold Stokowski, director of the Philadelphia symphony orchestra, who plays a lengthy film role with surprising ease and conviction, and Adolphe Menjou, who is in a role quite different from his usual type of parts. In addition to these two, Alice Brady breezes thru a short sequence in high glee, and Eugene Pallette, Mischa Auer and Billy Gilbert have important things to do and do them well.

The 'hundred men' of the title are members of a symphony orchestra of unemployed musicians whom Durbin is organizing and managing. Hans Kraly is credited with the original story.

Idea is that the unemployed artists in order to get sponsorship for a radio contract must obtain a conductor with an outstanding name of wide radio appeal. Stokowski, completing his regular subscription season, is unapproachable, but rebuffs which would discourage Napoleon mean nothing to the youngster.

Durbin, to Stokowski accompaniment, sings Mozart's 'Exultate' and the aria 'Libiamo ne' from *Traviata*.
□ 1937: Best Picture (Nomination)

. . . .

■ ONE IS A LONELY NUMBER

1972, 97 MINS, US ◇

Dir Mel Stuart   *Prod* Stan Margulies   *Scr* David Seltzer   *Ph* Michel Hugo   *Ed* David Saxon
Mus Michel Legrand   *Art Dir* Walter M. Simonds
● Trish Van Devere, Monte Markham, Janet Leigh, Melvyn Douglas, Jane Elliot, Jonathan Lippe (M-G-M)

One Is a Lonely Number is an excellent contemporary drama about the big and little problems affecting a divorced woman.

Trish Van Devere is the focal point of the story [from one by Rebecca Morris]. Suddenly abandoned by husband Paul Jenkins, she is forced into self-reliance for the first time in her life. It isn't always easy.

But Van Devere does get help, principally from the kindness of old store-keeper Melvyn Douglas; professional man-hater Janet Leigh; Jane Elliot, the heroine's best friend; and Maurice Argent, manager of the neighbourhood swimming pool where she finds employment as a life guard.

Van Devere, strikingly beautiful, projects a credible warmth, depth of character and a great deal of ladylike sensuality. Her romantic scenes with Monte Markham are as tasteful as they are most arousingly erotic.

. . . .

■ ONE MAGIC CHRISTMAS

1985, 88 MINS, US/CANADA ◇ ▣

Dir Phillip Borsos   *Prod* Peter O'Brian   *Scr* Thomas Meehan   *Ph* Frank Tidy   *Ed* Sidney Wolinsky
Mus Michael Conway Baker   *Art Dir* Bill Brodie
● Mary Steenburgen, Gary Basaraba, Harry Dean Stanton, Arthur Hill, Elizabeth Harnois, Robbie Magwood (Walt Disney/Silver Screen Partners II/Telefilm Canada)

One Magic Christmas represents an emotionally rewarding and artistically successful attempt to pull off the sort of uplifting family fare Hollywood used to do so well but lately has forgotten how to make.

Director Phillip Borsos keeps sentimentality nicely in check as he presents the sad Christmas season being faced by the Grainger family. Dad has been laid off, Mom is hardly managing to pay the bills, and they and the two kids are being evicted from their home just in time for the holidays.

Just when it appears things can't get any worse, they get very much worse indeed. The drama becomes intensely grim at midpoint, as Mom hits the absolute bottom-of-the-barrel. As has been seen periodically up to now, however, Mom has had an angel appointed to restore the proper spirit to her, and he quickly takes over to remedy matters.

Mary Steenburgen is realistically depressed for a long while, and is then very wonderfully won over to optimism and warmth.

The real find is six-year-old Elizabeth Harnois for the role of the little daughter who, while pathetically deprived of what any kid wants, doesn't give up on Mom.

. . . .

■ ONE MILLION B.C.

1940, 80 MINS, US ▣

Dir Hal Roach, Hal Roach Jr   *Prod* Hal Roach
Scr Mickell Novack, George Baker, Joseph Frickert, Grover Jones   *Ph* Norbert Brodine   *Ed* Ray Snyder

Mus Werner R. Heymann   *Art Dir* Charles D. Hall, Nicolai Remisoff
● Victor Mature, Carole Landis, Lon Chaney Jr, John Hubbard, Mamo Clark, Nigel de Brulier (Roach/United Artists)

One Million B.C. looks something like A.D.1910; it's that corny. Except for the strange-sounding grunts and monosyllabic dialog, it is also another silent. Hal Roach, who spent a lifetime making comedies, goes to the other extreme as producer of the prehistoric spectacle, filmed in Nevada. D.W. Griffith was associated with Roach in production of the film at the beginning but withdrew following dissension concerning casting and other angles. His name does not appear in the credits.

There isn't much sense to the action nor much interest in the characters. Majority of the animals fail to impress but the fight between a couple of lizards, magnified into great size, is exciting and well photographed. The ease with which some of the monsters are destroyed by man is a big laugh, notably the way one is subdued with a fishing spear. Knocking off a giant iguana is another audience snicker.

On occasion, also, the actions of the characters, including Victor Mature, bring a guffaw. He plays the part ox-like and the romantic interest, with Carole Landis on the other end, fails to ignite. Chaney Jr carves a fine characterization from the role of a tribal chieftain.

The story, pretty thin, relates to the way common dangers serve to wash up hostilities between the Rock and Shell clans, with a note of culture developed by the heroine (Landis) who astonishes the lads of the stone age when she sees to it that the women are to be served first, and the roast dinosaur (or whatever it is) is cut off in hunks with a rock knife, instead of torn off by the hands.

. . . .

■ ONE MILLION YEARS B.C.

1966, 100 MINS, UK ◇ ▣

Dir Don Chaffey   *Prod* Michael Carreras   *Scr* Michael Carreras   *Ph* Wilkie Cooper   *Ed* James Needs, Tom Simpson   *Mus* Mario Nascimbene   *Art Dir* Robert Jones
● Raquel Welch, John Richardson, Percy Herbert, Robert Brown, Martine Beswick, Jean Wladon (Hammer/Seven Arts)

Biggest novelty gimmick is that, despite four writers on screenplay [Mickell Novak, George Baker and Joseph Frickert from 1940 screenplay *One Million B.C.*, plus producer Michael Carreras], dialog is minimal, consisting almost entirely of grunts. Raquel Welch here gets little opportunity to prove herself an actress but she is certainly there in the looks department.

Don Chaffey does a reliable job directorially, but leans heavily on the ingenious special effects in the shape of prehistoric animals and a striking earthquake dreamed up by Ray Harryhausen. Simple idea of the film is of the earth as a barren, hostile place, one million years B.C., inhabitated by two tribes, the aggressive Rock People and the more intelligent, gentler Shell People.

John Richardson plays a Rock man who is banished after a fight with his gross father (Robert Brown). Wandering the land, battling off fearful rubber prehistoric monsters, he comes across the Shell People and falls for Welch, one of the Shell handmaidens. The two go off together to face innumerable other hazards.

. . . .

■ ONE NIGHT OF LOVE

1934, 98 MINS, US

Dir Victor Schertzinger   *Scr* S.K. Lauren, James Gow, Edmund North   *Ph* Joseph Walker   *Mus* Victor Schertzinger (adapt.)

● Grace Moore, Tullio Carminati, Lyle Talbot, Mona Barrie, Jessie Ralph, Luis Alberni (Columbia)

One Night of Love is basically an operatic film. It's the fact that the film is human, down to earth, that helps most. Even the operatic excerpts have all been carefully picked for popular appeal.

Story [by Dorothy Speare and Charles Beahan] is one of those convenient little yarns spun around the career of a singer (Grace Moore). She fails to win a radio contest so goes to Europe on her own, has usual student struggles, sings in a cafe, is discovered by Tullio Carminati, a great singing teacher. He drives her, mesmerises her, makes her into a star. She falls in love with him, is jealous of another girl singer, and almost upsets the applecart at the last minute of success at the Metropolitan debut in New York.

It's all handled carefully. Carminati, as the teacher-lover, is a perfect choice and manages to ease himself into a lot more attention than might be expected. Lyle Talbot is the other man for Moore and Mona Barrie is the other girl. Both do well enough. Jessie Ralph is excellent as the housekeeper.
□ 1934: Best Picture (Nomination)

● ●

■ **ONE NIGHT STAND**

1984, 94 MINS, AUSTRALIA ◇ ▽
Dir John Duigan   *Prod* Richard Mason   *Scr* John Duigan   *Ph* Tom Cowan   *Ed* John Scott   *Mus* William Motzing   *Art Dir* Ross Major
● Tyler Coppin, Cassandra Delaney, Jay Hackett, Saskia Post, Midnight Oil (Edgley)

It's New Year's Eve on a hot summer night in Sydney. Over a transistor radio comes the news nobody thought was possible: nuclear war has broken out in Europe and North America, and bombs have already dropped on US facilities in Australia: everyone is warned to stay where they are.

Thus begins a long, long night.

Pic builds inexorably to a truly shattering climax, yet doesn't rely on special effects or histrionics. Duigan seems to suggest that, in Australia at least, the world will end not with a bang nor exactly a whimper, but with a puzzled question-mark.

It's a daring approach but overall, and despite some rather strident acting early on, it does work.

● ●

■ **ONE OF OUR AIRCRAFT IS MISSING**

1942, 100 MINS, UK ▽
Dir Michael Powell   *Prod* John Corfield, Michael Powell, Emeric Pressburger   *Scr* Emeric Pressburger, Michael Powell   *Ph* Ronald Neame   *Ed* David Lean   *Art Dir* David Rawnsley
● Godfrey Tearle, Eric Portman, Hugh Williams, Bernard Miles, Pamela Brown, Hay Petrie (British National)

Aircraft is a full-length feature dealing with the flight of a crew of bombers which start from England to raid Stuttgart. The squadron all returns safely, except one which hits an obstruction and is entirely demolished. Then follows the story of what happened to the airmen.

The aforesaid bomber is returning from its raid on Stuttgart when it is hit and the crew tries to limp home. But over Holland they're compelled to bale out, landing in Dutch (occupied) territory, where the people protect them and give them disguises.

The six members of the Wellington are played by Godfrey Tearle, Eric Portman, Hugh Williams, Bernard Miles, Hugh Burden and Emrys Jones. A lot of Dutch people are recruited as natives of Holland, all of them excellent, not to mention Hay Petrie as the burgomaster. With the exception of Pamela Brown, all arrive solidly. Script, pro-

duction, direction and photography are splendid.

● ●

■ **ONE ON ONE**

1977, 98 MINS, US ◇ ▽
Dir Lamont Johnson   *Prod* Martin Hornstein   *Scr* Robby Benson, Jerry Segal   *Ph* Donald M. Morgan   *Ed* Robbe Roberts   *Mus* Charles Fox   *Art Dir* Sherman Loudermilk
● Robby Benson, Annette O'Toole, G.D. Spradlin, Gail Strickland, Melanie Griffith, James G. Richardson (Warner)

A trite and disappointing little film about a Los Angeles college basketball player. It follows the formula about the underdog-turned-hero but fails to ignite the emotions.

Robby Benson has an inarticulate, bumbling presence in this film as he blunders through the commercialized world of college athletics. His awkward performance slows down the film badly and makes it hard to empathize with him, despite the usually potent plot cliche of the little guy fighting back.

It's unbelievable that this nebbish would be pursued by such mature and attractive women as Annette O'Toole and Gail Strickland, both of whom have extended and embarrassing romantic scenes with Benson.

● ●

■ **ONE POTATO, TWO POTATO**

1964, 102 MINS, US
Dir Larry Peerce   *Prod* Sam Weston   *Scr* Raphael Hayes, Orville H. Hampton   *Ph* Andrew Laszlo   *Ed* Robert Fritch   *Mus* Gerald Fried
● Barbara Barrie, Bernie Hamilton, Richard Mulligan, Marti Merika, Robert Earl Jones (Cinema V/Weston-Bowalco)

Made in Ohio on a subscription basis for a reported $250,000, this is a tender, tactful look at miscegenation that speaks in human rather than polemic terms.

Set in a midwest US location (northern tier), it deals with a seemingly well-adjusted young Negro office worker who meets a young white divorcee who has a little girl. Their idyll grows slowly and gently as both react on normal planes with the color no apparent problem.

Then along comes the woman's first husband who has made his fortune after leaving her and demands the custody of the little girl. A sympathetic judge locates the girl in a good home, since he feels that as long as prejudice exists the little girl's life could be touched by it. All this is helped by fine delineation of character and added help from some new faces and the on-the-spot lensing.

Barbara Barrie has a striking presence and manages to mix integrity with need to etch a firm, moving character as the woman who finally finds the right man only to have her child taken away on racist principles. Bernie Hamilton is taking as the Negro husband who suddenly finds his manhood and very human liberty threatened by something that prevents him being a complete man.

Director Larry Peerce, for his first pic, has wisely told his story without many heavy symbolical and overdramatic embellishments.

● ●

■ **ONE SPY TOO MANY**

1966, 101 MINS, US ◇
Dir Joseph Sargent   *Prod* David Victor   *Scr* Dean Hargrove   *Ph* Fred Koenekamp   *Ed* Henry Berman   *Mus* Gerald Fried   *Art Dir* George W. Davis, Merrill Pye
● Robert Vaughn, David McCallum, Rip Torn, Dorothy Provine, Leo G. Carroll, Yvonne Craig (Arena/M-G-M)

Expanded from a *Man from U.N.C.L.E.* TV two-parter, *One Spy Too Many* zips along at a jazzy spy thriller pace.

Action and gadgetry are hung on a slender plot. Alexander, played by Rip Torn, is out to take over the world in the fashion of his Greek namesake. He hoists from the US Army Biological Warfare Division a tankful of its secret 'will gas', leaving a Greek inscription in the lab. International espionage agents Robert Vaughn and David McCallum begin to pursue Alexander and are joined in their efforts by his wife (Dorothy Provine), who is attempting to reach her husband in order to have him sign her divorce papers.

● ●

■ **ONE WAY PENDULUM**

1965, 90 MINS, UK
Dir Peter Yates   *Prod* Michael Deeley   *Scr* N.F. Simpson   *Ph* Denys Coop   *Ed* Peter Taylor   *Mus* Richard Rodney Bennett   *Art Dir* Reece Pemberton
● Eric Sykes, George Cole, Julia Foster, Jonathan Miller, Peggy Mount, Mona Washbourne (Woodfall)

Adapted from his own play by N. F. Simpson, what there is of a plot deals with an eccentric British family whose antics resemble normal behavior as Salvador Dali resembles Grandma Moses.

Papa (Eric Sykes) seeks change from his humdrum existence as an insurance clerk by erecting a do-it-yourself replica of the Old Bailey in his living room, only to find a trial underway when he gets it finished; the mother (Alison Leggatt repeating her stage role), seemingly the sane one, goes along with her oddly-behaviored family until she adds her own bit by engaging a charwoman (Peggy Mount) not to clean, but to eat the family's leftovers.

Nearly rational is daughter (Julia Foster), whose only concern is for what she considers a physical deformity – her arms don't reach her knees.

Peter Yates directs with a technique that treats comedy as deadly serious and is responsible for much of the antic spirit that keeps the film animated during most of its chaotic run.

● ●

■ **ONE, TWO, THREE**

1961, 115 MINS, US ▽
Dir Billy Wilder   *Prod* Billy Wilder   *Scr* Billy Wilder, I.A.L. Diamond   *Ph* Daniel L. Fapp   *Ed* Daniel Mandell   *Mus* Andre Previn   *Art Dir* Alexandre Trauner
● James Cagney, Horst Buchholz, Pamela Tiffin, Arlene Francis, Lilo Pulver, Howard St John (United Artists)

Billy Wilder's *One, Two, Three* is a fast-paced, high-pitched, hard-hitting, lighthearted farce crammed with topical gags and spiced with satirical overtones. Story of the mayhem that ensues when an emptyheaded Coca-Cola heiress on the loose in Berlin ties the knot with a card-carrying Communist, it's so furiously quick-witted that some of its wit gets snarled and smothered in overlap. But total experience packs a considerable wallop.

James Cagney is the chief exec of Coca-Cola's West Berlin plant whose ambitious promotion plans are jeopardized when he becomes temporary guardian of his stateside superiors's wild and vacuous daughter. The girl (Pamela Tiffin) slips across the border, weds violently anti-Yankee Horst Buchholz, and before long there's a bouncing baby Bolshevik on the way. When the home office head man decides to visit his daughter, Cagney masterminds an elaborate masquerade that backfires.

The screenplay, based on a one-act play by Ferenc Molnar, is outstanding. It pulls no punches and lands a few political and ideological haymakers on both sides of the Brandenburg Gate.

Cagney proves himself an expert farceur with a glib, full-throttled characterization. Although some of Buchholz delivery has more bark than bite, he reveals a considerable flair for comedy. Pretty Tiffin scores with a convincing display of mental density.

Another significant factor in the comedy is Andre Previn's score, which incorporates semi-classical and period pop themes (like *Saber Dance* and 'Yes, We Have No Bananas') to great advantage throughout the film.

■ ONE-EYED JACKS

1961, 137 MINS, US ◇ ▽
Dir Marlon Brando   *Prod* Frank P. Rosenberg
Scr Guy Trosper, Calder Willingham   *Ph* Charles
Lang Jr   *Ed* Archie Marshek   *Mus* Hugo Friedhofer
Art Dir Hal Pereira, J. McMillan Johnson
● Marlon Brando, Karl Malden, Pina Pellicer, Katy
Jurado, Ben Johnson, Slim Pickens (Paramount)

Charles Neider's novel, *The Authentic Death of Hendry Jones*, is the source of the tellingly direct screenplay. It is the brooding, deliberate tale of a young man (Marlon Brando) consumed by a passion for revenge after he is betrayed by an accomplice (Karl Malden) in a bank robbery, for which crime he spends five years (1880-85) in a Mexican prison.

His vengeful campaign leads him to the town of Monterey, where Malden has attained respectability and the position of sheriff, but romantic entanglements with Malden's stepdaughter (Pina Pellicer) persuade Brando to abandon his intention until the irresistibility of circumstance and Malden's own irrepressible will to snuff out the living evidence of his guilt draws the two men into a showdown.

It is an oddity of this film that both its strength and its weakness lie in the area of characterization. Brando's concept calls, above all, for depth of character, for human figures endowed with overlapping good and bad sides to their nature. In the case of the central characters – his own, Malden's, Pellicer's – he is successful. But a few of his secondary people have no redeeming qualities – they are simply arch-villains.

Brando creates a character of substance, of its own identity. It is an instinctively right and illuminating performance. Another rich, vivid variable portrayal is the one by Malden. Katy Jurado is especially fine as Malden's wife. Outstanding in support is Ben Johnson as the bad sort who leads Brando to his prey.

The $5 million-6 million production, framed against the turbulent coastline of the Monterey peninsula and the shifting sands and mounds of the bleak Mexican desert, is notable for its visual artistry alone.

■ ONION FIELD, THE

1979, 122 MINS, US ◇ ▽
Dir Harold Becker   *Prod* Walter Coblenz   *Scr* Joseph
Wambaugh   *Ph* Charles Rosher   *Ed* John W.
Wheeler   *Mus* Eumir Deodato   *Art Dir* Brian Eatwell
● John Savage, James Woods, Ted Danson, Ronny
Cox, Franklyn Seales, Priscilla Pointer
(Avco Embassy/Black Marble)

A highly-detailed dramatization of a true case, *The Onion Field* deals in its two hours with death and guilt; and the manipulation of the judicial system to pervert justice.

Set in 1963, two plainclothes cops on patrol in Hollywood stop a couple of suspicious-looking punks in a car. In a swift moment one of the bad guys pulls a gun and the cops are disarmed and kidnapped. They are taken to an onion field miles away and one is brutally murdered. The second makes his escape. The two killers are quickly arrested but each claims the other did the killing.

On this confusion the trials and re-trials drag on for years. Concurrently the survivor goes through bouts of guilt and is forced to resign from the force.

James Woods as the near-psychotic Powell is chillingly effective, creating a flakiness in the character that exudes the danger of a live wire near a puddle.

■ ONLY ANGELS HAVE WINGS

1939, 120 MINS, US ▽
Dir Howard Hawks   *Prod* Howard Hawks   *Scr* Jules
Furthman   *Ph* Joseph Walker, Elmer Dyer   *Ed* Viola
Lawrence   *Mus* Manuel Maciste, Dimitri Tiomkin
● Cary Grant, Jean Arthur, Richard Barthelmess, Rita
Hayworth, Thomas Mitchell (Columbia)

In *Only Angels Have Wings*, Howard Hawks had a story to tell and he has done it inspiringly well. Cary Grant is boss of the kindly Dutchman's decrepit airline. Grant takes up the planes only when it's too hazardous for the others. If the Dutchman can fly the mails regularly he's set for a juicy contract.

Jean Arthur is an American showgirl en route to Panama. She's excellent for the assignment.

Sub-plot has Richard Barthelmess coming on the scene with Rita Hayworth as his wife.

Baranca is the basic setting of this sub-tropical aviation romance [from an original story by Hawks] where treacherous mountain crags, capricious rainstorms and the like do their utmost to worst the mail plane service.

The Grant-Arthur cynicism and unyielding romantics are kept at a high standard.

■ ONLY GAME IN TOWN, THE

1970, 113 MINS, US ◇ ▽
Dir George Stevens   *Prod* Fred Kohlmar   *Scr* Frank D.
Gilroy   *Ph* Henri Decae   *Ed* John W. Holmes, William
Sands, Pat Shade   *Mus* Maurice Jarre
Art Dir Herman Blumenthal
● Elizabeth Taylor, Warren Beatty, Charles Braswell,
Hank Henry (20th Century-Fox)

The Only Game in Town is a rather mixed blessing. Elizabeth Taylor and Warren Beatty star as two Vegas drifters who find love with each other.

Film was shot at Studios de Boulogne in Paris, with second unit work in Las Vegas for some key exteriors.

Beatty delivers an engaging performance as a gambling addict, working off his debts as a saloon pianist for Hank Henry.

Frank D. Gilroy's script [based on his play] permits both stars to shine in solo and ensemble moments of hope, despair, recrimination, and sardonic humor. But the drama develops too sluggishly.

Montage sequences of Vegas niteries, all well shot and cut, break up the pacing, but also emphasize the dramatic vamping even more so, an inevitable result.

■ ONLY THE LONELY

1991, 102 MINS, US ◇ ▽
Dir Chris Columbus   *Prod* John Hughes, Hunt Lowry
Scr Chris Columbus   *Ph* Julio Macat   *Ed* Raja
Gosnell   *Mus* Maurice Jarre   *Art Dir* John Muto
● John Candy, Maureen O'Hara, Ally Sheedy, Kevin
Dunn, Milo O'Shea, Anthony Quinn (20th Century-Fox/
Hughes)

A lower-key *Marty* for the 1990s, *Only the Lonely* is a charming and well-observed romantic comedy about a single Chicago cop (John Candy) trying to break free from his smothering Irish mom (Maureen O'Hara, in her welcome return to the screen after 20 years). Performances are delightfully true and never descend into bathos or cheap sentiment.

O'Hara uses her native Dublin accent and her feistiest no-nonsense style to convey the mean-spirited, bigoted personality of Rose Muldoon.

This flinty immigrant widow, who's bullied her son all his life, routinely spews out invective against Italians, Greeks, Poles and Jews.

Candy is a sweet-natured fellow who yearns for something more out of life but is afraid to ask for it. His best friend (James Belushi) and his brother (Kevin Dunn) want him to stay single and everyone treats him like an overgrown baby. When he meets a shy mortuary cosmetician (Ally Sheedy), Candy begins to assert himself in ways that drive his mother to new lows of tart-tongued nastiness.

The neighborhood is enjoyably populated with such serio-comic types as the silver-tongued denizens of O'Neill's pub, (Bert Remsen and Milo O'Shea), and O'Hara's devastatingly sexy next-door neighbor (Anthony Quinn) whom she scorns as a 'Typical Greek' for besieging her with passion: 'Come to my bed. You will never leave.'

■ ONLY TWO CAN PLAY

1962, 106 MINS, UK ▽
Dir Sidney Gilliat   *Prod* Leslie Gilliat   *Scr* Bryan
Forbes   *Ph* John Wilcox   *Ed* Thelma Connell
Mus Richard Rodney Bennett   *Art Dir* Albert Witherick
● Peter Sellers, Mai Zetterling, Virginia Maskell,
Richard Attenborough, Kenneth Griffiths (British Lion)

Kingsley Amis' novel, *That Uncertain Feeling*, has had some of its cool sting extracted for the film version, but the result is a lively, middle-class variation along the lines of *The Seven Year Itch*.

Some of the humor is over-earthy and slightly lavatory, and the film never fully decides whether it is supposed to be light comedy, farce or satire. But it remains a cheerful piece of nonsense with some saucy dialog and situations capably exploited by Sellers and his colleagues.

He is a member of the staff of a Welsh public library. A white collar job. He is fed up and frustrated with the eternal prospect of living in a shabby apartment with a dispirited wife, two awful kids, peeling wallpaper, erratic plumbing and a dragon of a landlady. Into his drab life floats the bored, sexy young wife of a local bigwig and she makes a play for Sellers.

The fact that she can influence her spouse to get Sellers promotion is hardly in Sellers' mind. But what is in his mind never gets a chance of jelling. Their attempts at mutual-seduction are thwarted by babysitting problem, sudden return of the husband, intrusion of a herd of inquisitive cows when attempting a nocturnal roll.

Sellers adds another wily characterization to his gallery. His problems as frustrated lover carry greater weight because, from the beginning, he does not exaggerate or distort the role of the humble little librarian with aspirations. Mai Zetterling and Virginia Maskell provided effective contrasts as the two women in his life.

■ ONLY WHEN I LARF

1968, 103 MINS, UK ◇
Dir Basil Dearden   *Prod* Len Deighton, Brian Duffy
Scr John Salmon   *Ph* Anthony Richmond   *Ed* Fergus
McDonnell   *Mus* Ron Grainer   *Art Dir* John Blezard
● Richard Attenborough, David Hemmings, Alexandra
Stewart, Nicholas Pennell, Melissa Stribling (Paramount)

Only When I Larf is a pleasant little joke, based on a Len Deighton novel and rather less complicated than some of his other work, with sound, unfussy direction and witty, observed thesping.

Filmed in London, New York and Beirut, it has Richard Attenborough, David Hemmings and Alexandra Stewart as a con-trio. Situation arises whereby Attenborough and Hemmings fall out and seek to doublecross each other.

Mood is admirably set with the gang pulling off a slickly-planned con trick in a New York office. Talk is minimal, though the sript opens up into a more gabby talk-fest later, but dialog is usually pointed and crisp.

Attenborough plays an ex-brigadier and takes on various guises. His brigadier is a masterly piece of observation and the whole film has Attenborough at his considerable comedy best. Hemmings is equally effective as the discontented young whiz-kid lieutenant and Stewart, with little to do, manages to look both efficient and sexy.

■ ONLY WHEN I LAUGH

1981, 120 MINS, US ◇

Dir Glenn Gordon   *Prod* Roger M. Rothstein, Neil Simon   *Scr* Neil Simon   *Ph* David M. Walsh   *Ed* John Wright   *Mus* David Shire   *Art Dir* Albert Brenner
● Marsha Mason, Kristy McNichol, James Coco, Joan Hackett, David Dukes (Columbia)

Patrons expecting a skin-deep laughfest may be surprised at the unusually sombre shadows and heavy dramatics that make their way into this tale (a reworking of Simon's short-lived legit play, *The Gingerbread Lady*), though abundant humor still shines through.

Marsha Mason delivers a bravura performance as the film's centerpiece, a divorced actress who returns from a three-month drying out session at an alcoholic clinic to face a revitalized career both on the legit boards and as a mother to her long-estranged, 17-year-old daughter, well-played here by Kristy McNichol.

Core of the film is McNichol's attempt to reestablish a fulltime relationship with her mother, despite latter's previously boozy neglect and frequent social embarrassment. Storyline details Mason's juggling of those demands, along with the potential for renewed romance and career success (with former lover David Dukes, who's written their stormy affair into a strong Broadway vehicle for her).

The one-on-one encounters between Mason and McNichol, ranging from sisterly tomfoolery to intense emotional battling, are particularly strong. Their final scene of family rapprochement is not unrealistically rosy.

■ OPENING NIGHT

1978, 144 MINS, US ◇

Dir John Cassavetes   *Prod* Al Ruban   *Scr* John Cassavetes   *Ph* Tom Ruban   *Ed* Tom Cornwell   *Mus* Bo Harwood   *Art Dir* Brian Ryman
● Gena Rowlands, Ben Gazzara, John Cassavetes, Joan Blondell, Paul Stewart, Zohra Lampert (Faces)

With *Opening Night*, John Cassavetes, the cinematic poet of middle-class inner turmoil, explores the angst-ridden world of a famous actress on the brink of breakdown. Preparing a difficult role in a Broadway play, she witnesses the accidental death of a devoted fan, a traumatic event which causes her to re-examine her personal and professional relationships.

Gena Rowlands turns in a virtuoso performance as the troubled actress.

As with his other films, Cassavetes, who wrote and directed, puts a slice of life under the microscope

Across the board, he culls stunning performances from the entire cast, especially Joan Blondell as the writer whose play is being mounted.

But it is such a demanding work.

■ OPERATION CROSSBOW

1965, 118 MINS, US ◇ Ⓥ

Dir Michael Anderson   *Prod* Carlo Ponti   *Scr* Richard Imrie, Derry Quinn, Ray Rigby   *Ph* Erwin Hillier   *Ed* Ernest Walter   *Mus* Ron Goodwin   *Art Dir* Elliot Scott

● Sophia Loren, George Peppard, Trevor Howard, John Mills, Tom Courtenay, Richard Johnson (M-G-M)

Operation Crossbow is a sometimes suspenseful war melodrama said to be based upon British attempts to find and destroy Germany's development of new secret weapons – long-range rockets – in the early days of the Second World War. Ambitiously filmed in Europe and boasting production values which may seem to catch the spirit of the monumental effort, what the Carlo Ponti production lacks primarily is a cohesive story line.

Sophia Loren is in for little more than a bit, albeit a key character in one sequence. George Peppard plays the chief protagonist in this rambling tale of a British espionage mission, whose members impersonate German scientists believed dead, sent to locate and transmit information on the underground installation where Nazis are working on their deadly project.

Peppard acquits himself satisfactorily although unexplained is his flawless command of German so he can impersonate a German scientist.

■ OPPORTUNITY KNOCKS

1990, 105 MINS, US ◇

Dir Donald Petrie   *Prod* Mark R. Gordon, Christopher Meledandri   *Scr* Mitchel Katlin, Nat Bernstein   *Ph* Steven Poster   *Ed* Marion Rothman   *Mus* Miles Goodman   *Art Dir* David Chapman
● Dana Carvey, Robert Loggia, Todd Graff, Julia Campbell, Milo O'Shea, James Tolkan (Imagine/Brad Grey/Melendandri-Gordon)

Television and standup comic Dana Carvey's deft mimicry and physical comedy are used to the max in *Opportunity Knocks*, but pic's routine venture into action and romance genres subtracts from the laughs.

Carvey and con accomplice Todd Graff break, enter and take up residence in a luxurious suburban house. Carvey is mistaken for a housesitting friend by the mother of the house's owner (Doris Belack). Carvey heeds the advice of semiretired con artists Milo O'Shea and Sally Gracie, and starts a 'love con' with Julia Campbell, the earthy doctor daughter of Belack and Robert Loggia. Naturally, they fall in love.

Fortunately, the conventional screenplay and direction are frequently interrupted by Carvey's winsome shticking. Later, however, Carvey is expected to be a romantic lead, and the audience is expected to believe it. Filmmakers err on both counts.

■ OPTIMISTS OF NINE ELMS, THE

1974, 110 MINS, UK ◇ Ⓥ

Dir Anthony Simmons   *Prod* Adrian Gaye, Victor Lyndon   *Scr* Anthony Simmons, Tudor Gates   *Ph* Larry Pizer   *Ed* John Jympson   *Mus* Lionel Bart   *Art Dir* Robert Cartwright
● Peter Sellers, Donna Mullane, John Chaffey, David Daker, Marjorie Yates (Cheetah/Sagittarius)

Pic is a romanticized, Anglicized variant on [Vittorio De Sica's 1952 Italian classic] *Umberto D*, with Peter Sellers playing an aging vaudevillian whose meager income derives from sidewalk minstrelling with his equally-weary trained mutt. He tentatively befriends an 11-year-old girl and her six-year-old brother, opening their poverty-clouded eyes to a world of magical dreams while they offer him the blessing of human contact.

It all sounds like goo, and the film's last half-hour verges perilously close. But even at its worst *The Optimists* is acceptable family fare, and for much of its first 80 minutes it engagingly achieves a sense of fantasy.

Director-coscripter Anthony Simmons (on whose novel, *The Optimists of Nine Elms*, screenplay is based) obviously understands and relishes the unique world of childhood.

■ ORCA

1977, 92 MINS, US ◇ Ⓥ

Dir Michael Anderson   *Prod* Luciano Vincenzoni   *Scr* Luciano Vincenzoni, Sergio Donati   *Ph* Ted Moore   *Ed* Ralph E. Winters, John Bloom, Marion Rothman   *Mus* Ennio Morricone   *Art Dir* Mario Garbuglia
● Richard Harris, Charlotte Rampling, Will Sampson, Bo Derek, Keenan Wynn, Robert Carradine (De Laurentiis)

Orca is man-vs-beast nonsense. Some fine special effects and underwater camera work are plowed under in dumb story-telling.

Richard Harris is a shark-hunting seafarer who incurs the enmity of a superintelligent whale after harpooning the whale's pregnant mate.

We learn all about the whales from Charlotte Rampling, ever at the ready with scientific exposition, occasional voiceover and arch posing.

Assorted supporting players include Will Sampson, who complements Rampling's pedantic dialog with ancient tribal lore; Peter Hooten, Bo Derek and Keenan Wynn, a part of the Harris boat crew; Scott Walker as menacing leader of village fishermen who wish Harris would just leave their whale-harassed town.

■ ORDINARY PEOPLE

1980, 123 MINS, US ◇ Ⓥ

Dir Robert Redford   *Prod* Ronald L. Schwary   *Scr* Alvin Sargent   *Ph* John Bailey   *Ed* Jeff Kanew   *Mus* Marvin Hamlisch   *Art Dir* Phillip Bennett, J. Michael Riva
● Donald Sutherland, Mary Tyler Moore, Judd Hirsch, Timothy Hutton, Elizabeth McGovern, M. Emmet Walsh (Paramount/Wildwood)

A powerfully intimate domestic drama, *Ordinary People* represents the height of craftsmanship across the board. Robert Redford stayed behind the camera to make a remarkably intelligent and assured directorial debut that is fully responsive to the mood and nuances of the astute adaptation of Judith Guest's best seller.

While not ultimately downbeat or despairing, tale of a disturbed boy's precarious tightrope walk through his teens is played out with tremendous seriousness. Pic possesses a somber, hour-of-the-wolf mood, with characters forced to definitively confront their own souls before fadeout.

Dilemma is of a youth who has recently attempted suicide in remorse for not having saved his older brother from drowning.

Redford keenly evokes the darkly serene atmosphere of Chicago's affluent North Shore and effectively portrays this WASP society's predilection for pretending everything is okay even when it's not.
□ 1980: Best Picture

■ ORGANIZATION, THE

1971, 105 MINS, US ◇

Dir Don Medford   *Prod* Walter Mirisch   *Scr* James R. Webb   *Ph* Joseph Biroc   *Ed* Ferris Webster   *Mus* Gil Melle   *Art Dir* George B. Chan
● Sidney Poitier, Barbara McNair, Gerald S. O'Loughlin, Sheree North, Fred Beir, Allen Garfield (United Artists)

Sidney Poitier is back for third time around as Virgil Tibbs, the San Francisco homicide lieutenant, faced this time with combatting a worldwide dope syndicate.

The screenplay, generally highly polished, is a bit hazy occasionally in development, and Don Medford establishes a fast tempo in his lively direction. Pic's opening is a gem as stage is set for consequent action, skillfully enacted and drivingly constructed.

It's a heist of a furniture factory – front for crime ring – and seizure of $5 million in heroin by a group of young people taking law into their own hands to try to halt the drug sale that has been ruining the lives of relatives and friends. Tibbs is assigned case when the murdered body of the factory manager is found.

Poitier is confronted by a serious problem in police ethics as group calls him in, admitting robbery but denying the murder. Group asks his assistance, leaving them free to operate while they try their own methods.

....

■ **ORPHANS**

1987, 120 MINS, US ◇ Ⓥ
Dir Alan J. Pakula *Prod* Alan J. Pakula *Scr* Lyle Kessler *Ph* Donald McAlpine *Ed* Evan Lottman *Mus* Michael Small *Art Dir* George Jenkins
● Albert Finney, Matthew Modine, Kevin Anderson, John Kellogg (Lorimar)

The inherent dramatic insularity of Lyle Kessler's play about two urban outcast brothers and the Mephistophelian gangster who transforms their hermetic world is driven by the inspired energies of its principal cast.

Treat (Matthew Modine) and Phillip (Kevin Anderson) live in isolated squalor. Treat is a violent sociopath who ventures in to New York to steal and scavenge. Phillip is a recluse terrified of the world outside the house and the physically dominant older brother who keeps him there, a virtual prisoner of fear.

Control of self and one's destiny is the gospel of Harold (Albert Finney), a hard-drinking mobster whom Treat lures from a saloon to the house one night with the intention of holding him hostage for ransom. The tables are quickly turned, however, when the mysterious but expansive gunman offers these destitute marginals an opportunity for big money and a spiffy new life.

Modine does all he can to dominate the picture in a tangibly physical performance that seems to use madness as its method and to succeed on these terms more often than not. Anderson portrays Phillip with great sensitivity and an aching pathos that's free of mannered affectation. Finney permits himself to anchor the center between these two extremes.

....

■ **OSCAR, THE**

1966, 122 MINS, US ◇ Ⓥ
Dir Russell Rouse *Prod* Clarence Greene *Scr* Harlan Ellison, Russell Rouse, Clarence Greene *Ph* Joseph Ruttenberg *Ed* Chester W. Schaeffer *Mus* Percy Faith *Art Dir* Hal Pereira, Arthur Lonegan
● Stephen Boyd, Elke Sommer, Milton Berle, Eleanor Parker, Joseph Cotten, Jill St John (Greene-Rouse)

This is the story of a vicious, bitter, firstclass heel who rises to stardom on the blood of those close to him. Without a single redeeming quality, part played by Stephen Boyd is unsympathetic virtually from opening shots.

Clarence Green as producer and Russell Rouse as director are unrelenting in their development of the character, in screenplay on which they collabed with Harlan Ellison [based on Richard Sale's novel], and they make handsome use of the Hollywood background.

Boyd is surrounded by some offbeat casting which adds an interesting note. Milton Berle switches to dramatic role as a top Hollywood agent, and Tony Bennett, the singer, portrays a straight character, Boyd's longtime friend victimized by the star in his battle for success.

Boyd makes the most of his part, investing it with an audience-hate symbol which he never once compromises. Elke Sommer, as his studio-designer wife who is another of his victims, is chief distaff interest in a well-undertaken portrayal. Eleanor Parker excels in the rather thankless role of a studio talent scout and dramatic coach who discovers Boyd in NY.

An arresting impression is made by Hedda Hopper, playing herself.

....

■ **OSCAR WILDE**

1960, 98 MINS, UK
Dir Gregory Ratoff *Prod* William Kirby *Scr* Jo Eisinger *Ph* Georges Perinal *Ed* Tony Gibbs *Mus* Kenneth V. Jones
● Robert Morley, Phyllis Calvert, John Neville, Ralph Richardson, Dennis Price, Alexander Knox (Vantage)

This black-and-white version of the story of the poet-playwright-wit whose tragic downfall on homosexual charges was a scandal in Victorian times hit London screens just five days before *The Trials of Oscar Wilde*, a color job. It was produced swiftly but shows no signs of technical shoddiness, even though it was being edited up to a couple of hours before screening for the press.

Georges Perinal's lensing is effective and the atmosphere of Victorian London, Paris and the court scenes has been faithfully caught. The literate screenplay draws heavily on both Wilde's own epigrams and wisecracks but also on the actual documented evidence in the two celebrated court cases.

The picture starts unsatisfactorily but comes vividly to life when the court proceedings begin. The opening sequences are very sketchy and merely set the scene of Wilde as a celebrated playwright and his first meeting with the handsome father-hating young Lord Alfred Douglas, an association which was to prove his downfall.

Gregory Ratoff, as director, swiftly gets into his stride after the aforesaid uneasy start and, though the film is over-talky and over-stagey, it is a good and interesting job of work.

Robert Morley, who once made an effective stage Oscar Wilde, looks perhaps a little too old for the role but he gives a very shrewd performance, not only in the rich relish with which he delivers Wilde's bon mots but also in the almost frighteningly pathetic way in which he crumbles and wilts in the dock.

Ralph Richardson is also in memorable form as the brilliant Queen's Counsel, Sir Edward Carson, who mercilessly strips Wilde in court with his penetrating questions.

....

■ **OSTERMAN WEEKEND, THE**

1983, 102 MINS, US ◇ Ⓥ
Dir Sam Peckinpah *Prod* Peter S. Davis, William N. Panzer *Scr* Alan Sharp, Ian Masters *Ph* John Coquillon *Ed* Edward Abroms, David Rawlins *Mus* Lalo Schifrin *Art Dir* Robb Wilson King
● Rutger Hauer, John Hurt, Craig T. Nelson, Dennis Hopper, Chris Sarandon, Burt Lancaster (Davis-Panzer/20th Century-Fox)

Sam Peckinpah's *The Osterman Weekend* is a competent, professional but thoroughly impersonal meller which reps initial adaptation of a Robert Ludlum tome for the big screen.

CIA chief Burt Lancaster, who harbors presidential ambitions, recruits operative John Hurt to convince powerful TV journalist Rutger Hauer that several of his closest friends are actually Soviet agents. Hauer is about to host an annual weekend get-together with his buddies and their wives.

After Hurt has equipped the California ranch house with a warehouse-full of sophisticated surveillance gear, Hauer warily bids welcome to his guests, who include:

hot-tempered financier Chris Sarandon and his sexually unsatisfied wife (Cassie Yates); writer and martial arts expert Craig T. Nelson; doctor Dennis Hopper, and his wife, cocaine addict Helen Shaver.

After a videotape foul-up, the pals get wind of Hauer's suspicions of them, and the domestic situation rapidly deteriorates.

Hauer is solid as the off-balance but determined protagonist. Hurt effectively plays most of his role isolated from the others in his video command post, and Lancaster socks over his bookend cameo as the scheming CIA kingpin.

....

■ **OTHELLO**

1952, 91 MINS, MOROCCO
Dir Orson Welles *Prod* Orson Welles *Scr* Orson Welles *Ph* Anchise Brizzi, G.R. Aldo, Georgo Fanto, Obadan Troiani, Roberto Fusi *Ed* Jean Sacha, Renzo Lucidi, John Shepridge *Mus* Angelo Francesco Lavagnino, Alberto Barberis *Art Dir* Alexandre Trauner
● Orson Welles, Micheal MacLiammoir, Suzanne Cloutier, Robert Coote, Hilton Edwards, Fay Compton (Mercury)

After three years in the making, Orson Welles unveiled his *Othello* at the Cannes Film Festival in April 1952 to win the top award. Film is an impressive rendering of the Shakespearean tragedy.

Beginning is catchy in lensing, plasticity and eye appeal, but a bit murky in development. After the marriage of Othello and Desdemona over the protests of her father, the film takes a firm dramatic line and crescendos as the warped Iago brings on the ensuing tragic results. The planting of the jealousy seed in Othello is a bit sudden, but once it takes hold, the pic builds in power until the final death scene.

Micheal MacLiammoir is good as Iago, the jealous, twisted friend whose envy turns to hate and murder. Orson Welles gives the tortured Moor depth and stature.

Footage shot in Italy and Morocco is well matched photographically. Standout scenes are the murder of Roderigo in a Moroccan bath as the chase weaves through the steamy air and ends in general skewering and mayhem.

....

■ **OTHER, THE**

1972, 108 MINS, US ◇ Ⓥ
Dir Robert Mulligan *Prod* Robert Mulligan *Scr* Tom Tryon *Ph* Robert L. Surtees *Ed* Folmar Blangsted, O. Nicholas Brown *Mus* Jerry Goldsmith *Art Dir* Albert Brenner
● Uta Hagen, Diana Muldaur, Chris Udvarnoky, Martin Udvarnoky, Norma Connolly, Victor French (20th Century-Fox)

The apparently sluggish opening reels of *The Other* subsequently justify themselves among many other mind-engrossing plot twists in this occult shocker. The film [written by actor Tom Tryon from his first novel] is an outstanding example of topflight writing structure and dialog, enhanced to full fruition by a knowing director.

On a small Connecticut farm in 1935 a tragedy-stricken family is plagued further with a series of deaths. The story unfolds around, and from the viewpoint of, Diana Muldaur's two young identical-twin sons, expertly played by 10-year-olds Chris and Martin Udvarnoky. Martin is aloof, introverted, and a downbeat influence on Chris, whose more normal juvenile attributes and fantasies are nurtured lovingly by Hagen.

Tryon and Mulligan have seeded the story with many clues and visible occasions for misjudgment.

....

■ OTHER SIDE OF MIDNIGHT, THE

1977, 165 MINS, US ◇ Ⓥ

Dir Charles Jarrott *Prod* Frank Yablans *Scr* Herman
Raucher, Daniel Taradash *Ph* Fred J. Koenekamp
Ed Donn-Cambern, Harold F. Kress *Mus* Michel
Legrand *Art Dir* John DeCuir
● Marie-France Pisier, John Beck, Susan Sarandon,
Raf Vallone, Clu Gulager, Christian Marquand
(20th Century-Fox)

The film, is directed in somewhat predictable
style by Charles Jarrott. The script [from the
novel by Sidney Sheldon] seems awkwardly
pulled together, making for some weird time
jumps in the 1939-47 period even with the
help of sequence subtitles.

Inducted early into a life of making it on
her body, Marie-France Pisier sleeps her way
up to international film star status, all the
while paying out money to follow John Beck.

Beck meanwhile meets Susan Sarandon in
Washington, DC, whom he marries before
going off to the Pacific theater of war. Sarandon has enough troubles in his absence, but
when he comes back, her pull with boss Clu
Gulager lands Beck lots of jobs.

Pisier, from the mansions of rich Greek Raf
Vallone, fixes it so Beck has to turn to work
abroad, hiring on as her pilot so she can
degrade him.

Players, script and director have not failed
the project in this regard; Michel Legrand's
score is appropriately goopy.

■ OTHER SIDE OF THE MOUNTAIN, THE

1975, 101 MINS, US ◇

Dir Larry Peerce *Prod* Edward S. Feldman *Scr* David
Seltzer *Ph* David M. Walsh *Ed* Eve Newman
Mus Charles Fox *Art Dir* Philip Abramson
● Marilyn Hassett, Beau Bridges, Belinda J.
Montgomery, Nan Martin, William Bryant, Dabney
Coleman (Universal/Filmways)

This is a heartwarming love story – the true-
life tale of a desperately-injured 19-year-old
girl skier with such love for life she beats her
way back to a future of hope.

It's based on the tragic experience of Jill
Kinmont, a Bishop, Calif, girl who was a
shoo-in for a berth on the 1956 Winter Olympics team until she suffered her near-fatal accident while racing down the slopes in the
Snow Cup Race at Alta, Utah.

Script is from the biographical book, *A Long
Way Up*, by E.G. Valens, and personal reminiscences of the victim.

Film is a standout in every department,
perfect casting, fine acting, sensitive direction, imaginative photography and general
overall production all combining to give unusual strength to subject matter.

■ OTLEY

1969, 90 MINS, UK ◇

Dir Dick Clement *Prod* Bruce Cohn Curtis *Scr* Ian La
Frenais *Ph* Austin Dempster *Ed* Richard Best
Mus Stanley Myers *Art Dir* Carmen Dillon
● Tom Courtenay, Romy Schneider, Alan Badel, James
Villiers, Leonard Rossiter (Columbia)

Otley seeks to break away from over-done Ian
Fleming-like spy tales [of the period]. It
focuses on exploits of bumbling 'everyman
type' thrust into the espionage game.

Storyline is pegged around Tom Courtenay
unfortuitously present at an acquaintance's
London flat, when the latter is bumped off. It
soon evolves that the recently deceased was a
defector from a gang of state-secret smugglers, and now all parties concerned think
that Courtenay somehow knew as much as
his late friend.

Because of this, he is first kidnapped and
beaten up by Romy Schneider and her
cohorts, then after bumbling his way out of
their clutches, he is caught by the opposing
side and bounced about by them.

In seeking to avoid overheroics as well as
the pitfalls of parody, the film has an uneasy
lack of a point of view and fails to focus viewer's attention on any particular character or
plotline philosophy.

■ OUR DAILY BREAD

1934, 74 MINS, US

Dir King Vidor *Prod* King Vidor *Scr* King Vidor,
Elizabeth Hill Vidor *Ph* Robert Planck *Ed* Lloyd
Nossler *Mus* Alfred Newman
● Karen Morley, Tom Keene, John Qualen, Barbara
Pepper (Viking/United Artists)

King Vidor, who has the nerve to do unusual
things, has here brought to the screen a story
which deals with a throng of unemployed
who take up squatter rights on an abandoned
farm and turn it into a thriving communal
collective project. On the way they have
various difficulties chiefly from that ghoulish
visitor of farmlands, the drought.

When the drought has just about withered
the corn, and the young leader (Tom Keene)
of the collectives is nuts over a blonde
strumpet (Barbara Pepper), the colony is
aroused from the abyss of despondency for
one last effort.

It's a glorification of human will power
driving man beyond ordinary feats of endurance. Primitive, forceful, real and moving.

■ OUR GIRL FRIDAY

1953, 88 MINS, UK ◇

Dir Noel Langley *Prod* George Minter, Noel
Langley *Scr* Noel Langley *Ph* Wilkie Cooper
Ed John Seabourne *Mus* Ronald Binge *Art Dir* Fred
Pusey
● Joan Collins, George Cole, Kenneth More,
Robertson Hare, Hermione Gingold, Hattie Jacques
(Renown)

Three men and a girl stranded on a desert
island should be an obvious vehicle for a
spicy, sexy comedy, but this British effort
does not quite come up to expectations. The
story [from Norman Lindsay's novel, *The
Cautious Amorist*] has its moments of fun but
the dialog is often flat and forced. Much of
the film was lensed in the Spanish island of
Mallorca.

After a collision at sea, Joan Collins finds
herself on a desert island with George Cole, a
journalist; Kenneth More, a ship's stoker;
and Robertson Hare, an insufferable professor. For the sake of harmony, the three men
make a pact not to make a pass at the girl,
but two of them, Cole and Hare, rapidly succumb to her charms.

There is some lively competition among the
two swains for the privilege of being alone
with the girl. These incidents are the mainstay of the film's humor and inevitably the
joke proves to be a little protracted. There is
a delightful guest portrayal, taking only a
couple of minutes of screen time, from Hermione Gingold.

■ OUR MAN FLINT

1966, 107 MINS, US ◇ Ⓥ

Dir Daniel Mann *Prod* Saul David *Scr* Hal Fimberg,
Ben Starr *Ph* Daniel L. Fapp *Ed* William Reynolds
Mus Jerry Goldsmith *Art Dir* Jack Martin Smith, Ed
Graves
● James Coburn, Lee J. Cobb, Gila Golan, Edward
Mulhare, Benson Fong, Shelby Grant (20th Century-
Fox)

This Saul David production is a dazzling, ac-
tion-jammed swashbuckling spoof of Ian
Fleming's valiant counter-spy, who's given
more tools and gimmicks to pursue his craft
as he tracks down and destroys the perpetra-
tors of a diabolical scheme to take over the
world.

James Coburn takes on the task of being
surrounded by exotically-undraped beauts
and facing dangers which would try any man.
But he comes through unscathed, helped by a
dandy little specially-designed lighter which
has 83 separate uses, including such items as
being a derringer, two-way radio carrying
across oceans, blow-torch, tear gas bomb,
dart gun, you-name-it.

Assignment comes to him when three mad
scientists threaten the safety of the world by
controlling the weather, and he's selected by
ZOWIE (Zonal Organization on World
Intelligence Espionage) as the one man alive
who can ferret them out before they can put
their final threatened plan into work.

Lee J. Cobb has a field day as the exasperated American rep and head of ZOWIE who
cannot keep Flint in line according to recognized standards for espionage.

■ OUR MAN IN HAVANA

1960, 111 MINS, UK

Dir Carol Reed *Prod* Carol Reed *Scr* Grahame
Greene *Ph* Oswald Morris *Ed* Bert Bates
Mus Hermand Deniz
● Alec Guinness, Burl Ives, Maureen O'Hara, Ernie
Kovacs, Noel Coward, Ralph Richardson (Columbia)

Based on the Graham Greene novel, scripted
by that author, directed by Carol Reed, shot
mainly in colorful Cuba and acted by a star-
loaded cast headed by Alec Guinness, this
turns out to be polished, diverting entertainment, brilliant in its comedy but falling apart
towards the end when undertones of drama,
tragedy and message crop up.

Story concerns a mild-mannered and not
very successful vacuum-cleaner salesman in
Havana who needs extra money to send his
daughter to finishing school in Switzerland.
Against his will he is persuaded to become a
member of the British secret service. To hold
down his job, he is forced to invent mythical
sub-agents and concoct highly imaginative,
fictitious reports which he sends back to London. They are taken so seriously that two
assistants are sent to help him, and the web of
innocent deceit that he has spun gradually
mounts up to sinister and dramatic
consequences.

Greene has scripted his novel fairly faithfully, though the Catholic significance is only
lightly brought into the film. Reed sometimes
lets the story become woolly but has expert
control of a brilliant cast. Guinness is a perfect choice for the reluctant spy role, giving
one of his usual subtle, slyly humorous
studies.

But the standout thesping comes from Noel
Coward. From his first entrance, which is immediately after the credits, he dominates
every scene in which he appears. When he is
not on the screen, the audience is awaiting
him. He plays the boss of the Caribbean
network.

Another performance which steals a lot of
thunder from Guinness is that of Ralph
Richardson, who is Coward's boss stationed
in London. Between them, these two do a fine
job of joshing Britain's MI5.

■ OUR MOTHER'S HOUSE

1967, 104 MINS, UK ◇

Dir Jack Clayton *Prod* Jack Clayton *Scr* Jeremy
Brooks, Haya Harareet *Ph* Larry Pizer *Ed* Tom
Priestley *Mus* Georges Delerue *Art Dir* Reece
Pemberton
● Dirk Bogarde, Margaret Brooks, Pamela Franklin,
Louis Sheldon Williams, John Gugolka, Mark Lester (M-
G-M/Heron/Filmways)

Our Mother's House, a film about children but
not to be considered in any way a kiddie pic,
is a well-made look at family life and parenthood by seven destitute moppets. Dirk

Bogarde stars in an excellent performance as their long-lost legal father, who is not the total heel he seems; nor, for that matter are the kids all angels.

Julian Gloag's novel has been adapted into a good screenplay which develops neatly the accelerated maturing of children after the death of their long-ailing mother (Annette Carell).

Latter, object of adulation, is buried in the back yard, eldest child Margaret Brooks imposing her belief on others that this will eliminate orphanage fears. To all except eldest son Louis Sheldon Williams, she conceals existence of a father, Bogarde.

....

■ OUR TOWN

1940, 89 MINS, US ▽

Dir Sam Wood *Prod* Sol Lesser *Scr* Thornton Wilder, Frank Craven, Harry Chandlee *Ph* Bert Glennon *Ed* Sherman Todd *Mus* Aaron Copland *Art Dir* William Cameron Menzies, Harry Horner
● William Holden, Martha Scott, Fay Bainter, Beulah Bondi, Thomas Mitchell, Frank Craven (Lesser/United Artists)

The film version of Thornton Wilder's Pulitzer prize play *Our Town* is an artistic offering, utilizing the simple and philosophical form of the stage piece, excellently written, directed, acted and mounted.

The film version retains the story and essentials of the play. Developed at a deliberately slow tempo, the simple and unhurried life of a rural New England village of 2,200 souls is unfolded without attempt to point up dramatic highlights.

Frank Craven assumes his original stage role, that of the sideline commentator who introduces the characters and then appears briefly from time to time to bridge episodes with his homely and intimate comments.

The tale is divided into three periods, 1901, 1904, and 1913. It's a plain and homey exposition of life, romance, marriage and death in the New Hampshire town. More explicitly, it concerns the intimacies of two families, the adolescent and matured romance and married life of a boy and girl. Tragic ending of the play is switched for picture purposes, the girl taking a nightmare excursion through the village graveyard and visions of death while going through childbirth. The ethereal expedition, running about five minutes, is the one false note in the picture.

Lesser drew heavily on the original stage cast for the film version. Martha Scott delivers a sincerely warm portrayal as the girl, displaying a wealth of ability and personality. In addition to Scott and Craven, Arthur Allen and Doro Merande are from the stage group in their original roles, Allen particularly effective in his brief professor appearance describing the geographic structure of the countryside.

William Holden is fine as the boy; Fay Bainter and Beulah Bondi provide excellent mother portrayals; while Thomas Mitchell and Guy Kibbee are prominent as heads of the two households.
□ 1940: Best Picture (Nomination)

....

■ OUT OF AFRICA

1985, 150 MINS, US ◇ ▽

Dir Sydney Pollack *Prod* Sydney Pollack *Scr* Kurt Luedtke *Ph* David Watkin *Ed* Fredric Steinkamp, William Steinkamp, Pembroke Herring, Sheldon Kahn *Mus* John Barry *Art Dir* Stephen Grimes
● Meryl Streep, Robert Redford, Klaus Maria Brandauer, Michael Kitchen, Malick Bowens, Joseph Thiaka (Universal)

At two-and-a-half hours, *Out of Africa* certainly makes a leisurely start into its story. Just short of boredom, however, the picture picks up pace and becomes a sensitive, enveloping romantic tragedy.

Getting top billing over Robert Redford, Meryl Streep surely earns it with another engaging performance. Still, the film rarely comes to life except when Redford is around.

Ably produced and directed by Sydney Pollack, *Africa* is the story of Isak Dinesen, who wrote of her experiences in Kenya. Though Dinesen (real name: Karen Blixen) remembered it lovingly, hers was not a happy experience. Pic opens in 1914.

With one landscape after another, Pollack and lenser David Watkin prove repeatedly, however, why she should love the land so, but at almost travelog drag.

Eventually, Streep and husband Klaus Maria Brandauer split, leaving an opening for Redford to move in. True love follows, but not happiness because he's too independent to be tied down by a marriage certificate.
□ 1985: Best Picture

....

■ OUT OF SEASON

1975, 90 MINS, UK ◇

Dir Alan Bridges *Prod* Eric Bercovici, Reuben Bercovitch *Scr* Eric Bercovici, Reuben Bercovitch *Ph* Arthur Ibbetson *Ed* Peter Weatherly *Mus* John Cameron *Art Dir* Robert Jones
● Vanessa Redgrave, Cliff Robertson, Susan George (EMI/Lorimar)

Virtually a three-hander, *Out of Season* boasts topnotch performances by Vanessa Redgrave, Cliff Robertson and Susan George, a taut script and firstrate direction.

Though basic plot is that old chestnut about the dark stranger returning – after 20 years away – to visit an isolated hotel in an English seaside town, its handling is expert enough to avoid most of the pitfalls of the genre. And so is the acting.

Director Alan Bridges displays his ability to develop and hold obsessive situations, all hints and innuendos, and this ping pong match of the affections often has the suspense of a whodunit as audience tries to guess next move by the entangled mother, daughter, lover trio.

....

■ OUT OF THE BLUE

1980, 94 MINS, CANADA ◇ ▽

Dir Dennis Hopper *Scr* Leonard Yakir, Gary Jules Jouvenat *Ph* Marc Champion *Ed* Doris Dyck *Mus* Tom Lavin
● Linda Manz, Sharon Farrell, Dennis Hopper, Raymond Burr, Don Gordon (Robson Street)

Dennis Hopper directs and stars in this terse drama of what the 1970s drug culture and dregs of the counter-culture would have wrought on those easy riders who got off their bikes and tried to conform.

Linda Manz has tart authority as a streetwise 15-year-old. She had been in a terrible accident while driving with Hopper, her father, who plowed into a school bus stalled in the middle of the road, killing many of the kids.

Hopper has been sentenced to five years in prison. He has become a hero to his daughter, who has fantasised the late Elvis Presley into another hero.

Dramatically economical, pic captures urban overcrowding, personal problems and violence but sans excess. Hopper reportedly took over direction after film started but worked with the writer on changes to fit his own personal outlooks.

....

■ OUT OF THE PAST

1947, 95 MINS, US ▽

Dir Jacques Tourneur *Prod* Warren Duff *Scr* Geoffrey Homes *Ph* Nicholas Musuraca *Ed* Samuel E. Beetley *Mus* Roy Webb *Art Dir* Albert S. D'Agostino, Jack Okey

● Robert Mitchum, Jane Greer, Kirk Douglas, Rhonda Fleming, Richard Webb, Steve Brodie (RKO)

Out of the Past is a hardboiled melodrama [from the novel by Geoffrey Homes] strong on characterization. Direction by Jacques Tourneur pays close attention to mood development, achieving realistic flavor that is further emphasized by real life settings and topnotch lensing by Nicholas Musuraca.

Plot depicts Robert Mitchum as a former private detective who tries to lead a quiet, small-town life. Good portion of story is told in retrospect by Mitchum when his past catches up with him. Hired by a gangster to find a girl who had decamped with $40,000 after shooting the crook, Mitchum crosses her path in Acapulco, falls for her himself and they flee the gangster together.

Mitchum gives a very strong account of himself. Jane Greer as the baby-faced, charming killer is another lending potent interest. Kirk Douglas, the gangster, is believable and Paul Valentine makes role of henchman stand out. Rhonda Fleming is in briefly but effectively.

....

■ OUTCAST OF THE ISLANDS

1952, 102 MINS, UK

Dir Carol Reed *Prod* Carol Reed *Scr* W.E.C. Fairchild *Ph* John Wilcox *Ed* Bert Bates *Mus* Brian Easdale *Art Dir* Vincent Korda
● Ralph Richardson, Trevor Howard, Robert Morley, Kerima, Wendy Hiller, George Coulouris (London/British Lion)

Picture is based on the Joseph Conrad story, but the screenplay fails to capture the authentic atmosphere of the Far East in which the story is set. The backgrounds are genuine enough, but the plot is loosely constructed and the editing occasionally episodic.

The outcast is played by Trevor Howard. He is saved from the police, after being involved in a swindle, by the captain of a trading vessel who takes him to his island outpost. There, he doublecrosses his friend, tricks his partner and falls in love with the daughter of the blind native tribal chief.

Within that outline, the film concentrates on developing the shifting character of the outcast as a man without honor, without principle and without friends, yet having a devouring passion for the native girl.

Ralph Richardson, polished and dignified as usual, gives a sterling performance as the captain of the trading boat. Robert Morley chalks up another success as the captain's partner.

....

■ OUTFIT, THE

1973, 102 MINS, US ◇ ▽

Dir John Flynn *Prod* Carter De Haven *Scr* John Flynn *Ph* Bruce Surtees *Ed* Ralph E. Winters *Mus* Jerry Fielding *Art Dir* Tambi Larsen
● Robert Duvall, Karen Black, Joe Don Baker, Robert Ryan, Timothy Carey, Richard Jaeckel (M-G-M)

In *The Outfit* two relatively small time outside-the-law characters, stylishly handled by Robert Duvall and Joe Don Baker, drive off into the credits laughing gleefully. In their wake they leave countless stiffs, including crime-syndicate topper Robert Ryan, Duvall's girl friend (Karen Black), and a batch of other broken-boned face-smashed individuals who were caught up in pair's vengeance-motivated assault on organized crime.

John Flynn's simple screenplay [from a novel by Richard Stark] focuses on Duvall's explosive compulsion to square things with the mobsters who killed his brother as reprisal for their ripping off a bank controlled by the syndicate.

Flynn keeps the pace extremely fast and engaging. Duvall and Baker work smoothly together. Joanna Cassidy makes an attractive screen bow as Ryan's wife.

••••••••••••••••••••••••••••

■ OUTLAND

1981, 109 MINS, US ◇

Dir Peter Hyams   *Prod* Richard A. Roth   *Scr* Peter Hyams   *Ph* Stephen Goldblatt   *Ed* Stuart Baird   *Mus* Jerry Goldsmith   *Art Dir* Philip Harrison
● Sean Connery, Peter Boyle, Frances Sternhagen, Kika Markham (Warner/Ladd)

Outland is something akin to *High Noon* in outer space, a simple good guys-bad guys yarn set in the future on a volcanic moon of Jupiter.

While there are several mile-wide plot holes and one key under-developed main character, the film emerges as a tight, intriguing old-fashioned drama that gives audiences a hero worth rooting for.

It's clear from the beginning that newly arrived marshal Sean Connery is going to have his hands full. Soon into the action, a miner takes it upon himself to enter the deadly moon atmosphere without his spacesuit and literally fries before the audience's eyes.

Connery soon finds out that the miners are growing crazy due to an amphetamine they are taking that makes them produce more, but eventually destroys their brains. It doesn't take long to figure out that his rival (Peter Boyle), the smug general manager who basically runs the colony's operations, is involved in supplying the drug.

Writer-director Peter Hyams falls just short of providing the exciting payoff to the conflicts he so painstakingly sets up throughout the picture.

••••••••••••••••••••••••••••

■ OUTLAW, THE

1943, 124 MINS, US Ⓥ

Dir Howard Hughes   *Prod* Howard Hughes   *Scr* Jules Furthman   *Ph* Gregg Toland   *Ed* Wallace Grissell   *Mus* Victor Young
● Jack Buetel, Jane Russell, Thomas Mitchell, Walter Huston (Howard Hughes)

Beyond sex attraction of Jane Russell's frankly displayed charms, picture, according to accepted screen entertainment standards, falls short. Plot is based on legend Billy the Kid wasn't killed by the law but continued to live on after his supposed death.

Pace is series of slow-moving incidents making up continuous chase as directed by Howard Hughes and isn't quickened by the two hours running time, but slowness is not so much a matter of length as a lack of tempo in individual scenes.

This variation of the checkered film career of Billy the Kid has the outlaw joining forces with legendary Doc Holliday, played by Walter Huston, to escape the pursuing Sheriff Pat Garrett (Thomas Mitchell). Mixing strangely into the kid's life is Rio, Latin charmer, as portrayed by Russell.

Sex seldom rears its beautiful head in simonpure prairie dramas, but since this is an unorthodox, almost burlesque, version of tried and true desert themes, anything can and often does happen.

••••••••••••••••••••••••••••

■ OUTLAW BLUES

1977, 100 MINS, US ◇ Ⓥ

Dir Richard T. Heffron   *Prod* Steve Tish   *Scr* B.W.L. Norton   *Ph* Jules Brenner   *Ed* Danford B. Greene, Scott Conrad   *Mus* Charles Bernstein, Bruce Langhorne   *Art Dir* Jack Marty
● John Crawford, James Callahan, Michael Lerner, Steve Fromholz, Richard Lockmiller, Matt Clark (Warner)

Script takes Peter Fonda from prison, where he has developed a musical ability, to Texas

in pursuit of James Callahan, C&W name who has stolen the title song from Fonda.

Accidental shooting of Callahan in a scuffle launches a manhunt for Fonda by police chief John Crawford, mayoral candidate not about to be embarrassed at election time. Susan Saint James, one of Callahan's singing group, beds and befriends Fonda and, by clever p.r., makes him a major new platter star to be reckoned with by Michael Lerner, a music biz sharpie.

The film revolves into a series of chases, interleaved with some okay songs which Fonda is said to have sung himself. Story opts for the laughs and smiles which come easily in abundance.

••••••••••••••••••••••••••••

■ OUTLAW JOSEY WALES, THE

1976, 135 MINS, US ◇ Ⓥ

Dir Clint Eastwood   *Prod* Robert Daley   *Scr* Phil Kaufman, Sonia Chernus   *Ph* Bruce Surtees   *Ed* Ferris Webster   *Mus* Jerry Fielding   *Art Dir* Tambi Larsen
● Clint Eastwood, Chief Dan George, Sondra Locke, Bill McKinney, John Vernon, Paula Trueman (Warner)

The screenplay [based on the book *Gone to Texas* by Forrest Carter] is another one of those violence revues, with carnage production numbers slotted every so often and intercut with Greek chorus narratives by John Vernon and Chief Dan George.

Clint Eastwood is a Civil War era farmer whose family is murdered by brigands led by Bill McKinney; Vernon is a fellow counterguerrilla who is tricked into surrendering his men; George is an old Indian whom Eastwood encounters on the long trail of earthly retribution.

Eastwood's character meanders through the Middle West, disposing of antagonists by the dozen aided at times by George, Sam Bottoms, romantic interest Sondra Locke, latter's granny Paula Trueman and others.

••••••••••••••••••••••••••••

■ OUT-OF-TOWNERS, THE

1970, 97 MINS, US ◇ Ⓥ

Dir Arthur Hiller   *Prod* Paul Nathan   *Scr* Neil Simon   *Ph* Andrew Laszlo   *Ed* Fred Chulack   *Mus* Quincy Jones   *Art Dir* Charles Bailey
● Jack Lemmon, Sandy Dennis, Sandy Baron, Anne Meara, Robert Nichols, Ann Prestiss (Paramount/Jalem)

The Out-of-Towners is a total delight. Neil Simon's first modern original screen comedy stars Jack Lemmon and Sandy Dennis, an Ohio couple who become disillusioned with big-city life, New York style.

Lemmon and Dennis come to NY on one of those expense paid executive suite job interviews. In the course of 24 hours, they are stacked-up over the airport; diverted to Boston; lose their luggage; ride a food-less train to strike-bound and rainy NY; lose their Waldorf reservations; get held up; become involved in a police chase; escape mugging in Central Park; flee a mounted cop; and are asked to leave a church because of a TV rehearsal. Among other things.

Dennis and Lemmon are superb in comedy characterizations.

••••••••••••••••••••••••••••

■ OUTRAGE, THE

1964, 95 MINS, US

Dir Martin Ritt   *Prod* A. Ronald Lubin   *Scr* Michael Kanin   *Ph* James Wong Howe   *Ed* Frank Santillo   *Mus* Alex North   *Art Dir* George W. Davis, Tambi Larsen
● Paul Newman, Laurence Harvey, Claire Bloom, Edward G. Robinson, William Shatner, Howard Da Silva (M-G-M)

Outrage is adapted from the Fay and Michael Kanin Broadway play, *Rashomon*, which in turn was based on the Japanese film production of same tab. It is the story of a killing

of a Southern gentleman and the rape of his wife by a bloodthirsty bandit, told through the eyes of the three protagonists and then by a disinterested eye witness, each version differing.

Script unfolds in the American Southwest in the 1870s, a neat metamorphosis from the 12th-century Japan of the play and original Nipponese pic. Bandit character is retained, but the samurai character becomes a Southern gentleman of fine family (Laurence Harvey) who is travelling through the West with his wife (Claire Bloom) when set upon by a Mexican outlaw (Paul Newman).

Plot takes its form, opening on platform of a deserted railroad station as a prospector and a preacher, who is leaving the town a disillusioned man, recite to con-man Edward G. Robinson the trial of the outlaw a few days previously, when three people testify to three totally different accounts of what 'actually' happened.

Newman as the violent and passionate killer plays his colorful character with a flourish and heavy accent. Harvey has little to do in first three accounts except remain tied to a tree, his turn coming in fourth when the prospector tells how he and bandit are shamed by the wife into fighting for her. Bloom, who appeared in Broadway play, has her gamut during the four versions of her ravishment, running from pure innocence to her demand to the outlaw to kill her husband so she can go away with her new lover. In all, she delivers strongly, turning glibly from drama to comedy.

••••••••••••••••••••••••••••

■ OUTSIDER, THE

1979, 128 MINS, US ◇

Dir Tony Luraschi   *Scr* Tony Luraschi   *Ph* Ricardo Aronovitch   *Ed* Catherine Kelber   *Mus* Ken Thorne   *Art Dir* Franco Fumagalli
● Craig Wasson, Sterling Hayden, Patricia Quinn, Niall O'Brien, T.P. McKenna, Ray Macanally (Paramount/Cinematic Arts)

The Outsider represents the first attempt to get behind the incessant headlines and into the minds and motives at work on one of the longest-fought terrorist campaigns of the times – through an intelligent fictional story with an Irish setting.

A measure of the effectiveness of Craig Wasson's performance, as a young Irish-American inflamed to join the IRA by his grandfather's (Sterling Hayden) tales of fighting the Brits in the religion-charged cause of Irish nationalism, is that by the time he finally leaves Ireland as a disillusioned fugitive he looks – without artifice – 10 years older. What he's escaped is a neatly-plotted double trap by both the IRA and British army.

The strength of Tony Luraschi's features debut lies in its restraint.

••••••••••••••••••••••••••••

■ OUTSIDERS, THE

1983, 91 MINS, US ◇ Ⓥ

Dir Francis Coppola   *Prod* Fred Roos, Gray Frederickson   *Scr* Kathleen Knutsen Rowell   *Ph* Stephen H. Burum   *Ed* Anne Goursaud   *Mus* Carmine Coppola   *Art Dir* Dean Tavoularis
● C. Thomas Howell, Matt Dillon, Ralph Macchio, Patrick Swayze, Rob Lowe, Emilio Estevez (Zoetrope)

Francis Coppola has made a well acted and crafted but highly conventional film out of S.E. Hinton's popular youth novel, *The Outsiders*. Although set in the mid-1960s, pic feels very much like a 1950s drama about problem kids.

Screenplay is extremely faithful to the source material, even down to having the film open with the leading character and narrator. C. Thomas Howell, reciting the first lines of his literary effort while we see him writing them.

But dialog which reads naturally and evocatively on the page doesn't play as well on screen, and there's a decided difficulty of tone during the early sequences, as Howell and his buddies, (Matt Dillon and Ralph Macchio) horse around town, sneak into a drive-in and have an unpleasant confrontation with the Socs, rival gang from the well-heeled part of town.

When the Socs attack Howell and Macchio in the middle of the night, latter ends up killing a boy to save his friend, and the two flee to a hideaway in an abandoned rural church. It is during this mid-section that the film starts coming to life, largely due to the integrity of the performances by Howell and Macchio.

Howell is truly impressive, a bulwark of relative stability in a sea of posturing and pretense. Macchio is also outstanding as his doomed friend, and Patrick Swayze is fine as the oldest brother forced into the role of parent.

■ **OVER THE BROOKLYN BRIDGE**

1984, 106 MINS, US ◇ ⓥ

Dir Menahem Golan   *Prod* Menahem Golan, Yoram Globus   *Scr* Arnold Somkin   *Ph* Adam Greenberg   *Ed* Mark Goldblatt   *Mus* Pino Donaggio   *Art Dir* John Lawless

● Elliott Gould, Margaux Hemingway, Sid Caesar, Burt Young, Shelley Winters, Carol Kane (City)

Over the Brooklyn Bridge is producer-director Menahem Golan's love letter to New York City: a warm and pleasant romance similar to the type of films topliner Elliott Gould used to make in the early 1970s.

Screenplay by Arnold Somkin is short on laughs but very effective.

Gould stars as Alby Sherman, owner of a Brooklyn eatery who dreams of buying a posh restaurant on the East Side in midtown Manhattan. His love affair with an aristocratic Catholic girl from Philadelphia (Margaux Hemingway) raises the ire of his Jewish family, particularly the patriarch Uncle Benjamin (Sid Caesar), a women's underwear manufacturer who would rather have Alby marry his fourth cousin Cheryl (Carol Kane).

Gould and Hemingway are solid in the central roles, with standout support from a large cast. Caesar is very funny as a man who tries to run everyone else's lives for them. Kane is delightfully droll as the virginal intellectual whose demure exterior hides a rather kinky fantasy-sex life.

■ **OVER THE TOP**

1987, 93 MINS, US ◇ ⓥ

Dir Menahem Golan   *Prod* Menahem Golan, Yoram Globus   *Scr* Stirling Silliphant, Sylvester Stallone   *Ph* David Gurfinkel   *Ed* Don Zimmerman, James Symons   *Mus* Giorgio Moroder   *Art Dir* James Schoppe

● Sylvester Stallone, Robert Loggia, Susan Blakely, Rick Zumwalt, David Mendenhall, Chris McCarty (Cannon)

Sylvester Stallone muscles his way to the top of the heap in a beefy world of armwrestling in *Over the Top*. Routinely made in every respect, melodrama concerns itself as much with a man's effort to win the love of his son as it does with macho athletics..

Stallone, as a down-on-his-luck trucker named Lincoln Hawk, appears out of the blue to fetch his son when the latter graduates from military academy. Absent from both the kid's and mama Susan Blakely's lives for years, Stallone proposes a get-to-know-you truck ride back home to Los Angeles.

Little Michael (David Mendenhall) doesn't make things especially easy for his papa, his

military rigidity and formality providing a formidable barrier. At truckstops along the way, Stallone introduces his son to the thrills of armwrestling, and Michael's transformation from spoiled intellectual snot to future regular guy is well underway.

Stallone is sincere and soulful as a 'father who messed up pretty bad' and just wants his kid back, Mendenhall is a likable tyke, and justice is served in the end.

■ **OVERLANDERS, THE**

1946, 91 MINS, UK/AUSTRALIA

Dir Harry Watt   *Prod* Michael Balcon   *Scr* Harry Watt   *Ph* Osmond Borradaile   *Ed* Leslie Norman   *Mus* John Ireland

● Chips Rafferty, John Nugent Hayward, Daphne Campbell, Jean Blue (Ealing)

Producer Michael Balcon sent director Harry Watt to Australia with a mandate to make a picture representative of that continent. Watt spent five months soaking up the atmosphere. In the Federal Food Office, Controller Murphy explained of the greatest mass migration of cattle the world has ever known to get them out of reach of a probable Jap landing. Across 2,000 miles of heat and dust, drovers had battled with 500,000 head of cattle. Watt decided this would be the film's theme.

Story begins in 1942 at the tiny town of Wyndham, where meat works are destroyed, personnel evacuated, and Chips Rafferty, boss cattle drover, is told to shoot 1,000 head of prime beasts. He decides instead to overland them across 2,000 miles of tough going.

Epic trip lasts 15 months, and the adventures are graphic. Highlights are the breaking in of wild horses when their own had died from poison weed; the stampede with the men facing a charge of maddened cattle and the forced march across a mountain path with a sheer drop on one side.

■ **OVERLORD**

1975, 85 MINS, UK

Dir Stuart Cooper   *Prod* James Quinn   *Scr* Stuart Cooper, Christopher Hudson   *Ph* John Alcott   *Ed* Jonathan Gili   *Mus* Paul Glass

● Brian Stirner, Davyd Harries, Nicholas Ball, Julie Neesam, Sam Sewell (Imperial War Museum)

Overlord concentrates on a British youngster's World War II blitztime induction into the army, his brief training period and his early D-day death.

Pic has a lovely reminiscent feel for its period and the deceptively peaceful at-home backdrop to the war in the buildup phase to the Allied invasion of the Continent, with bombers taking off from the green fields of England, convoys of invasion troops crossing silent villages and, as a foretaste of deadlier things to come, rarely seen footage of dummy run rehearsals conducted along the coasts of Britain, eerily dramatic when glimpsed in hindsight on later events.

Youth's indoctrination, is very skillfully melded with real footage.

US director Stuart Cooper gives it the right understated, unheroic feel.

■ **OWL AND THE PUSSYCAT, THE**

1970, 98 MINS, US ◇ ⓥ

Dir Herbert Ross   *Prod* Ray Stark   *Scr* Buck Henry   *Ph* Harry Stradling   *Ed* Margaret Booth   *Mus* Richard Halligan   *Art Dir* Robert Wightman

● Barbra Streisand, George Segal, Robert Klein, Allen Garfield, Roz Kelly, Jacques Sandulescu (Columbia)

A zany, laugh-filled story of two modern NY kooks who find love at the end of trail of hilarious incidents.

Bill Manhoff's 1954 play, adapted here by Buck Henry, has been altered in that, as orig-

inally cast, one of the principals was white, the other black (on Broadway, Alan Alda and Diana Sands). Here it's two Bronx-Brooklyn Caucasian types, with Barbra Streisand giving it a Jewish Jean Arthur treatment and George Segal as an amiable, low-key foil.

The story is basically that of the out-of-work quasi-model and the struggling writer who cut up and down apartment corridors and in public to the astonishment of all others.

Streisand is a casual hooker, who first confronts Segal after he has finked on her activities to building superintendent Jacques Sandulescu. Their harangues then shift to apartment of buddy Robert Klein who decides it is better to leave with gal Evelyn Lang than lie awake listening.

One of her old scores turns out to be Jack Manning, Segal's intended father-in-law, but that plot turn blows up his affair and leads into the excellent climax we have been waiting for.

■ **OX-BOW INCIDENT, THE**

1943, 75 MINS, US ⓥ

Dir William A. Wellman   *Prod* Lamar Trotti   *Scr* Lamar Trotti   *Ph* Arthur Miller   *Ed* Allen McNeil   *Mus* Cyril J. Mockridge

● Henry Fonda, Dana Andrews, Mary Beth Hughes, Anthony Quinn, Jane Darwell, Harry Davenport (20th Century-Fox)

Screen version of the best-selling book [by Walter Van Tilburg Clark] depends too much on the hanging theme, developing this into a brutal closeup of a Nevada necktie party. Hardly a gruesome detail is omitted. Where the pleading by the three innocent victims doubtlessly was exciting on the printed page, it becomes too raw-blooded for the screen. Chief fault is that the picture over-emphasizes the single hanging incident of the novel, and there's not enough other action.

Western opus follows the escapades of two cowboys, played by Henry Fonda and Henry Morgan, in town after a winter on the range. They are tossed into the turmoil of the usually quiet western community which is aroused by the report of a cattleman's slaying by rustlers. A buddy of the supposedly slain rancher stirs the pot-boiling, and a posse is formed to get the culprits and handle them 'western style'. Remainder of story concerns efforts of the few law-abiding gentry to halt the lynching.

Fonda measures up to star rating, as one of the few level-headed cowhands. His brief scene with Mary Beth Hughes, the flashy belle of the village, following her sudden marriage, is topflight. He helps hold together the loose ends of the rather patent plot.

□ 1943: Best Picture (Nomination)

■ **PACIFIC HEIGHTS**

1990, 102 MINS, US ◇ ⓥ

Dir John Schlesinger   *Prod* Scott Rudin, William Sackheim   *Scr* Daniel Pyne   *Ph* Dennis E. Jones   *Ed* Mark Warner   *Mus* Hans Zimmer   *Art Dir* Neil Spisak

● Melanie Griffith, Matthew Modine, Michael Keaton, Mako, Nobu McCarthy, Laurie Metcalf (Morgan Creek)

The specter of a menace who invades one's home turf and can't be ousted is universally disturbing, and director John Schlesinger goes all out to make this creepy thriller-chiller as unsettling as it needs to be.

Story has babes-in-the-woods home buyers Patty (Melanie Griffith) and Drake (Matthew Modine) spending their every dime to restore an 1883 Victorian house in San Francisco, counting on the income from two downstairs apartments to meet the mortgage.

A nice Asian couple takes the one-bedroom, but the studio falls to reptilian Michael Keaton, who smoothtalks Modine into handing over a key without money up front. After he 'takes possession', it becomes clear they'll never see a dollar from this unnerving man. They encounter the shock of a legal system that's always on the renter's side.

First-time film scripter Daniel Pyne sets up a menacing cat-and-mouse game as sociopath Keaton plays the system to his advantage, finally provoking Modine into attacking him so he can go after his assets with a lawsuit. But pic loses its grip when it tips over into psycho-chiller territory.

Griffith lights up the screen as the kittenish but in-control Patty who lets her instincts be her guide when she takes off after Keaton on a one-woman crusade for justice.

PACIFIC PALISADES

1990, 94 MINS, FRANCE ◇

Dir Bernard Schmitt *Prod* Bernard Verley, Lise Fayolle *Scr* Marion Vernoux, Bernard Schmitt *Ph* Martial Barrault *Ed* Gilbert Namiand *Mus* Jean-Jacques Goldman, Roland Romanetti

● Sophie Marceau, Adam Coleman Howard, Anne Curry, Virginia Capers, Toni Basil (BVF/Sandor/Antenne 2)

Pacific Palisades is a transatlantic romance bringing Sophie Marceau to America for a change of climate (physical and emotional). She's in for some surprises, but the audience isn't. First feature by prize-winning vidclip helmer Bernard Schmitt sinks into the tar pits of culture shock cliches.

Marceau is a dissatisfied Parisian waitress who heads for LA on a bum job offer and finds herself living alone in a large modern suburban house. She's quickly exasperated and bored. Then she gets involved with the Canadian boyfriend (Adam Coleman Howard) of a Yank actress she initially was to have flown in with.

Despite the platitudes and plot inconsistencies, film is charmingly acted by Marceau in her first (mostly) English-lingo role. Howard is okay as the romantic interest whose idea of a hot date is a group outing to a hockey game.

PACK, THE

1977, 99 MINS, US ◇ Ⓥ

Dir Robert Clouse *Prod* Fred Weintraub, Paul Heller *Scr* Robert Clouse *Ph* Ralph Woolsey *Ed* Peter E. Berger *Mus* Lee Holdridge

● Joe Don Baker, Hope Alexander-Willis, Richard B. Shull, R.G. Armstrong, Ned Wertimer, Bibi Besch (Warner)

The Pack is a well-made and discreetly violent story of a pack of wild dogs menacing residents of a remote island.

The production, with Robert Clouse scripting Dave Fisher's novel and also directing, stars Joe Don Baker as a marine biologist who leads the humans' defense.

Strong story peg is habit of summer vacationers to abandon pets, but in this case, the stranded mutts band together in ferocious attack on people.

Clouse's attention to lighting and shadow adds an extra eerie feel to the proceedings. Fast cutaways from dog attacks create an unseen horror that makes for more fear than explicit footage otherwise might have achieved.

Given the simplistic script demands, Baker is very good. Hope Alexander-Willis, in film debut, comes across okay.

PACK UP YOUR TROUBLES

1932, 70 MINS, US

Dir George Marshall, Raymond McCarey *Prod* Hal Roach *Scr* H.M. Walker *Ph* Art Lloyd *Ed* Richard Currier

● Stan Laurel, Oliver Hardy, Donald Dillaway, Jacquie Lyn, Mary Carr, James Finlayson (M-G-M)

Seventy minutes of slapstick is a tall order for Laurel & Hardy and they hardly fill it. It's one of those hokum war farces with the numbskull L&H jazzing up the army as hapless rookies.

There's also a wartime buddy's girl baby whom the well-meaning L&H endeavor to return to her grandparents, a Mr and Mrs Smith. Trying to identify the Smiths through the city directory constitutes a major portion of that sort of pseudo-comedy.

One wonders why it wasn't kept to the confines of the usual twin-reeler as in the past.

PAD, THE (AND HOW TO USE IT)

1966, 86 MINS, US ◇

Dir Brian G. Hutton *Prod* Ross Hunter *Scr* Thomas C. Ryan, Ben Starr *Ph* Ellsworth Fredericks *Ed* Milton Carruth *Mus* Russ Garcia *Art Dir* Alexander Golitzen

● Brian Bedford, Julie Sommars, James Farentino, Edy Williams, Nick Navarro, Pearl Shear (Universal)

The Private Ear, which made up one half of the Peter Shaffer play, *The Private Ear and the Public Eye*, was a short but observant look at loneliness and the aborted effort of one shy male to communciate with the opposite sex. Ross Hunter's screen adaptation, thanks almost entirely to Shaffer's original dialog and the recreation by Brian Bedford of the shy young man he played in the New York production, recaptures much of the humor, compassion and wisdom of the legit production.

While the setting has been switched from an English flat to a Los Angeles rooming house, there is, basically, little difference between the storyline of the play and the film. Necessary expansion shows scenes only referred to in the play and adds a few extraneous characters. There is first rate playing by Julie Sommars as the gauche girl he covets and James Farentino as the Lothario friend who wrecks the timid type's plans.

PAGE MISS GLORY

1935, 92 MINS, US

Dir Mervyn LeRoy *Prod* Robert Lord *Scr* Delmer Daves, Robert Lord *Ph* George Folsey *Ed* William Clemens *Mus* Leo F. Forbstein (dir.) *Art Dir* Robert Haas

● Marion Davies, Pat O'Brien, Dick Powell, Mary Astor, Frank McHugh, Patsy Kelly (Cosmopolitan/Warner)

Same deficiency as in the play [by Joseph Schrank and Philip Dunning] occurs – the obvious. The farcical situations telegraph each ensuing denouement yards ahead. But the same fast and furious tempo, as in the play, does much to offset this fault. It's really a comedy Cinderella theme.

Marion Davies is the hotel chambermaid who is catapulted into being 'Down Glory', the mythical non-existent, composite beauty who cops a contest. Pat O'Brien and Frank McHugh are the broken-down promoters (slang for chiselers, although harmless guys in the main) who engineer the photographic compo girl into a $2,500 cash prize and a flock of offers.

When besieged by commercial sponsors for endorsements and newspapermen for interviews, Davies unconsciously walks from the

metamorphosis from the femme de chambre into the No. 1 US beaut. The farcical complications pile on with O'Brien (Chick Wiley) extricating himself ingeniously with each turn.

Davies does well by her generous comedy opportunities. Dick Powell, as a goofy stunt flyer, is well nigh wasted, virtually dragged in for his 'Page Miss Glory' title song [by Harry Warren and Al Dubin] duet with the star.

PAINT YOUR WAGON

1969, 166 MINS, US ◇ Ⓥ

Dir Joshua Logan *Prod* Alan Jay Lerner *Scr* Alan Jay Lerner, Paddy Chayevsky *Ph* William A. Fraker *Ed* Robert Jones *Mus* Frederick Loewe, Andre Previn *Art Dir* John Truscott

● Lee Marvin, Clint Eastwood, Jean Seberg, Ray Walston, Harve Presnell (Paramount)

Paint Your Wagon is the tale of a gold mining town in California in the 1840s – before it became a state and before there were many 'good' women in the territory.

Main story centres around a menage a trois. Lee Marvin, his pardner Clint Eastwood, and Marvin's wife (Jean Seberg) are the trio.

Director Joshua Logan has captured best the vastness and beauty of the country; the loneliness of men in womenless societies.

What the $17 million-plus film (from the 1951 Lerner-Loewe Broadway musical) lacks in a skimpy story line it makes up in the music and expert choreography. There are no obvious 'musical numbers'. All the songs, save one or two, work neatly, quietly and well into the script. The actors used their own voices, which are pleasant enough and add to the note of authenticity.

PAINTED VEIL, THE

1934, 83 MINS, US

Dir Richard Boleslavski *Prod* Hunt Stromberg *Scr* John Meehan, Salka Viertel, Edith Fitzgerald *Ph* William Daniels *Ed* Hugh Wynn *Mus* Herbert Stothart

● Greta Garbo, Herbert Marshall, George Brent, Warner Oland, Jean Hersholt, Beulah Bondi (M-G-M)

From almost any standpoint, *The Painted Veil* is a bad picture. It's clumsy, dull and long-winded. It's mostly the fault of the scripters. Yarn is so confused in the telling as to be almost hopeless. It deviates considerably from the original W. Somerset Maugham tale; that wouldn't be so bad if well done, but it emerges as neither film nor novel.

Yarn has Greta Garbo as the daughter of a Viennese professor (Jean Hersholt). A doctor in China (Herbert Marshall) comes a-visiting, asks her to marry him and she does, largely, it's indicated, because she wants to see China. Once they get to China she sits down to a constant and dangerous routine of wearing cockeyed hats that are an absolute menace

She meets George Brent, who doesn't seem to mind the hats. He flatters her for a while, then manages to get in a kiss. Hubby Marshall finds out, so he goes into the interior of China to clear up a bad cholera plague and drags her along, the idea seemingly being that may be both of them will catch the disease and die.

Garbo is but fair, although she doesn't get much chance to emote. Acting honors really go to Marshall.

PAJAMA GAME, THE

1957, 101 MINS, US ◇

Dir George Abbott, Stanley Donen *Prod* George Abbott, Stanley Donen *Scr* George Abbott, Richard Bissell *Ph* Harry Stradling *Ed* William Ziegler

Mus Richard Adler, Jerry Ross   *Art Dir* Malcolm Bert
● Doris Day, John Raitt, Carol Haney, Eddie Foy Jr, Reta Shaw, Barbara Nichols (Warner)

The inherent mobility and fluidity of *Pajama Game* as a stage property was such that this almost faithful transmutation into celluloid required little physical enhancement. But coproducers-codirectors George Abbott and Stanley Donen have not slighted the opportunities for size and scope when occasion warranted.

If the film version contains a shade more of social significance in the labor-engagement hassle, which was the springboard of the original Richard Bissell novel, *7¹/₂ Cents*, from which stems the romantic conflict between pajama factory superintendent John Raitt (who created the original stage role) and 'grievance committee chairman' Doris Day, it is a plus value because of the sturdy book.

Raitt is properly serious as the earnest factory executive and earnestly smitten with the blonde and beauteous Day. Day, always authoritative with a song, makes her chore even a shade more believable than Raitt. Carol Haney, recreating her soubret role opposite Eddie Foy Jr (also of the original stage cast), whams with 'Steam Heat', aided by Buzz Miller (stage original) and Kenneth LeRoy (substituting for Peter Gennaro of the Broadway cast).

● ●

■ PAJAMA PARTY

1964, 82 MINS, US ◇ ▼
Dir Don Weis   *Prod* James H. Nicholson, Samuel Z. Arkoff, Anthony Carras   *Scr* Louis M. Heyward   *Ph* Floyd Crosby   *Ed* Fred Feitshans, Eve Newman   *Mus* Les Baxter   *Art Dir* Daniel Haller
● Tommy Kirk, Annette Funicello, Elsa Lanchester, Jody McCrea, Buster Keaton, Dorothy Lamour (American International)

Exuberance of youth guns the action which twirls around a personable young Martian – Tommy Kirk – arriving on earth to pave the way for an invasion. He lands during a swimming party tossed by an eccentric wealthy widow (Elsa Lanchester), and immediately falls for Annette Funicello, girl-friend of widow's lug nephew (Jody McCrea).

Funicello displays an engaging presence and registers solidly. Kirk likewise shows class and Lanchester projects a rather zany character nicely. McCrea hams it up the way he should for such a part. Buster Keaton, playing an Indian, and Dorothy Lamour, dress store manager, sock over their roles.

● ●

■ PAL JOEY

1957, 112 MINS, US ◇ ▼
Dir George Sidney   *Prod* Fred Kohlmar   *Scr* Dorothy Kingsley   *Ph* Harold Lipstein   *Ed* Viola Lawrence, Jerome Thoms   *Mus* Richard Rodgers   *Art Dir* Walter Holscher
● Rita Hayworth, Frank Sinatra, Kim Novak, Barbara Nichols, Bobby Sherwood, Hank Henry (Columbia)

Pal Joey is a strong, funny entertainment. Dorothy Kingsley's screenplay, from John O'Hara's book, is skillful rewriting, with colorful characters and solid story built around the Richard Rodgers and Lorenz Hart songs. Total of 14 tunes are intertwined with the plot, 10 of them being reprised from the original. Others by the same team of cleffers are 'I Didn't Know What Time It Was', 'The Lady Is a Tramp', 'There's a Small Hotel' and 'Funny Valentine'.

Kingsley pulled some switches in shaping the [1940] legiter for the screen. Given a buildup to star status is the chorine from Albuquerque who becomes Joey's prey; Rita Hayworth (in the Vivienne Segal role) does the 'Zip' number that had been done by the herein-eliminated newspaper gal. There's not much terping, and the finale is happy ending stuff.

Frank Sinatra is potent. He's almost ideal as the irreverent, free-wheeling, glib Joey, delivering the rapid-fire cracks in a fashion that wrings out the full deeper-than-pale blue comedy potentials. Point might be made, though, that it's hard to figure why all the mice fall for this rat. Kim Novak is one of the mice (term refers to the nitery gals) and rates high as ever in the looks department but her turn is pallid in contrast with the forceful job done by Sinatra.

Hayworth, no longer the ingenue, moves with authority as Joey's sponsor and does the 'Zip' song visuals in such fiery, amusing style as to rate an encore. Standout of the score is 'Lady Is a Tramp'. It's a wham arrangement and Sinatra gives it powerhouse delivery.

● ●

■ PALE RIDER

1985, 115 MINS, US ◇ ▼
Dir Clint Eastwood   *Prod* Clint Eastwood   *Scr* Michael Butler, Dennis Shryack   *Ph* Bruce Surtees   *Ed* Joel Cox   *Mus* Lennie Niehaus   *Art Dir* Edward Carfagno
● Clint Eastwood, Michael Moriarty, Carrie Snodgress, Christopher Penn, Richard Dysart, Sydney Penny (Malpaso/Warner)

As he did in his Sergio Leone trilogy, Clint Eastwood portrays a nameless drifter, here called 'Preacher', who descends into the middle of a struggle between some poor, independent gold prospectors and a big company intent upon raping the beautiful land for all it's worth.

Borrowing from *Shane*, 'Preacher', so dubbed because he initially appears wearing a clerical collar, moves in with a group consisting of earnest Michael Moriarty, his somewhat reluctant lady friend Carrie Snodgress and her pubescent daughter Sydney Penny.

Preach pulls the threatened community together and inspires them to fight for their rights to the land rather than give up.

It's all been seen before, but Eastwood serves it up with authority, fine craftsmanship and a frequent sense of fun. This film is graced not only by an excellent visual look and confident storytelling, but by a few fine performances, led by Eastwood's own.

● ●

■ PALEFACE, THE

1948, 91 MINS, US ◇ ▼
Dir Norman Z. McLeod   *Prod* Robert L. Welch   *Scr* Edmund Hartmann, Frank Tashlin, Jack Rose   *Ph* Ray Rennahan   *Ed* Ellsworth Hoagland   *Mus* Victor Young   *Art Dir* Hans Dreier, Earl Hedrick
● Bob Hope, Jane Russell, Robert Armstrong (Paramount)

The Paleface is a smart-aleck travesty on the west, told with considerable humor and bright gags. Bob Hope has been turned loose on a good script.

Hope isn't all the film has to sell. There's Jane Russell as Calamity Jane, that rough, tough gal of the open west whose work as a government agent causes Hope's troubles, but whose guns save him from harm and give him his hero reputation. She makes an able sparring partner for the Hope antics, and is a sharp eyeful in Technicolor.

'Buttons and Bows' is top tune of the score's three pop numbers. Jay Livingston and Ray Evans cleffed and Hope renders as a plaintive love chant to Russell.

Script poses an amusing story idea – Hope as a correspondence school dentist touring the west in a covered wagon. He's having his troubles, but they're nothing compared to the grief that catches up with him when Calamity Jane seduces him into marriage so she can break up a gang smuggling rifles to the Indians.

● ●

■ PALM BEACH STORY, THE

1942, 96 MINS, US ▼
Dir Preston Sturges   *Prod* Paul Jones   *Scr* Preston Sturges   *Ph* Victor Milner   *Ed* Stuart Gilmore   *Mus* Victor Young
● Claudette Colbert, Joel McCrea, Mary Astor, Rudy Vallee, William Demarest, Sig Arno (Paramount)

This Preston Sturges production is packed with delightful absurdities. Claudette Colbert comes through with one of her best light comedy interpretations. She's strikingly youthful and alluring as the slightly screwball wife of five years standing, who, after seeing husband Joel McCrea out of debt, suddenly decides to seek a divorce, adventure and a bankroll for the husband she leaves behind.

Tongue-in-cheek spoofing of the idle rich attains hilarious proportions in scenes where Rudy Vallee, as John D. Hackensacker the Third, proposes to the errant wife and later woos her by singing to her to the accompaniment of a privately hired symphony orch big enough to fill the Radio City Music Hall pit.

McCrea plays it straight, for the most part, as the husband intent on winning his wife back.

● ●

■ PANDORA AND THE FLYING DUTCHMAN

1951, 122 MINS, UK ◇
Dir Albert Lewin   *Prod* Albert Lewin   *Scr* Albert Lewin   *Ph* Jack Cardiff   *Ed* Ralph Kemplen   *Mus* Alan Rawsthorne   *Art Dir* John Bryan
● James Mason, Ava Gardner, Nigel Patrick, Sheila Sim, Marius Goring, Mario Cabre (Kaufman/Lewin)

Albert Lewin produced, directed and did the story and script, keeping this film on an almost unrelieved level of sombre depression.

Lewin set his story in 1930 and filmed it on the coast of Spain. He gets into it with a flashback to explain the bodies of a man and woman found by fishermen off the coast.

Thanks to the presence of James Mason, the film has at least one distinctive histrionic touch. He plays the Dutchman of the title, a sea captain who, back in the 17th century, had been condemned to sail the oceans of the world until he found a woman willing to die for love. When this miracle occurs, his soul can find salvation.

Ava Gardner fares less distinctively as the girl who falls in love with this restless shade during one of the occasional brief periods allotted him to take on human form. Standout quality of the production is Jack Cardiff's color photography.

● ●

■ PANIC IN NEEDLE PARK, THE

1971, 110 MINS, US ◇ ▼
Dir Jerry Schatzberg   *Prod* Dominick Dunne   *Scr* Joan Didion, John Gregory Dunne   *Ph* Adam Holender   *Ed* Evan Lottman   *Art Dir* Murray P. Stern
● Al Pacino, Kitty Winn, Alan Vint, Richard Bright, Kiel Martin, Michael McClanathan

The Panic in Needle Park is a total triumph. Gritty, gutsy, compelling, and vivid to the point of revulsion, it is an overpowering tragedy about urban drug addiction. Director Jerry Schatzberg in only his second film becomes a major talent, while Al Pacino and Kitty Winn are terrific as a heroin-doomed couple.

Dominick Dunne produced on the streets of NY a drama so real that the persons and situations seem to have been caught in a documentary. James Mills' novel has been superbly adapted. The dialog is raw and uncompromising, yet artistic in its tragic-sardonic-ironic context.

Winn, introduced as a post-abortion discard of artist Raul Julia, takes up with Pacino, a drug pusher whose pretense of non-addiction soon fades away. She learns, and fast, the ropes of a strung-out world filled with young derelicts who steal, love, cheat, befriend and betray. This world is a jungle, ruled by instinctive addiction and passion, and it's just around everyone's corner now.

Pacino, after a brief mannered introduction, settles into his key role with terribly effective results. Winn is smash.

....

■ **PANIC IN THE CITY**

1968, 96 MINS, US ◇

Dir Eddie Davis   *Prod* Earle Lyon   *Scr* Eddie Davis, Charles E. Savage   *Ph* Alan Stensvold   *Ed* Terrell O. Morse   *Mus* Paul Dunlap   *Art Dir* Paul Sylos Jr
● Howard Duff, Linda Cristal, Stephen McNally, Nehemiah Persoff, Anne Jeffries, Oscar Beregi (United)

Panic in the City posits that a Communist operative in the US, acting independently of his Russian superiors, should be able to collect the material to construct an atomic bomb in Los Angeles. The panic of the title – there is talk of evacuating the city – never really happens thanks to the ingenious efforts of Howard Duff, an agent of the 'National' Bureau of Investigation.

It's all done perfunctorily and without any real distinction, but the low budget, necessitating real locations, makes possible the use of a great deal of LA

Nehemiah Persoff rather hysterically portrays the Commie fanatic, while Anne Jeffreys is his accomplice.

There are some sparks from Oscar Beregi's Czech scientist who assembles the bomb. Motorcycle vet Dennis Hooper has brief role of a murderer.

Development of the story is workmanlike enough, but disbelief sets in after Persoff goes batty by disobeying his superiors and deciding to explode the bomb.

....

■ **PANIC IN THE STREETS**

1950, 92 MINS, US
Dir Elia Kazan   *Prod* Sol C. Siegel   *Scr* Richard Murphy   *Ph* Joe MacDonald   *Ed* Harmon Jones   *Mus* Alfred Newman
● Richard Widmark, Paul Douglas, Barbara Bel Geddes, Jack Palance, Zero Mostel (20th Century-Fox)

This is an above-average chase meller. Tightly scripted and directed, it concerns the successful attempts to capture a couple of criminals, who are germ carriers, in order to prevent a plague and panic in a large city. The plague angle is somewhat incidental to the cops-and-bandits theme.

Story [by Edna and Edward Anhalt, adapted by Daniel Fuchs] opens harshly with three thieves stalking a man for his money and killing him to obtain it. The man has just arrived in New Orleans illegally and is suffering from a bubonic plague. His murderers, unknown to themselves, pick it up from him. The plot then concerns the efforts of the police, prodded by an alert Health Service officer, to locate and capture the slayers.

There is vivid action, nice human touches and some bizarre moments. Jack Palance gives a sharp performance.

....

■ **PANIC IN YEAR ZERO**

1962, 92 MINS, US
Dir Ray Milland   *Prod* Lou Rusoff, Arnold Houghland   *Scr* Jay Simms, John Morton   *Ph* Gil Warrenton   *Ed* William Austin   *Mus* Les Baxter   *Art Dir* Daniel Haller
● Ray Milland, Jean Hagen, Frankie Avalon, Mary Mitchel, Joan Freeman (American-International)

The aftermath of a nuclear attack is the subject pursued by this serious, sobering and engrossing film. The screenplay advances the theory that, in the event of a sudden wholesale outbreak of nuclear warfare, civilization will swiftly deteriorate into a decentralized

society of individual units, each necessarily hostile in relations with all others as part of a desperate struggle for self-preservation.

A family unit of four – father, mother and two teenaged children – is followed here in the wake of a series of initial nuclear blasts destroying Los Angeles and four other major US cities (excluding Washington – a rather astonishing oversight on the part of the unspecified enemy). The family is followed to an isolated cave in the hills where, thanks to the father's negative ingenuity, it remains until it is safe to come out.

Ray Milland manages capably in the dual task of director and star (he's the resourceful father), but it's safe to observe that he'd probably have done twice as well by halving his assignment, one way or the other.

....

■ **PAPER CHASE, THE**

1973, 111 MINS, US ◇ ⓥ
Dir James Bridges   *Prod* Robert C. Thompson, Rodrick Paul   *Scr* James Bridges   *Ph* Gordon Willis   *Ed* Walter Thompson   *Mus* John Williams   *Art Dir* George Jenkins
● Timothy Bottoms, Lindsay Wagner, John Houseman, Graham Beckel, Edward Herrmann (20th Century-Fox)

The Paper Chase has some great performances, literate screenwriting, sensitive direction and handsome production.

The tale of a young law school student, confused by his professional calling vs his inner evolution as a human being, seems timeless yet dated, too narrowly defined for broad audience empathy, and too often a series of sideways moving (though entertaining) thespian declamations.

James Bridges directs his own adaptation of the novel by John Jay Osborn Jr. Timothy Bottoms is excellent as the puzzled law student, Lindsay Wagner is very good as his girl, and John Houseman, the veteran legit and film producer-director-writer, is outstanding as a hard-nosed but urbane law professor.

The three players constitute the pervading plot triangle – Houseman the classroom dictator, Bottoms the uncertain supplicant, and Wagner, who plays Houseman's daughter.

....

■ **PAPER MASK**

1990, 118 MINS, UK ◇ ⓥ
Dir Christopher Morahan   *Prod* Christopher Morahan   *Scr* John Collee   *Ph* Nat Crosby   *Ed* Peter Coulson   *Mus* Richard Harvey   *Art Dir* Caroline Hanania
● Paul McGann, Amanda Donohoe, Frederick Treves, Tom Wilkinson, Barbara Leigh-Hunt, Jimmy Yuill (Film Four/Granada/British Screen)

Christopher Morahan's taut suspense thriller, from John Collee's novel about a young man who gets away with posing as an emergency room doctor in a British hospital, raises provocative questions about human pretense and the ruses of professional survival.

Pic focuses on a dissatisfied hospital worker, Matthew (Paul McGann), who seizes the chance to assume the identity of a promising young doctor after the other man dies in a car crash and his papers fall into Matthew's hands. Befriended by a competent and sympathetic nurse (Amanda Donohoe), he survives day by day. But the stakes are dramatically raised when he accidentally kills a doctor's wife with an overdose of anesthesia. To his astonishment, the hospital protects him, and in turn, itself.

Highly entertaining as a thriller-chiller, film is equally engrossing on a psychological level as it is always some aspect of the typically self-absorbed beings surrounding him that allows Matthew to pull off his deception.

....

■ **PAPER MOON**

1973, 101 MINS, US ⓥ
Dir Peter Bogdanovich   *Prod* Peter Bogdanovich   *Scr* Alvin Sargent   *Ph* Laszlo Kovacs   *Ed* Verna Fields   *Art Dir* Polly Platt
● Ryan O'Neal, Tatum O'Neal, Madeline Kahn, P.J. Johnson (Directors/Paramount/Saticoy)

Ryan O'Neal stars as a likeable con artist in the Depression midwest, and his real-life daughter, Tatum O'Neal, is outstanding as his nine-year-old partner in flim-flam. Joe David Brown's novel, *Addie Pray*, was the basis for Alvin Sargent's adaptation.

O'Neal arrives late at the funeral of a woman who was, or wasn't (as he claims), his wife, who has left a child of undetermined parentage but most determined character. Figuring to promote some fast money from locals for the kid, O'Neal finds the child more than adept in the shifty arts of selling Bibles to widows. Locked in uneasy but increasingly affectionate partnership, the O'Neals wend their way through the Kansas-Missouri farmlands.

Prominent among the large cast is Madeline Kahn, excellent as a carny stripper who captivates Ryan O'Neal. Tatum O'Neal makes a sensational screen debut.

....

■ **PAPER TIGER**

1975, 101 MINS, UK ◇
Dir Ken Annakin   *Prod* Euan Lloyd   *Scr* Jack Davies   *Ph* John Cabrera   *Ed* Alan Patillo   *Mus* Roy Budd   *Art Dir* Herbert Smith
● David Niven, Toshiro Mifune, Hardy Kruger, Ando, Ivan Desny, Irene Tsu (Levine)

Paper Tiger recalls the plots of vintage Shirley Temple vehicles in its cutesy relationship between English tutor David Niven and an 11-year-old Japanese moppet, (Ando), kidnapped together during turmoil in an unnamed Southeast Asian country.

Ando, like Temple, is dimpled, plucky, clever, and more resourceful than any of the adults in the story. He has a fresh, engaging personality, and it isn't his fault the camera moons over him at every opportunity.

Niven tries hard to breathe subtlety into his coward-turned-hero role, but is impeded by the lame screenplay and plodding direction. Toshiro Mifune, playing Ando's ambassador father, acts like his mind is elsewhere.

....

■ **PAPILLON**

1973, 150 MINS, US ◇ ⓥ
Dir Franklin J. Schaffner   *Prod* Robert Dorfmann, Franklin J. Schaffner   *Scr* Dalton Trumbo, Lorenzo Semple Jr   *Ph* Fred Koenekamp   *Ed* Robert Swink   *Mus* Jerry Goldsmith   *Art Dir* Anthony Masters
● Steve McQueen, Dustin Hoffman, Victor Jory, Don Gordon, Anthony Zerbe, Robert Deman (Allied Artists)

Henri Charriere's story of confinement in, and escape from, the infamous French Guiana prison colony was that of an ordeal. So is Franklin J. Schaffner's film version. For 150 uninterrupted minutes, the mood is one of despair, brutality, and little hope.

The script is very good within its limitations, but there is insufficient identification with the main characters. Steve McQueen, for example, says he has been framed for murdering a pimp; we do not see the injustice occur, hence have insufficient empathy.

Dustin Hoffman plays an urbane counterfeiter, a white collar criminal whose guilt is beyond question. Hoffman does an excellent job in portraying his character's adaptation to the corruptibilities of prison life.

The film begins with co-adaptor Dalton Trumbo (in an unbilled bit) addressing the latest shipload of prisoners consigned to the South American jungle horrors. He informs them they are henceforth nonhuman baggage. The oppressive atmosphere is so absolutely established within the first hour of the film that, in a sense, it has nowhere to go for the rest of the time.

The $13 million film was shot mostly in Spain and in Jamaica.

. . . .

■ PARADINE CASE, THE

1948, 131 MINS, US ⓥ

Dir Alfred Hitchcock *Prod* David O. Selznick *Scr* David O. Selznick *Ph* Lee Garmes *Ed* Hal C. Kern *Mus* Franz Waxman *Prod Des* J. McMillan Johnson

● Gregory Peck, Ann Todd, Charles Laughton, Charles Coburn, Louis Jourdan, Alida Valli (RKO/Selznick)

The Paradine Case offers two hours and 11 minutes of high dramatics.

Plot concerns murder of a blind man by his wife so she can marry her lover. Her attorney, believing in her not guilty plea, fights for her life. Himself infatuated with his client, the barrister plots and schemes to defeat justice but as dramatic events are brought out the truth is revealed. There are no flashback devices to clutter the trial and the audience gradually is let in on the facts as is the court as the hearing proceeds and emotions take hold. Charles Laughton gives a revealing portrait of a gross, lustful nobleman who presides at the trial.

Alfred Hitchcock's penchant for suspense, unusual atmosphere and development get full play. There is a deliberateness of pace, artful pauses and other carefully calculated melodramatic hinges upon which he swings the story and players. Selznick wrote the screenplay, adapted from the Robert Hichens novel by Alma Reville and James Bridie. It is a job that puts much emphasis on dialog and it's talk that punches. A very mobile camera helps give a feeling of movement to majority of scenes confined to the British courtroom as Hitchcock goes into the unfoldment of the highly dramatic murder trial.

Gregory Peck's stature as a performer of ability stands him in good stead among the extremely tough competition. As the barrister who defends Alida Valli, charged with the murder of her husband, he answers every demand of a demanding role. Ann Todd delights as his wife, giving the assignment a grace and understanding that tug at the emotions.

. . . .

■ PARADISE ALLEY

1978, 107 MINS, US ◇ ⓥ

Dir Sylvester Stallone *Prod* John F. Roach, Ronald A. Suppa *Scr* Sylvester Stallone *Ph* Laszlo Kovacs *Ed* Eve Newman *Mus* Bill Conti *Art Dir* John W. Corso

● Sylvester Stallone, Kevin Conway, Anne Archer, Joe Spinell, Armand Assante, Tom Waits (Force Ten)

Paradise Alley is *Rocky* rewritten by Damon Runyon. Set in New York's Hell's Kitchen area during the 1940s, it tells the uplifting tale of three brothers, played by Sylvester Stallone, Armand Assante, and Lee Canalito, and how they literally wrestle their way out of the ghetto.

It's an upbeat, funny, nostalgic film populated by colorful characters, memorable more for their individual moments than for their parts in the larger story.

Stallone proves a number of points with this film. First that he's a very capable director with a keen eye for casting. Second, he has a charming comic presence.

Paradise Alley shows off, once again, Stallone's ability as a writer. His sense of plot is old-fashioned – but it's also very commercial. The basic element is a hopeful loser who wants desperately to be a winner and triumphs.

The plot of this film is almost a throwaway. Three brothers, a dumb, beefy ice man (Canalito), a bitter crippled war veteran (Assante) and Stallone, the conman, all want to escape the slums. Stallone decides that Canalito's muscles in a wrestling ring are their ticket uptown.

. . . .

■ PARADISE, HAWAIIAN STYLE

1966, 87 MINS, US ◇ ⓥ

Dir Michael Moore *Prod* Hal Wallis *Scr* Allan Weiss, Anthony Lawrence *Ph* W. Wallace Kelley *Ed* Warren Low *Mus* Joseph J. Lilley *Art Dir* Hal Pereira, Walter Tyler

● Elvis Presley, Suzanna Leigh, James Shigeta, Donna Butterworth, Marianna Hill, Irene Tsu (Paramount)

Hal Wallis, who first brought Elvis Presley to the screen in 1956 and once before locationed in Hawaii (*Blue Hawaii*, 1961), returns singer to the island state in this gaily-begarbed and flowing musical.

Light script by Allan Weiss and Anthony Lawrence, based on former's original, serves more as a showcase for Presley's wares than as plottage but suffices to sock over the Presley lure. Star plays an airplane pilot with girl trouble, who loses one job after another when he becomes innocently embroiled. His troubles continue after he and James Shigeta team up for inter-island ferrying, with usual romanantic entanglements, fights and outbursts of song.

Michael Moore, making his directional bow after seven years with Wallis as an assistant, maintains a breezy pace and manages good performances from his cast.

. . . .

■ PARALLAX VIEW, THE

1974, 102 MINS, US ◇ ⓥ

Dir Alan J. Pakula *Prod* Alan J. Pakula *Scr* David Giler, Lorenzo Semple Jr *Ph* Gordon Willis *Ed* John W. Wheeler *Mus* Michael Small *Art Dir* George Jenkins

● Warren Beatty, Hume Cronyn, William Daniels, Paula Prentiss (Paramount)

The Parallax View is a partially-successful attempt to take a serious subject – a nationwide network of political guns for hire – and make it commercially palatable to the popcorn trade – via chases, fights, and lots of exterior production elements.

The adaptation of Loren Singer's novel follows newshawk Warren Beatty in his discovery of an assassination complex involving a security organization (called the Parallax Corp) which deliberately seeks out social misfits, dispatched by clients to murder political figures of various persuasions.

The story begins with the murder of Senator Bill Joyce, followed by the official investigation, after which many witnesses begin to die.

Paula Prentiss, very good as a prototype TV newshen, finally gets Beatty's interest aroused before her mysterious death.

Pakula's production and direction are lavish in physical details.

. . . .

■ PARAMOUNT ON PARADE

1930, 101 MINS, US ◇

Dir Dorothy Arzner, Victor Heerman, Ernst Lubitsch, Edward Sutherland, Otto Brower, Edwin H. Knopf, Lothar Mendes, Edmund Goulding, Rowland V. Lee, Victor Schertzinger, Frank Tuttle *Ph* Harry Fishbeck, Victor Milner *Ed* Merrill White *Art Dir* John Wenger

● Maurice Chevalier, Jean Arthur, Gary Cooper, Clara Bow, Jack Oakie, George Bancroft (Paramount)

Paramount on Parade links together with almost incredible smoothness achievements from the smallest technical detail to the greatest artistic endeavor. Interspersed throughout the 20 numbers are 11 songs, the work of 13 writers. Technicolor is used in seven of the numbers.

In color, setting and gracefulness of players and direction, the 'Dream Girl' number is outstanding.

But even with all the competition Maurice Chevalier comes through in first place. He is featured in three numbers and in two of these renders the song hits of the production. 'Sweeping the Clouds Away' is sung by him. Before this Chevalier appears in a sketch called 'A Park in Paris' which presents him as a gendarme among springtime activities.

Jack Oakie and Zelma O'Neal do a tapping special, in a gym. Clara Bow, in sailor garb, does her regular on the navy.

. . . .

■ PARASITE

1982, 85 MINS, US ◇ ⓥ

Dir Charles Band *Prod* Charles Band *Scr* Alan Adler, Michael Shoob, Frank Levering *Ph* Mac Ahlberg *Ed* Brad Arensman *Mus* Richard Band *Art Dir* Pamela Warner

● Robert Glaudini, Demi Moore, Luca Bercovici, James Davidson, Al Fann, Vivian Blaine (Embassy)

Parasite is a low-budget monster film which utilizes the 3-D process to amplify its shock effects.

Set in 1992, tale has a skimpy sci-fi peg of scientist Dr Paul Dean (Robert Glaudini) attempting to neutralize a strain of parasite he has developed for the government. Morbid premise is that the large, worm-like parasite is in his abdomen growing while he studies another specimen, racing to somehow avert his own death and save the world from millions of offspring.

Pic's raison d'etre is a set of frightening mechanical and sculpted monster makeup effects by Stan Winston. Convincing gore and sudden plunges at the camera are enhanced by Stereo Vision 3-D filming. Otherwise *Parasite* is lethargic between its terror scenes, making it a test of patience for all but the fanatical followers of horror cheapies.

. . . .

■ PARENT TRAP, THE

1961, 129 MINS, US ◇

Dir David Swift *Prod* Walt Disney *Scr* David Swift *Ph* Lucien Ballard *Ed* Philip W. Anderson *Mus* Paul Smith *Art Dir* Carroll Clark, Robert Clatworthy

● Hayley Mills, Maureen O'Hara, Brian Keith, Charlie Ruggles, Una Merkel, Leo G. Carroll (Walt Disney)

David Swift, whose writing, direction and appreciation of young Hayley Mills' natural histrionic resources contributed so much to *Pollyanna*, repeats the three-ply effort on this excursion, with similar success. Swift's screenplay, based on Erich Kastner's book, *Das doppelte Lottchen*, describes the nimble-witted method by which identical twin sisters (both played by Mills) succeed in reuniting their estranged parents after a 14-year separation during which the sisters were parted, unbeknownst to them, in opposite parental camps.

Mills seems to have an instinctive sense of comedy and an uncanny ability to react in just the right manner. Overshadowed, but outstanding in his own right, is Brian Keith as the father. Maureen O'Hara's durable beauty makes the mother an extremely attractive character.

. . . .

■ PARENTHOOD

1989, 124 MINS, US ◇ ⓥ

Dir Ron Howard *Prod* Brian Grazer *Scr* Lowell Ganz, Babaloo Mandel *Ph* Donald McAlpine *Ed* Michael Hill, Daniel Hanley *Mus* Randy Newman *Art Dir* Todd Hallowell

● Steve Martin, Mary Steenburgen, Dianne Wiest, Jason Robards, Rick Moranis, Tom Hulce (Imagine/Universal)

An ambitious, keenly observed, and often

very funny look at one of life's most daunting passages, *Parenthood*'s masterstroke is that it covers the range of the family experience, offering the points of view of everyone in an extended and wildly diverse middle-class family.

At its centre is over-anxious dad Steve Martin, who'll try anything to alleviate his eight-year-old's emotional problems, and Mary Steenburgen, his equally conscientious but better-adjusted wife.

Rick Moranis is the yuppie extreme, an excellence-fixated nerd who forces math, languages, Kafka and karate on his three-year-old girl, to the distress of his milder wife (Harley Kozak).

Dianne Wiest is a divorcee and working mother whose rebellious teens (Martha Plimpton and Leaf Phoenix) dump their anger in her lap.

Jason Robards is the acidic patriarch of the family whose neglectful fathering made his eldest son (Martin) grow up with an obsession to do better. The old man is forced to take another shot at fatherhood late in life when his ne'er-do-well, 27-year-old son (Tom Hulce) moves back in.

■ PARIS BLUES

1961, 98 MINS, US

Dir Martin Ritt   *Prod* Sam Shaw   *Scr* Walter Bernstein, Irene Kamp, Jack Sher   *Ph* Christian Matras   *Ed* Roger Dwyre   *Mus* Duke Ellington   *Art Dir* Alexandre Trauner
● Paul Newman, Joanne Woodward, Sidney Poitier, Louis Armstrong, Diahann Carroll, Serge Reggiani (United Artists/Pennebaker)

This reflects to some extent in form and technique the influence of the restless young Paris cinema colony, the environment in which the film was shot. But within its snappy, flashy veneer is an undernourished romantic drama of a rather traditional screen school.

The screenplay, based on a novel by Harold Flender, relates the romantic experiences of two expatriate US jazz musicians (Paul Newman and Sidney Poitier) and two American girls (Joanne Woodward and Diahann Carroll) on a two-week vacation fling in Paris. The men fall in love with the girls, then must weigh their philosophies and careers against their amour.

The screenplay fails to bring any true identity to the four characters. As a result, their relationships are vague and superficial. The film is notable for Duke Ellington's moody, stimulating jazz score. There are scenes when the drama itself actually takes a back seat to the music, with unsatisfactory results insofar as dialog is concerned. Along the way there are several full-fledged passages of superior Ellingtonia such as 'Mood Indigo' and 'Sophisticated Lady', and Louis Armstrong is on hand for one flamboyant interlude of hot jazz.

■ PARIS BY NIGHT

1989, 101 MINS, UK ◊ ⑦

Dir David Hare   *Prod* Patrick Cassavetti   *Scr* David Hare   *Ph* Roger Pratt   *Ed* George Akers   *Mus* Georges Delerue   *Art Dir* Anthony Pratt
● Charlotte Rampling, Michael Gambon, Robert Hardy, Iain Glen, Jane Asher (British Screen/Zenith/Film Four/Greenpoint-Pressman)

David Hare's second feature as a director is a handsomely produced, rather cold drama about the fall of a femme politician.

Although Clara Paige is at the top of the ladder, a high-profile, pro-Thatcher, Tory politico and member of the European parliament, she still finds other people's lives more attractive than her own. Her husband, Gerald (an MP) is a drunk she's come to despise.

On a high-level trip to Paris she meets with a young British businessman, Wallace, and starts an affair with him. Late at night, by the Seine, she's walking along when she sees Michael. Certain he's followed her, and that he's her anonymous caller, she tips him into the river, where he drowns.

What follows involves Clara's attempts to cover up her crime and her gradual realization that Michael, after all, was neither a blackmailer nor her telephone caller.

Hare handles it all with dry, often witty, precision, but with a slightly academic style. Ian Glen is miscast as the lover, and hardly comes across as a candidate for a passionate love affair.

■ PARIS, TEXAS

1984, 150 MINS, W. GERMANY/FRANCE ◊ ⑦

Dir Wim Wenders   *Prod* Don Guest   *Scr* Sam Shepard   *Ph* Robby Muller   *Ed* Peter Przygodda   *Mus* Ry Cooder   *Art Dir* Kate Altman
● Harry Dean Stanton, Nastassja Kinski, Dean Stockwell, Aurore Clement, Hunter Carson, Bernhard Wicki (Road/Argos)

Paris, Texas is a 'road movie' – an odyssey, if you will. It's a man's journey to self-recognition.

But what really impresses is the vision of writer-playwright Sam Shepard, upon whose *Motel Chronicles* short stories the original script was inspired and partially based.

Pic is the story of a man, Travis, wandering aimlessly along the Texas-Mexican border. Travis' brother in Los Angeles, Walt, is a billboard artist who took in the hero's boy four years ago when the mother literally left him on their doorstep.

Travis decides to win back the love of his son. Once he has done so, the pair's then off to Houston to find the missing mother, who works in a lonely-hearts kind of strip-joint.

Dean Stockwell as Walt is a standout, while Harry Dean Stanton as Travis only comes alive in the interim segments when he recovers his taste for humanity. Nastassja Kinski is hampered in a part that drags the film out interminably during a duolog with Stanton at the end.

■ PARIS TROUT

1991, 100 MINS, US ◊ ⑦

Dir Stephen Gyllenhaal   *Prod* Frank Konigsberg, Larry Sanitsky   *Scr* Pete Dexter   *Ph* Robert Elswit   *Ed* Harvey Rosenstock   *Mus* David Shire   *Art Dir* Richard Sherman
● Dennis Hopper, Barbara Hershey, Ed Harris, Ray McKinnon, Tina Lifford, Darnita Henry (Viacom)

Pete Dexter's haunting novel about an unspeakable crime in a simple Southern town circa 1949 is brought masterfully to life in *Paris Trout*, a mesmerizing, morbidly fascinating tale, with outstanding performances by Dennis Hopper, Barbara Hershey and Ed Harris.

Trouble begins when a young black man (Eric Ware) signs a note to buy a used car from Trout (Hopper). When the worthless car is wrecked the same day, he drops it off at Trout's store, declaring he won't pay. Trout and a hired gun head out to 'the hollow' to settle the debt. When the black man runs off, they enter the house and unload their pistols into his terrified mother and 12-year-old sister.

After his horrified wife (Hershey) visits the dying child at the clinic, Trout begins to humiliate and abuse her. He hires the town's crack lawyer (Ed Harris) to defend him, but the attorney becomes more and more disturbed by the case and Trout's lack of remorse.

Hopper, beefy and aged for the role and sporting a clipped redneck haircut, gives an extraordinary portrayal of the tortured madman. Hershey is marvelous in a mature, nuanced perf as the compassionate spouse struggling to maintain dignity.

■ PARRISH

1961, 140 MINS, US ◊

Dir Delmer Daves   *Prod* Delmer Daves   *Scr* Delmer Daves   *Ph* Harry Stradling Sr   *Ed* Owen Marks   *Mus* Max Steiner   *Art Dir* Leo K. Kuter
● Troy Donahue, Claudette Colbert, Karl Malden, Dean Jagger, Connie Stevens, Diane McBain (Warner)

Parrish is a long, plodding account of man vs monopoly in Connecticut's tobacco game.

Based on the novel by Mildred Savage, director Delmer Daves' screenplay is something of a cross between a rich man's *Tobacco Road* and a poor man's *A Place in the Sun*. Troy Donahue essays the title role of a poor young man who emerges from a laborer's toil in the Connecticut tobacco fields to challenge the dynasty of mighty land baron Karl Malden.

A number of romantic entanglements crop up to complicate this basic conflict, not the least of which are Donahue's bat-of-an-eyelash love affairs with Malden's daughter (Sharon Hugueny), his arch rival's (Dean Jagger's) daughter (Diane McBain) and a loose field girl (Connie Stevens) who gives illegitimate birth to the child of Malden's son (Hampton Fancher). Then there is the supreme complication: Malden's marriage to Donahue's mother (Claudette Colbert).

Donahue is handsome and has his moments, but lacks the animation and projection that is required to bring the title character, curiously vacant and elusive as written, into clearer focus. The picture's three principal veterans – Colbert, Malden and Jagger – do well, particularly Malden in spite of the exaggerated nature of his role.

■ PARTING GLANCES

1986, 90 MINS, US ◊ ⑦

Dir Bill Sherwood   *Prod* Yoram Mandel, Arthur Silverman   *Scr* Bill Sherwood   *Ph* Jacek Laskus   *Ed* Bill Sherwood   *Art Dir* John Loggia
● Richard Ganoung, John Bolger, Steve Buscemi (Rondo)

Parting Glances is bracingly forthright and believable in its presentation of an all-gay world within contempo New York City.

Set within a 24-hour period, Bill Sherwood's highly sophisticated pic centers around a series of farewell events for Robert (John Bolger), good-looking boyfriend of ultra-yuppie Michael (Richard Ganoung).

Robert, for reasons finally discovered by his lover, is leaving for a stint in Kenya, which will bring about the interruption, if not the end, of a six-year relationship.

Intertwined with this is Michael's very responsible dealing with his former lover Nick (Steve Buscemi), a caustic, cynical rock musician who has recently learned that he has AIDS.

Fortunately, film indulges in no special pleading, merely regarding the disease as another fact of gay life.

■ PARTNERS

1976, 96 MINS, CANADA ◊

Dir Dan Owen   *Prod* Chalmers Adams, Dan Owen   *Scr* Norman Snider, Dan Owen   *Ph* Marc Champion   *Ed* George Appleby   *Mus* Murray McLauchlan
● Denholm Elliott, Hollis McLaren, Michael Margotta, Lee Broker, Judith Gault, Robert Silverman (Clearwater)

Partners is a love story played off against a background of unscrupulous methods used by an American multi-national firm interested in buying out a large Canadian pulp and paper firm controlled by a very old moneyed family. Don Owen brings it off with elan and a few mystifying moments along the way.

A thief and dope smuggler, played with macho vigor by Michael Margotta, gets romantically and sexually involved with the daughter of the pulp and paper firm's owner and takes her along running dope across the US-Canada border.

Aside from Margotta, a fine performance by Denholm Elliott, and a jail scene vignette by actress Jackie Burroughs as a prostitute, the acting rarely rises above the superficial.

....

■ PARTNERS

1982, 93 MINS, US ◇ ▽
Dir James Burrows   *Prod* Aaron Russo   *Scr* Francis Veber   *Ph* Victor J. Kemper   *Ed* Danford B. Greene   *Mus* Georges Delerue   *Art Dir* Richard Sylbert
● Ryan O'Neal, John Hurt, Kenneth McMillan, Robyn Douglass, Jay Robinson, Denise Galik (Paramount)

Screenwriter/exec producer Francis Veber, who scored by spoofing one segment of the homosexual life-style in *La Cage aux Folles* and its sequel, this time tries to transfer his approach to a contemporary American setting. This production could loosely be termed *The Odd Couple Turns Gay and Joins the Police Force*, ultimately runs one very tired joke into the ground.

Essentially, this is the story of straight, macho detective Ryan O'Neal and closeted gay police office clerk John Hurt – an odd pair forced by their superior to go undercover and pose as a homosexual couple in order to trap the murderer of a male model.

Naturally, all the gays they encounter seem to either putter around displaying their limp wrists or swoon the moment O'Neal walks into a room. Hurt tries to be a crime solver, but is infinitely more content to bake a souffle or stare doe-eyed at O'Neal as he adoringly serves him breakfast in bed.

....

■ PARTY, THE

1968, 98 MINS, US ◇ ▽
Dir Blake Edwards   *Prod* Blake Edwards   *Scr* Blake Edwards, Tom Waldman, Frank Waldman   *Ph* Lucien Ballard   *Ed* Ralph Winters   *Mus* Henry Mancini   *Art Dir* Fernando Carrere
● Peter Sellers, Claudine Longet, Marge Champion, Steve Franken, Fay McKenzie (United Artists)

All the charm of two-reel comedy, as well as all the resulting tedium when the concept is distended to 10 reels, is evident in *The Party*.

The one-joke script, told in laudable, if unsuccessful, attempt to emulate silent pix technique, is dotted with comedy ranging from drawing-room repartee to literally, bathroom vulgarity.

Peter Sellers is a disaster-prone foreign thesp, who, in an amusing eight-minute prolog to titles, fouls up an important Bengal Lancer-type film location. His outraged producer (Gavin MacLeod) blackballs him to studio chief J. Edward McKinley, but, in a mixup, Sellers gets invited to a party at McKinley's home.

Production designer Fernando Carrere has done an outstanding job in creating, on the one set used, a super-gauge house of sliding floors, pools, centralized controls and bizarre trappings.

Besides Sellers, most prominent thesps are Claudine Longet, the romantic interest, and Steve Franken as a tipsy butler. Eventually it all becomes a big yawn.

....

■ PARTY GIRL

1958, 99 MINS, US ◇
Dir Nicholas Ray   *Prod* Joe Pasternak   *Scr* George Wells   *Ph* Robert Bronner   *Ed* John McSweeney   *Mus* Jeff Alexander   *Art Dir* William A. Horning, Randall Duell
● Robert Taylor, Cyd Charisse, Lee J. Cobb, John Ireland, Claire Kelly, Corey Allen (M-G-M

Party Girl is a straight melodrama of gangster days in Chicago, played straight. There is no effort to understand the phenomenon or to relate it to the times.

Robert Taylor plays a crippled lawyer, mouthpiece for gangster boss Lee J. Cobb. Taylor uses his disability to play on the sympathies of juries to get the mobster underlings, such as John Ireland, free of murder and mayhem charges he knows they are guilty of. He begins to be disturbed about his way of life when he meets Cyd Charisse, a dancer at a nightclub who picks up a little money occasionally at parties. Taylor sees he cannot censure Charisse for making money out of the mobs when he is doing the same thing himself. Taylor's breaking point comes when he is called on by Cobb to defend a psychopath mobster (Corey Allen).

The screenplay, based on a story by Leo Katcher, is intelligent and convincing, and Nicholas Ray's direction is good within the limits of the action.

Taylor carries considerable conviction as the attorney, suave and virile. Charisse's character has little background to supply her with any acting exercise, but she is interesting and, in two fine dance numbers, exciting. Lee J. Cobb contributes another of his somewhat flamboyant characterizations.

....

■ PARTY'S OVER, THE

1965, 94 MINS, UK
Dir Guy Hamilton   *Prod* Anthony Perry   *Scr* Mark Behm   *Ph* Larry Pizer   *Ed* John Bloom   *Mus* John Barry
● Oliver Reed, Clifford David, Ann Lynn, Catherine Woodville, Louise Sorel, Eddie Albert (Tricastle)

Censorship problems delayed release of *The Party's Over* for two years.

The tawdry yarn, loosely scripted by Mark Behm, concerns a young American girl, daughter of a tycoon, who comes to London and gets involved with a group of young Chelsea layabouts known as the 'Pack', a disillusioned bunch which lives only for kicks.

Eventually the girl disappears after one of the wildest parties, and is found dead. How she met her death, the events leading up to it and immediately after, which involve a mock funeral, a hint of necrophilia and a young man's suicide all merge into a pseudo-psychological and phony finale.

Performances are mostly routine, but there are a few that show distinct promise, notably Oliver Reed, as the arrogant, womanizing young misfit leader of the 'Pack', Clifford David, as a likeable American boy with a tricky role to which he brings a sense of humor, and Catherine Woodville, a standout as one of the few of the 'Pack' with any decent instincts left. Louise Sorel as the heroine is overly fey.

....

■ PASCALI'S ISLAND

1988, 104 MINS, UK ◇ ▽
Dir James Dearden   *Prod* Eric Fellner   *Scr* James Dearden   *Ph* Roger Deakins   *Ed* Edward Marnier   *Mus* Lock Dikker   *Art Dir* Andrew Mollo
● Ben Kingsley, Charles Dance, Helen Mirren, George Murcell, Sheila Allen (Avenue-Initial/Film Four Dearfilm)

Intrigue on a Turkish-occupied Greek island in 1908 is the theme of this mildly exotic British pic [based on the novel by Barry Unsworth] which, despite an eye-catching but mannered central performance from Ben Kingsley, looms as too languid and remote to make much impact.

Kingsley plays Pascali, a seedy little Turkish spy who's lived on the small island of Nisi for 20 years. The ever-watchful agent is a very minor cog in the crumbling Ottoman Empire, yet is filled with self-importance.

Sexually ambivalent, he carries a half-hearted torch for a comely, middle-aged Austrian painter, Lydia (Helen Mirren).

Enter Charles Dance as Bowles, a bronzed British adventurer professing to be an archeologist, actually planning to loot the island of its ancient treasures. Before long he's involved in an affair with Lydia, observed by the frustrated and jealous Pascali who is, perhaps, even more attracted to Bowles than to the woman. The stage is set for a final-reel tragedy.

Kingsley gives a technically impressive performance as the frustrated, bitter spy, but his mannerisms are becoming bothersome. Best is Mirren who still can disrobe to play a love scene with elegance and style; she brings much-needed warmth to an otherwise cold pic.

....

■ PASSAGE TO INDIA, A

1984, 163 MINS, UK ◇ ▽
Dir David Lean   *Prod* John Brabourne, Richard Goodwin   *Scr* David Lean   *Ph* Ernest Day   *Ed* David Lean   *Mus* Maurice Jarre   *Art Dir* John Box
● Judy Davis, Victor Banerjee, Peggy Ashcroft, James Fox, Alec Guinness, Nigel Havers (Columbia/HBO)

Fourteen years after his last film, David Lean returned to the screen with *A Passage to India*, an impeccably faithful, beautifully played and occasionally languorous adaptation of E.M. Forster's classic novel about the clash of East and West in colonial India.

Tale is set in 1928, a curious fact in that Forster's enduring novel was penned four years earlier. A young woman, Judy Davis, is taken from England to India by Peggy Ashcroft with the likely purpose of marrying the older woman's son Nigel Havers, the city magistrate of fictitious Chandrapore.

Intelligent and well brought up, Davis is not exactly a rebel, but chafes at the limitations and acute snobbery of the ruling British community.

Breaking the general rule against racial intermingling, local medic Victor Banerjee invites the ladies on an expedition to the nearby Marabar caves, an excursion which ends in tragedy when a bloodied Davis returns to accuse the bewildered, devastated Banerjee of having attempted to rape her in one of the caves.

Lean has succeeded to a great degree in the tricky task of capturing Forster's finely edged tone of rational bemusement and irony.

The outstanding set of performances here is led by Ashcroft, a constant source of delight as the wonderfully independent and frank Mrs Moore, and Davis, an Australian actress who has the rare gift of being able to look very plain (as the role calls for) at one moment and uncommonly beautiful at another.

☐ 1984: Best Picture (Nomination)

....

■ PASSAGE TO MARSEILLE

1944, 110 MINS, US ▽
Dir Michael Curtiz   *Prod* Hal B. Wallis   *Scr* Casey Robinson, John C. Moffitt   *Ph* James Wong Howe   *Ed* Owen Marks   *Mus* Max Steiner   *Art Dir* Carl Jules Weyl
● Humphrey Bogart, Michele Morgan, Claude Rains, Sydney Greenstreet, Peter Lorre, Helmut Dantine (Warner)

Yarn [from a novel by Charles Nordhoff and James Norman Hall], dedicated to the Fighting French, unwinds in a series of flashbacks, as related by a French liaison officer (Claude Rains) to an American newspaperman (John Loder), who seeks background for a story dealing with activities of these Frenchmen who are fighting, and flying, on the side of the Allies. Rains goes back many months in the telling, when a ship he was on picked up a group of men in a lifeboat in the Atlantic. The survivors admit, when pressed, that they are escaped prisoners from Devil's Island, who wish to return to France to fight for their country.

After the rescue, the freighter settles down to its normal routine, continuing back to Marseille, its destination, only to be disturbed again when the wireless crackles with the news of French surrender to the Nazis. The captain of the ship (Victor Francen) secretly orders its course changed toward England, but not before the fascist wireless operator radios the ship's position to a German patrol bomber.

Humphrey Bogart, as Matrac, a journalist whose opposition to the appeasers at the time of Munich resulted in his conviction on a trumped up charge of murder and treason and his banishment to Devil's Island, gives a forthright performance as one of the escaped convicts rescued by the freighter.

But the best job of all is done by Rains. Not only does he have the biggest part in the picture, but he captures practically all the acting honors in a film filled with good acting.

■ **PASSENGER, THE**

1975, 123 MINS, US ◇

Dir Michelangelo Antonioni   *Prod* Carlo Ponti
Scr Mark Peploe, Peter Wollen, Antonioni   *Ph* Luciano Tovoli   *Ed* Franco Arcali, Antonioni   *Art Dir* Piero Poletto
● Jack Nicholson, Maria Schneider, Jennie Runacre, Ian Hendry (M-G-M)

Jack Nicholson plays a seasoned TV newsman, adjusted to established limits yet conscious of his inadequacy in probing through the grim truth. Death of a British adventurer in a small north African hotel becomes a last chance for the newsman to scrap his own anguished identity and take on the mission of the dead man.

His new probe becomes a showdown with the merciless revolutionary currents and countercurrents in today's world.

It is not quite clear what part of Nicholson is courageous involvement in third world liberation, what part is a reaction to the disinterested passion of youth for justice or the ironic attrition of feared exposure by his estranged wife in London.

Nicholson plays the character with personal flair, as penetrating as Antonioni's handling of the film.

■ **PASSIONATE FRIENDS, THE**

1949, 91 MINS, UK

Dir David Lean   *Prod* Ronald Neame   *Scr* Eric Ambler   *Ph* Guy Green   *Ed* Geoffrey Foot
Mus Richard Addinsell   *Art Dir* John Bryan
● Anne Todd, Claude Rains, Trevor Howard (Cineguild/Rank)

Polished acting, masterly direction and an excellent script put *The Passionate Friends* in the top rank of class British productions. Eric Ambler's screenplay takes many liberties with the original H. G. Wells story, but he has built up a powerful dramatic situation on the triangle drama.

For the first half hour the story is related by means of a series of flashbacks, which inclines to some confusion, but it soon settles down to straightforward presentation with none of the dramatic effect being lost in the telling.

Ann Todd rises to new heights as the girl who forswears love for security and wealth. Hers is a flawless portrayal and ranks with the best seen in British pictures. Claude Rains, in the role of the banker husband, is a model of competence and Trevor Howard brings vigor and polish to the part of the lover.

■ **PASSOVER PLOT, THE**

1976, 108 MINS, US/ISRAEL ◇ Ⓥ

Dir Michael Campus   *Prod* Wolf Schmidt   *Scr* Millard Cohan, Patricia Knop   *Ph* Adam Greenberg   *Ed* Dov Hoenig   *Mus* Alex North   *Art Dir* Kuli Sander
● Harry Andrews, Hugh Griffith, Zalman King, Donald Pleasence, Scott Wilson, Dan Ades
(Atlas/Golan-Globus)

A disappointing film based on Hugh J. Schonfield's tampering-with-orthodoxy revisionist 1960s book on the life of Jesus Christ, *The Passover Plot*. The physically handsome production drains the vitality out of the Christ story through verbiage and overacting.

Schonfield's retelling of the New Testament depicts Jesus (or 'Yeshua', the Hebraic name used in the book and film) as a political revolutionary who contrives his own crucifixion as a plot against the Roman establishment.

Zalman King's Yeshua is an angry young man with little of the warmth and folk humor the character displays in the Bible texts. Far from seeming disrespectful, the film in fact errs on the side of excessive respect.

■ **PASSPORT TO PIMLICO**

1949, 84 MINS, UK Ⓥ

Dir Henry Cornelius   *Prod* Michael Balcon   *Scr* T.E.B. Clarke   *Ph* Lionel Banes, Cecil Cooney   *Ed* Michael Truman   *Mus* Georges Auric   *Art Dir* Roy Oxley
● Stanley Holloway, Barbara Murray, Raymond Huntley, Paul Dupuis, Jane Hylton, Hermione Baddeley (Ealing)

Sustained, lightweight comedy scoring a continual succession of laughs.

Story describes what happens when a wartime unexploded bomb in a London street goes off and reveals ancient documents and treasure which make the territory part of the duchy of Burgundy. Ration cards are joyfully torn up and customs barriers are put up by British.

The theme is related with a genuine sense of satire and clean, honest humor. The principal characters are in the hands of experienced players with Stanley Holloway leading the new government, Raymond Huntley the bank manager turned Chancellor of the Exchequer, Hermione Baddeley as the shopkeeper and Sydney Tafler as the local bookmaker.

■ **PASSWORD IS COURAGE, THE**

1962, 116 MINS, UK

Dir Andrew Stone   *Prod* Andrew Stone, Virginia Stone   *Scr* Andrew Stone   *Ph* Davis Boulton
Ed Noreen Ackland, Virginia Stone   *Art Dir* Wilfred Arnold
● Dirk Bogarde, Maria Perschy, Alfred Lynch, Nigel Stock, Reginald Beckwith (M-G-M)

Stone's screenplay, based on a biog of Sergeant-Major Charles Coward by John Castle, has pumped into its untidy 116 minutes an overdose of slapstick humour. Result is that what could have been a telling tribute to a character of guts and initiative, the kind that every war produces, lacks conviction.

Coward (Dirk Bogarde), a breezy, likeable character, becomes a prisoner of war and is dedicated to sabotaging and humiliating his German captors. As senior soldier in Stalag 8B, he rallies the other men to escape so that they can get back to fighting the Nazis. Coward's main problem is to make contact with the Polish underground to get maps, money, etc., before escaping through a 280-foot tunnel which the prisoners have laboriously built.

Bogarde gives a performance that is never less than competent, but never much more. The best male performance comes from Lynch, as Corporal Pope, a philosophical sol-

dier devoted to Coward. He is a composite of several characters in Coward's actual story. Maria Perschy, a personable Hungarian girl making her first appearance in a British film, brings some glamor to the film as the underground worker.

■ **PAT AND MIKE**

1952, 94 MINS, US Ⓥ

Dir George Cukor   *Prod* Lawrence Weingarten
Scr Ruth Gordon, Garson Kanin   *Ph* William Daniels
Ed George Boemler   *Mus* David Raksin   *Art Dir* Cedric Gibbons, Urie McCleary
● Spencer Tracy, Katharine Hepburn, Aldo Ray, William Ching, Sammy White, George Mathews (M-G-M)

The smooth-working team of Spencer Tracy and Katharine Hepburn spark the fun in *Pat and Mike*. Hepburn is quite believable as a femme athlete taken under the wing of promoter Tracy. Actress, as a college athletic instructor engaged to eager-beaver prof William Ching, enters an amateur golf tournament to prove to herself and to Ching that she is good. Deed attracts the attention of Tracy, who quick-talks her into signing a pro contract for a number of sports.

Film settles down to a series of laugh sequences of training, exhibitions and cross-country tours in which Hepburn proves to be a star.

Tracy is given some choice lines in the script and makes much of them in an easy, throwaway style that lifts the comedy punch.

■ **PAT GARRETT AND BILLY THE KID**

1973, 106 MINS [1989: 122 MINS], US ◇ Ⓥ

Dir Sam Peckinpah   *Prod* Gordon Carroll
Scr Rudolph Wurlitzer   *Ph* John Coquillon   *Ed* Roger Spottiswoode, Garth Craven, Robert L. Wolfe, Richard Halsey, David Berlatsky, Tony de Zarrara   *Mus* Bob Dylan   *Art Dir* Ted Haworth
● James Coburn, Kris Kristofferson, Bob Dylan, Richard Jaeckel, Katy Jurado, Jason Robards (M-G-M)

'It feels like times have changed,' mutters James Coburn as gunman-turned-sheriff Pat Garrett, now hot on the trail of erstwhile buddy, Billy the Kid (Kris Kristofferson).

Coburn offers more of his smiles as testimony to the wizardry of Old West dentistry, while Kristofferson ambles through his role with solid charm. Neither conveys the psychological tension felt between the two men whose lives diverge after years of camaraderie.

Bob Dylan makes his dramatic film debut in a part so peripheral (or so abridged by six film editors) as to make his appearance a trivial cameo. His acting is limited to an embarrassing assortment of tics, smirks, shrugs, winks and smiles.

The editing, faulted by the director, conceals the reported postproduction tinkering but also reduces such players as Jason Robards, Richard Jaeckel and Katy Jurado to walk-on status. [Peckinpah's original cut was finally released in 1989.]

■ **PATCH OF BLUE, A**

1965, 105 MINS, US

Dir Guy Green   *Prod* Pandro S. Berman, Guy Green
Scr Guy Green   *Ph* Robert Burks   *Ed* Rita Roland
Mus Jerry Goldsmith
● Sidney Poitier, Shelley Winters, Elizabeth Hartman, Wallace Ford, Ivan Dixon, Elisabeth Fraser (M-G-M)

A Patch of Blue is a touching contemporary melodrama, relieved at times by generally effective humor, about a blind white girl, rehabilitated from a dreary home by a Negro. Film has very good scripting plus excellent direction and performances, including an exceptional screen debut by Elizabeth Hartman as the gal.

P

Director Guy Green adapted Elizabeth Kata's *Be Ready with Bells and Drums*, and the ending, while positive, isn't sudsy. Hartman gives a smash interpretation to the role, and progresses most believably from an uneducated, unwanted and home-anchored maiden, to an upbeat, firmer grasp on what is to be her sightless maturity.

Sidney Poitier is excellent as he becomes her first true friend and gives her some self-assurance. She, of course, doesn't know he is Negro.

The domestic situation is grim, with Shelley Winters very good as Hartman's sleazy mother. Vet character actor Wallace Ford, Winters' dad, effectively blends personal frustration, shame and disappointment in his own daughter and pity for Hartman in limited footage.

■ **PATERNITY**

1981, 94 MINS, US ◇

Dir David Steinberg   *Prod* Lawrence Gordon, Hank Moonjean   *Scr* Charlie Peters   *Ph* Bobbie Byrne   *Ed* Donn Cambern   *Mus* David Shire   *Art Dir* Jack Collis

● Burt Reynolds, Beverly D'Angelo, Paul Dooley, Elizabeth Ashley, Lauren Hutton (Paramount)

There are several funny bits in *Paternity* a harmless enough romantic comedy that strangely has its strongest laughs in its least important scenes. But the basic story of a successful 44-year-old man who decides to fulfill his desire for fatherhood by pacting with a woman to have his child never comes across with much punch.

The idea behind the film is a charming one and Reynolds manages to evoke the sensitivity needed to make his character's desires seem believable. Charlie Peters' script comes through in odd moments, usually in the form of witty visual asides superfluous to the primary action. Much of the latter is also due to the hand of first time director David Steinberg, whose style clearly owes to his wonderfully snide point of view as a successful standup comic.

While Reynolds and D'Angelo make a nice enough onscreen couple, they just don't provide the sparks needed to light up a romantic comedy.

■ **PATHS OF GLORY**

1957, 87 MINS, US ▼

Dir Stanley Kubrick   *Prod* James B. Harris   *Scr* Stanley Kubrick, Calder Willingham, Jim Thompson   *Ph* George Krause   *Ed* Eva Kroll   *Mus* Gerald Fried   *Art Dir* Ludwig Reiber

● Kirk Douglas, Ralph Meeker, Adolphe Menjou, George Macready, Wayne Morris, Richard Anderson (United Artists)

Paths of Glory [based on the novel by Humphrey Cobb] is a starkly realistic recital of French army politics in 1916 during World War I. While the subject is well handled and enacted in a series of outstanding characterizations, it seems dated and makes for grim screen fare.

Story nub revolves around decision of the General Staff for a military unit commanded by George Macready, a general of the old school, to take an objective held for two years by the Germans. Knowing full well the impossibility of such an assault because of lack of manpower and impregnability of the position, the general nevertheless orders Kirk Douglas, colonel in command of the regiment, to make the suicidal attempt.

When his men either are driven back by enemy fire or are unable to leave the trenches, an unjust charge of cowardice against the men is lodged by the general and Douglas is ordered to arrange for three men to be selected to stand courtmartial, as an object lesson to whole army.

Stanley Kubrick in his taut direction catches the spirit of war with fine realism, and the futile advance of the French is exciting. He draws excellent performances, too, right down the line. Douglas scores heavily in his realization that his is a losing battle against the system, and Macready as the relentless general instilled with the belief that an order is an order, even if it means the death of thousands, socks over what may be regarded his most effective role to date.

■ **PATRICK**

1978, 110 MINS, AUSTRALIA ◇ ▼

Dir Richard Franklin   *Prod* Antony I. Ginnane, Richard Franklin   *Scr* Everett de Roche   *Ph* Don McAlpine   *Ed* Edward Queen-Mason   *Mus* Brian May   *Art Dir* Leslie Binns

● Susan Penhaligon, Robert Helpmann, Rod Mullinar, Bruce Barry, Julia Blake, Helen Heminway (Australian International)

Psychokinesis is a subject that can usually be relied upon to create some spectacular effects on screen, and as a result, occasionally the story and characters become subordinated. No so with *Patrick*, which is more a study in character reactions.

The denominative Patrick is introduced as a matricide who, after having done away with mom and her lover, is next seen in the intensive care section in a state of chronic, advanced – and, we're told – irreversible catatonic reaction: '160 pounds of limp meat hanging off a comatosed brain', says Dr Roget (Robert Helpmann).

Kathy Jacquard (Susan Penhaligon) is a recently estranged wife who returns to nursing to support herself. At Roget's clinic, as the newest member of the staff, she's given Patrick to watch over.

The patient falls in love with his nurse, which would be okay if he only had tonsillitis and was normal: Patrick is polyplegic and homicidal and possessed of this really terrific sixth sense which he uses spitefully.

The inert (and uncredited) lead, with help from Richard Franklin's shrewd direction, creates an incredible menace while the thesps surrounding him go through their action.

■ **PATRIOT, THE**

1928, 108 MINS, US

Dir Ernst Lubitsch   *Scr* Hans Kraley, Julian Johnson   *Ph* Bert Glennon   *Mus* Domenico Savino, Gerard Carbonara   *Art Dir* Hans Dreier

● Emil Jannings, Lewis Stone, Florence Vidor, Neil Hamilton, Harry Cording, Vera Voronina (Paramount)

Many elements combine to give *The Patriot* a valid claim to greatness. The magnificent performance of Emil Jannings as the mad Czar Paul alone. Besides Jannings the production has a whole array of assets. Story value is excellent, cast is almost flawless and the physical production is rich in beauty and fine graphic background.

Time is the late 18th century, and locale the richly picturesque atmosphere of the Russian court under Czar Paul, the insane emperor of all the Russias, idiot-monster of Nero-like proportions. Surrounded by murderous plots, the only creature the madman trusts is his minister of war, Count Pahlen (Lewis Stone).

The role of Pahlen is really the star part, and it is only Jannings' genius that holds up the character of the Czar. Stone gives a balanced and polished performance. Pahlen is pictured as a suave man of the world rather than the paragon of virtue as legendary heroes are usually presented. Character comes on the screen without heroics.

Pictorially the production is full of magnificent bits. One of the sets is the vast palace courtyard and long shots of soldiers moving through its intricate vistas, columns of foot soldiers with galloping horsemen weaving around dim corners and streaking across the snow-covered spaces, are stunning effects.

Sound effects are managed inconspicuously. There is no dialog.

☐ 1928/29: Best Picture (Nomination)

■ **PATSY, THE**

1964, 100 MINS, US ◇ ▼

Dir Jerry Lewis   *Prod* Ernest D. Glucksman   *Scr* Jerry Lewis, Bill Richmond   *Ph* Wallace Kelley   *Ed* John Woodcock   *Mus* David Raksin   *Art Dir* Hal Pereira, Cary Odell

● Jerry Lewis, Ina Balin, Everett Sloane, Phil Harris, Keenan Wynn, Peter Lorre (Paramount)

The Patsy's slim story line has its ups and downs, sometimes being hilarious, frequently unfunny.

Premise of a group of film professionals – a producer, director, writer-gagman, press agent and secretary – who have lost their star in a plane disaster and find another meal ticket by grabbing a hotel bellboy and building him to stardom, is an okay device for situations but lacks development – which might have made a better comedy.

Jerry Lewis also directs in the part, and as the patsy of this pack of hangers-on he indulges in his usual mugging and clowning, good for guffaws and enough nonsensical anticking to appeal to juve audiences especially.

Lewis as the simple-minded Stanley, 'discovered' as he is delivering ice to the forlorn group wondering how to salvage their own positions, socks over his customary brand of broad and nutty humor and gets good backing right down the line. Everett Sloane as the producer, Peter Lorre the director, Phil Harris the gagman, Keenan Wynn the p.a., and Ina Balin the secretary, deliver soundly.

Hedda Hopper plays herself in a nice scene, and others playing themselves in cameo roles are Ed Wynn, Rhonda Fleming, George Raft, Mel Torme.

■ **PATTON**

1970, 173 MINS, US ◇ ▼

Dir Franklin J. Schaffner   *Prod* Frank McCarthy   *Scr* Francis Ford Coppola, Edmund H. North   *Ph* Fred Koenekamp   *Ed* Hugh S. Fowler   *Mus* Jerry Goldsmith   *Art Dir* Urie McCleary, Gil Parrondo

● George C. Scott, Karl Malden, Michael Bates, Karl Michael Vogler, Edward Binns, Lawrence Dobkin (20th Century-Fox)

War is hell, and *Patton* is one hell of a war picture.

George C. Scott's title-role performance is outstanding and the excellent direction of Franklin J. Schaffner lends realism, authenticity, and sensitivity without ever being visually offensive, excessive or overdone in any area.

Patton is an amazingly brilliant depiction of men in war, revealing all facets of their character.

Film begins in North Africa, just before Gen George S. Patton Jr. takes over command in 1943 of an American component of an Anglo-American unit, decimated by German attack. It ends after the surrender of Germany, and Patton's relief from an occupation command because of embarrassing statements contrary to civilian and Allied policy.

☐ 1970: Best Picture

■ **PATTY HEARST**

1988, 108 MINS, US ◇ ▼

Dir Paul Schrader   *Prod* Marvin Worth   *Scr* Nicholas Kazan   *Ph* Bojan Bazelli   *Ed* Michael R. Miller   *Mus* Scott Johnson   *Art Dir* Jane Musky

● Natasha Richardson, William Forsythe, Ving Rhames, Frances Fisher, Jodi Long (Atlantic/Zenith)

Patty Hearst puts forth much less than its pretensions. Frequently wrapped in surrealistic stylization, film manages only to tell Hearst's side of her kidnapping ordeal.

Paralleling Hearst's book *Every Secret Thing*, on which Nicholas Kazan based the script, story quickly recounts Hearst's early life and picks up cinematically with her kidnaping.

Stuffed into a closet and blindfolded for nearly 50 days, Hearst is subjected to verbal abuse by the deranged band of self-styled revolutionaries that called themselves the Symbionese Liberation Army.

By the time Hearst is offered her freedom or membership in the SLA, one is bound to accept that the latter was chosen at least as much for survival as for any other motive.

In portraying Hearst, Natasha Richardson – daughter of Vanessa Redgrave and director Tony Richardson – is quite effective. She manages to convey all the sympathy clearly intended.

■ PAWNBROKER, THE

1964, 112 MINS, US

Dir Sidney Lumet   *Prod* Roger H. Lewis, Philip Langner   *Scr* Morton Fine, David Friedkin   *Ph* Boris Kaufman   *Ed* Ralph Rosenblum   *Mus* Quincy Jones   *Art Dir* Richard Sylbert
● Rod Steiger, Geraldine Fitzgerald, Brock Peters, Thelma Oliver, Jaime Sanchez, Marketta Kimbrell (Landau/Allied Artists)

The Pawnbroker [based on the novel by Edward Lewis Wallant] is a painstakingly etched portrait of a man who survived the living hell of a Nazi concentration camp and encounters further prejudice when he runs a pawnshop in Harlem.

Rod Steiger plays the embittered pawnbroker, and his personal credo is a reflection of his past experiences. He has lost his faith in God, the arts and sciences, he has no discriminatory feelings against white or colored man, but regards them all as human scum. Such is the character of the man whose pawnshop is actually a front for a Negro racketeer, whose main income comes from the slums and brothels.

There is little plot in the regular sense, but a series of episodes spanning just a few days of the present, which recall many harrowing experiences of the past. Some are absorbing, but others seem to lack the dramatic punch for which the director must have strived.

By the very nature of the subject, the pic is dominated by Steiger, and indeed virtually must stand or fall by his performance. He knows most of the tricks of the trade, and puts them to good use.

Although appearing only in three scenes, Geraldine Fitzgerald makes a deep impression as a welfare worker who almost succeeds in getting through to him, but at the last moment he refuses to weaken.

■ PEACEMAKER

1990, 90 MINS, US

Dir Kevin S. Tenney   *Prod* Andrew Lane, Wayne Crawford   *Scr* Kevin S. Tenney   *Ph* Thomas Jewitt   *Ed* Dan Duncin   *Mus* Dennis Michael Tenney   *Art Dir* Rob Sissman
● Robert Forster, Lance Edwards, Hilary Shephard, Robert Davi, Bert Remsen (Gibraltar/Mentone)

Peacemaker is an unexpected gem, a sci-fi action thriller that really delivers the goods despite an apparent low budget.

Inventive plot is a tale of two humanoid aliens (Robert Forster and Lance Edwards) who crash-land on Earth. One is an intergalactic serial killer, the other a police officer, or peacemaker. A simple set-up, except for one complication: both claim to be the cop.

Both aliens attempt to enlist the aid of assistant medical examiner Hilary Shepard, hoping she can help them find the key to the one functional space rover that survived their crash landing.

Peacemaker is a stunt extravaganza, a non-stop, fast-paced assemblage of chases, shoot-outs and explosions building to an impressive climax. Pic has a big-budget look throughout.

■ PEEPER

1975, 87 MINS, US

Dir Peter Hyams   *Prod* Irwin Winkler, Robert Chartoff   *Scr* W.D. Richter   *Ph* Earl Rath   *Ed* James Mitchell   *Mus* Richard Clements   *Art Dir* Albert Brenner
● Michael Caine, Natalie Wood, Kitty Winn, Thayer David, Liam Dunn, Dorothy Adams (20th Century-Fox)

Peeper is flimsy whimsy. In the can for a year after being made under the title *Fat Chance*, director Peter Hyams' limp spoof of a 1940s private-eye film stars Michael Caine as a fumbling gumshoe and Natalie Wood as a member of a mysterious wealthy family. Even in the cutdown 87-minute release version, the extremely handsome production shows far more care in physical details than artistic ones.

Keith Laumer's novel *Deadfall* (not to be confused with a 1968 Bryan Forbes film of that name, coincidentally starring Caine) was altered in tone and time by scripter W.D. Richter. Mimic artist Guy Marks opens the film by a Humphrey Bogart reading of the main credits over footage of a mysterious figure in an alley.

Story gets underway with Michael Constantine hiring Caine to find his long lost daughter so she will get his money. But comic assassins Timothy Agoglia Carey and Don Calfa keep popping up doing bad numbers on people.

Caine's search involves him with the odd Prendergast family, where bedridden neurotic mother Dorothy Adams, daughters Wood and Kitty Winn (one of whom may be Constantine's kid), and uncle Thayer David and household fixture Liam Dunn complicate the plot.

■ PEEPING TOM

1960, 109 MINS, UK

Dir Michael Powell   *Prod* Michael Powell   *Scr* Leo Marks   *Ph* Otto Heller   *Ed* Noreen Ackland   *Mus* Brian Easdale, Wally Scott   *Art Dir* Arthur Lawson
● Carl Boehm, Moira Shearer, Anna Massey, Maxine Audley, Shirley Anne Field, Jack Watson (Anglo-Amalgamated)

Anglo-Amalgamated unloaded around $560,000 on making *Peeping Tom*, the biggest load of coin it had ever invested in one picture. It's as well, for stripped of its color and some excellent photography plus imaginative direction by Michael Powell, the plot itself would have emerged as a shoddy yarn.

Story concerns a young man who, as a boy, was used as a guinea-pig by his father [played by Powell himself], a noted professor studying the symptoms of fear. The boy grows up to become an insane killer obsessed with the desire to photograph the terror on the faces of his victims as he kills them. He also has an unhealthy craving for peeping at young lovers, hence the title. In between these activities, he has a regular job as an assistant cameraman in a film studio and a part time job of photographing saucy pictures for sale on a seedy news-stand.

This mixed-up young man is played rather stolidly by Carl Boehm. It is more the fault of the screenplay than the actor himself that one gets only a very superficial glimpse into the workings of his mind. Anna Massey is charming as the girl who is one of his tenants and befriends him before she realizes that he is a

killer. Maxine Audley, as her blind mother, tackles a difficult, unrewarding role very well.

Brenda Bruce has a few good moments at the beginning of the film as a streetwalker who is his first victim while Moira Shearer is effective as another of his victims, an ambitious bit player who is murdered while he is pretending to give her a screen test on a deserted studio lot.

Powell has directed with imagination but he might well have tightened up the story line. The standout feature of *Peeping Tom* is some fascinating photography by Otto Heller, particularly in the film studio sequences. His use of color and shadow is most effective. Heller does much to give *Peeping Tom* a veneer which the story by Leo Marks does not entirely deserve.

■ PEE-WEE'S BIG ADVENTURE

1985, 90 MINS, US

Dir Tim Burton   *Prod* Robert Shapiro, Richard Gilbert Abramson   *Scr* Phil Hartman, Paul Reubens, Michael Varhol   *Ph* Victor J. Kemper   *Ed* Billy Weber   *Mus* Danny Elfman   *Art Dir* David L. Snyder
● Paul Reubens, Elizabeth Daily, Mark Holton, Diane Salinger, Judd Omen, Jon Harris (Aspen/Shapiro)

Children should love the film and adults will be dismayed by the light brushstrokes with which Paul Reubens (one of three credited screenwriters, but star-billed under his stage name, Pee-wee Herman) suggests touches of Buster Keaton and Eddie Cantor.

Pee-wee wakes up in a children's bedroom full of incredible toys, slides down a fire station-like brass pole, materializing in his trademark tight suit with white shoes and red bow-tie, proceeds to make a breakfast a la Rube Goldberg, and winds up in a front yard that looks like a children's farm.

It's a delicious bit, with Reubens making noises like a child, walking something like Chaplin, and remarkably drawing to adult viewers the joys and frustrations of being a kid. Rest of narrative deals with Pee-wee's unstoppable pursuit of his prized lost bicycle, a rambling kidvid-like spoof.

■ PEGGY SUE GOT MARRIED

1986, 104 MINS, US

Dir Francis Coppola   *Prod* Paul R. Gurian   *Scr* Jerry Leichtling, Arlene Sarner   *Ph* Jordan Cronenweth   *Ed* Barry Malkin   *Mus* John Barry   *Art Dir* Dean Tavoularis
● Kathleen Turner, Nicolas Cage, Barry Miller, Catherine Hicks, Joan Allen, Kevin J. O'Connor (Rastar/Tri-Star Delphi IV & V)

First-time scriptwriters have written a nice mix of sap and sass for Peggy Sue's (Kathleen Turner) character, a melancholy mother of two facing divorce who gets all dolled up in her 1950s-style ballgown to make a splash at her 25th high school reunion.

Sure enough, she's selected Prom Queen. In all the excitement, she collapses on stage – finding herself revived as an 18-year-old high school senior of the class of 1960.

Almost immediately, she realizes she's returned to her youth with all the knowledge and experience learned as an adult, quickly figuring out that she can alter the course of her future life by changing certain crucial decisions she made as a teenager.

The most important relationship for her is with steady boyfriend Charlie (Nicolas Cage), who she eventually marries, has two children by and only later seeks to divorce because of his infidelity.

What makes this treatment unique is that the jokes aren't so much derivative of pop culture, but are instead found in the learned wisdom of a middle-aged woman reacting to her own teenage dilemmas.

PEKING EXPRESS

1951, 85 MINS, US

Dir William Dieterle *Prod* Hal Wallis *Scr* John
Meredyth Lucas *Ph* Charles B. Lang Jr *Ed* Stanley
Johnson *Mus* Dimitri Tiomkin *Art Dir* Hal Pereira,
Franz Bachelin
● Joseph Cotten, Corinne Calvet, Edmund Gwenn,
Marvin Miller, Benson Fong (Paramount)

An excellent coating of intrigue and action
against an Oriental background provides
Peking Express with enough thriller
melodramatics to satisfy action-minded
audiences.

Considerable of the action [from a story by
Harry Hervey, adapted by Jules Furthman]
takes place aboard the Peking Express on a
run between Shanghai and Peking. Aboard
are Joseph Cotten, UN doctor on his way to
operate on the head of the Nationalist underground; Corinne Calvet, adventuress and old
flame of Cotten's; Edmund Gwenn, a priest;
Marvin Miller, black market operator; and
Benson Fong, rabid Commie newspaperman.

Action becomes rapid when Miller tips his
hands, has his bandits seize the train and the
principal passengers to hold as hostages so he
can secure the release of his son from the
underground.

Cotten does a credible job of his character,
keeping it unassuming but forceful. Calvet
makes an interesting charmer, and Gwenn is
excellent as the old priest. Miller's Chinese
heavy is expertly forced for hisses. Fong
impresses strongly as the reporter, a role that
takes him away from his usual light-comedy
characters.

PENDULUM

1969, 101 MINS, US ◇ ▽

Dir George Schaefer *Prod* Stanley Niss *Scr* Stanley
Niss *Ph* Lionel Lindon *Ed* Hugh S. Fowler
Mus Walter Scharf *Art Dir* Walter M. Simonds
● George Peppard, Jean Seberg, Richard Kiley,
Charles McGraw, Madeleine Sherwood, Robert F.
Lyons (Columbia)

Although the end result is a somewhat routine crime meller, *Pendulum* attacks head-on
the issue of individual liberties under the US
Constitution vs society as a whole. An excellent basic plot strain has been weakened by
potboiler elements.

The root idea is a nifty. George Peppard is
a police hero who rode to fame on the rape-
murder conviction of Robert F. Lyons. But
some sloppy gumshoe work precipitated a US
Supreme Court reversal, and ultimate dismissal of charges against the accused.

Then, Peppard himself is suspected of the
murder of his wife (Jean Seberg) and becomes a victim of a society, and its keepers,
who, while mouthing the principle that an
accused is innocent until he's proven guilty,
tends to think along reverse lines.

PENELOPE

1966, 94 MINS, US ◇

Dir Arthur Hiller *Prod* Arthur Loew Jr *Scr* George
Wells *Ph* Harry Stradling *Ed* Rita Roland *Mus* John
Williams *Art Dir* George W. Davis, Preston Ames
● Natalie Wood, Ian Bannen, Dick Shawn, Peter Falk,
Jonathan Winters, Lila Kedrova (M-G-M)

Penelope is one of those bright, delightfully-
wacky comedies. It's got a good – if light –
basic plot premise and plenty of glib laugh
lines and situations.

Script by George Wells [from a novel by
E.V. Cunningham] gives full sway to the
story of a young wife whose hobby is larceny.
Arthur Hiller's deft direction takes advantage
of the intended spirit and seizes upon every
opportunity for a romp.

Film opens with a little old lady holding up
a bank and getting away with $60,000 a few
hours after bank's official opening. She turns
out to be Natalie Wood, married to the
bank's prexy (Ian Bannen) and disguised
with a rubber mask which she doffs, along
with a distinguishing yellow suit, in ladies'
washroom.

Wood does a nimble job and turns in a gay
performance as well as being a nice clotheshorse for Edith Head's glamorous fashions.
Bannen is properly stuffy as her spouse. As
the psychoanalyst Dick Shawn is in his element in one of his zany characterizations and
Peter Falk socks over his role as police lieutenant assigned to the bank case.

PENITENTIARY

1979, 99 MINS, US ◇ ▽

Dir Jamaa Fanaka *Prod* Jamaa Fanaka *Scr* Jamaa
Fanaka *Ph* Marty Ollstein *Ed* Betsy Blankett
Mus Frankie Gaye *Art Dir* Adel Mazen
● Leon Isaac Kennedy, Thommy Pollard, Hazel Spears,
Badja Djola, Gloria Delaney, Chuck Mitchell (Gross)

A tough, disturbing and relatively
uncompromising look at contemporary
prison life, *Penitentiary* is a solid third feature
for Jamaa Fanaka and rates as one of
the 'blackest' pictures to come along since
the blaxploitation trend waned.

Circumstantial evidence lands lanky,
street-wise Leon Isaac Kennedy in prison.
Balance of power in his cell block, largely
inhabited by blacks, is dictated by brute
force, with the meanest, toughest inmates
lording it over the smaller (read sensitive)
ones with their fists. Bottom line in prison
relationships is sexual power, and Kennedy
avoids the dreaded fate of being used as a
'girl' only by beating up his cellmate.

The brutal realities of prison life are rendered with extreme believability, and a welcome lack of preachiness or liberal posturing.

PENNIES FROM HEAVEN

1981, 107 MINS, US ◇

Dir Herbert Ross *Prod* Nora Kaye, Herbert Ross
Scr Dennis Potter *Ph* Gordon Willis *Ed* Richard
Marks *Art Dir* Ken Adam, Fred Tuch, Bernie Cutler
● Steve Martin, Bernadette Peters, Christopher
Walken, Jessica Harper, Tommy Rall, John McMartin
(M-G-M/Hera)

Adapted by Dennis Potter from his acclaimed
six-part, 1978 BBC series of the same name,
film deliberately alienates viewer from the
first scene, which presents an unpleasant
Steve Martin attempting to force morning sex
on his mousy, unhappy wife, Jessica Harper.

Martin is a sheet-music salesman in De-
pression-ridden Chicago of 1934 whose 'real'
life consists of one squalid little scene after
another: he makes virginal schoolteacher
Bernadette Peters pregnant, after which she
loses her job and becomes a streetwalker in
the employ of pimp Christopher Walken.

Worked into this lugubrious, neo-Brechtian
tragedy are more than a dozen musical numbers of grave opulence. Purpose is to illustrate the idealism and innocence to which
Martin presumably aspires, with the vivid
contrast between the sunny escapism of 1930s
song lyrics and the somber dispiritedness of
the era from whence they came.

Almost as if he were directing Pinter, Herbert Ross has actors speak a line, then wait
two beats before delivering the next phrase.
Technique smothers such ordinarily lively
performers as Martin, Peters and Harper.

In short, this reportedly $19 million eso-
teric item is *Penny Gate*.

PENTHOUSE, THE

1967, 90 MINS, UK ◇

Dir Peter Collinson *Prod* Harry Fine *Scr* Peter
Collinson *Ph* Arthur Lavis *Ed* John Thumper
Mus John Hawksworth *Art Dir* Peter Mullins
● Suzy Kendall, Terence Morgan, Tony Beckley,
Norman Rodway, Martine Beswick (Tahiti-
Twickenham/Compton)

Story is one of those claustrophobic items
which find hero and heroine trapped in an
isolated apartment with a pair of deranged
hoodlums alternating physical and mental
bouts of sadism as they break down the couple's resistance.

But it's not what goes on but how it's developed that raised this item above the level of
other orgy-chiller entries. Peter Collinson's
script [from the play *The Meter Man* by C.
Scott Forbes] and direction work hand-in-
hand like a precision watch in milking a situation or line to the utmost before seguing, after a pause for breath, to the next crescendo
built-up.

The quality of the lines and the subtle yet
powerful impact of their content, plus the superbly controlled delivery by the cast, make
this a compelling – if at times inevitably distasteful – glimpse at some of the seamier
characteristics of the human being.

PEOPLE AGAINST O'HARA, THE

1951, 101 MINS, US

Dir John Sturges *Prod* William H. Wright *Scr* John
Monks Jr *Ph* John Alton *Ed* Gene Ruggiero
Mus Carmen Dragon *Art Dir* Cedric Gibbons,
James Basevi
● Spencer Tracy, Pat O'Brien, Diana Lynn, John
Hodiak, Eduardo Ciannelli, James Arness (M-G-M)

A basically good idea for a film melodrama
[from a novel by Eleazar Lipsky] is cluttered
up with too many unnecessary side twists and
turns, and the presentation is uncomfortably
overlong.

Plot premise finds Spencer Tracy, practicing civil law after pressure of criminal cases
had driven him to the bottle, taking on the
defense of James Arness, a young man he has
known since a boy, who has been charged
with murder. Arness has been neatly framed
for the killing, and asst district attorney John
Hodiak sees it as a cinch case. Despite careful
work by Tracy, he loses the case to Hodiak.

Arness is convicted, but Tracy does not
give up and finally convinces Hodiak and
homicide policeman Pat O'Brien there is still
a chance to prove the frame.

The picture has a number of very good
performances, sparked by the always sound
Tracy. O'Brien, Hodiak and Diana Lynn,
latter doing Tracy's daughter, have comparatively shorter footage, but each comes
through excellently.

PEOPLE THAT TIME FORGOT, THE

1977, 90 MINS, US ◇ ▽

Dir Kevin Connor *Prod* John Dark *Scr* Patrick Tilley
Ph Alan Hume *Ed* John Ireland, Barry Peters
Mus John Scott *Art Dir* Maurice Carter
● Patrick Wayne, Doug McClure, Sarah Douglas,
Dana Gillespie, Thorley Walters, Shane Rimmer
(American International)

Story of a small party headed by Patrick
Wayne seeking a marooned World War I
naval hero north of the ice barrier in the Arc-
tic. Film is second in Edgar Rice Burroughs'
Lost World trilogy lensed in the Canary
Islands and in Britain.

Special effects predominate the action as
Wayne and his group leave their ship in a
1918 amphibian through ice-cluttered water
and perilously lift over towering ice peaks,
are attacked by a giant pterodactyl and
forced to crash-land on the dusty island of
Caprona.

Again, special effects add to the suspense
as the group encounter all manner of
hair-raising beasties and erupting fire in

braving the dangers of the cavemen in an attempt to find their quarry. ◇

■ PEOPLE WILL TALK

1951, 109 MINS, US

Dir Joseph L. Mankiewicz *Prod* Darryl F. Zanuck *Scr* Joseph L. Mankiewicz *Ph* Milton Krasner *Ed* Barbara McLean *Mus* Alfred Newman (dir.) *Art Dir* Lyle Wheeler, George W. Davis
● Cary Grant, Jeanne Crain, Finlay Currie, Hume Cronyn, Walter Slezak, Sidney Blackmer
(20th Century-Fox)

Curt Goetz's play and film, *Dr Praetorius*, was used by Joseph L. Mankiewicz as the basis for his screenplay, and the script reflects his construction skill at melding drama. Serious aspects of the play, concerning a doctor who believes illness needs more than just medicinal treatment, have been brightened with considerable humor, and the camera adds enough scope to help overcome the fact that the picture's legit origin is still sometimes apparent.

Cary Grant is the doctor and Jeanne Crain the medical student who are the principals mixed up in the plot. Grant, facing charges of conduct unbecoming to his profession, finds time to become interested in Crain when she faints during a classroom lecture. He discovers she is pregnant, but when she tries to commit suicide, he proclaims the diagnosis a mistake and marries her.

Climax is hung on Grant's trial by the college board, and its more serious touches are carefully leavened with a lightness that makes it more effective.

Grant and Crain turn in the kind of performances expected of them and their work receives top support from the other members of the largish cast.

■ PERFECT

1985, 120 MINS, US ◇ ⓥ

Dir James Bridges *Prod* James Bridges *Scr* Aaron Latham, James Bridges *Ph* Gordon Willis *Ed* Jeff Gourson *Mus* Ralph Burns *Art Dir* Michael Haller
● John Travolta, Jamie Lee Curtis, Anne De Salvo, Marilu Henner, Laraine Newman, Mathew Reed
(Columbia/Delphi III)

Perfect pretends to be an old-fashioned love story dressed up in leotards, but more than anything else, it's a film about physical attraction. Set in the world of journalism, pic is guilty of the sins it condemns – superficiality, manipulation and smugness.

Formula is quite simple – a man must prove his worth to a reluctant woman – but problems with the plot and profession it's set in keep the affair from flowering.

Jamie Lee Curtis is an ex-Olympic-class swimmer turned aerobics instructor who was burned by a reporter and must be thawed out before she can enter into a relationship with star Travolta.

John Travolta is the heat, but before she can accept him, he must prove himself a decent fellow, something the film never really succeeds in doing. Character is a semi-autobiographical version of writer Aaron Latham, who based the script on a searing story he originally wrote for *Rolling Stone* and now seems to be exorcising here, feeling guilty for his ruthlessness.

Travolta cannot rescue his character, and he remains basically an unsympathetic figure. Curtis does cut quite a figure in her numerous aerobic outfits, and she does communicate a certain wounded pride and appeal.

■ PERFECT COUPLE, A

1979, 110 MINS, US

Dir Robert Altman *Prod* Robert Altman *Scr* Robert Altman, Allan Nicholls *Ph* Edmond L. Koons *Ed* Tony Lombardo *Mus* Allan Nicholls (prod.)
● Paul Dooley, Marta Heflin, Titos Vandis, Belita Moreno, Henry Gibson, Dimitra Arliss
(20th Century-Fox/Lion's Gate)

Immensely likeable in some parts, and a complete turn-off in others *Perfect Couple* reaffirms both Robert Altman's intelligence and his inaccessibility. The same theme turns up again here: the struggle of individuals to deal with forces and circumstances beyond their control.

In this instance, it's two different family structures. The linear family has Alex Theodopoulos (Paul Dooley) imprisoned in a suffocating , old-world Greek clan. Flip side is Sheila Shea (Marta Heflin), an elfin singer locked into a rock group/commune.

The couple meets through a videotape dating service (the kind of institution Altman loves to poke fun at) and have an on-again, off-again relationship complicated by both families.

■ PERFECT FRIDAY

1970, 94 MINS, UK ◇ ⓥ

Dir Peter Hall *Prod* Jack Smith *Scr* Anthony Grenville-Bell, C. Scott Forbes *Ph* Alan Hume *Ed* Rex Pyke *Mus* John Dankworth *Art Dir* Terence Marsh
● Ursula Andress, David Warner, Stanley Baker, Patience Collier, T.P. McKenna, David Waller
(De Grunwald)

No one else can steal $1 million with quite the flair of the British. A caper in point is *Perfect Friday* with Ursula Andress, Stanley Baker, and David Warner as a triangle of totally amoral thieves in a charming, ingenious and sexy bank job, tightly masterminded to the split-second, by director Peter Hall.

Andress and Warner play a casually-married couple, a vain, self-centered, modish and jet-setting playboy English lord and his Swiss wife, who live now, pay later, but at the moment are thoroughly bankrupt.

The gorgeously undressed Andress spends a great deal of the footage at maximum exposure, but also demonstrates a flair for low-key comedy. Warner is superb as the foppish young lord.

■ PERFECT STRANGERS

1945, 100 MINS, US

Dir Alexander Korda *Prod* Alexander Korda *Scr* Clemence Dane, Anthony Pelissier *Ph* Georges Perinal *Ed* E.B. Jarvis *Mus* Clifton Parker *Art Dir* Vincent Korda
● Robert Donat, Deborah Kerr, Glynis Johns, Ann Todd, Roland Culver
(London)

Perfect Strangers is a perfect stranger to modern technique, real life and smooth running. It appears too much like a museum piece.

The story is that of a young worker and his suburban wife, who find themselves respectively in the Royal Navy and the Wrens with the war's outbreak. Both benefit physically and mentally from the change. Donat shaves his moustache: Deborah Kerr puts on lipstick. Neither expects to like the other when they meet again but they do.

It's the type of yarn [an original story by Clemence Dane] that offers many possibilities of drama and situation, but all have been missed in this film. First you see Donat getting fit; then you see Kerr getting fit. Then you see Donat dancing; then you see Kerr dancing. Then you hear Donat telling his friends how dreary Kerr is; then you hear Kerr telling her friends how dreary Donat is. It seems to go on and on like this.

■ PERFECT STRANGERS

1950, 87 MINS, US ⓥ

Dir Bretaigne Windust *Prod* Jerry Wald *Scr* Edith Sommer *Ph* Peverell Marley *Ed* David Weisbart *Mus* Leigh Harline
● Ginger Rogers, Dennis Morgan, Thelma Ritter, Margalo Gillmore, Anthony Ross (Warner)

Cramming the Ben Hecht-Charles MacArthur legiter, *Ladies and Gentlemen*, into a fast-stepping film was a tough trick. It has been done admirably by scripter Edith Sommer and slammed home forcefully by director Bretaigne Windust.

Stars are spotted as jurors in a murder trial. Dennis Morgan is a married man with two children, Ginger Rogers a divorcee. They fall in love. Margalo Gillmore, whose husband has deserted her, holds out for the death sentence because the accused had asked his wife for a divorce before she was pushed, or fell, from a cliff. Suspense mounts neatly, hand-in-glove with the love story, to a gripping climax.

Picture is a top credit for producer Jerry Wald – different, provocative, adult. Morgan and Rogers are in top form.

■ PERSONAL BEST

1982, 122 MINS, US ◇ ⓥ

Dir Robert Towne *Prod* Robert Towne *Scr* Robert Towne *Ph* Michael Chapman *Ed* Bud Smith *Mus* Jack Nitzsche, Jill Fraser *Art Dir* Ron Hoobs
● Mariel Hemingway, Scott Glenn, Patrice Donnelly, Kenny Moore, Jim Moody, Kari Gosswiller
(Geffen/Warner)

Personal Best offers audiences a lot to like in solid characterizations, plus some shock that is a Robert Towne trademark. What they probably won't share, however, is his tedious fascination with physical perfection.

At his best, Towne handily overcomes the surface distractions of a lesbian relationship between two track stars (Mariel Hemingway and Patrice Donnelly). Though sometimes graphic, their intimacy is never self-conscious and Towne's sensitive pen creates two entirely believable characters in search of affection.

Towne is equally adept at drawing the two male characters, Scott Glenn as tough, domineering coach, and Kenny Moore, an ex-Olympic jock who becomes Hemingway's cushion once her crush on Donnelly is done.

Unfortunately, the vibrant personal scenes among these four are set against various track-and-field preparations for the Olympic trials. Towne has a love of slow motion that's employed as if he's afraid you might miss one, rippling muscle. Worse than that, when people aren't exercising, they are often talking about exercising.

■ PERSONAL SERVICES

1987, 105 MINS, UK ◇ ⓥ

Dir Terry Jones *Prod* Jim Bevan *Scr* David Leland *Ph* Roger Deakins *Ed* George Akers *Art Dir* Hugo Luczyc-Wyhowski
● Julie Walters, Alec McCowan, Shirley Stelfox, Danny Schiller, Tim Woodward, Victoria Hardcastle
(Vestron/Zenith)

For a pic about sex, *Personal Services* is remarkably unerotic. It deals with society's two-faced attitude to sex-for-sale in a humorous but essentially sad way, and is excellently acted and directed. Film is based on a real madam who became a household name as a result of a trial in 1986.

Pic tells the story of the transition of Christine Painter (a dominating performance by Julie Walters) from waitress to madam of Britain's most pleasant brothel, where the perversions are served up with a cooked breakfast and a cup of tea to follow. She looks

P

after the aged and infirm along with eminent clients, none of whom has a kink her girls can't cater to.

Julie Walters plays Christine as a charmingly vulgar yet benign madam, whose brothel-keeping career seemingly comes to an end when the police raid her London house during a Christmas party. At her trial she recognizes the judge as one of her regular clients.

Alex McCowan is excellent as her friend and business partner, a former pilot who proudly boasts of a World War II record of 207 missions over enemy territory in 'bra and panties'.

••••••••••••••••••••••••••••••••••

■ PERSONALS, THE

1982, 90 MINS, US ◇ ▼
Dir Peter Markle *Prod* Patrick Wells *Scr* Peter Markle *Ph* Peter Markle, Greg Cummins *Ed* Stephen E. Rivkin *Mus* Will Sumner
● Bill Schoppert, Karen Landry, Paul Elding, Michael Laskin, Vicki Dakil, Chris Forth (New World)

With a neutral title and a cast of unknowns, *The Personals* has little going for it other than that it's a terrific little picture.

Entire cast make their feature film debut, along with writer-director Peter Markle. Markle's story really isn't all that profound, but it's told with sincerity and humor.

Bill Schoppert is a true discovery as an average, balding, career-minded and funny fellow whose equally nice wife feels neglected and leaves him for another man. Reluctantly tossed back into the singles world. Schoppert resorts to placing a personal ad in a newspaper.

Initial result is a hilarious date with pushy Vicki Dakil, but he perseveres until he connects with Karen Landry, another neatly unassuming actress, and the result is love.

••••••••••••••••••••••••••••••••••

■ PET SEMATARY

1989, 102 MINS, US ◇ ▼
Dir Mary Lambert *Prod* Richard P. Rubinstein *Scr* Stephen King *Ph* Peter Stein *Ed* Michael Hill, Daniel Hanley *Mus* Elliot Goldenthal *Art Dir* Michael Z. Hanan
● Dale Midkiff, Fred Gwynne, Denise Crosby, Brad Greenquist, Michael Lombard (Paramount)

Pet Sematary marks the first time Stephen King has adapted his own book for the screen, and the result is undead schlock dulled by a slasher-film mentality – squandering its chilling and fertile source material.

The story hinges on a small family that comes to New England, moving into a vintage Americana house alongside a truck route. When Louis Creed (Dale Midkiff) finds his daughter's cat dead along the road, his elderly neighbor Jud (Fred Gwynne) takes him to a hidden Indian burial ground that brings the beast back to life.

The quiet madness that gradually leads Louis to try and bring a person back via the same process – despite the repeated warnings of a friendly ghost – isn't apparent in Mary Lambert's hastily assembled narrative.

King appears in a cameo as a minister presiding over a funeral. He also introduces some wan, recurrent humor in the form of the reappearing and grisly ghost (Brad Greenquist).

••••••••••••••••••••••••••••••••••

■ PETE KELLY'S BLUES

1955, 95 MINS, US ◇ ▼
Dir Jack Webb *Prod* Jack Webb *Scr* Richard L. Breen *Ph* Hal Rosson *Ed* Robert M. Leeds *Art Dir* Harper Goff, Field Gray
● Jack Webb, Janet Leigh, Edmond O'Brien, Peggy Lee, Andy Devine, Lee Marvin (Mark VII/Warner)

Jazz addicts (usually highly opinionated) may have a special interest in the musical frame. Beyond this special-interest factor is a melodramatic story that catches the mood of the Prohibition era. Jack Webb enacts a cornet player in a 1927 Kansas City speakeasy. Mostly it develops as a gangster picture (without the cops) with a Dixieland accompaniment.

Plot around which the music is woven has to do with the move-in into the band field by Edmond O'Brien, smalltime bootlegger-racketeer, and the abortive efforts at resistance made by Webb to protect his small outfit. Webb's understatement of his character is good and Peggy Lee scores a personal hit with her portrayal of a fading singer taken to the bottle.

••••••••••••••••••••••••••••••••••

■ PETE 'N' TILLIE

1972, 100 MINS, US ◇ ▼
Dir Martin Ritt *Prod* Julius J. Epstein *Scr* Julius J. Epstein *Ph* John Alonzo *Ed* Frank Bracht *Mus* John Williams *Art Dir* George Webb
● Walter Matthau, Carol Burnett, Geraldine Page, Barry Nelson, Rene Auberjonois, Lee H. Montgomery (Universal)

Pete 'n' Tillie is a generally beautiful, touching and discreetly sentimental drama-with-comedy, starring Walter Matthau and Carol Burnett as two lonely near-middleagers whose courtship, marriage, breakup and reunion are told with compassion through producer Julius J. Epstein's fine script and Martin Ritt's delicate direction.

Based on a Peter De Vries novella, *Witch's Milk*, screenplay neatly establishes the two main characters – Matthau as an awkward, pun-prone market researcher who covers his gaucheries with a sardonic veneer; and Burnett as a maturing woman beginning to harden into uneasy spinsterhood.

In particular, Burnett is the key to the film's viability by largely playing straight man to Matthau's ironies, so there is a smooth credible transition to the drama of later reels.

••••••••••••••••••••••••••••••••••

■ PETER IBBETSON

1935, 83 MINS, US
Dir Henry Hathaway *Prod* Louis D. Lighton *Scr* Vincent Lawrence, Waldemar Young *Ph* Charles Lang *Ed* Stuart Heisler *Mus* Ernst Toch *Art Dir* Hans Dreier, Robert Usher
● Gary Cooper, Ann Harding, John Halliday, Ida Lupino, Douglass Dumbrille, Doris Lloyd (Paramount)

From a technical standpoint, picture is just about tops, gaining so much weight in beauty and serenity that it almost overbears the incredulity of the story. George du Maurier wrote this story two generations earlier. It followed on his already successful first novel *Trilby* and was an even greater success. [Script also draws on the play by John Nathaniel Raphael.] Wallace Reid made a click film of it in the silent days.

Casting is not of the happiest. Gary Cooper was never meant to be a dreamy love-sick boy. When he tells the Duchess of Towers that she can't have things the way she wants them but the way he wants them, he's fine. When he lies dying in a stinking jail and dreams of wandering in Elysian lanes with his sweetheart – he's just not believable.

Ann Harding, on the other hand, as the duchess, is splendid. Ringlets have replaced the part down the center and the effect is startling.

John Halliday is the duke, a bit here but expertly played. Ida Lupino has a bit as Agnes and most definitely impresses.

••••••••••••••••••••••••••••••••••

■ PETER PAN

1953, 76 MINS, US ◇
Dir Hamilton Luske, Clyde Geronimi, Wilfred Jackson *Prod* Walt Disney *Scr* Ted Sears, Bill Peet, Joe Rinaldi, Erdman Penner, Winston Hibler, Milt Banta, Ralph Wright *Mus* Oliver Wallace
● (Walt Disney)

James M. Barrie's childhood fantasy, *Peter Pan*, many times legit-staged, and previously filmed with live actors, is a feature cartoon of enchanting quality.

The music score is fine, highlighting the constant buzz of action and comedy, but the songs are less impressive than usually encountered in such a Disney presentation.

The Barrie plot deals familiarly with a little boy (Peter Pan) who refused to grow up, preferring to remain a pixie in Never Never Land, and a little girl (Wendy) under paternal orders to pass into young ladyhood.

Before she does, however, she has one more night of childhood and, with Peter, Tinker Bell, and her two young brothers, John and Michael, pays a visit to the land of chimerical fantasy wherein dwell the comically-dreadful Captain Hook; the toadying Smee, who fawningly tends the pirate; the basso-voiced Indian chief; the popeyed, tick-tocking crocodile; and the beautiful mermaids and lost boys.

The voice of young Bobby Driscoll, and cartoon animation in his likeness, sell the Peter Pan character. Equally good are the voices of Kathryn Beaumont as Wendy; Hans Conried as the villainous Hook and the exasperated father, Mr Darling and Bill Thompson as the fawning Smee. Tom Conway dulcetly intones the narrated story bridges.

••••••••••••••••••••••••••••••••••

■ PETERSEN

1974, 103 MINS, AUSTRALIA ◇ ▼
Dir Tim Burstall *Prod* Tim Burstall *Scr* David Williamson *Ph* Robin Copping *Ed* David Bilcock *Mus* Peter Best *Art Dir* Bill Hutchinson
● Jack Thompson, Jacki Weaver, Joey Hohenfels, Amanda Hunt, George Mallaby, Arthur Dignam (Hexagon)

Tony Petersen (Jack Thompson) is an ex-electrician at university in pursuit of an arts degree. Married with two children, he's carrying on an affair with Patricia who, besides being a tutor in English at the university is also the wife of Associate Professor of English who is responsible for Petersen's studies.

Women find Petersen irresistible, and the attraction is mutual. He even actively participates in a public sex act protest by the University Women's Liberationists.

Plotwise pic is not too strong but has several meaningful meanderings. It contains some of playwright David Williamson's best writing yet. He's more disciplined and doesn't let the action get farcically out of hand and displays depths of sensitivity, humanity and gentleness mostly lacking previously.

••••••••••••••••••••••••••••••••••

■ PETE'S DRAGON

1977, 134 MINS, US ◇ ▼
Dir Don Chaffey *Prod* Ron Miller *Scr* Malcolm Marmorstein *Ph* Frank Phillips *Ed* Gordon D. Brenner *Mus* Irwin Kostal (sup.) *Art Dir* John B. Mansbridge, Jack Martin Smith
● Helen Reddy, Jim Dale, Mickey Rooney, Red Buttons, Shelley Winters, Sean Marshall (Walt Disney)

Pete's Dragon is an enchanting and humane fable which introduces a most lovable animal star (albeit an animated one). Budgeted at $11 million it was the most expensive film in the history of the Disney Studios, besting *Mary Poppins* by $4.5 million.

The pic's storyline is just a shell. This is a star vehicle and the headliner has been created with love and care by Disney animators headed by Ken Anderson and Don Blyth.

Elliott, the dumpy, clumsy, 12-foot tall mumbling dragon with the ability to go instantly invisible and the misfortune of setting the idyllic Maine town of Passamaquoddy even further back into the early 20th century, is a triumph.

●●●●●●●●●●●●●●●●●●●●●●●●●●●●●●

■ PETRIFIED FOREST, THE

1936, 75 MINS, US 🅥

Dir Archie L. Mayo *Scr* Charles Kenyon, Delmer Daves *Ph* Sol Polito *Ed* Owen Marks *Art Dir* John Hughes
● Leslie Howard, Bette Davis, Humphrey Bogart, Genevieve Tobin, Dick Foran, Joseph Sawyer (Warner)

The picture sticks closely to the legit script by Robert E. Sherwood. Playing the roles they created in the stage version are Leslie Howard and Humphrey Bogart – the former a soul-broken, disillusioned author, seeking, by wayfaring, to find some new significance in living, and the latter a killer, harried and surrounded by pursuers, revealing in his last moments a bewildered desperation which is not far removed from that of the writer.

The scenes in which the desperado holds court, as he awaits his own doom, over the group in the little Arizona gas station-barbecue stand are packed with skillfully etched drama and embroidered with appropriate touches of comedy.

Impressively enacted is the romance between Howard and Bette Davis which comes to flowering under the lowering brows and guns of the killer. The girl, daughter of the desert oasis' owner, longs for foreign climes and a chance to develop her talents as a painter. Howard, wishing to make this longing a reality, strikes a bargain with the gunman.

Davis gives a characterization that fetches both sympathy and admiration. Bogart's menace leaves nothing wanting. Well placed are the comedy relief bits which are allotted Charles Grapewin.

Warners made two endings for this picture. The happy ending had Howard recovering.

●●●●●●●●●●●●●●●●●●●●●●●●●●●●●●

■ PETULIA

1968, 103 MINS, UK ◇ 🅥

Dir Richard Lester *Prod* Raymond Wagner *Scr* Lawrence B. Marcus *Ph* Nicholas Roeg *Ed* Antony Gibbs *Mus* John Barry *Art Dir* Tony Walton
● Julie Christie, George C. Scott, Richard Chamberlain, Arthur Hill, Shirley Knight, Pippa Scott (Petersham-Wagner)

Petulia is an excellent romantic drama featuring the brief encounter of Julie Christie and George C. Scott. The bittersweet story vies for prominence with much commentary on materialistic aspects of society. Producer Raymond Wagner has complemented the story with strong production values, mainly from the Frisco locations.

Based on a John Haase novel, *Me and the Arch Kook Petulia*, the plot turns on the hectic, sometimes ecstatic affair between Christie, unhappy wife of sadistically weak Richard Chamberlain and Scott, just divorced from Shirley Knight and currently squiring Pippa Scott.

Arthur Hill and Kathleen Widdoes play a couple who try to patch things up between Knight and Scott, and Joseph Cotten has a few key scenes as Chamberlain's indulgent, overpowering father.

Scott's performance, in the face of a plot and film structure which could have relegated him to a reactive posture, is excellent. The natural emphasis is on Christie, who turns in a vital, versatile performance.

●●●●●●●●●●●●●●●●●●●●●●●●●●●●●●

■ PEYTON PLACE

1957, 166 MINS, US ◇

Dir Mark Robson *Prod* Jerry Wald *Scr* John Michael Hayes *Ph* William Mellor *Ed* David Bretherton *Mus* Franz Waxman
● Lana Turner, Hope Lange, Lee Philips, Lloyd Nolan, Arthur Kennedy, Russ Tamblyn (20th Century-Fox)

In leaning backwards not to offend, producer and writer have gone acrobatic.

On the screen is not the unpleasant sex-secret little town against which Grace Metalious set her story. These aren't the gossiping, spiteful, immoral people she portrayed. There are hints of this in the film, but only hints.

Under Mark Robson's direction, every one of the performers delivers a topnotch portrayal. Performance of Diane Varsi particularly is standout as the rebellious teenager Allison, eager to learn about life and numbed by the discovery that she is an illegitimate child. Also in top form in a difficult role is Hope Lange, stepdaughter of the school's drunken caretaker. As Varsi's mother, Lana Turner looks elegant and registers strongly.

Lee Philips is another new face as Michael Rossi, the school principal who courts the reluctant Turner. Pleasant looking, Philips has a voice that is at times high and nasal. Opposite Varsi, Russ Tamblyn plays Norman Page, the mama's boy, with much intelligence and appealing simplicity.

Robson's direction is unhurried, taking best advantage of the little town of Camden, Me, where most of the film was shot.
□ 1957: Best Picture (Nomination)

●●●●●●●●●●●●●●●●●●●●●●●●●●●●●●

■ PHANTASM

1979, 90 MINS, US ◇ 🅥

Dir Don Coscarelli *Prod* Don Coscarelli *Scr* Don Coscarelli *Ph* Don Coscarelli *Ed* Don Coscarelli *Mus* Fred Myrow, Malcolm Seagrave *Art Dir* S. Tyer
● Michael Baldwin, Bill Thornbury, Reggie Bannister, Kathy Lester, Angus Scrimm (Avco Embassy)

Pic opens with 13-year-old Mike Pearson (Michael Baldwin), who foolishly disobeys his older brother's orders not to attend the funeral of a close friend who, unbeknownst to everyone, was really stabbed by a woman after the two made love in a cemetery. Mike hides in the bushes during the ceremony and later happens to eye the villainous tall man (Angus Scrimm) loading the casket into a car.

Once inside the mausoleum, the fun begins, with Mike treated to a quite grisly murder courtesy of a futuristic flying silver sphere and the wrath of the tall man, who doesn't cotton to the kid's curiosity. Film then follows Mike, brother Jody (Bill Thornbury) and company as they attempt to unravel exactly what is going on.

Strong point of the feature is that it's played for both horror and laughs.

●●●●●●●●●●●●●●●●●●●●●●●●●●●●●●

■ PHANTASM II

1988, 90 MINS, US ◇ 🅥

Dir Don Coscarelli *Prod* Robert. A. Quezada *Scr* Don Coscarelli *Ph* Daryn Okada *Ed* Peter Teschner *Mus* Fred Myrow *Art Dir* Philip J.C. Duffin
● James Le Gros, Reggie Bannister, Angus Scrimm, Paula Irvine, Samantha Phillips (Universal)

Phantasm II is an utterly unredeeming, full-gore sequel to the original nine years earlier. The special effects horrors run amok here, with slimy, hissing apparitions constantly erupting from the bodies of the afflicted.

Story involves the morbid obsessions of two psychically connected teens, Mike (James Le Gros) and Liz (Paula Irvine). The pair are tortured in their dreams by The Tall Man (Angus Scrimm, reprising the role), a ghoulish mortician who wreaks evil via flying spheres that carve up people's faces.

Working out of his Morningside Mortuary, The Tall Man robs graves and hauls away corpses via a band of dwarves whose costumes look suspiciously like those of the Jawas in *Star Wars*.

All of this might be a hoot if molded in the right spirit, but in writer-director Don Coscarelli's hands it's incredibly morbid and meaningless.

●●●●●●●●●●●●●●●●●●●●●●●●●●●●●●

■ PHANTOM OF THE OPERA, THE

1925, 101 MINS, US ◇ ⊗ 🅥

Dir Rupert Julian *Scr* Raymond Schrock, Elliott J. Clawson, Tom Reed *Ph* Virgil Miller *Ed* Maurice Pivar *Art Dir* Charles D. Hall
● Lon Chaney, Mary Philbin, Norman Kerry, Arthur Edmund Carewe, Gibson Gowland (Universal)

It's reported the production cost approached $1 million, including over $50,000 for retakes, far above Universal's expectations. It's not a bad film from a technical viewpoint, but revolving around the terrifying of all inmates of the Grand Opera House in Paris by a criminally insane mind (Lon Chaney) behind a hideous face, the combination (from the novel by Gaston Leroux) makes a welsh rarebit look foolish as a sleep destroyer.

The love angle is in the persons of an understudy (Mary Philbin) whom the Phantom cherishes while she is also the sole thought of her military lover (Norman Kerry).

The girl is twice abducted by the Phantom to his cellar retreat, and the finish is built up by the pulling of levers, concealed buttons etc to make active secret doors, heat chambers, flooding passages and other appropriate devices. However, the kick of the picture is in the unmasking of the Phantom by the girl. It's a wallop.

Kerry is a colorless hero, Philbin contents herself with being pretty and becoming terrorized at the Phantom, and Chaney is either behind a mask or grimacing through his fiendish makeup.

●●●●●●●●●●●●●●●●●●●●●●●●●●●●●●

■ PHANTOM OF THE OPERA, THE

1930, 89 MINS, US ◇ 🅥

Dir Rupert Julian, Edward Sedgwick, (sound sequences) Ernst Laemmle *Scr* Elliott J. Clawson, Frank McCormack, Tom Reed *Ph* Charles Van Enger *Ed* Gilmore Walker, Edward Sedgwick *Art Dir* Charles D. Hall, Ben Carre
● Lon Chaney, Mary Philbin, Norman Kerry, Snitz Edwards, Arthur Edmund Carewe, Virginia Pearson (Universal)

In taking the old negative of *Phantom of the Opera*, U has even reproduced off-screen the voice of Lon Chaney in a few spots, besides scenes with Norman Kerry, Mary Philbin and others.

Dialog starts at the beginning. The big scene leading to the finish and capture of the Phantom is silent action. Synchronized score accompanies throughout with sound effects added to former silent scenes and singing obviously dubbed in for solos. This is particularly noticeable in a sequence where Philbin does a *Faust* favorite. Only scenes in color are a few of the opera and a masque ball but they are okay.

Only substitution in cast is Edward Martindel, talking the part played formerly by John Sainpolis. Others who appeared in the original picture, including John Miljan, are out through cutting of lesser scenes.

●●●●●●●●●●●●●●●●●●●●●●●●●●●●●●

■ PHANTOM OF THE OPERA

1943, 92 MINS, US ◇ 🅥

Dir Arthur Lubin *Prod* George Waggner *Scr* Eric Taylor, Samuel Hoffinstein *Ph* Hal Mohr *Mus* Edward Ward

● Nelson Eddy, Susanna Foster, Claude Rains, Jane Farrar, Hume Cronyn (Universal)

Phantom of the Opera is far more of a musical than a chiller, though this element is not to be altogether discounted, and holds novelty appeal. Story is about the mad musician who haunts the opera house and kills off all those who are in his protege's way towards becoming the headliner.

Tuneful operatic numbers and the splendor of the scenic settings in these sequences, combined with excellent group and solo vocalists, count heavily. Nelson Eddy, Susanna Foster and Jane Farrar (niece of operatic star Geraldine Farrar) score individually in singing roles and provide marquee dressing. Third act from [Friedrich von Flotow's opera] *Martha* and two original opera sketches based on themes from Chopin and Tchaikovsky have been skillfully interwoven.

Outstanding performance is turned in by Claude Rains as the musician who, from a fixation seeking to establish the heroine as a leading opera star, grows into a homicidal maniac. Eddy, Foster, and Edgar Barrier, as the Parisian detective, are awkward in movement and speech, though much like opera performers restricted by their medium.

■ PHANTOM OF THE OPERA, THE

1962, 84 MINS, UK ◇

Dir Terence Fisher *Prod* Anthony Hinds *Scr* John Elder *Ph* Arthur Grant *Ed* James Needs, Alfred Cox *Mus* Edwin Astley *Art Dir* Bernard Robinson, Don Mingaye
● Herbert Lom, Heather Sears, Thorley Walters, Michael Gough, Edward De Souza (Hammer)

Herbert Lom somewhat precariously follows in the macabre footsteps of Lon Chaney and Claude Rains. Switched to a London Opera House background, lushed up in color, with a new character, a dwarf rather confusingly brought in to supplement the sinister activities of The Phantom, it still provides a fair measure of goose pimples to combat some potential unwanted yocks.

Basically, the story remains the same. Baleful goings on backstage at the opera which suggest that the place is invaded by evil spirits. The evil spirit is, of course, the Phantom but he turns out to be a rather more sympathetic character than of old and much of his malignance is now switched to a new character, the dwarf, played effectively by Ian Wilson.

However, the atmosphere of brooding evil still works up to some effective highlights, with the terror of the heroine (Heather Sears) paramount, the bewilderment of the hero (Edward De Souza) and the eerie personality of the Phantom still motivating the action.

■ PHANTOM OF THE OPERA, THE

1989, 90 MINS, US ◇ Ⓥ

Dir Dwight H. Little *Prod* Harry Alan Towers *Scr* Duke Sandefur *Ph* Elemer Ragalyi *Ed* Charles Bornstein *Mus* Misha Segal *Art Dir* Tivada Bertalan
● Robert Englund, Jill Schoelen, Alex Hyde-White, Bill Nighy, Stephanie Lawrence (21st Century)

Not only are audiences unlikely to confuse this competent but flatly directed in Budapest production with Andrew Lloyd Webber's stage musical, or the classic Lon Chaney's silent, it also has precious little to do with Gaston Leroux's novel.

Opening in contemporary New York, this *Phantom* [based on a screenplay by Gerry O'Hara] starts with its heroine being hit on the head by a sandbag and mentally transported back to the mid-19th century for the bulk of the plot.

Set in London, rather than the Paris of Phantom tradition, this rendition seems faithful in broad outline to the original, save

for the fact that its tragic antihero is a Jack the Ripper-style maniac who apparently would rather kill the young soprano to whom he's devoted than kiss her.

Running about encased in makeup that makes him appear a kind of Jack Palance gone to seed, Robert England is his usual broad self. Yet gorehounds are bound to be disappointed. As the object of his decidedly mixed emotions, Jill Schoelen is pretty but vapid.

■ PHANTOM OF THE PARADISE

1974, 91 MINS, US ◇ Ⓥ

Dir Brian De Palma *Prod* Edward R. Pressman *Scr* Brian De Palma *Ph* Larry Pizer *Ed* Paul Hirsch *Mus* Paul Williams *Art Dir* Jack Fisk
● Paul Williams, William Finley, Jessica Harper, George Memmoli, Gerrit Graham (20th Century-Fox)

Phantom of the Paradise is a very good horror comedy-drama about a disfigured musician haunting a rock palace. Brian De Palma's direction and script makes for one of the very rare 'backstage' rock story pix, catching the garishness of the glitter scene in its own time.

The story takes novice songwriter William Finley through the despair of being ripped off by Paul Williams (excellent as a composite rock entrepreneur mogul), framed into prison, disfigured by an accident, and nearly betrayed anew by Williams who ostensibly sought reconciliation with Finley after the latter began haunting the Paradise rock house.

Part of phantom Finley's motivation is his distant love of Jessica Harper, whom he wants to sing his music in Williams' rock cantata production.

All the principals come across extremely well, especially Harper.

■ PHANTOM OF THE RUE MORGUE

1954, 83 MINS, US ◇

Dir Roy Del Ruth *Prod* Henry Blanke *Scr* Harold Medford, James R. Webb *Ph* J. Peverell Marley *Ed* James Moore *Mus* David Buttolph
● Karl Malden, Claude Dauphin, Patricia Medina, Steve Forrest, Allyn McLerie, Veola Vonn (Warner)

The horror in *Phantom of the Rue Morgue* is more to be taken lightly than seriously, since the shocker quality in Edgar Allen Poe's chiller tale, *Murders in the Rue Morgue*, has been dimmed considerably by the passage of time.

Murders and gory bodies abound in the Henry Blanke production, which gives fulsome attention to the bloody violence loosed by the title's phantom.

The script follows regulation horror lines in getting the Poe yarn on film and Roy Del Ruth's direction also is standard. Performances by Karl Malden, Claude Dauphin, Patricia Medina, Steve Forrest and the others fall into the same groove and none manages to rise above the material.

Malden is the mad scientist who has his trained ape destroy all pretty girls who spurn him. After Allyn McLerie, Veola Vonn and Dolores Dorn have died violent deaths, the rather stupid police inspector played by Dauphin figures Forrest, young professor of psychology, is the guilty party.

The 3-D color lensing by J. Peverell Marley is good, and puts the turn-of-the-century Paris scenes on display to full advantage.

■ PHAR LAP

1983, 118 MINS, AUSTRALIA ◇ Ⓥ

Dir Simon Wincer *Prod* John Sexton *Scr* David Williamson *Ph* Russell Boyd *Ed* Tony Paterson *Mus* Bruce Rowland *Art Dir* Larry Eastwood
● Tom Burlinson, Martin Vaughan, Judy Morris, Ron Leibman, Celia de Burgh, Vincent Ball (Edgley

Phar Lap was a champion Australian racehorse, a legend in his own lifetime, who met a mysterious death in California in 1932.

Film's one flaw is its opening: it begins with Phar Lap's illness and death, and while every schoolboy in Australia knows this is how the story ended, a little suspense might have been retained for overseas viewers. However, once the flashbacks begin and Phar Lap's story is told, the film takes off.

Tom Burlinson is very effective as the shy stable-boy who becomes devoted to the courageous horse. Martin Vaughan is impressive as the grimly determined trainer who leases the horse in the first place, as is Celia de Burgh, luminous as his loyal but neglected wife. Ron Leibman practically walks away with the picture as Davis, the smooth American horseowner, and Judy Morris is quietly effective as his naive, talkative wife.

■ PHILADELPHIA EXPERIMENT, THE

1984, 102 MINS, US ◇ Ⓥ

Dir Stewart Raffill *Prod* Douglas Curtis, Joel B. Michaels *Scr* William Gray, Michael Janover *Ph* Dick Bush *Ed* Neil Travis *Art Dir* Chris Campbell
● Michael Pare, Nancy Allen, Eric Christmas, Bobby Di Cicco, Kené Holliday
(New World/Cinema Group)

The Philadelphia Experiment had a lot of script problems in its development that haven't been solved yet, but final result is an adequate sci-fi yarn.

Problems with the pic are common to all stories with a time-warp twist but director Stewart Raffill and writers have kept *Philadelphia* reasonably simple.

In 1943, Michael Pare and Bobby Di Cicco are sailors aboard a destroyer that's the center of a secret radar experiment which goes awry, throwing them into 1984, seemingly cross-circuited into another experiment.

Befriended in the future by Nancy Allen, the pair obviously are a bit bemused at their surroundings before Di Cicco fades again into the past, leaving Pare to develop a romance with Allen and try to find his own way back in time.

■ PHILADELPHIA STORY, THE

1940, 112 MINS, US Ⓥ

Dir George Cukor *Prod* Joseph L. Mankiewicz *Scr* Donald Ogden Stewart *Ph* Joseph Ruttenberg *Ed* Frank Sullivan *Mus* Franz Waxman *Art Dir* Cedric Gibbons, Wade B. Rubottom
● Cary Grant, Katharine Hepburn, James Stewart, Ruth Hussey, John Howard, Roland Young (M-G-M)

It's Katharine Hepburn's picture, but with as fetching a lineup of thesp talent as is to be found, she's got to fight every clever line of dialog all of the way to hold her lead. Pushing hard is little Virginia Weidler, the kid sister, who has as twinkly an eye with a fast quip as a blinker light. Ruth Hussey is another from whom director George Cukor has milked maximum results to get a neat blend of sympathy-winning softness under a python-tongued smart-aleckness. As for Cary Grant, James Stewart and Roland Young, there's little to be said that their reputation hasn't established. John Howard, John Halliday and Mary Nash, in lesser roles, more than adequately fill in what Philip Barry must have dreamt of when he wrote the 1939 play.

The perfect conception of all flighty but characterful Main Line socialite gals rolled into one, Hepburn has just the right amount of beauty, just the right amount of disarray in wearing clothes, just the right amount of culture in her voice – it's no one but Hepburn.

Story is localed in the very social and comparatively new (for Philly, 1860) Main Line sector in the suburbs of Quakertown. Hepburn, divorced from Grant, a bit of rather useless uppercrust like herself, is about to marry a stuffed-bosom man of the people (Howard). Grant, to keep Henry Daniell, publisher of the mags *Dime* and *Spy* (*Time* and *Life*, get it?) from running a scandalous piece about Hepburn's father (Halliday), agrees to get a reporter and photog into the Hepburn household preceding and during the wedding. Stewart and Hussey are assigned and Grant, whose position as ex-husband is rather unique in the mansion, manages to get them in under a pretext. Everyone, nevertheless, knows why Stewart and Hussey are there and the repartee is swift.

When the acid tongues are turned on at beginning and end of the film it's a laugh-provoker from way down. When the discussion gets deep and serious, however, on the extent of Hepburn's stone-like character, the verbiage is necessarily highly abstract and the film slows to a toddle.
□ 1940: Best Picture (Nomination)

■ **PHYSICAL EVIDENCE**

1989, 99 MINS, US ◇ ⓥ
Dir Michael Crichton *Prod* Martin Ransohoff *Scr* Bill Phillips *Ph* John A. Alonzo *Ed* Glenn Farr *Mus* Henry Mancini *Art Dir* Dan Yarhi
● Burt Reynolds, Theresa Russell, Ned Beatty, Key Lenz, Ted McGinley (Columbia)

Burt Reynolds plays Joe Paris, a suspended detective who wakes up from a drunken binge to find himself the lead suspect in a murder investigation. His case is given to an assertive debutante (Theresa Russell) working in the public defender's office, whose obsession with the case begins to wreak havoc on her relationship with her yuppie, hot-tubbing fiance stockbroker (Ted McGinley).

Beyond that it's really anybody's guess as to what's going on, since the film [story by Steve Ransohoff] is so choppily assembled none of the various clues and innumerable suspects ever seem to lead anywhere.

Another major shortcoming is the woeful miscasting of Russell as the young attorney. Even with her hair tightly pulled back into an unflattering bun (to be literally and symbolically let down in quieter moments), Russell's uncommon onscreen beauty proves a distraction.

■ **PICCADILLY**

1929, 92 MINS, UK
Dir E.A. Dupont *Scr* Arnold Bennett *Ph* Werner Brandes *Ed* J.N. McConaughty *Mus* Eugene Contie
● Gilda Gray, Jameson Thomas, Anna May Wong, King Ho Chang, Cyril Ritchard, Charles Laughton (British International)

Piccadilly is virtually silent despite a useless prolog. It may have been added and contains its only dialog, badly done.

This Arnold Bennett story is set in a cabaret in Piccadilly. The owner of the class joint digs up a dancer from the scullery. It's Anna May Wong, a dishwasher whom the proprietor catches dancing for her companions.

In the cabaret are a couple of ballroom dancers, with Gilda Gray one of them. Business commences to fade and the house staff concludes the male dancer must have been the draw. With trade shot, the proprietor remembers the girl downstairs, calls her up and dresses her up, then falls for her.

Gray is so peeved she calls upon the Chinese dancer. The two women meet after the owner leaves. The audience apparently sees Gray shoot Wong, as the latter unsheaths a dagger.

Music is the usual medley of pop dance stuff, with the cabaret set about the best thing in the production. Camerawork on close-ups is excellent.

■ **PICKUP ON SOUTH STREET**

1953, 80 MINS, US
Dir Samuel Fuller *Prod* Jules Schermer *Scr* Samuel Fuller *Ph* Joe MacDonald *Ed* Nick De Maggio *Mus* Leigh Harline *Art Dir* Lyle R. Wheeler, George Patrick
● Richard Widmark, Jean Peters, Thelma Ritter, Murvyn Vye, Richard Kiley, Willis B. Bouchey (20th Century-Fox)

If *Pickup on South Street* makes any point at all, it's that there is nothing really wrong with pickpockets, even when they are given to violence, as long as they don't play footsie with Communist spies. Since this is at best a thin theme, *Pickup* for the most part falls flat on its face and borders on presumably unintended, comedy.

Film's assets are partly its photography, which creates an occasional tense atmosphere, and partly the performance of Thelma Ritter, the only halfway convincing figure in an otherwise unconvincing cast. As Moe, the tired but sharp-tongued old woman who sells ties and habitually informs on her underworld pals in order to collect enough money for a decent 'plot and stone', Ritter is both pathetic and amusing.

Story has Richard Widmark picking Jean Peters' purse in the subway. In the wallet he lifts are films of a secret chemical formula obtained by a Commie spy ring. Widmark's act is observed by two Federal agents who are shadowing Peters. Latter is instructed by her boyfriend-boss Richard Kiley to trace Widmark and get back the film.

Widmark is given a chance to repeat on his snarling menace characterization followed by a look-what-love-can-do-to-a-bad-boy act as Widmark's hard-boiled soul melts before Peters' romancing.

■ **PICKWICK PAPERS, THE**

1952, 109 MINS, UK ⓥ
Dir Noel Langley *Prod* George Minter *Scr* Noel Langley *Ph* Wilkie Cooper *Ed* Anne V. Coates *Mus* Antony Hopkins
● James Hayter, James Donald, Nigel Patrick, Kathleen Harrison, Joyce Grenfell, Donald Wolfit (Langley-Minter/Renown)

The adventures of Mr Pickwick (James Hayter) and his henchmen have been deftly adapted for the screen by Noel Langley. By its adherence to the original, the film is naturally episodic in character.

The picture follows the members of the Pickwick Club on their adventurous tour across England in search of knowledge and human understanding. The encounter with Mr Jingle (Nigel Patrick), the unscrupulous ne'er-do-well with the stilted turn of phrase; the famous literary fancy dress breakfast; the engagement of Sam Weller (Harry Fowler); the breach of promise suit brought against Mr Pickwick by his former housekeeper and his subsequent sojourn in Fleet prison are among the incidents.

In manner and appearance Hayter gives the impression of being the genuine article. His fellow members of the Pickwick Club are admirably played.

■ **PICNIC**

1955, 115 MINS, US ◇
Dir Joshua Logan *Prod* Fred Kohlmar *Scr* Daniel Taradash *Ph* James Wong Howe *Ed* Charles Nelson, William A. Lyon *Mus* George Duning *Art Dir* Jo Mielziner, William Flannery
● William Holden, Rosalind Russell, Kim Novak, Betty Field, Susan Strasberg, Cliff Robertson (Columbia)

This is a considerably enlarged *Picnic*, introducing new scope and style in flow of presentation without dissipating the mood and substance of the legiter by William Inge. The boards-to-screen transplanters correctly

refrained from making any basic changes. It's the story of a robust and shiftless showoff who, looking up an old college chum in a small town in Kansas, sets off various emotional responses among the small group of local inhabitants he encounters.

William Holden is the drifter, sometimes ribald, partly sympathetic and colorful and giving a forceful interpretation all the way.

Kim Novak is the town's No. 1 looker, and an emotional blank until muscle-man (and, to her, downtrodden) Holden proves an awakening force. Novak does right well.

Rosalind Russell, the spinster school teacher boarding with Novak's family, is standout.
□ 1955: Best Picture (Nomination)

■ **PICNIC AT HANGING ROCK**

1975, 115 MINS, AUSTRALIA ◇
Dir Peter Weir *Prod* Jim McElroy, Hal McElroy *Scr* Cliff Green *Ph* Russell Boyd *Mus* Bruce Smeaton *Art Dir* David Copping
● Rachel Roberts, Dominic Guard, Vivian Gray, Helen Morse, Kirsty Child, Anne Lambert (SAFC)

On a warm St Valentine's Day in 1900 some schoolgirls from a boarding school in Victoria picnic at nearby Hanging Rock. Four girls venture forth on their own; one, Edith, falls asleep and wakes to find the other three have taken off their shoes and stockings and are climbing higher.

The police are called to make an unsuccessful search. A young Englishman, Michael, also searches, spends the night alone by the rock and next day is found with a mysterious head wound but no memory of happenings. Later, one of the girls, Irma, is also found with a similar head wound and no memory of events.

Visually it probably is one of the most beautiful pix ever seen, with Aussie flora and fauna and wonderful blue skies. Everything has been carefully re-created with loving exactitude.

■ **PICTURE OF DORIAN GRAY, THE**

1945, 107 MINS, US ◇ (ONE SEQUENCE ONLY) ⓥ
Dir Albert Lewin *Prod* Pandro S. Berman *Scr* Albert Lewin *Ph* Harry Stradling *Ed* Ferris Webster *Mus* Herbert Stothart (dir.) [Mario Castelnuovo-Tedesco, Franz Waxman] *Art Dir* Cedric Gibbons, Hans Peters
● George Sanders, Hurd Hatfield, Donna Reed, Angela Lansbury, Peter Lawford (M-G-M)

The Picture of Dorian Gray, based upon the Oscar Wilde novel, represents an interesting experiment by Metro, reported to have cost over $2 million.

The morbid theme of the Wilde story is built around Gray: his contempt for the painting that was made of him, the fears of not retaining youth and, of course, the unregenerate depths to which Gray sinks.

In the adaptation by Albert Lewin, much of the offscreen narration, explaining among other things what is going on in Gray's mind may be too much for most to grasp.

Hurd Hatfield is pretty-boy Gray. He plays it with little feeling, as apparently intended, though he should have aged a little toward the end. George Sanders, misogynistic of mind and a cynic of the first water, turns in a very commendable performance. It's he who upsets the romance, ostensibly serious on Gray's part, which has developed with a cheap music hall vocalist. She's Angela Lansbury, who registers strongly and very sympathetically.

■ **PICTURE SHOW MAN, THE**

1977, 99 MINS, AUSTRALIA ◇
Dir John Power *Prod* Joan Long *Scr* Joan Long *Ph* Geoff Burton *Ed* Nick Beauman *Mus* Peter Best *Art Dir* David Copping

P

● Rod Taylor, John Meillon, John Ewart, Harold Hopkins, Patrick Cargill, Yelena Zigon (Limelight)

The Picture Show Man has an old-fashioned endearing quality. The story of an itinerant purveyor of motion picture entertainment in the country areas of Australia in the 1920s, it's cute without being cloying, and episodic without being disjointed.

Based on an unpublished manuscript, Joan Long's script has enough characterization to allow the actors a fair go at establishing themselves, yet keeps them well ordered enough to maintain the forward movement of the plot.

John Power's direction is firm without being thwarting and the result is that the good times being had on screen are conveyed to the audience and are affecting.

Rod Taylor's portrayal of the heavy is definitely lightweight.

■ PIED PIPER, THE

1972, 90 MINS, UK/W. GERMANY ◇ ⑫
Dir Jacques Demy *Prod* David Puttnam, Sandy Lieberson *Scr* Andrew Birkin, Jacques Demy, Mark Peploe *Ph* Peter Suschitzky *Ed* John Trumper *Mus* Donovan *Art Dir* Assheton Gorton
● Jack Wild, Donald Pleasence, John Hurt, Donovan, Michael Hordern, Roy Kinnear (Sagittarius/Goodtimes)

The Pied Piper, based on the 14th-century legend from Hamelin, has been filmed by the sensitive Jacques Demy as a sort of somber fairy tale and allegory. The results are commendable in ambition but uneven in execution.

In recreating the story of the minstrel who leads the rats out of Hamelin, but then leads its children away when the politicians fail to keep a promise, the writers started with one of folklore's greatest pre-sold subjects. However, the script seems more a series of broad, arch, low-comedy vignettes without a clear emphasis.

As a result, Donovan, in the title role, is in and out of the story, as is Jack Wild, cast as the crippled boy whose alchemist patron, Michael Hordern, cannot convince the town's elders of the connection between Black Plague and rats.

■ PIGEON THAT TOOK ROME, THE

1962, 101 MINS, US
Dir Melville Shavelson *Prod* Melville Shavelson *Scr* Melville Shavelson *Ph* Daniel L. Fapp *Ed* Frank Bracht *Mus* Allesandra Cicognini *Art Dir* Hal Pereira, Roland Anderson
● Charlton Heston, Elsa Martinelli, Harry Guardino, Salvatore Baccaloni, Gabriella Pollotta, Brian Donlevy (Paramount)

Melville Shavelson functions as producer, director and writer and shows good control in all three categories. This is a good-fun comedy and there's no incongruity in the fact that the setting is authentic-looking World War II Italy. His adaptation of *The Easter Dinner*, a novel by Donald Downes, has a wacky story that plays out amusingly well.

Interesting casting has to do with Charlton Heston who's an American infantry officer assigned to a cloak-and-dagger role in Rome before the Nazis decide to leave and the Yanks walk in. It comes to be that homing pigeons represent his contact with the Allies. His birds provide an Easter dinner for a local and friendly family who do not know they're partaking of a part of 'the American Air Force', as stated by one of the characters. Heston becomes replenished with German pigeons, gives them ankle bracelets with false war information, and one of these messengers heads unexpectedly to the Allies, instead of the enemy.

Heston plays the bewildered American officer with enough effectiveness to suggest

that he can be at home with cinematic mischief. Harry Guardino is Heston's radio man, a sort of funny fellow sidekick who becomes enamored of a local girl who happens to be pregnant by previous misfortune.

Elsa Martinelli is Heston's romantic vis-a-vis, not one easily won over but eventually, of course, they go hand in hand.

■ PILLOW TALK

1959, 105 MINS, US ◇ ⑫
Dir Michael Gordon *Prod* Ross Hunter, Martin Melcher *Scr* Stanley Shapiro, Maurice Richlin *Ph* Arthur E. Arling *Ed* Milton Carruth *Mus* Frank DeVol *Art Dir* Alexander Golitzen, Richard H. Riedel
● Rock Hudson, Doris Day, Tony Randall, Thelma Ritter, Nick Adams (Arwin/Universal)

Pillow Talk is a sleekly sophisticated production that deals chiefly with s-e-x. The principals seem to spend considerable time in bed or talking about what goes on in bed, but the beds they occupy are always occupied singly. There's more talk than action natch.

The plot (slight) of the amusing screenplay, from a story by Clarence Greene and Russell Rouse, is based on the notion that a telephone shortage puts Doris Day and Rock Hudson on a party line. Hudson is here a sophisticated man about town. Day displays a brace of smart Jean Louis gowns, and delivers crisply.

There is a good deal of cinema trickery in *Pillow Talk*. There are split screens; spoken thoughts by the main characters; and even introduction of background music orchestration for a laugh. It all registers strongly.

■ PIN UP GIRL

1944, 85 MINS, US ◇
Dir Bruce Humberstone *Prod* William LeBaron *Scr* Robert Ellis, Helen Logan, Earl Baldwin *Ph* Ernest Palmer *Ed* Robert Simpson *Mus* Emil Newman, Charles Henderson (dir.) *Art Dir* James Baseri, Joseph C. Wright
● Betty Grable, John Harvey, Martha Raye, Joe E. Brown (20th Century-Fox)

This is one of those escapist filmusicals which makes no pretenses at ultra-realism, and if you get into the mood fast that it's something to occupy your attention for an hour and a half. It's all very pleasing and pleasant.

Producer William LeBaron, director Bruce Humberstone and the cast, scripters, et al. have treated *Pin Up Girl* in uniform spirit. The Missouri gal who crashes the party of a welcome - to - a - Guadalcanal - hero (John Harvey) in one of New York's top niteries brooks no plot examination.

Right from the start, when Betty Grable is almost trapped in her gate-crashing she poses as a musicomedy actress, mounts the rostrum pronto and Charlie Spivak picks up the music cue and it all comes out all right. Just like that!

Joe E. Brown as the cafe prop and Martha Raye as his jealous star carry the low comedy against which are backgrounded expert hoofology by the Condos Bros, Spivak's stuff, rollerskating routines and the military finale.

In Technicolor Grable is a looker in pastel shades and spades. The costumes of the spec numbers have likewise been contrived for ultra-sartorial resplendence. All combined it makes for merry movie moments.

■ PINK FLAMINGOS

1974, 95 MINS, US ◇ ⑱
Dir John Waters *Scr* John Waters *Ph* John Waters *Ed* John Waters
● Divine, David Lochary, Mink Stole, Mary Vivian Pearce, Edith Massey, Danny Mills (Dreamland)

Divine, also known as Babs Johnson, is a

300 lb drag queen of grotesque proportions who holds the title 'the filthiest person in the world'. Vying for the title are Connie and Raymond Marble, who kidnap girls, impregnate them, and sell the children to lesbian couples in order to finance 'an inner city heroin ring' catering to high school students.

Around the above premise spins the nitwit plot of the poorly lensed 16mm picture *Pink Flamingo* – one of the most vile, stupid and repulsive films ever made.

Divine's Mama Edie, a huge mountain of adipose tissue, inhabits a playpen in the mobile home and performs coprophagy on the fresh product of a miniature poodle while 'How Much Is That Doggie in the Window' toodles on the soundtrack.

■ PINK FLOYD – THE WALL

1982, 99 MINS, UK ◇ ⑱
Dir Alan Parker *Prod* Alan Marshall *Scr* Roger Waters *Ph* Peter Biziou *Ed* Gerry Hamblyn *Art Dir* Brian Morris
● Bob Geldof, Christine Hargreaves, James Laurenson, Eleanor David, Bob Hoskins (M-G-M/United Artists/Tin Blue)

This $12 million production is not a concert film but an eye-popping dramatization of an audio storyline. Being a visual translation of a so-called 'concept' album, pic works extremely well in carrying over the somber tone of the LP.

The music is the core of the film, vocals subbing for the usual film dialog. But there's little need for dialog, since the visual treats offered by animation director Gerald Scarfe and photography director Peter Biziou tell the story.

Story centers around a frustrated, burned-out but successful rock star (Pink) who is near-suicidal and on the verge of insanity. His wife has left him for another man because of the interminable amount of time Pink spends on the road. When he contacts her by telephone, only to have the other man answer, his self-destruct mechanism begins its slow burn.

Powerful performance of Boomtown Rats lead singer Bob Geldof as Pink works to the pic's overall believability, despite its fantasy aura.

■ PINK PANTHER, THE

1964, 115 MINS, US ◇ ⑫
Dir Blake Edwards *Scr* Blake Edwards, Maurice Richlin *Ph* Philip Lathrop *Ed* Ralph E. Winters *Mus* Henry Mancini *Art Dir* Fernando Carrere
● David Niven, Peter Sellers, Robert Wagner, Capucine, Claudia Cardinale, Brenda DeBanzie (United Artists/Mirisch/GE)

This is film making as a branch of the candy trade, and the pack is so enticing that few will worry about the jerky machinations of the plot.

Quite apart from the general air of bubbling elegance, the pic is intensely funny. The yocks are almost entirely the responsibility of Peter Sellers, who is perfectly suited as a clumsy cop who can hardly move a foot without smashing a vase or open a door without hitting himself on the head.

The Panther is a priceless jewel owned by the Indian Princess Dala (Claudia Cardinale), vacationing in the Swiss ski resort of Cortina. The other principals are introduced in their various habitats, before they converge on the princess and her jewel.

Sellers' razor-sharp timing is superlative, and he makes the most of his ample opportunities. His doting concern for criminal wife (Capucine), his blundering ineptitude with material objects, and his dogged pursuit of the crook all coalesce to a sharp performance, with satirical overtones.

David Niven produces his familiar brand of debonair ease. Robert Wagner has a somewhat undernourished role. Capucine, sometimes awkward and over-intense as if she were straining for yocks, is nevertheless a good Simone Clouseau.

● ●

■ PINK PANTHER STRIKES AGAIN, THE

1976, 103 MINS, UK ◇ ⓥ

Dir Blake Edwards   *Prod* Blake Edwards   *Scr* Frank Waldman, Blake Edwards   *Ph* Harry Waxman   *Ed* Alan Jones   *Mus* Henry Mancini   *Art Dir* Peter Mullins
● Peter Sellers, Herbert Lom, Colin Blakely, Leonard Rossiter, Lesley-Anne Down, Burt Kwouk (United Artists)

The Pink Panther Strikes Again is a hilarious film about the further misadventures of Peter Sellers as Inspector Clouseau. Herbert Lom, Clouseau's nemesis in the police bureau, has had his character expanded into a Professor Moriarty-type fiend, which works just fine.

This time around, Lom is introduced nearly cured of his nervous collapse. But Sellers has assumed Lom's old chief inspector job, and when Lom escapes, Sellers is assigned to the case. Lom kidnaps scientist Richard Vernon who has a disappearing ray device; pitch is that Lom threatens world destruction unless Sellers is handed over to him for extermination.

Action proceeds smartly through plot-advancing action scenes, interleaved with excellent non-dialog sequences featuring Sellers and underscored superbly by Henry Mancini.

● ●

■ PINK STRING AND SEALING WAX

1945, 93 MINS, UK

Dir Robert Hamer   *Prod* Michael Balcon   *Scr* Diana Morgan, Robert Hamer   *Ph* Richard S. Pavey, R. Julius   *Ed* Michael Truman   *Mus* Norman Demuth   *Art Dir* Duncan Sutherland
● Mervyn Johns, Mary Merrall, Gordon Jackson, Sally Ann Howes, Googie Withers, Catherine Lacey (Ealing)

Bringing the England of the Victorian period to life is the best thing *Pink String and Sealing Wax* accomplishes. The black, high-necked, rustling Sunday-best bombazines which the church-going women wear contrast violently with the billowing cleavages of the bad women. The unrelenting tyranny of the lord and master of the respectable family is offset by the free-and-easy beatings-up the naughty gals receive at the hands of Cagney-ish husbands and sweethearts. In giving this side of English life, the picture (based on the West End stage hit by Roland Pertwee) is tops.

The bit players turn in performances so bright one wonders how come they aren't in the top billing. Catherine Lacey as a gin drunkard is superb. John Carol's warned-off jockey who loves 'em and leaves 'em without batting an eye is as smooth as the greasy cowlick draped over his forehead. Garry Marsh as the booze hound proprietor of the pub whom Withers rubs out with strychnine is Bill Sykes come to life.

● ●

■ PINOCCHIO

1940, 87 MINS, US ⓥ

Dir Ben Sharpsteen, Hamilton Luske   *Prod* Walt Disney   *Scr* Ted Sears, Webb Smith, Joseph Sabo, Otto Englander, William Cottrell, Aurelious Battaglia, Erdman Penner   *Mus* Leigh Harline
● (Walt Disney/RKO)

Pinocchio is a substantial piece of entertainment for young and old. Both animation and photography are vastly improved over Walt Disney's first cartoon feature, *Snow White*. Animation is so smooth that cartoon figures carry impression of real persons and settings rather than drawings.

Extensive use of the Disney-developed multiplane camera (first used moderately for *Snow White*) provides some ingenious cartoon photography, allowing for camera movement similar to dolly shots. Most startling effect is the jumpy landscape as seen through the eyes of a leaping Jiminy Cricket.

Opening is similar to *Snow White*, establishing at the start that this is a fairy tale. Jiminy, witty, resourceful and effervescing cricket, displays the title cover and first illustrations of the book with a dialog description introducing the old woodcarver, Geppetto, and his workshop. Place abounds with musical clocks and gadgets, pet kitten and goldfish – and the completed puppet whom he names Pinocchio. Geppetto's wish for a son on the wishing star is granted when the blue fairy appears and provides life for the puppet; with Jiminy Cricket appointed guardian of latter's conscience. Pinocchio soon encounters villainous characters and his impetuous curiosity gets him into a series of escapades.

Cartoon characterization of Pinocchio is delightful, with his boyish antics and pranks maintaining constant interest. Jiminy Cricket is a fast-talking character providing rich humor with wisecracks and witticisms. Kindly old Geppetto is a definitely drawn character while several appearances of Blue Fairy are accentuated by novel lighting effects. Picture stresses evil figures and results of wrongdoing more vividly and to greater extent than *Snow White*, and at times somewhat overplays these factors for children. This is minor, however.

● ●

■ PIRANHA

1978, 92 MINS, US ◇ ⓥ

Dir Joe Dante   *Prod* Jon Davison   *Scr* John Sayles   *Ph* Jamie Anderson   *Ed* Mark Goldblatt, Joe Dante   *Mus* Pino Donaggio   *Art Dir* Bill Mellin, Kerry Mellin
● Bradford Dillman, Heather Menzies, Kevin McCarthy, Keenan Wynn, Dick Miller, Barbara Steele (New World)

Since the title characters in *Piranha* are never actually seen (there's lots of speeded-up nibbling, but no closeups of the deadly Brazilian river munchers), the pic utilizes a lot of red dye in the water, and an auditory effect for the gnawing that sounds like an air-conditioner on the fritz.

What is different about *Piranha* is the unusual number of victims. Not only is the requisite slew of cameo performers dispatched quickly (Keenan Wynn, Kevin McCarthy, Bruce Gordon), but an entire camp full of school children, and a holiday crowd at a lakeside resort get chomped. This is one film where the fish win.

Heather Menzies plays an aggressive femme searching for missing persons, who enlists backwoods recluse Bradford Dillman in her cause. When they stumble on mad doctor McCarthy's mountain-top lab, they unwittingly release a generation of superhardy piranhas McCarthy was breeding for use in the Mekong Delta during the Vietnam war.

Barbara Steele turns up as a government scientist who hints the piranhas may be back for a sequel. Menzies is attractively competent, and Dillman does what he's supposed to, which isn't much. One yearns to have seen more of McCarthy and his lab, where a scaly homunculus is seen lurking about, but never explained.

● ●

■ PIRATE, THE

1948, 101 MINS, US ◇ ⓥ

Dir Vincente Minnelli   *Prod* Arthur Freed   *Scr* Albert Hackett, Frances Goodrich   *Ph* Harry Stradling   *Ed* Blanche Sewell   *Mus* Cole Porter, Lennie Hayton   *Art Dir* Cedric Gibbons, Jack Martin Smith
● Judy Garland, Gene Kelly, Walter Slezak, Gladys Cooper, Reginald Owen, Nicholas Brothers (M-G-M

The Pirate is escapist film fare. It's an eye and ear treat of light musical entertainment, garbing its amusing antics, catchy songs and able terping in brilliant color.

Gene Kelly and Judy Garland team delightfully in selling the dances and songs, scoring in both departments. The Cole Porter score is loaded with tunes that get over to the ear and the foot.

Adapted from the S. N. Behrman play, picture tells of the cloistered Latin girl about to fulfill an arranged wedding when she meets a travelling troupe of entertainers headed by Kelly. Title springs from fact that gal yearns for a fabulous pirate and sees him in the actor.

Vincente Minnelli's direction is light and seems to poke subtle fun at the elaborate musical ingredients and plot. The fact that *The Pirate* never takes itself too seriously adds to enjoyment, giving sharp point to some of the dialog in the script.

● ●

■ PIRATES

1986, 124 MINS, FRANCE/TUNISIA ◇ ⓥ

Dir Roman Polanski   *Prod* Tarak Ben Ammar   *Scr* Gerard Brach, Roman Polanski, John Brownjohn   *Ph* Witold Sobocinski   *Ed* Herve de Luze, William Reynolds   *Mus* Philippe Sarde   *Art Dir* Pierre Guffroy
● Walter Matthau, Damien Thomas, Richard Pearson, Cris Campion, Charlotte Lewis, Olu Jacobs (Carthago/Accent-Cominco)

Roman Polanski's *Pirates* is a decidedly underwhelming comedy adventure adding up to a major disappointment.

Pirates first was announced as a 1976 Polanski feature to star Jack Nicholson and Isabelle Adjani, before finally being produced (commencing in 1984) in Tunisia, Malta and the Seychelles, costing in excess of $30 million.

Walter Matthau gainfully essays the central role of Capt Thomas Bartholomew Red, a peg-legged British pirate captain with plenty of Long John Silver in his manner. Teamed with a handsome young French sailor (Cris Campion), Red is captured by Don Alfonso (Damien Thomas), captain of the Spanish galleon *Neptune*.

In a series of turnabout adventures, Red causes the *Neptune*'s crew to mutiny, takes the niece (Charlotte Lewis) of the governor of Maracaibo hostage, and steals a golden Aztec throne from the Spaniards.

Casting is unimpressive, with Matthau unable to carry the picture singlehandedly. Newcomer Campion projects a pleasant personality, more than can be said for Polanski's discovery Charlotte Lewis, thoroughly inexpressive here.

● ●

■ PIRATES OF PENZANCE, THE

1983, 112 MINS, US ◇ ⓥ

Dir Wilford Leach   *Prod* Joseph Papp, Timothy Burrill   *Scr* Wilford Leach   *Ph* Douglas Slocombe   *Ed* Anne V. Coates   *Mus* William Elliott (arr.)   *Art Dir* Elliot Scott
● Kevin Kline, Angela Lansbury, Linda Ronstadt, George Rose, Rex Smith, Tony Azito (Pressman/Universal)

Gilbert & Sullivan's durable *The Pirates of Penzance* has been turned into an elaborate screen musical by basically the same hands responsible for Joseph Papp's smash New York Shakespeare Festival and Broadway stage production, and result is a delight.

For the film, shot at Shepperton Studios in England, a charming artificiality of style was arrived at, which is most immediately apparent in Elliot Scott's beautifully witty production design.

Simple tale has orphan Rex Smith leaving, upon turning 21, the band of pirates with whom he's been raised. Upon hitting land, he encounters eight sisters and becomes smitten with one of them, Linda Ronstadt, Pirate King Kevin Kline is not about to let Smith go straight so easily, however, and informs him that, having been born on 29 February, he's actually only had five birthdays, and will therefore be obliged to remain with the gang until 1940 or so.

With the exception of Angela Lansbury, entertaining as the pirates' nursemaid and *aide-de-combat*, all principal cast members have repeated their Broadway performances here, and in exemplary fashion.

．．．．．．．．．．．．．．．．．．．．．．．．．．．

◼ PIT AND THE PENDULUM, THE

1961, 85 MINS, US ◇ Ⓥ

Dir Roger Corman *Prod* Roger Corman *Scr* Richard Matheson *Ph* Floyd Crosby *Ed* Anthony Carras *Mus* Les Baxter *Art Dir* Daniel Haller

● Vincent Price, John Kerr, Barbara Steele, Luana Anders, Antony Carbone (American International)

Pit and Pendulum is an elaboration of the short Poe classic about blood-letting in 16th-century Spain. The result is a physically stylish, imaginatively photographed horror film which, though needlessly corny in many spots, adds up to good exploitation.

The main problem is that Poe furnished scriptwriter Richard Matheson with only one scene – the spine-tingling climax – and Matheson has been hard put to come up with a comparably effective build-up to these last 10 or so minutes. He has removed the tale one generation beyond the time of the Spanish Inquisition (for reasons best known to himself) and contrived a plot involving an ill-fated nobleman slowly losing his mind because he thinks he accidentally buried his wife alive, just like his father did some years before – on purpose.

Actually Matheson's plotting isn't at all bad, but he has rendered it in some fruity dialog. If audiences don't titter, it's only because veteran star Vincent Price can chew scenery while keeping his tongue in his cheek.

While Matheson's script takes a good deal of time, including three extended flashbacks, to get to the denouement, it's almost worth it. The last portion of the film builds with genuine excitement to a reverse twist ending that might well have pleased Poe himself.

．．．．．．．．．．．．．．．．．．．．．．．．．．．

◼ PLACE FOR LOVERS, A

1969, 88 MINS, ITALY/FRANCE ◇

Dir Vittorio De Sica *Prod* Carlo Ponti, Arthur Cohn *Scr* Julian Halevy, Peter Baldwin, Ennio De Concini, Tonino Guerra, Cesare Zavattini *Ph* Pasquale De Santis *Ed* Adriana Novelli *Mus* Maurice De Sica *Art Dir* Piero Poletto

● Faye Dunaway, Marcello Mastroianni, Caroline Mortimer, Karin Engh (M-G-M/Ponti-Cohn)

With five scripters freely adapting a play [*Amanti*, by Brunello Rondi and Renaldo Cabieri] the result is bound to lack decision and this romantic drama comes out at times as somewhat sudsy and flabby. But with Vittorio De Sica's direction, the eye-pleasing atmosphere of the Italian Alps and Marcello Mastroianni and Faye Dunaway a good team as a pair of ill-starred lovers, there's enough pull.

Dunaway arrives to stay at a deserted elegant villa near Venice. She phones Mastroianni and he hotfoots it to the villa. Without quite understanding what gives, he is in the sack with Dunaway before the night's out.

Situations are often lethargically introduced and dialog is frequently stagey and mannered. But De Sica gets full measure out of the love interest with its moody background. Dunaway looks beautiful and enticing and Mastroianni is pleasantly cast as the infatuated lover.

．．．．．．．．．．．．．．．．．．．．．．．．．．．

◼ PLACE IN THE SUN, A

1951, 118 MINS, US

Dir George Stevens *Prod* George Stevens *Scr* Michael Wilson, Harry Brown *Ph* William C. Mellor *Ed* William Hornbeck *Mus* Franz Waxman *Art Dir* Hans Dreier, Walter Tyler

● Montgomery Clift, Elizabeth Taylor, Shelley Winters, Keefe Brasselle, Fred Clark, Raymond Burr (Paramount)

Theodore Dreiser's much-discussed novel of the 1920s, *An American Tragedy*, is here transposed to the screen for the second time by Paramount. The first version was made in 1930 by Josef Von Sternberg under the original title. This version, brought completely up to date in time and settings, is distinguished beyond its predecessor in every way. Montgomery Clift, Shelley Winters and Elizabeth Taylor give wonderfully shaded and poignant performances.

Tale is of a poor and lonely boy and girl who find comfort in each other. Unhappily, while the girl progresses to real love of the boy, he finds love elsewhere in a wealthy lass of a social set to which he'd like to become a part. His first attachment is not easily broken off, however, because the girl discovers herself pregnant. When she appears at a mountain lake resort where he is spending his vacation with the femme who has by this time become his fiancee, his confused emotions lead him to take her into a boat with intention of drowning her.

Winters plays the poor gal, Taylor the rich one. Clift at times seems overly-laconic.

☐ 1951: Best Picture (Nomination)

．．．．．．．．．．．．．．．．．．．．．．．．．．．

◼ PLACES IN THE HEART

1984, 102 MINS, US ◇ Ⓥ

Dir Robert Benton *Prod* Arlene Donovan *Scr* Robert Benton *Ph* Nestor Almendros *Ed* Carol Littleton *Mus* John Kander *Art Dir* Gene Callahan

● Sally Field, Lindsey Crouse, Ed Harris, Amy Madigan, John Malkovich, Danny Glover (Tri-Star)

Places in the Heart is a loving, reflective homage to his hometown by writer-director Robert Benton. Flawlessly crafted, Benton creates a full tapestry of life in Waxahachie, Texas circa 1935, but filmgoers may find his understated naturalistic approach lacking in dramatic punch.

Obviously drawing on his personal experiences and people he knew growing up, Benton remembers the rituals of everyday life: love, in all of its forms, birth and death.

Sally Field is solid in the lead role as a widowed mother, but she is not the strong unifying character that can tie the strands of Benton's script together.

Nestor Almendros' photography is not pretty, but high on feeling and atmosphere. It radiates a lived-in autumnal light.

☐ 1984: Best Picture (Nomination)

．．．．．．．．．．．．．．．．．．．．．．．．．．．

◼ PLAINSMAN, THE

1937, 112 MINS, US Ⓥ

Dir Cecil B. DeMille *Prod* Cecil B. DeMille *Scr* Waldemar Young, Lynn Riggs, Harold Lamb *Ph* Victor Milner, George Robinson *Ed* Anne Bauchens *Mus* George Anthei *Art Dir* Hans Dreier, Roland Anderson

● Gary Cooper, Jean Arthur, James Ellison, Charles Bickford, Helen Burgess, Porter Hall (Paramount)

The Plainsman is a big and a good western. It's cowboys and Indians on a broad, sweeping scale; not a *Covered Wagon* (1923) but majestic enough. Gary Cooper is Hickok, Jean Arthur is the historic Calamity Jane of his immediate associations, and James Ellison is a rather aggrandized Buffalo Bill. Opposite the latter is Helen Burgess as his bride. This perforce casts him as something of a musical comedy version of the plains scout whom history has pictured a much more grisly personality.

The spec appeal is in the redskin warfare. The sequence with the near burning-at-the-stake of Hickok in Yellow Hand's camp is tingling and the soldiers' holding out for several days against an almost overwhelming horde of Comanches, with some corking charging-through-the-water action, is another. Scripting [based on data from stories by Courtney Ryley Cooper and Frank J. Wilstack] and editing stand out favorably. Arthur is particularly endowed with some punch lines and pungent expletives as the hardy daughter.

．．．．．．．．．．．．．．．．．．．．．．．．．．．

◼ PLANES, TRAINS & AUTOMOBILES

1987, 93 MINS, US ◇ Ⓥ

Dir John Hughes *Prod* John Hughes *Scr* John Hughes *Ph* Don Peterman *Ed* Paul Hirsch *Mus* Ira Newborn *Art Dir* John W. Corso

● Steve Martin, John Candy, Laila Robbins, Michael McKean, Kevin Bacon (Paramount)

John Hughes has come up with an effective nightmare-as-comedy in *Planes, Trains & Automobiles*. Disaster-prone duo of Steve Martin and John Candy repeatedly recall a contemporary Laurel & Hardy as they agonizingly try to make their way from New York to Chicago by various modes of transport.

Man versus technology has been one of the staples of screen comedy since the earliest silent days, and Hughes makes the most of the format here packing as many of the frustrations of modern life as he can into this calamitous travelog of roadside America.

An ultimte situation comedy, tale throws together Martin, an ad exec, and Candy, a shower curtain ring salesman, as they head home from Manhattan to their respective homes in Chicago two days before Thanksgiving.

The problems start before they even get out of midtown. From there, it's a series of ghastly motel rooms, crowded anonymous restaurants, a sinister cab ride, an abortive train trip, an even worse excursion by rented car, some hitchhiking by truck, and, finally, a hop on the 'El' before sitting down to turkey.

．．．．．．．．．．．．．．．．．．．．．．．．．．．

◼ PLANET OF THE APES

1968, 112 MINS, US ◇ Ⓥ

Dir Franklin J. Schaffner *Prod* Arthur P. Jacobs *Scr* Michael Wilson *Ph* Leon Shamroy *Ed* Hugh S. Fowler *Mus* Jerry Goldsmith *Art Dir* Jack Martin Smith, William Creber

● Charlton Heston, Roddy McDowall, Kim Hunter, Maurice Evans, James Whitmore, James Daly (20th Century-Fox)

Planet of the Apes is an amazing film. A political-sociological allegory, cast in the mold of futuristic science-fiction, it is an intriguing blend of chilling satire, a sometimes ludicrous juxtaposition of human and ape mores, optimism and pessimism.

Pierre Boulle's novel, in which US space explorers find themselves in a world dominated by apes, has been adapted by Michael Wilson and Rod Serling.

The totality of the film works very well, leading to a surprise ending. The suspense, and suspension of belief, engendered is one of the film's biggest assets.

Charlton Heston, leader of an aborted space shot which propels his crew 20 centuries ahead of earth, is a cynical man who eventually has thrust upon him the burden of reasserting man's superiority over all other animals. At fadeout, he is the new Adam.

Key featured players – all in ape makeup – include Roddy McDowall and Kim Hunter, Maurice Evans, James Whitmore and James Daly.

■ PLATINUM BLONDE

1931, 82 MINS, US
Dir Frank Capra   *Scr* Jo Swerling, Dorothy Howell, Robert Riskin   *Ph* Joseph Walker   *Ed* Gene Milford
● Loretta Young, Robert Williams, Jean Harlow, Louise Closser Hale, Donald Dillaway, Reginald Owen (Columbia)

It's entertaining, has a lot of light, pleasing comedy and carries a cast that's tops. Robert Williams is a very likable character as a reporter who marries himself off to a snobbish society frail, and he plays it like a champ. Always displaying a fine screen presence and manner, Williams quickly ingratiates himself.

The newspaper background is prominent, and for once its 100% natural. The managing editor (Edmund Breese) with his hollering, swearing, affability and pride is aces.

The picture is with Williams all the way. It gives him a great break, and a pip scene, when after marrying the snooty plat (Jean Harlow) he renounces the whole gang in stiff language, taking ozone with the sob sister who all along has wanted it that way. Loretta Young runs third on footage and is somewhat missed.

■ PLATOON

1986, 120 MINS, US ◇ ⓥ
Dir Oliver Stone   *Prod* Arnold Kopelson   *Scr* Oliver Stone   *Ph* Robert Richardson   *Ed* Claire Simpson   *Mus* Georges Delerue   *Art Dir* Bruno Rubeo
● Tom Berenger, Willem Dafoe, Charlie Sheen, Forest Whitaker (Hemdale)

Platoon is an intense but artistically distanced study of infantry life during the Vietnam War. Writer-director Oliver Stone seeks to immerse the audience totally in the nightmare of the United States' misguided adventure, and manages to do so in a number of very effective scenes.

A Vietnam vet himself, Stone obviously had urgent personal reasons for making this picture, a fact that emerges instantly as green volunteer Charlie Sheen is plunged into the thick of action along the Cambodian border in late 1967.

Willem Dafoe comes close to stealing the picture as the sympathetic sergeant whose drugged state may even heighten his sensitivity to the insanity around him, and each of the members of the young cast all have their moments to shine.

□ 1986: Best Picture

■ PLAY DIRTY

1969, 117 MINS, UK ◇
Dir Andre de Toth   *Prod* Harry Saltzman   *Scr* Lotte Colin, Melvyn Bragg   *Ph* Edward Scaife   *Ed* Alan Osbiston   *Mus* Michel Legrand   *Art Dir* Tom Morahan
● Michael Caine, Nigel Davenport, Nigel Green, Harry Andrews, Bernard Archer (United/Lowndes)

Play Dirty is mainly the story of a small unit detailed to blow up a vital enemy fuel dump in the desert.

Main disappointment about the film [from an original story by George Marton] which has occasional crisp dialog and situations and two or three lively skirmishes is the performance of lead Michael Caine, who plays with an often tired and flat lack of expression which doesn't pump much blood into the dialog or action. He handles his role with intelligence but comes out second best to Nigel Davenport, a resourceful rogue with style.

Caine is cast as an inexperienced British army captain, detailed to lead reluctantly a small band of mercenaries into the desert to dispose of a vital enemy fuel dump.

Clash between Caine and Davenport is the main thread of the story and results in a fascinating relationship beween the two.

■ PLAY IT AGAIN, SAM

1972, 84 MINS, US ◇
Dir Herbert Ross   *Prod* Arthur P. Jacobs   *Scr* Woody Allen   *Ph* Owen Roizman   *Ed* Marion Rothman   *Mus* Billy Goldenberg   *Art Dir* Ed Wittstein
● Woody Allen, Diane Keaton, Tony Roberts, Jerry Lacy, Susan Anspach, Jennifer Salt (Paramount)

Woody Allen's 1969 legit comedy-starrer, *Play It Again, Sam*, has become on the screen 84 minutes of fragile fun. Allen and other key players from the stage version encore to good results. The placid direction of Herbert Ross keeps Allen in the spotlight for some good laughs, several chuckles and many smiles.

Allen's adaptation showcases his self-deprecating, and sometimes erratic, comedy personality. Ditched by wife Susan Anspach, who cannot stand his vicarious living of old Humphrey Bogart films, Allen is consoled by Diane Keaton and Tony Roberts, to the point that Keaton begins to fall for Allen. The interlude ends with a recreation of the final scene from Warners' *Cassablanca*. Jerry Lacy is most effective as the Bogart phantom who drops in from time to time.

■ PLAY MISTY FOR ME

1971, 102 MINS, US ◇ ⓥ
Dir Clint Eastwood   *Prod* Robert Daley   *Scr* Jo Helms, Dean Riesner   *Ph* Bruce Surtees   *Ed* Carl Pingitore   *Mus* Dee Barton   *Art Dir* Alexander Golitzen
● Clint Eastwood, Jessica Walter, Donna Mills, John Larch, Clarice Taylor, Don Siegel (Malpaso)

When it's not serving as an overdone travelog for the Monterey Peninsula-Carmel home environment of star, producer and debuting director Clint Eastwood, *Play Misty for Me* is an often fascinating suspenser about psychotic Jessica Walter, whose deranged infatuation for Eastwood leads her to commit murder. For that 80% of the film which constitutes the story, the structure and dialog create a mood of nervous terror which the other 20% nearly blows away.

Walter gives a superior performance as an unusual woman whose eccentricities are killing. Eastwood has selected excellent support: John Larch as a detective who nearly solves the case; Clarice Taylor, outstanding as a housekeeper; James McEachin as Eastwood's fellow-deejay on a (real) local radio station; Irene Hervey as a potential benefactor driven off by Walter's insults and director Don Siegel as a friendly bartender.

■ PLAYERS

1979, 120 MINS, US ◇ ⓥ
Dir Anthony Harvey   *Prod* Robert Evans   *Scr* Arnold Schulman   *Ph* James Crabe   *Ed* Randy Roberts   *Mus* Jerry Goldsmith   *Art Dir* Richard Sylbert
● Ali MacGraw, Dean-Paul Martin, Maximilian Schell, Pancho Gonzalez, Steve Guttenberg (Paramount)

Another love story in disguise, this time backgrounded against the tennis world, *Players* is disqualified by exec producer Arnold Schulman's wobbly script, a simpering performance by Ali MacGraw, and a preponderance of tennis footage.

Via backward glances, it's explained that Dean-Paul Martin, who at the film's beginning is pitted against Guillermo Vilas in the Wimbledon championships, rescues socialite Ali MacGraw from a car accident, is adopted by her, and eventually falls in love with her.

Only ace in *Players* is casting of Martin, who, in his first film role proves highly believable in both his tennis and dramatic scenes. Excellent support is offered by Pancho Gonzalez in a re-creation of his real-life role as a pro-turned-teacher.

■ PLAZA SUITE

1971, 114 MINS, US ◇ ⓥ
Dir Arthur Hiller   *Prod* Howard W. Koch   *Scr* Neil Simon   *Ph* Jack Marta   *Ed* Frank Braccht   *Mus* Maurice Jarre   *Art Dir* Arthur Lonergan
● Walter Matthau, Maureen Stapleton, Barbara Harris, Lee Grant (Paramount)

Neil Simon's excellent adaptation of his 1968 Broadway hit stars Walter Matthau in three strong characterizations of comedy-in-depth, teamed separately with Maureen Stapleton, Lee Grant and Barbara Harris.

Film opens with a 44-minute sketch featuring Stapleton as a nervous suburban wife who has taken her bridal suite at NY's Plaza Hotel while the paint dries at home. Hubby Matthau is a cool, jaded mate whose affair with secretary Louise Sorel is intuitively divined by the wife. Segment is the most dramatic, though filled with nervous comedy.

Middle episode is 33 minutes of lecherous farce, as Hollywood producer Matthau puts the make on Harris, a flame of 15 years past. She has become a reluctant matron of Tenafly, NJ. Some of the best laughs of the whole piece occur here.

Final 37 minutes involve father-of-the-bride Matthau, trying to coax frightened daughter Jenny Sullivan out of a locked hotel bathroom and into marriage to Thomas Carey. Grant is the harried mother. The comedy emphasis here is generally slapstick: raindrenched clothes; torn tails and stockings; broken furniture.

Each of the femme stars is given much screen time and the result not only is excellent spotlighting of their own talents, but also an adroit restraint on Matthau's presence.

■ PLEASE DON'T EAT THE DAISIES

1960, 111 MINS, US ◇
Dir Charles Walters   *Prod* Joe Pasternak   *Scr* Isobel Lennart   *Ph* Robert Bronner   *Ed* John MacSweeney   *Mus* David Rose   *Art Dir* George W. Davis, Hans Peters
● Doris Day, David Niven, Janis Paige, Spring Byington, Richard Haydn, Patsy Kelly (M-G-M)

Please Don't Eat The Daisies is a light and frothy comedy, and boff family fare. Pic is episodic
– as was the book by Jean Kerr – a series of highly amusing incidents strung together by a rather loose story thread, but this circumstance doesn't militate against interest. Charles Walters' direction maintains terrific pace.

Plotline is based on the adventures of Doris Day and David Niven after he turns to newspaper drama criticking during which they are forced out of their Gotham apartment and buy a monstrosity in the country – 70 miles from Broadway – where Day takes on community life while trying to modernize and make their new home livable. Janis Paige enters scene as a Broadway actress whom Niven pans in his very first review, which also incurs the enmity of his best friend, producer Richard Haydn.

Day delivers lustily and Niven makes hay with his critic's portrayal, for whom Paige goes on the make in a big way. Jack Weston also is good as a play-writing cabby.

■ PLENTY

1985, 124 MINS, US ◇ ⓥ
Dir Fred Schepisi   *Prod* Edward R. Pressman, Joseph Papp   *Scr* David Hare   *Ph* Ian Baker   *Ed* Peter Honess   *Mus* Bruce Smeaton   *Art Dir* Richard Macdonald
● Meryl Streep, Charles Dance, Tracey Ullman, John Gielgud, Sting, Ian McKellen (RKO/Pressman)

A picture possessing a host of first-class pedigrees, *Plenty* emerges as an absorbing and fastidiously made adaptation of David Hare's acclaimed play, but also comes off as cold and ultimately unaffecting.

Hare's ambitious drama, first staged in London in 1978, charts the growing social malaise of Western Europe and, specifically, Great Britain, over the years following the Second World War. He does this through the character of Susan Traherne, a difficult, unsettled, neurotic young woman who moves from idealism to frustration and madness in her passage through a succession of bleak political and personal events.

Pic opens with Susan, played by Meryl Streep, involved in derring-do with the Resistance in France during the war. She has a brief affair with commando Sam Neill, and no man can ever displace Neill from her mind.

Personally and historically, it's all downhill from there. Action is set principally in the British diplomatic world, and moves across a stage backdropped by post-war economic difficulties, Coronation Year, the Suez crisis and further developments in the Middle East.

. . . .

■ PLOT AGAINST HARRY, THE

1989, 80 MINS, US ♦ Ⓥ

Dir Michael Roemer   *Prod* Robert Young, Michael Roemer   *Scr* Michael Roemer   *Ph* Robert Young   *Ed* Terry Lewis, Georges Klotz   *Mus* Frank Lewin   *Art Dir* Howard Mandel

● Martin Priest, Ben Lang, Henry Nemo (King Screen)

The Plot against Harry is hilarious and often poignant. It was shot in 1969 but was held up because of a lack of completion funding. B&w pic is a sociological fossil of manners, mores and life in the 1960s.

Harry Plotnick (Martin Priest), a small-time Jewish numbers racketeer, gets released from prison and expects to pick up the gambling circuit he ran in his old neighborhood. His loyal schlemiel assistant/chauffeur Max, in cruising through his old turf in Manhattan, makes him realize the world has changed, and blacks and Hispanics now have dibs on his area.

In a farcical accident, Harry hits the rear end of a car carrying his ex-wife Kay and his ex-brother-in-law Leo and wife. Without missing a beat, Kay introduces Harry to the daughter he never saw, Margie (now pregnant), and her husband Mel, in an almost touching encounter.

As the story unfolds, Harry is faced with a new world and the gnawing lures of the solid middle-class family life that he's always eschewed.

The Plotnick family is boisterous, upfront, multilayered and Jewish in a way that Philip Roth would savor parodying. The cast is uniformly solid, delivering their sparklingly crisp dialog straight.

. . . .

■ PLOUGH AND THE STARS, THE

1937, 72 MINS, US

Dir John Ford   *Prod* Cliff Reid, Robert Sisk   *Scr* Dudley Nichols   *Ph* Joseph H. August   *Ed* George Hiveley   *Mus* Roy Webb

● Barbara Stanwyck, Preston Foster, Barry Fitzgerald, Denis O'Dea, Arthur Shields, Una O'Conner (RKO)

Story is an account of the Irish rebellion in 1916, a sanguinary outburst which failed of its purpose because the people were divided in allegiance, many Irish at the time fighting in France. It depicts the Irish character in various shadings of comedy, tragedy, sacrifice, selfishness and stupidity.

So many changes have been made in adapting this Sean O'Casey play to the screen that the tragic original has been modified into a romantic melodrama. Primarily the screen version is a woman's starring picture calling for an actress of considerably more gifts than Barbara Stanwyck here possesses. The altered story is the familiar theme that the men do the fighting and the women the weeping.

The opening shows the struggle and grief in a young bride's heart when her husband is selected by the citizen army to be the commandant of the fighting forces in Dublin. She has no interest in the uprising to free Ireland. Her world is her home.

These Irish boys are good looking, earnest and sincere. They take a tough licking but they're not quitters. Sympathy therefore is with the lads, which is one of the reasons Stanwyck has such a hard time holding up her end of the story.

In between there is humor and amusing characterization. Barry Fitzgerald has a joyful time in the role of Fluther, an Irish braggart. He is teamed with J.M. Kerrigan who is up to his usual high standard.

Preston Foster, opposite Stanwyck, fits nicely and his brogue comes easily. Only Stanwyck, of the entire cast, does not go Irish.

. . . .

■ PLOUGHMAN'S LUNCH, THE

1983, 100 MINS, US ♦ Ⓥ

Dir Richard Eyre   *Prod* Simon Relph, Ann Scott   *Scr* Ian McEwan   *Ph* Clive Tickner   *Ed* David Martin   *Mus* Dominic Muldowney   *Art Dir* Luciana Arrighi

● Jonathan Pryce, Tim Curry, Rosemary Harris, Frank Finlay, Charlie Dore, Bill Paterson (Greenpoint/Goldcrest/White)

Pic is set in the heartland of bourgeois England among its media creators and academic pontificators, and runs the period from the first spark of 1982's Falklands warlet to the victory speech of Prime Minister Margaret Thatcher at her party's gungho autumn shindig.

But those events are only a backdrop to the multi-layered story of a group of people who are either off the rails or suffering an acute lack of human commitment. It's a plot that could have turned out over-schematic, but Richard Eyre's strong directorial hand shows in delicately ambivalent performances from all players.

The film evidently springs from its author Ian McEwan's heart in characterizing the radio journalist played by Jonathan Pryce as lacking in virtue and understanding. His sins include political convictions that blow with the wind; neglect of a dying mother, leading on an older woman, and a fruitless infatuation with the TV researcher played by Charlie Dore.

Film reaches an astonishing climax during the Conservative party conference, where crew and cast filmed undercover.

. . . .

■ PLYMOUTH ADVENTURE

1952, 104 MINS, US ♦

Dir Clarence Brown   *Prod* Dore Schary   *Scr* Helen Deutsch   *Ph* William Daniels   *Ed* Robert J. Kern   *Mus* Miklos Rozsa   *Art Dir* Cedric Gibbons, Urie McCleary

● Spencer Tracy, Gene Tierney, Van Johnson, Leo Genn, Lloyd Bridges, Dawn Adams (M-G-M)

Metro has made *Plymouth Adventure*, the story of the Mayflower's perilous voyage to America [from a novel by Ernest Gebler], a large-scale sea spectacle.

The production, ably executed, puts more emphasis on the voyage itself and the attendant dangers than on developing the characters into flesh-and-blood people.

To Spencer Tracy falls the chore of enacting Captain Christopher Jones, the tough, earthy master of the Mayflower. Gene Tierney is the tragic Dorothy Bradford and Leo Genn her husband, the William Bradford later to become the first governor of the new colony. Van Johnson is John Alden, the carpenter who ships on the voyage and later marries Priscilla Mullins, played by Dawn Addams. They are all competent.

. . . .

■ POCKETFUL OF MIRACLES

1961, 136 MINS, US ♦ Ⓥ

Dir Frank Capra   *Prod* Frank Capra   *Scr* Hal Kanter, Harry Tugend   *Ph* Robert Bronner   *Ed* Frank P. Keller   *Mus* Walter Scharf   *Art Dir* Hal Pereira, Roland Anderson

● Glenn Ford, Bette Davis, Hope Lange, Arthur O'Connell, Peter Falk, Edward Everett Horton (United Artists)

The scenario, which alternates uneasily between wit and sentiment, is based on the 1933 *Lady for a Day*, which was adapted by Robert Riskin from a Damon Runyon story, and also directed by Frank Capra. It has to do with an impoverished apple-vender (Bette Davis) who would have her long lost daughter (Ann-Margret) believe that she is a lady of means. This is simple enough when the daughter is on the other side of the globe, but when she comes trotting over for a look-see, mama is in trouble.

Enter mama's favorite apple-polisher, influential Dave the Dude (Glenn Ford), who hastily sets up an elaborate masquerade with the aid of a horde of typical 1930s Runyonesque hoodlums who are hard as nails on the surface, but all whipped cream on the inside.

The picture seems too long, considering that there's never any doubt as to the outcome, and it's also too lethargic, but there are sporadic compensations of line and situation that reward the patience. Fortunately Capra has assembled some of Hollywood's outstanding character players for the chore.

For the romantic leads, he has Ford and Hope Lange. As a comedy team, they are no James Stewart-Jean Arthur (probably Capra's most formidable star-pairing), but they get by – particularly Ford. Lange is more suitable for serious roles. Davis has the meaty role of 'Apple Annie' and, except for a tendency to overemote in closeups, she handles it with depth and finesse.

The best lines in the picture go to Peter Falk, who just about walks off with the film when he's on.

. . . .

■ POINT BLANK

1967, 92 MINS, US ♦ Ⓥ

Dir John Boorman   *Prod* Judd Bernard, Robert Chartoff   *Scr* Alexander Jacobs, David Newhouse, Rafe Newhouse   *Ph* Philip H. Lathrop   *Ed* Henry Berman   *Mus* Johnny Mandel   *Art Dir* George W. Davis, Albert Brenner

● Lee Marvin, Angie Dickinson, Keenan Wynn, Carroll O'Connor, Lloyd Bochner, Michael Strong (M-G-M/Bernard-Winkler)

Point Blank is a violent, dynamic, thinly-scripted film. Lee Marvin stars as a double-crossed thief seeking vengeance, only to find he has again been used. Britisher John Boorman's first Hollywood pic is a textbook in brutality and a superior exercise in cinematic virtuosity.

Richard Stark's novel *The Hunter* is the basis for the screenplay, in which first five minutes recap Marvin's betrayal by best pal John Vernon and wife (Sharon Acker). The space-time jumps are lucid, effective, inventive, fluid – and repetitive. A hurry-and-wait sensation grows on a viewer as, once transposed from one scene to another, a dramatic torpor ensues at times, except for the hypo of choreographed brutality.

The futility of revenge is exemplified by the cyclic pattern of Marvin's movements, and Boorman's frequent cuts to the past overmake the point.

. . . .

■ POLICE ACADEMY

1984, 95 MINS, US ♦ Ⓥ

Dir Hugh Wilson   *Prod* Paul Maslansky   *Scr* Neal Israel, Pat Proft, Hugh Wilson   *Ph* Michael D. Margulies   *Ed* Robert Brown, Zach Staenberg

Mus Robert Folk   *Art Dir* Trevor Williams
● Steve Guttenberg, G.W. Bailey, George Gaynes, Michael Winslow, Kim Cattrall, Bubba Smith (Ladd)

Police Academy at its core is a harmless, innocent poke at authority that does find a fresh background in a police academy. Women in the film, such as Kim Cattrall as an Ivy League-type and Leslie Easterbrook as a busty sergeant, have almost nothing to do. Marion Ramsey as a timid-voiced trainee is fine in the film's most vivid female part.

Cowriter Hugh Wilson, makes his feature film debut as director, and his scenes are short and fragmentary. He gets a fresh comic performance from Michael Winslow as a walking human sound effects system (the film's most appealing turn).

Through it all, Steve Guttenberg is a likeable rogue in a role that's too unflappable to set off any sparks.

....

■ POLICE ACADEMY 3 BACK IN TRAINING

1986, 82 MINS, US ◇ ⓥ
Dir Jerry Paris   *Prod* Paul Maslansky   *Scr* Gene Quintano   *Ph* Robert Saad   *Ed* Bud Molin   *Mus* Robert Folk   *Art Dir* Trevor Williams
● Steve Guttenberg, Bubba Smith, David Graf, Michael Winslow, Marion Ramsey (Warner)

Cast of cartoon misfits is still basically intact and if *Police Academy 3* has any charm it's in the good-natured dopeyness of these people. No bones about it, these people are there to laugh at.

Leading the charge for the third time is Steve Guttenberg turning in another likable boy-next-door performance. His role, however, as the cute straight man seems a bit abbreviated, with the comic burden spread out among the cast. New additions Tim Kazurinsky and Bobcat Goldthwait as cadets are only intermittently amusing.

Plot has something to do with one of the two rival police academies being shut down by the penny-pinching governor (Ed Nelson). Bad guys led by Commandant Mauser (Art Metrano) try to sabotage the forces of virtue led by Commandant Lassard (George Gaynes).

....

■ POLLYANNA

1960, 133 MINS, US ◇
Dir David Swift   *Prod* Walt Disney   *Scr* David Swift   *Ph* Russell Harlan   *Ed* Frank Gross   *Mus* Paul Smith   *Art Dir* Carroll Clark, Robert Clatworthy
● Jane Wyman, Hayley Mills, Richard Egan, Karl Malden, Nancy Olson, Adolphe Menjou (Walt Disney)

In Walt Disney's *Pollyanna* Hayley Mills' work more than compensates for the film's lack of tautness and, at certain points, what seems to be an uncertain sense of direction. That the incredibly pre-World War I confectionery character (the glad girl, she was called) emerges normal and believably lovable is a tribute to Mills' ability and to writer-director David Swift's sane sensible approach to the familiar character from Eleanor H. Porter's novel.

Pollyanna is the tale of the little 12-year-old girl who plays the 'glad game' so well that she's soon got everyone she knows playing it. She's an orphan who lives with her aunt (Jane Wyman), the richest, most influential woman in a town which bears her name and sheepishly takes her advice and her charity. That is, until Pollyanna arrives.

Wyman, Richard Egan, Donald Crisp, Adolphe Menjou, Agnes Moorehead and Karl Malden are more than competent in key roles.

....

■ POLTERGEIST

1982, 114 MINS, US ◇ ⓥ
Dir Tobe Hooper   *Prod* Steven Spielberg, Frank Marshall   *Scr* Steven Spielberg, Michael Grais, Mark Victor   *Ph* Matthew F. Leonetti   *Ed* Michael Kahn   *Mus* Jerry Goldsmith   *Art Dir* James H. Spencer
● Craig T. Nelson, JoBeth Williams, Beatrice Straight, Dominique Dunne, Oliver Robins, Heather O'Rourke (M-G-M/United Artists)

Given the talents, *Poltergeist* is an annoying film because it could have been so much better. Certainly, the subject is interesting, a persistent parapsychological phenomenon that defies scientific explanation, yet refuses to go away.

But producer Steven Spielberg and the director Tobe Hooper, don't really care. They're fully content to demonstrate how well they can create the physical manifestations, plus a lot of standard sideshow horrors.

But the story is truly stupid, though well-acted. Craig T. Nelson and JoBeth Williams are the parents, living almost wall-to-wall with their neighbors in a suburban development. But when the furniture starts to fly around the room and the big tree in the yard gets hungry for the kids nobody ever seems to notice. Here you have a house in the middle of the street going berserk in Dolby Stereo and nobody calls the cops. But Williams is terrific as the mother, at first amused by the strange goings-on in her kitchen and later terrified when cute little Heather O'Rourke disappears into the walls. And Zelda Rubinstein walks off with the film as the miniature lady who comes to cleanse the house.

....

■ POLTERGEIST II

1986, 90 MINS, US ◇ ⓥ
Dir Brian Gibson   *Prod* Mark Victor, Michael Grais   *Scr* Mark Victor, Michael Grais   *Ph* Andrew Laszlo   *Ed* Thom Noble   *Mus* Jerry Goldsmith   *Art Dir* Ted Haworth
● JoBeth Williams, Craig T. Nelson, Heather O'Rourke, Oliver Robins, Zelda Rubinstein, Will Sampson (M-G-M)

It's another horrifying house party at the Freelings in *Poltergeist II*. Sequel finds the poor Freeling family a year later penniless and slightly crazed after their Cuesta Verde house was obliterated by poltergeists.

When Gramma dies, little Carol Anne's play telephone spontaneously rings with a call from 'the other side'.

This time around, co-scripters Mark Victor and Michael Grais (who wrote the first *Poltergeist* with Steven Spielberg) have the focus of evil in human form, in the perfectly cast, since deceased, Julian Beck.

Unlike the first film that focused all the action around the innocent blond and persecuted Carol Anne (Heather O'Rourke), juiciest moments in 'II' revolve around Craig Nelson playing a soppy drunk, a lustful husband (again to the warm JoBeth Williams), a loving father and a ghoulie-spewing monster.

....

■ POLYESTER

1981, 94 MINS, US ◇
Dir John Waters   *Prod* John Waters   *Scr* John Waters   *Ph* David Insley   *Ed* Charles Roggero   *Mus* Chris Stein   *Art Dir* Vincent Peranio
● Divine, Tab Hunter (New Line)

Baltimore-based underground filmmaker John Waters, famous for his midnight circuit hits like *Pink Flamingos*, surfaces in the pro ranks with *Polyester*, a fitfully amusing comedy of not so ordinary people. Waters' fabled shock tactics are toned down here.

Transvestite thesp Divine never steps out of character essaying the role of a housewife stuck with horrid children (Mary Garlington and Ken King) an unsympathetic husband (David Samson) and a truly evil mother (Joni Ruth White). As the episodic situation comedy unfolds, camp followers may enjoy Divine's eyerolling reactions but to the uninitiated most scenes play as overacted melodrama.

After a couple of silent teaser shots, Tab Hunter finally enters the picture after a full hour has elapsed. He is unable to fit into Waters' world, straining to overact and pull faces as the rest of the troupe and even extras do. His kissing Divine is about as offensive as film gets.

With nudity and explicit sex and violence absent, *Polyester* strains for a marketing gimmick by introducing 'Odorama.' After a cute scientist-in-lab prolog explaining the process, cheap gimmick turns out to be a scratch and sniff card handed out to the viewer, keyed manually to numbers flashed on the screen periodically during the film. It's a far cry from the fumes in the theatre gimmicks of Walter Reade's 1959 AromaRama and Mike Todd Jrs 1960 Smell-O-Vision.

....

■ POOL OF LONDON

1951, 85 MINS, UK
Dir Basil Dearden   *Prod* Michael Relph   *Scr* Jack Whittingham, John Eldridge   *Ph* Gordon Dines   *Ed* Peter Tanner   *Mus* John Addison   *Art Dir* Jim Morahan
● Bonar Colleano, Susan Shaw, Renee Asherson, Earl Cameron, Moira Lister, Max Adrian (Ealing)

The story of *Pool of London* spans just 48 hours when a cargo ship is in the London docks. The plot goes off at various tangents before finally converging on the basic dramatic theme of a manhunt following a holdup, murder and jewel robbery.

The central character, played by Bonar Colleano, is an over-confident, over-exuberant seaman who makes a bit of side money by small-time smuggling. He is tempted into the big coin by a gang of jewel thieves. Before he gets back to his boat, he finds that he has become implicated in a murder hunt and that he has landed his best friend, a colored boy, with the incriminating evidence.

While the main story is being developed, the film traces the warm attachment of the Negro seaman for a white girl. Although this is tastefully done, it has no bearing on the plot.

Colleano's role is a natural for him. He lives the part of the swaggering sailor, sure of himself until the moment of crisis. Earl Cameron gives a restrained and dignified performance as his friend.

....

■ POOR COW

1967, 101 MINS, UK ◇ ⓥ
Dir Ken Loach   *Prod* Joseph Janni   *Scr* Nell Dunn, Ken Loach   *Ph* Brian Probyn   *Ed* Roy Watts   *Mus* Donovan   *Art Dir* Bernard Sarron
● Carol White, Terence Stamp, John Bindon, Kate Williams, Queenie Watts, Malcolm McDowell (Vic/Anglo Amalgamated)

The film has a jolting opening, with Joy, the hapless heroine, shown in full detail giving birth to a baby, with the infant emerging from the womb in its natural state. This leads into a portrait of Joy, who has married a brutal crook (John Bindon) and, after he is nabbed by the cops, shacks up with another thief (Terence Stamp), a gentler type who is himself put inside.

The incidents of the plot are an excuse for an examination of promiscuous Joy. Left to fend for herself, she snatches happiness where she can find it.

Kenneth Loach uses an improvisatory technique in all this, and it largely works. Thesps were given the gist and trend of the dialog, and permitted to embroider it with their own words.

P

It is Carol White's film, and she scores with a flow of varied emotion, ranging from fetching happiness to a sudden spurt of tears in the final minutes, when she recalls straight to camera her affection for her baby.

....

■ POPE JOAN

1972, 101 MINS, UK ◇ ▽

Dir Michael Anderson *Prod* Kurt Unger *Scr* John Briley *Ph* Billy Williams *Ed* Bill Lenny *Mus* Maurice Jarre *Art Dir* Elliott Scott
● Liv Ullmann, Trevor Howard, Lesley-Anne Down, Jeremy Kemp, Olivia de Havilland, Maximilian Schell (Columbia/Big City/Command/Triple Eight)

Pope Joan deals with a female head of the Roman Catholic Church. Thanks to a screenplay that uses a modern-day story counterpart to suggest, apparently, that the theme is timely, this is too disjointed and rambling to make much sense.

The story is told as the ancient prototype of a modern female evangelist, torn between sex and salvation, whose religious fervor and bedroom capers more or less match those of her earlier counterpart.

She's 'adopted' in more ways than one by an artist-monk who eventually takes her to Greece as a male. They eventually wind up in Rome where her street preaching brings her to the attention of Leo XII, who takes her (him) on as a papal secretary, upped to cardinal and eventually his successor.

Liv Ulman as Pope Joan carries the film with Maximilian Schell and Franco Nero trailing behind.

[Version reviewed above is 132-minute one tradeshown in New York. The 111-minute UK version omits all modern sequences.]

....

■ POPE OF GREENWICH VILLAGE, THE

1984, 120 MINS, US ◇ ▽

Dir Stuart Rosenberg *Prod* Gene Kirkwood *Scr* Vincent Patrick *Ph* John Bailey *Ed* Robert Brown *Mus* Dave Grusin *Art Dir* Paul Sylbert
● Eric Roberts, Mickey Rourke, Daryl Hannah, Geraldine Page, Kenneth McMillan, Tony Musante (United Artists)

The Pope of Greenwich Village, set in Manhattan's Italian community, is a near-miss in its transition from novel [by Vincent Patrick] to film, setting forth an offbeat slice-of-life tale of small-time guys involved in big trouble.

Key protagonists are two young buddies (distantly related), Charlie (Mickey Rourke), a supervisor in a restaurant where Paulie (Eric Roberts) works as a waiter. Both are heavily in debt and headed nowhere, with the usual pipe dreams of escape.

Fired from their jobs at film's outset due to a misdeed by Paulie, the two of them seek a way out via a crime caper initiated by Paulie, involving an older man Barney (Kenneth McMillan) as safecracker.

....

■ POPEYE

1980, 114 MINS, US ◇ ▽

Dir Robert Altman *Prod* Robert Evans *Scr* Jules Feiffer *Ph* Giuseppe Rotunno *Ed* Tony Lombardo *Mus* Harry Nilsson *Art Dir* Wolf Kroeger
● Robin Williams, Shelley Duvall, Ray Walston, Paul L. Smith, Paul Dooley (Paramount/Walt Disney)

It is more than faint praise to say that *Popeye* is far, far better than it might have been, considering the treacherous challenge it presented. But avoiding disaster is not necessarily the same as success.

To the eye, Robin Williams is terrifically transposed into the squinting sailor with the bulging arms. But to the ear, his mutterings are not always comprehensible.

Popeye comes to the quaint village of Sweethaven in search of a father who abandoned him and this is his underlying motivation as he first meets Olive Oyl and acquires his own abandoned baby, Swee'pea.

That's just too much for a cartoon to carry, even with some generally good songs and a wacky, colorfully created town. Shelley Duvall makes a delightful Olive Oyl and Paul L. Smith a perfectly jealous Bluto.

....

■ POPI

1969, 115 MINS, US ◇ ▽

Dir Arthur Hiller *Prod* David B. Leonard *Scr* Tina Pine, Lester Pine *Ph* Andrew Laszlo *Ed* Anthony Ciccolini *Mus* Dominic Frontiere *Art Dir* Robert Gundlach
● Alan Arkin, Rita Moreno, Miguel Alejandro, Ruben Figueroa, John Harkins (United Artists)

Alan Arkin is cast as a Puerto Rican father, living in Spanish Harlem, whose fantastic plan to improve the lot of his two small sons backfires.

Arkin is given too much free rein for his very personal style, and is sometimes guilty of working a scene, meant to be poignant or even dramatic, for a laugh, which he usually gets. The undecided mood of the film works against it for any lasting impression on the viewer.

The character played by Arkin is the little man vs the big odds and he does what he can with it but the story is too much for him.

Script is riddled with illogical loopholes, some of which, hopefully, will only be apparent to those familiar with the Spanish Harlem scene.

Moreno is dropped midway through the film, but makes a good impression while she's on scene. If any viewer believes that Arkin would turn down such a doll, they'll believe the rest of the story.

....

■ PORGY AND BESS

1959, 136 MINS, US ◇

Dir Otto Preminger *Prod* Samuel Goldwyn *Scr* N. Richard Nash *Ph* Leon Shamroy *Ed* Daniel Mandell *Mus* George Gershwin *Art Dir* Oliver Smith
● Sidney Poitier, Dorothy Dandridge, Sammy Davis Jr, Pearl Bailey, Brock Peters, Diahann Carroll (Columbia)

As screen entertainment, *Porgy and Bess* retains most of the virtues and some of the libretto traits of the folk opera.

A novel [by DuBose and Dorothy Heyward] first in 1925 it became a play in 1927, running 217 performances for the Theatre Guild. The opera version of 1935, also for the Guild, eked out only 124 performances. It was not until the revival, after composer George Gershwin's death, that *Porgy and Bess* came into its own. The melodrama of a 1905 Charleston waterfront slum, which might otherwise have been forgotten, was elevated into a world favorite.

Porgy is a cripple and a beggar, who gets about drawn in a goat cart. Sidney Poitier makes him thoroughly believable though when he opens his voice to sing it is Robert McPherrin. Bess, the incompletely regenerate floozie, is Dorothy Dandridge, but the voice is Adele Addison. (Neither voice gets screen credit).

The love affair of this oddly-assorted pair has considerable humanity though Dandridge is perhaps too 'refined' to be quite convincing as the split-skirt, heroin-sniffing tramp.

Otto Preminger manipulates the characters in the Catfish Row to develop as much tension and pathos as the screenplay (fairly close to the original text) allows.

Many of the old slum life details of the stage production have been faded down. The racial stereotype dangers have been sterilized.

The handling of the music by conductor Andre Previn, including a three-minute over-ture before the story opens, is professional. Some liberties with the arrangements, in the de-operatizing direction, may irritate loyal followers of Gershwin who notice such matters.

....

■ PORKY'S

1981, 94 MINS, CANADA ◇

Dir Bob Clark *Prod* Don Carmody, Bob Clark *Scr* Bob Clark *Ph* Reginald H. Morris *Ed* Stan Cole *Mus* Carl Zittrer *Art Dir* Reuben Freed
● Dan Monahan, Mark Herrier, Wyatt Knight, Roger Wilson, Cyril O'Reilly, Tony Ganlos (Simon/Astral-Bellevue)

If, by chance, *Porky's* should prove to be Melvin Simon's swan song in the film industry, it will either be perceived as a thunderously rude exit or a titanic raspberry uttered to audiences everywhere.

Virtually every scene and dialog exchange constitutes a new definition of lewdness. Locker room humor reaches new heights (depths) here. Film cannot be faulted for lack of a driving force – simply, all these young Florida boys are itching to score and most of their time is spent in pursuit of said goal.

Title refers to a redneck establishment out in the Everglades known for its available women. After being embarrassingly turned away on their first visit, the boys return to wreak havoc on the joint, proving once and for all that violence will result when the sex drive is repressed.

....

■ PORKY'S II THE NEXT DAY

1983, 95 MINS, US ◇ ▽

Dir Bob Clark *Prod* Don Camody, Bob Clark *Scr* Roger E. Swaybill, Alan Ormsby, Bob Clark *Ph* Reginald H. Morris *Ed* Stan Cole *Mus* Carl Zittrer *Art Dir* Fred Price
● Dan Monahan, Wyatt Knight, Mark Herrier, Roger Wilson, Cyril O'Reilly, Tony Ganios (Simon-Reeves-Landsburg/Astral Bellevue Pathe)

Plot follows in the grand tradition of many early rock 'n' roll quickies, in which self-righteous upholders of comic morality attempted to stomp out the threat posed by the new primitive music. Replacing Chuck Mitchell's Porky as the heavy here is Bill Wiley's bigoted Rev. Bubba Flavel, who makes a crusade out of shutting down the school's Shakespeare festival due to the lewdness he finds strewn throughout the Bard's work.

Enlisted in his cause is the ample girls' gym teacher Miss Balbricker and the local contingent of the Ku Klux Klan, who are each the victims of two of the film's three 'big scenes'. Everyone who saw it remembers 'that scene' from the original. Here, some of the boys get back at Balbricker by sending a snake up into her toilet.

Director Bob Clark has not allowed success lead him astray into the dreaded realm of good taste.

....

■ PORTNOY'S COMPLAINT

1972, 101 MINS, US ◇ ▽

Dir Ernest Lehman *Prod* Ernest Lehman, Sidney Beckerman *Scr* Ernest Lehman *Ph* Philip Lathrop *Ed* Sam O'Steen, Gordon Scott *Mus* Michel Legrand *Art Dir* Robert F. Boyle
● Richard Benjamin, Karen Black, Lee Grant, Jack Somack, Jeannie Berlin, Jill Clayburgh (Warner)

The film version of *Portnoy's Complaint* is *not* trashy, tawdry, cheap, offensively vulgar, and pruriently titillating. Instead, it is a most effective, honest in context, necessarily strong and appropriately bawdy study in ruinous self-indulgence.

Besides adapting the Philip Roth novel into a lucid, balanced and moral screenplay, and

■ PORTRAIT OF JENNIE

1948, 86 MINS, US ◇ ⑦

Dir William Dieterle   *Prod* David O. Selznick   *Scr* Paul Osborn, Peter Berneis   *Ph* Joseph August   *Ed* William Morgan, Gerald Wilson   *Mus* Dimitri Tiomkin   *Prod Des* J. McMillan Johnson

● Joseph Cotten, Jennifer Jones, Ethel Barrymore, David Wayne, Lillian Gish (RKO/Selznick)

Portrait of Jennie is an unusual screen romance. The story of an ethereal romance between two generations is told with style, taste and dignity.

William Dieterle has given the story sensitive direction and his guidance contributes considerably toward the top performances from the meticulously cast players.

The script, by Paul Osborn and Peter Berneis, taken from Robert Nathan's novel, deals simply with an artist living in New York in the 1930s. His work lacks depth and it is only when he meets a strange child in the park one day that inspiration to paint people comes. The elfish quality of the child stimulates a sketch. It is appreciated by art dealers and he builds the child's physical being in his mind until the next time she appears he sees her as a girl just entering her teens. Her growth moves into college years and then as a graduate while he, meantime, is discovering she is a person who has been dead for years.

Jennifer Jones' performance is standout. Her miming ability gives a quality to the four ages she portrays – from a small girl through the flowering woman. Ingenuity in makeup also figures importantly in sharpening the portrayal.

Joseph Cotten endows the artist with a top performance, matching the compelling portrayal by Jones.

■ POSEIDON ADVENTURE, THE

1972, 117 MINS, US ⑦

Dir Ronald Neame   *Prod* Irwin Allen   *Scr* Stirling Silliphant, Wendell Mayes   *Ph* Harold E. Stine   *Ed* Harold F. Kress   *Mus* John Williams   *Art Dir* William Creber

● Gene Hackman, Ernest Borgnine, Red Buttons, Carol Lynley, Roddy McDowall, Stella Stevens (20th Century Fox)

The Poseidon Adventure is a highly imaginative and lustily-produced meller that socks over the dramatic struggle of 10 passengers to save themselves after an ocean liner capsizes when struck by a mammoth tidal wave created by a submarine earthquake.

It is a case of everything being upside down; in this reversed world of twisted ruin the principals' goal is the vessel's bottom where to break through may be some hope of survival.

The adaptation of the Paul Gallico novel plays up the tragic situation with a set of values which permits powerful action and building tension.

Chief protagonist is played by Gene Hackman, as a free-talking minister who keeps his cool and assumes leadership of the small group.

■ POSSE

1975, 92 MINS, US ◇

Dir Kirk Douglas   *Prod* Kirk Douglas   *Scr* William Roberts, Christopher Knopf   *Ph* Fred J. Koenekamp   *Ed* John W. Wheeler   *Mus* Maurice Jarre   *Art Dir* Lyle Wheeler

● Kirk Douglas, Bruce Dern, Bo Hopkins, James Stacy, Luke Askew, David Canary (Paramount/Bryna)

Posse is a good western, with Kirk Douglas as a cynical US marshal who eventually stumbles on his own political ambitions while tracking thief Bruce Dern under a strident law-and-order platform.

Story is a sort of conuluted *High Noon*, in which self-assured Douglas, complete with his own gang of deputies, manipulates a cowardly town which in the end turns its back on him. Dern, very effective as an escaped robber, ultimately capitalizes on Douglas' disloyalty to his men and escapes anew with a fully-trained crew which easily adapts to lawlessness.

Bo Hopkins, Luke Askew, Bill Burton, Louie Elias and Gus Greymountain are good as Douglas' assistants whom he plans to dump after becoming a US Senator from Texas.

■ POSSESSED

1947, 108 MINS, US

Dir Curtis Bernhardt   *Prod* Jerry Wald   *Scr* Silvia Richards, Ranald MacDougall   *Ph* Joseph Valentine   *Ed* Rudi Fehr   *Mus* Franz Waxman   *Art Dir* Anton Grot

● Joan Crawford, Van Heflin, Raymond Massey, Geraldine Brooks (Warner)

Joan Crawford cops all thesping honors in this production with a virtuoso performance as a frustrated woman ridden into madness by a guilt-obsessed mind. Actress has a self-assurance that permits her to completely dominate the screen even vis-a-vis such accomplished players as Van Heflin and Raymond Massey.

Heflin's part of a footloose engineer who romances his ladies with one eye on the railroad schedule is now drawn with equal sharpness. By sheer power of personal wit, however, Heflin infuses his role with charm and degree of credibility despite a lack of clear motivation for his behavior.

Unfolding via flashback technique, film opens with a terrific bang as the camera picks up Crawford wandering haggard and dazed through Los Angeles until she collapses. In the psychiatric ward of the local hospital, under narco-hypnosis, she relives the series of personal blows that ultimately reduced her to schizophrenia.

Despite its overall superiority, *Possessed* is somewhat marred by an ambiguous approach in Curtis Bernhardt's direction. Film vacillates between being a cold clinical analysis of a mental crackup and a highly surcharged melodramatic vehicle for Crawford's histrionics.

■ POSSESSION

1981, 127 MINS, FRANCE/W. GERMANY ◇

Dir Andrzej Zulawski   *Scr* Andrzej Zulawski, Frederic Tuten   *Ph* Bruno Nuytten   *Mus* Andrzej Korzynski

● Isabelle Adjani, Sam Neill, Heinz Bennent, Margit Carstensen, Michael Hogben (Oliane/Soma/Marianne)

Possession starts on a hysterical note, stays there and surpasses it as the film progresses. There are excesses on all fronts: in supposedly ordinary married life and then occult happenings, intricate political skulduggery with the infamous Berlin Wall as background – they all abound in this horror-cum-political-cum – psychological tale.

Sam Neill, New Zealand actor, returns home after a long absence. He has been on some sort of secret mission. After an ambiguous report to a commission he goes home to find his wife (Isabelle Adjani) acting strangely.

Neill hires a detective who tracks Adjani to an old house and a strange apartment. The detective gains entry and sees some sort of monster before Adjani slashes his throat with a broken bottle. Another sleuth gets the same treatment, and a bizarre mass of entrails encompass the men after they are killed.

Adjani is game as she plays the deranged, obsessed woman in high gear throughout. Pic's mass of symbols and unbridled, brilliant directing meld this disparate tale into a film that could get cult following on its many levels of symbolism and exploitation.

■ POSSESSION OF JOEL DELANEY, THE

1972, 105 MINS, UK ◇ ⑦

Dir Waris Hussein   *Scr* Matt Robinson, Grimes Grice   *Ph* Arthur Ornitz   *Ed* John Victor Smith   *Mus* Joe Raposo   *Art Dir* Peter Murton

● Shirley MacLaine, Michael Hordern, Edmundo Rivera Alvarez, Robert Burr, Miriam Colon, David Elliott (ITC)

The Possession of Joel Delaney is an unusual occult thriller [based on Ramona Stewart's novel]. Pic centers on a chic East Side society divorcee (Shirley MacLaine) who harbors an inordinate affection for her brother, Joel (Perry King), and attempts to save him when he is possessed by the spirit of a Puerto Rican friend fond of ritual beheadings.

Script eschews any serious attempt to explain the subject matter in conventional psychiatric terms, coming down on the side of ethnically-originated spiritualism. You believe it or you don't, ditto the rather murky sociological overtones that seem needlessly overemphasized.

Script overextends the build-up, making the final quarter a bit anti-climactic and slowing the pace, but the presence of MacLaine smooths over the rough spots.

■ POSTCARDS FROM THE EDGE

1990, 101 MINS, US ◇ ⑦

Dir Mike Nichols   *Prod* Mike Nichols, John Calley   *Scr* Carrie Fisher   *Ph* Michael Ballhaus   *Ed* Sam O'Steen   *Mus* Howard Shore (sup.), Carly Simon   *Art Dir* Patrizia Von Brandenstein

● Meryl Streep, Shirley MacLaine, Dennis Quaid, Gene Hackman, Richard Dreyfuss, Rob Reiner (Columbia)

Mike Nichols' film of Carrie Fisher's novel *Postcards from the Edge* packs a fair amount of emotional wallop in its dark-hued comic take on a chemically dependent Hollywood mother and daughter (Shirley MacLaine and Meryl Streep).

Streep's tour through Hollywood hell is signposted with many recognizable, on-target types: predatory macho creep (Dennis Quaid), sleazy business manager (Gary Morton), oafish producer (Rob Reiner), airheaded and roundheaded actress (Annette Bening) and sternly paternalistic director (Gene Hackman).

Refreshingly guileless in a role requiring casual clothing and no accent, Streep plays an overgrown child who's spent her life in her mother's shadow and has resorted to drugs to blunt her pain and boredom.

While casting of MacLaine in the role of an arch, ditzy, impossible stage mother is somewhat predictable, the actress gradually makes it her own until, stripped of her glamour in the climactic scene, she abandons the rampant egotism of the character to reveal the frightened creature underneath.

(Nichols insists, for the record, that the character isn't based on Fisher's mom, Debbie Reynolds, even though MacLaine's wick-

---

Introductory column (left, top)

producing handsomely on various locations, Ernest Lehman makes an excellent directorial debut. Richard Benjamin heads an outstanding cast.

Alexander Portnoy's hangup derives from heterosexual masturbation fantasies, and the first 44 minutes constitute the slap-happy, kinky exposition of his development. But what the story then pulls an audience into is the inevitable consequence.

P

edly salacious memories of life at Louis B. Mayer's M-G-M might suggest otherwise.)

● ●

■ POSTMAN ALWAYS RINGS TWICE, THE

1946, 110 MINS, US ⊙

Dir Tay Garnett   *Prod* Carey Wilson   *Scr* Harry Ruskin, Niven Busch   *Ph* Sidney Wagner   *Ed* George White   *Mus* George Bassman   *Art Dir* Cedric Gibbons, Randall Duell
● Lana Turner, John Garfield, Cecil Kellaway, Hume Cronyn, Audrey Totter (M-G-M)

The Postman Always Rings Twice is a controversial picture. The approach to lust and murder is as adult and matter-of-fact as that used by James M. Cain in his book from which the film was adapted.

It was box-office wisdom to cast Lana Turner as the sexy, blonde murderess, and John Garfield as the foot-loose vagabond whose lust for the girl made him stop at nothing. Each give to the assignments the best of their talents. Development of the characters makes Tay Garnett's direction seem slowly paced during first part of the picture, but this establishment was necessary to give the speed and punch to the uncompromising evil that transpires.

As in Cain's book, there will be little audience sympathy for the characters, although plotting will arouse moments of pity for the little people too weak to fight against passion and the evil circumstances it brings. The script is a rather faithful translation of Cain's story of a boy and girl who murder the girl's husband, live through terror and eventually make payment for their crime. The writing is terse and natural to the characters and events that transpire.

Cecil Kellaway, the husband, is a bit flamboyant at times in interpreting the character. Hume Cronyn is particularly effective as the attorney who defends the couple for murder.

● ●

■ POSTMAN ALWAYS RINGS TWICE, THE

1981, 123 MINS, US ◇

Dir Bob Rafelson   *Prod* Charles Mulvehill, Bob Rafelson   *Scr* David Mamet   *Ph* Sven Nykvist   *Ed* Graeme Clifford   *Mus* Michael Small   *Art Dir* George Jenkins
● Jack Nicholson, Jessica Lange, John Colico, Anjelica Huston (Paramount)

James M. Cain's 1934 novel attracted notoriety for its adulterous murder story, spiced with some fairly daring sequences for its day.

Because of the Hays Office, Hollywood couldn't touch the property until 1946, when MGM released a sanitized version with Lana Turner and John Garfield – and even that was greeted by some shock. For this remake, Bob Rafelson said he would shoot as an X but cut to an R.

But the final cut is limited to some fairly heavy groping, explicit shots of Jack Nicholson massaging the front of Jessica Lange's panties and a view of his head between her legs, suggesting more than is ever witnessed.

Stripped of its excess, Cain's yarn is essentially a morality tale of a Depression drifter who comes to work for a beautiful young woman and her older Greek husband. Falling madly in lust, they murder the old man, escape justice and then get their desserts in an ironical twist at the end.

In the key roles, Nicholson and Lange are excellent, as is Michael Lerner as their defense attorney.

In Cain's novel, once the couple escape punishment in court, she dies in an auto accident and he is wrongly executed for her murder, thus providing the justice. Rafelson throws this away for an ending that's not so neat.

● ●

■ POT CARRIERS, THE

1962, 84 MINS, UK

Dir Peter Graham Scott   *Prod* Gordon L.T. Scott   *Scr* T.J. Morrison, Mike Watts   *Ph* Erwin Hillier   *Ed* Richard Best   *Mus* Stanley Black   *Art Dir* Robert Jones
● Ronald Fraser, Paul Massie, Carol Lesley, Dennis Price, Davy Kaye, Alfred Burke (Associated British)

This lively slice of life in jail is a moderately unpretentious job but it shrewdly captures the atmosphere of the locale, neatly blends comedy and drama and offers some sharp thesping. Screenplay has been adapted by T. J. Morrison and Mike Watts from the latter's play. Pic title is used to spotlight one of the supreme indignities of prison.

Paul Massie plays a first offender sentenced to a year's jail for grievous bodily harm, after slugging another man in a jealous tiff with his girl friend. Assigned to the Kitchen Gang, he quickly settles down to the routine and joins in the 'fiddling' which is highly organized among the prisoners, which mainly consists of stealing chow from the kitchens and swapping it for luxuries which another member of the gang lifts from the officers' mess.

In a large, mainly male cast, there are some notable bits of thesping, biggest impact being made by Ronald Fraser as the 'trusty' who is the kingpin among the fiddlers. Paul Massie is a likeable, straightforward hero.

● ●

■ POWER, THE

1968, 108 MINS, US ◇

Dir Bryon Haskin   *Prod* George Pal   *Scr* John Gay   *Ph* Ellsworth Fredricks   *Ed* Thomas J. McCarthy   *Mus* Miklos Rozsa   *Art Dir* George W. Davis, Merrill Pye
● George Hamilton, Suzanne Pleshette, Richard Carlson, Yvonne De Carlo, Earl Holliman, Arthur O'Connell (M-G-M)

Somewhere along the way something misfired. What started out as an ingenious, imaginative sci-fi premise developed into a confusing maze of cloudy characters, motivations and events in its development.

George Pal production carries plenty of suspense as audience hopefully awaits a logical conclusion, but in final wrapup the spectator is left wondering what it's all about.

Screenplay, based on the Frank M. Robinson novel, is set among a group of scientists engaged in human endurance research. It is discovered that one among them has a super-intelligence, possibly a mind of the next evolution, so strong it controls the others' minds. As murder starts, George Hamilton, one of the scientists, undertakes to learn the identity of The Power, while himself a suspect by the police.

Byron Haskin's direction is limited by script but he manages tension as yarn builds to its finale. Hamilton is okay in his role and Suzanne Pleshette, in part of his geneticist girl-friend, is easy on the eye. Balance of cast are as good as roles will allow.

● ●

■ POWER

1986, 111 MINS, US ◇ Ⓥ

Dir Sidney Lumet   *Prod* Reene Schisgal, Mark Tarlov   *Scr* David Himmelstein   *Ph* Andrzej Bartkowiak   *Ed* Andrew Mondshein   *Mus* Cy Coleman   *Art Dir* Peter Larkin
● Richard Gere, Julie Christie, Gene Hackman, Kate Capshaw, Denzel Washington, E.G. Marshall (Lorimar/Polar)

Not so much about power as about p.r., this facile treatment of big-time politics and media, featuring Richard Gere as an amoral imagemaker, revolves around the unstartling premise that modern politicians and their campaigns are calculatedly packaged for TV. In spite of relentless jet-propelled location

hopping that helps to stave off boredom, *Power* never gets airborne.

Pete St John (Gere) is a peripatetic public relations wiz whose services practically guarantee political success. His ex-wife (Julie Christie) and alcoholic former mentor Wilfred Buckley (Gene Hackman) both remember Pete when the kid had ideals. He's dumped them both but they still care for him. All that remains to be seen is if Pete will find some sort of redemption.

● ●

■ POWER AND THE GLORY, THE

1933, 73 MINS, US

Dir William K. Howard   *Prod* Jesse L. Lasky   *Scr* Preston Sturges   *Ph* James Wong Howe   *Mus* Louis De Francesco (dir.)   *Art Dir* Max Parker
● Spencer Tracy, Colleen Moore, Ralph Morgan, Helen Vinson, Clifford Jones, Henry Kolker (Fox)

Jesse L. Lasky's production for Fox, is unique through its 'narratage' style of cinematurgy. Its treatment has been consummately developed by director William K. Howard and scenarist Preston Sturges. The four principal characters are performed by Spencer Tracy, who has never done better; Colleen Moore, whose come-back is distinguished; Ralph Morgan, ever-effective; and Helen Vinson, at her best.

Film starts with its ending – the ecclesiastic services for the dead. Showing the finale of the life span of your central character is something that is by no means easy to offset. And that's where the 'narratage' comes in. Morgan is the narrator, detailing the highlights in the career of his friend (Tracy) who, even in death, is much maligned.

Morgan undertakes to show that Tracy, who fought his way up from an ignorant, unschooled trackwalker to the presidency of railroads, and a tycoon of industry, was not the bad egg everybody painted. He argues that his strike-breaking methods, which cost many railroad workers' lives, had another element to it; that his turning out his first wife (Moore) in favor of Vinson might have had extenuating circumstances, etc.

It's well done in every respect. Casting right down the line is punchy for performance. Howard's direction is truly unique and distinguished. His favorite camera-man. James Wong Howe, manifests indubitable artistry.

● ●

■ PREDATOR

1987, 107 MINS, US ◇ Ⓥ

Dir John McTiernan   *Prod* Lawrence Gordon, Joel Silver, John Davis   *Scr* Jim Thomas, John Thoma   *Ph* Donald McAlpine   *Ed* John F. Link, Mark Helfrich   *Mus* Alan Silvestri   *Art Dir* John Vallone
● Arnold Schwarzenegger, Carl Weathers, Elpidia Carrillo, Bill Duke, Jesse Ventura, Sonny Landham (20th Century-Fox/Amercent/American Entertainment)

Predator is a slightly above-average actioner that tries to compensate for tissue-thin-plot with ever-more-grisly death sequences and impressive special effects.

Arnold Schwarzenegger plays Dutch, the leader of a vaguely defined military rescue team that works for allied governments. Called into a US hot spot somewhere in South America, he encounters old buddy Dillon (Carl Weathers), who now works for the CIA.

The unit starts to get decimated in increasingly garish fashion by an otherworldly Predator. Enemy is a nasty, formidable foe with laser powers.

Schwarzenegger, while undeniably appealing, still has a character who's not quite real. While the painted face, cigar, vertical hair and horizontal eyes are all there, none of the humanity gets on the screen, partly because of the sparse dialog.

Weathers can't breathe any life into the cardboard character of Dillon, who goes from being unbelievably cynical to unbelievably heroic in about five minutes.

Director John McTiernan relies a bit too much on special effects 'thermal vision' photography, in looking through the Predator's eyes, while trying to build tension before the blood starts to fly.

- -

■ PREDATOR 2

1990, 108 MINS, US ◇ ⓥ

Dir Stephen Hopkins   *Prod* Lawrence Gordon, Joel Silver, John Davis   *Scr* Jim Thomas, John Thomas   *Ph* Peter Levy   *Ed* Mark Goldblatt   *Mus* Alan Silvestri   *Art Dir* Lawrence G. Paull
● Danny Glover, Gary Busey, Ruben Blades, Maria Conchita Alonso, Bill Paxton, Kevin Peter Hall (20th Century-Fox)

While the film doesn't achieve the same thrills of the final 45 minutes of *Predator* in terms of overall excitement, it outdoes its first safari in start-to-finish hysteria. The real star is the pic's design. Writers don't waste much time on character development.

The setting is Los Angeles, 1997, where outgunned cops face hordes of Jamaican, Colombian and other assorted drug dealers who rule the streets. It's a balmy 109 degrees in the globally warmed basin, where Danny Glover heads a dedicated, ethnically mixed group of cops who are more than a little confused as the drug dealers start turning up dead in droves. The plot thickens when a fed (Gary Busey) comes in to take charge of the investigation.

Centerpiece is, again, a massive alien gifted with the strange weaponry and camouflage abilities like his kinsman that, it's told, had visited the planet 10 years earlier.

The pace of the film is absolutely frenetic. An awe-inspiring set in the closing sequence recalls the climactic moment in *Aliens*.

- -

■ PRESENTING LILY MARS

1943, 106 MINS, US ⓥ

Dir Norman Taurog   *Prod* Joseph Pasternak   *Scr* Richard Connell, Gladys Lehman   *Ph* Joseph Ruttenberg   *Ed* Albert Akst   *Mus* George Stoll (dir.)
● Judy Garland, Van Heflin, Fay Bainter, Marta Eggerth, Richard Carlson (M-G-M)

Presenting Lily Mars spotlights Judy Garland and Van Heflin in a stage Cinderella yarn that supplies minor switches to regulation formula, but mainly depends on performances, direction and musical mounting, to carry it through.

Story is a typical Cinderella tale, with Garland an aspiring and stagestruck youngster who attempts to catch attention of producer Van Heflin in a small Indiana town. She makes a pest of herself for 40 minutes of the running time until she follows him into New York, gets a job in his new show, and eventually falls in love with the producer.

Heflin adequately handles the asignment of the young producer who eventually falls in love with Garland. Latter delivers in her usual effective style as the aspiring actress, putting across her numbers in top fashion.

Bob Crosby band is on for one tune in a nightspot where Garland heads for the mike to sing a song, while Tommy Dorsey and his ork appears for the finale accompaniment to song and dance by Miss Garland.

- -

■ PRESIDENT'S ANALYST, THE

1967, 103 MINS, US ◇ ⓥ

Dir Theodore J. Flicker   *Prod* Stanley Rubin   *Scr* Theodore J. Flicker   *Ph* William A. Fraker   *Ed* Stuart Pappe   *Mus* Lalo Schifrin   *Art Dir* Pato Guzman

● James Coburn, Godfrey Cambridge, Severn Darden, Joan Delaney, Pat Harrington, Barry Maguire (Paramount/Panpiper)

The President's Analyst is a superior satire on some sacred cows, principally the lightly camouflaged FBI, hippies, psychiatry, liberal and conservative politics – and the telephone company.

Inventive story peg – James Coburn starring as the personal analyst to the President of the US – is fleshed out with hilarious incidents which zero in on, and hit, their targets.

William Daniels scores as an upper-middle class compulsive liberal, whose family practices marksmanship, karate and eaves-dropping because of right-wing neighbours.

Barry Maguire and Jill Banner are hippies, and Banner's sex scene with Coburn – in fields of flowers right out of some cosmetics teleblurb – is a comedy highlight in which several foreign and domestic spies kill each other off as they plot Coburn's demise.

- -

■ PRESIDENT'S LADY, THE

1953, 96 MINS, US ⓥ

Dir Henry Levin   *Prod* Sol C. Siegel   *Scr* John Patrick   *Ph* Leo Tover   *Ed* William B. Murphy   *Mus* Alfred Newman   *Art Dir* Lyle R. Wheeler, Leland Fuller
● Susan Hayward, Charlton Heston, John McIntire, Fay Bainter, Ralph Dumke (20th Century-Fox)

The dramatic story of a lady's influence on the life of a great man invariably makes for interesting filming, and in the case of Andrew Jackson, the seventh president of the United States, 20th-Fox has created a particularly moving narrative. Based on Irving Stone's bestselling novel, *Lady* covers more than 40 years in the life of the famed Indian fighter and general.

It covers the period when the young Tennessee lawyer is Attorney General, through his battles with the Indians – and, more importantly, through the period of courting and marriage with Rachel Donelson Robards. It is the story of Jackson being forced to fight his way up the political ladder with the stigma of adultery plaguing him along the way.

Through it all, Charlton Heston supplies the kind of ammunition to this film that is as loaded as any carbine slung across his broad shoulders. It is a forthright steely-eyed portrayal. Susan Hayward gives the pic a simple, sustained performance in addition to physical beauty. John McIntire plays Jackson's longtime friend and law partner, and he gives the role neat shading in a distinctly lesser role.

- -

■ PRESIDIO, THE

1988, 97 MINS, US ◇ ⓥ

Dir Peter Hyams   *Prod* D. Constantine Conte   *Scr* Larry Ferguson   *Ph* Peter Hyams   *Ed* James Mitchell   *Mus* Bruce Boughton   *Art Dir* Albert Brenner
● Sean Connery, Mark Harmon, Meg Ryan, Jack Warden, Mark Blum (Paramount)

Sean Connery and Mark Harmon go head to head as an Army provost marshal and a San Francisco cop who clash jurisdictions and styles in the investigation of an MP's murder.

Naturally, there's a backstory – they'd locked horns earlier when Connery was Harmon's c.o. in the military – and a complication – Harmon gets involved with Connery's frisky and equally willful daughter (Meg Ryan).

Tug-of-war for dominance among the trio provides the interest in an otherwise ordinary crime story, as Harmon and Connery end up working to piece together clues in a convoluted smuggling caper.

Along the way there are three very splashy action sequences – a car chase through the army base and the streets of S.F., a footrace through crowded Chinatown and the final, treacherous shootout in a water bottling

plant that becomes as hairy as the swamps of 'Nam.

- -

■ PRESUMED INNOCENT

1990, 127 MINS, US ⓥ

Dir Alan J. Pakula   *Prod* Sydney Pollack, Mark Rosenberg   *Scr* Frank Pierson, Alan J. Pakula   *Ph* Gordon Willis   *Ed* Evan Lottman   *Mus* John Williams   *Art Dir* George Jenkins
● Harrison Ford, Brian Dennehy, Raul Julia, Bonnie Bedelia, Paul Winfield, Greta Scacchi (Mirage/Warner)

Honed to a riveting intensity by director Alan Pakula and featuring the tightest script imaginable, *Presumed Innocent* is a demanding, disturbing javelin of a courtroom murder mystery.

Hewing closely to Scott Turow's bestselling 1987 novel, the harrowing tale unfolds with nary a wasted step, as deputy prosecutor and family man Rusty Sabich (Harrison Ford) arrives at work to learn his beautiful colleague Carolyn Polhemus (Greta Scacchi) has been brutally murdered. Forced to lead the investigation by his longtime boss Raymond Horgan (Brian Dennehy), who's in a deep sweat over his re-election campaign, Sabich can scarcely admit he'd had an affair with the dead attorney. But his pained, steely cool wife (Bonnie Bedelia) knows, and she's none too sympathetic or forgiving about it.

Sabich is then confronted by rat-like ex-colleague Tommy Molto (Joe Grifasi), who's part of an opposing campaign for the chief prosecutor's office. Molto swears Sabich was at Carolyn's apartment the night of the murder. Before long Sabich is embroiled in a grand jury investigation that spurs his politically frightened boss to turn on him. With a sly, magnetic Raul Julia brought in as Sabich's crafty defense lawyer, one never knows, until pic's astonishing denouement, whether Sabich did the deed or not.

Ford, in a very mature, subtle, lowkey performance, pulls off the difficult feat of making it impossible to be sure. Bedelia is wondrously controlled, and Scacchi, sans any hint of a European accent, is convincing and seductive.

- -

■ PRETTY BABY

1978, 109 MINS, US ◇ ⓥ

Dir Louis Malle   *Prod* Louis Malle   *Scr* Polly Platt   *Ph* Sven Nykvist   *Ed* Suzanne Baron, Suzanne Fenn   *Mus* Jerry Wexler   *Art Dir* Trevor Williams
● Keith Carradine, Susan Sarandon, Brooke Shields, Frances Faye, Antonio Fargas, Gerrit Graham (Paramount)

The Louis Malle-Polly Platt collaboration on *Pretty Baby* has yielded an offbeat depiction of life in New Orleans' Storyville red-light district circa 1917, as experienced by a lifelong resident – a 12-year-old girl. The film is handsome, the players nearly all effective, but the story highlights are confined within a narrow range of ho-hum dramatization.

The time of the plot is just before Josephis Davids, Secretary of the US Navy, closed Storyville as a bad influence; the black musicians who found employment in the brothels there drifted north to Kansas City, Memphis and Chicago, later east to NY, and thereby changed forever the direction and the fabric of American popular music. But that potentially strong film plot is not what's here.

Instead, Malle and Platt [using material in *Storyville* by Al Rose] have created a placid milieu in the barrelhouse owned by Frances Faye. There, Susan Sarandon is one of the girls who, in residence, has given birth to a child, in this case Brooke Shields, who gives either an extraordinarily subtle or else a totally perplexed performance as a pre-teenager whose entire world is that of the brothel.

Keith Carradine is cast as a catatonic photographer who only likes to shoot portraits of the girls. Eventually Shields and Carradine live together, but the relationship ends when Sarandon, who left to marry a customer, returns in respectability to claim the under-age child. That's it.

■ **PRETTY BOY FLOYD**

1960, 96 MINS, US

Dir Herbert J. Leder   *Prod* Monroe Sachson
Scr Herbert J. Leder   *Ph* Chuck Austin   *Ed* Ralph Rosenblum   *Mus* Del Sirino, William Sanford
● John Ericson, Barry Newman, Joan Harvey, Carl York, Phil Kenneally (Le-Sac)

This is a grim, almost sadistic reworking of the tale of the Oklahoma farm boy who won fame and ill-fortune in the early 1930s. It points a glib moral (crime does not pay) without ever presenting anything more than a few superficial reasons for the phenomenon that Pretty Boy Floyd represented. Script says Floyd had a bad temper and was igno-rant. Period.

John Ericson does a good job in the role and is backed by a competent group of New York actors, few of whom have been on the screen before. (Film was shot entirely at Gold Medal Studios in the Bronx.) Low budget of the pic shows through from time to time, but actually seems to help create an appropri-ately seedy and sordid atmosphere.

Script first picks up Floyd when he is mak-ing a desultory attempt to go straight as an oil-field worker. Bounced when it's revealed that he served time for armed robbery in St Louis, Floyd picks up a life of crime again with an old cellmate. He soon branches out on his own and becomes the terror of the Middle West.

The film shows numerous of Floyd's bank holdups, as well as the famous 'Kansas City Massacre', in which Floyd and two others gunned to death two FBI men and a pol-iceman who were transferring a brother hood to prison. Same incident, as well as Floyd's eventual demise at the hands of the G-Men, are in *The FBI Story*.

■ **PRETTY IN PINK**

1986, 96 MINS, US ◇ ⓥ

Dir Howard Deutch   *Prod* Lauren Shuler   *Scr* John Hughes   *Ph* Tak Fujimoto   *Ed* Richard Marks   *Mus* Michael Gore   *Art Dir* John W. Corso
● Molly Ringwald, Harry Dean Stanton, Jon Cryer, Andrew McCarthy, Annie Potts, James Spader (Paramount)

Pretty in Pink is a rather intelligent (if not ter-ribly original) look at adolescent insecurities.

Like scores of leading ladies before her, Molly Ringwald is the proverbial pretty girl from the wrong side of the tracks, called to a motherless life with down-on-his-luck dad (Harry Dean Stanton) and the misfortune to have to attend high school where the rich kids lord it over the poor.

That's enough to make any young lady insecure, even before the wealthy nice guy (Andrew McCarthy) asks her to the senior prom. Teased by his rich pals for slumming, McCarthy is also a bundle of uncertainties.

Moving predictably, none of this is unique drama. In the end, the wrong guy still gets the girl, which is a lesson youngsters might as well learn early.

■ **PRETTY MAIDS ALL IN A ROW**

1971, 95 MINS, US ◇

Dir Roger Vadim   *Prod* Gene Roddenberry   *Scr* Gene Roddenberry   *Ph* Charles Rosher   *Ed* Bill Brame   *Mus* Lalo Schifrin   *Art Dir* George W. Davis, Preston Ames
● Rock Hudson, Angie Dickinson, Telly Savalas, John David Carson, Roddy McDowall, Keenan Wynn (M-G-M)

Pretty Maids All in a Row, Roger Vadim's first US-made film, is apparently intended as a sort of genteel black murder-sex comedy. Gene Roddenberry's production careers through 95 minutes of juvenile double entendre and pratfall. Rock Hudson stars as a married high-school guidance counseller who gets to know his girl students in the aca-demic and Biblical sense, and eventually has to kill several to keep them quiet.

The unravelling of the murders (but not to an audience, which knows early what's up) parallels another story line: John David Car-son's post-acne, pre-adult shy-guy character which blossoms under the careful attention of Angie Dickinson, the constant nymph. Car-son does extremely well in the best developed characterization in the script.

Whatever substance was in the original [novel by Francis Pollini] or screen concept has been plowed under, leaving only super-ficial, one-joke results.

■ **PRETTY POISON**

1968, 89 MINS, US ◇ ⓥ

Dir Noel Black   *Prod* Marshal Backlar, Noel Black
Scr Lorenzo Semple Jr   *Ph* David Quaid   *Ed* William Ziegler   *Mus* Johnny Mandel   *Art Dir* Jack Martin Smith, Harold Michelson
● Anthony Perkins, Tuesday Weld, Beverly Garland, John Randolph, Dick O'Neill, Clarice Blackburn (20th Century-Fox)

Pretty Poison is an attempt at low-key psycho-logical terror. Anthony Perkins, a mentally unhealthy resident of his own fantasies, finds in Tuesday Weld a more than willing pupil. Awkwardly begun and tediously developed, the film [from a novel by Stephen Geller] goes too much off the track.

A prolog and a quasi-epilog sequence es-tablish Perkins as a disobedient parolee from confinement for arson-murder. Main body of the story, all shot on location in Massachu-setts, concerns his play-acting and sexual playing with Weld, restless daughter of the widowed Beverly Garland.

From an innocent-looking teenager, Weld progresses to a cold, pathological killer and betrayor, escaping justice while pitiable Per-kins, probably less deranged than she, falls victim to her superior depravity.

Perkins does a creditable job in a difficult part. So much of his earlier dialog might lead to disastrous guffaws that merely avoiding this trap must be credited to him and the director.

■ **PRETTY POLLY**

1967, 102 MINS, UK ◇

Dir Guy Green   *Prod* George W. George, Frank Granat   *Scr* Willis Hall, Keith Waterhouse   *Ph* Arthur Ibbetson   *Ed* Frank Clarke   *Mus* Michel Legrand   *Art Dir* Peter Mullins
● Hayley Mills, Trevor Howard, Shashi Kapoor, Brenda de Banzie, Dick Patterson, Kalen Lui (Universal)

Hayley Mills (as Polly) goes on vacation with a rich, disagreeable aunt to Singapore. Frum-pish, bespectacled and lumpily dressed, she timidly obeys her aunt's constant demands for attention and looks suitably badgered.

But the relation dies from taking a swim too soon after a heavy lunch, and this sparks off the transformation scene. Polly is encouraged by an Indian acting as guide and helpmate to have her hair done, exchange her glasses for contact lenses, and indulge in a riot of makeup. She emerges as a siren.

Derived from a Noel Coward short story – itself written in the vein of Somerset Maugham – the script goes all out for senti-ment, and, on its undemanding level, achieves it.

■ **PRETTY WOMAN**

1990, 117 MINS, US ◇ ⓥ

Dir Garry Marshall   *Prod* Arnon Milchan, Steven Reuther   *Scr* J.F. Lawton   *Ph* Charles Minsky   *Ed* Priscilla Nedd   *Mus* James Newton Howard   *Art Dir* Albert Brenner
● Richard Gere, Julia Roberts, Ralph Bellamy, Jason Alexander, Laura San Giacomo, Hector Elizondo (Touchstone)

J.F. Lawton's formula screenplay owes plenty to *Pygmalion*, *Cinderella* and *The Owl and the Pussycat* in limning a fairy tale of a prosti-tute with a heart of gold who mellows a stuffy businessman.

Pic's first two reels are weak, as corporate raider Richard Gere is unconvincingly thrown together with streetwalker Julia Roberts when he seeks directions to Beverly Hills. Seducing this reluctant john, she's im-probably hired by Gere to spend the week with him as escort since he's split up with his girlfriend. Her price tag is $3,000; film's cryp-tic shooting title was *3000*.

Film blossoms along with Roberts, when she doffs her unflattering Carol Channing blond wig to get natural and embark on a massively entertaining (and class conscious) shopping adventure on Rodeo Drive. Roberts handles the transition from coarse and gawky to glamorous with aplomb.

Pic's casting is astute, with Gere under-playing like a sturdy ballet star who hoists the ballerina Roberts on his shoulders. Sex-iest routine has Gere playing solo-jazz piano late at night in the hotel ballroom and joined for a tryst by Roberts. Supporting cast is outstanding.

■ **PRICK UP YOUR EARS**

1987, 108 MINS, UK ◇ ⓥ

Dir Stephen Frears   *Prod* Andrew Brown   *Scr* Alan Bennett   *Ph* Oliver Stapleton   *Ed* Mick Audsley   *Mus* Stanley Myers   *Art Dir* Hugo Luczyc-Wyhowski
● Gary Oldman, Alfred Molina, Vanessa Redgrave, Wallace Shawn, Julie Walters (Civilhand/Zenith)

Though selling itself as a biography of con-troversial young British playwright Joe Orton, who was murdered in 1967, *Prick Up Your Ears* actually says very little about Orton the author, but deals almost totally with his relationship with Kenneth Halliwell, his lover and bludgeon killer.

Orton and Halliwell met at the Royal Academy of Dramatic Art. The inarticulate Orton fell for the seemingly sophisticated Halliwell, and for a while the pic dwells on Orton's promiscuity, at a time when homo-sexuality was still illegal in the UK. Sud-denly, after years of obscurity, Orton becomes an overnight success.

The script [based on the biography by John Lahr] is witty, the direction fluid, with one of the homosexual orgy scenes in a public toilet almost balletic, and the depiction of the lov-ers' life in their flat suitably claustrophobic.

Gary Oldman is excellent as Orton, right down to remarkable resemblance, while Alfred Molina creates both an amusing and tormented Halliwell. Vanessa Redgrave takes top honors, though, as a compassionate and benign agent.

■ **PRIDE AND PREJUDICE**

1940, 117 MINS, US ⓥ

Dir Robert Z. Leonard   *Prod* Hunt Stromberg
Scr Aldous Huxley, Jane Murfin   *Ph* Karl Freund   *Ed* Robert J. Kern   *Mus* Herbert Stothart
● Greer Garson, Laurence Olivier, Mary Boland, Edna May Oliver, Edmund Gwenn, Maureen O'Sullivan (M-G-M)

Metro reaches into the remote corners of the library bookshelf for this old-time novel about English society and the vicissitudes of a

British mother faced with the task of marrying off five daughters in a limited market. *Pride and Prejudice* was written by Jane Austen in 1793. As a film it possesses little of general interest, except as a co-starring vehicle for Greer Garson and Laurence Olivier.

Any novel which survives more than a century possesses unusual qualities, and *Pride and Prejudice* qualifies chiefly because of the characterization of Elizabeth Bennet (Garson), eldest of the eligible sisters and a rather daring young woman with ideas of feminism far in advance of her contemporaries. In the screenplay she is trimmed to fit into a yarn about a family, rather than about an unusual and courageous girl. In consequence, the film is something less than satisfactory entertainment, despite lavish settings, costumes, and an acting ensemble of unique talent.

Olivier appears very unhappy in the role of Darcy, rich young bachelor, who is first spurned and then forgiven for his boorishness, conceit and bad manners.

There are some good performances. Mary Boland is a fluttering, clucking mother of a brood of young women whose aim is matrimony. Edna May Oliver, as the dominant Lady Catherine, comes on the scene late in the story and makes for some much needed merriment. Melville Cooper does a good comedy bit and the other Bennet sisters, as played by Maureen O'Sullivan, Ann Rutherford, Marsha Hunt and Heather Angel, provide charm and pulchritude.

••••••••••••••••••••••••••••••

■ PRIDE AND THE PASSION, THE

1957, 132 MINS, US ◇ ⓥ

Dir Stanley Kramer   *Prod* Stanley Kramer   *Scr* Edna Anhalt, Edward Anhalt   *Ph* Franz Planer   *Ed* Frederic Knudtson, Ellsworth Hoagland   *Mus* Georg Antheil   *Art Dir* Fernando Carrere

● Cary Grant, Frank Sinatra, Sophia Loren, Theodore Bikel (United Artists)

This is Stanley Kramer's powerful production of C.S. Forester's sweeping novel, *The Gun*, about the Spanish 'citizens' army' that went to battle against the conquering legions of the French in 1810. The picture was in preparation and production in Spain for a year and a half.

It is the story of the band of guerillas who come upon an oversized cannon that is abandoned by the retreating Spanish army. All things revolve around the huge weapon; it becomes symbolic of the spirit and courage of the Spanish patriots and their leader (Frank Sinatra).

From this point on *Passion* focuses on this unlikely army seeking to make its way to the French stronghold at Avila against incredibly tall odds. Their ally is Cary Grant, a British naval officer assigned to retrieve the gun for use against Napoleon's forces.

Sophia Loren is Sinatra's sultry and inflammable mistress with beaucoup accent on the decollete. At first hostile toward Grant, she comes to recognize his pro-Spanish motives and veers to him romantically. They make for an engaging trio.

Top credit must go to the production. The panoramic, longrange views of the marching and terribly burdened army, the painful fight to keep the gun mobile through ravine and over waterway – these are major plusses.

••••••••••••••••••••••••••••••

■ PRIDE OF THE MARINES

1945, 119 MINS, US

Dir Delmer Daves   *Prod* Jerry Wald   *Scr* Albert Maltz, Marvin Borowsky   *Ph* Peverell Marley, Robert Burks   *Ed* Owen Marks   *Mus* Franz Waxman   *Art Dir* Leo Kuter

● John Garfield, Eleanor Parker, Dane Clark, Ann Doran, John Ridgely, Rosemary De Camp (Warner)

Pride of the Marines is a two-hour celluloid

saga [from a story by Roger Butterfield] which as an entertainment film with a forceful theme, so punchy that its 'message' aspects are negligible, is a credit to all concerned.

The simple story of Al Schmid, real-life marine-hero of Guadalcanal, is the story of American patriotism and heroism which is unheroic in its simple forthrightness; American pride in defending our way of life; American guts; and also a distorted sense of foolish pride, born of stubbornness, when the blinded Al Schmid rebels at returning to his loved ones because he 'wants nobody to be a seeing-eye dog for me'.

As unfolded it's a heart-tugging, sentimentally heroic tale. John Garfield as the brittle Al Schmid, ex-machinist now Marine-hero, albeit blinded, gives a vividly histrionic performance. He is buoyed plenty by Dane Clark and Anthony Caruso, with Eleanor Parker as the No 1 femme.

••••••••••••••••••••••••••••••

■ PRIDE OF THE YANKEES, THE

1942, 120 MINS, US ⓥ

Dir Sam Wood   *Prod* Sam Goldwyn   *Scr* Jo Swerling, Herman J. Mankiewicz   *Ph* Rudolph Mate   *Ed* Daniel Mandell   *Mus* Leigh Harline   *Art Dir* William Cameron Menzies

● Gary Cooper, Teresa Wright, Babe Ruth, Walter Brennan, Dan Duryea, Elsa Jansen (RKO/Goldwyn)

Sam Goldwyn has produced a stirring epitaph on Lou Gehrig. For baseball and non-baseball fan alike, this sentimental, romantic saga of the NY kid who rose to the baseball heights and later met such a tragic end is well worth seeing. Clever fictionizing and underplaying of the actual sport in contrast to the more human, domestic side of the great ballplayer make the film good for all audiences.

Gary Cooper makes his Gehrig look and sound believable from the screen.

To the credit of the screenwriters, and Paul Gallico who wrote the original, no attempt is made to inject color into the characterization of Gehrig. He's depicted for what he was, a quiet, plodding personality who strived for and achieved perfection in his profession.

☐ 1942: Best Picture (Nomination)

••••••••••••••••••••••••••••••

■ PRIEST OF LOVE

1981, 125 MINS, UK ◇

Dir Christopher Miles   *Prod* Christopher Miles, Andrew Donally   *Scr* Alan Plater   *Ph* Ted Moore   *Ed* Paul Davies   *Mus* Joseph James   *Art Dir* Ted Tester, David Brockhurst

● Ian McKellen, Janet Suzman, Ava Gardner, Penelope Keith, Jorge RiveroJohn Gielgud (Milesian)

Priest of Love is an impressively mounted and acted biopic [from a book by Harry T. Moore] dealing with the later years in the life of author D.H. Lawrence. Reunited with screenwriter Alan Plater who wrote his filmization of Lawrence's *The Virgin and the Gypsy*, director Christopher Miles takes a somewhat removed and cool look at his subject.

Picture opens in 1924 with Lawrence (Ian McKellen), wife Frieda (Janet Suzman) and their friend Dorothy Brett (Penelope Keith) enroute to Taos, New Mexico, for a self-imposed exile at the home of art patroness Mabel Dodge Luhan (Ava Gardner). Back in Britain, his books have been banned by the censor Herbert Muskett (an effetiely stern cameo by John Gielgud).

Key scenes involve the fearless duo pushing relentlessly for the truth in a sexual manifesto in literature and tasteful scenes indicating his bisexuality (with a youth nude bathing at an Italian seashore) and relentless selfishness in inviting Dorothy to bed and then spurning her suddenly.

Too infrequently seen in films, McKellen gives a bravura performance, all the more re-

markable for its avoidance of easy empathy. Veteran of a one-woman show on stage as Frieda, Janet Suzman is given her head by Miles and turns in a flamboyant, explosive turn which prevents the film from being dominated by McKellen.

••••••••••••••••••••••••••••••

■ PRIME CUT

1972, 86 MINS, US ◇ ⓥ

Dir Michael Ritchie   *Prod* Joe Wizan   *Scr* Robert Dillon   *Ph* Gene Polito   *Ed* Carl Pingitore   *Mus* Lalo Schifrin   *Art Dir* Bill Malley

● Lee Marvin, Gene Hackman, Angel Tompkins, Gregory Walcott, Sissy Spacek, Janit Baldwin (Cinema Center)

Prime Cut is another contemporary underworld bloodletting, which is drawn, quartered and ground according to an overused recipe for hash. Lee Marvin and Gene Hackman provide the dressing along with the scenery of Calgary.

Writer Robert Dillon sends collection-agent Marvin to Eddie Egan, a Chi gangster who no longer is getting his cut from Hackman, a Kansas cattle king who also deals in dope and girls, among whom are Sissy Spacek and Janit Baldwin.

Director Michael Ritchie moves the pawns about inventively and with sterile precision.

There are no serious dramatic demands made of the players. Marvin and Hackman do this sort of thing all the time. Spacek and Baldwin look good in their feature debut and Gregory Walcott is most effective as a supersadist.

••••••••••••••••••••••••••••••

■ PRIME OF MISS JEAN BRODIE, THE

1969, 116 MINS, UK ◇ ⓥ

Dir Ronald Neame   *Prod* Robert Fryer   *Scr* Jay Presson Allen   *Ph* Ted Moore   *Ed* Norman Savage   *Mus* Rod McKuen   *Art Dir* John Howell

● Maggie Smith, Robert Stephens, Pamela Franklin, Gordon Jackson, Jane Carr (20th Century-Fox)

Maggie Smith's tour-de-force performance as a school-teacher slipping into spinsterhood is one of several notable achievements in this sentimental and macabre personal tragedy.

Jay Presson Allen adapted her own play [based on a novel by Muriel Spark]. The story, set in 1930s Edinburgh, treats in a tenderly savage way the decline of an age-resisting school-marm who lives too vicariously through a select group of prodigy-stooges. The telling involves elements of warm humor, biting sarcasm, pity, contempt, betrayal, and despair.

Smith's performance is a triumph. Other cast principals, all of whom project excellent performances, include Robert Stephens, the art teacher, Pamela Franklin, cast as a mysteriously-adult child and the eventual betrayor of Smith, and Gordon Jackson is impressive as the pitiable, gutless music teacher. Celia Johnson's key adversary role as the school head-mistress comes off magnificently.

••••••••••••••••••••••••••••••

■ PRINCE AND THE PAUPER, THE

1937, 115 MINS, US ⓥ

Dir William Keighley   *Prod* Robert Lord   *Scr* Laird Doyle   *Ph* Sol Polito   *Ed* Ralph Dawson   *Mus* Erich Wolfgang Korngold

● Errol Flynn, Claude Rains, Henry Stephenson, Barton MacLane, Billy Mauch, Bobby Mauch (Warner)

Of all his stories, Mark Twain loved best *The Prince and the Pauper*. Produced with sincerity and lavishness, this film [from a dramatised version by Catherine C. Cushing] is a costume picture minus any romance whatsoever.

In this film are the Mauch Twins, in addition to Errol Flynn, who is at his best in romantic, swashbuckling roles. But there is no girl opposite Flynn. So it's just the story of the Tudor Prince who exchanges places with a beggar boy, and regains his throne on Coronation Day through the heroism of a dashing soldier of fortune.

Such interest as the film contains could have been heightened by some drastic trimming in the early scenes, so that Flynn's entrance might have been moved up. He does Miles Hendon with the proper dash and spirit. The Mauch boys play their contrasting parts with earnestness if not too much skill. Claude Rains as Hertford; Montagu Love as Henry VIII, and Barton MacLane as John Canty, are fiercely melodramatic.

It doesn't seem that William Keighley, in his direction, has captured sufficient sympathy for the two youngsters to compensate for the romantic loss in having no fiancee for Flynn. The fragile plot scarcely holds together a full-length screenplay.

■ **PRINCE AND THE PAUPER, THE**

1977, 121 MINS, UK ◇ ⓥ
Dir Richard Fleischer   *Prod* Pierre Spengler
Scr George Macdonald Frazer   *Ph* Jack Cardiff
Ed Ernest Walter   *Mus* Maurice Jarre   *Art Dir* Tony Pratt
● Oliver Reed, Raquel Welch, Mark Lester, Ernest Borgnine, George C. Scott, Rex Harrison (Salkind)

Some of the irony and wit of Mark Twain's original fable about an English prince's switch with his poor lookalike has been lost or subdued, but this edition of *The Prince and the Pauper* [from an original screenplay by Berta Dominguez and Pierre Spengler, based on Twain's novel] still makes for satisfactory entertainment.

Lester as the prince trades identities with Mark Lester the pauper and is then banished from the castle and launched into an eye- and heart-opening odyssey around medieval England, finding it to be no Camelot but a land of wretched poor and persecuted.

As the pauper, meantime, he not only swoons over young Lady Jane but also breathes a refreshing humanity into the court of ruthless King Henry.

■ **PRINCE AND THE SHOWGIRL, THE**

1957, 117 MINS, US ◇ ⓥ
Dir Laurence Olivier   *Prod* Laurence Olivier
Scr Terence Rattigan   *Ph* Jack Cardiff   *Ed* Jack Harris   *Mus* Richard Addinsell   *Art Dir* Carmen Dillon
● Marilyn Monroe, Laurence Olivier, Sybil Thorndike, Richard Wattis, Jeremy Spenser, Paul Hardwick (Monroe/Warner)

This first indie production of Marilyn Monroe's company is a generally pleasant comedy, but the pace is leisurely. Filmed in London with a predominantly British cast, the film is not a cliche Cinderella story as its title might indicate.

Based on Terence Rattigan's play *The Sleeping Prince*, the story takes place in London in 1911 at the time of the coronation of King George V. Laurence Olivier and his entourage, including his son, the boy king of the Balkan country, and the queen dowager, Olivier's mother-in-law, come to London for the ceremonies. The regent's roving eye alights on Monroe and the British Foreign Office, apprehensive of the delicate balance of power in the Balkan area, makes a determined effort to give the regent what he wants.

To Olivier's credit as producer, director and performer, he achieves the utmost from his material. His own performance as the stuffy regent is flawless. The part of the seemingly naive showgirl is just right for Monroe; she shows a real sense of comedy and can command a laugh with her walk or with an expression.

Sybil Thorndike is excellent as the hard-of-hearing not-quite-there dowager; Jeremy

Spenser, who bears a remarkable resemblance to the young king, and Richard Wattis is properly harassed as the British Foreign office representative.

■ **PRINCE JACK**

1984, 100 MINS, US ◇ ⓥ
Dir Bert Lovitt   *Prod* Jim Milio   *Scr* Bert Lovitt   *Ph* Hiro Narita   *Ed* Janice Hampton   *Mus* Elmer Bernstein   *Art Dir* Michael Corenblith
● Robert Hogan, James F. Kelly, Kenneth Mars, Lloyd Nolan, Cameron Mitchell, Robert Guillaume (LMF)

Prince Jack is an ambiguous little indie mock documentary about key events and private encounters during the Kennedy years. The ambiguity lies in writer-director Bert Lovitt's wavering between depicting Jack Kennedy as a tough wheeler-dealer and a politician of the grandest vision.

Towards the end, the Cuban missile crisis is solved with Martin Luther King as a go-between.

King is made to be the only thoroughly likable and almost all-around popular guy in this feature, and he is played with cool and quiet charm by Robert Guillaume.

It would seem that the greater policy decisions are depicted fairly correctly (Ole Miss, The Bay of Pigs), while most of the Inner Sanctum private talks in the Oval Office of the White House are obviously based on hearsay and guesswork.

■ **PRINCE OF DARKNESS**

1987, 101 MINS, US ◇ ⓥ
Dir John Carpenter   *Prod* Larry Franco   *Scr* Martin Quatermass [=John Carpenter]   *Ph* Gary B. Kibbe   *Ed* Steve Mirkovich   *Mus* John Carpenter, Alan Howarth   *Art Dir* Daniel Lomino
● Donald Pleasence, Jameson Parker, Victor Wong, Lisa Blount, Dennis Dun, Susan Blanchard (Alive/Universal)

The Great Satan doesn't just reside in man's heart of darkness. Instead he lives in an opposite dimension, and manifests himself in this world in...bugs. That's about the extent of the horror that John Carpenter conjures up in *Prince of Darkness*.

Carpenter spends so much time turning the screws on the next scare that he completely forsakes his actors, who are already stranded with a shoddy script.

Story takes place in LA, where physics prof Birack (Victor Wong) takes his graduate class to an abandoned church in the middle of the city. He's summoned there by a priest (Donald Pleasence, who seems to have some secret sorrow), who has discovered inside the church a secret canister, guarded for hundreds of years by a forgotten sect of the Catholic church, the Brotherhood of Sleep.

Canister itself, which is supposed to be the embodiment of all evil, mostly looks like a green slime lava lamp. It starts sliming various students and turning them into zombies, so they can go out and wreak even more havoc.

None of the ensemble really stand out, with lovers Jameson Parker and Lisa Blount never getting a real chance to develop their relationship, and Dennis Dun's Walter completely robbed of his charm through his stilted delivery of equally wooden lines.

■ **PRINCE OF THE CITY**

1981, 167 MINS, US ◇
Dir Sidney Lumet   *Prod* Burtt Harris   *Scr* Jay Presson Allen, Sidney Lumet   *Ph* Andrzej Bartkowiak   *Ed* John J. Fitzstephens   *Mus* Paul Chihara   *Art Dir* Tony Walton
● Treat Williams, Jerry Orbach, Bob Balaban, Lindsay Crouse (Warner/Orion)

The film is a concentrated, unrelievedly serious and cerebrally involving entry, exhaustively detailing the true-life saga of a Gotham detective who turned Justice Dept informer to eke out widespread corruption in his special investigating unit during the 1960s.

Treat Williams is outstanding as the young, gung-ho cop who is courted by federal investigators and finds himself on a conscience-wracking approach-avoidance track that finally leads him to accept the informant role.

As Federal pressure for indictments mounts, however, matters quickly career out of control and Williams is cajoled, manipulated and ultimately blackmailed into spilling everything, while friends spurn him or commit suicide, his protectors are promoted upstairs, Mafiosi attempt buying him off, then try bumping him off, and the Feds barely agree not to prosecute him for his own past sins.

Within a nightmarish, frequently Kalkaesque atmosphere of intense danger and uncontrollable conscience, the film paints a world where law and morality are only relative commodities.

Director Sidney Lumet is in firm control of the sprawling canvas, showing in spades his ability to harness intense energy and almost uniformly top-rate performances from a cannily-cast stable of solid character actors.

■ **PRINCE VALIANT**

1954, 100 MINS, US ◇ ⓥ
Dir Henry Hathaway   *Prod* Robert L. Jacks   *Scr* Dudley Nichols   *Ph* Lucien Ballard   *Ed* Robert Simpson   *Mus* Franz Waxman
● James Mason, Janet Leigh, Robert Wagner, Debra Paget, Sterling Hayden, Victor McLaglen (20th Century-Fox)

The cartoon strip hero comes to the screen as a good offering for fans who dote on the fanciful derring-do of the Arthurian period.

Harold Foster's King Features strip gives an imaginative action basis for Robert L. Jacks' production guidance and the direction by Henry Hathaway. Although the picture comes in a bit overlength, the direction and Dudley Nichols' scripting combine to bring it off acceptably against some rather dazzling settings, including authentic castles and sites actually lensed in England.

Heading the star list is James Mason, who plays Sir Brack, pretender to King Arthur's throne. His dirty work is excellent, whether thinking up ambushes for Robert Wagner, in the title role, or engaging the young hero in joust or broadsword combat. The way he and Mason have at each other in the climaxing duel puts a topnotch action capper on the tale.

The plot finds Wagner in exile with his royal parents after their throne was seized by Primo Carnera. The Viking prince goes to King Arthur's court, becomes a squire to Sir Gawain, falls in love with Janet Leigh and, eventually, is able to put the finger on Mason as the mysterious Black Knight.

■ **PRINCESS BRIDE, THE**

1987, 98 MINS, US ◇ ⓥ
Dir Rob Reiner   *Prod* Andrew Scheinman, Rob Reiner   *Scr* William Goldman   *Ph* Adrian Biddle   *Ed* Robert Leighton   *Mus* Mark Knopfler   *Art Dir* Norman Garwood
● Cary Elwes, Mandy Patinkin, Chris Sarandon, Christopher Guest, Wallace Shawn (Act III/20th Century-Fox)

Based on William Goldman's novel, this is a post-modern fairy tale that challenges and affirms the conventions of a genre that may

477

not be flexible enough to support such horseplay.

It also doesn't help that Cary Elwes and Robin Wright as the loving couple are nearly comatose and inspire little passion from each other, or the audience.

Bound together by their love at tender age, young Westley (Elwes) then stableboy, falls in love with his beautiful mistress (Wright), but they're separated when he goes off to sea on a mission. After years of grieving for him she becomes betrothed to the evil Prince Humperdinck (Chris Sarandon) who masterminds her kidnaping to strengthen his own position in the kingdom.

First off, Westley must defeat a trio of kidnapers headed by the diminutive, but slimy, Wallace Shawn. His accomplices are the kind-hearted giant Fezzik (Andre The Giant) and Inigo Montoya, a Spanish warrior (Mandy Patinkin) out to avenge the murder of his father.

Patinkin especially is a joy to watch and the film comes to life when his longhaired, scruffy cavalier is on screen.

························

■ **PRISON**

1988, 102 MINS, US ◇ ▽

Dir Renny Harlin *Prod* Irwin Yablans *Scr* C. Courtney Joyner *Ph* Mac Ahlberg *Ed* Ted Nicolaou *Mus* Richard Band *Art Dir* Phillip Duffin
● Lane Smith, Viggo Mortensen, Chelsea Field, Andre De Shields, Lincoln Kilpatrick (Empire)

Starring as the prison in this rough penal pic with its special effects-laden horror story is the 87-year-old Wyoming State Penitentiary, which has attracted tourists rather than cons since 1981. The structure takes on all the menace of the house in *Amityville Horror* or hotel in *The Shining*.

The crumbling stone fortress is grounds for revenge because, as aged inmate Cresus (Lincoln Kilpatrick) points out toward the end, 'things won't stay buried.' It turns out that in 1964 guard Ethan Sharpe (Lane Smith) watched an innocent man fry in the electric chair.

Sharpe, now a warden, is appointed to the prison's helm despite recurrent nightmares brought on by a guilty conscience. The wronged convict's evil spirit is mad enough to eliminate a few of the new guards and inmates.

Viggo Mortensen plays Burke, a James Dean type antihero spared death but not a lot of bumps and bruises. His resemblance to the electrocuted con apparently is just a coincidence in the screenplay of producer Irwin Yablans' story.

························

■ **PRISONER, THE**

1955, 94 MINS, UK ▽

Dir Peter Glenville *Prod* Vivian A. Cox, Sydney Box *Scr* Bridget Boland *Ph* Reg Wyer *Ed* Freddie Wilson *Mus* Benjamin Frankel
● Alec Guinness, Jack Hawkins, Wilfrid Lawson, Jeanette Sterke, Ronald Lewis, Raymond Huntley (Columbia)

Closely following the Bridget Boland play, this British filmization retains the essentials of this stark and dramatic narrative with Alec Guinness repeating his original role of the cardinal held on a phoney charge of treason.

In her own adaptation, Boland has broadened the canvas of her subject, particularly to include background atmosphere of unrest in the capital while the cardinal is held without charge.

Peter Glenville's studied direction is a technical achievement, although the film just fails to achieve the anticipated emotional impact. The acting, however, is exceptionally high. The flawless performance by Guinness is matched by a superb portrayal by Jack Haw-

kins. But both of these stars find their equal in Wilfrid Lawson's interpretation of the jailor.

························

■ **PRISONER OF SECOND AVENUE, THE**

1974, 98 MINS, US ◇ ▽

Dir Melvin Frank *Prod* Melvin Frank *Scr* Neil Simon *Ph* Philip Lathrop *Ed* Bob Wyman *Mus* Marvin Hamlisch *Art Dir* Preston Ames
● Jack Lemmon, Anne Bancroft, Gene Saks, Elizabeth Wilson, Florence Stanley, Macine Stuart (Warner)

Neil Simon's play *The Prisoner of Second Avenue* has Jack Lemmon and Anne Bancroft as a harried urban couple. The film is more of a drama with comedy, for the personal problems as well as the environmental challenges aren't really funny, and even some of the humor is forced and strident.

Lemmon has done prior Simon plots on the screen, and he has the same basic character down cold. Bancroft demonstrates a fine versatility in facing the script demands. Atop the couple's problems in their apartment comes Lemmon's axing after many years on the job.

Gene Saks, Elizabeth Wilson and Florence Stanley do well as Lemmon's brother and sisters, while Ed Peck, the hostile upstairs neighbor, and Ivor Francis, Lemmon's taciturn shrink, head a good supporting cast.

························

■ **PRISONER OF SHARK ISLAND, THE**

1936, 95 MINS, US ▽

Dir John Ford *Prod* Darryl F. Zanuck *Scr* Nunnally Johnson *Ph* Bert Glennon *Ed* Jack Murray *Mus* Hugo Friedhofer, R.H. Bassett *Art Dir* William Darling
● Warner Baxter, Gloria Stuart, Claude Gillingwater, Arthur Byron, Harry Carey, Francis Ford (20th Century-Fox)

Warner Baxter as Dr Samuel A. Mudd, 'America's Jean Valjean' of the post-Civil War hysteria, turns in a capital performance as the titular prisoner of 'America's Devil's Island'.

The sympathetic trouping of Gloria Stuart as Dr Mudd's plucky wife who constantly endeavors to win back biased public favor for her unjustly condemned husband, plus the effective injection of a new kid charmer (Joyce Kay) as their baby daughter does much to achieve some mixed sympathies, but by and large it's a film for the men.

Not wholly a figment of Hollywood imagination, the saga of Dr Mudd is founded on fact. Baxter's woes start when he unknowingly sets the broken leg of John Wilkes Booth, Lincoln's assassin. Accused of conspiracy in the crime, he is court-martialed and, of eight co-defendants, three are hung and Dr Mudd is among those committed to Shark Island for life.

Casting is tiptop. John Carradine stands out as a new face among especially sinister heavies, a highly effective villyun. Frank McGlynn Sr, in his Abraham Lincoln personation is, as ever, realistic in dignified portrayal and uncanny resemblance to the martyred liberator.

························

■ **PRISONER OF ZENDA, THE**

1922, 130 MINS, US ⊗

Dir Rex Ingram *Prod* Rex Ingram *Scr* Mary O'Hara *Ph* John F. Seitz
● Lewis Stone, Alice Terry, Robert Edeson, Stuart Holmes, Barbara La Marr, Lois Lee (Metro)

To say that Rex Ingram and a remarkably good company of screen players have made the very utmost of the possibilities of Anthony Hope's novel about sums up this venture. It is the kind of romance that never stales – fresh, genuine, simple and wholesome. Indeed this screen translation is more

profoundly interesting than either the novel or the Edward Rose stage play.

Ingram built a spacious ballroom with an atmosphere of unobtrusive splendor. For once you get the illusion that it is a royal ball and not a movie mob scene.

Another bit of finesse is the choice of the hero and heroine, in Lewis Stone, who makes no pretence to Apollo-like beauty, and Alice Terry who makes a Princess Flavia of surpassing blonde loveliness in her regal robes.

The close-ups of all the characters are done in a misty dimness that gives them a remoteness that inspires the imagination. Some of the landscapes are handled in like manner and throughout the photography is marked.

························

■ **PRISONER OF ZENDA, THE**

1937, 100 MINS, US ▽

Dir John Cromwell *Prod* David O. Selznick *Scr* John L. Balderston, Wells Root, Donald Ogden Stewart *Ph* James Wong Howe *Ed* Hal C. Kern, James E. Newcom *Mus* Alfred Newman
● Ronald Colman, Madeleine Carroll, Douglas Fairbanks Jr, Mary Astor, C. Aubrey Smith, Raymond Massey (Selznick/United Artists)

Zenda is hokum of the 24-carat variety [from Anthony Hope's novel, dramatized by Edward Rose]; a sheer piece of romantic nonsense about a mythical European kingdom, a struggle for possession of a throne between a dissolute true heir and an ambitious stepbrother with larcenous inclinations; a lovely blonde princess; a swashbuckling duke, who bends with the political wind, and a young Englishman, on his annual outing, who is persuaded to impersonate the king.

Cromwell's direction is excellent. His opening scenes in the Balkan capital are as casual as a travelog, and his players assume lifelike characterizations through a series of intimate, human situations.

Colman (who plays the dual role of Englishman and King) has the ability to make a full dress court uniform appear as comfortable as a suit of pajamas. He never trips over his sword, or loosens his collar for air. Madeleine Carroll in all her blonde loveliness is quite receptive to impassioned protestations, so the romance has a touch of verity.

It's a close race between Colman and Fairbanks Jr, who plays Rupert of Hentzau for top acting honours. Best femme part is the scheming Antoinette, which Mary Astor is inclined to underplay.

························

■ **PRISONER OF ZENDA, THE**

1952, 100 MINS, US ◇ ▽

Dir Richard Thorpe *Prod* Pandro S. Berman *Scr* John L. Balderston, Noel Langley *Ph* Joseph Ruttenberg *Ed* George Boemler *Mus* Alfred Newman
● Stewart Granger, Deborah Kerr, James Mason, Louis Calhern, Jane Greer, Lewis Stone (M-G-M)

Fanciers of costumed swashbucklers will find this remake of the venerable *Prisoner of Zenda* a likeable version. The third time around for the yarn [adapted by Wells Root from the novel by Anthony Hope] this time it wears Tehnicolor dress, and has lavish physical appurtenances.

Plot deals with an Englishman who goes on a holiday to the small kingdom of Ruritania and gets involved in a royal impersonation and a love affair with a beautiful princess. Stewart Granger is the hero, dualing as the Englishman and the king he impersonates, and gives the roles the proper amount of dashing heroics.

Opposite him is Deborah Kerr, the lovely princess, and her looks and ability to wear period gowns are just what the part requires. James Mason scores as Rupert of Hentzau, making the character a rather likeable heavy.

Lewis Stone, who played the dual role in the original 1922 version of the story, appears briefly in this one as a cardinal.

■ PRIVATE BENJAMIN

1980, 109 MINS, US ◇ ▼
Dir Howard Zieff *Prod* Nancy Meyers, Charles Shyer, Harvey Miller *Scr* Nancy Meyers, Charles Shyer, Harvey Miller *Ph* David M. Walsh *Ed* Sheldon Kahn *Mus* Bill Conti *Art Dir* Robert Boyle
● Goldie Hawn, Eileen Brennan, Armand Assante, Sam Wanamaker, Harry Dean Stanton, Robert Webber (Warner/Meyers-Shyler-Miller)

Goldie Hawn's venture in producing her own film is actually a double feature – one is a frequently funny tale of an innocent who is conned into joining the US Army and her adventures therein; the other deals with the same innocent's personality problems as a Jewish princess with only an intermittent chuckle to help out.

The trouble may be with the use of too many screenwriters who have been told to always keep their star's image uppermost in their scribblings. But she's not so gifted that she can carry a heavy load of indifferent material on her own two little shoulders, without considerable sagging.

Another script problem is that the supporting characters are, even when they start out sympathetically, turned into unlikeable types.

■ PRIVATE FILES OF J. EDGAR HOOVER, THE

1977, 112 MINS, US ◇ ▼
Dir Larry Cohen *Prod* Larry Cohen *Scr* Larry Cohen *Ph* Paul Glickman *Ed* Christopher Lebenzon *Mus* Miklos Rozsa *Art Dir* Cathy Davis
● Broderick Crawford, Jose Ferrer, Michael Parks, Ronee Blakely, Rip Torn, Celeste Holm (Larco)

According to Larry Cohen, who wrote, produced and directed this $3 million look at America's top cop, J. Edgar Hoover was a public relations gimmick. As a vindictive, puritanical paranoid he shipped agents off to Knoxville for reading *Playboy* magazine. Privately, he was a mama's boy and a homosexual who got his jollies by sitting in the dark with a bottle of bourbon and a tape recorder playing the sounds of a powerful government official's hotel liaisons.

This may be the motion picture industry's first historical horror story. Cohen has adopted two visual styles. There's the 'backlot look' used to reenact great moments in J. Edgar Hoover's life, like the shooting of John Dillinger in front of the Biograph Theatre in Chicago and Hoover's first arrest.

Then there's the documentary look: Hoover in the FBI building; that's the real FBI building. Hoover in the apartment of his lifelong friend Lionel McCoy; that's the real McCoy's apartment.

He also knew enough to cast Broderick Crawford in the lead. As Hoover, the jowly Crawford turns in a fine performance. However, the remainder of the performances, starting with Michael Parks' Robert Kennedy, are grotesque attempts to mimic well known public officials.

■ PRIVATE FUNCTION, A

1984, 93 MINS, UK ◇ ▼
Dir Malcolm Mowbray *Prod* Mark Shivas *Scr* Alan Bennett *Ph* Tony Pierce-Roberts *Ed* Barrie Vince *Mus* John Du Prez *Art Dir* Stuart Walker
● Michael Palin, Maggie Smith, Liz Smith, Denholm Elliott, Richard Griffiths, John Normington (HandMade)

Pic is set in 1947, at a time of national rejoicing over a royal wedding and hardship caused by food rationing. Plot evolves out of a plan hatched by a group of town notables to fatten up a secret pig for festive devouring on the wedding night.

Central characters are a husband and wife team played by Maggie Smith and Michael Palin. She's a bullying wife anxious to reach the social highspots in the Yorkshire village where he works as a foot doctor. Their domestic crises are made more complex and amusing by the presence of a greedy mother (Liz Smith) who lives in terror of being put away.

Director Malcolm Mowbray neatly orchestrates the resulting drama, and points up the class antagonisms at play.

■ PRIVATE LESSONS

1981, 87 MINS, US ◇
Dir Alan Myerson, [James Fargo] *Prod* R. Ben Efraim *Scr* Dan Greenburg *Ph* Jan De Bont *Ed* Fred Chulack
● Sylvia Kristel, Howard Hesseman, Ron Foster, Eric Brown (Jensen Farley)

Private Lessons is a novelty comedy limning an adolescent boy's introduction to sex via his worldly European housekeeper. Suffering from a rickety structure that reflects extensive production problems (James Fargo directed additional footage sans credit), picture has a sustained air of amorality which is quite unusual for US films.

Story is set at a ritzy mansion in idyllic Arizona during summer vacation, with premise of Mr Fillmore (Ron Foster) leaving orders that his beautiful housekeeper (Sylvia Kristel) initiate his 15-year-old son Philly (Eric Brown) to sex before he returns from a business trip.

Dan Greenburg's script from his own novel [*Philly*] is very effective in presenting an innocent youth's point-of-view confronted with the sexual stimuli that pervade modern society. Inability to flesh out this central notion into a feature-length screenplay is a pity, but *Private Lessons* should satisfy general audiences with its diversions of frequent nudity, softcore sex, dominant rock music score and gags.

As Philly, Brown successfully carries the picture with a warm performance. Kristel is a beautiful dream-woman, but play-acting role here does not tap her thesping abilities. Although Kristel bares her breasts frequently, an unmatched stunt double [Judy Helden] is used for her disconcertingly in several of the nude scenes.

■ PRIVATE LIFE OF DON JUAN, THE

1934, 89 MINS, UK
Dir Alexander Korda *Prod* Alexander Korda *Scr* Frederick Lonsdale, Lajos Biro *Ph* Georges Perinal, Robert Krassker *Ed* Harold Young, Stephen Harrison *Mus* Mischa Spoliansky, Arthur Wimperis, Arthur Benjamin *Art Dir* Vincent Korda
● Douglas Fairbanks, Merle Oberon, Binnie Barnes, Joan Gardner, Benita Hume, Barry Mackay (London/United Artists)

Douglas Fairbanks' prime portrayal is as the antiquated knight who is finally disillusioned as the arch-heartbreaker when he must bow to his years and recognize that his amorous porch-climbing career is finis.

But the film holds more than that. There are many fine lights and shadings to get over the fact that the susceptible Seville femmes, who were not loath to two-timing their senors, had glorified Don Juan into an almost mythical figure.

Fairbanks is first introduced as a bit weary and slightly ill cavalier. All the faithful illusion is maintained to impress upon the viewer that he is still the real Don Juan of history, excepting that he happens to have become a bit fatigued. His faithful retainer, his cook, his masseur, all his aides, are shown jealously watching over him.

There's even planted the premise of Fairbanks being irked with the wife (Benita Hume) whom, he complains, has been too possessive of late; so much so that it's been cramping his style.

Fairbanks, stacked beside some nifty lookers – Merle Oberon, Binnie Barnes, Joan Gardner, Hume, Patricia Hilliard, Diana Napier, Natalie Lelong (Princess Paley), Betty Hamilton, Toto Koopman, Spencer Trevor, Nancy Jones and Florence Wood – makes for an incongruous impression.

Georges Perinal, Rene Clair's ace camera-grinder, in this, his first away from French productions, has fashioned some fine stuff.

■ PRIVATE LIFE OF HENRY VIII, THE

1933, 96 MINS, UK
Dir Alexander Korda *Prod* Alexander Korda *Scr* Lajos Biro, Arthur Wimperis *Ph* Georges Perinal *Ed* Stephen Harrison *Mus* Kurt Schroeder (dir.) *Art Dir* Vincent Korda
● Charles Laughton, Binnie Barnes, Merle Oberon, Elsa Lanchester, Wendy Barrie, Robert Donat (London/United Artists)

Unquestionably the perfect pick for the part, it must also be said that Charles Laughton is aided no little by the script, more generous to the character of Henry VIII than most of his biographers. The corpulent ruler is here made rather a jolly old soul and, for those who may have forgotten, it can be said that he had six wives, of whom the picture concerns itself with five. A couple are inclined to beat about the royal bush, so they thereby lose their heads for being promiscuous.

Laughton is happily supported right down the line, especially by Merle Oberon, Binnie Barnes, Robert Donat and Elsa Lanchester. The fair Barnes shares with Lanchester the major portion of footage devoted to the wives while Oberon is a British edition of Fay Wray.

Of comedy highlights audiences will probably like best the card game between Henry and Anne of Cleves (Lanchester), in which she takes him for almost half his kingdom, and the ruler at the banquet table. It being the open season for belching, Laughton demonstrates that he is equally as adept in this as at giving the 'berry [*If I Had a Million*, 1932].
□ 1932/33: Best Picture (Nomination)

■ PRIVATE LIFE OF SHERLOCK HOLMES, THE

1970, 125 MINS, UK ◇ ▼
Dir Billy Wilder *Prod* Billy Wilder *Scr* Billy Wilder, I.A.L. Diamond *Ph* Christopher Challis *Ed* Ernest Walter *Mus* Miklos Rozsa *Art Dir* Tony Inglis
● Robert Stephens, Colin Blakely, Irene Handl, Stanley Holloway, Christopher Lee, Genevieve Page (United Artists)

Billy Wilder's enterprise is a strange one because of its shift in directions from quite good satire to straight spy stuff. It is in large part old-fashioned, in that it's mile-wide and ancient-history Sherlock Holmes, but it's also handsomely produced and directed with incisiveness by Wilder.

Robert Stephens is the detective consultant, the man from Baker Street who fakes a story about his being not all masculine to duck out on an assignment from a Russian ballerina. But is he really faking? Stephens plays Sherlock in rather gay fashion under Wilder's tongue-in-cheek direction.

Colin Blakely is Dr John H. Watson; a performer who plays it broad and bright.

The dialog is crisp and amusing, Wilder and I.A.L. Diamond having a way with such matters.

■ **PRIVATE LIVES OF ELIZABETH AND ESSEX, THE**

1939, 106 MINS, US ◇ ⓥ
Dir Michael Curtiz   *Prod* Hal B. Wallis   *Scr* Norman Reilly Raine, Aeneas MacKenzie   *Ph* Sol Polito, W. Howard Greene   *Ed* Owen Marks   *Mus* Erich Wolfgang Korngold   *Art Dir* Anton Grot
● Bette Davis, Errol Flynn, Olivia de Havilland, Vincent Price, Donald Crisp, Alan Hale (Warner)

The Private Lives of Elizabeth and Essex is a lavishly-produced historical drama, the first picture to be released using the new fast Technicolor negative, and improved processing methods.

Bette Davis dominates the production at every turn as Elizabeth, virgin queen of England. Her delineation would indicate that Davis did much personal research.

Picture is a film version of Maxwell Anderson's *Elizabeth the Queen*. Story details the intimate May-and-December love affair of youthful Lord Essex (Errol Flynn) and matronly Queen Elizabeth. Both are headstrong and stubborn; each is ambitious to rule England.

Picture has its slow spots, particularly the excursion of Essex to Ireland to subdue Tyrone (Alan Hale). At times the dialog becomes brittle, and direction grooves into stagey passages that could have been lightened. Minor shortcomings, however, in the general excellence of the production.

■ **PRIVATE POTTER**

1963, 89 MINS, UK
Dir Caspar Wrede   *Prod* Ben Arbeid   *Scr* Ronald Harwood, Caspar Wrede   *Ph* Arthur Lavis   *Ed* John Pomeroy   *Mus* George Hall
● Tom Courtenay, James Maxwell, Ralph Michael, Brewster Mason, Ronald Fraser, Mogens Wieth (M-G-M)

This film is an egghead pic that doesn't quite come off. Yarn has a strong, imaginative idea but tails away inconclusively and falls between two stools, not quite arty, not quite commercial.

Tom Courtenay plays an inexperienced young soldier who screams in terror while on patrol that is tracking down a terrorist leader on a Mediterranean island. As a result, the mission misfires and a colleague is killed. The young soldier excuses himself with the plea that he saw a vision of God. Question that arises is whether he is to be court-martialled for cowardice or whether, in fact, he did have this religious experience. And, if so, whether or not he should be punished.

It is the conflicting clash of army regulations and men's consciences which intrigue. But the young solider's character is never clearly defined and the film eventually flounders in speculation and conjecture.

Courtenay acts with some imagination but best performance comes from James Maxwell, as his commanding officer. Gradually he begins to believe in the lad's story and then his own conscience starts to interfere. Ralph Michael, as the padre; Brewster Mason, as the brigadier, who lives by army regulations; and Ronald Fraser, as a cheery doctor, also give vivid performances.

■ **PRIVATE'S PROGRESS**

1956, 102 MINS, UK ⓥ
Dir John Boulting   *Prod* John Boulting, Roy Boulting   *Scr* Frank Harvey, John Boulting   *Ph* Eric Cross   *Ed* Anthony Harvey   *Mus* John Addison
● Richard Attenborough, Dennis Price, Terry-Thomas, Ian Carmichael, Peter Jones, William Hartnell (Charter/British Lion)

As a lighthearted satire on British army life during the last war, *Private's Progress* has

moments of sheer joy based on real authenticity. But it is not content to rest on satire alone and introduces an unreal melodramatic adventure which robs the story of much of its charm. The Boulting Brothers obviously felt there must be some point to the plot and they've added an adventure tailpiece in which a War Office brigadier invades enemy territory to bring back valuable art treasures to Britain.

The basic comedy, however, derives from the depiction of the typical misfit into the army way of life. Ian Carmichael is shown as the earnest university student who interrupts his studies to join the forces. He is a lamentable failure.

Many weaknesses of the yarn are surmounted by the allround performances of the cast. Carmichael does remarkably well. Richard Attenborough is in confident mood as a private who soon gets to know his way around. Dennis Price gives a smooth study as the brigadier.

■ **PRIVILEGE**

1967, 103 MINS, UK ◇ ⓥ
Dir Peter Watkins   *Prod* John Heyman   *Scr* Norman Bogner   *Ph* Peter Suschitzky   *Ed* John Trumper   *Mus* Mike Leander   *Art Dir* Bill Brodie
● Paul Jones, Jean Shrimpton, Mark London, William Job (Rank-Universal/World-Film/Memorial)

In *Privilege*, Paul Jones, erstwhile singer with the Manfred Mann Group, makes his acting debut. Maybe it's the fault of writer, director or both but Jones plays the role of the bewildered, disillusioned singer on one note of unanimated distaste.

Trouble with *Privilege* is that it cannot make up its mind whether it's a crusading film for the intelligentsia or a snide, 'with it' comedy.

A coalition government encourages the violence of the act of pop idol Steve Shorter (Jones) as a means of guiding the violence of Britain's youth into controllable channels. Then, cynically, it's decided that his image must be changed and he is taken from the ordinary scene of putting over national-interest commercials and selling consumer-goods to his worshipping fans and exploited by the Church as a kind of godlike hot gospeller.

But the best angles of the pic are those which turn a cynical and only too accurate searchlight on the pop music scene and those who batten on a minimal talent, plus the gullibity of the fans.

■ **PRIZE, THE**

1963, 135 MINS, US ◇
Dir Mark Robson   *Prod* Pandro S. Berman   *Scr* Ernest Lehman   *Ph* William H. Daniels   *Ed* Adrienne Fazan   *Mus* Jerry Goldsmith   *Art Dir* George W. Davis, Urie McCleary
● Paul Newman, Edward G. Robinson, Elke Sommer, Diane Baker, Micheline Presle, Gerard Oury (M-G-M)

Stockholm during Nobel week is the setting for Irving Wallace's smorgasbord novel. In Ernest Lehman's Hitchcockeyed screenplay, seven selected prizewinners convene to receive the award. The man from literature (Paul Newman) senses something amiss in the behavior and physique of the man from physics (Edward G. Robinson), proceeds to snoop around for clues and ends up in a wild goose chase, with himself as the goose who almost gets cooked.

The Prize is a suspense melodrama played for laughs. Trouble is the basic comedy approach clashes with the political-topical framework of the story. Although limited as a comic actor and confronted here with a rather difficult and unsubstantial character to portray, Newman tackles his task with sufficient vivacity to keep an audience con-

cerned for his welfare and amused by his antics. Robinson achieves a persuasive degree of contrast in his dual role.

Elke Sommer, as an attache who gets attached to Newman, hasn't a very scintillating role, but has the looks to make that a secondary issue.

Mark Robson's direction generates a lot of excitement, humor and suspense in spots, but this is offset by hokey elements, occasional exaggerations and stripping of dramatic gears as the film fluctuates between its incompatible components.

■ **PRIZE OF ARMS, A**

1962, 105 MINS, UK
Dir Cliff Owen   *Prod* George Maynard   *Scr* Paul Ryder   *Ph* Gilbert Taylor, Gerald Gibbs   *Ed* John Jympson   *Mus* Robert Sharples   *Art Dir* Jim Morahan, Bernard Sarron
● Stanley Baker, Helmut Schmid, Tom Bell, Tom Adams, Anthony Bate (R.L.C./British Lion/Bryanston)

Stanley Baker's carefully laid scheme for knocking off a $700,000 army payroll seems unnecessarily complicated. This seems to shriek out for mishaps. But Paul Ryder's screenplay [from an original story by Nicolas Roeg and Kevin Kavanagh] is smoothly efficient even though audiences are too often left in the dark about detail. Baker plays an ex-army captain who has been cashiered for Black Market activities in Hamburg. While in the army he has dreamed up a perfect plan for revenge (and to get rich). He has enlisted the help of Helmut Schmid, an explosives expert, and Tom Bell, a daring but edgy young man.

Baker learns that an army is preparing to go abroad at the time of the Suez crisis. He realizes that when troops are on the move abroad they have to take money with them. The trio plan to hijack the dough while the forces are moving towards the docks.

Baker, Schmid and Bell play the three leads confidently, with Baker particularly on the ball in the type of harsh tough part that he plays so often and so well. But the thesping of the three stars is given greater impact by the strength of a long list of character and feature actors as officers, other ranks, detectives, etc.

■ **PRIZZI'S HONOR**

1985, 129 MINS, US ◇ ⓥ
Dir John Huston   *Prod* John Foreman   *Scr* Richard Condon, Janet Roach   *Ph* Andrzej Bartkowiak   *Ed* Rudi Fehr, Kaja Fehr   *Mus* Alex North   *Art Dir* Dennis Washington
● Jack Nicholson, Kathleen Turner, Robert Loggia, William Hickey, John Randolph, Anjelica Huston (ABC)

John Huston's *Prizzi's Honor* packs love, sex, and murder – and dark comedy – into a labyrinthine tale.

Based on the novel by Richard Condon, plot centers on the tragic-comedy that results when a hit man for a powerful crime family (Jack Nicholson) falls hard for a svelte blonde (Kathleen Turner) who turns out to be his female counterpart in hired killings.

Picture is a stretch for Nicholson, who speaks in a street-tough, accented gangsterese that initially takes some getting used to, but shortly becomes totally convincing. Turner manages to use her loveliness to jolting results when she finally turns her gun on a pair of victims in an apartment hallway.

Even more monstrous, in a deceptive way, is the character played by Anjelica Huston, who is the black sheep of the powerful clan, but who maneuvers the plot in insidious ways, all of them tied to the fact that she harbors a lost love for Nicholson.
□ 1985: Best Picture (Nomination)

■ PRODUCERS, THE

1968, 100 MINS, US ◇ Ⓥ

Dir Mel Brooks   *Prod* Sidney Glazier   *Scr* Mel Brooks   *Ph* Joseph Coffey   *Ed* Ralph Rosenbloom   *Mus* John Morris   *Art Dir* Chuck Rosen

● Zero Mostel, Gene Wilder, Kenneth Mars, Estelle Winwood, Dick Shawn, Christopher Hewitt (Embassy)

Mel Brooks has turned a funny idea into a slapstick film, thanks to the performers, particularly Zero Mostel.

Playing a Broadway producer of flops who survives (barely) by suckering little old ladies, he teams with an emotionally retarded accountant portrayed by Gene Wilder in a scheme to produce a flop. By selling 25,000% of production, they figure to be rich when it flops. For the twist, the musical comedy *Springtime for Hitler*, penned by a shell-shocked Nazi, is a smash.

The film is unmatched in the scenes featuring Mostel and Wilder alone together, and several episodes with other actors are truly rare. When the producers approach the most atrocious director on Broadway, they find Christopher Hewitt in drag exchanging catty comments with his secretary (Andreas Voutsinas).

Estelle Winwood is a winner as a salacious little old lady, and Kenneth Mars has his moments as the Nazi scripter.

■ PROFESSIONALS, THE

1966, 116 MINS, US ◇ Ⓥ

Dir Richard Brooks   *Prod* Richard Brooks   *Scr* Richard Brooks   *Ph* Conrad Hall   *Ed* Peter Zinner   *Mus* Maurice Jarre   *Art Dir* Edward Haworth

● Burt Lancaster, Lee Marvin, Robert Ryan, Jack Palance, Claudia Cardinale, Ralph Bellamy (Columbia)

The Professionals is a well-made actioner, set in 1917 on the Mexican-US border, in which some soldiers of fortune rescue the reportedly kidnapped wife of an American businessman. Exciting explosive sequences, good overall pacing and acting overcome a sometimes thin script.

Richard Brooks' adaptation of Frank O'Rourke's novel, *A Mule for the Marquesa*, depicts the strategy of Lee Marvin and cohorts, sent by gringo Ralph Bellamy into the political turmoil of Mexico to rescue his missing wife, Claudia Cardinale, known to be secreted in the brigand village of Jack Palance. Latter only a few years earlier had achieved a transient victory in the Revolution with the help of Marvin and Burt Lancaster.

Quiet and purposeful, Marvin underplays very well as the leader of the rescue troop. Robert Ryan, who loves animals, is in the relative background, as is Woody Strode, Negro-Indian scout and tracker. Lancaster is the most dynamic of the crew, as a light-hearted but two-fisted fighter.

■ PROM NIGHT

1980, 91 MINS, US ◇ Ⓥ

Dir Paul Lynch   *Prod* Peter Simpson   *Scr* William Gray   *Ph* Robert New   *Ed* Brian Ravok   *Mus* Carl Zittrer, Paul Zaza   *Art Dir* Reuben Freed

● Leslie Nielsen, Jamie Lee Curtis, Casey Stevens, Eddie Benton (Simcom)

Borrowing shamelessly from *Carrie* and any number of gruesome exploitationers pic [from a story by Robert Gunza Jr] manages to score a few horrific points amid a number of sagging moments.

It opens with the falling death of a 10-year-old girl brought on by unmerciful teasing on the part of four of her peers. It's six years later and prom night for the surviving kiddies and each is slated to meet an unsavory fate due to past exploits – unbeknownst to anyone.

Once the masked killer gets going it becomes a guessing game of who is the ax-wielding avenger and which, if any, victims will escape.

Director Paul Lynch seems to capture the spirit of the genre here, but spends a little too much time setting up each murder, thus eliminating some suspense.

■ PROMISE, THE

1979, 97 MINS, US Ⓥ

Dir Gilbert Cates   *Prod* Fred Weintraub, Paul Heller   *Scr* Gary Michael White   *Ph* Ralph Woolsey   *Ed* Peter E. Berger   *Mus* David Shire   *Art Dir* William Sandell

● Kathleen Quinlan, Stephen Collins, Beatrice Straight, Laurence Luckin, Michael O'Hare, Bibi Besch (Universal)

The title of this romantic melodrama, has to do with a buried necklace and the promise of undying love and faith in each other made by a young architectural student and a girl student.

The girl is severely injured in an auto accident and the boy is unconscious for some time, during which his mother – a female building tycoon – persuades the girl to undergo some very expensive plastic surgery and seek a new life elsewhere. She tells her son the girl is dead.

The scene changes to California. The girl, a promising artist, has for reasons known only to herself, switched to photography. She's an overnight success and is sought by the young architect who's building a medical center. Does he recognize her?

Kathleen Quinlan, is pretty convincing as the painter/photographer and a new, very handsome, young leading man is added to the Hollywood scene with Stephen Collins as the architect.

■ PROMISE HER ANYTHING

1966, 96 MINS, UK/US ◇

Dir Arthur Hiller   *Prod* Stanley Rubin   *Scr* William Peter Blatty   *Ph* Douglas Slocombe   *Ed* John Shirley   *Mus* Lyn Murray   *Art Dir* Wilfrid Shingleton

● Warren Beatty, Leslie Caron, Bob Cummings, Keenan Wynn, Hermione Gingold, Lionel Stander (Seven Arts/Stark/Paramount)

Promise Her Anything is a light, refreshing comedy-romance, set in Greenwich Village but filmed in England, which satirizes both child psychology and nudie pix in a tasteful, effective manner. Well-paced direction of many fine performances, generally sharp scripting and other good production elements add up to a satisfying comedy.

An Arne Sultan-Marvin Worth story has been adapted into what is basically a romantic triangle. Leslie Caron, with a precocious baby boy but no hubby, hopes to connect with her employer, child psychologist Bob Cummings who, in private life, abhors moppets. Caron's neighbor (Warren Beatty) wants her, although he is careful to conceal his profession – making mail-order nudie films.

Director Arthur Hiller has overcome a basic problem: specifically, that Caron and Beatty are not known as film comics. His fine solution has been to spotlight baby Michael Bradley in the first 30 minutes, when Caron is establishing an easy audience rapport, while Beatty slides into a likeable groove via energetic tumbles and other manifestations of youthful enthusiasm.

■ PROPHECY

1979, 102 MINS, US ◇ Ⓥ

Dir John Frankenheimer   *Prod* Robert L. Rosen   *Scr* David Seltzer   *Ph* Harry Stradling Jr   *Ed* Tom Rolf   *Mus* Leonard Rosenman   *Art Dir* William Craig Smith

● Talia Shire, Robert Foxworth, Armand Assante, Richard Dysart, Victoria Racimo, Tom McFadden (Paramount)

Director John Frankenheimer has made a frightening monster movie that people could laugh at for generations to come, complete with your basic big scary thing, cardboard characters and a story so stupid it's irresistible.

Once again, the real villain is Careless Mankind. Only this time, it isn't Atomic Fallout that's creating giant ants and killer cockroaches but Industrial Pollution.

Among the performers, only Armand Assante as an Indian leader gets half-a-chance to show his talent and Talia Shire is reduced to a whining wimp. Leonard Rosenman's score cheats constantly, building to frightening moments that don't happen.

■ PROTECTOR, THE

1985, 95 MINS, US ◇ Ⓥ

Dir James Glickenhaus   *Prod* David Chan   *Scr* James Glickenhaus   *Ph* Mark Irwin   *Ed* Evan Lottman   *Mus* Ken Thorne   *Art Dir* William F. De Seta, Oliver Wong

● Jackie Chan, Danny Aiello, Roy Chiao, Victor Arnold, Kim Bass, Richard Clarke (Golden Harvest/Warner)

Jackie Chan and Danny Aiello head for Hong Kong to track down a drug kingpin who has kidnapped the daughter of his estranged business partner.

A furious barroom shootout at the outset is immediately followed by a speedboat chase in New York harbor that rivals James Bond pictures for elaborate thrills.

What also puts matters on the right track is the tongue-in-cheek humor running throughout. Chan and Aiello both sail through the farfetched action with insouciance and aplomb as they infuriate their superiors by wreaking havoc wherever they go and knock off enough baddies to momentarily put a dent in Hong Kong's population figures.

Chan indulges in almost superhuman acrobatics every 15 minutes or so, running up walls, pole-vaulting and swinging from sampan to sampan in the harbor and generally putting his karate expertise to good use.

■ PROTOCOL

1984, 96 MINS, US ◇ Ⓥ

Dir Herbert Ross   *Prod* Anthea Sylbert   *Scr* Buck Henry   *Ph* William A. Fraker   *Ed* Paul Hirsch   *Mus* Basil Poledouris   *Art Dir* Bill Malley

● Goldie Hawn, Chris Sarandon, Richard Romanus, Andre Gregory, Gail Strickland, Cliff De Young (Warner)

Goldie Hawn's insistence on Saying Something Important takes a lot of the zip out of *Protocol*, but the light comedy still has its moments for the forgiving.

One big problem here is an oh-so-obvious effort to reinvent the formula that boosted *Private Benjamin* to the heights. Here she's a sweet, unsophisticated cocktail waitress hurdled into the unfamiliar world of Washington diplomacy and Mideast travail.

In *Benjamin*, Hawn's main adversary was a woman captain (Eileen Brennan) and ill-intentioned men; here, it's Gail Strickland as a devious, plotting protocol officer and more ill-intentioned men.

Formula doesn't work as well in *Protocol*, partly because Strickland and gang aren't as much fun to foil as Brennan's bunch was.

■ PROUD REBEL, THE

1958, 100 MINS, US ◇

Dir Michael Curtiz   *Prod* Samuel Goldwyn Jr   *Scr* Joe Petracca, Lillie Hayward   *Ph* Ted McCord   *Ed* Aaron Stell   *Mus* Jerome Moross   *Art Dir* McClure Capps

● Alan Ladd, Olivia de Havilland, Dean Jagger, David Ladd, Cecil Kellaway, John Carradine (Buena Vista)

Warmth of a father's love and faith, and the devotion of a boy for his dog, are the stand-out ingredients of this suspenseful and fast-action post-Civil War yarn. Michael Curtiz, too, has achieved fine feeling in his direction of the screenplay, based on an original by James Edward Grant, and is backed by some fine color photography.

It's the characterizations that hold forth most strongly, topped perhaps by the very appealing performance of David Ladd, star's 11-year-old son who plays Alan Ladd's boy in the pic. Youngster has been shocked mute during Union forces' sacking of Atlanta during the war, when he saw his mother killed and his home destroyed by fire, and it's Alan Ladd's dogged wandering of the land to find a doctor who can cure his son which motivates plot.

Action unfolds in a small Southern Illinois community, where Ladd is drawn into a fight with the two sons of Dean Jagger, a big sheep-raiser; the payment of his fine after his arrest by Olivia de Havilland, a lonely farmwoman whose property is coveted by Jagger; and Ladd working out this fine on the farm.

● ●

■ PROVIDENCE

1977, 110 MINS, FRANCE ◇ ⓥ

Dir Alain Resnais *Prod* Action Films-SFP *Scr* David Mercer *Ph* Ricardo Arnovitch *Ed* Albert Jurgenson *Mus* Miklos Rozsa *Art Dir* Jacques Saulnier
● Dirk Bogarde, Ellen Burstyn, John Gielgud, David Warner, Elaine Stritch, Cyril Luckham (Action/SFP)

A striking amalgam of the literary and theatrical approach in scripting; that is, sharp talk, highblown scenes of personal revelation and general politico asides; has been turned into an unusual visual tour-de-force by French director Alain Resnais.

It is a riveting pic pictorially, offering dense insights into the flights of imagination of a supposedly dying writer of perhaps some faddish fame.

The style is impeccable as the film sashays from the novelist's feverish, drunken ramblings about his new novel, putting his family into it, and commenting on them.

John Gielgud's mellifluous or impassioned delivery as the writer is extraordinary; as well as Dirk Bogarde as the son, a cold, internally-wounded man who cannot show emotion.

● ●

■ PROWLER, THE

1951, 92 MINS, US

Dir Joseph Losey *Prod* S.P. Eagle [= Sam Spiegel] *Scr* Hugo Butler *Ph* Arthur Miller *Ed* Paul Weatherwax *Mus* Lyn Murray *Art Dir* Boris Leven
● Van Heflin, Evelyn Keyes, John Maxwell, Katherine Warren, Emerson Treacy, Madge Blake (Horizon/United Artists)

Combination of illicit love, murder and premarital relations makes *The Prowler* a bawdy, daring story [from an original by Robert Thoeren and Hans Wilhelm].

Van Heflin makes the most of an unsympathetic role, that of a cop who steals the love of a woman (Evelyn Keyes) who had called the police when she saw a prowler peering through her bathroom window. Keyes, as the woman, wife of an all-night disk jockey, also has an unsympathetic part, as a gal wooed and won by Heflin behind her husband's back.

Pic builds to an exciting climax in a desert ghost town, where Heflin has taken Keyes, now his wife, to have her baby in order to avoid publicity.

● ●

■ PRUDENCE AND THE PILL

1968, 92 MINS, US

Dir Fielder Cook *Prod* Kenneth Harper, Ronald J. Kahn *Scr* Hugh Mills *Ph* Ted Mocre *Ed* Norman Savage *Mus* Bernard Ebbinghouse *Art Dir* Wilfrid Shingleton
● Deborah Kerr, David Niven, Judy Geeson, David Dundas, Vickery Turner, Hugh Armstrong (20th Century-Fox)

Deborah Kerr and David Niven team as a couple which winds up married to others.

Hugh Mills wrote the book, and adapted it for films. Basic flaw in the screenplay, which the generally excellent acting and direction cannot entirely overcome, is the rambling from one set of interesting characters to another.

Obvious attempt was to incorporate a lot of unique personalities, all affected by the pill and changing sex customs, but the result is a lack of unity. The whole film, then, is less than the sum of its parts.

Film is more than a one-joke script – the secret switching of birth control pills so that the wrong people get pregnant – and to the credit of the pic, this is not a tasteless recurring incident.

Title art designed by Richard Williams is a great sendoff to the film, in its semi-Victorian atmosphere on which modern characters intrude. The parallel between old-fashioned genteel marriage and contemporary assaults thereon, is drawn most cleverly.

● ●

■ PSYCHO

1960, 109 MINS, US ⓥ

Dir Alfred Hitchcock *Prod* Alfred Hitchcock *Scr* Joseph Stefano *Ph* John L. Russell *Ed* George Tomasini *Mus* Bernard Herrmann *Art Dir* Joseph Hurley, Robert Clatworthy, George Milo
● Anthony Perkins, Janet Leigh, Vera Miles, John Gavin, Martin Balsam, John McIntire (Paramount)

Alfred Hitchcock is up to his clavicle in whimsicality and apparently had the time of his life in putting together *Psycho*. He's gotten in gore, in the form of a couple of graphically-depicted knife murders, a story that's far out in Freudian motivations, and now and then injects little amusing plot items that suggest the whole thing is not to be taken seriously.

Anthony Perkins is the young man who doesn't get enough exorcise (repeat exorcise) of that other inner being. Among the victims are Janet Leigh, who walks away from an illicit love affair with John Gavin, taking with her a stolen $40,000, and Martin Balsam, as a private eye who winds up in the same swamp in which Leigh's body also is deposited.

John McIntire is the local sheriff with an unusual case on his hands, and Simon Oakland is the psychiatrist. Perkins gives a remarkably effective in-a-dream kind of performance as the possessed young man. Others play it straight, with equal competence.

Joseph Stefano's screenplay, from a novel by Robert Bloch, provides a strong foundation for Hitchcock's field day. And if the camera, under Hitchcock's direction, tends to over-emphasize a story point here and there, well, it's forgivable.

● ●

■ PSYCHO II

1983, 113 MINS, US ◇ ⓥ

Dir Richard Franklin *Prod* Hilton A. Green *Scr* Tom Holland *Ph* Dean Cundey *Ed* Andrew London *Mus* Jerry Goldsmith *Art Dir* John W. Corso
● Anthony Perkins, Vera Miles, Meg Tilly, Robert Loggia, Dennis Franz, Hugh Gillin (Universal/Oak Industries)

Psycho II is an impressive, 23-years-after followup to Alfred Hitchcock's 1960 suspense classic.

New story, set 22 years later, has Norman Bates (Anthony Perkins) released from a mental institution on the petition of his psychiatrist, Dr Raymond (Robert Loggia), over the objections of Lila Loomis (Vera Miles) whose sister he murdered (Janet Leigh in the first film).

Securing a job as cook's assistant at a local diner, Bates is befriended by a young waitress Mary (Meg Tilly) who moves into his house as an empathetic companion. A series of mysterious murders ensue, beginning with the killing of the obnoxious manager Toomey (Dennis Franz), who has turned the Bates family business into a hot-sheets motel.

Director Richard Franklin deftly keeps the suspense and tension on high while dolling out dozens of shock-of-recognitions shots drawn from the audience's familiarity with *Psycho*.

Reprising his famous role, Perkins is very entertaining, whether stammering over the pronunciation of 'cutlery' or misleading the audience in both directions as to his relative sanity.

● ●

■ PSYCHO III

1986, 96 MINS, US ◇ ⓥ

Dir Anthony Perkins *Prod* Hilton A. Green *Scr* Charles Edward Pogue *Ph* Bruce Surtees *Ed* David Blewitt *Mus* Carter Burwell *Art Dir* Henry Bumstead
● Anthony Perkins, Diana Scarwid, Jeff Fahey, Roberta Maxwell, Hugh Gillin, Lee Garlington (Universal)

A few amusing little notions are streched to the point of diminishing returns in *Psycho III*.

Opening sequence is a full-fledged homage to Alfred Hitchcock's *Vertigo* and helps set the comic, in-joke tone of the rest of the picture. Unhappy novice Diana Scarwid is all set to jump from a church belltower but, in an effort to save her, one of the nuns falls to her death instead.

Scarwid flees in distress, is given a ride through the desert by aspiring musician Jeff Fahey, and where should the unlikely and unsuspecting duo wind up but the Bates Motel.

The whole enterprise is dependent almost entirely upon self-referential incidents and attitudes for its effect, and it eventually becomes wearying.

Main pleasure of the picture stems from Anthony Perkins' amusing performance.

● ●

■ PUBERTY BLUES

1981, 97 MINS, AUSTRALIA ◇

Dir Bruce Berseford *Prod* John Long, Margaret Kelly *Scr* Margaret Kelly *Ph* Don McAlpine *Ed* Bill Anderson *Mus* Les Gock *Art Dir* David Copping
● Nell Schofield, Jad Capelja, Geoff Rhoe, Tony Hughes, Sandy Paul (Limelight)

Puberty Blues is a leisurely, entertaining tale about a group of teenagers fumbling, fighting and fretting their way through adolescence.

Puberty Blues is based on a book of the same name, published in 1979, by Sydney teenagers Kathy Lette and Gabrielle Carey, who also wrote for local newspapers and magazines under the intriguing pseudonym, the Salami Sisters.

Set in the middle-class suburb of Cronulla, one of Sydney's southern beaches, the story focusses on Debbie and Sue, two girls of fairly average looks, intelligence and upbringing. Opening passages show them falling in with one of the school gangs, cheating in exams, smoking in the toilets, getting drunk, and pairing off with boyfriends.

Film gains more momentum when Debbie fears she is pregnant, her boyfriend Garry cannot cope, he seeks refuge in heroin, and dies of an overdose. To offset the bleakness, the pic is laced with Debbie's witty observations and humorous interludes.

Working with a young, inexperienced cast, Beresford has drawn some remarkable performances. Nell Schofield, 17, is particularly impressive as Debbie, an intuitive player with tangible screen presence.

●●●●●●●●●●●●●●●●●●●●●●●●●●●●●●●●

■ PUBLIC ENEMY, THE

1931, 83 MINS, US Ⓥ
Dir William Wellman *Scr* Kubec Glasmon, John Bright, Harvey Thew *Ph* Dev Jennings *Ed* Ed McCormick *Art Dir* Max Parker
● James Cagney, Edward Woods, Donald Cook, Joan Blondell, Jean Harlow, Beryl Mercer (Warner)

There's no lace on this picture. It's raw and brutal. It's low-brow material given such workmanship as to make it high-brow. To square everything there's a foreword and postscript moralizing on the gangster as a menace to the public welfare.

Pushing a grapefruit into the face of the moll (Mae Clarke) with whom he's fed up, socking another on the chin for inducing him to her for the night while he's drunk, and spitting a mouthful of beer into the face of a speakeasy proprietor for using a rival's product are a few samples of James Cagney's deportment as Tom, a tough in modern gangster's dress.

The story traces him and Matt (Edward Woods) from street gamins in 1909 as a couple of rowdy neighbourhood boys. Titles then designate lapses in time of 1915, 1917 and finally 1920. During this interim they've killed a cop on their first big job, and both kids are set to go the hard way.

The comedy in the picture, as well as the rough stuff, is in the dialog and by-play with the dames who include, besides Clarke, Joan Blondell and Jean Harlow. Harlow better hurry and do something about her voice. She doesn't get the best of it alongside Clarke and Blondell, who can troupe.

●●●●●●●●●●●●●●●●●●●●●●●●●●●●●●●●

■ PUMP UP THE VOLUME

1990, 105 MINS, US/CANADA ◇ Ⓥ
Dir Allan Moyle *Prod* Rupert Harvey, Sandy Stern *Scr* Allan Moyle *Ph* Walt Lloyd *Ed* Wendy Bricmont, Ric Keeley, Kurt Hathaway *Art Dir* Bruce Bolander
● Christian Slater, Samantha Mathis, Ellen Greene, Scott Paulin, Cheryl Pollack, Annie Ross (New Line/SC Entertainment)

Writer-director Allan Moyle's story about a shy high school student who galvanizes an Arizona suburb with a rebellious pirate radio show has rambunctious energy and defiant attitude.

Christian Slater is first-rate as a bright but alienated student who feels trapped and disconnected in a suburban 'whitebread land' where 'everything is sold out.' Everything includes his father (Scott Paulin), a former 1960s radical who has bought into the yuppie dream.

Slater's rebellious late-night broadcasts soon make him a hero and stir up the dormant anger of other alienated kids. But one night his talk-radio antics go out of control.

Moyle resolves things in favor of love and justice, but his ending resolutely refuses to sell out the movie's angry stance against complacency. Slater handles numerous monolog scenes with conviction and charisma. Newcomer Samantha Mathis (as Nora, who falls in love with Slater's disembodied voice) and Paulin show a good grasp of their characters.

●●●●●●●●●●●●●●●●●●●●●●●●●●●●●●●●

■ PUMPING IRON

1977, 85 MINS, US ◇ Ⓥ
Dir George Butler, Robert Fiore *Prod* George Butler, Jerome Gary *Scr* George Butler *Ph* Robert Fiore *Ed* Larry Silk, Geof Bartz *Mus* Michael Small
● Arnold Schwarzenegger, Lou Ferrigno, Matty Ferrigno, Ken Waller, Franco Columbu, Mike Katz (Cinema 5)

The life of a weightlifter who takes himself seriously is, ultimately, as lonely as that of a ballet dancer. He knows that if he's serious about his profession it means a daily, dedicated routine of exercises so that any gains won are not lost.

What this film documentary, based on George Butler and Charles Gaines' book, *Pumping Iron*, does not tell the viewer, however, is what lies beyond the peak of success.

The most fascinating aspect of this film is the dedicated training that turns average-built young men (frequently they refer to themselves as weaklings in their early youth) into superbly-created physical edifices.

The film, while spotlighting Arnold Schwarzenegger, also treats with other competitors, preparing for the Mr Universe and Mr Olympia contests.

●●●●●●●●●●●●●●●●●●●●●●●●●●●●●●●●

■ PUMPING IRON II THE WOMEN

1985, 107 MINS, US ◇ Ⓥ
Dir George Butler *Prod* George Butler *Scr* Charles Gaines, George Butler *Ph* Dyanna Taylor *Ed* Paul Barnes, Susan Crutcher, Jane Kurson *Mus* David McHugh, Michael Montes
● Lori Bowen, Carla Dunlap, Bev Francis, Rachel McLish, Kris Alexander, Lydia Cheng (Pumping Iron/White Mountain/Bar Belle)

This enjoyable, slickly conceived documentary on the subculture of women's bodybuilding could have been better had director George Butler tempered his penchant for camera's eye detachment with some analytical and repertorial sweat.

Although he succeeds fairly well in exploiting the inherent drama of the 1983 Caesars Palace World Cup Championship for women bodybuilders, Butler is too content to let the alluring amazons speak for themselves on the film's central question: what is femininity and how far many women go in liberating themselves from stereotypes before confronting immovable cultural resistance?

The question is embodied graphically by Australian power-lifter Bev Francis, whose awesome, spectacularly mannish physique will be matched in a great flex-off against the wiry, compelling developed bodies of the best 'feminine' bodybuilders. These include smug, shrewd defending champ Rachel McLish; the appealingly articulate Carla Dunlap, who's the only black woman in the group; and Lori Bowen, a humble girl from Texas who idolizes the aloof McLish and plans to use her prize money to free her boyfriend from his male go-go dancer's gig.

●●●●●●●●●●●●●●●●●●●●●●●●●●●●●●●●

■ PUMPKIN EATER, THE

1964, 118 MINS, UK
Dir Jack Clayton *Prod* James Woolf *Scr* Harold Pinter *Ph* Oswald Morris *Ed* James Clark *Mus* Georges Delerue *Art Dir* Edward Marshall
● Anne Bancroft, Peter Finch, James Mason, Cedric Hardwicke, Richard Johnson, Eric Porter (Columbia/Romulus)

Harold Pinter's screenplay is based on a witty novel by Penelope Mortimer, and his script vividly brings to life the principal characters in this story of a shattered marriage, though Pinter's resort to flashback technique is confusing in the early stages. Jack Clayton's direction gets off to a slow, almost casual start, but the pace quickens as the drama becomes more intense,

Anne Bancroft is exceptionally good. She plays the mother of several young children who leaves her second husband to marry Peter Finch, a scriptwriter with a promising career ahead. And as he succeeds in his work, so she becomes aware of his increasing infidelities and she becomes a case for psychiatric treatment. The role may sound conventional enough, but not as played by Bancroft; she adds a depth and understanding which puts it on a higher plane.

Peter Finch's performance is a mature interpretation, and always impressive. To him, casual infidelities are the natural prerequisites of a successful writer.

Notwithstanding the scope offered by those two roles, James Mason stands out in a much smaller part. He plays a deceived husband with a sinister, malevolent bitterness, to provide one of the acting highlights of the picture.

●●●●●●●●●●●●●●●●●●●●●●●●●●●●●●●●

■ PUNCH AND JUDY MAN, THE

1963, 96 MINS, UK
Dir Jeremy Summers *Prod* Gordon L. T. Scott *Scr* Philip Oakes, Tony Hancock *Ph* Gilbert Taylor *Ed* Gordon Pilkington *Mus* Derek Acott, Don Banks
● Tony Hancock, Sylvia Syms, Ronald Fraser, Barbara Murray, John Le Mesurier, Hugh Lloyd (Macconkey)

Tony Hancock's second film produces many amusing sequences, but it fails to jell. Story line is too slight. Result is a series of spasmodic incidents which Hancock has, largely, to carry on his own personality, despite being surrounded by some firstclass character actors.

Hancock plays a Punch and Judy man at a seaside resort which is ruled over by a snobbish mayor. Hancock's marriage is foundering, since he fights the snobbery while his social climbing wife (Sylvia Syms) is anxious for him to mend his ways so that she can move into the local big league. Climax is the gala held to celebrate the 60th anni of the resort.

Director Jeremy Summers makes good use of the closeup to put over Hancock's expressive mug, and devotees of the comic will get a generous quota of giggles. But either Summers or the editor, or maybe both, have failed to keep the film on a taut and even keel.

Syms, as Hancock's disgruntled wife, takes her few opportunities avidly. Ronald Fraser shines as the officious mayor. Eddie Byrne chips in with a neat cameo as an ice cream assistant and Barbara Murray, as a socialite and guest of honor at the gala, pin-points once more that she is a sadly underrated femme in pix.

●●●●●●●●●●●●●●●●●●●●●●●●●●●●●●●●

■ PUNISHER, THE

1990, 90 MINS, US/AUSTRALIA ◇ Ⓥ
Dir Mark Goldblatt *Prod* Robert Kamen *Scr* Boaz Yakin *Ph* Ian Baker *Ed* Tim Wellburn *Mus* Dennis Dreith *Art Dir* Norma Moriceau
● Dolph Lundgren, Louis Gossett Jr, Jeroen Krabbe, Kim Miyori, Bryan Marshall, Nancy Everhard (New World)

With origins in a Marvel Comics character, *The Punisher* is, as might be expected, two-dimensional. The Punisher has killed 125 people before the film even begins, and the ensuing 90 minutes are crammed with slaughters of every conceivable kind. Pic was the only product of the New World offshoot Down Under.

Story involves an ex-cop whose wife and children were murdered by the mafia in New York. He hides from civilization in the city's sewers and for five years he's been killing the various heads of the mob families in nonstop vengeance.

Another party comes to play – the Japanese mafia headed by the glamorous, stony cold Lady Tanaka. The Punisher is quite content to see his enemies slaughter each other until the Japanese kidnap the locals' children.

Dolph Lundgren looks just as if he's stepped out of a comic book. Thankfully, he breezes through the B-grade plot with tongue firmly placed in cheek.

••••••••••••••••••••••••••••••

■ **PUNISHMENT PARK**

1971, 88 MINS, US ◇

Dir Peter Watkins *Scr* Peter Watkins *Ph* Joan Churchill *Ed* Peter Watkins *Mus* Paul Motian
● Paul Alelyanes, Carmen Argenziano, Stan Armsted, Harold Beaulieu, Jim Bohan, Kerry Cannon (Francoise)

Like the same director's *The War Game*, this pic apparently is set in the indeterminate future. It is presented in the guise of a live TV documentary complete with camera jerks, microphones and lights in full view.

Escalation of Asian wars is pre-supposed with intensified tensions between the larger international powers and the increase of anti-war propaganda and demonstrations of draft evaders.

Those youthful rebels coming before tribunals on conscientious and other grounds are given the choice of serving penal sentences or a three-days endurance test in Punishment Park, situated in Southern California.

The rules are that 'corrective groups' are given three days to reach, on foot, an American flag 57 miles away. They are allowed two to three hours' start, after which the National Guard hounds them out. If they manage to reach the flag in the alloted time they will be given their freedom. The journey they have to traverse is over desert territory in temperatures rising above the 100-degree mark by day and cold by night.

The pic deftly switches back and forth from the members of one such corrective group, the armed forces and seven different offenders being tried by a quasi-judicial tribunal.

••••••••••••••••••••••••••••••

■ **PUPPET ON A CHAIN**

1971, 98 MINS, UK ◇ ⓥ

Dir Geoffrey Reeve *Prod* Kurt Unger *Scr* Alistair MacLean *Ph* Jack Hildyard *Ed* Bill Lenny *Mus* Piero Piccioni
● Sven-Bertil Taube, Barbara Parkins, Alexander Knox, Patrick Allen, Vladek Sheybal, Penny Casdagli (Unger)

Puppet on a Chain could be remembered as the film with the speedboat chase. Don Sharp, who was engaged specially to direct this sequence, has in no way spared the boats as the hero relentlessly pursues the villain through the canals of Amsterdam. Regrettably the standard of this sequence is not reflected in the rest of the film.

Sven-Bertil Taube plays a US narcotics agent seeking the headquarters of a drug syndicate in Amsterdam aided by his undercover assistant, Maggie (Barbara Parkins). Wherever they go sudden death is never far behind. The trail leads to a religious order and an island castle.

Alistair MacLean scripted his own story. There is all the action, implausible happenings, violent rough housing and mystery that distinguishes so much of his work, but he has created little sympathy for the characters.

••••••••••••••••••••••••••••••

■ **PURPLE HEARTS**

1984, 115 MINS, US ◇ ⓥ

Dir Sidney J. Furie *Prod* Sidney J. Furie *Scr* Rick Natkin, Sidney J. Furie *Ph* Jan Kiesser *Ed* George Grenville *Mus* Robert Folk *Art Dir* Francisco Balangue
● Ken Wahl, Cheryl Ladd, Stephen Lee, David Harris, Cyril O'Reilly, Lane Smith (Ladd)

Purple Hearts is a systematically simple love story set against the Vietnam War, with the action largely overwhelming the romantic time-outs.

Ken Wahl is a handsome young and dedicated doctor in Vietnam where he meets a beautiful young and dedicated nurse (Cheryl Ladd). They fall in love. Between kisses, they assure each other that they hope one day to return Stateside and do medical good together forever. But then he's killed – but no he isn't – and then she's killed – but (fill in the blank) – and it looks like they may never live happily ever after.

Wahl is solid in the lead and Ladd hangs in there in a less demanding part.

••••••••••••••••••••••••••••••

■ **PURPLE RAIN**

1984, 104 MINS, US ◇ ⓥ

Dir Albert Magnoli *Prod* Robert Cavallo, Joseph Ruffalo, Steven Fargnoli *Scr* Albert Magnoli, William Blinn *Ph* Donald L. Thorin *Ed* Albert Magnoli, Ken Robinson *Mus* Michel Colombier *Art Dir* Ward Preston
● Prince, Apollonia Kotero, Morris Day, Olga Karlatos, Clarence Williams III, Jerome Benton (Warner)

Playing a character rooted in his own background, and surrounded by the real-life members of his Minneapolis-based musical 'family', rock star Prince makes an impressive feature film debut in *Purple Rain*, a rousing contemporary addition to the classic backstage musical genre.

Director Albert Magnoli gets a solid, appealing performance from Prince, whose sensual, somewhat androgynous features are as riveting on film as they are on a concert stage. Femme love interest Apollonia Kotero is a beautiful, winsome presence.

Custom-tailored vehicle for the rocker spins the familiar tale of a youngster who escapes the sordid confines of his family life through music, ultimately becoming the better man and musician.

••••••••••••••••••••••••••••••

■ **PURPLE ROSE OF CAIRO, THE**

1985, 82 MINS, US ◇ ⓥ

Dir Woody Allen *Prod* Robert Greenhut *Scr* Woody Allen *Ph* Gordon Willis *Ed* Susan E. Morse *Mus* Dick Hyman *Art Dir* Stuart Wurtzel
● Mia Farrow, Jeff Daniels, Danny Aiello, Dianne Wiest, Van Johnson, Zoe Caldwell (Orion)

Tale is a light, almost frivolous treatment of a serious theme, as Woody Allen here confronts the unalterable fact that life just doesn't turn out the way it does (or did) in Hollywood films. For all its situational goofiness, pic is a tragedy, and it's too bad Allen didn't build up the characters and drama sufficiently to give some weight to his concerns.

Allen introduces Depression-era waitress Mia Farrow, a hopeless film buff so consumed by motion picture gossip and fantasies she can barely hold down her job.

Her husband (Danny Aiello) is a complete boor, so she spends all her free time seeing films over and over again until Tom Baxter (Jeff Daniels), a character in a fictional RKO epic *The Purple Rose of Cairo*, stops the action, starts speaking to Farrow directly from the screen, and, fed up with repeating the same action time after time, steps out of the film and asks to be shown something of real life.

Mia Farrow is excellent again under Allen's direction, and at certain times (especially when lying to her husband) begins to sound like him. Jeff Daniels is okay as the bland 1930s adventurer come to life, although he's rather restricted by role's unavoidable thinness.

••••••••••••••••••••••••••••••

■ **PURSUED**

1947, 100 MINS, US ⓥ

Dir Raoul Walsh *Prod* Milton Sperling *Scr* Niven Busch *Ph* James Wong Howe *Ed* Christian Nyby *Mus* Max Steiner *Art Dir* Ted Smith
● Teresa Wright, Robert Mitchum, Judith Anderson, Dean Jagger, Harry Carey Jr (Warner/United States)

Pursued is potent frontier days western film fare. Standout in picture is suspense generated by the original script and Raoul Walsh's direction. It builds the western gunman's death walk to high moments of thrill and action. Strong casting also is a decided factor in selling the action wares. Production makes use of natural outdoor backgrounds supplied by New Mexico scenery, lending air of authenticity that is fully captured by the camera.

There are psychological elements in the script, depicting the hate that drives through a man's life and forces him into unwanted dangers. Robert Mitchum is the victim of that hate, made to kill and fear because of an old family feud. His role fits him naturally and he makes it entirely believable. Teresa Wright upholds the femme lead with another of her honestly valued, talented portrayals that register sincerity.

Plot motivation stems from feuding between the Callums and the Rands. Feud starts when Dean Jagger, a Callum, wipes out Mitchum's family because a Callum girl dared love Mitchum's father.

Among memorable moments is the stalking of Mitchum by the Callums as he spends his wedding night with a bride who also had just tried to kill him.

••••••••••••••••••••••••••••••

■ **PUTNEY SWOPE**

1969, 84 MINS, US ◇ ⓥ

Dir Robert Downey *Scr* Robert Downey *Ph* Gerald Cotts *Ed* Bud Smith *Mus* Charley Cuva *Art Dir* Gary Weist
● Stanley Gottlieb, Allan Garfield, Arnold Johnson, Laura Greene, Ramon Gordon (Herold)

What happens when black militants take over a large Manhattan advertising agency is the basis for a comic satire on black racial identity and the dollar sign on the American altar of success.

The situations include political caricature, but disappointedly nothing much beyond marginal interest occurs. The comedy is only intermittently funny and the satire is mostly shallow and obvious.

Putney Swope is the only black member of an ad agency. By happenstance he is elected to head the firm after the previous chairman dies.

Director Robert Downey's sense of the ridiculous is employed in a spotty, punchline kind of comic usage. The sharp individual parts do not build to anything and the film, as a piece, is more often dull than exciting, less revealingly witty then merely clever.

••••••••••••••••••••••••••••••

■ **PUZZLE OF A DOWNFALL CHILD**

1970, 104 MINS, US ◇

Dir Jerry Schatzberg *Prod* Paul Newman, John Foreman *Scr* Adrien Joyce [=Carolyn Eastman] *Ph* Adam Holender *Ed* Evan Lottman *Mus* Michael Small *Art Dir* Richard Bianchi
● Faye Dunaway, Barry Primus, Viveca Lindfors, Barry Morse, Roy Scheider (Universal)

Puzzle of a Downfall Child, stars Faye Dunaway as a confused high-fashion model with severe emotional problems, most never resolved. Unfortunately, the film is marked by cinema-verite chic though Dunaway makes the most of a tour-de-force opportunity.

Plot takes a riches-to-rags course, Dunaway entering as the latest hot model, insecure in frustrating relationships with photographer Barry Primus and well-to-do Roy Scheider. Dunaway tells her story to Primus in flashback in her seacoast cabin refuge from mental breakdown, professional decline and personal unfulfillment.

The character first garners wholesome pity, but the plot development soon banishes her to bathos and finally boredom.

••••••••••••••••••••••••••••••

Q

PYGMALION

1938, 96 MINS, UK ⓥ

Dir Anthony Asquith, Leslie Howard *Prod* Gabriel Pascal *Scr* W.P. Lipscomb, Cecil Lewis *Ph* Harry Stradling *Ed* David Lean *Mus* Arthur Honegger *Art Dir* Laurence Irving

● Wendy Hiller, Leslie Howard, Wilfred Lawson, Marie Lohr, Scott Sunderland, Jean Cadell (Pascal)

Smartly produced, this makes an excellent job of transcribing George Bernard Shaw, retaining all the key lines and giving freshness to the theme. The speed of the first half contrives to show up the anti-climax, the play subsequently petering out in a flood of clever talk. But it's still a Cinderella story, which is one of the most reliable subjects for drama.

Leslie Howard's performance is excellent in its comedy. It's vital and at times dominating. Wendy Hiller carries off a difficult part faultlessly. She never loses sight of the fact that this is a guttersnipe on whom culture has been imposed; the ambassador's reception, where she moves like a sleepwalker, is eloquent of this, and even in the final argument the cockney is always peeping through the veneer.

Wilfred Lawson's Doolittle is only a shadow of the part G.B.S. wrote, but his moral philosophies could obviously not have been put on the screen in toto without gumming up the action. As it is he presents a thoroughly enjoyable old reprobate.

□ 1938: Best Picture (Nomination)

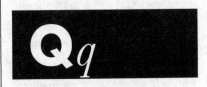

Q – THE WINGED SERPENT

1982, 92 MINS, US ◇ ⓥ

Dir Larry Cohen *Prod* Larry Cohen *Scr* Larry Cohen *Ph* Armando Crespi *Ed* Armand Lebowitz *Mus* Robert Ragland

● Michael Moriarty, David Carradine, Candy Clark, Richard Roundtree, Malachi McCourt (Arkoff)

Q – The Winged Serpent is a delightful science-fiction winner. Larry Cohen's tale of a religious bird of prey terrorizing New York City has wit, style and an above average script for the genre.

Story centers on Michael Moriarty, an ex-junkie who drives getaway cars for the mob. He takes refuge in the Chrysler Building's summit, where he stumbles onto the title character's lair complete with a large unhatched egg.

In the meantime, the green bird has been having a merry feed of workmen and apartment dwellers in the city's high rises. Policeman David Carradine links the arrival of the monster to a series of bizarre ritual killings where the victims are literally skinned alive.

The Winged Serpent has great fun mixing realistic settings with political satire and a wild yarn. Writer-director Cohen has a bagful of tricks and a wild sense of the bizarre to lend the project.

The picture belongs to the bird and Moriarty, and the latter assays his loser with relish.

Q PLANES

1939, 82 MINS, UK

Dir Tim Whelan *Prod* Irving Asher, Alexander Korda *Scr* Ian Dalrymple, Brock Williams, Jack Whittingham, Arthur Wimperis *Ph* Harry Stradling *Mus* Muir Mathieson (dir.) *Art Dir* Vincent Korda

● Laurence Olivier, Ralph Richardson, Valerie Hobson (Harefield/London)

Q Planes is an aviation picture, but not heavy on heroics. Even in the final rescue sequence, melodramatically carried to the timber line of hokum, there is a refreshing tongue-in-cheek attitude. Whole thing is bright, breezy and flavorsome. Starts off as a newsreel, showing government buildings and streets in London.

The acting honors go – and at a gallop – to Ralph Richardson, playing a Scotland Yard eccentric. Director Tim Whelan is entitled to full credit for a generally fast-paced and well-integrated entertainment.

Plot concerns the use of a salvage ship anchored at sea to capture army airplanes on their test flights. All of the crew speak with German accents and little doubt is left as to who the villains are.

Valerie Hobson, as a newspaper-woman and sister of the Scotland Yard eccentric, provides the romantic touch.

Q&A

1990, 132 MINS, US ◇ ⓥ

Dir Sidney Lumet *Prod* Arnon Milchan, Burtt Harris *Scr* Sidney Lumet *Ph* Andrzej Barthkowiak *Ed* Richard Cirincione *Mus* Ruben Blades *Art Dir* Philip Rosenberg

● Nick Nolte, Timothy Hutton, Armand Assante, Patrick O'Neal, Lee Richardson, Jenny Lumet (Regency/Odyssey)

Director Sidney Lumet grabs a tiger by the tail with *Q&A*, a hard-hitting thriller that takes on weighty topics of racism and corruption in the New York City justice system.

Working from Edwin Torres' novel, Lumet has scripted in concise, suspenseful fashion, opening with cop Nick Nolte ruthlessly killing a Latino drug dealer outside an after-hours club and then intimidating witnesses on the scene. As his first job as a new assistant d.a., Timothy Hutton is summoned by his cooly evil boss Patrick O'Neal (a man with unbridled political ambitions) to do a routine investigation, writing up a Q&A with Nolte and other principal players. He's obviously the fall guy. Key to film's success is how the case gradually uncovers new layers of corruption and insidious racism, with escalating awareness (and danger) for Hutton.

Nolte is outstanding, bringing utter conviction to the stream of racist and sexist epithets that pour from his good ole boy lips.

QUADROPHENIA

1979, 120 MINS, UK ◇ ⓥ

Dir Franc Roddam *Prod* Roy Baird, Bill Curbishley *Scr* Dave Humphries, Martin Stellman, Franc Roddam *Ph* Brian Tufano *Ed* Mike Taylor *Mus* Pete Townshend *Art Dir* Simon Holland

● Phil Daniels, Mark Wingett, Toyah Wilcox, Sting, Leslie Ash (The Who)

Set in 1963, when rival image-cults among young Britishers led to a wave of crowd-fights in normally staid seaside resorts, the picture [based on the record album *Quadrophenia* by Pete Townshend] plots the plight of one pill-popping, fashion-mad 'Mod' who abandons himself completely to the gang-identity.

After fighting the enemy 'Rockers' (denoted by black leather, motorbikes and beer) in a disorderly clash on Brighton beach, and being arrested for the cause, he swiftly discovers the hollowness of the whole image thing.

It's a tribute to helmer Franc Roddam's simple, restrained direction that the downbeat ending, when the jobless, exhausted kid is left in the advanced state of schizophrenia implied by the title, succeeds in being climactic.

Sting, as the weekend super-Mod whose image collapses when he's revealed to work as a bellhop, cuts a slick dash in the dancehall sequences.

QUALITY STREET

1937, 84 MINS, US

Dir George Stevens *Prod* Pandro S. Berman *Scr* Mortimer Offner, Allan Scott *Ph* Robert De Grasse *Ed* Henry Berman *Mus* Roy Webb

● Katharine Hepburn, Franchot Tone, Eric Blore, Fay Bainter, Cora Witherspoon, Joan Fontaine (RKO)

Of a dramatic texture which never was too strong even in the theatre, *Quality Street* is a theatrical memory involving Maude Adams in a J.M. Barrie piece. It was not rated among her best. Incredibly romantic and farcical, the idea of a 30-year-old woman deceiving her sweetheart into believing she is her own niece of 16 was tough going for the horse-and-buggy patrons of 1901.

It is a film full of effort. The settings are of a charming London residential spot, the gardens are charmingly arranged, and the costumes are charming beyond description. The dialog tries to be charming, too. The men in the cast, headed by Franchot Tone, are soldiers in England's army which smashed Napoleon. They're not so charming as quaint. Napoleon must have been a pushover and history is all wrong.

Working from a script possessing neither imagination nor ingenuity, George Stevens is limited in his direction.

QUARE FELLOW, THE

1962, 90 MINS, UK

Dir Arthur Dreifuss *Prod* Anthony Havelock-Allen *Scr* Arthur Dreifuss *Ph* Peter Hennessy *Ed* Gitta Zadek *Mus* Alexander Faris *Art Dir* Ted Marshall

● Patrick McGoohan, Sylvia Syms, Walter Macken, Dermot Kelly, Arthur O'Sullivan (British Lion)

Based on Brendan Behan's play, this is an all-out protest against capital punishment. It is downbeat entertainment but honest and has the benefit of a sterling cast, virtually all Irish. It has also been shot entirely in a Dublin prison and on location.

Patrick McGoohan is a young man from the Irish backwoods who takes up his first appointment as a jail warder with lofty ideals. Criminals must be punished for the sake of society is his inflexible theory and that also embraces capital punishment. But when he arrives he is shaken by the prison atmosphere.

Two men are awaiting the noose. One is reprieved but hangs himself. That shakes McGoohan. He meets the young wife (Sylvia Syms) of the other murderer and his convictions totter still more when he hears precisely what caused her husand to murder his brother. Mostly, though, he is influenced by a veteran warder (Walter Macken) who believes that capital punishment is often a worse crime than the original offence.

The Quare Fellow (Irish prison slang for a guy due to be topped) is mostly a study of men's conscience and convictions. Such thin storyline as there is hinges on whether the murderer will be reprieved.

The film, a mixture of grim humor and cynical starkness, brings out the clamminess and misery of prison life, and is helped by the grey lensing of Peter Hennessy.

QUARTET

1948, 120 MINS, UK ⓥ

Dir Ken Annakin, Arthur Crabtree, Harold French, Ralph Smart *Prod* Anthony Darnborough *Scr* R.C. Sherriff *Ph* Ray Elton, Reg Wyer *Ed* A. Charles Knott, Jean Barker *Mus* John Greenwood *Art Dir* George Provis, Cedric Dalve

● Basil Radford, Naunton Wayne, Dirk Bogarde,

Bernard Lee, Cecil Parker, Nora Swinburne (Rank/Gainsborough)

Of the four stories [from originals by Somerset Maugham] that make up the film, the first and last are the most intriguing. *The Facts of Life* is a superbly told piece of a 19-year-old who disregards his father's advice on his first trip to Monte Carlo and outwits an obvious adventuress, and *The Colonel's Lady* is a delightful yarn of a colonel's wife who causes much embarrassment to her husband by the publication of a book of verse purporting to describe her romantic experiences.

The intermediate two, while lacking the high level of the first and last, are certainly more than potboilers. An undergraduate son of a member of the landed gentry, who hopes to become a professional pianist, provides the melodramatic theme of *The Alien Corn*, while *The Kite* is an unusual story of a simple young man, very much under his mother's domination, who put his kite-flying before his wife and cheerfully goes to gaol when she wrecks his latest invention.

••••••••••••••••••••••••••••••••

■ **QUARTET**

1981, 100 MINS, UK/FRANCE ◇

Dir James Ivory   *Prod* Ismael Merchant   *Scr* Ruth Prawer Jhabvala   *Ph* Pierre Lhomme   *Ed* Humphrey Dixon   *Mus* Richard Robbins

● Alan Bates, Maggie Smith, Isabelle Adjani, Anthony Higgins, Suzanne Flon, Pierre Clements (Lyric/Merchant Ivory)

Quartet is an elegant tale of a pretty, innocent but resilient woman set in the Paris of the late 1920s. Director James Ivory takes his usual aloofly observant distance and the film's love triangle loses some drastic impetus. The seething Paris bohemian backdrop of the era is used only in a token way.

Isabelle Adjani is married to a young Pole who, arrested when he gets mixed up in nefarious art dealings, is sentenced to a year in prison.

She is left alone and penniless. A noted English agent, played by Alan Bates with massive solemnity, had taken a shine to her after meeting her in the expatriate circles of Paris residents. He asks her to move in with him and his wife.

The latter is an edgy, middle-aged painter limned with asperity by Maggie Smith. Other girls had stayed there and she indulged her husband's sensuality to keep him. Adjani at first spurns Bates's advances but gives in though she still loves her husband.

Overall, a lowkey film. Based on Jean Rhys' book, the script uses her spare style.

••••••••••••••••••••••••••••••••

■ **QUATERMASS EXPERIMENT, THE**

1955, 81 MINS, UK ⓥ

Dir Val Guest   *Prod* Anthony Hinds   *Scr* Val Guest, Richard Landau   *Ph* Jimmy Harvey   *Ed* James Needs   *Mus* James Bernard   *Art Dir* J. Elder Wills

● Brian Donlevy, Jack Warner, Richard Wordsworth, David King-Wood, Gordon Jackson, Lionel Jeffries (Hammer)

Taken from a BBC television play, *The Quatermass Experiment* is an extravagant piece of science fiction, based on the after-effects of an assault on space by a rocket ship. Despite its obvious horror angles, production is crammed with incident and suspense.

Brian Donlevy (in the title role) is the scientist who designs a new rocket that is sent hurtling into space with three men on board. It crash lands in a small English village, with only one survivor. The mystery is what happened to the other two who have disappeared without trace although the rocket ship remained air sealed.

This is unrelieved melodrama. It draws its entertainment from a series of wildly im-

probable happenings. There is an occasional over-plus of horror closeups of the victims.

Donlevy plays the scientist with a grim and ruthless conviction.

••••••••••••••••••••••••••••••••

■ **QUEEN CHRISTINA**

1933, 100 MINS, US

Dir Rouben Mamoulian   *Prod* Walter Wanger   *Scr* S. N. Behrman, Salka Viertel, H. M. Harwood   *Ph* William Daniels   *Ed* Blanche Sewell   *Mus* Herbert Stothart   *Art Dir* Alexander Toluboff

● Greta Garbo, John Gilbert, Ian Keith, Lewis Stone, Elizabeth Young, C. Aubrey Smith (M-G-M)

Chief fault with *Christina* is its lethargy. It is slow and ofttimes stilted. This is perhaps good cinematic motivation to establish the contrast between the queen, who has been reared as a boy to succeed to the Swedish throne, and the episode in the wayside inn where she shares her room with the new Spanish envoy who had mistaken her for a flip Nordic youth.

The buildup of the romance fol-de-rol, after the major climactic clinch, is a bit DeMille-Stroheim. Greta Garbo, in this sequence, for example, consumes beaucoup footage caressing sundry pieces of furniture, fixtures and plaques in the room, in a self-expressed purpose of memorizing every aspect thereof and when John Gilbert asks her, 'What are you doing?' sympathetically, the audience isn't quite as understanding.

The background is an obviously romantic admixture of history and fiction [story by Salka Viertel and Margaret P. Levino], touching lightly on the protestations of the A. D. 1600 Protestant Sweden's nationals against their queen's alliance with a Catholic from Spain. Gilbert is the Spanish envoy who has come to Stockholm on the expressly diplomatic and amorous mission of asking for the queen's hand in marriage to his king, the Spanish ruler.

Garbo's performance is too often apace of the script's lethargy, but as often, and more, in glamorous keeping with the romantic highlights. Her regal impression is convincing, which counts for plenty.

That goes for almost every character, from the humble peasants who are called upon to manifest their deep-rooted loyalty to the Crown in words, to the members of the royal court.

••••••••••••••••••••••••••••••••

■ **QUEEN KELLY**

1929, 96 MINS, US ⓣ

Dir Erich Von Stroheim   *Prod* Gloria Swanson   *Scr* Erich Von Stroheim   *Ph* Gordon Pollock, Paul Ivano   *Ed* Viola Lawrence   *Mus* Adolph Tandler   *Art Dir* Harold Miles

● Gloria Swanson, Seena Owen, Walter Byron, Wilhelm Von Brincken, Madge Hunt, Wilson Benge (Gloria/United Artists)

Queen Kelly, which Erich Von Stroheim originally wrote as *The Swamp*, was the director's eighth silent picture and was undertaken at the behest of Gloria Swanson. Best guess is that Von Stroheim's full scenario would have played for at least five hours' running time. Film was in production less than three months, from 1 November 1928 to 21 January 1929, when Swanson, finally fed up with her director's excesses, told financier Joseph Kennedy to shut it down after an expenditure of $800,000.

Since *Queen Kelly* was shot in sequence, what exists of it plays very smoothly and coherently up through its arbitrary, but dramatically valid, conclusion. Set in the sort of fin-de-siecle Ruritanian principality usually favored by the director, tale presents the mad young Queen Regina (Seena Owen) forcing the playboy Prince Wolfram (Walter Byron) into a royal marriage.

Far from resigned to a life of amorous activity, Wolfram encounters a troup of convent girls while on cavalry drill in the country and, in a legendary scene, meets Kitty Kelly (Gloria Swanson).

As planned by the director, film would have continued ever-deeper into grand melodrama until, coming full circle, Kitty would truly have become Queen Kelly along with Wolfram, displacing Regina on the throne.

Version of the film released minimally in Europe and South America in the early 1930s ended with Kitty successfully committing suicide. Footage of her in a bordello in German East Africa was not discovered until 1963. The music score by Adolph Tandler, which was written for Swanson's 1931–32 version, was discovered on a nitrate soundtrack for use in this edition. [Version reviewed is a complete-as-possible reconstruction in 1985.]

••••••••••••••••••••••••••••••••

■ **QUEEN OF OUTER SPACE**

1958, 80 MINS, US ◇

Dir Edward Bernds   *Prod* Ben Schwalb   *Scr* Charles Beaumont   *Ph* William Whitley   *Ed* William Austin   *Mus* Marlin Skiles   *Art Dir* David Milton

● Zsa Zsa Gabor, Eric Fleming, Laurie Mitchell, Paul Birch, Patrick Waltz, Barbara Darrow (Allied Artists)

Most of the female characters in *Queen of Outer Space* look like they would be more at home on a Minsky runway than the Cape Canaveral launching pad, but Ben Schwalb's production [based on a story by Ben Hecht] is a good-natured attempt to put some honest sex into science-fiction.

The year is 1985, and Eric Fleming, Patrick Waltz and Dave Willock are US officers in charge of a space ship assigned to check on an American satellite space station. They are deflected from their course by mysterious energy rays from the planet Venus, where their ship is eventually wrecked. Taken prisoner by a malignant queen (Laurie Mitchell), they are about to be destroyed, when they are rescued by a pro-masculine group headed by Zsa Zsa Gabor.

The cast is predominantly feminine and attractively garbed in the brief raiment that appears to be customary on other planets. Gabor makes a handsome leading lady, romanced by Fleming and the others lend the necessary ingredients to their roles.

••••••••••••••••••••••••••••••••

■ **QUEEN OF SPADES, THE**

1949, 95 MINS, UK ⓥ

Dir Thorold Dickinson   *Prod* Anatole de Grunwald   *Scr* Rodney Ackland, Arthur Boys   *Ph* Otto Heller, Gus Drisse, Val Stewart   *Ed* Hazel Wilkinson   *Mus* Georges Auric   *Art Dir* Oliver Messel

● Anton Walbrook, Edith Evans, Yvonne Mitchell, Ronald Howard (Associated British Pathe)

Opulence of Imperial Russia at the beginning of the 19th century provides a colorful background for this filmization of Alexander Pushkin's short story, which brings to the screen a legend of gambling and intrigue.

Central character in the story is a captain of the Engineers. He cannot afford to gamble but is prepared to stake his all on a secret formula believed to have been passed on to a certain countess. Countess dies, but believing he has received a message from the dead, the captain goes to a gambling table and challenges his rival in love.

Outstanding performance comes from Edith Evans, making her screen debut. Her interpretation of the old grotesque countess is almost terrifying in its realism, and she dominates the screen from her first entry until her death. Anton Walbrook, and Ronald Howard as his rival in love, lack color.

••••••••••••••••••••••••••••••••

Q

QUERELLE

1982, 120 MINS, W. GERMANY/FRANCE ◇ Ⓥ

Dir Rainer Werner Fassbinder *Scr* Rainer Werner Fassbinder *Ph* Xaver Schwarzenberger *Ed* Juliane Lorenz *Mus* Peer Raben *Art Dir* Rolf Zehetbauer
● Brad Davis, Franco Nero, Jeanne Moreau, Laurent Malet, Hanno Poschl, Gunther Kaufman (Planet/Gaumont)

The last film of Rainer Werner Fassbinder is, unfortunately, disappointing. His attempt to put the mystical homosexual world of French writer Jean Genet on film is ultimately tedious.

There is curio value in this strange tale of a young sailor, Querelle, who fascinates all who come in contact with him but who seems more absorbed in himself.

It seems to be set in the 1930s but is timeless and stylized. A boat on which Querelle works pulls into a port in Brest, France. Film is all studio work without any pretense at realism. It ties up at a jetty which has a bar and a bordello run by Jeanne Moreau. Querelle, played with a sort of dreamlike intensity by Brad Davis, is soon mixed up in this strange world.

....

QUEST FOR FIRE

1981, 97 MINS, FRANCE/CANADA ◇

Dir Jean-Jacques Annaud *Prod* Denis Heroux, John Kemeny, Jacques Dorfmann, Vera Belmont *Scr* Gerard Brach *Ph* Claude Agostini *Ed* Yves Langlois *Mus* Philippe Sarde *Art Dir* Brian Morris
● Everett McGill, Rae Dawn Chong, Ron Perlman, Nameer El Kadi, Gary Schwartz, Kurt Schiegel (ICC/Belstar/Stephan)

Jean-Jacques Annaud's *Quest for Fire* is an engaging prehistoric yarn that happily never degenerates into a club and lion skin spinoff of *Star Wars* and resolutely refuses to bludgeon the viewer with facile or gratuitous effects.

Despite four years of effort, a $12 million budget, grueling location shooting in Kenya, Scotland, Iceland and Canada, hundreds of masks and costumes and a herd of difficult elephants (making their screen apperance as mammoths), Annaud and his collaborators have brought off a polished entertainment.

Technical advisor Anthony Burgess invented special primitive jargons for the occasion, which are used in moderation and don't jar comically on the ears.

Gerard Brach's screenplay is loosely based on Jean-Henri Rosny the Elder's *La guerre du feu* (1911), a classic of French language popular literature. He also introduces a female character as a major dramatic and emotional pivot.

Three warriors of a primitive homo sapiens tribe are sent out to find a source of fire after their old pilot lights are extinguished during an attack by a group of unneighborly Neanderthals. After numerous adventures they find a fire amongst a cannibal tribe, but also learn how to produce it when they are led to an advanced human community by a young girl whom they've saved from the cannibals.

Annaud wisely uses mimes, dancers, acrobats and stuntmen for many of the secondary and extra roles. Under the guidance of anthropologist Desmond Morris, they provide credible physical expression and their excellent masks and makeup.

Everett Gill New York stage actor Ron Perlman, and Turkish-born Nameer El Kadi etch engaging portraits as the three early homo sapiens, but the best performance comes from 20-year-old Rae Dawn Chong (daughter of comic Tommy Chong), unaffectedly radiant as the tribal nymphet who teaches them how to make a fire and eventually mates with Gill (after showing him how to make love face-to-face).

....

QUICK CHANGE

1990, 88 MINS, US ◇ Ⓥ

Dir Howard Franklin, Bill Murray *Prod* Robert Greenhut, Bill Murray *Scr* Howard Franklin *Ph* Michael Chapman *Ed* Alan Heim *Mus* Randy Edelman *Art Dir* David Gropman
● Bill Murray, Geena Davis, Randy Quaid, Jason Robards, Bob Elliott (Warner/Devoted)

Bill Murray delivers a smart, sardonic and very funny valentine to the rotten Apple in *Quick Change*. Pic became Murray's directing debut (he shares the chores with screenwriter Howard Franklin) after he and Franklin became too attached to the project to bring anyone else in. Material, based on Jay Cronley's book, is neither ambitious nor particularly memorable, but it's brought off with a sly flair that makes it most enjoyable.

Murray plays a fed-up New Yorker who enlists his girlfriend (Geena Davis) and lifelong pal (Randy Quaid) in a bank heist so they can get outta town. Hold-up, which nets $1 million and a very nice watch, sets off a carnival of police and crowd reaction in the New York streets, but none of it flaps the dynamite-rigged Murray.

With Jason Robards as a crusty police inspector who's as crazily sharp as *Twin Peaks* agent Cooper, pic offers some crazy little set-pieces in a manic game of chase. Pic is so thick with gritty, tired, scuzzy NY atmosphere viewer wants to scrape it off the skin.

Only in the final reel do things feel broadly contrived, concurrent with pic's move from NY locations to a Florida soundstage for airport shooting.

....

QUICK MILLIONS

1931, 69 MINS, US

Dir Rowland Brown *Scr* Courtenay Terrett, Rowland Brown, John Wray *Ph* Joseph August *Ed* Harold Schuster *Art Dir* Duncan Cramer
● Spencer Tracy, Marguerite Churchill, Sally Eilers, Robert Burns, John Wray, Warner Richmond (Fox)

Another gangster story, but written down to the bone and directed for everything it contains.

For continuity and cutting the studio handed Brown a bonus of $1,000. It's Rowland Brown's first picture. Previously he was a Fox contract writer. His co-author on this story, like himself, is a former newspaper reporter. Courtenay Terrett once wrote a story called *Only Saps Work*, and Paramount took it along with Terrett.

The background of *Quick Millions* is similar and takes the eye through a cleverly-knit panorama of racketeering as the yoke is laid on big business interests.

Story, after a fashion, gives an inside on how racketeers prey on organized business. In brief, it recounts the tale of a tough truck driver, with ideas, who climbs to the top, even socially, through forcing contractors into the right corner, only to topple from his throne at the hands of rival gangsters after turned down by the girl, a contractor's daughter. Simple, but the force, interest, suspense and the benefit of capable workmanship.

Spencer Tracy is excellent. Sally Eilers looks well at all times, and that's about all she has to do. Marguerite Churchill, as the former sweetheart, has the better of it from a script viewpoint. Robert Burns, Warner Richmond and George Raft are good gangster types. Contractor racket victim John Wray, who did the added dialog, oke.

....

QUIET AMERICAN, THE

1958, 120 MINS, US

Dir Joseph L. Mankiewicz *Prod* Joseph L. Mankiewicz *Scr* Joseph L. Mankiewicz *Ph* Robert Krasker *Ed* William Hornbeck *Mus* Mario Nascimbene *Art Dir* Rino Mondinello
● Audie Murphy, Michael Redgrave, Claude Dauphin, Giorgia Moll, Kerima, Bruce Cabot (United Artists/Figaro)

In adapting Graham Greene's bitter and cynical *The Quiet American* into a motion picture, Joseph L. Mankiewicz has allowed himself the luxury of turning the screen into a debating society. It might have paid off had he retained the central character of the American in the book who, in Greene's version, represented all the determined bungling of American foreign policy. As it turns out, the film – shot in Vietnam and at Cinecitta Studios in Rome – is an overlong, overdialogued adaptation, concerned with the pros and cons of a Third Force in Asia.

Story follows the line of the book, but with the all-important difference that the character of the American, played without much depth by Audie Murphy, has been drained of meaning, giving the whole picture a pro-American slant. Murphy here doesn't represent the US government, but merely works for a private US aid mission. In other words, his ideas of a Third Force standing between Communism and French Colonialism are his own.

It's one long flashback from the moment Murphy is found murdered and Michael Redgrave, playing a British correspondent, is asked by French inspector Claude Dauphin to identify him. Dauphin gradually unspools the sometimes obscure story.

Love interest in the film is pretty newcomer Giorgia Moll who lives with Redgrave but leaves him for the younger Murphy. Running throughout is the clashing of views between Redgrave and Murphy.

Redgrave's moody portrayal of the neurotic aging Britisher hiding personal anxieties under a mask of cynicism makes the whole thing worthwhile.

The Quiet American has been photographed skillfully, though the number of scenes showing off Vietnam (the story is laid in 1952, before the partition) isn't very large.

....

QUIET DAYS IN CLICHY

1970, 100 MINS, DENMARK

Dir Jens-Jorgen Thorsen *Scr* Jens-Jorgen Thorsen *Ph* Jesper Hom *Ed* Anker *Mus* Country Joe McDonald, Ben Webster, Andy Sunstrom
● Louise White, Paul Valjean, Wayne John Rodda, Ulla Lemvigh-Muller, Susanne Krage (SBA)

This is a true-to-the-letter re-telling of Henry Miller's memoir about Montmartre life, with very little food and many, many women.

Director Jens-Jorgen Thorsen shows both technical skill and madcap humor and, furthermore, knows more than a little about the loneliness dimension of Miller's work.

Paul Valjean looks like the popular image of Henry Miller, easygoing, nice, lecherous, hungry and full of fun. Among the girls who indulge in unlimited frontal nudity, Louise White, Ulla Lemvigh-Muller and Susanne Krage have the rather spectacular achievement of making the audience remember their faces as well as their bodies.

....

QUIET MAN, THE

1952, 129 MINS, US ◇ Ⓥ

Dir John Ford *Prod* John Ford, Merian C. Cooper *Scr* Frank S. Nugent *Ph* Winton C. Hoch *Ed* Jack Murray *Mus* Victor Young *Art Dir* Frank Hotaling
● John Wayne, Maureen O'Hara, Victor McLaglen, Barry Fitzgerald, Ward Bond, Mildred Natwick (Argosy/Republic)

This is a robust romantic drama of a native-born's return to Ireland. Director John Ford took cast and cameras to Ireland to tell the story [by Maurice Walsh] against actual backgrounds.

Wayne is the quiet man of the title, returning to the land of his birth to forget a life of struggle and violence. In Inisfree, Wayne buys the cottage where he was born, immediately arousing the ire of Victor McLaglen, a well-to-do farmer who wanted the property himself.

His next mistake is to fall for Maureen O'Hara, McLaglen's sister. Custom decrees the brother must give consent to marriage, so Wayne's suit is hopeless until newly-made friends are able to trick McLaglen long enough to get the ceremony over with. Safely married, Wayne finds himself with a bride but not a wife.

Despite the length of the footage, film holds together by virtue of a number of choice characters, the best of which is Barry Fitzgerald's socko punching of an Irish type. Wayne works well under Ford's direction, answering all demands of the vigorous, physical character.

□ 1952: Best Picture (Nomination)

．．．．．．．．．．．．．．．．．．．．．．．．．．．

■ QUIGLEY DOWN UNDER

1990, 119 MINS, US ◇ Ⓥ

Dir Simon Wincer *Prod* Stanley O'Toole *Scr* John Hill *Ph* David Eggby *Ed* Adrian Carr, Peter Burgess *Mus* Basil Poledouris *Art Dir* Ross Major
● Tom Selleck, Laura San Giacomo, Alan Rickman, Chris Haywood, Ron Haddrick, Tony Bonner (M-G-M/Pathe)

Quigley Down Under is an exquisitely crafted, rousing Western made in Oz.

Script was written for Steve McQueen in the 1970s, then developed in 1984, Rick Rosenthal to helm; project was reactivated in 1986 with Lewis Gilbert scheduled to direct.

Tom Selleck is in the title role as a sharp-shooter from the American West who answers villain Alan Rickman's ad and heads to Fremantle in Western Australia. Quigley is informed that he's been hired to kill aborigines with his longrange, custom-made rifle as part of Rickman's campaign of genocide, encouraged by the local authorities.

Selleck's violent response to the request begins a vendetta in which Rickman has him left for dead in the middle of nowhere. Along for the ensuing survival trek is Laura San Giacomo, a fellow American haunted by the death of her child in a Commanche raid.

Selleck has his best bigscreen casting so far here (not counting the missed opportunity to be Indiana Jones). He's thoroughly convincing with his custom-made rifle and low-key manner. San Giacomo comes into her own as the feisty heroine. Rickman is a perfectly hissable villain.

．．．．．．．．．．．．．．．．．．．．．．．．．．．

■ QUILLER MEMORANDUM, THE

1966, 103 MINS, UK ◇ Ⓥ

Dir Michael Anderson *Prod* Ivan Foxwell *Scr* Harold Pinter *Ph* Erwin Hiller *Ed* Frederick Wilson *Mus* John Barry *Art Dir* Maurice Carter
● George Segal, Alec Guinness, Max von Sydow, Senta Berger, George Sanders, Robert Helpmann (Rank)

The Quiller Memorandum, based on a novel by Adam Hall (pen name for Elleston Trevor) and with a screenplay by Harold Pinter, deals with the insidious upsurge of neo-Nazism in Germany. It relies on a straight narrative storyline, simple but holding, literate dialog and well-drawn characters.

Set largely on location in West Berlin, it has George Segal brought back from vacation to replace a British agent who has come to a sticky end at the hands of a new infiltrating group of Nazis. His job is to locate their headquarters. He does this in a lone-wolf way, refusing to be hampered by bodyguards. En route he has some edgy adventures.

Segal plays Quiller with a laconic but likeable detachment, underlining the loneliness and lack of relaxation of the agent, who can-

not even count on support from his own side. Alec Guinness never misses a trick in his few scenes as the cold, witty fish in charge of Berlin sector investigations. Max von Sydow plays the Nazi chief quietly but with high camp menace.

．．．．．．．．．．．．．．．．．．．．．．．．．．．

■ QUINTET

1979, 100 MINS, US ◇ Ⓥ

Dir Robert Altman *Prod* Robert Altman *Scr* Frank Barhydt, Robert Altman, Patricia Resnick *Ph* Jean Boffety *Ed* Dennis M. Hill *Mus* Tom Pierson *Art Dir* Leon Ericksen
● Paul Newman, Vittorio Gassman, Fernando Rey, Bibi Andersson, Brigitte Fossey, Nina Van Pallandt (20th Century-Fox)

Here's another one for Robert Altman's inner circle.

In one of the few obvious points about the picture [based on a story by Altman, Lionel Chetwynd and Patricia Resnick], the title refers to a game popular in some future city (Montreal?) that's slowly dying in a new Ice Age. Though the finer details are anybody's guess, the game involves five players trying to eliminate each other, plus a sixth who comes late to the board.

Paul Newman arrives in the city with his young pregnant bride (Brigitte Fossey) and finds some of the citizens playing the game for real, with Fernando Rey as referee. After losing his bride to a bomb, Newman is drawn into the game.

Before it's over, there have been two bloody throat slashings, a hand bursting open in a fire and one vigorous stabbing.

．．．．．．．．．．．．．．．．．．．．．．．．．．．

■ QUO VADIS

1951, 171 MINS, US ◇ Ⓥ

Dir Mervyn LeRoy *Prod* Sam Zimbalist *Scr* John Lee Mahin, S. H. Behrman, Sonya Levien *Ph* Robert Surtees, William V. Skall *Ed* Ralph E. Winters *Mus* Miklos Rozsa *Art Dir* Cedric Gibbons, William Horning, Edward Carfagno, Hugh Hunt
● Robert Taylor, Deborah Kerr, Leo Genn, Peter Ustinov, Patricia Laffan, Finlay Currie (M-G-M)

Quo Vadis is a super-spectacle in all its meaning. That there are shortcomings [in this fourth version of the tale] even Metro must have recognized and ignored in consideration of the project's scope. The captiousness about the story line, some of the players' wooden performances in contrast to the scenery-chewing of Peter Ustinov (Nero), are part and parcel of any super-spectacular.

The contrast, of course, is sharp in that Leo Genn's slick underplaying makes Ustinov's sybarite conception of Nero that much more out of focus with realities. But the Polish novelist, Henryk Sienkiewicz, intended to contrast the glory that was Rome and the splendor that was Nero's court with the travails of the early Christians.

While the Romans worship their idols and vestal virgins, while Nero rules a still-lush if decadent court in its final stage of cowardice, wickedness and degeneracy, Robert Taylor is shown leading his victorious Roman troops down the Appian Way. Deborah Kerr, as a Christian hostage, is the vis-a-vis. Genn, as the suave Petronius, who constantly derides the stupid Nero, has Marina Berti, a beauteous slave girl, as his romantic opposite.

There are no ups and downs on the spectacular values that comprise the Circus of Nero, the profligate court scenes, the marching armies, the racing chariots, the burning of Rome, the shackled captives under Roman rule, the pagan ceremonies, the secret Christian meetings, the gladiators unto the death to amuse Nero's court, and the climax as the Christian martyrs face the unleashed lions in the great Circus of Nero.

□ 1951: Best Picture (Nomination)

．．．．．．．．．．．．．．．．．．．．．．．．．．．

■ RABID

1977, 91 MINS, CANADA ◇ Ⓥ

Dir David Cronenberg *Prod* John Dunning *Scr* David Cronenberg *Ph* Rene Verzier *Ed* Jean Lafleur *Art Dir* Claude Marchand
● Marilyn Chambers, Frank Moore, Joe Silver, Howard Ryshpan, Patricia Gage, Susan Roman (Cinema Entertainment)

Rabid, as the dictionary explains means both 'affected with rabies' and 'extremely violent'. Using both definitions, *Rabid*, is so accurately titled that this one world tells all. Here is an extremely violent, sometimes nauseating, picture about a young woman affected with rabies, running around Montreal infecting others.

Marilyn Chambers, the Whilone Procter & Gamble Ivory Snow girl turned porno film actress, plays the infected one – sort of a cross between Typhoid Mary with rabies and a vampire.

On the one side in the urban jungle are human animals, foaming at the mouth, biting each other in shopping malls, operating rooms and subway cars. On the other side are animals of another sort shooting down those salivating the green foam.

．．．．．．．．．．．．．．．．．．．．．．．．．．．

■ RACHEL AND THE STRANGER

1948, 92 MINS, US

Dir Norman Foster *Prod* Richard H. Berger *Scr* Waldo Salt *Ph* Maury Gertsman *Ed* Les Millbrook *Mus* Roy Webb *Art Dir* Albert S. D'Agostino, Jack Okey, Walter E. Keller
● Loretta Young, William Holden, Robert Mitchum, Gary Gray (RKO)

Mood of the picture is pleasant but is so even that interest isn't too strong. Dangers of pioneering in a wilderness, vaguely referred to as the northwest, could have been more excitingly depicted. Single incident of excitement – a strong one – is put off until the finale and has a socko Indian raid on a settler's homestead in the wilds.

Otherwise, narrative maintains its even pace in telling story of a pioneer who buys a bride to do the chores and teach niceties of life to his motherless son. The bride is only a servant until a hunter, friend of the groom, appears and makes a play for her.

William Holden enacts the dour settler, so deeply in love with his dead wife he fails to appreciate, or even notice, the charms of his new bondswoman bride. Loretta Young has only two costume changes and her makeup is true to role, but she makes some glamour shine through. Robert Mitchum is the aimlessly wandering hunter.

．．．．．．．．．．．．．．．．．．．．．．．．．．．

■ RACHEL PAPERS, THE

1989, 95 MINS, UK ◇ Ⓥ

Dir Damian Harris *Prod* Andrew S. Karsch *Scr* Damion Harris *Ph* Alex Thomson *Ed* David Martin *Mus* Chaz Jenkel *Art Dir* Andrew McAlpine
● Dexter Fletcher, Ione Skye, Jonathan Pryce, James Spader, Bill Patterson, Michael Gambon (Initial/Longfellow)

Charles Highway is a 19-year-old with no money problems who maps out his sexual conquests via his desktop. He meets beautiful American Rachel Noyce, also 19. It's love at first sight, but she already has a boyfriend.

After a bit of frustration, he sends her a funny love message on videotape, and she comes around. They have a steamy, passionate affair, of which he tires all too soon. They part. End of story.

The basic material is as old as the hills, but Martin Amis, who wrote the original novel some 15 years earlier, explored it in fresh directions. Director Damaian Harris' isn't able to capture the book's special charms, and resorts to having his young hero address the camera to keep the viewer in the picture. Unfortunately, Dexter Fletcher is rather too self-conscious here, and makes Charles a less than endearing hero. On the other hand, Ione Skye seizes her chances as Rachel and gives a glowingly sensual performance. Their lengthy loves scenes together, often in a bathtub, are certainly steamy.

■ RACHEL, RACHEL

1968, 101 MINS, US ◇ ⓥ
Dir Paul Newman *Prod* Paul Newman *Scr* Stewart Stern *Ph* Gayne Rescher *Ed* Dede Allen *Mus* Jerome Moross *Art Dir* Robert Gundlach
● Joanne Woodward, James Olson, Kate Harrington, Estelle Parsons, Donald Moffatt, Terry Kiser (Warner/Seven Arts)

Rachel, Rachel is a low-key melodrama starring Joanne Woodward as a spinster awakening to life. Produced austerely by Paul Newman, who also directs with an uncertain hand, it marks Newman's feature debut in these non-acting capacities. Offbeat film moves too slowly to an upbeat, ironic climax.

Margaret Laurence's novel, *A Jest of God*, has been adapted into an episodic, halting screenplay which not only conveys the tedium of Woodward's adult life but also, unfortunately, takes its time in so doing.

There is very little dialog – most of which is very good – but this asset makes a liability out of the predominantly visual nature of the development, which in time seems to become redundant, padded and tiring.

James Olson, a childhood friend who has returned for a visit, provides Woodward with an alternative. Believing herself pregnant by Olson, she determines to have the child.

Direction is awkward. Were Woodward not there film could have been a shambles.
□ 1968: Best Picture (Nomination)

■ RACING WITH THE MOON

1984, 108 MINS, US ◇ ⓥ
Dir Richard Benjamin *Prod* Alain Bernheim, John Kohn *Scr* Steven Kloves *Ph* John Bailey *Ed* Jacqueline Cambas *Mus* Dave Grusin *Art Dir* David L. Snyder
● Sean Penn, Elizabeth McGovern, Nicolas Cage, John Karlen, Rutanya Alda, Kate Williamson (Paramount/Jaffe-Lansing)

Racing with the Moon is a sweet, likable film that doesn't contain the usual commercial elements normally expected these days in youth pics. Working in a more straightforward, serious mode, Richard Benjamin confirms the directorial promise he displayed in *My Favorite Year*, and Sean Penn and Elizabeth McGovern are good as the romantic leads.

Time frame is Christmas of 1942, and Penn and his rowdy buddy Nicolas Cage have just a few weeks left until they join the Marines. Penn becomes dazzled by a new face in the California coastal town, McGovern, whom he takes to be a rich girl since she lives up in the 'Gatsby' mansion. While, a wrong-side-of-the-tracks type, Cage gets his g.f. pregnant, and after a disastrous, but wonderfully staged, attempt to hustle some sailors at pool, Penn forces himself to enlist McGovern's help in raising $150 for an abortion for his friend's gal.

First-time scenarist Steven Kloves has created two nice leading characters, nicely essayed by Penn and McGovern.

Benjamin shows a consistently generous attitude toward his characters and an inclination to emphasize their most exemplary traits.

■ RACKET, THE

1928, 70 MINS, US ⊗
Dir Lewis Milestone *Prod* Howard Hughes *Scr* Bartlett Cormack
● Thomas Meighan, Marie Prevost, Louis Wolheim, George Stone, John Darrow, 'Skeets' Gallagher (Paramount/Caddo)

A good story, plus good direction, plus a great cast and minus dumb supervision, is responsible for another great underworld film.

Thomas Meighan has his best role in years as Captain McQuigg, and Louis Wolheim, as Nick Scarsi, adds to a screen rep that has already labeled him the best character heavy, the one-eyed monster has ever pecked at.

The Racket, like all great pictures, started with a great yarn and a director alive to its possibilities. It grips your interest from the first shot to the last, and never drags for a second. It's another tale of the underworld, a battle of wills and cunning between an honest copper and a gorilla who has the town in his lap.

Tom Miranda was given wide latitude with slang and gun chatter and the result is the most authentic set of titles that have graced an underworld picture to date. The gorillas talk as they should and not as some lamebrained obstructionist thinks they should. They don't go to jail – they go to the can – and without those diagrams the average super wants with any title in vernacular.

And shades of Beverly Hills, there's no love interest! Imagine a hero who doesn't cop a moll in the last ten feet.

Boy, page the millenium!
□ 1927/28: Best Picture (Nomination)

■ RADIO DAYS

1987, 85 MINS, US ◇ ⓥ
Dir Woody Allen *Prod* Robert Greenhut *Scr* Woody Allen *Ph* Carlo Di Palma *Ed* Susan E. Morse *Mus* Dick Hyman *Art Dir* Santo Loquasto
● Mia Farrow, Seth Green, Julie Kavner, Josh Mostel, Michael Tucker, Dianne Wiest (Orion)

Although lacking the bite and depth of his best work, *Radio Days* is one of Woody Allen's most purely entertaining pictures. It's a visual monolog of bits and pieces from the glory days of radio and the people who were tuned in.

Rockaway Beach, a thin strip of land on the outskirts of New York City is where young Joe (Seth Green) and his family live in not-so splendid harmony and for entertainment and escape to listen to the radio. Set at the start of World War II, it's a world of aunts and uncles all living on top of each other and the magical events and people, real and imagined, that forever shape one's young imagination.

Radio Days is not simply about nostalgia, but the quality of memory and how what one remembers informs one's present life.

Dianne Wiest is delicious as an aunt who is desperate to find a husband but somehow keeps meeting Mr Wrong. The robust Masked Avenger is, in real life, the diminutive Wallace Shawn. Mia Farrow is a none-too-bright cigaret girl with a yen for stardom who magically transforms her life.

■ RAFFERTY AND THE GOLD DUST TWINS

1975, 91 MINS, US ◇
Dir Dick Richards *Prod* Michael Gruscoff, Art Linson *Scr* John Kaye *Ph* Ralph Woolsey *Ed* Walter Thompson *Mus* Artie Butler *Art Dir* Joel Schiller

● Alan Arkin, Sally Kellerman, Mackenzie Phillips, Alex Rocco, Charles Martin Smith, Harry Dean Stanton (Warner)

Rafferty and the Gold Dust Twins is another sterile Warner Bros. comedy-drama about the 'little people' of America, as seen through the eyes of Beverly Hills and Upper Manhattan. Alan Arkin stars as a loutish bumbler, fraudulently kidnapped by Sally Kellerman and teenager Mackenzie Phillips, into an odyssey through many lower class southwest locations.

Arkin's stereotyped Everyman clod meshes awkwardly with spaced-out Kellerman's formula characterization, thereby throwing interest by default to Phillips (the mature moppet of *American Graffiti* in another good streetwise role).

Harry Dean Stanton in a very good part as an embittered yahoo, and Charlie Martin Smith (also from *Graffiti* are among the more effective supporting players.

■ RAFFLES

1930, 70 MINS, US
Dir Harry D'Arrast, George Fitzmaurice *Prod* Samuel Goldwyn *Scr* Sidney Howard *Ph* George Barnes, Gregg Toland *Ed* Stuart Heisler *Art Dir* William, Cameron Menzies, Park French
● Ronald Colman, Kay Francis, David Torrence, Frances Dade (Goldwyn)

The old-fashioned artifices of the [original 1899 novel *The Amateur Cracksman* by E.W. Hornung and its subsequent dramatization] are incidental. The essence of its interest is a rascal so captivating that you are pleased to see him emerge triumphant, though guilty, from his brush with Scotland Yard.

Picture version capitalizes such instinctive feeling, by actually having the defeated Inspector K. McKenzie take his final trimming with a philosophical grin.

Kay Francis is a happy choice – an actress with that suggestion of reserve vitality that makes her stand out strongly.

Comedy sequences supplied by Alison Skipworth and Frederick Kerr, the sentimental British dowager and her absurd spouse, have a good deal of freshness and reality. In like manner, the picture's atmosphere impresses as thoroughly authentic.

■ RAGE

1966, 103 MINS, US/MEXICO ◇ ⓥ
Dir Gilberto Gazcon *Prod* Gilberto Gazcon *Scr* Teddi Sherman, Gilberto Gazcon, Fernando Mendez *Ph* Rosalio Solano *Ed* Carlos Savage, Walter Thompson *Mus* Gustavo Cesar Carreon
● Glenn Ford, Stella Stevens, David Reynoso, Armando Silvestre, Ariadna Wellter, Jose Elias Moreno (Schenck/Jalisco)

Rage, a joint Mexican-American production lensed entirely below the Border, is a moderately interesting story of a doctor's frantic race against time to reach a hospital for the Pasteur treatment against rabies.

Glenn Ford and Stella Stevens are the only Americans in cast, balance recruited wholly from Mexican ranks. Although Mexican-made, pic was shot in English.

Ford plays a guilt-ridden physician half-bent upon self-destruction, haunted by memory of the death of his wife and child, for which he blames himself. His base of operations is a construction camp practically in the wilderness. Nipped by his pet dog, he finds later it has rabies, and figures he has only about 48 hours to reach a medical center where he may be treated. With Stevens, a hooker who has been in the camp, he races thru desert and mountain in an attempt to reach the hospital.

Good suspense is worked up in situation and writer-director Gilberto Gazcon maintains mood realistically. Ford etches a rugged characterization, particularly as panic begins to take hold in what appears to be a hopeless effort in reaching the hospital in time.

● ●

■ RAGE

1972, 99 MINS, US ◇ Ⓥ

Dir George C. Scott   *Prod* Fred Weintraub   *Scr* Philip Friedman, Dan Kleinman   *Ph* Fred Koenekamp   *Ed* Michael Kahn   *Mus* Lalo Schifrin   *Art Dir* Frank Sylos
● George C. Scott, Richard Basehart, Martin Sheen, Barnard Hughes, Nicolas Beauvy, Paul Stevens (Warner/Weintraub)

Rage is a sluggish, tried and tiring melodrama, starring George C. Scott, in his directorial debut, as a father wreaking vengeance for the death of his son after a chemical warfare experimental accident. Though largely a western states exterior film, the plot is a stagey, talky effort reminiscent of a 1950s TV anthology drama.

Writers start on a promising track – establishing widower Scott's relationship with son Nicolas Beauvy, and engendering suspense when the boy and the family cattle suddenly begin to drop like flies. Even further, the efforts of the US Army and other government officials to hush the goof from press and Scott are dramatized in an all-too-credible way. But the story resolution becomes a shambles as Scott begins killing and blowing up installations.

● ●

■ RAGE TO LIVE, A

1965, 101 MINS, US

Dir Walter Grauman   *Prod* Lewis J. Rachmil   *Scr* John T. Kelley   *Ph* Charles Lawton   *Ed* Stuart Gilmore   *Mus* Nelson Riddle   *Art Dir* James Sullivan
● Suzanne Pleshette, Bradford Dillman, Ben Gazzara, Peter Graves, Bethel Leslie, James Gregory (Mirisch/United Artists)

In this banal transfer from tome to film, the characters in John O'Hara's *A Rage to Live* have retained their two-dimensional unreality in a country-club setting. Nympho heroine goes from man to man amidst corny dialog and inept direction which combine to smother all thesps.

Director Walter Grauman achieves little with the players, nor does he attempt to hypo visual interest via technical gimmicks.

Thesps share the guilt. Suzanne Pleshette misses as the nympho who is dressed to the nines in an eye-catching Howard Shoup wardrobe. Bradford Dillman, the love in her life (as opposed to the men in her bed), is wasted on Rover-boy lines. Ben Gazzara, the boy-who-worked-his-way-up, has little of the animal magnetism which is supposed to have rocked the pair's marriage boat.

● ●

■ RAGGEDY MAN

1981, 94 MINS, US ◇

Dir Jack Fisk   *Prod* Burt Weissbourd, William D. Wittliff   *Scr* William D. Wittliff   *Ph* Ralf Bode   *Ed* Edward Warschilka   *Mus* Jerry Goldsmith   *Art Dir* John Lloyd
● Sissy Spacek, Eric Roberts, Sam Shepard, William Sanderson, Tracey Walter (Universal)

Directed by husband Jack Fisk (his first feature), Sissy Spacek plays a spunky divorcee, struggling to raise two young boys and stuck in a hopeless job as a small-town telephone operator tied to the switchboard in her house.

The setting is Texas in 1944 and Fisk, along with art director John Lloyd and costumer Joe I. Tompkins, has done a superb job in creating a faithful environment, down to the smallest detail. (Fisk was previously an art director.)

Enter sailor Eric Roberts in a rainstorm, knocking on the door to use the phone. After a night on the porch, Roberts spends a warmhearted day with Spacek and the lads (Henry Thomas and Carey Hollis Jr). Gradually, warmth turns to heat in Spacek's bed.

Roberts is a terrific match for Spacek and their building romance sparkles. But she abruptly sends him packing and, after a tearful farewell, Roberts is seen no more.

With Roberts gone, the film turns mean as William Sanderson and Tracey Walter – both ably playing their redneck roles – make their move on Spacek. This is standard stuff and hardly worth Spacek's talents.

● ●

■ RAGGEDY RAWNEY, THE

1988, 102 MINS, UK ◇ Ⓥ

Dir Bob Hoskins   *Prod* Bob Weis   *Scr* Bob Hoskins, Nicole De Wilde   *Ph* Frank Tidy   *Ed* Alan Jones   *Mus* Michael Kamen   *Art Dir* Jiri Matolin
● Bob Hoskins, Dexter Fletcher, Zoe Nathenson, Dave Hill, Ian Dury (HandMade)

Bob Hoskins brings to the screen an intriguing and particularly insightful perspective on the horrors suffered by the innocent amidst warfare.

Heading an ensemble cast as Darky, Hoskins plays the gritty leader of a gypsy-like band of refugees on the run from a war purposely set in an unspecified period somewhere in Europe.

A young soldier named Tom (Dexter Fietcher) deserts after an attack on his unit sends him into a panic.

By the time he catches up with Darky, et al, Tom is deemed to be a 'rawney' – a person who is half-mad and half-magic. The film then opens its direct passageway into this closed community of near medieval attitudes, with fears of evil spirits and the unknown.

● ●

■ RAGING BULL

1980, 119 MINS, US ◇ Ⓥ

Dir Martin Scorsese   *Prod* Irwin Winkler, Robert Chartoff, Peter Savage   *Scr* Paul Schrader, Mardik Martin   *Ph* Michael Chapman   *Ed* Thelma Schoonmaker   *Art Dir* Gene Rudolf
● Robert De Niro, Cathy Moriarty, Joe Pesci, Frank Vincent (United Artists)

Martin Scorsese makes pictures about the kinds of people you wouldn't want to know. In his mostly b&w biopic of middleweight boxing champ Jake La Motta, *Raging Bull*, the La Motta character played by Robert De Niro is one of the most repugnant and unlikeable screen protagonists in some time.

But the boxing sequences are possibly the best ever filmed, and the film captures the intensity of a boxer's life with considerable force.

Scorsese excels at whipping up an emotional storm but seems unaware that there is any need for quieter, more introspective moments in drama.

The relentless depiction of the downward slide of La Motta from a trim contender in 1941 to a shockingly bloated slob introducing strippers in a sleazy nightclub in 1964 has the morbid quality of a German expressionist film. By the time De Niro – who actually gained 50 pounds for the latter scenes – sits at a dressing-room mirror looking at his puffy face, he's become as grotesque as Emil Jannings in *The Blue Angel*.

Aside from the customary genre plot of a boxer selling out to the mob, what seems to be on the minds of Scorsese and his screenwriters is an exploration of an extreme form of Catholic sadomasochism.
☐ 1980: Best Picture (Nomination)

● ●

■ RAGING MOON, THE

1971, 110 MINS, UK ◇ Ⓥ

Dir Bryan Forbes   *Prod* Bruce Cohn Curtis   *Scr* Bryan Forbes   *Ph* Tony Imi   *Ed* Timothy Gee   *Mus* Stanley Myers   *Art Dir* Robert Jones
● Malcolm McDowell, Nanette Newman, Georgia Brown, Bernard Lee, Gerald Sim, Michael Flanders (M-G-M/EMI)

The Raging Moon is a tender love story woven round a delicate situation, but it has some good tangy dialog and some funny situations.

Early situations are broad and a bit bawdy but purpose is to establish the rough-and-ready character of the young hero (a bit of a yobbo, though with a yearning to write) and his background. He's a carefree boy with the birds, crazy about football and with little respect for his elders. Injured in a football match he loses the use of his legs. He lands up in a home for cripples. He's surly, resentful and a pain to the rest of the inmates who've learned to live with their misfortune.

But at the home he meets and falls in love with a girl who has been wheelchaired for six years. Slowly, their relationship blossoms.

Bryan Forbes' dialog is punchy, perceptive and very understanding of human problems. He has also worked up an excellent cast. Malcolm McDowell handles the two or three facets of the hero with strong facility. Nanette Newman has a stunning warmth and radiance that communicates.

● ●

■ RAGMAN'S DAUGHTER, THE

1972, 94 MINS, UK ◇

Dir Harold Becker   *Prod* Harold Becker, Souter Harris   *Scr* Alan Sillitoe   *Ph* Michael Seresin   *Ed* Antony Gibbs   *Mus* Kenny Clayton   *Art Dir* David Brockhurst
● Simon Rouse, Victoria Tennant, Patrick O'Connell, Leslie Sands, Rita Howard, Brian Murphy (Penelope/Harpoon)

Slow-paced but poignant pic based on an Alan Sillitoe novel which captures both the lyricism and grime of the Nottingham area. Carefully avoiding the pitfalls of the motor-cycle thug genre, director Harold Becker weaves a bitter-sweet love affair between a petty teenage thief and the daughter of a wealthy rag dealer. Touches of humor and implied social comment, plus imaginative location lensing, give a ring of authenticity and honesty.

Both Simon Rouse and Patrick O'Connell, as the younger and older Tony, put in superb, convincing jobs of thesping as outcasts of society. Sillitoe steers clear of moralizing, and even social issues inherent in the relationship between the protagonists is made subservient to a broader concern for lost youth and the joys of yesteryear.

● ●

■ RAGTIME

1981, 155 MINS, US ◇

Dir Milos Forman   *Prod* Dino De Laurentiis   *Scr* Michael Weller   *Ph* Miroslav Ondricek   *Ed* Anne V. Coates, Antony Gibbs, Stanley Warnow   *Mus* Randy Newman   *Art Dir* John Graysmark
● James Cagney, Brad Dourif, Elizabeth McGovern, Pat O'Brien, Donald O'Connor, Mandy Patinkin (Paramount/De Laurentiis)

The page-turning joys of E.L. Doctorow's bestselling *Ragtime*, which dizzily and entertainingly charted a kaleidoscopic vision of a turn-of-century America in the midst of intense social change, have been realized almost completely in Milos Forman's superbly crafted screen adaptation.

Within a myriad of characters who include the likes of Evelyn Nesbit, Stanford White, Booker T. Washington and J. Pierpont Morgan, the film charts the syncopated social forces that truly ushered in 20th-century

America by pivoting them around a nameless upper-crust family unexpectedly caught up in the maelstrom.

Overriding focus of the film is on the travails of a fictional black ragtime pianist (Howard E. Rollins), whose common-law wife (Debbie Allen) is taken in by The Family after she abandons her newborn child in their garden.

Juggling the scores of characters that Doctorow intertwined in his quirky blend of historical and fictional people and events, Forman and scripter Michael Weller were forced into some occasional truncation and shortcutting, but ultimately win the chess game hands down.

....

■ RAIDERS OF THE LOST ARK

1981, 115 MINS, US ◇

Dir Steven Spielberg   *Prod* Frank Marshall
Scr Lawrence Kasdan   *Ph* Douglas Slocombe
Ed Michael Kahn   *Mus* John Williams   *Art Dir* Norman Reynolds
● Harrison Ford, Karen Allen, Denholm Elliott, Paul Freeman, Alfred Molina (Paramount)

'Raiders of the Lost Ark' is the stuff that raucous Saturday matinees at the local Bijou once were made of, a crackerjack fantasy-adventure.

Steeped in an exotic atmosphere of lost civilizations, mystical talismans, gritty mercenary adventurers, Nazi arch-villains and ingenious death at every turn, the film is largely patterned on the serials of the 1930s, with a large dollop of Edgar Rice Burroughs.

Story [by George Lucas and Philip Kaufman] begins in 1936 as Indiana Jones (Harrison Ford), an archeologist and university professor who's not above a little mercenary activity on the side, plunders a South American jungle tomb. He secures a priceless golden Godhead, only to have it snatched away by longtime archeological rival Paul Freeman, now employed by the Nazis.

Back in the States, Ford is approached by US intelligence agents who tell him the Nazis are rumored to have discovered the location of the Lost Ark of the Covenant (where the broken 10 Commandments were sealed). The ark is assumed to contain an awesome destructive power.

Ford's mission is to beat the Germans to the ark.

Director Stephen Spielberg has deftly veiled proceedings in a sense of mystical wonder that makes it all the more easy for viewers to suspend disbelief and settle back for the fun.

....

■ RAILWAY CHILDREN, THE

1970, 108 MINS, UK ◇

Dir Lionel Jeffries   *Prod* Robert Lynn   *Scr* Lionel Jeffries   *Ph* Arthur Ibbetsen   *Ed* Teddy Darvas
Mus Johnny Douglas   *Art Dir* John Clark
● Dinah Sheridan, Bernard Cribbins, William Mervyn, Iain Cuthbertson, Jenny Agutter, Sally Thomsett (EMI)

Story, from E. Nesbitt's w.k. novel set in the Edwardian age, concerns a well-to-do family whose life's turned upside down when the father (something in the Foreign Office) is unjustly jailed. The family, in straitened circumstances, go to live on the Yorkshire moors.

They soon adapt to the new life, make friends with the goodhearted villagers, and particularly with a well-to-do gent whom they enlist to help clear their father.

The village is near a railway and this becomes the centre of their activities with the local porter and general railway factotum becoming one of their most useful allies.

Much of the film's success depends on the trio of children. Eldest is played with grave confidence by snub-nosed Jenny Agutter.

....

■ RAIN

1932, 92 MINS, US

Dir Lewis Milestone   *Prod* Lewis Milestone
Scr Maxwell Anderson, Lewis Milestone   *Ph* Oliver Marsh   *Ed* W. Duncan Mansfield   *Art Dir* Richard Day
● Joan Crawford, Walter Huston, William Gargan, Guy Kibbee, Walter Catlett, Beulah Bondi (Milestone/United Artists)

It turns out to be a mistake to have assigned the Sadie Thompson role to Joan Crawford. The dramatic significance of it all is beyond her range. As for producer-director Lewis Milestone's shortcomings as an entrepreneur, the outcome is equally to be laid at his doorstep [in this version of the play by John Cotton and C. Randolph from the story by W. Somerset Maugham].

The 92 minutes to achieve the climactic finale, where the salvationist succumbs to the flesh, is too long a period to reach the fairly obvious. It then becomes the burden of the Sadie Thompson, Davidson (Walter Huston) and other characters to sustain matters through their own personal impressions. And it's all so talky.

Apart from that, Milestone goes in for the impressionistic rain thing too much with camera angles.

Huston must have felt as ridic as were some of his lines when he had to utter them during production.

Joan Crawford's getup as the light lady is extremely bizarre. Pavement pounders don't quite trick themselves up as fantastically as all that.

....

■ RAIN MAN

1988, 140 MINS, US ◇

Dir Barry Levinson   *Prod* Mark Johnson   *Scr* Ronald Bass, Barry Morrow   *Ph* John Seale   *Ed* Stu Linder   *Mus* Hans Zimmer   *Art Dir* Ida Random
● Dustin Hoffman, Tom Cruise, Valerie Golino, Jerry Molen, Jack Murdock (Guber-Peters/United Artists)

Raymond Babbitt (Dustin Hoffman) is an autistic savant, a person extremely limited in some mental areas and extremely gifted in others. His younger brother, hard-driving luxury car dealer Charlie Babbitt (Tom Cruise), has his limitations too – mostly in the areas of kindness and understanding.

Unaware of Raymond's existence until his estranged father dies, Charlie is brought up short when he learns the old man's entire $3 million fortune has been willed to his brother.

Charlie shanghais him, without regard for his welfare, into a cross-country trip to LA, dangling a Dodger game as bait. Meanwhile, he threatens Raymond's guardian, the bland Dr. Bruner (Jerry Molen), with a custody battle unless he hands over half the fortune.

Director Barry Levinson lingers long on the road trip segment, building the relationship between the brothers degree by degree. Result is lightly engrossing.

By the last third, pic [based on a story by Barry Morrow] becomes quite moving as these two isolated beings discover a common history and deep attachment.

It's a mature assignment for Cruise and he's at his best in the darker scenes. Hoffman achieves an exacting physical characterization of Raymond, from his constant nervous movements to his rigid, hunched shoulders and childish gait.

□ 1988: Best Picture

....

■ RAIN PEOPLE, THE

1969, 101 MINS, US ◇

Dir Francis Coppola   *Prod* Bart Patton, Ronald Colby   *Scr* Francis Coppola   *Ph* Wilmer Butler   *Ed* Blackie Malkin   *Mus* Ronald Stein   *Art Dir* Leon Ericksen
● James Caan, Shirley Knight, Robert Duvall, Marya Zimmet, Tom Aldredge (Warner/Seven Arts/Coppola)

Writer-director Francis Coppola, scrutinizing the flight of a neurotic young woman and her efforts to assist a brain-damaged ex-football player, has developed an overlong, brooding film incorporating some excellent photography. Often lingering too long on detail to build effects, he manages to lose character sympathy.

Shirley Knight, in a neurotic panic because she dreads the ties of domesticity, runs away from her Long Island home and husband. She phones him from the Pennsylvania Turnpike to tell him she is pregnant and has to get away from home.

She picks up James Caan, an ex-football hero whose brain was damaged in a college game, who is hitchhiking to West Virginia to work for the father of a girlfriend from school.

....

■ RAINMAKER, THE

1956, 121 MINS, US ◇

Dir Joseph Anthony   *Prod* Hal Wallis   *Scr* N. Richard Nash   *Ph* Charles Lang Jr   *Ed* Warren Low   *Mus* Alex North   *Art Dir* Hal Pereira, Walter Tyler
● Burt Lancaster, Katharine Hepburn, Wendell Corey, Lloyd Bridges, Earl Holliman, Cameron Prud'homme (Paramount)

The N. Richard Nash play has been fashioned into a solid screen entertainment. With Burt Lancaster turning in perhaps his most colorful performance and Katharine Hepburn offering a free-wheeling interpretation of a spinster in search of romance, the adaptation is a click show all around.

Nash's own screenplay stays close to the original, establishing the title character right at the start and then moving into the story of how the smooth-talking fraud pretends to bring rain to a drought-stricken ranch area. It's humorously and imaginatively done against unusually effective sets.

Locale is the southwestern town of Three Point where Lancaster sets out to pick up $100 on his promise of bringing a vitally-needed downpour. He comes into contact with rancher Cameron Prud'homme and his family, comprising Hepburn as the daughter, two sons, Lloyd Bridges, who's stern and practical, and Earl Holliman, a clumsy, likeable youngster.

That's the setup. Lancaster, although he's obviously a con artist, is permitted to live in Prud'homme's tack house and work his rain magic. He convinces Hepburn that she's pretty, and not plain as Bridges insists.

....

■ RAINS CAME, THE

1939, 100 MINS, US

Dir Clarence Brown   *Prod* Darryl F. Zanuck   *Scr* Philip Dunne, Julien Josephson   *Ph* Arthur Miller   *Ed* Barbara McLean   *Mus* Alfred Newman   *Art Dir* William Darling, George Dudley
● Myrna Loy, Tyrone Power, George Brent, Jane Darwell, Brenda Joyce, Maria Ouspenskaya (20th Century-Fox)

Liberties have been taken with [Louis Bromfield's] original novel, resulting in switching some of the original characterizations or intent, but under production code restrictions, and to conform with the mass market of film entertainment, it merges as a competent job.

Newcomer Brenda Joyce, cast as the daughter of social-climbing missionaries, rings the bell throughout with a consistent performance as a forthright romantic adolescent, stuck on George Brent. Latter is the wastrel, of good British family, who has been dawdling in Ranchipur for years on an art assignment.

His best friend is the enlightened young Dr-Major Rama Safti, who is blind to any romantic deviations, in his intensive medical duties, until Myrna Loy comes on the scene.

RAINS OF RANCHIPUR, THE

1955, 104 MINS, US ◇

Dir Jean Negulesco *Prod* Frank Ross *Scr* Merle Miller *Ph* Milton Krasner *Ed* Dorothy Spencer *Mus* Hugo Friedhofer *Art Dir* Lyle Wheeler, Addison Hehr
● Lana Turner, Richard Burton, Fred MacMurray, Joan Caulfield, Michael Rennie (20th Century-Fox)

Louis Bromfield's *The Rains Came*, brought to the screen once before by 20th-Fox in 1939, is filmed this time with Lana Turner as the titled trollop.

However, the cast itself hardly comes alive. Only sturdy performances are turned in by Richard Burton and Eugenie Leontovich.

Turner, as Edwina (Lady Esketh) has the role of a temptress down pat, perhaps too much so. She's good in a couple of scenes, indifferent in most of them and almost embarrassing in some. Burton's portrayal of Dr Safti, the dedicated Indian doctor, who falls in love with Turner, has strength and conviction and is underplayed intelligently. As the Maharani, Leontovich has dignity, and the scenes between her and Burton are definite assets to the picture.

RAINTREE COUNTY

1957, 187 MINS, US ◇

Dir Edward Dmytryk *Prod* David Lewis *Scr* Millard Kaufman *Ph* Robert Surtees *Ed* John Dunning *Mus* Johnny Green *Art Dir* William A. Horning, Urie McCleary
● Montgomery Clift, Elizabeth Taylor, Eva Marie Saint, Nigel Patrick, Lee Marvin, Rod Taylor (M-G-M)

Raintree County, one of the biggest and costliest (estimated at $5 million) productions from Metro since its release of David O. Selznick's *Gone with the Wind*, was lensed via the Camera 65 process (65mm negative is used and reduced to 35mm for release prints). It is a study of emotional conflicts set against the Civil War turmoil, and done with pictorial sweep.

Story unfolds against a background of historic events – the war, Abraham Lincoln's election, the Northern abolition movement, Southern secession, etc. Metro shot on location near Danville, Ky, for the most part.

The settings at the start is Raintree County, Indiana, where Montgomery Clift and Eva Marie Saint are blissfully in love and looking ahead to life together. Elizabeth Taylor, whose troubled mind is later revealed, comes as a visitor from New Orleans and woos Clift away from Saint and into marriage.

They take up residence in the Deep South where the slavery issue is exposed to Clift, who abhors it, and the couple return to Raintree. At first distressed by the upheaval of the times, Taylor eventually becomes insane. Taking her young son with her, she runs again to her native Dixie. Clift enters the Union Army.

Under Edward Dmytryk's direction, this adaption of Ross Lockridge Jr's novel unfolds fairly interestingly but slowly. Picture lacks highlight material; even the war scenes don't quite have the necessary impact and the relationship between Taylor and Clift could have been charged up more.

RAISE THE TITANIC

1980, 102 MINS, UK ◇ ⓥ

Dir Jerry Jameson *Prod* William Frye *Scr* Adam Kennedy *Ph* Matthew F. Leonetti *Ed* J. Terry Williams, Robert F. Shugrue *Mus* John Barry *Art Dir* John F. DeCuir
● Jason Robards, Richard Jordan, Alec Guinness, David Selby, Anne Archer, M. Emmet Walsh (ITC)

Raise the Titanic wastes a potentially intriguing premise with dull scripting, a lackluster cast, laughably phony trick work, and clunky direction. Half of the running time (at least) is devoted to underwater miniature shots of submarines and other apparatus trying to dislodge the long-lost luxury liner *Titanic* from its deepsea resting place.

The ridiculously expository screenplay [adapted by Eric Hughes from the novel by Clive Cussler] repeatedly explains what will happen, why it's happening, and how it's going to happen.

The actors adopt various strategies for coping with their unspeakable dialog and cardboard characterizations. Alec Guinness provides a dramatic highlight with a lovely scene as a retired old salt who served on the *Titanic*'s crew.

RAISING ARIZONA

1987, 94 MINS, US ◇ ⓥ

Dir Joel Coen *Prod* Ethan Coen *Scr* Ethan Coen, Joel Coen *Ph* Barry Sonnenfeld *Ed* Michael R. Miller *Mus* Carter Burwell *Art Dir* Jane Musky
● Nicolas Cage, Holly Hunter, Trey Wilson, John Goodman, William Forsythe (Circle/Pedas/Berenholtz)

Pic is the Coen Brothers' twisted view of family rearing in the American heartlands and full of quirky humor and off-the-wall situations as their debut effort, *Blood Simple*. The film captures the surrealism of everyday life. Characters are so strange here that they seem to have stepped out of late-night television, tabloid newspapers, talk radio and a vivid imagination.

Nicolas Cage and Holly Hunter are the off-center couple at the center of the doings. Cage is a well-meaning petty crook with a fondness for knocking off convenience stores. Hunter is the cop who checks him into prison so often that a romance develops.

They soon learn marriage is 'no Ozzie and Harriet Show' and when she learns she can't have kids or adopt them, they do the next logical thing – steal one.

Loosely structured around a voice-over narration by Cage, *Raising Arizona* is as leisurely and disconnected as *Blood Simple* was taut and economical. While film is filled with many splendid touches and plenty of yocks, it often doesn't hold together as a coherent story.

While Cage and Hunter are fine as the couple at sea in the desert, pic sports at least one outstanding performance from John Goodman as the con brother who wants a family too.

RAKE'S PROGRESS, THE

1945, 110 MINS, UK ⓥ

Dir Sidney Gilliat *Prod* Sidney Gilliat, Frank Launder *Scr* Sidney Gilliat, Frank Launder *Ph* Wilkie Cooper, Jack Asher *Ed* Thelma Myers *Mus* William Alwyn *Art Dir* Norman Arnold
● Rex Harrison, Lilli Palmer, Godfrey Tearle, Jean Kent, Griffith Jones (Individual)

This is probably one of the finest films to come out of a British studio. Superb as Rex Harrison and Lilli Palmer are, their individual performances are equalled by many others in the big cast. The script is racy in dialogue.

Direction by Sidney Gilliat who with Frank Launder, also wrote [from a story by Val

Valentine] and produced the picture, is virtually flawless. The independent company [Individual Productions] was formed by Gilliat and Launder when these two experienced scriptwriters got tired of working for a salary and threw up their jobs with Gainsborough.

RALLY 'ROUND THE FLAG, BOYS!

1958, 106 MINS, US ◇

Dir Leo McCarey *Prod* Leo McCarey *Scr* Claude Binyon, Leo McCarey *Ph* Leon Shamroy *Ed* Louis Loeffler *Mus* Cyril J. Mockridge *Art Dir* Lyle Wheeler, Leland Fuller
● Paul Newman, Joanne Woodward, Joan Collins, Jack Carson, Dwayne Hickman, Tuesday Weld (20th Century-Fox)

This is a bedroom farce of split-level thinking in split-level housing. The film version of Max Shulman's bestseller is unmistakably a Leo McCarey picture. Some of the gags are elaborate and as carefully timed as a dance sequence.

The plot is simple. Paul Newman and Joanne Woodward are the couple (two children), living in Fairfield County, Conn. They have, in the delicate phrase, drifted apart. Newman is all for drifting right back, but Woodward is so busy organizing their town into a community as neat, tidy and efficient as their modern kitchen, she can't find the time. Enter the Temptress, or third angle of triangle. She is Joan Collins.

McCarey is working here with players – Newman, Woodward and Collins – who did only incidental film comedy up to this one. They are called upon to slam into opening doors, swing from chandeliers, do the dropped pants bit (in Newman's case), takes and double-takes. Jack Carson, of course, is a past-master at the slow burn, and volcanic reaction, and more than holds his own.

RAMBO
FIRST BLOOD PART II

1985, 95 MINS, US ◇ ⓥ

Dir George Pan Cosmatos *Prod* Buzz Feitshans *Scr* Sylvester Stallone, James Cameron *Ph* Jack Cardiff *Ed* Mark Goldblatt, Mark Helfrich *Mus* Jerry Goldsmith *Art Dir* Bill Kenney
● Sylvester Stallone, Richard Crenna, Charles Napier, Julia Nickson, Steven Berkoff, Martin Kove (Tri-Star)

This overwrought sequel to the popular *First Blood* (1982) is one mounting fireball as Sylvester Stallone's special operations veteran is sprung from a prison labor camp by his former Green Beret commander (Richard Crenna) to find POWs in Vietnam.

That the secret mission is a cynical ruse by higher-ups which is meant to fail heightens Stallone's fury while touching off a provocative political theme: a US government that wants to forget about POWs and accommodate the public at the same time.

The charade on the screen, which is not pulled off, is to accept that the underdog Rambo character, albeit with the help of an attractive machine-gun wielding Vietnamese girl (Julia Nickson), can waste hordes of Vietcong and Red Army contingents enroute to hauling POWs to a Thai air base in a smoking Russian chopper with only a facial scar (from a branding iron-knifepoint) marring his tough figure.

Steven Berkoff is a twisted and nominally chilly Russian advisor, but his performance is essentially the same nasty thing he did in *Octopussy* and *Beverly Hills Cop*.

RAMBO III

1988, 101 MINS, US ◇ ⓥ

Dir Peter Macdonald *Prod* Buzz Feitshans *Scr* Sylvester Stallone, Sheldon Lettich *Ph* John Stanier *Ed* James Symons, Andrew London, O.

Nicholas Brown, Edward A. Warschilka   *Mus* Jerry Goldsmith   *Art Dir* Billy Kenney
● Sylvester Stallone, Richard Crenna, Marc de Jonge, Kurtwood Smith, Spiros Focas (Carolco)

Rambo III stakes out a moral high ground for its hero missing or obscured in the previous two pictures. In the Soviets' heinous nine-year occupation of Afghanistan, this mythic commando and quintessential outsider is enlisted in a cause that – glasnost notwith-standing – is indisputably righteous.

Indeed, as this chapter opens, the character of John Rambo has been demilitarized and transported to exotic self-exile in Thailand, where he lives in a Buddhist monastery and supports himself by engaging in slam-bang mercenary martial arts contests.

Richard Crenna has come halfway around the world to Bangkok to ask Stallone for pay-back – Rambo's participation in a clandes-tine operation to destroy a 'brutal' Russian general who rules a remote province in occu-pied Afghanistan.

The battle scenes in *Rambo III* are explo-sive, conflagratory tableaux that make for wrenching, frequently terrifying viewing. Always at ground zero in the chaos is Rambo – gloriously, inhumanly impervious to fear and danger – whose character is inhabited by Stallone with messianic intensity.

．．．．．．．．．．．．．．．．．．．．．．．．

■ RANCHO NOTORIOUS

1952, 89 MINS, US ◇ Ⓥ

Dir Fritz Lang   *Prod* Howard Welsch   *Scr* Daniel Taradash   *Ph* Hal Mohr   *Ed* Otto Ludwig   *Mus* Emil Newman   *Art Dir* Robert Priestley
● Marlene Dietrich, Arthur Kennedy, Mel Ferrer, Lloyd Gough, Gloria Henry, William Frawley (Fidelity/RKO)

This Marlene Dietrich western has some of the flavor of the old outdoor classics (like the actress's own onetime *Destry Rides Again* with-out fully capturing their quality and magic. The characters play the corny plot straight; directing keeps the pace lively and inter-esting, and the outdoor shots, abetted by the constant splash of color, are eye-arresting. Dietrich is as sultry and alluring as ever.

Plot, starting off in a little Wyoming town in the 1870s, finds a young femme brutally assaulted and killed on the eve of her wed-ding and her embittered cowboy lover (Arthur Kennedy) riding off to find and kill the unknown murderer. The trail first leads to Frenchy Fairmount (Mel Ferrer), a flashy outlaw, and then to Chuck-a-Luck, the ranch run by Altar Keane (Dietrich), one-time fab-ulous saloon entertainer.

Dietrich is a dazzling recreation of the old-time saloon mistress, and handles her song, 'Get Away, Young Man', with her usual throaty skill.

．．．．．．．．．．．．．．．．．．．．．．．．

■ RANDOM HARVEST

1942, 125 MINS, US Ⓥ

Dir Mervyn LeRoy   *Prod* Sidney Franklin
Scr Claudine West, George Froeschel, Arthur Wimperis   *Ph* Joseph Ruttenberg   *Ed* Harold F. Kress   *Mus* Herbert Stothart
● Ronald Colman, Greer Garson, Susan Peters, Henry Travers, Reginald Owen (M-G-M)

The film transcription of James Hilton's novel *Random Harvest*, under Sidney Frank-lin's production and Mervyn LeRoy's direc-tion, achieves much more than average importance.

Ronald Colman plays Charles Rainier, prosperous Briton who loses his memory as result of shellshock in the First World War. As the film opens he is a mental case in an asylum where efforts are being made to res-tore his memory. He wanders off, eluding officers of the sanatorium.

Colman gives a fine performance but is not quite the romantic type that he was years

ago. In fact, he looks older than he should have been for film expediency.

Greer Garson, more charming and seduc-tive than ever, is an important mainstay of the picture. Essaying a highly sympathetic role, she overshadows Colman.

□ 1942: Best Picture (Nomination.)

．．．．．．．．．．．．．．．．．．．．．．．．

■ RANSOM

1975, 97 MINS, UK ◇

Dir Casper Wrede   *Prod* Peter Rawley   *Scr* Paul Wheeler   *Ph* Sven Nykvist   *Ed* Thelma Connell   *Mus* Jerry Goldsmith   *Art Dir* Sven Wickman
● Sean Connery, Ian McShane, Norman Bristow, John Cording, Isabel Dean, William Fox (Lion/20th-Century Fox)

Connery is billed above the title as the head of a government security agency trying to cope with plane-hijacking terrorists. Rather curiously, Connery works for the government of 'Scandinavia', not Norway where most of the pic was filmed, but in any event at no time does he lose his Scottish brogue.

The terrorists are holding the British am-bassador in exchange for their own release and that of some cohorts held by Britain. A squad of accomplices headed by McShane commandeer a loaded passenger jet as it lands at Oslo, and the cat and mouse game begins.

As a match of wits, the ensuing tale doesn't amount to much. But along with plot inge-nuity, what's glaringly missing is even the briefest exploration of the terrorists and their psychology.

．．．．．．．．．．．．．．．．．．．．．．．．

■ RARE BREED, THE

1966, 97 MINS, US ◇ Ⓥ

Dir Andrew V. McLaglen   *Prod* William Alland
Scr Ric Hardman   *Ph* William H. Clothier   *Ed* Russell F. Schoengarth   *Mus* John Williams   *Art Dir* Alexander Golitzen, Alfred Ybarra
● James Stewart, Maureen O'Hara, Brian Keith, Juliet Mills, Don Galloway, David Brian (Universal)

Based on the actual intro of white-faced Hereford cattle from England to the US west-ern ranges, *The Rare Breed* is a generally suc-cessful fictionalized blend of violence, romance, comedy, inspiration and oater Americana.

Ric Hardman's good – if overly wide-rang-ing – script takes as a point of departure the phasing out of the longhorn by the 'rare' (circa 1884) Hereford stock from England. As the drama unfolds, rugged animal survival problems dissolve into human conflicts.

For almost half of the running time the plot concerns the stubborn determination of widowed Maureen O'Hara and daughter Juliet Mills to deliver a bull for breeding purposes. Opposing factors include James Stewart, intially a drifter who agrees, although reluctantly, to swindle the gals via Alan Caillou's bribe, with two conspirators, Jack Elam and Harry Carey Jr.

Second half is virtually another pic, with quietly-stubborn O'Hara pitted against Brian Keith in a sort of Anna-and-the-King-of-Siam byplay.

．．．．．．．．．．．．．．．．．．．．．．．．

■ RATBOY

1986, 104 MINS, US ◇ Ⓥ

Dir Sondra Locke   *Prod* Fritz Manes   *Scr* Rob Thompson   *Ph* Bruce Surtees   *Ed* Joel Cox   *Mus* Lennie Niehaus   *Art Dir* Edward Carfagno
● Sondra Locke, Robert Townsend, Christopher Hewett, Larry Hankin, Sydney Lassick, Gerrit Graham (Malpaso)

Yet another picture about how a semi-human, quasi-alien being just can't fit in among earthlings, *Ratboy* can boast of some modest virtues, but is simply too mild on all

counts to carry much impact. Oddball first feature from Sondra Locke, who also stars as an out-of-work journalist, deals with eccen-tric, desperate individuals but in a rather straightforward, unobsessed manner.

The origins of the title character are never investigated or explained. Indeed, after the terrified little bugger is trapped by some tran-sients, he is just blithely manipulated and used by a succession of hustlers who can't put their greed and self-interests on hold long enough to even inquire where the tiny one came from or how he got that way.

Acting tends to the broad side, and Rat-boy's nose twitching is cute.

．．．．．．．．．．．．．．．．．．．．．．．．

■ RATTLE OF A SIMPLE MAN

1964, 96 MINS, UK Ⓥ

Dir Muriel Box   *Prod* William Gell   *Scr* Charles Dyer
Ph Reg Wyer   *Ed* Frederick Wilson   *Mus* Stanley Black   *Art Dir* Robert Jones
● Harry H. Corbett, Diane Cilento, Thora Hird, Michael Medwin, Charles Dyer, Hugh Futcher (Associated British)

Most of the charm and tenderness that oc-casionally illuminated Charles Dyer's suc-cessful play has been lost in this coarsened, fatuous film. Only a lively, vivid performance by Diane Cilento in a contrived role holds much interest, though a sound cast does spar-tan work in juggling the sparse material. Dyer, has broadened his intimate little play for the benefit of the screen and has heaved most of its values into the trash can.

A bunch of football fans from the North of England, characteristically drawn as noisy, boozing, lecherous nitwits, comes to London for the Cup Final and a night out among the sleazy bright lights. One of them (Harry H. Corbett), a particulary gormless, repressed, mother-ridden oaf, is conned into a bet with his pals. He wagers his motorbike that he'll have an affair with a goodlooking, blonde tart that he picks up in Soho drinking club.

The bedroom rendezvous is a pitiable farce in which he fails to take the opportunities cheerfully flung at him by the goodtime girl. Instead he weaves dreams of real love about the goldenhearted little prostie.

．．．．．．．．．．．．．．．．．．．．．．．．

■ RAW DEAL

1986, 106 MINS, US ◇ Ⓥ

Dir John Irvin   *Prod* Martha Schumacher   *Scr* Gary M. DeVore, Norman Wexler   *Ph* Alex Thomson   *Ed* Anne V. Coates   *Mus* Cinemascore
Art Dir Giorgio Postiglione
● Arnold Schwarzenegger, Kathryn Harrold, Sam Wanamaker, Paul Shenar, Robert Davi, Ed Lauter (De Laurentiis/International)

Comic book crime meller suffers from an irre-deemably awful script, and even director John Irvin's engaging sense of how absurd the proceedings are can't work an alchemist's magic.

Bald exposition sees former FBI man, Arnold Schwarzenegger, now rather im-plausibly a southern sheriff, recruited to infil-trate Chicago's biggest mob, which has been rubbing out men scheduled to testify against it. The big man impresses kingpin Sam Wanamaker with his brain and lieutenant Paul Shenar (as well as tarty Kathryn Har-rold) with his brawn, and soon wins himself a job with the gang.

Cast members do what's necessary, but have all been seen to better advantage on other occasions.

．．．．．．．．．．．．．．．．．．．．．．．．

■ RAWHIDE

1951, 87 MINS, US Ⓥ

Dir Henry Hathaway   *Prod* Samuel G. Engel
Scr Dudley Nichols   *Ph* Milton Krasner   *Ed* Robert Simpson   *Mus* Sol Kaplan

● Tyrone Power, Susan Hayward, Hugh Marlowe, Dean Jagger, Edgar Buchanan, Jack Elam (20th Century-Fox)

Maximum suspense for a western is generated in this Tyrone Power-Susan Hayward costarrer. Despite a strongly-told story, however, picture isn't the proper vehicle for Power, who is wasted in part and comes off second best to a number of other players.

Power and Hayward are held prisoners at a stagecoach station in the early west by Hugh Marlowe, an escaped murderer from a prison in the territory, and his three companions, who are waiting to rob the eastbound stage next day which carries $100,000 in gold. Power is employed at station, and Hayward is there with her infant niece only until she can catch the next stage east.

Acting honors are about evenly divided between femme star and Marlowe, both in hardboiled parts. Jack Elam, too, fares particularly favorably as woman-hungry escaped con, member of Marlowe's pack, and Edgar Buchanan, Dean Jagger and George Tobias likewise are effective. Power is never permitted a chance as a hero.

························

■ RAZORBACK

1984, 94 MINS, AUSTRALIA ◇ ⓥ

Dir Russell Mulcahy   *Prod* Hal McElroy   *Scr* Everett De Roche   *Ph* Dean Semler   *Ed* Bill Anderson   *Mus* Iva Davies   *Art Dir* Bryce Walmsley
● Gregory Harrison, Arkie Whiteley, Bill Kerr, Chris Haywood, David Argue, Judy Morris (McElroy & McElroy)

A razorback is a particularly nasty species of feral pig, vicious and brainless, which is found in Australia's outback. Production involves a giant of the species which runs amok with spectacular abandon.

Screenplay by Everett De Roche, an experienced writer of thrillers, from a book by Peter Brennan, starts with a bang: Jake Cullen (Bill Kerr) is minding his grandchild in his isolated homestead when the place is attacked by the unseen porker who wounds the old man and disappears with the infant.

The distraught granddad is brought to trial for killing the kid, but acquitted, and he becomes obsessed with getting the giant beast.

Enter Judy Morris who plays an American TV journalist who arrives in this remote spot to do a story on the slaughter of the kangaroos.

She becomes the next victim of the razorback. But her husband, Carl (Gregory Harrison), doesn't believe she fell down a mine shaft, the story put out by the locals.

The plot may be a bit familiar, but *Razorback* is no quickie: it's an extremely handsome production, beautifully shot by Dean Semler.

························

■ RAZOR'S EDGE, THE

1946, 146 MINS, US ⓥ

Dir Edmund Goulding   *Prod* Darryl F. Zanuck   *Scr* Lamar Trotti   *Ph* Arthur Miller   *Ed* J. Watson Webb   *Mus* Alfred Newman   *Art Dir* Richard Day, Nathan Juran
● Tyrone Power, Gene Tierney, John Payne, Anne Baxter, Clifton Webb, Herbert Marshall (20th Century-Fox)

The Razor's Edge has everything for virtually every type of film fan. Fundamentally it's all good cinematurgy. It's a moving picture that moves.

The romance is more than slightly on the sizzling side. Tyrone Power, as the flyer who can't find himself, is always seeking goodness and spurns the easy life offered him by the more than casually appealing Gene Tierney. It reaches a climax after they play the Paris nitery belt from Montmartre to Montparnasse, and when back in Chicago she loses sight of him and marries John Payne there is

the unashamed confession of a lasting love which Power spurns.

For all its pseudo-ritualistic aura the film is fundamentally a solid love story. Tierney is the almost irresistibly appealing femme and completely depicts all the beauty and charm endowed her by Maugham's characterization. Anne Baxter walks off with perhaps the film's personal bit as the dipso, rivaled only by Clifton Webb's effete characterization as the dilettante rich uncle.

Herbert Marshall introduces a new cinematic technique – as it was in the original novel – of playing the author W. Somerset Maugham who thus integrates himself into the story by name identity instead of the conventional first-person (but invariably fictiously identified) characterization.
□ 1946: Best Picture (Nomination)

························

■ REACH FOR GLORY

1962, 80 MINS, UK

Dir Philip Leacock   *Prod* John Kohn, Jud Kinberg   *Scr* John Kohn, Jud Kinberg   *Ph* Bob Huke   *Ed* Frederick Wilson   *Mus* Bob Russell   *Art Dir* John Blezard
● Michael Anderson Jr., Martin Tomlinson, Oliver Grimm, Harry Andrews, Kay Walsh (Gala/Blazer)

In this tale about a group of adolescent boys at a military school in Britain during the last war, the themes of racism, war hate and its effect on youth, conscientious objection and the consequences of parental weakness on youth are all touched on.

Film is well meaning, tightly and economically made but still lacks the edge of the necessary impact. Result is a diffuse pic which is interesting but does not emerge a heavyweight.

A group of London youths chafe in a country school to which they have been evacuated. The war fills them with dreams of glory and a desire for action that is unfortunately turned to gang warfare, spartan, cabalistic rituals, anti-semitism and general unruliness. Into this comes a refugee Jewish boy from Germany.

Shame at conscientious objectors is also worked in via a brother of one of the boys and false accusations of budding homosexuality.

························

■ REACH FOR THE SKY

1956, 136 MINS, UK ⓥ

Dir Lewis Gilbert   *Prod* Daniel M. Angel   *Scr* Lewis Gilbert   *Ph* Jack Asher   *Ed* John Shirley   *Mus* John Addison   *Art Dir* Bernard Robinson
● Kenneth More, Muriel Pavlow, Lyndon Brook, Lee Patterson, Alexander Knox, Dorothy Alison (Rank/Pinnacle)

First and foremost, this is a story of courage, showing a man's triumph over physical disability and every obstacle raised to curtail his normal activities. Adapted from the biography [*The Story of Douglas Bader*] by his fellow pilot Paul Brickhill, it covers the career of Douglas Bader who, after losing both legs in a plane crash while stunting, succeeds in rejoining the RAF to become a Wing Commander in the last world war and one of the aces in the Battle of Britain.

From the cocky young recruit's first day at the training station through all the gay comradeship and hazards of flying, Kenneth More (Bader) depicts with unerring skill the humor, friendliness and supreme fortitude of one of the war's most honored heroes.

His determination to take up life where it nearly left off and return to the only job he knows, is shown without heroics. And this enhances its dramatic value. Every Air Force taboo on his disability is finally overcome and he gets airborne again with the outbreak of war.

Lyndon Brook plays the staunch friend who has to break the news to Bader of his afflic-

tion. Alexander Knox is quietly effective as the surgeon.

························

■ REAL GENIUS

1985, 104 MINS, US ◇ ⓥ

Dir Martha Coolidge   *Prod* Brian Grazer   *Scr* Neal Israel, Pat Proft, Peter Torokvei   *Ph* Vilmos Zsigmond   *Ed* Richard Chew   *Mus* Thomas Newman   *Art Dir* Josan F. Russo
● Val Kilmer, Gabe Jarret, Michelle Meyrink, William Atherton, Jonathan Gries, Patti D'Arbanville (Tri-Star)

Real Genius is *Police Academy* with brains. Setting the proceedings at a think tank for young prodigies seems a curious choice as most of the humor of the film comes out of character rather than place. Val Kilmer, punning his way through his senior year at Pacific Tech, is hardly convincing as a world-class intellect.

Plot about creating a portable laser system for the Air Force under the tutelage of campus creep Professor Hathaway (William Atherton) has the authority of an old Abbott and Costello film. Theme about the exploitation of these youthful minds is lost in a sea of sight gags.

What lifts the production above the run-of-the-mill is swift direction by Martha Coolidge, who has a firm grasp over the manic material.

························

■ RE-ANIMATOR

1985, 86 MINS, US ◇ ⓥ

Dir Stuart Gordon   *Prod* Brian Yuzna   *Scr* Dennis Paoli, William J. Norris, Stuart Gordon   *Ph* Mac Ahlberg   *Ed* Lee Percy   *Mus* Richard Band   *Art Dir* Robert A. Burns
● Jeffrey Combs, Bruce Abbott, Barbara Crampton, Robert Sampson, David Gale, Gerry Black (Re-Animated)

Re-Animator, is based on an H.P. Lovecraft tale [*Herbert West – The Re-Animator*] about a crazy scientist who brings dead bodies back to life with a special serum. Trouble is, they come back violent and ready to kill.

Herbert West (Jeffrey Combs) is the inventor who, like horror film scientists from time immemorial, is too batty to realize the consequences of his actions. Romantic leads are Bruce Abbott and Barbara Crampton, latter a looker who, at the pic's climax, is strapped naked to a lab table as an object of the lusts of a hateful admirer, who by this time literally has lost his head.

Pic has a grisly sense of humor, and sometimes is *so* gross and over the top the film tips over into a kind of bizarre comedy.

························

■ REAP THE WILD WIND

1942, 124 MINS, US ⓥ

Dir Cecil B. DeMille   *Prod* Cecil B. DeMille   *Scr* Alan LeMay, Charles Bennett, Jesse Lasky Jr   *Ph* Victor Milner, William V. Skall   *Ed* Anne Bauchens   *Mus* Victor Young
● Ray Milland, John Wayne, Paulette Goddard, Raymond Massey, Robert Preston, Susan Hayward (Paramount)

Reap the Wild Wind is a melodrama of Atlantic coastal shipping in the windjammer days, 100 years ago. It is a film possessing the spectacular sweep of colorful backgrounds which characterize the Cecil DeMille type of screen entertainment.

After a short foreword by DeMille, the picture opens with scenes of a hurricane, shipwreck and struggle for bounty among the salvage workers. This melodramatic tempo is too swift to be maintained. Various angles of plot and contest necessarily must be introduced. The pacing is uneven.

Towards the end, however, the action quickens. There is a unique filming of an

R

undersea battle between a giant squid, of octopus descent, and the two male protagonists. Despite its obvious make-believe, it is shrewd filming, realistic and thrilling.

The production is a visual triumph. Some of the marine scenes are breathtaking. There is skillful blending of process photography.

REAR WINDOW

1954, 112 MINS, US ◇ Ⓥ
Dir Alfred Hitchcock   Prod Alfred Hitchcock   Scr John Michael Hayes   Ph Robert Burks   Ed George Tomasini   Mus Franz Waxman   Art Dir Hal Pereira, Joseph MacMillan Johnson
● James Stewart, Grace Kelly, Wendell Corey, Thelma Ritter, Raymond Burr, Judith Evelyn (Paramount)

A tight suspense show is offered in *Rear Window*, one of Alfred Hitchcock's better thrillers. Hitchcock combines technical and artistic skills in a manner that makes this an unusually good piece of murder mystery entertainment. A sound story by Cornell Woolrich and a cleverly dialoged screenplay provide a solid basis for thrill-making.

Hitchcock confines all of the action to a single apartment-courtyard setting and draws nerves to snapping point in developing the thriller phases of the plot.

James Stewart portrays a news photographer confined to his apartment with a broken leg. He passes the long hours by playing peeping-tom on the people who live in the other apartments overlooking the courtyard. In one of the apartments occupied by Raymond Burr and his invalid, shrewish wife Stewart observes things that lead him to believe Burr has murdered and dismembered the wife.

Adding to the grip the melodrama has on the audience is the fact that virtually every scene is one that could only be viewed from Stewart's wheelchair, with the other apartment dwellers seen in pantomime action through the photog's binoculars or the telescopic lens from his camera.

The production makes clever use of natural sounds and noises throughout.

REBECCA

1940, 130 MINS, US Ⓥ
Dir Alfred Hitchcock   Prod David O. Selznick   Scr Robert E. Sherwood, Joan Harrison   Ph George Barnes   Ed Hal C. Kern, James E. Newcom   Mus Franz Waxman   Art Dir Lyle Wheeler
● Laurence Olivier, Joan Fontaine, George Sanders, Judith Anderson, Nigel Bruce, Reginald Denny (Selznick/United Artists)

Picture is noteworthy for its literal translation of Daphne du Maurier's novel to the screen, presenting all of the sombreness and dramatic tragedy of the book.

Alfred Hitchcock pilots his first American production with capable assurance and exceptional understanding of the motivation and story mood. Despite the psychological and moody aspects of the tale throughout its major footage, he highlights the piece with several intriguing passages that display inspired direction.

Olivier provides an impressionable portrayal as the master of Manderley, unable to throw off the memory of his tragic first marriage while trying to secure happiness in his second venture. Joan Fontaine is excellent as the second wife, carrying through the transition of a sweet and vivacious bride to that of a bewildered woman marked by the former tragedy she finds hard to understand.

Supporting cast has been selected with careful attention to individual capabilities. Judith Anderson is the sinister housekeeper and confidante of the former wife; George Sanders is personable in portrayal of the despicable Jack Flavell; and Reginald Denny is

Crawley, the estate manager and pal of Olivier. Florence Bates provides many light moments in the early portion as a romantically-inclined dowager.
□ 1940: Best Picture

REBECCA OF SUNNYBROOK FARM

1917, 74 MINS, US ⊗ Ⓥ
Dir Marshall Neilan   Scr Frances Marion   Ph Walter Stradling
● Mary Pickford, Eugene O'Brien, Helen Jerome Eddy, Charles Ogle, Marjorie Daw, Mayme Kelso   (Artcraft)

Rebecca of Sunnybrook Farm moves along in perfect unison, devoid of padding, minus the wastage of one foot of film, engrossing and impressive, yet with perfect accord in its relation to suspense and cumulative appeal.

In adapting the Kate Douglas Wiggin book for the screen, Frances Marion wrought well. The original story has been retained, with the necessary elaboration. Compared with the dramatic production, which was excellently done, the screen version seems magnitudinous. The story is of Rebecca, a member of a large family, who is sent to the home of her aunts for rearing, ultimately inheriting their estate, and, incidentally, marrying the finest young man in the town. It attained its great popularity through its fidelity in picturing the atmosphere of New England.

Mary Pickford plays as she never played before, varying lights and shades to elicit the major interest, tearful at one moment and laughing the next. Her support is flawless, embodying many artists of repute.

REBECCA OF SUNNYBROOK FARM

1938, 80 MINS, US Ⓥ
Dir Allan Dwan   Prod Raymond Griffith   Scr Karl Tunberg, Don Ettlinger   Ph Arthur Miller   Ed Allen McNeil   Mus Arthur Lange (dir.)   Art Dir Bernard Herzbrun, Hans Peters
● Shirley Temple, Randolph Scott, Jack Haley, Gloria Stuart, Helen Westley, Bill Robinson (20th Century-Fox)

Shirley Temple proves she's a great little artist in this one. The rest of it is synthetic and disappointing. Why they named it *Rebecca of Sunnybrook Farm* is one of those mysteries. The only resemblance to Kate Douglas Wiggins' charming comedy is a load of hay, a litter of pigs and Bill Robinson's straw hat.

More fitting title would be *Rebecca of Radio City*. The story is about a talented stage child who wins a broadcasting moppet contest, then is lost to the advertising agency in the shuffle and rediscovered at Aunt Mirandy's farm. The supporting characters, mostly unsympathetic, over-drawn and exaggerated, are familiar types.

Randolph Scott and Jack Haley try to get some excitement and suspense into the search for Shirley. Slim Summerville and Helen Westley manage a few laughs from the old situation of sulking sweethearts.

REBEL, THE

1961, 105 MINS, UK ◇
Dir Robert Day   Prod W.A. Whittaker   Scr Alan Simpson, Ray Galton   Ph Gilbert Taylor   Ed Richard Best   Mus Frank Cordell   Art Dir Robert Jones
● Tony Hancock, George Sanders, Paul Massie, Margit Saad, Gregoire Aslan, Irene Handl (Associated British)

Tony Hancock's TV writers, Alan Simpson and Ray Galton, scripted this, and they knew their man's idiosyncrasies intimately. He's the little man, slightly at war with himself and his fellows, but quick to grasp an opportunity for getting on.

In *The Rebel*, he is a downtrodden London city clerk, fed up with the daily round, and with a yen to be a sculptor. Unfortunately, he's very unskilled. Eventually, he blows his top, throws up his job and sets up shop as an existentialist painter in Paris. He talks himself into being accepted on the Left Bank as the leader of a new movement in art. Then an art connoisseur boobs. He exhibits the paintings of Hancock's roommate, thinking they are Hancock's work. The misfit becomes a national figure.

Among several amusing scenes are those when Hancock revolts against his office boss, an existentialist Left Bank party, Hancock's visit to the yacht of a Greek millionaire where he is commissioned to sculpt the tycoon's vamp wife, a colorful carnival party aboard the yacht and Hancock 'painting' a picture by daubing paint on a canvas and then bicycling over it.

REBEL WITHOUT A CAUSE

1955, 111 MINS, US ◇ Ⓥ
Dir Nicholas Ray   Prod David Weisbart   Scr Stewart Stern   Ph Ernest Haller   Ed William Zeigler   Mus Leonard Rosenman
● James Dean, Natalie Wood, Corey Allen, Sal Mineo, Dennis Hopper, Jim Backus (Warner)

Here is a fairly exciting, suspenseful and provocative, if also occasionally far-fetched, melodrama of unhappy youth on another delinquency kick. The film presents a boy whose rebellion against a weakling father and a shrewish mother expresses itself in boozing, knife-fighting and other forms of physical combat and testing of his own manhood.

Although essentially intent upon action, director Nicholas Ray, who sketched the basic story, does bring out redeeming touches of human warmth. There is as regards the hero, if not as regards the highschool body generally, a better-than-average-for-a-psychological thriller explanation of the core of confusion in the child.

James Dean is very effective as a boy groping for adjustment to people. His actor's capacity to get inside the skin of youthful pain, torment and bewilderment is not often encountered.

Natalie Wood as the girl next door also shows teenage maladjustment. She, too, asks more of her father than he can give.

RECKLESS MOMENT, THE

1949, 81 MINS, US
Dir Max Ophuls   Prod Walter Wanger   Scr Henry Garson, Robert W. Souerberg   Ph Burnett Guffey   Ed Gene Hawlick   Mus Hans J. Salter
● James Mason, Joan Bennett, Geraldine Brooks, Henry O'Neill (Columbia)

A tense melodrama projecting good mood and suspense has been fashioned out of Elisabeth Sanxay Holding's mag yarn, 'The Blank Wall'. Matter-of-fact technique used in the script and by Max Ophuls' direction doesn't permit much warmth to develop for the characters. Production gains in authentic values by using the seaside resort of Balboa and commercial sections of Los Angeles.

Plot wrings out suspense in its concern with a mother who becomes involved in murder and blackmail to save her daughter from the consequences of a romance with an unsavory older man.

James Mason's ability as an actor makes his assignment as a blackmailer very substantial and Joan Bennett shows up exceptionally well in a part that is tinged with coldness despite the fact it deals with a mother's concern and Henry O'Neill is good as the grandfather.

■ RECKONING, THE

1970, 109 MINS, UK ◇

Dir Jack Gold   *Prod* Ronald Shedlo   *Scr* John McGrath   *Ph* Geoffrey Unsworth   *Ed* Peter Weatherley   *Mus* Malcolm Arnold   *Art Dir* Ray Simm
● Nicol Williamson, Rachel Roberts, Ann Bell, Zena Walker, Paul Rogers, Gwen Nelson (Columbia)

The Reckoning is the story of a ruthless man, who rises from a Liverpool slum to the upper strata of cutthroat big business in London. Actually a character study of a man totally without morals or ethics, it is interesting in its treatment and for Nicol Williamson's performance in a hard-hitting role.

Filmed in story's actual locale, script is based on Patrick Hall's novel, *The Harp That Once*.

Scene segues from fashionable London, where Williamson, as an ambitious and aggressive businessman, is married to a woman he doesn't love and is stymied from rising in his job by politics, to Liverpool. He is called there when his father is dying.

Williamson is entirely believable in his part, displaying a dominant personality and a flair for punching over his role.

Rachel Roberts is realistic as a married woman Williamson picks up at a wrestling match the night his father dies.

■ RED BADGE OF COURAGE, THE

1951, 68 MINS, US ⓥ

Dir John Huston   *Prod* Gottfried Reinhardt   *Scr* John Huston   *Ph* Harold Rosson   *Ed* Ben Lewis   *Mus* Bronislau Kaper   *Art Dir* Cedric Gibbons, Hans Peters
● Audie Murphy, Bill Mauldin, John Dierkes, Royal Dano, Arthur Hunnicutt, Douglas Dick (M-G-M)

This is a curiously moody, arty study of the psychological birth of a fighting man from frightened boy, as chronicled in Stephen Crane's novel *The Red Badge of Courage*.

Pic follows two figures during the days of the War Between the States. They are Audie Murphy, the youth who goes into his first battle afraid but emerges a man, and Bill Mauldin, on whom the same fears and misgivings have less sensitive impact.

Rather than any clearly defined story line, picture deals with a brief few hours of war and the effect it has on the few characters with which the script is concerned. Within the limited format, director John Huston artfully projects the characters to capture a seemingly allegorical mood of all wars and the men involved in them. His battle scene staging has punch and action, and his handling of the individual players makes them stand out. Narration, taken directly from the text of Crane's story, does a great deal to make clear the picture's aims.

There is an unbilled guest appearance by Andy Devine as a cheery soldier who lets God do his worrying, and it makes a single scene stand out.

■ RED DANUBE, THE

1949, 119 MINS, US

Dir George Sidney   *Prod* Carey Wilson   *Scr* Gina Kaus, Arthur Wimperis   *Ph* Charles Rosher   *Ed* James E. Newcom   *Mus* Miklos Rozsa
● Walter Pidgeon, Ethel Barrymore, Peter Lawford, Angela Lansbury, Janet Leigh, Louis Calhern (M-G-M)

In *The Red Danube* [from the novel *Vespers in Vienna* by Bruce Marshall], Metro aims a haymaker at Soviet repatriation methods in Europe and general Communist ideology, but the punch lands short of the mark.

Film might have been rescued by a more winning portrayal of its pro-democratic forces. But Walter Pidgeon, who limns a Brit-ish army colonel engaged in fulfilling the western allies' commitment to repatriate forcibly all refugees from Russia, is hamstrung for too many reels by calloused and blundering doings. His adjutant, Peter Lawford, is depicted as a peculiarly capri cious character.

Scene of the struggle is Vienna, circa 1945, where Pidgeon is billeted in a convent. Here much tedious religious talk is generated between the colonel, a professed unbeliever, and the mother-superior (Ethel Barrymore) on the pros and cons of organized religion.

Chief pawn is a ballerina (Janet Leigh) beloved by Lawford. Pidgeon turns over the ballerina on the promise she will not be mistreated.

■ RED DAWN

1984, 114 MINS, US ◇ ⓥ

Dir John Milius   *Prod* Buzz Feitshans, Barry Beckerman   *Scr* Kevin Reynolds, John Milius   *Ph* Ric Waite   *Ed* Thom Noble   *Mus* Basil Poledouris   *Art Dir* Jackson De Govia
● Patrick Swayze, C. Thomas Howell, Ron O'Neal, William Smith, Powers Booth, Charlie Sheen (M-G-M/UA)

Red Dawn charges off to an exciting start as a war picture and then gets all confused in moralistic handwriting, finally sinking in the sunset.

Sometime in the future, the United States stands alone and vulnerable to attack, abandoned by its allies. Rather than an all-out nuclear war Soviet and Cuban forces bomb selectively and then launch a conventional invasion across the southern and northwest Boleroborders.

Dawn takes place entirely in a small town taken by surprise by paratroopers. Grabbing food and weapons on the run, a band of teens led by Patrick Swayze and C. Thomas Howell makes it to the nearby mountains as the massacre continues below.

Swayze, Howell and the other youngsters are all good in their parts.

■ RED DUST

1932, 83 MINS, US ⓥ

Dir Victor Fleming   *Scr* John Lee Mahin   *Ph* Harold Rosson   *Ed* Blanche Sewell
● Clark Gable, Jean Harlow, Gene Raymond, Mary Astor, Donald Crisp, Tully Marshall (M-G-M)

Familiar plot stuff, but done so expertly it almost overcomes the basic script shortcomings and the familiar hot-love-in-the-isolated-tropics theme [from the play by Wilson Collison].

This time it's a rubber plantation in Indo-China, bossed by Clark Gable. Jean Harlow is the Sadie Thompson of the territory. Enter Gene Raymond and Mary Astor on Raymond's initial engineering assignment. Gable makes a play for Astor and it looks like the young husband will have his ideals shattered when circumstances cause Gable to send them both back to a more civilized existence, with more conventional standards, leaving Harlow as a more plausible (and, for audience purposes, more acceptable) playmate.

It's as simple as all that, basically. Astor is oke in the passive virtuous moments, but falls down badly on the clinches, sustained only by Gable. As the putteed, unshaven he-man rubber planter Gable's in his element, sustaining an unsympathetic assignment until it veers about a bit.

Harlow's elementary conception of moral standards, so far as the decent kid explorer (Raymond) is concerned, sort of gilds her lily of the fields assignment. She plays the light lady to the limit, however, not overdoing anything.

■ RED HEAT

1988, 103 MINS, US ◇ ⓥ

Dir Walter Hill   *Prod* Walter Hill, Gordon Carroll   *Scr* Harry Kleiner, Walter Hill, Troy Kennedy Martin   *Ph* Matthew F. Leonetti   *Ed* Freeman Davies, Carmel Davies, Donn Aron   *Mus* James Horner   *Art Dir* John Vallone
● Arnold Schwarzenegger, James Belushi, Peter Boyle, Ed O'Ross, Larry Fishburne (Carolco/Lone Wolf/Oak)

Red Heat has earned a place in the history books as the first entirely American-produced film to have been permitted to lens in the USSR, even if location work was essentially limited to establishing shots.

Entire early Moscow section (shot mostly in Budapest) establishes the notion that one of the prices the East will pay for opening up is an increase in the Western disease of drug dealing. A particularly loathesome practitioner in the field named Viktor (Ed O'Ross) manages to slip through the fingers of the Red Army's top enforcer (guess who) and heads for Chicago.

In full uniform, Arnold Schwarzenegger arrives at O'Hare Airport, where he is greeted by two working stiffs from the Chicago Police Dept, James Belushi and Richard Bright. Belushi is assigned to keep tabs on the terminator as the latter tracks down Viktor.

Schwarzenegger, who when he dons a green suit is dubbed 'Gumby' by Belushi, is right on target with his characterization of the iron-willed soldier, and Belushi proves a quicksilver foil.

■ RED HOUSE, THE

1947, 100 MINS, US ⓥ

Dir Delmer Daves   *Prod* Sol Lesser   *Scr* Delmer Daves   *Ph* Bert Glennon   *Ed* Merrill White   *Mus* Miklos Rozsa   *Art Dir* McClure Capps
● Edward G. Robinson, Lon McCallister, Judith Anderson, Allene Roberts, Julie London, Rory Calhoun (United Artists)

The Red House is an interesting psychological thriller [based on the novel by George Agnew Chamberlain], with its mood satisfactorily sustained throughout the pic. Film, however, has too slow a pace, so that the paucity of incident and action stands out sharply, despite good performances by Edward G. Robinson, Judith Anderson, Allene Roberts, Lon McCallister and others.

Film has a simple, rustic quality in scripting, setting and characterization.

Pic, however, is built on a single thread, and takes too long in getting to its climax. It ends on something of a macabre note, and throughout it has several false touches – a muscle-brained young woodsman being in possession of $750; entrusting the money to a flighty girl to buy him a bond with it, etc.

Robinson has supplied himself with a fat part that suits his talents and to which he gives his best efforts. He's cast as a farmer, living with a sister and an adopted daughter in an isolated area of a small community, further withdrawn from the community by his strange, gloomy moods. Part of his property is a wooded area to which no one can go; the farmer even employs a young woodsman to keep trespassers out by gunfire if necessary. A young hired hand comes to work on the farm, is intrigued by the wooded area, and enters it, to meet with several mishaps.

■ RED LINE 7000

1965, 118 MINS, US ◇

Dir Howard Hawks   *Prod* Howard Hawks   *Scr* George Kirgo   *Ph* Milton Krasner   *Ed* Stuart Gilmore, Bill Brame   *Mus* Nelson Riddle
● James Caan, Laura Devon, Gail Hire, Charlene Holt, John Robert Crawford, Marianna Hill (Paramount)

Script by George Kirgo, based on a story by

director Howard Hawks, centers on three sets of characters as they go about their racing and lovemaking. Trio of racers are members of a team operating out of Daytona, Fla, their individual lives uncomplicated until three femmes fall in love with them. In a thrilling climax, one of the drivers, overcome with jealousy, causes another to crash but miraculously his life is saved.

Making excellent impressions are Laura Devon, Gail Hire and Marianna Hill, as girlfriends of the three daredevils of the track. James Caan, John Robert Crawford and James Ward in these roles are effective.

Hawks is on safe ground while his cameras are focused on race action. His troubles lie in limning his various characters in their more intimate moments. Title refers to an engine speed beyond which it's dangerous to operate a race car, perhaps symbolic of what Hawks wanted to achieve in the emotions of his players.

....

■ RED PONY, THE

1949, 89 MINS, US ◇ Ⓥ

Dir Lewis Milestone   *Prod* Charles K. Feldman, Lewis Milestone   *Scr* John Steinbeck   *Ph* Tony Gaudio   *Ed* Harry Keller   *Mus* Aaron Copland
● Myrna Loy, Robert Mitchum, Louis Calhern, Shepperd Strudwick, Peter Miles, Beau Bridges (Republic)

Lewis Milestone's filmization of a novelette by John Steinbeck has been pieced together with taste and fidelity. It has, however, stumbled over one obstacle. The secondary theme, an attempt to etch the emotional complexities of the grownups that surround the boy is slack-paced and sketchily drawn.

Boy-and-pony theme owes much of its compassion and winning graces to a fine and sensitive performance by Peter Miles. As Billy Buck, the hired man, Robert Mitchum underscores a likeable role.

Neither Myrna Loy nor Shepperd Strudwick are as satisfactory as the boy's parents. Since it is their lot to go through some pretty tedious bits of business, script and direction are undoubtedly more at fault than their thesping efforts.

....

■ RED RIVER

1948, 126 MINS, US Ⓥ

Dir Howard Hawks   *Prod* Charles K. Feldman   *Scr* Borden Chase, Charles Schnee   *Ph* Russell Harlan   *Ed* Christian Nyby   *Mus* Dimitri Tiomkin   *Art Dir* John Datu Arensma
● John Wayne, Montgomery Clift, Joanne Dru, Walter Brennan, Coleen Gray, John Ireland (United Artists)

Howard Hawks' production and direction give a masterful interpretation to a story of the early west and the opening of the Chisholm Trail, over which Texas cattle were moved to Abilene to meet the railroad on its march across the country.

Also important to *Red River* is the introduction of Montgomery Clift. Clift brings to the role of Matthew Garth a sympathetic personality that invites audience response.

Hawks has loaded the film with mass spectacle and earthy scenes. His try for naturalness in dialog between principals comes off well. The staging of physical conflict is deadly, equalling anything yet seen on the screen. Picture realistically depicts trail hardships; the heat, sweat, dust, storm and marauding Indians that bore down on the pioneers. Neither has Hawks overlooked sex, exponents being Joanne Dru and Coleen Gray.

Picture is not all tough melodrama. There's a welcome comedy relief in the capable hands of Walter Brennan. He makes his every scene stand out sharply, leavening the action with chuckles while maintaining a character as rough and ready as the next.

Sharing co-director credit with Hawks is Arthur Rosson. The pair have staged high excitement in the cattle stampedes and other scenes of mass action.

....

■ RED SHOES, THE

1948, 134 MINS, UK ◇ Ⓥ

Dir Michael Powell, Emeric Pressburger   *Prod* Michael Powell, Emeric Pressburger   *Scr* Michael Powell, Emeric Pressburger   *Ph* Jack Cardiff, Christopher Challis   *Ed* Reginald Mills   *Mus* Brian Easdale   *Art Dir* Hein Heckroth, Arthur Lawson
● Anton Walbrook, Marius Goring, Moira Shearer, Leonide Massine, Robert Helpmann, Ludmilla Tcherina (Archers)

For the first 60 minutes, this is a commonplace backstage melodrama, in which temperamental ballerinas replace the more conventional showgirls. Then a superb ballet of the Red Shoes, based on a Hans Andersen fairy tale, is staged with breathtaking beauty out-classing anything that could be done on the stage. It is a colorful sequence, full of artistry, imagination and magnificence. The three principal dancers, Moira Shearer, Leonide Massine and Robert Helpmann, are beyond criticism.

Then the melodrama resumes, story being about the love of a ballerina for a young composer thus incurring the severe displeasure of the ruthless Boris Lermontov, guiding genius of the ballet company.

Although the story may be trite, there are many compensations, notably the flawless performance of Anton Walbrook, whose interpretation of the role of Lermontov is one of the best things he has done on the screen. Shearer, glamorous redhead, shows that she can act as well as dance, while Marius Goring, polished as ever, plays the young composer with enthusiasm.

Other assets that can be chalked up are the wide variety of interesting locations – London, Paris, Monte Carlo, magnificent settings, firstclass Technicolor and some brilliant musical scores played by the Royal Philharmonic Orchestra with Thomas Beecham as conductor.

□ 1948: Best Picture (Nomination)

....

■ RED SONJA

1985, 89 MINS, US ◇ Ⓥ

Dir Richard Fleischer   *Prod* Christian Ferry   *Scr* Clive Exton, George MacDonald Fraser   *Ph* Giuseppe Rotunno   *Ed* Frank J. Urioste   *Mus* Ennio Morricone   *Art Dir* Danilo Donati
● Brigitte Nielsen, Arnold Schwarzenegger, Sandahl Bergman, Paul Smith, Ernie Reyes Jr, Ronald Lacey (M-G-M/United Artists)

Red Sonja [based on stories by Robert E. Howard] returns to those olden days when women were women and the menfolk stood around with funny hats on until called forth to be whacked at.

Except, of course, for Arnold Schwarzenegger, whose Kalidor creation has just enough muscles to make him useful to the ladies, but not enough brains to make him a bother, except that he talks too much.

To her credit in the title role, Brigitte Nielsen never listens to a word he has to say, perhaps because she has an unfortunate tendency to address her as 'Sony-uh.' Nielsen wants to revenge her sister and find the magic talisman all on her own with no help from Kalidor, though she does think it's kind of cute when he wades into 80 guys and wastes them in an effort to impress her.

....

■ RED SUN

1971, 115 MINS, FRANCE ◇ Ⓥ

Dir Terence Young   *Prod* Robert Dorfmann   *Scr* L. Koenig, D.B. Petitclerc, W. Roberts, L. Roman   *Ph* Henri Alekan   *Ed* Johnny Dwyre   *Mus* Maurice Jarre

● Charles Bronson, Ursula Andress, Toshiro Mifune, Alain Delon, Capucine (Corona/Oceania)

East is East and West is West, but the twain meets in this actionful oater with Japanese actor Toshiro Mifune matching sword and wits with Yank Charles Bronson and Frenchman Alain Delon.

Mifune is a Samurai accompanying the Japanese ambassador in a trek across the West to Washington in the mid-19th century to deliver a jeweled, golden sword to the US president. On the way the train is held up by Bronson and Delon, but the latter doublecrosses Bronson and also kills a samurai friend of Mifune and takes the sword. Mifune's code requires he find the sword and kill Delon.

Mifune is his towering, glowering self in his rich samurai garb and his sword matches the guns. Bronson is relaxed and effective as the bandit with some honor within his own life. Ursula Andress is decorative as the wily prostie, out to make a killing to get out of her life of bondage.

Young lays on the action and blood with some interludes in the growing friendship between Bronson and Mifune.

....

■ RED TENT, THE

1971, 121 MINS, ITALY/USSR ◇ Ⓥ

Dir Mikhail Kalatozov   *Prod* Franco Cristaldi   *Scr* Ennio De Concini, Richard Adams   *Ph* Leonid Kalashnikov   *Ed* Peter Zinner   *Mus* Ennio Morricone   *Art Dir* Giancarlo Bartolini Salimboni, David Vinitsky
● Sean Connery, Claudia Cardinale, Hardy Kruger, Peter Finch, Massimo Girotti, Luigi Vannucchi (Vides/Mosfilm)

This first Italo-Russian coproduction deals with the 1928 rescue of an Italian Polar expedition stranded by a dirigible crash. Some spectacularly beautiful Arctic footage, plus an exciting personal story of survival, make the production compelling and suspenseful.

Framework of the script is metaphysical; a sort of rugged adventure yarn in a Jean-Paul Sartre setting. Peter Finch plays General Nobile, an Italian Arctic explorer who is lost in the North Atlantic wastes. Years later, his nightmares about the incident summon up phantoms of those involved with him.

Sean Connery plays Roald Amundsen, a fellow explorer who died in search for Finch; Claudia Cardinale plays a nurse who was in love with one of Finch's crew; and Hardy Kruger is a daredevil rescue pilot whose motivations in rescuing Finch before his men creates an international scandal.

Connery plays an aged man very convincingly. Kruger and Cardinale supply key plot motivations, but the heaviest burden is on Finch; he is excellent in a characterization which demands many moods, many attitudes.

....

■ RED-HEADED WOMAN

1932, 74 MINS, US

Dir Jack Conway   *Scr* Anita Loos   *Ph* Harold Rosson   *Ed* Blanche Sewell
● Jean Harlow, Chester Morris, Lewis Stone, Leila Hyams, Una Merkel, Henry Stephenson (M-G-M)

The outstanding fact is that M-G-M has turned out an interesting dissertation on a thoroughly provocative subject. Jean Harlow, hitherto not highly esteemed as an actress, gives an electric performance.

Ethics of the subject are sufficient to make a church deacon gulp and stammer. Heroine (Harlow) is a home wrecker, a vicious vamp and a destroyer of peace, and the wages of sin in her case are paid in the final close-up in strange and wonderful coin.

Picture is handled with a curious blending of bluntness and subtlety. Some of the 'vamping' sequences, and there are plenty of them, are torrid. But the overall effect is conveyed with a great deal of fancy skating over very thin ice and its very candor is disarming.

. . . .

■ REDS

1981, 200 MINS, US ◇

Dir Warren Beatty   *Prod* Warren Beatty   *Scr* Warren Beatty, Trevor Griffiths   *Ph* Vittorio Storaro   *Ed* Dede Allen, Craig McKay   *Mus* Stephen Sondheim, Dave Grusin   *Art Dir* Richard Sylbert
● Warren Beatty, Dian Keaton, Jerzy Kosinski, Jack Nicholson, Maureen Stapleton, Edward Herrmann (Paramount)

Warren Beatty's *Reds* is a courageous and uncompromising attempt to meld a high-level socio-political drama of ideas with an intense love story, but it is ultimately too ponderous.

More than just the story of American journalist-activist John Reed's stormy romantic career with writer Louise Bryant, a kinetic affair backdropped by pre-World War I radicalism and the Russian Revolution, the film is also, to its eventual detriment, structured as a Marxist history lesson.

First half of the film, though it takes an inordinant amount of time and detail to do it, does an intelligent job of setting both the political and emotional scene. Beginning in 1915, Reed (Beatty) is introduced as an idealistic reporter of decidedly radical bent who meets Portland writer Bryant (Diane Keaton) and persuades her to join him in New York within a tight-knit radical intellectual salon that includes the likes of playwright Eugene O'Neill (Jack Nicholson), anarchist-feminist Emma Goldman (Maureen Stapleton) and radical editor Max Eastman (Edward Herrmann).

Their on-again, off-again affair – which challenges their respective claims of emotional liberation – survives Keaton's brief fling with Nicholson and they marry.

But Beatty's inability to resist the growing socialist bandwagon strains them yet again and Keaton ships off to cover the French battlefront and begin life afresh. En route to cover the upcoming conflagration in Russia, Beatty persuades her to join him – in professional, not emotional status – and in Petrograd, the revolutionary fervor rekindles their romantic energies as well.

Reds bites off more than an audience can comfortably chew. Constant conflicts between politics and art, love and social conscience, individuals versus masses, pragmatism against idealism, take the form of intense and eventually exhausting arguments that dominate the script by Beatty and British playwright Trevor Griffiths.

As director, Beatty has harnessed considerable intensity into individual confrontations but curiously fails to give the film an overall emotional progression.

. . . .

■ REFLECTIONS IN A GOLDEN EYE

1967, 109 MINS, US ◇ Ⓥ

Dir John Huston   *Prod* Ray Stark   *Scr* Chapman Mortimer, Gladys Hill   *Ph* Aldo Tonti   *Ed* Russell Lloyd   *Mus* Toshiro Mayuzumi   *Art Dir* Stephen Grimes
● Elizabeth Taylor, Marlon Brando, Brian Keith, Julie Harris, Robert Forster, Zorro David (Warner/Seven Arts)

Carson McCullers' novel, *Reflections in a Golden Eye*, about a latent homosexual US Army officer in the pre Second World War period, has been turned into a pretentious melodrama by director John Huston.

Adaptation features six disparate characters: Marlon Brando, the latent homosexual; his wife, Elizabeth Taylor, a practicing heterosexual – practicing with Brian Keith,

whose own wife, Julie Harris, once cut off her breasts with scissors after unfortunate childbirth; Robert Forster, young fetishist and exhibitionist; Zorro David, Harris' fey houseboy. Also prominent are a host of sex symbols, and some salty expressions.

Brando struts about and mugs as the stuffy officer, whose Dixie dialect is often incoherent. Taylor is appropriately unaware of her husband's torment. Her dialect also obscures some vital plot points.

The most outstanding and satisfying performance is that of Brian Keith. This versatile actor is superb as the rationalizing and insensitive middle-class hypocrite.

. . . .

■ REINCARNATION OF PETER PROUD, THE

1975, 104 MINS, US ◇

Dir J. Lee Thompson   *Prod* Frank P. Rosenberg   *Scr* Max Ehrlich   *Ph* Victor J. Kemper   *Ed* Michael Anderson   *Mus* Jerry Goldsmith   *Art Dir* Jack Martin Smith
● Michael Sarrazin, Jennifer O'Neill, Margot Kidder, Cornelia Sharpe, Paul Hecht, Tony Stephano (American International)

Reincarnation of Peter Proud embodies all the thrills of Max Ehrlich's bestseller, plus an oustandingly rich performance from Margot Kidder. Only weakness still is story's sudden and unsatisfactory ending.

Michael Sarrazin from the start almost, realizes that some unknown person is within him. Tracing scenes from his dreams, he ventures to small Massachusetts town where Kidder had murdered philandering husband, briefly but ably played by Stephano.

Sarrazin is best in contending with the semi incestuous love affair that develops between him and Jennifer O'Neill. Her best moments, too, come in the clinches that do-don't take place between two obviously attracted, and otherwise eligible, young lovers.

. . . .

■ REIVERS, THE

1969, 107 MINS, US ◇ Ⓥ

Dir Mark Rydell   *Prod* Irving Ravetch, Arthur Kramer   *Scr* Irving Ravetch, Harriet Frank Jr   *Ph* Richard Moore   *Ed* Tom Stanford   *Mus* John Williams   *Art Dir* Charles Bailey, Joel Schiller
● Steve McQueen, Sharon Farrell, Rupert Crosse, Mitch Vogel, Clinton James, Will Geer (Solar/Cinema Center)

The Reivers is a nice bawdy film, sort of Walt Disney with an adult rating. Imagine a charming nostalgia-soaked family-type film about a winsome 11-year-old in turn-of-the-century Mississippi who gets himself cut up in a Memphis bordello defending the good name of a lovely professional lady.

The film is an adaptation of William Faulkner's last novel.

Mitch Vogel, as the kid, is appealing, subtle and sensitive, hovering between freckle-faced moppet and sexual puberty.

He is led astray by the family handy man and resident rogue Steve McQueen who gives a lively ribald characterization.

Completing the triumvirate of 'Reivers', an old word that means 'thieves', is Rupert Crosse. He is a humorously light-hearted but sardonically mocking dude.

In a gleaming gold Winton Flyer the three steal off to Memphis, and the end of innocence for the boy.

. . . .

■ RELUCTANT DEBUTANTE, THE

1958, 96 MINS, US ◇

Dir Vincente Minnelli   *Prod* Pandro S. Berman   *Scr* William Douglas Home   *Ph* Joseph Ruttenberg   *Ed* Adrienne Fazan   *Mus* Eddie Warner (arr.)   *Art Dir* A.J. d'Eaubonne
● Rex Harrison, Kay Kendall, John Saxon, Sandra Dee, Angela Lansbury, Diane Clare (M-G-M/Avon)

The Reluctant Debutante is refreshing and prettily dressed, a colorful, saucy film version of the William Douglas Home stage trifle.

Debutante is the story of London's social 'season', a time when bright and not-to-bright 17-year-olds make their debuts in society, carrying on at one deb's ball after another. Rex Harrison and Kay Kendall, as newly married on screen as off, invite his American daughter (by a former marriage) for a British visit that results in the girl's coming out socially.

As played by Sandra Dee, the teenager is bored with English stiffs but falls madly for an American drummer (John Saxon) who's tabbed with a most dubious reputation. Mixed-up telephone calls, embarrassing situations and advances – both wanted and unwanted – follow with rapidity.

Harrison is suavely disturbed as the father. Dee proves a rather good actress who maintains a lively character throughout, and Saxon lends a fine boyish charm to the proceedings. But it's really Kendall's picture, and she grabs it with a single wink. She's flighty and well-meaning, snobbish and lovable.

. . . .

■ REMBRANDT

1936, 85 MINS, US Ⓥ

Dir Alexander Korda   *Prod* Alexander Korda   *Scr* Carl Zuckmayer, June Head, Arthur Wimperis   *Ph* Georges Perinal   *Ed* Francis Lyon, William Hornbeck   *Mus* Geoffrey Toye   *Art Dir* Vincent Korda
● Charles Laughton, Gertrude Lawrence, Elsa Lanchester, Walter Hudd, Roger Livesey, John Bryning (London)

An idealized film biography of the life of the famous painter. Story begins at the height of Rembrandt's fame, during his lifetime, and carries on to his solitary, poverty-stricken old age. Despite a cast of two score principals, it is a one-part production, with but one scene in the entire film in which the star does not play the central character.

It was an inspiration to film many of the scenes with a suggestion of the lighting for which Rembrandt is famous in his paintings.

Forty principals were requisitioned from the best artists the British legitimate stage has to offer. If some of them, like Gertrude Lawrence and Elsa Lanchester, stand out from the others, it is only because they have more extensive and showier roles.

Despite all this artistic and technical assistance, Charles Laughton is far from satisfactory. According to the story, he is never interested in anything relating to finance or the ordinary rules of domestic economy. The only tragic things in his life are the deaths of his two wives. On neither occasion does Laughton express the overwhelming sorrow the story calls for.

. . . .

■ REMEMBER MY NAME

1978, 95 MINS, US ◇

Dir Alan Rudolph   *Prod* Robert Altman   *Scr* Alan Rudolph   *Ph* Tak Fujimoto   *Ed* Thomas Walls, William A. Sawyer   *Mus* Alberta Hunter
● Geraldine Chaplin, Anthony Perkins, Moses Gunn, Berry Berenson, Jeff Goldblum, Timothy Thomerson (Lion's Gate)

Remember My Name is an attempt to make what Alan Rudolph calls a 'contemporary blues fable'. Whatever the generic goal, the end product is an incomprehensible melange of striking imagery, obscure dialog, a powerful score, and a script that doesn't know how to go from A to B.

Anthony Perkins is a construction worker married to Berry Berenson. Geraldine Chaplin arrives on the scene and begins a

R

petty harassment of the couple, which gradually turns more sinister.

It develops that Chaplin is an ex-convict, recently sprung from a 12-year sentence for murder. She got a job in a nearby five-and-dime store managed by Jeff Goldblum (whose mother is still doing time), where she terrorizes store clerk Alfre Woodard and Goldblum. Chaplin also gets a room in a run-down apartment building managed by Moses Gunn, with whom she has a brief liaison.

If done on a traditional, linear level, *Remember My Name* might have induced some interest as a moderate chiller with emotional undertones. In Rudolph's infuriatingly oblique style, however, it becomes an irritating and puzzling affair that insults, rather than teases, the viewer.

■ RENT-A-COP

1988, 95 MINS, US ◇ ▼

Dir Jerry London *Prod* Raymond Wagner *Scr* Dennis Shryack, Michael Blodgett *Ph* Giuseppe Rotunno *Ed* Robert Lawrence *Mus* Jerry Goldsmith *Art Dir* Tony Masters

● Burt Reynolds, Liza Minelli, James Remar, Richard Masur, Dionne Warwick (Kings Road)

Pic, a cheesy little crime thriller, starts off promisingly as a sort of followup to Burt Reynolds' *Sharky's Machine*, with him working again with fellow cop Bernie Casey on a big drug bust. Nutcase James Remar wipes everybody out except Reynolds, who is suspected of being crooked and bounced from the force.

He gets work as a 'rent-a-cop', undercover (dressed as a Santa Claus) in a department store. In an awkwardly staged but key subplot, Liza Minnelli, as a Chicago hooker, has been saved from Remar by Reynolds and now attaches herself to him for protection.

Reynolds looks bored and is boring here, with an ill-fitting toupe that is downright embarrassing from one closeup angle. Minnelli is a lot of fun as the flamboyant prostie. Dionne Warwick is thoroughly wasted here as head of a callgirl ring. Remar is laughably hammy as the narcissistic killer.

■ REPO MAN

1984, 94 MINS, US ◇ ▼

Dir Alex Cox *Prod* Jonathan Wacks *Scr* Alex Cox *Ph* Robby Muller *Ed* Dennis Dolan *Mus* Steve Hufsteter, Tito Larrna, Los Plugz, Iggy Pop *Art Dir* J. Rae Fox, Linda Burbank

● Harry Dean Stanton, Emilio Estevez, Olivia Barash, Tracey Walter, Sy Richardson, Vonetta McGee (Edge City)

Repo Man has the type of unerring energy that leaves audiences breathless and entertained. While the title, referring to the people who repossess cars from those behind on their payments, might suggest a low-budget, gritty, realistic venture, the truth exists somewhat on the other end of the spectrum.

The more conventional aspects of the script deal with an aimless young man, wonderfully underplayed by Emilio Estevez, who falls in with a crowd of repo men and takes to the 'intense' lifestyle with ease.

Director-writer Alex Cox establishes the offbeat nature of the film from the start. In the opening scene, a state trooper stops a speeder and on a routine check of his trunk is blasted by a flash of light leaving him merely a smoldering pair of boots. This aspect of the story, centering on a 1964 Chevy Malibu, begins to have significance only later.

The initial plot thrust involves Otto Maddox (Estevez) and Bud (Harry Dean Stanton), the veteran repo man who teaches him the ropes.

However, these are certainly tame facets as a story of alien invaders evolves.

The ever reliable Stanton turns in yet another indelible portrait of a seamy lowlife while Estevez registers as a charismatic and talented actor.

■ REPORT TO THE COMMISSIONER

1975, 112 MINS, US ◇

Dir Milton Katselas *Prod* Mike Frankovich *Scr* Abby Mann, Ernest Tidyman *Ph* Mario Tosi *Ed* David Blewitt *Mus* Elmer Bernstein *Art Dir* Robert Clatworthy

● Michael Moriarty, Yaphet Kotto, Susan Blakely, Hector Elizondo, William Devane, Richard Gere (United Artists)

Report to the Commissioner is a superb suspense drama of the tragic complexities of law enforcement.

Based on the novel by James Mills, it tells in flashback why Michael Moriarty, an idealistic new dectective, is being harassed to provide an alibi for the death of Susan Blakely, an undercover narc killed accidentally in the pad she shares with bigtime dealer Tony King. Hector Elizondo and Michael McGuire are medium-level detectives whose ambitions overcome their adherence to procedure, and lay the foundations for Moriarty's unexpected fate. Yaphet Kotto, in an outstanding performance, is Moriarty's senior partner. Richard Gere is very good as a smalltime pimp.

■ REPULSION

1965, 104 MINS, UK ▼

Dir Roman Polanski *Prod* Gene Gutowski *Scr* Roman Polanski, Gerard Brach *Ph* Gil Taylor *Ed* Alastair McIntyre *Mus* Chico Hamilton *Art Dir* Seamus Flannery

● Catherine Deneuve, Ian Hendry, John Fraser, Patrick Wymark, Yvonne Furneaux, Renee Houston (Compton/Tekli)

Repulsion is a classy, truly horrific psychological drama in which Polish director Roman Polanski draws out a remarkable performance from young French thesp, Catherine Deneuve. Polanski, who wrote the original screenplay with Gerard Brach, uses his technical resources and the abilities of his thesps to build up a tense atmosphere of evil.

A notable plus is Polanski's use of sound. There are two brief sequences, for instance, when the young heroine tosses in her bed as she listens to the muted sound of her sister and her lover in the next room. The moans and ecstatic whimperings of the love act is a dozen times more effective and sensual than any glimpse of the lovers in bed.

Deneuve is a youngster working in a beauty shop, a deliberately sharp contrast to the drab apartment which she shares with her flighty elder sister. The girl is sexually repressed, deeply attracted to the thought of men but at the same time loathing the thought of them. Her daydreaming grows into erotic sexual fantasies, and when her sister and boyfriend leave her for a few days while they go on an Italian vacation, her loneliness and imagination take hold and insanity sets in.

Deneuve, without much dialog, handles a very difficult chore with insight and tact. John Fraser plays her would-be boyfriend likeably.

■ REQUIEM FOR A HEAVYWEIGHT

1962, 85 MINS, US

Dir Ralph Nelson *Prod* David Susskind *Scr* Rod Serling *Ph* Arthur J. Ornitz *Ed* Carl Lerner *Mus* Laurence Rosenthal *Art Dir* Burr Smidt

● Anthony Quinn, Jackie Gleason, Mickey Rooney, Julie Harris, Stan Adams, Cassius Clay (Columbia)

Rod Serling's poignant portrait of the sunset

of a prizefighter has lost some of its dramatic weight in the transition from the very small to the very large screen. However, it still packs considerable punch as a character study, although its action has slowed to where the plot padding is often obvious.

Some of the casting, no doubt done for authenticity and atmosphere, has boomeranged. Julie Harris plays her employment counselor as though she never really believed in the character. Casting actual boxing personalities is atmospheric but distracting and often ludicrous, particularly an amateurish bit by Jack Dempsey.

The performances of Quinn and Gleason are equally matched and carry the picture, no small chore. Quinn's punchy, inarticulate behemoth is so painfully natural that one winces when he feels pain, whether to his body or his feelings. Gleason is amazingly fine. He's weak, crafty, shiftly and still a little pathetic.

Mickey Rooney, hampered with some bad makeup, is warm and sympathetic as Army, the trainer, but doesn't really shine except for one card-playing scene. It's the only funny bit in the pic and he steals it from under Gleason's nose. The plot contains some glaring implausibilities.

■ RESCUERS, THE

1977, 76 MINS, US ◇

Dir Wolfgang Reitherman *Prod* Wolfgang Reitherman *Scr* Larry Clemmons, Ken Anderson, Vance Gerry, David Michener, Burny Mattinson, Frank Thomas, Fred Lucky, Ted Berman, Dick Sebast *Ed* James Melton, Jim Koford *Mus* Artie Butler *Art Dir* Don Griffith

● (Walt Disney)

Four years of work were invested on this $7.5 million production and the expense, care, and expertise shows.

An admirably simple story [suggested by *The Rescuers* and *Miss Bianca* by Margery Sharp] about two mice (voiced by Bob Newhart and Eva Gabor) who embark on a quest to rescue a kidnapped orphan girl (Michelle Stacy) from the clutches of an evil witch (Geraldine Page).

There's real terror in the story, and the Gothic setting of the swamp where the girl is held captive; the maudlin pitfalls of the plot are avoided through deft use of humor, and the plucky character of the young captive.

Among the most memorable sequences are two hilarious ascents by a goofy bird named Orville, who takes the mice on their rescue mission.

■ RESTLESS YEARS, THE

1958, 86 MINS, US

Dir Helmut Kautner *Prod* Ross Hunter *Scr* Edward Anhalt *Ph* Ernest Laszlo *Ed* Al Joseph *Mus* Joseph Gershenson *Art Dir* Alexander Golitzen, Philip Barber

● John Saxon, Sandra Dee, Teresa Wright, James Whitmore, Luana Patten, Margaret Lindsay (Universal)

A touching account of adolescence and some of its problems as compounded by adult density, *The Restless Years* is based on Patricia Joudry's play, *Teach Me How to Cry*. In almost the first line of dialog, Sandra Dee is described as an illegitimate child. Her problems arise out of this and the fact that her unwed mother (Teresa Wright) has never recovered from the desertion by the father.

Everyone in town, apparently, knows the story except Dee. The girl begins to grow up when a new boy in town (John Saxon), who doesn't know or doesn't care about local gossip and prejudice, meets her and falls in love. His life is complicated by his luckless father (James Whitmore) who has come back to his home town to achieve the success that has eluded him elsewhere.

It is a period piece, with the dressmaker mother of an illegitimate child, and would have been more plausible if it had been played in period. But granting this, it has a feeling of poetry and sensitivity. Dee gives the picture its strongest sense of reality.

■ **RESURRECTION**

1980, 103 MINS, US ◇ ▼

Dir Daniel Petrie   *Prod* Renee Missel, Howard Rosenman   *Scr* Lewis John Carlino   *Ph* Mario Tosi   *Ed* Rita Roland   *Mus* Maurice Jarre   *Art Dir* Paul Sylbert

● Ellen Burstyn, Sam Shepard, Richard Farnsworth, Roberts Blossom (Universal)

Resurrection, an unusual supernatural drama about a faith healer, gives Ellen Burstyn a shot at a tour-de-force performance, but never comes into strong enough focus dramatically or philosophically.

The overly prosaic style of director Daniel Petrie and the underdeveloped screenplay inhibit her from exerting her full range of emotions.

She begins as a housewife who gives her husband a sports car, only to have it cause his death in a crash which leaves her legs paralyzed. During her laborious recovery period, she discovers that her close brush with death has given her the power of healing by the laying on of hands.

There is commendably little sensationalism, but not enough thoughtful exploration. Petrie's filming makes the pic resemble a soap opera.

■ **RETURN FROM THE ASHES**

1965, 108 MINS, UK

Dir J. Lee Thompson   *Prod* J. Lee Thompson   *Scr* Julius Epstein   *Ph* Christopher Challis   *Ed* Russell Lloyd   *Mus* John Dankworth   *Art Dir* Michael Stringer

● Maximilian Schell, Samantha Eggar, Ingrid Thulin, Herbert Lom, Talitha Pol, Vladek Sheybal (Mirisch/United Artists)

Return from the Ashes does not always reach its mark as a thriller. The production, filmed in England, carries the makings of a suspenseful melodrama but in development is early contrived.

The screenplay based on a novel by Hubert Monteilhet builds around a plot for the perfect murder by an unscrupulous Polish chess master married to one woman and in love with her stepdaughter. Set in Paris at the close of Second World War, when the wife, a Jewess, returns from tortured internment in Dachau to find her husband living with the younger woman, plottage concerns the Pole's passion for money as he does away first with one, then the other femme, to accomplish his goal.

Thompson, who also directs, establishes a tense mood frequently, but level of interest suffers from character fuzziness which occasionally clouds the issue.

Maximilian Schell delivers strongly in a blackhearted role, lending credence to the character through constantly underplaying his scenes. Samantha Eggar displays dramatic aptitude as the amoral stepdaughter, Fabi, whose entry into her bath provides one of the highlights of the film.

■ **RETURN FROM WITCH MOUNTAIN**

1978, 93 MINS, US ◇ ▼

Dir John Hough   *Prod* Ron Miller   *Scr* Malcolm Marmorstein   *Ph* Frank Phillips   *Ed* Bob Bring   *Mus* Lalo Schifrin   *Art Dir* John B. Mansbridge, Jack Senter

● Bette Davis, Christopher Lee, Kim Richards, Ike Eisenmann, Jack Soo, Anthony James (Walt Disney)

Kim Richards and Ike Eisenmann reprise their roles from *Escape to Witch Mountain* (1975) as sister and brother from another world, this time back on Earth for a vacation, courtesy of space traveler Uncle Bene (Denver Pyle). Siblings get a quick test of their psychic powers as mad scientist Christopher Lee and accomplice Bette Davis are testing their mind-control device on henchman Anthony James – when Eisenmann saves James from falling off a building by anti-gravity display, Lee sees the youngster as his meal ticket to world power.

Film is basically a chase caper, as Richards tries to find her brother, aided by a junior bunch of Dead End kids, Christian Juttner, Brad Savage, Poindexter and Jeffrey Jacquet. Despite an extrasensory link between the siblings (they communicate via telepathy, and can also make objects move at will), Lee has Eisenmann strait-jacketed with his device, so he can use youngster's 'molecular reorganization' powers to his own purposes.

Eisenmann and Richards have matured considerably since original. Lee makes one of the best Disney villains in years, but Davis doesn't quite click as his partner in crime.

■ **RETURN HOME**

1990, 87 MINS, AUSTRALIA ◇

Dir Ray Argall   *Prod* Cristina Pozzam   *Scr* Ray Argall   *Ph* Mandy Walker   *Ed* Ken Sallows   *Mus* Joe Camilleri   *Art Dir* Kerith Homes

● Dennis Coard, Frankie J. Holden, Ben Mendelsohn, Micki Camilleri, Rachel Rains (Musical)

Cinematographer Ray Argall makes an assured crossover to the director's chair with *Return Home*. The low-key performances perfectly fit the mood Argall is aiming for.

Newcomer Dennis Coard plays Noel, a successful big city insurance broker, whose personal life appears to be in tatters after a recent divorce. He decides to go home, back to the beachside suburb in Adelaide where he grew up at his father's gas station with older brother, Steve.

Steve (Frankie J. Holden) still runs the gas station, in partnership with his hard-working wife, Judy (Micki Camilleri), but things aren't going well. The other principal character in the film is Gary (Ben Mendelsohn), Steve's teenage mechanic, a well-meaning, awkward youth who's had a falling out with Wendy (Rachel Rains), his girlfriend.

Noel hangs out with Steve, Gary and Judy; he observes their lives, and evidently sees in them what he's lost in his own world of the rat race.

■ **RETURN OF A MAN CALLED HORSE, THE**

1976, 125 MINS, US ◇ ▼

Dir Irvin Kershner   *Prod* Terry Morse Jr   *Scr* Jack De Witt   *Ph* Owen Roizman   *Ed* Michael Kahn   *Mus* Laurence Rosenthal   *Art Dir* Stewart Campbell

● Richard Harris, Gale Sondergaard, Geoffrey Lewis, Bill Lucking, Jorge Luke, Claudio Brook (United Artists)

The Return of a Man Called Horse is a visually stunning sequel, again starring Richard Harris as an English nobleman who this time returns to the American west to save his adopted Indian tribe from extinction.

Irvin Kershner's film is handsome, leisurely, placid to the point of being predictable but dotted with some action highlights; in particular, Harris encores a physical torture-ritual, explicit enough to drive some audiences to the concession stand.

Jack De Witt wrote the original *Horse* script from a Dorothy M. Johnson story, published in 1950 in the old *Collier's* mag.

De Witt herein has extended the story, bringing Harris back west again to find his tribe wasted and dispossessed by land poacher Geoffrey Lewis.

■ **RETURN OF DR. FU MANCHU, THE**

1930, 73 MINS, US

Dir Rowland V. Lee   *Scr* Florence Ryerson, Lloyd Corrigan   *Ph* Archie J. Stout

● Warner Oland, Neil Hamilton, Jean Arthur, O.P. Heggie, William Austin, Evelyn Hall (Paramount)

Another chapter in the lurid melodramatic series made more or less from the detective stories by Sax Rohmer, English writer. As a picture it's absurd.

Picture has a brisk opening. Fu Manchu (Warner Oland) having been apparently killed in the previous picture, it became necessary to bring him to life again in an elaborate Chinese funeral. The archdemon escapes from his own coffin by a spring door, while an Oriental attendant is sealing the casket with molten lead. He takes up the trail of Dr Petrie all over and the story becomes a checker game between the wily Celestial and the super detective, Nayland Smith.

Picture has a nicely staged wedding scene with Jean Arthur looking remarkably beautiful as the bride. Neil Hamilton does all that is possible to hold up the puppet role of the hero and O.P. Heggie is once more the super-human cool Inspector Nayland Smith.

■ **RETURN OF FRANK JAMES, THE**

1940, 92 MINS, US ◇ ▼

Dir Fritz Lang   *Prod* Kenneth Macgowan   *Scr* Sam Hellman   *Ph* George Barnes, William V. Skall   *Ed* Walter Thompson   *Mus* David Buttolph   *Art Dir* Richard Day, Wiard B. Ihnen

● Henry Fonda, Gene Tierney, Jackie Cooper, John Carradine, Henry Hull, J. Edward Bromberg (20th Century-Fox)

Jesse James, under the sponsorship of 20th Century-Fox, was murdered a year ago by those cowards, the Ford brothers. This season, with vengeance rankling in his breast, Jesse James' older brother, Frank, returns to even the score. That he does, in obedience to Sam Hellman's script, but it's pretty slow stuff in the telling. Frank's no cinematic match for Jesse, which appears to be Will Hays' fault more than anyone else's. Rule 16a in the book is that a bad man can't be a hero. Which leaves Hellman in the paradoxical position of having Frank responsible for deaths of three men who never so much as tasted a single slug from his six-shooter. Effort to put wings on Frank is too much. Angelic aspect bogs the plot and instead of flying it can do no better than plod for a slow 92 minutes.

From standpoint of production and cast, Darryl Zanuck has spared nary a horse. It's filled with ah-evoking outdoor scenes and nostalgically-impressive western streets and indoor sets. Henry Fonda, underplaying Jesse James' older brother, Frank, in typical quiet style, is impressive; Jackie Cooper, as his kid buddy, shows a maturing dramatic sense although the pout is still there; Henry Hull, as a southern newspaper editor, overacts like no one else can, but is tremendously appealing despite it; John Carradine is a duly hissable villain as Bob Ford; J. Edward Bromberg earns laughs as a dumb railroad detective; and Donald Meek, Eddie Collins and George Barbier are, as usual, good for smiles.

Only member of the cast with whom fault can be found is Gene Tierney, making her film debut. Tierney's plenty pretty but for oomph she just isn't. Playing the role of a naive gal reporter to whom Frank takes a fancy, she seems to just lack what it takes to make an impression on the screen.

RETURN OF SWAMP THING, THE

1989, 88 MINS, US ◇ Ⓥ

Jim Wynorski   Prod Ben Melniker, Michael Uslan   Scr Derek Spencer, Grant Morris   Ph Zoran Hockstalter   Ed Leslie Rosenthal   Mus Church Cirino   Art Dir Robb Wilson King
● Louis Jourdan, Heather Locklear, Sarah Douglas, Dick Durock, Ace Mask, Joey Sagal (Lightyear)

The Return of Swamp Thing is scientific hokum without the fun. Second attempt to film the DC Comics character will disappoint all but the youngest critters.

They may be entertained by watching crossbred creatures squirm helplessly or buy into the Swamp Thing's (Dick Durock) instant love for Heather Locklear. He's a plant; she's a vegetarian.

Pic is set against a backdrop of evil where Dr Arcane (Louis Jourdan) has turned the disco-looking basement of his ante-bellum mansion into a mutant lab inhabited by failed experiments as he tries to discover the genetic equivalent of the Fountain of Youth.

The Swamp Thing escaped, but most of his more unfortunate distant cousins of the Petri dish have not, like the cockroach/man stuck on his back flailing his legs while Drs Lana Zurrell and Rochelle (Sarah Douglas and Ace Mask, respectively) lament another misfire.

Locklear arrives at the scene to confront Jourdan, her evil stepfather, who has never quite adequately explained her mother's mysterious death.

It doesn't take a genius to figure out Mom's fate, though it take the dense Locklear character an hour and a half.

RETURN OF THE JEDI

1983, 133 MINS, US ◇ Ⓥ

Dir Richard Marquand   Prod Howard Kazanjian   Scr Lawrence Kasdan, George Lucas   Ph Alan Hume   Ed Sean Barton, Marcia Lucas, Duwayne Dunham   Mus John Williams   Art Dir Norman Reynolds
● Mark Hamill, Harrison Ford, Carrie Fisher, Billy Dee Williams, Anthony Daniels, Peter Mayhew (Lucasfilm/20th Century-Fox)

Jedi is the conclusion of the middle trilogy of George Lucas' planned nine-parter and suffers a lot in comparison to the initial Star Wars [1977], when all was fresh. One of the apparent problems is neither the writers nor the principal performers are putting in the same effort.

Telegraphed in the preceding The Empire Strikes Back [1980], the basic dramatic hook this time is Mark Hamill's quest to discover – and do something about – the true identity of menacing Darth Vader, while resisting the evil intents of the Emperor (Ian McDiarmid).

Hamill is not enough of a dramatic actor to carry the plot load here, especially when his partner in so many scenes is really little more than an oversized gas pump, even if splendidly voiced by James Earl Jones.

Even worse, Harrison Ford, who was such an essential element of the first two outings, is present more in body than in spirit this time, given little to do but react to special effects. And it can't be said that either Carrie Fisher or Billy Dee Williams rise to previous efforts.

But Lucas and director Richard Marquand have overwhelmed these performer flaws with a truly amazing array of creatures, old and new, plus the familiar space hardware.

RETURN OF THE LIVING DEAD, THE

1985, 90 MINS, US ◇ Ⓥ

Dir Dan O'Bannon   Prod Tom Fox   Scr Dan O'Bannon   Ph Jules Brenner   Ed Robert Gordon   Mus Matt Clifford   Art Dir William Stout
● Clu Gulager, James Karen, Don Calfa, Thom Mathews, Beverly Randolph, John Philbin (Hemdale/Fox)

Early on here, one character asks another if he's seen the original Night of the Living Dead, then goes on to explain that the 1968 film altered the facts concerning a real-life zombie attack on the local populace.

Virtually the entire action of the rather threadbare production [from a story by Rudy Ricci, John Russo and Russell Streiner] shuttles among three locations – a medical supply warehouse, where numerous zombies have been sent by the Army; a nearby mortuary; and an adjacent cemetery, where a bunch of punks frolic before being chased out by corpses risen from their graves.

From then on, it's the same old story, as unusually vigorous, athletic zombies besiege the motley bunch of human beings holed up in the vicinity and eat the brains of anyone they get their hands on.

Director Dan O'Bannon deserves considerable credit for creating a terrifically funny first half-hour of exposition, something in which he is greatly aided by the goofball performance of James Karen as a medical supply know-it-all.

RETURN OF THE MUSKETEERS, THE

1989, 94 MINS, UK/FRANCE/SPAIN ◇ Ⓥ

Dir Richard Lester   Prod Pierre Spengler   Scr George MacDonald Fraser   Ph Bernard Lutic   Ed John Victor Smith   Mus Jean-Claude Petit   Art Dir Gil Arrondo
● Michael York, Oliver Reed, Frank Finlay, C. Thomas Howell, Richard Chamberlain, Kim Cattrall (Burrill/Filmdebroc/Cine 5/Iberoamericana)

In 1974 Richard Lester boosted his then-flagging career with The Three Musketeers and its sequel The Four Musketeers, lavish swashbucklers with a comic touch. His attempt at a comeback is, sadly, a stillborn event which looks as tired as its re-assembled cast.

It's 20 years since the four musketeers ordered the execution of the evil Milady De Winter. But now King Charles is dead, and his son Louis, a 10-year-old, reigns with his mother (a reprise by Geraldine Chaplin).

D'Artagnan (Michael York) is assigned to bring together his three former comrades to fight for the Queen and Cardinal. He quickly recruits Porthos (Frank Finlay) and Athos (Oliver Reed), together with the latter's son, Raoul (C. Thomas Howell); however, Aramis (Richard Chamberlain), now a womanizing Abbe, is reluctant to join the band.

There follows a complicated and sometimes hard to follow plot [from Alexandre Dumas' Twenty Years After] involving a failed attempt to rescue King Charles I of England from execution. According to this, the executioner of the king was actually Justine (Kim Cattrall), evil daughter of Milady, who's intent on avenging herself on the four musketeers who she blames for the death of her mother.

Pic is dedicated to Roy Kinnear, whose accidental death during production must have cast a pall over the entire project.

RETURN OF THE PINK PANTHER, THE

1975, 115 MINS, UK ◇

Dir Blake Edwards   Prod Blake Edwards   Scr Frank Waldman, Blake Edwards   Ph Geoffrey Unsworth   Ed Tom Priestley   Mus Henry Mancini   Art Dir Peter Mullins
● Peter Sellers, Christopher Plummer, Catherine Schell, Herbert Lom, Peter Arne, Gregoire Aslan (United Artists)

The Return of the Pink Panther establishes Peter Sellers once again as the bane of the existence of chief detective Herbert Lom, who is forced to reinstate Sellers when the Pink Panther diamond is stolen from its native museum by a mysterious burglar.

Suspicion falls on Christopher Plummer, ostensibly retired phantom jewel thief who decides he must catch the real culprit to save himself. Catherine Schell plays Plummer's wife, who turns out to be a decoy in more ways than one.

Sellers' work takes him into contact with Peter Arne and Gregoire Aslan, native police under pressure from general Peter Jeffrey to find the gem: with befuddled concierge Victor Spinetti and perplexed bellboy Mike Grady, both at a posh Swiss resort hotel; and periodically with his valet Cato, played by Burt Kwouk.

All hands seem to be having a ball, especially Schell, whose unabashed amusement at Clouseau's seduction attempts often matches an audience's hilarity.

RETURN OF THE SECAUCUS SEVEN

1980, 110 MINS, US ◇ Ⓥ

Dir John Sayles   Prod Jeffrey Nelson, William Aydelott   Scr John Sayles   Ph Austin de Besche   Ed John Sayles   Mus K. Mason Daring
● Mark Arnott, Gordon Clapp, Maggie Cousineau, Brian Johnston, Adam LeFevre, John Sayles (Salsipuedes)

John Sayles has fashioned an admirable post-mortem of the 1960s student left. Virtually the whole cast and crew make their feature debut here, and while not all the work is on an entirely professional level, earnestness and intelligence of the enterprise carry the day.

Structured like a well-built three-act play, drama is set at eight-year reunion of seven student activists who were arrested together in Secaucus, NJ on their way to a Washington demonstration. As old cohorts and a few new companions gather at the New Hampshire farm of one of the couples, complicated history of romantic relationships within the group begins to be unravelled. A diagram of past and present liaisons would prove as dense as that for any soap opera.

Film is virtually wall-to-wall talk, all of it interesting and much of it rather witty.

RETURN OF THE SOLDIER, THE

1982, 102 MINS, UK ◇ Ⓥ

Dir Alan Bridges   Prod Anne Skinner, Simon Relph   Scr Hugh Whitemore   Ph Stephen Goldblatt   Ed Laurence Mery Clark   Mus Richard Rodney Bennett   Art Dir Luciana Arrighi
● Julie Christie, Alan Bates, Glenda Jackson, Ann-Margret, Ian Holm, Frank Finlay (Brent Walker)

Alan Bates comes home from World War I with shell shock and is partly amnesiac. He does not remember his wife, played by Julie Christie with overdone snobbishness, but does recall a lower-class girl (Glenda Jackson) he loved as a young man and his doting cousin, latter played with feeling by Ann-Margret.

Christie allows Bates to see Jackson, now married and a bit dowdy. However the love is still there. A psychiatrist warns that bringing Bates back to normal might be dangerous, for he is probably concealing the tragedy of the death of his child from himself.

Stereotyped characters may have been more alive when the book [by Rebecca West] was written castigating the hollowness of a certain British class system. Today it is more quaint than anything else and fails to find the depth in these people to make them timeless.

RETURN TO OZ

1985, 110 MINS, US ◇ Ⓥ

Dir Walter Murch   Prod Paul Maslansky   Scr Walter Murch, Gill Dennis   Ph David Watkin   Ed Leslie Hodgson   Mus David Shire   Art Dir Norman Reynolds
● Nicol Williamson, Jean Marsh, Fairuza Balk, Piper Laurie, Matt Clark, Sean Barrett (Walt Disney/Silver Screen Partners II)

Return to Oz is an astonishingly somber, melancholy and, sadly, unengaging trip back to a favorite land of almost every American's youth. Straight dramatic telling of little Dorothy's second voyage to the Emerald City [based on *The Land of Oz* and *Ozma of Oz* by L. Frank Baum] employs an amusement park-full of imaginative characters and special effects, but a heaviness of tone and absence of narrative drive prevent the flights of fancy from getting off the ground.

Opening finds Dorothy back at home in Kansas but unable to sleep because of disturbing memories of her recent trip. Reacting harshly, Aunt Em and Uncle Henry decide the girl has become deranged and send her to a clinic to receive electroshock therapy from sinister nurse Jean Marsh and doctor Nicol Williamson.

After nearly a half-hour of these nightmarish goings-on, Dorothy and her talking chicken Billina are delivered to Oz, but not a very inviting section of it. Landed on the edge of the Deadly Desert, Dorothy soon discovers the Yellow Brick Road in disrepair, the Emerald City in ruins and her companions from the previous trip turned to stone.

Along the way, as before, Dorothy accumulates some helpful friends.

■ RETURN TO PARADISE

1953, 90 MINS, US ◇

Dir Mark Robson *Prod* Theron Warth *Scr* Charles Kaufman *Ph* Winton C. Hoch *Ed* Daniel Mandell *Mus* Dimitri Tiomkin
● Gary Cooper, Roberta Haynes, Barry Jones, Moira MacDonald, John Hudson (Aspen)

The simplicity of authentic Samoan settings provides a strong, appealing background for this leisurely, idyllic, romantic drama, based on the *Mr Morgan* portion of James A. Michener's bestselling *Return to Paradise*.

Gary Cooper protrays Morgan, a casual soldier of fortune taking his ease in the unhurried life of the island paradises. On one atoll where he decides to stay awhile, an island beauty attracts his attention to set the romance of the piece. For conflict there is the domination of the island and the natives by a missionary, a man who has forgotten the Bible teaches more than hellfire and damnation.

Cooper's delivery of the foot-loose South Seas wanderer is in his easy-going, understated style of histrionics and just right for the character and for the mood aimed by Mark Robson's direction. Opposite him is Roberta Haynes as the native girl, Maeva. Barry Jones makes his portrayal of the zealot, Pastor Cobbett, a performance gem. Moira MacDonald, three-quarters Polynesian and recruited in Samoa for the role, has natural appeal as the daughter.

Music is an important part of the production both in the native numbers recorded in the islands, where all of the lensing took place, and that cleffed by Dimitri Tiomkin.

■ RETURN TO PEYTON PLACE

1961, 123 MINS, US ◇

Dir Jose Ferrer *Prod* Jerry Wald *Scr* Ronald Alexander *Ph* Charles G. Clarke *Ed* David Bretherton *Mus* Franz Waxman *Art Dir* Jack Martin Smith, Hans Peters
● Carol Lynley, Jeff Chandler, Eleanor Parker, Mary Astor, Tuesday Weld, Robert Sterling (20th Century-Fox)

Basically *Return to Peyton Place* is a high-class soap opera. The screenplay preserves the nature of Grace Metalious' novel, alternately building three or four separate but related story veins into individual crescendos, then welding the moving parts into a single grand climax in which everything falls neatly into place.

The basic stories are: (1) Carol Lynley's, as they tyro novelist whose close-to-home fiction

produces civic repercussions and whose romantic relations with her editor-publisher (Jeff Chandler) accelerate her maturity; (2) Tuesday Weld's, as the emotionally-troubled girl whose past misfortunes are soothed when Lynley's book sheds new light into the matter; and (3) Mary Astor's, as a super-possessive Peyton Place mother who attempts to wreck the marriage of her son.

Jose Ferrer's direction of this material is deliberate, but restrained and perceptive. The cast is a blend of polished veterans and young players. The lovely Lynley does a thoroughly capable job, although a shade more animation would have been desirable. But it is the veteran Astor who walks off with the picture.

■ REUBEN, REUBEN

1983, 101 MINS, US ◇ ⓥ

Dir Robert Ellis Miller *Prod* Walter Shenson, Julius J. Epstein *Scr* Julius J. Epstein *Ph* Peter Stein *Ed* Skip Lusk *Mus* Billy Goldenberg *Art Dir* Peter Larkin
● Tom Conti, Kelly McGillis, Roberts Blossom, Cynthia Harris, E. Katherine Kerr, Joel Fabiani (20th Century-Fox/Taft Entertainment)

About a leching, alcoholic Scottish poet making the New England campus circuit, *Reuben, Reuben* is exceptionally literate, with lines that carom with wit from the superb adaptation by Julius J. Epstein of a 1964 Peter De Vries novel. Epstein, with De Vries' blessing, merged three separate stories in the novel into the character of the rascal poet on the slide.

Helmsman Robert Ellis Miller draws solid performances from debuting actress Kelly McGillis, whose chic blonde Vassar looks interestingly contrast, in this case, with her character's farmyard roots. She becomes the all-consuming obsession of Tom Conti as he lurches from one bottle and bed to another. Two of his sexual conquests on the poet's college town circuit are nicely and avariciously played by Cynthia Harris and E. Katherine Kerr.

But the film is a tour-de-force act for Conti (in his first US-made film) and he captures the vulnerability of a man whose plunge into darkness suggests the emotional time most closely associated with 4 a.m.

■ REUNION

1989, 110 MINS, FRANCE/W. GER/UK ◇ ⓥ

Dir Jerry Schatzberg *Prod* Anne Francois *Scr* Harold Pinter *Ph* Bruno de Keyzer *Ed* Martine Barraque *Mus* Philippe Sarde *Art Dir* Alexandre Trauner
● Jason Robards, Christian Anholt, Samuel West, Francois Fabian, Maureen Kewin, Barbara Jefford (Ariane/FR3/NEF/Vertriebs/CLG/Tac/Arbo/Maran)

This enormously impressive film ranks as one of the best of countless pics dealing with the rise of Nazism in Germany in the early 1930s.

Based on Fred Uhlman's autobiographical novel, drama is set in Stuttgart in 1933 and deals with the growing friendship between two schoolboys from different backgrounds: Hans (Christian Anholt), son of a Jewish doctor and World War I vet who, till now, was considered a pillar of the community; and the aristocratic Konrad (Samuel West), who's led a sheltered life, taught by private tutors, and who finds himself stimulated by the intelligent, sensitive Hans.

At the beginning of the year, portents of what's to come are few: small groups of Nazis march in the streets; a friend advises Hans' father to leave before Hitler takes over. Gradually, as the year progresses, the Fascist movement takes hold.

The long central part of the film is framed by a present-day narrative in which Hans, now Henry Strauss (Jason Robards), decides to return to Stuttgart to locate his parents'

grave and to discover what happened to his old friend.

Director Jerry Schatzberg has made what probably is his best film to date, a sober, thoughtful pic that recreates a seemingly authentic world of 56 years ago.

■ REVENGE

1990, 124 MINS, US ◇ ⓥ

Dir Tony Scott *Prod* Hunt Lowry, Stanley Rubin *Scr* Jim Harrison, Jeffrey Fiskin *Ph* Jeffrey Kimball *Ed* Chris Lebenzon *Mus* Jack Nitzsche *Art Dir* Michael Seymour, Benjamin Fernandez
● Kevin Costner, Anthony Quinn, Madeleine Stowe, Sally Kirkland, James Gammon, Miguel Ferrer (Rastar)

This far-from-perfect rendering of Jim Harrison's shimmering novella has a romantic sweep and elemental power that ultimately transcend its flaws. It's a contempo tale of a doomed love triangle in lawless Mexico.

As J. Cochran, a hotshot Navy pilot who retires after 12 years, Kevin Costner heads down to Puerto Vallarta for recreation at the home of a wealthy sportsman friend, Tibey (Anthony Quinn) and is right away smitten with his host's gorgeous and unhappy wife Miryea (Madeleine Stowe). Despite his friend's graciousness and reputation as a cold-blooded killer, Cochran takes the suicide plunge into passion, running off with Miryea for a sexual idyll.

The much-fiddled-with footage was eventually pasted into its current form, and though much is lost, the tale's simplicity, grace and subtlety shine through. All three elements of the love triangle are compelling, and as a crucial fourth character Mexico performs radiantly.

Stowe is a great screen beauty she is certainly a match for Costner's charisma. The magnificent Quinn as a political puppeteer is so rich and sympathetic that he threatens to steal away the audience despite his brutality.

■ REVENGE OF FRANKENSTEIN, THE

1958, 89 MINS, UK ◇ ⓥ

Dir Terence Fisher *Prod* Anthony Hinds *Scr* Jimmy Sangster, H. Hurford Janes *Ph* Jack Asher *Ed* Alfred Cox, James Needs *Mus* Leonard Salzedo *Art Dir* Bernard Robinson
● Peter Cushing, Francis Matthews, Eunice Gayson, Michael Gwynn, John Welsh, Lionel Jeffries (Hammer)

Made by the same team as *The Curse of Frankenstein*, this is a high grade horror film.

Peter Cushing, as the famed medical experimenter, is still determined to make a monster, although that is not how he would put it. Despite official pressure, Frankenstein is again collecting bits of bone and tissue, muscle and blood, to put together a man of his creation. Again he succeeds, but again something goes wrong and his creature – through brain damage – becomes a cannibal, slavering blood and saliva.

The production is a rich one. The screenplay is well-plotted, peopled with interesting characters, aided by good performances from Francis Matthews as Cushing's chief assistant and others.

■ REVENGE OF THE NINJA

1983, 88 MINS, US ◇ ⓥ

Dir Sam Firstenberg *Prod* Menahem Golan, Yoram Globus *Scr* James R. Silke *Ph* David Gurfinkel *Ed* Michael J. Duthie, Mark Helfrich *Mus* Rob Walsh, W. Michael Lewis, Laurin Rinder *Art Dir* Paul Staheli
● Sho Kosugi, Keith Vitali, Virgil Frye, Arthur Roberts, Mario Gallo, Grace Oshita (Cannon)

Revenge of the Ninja is an entertaining martial arts actioner, following up *Enter the Ninja* (1981) but lacking that film's name players and Far East locale.

R

After a brief intro set in Japan, where Cho Osaki (Sho Kosugi) witnesses most of his family wiped out by black-clad ninjas, action shifts to an unidentified US locale (filmed in Salt Lake City) six years later. Osaki, with his surviving child and its grandma, runs a gallery featuring imported Japanese dolls, which unbeknownst to him is a front for heroin smuggling run by his pal Braden (Arthur Roberts). Braden is involved with an unscrupulous US mobster Caifano (Mario Gallo).

Revenge occurs when Braden kills grannie, kidnaps the child Kane (Kane Kosugi) and later kills Osaki's best friend, martial arts expert Dave Hatcher (Keith Vitali). Fine fight choreography by Kosugi, including fast and often funny moves by him, keeps the film cooking.

．．．．．．．．．．．．．．．．．．．．．．．．．．．．．．．．

■ REVENGE OF THE PINK PANTHER

1978, 98 MINS, US ◇ ⓥ

Dir Blake Edwards *Prod* Blake Edwards *Scr* Frank Waldman, Ron Clark, Blake Edwards *Ph* Ernie Day *Ed* Alan Jones *Mus* Henry Mancini *Art Dir* Peter Mullins
● Peter Sellers, Herbert Lom, Dyan Cannon, Robert Webber, Burt Kwouk, Paul Mullins (United Artists)

Revenge of the Pink Panther isn't the best of the continuing film series, but Blake Edwards and Peter Sellers on a slow day are still well ahead of most other comedic filmmakers.

This time out, Sellers tracks down an international drug ring. Herbert Lom also encores as Sellers' nemesis and Dyan Cannon is delightful as the resourceful discarded mistress of dope smuggler industrialist Robert Webber.

The screenplay, from an Edwards story, is a paradoxical embarrassment of riches: Sellers, faithful servant Burt Kwouk, Lom, Cannon, etc, each alone and also in various combinations, are too much for a simple story line. The result is that the plot roams all over the map, trying to cover all the bases but in totality adding up to less than the parts.

．．．．．．．．．．．．．．．．．．．．．．．．．．．．．．．．

■ REVERSAL OF FORTUNE

1990, 120 MINS, US ◇ ⓥ

Dir Barbet Schroeder *Prod* Edward R. Pressman, Oliver Stone, Elon Dershowitz, Nicholas Kazan *Scr* Nicholas Kazan *Ph* Luciano Tovoli *Ed* Lee Percy *Mus* Mark Isham *Art Dir* Mel Bourne
● Jeremy Irons, Glenn Close, Ron Silver, Anabella Sciorra, Uta Hagen, Fisher Stevens (Warner/Shochiku Fuji/Sovereign)

Reversal of Fortune turns the sensational Claus von Bulow case into a riveting film. The story [from the book by Alan Dershowitz] of the Newport society figure's trial, conviction and acquittal on appeal for the attempted murder of his wealthy wife is presented here in an absorbing, complex mosaic.

Jeremy Irons gives a memorable performance as the inscrutable European blueblood emigre. Cast in perfect apposition is Ron Silver, seizing with dynamic gusto the role of a career in which as von Bulow's passionately idealistic but streetwise defense attorney, Harvard law professor Dershowitz.

Glenn Close is typically excellent in the smaller but pivotal role of Sunny von Bulow, who narrates the story and appears in flashbacks.

On one level, *Reversal of Fortune* deals with the impossibility of knowing the truth about the unknowable. Was von Bulow guilty of injecting his wife with a near-fatal dose of insulin? Was he framed by Sunny's maid (Uta Hagen) or family? Or did the profoundly unhappy woman attempt suicide?

On other levels, it is a finely detailed manners study of the superwealthy, a drama of conflicting principles and values and an engrossing legal detective story.

．．．．．．．．．．．．．．．．．．．．．．．．．．．．．．．．

■ REVOLUTION

1986, 125 MINS, UK/NORWAY ◇ ⓥ

Dir Hugh Hudson *Prod* Irwin Winkler *Scr* Robert Dillon *Ph* Bernard Lutic *Ed* Stuart Baird *Mus* John Corigliano *Art Dir* Assheton Gorton
● Al Pacino, Donald Sutherland, Nastassja Kinski, Joan Plowright, Steven Berkoff, Annie Lennox (Goldcrest/Viking)

Watching *Revolution* is a little like visiting a museum – it looks good without really being alive. The film doesn't tell a story so much as it uses characters to illustrate what the American Revolution has come to mean. Despite attempting to reduce big events to personal details, *Revolution* rarely works on a human scale.

While intimate story of Tom Dobb (Al Pacino) and his son Ned (Dexter Fletcher, Sid Owen as young Ned) and Tom's love for renegade aristocrat Daisy McConnahay (Nastassja Kinski) is full of holes, the larger canvas is staged beautifully.

Unfortunately, against this well-drawn background the small story that is meant to serve as a way into the drama for viewers looks too much like an historical reenactment.

Performances fail to elevate the material with only Pacino, Fletcher and Owen giving their characters a personal touch. Donald Sutherland is wasted and distant as an English officer, partially because it is nearly impossible to understand what he's saying through his thick brogue.

．．．．．．．．．．．．．．．．．．．．．．．．．．．．．．．．

■ REWARD, THE

1965, 91 MINS, US ◇

Dir Serge Bourguignon *Prod* Aaron Rosenberg *Scr* Serge Bourguignon, Oscar Millard *Ph* Joe MacDonald *Ed* Robert Simpson *Mus* Elmer Bernstein *Art Dir* Jack Martin Smith, Robert Boyle
● Max von Sydow, Yvette Mimieux, Efrem Zimbalist Jr, Gilbert Roland, Emilio Fernandez, Nino Castelnuovo (Arcola/20th Century-Fox)

The Reward for a fugitive and its effects on a group thrown together by fate comprise the theme of this moody, somewhat uneven, desert meller. Some good acting and excellent production values bolster a plot that fizzes out in final reel.

Director Serge Bourguignon and Oscar Millard adapted Michael Barrett's tome which crash lands crop-duster Max von Sydow in a boondocks Mexican town coincident with the passing through of Efrem Zimbalist Jr, latter on the lam from a murder rap and accompanied by Yvette Mimieux. Sydow cues police inspector Gilbert Roland to the price on Zimbalist's head, and the slow chase is on, leading to uneventful and unresisted capture.

About 40 per cent of the film has elapsed before plot begins to move when brutal, sadistic police sergeant Emilio Fernandez finds out there's a reward and starts to dominate the group.

Sydow gives a lethargic performance despite a role that is basically passive. He talks little, then in gutteral tones, but mostly reacts sluggishly to events.

．．．．．．．．．．．．．．．．．．．．．．．．．．．．．．．．

■ RHAPSODY IN BLUE

1945, 130 MINS, US

Dir Irving Rapper *Prod* Jesse L. Lasky *Scr* Howard Koch, Elliot Paul *Ph* Sol Polito, Merritt Gerstad *Ed* Folmer Blangsted *Mus* Leo F. Forbstein (dir.) *Art Dir* Anton Grot, John B. Hughes
● Robert Alda, Joan Leslie, Alexis Smith, Charles Coburn, Oscar Levant, Albert Basserman (Warner)

Those who knew George Gershwin and the Gershwin saga may wax slightly vociferous at this or that miscue, but as cinematurgy, designed for escapism and entertainment, no matter the season, *Rhapsody in Blue* can't miss.

The years have certainly lent enhancement to his music, and the glib interplay of names such as Otto Kahn, Jascha Heifetz, Maurice Ravel, Walter Damrosch and Rachmaninov (all of whom are impersonated) lend conviction to the basic yarn [from a story by Sonya Levien] of the New York East Side boy whose musical genius was to sweep the world.

Robert Alda plays Gershwin and makes him believable. Herbert Rudley as Ira Gershwin is perhaps more believable to the initiate, looking startlingly like the famed lyricist brother of the composer, but young Alda, a newcomer, makes his role tick as the burningly ambitious composer who is constantly driving himself.

Oscar Levant as Oscar Levant can't miss, and he doesn't here. He has the meatiest, brilliant lines and whams over the titular *Rhapsody in Blue* and Concerto in F with virtuosity and authority as befits a real-life confidante of the late composer.

．．．．．．．．．．．．．．．．．．．．．．．．．．．．．．．．

■ RHINESTONE

1984, 111 MINS, US ◇ ⓥ

Dir Bob Clarke *Prod* Howard Smith, Marvin Worth *Scr* Phil Alden Robinson, Sylvester Stallone *Ph* Timothy Galfas *Ed* Stan Cole, John Wheeler *Mus* Dolly Parton *Art Dir* Robert Boyle
● Sylvester Stallone, Dolly Parton, Richard Farnsworth, Ron Leibman, Tim Thomerson, Steven Apostle Pec (20th Century-Fox)

Effortlessly living up to its title, *Rhinestone* is as artificial and synthetic a concoction as has ever made its way to the screen.

Directed in low-down, good-spirited vulgar fashion by Bob Clark, film is a genuine oddball. Sylvester Stallone's character, that of a Gotham cabbie whom singer Dolly Parton bets she can turn into a convincing country crooner in two weeks' time, is like no one ever encountered on earth before.

Uncouth loudmouth, has no discernible talents whatsoever, so it's an uphill battle when Parton takes him down home to Tennessee to try to pump some real country feeling into his bulging veins.

Neither Stallone nor Parton stray at all from their past personae.

．．．．．．．．．．．．．．．．．．．．．．．．．．．．．．．．

■ RICH AND FAMOUS

1981, 117 MINS, US ◇

Dir George Cukor *Prod* William Allyn *Scr* Gerald Ayres *Ph* Don Peterman *Ed* John F. Burnett *Mus* Georges Delerve *Art Dir* Jan Scott
● Jacqueline Bisset, Candice Bergen, Meg Ryan, David Selby, Hart Bochner (M-G-M)

While not without its problems, *Rich and Famous* is an absorbing drama of some notable qualities, the greatest of which is a gutsy, fascinating and largely magnificent performance by Jacqueline Bisset. Tale delineating the friendship of two smart, creative ladies over a period of two decades makes for 'women's picture' in the best sense of the term.

Plot dynamics of Gerald Ayres' imaginative, very modern updating of John Van Druten's 1940 play *Old Acquaintance* rather closely follow those of Warner Brothers' solid 1943 film version, which starred Bette Davis and Miriam Hopkins. Bisset and Bergen essay college chums whose lives intersect at crucial points over the years.

A recurrent spot in which the pic seems to miss its potential is the occasional confrontation scene in which the ladies have at it in shouting cat fights. These abusive sessions invariably deal with the essence of their relationship, but they have been directed at such a fast pace that the emotional depth-charges fizzle out on the surface.

For a bright, sophisticated piece such as this, particularly one under the guidance of the irrepressibly elegant Goerge Cukor, the somewhat harsh, murky visual style is suprising. Cukor took over the production on short notice when original director Robert Mulligan was replaced after four days' lensing (none of the latter's footage remains).

....

■ RICHARD PRYOR ... HERE AND NOW

1983, 94 MINS, US ◇ ⓥ

Dir Richard Pryor *Prod* Bob Parkinson, Andy Friendly *Scr* Richard Pryor *Ph* Vincent Singletary, Kenneth A. Patterson, Joe Epperson, Tom Geren, Johnny Simmon, Dave Landry *Ed* Raymond Bush
● Richard Pryor (Columbia)

As a concert film, *Richard Pryor ... Here and Now* should attract and please those who appreciate him as a standup comic. But beyond the ample laughs, there is a beautiful monolog that's so painfully acute it would entrance even those who never laugh at his other stuff.

His third concert film, *Here and Now* is a mixture of the ones done before and after the fire that almost killed him. Drug-free and still grateful for a second chance, Pryor remains much more mellow, but less self-examining and contemplative than in *Live on Sunset Strip* (1982).

Some of the hostility and bite have returned, though well under control. On top of the laughs, he also displays a deepening sympathy for those doomed by substances.

....

■ RICHARD PRYOR LIVE ON THE SUNSET STRIP

1982, 82 MINS, US ◇ ⓥ

Dir Joe Layton *Prod* Richard Pryor *Scr* Richard Pryor *Ph* Haskell Wexler *Ed* Sheldon Kahn *Mus* Harry R. Betts *Art Dir* Michael Baugh
● Richard Pryor (Columbia/Rastar)

This is not a film in any respect, except to note the medium Richard Pryor's stand-up routine was captured on in two nights at the Palladium in 1981. Director Joe Layton and cameraman Haskell Wexler make no noticeable contributions and often fail to solve the problems of concert lensing.

But Pryor is truly amazing and that's all that counts. After a number of roles in successful pictures, he brings an acting ability to his stage routine that enhances his well-established talent for caricature. What this allows him to do is pull the audience into moments of genuine emotion, then clobber them suddenly with a hilarious switch.

By far the best comes with a candid discussion of his drug addiction that culminates in the freebase explosion that almost killed him.

....

■ RICHARD III

1955, 160 MINS, UK ◇ ⓥ

Dir Laurence Olivier, Anthony Bushell *Prod* Laurence Olivier *Scr* Laurence Olivier *Ph* Otto Heller *Ed* Helga Cranston *Mus* William Walton *Art Dir* Roger Furse, Carmen Dillon
● Laurence Olivier, John Gielgud, Claire Bloom, Ralph Richardson, Alec Clunes, Stanley Baker (London)

The Bard pulled no punches in his dramatization of *Richard III*, and Laurence Olivier's filmization likewise portrays him as a ruthless and unscrupulous character, who stops at nothing to obtain the throne. The murder of his brother Clarence (John Gielgud), the betrayal of his cousin, Buckingham (Ralph Richardson), the suffocation of the princes in

the Tower are among the unscrupulous steps in the path of Richard's crowning, which are staged with lurid, melodramatic conviction.

At all times Shakespeare's poetry, impeccably spoken by this outstanding cast, heightens the dramatic atmosphere. The production, and notably Roger Furse's decor, is consistently spectacular. The climactic battle sequences rival the pageantry of *Henry V*.

Running Olivier's performance a very close second is Richardson's scheming Buckingham. Another distinguished performance is contributed by Gielgud as Clarence.

....

■ RIDE IN THE WHIRLWIND

1966, 82 MINS, US ◇ ⓥ

Dir Monte Hellman *Prod* Monte Hellman, Jack Nicholson *Scr* Jack Nicholson *Ph* Gregory Sandor *Mus* Robert Drasnin
● Cameron Mitchell, Jack Nicholson, Tom Filer, Millie Perkins, Katherine Squire, George Mitchell (Hellman-Nicholson)

Monte Hellman's *Ride in the Whirlwind* is a flat, woodenly acted western with mild suspense that never grabs. Part of the fault is with Jack Nicholson's script, which is little more than a promising plot line rather than a fully developed scenario. Nicholson also plays the lead, but since Nicholson the writer has little to say, Nicholson the actor has even less.

Hellman never exploits the full potential of the situations. A trio of uncommunicative saddle tramps – Nicholson, Cameron Mitchell, Tom Filer – stumble on a motley gang holed up in a mountain shack after a stage coach robbery. For reasons never adequately explained, the one-eyed gang leader is downright cordial to the cow pokes.

They spend the night, and in the morning find themselves surrounded by a posse of vigilantes that is going to string them up first and ask questions later.

In the getaway Filer is shot down and Mitchell and Nicholson have to climb up a sheer canyon.

Not one of the characters emerges from the flatness of the screen, and to a man they move and talk like animated cigar store Indians.

....

■ RIDE LONESOME

1959, 74 MINS, US ◇

Dir Budd Boetticher *Prod* Budd Boetticher *Scr* Burt Kennedy *Ph* Charles Lawton Jr *Ed* Jerome Thoms *Mus* Heinz Roemheld
● Randolph Scott, Karen Steele, Parnell Roberts, James Best, Lee Van Cleef, James Coburn (Ranown)

Ride Lonesome has Randolph Scott as a bounty hunter whose interest in a young murderer (James Best) seems to be solely the money he will collect for his delivery. Along the way, he picks up a young widow (Karen Steele), and two feckless outlaws (Parnell Roberts and James Coburn). Soon Best's brother, (Lee Van Cleef) is trailing them with his own band, intent on rescuing Best.

Ride Lonesome has several good plots and sub-plots going for it, creating a chase melodrama that is often a chase-within-a-chase. Scriptwriter Burt Kennedy has used genuine speech of the frontier and some offhand, often rather grim humor, to give the screenplay additional interest where the pursuit portions necessarily lag. Boetticher and his cast handle it well, only occasionally overreaching in brief scenes where Steele's sex seems stressed beyond reason.

Scott does a good job as the taciturn and misunderstood hero, but the two standouts are Best as the giggling killer and Roberts as the sardonic outlaw who wants to get away to a new start.

....

■ RIDE THE HIGH COUNTRY

1962, 94 MINS, US ◇ ⓥ

Dir Sam Peckinpah *Prod* Richard E. Lyons *Scr* N.B. Stone Jr *Ph* Lucien Ballard *Ed* Frank Santillo *Mus* George Bassman *Art Dir* George W. Davis, Leroy Coleman
● Randolph Scott, Joel McCrea, Mariette Hartley, Edgar Buchanan, Ron Starr, Warren Oates (M-G-M)

The old saying 'you can't make a silk purse out of a sow's ear' rings true for Metro-Goldwyn-Mayer's artistic western *Ride the High Country*. It remains a standard story, albeit with an interesting gimmick and some excellent production values.

Scott and McCrea play their ages in roles that could well be extensions of characters they have each played in countless earlier films. They are quick-triggered ex-lawmen, former famed 'town-tamers' whom life has passed by and who are now reduced to taking jobs as guards for a gold shipment. They engage in one last battle – over a woman and involving a youth who epitomizes their own youth.

It is Sam Peckinpah's direction, however, that gives the film greatest artistry. He gives N. B. Stone Jr.'s script a measure beyond its adequacy, instilling bright moments of sharp humor and an overall significant empathetic flavor.

....

■ RIDE, VAQUERO

1953, 91 MINS, US ◇

Dir John Farrow *Prod* Stephen Ames *Scr* Frank Fenton *Ph* Robert Surtees *Ed* Harold F. Kress *Mus* Bronislau Kaper *Art Dir* Cedric Gibbons, Arthur Lonergan
● Robert Taylor, Ava Gardner, Howard Keel, Anthony Quinn, Kurt Kasznar, Jack Elam (M-G-M)

Locale of the production is southwest Texas, a territory around Brownsville, that is under the thumb of a group of outlaw gangs controlled by Anthony Quinn and his lieutenant (Robert Taylor). When Howard Keel tries to found a cattle empire and brings in settlers, the outlaws fight back, knowing they will be through if civilization comes to the land.

John Farrow's direction stirs up plenty of violent action as he plays off the story. While the script is a bit vague in development of some of the personalities, overall effect is okay for the outdoor fan, although more critical audiences would have liked less obscurity. Keel brings Ava Gardner, his bride, to his new homestead, only to find it a smoking ruin as the result of a Quinn-directed raid. Keel builds again, stronger this time, after he fails to unite the townspeople and the sheriff against the outlaw. When the new home is ready, Quinn's forces attack.

Taylor is very good in selling the quiet menace of his character, and Quinn stands out as the flamboyant outlaw leader. Gardner provides physical beauty to a character that is not as well stated as it could have been. Keel does well by his determined, foolhardy character.

....

■ RIFF-RAFF

1991, 92 MINS, UK ◇ ⓥ

Dir Ken Loach *Prod* Sally Hibbin *Scr* Bill Jesse *Ph* Barry Ackroyd *Ed* Jonathan Morris *Mus* Stewart Copeland *Art Dir* Martin Johnson
● Robert Carlyle, Emer McCourt, Jimmy Coleman, Ricky Tomlinson, Willie Ross, Derek Young (Parallax/Film Four)

Riff-Raff, a sprightly ensemble comedy about workers on a London building site, will surprise those who think Brit helmer Ken Loach can crank out only political items. Semi-improvised pic is strong on yocks and easy to digest.

Central character is Stevie (Robert Carlyle), a young Glaswegian just out of stir,

R

who's come south and got a job converting a closed-down hospital into luxury apartments. His co-workers are from all over – Liverpudlians, Geordies (natives of Newcastle), West Indians. They're breaking every regulation in the book and running scams on the side. Home is a squat in a dingy council block.

After Stevie meets Susan (Emer McCourt), a drifter from Belfast who's trying to make it as a singer, they move in together and make a go of it in the big city. Story yo-yos between their fragile relationship and the shenanigans on the building site.

Fruity script by onetime laborer Bill Jesse (who died in 1990 just before the pic was completed) catches the wisecracking flavor of navvy repartee. Comedic tone also spills over into the love story. Thesping by no-name cast is strong and clearly benefits from Loach's insistence that all actors have building-site experience.

■ RIGHT STUFF, THE

1983, 192 MINS, US ◇ ⓥ

Dir Philip Kaufman   *Prod* Robert Chartoff, Irwin Winkler   *Scr* Philip Kaufman   *Ph* Caleb Deschanel   *Ed* Glenn Farr, Lisa Fruchtman, Stephen A. Rotter, Tom Rolf, Douglas Stewart   *Mus* Bill Conti   *Art Dir* Geoffrey Kirkland
● Sam Shepard, Scott Glenn, Ed Harris, Dennis Quaid, Fred Ward, Barbara Hershey (Ladd Company)

The Right Stuff is a humdinger. Full of beauty, intelligence and excitement, this big-scale look at the development of the US space program and its pioneering aviators provides a fresh, entertaining look back at the recent past. Film version of Tom Wolfe's best selling revisionist history was some three years in the making.

Tale spans 16 years, from ace test pilot Chuck Yeager's breaking of the sound barrier over the California desert to Vice-President Johnson's welcoming of the astronauts to their new home in Houston with an enormous barbecue inside the Astrodome. Telling takes over three hours, but it goes by lickity-split under Philip Kaufman's direction and is probably the shortest-seeming film of its length ever made.

Emblematic figure here is Yeager, played by a taciturn Sam Shepard. As the ace of aces who was passed by for astronaut training due to his lack of college degree, Yeager, for Kaufman as for Wolfe, is the embodiment of 'the right stuff', that ineffable quality which separates the men from the boys, so to speak.
□ 1983: Best Picture (Nomination)

■ RING, THE

1952, 79 MINS, US

Dir Kurt Neumann   *Scr* Irving Shulman   *Ph* Russell Harlan   *Ed* Bruce B. Pierce   *Mus* Herschel Burke Gilbert
● Gerald Mohr, Rita Moreno, Lalo Rios, Robert Arthur, Robert Osterloh, Jack Elam (King Bros/United Artists)

Efforts of a young boxer to fight his way up from preliminaries to main bout stature provides a sock setting for a well-spun yarn [from a novel by Irving Shulman] of discrimination on the Coast against the Mexican-Americans.

Accent is on realism. Pic pinpoints the discriminatory line without relying on any hysterical sequences. The message hits home with such effectively underplayed scenes as tourists gazing at 'those lazy Mexicans', brushoff of a group of Mexican-American boys by a waitress in a Beverly Hills eatery and the turndown of a young couple at a skating rink gate because it wasn't 'Mexican Night'. The prizefighting scenes, too, are executed graphically.

Cast is headed by Gerald Mohr, the manager; Lalo Rios, the boxer, and Rita Moreno.

■ RING OF BRIGHT WATER

1969, 107 MINS, UK ◇ ⓥ

Dir Jack Couffer   *Prod* Joseph Strick   *Scr* Jack Couffer, Bill Travers   *Ph* Wolfgang Suschitzky   *Ed* Reginald Mills   *Mus* Frank Cordell   *Art Dir* Ken Ryan
● Bill Travers, Virginia McKenna, Roddy McMillan, Jameson Clark, Jean Taylor-Smith (Palomar)

Bill Travers and Virginia McKenna followed up their success in *Born Free* with an engaging film about an otter. It is a semi-documentary, based on Gavin Maxwell's autobiographical bestseller, *Ring of Bright Water*.

Story concerns a London civil servant, anxious to get out of the rat race to write. He makes his decision when he acquires Mij, a young otter, as a pet and finds that keeping the charming but mischievous mammal in a London apartment is frought with headaches. So he and Mij depart for a lonely coastal village in the Highlands where they settle down contentedly in a ramshackle crofter's cottage.

Travers and McKenna unselfishly subdue their performances to the star demands of the lolloping young rascal, Mij, but keep the interest firmly alive by their tactful playing.

■ RIO BRAVO

1959, 140 MINS, US ◇ ⓥ

Dir Howard Hawks   *Prod* Howard Hawks   *Scr* Jules Furthman, Leigh Brackett   *Ph* Russell Harlan   *Ed* Folmar Blangsted   *Mus* Dimitri Tiomkin   *Art Dir* Leo K. Kuter
● John Wayne, Dean Martin, Ricky Nelson, Angie Dickinson, Walter Brennan, Ward Bond (Armada)

Rio Bravo is a big, brawling western. Script based on the B. H. McCampbell short story, gets off to one of the fastest slam-bang openings on record. Within 90 seconds Wayne, a fast-shooting sheriff, is clubbed, another man knocked out and a third man murdered.

Plot thereafter revolves around Wayne's attempts to hold the murderer, brother of the most powerful rancher in the area, until the arrival some days hence of the US marshal. He's up against the rancher utilizing gunman tactics to free the jailed killer.

Producer-director Howard Hawks makes handsome use of force in logically unravelling his hard-hitting narrative, creating suspense at times and occasionally inserting lighter moments to give variety. Wayne delivers a faithful portrayal of the peace officer who must fight his battle with the aid of only two deputies. One of these is Dean Martin, his ex-deputy who attempts to kick off a two-year drunk to help his friend. The other deputy is Walter Brennan, a cantankerous old cripple assigned to guard the prisoner in the jail.

In for distaff interest and with more legitimate footage than usual in a western is Angie Dickinson, a looker fashioned into an important key character who delivers in every way.

■ RIO CONCHOS

1964, 105 MINS, US ◇ ⓥ

Dir Gordon M. Douglas   *Prod* David Weisbart   *Scr* Joseph Landon, Clair Huffaker   *Ph* Joe MacDonald   *Ed* Joseph Silver   *Mus* Jerry Goldsmith   *Art Dir* Jack Martin Smith, William Geber
● Richard Boone, Stuart Whitman, Tony Franciosa, Wende Wagner, Warner Anderson, Edmond O'Brien (20th Century-Fox)

Rio Conchos is a big, tough, action-packed slam-bang western with as tough a set of characters as ever rode the sage. It is Old West adventure at its best.

Producer David Weisbart has woven fanciful movement along with lush settings via on-the-spot color lensing in Arizona. To this, Gordon Douglas has added his own version of what a lusty western should be in the direction, getting the most from a batch of colorful characters. Music score by Jerry Goldsmith is a particularly valuable asset in striking a fast mood from the opening scene.

Script by Joseph Landon and Clair Huffaker, adapted from latter's novel, limns the quest of four men for 2,000 stolen repeating rifles that a group of former Confederate soldiers have been running to the Apaches. Quartet is composed of Stuart Whitman, a cavalry captain, who heads the party; Richard Boone, an ex-reb who hates Apaches; Tony Franciosa, a Mexican gigolo-type killer whom the army was about to hang; and Jim Brown, a cavalry corporal. Their destination is the camp of a demented Confederate gun-runner (Edmond O'Brien) who wants vengeance on the North for the South's defeat.

Whitman acquits himself excellently in his tough role but interest principally lies in characters played by Boone and Franciosa, both killers and a director's dream. Brown, too, handles himself well, and Vito Scotti, as a laughing bandit, registers particularly in his brief menacing role before being killed.

■ RIO GRANDE

1950, 105 MINS, US ⓥ

Dir John Ford   *Prod* John Ford, Merian C. Cooper   *Scr* James Kevin McGuinness   *Ph* Bert Glennon   *Ed* Jack Murray   *Mus* Victor Young
● John Wayne, Maureen O'Hara, Ben Johnson, Claude Jarmon Jr, Harry Carey Jr, Victor McLaglen (Republic/Argosy)

Rio Grande is filmed outdoor action [based on a *SatEvePost* story by James Warner Bellah] at its best, delivered in the John Ford manner.

John Wayne's devotion to military oath had led him, some 15 years back, to destroy the plantation home of his southern-born wife during the war between the states. He is now a lonely man, fighting Indians in the west. To his fort comes his young son, Claude Jarman Jr whom he has not seen in 15 years.

Into this setup of rugged living, endangered daily by marauding Indians, comes Maureen O'Hara, Wayne's estranged wife, determined to take the son back.

Comedy touches are introduced by Victor McLaglen as the top sergeant, a role he has performed in other Ford pictures.

■ RIO LOBO

1970, 114 MINS, US ◇ ⓥ

Dir Howard Hawks   *Prod* Howard Hawks   *Scr* Leigh Brackett, Burton Wohl   *Ph* William Clothier   *Ed* John Woodcock   *Mus* Jerry Goldsmith   *Art Dir* Robert Smith
● John Wayne, Jorge Rivero, Jennifer O'Neill, Jack Elam, Chris Mitchum, Victor French (Malabar/Cinema Center)

Rio Lobo is the sort of western that John Wayne and producer-director Howard Hawks do in their sleep. But by no stretch of nostalgia does it match such previous Wayne-Hawks epics as *Red River* or *Rio Bravo*.

Leigh Brackett and Burton Wohl's script, based on Wohl's story, is by the numbers. In the Civil War, Wayne is a Union colonel – an ex-Texas Ranger, of course – who keeps losing army gold shipments to Confederate guerrillas led by Jorge Rivero and Chris Mitchum. He captures them, but they won't tell him who the traitors are who have been tipping them off about the gold.

From than on it is the same plot that has been worked over since the silent days of Bronco Billy with no new surprises.

Hawks' direction is as listless as the plot.

RIO RITA

1942, 91 MINS, US

Dir S. Sylvan Simon   *Prod* Pandro S. Berman
Scr Richard Connell, Gladys Lehman   *Ph* George
Folsey   *Ed* Ben Lewis   *Mus* Herbert Stothart (dir)
● Bud Abbott, Lou Costello, Kathryn Grayson, John
Carroll, Patricia Dane, Tom Conway (M-G-M)

Like all Abbott and Costello entries. Without
them it would be so much celluloid. So far as
the oft-filmed version of the former Ziegfeld
stage musical is concerned, Metro uses but
the original title song and the 'Rangers'
number.

Script relies principally on a Nazi espionage story. The plot has to do with mysterious
radiocasts to a foreign power; the manager
(Tom Conway) of the heroine's (Kathryn
Grayson) hotel is really a Nazi spy; his girl
friend Patricia Dane is (or isn't) a G-woman
in disguise (the plot's confusing on this
point), and Abbott and Costello, along with
hero John Carroll, save the day in the nick.
It's that kind of a plot.

Director S. Sylvan Simon has spaced the
A&C nonsensities with a good sense of timing
to properly break up the hoke. There are a
couple of reprises on some of the business,
but withal the 91 minutes pace well.

RIOT

1968, 96 MINS, US ◇

Dir Buzz Kulik   *Prod* William Castle   *Scr* James Poe
Ph Robert B. Hauser   *Ed* Edwin H. Bryant
Mus Christopher Komeda   *Art Dir* Paul Sylbert
● Jim Brown, Gene Hackman, Mike Kellin, Gerald S.
O'Loughlin, Ben Carruthers (Paramount)

Riot is a good prison programmer produced
with authenticity inside Arizona State Prison.
Jim Brown and Gene Hackman are leaders of
a convict revolt which paralyzes prison routine and unleashes some violent passions.
Buzz Kulik's direction is better in the forward plot thrusts than in the many repetitious stretches, not at all alleviated by a
pedestrian ballad reprised much too often.

Ex-convict Frank Elli's book, *The Riot*, has
been adapted into a wandering script which
lacks a definite cohesion. Concept vacillates
between apparent attempt to tell a straightforward escape story, and temptation to
linger and exploit violence. No social document, this; but not a potboiler, either.

Hackman, Mike Kellin and a freaked-out
psychotic con, played by Ben Carruthers,
launch a minor riot as prelude to escape.

Brown's immensely strong screen presence
is manifest. Hackman gives the best performance as an equivocating, cynical manipulator
of crowd psychology. Carruthers is too
unrestrained.

RIOT IN CELL BLOCK 11

1954, 80 MINS, US Ⓥ

Dir Don Siegel   *Prod* Walter Wanger   *Scr* Richard
Collins   *Ph* Russell Harlan   *Ed* Bruce B. Pierce
Mus Herschel Burke Gilbert
● Neville Brand, Emile Meyer, Frank Faylen, Leo
Gordon, Robert Osterloh, Paul Frees (Allied Artists)

Riot in Cell Block 11 is a hard-hitting, suspenseful prison thriller.

The pros and cons of prison riots are stated
articulately in the Richard Collins screen
story, and producer Walter Wanger uses a realistic, almost documentary, style to make his
point for needed reforms in the operation of
penal institutions.

The picture doesn't use formula prison
plot. There's no inmate reformed by love or
fair treatment, nor unbelievable boy-meets-
girl, gets-same angle. Nor are there any
heroes and heavies of standard pattern.
Instead, it deals with a riot, how it started
and why, what was done to halt it, the capit-
ulations on both sides.

The points for reform made in the Wanger
production cover overcrowding housing, poor
food, the mingling of mentally well and mentally sick prisoners, the character-corroding
idleness of men caged in cell blocks.

A standout performance is given by Emile
Meyer, the warden who understands the prisoners' problems.

RISKY BUSINESS

1983, 96 MINS, US ◇ Ⓥ

Dir Paul Brickman   *Prod* Jon Avnet   *Scr* Paul
Brickman   *Ph* Reynaldo Villalobos, Bruce Surtees
Ed Richard Chew   *Mus* Tangerine Dream
Art Dir William J. Cassidy
● Tom Cruise, Rebecca De Mornay, Curtis Armstrong,
Bronson Pinchot, Raphael Sbarge, Joe Pantoliano
(Geffen)

Risky Business is like a promising first novel,
with all the pros and cons that come with that
territory.

High schooler Tom Cruise could literally
be a next-door neighbor to Timothy Hutton
in *Ordinary People* on Chicago's affluent suburban North Shore. That changes virtually
overnight, however, when he meets sharp-
looking hooker Rebecca De Mornay. On the
lam from her slimy pimp, she shacks up in
Cruise's splendid home while his parents are
out of town and, since he's anxious to prove
himself as a Future Enterpriser in one of his
school's more blatantly greed-oriented
programs, convinces him to make the house
into a bordello for one night.

Ultimately, pic seems to endorse the bottom line, going for the big buck. In fact, not
only is Cruise rewarded financially for setting
up the best little whorehouse in Glencoe, but
it gets him into Princeton to boot. Writer-
director Paul Brickman can therefore be
accused of trying to have it both ways, but
there's no denying the stylishness and talent
of his direction.

RITA, SUE AND BOB TOO

1987, 95 MINS, UK ◇ Ⓥ

Dir Alan Clarke   *Prod* Sandy Lieberson   *Scr* Andrea
Dunbar   *Ph* Ivan Strasburg   *Ed* Stephen Singleton
Mus Michael Kamen
● Michelle Holmes, Siobhan Finneran, George
Costigan, Lesley Sharp, Willie Ross, Patti Nicholls
(Film Four/Umbrella/British Screen)

Rita, Sue and Bob Too is a sad-funny comedy
about sex and life in the Yorkshire city of
Bradford.

Rita and Sue are two schoolgirls who sometimes babysit for a well-off couple, Bob and
Michelle. In the film's opening sequence, the
odious yet somehow charming Bob, a real-
estate agent, gives the girls a lift home, but
stops off first on the moors above the city and
without preliminaries, proposes sex with
them. The girls are agreeable, with Sue taking the first turn on the reclining seat in Bob's
Rover.

Immediately screenwriter Andrea Dunbar
[who adapted the film from her own plays
The Arbor and *Rita, Sue and Bob Too*] injects a
completely convincing mixture of raunchy
comedy and sadness.

Rita and Sue, splendidly played by Siobhan
Finneran and Michelle Holmes, are pathetic
figures as they trip along in their tight miniskirts, but they're lively and funny. George
Costigan makes Bob a charming character,
despite his ingrained seediness.

RITZ, THE

1976, 90 MINS, US ◇ Ⓥ

Dir Richard Lester   *Prod* Denis O'Dell   *Scr* Terrence
McNally   *Ph* Paul Wilson   *Ed* John Bloom   *Mus* Ken
Thorne   *Art Dir* Phillip Harrison

● Jack Weston, Rita Moreno, Jerry Stiller, Kaye
Ballard, F. Murray Abraham, Paul B. Price (Warner)

Depending on where one's taste lies,
The Ritz is either esoteric farce for the urban
cosmopolite, or else one long tasteless and
anachronistic 1950-ish 'gay' joke, shot at
England's Twickenham Studios in 25 days.

Terrence McNally adapted his 1975 play
about assorted mistaken identities and
hangups in a NY gay steambath (including
Broadway cast originals).

McNally's story has Weston fingered for
rubout by dying father-in-law George
Coulouris. Escaping from the midwest, Jack
Weston heads for a notorious Gotham gay
bath, figuring that avenging brother-in-law
Jerry Stiller will never find him.

But the plan doesn't figure on the gangland
family's diversified business interests, nor on
the ingenuity of Weston's wife, played by
Kaye Ballard.

Classic farce construction provides the
expected physical action.

RIVER, THE

1938, 30 MINS, US

Dir Pare Lorentz   *Scr* Pare Lorentz   *Ph* Pare Lorentz
Ed Stacy Woodward, Floyd Crosby, Willard Van Dyke
Art Dir Virgil Thomson (Farm Security Administration)

● This is the second film produced by the
Farm Security Administration, previous one
having been *The Plough That Broke the Plains*,
also written and directed by Pare Lorentz,
with musical score by Virgil Thomson. It's a
more arresting, more compelling job than the
previous effort, although still failing to
encompass the subject entirely.

Documentary pic seeks to tell the story of
the Mississippi river, its sources, its majestic
course, its destination, its uses and abuse by
heedless man, and its relentless retaliation.

As the narrator [Thomas Chalmers] states,
the Mississippi is the most nearly perfect
river in the world, and something of that
mighty quality infests the film. Film impressively depicts the beauty and the power of the
river, how it has been squandered and destroyed, how terrible has been the inevitable
result. But it fails to tie its interrelated parts
into a whole that is entirely clear or convincing. It skips from fact to fact, argument to
argument, but doesn't quite weave a perfect
pattern.

Thomson's score, blended from symphonic
sources, ballads, spirituals and original compositions, highlights the film dramatically.
Narrative is vividly effective, being a composite of straight description and exposition
and poetic prose.

RIVER, THE

1951, 99 MINS, INDIA/US ◇ Ⓥ

Dir Jean Renoir   *Prod* Kenneth McEldowney
Scr Rumer Godden, Jean Renoir   *Ph* Claude Renoir
Ed George Gale   *Mus* M.A. Partha Sarathy
Art Dir Eugene Lourie, Bansi Chandragupta
● Nora Swinburne, Esmond Knight, Arthur Shields,
Thomas E. Breen, Patricia Walters, Adrienne Corri
(Oriental-International/United Artists)

Jean Renoir's *The River* is a sort of animated
geographic, in color, of life on the Ganges
River in West Bengal. It is a distinctive story
of adolescent love, with a philosophy that life
flows on just as the river.

This is a beautiful picture, and certainly
neither Technicolor nor India ever looked
better. Throughout it is ablaze with vivid,
contrasting colors. But one never feels the
real India and rather suspects that this is a
highly glamorized version.

The story tells how the life of a British
family (the family runs a jute mill) is interrupted by the appearance of one Capt John
on a visit to his cousin, Mr John, a neighbor.

R

Two young teenagers fall as madly in love with Capt John, who lost a leg in the last war, as their newly-awakened emotions will allow. But Capt John is too busy being a lost soul to take them seriously.

Although the drama too frequently seems merely an afterthought, a sort of excuse upon which to build a lush panorama of India, the characters are completely credible. Exception is Thomas Breen as Capt John. He has the appearance of one who might excite the immature emotions of the three young ladies, but hasn't the ability to appear convincing. Outstanding is Radha, whose ritual dance of love with the god Krishna highlights the pic.

■ RIVER, THE

1984, 122 MINS, US ◇ ⓥ
Dir Mark Rydell *Prod* Edward Lewis, Robert Cortes
Scr Robert Dillon, Julian Barry *Ph* Vilmos Zsigmond
Ed Sidney Levin *Mus* John Williams *Art Dir* Charles Rosen
● Mel Gibson, Sissy Spacek, Shane Bailey, Becky Jo Lynch, Scott Glenn, Don Hood (Universal)

The River puts fundamental American values to the test in a society that has come unglued. Stripped down to the bare essentials few people actually ever come into contact with, pic remains a rather private ordeal observed from the outside looking in. There is a victory at the end, but not a sense of lasting triumph

Setting the tone is the Garvey family battling the flood waters of the river to save their farm. Farmers are forced to sell off their land with hungry wolf businessman Joe Wade (Scott Glenn) waiting to pick up the pieces.

Glenn, as the silver-spoon kid and Spacek's former lover, is the film's most complex creation. Though he is the malignancy behind much of the farmers' troubles, director Mark Rydell allows him to maintain a level of humanity.

■ RIVER OF NO RETURN

1954, 90 MINS, US ◇ ⓥ
Dir Otto Preminger *Prod* Stanley Rubin *Scr* Frank Fenton *Ph* Joseph LaShelle *Ed* Louis Loeffler
Mus Cyril J. Mockridge
● Robert Mitchum, Marilyn Monroe, Rory Calhoun, Tommy Rettig, Murvyn Vye, Douglas Spencer (20th Century-Fox)

The striking beauties of the Canadian Rockies co-star with the blonde charms of Marilyn Monroe and the masculine muscles of Robert Mitchum in *River of No Return*.

The competition between scenic splendors of the Jasper and Banff National Parks and entertainment values finds the former finishing slightly ahead on merit, although there's enough rugged action and suspense moments to get the production through its footage. In between the high spots, Otto Preminger's directorial pacing is inclined to lag, so the running time seems overlong.

Mitchum and Tommy Rettig, playing father and son, pull Monroe and Rory Calhoun from a river that races by their wilderness farm. Calhoun is trying to get to a settlement to file a gold claim he has won dishonestly at cards and Monroe is along because she expects to marry him. Calhoun steals Mitchum's horse and gun and rides off, leaving the others at the mercy of warring Indians. Man, woman and boy take to the river on a raft to escape the redskins.

■ RIVER'S EDGE

1986, 99 MINS, US ◇ ⓥ
Dir Tim Hunter *Prod* Sarah Pillsbury, Midge Sanford
Scr Neal Jimenez *Ph* Frederick Elmes *Ed* Howard Smith, Sonya Sones *Mus* Jurgen Knieper *Art Dir* John Moto
● Crispin Glover, Keanu Reaves, Ione Skye, David Roebuck, Dennis Hopper (Hemdale)

Tim Hunter's *River's Edge* is an unusually downbeat and depressing youth pic.

The setting is a small town, presumably in Oregon. Pic opens with 12-year-old Tim destroying his kid sister's doll and then spotting high-schooler Samson sitting on the river bank with the naked body of a girl he's just murdered. Tim's reaction is to steal a couple of cans of beer for the killer.

But they're really nice at heart, the film seems to be saying. They have to cope with broken homes and the threat of the Bomb, otherwise they wouldn't be so hopeless.

As group leader Layne, Crispin Glover could have used more restraint: he gives a busy, fussy performance. Others in the cast are more effective, with young Joshua Miller particularly striking as the awful child, Tim.

■ ROAD GAMES

1981, 100 MINS, AUSTRALIA ◇
Dir Richard Franklin *Prod* Richard Franklin
Scr Everett DeRoche *Ph* Vincent Monton *Ed* Edward McQueen-Mason *Mus* Brian May *Art Dir* Jon Dowding
● Stacy Keach, Jamie Lee Curtis, Marion Edward, Grant Page (Quest)

'*Road Games*' is an above-average suspenser concerning an offbeat truck driver who winds up stalking a murderer. Stacy Keach's characterization of the amusing, poetry-spouting man is particularly endearing but the film builds all too effectively to a rather disappointing climax.

Keach limns an independent trucker in Melbourne assigned to deliver a major shipment of pork to Perth. Amid cracking jokes, concocting stories about the inhabitants of passing cars and fantasizing about pretty girls (all to the deadpan of his pet dog), he becomes suspicious of the driver of a green van.

Through a series of clues he begins to realize the guy is actually a killer of young women the police have been looking for. Neither the police nor anyone else will listen to Keach so he eventually decides to get the guy himself.

Jamie Lee Curtis appears midway through as an heiress hitchhiker who befriends Keach while looking for some diversion from everyday life.

■ ROAD TO BALI

1952, 91 MINS, US ◇ ⓥ
Dir Hal Walker *Prod* Harry Tugend *Scr* Frank Butler, Hal Kanter, William Morrow *Ed* Archie Marshek *Mus* Joseph J. Lilley (dir.) *Art Dir* Hal Pereira, Joseph McMillan Johnson
● Bob Hope, Bing Crosby, Dorothy Lamour, Murvyn Vye, Peter Coe, Leon Askin (Paramount)

Bing Crosby, Bob Hope and Dorothy Lamour are back again in another of Paramount's highway sagas, with nonsensical amusement its only destination. Five songs are wrapped up in the production.

Needing a job, Crosby and Hope hire out to Murvyn Vye, a South Seas island prince, as divers, sail for Vye's homeland and meet Princess Lamour, which is excuse enough for her to sing 'Moonflowers', later reprised as the finale tune.

There's no story to speak of in the script [from a story by Frank Butler and Harry Tugend] but the framework is there on which to hang a succession of amusing quips and physical comedy dealing with romantic rivalry and chuckle competition between the two male stars. It also permits some surprise guest star appearances, such as the finale walkon of Jane Russell; Humphrey Bogart pulling the African Queen through Africa.

■ ROAD TO HONG KONG, THE

1962, 91 MINS, UK
Dir Norman Panama *Prod* Melvin Frank
Scr Norman Panama, Melvin Frank *Ph* Jack Hildyard *Ed* John Smith, Alan Osbiston *Mus* Robert Farnon *Art Dir* Roger Furse
● Bing Crosby, Bob Hope, Joan Collins, Dorothy Lamour, Robert Morley, Felix Aylmer (United Artists/Melnor)

The seventh *Road* comedy, after a lapse of seven years, takes the boys on a haphazard trip to a planet called Plutonius, though this only happens as a climax to some hilarious adventures in Ceylon and Hong Kong.

It's almost useless to outline the plot. But it involves Crosby and Hope as a couple of flop vaudevillians who turn con men. Somewhere along the line, Hope loses his memory and that, in a mysterious manner, leads them to involvement with a mysterious spy (Joan Collins) a secret formula and a whacky bunch of thugs called the Third Echelon, led by Robert Morley.

The script is spiced with a number of private jokes (golf, Hope's nose, Crosby's dough, reference to gags from previous *Road* films) but not enough to be irritating. Major disappointment is Joan Collins, who though an okay looker, never seems quite abreast of the comedians. Lamour plays herself as a vaude artist who rescues the Crosby-Hope team from one of their jams.

As guest artists, Frank Sinatra and Dean Martin help to round off the film. David Niven appears for no good reason, while the best interlude is that of Peter Sellers. He plays a native medico, examining Hope for amnesia and it is a brilliantly funny cameo.

■ ROAD TO MOROCCO

1942, 83 MINS, US ⓥ
Dir David Butler *Prod* Paul Jones *Scr* Frank Butler, Don Hartman *Ph* William Mellor *Ed* Irene Morra
● Bing Crosby, Bob Hope, Dorothy Lamour, Anthony Quinn, Vladimir Sokoloff, Dona Drake (Paramount)

Morocco is a bubbling spontaneous entertainment without a semblance of sanity; an uproarious patchquilt of gags, old situations and a blitz-like laugh pace that never lets up for a moment. It's Bing Crosby and Bob Hope at their best, with Dorothy Lamour, as usual, the pivotal point for their romantic pitch.

The story's absurdities, all of which are predicated on Crosby and Hope as shipwrecked stowaways cast ashore on the coast of North Africa, at no time weave a pattern of restraint. It's just a madcap holiday for the fun-makers.

The scripters, along with everyone else associated with the production, must surely have realized, of course, that the yarn couldn't be played straight. The result is some unorthodox film-making that finds both male stars making dialogistic asides that kid, for instance, some of the film's 'weaknesses' or, in other cases, poke fun at various objects that aren't even remotely associated with the picture.

■ ROAD TO RIO

1947, 100 MINS, US ⓥ
Dir Norman Z. McLeod *Prod* Daniel Dare
Scr Edmund Beloin, Jack Rose *Ph* Ernest Laszlo
Ed Ellsworth Hoagland *Mus* Robert Emmett Dolan
Art Dir Hans Dreier, Earl Hedrick
● Bing Crosby, Bob Hope, Dorothy Lamour, Gale Sondergaard (Paramount)

There are no talking animals in this to prep

uproarish see-hear gags, but a capable substitute is a trumpet that blows musical bubbles. Stunt pays off as one of a number of top, hard-punching laugh-getters. Norman Z. McLeod's direction blends the music and comedy into fast action and sock chuckles that will please followers of the series.

Bing Crosby and Bob Hope repeat their slaphappy characters in the Edmund Beloin-Jack Rose plot. Opening establishes the boys, as usual, in trouble and broke. When they set a circus on fire, pair escape by taking refuge on a ship heading for Rio. It doesn't take them long to discover a damsel in distress (Dorothy Lamour) and action centers around their efforts to save her from a wicked aunt and a forced marriage.

■ ROAD TO SINGAPORE

1940, 84 MINS, US

Dir Victor Schertzinger   *Prod* Harlan Thompson
Scr Don Hartman, Frank Butler, Harry Hervey
Ph William C. Mellor   *Ed* Paul Weatherwax
Mus Victor Young   *Art Dir* Hans Dreier, Robert Odell
● Bing Crosby, Bob Hope, Dorothy Lamour, Charles Coburn, Anthony Quinn, Jerry Colonna (Paramount)

Initial teaming of Bing Crosby and Bob Hope in *Road to Singapore* provides foundation for continuous round of good substantial comedy of rapid-fire order, swinging along at a zippy pace. Contrast is provided in Crosby's leisurely presentation of situations and dialog, in comparison to the lightning-like thrusts and parries of Hope. Neat blending of the two brands accentuates the comedy values for laugh purposes.

Story is a light framework on which to drape the situations for Crosby and Hope, with Dorothy Lamour providing decorative character of a native gal in sarong-like trappings. Crosby is the adventurous son of a shipping magnate, who refuses to sit behind a desk. He walks out on both father and a socialite fiancee to ship to the South Seas with sailor-buddy Hope. Lamour moves in with the pair, and from there on it's a happy mixture of both making passes for the native beauty, while they struggle to raise the necessary coin to live in comfort on the island. Crosby eventually gets the girl, but not until the trio romps through some zany adventures.

■ ROAD TO UTOPIA

1945, 90 MINS, US Ⓥ

Dir Hal Walker   *Prod* Paul Jones   *Scr* Norman Panama, Melvin Frank   *Ph* Lionel Lindon, Gordon Jennings, Farciot Edouart   *Ed* Stuart Gilmore
Mus Leigh Harline   *Art Dir* Hans Dreier, Roland Anderson
● Bing Crosby, Bob Hope, Dorothy Lamour, Robert Benchley, Hillary Brooke, Douglass Dumbrille (Paramount)

Bob Benchley is cut into an upper corner of various shots making wisecracks, first being that 'this is how not to make a picture'. Others are in the same groove, while additional off-the-path gags include Bob Hope and Dorothy Lamour in a kissing scene, topped by Hope's aside to the audience: 'As far as I'm concerned the picture is over right now'. Another is a guy walking across a scene asking Bing Crosby and Hope where Stage 8 is.

Action is laid in the Klondike of the gold rush days. On their way there, scrubbing decks because they'd lost their money, Crosby and Hope come upon a map leading to a rich gold mine. It had been stolen from Lamour's father by two of the toughest badmen of Alaska. Lamour goes to the Klondike in search of them.

Technically picture leaves nothing to be desired. Paul Jones, producer, and Hal

Walker, who directed, make a fine combination in steering and in the production value provided. Performances by supporting cast are all good.

■ ROAD TO ZANZIBAR

1941, 89 MINS, US

Dir Victor Schertzinger   *Prod* Paul Jones   *Scr* Frank Butler, Don Hartman   *Ph* Ted Tetzlaff   *Ed* Alma MacRorie   *Mus* Victor Young (dir.)
● Bing Crosby, Bob Hope, Dorothy Lamour, Una Merkel, Jean Marsh, Eric Blore (Paramount)

Zanzibar is Paramount's second coupling of Bing Crosby, Bob Hope and Dorothy Lamour. Although picture has sufficient comedy situations and dialog between its male stars, it lacks the compactness and spontaneity of its predecessor.

The story framework is pretty flimsy foundation for hanging the series of comedy and thrill situations concocted for the pair. It's a fluffy and inconsequential tale, with Crosby-Hope combo, doing valiant work to keep up interest.

Pair are stranded in South Africa, with Crosby the creator of freak sideshow acts for Hope to perform. With his saved passage money back to the States, Crosby buys a diamond mine, which is quickly sold by Hope for profit. Then pair start out on strange Safari with Lamour and Una Merkel, pair of Brooklyn entertainers, pursuing a millionaire hunter.

Comedy episodes generally lack sparkle and tempo, and musical numbers are also below par for a Crosby picture.

■ ROAR

1981, 102 MINS, US ◇

Dir Noel Marshall   *Prod* Noel Marshall, Charles Sloan, Jack Rattner   *Scr* Noel Marshall   *Ph* Jan De Bont
Mus Dominic Frontiere   *Art Dir* Joel Marshall
● Tippi Hedren, Noel Marshall, John Marshall, Melanie Griffith, Jerry Marshall, Kyalo Mativo (Marshall)

The noble intentions of director-writer-producer Noel Marshall and his actress-wife Tippi Hedren shine through the faults and short-comings of *Roar*, their 11-year, $17 million project – touted as the most disaster-plagued pic in Hollywood history.

Given the enormous difficulties during production – a devastating flood, several fires, an epidemic that decimated the feline cast and numerous injuries to actors and crew, it's a miracle that the pic was completed.

Here is a passionate plea for the preservation of Arican wildlife meshed with an adventure-horror tale which aims to be a kind of *Jaws* of the jungle. If it seems at times more like *Born Free* gone berserk, such are the risks of planting the cast in the bush (actually the Marshalls' ranch in Soledad Canyon in California), surrounded by 150 untrained lions, leopards, tigers, cheetahs and other big cats, not to mention several large and ill-tempered elephants.

Thin plot has Hedren and her three children trekking to Africa to reunite with Marshall, an eccentric scientist who's been living in a three-story wooden house in the jungle with his feline friends, an experiment to show that humans and beasts can happily coexist.

Hedren and her daughter Melanie Griffith have proved their dramatic ability elsewhere: here they and their costars are required to do little more than look petrified.

■ ROARING TWENTIES, THE

1939, 106 MINS, US Ⓥ

Dir Raoul Walsh   *Prod* Samuel Bischoff   *Scr* Jerry Wald, Richard Macaulay, Robert Rossen   *Ph* Ernest Haller   *Ed* Jack Killifer   *Mus* Heinz Roemheld   *Art Dir* Max Parker

● James Cagney, Humphrey Bogart, Priscilla Lane, Gladys George, Frank McHugh, Paul Kelly (Warner)

This is a partially true gangster melodrama from the pen of Mark Hellinger. As a seasoned Broadway columnist Hellinger well remembered the dizzy times that gave birth to such illegal hot spots as the Hotsy-Totsy, Dizzy, Black Bottom, etc. Above all, he had intimate knowledge of the El Fay, the Del Fey and the Guinan clubs, and the Texas Guinan-Larry Fay operation thereof. He has thinly disguised them as the central figures of this yarn, in a good many instances spilling some inside facts, but the blow-off (for the sake of better picture entertainment) is certainly fictionized.

Because of James Cagney and the story's circumstances, *The Roaring Twenties* is reminiscent of *Public Enemy*. Story and dialog are good. Raoul Walsh turns in a fine directorial job; the performances are uniformly excellent.

■ ROBBERY

1967, 114 MINS, UK ◇ Ⓥ

Dir Peter Yates   *Prod* Stanley Baker, Michael Deeley
Scr Edward Boyd, Peter Yates, George Markstein
Ph Douglas Slocombe   *Ed* Reginald Beck
Mus Johnny Keating   *Art Dir* Michael Seymour
● Stanley Baker, Joanna Pettet, James Booth, Frank Finlay, Barry Foster, William Marlowe (Paramount)

This precision-tooled suspense thriller turns many of the traditional ingredients that usually go into this kind of film inside out and manages to come up with a tight, well paced, highly entertaining pic.

For a brisk start there's a car robbery and the maneuvres of the robbers in London streets consume the first 20 minutes, during which there is no dialog but a thumping good score by Johnny Keating which adds to the unexplained incidents. The cleverly executed theft is followed by a roller-coaster car chase.

Peter Yates directs with a sense of authenticity and detail which makes the viewer both detached and increasingly curious concerning the various incidents involved in blue-printing and executing the robbery of £3 million from a British mail train.

■ ROBBERY UNDER ARMS

1957, 99 MINS, UK ◇

Dir Jack Lee   *Prod* Joseph Janni   *Scr* Alexander Baron, W.P. Lipscomb   *Ph* Harry Waxman
Ed Manuel Del Campo   *Mus* Matyas Seiber   *Art Dir* Alex Vetchinsky
● Peter Finch, Ronald Lewis, Laurence Naismith, Maureen Swanson, David McCallum, Jill Ireland (Rank)

Set in Australia of a 100 years earlier, *Robbery under Arms* is a well-made straightforward drama. The story, based on a Victorian novel [by Rolf Boldrewood] has Peter Finch as Captain Starlight, a virile, likeable rogue who runs a gang of bushrangers. In search of adventure, Ronald Lewis and David McCallum join the gang which includes their father. When the two attempt to break away and lead honest lives they find that they've lost their chance.

Jack Lee's direction splendidly captures the Australian atmosphere. He indulges in no frills. Lee is admirably supported by lenser Harry Waxman who fills the screen with sweeping camerawork, suggesting the vastness of the Australian canvas.

In the star role, Finch has a comparatively small role but he plays it with a swagger which is highly effective. Good opportunities are given to the brothers, Lewis and McCallum. The distaff side plays second fiddle to the men in this action meller, but Maureen Swanson, in an undeveloped role as a fiery, possessive young woman who sets her amorous sights on Lewis, has a real opportunity.

································

■ ROBE, THE

1953, 135 MINS, US ◇ Ⓥ
Dir Henry Koster   *Prod* Frank Ross   *Scr* Philip Dunne
Ph Leon Shamroy   *Ed* Barbara McLean   *Mus* Alfred Newman   *Art Dir* Lyle R. Wheeler, George W. Davis
● Richard Burton, Jean Simmons, Victor Mature, Michael Rennie, Jay Robinson, Dean Jagger (20th Century-Fox)

The Robe was 10 years coming, first under RKO aegis when producer Frank Ross was there. It is a big picture in every sense of the word. One magnificent scene after another, under the [new] anamorphic CinemaScope technique, unveils the splendor that was Rome and the turbulence that was Jerusalem at the time of Christ on Calvary.

The homespun robe worn by Jesus is the symbol of Richard Burton's conversion when the Roman tribune realizes he carried out the crucifixion of a holy man at Pontius Pilate's orders. Victor Mature is the Greek slave for whom Burton outbid the corrupt Caligula (Jay Robinson), the Roman prince regent.

Lloyd C. Douglas' original bestseller is a fictionized novel of Scriptural times, and thus Jean Simmons is cast as the love interest who, as the ward of the Emperor Tiberius (Ernest Thesiger), spurns her destiny as the betrothed of the Prince Regent for the love of Marcellus Gallio (Burton).

The performances are consistently good. Simmons, Burton and Mature are particularly effective, and Betta St John, Dean Jagger, Michael Rennie, Torin Thatcher and Ernest Thesiger likewise standout in the other more prominent roles. Jeff Morrow's heavy is good, and the sword duel between him and Burton a highlight.

The slave market, the freeing of the Greek slave from the torture rack, the Christians in the catacombs, the dusty plains of Galilee, the Roman court splendor and that finale 'chase' (with the four charging white steeds head-on into the camera creating a most effective 3-D illusion) are standouts.

The Robe reportedly cost $4.5 million, of which close to $1 million may date back to producer Frank Ross' investiture under the original RKO banner. With or without the hidden charges it looks almost all of it.

☐ 1953: Best Picture(Nomination)

································

■ ROBIN AND MARIAN

1976, 106 MINS, UK ◇ Ⓥ
Dir Richard Lester   *Prod* Denis O'Dell   *Scr* James Goldman   *Ph* David Watkin   *Ed* John Victor Smith
Mus John Barry   *Art Dir* Michael Stringer
● Sean Connery, Audrey Hepburn, Robert Shaw, Richard Harris, Nicol Williamson, Denholm Elliott (Columbia/Rastar)

Robin and Marian is a disappointing and embarrassing film: disappointing, because Sean Connery, Audrey Hepburn, the brilliant Robert Shaw, Richard Harris and a screenplay by James Goldman ought to add up to something even in the face of Richard Lester's flat direction; embarrassing, because the incompatible blend of tongue-in-cheek comedy, adventure and romance gives the Robin Hood-revisited film the grace and energy of a geriatrics' discotheque.

Connery's Robin and Nicol Williamson's Little John return to England after Harris' King Richard dies abroad; back home, Shaw's Sheriff of Nottingham is still in office, now nominally subservient to nobleman Kenneth Haigh who was appointed by Ian Holm's bad King John. Hepburn's Marian has retired to a nunnery, eventually becoming Mother Superior there when Robin didn't return from the Crusades.

The idea of picking up the Robin Hood legend 20 years later seems okay at first consideration, but Goldman and Lester never got beyond the premise.

································

■ ROBIN AND THE SEVEN HOODS

1964, 123 MINS, US ◇ Ⓥ
Dir Gordon M. Douglas   *Prod* Frank Sinatra
Scr David R. Schwartz   *Ph* William H. Daniels   *Ed* Sam O'Steen   *Mus* Nelson Riddle   *Art Dir* LeRoy Deane
● Frank Sinatra, Dean Martin, Sammy Davis Jr, Peter Falk, Bing Crosby, Edward G. Robinson (Warner)

Robin and the Seven Hoods is a spoof on gangster pix of bygone days sparked by the names of Frank Sinatra, Dean Martin and Bing Crosby. The daffy doings of Chicago's hoodlums during the Prohibition era in a battle for leadership of the rackets backdrops action which usually is on the slightly wacky side.

Scripter David R. Schwartz takes the legend of Robin Hood and his merrie men and retailors it loosely to the frolickings of Sinatra and his pack. In some measure the parallel is successful, at least as basis for a premise which gives the plot a gimmick springboard as Sinatra, as Robbo, the good-hearted hood, takes from the rich to give to the poor.

Yarn opens in 1928 with the gangster king-pin of the day – Edward G. Robinson doing a cameo bit here – guest of honor at a lavish birthday party. After a sentimental rendition of 'For He's a Jolly Good Fellow' by the assembled company of hoods, they shoot Robinson dead.

Thereafter it's for grabs as Peter Falk has himself elected as the new Number One, and Sinatra arrives to warn him to keep out of his territory.

Performance-wise, Falk comes out best. His comic gangster is a pure gem. Sinatra of course, is smooth and Crosby in a 'different' type of role rates a big hand.

································

■ ROBIN HOOD PRINCE OF THIEVES

1991, 138 MINS, US ◇ Ⓥ
Dir Kevin Reynolds   *Prod* John Watson, Pen Densham, Richard B. Lewis   *Scr* Pen Densham, John Watson
Ph Doug Milsome   *Ed* Peter Boyle   *Mus* Michael Kamen   *Art Dir* John Graysmark
● Kevin Costner, Morgan Freeman, Mary Elizabeth Mastrantonio, Christian Slater, Alan Rickman, Sean Connery (Morgan Creek)

Kevin Costner's *Robin Hood* is a Robin of wood. Murky and uninspired, this $50 million rendition bears evidence of the rushed and unpleasant production circumstances that were much reported upon. At the same time, this seriously intended, more realistically motivated revision of the Robin myth may have diminished the hero, but it hasn't destroyed him.

Lackluster script, from a story by Pen Densham, begins in the year 1194 in Jerusalem, where Robin leads a prison uprising and escapes with a Moor, Azeem (Morgan Freeman). Retreating from the Crusades, the pair head for England, where they find that Robin's father has been slain by the Sheriff of Nottingham (Alan Rickman), who is attempting to eliminate all resistance and perhaps make a play for the throne in the absence of King Richard.

To avenge his father's death, Robin joins up with Little John and the latter's band of outsiders in a safe enclave in Sherwood Forest. Major setpiece is the sheriff's attack on the outlaws' hippie-like compound, which decimates the group. But Robin is able to lead a counterattack on Nottingham Castle.

The best that can be said for Costner's performance is that it is pleasant. At worst, it can be argued whether it is more properly described as wooden or cardboard.

Looking beautiful and sporting an accent that comes and goes, Mary Elizabeth Mastrantonio makes a sprightly, appropriately feisty Marian. Of the Americans, Christian Slater is most successful at putting on an English accent, and he has some spirited moments as Will Scarlett.

As the 'painted man' who accompanies Robin in gratitude for his life having been saved, Freeman is a constant, dominant presence. As the sheriff, Rickman goes way over the top, emoting with facial and vocal leers. It's a relief whenever this resourceful thesp is on-screen, such is the energy and brio he brings to the proceedings. An unbilled Sean Connery shows up at the very end as King Richard to give his blessing to Robin and Marian's marriage.

································

■ ROBOCOP

1987, 103 MINS, US ◇ Ⓥ
Dir Paul Verhoeven   *Prod* Arne Schmidt   *Scr* Edward Neumeier   *Ph* Jost Vacano   *Ed* Frank J. Drioste
Mus Basil Poledouris   *Art Dir* William Sandell
● Peter Weller, Nancy Allen, Ronny Cox, Kurtwood Smith (Davison)

RoboCop is a comic book movie that's definitely not for kids. The welding of extreme violence with four-letter words is tempered with gut-level humor and technical wizardry.

Roller-coaster ride begins with the near-dismemberment of recently transferred police officer Murphy (Peter Weller), to the southern precinct of the Detroit Police Dept in the not-too-distant future.

There are three organizations inextricably wound into Detroit's anarchical society – the police, a band of sadistic hoodlums, and a multinational conglomerate which has a contract with the city to run the police force.

Weller is blown to bits just at the time an ambitious junior exec at the multinational is ready to develop a prototype cyborg – half-man, half-machine programmed to be an indestructable cop. Thus Weller becomes RoboCop, unleashed to fell the human scum he encounters, not the least among them his killers.

As sicko sadists go, Kurtwood Smith is a well-cast adversary. Nancy Allen as Weller's partner (before he died) provides the only warmth in the film, wanting and encouraging RoboCop to listen to some of the human spirit that survived inside him. *RoboCop* is as tightly worked as a film can be, not a moment or line wasted.

································

■ ROBOCOP 2

1990, 118 MINS, US ◇ Ⓥ
Dir Irvin Kershner   *Prod* Jon Davison   *Scr* Frank Miller, Walon Green   *Ph* Mark Irwin   *Ed* William Anderson
Mus Leonard Rosenman   *Art Dir* Peter Jamison
● Peter Weller, Nancy Allen, Dan O'Herlihy, Belinda Bauer, Tom Noonan, Galyn Gorg (Orion)

This ultraviolent, nihilistic sequel has enough technical dazzle to impress hardware fans, but obviously no one in the Orion front office told filmmakers that less is more.

The future is represented by a crumbling Detroit (actually filmed like the original in Texas), dominated by Dan O'Herlihy's Omni Consumer Products company. He's set to foreclose on loans and literally take possession of Motown. Standing in his way is a loose cannon, drug magnate/user Tom Noonan, whose goal is to flood society with designer versions of his drug Nuke.

Peter Weller as RoboCop must defeat both factions while effeminate mayor Willard Pugh gets in the way. Noonan is reconstituted as Robocop 2 by O'Herlihy's sexy assistant Belinda Bauer, providing the film's final half hour of great special effects as an end in themselves.

Gabriel Damon as a precocious 12-year-old gangster is the best thing in the picture.

. . . .

■ ROBOT MONSTER

1953, 62 MINS, US ⓥ
Dir Phil Tucker   *Prod* Phil Tucker   *Scr* Wyott Ordung
Ph Jack Greenhalgh   *Ed* Bruce Schoengarth
Mus Elmer Bernstein
● George Nader, Claudia Barrett, Selena Royle, Gregory Moffett, John Mylong, Pamela Paulson (Three Dimensional)

Judged on the basis of novelty, as a showcase for the Tru-Stereo Process, *Robot Monster* comes off surprisingly well, considering the extremely limited budget ($50,000) and schedule on which the film was shot.

The Tru-Stereo Process (3-D) utilized here is easy on the eyes, coming across clearly at all times. To the picture's credit no 3-D gimmicks were employed.

Beating Arch Oboler's *Five* [1951] by one survivor, yarn here concerns itself with the last six people on earth – all pitted against a mechanical monster called Ro-Man, sent from another planet whose 'people' are disturbed by strides being made on earth in the research fields of atomic development and space travel.

Sextet – a famed scientist, his wife, assistant, daughter and two children – are protected from Ro-Man's supersonic death ray by anti-biotic serum.

Of the principals, George Nader, as the aide who falls in love with and eventually marries the scientist's daughter in a primitive ceremony, fares the best. Selena Royle also comes across okay, but of the others the less said the better.

. . . .

■ ROCK AROUND THE CLOCK

1956, 76 MINS, US ⓥ
Dir Fred F. Sears   *Prod* Sam Katzman   *Scr* Robert Kent, James B. Gordon   *Ph* Benjamin H. Kline   *Ed* Saul A. Goodkind, Jack W. Ogilvie   *Mus* Fred Karger (sup.)
● Bill Haley and The Comets, The Platters, Tony Martinez and His Band, Freddie Bell and His Bellboys, Alan Freed, Lisa Gaye (Clover/Columbia)

Rock around the Clock takes off to a bouncy little beat and never lets up for 76 minutes of foot-patting entertainment. Bill Haley and The Comets set the beat with nine of their record favorites, including the title tune, 'Razzle Dazzle', 'Happy Baby', 'See You Later, Alligator', 'Rudy's Back' and others. Freddie Bell and His Bellboys are on for two solid numbers, 'Giddy Up, Ding Dong' and 'We're Gonna Teach You to Rock'.

Fred F. Sears' direction has excellent pace and keeps interest going with a story that tells how a band manager finds the Haley Comets in the mountains and brings dancing back to ballrooms throughout the country.

Johnny Johnston is likeable as the manager, while Alix Talton is a cool chick as a big band booker who tries unsuccessfully to get her matrimonial hooks in him. Film is a particularly strong showcasing for Lisa Gaye, who plays the rock and roll dancer with The Comets. Her terping's good and that figure the dance costumes display commands added interest.

. . . .

■ ROCKETEER, THE

1991, 108 MINS, US ◇ ⓥ
Dir Joe Johnston   *Prod* Lawrence Gordon, Charles Gordon, Lloyd Levin   *Scr* Danny Bilson, Paul De Meo   *Ph* Hiro Narita   *Ed* Arthur Schmidt   *Mus* James Horner   *Art Dir* Jim Bissell
● Bill Campbell, Jennifer Connelly, Alan Arkin, Timothy Dalton, Paul Sorvino, Ed Lauter (Disney/Gordon/Silver Screen Partners IV)

Based on a comic ['graphic novel' by Dave

Stevens] unveiled in 1981, this $40 million adventure fantasy puts a shiny polish on familiar elements: airborne hero, damsel in distress, Nazi villains, 1930s Hollywood glamor, dazzling special effects.

Elaborate opening sequence has an ace pilot (Bill Campbell) testing a new racing plane over LA skies in 1938 while, on the ground below, hoods and Feds in speeding cars shoot it out after robbery of a mysterious device.

Developed by none other than Howard Hughes, the invention makes its way into the pilot's hands, but it's coveted by a dashing star of swashbuckling films who also happens to be a dedicated Nazi (Timothy Dalton). Although he has hired thugs led by Paul Sorvino to recover the priceless device, Dalton has his own ideas about getting at Campbell through his gorgeous g.f. (Jennifer Connelly).

The object of intense interest is a portable rocket pack which, if strapped to one's back, can send its wearer zipping around almost as fast, if not as quietly, as Superman.

Newcomer Campbell exhibits the requisite grit and all-American know-how, but the lead role is written with virtually no humor or subtext. Those around him come off to better advantage, notably Dalton as the deliciously smooth, insidious Sinclair; Sorvino and Alan Arkin, with the latter as the Rocketeer's mentor; Terry O'Quinn as Hughes; and the lovely, voluptuous Connelly.

. . . .

■ ROCKING HORSE WINNER, THE

1949, 96 MINS, UK ⓦ
Dir Anthony Pelissier   *Prod* John Mills   *Scr* Anthony Pelissier   *Ph* Desmond Dickinson   *Ed* John Seabourne   *Mus* William Alwyn
● Valerie Hobson, John Howard Davies, Ronald Squire, John Mills (Two Cities)

There has rarely been a more faithful adaptation of an original, with the exception of the ending, which was added at the request of the censor.

In following the original D. H. Lawrence short story, Anthony Pelissier, who scripted as well as directed, has developed the story of an extravagant mother as seen through the eyes of a sensitive child. How to raise the cash to bring the family out of debt and anxiety is the problem preying on the youngster's mind.

Then, gradually, the boy realizes he has a facility for picking winners in horse races and in secret association with the family handyman, later joined by a sporting uncle, has an astonishing run of good luck.

John Howard Davies plays the sensitive lad with a skill and sincerity which would do credit to a seasoned trouper. Valerie Hobson is fine as the mother.

. . . .

■ ROCKY

1976, 119 MINS, US ◇ ⓥ
Dir John G. Avildsen   *Prod* Irwin Winkler   *Scr* Sylvester Stallone   *Ph* James Crabe   *Ed* Richard Halsey, Scott Conrad   *Mus* Bill Conti   *Art Dir* Bill Cassidy
● Sylvester Stallone, Talia Shire, Burt Young, Carl Weathers, Burgess Meredith, Thayer David (United Artists)

Sylvester Stallone stars in his own screenplay about a minor local boxer who gets a chance to fight a heavyweight championship bout.

Stallone's title character is that of a near-loser, a punchy reject scorned by gym owner Burgess Meredith, patronized by local loan shark Joe Spinell, rebuffed by plain-Jane Talia Shire whose brother, Burt Young, keeps engineering a romantic match.

Rocky would have remained in this rut, had not heavyweight champ Carl Weathers come up with the Bicentennial gimmick of fighting a sure-ringer, thereby certifying the American Dream for public consumption.

En route all this, Stallone brings out the best in Shire, exposes the worst in Young and generally gets his life together.
□ 1976: Best Picture

. . . .

■ ROCKY HORROR PICTURE SHOW, THE

1975, 100 MINS, UK ◇
Dir Jim Sharman   *Prod* Michael White   *Scr* Jim Sharman, Richard O'Brien   *Ph* Peter Suschitzky   *Ed* Graeme Clifford   *Mus* Richard O'Brien   *Art Dir* Terry Ackland Snow
● Tim Curry, Susan Sarandon, Barry Bostwick, Richard O'Brien, Jonathan Adams, Nell Campbell (20th Century Fox)

The Rocky Horror Picture Show is adapted from a rock stage musical of same title set in a spooky castle deep in the heart of Ohio. Into it on a rain-swept night stumble affianced Janet and Brad, wholesome straights, hoping to find a telephone, but finding instead the earthy lair of some weirdos from the planet Transylvania. Chief freak therein is the bisexual Frank N. Furter, played with relish by Tim Curry, who first seduces Janet and then conquers Brad.

The plot mixture also includes Curry's 'monster' creation, rippling-muscled Rocky; a revenging scientist; Riff Raff, Curry's hunch-backed lackey; and assorted groupies of which Magenta and Columbia (Patricia Quinn and Nell Campbell) are most prominent.

Overall, however, most of the jokes that might have seemed jolly fun on stage now appear obvious and even flat. The sparkle's gone.

. . . .

■ ROCKY II

1979, 119 MINS, US ◇ ⓥ
Dir Sylvester Stallone   *Prod* Irwin Winkler, Robert Chartoff   *Scr* Sylvester Stallone   *Ph* Bill Butler   *Ed* Danford B. Greene   *Mus* Bill Conti   *Art Dir* Richard Berger
● Sylvester Stallone, Talia Shire, Burt Young, Carl Weathers, Burgess Meredith (United Artists)

Rocky II follows much the same theme as its predecessor – that is fighter Rocky Balboa's path to a stab at the heavyweight crown. In its boxing and training scenes *Rocky II* packs much of the punch the original did, complete with an exciting pugilistic finale that's even better than its predecessor.

However, in an attempt to tell the new story – that of Rocky's adjustment to near-success and an attempt to lead a non-boxing life – the plot tends to drag and the picture takes on a murky quality.

Luckily, director, actor and scripter Sylvester Stallone and producers Irwin Winkler and Robert Chartoff know from experience audiences love to root for the underdog and have concocted an irresistible final 30 minutes.

. . . .

■ ROCKY III

1982, 99 MINS, US ◇ ⓥ
Dir Sylvester Stallone   *Prod* Irwin Winkler, Robert Chartoff   *Scr* Sylvester Stallone   *Ph* Bill Butler   *Ed* Don Zimmerman, Mark Warner   *Mus* Bill Conti   *Art Dir* Ronald Kent
● Sylvester Stallone, Carl Weathers, Mr T, Talia Shire, Burt Young, Burgess Meredith (M-G-M-/United Artists)

The real question with *Rocky III* was how Sylvester Stallone could twist the plot to make an interesting difference. He manages.

Revisiting the champ three years after the big victory, we find him and wife Talia Shire happily married with a son, a big house, lots of money and media attention after successfully defending his title 10 times.

But Clubber Lang, menacingly and beautifully played by Mr T, is also tough and hun-

R

gry for a title shot. Ailing Burgess Meredith tells Stallone he's no longer a match for T and should retire gracefully. But Stallone insists on proving himself and quickly goes down for the count under T's hammering.

Though lion-hearted and iron-jawed, it's obvious now that Stallone has never been a very skilled boxer. But Carl Weathers steps in to teach and train him, if Stallone can work up the will.

As usual, Stallone the writer-director is less successful in handling all the dramatic interims than staging the battles.

. . . .

■ ROCKY IV

1985, 91 MINS, US ◇ ⓥ
Dir Sylvester Stallone *Prod* Robert Chartoff, Irwin Winkler *Scr* Sylvester Stallone *Ph* Bill Butler *Ed* Don Zimmerman, John W. Wheeler *Mus* Vince DiCola *Art Dir* Bill Kenney
● Sylvester Stallone, Talia Shire, Burt Young, Carl Weathers, Brigitte Nielsen, Dolph Lundgren (United Artists)

Sylvester Stallone is really sloughing it off shamelessly in *Rocky IV*, but it's still impossible not to root for old Rocky Balboa to get up off the canvas and whup that bully one more time.

Beyond its visceral appeal, *Rocky IV* is truly the worst of the lot, though Stallone himself is more personable in this one and that helps. Dolph Lundgren is the most contrived opponent yet and that hurts.

Lundgren, an almost inhuman giant fighting machine created in Russian physical-fitness labs, comes to the US to challenge the champ, but is first taken on by Apollo Creed (Carl Weathers), anxious to prove himself one last time.

So it's on to Moscow where, surprise, surprise, it's going to take a lot of training to get Stallone in shape for the Soviet. Though it really makes no difference, the story gets truly dumb at this point.

Lundgren, according to the digital readout, has developed a punch of 2,000 p.s.i., which should be enough to send Rocky back to Philadelphia without a plane. Once the fight starts, however, there's no way Rocky fans can resist getting caught up in it, predictable and preposterous though it be.

. . . .

■ ROCKY V

1990, 104 MINS, US ◇ ⓥ
Dir John G. Avildsen *Prod* Irwin Winkler, Robert Chartoff *Scr* Sylvester Stallone *Ph* Steven Poster *Ed* John G. Avildsen, Michael N. Knue *Mus* Bill Conti *Art Dir* William J. Cassidy
● Sylvester Stallone, Talia Shire, Burt Young, Sage Stallone, Burgess Meredith, Tommy Morrison (United Artists)

When the underdog always wins he's not much of an underdog anymore, and the narrative cartwheels Sylvester Stallone has turned over the years to put Rocky in that position have peeled away the novelty.

So it is with *Rocky V*. Stallone again scripted and continues to evince a thudding lack of storytelling subtlety, sinking to a new low with the ending, which seems inspired by championship wrestling.

Stallone positively goes wild with cliches here: Rocky left broke by mismanagement of his fortune, a Don King-like promoter (Richard Gant) pressuring Rocky to fight again, strained relations between Rocky and his son (real-life son Sage) because of Rocky's tutelage of a young boxer (Tommy Morrison) who ultimately turns on him.

The central problem is that Rocky suffers brain damage from his various beatings in the ring, making it risky for him ever to fight again.

Burt Young has his moments as the slobbish Paulie. Talia Shire has become shrill and annoying as Adrian. Gant is perfectly hissable as Duke. Boxer-turned-actor Morrison is serviceable as the ham-fisted heavy. Bill Conti's score remains the series' greatest asset.

. . . .

■ ROGER AND ME

1989, 90 MINS, US ◇ ⓥ
Dir Michael Moore *Prod* Michael Moore *Ph* Chris Beaver, John Prusak, Kevin Rafferty, Bruce Schermer *Ed* Wendey Stanzler, Jennifer Berman
● (Dog Eat Dog)

Roger and Me is a cheeky and smart indictment against General Motors for closing its truck plant in Flint, Mich, throwing 30,000 employees out of work and, as a result, leaving many neighborhoods abandoned.

Michael Moore, a Flint native who recalls the prosperous 'Great American Dream' days of his 1950s childhood, launches a one-man documentary crusade to bring GM chairman Roger Smith back to town. He wants Smith to see the human tragedy caused by the plant closing.

He interviews fired workers, shows decaying houses across the city and two grandiose schemes to reactivate the town: the opening of a Hyatt Regency hotel and a huge shopping mall. Both fail quickly for lack of business. Tourists don't come to Flint.

Intercut are scenes of the town's rich, who seem oblivious to the plight of their fellow citizens and wonder what the fuss is about.

Pic is one-sided, for sure, but Moore makes no pretense otherwise. The irony of the title pervades the piece.

. . . .

■ ROLLERBALL

1975, 129 MINS, US ◇
Dir Norman Jewison *Prod* Norman Jewison *Scr* William Harrison *Ph* Douglas Slocombe *Ed* Antony Gibbs *Mus* Andre Previn (sup.) *Art Dir* John Box
● James Caan, John Houseman, Maud Adams, John Beck, Moses Gunn, Pamela Hensley (United Artists)

Norman Jewison's sensational futuristic drama about a world of Corporate States stars James Caan in an excellent performance as a famed athlete who fights for his identity and free will. The $5 million film was made in Munich and London.

The year is 2018, and the world has been regrouped politically to a hegemony of six conglomerate cartels. There is total material tranquility: no wars, no poverty, no unrest – and no personal free will and no God.

The ingenious way of ventilating human nature's animal-violence residual content is the world sport of rollerball, a combination of roller derby, motorcycle racing and basketball where violent death is part of the entertainment. Caan is a long-standing hero of the sport, becoming dangerously popular. He is ordered to retire. He refuses. Tilt.

The very fine music track was supervised and conducted by Andre Previn, utilizing excerpts from Bach, Shostakovich, Tschaikovsky and Albinoni/Giazotto, plus original Previn work which included the corporate anthems which begin each game.

The performances of the principals are uniformly tops. Besides the great work of Caan, John Houseman and Ralph Richardson, John (as head of the corporation) Beck is excellent as the model yahoo jock. As the women in Caan's life, Maud Adams, Pamela Hensley and Barbara Trentham step right out of today's deodorant and cosmetics teleblurbs – just the way they're supposed to be when life imitates consumer advertising imagery.

■ ROLLERCOASTER

1977, 119 MINS, US ◇ ⓥ
Dir James Goldstone *Prod* Jennings Lang *Scr* Richard Levinson, William Link *Ph* David M. Walsh *Ed* Edward A. Biery, Richard Sprague *Mus* Lalo Schifrin *Art Dir* Henry Bumstead
● George Segal, Richard Widmark, Timothy Bottoms, Henry Fonda (Universal)

Timothy Bottoms is a subdued maniac with a plan to blackmail $1 million from a group of amusement park owners.

Pic's plot is simple and uncluttered. There is a madman on the loose, one with a thorough knowledge of bombs, rollercoasters and electronics. From a short scene early on, there is a hint that he served in Vietnam, which is supposed to partly account for his instability. His sole objective is cash.

Bottoms and the man trying to outsmart him (George Segal) are adversaries who develop a mutual respect and, in a sense, a rapport.

Pic's taut opening 20 minutes depict the major catastrophe – bombing of a rollercoaster track and the subsequent derailing of the cars.

The rollercoaster rides are the picture's highlights and they are fabulous.

. . . .

■ ROLLING THUNDER

1977, 99 MINS, US ◇ ⓥ
Dir John Flynn *Prod* Lawrence Gordon *Scr* Paul Schrader, Heywood Gould *Ph* Jordon Croneweth *Ed* Frank P. Keller *Mus* Barry DeVorzon *Art Dir* Steve Berger
● William Devane, Tommy Lee Jones, Linda Haynes, Lisa Richards, Dabney Coleman, James Best (AIP)

Excellent cast performs well, but not well enough and Paul Schrader's story is strong, but not strong enough. In sum, it neither rolls nor thunders.

With coscripter Heywood Gould, Schrader follows an embittered loner to a bloody conclusion. After eight years of torture as a prisoner of war, William Devane returns to a grateful San Antonio where he receives a hero's welcome, except at home where wife Lisa Richards has fallen in love with his friend Lawrason Driscoll.

But neither the good nor the ill has much impact on Devane, who left all emotion behind in the prison camp. And even though he has a hard time animating a wooden character, Devane succeeds in making the first half of the picture the best, creating a believable reflection of the difficult adjustments of real POWs.

. . . .

■ ROLLOVER

1981, 118 MINS, US ◇
Dir Alan J. Pakula *Prod* Bruce Gilbert *Scr* David Shaber *Ph* Giuseppe Rotunno *Ed* Evan Lottman *Mus* Michael Small *Art Dir* George Jenkins
● Jane Fonda, Kris Kristofferson, Hume Cronyn, Josef Sommer, Bob Gunton, Jodi Long (Orion/Warner)

Although elegantly appointed and possessed of a provocative theme, *Rollover* is a fundamentally disappointing political-romantic thriller [from a story by David Shaber, Howard Kohn and David Weir] set in the rarified world of international high finance.

Coiffed and gowned to the hilt, Jane Fonda plays a former film star whose corporate bigwheel husband is mysteriously murdered. Bank troubleshooter Kris Kristofferson is called in to try to right the ailing firm, quickly begins consoling the widow by night as well as by day and soon accompanies her to Saudi Arabia to firm a deal for venture capital, which, while giving Fonda the board chairmanship, also hands the Arabs the final financial trump card.

Eventually transpires that the Arabs decide not to 'rollover', or redeposit, their huge sums in the bank, which sends the banking community, Wall Street and the entire international financial network into chaos.

It's a scary theme, and Pakula's previously displayed expertise at conveying pervasive paranoia triggered by massive conspiracies at high levels is perfectly in tune with the story's aims. But there's a certain lack of reality, cued in part by numerous melodramatic contrivances.

■ ROMAN HOLIDAY

1953, 118 MINS, US

Dir William Wyler   *Prod* William Wyler   *Scr* Ian McLellan Hunter, John Dighton   *Ph* Franz Planer, Henri Alekan   *Ed* Robert Swink   *Mus* Georges Auric   *Art Dir* Hal Pereira, Walter Tyler
● Gregory Peck, Audrey Hepburn, Eddie Albert, Hartley Power, Harcourt Williams (Paramount)

This William Wyler romantic comedy-drama [from a story by Ian McLellan Hunter] is the Graustarkian fable in modern dress, plus the Cinderella theme in reverse. He times the chuckles with a never-flagging pace, puts heart into the laughs, endows the footage with some boff bits of business and points up some tender, poignant scenes in using the smart script and the cast to the utmost advantage.

The aged face of the Eternal City provides a contrast to the picture's introduction of a new face, Audrey Hepburn, British ingenue who made an impression with the legit-goers in *Gigi*. Gregory Peck, in the role of American newspaperman, figures importantly in making the picture zip along engrossingly. Eddie Albert makes a major comedy contribution as a photog who secretely lenses the princess during the 24 hours she steals away from the dull court routine.

The fine script deals with a princess who rebels against the goodwill tour she is making of Europe after arriving in Rome. The adventures she encounters with Peck during the day and evening are natural and amusing. After this day of fun is over the princess and the reporter are in love, but each knows nothing can come of the Roman holiday.

All the interiors, except those in the Palazzos Brancaccio and Colonna, were lensed in Rome's Cinecitta Studios, while exteriors put on film many landmarks of the city.
□ 1953: Best Picture (Nomination)

■ ROMAN SCANDALS

1933, 93 MINS, US

Dir Frank Tuttle, Busby Berkeley   *Prod* Samuel Goldwyn   *Scr* George S. Kaufman, Robert Sherwood, William Anthony McGuire, Arthur Sheekman, Nat Perrin, George Oppenheimer   *Ph* Ray June, Gregg Toland   *Ed* Stuart Heisler   *Art Dir* Richard Day
● Eddie Cantor, Ruth Etting, Gloria Stuart, David Manners, Verree Teasdale, Edward Arnold (Goldwyn/United Artists)

Comedy high spots and moments of exotic beauty in production retrieve a sometimes ineffective Eddie Cantor vehicle. Subject matter is the hokiest kind of hoke.

Best of the bits has Cantor as the Roman emperor's food taster trying to stall off the queen's plot to poison her royal spouse and struggling at the same time with a stubborn attack of hiccoughs. Hilarity of Cantor's buffoonery lies in the dignity of the stately surroundings of the Roman court and the straight playing of the supporting cast.

Background of imperial Rome is made to order for spectacle, and the producer has made the most of it. There is a long sequence in a swank Roman women's bath, elaborated and built for pictorial effect to the last extreme. This sequence is the elaborate incidental to one of the song numbers,

'Keep Young and Beautiful', which gets a remarkably intricate build-up for the Cantor rendering in blackface.

Cantor is almost constantly on the screen for all of the hour and a half, and it's practically impossible for any funmaker to sustain top speed that length of time.

David Manners stands out in the cast, one of the few Hollywood actors who can look genuine in Roman toga. His satisfying playing of the leading straight role does a lot to sharpen the comedy angle. Gloria Stuart and Verree Teasdale in the top femme parts make an eyeful, the one blonde and the other brunette.

■ ROMAN SPRING OF MRS. STONE, THE

1962, 103 MINS, UK

Dir Jose Quintero   *Prod* Louis de Rochemont   *Scr* Gavin Lambert   *Ph* Harry Waxman   *Ed* Ralph Kemplen   *Mus* Richard Addinsell   *Prod Des* Roger Furse
● Vivien Leigh, Warren Beatty, Coral Browne, Jill St John, Lotte Lenya, Jeremy Spenser (Warner)

Vivien Leigh is the star of this gloomy, pessimistic portrait of the artist as a middle-aged widow, from Tennessee Williams' only novel. She portrays a lonely, uncertain ex-actress who has given up her profession and her past to settle in Rome following the sudden death of her wealthy husband. However reluctantly, she soon falls prey to the interests of the fortune-hunting parasites and pimps of Rome who seek monetary rewards in return for romantic favors.

But Leigh has the misfortune to fall in love with her 'young man' (Warren Beatty), who convincingly feigns amour, then flutters away on another attractive assignment provided by agent-panderer Lotte Lenya.

Leigh gives an expressive, interesting delineation – projecting intelligence and femininity, as always. Mrs Stone, however, is no Blanche DuBois. There's less to work with. Although every once in a while a little Guido Panzini creeps into his Italo dialect and Marlon Brando into his posture and expression, Beatty gives a fairly convincing characterization of the young, mercenary punk-gigolo. Lenya is frighteningly sinister as the cunning pimpette.

■ ROMANCING THE STONE

1984, 105 MINS, US

Dir Robert Zemeckis   *Prod* Michael Douglas, Jack Brodsky, Joel Douglas   *Scr* Diane Thomas   *Ph* Dean Cundey   *Ed* Donn Cambern, Frank Morriss   *Mus* Alan Silvestri, Eddy Grant   *Art Dir* Lawrence G. Paull
● Michael Douglas, Kathleen Turner, Danny DeVito, Zack Norman, Alfonso Arau, Manuel Ojeda (El Corazon/20th Century-Fox)

Living alone with her cat, Kathleen Turner writes romantic novels and cries over the outcome, assuring friend Holland Taylor that one day the writer's life will pick up for real.

Naturally, Turner receives a package mailed from South America just ahead of sister's phone call that she's been kidnapped and will die if Turner doesn't deliver the contents of the package south of the border as soon as possible.

Heading for the jungles in her high heels, Turner is like a lot of unwitting screen heroines ahead of her, guaranteed that her drab existence is about to be transformed – probably by a man, preferably handsome and adventurous. Sure enough, Michael Douglas pops out of the jungle.

The expected complications are supplied by the kidnappers, Danny DeVito and Zack Norman.

■ ROMANOFF AND JULIET

1961, 103 MINS, US

Dir Peter Ustinov   *Prod* Peter Ustinov   *Scr* Peter Ustinov   *Ph* Robert Krasker   *Ed* Renzo Lucidi   *Mus* Mario Nascimbene   *Art Dir* Alexandre Trauner
● Peter Ustinov, Sandra Dee, John Gavin, Akim Tamiroff, Suzanne Cloutier, John Phillips (Universal)

Some of the satiric toxin has gone out of Peter Ustinov's *Romanoff and Juliet* in its cinemetamorphosis, but enough of the comic chemistry remains. Ustinov has managed not only to retain the lion's share of his tongue-in-cheek swing at political hyprocisy, diplomatic pomposity and general 20th-century lack of harmony or philosophical perspective, but he has added several noteworthy observations.

His performance as the general of Concordia, a tiny mock republic feverishly wooed by Russia and the US to solicit its vital UN vote, is a beautiful blend of outrageous mugging and sly comment. When he's on, the picture's at its best. Sandra Dee and John Gavin costar as daughter and son of the US and Russian ambassadors to Concordia, whose romance and marriage ultimately blots out the political crisis, representing Ustinov's love-and-laughter platform for harmonious international relations.

■ ROMANTIC ENGLISHWOMAN, THE

1975, 115 MINS, UK/FRANCE

Dir Joseph Losey   *Prod* Daniel M. Angel   *Scr* Thomas Wiseman, Tom Stoppard   *Ph* Gerry Fisher   *Mus* Richard Hartley
● Glenda Jackson, Michael Caine, Helmut Berger, Beatrice Normand, Nathalie Delon, Michel Lonsdale (DIAL/Meric-Matalon)

Joseph Losey has concocted a low-key, sitcom-type pic [from the book by Thomas Wiseman] using the familiar theme of an unsatisfied, well-heeled married woman with a child on a romantic escapade.

Glenda Jackson plays in her clipped, cold way as she is off to the German bath and gambling site of Baden-Baden at the start of the pic. There she notices Helmut Berger who is noted as smuggling in heroin which he inanely stashes in a rain drain and which is later washed away.

In Britain the husband, Michael Caine, invites him to stay. Eventually she and Berger are caught necking by Caine and she runs off after Berger.

Pic remains disappointing in its cocktail of satire, intrigue and romantic comedy-drama that do not quite jell.

■ ROME EXPRESS

1932, 94 MINS, UK

Dir Walter Forde   *Prod* Michael Balcon   *Scr* Sidney Gilliat, Clifford Grey, Frank Vosper, Ralph Stock   *Ph* Gunther Krampf   *Ed* Frederick Y. Smith   *Art Dir* A. L. Mazzei
● Conrad Veidt, Esther Ralston, Joan Barry, Cedric Hardwicke, Frank Vosper, Hugh Williams (Gaumont-British)

The acting and casting call attention to *Rome Express*. A combination of *Grand Hotel* and *Shanghai Express*, nevertheless it is original in conception and execution. Casting is superb and the players all excellent.

Conrad Veidt does an unusually good job as Zurta, a criminal, and Frank Vosper makes a human being of Jolif, the head of the French Surete.

Story is laid entirely on a train which travels out of Paris. Veidt and Hugh Williams are adventurers chasing Donald Calthrop, who double-crossed them after stealing a famous painting. Also on the train are Joan Barry and Harold Huth, married but not traveling with their legal mates; Esther Ralston, a film star, and her American manager, Finlay Currie; as also Cedric Hardwicke, a philanthropist, and his secretary (Eliot Makeham); and Vosper, head of the French police. Search for the picture leads to murder, with all those above named involved. Theft, murder and explanation unravel before the train ends its run.

. . . .

■ ROMEO AND JULIET

1936, 130 MINS, US

Dir George Cukor   *Prod* Irving Thalberg   *Scr* Talbot Jennings   *Ph* William Daniels   *Ed* Margaret Booth   *Mus* Herbert Stothart   *Art Dir* Cedric Gibbons, Oliver Messel
● Norma Shearer, Leslie Howard, John Barrymore, Edna May Oliver, Basil Rathbone, C. Aubrey Smith (M-G-M)

Romeo and Juliet is a faithful and not too imaginative translation to the screen of the William Shakespeare play.

Romeo and Juliet is a love-story tragedy, requiring precise pace in order that the beauty of its poetry shall be thoroughly grasped. The fine lyric qualities have been retained, and from that point of view there is every reason to laud the production as successful. In accomplishing this worthy purpose, however, the tempo is a beat or two slower than the familiar methods of modern story telling.

Surprisingly few liberties have been taken with the original text. Preparation for the screen was confined chiefly to condensation.

Norma Shearer adds an important portrait to her gallery of roles. She never conveys the impression that she is getting a great kick out of the part, and her restraint aids her conception of the characterization of the daughter of the Capulets, a child of 14.

The famous balcony love scene with Leslie Howard is played sincerely and beautifully. She makes the final tragic moments of the play convincing and moving.

Against her child-like figure, Howard and Ralph Forbes, rival suitors, appear years her senior. Howard's Romeo is a forthright young man of considerable determination, rather than a headstrong, impassioned young lover. But what illusion is lost in looks, Howard adequately makes up in speech. His lines are clearly spoken.

After a rather hesitant beginning John Barrymore makes a real, live person out of Mercutio. His opening scenes are hurried, noisy and indistinct. But the passages preceding and following the fatal duel with Basil Rathbone (Tybalt) are exciting and thrilling. Barrymore plays in the grand manner, which the part allows.
□ 1936: Best Picture (Nomination)

. . . .

■ ROMEO AND JULIET

1968, 152 MINS, ITALY/UK ◇ ⓥ

Dir Franco Zeffirelli   *Prod* Dino De Laurentiis   *Scr* Franco Brusati, Masolino D'Amico   *Ph* Pasquale de Santis   *Ed* Reginald Mills   *Mus* Nino Rota   *Art Dir* Luciano Puccini
● Olivia Hussey, Leonard Whiting, Milo O'Shea, Michael York, John McEnery, Pat Heywood (Verona/De Laurentiis/British Home Entertainments)

Shot entirely in Italy, director Franco Zeffirelli has conjured up a very good eyeful, with splendid use of color in costumes and backgrounds.

Street and fight sequences give film plenty of movement, allied with bold effective cuts in the Bard's text. Zeffirelli has tried, and often succeeds, in giving the film an up-to-date feeling.

Neither Olivia Hussey nor Leonard Whiting has the experience, looks or vital personality to rise to the pinnacles of the star-cross'd lovers. Dramatic highlights are stilted and much of the verse flat to the ear. Rarely will audiences be moved to throat-gulping by the plight of the young couple.

For all Hussey's prettiness and Whiting's shy charm it is clear that they do not understand one tenth of the meaning of their lines and it is a drawback from which the film cannot recover. The young leads are surrounded by some excellent pro performers, which helps them, but also shows up their inadequacies.
□ 1968: Best Picture (Nomination)

. . . .

■ ROOKIE, THE

1990, 121 MINS, US ◇ ⓥ

Dir Clint Eastwood   *Prod* Howard Kazanjian, Steven Siebert, David Valdes   *Scr* Boaz Yakin, Scott Spiegel   *Ph* Jack N. Green   *Ed* Joel Cox   *Mus* Lennie Niehaus   *Art Dir* Judy Cammer
● Clint Eastwood, Charlie Sheen, Raul Julia, Sonia Braga, Tom Skerritt, Lara Flyn Boyle (Malpaso/Warner)

Overlong, sadistic and stale even by the conventions of the buddy pic genre, Clint Eastwood's 'The Rookie' is actually *Dirty Harry 5¹⁄₂* since Eastwood's tough-as-nails cop Nick Pulovski could just as easily be named Harry Callahan, and his penchant for breaking in partners (and getting them killed) is a holdover from Harry's first three patrols.

This time, however, the troubles lie in partner Charlie Sheen, a rich kid working out childhood guilt and hostility against his parents by playing policeman. Pair pursues a stolen-car ring operated by ruthless thief Raul Julia and sweaty henchwoman Sonia Braga (in a nearly non-verbal role). Pulovski is taken hostage, and Sheen's character has to find himself by, essentially, disregarding all conventional legal channels and destroying as much property as possible.

The normally brilliant Julia lapses into and out of a bad German accent, Braga has just a window-dressing bad-girl role, and *Twin Peaks*' Lara Flynn Boyle is Sheen's blandly drawn girlfriend. Eastwood the actor seems rightfully bored with the material, while Sheen continues to hammer away at his own tough-guy rep with only marginal success.

. . . .

■ ROOM AT THE TOP

1959, 117 MINS, UK ⓥ

Dir Jack Clayton   *Prod* John Woolf, James Woolf   *Scr* Neil Paterson   *Ph* Freddie Francis   *Ed* Ralph Kemplen   *Mus* Mario Nascimbene
● Laurence Harvey, Simone Signoret, Heather Sears, Donald Wolfit, Donald Houston, Hermione Baddeley (Remus)

Room at the Top, based on John Braine's best-selling novel, is an adult, human picture. Neil Paterson's literate, well-molded screenplay is enhanced by subtle, intelligent direction from first-timer Jack Clayton and a batch of top-notch performances.

Laurence Harvey takes a job as an accountant in the local government offices of a North Country town. He is an alert young man with a chip on his shoulder because of his humble background. He quickly finds that the small town is virtually controlled by a self-made millionaire and is dominated by those with money and power. Harvey is determined to break down this class-consciousness and sets his cap at the millionaire's daughter. At the same time he is irresistibly drawn to an unhappily married Frenchwoman (Simone Signoret) with whom he has a violent affair.

The Clayton touch produces some fine scenes. These include the young girl's first capitulation to Harvey, the manner in which the millionaire stresses his power over the young upstart, the love scenes between Harvey and Simone Signoret and their quarrel and parting. Above all, Clayton never loses the authentic 'small town' atmosphere.

Harvey makes a credible figure of the young man, likeable despite his weaknesses, torn between love and ambition, and he brings strength and feeling to his love scenes with Signoret. She gives perhaps, the best performance in a capital all-round cast. Heather Sears has less opportunity as the young girl.
□ 1959: Best Picture (Nomination)

. . . .

■ ROOM WITH A VIEW, A

1986, 115 MINS, UK ◇ ⓥ

Dir James Ivory   *Prod* Ismail Merchant   *Scr* Ruth Prawer Jhabvala   *Ph* Tony Pierce-Roberts   *Ed* Humphrey Dixon   *Mus* Richard Robbins   *Art Dir* Gianni Quaranta, Brian Ackland-Snow
● Maggie Smith, Helena Bonham Carter, Denholm Elliott, Julian Sands, Daniel Day Lewis, Simon Callow (Merchant-Ivory/Goldcrest)

A thoroughly entertaining screen adaptation of novelist E.M. Forster's comedy of manners about the Edwardian English upper class at home and abroad, distinguished by superb ensemble acting, intelligent writing and stunning design.

Set in 1907, *A Room with a View* moves between a pensione in Florence, Italy where a well-to-do young English lady, Lucy Honeychurch (Helena Bonham Carter) is traveling on the type of compulsory horizon-broadening tour that was the prerogative of her class, chaperoned by her fussy, punctilious aunt Charlotte (Maggie Smith), and the insular Surrey countryside where she lives with her mother (Rosemary Leach).

James Ivory's direction makes what might have been a talky period piece in lesser hands a consistently engaging study of the mores and morality of a bygone time.
□ 1986: Best Picture (Nomination)

. . . .

■ ROOSTER COGBURN

1975, 107 MINS, US ◇

Dir Stuart Millar   *Prod* Hal B. Wallis   *Scr* Martin Julien   *Ph* Harry Stradling Jr   *Ed* Robert Swink   *Mus* Laurence Rosenthal   *Art Dir* Preston Ames
● John Wayne, Katharine Hepburn, Anthony Zerbe, Richard Jordan, John McIntyre, Strother Martin (Universal)

Rooster Cogburn has the exciting charisma of John Wayne and Katharine Hepburn, plus the memories of Wayne's Oscar-winning performance in *True Grit*.

The title is based on the character from Charles Portis' novel *True Grit*, which picks up judge John McIntyre after another trigger-happy foulup. But outlaw Richard Jordan and gang, aided by Anthony Zerbe, Wayne's onetime scout, is acting up, causing several deaths including that of preacher Jon Lormer, survived by spinster daughter Hepburn and Indian lad Richard Romancito. Latter pair join reinstated marshal Wayne to track down the bad guys.

A little artfulness, a little creativity, a little subtlety could work wonders. Like Jordan not chewing up the scenery like a silent pix heavy. Like Hepburn and Wayne not doing a frontier version of The Bickersons. Like not shoe-horning *The African Queen* plot line into this script.

. . . .

■ ROOTS OF HEAVEN, THE

1958, 130 MINS, US ◇

Dir John Huston   *Prod* Darryl F. Zanuck   *Scr* Romain Gary, Patrick Leigh-Fermor   *Ph* Oswald Morris   *Ed* Russell Lloyd   *Mus* Malcolm Arnold   *Art Dir* Stephen Grimes, Raymond Gabutti
● Errol Flynn, Juliette Greco, Trevor Howard, Eddie Albert, Orson Welles, Herbert Lom (20th Century-Fox)

The Roots of Heaven has striking pictorial aspects, some exciting performances and builds to a pulsating climax of absorbing tension. Unfortunately, these plus factors almost all come in the second half of the picture.

The locale of the screenplay, from Romain Gary's novel, is French Equatorial Africa. Trevor Howard, whose presence is never completely explained, is launching a campaign to save the elephants of Africa. He believes they are threatened with extinction from big game hunters, ivory poachers and the encroachment of civilization. When he tries to get signers of his petition to outlaw the killings, he is rebuffed on all fronts.

Howard gets only two signatures. One is from Errol Flynn, an alcoholic British ex-officer, and the other is from Juliette Greco, a prostitute. So Howard decides on a campaign of harassment of the hunters and his counter-attack attracts the attention of a safari-ing American TV personality, Orson Welles; a Danish scientist, Friedrich Ledebur; a German nobleman, Olivier Hussenot, and some natives who propose to use Howard as a symbol of their own resistance to colonial law and practice.

Director John Huston has staged his exterior scenes superbly. Full advantage is taken here of the arduous African locations. Howard gives a fine performance and is responsible for conveying as much as comes across of the tricky theme. Flynn plays the drunken officer competently but without suggesting any latent nobility or particular depth. Greco is interesting without being very moving. Orson Welles in a brief bit (reportedly done as a favor to producer Darryl F. Zanuck) is a pinwheel of flashing vigor, his evil to be lamented.

● ●

■ **ROPE**

1948, 80 MINS, US ◇ ⓥ

Dir Alfred Hitchcock   *Prod* Alfred Hitchcock
Scr Arthur Laurents, Hume Cronyn   *Ph* Joseph Valentine, William V. Skall   *Ed* William H. Ziegler
Mus David Buttolph   *Art Dir* Perry Ferguson
● James Stewart, John Dall, Farley Granger, Cedric Hardwicke, Constance Collier (Warner/Transatlantic)

Hitchcock could have chosen a more entertaining subject with which to use the arresting camera and staging technique displayed in *Rope*. Theme is of a thrill murder, done for no reason but to satisfy a sadistical urge and intellectual vanity. Plot has its real-life counterpart in the infamous Loeb-Leopold case, and is based on the play by Patrick Hamilton.

Feature of the picture is that story action is continuous without time lapses. Action takes place within an hour-and-a-half period and the film footage nearly duplicates the span, being 80 minutes. It is entirely confined to the murder apartment of two male dilettantes, intellectual morons who commit what they believe to be the perfect crime, then celebrate the deed with a ghoulish supper served to the victim's relatives and friends from atop the chest in which the body is concealed.

To achieve his effects, Hitchcock put his cast and technicians through lengthy rehearsals before turning a camera.

James Stewart, as the ex-professor who first senses the guilt of his former pupils and nibbles away at their composure with verbal barbs, does a commanding job. John Dall stands out as the egocentric who masterminds the killing and ghoulish wake. Equally good is Farley Granger as the weakling partner in crime.

● ●

■ **ROSARY MURDERS, THE**

1987, 105 MINS, US ◇ ⓥ

Dir Fred Walton   *Scr* Elmore Leonard, Fred Walton
Ph David Golia   *Ed* Sam Vitale   *Mus* Bobby Laurel, Don Sebesky
● Donald Sutherland, Charles Durning, Josef Sommer, Belinda Bauer (Goldwyn)

A string of a half-dozen murders committed by someone with a grudge against the Catholic Church, his victims being nuns and priests in a Detroit parish, is lacking in suspense or dramatic buildup, and what should have been the final climatic sequences are as flat as a holy wafer.

Pic revolves mostly around a priest, Father Koesler, who sets about trying to solve the murders while the police seem to be twiddling their thumbs. The priest turns sleuth after the murderer drops a few clues to him during a confessional box session. As a man of the cloth, latter can't tip off the police or probable victims because of his secrecy vows.

Donald Sutherland puts in a good performance as the liberal-minded investigating priest, and Charles Durning is fine as the hard-line father superior.

● ●

■ **ROSE, THE**

1979, 134 MINS, US ◇ ⓥ

Dir Mark Rydell   *Prod* Marvin Worth   *Scr* Bill Kerby, Bo Goldman   *Ph* Vilmos Zsigmond   *Ed* Robert L. Wolfe   *Mus* Paul A. Rothchild   *Art Dir* Richard MacDonald
● Bette Midler, Alan Bates, Frederic Forrest, Harry Dean Stanton, Barry Primus, David Keith (20th Century-Fox)

Producers haven't flinched from picking the scabs off the body of 1960s rock-and-roll. While there are certainly similarities to the tragic story of Janis Joplin, *The Rose* emerges as its own self-contained tale.

What's puzzling is that the screenwriters have chosen to dwell solely on the downward career spiral of Bette Midler's character, known on and off-stage as The Rose.

Revolving around the star are various satellites, including boyfriend Frederic Forrest, manager Alan Bates and road manager Barry Primus.

Result is an ultra-realistic look at the infusion of money, sex, drugs and booze into the simple process of singing a song, a chore Midler does faultlessly in several excellent concert sequences.

● ●

■ **ROSE OF WASHINGTON SQUARE**

1939, 90 MINS, US

Dir Gregory Ratoff   *Prod* Nunnally Johnson
Scr Nunnally Johnson   *Ph* Karl Freund   *Ed* Louis Loeffler   *Mus* Louis Silvers (dir)   *Art Dir* Richard Day, Rudolph Sternad
● Tyrone Power, Alice Faye, Al Jolson, William Frawley, Joyce Compton (20th Century-Fox)

Of the three co-stars this is Al Jolson's picture. But it's not much of a filmusical. It's primarily a story deficiency. Nunnally Johnson did the screenplay and production, although original by John Larkin and Jerry Horwin is as much to blame.

A major, solo title emphasizes that the plot structure is fictional. However, the Fannie Brice-Nicky Arnstein saga is an incidental to a show business romance where Al Jolson (billed as Ted Cotter, but he might just as well have been called Jolson) is the altruistic patron of the beauteous and talented Alice Faye. She in turn is stuck on the wrong-guy character played by Tyrone Power.

Faye is still plenty on the s.a. side, excepting for a few camera angles that don't flatter her chin-line. Power's vacillating characterization is a missout.

● ●

■ **ROSE TATTOO, THE**

1955, 117 MINS, US

Dir Daniel Mann   *Prod* Hal Wallis   *Scr* Tennessee Williams   *Ph* James Wong Howe   *Ed* Warren Low
Mus Alex North   *Art Dir* Hal Pereira, Tambi Larsen

● Anna Magnani, Burt Lancaster, Marisa Pavan, Ben Cooper, Jo Van Fleet, Virginia Grey (Paramount)

The Rose Tattoo creates a realistic Italiano atmosphere in the bayou country of the south, establishes vivid characters with one glaring exception and dwells upon a story that is important only because it gives its key character a jumping-off point for fascinating histrionics.

Anna Magnani gives *Tattoo* its substance; she's spellbinding as the signora content with the memory of the fidelity of her husband until she discovers he had a blonde on the side before his banana truck carried him to death.

The characters inspire little sympathy. Magnani has animalistic drive and no beauty. Burt Lancaster, as the village idiot by inheritance, is called upon to take on a role bordering on the absurd.

Otherwise Daniel Mann does fine in the directing. He provides pace where some situations might have been static.

☐ 1955: Best Picture (Nomination)

● ●

■ **ROSEBUD**

1975, 126 MINS, US ◇

Dir Otto Preminger   *Prod* Preminger   *Scr* Erik Lee Preminger   *Ph* Denys Coop   *Ed* Peter Thornton
Mus Laurent Petitgirard   *Art Dir* Michael Seymour
● Peter O'Toole, Richard Attenborough, Cliff Gorman, Claude Dauphin, John V. Lindsay, Peter Lawford (United Artists)

Political tumult story, involving Palestine Liberation Organization terrorist kidnapping, is a bland and unexciting film. Peter O'Toole heads the cast as a Briton, secret agenting for the U.S., who sorts out the crisis.

An episodic collage of long sequences which cross cut between the yacht heist of five young wealthy girls, and the efforts of their families and police to track down their kidnappers. O'Toole (who replaced Robert Mitchum after shooting began) is recruited from his CIA cover as a *Newsweek International* reporter to locate the girls and the PLO group.

O'Toole's is among the few strong performances, but that isn't saying much. As a foreign policy document, *Rosebud* at least will not cause controversy, because as a motion picture, it's a crashing bore.

● ●

■ **ROSELAND**

1977, 103 MINS, US ◇ ⓥ

Dir James Ivory   *Prod* Ismail Merchant   *Scr* Ruth Prawere Jhabvala   *Ph* Ernest Vincze   *Ed* Humphrey Dixon, Richard Schmiechen   *Mus* Michael Gibson
● Teresa Wright, Lou Jacobi, Don de Natale, Louise Kirtland, Geraldine Chaplin, Helen Gallagher (Merchant-Ivory)

There is romance to the notion that our buildings will outlast us, that our passions will be seen and remembered within the walls while we go on our way to our just desserts. That is the emotional underpinning of *Roseland*, a clean, well-lighted ballroom of New York's West Side.

Standout is Lilia Skala, playing an elderly German woman with the bearing of Bismarck, who confides to her sleepy Peabody (a Roseland dance) partner, David Thomas, that she has had to do cleaning and work as a cook at Schrafft's to pay her way.

Second tale of a gigolo, nicely crafted by Christopher Walken, is of his failure to separate himself from Joan Copeland, excellent in her portrayal of a lonely and dying woman now buying what her faded glamor once commanded.

● ●

ROSEMARY'S BABY

1968, 134 MINS, US ◇ Ⓥ

Dir Roman Polanski   *Prod* William Castle   *Scr* Roman
Polanski   *Ph* William Fraker   *Ed* Sam O'Steen, Bob
Wyman   *Mus* Christopher Komeda   *Art Dir* Richard
Sylbert

● Mia Farrow, John Cassavetes, Ruth Gordon, Sidney
Blackmer, Maurice Evans, Ralph Bellamy (Paramount)

Several exhilarating milestones are achieved
in *Rosemary's Baby*, an excellent film version of
Ira Levin's diabolical chiller novel. Writer-
director Roman Polanski has triumphed in
his first US-made pic. The film holds attention without explicit violence or gore.

Mia Farrow and John Cassavetes, a likeable young married couple, take a flat in a
rundown New York building. Ralph Bellamy, an obstetrician prescribing some
strange pre-natal nourishment for Farrow
and Maurice Evans, Farrow's sole ally, who
dies a mysterious death, as well as Charles
Grodin, enter the plot at adroit intervals.

The near-climax – Farrow has been
drugged so as to conceive by Satan – and the
final wallop make for genuine cliff hanger
interest.

Farrow's performance is outstanding. Cassavetes handles particularly well the difficult
projection of a husband as much in love with
his wife as with success. Neighbour Ruth
Gordon is pleasantly unrestrained in her
pushy self-interest, quite appropriate herein,
while other principals score solidly.

ROSENCRANTZ AND GUILDENSTERN ARE DEAD

1991, 118 MINS, UK Ⓥ

Dir Tom Stoppard   *Prod* Michael Brandman, Emanuel
Azenberg   *Scr* Tom Stoppard   *Ph* Peter Biziou
Ed Nicolas Gaster   *Mus* Stanley Myers
Art Dir Vaughan Edwards

● Garry Oldman, Tim Roth, Richard Dreyfuss, Iain
Glen, Joanna Roth, Donald Sumpter (Brandenberg)

Marking his debut as director, playwright
Tom Stoppard takes two marginal characters
from Shakespeare's *Hamlet*, and places them
at the center of a comedy-drama, while the
major characters of the play – Hamlet, Ophelia, Claudius and the rest – are only part of
the background.

Rosencrantz and Guildenstern are never
certain about what's going on in Elsinore.
They overhear crucial conversations and
encounters, they talk briefly to the King and
to Hamlet, and, in the end, they accompany
Hamlet on a voyage to England, but they're
never a part of the central drama.

Stoppard's 1967 play has been seen as a
mixture of Samuel Beckett and Shakespeare,
but on film, he adds cinematic references so
that the two protagonists, with their endless
word games, come across as a mixture of Abbott & Costello (the 'Who's On First' routine) and Laurel and Hardy (with the clumsy
Rosencrantz forever annoying and frustrating
the superior Guildenstern). There's also a
touch of Monty Python in the zaniness of the
characters and their verbal and visual antics.

Gary Oldman and Tim Roth are splendid
in their roles. Oldman plays his character as
a shrewd simpleton, and Roth plays his as a
man who thinks he's clever, but really isn't.
Also giving a formidable performance is
Richard Dreyfuss as the leader of a band of
strolling players.

ROUGH CUT

1980, 112 MINS, US ◇ Ⓥ

Dir Don Siegel   *Prod* David Merrick   *Scr* Francis Burns
[= Larry Gelbart]   *Ph* Freddie Young   *Ed* Doug
Stewart   *Mus* Nelson Riddle   *Art Dir* Ted Haworth

● Burt Reynolds, Lesley-Anne Down, David Niven,
Patrick Magee, Joss Ackland, Timothy West (Paramount)

Rough Cut emerges as an undistinctive, frothy

romantic comedy that will charm a few and
probably miss the eye of many. Love match
of Burt Reynolds and Lesley-Anne Down
works only in selected spots and frame of the
story, intrigue over a $30 million diamond
heist, is hard-pressed to sustain interest.

Blake Edwards was originally scheduled to
direct the picture for David Merrick in 1977
with Larry Gelbart scripting and Reynolds
top-lining. Edwards eventually bowed out
and Reynolds took on other films until Don
Siegel was signed to helm in 1979. Siegel was
fired and rehired by Merrick and pic finally
wound.

Trouble began when Merrick decided he
wanted a new ending and Siegel insisted he
had the final cut. Result was Merrick hiring
Robert Ellis Miller to shoot a fourth finale.

Problem seems to lie in much of the dialog,
which comes across as both wooden and
contrived. Reynolds and Down do what they
can but their attempts at witty banter never
appear natural.

ROUGH NIGHT IN JERICHO

1967, 102 MINS, US ◇

Dir Arnold Laven   *Prod* Martin Rackin   *Scr* Sydney
Boehm, Marvin H. Albert   *Ph* Russell Metty   *Ed* Ted J.
Kent   *Mus* Don Costa   *Art Dir* Alexander Golitzen,
Frank Arrigo

● Dean Martin, George Peppard, Jean Simmons, John
McIntire, Slim Pickens, Don Galloway (Universal)

Most unusual aspect about this production is
offbeat casting of Dean Martin as a heavy
without a single redeeming quality. George
Peppard is the hero. Both are embroiled in a
bloody and violent western.

Plotwise, *Rough Night in Jericho* frequently
carries a nebulous story line, particularly in
limning the actions of Martin, onetime lawman turned vicious town boss. Screenplay,
an adaptation of Marvin H. Albert's novel
The Man in Black, is lacking in the suspense
one expects from a big league western but
regulation action is there in good measure.

Peppard plays a former deputy US marshal
who becomes involved in the affairs of the
town of Jericho – and Martin – when he
arrives with John McIntire, onetime marshal
whom he once served under. Latter has come
to help Jean Simmons save her stage line,
coveted by Martin, who also wants its femme
owner.

'ROUND MIDNIGHT

1986, 133 MINS, FRANCE/US ◇ Ⓥ

Dir Bertrand Tavernier   *Prod* Irwin Winkler
Scr Bertrand Tavernier, David Rayfiel   *Ph* Bruno de
Keyzer   *Ed* Armand Psenny   *Mus* Herbie Hancock
Art Dir Alexandre Trauner

● Dexter Gordon, Francois Cluzet, Gabrielle Haker,
Sandra Reaves-Phillips, Lonette McKee, Christine Pascal
(Little Bear/PECF/Warner)

'Round Midnight is a superbly crafted music
world drama in which Gallic director
Bertrand Tavernier pays a moving dramatic
tribute to the great black musicians who lived
and performed in Paris in the late 1950s. The
$3 million film is dedicated to jazz giants Bud
Powell and Lester Young, the composite
inspiration for the story's central personage.

With his American co-scripter, David Rayfiel, Tavernier has placed deftly the themes of
cultural roots, affinities and distances at the
heart of the screenplay, which dramatizes the
friendship between an aging jazz saxophonist, who has accepted an engagement at
the legendary Blue Note club in Saint-
Germain-des-Pres, and a passionate young
French admirer who is ready to make personal sacrifices to help his idol.

Tavernier cast a non-professional in the
central role: Dexter Gordon, the 63-year-old
jazz veteran whom Tavernier has long

admired. With his hoarse, hesitant diction
and his lanky shuffle, Gordon fills the part of
the world-weary artist with his own jagged
warmth.

Film is no less a treat for the eye as for the
ear. Shot almost entirely in the Epinay
studios north of Paris, production is vividly
designed by veteran Alexandre Trauner.

ROXANNE

1987, 107 MINS, US ◇ Ⓥ

Dir Fred Schepisi   *Prod* Michael Rachmil, Daniel
Melnick   *Scr* Steve Martin   *Ph* Ian Baker   *Ed* John
Scott   *Mus* Bruce Smeaton   *Art Dir* Jack DeGovia

● Steve Martin, Daryl Hannah, Rick Rossovich, Shelley
Duvall (Columbia)

As a reworking of Edmond Rostand's play
Cyrano de Bergerac, the only reason to see the
film is for a few bits of inspired nonsense by
Steve Martin as the nosey lover. Written by
Martin to suit his special talent for sight gags,
this Cyrano, called CB here, is just a wild and
crazy guy with a big nose and a gift for gab.

The central plot device of the play, in which
a true love writes letters to help another
suitor with the same woman he doesn't love
as much, is here adapted to a small ski community in Washington State where Martin is
fire chief.

The film is barely underway when Roxanne
(Daryl Hannah) is out of her clothes and
locked out of her house. When CB comes to
the rescue it's love at first sight, but his
enlarged proboscis disqualifies him as a
serious suitor, or so he thinks.

Instead, Roxanne turns her attentions to
Chris (Rick Rossovich), a new recruit on the
fire department who is all but rendered dumb
in front of women. Eventually, Roxanne
learns Rossovich is only after her body and
realizes Martin loves her truly.

Aussie director Fred Schepisi, who has
elsewhere handled much rougher material,
does a professional job of creating a breezy
atmosphere, but in the end it's hopelessly
sappy stuff.

ROXIE HART

1942, 72 MINS, US

Dir William A. Wellman   *Prod* Nunnally Johnson
Scr Nunnally Johnson   *Ph* Leon Shamroy   *Ed* James B.
Clark   *Mus* Alfred Newman

● Ginger Rogers, Adolphe Menjou, George
Montgomery, Lynne Overman, Nigel Bruce, Phil Silvers
(20th Century-Fox)

Maurine Watkins' play [*Chicago*] of a girl
who basks in the publicity spotlight for a brief
period when accused of murder is broadly
embellished via the screenplay by Nunnally
Johnson and direction by William Wellman.

Picture aims solely for adult attention. Ginger Rogers is the girl who stands trial for
murder committed by her husband, after getting buildup on publicity values by cynical
crime reporter Lynne Overman. Banner-
lined all over town, Roxie becomes an enthusiastic stooge for the press, court and slick
mouthpiece (Adolphe Menjou).

Ginger Rogers does well as the tough girl
who is dazzled by the sudden attention, but
seems to overdo her characterization at
several points. Menjou is excellent as the
theatric and wily criminal mouthpiece who
craftily steers the judge and jury to the proper
verdict.

ROYAL FLASH

1975, 121 MINS, UK ◇

Dir Richard Lester   *Prod* David B. Picker, Denis O'Dell
Scr George McDonald Fraser   *Ph* Geoffrey
Unsworth   *Ed* John Victor Smith   *Mus* Ken Thorne
Art Dir Terence Marsh

● Malcolm McDowell, Alan Bates, Florinda Bolkan, Oliver Reed, Britt Ekland, Lionel Jeffries (20th Century-Fox)

Royal Flash is a royal pain. Richard Lester's formula period comedy style [adapted by George MacDonald Fraser from his novel], as enduring as it is not particularly endearing, achieves its customary levels of posturing silliness.

Malcolm McDowell, fleeing a bordello raid, falls in with Florinda Bolkan, playing Lola Montez, in turn alienating Oliver Reed's Otto von Bismarck. The latter, with accomplice Alan Bates and hit-men Lionel Jeffries and Tom Bell, force McDowell to impersonate a Prussian nobleman for purposes of marriage to duchess Britt Ekland. Complex political, sexual and survival strategies lurch the plot forward.

The players are as competent as the film allows, and their work in other films is proof of their talent.

● ●

■ ROYAL HUNT OF THE SUN, THE

1969, 121 MINS, UK ◇
Dir Irving Lerner   *Prod* Eugene Frenke, Philip Yordan
Scr Philip Yordan   *Ph* Roger Barlow   *Ed* Peter Parasheles   *Mus* Marc Wilkinson   *Art Dir* Eugene Lourie
● Robert Shaw, Christopher Plummer, Nigel Davenport, Michael Craig, Leonard Whiting, Andrew Keir (Rank)

Based on Peter Shaffer's rich, imaginative play, *Royal Hunt of the Sun* is a film that's striking in many ways, visually and literately.

It has many plusses, notably a standout duo of performances by Robert Shaw and Christopher Plummer and some very sound supporting and an intelligent top-drawer script by Philip Yordan.

Story concerns General Francisco Pizarro, Spanish soldier of fortune who, for the third time penetrates Peru, the Land of the Sun, in search of the Kingdom of Gold. He leads a small, ill-equipped band with which to tackle the forces of the Inca.

Shaw powerfully portrays the conquistador and his varying and complicated moods of violence, sadness, despair, anger and puzzlement. Plummer is particularly outstanding in the tricky role of King Atahuallpa, though not always entirely audible due to the curious accent he affects.

● ●

■ ROYAL WEDDING

1951, 93 MINS, US ◇ Ⓥ
Dir Stanley Donen   *Prod* Arthur Freed   *Scr* Alan Jay Lerner   *Ph* Robert Planck   *Ed* Albert Akst
Mus Johnny Green (dir.)
● Fred Astaire, Jane Powell, Peter Lawford, Sarah Churchill, Keenan Wynn, Albert Sharpe (M-G-M)

This is an engaging concoction of songs and dances in a standard musical framework, brightly dressed in color to show off its physical attributes.

Score uses up nine tunes to back the singing and terping, and two of the numbers are sock enough to almost carry the picture by themselves. They are Astaire's solo dance on a ceiling, upside-down, and the teaming with Powell in a sort of Frankie-and-Johnny-apache-hepcat presentation that will click with audiences.

The ceiling stepping to the Burton Lane-Alan Jay Lerner 'You're All the World to Me' combines technical magic and Astaire's foot wizardry into a potent novelty. 'How Could You Believe Me' sets up the earthy Astaire-Powell delivery of the other outstanding musical sequence.

Light plot sees Astaire and Powell as a brother-sister team of Broadway musical stars. They go to London to open their show during the period when preparations are being made for the royal marriage. In between presentation of the musical numbers, Astaire falls in love with Sarah Churchill, show hoofer, and Powell catches the love bug from Peter Lawford, an English lord-romeo.

● ●

■ R.P.M.
REVOLUTIONS PER MINUTE

1970, 92 MINS, US ◇ Ⓥ
Dir Stanley Kramer   *Prod* Stanley Kramer   *Scr* Erich Segal   *Ph* Michel Hugo   *Ed* William A. Lyon
Mus Barry DeVorzon, Perry Botkin Jr   *Art Dir* Robert Clatworthy
● Anthony Quinn, Ann-Margret, Gary Lockwood, Paul Winfield, Graham Jarvis, Alan Hewitt (Columbia)

Subtitled 'Revolutions Per Minute', this campus crisis meller slowly spins its improbable wheels to the climactic production number involving a student riot.

Anthony Quinn stars as an harassed college president, Ann-Margret is his plot-irrelevant young mistress, and Gary Lockwood is a student radical. The treatment is deja vu, Eric Segal's script is replete with glib one-liners but lacking real story fibre, and Kramer's direction is dull.

Quinn is introduced as a 53-year-old professor, risen to his post from Spanish Harlem and popular with his students. At the outset, the current college head has thrown in the towel as students have occupied the Administration Bldg, housing a big computer.

Lockwood, along with Paul Winfield, are the radical student leaders.

● ●

■ RUBY

1977, 84 MINS, US ◇ Ⓥ
Dir Curtis Harrington   *Prod* George Edwards
Scr George Edwards, Barry Schneider   *Ph* William Mendenhall   *Ed* Bill McGee   *Mus* Don Ellis
● Piper Laurie, Stuart Whitman, Roger Davis, Janit Baldwin, Crystin Sinclaire, Paul Kent (Dimension/Krantz)

In the cookbook school of filmmaking *Ruby* is strictly leftovers. Begin with a hunk of the occult. Add a cup of 1950s nostalgia, some hardboiled detective, a dash of camp from old horror movies and sprinkle with violence.

Most of the pic's action takes place around Ruby's Drive-In. Piper Laurie is the one-time gun moll and wife of a big-time mobster. She now owns a drive-in staffed by 'associates' of her dead husband. He was gunned down 16 years ago when someone finked on him, but his spirit is back to haunt the drive-in.

He gets the job done: a projectionist is strangled with film; a concession stand attendant stuffed into a soda machine; and the dead mobster's daughter afflicted with a case of the shaking bed.

Performances are generally poor.

● ●

■ RUBY GENTRY

1952, 82 MINS, US Ⓥ
Dir King Vidor   *Prod* Joseph Bernhard   *Scr* Silvia Richards   *Ph* Russell Harlan   *Ed* Terry Morse
Mus Heinz Roemheld
● Jennifer Jones, Charlton Heston, Karl Malden, Tom Tully, James Anderson, Josephine Hutchinson (Bernhard-Vidor/20th Century-Fox)

This is a bold, adult drama laying heavy stress on sex, a story of fleshy passions in the tidewater country of North Carolina.

Vidor belts over the blatantly sensual Arthur Fitz-Richard story. It's a sordid type of drama, with neither Jennifer Jones nor Charlton Heston gaining any sympathy in their characters.

Story starts with the animal attraction between Jones, from the wrong side of the tracks, and Heston, purse-poor southern gent who willingly trifles in the swamp but for marriage chooses Phyllis Avery's wealthy, properly-bred girl, so he can rebuild his family fortunes.

With a legal mating with Heston impossible, Jones turns to the friendship of Malden and his bedridden wife (Josephine Hutchinson). After the latter dies, she accepts Malden's proposal and they are married. Society refuses to accept his bride.

Jones goes through much of the footage in skin-tight levis, of which she and careful camera angles and lighting make the most.

● ●

■ RUGGLES OF RED GAP

1923, 89 MINS, US ⊗
Dir James Cruze   *Scr* Walter Woods, Anthony Coldeway   *Ph* Karl Brown
● Edward Everett Horton, Ernest Torrence, Lois Wilson, Fritzi Ridgeway, Charles Ogle, Louise Dresser (Paramount)

Here is a great comedy novel [by Harry Leon Wilson] made into a delightful feature picture.

The adaptation is literal in that it reproduces the effect of the original story with no forced interpolations and a full use of the material. The acting is a triumph of team work.

Ernest Torrence's Cousin Egbert is a gem, a bit of comic characterization that hasn't a suspicion of clowning.

Edward Horton's Ruggles is a fitting companion piece. This most British of British valets is almost as good fun in the film as he was in the book.

One of the things that go to make the whole picture delightful is the absence of hokum. Ruggles is as far from the familiar comic picture of the English valet as could be. He is just an embarrassed automaton hedged about by his own class consciousness and prejudices and stunned by the strange people he is thrown among. He is actually a likeable human being.

Lois Wilson plays 'the Kenner woman' with her invariable charm while Louise Dresser, is abundantly convincing as the formidable Mrs Ellie, wife and general manager of Cousin Egbert

● ●

■ RUGGLES OF RED GAP

1935, 90 MINS, US Ⓥ
Dir Leo McCarey   *Prod* Arthur Hornblow Jr
Scr Walter De Leon, Harlan Thompson, Humphrey Pearson   *Ph* Alfred Gilks   *Ed* Edward Dmytryk
Mus Ralph Rainger   *Art Dir* Hans Dreier, Robert Odell
● Charles Laughton, Mary Boland, Charles Ruggles, ZaSu Pitts, Roland Young, Leila Hyams (Paramount)

Leo McCarey has turned out a fast and furiously funny film which is a perfect example of what smart handling behind the camera can do. Original novel [by Harry Leon Wilson] has been made as a film twice before, once by Essanay (1918) and by Paramount (1923). But this time the yarn is handled from a completely fresh standpoint – with gratifying results.

Story is a bit dated. It plants Elmer (Charlie Ruggles) and his wife (Mary Boland) in Paris. They play poker with the Earl of Burnstead (Roland Young) and win his butler, Ruggles (Charles Laughton). They take him back to Red Gap, state of Washington. There Ruggles is mistaken for a British army captain and becomes a celebrity. That gives him the idea of freedom and standing on his own. He falls in love with Mrs Judson (ZaSu Pitts) and opens a restaurant.

Laughton turns in a performance that will surprise some and widen his appeal by far. He's played comedy before (*Henry VIII*), but here he is doing it differently. It's not satire; it's not a pathological character study. Just plain comedy.
□ 1935: Best Picture (Nomination)

● ●

R

RULING CLASS, THE

1972, 154 MINS, UK ◇ ⓥ

Dir Peter Medak *Prod* Jules Buck, Jack Hawkins
Scr Peter Barnes *Ph* Ken Hodges *Ed* Ray Lovejoy
Mus John Cameron *Art Dir* Peter Murton
● Peter O'Toole, Alastair Sim, Arthur Lowe, Harry Andrews, Coral Browne, Michael Bryant (Keep)

Peter Medak's *Ruling Class*, based on Peter Barnes' play of same name and scripted by the author, is a biting indictment of the so-called upper strata (British and/or other) of the old school tie thing.

Barnes' amusing but hardhitting script doesn't tell as well as it plays in recounting the rise to the House of Lords of the allegedly insane 14th Earl of Gurney, who very topically believes he's J.C. and whose unamused family wants wants him back in the nuthouse – once he's fathered the child through which they hope to get their greedy hands back on the estate the Earl has unexpectedly inherited.

Symbols are up for grabs, of course, but pic avoids usual message film pitfalls in coming across almost throughout with amusing tongue-in-cheek finesse alternating with hilarious stretches.

RUMBLE FISH

1983, 94 MINS, US ◇ ⓥ

Dir Francis Coppola *Prod* Fred Roos, Doug Claybourne *Scr* S. E. Hinton, Francis Coppola
Ph Stephen H. Burum *Ed* Barry Malkin *Mus* Stewart Copeland *Art Dir* Dean Tavoularis
● Matt Dillon, Mickey Rourke, Diane Lane, Dennis Hopper, Diana Scarwid, Vincent Spano (Zoetrope)

Rumble Fish is another Francis Coppola picture that's overwrought and overthought with camera and characters that never quite come together in anything beyond consistently interesting. Beautifully photographed in black and white by Stephen H. Burum, the picture [from the novel by S. E. Hinton] really doesn't need all the excessive symbolism Coppola tries to cram into it.

For those who want it, however, *Fish* is another able examination of teenage alienation, centered around two brothers who are misfits in the ill-defined urban society they inhabit.

One, Matt Dillon, is a young tough inspired to no good purposes by an older brother, Mickey Rourke, once the toughest but now a bit of an addled eccentric, though remaining a hero to neighborhood thugs.

Dillon and Rourke turn in good performances as does Dennis Hopper as their drunken father and Diane Lane as Dillon's dumped-on girlfriend.

Title and a lot of the symbolism stem from Siamese fighting fish (photographed in color composite shots) which are unable to coexist with their fellows, or even an image of themselves.

RUN FOR THE SUN

1956, 98 MINS, US ◇

Dir Roy Boulting *Prod* Harry Tatelman *Scr* Dudley Nichols, Roy Boulting *Ph* Joseph La Shelle *Ed* Fred Knudtsen *Mus* Fred Steiner
● Richard Widmark, Trevor Howard, Jane Greer, Peter Van Eyck, Carlos Henning, Juan Garcia (Russ-Field)

Film is a chase feature in practically all phases. Jane Greer, news mag staffer, comes to Mexico to find Richard Widmark, writer-adventurer, to find why he's given up writing. She falls for her news quarry and then the plane in which she is flying with him crashes in the jungle.

The couple is rescued by Trevor Howard and Peter Van Eyck, a mysterious pair.

When Widmark discovers their true identities as war criminals hiding out from trial and punishment, it becomes a murderous game through the jungle.

The four principals enact their roles exceptionally well. Pic is based on Richard Connell's story *The Most Dangerous Game* [filmed in 1932], but there is virtually no resemblance to that old thriller in the final results.

RUN OF THE ARROW

1957, 86 MINS, US ◇

Dir Samuel Fuller *Prod* Samuel Fuller *Scr* Samuel Fuller *Ph* Joseph Biroc *Ed* Gene Fowler Jr
Mus Victor Young *Art Dir* Albert S. D'Agostino, Jack Okey
● Rod Steiger, Sarita Montiel, Brian Keith, Ralph Meeker, Jay C. Flippen, Charles Bronson (RKO)

Yankee-hating Southerner goes west after the Civil War to join the Sioux in their uprising against the US. Slow in takeoff, action becomes pretty rough at times.

Production is strong on visual values to bolster Samuel Fuller's sometimes meandering screenplay highlighting Rod Steiger as Southerner taken into the tribe after he survives the run-of-the-arrow torture ordeal. Forceful use is made of Indians and their attacks on the whites to give unusual color to feature, which additionally has Sarita Montiel, Spanish actress, in as Steiger's Indian wife [dubbed by Angie Dickinson].

On debit side, Steiger frequently lapses from Southerner into Irish dialect, and footage occasionally is impeded by irrelevant sequences. Steiger is never sympathetic and character itself is not clearly defined, though actor endows his character with vigor.

RUN WILD, RUN FREE

1969, 100 MINS, UK ◇

Dir Richard C. Sarafian *Prod* John Danischewsky
Scr David Rook *Ph* Wilkie Cooper *Ed* Geoffrey Foot *Mus* David Whitaker *Art Dir* Ted Tester
● John Mills, Sylvia Sims, Bernard Miles, Mark Lester, Gordon Jackson, Fiona Fullerton (Columbia)

This sensible and sensitive film, is handled with care and obvious affection. Heavy on the melodrama and profound in the study of characters through outstanding performances by John Mills and Mark Lester, feature is an honestly moving film.

Young Lester registers an excellent performance as an introverted, psychosomatically mute lad growing up on the moors of England.

Lester's meeting with a wild, white colt concurrent with his initial acquaintance with moorman Mills, (a retired army colonel), provides a setup for interaction bween the three that is basis for the film.

David Rook's film adaptation of his own novel is particularly good in that it sentimentalizes without getting sticky and his concise dialog and sensible placement of incidents eliminates any story lag.

RUNAWAY

1984, 100 MINS, US ◇ ⓥ

Dir Michael Crichton *Prod* Michael Rachmil
Scr Michael Crichton *Ph* John A. Alonzo *Ed* Glenn Farr *Mus* Jerry Goldsmith *Art Dir* Douglas Higgins
● Tom Selleck, Cynthia Rhodes, Gene Simmons, Kirstie Alley, Stan Shaw, Joey Cramer (Tri-Star/Delphi III)

Tom Selleck, with a cop's short haircut and playing a workaday stiff who's afraid of heights, cuts a less dashing but more accessible figure in *Runaway* than in prior pictures. However, this Michael Crichton robotic nightmare is so trite that the story seems lifted from Marvel Comics, with heat-seeking bullets and a villain so bad he would be fun if

the film wasn't telling us to take this near-futuristic adventure with a straight face.

Selleck's fem police partner Cynthia Rhodes, is an over-achiever and formula romantic foil to Selleck, who's a single parent raising a son. Departure may be fresh for Selleck but the comparative lack of his trade-marked sardonic humor does cost the pic.

RUNAWAY TRAIN

1985, 111 MINS, US ◇ ⓥ

Dir Andrei Konchalovsky *Prod* Menahem Golan, Yoram Globus *Scr* Djordje Milicevic, Paul Zindel, Edward Bunker *Ph* Alan Hume *Ed* Henry Richardson *Mus* Trevor Jones *Art Dir* Stephen Marsh
● Jon Voight, Eric Roberts, Rebecca DeMornay, Kyle T. Heffner, John P. Ryan, T.K. Carter (Cannon/Northbrook)

Runaway Train is a sensational picture. Wrenchingly intense and brutally powerful, Andrei Konchalovsky's film rates as a most exciting action epic and is fundamentally serious enough to work strongly on numerous levels.

An exercise in relentless, severe tension, tale begins with a prison drama, then never lets up as it follows two escaped cons as they become inadvertent passengers on some diesel units that run out of control through the Alaskan wilderness.

The two desperate men who find themselves joined by a young lady, are tracked throughout their headlong journey by railroad officials bent on avoiding a crash.

Jon Voight brilliantly portrays a two-time loser determined never to return to prison after his third breakout.

Pic is based upon [an unfilmed] screenplay by Akira Kurosawa, and bears imprint of the renowned Japanese director.

Younger con Eric Roberts impressively manages to hold his own under the demanding circumstances, and Rebecca DeMornay works herself well into the essentially all-male surroundings.

RUNNER STUMBLES, THE

1979, 99 MINS, US ◇ ⓥ

Dir Stanley Kramer *Prod* Stanley Kramer *Scr* Milan Stitt *Ph* Laszlo Kovacs *Ed* Pembroke J. Herring
Mus Ernest Gold *Art Dir* Al Sweeney Jr
● Dick Van Dyke, Kathleen Quinlan, Maureen Stapleton, Ray Bolger, Tammy Grimes, Beau Bridges (Stanley Kramer)

Based on an actual murder case in 1927 where a priest was accused of killing a nun he was in love with, subject matter is celibacy in the Catholic church, and presented in such a way that, at times, it appears like the best of the old-fashioned 1940s tear jerkers complete with overly lush sound track.

Yet *Runner* ultimately emerges as more than melodrama because director Stanley Kramer puts equal emphasis on the priest (Dick Van Dyke) and how he grapples with his love for God and this woman (Kathleen Quinlan) in his life.

Throughout, the film is paced by fine performances, especially Van Dyke as Father Rivard, Quinlan as Sister Rita and Maureen Stapleton as Van Dyke's housekeeper.

RUNNERS

1983, 110 MINS, UK ◇ ⓥ

Dir Charles Sturridge *Prod* Barry Hanson
Scr Stephen Poliakoff *Ph* Howard Atherton *Ed* Peter Coulson *Mus* George Fenton *Art Dir* Arnold Chapkis
● James Fox, Jane Asher, Kate Hardie, Robert Lang, Eileen O'Brien, Ruti Simon (Hanstoll/Goldcrest)

There are a lot of interesting ideas in *Runners*, but they're never really shaped into a coherent film. It's evident that directing

Brideshead Revisited, the rambling TV series with which helmer Charles Sturridge secured international acclaim, was not the best education in cinematic structure.

The meandering plot follows a father, played by James Fox, who searches for his daughter long after everyone else, including his wife, have given up. Tracking her down to a car hire firm, rather than some perverse religious sect as he had expected, he is horrified at her reluctance to return.

Along the way, the father strikes up with a woman from a different social class who is hunting for her son. There are some interesting nuances in this relationship, but eventually it is the trival details of the hunt that dominate the screen.

One is two thirds of the way through the film before the question is even raised of why this girl fled. Fox and Jane Asher give as much to the roles as they can.

■ **RUNNING MAN, THE**

1963, 103 MINS, UK ◇
Dir Carol Reed *Prod* Carol Reed *Scr* John Mortimer *Ph* Robert Krasker *Ed* Bert Bates *Mus* William Alwyn
● Laurence Harvey, Lee Remick, Alan Bates, Felix Aylmer, Eleanor Summerfield (Columbia)

The story of the man who poses as dead in order that his 'widow' can pick up the insurance money is not exactly new. But director Carol Reed makes it holding entertainment.

Based on Shelley Smith's novel *Ballad of a Running Man*, John Mortimer has written a smart script, with the three principal characters well delineated. Interiors were shot at Ardmore Studios, Ireland, but main locations were lensed in Spain.

Film opens with a memorial service for Laurence Harvey, believed drowned following a glider accident. Solemnly his wife (Lee Remick) accepts the sympathy of friends. But soon Harvey turns up, larger than life, and sets in motion their plan to collect $140,000.

The claim goes through and the wife joins Harvey in Spain where she finds that he has assumed the identity of an Australian millionaire and is already plotting to pull off another insurance swindle.

Harvey has a role that suits him admirably, allowing him to run the gamut of many moods. Remick is also admirable as the young, pretty wife. Hers is a difficult part suggesting acute tension as she wavers between Harvey and Alan Bates, who has fallen for her and to whom she gives in one afternoon.

Bates, in the less flashy role of an insurance agent, ostensibly playing detective, is first-class. He plays on a quiet, yet strong, note and is a most effective contrast to the flamboyance of Harvey.

■ **RUNNING MAN, THE**

1987, 101 MINS, US ◇ ▼
Dir Paul Michael Glaser *Prod* Tim Zinnemann, George Linder *Scr* Stephen E. de Souza *Ph* Tom Del Ruth *Ed* Mark Roy Warner, Edward A. Warschilka, John Wright *Mus* Harold Faltermeyer *Art Dir* Jack T. Collis
● Arnold Schwarzenegger, Maria Conchita Alonso, Richard Dawson, Yaphet Kotto, Jim Brown, Jesse Ventura (Tri-Star/Taft/Barish/HBO)

Pic, based on a novel by Richard Bachman (Stephen King), opens in 2017 when the world, following a financial collapse, is run by a police state, with TV a heavily censored propaganda tool of the government. Arnold Schwarzenegger is Ben Richards, a helicopter pilot who disobeys orders to fire on unarmed people during an LA food riot. He's slapped in prison and escapes 18 months later with pals Yaphet Kotto and Marvin J. McIntyre.

Producer-host of the popular TV gameshow *The Running Man* Damon Killian (Richard Dawson) orders Richards up as his next contestant and he is duly captured and made a runner in this lethal (and fixed) gladiatorial contest for the masses.

Format works only on a pure action level, with some exciting, but overly repetitious, roller-coaster style sequences of runners hurtling into the game through tunnels on futuristic sleds. Bloated budget was $27 million.

Schwarzenegger sadistically dispatches the baddies, enunciating typical wisecrack remarks (many repeated from his previous films), but it's all too easy, despite the casting of such powerful presences as Jim Brown and former wrestlers Jesse Ventura and Prof. Toru Tanaka.

■ **RUNNING ON EMPTY**

1988, 116 MINS, US ◇ ▼
Dir Sidney Lumet *Prod* Amy Robinson, Griffin Dunne *Scr* Naomi Foner *Ph* Gerry Fisher *Ed* Andrew Mondshein *Mus* Tony Mottola *Art Dir* Philip Rosenberg
● Christine Lahti, River Phoenix, Judd Hirsch, Martha Plimpton, Jonas Arby (Lorimar/Double Play)

The continuing shock waves emitted by the cataclysmic events of the 1960s are dramatized in fresh and powerful ways in *Running On Empty*, a complex, turbulent tale told with admirable simplicity. Film successfully operates on several levels – as study of the primacy of the family unit, an anguished teen romance, a coming-of-age story and a look at what happened to some political radicals a generation later.

The two central adult characters are Weathermen-like urban bombers who have been living underground since 1971.

Arthur and Annie Pope (Judd Hirsch and Christine Lahti) have been on the FBI's most-wanted list since bombing a university defense research installation, an act that blinded a janitor. Their life since then has required them to be as unobtrusively middle-class as possible, and to be able to pick up and leave for a new destination on a moment's notice.

Son Danny (River Phoenix), now 17, is quickly recognized by the local music teacher as an exceptionally promising pianist, and is nudged along toward an eventual audition for Juilliard. At the same time, Danny slowly commences an edgy but potent first love with the teacher's daughter Lorna (Martha Plimpton).

Superior screenplay keeps the focus intimate, forcing the head of the family to face the prospect of the family's breakup so that his son can pursue his own talents and interests.

■ **RUNNING SCARED**

1986, 106 MINS, US ◇ ▼
Dir Peter Hyams *Prod* David Foster, Lawrence Turman *Scr* Gary DeVore, Jimmy Huston *Ph* Peter Hyams *Ed* James Mitchell *Mus* Rod Temperton *Art Dir* Albert Brenner
● Gregory Hines, Billy Crystal, Steven Bauer, Darlanne Fluegel, Joe Pantoliano, Jimmy Smits (M-G-M)

Gregory Hines and Billy Crystal are undercover cops too cool for words. As elsewhere, drugs keep flowing into Chicago as through open floodgates, and Hines and Crystal are concerned particularly with aborting the career of aspiring Spanish godfather Jimmy Smits.

Nonstop banter between the two stars is rowdy, intimate, natural and often very funny. The men seem like real soul mates who have been together for years and still manage to maintain mutual respect and competition in equal measure.

Well-paced pic is punctuated with the usual shootouts, confrontations with superiors, street talk and low-life bad guys that come with the territory, as well as the inevitable stops-out climax in which hundreds of rounds of ammo are discharged.

■ **RUSH TO JUDGMENT**

1967, 122 MINS, US
Dir Emile de Antonio *Prod* Mark Lane, Emile de Antonio *Scr* Mark Lane *Ph* Robert Primes *Ed* Daniel Drasin
● (Impact Films/Judgment)

Lawyer Mark Lane, whose 'brief for the defense' of Lee Harvey Oswald was in the no 1 non-fiction best-seller position for several months, converted his material into a film of the same name, *Rush to Judgment*. For many it will seem a convincing pic, opening up severe doubts about the thoroughness and even integrity of the Warren Commission's [investigation into the assassination of President Kennedy].

Rush to Judgment is sober and unexcited, making its points with quiet and controlled definiteness, sans hysterics or frenzied accusations. Lane and collaborator Emile de Antonio have let their material present itself, utilizing wryness as their main weapon to sow seeds of doubt.

Point of the film is neatly summed up by one interviewee: 'The Warren Commission, I think, had to report in their book what they wanted the world to believe . . . It had to read like they wanted it to read. They had to prove that Oswald did it alone.'

■ **RUSSIA HOUSE, THE**

1990, 123 MINS, US ◇ ▼
Dir Fred Schepisi *Prod* Paul Maslansky, Fred Schepisi *Scr* Tom Stoppard *Ph* Ian Baker *Ed* Peter Honess *Mus* Jerry Goldsmith *Art Dir* Richard MacDonald
● Sean Connery, Michelle Pfeiffer, Roy Scheider, James Fox, Klaus Maria Brandauer, Ken Russell (Pathe)

John le Carré's glasnost-era espionage novel has been turned into intelligent adult entertainment, but somber tone, utter lack of action and sex, and complexity of plot tilts this mainly to upscale audience.

The film is the first US non-coproduction to be shot substantially in the USSR.

Sean Connery plays Barley Blair, a boozy, inconoclastic London publisher to whom a highly sensitive manuscript is sent via a Moscow book editor named Katya (Michelle Pfeiffer). Intercepted by British authorities, the text, authored by a leading physicist, purports to lay out the facts about Soviet nuclear capabilities in devastating detail.

Over his protestations, Blair is sent to Moscow in his role as prospective publisher to meet the writer, the mysterious Dante (Klaus Maria Brandauer), determine his reliability and put more questions to him. His intermediary is the beautiful Katya with whom he falls in love.

As the flawed, unreliable publisher, Connery is in top form. Pfeiffer's Katya is a much more guarded figure. Her Russian accent proves very believable but she has limited notes to play.

Most of the supporting roles are one-dimensional British or US intelligence types, but James Fox, Roy Scheider, John Mahoney and Michael Kitchen embody them solidly and with wit when possible. Director Ken Russell amusingly hams it up as an impishly aggressive spy master. Brandauer is strong as always in his brief appearance as the charismatic Dante.

S

■ RUSSIANS ARE COMING! THE RUSSIANS ARE COMING!, THE

1966, 124 MINS, US ◇ ▽

Dir Norman Jewison *Prod* Norman Jewison
Scr William Rose *Ph* Joseph Biroc *Ed* Hal Ashby, J.
Terry Williams *Mus* Johnny Mandel *Art Dir* Robert F.
Boyle
● Carl Reiner, Eva Marie Saint, Alan Arkin, Brian Keith,
Jonathan Winters, Theodore Bikel (Mirisch/United
Artist)

The Russians Are Coming! The Russians Are Coming! is an outstanding cold-war comedy depicting the havoc created on a mythical Massachusetts island by the crew of a grounded Russian sub.

Nathaniel Benchley's novel *The Off-Islanders* got its title from New England slang for summer residents, herein top-featured Carl Reiner, wife Eva Marie Saint, and their kids, Sheldon Golomb and Cindy Putnam.

Basically, story concerns aftermath of an accidental grounding of the Russian sub by overly curious skipper Theodore Bikel, who sends Alan Arkin ashore in charge of a landing party to get a towing boat. The wild antics which follow center around sheriff Brian Keith, sole resident who manages to keep cool except when arguing with Paul Ford, firebrand civil defense chief (self appointed) who arms himself to repel the 'invasion' with a sword and an American Legion cap.

Arkin, in his film bow, is absolutely outstanding as the courtly Russian who kisses a lady's hand even as he draws a gun.

English music hall vet Tessie O'Shea, also in film debut, is very good as the island's telephone operator who contributes to the spread of the 'invasion' rumors, and her scenes with Reiner, in which they are lashed together and attempt to escape, is a comedy highlight.
☐ 1966: Best Picture (Nomination)

■ RUTHLESS PEOPLE

1986, 93 MINS, US ◇ ▽

Dir Jim Abrahams, David Zucker, Jerry Zucker
Prod Michael Peyser *Scr* Dale Launer *Ph* Jan
DeBont *Ed* Arthur Schmidt *Mus* Michel Colombier
Art Dir Donald Woodruff
● Danny DeVito, Bette Midler, Judge Reinhold, Helen
Slater, Anita Morris, Bill Pullman (Touchstone/Silver
Screen)

Ruthless People is a hilariously venal comedy about a kidnapped harridan whose rich husband won't pay for her return.

In short, impoverished couple Judge Reinhold and Helen Slater kidnap Bel-Air princess Bette Midler because her mercenary husband, played by Danny DeVito, has ripped off Slater's design for spandex miniskirts.

There is much, much more to it than that, as screenwriter Dale Launer cleverly builds twist upon complication to a point where practically everyone in the cast is writhing in frustration and mystification as they wonder whether their latest opportunistic scheme is going to work.

Midler, when first glimpsed, is an absolute fright who looks like a cross between Cyndi Lauper and Divine. After terrorizing her kidnappers, she embarks upon an energetic self-improvement program, and not surprisingly emerges with the upper hand.

■ RYAN'S DAUGHTER

1970, 194 MINS, UK ◇ ▽

Dir David Lean *Prod* Anthony Havelock-Allan
Scr Robert Bolt *Ph* Freddie Young *Ed* Norman
Savage *Mus* Maurice Jarre *Art Dir* Stephen Grimes
● Robert Mitchum, Trevor Howard, Sarah Miles,
Christopher Jones, John Mills, Leo McKern
(M-G-M/Faraway)

Ryan's Daughter is a brilliant enigma, brilliant, because director David Lean achieves to a marked degree the daring and obvious goal of intimate romantic tragedy along the rugged geographical and political landscape of 1916 Ireland; an enigma, because overlength of perhaps 30 minutes serves to magnify some weaknesses of Robert Bolt's original screenplay, to dissipate the impact of the performances, and to overwhelm outstanding photography and production.

Robert Mitchum gives a stolid performance as an aloof widower, a schoolteacher returning from a Dublin trip to whom Sarah Miles pours out her conception of love. United in marriage, pair never achieve a full sexual-spiritual union – he is 20 years her senior, she is immature. Arrival of shell-shocked Christopher Jones to take over the British occupation garrison cues an illicit affair.

As the townsfolk become more scandalized by the affair between Jones and Miss Miles, she is eventually stripped and shorn as an adulterer and a wrongly-convicted informer.

Trevor Howard gives an assured performance as a knowing local priest; John Mills might be a technical tour de force as a Quasimodo-like town idiot, but the character is overdrawn and often jarring to story-telling; other supporting players, many drawn from the Irish stage, are very good.

S s

■ SABOTEUR

1942, 100 MINS, US ▽

Dir Alfred Hitchcock *Prod* Frank Lloyd *Scr* Peter
Viertel, Joan Harrison, Dorothy Parker *Ph* Joseph
Valentine *Ed* Otto Ludwig *Mus* Frank Skinner *Art
Dir* Jack Otterson
● Priscilla Lane, Robert Cummings, Norman Lloyd,
Otto Kruger, Murray Alper, Alma Kruger (Universal)

Saboteur is a little too self-consciously Hitchcock. Its succession of incredible climaxes, its mounting tautness and suspense, its mood of terror and impending doom could have been achieved by no one else. That is a great tribute to a brilliant director. But it would be a greater tribute to a finer director if he didn't let the spectator see the wheels go round, didn't let him spot the tricks – and thus shatter the illusion, however momentarily.

Like all Hitchcock films, *Saboteur* is excellently acted. Norman Lloyd is genuinely plausible as the ferret-like culprit who sets the fatal airplane factory on fire. Robert Cummings lacks variation in his performance of the thick-headed, unjustly accused worker who crosses the continent to expose the plotters and clear himself; but his directness and vigor partly redeem that short-coming.

There is the customary Hitchcock gallery of lurid minor characters, including a group of circus freaks, a saboteur whose young son has the macabre habit of breaking his toys, and a monstrous butler with a sadistic fondness for a blackjack.

■ SABRINA

1954, 112 MINS, US ▽

Dir Billy Wilder *Prod* Billy Wilder *Scr* Billy Wilder,
Samuel Taylor, Ernest Lehman *Ph* Charles Lang
Ed Arthur Schmidt *Mus* Frederick Hollander
● Humphrey Bogart, Audrey Hepburn, William
Holden, Walter Hampden, John Williams, Martha Hyer
(Paramount)

A slick blend of heart and chuckles makes *Sabrina* a sock romantic comedy. Script is long on glibly quipping dialog, dropped with a seemingly casual air, and broadly played situations. The splendid trouping delivers them style. Leavening the chuckles are tugs at the heart.

Basically, the plot's principal business is to get Audrey Hepburn, daughter of a chauffeur in service to an enormously wealthy family, paired off with the right man. She's always been in love with playboy William Holden, but ends up with Humphrey Bogart, the austere, businessman brother.

The fun is in the playing. Bogart is sock as the tycoon with no time for gals until he tries to get Hepburn's mind off Holden. The latter sells his comedy strongly, wrapping up a character somewhat offbeat for him. Hepburn again demonstrates a winning talent for being 'Miss Cinderella'.

■ SADIE McKEE

1934, 90 MINS, US

Dir Clarence Brown *Prod* Lawrence Weingarten
Scr John Meehan *Ph* Oliver T. Marsh *Ed* Hugh
Wynn *Art Dir* Cedric Gibbons, Frederic Hope
● Joan Crawford, Gene Raymond, Franchot Tone,
Edward Arnold, Esther Ralston, Akim Tamiroff (M-G-M)

Sadie McKee is the Cinderella theme all over again, plus an s.a. angle through the stellar player of the titular role encountering three major romances in the persons of the featured male trio in support – Franchot Tone, Gene Raymond and Edward Arnold.

Basically it's the story [from the *Liberty* magazine serial by Vina Delmar] of the housemaid (Joan Crawford) who marries the boss of the manor, but not until after he comes humbly to her, and after she has experienced turbulent affairs with the other two.

That her major attachment to Arnold is obviously a mercenary marriage is sufficiently well built up to make it almost sympathetic, in view of the goading of the supercilious young master (Tone) of the household in which Sadie's mother is the cook.

Raymond is cast as the No. 1 sweetie who, according to Tone, is a no-good guy, but who is the major romance interest even after he runs out with a vaudeville single (well played by Esther Ralston).

The playing is expert throughout, so much so that in its realism it perhaps makes the star suffer a bit, particularly at the hands of Arnold whose bluff, constantly inebriated performance almost steals the picture.

■ SADIE THOMPSON

1928, 94 MINS, US ⊗ ▽

Dir Raoul Walsh *Scr* Raoul Walsh, C. Gardner
Sullivan *Ph* Oliver Marsh, George Barnes, Robert
Kurrle *Ed* C. Gardner Sullivan *Art Dir* William
Cameron Menzies
● Lionel Barrymore, Gloria Swanson, Blanche
Friderici, Raoul Walsh, Charles Lane, Florence Midgley
(United Artists)

Program credits make no reference to *Rain* the play, the picture having been adapted from the 'original story' by W. Somerset Maugham. However, the presentation conveys the idea of *Rain* by a stereoptican downpour effect prior to and through the opening titles.

The scene in which Hamilton enters Sadie's room during the night is not more than barely hinted at, finishing with Lionel Barrymore standing at the door. For a few previous feet is shown his mental struggle to overcome Sadie's physical attraction for him, but nothing more than a faltering hand reaching out to stroke her hair is flashed.

Sadie's costume, her struggle to articulate above and over a wad of rum and her familiarity with the Marines is sufficient to establish her character at the beginning. But there's likely to be a wide difference of opinion on Gloria Swanson's interpretation of the role.

Barrymore's performance is okay and Raoul Walsh, assuming the double duties of actor and director, does well by both. He plays O'Hara with whom Sadie eventually sails away. Charles Lane makes a minor bit count, and Blanche Friderici rises to her occasion late in the running.

● ●

■ **SAFE PLACE, A**

1971, 94 MINS, US ◇

Dir Henry Jaglom   *Prod* Bert Schneider   *Scr* Henry Jaglom   *Ph* Dick Kratina   *Ed* Pieter Bergema
● Tuesday Weld, Orson Welles, Jack Nicholson, Philip Proctor, Gwen Welles, Dov Lawrence (BBS/Columbia)

Tuesday Weld is the child-like woman in whose silly pussycat consciousness the backward, forward, now it's now, now it isn't now action takes place. In her one clear decision she is casually cruel to the young man (Philip Proctor) who adores her while receptive to the curiously charming drop-by-without-calling stud played by Jack Nicholson.

Weld has many scenes in the park with an itinerant magician, supposedly a father image. Of the many weirdo roles played in his time by Orson Welles this may be the prize example.

Unrelated to the story in Weld's head is hippie girl's rambling account of her feelings adroitly soliloquized by Gwen Welles. This is rather touching, quite lucid and uninterrupted, though wildly neurotic.

All this deliberate experimentation puts a heavy burden upon the viewer. Hardly a scene is fully played out, hardly an explanation provided. It would seem that writer-director Henry Jaglom has plunged in over his own depth. It is like a gymnastic symphony conductor over-personalizing the music.

● ●

■ **SAFETY LAST**

1923, 77 MINS, US ⊗ ▽

Dir Fred Newmeyer, Sam Taylor   *Scr* Hal Roach, Sam Taylor, Tim Whelan, H.M. Walker   *Ph* Walter Lundin   *Ed* Thomas J. Crizer   *Art Dir* Fred Guiol
● Harold Lloyd, Mildred Davis, Bill Strother, Noah Young, Westcott B. Clarke, Mickey Daniels (Roach)

This Harold Lloyd high-class low comedy has thrills as well as guffaws. It leads up to big shrieks through Lloyd apparently climbing the outside wall to the top or 12th floor of a building, probably in Los Angeles. This bit is chockerblock with trick camera work but skilfully done.

The comedy business of the department store where Lloyd is a clerk nearly equals the remainder.

Lloyd as a small town boy leaves his sweetheart in the country, going to the city and obtains a $15-a-week position as a counter jumper. Back home the girl receives a little cheap piece of jewelry and believes Lloyd has made the great success he said he would in the big city. Upon the advice of her mother she goes there.

Lloyd, in an attempt to have her think he is the boss instead of a clerk, wanders into all kinds of complications. It leads up to the building climbing, a plan suggested by the clerk to the general manager as a means of obtaining publicity for the firm.

● ●

■ **SAHARA**

1943, 85 MINS, US ▽

Dir Zoltan Korda   *Prod* Harry Joe Brown   *Scr* John Howard Lawson, Zoltan Korda   *Ph* Rudolph Mate   *Ed* Charles Nelson   *Mus* Miklos Rozsa
● Humphrey Bogart, Bruce Bennett, Lloyd Bridges, Rex Ingram, J. Carrol Naish, Dan Duryea (Columbia)

Story background displays Libyan desert fighting in 1942, when the British were hurled back to the El Alamein line. It vividly focuses attention on exploits of an American tank crew headed by Humphrey Bogart to escape the onrushing Nazis, and battles against desert sands and lack of water.

Picture gets off to a fast start, with Bogart heading his 28-ton tank south on the desert in drive to regain the British lines. Along the way he picks up six Allied stragglers; Sudenese soldier Rex Ingram with latter's Italian prisoner, J. Carrol Naish; and a downed Nazi pilot (Kurt Krueger). Bogart pushes on with his assorted passengers to reach a water hole at an old desert fort which provides a trickle but enough to sustain the group. Nazi motorized battalion also heads for the water supply.

Script [adapted by James O'Hanlon from a story by Philip MacDonald] is packed with pithy dialog, lusty action and suspense, and logically and well-devised situations avoiding ultra-theatrics throughout. It's an all-male cast, but absence of romance is not missed in the rapid-fire unfolding of vivid melodrama.

● ●

■ **SAHARA**

1983, 104 MINS, US ◇ Ⓥ

Dir Andrew V. McLaglen   *Prod* Menahem Golan, Yoram Globus   *Scr* James R. Silke   *Ph* David Gurfinkel   *Mus* Ennio Morricone   *Art Dir* Luciano Spadoni
● Brooke Shields, Lambert Wilson, Horst Buchholz, John Rhys-Davies, Ronald Lacey, John Mills (Cannon)

Coproducer Menahem Golan reportedly hatched the idea for *Sahara* when Mark Thatcher, son of the British prime minister, disappeared in the desert during an international car rally.

An old fashioned B-grade romantic adventure, directed in pedestrian fashion by Andrew V. McLaglen, *Sahara* is lamentably low on excitement, laughs and passion.

Screenplay, set in 1927, has Brooke Shields as heiress to a car company who promises her dying daddy that she'll win the world's toughest endurance rally driving the car he designed. Wily Brooke disguises herself as a man, complete with wig and moustache.

Soon after the race starts, she discards her disguise and reverts to Brooke the beautiful, only to receive a beating and a mouthful of sand when she's captured by Arab thug John Rhys-Davies. Handsome sheikh Lambert Wilson saves her from his clutches and falls mildly in love with her.

Director McLaglen and most everyone else treat it all tongue in cheek.

● ●

■ **SAILOR FROM GIBRALTAR, THE**

1967, 89 MINS, UK

Dir Tony Richardson   *Prod* Oscar Lewenstein, Neil Hartley   *Scr* Christopher Isherwood, Don Magner, Tony Richardson   *Ph* Raoul Coutard   *Ed* Anthony Gibbs   *Mus* Antoine Duhamel   *Art Dir* Marilena Aravantinou
● Jeanne Moreau, Ian Bannen, Vanessa Redgrave, Zia Moyheddin, Hugh Griffith, Orson Welles (Lopert Pictures)

The novels of Marguerite Duras are frequently no more than lengthy short stories – and not too strong on the narrative side. With such interpreters as Christopher Isherwood and Tony Richardson (neither famous for clarity of intent) plus Don Magner, the ensuing screenplay is replete with repetitive sequences.

A Britisher (Ian Bannen) and his mistress (Vanessa Redgrave) are on an Italian holiday which quickly becomes evident will be their last. She's still hungry for him but he can't stand her but isn't brave enough to send her away.

When a mysterious woman on a yacht (Jeanne Moreau) crosses their path, his greed (both sexual and practical) provides the impetus to ditch his mistress and make a fast pass at the yachtswoman.

Orson Welles is wasted on a brief bit as an information peddler and Hugh Griffith is only slightly better as a white hunter and guide. Redgrave is touching and believably irritating in her brief role. The rest of the cast walk through their parts like somnambulists.

● ●

■ **SAILOR TAKES A WIFE, THE**

1946, 92 MINS, US

Dir Richard Whorf   *Prod* Edwin H. Knopf   *Scr* Chester Erskine, Anne Morrison Chapin, Whitfield Cook   *Ph* Sidney Wagner   *Ed* Irvine Warburton   *Mus* Johnny Green   *Art Dir* Cedric Gibbons, Edward Carfagno
● Robert Walker, June Allyson, Hume Cronyn, Audrey Totter, Eddie 'Rochester' Anderson (M-G-M)

The Sailor Takes a Wife stage play has been given light, broad screen treatment. Production isn't elaborate but has polish, the direction is smooth, and the cast gets the best from the comedy situations.

Robert Walker and June Allyson head the funning, making the antics and complications around which the plot revolves delightful. Story is on the light side and laughs are mostly situation, but Richard Whorf's direction keeps it on the move. Plot deals with a sailor and a girl who meet and marry, all in one evening, and subsequent efforts to adjust themselves to marital status.

Bride's first disappointment comes when her husband is discharged almost immediately, leaving her with a civilian instead of the hero she expected. Further complications develop when Walker, searching for a job, becomes entangled innocently with a romantically-inclined foreign femme menace, brightly played by Audrey Totter.

● ●

■ **SAILOR WHO FELL FROM GRACE WITH THE SEA, THE**

1976, 104 MINS, UK ◇ Ⓥ

Dir Lewis John Carlino   *Prod* Martin Poll   *Scr* Lewis John Carlino   *Ph* Douglas Slocombe   *Ed* Anthony Gibbs   *Mus* John Mandel   *Art Dir* Ted Haworth
● Sarah Miles, Kris Kristofferson, Jonathan Kahn, Margo Cunningham, Earl Rhodes, Paul Tropea (Avco Embassy)

With a quartet of fine characters and performances, *The Sailor Who Fell from Grace with the Sea* could have ventured just about anywhere – except where writer-director Lewis John Carlino takes it in an effort to remain faithful to Yukio Mishima's novel.

Cultural differences still remain in this increasingly homogenized world and the prime problem with *Sailor* is trying to transfer decidedly Oriental ideas about honor, order and death into an English countryside.

Mishima's novel was about a Japanese widow who falls in love with a sailor. At first attracted to the sailor as an honorable symbol, her 13-year-old son defends him before his gang of idealistic schoolmates. But when the sailor leaves the sea to marry, the boy and his gang feel betrayed and plot to kill him to restore his purity.

On film, the story won't settle down with these upper-class young English lads.

● ●

■ **SAILOR'S RETURN, THE**

1978, 112 MINS, UK ◇

Dir Jack Gold   *Prod* Otto Plaschkes   *Scr* James Saunders   *Mus* Carl Davis
● Tom Bell, Shope Shodeinde, Mick Ford, Paola Dionisotti, George Costigan, Clive Swift (Ariel/NFFC)

Set in the early reign of Queen Victoria (1819-1901), story, adapted from David

Garnett's novel, is about a sailor who returns home to England with a bride from the black Kingdom of Dahomey in West Africa.

It's her dowry, a treasure of pearls, that sets them up in business with an inn for thirsty passers-by in a lush English countryside. But her color and the presence of a black son set them off from intolerant neighbors, despite some support from friends in the area.

Conflicts with the sailor's sister, the local pastor (who preaches hell fire), and prejudiced visitors to the inn lead to slow alienation in a foreign land.

Tom Bell scores as the sailor Targett, and Shope Shodeinde (a native Nigerian) as the African princess brings credibility but hardly sparkle to Tulip, a lively flower that must slowly wither in a foreign climate with the accumulation of disappointments and unawaited hostility.

■ SAINT IN LONDON, THE

1939, 72 MINS, UK ▼
Dir John Paddy Carstairs   *Scr* Lynn Root, Frank Fenton   *Ph* Claude Friese-Greene
● George Sanders, Sally Gray, David Burns, Athene Seyler (RKO)

This is a workmanlike job. Previous *Saint* pix, with George Sanders in his standard role, were made in Hollywood.

Plot [from the novel *The Million Pound Day* by Leslie Charteris] revolves around an organization of international counterfeiters. The Saint aids Scotland Yard in rounding up a gang that's ready to foist upon the public $5 million worth of banknotes printed in England for a Continental country. The Saint's chief assistants are Sally Gray and David Burns. Burns almost steals the picture with another inimitable hick crook role. Sanders is excellent, as usual.

Direction is alert, with some photography being excellent.

■ SAINT JACK

1979, 112 MINS, US ◇ ▼
Dir Peter Bogdanovich   *Prod* Roger Corman
Scr Howard Sackler, Paul Theroux, Peter Bogdanovich   *Ph* Robby Muller   *Ed* William Carruth
Art Dir David Ng
● Ben Gazzara, Denholm Elliott, James Villiers, Joss Ackland, Rodney Bewes, Lisa Lu
(New World/Playboy/Shoals Creek-Copa de Oro)

Shot entirely on location in Singapore, the film (produced by Roger Corman, who gave Bogdanovich his start of *The Wild Angels* in 1964) is extremely well crafted, finely acted, and conjures up a positively intriguing milieu.

At bottom line, though, it's essentially a character study – Ben Gazzara excels as a pimp with a heart of gold – told in a mood that begins with a twinkling-eyed bawdiness, but becomes progressively more sombre and even nihilistic.

Based on Paul Theroux's novel, the film is laid in 1971, putting its exclusive focus on Gazzara, an expatriate US hustler-type who jumps ship and uses the cover of a local provision broker to operate a freelance prostitution ring.

The script is a good one, gutsy and sometime very funny.

■ SAINT JOAN

1957, 110 MINS, US ▼
Dir Otto Preminger   *Prod* Otto Preminger
Scr Graham Greene   *Ph* Georges Perinal   *Ed* Helga Cranston   *Mus* Mischa Spolianksy   *Art Dir* Roger Furse
● Jean Seberg, Richard Widmark, Richard Todd, Anton Walbrook, John Gielgud, Felix Aylmer (United Artists)

Otto Preminger showed courage when he decided to make G.B. Shaw's *Saint Joan* into a film and to star an unknown of next to no theatrical experience in the role. Jean Seberg of Marshalltown, Iowa, makes a sincere effort, but her performance rarely rises above the level of the Iowa prairie.

Seberg is helped most by her appealing looks. She has a fresh, unspoiled quality and she photographs well. But Shaw's Joan is more than just an innocent country maiden.

In vivid contrast, Preminger surrounds her with a supporting cast that performs brilliantly. Richard Widmark plays the idiot Dauphin with gusto though he at times over-acts the part. Richard Todd as Dunois; Anton Walbrook as Cauchon, the Bishop of Beauvais, and Felix Aylmer, the Inquisitor.

It is John Gielgud who stands out with a brilliant performance as the politically-minded Earl of Warwick, determined to get Joan to the stake, though contemptuous of the Church's winded arguments of 'heretic' vs 'witch'.

Graham Greene wrote the screenplay, and while it is somewhat toned down, and probably less anti-clerical than the Shaw original, it still retains the essentials of the Shaw classic.

■ SALLY IN OUR ALLEY

1931, 77 MINS, UK
Dir Maurice Elvey   *Scr* Basil Dean   *Ph* Miles Malleson, Alma Reville, Archie Pitt
● Gracie Fields, Ian Hunter, Florence Desmond, Fred Groves, Gibb McLaughlin (Associated Talking Pictures/Radio)

Gracie Fields doesn't exactly suggest sufficient sympathy to hold the romantic lead, but her eccentric singing and dialect-gagging records well.

Story [from the play *The Likes of 'Er* by Charles McEvoy] tells how a Lancashire girl refuses to marry because her boy friend is reported killed in the war, although actually he isn't dead but pretends to be because he's crippled. She makes a hit serving and singing in a coffee shop.

Atmosphere is good generally. Introduction of the songs is resourceful and some of the gags are quite good. Dialog is pert on English comedy lines. But the whole canvas is very small and the footage seems very long.

Fields is just Fields as in vaude, but lacking aggressiveness. Ian Hunter has more repose and acting ability than the rest, while new-comer Florence Desmond troupes well in an utterly unsympathetic role.

■ SALLY, IRENE AND MARY

1938, 86 MINS, US
Dir William A. Seiter   *Prod* Darryl F. Zanuck
Scr Harry Tugend, Jack Yellen   *Ph* Peverell Marley
Ed Walter Thompson   *Mus* Arthur Lange (dir.)
Art Dir Bernard Herzbrun, Rudolph Sternad
● Alice Faye, Tony Martin, Fred Allen, Jimmy Durante, Gregory Ratoff, Joan Davis (20th Century-Fox)

Sally, Irene and Mary is another in the Darryl F. Zanuck formula of vaudscreen musicals, skillfully blending the variety components and dovetailing them into an amiable entertainment [from an original story by Karl Tunberg and Don Ettlinger, suggested by a play by Edward Dowling and Cyrus Wood].

Fred Allen marks his second big league picture work since he became a radio name. He foils with and for Jimmy Durante, both proving an efective team throughout with a running gag sequence.

It's the vocal prowess of Tony Martin and Alice Faye, Mr and Mrs in private life and the romance interest here, that does much to sustain the interest.

Gregory Ratoff as an amorous baron, the gangling Joan Davis with her standard comedy hokum, notably a gypsy sequence, Durante as a white wing gone impresario, and a runaway show boat (finale) are the comedy highlights. Plus of course Allen's own stacato line-reading, cast as a shoestring agent. He's foiled principally in this respect by Louise Hovick, nee Gypsy Rose Lee, doing a sleeker, brunet Mae West.

■ SALOME

1953, 102 MINS, US ◇ ▼
Dir William Dieterle   *Prod* Buddy Adler   *Scr* Harry Kleiner   *Ph* Charles Lang   *Ed* Viola Lawrence
Mus George Duning, Daniele Amfitheatrof   *Art Dir* John Meehan
● Rita Hayworth, Stewart Granger, Judith Anderson, Cedric Hardwicke, Alan Badel (Columbia/Beckworth)

The story by Jesse L. Lasky Jr and the screenplay by Harry Kleiner, change and embroider the Biblical tale of the girl who danced for King Herod and caused the beheading of John the Baptist. More their own interpretation than a factual chronicle of the religious story, it is a vehicle especially slanted for Rita Hayworth.

Film opens by establishing King Herod's superstitious fear of John the Baptist and his protection of the prophet, despite the insistence of his queen, Herodias, that the holy man be slain for talking against the throne. Opening also finds Salome, Herod's step-daughter, banished from Rome because Caesar's nephew wants to marry her. During the trip back to Galilee, she vents her spite against all Romans on Commander Claudius, played by Stewart Granger, even though they are attracted to each other. Salome finds Galilee in a state of unrest and, egged on by her wicked mother, Herodias, tries to enlist Claudius' aid in doing away with the prophet.

Hayworth, who has never been better photographed, injects excellent dramatic values and wears the clinging Roman costumes to advantage. Her dance, staged by Valerie Bettis, packs plenty of s.a. Granger gives an easy, assured masculine portrayal to his central role, and when he and Miss Hayworth are on together the picture has a decided lift.

■ SALT OF THE EARTH

1954, 94 MINS, US ▼
Dir Herbert J. Biberman   *Prod* Paul Jarrico
Scr Michael Wilson   *Ph* [uncredited]
Ed [uncredited]   *Mus* Sol Kaplan
● Rosaura Revueltas, Juan Chacon, Will Geer, David Wolfe, Mervin Williams, David Sarvis (Independent/International Union of Mine, Mill & Smelter Workers)

Salt of the Earth is a good, highly dramatic and emotion-charged piece of work that tells its story straight. It is, however, a propaganda picture which belongs in union halls rather than theatres.

It is a bitter tale that Michael Wilson has concocted and the large cast acts it out with a conviction that obviously didn't require much prompting. The story concerns Mexican miners in a small New Mexican mining community, Zinc Town. A series of mine accidents prompts a strike. The company attempts to break it via acts of intimidation that include arrest and brutality.

Director Herbert J. Biberman was one of the Unfriendly Ten who served a five-months jail sentence for contempt of Congress. Producer Paul Jarrico also was in trouble with Congress.

Yet as a piece of film artistry, *Salt* achieves moments of true pictorial excellence. Rosaura Revueltas, a Mexican actress playing the wife of the strike leader, gives a taut, impressive performance that has real dimension. Juan

Chacon, a union leader in real life, turns in a creditable acting job.

Biberman's direction achieves distinctive quality. He concentrates on misery and violence and anger with a stark determination and a flair for realism that is designed to do much more than rouse sympathy.

■ SALVADOR

1986, 123 MINS, US ◇ Ⓥ
Dir Oliver Stone *Prod* Gerald Green, Oliver Stone
Scr Oliver Stone, Richard Boyle *Ph* Robert Richardson *Ed* Claire Simpson *Mus* Georges Delerue *Art Dir* Bruno Rubeo
● James Woods, James Belushi, Michael Murphy, John Savage, Elpedia Carrillo, Tony Plana (Hemdale)

The tale of American photojournalist Richard Boyle's adventures in strife-torn Central America, *Salvador* is as raw, difficult, compelling, unreasonable, reckless and vivid as its protagonist.

James Woods portrays the real-life Boyle, who at the outset is shown to be at his lowest ebb as a virtual bum and professional outcast in San Francisco.

With no particular prospects, he shanghais fun-loving buddy James Belushi for the long drive down to (El) Salvador, where Woods has left behind a native girlfriend and where he thinks he might be able to pick up some freelance work.

The film has an immediacy, energy and vividness that is often quite exciting, and the essential truth of much of what director Oliver Stone has put on display will prove bracing for many viewers.

■ SAME TIME, NEXT YEAR

1978, 119 MINS, US ◇ Ⓥ
Dir Robert Mulligan *Prod* Walter Mirisch, Morton Gottlieb *Scr* Bernard Slade *Ph* Robert Surtees *Ed* Sheldon Kahn *Mus* Marvin Hamlisch *Art Dir* Henry Bumstead
● Ellen Burstyn, Alan Alda, Ivan Bonar (Universal)

Same Time, Next Year is a textbook example of how to successfully transport a stage play to the big screen. The production of Bernard Slade's play, sensitively directed by Robert Mulligan, is everything you'd want from this kind of film. And it features two first class performances by Ellen Burstyn and Alan Alda.

The picture opens in 1951 at a resort in northern California. Burstyn, a 24-year-old Oakland housewife, and Alda, a 27-year-old accountant from New Jersey, meet over dinner, get along and have a fling. The next morning they wake up in the same bed, talk about what's happened, realize that while they're both happily married with six children between them, they're in love.

They make a pact to meet at the same resort every year, which is just what they do and is just what the film is about. We see the two every five or six years as they adjust to the changes time brings.

What always remains through the years is the deep affection the two share. It's nice to see a film about two people who like each other this deeply.

■ SAMMY AND ROSIE GET LAID

1987, 100 MINS, UK ◇ Ⓥ
Dir Stephen Frears *Prod* Tim Bevan, Sarah Radclyffe *Scr* Hanif Kureishi *Ph* Oliver Stapleton *Ed* Mick Audsley *Mus* Stanley Myers *Art Dir* Hugo Luczyc Wyhowski
● Shashi Kapoor, Claire Bloom, Ayub Khan Din, Frances Barber, Roland Gift (Cinecom/Film Four)

Cynical and brutally unsentimental in outlook, *Sammy and Rosie Get Laid*, brings the force of an accelerated cinematic attack to bear upon its complex thematic juxtaposition of sexual warfare, cross-cultural dislocation, racism and the ruthlessness of power.

With relentless momentum director Stephen Frears unfolds the story of Sammy, (Ayub Khan Din), the hedonistic, thoroughly English son of a prominent Pakistani politician. Sammy, who scrapes out a living as an accountant, lives in a dangerous and decaying black neighborhood with his wife Rosie (Frances Barber), a sexually adventurous feminist journalist.

Change enters their lives with the arrival of Rafi (Shashi Kapoor), Sammy's long-lost father who has been forced to flee his political enemies in Pakistan. Rafi attempts to buy his way back into the affection of his son and that of a beautiful and sensitive Englishwoman, Alice (Claire Bloom) whom he also cruelly abandoned in his self-centered quest for power in the East.

Frears levitates the film's harsh realism with a fantastical counterpoint in touches like the ghost of a tortured labor leader who haunts Rafi from the outset, and a band of gypsy buskers who serenade the ongoing anarchy.

■ SAMMY GOING SOUTH

1963, 128 MINS, UK ◇
Dir Alexander Mackendrick *Prod* Michael Balcon *Scr* Denis Cannan *Ph* Edwin Hillier *Ed* Jack Harris *Mus* Tristram Cary
● Edward G. Robinson, Fergus McClelland, Constance Cummings, Harry H. Corbett, Paul Stassino, Zia Moyheddin (British Lion/Bryanston Seven Arts)

Pic is based on an uneasy, incredible idea [from a novel by W.H. Canaway]. A 10-year-old youngster (Fergus McClelland) is orphaned when his parents are killed in an air raid during the Suez crisis. In a blur he remembers that he has an Aunt Jane in Durban and that Durban is in the South. So he sets out, armed only with a toy compass.

He meets a Syrian peddler who sees in the kid a chance of a reward from Aunt Jane. He meets a rich American tourist but escapes her greedy clutches. Not until he meets up with a grizzled old diamond smuggler (Edward G. Robinson) does the film flicker into some spark of human interest. The old man and the moppet strike up a splendid friendship.

Mackendrick's films usually strike an attitude and have intuition on points of views. Relationships between his key characters are usually more clearly defined and worked on than in this. With the exception of Robinson, looking like a slightly junior Ernest Hemingway, and Paul Stassino, as a glib crook of a guide, the others are cardboard.

■ SAMSON AND DELILAH

1949, 120 MINS, US ◇ Ⓥ
Dir Cecil B. DeMille *Prod* Cecil B. DeMille *Scr* Jesse L. Lasky Jr, Frederic M. Frank *Ph* George Barnes *Ed* Anne Bauchens *Mus* Victor Young
● Hedy Lamarr, Victor Mature, George Sanders, Angela Lansbury, Henry Wilcoxon, Russ Tamblyn (Paramount)

Cecil B. DeMille has again dipped into the Bible for his material, made appropriately dramatic revisions in the original, and turned up with a DeMille-size smash.

The scriptwriters have woven from the abbreviated biblical telling of the Samson legend a lusty action story with a heavy coating of torrid-zone romance. Dozens of bit players and extras in tremendous, sweeping sets give size to the picture.

Victor Mature fits neatly into the role of the handsome but dumb hulk of muscle that both the Bible and DeMille make of the Samson character. Hedy Lamarr never has been more eye-filling and makes of Delilah a convincing minx. George Sanders gives a pleasantly light flavor of satirical humor to the part of the ruler, while Henry Wilcoxon is duly rugged as the military man.

The picture is claimed to have cost $3 million and looks well like it might have run considerably more than that.

■ SAN DEMETRIO-LONDON

1943, 93 MINS, UK
Dir Charles Frend *Prod* Michael Balcon *Scr* Robert Hamer, Charles Frend *Ph* Ernest Palmer *Ed* Eily Boland *Mus* John Greenwood
● Walter Fitzgerald, Mervyn Johns, Ralph Michael, Robert Beatty, Gordon Jackson (Ealing)

Whether wittingly or accidentally, the presentation of this epic tale of the British Merchant Marine omits the customary cast of characters in the screen credits. Thus does it emphasize the genuineness of the personalities concerned in the unfolding of a gripping drama.

So one prefers to believe the man who plays the skipper of the *San Demetrio* is Captain Waite in person, just as the tough, nameless Texan who joins the tanker in Galveston is a tough Texan imbued with the idea of Britain's needing help to win the war.

If the chief engineer – who performs miracles in the half-flooded, fire-swept engine room by not only restarting the engines, but by cooking a pailful of potatoes in live steam from a leaking valve – is not a c.e. in real life, it really doesn't make any difference. And this goes for all of them, from the bosun to the kid apprentice whose first voyage it is.

Much credit must go to Michael Balcon, the producer, and Charles Frend, who directed. How much F. Tennyson Jesse's official account on salvaging the *San Demetrio*, after she had been abandoned for two days and nights 900 miles from her port, helped Robert Hamer and the director in their writing of the script can only be surmised, but the dialog is unvaryingly authentic.

■ SAN FRANCISCO

1936, 115 MINS, US Ⓥ
Dir W.S. Van Dyke *Prod* John Emerson, Bernard Hyman *Scr* Anita Loos *Ph* Oliver T. Marsh *Ed* Tom Held *Mus* Herbert Stothart
● Clark Gable, Jeanette MacDonald, Spencer Tracy, Jack Holt, Jessie Ralph, Ted Healy (M-G-M)

An earthquake noisy and terrifying, is *San Francisco*'s forte. Quake occurs after more than an hour and up to then the picture is distinguished chiefly for its corking cast and super-fine production.

Story basically follows the outline traced previously by Warner's *Frisco Kid* and Goldwyn's *Barbary Coast* [both 1935] although this one tends more to the musical through the constant singing of Jeanette MacDonald.

Lone incongruous note is the remarkable survival of Clark Gable after a whole wall has toppled over on him. His survival is necessary, to complete the picture, but it might have been made easier to believe.

As were James Cagney and Edward G. Robinson before him, Gable is 'king' of the Barbary Coast, and like his predecessors, his reformation is the essence of the plot [story by Robert Hopkins]. Only this guy is tougher; it takes the earthquake to cure him. As Blackie Norton he operates a prosperous gambling joint and beer garden. The closest friend of this godless soul is a priest, who doesn't try to reform Blackie but always hopes for the best.

MacDonald enters as a Denver choir singer who's in Frisco looking for work. From the show at Blackie Norton's she graduates to grand opera under the sponsorship of Blackie's political rival.

Spencer Tracy plays a priest, and it's the most difficult role in the picture. His slang – he calls Gable 'mug' and 'sucker' good naturedly – is the sort usually associated with men of lesser spiritual quality.
□ 1936: Best Picture (Nomination)
....

■ **SAN QUENTIN**

1946, 66 MINS, US
Dir Gordon M. Douglas *Prod* Martin Mooney
Scr Lawrence Kimble, Arthur A. Ross, Howard J. Green *Ph* Frank Redman *Ed* Marvin Coil *Mus* Paul Sawtell *Art Dir* Albert S. D'Agostino, Lucius O. Croxton
● Lawrence Tierney, Barton MacLane, Harry Shannon, Marian Carr, Carol Forman, Richard Powers (RKO)

Gordon M. Douglas whips together this tale of reformation leagues within prisons with plenty of movement, spotting action and development without a slow moment. Lawrence Tierney, as a prisoner of San Quentin, now reformed and just discharged from honorable army service, acquits himself capably, making role believable all the way.

Plot frames its melodramatics around efforts of Harry Shannon, San Quentin warden, to keep his prisoners' welfare league going in the face of opposition. Taking a group of prisoners to San Francisco to speak to a newspaper club, Shannon is wounded and others killed when a supposedly reformed inmate arranges an escape. To clear the warden's plan and make life better for majority of prisoners Tierney goes on a manhunt for Barton MacLane, the killer.
....

■ **SAND CASTLE, THE**

1961, 70 MINS, US ◇
Dir Jerome Hill *Prod* Jerome Hill *Scr* Jerome Hill *Ph* Lloyd Ahern *Ed* Julia Knowlton, Henri A. Sundquist *Mus* Alec Wilder
● Barrie Cardwell, Laurie Cardwell, George Dunham, Maybelle Nash, Erica Speyer (De Rochemont/Noel)

This delightful, fanciful look at the world and its people as we might like them to be is the complete work of Jerome Hill who previously made the notable documentary *Albert Schweitzer*.

A little boy and his sister (Barrie and Laurie Cardwell) start the day's activities as their mother leaves them on the beach to play. Slowly but in ever-increasing numbers, other people begin to arrive: the painter (George Dunham) who must change his picture as the people obscure his view; the eccentric old lady (Maybelle Nash) who brings her bird in its cage and sits beneath a large canopy; the angler, the diver, the fat man and the blonde who worship the sun.

Oblivious to them all, the boy starts to build a large sand castle in the shape of a fort, helped by his sister who fetches driftwood and shells. The others gather round and admire his work. There is no dialog, only incidental and amusing conversation.

Nothing is overstated and none of the characters is overdrawn or derivative. The mood is always one of gentleness, charm and tranquility. As the afternoon ends everyone goes home and the boy and his sister fall asleep by their castle to dream (in color) of being within its walls where they meet cut-out puppets (also the work of Hill) of the people who were on the beach.
....

■ **SAND PEBBLES, THE**

1966, 193 MINS, US ◇ ▼
Dir Robert Wise *Prod* Robert Wise *Scr* Robert Anderson *Ph* Joseph MacDonald *Ed* William Reynolds *Mus* Jerry Goldsmith *Art Dir* Boris Leven
● Steve McQueen, Richard Attenborough, Richard Crenna, Candice Bergen, Marayat Andriane, Mako (Argyle/Solar/20th Century-Fox)

Out of the 1926 political and military turmoil in China, producer-director Robert Wise has created a sensitive, personal drama, set against a background of old style US Navy gunboat diplomacy. *The Sand Pebbles*, based on the novel by Richard McKenna, is a handsome production, boasting some excellent acting characterizations.

Steve McQueen looks and acts the part he plays so well – that of a machinist's mate with nine years of navy service. Richard Crenna likewise is authentic as the gunboat captain, a young lieutenant who speaks the platitudes of leadership with a slight catch in his throat, due to lack of practical experience.

The title derives from a language perversion of San Pablo, formal name of the gunboat on Yangtze river patrol. Among the crew is Richard Attenborough, very believable in his role as a sailor who falls in love with newcomer Marayat Andriane in a tragic bi-racial romance. Her performance is sensitive.

The major drawback to the film as a whole is a surfeit of exposition, mainly in the second half. Every scene is in itself excellent, but unfortunately the overall dramatic flow of the pic suffers in the end.
□ 1966: Best Picture (Nomination)
....

■ **SANDERS OF THE RIVER**

1935, 98 MINS, UK ▼
Dir Zoltan Korda *Prod* Alexander Korda *Scr* Lajos Biro, Jeffrey Dell *Ph* Georges Perinal *Ed* Charles Crichton *Mus* Mischa Spoliansky *Art Dir* Vincent Korda
● Leslie Banks, Paul Robeson, Nina Mae McKinney, Robert Cochran, Martin Walker, Allan Jeayes (London/United Artists)

Story of an African colony is an immense production, done for the greater part with deft direction, played with distinction by two main characters. Leslie Banks and Paul Robeson carry the greater part of this tale of a British commissioner who rules an African sector through commanding both fear and respect.

The story [from an original by Edgar Wallace] is simple. Sanders (Banks) is in charge of a large section in the British African possessions. He makes a minor chief of Bosambo (Robeson), an engaging fugitive from prison, revealing the excellence of his judgment of men. Mofolabo, known as 'the old king', is in an inaccessible section of the district and gives much trouble. When Sanders goes out on leave to get married, rum runners send word through the district that Sanders is dead, inciting the king to fresh depredations. But Sanders has gone only as far as the coast when he hears of the trouble, and comes back.

There are some nicely staged mob scenes, mostly ceremonials, with a remarkable male muscle dancer and a small regiment of natives who appear to be genuine. Robeson gets two of the songs [lyrics by Arthur Wimperis], with the third going to Nina Mae McKinney, a lullaby set against a humming harmonic background.
....

■ **SANDPIPER, THE**

1965, 115 MINS, US ◇ ▼
Dir Vincente Minnelli *Prod* Martin Ransohoff *Scr* Dalton Trumbo, Michael Wilson *Ph* Milton Krasner *Ed* David Bretherton *Mus* Johnny Mandel *Art Dir* George W. Davis, Urie McCleary
● Elizabeth Taylor, Richard Burton, Eva Marie Saint, Charles Bronson, Robert Webber, James Edwards (M-G-M)

The Sandpiper is the story of a passing affair between an unwed nonconformist and a married Episcopalian minister who is headmaster of a private boys school attended by femme's

nine-year-old son. Original by Martin Ransohoff, who produced, is trite and often ponderous in its philosophizing by the two principals, and picture is further burdened by lack of any fresh approach.

Under Vincente Minnelli's leisurely but dramatic direction, the screenplay opens on Elizabeth Taylor as a budding artist whose young son is taken away from her after lad's brush with the law and sent to the school run by Richard Burton. Latter becomes interested in her although ostensibly happily wed to Eva Marie Saint, mother of his twin teenage sons.

Burton probably comes off best with a more restrained performance, although Taylor plays well enough a role without any great acting demands.

Eva Maria Saint gets the most out of a comparatively brief appearance, most of her drama confined to her reaction upon Burton's confession. Morgan Mason, son of Pamela and James Mason, makes a nice impression as Taylor's son.
....

■ **SANDS OF IWO JIMA**

1949, 110 MINS, US ▼
Dir Allan Dwan *Prod* Edmund Grainger *Scr* Harry Brown, James Edward Grant *Ph* Reggie Lanning *Ed* Richard L. Van Enger *Mus* Victor Young
● John Wayne, John Agar, Adele Mara, Forrest Tucker, Wally Cassell, Richard Webb (Republic)

This is a vast saga of a marine platoon whose history is traced from its early combat training through its storming of Iwo Jima's beaches to the historic flag-raising episode atop the sandy atoll. It's loaded with the commercial ingredients of blazing action, scope and spectacle, but it falls short of greatness because of its sentimental core and its superficial commentary on the war.

Best portions of this pic are the straight battle sequences, many of which were made up of footage taken at the actual fighting at Tarawa and Iwo Jima.

John Wayne stands head and shoulders above the rest of the cast, and not only physically, as the ruthlessly efficient marine sergeant. He draws a powerful portrait of a solider with the job of making plain joes into murdering machines.
....

■ **SANDS OF THE KALAHARI**

1965, 119 MINS, UK ◇
Dir Cy Endfield *Prod* Joseph E. Levine *Scr* Cy Endfield *Ph* Erwin Hillier *Ed* John Jympson *Mus* John Dankworth
● Stuart Whitman, Stanley Baker, Susannah York, Harry Andrews, Theodore Bikel, Nigel Davenport (Paramount/Levine)

Cy Endfield, co-producer, director and scripter of the long film (made almost entirely on location in Africa), wisely makes the camera as important as anyone in the cast, emphasizing the savagery that is throughout. Although Endfield has been lucky with his casting, some members too quickly betray symptoms of scenery chewing.

A planeload of assorted types crashes in the desert and the rest of the film deals with their efforts to survive. It's some time before a villain is unveiled and, even then, the viewer's faith gets a few shakes. Susannah York, as the only female in the cast, gets plenty of exposure. Stuart Whitman, a gunhappy survivalist, and Stanley Baker, a nondescript loser, are the only main characters. Unbilled but colorful are assorted natives, animals and insects.

Entertainment, pure and simple [from a novel by William Mulvihill], was evidently what the filmmakers aimed for and that's the target they hit.
....

■ SANDWICH MAN, THE

1966, 95 MINS, UK ◇

Dir Robert Hartford-Davis *Prod* Peter Newbrook
Scr Michael Bentine, Robert Hartford-Davis *Ph* Peter Newbrook *Ed* Peter Taylor *Mus* Mike Vickers
● Michael Bentine, Dora Bryan, Harry H. Corbett, Bernard Cribbins, Diana Dors, Ian Hendry (Titan)

The Sandwich Man is like a documentary in drag. Michael Bentine, who wrote the screenplay with the director, Robert Hartford-Davis, seeks to give a picture of London and some of the wayout, curious behaviour of its inhabitants through the eyes of a sandwichboard man who, wandering the streets, has a load of opportunity of observing, and of getting implicated. Not a bad idea and, filmed on location entirely, it gives director and cameraman Peter Newbrook a swell chance of bringing London to life. But in the countdown, a film has either got to be a feature pic or a 'doc' primarily.

A loosely scribed romance between a young car salesman and a model, and the fact that on this day Bentine's prize racing pigeon is competing in an important race are the only two highly slim 'plotlines'. For the remainder, Bentine (dressed as a dude sandwichboard man) wanders around observing the odd things happening around him.

Bentine has an amiable personality that deserves further screen exposure.

■ SANTA CLAUS

1985, 112 MINS, US ◇ ⊗

Dir Jeannot Szwarc *Prod* Ilya Salkind, Pierre Spengler *Scr* David Newman *Ph* Arthur Ibbetson
Ed Peter Hollywood *Mus* Henry Mancini
Art Dir Anthony Pratt
● David Huddleston, Dudley Moore, John Lithgow, Judy Cornwell, Christian Fitzpatrick, Carrie Kei Heim (Salkind/Santa Claus)

Santa Claus is a film for children of all ages, but will probably skew best toward infancy or senility.

Oddly enough, even Scrooge himself might adore the first 20 minutes when *Santa* develops a charming attitude, lovely special effects and a magical feeling that the audience may indeed be settling down for a warm winter's eve.

After that, however, the picture becomes Santa Meets Son of Flubber or something in a mad rush to throw in whatever might appeal to anybody. Bah, humbug.

David Huddleston is a perfect Claus, first introduced several centuries ago as a woodcutter who delights in distributing Christmas gifts to village children. Wondrously, Mr and Mrs Claus awake to discover they are at the North Pole, where their arrival is excitedly hailed by elves led by Dudley Moore.

Moore manufactures a batch of bad toys and, sorry to have disappointed Santa, flees to 20th Century New York City, where he ends up working in a crooked toy factory run by John Lithgow, saddled with an absolutely horrible, cigar-sucking performance as a greedy corporate monster.

■ SAPPHIRE

1959, 92 MINS, UK ◇ ⊗

Dir Basil Dearden *Prod* Michael Relph, Basil Dearden *Scr* Janet Green *Ph* Harry Waxman
Ed John Guthridge *Mus* Philip Green
● Nigel Patrick, Yvonne Mitchell, Michael Craig, Paul Massie, Bernard Miles, Earl Cameron (Rank)

Sapphire is a well-knit pic showing how the police patiently track down a murderer. But, though obviously inspired by 1958's outbreak of color-bar riots in London and Nottingham, it ducks the issue, refusing to face boldly up to the problem. It eventually adds up merely to another whodunit.

Victim of a savage murder in a London open space is attractive music student Sapphire (Yvonne Buckingham). The girl is revealed as having a dual personality. As well as being a student, she is also a good-time girl with a love for the bright lights. She is pregnant after an affair with a young man with a brilliant career as architect awaiting him.

Director Basil Dearden has a very effective cast. Nigel Patrick is fine as a suave, polite but ruthlessly efficient cop. Michael Craig, his assistant, is equally good as a less tolerant man who, for some unexplained reason, loathes coloured people. But perhaps the best performance of all is that of Earl Cameron as an intelligent, tolerant Negro doctor who is the brother of the slain girl. Cameron brings immense dignity to a small role.

■ SARABAND FOR DEAD LOVERS

1948, 96 MINS, UK ◇

Dir Basil Dearden, Michael Relph *Prod* Michael Balcon *Scr* John Dighton, Alexander Mackendrick
Ph Douglas Slocombe *Ed* Michael Truman *Mus* Alan Rawsthorne *Art Dir* Jim Morahang, William Kellner
● Stewart Granger, Joan Greenwood, Flora Robson, Francoise Rosay, Anthony Quayle, Frederick Valk (Ealing)

Colorful production, magnificent settings and costumes enhanced by unobtrusive use of Technicolor and a powerful melodramatic story of court intrigue at the House of Hanover in the early 18th century, add up to a firstrate piece of hokum entertainment.

Taken from Helen Simpson's novel, the screenplay sincerely captures the atmosphere of the period. It tells the poignant story of the unhappy Princess Dorothea, compelled to marry against her will the uncouth Prince Louis to strengthen his title to the kingship of England.

Without undue sentiment, and with emotion in the right key, the plot unfolds against the fascinating background of the Hanoverian court, with its intrigue and tragedies, its romances and miseries.

Reality is established by the excellent characterization of a well-chosen cast. Stewart Granger, as the Swedish Count Konigsmark, gives a performance that ranks with his best. Joan Greenwood is charming and colorful as the hapless Dorothea. Flora Robson is merciless as the arch intriguer at the court.

■ SARATOGA

1937, 90 MINS, US

Dir Jack Conway *Prod* Bernard H. Hyman, John Emerson *Scr* Anita Loos, Robert Hopkins *Ph* Ray June *Ed* Elmo Veron *Mus* Edward Ward
● Jean Harlow, Clark Gable, Lionel Barrymore, Frank Morgan, Walter Pidgeon, Una Merkel (M-G-M)

Saratoga, a story of the thoroughbreds and the men and women who follow the horses around the circuit, is a glamorous comedydrama which the late Jean Harlow was completing, as co-star with Clark Gable. The few scenes remaining to be made at the time of her death were photographed with an alternate in her part, and done with such skill that audiences will not easily distinguish the substitution.

Anita Loos and Robert Hopkins, who collaborated on *San Francisco*, have gone behind the scenes at racetracks and breeding farms to tell a story of human interest. Gable plays a bookmaker in a breezy, horsey manner. Harlow is the daughter in a family which has bred and raced horses for generations. She takes her small inheritance and wagers on the horses. She is prompted to this in an effort to win enough to repurchase the family breeding farm from Gable, who holds the mortgage to cover losses incurred by her father.

Harlow's performance is among her best. She has several rowdy comedy passages with

Gable which are excellently done. The performances of Lionel Barrymore (as the grandfather), Una Merkel (an itinerant follower of the horses), and Frank Morgan (as a turf neophyte) are splendid.

■ SARATOGA TRUNK

1943, 135 MINS, US

Dir Sam Wood *Prod* Hal B. Wallis *Scr* Casey Robinson *Ph* Ernest Haller *Ed* Ralph Dawson
Mus Max Steiner *Art Dir* Fred MacLean
● Gary Cooper, Ingrid Bergman, Flora Robson (Warner)

Story has color, romance, adventure, and not a little s.a. Ingrid Bergman is the beautiful albeit calculating Creole, and Gary Cooper is very effective in the plausible role of a droll, gamblin' Texan who has the romantic hex on the headstrong Creole. Flora Robson is capitally cast as her body-servant and Jerry Austin does a bangup job as the dwarf who, with the mulatto servant, make a strange entourage.

The 1875 period, and the New Orleans and Saratoga locales, combine into a moving story as Bergman returns from Paris to avenge her mother's 'shame'. That this is a spurious sentimentality, considering she was born out of wedlock, and her father's family sought to banish her virtually to France, is beside the point. Bergman, as fetching in a brunette wig as in her natural lighter tresses, takes command in every scene. She sparks the cinematurgy, a vital plus factor considering Cooper's laconic personation, and the sultry reticence of her two curious servants.

The two major geographical segments – her native NO and the fertile Saratoga – are replete with basic action and never pall.

■ SATAN BUG, THE

1965, 114 MINS, US ◇ ⊗

Dir John Sturges *Prod* John Sturges *Scr* James Clavell, Edward Anhalt *Ph* Robert Surtees *Ed* Ferris Webster *Mus* Jerry Goldsmith
● George Maharis, Richard Basehart, Anne Francis, Dana Andrews, Edward Asner, Frank Sutton (Mirisch-Kappa)

The Satan Bug is a superior suspense melodrama and should keep audiences on the edge of their seats despite certain unexplained, confusing elements which tend to make plot at times difficult to follow.

Based on a novel by Ian Stuart (nom de plume for Britisher Alistair MacLean), producer-director John Sturges builds his action to a generally chilling pace after a needlesslyslow opening which establishes America's experiments in bacteriological warfare at a highly-secret top-security research installation in the desert. The scientist who develops the deadly virus known as the Satan Bug, so lethal it can cause instant death over great areas, is murdered and flasks containing the liquid mysteriously spirited out of the lab.

Script projects George Maharis as a former Army Intelligence officer recalled to find the virus before it can be put to the use threatened by a millionaire paranoiac who masterminded the theft and claims to hate war.

Maharis makes a good impression as the investigator, although his character isn't developed sufficiently – a fault also applying to other principals – due to overspeedy editing in an attempt to narrate story at fever pitch.

■ SATAN MET A LADY

1936, 74 MINS, US

Dir William Dieterle *Scr* Brown Holmes *Ph* Arthur Edeson *Ed* Warren Low *Art Dir* Max Parker
● Bette Davis, Warren William, Alison Skipworth, Arthur Treacher, Winifred Shaw, Marie Wilson (Warner)

S

This is an inferior remake of *The Maltese Falcon*, which Warner produced in 1931. Many changes have been made [to the novel by Dashiell Hammett], in story structure as well as title, but none is an improvement.

Bette Davis is dropped to featured billing rank in this one, on an equal basis with Warren William, and both under the title. But as for importance in the story, Davis has much less to do than at least one other femme member of the cast.

Where the detective of *Maltese Falcon* and his activities were natural and amusing, he and his satiric crime detection are now forced and unnatural.

Among items changed are the names of the characters as well as a few of the characters themselves. Sam Spade, played by Ricardo Cortez in the original, is now Ted Shane as played by Warren William. The plaster bird is now a ram's horn. There's hardly any mystery in this version. The comedy isn't strong enough to fill the bill.

William tries hard to be gay as the eccentric private cop and his performance is all that keeps the picture moving in many lagging moments. Marie Wilson has a tendency to muff her best chances through overstressing.

....

■ **SATAN NEVER SLEEPS**

1962, 133 MINS, US ◇

Dir Leo McCarey   *Prod* Leo McCarey   *Scr* Claude Binyon, Leo McCarey   *Ph* Oswald Morris   *Ed* Gordon Pilkington   *Mus* Richard Rodney Bennett   *Art Dir* Tom Morahan

● William Holden, Clifton Webb, France Nuyen, Athene Seyler, Martin Benson, Weaver Lee (20th Century-Fox)

China in its critical year of 1949 is the setting of the screenplay, from a novel by Pearl S. Buck. Cornered in this moment of imminent national alteration to Communism are two Catholic priests, played by Clifton Webb and William Holden, the latter adoringly but hopelessly pursued by a Chinese maiden (France Nuyen). The priests are soon imprisoned by the local People's Party leader (Weaver Lee), who also rapes the girl.

Lee eventually see the light when: (1) Nuyen given birth to his child, (2) his parents are murdered by the Reds, (3) he is reprimanded and demoted for personal ambition and leniency. More occurs in the final 15 minutes of this picture than in the preceding 118.

Holden is a kind of leather-jacketed variation of Bing Crosby's sweatshirted Father O'Malley and Webb a wry, caustic version of Barry Fitzgerald's Father Fitzgibbon in Leo McCarey's *Going My Way* (1944). Nuyen plays vivaciously as the sweet nuisance. The villains are absurdly all black. Outdoor locations in England and Wales pass acceptably for China.

....

■ **SATURDAY NIGHT AND SUNDAY MORNING**

1960, 89 MINS, UK

Dir Karel Reisz   *Prod* Tony Richardson, Harry Saltzman   *Scr* Alan Sillitoe   *Ph* Freddie Francis   *Ed* Seth Holt   *Mus* Johnny Dankworth

● Albert Finney, Shirley Anne Field, Rachel Roberts, Hylda Baker, Norman Rossington, Bryan Pringle (Woodfall/Bryanston)

Alan Sillitoe's novel is produced, directed and acted with integrity and insight. This is a good, absorbing but not very likeable film.

The hero is a Nottingham factory worker who refuses to conform. He hates all authority but protests so blunderingly. His attitude is simple: 'What I want is a good time. The remainder is all propaganda.' Through the week he works hard at his lathe. In his spare time – Saturday night and Sunday morning (and a couple of evenings) – he comes into his own. Liquor and women.

Sillitoe does a good job with his first screenplay, though, necessarily, much of the motive and the thinking of his characters has been lost in the adaptation. Director Karel Reisz' experience in documentaries enables him to bring a sharp tang and authenticity to the film. The locations and the interiors have caught the full atmosphere of a Midland industrial town.

The central figure is cocky, violent and selfish, yet at times almost pathetically likeable. Albert Finney, in his first major screen performance, handles scenes of belligerence and one or two love scenes with complete confidence and is equally effective in quieter moments. On a par is the performance of Rachel Roberts as the married woman carrying on a hopeless affair with Finney. Shirley Anne Field, as the conventional young woman who eventually snares Finney, is appropriately pert.

....

■ **SATURDAY NIGHT FEVER**

1977, 119 MINS, US ◇ Ⓥ

Dir John Badham   *Prod* Robert Stigwood   *Scr* Norman Wexler   *Ph* Ralph D. Bode   *Ed* David Rawlins   *Mus* Barry Gibb, Robin Gibb, Maurice Gibb, David Shire   *Art Dir* Charles Bailey

● John Travolta, Karen Lynn Gorney, Barry Miller, Joseph Cali, Paul Pape, Bruce Ornstein (Paramount)

John Travolta stars as an amiably inarticulate NY kid who comes to life only in a disco environment. The clumsy story lurches forward through predictable travail and treacle, separated by phonograph records (or vice versa). John Badham's direction is awkward.

Coloring-book plot lines give Travolta a bad homelife (Val Bisoglio's father is an ethnic horror story), a formula gang of buddies, an available 'bad' girl (Donna Pescow), an elusive 'good' girl (Karen Lynn Gorney) plus lots of opportunity to boogie on the dance floor and make out in automobile back seats.

Between original music by Barry, Robin and Maurice Gibb plus David Shire, and familiar platter hits, the film usually has some rhythm going on in the background.

....

■ **SATURN 3**

1980, 88 MINS, UK ◇ Ⓥ

Dir Stanley Donen   *Prod* Stanley Donen, Martin Starger   *Scr* Martin Amis   *Ph* Billy Williams   *Ed* Richard Marden   *Mus* Elmer Bernstein   *Art Dir* Stuart Craig

● Farrah Fawcett, Kirk Douglas, Harvey Keitel, Ed Bishop (Grade-Kastner)

Somewhere in deepest, darkest space, Kirk Douglas and Farrah Fawcett jog around through a space station that looks suspiciously like Bloomingdale's after closing. The pair are scientists doing important work, when bad guy Harvey Keitel shows up.

Douglas is sprightly, but he has to handle some pretty awful lines in this Martin Amis script [from a story by John Barry]. Keitel's dialog, if quoted, would be on a par.

Life goes on in this shopping mall of lights till Keitel builds Hector, the mad robot, whose tubes and hubcaps develop goose-bumps for Farrah.

Best scene in the entire effort is Hector's resurrection after he has been dismantled for being randy. The parts find each other and reconnect which is more than this film does.

....

■ **SAVAGES**

1972, 105 MINS, US ◇ Ⓥ

Dir James Ivory   *Prod* Ismail Merchant   *Scr* James Ivory, George Swift Trow, Michael O'Donoghue   *Ph* Walter Lassally   *Ed* Kent McKinney   *Mus* Joe Raposo   *Art Dir* Charles E. White III, Michael Doret

● Louis J. Stadlen, Anne Francine, Thayer David, Susan Blakely, Russ Thacker, Salome Jens (Angelika/Merchant-Ivory)

Savages, first US film by producer Ismail Merchant and director James Ivory, is about members of a primitive tribe who are lured by the appearance of a rolling croquet ball to an old deserted mansion where they dress in clothes and take on 'civilized' societal behavior, only to return to the forest and their primitive behavior the following morning.

The playing has flair and grace, sans woodenness from everyone, with Walter Lassally's excellently balanced b&w lensing for the primitive days and color for the so-called civilized times a great asset, as are the editing and music. The only carp might be a tendency to overplay an act.

But no denying an almost hypnotic charm and fascination in this offbeat, insouciant look at mankind and his climb to civilization and fall.

....

■ **SAVAGE EYE, THE**

1959, 68 MINS, US

Dir Ben Maddow, Sidney Meyers, Joseph Strick   *Prod* Edward Harrison   *Ph* Jack Couffer, Helen Leavitt, Haskell Wexler   *Mus* Leonard Rosenman

● Barbara Baxley, Herschel Bernardi, Jean Hidey, Elizabeth Zemach (City)

Fascinating and uncompromising semi-documentary impressively put together as an obvious labor of love by three talented American film-makers.

Story of a divorced woman's attempts to readjust to a single life affords an excellent opportunity to dissect some frightening and depressing panoramas of modern existence. From the woman's first arrival at a big-city airport (site of most of shooting is Los Angeles, but no effort has been made to establish a specific locale), pic moves into her first visual impressions of the city, its seamy side, its bars and drunks, its beauty parlors lined with elderly women, its store windows, and above all, its people.

Subsequent portions of the film feature, among other things, the detailed horror of a nose-bobbing operation, the bloodthirsty behaviour of men and women at boxing and wrestling matches, a detailed and critically observed striptease sequence, complete with leering spectators, a cruelly fascinating sequence shot during a faith-healing service, and a harrowing and nightmarish bit depicting a pervert's party.

Wealth of material is linked by presence of the key character, caught on her search for warmth and companionship, and by a spoken commentary (well-mouthed by Gary Merrill) in the form of a dialogue between the woman and an imaginary poet.

Footage, shot over a span of several years, boasts much expertly and realistically photographed (some of it hidden-camera) material. It's slickly integrated and matched with recreated sequences to bring about a true-looking patina.

....

■ **SAVAGE INNOCENTS, THE**

1960, 111 MINS, UK/ITALY/US ◇ Ⓥ

Dir Nicholas Ray   *Prod* Joseph Janni, Maleno Malenotti   *Scr* Hans Ruesch   *Ph* Aldo Tonti, Peter Hennessy   *Ed* Ralph Kemplen   *Mus* Angelo Francesco Lavagnino   *Art Dir* Don Ashton

● Anthony Quinn, Yoko Tani, Peter O'Toole, Marie Yang, Francis De Wolff, Anthony Chin (Rank/Malenotti/Paramount)

The Savage Innocents is a polyglot pic. Financial responsibility was carved up between Britain, America and Italy. Rank chipped in with a third of the $1.5 million budget and Pinewood studios and British technicians were

525

used; Italy, through producer Maleno Male-notti, has a third stake; America (Paramount release) supplied the remainder. There's a Yank director and screenplay writer, Nicholas Ray; America's Anthony Quinn is the main star, while the [Japanese] femme lead Yoko Tani comes from Paris.

Remainder of the cast is drawn from various countries. Shooting, apart from Pine-wood, took place in Hudson Bay and Green-land. Somewhere along the line Denmark gets an honorable mention among the credits.

Two undeniable things stand out. Art director and editor have done a standout job in matching and cutting so that it is virtually impossible to decide where Pinewood began and Canada came in. Secondly, the chief lensers have turned out some brilliant camerawork with color sweeping superbly across the widescreen.

The problem is whether the yarn [based on Hans Ruesch's novel *Top of the World*] stands up. For long sessions it is a documentary of life in the Eskimo belt. The story line is simple. It concerns a powerful, good humored hunter (Quinn) who spends the early stages of the film deciding which of two young women he wishes to make his wife. Second half becomes melodrama when he accidentally murders a missionary.

The memorable moments are those of Quinn hunting down foxes, bears, seals, walruses and the majesty of the bleak wastes, the ice, the storms and primitive living conditions. The human element doesn't come out of it quite so well.

Quinn, mainly talking pidgin English-cum-Eskimo, comes out as an authentic Eskimo. Tani is a delight as the woman. Peter O'Toole is firstrate as a tough trooper.

••••••••••••••••••••••••••••••••

■ SAVAGE STREETS

1984, 93 MINS, US ◇ ⊕

Dir Danny Steinmann   *Prod* John C. Strong III
Scr Norman Yonemoto, Danny Steinmann   *Ph* Stephen Posey   *Ed* Bruce Stubblefield, John O'Conner
Mus Michael Lloyd, John D'Andrea   *Art Dir* Ninkey Dalton
● Linda Blair, John Vernon, Robert Dryer, Johnny Venocur, Sal Landi, Scott Mayer (Savage Street)

Linda Blair toplines as Brenda, an LA girl who turns vigilante when her mute younger sister Heather (Linnea Quigley) is brutally gang-raped by a local gang of toughs.

Pic unfolds as a tough update of the juvenile delinquency B-pictures of the 1950s, incorporating ineffectual adult authorities (John Vernon as the hardnosed but powerless high school principal), warring groups of dislikeable good kids and gangs of punks.

The uncensored approach pays off in deliciously vulgar dialog and well-directed confrontation scenes.

Blair emerges here as a tawdry, delightfully trashy sweater girl in a league with 1950s B-heroines such as Beverly Michaels, Juli Reding and Mamie Van Doren.

••••••••••••••••••••••••••••••••

■ SAVAGE, THE

1953, 95 MINS, US ◇

Dir George Marshall   *Prod* Mel Epstein   *Scr* Sydney Boehm   *Ph* John F. Seitz   *Ed* Arthur Schmidt
Mus Paul Sawtell   *Art Dir* Hal Pereira, William Flannery
● Charlton Heston, Susan Morrow, Peter Hanson, Joan Taylor, Richard Rober, Donald Porter (Paramount)

This tale of Indian fighting travels in fairly devious circles to relate a standard story [from a novel by L.L. Foreman]. However, it has excellent outdoor photography and liberal amounts of Indian fighting scenes.

Charlton Heston has a fairly confused role which forces the story to travel unnecessarily in circles. He plays Warbonnet, a white lad who has been brought up as an Indian following the massacre of his father by Crow

Indians. Living with a tribe in the Sioux confederation, Heston knows how to knock off a Crow scalp, but his major problem comes when he has to choose on which side he'll fight in the impending war between the paleface and the Indians.

The femme interest is slight, with Susan Morrow as the belle of the army fort. Joan Taylor as an Indian maid is Morrow's major competition for Heston's affection.

Peter Hanson and Richard Rober do well in major white roles while Indians are staunchly portrayed by Ian MacDonald and Donald Porter. One of the more colorful enactments is by Milburn Stone as a corporal who befriends Heston.

••••••••••••••••••••••••••••••••

■ SAVE THE TIGER

1973, 99 MINS, US ◇ ⊕

Dir John G. Avildsen   *Prod* Steve Shagan   *Scr* Steve Shagan   *Ph* Jim Crabe   *Ed* David Bretherton
Mus Marvin Hamlisch   *Art Dir* Jack Collis
● Jack Lemmon, Jack Gilford, Laurie Heinemann, Norman Burton, Patricia Smith, Thayer David (Filmways)

Save the Tiger is an intellectual exploitation film which ostensibly lays bare the crass materialism of the age. Producer-writer Steve Shagan's script stars Jack Lemmon in an off-beat casting as a pitiable businessman trapped in his own life-style.

Partnered with Jack Gilford in the garment business, Lemmon finds his finances so strapped that he decides to hire a professional arsonist to have what used to be called 'a successful fire' in one of his factories. This trauma occurs on fashion-show day, when lecherous out-of-town buyer Norman Burton demands some call-girl kinkiness and has a coronary attack.

The closest thing to a point of reference is in Gilford's character, who, after the successful fashion line showing, berates Lemmon's ethics. Latter makes a facile comeback, thereby returning the plot to its free-form, floating exploitation of seaminess.

There is a lot of mature, untapped ability on display in Lemmon's performance. Gilford delivers an outstanding performance, beyond the fact that his is the sole voice of sanity. Patricia Smith is excellent as Lemmon's wife.

••••••••••••••••••••••••••••••••

■ SAVING GRACE

1986, 112 MINS, US ◇ ⊕

Dir Robert M. Young   *Prod* Herbert F. Solow
Scr David S. Ward   *Ph* Reynaldo Villalobos   *Art Dir* Giovanni Natalucci
● Tom Conti, Fernando Rey, Erland Josephson, Giancarlo Giannini, Donald Hewlett, Angelo Evans (Embassy)

This may be the first comedy ever about a Pope running away from office – for a short, private spree in the country among the real people whose shepherd he is supposed to be, sans the bureaucratic interference of the Vatican hierarchy.

Tom Conti may be a little young and literally too light on his feet to play a Pope, but he is too good an actor not to make the best of it, eliciting lots of personal sympathy even when not quite convincing as a High Pontiff.

Fernando Rey, Erland Josephson and Donald Hewlett are an amusing trio of Cardinals covering for their boss in his absence. Giancarlo Giannini is effective as a mysterious goat-herd of few words, and Angelo Evans displays plenty of vitality as a tough-acting kid with a good heart.

••••••••••••••••••••••••••••••••

■ SAYONARA

1957, 147 MINS, US ◇ ⊕

Dir Joshua Logan   *Prod* William Goetz   *Scr* Paul Osborn   *Ph* Ellsworth Fredricks   *Ed* Arthur P. Schmidt, Philip W. Anderson   *Mus* Franz Waxman   *Art Dir* Ted Haworth

● Marlon Brando, Red Buttons, Ricardo Montalban, Patricia Owens, Martha Scott, James Garner (Warner)

Sayonara, based on the James A. Michener novel, is a picture of beauty and sensitivity. Amidst the tenderness and the tensions of a romantic drama, it puts across the notion that human relations transcend race barriers. Joshua Logan's direction is tops.

Though strongly supported, particularly by Red Buttons, it's Marlon Brando who carries the production. As Major Gruver, the Korean war air-ace, Brando affects a nonchalant Southern drawl that helps set the character from the very start. He is wholly convincing as the race-conscious Southerner whose humanity finally leads him to rebel against army-imposed prejudice.

Story has combat-fatigued Brando transferred to Kobe for a rest and to meet his State-side sweetheart (Patricia Owens), daughter of the commanding general of the area. They find things have changed and the sensitive, well-educated girl is no longer sure she wants to marry Brando. He in turn is upset because Airman Joe Kelly, played by Buttons, wants to marry a Japanese (Miyoshi Umeki).

Brando meets a beautiful Japanese actress-dancer (Miiko Taka) and gradually falls deeply in love with her. When Buttons and his wife, in desperation, commit suicide, Brando realizes that, regardless of the consequences, he must marry Taka.

Taka plays the proud Hana-ogi, the dedicated dancer, who starts by hating the Americans whom she sees as robbing Japan of its culture and ends in Brando's arms. Apart from being beautiful she's also a distinctive personality and her contribution rates high.

☐ 1957: Best Picture (Nomination)

••••••••••••••••••••••••••••••••

■ SCALPHUNTERS, THE

1968, 102 MINS, US ◇ ⊕

Dir Sydney Pollack   *Prod* Jules Levy   *Scr* William Norton   *Ph* Duke Callaghan, Richard Moore   *Ed* John Woodcock   *Mus* Elmer Bernstein   *Art Dir* Frank Arrigo
● Burt Lancaster, Shelley Winters, Telly Savalas, Ossie Davis, Armando Silvestre (United Artists)

In artistic terms, *The Scalphunters* is hard to describe: a satirical, slapstick, intellectual drama, laced with civil rights overtones, and loaded with recurring action scenes. Burt Lancaster and Shelley Winters provide marquee dressing.

Story topcasts Lancaster as a fur trapper, robbed of his skins by Indian chief Armando Silvestre who swaps cultured Negro ex-slave Ossie Davis. Telly Savalas heads a crew of scalphunters, with Winters as mistress to Savalas. Lancaster and Davis pursue the scalphunters.

The whole ensemble works to a remarkable degree. Lancaster and Davis work particularly well together, ditto Savalas and Winters. There are talky periods of slow pace, but they are terminated before undue damage has been done.

••••••••••••••••••••••••••••••••

■ SCANDAL

1989, 114 MINS, UK/US ◇ ⊕

Dir Michael Caton-Jones   *Prod* Stephen Woolley
Scr Michael Thomas   *Ph* Mike Molley   *Ed* Angus Newton   *Mus* Carl Davis   *Art Dir* Simon Holland
● John Hurt, Joanne Whalley-Kilmer, Bridget Fonda, Ian McKellen, Leslie Phillips, Britt Ekland (Palace/British Screen/Miramax)

In 1963 the sensational revelations that a good-time girl had been having affairs with a British cabinet minister and a Soviet naval attache shocked the UK and helped bring down the Conservative government. *Scandal* reexamines the controversy.

Man-about-town Stephen Ward (John Hurt) meets young showgirl Christine Keeler (Joanne Whalley-Kilmer) and decides to transform her into a glamorous sophisticate.

Ward is delighted when Soviet naval attache Ivanov (Jeroen Krabbe) takes a shine to Whalley-Kilmer, though at the same time cabinet minister John Profumo (Ian McKellen), the secretary of state for war, falls for her.

McKellen is forced to resign and Hurt is eventually arrested and charged with living on the earnings of prostitutes.

Hurt is excellent as the charming but shallow Ward.

Whalley-Kilmer looks the part, but seems happier with the humorous and ironic parts of the script. American Bridget Fonda – with an admirable British accent – is perfect.

. . . .

■ SCANNERS

1981, 102 MINS, CANADA ◇

Dir David Cronenberg   *Prod* Claude Heroux
Scr David Cronenberg   *Ph* Mark Irwin   *Ed* Ron Sanders   *Mus* Howard Shore   *Art Dir* Carol Spier
● Stephen Lack, Jennifer O'Neill, Patrick McGoohan, Michael Ironside (Filmplan)

'*Scanners*' offers at least one literally eye-popping moment and another that can only be called mind-blowing.

A variation on the pod people of *Invasion of the Body Snatchers* in that they cannot readily be distinguished from normal humans, scanners are telepathic curiosities who, like Sissy Spacek's Carrie, are able to zap people and things at will.

There are good scanners and bad scanners and one, Stephen Lack, who is in between and finds himself recruited by scientist Patrick McGoohan to infiltrate the evil group and track down the chief baddie, who has Hitlerian aspirations for his band of psychic gangsters.

Following the pattern of many effects-oriented low-budgeters, story settles into low gear after the opening reel, in which a man's head explodes on camera.

All this should give fans of David Cronenberg's previous pix their money's worth, although lack of any rooting interest vitiates any possible suspense and highly elegant visual style works against much shock value. Ending is also a bit puzzling.

. . . .

■ SCARAMOUCHE

1952, 115 MINS, US ◇ Ⓥ

Dir George Sidney   *Prod* Carey Wilson   *Scr* Ronald Millar, George Froeschel   *Ph* Charles Rosher
Ed James E. Newcom   *Mus* Victor Young   *Art Dir* Cedric Gibbons, Hans Peters
● Stewart Granger, Eleanor Parker, Janet Leigh, Mel Ferrer, Henry Wilcoxon, Nina Foch (M-G-M)

Metro's up-to-date version of *Scaramouche* bears only the most rudimentary resemblance to its 1923 hit or to the Rafael Sabatini novel on which they both were based. Pic never seems to be quite certain whether it is a costume adventure drama or a satire on one.

The highly-complex Sabatini plot has been greatly simplified for present purposes. It finds the French Revolution all but eliminated from the story, because of the inevitable Red analogy were the hero allowed to spout the 1789 theme of 'Liberty, Equality, Fraternity'.

Granger is a brash young man who is determined to avenge the death of a friend at the hand of nobleman Mel Ferrer, the best swordsman in France. Stewart Granger has to keep under cover until he gets in enough lessons with the weapon to take on Ferrer. Just in the nick, (a) he's elected to the French assembly, so he doesn't have to hide out anymore; (b) he discovers Miss Leigh is not his

sister, so he can grab her, and (c) the marquis is really his brother. That leaves everyone mildly happy except Miss Parker, who, when last seen is being hauled into a bedroom by Napoleon.

. . . .

■ SCARECROW

1973, 112 MINS, US ◇ Ⓥ

Dir Jerry Schatzberg   *Prod* Robert M. Sherman
Scr Garry Michael White   *Ph* Vilmos Zsigmond
Ed Evan Lottman   *Mus* Fred Myrow   *Art Dir* Al Brenner
● Gene Hackman, Al Pacino, Dorothy Tristan, Ann Wedgeworth, Richard Lynch, Eileen Brennan (Warner)

Scarecrow is a periodically interesting but ultimately unsatisfying character study of two modern drifters. Gene Hackman is excellent as a paroled crook with determined plans for the future, but Al Pacino is shot down by the script which never provides him with much beyond freaky second-banana status.

Script seems an attempt to update Runyonesque characters and situations to the seamy 1970s.

Hackman and Pacino meet in the California countryside. The former is gruff, eccentric, crude and volatile. The latter is likeable, weak, but sufficiently put together to return to Detroit to the wife and child he abandoned years earlier.

In their travels, pair encounter several extremely well-cast and most effective characters.

. . . .

■ SCARECROW, THE

1982, 87 MINS, NEW ZEALAND ◇

Dir Sam Pillsbury   *Prod* Rob Whitehouse   *Scr* Sam Pillsbury, Michael Heath   *Ph* James Bartle   *Ed* Ian John   *Mus* Andrew Hagen, Morton Wilson, Phil Broadhurst   *Art Dir* Neil Angwin
● Jonathan Smith, Daniel McLaren, Stephen Taylor, Des Kelly, Tracy Mann, John Carradine (Oasis/NZNFU)

As did the novel on which it is based, *The Scarecrow* sets up its own category, which is a kind of hillbilly Gothic thriller. The bizarre events are seen through the eyes of Ned, and the impact on a small New Zealand country township, circa 1953, of the quintessential evil stranger, embodied by the smooth-talking itinerant side-show magician and hypnotist, Salter.

Evil the stranger may be, but he is also the flame that brings to the boil the town's stew of lust and perversion that has been simmering all along.

Events are commented upon by the off-screen voice of Ned, now grown older but still talking in the overblown phrases of a lad who has read too many cheap adventure thrillers. It is an effective part of this device, however, carried over from the original novel by Ronald Hugh Morrieson, that highly unpleasant undertones exist, such as necrophilia and senile sexuality.

The central role of Salter himself is given the full saturnine treatment by John Carradine, abetted by ominous lighting and sound effects at every turn.

. . . .

■ SCARFACE

1932, 90 MINS, US Ⓥ

Dir Howard Hawks   *Prod* Howard Hughes   *Scr* Ben Hecht, W. R. Burnett, John Lee Mahin, Seton I. Miller   *Ph* Lee Garmes, L. William O'Connell   *Ed* Edward Curtiss   *Mus* Adolph Tandler, Gustav Arnheim   *Art Dir* Harry Olivier
● Paul Muni, Ann Dvorak, Karen Morley, George Raft, Boris Karloff, Osgood Perkins (Hughes/United Artists)

Scarface contains more cruelty than any of its gangster picture predecessors, but there's a squarer for every killing. The blows are always softened by judicial preachments and sad endings for the sinners.

There is none of the *Public Enemy*'s tracing the mug from boyhood to blame the environment for the cause this time. Paul Muni is a bad one in the first spin of the spindle, murdering a gent while he (Muni) is still just an introductory shadow on the wall. He whistles an operatic aria before shooting his cannon, which signalizes when he's going to kill somebody from then on.

Plot traces the rise of Scarface from the position of bodyguard for an early district beer baron to the booze chief of the whole city. Along the way he overthrows his employer and later has him slain. He even cops the boss' girl. She's a wicked blonde with a love for gunmen and gunfire, and she of all the gang is left unpunished at the finish.

George Raft gets most of the sympathy for his Rinaldo. He talks little and habitually tosses a coin while doing most of his pal's private gat work. Karen Morley has to fight an apparently natural air of refinement to get into the moll atmosphere, but she makes her part sit up and talk. Ann Dvorak is okay as Scarface's kid sister.

. . . .

■ SCARFACE

1983, 170 MINS, US ◇ Ⓥ

Dir Brian De Palma   *Prod* Martin Bregman, Peter Saphier   *Scr* Oliver Stone   *Ph* John A. Alonzo
Ed Jerry Greenberg, David Ray   *Mus* Giorgio Moroder   *Art Dir* Ed Richardson
● Al Pacino, Steven Bauer, Michelle Pfeiffer, Mary Elizabeth Mastrantonio, Robert Loggia, F. Murray Abraham (Universal)

Scarface is a grandiose modern morality play, excessive, broad and operatic at times.

Film's origins lie in the 1932 Howard Hughes production directed by Howard Hawks and adapted by Ben Hecht from the novel by Armitage Trail. Contours of the saga are very similar to those of the original, as the nearly three-hour effort charts the rise and fall of an ambitious young thug who for awhile becomes the biggest shot in gangsterdom, but ultimately is just too dumb to stay at the top.

Docu prolog recounts how some 25,000 criminals entered the United States in 1980 during the boatlift from Mariel Harbor in Cuba. Among them, per this fiction, was one Tony Montana (Al Pacino), who impresses local Miami kingpin Robert Loggia. Thanks to the fact that he has nerves of steel and ice in his veins, Pacino moves up fast in the underworld and establishes a crucial personal link with Bolivian cocaine manufacturer Paul Shenar.

All this is brought off by scripter Oliver Stone and director Brian De Palma in efficient, sometimes stylish fashion.

Performances are all extremely effective, with Pacino leading the way. Michelle Pfeiffer does well with a basically one-dimensional role as a blonde WASP goddess. Shenar is outstanding as the cool, well-bred Bolivian.

. . . .

■ SCARLET EMPRESS, THE

1934, 104 MINS, US

Dir Josef von Sternberg   *Scr* Manuel Komroff   *Ph* Bert Glennon   *Mus* John M. Leopold, W. Frank Harling (arr.)   *Art Dir* Hans Dreier, Peter Ballbusch, Richard Kollorsz
● Marlene Dietrich, John Lodge, Sam Jaffe, Louise Dresser, Maria Sieber, C. Aubrey Smith (Paramount)

The greatest trouble with *Scarlet Empress* is, at the same time, its greatest weakness. Josef von Sternberg becomes so enamoured of the pomp and flash values that he subjugates everything else to them. That he succeeds as well as he does is a tribute to his artistic genius and his amazingly vital sense of photogenic values.

Marlene Dietrich has never been as beautiful as she is here. Again and again she is photographed in closeups, under veils and behind thin mesh curtains and always breathtakingly. But never is she allowed to become really alive and vital. She is as though enchanted by the immense sets through which she stalks.

She is first picked up as a baby and a cute touch has this sequence being acted by her baby, Maria Sieber. Then she's the young German princess affianced to the far-off Russian and sent to the foreign court. She is innocent, wide-eyed, unsuspecting. And, of course, she is an easy mark for all the viciousness and grossness she soon finds herself surrounded with. Wedded to the mad crown prince she is slowly driven into the arms of other men.

Film is claimed based on a diary of Catherine II which, perhaps, forgives its choppiness and episodic quality. Sternberg uses a minimum of dialog and goes back to the silent film method of titles to explain action.

························

■ **SCARLET PIMPERNEL, THE**

1934, 98 MINS, UK Ⓥ

Dir Harold Young *Prod* Alexander Korda *Scr* S.N. Behrman, Robert Sherwood, Arthur Wimperis, Lajos Biro *Ph* Harold Rosson *Ed* William Hornbeck *Mus* Arthur Benjamin *Art Dir* Vincent Korda

● Leslie Howard, Merle Oberon, Raymond Massey, Nigel Bruce, Bramwell Fletcher, Joan Gardner (London Films/United Artists)

An intriguing adaptation of a noted novel, the English-made *Pimpernel* is distinguished by a splendid cast and productional mounting that rates with Hollywood's best.

Leslie Howard's performance in the title role is not only up to the Howard standard, but so fine that an extraordinary production job was required to prevent this from being a monolog film.

As the Scarlet Pimpernel, an English nobleman who seeks to rescue the aristocrats of France from Robespierre's guillotine, Howard essays what amounts to a dual role. At home a foppish, affected clotheshorse; abroad, a gallant adventurer playing a dangerous game.

With the story in his favor, Howard has the acting edge all the way, so it was only by their own efforts that the supporting players could stand out. As Chauvelin, the villain of the piece, Raymond Massey turns in a gem of a performance.

Co-starred with Howard is Merle Oberon, the slant-eyed knockout. Portraying Lady Blakeley, a tragic young woman who nearly betrays her husband, Oberon is confined by script limitations to sad moments only.

Enough of Baroness Orczy's novel is retained to make the picture plot recognizable to the book readers.

························

■ **SCARLET STREET**

1946, 96 MINS, US Ⓥ

Dir Fritz Lang *Prod* Walter Wanger *Scr* Dudley Nichols *Ph* Milton Krasner *Ed* Arthur Hilton *Mus* Hans J. Salter *Art Dir* Alexander Golitzen, John B. Goodman

● Edward G. Robinson, Joan Bennett, Dan Duryea (Universal/Diana)

Fritz Lang's production and direction ably project the sordid tale of the romance between a Milquetoast character and a golddigging blonde. Script [based on a French novel, play and film] is tightly written by Dudley Nichols and is played for sustained interest and suspense by the cast.

Edward G. Robinson is the mild cashier and amateur painter whose love for Joan Bennett leads him to embezzlement, murder

and disgrace. Two stars turn in top work to keep the interest high, and Dan Duryea's portrayal of the crafty and crooked opportunist whom Bennett loves is a standout in furthering the melodrama.

························

■ **SCENES FROM A MALL**

1991, 87 MINS, US ◇ Ⓥ

Dir Paul Mazursky *Prod* Paul Mazursky *Scr* Roger L. Simon, Paul Mazursky *Ph* Fred Murphy *Ed* Stuart Pappe *Mus* Marc Shaiman *Art Dir* Pato Guzman

● Bette Midler, Woody Allen, Bill Irwin, Daren Firestone, Rebecca Nickels, Paul Mazursky (Touchstone/Silver Screen Partners IV)

Paul Mazursky's 14th film as director is a cozy, insular middle-aged marital comedy that's about as deep and rewarding as a day of mall-cruising.

Talents of Bette Midler and Woody Allen seem misspent in roles as cuddly but squabbling spouses. Pic's title, a takeoff on Ingmar Bergman's *Scenes from a Marriage*, should be consumers' first clue as to what's in store.

Midler and Allen are a Hollywood Hills-dwelling twin-career couple of the 1990s. He's a successful sports lawyer; she's a psychologist who's written a high-concept book on how to renew a marriage. They pack their kids off for a ski weekend and head for the Beverly Center mall to spend their 16th anniversary indulging their every whim.

Allen drops the bombshell that he's just ended a six-month affair with a 25-year-old. Midler confesses to an ongoing affair with a Czechoslovakian colleague, played by Mazursky. These emotional storms never achieve any veracity. They seem like just another indulgence on the part of the pampered, secure spouses.

Pic shot exteriors at the Beverly Center and moved to a mall in Stamford, Conn, for two weeks of interior filming. For the remainder, a huge, two-story replica mall was constructed at Kaufman Astoria Studios, NY, and 2,600 New York extras were outfitted in LA garb.

························

■ **SCENES FROM THE CLASS STRUGGLE IN BEVERLEY HILLS**

1989, 102 MINS, US ◇ Ⓥ

Dir Paul Bartel *Prod* J. C. Katz *Scr* Bruce Wagner *Ph* Steven Fierberg *Ed* Alan Toomayan *Mus* Stanley Myers *Art Dir* Alex Tavoularis

● Jacqueline Bisset, Ray Sharkey, Robert Beltran, Mary Woronov, Ed Begley Jr, Wallace Shawn (North Street)

Scenes from the Class Struggle in Beverley Hills is a lewd delight. In top form here, director Paul Bartel brings a breezy, sophisticated touch to this utterly outrageous sex farce and thereby renders charming even the most scabrous moments in Bruce Wagner's very naughty screenplay [from a story by him and Bartel].

Script is structured in the manner of a classical French farce, and features more seductions and coitus interuptus than a season of soap operas. Hoity-toity divorcee Mary Woronov is having her house fumigated and so, with her sensitive son, checks in for the weekend next door at the home of former sitcom star Jacqueline Bisset, whose husband has just kicked the bucket.

Joining the menagerie of the filthy rich are Woronov's pretentious playwright brother Ed Begley Jr, his brand-new sassy black wife Arnetia Walker, Woronov's crazed ex-husband Wallace Shawn, Bisset's precocious daughter Rebecca Schaeffer, 'thinologist' Bartel and, in a surprisingly real apparition, Bisset's late hubby, Paul Mazursky.

Droll tone is set at the outset by the quaintly 1950s titles and Stanley Myers' witty score, and the comic champagne is kept bubbly with only the most momentary of missteps.

························

■ **SCENT OF MYSTERY**

1960, 125 MINS, US ◇

Dir Jack Cardiff *Prod* Michael Todd Jr *Scr* William Roos *Ph* John Von Kotze *Mus* Mario Nascimbene

● Denholm Elliott, Peter Lorre, Paul Lukas, Peter Arne, Beverley Bentley, Leo McKern (Todd)

Scent of Mystery is carefully planned to synchronize scents with action in the film. Unlike Aromarama, which hit the market (in Manhattan) first, the script is designed with the smells in mind. In the Aromarama presentation, a documentary dealing with Red China, the odors were added as an afterthought.

The dispensing systems are different. In Smell-O-Vision, developed by the Swiss-born Hans Laube, the odors are piped via plastic tubing – a mile of tubing at Chicago's Cinestage Theatre – to individual seats, the scents being triggered automatically by signals on the film's soundtrack. The Aromarama smells are conveyed through the theatre's regular air ventilating system. The Smell-O-Vision odors are more distinct and recognizable and do not appear to linger as long as those in Aromarama.

Reaction of those at the Smell-O-Vision premiere was mixed. Of those queried, not all claimed to have whiffed the some 30 olfactions said to have been distributed during the course of the film. A number of balcony smellers said the aroma reached them a few seconds after the action on the screen. Other balcony dwellers said they heard a hissing sound that tipped off the arrival of a smell. Among the smells that clicked were those involving flowers, the perfume of the mystery girl in the film, tobacco, orange, shoe polish, port wine (when a man is crushed to death by falling casks), baked bread, coffee, lavender, and peppermint.

Utilizing the 70 mm Todd Process, a similar but technically different process, from Todd-AO, the picture – with or without the smells – is a fun picture, expertly directed by Jack Cardiff. It has many elements that are derivative of a Hitchcock chase film, the late Mike Todd's *Around the World in 80 Days*, and the Cinerama travelog technique.

It wanders all over the Spanish landscape, covering fiestas, the running of the bulls ceremony, native dances, street scenes of Spanish cities and towns. The travelog is neatly integrated as part of the chase as Denholm Elliott, as a very proper Englishman on Spanish holiday, plays a sort of Don Quixote character who boldly stumbles through the cities and countryside as a self-appointed protector of a damsel in distress. He is accompanied by a philosophical taxi driver, neatly portrayed by Peter Lorre. Paul Lukas is properly sinister as a mysterious hired assassin.

Cardiff has wisely directed the film with a tongue-in-cheek quality. Diana Dors is seen briefly (time and costume) on a Spanish beach and Elizabeth Taylor is present at the denouement in a non-speaking role. Although smell plays an important part in Elliott's uncovering of the villain, the audience need not necessarily be involved in the odor – the recognition of a man's tobacco.

························

■ **SCHOOL FOR SCOUNDRELS**

1960, 94 MINS, UK Ⓥ

Dir Robert Hamer *Prod* Hal E. Chester *Scr* Patricia Moyes, Hal E. Chester, Peter Ustinov *Ph* Edwin Hillier *Ed* Richard Best *Mus* John Addison *Art Dir* Terence Verity

● Ian Carmichael, Terry-Thomas, Alastair Sim, Janette Scott, Dennis Price, Peter Jones (Guardsman)

The gentle art of getting and remaining 'one up' on the next fellow, so painstaking chronicled by British humorist Stephen Potter in his series of books, is engagingly translated to

S

the screen in this delicate English comedy. Those familiar with Potter's spoofs (*Lifemanship, Gamesmanship, Oneupmanship*) will get the biggest boot out of *School for Scoundrels*.

Although it is virtually impossible to capture Potter's many intimate ironies, the scenarists have successfully caught the essence of the author's maxim – 'How to Win Without Actually Cheating!' (as the film is subtitled).

Alastair Sim personifies the master lifeman down to the minutest detail – a brilliant performance. Ian Carmichael is a delight as the pitifully inept wretch who undergoes metamorphosis at Sim's finishing school for social misfits, and Terry-Thomas masterfully plummets from one-up to one-down as his exasperated victim.

Janette Scott, a fresh, natural beauty, charmingly plays the object of their attention. Unfortunately for Dennis Price and Peter Jones, they are involved in the weakest passage of the film – a none-too-subtle used car sequence that will disturb Potter purists.

■ SCORPIO

1973, 114 MINS, US ◇ ⊽

Dir Michael Winner *Prod* Walter Mirisch *Scr* David W. Rintels, Gerald Wilson *Ph* Robert Paynter *Ed* Freddie Wilson *Mus* Jerry Fielding *Art Dir* Herbert Westbrook

● Burt Lancaster, Alain Delon, Paul Scofield, John Colicos, Gayle Hunnicutt, J.D. Cannon (Scimitar/United Artists)

Despite its anachronistic emulation of mid-1960s cynical spy mellers, *Scorpio* might have been an acceptable action programmer if its narrative were clearer, its dialog less 'cultured' and its visuals more straightforward.

Pic opens with the assassination of an Arab government official, but his identity and relationship to the protagonists remain puzzlements beyond the film's conclusion. Even more irritating is nearly total confusion about other characters' occupations or moral positions.

Ultimately, pic settles down into the usual is-he-or-isn't-he-a-double-agent gimmick, with CIA-blackmailed Alain Delon pursuing supposed Soviet defector Burt Lancaster from Washington to Europe. While ducking his would-be assassin, Lancaster takes refuge in the Viennese home of Paul Scofield, a Russian agent.

■ SCOTT JOPLIN

1977, 96 MINS, US ◇

Dir Jeremy Paul Kagan *Prod* Stan Hough *Scr* Christopher Knopf *Ph* David M. Walsh *Ed* Patrick Kennedy *Mus* Scott Joplin *Art Dir* William H. Hiney

● Billy Dee Williams, Clifton Davis, Margaret Avery, Eubie Blake, Godfrey Cambridge, Seymour Cassel (Motown/Universal)

Universal Pictures owed a large debt to Scott Joplin – whose ragtime music was a key factor in the enormous success of *The Sting* – and the studio paid back the debt with *Scott Joplin*, a biopic starring Billy Dee Williams originally intended for TV.

Williams is fine, and the film has a lot of verve and intensity, but the story of Joplin's life is so grim it makes the film a real downer.

Scott Joplin is buoyant fun for the first half but then becomes a harrowing ordeal when Joplin learns he has syphilis. He turns into a desperate wreck, forsaking his popular ragtime tunes to write an opera, 'Treemonisha,' which wasn't performed until 1975.

But the second half of the film makes too many wobbly jumps over periods of Joplin's life to satisfy dramatically.

■ SCOTT OF THE ANTARCTIC

1948, 111 MINS, UK ◇ ⊽

Dir Charles Frend *Prod* Michael Balcon *Scr* Walter Meade, Ivor Montagu, Mary Hayley Bell *Ph* Jack Cardiff, Osmond Borrodaile, Geoffrey Unsworth *Ed* Peter Tanner *Mus* Ralph Vaughan Williams *Art Dir* Arne Akermark

● John Mills, Harold Warrender, Derek Bond, Reginald Beckwith, James Robertson Justice, Kenneth More (Ealing)

Scott of the Antarctic should be not only a magnificent eye-filling spectacle but also a stirring adventure. But the director's affinity to the documentary technique robs the subject of much of its intrinsic drama.

Pic's greatest asset is the superb casting of John Mills in the title role. Obviously playing down the drama on directorial insistence, Mills' close resemblance to the famous explorer makes the character come to life.

Scott's discovery that he has been beaten in the race to the South Pole should be a piece of poignant and moving drama. Instead, the five members of the expedition look very resolute, and very British, and philosophically begin the long trail home. Although depicted with fidelity, the agonies of the explorers on their homeward trek are presented with inadequate dramatization, with the result that the audience isn't emotionally affected.

■ SCREWBALLS

1983, 90 MINS, US ◇ ⊽

Dir Rafal Zielinski *Prod* Maurice Smith *Scr* Jim Wynorski, Linda Shayne *Ph* Miklos Lente *Ed* Brian Ravok *Mus* Tim McCauley *Art Dir* Sandra Kybartas

● Peter Keleghan, Lynda Speciale, Alan Daveau, Kent Deuters, Jason Warren, Linda Shayne (New World)

Screwballs is a poor man's *Porky's*. This compendium of horny high school jokes set in 1965 is full of youthful exuberance and proves utterly painless to watch, but it is so close in premise and tone to its model that negative comparisons can't help but be drawn.

Five lads receive detentions for such infractions as posing as a doctor during girls' breast examinations and straying into the gals' locker room. Responsible for the boys' plight is snooty homecoming queen Purity Busch, evidently the only female virgin left at the school. Five guys dedicate themselves to de-purifying her, and remainder of the film describes their goonlike attempts on her innocence.

Film was lensed in Toronto, which can only make one wonder why all these studies of randy young Americans come from north of the border.

■ SCROOGE

1970, 118 MINS, UK ◇ ⊽

Dir Ronald Neame *Prod* Robert H. Solo *Scr* Leslie Bricusse *Ph* Oswald Morris *Ed* Peter Weatherly *Mus* Leslie Bricusse *Art Dir* Bob Cartwright

● Albert Finney, Alec Guinness, Edith Evans, Kenneth More, Laurence Naismith, Michael Medwin (Cinema Center/Waterbury)

Scrooge is a most delightful film in every way, made for under $5 million in direct costs at England's Shepperton Studios. Albert Finney's remarkable performance in the title role; executive producer Leslie Bricusse's fluid adaptation of the Charles Dickens classic, *A Christmas Carol*, plus his unobtrusive complementary music and lyrics; and Ronald Neame's delicately controlled direction which conveys, but does not force, all the inherent warmth, humor and sentimentality.

An excellent cast of key supporting players enhances both the artistry of the film and its universal appeal: Alec Guinness, as Marley's ghost and, Edith Evans and Kenneth More, respectively, as the Ghosts of Christmas Past and Present.

Finney's performance as cold-hearted Scrooge is a professional high-water mark.

■ SCUM

1979, 96 MINS, UK ◇ ⊽

Dir Alan Clarke *Prod* Davina Belling *Scr* Roy Minton *Ph* Phil Meheux *Ed* Mike Bradsell *Art Dir* Mike Porter

● Ray Winstone, Mick Ford, John Judd, Phil Daniels (Boyd's)

Given that *Scum*, a relentlessly brutal slice of British reform school life, is strongly directed by Alan Clarke, and acted with admirable conviction, it is a pity that the hard-hitting screenplay is more passionate tract than powerful entertainment.

Its appeal could have been wider with more dramatic light and shade, and its message more likely to find its mark if the basic point – that a youth penitentiary can kill, not cure – had been made through more investigative character-study, instead of via a catalog of horrific events.

Significantly, the plot of a 'trainee' (young offender) whose means of survival in the corrupt reformatory is to become top dog by meeting violence with violence started life as a BBC-TV play. Although filmed, it was never aired on account of its alleged bias and unpalatability.

■ SEA GULL, THE

1968, 141 MINS, UK ◇

Dir Sidney Lumet *Prod* Sidney Lumet *Ph* Gerry Fisher *Ed* Alan Heim *Art Dir* Tony Walton

● James Mason, Vanessa Redgrave, Simone Signoret, David Warner, Harry Andrews, Denholm Elliott (Warner/Seven Arts)

The Sea Gull is a sensitive, well-made and abstractly interesting period pic. Downbeat eternal verities – frustration, unrequited love, etc. – are projected admirably by a cast featuring James Mason, Simone Signoret (both in memorable performances), Vanessa Redgrave and David Warner.

Setting is a rural Russian house, where bailiff Ronald Radd, his wife Eileen Herlie and daughter Kathleen Widdoes seek to create a pleasant climate for the final years of Harry Andrews, a retired official who apparently has endured a life of frustration. Andrews herein is a cliche, crotchety old fool. His performance is the poorest one in the film.

Signoret, Andrews' sister, has descended for a visit, trailed by her current lover, Mason, a popular hack writer. Redgrave, a neighborhood girl, becomes entranced with Mason.

The deliberate adherence to the Chekhov's script necessarily retains the somewhat old-fashioned character motivations and plot structures.

Director Sydney Lumet has created an appropriately somber mood.

■ SEA GYPSIES, THE

1978, 101 MINS, US ◇ ⊽

Dir Stewart Raffill *Prod* Joseph C. Raffill *Scr* Stewart Raffill *Ph* Thomas McHugh *Ed* Dan Greer *Mus* Fred Steiner

● Robert Logan, Mikki Jamison-Olsen, Heather Rattray, Cjon Damitri Patterson, Shannon Saylor (Raffill)

The Sea Gypsies is a sometimes touching, sometimes frightening adventure tale about a father, his two daughters, a female photojournalist, and a stowaway who set off on a round-the-world sail and wind up stranded on a desert island off the coast of Alaska.

It's a superior effort in every way – credible story, effective acting, first rate technical credits. Thomas McHugh's photography is worthy of picture postcards and Stewart Raffill's direction is expertly paced.

Loosely adapted by the director from a true story about a group of animal trainers and actors sailing from Jamaica to California, the plot opens with Robert Logan about to embark on his voyage with his two daughters (Heather Rattray and Shannon Saylor).

The trip is being financed partly by a magazine and Logan is waiting for the correspondent to arrive – the male correspondent who is also a crack sailor – when his replacement shows up. She's an attractive, ambitious female journalist (Mikki Jamison-Olsen).

A storm hits, the ship goes down and suddenly it's survival time off the coast of Alaska.

■ **SEA HAWK, THE**

1924, 129 MINS, US ⊗

Dir Frank Lloyd   *Scr* J.G. Hawks, Walter Anthony   *Ph* Norbert Brodine   *Ed* Edward M. Roskam   *Art Dir* Stephen Goosson, Fred Gabourie

● Milton Sills, Enid Bennett, Lloyd Hughes, Wallace MacDonald, Marc MacDermott, Wallace Beery (First National)

This picture has no end of entertainment value. It is just as thrilling and gripping as reading one of Rafael Sabatini's books; all of the punch of that author's writings has been brought to the screen.

There's action aplenty. It starts in the first reel and holds true to the last minute. Milton Sills, who is featured together with Enid Bennett, comes into his own in this production, and Bennett also scores tremendously. One must, however, not overlook Wallace Beery, a low comedy ruffian, who wades right through the story.

Frank Lloyd, who directed, is to be considered with the best that wield a megaphone. *The Sea Hawk* cost around $800,000. The properties used alone cost $135,000. The picture looks it.

■ **SEA HAWK, THE**

1940, 127 MINS, US ▼

Dir Michael Curtiz   *Prod* Hal B. Wallis, Henry Blanke   *Scr* Howard Koch, Seton I. Miller   *Ph* Sol Polito   *Ed* George Amy   *Mus* Erich Wolfgang Korngold   *Art Dir* Anton Grot

● Errol Flynn, Brenda Marshall, Claude Rains, Flora Robson, Donald Crisp, Alan Hale (Warner)

The Sea Hawk retains all of the bold and swashbuckling adventure and excitement of its predecessor, turned out for First National by Frank Lloyd in 1923. But the screenplay of the new version is expanded to include endless episodes of court intrigue during the reign of Queen Elizabeth that tend to diminish the effect of the epic sweep of the high seas dramatics. When the script focuses attention on the high seas and the dramatic heroics of the sailors who embarked on daring raids against Spanish shipping, the picture retains plenty of excitement.

Story traces the adventures of the piratical sea fighter (Errol Flynn), commander of a British sailing ship that preys on Spanish commerce in the late 16th century. Colorful and exciting sea battle at the start, when Flynn's ship attacks and sinks the galleon of the Spanish ambassador, comes too early and is never topped by any succeeding sequences. Then follows extensive internal politics of Elizabeth's court, with the queen secretly condoning Flynn's buccaneering activities.

Little credit can be extended to the overwritten script, with long passages of dry and uninteresting dialog, or to the slow-paced, uninspiring direction by Michael Curtiz. Errol Flynn fails to generate the fire and dash necessary to successfully put over the role of the buccaneer leader, although this lack

might partially be attributed to the piloting. Flora Robson gets attention in the role of Queen Elizabeth.

The Sea Hawk is a big budget production with reported cost set around $1.75 million. Expenditure is easily seen in the large sets, sweeping sea battles and armies of extras used with lavish display. From a production standpoint, the picture carries epic standards, but same cannot be said for the story.

■ **SEA OF LOVE**

1989, 112 MINS, US ◇ ▼

Dir Harold Becker   *Prod* Martin Bregman, Louis A. Stoller   *Scr* Richard Price   *Ph* Ronnie Taylor   *Ed* David Bretherton   *Mus* Trevor Jones   *Art Dir* John Jay Moore

● Al Pacino, Ellen Barkin, John Goodman, Michael Rooker, William Hickey (Universal)

Sea of Love is a suspenseful film noir boasting a superlative performance by Al Pacino as a burned-out Gotham cop.

Handsome production benefits from a witty screenplay limning the bittersweet tale of a 20-year veteran NYC cop (Pacino) assigned to a case tracking down the serial killer of men who've made dates through the personal columns.

He teams up with fellow cop John Goodman to set a trap for the murderer. Clues point to a woman being the killer.

Early on, Ellen Barkin appears as one of the suspects, but after an initial rebuff Pacino is smitten with her and crucially decides not to get her fingerprints for analysis. Pic builds some hair-raising twists and turns as the evidence mounts pointing to her guilt, climaxing in a surprising revelation.

Pacino here brings great depth to the central role. A loner with retirement after 20 years facing him, this cop is a sympathetic, self-divided individual and Pacino makes his clutching at a second chance with femme fatale Barkin believable.

■ **SEA WOLF, THE**

1941, 98 MINS, US ▼

Dir Michael Curtiz   *Prod* Henry Blanke   *Scr* Robert Rossen   *Ph* Sol Polito   *Ed* George Amy   *Mus* Erich Wolfgang Korngold

● Edward G. Robinson, Ida Lupino, John Garfield, Alexander Knox, Barry Fitzgerald (Warner)

Jack London's famous hellship sails for another voyage over the cinematic seas in this version of *The Sea Wolf*. Edward G. Robinson steps into the role of the callous and inhuman skipper, Wolf Larsen.

John Garfield signs on to the sailing schooner to escape the law. Ida Lupino (also a fugitive) and the mild-mannered novelist (Alexander Knox) are rescued from a sinking ferryboat in San Francisco bay. Robinson is the dominating and cruel captain who takes fiendish delight in breaking the spirits of his crew and unwilling passengers.

Robinson provides plenty of vigor and two-fisted energy to the actor-proof role of Larsen, and at times is over-directed. Garfield is the incorrigible youth whose spirit cannot be broken, and is grooved to his familiar tough characterization of previous pictures. Lupino gives a good account of herself in the rough-and-tumble goings on, but the romantic angle is under-stressed in this version.

Michael Curtiz directs in a straight line, accentuating the horrors that go on during the voyage of the *Ghost*.

■ **SEA WOLVES, THE**

1980, 120 MINS, UK ◇ ▼

Dir Andrew V. McLaglen   *Prod* Evan Lloyd   *Scr* Reginald Rose   *Ph* Tony Imi   *Ed* John Glen   *Mus* Roy Budd   *Art Dir* Syd Cain

● Gregory Peck, Roger Moore, David Niven, Trevor Howard, Patrick MacNee (Lorimar/Rank)

How a band of pip-pip British civilians rallied to King and country, tucked in their pot bellies and knocked out a German spy nest that was playing havoc with wartime Allied shipping in the Indian Ocean.

Touted as 'the last great untold action story of the war', film was scripted by Reginald Rose from James Leasor's novel *The Boarding Party*.

Sea Wolves is unabashed flag-waving, a salute to the Calcutta Light Horse, a part-time regiment whose membership consisted mainly of colonial business types way past draft age but recruited as volunteers for the destruction of three German freighters interned in coastal waters off the then-neutral Portuguese colony of Goa.

Gregory Peck's a Britisher in this one, but the affected accent won't fool anyone. He and Roger Moore are regular army. The stiff-uppered civvy retreads, headed by David Niven, include Trevor Howard and Patrick MacNee.

■ **SEALED CARGO**

1951, 90 MINS, US

Dir Alfred Werker   *Prod* Samuel Bischoff, Warren Duff   *Scr* Dale Van Every, Oliver H.P. Garrett, Roy Huggins   *Ph* George E. Diskant   *Ed* Ralph Dawson   *Mus* Roy Webb

● Dana Andrews, Claude Rains, Carla Balenda, Philip Dorn, Onslow Stevens, Skip Homeier (RKO)

Story of adventure at sea during the Second World War [from Edmund Gilligan's *Gaunt Woman*], involving Yankee fishermen and Nazi submarines, has some fanciful exploits and not-too-believable intrigue, but it hangs together for most of the pic.

Dana Andrews plays the skipper of a New England fishing ship which comes across a shell-riddled square-rigger, *The Gaunt Woman*, off Newfoundland. Master of the floundering craft (Claude Rains) gets the smaller boat to tow his vessel to an isolated village in Newfoundland, where Andrews discovers that it is actually crammed with torpedoes and serves as the mother ship for German U-boats. Problem is one of blowing up the *Woman* without at the same time wiping out the village. Further complication is that Carla Balenda, one of Andrews' passengers, has been taken as hostage by Rains.

Andrews handles his role in convincing fashion. Rains clicks in his characterization of the German officer, getting across his menacing aspect underneath his quiet, cultured front.

■ **SEANCE ON A WET AFTERNOON**

1964, 116 MINS, UK ▼

Dir Bryan Forbes   *Prod* Richard Attenborough, Bryan Forbes   *Scr* Bryan Forbes   *Ph* Gerry Turpin   *Ed* Derek York   *Mus* John Barry   *Art Dir* Ray Simms

● Kim Stanley, Richard Attenborough, Nanette Newman, Patrick Magee, Mark Eden (Rank/Allied Film Makers)

This is a skilful and, on many counts, admirable picture. Bryan Forbes' writing and direction create an aptly clammy atmosphere and he's backed by some shrewd thesping.

Onus of the acting falls heavily on Kim Stanley and Richard Attenborough. Yet though she is an exciting actress to watch, she is much Method, and technicalities occasionally get in the way.

It throws extra responsibility on Attenborough as her weak, loving and downtrodden husband. Here is a splendid piece of trouping which rings true throughout.

The star is a medium of dubious authenticity, who inveigles her spouse into a nutty plan which she confidently believes will give her the recognition due to her. Idea is to 'borrow' a child, make out it has been kidnapped, collect the ransom loot and wait for the story to pump up to front page sensation. Then she aims to hold a seance and reveal clues which will enable the cops to find the child unharmed.

The film throughout is pitched in sombre key with much macabre reference to a son that the couple never had but in whom Stanley implicitly believes. The dankness of the house in which her shabby machinations evolve is well caught, thanks to deft artwork and Gerry Turpin's searching camera.

Forbes' well-written, imaginative script [from the novel by Mark McShane] is a study in grey, abetted by the fine lensing of Turpin. An exciting, ingenious highspot involves complicated production when Attenborough is due to collect the ransom money. It was shot with hidden cameras in Leicester Square and Piccadilly at London's busiest hour. Result is an air of intense, exciting realism. So realistic, in fact, that parts of it had to be reshot. Without realizing that a film was being shot, the negative revealed several w.k. characters such as John Gielgud captured while strolling in London about their daily business.

SEARCH FOR PARADISE

1957, 120 MINS, US ◇

Dir Otto Lang   *Prod* Lowell Thomas   *Scr* Lowell Thomas, Otto Lang, Prosper Buranelli   *Ph* Harry Squire, Jack Priestley   *Ed* Lovel S. Ellis, Harvey Manger   *Mus* Dimitri Tiomkin
● Lowell Thomas, James S. Parker, Christopher Young (Cinerama)

The fourth Cinerama sticks almost slavishly to established formulae. Once more strange lands are 'seen' by two selected 'tourists' this time a make-believe air force major (Christopher Young) and sergeant (James S. Parker) who, at the payoff, decide that they'll sign up for another hitch, the air force itself being the ultimate paradise.

The beginning of the picture is cornily contrived. An Associated Press newsmachine is seen ticking out a bulletin that Lowell Thomas is one of three ambassadors just appointed to represent Washington at the coronation durbar of King Mahendra of Nepal.

The several stops of *Search* are all way-stations en route to Nepal. The picture centres upon the approach to and environs of the Himalayas, world's greatest peaks, truthfully described as a region of mystery, age, mysticism and Communistic intrigue.

Lowell picks up the major and the sarge in the Vale of Kashmir, a plausible paradise indeed, especially its Shalimar Gardens. The visit at Nepal is the big sequence. And a stunning display of oriental pomp it is. This segment is a genuine peep into dazzling fantasy and a true coup for Cinerama and Thomas.

SEARCHERS, THE

1956, 119 MINS, US ◇ Ⓥ

Dir John Ford   *Prod* Merian C. Cooper, C.V. Whitney   *Scr* Frank S. Nugent   *Ph* Winton C. Hoch   *Ed* Jack Murray   *Mus* Max Steiner   *Art Dir* Frank Hotaling, James Basevi
● John Wayne, Jeffrey Hunter, Vera Miles, Ward Bond, Natalie Wood, Hank Worden (Whitney/Warner)

The Searchers is a western in the grand scale – handsomely mounted and in the tradition of *Shane*. The VistaVision-Technicolor photographic excursion through the southwest – presenting in bold and colorful outline the arid country and areas of buttes and giant rock formations – is eyefilling and impressive.

Yet *The Searchers* is somewhat disappointing. There is a feeling that it could have been

so much more. Overlong and repetitious, there are subtleties in the basically simple story that are not adequately explained.

There are, however, some fine vignettes of frontier life. The picture involves a long, arduous trek through primitive country by two men in search of nine-year-old girl kidnapped by hostile Comanche Indians.

Wayne, the uncle of the kidnapped girl, is a bitter, taciturn individual throughout and the reasons for his attitude are left to the imagination of the viewer.

His bitterness toward the Indians is understandable. They massacred his brother's family (except for the kidnapped girl) and destroyed the ranch. He feels the girl has been defiled by the Indians during her years with them and he is determined to kill her.

Wayne's partner in the search is Jeffrey Hunter, who is also involved in labored attempts at comedy relief.

Wayne is fine in the role of the hard-bitten, misunderstood, and mysterious searcher and the rest of the cast acquits itself notably, including Hunter and Miles.

SEBASTIAN

1968, 100 MINS, UK ◇ Ⓥ

Dir David Greene   *Prod* Herbert Brodkin, Michael Powell   *Scr* Gerald Vaughn-Hughes   *Ph* Gerry Fisher   *Ed* Brian Smedley-Aston   *Mus* Jerry Goldsmith   *Art Dir* Wilfrid Shingleton
● Dirk Bogarde, Susannah York, Lilli Palmer, John Gielgud, Janet Munro, Ronald Fraser (Paramount/Maccius)

Very good direction, acting and dialog are apparent in *Sebastian*, but a fatal flaw in basic plotting makes this production just a moderately entertaining Cold War comedy-drama.

The amusing, and not so amusing, pressures on persons who break foreign government secret codes are potent angles for a strong film, but, herein, story touches so many bases that it never really finds a definite concept.

Leo Marks' original screen story, scripted by Gerald Vaughn-Hughes, depicts Dirk Bogarde as a daffy math genius in cryptography. Susannah York, a new recruit to the code force, breaks down his romantic reserve.

Lilli Palmer, as a politically-suspect coder, and John Gielgud, an Intelligence chief, add lustre. Janet Munro scores very well as a boozy fading pop singer who, with Ronald Fraser, attempts to compromise Bogarde's security clearance.

Despite all the plus elements, film wanders about in its unfolding. Short, tight scenes of good exposition are broken by recurring transitional sequences which add up to an apparent padding effect.

SECONDS

1966, 108 MINS, US ◇

Dir John Frankenheimer   *Prod* John Frankenheimer, Edward Lewis   *Scr* Lewis John Carlino   *Ph* James Wong Howe   *Ed* Ferris Webster, David Webster   *Mus* Jerry Goldsmith   *Art Dir* Ted Howarth
● Rock Hudson, Salome Jens, John Randolph, Will Geer, Jeff Corey, Richard Anderson (Paramount)

US suburbia boredom is treated in an original manner in this cross between a sci-fi opus, a thriller, a suspense pic and a parable on certain aspects of American middle-class life.

A middleaged man has lost contact with his wife. His only daughter is married and gone. Even his work, which was his mainstay in life, seems to pall. Into this comes a strange call from a supposedly dead friend to come to a certain place.

He finds himself in a mysterious big business surgery corporation with some disquieting features of a room full of listless men. He is told he can be redone surgically to become

a young man and start life over again. He decides to go through with it and after surgery wakes up as Rock Hudson.

This has some intriguing aspects on the yearning for youth and a chance to live life over again by many men. But this Faustian theme is barely touched on and the hero's tie with the past is also somewhat arbitrary. Film [from the novel by David Ely] does not quite come off as a thriller, sci-fi adjunct or philosophical fable.

SECRET AGENT, THE

1936, 83 MINS, UK Ⓥ

Dir Alfred Hitchcock   *Prod* Michael Balcon   *Scr* Charles Bennett, Ian Hay, Jesse Lasky Jr   *Ph* Bernard Knowles   *Ed* Charles Frend   *Mus* Louis Levy   *Art Dir* Otto Wrendorff, Albert Jullion
● Madeleine Carroll, Peter Lorre, John Gielgud, Robert Young, Percy Marmont, Lilli Palmer (Gaumont-British)

Secret Agent dallies much on the way but rates as good spy entertainment, suave story telling, and, in one particular case, brilliant characterization. This is the role of the Mexican hired killer as played by Peter Lorre. Director Alfred Hitchcock has done well at lending the tale's grim theme [from the play by Campbell Dixon, based on the novel *Ashenden* by W. Somerset Maugham] with deftly fashioned humor, appropriate romantic interplay and some swell outdoor photography.

More critical element will find the part of Madeleine Carroll somewhat straining credulity. The film has her philandering at the game of espionage and out of sheer ineptitude pulling one of the major coups of the service. Likewise unconvincing is the overly sensitive conduct in which her co-spy (John Gielgud) indulges once he is bitten by love.

Production maintains an easy-going pace almost throughout, with most of the action cast against the background of the Swiss Alps. Gielgud is assigned to Switzerland to prevent a German spy from getting back into pro-German territory. To do the actual killing, Lorre, a Mexican with a juvenile sense of fun but a boundless enthusiasm for playing the knife upon humans, is sent along. Arriving on the scene, Gielgud finds that Carroll had been matched with him for the job, with the pair to pose as man and wife.

SECRET BEYOND THE DOOR, THE

1947, 98 MINS, US

Dir Fritz Lang   *Prod* Walter Wanger   *Scr* Silvia Richards   *Ph* Stanley Cortez   *Ed* Arthur Hilton   *Mus* Miklos Rozsa   *Art Dir* Max Parker
● Joan Bennett, Michael Redgrave, Anne Revere (Universal/Diana)

Film carries the Diana Productions label, a combo of Walter Wanger, Fritz Lang and Joan Bennett who have been responsible for several other Diana thrillers. It is arty, with almost surrealistic treatment in camera angles, story-telling mood and suspense, as producer-director Lang hammers over his thrill points.

Co-starring with Bennett is Michael Redgrave. He disappoints as the man with an anti-woman complex who nearly murders his wife before finding out what his trouble is. Bennett is good as the rich, useless society girl who finds a love so strong she would rather die than give it up.

Mental complexities of the principals makes it sometimes hard to sort out the various motivations used to spin the tale. It's based on a story by Rufus King, scripted by Silvia Richards. Such psychiatric tricks as mental cases who recoil at locked doors, lilacs, or become oddly stimulated by physical combat and looks are some of the suspense devices.

■ SECRET CEREMONY

1968, 109 MINS, UK ◇ ⓥ

Dir Joseph Losey   *Prod* John Heyman, Norman
Priggen   *Scr* George Tabori   *Ph* Gerald Fisher
Ed Reginald Beck   *Mus* Richard Rodney Bennett
Art Dir Richard MacDonald
● Elizabeth Taylor, Mia Farrow, Robert Mitchum,
Peggy Ashcroft, Pamela Brown (Universal)

Robert Mitchum is featured in this macabre
tale [from a short story by Marco Denevi] of
mistaken identity, psychological and sexual
needs, ultimate suicide and murder. Moody,
leisurely developed and handsomely produced, it was made at England's Elstree
Studios.

Mia Farrow, playing a wealthy, demented
and incest-prone nympho, appears to have
kidnapped Elizabeth Taylor, in the role of an
aging prostitute. As things turn out, Taylor
does not mind being mistaken for Farrow's
deceased mother; instead, she gradually, but
fitfully, eases into the child's desired mold.

Only the return of Mitchum, the girl's stepfather with a libertine reputation, cues the
revelation that Farrow is a sexual psychotic
whose seduction of Mitchum helped ruin her
mother's marriage.

Performances are generally good: Farrow's
via an emphasis on facial expressions, Taylor's via a salutary toning down of her shriek-
ing-for-speaking tendencies, and Mitchum's
casual, stolid projection.

■ SECRET LIFE OF AN AMERICAN WIFE, THE

1968, 93 MINS, US ◇ ⓥ

Dir George Axelrod   *Prod* George Axelrod
Scr George Axelrod   *Ph* Leon Shamroy   *Ed* Harry
Gerstad   *Mus* Billy May   *Art Dir* Jack Martin Smith
● Walter Matthau, Anne Jackson, Patrick O'Neal, Edy
Williams, Richard Bull (20th Century-Fox/Charlton)

The Secret Life of an American Wife, as the title
might indicate, is a light sophisticated marital farce. Basic idea, which sometimes takes
on the aspect of a French romp, takes a
comedy look at sex in the person of a 34-year-
old Connecticut wife who thinks she's gone to
pot and lost all her appeal. More skillful
development might have heightened impact
of her deciding to do something about it, but
overall the tale is amusing.

George Axelrod production, which he also
wrote and directed, actually is a one-woman
show with a couple of male characters tossed
in for necessary consequence.

Even when such a past master at comedy as
Walter Matthau, in role of a top film star on
whom Anne Jackson tries her wiles, enters,
the unfoldment is focused on her.

Jackson is enticing as the wife of a public
relations man, Patrick O'Neal, who must
cater to his top client, Matthau, whenever
latter comes to NY from Hollywood for a
round of frolic.

Matthau turns on all the faucets in his delineation of the thesp, who spends most of his
scenes in pajama bottoms and a towel.

■ SECRET LIFE OF WALTER MITTY, THE

1947, 108 MINS, US ◇ ⓥ

Dir Norman Z. McLeod   *Prod* Samuel Goldwyn
Scr Ken Englund, Everett Freeman   *Ph* Lee Garmes
Ed Monica Collingwood   *Mus* David Raksin   *Art
Dir* George Jenkins, Perry Ferguson
● Danny Kaye, Virginia Mayo, Boris Karloff, Fay
Bainter (RKO/Goldwyn)

Some of the deepest-dyed Thurber fans may
squeal since there's naturally considerable
change from the famed short story on which
the screenplay is built. There's a basic switch
in the plot that has been concocted around
the Mitty daydreams. Thurber's whole conception of Mitty was an inconsequential fellow from Perth Amboy, NJ, to whom nothing
– but nothing – ever happened and who, as a

result, lived a 'secret life' via his excursions
into daydreaming. In contrast, the picture
builds a spy-plot around Mitty that is more
fantastic than even his wildest dream.

Danny Kaye reveals a greater smoothness
and polish thespically and a perfection of timing in his slapstick than has ever been evident
in the past.

Exceedingly slick job is done on the segues
from the real-life Mitty into the dream sequences. Mitty's fantasies carry him through
sessions as a sea captain taking his schooner
through a storm, a surgeon performing a
next-to-impossible operation, an RAF pilot, a
Mississippi gambler, a cowpuncher and a hat
designer. They're all well-loaded with satire,
as is the real-life plot with pure slapstick.

Virginia Mayo is the beautiful vis-a-vis in
both the real-life spy plot, and the dreams.
She comes a commendable distance thespically in this picture. Karloff wins heftiest yaks
in a scene in which he plays a phony psychiatrist convincing Mitty he's nuts.

■ SECRET OF MY SUCCESS, THE

1965, 112 MINS, UK ◇

Dir Andrew L. Stone   *Prod* Virginia Stone, Andrew L.
Stone   *Scr* Andrew L. Stone   *Ph* David Boulton
Ed Virginia Stone, Noreen Ackland   *Mus* Lucien
Cailliet, Derek New, Joao Baptista Laurenco,
Christopher Stone
● Shirley Jones, Stella Stevens, Honor Blackman,
James Booth, Lionel Jeffries, Amy Dolby (M-G-M)

There are several capable players in *Secret of
My Success*, many of them from the British studios. But the screenplay Andrew L. Stone has
whipped up is too much of a handicap, and
what might have been a bright, little British
comedy turns out to be neither comedy nor
melodrama.

Three almost separate yarns are employed
to trace the rise of a lowly English town constable to position of ruler in a mythical Latin-
American country.

Initial episode details how his understanding of a comely, little village dressmaker
(Stella Stevens), while only a town constable,
wins a promotion to police inspector. The
curvaceous, red-haired Stevens puts this
across despite all its implausibilities, such as
hiding the body of her slain husband.

Booth's first big job as police inspector
shows him becoming involved with a baroness. This little tale tells about the breeding of
giant spiders until they become as big as
over-sized bulldogs – and large enough to
crush a man to death.

Another sharp maneuver by his mother
wins Booth the job of liaison officer to the
president of Guanduria, Latin-American
mythical land. By helping Shirley Jones, who
is secretly plotting a revolution, he winds up
as new ruler of this country.

■ SECRET OF MY SUCCESS, THE

1987, 110 MINS, US ◇ ⓥ

Dir Herbert Ross   *Prod* Herbert Ross   *Scr* Jim Cash,
Jack Epps, A.J. Carothers   *Ph* Carlo Di Palma   *Ed* Paul
Hirsch   *Mus* David Foster   *Art Dir* Edward Pisoni, Peter
Larkin
● Michael J. Fox, Helen Slater, Richard Jordan,
Margaret Whitton, John Pankow, Christopher Murney
(Rastar)

The Secret of My Success is a bedroom farce with
a leaden touch, a corporate comedy without
teeth. What it does have is Michael J. Fox in
a winning performance as a likable hick out
to hit the big time in New York.

Fresh off the bus from Kansas, Brantley
Foster (Fox) doesn't want to return until he
has a penthouse, jacuzzi, a beautiful girlfriend and a private jet he can go home in.
His ideals are a yuppie's dream.

Fox encounters the predictable crime-
infested corners of New York and his squalid

apartment is furnished with roaches and rats.
When he meets his dream girl (Helen Slater),
he is literally thunderstruck.

After young Brantley lands a job in the
mailroom of an anonymous NY corporation
his big chance comes when he takes over an
abandoned office and sets himself up as a
young exec.

Fox, in spite of his inherent charm, lacks a
genuine personality and is neither country
bumpkin nor city sharpie. Consequently, the
film lacks a consistent tone or style.

■ SECRET OF NIMH, THE

1982, 82 MINS, US ◇ ⓥ

Dir Don Bluth   *Prod* Don Bluth, Gary Goldman, John
Pomeroy   *Scr* Don Bluth, Gary Goldman, John
Pomeroy, Will Finn   *Ed* Jeffrey Patch   *Mus* Jerry
Goldsmith
● (M-G-M/United Artists)

The Secret of NIMH is a richly animated and
skillfully structured film created by former
Disney animators Don Bluth, Gary Goldman
and John Pomeroy. As craft, their first
feature film is certainly an homage to the best
of an age ago. Every character moves fluidly
and imaginatively against an extravaganza of
detailed background and dazzling effects, all
emboldened by fascinating colored textures.

The story is simple. A mother mouse
(voiced by Elizabeth Hartman) is simply trying to find a new home for her brood before
the old one is destroyed by spring plowing.
Her task is complicated by the severe illness
of a son, too sick to move.

Beyond that, the layers pile high. On the
light side there's the comedy of Dom DeLuise
as a clumsy crow who tries to help. At the
worst are a pack of rats led for good and ill by
Derek Jacobi, Peter Strauss and Paul Shenar,
all influenced by some modern-day sci-fi
mind-bending, mixed with old-fashioned
sorcery. John Carradine also serves well as a
menacing but helpful great owl, full of
wisdom and woe.

■ SECRET OF SANTA VITTORIA, THE

1969, 134 MINS, US ◇

Dir Stanley Kramer   *Prod* Stanley Kramer   *Scr* William
Rose, Ben Maddow   *Ph* Giuseppe Rotunno
Ed William Lyon, Earle Herdan   *Mus* Ernest Gold   *Art
Dir* Robert Clatworthy
● Anthony Quinn, Anna Magnani, Virna Lisi, Hardy
Kruger, Sergio Franchi, Giancarlo Giannini (United
Artists)

The Secret of Santa Vittoria comes near being a
dramatic knockout, so tempered with humor
and understanding that it also becomes an
idyll of war and Italian peasantry. Carrying
charm, suspense, romance, the production
offers Anthony Quinn at his seasoned best, a
plot and unfoldment that holds the spectator.

Based on the Robert Crichton bestseller, its
story – said to be true and to have become a
legend – is simple. The people of a hill town
in northern Italy are suddenly thrown into
shock when apprised that a detachment of
the retreating German army is to descend on
their town to confiscate all their wine, their
very life blood.

Screenplay painstakingly develops this
conflict, to which Stanley Kramer's direction
adds fascinating character evolvement and
ingenious invention.

■ SECRET PEOPLE

1952, 96 MINS, UK

Dir Thorold Dickinson   *Prod* Sidney Cole   *Scr* Thorold
Dickinson, Wolfgang Wilhelm   *Ph* Gordon Dines
Ed Peter Tanner   *Mus* Roberto Gerhard   *Art
Dir* William Kellner
● Valentina Cortese, Serge Reggiani, Charles Goldner,
Audrey Hepburn, Megs Jenkins, Athene Seyler (Ealing)

S

Secret People is a hackneyed story of political agents working against a tyrannical dictator, dressed up with all the familiar cliches to make a dull and rather confusing offering.

The yarn has a prewar setting, opening in London in 1930 with the arrival of two girls whose father has been killed by a European dictator. Story skips seven years, when the two girls together with the Italian cafe owner who has adopted them, spend a weekend in Paris. There, the older girl runs into the boy she left behind at home to carry on her father's work. He follows her to London, and compels her to act as an accomplice in an attempt on the dictator's life.

Audrey Hepburn, in a minor role combines beauty with skill, particularly in two dance sequences.

■ **SECRET PLACES**

1984, 96 MINS, UK ◇ ⓥ
Dir Zelda Barron   *Prod* Simon Relph, Ann Skinner   *Scr* Zelda Barron   *Ph* Peter MacDonald   *Ed* Laurence Mery-Clark   *Mus* Michel Legrand   *Art Dir* Eileen Diss
● Marie-Therese Relin, Tara MacGowran, Claudine Auger, Jenny Agutter, Cassie Stuart, Anne-Marie Gwatkin (Skreba/Virgin)

Secret Places is a pleasing evocation of schoolgirl life in England during World War II.

Based on a novel by Janice Elliott, the film recounts the initially hostile response of a group of adolescents to the enrollment of Laura Meister, a German refugee, in their all-girl school. Gradually her exotically winning ways and intelligence secure her enrollment in the select circle which gathers in 'secret places'. Things turn sour, however, when a girl's father is killed in battle.

The plot relates the psychological pressures which lead to Laura's attempted suicide.

Marie-Therese Relin captures the gestures and looks of a girl whose emotional resilience conceals suffering. Tara MacGowran is right on as a repressed English girl.

■ **SECRET POLICEMAN'S BALL, THE**

1980, 91 MINS, UK ◇ ⓥ
Dir Roger Graef   *Prod* Roger Graef, Thomas Schwalm   *Ph* Ernest Vincze, Clive Tickner, Pascoe MacFarlane   *Ed* Thomas Schwalm
● John Cleese, Peter Cook, Eleanor Bron, Pete Townshend, Rowan Atkinson, Michael Palin (Document/Amnesty International)

Roger Graef's film record of this year's Amnesty International benefit show at Her Majesty's Theatre, London, is primarily aimed at the tube.

John Cleese, Michael Palin and Terry Jones of the *Monty Python* team appear in various sketches; guitarist Pete Townshend plays acoustic versions of a couple of The Who's repertoire, joined on one by classical picker John Williams; Peter Cook (sans Dudley Moore) renders a takeoff of one of the local hits of 1979 – the judge's summing-up in the trial of Liberal politician Jeremy Thorpe; and Billy Connolly, Clive James and Eleanor Bron, among others, contribute solo spots. All gave their services free.

There is no backstage material in *The Secret Policeman's Ball*, which is a disappointment. The earlier such venture, *Pleasure at Her Majesty's* [1976], included footage of hasty rehearsals and dressing-room neurosis, which leavened the laugh-lump with an extra dimension.

■ **SECRET POLICEMAN'S OTHER BALL, THE**

1982, 99 MINS, UK ◇ ⓥ
Dir Julian Temple   *Prod* Martin Lewis, Peter Walker   *Scr* Marty Feldman, Michael Palin, Martin Lewis, and members of the cast   *Ph* Oliver Stapleton   *Ed* Geoff Hogg

● Rowan Atkinson, Alan Bennett, John Cleese, Billy Connolly, Victoria Wood, Eric Clapton (Amnesty International)

The second filmed record of the bi-annual Amnesty International fundraiser in London. *The Secret Policeman's Other Ball* is a thoroughly entertaining concert pic. As irreverent and clever as its title, show boasts comic talents from *Monty Python, Beyond the Fringe* and *Not the Nine O'Clock News* and therefore does require a taste for British humor.

Some of the humor slides over into tastelessness, but most of it is rousing fun in the tradition of the groups from which these performers have sprung. Particularly hilarious are a *Top of the Form* quiz show take-off in which the moderator gets the correct answers mixed up, and a deadpan, coming-out-of-the-closet sexual confession by Alan Bennett.

■ **SECRET WAR OF HARRY FRIGG, THE**

1968, 110 MINS, US ◇ ⓥ
Dir Jack Smight   *Prod* Hal Chester   *Scr* Peter Stone, Frank Tarloff   *Ph* Russell Metty   *Ed* Terry Williams   *Mus* Carlo Rustichelli   *Art Dir* Alexander Golitzen, Henry Bumstead
● Paul Newman, Sylva Koscina, Tom Bosley, Andrew Duggan, John Williams, Werner Peters (Universal/Albion)

The Secret War of Harry Frigg is an amusing World War II comedy starring Paul Newman as a dumb army private sent to rescue five Axis-held Allied generals. Strong story premise, excellent supporting cast and generally good dialog work to smooth over sometimes static direction and sluggish pacing.

Frank Tarloff's original story, scripted by author and Peter Stone, concerns the exploits of the title character as he effects the eventual rescue of five top brass from Italian-German incarceration. Newman plays a perennial goof-off, who achieves a measure of self-confidence and maturity under pressure. Sympathy is with him all the way.

Carrying the main comedy load are the five captured generals – Andrew Duggan, Tom Bosley, John Williams, Charles D. Gray, Jacques Roux – plus their Italo captor, Vito Scotti, and James Gregory, the US general.

There are many smiles, and some strong laughs, in the pic, result of which audience will probably emerge feeling lifted, if never consistently nor hilariously diverted.

■ **SEDUCTION OF JOE TYNAN, THE**

1979, 107 MINS, US ◇ ⓥ
Dir Jerry Schatzberg   *Prod* Martin Bregman   *Scr* Alan Alda   *Ph* Adam Holender   *Ed* Evan Lottman   *Mus* Bill Conti   *Art Dir* David Chapman
● Alan Alda, Barbara Harris, Meryl Streep, Rip Torn, Melvyn Douglas (Universal)

Adroitly combining humor and intimate drama, *Joe Tynan* joins that list of exemplary Washington-set pix, including *Advise and Consent* and *The Best Man*.

In large part, the credit goes to Alan Alda, whose portrayal in the title role is no less complex and multi-faceted than his screenplay. Joe Tynan is a familiar political figure: the young, handsome liberal Senator who rides upward on the coat-tails of a few big media victories. Alda assumes the pasted-on smile, the hearty handshake and breezy confidence of a politico with immense ease. He seems to have been born for the role.

Less often explored is the price paid for such double-edged success, and this is where *Joe Tynan* excels. As Alda's intelligent and frustrated wife, Barbara Harris gives the performance of her career.

■ **SEE NO EVIL, HEAR NO EVIL**

1989, 103 MINS, US ◇ ⓥ
Dir Arthur Hiller   *Prod* Marvin Worth   *Scr* Earl Barret, Arne Sultan, Eliot Wald, Andrew Kurtzman, Gene Wilder   *Ph* Victor J. Kemper   *Ed* Robert C. Jones   *Mus* Stewart Copeland   *Art Dir* Robert Gundlach
● Richard Pryor, Gene Wilder, Joan Severance, Kevin Spacey, Kirsten Childs (Tri-Star)

With Richard Pryor and Gene Wilder in the lead roles, *See No Evil, Hear No Evil* could only be a broadly played, occasionally crass, funny physical comedy.

How the blind Pryor ends up working for the deaf Wilder at a Manhattan lobby newsstand really is inconsequential, since neither their first encounter, nor anything that follows, is believable for a minute, including the thing that binds them in the first place – how each denies his limitations.

While Wilder's back is turned, a customer is shot in the back. Pryor is out on the curb listening for the New York *Daily News* to make its morning drop – so he misses hearing anything inside.

By the time Wilder turns around, he's only able to catch a glimpse of the assailant's (Joan Severance) sexy games. Pryor has missed it all, though he does manage to catch a whiff of Severance's perfume before she slips by him onto the crowded street.

The cops arrive and, in predictable fashion, arrest the only suspects around, the two numbskulls who couldn't possibly coordinate anything, much less a murder.

■ **SEE YOU IN THE MORNING**

1989, 119 MINS, US ◇ ⓥ
Dir Alan J. Pakula   *Prod* Alan J. Pakula   *Scr* Alan J. Pakula   *Ph* Donald McAlpine   *Ed* Evan Lottman   *Art Dir* George Jenkins
● Jeff Bridges, Alice Krige, Farrah Fawcett, Drew Barrymore, Lukas Haas (Lorimar)

See You in the Morning is a bad dream for those who've admired Alan J. Pakula's best work.

Pakula produced, wrote and directed the semi-autobiographical story of a man torn between two families and two marriages.

Jeff Bridges is a Manhattan psychiatrist who tries earnestly to fit in with his new life with second wife Beth (Alice Krige) and her two kids, while remaining the most decent of dads to his own two kids. Their mother is played by Farrah Fawcett.

As dull as this sounds, it's even more boring to watch. At just under two hours, it seems nearly interminable.

Pakula tried too hard to make this into a romantic comedy. Bridges' character jokes to avoid talking about his feelings (some shrink!) while Krige is the guilt-ridden martyr type.

■ **SEMI-TOUGH**

1977, 107 MINS, US ◇ ⓥ
Dir Michael Ritchie   *Prod* David Merrick   *Scr* Walter Bernstein   *Ph* Charles Rosher Jr   *Ed* Richard A. Harris   *Mus* Jerry Fielding   *Art Dir* Walter Scott Herndon
● Burt Reynolds, Kris Kristofferson, Jill Clayburgh, Robert Preston, Bert Convy, Roger E. Mosley (United Artists)

Semi-Tough begins as a bawdy and lively romantic comedy about slap happy pro football players, then slows down to a too-inside putdown of contemporary self-help programs.

Stars Burt Reynolds, Kris Kristofferson and Jill Clayburgh are all excellent within the limits of the zigzag Walter Bernstein script and Michael Ritchie's ambivalent direction.

Dan Jenkins' book was adapted by Bernstein to tell of pals Reynolds and Kristofferson, members of a flashy team owned by eccentric Robert Preston, whose daughter (Clayburgh) roommates with the two guys. She tilts romantically towards Kristofferson, whose personality has become more assured after undergoing training by Bert Convy.

··

■ SENATOR WAS INDISCREET, THE

1947, 86 MINS, US ⓥ
Dir George S. Kaufman   *Prod* Nunnally Johnson
Scr Charles MacArthur   *Ph* William Mellor
Ed Sherman A. Rose   *Mus* Daniele Amfitheatrof   *Art Dir* Bernard Herzbrun, Boris Leven
● William Powell, Ella Raines, Arleen Whelan, Charles D. Brown, Peter Lind Hayes, Myrna Loy (Universal)

Director George S. Kaufman manifests pace and polish in a fast-moving bit of fluff about a flannel-mouth Solon whose presidential aspirations become complicated when he loses an incriminating diary wherein he had recorded every step taken by his political backers in the past 30 days. Topper finds William Powell (in the title role) in native South Seas garb and his 'queen' is the unbilled Myrna Loy – a frank takeoff on the Crosby-Hope technique of 'surprise' tongue-in-cheek fadeouts.

Powell does a fine job as the stuffy dimwit of a senator who was not stupid enough not to record his political machine's machinations. He uses that as a club over Charles D. Brown, who does a capital job as the bullying political boss. Ella Raines is the newspaper gal who rightly suspects Arleen Whelan got away with the diary as a favor to her beau, who too has political ambitions in opposition to the senator.

Casting is good down the line, and there are many nice little touches (such as that autographed, oversize postage stamp whereon George Washington 'thanks' p.a. Peter Lind Hayes for 'putting me on the stamp').

··

■ SEND ME NO FLOWERS

1964, 100 MINS, US ◇ ⓥ
Dir Norman Jewison   *Prod* Harry Keller   *Scr* Julius Epstein   *Ph* Daniel L. Fapp   *Ed* J. Terry Williams
Mus Frank DeVol   *Art Dir* Alexander Golitzen, Robert Clatworthy
● Rock Hudson, Doris Day, Tony Randall, Paul Lynde, Hal March, Edward Andrews (Universal)

Send Me No Flowers doesn't carry the same voltage, either in laughs or originality, as Doris Day and Rock Hudson's two previous entries, *Pillow Talk* (1959) and *Lover Come Back* (1961).

Adapted from the Broadway play by Norman Barasch and Carroll Moore, the thin story line romps around Hudson, a hypochondriac, overhearing his doctor discussing the fatal symptoms of another patient and believing them to be his own. In the belief he has only a few weeks to live, he sets about trying to find a suitable man to take his place as Day's husband.

Norman Jewison in his direction weaves his characters in and out of this situation as skillfully as the script will permit, having the benefit, of course, of seasoned thesps in such roles. Day is quite up to the demands of her part, indulging in a bit of slapstick in the opening sequence as she's locked out of the house in her nightgown, arms loaded with eggs and milk bottles. Hudson plays his character nobly.

Tony Randall, costarred with the pair in the other two films, again plays Hudson's pal, this time his next door neighbor, who takes his friend's expected fate even harder than the soon-to-be-deceased and goes on a threeday drunk.

··

■ SENDER, THE

1983, 91 MINS, UK ◇ ⓥ
Dir Roger Christian   *Prod* Edward S. Foldman
Scr Thomas Baum   *Ph* Roger Pratt   *Ed* Alan Strachan   *Mus* Trevor Jones   *Art Dir* Steve Spence, Charles Bishop
● Kathryn Harrold, Zeljko Iranek, Shirley Knight, Paul Freeman, Sean Hewitt, Harry Ditson (Paramount/Kingsmere)

The Sender is a superbly-crafted modern horror picture, credibly using telepathic communication as its premise for creating nightmarish situations.

Thomas Baum's screenplay concerns a suicidal young amnesiac (Zeljko Ivanek) near the fictional town of Corinth, Georgia. Taken to a psychiatric clinic, he establishes a telepathic link with his psychiatrist Gail Farmer (Kathryn Harrold), causing her to experience involuntarily his violent nightmares.

The 'sender' cannot control his telepathic powers, and when Dr Denman (Paul Freeman), Farmer's superior, subjects him to shock treatment and surgical experiments, he sends telepathic images of horror which disrupt the entire hospital. Farmer, who is visited by the sender's mysterious mother Jerolyn (Shirley Knight), tries to cure him.

Cast is good within script limitations, as Harrold represents an attractive, sympathetic heroine and Ivanek a mesmerizing, troubled youngster.

··

■ SENTINEL, THE

1977, 91 MINS, US ◇ ⓥ
Dir Michael Winner   *Prod* Michael Winner
Scr Michael Winner   *Ph* Dick Kratina   *Ed* Bernard Gribble, Terence Rawlings   *Mus* Gil Melle
Art Dir Philip Rosenberg
● Chris Sarandon, Christina Raines, Martin Balsam, John Carradine, Jose Ferrer, Ava Gardner (Universal)

The Sentinel is a grubby, grotesque excursion into religioso psychodrama, notable for uniformly poor performances by a large cast of familiar names and direction that is hysterical and heavy-handed.

The story [from Jeffrey Knovitz' novel] is based on the familiar device of taking some innocent (in this case, Cristina Raines, whose performance is miserable), confronted with kooky situations and characters whose motives are unclear except that the innocent seems to be losing mental control.

Raines, cast as a fashion model, has some mighty formidable plot adversaries: fiance Chris Sarandon, amusingly trying to play a successful lawyer; weird neighbors like Burgess Meredith, in ludicrous overacting job; also pushy lesbian Sylvia Miles and lover Beverly D'Angelo.

··

■ SEPARATE TABLES

1958, 98 MINS, US ⓥ
Dir Delbert Mann   *Prod* Harold Hecht   *Scr* Terence Rattigan, John Gay   *Ph* Charles Lang Jr   *Ed* Marjorie Fowler, Charles Ennis   *Mus* David Raksin   *Art Dir* Edward Carrere
● Rita Hayworth, Deborah Kerr, David Niven, Wendy Hiller, Burt Lancaster, Gladys Cooper (United Artists/Hecht-Hill-Lancaster)

As a play, *Separate Tables* consisted of two separate vignettes set against the same English boarding house and served as an acting tour de force for Eric Portman and Margaret Leighton. Much of the appeal of Terence Rattigan's play was due to the remarkable change in characterization they were able to make as they assumed different roles in each of the segments. Rattigan and John Gay have masterfully blended the two playlets into one literate and absorbing full-length film.

Basically, story is a character study of a group of residents of the small British seaside town of Bournemouth, described in the film as a tourist spot in the summer and haven for the lonely and the desperate in the winter. The majority of the residents are tortured by psychological problems and unhappy pasts. As a phoney major, with a madeup Sandhurst background, David Niven gives one of the best performances of his career. Deborah Kerr is excellent as a plain, shy girl completely cowed by a domineering and strong mother, finely portrayed by Gladys Cooper.

A separate but integrated story concerns Burt Lancaster, Rita Hayworth and Wendy Hiller. As a writer hurt by life and living a don't-care existence at the out-of-the-way hotel, Lancaster turns in a shaded performance. Hayworth is equally good as his former wife whose narcissism and desire to dominate men leads to Lancaster's downfall. Hiller is the efficient manager of the hotel who finds her romance with Lancaster shattered on the arrival of his physically attractive and fashionable ex-wife.
☐ 1958: Best Picture (Nomination)

··

■ SEPTEMBER

1987, 82 MINS, US ◇ ⓥ
Dir Woody Allen   *Prod* Robert Greenhut   *Scr* Woody Allen   *Ph* Carlo D. Palma   *Ed* Susan E. Morse
Art Dir Santo Loquasto
● Denholm Elliott, Dianne Wiest, Mia Farrow, Elaine Stritch, Sam Waterston, Jack Warden (Orion)

September sees Woody Allen in a compellingly melancholy mood, as he sends four achingly unhappy younger people and two better adjusted older ones through a grim story drenched with Chekhovian overtones.

Set entirely within the lovely Vermont country home of Mia Farrow at summer's end, tale is constructed around a pattern of unrequited, mismatched infatuations that drive the high-strung, intellectual characters to distraction. Neighbor Denholm Elliott loves Farrow, Farrow is a goner for guesthouse occupant Sam Waterston, and Waterston is nuts for Farrow's best friend Dianne Wiest, who is married.

Also visiting are Farrow's mother, a former screen star and great beauty played by Elaine Stritch, and the latter's husband, physicist Jack Warden.

So it goes, a merry-go-round of frustration, resentment, heartbreak, disappointment and bitterness, described in brittle, often piercing terms in Allen's dialog. Happily, the air is cleared on occasion by the outrageous Stritch, whose rowdy, forthright comments never fail to lighten the mood and provide genuine amusement.

This is the film Allen largely reshot with a significantly altered cast after feeling dissatisfied with his first version. Originally, Maureen O'Sullivan, Farrow's real mother, played the role finally filled by Stritch. Sam Shepard, then, briefly, Christopher Walken, had Waterston's part, and Elliott was first cast as the actress' husband, with Charles Durning in the role of the neighbor.

··

■ SERGEANT, THE

1968, 107 MINS, US ◇
Dir John Flynn   *Prod* Richard Goldstone   *Scr* Dennis Murphy   *Ph* Henri Persin   *Ed* Charles Nelson, Francoise Diot   *Mus* Michel Magne   *Art Dir* Willy Holt
● Rod Steiger, John Phillip Law, Ludmila Mikael, Frank Latimore, Elliott Sullivan (Warner/Seven Arts)

Dennis Murphy's novel reaches the screen as a moving production, filmed with sensitivity by debuting director John Flynn, and with robust, appropriately grim physical values. Rod Steiger's title-role performance is generally excellent, and John Phillip Law hits the mark, as the would-be mark.

To say that this is a story about a homosexual is like claiming that an iceberg floats com-

S

pletely on the surface of water. The pic is about a total, pervading enslavement of one person to another.

A five-minute prolog, in black-and-white for good contrast, establishes Steiger as a hero during the 1944 liberation of France. The heroic deed included the strangling of a helpless, disarmed German soldier. His death grip on the younger man betrays a latent homosexuality.

Time shifts under titles to 1952, with Steiger reporting as first sergeant at a US base in rural France. He effectively seizes command, and works to shape up the slovenly unit. Law attracts Steiger's attention. Practically dragooned into the company office, Law falls increasingly under the thrall of Steiger.

Story threads are strongly woven, through Murphy's own fine adaptation of his book as well as Flynn's incisive direction.

· ·

■ SERGEANT YORK

1941, 134 MINS, US

Dir Howard Hawks *Prod* Jesse L. Lasky, Hal B. Wallis *Scr* Abem Finkel, Harry Chandlee, Howard Koch, John Huston *Ph* Sol Polito *Mus* Max Steiner
● Gary Cooper, Walter Brennan, Joan Leslie, Ward Bond (Warner)

For more than 20 years studios sought permission to film the heroic World War deeds of Sergeant York. And for as long a period York refused the necessary cooperation for a film of his heroism on the early morning of 8 October 1918, when he single-handed killed 20 Germans and compelled the surrender of 132 of the enemy in the Argonne sector.

Lauded, praised, awarded the Congressional Medal of Honor, York side-stepped all proffers to benefit from the acclaim. He returned from army service to his home in Pall Mall, Tenn, where he devoted himself to farming and educational work.

It is film biography at its best. The writers have paid more attention to character, and the backgrounds and associations which create it, than to incident.

For Gary Cooper the role is made to order. He convincingly portrays the youthful backwoodsman, unruly as a youth, who in time gains mastery over his wildness. The romantic passages played with Joan Leslie are tender and human. But Cooper is best, perhaps, in the scenes of early camp training when his marksmanship, learned in the woods, attracts attention. Among the featured players the reliable Walter Brennan is splendid as the combination village pastor and storekeeper.
□ 1942: Best Picture (Nomination)

· ·

■ SERGEANTS 3

1962, 113 MINS, US ◇

Dir John Sturges *Prod* Frank Sinatra *Scr* W.R. Burnett *Ph* Winton Hoch *Ed* Ferris Webster *Mus* Billy May *Art Dir* Frank Hotaling
● Frank Sinatra, Dean Martin, Sammy Davis Jr, Peter Lawford, Joey Bishop (United Artists)

Sergeants 3 is warmed-over *Gunga Din* a westernized version of that screen epic, with American-style Indians and Vegas-style soldiers of fortune. The essential differences between the two pictures, other than the obvious one of setting, is that the emphasis in *Gunga* was serious, with tongue-in-cheek overtone, whereas the emphasis in *Sergeants* is tongue-in-cheek, with serious overtones.

Although, unaccountably, no mention is made of the obvious source in the screen credits. W. R. Burnett's screenplay not only owes its existence to that story, but adheres to it faithfully, with one noteworthy exception – *Gunga* does not die for his heroism. It's peaches and cream all the way.

The 'Big Three' of Sinatra, Martin and Lawford reenact the parts played in the original by Cary Grant, Victor McLaglen and Douglas Fairbanks Jr. Of the three, Martin seems by far the most animated and comfortable, Sinatra and Lawford coming off a trifle too businesslike for the irreverent, look-ma-we're-cavalrymen approach.

· ·

■ SERPENT AND THE RAINBOW, THE

1988, 98 MINS, US ◇ ▼

Dir Wes Craven *Prod* David Ladd, Doug Claybourne *Scr* Richard Maxwell, A.R. Simoun *Ph* John Lindley *Ed* Glenn Farr *Mus* Brad Fiedel *Art Dir* David Nichols
● Bill Pullman, Cathy Tyson, Zakes Mokae, Paul Winfield, Brent Jennings (Universal)

Wes Craven's *The Serpent and the Rainbow* is a better-than-average supernatural tale [inspired by Wade Davis' book] that offers a few good scares but gets bogged down in special effects. Film is intriguingly eerie as long as it explores the secrets of voodoo in a lush Haitian setting alive with mysteries of the spirit.

Dennis Alan (Bill Pullman), a Harvard anthropologist looking for a magic zombie powder at the behest of an American drug company, is sort of a second-rate Indiana Jones.

In Haiti, Alan gets involved with psychiatrist Marielle Celine (Cathy Tyson) who is battling the cumulative effects of deep-rooted black magic, religion and everyday mental illness.

Opposing the more progressive Marielle are the reactionary political and supernatural forces of police chief Dargent Peytraud, played with evil zeal by Zakes Mokae. Speaking out of the side of his gold-toothed mouth, Mokae walks a narrow line between being truly frightening and truly hilarious.

Special effects are well done, but fail to capture the creepy undercurrents of voodoo.

· ·

■ SERPENT OF THE NILE

1953, 81 MINS, US ◇

Dir William Castle *Prod* Sam Katzman *Scr* Robert E. Kent *Ph* Henry Freulich *Ed* Gene Havlick *Mus* Mischa Bakaleinikoff *Art Dir* Paul Palmentola
● Rhonda Fleming, William Lundigan, Raymond Burr, Jean Byron, Michael Ansara, Julie Newmar (Columbia)

Producer Sam Katzman dusts off some incidents in the life and loves of Cleopatra for mediocre results in *Serpent of the Nile*. Much of the difficulty is the lack of credibility in the script. Its treatment of Mark Anthony's rise to power following Caesar's assassination and subsequent fall, when subjected to the wiles of Cleopatra, is seldom convincing. This slice of Roman history is played straight.

Yarn has Raymond Burr, as Anthony, proposing an alliance between Rome and wealthy Egypt, which is ruled by Rhonda Fleming as Cleopatra. Thoroughly unscrupulous, she schemes to eliminate Burr and place herself on the throne of Rome. Her plan, however, is nipped by William Lundigan, Burr's lieutenant, who brings the Roman legions to Alexandria.

Burr's Anthony is a wishywashy individual whose love for drink and infatuation for Fleming makes him lose his sense of logic. She, on the other hand, fails to impress as the Egyptian beauty, primarily due to the stilted dialog. Lundigan, too, has his moments of vacillation. But, fortunately, his portrayal shows enough virility and drive to meet the combat requirements the role demands.

· ·

■ SERPENT'S EGG, THE

1977, 120 MINS, W. GERMANY/US ◇ ▼

Dir Ingmar Bergman *Prod* Dino De Laurentiis *Scr* Ingmar Bergman *Ph* Sven Nykvist *Ed* Petra von Oelffen *Mus* Rolf Wilhelm *Art Dir* Rolf Zehetbauer
● Liv Ullmann, David Carradine, Gert Frobe, Heinz Bennent, James Whitmore (Rialto/De Laurentiis)

The Serpent's Egg, Ingmar Bergman's first English-language feature and his first film made outside his home country, bears the master's stamp right from the beginning in a superior collaboration with cinematographer Sven Nykvist and production designer Rolf Zehetbauer.

The latter has recreated a Berlin of a poverty-ridden, fear-stricken early 1920s that is much more than paint-deep. Also, Bergman makes his actors, with one fatal exception (David Carradine), work their individualities into the grandest of ensemble playing.

The Serpent's Egg lacks both the strength and depth of Bergman's major work. By going outwardly international, the master becomes perilously close to becoming shallow as well.

· ·

■ SERPICO

1973, 129 MINS, US ◇ ▼

Dir Sidney Lumet *Prod* Martin Bregman *Scr* Waldo Salt, Norman Wexler *Ph* Arthur J. Ornitz *Ed* Dede Allen, Richard Marks *Mus* Mikis Theodorakis *Art Dir* Charles Bailey
● Al Pacino, John Randolph, Jack Kehoe, Biff McGuire, Barbara Eda-Young, Cornelia Sharpe (De Laurentiis/Artists Entertainment)

Serpico is based on the actual experiences of an honest NY policeman who helped expose corruption. Al Pacino's performance is outstanding. Sidney Lumet's direction adeptly combines gritty action and thought-provoking comment.

The real-life Frank Serpico, who climaxed an 11-year police career by blowing the lid on departmental corruption, told his story first through a book collaboration with Peter Maas.

Pacino dominates the entire film. His inner personal torment is vividly detailed, manifested first in the breakup of an affair with Cornelia Sharpe and later, much more terribly, in the wreck of his love for Barbara Eda-Young.

A very large cast exemplifies the assorted attitudes with which Pacino must deal.

· ·

■ SERVANT, THE

1963, 117 MINS, UK ▼

Dir Joseph Losey *Prod* Joseph Losey, Norman Priggen *Scr* Harold Pinter *Ph* Douglas Slocombe *Ed* Reginald Mills *Mus* John Dankworth *Art Dir* Ted Clements
● Dirk Bogarde, Sarah Miles, Wendy Craig, James Fox (Springbok)

The Servant is for the most part strong dramatic fare, though the atmosphere and tension is not fully sustained to the end. Harold Pinter's screenplay based on the Robin Maugham novel is distinguished by its literacy and sharp incisive dialog.

Dirk Bogarde plays a manservant who is hired by a young and elegant man about town to run a house he has just bought in a fashionable part of London, and who, almost imperceptibly, begins to dominate his master.

Up to the point where the servant gains supremacy, Joseph Losey's direction is first class, despite a few conventional shots which are used to gain effect. The last segment of the story, which puts some strain on credibility, is less convincing and, therefore, less satisfying. But the relationship of master and servant, with its underlying suggestion of homosexuality is sensitively handled.

Bogarde not only looks the part, but plays it with natural assurance. There is also a noteworthy performance from James Fox, who assuredly suggests the indolent young man about town. The two main femme roles are also expertly played, Sarah Miles making a highly provocative and sensuous maid, and Wendy Craig giving a contrasting study as the fiancee who is overwhelmed by events she cannot control.

■ SESAME STREET PRESENTS: FOLLOW THAT BIRD

1985, 88 MINS, US ◇ ▾
Dir Ken Kwapis *Prod* Tony Garnett *Scr* Tony Geiss, Judy Freudberg *Ph* Curtis Clark *Ed* Stan Warnow, Evan Landis *Mus* Van Dyke Parks, Lennie Niehaus *Art Dir* Carol Spier
● Caroll Spinney, Jim Henson, Frank Oz, Paul Bartel, Sandra Bernhard, John Candy (Warner/Children's Television Workshop/World Film Services)

Simple premise has the slightly goofy yellow, eight-foot fowl Big Bird taken away from Sesame Street by the officious Miss Finch so he can grow up among his own kind, a bird family named the Dodos, in Oceanview, Ill.

The Dodos are a bunch of loons, however, so B.B. begins the long trek back to New York on foot, while the Sesame Street gang mobilizes in assorted vehicles to find its dear friend.

En route, B.B. has a pleasant encounter with country singing truck driver Waylon Jennings, but a distinctly nasty one with the Sleaze Brothers (SCTV's Joe Flaherty and Dave Thomas), unscrupulous amusement park operators who abduct B.B. for their own nefarious purposes.

All turns out for the best, of course, and spicing things up along the way are Chevy Chase and Kermit The Frog as TV newscasters, Sandra Bernhard and Paul Bartel as the proprietors of a lowdown roadside diner, and John Candy as a motorcycle cop.

■ SEVEN BRIDES FOR SEVEN BROTHERS

1954, 102 MINS, US ◇ ▾
Dir Stanley Donen *Prod* Jack Cummings *Scr* Albert Hackett, Frances Goodrich, Dorothy Kingsley *Ph* George Folsey *Ed* Ralph E. Winters *Mus* Adolph Deutsch (dir.)
● Howard Keel, Jeff Richards, Russ Tamblyn, Tommy Rall, Jane Powell, Julie Newmar (M-G-M)

This is a happy, hand-clapping, foot-stomping country type of musical with all the slickness of a Broadway show. Johnny Mercer and Gene de Paul provide the slick, showy production with eight songs, all of which jibe perfectly with the folksy, hillbilly air maintained in the picture. Howard Keel's robust baritone and Jane Powell's lilting soprano make their songs extremely listenable.

A real standout is the acrobatic hoedown staged around a barn-raising shindig, during which six of the title's seven brothers vie in love rivalry with the town boys for the favor of the mountain belles.

With tunes and terping taking up so much of the footage there isn't too much for Stanley Donen to do except direct the story bridges between the numbers.

It's the story of seven brothers living on a mountain farm. The eldest gets a bride and the others decide likewise, steal their maidens and after a snowed-in winter, the girls' parents mastermind a mass shot-gun wedding.

The long and the short of the teaming of Keel and Powell is that the pairing comes off very satisfactorily, vocally and otherwise. The brothers are all good, with Russ Tamblyn standing out in particular for performance and his dance work.
□ 1954: Best Picture (Nomination)

■ SEVEN DAYS IN MAY

1964, 120 MINS, US ▾
Dir John Frankenheimer *Prod* Edward Lewis *Scr* Rod Serling *Ph* Ellsworth Fredericks *Ed* Ferris Webster *Mus* Jerry Goldsmith *Art Dir* Cary Odell
● Burt Lancaster, Kirk Douglas, Fredric March, Ava Gardner, Edmond O'Brien, Martin Balsam (Paramount/Seven Arts)

A combination of competents has drawn from the novel of the same title a strikingly dramatic, realistic and provocatively topical film in *Seven Days in May*. Fletcher Knebel-Charles W. Bailey II's book detailed a military plot to overthrow the government of the United States 'in the not-too-distant future'.

What *Seven Days in May* undertakes is the proposition that extremists could reach the point where they'd try to uproot the present form of government. Such a man is Gen. James M. Scott, played with authority by Burt Lancaster. He's a member of the Joint Chiefs of Staff, burning with patriotic fervor and seeking to 'save' the country from the perils of a just-signed nuclear pact with Russia. He enlists the support of fellow chiefs. Their plan of seizure is to be consummated in seven days in May.

The performances are excellent down the line, under the taut and penetrating directorial guidance of John Frankenheimer. Kirk Douglas is masterfully cool and matter of fact as Scott's aide, utterly devoted until he comes to be suspicious. He goes to the president with information that has got to be checked out in those fateful seven days.

Edmund O'Brien is standout as a southern senator with an addiction to bourbon and an unfailing loyalty to the president. Ava Gardner works out well enough as the Washington matron who has had an affair with Lancaster and is amenable to a go with Douglas.

■ SEVEN DAYS TO NOON

1950, 94 MINS, UK
Dir John Boulting *Prod* Roy Boulting *Scr* Frank Harvey, Roy Boulting *Ph* Gilbert Taylor *Ed* Roy Boulting *Mus* John Addison
● Barry Jones, Olive Sloane, Andre Morell, Sheila Manahan, Hugh Cross, Joan Hickson (London/Boulting)

Much of the pic was lensed on location in the London area. Focal point of the plot is an ultimatum sent to the prime minister by an atom scientist who becomes mentally deranged because his work is being used for destruction, not for mankind's benefit. He warns that unless atomic bomb production ceases by noon the following Sunday (the letter is received on the Monday morning), he will, himself, blow up all of London with a bomb he has stolen.

Barry Jones' interpretation of the scientist is intelligent. His clearly defined portrait of the man no one understands is a moving piece of acting. Principal female role, which is generously filled with comedy lines, is taken by Olive Sloane. She plays a former showgirl with rare gusto.

■ 711 OCEAN DRIVE

1950, 102 MINS, US
Dir Joseph H. Newman *Prod* Frank N. Seltzer *Scr* Richard English, Francis Swan *Ph* Franz Planer *Ed* Bert Jordan *Mus* Sol Kaplan
● Edmond O'Brien, Joanne Dru, Donald Porter, Sammy White, Otto Kruger (Columbia)

Story concerns a telephone worker (Edmund O'Brien) with a knack for electrons who joins a syndicate and expands its operations with his inventions. When the syndicate chief is killed, he takes charge of the organization, and runs into the opposition of an eastern

syndicate. The bigger outfit makes overtures which he rejects until he meets Joanne Dru, the wife of one of the eastern leaders.

Operations of the syndicates are given a realistic touch by the screenplay, and Joseph H. Newman's direction keeps action at a fast pace. O'Brien is excellent as the hot-tempered, ambitious young syndicate chief.

■ SEVEN NIGHTS IN JAPAN

1976, 104 MINS, UK/FRANCE ◇ ▾
Dir Lewis Gilbert *Prod* Lewis Gilbert *Scr* Christopher Wood *Ph* Henri Decae *Ed* John Glen *Mus* David Hentschel
● Michael York, Hidemi Aoki, Charles Gray, Ann Lonnberg, Eleonore Hirt, James Villiers (EMI/Paramount)

Seven Nights in Japan is a beautifully-photographed pastiche bearing little true resemblance to the enigmatic life of bustling Tokyo, where it was lensed.

Simplistic plot details the implausible romance between a royal prince (Michael York) who is serving as a naval officer, and a petite Japanese bus guide (Hidemi Aoki) whom he meets when his ship visits Japan. There are also some ludicrous attempts to kill the prince made by a fanatical gang of bungling political cut-throats.

Christopher Wood's script is sadly lacking in humor and pace and the storyline can only be labeled corny and unreal. York's acting is suitably princelike although never exceptional while Aoki has occasional moments.

■ SEVEN UPS, THE

1973, 103 MINS, US ◇ ▾
Dir Philip D'Antoni *Prod* Philip D'Antoni *Scr* Albert Ruben, Alexander Jacobs *Ph* Urs Furrer *Ed* Jerry Greenberg, Stephen A. Rotter, John C. Horger *Mus* Don Ellis *Art Dir* Ed Wittstein
● Roy Scheider, Victor Arnold, Jerry Leon, Ken Kercheval, Tony Lo Bianco, Larry Haines (20th Century-Fox)

The Seven Ups is a serviceable dualer about some underground cops who get caught in a series of gangland kidnappings. Produced by debuting director Philip D'Antoni in NY, the film features, at midpoint, a complicated and extravagant car chase which must have taxed the ingenuity of the director and that of stunt coordinator Bill Hickman. Roy Scheider heads an okay cast in a fair script.

Plot finds Scheider, Victor Arnold, Jerry Leon and Ken Kercheval members of a special NYPD unit which operates in unorthodox methods. Tony Lo Bianco plays an informant who uses Scheider's loan shark list to set up his own kidnap operation.

Scheme backfires with Kercheval's surprise death. That event sets off Scheider into a spree of lawless law enforcement which on the screen always turns out right.

■ 7 WOMEN

1965, 88 MINS, US ◇
Dir John Ford *Prod* John Ford, Bernard Smith *Scr* Janet Green, John McCormick *Ph* Joseph LaShelle *Ed* Otho S. Lovering *Mus* Elmer Bernstein *Art Dir* George W. Davis, Eddie Imazu
● Anne Bancroft, Sue Lyon, Margaret Leighton, Flora Robson, Mildred Dunnock, Betty Field (M-G-M)

7 Women is a run-of-the-mill story of an isolated American mission in North China whose serenity is rudely shattered by a ravaging Mongolian barbarian and his band of cutthroats. Production is set in 1935, when the Chinese-Mongolian border was a lawless, violent land dominated by bandits, and takes its title from the seven femmes trapped in mission and subjected to gross indignities.

Ford directs from script based on a short story *Chinese Finale* by Norah Lofts and manages regulation treatment. While yarn attempts to tell the relationships of the septet – generally an uninteresting lot – most of the attention focuses necessarily upon Anne Bancroft, a recently-arrived doctor whose worldly cynicism brings her into conflict with the rigid moral concepts of mission's head, portrayed by Margaret Leighton. Bancroft endows character with some authority, and Mike Mazurki is properly brutal as the huge bandit leader.

Leighton acquits herself well in an intolerant, self-righteous role.

•••••••••••••••••••••••••••••••••

■ 7 WONDERS OF THE WORLD

1956, 120 MINS, US ◇

Dir Ted Tetzlaff, Andrew Marton, Tay Garnett, Paul Mantz, Walter Thompson   *Prod* Lowell Thomas   *Scr* Prosper Buranelli, William Lipscomb   *Ph* Harry Squire, Gayne Rescher   *Ed* Harvey Manger, Jack Murray   *Mus* Emil Newman, David Raksin, Jerome Moross
● (Stanley Warner/Cinerama)

While the titular *7 Wonders of the World* might be pointed to captiously as a misnomer, [this third Cinerama production] is a resourceful kickoff for an airlift from Manhattan through 32 countries in 120 minutes. The Sphinx and the Pyramids are pointed to as the sole remainders of the seven ancient wonders and the unfolding is a modern odyssey.

Emerging from the aerial hedgehop of local geographical closeups is a religioso pageantry which includes an exposition of Israel's renaissance; the final ceremonies of the Marian Year, culminating in the Papal blessing and a first-time lighting of Saint Peter's for motion pictures; and a curtsy to the Protestant church, back in the US with a typical American countryside scene. Buddhist priests and Benares (India) temple dancers blend with scenes of African tribal dances and a glorified Japanese geisha line that looks more Leonidoff than authentic Fujiyama.

7 Wonders of the World is at its best when the old and the modern are shown in sharp juxtaposition.

•••••••••••••••••••••••••••••••••

■ SEVEN YEAR ITCH, THE

1955, 105 MINS, US ◇ Ⓥ

Dir Billy Wilder   *Prod* Billy Wilder, Charles K. Feldman   *Scr* George Axelrod, Billy Wilder   *Ph* Milton Krasner   *Ed* Hugh S. Fowler   *Mus* Alfred Newman   *Art Dir* Lyle Wheeler, George W. Davis
● Marilyn Monroe, Tom Ewell, Evelyn Keyes, Sonny Tufts, Robert Strauss, Victor Moore (20th Century-Fox)

The film version of *The Seven Year Itch* bears only a fleeting resemblance to George Axelrod's play of the same name on Broadway. The screen adaptation concerns only the fantasies, and omits the acts, of the summer bachelor, who remains totally, if unbelievably, chaste. Morality wins if honesty loses, but let's not get into that. What counts is that laughs come thick and fast, that the general entertainment is light and gay.

The performance of Marilyn Monroe is baby-dollish as the dumb-but-sweet number upstairs who attracts the eye of the guy, seven years married and restless, whose wife and child have gone off for the summer. The acting kudos belongs to Tom Ewell, a practiced farceur and pantomimist who is able to give entire conviction to the long stretches of soliloquy, a considerable test of Ewell's technique.

•••••••••••••••••••••••••••••••••

■ SEVEN-PER-CENT SOLUTION, THE

1976, 113 MINS, UK ◇ Ⓥ

Dir Herbert Ross   *Prod* Herbert Ross   *Scr* Nicholas Meyer   *Ph* Oswald Morris   *Ed* William Reynolds, Chris Barnes   *Mus* John Adison   *Art Dir* Ken Adam

● Alan Arkin, Vanessa Redgrave, Robert Duvall, Nicol Williamson, Laurence Olivier, Joel Grey (Universal)

The Seven-Per-Cent Solution is an outstanding film. Producer-director Herbert Ross and writer Nicholas Meyer, adapting his novel, have fashioned a most classy period crime drama.

The concept is terrific, in that Sherlock Holmes (Nicol Williamson), while a patient of Sigmund Freud (Alan Arkin), becomes his analyst's partner as both apply their specialized abilities in the parallel solution of a kidnap crime. Simultaneously, there is resolved Holmes' own childhood trauma which has motivated his lifelong enmity towards Professor Moriarty.

The title takes its name from a dope mixture used by Holmes in his addiction. Dr Watson, his faithful friend, gets Holmes' brother Mycroft (Charles Gray) and mild-mannered Moriarty (Laurence Olivier) to trick Holmes to Vienna where Freud can treat him.

Holmes agrees to a powerful withdrawal regimen, which dissolves story wise into the introduction of Vanessa Redgrave, a former Freud patient cured of her own addiction, but now apparently in relapse. Holmes becomes intrigued with Redgrave's plight, as does Freud, and both pursue the matter.

•••••••••••••••••••••••••••••••••

■ SEVENTH CROSS, THE

1944, 111 MINS, US

Dir Fred Zinnemann   *Prod* Pandro S. Berman   *Scr* Helen Deutsch   *Ph* Karl Freund   *Ed* Thomas Richards   *Mus* Roy Webb   *Art Dir* Cedric Gibbons, Leonid Vasian
● Spencer Tracy, Signe Hasso, Hume Cronyn, Jessica Tandy, Agnes Moorehead (M-G-M)

Cross tells the story of seven men who escape from a concentration camp, and it follows the death or capture of six of them. Upon their escape the camp's commandant has ordered seven trees stripped and crosses nailed to them. It is his plan, as each fugitive is caught, to pinion them to the crosses and let them die of exposure.

And so this becomes the story of the seventh cross – the one that was never occupied. It is the story of George Heisler, who makes good his escape amid a web of almost unbelievable circumstances. The sheer fancy, as he eludes the Gestapo at every turn, is gripping drama.

This is a film of fine performances. There are one or two characterizations that might possibly eclipse that of the central one, played by Spencer Tracy, who, as usual, underplays and gives one of his invariably creditable portrayals.

•••••••••••••••••••••••••••••••••

■ 7TH DAWN, THE

1964, 123 MINS, UK ◇

Dir Lewis Gilbert   *Prod* Charles K. Feldman, Karl Tunberg   *Scr* Karl Tunberg   *Ph* Frederick A. Young   *Ed* John Shirley   *Mus* Riz Ortolani   *Prod Des* John Stoll
● William Holden, Susannah York, Capucine, Tetsuro Tamba, Michael Goodliffe, Allan Cuthbertson (United Artists)

Set in the Malayan jungle, circa 1945, the pic uses as its background a three-way struggle between Communist-inspired Malayan terrorists, British governors and the people of Malaya along with outsiders who have vested interests in the country. All are interested in freedom for the place but their motives vary considerably.

Pivotal characters in the film each represent a faction, a fact which leads to some rather predictable problems and solutions as time passes. Personal relationships aren't helped much either by co-producer Karl Tunberg's screenplay, based on Michael Keon's novel *The Durian Tree*. Although the

script moves fairly fluently through the action passages, harmful slowdowns develop during personal moments between the characters.

William Holden handles himself in credible fashion as a Yank co-leader of local guerilla forces during World War II who stays on after the war's end to become a major local land owner and who gets involved in the new politics because of his old-time friendshp for the leader of the Red terrorists, played by Tetsuro Tamba. Holden is further involved because of his mistress, a Malayan loyalist portrayed by Capucine. These three had worked together on the same side during the previous combat. For further plot there's the blonde and attractive daughter of the British governor, a role essayed by Susannah York.

•••••••••••••••••••••••••••••••••

■ SEVENTH VEIL, THE

1945, 94 MINS, UK Ⓥ

Dir Compton Bennett   *Prod* Sydney Box   *Scr* Muriel Box, Sydney Box   *Ph* Reginald Wyer, Bert Mason   *Ed* Gordon Hales   *Mus* Benjamin Frankel   *Art Dir* Jim Carter
● James Mason, Ann Todd, Herbert Lom, Albert Lieven, Hugh McDermott (Sydney Box/Ortus)

Title refers to the screen every human uses to hurdle his innermost thoughts. Like Salome, ordinary people will remove one or two – or more veils for the benefit of friends, sweethearts, spouses. But unlike Salome, nobody ever sheds the seventh veil. How Ann Todd is made to do this is the backbone of the pic – and its achievement is filmed magnificently.

Apart from the engrossing story (of the merciless discipline to which a teenage, sensitive orphan is subjected by a grim bachelor guardian) as it surges swiftly to its tremendous climax, there is a feast of harmony by the London Symphony Orchestra, conducted by Muir Mathieson, accompanying an unidentified piano virtuoso [Eileen Joyce] – ostensibly Todd.

•••••••••••••••••••••••••••••••••

■ 7TH VOYAGE OF SINBAD, THE

1958, 89 MINS, UK ◇ Ⓥ

Dir Nathan Juran   *Prod* Charles H. Schneer   *Scr* Kenneth Kolb   *Ph* Wilkie Cooper   *Ed* Edwin Bryant   *Mus* Bernard Herrmann   *Art Dir* Gil Parronda
● Kerwin Mathews, Kathryn Grant, Richard Eyer, Torin Thatcher, Alec Mango, Danny Green (Morningside/Columbia)

Just about every trick in the book – including one called Dynamation, i.e. the animation of assorted monsters, vultures, skeletons, etc – has been used to bring a vivid sort of realism to the various and terrifying hazards which Sinbad encounters on his voyage and in his battle with Sokurah the magician. Add to this a love story, interrupted when the princess Parisa is shrunk to inch-size by the magician, and what emerges is a bright, noisy package.

Kerwin Mathews makes a pleasant Sinbad, acting the part with more restraint than bravura; Kathryn Grant is pretty as the princess; Torin Thatcher has a fittingly evil look as the magician; Richard Eyer is cute as the Genie; Alec Mango has dignity as the Caliph.

But this isn't the sort of film in which performances matter much. It's primarily entertainment for the eye, and the action moves swiftly and almost without interruption. Ray Harryhausen, who was responsible for visual effects, emerges as the hero of this piece.

•••••••••••••••••••••••••••••••••

■ SEVERED HEAD, A

1971, 98 MINS, UK ◇

Dir Dick Clement   *Prod* Alan Ladd Jr   *Scr* Frederic Raphael   *Ph* Austin Dempster   *Ed* Peter Weatherley   *Mus* Stanley Myers   *Art Dir* Richard Macdonald
● Lee Remick, Richard Attenborough, Ian Holm, Claire Bloom, Jennie Linden, Clive Revill (Gershwin-Kantner)

This is a very upper-class and intellectually snobbish film about 'civilized copulation'. It's based on Iris Murdoch's novel (subsequently dramatized by Murdoch and J.B. Priestley).

It's the writing, direction (by Dick Clement) and acting that gives it stylish panache. The mattress merry-go-round has a great game of musical chairs among its cast. Ian Holm plays Martin Lynch-Gibbon, a wine taster, with a mistress played by Jennie Linden. Holm's wife (Lee Remick), a predatory nympho, is having an affair with her husband's best friend, psychologist Richard Attenborough, who is also sexually involved with his sister, Claire Bloom ('She's only my half sister,' he explains apologetically, but with little conviction).

Cast, all round, is very good, with Holm, the fall guy, excellent. Attenborough gives the psychiatrist a nicely humored pomposity, and Clive Revill, as Holm's sculptor brother, brings his usual breeziness to one of the few extrovert roles.

On the distaff side Remick makes the least impact, at times becoming tediously fluffy. Linden is strong and loving as the mistress who's shuffled around like a pawn and Bloom scores heavily as the menacing, enigmatic egghead.

■ **SEX AND THE SINGLE GIRL**

1964, 114 MINS, US ◇

Dir Richard Quine *Prod* Richard Quine *Scr* Joseph Heller, David R. Schwartz *Ph* Charles Lang *Ed* David Wages *Mus* Neal Hefti *Art Dir* Cary Odell
● Tony Curtis, Natalie Wood, Henry Fonda, Lauren Bacall, Mel Ferrer, Edward Everett Horton (Quine-Reynard/Warner)

Helen Gurley Brown's how-to-do-it book for single girls is takeoff point for story by Joseph Hoffman, scripted by Joseph Heller and David R. Schwartz. Natalie Wood is Dr Helen Brown of International Institute of Advanced Marital and Pre-Marital Studies, who is target of scandal mag editor Tony Curtis. Curtis is bent on exposing her to be 23-year-old virgin without background for advising single girls about sex.

Curtis poses as his neighbor, Henry Fonda, who has monumental wife trouble, and goes to Wood for advice. Inevitably, they fall for one another with Wood ignorant of Curtis' identity as ogre out to ruin her career.

As usual in this type of farce, male and female leads have fewer comic lines than supporting players. But Curtis registers exceptionally well when detailing supposed marital problems to adviser. His timing in confessing to 'inadequacies' shows great comic talent. And one of funniest bits in pic comes when poised, self-assured 'Dr Brown' finds she has romantic problem of own, crumples into tears and places long-distance call to 'Mother'.

Fonda and Bacall as warring husband and wife also serve up effective scenes as they battle over Fonda's non-existent wild life as head of Sexy Sox Inc.

Edward Everett Horton shines as boss of Curtis' mag, who harangues aides to make publication 'the most disgusting scandal sheet the human mind can recall'.

■ **SEX, LIES, AND VIDEOTAPE**

1989, 101 MINS, US ◇ ⊙

Dir Steven Soderbergh *Prod* Robert Newmyer, John Hardy *Scr* Steven Soderbergh *Ph* Walt Lloyd *Ed* Steven Soderbergh *Mus* Cliff Martinez *Art Dir* Joanne Schmidt
● James Spader, Andie MacDowell, Peter Gallagher, Laura San Giacomo (Outlaw)

This is a sexy, nuanced, beautifully con-

trolled examination of how a quartet of people are defined by their erotic impulses and inhibitions.

Imaginatively presented opening intercuts the embarrassed therapy confessions of young wife Andie MacDowell with the impending arrival in town of James Spader, a mysterious stranger type who was a college chum of MacDowell's handsome husband (Peter Gallagher).

Given MacDowell's admissions that she and Gallagher are no longer having sex, it would seem that Spader is walking into a potentially provocative situation.

He drops a bombshell by revealing that he is impotent, seemingly scratching any developments on that end. Meanwhile Gallagher has been conducting a secret affair with his wife's sexy wild sister (Laura San Giacomo).

Pic is absorbing and titillating because nearly every conversation is about sex and aspects of these attractive people's relationships. Several steamy scenes between Gallagher and San Giacomo, and some extremely frank videotapes featuring women speaking about their sex lives, turn the temperature up even more.

Lensed on location in Baton Rouge, La, for $1.2 million, production looks splendid.

■ **SEXTETTE**

1978, 91 MINS, US ◇ ⊙

Dir Ken Hughes *Prod* Daniel Briggs, Robert Sullivan *Scr* Herbert Baker *Ph* James Crabe *Ed* Argyle Nelson *Mus* Artie Butler *Art Dir* James F. Claytor
● Mae West, Timothy Dalton, Dom DeLuise, Tony Curtis, Ringo Starr, George Hamilton (Briggs-Sullivan)

Sextette is a cruel, unnecessary and mostly unfunny musical comedy. Mae West made the mistake in 1970 of returning to the screen after a 26-year absence in *Myra Breckenridge*, and she's blundered again.

The screenplay, based on a play by West, concerns a sexy Hollywood movie star who has married a young British nobleman. It's her sixth marriage and in the course of attempting to consummate the liaison she's interrupted by numbers four and five, fans, newspapermen, Rona Barrett, an American gymnastic team and a group of international diplomats meeting at her London hotel.

She's also in the middle of dictating her memoirs when the tape of her recorded autobiography gets out of her hands, a fate which could shorten her latest marriage.

West is on screen for most of the film, mostly attempting Mae West imitations and lip-syncing a series of undistinguished musical numbers. It's an embarrassing attempt at camp from the lady who helped invent the word.

Only Dom DeLuise is occasionally amusing as West's agent. The remainder of the cast – Tony Curtis as a Soviet delegate to the peace conference, Timothy Dalton as West's new husband, Ringo Starr and George Hamilton as former husbands, among others – hardly enhance their reputations.

■ **SGT. PEPPER'S LONELY HEARTS CLUB BAND**

1978, 111 MINS, US ◇ ⊙

Dir Michael Schultz *Prod* Robert Stigwood *Scr* Henry Edwards *Ph* Owen Roizman *Ed* Christopher Holmes *Art Dir* Brian Eatwell
● Peter Frampton, Barry Gibb, Robin Gibb, Maurice Gibb, Frankie Howerd, Paul Nicholas (Universal)

Sgt. Pepper's Lonely Hearts Club Band will attract some grown-up flower children of the 1960s who will soon find the Michael Schultz film to be a totally bubblegum and cotton candy melange of garish fantasy and narcissism. The production crams nearly 30 songs, largely by The Beatles, into newly-recorded

versions tailored for stars Peter Frampton and The Bee Gees.

Plot has Frampton as the grandson of the earlier Sgt Pepper who carries on the family band tradition with a modern-sound in partnership with The Bee Gees. Story introduces a lot of freakish characters out to steal the band's instruments which, somehow, make Heartland, USA, a dream of a small town. They don't succeed, though there's enough teeny-bopper-teasing naughtiness to amuse and thrill the target audience. Donald Pleasance, one of the heavies, plays a music biz wizard whose fictional trademark is that of producer Robert Stigwood's organization.

Near the end of the 111-minute film, when all wrongs have been righted, there's a celebrity olio in which many familiar names appear to be singing happily. The sound of this isn't any more lifelike than much of the preceding singing.

■ **SHADOW OF A DOUBT**

1943, 106 MINS, US ⊙

Dir Alfred Hitchcock *Prod* Jack Skirball *Scr* Thornton Wilder, Sally Benson, Alma Reville *Ph* Joseph Valentine *Ed* Milton Carruth *Mus* Dimitri Tiomkin *Art Dir* John B. Goodman, Robert Boyle
● Joseph Cotten, Teresa Wright, MacDonald Carey, Patricia Collinge, Hume Cronyn (Universal)

The suspenseful tenor of dramatics associated with director Alfred Hitchcock is utilized here to good advantage in unfolding a story [by Gordon McDonell] of a small town and the arrival of what might prove to be a murderer. Hitchcock poses a study in contrasts when the world-wise adventurer (Joseph Cotten) eludes police in Philadelphia to journey to his sister's home and family in the small California town of Santa Rosa. His deb-age niece (Teresa Wright), is not only named young Charlie after her uncle, but knows there's a mental contact somewhere along the line. Amid the typical small-town family life, she intuitively feels that Cotten has a guilty conscience, and finally ties the ends together to cast suspicion on him as a murderer and fugitive.

Hitchcock deftly etches his small-town characters and homey surroundings. Wright provides a sincere and persuasive portrayal as the girl, while Cotten is excellent as the motivating factor in the proceedings. Strong support is provided by Henry Travers, Patricia Collinge, Edna May Wonacott and Charles Bates. Hume Cronyn gets attention as the small-town amateur sleuth.

■ **SHADOWS**

1961, 84 MINS, US

Dir John Cassavetes *Prod* Maurice McEndree, Seymour Cassel *Scr* [improvised] *Ph* Erich Kolmar *Ed* Len Appleson, Maurice McEndree *Mus* Charlie Mingus, Shifi Hadi *Art Dir* Randy Liles, Bob Reeh
● Lelia Goldoni, Ben Carruthers, Tony Ray, Hugh Hurd, Rupert Crosse, Tom Allen (McEndree-Cassel)

First made in 16mm as an exercise in improvisation by a group of actors directed by John Cassavetes, a.w.k. thesp himself, *Shadows* was then filled out and blown up to 35mm under the supervision of two producers. It came in for $40,000, and a showing at the British Film Institute got it raves and an advance from British Lion of $25,000.

A brother and sister who look white have a brother who is completely Negro. The film dwells on the dramatic interludes in their lives and the inevitable race problems. The girl is 20 and unsure of her emotions until her first affair is marred by a cowardly reaction to the revelation of her color by her lover. The white-looking brother drifts through various adventures with too unanchored white friends, and the Negro brother is a singer

S

accepting his fate of trying to work in low dive shows and getting along with his edgy sister and brother.

Nothing rings false in the film. Though the narrative is rambling it strikes solid truths and dimension in showing people living and reacting in a manner which is dictated from within rather than forced on them by a script. Pic, in its improvised form, has actors working from general situations within an agreed outline.

Lella Goldoni has nervous charm, guile and vulnerability as the girl, Ben Carruthers possesses the sullen violence of solitude and indecision, and Hugh Hurd has warmth and understanding as the breadwinning brother. Cassavetes has given this form and a point of view without trying to solve anything but letting the characters express themselves. There is no attempt at technique but the story and action carries itself and New York is an essential part of this unique film.

■ **SHAFT**

1971, 98 MINS, US ◇ ▼
Dir Gordon Parks   *Prod* Joel Freeman   *Scr* John D.F. Black   *Ph* Urs Furrer   *Ed* Hugh A. Robertson   *Mus* Isaac Hayes
● Richard Roundtree, Moses Gunn, Gwenn Mitchell, Christopher St John, Charles Cioffi, Lawrence Pressman (M-G-M)

Take a formula private-eye plot, update it with all-black environment, and lace with contemporary standards of on-and off-screen violence, and the result is *Shaft*. It is directed by Gordon Parks with a subtle feel for both the grit and the humanity of the script.

Ernest Tidyman's novel, adapted by himself and John D.F. Black, concerns the kidnap by the Mafia of Sherri Brewer, daughter of Harlem underworld boss Moses Gunn. Richard Roundtree, as a black Sam Spade, is hired by Gunn to find her. Understanding but tough white cop Charles Cioffi, whose outstanding characterization singlehandedly upgrades the plot from strictly racial polemic, works with Roundtree in avoiding a gangland confrontation which, to outsiders, would appear to be a racial war.

In his second feature film after a long career as a still photographer, Parks shows some excellent story-telling form, with only minor clutter of picture-taking-for-its-own-sake.

■ **SHAGGY DOG, THE**

1959, 101 MINS, US
Dir Charles Barton   *Prod* Walt Disney   *Scr* Bill Walsh, Lillie Hayward   *Ph* Edward Colman   *Ed* James D. Ballas   *Mus* Paul Smith
● Fred MacMurray, Jean Hagen, Tommy Kirk, Annette Funicello, Tim Considine, Kevin Corcoran (Walt Disney)

The Shaggy Dog, said to be the first live action film by Walt Disney set in the present, is about what's called 'shape-shifting'. According to the screenplay suggested by Felix Salten's *The Hound of Florence*, there used to be a great deal of shifting of shapes, from man to beast and sometimes back.

There are a good many laughs on this simple premise and the script's exploitation of them. The only time the film falters badly is in its choice of a gimmick to get the boy-who-turns-into-a-dog turned back, for good and all, into a boy. According to the legend, it takes an act of heroism on the part of the shifting shape to be restored.

Fred MacMurray plays the father of the two boys, Tommy Kirk and Kevin Corcoran. MacMurray himself is a mailman physically allergic to dogs. Young Kirk accidentally transforms himself into a large, shaggy sheep dog when he comes into possession of a spell-casting ring once owned by the Borgias.

Where MacMurray has a good line, he shows that he has few peers in this special field of comedy. Jean Hagen, as his wife, is pretty and pleasant in a more or less straight role, while the two boys handle their comedy nicely.

■ **SHAKE HANDS WITH THE DEVIL**

1959, 104 MINS, US
Dir Michael Anderson   *Prod* Michael Anderson   *Scr* Ivan Goff, Ben Roberts   *Ph* Erwin Hillier   *Ed* Gordon Pilkington   *Mus* William Alwyn   *Art Dir* Tom Morahan
● James Cagney, Don Murray, Dana Wynter, Glynis Johns, Michael Redgrave, Sybil Thorndike (United Artists/Pennebaker)

A strong and unusual story has been diluted in its telling. The theme is that those who 'shake hands with the devil' often find they have difficulty getting their hands back. Two such, in the screenplay from the novel by Rearden Conner, are James Cagney and Don Murray.

Against a background of the 1921 Irish Rebellion, Cagney is a professor of medicine at a Dublin university, and Murray, an American veteran of World War I, is his student. Cagney is also a 'commandant' of the underground, and Murray's father, an Irish patriot, was killed while working with Cagney.

It is Cagney who wants to continue the terror when the leader of the Irish independence movement (Michael Redgrave) works out a treaty with the British that eventually leads to freedom.

The principals, paced by Cagney, are interesting and sometimes moving. But they seem posed against the Irish background, rather than part of it. The supporting cast looms larger than it should. Sybil Thorndike, for instance, as a titled Irish lady lending her name and fierce old heart to the cause, is fine. Redgrave has dignity and strength in his few scenes.

Erwin Hillier's camerawork is good, creating a grim, gray Ireland that is a natural setting for the sanguine struggle.

■ **SHAKESPEARE-WALLAH**

1965, 125 MINS, INDIA/US ▼
Dir James Ivory   *Prod* Ismail Merchant   *Scr* Ruth Prawer Jhabvala, James Ivory   *Ph* Subrata Mitra   *Ed* Amit Bose   *Mus* Satyajit Ray
● Shashi Kapoor, Felicity Kendal, Geoffrey Kendal, Laura Liddell, Madhur Jaffrey (Merchant-Ivory)

Shakespeare-Wallah is officially designated an Indian-American coproduction, though the official credits do not name the US associates, apart from the Californian-born director, James Ivory.

The English language production is the story of a touring theatrical company specializing in Shakespearean production which has seen better days. It's a struggle to keep the company going which was founded by Tony and Carla Buckingham (Geoffrey Kendal and Laura Liddell) who are totally dedicated, and expect the same from all around, and particularly from their daughter Lizzie, who is currently enamored of an Indian playboy, who is also indulging in some extra-curricular activities with an Indian actress in the company.

The pace of the production is always too leisurely, and some of the Shakespearean excerpts could advantageously be cut. Nevertheless, there is a naive charm to the production.

There is also a very confident performance by Shashi Kapoor, as the Indian playboy. Felicity Kendal is a pert newcomer with an ingenuous style. Madhur Jaffrey ably completes the cast as the Indian actress.

■ **SHALAKO**

1968, 118 MINS, UK ◇ ▼
Dir Dmytryk   *Prod* Evan Lloyd   *Scr* J.J. Griffith, Hal Hopper, Scot Finch   *Ph* Ted Moore   *Ed* Bill Blunden   *Mus* Robert Farnon
● Sean Connery, Brigitte Bardot, Peter Van Eyck, Stephen Boyd, Honor Blackman, Jack Hawkins (Kingston/Palomar)

Though purporting to take place in New Mexico during the 19th century, this $5 million film was actually shot on location in Almeria, Spain, but doesn't look it.

Based on Louis L'Amour's novel, it's a 19th-century story of an aristocratic, 'dude' hunting safari from Europe which is led into Apache territory by its double crossing 'white' hunter and given a hard time by the redskins.

Shalako (Sean Connery) comes across the camp when he rescues one of them (Brigitte Bardot) from Indians and has to pit his wits and resource, not only against the Apaches but against members of the expedition, before he manages to save the party from complete destruction.

Jealousy, obstinacy, greed and roguery all emotionally stir up trouble for the hunters.

The film is a slow starter while the various characters are being established and has an over-abrupt and inconclusive ending.

Intriguing are the relationships between members of the hunting party.

■ **SHALL WE DANCE**

1937, 101 MINS, US ▼
Dir Mark Sandrich   *Prod* Pandro S. Berman   *Scr* Allan Scott, Ernest Pagano   *Ph* David Abel   *Ed* William Hamilton   *Mus* Nathaniel Shilkret   *Art Dir* Van Nest Polglase, Carroll Clarke
● Fred Astaire, Ginger Rogers, Edward Everett Horton, Eric Blore, Jerome Cowan, Ketti Gallian (RKO)

Shall We Dance, the seventh in the Astaire-Rogers series, is a standout because the script affords Astaire a legitimate excuse for a change of pace in his dancing, the comedy is solid, and this is the best cutting job an Astaire picture has enjoyed in a long time. This latter item is important as it had begun to look as if the studio couldn't decide whether Astaire was making musicals or operettas.

There have been others in the string which have had stronger tunes, superior punch laughs, and packed more dynamite in Astaire's own specialties, yet seldom have these ingredients been made to fit so evenly. All six songs [by George and Ira Gershwin], one more than usual, have been nicely spotted with no attempt to overplay any of them. Nor is there a bad ditty in the batch.

Basically the story [*Watch Your Step* by Lee Loeb and Harold Buchman, adapted by P.J. Wolfson] is of a ballet dancer (Astaire) who would rather be a hoofer. Romantically the script ties him into a complicated affinity with Ginger Rogers who is a musical comedy star. The rumors of their marriage grow to such proportion it forces them to secretly wed with the understanding of an immediate divorce. In locale the yarn starts in Paris, spends some time en route to the US and finishes in New York.

Astaire's stock company has been re-assembled, hence the comedy is in the hands of Edward Horton, as Astaire's manager, and Eric Blore, as a Manhattan maitre d'hotel.

■ **SHAMPOO**

1975, 109 MINS, US ◇
Dir Hal Ashby   *Prod* Warren Beatty   *Scr* Robert Towne, Warren Beatty   *Ph* Laszlo Kovacs   *Ed* Robert C. Jones   *Mus* Paul Simon   *Art Dir* Richard Sylbert
● Warren Beatty, Julie Christie, Goldie Hawn, Lee Grant, Jack Warden, Tony Bill (Columbia)

Late 1960s story about the ultimate emotional sterility and unhappiness of a swinger emerges as a mixed farcical achievement.

Warren Beatty is a Beverly Hills hairdresser who turns onto all his customers including Lee Grant, bored wife of Jack Warden (latter in turn keeping Julie Christie on the side), while Beatty's current top trick is Goldie Hawn.

All the excellent creative components do not add up to a whole. There are, however, strong elements in the film. Warden's performance is outstanding. He makes the most of a script and direction which gives his character much more dimension than the prototype cuckold. Also, Hawn's excellent delineation of a bubbly young actress has a solid undertone of sensitivity which culminates in her quiet dismissal of Beatty from her home and her heart.

● ●

■ **SHAMUS**

1973, 98 MINS, US ◇ ⓥ
Dir Buzz Kulik   *Prod* Robert M. Weitman   *Scr* Barry Beckerman   *Ph* Victor J. Kemper   *Ed* Walter Thompson   *Mus* Jerry Goldsmith   *Art Dir* Philip Rosenberg
● Burt Reynolds, Dyan Cannon, John Ryan, Joe Santos, Georgio Tozzi, Ron Weyand (Columbia)

Shamus is a confusing, hardbiting meller of a tough private eye. Burt Reynolds plays a rough-hewn and alert character who has turned to private investigation in his tough Brooklyn neighborhood instead of laying in with the mob. Filming was done on actual locations, which lends an emphatic authenticity to backgrounds.

Star carries the narrative niftily as he's called in by a multi-millionaire to ferret out the indentity of the person who bumped off a man who stole a fortune in diamonds owned by a tycoon. But thereafter scripter Barry Beckerman drags in an assortment of mostly-unexplained characters but some dandy rough work – and finales in a fine fog. Perhaps something was lost in translation to the screen.

● ●

■ **SHANE**

1953, 118 MINS, US ⓥ
Dir George Stevens   *Prod* George Stevens   *Scr* A.B. Guthrie Jr, Jack Sher   *Ph* Loyal Griggs   *Ed* William Hornbeck, Tom McAdoo   *Mus* Victor Young   *Art Dir* Hal Pereira, Walter Tyler
● Alan Ladd, Jean Arthur, Van Heflin, Brandon deWilde, Jack Palance, Ben Johnson (Paramount)

This is by no means a conventional giddyap oater feature, being a western in the truer sense and ranking with some of the select few that have become classics in the outdoor field.

Director George Stevens handles the story and players with tremendous integrity. Alan Ladd's performance takes on dimensions not heretofore noticeable in his screen work. Van Heflin commands attention with a sensitive performance, as real and earnest as the pioneer spirit he plays. The screenplay is A.B. Guthrie, Jr's first, as is the novel of Jack Schaefer.

Plot is laid in early Wyoming, where a group of farmer-settlers have taken land formerly held by a cattle baron. Latter resents this intrusion on the free land and the fences that come with the setting down of home roots. His fight is against Heflin chiefly, who is the driving force that keeps the frightened farmers together. Just when it seems the cattle man may eventually have his way, a stranger, known only as Shane, rides on to Heflin's homestead, is taken in and becomes one of the settlers, as he tries to forget his previous life with a gun.

Jean Arthur plays the role of Heflin's wife, who is attracted to the stranger. A standout is the young stage actor, Brandon deWilde, who brings the inquisitiveness and quick hero worship of youth to the part of Heflin's son. Jack Palance, with short but impressive footage, is the hired killer.

Wyoming's scenic splendors against which the story is filmed are breathtaking. Sunlight, the shadow of rain storms and the eerie lights of night play a realistic part in making the picture a visual treat.

☐ 1953: Best Picture (Nomination)

● ●

■ **SHANGHAI EXPRESS**

1932, 80 MINS, US
Dir Josef von Sternberg   *Scr* Jules Furthman   *Ph* Lee Garmes   *Mus* W. Franke Harling   *Art Dir* Hans Dreier
● Marlene Dietrich, Clive Brook, Anna May Wong, Warner Oland, Eugene Pallette, Lawrence Grant (Paramount)

Josef von Sternberg, the director, has made this effort interesting through a definite command of the lens. As to plot structure and dialog, *Shanghai Express* runs much too close to old meller and serial themes to command real attention. The finished product is an example of what can be done with a personality and photogenic face such as Marlene Dietrich possesses to circumvent a trashy story.

The script [from a story by Harry Hervey] relates how the heroine became China's most famed white prostitute, who meets her former English fiance (Clive Brook) on board train. The man has become a medical officer in the British Army. With a revolution going on, Warner Oland turns out to be the rebel leader, has the train held up and in looking for a hostage, to guarantee the return of his chief lieutenant captured by the Chinese forces, he picks Brook.

To save Brook's eyes being burned from his head, Shanghai Lily promises to become mistress of the revolutionary, leading to further misunderstandings between the central pair.

For counter-interest there is Eugene Pallette as an American gambler among the passengers, Louise Closser Hale as a prim boarding housekeeper, Gustav von Seyffertitz as a dope smuggling invalid, Lawrence Grant as a fanatical missionary, and Emile Chautard as a disgraced French officer wearing his uniform without authority.

It can't be said that either Dietrich or Brook gives an especially good performance. The British actor is unusually wooden, while Dietrich's assignment is so void of movement as to force her to mild but consistent eye rolling.

☐ 1931/32: Best Picture (Nomination)

● ●

■ **SHANGHAI GESTURE, THE**

1941, 97 MINS, US ⓥ
Dir Josef von Sternberg   *Prod* Arnold Pressburger   *Scr* Karl Vollmoeller, Geza Herczeg, Jules Furthman, Josef von Sternberg   *Ph* Paul Ivano   *Ed* Sam Winston   *Mus* Richard Hageman   *Art Dir* Boris Leven
● Gene Tierney, Victor Mature, Ona Munson, Walter Huston, Phyllis Brooks, Albert Basserman (United Artists)

Thirty-one film treatments on [John Colton's play] *Shanghai Gesture* were submitted without success to the Hays Office. Producer Arnold Pressburger finally slipped through a treatment for a go-ahead signal – to at least bring the original title and the Oriental background of the polyglot Asiatic metropolis to the screen.

Stripped of the sensational elements of *Gesture* at the time it was produced on the stage, the resultant film version is a rather dull and hazy drama of the Orient.

Mother Gin Sling (Ona Munson) is the operating brains of a gambling casino, case-hardened through her struggles up the ladder. When property in the district is bought

up by Walter Huston, English financier, and the Mother is told to fold, she goes out to get the goods on her enemy in typical Oriental fashion. Result is Gin Sling's manipulation of Huston's daughter (Gene Tierney) onto a downward path; Gin Sling's accusation of his desertion years before; and his rebuttal that the girl she has ruined is actually her daughter.

Victor Mature, as the matter-of-fact Arab despoiler of Tierney's honor, provides a standout performance. Huston's abilities are lost in the jumble, while Munson cannot penetrate the masklike makeup arranged for her characterization.

● ●

■ **SHANGHAI SURPRISE**

1986, 97 MINS, UK/US ◇ ⓥ
Dir Jim Goddard   *Prod* John Kohn   *Scr* John Kohn, Robert Bentley   *Ph* Ernie Vincze   *Ed* Ralph Sheldon   *Mus* George Harrison, Michael Kamen   *Art Dir* Peter Mullins
● Sean Penn, Madonna, Paul Freeman, Richard Griffiths, Philip Sayer (M-G-M/Handmade/Vista)

Tale [from the novel *Faraday's Flowers* by Tony Kenrick] is a phony, thoroughgoing concoction. A missionary (Madonna) enlists the services of a down-and-out, would-be adventurer (Sean Penn) to help her track down a substantial supply of opium that disappeared under mysterious circumstances a year before, in 1937, during the Japanese occupation of China.

The blood-stirring premise provides the excuse for any number of encounters with exotic and shady characters who would have been right at home in Warner Bros foreign intrigue mellers of the 1940s.

But centerstage is the completely illogical relationship between the hustler and missionary. Penn seems game and has energy while Madonna can't for a moment disguise that her character makes no sense at all.

● ●

■ **SHARKY'S MACHINE**

1981, 119 MINS, US ◇
Dir Burt Reynolds   *Prod* Hank Moonjean   *Scr* Gerald Di Pego   *Ph* William A. Fraker   *Ed* William Gardeau   *Mus* Al Capps   *Art Dir* Walter Scott Herndon
● Burt Reynolds, Vittorio Gassman, Rachel Ward, Charles Durning (Orion/Warner)

Directing himself in *Sharky's Machine*, Burt Reynolds has combined his own macho personality with what's popularly called mindless violence to come up with a seemingly guaranteed winner [from a novel by William Diehl].

Not surprisingly, Reynolds is 'Sharky' and the 'machine' is police parlance for a team of fellow cops working with him. They are all good policemen, but for one reason or another have been relegated to unchallenging assignments, mainly in the cesspool of the vice squad.

But a hooker's murder brings Reynolds within sniffing distance of big time shenanigans involving gubernatorial candidate Earl Holliman, crime boss Vittorio Gassman and high-priced call girl Rachel Ward.

Staking out Ward's apartment, actor Reynolds surrenders to an infatuation with her that director Reynolds has an intersting time developing.

By the time Reynolds gets a couple of fingers sliced off by Darryl Hickman and Co, all characterization is gone and it's just a matter then of who runs out of bullets first.

● ●

■ **SHE**

1965, 104 MINS, UK ◇
Dir Robert Day   *Prod* Michael Carreras   *Scr* David T. Chantler   *Ph* Harry Waxman   *Ed* James Needs, Eric Boyd-Perkins   *Mus* James Bernard   *Art Dir* Robert Jones

S

● Ursula Andress, Peter Cushing, Bernard Cribbins, John Richardson, Christopher Lee, Andre Morell (Seven Arts/Hammer)

Fourth filming of H. Rider Haggard's fantasy adds color and widescreen to special effects, all of which help overcome a basic plot no film scripter has yet licked.

Ursula Andress is sole-starred as the immortal She, cold-blooded queen Ayesha of a lost kingdom who pines for return of the lover she murdered eons ago. In David T. Chantler's okay script, it turns out that John Richardson is the look-alike lover, footloose in Palestine after the First World War with buddies Peter Cushing and Bernard Cribbins.

High priest Christopher Lee and servant girl Rosenda Monteros are emissaries who spot Richardson's resemblance, triggering a desert trek by the three men to Kuma land. Cushing and Cribbins keep their senses, while Richardson falls under Andress' spell.

Director Robert Day's overall excellent work brings out heretofore unknown depths in Andress' acting. Role calls for sincere warmth as a woman in love, also brutal cruelty as queen, and she convinces.

All other players are good in routine roles, particularly Monteros as the competing love interest who loses her man and her life. Christopher Lee is also effective as the loyal priest whom Ayesha kills.

■ SHE DONE HIM WRONG

1933, 65 MINS, US
Dir Lowell Sherman   *Scr* Harvey Thew, John Bright   *Ph* Charles Lang   *Mus* Ralph Rainger
● Mae West, Cary Grant, Gilbert Roland, Noah Beery Sr, Rafaela Ottiano, David Landau (Paramount)

Atmospherically, *She Done Him Wrong* is interesting since it takes audiences back to the 1890s and inside a Bowery free-and-easy, but mostly following a few highlights in the career of Diamond Lou, nee Lil.

Director Lowell Sherman turns in a commendable job. He tackles the script with a tongue-in-cheek attitude that takes nothing too seriously, and he restrains Mae West from going too far.

The locale, the clothes and the types are interesting, and so is West in her picture hats, straight jacket gowns and with so much jewelry that she looks like a Knickerbocker ice plant.

Deletions in the script from its original 1928 legit form [*Diamond Lil* by Mae West] are few, with only the roughest of the rough stuff out. White slavery angle is thinly disguised, with the girls instead shipped to Frisco to pick pockets. Character titles are changed only slightly, such as from Lil to Lou, etc. The swan bed is in, but for a flash only, with Mae doing her stuff on the chaise lounge in this version.

Numerous ex-vaudevillians besides West in the cast, including Cary Grant, the soul-saver; Fuzzy Knight, who whips a piano, and Grace La Rue. The latter, who headlined when West was chasing acrobats in the No. 2 spot, has a bit. Rafaela Ottiano, who does Rita, is a carry-over from the original legit cast.

With this strong line-up and others, including Gilbert Roland, Noah Beery, David Landau and Owen Moore as background, they're never permitted to be anything more than just background. West gets all the lens gravy and full figure most of the time.
□ 1932/33: Best Picture (Nomination)

■ SHE WORE A YELLOW RIBBON

1949, 103 MINS, US ◇ Ⓥ
Dir John Ford   *Prod* John Ford, Merian C. Cooper   *Scr* Frank Nugent, Laurence Stallings   *Ph* Winton Hoch, Charles Boyle   *Ed* Jack Murgay   *Mus* Richard Hageman

● John Wayne, Joanne Dru, John Agar, Ben Johnson, Victor McLaglen, Mildred Natwick (RKO/Argosy)

She Wore a Yellow Ribbon is a western meller done in the best John Ford manner.

Drama of the undermanned US Cavalry post far out in the Indian country is centered on a veteran captain about to retire. It develops into a saga of the cavalry, its hard-bitten men, loyal wives and usual intrigues. The tale moves along easily as it shows how the troop surmounts the Indian peril. There's hardly a breather from the time the audience is tipped that John Wayne is soon retiring as cavalry captain til he finalizes his last dramatic moment.

Wayne wears well in this somewhat older characterization. He makes the officer an understanding, two-fisted guy without overdoing it. Victor McLaglen gives the production tremendous lift as the whisky-nipping non-com.

■ SHE-DEVIL

1989, 99 MINS, US ◇ Ⓥ
Dir Susan Seidelman   *Prod* Jonathan Brett, Susan Seidelman   *Scr* Barry Strugatz, Mark R. Burns   *Ph* Oliver Stapleton   *Ed* Craig McKay   *Mus* Howard Shore   *Art Dir* Santo Loquasto
● Meryl Streep, Roseanne Barr, Ed Begley Jr, Linda Hunt, Sylvia Miles (Orion)

A dark and gleeful revenge saga set in a world of unfaithful husbands and unfair standards of beauty, *She-Devil* [from Fay Weldon's novel *The Life and Loves of a She Devil*] offers a unique heroine in Ruth Patchett (Roseanne Barr), a dumpy but dedicated housewife afflicted with a conspicuous facial mole and an uninterested husband (Ed Begley Jr).

When Begley, an accountant, strays into the arms of a fabulously wealthy and affected romance novelist (Meryl Streep), Barr puts up with it – to a point.

However, when Begley, bags more or less packed, sets her blood boiling with crude put-downs, Barr clicks into an inspired attack mode, first by blowing up the house, then by dumping off the children at his love nest on her way to Whereabouts Unknown, then by ingeniously dismantling his career.

The casting is a real coup, with Barr going her everywoman TV persona one better by breaking the big screen heroine mold, and Streep blowing away any notion that she can't be funny.

■ SHEIK, THE

1921, 100 MINS, US ⊗
Dir George Melford   *Scr* Monte M. Katterjohn   *Ph* William Marshall
● Anges Ayres, Rudolph Valentino, Adolphe Menjou, Walter Long, Lucien Littlefield, George Waggner (Paramount)

Edith M. Hull's novel, preposterous and ridiculous as it was, won out because it dealt with every caged woman's desire to be caught up in a love clasp by some he-man who would take the responsibility and dispose of the consequences, but Monte M. Katterjohn's scenario hasn't even that to recommend it. He has safely deleted most of the punch, and what they missed George Melford manages by inept direction of the big scenes.

Lady Diana has gone alone into the desert with a native guide only to be captured by a young sheik and he detains her in his palace of a tent, and that is all.

The acting could not be worse than the story, but it is bad enough. Valentino is revealed as a player without resource. He depicts the fundamental emotions of the Arabian sheik chiefly by showing his teeth and rolling his eyes, while Agnes Ayres looks too

matronly to lend much kick to the situation in which she finds herself.

■ SHE'LL BE WEARING PINK PAJAMAS

1985, 90 MINS, UK ◇ Ⓥ
Dir John Goldschmidt   *Prod* Tara Prem, Adrian Hughes   *Scr* Eva Hardy   *Ph* Clive Tickner   *Ed* Richard Key   *Mus* John du Prez   *Art Dir* Colin Pocock
● Julie Walters, Anthony Higgins, Jane Evers, Janet Henfrey, Paula Jacobs, Penelope Nice (Film Four/Pink Pajamas)

She'll Be Wearing Pink Pajamas is about a group of British women from mixed backgrounds who gather together, awkwardly at first, but eventually confide in each other and reveal their innermost secrets and problems.

After a slightly off-key opening, in which the characters are introed, we're into the setting of an outdoor survival course for women only, a week-long exercise designed to push the participants physically as far as they can go. The intimate discussions that follow take place against outdoor backgrounds, filmed in England's beautiful Lake District, as the women ford streams, climb mountains, canoe, swing on ropes, or go on a marathon hike.

There's one man around (Anthony Higgins), but he's almost an intrusion. The women are a lively and well-differentiated lot, and there is a bevy of fine actresses playing them. Standout is Julie Walters as a bouncy type who proves surprisingly weak in the crunch.

■ SHELTERING SKY, THE

1990, 137 MINS, UK/ITALY ◇ Ⓥ
Dir Bernardo Bertolucci   *Prod* Jeremy Thomas   *Scr* Mark Peploe, Bernardo Bertolucci   *Ph* Vittorio Storaro   *Ed* Gabriella Cristiani   *Mus* Ryuichi Sakamoto, Richard Horowitz   *Art Dir* Gianni Silvestri
● John Malkovich, Debra Winger, Campbell Scott, Jill Bennett, Timothy Spall, Eric Vu-An (Thomas)

Paul Bowles' classic 1949 novel of a journey into emptiness has been visualized with intense beauty by the creative team of *The Last Emperor*. But those who haven't read the book will be left bewildered.

John Malkovich and Debra Winger play Port and Kit Moresby, Americans traveling without destination or itinerary in postwar North Africa. Their 10-year marriage is unraveling while their opportunistic companion, Tunner (Campbell Scott), looks on.

They press on through Tangiers, Niger and Algeria, moving with a perverse sense of purpose further from comfort, ego and the signposts of the familiar. Pic boils down to the existential love story between Kit and Port, who are groping through the ruins of their infidelities toward whatever is left between them when all is lost.

In a marvelous directorial conceit, Bowles himself, 80 years old, watches his characters from a seat in a Tangiers cafe.

Malkovich is an excellent choice as Port, his shifting, centaur-like physicality filling in for the interior life the screen can't provide. Aside from her resemblance to writer Jane Bowles, who inspired Kit, Winger is less interesting to watch.

At the end, familiar language completely disappears, as shell-shocked Kit wanders into the desert and becomes a sex slave to the wandering Tuareg leader Belqassim (played by Eric Vu-An of the Paris Ballet).

■ SHENANDOAH

1965, 105 MINS, US ◇ Ⓥ
Dir Andrew V. McLaglen   *Prod* Robert Arthur   *Scr* James Lee Barrett   *Ph* William H. Clothier   *Ed* Otho Lovering   *Mus* Frank Skinner   *Art Dir* Alexander Golitzen, Alfred Sweeney

● James Stewart, Doug McClure, Glenn Corbett, Patrick Wayne, Rosemary Forsyth, Katharine Ross (Universal)

Shenandoah centers upon one person, a sort of behind-the-scenes glimpse of one man's family in Virginia during the Civil War.

Screenplay focuses on Stewart, a prosperous Virginia farmer in 1863 who completely ignores the strife raging around him. A widower, he has raised his family of six sons and one daughter to be entirely self-contained. Not believing in slavery, he wants no part in a war based upon it, providing the conflict does not touch either his land or his family. When his youngest, a 16-year-old boy whose mother died giving birth and who therefore occupies a particular spot in the father's heart, is captured as a Reb by Unionists, the farmer then makes the war his own business.

Stewart, seldom without a cigar butt in the corner of his mouth, endows his grizzled role with warm conviction.

Battle sequences are well integrated with the family's efforts to lead a normal life, and Andrew McLaglen is responsible for some rousing hand-to-hand action between the Blue and the Grey.

● ●

■ SHERIFF OF FRACTURED JAW, THE

1958, 100 MINS, UK ◇

Dir Raoul Walsh   *Prod* Daniel M. Angel   *Scr* Arthur Dales   *Ph* Otto Heller   *Ed* John Shirley   *Mus* Robert Farnon   *Art Dir* Bernard Robinson
● Kenneth More, Jayne Mansfield, Robert Morley, Ronald Squire, Henry Hull, Bruce Cabot (20th Century-Fox)

The starring combo of Jayne Mansfield and Kenneth More merge like bacon and eggs, and the result is a wave of yocks. Raoul Walsh directs this cheerful skit about the wild, woolly west with vigor and pace. He gives little time to remind the audience that many of the situations are predictable and that the brisk screenplay [from a story by Jacob Hay] occasionally needs an upward jolt from the skill of the leading thesps.

Yarn starts off in London at the turn of the century. More has inherited a fading gunsmith business. Reading that there is a spot of bother in the Wild West he decides that that's the place to sell his guns. So this dude salesman (walking stick, brown derby and strictly West End suiting) nonchalantly sets off with some samples, and all the confidence in the world.

It's not long before he is up to his surprised eyebrows in trouble. He becomes involved with Injuns, two warring sets of cowboys and with Mansfield, the pistol-packing boss of a saloon. He is conned into becoming the sheriff of the one-horse town of Fractured Jaw.

More's immaculate throwaway line of comedy gets full rein. With polite manners, impeccable accent and a brash line of action, he leaves the locals in doubt as to whether he is the biggest fool or the bravest man ever to hit their territory. Mansfield gives More hearty support, looks attractive in a big, bosomy way and sings two or three numbers very well. The film was made in Spain and at Pinewood, but the locations have an authentic western air.

● ●

■ SHERLOCK, JR.

1924, 48 MINS, US ⊗

Dir Buster Keaton   *Scr* Jean Havez, Joseph Mitchell, Clyde Bruckman   *Ph* Elgin Lessley, Byron Houck   *Art Dir* Fred Gabourie
● Buster Keaton, Kathryn McGuire, Ward Crane, Joseph Keaton (Keaton/Metro)

This Buster Keaton feature length comedy is about as unfunny as a hospital operating room.

The picture has all the old hoke in the world in it. That ranges from a piece of business with a flypaper to a money-changing bit and, for added good measure, a chase. There are, in fact, two chases; but neither can for a single second hold a candle to Harold Lloyd. In comparison they appear child's play.

There is one piece of business, however, that is worthy of comment. It is the bit where Buster as a motion-picture machine operator in a dream scene walks out of the booth and into the action that is taking place on the screen of the picture that he is projecting. That is clever. The rest is bunk.

● ●

■ SHE'S GOTTA HAVE IT

1986, 100 MINS, US ⓥ

Dir Spike Lee   *Prod* Shelton J. Lee   *Scr* Spike Lee   *Ph* Ernest Dickerson   *Ed* Spike Lee   *Mus* Bill Lee   *Art Dir* Wynn Thomas
● Tracy Camilla Jones, Redmond Hicks, John Terrell, Spike Lee (Forty Acres/Mule Filmworks)

This worthy but flawed attempt to examine an independent young woman of the 1980s was lensed, in Super 16mm, in 15 days but doesn't appear jerrybuilt.

All the elements of an interesting yarn are implicit here – save one: a compelling central figure (played by Tracy Camilla Johns). The young woman who's the focus of the pic is, clearly, trying to find herself. She juggles three beaus, fends off a lesbian's overtures and consults a shrink to determine if she's promiscuous or merely a lady with normal sexual appetites.

The three beaus, an upscale male model, a sensitive sort and a funny street flake, all essayed nicely by, respectively, John Terrell, Spike Lee and Redmond Hicks, serve to keep the scenario moving with interest.

● ●

■ SHINING, THE

1980, 146 MINS, US ◇ ⓥ

Dir Stanley Kubrick   *Prod* Stanley Kubrick   *Scr* Stanley Kubrick, Diane Johnson   *Ph* John Alcott   *Ed* Ray Lovejoy   *Mus* Bartok   *Art Dir* Roy Walker
● Jack Nicholson, Shelley Duvall, Danny Lloyd, Scatman Crothers, Barry Nelson, Anne Jackson (Warner)

With everything to work with, director Stanley Kubrick has teamed with jumpy Jack Nicholson to destroy all that was so terrifying about Stephen King's bestseller.

In his book, King took a fundamental horror formula – an innocent family marooned in an evil dwelling with a grim history – and built layers of ingenious terror upon it. The father is gradually possessed by the demonic, desolate hotel.

With dad going mad, the only protection mother and child have is the boy's clairvoyance – his 'shining' – which allows him an innocent understanding and some ability to outmaneuver the devils.

But Kubrick sees things his own way, throwing 90% of King's creation out.

The crazier Nicholson gets, the more idiotic he looks. Shelley Duvall transforms the warm sympathetic wife of the book into a simpering, semi-retarded hysteric.

● ●

■ SHIP OF FOOLS

1965, 148 MINS, US ⓥ

Dir Stanley Kramer   *Prod* Stanley Kramer   *Scr* Abby Mann   *Ph* Ernest Lazlo   *Ed* Robert C. Jones   *Mus* Ernest Gold
● Vivien Leigh, Simone Signoret, Jose Ferrer, Lee Marvin, Oskar Werner, Elizabeth Ashley (Columbia)

Director-producer Stanley Kramer and scenarist Abby Mann have distilled the essence of Katherine Anne Porter's bulky novel in a

film that appeals to the intellect and the emotions.

As screen entertainment *Ship of Fools* is intelligent and eminently satisfying most of the time. The human cargo aboard the German ship *Vera* sailing from Vera Cruz to Bremerhaven (1933) is a cross-section of mass humanity that a landlubber can encounter in any metropolis.

All of the principals give strong performances from the aggressive interpretation by Jose Ferrer as a loathsome disciple of the emerging Hitlerian new order to Vivien Leigh as a fading American divorcee who gets her kicks out of leading on admirers and throwing cold water on their burning desires.

Of equal importance to the main stream of this drama, and also astutely attuned, are the contributions by Simone Signoret in the role of La Condesa and Oskar Werner as Dr Schumann, the ship's doctor.

Also impressive are George Segal and Elizabeth Ashley as young lovers whose intellects and emotions seem to be always warring against the animal magnetism that draws them together.

□ 1965: Best Picture (Nomination)

● ●

■ SHIRLEY VALENTINE

1989, 108 MINS, UK ◇ ⓥ

Dir Lewis Gilbert   *Prod* Lewis Gilbert   *Scr* Willy Russell   *Ph* Alan Hume   *Ed* Lesley Walker   *Mus* George Hadjinasios, Willy Russell   *Art Dir* John Stoll
● Pauline Collins, Tom Conti, Alison Steadman, Julia McKenzie, Joanna Lumley, Bernard Hill (Paramount)

Shirley Valentine is an uneven but generally delightful romantic comedy that has as its lead the irresistible Pauline Collins.

Collins *is* Shirley Valentine, the perfect match of actress and character. She starred in the one-woman show for more than a year on stage, first in a London West End production, then on Broadway.

The legit work was a monolog in which Collins, a middle-aged Liverpool housewife who yearns to drink 'a glass of wine in a country where the grape is grown,' described other characters and gave them life through her fanciful imagery.

In Willy Russell's film adaptation, *Shirley Valentine* becomes a full-blown location shot with those and other characters now cast as separate speaking parts, mostly by other terrific British actors. Tom Conti is barely recognizable here playing a very convincing swarthy Greek tavern keeper whose specialty is the romantic sail to a secluded cove.

Shirley Valentine-Bradshaw, the mildly sour Liverpool housewife, was more entertaining than Shirley Valentine, the contented reborn woman. Even so, it would be impossible not to smile along with this very happy person as the curtain/sunset falls.

● ●

■ SHIVERS

1975, 88 MINS, CANADA ◇ ⓥ

Dir David Cronenberg   *Prod* Ivan Reitman   *Scr* David Cronenberg   *Ph* Robert Saad   *Ed* Patrick Dodd   *Mus* Ivan Reitman (sup.)
● Paul Hampton, Joe Silver, Lynn Lowry, Alan Migicovsky, Susan Petrie, Barbara Steele (DAL/Reitman)

Shivers, a low-budget Canadian production, is a silly but moderately effective chiller about creeping parasites that systematically (and comically) 'infect' an entire highrise population with nothing less than sexual hysteria.

Premise of pic is a bit shaky. A mad doctor who believes in matter over mind has implanted in his teenage mistress a strange parasite that brings out the basest of human impulses. He's not the only one she fools

S

around with, so before long, the 'disease' is spreading like crazy.

The star of the movie is special effects and makeup man Joe Blasco, whose bloody, disgusting-looking crawlers are seen climbing out of people's throats as well as highrise plumbing to attack innocents.

• •

■ SHOCK CORRIDOR

1963, 101 MINS, US ⓥ

Dir Samuel Fuller   *Prod* Samuel Fuller   *Scr* Samuel Fuller   *Ph* Stanley Cortez   *Ed* Jerome Thoms   *Mus* Paul Dunlap   *Art Dir* Eugene Lourie

● Peter Breck, Constance Towers, Gene Evans, James Best, Hari Rhodes, Larry Tucker (Allied Artists)

Samuel Fuller's thin plot has a newspaperman (Peter Breck) contriving, with the aid of a psychiatrist no less, to get himself committed to a mental ward in order to identify a murderer known only to the inmates and whom the police have been unable to detect.

Within all this lurks three points about Americana, each embodied in characters the fourth-estater encounters in the hospital. A Communist-brainwashed and subsequently disgraced Korean war vet (James Best) is the mouthpiece through which Fuller pleads for greater understanding of such unfortunate individuals.

Likewise, a Negro (Hari Rhodes) supposed to have been the first to attend an all-white Southern university serves to make the point that it takes enormous emotional stamina to play the role of the martyr in social progress. And the character of a renowned physicist (Gene Evans) whose mind has deteriorated into that of a six-year-old enables Fuller to get in some digs against bomb shelters and America's participation in the space race.

But all these points go for naught because the film is dominated by sex and shock superficialities. Among the gruelling passages are a striptease and an attack on the hero in a locked room by half-a-dozen nymphos.

The dialog is unreal and pretentious, and the direction is heavyhanded, often mistaking sordidness for realism. The performers labor valiantly, but in vain. Those most prominent are Breck, who really gets his lumps and earns his pay, and Constance Towers as his stripper girl friend.

• •

■ SHOCK TO THE SYSTEM, A

1990, 87 MINS, US ⓥ

Dir Jan Egleson   *Prod* Patrick McCormick   *Scr* Andrew Klavan   *Ph* Paul Goldsmith   *Ed* Peter C. Frank, William A. Anderson   *Mus* Gary Chang   *Art Dir* Howard Cummings

● Michael Caine, Elizabeth McGovern, Peter Riegert, Swoosie Kurtz, Will Patton, John McMartin (Corsair)

A Shock to the System is a very dark comedy about escaping the current rat race via murder. Unsympathetic, poorly motivated central character [from a novel by Simon Brett] and flat direction nullify Michael Caine's reliable thesping.

Caine is cast as a Britisher working for a NY firm who's passed over for the post of marketing department head when John McMartin (in an affecting performance) is forced to take early retirement. Upstart Peter Riegert (way too sympathetic for the role) gets the job instead and starts throwing his weight around.

After doing away with wife Swoosie Kurtz by rigging faulty electric wiring in the basement, he blows up Riegert (and obnoxious assistant Philip Moon) on his sailboat. Plodding Connecticut cop Will Patton discovers plenty of clues.

Jan Egleson's direction slows to a snail's pace during the middle reels and lacks the style of the classics in this genre.

• •

■ SHOCKER

1989, 110 MINS, US ⓥ

Dir Wes Craven   *Prod* Marianne Maddalena, Barin Kumar   *Scr* Wes Craven   *Ph* Jacques Haitkin   *Ed* Andy Blumenthal   *Mus* William Goldstein   *Art Dir* Cynthia Kay

● Michael Murphy, Peter Begg, Mitch Pileggi, Cami Cooper, Richard Brooks (Alive/Universal)

At first glance (or at least for the first 40 minutes) *Shocker* seems a potential winner, an almost unbearably suspenseful, stylish and blood-drenched ride courtesy of writer-director Wes Craven's flair for action and sick humour.

As it continues, however, the camp aspects simply give way to the ridiculous while failing to establish any rules to govern the mayhem. The result is plenty of unintentional laughs.

The obtuse story has Horace Pinker (Mitch Pileggi), already a mass killer of several families, slaying the foster family of Jonathan (Peter Berg) and his police captain father (Michael Murphy). Jonathan 'sees' the events in a prescient dream that indicates he's linked to the murderer.

That leads the police to Pinker's door, and after a series of misadventures he's caught and executed. But Horace lives on after the execution as a disembodied malevolent spirit who strikes out by possessing others.

• •

■ SHOES OF THE FISHERMAN, THE

1968, 162 MINS, US ◇ ⓥ

Dir Michael Anderson   *Prod* George Englund   *Scr* John Patrick, James Kennaway   *Ph* Erwin Hillier   *Ed* Ernest Walter   *Mus* Alex North   *Art Dir* George W. Davis, Edward Carfagno

● Anthony Quinn, Laurence Olivier, Oskar Werner, David Janssen, Vittorio De Sica, Leo McKern (M-G-M)

Anthony Quinn plays a future Pope of Russian extraction who would, if necessary, strip the Roman Catholic Church of its material wealth in order to avoid nuclear world war. Occasionally awkward script structure and dialog, and overall sluggish pacing do not substantially blunt the impact of the basic story (from Morris L. West's novel), as interpreted by an excellent international cast.

It starts with Quinn as a 20-year inmate of a Siberian slave labor camp, and ends with his public Coronation promise as the new Pope to spend the Church's wealth.

Laurence Olivier, as the Russian premier, had ordered Quinn's release from religious persecution, and ultimate dispatch to Rome. Quinn's performance is excellent. That experience-lined face suggests 20 years of Siberian enslavement, even if the script has him returning to urbane society with a bit too much facility.

Olivier, along with Frank Finlay and Clive Revill, are superior in projecting not unsympathetic Russian politicians.

• •

■ SHOGUN

1981, 150 MINS, US ◇

Dir Jerry London   *Prod* Eric Bercovici   *Scr* Eric Bercovici   *Ph* Andrew Laszlo   *Ed* Bill Luciano, Jerry Young, Benjamin A. Weissman, Donald R. Rode   *Mus* Maurice Jarre   *Art Dir* Joseph R. Jennings

● Richard Chamberlain, Toshiro Mifune, Yoko Shimada, Alan Badel, Michael Hordern (Paramount)

In *Shogun*, East meets West in a period clash of swords and culture, but with scarcely the wit, style, dramatic tension or plausibility to justify a running time of 150 tiresome minutes for this spinoff from the James Clavell novel as recut from the eight-hour Paramount TV miniseries.

Richard Chamberlain and Toshiro Mifune are top-featured in this bilingual (and subtitled) tale of 17th-century Japanese political intrigue with praiseworthy professional dig-

nity, the former as a shipwrecked Englishman, the latter as one of the tribal chieftains vying for the title and power of shogun, or supreme Godfather. The whole shebang was lensed on locations in Japan.

Yoko Shimada projects a Dresden-doll appeal as an aristocratic lady who, besides helping Chamberlain bridge the culture gap, enters into forbidden love, thereby telegraphing her doom.

Producer Eric Bercovici's script on the big screen proves only too difuse and confusing to do anything like justice to either the romance, any other relationship or indeed the wider canvas of betrayal, barbarism and warlord ritual posturing.

• •

■ SHOOT THE MOON

1982, 124 MINS, US ◇ ⓥ

Dir Alan Parker   *Prod* Alan Marshall   *Scr* Bo Goldman   *Ph* Michael Seresin   *Ed* Gerry Hambling   *Art Dir* Geoffrey Kirkland

● Albert Finney, Diane Keaton, Karen Allen, Peter Weller, Dana Hill, Viveka Davis (M-G-M/United Artists)

A number of high-powered artists fail to coalesce their talents in *Shoot the Moon* a grim drama of marital collapse which proves disturbing and irritating by turns.

Noisy pic belongs almost entirely to toplined Albert Finney and Diane Keaton, who play affluent serious writer and housewife, respectively, and parents of four girls. First act is devoted to couple hitting absolute rock bottom, with nothing to do but for Finney to walk out into the arms of g.f. Karen Allen.

Attempting to handle the situation in civilized fashion, pair agrees that Finney can spend a reasonable amount of time with the girls, which allows Finney to catch glimpses of his wife's slow-cooking affair with a construction worker.

Forced to 'control' himself much of the time, Finney is a walking time bomb, exploding horrendously on one occasion before the climax when he beats his most troublesome daughter. Stripped of most of her charm and sometimes brutally photographed, Keaton is more erratic.

• •

■ SHOOT TO KILL

1988, 110 MINS, US ◇ ⓥ

Dir Roger Spottiswoode   *Prod* Ron Silverman, Daniel Petrie Jr.   *Scr* Harv Zimmel, Michael Burton, Daniel Petrie Jr.   *Ph* Michael Chapman   *Ed* Garth Craven, George Bowers   *Mus* John Scott   *Art Dir* Richard Sylbert

● Sidney Poitier, Tom Berenger, Kirstie Alley, Clancy Brown, Richard Masur (Touchstone/Silver Screen Partners III)

Everybody, including the audience, gets a good workout in *Shoot to Kill*, a rugged, involving manhunt adventure [story by Harv Zimmel] in which a criminal leads his pursuers over what is perhaps the most challenging land route out of the United States.

Sidney Poitier establishes his authority immediately as a veteran FBI man in San Francisco who, despite handling the crisis with calm assuredness, cannot prevent the getaway of a jewel thief who kills hostages on a foggy night on Frisco Bay.

Another shooting of a similar type takes Poitier up to the Pacific Northwest, where he is forced to engage the services of tough backwoodsman Tom Berenger to lead him up into the mountains to apprehend the villain before he makes it over the border into Canada.

A self-styled macho hermit, Berenger considers Poitier a cityfied softy incapable of making it in the mountains. This sets up a cliched enmity between the two men that one knows will have to be broken down, but not without some predictable jibes at Poitier's awkwardness outdoors and some revelations of Berenger's own vulnerabilities.

Poitier, 63 when the film was shot, looks little more than 40. The actor's directness and easiness on the screen are refreshing, his humor self-deprecating and understated.

Berenger solidly fills the bill as the confident mountain man, and Kirstie Alley, despite the extreme limitations of her role, proves entirely believable as his female counterpart. British Columbia locations give the film tremendous scenic impact.

■ **SHOOTING PARTY, THE**

1984, 106 MINS, UK ◇ Ⓥ

Dir Alan Bridges *Prod* Geoffrey Reeve *Scr* Julian Bond *Ph* Fred Tammes *Ed* Peter Davies *Mus* John Scott *Art Dir* Morley Smith

● Edward Fox, Cheryl Campbell, James Mason, Dorothy Tutin, John Gielgud, Frank Windsor (Reeve)

A handsome historical homage to the proprieties and values of pre-First World War landed aristocracy in England, *The Shooting Party* revolves around a holiday spent on an estate in 1913, as an era ends.

Julian Bond's adaptation of the novel [by Isabel Colegate] incorporates enough to make a promising miniseries.

James Mason as Sir Randolph is as worldweary as he is tired of his genuinely tiresome guests. Thesp credits resemble a Who's Who of the British stage, with John Gielgud eclipsing the gentry in a brief appearance as a pamphleteering defender of animal rights, opposed to slaughter as amusement.

Director Alan Bridges is very good at handling a story that tries to distinguish between the nobility and what is truly noble.

■ **SHOOTIST, THE**

1976, 99 MINS, US ◇ Ⓥ

Dir Don Siegel *Prod* Mike Frankovich, William Self *Scr* Miles Hood Swarthout, Scott Hale *Ph* Bruce Surtees *Ed* Douglas Stewart *Mus* Elmer Bernstein *Art Dir* Robert Boyle

● John Wayne, Lauren Bacall, Ron Howard, Bill McKinney, James Stewart, Richard Boone (De Laurentiis)

The Shootist stands as one of John Wayne's towering achievements. Don Siegel's terrific film is simply beautiful, and beautifully simple, in its quiet, elegant and sensitive telling of the last days of a dying gunfighter at the turn of the century. Wayne and Lauren Bacall are both outstanding.

The time is 1901. Wayne a prairie-hardened gunfighter, rides into the new century where Carson City is in segue to modern civilization. Saloon shootouts still occur; Hugh O'Brian's card dealing is still not to be challenged.

Wayne's trip is to town doctor James Stewart, who confirms a cancer diagnosis. Atop this comes an emerging tenderness between Wayne and Bacall which is articulated in careful politeness and the artful exchange of expressions that evoke memories of great silent films.

■ **SHOP AROUND THE CORNER, THE**

1940, 97 MINS, US Ⓥ

Dir Ernst Lubitsch *Prod* Ernst Lubitsch *Scr* Samson Raphaelson *Ph* William Daniels *Ed* Gene Ruggiero *Mus* Werner R. Heymann *Art Dir* Cedric Gibbons, Wade B. Rubottom

● Margaret Sullavan, James Stewart, Frank Morgan, Joseph Schildkraut, Felix Bressart (M-G-M)

Although picture carries the indelible stamp of Ernst Lubitsch at his best in generating humor and human interest from what might appear to be unimportant situations, it carries further to impress via the outstanding

characterizations by Margaret Sullavan and James Stewart in the starring spots. Sullavan's portrayal is light and fluffy – in contrast to the seriousness of Stewart in both business and romance.

The supporting cast is very well-balanced. In the compact group is Frank Morgan, as the owner-operator of the small gift shop in Budapest, and his staff including Joseph Schildkraut, Sara Haden, Felix Bressart, William Tracy, Inez Courtney and Charles Smith.

The story [based on Nikolaus Laszlo's play] might be termed a small edition of *Grand Hotel*, with practically all of the action taking place in the small shop. Stewart, senior clerk, confides to Bressart that he is corresponding with a girl (Sullavan) through a newspaper ad, and takes the affair with the unknown very seriously. Sullavan arrives to apply for a job and, after being turned down by Stewart, is hired by Morgan.

From that point on it's an intimate tale of the store and its workers. Story swings along at fast pace.

■ **SHOPWORN ANGEL, THE**

1938, 85 MINS, US

Dir H.C. Potter *Prod* Joseph L. Mankiewicz *Scr* Waldo Salt *Ph* Joseph Ruttenberg *Ed* W. Donn Hayes *Mus* Edward Ward *Art Dir* Cedric Gibbons, Joseph C. Wright

● Margaret Sullavan, James Stewart, Walter Pidgeon, Hattie McDaniel, Nat Pendleton, Alan Curtis (M-G-M)

Original of *Shopworn Angel* first appeared about 20 years earlier as a *Saturday Evening Post* story by Dana Burnet. Paramount filmed it (partly in sound) in 1929, with Nancy Carroll, Gary Cooper and Paul Lukas. In general, this remake follows the original story with reasonable faithfulness. It's still the wartime yarn about the crafty Broadway chorine who meets a Texas rookie on his way to France and, when he falls for her, marries him rather than disillusion him.

The present version seems a softer one, without the stark edges of the original and as a result less absorbing. Instead of the cool schemer played by Nancy Carroll, the chorine is now generous and warm-hearted. The girl's lover is no longer the menace of the earlier version, but is now the typical Walter Pidgeon man-who-doesn't-get-the-girl.

It is only occasional credible screen drama. As the girl, Margaret Sullavan turns in a powerful performance. Her playing is pliant, has depth and eloquence.

James Stewart is a natural enough rookie but there's little characterization in his performance.

■ **SHORT CIRCUIT**

1986, 98 MINS, US ◇ Ⓥ

Dir John Badham *Prod* David Foster, Lawrence Turman *Scr* S.S. Wilson, Brent Maddock *Ph* Nick McLean *Ed* Frank Morriss *Mus* David Shire *Art Dir* Dianne Wager

● Ally Sheedy, Steve Guttenberg, Fisher Stevens, Austin Pendleton, G.W. Bailey, Brian McNamara (Tri-Star/PSO)

Short Circuit is a hip, sexless sci-fi sendup featuring a Defense Dept robot who comes 'alive' to become a pop-talking peacenik.

Robot is the one-dimensional No. 5, the ultimate weapon designed by playful computer whiz Dr Newton Crosby (Steve Guttenberg).

By a fluke, No. 5 gets short-circuited and begins to malfunction. It finds itself outside the high-security Nova compound in a chase that lands it on top of a natural foods catering truck and under the influence of its sweet but tough animal-loving owner, Stephanie (Ally

Sheedy). Scripters get credit for some terrific dialog that would have been a lot less disarming if not for the winsome robot and Sheedy's affection for it. Guttenberg plays his best goofy self.

■ **SHORT CIRCUIT 2**

1988, 110 MINS, US ◇ Ⓥ

Dir Kenneth Johnson *Prod* David Foster, Lawrence Turman *Scr* S.S. Wilson, Brent Maddock *Ph* John McPherson *Ed* Conrad Buff *Mus* Charles Fox *Art Dir* Bill Brodie

● Fisher Stevens, Michael McLean, Cynthia Gibb, Jack Weston, Dee McCafferty (Turman–Foster/Tri-Star)

Mild and meek, *Short Circuit 2* has an uncomplicated sweetness as a successful followup to the original robot kiddie comedy.

'Johnny Five' makes his way to the Big City, where protector Fisher Stevens struggles to make ends meet hawking toy models of his mechanical wonder on the street.

Cutie-pie store employee Cynthia Gibb needs to bring a novel item to her shelves, and sends Stevens and self-styled entrepreneur Michael McKean into instant action by ordering 1,000 of the little of the little buggers for the Christmas season. Underhanded banker Jack Weston has some other ideas for the tireless automaton, scheming to kidnap it and press it into service stealing some priceless jewels from a safe deposit box.

Although derivative, the robot, made up of all manner of spare electronic parts, remains charming, and kids will undoubtedly find delightful scenes in which Number Five jumps around from place to place and sails through the air amid the skyscrapers of Toronto.

The film is set in a generic US metropolis, complete with American flags and a citizenship swearing-in ceremony. However, the city is constantly recognizable as Toronto.

■ **SHORT TIME**

1990, 97 MINS, US ◇ Ⓥ

Dir Gregg Champion *Prod* Todd Black *Scr* John Blumenthal, Michael Berry *Ph* John Connor *Ed* Frank Morriss *Mus* Ira Newborn *Art Dir* Michael Bolton

● Dabney Coleman, Matt Frewer, Teri Garr, Barry Corbin (Gladden)

Anyone trying to make a black comedy should be made to watch the classic *Harold & Maude* about 20 times before venturing into what too often is a sorely misused genre. Gregg Champion's extensive work as a second-unit director evidently hasn't prepared him for dealing with the nuances of human emotion. His idea of humor in this uneasy cross between farce and disease-of-the-week melodrama is to pile the desperate Dabney Coleman into a police car and have him crash into about half of the vehicles in Seattle before angrily stepping out in one piece.

Champion wants to turn Coleman's dilemma from farce into genuine emotion as the film progresses, but the character's callous disregard of other people's lives in his own quest for death makes him impossible to care about when the soapy music begins. He's otherwise a seemingly decent guy who has alienated wife Teri Garr, typecast as a drab but understanding featherhead.

The real problem is the subplot about a black bus driver (Deejay Jackson), whose urine sample has been mixed up with Coleman's, and who's really the one dying of a rare blood disorder but doesn't realize it.

■ **SHOT IN THE DARK, A**

1964, 103 MINS, US ◇ Ⓥ

Dir Blake Edwards *Prod* Blake Edwards *Scr* Blake Edwards, William Peter Blatty *Ph* Christopher Challis *Ed* Ralph E. Winters, Bert Bates *Mus* Henry Mancini *Art Dir* Michael Stringer

● Peter Sellers, Elke Sommer, Herbert Lom, George Sanders, Graham Stark, Douglas Wilmer (Mirisch/United Artists)

Based upon the French farce authored by Marcel Achard and adapted to the American stage by Harry Kurnitz, director Blake transforms Peter Sellers' role from a magistrate, whose activities were limited to judicial chambers, into Inspector Clouseau, where more movement and greater area are possible. 'Give me 10 men like Clouseau, and I could destroy the world!' his superior exclaims in despair, summing up the character played by Sellers, sent to investigate a murder in the chateau of a millionaire outside Paris.

When this chief inspector, portrayed by Herbert Lom, attempts to take him off the case, powers above return him to his investigations which revolve about chief suspect Elke Sommer, a French maid, whom the dick is convinced is innocent.

The chores takes him to a nudist camp, a tour of Parisian nightclubs, where dead bodies are left in his wake, and to his apartment, where one of the funniest seduction scenes ever filmed unfolds to the tune of three in a bed and an exploding time bomb. It's never completely clear whether the detective solves his case in a windup that doesn't quite come off.

Sometimes the narrative is subordinated to individual bits of business and running gags but Sellers' skill as a comedian again is demonstrated, and Sommer, in role of the chambermaid who moves all men to amorous thoughts and seduction, is pert and expert. Lom gives punch and humor to star's often distraught superior, George Sanders lends polish as the millionaire and Graham Stark excels as Sellers' dead-pan assistant.

· ·

■ SHOULDER ARMS

1918, 36 MINS, US ⊗

Dir Charles Chaplin *Prod* Charles Chaplin
Scr Charles Chaplin *Ph* Rollie Totheroh *Mus* Charles Chaplin
● Charles Chaplin, Edna Purviance, Sydney Chaplin, Loyal Underwood, Henry Bergman, Albert Austin (First National)

In *Shoulder Arms* Chaplin is a doughboy. At the finish he captures the Kaiser, Crown Prince and Hindenburg.

At the opening he is the most awkward member of an awkward drilling squad. His trouble with his feet is terrific. After a long hike, Chaplin has heroic dreams of what he accomplishes as a private in the trenches over there.

Chaplin wrote and directed the story. His camouflage as a small tree, during which he runs through a wood is one of the best and most original pieces of comedy work ever put on a screen. There is some slapstick, laughably worked in, also pie-throwing with limburger cheese substituted. That occurs in the trenches.

The trenches are good production bits. There is fun also in the dug-out, with the water, and a floating candle burning one of the boys' exposed toes.

Shoulder Arms includes much more action than generally found in a Chaplin comedy. With Chaplin in uniform without his derby hat and cane, it says that Charlie Chaplin is a great film comedian.

· ·

■ SHOUT, THE

1978, 87 MINS, UK ◇ Ⓥ

Dir Jerzy Skolimowski *Prod* Jeremy Thomas
Scr Michael Austin, Jerzy Skolimowski *Ph* Mike Molloy *Ed* Barrie Vince *Mus* Rupert Hine, Anthony Banks, Michael Rutherford *Art Dir* Simon Holland

● Alan Bates, Susannah York, John Hurt, Robert Stephens, Tim Curry, Julian Hough (Recorded Picture)

Polish director Jerzy Skolimowski has been able to create a gripping film [from a story by Robert Graves] that holds attention most of the way through its economical length. It probes a couple beset by a catalyst that breaks their seemingly surface contentment. Film is told by Alan Bates during a cricket match in an asylum.

Bates, a tramp-like figure, accosts a man (John Hurt) outside a church one day. It is a small town and Bates gets invited to dinner and stays. He tells strange tales of how he lived with Australian aborigines and killed his own children when he left and how he learned how to cast various spells, especially a shout that can kill.

Flash forwards indicate Bates will disrupt the couple with one problem of the man apparently dallying with the wife of the local shoemaker.

Hurt is an electronic music composer and his work counterpoints Bates's shout in a way. The story builds as the listener becomes apprehensive. It crescendos as Bates, in the tale, reduces the wife to his whims.

· ·

■ SHOUT AT THE DEVIL

1976, 147 MINS, UK ◇ Ⓥ

Dir Peter Hunt *Prod* Michael Klinger *Scr* Wilbur Smith, Stanley Price, Alistair Reid *Ph* Mike Reed *Ed* Michael Duthie *Mus* Maurice Jarre *Art Dir* Syd . Cain

● Lee Marvin, Roger Moore, Barbara Parkins, Ian Holm, Rene Kolldehoff, Horst Janson (Hemdale)

A nice sprawling, basic, gutsy and unsophisticated film, which displays its reported $7 million budget on nearly every frame.

Based on a Wilbur Smith (*Gold*) novel, script is a pastiche of almost every basic action-suspense ingredient known to the cinema.

Exotic tropical settings, man-eating crocodiles, air and sea combat, shipwreck, big game hunting, natives on a rampage, ticking time bombs, rape and fire, malaria, they're all there and then some.

Basic ingredients have to do with a successful attempt to put permanently out of action a crippled World War I German battle cruiser holed up for repairs in a remote South East African river delta.

The oddball opposites-attract relationship between Lee Marvin and Roger Moore generally works very well indeed, and the constantly imbibing Irisher and the contrastingly 'straight' Britisher make good foils. The motivating love story linking Moore and Barbara Parkins is rarely involving and convincing.

· ·

■ SHOW BOAT

1936, 110 MINS, US Ⓥ

Dir James Whale *Prod* Carl Laemmle Jr *Scr* Oscar Hammerstein II *Ph* John J. Mescall *Ed* Ted Kent, Bernard Burton *Mus* Victor Baravelle (dir.) *Art Dir* Charles D. Hall

● Irene Dunne, Allan Jones, Charles Winninger, Paul Robeson, Helen Morgan, Helen Westley (Universal)

Show Boat, Universal's second talkerized version, is a smash filmusical. Basic tender romance [from Edna Ferber's novel] between Magnolia (Irene Dunne) and Gaylord Ravenal (Allan Jones), romantic wastrel of the Mississippi river banks, has been most effectively projected by this reproduction of the classic [1927] Edna Ferber-Oscar Hammerstein II-Jerome Kern operetta.

The now classic songs, 'Make Believe', 'Ol' Man River', 'Can't Help Lovin' That Man', 'Why Do I Love You', 'Bill' and 'You Are Love', as the duet thematic have been

retained and three new numbers, all in a novelty vein, have been added.

Dunne and Jones are superb in the roles originally created by Norma Terriss and Howard Marsh. Charles Winninger in his original Captain Andy role is, as ever, engaging; Helen Morgan is the same Julie as in the Ziegfeld original; Paul Robeson has Jules Bledsoe's basso opportunities with 'Ol' Man River'; Helen Westley has the original Edna Mae Oliver assignment and delivers adequately, if a bit morosely, lacking the subtle brittleness of the Oliver interpretation.

Dunne maintains the illusion of her Magnolia throughout – from her own secluded girlhood; into sudden stardom on the Cotton Blossom; and later, as a more mature artist, carrying the torch for the disappeared Ravenal and rearing her own child into professional prominence.

Robeson's 'Ol' Man river' is perhaps the single song highlight, although some may be captious a bit over the camera angles illustrating 'totin' the bales' and 'landing in jail'.

· ·

■ SHOW BOAT

1951, 107 MINS, US ◇ Ⓥ

Dir George Sidney *Prod* Arthur Freed *Scr* John Lee Mahin *Ph* Charles Rosher *Ed* John Dunning *Mus* Jerome Kern *Art Dir* Cedric Gibbons, Jack Martin Smith

● Kathryn Grayson, Howard Keel, Ava Gardner, Joe E. Brown, Marge Champion, Gower Champion (M-G-M)

Show Boat started beguiling audiences back in 1927, when it was first brought to the Broadway stage after a Philadelphia tryout. Since then, in many legit versions and in two previous film treatments, it has continued that beguilement.

There has been no tampering with the basic line of the Edna Ferber novel, from which Jerome Kern and Oscar Hammerstein II did the original musical. There are a few changes in this latest film version, the first in color, and an introduction of the finale in a time span much shorter than the original.

'Ol' Man River', 'Make Believe', 'Why Do I Love You', 'You Are Love', 'My Bill', and 'Can't Help Lovin' That Man' are Kern tunes that lose nothing in the passing of the years. With voices of such show-tune ableness as Kathryn Grayson and Howard Keel to sing them they capture the ear and tear at the emotions.

Grayson is a most able Magnolia, the innocent show boat girl who runs off with the dashing gambler (Keel), finds her marriage wrecked by his love of lady chance, goes back to the show boat to have her child and then reconciles with the wandering mate after a few years.

Ava Gardner is the third star, bringing to her role of Julie, the mulatto who is kicked off the Cotton Blossom because of early southern prejudice, all the physical attributes it needs to attract attention.

There is an amazing amount of freshness instilled into the picture by Marge and Gower Champion, young dance team who handle the roles of Ellie May and Frank Schultz, show boat terpers. The other big song moment is William Warfield's rich baritoning of 'Ol' Man River'.

· ·

■ SHOW PEOPLE

1928, 63 MINS, US

Dir King Vidor *Scr* Wanda Tuchock, Ralph Spence *Ph* John Arnold *Ed* Hugh Wynn *Art Dir* Cedric Gibbons

● Marion Davies, William Haines, Dell Henderson, Paul Ralli, Tenen Holtz, Harry Gribbon (M-G-M)

As an entertainment *Show People* is a good number. It has laughs, studio atmosphere galore, intimate glimpses of various stars, considerable Hollywood geography, and just enough sense and plausibility to hold it together.

As a document of Hollywood it presents some peculiar angles. When Peggy Pepper (Marion Davies) gets the w.k. swell head she is seen to be the complacent girlfriend of her leading man, an insufferably conceited stuffed shirt. The odd part of this leading man character is that he (Paul Ralli) looks, dresses and acts like John Gilbert, star of the company which produced the picture. The satire seems pretty sharply pointed at times.

Davies is obviously mimicking the peculiar pucker of the lips identified with Mae Murray, former M-G-M star. However, at other times the story suggests the career of Gloria Swanson, particularly with emphasis upon the custard pie gal becoming an emotional actress. Bebe Daniels is also suggested.

SHUTTERED ROOM, THE

1966, 99 MINS, UK ◇

Dir David Greene *Prod* Phillip Hazelton *Scr* D.B. Ledrov, Nathaniel Tanchuck *Ph* Ken Hodges *Ed* Brian Smedley-Aston *Mus* Basil Kirchin *Art Dir* Brian Eatwell

● Gig Young, Carol Lynley, Oliver Reed, Flora Robson, William Devlin, Bernard Kay (Seven Arts)

With a good quota of shudders and a neat suggestion of evil throughout, this is an efficient entry in a somewhat oldfashioned vein of melodrama. Although supposedly taking place in New England, the locations are blatantly British scenery.

Susannah Kelton (Carol Lynley) has inherited an old millhouse on a remote island, and turns up there with husband Mike (Gig Young) to take possession. A prolog already has warned that there's a mad dame locked up in an upper story. Ethan (Oliver Reed), who heads a mischievous gang of layabouts, surveys her with a morose and lascivious eye.

The script is adequate in the plotting but feeble in the dialog department, sparking off untoward laffs in the wrong places. Lynley is competently scared throughout. And Reed brings a brooding touch of lechery to the over-excited Ethan.

SHY PEOPLE

1987, 118 MINS, US ◇ Ⓥ

Dir Andrei Konchalovsky *Prod* Menahem Golan, Yoram Globus *Scr* Gerard Brach, Andrei Konchalovsky, Marjorie David *Ph* Chris Menges *Ed* Alain Jakubowicz *Mus* Tangerine Dream *Art Dir* Steve Marsh

● Jill Clayburgh, Barbara Hershey, Martha Plimpton, Merritt Butrick, John Philbin (Cannon)

Cosmopolitan writer Diana Sullivan (Jill Clayburgh) lives in splendid disharmony in New York with her teenage daughter Grace (Martha Plimpton). Clayburgh is totally in her element as a spoiled middle-age woman trying to cope with her too-hip daughter.

They are soon out of their element, though, when they travel to Louisiana. It is not simply a case of invaders from civilization soiling a pure culture; story is deepened by the exploration of family ties.

What they find when they arrive is Ruth Sullivan (Barbara Hershey), the matriarch of a family of three sons, one of whom is kept in a cage and seems half retarded, plus a pregnant daughter (Mare Winningham).

Director Andrei Konchalovsky and cinematographer Chris Menges offer a slow and seductive descent into this world of alligators and primordial beauty.

Clayburgh gives one of her best performances and seems right at home with the ticks and self-centered mannerisms of a modern woman. Plimpton nearly steals the show with

her mixture of girlish brashness and suggestive sexuality.

SIBLING RIVALRY

1990, 88 MINS, US ◇ Ⓥ

Dir Carl Reiner *Prod* David V. Lester, Don Miller, Liz Glotzer *Scr* Martha Goldhirsh *Ph* Reynaldo Villalobos *Ed* Bud Molin *Mus* Jack Elliott *Art Dir* Jeannine Claudia Oppewall

● Kirstie Alley, Bill Pullman, Carrie Fisher, Jami Gertz, Scott Bakula, Sam Elliott (Castle Rock/Nelson)

In her first solo-starring vehicle, Kirstie Alley – who plays the creatively stifled wife of a stuffy young doctor (Scott Bakula) – comes into her own with a flamboyant, highly physical performance.

Her adulterous hop in the sack with mystery hunk Sam Elliott results in his death by heart attack after strenuous lovemaking. What follows involves three sets of siblings: Alley and her slightly ditzy younger sister and rival (Jami Gertz); weird vertical blinds salesman Bill Pullman as the black sheep younger brother of upwardly mobile cop Ed O'Neil; and the massive clan of doctors comprising Bakula, his sister (Carrie Fisher) and brother (Elliott).

The surprise that Elliott turns out to be Alley's brother-in-law is effectively developed and launches several hilarious setpieces. Pullman and Alley are united in crime after Pullman thinks *he* accidentally killed Elliott with his vertical blinds equipment. Both he and Alley attempt to cover up the fatality as a suicide.

Though the rushed happy ending doesn't ring true, *Sibling Rivalry* creates a cheerful mood from morbid material. Carl Reiner directs swiftly and efficiently, getting maximum yocks out of borderline vulgar content.

SICILIAN, THE

1987, 115 MINS, US ◇ Ⓥ

Dir Michael Cimino *Prod* Michael Cimino, Joann Carelli *Scr* Steve Shagan *Ph* Alex Thomson *Ed* Francoise Bonnot *Mus* David Mansfield *Art Dir* Wolf Kroeger

● Christopher Lambert, Terence Stamp, Joss Ackland, John Turturro, Barbara Sukowa, Ray McAnally (Gladden/20th Century-Fox)

The Sicilian represents a botched telling of the life of postwar outlaw leader Salvatore Giuliano. Just who contributed to what parts of the botching remain a mystery, since uncredited hands cut 30 minutes from the version director Michael Cimino delivered. [The 145-minute version was later released on video, and theatrically in Europe.]

Cimino seems to be aiming for an operatic telling of the short career of the violent 20th-century folk hero [based on Mario Puzo's novel], but falls into an uncomfortable middle ground between European artfulness and stock Hollywood conventions.

Saga served as the basis of Francesco Rosi's 1962 *Salvatore Giuliano*, and has at its core a popular young man who, working from the mountains, employs increasingly excessive means to further his dream of achieving radical land distribution from the titled estate owners to the peasants.

Giuliano unhesitatingly kills anyone he thinks has betrayed him, and maintains a semi-adversarial, curiously equivocal relationship with both the Catholic Church and the all-powerful Mafia.

In the lead, Christophe (billed in US projects as Christopher) Lambert betrays little inner conflict or sense of thought, and simply does not make Giuliano interesting.

Coming off by far the best is Joss Ackland, who makes the Mafia chieftain a warm, sympathetic man one enjoys being around. Richard Bauer makes a strong impression as

an adviser and go-between for Giuliano and the Mafia, and Giulia Boschi is strikingly, seriously beautiful as the hero's wife.

SID AND NANCY

1986, 111 MINS, UK ◇ Ⓥ

Dir Alex Cox *Prod* Eric Fellner *Scr* Alex Cox, Abbe Wool *Ph* Roger Deakins *Ed* David Martin *Mus* The Pogues, Pray for Rain *Art Dir* Andrew McAlpine

● Gary Oldman, Chloe Webb, David Hayman (Embassy/Zenith/Initial)

Sid and Nancy is the definitive pic on the punk phenomenon. The sad, sordid story of Sid Vicious, a lead member of The Sex Pistols, and his relationship with his American girlfriend, Nancy Spungen, is presented by Alex Cox without flinching. Authenticity is the film's major asset.

It's a world of drugs and booze, with sex lagging behind in interest for the most part. But grim as much of the film is, it's not without humor.

With his unwashed hair sticking out at all angles, his pale face and brash British accent, Gary Oldman fits the part like a glove. Chloe Webb doesn't spare her looks as the ravaged, shrill Nancy. Both actors are beyond praise.

The film's dialog is extremely rough, the settings sordid, the theme of wasted lives (and talent?) depressing. But *Sid and Nancy* is a dynamic piece of work, which brings audiences as close as possible to understanding its wayward heroes.

SIDDHARTHA

1972, 95 MINS, US ◇

Dir Conrad Rooks *Prod* Conrad Rooks *Scr* Conrad Rooks *Ph* Sven Nykvist *Ed* Willy Kemplen *Art Dir* Malcolm Golding

● Shashi Kapoor, Simi Garewal, Romesh Sharma, Pinchoo Kapoor, Zul Vellani, Amrik Singh (Lotus)

Conrad Rooks' second pic, *Siddhartha*, based on the 1922 book by Hermann Hesse, takes place 2,500 years ago in India. It is about a well-to-do young Brahmin who feels he must leave home and find himself and also echoes a man questing for nirvana in a confused society.

Rooks has chosen to give this a surface elegance which sometimes robs the film of its needed earthiness and sensuality in its love angle and more robustness in detailing the vagaries of social aspects and values at the time. But it does have a fine photographic beauty in the hands of Swedish lenser Sven Nykvist.

Siddhartha, after leaving his father, roams with a friend for years, with a group of holy men. Then he meets a great teacher who preaches the need for one's own way to inner harmony who may be the Buddha himself.

SIESTA

1987, 97 MINS, US ◇ Ⓥ

Dir Mary Lambert *Prod* Gary Kurfirst *Scr* Patricia Louisianna Knop *Ph* Bryan Loftus *Ed* Glenn A. Morgan *Mus* Marcus Miller *Art Dir* John Beard

● Ellen Barkin, Gabriel Byrne, Julian Sands, Isabella Rossellini, Martin Sheen, Alexei Sayle (Lorimar/Siren/Palace)

First feature film by Mary Lambert, best known for her Madonna videos, is a densely packed portrait of a beautiful, disturbed woman at the end of her rope. Told in a fragmented, time-jumping style, this subjective, hallucinatory recollection of a five-day descent into hell sustains intense interest throughout, to a great extent because of Ellen Barkin's extravagantly fine performance in the leading role.

In its elaborate, jigsaw-puzzle way, film tells of how Barkin, a daredevil skydiver, impulsively leaves her home and husband in Death Valley for a quick trip to Spain to find the man she still loves, trapeze artist Gabriel Byrne, who also has married someone else, Isabella Rossellini.

Although due back in California imminently for a big commercial payday, Barkin lets her desire for Byrne prolong her Spanish sojourn past the deadline. She falls in with a dissolute, aimless English crowd led by Julian Sands and Jodie Foster and finally becomes utterly lost and delirious, helpless at the hands of filthy-minded taxi driver Alexi Sayle.

Byrne puts on a continuous smoldering act as the sought-after lover, Martin Sheen is all congenial American hype as Barkin's abandoned husband, and Jodie Foster, as a snooty but friendly socialite, has fun with a British accent.

■ SIGN OF THE CROSS, THE

1932, 115 MINS, US

Dir Cecil B. DeMille   *Prod* Cecil B. DeMille
Scr Waldemar Young, Sidney Buchman   *Ph* Karl Struss   *Ed* Anne Bauchens   *Mus* Rudolph Kopp
● Fredric March, Claudette Colbert, Elissa Landi, Charles Laughton, Ian Keith (Paramount)

Religion triumphant over paganism. And the soul is stronger than the flesh. Religion gets the breaks, even though its followers all get killed in this picture. It's altogether a moral victory.

For example, the handsome Prefect of Rome (Fredric March) sees that he can't get to first base with the Christian maiden (Elissa Landi), so he calls in the village temptress, Ancaria (Joyzelle Joyner), for help. Ancaria is described as the hottest gal in town. 'The most versatile' is the phrase used. She uses her arts on Landi. In the street the other Christian martyrs are marching to their doom, singing hymns bravely as they go. Their chants disrupts and finally drowns out the temptress' routine, and she strikes the unmoved Landi in the face. Then, having lost, she walks.

Besides Ancaria, there is Charles Laughton's expert Nero, who doubles as the degenerate emperor and musical pyromaniac as Rome burns. Most of the last half is taken up with a bloody festival staged by crazy Caesar in the arena.

Cast is uniformly good, but only one exceptional performance is registered. That's Laughton's. With utmost subtlety and a minimum of effort he manages to get over his queer character before his first appearance is a minute old.

Claudette Colbert [as Poppaea] and Landi and March and Ian Keith [as Tigellinus] are called upon chiefly to look their parts, and they manage. Frequently some badly written and often silly dialog holds them down.

■ SIGN OF THE PAGAN

1954, 91 MINS, US ◇

Dir Douglas Sirk   *Prod* Albert J. Cohen   *Scr* Oscar Brodney   *Ph* Russell Metty   *Ed* Milton Carruth, Al Clark   *Mus* Frank Skinner, Hans J. Salter   *Art Dir* Alexander Golitzen, Emrich Nicholson
● Jeff Chandler, Jack Palance, Ludmilla Tcherina, Rita Gam, Jeff Morrow, George Dolenz (Universal)

Unlike most screen spectacles, *Sign of the Pagan*'s running time is a tight 91 minutes, in which the flash of the Roman Empire period is not permitted to slow down the telling of an interesting action story.

Plot deals with Attila the Hun, the Scourge of God, and his sweep across Europe some 1,500 years ago. Particularly noteworthy is the treatment of the barbarian in writing and direction, and in the manner in which Jack Palance interprets the character. Instead of a

straight, all-evil person, he is a human being with some good here and there to shade and make understandable the bad.

Douglas Sirk's direction of the excellent script catches the sweep of the period portrayed without letting the characters get lost in spectacle. Representing good in the plot is Jeff Chandler, centurion made a general by his princess, Ludmilla Tcherina, to fight off Attila's advancing hordes.

With Palance scoring so solidly in his role of Attila, he makes the other performers seem less colorful, although Chandler is good as Marsian.

■ SILENCE OF THE LAMBS, THE

1991, 118 MINS, US ◇ ⓥ

Dir Jonathan Demme   *Prod* Edward Saxon, Kenneth Utt, Ron Bozman   *Scr* Ted Tally   *Ph* Tak Fujimoto
Ed Craig McKay   *Mus* Howard Shore   *Art Dir* Kristi Zea
● Jodie Foster, Anthony Hopkins, Scott Glenn, Ted Levine, Brooke Smith, Diane Baker (Orion/Strong Heart)

Skillful adaptation of Thomas Harris' bestseller intelligently wallows in the fascination for aberrant psychology and pervese evil.

Sharp script charts tenacious efforts of young FBI recruit Clarice Starling (Jodie Foster) to cope with the appalling challenges of her first case. Confounded by a series of grotesque murders committed by someone known only as 'Buffalo Bill', bureau special agent Jack Crawford (Scott Glenn) asks his female protege to seek the help of the American prison system's No. 1 resident monster in fashioning a psychological profile of the killer.

Dr Hannibal Lecter (Anthony Hopkins) has been kept in a dungeon-like cell for eight years, and while officious doctors and investigators can get nothing out of him, he is willing to play ball with this attractive new inquisitor. Lecter gives Starling clues as to the killer's identity in exchange for details about her past.

Just as it seems the noose is tightening around the killer, Lecter, in a remarkably fine suspense sequence, manages an unthinkable escape.

Plot is as tight as a coiled rattler. Foster fully registers the inner strength her character must summon up. Scott Glenn is a very agreeable surprise as the FBI agent who takes a chance by putting his young charge on the case. Hopkins, helped by some highly dramatic lighting, makes the role the personification of brilliant, hypnotic evil, and the screen jolts with electricity whenever he is on.

■ SILENCERS, THE

1966, 103 MINS, US ◇ ⓥ

Dir Phil Karlson   *Prod* Irving Allen   *Scr* Oscar Saul
Ph Burnett Guffey   *Ed* Charles Nelson   *Mus* Elmer Bernstein   *Art Dir* Joe Wright
● Dean Martin, Stella Stevens, Daliah Lavi, Victor Buono, Arthur O'Connell, Cyd Charisse (Meadway/Claude/Columbia)

Dean Martin – as Matt Helm, ace of the American counter-espionage agency, ICE – succeeds in a kind of lover-boy way in taking his place up there with such stalwarts as Sean Connery, James Coburn and David Niven.

Produced by Irving Allen and directed by Phil Karlson, both utilizing shock technique, the fastdriving screenplay is based on two of Donald Hamilton's Matt Helm books, *The Silencers* and *Death of a Citizen*.

Plot focuses on a Chinese agent (Victor Buono) who masterminds a ring that plans to divert a US missile so it will destroy Alamogordo, New Mexico, thus creating wide devastation and atomic fallout leading perhaps to global war. All Matt Helm has to do is halt this catastrophe.

Starring with Martin are Stella Stevens and Daliah Lavi. Stevens does herself proud as a mixed-up living doll who can stumble over her own shadow. Lavi is a femme fatale, Martin's ever-lovin' spymate who comes up with a big surprise for him. The glamor department is further repped by Cyd Charisse as a dancer killed by the mob as she's dancing.

■ SILENT ENEMY, THE

1958, 112 MINS, UK ⓥ

Dir William Fairchild   *Prod* Bertram Ostrer
Scr William Fairchild   *Ph* Otto Heller   *Ed* Alan Osbiston   *Mus* William Alwyn   *Art Dir* Bill Andrews
● Laurence Harvey, Dawn Addams, Michael Craig, John Clements, Sidney James, Alec McCowen (Romulus)

The Secret Enemy [from the book *Commander Crabb* by Marshall Pugh] tells the remarkable story of Lieutenant Crabb, a young naval bomb disposal officer, whose exploits in leading frogmen against the Italians earned him a George Medal. It makes smooth, impressive drama, done without heroics, but with excitement.

Laurence Harvey arrives in Gibraltar in 1941 to tackle the Italian menace that is striking successfully at key shipping in the area. With courage and determination, he becomes an experienced diver. Harvey is brash, intolerant of red tape, but fired with drive.

Without permission, Harvey and Michael Craig, one of the seamen, slip across to Spain and discover that the enemy base is in an interned Italian ship. The hull has been converted so that the frogmen can come and go underwater without being seen.

The impatience of the men as they wait to strike, the rigorous training and, above all, the feeling of men doing a thankless and arduous job with a quiet sense of duty are all admirably portrayed. The remarkable underwater scenes give this polished film a sock impact.

■ SILENT MOVIE

1976, 86 MINS, US ◇ ⓥ

Dir Mel Brooks   *Prod* Michael Hertzberg   *Scr* Mel Brooks, Ron Clark, Rudy DeLuca, Barry Levinson
Ph Paul Lohmann   *Ed* John C. Howard, Stanford C. Allen   *Mus* John Morris   *Art Dir* Al Brenner
● Mel Brooks, Marty Feldman, Dom DeLuise, Bernadette Peters, Sid Caesar, Harold Gould (20th Century-Fox)

It took a lot of chutzpah for Mel Brooks to make *Silent Movie* a film with only one word of dialog in an almost non-stop parade of sight gags.

Brooks, Marty Feldman, and Dom DeLuise head the cast as a has-been director and his zany cronies, conning studio chief Sid Caesar into making their silent film as a desperate ploy to prevent takeover of the studio by the Engulf & Devour conglomerate, headed by villainous Harold Gould. The parallels with realities are drolly satiric.

The slender plot of *Silent Movie* [from a story by Ron Clark] is basically a hook for slapstick antics, some feeble and some very fine (notably a wonderful nightclub tango with Anne Bancroft). Harry Ritz, Charlie Callas, Henny Youngman, and the late Liam Dunn are standouts.

■ SILENT PARTNER, THE

1979, 103 MINS, CANADA ◇ ⓥ

Dir Daryl Duke   *Prod* Joel B. Michaels, Stephen Young   *Scr* Curtis Hanson   *Ph* Billy Williams
Mus Oscar Peterson   *Art Dir* Trevor Williams
● Susannah York, Christopher Plummer, Elliott Gould, Celine Lomez, Ken Pogue, John Candy (EMC)

The *Silent Partner* is one of the films that run the gamut from intrigue to violence. Filmed entirely in Toronto, it's an independently financed film which won six Canadian Film Awards.

Christopher Plummer plays the villain in for a change – a bank robber. Elliott Gould is a bank clerk who finds out that Plummer, dressed in a Santa Claus suit, plans a robbery. Susannah York is a bank employee under pressure from Plummer and newcomer Celine Lomez is a cohort of Plummer.

The story [from the novel *Think of a Number* by Anders Bodelson] has Gould, a teller in a branch office, get suspicious when it is the Christmas season and the bank is filled with shoppers. The robber hits and Gould's alertness inspires him to hide $50,000 in a lunch box with the police believing that the robber has all the loot.

- -

■ SILENT PLAYGROUND, THE

1964, 75 MINS, UK
Dir Stanley Goulder *Prod* George Mills *Scr* Stanley Goulder *Ph* Martin Curtis *Ed* Peter Musgrave *Mus* Tristram Cary *Art Dir* Maurice Pelling
● Roland Curram, Bernard Archard, Jean Anderson, Ellen McIntosh (Focus/British Lion)

Brought in in 24 days at a modest $75,000, with entire location shooting and a little known cast, this is quality production. Writer-director Stanley Goulder had documentary experience but this is his first feature work. His screenplay is taut, economic and natural in dialog and his direction is unfussy and alert.

The story, which has a useful reminder to parents and moppets, 'never take sweets from a stranger', concerns a mentally retarded youth who loves kids. Returning from the hospital where he is an out-patient he hands out highly colored barbiturate tablets to youngsters in a cinema matinee queue. End of show finds a number of unconscious children slumped in their seats. All are dangerously ill. Then begins the patient fight for their lives at the local hospital, while the police hunt for the donor of the tablets.

- -

■ SILENT RAGE

1982, 100 MINS, US ◇ ⓥ
Dir Michael Miller *Prod* Anthony B. Unger *Scr* Joseph Fraley *Ph* Robert Jessup, Neil Roach *Ed* Richard C. Meyer *Mus* Peter Bernstein, Mark Goldenberg *Art Dir* Jack Marty
● Chuck Norris, Ron Silver, Steven Keats, Toni Kalem, William Finley, Brian Libby (Unger/Topkick)

Silent Rage seems as if it were made with a demographics sampler entitled '10 Sleazy Ways to Cash in on the Exploitation Market'. The result is a combination horror-kung fu-oater-woman in peril-mad scientist film with more unintentional laughs than possible in the space of 100 minutes.

The scenario goes something like this – a sweaty, crazy young man chops a woman and another man to death. Our hero of the day, Chuck Norris (the sheriff), catches him but the guy is shot by some over-anxious law enforcers.

The run-of-the-mill crime story? Of course, not. One of the hospital surgeons happens to be a mad scientist who has been working on a formula to speed up the human healing process. All he needs is a human guinea pig. Now we have a murderer who is not only crazy but indestructible.

- -

■ SILENT RUNNING

1972, 89 MINS, US ◇ ⓥ
Dir Douglas Trumbull *Prod* Michael Gruskoff *Scr* Deric Washburn, Michael Cimino, Steven Bocho *Ph* Charles F. Wheeler *Ed* Aaron Stell *Mus* Peter Schickele
● Bruce Dern, Cliff Potts, Ron Rifkin, Jesse Vint (Universal)

Silent Running depends on the excellent special effects of debuting director Douglas Trumbull and his team and on the appreciation of a literate but broadly entertaining script. Those being the highlights, they are virtually wiped out by the crucial miscasting of Bruce Dern. As a result, the production lacks much dramatic credibility and often teeters on the edge of the ludicrous.

Dern and three clod companions man a space vehicle in a fleet of airships containing vegetation in case the earth again can support that type of life. But the program is scuttled, all hands are recalled, but Dern decides to mutiny. In the process, he kills his three shipmates and goes deeper into space. His only companions are two small robots, whose life-like qualities are rather touching.

- -

■ SILK STOCKINGS

1957, 117 MINS, US ◇ ⓥ
Dir Rouben Mamoulian *Prod* Arthur Freed *Scr* Leonard Gershe, Leonard Spigelgass *Ph* Robert Bronner *Ed* Harold F. Kress *Mus* Cole Porter *Art Dir* William A. Horning, Randall Duell
● Fred Astaire, Cyd Charisse, Janis Paige, Peter Lorre, Joseph Buloff, Jules Munshin (M-G-M)

Silk Stockings has Fred Astaire and Cyd Charisse, the music of Cole Porter and comes off as a top-grade musical version of Metro's 1939 *Ninotchka*. Adapted from the [1955] Broadway musical adaptation of same tag, film has two new Porter songs and a total of 13 numbers. Astaire enacts an American film producer in Paris who falls for the beautiful Commie when she arrives from Moscow to check on the activities of three Russian commissars.

Rouben Mamoulian in his deft direction maintains a flowing if over-long course. Musical numbers are bright, inserted naturally, and both Astaire and Charisse shine in dancing department, together and singly. Choreography is by Hermes Pan (Astaire numbers) and Eugene Loring (others).

Janis Paige shares top honors with the stars for a knock-'em-dead type of performance, George Tobias has a few good moments as a Commie chief, and commissar trio Peter Lorre, Jules Munshin and Joseph Buloff are immense.

- -

■ SILKWOOD

1983, 128 MINS, US ◇ ⓥ
Dir Mike Nichols *Prod* Mike Nichols, Michael Hausman *Scr* Nora Ephron, Alice Arlen *Ph* Miroslav Ondricek *Ed* Sam O'Steen *Mus* Georges Delerue *Art Dir* Patrizia von Brandenstein
● Meryl Streep, Kurt Russell, Cher, Craig T. Nelson, Diana Scarwid, Fred Ward (ABC)

A very fine biographical drama, *Silkwood* concerns Karen Silkwood, a nuclear materials factory worker who mysteriously died just before she was going to blow the whistle on her company's presumed slipshod methods and cover-ups.

A lowdown, spunky and seemingly uneducated Southern gal whose three kids live elsewhere with their father, Silkwood works long hours at a tedious job which presents the constant threat of radiation contamination.

Her home life is rather more unconventional, as she shares a rundown abode with two coworkers, b.f. Kurt Russell and a lesbian friend, Cher.

The complexion of their domestic life takes a turn when blonde cowgirl beautician Diana Scarwid moves in with Cher, and at work, Silkwood finds herself increasingly at odds with management after she becomes involved

with a union committee fighting decertification of the union at the plant.

Silkwood's death in 1974 was officially ruled an accident, but the story became a cause celebre in the media and among anti-nuke proponents.

- -

■ SILVER BEARS

1978, 113 MINS, US ◇ ⓥ
Dir Ivan Passer *Prod* Alex Winitsky, Arlene Sellers *Scr* Peter Stone *Ph* Anthony Richmond *Ed* Bernard Gribble *Mus* Claude Bolling *Art Dir* Edward Marshall
● Michael Caine, Cybill Shepherd, Louis Jourdan, Stephane Audran, Tom Smothers, David Warner (Columbia)

Director Ivan Passer has assembled a rather talented squad of performers, then marched them through a minefield, losing all hands in an attack on an uncertain objective.

Michael Caine goes to Switzerland to set up a bank for mobster Martin Balsam, with the help of Louis Jourdan running swindle one against them. Caine and Jourdan get involved with Stephane Audran and David Warner's swindle two silver-mine in Iran.

Adapted from Paul E. Erdman's novel about international finance, Peter Stone's script keeps the air filled with multi-million dollar figures, confounded hourly but yielding no interest.

Unceasingly cynical, the film lacks a single sympathetic character worth caring about. Everybody lies; everybody swindles; and all the bad guys – and girl – win in the end.

- -

■ SILVER CHALICE, THE

1954, 142 MINS, US ◇ ⓥ
Dir Victor Saville *Prod* Victor Saville *Scr* Lesser Samuels *Ph* William V. Skall *Ed* George White *Mus* Franz Waxman *Art Dir* Rolf Gerard, Boris Leven
● Virginia Mayo, Pier Angeli, Jack Palance, Paul Newman, Natalie Wood, Joseph Wiseman (Warner)

Like the Thomas B. Costain book, the picture is overdrawn and sometimes tedious, but producer-director Victor Saville still manages to instill interest in what's going on, and even hits a feeling of excitement occasionally.

The picture introduces Newman who handles himself well before the cameras. Helping his pic debut is Pier Angeli, and it is their scenes together that add the warmth to what might otherwise have been a cold spectacle.

The plot portrays the struggle of Christians to save for the future the cup from which Christ drank at the Last Supper. On the side of the Christians is a Greek sculptor, played by Newman, who is fashioning a silver chalice to hold the religious symbol. On the side of evil are the decadent Romans, ruled over by an effete Nero, and Simon, the magician (a real character), played by Jack Palance, who wants to use the destruction of the cup to further his own rise to power.

- -

■ SILVER CITY

1984, 101 MINS, AUSTRALIA ◇ ⓥ
Dir Sophia Turkiewicz *Prod* Joan Long *Scr* Thomas Keneally, Sophia Turkiewicz *Ph* John Seale *Ed* Don Saunders *Mus* William Motzig *Art Dir* Igor Nay
● Gosia Dobrowolska, Ivar Kants, Anna Jemison, Steve Bisley, Debra Lawrance, Ewa Brok (Limelight)

A passionate love story set against a background of post-war European immigration into Australia is the theme of *Silver City*, an extremely handsome production which introduces vibrant new actress Gosia Dobrowolska.

She plays Nina, a young Polish girl who arrives, bereaved and alone, in Australia in 1948 and becomes one of thousands of citizens of so-called Silver City, a migrant camp

S

outside Sydney. There she meets a fellow Pole, Julian, a former law student, and falls in love with him although he's married to one of her best friends.

This is a film for anyone who has ever left the country of their birth to start a new life in a strange land.

The background to this affair is vividly etched in. Director Sophia Turkiewicz, came to Australia from Poland aged three with her mother, which has provided her with rich material for her first feature.

■ SILVER DREAM RACER

1980, 111 MINS, UK ◇ ⓥ

Dir David Wickes   *Prod* Rene Dupont   *Scr* David Wickes   *Ph* Paul Beeson   *Ed* Peter Hollywood   *Mus* David Essex, John Cameron   *Art Dir* Malcolm Middleton

● David Essex, Beau Bridges, Cristina Raines, Harry H. Corbett, Diane Keen, Lee Montague (Rank/Wickes)

It's about motorcycle racing. But among all the biking footage in a yarn about a 'revolutionary' prototype which challenges and, natch, licks all world championship comers, there's not one memorable shot of the machine in action.

That's a big pity, as the model – a genuine prototype built by Britisher Barry Hart – will certainly whet the appetites of two-wheel fans. But the film's action sequences prove generally disappointing.

Plot is routine, but no worse than many, and the acting does favors for the dialog. Popstar David Essex is a natural as the ingenuous-looking Cockney fellow who can turn on a sneer when needed. Beau Bridges is fine as the loud-mouthed American Goliath against whom David pits his derided British mount.

■ SILVER STREAK

1976, 113 MINS, US ◇ ⓥ

Dir Arthur Hiller   *Prod* Thomas L. Miller, Edward K. Milkis   *Scr* Colin Higgins   *Ph* David M. Walsh   *Ed* David Bretherton   *Mus* Henry Mancini   *Art Dir* Alfred Sweeney

● Gene Wilder, Jill Clayburgh, Richard Pryor, Patrick McGoohan, Ned Beatty, Clifton James (20th Century-Fox)

While falling short of its comedy promise (except when Richard Pryor is on the screen), *Silver Streak* is an okay adventure comedy starring Gene Wilder on the lam from crooked art thieves aboard a trans-continental train.

Wilder, mild-mannered book executive, boards a train for a leisurely trip from Los Angeles to Chicago. Jill Clayburgh, in adjoining compartment, works for an art scholar whose research will expose the fakery of Patrick McGoohan, urbane and despicable villain of the George Sanders-Basil Rathbone school.

Only when Pryor enters the film is there some long-overdue snap and zest. Wilder and Pryor are great together.

■ SILVERADO

1985, 132 MINS, US ◇ ⓥ

Dir Lawrence Kasdan   *Prod* Lawrence Kasdan   *Scr* Lawrence Kasdan, Mark Kasdan   *Ph* John Bailey   *Ed* Carol Littleton   *Mus* Bruce Broughton   *Art Dir* Ida Random

● Kevin Kline, Scott Glenn, Kevin Costner, Danny Glover, John Cleese, Rosanna Arquette (Columbia)

Rather than relying on legendary heroes of Westerns past, writer-director Lawrence Kasdan with his brother Mark have used their special talent to create a slew of human scale characters against a dramatic backdrop borrowing from all the conventions of the genre. *Silverado* strikes an uneasy balance between the intimate and naturalistic with concerns that are classical and universal.

Drifters Paden (Kevin Kline) and Emmett (Scott Glenn) join fates in the desert and follow their destiny to Silverado where they tangle with the McKendrick clan. Along the way they meet up with Glenn's gun happy brother Jake (Kevin Costner) who they break from a jail guarded by Sheriff Langston (John Cleese).

Modern element in the stew is introduction of Danny Glover, an itinerant black returning to Silverado to rejoin what's left of his family.

On the other side of the fence is arch villain Cobb, sheriff of Silverado and puppet of the McKendricks. As Cobb, Brian Dennehy is an actor born to be in Westerns, so powerful is his sense of destruction. Other performances, especially Kline and Glenn, are equally strong.

Real rewards of the film are in the visuals and rarely has the West appeared so alive, yet unlike what one carries in one's mind's eye. Ida Random's production design is thoroughly convincing in detail.

■ SIN OF HAROLD DIDDLEBOCK, THE

1947, 90 MINS, US ⓥ

Dir Preston Sturges   *Prod* Preston Sturges   *Scr* Preston Sturges   *Ph* Robert Pittack   *Ed* Tom Neff   *Mus* Werner Heymann   *Art Dir* Robert Usher

● Harold Lloyd, Raymond Walburn, Franklin Pangborn, Margaret Hamilton, Edgar Kennedy (California)

Attired in the same strawhat and black-rimmed specs in his silent flickers, neither Harold Lloyd's person nor his comedy has changed much. As an added lure, director Preston Sturges has incorporated into the first 10 minutes of the film an actual sequence from Lloyd's *The Freshman* which the comedian made in 1923.

Film segues expertly from the *Freshman* footage to the new product, showing Raymond Walburn, as an enthusiastic alumnus now head of a top ad agency, promising Lloyd a job for having won the game. Lloyd takes the job after graduation but is stuck immediately into a minor bookkeeper's niche, where he remains forgotten for 22 years. Walburn finally remembers him long enough to fire him – which is where the fun starts.

Abetted by some excellent dialog from Sturges' pen, Lloyd handles his role in his usual funny fashion. One sequence, in which he dangles from a leash 80 stories above the sidewalk, with the other end of the leash tied to a nervous lion, is standout.

■ SINBAD AND THE EYE OF THE TIGER

1977, 112 MINS, US ◇ ⓥ

Dir Sam Wanamaker   *Prod* Charles H. Schneer, Ray Harryhausen   *Scr* Beverley Cross   *Ph* Ted Moore   *Ed* Roy Watts   *Mus* Roy Budd   *Art Dir* Geoffrey Drake

● Patrick Wayne, Taryn Power, Margaret Whiting, Jane Seymour, Patrick Troughton, Kurt Christian (Columbia/Schneer)

The plot takes Patrick Wayne, as Sinbad, on a quest to free a prince (Damien Thomas) from the spell of evil sorceress Margaret Whiting. Thomas has quite a dilemma, in that he's turned into a baboon and is fast losing all vestiges of human behavior.

Along for the odyssey are a couple of young cuties (Taryn Power and Jane Seymour) who keep their modest demeanor while wearing scanty outfits.

The plot scenes are hammy beyond belief. Whiting is a particular offender with her all-stops-out villainy.

When the fantasy creatures have center stage, the film is enjoyable to watch. Such beasties as skeletons, a giant bee and an outsized walrus, are marvelously vivified by Ray Harryhausen.

Most of the studio work was done in England, with locations in Spain, Malta, and the Mediterranean.

■ SINBAD THE SAILOR

1947, 116 MINS, US ◇ ⓥ

Dir Richard Wallace   *Prod* Stephen Ames   *Scr* John Twist   *Ph* George Barnes   *Ed* Sherman Todd, Frank Doyle   *Mus* Roy Webb   *Art Dir* Albert S. D'Agostino, Carroll Clark

● Douglas Fairbanks Jr, Maureen O'Hara, Walter Slezak, Anthony Quinn, Jane Greer (RKO)

The sterling adventures of Sinbad as a sailing man and as a romancer are garbed in brilliant color in this RKO production.

Cast values match production elegance. Douglas Fairbanks Jr matches do-and-dare antics of his father. He measures up to the flamboyance required to make Sinbad a dashing fictional hero. Maureen O'Hara lends shapely presence as the heroine.

Story concerns Sinbad's mythical eighth adventure wherein he seeks a fabulously rich island and the love of an Arabian Nights beauty. Major production fault is that dialog and main story points are obscure, making intelligent following of plot difficult. Principal opponents to Sinbad's search are Walter Slezak and Anthony Quinn. Former's character is never clearly explained, and latter's role also is obscured in the writing.

■ SINCE YOU WENT AWAY

1944, 158 MINS, US ⓥ

Dir John Cromwell   *Prod* David O. Selznick   *Scr* David O. Selznick   *Ph* Stanley Cortez, Lee Garmes   *Ed* Hal C. Kern   *Mus* Max Steiner, Louis Forbes   *Art Dir* William L. Pereira

● Claudette Colbert, Jennifer Jones, Joseph Cotten, Shirley Temple, Monty Woolley, Robert Walker (United Artists/Selznick)

As David O. Selznick screenplayed his own production, from Margaret Buell Wilder's book, *Since You Went Away* is a heart-warming panorama of human emotions, reflecting the usual wartime frailties of the thoughtless and the chiseler, the confusion and uncertainty of young ideals and young love, all of it projected against a panorama of utterly captivating home love and life in the wholesome American manner.

Claudette Colbert is the attractive, understanding mother of Jennifer Jones, 17, and Shirley Temple, in her earliest teens, all of whom adore their absent husband and father, Timothy, a captain off to the wars. The father is never shown; only his photo in officer's uniform, along with closeups of other domestic memorabilia.

True, Selznick's continuity has given director John Cromwell an episodic script, but it is this narrative form which makes for so much audience-appeal. Each sequence is a closeup, a character study, a self-contained dramalet.
☐ 1944: Best Picture (Nomination)

■ SINFUL DAVEY

1969, 95 MINS, UK ◇

Dir John Huston   *Prod* William N. Graf   *Scr* James R. Webb   *Ph* Freddie Young, Edward Scaife   *Ed* Russel Lloyd   *Mus* Ken Thorne   *Art Dir* Stephen Grimes

● John Hurt, Pamela Franklin, Nigel Davenport, Ronald Fraser, Robert Morley (Mirisch)

Sinful Davey is a bland, lethargic period comedy about a 19th-century teenage highwayman. A competent cast and a good James R. Webb screenplay are shot down by the club-footed, forced direction of John Huston, who seems to think that comedy is chatter, alternating with pratfall running and jumping.

Webb, it is said, discovered the ancient diary of David Haggart, subject of the piece, and the writer has, indeed, fashioned a good episodic story.

John Hurt has the title role, and other principal players include Nigel Davenport, a dedicated cop and Ronald Fraser and Fidelma Murphy, as Hurt's two genial associates in a series of daring robberies.

The script and cast, plus uniformly excellent below-the-line staffers are present, but the project founders on Huston's work.

■ SINGER NOT THE SONG, THE

1961, 132 MINS, UK ◇ ⓥ

Dir Roy Baker *Prod* Roy Baker *Scr* Nigel Balchin *Ph* Otto Heller *Ed* Roger Cherrill *Mus* Philip Green *Art Dir* Alex Vetchinsky

● Dirk Bogarde, John Mills, Mylene Demongeot, Laurence Naismith (Rank)

As a dialectic discussion hinged on the Roman Catholic religion, this can only be accepted as flippant. As a romantic drama, it must be agreed that it is glossy, but overcontrived. Yet, somehow, the thesping of the two principals, John Mills and Dirk Bogarde, prevents the screen version of Audrey Erskine Lindop's novel (shot in Spain) from falling between these two spacious schools.

Mills is a dedicated Roman Catholic priest who comes to the tiny community of Quantana, Mexico, to replace an older priest who is worn out from battling with the murderous, marauding gang of bandits led by Anacleto (Bogarde). To intimidate the newcomer, Bogarde's gang sets out on a series of murders by the alphabetical method.

Priest Mills, resolutely deciding to break Bogarde's power, shows a struggle in which the two gain mutual respect, though their religious opinions clash badly. The unscrupulous, cynical bandit realizes, though in a manner not explained very convincingly, that a local belle (Mylene Demongeot) is in love with the priest and he with her. He uses this knowledge to create a situation that puts the priest in a moral dilemma.

Mills and Bogarde have some excellent acting encounters, though their accents, like those of many others, strike odd notes in the Mexican atmosphere.

■ SINGIN' IN THE RAIN

1952, 102 MINS, US ◇ ⓥ

Dir Gene Kelly, Stanley Donen *Prod* Arthur Freed *Scr* Betty Comden, Adolph Green *Ph* Harold Rosson *Ed* Adrienne Fazan *Mus* Lennie Hayton (dir.) *Art Dir* Cedric Gibbons, Randall Duell

● Gene Kelly, Donald O'Connor, Debbie Reynolds, Jean Hagen, Millard Mitchell, Cyd Charisse (M-G-M)

Musical has pace, humor and good spirits a-plenty, in a breezy, good-natured spoof at the film industry itself. The 1927 era, with advent of the talkies, lends itself to some hilarious slapstick, of which the film takes excellent advantage.

Story has Gene Kelly and Jean Hagen as a team of romantic film favorites of the silents, and the studio's problem of translating their popularity to the talkies because of Hagen's high-pitched, squeaky voice. Problem is complicated further by Kelly falling in love with a nitery chorine (Debbie Reynolds), and Hagen's jealous tantrums and knifings. Donald O'Connor plays the boyhood pal and early-vaude days teammate of Kelly, as well as his present studio mentor.

Kelly's dancing is standout, whether in the 'Singin' in the Rain' and other solos; in the duo dance numbers with O'Connor, such as the vaudeville routine, 'Fit As a Fiddle', or the diction lesson, or in trios with O'Connor and Reynolds as in 'Good Morning'. Reynolds is a pretty, pert minx, with a nice singing voice and fine dancing ability. O'Connor has the film's highspot with a solo number, 'Make 'Em Laugh'. The guy appears to kill himself with his acrobatics and pratfalls over a cluttered studio set.

■ SINGING NUN, THE

1966, 96 MINS, US ◇

Dir Henry Koster *Prod* John Beck, Hayes Goetz *Scr* Sally Benson, John Furia Jr *Ph* Milton Krasner *Ed* Rita Roland *Mus* Harry Sukman *Art Dir* George W. Doris, Urie McCleary

● Debbie Reynolds, Ricardo Montalban, Greer Garson, Agnes Moorehead, Chad Everett, Katharine Ross (M-G-M)

The Singing Nun, patently designed to cash in on the story of the Belgian nun Soeur Sourire and her song 'Dominique', carries an expectancy not always realized. Fictionized approach to the truelife character – necessitated by agreement with Catholic church authorities not to make pictures autobiographical – resultantly loses in the transition, and while there are engaging musical interludes what emerges is slight and frequently slow-moving.

The production unfolds mostly in the small Samaritan House, situated in a slum section of Brussels, where the young Dominican nun carries on her work with children and study preparatory to an African missionary assignment. In this role, Debbie Reynolds expertly warbles a dozen numbers to her own guitar accompaniment, some nine of the songs composed by the Belgian sister.

■ SINK THE BISMARCK!

1960, 97 MINS, UK

Dir Lewis Gilbert *Prod* John Brabourne *Scr* Edmund H. North *Ph* Christopher Challis *Ed* Peter Hunt *Mus* Clifton Parker *Art Dir* Arthur Lawson

● Kenneth More, Dana Wynter, Carl Mohner, Laurence Naismith, Geoffrey Keen, Michael Hordern (20th Century-Fox)

Sink The Bismarck! is a first-rate film re-creation of a thrilling historical event. The screenplay is taken from a book by C. S. Forester. It concentrates almost entirely on three playing areas. These are the subterranean London headquarters of the British admiralty, where the battle is plotted and directed; aboard the Germans' 'unsinkable' battleship, the *Bismarck;* and on board the various British vessels called into pursuit of the Nazi raider.

The film opens with the chilling news that the *Bismarck* has escaped the British naval blockade and is loose in the North Atlantic. After it sinks the *Hood*, considered the greatest battleship in the world, it appears nothing can stop it from rendezvousing with its sister ships holed up at Brest.

Some of the dialog is a little high-flown, with the British at times too aware of the historical importance of the event. The Germans, on the other hand, tend to be Nazi caricatures.

Kenneth More plays the British captain who directs the battle to catch the *Bismarck* with his customary and effective taciturnity. Dana Wynter is a helpful note as the WREN officer who is his aide. Carl Mohner manages some character as the German officer commanding the Bismarck.

■ SISTERS

1973, 92 MINS, US ◇ ⓥ

Dir Brian De Palma *Prod* Edward R. Pressman *Scr* Brian De Palma, Louisa Rose *Ph* Gregory Sandor *Ed* Paul Hirsch *Mus* Bernard Herrmann *Art Dir* Gary Weist

● Margot Kidder, Jennifer Salt, Charles Durning, Bill Finley, Lisle Wilson, Bernard Hughes (American International)

Sisters is a good psychological murder melodrama, starring Margot Kidder as the schizoid half of Siamese twins, and Jennifer Salt as a news hen driven to terror in her investigation of a bloody murder. Brian De Palma's direction emphasizes exploitation values which do not fully mask script weakness.

Kidder, paired with Lisle Wilson on a TV game show (neatly satirized in opening scene), later invites him over for the night. Next morning, in a nervous state and after a voiceover dialog in French with another person never seen, Kidder slashes Wilson with a butcher knife.

Salt views the murdered man's agonies from a nearby window, and doggedly pursues the case despite incredulity of detective Dolph Sweet but with assistance of private eye Charles Durning.

■ SISTERS, THE

1938, 95 MINS, US

Dir Anatole Litvak *Prod* Anatole Litvak *Scr* Milton Krims *Ph* Tony Gaudio *Ed* Warren Low *Mus* Max Steiner *Art Dir* Carl Jules Weyl

● Errol Flynn, Bette Davis, Anita Louise, Ian Hunter, Donald Crisp, Beulah Bondi (Warner)

Adapted from Myron Brinig's bestseller, this film has the sweep of a virtual cavalcade of early 20th-century American history. Plot starts out with three sisters, daughters of a small Montana town druggist, getting ready for a dance, staged to hear returns on the national election that swept Roosevelt into a second term as president. It closes four years later as the same family prepares again for another election ball, this time to hail Taft as new president.

Totally different marriages of the three girls are clearly set out, with highlights in their wedded lives taking the happy sisters often close to the brink of matrimonial smashup but always managing to surmount trying difficulties.

Most of the interest centres on Louise (Bette Davis) who elopes with Frank Medlin (Errol Flynn), sports scribe. This case of love-at-first sight works out satisfactorily until the newspaperman, hampered by domestic ties and unwillingness to buckle down as an author, takes to heavy imbibing.

Davis turns in one of her most scintillating performances. Flynn's happy-go-lucky reporter is a vivid portrayal although his slight English accent seems incongruous. Anita Louise makes a delightful flirty daughter who finally weds the elderly wealthy man in her commmunity while Jane Bryan is adequate as the more conservative sister who decides that safety in matrimony is represented by the dull town banker's son.

■ SITTING DUCKS

1979, 90 MINS, US ◇ ⓥ

Dir Henry Jaglom *Prod* Meira Attia Dor *Scr* Henry Jaglom *Ph* Paul Glickman *Mus* Richard Romanus

● Michael Emil, Zack Norman, Patrice Townsend, Richard Romanus, Irene Forrest, Henry Jaglom (Sunny Side Up)

Rather loopy story serves basically to provide a framework for several fabulous character riffs and to give a little momentum to any number of enjoyable crazy situations.

Two small-time hustlers make off with loot siphoned off from a gambling syndicate for which one works, and majority of the running time is devoted to their haphazard drive down the eastern seaboard to reach a plane that will carry them to a life of kings in Central America.

Along the way, hyped-up pair, acted in a marvel of improvisational style by Michael Emil and Zack Norman, meet up with two young ladies who hitch on for the wild ride.

Interplay among the four constitutes the meat of the film, and every line and every scene springs spontaneously off the screen as if they're being played for the first time.

• •

■ SITTING PRETTY

1933, 80 MINS, US
Dir Harry Joe Brown   *Prod* Charles R. Rogers
Scr Jack McGowan, S. J. Perelman, Lou Breslow
Ph Milton Krasner
● Jack Oakie, Jack Haley, Ginger Rogers, Thelma Todd, Gregory Ratoff, Lew Cody (Paramount)

Sitting Pretty's assets are a youthful trio of leads, some fast dialog, a swell score and direction that hits a pace from the start and sustains it to the finish.

The good old triangle provides a foundation for the action [from a story suggested by Nina Wilcox Putnam]. But that foundation is neatly upholstered by the cast, the music, the girls and the staging. Story takes Jack Oakie and Jack Haley to Hollywood as a songwriting team. Back in New York they're told to go west by Mack Gordon, who plays a music publisher in the film and who, with his partner Harry Revel, wrote the score. Ginger Rogers slips in as a kindhearted lunch-wagon proprietress whom the boys happen to touch while hitch-hiking westward.

For Oakie it's quite familiar ground; again he's the fresh guy who goes swell-headed from success, then becomes a nice but deflated fellow at the finish. For Haley this is his first really important screen assignment. Rogers hasn't an opportunity to get a good lick at the ball, being hemmed in by story limitations, but she looks good.

Gregory Ratoff plays a Hollywood agent, and through this dialectician and Lew Cody, as a picture producer, the dialog gets in some satirical inside studio stuff that's broad enough to be understood by almost anybody.

• •

■ SITTING TARGET

1972, 93 MINS, UK ◇
Dir Douglas Hickox   *Prod* Barry Kulick   *Scr* Alexander Jacobs   *Ph* Ted Scaife   *Ed* John Glen   *Mus* Stanley Myers   *Art Dir* Jonathan Barry
● Oliver Reed, Jill St John, Ian McShane, Edward Woodward, Frank Finlay, Freddie Jones (M-G-M)

Sitting Target is a picture of brutish violence. Its story of a British prison break by a hardened, jealousy-ridden convict to kill the wife he believes unfaithful has been recounted with no holds barred.

The screenplay [from a novel by Laurence Henderson] sometimes is difficult to follow, but Douglas Hickox' tense direction keeps movement at top speed. Obsession of con to get to his wife, who has revealed she is pregnant and wants a divorce, is a motivating theme – built with growing suspense. Jill St John becomes the sitting target for Oliver Reed as the convicted murderer who smashes his way to freedom and stalks his prey.

Actual scenes lensed in two Irish prisons give film a grimly authentic atmosphere and the escape of Reed and two other cons is spectacularly depicted.

• •

■ 633 SQUADRON

1964, 94 MINS, UK
Dir Walter Grauman   *Prod* Cecil F. Ford   *Scr* James Clavell, Howard Koch   *Ph* Edward Scaife, John Wilcox   *Ed* Bert Bates   *Mus* Ron Goodwin
Art Dir Michael Stringer
● Cliff Robertson, George Chakiris, Maria Perschy, Harry Andrews, Donald Houston, Michael Goodliffe (United Artists)

Cinematically, *633 Squadron* is a spectacular achievement, a technically explosive depiction of an RAF unit's successful but costly mission to demolish an almost impregnable

Nazi rocket fuel installation in Norway. The production, filmed in its entirety in England, contains some rip-roaring aerial action. Unfortunately, this technical prowess is not matched by the drama it adorns.

The characters of the scenario from the novel by Frederick E. Smith are somewhat shallowly drawn and fall into rather familiar war story molds and behavior patterns.

Cliff Robertson skillfully rattles off the leading assignment, that of a Yank wing commander whose squadron is chosen for the dangerous mission. George Chakiris is adequate though miscast and rather colorless as a Norwegian resistance leader who is to pave the way for the vital bombing raid. Maria Perschy supplies decorative romantic interest as Chakiris' sister and eventually Robertson's girl.

• •

■ SIX WEEKS

1982, 107 MINS, US ◇ ▼
Dir Tony Bill   *Prod* Peter Guber, Jon Peters   *Scr* David Seltzer   *Ph* Michael D. Margulies   *Ed* Stu Linder   *Mus* Dudley Moore   *Art Dir* Hilyard Brown
● Dudley Moore, Mary Tyler Moore, Katherine Healy, Shannon Wilcox, Bill Calvert, Joe Regalbuto (PolyGram/Universal)

A sort of moppet *Love Story*, *Six Weeks* is an unabashed tearjerker aimed directly at the hearts of the mass audience.

Story [from the novel by Fred Mustard Stewart] for the most part takes place in the rarified, monied atmosphere of upper-class LA and NY as leukemia-stricken Katherine Healy is the 12-year-old daughter of cosmetics tycoon Mary Tyler Moore and has admittedly had all the advantages in life, except for a father.

Daddy figure comes along in the person of California Congressional candidate Dudley Moore. Healy takes an immediate shine to the likable politician, so much so that she insists upon working for his campaign.

In the middle of his campaign, Moore chucks everything for a whirlwind weekend in Gotham, where he 'miraculously' manages to get ballet-addict Healy cast in a children's production of *The Nutcracker*.

Such material could have been insufferable, but scripter David Seltzer and Tony Bill, displaying growing assurance in his second directorial outing, have generally stayed on the tightrope between shameless emotional manipulation and undue restraint.

• •

■ SIXTEEN CANDLES

1984, 93 MINS, US ◇ ▼
Dir John Hughes   *Prod* Hilton A. Green   *Scr* John Hughes   *Ph* Bobby Byrne   *Ed* Edward Warschilka   *Mus* Ira Newborn   *Art Dir* John W. Corso
● Molly Ringwald, Anthony Michael Hall, Michael Schoeffling, Paul Dooley, Justin Henry, Liane Curtis (Universal)

Cream puff of a teen comedy about the miseries of a girl turning 16 turns out to be an amiable, rather goldilocked film. Tone of the film, despite some raw language, brief nudity in the shower and carnage at a high school party, actually suggests the middle America of a Norman Rockwell *Saturday Evening Post* cover.

For the girls, there's Molly Ringwald as the film's angst-ridden centerpiece. Ringwald is engaging and credible. For the boys, there's a bright, funny performance by Anthony Michael Hall, a hip freshman wimp called Ted the Geek. There's also a darkly handsome high school heartbreak kid (Michael Schoeffling), a merciful brisk pace, some quick humor (visual and verbal), and a solid music track.

• •

■ SIXTH AND MAIN

1977, 103 MINS, US ◇
Dir Christopher Cain   *Prod* Christopher Cain
Scr Christopher Cain   *Ph* Hilary John Brown   *Ed* Ken Johnson   *Mus* Bob Summers
● Leslie Nielsen, Roddy McDowall, Beverly Garland, Leo Penn, Joe Maross, Bard Stevens (National Cinema)

Sixth and Main is a very professionally made lowbudgeter which succeeds to a great extent in exploring the emotions underneath the skin of the cliche skid row character. Christopher Cain wrote, produced and directed the pic, starring Leslie Nielsen as a talented dropout and Roddy McDowall as a crippled street person.

The film is earthy without being vulgar, though script at times veers too far into the preachy and meller realm.

Plot takes Beverly Garland, a slumming literary type, to downtown LA to absorb atmosphere for a book. She stumbles onto Nielsen, who hardly ever speaks but lives in a junked trailer full of promising manuscripts. With help from literary critic Joe Maross, she tries to promote Nielsen as a new find.

• •

■ SKIN DEEP

1978, 103 MINS, NEW ZEALAND ◇ ▼
Dir Geoff Steven   *Prod* John Maynard   *Scr* Piers Davies, Roger Horrocks, Geoff Steven   *Ph* Leon Narby
● Jim Macfarlane, Ken Blackburn, Alan Jervis, Grant Tilly, Bill Johnson, Arthur Wright (Phase Three)

Skin Deep, New Zealand's long-awaited breakthrough film, is a soberly-paced but absorbing tale of a small country town which is making its bid, via a publicity campaign, to attract tourists and industry.

When a masseuse is imported from the nearest big city and Vic's Gym becomes a massage parlor and sauna the inevitable happens. Many local males are anxious to try the parlor-style sex that previously they had only read about, and the respectable matrons pressure the police to shutter the den of vice.

An excellent script and three-dimensional characters flesh out this skeleton. Central to the theme and payoff is Sandra Ray (Deryn Cooper), the masseuse who, though she still emits plenty of erotic voltage, has had enough of the sex side of the business.

Leading the parade of straying husbands on the prowl for parlor extras is Bob Warner, (Ken Blackburn) chairman of the fund-raising group, the town's leading business man and the first to run for cover when the squeeze comes on the massage establishment.

• •

■ SKIN DEEP

1989, 101 MINS, US ◇ ▼
Dir Blake Edwards   *Prod* Tony Adams   *Scr* Blake Edwards   *Ph* Isidore Mankofsky   *Ed* Robert Pergament   *Mus* Ivan Neville, Don Grady   *Art Dir* Rodger Maus
● John Ritter, Vincent Gardenia, Alyson Reed, Joel Brooks, Julianne Phillips, Raye Hollit (Morgan Creek/BECO)

Blake Edwards' *Skin Deep* finds the director centering again on the trials and tribulations of his favourite kind of character – the charming, womanizing sot. Fortunately, he freshens up his trademark formula by satirizing the most contemporary of current social practices: safe sex.

John Ritter is a dissipated writer with writer's block who is always to be found with a drink in his hand and an eye on a potential sexual conquest.

Ritter is married to a pretty (and pretty dull) newscaster (Alyson Reed) who is smart enough, however, to boot her husband out when she finds him in bed with her hairdresser (Julianne Phillips).

■ SKIP TRACER

1977, 93 MINS, CANADA
Dir Zale Dalen   *Prod* Laara Dalen   *Ph* Ron Oreiux
● David Petersen (Highlights/CFDC)

Skip Tracer, as its title implies, is an account of the methods of persons employed to recover automobiles, television sets, furniture or whatever on which the time-purchase buyers have defaulted.

Film emerges as one of the best ever turned out in British Columbia, though none of the players are known and all were recruited from Vancouver legit stage troupes. Film was made on a low budget of $145,000.

David Petersen, the central figure, the poker-faced, epitome of a hardhearted, alibi-contemptuous sleuth. Supporting players also believable.

There is a slow pace and a lack of action, but the film involves the viewer.

■ SKIPPY

1931, 85 MINS, US
Dir Norman Taurog   *Scr* Joseph L. Mankiewicz, Norman McLeod, Don Marquis
● Jackie Cooper, Robert Coogan, Mitzi Green, Jackie Searl, Willard Robertson, Enid Bennett (Paramount)

All credit to the kid players, director Norman Taurog, and the adapters for taking Percy Crosby's newspaper comic strip [co-written with Sam Mintz] and making it readable and moving in scenario form.

When Skippy (Jackie Cooper) is so sorely depressed over the death of his poor kid-pal's dog, he turns down supper and goes up to his bed to cry. The two kids had tried so hard to dig up the coin for his release from the moronic dogcatcher's pound.

To get the $3 for the license they tried everything from staging a show and running out on the musicians after promoting a buck from Mitzi Green to let her play the lead, to selling lemonade for a cent a drink.

When Skippy's father gives him the promised bike to ease his sorrow, Skippy trades it for Mitzi's dog. Sooky (Robert Coogan) already had gotten a new mutt meanwhile, making it a bad deal for Skippy, but Skippy's father makes the ending happy.

Cooper's playing could not be improved upon. He does everything well, never camera-conscious and never suggesting it's only a picture. The small and young Coogan boy is cute in every sense. His voice jibes with his looks and manner so well it makes him doubly cute. In contributing some valuable 'heavy' aid to this talker, Jackie Searl plays his boyish assignment as well as John Barrymore ever played a lover.

□ 1930/31: Best Picture (Nomination)

■ SKY RIDERS

1976, 91 MINS, US ◇ Ⓥ
Dir Douglas Hickox   *Prod* Terry Morse Jr   *Scr* Jack DeWitt, Stanley Mann, Garry Michael White
Ph Ousama Rawi   *Ed* Malcolm Cooke   *Mus* Lalo Schifrin   *Art Dir* Terry Ackland-Snow
● James Coburn, Susannah York, Robert Culp, Charles Aznavour, Werner Pochath, Zou Zou (20th Century-Fox)

Hang gliding stunts provide most of the interest in *Sky Riders* filmed in Greece. The political terrorism story line is a familiar one and the screenplay is synthetic formula stuff, but the stunt work is good.

Simple plot has footloose pilot James Coburn masterminding the rescue of Susannah York and her two children after bungling police operation led by Charles Aznavour doesn't produce results.

The film provoked an international incident when a Greek electrician died in an explosion accident. Ironically, no one was seriously injured in the aerial scenes. Producer Terry Morse Jr was arrested, exec producer Sandy Howard was detained in Greece for several weeks, and a $250,000 out-of-court settlement was made.

■ SKY WEST AND CROOKED

1966, 102 MINS, UK ◇ Ⓥ
Dir John Mills   *Prod* Jack Hanbury   *Scr* Mary Hayley Bell, John Prebble   *Ph* Arthur Ibbetson   *Ed* Gordon Hales   *Mus* Malcolm Arnold   *Art Dir* Carmen Dillon
● Hayley Mills, Ian McShane, Laurence Naismith, Geoffrey Bayldon, Annette Crosbie, Norman Bird (Rank)

It's a family affair with Hayley Mills starring, poppa John Mills doing his first directorial stint and his wife Mary (who writes professionally as Mary Hayley Bell), sharing the screenplay with John Prebble from her own story.

Hayley Mills portrays a village girl who is a misfit because of simplicity, the result of an accident which resulted in the death of her boy playmate and her own wounding.

The adults around the village tolerantly regard her as slightly idiotic, with her morbid obsession with death which causes her to be at her happiest when playing in the local graveyard and in burying dead pets in consecrated ground.

This naive yarn is rescued from bathos by the evident sincerity of both star and director and by a very convincing portrayal of village life, highlighted by some excellent photography by Arthur Ibbetson. John Mills has played safe in his first directing experiment and the result, while often stodgy, suggests that he knows his way around a directorial chair.

■ SKYJACKED

1972, 100 MINS, US ◇
Dir John Guillermin   *Prod* Walter Seltzer   *Scr* Stanley R. Greenberg   *Ph* Harry Stradling Jr   *Ed* Robert Swink   *Mus* Perry Botkin Jr   *Art Dir* Edward C. Carfagno
● Charlton Heston, Yvette Mimieux, James Brolin, Claude Akins, Jeanne Crain, Susan Dey (M-G-M)

Charlton Heston and Yvette Mimieux star as pilot and stewardess respectively of a jetliner seized by James Brolin. John Guillermin's fastpaced direction makes the most of a large group of top performers.

Stanley R. Greenberg's adaptation of David Harper's novel, *Hijacked*, establishes early and sustains throughout the diverse personal interactions of literally dozens of characters. The dramatic device of trapping a motley group is a venerable but effective blue-print, herein made all the more compelling by a contemporary social phenomenon.

Heston is a most effective leader as the plane captain suddenly faced with a lipstick-scrawled demand for a course change to Anchorage, Alaska, where Claude Akins as a ground controller heightens the suspense of a delicate landing maneuver.

■ SLAM DANCE

1987, 99 MINS, US/UK ◇ Ⓥ
Dir Wayne Wang   *Prod* Rupert Harvey, Barry Opper   *Scr* Don Opper   *Ph* Amir Mokri   *Ed* Lee Percy   *Mus* Mitchell Froom   *Art Dir* Eugenio Zanetti
● Tom Hulce, Mary Elizabeth Mastrantonio, Virginia Madsen, Millie Perkins, Adam Ant, Harry Dean Stanton (Island/Zenith/Sho)

Slam Dance is like junk food. It's brightly packaged, looks good and satisfies the hunger for entertainment, but it isn't terribly nourishing or well-made.

Tom Hulce is underground cartoonist C.C. Drood, a man whose life has come apart cheerfully at the seams. He's separated from his wife (Mary Elizabeth Mastrantonio) and daughter (Judith Barsi), though he still imagines them back together as a family.

Drood's the kind of man who never lets a little thing like marriage stand in the way of a good time or a hot romance with the beautiful and mysterious Yolande (Virginia Madsen). Only one day Yolande turns up dead and Drood's the prime suspect.

Mastrantonio is lovely as always, but without direction. Madsen fares even worse and has virtually nothing to do but look glamorous in a few scenes.

Adam Ant decorates the screen as Drood's two-timing buddy, but basically he's just along for the ride. What really holds the film together is Hulce's loosey-goosey performance which sets the tempo for the action.

■ SLAP SHOT

1977, 123 MINS, US ◇ Ⓥ
Dir George Roy Hill   *Prod* Robert J. Wunsch, Stephen Friedman   *Scr* Nancy Dowd   *Ph* Victor Kemper   *Ed* Dede Allen   *Mus* Elmer Bernstein   *Art Dir* Henry Bumstead
● Paul Newman, Strother Martin, Michael Ontkean, Jennifer Warren, Lindsay Crouse, Jerry Houser (Universal)

Like the character played by Paul Newman in *Slap Shot*, director George Roy Hill is ambivalent on the subject of violence in professional ice hockey. Half the time Hill invites the audience to get off on the mayhem, the other half of the time he decries it.

Screenwriter Nancy Dowd, who drew on the experiences of her hockey-playing brother Ned Dowd (pic's tech advisor and a bit player), had the originality to deal with an offbeat milieu that has been rarely treated by American films.

What Dowd seems to have had in mind was a satire of American rowdyism, as brought out in the adolescent antics of this sleazy minor league Pennsylvania hockey team, of which Newman is player-coach.

Interspersed with the roughhouse rink action are scenes delineating the confused sexual liaisons of Newman and the others.

■ SLAUGHTER ON TENTH AVENUE

1957, 103 MINS, US
Dir Arnold Laven   *Prod* Albert Zugsmith   *Scr* Lawrence Roman   *Ph* Fred Jackman   *Ed* Russell F. Schoengarth   *Mus* Herschel Burke Gilbert (arr.)   *Art Dir* Alexander Golitzen, Robert E. Smith
● Richard Egan, Jan Sterling, Dan Duryea, Julie Adams, Walter Matthau, Charles McGraw (Universal)

Slaughter on Tenth Avenue, the title of Richard Rodgers' ballet music from *On Your Toes*, is effectively employed for a hard-hitting and commendable film about racketeering on the New York waterfront. The picture is adapted from a book entitled *The Man Who Rocked the Boat* by William J. Keating and Richard Carter.

Since Keating was a NY assistant district attorney whose true-life experiences with waterfront gangs are recorded in the book, the film has a quiet, documentary flavor and contains a minimum of the false heroics that usually appear in pictures of this type.

The story presents Richard Egan as Keating, a young assistant DA who has been assigned to a shooting case stemming from waterfront conflicts. Mickey Shaughnessy, an honest longshoreman, is shot because of his efforts to eliminate the gangster elements from the docks. Shaughnessy, his wife (Jan Sterling) and his supporters at first follow the underworld code of not revealing the identity of the triggermen. However, Keating is persistent.

Egan is convincing as the at-first-wide-eyed and then tough assistant DA from the Pennsylvania coal country. Sterling is excellent as Shaughnessy's tough yet tender and understanding wife.

■ **SLAUGHTERHOUSE-FIVE**

1972, 104 MINS, US ◇ ▽
Dir George Roy Hill   *Prod* Paul Monash   *Scr* Stephen Geller   *Ph* Miroslav Ondricek   *Ed* Dede Allen   *Mus* Glenn Gould   *Art Dir* Alexander Golitzen, George Webb
● Michael Sacks, Ron Leibman, Eugene Roche, Sharon Gans, Valerie Perrine, Roberts Blossom (Universal/Vanadas)

Slaughterhouse-Five is a mechanically slick, dramatically sterile commentary about World War II and afterward, as seen through the eyes of a boob Everyman. Director George Roy Hill's arch achievement emphasizes the diffused cant to the detriment of characterizations, which are stiff, unsympathetic and skin-deep.

Stephen Geller's adaptation of Kurt Vonnegut Jr's novel *Slaughterhouse-Five or The Children's Crusade* is in an academic sense fluid and lucid. Michael Sacks in his screen debut plays Billy Pilgrim, the luckless loser who always seems to be in the wrong place at the wrong time.

The story jumps around from its beginning in World War II where as a dumb draftee Pilgrim becomes a prisoner of war in Germany.

In the postwar period, Pilgrim moves into the orbits of overweight wife and predictable offspring.

■ **SLEEPER**

1973, 88 MINS, US ◇ ▽
Dir Woody Allen   *Prod* Jack Grossberg   *Scr* Woody Allen, Marshall Brickman   *Ph* David M. Walsh   *Ed* Ralph Rosenbloom   *Art Dir* Dale Hennesy
● Woody Allen, Diane Keaton, John Beck, Mary Gregory, Don Keefer, Don McLiam (United Artists/Rollins-Joffe)

Woody Allen's *Sleeper*, is a nutty futuristic comedy, with Allen brought back to life 200 years hence to find himself a wanted man in a totally regulated society. Diane Keaton again plays his foil, and both are hilarious. The Dixieland music score [played by Allen with the Preservation Hall Jazz Band and New Orleans Funeral & Ragtime Orchestrà] is just one more delightful non sequitur.

Story opens with Bartlett Robinson and Mary Gregory, two underground scientists, restoring Allen to life from a two-century deep freeze after sudden death from a minor operation. Allen is hunted as an alien. In the course of avoiding capture he becomes first a robot servant to Keaton, later her captor, then rescuer, finally her lover in a fadeout clinch.

The film is loaded with throwaway literacy and broad slapstick, and while it fumbles the end, the parade of verbal and visual amusement is pleasant as long as it lasts.

The star teaming resembles, on a much more advanced basis, the Bob Hope pix of the 1940s in which he starred with some gorgeous leading women in a series of improbable but delightful escapades.

■ **SLEEPING BEAUTY**

1959, 75 MINS, US ◇ ▽
Dir Clyde Geronimi   *Prod* Walt Disney   *Scr* Erdman Penner   *Ed* Roy M. Brewer Jr, Donald Halliday   *Mus* George Bruns (adapt.)
● (Walt Disney)

Sleeping Beauty, adapted from the Charles Perrault version of the fairy tale (and reportedly costing $6 million), is no surprise in its familiar outlines. It's the story of Princess Aur-

ora, who is put under a spell at birth by the bad fairy, Maleficent. She is to prick her finger on a spinning wheel and die before she grows up. But the good fairies, Flora, Fauna and Merryweather, are able to amend the curse. The princess shall not die, but shall fall into a deep sleep. She will be awakened by her true love, Prince Philip.

Mary Costa's rich and expressive voice for the title character gives substance and strength to it. The music is an adaptation of Tchaikovsky's *Sleeping Beauty* ballet, and it is music – where adapted for song – that requires something more than just a pleasant voice. Bill Shirley, as the prince, contributes some good vocal work. His cartoon character is considerably more masculine than Disney heroes usually are.

Some of the best parts of the picture are those dealing with the three good fairies, spoken and sung by Verna Felton, Barbara Jo Allen and Barbara Luddy.

The picture was shot in Technirama and Technicolor, and then, when completed, printed for 70mm on special printer lenses developed for Disney by Panavision. Disney gives credit to more than 70 contributors on *Sleeping Beauty*. Clyde Geronimi was supervising director, and Eric Larson, Wolfgang Reitherman and Les Clark, the sequence directors.

■ **SLEEPING CITY, THE**

1950, 85 MINS, US
Dir George Sherman   *Prod* Leonard Goldstein   *Scr* Jo Eisinger   *Ph* William Miller   *Ed* Frank Gross   *Mus* Frank Skinner
● Richard Conte, Coleen Gray, Richard Taber, Peggy Dow, Alex Nicol (Universal)

The production, storied in the corridors of NY's Bellevue hospital – and actually filmed at Bellevue – recruited a New York stage cast in the main to back up the stars, Richard Conte and Coleen Gray, in telling a yarn of intrigue and murder. Only, as Conte points up in a foreword, none of these actually happened at Bellevue.

Sleeping City tells of two deaths in which the hospital is involved. Both victims are interns. Both, because of meagre wages that all interns receive, are forced to steal narcotics from the hospital stocks and sell them to pay off gambling debts. Both have become linked with an unknown bookmaker. Conte plays a member of the police confidential squad who is planted in the hospital as an intern to uncover the mystery.

Conte gives his usually plausible performance. Gray looks attractive as the nurse, though her characterization doesn't call for much thesping ability.

■ **SLEEPING DOGS**

1977, 107 MINS, NEW ZEALAND ◇ ▽
Dir Roger Donaldson   *Prod* Roger Donaldson   *Scr* Ian Mune, Arthur Baysting   *Ph* Michael Sarasin   *Ed* Ian John   *Mus* Murray Grindlay
● Sam Neill, Bernard Kearns, Nevan Rowe, Ian Mune, Ian Watkin, Don Selwyn (Aardvark)

Sleeping Dogs has sharp directional flair evident, particularly in the action segments, taut performances by the large cast and a handsome technical gloss in all departments.

When the pictures are left to tell the story they do it with great visual impact. The script is less successful.

The story is a political thriller [from the novel *Smith's Dream* by Karl Stead], set in New Zealand of the near future, and sees the small democracy taken over by the rightist party in power, via rigged shooting at a street demonstration. Overnight a police state is set up, and a counter-revolutionary force of freedom-fighters starts hitting back.

As Smith, Sam Neill is natural. He projects the right intensity for a man caught up in an Orwellian nightmare.

■ **SLEEPING WITH THE ENEMY**

1991, 98 MINS, US ◇ ▽
Dir Joseph Ruben   *Prod* Leonard Goldberg   *Scr* Ronald Bass   *Ph* John W. Lindley   *Ed* George Bowers   *Mus* Jerry Goldsmith   *Art Dir* Doug Kraner
● Julia Roberts, Patrick Bergin, Kevin Anderson, Elizabeth Lawrence (20th Century-Fox)

In *Sleeping with the Enemy*, a chilling look at marital abuse gives way to a streamlined thriller [from the novel by Nancy Price] delivering mucho sympathy for imperiled heroine Julia Roberts and screams aplenty as she's stalked by her maniacal husband.

Laura (Roberts) appears to be a perfect doll wife dwelling in an isolated Cape Cod beach manse with successful financial consultant Martin (Patrick Bergin). In fact, he's an overbearing control freak.

She's actually been plotting her escape for a long time. One night she gets her chance, slipping off a sailboat during a storm and swimming ashore while her husband believes she's drowned.

But Martin comes up with enough peculiar clues to believe he's been had. Soon after Laura, who's renamed herself Sara Wates, is ensconced in an idyllic Iowa college town and forging a friendship with a sweet-natured drama teacher (Kevin Anderson), the menacing Martin is on the trail.

Ironically, it's Laura's poor, blind, stroke-ridden mother (Elizabeth Lawrence) who points Martin toward her door, and once there in indulges in some unique forms of fetishistic terrorism.

Roberts is terrific in a layered part. Anderson brings an edge to the nice-guy-next-door role, and the dark, dashing Bergin is chillingly twisted.

■ **SLENDER THREAD, THE**

1965, 98 MINS, US
Dir Sydney Pollack   *Prod* Stephen Alexander   *Scr* Stirling Silliphant   *Ph* Loyal Griggs   *Ed* Thomas Stanford   *Mus* Quincy Jones   *Art Dir* Hal Pereira, Jack Poplin
● Sidney Poitier, Anne Bancroft, Telly Savalas, Steven Hill, Edward Asner, Indus Arthur (Athene/Paramount)

The Slender Thread, suggested by a 29 May 1964 *Life* magazine article by Shana Alexander (wife of producer) of an actual occurrence, is supercharged with emotion and dramatic overtones. As a showy vehicle for talents of Sidney Poitier and Anne Bancroft, the production offers mounting tension, but good as the picture is it could have been improved through more lucid writing.

Story is of a distraught woman who has taken an overdose of barbiturates and phones a clinic. Film takes its title from the telephone line which suddenly becomes a slender thread by means of which Poitier, a college student volunteer who answers femme's call, must try to save her life without breaking the connection.

Poitier who remains on the telephone almost the entire unreeling of picture, delivers a compelling performance, matched by Bancroft as the tortured wife and mother who attempts suicide when she sees her marriage of 12 years going down the drain.

Film is kept on a realistic level. The two stars never meet, their sole contact strictly telephonic.

■ **SLEUTH**

1973, 138 MINS, UK ◇ ▽
Dir Joseph L. Mankiewicz   *Prod* Morton Gottlieb   *Scr* Anthony Shaffer   *Ph* Oswald Morris   *Ed* Richard Marden   *Mus* John Addison   *Art Dir* Ken Adam

● Laurence Olivier, Michael Caine (Palomar/20th Century Fox)

Joseph L. Mankiewicz' film version of *Sleuth* is terrific. Anthony Shaffer's topnotch screenplay of his legit hit provides Laurence Olivier and especially Michael Caine with two of their best roles.

Olivier is outstanding as the famed mystery novelist and society figure who is galled at the prospect of losing his wife to Caine. Latter is sensational as the lower-class tradesman (hairdresser) who eventually proves himself worthy of playing the game of cat-and-mouse with which Olivier seeks to avenge his honor.

Ken Adam's outstanding production design, replete with the automated gadgetry with which Olivier's character enjoys his private games, contributes mightily to the overall achievement.

● ●

■ **SLIPPER AND THE ROSE, THE THE STORY OF CINDERELLA**

1976, 146 MINS, UK ◇ ⑫

Dir Bryan Forbes *Prod* Stuart Lyons *Scr* Bryan Forbes, Richard M. Sherman, Robert B. Sherman *Ph* Tony Imi *Ed* Timothy Gee *Mus* Richard M. Sherman, Robert B. Sherman *Art Dir* Raymond Simm
● Richard Chamberlain, Gemma Craven, Annette Crosbie, Edith Evans, Christopher Gable, Michael Hordern (Paradine)

What script has managed to do so surprisingly well is first of all to modernize the classic Cinderella tale, making it entertaining and (almost) believable for adults while preserving basic pattern and texture of the original for the youngsters.

Richard Chamberlain makes a believable, feet-on-the-ground Prince, Gemma Craven is a pretty and very effective Cinderella.

Michael Hordern steals many a scene as the king, in a very good performance; Kenneth More has great moments as the chamberlain; while Edith Evans thefts the scenes she's in with some irresistible windup oneliners.

Physical facets, from eye-popping Pinewood Studio sets to the lushly romantic Austrian exteriors, are standout.

● ●

■ **SLIPSTREAM**

1989, 101 MINS, UK ◇ ⑮

Dir Steven Lisberger *Prod* Gary Kurtz *Scr* Tony Kayden *Ph* Frank Tidy *Ed* Terry Rawlings *Mus* Elmer Bernstein *Art Dir* Andrew McAlpine
● Mark Hamill, Bob Peck, Bill Paxton, Kitty Aldridge, Ben Kingsley, F. Murray Abraham (Entertainment)

British-made sci-fi adventure romp *Slipstream* is one of those films that had potential, but unfortunately it doesn't make the grade.

Slipstream seems to be making some kind of ecological message; the film's version of Earth [from a story by Sam Clemens] is a place ruined by pollution with the planet washed clean by a river of wind called the 'Slipstream.'

Lawman Mark Hamill and his partner Kitty Aldridge capture Bob Peck, who's wanted for murder. When adventurer Bill Paxton discovers there is a price on Peck's head he snatches him and makes his escape down the Slipstream.

They come across a cult of religious fanatics who worship the wind, led by Ben Kingsley. One of the cult (Eleanor David) falls for Peck – even though it turns out he is an android.

Strong points are the stunning locations (Turkey and the Yorkshire moors), the performances by Hamill and Aldridge, plus impressive aircraft and technical effects. Kingsley and F. Murray Abraham have virtual walk-on parts.

● ●

■ **SLITHER**

1973, 98 MINS, US ◇ ⑦

Dir Howard Zieff *Prod* Jack Sher *Scr* W.D. Richter *Ph* Laszlo Kovacs *Ed* David Bretherton *Mus* Tom McIntosh *Art Dir* Dale Hennesy
● James Caan, Peter Boyle, Sally Kellerman, Louise Lasser, Allen Garfield, Richard B. Shull (M-G-M)

Slither is, in effect, an excellent, live-action, feature-length counterpart to a great old Warner Bros cartoon. That is to say, a combination of physical and visual madness overlaid with satirical, throwaway sophistication which ends up its caper plot while nourishing it to the full..

W.D. Richter's first produced script is a smash achievement in structure and dialog. James Caan is superb as a likeable paroled car thief whose incidental friendship with Richard B. Shull, an embezzler, leads him into contact with a bizarre set of characters, some in search of a concealed fortune, others determined to thwart the treasure hunt.

The characters road-run over the countryside, where a couple of ominous black vans and several ordinary-looking businessmen create a mood of latent terror.

● ●

■ **SLOW DANCING IN THE BIG CITY**

1978, 101 MINS, US ◇

Dir John G. Avildsen *Prod* Michael Levee, John G. Avildsen *Scr* Barra Grant *Ph* Ralf Bode *Ed* John G. Avildsen *Mus* Bill Conti *Art Dir* Henry Shrady
● Paul Sorvino, Anne Ditchburn, Nicolas Coster, Anita Dangler, Hector Jaime Mercado, Thaao Penghlis (United Artists)

Slow Dancing in the Big City has so much heart John Avildsen's aorta is showing.

Barra Grant's story is a simple boy meets girl tale, or in this case, dancer meets columnist. Anne Ditchburn, a lovely dancer and choreographer, meets Paul Sorvino, the columnist.

Sorvino seems to do a good job in any picture under any conditions and he's just terrific here. Ditchburn is promising, but the post-production looping is downright dreadful and interferes not just with her performance but with the flow of the film.

A number of dancing scenes featuring Ditchburn – performances, rehearsals and a solo on the roof of a Manhattan apartment – are among the production's high points.

The film has two plots moving along side by side although the focus clearly is on the Ditchburn-Sorvino relationship. The second genuinely touching plot concerns a young ghetto kid Sorvino is writing about and his struggle to overcome the harsh city.

What's a shame about *Slow Dancing* is that somewhere on the cutting room floor probably is a fine film.

● ●

■ **SLUMBER PARTY MASSACRE**

1982, 84 MINS, US ◇ ⑱

Dir Amy Jones *Prod* Amy Jones, Aaron Lipstadt *Scr* Rita Mae Brown *Ph* Steve Posey *Ed* Wendy Allan *Mus* Ralph Jones *Art Dir* Pam Canzano
● Michele Michaels, Robin Stille, Michael Villela, Andre Honore (Santa Fe)

Besides its obviously catchy title, *Slumber Party Massacre* is an entertaining terror thriller, with the switch that distaff filmmakers handle the 'young women in jeopardy' format.

Set in Venice, Cal, pic concerns high school girls having a sleep-over party, with 'let's scare 'em' antics by the boyfriends. Meanwhile, a mad killer is in the vicinity, wasting kids of both sexes in bloody fashion with a portable drill and various wicked knives.

Out of traditional horror material consisting of red herrings, sudden shock movements into frame, etc, helmer Amy Jones develops

some very stylish sequences. Notable is a complex mid-film montage mixing (with matched compositions) a horror film on TV, actual killings by the nut, and the sister chatting humorously on the phone.

● ●

■ **SMALL BACK ROOM, THE**

1949, 106 MINS, UK

Dir Michael Powell, Emeric Pressburger *Prod* Michael Powell, Emeric Pressburger *Scr* Michael Powell, Emeric Pressburger, Nigel Balchin *Ph* Christopher Challis *Ed* Clifford Turner, Reginald Mills *Mus* Brian Easdale *Art Dir* Hein Heckroth
● David Farrar, Kathleen Byron, Jack Hawkins, Cyril Cusack, Sidney James, Leslie Banks (London/Archers)

Central character in the plot [from a novel by Nigel Balchin] is Sammy Rice, scientist and research worker, whose lame foot has made him a complex individual. Although becoming extremely unpopular by his frank and adverse comments on a new type of anti-tank gun, he redeems himself by dismantling a booby bomb which is the enemy's latest secret weapon.

It is this latter scene which is by far the high spot of the production, and although it is a long time coming it is handled to extract every ounce of suspense from it. In scenes like that the drama becomes real and satisfying but the same reaction isn't forthcoming in the highly imaginative sequence in which the complex Sammy seeks solace in whisky.

● ●

■ **SMALL TOWN GIRL**

1936, 95 MINS, US

Dir William Wellman *Prod* Hunt Stromberg *Scr* John Lee Mahin, Edith Fitzgerald *Ph* Charles Rosher *Ed* Blanche Sewell *Mus* Herbert Stothart, Edward Ward *Art Dir* Cedric Gibbons, Arnold Gillespie
● Janet Gaynor, Robert Taylor, Binnie Barnes, Lewis Stone, Andy Devine, James Stewart (M-G-M)

Small Town Girl is romance with nice comedy sequences and with a well-balanced cast headed by Janet Gaynor and Robert Taylor.

Ben Ames Williams' novel gives a few neat twists to the ancient plot of the obscure Cinderella who marries into the wealthy family. All the time-tested and easy-to-foresee elements are present, including the hoity-toity sweetheart who is bad for the character and the career of the silver-spoon kid who is ultimately brought onto the right track by the wholesome influence exponent.

Picture has tempo and humanity. There is a skillful blending of the sentimentality and the giggles. On the acting end it's a smacko assignment for Gaynor and she displays considerable authority in her performance.

Taylor looks like the dames like him to look, and he acts like the boys can okay him. Binnie Barnes makes a provocative off-type vixen.

● ●

■ **SMALL TOWN GIRL**

1953, 93 MINS, US ◇

Dir Leslie Kardos *Prod* Joe Pasternak *Scr* Dorothy Cooper, Dorothy Kingsley *Ph* Joseph Ruttenberg *Ed* Albert Akst *Mus* Andre Previn (dir.) *Art Dir* Cedric Gibbons, Hans Peters
● Jane Powell, Farley Granger, Ann Miller, S.Z. Sakall, Robert Keith, Bobby Van (M-G-M)

Small Town Girl packages an engaging round of light musical comedy and a plot [from a story by Dorothy Cooper] with just enough substance to hold the attention without wearing. Jane Powell and Farley Granger are the chief exponents of young love and both carry a major portion of the entertainment to excellent results. However, it is the spotlighting of young Bobby Van in a song-dance-comedy spot that impresses the most.

However, Van doesn't grab all the dance footage. Shapely Ann Miller exposes her gams in two hot production pieces. 'I've Gotta Hear That Beat', flashily staged by Busby Berkeley, and 'My Gaucho', a piece of south-of-the-border rhythm that she makes pay off. Both tunes were written by Nicholas Brodszky and Leo Robin.

Granger is a rich playboy who makes the mistake of speeding through a small town in which Robert Keith is judge. He's jailed for 30 days, thus breaking up his elopement with showgirl Miller. Granger makes happy time, though, with Powell, Keith's daughter, even talking her and Chill Wills, jailer, into letting him out for a night in New York. She goes along to insure his return, and love blooms, breaking up the hopes of S.Z. Sakall that his son, Van, will eventually marry the gal and settle down to clerking job instead of dreaming of the NY stage.

■ SMALL TOWN IN TEXAS, A

1976, 95 MINS, US ◇ Ⓥ

Dir Jack Starrett   *Prod* Joe Solomon   *Scr* William Norton   *Ph* Bob Jessup   *Ed* John C. Horger, Larry L. Mills, Jodie Copelan   *Mus* Charles Bernstein   *Art Dir* Elayne Ceder
● Timothy Bottoms, Susan George, Bo Hopkins, Art Hindle, John Karlen, Morgan Woodward (CoCaCo)

Plot picks up Timothy Bottoms en route home from a prison stretch to reunite with girl friend Susan George and their out of wedlock son, also to contemplate revenge on Bo Hopkins, who busted him on a pot charge and is now involved with George.

The film jettisons believability to concentrate on stunt crashes and explosions. Bottoms' character is overly obtuse even for an embittered ex-con and pointlessly risks the lives of George and their son.

Bo Hopkins acts rings around Bottoms. He does an excellent job of conveying the sheriff's unsettling mixture of boyish charm and viciousness. George is okay in another over-wrought part. Buck Fowler is a standout in the supporting cast as a grizzled old moonshiner who gleefully joins the chase.

■ SMALL WORLD OF SAMMY LEE, THE

1963, 107 MINS, UK

Dir Ken Hughes   *Prod* Frank Godwin   *Scr* Ken Hughes   *Ph* Wolfgang Suschitzky   *Ed* Henry Richardson   *Mus* Kenny Graham
● Anthony Newley, Julia Foster, Robert Stephens, Wilfrid Brambell, Warren Mitchell, Miriam Karlin (British Lion/Bryanston Seven Arts)

Originally an award-winning teleplay by Ken Hughes the film has been pumped up to feature length, perhaps at overlength. Though highly overcoloured, it remains a sharp, snide commentary on the sleazy side of Soho, and emerges as a firstclass vehicle for Anthony Newley.

Newly, a fugitive from the East End, is the smart-aleck emcee of one of the shabby stripperies which grind through the day for the benefit of jaded business man and alcoholic layabouts. Newley, between churning out tired, near-blue gags and introducing the peelers, is an inveterate poker and horse player. The story consists entirely of his efforts to raise $840 in five hours to pay off a gangster-bookie who is threatening to cut him up if he doesn't deliver the loot on time.

Hughes' uninhibited screenplay is incisive and tart while his direction has the deft assurance of a man who is realing with his own idea and knows what he wants as the end product. His cameras stray restlessly around the seamier parts of Soho and the East End.

Newley gives a restless, intelligent and perceptive performance as the little fish floundering in a pond that is too deep for him. Few of the supporting actors have much opportunity to make great impact but some register

brilliantly. Notably, Warren Mitchell as Newley's East End delicatessen store-owner brother. Miriam Karlin turns up in this sequence but all too briefly. Robert Stephens provides a sly picture of the odious clubowner.

■ SMALLEST SHOW ON EARTH, THE

1957, 81 MINS, UK Ⓥ

Dir Basil Dearden   *Prod* Michael Relph   *Scr* William Rose, John Eldridge   *Ph* Douglas Slocombe   *Ed* Oswald Hafenrichter   *Mus* William Alwyn   *Art Dir* Allan Harris
● Bill Travers, Virginia McKenna, Leslie Phillips, Peter Sellers, Margaret Rutherford, Bernard Miles (British Lion)

William Rose, who scripted *Genevieve*, has fashioned a shrewd and bright comedy around the exhibition side of motion pictures. The centre of interest is a small, derelict picture house inherited by a young struggling writer.

The theatre, in a small, smelly provincial town, is adjacent to the mainline railroad station. The staff comprises three ancients – Margaret Rutherford, who played the piano in the silent days, but now sits at the cash desk; Peter Sellers, the boothman with a weakness for whisky; and Bernard Miles, a doorman and general handyman.

When Bill Travers and Virginia McKenna inherit the theatre, their immediate reaction is to sell out to the opposition, who had made a substantial offer to the previous owner. But the offer now forthcoming would not even be adequate to meet the inherited debts, so they set about on a big bluff, pretending to re-open in the hope that the bids will be bettered.

The film is loaded with delightful touches, and there's one prolonged laughter sequence when the projectionist is on a drinking bout and Bill Travers takes over the booth.

■ SMASH PALACE

1981, 100 MINS, NEW ZEALAND ◇

Dir Roger Donaldson   *Prod* Roger Donaldson   *Scr* Roger Donaldson   *Ph* Graeme Cowley   *Ed* Mike Horton   *Mus* Sharon O'Neill   *Art Dir* Reston Griffiths
● Bruno Lawrence, Anna Jemison, Greer Robson, Keith Aberdein, Les Kelly (Aadvark)

Smash Palace is a thoroughly remarkable drama about a marital break-up which erupts into an impulsive kidnapping of a child by its father and a totally-believable escalation to the brink of tragedy.

Roger Donaldson's handling of actors is excellent, and his visual control constantly enthralling. The eponymous location is a vast junk-yard of cars, established by Al Shaw's father, and now the panier of hope for Al, a former Grand Prix driver, returned to a remote New Zealand country town with a pregnant French wife.

However, his wife has, during the ensuing eight years, grown increasingly dissatisfied, and the early scenes economically establish the deeper reasons. The script's expositional sequences are neatly handled, making the character development logically part of the narrative.

With strong performances by both Bruno Lawrence and Anna Jemison to work with, the director has effectively created a reality to the tension that goes beneath the surface – or as it might be said: has re-created real life on film.

■ SMASHING TIME

1967, 96 MINS, UK ◇

Dir Desmond Davis   *Prod* Roy Millichip, Carlo Ponti   *Scr* George Melly   *Ph* Manny Wynn   *Ed* Barry Vince   *Mus* John Addison   *Art Dir* Ken Bridgeman
● Rita Tushingham, Lynn Redgrave, Michael York,

Anna Quayle, Irene Handl, Ian Carmichael (Paramount/Solmur)

Starring Rita Tushingham and Lynn Redgrave as a pair of girls from the north of England who go to London to explore its glittery side – and have themselves a smashing time – the writer and producers display an amazing memory of Hollywood film.

Femmes play Laurel and Hardy characters, Tushingham as the bewildered Stan, Redgrave the aggressive Oliver. George Melly's original screenplay might be the further misadventures of the Hollywood comics in change-of-sex garb.

Extensive use is made of a swinging London background, with many of its characters, particularly the fey. Desmond Davis' direction, when it isn't focusing on hoary routines, is fast in limning the conglomerate situations in which femmes are plunged, Lynn becoming a recording star, Rita a top fashion photographer's model. With their usual flair for disaster, both find themselves out.

■ SMILE

1975, 113 MINS, US ◇

Dir Michael Ritchie   *Prod* Ritchie   *Scr* Jerry Belson   *Ph* Conrad Hall   *Ed* Richard Harris   *Mus* Daniel Osborn, Leroy Holmes, Charles Chaplin
● Bruce Dern, Barbara Feldon, Michael Kidd, Geoffrey Lewis, Nicholas Pryor, Colleen Camp (United Artists)

Smile is a hilarious but ultimately shallow putdown of teenage beauty contests. Jerry Belson's original script depicts the climactic days of a statewide beauty competition, where a group of adolescent girls get caught up in the melange of mercantilism, boosterism and backstage politics attendant to such tribal rites.

The uniformly excellent performances come from Bruce Dern, a compulsively upbeat smalltown mobile home dealer and chief judge of the contest; Barbara Feldon, perfect as an 'active' woman whose marriage to Nicholas Pryor is in a shambles; Geoffrey Lewis, very effective as pageant president; and Michael Kidd, imported bigtime choreographer whose career is in a slump.

Titles employ Nat Cole's old hit record of 'Smile'.

■ SMOKEY AND THE BANDIT

1977, 96 MINS, US ◇ Ⓥ

Dir Hal Needham   *Prod* Mort Engelberg   *Scr* James Lee Barrett, Charles Shyer, Alan Mandel   *Ph* Bobby Byrne   *Ed* Walter Hanneman, Angelo Ross   *Mus* Bill Justis, Jerry Reed, Dick Feller   *Art Dir* Mark Mansbridge
● Burt Reynolds, Sally Field, Jerry Reed, Jackie Gleason, Mike Henry, Paul Williams (Universal/Rastar)

Burt Reynolds stars as a bootlegger-for-kicks who, with Jerry Reed and Sally Field, outwit zealous sheriff Jackie Gleason.

The plot is simple: rich father-son team of blowhards Pat McCormick and Paul Williams offer a reward if Reynolds will truck a load of Coors beer from Texas to Georgia; Reynolds and buddy Reed race to meet the deadline: Field complicates matters as a not-yet-bride who flees beau Mike Henry, son of outraged Gleason, who then chases them all across the southeast.

There is a parade of roadside set pieces involving many different ways to crash cars. Overlaid is citizens band radio jabber (hence, the title) which is loaded with downhome gags. Field is the hottest element in the film.

■ SMOKEY AND THE BANDIT II

1980, 101 MINS, US ◇ Ⓥ

Dir Hal Needham   *Prod* Hank Moonjean   *Scr* Jerry Belson, Brock Yates   *Ph* Michael Butler   *Ed* Donn Cambern, William Gordean   *Mus* Snuff Garrett (sup.)   *Art Dir* Henry Bumstead

● Burt Reynolds, Jackie Gleason, Sally Field, Dom DeLuise, Jerry Reed (Universal/Rastar/Mort Engelberg)

Sally Field tells Burt Reynolds in *Smokey and the Bandit II* that he is no longer having fun doing what used to come naturally. This stale sequel seems to be evidence of going through the motions for money instead of fun.

Smokey II [from a story by Michael Kane] concentrates on sluggish and mostly over-done attempts at roadside comedy skits, and it doesn't even bother to have Reynolds and Field play the same characters they played so engagingly in the original.

Here, Reynolds is hired to haul a pregnant elephant to the Republican convention. The heavy reliance on elephant gags quite literally slows down the film.

Ironically, the best part of the film is the unusual end credit sequence, which shows the actors having fun when they blow lines in outtakes.

· ·

■ SNAKE PIT, THE

1948, 107 MINS, US
Dir Anatole Litvak   *Prod* Anatole Litvak, Robert Bassler   *Scr* Frank Partos, Millen Brand   *Ph* Leo Tover   *Ed* Dorothy Spencer   *Mus* Alfred Newman   *Art Dir* Lyle R. Wheeler, Joseph C. Wright
● Olivia de Havilland, Mark Stevens, Leo Genn, Celeste Holm, Helen Craig, Leif Erickson (20th Century-Fox)

The Snake Pit is a standout among class melo-dramas. Based on Mary Jane Ward's novel, picture probes into the processes of mental illness with a razor-sharp forthrightness, giv-ing an open-handed display of the make-up of bodies without minds and the treatments used to restore intelligence. Clinical detail is stated with matter-of-fact clarity and be-comes an important part of the melodramatics.

Olivia de Havilland is a young bride who goes insane and is committed to an institu-tion for treatment. An understanding medico (Leo Genn) uses kindness and knowledge of mental ills to restore her. Just as a cure seems possible, she again plunges into a mental snake pit and starts all over on the road to insanity.

De Havilland's performance is top gauge. Genn goes about his part of the doctor with a quietness that gives it strength and Mark Ste-vens is excellent as De Havilland's husband.
☐ 1948: Best Picture (Nomination)

· ·

■ SNOW WHITE AND THE SEVEN DWARFS

1937, 80 MINS, US ◇
Dir David Hand   *Prod* Walt Disney   *Scr* Ted Sears, Otto Englander, Earl Hurd, Dorothy Ann Blank, Richard Creedon, Dick Rickard, Merrill De Maris, Webb Smith   *Mus* Frank Churchill, Paul Smith, Leigh Harline (arr.)   *Art Dir* Charles Philippi, High Hennesy, Terrell Stapp, McLaren Stewart, Harold Miles, Tom Codrick, Gustaf Tenggren, Kenneth Anderson, Kendall O'Connor, Hazel Sewell
● (Disney/RKO)

Wal Disney's *Snow White and the Seven Dwarfs*, seven reels of animated cartoon in Tech-nicolor, unfolds an absorbingly interesting and, at times, thrilling entertainment.

More than two years and $1 million were required by the Disney staff, under David Hand's supervision, to complete the film. In a foreword Disney pays a neat compliment to animators, designers and musical composers whose united efforts have produced a work of art. No less than 62 staff names are flashed in the credit titles as being responsible for various divisions of the job.

The opening shows the cover of Grimm's book of tales. Soon all the characters assume lifelike personalities. Snow White is the em-bodiment of girlish sweetness and kindness, exemplified in her love for the birds and the small animals of the woods that are her friends and, as it subsequently develops, her rescuers. The queen is a vampish brunet, of homicidal instincts, who consorts with black magic and underworld forces of evil. And the seven little dwarfs, Doc, Grumpy, Dopey, Sleepy, Happy, Sneezy and Bashful, are the embodiments of their nametags, a merry crew of masculine frailities.

Pastel shades predominate in the Tech-nicolor and there is an absence of garish, bril-liant colorings.

Sound plays an important part in the pro-duction and the synchronization of words to the moving lips of the characters is worked out perfectly.

· ·

■ SNOWBALL EXPRESS

1972, 99 MINS, US ◇ ⊛
Dir Norman Tokar   *Prod* Ron Miller   *Scr* Don Tait, Jim Parker, Arnold Margolin   *Ph* Frank Phillips   *Ed* Robert Stafford   *Mus* Robert F. Brunner   *Art Dir* John B. Mansbridge, Walter Tyler
● Dean Jones, Nancy Olson, Harry Morgan, Keenan Wynn, Johnny Whitaker, Kathleen Cody (Walt Disney)

The Disney trademark of wholesome enter-tainment is immediately discernible in this comedy focusing on a young family man inheriting a derelict resort hotel in Colorado.

Dean Jones, a veteran of Disney films, plays the insurance accountant who quits the Man-hattan rat race when he's informed he has been willed the estate of a distant uncle in the Rockies, principal asset of which is the Grand Imperial Hotel.

Based on the book *Chateau Bon Vivant*, by Frankie and John O'Rear, narrative under Norman Tokar's deft direction follows Jones' efforts at making a go of a bad deal. High-lights of film are the various ski sequences and a nightmarish snowmobile race.

Jones delivers as usual in a slightly frus-trated character and Nancy Olson, as his wife, lends piquancy as she gradually throws in with Jones on his project.

· ·

■ SNOWS OF KILIMANJARO, THE

1952, 113 MINS, US ◇ ⊛
Dir Henry King   *Prod* Darryl F. Zanuck   *Scr* Casey Robinson   *Ph* Leon Shamroy   *Ed* Barbara McLean   *Mus* Bernard Herrmann   *Art Dir* Lyle Wheeler, John De Cuir
● Gregory Peck, Susan Hayward, Ava Gardner, Hildegarde Neff, Leo G. Carroll, Torin Thatcher (20th Century-Fox)

A big, broad screen treatment has been given to Ernest Hemingway's *The Snows of Kiliman-jaro*. The script broadens the 1927 short story considerably without losing the Hemingway penchant for the mysticism behind his virile characters and lusty situations.

·Ava Gardner makes the part of Cynthia a warm, appealing, alluring standout. Gregory Peck delivers with gusto the character of the writer who lies dangerously ill on the plain at the base of Kilimanjaro, highest mountain in Africa, and relives what he believes is a mis-spent life. Susan Hayward is splendid, particularly in the dramatic closing sequence, in the less colorful role of Peck's wife.

The location-lensed footage taken in Paris, Africa, the Riviera and Spain add an import-ant dress to the varied sequences. The Paris street and cafe scenes, the music and noise, are alive. The African-lensed backgrounds are brilliant, as are those on the Riviera and in Spain.

· ·

■ S.O.B.

1981, 121 MINS, US ◇
Dir Blake Edwards   *Prod* Blake Edwards, Tony Adams   *Scr* Blake Edwards   *Ph* Harry Stradling   *Ed* Ralph E. Winters   *Mus* Henry Mancini   *Art Dir* Roger Maus
● Julie Andrews, William Holden, Marisa Berenson, Larry Hagman, Robert Loggia, Robert Vaughn (Paramount/Lorimar)

S.O.B. is one of the most vitriolic – though only occasionally hilarious – attacks on the Tinseltown mentality ever.

Taking its core from part of director Blake Edwards' own battle-weary Hollywood career, pic is structured as an arch fairy tale, spinning the chronicle of a top-grossing pro-ducer (Richard Mulligan) whose latest $30 million musical extravaganza is hailed by the world as the b.o. turkey of the century, rele-gating him to has-been status overnight.

With Julie Andrews as his pure-as-driven snow imaged wife prompted finally to leave him for good, while production chief Robert Vaughn plots how to salvage the pic by mass-ive, contract-bending recutting, Mulligan tries several failed variations on the suicide route until a mid-orgy epiphany tells him to cut and reshoot the G-rated failure into an opulent softcore porno fantasy.

Black comedy is a tough commodity to sus-tain and, after a broad start, Edwards quickly finds a deft balance that paints a cockeyed, self-contained world that comfortably sup-ports its exaggerated characters. Unhappily, about midway through the pic, the tone be-comes less certain (especially when it strains for seriousness) and styles begin to switch back and forth.

· ·

■ SO BIG

1953, 101 MINS, US
Dir Robert Wise   *Prod* Henry Blanke   *Scr* John Twist   *Ph* Ellsworth Fredericks   *Ed* Thomas Reilly   *Mus* Max Steiner   *Art Dir* John Beckman
● Jane Wyman, Sterling Hayden, Nancy Olson, Steve Forrest, Elizabeth Fraser, Martha Hyer (Warner)

This is the third time around for Edna Fer-ber's Pulitzer Prize-winning novel. It was made as a silent film by First National back in 1925 and as a talker by Warner Bros in 1932. Jane Wyman handles the emotional histrionics in this re-make.

So Big is big and sprawling, covering a period of some 25 years. Its basic flaw is that it attempts to cover too much, resulting in an episodic quality and in flat surface characters.

Wyman is superb in transition from the young girl with the aristocratic background to the widow of a Dutch truck farmer. Noth-ing stops Selina's nobility from the time she arrives in the Dutch community outside of Chicago as a young schoolteacher to the moment her son decides to return to his drawing board. She takes poverty, back-breaking farm work, widowhood and dis-appointment serenely, philosophically and with dignity.

Sterling Hayden scores as the unlearned, rugged yet gentle farmer who wins the schoolteacher. Nancy Olson is appropriately flippant and understanding as the Paris-trained artist who values true creativeness over financial success. Steve Forrest, as Seli-na's architect-son, wrestles neatly with the money versus art problem.

Ellsworth Fredericks' camera has success-fully captured the drudgery of the farm, the excitement of the market place, and the splendor and gaudiness of the rich in 1900 Chicago.

· ·

■ SO FINE

1981, 91 MINS, US ◇
Dir Andrew Bergman   *Prod* Mike Lobell   *Scr* Andrew Bergman   *Ph* James A. Contner   *Ed* Alan Helm   *Mus* Ennio Morricone   *Art Dir* Santo Loquasto
● Ryan O'Neal, Jack Warden, Mariangela Melato, Richard Kiel, Fred Gwynne (Warner)

S

So Fine is quite all right. Andrew Bergman, screenwriter on *Blazing Saddles* and *The In-Laws*, has come up with a somewhat less zany concoction this time but makes an impressively sharp directorial debut highlighted by some good bedroom farce.

Ryan O'Neal is a Shakespeare-spouting English professor implausibly recruited into his father Jack Warden's faltering dressmaking firm upon the unchallengeable demand of Big Eddie, played by the 7' 2" Richard Kiel.

Latter's petite wife, Mariangela Melato, quickly corrals O'Neal into the sack (while Kiel's in it too, no less) and, in his best bumbling manner, O'Neal inadvertently hits upon a new fashion discovery – skin-tight jeans with seethrough behinds.

Despite his smashing success in the garment district, O'Neal retreats to the world of academia but is pursued by Melato, who in turn is followed by the jealous Big Eddie. It all ends up in a slapstick, amateur hour operatic production of Verdi's *Otello* reminiful of, among other things, *A Night at the Opera*.

SO LONG AT THE FAIR

1950, 84 MINS, UK

Dir Terence Fisher, Antony Darnborough *Prod* Sidney Box *Scr* Anthony Thorne, Hugh Mills *Ph* Reginald Wyer *Ed* Gordon Hales *Mus* Benjamin Frankel
● Jean Simmons, Dirk Bogarde, David Tomlinson, Honor Blackman, Cathleen Nesbitt, Felix Aylmer (Gainsborough/Rank)

The pic is a good workmanlike British thriller, not in the top bracket. Setting for the film is the Paris exhibition of 1889.

The story opens as Vicky Barton (Jean Simmons) arrives in Paris with her brother (David Tomlinson). After a festive first night, they return to their hotel eager to participate in the revels of the following day. But the next morning, the brother disappears. At the hotel they insist that the girl came alone and both the British consul and the chief of police find it hard to accept her story.

Despite the strong plot, the film never succeeds in developing a tense atmosphere. Picture has a good all-round cast. Simmons turns in a smooth performance. Dirk Bogarde displays a keen determination as the young artist who helps her unravel the mystery.

SO PROUDLY WE HAIL!

1943, 126 MINS, US

Dir Mark Sandrich *Prod* Mark Sandrich *Scr* Allan Scott *Ph* Charles Lang *Ed* Ellsworth Hoagland *Mus* Miklos Rozsa
● Claudette Colbert, Paulette Goddard, Veronica Lake, George Reeves, Barbara Britton, Sonny Tufts (Paramount)

Mark Sandrich's *So Proudly We Hail!* is a saga of the war-front nurse and her heroism under fire. As such it glorifies the American Red Cross and presents the wartime nurse, in the midst of unspeakable dangers, physical and spiritual, in a new light.

Director-producer Sandrich and scripter Allen Scott have limned a vivid, vital story. It's backgrounded against a realistic romance of how a group of brave American Nightingales came through the hellfire to Australia and thence back to Blighty.

Done in flashback manner, with Claudette Colbert rapidly sinking physically, the saga of their travail pitches to the situation where, out of the past, a love letter from her officer-lover finally brings her back on the road to recovery. Paulette Goddard does a capital job as running mate, and Veronica Lake is the sullen nurse who finally sees the light.

Sonny Tufts walks off with the picture every time he's on. As Kansas, the blundering ex-footballer, he's Goddard's vis-a-vis.

George Reeves isn't as effective as the romantic opposite to Colbert.

SOAPDISH

1991, 95 MINS, US ◇ ⓥ

Dir Michael Hoffman *Prod* Aaron Spelling, Alan Greisman *Scr* Robert Harling, Andrew Bergman *Ph* Ueli Steiger *Ed* Garth Craven *Mus* Alan Silvestri *Art Dir* Eugenio Zanetti
● Sally Field, Kevin Kline, Robert Downey Jr, Cathy Moriarty, Whoopi Goldberg, Carrie Fisher (Paramount)

Soapdish aims at a satiric target as big as a Macy's float and intermittently hits it. Sally Field and Kevin Kline play a feuding pair of romantically involved soap opera stars in this broad but amiable sendup of daytime TV.

Field, the reigning 'queen of misery' on the sudser *The Sun Also Sets*, is at the peak of her glory but is going to pieces emotionally. Amazonian harpy Cathy Moriarty is scheming to take over the show by using her sexual wiles to convince the slimy producer (Robert Downey Jr) to have Field's character destroy her popularity by committing some unspeakable crime.

To drive Field even more off the edge, Downey surprises her by bringing back her long-ago flame, Kevin Kline, whom she had thrown off the show in 1973. Whoopi Goldberg, the show's jaded head writer, flips when told Kline is coming back because his character was written out by having him decapitated in a car crash.

Field works hard and shows an expert sense of comic timing, but the grittily down-to-earth acting persona Field has developed now makes her seem a bit too reasonable for the zany demands of this script.

Kline is utterly marvelous as a sort of low-rent John Barrymore type, boozing and carousing his way through the ranks of worshipful young actresses. Moriarty, who acts as if she's been staying up late studying Mary Woronov pics, is a scream as Field's deep-voiced, hate-consumed rival.

SOCIETY

1989, 99 MINS, US ◇ ⓥ

Dir Brian Yuzna *Prod* Keith Walley *Scr* Woody Keith, Rick Fry *Ph* Rick Fichter *Ed* Peter Teschner *Mus* Mark Ryder, Phil Davies *Art Dir* Matthew C. Jacobs
● Billy Warlock, Devin Devasquez, Evan Richards, Ben Meyerson, Connie Danese, Patrice Jennings (Wild Street)

Society is an extremely pretentious, obnoxious horror film that unsuccessfully attempts to introduce kinky sexual elements into extravagant makeup effects.

Teen Billy Warlock is thought to be paranoid by everyone, including his shrink, when he starts suspecting not only that he must have been adopted but also that his parents are having incestuous orgies with his sister.

Following many strange occurrences, red herrings and repetitive nudges about the class system and 'fitting into society', it's finally revealed that rich and powerful folk really are some sort of undead monsters preying on Billy and all us other have-nots.

Sickening climax, notable for its poor continuity, is a sexual orgy called shunting, in which makeup expert Screaming Mad George indulges in what's credited as 'surrealistic makeup effects.'

Sole bright spot is a very sexy turn by former Playboy magazine model Devin Devasquez.

SODOM AND GOMORRAH

1962, 153 MINS, ITALY ◇ ⓥ

Dir Robert Aldrich *Prod* Goffredo Lombardo, Joseph E. Levine *Scr* Hugo Butler, Giorgio Prosperi *Ph* Silvano Ippoliti, Mario Montuori, Cyril Knowles

Ed Peter Tanner *Mus* Miklos Rozsa *Art Dir* Ken Adam
● Stewart Granger, Pier Angeli, Stanley Baker, Anouk Aimee, Rossana Podesta, Claudia Mori (20th Century-Fox/Titanus)

Director Robert Aldrich has said, 'Every director ought to get one Biblical film out of his system, but there's not very much that you can do about this sort of picture.' Too true. Net: *Sodom and Gomorrah* has many of the faults of the Biblical epic, but many good qualities.

Storyline concerns Lot's pilgrimage to the Valley of Jordan with the Hebrews. They set up camp in the valley but are almost immediately involved in a bitter clash between the Helamites, who covet the wealth of Sodom and Gomorrah, two cesspools of depravity, ruled over by the cold, beautiful, unscrupulous Queen Bera who, incidentally, is being doublecrossed for power by her scheming brother.

Stewart Granger makes a distinguished, solemn and sincere figure of Lot and Stanley Baker, as the treacherous Prince of Sodom, is sufficiently sneaky though he has only a couple of highspots in his role. Anouk Aimee is an impressively sinister Queen, Pier Angeli has some moments of genuine emotion as Lot's wife and Rossana Podesta and Claudia Mori play the shadowy roles of Lot's daughters adequately.

SOLDIER BLUE

1970, 112 MINS, US ◇ ⓥ

Dir Ralph Nelson *Prod* Harold Loeb, Gabriel Katzka *Scr* John Gay *Ph* Robert Hauser *Ed* Alex Beaton *Mus* Roy Budd *Art Dir* Frank Arrigo
● Candice Bergen, Peter Strauss, Donald Pleasence, John Anderson, Jorge Rivero, Dana Elcar (Avco Embassy)

Screenplay, from Theodore V. Olsen's novel, *Arrow in the Sun*, deals with the attempt of US soldier Honus Gant (Peter Strauss), the 'soldier blue' of the title, and a white woman who had been kidnapped by Indians two years before (Candice Bergen) to stay alive until they can reach an army outpost.

The major portion of the film deals with the pair's trek. Their misadventures include encountering white man Isaac Cumber (Donald Pleasence) who is en route to the Cheyennes to sell them guns for the gold they stole from the paymaster and who takes the pair prisoners. Finally, Bergen goes on ahead for help but discovers the Army's plot to wipe out the Indians, and she warns them.

SOLDIER IN THE RAIN

1963, 87 MINS, US ⓥ

Dir Ralph Nelson *Prod* Martin Jurow *Scr* Maurice Richlin, Blake Edwards *Ph* Philip Lathrop *Ed* Ralph Winters *Mus* Henry Mancini *Art Dir* Phil Barber
● Jackie Gleason, Steve McQueen, Tuesday Weld, Tony Bill, Tom Poston, Ed Nelson (Allied Artists)

One might classify the film a fairy tale in khaki. The screenplay out of a novel by William Goldman relates the bittersweet tale of two modern army buddies – a smooth operating master sergeant (Jackie Gleason) who has found a home in the service, and his hero-worshipping protege (Steve McQueen), a supply sergeant who is about to return to civvies and hopes Gleason will join him in private enterprise on the outside.

There are several sudden, and vigorous, bursts of comedy dialog, principally exchanges between Gleason, who has a complex about his bulk, and Tuesday Weld, who plays a basically sweet but dumb and ingeniously tactless 18-year-old whose idea of a compliment is to refer to him as a 'fat Randolph Scott'. But such mirth is only spasmodic and is snowed under by a sentimental approach that misfires.

McQueen is a kind of southern-fried boob who reminds one of Clem Kadiddlehoffer. The style of portrayal is exaggerated and un-natural. Gleason fares better with a re-strained approach, through which his natural endomorphic vitality seeps through. Weld is a standout with her convincing portrait of the classic dizzy blonde as a teenager. Tony Bill scores as McQueen's screwball sidekick.

The screenplay's ups and downs seem to have engulfed director Ralph Nelson. He has capitalized on the scattered bright spots, but has failed to detect or delete the artificiality of McQueen's approach.

. . . .

■ SOLDIER'S STORY, A

1984, 101 MINS, US ◇ ⓥ
Dir Norman Jewison   *Prod* Norman Jewison, Ronald L. Schwary, Patrick Palmer   *Scr* Charles Fuller   *Ph* Russell Boyd   *Ed* Mark Warner, Caroline Bigglestaff   *Mus* Herbie Hancock   *Art Dir* Walter Scott Herndon
● Howard E. Rollins Jr., Adolph Caesar, Dennis Lipscomb, Art Evans, Denzil Washington, Larry Riley (Caldix)

A Soldier's Story is a taut, gripping film which features many of the old fashioned virtues of a good Hollywood production – brilliant ensemble acting, excellent production values, a crackling script (adapted from the Pulitzer Prize winning *A Soldier's Play* [1981] by its author, Charles Fuller), fine direction and a liberal political message.

Howard Rollins Jr plays Captain Daven-port, a prideful black army attorney called into Fort Neal, La, to investigate the murder of Sgt Waters (Adolph Caesar). Rollins' arrival at this holding tank for black soldiers is cause for racial strife on both sides of the fence – the white officers are contemptuous and the black soldiers are proud.

Film is structured around a series of flashbacks as Rollins interviews the team members who represent a variety of black experience and attitudes.
□ 1984: Best Picture (Nomination)

. . . .

■ SOLDIERS THREE

1951, 91 MINS, US
Dir Tay Garnett   *Prod* Pandro S. Berman   *Scr* Marguerite Roberts, Tom Reed, Malcolm Stuart Boylan   *Ph* William Mellor   *Ed* Robert J. Kern   *Mus* Adolph Deutsch   *Art Dir* Cedric Gibbons, Malcolm Brown
● Stewart Granger, Walter Pidgeon, David Niven, Robert Newton, Cyril Cusack, Greta Gynt (M-G-M)

Three scripters worked on the story, loosely based on Rudyard Kipling, but come up with nothing more than a string of incidents involving three soldiers in India (Stewart Granger, Robert Newton and Cyril Cusack). Trio's off-limits antics, such as drunken brawl-ing, add to the hot water in which their colonel (Walter Pidgeon) finds himself and do nothing to calm the colonel's aide (David Niven). Antics do, however, enliven the film's footage and save it from missing altogether.

Granger is very likeable in his comedy role, and his two cohorts, Newton and Cusack, do their full share in getting laughs. Niven also is good as the slightly stuffy aide who leads the pants-losing patrol. Pidgeon, as a colonel with worries, forgets his broad British bum-bling occasionally, but this fits with general development.

. . . .

■ SOLOMON AND SHEBA

1959, 141 MINS, US ◇ ⓥ
Dir King Vidor   *Prod* Ted Richmond   *Scr* Anthony Veillier, Paul Dudley, George Bruce   *Ph* Freddie Young   *Ed* John Ludwig   *Mus* Mario Nascimbene

Art Dir Richard Day, Alfred Sweeney, Luis Perez Espinosa
● Yul Brynner, Gina Lollobrigida, George Sanders, David Farrar, Marisa Pavan (United Artists)

The tab for this expensive production was unexpectedly hiked when Tyrone Power died in mid-production (although insurance covered much) and the subsequent hiring of Yul Brynner necessitated new writing as well as new shooting. A figure of over $5 million, judging by the spectacle, color and location expenses in Spain seems a reasonable one.

The story concerns the clash between Solo-mon and his brother Adonijah when King David crowns the poet-philosopher instead of the warrior. From then on it's political intrigue, with Egypt conniving with Sheba to bring down Israel, which is flourishing under the wise rule of Solomon, and the treacherous manner in which the Queen of Sheba under-mines Solomon but falls in love with him in the process.

The fascinating clash between the two brothers is only spasmodically developed and, inevitably, plays second fiddle to the re-lationship between the queen and her infat-uated target. Often what should have been a moving, gripping romance turns out to be lit-tle more than an affair between a couple of people at the local golf club.

There are some magnificent production scenes. Three startlingly effective battle se-quences, the stoning of Sheba, her arrival in Jerusalem, the terrifying wrath of God which razes the Temple of Jehova and Sheba's God of Love, the scene where Solomon gives judg-ment over the baby, the sight of the plains of Israel made bleak and arid and, above all, the startling dance-ritual to the God of Love which develops into an orgy.

Gina Lollobrigida virtually portrays three different Shebas. First, the arrogant, fiery, ambitious Queen; then the voluptuous, wily, seductress; finally, the Sheba who involuntar-ily falls in love with the King and risks all by denouncing her own gods.

Lollobrigida not only looks stunning but shows the queen to be a woman of sharp brain as well as sensual beauty. Brynner, sur-prisingly subdued, also does a fine job in pre-senting a Solomon who credibly suggests a singer of songs, yet finally is a man of ordin-ary flesh and blood who cannot resist Sheba.

. . . .

■ SOME CAME RUNNING

1958, 137 MINS, US ◇ ⓥ
Dir Vincente Minnelli   *Prod* Sol C. Siegel   *Scr* John Patrick, Arthur Sheekman   *Ph* William H. Daniels   *Ed* Adrienne Fazan   *Mus* Elmer Bernstein   *Art Dir* William A. Horning, Urie McCleary
● Frank Sinatra, Dean Martin, Shirley MacLaine, Martha Hyer, Arthur Kennedy, Nancy Gates (M-G-M)

The story is pure melodrama, despite the intention of the original novel's author, James Jones, to invest it with greater stature. But the integrity with which the film is han-dled by all its contributors lifts it at times to tragedy. Jones' novel has been stripped to essentials in the screenplay, and those are presented in hard clean dialog and incisive situations.

Frank Sinatra is an ex-serviceman and ex-novelist who returns to his home town, unwitting and unwilling, when he gets drunk in Chicago and is shipped back unconscious on a bus. Accompanying him is Shirley MacLaine who is generally unwitting but never unwilling, a good-natured tart with no pretensions.

Sinatra can't stand his brother (Arthur Kennedy) or the brother's wife (Leora Dana) but he falls deeply in love with a friend of theirs (Martha Hyer). He meets a pal (Dean Martin) who becomes an ally, and he be-comes involved in the personal life of his niece (Betty Lou Keim).

The title, incidentally, is taken from St Mark, and is construed to mean that some have come running to find the meaning of life, but are prevented from finding it by obsession with materialism.

Sinatra gives a top performance, sardonic and compassionate, full of touches both instinctive and technical. It is not easy, either, to play a man dying of a chronic ill-ness and do it with grace and humor, and this Martin does without faltering.

MacLaine isn't conventionally pretty. Her hair looks like it was combed with an egg-beater. But she elicits such empathy and humor that when she offers herself to Sinatra she seems eminently worth taking.

. . . .

■ SOME KIND OF HERO

1982, 97 MINS, US ◇ ⓥ
Dir Michael Pressman   *Prod* Howard W. Koch   *Scr* James Kirkwood, Robert Boris   *Ph* King Baggot   *Ed* Christopher Greenbury   *Mus* Patrick Williams   *Art Dir* James L. Schoppe
● Richard Pryor, Margot Kidder, Ray Sharkey, Ronny Cox, Lynne Moody, Olivia Cole (Paramount)

Some Kind of Hero is yet another example of how Richard Pryor can take a mediocre film and elevate it to the level of his extraordinary talents.

Something went awry in the adaptation of James Kirkwood's novel to the screen, for Pryor's performance is truly a class piece of acting, playing a likable enough fellow who loses everything but his sense of humor dur-ing five years in a Vietnamese prison camp.

During this tenure, he establishes a loving friendship with hot-tempered POW Ray Sharkey. When Sharkey becomes deathly ill, Pryor signs a denouncement of US activities in the war to get the North Vietnamese to provide proper medical attention. Action then shifts to Pryor's return to the US, where the act comes back to haunt him.

Pryor's only luck is meeting Beverly Hills prostitute Margot Kidder, who gives him some loving encouragement and considers him something more than just another customer.

With Kidder's role almost as limited as Sharkey's, latter portion of the story pretty much falls apart as Pryor is torn between good and bad.

. . . .

■ SOME LIKE IT HOT

1959, 105 MINS, US ⓥ
Dir Billy Wilder   *Prod* Billy Wilder   *Scr* Billy Wilder, I.A.L. Diamond   *Ph* Charles Lang   *Ed* Arthur Schmidt   *Mus* Adolph Deutsch
● Marilyn Monroe, Tony Curtis, Jack Lemmon, George Raft, Pat O'Brien, Joe E. Brown (Ashton/Mirisch)

Some Like It Hot is a whacky, clever, farcical comedy that starts off like a firecracker and keeps on throwing off lively sparks till the very end.

Story revolves around the age-old theme of men masquerading as women. Tony Curtis and Jack Lemmon escape from a Chicago nightclub that's being raided, witness the St. Valentine's day massacre and 'escape' into the anonymity of a girl band by dressing up as feminine musicians. This leads to the obvious complications, particularly since Curtis meets Marilyn Monroe (ukulele player, vocalist and gin addict) and falls for her. Lemmon, in turn, is propositioned by an addle-brained millionaire (Joe E. Brown).

A scene on a train, where the 'private' pull-man berth party of Lemmon and Monroe in her nightie is invaded by guzzling dames, represents humor of Lubitsch proportions. And the alternating shots of Monroe trying to stimulate Curtis on a couch, while Lemmon and Brown live it up on the dance floor, rate as a classic sequence.

Marilyn has never looked better. Her performance as Sugar, the fuzzy blonde who likes saxophone players 'and men with glasses', has a deliciously naive quality. It's a tossup whether Curtis beats out Lemmon or whether it goes the other way round. Both are excellent.

Curtis has the upper hand because he can change back and forth from his femme role to that of a fake 'millionaire' who woos Monroe. He employs a takeoff on Cary Grant, which scores with a bang at first, but tends to lose its appeal as the picture progresses.

Lemmon draws a choice assignment. Some of the funniest bits fall to him, such as his announcement that he's 'engaged' to Brown.

But, in the final accounting, this is still a director's picture and the Wilder touch is indelible. If the action is funny, the lines are there to match it.

••••••••••••••••••••••••••••••

■ SOME PEOPLE

1962, 93 MINS, UK ◇

Dir Clive Donner *Prod* James Archibald *Scr* John Eldridge *Ph* John Wilcox *Ed* Fergus McDonell *Mus* Ron Grainer *Art Dir* Reece Pemberton
● Kenneth More, Ray Brooks, Annika Wills, Angela Douglas, David Andrews, David Hemmings (Anglo Amalgamated)

This one is something of a hybrid. It is designed as a feature entertainment film, a peek at the problems of modern youth in danger of becoming delinquents. As such it stands up as reasonable entertainment. But also planted firmly in the film, some unabashed propaganda for the Duke of Edinburgh's Award Scheme for youth.

The pic is set in the industrial town of Bristol. Three lads are part of a gang of ton-up motorcyclists. Involved in an accident, they are banned from driving. Then, out of sheer boredom, they become potential young hoods. Luckily, they become involved with Kenneth More, playing a voluntary church choirmaster. He gives them the opportunity of rehearsing their rock 'n' roll combo. And gradually, they become interested in the new pursuits that the Duke's scheme has to offer youngsters of initiative.

John Eldridge's storyline is loose. Clive Donner's direction is leisurely but affectionate.

More handles the role of the sympathetic choirmaster with his usual, easy charm. But the revelation is in the performances of some of the youngsters. Ray Brooks, David Andrews and David Hemmings play the three main teenagers with authority. Angela Douglas is pretty provocative as a young blonde who can handle a song and a boy with equal assurance.

••••••••••••••••••••••••••••••

■ SOMEBODY UP THERE LIKES ME

1956, 112 MINS, US Ⓥ

Dir Robert Wise *Prod* Charles Schnee *Scr* Ernest Lehman *Ph* Joseph Ruttenberg *Ed* Albert Akst *Mus* Bronislau Kaper *Art Dir* Cedric Gibbons, Malcolm Brown
● Paul Newman, Pier Angeli, Everett Sloane, Eileen Heckart, Sal Mineo, Harold J. Stone (M-G-M)

Somebody Up There Likes Me is a superbly done, frank and revealing film probe of Rocky Graziano, the East Side punk who overcame a lawless beginning to win respect and position as middle-weight champion of the world.

Paul Newman's talent is large and flexible, revealing an approach to the Graziano character that scores tremendously.

In the latter half, when Norma Unger, played with beautiful sensitivity by Pier Angeli, comes into his life, the audience is back on his side, pulling for him to shake off the past, and literally cheering him on in that potently staged championship match with

Tony Zale. Credit for this stirring climax and its authenticity must be shared by technical adviser Johnny Indrisano and Courtland Shepard, who fights like a true-to-life Zale.

Numbered among the featured and supporting cast are Everett Sloane, great as the manager Irving Cohen; Eileen Heckart, exceptionally fine as Graziano's mother; Harold J. Stone, almost uncomfortably real as the wine-sodden father; and Sal Mineo, excellent as the street chum who shared Graziano's early ways.

••••••••••••••••••••••••••••••

■ SOMEONE TO LOVE

1987, 109 MINS, US ◇ Ⓥ

Dir Henry Jaglom *Prod* M.H. Simonsons *Scr* Henry Jaglom *Ph* Hanania Baer
● Orson Welles, Henry Jaglom, Andrea Marcovicci, Michael Emil, Sally Kellerman, Oja Kodar (Rainbow)

Someone To Love represents Henry Jaglom's alternately engaging and chaotic rumination on loneliness and aloneness in the 1980s. A serio-comic psycho-drama in which the filmmaker calls upon his friends to explore why he and they have problems with commitment or finding the right mate, pic is blessed with an almost overwhelming final screen appearance by Orson Welles.

Jaglom plays himself, a director so frustrated at his girlfriend Andrea Marcovicci's unwillingness to settle down he decides to devote an entire feature to what he perceives as a general malaise of his generation.

Without revealing his intentions, Jaglom invites many friends to a St Valentine's Day party who are somewhat taken aback by their host's desire to scrutinize their innermost feelings and insecurities with a camera, and some bow out.

Orson Welles, who appeared in Jaglom's first feature, *A Safe Place* (1971), returns here to act as the younger man's mentor and provocateur as he sits in the back of the theater smoking a cigar and delivering stunningly perceptive and intellectually far-ranging comments.

Also notable is Welles' longtime companion Oja Kodar, who portrays a visiting Yugoslavian woman with particularly sensitive and personal things to say about being a woman alone. Marcovicci gets to sing impressively and aggravate Jaglom, Sally Kellerman gives a vivid account of what one imagines Sally Kellerman to be like, and Michael Emil here gets his usual humorous philosophical ramblings thrown back in his face for a change.

••••••••••••••••••••••••••••••

■ SOMEONE TO WATCH OVER ME

1987, 106 MINS, US ◇ Ⓥ

Dir Ridley Scott *Prod* Thierry de Ganay *Scr* Howard Franklin *Ph* Steven Poster *Ed* Claire Simpson *Mus* Michael Kamen *Art Dir* Jim Bissell
● Tom Berenger, Mimi Rogers, Lorraine Bracco, Jerry Orbach, John Rubinstein, Andreas Katsulas (Columbia)

Someone to Watch Over Me is a stylish and romantic police thriller which manages, through the sleek direction of Ridley Scott and persuasive ensemble performances, to triumph over several hard-to-swallow plot developments.

Tom Berenger portrays Mike Keegan, a happily married NY cop from the Bronx who has just been promoted to detective and finds himself assigned on the night shift to protect socialite Claire Gregory (Mimi Rogers), witness to a brutal murder.

Heinous killer Joey Venza, played with economical nuance and menace by Andreas Katsulas, tracks Gregory down at the Guggenheim Museum and terrorizes her in the ladies' room while Keegan is distracted. Though he subsequently chases Venza down

and effects the collar, failure to read the goon his rights results in Venza back on the street and Gregory marked for death.

Berenger carries the film handily, utterly convincing as the working class stiff out of his element accompanying Rogers through her elegant apartment or posh parties. Rogers is alluring as the romantic interest, recalling the sharpness and beauty of Laraine Day, while wife, Lorraine Bracco, is fully sympathetic and easily has the viewer siding against the two leads during their hanky-panky segments.

••••••••••••••••••••••••••••••

■ SOMETHING WICKED THIS WAY COMES

1983, 94 MINS, US ◇ Ⓥ

Dir Jack Clayton *Prod* Peter Vincent Douglas *Scr* Ray Bradbury *Ph* Stephen H. Burum *Ed* Argyle Nelson *Mus* James Horner *Art Dir* Richard MacDonald
● Jason Robards, Jonathan Pryce, Diane Ladd, Pam Grier, Royal Dano, Vidal Peterson (Walt Disney/Bryna)

Film version of Ray Bradbury's popular novel *Something Wicked This Way Comes* must be chalked up as something of a disappointment. Possibilities for a dark, child's view fantasy set in rural America of yore are visible throughout the $20 million production but various elements have not entirely congealed into a unified achievement.

Location scenes shot in an astonishingly beautiful Vermont autumn stand in for early 20th century Illinois, where two young boys are intrigued by the untimely arrival of a mysterious carnival troupe. By day, fairgrounds seem innocent enough, but by night they possess a strange allure which leads local inhabitants to fall victim to their deepest desires.

Thanks to the diabolical talents of carnival leader Mr Dark, played by the suitably sinister Jonathan Pryce, these wishes can be granted, but at the price of becoming a member of the traveling freak show. Mr Dark decides that little Will and Jim would make excellent recruits and pursues them vigilantly until the apocalyptic finale.

••••••••••••••••••••••••••••••

■ SOMETHING WILD

1986, 113 MINS, US ◇ Ⓥ

Dir Jonathan Demme *Prod* Jonathan Demme, Kenneth Utt *Scr* E. Max Frye *Ph* Tak Fujimoto *Ed* Craig McKay *Mus* John Cale, Laurie Anderson *Art Dir* Norma Moriceau
● Jeff Daniels, Melanie Griffith, Ray Liotta, Margaret Colin, Tracey Walter, Dana Preu (Religioso Primitiva)

Conceptually and stylistically compelling under Jonathan Demme's sometimes striking direction, this offbeat thriller is about an unlikely couple on the run.

First-time screenwriter E. Max Frye's story sees superyuppie Jeff Daniels being picked up by hot number Melanie Griffith at a luncheonette, driven out to New Jersey and, before he knows what's happening, being handcuffed to a bed and ravished by this crazy lady.

Everything changes at her highschool reunion, however, as Griffith's ex-con husband makes an unexpected appearance and proceeds to change the couple's joyride into a nightmare. From this point on, Demme and Frye adroitly tighten the screws as the focus shifts from Griffith to the showdown between the two utterly different men vying for her attentions.

Daniels does a good job in transforming himself from straitlaced good boy to loosened up, wised-up man. Griffith is provocative enough, but falls a little short in putting across all the aspects of this complicated woman.

••••••••••••••••••••••••••••••

■ SOMETIMES A GREAT NOTION

1971, 114 MINS, US ◇ ▽

Dir Paul Newman   *Prod* John C. Foreman   *Scr* John Gay   *Ph* Richard Moore   *Ed* Bob Wyman   *Mus* Henry Mancini   *Art Dir* Philip Jefferies
● Paul Newman, Henry Fonda, Lee Remick, Michael Sarrazin, Richard Jaeckel, Linda Lawson (Universal)

Sometimes a Great Notion is a good, if plot-sprawling, outdoor action film set in Northwest lumber country, about a family of individualists fighting a town and a union. Paul Newman directed, produced, and stars as the crown prince to family patriarch Henry Fonda.

John Gay's adaptation of Ken Kesey's novel tries to balance the intellectual angles – Fonda's rigorous adherence to a principle, Newman's unending follow-through after disaster, and Michael Sarrazin's maturity from a self-indulgent drop-out. The result is rather good – a sort of contemporary 'western' in the timber territory.

Fonda's performance is perhaps his first in a crotchety characterization; there is an artistic overrun, however, which makes the character seem semi-senile instead of rock-ribbed noble. Lee Remick is too chic and sophisticated for her nothing part as Newman's concerned wife.

Sarrazin and Newman come off the best, the latter again in the kind of believable melodramatic role which first made him a star, the former in a demanding role which begins with drop-out petulance mixed with fraternal enmity.

■ SOMEWHERE IN TIME

1980, 103 MINS, US ◇ ▽

Dir Jeannot Szwarc   *Prod* Stephen Deutsch   *Scr* Richard Matheson   *Ph* Isidore Mankofsky   *Ed* Jeff Gourson   *Mus* John Barry   *Art Dir* Seymour Klate
● Christopher Reeve, Jane Seymour, Christopher Plummer, Teresa Wright, Bill Erwin, Sean Hayden (Universal/Rastar)

A charming, witty, passionate romantic drama about a love transcending space and time, *Somewhere In Time* is an old-fashioned film in the best sense of that term. Which means it's carefully crafted, civilized in its sensibilities, and interested more in characterization than in shock effects.

In the finely wrought screenplay by veteran fantasy writer Richard Matheson, based on his own novel *Bid Time Return*, Christopher Reeve is a young Chicago playwright who becomes mysteriously fascinated by a 1912 photo of a stage actress (Jane Seymour).

Reeve is drawn to a hotel on Mackinac Island in Michigan, where it transpires they actually did meet and have an affair at the time the photo was taken.

Seymour is lovely and mesmerizing enough to justify Reeve's grand romantic obsession with her.

■ SON OF PALEFACE

1952, 95 MINS, US ◇ ▽

Dir Frank Tashlin   *Prod* Robert L. Welch   *Scr* Frank Tashlin, Robert L. Welch, Joseph Quillan   *Ph* Harry J. Wild   *Ed* Eda Warren   *Mus* Lyn Murray
● Bob Hope, Jane Russell, Roy Rogers, Bill Williams, Lloyd Corrigan, Paul E. Burns (Paramount)

A free-wheeling, often hilarious, rambunctious followup to *The Paleface*. It is the broadest kind of slapstick, drawing advantageously on the silent-day masters of the pratfalls.

Plot finds Roy Rogers and Lloyd Corrigan, government agents, assigned to the case of running down 'The Torch', a bandit and gang that is looting gold shipments and then mysteriously disappearing. The job is complicated by the appearance in the small western town of Sawbuck Pass of Hope, the Harvard grad son of the late Paleface Potter.

A supercilious, cowardly braggart, Hope complicates matters temporarily until the agents decide to use him to confirm their suspicions that Jane Russell, the long-legged, amorous keeper of the Dirty Shame saloon, is the leader of the robbers.

■ SONG OF BERNADETTE, THE

1943, 158 MINS, US ▽

Dir Henry King   *Prod* William Perlberg   *Scr* George Seaton   *Ph* Arthur Miller   *Ed* Barbara McLean   *Mus* Alfred Newman
● Jennifer Jones, Charles Bickford, Gladys Cooper, Vincent Price, Lee J. Cobb, Anne Revere (20th Century-Fox)

Song of Bernadette is an absorbing, emotional and dramatic picturization of Franz Werfel's novel. Film version is a warming and intimate narrative of godly visitation on the young girl of Lourdes which eventuated in establishment of the Shrine at Lourdes, a grotto for the divine healing of the lame and halt.

Sensitively scripted and directed in best taste throughout, *Bernadette* unfolds in leisurely fashion with attention held through deft characterizations and incidents, rather than resort to synthetic dramatics. Many times during the extended running time there are sideline episodes inserted, but even these fail to lessen intense attention to the major theme.

Cast is expertly selected, and even the one-shot bits click solidly in fleeting footage. Jennifer Jones, in title role, delivers an inspirationally sensitive and arresting performance. Wistful, naive, and at times angelic, Jones takes command early to hold control as the motivating factor through the lengthy unfolding.

Despite the deeply religious tone of the dramatic narrative, theme is handled with utmost taste and reverence.

☐ 1943: Best Picture (Nomination)

■ SONG OF CEYLON

1935, 39 MINS, UK

Dir Basil Wright   *Prod* John Grierson   *Ph* Basil Wright   *Mus* Walter Leigh
(Ceylon Tea Production Board)

This thoroughgoing four-reel travelog on Ceylon attemps to dig down deep and cinematically explain the country and its people in more thorough manner than customarily encountered. Unfortunately it is just a shade too arty.

Had some of the hard-headed realistic *March of Time* approach been used, film would have come off much better. As it stands, the fancy and at time fantastic treatment will largely mystify audiences. In view of the splendid camerawork and some of the sequences, notably the native dances and religious devotions to Buddha, pic should have been aimed at the general public.

Effort to explain the economics and commerce of Ceylon is badly muddled through extensive use of vague or bewildering symbolisms. [Film is narrated by Lionel Wendt.]

■ SONG OF SCHEHERAZADE

1947, 105 MINS, US ▽

Dir Walter Reisch   *Prod* Edward Kaufman   *Scr* Walter Reisch   *Ph* Hal Mohr, William V. Skall   *Ed* Frank Goss   *Mus* Rimsky-Korsakov, Miklos Rozsa (adapt.)   *Art Dir* Jack Olterson
● Yvonne De Carlo, Brian Donlevy, Jean-Pierre Aumont, Eve Arden (Universal)

The music of Rimsky-Korsakov and eye value of brilliant color give *Song of Scheherazade* entertainment elements not otherwise found in the fluffy, ineptly directed and played story. Score contains 10 Rimsky-Kor-sakov tunes, ably adapted to the screen by Miklos Rozsa.

Basis for display of composer's muscle is his supposed escapades during a week in Spanish Morocco. Story has a comic-opera flavor, and Walter Reisch's direction of his own script often wavers in the treatment of plot elements and characters. Adding to ludicrous spots are a variety of accents, topped by the Broadwayese and 20th-century flippancy tossed into the 1865 period by Eve Arden. Plot purports to be based on an incident in Rimsky-Korsakov's life, when he was a midshipman in the Russian Navy, and is aimed at showing the influence the background had on his music.

Jean-Pierre Aumont plays the young composer. Yvonne De Carlo is the Spanish dancer with whom he falls in love during the week's adventuring. Brian Donlevy does a chain-smoking captain of the training ship who tries to make his students the pride of the Russian navy.

■ SONG OF THE ISLANDS

1942, 73 MINS, US ◇ ▽

Dir Walter Lang   *Prod* William Le Baron   *Scr* Joseph Schrank, Robert Pirosh, Robert Ellis, Helen Logan   *Ph* Ernest Palmer   *Ed* Robert Simpson   *Mus* Mack Gordon
● Betty Grable, Victor Mature, Jack Oakie, Thomas Mitchell, Hilo Hattie (20th Century-Fox)

Song of the Islands is a spontaneous and breezy mixture of comedy, song, dance and romance – set in Hawaiian atmosphere.

There's plenty of color, a load of romance, and sufficient comedy ladled out in generally broad style to carry audience interest.

Story is only a light and fragile framework on which to hang the various sequences. Betty Grable is the daughter of Thomas Mitchell, philosophical Irish beachcomber, who owns a portion of a small island in the Hawaiian group and treats the natives with consideration.

Victor Mature sails in to visit his father's cattle ranch on the other side of the island, and immediately romance gets under way.

Liberal potions of surefire comedy are supplied by Jack Oakie, who has a field day in by-play with buxom native maid (Hilo Hattie). Fast-paced script is enhanced by consistently zippy direction by Walter Lang.

■ SONG TO REMEMBER, A

1945, 110 MINS, US ◇ ▽

Dir Charles Vidor   *Prod* Sidney Buchman, Louis F. Edelman   *Scr* Sidney Buchman   *Ph* Tony Gaudio   *Ed* Charles Nelson   *Mus* Miklos Rozsa (adapt.)   *Art Dir* Lionel Banks, Van Nest Polglase
● Paul Muni, Merle Oberon, Cornel Wilde, Stephen Bekassy, George Coulouris (Columbia)

Based on the colorful – though brief – life of Polish composer Frederic Chopin, picture is a showmanly presentation of intimate drama and music.

Plot [from a story by Ernst Marischka] introduces Chopin as a prodigy at 11, with Paul Muni the old music master who easily recognizes his genius. When 22, the student and teacher flee to Paris after Chopin refuses to perform for the Russian governor. Young Franz Liszt befriends the newcomer and is directly responsible in getting him recognition.

Brilliant performances are generally turned in by the cast, with Muni provoking maximum interest with his portrayal of the music teacher. Cornel Wilde is spotlighted as Chopin and establishes himself as a screen personality. Merle Oberon clicks as the cold and calculating writer.

Jose Iturbi contributes importantly in the overall with his background playing of numerous Chopin compositions. Wilde does

S

a fine job of keyboard manipulations and the visual and sound components blend accurately for realist effect.

Reproduction of the piano passages is the best of its kind that has so far been accomplished, and credit for the achievement must go to John Livadary and the entire Columbia sound department.

■ SONGWRITER

1984, 94 MINS, US ◇ ▼
Dir Alan Rudolph *Prod* Sydney Pollack *Scr* Bud Shrake *Ph* Matthew Leonetti *Ed* Stuart Pappe *Mus* Larry Cansler *Art Dir* Joel Schiller
● Willie Nelson, Kris Kristofferson, Melinda Dillon, Rip Torn, Lesley Ann Warren (Tri-Star)

Songwriter is a good-natured film that rolls along on the strength of attitudes and poses long ago established outside the picture by its stars, Willie Nelson and Kris Kristofferson, basically playing themselves disguised as fictional characters.

Brief opening collage establishes the younger days of Doc Jenkins (Nelson) and Blackie Buck (Kristofferson) as a performing duo before they go their semi-separate ways and revert to character.

Doc Jenkins is the saint of country music, loved and respected by everyone. Luckily Nelson has enough of a screen presence to support his deification. As Blackie Buck, Kristofferson is still the outlaw with a heart of gold, but who will probably never grow up and settle down.

Director Alan Rudolph, who took over for Steve Rash two weeks into the filming, is best at working with actors, and Lesley Ann Warren, in particular, is radiant as an up-and-coming, but reluctant country/western singer.

■ SONS AND LOVERS

1960, 99 MINS, UK
Dir Jack Cardiff *Prod* Jerry Wald *Scr* Gavin Lambert, T.E.B. Clarke *Ph* Freddie Francis *Ed* Gordon Pilkington
● Trevor Howard, Dean Stockwell, Wendy Hiller, Mary Ure, Heather Sears, William Lucas (20th Century-Fox)

Sons and Lovers is a well-made and conscientious adaptation of D. H. Lawrence's famed novel, smoothly directed by Jack Cardiff and superbly acted by a notable cast.

Gavin Lambert and T. E. B. Clarke collaborated in producing a literate screenplay, though not entirely recapturing the atmosphere of the Nottinghamshire mining village so vividly described in the original. Also there is a tendency to portray the mother as an overly selfish, possessive and nagging woman. Even Wendy Hiller's flawless performance cannot make her a sympathetic character.

Many of the exteriors were filmed on location outside Nottingham, and their authenticity is a plus factor. Against the background of the grimy mining village is unfolded the story of a miner's son with promising artistic talents who is caught up in continual conflict between his forthright father and possessive mother. He sacrifices a chance to study art in London, gives up the local farm girl he loves, and eventually becomes entangled with a married woman separated from her husband.

Easily the outstanding feature of the production is the powerful performance by Trevor Howard, as the miner. He gives a moving and wholly believable study of a man equally capable of tenderness as he is of being tough. He looks the character, too. Dean Stockwell puts up a good showing as the son, and makes a valiant try to cope with the accent.
□ 1960: Best Picture (Nomination)

■ SONS OF KATIE ELDER, THE

1965, 120 MINS, US ◇ ▼
Dir Henry Hathaway *Prod* Hal Wallis *Scr* William H. Wright, Allan Weiss, Harry Essex *Ph* Lucien Ballard *Ed* Warren Low *Mus* Elmer Bernstein *Art Dir* Hal Pereira, Walter Tyler
● John Wayne, Dean Martin, Martha Hyer, Michael Anderson Jr, Earl Holliman, Denis Hopper (Paramount)

Talbot Jennings' story tells of four brothers – John Wayne a notorious gunslinger, Dean Martin a gambler – who return to their Texas home to attend their mother's funeral and remain to fight the town.

Two stars are joined by Earl Holliman and Michael Anderson Jr, latter the kid brother, in family setup. The three older brothers are prodigals who left home years before. The mother is never shown, but her influence is felt throughout the film as the three seniors decide that the best monument they can erect for their mother is to send her last-born back to college.

Drama takes form as the brothers decide to stay long enough to learn who murdered their father six months previously, look into the situation of their mother losing her ranch to a townsman, and a grim young deputy sheriff learning Martin is wanted for murder and deciding to bring the brothers in.

Wayne delivers one of his customary rugged portrayals, a little old, perhaps, to have such a young brother as Anderson but not so old that he lacks the attributes of a gunman. Martin, who plays his part with a little more humor than the others, is equally effective in a hardboiled characterization.

■ SOPHIE'S CHOICE

1982, 157 MINS, US ◇ ▼
Dir Alan J. Pakula *Prod* Alan J. Pakula, Keith Barish *Scr* Alan J. Pakula *Ph* Nestor Almendros *Ed* Evan Lottman *Mus* Marvin Hamlisch *Art Dir* George Jenkins
● Meryl Streep, Kevin Kline, Peter MacNicol, Rita Karin, Stephen D. Newman, Josh Mostel (ITC)

Sophie's Choice is a handsome, doggedly faithful and astoundingly tedious adaptation of William Styron's best-seller.

Set in 1947, tale has young aspiring writer Stingo, (Peter MacNicol), a southern lad, taking a room in a comfortable house in which also dwell Sophie (Meryl Streep), a Polish former Catholic, and her exuberant, changeable, Jewish lover, Nathan Landau (Kevin Kline). Three become best of friends, although at times Nathan turns on the other two, leaving Stingo to console Sophie and hear some of her painful confessions about her pre-war life and incarceration by the Nazis.

Ever so slowly, it comes clear that Sophie has lied about many things, notably her father. After 90 minutes, film flips into a half-hour, subtitled, sepiatoned flashback to portray Sophie's tenure as secretary to the commanding officer at Auschwitz.

Streep, Kline and MacNicol all give it a good shot individually, but they never coalesce into the close, warm trio called for by the story.

■ SORCERER

1977, 121 MINS, US ◇
Dir William Friedkin *Prod* William Friedkin *Scr* Walon Green *Ph* John M. Stephens, Dick Bush *Ed* Bud Smith *Mus* Charlie Parker *Art Dir* John Box
● Roy Scheider, Bruno Cremer, Francisco Rabal, Amidou, Ramon Bieri, Peter Capell (Universal/Paramount)

William Friedkin's *Sorcerer* is a painstaking, admirable, but mostly distant and uninvolving suspenser based on the French classic *The Wages of Fear* [from the novel by Georges Arnaud]. Friedkin vividly renders the experience of several men driving trucks loaded with nitro through the South American jungle.

The drivers are Roy Scheider, Bruno Cremer, Amidou and Francisco Rabal.

The story has a strong existential feeling, desperate men staking their lives on a suicidal mission because they have no other way of making a living.

But despite the opening scenes – of Scheider involved in a New Jersey robbery, Cremer in a French bank scandal, and Amidou in an Arab terrorist incident – the film fails to bring them alive as people.

■ SORCERERS, THE

1967, 86 MINS, UK ◇ ▼
Dir Michael Reeves *Prod* Patrick Curtis, Tony Tenser *Scr* Michael Reeves, Tom Baker *Ph* Stanley Long *Ed* Ralph Sheldon *Mus* Paul Ferris *Art Dir* Tony Curtis
● Boris Karloff, Catherine Lacey, Ian Ogilvy, Elizabeth Ercy, Victor Henry, Susan George (Tigon)

Boris Karloff brings his familiar adroit horror touch to the role of an aging somewhat nutty ex-stage mesmerist who aims to complete his experiments by dominating the brain of a young subject. Karloff himself is dominated by his wife (Catherine Lacey), who was his stage assistant.

Karloff persuades Ian Ogilvy, who plays a feckless, slightly moody youth, to become the subject for his experiments. Initial experiments work well as Karloff sees in the youth a tool who may be able to benefit mankind under his influence. But Karloff's wife, motivated by greed, insists that the lad should work for their benefit for a while.

■ SORRY, WRONG NUMBER

1948, 89 MINS, US ▼
Dir Anatole Litvak *Prod* Hal Wallis *Scr* Lucille Fletcher *Ph* Sol Polito *Ed* Warren Low *Mus* Franz Waxman *Art Dir* Hans Dreier, Earl Hedrick
● Barbara Stanwyck, Burt Lancaster, Ann Richards, Wendell Corey, Ed Begley (Paramount)

Sorry, Wrong Number is a real chiller. Film is a fancily dressed co-production by Hal B. Wallis and Anatole Litvak. Pair has smoothly coordinated efforts to give strong backing to the Lucille Fletcher script, based on her radio play.

Plot deals with an invalid femme who overhears a murder scheme through crossed telephone lines. Alone in her home, the invalid tries to trace the call. She fails, and then tries to convince the police of the danger. She gradually comes to realize that it is her own death that is planned.

Barbara Stanwyck plays her role of the invalid almost entirely in bed. Her reading is sock, the actress giving an interpretation that makes the neurotic, selfish woman understandable. Same touch is used by Burt Lancaster to make audiences see through the role of the invalid's husband and how he came to plot her death.

Considerable emphasis is placed on the score by Franz Waxman to heighten the gradually mounting suspense. Sol Polito uses an extremely mobile camera for the same effect, sharpening the building terror with unusual angles and lighting.

■ SOUL MAN

1986, 101 MINS, US ◇ ▼
Dir Steve Miner *Prod* Steve Tisch *Scr* Carol Black *Ph* Jeffrey Jur *Ed* David Finfer *Mus* Tom Scott *Art Dir* Gregg Fonseca
● C. Thomas Howell, Arye Gross, Rae Dawn Chong, James Earl Jones, Melora Hardin, Leslie Nielsen (Balcour/Tisch)

This social farce is excellently written, fast paced and intelligently directed.

Film is hilarious throughout as initial screenplay by Carol Black consistently engages via fable-like tale of a white man (C. Thomas Howell) darkening his skin in order to win a law-school scholarship intended for a black.

Director Steve Miner skillfully guides pic through visually compelling scenes, producing a comedic review of the state of America's racist attitudes.

Howell as the white-turned-black law student is just effective enough to be believable. As Howell's close buddy, Arye Gross delivers gifted and energized screen humor. Rae Dawn Chong is wholly natural and intellectually appealing. Her reluctant romantic involvement with Howell focuses his ultimate moral dilemma over the skin deception.

■ SOUND AND THE FURY, THE

1959, 115 MINS, US ◇

Dir Martin Ritt *Prod* Jerry Wald *Scr* Irving Ravetch, Harriet Frank Jr *Ph* Charles G. Clarke *Ed* Stuart Gilmore *Mus* Alex North
● Yul Brynner, Joanne Woodward, Margaret Leighton, Stuart Whitman, Ethel Waters, Jack Warden (20th Century-Fox)

Sound and the Fury is a provocative and sensitively-executed study of the decadent remnants of an erstwhile eminent family of a small southern town. The characters of the William Faulkner allegorical novel are a lost generation whose heritage is only the family name. They represent skid-row morality.

The Compsons are two brothers, one a weak alcoholic and the other a mute idiot (John Beal and Jack Warden), and a sister (Margaret Leighton) who has a long history of promiscuity. Their father, before his own death and following the death of his wife, had taken on a second mate and a stepson, Yul Brynner. Latter in turn has taken on the Compson name and rules as master over a decrepit estate and his wretched second-hand relatives. Subject to his control also is Joanne Woodward, cast as Miss Leighton's youthful, illegitimate daughter.

Woodward gives firm conviction to the part of the girl who cries out desperately for the love and affection she can't find in her own home and, somewhat giddily, takes up with a crude mechanic.

Leighton is remarkably realistic as the washed-out hag who had abandoned her daughter at childbirth and now has returned for refuge from a world (of men) no longer holding out hands to her.

Brynner is every inch the household tyrant. He's a fierce domineering personality, bent on keeping the family together so that the name he has adopted will not lose all its social value. Brynner has subtly shaded the character with maximum skill, eventually emerging from Woodward's bitter and cold keeper to benefactor concerned with her integrity and, it's suggested, a closer role in her future. Pygmalion or in-law uncle with an incestuous drive?

■ SOUND BARRIER, THE

1952, 118 MINS, UK

Dir David Lean *Prod* David Lean *Scr* Terence Rattigan *Ph* Jack Hildyard *Ed* Geoffrey Foot *Mus* Malcolm Arnold *Art Dir* Vincent Korda
● Ralph Richardson, Ann Todd, Nigel Patrick, John Justin, Dinah Sheridan, Joseph Tomelty (London/British Lion)

Technically, artistically and emotionally, this is a topflight British offering.

Dwarfing the individual performers, good though they are, are the magnificent air sequences, with impressive and almost breath-taking dives by the jet as it attempts to crash the sound barrier.

The visionary in the film is superbly played by Ralph Richardson. His ambition to make the first faster-than-sound plane has brought him nothing but grief and disaster. He sees his only son killed on his first solo try; he accepts the estrangement of his daughter (Ann Todd) when his son-in-law (Nigel Patrick) crashes while making the first attempt to crash the barrier.

Ann Todd's portrayal of the daughter correctly yields the emotional angle.

David Lean's direction is bold and imaginative.

■ SOUND OF MUSIC, THE

1965, 173 MINS, US ◇ Ⓥ

Dir Robert Wise *Prod* Robert Wise *Scr* Ernest Lehman *Ph* Ted McCord *Ed* William Reynolds *Mus* Richard Rodgers *Art Dir* Boris Leven
● Julie Andrews, Christopher Plummer, Eleanor Parker, Richard Haydn, Peggy Wood, Charmian Carr (20th Century-Fox)

The magic and charm of the Rodgers-Hammerstein-Lindsay-Crouse 1959 stage hit are sharply blended in this filmic translation. The Robert Wise production is a warmly-pulsating, captivating drama set to the most imaginative use of the lilting R-H tunes, magnificently mounted and with a brilliant cast headed by Julie Andrews and Christopher Plummer.

Wise drew on the same team of creative talent associated with him on *West Side Story* to convert the stage property, with its natural physical limitations, to the more expansive possibilities of the camera.

For the story of the Von Trapp family singers, of the events leading up to their becoming a top concert attraction just prior to the Second World War and their fleeing Nazi Austria, Wise went to the actual locale, Salzburg, and spent 11 weeks limning his action amidst the pageantry of the Bavarian Alps.

Against such background the tale of the postulant at Nonnberg Abbey in Salzburg who becomes governess to widower Captain Von Trapp and his seven children, who brings music into a household that had, until then, been run on a strict naval office regimen, with no frivolity permitted, takes on fresh meaning.

Andrews endows her role of the governess who aspires to be a nun, but instead falls in love with Navy Captain Von Trapp and marries him, with fine feeling and a sense of balance which assures continued star stature. Plummer also is particularly forceful as Von Trapp, former Austrian Navy officer who rather than be drafted into service under Hitler prefers to leave his homeland.

Playing the part of the baroness, whom the captain nearly married, Eleanor Parker acquits herself with style.

□ 1965: Best Picture

■ SOUNDER

1972, 105 MINS, US ◇ Ⓥ

Dir Martin Ritt *Prod* Robert B. Radnitz *Scr* Lonne Elder III *Ph* John Alonzo *Ed* Sid Levin *Mus* Taj Mahal *Art Dir* Walter Herndon
● Cicely Tyson, Paul Winfield, Kevin Hooks, Carmen Mathews, Taj Mahal, Janet MacLachlan (20th Century Fox)

Sounder is an outstanding film. The superb production depicts the heart-warming and character-building struggles of a poor black sharecropper family in the Depression era. Martin Ritt's masterful direction, an excellent adaptation [from William H. Armstrong's novel], and a uniformly terrific cast make this a film which transcends space, race, age and time. Ritt's sensitive, gentle and delicate style is mated well with script and cast.

Appearing in his first major theatrical role is Kevin Hooks, excellent as the eldest son who assumes the challenges of manhood when his father (Paul Winfield) is sentenced to a year at hard labor for stealing some food for his family.

Winfield is a smash in combining youth and mature virility into a figure of parental authority and parental love. His scenes with Hooks are magnificent, as are his interactions with Cicely Tyson as his wife.

□ 1972: Best Picture (Nomination)

■ SOURSWEET

1989, 110 MINS, UK ◇

Dir Mike Newell *Prod* Roger Randall-Cutler *Scr* Ian McEwan *Ph* Michael Gerfath *Ed* Mick Audsley *Mus* Richard Hartley *Art Dir* Adrian Smith
● Sylvia Chang, Danny Dun, Jodi Long, Soon-Tech Oh, William Chow (First/British Screen/Zenith)

Soursweet is an aptly titled charmer about a Chinese family living in a dismal suburb of London. Pic sympathetically explores the insidious ways in which Chinese emigrants have to adapt to life in Britain after moving to London from Hong Kong.

Adapted from Timothy Mo's novel, the film opens with an elaborate wedding ceremony for a young couple (Sylvia Chang, Danny Dun) held on the outskirts of Hong Kong. Shortly after, the couple moves to London, where Dun finds work as a waiter in a crowded Chinatown restaurant.

Dun goes through a period in which he becomes indebted to a seedy moneylender who works for one of the two gangs who seem to control the Chinatown underworld. The couple soon moves to the suburbs, where they start a modest Chinese restaurant in a rented house. After a slow start, the place prospers, and gradually friendly links are formed with the locals.

It's the small details that are most significant. The way a little boy discovers at school that the Chinese way of fighting, taught to him by his mother, is considered unfair. Or the way traditional Chinese customs give way in the face of British culture and lifestyle; french fries replace noodles.

■ SOUTH PACIFIC

1958, 170 MINS, US ◇ Ⓥ

Dir Joshua Logan *Prod* Buddy Adler *Scr* Paul Osborn *Ph* Leon Shamroy *Ed* Robert Simpson *Mus* Richard Rodgers *Art Dir* Lyle R. Wheeler, John DeCuir, Walter M. Scott, Paul S. Fox
● Rossano Brazzi, Mitzi Gaynor, John Kerr, Ray Walston, Juanita Hall, France Nuyen (20th Century-Fox/South Pacific Enterprises/Magna)

South Pacific is a compelling entertainment. The songs, perennial favorites, are mated to a sturdy James A. Michener story. Combination boffo.

Mitzi Gaynor is no Mary Martin but there are millions who never saw the original Nellie Forbush. Rossano Brazzi may be no Ezio Pinza but the late, great Metropolitan Opera basso profundo hasn't the global b.o. impact of the Italian film-star-gone-Hollywood. Besides, Giorgio Tozzi's dubbed basso has been skillfully integrated into the Brazzi brand of romantic antics.

The histrionics are effective throughout and of high standard. John Kerr (vocally dubbed by Bill Lee) is the right romantic vis-a-vis for Eurasian beauty France Nuyen, daughter of the bawdy 'Bloody Mary' whom Juanita Hall recreates for the screen. She's of the Broadway original and like most of the other principals has been given a vocal stand-in (Muriel Smith, but unbilled; Tozzi alone gets screen credit as Brazzi's ghost voice). Ray Walston

S

is capital as the uninhibited seabee Luther Billis, recreating the role he did in the road company and in London.

Gaynor is uneven in her overall impact. She is in her prime with 'Honey-Bun' in that captivating misfit sailor's uniform, and she is properly gay and buoyant and believable in 'Wonderful Guy'. In other sequences she is conventional. No dubbee she, Gaynor's song-and-dance is essentially very professional.

Brazzi is properly serious of mien and earnest in his love protestations. The seabees are forthrightly dame-hungry; and there is enough cheesecake among the nurses corps to decorate the beachhead. Their treatment of 'Nothing Like a Dame' is standout.

From 'Some Enchanted Evening' to 'My Girl Back Home', it's a surefire score. It's probably the greatest galaxy of popular favorites from a single show in the history of musical comedy. 'Home' was originally in the legit score, was eliminated for show's length but, a favorite with R&H, reinstated into the film version.

All the other credits are topflight – the Alfred Newman baton, the Ken Darby musical assist, and all that goes with this $5 million spectacle.

．．．．．．．．．．．．．．．．．．．．．．．．．．．．

■ SOUTH RIDING

1938, 91 MINS, UK ⓥ

Dir Victor Saville   *Prod* Victor Saville   *Scr* Ian Dalrymple, Donald Bull   *Ph* Harry Stradling   *Ed* Hugh Stewart, Jack Dennis   *Mus* Richard Addinsell   *Art Dir* Lazare Meerson

● Edna Best, Ralph Richardson, Edmund Gwenn, Ann Todd, John Clements, Marie Lohr (London)

There are enough requisites in this English melodrama [from a novel by Winifred Holtby] to excite attention. It is fairly familiar matter – the spoiled child whose father fears she will grow up to be like her stark-mad mother, the conniving contractor and real estate operator, and the country gentleman whose intense love of his estate nearly enables the crooked plot to hatch. But all of this has been heightened by original twirls of acting and direction.

Many incidental plot threads are dragged in at the sacrifice of more vital episodes. An example is the flashback to show how the estate owner's wife became demented, obviously to display Ann Todd's histrionics.

The affair the week-kneed councilman is supposed to have had with a country damsel is not obvious enough for average American audiences.

Edna Best is tops in the film as the school teacher. Ralph Richardson contributes one of his finer thespian jobs as the country gentleman. John Clements, who resembles Gary Cooper, also is top flight as the ambitious young councilman. Glynis Johns, in the role of the headstrong daughter of the wealthy estate holder, shows promise.

Title of film, derives from a supposed judicial district. Actually there is no 'South' Riding, the other divisions being East, West and North.

．．．．．．．．．．．．．．．．．．．．．．．．．．．．

■ SOUTH SEAS ADVENTURE

1958, 120 MINS, US ◇

Dir Carl Dudley, Richard Goldstone, Francis D. Lyon, Walter Thompson, Basil Wrangell   *Prod* Carl Dudley, Richard Goldstone   *Scr* Charles Kaufman, Joseph Ansen, Harold Medford   *Ph* John F. Warren, Paul Hill   *Ed* Frederick Y. Smith, Walter Stern   *Mus* Alex North   *Art Dir* Dan Cathcart, Ray Morris, Eric Thompson

● (Cinerama)

If *South Seas Adventure* were not No. 5 in a sequence of [three-camera Cinerama] travelogs its merits would no doubt seem more estimable. Here again is the airplane ride over the snow, the ocean, the endless prairie. Glacial

and other geologic wonders, raging waters and smouldering volcanic mud are again glanced. There is even once again the ride in the amusement park.

Yet the voyage by liner, schooner and aircraft adds up to a fairly diverting if not very exciting journey. Cinerama still conveys its unique brand of pictorial experience, though distortion and seams persist.

Continuity is pretty straightforward, dotted with a few giggles but eschewing the purple prose, and especially the built-in songplugs and private exploitation which marred *Search for Paradise*.

Some confusion results from the use of a main narrator, Orson Welles, but spelled off in different sequences by three other narrators, Shepherd Menken, Walter Coy, Ted de Corsia. Alex North's score stays in the background, where it belongs, most of the time, but in some of the flying and Australian scenes, notably the demented steeplechase of the kangaroos, the music comes forward strongly and imaginatively.

This is an updated and primarily respectable South Seas in which Paul Gauguin is only a name and cannibalism, beach-combing, Somerset Maugham, Robert Louis Stevenson and J.C. Furnas tales are not on the screen. Big physical thrill among the islands is the jump off the bamboo tower by the natives of the New Hebrides, the fall being broken by vine ropes attached to the men's ankles.

．．．．．．．．．．．．．．．．．．．．．．．．．．．．

■ SOUTHERN COMFORT

1981, 100 MINS, US ◇

Dir Walter Hill   *Prod* David Giler   *Scr* Michael Kane, Walter Hill, David Giler   *Ph* Andrew Laszlo   *Ed* Freeman Davies   *Mus* Ry Cooder   *Art Dir* John Vallone

● Keith Carradine, Powers Boothe, Fred Ward, Franklyn Seales, T.K. Carter (20th Century-Fox)

An arresting exercise in visual filmmaking and a tautly told suspenser about men out of their depths in the Louisiana swamps, *Southern Comfort* is hardly a cinematic equivalent of the libation of the same name. It's an elemental drama of survival in a threatening environment, and the traditional themes of group camaraderie and mutual support are turned inside out.

Set in 1973, tale presents nine National Guard members, weekend soldiers, heading out into the bayou for practice maneuvers. They make the mistake of appropriating some canoes belonging to local Cajuns, and when the densest of the group commits the lunacy of firing (blanks) at some native pursuers the ill-prepared unit finds itself in a virtual state of war with forbidding area's inhabitants.

Pic is most exciting as a visual experience, as Walter Hill once again proves himself a consummate filmmaker with a great talent for mood, composition and action choreography. Also outstanding is Ry Cooder's unusual score, which makes use of spare, offbeat instrumentation as well as some authentic Cajun music. Acting-wise, this is an ensemble piece, and all hands contribute strongly.

．．．．．．．．．．．．．．．．．．．．．．．．．．．．

■ SOUTHERNER, THE

1945, 91 MINS, US ⓥ

Dir Jean Renoir   *Prod* David L. Loew, Robert Hakim   *Scr* Jean Renoir, Hugo Butler   *Ph* Lucien Andriot   *Ed* Gregg Tallas   *Mus* Werner Janssen   *Art Dir* Eugene Lourie

● Zachary Scott, Betty Field, Beulah Bondi, Percy Kilbride, J. Carrol Naish (United Artists)

There is something distressing about the haphazards of the soil's human migrants, and all the squalor that one associates with their condition is brought to *The Southerner*. An adap-

tation from the George Sessions Perry novel, *Hold Autumn in Your Hand*, this film conjures a naked picture of morbidity. It may be trenchant realism, but these are times when there is a greater need. Escapism is the word.

The Southerner creates too little hope for a solution to the difficulties of farm workers who constantly look forward to the day when they can settle forever their existence of poverty with a long-sought harvest – a harvest that invariably never comes.

This is, specifically, the story of Sam and Nona, and their struggle to cultivate the rich earth of their mid-west farm. It is a farm beset by liabilities, of which lack of money and food are no small factors. Their home is a patchwork of sagging planks and misguided faith.

Zachary Scott and Betty Field give fine performances, as do Beulah Bondi, the grandmother, Percy Kilbride, Charles Kemper and J. Carrol Naish.

．．．．．．．．．．．．．．．．．．．．．．．．．．．．

■ SOYLENT GREEN

1973, 97 MINS, US ◇ ⓥ

Dir Richard Fleischer   *Prod* Walter Seltzer, Russell Thatcher   *Scr* Stanley R. Greenberg   *Ph* Richard H. Kline   *Ed* Samuel E. Boetley   *Mus* Fred Myrow   *Art Dir* Edward C. Carfagno

● Charlton Heston, Leigh Taylor-Young, Chuck Connors, Joseph Cotten, Brock Peters, Edward G. Robinson (M-G-M)

The somewhat plausible and proximate horrors in the story of *Soylent Green* carry the production over its awkward spots to the status of a good futuristic exploitation film.

The year is 2022, the setting NY City, where millions of over-populated residents exist in a smog-insulated police state, where the authorities wear strange-looking foreign uniforms (not the gray flannel suits which is more likely the case), and where real food is a luxury item. Charlton Heston is a detective assigned to the assassination murder of industrialist Joseph Cotten, who has discovered the shocking fact that the Soylent Corp, of which he is a director, is no longer capable of making synthetic food from the dying sea. The substitute – the reconstituted bodies of the dead.

The character Heston plays is pivotal, since he is supposed to be the prototype average man of the future who really swallows whole the social system. Edward G. Robinson, his investigative aide, reminisces about the old days – green fields, flowers, natural food, etc. But the script bungles seriously by confining Heston's outrage to the secret of Soylent Green.

．．．．．．．．．．．．．．．．．．．．．．．．．．．．

■ SPACEBALLS

1987, 96 MINS, US ◇ ⓥ

Dir Mel Brooks   *Prod* Mel Brooks   *Scr* Mel Brooks, Thomas Meehan, Ronny Graham   *Ph* Nick McLean   *Ed* Conrad Buff   *Mus* John Morris   *Art Dir* Terence Marsh

● Mel Brooks, John Candy, Rick Moranis, Bill Pullman, Daphne Zuniga (M-G-M/Brooksfilm)

Mel Brooks will do anything for a laugh. Unfortunately, what he does in *Spaceballs*, a misguided parody of the *Star Wars* adventures, isn't very funny.

Pic features Bill Pullman as Lone Starr and Daphne Zuniga as Princess Vespa, former a composite of Harrison Ford and Mark Hamill, latter a Carrie Fisher clone. Pullman's partner is John Candy as Barf, a half-man, half-dog creature who is his own best friend. Equipped with a constantly wagging tale and furry sneakers, Barf is one of the better comic creations here.

The plot about the ruthless race of Spaceballs out to steal the air supply from the planet Druidia is more cliched than the original. Brooks turns up in the dual role of President Skroob of Spaceballs and the all-knowing, all-powerful Yogurt.

Brooks' direction is far too static to suggest the sweeping style of the *Star Wars* epics and pic more closely resembles Flash Gordon programmers. Aside from a few isolated laughs *Spaceballs* is strictly not kosher.

● ●

■ SPACECAMP

1986, 107 MINS, US ◇ ▼
Dir Harry Winer *Prod* Patrick Bailey *Scr* W.W. Wicket, [= Clifford Green, Ellen Green], Casey T. Mitchell *Ph* William A. Fraker *Ed* John W. Wheeler, Timothy Board *Mus* John Williams *Art Dir* Richard MacDonald
● Kate Capshaw, Lea Thompson, Kelly Preston, Larry B. Scott, Leaf Phoenix, Tate Donovan (ABC)

SpaceCamp is a youthful view of outer space set at the real-life United States Space Camp in Huntsville, Alabama for aspiring young astronauts. Pic never successfully integrates summer camp hijinks with outer space idealism to come up with a dramatically compelling story.

Hampered by cliché-ridden dialog, performances suffer from a weightlessness of their own. Kate Capshaw as the instructor and one trained astronaut to make the flight neither looks nor acts the part of a serious scientist.

As for the kids, Tate Donovan as the shuttle commander-in-training is uninteresting and Lea Thompson as his would-be girlfriend is too young and naive for words, even the ones she's given.

● ●

■ SPANISH GARDENER, THE

1957, 97 MINS, UK ◇
Dir Philip Leacock *Prod* John Bryan *Scr* Lesley Storm, John Bryan *Ph* Christopher Challis *Ed* Reginald Mills *Mus* John Veale *Prod Des* Maurice Carter
● Dirk Bogarde, Jon Whiteley, Michael Hordern, Cyril Cusack, Maureen Swanson, Bernard Lee (Rank)

A.J. Cronin's novel of a minor diplomat with considerable academic qualifications, but without human understanding, translates into absorbing screen entertainment. It is a leisurely told story with colorful Spanish backgrounds.

Michael Hordern is the diplomat separated from his wife, continually passed up for promotion, who insists that his son is delicate, cannot join other children in games or at school and is denied every form of companionship. Dirk Bogarde is hired as a gardener and his friendly attitude to the kid sparks a violent jealousy in the father.

Bogarde gives a polished, restrained study as the Spanish gardener whose motives in befriending the boy are completely misunderstood. Jon Whiteley's moppet is a keenly sensitive portrayal. Cyril Cusack, as a sinister valet, and Maureen Swanson, as the gardener's girl friend, top a good supporting cast.

● ●

■ SPARROWS CAN'T SING

1963, 94 MINS, UK
Dir Joan Littlewood *Prod* Donald Taylor *Scr* Joan Littlewood, Stephen Lewis *Ph* Max Greene, Desmond Dickinson *Ed* Oswald Hafenrichter *Mus* Stanley Black
● James Booth, Barbara Windsor, Roy Kinnear, Avis Bunnage, George Sewell, Barbara Ferris (Carthage)

For her first essay in pix, Joan Littlewood plays fairly safe. The film is based on a play that she staged at the Theatre Workshop. She and the author of the play (Stephen Lewis) collaborated on the loose screenplay and Littlewood surrounds herself with most of the Workshop cast. She also operates almost

entirely on location in the East End that she knows and clearly loves so well.

The storyline is disarmingly slight. James Booth plays a tearaway merchant seaman who comes back to his East End home after two years afloat to find that his home had been torn down during replanning and his wife (Barbara Windsor) has found herself another nest with a local bus driver. His arrival strikes uneasiness in the hearts of the locals, who know his uncertain temper. But Booth sets out to find his wife and collect his conjugal rights.

This could have been played for drama or even tragedy. The screenplay writers and Littlewood's direction beckon to the brighter and breezier slant and, though there is a sober side to the film, this is mostly played for yocks. Much of the dialog, which is rather salty, appears to have been made up off the cuff of the players. This shows up dangerously in the intimate scenes, but gives gusto to others.

Booth is a striking personality, a punchy blend of toughness, potential evil and irresistible charm. Barbara Windsor (who also chants the Lionel Bart title song) is a cute young blonde who teeters delightfully through her role, on stiletto heels and with a devastating sense of logic.

● ●

■ SPAWN OF THE NORTH

1938, 105 MINS, US
Dir Henry Hathaway *Prod* Albert Lewin *Scr* Jules Furthman, Talbot Jennings *Ph* Charles Lang *Ed* Ellsworth Hoagland *Mus* Dimitri Tiomkin
● George Raft, Henry Fonda, Dorothy Lamour, Akim Tamiroff, John Barrymore, Louise Platt (Paramount)

Impressive scenes of the Alaskan waters, backgrounded by towering glaciers which drop mighty icebergs into the sea, imperiling doughty fishermen and their frail craft, lift *Spawn of the North* into the class of robust out-of-door films where the spectacular overshadows the melodrama.

The plot [story by Barrett Willoughby] recounts the battles between licensed fishermen and pirates who steal the catch from the traps which are set for salmon at spawning time. George Raft and Henry Fonda, boyhood friends, are members of opposing factions, the former having fallen in with Russian thieves.

Merit of the film is in the persuasive and authentic photographic record of Alaskan life and customs. Akim Tamiroff is a truly menacing pirate with a black heart and no regard for law and order. John Barrymore is an amusing small town editor and Lynne Overman makes a cynical role standout by his gruff humor.

● ●

■ SPEAKING PARTS

1989, 92 MINS, CANADA ◇ ▼
Dir Atom Egoyan *Scr* Atom Egoyan *Ph* Paul Sarossy *Ed* Bruce McDonald *Mus* Mychael Danna *Art Dir* Linda Del Rosario
● Michael McManus, Arsinee Khanjian, Gabrielle Rose, David Hemblen, Patricia Collins (Ego)

Speaking Parts, the third feature from Toronto's Atom Egoyan, is a brooding, personal effort, adroitly blending film and video, but with mixed results overall.

Hero cleans hotel rooms, sexually services female clients off screen on orders from the housekeeper, but seeks a speaking part in films after playing extra roles.

He spurns advances from an equally brooding hotel laundry worker and persuades a scriptwriter guest to advance him for the role as her dead brother in a forthcoming pic.

That she does to a producer, who is seen almost throughout on a video screen communicating with his staff.

Meanwhile, the laundry worker replays videos of the would-be-actor's bit part scenes at home and attaches herself to a vidstore owner who tapes a sexual orgy and a wedding.

● ●

■ SPECIAL AGENT

1949, 70 MINS, US
Dir William C. Thomas *Prod* William H. Pine, William C. Thomas *Scr* Lewis R. Foster, Whitman Chambers *Ph* Ellis Carter *Ed* Howard Smith *Mus* Lucien Cailliet
● William Eythe, George Reeves, Laura Elliot, Paul Valentine (Paramount)

Special Agent draws its melodramatic meat from an actual case in the files of the railroads' special agent division. Script tells of a daring express car robbery by two brothers and the painstaking way the special agents go about bringing the crooks to justice. Direction by William C. Thomas achieves a good documentary flavor in the thrills, concentrating footage mostly on the agents and their work.

William Eythe pleases as the young agent stationed in a small California town. For romance there is Laura Elliot, daughter of the engineer killed in the robbery.

George Reeves and Paul Valentine depict the heavies who, in tackling their first major crime, loot a train of a $100,000 payroll. Reeves is good but Valentine is a bit too mannered as the trigger-happy killer.

● ●

■ SPELLBOUND

1945, 116 MINS, US ▼
Dir Alfred Hitchcock *Prod* David O. Selznick *Scr* Ben Hecht, Angus MacPhail *Ph* George Barnes *Ed* William Ziegler, Hal C. Kern *Mus* Miklos Rozsa *Art Dir* James Basevi, John Ewing
● Ingrid Bergman, Gregory Peck, Rhonda Fleming, Leo G. Carroll, Norman Lloyd (United Artists)

David O. Selznick devised unique production values for this Alfred Hitchcock-directed version of a psychological mystery novel. (*The House of Dr Edwardes*, written by Hilary St George Saunders).

The story, employing as it does psychiatry and psychoanalysis in a murder mystery, would not lend itself for anything but a skillfully blended top budget production.

Gregory Peck, suffering from amnesia, believes that he committed a murder but has no memory of the locale or circumstances surrounding the crime. Ingrid Bergman as a psychiatrist in love with Peck tries desperately to save him from punishment for the crime she is certain he could not have committed, and in doing so risks her career and almost her life.

Salvador Dali designed the dream sequence with all the aids of futurism and surrealism in his sets. The sets, chairs and tables have human legs and roofs slope at 45-degree angles into infinity.

Alfred Hitchcock handles his players and action in suspenseful manner and, except for a few episodes of much scientific dialogue, maintains a steady pace in keeping the camera moving.
□ 1945: Best Picture (Nomination)

● ●

■ SPENCER'S MOUNTAIN

1963, 121 MINS, US ◇
Dir Delmer Daves *Prod* Delmer Daves *Scr* Delmer Daves *Ph* Charles Lawton *Ed* David Wages *Mus* Max Steiner
● Henry Fonda, Maureen O'Hara, James MacArthur, Donald Crisp, Wally Cox, Mimsy Farmer (Warner)

Delmer Daves chooses the majestic Grand Teton's to background a quite ordinary, but generally enjoyable and often emotionally moving comedy-drama about a large, simple, hardworking family and its joys and disappointments from the cradle to the grave.

Daves, working from a novel (laid in Blue Ridge Mountain Country) by Earl Hamner Jr, views the Spencers idealistically – the family that pulls together and walks straight.

Daves' script plays better than it sounds in synopsis for it is the interplay and incidents that spark humor and warmth, sentiment and a bit of boisterousness in the story which is motivated by the desire of uneducated parents to fulfill their son's desire for a college education when all that the father earns is required to keep food on the table for a brood of nine youngsters, plus husband-wife and grandparents.

With less ingratiating and expert performers than Henry Fonda and Maureen O'Hara as the central characters the chances are Daves might have found himself in trouble. Fonda, in particular, can take what easily could have been an ordinary hayseed and invest such a role with depth, purposefulness and dignity.

● ●

■ SPHINX

1981, 117 MINS, US ◇

Dir Franklin J. Schaffner   *Prod* Stanley O'Toole
Scr John Byrum   *Ph* Ernest Day   *Ed* Robert E. Swink, Michael F. Anderson   *Mus* Michael J. Lewis   *Art Dir* Terence Marsh

● Lesley-Anne Down, Frank Langella, Maurice Ronet, John Gielgud, Saeed Jaffrey (Orion)

This film is an embarrassment. Contempo *Perils of Pauline* sees earnest, dedicated Egyptologist Lesley-Anne Down through countless situations of dire jeopardy as she travels from Cairo to Luxor's Valley of the Kings in pursuit of a mysterious tomb of riches, which also holds great interest for black marketeers.

Along the way, lovely Lesley-Anne is almost murdered after witnessing John Gielgud's demise, caught off guard not once, not twice, but three times in her hotel room, shot at as a matter of course, nearly raped by a prison guard, held at knifepoint, thrown into a dark dungeon inhabited by decomposed corpses, attacked by bats, chased by a car, shot at again and finally nearly buried as the tomb's ceiling comes crashing down.

In all, she screams gasps and exclaims 'My God!' more often than any heroine since Jamie Lee Curtis in her collected horror films.

Franklin J. Schaffner's steady and sober style is helpless in the face of the mounting implausibilities.

● ●

■ SPIES LIKE US

1985, 109 MINS, US ◇ ▽

Dir John Landis   *Prod* Brian Grazer, George Folsey Jr   *Scr* Dan Aykroyd, Lowell Ganz, Babaloo Mandel
Ph Robert Paynter   *Ed* Malcolm Campbell   *Mus* Elmer Bernstein   *Art Dir* Peter Murton

● Chevy Chase, Dan Aykroyd, Steve Forrest, Donna Dixon, Bruce Davison, William Prince (Warner)

Teamed together for the first time in *Spies Like Us*, Chevy Chase and Dan Aykroyd need a subteen audience for their juvenile humor.

Spies is not very amusing. Though Chase and Aykroyd provide moments, the overall script thinly takes on eccentric espionage and nuclear madness, with nothing new to add.

Chase and Aykroyd are a couple of bumbling bureaucrats with aspirations for spy work, but no talent for the job. They unknowingly are chosen for a mission, however, because they will make expendable decoys for a real spy team headed by pretty Donna Dixon.

Much of the time, Aykroyd is fooling with gadgets, Chase is fooling with Dixon and

director John Landis is fooling with half-baked comedy ideas.

● ●

■ SPIRAL ROAD, THE

1962, 145 MINS, US ◇

Dir Robert Mulligan   *Prod* Robert Arthur   *Scr* Neil Paterson, John Lee Mahin   *Ph* Russell Harlan
Ed Russell F. Schoengarth   *Mus* Jerry Goldsmith   *Art Dir* Alexander Golitzen, Henry Bumstead

● Rock Hudson, Burl Ives, Gena Rowlands, Geoffrey Keen, Neva Patterson (Universal)

Being uninspired, *The Spiral Road* is the uninspiring tale of an atheist's conversion to God. The picture, moreover, takes the devil's own time getting down to cases and the resolution; and of its numerous defects, prolonged length is a major infirmity of this chronicle of jungle medicine in Java as practiced by the Dutch.

A novel by Dutch author Jan de Hartog is the source for the flabby screenplay. It concerns an opportunist, gainsaying freshman medic (Rock Hudson) and his determination to ride to scientific fame on the research of a seasoned jungle physician (Burl Ives). Hudson's arrogance and cynicism are played against sundry goodhearts – his suffering wife (Gena Rowlands), the Salvation Army man (Geoffrey Keen), and highminded types who constitute his superiors in the government medical mission.

● ●

■ SPIRAL STAIRCASE, THE

1946, 83 MINS, US ▽

Dir Robert Siodmak   *Prod* Dore Schary   *Scr* Mel Dinelli   *Ph* Nicholas Musuraca   *Ed* Harry Marker, Harry Gerstad   *Art Dir* Albert S. D'Agostino, Jack Okey

● Dorothy McGuire, George Brent, Ethel Barrymore, Kent Smith, Rhonda Fleming (RKO)

This is a smooth production of an obvious, though suspenseful murder thriller, ably acted and directed. Mood and pace are well set, and story grips throughout.

Mel Dinelli has done a tight, authentic-sounding script of a mass-murder story [based on Ethel Lina White's novel, *Some Must Watch*] set in a small New England town of 1906. Director Robert Siodmak has retained a feeling for terror throughout the film by smart photography, camera angles and sudden shifts of camera emphasis, abetted in this job by a choice performance of his cast. Film lacks the leaven of a little humor, but interest never wanes.

Dorothy McGuire's stature as actress is increased by her performance as a maid-servant bereft of speech since childhood, and Ethel Barrymore's list of pic-portraits will get another gold-framer from her role of bedridden wealthy eccentric. McGuire's portrayal of a tongue-tied girl in love; the pathos of her dream wedding-scene; her terror when pursued by the murderer – are all etched sharply for unforgettable moments. Barrymore's awareness from her bedchamber of the insanity and murder going on about her is also acutely set, to give distinction to her part.

● ●

■ SPIRIT OF ST. LOUIS, THE

1957, 135 MINS, US ◇ ▽

Dir Billy Wilder   *Prod* Leland Hayward   *Scr* Billy Wilder, Wendell Mayes   *Ph* Robert Burks, J. Peverell Marley   *Ed* Arthur P. Schmidt   *Mus* Franz Waxman   *Art Dir* Art Loel

● James Stewart, Murray Hamilton, Patricia Smith, Bartlett Robinson (Warner)

Although lacking the elaborate production trappings that would automatically mirror a multi-million dollar budget, an extensive shooting schedule and painstaking care went into this picture. It's Class A picture-making yet doesn't manage to deliver entertainment

wallop out of the story about one man in a single-engine plane over a 3,610-mile route.

Spirit is a James Stewart one-man show. He portrays Charles Lindbergh with a toned-down performance intended as consistent with the diffident (i.e. non-communicative) nature of the famed aviator. The story development tends to focus on the personal side of the 1927 hero, as much as it does on the flight itself, and Stewart comes off with sort of an appropriate, shy amiability.

The flashback technique is used frequently to convey some of Lindbergh's background, such as his days as a mail pilot, an amusing bit re his first encounter with the air force, his barnstorming stunts, etc.

● ●

■ SPLASH

1984, 111 MINS, US ◇ ▽

Dir Ron Howard   *Prod* Brian Grazer   *Scr* Lowell Ganz, Babaloo Mandel, Bruce Jay Friedman   *Ph* Don Peterman   *Ed* Daniel P. Hanley, Michael Hill   *Mus* Lee Holdridge   *Art Dir* Jack T. Collis

● Tom Hanks, Daryl Hannah, John Candy, Eugene Levy, Dody Goodman, Shecky Greene (Touchstone)

Touchstone Films takes the plunge with surprisingly charming mermaid yarn notable for winning suspension of disbelief and fetching by-play between Daryl Hannah and Tom Hanks.

Although film is a bit uneven, production benefits from a tasty look, an airy tone, and a delectable, unblemished performance from Hannah who couldn't be better cast if she were Neptune's daughter incarnate. Hanks, as a Gotham bachelor in search of love, makes a fine leap from sitcom land, and John Candy as an older playboy brother is a marvelous foil.

The mermaid's fin materializes into human legs when she leaves the water and, a la Lady Godiva, blonde tresses covering her breasts. Screenplay is marred by some glaring loopholes in its inner structure but story is a sweet takeoff on the innocence mythology and sensuality associated with mermaids.

● ●

■ SPLENDOR

1935, 77 MINS, US

Dir Elliott Nugent   *Prod* Samuel Goldwyn   *Scr* Rachel Crothers   *Ph* Gregg Toland   *Ed* Margaret Clancey   *Mus* Alfred Newman   *Art Dir* Richard Day

● Miriam Hopkins, Joel McCrea, Paul Cavanaugh, Helen Westley, Billie Burke, David Niven (Goldwyn/ United Artists)

Here is a rare combination of a well-written story, interpreted in skilled and sympathetic action under able and understanding direction. This is the film Rachel Crothers specially authored for Goldwyn on a royalty and guarantee basis.

Miriam Hopkins marries Joel McCrea while he is south on a business trip, and he proudly bring her home, not realizing that his ambitious mother (Helen Westley) is looking to a marriage with an heiress (Ruth Weston).

Hopkins gets small welcome from her in-laws, and even McCrea is a bit impatient with her because of his own perplexities. His father and grandfather amassed money, apparently without effort. He doesn't seem able to realize why he cannot.

Paul Cavanaugh, a distant relative, takes an interest in the young wife and things become easier for her. The old lady looks to her to use her influence in behalf of McCrea. She virtually forces the girl into an affair.

Helen Westley, as the mother, is the dominant figure. Her cold-blooded, merciless nagging of the girl is as well played as it has been written. Hopkins is not altogether at ease as the sweet young thing in the first few scenes, but later she doesn't miss a chance. Paul Cavanaugh is admirable.

● ●

■ SPLENDOR IN THE GRASS

1961, 124 MINS, US ◇ ⓥ
Dir Elia Kazan *Prod* Elia Kazan *Scr* William Inge
Ph Boris Kaufman *Ed* Gene Milford *Mus* David
Amram *Art Dir* Richard Sylbert
● Natalie Wood, Warren Beatty, Pat Hingle, Audrey
Christie, Barbara Loden, Fred Stewart (Warner)

Elia Kazan's production of William Inge's original screenplay covers a forbidding chunk of ground with great care, compassion and cinematic flair. Yet there is something awkward about the picture's mechanical rhythm. There are missing links and blind alleys within the story. Too much time is spent focusing on characters of minor significance.

Inge's screenplay deals with a young couple deeply in love but unable to synchronize the opposite polarity of their moral attitudes. Their tragedy is helped along by the influence of parental intervention. The well-meaning parents (his father, her mother, both of whom completely dominate their more perceptive mates), in asserting their inscrutable wills upon their children, lead them into a quandary. The children cannot consummate their relationship, either sexually or maritally.

Natalie Wood and Warren Beatty (whom the picture 'introduces') are the lovers. Although the range and amplitude of their expression is not always as wide and variable as it might be, both deliver convincing, appealing performances. The real histrionic honors, though, belong to Audrey Christie, who plays Wood's mother, and Pat Hingle, as Beatty's father. Both are truly exceptional, memorable portrayals.

Barbara Loden does an interesting job in a role (Beatty's 'flapper sister') that is built up, only to be sloughed off at the apex of its development. Fred Stewart is excellent as Wood's father.

Exteriors for the picture were shot in New York State, and the countryside looks a little lush for Kansas, which is the setting of the drama. David Amram's romantic theme is hauntingly beautiful. There's an exceptional job of costuming by Anna Hill Johnstone. The clothes are not only faithful to the two eras (late 1920s, early 1930s) covered, but they are attractive on the people who wear them.

■ SPRING AND PORT WINE

1970, 101 MINS, UK ◇
Dir Peter Hammond *Prod* Michael Medwin *Scr* Bill
Naughton *Ph* Norman Warwick *Ed* Fergus
McDonell *Mus* Douglas Gamley *Art Dir* Reece
Pemberton
● James Mason, Susan George, Diana Coupland,
Rodney Bewes, Hannah Gordon, Len Jones (Memorial)

Set in the mill area of Lancashire and its moors (though lacking most of the cliche Lancashire gags and mannerisms), this is the story [from the play by Bill Naughton] of a generation clash in a small family and the points of view of both parents and children are fairly, compassionately and interestingly brought out.

James Mason plays the patriarch of the family, a kindly but stubborn man who brings up his family with a startling strictness. Remembering his own youth he is determined the house he reigns over shall not be such a mess.

Chief rebel is the high-spirited Susan George whose refusal to eat a herring for tea sparks off a handful of situations that remind Mason that 'you can spend a lifetime creating a family and break it up in a weekend.'

■ SPRING IN PARK LANE

1948, 91 MINS, UK
Dir Herbert Wilcox *Prod* Herbert Wilcox
Scr Nicholas Phipps *Ph* Max Greene *Ed* F. Clarke
Mus Robert Farnon *Art Dir* Bill Andrews
● Anna Neagle, Michael Wilding, Tom Walls, Peter
Graves, Nicholas Phipps, Nigel Patrick (British Lion)

Great merit of the story is that it seems like a happy improvisation. None of the elaborate and necessary scaffolding is apparent, and when Michael Wilding as a younger son of a noble family, needing money for a return trip to New York, becomes a temporary footman in a Park Lane mansion, he is immediately accepted as such by the audience. And since Anna Neagle plays a secretary in the same house, everybody knows it will be love at first sight and that sooner or later the two will march altarwards.

It's a story in which the trimmings and incidentals are all-important. The gay harmless fun poked at the film stars, the dinner party bore, the housekeeper to whom bridge is a religion, the footman cutting in to dance or discussing art with his boss – incident upon incident carry merry laughter through the picture.

■ SPY IN BLACK, THE

1939, 82 MINS, UK ⓥ
Dir Michael Powell *Prod* Irving Asher *Scr* Emeric
Pressburger *Ph* Bernard Browne *Ed* William
Hornbeck, Hugh Stewart *Mus* Miklos Rozsa
Art Dir Vincent Korda
● Conrad Veidt, Sebastian Shaw, Valerie Hobson,
Marius Goring, June Duprez, Mary Morris
(Harefield/Korda)

The Spy in Black is a praiseworthy film on international espionage during World War I.

The plot [adapted by Roland Pertwee from a novel by J. Storer Clouston], while necessarily melodramatic, is always within the range of possibility. Conrad Veidt, as captain of a German submarine, receives instructions to proceed to the Orkney Islands, where he's to meet a woman spy, from whom he's to take orders. She instructs him to sink 15 British ships cruising off the coast of Scotland, and contacts him with a discharged traitorous lieutenant of the British Navy.

Veidt has a strong role for which he's admirably suited. Sebastian Shaw is excellent as the English naval officer. Valerie Hobson, as the other spy, is creditable.

■ SPY WHO CAME IN FROM THE COLD, THE

1966, 112 MINS, UK ⓥ
Dir Martin Ritt *Prod* Martin Ritt *Scr* Paul Dehn, Guy
Trosper *Ph* Oswald Morris *Ed* Anthony Harvey
Mus Sol Kaplan *Art Dir* Hal Pereira, Tambi Larsen
● Richard Burton, Claire Bloom, Oskar Werner, Sam
Wanamaker, George Voskovec, Rupert Davies (Salem/
Paramount)

The Spy Who Came in from the Cold is an excellent contemporary espionage drama of the Cold War which achieves solid impact via emphasis on human values, total absence of mechanical spy gimmickry, and perfectly controlled underplaying. Filmed at Ireland's Ardmore Studios and England's Shepperton complex, the production boasts strong scripting, acting, direction and production values.

Film effectively socks over the point that East-West espionage agents are living in a world of their own, apart from the day-to-day existence of the millions whom they are serving.

Other fictional spies operate with such dash and flair that the erosion of the spirit is submerged in picturesque exploits and intricate technology. Not so in this adaptation of John Le Carre's novel in which Richard Burton 'comes in from the cold' – meaning the field

operations – only to find himself used as a pawn in high-level counter-plotting.

Burton fits neatly into the role of the apparently burned out British agent, ripe for cultivation by East German Communist secret police as a potential defector.

■ SPY WHO LOVED ME, THE

1977, 125 MINS, UK ◇ ⓥ
Dir Lewis Gilbert *Prod* Albert R. Broccoli
Scr Christopher Wood, Richard Maibaum *Ph* Claude
Renoir *Ed* John Glen *Mus* Marvin Hamlisch
Art Dir Peter Lamont
● Roger Moore, Barbara Bach, Curt Jurgens, Richard
Kiel, Caroline Munro, Walter Gotell (United Artists/Eon)

As always, story and plastic character are in the service of comic strip parody, an excuse to star the prop department, set designer, stunt arrangers, the optical illusion chaps, and such commercial suppliers as the maker of the sporty Lotus car, a lethal job that also converts to an underwater craft.

When British and Russian nuclear subs start to mysteriously vanish, two agents are assigned by their collaborating governments to jointly crack the case.

Curt Jurgens' arsenal includes the film's gimmick character, a monster human known as 'Jaws', played with robotic finesse by Richard Kiel.

The big action sequences were shot on a specially-built stage with tank at Pinewood Studios outside London.

■ SPY WITH MY FACE, THE

1966, 86 MINS, US ◇
Dir John Newland *Prod* Sam Rolfe *Scr* Clyde Ware,
Joseph Calvelli *Ph* Fred Koenekamp *Ed* Joseph
Dervin *Mus* Morton Stevens *Art Dir* George W.
Davis, Merrill Pye
● Robert Vaughn, Senta Berger, David McCallum, Leo
G. Carroll, Michael Evans, Sharon Farrell (M-G-M)

The Spy With My Face, new version of an old *Man From U.N.C.L.E.* episode, is perhaps most garbled, plotwise, of any entry on the [mid-1960s] spymelodrama cycle. Thrush, that band of murderous renegades that would rule the world and is constantly combating U.N.C.L.E., fixes up one of its agents to be the exact double of Napoleon Solo, the good-guy, and nearly succeeds in its purpose – whatever that is.

New footage was added to the original TV segment hour's length to bring it up to 86 minutes for theatrical release.

Film loses sight of story line, which has something to do with transporting a new combination to a vault in Switzerland containing a scientific secret of world import. Vaughn plays his double role straight, and Senta Berger is in as a beauteous she-spy. Femme honors, however go to Sharon Farrell as a cute sexpot. David McCallum appears in his familiar sidekick role, as does Leo G. Carroll as U.N.C.L.E. topper, and Michael Evans is the smooth heavy.

■ SQUEEZE, THE

1977, 106 MINS, UK ◇ ⓥ
Dir Michael Apted *Prod* Stanley O'Toole *Scr* Leon
Griffiths *Ph* Dennis Lewiston *Ed* John Shirley
Mus David Hentschel *Art Dir* William McCrow
● Stacy Keach, Freddie Starr, Edward Fox, Stephen
Boyd, David Hemmings, Carol White (Warner)

There's nothing to distinguish *The Squeeze* from routine crime drama in which retribution triumphs. Stacy Keach plays a busted cop fighting the booze habit and some murderous thugs at the same time.

Keach suffers some nasty lumps and sundry humiliations, all in the cause of Edward Fox as a security film exec whose wife and kid are hostages against a million-dollar-plus payoff. Carol White is the terrorized wife, with the complication that she's also Keach's former spouse.

Directed on locations in London by Michael Apted, pic has little in the way of style and no great surprises. It does, however, have a kind of gratuitous nasty tone, as evidenced when the thugs holding White captive force her to perform a strip.

● ●

■ **SQUIRM**

1976, 93 MINS, US ◇ ⓥ

Dir Jeff Lieberman   *Prod* George Manasse   *Scr* Jeff Lieberman   *Ph* Joseph Mangine   *Ed* Brian Smedley
Mus Robert Prince   *Art Dir* Henry Shrady
● John Scardino, Patricia Pearcy, R.A. Dow, Jean Sullivan, Peter MacLean, Fran Higgins (American International)

Squirm is an average shock meller about some rampaging sand worms in the Georgia sticks, claimed to be derived from an actual occurrence on 29 September 1975. Some genuine creepy special effects are offset by clumsy and amateurish low-budget location production, yet there is an admirable earnestness to the effort.

Story kicker is an electrical storm which downs power lines, with runaway juice charging the wet mud and driving out the 10-18-inch sand worms of the area. They are hungry and angry. They are also effective.

City slicker John Scardino visits local Patricia Pearcy, eldest daughter of widow Jean Sullivan. Sheriff Peter MacLean doesn't believe in the worm plague, but becomes one of its victims.

● ●

■ **ST. ELMO'S FIRE**

1985, 108 MINS, US ◇ ⓥ

Dir Joel Schumacher   *Prod* Lauren Shuler   *Scr* Joel Schumacher, Carl Kurlander   *Ph* Stephen H. Burum
Ed Richard Marks   *Mus* David Foster   *Art Dir* William Sandell
● Rob Lowe, Demi Moore, Andrew McCarthy, Judd Nelson, Ally Sheedy, Emilio Estevez (Columbia-Delphi IV/Channel)

St. Elmo's Fire is all about a group of recent college graduates in Washington who were always the best of friends but now are drifting apart as real life approaches, discovering various reasons why they are so individually obnoxious.

Rob Lowe is a saxophone player who refuses to assume any adult responsibility. The rest of the gang befriends him, especially virginal Mare Winningham, who's a social worker by trade anyway.

The other major problem is beautiful, coked-out Demi Moore who lives in a pink apartment, sleeps with her boss and calls her friends with wee-hour problems.

There's also yuppie Capitol Hill aide Judd Nelson, a Democrat turned Republican because the pay is better, and his live-in [Ally Sheedy] who won't marry him but has reason to resent his cheating.

Making them all look good by comparison is Emilio Estevez. He spots medical student Andie MacDowell and decides he must marry her despite her absolute lack of interest.

Beyond occasional mutterings of words like 'love' and 'beer,' there's never any explanation in the dialog that would hint at motivation.

● ●

■ **ST. IVES**

1976, 93 MINS, US ◇ ⓥ

Dir J. Lee Thompson   *Prod* Pancho Kohner, Stanley Canter   *Scr* Barry Beckerman   *Ph* Lucien Ballard
Ed Michael F. Anderson   *Mus* Lalo Schifrin
Art Dir Philip M. Jefferies

● Charles Bronson, John Houseman, Jacqueline Bisset, Maximilian Schell, Harry Guardino, Harris Yulin (Warner)

St. Ives merely confirms a point: eliminate gratuitous, offensive and overdone violence from a dull and plodding film story, and all you've got left is a dull and plodding film.

The production stars Charles Bronson as an ex-police reporter involved with wealthy crime dilettante John Houseman and partner Jacqueline Bisset. J. Lee Thompson's direction is functional.

Barry Beckerman wrote the script from an Oliver Bleeck novel, *The Procane Chronicle*. Plot injects Bronson as go-between in recovery for some stolen Houseman papers, but every time the ransom is to be delivered, somebody dies.

Plot progress is marred by lots of month-old red herrings. Film is careful to show that Bronson's character doesn't need pistols.

● ●

■ **ST. VALENTINE'S DAY MASSACRE, THE**

1967, 100 MINS, US ◇ ⓥ

Dir Roger Corman   *Prod* Roger Corman   *Scr* Howard Browne   *Ph* Milton Krasner   *Ed* William B. Murphy
Mus Fred Steiner   *Art Dir* Jack Martin Smith, Philip Jeffries
● Jason Robards, George Segal, Ralph Meeker, Jean Hale, Clint Ritchie, Frank Silvera (20th Century-Fox)

The film is a slam-bang, gutsy recreation of *The St. Valentine's Day Massacre*, a 1929 gangland sensation of Chicago. Well-written, and presented in semi-documentary style, it features Jason Robards as Al Capone. Salty dialog and violence are motivated properly, and solid production values recreate a bygone era.

Robards is excellent as Capone, and Ralph Meeker, as Moran, is equally chilling. A large cast spotlights George Segal, who with brother David Canary act as Meeker's ace gunmen.

Clint Ritchie, playing in very good fashion the ever-smiling, dapper Jack McGurn, one of Capone's key aides, is placed by his boss in charge of eliminating Moran and his mob. Latter – through a stroke of fate – escaped the bloodbath, and Capone was never proven the man behind it all.

● ●

■ **STAGE DOOR**

1937, 83 MINS, US/UK ⓥ

Dir Gregory La Cava   *Prod* Pandro S. Berman
Scr Morrie Ryskind, Anthony Veiller   *Ph* Robert de Grasse   *Ed* William Hamilton   *Mus* Roy Webb
● Katharine Hepburn, Ginger Rogers, Adolphe Menjou, Gail Patrick, Constance Collier, Andrea Leeds (RKO)

It isn't *Stage Door*, as written [for the stage] by Edna Ferber and George S. Kaufman. Instead, it is a hall bedroom view of aspiring young actresses who live in a New York theatrical boarding house and vent their bitterness against the economic uncertainties of legit employment in sharp and cutting repartee. It is funny in spots, emotionally effective occasionally, and generally brisk and entertaining.

Whether it was Gregory La Cava or Pandro S. Berman, the producer, who decided to throw away the play and write a new script on the old idea that there is a broken heart for every light on Broadway, is beside the point.

Story revolves around one of the minor characters, a talented young actress of promise unable to withstand the pressure of constant casting disappointment. Part is played for all it's worth by Andrea Leeds.

Opening shows the inhabitants of a rooming house in the West 40s. They're a high strung, noisy bevy of showgirls, nightclub dancers and embryo dramatic timber. Dialog

is caustic as they comment on each other and the passing world of show business. Ginger Rogers does a floor specialty in a night club which gives her an introduction to Adolphe Menjou, a hardboiled theatrical producer and femme despoiler.

Katharine Hepburn, stagestruck daughter of a wealthy westerner, becomes Ginger's roommate at the boarding house. Former's father, in the hope he can ndiscourage her theatrical career, anonymously finances a Menjou dramatic production, with Hepburn in the lead.

Rogers has more to do than Hepburn, but her part is less clearly defined. As a sharpshooter with the snappy reply she scores heavily. Her dancing is limited to a short floor number.

□ 1937: Best Picture (Nomination)

● ●

■ **STAGE DOOR CANTEEN**

1943, 132 MINS, US ⓥ

Dir Frank Borzage   *Prod* Sol Lesser   *Scr* Delmer Daves   *Ph* Harry Wild   *Ed* Hal Kern   *Mus* Freddie Rich
● Cheryl Walker, William Terry, Marjorie Riordan, Lon McCallister, Margaret Early, Michael Harrison (United Artists)

What stood a good chance of emerging a 'big short' under less skillful hands than Sol Lesser proves a sock filmusical of great stature. It has a cast that reads like an out-of-this-world benefit, and a romance as simple as Elsie Dinsmore – and the blend is plenty boffo.

Stage Door Canteen is a skilful admixture by two casts, in itself a departure. One cast projects the simple love story – Eileen and her 'Dakota'; Jean and her 'California'; Ella Sue and her 'Texas'; Mamie and her 'Jersey'. Another cast comprises the Stars of the Stage Door Canteen, and but few of them do walkthrough parts.

Plausibly and smoothly, these stars are introduced into their natural habitat, the Stage Door Canteen on West 44th Street, just off Broadway, where Lunt and Fontanne and Vera Gordon, Sam Jaffe, George Raft and Allen Jenkins, Ned Sparks, Ralph Morgan and Hugh Herbert – these, among others, are shown doing their menial back-in-the-kitchen chores. Then, up front, performing for the visiting men in uniform, gobs, doughboys, marines – no officers – is paraded a galaxy of talent that's a super-duper, all-star array which reads like a casting agent's dream of paradise.

Thus are paraded six bands – Basie, Cugat, Goodman, Kyser, Lombardo and Martin, in sock specialties all.

And, to project the mechanics of the canteen, showing the officer-of-the-day, the senior hostesses, the dancing junior hostesses, or as part of the plot motivation (as with Katharine Cornell's skillful bit of *Romeo and Juliet*, and Paul Muni's part as rehearsing his own play), there are introduced another array of stars and legit personalities: Helen Hayes, Ina Claire, Tallulah Bankhead, Vinton Freedley, Merle Oberon, Brock Pemberton, Katherine Hepburn and the others are intertwined into the lonely-soldier-boy-meets-romantic-stage-girl plot.

Scripter Delmer Daves does a deft writing job, and Frank Borzage's direction smoothly splices the sum total into a very palatable cohesive entity.

● ●

■ **STAGE FRIGHT**

1950, 110 MINS, US/UK ⓥ

Dir Alfred Hitchcock   *Prod* Alfred Hitchcock
Scr Whitfield Cook, Alma Reville, James Bridie
Ph Wilkie Cooper   *Ed* Edward Jarvis   *Mus* Leighton Lucas   *Art Dir* Terence Verity
● Jane Wyman, Marlene Dietrich, Michael Wilding,

Richard Todd, Kay Walsh, Alastair Sim (Warner/Associated British)

Alfred Hitchcock doesn't stress melodrama throughout. He plays a surprising number of sequences strictly for lightness. Also, he has a choice cast to put through its paces, and there's not a bad performance anywhere. The dialog has purpose, either for a chuckle or a thrill, and the pace is good.

Jane Wyman is a drama student who is sought out by a friend (Richard Todd) who is fleeing from the charge of murdering Marlene Dietrich's husband. Wyman and her father (Alistair Sim) hide Todd and attempt to prove Dietrich is guilty of the crime.

Wyman is delightful as embryo actress but the choice femme spot goes to Dietrich.

Michael Wilding clicks as a debonair detective.

■ STAGE STRUCK

1958, 95 MINS, US ◇ ⑦
Dir Sidney Lumet   *Prod* Stuart Millar   *Scr* Ruth Goetz, Augustus Goetz   *Ph* Franz Planer, Maurice Hartband   *Ed* Stuart Gilmore   *Mus* Alex North   *Art Dir* Kim Edgar Swados
● Henry Fonda, Susan Strasberg, Joan Greenwood, Herbert Marshall, Christopher Plummer, Patricia Englund (RKO)

Stage Struck weaves another variation on the wellworn tale of the eager young actress who can't persuade anyone on Broadway to give her a job until the star flounces out on the eve of opening night. The tyro steps into the star's shoes, knocks the audience right out of its red plush seats; veterans backstage murmur, 'that's showbiz,' and the camera pans slowly away from a solitary figure standing in the middle of an empty theatre; music up and out. It's a remake of *Morning Glory*, a yesteryear [1933] Katherine Hepburn starrer.

Susan Strasberg plays the would-be actress who hounds producer Henry Fonda for a chance. He is intrigued by the girl but not as an actress and turns her down. Not so his playwright (Christopher Plummer), who sees her both as actress and romantic opposite. When the star of their show (Joan Greenwood) makes a temperamental exit, Plummer has Strasberg set to take over her role and she does with plot-predictable ease and success.

Strasberg occupies a major portion of the footage in this screenplay from a Zoe Akins play. She is not a conventional screen beauty but her face is expressive and lively. Fonda plays with his customary quiet authority and disarming command and Herbert Marshall limns a warming portrait as a stage veteran. Greenwood gives the rampaging star the Bankhead bit and very funny she is. Plummer has considerable depth to his playing.

Camerawork is striking, notably in the Central Park scene, a setting of a Greenwich Village street, dawn in Times Square, and the interiors of the theatre (actually the National on 41st Street).

■ STAGECOACH

1939, 95 MINS, US ⑦
Dir John Ford   *Prod* Walter Wanger   *Scr* Dudley Nichols   *Ph* Bert Glennon   *Ed* Dorothy Spencer, Walter Reynolds   *Mus* Leo Shuken, John Leipold, Richard Hageman, W. Franke Harling, Louis Gruenberg
● Claire Trevor, John Wayne, Andy Devine, Thomas Mitchell, George Bancroft, John Carradine (United Artists)

Directorially, production [based on Ernest Haycox' *Collier's* magazine story, *Stage to Lordsburg*] is John Ford in peak form, sustaining interest and suspense throughout, and presenting exceptional characterizations. Picture is a display of photographic grandeur.

It's the adventures of a group aboard a stagecoach between two frontier settlements during the sudden uprising of the Apaches. Situation is a *Grand Hotel* on wheels.

There's Claire Trevor, dance hall gal forced to leave town; driver, Andy Devine; gambler, John Carradine; inebriated frontier medic, Thomas Mitchell; marshall, George Bancroft; wife of an army officer en route to his post, Louise Platt; whiskey salesman, Donald Meek, and absconding banker, Berton Churchill. John Wayne, recently escaped from prison, is picked up on the road shortly after the start.

In maintaining a tensely dramatic pace all the way, Ford still injects numerous comedy situations, and throughout sketches his characters with sincerity and humaneness. It's absorbing drama without the general theatrics usual to picturizations of the early west.

The running fight between the stagecoach passengers and the Apaches has been given thrilling and realistic presentation by Ford. In contrast, the hacienda sequence is an extremely tender episode.
□ 1939: Best Picture (Nomination)

■ STAGECOACH

1966, 114 MINS, US ◇
Dir Gordon M. Douglas   *Prod* Martin Rackin   *Scr* Joseph Landon   *Ph* William H. Clothier   *Ed* Hugh S. Fowler   *Mus* Jerry Goldsmith   *Art Dir* Jack Martin Smith, Herman A. Blumenthal
● Ann-Margret, Red Buttons, Michael Connors, Alex Cord, Bing Crosby, Bob Cummings (20th Century-Fox)

New version of *Stagecoach* derives from a 1939 Walter Wanger production for United Artists, written by Dudley Nichols from a 1937 short story by Ernest Haycox.

Film kicks off with a gory two-minute sequence establishing the brutality of Indians on the warpath, the menace which hangs over subsequent developments, after which the stagecoach starts loading its motley passenger crew. Ann-Margret is quite good as the saloon floozy bad-mouthed out of town under US Army pressure by John Gabriel. Bing Crosby, the boozy medic, is a similar victim of Gabriel's incorrect evaluation of a drunken brawl.

Bob Cummings, the gutless bank clerk absconding with a large payroll, is excellent. Cummings delivers much depth, evoking pity and sympathy. He makes an excellent heavy.

To Alex Cord goes the choice John Wayne role of Ringo, framed into prison by land-grabbing Keenan Wynn. Cord underplays very well, and conveys the stubborn determination to avenge his dead father and brother, killed by Wynn, which sustained him during a sadistic incarceration from which he has escaped to join the stage.

Artist Norman Rockwell, who designed pic's logo and painted the perceptive talent portraits used in end titles and exploitation, appears briefly in an early saloon scene.

■ STAGESTRUCK

1936, 90 MINS, US ⑦
Dir Busby Berkeley   *Scr* Tom Buckingham, Pat C. Flick   *Ph* Byron Haskin
● Dick Powell, Joan Blondell, Warren William, Frank McHugh, Jeanne Madden, Carol Hughes (Warner)

Even though it makes an attempt to poke fun at the show-must-go-on thing, *Stage Struck* is cut from the same old pattern, gravitating between moments of sizzling comedy and long stretches of dull palaver.

Picture takes a pretzel-like course in recounting the conventional yarn [by Robert Lord] about the unknown kid who makes good as the last-minute fill-in for the show's star. Musical interludes [songs by E.Y. Harburg and Harold Arlen] are kept down to the minimum.

With her material anything but surefire, Joan Blondell unlimbers a likable grade of comedy. Hers is the part of the dame whose only claim to fame is a penchant for drilling her troublesome boy friends and the newsprint attention that goes with such incidents. She backs herself to the lead part in a musical show where Dick Powell functions as director. A clash of temperaments ends that venture and the pair meet again in her next bit of angeling.

Paired with Powell for the romantic byplay, Jeanne Madden does okay for a starter.

■ STAIRCASE

1969, 101 MINS, US ◇ ⑦
Dir Stanley Donen   *Prod* Stanley Donen   *Scr* Charles Dyer   *Ph* Christopher Challis   *Ed* Richard Marden   *Mus* Dudley Moore   *Art Dir* Willy Holt
● Richard Burton, Rex Harrison, Cathleen Nesbitt, Beatrix Lehmann, Gordon Heath, Stephen Lewis (20th Century-Fox)

Staircase, investigating lonely, desperate lives of two aging male homosexuals in a drab London suburb, comes uncomfortably close to being depressing. Caustic wit, splendid photography and fine direction serve only to point up weary plight of the middleaged pair who cling to one another even while they clash.

Homosexuality, though predominant influence of storyline [from the play by Charles Dyer], is not central theme of screenplay. Its basis is urgent need of neurotic individuals for consolation.

Harrison as the flighty dagger-tongued roommate of fellow 'hair stylist' Burton offers portrait of a bitter, disenchanted man living in terror of being alone. Burton, almost stoic, commands respect and, at the same time, sympathy. Harrison and Burton have dared risky roles and have triumphed.

■ STAKEOUT

1987, 115 MINS, US ◇ ⑦
Dir John Badham   *Prod* Jim Kouf, Cathleen Summers   *Scr* Jim Kouf   *Ph* John Seale   *Ed* Tom Rolf, Michael Ripps   *Mus* Arthur B. Rubinstein   *Art Dir* Philip Harrison
● Richard Dreyfuss, Emilio Estevez, Madeleine Stowe, Aidan Quinn, Dan Lauria (Touchstone/Silver Screen Partners II)

Stakeout is a slick, sure-footed entertainment, one part buddy comedy and one part police actioner stitched together with a dash of romance.

Richard Dreyfuss is a reckless cop whose life is unraveling slowly. While he's on familiar ground talking his way out of tight spots and jousting with partner Emilio Estevez, when the plot calls for rough stuff, it's a stretch he doesn't make.

As the more stable, but still mischievous anchor of the pair, Estevez is likable, if a bit flat. He's not an actor with a great gift for comedy, and many of his exchanges with Dreyfuss lack chemistry.

As Seattle cops (the film was shot in Vancouver), the wisecracking duo is assigned to a routine stakeout where they are supposed to wait for an escaped con (Aidan Quinn) to contact his ex-girlfriend (Madeleine Stowe). Dreyfuss is not a man to wait around for something to happen and, as he barrels into the case, he falls in love with Stowe.

■ STALAG 17

1953, 119 MINS, US ⑦
Dir Billy Wilder   *Prod* Billy Wilder   *Scr* Billy Wilder, Edwin Blum   *Ph* Ernest Laszlo   *Ed* George Tomasini   *Mus* Franz Waxman   *Art Dir* Hal Pereira, Franz Bachelin

S

● William Holden, Don Taylor, Otto Preminger, Robert Strauss, Harvey Lembeck, Peter Graves (Paramount)

The legit hit about GI internees in a Nazi prison camp during the Second World War is screened as a lusty comedy-melodrama, loaded with bold, masculine humor and as much of the original's uninhibited earthiness as good taste and the Production Code permit.

Producer-director Billy Wilder, who did the screen adaptation of the Donald Bevan-Edmund Trzcinski play with Edwin Blum, uses a suspense approach with plenty of leavening humorous byplay springing from the confinement of healthy young males. Nub of the plot is the uncovering of an informer among the GIs in a particular barracks and up to the time his identity is revealed there is plenty of tenseness in the footage.

Opening shows the death of two GIs while attempting a well-plotted escape and the sudden realization there is an informer in their midst. Suspicion fastens on William Holden, a cynical character trying to make the best of his prison lot. When Don Taylor is temporarily moved into the barracks and just as quickly revealed as the American who blew up an ammunition train, the prisoners decide Holden is their man and beat him unmercifully.

Otto Preminger is the third star, playing the camp commander, with obvious relish for its colorful cruelty. Laugh standouts are Robert Strauss, the dumb Stosh of the play and Harvey Lembeck as Harry, the only slightly brighter pal of Stosh.

■ **STALKING MOON, THE**

1969, 109 MINS, US ◇ ⓥ

Dir Robert Muligan *Prod* Alan J. Pakula *Scr* Alvin Sargent *Ph* Charles Lang *Ed* Aaron Stell *Mus* Fred Karlin *Art Dir* Roland Anderson, Jack Poplin
● Gregory Peck, Eva Marie Saint, Robert Forster, Noland Clay, Nathaniel Narciso (National General)

The Stalking Moon seemingly was meant to be a chilling suspenser, framed in a western environment. It does not achieve this goal, because of clumsy plot structuring and dialog and limp direction, which produces tedious pacing.

Theodore V. Olsen's novel, scripted by Alvin Sargent, has Gregory Peck retiring as a vet Indian scout with the US Army. In an Indian round-up, Eva Marie Saint appears, with son Noland Clay. Years before, she was kidnapped and impressed into squaw service by Nathaniel Narciso. Peck takes her and the boy to his retirement ranch, but the Indian brave stalks them.

Forgetting the oater atmosphere (which is supposed to be secondary) film doesn't cut it as a suspenser. Saint, although perhaps as stolid as a frightened Indian slave-woman might be, is not able to project her determined flight from the range territory.

Kid Clay just stares at everything. Dialog is spare and vapid.

■ **STAND BY ME**

1986, 87 MINS, US ◇ ⓥ

Dir Rob Reiner *Prod* Bruce A. Evans, Raynold Gideon, Andrew Scheinman *Scr* Raynold Gideon, Bruce A. Evans *Ph* Thomas Del Ruth *Ed* Robert Leighton *Mus* Jack Nitzsche *Art Dir* Dennis Washington
● Wil Wheaton, River Phoenix, Corey Feldman, Jerry O'Connell, Richard Dreyfuss, Kiefer Sutherland (Act III)

Stand by Me falls somewhat short of being a firstrate 'small' picture about adventurous small-town adolescent boys, although director Rob Reiner is to be lauded for coming close. Formerly titled *The Body*, based on a novella of the same name by Stephen King, it is the experiences of four youths on a two-day trek through the woods around their home-

town of Castle Rock, Oregon, to find the yet-undiscovered body of a dead teenager reported missing for several days.

Film opens very slowly with the extraneous narration of grownup writer Richard Dreyfuss reminiscing on that certain summer of 1959 between sixth and seventh grades that he spent with three close buddies as they sought to become heroes in each other's and the town's eyes.

Scripters have written inspired dialog for this quartet of plucky boys at that hard-to-capture age when they're still young enough to get scared and yet old enough to want to sneak smokes and cuss.

Leading the cast is the introspective, sensitive 'brain' of the bunch, Gordie Lachance (Wil Wheaton). His somber personality is matched by best friend Chris Chambers (River Pheonix), a toughie who is an abused child; Teddy Dechamp (Corey Feldman), the loony kid of an institutionalized father; and the perfectly named wimp, Vern Tessie, the chubby kid who everyone else enjoys poking fun at.

■ **STANLEY & IRIS**

1990, 102 MINS, US ◇ ⓥ

Dir Martin Ritt *Prod* Arlene Sellers, Alex Winitsky *Scr* Harriet Frank Jr, Irving Ravetch *Ph* Donald McAlpine *Ed* Sidney Levin *Mus* John Williams *Art Dir* Joel Schiller
● Jane Fonda, Robert De Niro, Swoosie Kurtz, Martha Plimpton (Lantana/M-G-M)

The elements are in place but they don't add up to great drama in this well-meant effort to personalize the plight of illiterate people.

Project reunites director Martin Ritt with screenwriting team that produced the Oscar-winning *Norma Rae*, which also had a working-class setting and underdog social concern. *Stanley & Iris* [from the novel *Union Street* by Pat Barker] features Robert De Niro's plight as an illiterate cook but proves too small for a feature film framework.

Jane Fonda plays Iris, a recent widow still struggling with grief while trying to support a whole household. She catches the eye of Stanley Cox, a cafeteria cook who at middle age has never learned to read or write. Fired by his boss for being potentially dangerous, Stanley no longer can afford to care properly for the aging father who lives with him. When the old man dies, Stanley finally confronts his fears and asks Iris to teach him to read.

Fonda has some trouble evoking a woman whose life would have dropped her off at such a humble station. De Niro, as a quiet, prideful man who feels foolish and like 'a big dummy' trying to learn, does in fact come across as self-consciously awkward and a tad silly, though his performance includes some muted, winning comedy.

■ **STAR, THE**

1952, 90 MINS, US

Dir Stuart Heisler *Prod* Bert E. Friedlob *Scr* Katherine Albert, Dale Eunson *Ph* Ernest Laszlo *Ed* Otto Ludwig *Mus* Victor Young *Art Dir* Boris Levin
● Bette Davis, Sterling Hayden, Natalie Wood, Warner Anderson, Minor Watson, June Travis (Friedlob/20th Century-Fox)

A strong performance by Bette Davis, in a tailor-made role, gives a lift to *The Star* that it might not have had otherwise.

There is a 'tradey' feel to the story, as befits the backstage Hollywood plot. Opening finds Davis sulking outside an auction house that is selling her last possessions to pay her creditors. A meeting there with her agent-friend (Warner Anderson) and a pitch for him to get her another picture fails. She gets drunk, is arrested and bailed out by a boating man (Sterling Hayden).

Hayden tries to get her to forget a film career and become a normal, natural woman. She tries, but fails at holding a department store job, and wangles a screen test from a kindly producer.

With most of the footage concentrating on Davis' character, there isn't too much for the other players to do.

■ **STAR!**

1968, 165 MINS, US ◇

Dir Robert Wise *Prod* Saul Chaplin *Scr* William Fairchild *Ph* Ernest Laszlo *Ed* William Reynolds *Art Dir* Boris Leven
● Julie Andrews, Richard Crenna, Michael Craig, Daniel Massey, Robert Reed, Bruce Forsyth (20th Century-Fox)

Julie Andrews' portrayal of the late, great musicomedy idol, Gertrude Lawrence, occasionally sags between musical numbers but the cast and team of redoubtable technical contributors have helped to turn out a pleasing tribute to one of the theatre's most admired stars.

It gives a fascinating coverage of Lawrence's spectacular rise to showbiz fame, and also a neatly observed background of an epoch now gone.

The film has, as its framework, the star sitting in with a TV producer watching a supposed black-and-white TV documentary of her career.

It's a tricky but meaty role, but even those intimate with Lawrence's work and personality will quickly settle for accepting, in Andrews' carefully built-up performance, the illusion that they're watching Lawrence. Andrews, however, tends to overdo the cockney hoydenishness in the early stages.

Humor is more witty than boisterously funny, while the 17 musical numbers are staged in polished fashion.

■ **STAR CHAMBER, THE**

1983, 109 MINS, US ◇ ⓥ

Dir Peter Hyams *Prod* Frank Yablans *Scr* Roderick Taylor, Peter Hyams *Ph* Richard Hannah *Ed* Jim Mitchell *Mus* Michael Small *Art Dir* Bill Malley
● Michael Douglas, Hal Holbrook, Yaphet Kotto, Sharon Gless, James B. Sikking, Joe Regalbuto (20th Century-Fox)

Producer and director exhibit an excess of faith in today's educational system if they think the bulk of today's filmgoing audience will know the title's 15th-century derivation as an extra-judicial body.

Chamber does start out on an important note. The US criminal justice system is not only collapsing but what's left has been perverted until the victims of crime have no hope of satisfaction nor protection.

As a decent, conscientious judge, Michael Douglas deals with the problem daily, forced by straining legal precedent to free the obviously 'guilty'.

Severely stricken by one event, Douglas turns to his friend and mentor, Hal Holbrook, who is secretly part of a group of judges who mete out their own fatal sentences on criminals who've been through their real courts and gone free.

Getting to this point in the film, there's a pleasure in rediscovering intelligent dialog, ably provided by Hyams and Roderick Taylor. But the talk is haunted by concern that this intellectual morass cannot be solved within the confines of cinema.

■ **STAR 80**

1983, 102 MINS, US ◇ ⓥ

Dir Bob Fosse *Prod* Wolfgang Glattes, Kenneth Utt *Scr* Bob Fosse *Ph* Sven Nykvist *Ed* Alan Helm *Mus* Ralph Burns *Art Dir* Jack G. Taylor Jr.

● Mariel Hemingway, Eric Roberts, Cliff Robertson, Carroll Baker, Roger Rees, David Clennon (Ladd Company)

Bob Fosse takes another look at the underside of the success trip in *Star 80*, an engrossing, unsentimental and unavoidably depressing account of the short life and ghastly death of Playmate-actress Dorothy Stratten.

Stratten was a sweet, voluptuous blonde who became a popular Playmate of the Year in Playboy, appeared in a few films, all of which are forgettable except for Peter Bogdanovich's *They All Laughed* (1981), and was brutally killed by her estranged husband in a murder-suicide in 1980.

As played here by Mariel Hemingway, Stratten is a virginal, extremely insecure teenager – almost a baby, really – in Vancouver who is swooped down upon by smalltime hustler Paul Snider. Although doubtlessly in love with his discovery, Snider uses Stratten as his ticket to the big time in LA.

Give Stratten's passivity and pliability, histrionics fall to the Snider character, and Eric Roberts gives a startlingly fine performance as this pathetic loser.

■ **STAR IS BORN, A**

1937, 111 MINS, US ⓥ

Dir William A. Wellman   *Prod* David O. Selznick
Scr William A. Wellman, Robert Carson, Dorothy Parker, Alan Campbell   *Ph* W. Howard Greene   *Ed* Hal C. Kern   *Mus* Max Steiner   *Art Dir* Lansing C. Holden
● Janet Gaynor, Fredric March, Adolphe Menjou, May Robson, Andy Devine, Lionel Stander (Selznick/United Artists) ·

Although not the first film which has attempted to capitalize the international reputation of Hollywood, it is unquestionably the most effective one yet made. The highly commendable results are achieved with a minimum of satiric hokum and a maximum of honest story telling.

Film is photographed throughout in Technicolor. Several scenes impress on sheer beauty and composition – a view of the California desert backed by snow-capped mountains, a garden landscape with swans in the foreground, a Pacific sunset towards which the broken screen idol swims to his tragic death. Colors of the interiors are soft and subdued.

Story relates the experiences of a young girl who rises to cinema fame while her husband, having touched the heights, is on a swift descent. Love is the heroine; alcohol, the villain.

Janet Gaynor gives to her role, the small town girl who makes good, a characterization of sustained loveliness. She is equally as good in the comedy passages.

The same, without reservation, may be said for Fredric March and the manner in which he plays the passe star, Norman Maine. He creates a finely drawn portrait of weakness without viciousness, a demoralization which reminds of George Hurstwood in Theodore Dreiser's novel *Sister Carrie*.

Others in the cast also are excellent, including Adolphe Menjou, who plays a producer; Lionel Stander, as a studio publicity man; Andy Devine, an assistant director, and May Robson.
☐ 1937: Best Picture (Nomination)

■ **STAR IS BORN, A**

1954, 182 MINS, US ◇ ⓥ

Dir George Cukor   *Prod* Sid Luft   *Scr* Dorothy Parker, Alan Campbell, Robert Carson   *Ph* Sam Leavitt
Mus Ray Heindorf   *Art Dir* Malcolm Bert
● Judy Garland, James Mason, Jack Carson, Charles Bickford, Tom Noonan, Lucy Marlow (Warner/Transcona)

A Star Is Born was a great 1937 moneymaker

and it's an even greater picture in its filmusical transmutation.

Unfolded in the showmanly adaptation is a strong personal saga which somehow becomes, in a sense, integrated into the celluloid plot. The reel and the real-life values sometimes play back and forth, in pendulum fashion, and the unspooling is never wanting for heart-wallop and gutsy entertainment values.

Judy Garland glitters with that stardust which in the plot the wastrel star James Mason recognizes. And her loyalties are as Gibraltar amidst the house of cards which periodically seem to collapse around her and upon him.

From the opening drunken debacle at the Shrine benefit to the scandalous antics of a hopeless dipsomaniac when his wife (Garland) wins the Academy Award, there is an intense pattern of real-life mirrorings.

Integrated into the arresting romance-with-music is perhaps the best inside stuff on the Hollywood film production scene that has ever been publicly projected.

Whatever the production delays, which allegedly piled up a near-$5 million production cost, the end-results are worth it.

■ **STAR IS BORN, A**

1976, 140 MINS, US ◇ ⓥ

Dir Frank Pierson   *Prod* Jon Peters   *Scr* John Gregory Dunne, Joan Didion, Frank Pierson   *Ph* Robert Surtees   *Ed* Peter Zinner   *Art Dir* Polly Platt
● Barbra Streisand, Kris Kristofferson, Paul Mazursky, Gary Busey, Oliver Clark, Vanetta Fields (Warner)

A Star is Born has the rare distinction of being a superlative remake. Film rightfully credits the original William Wellman-Robert Carson story on which David O. Selznick mounted his 1937 version, the first to use this title.

Plot picks up Kris Kristofferson past his rock superstar prime, unable or unwilling to make his tour commitments, raising hell and alienating people. His success has become a machine, supervised by Paul Mazursky (as a smooth rock music manager), kept in line by Gary Busey, and attended to by Sally Kirkland, Joanne Linville and others who typify the coterie that comes with fame.

Barbra Streisand is discovered in a tacky nitery, singing with Vanetta Fields and Clydie King.

■ **STAR OF MIDNIGHT**

1935, 90 MINS, US ⓥ

Dir Stephen Roberts   *Prod* Pandro S. Berman
Scr Howard J. Green, Anthony Veiller, Edward Kaufman   *Ph* J. Roy Hunt   *Ed* Arthur Roberts
Mus Max Steiner
● William Powell, Ginger Rogers, Paul Kelly, Gene Lockhart, Ralph Morgan, Leslie Fenton (RKO)

Star of Midnight is a non-camouflaged follow-up on *The Thin Man* (1934), although made by a different producer [from the novel by Arthur Somers Roche]. It hits a similar merry comedy-drama stride and attains practically the same effectiveness as screen entertainment.

William Powell is once more the happy-go-lucky master sleuth, brought into the case against his wishes and better judgment, but solving it just the same. His romance this time is not so adult, but equally humorous, and, with Ginger Rogers opposite, always interesting.

The mystery is double-barrelled, concerning the disappearance of a show's leading woman and the killing of a Broadway columnist. Powell unravels both in the customary ingenious manner, to the consternation and despite the interference of the regularly assigned policemen. As did Myrna Loy in *Thin Man*, Rogers here helps him consider-

ably. She looks like a million, troupes splendidly and wears a pictureful of class clothes.

Smart dialog containing a good share of genuine laughs keeps Powell and Rogers occupied most of the time when they are not mystery-solving or drinking.

■ **STAR SPANGLED RHYTHM**

1943, 99 MINS, US

Dir George Marshall   *Prod* Joseph Sistrom   *Scr* Harry Tugend   *Ph* Leo Tover   *Ed* Arthur Schmidt
Mus Robert Emmett Dolan
● Victor Moore, Betty Hutton, Eddie Bracken, Anne Revere, Walter Abel (Paramount)

Except for a few gags and situations, *Rhythm* has essentially nothing new in it. But neither has a Christmas tree. Yet both bring good cheer because of the way they're dressed up. The whole thing, as Harry Tugend has written it and George Marshall directed it, is fresh, alive and full of bounce.

It's a gay and good-humored tune-pic, but on the grand scale, grand because of the personalities who wander in and out of the pic, because of the seven listenable tunes, because of the general lavishness of the production and because of the downright gaiety of the whole affair.

Best of all, most of the flock of stars do much better than the usual smile and a couple of lines. Among the names whose contribution to the film deserves more than perfunctory billing are Bing Crosby, Bob Hope, Dorothy Lamour, Paulette Goddard, Veronica Lake, Mary Martin, Victor Moore, Betty Hutton and Eddie Bracken.

Scaffolding for this galaxy is the arrival at San Pedro of Bracken and a pile of his navy shipmates. Bracken's father (Victor Moore) is a former hoss opry star who's now a gateman at the Paramount lot. Rather than disclose this comedown to Bracken, Hutton convinces Moore that he should say he's head of the studio. Bracken thereupon brings his shipmates to the lot (promising each of them a 24-karat Par blonde) and Moore has to attempt to play the big-shot that his son has billed him.

■ **STAR STRUCK**

1982, 102 MINS, AUSTRALIA ◇ ⓥ

Dir Gillian Armstrong   *Prod* David Elfick, Richard Brennan   *Scr* Stephen Maclean   *Ph* Russell Boyd
Ed Nicholas Beauman   *Mus* Mark Moffatt
Art Dir Brian Thomson
● Jo Kennedy, Ross O'Donovan, Pat Evison, Margo Lee, Max Cullen, Ned Lander (Palm Beach)

Picture is a raucous, 'let's put on a show' musical with a punk rock beat. Story centers on an enterprising 14-year-old entrepreneur Ross O'Donovan who has big career plans for his cousin, singer Jo Kennedy. Grooming (?) her in the punk mode, O'Donovan has his sights on copping first prize on a New Year's television talent show.

However, he can't get the attention of a powerful Sydney disk jockey until he stages a daring balancing tightrope stunt for Kennedy. Suddenly, she's a media star quickly homogenized for home consumption.

Meanwhile, the family hotel-bar is on the verge of bankruptcy. The $25,000 talent prize becomes all-important to save the failing establishment.

Script is pure fantasy material offering director Gillian Armstrong the opportunity to send-up the likes of Busby Berkeley and Garland-Rooney musicals. The film certainly doesn't lack energy. Camerawork by Russell Boyd is glossy and fluid and song-and-dance routines are loud and splashy. Regrettably, the choreography is uninspired.

■ STAR TREK
THE MOTION PICTURE

1979, 132 MINS, US ◇

Dir Robert Wise   *Prod* Gene Roddenberry
Scr Harold Livingston   *Ph* Richard H. Kline   *Ed* Todd
Ramsay   *Mus* Jerry Goldsmith   *Art Dir* Harold
Michelson
● William Shatner, Leonard Nimoy, DeForest Kelley,
George Takei, James Doohan, Persis Khambatta
(Paramount)

The *Enterprise* has been completely recondi-
tioned during a two-year drydock, but must
be prematurely dispatched to intercept an
Earth-bound attacker.

William Shatner's Kirk is told to lead the
mission along with other show regulars.

Upshot is a search-and-destroy thriller
[based on a story by Alan Dean Foster] that
includes all of the ingredients the TV show's
fans thrive on: the philosophical dilemma
wrapped in a scenario of mind control,
troubles with the space ship, the dependable
and understanding Kirk, the ever-logical
Spock, and suspenseful take with twist
ending. Touches of romance and corn also
dot this voyage.

But the expensive effects (under supervision of Douglas Trumbull) are the secret of
this film, and the amazing wizardry throughout would appear to justify the whopping
budget. Jerry Goldsmith's brassy score is the
other necessary plus.

■ STAR TREK II
THE WRATH OF KHAN

1982, 113 MINS, US ◇ Ⓥ

Dir Nicholas Meyer   *Prod* Robert Sallin   *Scr* Jack B.
Sowards   *Ph* Gayne Rescher   *Ed* William P.
Dornisch   *Mus* James Horner, Alexander Courage
Art Dir Joseph R. Jennings
● William Shatner, Leonard Nimoy, DeForest Kelley,
Ricardo Montalban, James Doohan, Walter Koenig
(Paramount)

Star Trek II is a very satisfying space
adventure, closer in spirit and format to the
popular TV series than to its big-budget
predecessor.

Story is nominally a sequel to the TV episode *Space Seed*, with Starship Reliant captain
Terrell (Paul Winfield) and Commander
Chekov (Walter Koenig) incorrectly landing
on a planet on an exploration mission. This
allows the evil Khan (Ricardo Montalban)
who was marooned there with his family and
crew 15 years before by Kirk (William
Shatner), to take over the Reliant and vow
revenge on Kirk.

Admiral Kirk is coaxed to take command
once again of the Starship *Enterprise* on a
training mission, travels to the Regula space
station on a rescue mission. Dr Carol Marcus
(Bibi Besch) and her (and Kirk's) son David
(Merritt Butrick) have been working there on
the Genesis Project, to convert barren planets
into Eden-like sources of life. Khan has stolen
the Genesis Effect equipment.

Final reel is a classic of emotional
manipulation: Spock unhesitatingly calcu-
lates that he must sacrifice himself to save the
Enterprise crew.

■ STAR TREK III
THE SEARCH FOR SPOCK

1984, 105 MINS, US ◇ Ⓥ

Dir Leonard Nimoy   *Prod* Harve Bennett   *Scr* Harve
Bennett   *Ph* Charles Correll   *Ed* Robert F. Shugrue
Mus James Horner, Alexander Courage   *Art Dir* John
E. Chilberg II
● William Shatner, DeForest Kelley, James Doohan,
George Takei, Walter Koenig, Leonard Nimoy
(Paramount)

Star Trek III is an emotionally satisfying science fiction adventure. Dovetailing neatly

with the previous entry in the popular series
Star Trek II, film centers upon a quest to
seemingly bring Spock (Leonard Nimoy), the
noble science officer and commander who
selflessly gave his life to save 'the many', back
to life.

Spock's friend, Admiral Kirk (William
Shatner) is visited by Spock's Vulcan father
(Mark Lenard), who informs him that
Spock's living spirit may still be alive via a
mindmeld with one of Kirk's crew and must
be taken to the planet Vulcan to be
preserved.

Kirk discovers who the 'possessed' crew
member is, and with his other shipmates,
steals the Enterprise out of its dock and sets
off for Vulcan.

■ STAR TREK IV
THE VOYAGE HOME

1986, 119 MINS, US ◇ Ⓥ

Dir Leonard Nimoy   *Prod* Harve Bennett   *Scr* Harve
Bennett, Steve Meerson, Peter Krikes, Nicholas Meyer
Ph Don Peterman   *Ed* Peter E. Berger   *Mus* Leonard
Rosenman   *Art Dir* Jack T. Collis
● William Shatner, Leonard Nimoy, DeForest Kelley,
James Doohan, Catherine Hicks, George Takei (Bennett)

Latest excursion is warmer, wittier, more
socially relevant and truer to its TV origins
than prior odysseys.

This voyage finds the crew earthbound but
they find the galaxy dark and messages from
Earth distorted. Spock locates the source of
the trouble in the bleating, eerie sounds of an
unidentified probe and links them to a cry
from the Earth's past that has long been
silenced.

Scripters employ successful use of time
travel.

Spock (Leonard Nimoy) and Kirk (William
Shatner) play off each other in a sort of deadpan futuristic version of Hope and Crosby
with Nimoy, surprisingly, as the awkward
one relying on Shatner's smooth talking to
win the help of a zealous save-the-whales
biologist (Catherine Hicks) in capturing a
couple of specimens.

■ STAR TREK V
THE FINAL FRONTIER

1989, 106 MINS, US ◇ Ⓥ

Dir William Shatner   *Prod* Harve Bennett   *Scr* David
Loughery   *Ph* Andrew Laszlo   *Ed* Peter Berger
Mus Jerry Goldsmith   *Art Dir* Herman Zimmerman
● William Shatner, Leonard Nimoy, DeForest Kelley,
James Doohan, Nichelle Nichols, George Takei
(Paramount)

Even diehard Trekkies may be disappointed
by *Star Trek V*. Coming after Leonard
Nimoy's delightful directorial outing on *Star
Trek IV*, William Shatner's inauspicious feature directing debut is a double letdown.

A major flaw in the story [by Shatner,
Harve Bennett and David Loughery] is that
it centers on an obsessive quest by a character who isn't a member of the Enterprise
crew, a renegade Vulcan played by Laurence
Luckinbill in Kabuki-like makeup. The
crazed Luckinbill kidnaps the crew and
makes them fly to a never-before-visited planet at the centre of the galaxy in quest of the
Meaning of Life.

Better they should have stayed home and
watched reruns of the TV series, which had a
lot more to say about the meaning of life.

Shatner, rises to the occasion, however, in
directing a dramatic sequence of the mystical
Luckinbill teaching Nimoy and DeForest
Kelley to re-experience their long-buried
traumas. The re-creations of Spock's rejection by his father after his birth and Kelley's
euthanasia of his own father are moving highlights.

■ STAR WARS

1977, 121 MINS, US ◇ Ⓥ

Dir George Lucas   *Prod* Gary Kurtz   *Scr* George
Lucas   *Ph* Gilbert Taylor   *Ed* Paul Hirsch, Marcia
Lucas, Richard Chew   *Mus* John Williams   *Art Dir* John
Barry
● Mark Hamill, Harrison Ford, Carrie Fisher, Peter
Cushing, Alec Guinness, Anthony Daniels
(20th Century-Fox)

Star Wars is a magnificent film. George Lucas
set out to make the biggest possible adventure fantasy out of his memories of serials and
older action epics, and he succeeded
brilliantly.

The superb balance of technology and
human drama is one of the many achievements: one identifies with the characters
and accepts, as do they, the intriguing
intergalactic world in which they live.

Carrie Fisher is delightful as the regal, but
spunky princess on a rebel planet who has
been kidnapped by Peter Cushing, would-be
ruler of the universe. Mark Hamill is
excellent as a farm boy who sets out to rescue
Fisher in league with Alec Guinness, last
survivor of a band of noble knights.

Harrison Ford is outstanding as a likeable
mercenary pilot.
□ 1977: Best Picture (Nomination)

■ STARDUST

1974, 113 MINS, UK ◇ Ⓥ

Dir Michael Apted   *Prod* David Puttnam, Sandy
Lieberson   *Scr* Ray Connolly   *Ph* Tony Richmond
Ed Mike Bradsell   *Mus* Dave Edmunds, David
Puttnam (arr.)
● David Essex, Adam Faith, Larry Hagman, Ines Des
Longchamps, Rosalind Ayres, Marty Wilde
(EMI/Goodtimes)

Several members of the team that put
together the highly successful *That'll Be the
Day* [1973] are associated with this much
more elaborate and ambitious followup.

Singer-guitarist Jim Maclaine (David
Essex), seen on the verge of maturity and
foretasting fame and fortune at the end of
Day, is followed here on his rapid rise and fall
as the eventual star of a heterogeneous pop
group, the Stray Cats, as it makes it first in
the nabes, then in the UK, US and the world.

Enroute, pic details the loves, joys and
tribulations, hardships and achievements,
jealousies, superficialities and hypocrisies, as
well as – and importantly – the damning
effect of drugs, of the music scene glimpsed
from the lowest beginnings to number one
position in the global charts.

■ STARDUST MEMORIES

1980, 89 MINS, US ◇

Dir Woody Allen   *Prod* Robert Greenhut   *Scr* Woody
Allen   *Ph* Gordon Willis   *Ed* Susan E. Morse
Art Dir Santo Loquasto
● Woody Allen, Charlotte Rampling, Marie-Christine
Barrault, Jessica Harper, Amy Wright, Tony Roberts
(United Artists)

While Woody Allen teased with autobiography in *Manhattan* and *Annie Hall* he drops
all pretense here. No effort is made to pretend
that his character of Sandy Bates is anybody
but Allen himself – a filmmaker first adored
for wacky comedies, then gradually appreciated as a cinematic genius.

But Bates-Allen thinks those who like his
early comedies more than his later 'deeper'
pictures are buffoons; he thinks those who try
to sift through the meaning of his later works
are intellectual lamebrains and he makes
clear that any attempt to analyze *Stardust
Memories* itself would be the height of
pompous pretension.

Though there are laughs along the way,
this is a truly mean-spirited picture. Once a

sympathetic nebbish, Allen here sees himself as a put-upon, embittered genius, disdainful of everything around him.

••••••••••••••••••••••••••••••••

■ **STARMAN**

1984, 115 MINS, US ◇ ⑱

Dir John Carpenter   *Prod* Larry J. Franco   *Scr* Bruce A. Evans, Raynold Gideon   *Ph* Donald M. Morgan   *Ed* Marion Rothman   *Mus* Jack Nitzsche   *Art Dir* Daniel Lomino

● Jeff Bridges, Karen Allen, Charles Martin Smith, Richard Jaeckel, Robert Phalen, Tony Edwards (Columbia-Delphi II)

There is little that is original in *Starman*, but at least it has chosen good models As amalgam of elements introduced in *Close Encounters of the Third Kind*, *E.T.* and even *The Man Who Fell to Earth*, *Starman* shoots for the miraculous and only partially hits its target.

The Starman (Jeff Bridges) arrives much like 'E.T.' – an alien in a hostile environment – but in an elaborate transformation scene he assumes human form. The body he chooses for his sojourn on Earth happens to belong to the dead husband of Jenny Hayden (Karen Allen) who lives alone in a remote section of Wisconsin.

Bridges and Allen set off on a trip across the country to Arizona where the Starman must make his connection to return home.

••••••••••••••••••••••••••••••••

■ **STARS LOOK DOWN, THE**

1939, 104 MINS, UK ⑱

Dir Carol Reed   *Prod* Isadore Goldsmith   *Scr* J.B. Williams   *Ph* Mutz Greenbaum   *Ed* Reginald Beck   *Art Dir* James Carter

● Michael Redgrave, Margaret Lockwood, Emlyn Williams, Nancy Price, Edward Rigby, Cecil Parker (Grafton/Grand National)

The Stars Look Down is a visual education on British mining. A picturization of a subject long an uncomfortable wedge in the English social-political scheme, *Stars* would merit laurels alone for a faithful and gripping treatment. But film goes for more; it is a splendid dramatic portrait of those who burrow for the black diamond in England's northland. Direction is of class standing and picture is mounted with exactness of detail and technique.

Adopted from A.J. Cronin's novel of the mining town from where two sons seek different roads to success, one returning to foster misery, the other to fight on for its alleviation, film unrolls at steady pace a wealth of dramatic incident.

There are some gaps where treatment is not on par with dramatic situation. The Emlyn Williams part, the focal point of the tragedy, is under-developed, but director Carol Reed has guided well a cast that exacts the utmost generally. Michael Redgrave, as son of the strike-leader (Williams), a ne'er-do-well, and Margaret Lockwood, as a slut, share the starring honors.

••••••••••••••••••••••••••••••••

■ **STARTING OVER**

1979, 106 MINS, US ◇ ⑱

Dir Alan J. Pakula   *Prod* Alan J. Pakula   *Scr* James L. Brooks   *Ph* Sven Nykvist   *Ed* Marion Rothman   *Mus* Marvin Hamlisch   *Art Dir* George Jenkins

● Burt Reynolds, Jill Clayburgh, Candice Bergen, Charles Durning, Frances Sternhagen, Austin Pendleton (Paramount/Brook)

Starting Over takes on the subject of marital dissolution from a comic point of view, and succeeds admirably, wryly directed by Alan J. Pakula, and featuring an outstanding cast.

In fact, *Starting Over* [from the novel by Dan Wakefield] favorably evokes the screwball

comedies of the 1930s and the heyday of American screen comedy.

Burt Reynolds plays a mild-mannered writer unwillingly foisted into a 'liberated' condition by spouse Candice Bergen, feeling her feminine oats as a songwriter. Fleeing to Boston and protection of relatives Charles Durning and Frances Sternhagen, he meets spinster schoolteacher Jill Clayburgh, and the off-and-on romance begins.

With unfailing comic timing Reynolds is the core of the film, and underplays marvellously.

••••••••••••••••••••••••••••••••

■ **STATE FAIR**

1945, 100 MINS, US ◇

Dir Walter Lang   *Prod* William Perlberg   *Scr* Oscar Hammerstein II   *Ph* Leon Shamroy   *Ed* J. Watson Webb   *Mus* Richard Rodgers   *Art Dir* Lyle R. Wheeler, Lewis Creber

● Jeanne Crain, Dana Andrews, Dick Haymes, Vivian Blaine, Charles Winninger, Fay Bainter (20th Century-Fox)

The Phil Stong novel, which Oscar Hammerstein II authored for the lastest screen version [adapted by Sonya Levien and Paul Green], is still a boy-meets-girl yarn that has lost none of the flavor of the years. And notably distinctive in the telling is the frequent punctuation of the story by the Rodgers-Hammerstein tunes. Otherwise, the yarn is still the one of midwest rustication, concerning mainly the hoopla attendant to the annual state fair, at which products, from pickles to hogs, are displayed for judging and prizes.

Jeanne Crain and Dick Haymes are the Frake progeny, and Dana Andrews is the newspaper reporter who covers the fair and is the other half of the Crain romantic attachment. Haymes and Blaine handle the other romantic situation. Fay Bainter is the mother.

The film's top tune is 'That's for Me', featured by Blaine in a bandstand sequence. It's a sock ballad. Not too far behind is another, 'It Might as Well Be Spring', sung by Crain. 'It's a Grand Night for Singing', by Haymes, is another. The tunes are whammo from both lyrical and melody content, made evident by the allotment of one to each of the three singing principals.

••••••••••••••••••••••••••••••••

■ **STATE FAIR**

1962, 118 MINS, US ◇ ⑱

Dir Jose Ferrer   *Prod* Charles Brackett   *Scr* Richard Breen   *Ph* William C. Mellor   *Ed* David Bretherton   *Mus* Richard Rodgers   *Art Dir* Jack Martin Smith, Walter M. Simonds

● Pat Boone, Bobby Darin, Pamela Tiffin, Ann-Margret, Tom Ewell, Alice Faye (20th Century-Fox)

This marks the third time around (1933, 1945) on the screen for this vehicle. To the five original R&H refrains retained in this version, five new numbers with both music and lyrics by Richard Rodgers have been added. The old songs are still charming, but they are not rendered with quite the zest and feeling of the 1945 cast.

Richard Breen's updated, reset (from Iowa to Texas) scenario isn't otherwise appreciably altered from the last time out. Same three love affairs are there (involving four people and two Hampshire hogs). Same brandy-spiked mince meat episode. Fairgrounds, however, have been switched to Dallas, and there's something crass and antiseptic about the atmosphere – a significant loss.

None of the four young stars comes off especially well. Pat Boone and Bobby Darin emerge rather bland and unappealing. Pamela Tiffin's range of expression seems rather narrow on this occasion. Of the four,

Ann-Margret makes perhaps the most vivid impression, particularly during her torrid song-dance rendition of 'Isn't It Kind of Fun', the film's big production number.

••••••••••••••••••••••••••••••••

■ **STATE FAIR**

1933, 80 MINS, US

Dir Henry King   *Prod* Winfield Sheehan   *Scr* Paul Green, Sonya Levien   *Ph* Hal Mohr   *Ed* R. W. Bischoff   *Mus* Ray Flynn   *Art Dir* Duncan Cramer

● Will Rogers, Janet Gaynor, Lew Ayres, Sally Eilers, Norman Foster, Louise Dresser (Fox)

Based on Phil Stong's bestseller written around a country fair, Henry King has nicely caught the spirit of the simple story and has turned in a production that has the charm of naturalness and the virtue of sincerity.

No villain, little suspense, but a straightforward story of a rural family who find their great moments at the state fair, where paterfamilias captures the title for his prize hog, the mother makes a clean sweep in the pickle entries, the boy gets his first vicarious but satisfying taste of romance, and the girl finds a more lasting love.

Of chief interest is the debut of a new romance team in Janet Gaynor and Lew Ayres. His rather flippant style gives a needed tang to situations which sometimes in the past have been too saccharine. It is a charming romance between these two. There is interest, too, in the less wholesome romance of the boy with the girl of the acrobatic act. Norman Foster and Sally Eilers handle this capably, while there is just enough of Will Rogers' quaint humor and Louise Dresser's country dame to temper the more hectic moments.

For a moment Victor Jory steals the screen as the concession owner who gypped young Frake (Foster) the year before and smilingly prepares to repeat, only to find that his erstwhile victim has spent the twelve-month interval in practising to ring the prizes and is practically a dead shot. There is even a humorous twist to the porcine romance of Blue Boy, the prize hog, who comes to life only when he meets Esmeralda, the red-headed sow.

☐ 1932/33: Best Picture (Nomination)

••••••••••••••••••••••••••••••••

■ **STATE OF GRACE**

1990, 134 MINS, US ◇ ⑱

Dir Phil Joanou   *Prod* Ned Dowd, Randy Ostrow, Ron Rotholz   *Scr* Dennis McIntyre   *Ph* Jordan Cronenweth   *Ed* Claire Simpson   *Mus* Ennio Morricone   *Art Dir* Patrizia Von Brandenstein, Doug Kraner

● Sean Penn, Ed Harris, Gary Oldman, Robin Wright, John Turturro, Burgess Meredith (Cinehaus/Orion)

State of Grace is a handsomely produced, mostly riveting, but ultimately overlong and overindulgent gangster picture.

Sean Penn plays Terry, one of New York's Irish residents who grew up in Hell's Kitchen with his friends, brothers Frankie (Ed Harris) and Jackie (Gary Oldman) and their sister, Kathleen (Robin Wright), with whom he was once in love.

Terry's been away from New York for 12 years, but now he returns and signs up with the Irish mob headed by the ruthless Frankie. He also resumes his passionate relationship with Kathleen. Terry isn't all he seems, and in fact he's an undercover cop assigned to get the goods on Frankie.

Penn is excellent as Terry, who drinks too much and who ultimately gets too personally involved with his mission. Harris is a malevolent Frankie, who carries out his executions personally. Oldman is suitably manic as the unstable younger brother. Wright, though she gives a glowing performance as Kathleen, seems to belong to an altogether different movie.

....

■ **STATE OF THE UNION**

1948, 121 MINS, US ⓥ
Dir Frank Capra   *Prod* Frank Capra   *Scr* Anthony Veiller, Myles Connolly   *Ph* George J. Folsey   *Ed* William Hornbeck   *Mus* Victor Young
● Spencer Tracy, Katharine Hepburn, Van Johnson, Angela Lansbury, Adolphe Menjou (M-G-M/Liberty)

The hit Broadway play by Howard Lindsay and Russel Crouse has been expanded somewhat in the screen adaptation, a broadening that makes the best use of screen technique. Dialog has headline freshness, and a stinging bite when directed at politicians, the normal voter and the election scene.

Plot deals with a power-mad femme newspaper publisher who picks up a selfmade plane magnate and shoves him towards the White House to satisfy her own interests. The candidate begins to lose his commonsense when the political malarkey soaks in and only is saved by his frank and honest wife.

Cast is loaded with stalwarts who deliver in top form. The fact that it's pat casting only helps to insure the payoff. Spencer Tracy fits his personality to the role of the airplane manufacturer who becomes a presidential aspirant. It's a sock performance. Katharine Hepburn makes much of the role of Tracy's wife, giving it understanding and warmth that register big. Van Johnson shines as the columnist turned political press agent. It's one of his better performances.

Capra's direction punches over the pictorial expose of US politics and candidate manufacturers, the indifference of the average voter, and the need for more expression of true public opinion at the polls.

....

■ **STATION SIX-SAHARA**

1964, 97 MINS, UK
Dir Seth Holt   *Prod* Victor Lyndon   *Scr* Bryan Forbes, Brian Clemens   *Ph* Gerald Gibbs   *Ed* Alastair McIntyre   *Mus* Ron Grainer   *Art Dir* Jack Stephens
● Carroll Baker, Peter Van Eyck, Ian Bannen, Denholm Elliott, Jorg Felmy, Mario Adorf (Allied Artists)

Station Six-Sahara is a sex melodrama [from the play, *Men without a Past*, by Jacques Maret], filmed in the Libyan desert with Carroll Baker. Story premise of a sexpot arriving at an isolated desert oil pipeline station where five lonely men have only thing in common – the nagging need for a woman – is generally well developed.

Good interest is early sustained despite fact that Baker does not appear for first 42 minutes. Limited confines of the rude station settings puts emphasis strictly upon yarn unfoldment and permits director Seth Holt to display his helming mettle while audience awaits entrance of femme star, only woman in cast. With her entry into plot, when a car roars out of the night and eager hands, after it crashes, lift her seductive figure out of the wreckage, attention picks up perceptibly as the men react in varying degrees and kind to her presence.

Baker, in what amounts actually to a smaller role, feelingly delineates this key character and makes her work count. Peter Van Eyck, in charge of the station which he operates with typical cold Teutonic efficiency, is smooth and convincing. Jorg Felmy, another German with icy self-control, underplays his role for excellent effect. Ian Bannen, a Scotsman with a sour sense of humor, and Denholm Elliott, a paperspined Englishman who lives on memories of the desert war in World War II, persuasively portray their respective parts.

....

■ **STAY HUNGRY**

1976, 102 MINS, US ◇ ⓥ
Dir Bob Rafelson   *Prod* Harold Schneider   *Scr* Charles Gaines, Bob Rafelson   *Ph* Victor Kemper   *Ed* John F. Link II   *Mus* Bruce Langhorne   *Art Dir* Toby Carr Rafelson
● Jeff Bridges, Sally Field, Arnold Schwarzenegger, R.G. Armstrong, Robert Englund, Helena Kallianiotes (United Artists)

Stay Hungry features an excellent Jeff Bridges as a spoiled but affable rich young Alabama boy who slums his way to maturity through relationships with street-smart characters.

Bridges gets involved in a big urban real estate scheme with Joe Spinell and cohorts, all buying up small plots for a major development. But R.G. Armstrong's second-rate gym can't be had, so Bridges decides to infiltrate.

There he falls for Sally Field and also is exposed to the barbell denizens who include real-life bodybuilding champ Arnold Schwarzenegger, good-natured staffer Robert Englund, uptight ladies instructor Helena Kallianiotes and amiable attendant Roger E. Mosely.

All these characters conflict with Bridges' family and social circle. But underneath it all is a lurching and poorly defined film concept.

....

■ **STAYING ALIVE**

1983, 96 MINS, US ◇ ⓥ
Dir Sylvester Stallone   *Prod* Robert Stigwood, Sylvester Stallone   *Scr* Sylvester Stallone, Norman Wexler   *Ph* Nick McLean   *Ed* Don Zimmerman, Mark Warner   *Mus* The Bee Gees   *Art Dir* Robert F. Boyle
● John Travolta, Cynthia Rhodes, Finola Hughes, Steve Inwood, Julie Bovasso (Stigwood/Paramount)

The bottom line is that *Staying Alive* is nowhere as good as its 1977 predecessor, *Saturday Night Fever.*

When last heard from, John Travolta's Tony Manero had left Brooklyn for an uncertain future in Manhattan. Now, he's on the rounds of casting calls and auditions for Broadway dance shows.

He's also got a comfortable but uncommitted relationship going with fellow struggling dancer and sometime saloon singer Cynthia Rhodes, who loves him a lot. Nevertheless, Travolta doesn't think twice about her feelings when he spots alluring British dancer Finola Hughes and hooks up with her while winning a background role in a show in which she will be starring.

By close to showtime, Travolta and Hughes loathe each other, and she's none too pleased when this unknown upstart manages to replace her faltering costar in the male lead of the production. The show, entitled *Satan's Alley*, emerges as an opening night smash, and Tony Manero is a success at last.

....

■ **STAYING TOGETHER**

1989, 91 MINS, US ◇ ⓥ
Dir Lee Grant   *Prod* Joseph Feury   *Scr* Monte Merrick   *Ph* Dick Bush   *Ed* Katherine Wenning   *Art Dir* W. Steven Graham
● Sean Astin, Stockard Channing, Melinda Dillon, Jim Haynie, Levin Helm (Feury)

Staying Together, a sincerely made coming-of-age tale, serves up familiar homilies about family values in changing small-town America and the indomitable power of love.

In a bucolic town somewhere in South Carolina, Mr and Mrs McDermott and their three strapping sons run a self-named home-cooked-chicken restaurant. Mom is a tower of strength and a paragon of understanding; dad is gruff but caring, and the brothers confine their red-blooded oats-sowing, boozing and pot-smoking to their off hours.

The yuppies have landed and pop McDermott takes an offer he can't refuse for the restaurant and its choice land site.

Middle sibling Brian (essayed by Tom Cruise–John Travolta hybrid Tim Quill) has been having an affair with an older woman who's championing the developers' cause. When his dad decides to cash in, the hot-tempered kid denounces pop, leaves home and talks his way into a job on the condo construction site.

Lee Grant and screenwriter Monte Merrick push all the preprogrammed melodrama buttons, including prodigal son Brian's too-late-to-say-goodbye dash to the hospital.

....

■ **STEALING HEAVEN**

1989, 110 MINS, UK/YUGOSLAVIA ◇ ⓥ
Dir Clive Donner   *Prod* Simon MacCorkindale, Andros Epaminondas   *Scr* Chris Bryant   *Ph* Mikael Salomon   *Ed* Michael Ellis   *Mus* Nick Bicat   *Art Dir* Voytek
● Derek de Lint, Kim Thomson, Denholm Elliott, Bernard Hepton, Kenneth Cranham, Rachel Kempson (Amy/Jadran)

This handsome historical pageant attempts to tell the 'true story' behind one of history's most famous romances, that of 12th-century French philosopher Pierre Abelard and his beloved Heloise which has survived through the ages in the exchange of letters between them, each of them shut off from the world in another convent.

Chris Bryant's script, based on Marion Meade's novel, pushes toward a sharp and witty, anticlerical, feminist tract. Abelard shuns emotional commitments as dangerous to his intellectual capacities. Fulbert, Heloise's uncle, is a mercenary bigot who looks for the best deal on his niece; and Heloise is the smart, intelligent and unconventional girl with the courage to assume responsibility for her feelings.

....

■ **STEAMBOAT BILL, JR**

1928, 65 MINS, US ⊗ ⓥ
Dir Charles F. Reisner   *Prod* Joseph M. Schenck   *Scr* Carl Harbaugh   *Ph* Dev Jennings, Bert Haines
● Buster Keaton, Ernest Torrence, Tom McGuire, Marion Byron, Tom Lewis (United Artists)

The last comedy Buster Keaton made under his United Artists contract, it was held back for several months, getting itself concerned in several wild rumors. Whatever may have been the real reason why United Artists took its time about releasing this one, it had nothing to do with quality, for it's a pip of a comedy. It's one of Keaton's best.

The story concerns the efforts of an old hard-boiled river captain (Ernest Torrence), to survive on the river in the face of opposition from a brand new modern rival boat, put in commission by his rival (Tom McGuire). The old-timer hasn't seen his son since he was an infant. The son arrives (Keaton), and things begin to happen, fast and furiously.

The son falls in love with the daughter of the rival owner. Matters reach a climax when the old tub of Steamboat Bill is condemned. In a rage, he confronts his rival and accuses him of robbing him. A battle ensues.

An excellent cast gives Keaton and Torrence big league support. Tom Lewis as the first mate, McGuire as the rival owner and Marion Byron as the girl contribute heavily. The windstorm is a gem and the river stuff interesting and colorful.

....

■ **STEEL**

1980, 99 MINS, US ◇ ⓥ
Dir Steve Carver   *Prod* Peter S. Davis, William N. Panzer   *Scr* Leigh Chapman   *Ph* Roger Shearman   *Ed* David Blewitt   *Mus* Michel Colombier   *Art Dir* Ward & Preston
● Lee Majors, Jennifer O'Neill, Art Carney, George Kennedy, Harris Yulin (Davis-Panzer/New Line)

Steel began lensing in Lexington, Kentucky, in 1978 and during production famed stuntman A.J. Bakunis died doing a tricky maneuver (pic is dedicated to him).

Lee Majors stars and exec produced and his well-crafted, restrained portrayal as the leader of the constructioners provides a solid base for a series of involving relationships.

There is an explosion and George Kennedy, the good-hearted company owner, plunges to a tragic death. Daughter Jennifer O'Neill is then left to take on the task of completing the project. Kennedy's friend Art Carney suggests O'Neill search out Majors to coordinate the job, and he rounds up the most famous workers in the business.

What unravels is a rightly-directed story and true-to-life character study of endearing personalities interacting against outside forces.

························

■ STEEL HELMET, THE

1951, 84 MINS, US

Dir Samuel Fuller *Prod* Samuel Fuller *Scr* Samuel Fuller *Ph* Ernest W. Miller *Ed* Philip Cahn *Mus* Paul Dunlap *Art Dir* Theobald Holsopple
● Gene Evans, Robert Hutton, Richard Loo, Steve Brodie, James Edwards, William Chun (Deputy/Lippert)

The Steel Helmet pinpoints the Korean fighting in a grim, hardhitting tale that is excellently told.

A veteran top sergeant is the sole survivor of a small patrol, bound and murdered by North Koreans. He and a young native boy, who freed him, start back for the lines. They are soon joined by a Negro medic, sole survivor of another group. Trio encounters a patrol of green GIs, help them out of an ambush and go along to establish an observation post in a Korean temple. There they help direct artillery fire and capture a North Korean major hiding out in the temple.

Film serves to introduce Gene Evans as the sergeant, a vet of World War II, a tough man who is interested in staying alive, and hardened to the impact of warfare. Robert Hutton, conscientious objector in the last war but now willing to fight against communism; Steve Brodie, the lieutenant who used pull to stay out of combat previously; James Edwards, the Negro medic, and Richard Loo, a heroic Nisei, are the other principals who add to the rugged realism.

························

■ STEEL MAGNOLIAS

1989, 118 MINS, US ◇ Ⓥ

Dir Herbert Ross *Prod* Ray Stark *Scr* Robert Harling *Ph* John A. Alonzo *Ed* Paul Hirsch *Mus* Georges Delerue *Art Dir* Gene Callahan
● Sally Field, Dolly Parton, Shirley MacLaine, Daryl Hannah, Olympia Dukakis, Julia Roberts (Rastar/Tri-Star)

Robert Harling's play was set solely in the beauty parlor where his heroines – a group of the liveliest, warmest Southern women imaginable – gather to dish dirt, crack jokes, do hair and give one another some solid, postfeminist emotional support. In opening up his own play for the screen, Harling has made actual characters of the menfolk only talked about in the play.

As Sally Field's troubled yet ever-hopeful seriously diabetic daughter, Julia Roberts has real freshness and charm of the sort that can't be faked.

As the beauty shop owner around whom all the action swirls, Dolly Parton is thoroughly in her element. Wisely she remains in character as a particular good ole gal – with the Dolly fans love peeking out from underneath.

Shirley MacLaine is a nicely bridled caricature as the town curmudgeon. She looks a

wreck, talks trash and obviously loves every minute of it.

As her partner in hamming-as-an-art-form, Olympia Dukakis just about walks away with the picture, even though she's never the center of attention in any of the film's scenes.

Daryl Hannah, not unexpectedly, has her hands full keeping up with this company as a gawky, nerdish beautician's assistant.

Field does some spectacular underplaying through the bulk of the action, revealing layer after layer of the feelings of this kindly tempered, deeply worried mother.

························

■ STEEL TRAP, THE

1952, 84 MINS, US

Dir Andrew L. Stone *Prod* Bert E. Friedlob *Scr* Andrew L. Stone *Ph* Ernest Laszlo *Ed* Otto Ludwig *Mus* Dimitri Tiomkin
● Joseph Cotten, Teresa Wright, Eddie Marr, Aline Towne, Bill Hudson (Thor/20th Century-Fox)

Andrew Stone's direction of his own story emphasizes suspense that is leavened with welcome chuckles of relief in telling the improbable but entertaining events.

Joseph Cotten is a minor bank exec who succumbs to a larcenous impulse and lays plans to heist $1 million when the bank closes on Friday, take off via plane with his wife for Brazil, where there is no extradition treaty with the States. Suspense continues to mount as Cotten encounters such frustrating difficulties as passport trouble, delays in plane transportation from Los Angeles to New Orleans that cause him to miss the Saturday plane to Brazil and, finally, customs curiosity that reveals to his wife he is a thief.

Cotten is very good, and Wright is capable as the wife.

························

■ STEELYARD BLUES

1973, 92 MINS, US ◇ Ⓥ

Dir Alan Myerson *Prod* Tony Bill, Michael Phillips, Julia Phillips *Scr* David S. Ward *Ph* Laszlo Kovacs, Steven Larner *Ed* Donn Cambern, Robert Grovenor *Mus* Nick Gravenites, Paul Butterfield, David Shire *Art Dir* Vincent Cresciman
● Jane Fonda, Donald Sutherland, Peter Boyle, Garry Goodrow, Howard Hesseman, John Savage (Warner)

Steelyard Blues is an erratically amusing slapstick comedy about non-conformists.

Screenplay spotlights Donald Sutherland as ring-leader of some drop-outs which also include kid brother John Savage and Peter Boyle, who does a hilarious takeoff of Marlon Brando's *The Wild One* image. Jane Fonda is the town hooker whose customers include most of the city hall, including Sutherland's prime-adversary, his older brother Howard Hesseman, a politically ambitious DA.

The drop-outs focus their energies on restoring an old US Navy amphibian plane, and their search for spare parts leads to a climactic raid on a nearby naval air station.

Like many other films, this one suffers from a lingering late 1960s social-protest plot fibre, the result being an odd combination of nostalgia and anachronism.

························

■ STELLA

1990, 114 MINS, US ◇ Ⓥ

Dir John Erman *Prod* Samuel Goldwyn Jr *Scr* Robert Getchell *Ph* Billy Williams *Ed* Jerrold L. Ludwig *Mus* John Morris *Art Dir* James Hulsey
● Bette Midler, John Goodman, Trini Alvarado, Stephen Collins, Marsha Mason, Eileen Brennan (Touchstone/Goldwyn)

The semitragic *Stella Dallas* shows her years in this hopelessly dated and ill-advised remake.

The idea of a lower-class mother who selflessly sends her daughter off to her upper-

crust dad and his new wife – all so daughter can land the right beau – must sound like nails on a blackboard to Equal Rights Amendment proponents, and Bette Midler's ballsy wit completely misses the redeeming lower-class yearning Barbara Stanwyck gave the 1937 role.

All of the significant changes in the story come early, as Stella (Midler) meets a young doctor (Stephen Collins) while tending bar and quickly gets pregnant by him. She refuses his half-hearted offfer of marriage as well as any financial help, letting him run off to New York while she raises their daughter (Trini Alvarado) on her own.

Erman and writer Robert Getchell try to inject some levity into the maudlin proceedings. On that front they largely succeed, thanks primarily to the winning performance by John Goodman as Stella's long-suffering admirer Ed as well as Midler's natural comic flair.

························

■ STELLA DALLAS

1925, 108 MINS, US ⊗ Ⓥ

Dir Henry King *Prod* Samuel Goldwyn *Scr* Frances Marion *Ph* Arthur Edeson *Ed* Stuart Heisler *Art Dir* Ben Carre
● Belle Bennett, Ronald Colman, Alice Joyce, Jean Hersholt, Lois Moran, Douglas Fairbanks Jr. (Goldwyn/United Artists)

A mother picture. Not a great picture, but a great mother picture. Its sentiment is terrific. Henry King tells his story simply and directly without dramatics, gauging the extent to which he can play upon such an emotional subject to a nicety. In this he is helped by two magnificent performances by Belle Bennett and Lois Moran.

If ever there were a two-character picture this is it. Both characters are women, mother and daughter. It tells of a mother who eliminates herself so that her child may enjoy the advantages of which the girl will not partake while knowing that her mother has no one to whom she can turn.

Moran convinces in what practically amounts to three roles, as she plays the daughter at 10, 13 and as a young woman. Excellent in each, her performance is something of a revelation. Bennett, makes something of a cinema comeback in this release.

Alice Joyce makes a splendid contrast, while Ronald Colman is limited in his activities. Jean Hersholt is prominent among the secondary players, with young Douglas Fairbanks Jr acquitting himself creditably in his brief footage.

························

■ STELLA DALLAS

1937, 104 MINS, US ◇

Dir King Vidor *Prod* Samuel Goldwyn *Scr* Harry Wagstaff Gribble, Gertrude Purcell *Ph* Rudolph Mate *Ed* Sherman Todd *Mus* Alfred Newman *Art Dir* Richard Day
● Barbara Stanwyck, John Boles, Anne Shirley, Barbara O'Neil, Alan Hale, Marjorie Main (Goldwyn/Unfited Artists)

Producer Samuel Goldwyn made the film first in 1925 and did mighty well by the results. *Stella Dallas* is chiefly a tear-jerker of A ranking.

In producing this picture Goldwyn pretty much followed his original, bringing it, however, a bit more up-to-date. Thus the sock scenes are still the same ones. These are, especially, a scene between Barbara Stanwyck and Anne Shirley in a train when the former has just heard playmates of the latter criticize the mother as a millstone around the child's head; a scene between the girl and her father, and the woman he wants to marry; and a scene between the mother and daughter at a birthday party to which no one has shown up because of one of the mother's indiscretions.

The story [from the novel by Olive Higgins Prouty] itself is a simple enough one, not so much of mother love as the difficulties of a young girl whose parents are at extremes in the social world. It isn't overdone.

There are few faults to be pointed. Only one which is obvious is that Stanwyck is permitted to go entirely too far in costuming in her latter scenes. Especially when it is considered that the mother makes all the daughter's clothes and these are in rare good taste.

．．．．．．．．．．．．．．．．．．．．．．．．．

■ STEPFORD WIVES, THE

1975, 114 MINS, US ◇

Dir Bryan Forbes *Prod* Edgar J. Scherick *Scr* William Goldman *Ph* Owen Roizman *Ed* Timothy Gee *Mus* Michael Small *Art Dir* Gene Callahan
● Katharine Ross, Paula Prentiss, Peter Masterson, Nanette Newman, Patrick O'Neal, Tina Louise (Palomar/Columbia)

Bryan Forbes' filmization of Ira Levin's *The Stepford Wives* is a quietly freaky suspense-horror story.

Katharine Ross (in an excellent and assured performance), husband Peter Masterson and kids depart NY's urban pressures to a seemingly bovine Connecticut existence. Trouble is, Ross and new friend Paula Prentiss (also excellent) find all the other wives exuding sticky hairspray homilies and male chauvinist fantasy responses. When Prentiss finally changes her attitude, Ross panics but cannot escape.

Patrick O'Neal heads a local men's club that somehow is involved in the unseen, sluggishly developed but eventually exciting climax.

The black humor and sophistication of the plot is handled extremely well.

．．．．．．．．．．．．．．．．．．．．．．．．．

■ STEPPENWOLF

1974, 105 MINS, US ◇

Dir Fred Haines *Prod* Melvin Fishman, Richard Herland *Scr* Fred Haines *Ph* Tomislav Pinter *Ed* Irving Lerner *Mus* George Gruntz *Art Dir* Leo Karen
● Max von Sydow, Dominique Sanda, Pierre Clementi, Carla Romanelli, Roy Bosier, Alfred Baillou (Sprague)

Four decades after publication, *Steppenwolf* sold some 1.5 million paperbacks to a young audience suddenly attracted to Herman Hesse. Film remains just as subjective and essentially plotless as the book, but director Fred Haines seems fully in control.

Film has a rich appearance far beyond its $1.2 million budget. The weird effects produced from a sophisticated, electronic video mix allow Haines to translate Hesse's abstractions faithfully, if such a thing is at all possible.

Haines was equally careful in casting Max von Sydow as Harry Haller, the misanthrope who opts for one last try at life before reaching 50 and a preplanned suicide. Whether it's madness, drugs or love that envelopes him remains as mysterious in pic, but von Sydow makes the journey remarkable.

．．．．．．．．．．．．．．．．．．．．．．．．．

■ STEREO

1969, 63 MINS, CANADA

Dir David Cronenberg *Prod* David Cronenberg *Scr* David Cronenberg *Ph* David Cronenberg *Ed* David Cronenberg
● Ron Mlodzik, Jack Messinger, Iain Ewing, Clara Mayer, Paul Mulholland, Arlene Mlodzik (Emergent)

Lensed for a paltry $3,500, *Stereo* is the initial feature film effort by David Cronenberg.

Shot in black-and-white wihout synch sound, *Stereo* carries built-in liabilities thanks to its technical limitations and aesthetic

idiosyncracies. Basically a student effort (Cronenberg was 26), pic tests the viewer's patience and endurance even with its hour's running time due to its emphatically dry, scientific narration and deliberate emotional distancing.

Film abstractly examines the situation at the Canadian Academy for Erotic Inquiry, where eight individuals have been subjected to telepathic surgery. As the narrator drones on the operation, alternately strange and static scenes are presented which only occasionally bear any relation to the words being spoken.

．．．．．．．．．．．．．．．．．．．．．．．．．

■ STERILE CUCKOO, THE

1969, 108 MINS, US ◇ ⓥ

Dir Alan J. Pakula *Prod* Alan J. Pakula *Scr* Alvin Sargent *Ph* Milton R. Krasner *Ed* Sam O'Steen, John W. Wheeler *Mus* Fred Karlin
● Liza Minnelli, Wendell Burton, Tim McIntire, Elizabeth Harrower, Austin Green (Paramount)

The Sterile Cuckoo is a kook named Pookie, a wacky, wisecracking motherless, outrageously adorable, collegiate gamin [from a novel by Jack Nichols] who comes on like gangbusters. Liza Minnelli plays the role, and her fragile, funny freshman love affair with an undergraduate entomologist (Wendell Burton in his first screen role) is in a class by itself.

A first affair in a ramshackle upstate New York motel becomes high comedy with the hot-to-trot vamp Minnelli prodding the nervous-in-the-service Burton, who keeps his mackinaw buttoned up to the chin while she strips down.

It is Minnelli's one-woman show. The 21-year-old Burton is not so much her costar as her straight man.

．．．．．．．．．．．．．．．．．．．．．．．．．

■ STEVIE

1978, 102 MINS, UK ◇ ⓥ

Dir Robert Enders *Prod* Robert Enders *Scr* Hugh Whitemore *Ph* Freddie Young *Ed* Peter Tanner *Mus* Patrick Gowers *Art Dir* Bob Jones
● Glenda Jackson, Mona Washbourne, Alec McCowen, Trevor Howard (Bowden)

Stevie is a well-acted and literate, but also talky and claustrophobic screen biography of British poet and novelist Stevie Smith. Glenda Jackson stars in the title role and her performance – in fact, the entire style of the film – seems better suited to the stage than the big screen.

Robert Enders, who directed from Hugh Whitemore's script of his own play, has adopted a visual style better suited to a tele-film than a theatrical feature. Most of the picture takes place inside a suburban residence Smith shared with her aunt, portrayed by Mona Washbourne in a charming and sympathetic performance.

By limiting the action to that one setting the film becomes stifling. Too much of Smith's life is described by Jackson in reminiscenses to her aunt, confessions into the camera, or recitations of her poetry, rather than re-enacted.

Only other characters are Alec McCowen as a boyfriend of Jackson and Trevor Howard as companion who also comments on the poet's life and work.

．．．．．．．．．．．．．．．．．．．．．．．．．

■ STICKY FINGERS

1988, 97 MINS, US ◇ ⓥ

Dir Catlin Adams *Prod* Catlin Adams, Melanie Mayron *Scr* Catlin Adams, Melanie Mayron *Ph* Gary Thieltges *Ed* Bob Reitano *Mus* Gary Chana *Art Dir* Jessica Scott-Justice
● Helen Slater, Melanie Mayron, Danitra Vance, Eileen Brennan, Carol Kane (Hightop)

Sticky Fingers is a snappy, offbeat urban comedy about two NY gal pals – starving artist types – who get caught up in the shopping spree of a lifetime. Too bad the money isn't theirs.

Story, cowritten by debut director Catlin Adams and Melanie Mayron, casts Mayron and Helen Slater as struggling musicians on the verge of eviction from their NY walkup until a bagful of drug money – nearly a million bucks – lands in their laps. They've been asked to 'mind it' for a spacey friend-of-a-friend (Loretta Devine) who's clearing out of town in a hurry.

Initially panicked, they wind up using it to pay their rent; then to replace their instruments. As days pass, the urge to spend becomes insatiable, and they give in with gusto.

Memorable supporting roles abound, including Danitra Vance as a fellow musician and Stephen McHattie as a tough but romantic undercover cop posing as a parking lot attendant across from their building.

Eileen Brennan is right on as the ailing landlady and Carol Kane delightful as her sister, who has a romance with the cop. Christopher Guest is near perfect as Mayron's uncertain boyfriend, a newly published novelist pursued by a spooky ex-girlfriend (Gwen Welles).

．．．．．．．．．．．．．．．．．．．．．．．．．

■ STILL OF THE NIGHT

1982, 91 MINS, US ◇ ⓥ

Dir Robert Benton *Prod* Arlene Donovan *Scr* Robert Benton *Ph* Nestor Almendros *Ed* Jerry Greenberg *Mus* John Kander *Art Dir* Mel Bourne
● Roy Scheider, Meryl Streep, Jessica Tandy, Joe Grifasi, Sara Botsford, Josef Sommer (M-G-M/United Artists)

It comes as almost a shock to see a modern suspense picture that's as literate, well acted and beautifully made as *Still Of The Night*. Despite its many virtues, however, Robert Benton's film has its share of serious flaws, mainly in the area of plotting.

Roy Scheider effectively plays an introspective New York shrink whose own life becomes endangered after one of his patients is found murdered. Prime suspect may well be Meryl Streep, the neurotic mistress of the dead man whose distressed, unpredictable behavior represents the source of most of the film's mystery.

Perpetually moving around physically, mentally and emotionally, Streep slowly insinuates herself into Scheider's relatively uneventful life.

Benton has fashioned as gorgeously crafted a suspense piece as one could ask for. High marks also go to supporting players, particularly Josef Sommer as the murdered man who appears in flashback, and Joe Grifasi as the persistent cop.

．．．．．．．．．．．．．．．．．．．．．．．．．

■ STING, THE

1973, 127 MINS, US ◇ ⓥ

Dir George Roy Hill *Prod* Tony Bill, Michael Phillips, Julia Phillips *Scr* David S. Ward *Ph* Robert Surtees *Ed* William Reynolds *Mus* Marvin Hamlisch (adapt.) *Art Dir* Henry Bumstead
● Paul Newman, Robert Redford, Robert Shaw, Charles Durning, Ray Walston, Eileen Brennan (Universal/Zanuk-Brown)

Paul Newman and Robert Redford are superbly re-teamed as a pair of con artists in Chicago of the 1930s, out to fleece a bigtime racketeer brilliantly played by Robert Shaw.

Script establishes Redford as a novice con artist, apprentice to Robert Earl Jones who is murdered when one of their marks turns out to be a cash runner for Shaw's regional syndicate. Ambition plus revenge leads Redford to Newman, an acknowledged master of the con trade who rounds up Eileen Brennan,

Harold Gould, Ray Walston and John Heffernan to fake a bookie joint operation to snare Shaw in a major bet.

The three stars make all the difference between simply a good film and a superior one. Newman's relationship with Brennan (in a sensational supporting role) rounds out his characterization of an old pro making his last big score. Redford really turns to and works superbly. Shaw's taciturn menace commands attention even when he is simply part of a master shot.

The film comes to a series of startling climaxes, piled atop one another with zest. In the final seconds the audience realizes it has been had, but when one enjoys the ride, it's a pleasure.
□ 1973: Best Picture

■ STING II, THE

1983, 102 MINS, US ◇ Ⓥ
Dir Jeremy Paul Kagan   *Prod* Jennings Lang
Scr David S. Ward   *Ph* Bill Butler   *Ed* David Garfield
Mus Lalo Schifrin   *Art Dir* Edward C. Carfagno
● Jackie Gleason, Mac Davis, Teri Garr, Karl Malden, Oliver Reed, Bert Remsen (Universal)

Stars Jackie Gleason and Mac Davis come nowhere close to evoking the charming onscreen qualities of Paul Newman and Robert Redford. Combined with the slow pace and overdone exposition, *The Sting II* is mostly just a chore to watch.

Though screenwriter David S. Ward concocts as viable a story as he did in the original, the trouble is there is still an original.

Gleason plays the master con man out to make a big score with the help of fellow huckster Davis. The chief patsy is tacky nightclub owner Karl Malden while Oliver Reed does a less than distinctive turn as a mysterious gangster watching it all happen.

So much of the intricate plot is explained in dialog that the first half of the film often seems like someone reading an instruction book. Exception is Teri Garr, who provides what little life there is as a slick, seasoned trickster who becomes involved in the scam.

The second half picks up a bit as the plan goes into effect and this is where the performances come into play.

■ STIR CRAZY

1980, 111 MINS, US ◇ Ⓥ
Dir Sidney Poitier   *Prod* Hannah Weinstein   *Scr* Bruce Jay Friedman   *Ph* Fred Schuler   *Ed* Harry Keller
Mus Tom Scott   *Art Dir* Alfred Sweeney
● Gene Wilder, Richard Pryor, Jobeth Williams, Georg Stanford Brown (Columbia)

Story setup has down-on-their-luck New Yorkers Richard Pryor and Gene Wilder deciding to blow the city for what they think are the promising shores of California. Driving cross-country they land in a small town where they take a job dressing up as woodpeckers in a local bank in order to make some cash. Two baddies they met in a bar use the woodpecker suits to rob the bank, leaving Pryor and Wilder 120-year prison sentences and no alibi.

Majority of the action focuses on the antics of prison life, with Pryor and Wilder at the center of a group of fairly stereotypical jail characters.

Director Sidney Poitier's chief role seems to be providing enough space for Pryor and Wilder to do their schtick without going too far afield from the scant storyline.

■ STITCH IN TIME, A

1963, 94 MINS, UK
Dir Robert Asher   *Prod* Hugh Stewart   *Scr* Jack Davies   *Ph* Jack Asher   *Ed* Gerry Hambling
Mus Philip Green

● Norman Wisdom, Edward Chapman, Jeannette Sterke, Jerry Desmonde, Jill Melford (Rank)

This gains by economizing on plot, but devises a string of farcical events that put the pint-sized Norman Wisdom through the full pratfalling routine. The thin thread linking the scenes has Wisdom as a hapless butcher's assistant causing constant commotion in a hospital, where his employer is undergoing surgery for a swallowed watch. He gets banned from the place by the hospital boss, Sir Hector (Jerry Desmonde), and the remainder of the running time is taken up by his bizarre attempts to regain entry.

The sketches follow each other thick and fast, and leave no time to brood over their naivety. Jack Davies's script is the sixth for the comedian, and he knows the strength and limitations of the star. For sophisticated palates, Wisdom is mechanical, and he plays up the sentiment of the 'little man' up against authority to cloying effect.

■ STOLEN LIFE, A

1946, 100 MINS, US
Dir Curtis Bernhardt   *Prod* Bette Davis   *Scr* Catherine Turney   *Ph* Sol Polito, Ernest Haller   *Ed* Rudi Fehr
Mus Max Steiner   *Art Dir* Robert M. Haas
● Bette Davis, Glenn Ford, Dane Clark, Walter Brennan (Warner/BD)

Story [from a novel by Karel J. Benes] unfolds leisurely in telling of a sister who assumes her twin's identity in order to find love.

Bette Davis appears as a sweet, sincere, artistic girl, and as this girl's man-crazy sister. When the latter, by trickery, marries man with whom former has fallen in love and is later drowned in a boating accident, the sweet girl takes on her sister's identity in a try for happiness. Script spends a great deal of footage establishing life in New England summer resorts. Since it is a woman's story, dialog hands plenty of cliches to male players, particularly to Glenn Ford as the man in love with both sisters.

Dane Clark appears briefly in role of rude artist. Role is difficult and not a fortunate one for Clark. Walter Brennan gives a good character reading to his part of a salty old down'easter.

Special photography for dual role played by Davis is the best yet. At no time is double exposure or other tricks used to bring the characters together in scenes apparent. Credit for trick work goes to Willard Van Enger and Russell Collings.

■ STONE BOY, THE

1984, 93 MINS, US ◇ Ⓥ
Dir Christopher Cain   *Prod* Joe Roth, Ivan Bloch
Scr Gina Berriault   *Ph* Juan Ruiz-Anchia   *Ed* Paul Rubell   *Mus* James Horner   *Art Dir* Joseph G. Pacelli
● Robert Duvall, Jason Presson, Frederic Forrest, Glenn Close, Wilford Brimley, Gail Youngs (TLC)

Director Chris Cain, in only his second feature, draws a remarkably restrained and moving performance from debuting child actor Jason Presson, who plays central role of a 12-year-old brother who accidentally and tragically slays his older, beloved brother with a shotgun in the opening moments of the film.

Production's sorrowful subject matter as family is rendered dazed and grief-stricken by the death of the older son, while young responsible brother retreats behind a wall of guilt, never lapses into sentimentality or melodrama.

Robert Duvall unthinkingly compounds the misery of his son by fostering a family attitude that denies the boy communication.

The Stone Boy, in its inarticulate characters whose feelings tear them apart, is a singular and highly accessible film.

■ STONE KILLER, THE

1973, 95 MINS, US ◇ Ⓥ
Dir Michael Winner   *Prod* Michael Winner
Scr Gerald Wilson   *Ph* Richard Moore   *Ed* Frederick Wilson   *Mus* Roy Budd   *Art Dir* Ward Preston
● Charles Bronson, Martin Balsam, David Sheiner, Norman Fell, Ralph Waite, Stuart Margolin (Columbia/De Laurentiis)

The Stone Killer [adapted by Gerald Wilson from John Gardiner's novel, *A Complete State of Death*], is a confused, meandering crime potboiler, starring Charles Bronson as a tough detective who starts out on a low-level gangster case only to find upper Mafia echelon also are involved. The story and direction reach for so many bases that the end result is a lot of cinema razzle-dazzle without substance.

Bronson is discovered killing a NY ghetto punk, his overkill enough to banish him to the LA Police Dept, a plot point which may strike some as unintentionally amusing. Eventually it becomes clear that Martin Balsam, a prototype hood of the Prohibition era, is planning massacre-revenge for a 40-year old shootout which introduced non-Sicilian elements to organized crime.

■ STORM, THE

1930, 76 MINS, US
Dir William Wyler   *Scr* Wells Root   *Ph* Alvin Wyckoff
● Lupe Velez, Paul Cavanaugh, William Boyd, Alphonz Ethier, Ernie S. Adams (Universal)

The Storm served on two former occasions as a silent, in 1916 for Paramount and in 1922 for U. Lupe Velez is a French smuggler's daughter who is left with a friendly trapper by her father just before a bullet from a mountie's gun lays him low. She plays with an accent that is a cross between Spanish and French, half the time doing a flashing Spanish senorita, the other half a piquant young demoiselle.

Story [from a play, *Men without Skirts*, by Langdon McCormick] is that of a trapper-miner and his best friend who develop a bad jealousy between each other for the girl ward left with the former. They both lean heavily toward the girl, finally hating each other.

Shots of the girl in the river attempting to rescue her father from Mounties are very cleverly done. The old man's leap from a cliff, and their race down the river until the canoe capsizes, is also fairly thrilling stuff expertly photographed.

■ STORM BOY

1976, 88 MINS, AUSTRALIA ◇
Dir Henri Safran   *Prod* Matt Carroll   *Scr* Sonia Borg
Ph Ken Hammond   *Ed* G. Turney-Smith   *Mus* Michael Carlos   *Art Dir* David Copping
● Greg Rowe, Peter Cummins, David Gulpilil, Judy Dick, Tony Allison, Michael Moody (SAFC)

Storm Boy is a gem of a film. Modestly and carefully made, it is a skillful adaptation of a kid's book by Colin Thiele.

Mike (Greg Rowe) is the 10-year-old son of Tom, (Peter Cummins) a wifeless fisherman who inhabits a shanty on the beach and ekes out a living selling his catch to the fishmonger in the nearest town.

They live near a bird sanctuary, and a chance meeting with an aborigine (David Gulpilil) affects Mike's life, and gives him the name Storm Boy. Fingerbone Bill is also a rejector of society, his tribe has cast him out and he lives a nomadic life pretty much along the lines of his ancestors. And he has retained the mystical insights of his forebears.

Storm Boy is certainly a kid-flick, but it's one that'll get to the adults, too.

For a first feature, Paris-born director Henri Safran shows a sure hand. Final kudos to composer, Michael Carlos, for an evocative score.

. . . .

■ STORMY WEATHER

1943, 77 MINS, US ⓥ

Dir Andrew Stone *Prod* William LeBaron
Scr Frederick Jackson, Ted Koehler *Ph* Leon Shamroy, Fred Sersen, Benny Carter *Ed* James B. Clark
● Lena Horne, Bill Robinson, Fats Waller, Dooley Wilson, Cab Calloway, Katherine Dunham (20th Century-Fox)

Stormy Weather is chockful of the cream-of-the-crop colored talent, with a deft story skein to hold it together. Bill Robinson and Lena Horne top the cast. It's a tribute to the affection in which Bojangles is held that the story plot is glossed over in favor of all the other components.

Story nicely spans both wars. Lt Jim Europe's band is marching up 5th Ave in a riotous homecoming. Dooley Wilson, Robinson and the others have come back from the wars. The big Harlem hoopla thus projects Lena Horne who takes a liking immediately to Robinson. Her partner (Babe Wallace) is the menace, a conceited professional.

Story is told via the flashback formula. A 25th Anniversary Number of *Theatre World* holds the plot together. The special edition is in tribute to the great trouper, Robinson. Surrounding him are the neighbors' children on his comfortable, handsome front porch.

Via the *Theatre World* anniversary number, Robinson continues crossing and re-crossing paths with Horne, in and out of shows, Hollywood filmusicals, etc, with Cab Calloway, Katherine Dunham and her expert troupe of ballet dancers, Fats Waller, the Nicholas Bros, plus others.

. . . .

■ STORY OF G.I. JOE, THE

1945, 109 MINS, US

Dir William A. Wellman *Prod* Lester Cowan *Scr* Leopold Atlas, Guy Endore *Ph* Russell Metty *Ed* Otto Lovering, Albrecht Joseph *Mus* Ann Ronell, Louis Applebaum *Art Dir* James Sullivan, David Hall
● Burgess Meredith, Robert Mitchum, Freddie Steele, Wally Cassell (United Artists)

From where the civilian sits, this seems the authentic story of GI Joe – that superb, slugging human machine, the infantryman, without whom wars cannot be won. Add to authentic story handling a production that's superb, casting and directing that's perfect, and a sock star supported by a flawless group of artists.

From the moment the infantrymen are picked out by the camera at 'blanket drill' in the African desert until the last shot on the open highway to Rome, it's the foot-slogging soldier who counts most in this film. Real-life GI diarist Ernie Pyle is there, very much. He is ever present. But as conceived by the scripters, directed by William A. Wellman, and acted by Burgess Meredith, Pyle is not the war but a commentary on it – which is as it should be.

Meredith, playing the simple little figure that's Pyle, is felt in every scene, his impact carrying over from the preceding sequences.

But without support, Meredith for all his worth could not have made this the great picture it is. Robert Mitchum is excellent as the lieutenant who, in the film, grows to a captaincy. Freddie Steele is tops as the tough sergeant who finally cracks up when he hears his baby's voice on a disc mailed from home. Wally Cassell as the Lothario of the com-

pany, and all the others – professionals as well as real-life GIs who helped make the pic – are excellent.

. . . .

■ STORY OF MANKIND, THE

1957, 99 MINS, US ◇

Dir Irwin Allen *Prod* Irwin Allen *Scr* Irwin Allen, Charles Bennett *Ph* Nicholas Musuraca *Ed* Roland Gross, Gene Palmer *Mus* Paul Sawtell *Art Dir* Art Loel
● Ronald Colman, Vincent Price, Agnes Moorehead, Peter Lorre, Dennis Hopper, Virginia Mayo (Cambridge/Warner)

Hendrik Willem Van Loon's monumental *Story of Mankind* has been brought to the screen in a name-dropping production that provides a kaleidoscope of history from Pleistocene man to Plutonium man. In the process, however, producer-director Irwin Allen seems unable to decide whether to do a faithful history of man's development into a thinking being, a debate on whether man's good outweighs his evil, or a compilation of historical sagas with some humor dragged in for relief.

As a peg on which to hang the panorama, screenplay convokes the 'High Tribunal of Outer Space' upon news that man has discovered the Super-H bomb 60 years too soon. The problem is whether to halt the scheduled explosion and thereby save mankind or let it go off and exterminate the human race. To reach a decision, the tribunal permits both the Devil and the Spirit of Man to give evidence as to man's fitness to continue.

In the dreary cataloguing of man's crimes against humanity, the Devil makes a much better case.

Best of the portrayals is Agnes Moorehead's Queen Elizabeth and Cedric Hardwicke turns in a good performance as the High Judge. Ronald Colman is a dignified personification of the Spirit of Man and Vincent Price is the sophisticated, sneering embodiment of Old Scratch.

Peter Lorre brings some conviction to the role of Nero, Dennis Hopper is moodily appropriate as Napoleon and Virginia Mayo looks the part of Cleopatra. Hedy Lamarr is miscast as Joan (yes, of Arc) in one of the few other key parts, some of the 'stars' being on and off the screen so rapidly as to go unrecognized.

. . . .

■ STORY OF ROBIN HOOD, THE

1952, 83 MINS, UK ◇ ⓥ

Dir Ken Annakin *Prod* Perce Pearce *Scr* Lawrence E. Watkin *Ph* Guy Green *Ed* Gordon Pilkington *Mus* Clifton Parker *Art Dir* Carmen Dillon, Arthur Lawson
● Richard Todd, Joan Rice, Peter Finch, James Hayter, James Robertson Justice, Martita Hunt (Walt Disney/RKO)

For his second British live-action production, Walt Disney took the legend of Robin Hood and translated it to the screen as a superb piece of entertainment, with all the action of a western and the romance and intrigue of a historical drama.

Despite his modest stature, Richard Todd proves to be a first-rate Robin Hood, alert, dashing and forceful, equally convincing when leading his outlaws against Prince John as he is in winning the admiration of Maid Marian. Although a comparative newcomer to the screen, Joan Rice acts with charm and intelligence.

James Hayter as Friar Tuck, Martita Hunt as the queen, Peter Finch as the sheriff, James Robertson Justice as Little John, Bill Owen as the poacher, and Elton Hayes as the minstrel are in the front rank.

. . . .

■ STORY OF RUTH, THE

1960, 132 MINS, US ◇

Dir Henry Koster *Prod* Samuel G. Engel *Scr* Norman Corwin *Ph* Arthur E. Arling *Ed* Jack W. Holmes *Mus* Franz Waxman *Art Dir* Lyle R. Wheeler, Franz Bachelin
● Stuart Whitman, Tom Tryon, Peggy Wood, Viveca Lindfors, Jeff Morrow, Elana Eden (20th Century-Fox)

The Story of Ruth is a refreshingly sincere and restrained Biblical drama, a picture that elaborates on the romantic, political and devotional difficulties encountered by the Old Testament heroine. Yet, for all its obvious high purpose, bolstered by several fine performances, there is a sluggishness that is disturbing.

The screenplay describes the heroine's activities from her youthful indoctrination as a Moabite priestess through her marriage to the Judean, Boaz. Along the way it dramatizes her romance with the kindly Mahlon, his violent death, her conversion to Judaism and flight with Mahlon's mother, Naomi, to Bethlehem, where she encounters religious persecution and becomes embroiled in a romantic triangle.

Although the screenplay wisely avoids archaic phrases, director Henry Koster has not always succeeded in side-stepping stereotyped biblical-pic posturing and mannerisms among his players, and is inclined to anticipate mysterious character knowledge in a few instances. But he has coaxed several very effective portrayals out of his principals.

The film introduces Elana Eden in the title role. She gives a performance of dignity, projecting an inner strength through a delicate veneer. The picture is helped by veteran Peggy Wood's excellent characterization of Naomi. Her timing is always sharp. Tom Tryon establishes a pleasing screen personality with a vigorous delineation of Mahlon. Franz Waxman's music is typically biblical in tone and tempo.

. . . .

■ STORY OF VERNON AND IRENE CASTLE, THE

1939, 96 MINS, US ⓥ

Dir H.C. Potter *Prod* George Haight *Scr* Richard Sherman *Ph* Robert de Grasse *Ed* William Hamilton *Mus* Victor Baravelle *Art Dir* Van Nest Polglase, Perry Ferguson
● Fred Astaire, Ginger Rogers, Edna May Oliver, Walter Brennan (RKO)

The Story of Vernon and Irene Castle is top-flight cinematic entertainment. It's another switch on the backstage story, this time dealing with a much-in-love married pair of ballroomologists catapulted from dire straits in Paris into international acclaim and fortune.

The medley of some 40 yesteryear pops is the common denominator for all types of audiences.

Irene Castle technically-advised. Her published memoirs, *My Husband* and *My Memories*, are the story background [adapted by Oscar Hammerstein and Dorothy Yost] of the film. Her personal life story has been seemingly transmuted into celluloid with considerable faithfulness and a minimum of bombast or heroics.

Their success story dates from the time that the shrewd Maggie Sutton (Edna May Oliver) gets them an audition at the Cafe de Paris. Comes the war, however, and Castle enlists in the Canadian Royal Flying Corps, and meets untimely death as a flying instructor.

Rogers and Fred Astaire are excellent as the Castles.

. . . .

■ STRAIGHT TIME

1978, 114 MINS, US ◇ ▼
Dir Ulu Grosbard   *Prod* Stanley Beck, Tim Zinnemann
Scr Alvin Sargent, Edward Bunker, Jeffrey Boam
Ph Owen Roizman   *Ed* Sam O'Steen, Randy Roberts
Mus David Shire   *Art Dir* Stephen Grimes
● Dustin Hoffman, Theresa Russell, Gary Busey, Harry
Dean Stanton, M. Emmet Walsh, Rita Taggart
(First Artists/Sweetwall)

Straight Time is a most unlikeable film because
Dustin Hoffman, starring as a paroled and
longtime criminal, cannot overcome the
essentially distasteful and increasingly
unsympathetic elements in the character.
Ulu Grosbard's sluggish direction doesn't
help.

Apparent plot peg [from Edward Banker's
novel *No Beast so Fierce*] is that a parolee suffers so many indignities that a return to crime
is easier.

Viewers are asked initially to believe that
M. Emmet Walsh, the assigned parole
officer, is a sadistic person who delights in
hassling his charges. But given the circumstances, he does not emerge as a heavy.
Indeed, Hoffman's too-easy lapse into his old
ways absolves any blame on The System.
Hoffman's character would have defied the
parole supervision of a saint.

Theresa Russell is very good as Hoffman's
girl; Harry Dean Stanton is excellent as a
reformed hood who (nobody explains why) is
being suffocated in the life of a successful
suburban businessman; Gary Busey is good
as a weak ex-con who bungles a climactic
robbery plan.

■ STRAIT-JACKET

1963, 93 MINS, US ▼
Dir William Castle   *Prod* William Castle   *Scr* Robert
Bloch   *Ph* Arthur Arling   *Ed* Edwin Bryant   *Mus* Van
Alexander   *Art Dir* Boris Leven
● Joan Crawford, Diane Baker, Leif Erickson, Howard
St John, John Anthony Hayes, George Kennedy
(Columbia)

Strait-Jacket could be summoned up as a chip
off the old Bloch. Writer Robert Bloch's *Psycho*, that is. In crossing the basic plot design
of that 1960 Bloch-buster with the instrument
of murder (the axe) and at least one of the
ramifications of the celebrated Lizzie Borden
case, Bloch has provided the grisly ingredients for producer-director William Castle to
concoct some marketable 'chop' suey.

Heads really roll in this yarn, which commences with a dual hatchet job on a cheating
husband and his lady friend who are discovered bedrooming by the wife (Joan
Crawford), whose three-year-old daughter
witnesses in horror the 40 some odd whacks
per victim administered by her mother. Mom
goes to the insane asylum and daughter
grows up into Diane Baker. They are reunited 20 years later when mom is released.

Crawford does well by her role, delivering
an animated performance. Baker is pretty
and histrionically satisfactory as her
daughter. Some of Castle's direction is stiff
and mechanical, but most of the murders are
suspensefully and chillingly constructed.

■ STRANGE AFFAIR, THE

1968, 102 MINS, UK ◇
Dir David Greene   *Prod* Howard Harrison, Stanley
Mann   *Scr* Stanley Mann   *Ph* Alex Thomson
Ed Brian Smedley-Aston   *Mus* Basil Kirchin   *Art
Dir* Brian Eatwell
● Michael York, Jeremy Kemp, Susan George, Jack
Watson, David Glaisyer, Richard Vanstone (Paramount)

Michael York is the 'Strange' involved in an
affair which finds Scotland Yard sergeant
Pierce (Jeremy Kemp) trying to nail a trio of
dangerous criminals and drug peddlers.

Frustrated in various attempts at getting

legal evidence, Kemp in desperation resorts
to blackmailing Strange, who's been caught
in a compromising situation with a girl, into
planting a drug packet on one of the trio during a search.

Situation provides opportunities for some
subsurface characterizations of the two men
torn by different concepts of duty.

There are no lags in the action, with Stanley Mann's literate script [from a novel by
Bernard Toms] ringing true all the way, just
as it provides an amusing change of pace in
the tryst linking Strange with an ebullient
hippie played by Susan George.

York makes a very sympathetic person out
of Strange. Kemp is suitably harassed and
obsessed as the duty-first plainclothesman,
while Jack Watson, David Glaisyer and
Richard Vanstone are properly sneery as the
baddies. It is, however, George who captures
most attention in a very appealing
performance.

■ STRANGE ALIBI

1941, 63 MINS, US
Dir D. Ross Lederman   *Scr* Kenneth Gamet   *Ph* Allen
G. Siegler   *Ed* Frank Magee
● Arthur Kennedy, Joan Perry, Howard da Silva,
Florence Bates (Warner/First National)

This rates high among the average run of B
mellers. It's an evidence of Warners' crime-
and-punishment actioners working at an all-
out peak. Everything in it has been seen
before – particularly the sets – but the
concoction has been tossed together again
under director D. Ross Lederman to become
a speedy and delectable dish.

Plot [from a story by Leslie T. White] is far
from new. Unfortunately, Lederman has had
to dive into the stock barrel for a load of trite
court and prison stuff which bogs the picture
right down in the center.

Arthur Kennedy plays a detective who
arranges with his chief for a publicized break
between them so that he can go over to the
mob. Racket guys find out he's not playing
them straight and kill the chief, planting the
murder on Kennedy, who is sent up for life.
He breaks from prison and very neatly
squares himself for fadeout clinch.

Kennedy does a nice job when not stilted
by the B-picture dialog.

■ STRANGE BEDFELLOWS

1964, 99 MINS, US ◇
Dir Melvin Frank   *Prod* Melvin Frank   *Scr* Melvin
Frank, Michael Pertwee   *Ph* Leo Tover   *Ed* Gene
Milford   *Mus* Leigh Harline   *Art Dir* Alexander
Golitzen, Joseph Wright
● Rock Hudson, Gina Lollobrigida, Gig Young,
Edward Judd, Terry-Thomas, Arthur Haynes (Panama-
Frank/Universal)

Strange Bedfellows is another of those romantic
marital comedies, based primarily on misunderstandings. Critics for the thinking man
may scoff at the plot, which derives much of
its drama from ancient device of each character not quite understanding what the others
are up to. But story line differs enough so that
it isn't simple carbon of all the Rock Hudson-
Tony Randall-Doris Day comedies.

Hudson is a trifle solemn as London-based
US oil executive who can rise to extreme top
echelon if his corporate image is white-
washed. This means he must patch up seven-
year marriage to Gina Lollobrigida, who
more than compensates for Hudson's stuffiness by her enthusiastic rapport with zany
causes.

But the unabashed comedians steal the
show. Probably the funniest bit has Arthur
Haynes and David King as taxidrivers with
Hudson and Gina in their respective vehicles.
The estranged lovers try to communicate

with one another by way of two-way cab
radio, with hilarity resulting from cabbies
garbling of messages.

■ STRANGE CARGO

1940, 111 MINS, US
Dir Frank Borzage   *Prod* Joseph L. Mankiewicz
Scr Lawrence Hazard   *Ph* Robert Planck   *Ed* Robert J.
Kern   *Mus* Franz Waxman
● Joan Crawford, Clark Gable, Ian Hunter, Peter
Lorre, Paul Lukas, Albert Dekker (M-G-M)

Strange Cargo is a strange melodramatic concoction [from a book by Richard Sale] that
endeavors to mix the adventures of an escaping group of convicts from a tropical island
prison with religious preachment through
inclusion of a mysterious stranger with
Christ-like attributes. The attempt is not successful. Combined with this fault is a slow,
ploddy technique on the directing side, overlong footage and many dragging passages.

In accentuating the individual spiritual redemptions of the various convict members of
the escaping group, story builds up with
some rather strong talk and ridicule of the
Bible, its passages and teachings.

Story, in attempt to dovetail stark and
dangerous adventure with a religious motif,
does not jell to any degree of consistency.
Shortly after establishing the prison setting,
the convicts escape and struggle through jungle, swamp and sand to reach a hidden boat.
Clark Gable saves Joan Crawford from the
clutches of a designing miner en route, and
takes her along. It's a strange group aboard
the small open sailboat, the stranger (Ian
Hunter) dominating with his quiet though
definite manner.

Crawford is provided with a particularly
meaty role as the hardened dance hall gal
who falls hard for the tough convict. Gable is
vigorous in his portrayal of the self-appointed
head of the escaping convicts, a far from sympathetic assignment, and he is overshadowed
by the reserved but strong-willed Hunter as
the redeemer of the tough souls assembled in
the small boat.

■ STRANGE INTERLUDE

1932, 110 MINS, US
Dir Robert Z. Leonard   *Scr* Bess Meredyth, C. Gardner
Sullivan   *Ph* Lee Garmes   *Ed* Margaret Booth
● Norma Shearer, Clark Gable, Alexander Kirkland,
Ralph Morgan, Robert Young, May Robson (M-G-M)

Norma Shearer who shoulders the brunt of
the histrionic burden, somehow misses in a
vacillating characterization which was made
necessarily so, for censor purposes alone, if
nothing else. As for Clark Gable, he is
eclipsed by Alexander Kirkland as the weak
husband of the heroine and Ralph Morgan as
the mawk with the mother fixation.

Through their life's span, as the story
proceeds into old age, when Nina Leeds
(Shearer) sees her illegitimate son moulded
to conform with her life's ideas, the episodic,
transitory cinematurgy is as much a credit to
the hairdressers and the makeup staff on the
Metro lot as to Shearer, Gable, Kirkland and
Morgan. The makeup is excellent but the
make-believe isn't.

No question that the devitalizing of the
[1928–29 Pulitzer Prize play by Eugene]
O'Neill has much to do with it. The formula
cinematic contrivances employed to pitch
emotions falsely, to misfit climaxes, are very
apparent.

The O'Neill asides, in screen treatment,
might be said to be somewhat of an improvement over the stage original. The actual
words are uttered, and then the subconscious
thoughts are voiced by the same player on the
soundtrack (with a different inflection, of
course).

STRANGE LOVE OF MARTHA IVERS, THE

1946, 113 MINS, US ⊗
Dir Lewis Milestone   *Prod* Hal Wallis   *Scr* Robert
Rossen   *Ph* Victor Milner   *Ed* Archie Marshek
Mus Miklos Rozsa   *Art Dir* Hans Dreier, John Meehan
● Barbara Stanwyck, Van Heflin, Lizabeth Scott, Kirk
Douglas (Paramount)

Story is a forthright, uncompromising presentation of evil, greedy people and human weaknesses. Characters are sharply drawn in the Robert Rossen script, based on Jack Patrick's original story, and Lewis Milestone's direction punches home the melodrama for full suspense and excitement.

Prolog opening establishes the murder of a bullying aunt by her young niece. Deed is witnessed by the son of the girl's tutor, but is blamed on an unknown prowler. Coverup moves the tutor and son into a position of power in the girl's household. Story then picks up 18 years later with the accidental return to the town of another of the girl's childhood friends. Return panics Barbara Stanwyck and Kirk Douglas, now grown up and married, who fear the friend was also a witness of the early killing.

Character portrayed by Stanwyck is evil and she gives it a high-caliber delineation. Douglas makes his weakling role interesting, showing up strongly among the more experienced players. Best performance honors, though, are divided between Heflin and Scott, latter as a Heflin pickup.

STRANGE VENGEANCE OF ROSALIE, THE

1972, 107 MINS, US ◇
Dir Jack Starrett   *Prod* John Kohn   *Scr* Anthony
Greville-Bell, John Kohn   *Ph* Ray Parslow   *Ed* Thom
Noble   *Mus* John Cameron   *Art Dir* Roy Walker
● Bonnie Bedelia, Ken Howard, Anthony Zerbe (20th
Century-Fox/Cinecrest)

The Strange Vengeance of Rosalie is an offbeat film, centered around the fascinating, although admittedly preposterous, situation of a lonely adolescent part-Indian girl (Bonnie Bedelia), naive and emotionally disturbed, who hitches a ride with a traveling salesman (Ken Howard) and leads him to her isolated ramshackle cabin in New Mexico, where she lets the air out of the tires of his car, breaks his leg and holds him captive.

Pic generally holds together on strength of engaging performances and a fair amount of tension throughout, but the mixture of serious suspenseful drama (tinged with an ever-present air of impending violence) and humorous repartee between the characters doesn't jell.

STRANGER, THE

1946, 94 MINS, US ⊗
Dir Orson Welles   *Prod* S.P. Eagle [= Sam Spiegel]
Scr Anthony Veiller   *Ph* Russell Metty   *Ed* Ernest
Nims   *Mus* Bronislau Kaper   *Art Dir* Perry Ferguson
● Orson Welles, Edward G. Robinson, Loretta Young,
Philip Merivale, Richard Long (RKO/International)

The Stranger is socko melodrama, spinning an intriguing web of thrills and chills. Director Orson Welles gives the production a fast, suspenseful development, drawing every advantage from the hard-hitting script from the Victor Trivas story. Plot moves forward at a relentless pace in depicting the hunt of the Allied Commission for Prosecution of Nazi War Criminals for a top Nazi who has removed all traces of his origin and is a professor in a New England school. Edward G. Robinson is the government man on his trail. Loretta Young is the New England girl who becomes the bride of the Nazi.

Story opens in Germany, where a Nazi is

allowed to escape in belief he will lead the way to former head of a notorious prison camp. Chase moves across Europe to the small New England town where Welles is marrying Young. When the escaped Nazi contacts him, Welles strangles him and buries the body in the woods. From then on the terror mounts as Robinson tries to trap Welles into revealing his true identity.

A uniformly excellent cast gives reality to events that transpire. The three stars, Robinson, Young and Welles, turn in some of their best work, the actress being particularly effective as the misled bride.

STRANGER THAN PARADISE

1984, 95 MINS, US ⊗
Dir Jim Jarmusch   *Prod* Sara Driver   *Scr* Jim
Jarmusch   *Ph* Tom DiCillo   *Ed* Jim Jarmusch, Melody
London   *Mus* John Lurie
● John Lurie, Ester Balint, Richard Edson, Cecilia Stark
(Cinesthesia-Grokenberger)

Stranger than Paradise is a bracingly original avant-garde black comedy. Begun as a short which was presented under the same title at some earlier festivals, film has been expanded in outstanding fashion by young New York writer-director Jim Jarmusch.

Simple narrative starts with self-styled New York hipster Willie (John Lurie) being paid a surprise, and quite unwelcome, visit by Hungarian cousin Eva (Ester Balint). But when she finally leaves after 10 days, there seems to be a strange sort of affection between them.

Since plot doesn't count for much here, the style takes over, and Jarmusch has made such matters as camera placement, composition (in stunning black-and-white) and structure count for a lot.

STRANGERS IN THE CITY

1962, 80 MINS, US
Dir Rick Carrier   *Prod* Rick Carrier   *Scr* Rick Carrier
Ph Rick Carrier   *Ed* Stan Russell   *Mus* Bob Prince
● Robert Gentile, Camilo Delgado, Rosita De Triana,
Creta Margos, Robert Corso (Embassy/Carrier)

A first film by Yank Rick Carrier, this shows a Puerto Rican family in a Manhattan slum. The father is a vain, proud man with a lack of understanding of America or his family – and he has just lost his job. His teenage son and daughter go to look for work but he orders his wife to stay home. The boy runs into local racism and general hoodlumism as a delivery boy while the girl, a beauty, is used by factory workers and then becomes a sort of call girl for a dressmaker.

It may sound overly melodramatic, but this has a neat insight into NY life, as this producer sees it. Though this pic shows mainly bigoted people, it also depicts how their own weaknesses help betray this family. Much of the wickedness is from plain ignorance.

Some of the acting is skimpy. But Robert Gentile, as the son; Creta Margos, as his pliant comely sister; Rosita De Triana, as the anguished mother and Robert Corso, as the foppish gang leader, are standout.

STRANGER'S KISS

1983, 94 MINS, US ◇ ⊗
Dir Matthew Chapman   *Prod* Doug Dilge
Scr Matthew Chapman, Blaine Novak   *Ph* Mikail
Suslov   *Ed* William Carruth   *Mus* Gato Barbieri
● Peter Coyote, Victoria Tennant, Blaine Novak, Dan
Shor, Richard Romanus, Linda Kerridge (White)

Stranger's Kiss is a glowing homage to 1950s melodrama set in the film world. Though shot on a modest budget, picture has a lush look aided by strong artistic and technical contributions.

The love triangle tale is mirrored in both the real life and film-within-a-film structure of the production. Principals are Carole Redding (Victoria Tennant), a young woman kept by a gangster (Richard Romanus) who agrees to finance the film's film and costar, Stevie Blake (Blaine Novak, who also cowrote the script), a hustler who soon becomes consumed by Carole's mysterious background.

Stanley (Peter Coyote), the director, keeps Stevie in the dark to capitalize on his emotions. Both stories concern a boxer and a dancehall girl who fall in love but her past debt to a hoodlum threatens to destroy the relationship. Plot is reminiscent of Stanley Kubrick's *Killer's Kiss* and several other low budget items circa 1955, the setting of the picture.

Tennant is radiant as Carole with a genuine screen presence suited to her role. In sharp contrast, Novak has a forceful presence which demands our attention and eventually wins our affection.

STRANGERS ON A TRAIN

1951, 100 MINS, US ⊗
Dir Alfred Hitchcock   *Prod* Alfred Hitchcock
Scr Raymond Chandler, Czenzi Ormonde   *Ph* Robert
Burks   *Ed* William H. Zeigler   *Mus* Dimitri Tiomkin
Art Dir Ted Haworth
● Farley Granger, Robert Walker, Ruth Roman, Leo G.
Carroll, Patricia Hitchcock, Laura Elliott (Warner)

Given a good basis for a thriller in the Patricia Highsmith novel and a first-rate script, Hitchcock embroiders the plot into a gripping, palm-sweating piece of suspense.

Story offers a fresh situation for murder. Two strangers meet on a train. One is Farley Granger, separated from his tramp wife (Laura Elliott) and in love with Ruth Roman. The other is Robert Walker, a neurotic playboy who hates his rich father. Walker proposes that he will kill Elliott if Granger will do away with the father. Granger treats the proposal as a bad joke but Walker is serious.

Latter stalks down Elliott in an amusement park and strangles her. He then starts chasing Granger to make him fulfill the other end of the bargain.

Performance-wise, the cast comes through strongly. Granger is excellent as the harassed young man innocently involved in murder. Roman's role of a nice, understanding girl is a switch for her, and she makes it warmly effective. Walker's role has extreme color, and he projects it deftly. Elliott stands out briefly as the victim, and Patricia Hitchcock (the director's daughter) also registers.

STRANGER'S RETURN

1933, 88 MINS, US
Dir King Vidor   *Prod* King Vidor   *Scr* Brown Holmes,
Phil Stong   *Ph* William Daniels   *Ed* Dick Fantl
Art Dir Frederic Hope
● Lionel Barrymore, Miriam Hopkins, Franchot Tone,
Stuart Erwin, Irene Hervey, Beulah Bondi (M-G-M)

It is the story [from the novel by Phil Stong] of a New York girl who goes west after she leaves her husband, finds a new love, but loses out when the hero leaves to avoid temptation since he does not want to injure his wife and son, despite his greater love for his new idol.

Supplementing, or rather overshadowing the love interest, is a rare well-written story of a somewhat eccentric old farmer plagued by his fortune-seeking relatives who hover about the farm waiting the death of their prospective victim.

As the farmer Lionel Barrymore has a role he fits. Even his false whiskers are forgiven. Barrymore carries the bulk of the story.

Miriam Hopkins is not as fortunate. She is natural for the greater part, but fails at times in the lighter phases.

Franchot Tone is a likable hero, always in command of his scenes. No faulty performance in the entire cast.

● ●

■ STRANGERS WHEN WE MEET

1960, 117 MINS, US ◇ ▼

Dir Richard Quine   *Prod* Richard Quine   *Scr* Evan Hunter   *Ph* Charles Lang Jr   *Ed* Charles Nelson   *Mus* George Dunning   *Art Dir* Ross Bellah

● Kirk Douglas, Kim Novack, Ernie Kovacs, Barbara Rush, Walter Matthau, Virginia Bruce (Bryna-Quine/ Columbia)

A pictorially attractive but dramatically vacuous study of modern-style infidelity, *Strangers When We Meet* is easy on the eyes but hard on the intellect. A bunch of maladjusted suburbanites are thrown together in Evan Hunter's screenplay (from his novel), and what comes out is an old-fashioned soap opera.

Brilliant architect Kirk Douglas is upset because his spouse (Barbara Rush) is overly concerned with balancing the family budget. Meanwhile, housewife Kim Novak is disturbed over being taken for granted by her undersexed mate (John Bryant). Out of this germ of marital instability, a feverishly passionate affair blossoms between Douglas and Novak via a series of trysts. But unstable, sharp-eyed neighbor Walter Matthau, putting two and two together and coming up with an odd number, decides to even things up by getting into the act.

It is a rather pointless, slow-moving story, but it has been brought to the screen with such skill that it charms the spectator into an attitude of relaxed enjoyment, much the same effect as that produced by a casual daydream fantasy. Douglas does well by his role, and Novak brings to hers that cool, style-setting attitude that is her trademark.

● ●

■ STRANGLER, THE

1964, 89 MINS, US ▼

Dir Burt Topper   *Prod* Samuel Bischoff, David Diamond   *Scr* Bill S. Ballinger   *Ph* Jacques Marquette   *Ed* Robert Eisen   *Mus* Marlin Skiles   *Art Dir* Hal Pereira, Eugene Lourie

● Victor Buono, David McLean, Diane Sayer, Davey Davison, Ellen Corby (Allied Artists)

Bill S. Ballinger's scenario describes the latter phases of the homicidal career of a paranoid schizophrenic (Victor Buono) whose hatred of women has been motivated by a possessive mother who has completely warped his personality. His fetish for dolls ultimately betrays him to the police just as he is in the act of applying the coup de grace to distaff victim No. 11.

Dramatically skillful direction by Burt Topper and a firm level of histrionic performances help *The Strangler* over some rough spots and keep the picture from succumbing to inconsistencies of character and contrivances of story scattered through the picture.

Bueno for Buono, a convincing menace all the way. There's always a place on the screen for a fat man who can act, and Buono has the avoirdupois field virtually to himself.

● ●

■ STRAPLESS

1990, 97 MINS, UK ◇ ▽

Dir David Hare   *Prod* Rick McCallum   *Scr* David Hare   *Ph* Andrew Dunn   *Ed* Edward Marnier   *Mus* Nick Bicat   *Art Dir* Roger Hall

● Blair Brown, Bruno Ganz, Bridget Fonda, Alan Howard, Michael Gough, Hugh Laurie (Granada/Film Four)

Writer-director David Hare's third feature centers on the concerns of a middle-aged professional woman whose personal problems relate to wider political and social issues in Britain today.

This time the central character is an American, Dr Lillian Hempel (Blair Brown), who's lived in Britain for 12 years. While on vacation in Portugal she meets an apparently wealthy stranger, Raymond Forbes (Bruno Ganz), who woos her but fails to get her into his bed.

Back in London, Forbes continues his courtship, begging Lillian to marry him. They marry secretly, and soon after he simply disappears. Lillian discovers he already has a wife and son, also abandoned.

Lillian's serious, well-ordered life is contrasted with her flighty younger sister Amy (Bridget Fonda), who has a series of Latin lovers and gets pregnant by one of them.

Meanwhile, Lillian gradually is being drawn toward political activism as the British government's health service cutbacks begin to hurt.

Strapless (so-named because both the sisters wind up with no visible means of support) is an intelligent, ironic, multi-layered drama that's consistently intriguing. Performances are impeccable.

● ●

■ STRAW DOGS

1971, 118 MINS, UK ◇ ▼

Dir Sam Peckinpah   *Prod* Daniel Melnick   *Scr* David Zelag Goodman, Sam Peckinpah   *Ph* John Coquillon   *Ed* Paul Davies   *Mus* Jerry Fielding   *Art Dir* Ray Simms

● Dustin Hoffman, Susan George, Peter Vaughan, T.P. McKenna, Del Henney, Colin Welland (ABC)

Director Sam Peckinpah indulges himself in an orgy of unparalleled violence and nastiness with undertones of sexual repression in this production.

Dustin Hoffman appears as a quiet American mathematician who has married a lively, sexy English girl, played by Susan George, and goes to live on their isolated West Country farm. They get on reasonably well with a moronic assortment of locals, most of whom are heavy drinkers. Some are sexually repressed and the wife is seduced while her husband is hunting.

When the village dolt accidentally kills a teenage mini-skirted flirt he takes refuge at the farm. Hoffman refuses to give him to the enflamed villagers. Count is lost of the gruesome killings and bestialities that ensue.

The script relies on shock and violence to tide it over weakness in development, shallow characterization and lack of motivation. Hoffman scores as the easy-going American who rises to heights of belligerence when he considers the dolt is being wronged.

● ●

■ STRAWBERRY BLONDE

1941, 98 MINS, US ▼

Dir Raoul Walsh   *Prod* William Cagney   *Scr* Julius J. Epstein, Philip G. Epstein   *Ph* James Wong Howe   *Ed* William Holmes   *Mus* Heinz Roemheld

● James Cagney, Olivia de Havilland, Rita Hayworth, Jack Carson, Alan Hale, George Tobias (Warner)

Warners dips into the Gay Nineties period with this second film version of James Hagan's play, *One Sunday Afternoon*. Paramount turned out the original picture back in 1933 with Gary Cooper starred.

This entry of the Hagan play switches the locale to New York; otherwise it sticks close to the original. Story is told in retrospect. James Cagney is a struggling dentist with few patients, when an emergency call comes to pull a molar of his worst enemy, and he figures to give the latter a good dose of gas. While waiting for the patient's arrival, yarn goes back 10 years, when Cagney was enamored of the neighborhood's 'strawberry blonde'.

Jilted, he conveniently marries the loving and understanding nurse (Olivia de Havilland) but through the years carries a hate for the man who victimized him and stole his first girl. But he again meets the girl of his memories, finds her a nagging nuisance, and figures his enemy has had sufficient punishment through the years. It's then that he realizes he has the perfect wife.

Cagney and de Havilland provide topnotch performances that do much to keep up interest in the proceedings. Rita Hayworth is an eyeful as the title character, while Jack Carson is excellent as the politically ambitious antagonist of the dentist.

● ●

■ STREAMERS

1983, 118 MINS, US ◇ ▽

Dir Robert Altman   *Prod* Nick J. Mileti, Robert Altman   *Scr* David Rabe   *Ph* Pierre Mignot   *Ed* Norman Smith   *Mus* Stephen Foster   *Art Dir* Wolf Kroeger

● Matthew Modine, Michael Wright, Mitchell Lichtenstein, David Allen Grier, Albert Macklin, Guy Bond (United Artists Classics)

Streamers is a highly stylized set of theatricals describing an existentialist hell among a small group of men in a military barracks.

Apart from allowing the camera to occasionally peek through a curtain, writer David Rabe and director Robert Altman have their 1965 soldiers await orders to go to Vietnam and spending the waiting time either lying around on their bunks or returning drunk from saloon or whorehouse outings. They mostly taunt each other with tales of their own past history, but the taunts are socially, racially and sexually loaded, two of the soldiers being black, a third being an Ivy League homosexual and the fourth an intellectual 'from the sticks'.

Things explode in blood-gushing violence and general sadness when the possibilities have been exhausted in this overlong, overemphatic film.

● ●

■ STREET SCENE

1931, 80 MINS, US ▼

Dir King Vidor   *Prod* Samuel Goldwyn   *Scr* Elmer Rice   *Ph* George Barnes   *Ed* Hugh Bennett   *Mus* Alfred Newman   *Art Dir* Richard Day

● Sylvia Sidney, William Collier Jr., Estelle Taylor, Max Montor, David Landau, Russell Hopton (Goldwyn/United Artists)

Street Scene comes upon the screen in faithful reproduction of the stage play. Author Elmer Rice went to Hollywood and had a supervisory hand in the filming and nearly a dozen of the characters are played by the same actors who appeared in the first New York production.

Principal setting is almost a reproduction of the stage locale, even to the scaffolding of the construction job adjoining the tenement house in the West 60s of New York.

Picture opens on a sequence of city life with the introduction of a crashing symphonic musical setting, rather in the Gershwin manner, symbolizing the breadth and scope of the subject.

Sylvia Sidney gives an even, persuasive performance in a role for which she is particularly fitted, typifying the tragedy of budding girlhood cramped by sordid surroundings. Even her lack of formal beauty intensifies the pathos of the character. Young William Collier Jr. makes a splendid opposite to the heroine, playing his quieter scenes with true emphasis and rising to the swifter tempo with satisfying vigor.

In a purely acting sense the honors go to Beula Bondi, as the malicious scandalmonger of the tenement, playing the part she created on the stage, and playing it to the hilt.

● ●

S

STREETCAR NAMED DESIRE, A

1951, 125 MINS, US 🅥

Dir Elia Kazan   *Prod* Charles K. Feldman   *Scr* Oscar Saul   *Ph* Harry Stradling   *Ed* David Weisbart   *Mus* Alex North   *Art Dir* Richard Day
● Vivien Leigh, Marlon Brando, Kim Hunter, Karl Malden, Rudy Bond, Nick Dennis (Feldman)

Tennessee Williams' exciting Broadway stage play – winner of the Pulitzer Prize and New York Drama Critics award during the 1947-48 season – has been screenplayed into an even more absorbing drama of frustration and stark tragedy. With Marlon Brando essaying the part he created for the Broadway stage, and Vivien Leigh as the morally disintegrated Blanche DuBois (originated on Broadway by Jessica Tandy). *A Streetcar Named Desire* is thoroughly adult drama, excellently produced and imparting a keen insight into a drama whose scope was, of necessity, limited by its stage setting.

Pic is a faithful adaptation from the original play. It is the story of Blanche DuBois, a faded Mississippi teacher, who seeks refuge with a sister in the old French Quarter of New Orleans. Because her presence intrudes on the husband-wife relationship, the husband, a crude brutal young Polish-American, immediately becomes hostile to the visitor. He also suspects she's lying about her past. It is this hostility that motivates the story's basic elements. Stanley Kowalski (Brando), the husband, embarks on a plan to force his sister-in-law from his home.

Leigh gives a compelling performance in telling the tragedy of Blanche DuBois. Brando at times captures strongly the brutality of the young Pole but occasionally he performs unevenly in a portrayal marked by frequent garbling of his dialog. Kim Hunter and Karl Malden are excellent, as Blanche's sister and frantic suitor.
☐ 1951: Best Picture (Nomination)

STREETS

1990, 83 MINS, US ◇ 🅥

Dir Katt Shea Rubin   *Prod* Andy Rubin   *Scr* Katt Shea Rubin, Andy Rubin   *Ph* Phedon Papamichael   *Ed* Stephen Mark   *Mus* Aaron Davis   *Art Dir* Virginia Lee
● Christina Applegate, David Mendenhall, Eb Lottimer, Patrick Richwood, Alan Stock (Concorde)

Despite its B-film framework involving a maniacal killer stalking street kids, *Streets* transcends its genre with a gritty and affecting portrait of a teenage throwaway struggling to exist in LA's demimonde. Director Katt Shea Ruben, who scripted with her producer-husband Andy Ruben, clearly had more ambitious things in mind than just another Concorde thriller in which nubile girls are stalked and murdered.

Christina Applegate's solid performance in her first starring feature as the jaded but still sensitive Dawn, who sells sex to survive and shoots up heroin to get through the day, speaks volumes about the scuzzy side of LA life. Working with a minimal budget and a 19-day shooting sked, Ruben conjures up an impressive, subtly fantastic atmosphere.

Yet since this is a Roger Corman production, neorealism isn't enough, and there has to be a psycho killer (vampirish policeman Eb Lottimer), who preys on street kids and becomes obsessed with eliminating Applegate. Although without much insight into the character of the killer, *Streets* has a compelling pattern of visual suspense.

STREETS OF FIRE

1984, 94 MINS, US ◇ 🅥

Dir Walter Hill   *Prod* Lawrence Gordon, Joel Silver   *Scr* Walter Hill, Larry Gross   *Ph* Andrew Laszlo   *Ed* Freeman Davies, Michael Ripps   *Mus* Ry Cooder   *Art Dir* John Vallone

● Michael Pare, Diane Lane, Rick Moranis, Amy Madigan, Willem Dafoe, Deborah Van Valkenburgh (Universal/RKO)

Assembled by the team that created *48HRS.* [1982], pic is a pulsing, throbbing orchestration careening around the rescue of a kidnapped young singer. The decor is urban squalor.

Movie has 10 original songs and musically the movie is continually hot, with lyrics charting the concerns of the narrative line, simplistic as it is.

Film also has undeniable texture. Smoke, neon, rainy streets, platforms of elevated subway lines, alleys and warehouses create an urban inferno in an unspecified time and place.

Diane Lane, whose singing voice is dubbed, looks great and is cast expertly. So are Willem Dafoe and Lee Ving.

Briefly seen as a stripper-dancer in the Bombers' hangout is Marine Jahan, who was the uncredited dancer in *Flashdance*.

STREETS OF GOLD

1986, 95 MINS, US ◇ 🅥

Dir Joe Roth   *Prod* Joe Roth   *Scr* Heywood Gould, Richard Price, Tom Cole   *Ph* Arthur Albert   *Ed* Richard Chew   *Mus* Jack Nitzsche   *Art Dir* Marcos Flaksman
● Klaus Maria Brandauer, Adrian Pasdar, Wesley Snipes, Angela Molina (Ufland/Roth)

Streets of Gold is a likable, but hardly compelling story of not one, but two kids trying to box their way out of the slums.

Klaus Maria Brandauer is at the center of the ring, playing a Russian Jew and former boxing champion who was banned from competing for the Soviet team because of his religion – so he emigrated to the US and now works as a dishwasher and gets drunk a lot.

A brash Irish tough named Timmy Doyle (Adrian Pasdar) is so impressed that this middle-aged and seemingly out-of-shape lunk can so easily humiliate an athlete half his age, he seeks him out the next day, and asks him to be his coach.

Streets of Gold is paved with credibly gritty scenes, but the end result comes off as a highbrow boxing training film.

STRIKE IT RICH

1990, 84 MINS, UK/US ◇ 🅥

Dir James Scott   *Prod* Christine Oestreicher, Graham Easton   *Scr* James Scott, Richard Rayner, Julian Mitchell, Dick Vosburgh   *Ph* Robert Paynter   *Ed* Thomas Schwalm   *Mus* Shirley Walker, Cliff Eidelman   *Art Dir* Christopher Hobbs
● Robert Lindsay, Molly Ringwald, John Gielgud, Max Wall, Simon de la Brosse, Michel Blanc (Flamingo/Ideal/British Screen/BBC)

Strike It Rich is a poorly directed piece of light (i.e. low calorie) entertainment. Helmer James Scott closely follows the letter of Graham Green's 1955 novella *Loser Takes All*. He adds an opening reel (shot partly in black & white) that fleshes out the romance of accountant Robert Lindsay and half-his-age Molly Ringwald, portraying a British lass raised in America after being evacuated during the Blitz.

Unfortunately, the Greene material is merely a trifle that would have needed the talents and charm of say, Stanley Donen, Kenneth More and Audrey Hepburn in the 1950s to constitute a viable theatrical feature. As executed here, it's hopelessly old-fashioned, remote and even fusty.

There's no chemistry between the stars. Ringwald's frequently flat line readings are a drag. Lindsay's screen career remains stillborn. Gielgud's role is just a brief walkthrough.

STRIPES

1981, 103 MINS, US ◇

Dir Ivan Reitman   *Prod* Ivan Reitman, Dean Goldberg   *Scr* Leo Blum, Dean Goldberg   *Ph* Bill Butler   *Ed* Eva Ruggiero, Michael Laciano   *Mus* Elmer Bernstein   *Art Dir* James Spencer
● Bill Murray, Harold Ramis, Warren Oates, Sean Young, John Candy, P.J. Soles (Columbia)

Stripes is a cheerful, mildly outrageous and mostly amiable comedy pitting a new generation of enlistees against the oversold lure of a military hungry for bodies and not too choosy about what it gets. There's little in the way of art or comic subtlety here, but the film really seems to work.

Bill Murray, who worked under Ivan Reitman in *Meatballs*, is an aimless layabout whose Sad Sack life prompts him to consider the army as a last-ditch passport to the career, romances, travels and other delights painted in those glossy federal commercials.

Predictably, after he cons buddy Harold Ramis into enlisting, the sexy ads quickly prove to be Madison Avenue fiction, with basic training – under the grizzled glare of drill sergeant Warren Oates – taking the place of fraternity hell week as Murray heads deeper into trouble, cued by his amiably arrogant smart-assedness.

Apart from Murray's focal presence, Ramis and obese John Candy are wildly funny, with Oates treading a good balance between grizzly humor and military convictions (which the film, surprisingly, winds up more honoring than knocking).

STRIPPER, THE

1963, 95 MINS, US

Dir Franklin J. Schaffner   *Prod* Jerry Wald   *Scr* Meade Roberts   *Ph* Ellsworth Fredericks   *Ed* Robert Simpson   *Mus* Jerry Goldsmith   *Art Dir* Jack Martin Smith, Walter M. Simonds
● Joanne Woodward, Richard Beymer, Claire Trevor, Carol Lynley, Robert Webber, Gypsy Rose Lee (20th Century-Fox)

This final film by Jerry Wald is an unsuccessful attempt to convert William Inge's 1959 Broadway flop, *A Loss of Roses*, into a substantial and appealing motion picture. Like the play, the film has its merits, but they are only flashes of magic in a lacklustre package. Joanne Woodward's performance in a role expanded to focal prominence in the film is one of them.

The story is set in traditional Inge country – a small town in Kansas – more specifically the modest residence of two characters into those humdrum lives comes Woodward, stranded by the abrupt deterioration of the little magician's unit of which she is a part.

She is taken in by an old friend (Claire Trevor) now a widow who lives with her son (Richard Beymer), an ardent but inexperienced lad. There are attempts to make something of the mother-son relationship, but the two characters are never properly clarified, and remain two-dimensional. At any rate, Beymer fancies himself in love with the visitor and has a one-night affair with the fading, desperately accommodating and romantically vulnerable would-be actress.

Histrionic honors go hands down to the animated Woodward, who rivets attention and compassion to herself throughout with a farceful and vivacious portrayal of the goodhearted but gullible girl. Beymer is adequate, little more, in the rather baffling role of the lad.

Lovely Carol Lynley is wasted in a thankless role which requires mostly a photogenic rear anatomy for walking away shots. Woodward's rear gets a big photographic play, too.

Franklin Schaffner's direction tends to be a bit choppy, uneven and, in spots, heavyhanded or unobservant. Jerry Goldsmith's score has sparkle and character, and is obtrusive in a constructive manner – when a musical lift is needed to enliven the going.

• •

■ STROMBOLI

1950, 81 MINS, ITALY/US ▼

Dir Robert Rossellini   *Prod* Ingrid Bergman, Roberto Rossellini   *Scr* Roberto Rossellini, Art Cohn, Renzo Cesana, Sergio Amidei, Gianpaolo Callegari   *Ph* Otello Martelli   *Ed* Roland Gross, Jolanda Benvenuti   *Mus* Renzo Rossellini
● Ingrid Bergman, Mario Vitale, Renzo Cesana, Mario Sponzo (Be-Ro/RKO)

Director Roberto Rossellini purportedly denied responsibility for the film, claiming the American version was cut by RKO beyond recognition. Cut or not cut, the film reflects no credit on him. Given elementary-school dialog to recite and impossible scenes to act, Ingrid Bergman's never able to make the lines real nor the emotion sufficiently motivated to seem more than an exercise.

So many morally-questionable scenes apparently had to be removed that RKO found it necessary to insert a great deal of detail in other actions to stretch the film to its 81-minute length [from its original 107 minutes].

The only visible touch of the famed Italian director is in the hard photography, which adds to the realistic, documentary effect of life on the rocky, lava-blanketed island. Rossellini's penchant for realism, however, does not extend to Bergman. She's always fresh, clean and well-groomed.

The story is of a girl (Bergman) in an Italian displaced persons camp who marries a native fisherman (Mario Vitale) of Stromboli so that she may be released. Miss Bergman hates it from the start, but she does grow to love her man.

Language of the pic is a bit confusing. Bergman, on an Italian isle, speaks English with a Swedish accent. Vitale's voice has been dubbed and there's little strain in deciphering his English. Renzo Cesana as the priest does the best thespic job in the pic.

• •

■ STRONGEST MAN IN THE WORLD, THE

1975, 92 MINS, US ◇

Dir Vincent McEveety   *Prod* Bill Anderson   *Scr* Joseph L. McEveety, Herman Groves   *Ph* Andrew Jackson   *Ed* Cotton Warburton   *Mus* Robert F. Brunner   *Art Dir* John B. Mansbridge, Jack Senter
● Kurt Russell, Joe Flynn, Eve Arden, Cesar Romero, Phil Silvers, Dick Van Patten (Walt Disney)

The students of Medfield College unintentionally zap the laws of nature with unexpected and sometimes hilarious results. Through a lab accident, they concoct a scientific formula which gives people superhuman strength, a spoof on vitality and energy claims of cereal companies.

The script rivets on situation of the school's reputation and financial stability tied in with sale of the formula to a cereal outfit and participating in an intercollegiate weight-lifting contest. The other team is sponsored by a rival cereal concern, acknowledged the No. 1 because of its previous success in out-publicizing the merits of its product.

Joe Flynn, who died just after pic was finished, is the sputtering college dean, faced with the threat by the college board that he's through unless he can create a financial turnaround and Kurt Russell is the student responsible for the formula and Cesar Romero cops a hand as the slick heavy.

• •

■ STUD, THE

1978, 90 MINS, UK ◇ ▼

Dir Quentin Masters   *Prod* Ronald S. Kass   *Scr* Jackie Collins   *Ph* Peter Hannan   *Ed* David Camplin   *Mus* Sammy Cahn, Biddu   *Art Dir* Michael Bastow

● Joan Collins, Oliver Tobias, Emma Jacobs, Sue Lloyd, Walter Gotell, Mark Burns (Brent Walker)

The Stud goes a long way toward transcending the softcore sexpo genre, but ultimately doesn't quite make it. It's a shame because the producers have obviously tried hard to avoid low-budget seediness of routine skinflicks.

Based on the novel by Jackie Collins (sister of Joan, who toplines) the $1 million production has Oliver Tobias in title role as a virile manager of a London nitery.

Joan Collins is the lady who pulls the strings to manipulate him as her own sexual marionette. Her husband (Walter Gotell) owns the nightclub and if the stud wants to keep his perquisites he must toe the line and keep the lady happy. And quite a few others, too.

Tobias is short on sensitivity and would-be Lotharios seeking useful tips might be excused for wondering what, apart from rakish good looks, is the secret of his success in persuading so many eligibles into the sack. He, in fact, seems faintly embarrassed about the whole thing. Collins sails through her part giving just what was demanded but adding no dimension.

• •

■ STUDENT PRINCE, THE

1927, 105 MINS, US ⊗

Dir Ernst Lubitsch   *Scr* Hans Kraly, Marian Ainslee, Ruth Cummings   *Ph* John Mescall   *Ed* Andrew Marton   *Art Dir* Cedric Gibbons, Richard Day
● Ramon Novarro, Norma Shearer, Jean Hersholt, Gustav von Seyffertitz, Philippe De Lacy (M-G-M)

Ernst Lubitsch took his tongue out of his cheek when he directed this special [based on the 1924 operetta by Dorothy Donnelly and Sigmund Romberg from the novel by Wilhelm Meyer-Förster]. He had to, and in doing so he also took any kick right out of the picture, if any were there in the script for him. It's not farce and it's not drama. Just a pretty love story of peaches and cream.

The Student Prince concerns an heir to a throne who is forced to give up his love for a tavern maid because of duty to his country. And on the point of the Prince marrying the Princess his dead uncle had selected, the film ends.

The claim is that it took a year to make this feature, yet this doesn't show. Productionally there are some rich interiors counterbalanced by a sprinkling of back drops on exteriors.

But nothing can stand off Ramon Novarro's facial makeup. This is ghastly under certain lighting conditions and at no time allows him to completely spin the illusion of the character he is playing. Shearer's personal efforts are a highlight and Jean Hersholt stands a good chance of outlasting both in the memory.

• •

■ STUDS LONIGAN

1960, 103 MINS, US ▼

Dir Irving Lerner   *Prod* Philip Yordan   *Scr* Philip Yordan   *Ph* Arthur H. Feindel, Haskell P. Wexler   *Ed* Verna Fields   *Mus* Jerry Goldsmith   *Art Dir* Jack Poplin
● Christopher Knight, Frank Gorshin, Helen Westcott, Dick Foran, Venetia Stevenson, Jack Nicholson (United Artists)

Compressing James T. Farrell's respected trilogy into a 103-minute film doesn't come off. *Studs Lonigan* is an earnest attempt gone wrong, partially in overly-artistic conception, but principally through incoherent execution complicated by undisciplined histrionics.

Philip Yordan's scenario is quite faithful to Farrell's book, which centers its attention on the essentially decent hero who struggles against slum life of Chicago's South Side district in the 1920s. Christopher Knight, as the

hero, has a disquieting tendency toward facial contortion and responsive exaggeration. The role is an extremely demanding one for any actor, let alone a newcomer to the screen.

The three standouts in the large cast are Frank Gorshin, Helen Westcott and Dick Foran. Gorshin has an instinctive ability to generate a natural reaction. Westcott creates a figure of pathos and dimension, despite the fact that Yordan's screenplay leaves the character she is playing – the loveless schoolteacher who becomes Stud's secret counsel and companion – essentially undeveloped and unexplored. Foran comes through admirably in the role of Stud's decent father.

Lensman Arthur H. Feindel and special photographic consultant Haskell P. Wexler have chosen an unusual assortment of sharp, tilted angles at which to place the camera. In combination with some unusual shading effects, this emphasis on startling composition is clever, but frequently distracting.

• •

■ STUFF, THE

1985, 93 MINS, US ◇ ▼

Dir Larry Cohen   *Prod* Paul Kurta   *Scr* Larry Cohen   *Ph* Paul Glickman   *Ed* Armond Lebowitz   *Art Dir* Marleen Marta, George Stoll
● Michael Moriarty, Andrea Marcovicci, Paul Sorvino, Scott Bloom, Garrett Morris, Danny Aiello (Larco/New World)

The Stuff is sci-fi with no hardware but lots of white goo. It's a certified Larry Cohen film that seems to fly right out of the 1950s horror genre. It also has an underlying humor about it, plays around with satirizing fast foods, and cloaks a sly little subtext about people who ingest stuff they know is not good for them.

What's not to like? The film enjoys a larky sense of innocence, some hideous gaping mouths full of a curdling, parasitic menace, and a fey performance by Michael Moriarty as an industrial saboteur who, along with Andrea Marcovicci and little Scott Bloom, track down the scourge of the countryside and the heavies.

It also benefits from a hilarious performance played straight by Paul Sorvino as a self-styled paramilitary nut. The 11-year-old Bloom is appealing, while Garrett Morris as a chocolate cookie mogul and Danny Aiello as Vickers lend flavor in support.

• •

■ STUNT MAN, THE

1980, 129 MINS, US ◇ ▼

Dir Richard Rush   *Prod* Richard Rush   *Scr* Lawrence B. Marcus   *Ph* Mario Tosi   *Ed* Jack Hofstra, Caroline Ferriol   *Mus* Dominic Frontiere   *Art Dir* James Schoppe
● Peter O'Toole, Steve Railsback, Barbara Hershey, Allen Goorwitz, Alex Rocco, Sharon Farrell (Simon)

Offbeat tale, based on Paul Brodeur's 1970 novel, has Vietnam vet Steve Railsback on the lam and accepting refuge from both benevolent and sinister film director Peter O'Toole, who puts the fugitive through some highly dangerous paces as a stunt man while shielding him from the cops.

Lawrence B. Marcus and adaptor-director Richard Rush are least successful in making fully credible the relationship between Railsback and film-within-the-film star Barbara Hershey, with his disillusionment upon discovering that she once had a fling with O'Toole playing as particularly unconvincing.

O'Toole is excellent in his best, cleanest performance in years. He smashingly delineates an omnipotent, godlike type whose total control over those around him makes him seem almost unreal.

• •

S

■ **STUNTS**

1977, 90 MINS, US ◇ Ⓥ

Dir Mark L. Lester   *Prod* Raymond Lofaro, William Panzer   *Scr* Dennis Johnson, Barney Cohen   *Ph* Bruce Logan   *Ed* Corky Ehlers   *Mus* Michael Kamen
● Robert Forster, Fiona Lewis, Joanna Cassidy, Darrell Fetty, Bruce Glover, Jim Luisi (New Line/Fleischman)

Robert Forster is excellent as an ace stuntman who thwarts a maniac stalking a film crew making a police actioner on an oceanside location in San Luis Obispo, Calif.

This is a tight-lipped actioner about a male group involved in a dangerous trade, with sexy female camp followers admitted to the group once they accept the code of grace under pressure.

There is much emphasis on expertise, emotional control, and the details of the craft, which are shown in docu-like style. The action scenes alternate with more relaxed character interplay in a motel and a bar, where the concept of expertise is translated into personal relationships.

Fiona Lewis is the prime romantic interest, a groupie journalist who initially causes friction in the group.

....

■ **SUDDEN IMPACT**

1983, 117 MINS, US ◇ Ⓥ

Dir Clint Eastwood   *Prod* Clint Eastwood   *Scr* Joseph C. Stinson   *Ph* Bruce Surtees   *Ed* Joel Cox   *Mus* Lalo Schifrin   *Art Dir* Edward Carfagno
● Clint Eastwood, Sondra Locke, Pat Hingle, Bradford Dillman, Paul Drake, Audrie J. Neenan (Warner)

The fourth entry in the lucrative *Dirty Harry* series, *Sudden Impact* is a brutally hard-hitting policier which casts Clint Eastwood as audiences like to see him, as the toughest guy in town.

Sudden Impact sends Harry out of his normal jurisdiction in San Francisco to research a case with connections to coastal San Paulo. While there, he bumps into Sondra Locke, who is extracting her own brand of vengeance on a group of individuals who, some years back, savagely raped both her and her younger sister.

Local police chief Pat Hingle tries to bar Harry from behaving as usual in his community, but that doesn't prevent a slew of shootings.

This is the first entry in the series to have been directed by Eastwood himself, and action is put over with great force, if also with some obviousness. Locke looks astonishingly like Tippi Hedren did in Hitchcock's *Marnie* and, with the exception of a sympathetic black cop played by Albert Popwell, nearly everyone else in the cast represents a menace to Harry in one way or another.

....

■ **SUDDENLY, LAST SUMMER**

1959, 112 MINS, US Ⓥ

Dir Joseph L. Mankiewicz   *Prod* Sam Spiegel   *Scr* Gore Vidal, Tennessee Williams   *Ph* Jack Hildyard   *Ed* William W. Hornbeck, Thomas G. Stanford   *Mus* Buxton Orr, Malcolm Arnold
● Elizabeth Taylor, Katharine Hepburn, Montgomery Clift, Albert Dekker, Mercedes McCambridge, Gary Raymond (Columbia)

Perversion and greed, Tennessee Williams' recurrent themes, are worked over again in *Suddenly Last Summer*. The play was concerned with homosexuality and cannibalism. The cannibalism has been dropped, or muted, in the film version. It has some very effective moments, but on the whole it fails to move.

Perhaps the reason is that what was a long one-act play has been expanded in the screenplay to a longish motion picture. Nothing that's been added is an improvement on the original; they stretch the seams of the original fabric without strengthening the seamy aspects of the story.

The story is that of a doting mother (Katharine Hepburn) and her son. The son was a homosexual and his mother his procuress. When she had passed the age when she could function effectively in this capacity, he enlisted the services of his beautiful cousin, Elizabeth Taylor.

The question is whether Taylor is fancifully insane or ruthlessly sane. Hepburn wants a lobotomy performed on Taylor, to excise the memory of the son's death, by detaching a portion of the brain. It is the job of Montgomery Clift, as the neuro-surgeon who would perform the operation, to decide if Taylor is deranged as Hepburn insists.

Hepburn is dominant, making her brisk authority a genteel hammer relentlessly crushing the younger woman. Taylor is most effective in her later scenes, although these have been robbed of their original theatricality. Clift is little more than straight man to the two ladies.

Although Joseph L. Mankiewiez' direction is inventive in giving the essentially static narrative some movement and rhythm, it must be faulted for blunting Taylor's final scene so it fails to match Hepburn's opening monolog. (The play was actually only two monologs of almost equal power and length.)

....

■ **SUFFERING BASTARDS**

1990, 89 MINS, US ◇ Ⓥ

Dir Bernard McWilliams   *Prod* Tom Mangan, Neil Hodges, George F. Andrews   *Scr* Bernard McWilliams, John C. McGinley   *Ph* Neil Hodges   *Ed* Steve Wang   *Mus* Dan Di Paola
● John C. McGinley, David Warshofsky, Pam LaTesta, Rene Rivera, Eric Bogosian (Cinelux)

Bernard McWilliams' demented comedy *Suffering Bastards*, shot on a shoestring, soars with sheer zaniness and outrageous invention.

Womanizing Buddy Johnson (John C. McGinley) and his brother Al (David Warshofsky) sing and swing in their mother's tawdry Atlantic City nightclub. The irrepressible brothers, who bear as much resemblance to each other as Laurel did to Hardy, find the club taken over by a smooth-talking swindler.

Out of a job, but vowing to Mommy (a delectable Pam LaTesta) they'll buy the club back someday, they find employment in a sinister warehouse. Buddy's irresponsible flirting with the secretary makes a permanent enemy out of her violent boyfriend, Bernard (fine Rene Rivera), a Hispanic hitman who becomes their undefeatable, hilarious nemesis.

Scripters take galiardic humor one notch up the sophistication ladder, mixing sight gags with a deadpan offscreen narrator. McGinley and Warshofsky carry off their roles with unrepentant relish.

....

■ **SUGARLAND EXPRESS, THE**

1974, 109 MINS, US ◇ Ⓥ

Dir Steven Spielberg   *Prod* Richard D. Zanuck, David Brown   *Scr* Hal Barwood, Matthew Robbins   *Ph* Vilmos Zsigmond   *Ed* Edward M. Abroms, Verna Fields   *Mus* John Williams   *Art Dir* Joseph Alves Jr
● Goldie Hawn, Ben Johnson, Michael Sacks, William Atherton, Gregory Walcott, Harrison Zanuck (Universal)

The Sugarland Express begins and plays for much of its length as a hilarious madcap caper chase comedy.

Goldie Hawn stars as a young mother who helps husband William Atherton escape from prison so they may rescue their baby from involuntary adoption. Unfortunately, the film degenerates in final reels to heavy-handed social polemic and sound-and-fury shootout.

Based on an actual event in Texas in 1969, the screenplay is by Hal Barwood and Matthew Robbins, from a story by them and feature-debuting director Steven Spielberg. Besides some excellent major characterizations – Michael Sacks as a patrol car officer whom they kidnap, and Ben Johnson, outstanding as a police captain – the comedic impact is enhanced by terrific visual staging.

....

■ **SULLIVAN'S TRAVELS**

1941, 90 MINS, US Ⓥ

Dir Preston Sturges   *Prod* Paul Jones   *Scr* Preston Sturges   *Ph* John Seitz, Farciot Edouard   *Ed* Stuart Gillmore   *Mus* Leo Shuken
● Joel McCrea, Veronica Lake, William Demarest, Franklin Pangborn, Porter Hall, Eric Blore (Paramount)

Sullivan's Travels is a curious but effective mixture of grim tragedy, slapstick of the Keystone brand and smart, trigger-fast comedy.

It is written and directed by Preston Sturges, who springs a flock of surprises as he flits from slapstick to stark drama, from high comedy to a sequence of the Devil's Island prison type of stuff, into romantic spells, some philosophy and, in effect, all over the place without warning.

He ties it all together neatly, however, and keeps his audience on the go and on edge. Sturges' dialog is trenchant, has drive, possesses crispness and gets the laughs where that is desired.

Hollywood director Joel McCrea, anxious to produce *Oh, Brother, Where Art Thou?*, an epic of hard times and troubles, disguises himself as a hobo and goes out to look for troubles, finding plenty for himself. He picks up Veronica Lake on the way and they travel the rails together, she in boy's clothes.

A fine cast has been assembled around McCrea and Lake. Latter supplies the sex appeal and does a good acting job. McCrea, in the lap of luxury as a Hollywood director one minute, and a bum the next, turns in a swell performance.

....

■ **SUMMER AND SMOKE**

1961, 120 MINS, US ◇

Dir Peter Glenville   *Prod* Hal Wallis   *Scr* James Poe, Meade Roberts   *Ph* Charles Lang Jr   *Mus* Elmer Bernstein   *Art Dir* Hal Pereira, Walter Tyler
● Laurence Harvey, Geraldine Page, John McIntire, Una Merkel, Rita Moreno, Thomas Gomez (Paramount)

Peter Glenville, who guided Tennessee Williams' play in Britain, gives this pic version a solid delineation, effectively guiding his cast, and giving several scenes heightened impact by cutting them off short, allowing effect to follow into next sequence. Throughout most of the first half, he has also successfully disengaged film from its stage format.

Performances are almost uniformly excellent, though Geraldine Page walks off with top honors in a repeat of her 1952 stage role as Alma Winemiller, the repressed spinster. Laurence Harvey, perhaps a bit young to play her opposite number, John, perhaps a bit too continental as a bayou boy, is nevertheless very good, and gives a solid and believable rendering of the ne'er-do-well who reforms.

Una Merkel (again a repeat of her stage role) cuts herself a memorable cameo in a relatively small part, while Rita Moreno as the dance hall girl, Thomas Gomez as her father, John McIntire as the boy's pa, all give their supporting roles an effective reading. Earl Holliman is standout in a brief one-sequence appearance as the traveling salesman in the finale. An extra nod must go also to Pamela Tiffin, who as Nellie adds a pro flair to dazzling youthful beauty. It's her first screen role.

....

■ SUMMER HOLIDAY

1948, 92 MINS, US ◇

Dir Rouben Mamoulian *Prod* Arthur Freed
Scr Frances Goodrich, Albert Hackett, Irving Brecher,
Jean Holloway *Ph* Charles Schoenbaum *Ed* Albert
Akst *Mus* Harry Warren, Ralph Blane *Art Dir* Cedric
Gibbons, Jack Martin Smith
● Mickey Rooney, Gloria DeHaven, Walter Huston,
Frank Morgan, Agnes Moorehead, Marilyn Maxwell
(M-G-M)

The Eugene O'Neill play, *Ah. Wilderness* with
its account of a turn-of-the-century small-
town New England family, provides admirable setting, story, color and mood for the
musical numbers and script. The musical
numbers, tastefully chosen and skillfully
staged, are not spotted arbitrarily, but stem
naturally from the situations.

For example, the film is introduced by a
song called 'It's Our Home Town'. Walter
Huston sings the first chorus, as the newspaper publisher, with the other characters
taking it up to identify themselves and plant
the general story line.

The story emphasizes the puppy-love
romance between the publisher's son and girl
across the street. Respectively Mickey
Rooney and Gloria DeHaven. Except for
some laughable mugging by the former, they
make an appealing pair, and their musical
numbers are nicely done.

Huston is fine as the understanding Nat
Miller, the boy's father. Frank Morgan
achieves a nice blend of comedy and pathos
as Uncle Sid.

Mamoulian's direction has style, is well
paced and without sacrificing story credibility makes the songs stand out.

■ SUMMER HOLIDAY

1963, 109 MINS, UK ◇ ▽

Dir Peter Yates *Prod* Kenneth Harper *Scr* Peter
Myers, Ronald Cass *Ph* John Wilcox *Ed* Jack Slade
Mus Stanley Black
● Cliff Richard, Lauri Peters, Melvyn Hayes, Una
Stubbs, The Shadows (Elstree)

Peter Myers and Ronald Cass have provided
a screenplay which is short on wit but anyway is simply a valid excuse for a light-
hearted jaunt through sunny Europe. Cliff
Richard and three mechanic buddies set out
for a European holiday in a borrowed double-
decker London bus. They pick up (in quite
the nicest way) three stranded girls, a cabaret
act en route to Athens. The boys decide to
make Athens their objective.

They also encounter a troupe of wandering
entertainers and a stowaway in the shape of a
young boy. 'He' turns out to be an American
girl tele singer, fleeing from the professional
demands of her dragon of a mother and her
agent.

From this thin thread of yarn, songs, situations and dance routines arise fairly naturally. Even when dragged in, they add a lot
to the excitement. Richard has a warm
presence and sings and dances more than
adequately.

Lauri Peters is pleasant as the young Yank
heroine and romantic interest, and Melvyn
Hayes has a sharp comic talent.

Highlighted throughout are production
sequences which are put over shrewdly by
director Peter Yates and into which
choreographer Herbert Ross pumps an
exuberant American expertise.

Myers and Cass have written seven numbers and others including Richard have contributed another nine. Filmed largely in
France and Greece, the editing and backgrounds give an impression of a continuous
trip across Europe.

■ SUMMER MADNESS

1955, 100 MINS, UK ◇

Dir David Lean *Prod* Ilya Lopert *Scr* H.E. Bates,
David Lean *Ph* Jack Hildyard *Ed* Peter Taylor
Mus Alessandro Cicognini *Art Dir* Vincent Korda
● Katharine Hepburn, Rossano Brazzi, Isa Miranda,
Darren McGavin, Mari Aldon, Jeremy Spenser
(Lopert/London)

Summer Madness, made in Venice during the
summer of 1954, is a loose adaptation of
Arthur Laurents' stage play, *Time of the
Cuckoo*. With Katharine Hepburn in the role
originated by Shirley Booth and with the
scenic beauties of the canal city, the film
stacks up as promising entertainment – with
some reservations. There is a lack of cohesion
and some abruptness in plot transition without a too-clear buildup. Lesser characterizations, too, are on the sketchy side.

Covering these flaws is a rich topsoil of
drama as the proud American secretary
who hits Venice as a tourist falls for and is
disillusioned by the middle-aged Italian
charmer.

Rossano Brazzi, as the attractive vis-a-vis,
scores a triumph of charm and reserve.
Hepburn turns in a feverish acting chore of
proud loneliness.

■ SUMMER OF '42

1971, 102 MINS, US ◇ ▽

Dir Robert Mulligan *Prod* Richard A. Roth
Scr Herman Raucher *Ph* Robert Surtees *Ed* Folmar
Blangsted *Mus* Michel Legrand *Art Dir* Albert
Brenner
● Jennifer O'Neill, Gary Grimes, Jerry Houser, Oliver
Conant, Katherine Allentuck, Christopher Norris
(Warner)

The emotional and sexual awakening of teenagers is a dramatic staple. Robert Mulligan's
Summer of '42 has a large amount of charm
and tenderness; it also has little dramatic
economy and much eye-exhausting
photography which translates to forced and
artificial emphasis on a strungout story.

Script tells of that long-ago summer, way
out on Long Island, when Gary Grimes had
his first sexual-romantic experience with war-
widowed Jennifer O'Neill. His two pals
(Jerry Houser and Oliver Conant), begin and
end the film not yet matured. For Houser, the
easy charms of Christopher Norris still
suffice, but the younger Conant literally
disappears from the plot when the prospects
of action instead of talk presents itself.

The three boys come across well, particularly Grimes. Houser's character is more
coarse, even obnoxious at times, and he plays
it well to help set off Grimes' more introspective nature. O'Neill is wooden and stilted,
though her lines are few so the handicap does
not unduly mar the film.

■ SUMMER PLACE, A

1959, 130 MINS, US ◇

Dir Delmer Daves *Prod* Delmer Daves *Scr* Delmer
Daves *Ph* Harry Stradling *Ed* Owen Marks
Mus Max Steiner
● Richard Egan, Dorothy McGuire, Sandra Dee,
Arthur Kennedy, Troy Donahue, Constance Ford
(Warner)

A Summer Place is one of those big, emotional,
slickly-produced pictures that bite off a great
deal more than they can chew and neatly dispose of their intense, highly-dramatic
melange by dropping their characters into
slots clearly marked 'good' and 'bad'.

In his capacity as writer [from the novel by
Sloan Wilson] and director, Delmer Daves
has missed the mark by a mile. His characters, anguished most of the time, are unreal
and totally devoid of depth. The film runs at
least 20 minutes too long and has a tendency

to use dialog to preach what should be
implied.

Millionaire Richard Egan, his wife (Constance Ford) and daughter (Sandra Dee)
arrive on a small island off the New England
coast where, 20 years ago, Egan was a lifeguard and had an affair with Dorothy
McGuire, who subsequently married Arthur
Kennedy, the impoverished owner of a summer mansion. Egan has an affair with
McGuire, which is discovered, and divorces
result. Meanwhile, Dee and Kennedy's son
(Troy Donahue) have fallen in love but are
broken up by Dee's mother.

With the single exception of McGuire, who
comes through with a radiant performance
and is lovely to look at, the cast does an average job. Egan is wooden. Dee has a conventionally pretty face, but it's only in one scene
(when she becomes hysterical) that the director gets her to emote. Donahue is handsome,
but little more. Kennedy is good as a combination snob and drunk, but he fights some
pretty tough lines.

■ SUMMER STOCK

1950, 108 MINS, US ◇ ▽

Dir Charles Walters *Prod* Joe Pasternak *Scr* George
Wells, Sy Gomberg *Ph* Robert Planck *Ed* Albert
Akst *Mus* Johnny Green, Saul Chaplin (dirs.)
● Judy Garland, Gene Kelly, Eddie Bracken, Gloria De
Haven, Phil Silvers (M-G-M)

Summer Stock showcases M-G-M's two top
musical stars, Judy Garland and Gene Kelly.
It has a light, gay air, including nine tunes,
some used for dance numbers. Story portion
is never allowed to intrude much.

The background is a New England farm
setting. Garland is the farmerette. Her younger sister (Gloria De Haven) brings a troupe
of would-be thespians to the farm and they
take over the barn to stage a new musical
written by Kelly. Not only is Garland upset
at such an invasion, so is the whole village of
New Englanders.

Setup provides ample excuse for ringing in
most of the musical numbers, although not
justifying the finale that sees a production
that would do credit to Broadway being
staged in a barn by a group of impoverished
actors.

■ SUMMER STORY, A

1988, 95 MINS, UK/US ◇ ▽

Dir Piers Haggard *Prod* Danton Rissner
Scr Penelope Mortimer *Ph* Kenneth MacMillan
Ed Ralph Sheldon *Mus* Georges Delerue *Art Dir* Leo
Austin
● Imogen Stubbs, James Wilby, Kenneth Colley,
Sophie Ward, Susannah York (ITC)

A Summer Story is a beautifully made pastoral
romance, skillfully adapted from a John Galsworthy story, *The Apple Tree*.

Screen version is set in Devon in 1902, portraying the ill-fated romance one summer between weak-willed young barrister Ashton
(James Wilby, perfectly cast) and a lovely
country lass Megan (newcomer Imogen
Stubbs).

Holed up at a country farm on holiday due
to a sprained ankle, Ashton procrastinates,
delaying his departure due to a crush on
Megan. Shortly after they consummate the
relationship, he heads for home via the resort
at Torquay and procrastinates again, lolling
with a beautiful sister (Sophie Ward) of an
old school chum he meets there rater than
returning quickly to fetch Megan as
promised.

Stage actress Stubbs is a real find as the
heartbroken heroine, bringing a modern
strength to the period role, while Wilby is a
sympathetic version of the archetypal weak
young aristocrat.

SUMMER WISHES, WINTER DREAMS

1973, 87 MINS, US ◇ ⓥ

Dir Gilbert Cates   *Prod* Jack Brodsky   *Scr* Stewart
Stern   *Ph* Gerald Hirschfeld   *Ed* Sidney Katz
Mus Johnny Mandel   *Art Dir* Peter Dohanos
● Joanne Woodward, Martin Balsam, Sylvia Sidney,
Dori Brenner (Columbia/Rastar)

Summer Wishes, Winter Dreams begins with idle
chatter between Joanne Woodward and her
mother Sylvia Sidney about lunch and tea.
Fifteen minutes later the two are still debating whether to have broiled chicken and fritters. And 80 minutes later – long after mother
is gone with a heart attack – Woodward and
husband Martin Balsam are reminiscing
about the macaroons in Atlantic City.

After one of her routine days is interrupted
by the sudden death of mother, Woodward
takes off for Europe with Balsam. Now the
focus shifts from her woes to his as he
searches for the only place his life had drama:
28 years earlier at Bastogne. He recalls the
horror of two frightened days under attack,
staring at the bodies of three young Germans
he had killed, and the abandoned prayer he
made that he would never be ungrateful for
life if allowed to hold onto it.

Performances by Woodward, Balsam and
Sidney (her first pic in 17 years) are first-rate,
and they create genuinely tender moments.
But only those past 40 and approaching 50 or
more are likely to feel the depth.

SUMMERFIELD

1977, 95 MINS, AUSTRALIA ◇

Dir Ken Hannam   *Prod* Pat Lovell   *Scr* Cliff Green
Ph Mike Molloy   *Ed* Sarah Bennet   *Mus* Bruce
Smeaton   *Art Dir* Grace Walker
● Nick Tate, John Walters, Elizabeth Alexander,
Michelle Jarman, Charles Tingwell, Geraldine Turner
(Clare Beach)

A good-looking mystery, *Summerfield* is not
unlike an Australian version of Hitchcock's
The Birds in the opening sequences. It starts
slowly, introducing the characters while at
the same time establishing an undefined
menace in the locale – a remote island
community off the coast of Victoria.

Nick Tate is the replacement schoolteacher
– his successor has disappeared in strange
circumstances – and he unravels the intricacies of the local society. The atmosphere is
heavy with xenophobic responses by the
denizens of the area, and there is a generally
overpowering feeling of mendacity and
tightly-inbred coverup.

Gradually he picks up clues to what everybody is not talking about. And, of course,
once he starts, his curiosity gets the better of
him and impetus takes over.

SUN ALSO RISES, THE

1957, 129 MINS, US ◇

Dir Henry King   *Prod* Darryl F. Zanuck   *Scr* Peter
Viertel   *Ph* Leo Tover   *Ed* William Mace   *Mus* Hugo
Friedhofer   *Art Dir* Lyle R. Wheeler, Mark-Lee Kirk
● Tyrone Power, Ava Gardner, Mel Ferrer, Errol Flynn,
Eddie Albert, Juliette Greco (20th Century-Fox)

In undertaking the transmutation into screen
fare of the novel which first escalatored
Ernest Hemingway to renown, producer
Darryl F. Zanuck doesn't gloss over key plot
twist that Tyrone Power plays an impotent
newspaperman in frustrated love with Ava
Gardner, who plays Lady Brett Ashley. But
the script drags along their 'love affair'
instead of propelling it. Thus the yarn never
comes off either as a love story or a definitive
study of the 'lost generation'.

Performances are mixed. Power is on the
wooden side, his character never wholly
believable. Gardner turns in a far more sympathetic and credible performance. Mel

Ferrer never quite achieves the hangdog
aspect required of his role. Errol Flynn and
Eddie Albert turn in topflight characterizations as drunken members of the gambling
expatriates. Flynn registers especially well.

SUNBURN

1979, 99 MINS, US ◇ ⓥ

Dir Richard C. Sarafian   *Prod* John Daly, Gerald
Green   *Scr* John Daly   *Ph* Alex Phillips Jr   *Ed* Geoff
Foot   *Mus* John Cameron   *Art Dir* Ted Tester
● Farrah Fawcett, Charles Grodin, Art Carney, Joan
Collins, Eleanor Parker, Keenan Wynn (Paramount)

Sunburn exists for no other reason than to
provide a vehicle for Farrah Fawcett.

Confection [from the book *The Bind* by
Stanley Ellin] has Fawcett as a Gotham
model posing as Charles Grodin's wife as he
sleuths around chic Acapulco settings
investigating the mysterious death of an
industrialist on behalf of an insurance
company stuck with a $5 million claim.

Scenes devoted to real plot movement are
few and far between in script's first hour,
since Fawcett's character is mostly irrelevant
and has to be given something to do, like
being scared by a lizard entering her
bedroom.

Grodin works overtime to carry the picture
and does so marvelously, displaying a savvy
low-key comedy style. Grodin and
Joan Collins share a farcical seduction scene
that's a small comic gem.

SUNDAY BLOODY SUNDAY

1971, 110 MINS, UK ◇ ⓥ

Dir John Schlesinger   *Prod* Joseph Janni
Scr Penelope Gilliatt   *Ph* Billy Williams   *Ed* Richard
Marden   *Art Dir* Norman Dorme
● Glenda Jackson, Peter Finch, Murray Head, Peggy
Ashcroft, Maurice Denham, Vivian Pickles
(United Artists)

John Schlesinger's *Sunday Bloody Sunday* is a
low-keyed, delicately-poised recital of tri-
angular love in which Glenda Jackson and
Peter Finch share the affections of AC-DC
Murray Head. The visible sexplay, however,
is diffident, the storyline sparse. Observation
and character are all.

The story's bi-sexual triangle differs in that
it's not menage-a-trois stuff. Head goes from
one pad to the other. Scripter Penelope Gilliatt with nice economy of dialog, is herein
observing the emotional incompleteness of
people and how they try to cope.

Jackson is a career femme on the rebound
(separated from husband), Finch is a Jewish
doctor, and Head, youngest of the trio, is a
sculptor-designer oscillating between homo
and hetero affairs and career.

Sequence after vignette after sequence
larded with deft little touches, all add to this
story's cumulative message, namely that half
a loaf is often better than none.

SUNDAY IN NEW YORK

1963, 105 MINS, US ◇

Dir Peter Tewksbury   *Prod* Everett Freeman
Scr Norman Krasna   *Ph* Leo Tover   *Ed* Fredric
Steinkamp   *Mus* Peter Nero   *Art Dir* George W.
Davis, Edward Carfagno
● Cliff Robertson, Jane Fonda, Rod Taylor, Robert
Culp, Jim Backus, Jo Morrow (M-G-M)

Norman Krasna's screenplay, from his
Broadway legiter, doesn't really get rolling
until it has virtually marked time for almost
an hour, but once it gets up this head of
steam the entire complexion of the picture
seems to change.

The story has to do with the sudden arrival
at her brother's apartment in New York of an
Albany maiden (Jane Fonda) who's fretting

over that age-old puzzler – should a girl
before marriage? By now, she has alienated
herself from a well-heeled hometown beau
(Robert Culp) upon whom she had matrimonial designs. Big brother (Cliff Robertson),
an airline pilot, lauds the virtuous life, but
when sis subsequently discovers flimsy negligee in his closet, she impulsively attempts to
seduce the nearest male (Rod Taylor), a
young newspaperman.

The entire cast is equal to the challenge.
Best of the lot is Taylor, who delivers a warm,
flexible and appealing performance as the
young journalist. Fonda, showing more
becoming restraint on this outing, scores
comedically and romantically as the forward-
thinking lass. Robertson is convincing and
chips in some highly amusing reactions as her
generally befuddled pilot-brother.

SUNDAY TOO FAR AWAY

1975, 90 MINS, AUSTRALIA ◇

Dir Ken Hannam   *Scr* John Dingwall   *Ph* Geoffrey
Burton
● Jack Thompson, Max Cullen, Reg Lye, John Ewart
(SAFC)

Sheep shearers are journeymen who go about
to the sheep farms, and, through a contractor, skim off the wool in backbreaking, dreary
work. This, of course, leads to a sort of rivalry
to remove some of the strain.

Foley (Jack Thompson) is a solid chap who
would like to quit after his present job. But
apparently that is not to be. The cutting of
prices for shearers leads to a strike after the
odyssey of their last contract. They finally
win it.

Pic may have resemblances to oaters in its
place and hardbitten characters, the brawls
and the landscapes. But this has a directorial
ease that gets over a rather flat intro to create
an extraordinary insight into men at work.

SUNDOWN

1941, 90 MINS, US ⓥ

Dir Henry Hathaway   *Prod* Walter Wanger   *Scr* Barre
Lyndon   *Ph* Charles Lang   *Ed* Dorothy Spencer
Mus Miklos Rozsa
● Gene Tierney, Bruce Cabot, George Sanders, Carl
Esmond, Cedric Hardwicke, Dorothy Dandrige
(United Artists)

An adventurous melodrama, unfolded in a
colonial outpost of British East Africa, *Sundown* is an interesting tale of its type. Locale is
cinematically fresh, the Kenya country near
the Abyssinian border. Barre Lyndon's
screenplay of own *SatEvePost* story neatly
mixes informative material of conditions with
interesting drama of conditions on East African front; while Henry Hathaway directs in
straight line to hold audience attention, and
accentuate the dramatic highlights en route.

Story details the British administration of
colonies, and the far-reaching efforts of Nazi
agents to foment native uprisings against the
British. Bruce Cabot is local commissioner of
Manieka, being joined by army officer
George Sanders, who is detailed to uncover
gun-running plot to natives. Carl Esmond,
secret Nazi agent, arrives posing as mining
engineer; also Gene Tierney, operator of
large caravans and network of native trading
posts.

SUNDOWNERS, THE

1950, 65 MINS, US ◇ ⓥ

Dir George Templeton   *Prod* Alan LeMay   *Scr* Alan
LeMay   *Ph* Winton C. Hoch   *Ed* Jack Ogilvie   *Mus* Al
Colombo
● Robert Preston, Robert Sterling, Chill Wills, John Litel,
Cathy Downs, John Barrymore Jr (Eagle Lion/LeMay-
Templeton)

Story pits brother against brother to bring to a conclusion its account of a feud between rival cattlemen. Before that finale, tension is kept alive by cattle raids, gun battles and the constant fight of wills between a brother trying to carve a ranch and home from his section of Texas land and an older brother who dominates.

Interesting is the film debut of John Barrymore Jr. He does well by his role of a kid who idolizes his bad, eldest brother but is held in line by the middle kin (Robert Sterling). Latter makes his footage count. Robert Preston gets his teeth into the colorful role of the daring, dashing eldest member of the Cloud family, and will be liked despite his bad ways.

....

■ **SUNDOWNERS, THE**

1960, 133 MINS, US ◇ ▼

Dir Fred Zinnemann *Prod* Fred Zinnemann
Scr Isobel Lennart *Ph* Jack Hildyard *Ed* Jack Harris
Mus Dimitri Tiomkin *Art Dir* Michael Stringer
● Deborah Kerr, Robert Mitchum, Peter Ustinov, Glynis Johns, Dina Merrill, Chips Rafferty (Warner)

Jon Cleary's novel is the basic source from which director Fred Zinnemann's inspiration springs. Between Cleary and Zinnemann lies Isobel Lennart's perceptive, virile screenplay, loaded with bright, telling lines of dialog and gentle philosophical comment. But, fine as the scenario is, it is Zinnemann's poetic glances into the souls of his characters, little hints of deep longings, hidden despairs, indomitable spirit that make the picture the achievement it is.

On paper, the story sounds something short of fascinating. It tells of a 1920s Irish-Australian sheepdrover (Robert Mitchum) whose fondness for the freedom of an itinerant existence clashes with the fervent hope of settling-down shared by his wife (Deborah Kerr) and his son (Michael Anderson Jr). The wife, in an effort to raise funds for a down-payment on a farm, persuades her husband to accept stationary employment as a shearer.

Mitchum's rugged masculinity is right for the part. There are moments when he projects a great deal of feeling with what appears to be a minimum of effort. Kerr gives a luminous and penetrating portrayal of the faithful wife, rugged pioneer stock on the outside, wistful and feminine within. There is one fleetingly eloquent scene at a train station, in which her eyes meet those of an elegant lady traveller, that ranks as one of the most memorable moments ever to cross a screen.

Peter Ustinov, as a whimsical, learned bachelor who joins the family and slowly evolves into its 'household pet,' gives a robust, rollicking performance. Glynis Johns is a vivacious delight as a hotelkeeper who sets her sights on matrimonially-evasive Ustinov.

Art, photographic and technical skills are extremely well represented by the craftsmen assembled in the bush country of Australia and at Elstree Studios in London.

□ 1960: Best Picture (Nomination)

....

■ **SUNRISE**

1927, 95 MINS, US ⊗

Dir F.W. Murnau *Scr* Carl Mayer, Katherine Hilliker, H.H. Caldwell *Ph* Charles Rosher, Karl Struss
Ed Katherine Hilliker, H.H. Caldwell, Harold Schuster
Mus Hugo Riesenfeld *Art Dir* Rochus Gliese
● George O'Brien, Janet Gaynor, Margaret Livingston (Fox)

Sunrise is a distinguished contribution to the screen, made in this country, but produced after the best manner of the German school. In its artistry, dramatic power and graphic suggestion it goes a long way toward realizing the promise of this foreign director in his former works, notably *Faust*.

What director F.W. Murnau has tried to do is to crystallize in dramatic symbolism those conflicts, adjustments, compromises and complexities of man-and-woman mating experiences that ultimately grow into an endearing union.

Many elements enter into the success of this ambitious effort. Murnau reveals a remarkable resourcefulness of effects; the playing of George O'Brien and Janet Gaynor and their associates is generally convincing.

The incidental music blends smoothly, suggesting the mood of the scene, but without intruding into the conscientiousness. In many scenes (honking autos, when dreaming lovers block a street, is a case in point) sound effects are introduced. This has been managed with skill.

All these things lay upon a story [by Herman Sadermann] as simple as it is human. The Woman from the City snares a young farmer. Under her hypnotism he listens to a plan to drown the young wife, sell the farm and go off to the city.

....

■ **SUNRISE AT CAMPOBELLO**

1960, 144 MINS, US ▼

Dir Vincent J. Donehue *Prod* Dore Schary *Scr* Dore Schary *Ph* Russell Harlan *Ed* George Boemler
Mus Franz Waxman
● Ralph Bellamy, Greer Garson, Hume Cronyn, Jean Hagen, Ann Shoemaker, Tim Considine (Warner)

In the journey from stage to screen this chapter from the life of Franklin Delano Roosevelt loses none of its poignant and inspirational qualities, none of its humor and pathos. Dore Schary, as author-producer of the play and the film, can take just pride in this grandslam feat. And this satisfaction is to be shared also by Ralph Bellamy, whose brilliant portrayal of Roosevelt, and Vincent J. Donehue, the director, clicked so resoundingly on Broadway.

The period is 1921, when polio shatters a joyous family vacation on the island retreat of Campobello, to 1924, when Roosevelt re-emerged in public to put in Al Smith's name as a presidential hopeful at the Democratic convention and in the process, lit his own political star.

Campobello opened a new career for Schary as a playwright in 1958, shortly after he exited as production head of M-G-M. The film is also a brilliant new showcase for Greer Garson. She comes through as Eleanor Roosevelt with a deeply moving, multifaceted characterization.

There is a third tower of strength in the person of Hume Cronyn as Louis Howe, the wizened, asthmatic, devoted friend and political Svengali to Roosevelt. There is, considering the sober nature of the subject, a surprising amount of humor in *Campobello* and a good measure of it is deftly generated by Cronyn.

Franz Waxman's score makes a big contribution, notably to the convention sequence. Pic begins with an overture, about eight minutes, of melodious oldtimers.

....

■ **SUNSET**

1988, 106 MINS, US ◇ ▼

Dir Blake Edwards *Prod* Tony Adams *Scr* Blake Edwards *Ph* Anthony B. Richmond *Ed* Robert Pergament *Mus* Henry Mancini *Art Dir* Rodger Maus
● Bruce Willis, James Garner, Malcolm McDowell, Mariel Hemingway, Kathleen Quinlan, Jennifer Edward (Hudson Hawk/Tri-Star)

Sunset is a silly Hollywood fiction, unconvincing in all but a couple of its details. Premise of teaming up righteous cowboy star Tom Mix and real-life lawman Wyatt Earp to solve an actual murder case may have looked good on paper, but it plays neither amusingly nor excitingly.

Despite the tough guy charm he has exhibited elsewhere, Bruce Willis is one of the least likely choices imaginable to play Mix, perhaps the top Western star of the 1920s.

That's just the beginning of the film's lack of plausibility, even on its own terms. The notion of English, Chaplin-like former star (Malcolm McDowell) becoming the venal head of a studio bears no resemblance to anything that ever occurred in Hollywood while the idea of multiple murders taking place at the first Academy Awards ceremony is nasty and far-fetched.

Fortunately, there is James Garner as Earp as relief from all the nonsense around him. In fact, the man from Tombstone seems a little too sophisticated and at ease in Tinseltown, but the actor's natural charm and fine sense of one-upmanship wins the day in virtually all his scenes.

....

■ **SUNSET BLVD.**

1950, 110 MINS, US

Dir Billy Wilder *Prod* Charles Brackett *Scr* Charles Brackett, Billy Wilder, D.M. Marshman Jr *Ph* John F. Seitz *Ed* Arthur Schmidt *Mus* Franz Waxman
● William Holden, Gloria Swanson, Erich von Stroheim, Nancy Olson, Cecil B. DeMille, Buster Keaton (Paramount)

Sunset Blvd. is a backstage melodrama using a filmland, instead of a legit, locale. It is tied in with a pseudo-expose of Hollywood.

The expose of the land of the swimming pool opens with a shot of a dead man floating in the plunge of a Beverly Hills mansion. The voice of the dead man then narrates the story, going back six months to explain why he eventually reached such a sorry state. He is a young writer with a few minor credits and many creditors.

He finds refuge in what he believes to be an abandoned mansion. It is occupied by a former great femme star. She takes a fancy to the young man, employs him to write a script that will return her to past glory. The association segues into an affair.

Performances by the entire cast, and particularly William Holden and Gloria Swanson, are exceptionally fine. Swanson, returning to the screen after a very long absence, socks hard with a silent-day technique to put over the decaying star she is called upon to portray. Erich von Stroheim, as her butler and original discoverer, delivers with excellent restraint.

The other performer rating more than a mention is Cecil B. DeMille. He plays himself with complete assurance in one of the few sympathetic roles.

□ 1950: Best Picture (Nomination)

....

■ **SUNSHINE BOYS, THE**

1975, 111 MINS, US ◇

Dir Herbert Ross *Prod* Ray Stark *Scr* Neil Simon
Ph David M. Walsh *Ed* Margaret Booth, John F. Burnett *Mus* Harry V. Lojewski (sup.) *Art Dir* Albert Brenner
● Walter Mathau, George Burns, Richard Benjamin, Lee Meredith, Carol Arthur, Rosetta Le Noire (M-G-M)

The Sunshine Boys is an extremely sensitive and lovable film version of Neil Simon's play, with Walter Matthau and George Burns outstanding in their starring roles as a pair of long-hostile vaudeville partners.

Matthau, with some complex makeup artistry atop his own brilliant talent, gives the Willy Clark character its full dimension of rascality, stubborness, heart, pride and, eventually, humility. Burns, returning to pix, provides in his standout performance the right complementing aspects to the pair's love-hate relationship spanning 43 years.

Richard Benjamin, the nephew-agent who is the catalyst of their reconciliation, serves to ventilate audience responses to the principals' behavior while simultaneously creating an independent characterization all his own.

Apart from the incidental title music, there is no score, which seems the proper decision. Matthau, Burns, Benjamin and the story need no musical accent.

● ●

■ SUPERFLY

1972, 96 MINS, US ◇ ▼

Dir Gordon Parks Jr   *Prod* Sig Shore   *Scr* Phillip Fenty   *Ph* James Signorelli   *Ed* Bob Brady   *Mus* Curtis Mayfield

● Ron O'Neal, Carl Lee, Sheila Frazier, Julius W. Harris, Charles McGregor, Nate Adams (Warner)

Best that can be said for this quickie is its unpretentiousness in not seeking any pseudo-sociological meaning or theme, or assuming any airs that one is supposed to be enriched or provoked by it all. It's strictly action-adventure, alternating, like clockwork, drugs-sex-violence for its duration with hardly a plot line to hold it together.

Cast handles the simple characterizations adequately, with Ron O'Neal heading as Superfly, sluggin', lovin', needlin' and philosophizing his way through the tale of the pusher with heart of gold, wanting to get out – but only after making his easy $1 million. Supporting convincingly are Carl Lee, Julius W. Harris as Scatter and Charles McGregor as Fat Freddie.

Sheila Frazier and Polly Niles offer the sex interests, including a breast or two when things get otherwise dull.

● ●

■ SUPERGIRL

1984, 114 MINS, UK ◇ ▼

Dir Jeannot Szwarc   *Prod* Timothy Burrill   *Scr* David Odell   *Ph* Alan Hume   *Ed* Malcolm Cooke   *Mus* Jerry Goldsmith   *Art Dir* Richard Macdonald

● Faye Dunaway, Helen Slater, Peter O'Toole, Peter Cook, Brenda Vaccaro, Mia Farrow (Artistry/Cantharus)

Supergirl is Kara, Superman's cousin, who journeys from her home on the planet of Argo to Earth to recover the missing Omegahedron Stone, life-force of her world, which has fallen into the clutches of the evil Selena (Faye Dunaway), a power-hungry sorceress.

Landing near an exclusive boarding school for young ladies, Kara quickly adopts the name of Linda Lee and finds herself rooming with Lois Lane's kid sister, Lucy (Maureen Teefy).

Rest of pic represents a struggle between the good of Supergirl and the evil of Selena with, as is usually the case, evil being a lot more fun.

Dunaway has a ball as Selena, and her enjoyably over-the-top handling of the part could merit cult attention. She's ably backed by Brenda Vaccaro as her incredulous assistant, and Peter Cook as her sometime lover and math teacher at the girls' school.

Peter O'Toole makes a modest impression as Supergirl's friend and mentor, while Mia Farrow and Simon Ward, as her parents, have even smaller roles than Susannah York and Marlon Brando in the first *Superman*.

Helen Slater is a find: blonde as Supergirl, dark-haired as Linda Lee, she's an appealing young heroine in either guise. Screenplay is filled with witty lines and enjoyable characters, but Jeannot Szwarc's direction is rather flat.

● ●

■ SUPERMAN

1978, 143 MINS, US ◇ ▼

Dir Richard Donner   *Prod* Pierre Spengler   *Scr* Mario Puzo, David Newman, Leslie Newman, Robert Benton   *Ph* Geoffrey Unsworth   *Ed* Stuart Baird   *Mus* John Williams   *Art Dir* John Barry

● Marlon Brando, Gene Hackman, Christopher Reeve, Margot Kidder, Ned Beatty, Glenn Ford (Warner/Salkind)

Magnify James Bond's extraordinary physical powers while curbing his sex drive and you have the essence of *Superman*, a wonderful, chuckling, preposterously exciting fantasy.

Forget Marlon Brando who tops the credits. As Superman's father on the doomed planet Krypton, Brando is good but unremarkable.

As both the wholesome man of steel and his bumbling secret identity Clark Kent, Christopher Reeve is excellent. As newswoman Lois Lane, Margot Kidder plays perfectly off both of his personalities.

Tracing the familiar cartoon genesis, film opens with spectacular outer-space effects and the presentation of life on Krypton where nobody believes Papa Brando's warnings of doom. So he and wife Susannah York ship their baby son on his way to Earth.

Striking terra firma, the baby is found by Glenn Ford and Phyllis Thaxter who take him for their own. But the time must ultimately come when Superman's powers for good are revealed to the world and his debut becomes a wild night, beginning with Lane's rescue from a skyscraper, the capture of assorted burglars and the salvation of the president's airplane.

Lurking in wacky palatial splendor in the sewers beneath Park Ave, supercriminal Gene Hackman views this caped arrival as a superthreat befitting his evil genius.

● ●

■ SUPERMAN II

1981, 127 MINS, UK ◇ ▼

Dir Richard Lester   *Prod* Pierre Spengler   *Scr* Mario Puzo, David Newman, Leslie Newman   *Ph* Geoffrey Unsworth, Robert Paynter   *Ed* John Victor-Smith   *Mus* Ken Thorne   *Art Dir* John Barry, Peter Murton

● Christopher Reeve, Gene Hackman, Margot Kidder, Ned Beatty, Terence Stamp, Sarah Douglas (International/Salkind)

For all the production halts, setbacks, personnel changeovers and legal wrangling that paved its way to the screen, *Superman II* emerges as a solid, classy, cannily constructed piece of entertainment which gets down to action almost immediately.

Although original plans called for lensing the first two *Superman* features simultaneously, the sequel is reportedly 80% newly shot footage.

The film does an especially good job of picking up the strings of unexplored characters and plot seeds left dangling from the first pic, taking its core plot from the three Kryptonian villains – Terence Stamp, Jack O'Halloran and Sarah Douglas – briefly glimpsed in the first pic. Here, they're liberated from perpetual imprisonment in a bizarre time-warp by an H-bomb explosion in outer space.

The film builds quickly to a climactic battle between Christopher Reeve and the three supervillains in mid-town Manhatten.

● ●

■ SUPERMAN III

1983, 123 MINS, UK ◇ ▼

Dir Richard Lester   *Prod* Pierre Spengler   *Scr* David Newman, Leslie Newman   *Ph* Robert Paynter   *Ed* John Victor Smith   *Mus* Ken Thorne   *Art Dir* Peter Murton

● Christopher Reeve, Richard Pryor, Robert Vaughn, Annette O'Toole, Annie Ross, Margot Kidder (Salkind/Dovemead)

Superman III emerges as a surprisingly soft-cored disappointment. Putting its emphasis on broad comedy at the expense of ingenious plotting and technical wizardry, it has

virtually none of the mythic or cosmic sensibility that marked its predecessors.

The film begins with a hilarious pre-credits sequence in which Richard Pryor, an unemployed 'kitchen technician', decides to embark on a career as a computer programmer. Robert Vaughn, a crooked megalomaniac intent on taking over the world economy, dispatches Pryor to a small company subsid in Smallville, where he programs a weather satellite to destroy Colombia's coffee crop (and make a market-cornering killing for Vaughn).

Foiled by Superman (Christopher Reeve), Pryor uses the computer to concoct an imperfect form of Kryptonite – using cigarette tar to round out the formula. The screenplay opts for the novelty of using the Kryptonite to split the Clark Kent/Superman persona into two bodies, good and evil.

Most of the action relies on explosive pyrotechnics and careening stuntpersons. At the romantic level, the film does paint a nice relationship between Reeve (as Kent) and his onetime crush Annette O'Toole.

● ●

■ SUPERMAN IV
THE QUEST FOR PEACE

1987, 89 MINS, US ◇ ▼

Dir Sidney J. Furie   *Prod* Menahem Golan, Yoram Globus   *Scr* Lawrence Konner, Mark Rosenthal   *Ph* Ernest Day   *Ed* John Shirley   *Mus* John Williams   *Art Dir* John Graysmark

● Christopher Reeve, Gene Hackman, Jackie Cooper, Mariel Hemingway, Jon Cryer, Margot Kidder (Cannon/Warner)

Opening sequence shows Superman has picked up the spirit of glasnost as he flies into space to rescue an imperiled cosmonaut and utters his first lines of the picture in Russian.

Superman's newly assumed mission sees him addressing the United Nations to tell the world he personally is going to remove all nuclear weapons from the face of the earth.

Meanwhile, Lex Luthor (Gene Hackman) has created an evil clone of Superman called Nuclear Man, who wreaks havoc with famous landmarks around the world and does savage battle with the hero on the face of the moon until Superman discovers his nemesis' single flaw.

The earlier films in the series were far from perfect, but at their best they had some flair and agreeable humor, qualities this one sorely lacks. Hackman gets a few laughs, but has less to work with than before, and everyone else seems to be just going through the motions and having less fun doing so.

● ●

■ SUPERVIXENS

1975, 105 MINS, US ◇

Dir Russ Meyer   *Prod* Russ Meyer   *Scr* Russ Meyer   *Ph* Russ Meyer   *Ed* Russ Meyer   *Mus* William Loose   *Art Dir* Michael Levesque

● Shari Eubank, Charles Pitts, Charles Napier, Uschi Digard, Henry Rowland, Christy Hartburg (September 19)

Russ Meyer's *Supervixens* is an overlong and overly violent skin pic whose interest lies in its pretentions to be more than a skin film.

The story involves a gas-station attendant, Clint (Charles Pitts) whose foul-mouthed girlfriend is, successively stabbed, beaten, drowned and electrocuted by a brutish cop (Charles Napier) with Clint getting the blame. Fleeing town, he has sexual encounters with a succession of busty amazons, then falls for Supervixen (Shari Eubank) whom he must eventually rescue from a sick cop (Napier again). It's all very low on camp and high on blood.

The film is technically slick and the acting is competent.

● ●

■ SUPPORT YOUR LOCAL GUNFIGHTER

1971, 92 MINS, US ◇

Dir Burt Kennedy   *Prod* Bill Finnegan   *Scr* James
Edward Grant   *Ph* Harry Stradling   *Ed* Bill Gulick
Mus Jack Elliot, Allyn Ferguson   *Art Dir* Phil Barber
● James Garner, Suzanne Pleshette, Jack Elam, Joan
Blondell , Harry Morgan, Marie Windsor
(Cherokee/Brigade)

Burt Kennedy's follow-up to *Support Your
Local Sheriff* has James Garner escaping from
the clutches of Marie Windsor, only to
become mistaken by competing mine-owners
Harry Morgan and John Dehner for a hired
gun, played in finale cameo by Chuck Connors. Jack Elam again is excellent in role of a
befuddled but willing accomplice to Garner's
maneuvers. Joan Blondell is good as a
bordello queen, and Henry Jones scores as a
nosy gossip.

Suzanne Pleshette starts out a bit too strong
as a tom-boy, but eventually settles in. There
are a few hefty laughs, many chuckles, a few
smiles, and some cold gags.

A.D. Flowers' special explosive effects
punch up some of the action sequences, and
Elam's curtain-narration speech, where he
describes how he went on to become a big
star of Italian westerns, brings the 92 minutes
to a good finish.

■ SUPPORT YOUR LOCAL SHERIFF

1969, 96 MINS, US ◇ Ⓥ

Dir Burt Kennedy   *Prod* William Bowers   *Scr* William
Bowers   *Ph* Harry Stradling   *Ed* George Brooks
Mus Jeff Alexander   *Art Dir* Leroy Coleman
● James Garner, James Hackett, Walter Brennan,
Harry Morgan, Jack Elam, Bruce Dern (United Artists/
Cherokee)

Support Your Local Sheriff uses as the basis for
its comedy the many cliches that have
become part and parcel of the Western genre.

Whether it's the town dominated by a tyrant, the never-missing gunfighter, the absolutely pure hero, the chaste but unchased
maiden, the growth of the territory – they're
all dealt with and done under, by demolishing dialogue or just enough exaggeration to
point up the ridiculous in even the most respectable circumstances.

James Garner is delightful as the 'stranger'
riding into town on his way to Australia, so
modest, yet so perfect in his various abilities –
never missing a shot, turning the town derelict into his deputy, outthinking the Danbys (a
superb quartet of villains) outwitting the
attempts of the mayor's daughter to land him
until he's ready.

The action almost never moves beyond the
tiny town's limits, and the community itself
seems just enough exaggerated to let the
audience know that it's not to be taken
seriously.

■ SUPPOSE THEY GAVE A WAR AND NOBODY CAME?

1970, 113 MINS, US ◇ Ⓥ

Dir Hy Averback   *Prod* Fred Engel   *Scr* Don McGuire,
Hal Captain   *Ph* Burnett Guffey   *Ed* John F. Brunett
Mus Jerry Fielding   *Art Dir* Jack Poplin
● Brian Keith, Tony Curtis, Ernest Borgnine, Ivan Dixon,
Suzanne Pleshette, Tom Ewell (ABC)

A meandering comedy about three old-time
army tankmen in a non-combatant missile
base at war with the southern redneck town
in which it is located.

Main problem is that Hy Averback's direction and the screenplay, both of which have
their moments, never focus and decide if it is
a comedy, serious drama or farce.

Ernest Borgnine is the heavy-handed
southern sheriff. Tony Curtis keeps it light-
hearted, but nevertheless convincing, as 'a
middle-aged, paunchy garrison soldier who
thinks he is Warren Beatty'.

Suzanne Pleshette, a wise-cracking, self-
proclaimed 'beer hustler', is very real, and
her handling of tough snappy dialog makes
her appearances some of the best scenes in
the film, especially in those with Curtis.

■ SURVIVORS, THE

1983, 102 MINS, US ◇ Ⓥ

Dir Michael Ritchie   *Prod* William Sackheim
Scr Michael Leeson   *Ph* Billy Williams   *Ed* Richard A.
Harris   *Mus* Paul Chihara   *Art Dir* Gene Callahan
● Walter Matthau, Robin Williams, Jerry Reed, James
Wainwright, Kristen Vigard, Annie McEnroe
(Delphi/Rastar)

An aimless, unfocused social comedy, *The
Survivors* misfires on just about every level,
finding what laughs it has to offer solely in
the personal performing talents of Walter
Matthau and Robin Williams.

Exec Williams and gas station owner
Matthau both become unemployed at the
outset, and through a bizarre coincidence are
thrown together as intended victims of
professional hitman Jerry Reed.

Confronted with the threat of another
attack by Reed, Williams becomes a
maniacal gun enthusiast and joins a survival
training unit run in the snowy mountains by
James Wainwright.

It feels as though the script, such as it was,
was tossed out the window once action moves
to the New Hampshire compound. All of
Williams' dialog from this point on sounds
like lifts from crazed comic monologs he
might deliver onstage. Matthau at least
makes things watchable thanks to his
masterful comic timing.

■ SUSAN LENOX
HER FALL AND RISE

1931, 75 MINS, US

Dir Robert Z. Leonard   *Scr* Wanda Tuchock, Zelda
Sears, Leon Gordon, Edith Fitzgerald   *Ph* William
Daniels   *Ed* Margaret Booth
● Greta Garbo, Clark Gable, Jean Hersholt, John
Miljan, Alan Hale (M-G-M)

Not the least of this film's assets is the title,
carrying the prestige of a novel that was a
sensation upon its publication. What David
Graham Phillips wrote as a protest against
narrow-minded respectability has evolved in
the filming into a hot romance based on sexual antagonism.

The picture provides Greta Garbo with a
role of destiny-hounded woman, not altogether unlike her Anna Christie, and adds to
the Garbo gallery another impressive
portrait.

The Garbo Susan is a glamorous figure, a
vital Swedish immigrant girl who flees her
ignorant, self-righteous foster parents in a
raging storm to take refuge with a prepossess-
ing young engineer (Clark Gable). The
young pair fall in love. Out of the curious sexual antagonism that seems to be generated by
their passion she goes her errant way to
become a famous courtesan, while he sinks
from bad to worse to the finality of a South
Seas beachcomber.

Teaming with the great Garbo, of course,
marks the peak of Gable's vogue. He appears
to excellent purpose here, playing with agreeable urbanity and giving a performance that
blends effectively into the whole atmosphere.

■ SUSAN SLADE

1961, 116 MINS, US ◇

Dir Delmer Daves   *Prod* Delmer Daves   *Scr* Delmer
Daves   *Ph* Lucien Ballard   *Ed* William Ziegler
Mus Max Steiner   *Art Dir* Leo K. Kuter
● Troy Donahue, Connie Stevens, Dorothy McGuire,
Lloyd Nolan, Bert Convy (Warner)

Susan Slade, though slickly produced and attractively peopled, weighs in as little more
than a plodding and predictable soap opera.
It is, however, a telling showcase for Connie
Stevens.

The screenplay by Delmer Daves, who also
produced and directed as is his custom, is
from the novel by Doris Hume. Yarn has a
chicken way of evading its real issues by ush-
ering in devastatingly convenient melodramatic swerves at key moments.

Stevens enacts the innocent, virginal
daughter of a devoted family man and engineer (Lloyd Nolan) who returns with his brood
to luxury in the States after 10 years of service
on a project in remote Chile. The girl
promptly falls madly in love and finds herself
with child but without husband.

The family then tries a fake by moving to
Guatemala, where Nolan dies and his wife
(Dorothy McGuire) supposedly bears the
child. The story returns to the US and boils
down to the inevitable triangle. Who is
worthy of Stevens' love – junior tycoon Bert
Convy or poor stable operator Troy
Donahue?

Pretty Stevens comes on like gangbusters,
and Lucien Ballard's misty, flattering
close-up photography is her ally from start to
finish. Donahue gives a wooden performance.
Veterans Nolan and McGuire emote with
sincerity.

The film was lensed in dazzlingly scenic
places such as the Carmel coastline and San
Francisco.

■ SUSPECT

1987, 121 MINS, US ◇ Ⓥ

Dir Peter Yates   *Prod* Daniel A. Sherkow   *Scr* Eric
Roth   *Ph* Billy Williams   *Ed* Ray Lovejoy
Mus Michael Kamen   *Art Dir* Stuart Wurtzel
● Cher, Dennis Quaid, Liam Neeson, John Mahoney,
Joe Mantegna (Tri-Star)

Art imitates art – and not very well – in Peter
Yates' gimmicky suspense drama sabotaged
by a flimsy script full of cliches. Dennis
Quaid valiantly struggles to breathe life into
the matter, but comes up short when a surprise ending packs little punch because the
audience knows in the first five minutes the
prime suspect can't be guilty.

Cher stars as Kathleen Riley, a hard-working Washington, DC public defender unlike
any ever seen before. A day before taking a
long-needed vacation, she's given a defendant charged with the brutal murder of a Justice Dept staffer. Carl Wayne Anderson
(Liam Neeson) has everything working
against him: a Vietnam vet, he was rendered
deaf and speechless by the psychological toll
of the war, and he's homeless – he *has* to be
innocent.

Just when it seems the entire film is going to
be suffocated by liberal piety, Quaid shows
up as Dairy State lobbyist Eddie Sanger, so
persuasive that he's 'dangerous'. Sanger is
called in for jury duty and sparks begin to fly
when he faces off against Cher in the courtroom. Scenes with the two of them are the
best in the film, but there aren't enough.

■ SUSPICION

1941, 102 MINS, US Ⓥ

Dir Alfred Hitchcock   *Prod* Alfred Hitchcock
Scr Samson Raphaelson, Joan Harrison, Alma Reville
Ph Harry Stradling   *Ed* William Hamilton   *Mus* Franz
Waxman   *Art Dir* Van Nest Polglase
● Cary Grant, Joan Fontaine, Cedric Hardwicke, Nigel
Bruce, May Whitty, Isabel Jeans (RKO)

Alfred Hitchcock's trademarked cinematic
development of suspenseful drama, through
mental emotions of the story principals, is
vividly displayed in *Suspicion*, a class production [from the novel *Before the Fact* by

S

Francis Iles] provided with excellence in direction, acting and mounting.

Joan Fontaine successfully transposes to the screen her innermost emotions and fears over the wastrel and apparently-murderous antics of her husband. Cary Grant, turns in a sparkling characterization as the bounder who continually discounts financial responsibilities and finally gets jammed over thefts from his employer.

Unfolded at a leisurely pace, Hitchcock deftly displays the effect of occurrences on the inner emotions of the wife. Protected girl of an English country manor, Fontaine falls in love and elopes with Grant, an impecunious and happy-go-lucky individual, who figured her family would amply provide for both of them. Deeply in love, she overlooks his monetary irresponsibilities until discovery that he has stolen a large sum from an estate, and prosecution and exposure looms.

☐ 1942: Best Picture (Nomination)

· ·

■ SVENGALI

1931, 79 MINS, US ⊛
Dir Archie Mayo   *Scr* J.G. Alexander   *Ph* Barney McGill
● John Barrymore, Marian Marsh, Bramwell Fletcher, Donald Crisp, Lumsden Hare, Carmel Myers (Warner)

Formerly well known as *Trilby* via famed novel [by George Du Maurier] and stage interpretations, the studio renamed it to designate the villainous hypnotist as the leading character.

Story, of course, is well known, but Svengali (John Barrymore) here makes it clear that Trilby (Marian Marsh), the model has been the house guest of several artists so that her desire to become legally attached to the pursuing young Englishman is not going to be without family difficulties. He hypnotizes her into running away with him and also into a career as a concert star.

Barrymore's playing is interesting, sterling and in broad strokes. Marsh takes a change for the better on looks in the late footage, but flashes nothing unusual histrionically.

· ·

■ SWALLOWS AND AMAZONS

1974, 92 MINS, UK ◇ ⊛
Dir Claude Whatham   *Prod* Richard Pilbrow   *Scr* David Wood   *Ph* Denis Lewiston   *Ed* Michael Bradsell   *Mus* Wilfred Josephs   *Art Dir* Simon Holland
● Virginia McKenna, Ronald Fraser, Brenda Bruce, Jack Woolgar, John Franklyn-Robbins, Simon West (EMI/Theatre Projects)

This charming, delightful, beautifully-made film for both adults and children is faithfully based on the 1929 children's classic by Arthur Ransome. In the deft screenplay by David Wood, the essential plot involving four children (the Swallows) on holiday in the Lake District, and their friendly rivalry with two tomboy girls (the Amazons) is simple but absorbing, and captures the spirit of the period.

Their activities take place on and around the water, with the picturesque landscape caught in pastel shades by Denis Lewiston. Virginia McKenna and Ronald Fraser are seen briefly but register well, especially Fraser as the peppery but sympathetic uncle, living on a houseboat. The main burden is carried by the child actors, who all enter into the spirit of the proceedings with naturalness and enthusiasm.

· ·

■ SWAN, THE

1956, 107 MINS, US ◇
Dir Charles Vidor   *Prod* Dore Schary   *Scr* John Dighton   *Ph* Joseph Ruttenberg, Robert Surtees   *Ed* John Dunning   *Mus* Bronislau Kaper
● Grace Kelly, Alec Guinness, Louis Jourdan, Agnes Moorehead, Jessie Royce Landis, Brian Aherne (M-G-M)

Delightful make-believe of Ferenc Molnar's venerable play *The Swan* makes for a genteel picture about genteel people in a never-never world of crowns, titles and luxury living. There's subtle humor and broad humor, and several scenes that reach right into the heart.

Costarring with Grace Kelly is Alec Guinness, who adds the correct, modified comedy touch to his role of the crown prince who, regardless of what audiences might want, must end up with the princess, and Louis Jourdan, who adds a feeling romantic flavor to his character of the commoner-tutor who dares to love the princess. Kelly shines right along with her male stars as the princess.

A standout romantic sequence occurs during a ball welcoming the crown prince. The tutor and Kelly fall in love right before your eyes as they dance to 'The Swan Waltz'.

Abetting the star trio with sock support in featured roles are Jessie Royce Landis, Kelly's mother; Brian Aherne, as the monk; Estelle Winwood, the pixilated, not-bright old maid sister of Landis and Agnes Moorehead, the strident queen mother.

· ·

■ SWARM, THE

1978, 116 MINS, US ◇ ⊛
Dir Irwin Allen   *Prod* Irwin Allen   *Scr* Stirling Silliphant   *Ph* Fred J. Koenekamp   *Ed* Harold F. Kress   *Mus* Jerry Goldsmith   *Art Dir* Stan Jolley
● Michael Caine, Katharine Ross, Richard Widmark, Richard Chamberlain, Olivia de Havilland, Ben Johnson (Warner)

Killer bees periodically interrupt the arch writing, stilted direction and ludicrous acting in Irwin Allen's disappointing and tired non-thriller.

Stirling Silliphant gets writing credit, based on an Arthur Herzog novel. It's the kind of screenplay where characters who supposedly are familiar with certain technical work spend most of their time explaining it to each other.

Then there's the sub-plot romance between schoolmarm Olivia de Havilland (with the worst phony southern accent imaginable) and either Fred MacMurray or Ben Johnson.

Michael Caine heads the cast as a scientist who must contend with killer bees as well as with Richard Widmark, once again playing one of those cardboard military officers. Lots of other familiar names crop up.

Allen was smarter on *The Towering Inferno* to have a partner handling the dramatic sequences. By the time the bees get to Houston, and the city is torched, few will care.

· ·

■ SWASHBUCKLER

1976, 101 MINS, US ◇
Dir James Goldstone   *Prod* Jennings Lang   *Scr* Jeffrey Bloom   *Ph* Philip Lathrop   *Ed* Edward A. Biery   *Mus* John Addison   *Art Dir* John Lloyd
● Robert Shaw, James Earl Jones, Peter Boyle, Genevieve Bujold, Beau Bridges, Anjelica Huston (Universal)

An uneven picture which is splotchy in the form it tries to emulate, and vacuous in the substance.

Jeffrey Bloom is given sole screenplay credit and Paul Wheeler sole story credit, for the coloring-book plot and formula characters as follows: genial lead pirates, Robert Shaw and James Earl Jones; wicked colonial governor, Peter Boyle; wronged noblelady, Genevieve Bujold; wronged noblelady's noble father, Bernard Behrens; and foppish soldier, Beau Bridges.

There's no sincerity in *Swashbuckler*. There's not even a consistent approach. This tacky

pastepot job can't make up its mind whether it is serious, tongue-in-cheek, satirical, slap-stick, burlesque, parody or travesty; but be assured it's all of the above.

· ·

■ SWEENEY!

1977, 97 MINS, UK ◇ ⊛
Dir David Wickes   *Prod* Ted Childs   *Scr* Ranald Graham   *Ph* Dusty Miller   *Ed* Chris Burt   *Mus* Denis King   *Art Dir* Bill Alexander
● John Thaw, Dennis Waterman, Barry Foster, Ian Bannen, Colin Welland, Diane Keen (Euston)

Regular TV series topliners John Thaw and Dennis Waterman as two cops drift through Ranald Graham's occasionally witty screenplay with no special flair following the unlikely storyline.

Oil and its sway on the world's political and economic situation is the plot. Ian Bannen plays a steely-eyed alcoholic government minister and easily gives the best performance of the pic, while Barry Foster, an English actor, is unconvincing as an American press agent whose accent-slip is constantly showing.

David Wickes' direction and Chris Burt's editing produce a dull package.

The TV show [created by Ian Kennedy Martin] packed a certain authenticity. This theatrical version, must put the concept back into the realms of the fairy story class.

· ·

■ SWEENEY 2

1978, 108 MINS, UK ◇ ⊛
Dir Tom Clegg   *Prod* Ted Childs   *Scr* Troy Kennedy Martin   *Ph* Dusty Miller   *Ed* Chris Burt   *Mus* Tony Hatch   *Art Dir* Bill Alexander
● John Thaw, Dennis Waterman, Denholm Elliott, Georgina Hale, Nigel Hawthorne, Lewis Fiander (Euston)

Sweeney 2 is excellent British cops and robbers stuff in which a special squad of Scotland Yard detectives ultimately crack and demolish a gang of bank robbers whose hallmarks include goldplated shotguns. Good action well-spaced and paced; good characterization played with finesse; a witty script and stylish direction all lend the production a degree of distinction.

Thesping is good to excellent. John Thaw is credible and appealing as the hardbitten cop who leads the police team on the case. Also notably fine are Denholm Elliott as a corrupt police officer who lands in the jug, Dennis Waterman as Thaw's number two, and Georgina Hale as a pickup promoted by the unattached Thaw.

· ·

■ SWEET BIRD OF YOUTH

1962, 120 MINS, US ◇ ⊛
Dir Richard Brooks   *Prod* Pandro S. Berman   *Scr* Richard Brooks   *Ph* Milton Krasner   *Ed* Henry Berman   *Mus* Harold Gelman (sup.)   *Art Dir* George W. Davis, Urie McCleary
● Paul Newman, Geraldine Page, Shirley Knight, Ed Begley, Rip Torn (M-G-M)

Sweet Bird of Youth is a tamer and tidied but arresting version of Tennessee Williams' Broadway play. It's a glossy, engrossing hunk of motion picture entertainment, slickly produced by Berman.

In altering the playwright's Dixie climax (castration of the hero) Brooks has slightly weakened the story by damaging character consistency and emotional momentum. But he has accomplished this revision as if winking his creative eye at the 'in' audience.

Four members of the original Broadway cast re-create their roles: Newman, Page, Torn and Sherwood. Newman brings thrust and vitality to the role, but has some overly-mannered moments that distract.

But this is Page's picture. She draws the best, wittiest and most acid lines and the most colorful character and what she does with this parley is a lesson in the art of acting. Her portrayal of the fading actress seeking substitute reality in drink, sex and what have you to offer is a histrionic classic. Shirley Knight is sympathetic and attractive as the distraught daughter of a corrupt political boss, and Ed Begley is outstanding in a perceptive portrayal of the latter.

....

■ SWEET CHARITY

1969, 157 MINS, US ◇ ⦻

Dir Bob Fosse *Prod* Robert Arthur *Scr* Peter Stone *Ph* Robert Surtees *Ed* Stuart Gilmore *Mus* Cy Coleman *Art Dir* Alexander Golitzen, George C. Webb

● Shirley MacLaine, John McMartin, Ricardo Montalban, Sammy Davis Jr, Chita Rivera, Paula Kelly (Universal)

Sweet Charity is, in short, a terrific musical film. Based on the 1966 legituner, extremely handsome and plush production accomplishes everything it sets out to do.

Elements of comedy, drama, pathos and hope blend superbly with sure fire entertainment values, stylishly and maturely planned and executed.

The story involves a gullible woman, of relatively low station in life, who refuses to believe that tomorrow does not hold a promise of happiness.

Shirley MacLaine is a dance-hall hostess who, at the outset, has just been sloughed off by a gigolo. An accidental encounter with an Italian screen idol, played superbly by Ricardo Montalban, precedes a blossoming romance with John McMartin.

MacLaine's unique talents as a comic tragedienne are set off to maximum impact.

The film strikes the correct balance between escapist fantasy and hard reality. MacLaine's working environment is sleazy, but romantic adventures occur in believable settings – a lavish apartment, a street, a rooftop, a restaurant, a discotheque.

Fosse's staging of the musical numbers is outstanding. Atop his remembered style is a brilliant, film-oriented appreciation of the emphasis possible only with camera and movieola.

....

■ SWEET DREAMS

1985, 115 MINS, US ◇ ⦻

Dir Karel Reisz *Prod* Bernard Schwartz, Charles Mulvehill *Scr* Robert Getchell *Ph* Robbie Greenberg *Ed* Malcolm Cooke *Mus* Charles Gross *Art Dir* Albert Brenner

● Jessica Lange, Ed Harris, Ann Wedgeworth, David Clennon, James Staley, Gary Basabara (HBO/Silver Screen)

Clearly the coal miner's daughter's cousin by both birthright and ambition, *Sweet Dreams* upholds the family honor quite well, with Jessica Lange's portrayal of country singer Patsy Cline certainly equal to Sissy Spacek's Oscar-winning recreation of Loretta Lynn.

The film slants Cline's biography toward romance as likeable redneck Harris meets Lange at a roadside inn and their initially blissful marriage tackles the rough, upward climb to stardom, with many a shabby waystop. Apart from the deftly interwoven singing sequences, most of Cline's career takes place off-camera.

Instead, *Dreams* deals with what could have been any marriage of its time and place: an ambitious, independent wife – a bit too sassy and sharp-tongued at times – versus an essentially loving working stiff, whose macho insecurities inspire him to too much booze, a little infidelity and boorish brutality.

....

■ SWEET HUNTERS

1969, 115 MINS, PANAMA [FRANCE] ◇

Dir Ruy Guerra *Prod* Claude Giroux *Scr* Ruy Guerra, Philippe Dumarcay, Gerard Zinzz *Ph* Ricardo Aronovitch *Ed* Kenout Peltier *Art Dir* Bernard Evein

● Sterling Hayden, Maureen McNalley, Susan Strasberg, Stuart Whitman, Andrew Hayden (General)

A moody, brooding tale of a growingly alienated family on an isolated island whose actions are catalyzed by the news that an escaped prisoner could be heading for the isle. Pic tries for interior landscapes to be reflected by the bleak natural surroundings but falters between romantic mannerism and literary-hued melodrama.

Film does have stunning lensing and visual intensity and some good acting. But direction has a tendency to linger too lovingly on isolated scenes.

Maureen McNalley plays the wife with chilling lassitude. Her husband is played by Sterling Hayden who seems so taken by his interest in migrating birds that when he finds his wife with the prisoner he can only talk about the birds to the exhausted, dying man.

[Though carrying a Panamanian tag, pic was made by Claude Giroux's company, entirely in France.]

....

■ SWEET LIBERTY

1986, 107 MINS, US ◇ ⦻

Dir Alan Alda *Prod* Martin Bregman *Scr* Alan Alda *Ph* Frank Tidy *Ed* Michael Economou *Mus* Bruce Broughton *Art Dir* Ben Edwards

● Alan Alda, Michael Caine, Michelle Pfeiffer, Bob Hoskins, Lise Hilboldt, Lillian Gish (Universal)

Comedic potential is too rarely realized in this story of a college professor who watches filming of his historical tome become bastardized by Hollywood into a lusty romp.

Playing their true ages are Alan Alda as college professor Michael Burgess who teaches history of the American Revolution, and Michael Caine as boxoffice draw Elliot James.

When the film company arrives on location in bucolic Sayeville, Alda falls for leading lady Faith Healy (Michelle Pfeiffer), at the same time stringing along girlfriend Gretchen Carlsen (Lise Hilboldt).

The Hollywood cast and crew look and act the part, notably the macho stuntmen out to strut their stuff, as do the townsfolk who appear eager to do something other than endure another stifling Southern summer.

....

■ SWEET MOVIE

1974, 99 MINS, FRANCE/CANADA ◇ ⦻

Dir Dusan Makevejev *Scr* Dusan Makevejev *Ph* Pierre Lhomme *Ed* Yann Dedet *Mus* Manos Hadjidakis

● Carole Laure, Pierre Clementi, Anna Pruchnal, Sami Frey, Jane Mallet, John Vernon (VM/Mojack/Maran)

Sweet Movie is literally sweet, with lovemaking in a bed of sugar and a girl being bathed in chocolate for advertising purposes. But it also has an underpinning of scatology and a zany look at sensuality. Neither hard nor softcore. Yugoslav filmmaker Dusan Makevejev's first pic in the West, is provocative but also arbitrary.

It begins as broad funny satire on the richest man in the world looking for a virgin to marry and then goes into the girl's hegira as she finds personal sensual liberation with a revolutionary type woman who plows the rivers in a boat called Survival with a giant head of Karl Marx on its prow.

The virgin, played with winsome innocence and then phlegmatic and eventual awakening by Carole Laure, finds her rich husband has a golden phallus.

....

■ SWEET NOVEMBER

1968, 114 MINS, US ◇

Dir Robert Ellis *Prod* Jerry Gershwin, Elliott Kastner *Scr* Herman Raucher *Ph* Daniel L. Fapp *Ed* James Heckett *Mus* Michael Legrand *Art Dir* John Lloyd

● Sandy Dennis, Anthony Newley, Theodore Bikel, Burr DeBenning, Sandy Baron, Marj Dusay (Warner/Seven Arts)

Sweet November is a love story with a charming, almost fragile and slightly nebulous premise.

Sandy Dennis and Anthony Newley are the stars and each is outstanding in a strongly characterized role. They are called upon to engage in what some may regard as an overabundance of dialog, which lends more an aspect of a stage play than a motion picture, but this fits the mood and the tenor of the plot. Plot itself, which deals with a quixotic Brooklyn girl, is curiously motivated but interesting in its fulfillment.

Herman Raucher's original screenplay focuses on the girl who takes to her heart – and her flat – for a month at a time some man with a problem. In doing so, she seeks to ease her own troubles, which may mean the end of her life at any time, but the man always leaves her as a changed human being.

Dennis is delightful in role of the kindly femme and Newley shades his performance with subtle comedy.

....

■ SWEET REVENGE

1990, 93 MINS, US/FRANCE ◇ ⦻

Dir Charlotte Brandstrom *Prod* Monique Annaud *Scr* Janet Bromwell *Ph* Olivier Gueneau *Ed* Marie-Sophie Gally *Mus* Didier Vasseur *Art Dir* Francoise Benoit-Fresco

● Rosanna Arquette, Carrie Fisher, John Sessions, Francois Eric Gendron, Myriam Moszko, John Hargreaves (Chrysalide/Canal Plus)

Sweet Revenge is a stab at old-fashioned screwball romantic comedy that comes off only half-heartedly because Americanized Swedish-French helmer Charlotte Brandstrom works from a screenplay that relies on squeaky contrivances in every twist of its convoluted plot.

Carrie Fisher plays Linda Michaels, a Paris-based corporation lawyer, who pays out-of-work actress Kate Williams (Rosanna Arquette) to trap her ex-husband John (England's dark and curly-headed John Sessions), a struggling writer, into a mock marriage so that Linda can get out of paying him the alimony awarded him. The actress and the writer, of course, fall in real love right away.

Sweet Revenge has a neat production dress but uses the attractions of its Paris locations in a distracted way. Romance, in other words, is served up pretty cold throughout although Arquette and Sessions do kindle a flickering flame convincingly for a few moments.

....

■ SWEET RIDE, THE

1968, 111 MINS, US ◇

Dir Harvey Hart *Prod* Joe Pasternak *Scr* Tom Mankiewicz *Ph* Robert B. Hauser *Ed* Philip W. Anderson *Mus* Pete Rugolo *Art Dir* Jack Martin Smith, Richard Day

● Tony Franciosa, Michael Sarrazin, Jacqueline Bisset, Bob Denver, Michael Wilding, Michael Carey (20th Century-Fox)

The Sweet Ride could sum up as *Hell's Angels' Bikini Beach Party in Valley of the Dolls near Peyton Place.* Though well-mounted and interesting in the spotlighting of Michael Sarrazin and Jacqueline Bisset, overall result is a flat programmer, with ragged scripting, papier mache characters and routine direction.

Tony Franciosa is a beach-bum tennis hustler who is a sort of god to Malibu pad-mates

S

Sarrazin and draft-dodging musician Bob Denver. Their life is a ball, we are told, interrupted only by neighbor Lloyd Gough, who keeps yelling about the decline of morals.

Enter Bisset, who has a running, masochistic affair with producer Warren Stevens. She takes to Sarrazin, though Charles Dierkop, a recurring motorcycle bum, gets an inordinate amount of attention from Bisset.

William Murray's novel has been adapted by Tom Mankiewicz into a contrived, unbelievable script about the Malibu-Hollywood young set, which supposedly 'tells it like it is.' It succeeds both in talking down to young people, and talking up to older folks.

● **SWEET SMELL OF SUCCESS**

1957, 96 MINS, US ⓥ
Dir Alexander Mackendrick   *Prod* James Hill
Scr Clifford Odets, Ernest Lehman   *Ph* James Wong Howe   *Mus* Elmer Bernstein   *Art Dir* Edward Carrere
● Burt Lancaster, Tony Curtis, Susan Harrison, Marty Milner, Sam Levene, Barbara Nichols (United Artists)

James Hill's production, locationed in Manhattan, captures the feel of Broadway and environs after dark. It's a no-holds-barred account of the sadistic fourth estater played cunningly by Burt Lancaster.

Failure to comply with his wishes means a broken career. Breaks in his column sustain the pressagent but for the mentions there are certain favors to be granted. To the p.a., the columnist's dictates are law; if the favors include framing a young musician on a narcotics rap, that's all right, too.

Flaw in *Success* concerns the newspaperman's devotion to his sister. It's not clear why he rebels at her courtship with a guitarist, who appears to be a nice kid.

Tony Curtis as the time-serving publicist comes through with an interesting performance, although somehow the character he plays is not quite all the heel as written.

Susan Harrison is 'introduced' in the picture and comes off well as the sister. She has a fetching beauty and shows easiness in handling the assignment.

● **SWEET WILLIAM**

1980, 92 MINS, UK ◇ ⓥ
Dir Claude Whatham   *Prod* Jeremy Watt, Don Boyd
Scr Beryl Bainbridge   *Ph* Les Young   *Ed* Peter Coulson   *Art Dir* Eileen Diss
● Sam Waterston, Jenny Agutter, Anna Massey, Tim Pigott-Smith, Geraldine James (Kendon)

Nice, ordinary English girl Jenny Agutter meets wild, romantic Scots divorcee Sam Waterston. Sadly for her – though the tone is never more than just slightly bitter-sweet – his romantic nature includes having a wildly on-off relationship with the truth. He's a wolf with two not-so-ex-wives, and a compulsion to bed down her friends, neighbors and anything else he sees move.

Adapted from her own novel by Beryl Bainbridge, the screenplay is diligent without being distinguished. The same goes for Claude Whatham's direction, which tends to prefer lingering realism to dramatic pace, and thus to set up apparent significance where there is none.

Agutter is well cast, and good in that her seduction by the outlandish Waterston is entirely believable.

● **SWEETIE**

1989, 97 MINS, AUSTRALIA ◇ ⓥ
Dir Jane Campion   *Prod* John Maynard   *Scr* Jane Campion, Gerard Lee   *Ph* Sally Bongers   *Ed* Veronica Heussler   *Mus* Martin Armiger   *Art Dir* Peter Harris
● Genevieve Lemon, Karen Colston, Tom Lycos, Jon Darling, Dorothy Barry (Arenafilm)

Sweetie is an original, audacious tragicomedy about two sisters, one who's afraid of trees but believes in fortune tellers, the other who's plump and plain and eager to make her mark in showbiz.

At the beginning, focus is on Kay (Karen Colston) who works in an undefined factory in the inner city. She becomes convinced that a man described by a fortune teller as the man of her life is Louis (Tom Lycos), who just became engaged to a workmate. Kay sets about seducing him (in the factory parking lot) and before long they're living together in a rundown house in an unfashionable part of town.

Enter Dawn (Genevieve Lemon), known as Sweetie, Kay's sister, who with her drugged-out boyfriend Bob (Michael Lake) simply breaks into the house and moves into the spare room.

Genevieve Lemon is so good as the overweight, slow-witted Sweetie that her part seems too small. Karen Colson is fine as the sensitive, constantly nervous Kay. As Sweetie's tacky, somnolent boyfriend, Michael Lake steals his scenes.

● **SWIMMER, THE**

1968, 94 MINS, US ◇ ⓥ
Dir Frank Perry   *Prod* Frank Perry, Roger Lewis
Scr Eleanor Perry   *Ph* David L. Quaid, Michael Nebbia   *Ed* Sidney Katz, Carl Lerner, Pat Somerset   *Mus* Marvin Hamlisch   *Art Dir* Peter Dohanos
● Burt Lancaster, Janet Landgard, Janice Rule, Diana Van Der Vlis, Tony Bickley, Joan Rivers (Columbia/Horizon-Dover)

Burt Lancaster stars as a suburban bum who, in retracing his steps from pool to pool, illuminates the causes of his downfall. The stylized, episodic, moody film, based on John Cheever's dramatic fantasy, is something of a minor triumph in collaborative filmmaking.

Lancaster, in swim trunks throughout, pops up on a sunny Sunday morning at a suburban poolside, miles away from his house, and decides to 'swim' home by visiting at each neighbor's house. Each self-contained sequence adds indirect light to Lancaster himself; he is compulsively gregarious, compulsively youthful, compulsively sexual, compulsively self-deluded. Film is the story of a moral hangover, with the sobered-up bewildered man retracing his steps to see what he has done.

Without detailing the large cast, suffice it to say that performances, direction and writing hit the target. Lancaster emerges with a strong achievement, that of a pitiable middle-aged Joe College.

● **SWIMMING TO CAMBODIA**

1987, 87 MINS, US ◇ ⓥ
Dir Jonathan Demme   *Prod* R.A. Shafransky
Scr Spalding Gray   *Ph* John Bailey   *Ed* Carol Littleton   *Mus* Laurie Anderson   *Art Dir* Sandy McLeod
● Spalding Gray (Demme)

Witnessed in its original SoHo incarnation as a staged monolog, Spalding Gray's free-associating recollection of his experiences in Thailand during the making of *The Killing Fields* had an exhilarating immediacy which is mostly absent in this compressed filmed performance of *Swimming to Cambodia*.

Addressing a live audience from a seat at a bare table, the emotionally expansive, anti-heroic raconteur skillfully fosters an illusion of spontaneous, confessional intimacy.

Recreating a dislocating culture-shocked odyssey that takes him from the surreal flesh-pots of Bangkok to a nearly suicidal quest for a 'perfect moment' at a spectacularly paradisical Thai beach, Gray elicits compassion

and universal recognition for his serio-comic search for self.

● **SWING HIGH, SWING LOW**

1937, 92 MINS, US ⓥ
Dir Mitchell Leisen   *Prod* Arthur Hornblow Jr
Scr Virginia Van Upp, Oscar Hammerstein II   *Ph* Ted Tetzlaff   *Ed* Eda Warren   *Mus* Boris Morros (dir.)
● Carole Lombard, Fred MacMurray, Charles Butterworth, Jean Dixon, Dorothy Lamour, Franklyn Pangborn (Paramount)

Swing High, Swing Low is a switch on the old George Manker Watters-Arthur Hopkins play, *Burlesque*. Instead of the burlesque comic, Skid Johnson, of the putty-nose, whom the late Hal Skelly glorified in the Broadway original and in the first filmization (called *Dance of Life*, 1929), the switch to a Panama honky-tonk and a class NY cafe is as ultra-modern as the sweet-hot trumpeting which is the keynote of Fred MacMurray's expert performance.

As an ex-Canal Zone soldier who can toot a mean horn, which carries him from Mama Murphy's Panama joint to the Hollywood version of an El Morocco type of class place, MacMurray, ably foiled by Carole Lombard, does much to sustain a story, which, in spots, looms as a bit dated.

Sagas about kings of the nite clubs who, when they start to skid, go down fast, have become a bit familiar, as has also the basic triangle situation when MacMurray goes the whoopee route and Lombard ultimately comes back to resurrect him from the sloughs. However, expert trouping by both more than sustains the story requirements.

MacMurray's off-screen hot lips are two boys from Victor Young's band, Frank Zinziv and William Candreva, and their triple-tongue and other horn intricacies are somethin'! Young with Phil Boutelje, of the Par musical corps, does an expert job on the arrangements.

● **SWING SHIFT**

1984, 100 MINS, US ◇ ⓥ
Dir Jonathan Demme   *Prod* Jerry Bick   *Scr* Rob Morton [= Ron Nyswaner, Bo Goldman, Nancy Dowd]   *Ph* Tak Fujimoto   *Ed* Craig McKay
Mus Patrick Williams   *Art Dir* Peter Jamison
● Goldie Hawn, Kurt Russell, Christine Lahti, Fred Ward, Ed Harris, Holly Hunter (Lantana/Warner)

With all the heartwarming heroics to choose from on the homefront in World War II, *Swing Shift* tries instead to twist some consequence out of a tawdry adulterous tryst by a couple of self-centered sneaks. But the writing and acting are too flat for the challenge.

Goldie Hawn and Ed Harris are your basic nice young couple living modestly in a Santa Monica cottage until Pearl Harbor demands he immediately volunteer. Hawn fretfully sees him off to war and somewhat timidly goes to work at an aircraft factory where she draws the immediate romantic interest of Kurt Russell.

Bearded by Hawn's neighbor/coworker Christine Lahti, the lovers spend the war having loads of fun, dancing, smooching, bedding and riding with the top down.

But Harris eventually comes home for a happy ending.

● **SWING TIME**

1936, 103 MINS, US ⓥ
Dir George Stevens   *Prod* Pandro S. Berman
Scr Howard Lindsay, Allan Scott   *Ph* David Abel
Ed Henry Berman   *Mus* Nathaniel Shilkret (dir.)
Art Dir Van Nest Polglase, Carroll Clark
● Fred Astaire, Ginger Rogers, Victor Moore, Helen Broderick, Erick Blore, Betty Furness (RKO)

Swing Time is another winner for the Fred Astaire-Ginger Rogers combo. It's smart, modern, and impressive in every respect, from its boy-loses-girl background to its tunefulness, dancipation, production quality and general high standards.

There are six Jerome Kern tunes (Dorothy Fields' clever lyrics don't retard the motivation, either) and while perhaps a bit more sprightly in general tenor than the quasi-operetta score of Kern's previous *Roberta* (1935) for the same team, the tunes as usual have substance and quality.

'The Way You Look Tonight' is the ballad outstander, although not over-plugged and first introduced in her boudoir after Astaire and his pop (Victor Moore) are shown picketing Ginger Rogers and Helen Broderick's rooms as being 'unfair' to them.

Finale number, after the pash maestro (Georges Metaxa) seemingly breaks up the romance, is 'Never Gonna Dance', perhaps the best tune of the score, with its sweet-swing tempo.

This is Goerge Stevens' first directorial chore for Astaire-Rogers and also his first film musical on the RKO lot. Young megger (nephew of Ashton Stevens, the Chicago dramatic critic) does a highly competent job considering everything. He's also credited for suggesting the *Swing Time* title which Astaire's personal endorsement finally clinched after *Never Gonna Dance* was agreed upon, more or less officially, as the release title.

■ **SWINGER, THE**

1966, 81 MINS, US ◇
Dir George Sidney   *Prod* George Sidney
Scr Lawrence Roman   *Ph* Joseph Biroc   *Ed* Frank Santillo   *Mus* Marty Paich   *Art Dir* Hal Pereira, Walter Tyler
● Ann-Margret, Tony Franciosa, Robert Coote, Yvonne Romain, Horace McMahon, Nydia Westman (Paramount)

The Swinger is a very amusing original screen comedy which satirizes nudie books and magazines. The colorful, tuneful George Sidney production utilizes outstanding post-production skills to enhance impact of hip scripting and good performances.

Ann-Margret's best screen work derives from Sidney's direction, which herein spotlights her singing-dancing talents. She is an aspiring mag writer who, unable to sell straight material, fakes her autobiog in the form of a mish-mash of lurid paperback plots. Tony Franciosa, the editor, swallows the bait and tries to reform her, while nudie mag publisher Robert Coote seeks to exploit the gal.

A two-minute terp scene by Ann-Margret, to a rhythmic title tune by Andre and Dory Previn, precedes main title. Pic then opens with a hilarious tour of L.A., featuring non-sequitur narration by Coote to some jazzy picture editing. David Winters choreographed the terp sequences, one of which is a rather sexy bit in which Ann-Margret, in a fake orgy, rolls about on canvas with her body covered with paint.

■ **SWISS FAMILY ROBINSON**

1960, 126 MINS, US ◇ Ⓥ
Dir Ken Annakin   *Prod* Bill Anderson   *Scr* Lowell S. Hawley   *Ph* Harry Waxman   *Ed* Peter Baita   *Mus* William Alwyn   *Art Dir* Peter Boita
● John Mills, Dorothy McGuire, James MacArthur, Janet Munro, Sessue Hayakawa, Cecil Parker (Walt Disney)

The rather modest 1813 Johann Wyss tale has been blown up to prodigious proportions. The essence and the spirit of the simple, intriguing story of a marvelously industrious family is all but snuffed out, only spasmodically flickering through the ponderous approach.

The Robinson family seems to be enjoying a standard of living that would be the envy of an average modern family. Their famous tree house is almost outrageously comfortable (running water, no less), and seems to pop up overnight with virtually no effort. In fact, the element of time and realistic effort, so vital to the overall perspective, is consistently vague in this version. It seems to be happening in a matter of days, not decades. The climactic scrape with a band of Oriental buccaneers is the crushing blow to any semblance of credulity.

Photographically, it is a striking achievement. Through Harry Waxman's lens have been captured some compelling views of Tobago island in the West Indies. Several sequences have a heap of genuine excitement, particularly the opening raft scene in which the family battles treacherous ocean currents to get from wrecked ship to island. These aspects add excitement and interest but don't make up for the all-important loss of the story's basic values. The acting is generally capable, but hardly memorable.

■ **SWITCH**

1991, 103 MINS, US ◇ Ⓥ
Dir Blake Edwards   *Prod* Tony Adams   *Scr* Blake Edwards   *Ph* Dick Bush   *Ed* Robert Pergament   *Mus* Henry Mancini   *Art Dir* Roger Maus
● Ellen Barkin, Jimmy Smits, JoBeth Williams, Lorraine Bracco, Tony Roberts, Lysette Anthony (HBO/Cinema Plus/BECO)

Switch is a faint-hearted sex comedy that doesn't have the courage of its initially provocative convictions. Undemanding audiences will get a few laughs from the notion of a man parading around in Ellen Barkin's body. Ladykiller Steve Brooks (Perry King) accepts an invitation for a hot tub frolic with three of his old girlfriends, only to be murdered by them for his innumerable emotional crimes against women over the years. Steve is given a chance to escape a fiery fate by returning to Earth and finding just one woman who genuinely likes him. Only catch is that he will henceforth inhabit the body of a woman, and that of an uncommonly sexy one.

Masquerading as the disappeared man's long-lost half-sister, 'Amanda' manages to hold on to Steve's old job at a high-powered ad agency, hangs out with Steve's best friend Jimmy Smits and intimidates the murder ringleader, JoBeth Williams, into assisting her in dressing.

Things look like they'll shift into high gear when Amanda meets cosmetics queen Lorraine Bracco, a lesbian, and decides to seduce her into transferring her big account to the agency. Unfortunately, pic chickens out from this point on, to dismaying ends.

Barkin is clearly game for anything the director wants her to do, including extensive physical clowning, but mugs and overdoes the grimacing and macho posturing. Smits and Bracco are smooth enough.

■ **SWORD AND THE SORCERER, THE**

1982, 100 MINS, US ◇ Ⓥ
Dir Albert Pyun   *Prod* Brandon Chase, Marianne Chase, Tom Karnowski, John Stuckmeyer   *Scr* Albert Pyun, Tom Karnowski, John Stuckmeyer   *Ph* Joseph Mangine   *Ed* Marshall Harvey   *Mus* David Whitaker   *Art Dir* George Costello
● Lee Horsley, Kathleen Beller, Simon MacCorkindale, George Maharis, Richard Lynch, Nina Van Pallandt (Chase)

Combine beaucoup gore and an atrocity-a-minute action edited in fastpace style. Then, toss in a scantily clad cast of none-too-talented performers mouthing dimwitted dialog and garnish with a touch of medieval gibberish. The result would be something resembling *The Sword and the Sorcerer*.

The plot is needlessly complicated by a truly lackluster script. Stripped to essentials, which the cast often does in this pseudo epic, *Sword* is about the retaking by a group of ragtag medievalists of a once peaceable kingdom sadistically ruled by an evil knight named Cromwell.

Lee Horsley grins a lot as the leader of the rebels, who turns out to be the long-banished son of the old and virtuous king. Simon MacCorkindale grimaces a good deal as a royal pretender.

For trivia fans, Nina Van Pallandt plays the good queen who's dispatched quickly and mercifully since her performance is nothing to boast of.

■ **SYLVIA**

1965, 115 MINS, US
Dir Gordon Douglas   *Prod* Martin H. Poll   *Scr* Sydney Boehm   *Ph* Joseph Ruttenberg   *Ed* Frank Bracht   *Mus* David Raksin   *Art Dir* Hal Pereira, Roland Anderson
● Carroll Baker, George Maharis, Joanne Dru, Peter Lawford, Viveca Lindfors, Edmond O'Brien (Paramount)

Sylvia is the story of a prostitute who turns to decency. The production is episodic until its closing reels, covering a period of 14 to 15 years as a private investigator digs into her obscure past to learn who she really is; consequently, considerable dramatic impact is lost due to film's rambling flashback treatment.

Carroll Baker is joined in stellar spot by George Maharis as the private eye who ultimately falls in love with the woman he is tracing. Actually, although hers is the motivating character, top honours go to Maharis for a consistently restrained performance which builds, while actress suffers somewhat from the spotty nature of her haphazard part.

Under Gordon Douglas' telling direction of Sydney Boehm's screenplay based on the E.V. Cunningham novel, sequences limning title character's part are generally individually strongly etched.

Ann Sothern as a blowsy cashier in a penny arcade where Sylvia once worked is a definite standout. Viveca Lindfors likewise scores as a Pittsburgh librarian.

■ **SYLVIA SCARLETT**

1936, 90 MINS, US Ⓥ
Dir George Cukor   *Prod* Pandro S. Berman
Scr Gladys Unger, John Collier, Mortimer Offner   *Ph* Joseph August   *Ed* Jane Loring   *Mus* Roy Webb
● Katherine Hepburn, Cary Grant, Brian Aherne, Edmund Gwenn, Natalie Paley, Dennie Moore (Radio)

Silvia Scarlett is puzzling in its tangents and sudden jumps, plus the almost poetic lines that are given to Katherine Hepburn. At moments the white [from the novel by Compton MacKenzie] skirts the border of absurdity.

Mistake seems to have been in not sticking to a broad vein of comedy. In the serious passages, notably the half-crazy jealousy of the father (Edmund Gwenn) for his young and helter-skelter wife (Dennie Moore) there is little preparation in the audience's mind for anything so serious as a suicide.

Perhaps it is not valid to ask whether anybody would really fail to suspect the true sex of such a boy as Hepburn looks and acts. But while carrying this off well enough, she shines brightest and is most likeable in the transition into womanhood inspired by her meeting with an artist (Brian Aherne).

Cary Grant, doing a petty English crook with a Soho accent, practically steals the picture. This is especially true in the earlier sequences. A scene in an English mansion to which Hepburn, Grant and Gwenn have gone for purposes of robbery is dominated by Grant.

The picture is half-whimsical, almost allegorical, and with the last half having a dream-worldish element that's hard to define, and equally hard to understand.

●●●●●●●●●●●●●●●●●●●●●●●●●●●

■ SYMPHONY OF SIX MILLION

1932, 92 MINS, US

Dir Gregory La Cava   *Prod* David O. Selznick, Pandro S. Berman   *Scr* Bernard Schubert, J. Walter Ruben, James Seymour   *Ph* Leo Tover   *Ed* Archie Marshek   *Mus* Max Steiner   *Art Dir* Carroll Clark
● Irene Dunne, Ricardo Cortez, Gregory Ratoff, Anna Appel, Lita Chevret, Noel Madison (RKO)

This is a story [by Fannie Hurst] of a brilliant Jewish surgeon who loses his nerve when his family virtually forces him to operate on his father for a brain tumor. The father dies on the table and the boy goes to pieces, vowing he will never touch an instrument again. His faith in himself is restored when he successfully performs a delicate spinal operation on the girl he loves. She has deliberately endangered her own life to force him to action.

It is an all-Jewish film which could have stood more attention as to racial contrasts for general appeal. Only now and then do the characters become human, but all have at least one fine moment of sincerity. Gregory Ratoff gets his big chance in the scene of the redemption of the firstborn. Anna Appel, as the mother, gets her scene early in the play when she persuades her son to move uptown to a fashionable practice and wealth.

Ricardo Cortez is generally good as the young surgeon. Irene Dunne is meaningless, appearing but seldom and then always in forced and unreal situations.

●●●●●●●●●●●●●●●●●●●●●●●●●●●

■ SYNANON

1965, 105 MINS, US

Dir Richard Quine   *Prod* Richard Quine   *Scr* Ian Bernard, S. Lee Pogostin   *Ph* Harry Stradling   *Ed* David Wages   *Mus* Neal Hefti
● Edmond O'Brien, Chuck Connors, Stella Stevens, Alex Cord, Richard Conte, Eartha Kitt (Columbia)

Synanon is a fictionized semi-documentary of a rehabilitation home for drug addicts on the beachfront of Santa Monica, Calif, where almost miraculous cures are said to be achieved. As backdrop for a dramatic story it is grim, hard-hitting and sometimes shocking.

Producer-director Richard Quine moved his cameras to the actual locale to ensure authenticity in this story of Synanon House, established by Charles E. Dederich, an ex-alcoholic, in 1958.

Edmond O'Brien enacts the character of Dederich (who acted as technical advisor), plagued by debts and civil opposition as he goes about his seemingly thankless task of trying to bring lives back from the brink.

O'Brien's performance is smooth and convincing and lends strength to the character he portrays. Cord registers decisively in an unsympathetic role, and Stella Stevens is persuasive as a hooker, with a great love for her five-year-old son.

●●●●●●●●●●●●●●●●●●●●●●●●●●●

■ SYSTEM, THE

1964, 90 MINS, UK

Dir Michael Winner   *Prod* Kenneth Shipman   *Scr* Peter Draper   *Ph* Nicolas Roeg   *Ed* Fred Burnley   *Mus* Stanley Black   *Art Dir* Geoffrey Tozer
● Oliver Reed, Jane Merrow, Barbara Ferris, Julia Foster, David Hemmings, Derek Nimmo (B.L.C./Bryanston)

The System is a slight anecdote, not explored as fully as it might have been, but made

worthwhile by some bright direction, lensing and acting from young, eager talent.

Screenplay concerns the activities of a bunch of local lads at a seaside resort who every summer work a system by which they 'take' the holidaying femmes for a light-hearted emotional ride. There's nothing vicious about it. It's simply young men in search of goodtime romances that will have to make do in their memories during the dreary offseason winter months.

Tinker (Oliver Reed), a young beach photographer, is leader of the 'come up and see my pad' gang. The film tells how, one summer, he himself gets taken. He falls heavily in love with a well-loaded, well-stacked fashion model, and that's against the 'rules', even when the girl reciprocates.

This thin yarn is an adroitly spun concoction of comedy, sentiment and pathos which, however, needs a strong sub-plot to sustain interest. Scripter Peter Draper has decked out his situations with some neat dialog, mostly of the flip-talk variety, but there are one or two moments of genuine emotional depth between the young lovers.

●●●●●●●●●●●●●●●●●●●●●●●●●●●

T t

■ TABLE FOR FIVE

1983, 122 MINS, US ◇ ▼

Dir Robert Lieberman   *Prod* Robert Schaffel   *Scr* David Seltzer   *Ph* Vilmos Zsigmond   *Ed* Michael Kahn   *Mus* Miles Goodman, John Morris   *Art Dir* Robert F. Boyle
● Jon Voight, Richard Crenna, Marie-Christine Barrault, Millie Perkins, Roxana Zal, Robby Kiger (CBS Theatrical)

Well-written drama concerns an errant father who takes his three children on an ocean voyage in an effort to close the gap that's grown between them. Pic earns most of its emotional points honestly and will touch most anyone who's ever taken the responsibilities of parenting seriously, either in fact or theoretically.

At the opening, Jon Voight's kids have lived with their mother (Millie Perkins) and her new man, attorney Richard Crenna, for several years. Voight swoops into New York to take the moppets off on a luxurious sea cruise with the promise of a new-found sense of responsibility.

But Voight quickly realizes that he really doesn't know how to communicate with the kids who, for their part, resent the fact he's more interested in chasing blondes in the bar than hanging out with them.

Despite the attempted interference of his sharp daughter, Voight manages to initiate a shipboard romance with a sympathetic French woman, Marie-Christine Barrault.

●●●●●●●●●●●●●●●●●●●●●●●●●●●

■ TABU

1931, 81 MINS, US

Dir F.W. Murnau   *Prod* Robert J. Flaherty, F.W. Murnau   *Scr* Robert J. Flaherty, F.W. Murnau   *Ph* Floyd Crosby, Robert J. Flaherty   *Mus* Hugo Riesenfeld
● Reri, Matahi, Hitu, Jean, Jules, Kong Ah (Paramount)

A strong love story in a South Seas background, with South Sea natives rather than regular actors.

The title, *Tabu*, means death. It's the fate that hangs over the romantic leads who flee from a distant isle and its barbaric customs after a girl has been handed over to Tabu, ruler of one of the islands, as 'the chosen one'. Along with her goes the dictum, 'no man

must touch her or cast eyes of desire upon her'.

Matahi rescues the girl, Reri, from a schooner at the propitious moment, just as she is to be taken away. They flee to an island that flourishes in the pearl trade and has been penetrated to a greater extent by white men. Here Matahi becomes famous as a pearl diver, but finally Tabu turns up to claim the girl, threatening the Tabu sign (or death) on Matahi if she doesn't come along with him.

About 90% of the footage is devoted to the romantic leads, their happiness, troubles, heartaches, etc. Against this, there is a little native life – fishing, diving, waterfalls, mode of living, etc, as was brought but to a far greater extent in *Moana*.

Tabu is a silent, with synchronization and sound effects, but difficult to figure out whether some of the effects and the singing, as well as native music, were dubbed over or not.

●●●●●●●●●●●●●●●●●●●●●●●●●●●

■ TAI-PAN

1986, 127 MINS, US ◇ ▼

Dir Daryl Duke   *Prod* Raffaella De Laurentiis   *Scr* John Briley, Stanley Mann   *Ph* Jack Cardiff   *Mus* Maurice Jarre   *Art Dir* Tony Masters
● Bryan Brown, Joan Chen, John Stanton, Tom Guinee, Bill Leadbitter, Russell Wong (De Laurentiis)

Tai-Pan is a historical epic [from James Clavell's novel] lost somewhere between 19th-century Hong Kong and 20th-century Hollywood. Despite flashes of brilliance and color, *Tai-Pan* fails to evoke a mysterious and moving world as a back-drop to its romantic drama. Director Daryl Duke and his team have made an attractive shell but failed to put in any heart.

As the Tai-Pan, or trade leader of the European community, first in Canton and then later in Hong Kong, Aussie thesp Bryan Brown looks the part well enough, but lacks charisma.

Within the exotic setting the story is actually rather conventional. Brown is opposed by arch villains Brock (John Stanton) and his son Gorth (Bill Leadbitter) for the control of the trading rights. At the same time there is considerable politicking going on with the Chinese over the opium trade and the British over trade regulations.

Film presents a good deal of romancing, between Brown and his lovely Chinese concubine May-May (Joan Chen) and several other women who seem to have a bottomless supply of revealing costumes.

●●●●●●●●●●●●●●●●●●●●●●●●●●●

■ TAKE A GIRL LIKE YOU

1970, 101 MINS, UK ◇

Dir Jonathan Miller   *Prod* Hal Chester   *Scr* George Melly   *Ph* Dick Bush   *Ed* Jack Harris   *Mus* Stanley Myers
● Noel Harrison, Oliver Reed, Hayley Mills, Sheila Hancock, John Bird, Aimi MacDonald (Columbia)

Take a movie like this. It's about a virgin (Hayley Mills) and a guy (Oliver Reed) who is trying to make her, can't, and is obsessed about it. That's all there is to it.

Basically, it is not a bad little English kitchen-sink drama with some strong but low-key performances, but a lack of sense of humor, generally wearisome development, and a downbeat ending.

At the core of George Melly's script, based on Kingsley Amis' novel, is the whole dreary ritual of a boy and girl in conflict about sex.

Jonathan Miller's direction is competent, not without its occasional humor and bright spots, but they are too occasional, and what should be a comedy is essentially heavy and melodramatic.

●●●●●●●●●●●●●●●●●●●●●●●●●●●

■ TAKE A HARD RIDE

1975, 103 MINS, US ◇

Dir Anthony M. Dawson [= Antonio Margheriti]
Prod Harry Bernsen *Scr* Eric Bercovici, Jerry Ludwig
Ph Riccardo Pallotini *Ed* Stanford C. Allen *Mus* Jerry
Goldsmith *Art Dir* Julio Molina
● Jim Brown, Lee Van Cleef, Fred Williamson,
Catherine Spaak, Jim Kelly, Barry Sullivan (20th-Century
Fox)

Take a Hard Ride is a poly-formula period
western dual bill item for the popcorn belt.
Jim Brown heads cast as a wrangler hunted
for the $86,000 in cash he is returning to his
late employer's widow. Lots and lots of
people get killed in Harry Bernsen's location
production shot in the Canary Islands.

The script mixes several potboiler genres:
Brown, gambler Fred Williamson and mute
Jim Kelly contribute black and karate elements; Lee Van Cleef provides the Italoater
menace as a callous bounty hunter; Catherine Spaak is briefly encountered and
dropped on the trail, not before adding a
Continental touch; crooked sheriff Barry Sullivan and Dana Andrews, in a cameo as
Brown's boss, are in more conventional oater
roles.

Second unit director and stunt boss Hal
Needham jazzes up the pace with several offbeat highlights.

■ TAKE HER, SHE'S MINE

1963, 98 MINS, US ◇

Dir Henry Koster *Prod* Henry Koster *Scr* Nunnally
Johnson *Ph* Lucien Ballard *Ed* Marjorie Fowler
Mus Jerry Goldsmith *Art Dir* Jack Martin Smith,
Malcolm Brown
● James Stewart, Sandra Dee, Audrey Meadows,
Robert Morley, Philippe Forquet, John McGiver
(20th Century-Fox)

The screen version of *Take Her, She's Mine* is
an improvement over the Phoebe and Henry
Ephron stage play from which it springs,
even though several of the revisions and additions dreamed up by scenarist Nunnally
Johnson are contrived and far from fresh.

The difficulty encountered by an older generation in comprehending the behavior of a
younger generation is the business explored
in this comedy. More specifically, one father's (James Stewart) trials and tribulations
when he packs his precious daughter (Sandra
Dee) off to college and observes, in long distance dismay with an occasional globe-trot
for closer inspection, her transition from
adolescent to young woman.

An occasional dash of the *Tammy* whammy
seeps into Dee's characterization, but on the
whole she's effective. Audrey Meadows, a
gifted comedienne, is wasted in the bland and
barren role of Stewart's wife. Robert Morley,
though in the somewhat irrelevant role of a
jaded Britisher, has some of the best lines in
the film. Jerry Goldsmith contributes a
whimsical score, especially helpful in a costume party sequence that needs all the help it
can get.

■ TAKE ME OUT TO THE BALL GAME

1949, 83 MINS, US ◇ ⊽

Dir Busby Berkeley *Prod* Arthur Freed *Scr* Harry
Tugend, George Wells *Ph* George Folsey
Ed Blanche Sewell *Mus* Adolph Deutsch
● Frank Sinatra, Esther Williams, Gene Kelly, Betty
Garrett, Edward Arnold, Jules Munshin (M-G-M)

Take Me Out to the Ball Game, backgrounded
by an early-day baseball yarn, is short on
story, but has some amusing moments—and
Gene Kelly.

Aided by Technicolor, Esther Williams is
an eyeful, and Frank Sinatra cavorts pleasantly as shortstop Kelly's second baseman.

Jules Munshin and Betty Garrett are the
comedy relief, and the overall combination of
talents is actually worthier of better material.

The yarn is about a couple of singing-dancing major league ball-players and the complications in which they become involved when
they meet some gamblers and Williams,
owner of the club. There is no pretense that
Ball Game is anything more than a romp for
Kelly's virtuosity.

■ TAKE THE MONEY AND RUN

1969, 85 MINS, US ◇ ⊽

Dir Woody Allen *Prod* Charles H. Joffe *Scr* Woody
Allen, Mickey Rose *Ph* Lester Shorr *Ed* James T.
Heckert *Mus* Marvin Hamlisch *Art Dir* Fred Harpman
● Woody Allen, Janet Margolin, Marcel Hillaire,
Jacquelyn Hyde, Lonny Chapman (Palomar)

A few good laughs in an 85-minute film do
not a comedy make. Woody Allen's *Take the
Money and Run*, basically a running gag about
hero Allen's ineptitude as a professional
crook, scatters its fire in so many directions it
has to hit at least several targets. But satire
on documentary coverage of criminal flop is
over-extended and eventually tiresome.

Bright spots are interviews with parents-in-
disguise Ethel Sokolow and Henry Leff; Janet
Margolin, as wife, and prison psychiatrist
Don Frazier also deliver yocks.

Margolin turns in a neat performance as
Allen's wife.

Allen, both as director and actor, sustains
his own characterization. In such scenes as
robbery when he can't convince bank personnel they are being robbed, or in chain gang's
visit to farmhouse, he creates genuinely funny
moments.

■ TAKING CARE OF BUSINESS

1990, 103 MINS, US ◇ ⊽

Dir Arthur Hiller *Prod* Geoffrey Taylor *Scr* Jill
Mazursky, Jeffrey Abrams *Ph* David M. Walsh
Ed William Reynolds *Mus* Stewart Copeland
Art Dir Jon Hutman
● James Belushi, Charles Grodin, Anne DeSalvo, Loryn
Locklin, Veronica Hamel, Hector Elizondo
(Hollywood/Silver Screen Partners IV)

Charles Grodin and James Belushi come
together too late in the plot to prevent a poky
start for *Taking Care of Business*, but their
mutual chemistry eventually kicks in some
jovial jousting. Brash Belushi and befuddled
Grodin are perfect casting for yarn about a
likable escaped con who assumes the identity
of a stuffy, overworked ad agency exec.

At the start, Belushi is still in county jail,
and there's some fun as he high-fives it with
fellow inmates and torments warden Hector
Elizondo. Mostly familiar schtick. Ditto Grodin's intro as he fusses with his workload and
neglects wife Victoria Hamel. Though
Belushi is set for release in days, he can't wait
to see the World Series so he escapes just as
Grodin arrives in LA to pitch his agency to a
Japanese tycoon.

At the airport, Grodin loses his time-plan-
ning book – *Business* is one long commercial
itself for a particular brand (Filofax, as pic is
titled in the UK) – and Belushi finds it. Setting himself up in a Malibu mansion, Belushi
proceeds to live Grodin's life just the opposite
of how the businessman would do it, romancing the boss's daughter (played with sexy
feistiness by Loryn Locklin), beating the
potential client (Mako) at tennis, criticizing
his products and making sexist remarks to
fierce, feminist exec (Gates McFadden).

Inevitably, Grodin catches up with Belushi
and the farcical convolutions multiply with
the arrival of Hamel. As the action picks up,
so does the dialog.

■ TAKING OF PELHAM ONE TWO THREE, THE

1974, 104 MINS, US ⊽

Dir Joseph Sargent *Prod* Gabriel Katzka, Edgar J.
Scherick *Scr* Peter Stone *Ph* Owen Roizman
Ed Jerry Greenberg *Mus* David Shire *Art Dir* Gene
Rudolf
● Walter Matthau, Robert Shaw, Martin Balsam,
Hector Elizondo, Earl Hindman, James Broderick
(Palomar/Palladium)

The Taking of Pelham One Two Three is a good
action caper about a subway car heist under
the streets of Manhattan. Walter Matthau
heads the cast as a Transit Authority detective matching wits with the hijackers headed
by Robert Shaw. Joseph Sargent's direction
is fast but the major liability is Peter Stone's
screenplay which develops little interest in
either Matthau or Shaw's gang, nor the
innocent hostages.

Shaw, Martin Balsam, Hector Elizondo
and Earl Hindman seize a subway car,
named for the starting station on the line and
its time of departure, and demand $1 million.
Matthau is on duty at subway communications h.q. and deals with Shaw over voice
radio all the while fending off the Archie
Bunker types with whom he works.

A sidebar characterization is that of Lee
Wallace as the mayor, a travesty of a role
played for silly laughs.

Shaw is superb in another versatile
characterization.

■ TAKING OFF

1971, 92 MINS, US ◇ ⊚

Dir Milos Forman *Prod* Alfred W. Crown *Scr* Milos
Forman, John Guare, Jean-Claude Carriere
Ph Miroslav Ondricek *Ed* John Carter *Art Dir* Robert
Wightman
● Lynn Carlin, Buck Henry, Linnea Heacock, Georgia
Engel, Tony Harvey, Audra Lindley (Universal)

Taking Off is a very compassionate, very
amusing contemporary comedy about a NY
couple whose concern for a drop out daughter
is matched by her astonishment at their
social mores. Milos Forman's first US-made
film shows him to be a director who can depict the contradictions of human nature while
avoiding tract, harangue and polemics.

The plot peg is the flight to Greenwich
Village of Linnea Heacock, who's seeking
something not provided in her home life.
Lynn Carlin and Buck Henry (as the
parents) enliven the many motivated and
developing sequences: initial search for the
girl conducted with friends Tony Harvey and
Georgia Engel; a large meeting of discarded
parents where Vincent Schiavelli turns them
all on to marijuana; and a funny strip poker
game at home which ends abruptly when the
runaway girl calmly appears from her
bedroom.

Henry tackles his first big screen role and
achieves superb results. Carlin seems not an
actress in a part, but a real mother, caught by
candid camera, who doesn't know whether to
laugh or cry about a family crisis.

■ TALE OF TWO CITIES, A

1935, 121 MINS, US ⊽

Dir Jack Conway *Prod* David O. Selznick *Scr* W.P.
Lipscomb, S.N. Behrman *Ph* Oliver T. Marsh
Ed Conrad A. Nervig *Mus* Herbert Stothart
● Ronald Colman, Elizabeth Allan, Edna May Oliver,
Reginald Owen, Basil Rathbone, Blanche Yurka
(M-G-M)

Metro achieves in *A Tale of Two Cities* a
screen classic. The two yawning pitfalls of
spectacle and dialog have been adroitly
evaded. The fall of the Bastille [directed by
Val Lewton and Jacques Tourneur] is
breathtaking but it is given no greater valu-

ation than its influence on the plot [from the novel by Charles Dickens] warrants.

The rabble at the guillotine is blood-chilling in its ferocity, but not for a moment does it overlie the principals, waiting in the shadow of the bloody platform for their turn to come. In the dialog the lines are neither the often stilted phrases of the book, nor yet the colloquial language of today.

Ronald Colman makes his Carton one of the most pathetic figures in the screen catalog. Gone are his drawing room mannerisms, shaved along with his moustache. Henry B. Walthall is good as Manette and Blanche Yurka magnificent as the vengeful Mme De Farge.

The others all are good, each in proportion to assignment, with Elizabeth Allan suffering somewhat from necessity for being so typically a Dickens' heroine.
□ 1936: Best Picture (Nomination)

■ TALE OF TWO CITIES, A

1958, 117 MINS, UK ⓥ
Dir Ralph Thomas   *Prod* Betty E. Box   *Scr* T.E.B. Clarke   *Ph* Ernest Steward   *Ed* Alfred Roome   *Mus* Richard Addinsell   *Art Dir* Carmen Dillon
● Dirk Bogarde, Dorothy Tutin, Cecil Parker, Marie Versini, Stephen Murray, Rosalie Crutchley (Rank)

Set against the Storming of the Bastille, *Cities* is primarily a character study of a frustrated young lawyer who fritters his life away in drink until the moment when he makes everything worthwhile by a supreme sacrifice for the girl he loves. Dirk Bogarde brings a lazy charm and nonchalance to the Sydney Carton role but tends to play throughout in a surprisingly minor key.

Leading femme is Dorothy Tutin, whose role does not strain her thesping ability. Cecil Parker, as a banker; Athene Seyler, as Tutin's fussy companion; and Stephen Murray, as Dr Manette, all have meaty portrayals which they handle with authority.

But it is among some of the other characterizations that there is most to admire, notably new young actress Marie Versini. Playing a young servant girl who becomes a victim of Madame Guillotine, Versini brings a beautiful restraint and appeal to her task.

Among other standout performances are those by Donald Pleasence, as an unctuous spy; Christopher Lee, as a sadistic aristocrat; and Duncan Lamont, as one of the leaders of the revolution. Rosalie Crutchley also makes notable impact with a brilliant study in malevolence as his vengeful wife.

■ TALES FROM THE DARKSIDE THE MOVIE

1990, 93 MINS, US ◇ ⓥ
Dir John Harrison   *Prod* Richard P. Rubinstein, Mitchell Galin   *Scr* Michael McDowell, George A. Romero   *Ph* Robert Draper   *Ed* Harry B. Miller   *Mus* Donald A. Rubinstein, Jim Manzie, Pat Regan, Chaz Jankel, John Harrison   *Art Dir* Ruth Ammon
● Deborah Harry, Christian Slater, Rae Dawn Chong, James Remar, David Johansen, Steve Buscemi (Paramount)

Tales from the Darkside is significantly gorier than its namesake TV series, and has better production values.

Structure is a lift from Scheherazade in *1,001 Nights*, as Deborah Harry prepares to cook little boy Matthew Lawrence, he delays his fate by telling her a trio of horror stories.

Most ambitious segment, *Beetlejuice* writer Michael McDowell's *Lover's Vow* is saved for last: Gotham artist James Remar witnessing a barman's extremely gory murder by a gargoyle come to life. To save his skin he vows to the gargoyle not to tell anyone what happened, but after meeting beautiful Rae Dawn Chong, romancing her and marrying her, 10

years later he spills the beans with tragic results. Sexy and sinister Chong is a delight in this one.

Other segments are more routine. George A. Romero's adaptation of a Stephen King story is punched up by casting David Johansen as a hit man assigned to kill a black cat by drug tycoon William Hickey. Curtainraiser is a corny but effective tale from the creator of Sherlock Holmes: college student Steve Buscemi bringing an ancient mummy back to life for revenge with ironic results.

■ TALES OF BEATRIX POTTER

1971, 90 MINS, UK ◇ ⓥ
Dir Reginald Mills   *Prod* John Brabourne, Richard Goodwin   *Scr* Richard Goodwin, Christine Edzard   *Ph* Austin Dempster   *Ed* John Rushton   *Mus* John Lanchbery   *Art Dir* John Howell
● Frederick Ashton, Alexander Grant, Ann Howard, Wayne Sleep, Michael Coleman, Lesley Collier (M-G-M/EMI)

The production partners, John Brabourne and Richard Goodwin and director Reginald Mills, conceived the happy notion of having Beatrix Potter's animals represented by members of the Royal Ballet and the result is 90 minutes of style, fun and enchantment.

Film's opener introduces Erin Geraghty as the introverted young Beatrix in her gloomy Victorian home. But then the animals take over. There's little point in detailing the various stories – the adventures of The Bad Mice, the jaunty capers of Jeremy Fisher, how Jemima Puddle-Duck escapes a fate worse than death at the paws of The Fox, etc. The point is that the episodes skip merrily along, the choreography by Frederick Ashton blends splendidly with Reginald Mills' direction and John Lanchbery's bright, if tinkly, music has the right lilting note. But the whole thing might have fallen apart but for the lifelike masks designed by Rostislav Doboujinsky and Christine Edzard's gay costumes.

■ TALES OF HOFFMAN, THE

1951, 138 MINS, UK ◇
Dir Michael Powell, Emeric Pressburger   *Prod* Michael Powell, Emeric Pressburger   *Scr* Michael Powell, Emeric Pressburger   *Ph* Christopher Challis   *Ed* Reginald Mills   *Art Dir* Arthur Lawson
● Moira Shearer, Robert Rounseville, Robert Helpmann, Pamela Brown, Frederick Ashton, Leonide Massine (Archers/London)

Michael Powell and Emeric Pressburger follow up their sock *Red Shoes* ballet picture with as distinguished an opera-ballet film in *Tales of Hoffman*. The Jacques Offenbach fantasy opera has been transformed to the screen with great imagination and taste, with an unusual amount of inventiveness and effects, for a lush, resplendent production that's a treat to eye and ear.

Hoffman is a better picture than *Shoes*, with more imagination and story structure. But the story lines in the second and third episodes are confusing, except perhaps to the inveterate operagoer. *Hoffman* lacks the everyday romance of *Shoes*, is sung throughout instead of having spoken dialog, and lacks humor.

Film is a brilliant integration of dance, story and music. Fantastic nature of its story is brought out more sharply by the excellent use of Technicolor.

Prolog has Hoffman (Robert Rounseville) watching a ballet and in love with the prima ballerina, Stella (Moira Shearer), who appears to him as the embodiment of his past loves. When he thinks Stella has spurned him, he moons in a tavern, and relates to a group of students 'the three tales of my folly of love'.

One concerns the time, in Paris, when he fancied himself in love with Olympia

(Shearer), who turned out to be a life-size doll created by a magician. Second act, set in Venice, has Hoffman bewitched by a beautiful courtesan, Giulietta (Ludmilla Tcherina), whose master is trying to acquire Hoffman's soul through the girl. Third act, set on a Grecian isle, has Hoffman in love with Antonia (Ann Ayars), daughter of a singer and conductor, who is in danger of dying from consumption if she herself attempts to sing.

Shearer, Robert Helpmann, Ludmilla, Tcherina and Leonide Massine, all of them dancers who appeared in *Red Shoes*, are distinguished again here.

■ TALES OF MANHATTAN

1942, 117 MINS, US
Dir Julien Duvivier   *Prod* Boris Morros, S.P. Eagle [= Sam Spiegel]   *Scr* Ben Hecht, Ferenc Molnar, Donald Ogden Stewart, Samuel Hoffenstein, Alan Campbell, Ladislas Fodor, L. Vadnai, L. Gorog, Lamar Trotti, Henry Blankfort   *Ph* Joseph Walker   *Ed* Robert Bischoff   *Mus* Sol Kaplan
● Charles Boyer, Rita Hayworth, Ginger Rogers, Henry Fonda, Charles Laughton, Edward G. Robinson (20th Century-Fox)

In *Tales of Manhattan* the hero is an expensive dress coat, which bears a curse, and the film recounts the fortunes and misfortunes of those who wear or come in possession of it. It was originally made for Charles Boyer, playing a Broadway matinee idol, and winds up as scarecrow on a poor old Negro's farm.

The expanse of acting and writing talent may have been too much for Julien Duvivier, a fine foreign director, for he comes up with very few original touches in this picture. Some of the sequences he appears to have permitted to go along on their momentum.

Despite the plenitude of costly stars, featured players and writers, Boris Morros and S.P. Eagle [= Sam Spiegel] brought the film in for slightly more than $1 million, not high considering all the credits.

■ TALES OF ORDINARY MADNESS

1981, 107 MINS, ITALY ◇
Dir Marco Ferreri   *Scr* Sergio Amidei, Marco Ferreri, Anthony Fourtz   *Ph* Tonino Delli Colli   *Ed* Ruggero Mastroianni   *Mus* Philippe Sarde
● Ben Gazzara, Ornella Muti, Susan Tyrrell, Tanya Lopert (23 Giugno/Ginis)

Marco Ferreri, the anarchically-inclined 'Italo' filmmaker who has delved into the human psyche often in its mainly frustrated, exploited aspects in today's world, seems to have found a kindred spirit in the stories of the 1960s Yank sub-culture writer-poet Charles Bukowski. Film is a distillation of Ferreri's themes.

Ben Gazzara, in a knowing characterization of a poet (Charles) searching for the essence of love though primarily self-destructive and half believing in its redemptive powers, is first seen giving a philosophical comic talk in some foreign university on a tour. Going back to a dressing room, he finds a Lolita-like runaway who steals his money when he falls asleep.

He goes back to LA to write, drink and keep searching for women in a sort of adventurous series of escapades reminiscent of Henry Miller but not as self-indulgent and sex-for-its-own sake as the writings of Miller.

One day a sexy-looking blonde catches his eye in the street and he follows her. He finds her house and goes in to be suddenly devoured by her sexually but then turned over to the police for molesting her. Susan Tyrrell is effective in her sexual quirkiness.

Charles is freed and joins the tramp wino world for a while. Then home again to write and dry out. He also comments on the action along the way.

●●●●●●●●●●●●●●●●●●●●●●●●●●●●●●●●

■ **TALK OF THE TOWN**

1942, 110 MINS, US ▼

Dir George Stevens   *Prod* George Stevens   *Scr* Irwin Shaw, Sidney Buchman   *Ph* Ted Tetzlaff   *Ed* Otto Meyer   *Mus* Frederick Hollander
● Cary Grant, Jean Arthur, Ronald Colman, Edgar Buchanan, Glenda Farrell, Rex Ingram (Columbia)

Case of Cary Grant, the outspoken factory town, soapbox 'anti' worker, being tried for arson and the death of factory foreman in the blaze, serves as a vehicle to introduce a pert schoolteacher (Jean Arthur) and a law school dean (Ronald Colman) in a procession of comedy dissertations on law, in theory and practice. Plot has Grant escaping before his trial is completed and seeking refuge in the schoolmarm's home.

Story [from one by Sidney Harmon, adapted by Dale Van Every] doesn't give Grant quite enough to do, with plenty of meaty lines and situations handed Colman, who manages the transition from the stuffy professor to a human being with the least amount of implausibility.

George Stevens' direction is topflight for the most part. Transition from serious or melodramatic to the slap-happy and humorous sometimes is a bit awkward, but in the main it is solid escapist comedy.
□ 1942: Best Picture (Nomination)

●●●●●●●●●●●●●●●●●●●●●●●●●●●●●●●●

■ **TALK RADIO**

1988, 110 MINS, US ◇ ▼

Dir Oliver Stone   *Prod* Edward R. Pressman, A. Kitman Ho   *Scr* Eric Bogosian, Oliver Stone   *Ph* Robert Richardson   *Ed* David Brenner   *Mus* Stewart Copeland   *Art Dir* Bruno Rubeo
● Eric Bogosian, Alec Baldwin, Ellen Greene, Leslie Hope, John C. McGinley (Cineplex Odeon/Ten Four)

Talk Radio casts a spotlight on the unpalatable underside of American public opinion, and turns up an unlimited supply of anger, hatred and resentment in the process.

Known in theatrical circles as a monologist and performance artist, Eric Bogosian debuted the initial incarnation of *Talk Radio* in Portland, Ore, in 1985. For the screenplay, he and director Oliver Stone worked in material relating to Alan Berg, the Denver talkshow host murdered by neo-Nazis in 1984, and also created a flashback to illuminate their antihero's personal background and beginnings in the radio game.

Most of the film, however, unfolds in the modern studio of KGAB, a Dallas station from which the infamous Barry Champlain (Bogosian) holds forth. Young, caustic, rude, insulting, grandstanding, flippant and mercilessly cruel, the talkshow host spews vitriol impartially on those of all races, colors and creeds and spares the feelings of no one.

Champlain draws out the nighttime's seamiest denizens from under their rocks, fringe characters with access to the airwaves.

A dramatic structure has been imposed on the proceedings by the arrival of a radio syndicator who wants to take Champlain's show nationwide. At the same time, Champlain's ex-wife Ellen (Ellen Greene) arrives in town, which occasions a look back at the man's origins.

Bogosian commands attention in a patented tour-de-force. Supporting performances are all vividly realized, notably Michael Wincott's drug-crazed Champlain fan invited to the studio for a tete-a-tete with the host.

●●●●●●●●●●●●●●●●●●●●●●●●●●●●●●●●

■ **TALL GUY, THE**

1989, 92 MINS, UK ◇ ▼

Dir Mel Smith   *Prod* Paul Webster   *Scr* Richard Curtis   *Ph* Adrian Biddle   *Ed* Dan Rae   *Mus* Peter Brewis   *Art Dir* Grant Hicks
● Jeff Goldblum, Emma Thompson, Rowan Atkinson, Emil Wolk, Geraldine James (LWT/Virgin/Working Title)

The Tall Guy is a cheery, ingratiating romantic comedy with Jeff Goldblum putting in a stellar performance as a bumbling American actor in London whose career and romantic tribulations are suddenly transformed into triumphs.

At the outset, Yank thesp Goldblum has been performing in the West End for several years as straight man to popular comic Rowan Atkinson. The insecure goof-ball is earning a living but going nowhere fast when he comes under the care of hospital nurse Emma Thompson.

Immediately smitten, Goldblum spends the time between weekly visits for injections desperately concocting ways to ask her out.

Throughout the entire film, the relationship evolves winningly, with so much believable give-and-take, mutual ribbing and support that one roots for it heavily.

As soon as he has discovered domestic bliss, however, Goldblum is sacked by Atkinson, who resents anyone else in his show getting a laugh, and is thrust into the forbidding world of the unemployed actor.

The fresh, alert performances add enormously to the polished sparkle of the script. Goldblum is in splendid form as the eternally naive American abroad. Thompson makes a wonderfully poised foil for her leading man's volubility. British favorite Atkinson has a great time enacting the most vain and mean-spirited of stars, and Hugh Thomas elicits quite a few laughs in his brief appearance as a wild-eyed medic.

●●●●●●●●●●●●●●●●●●●●●●●●●●●●●●●●

■ **TALL MEN, THE**

1955, 122 MINS, US ◇ ▼

Dir Raoul Walsh   *Prod* William A. Bacher, William B. Hawks   *Scr* Sydney Boehm, Frank Nugent   *Ph* Leo Tover   *Ed* Louis Loeffler   *Mus* Victor Young   *Art Dir* Lyle Wheeler, Mark-Lee Kirk
● Clark Gable, Jane Russell, Robert Ryan, Cameron Mitchell, Emile Meyer (20th Century-Fox)

They must have had *The Tall Men* in mind when they invented CinemaScope. It's a big, robust western that fills the wide screen with a succession of panoramic scenes of often incredible beauty.

This is the Clark Gable of old in a role that's straight up his alley – rough, tough, quick on the draw and yet with all the 'right' instincts. The vet actor seems to enjoy himself thoroughly and he is equally at ease in the saddle as in his swap-a-quip dialog with Jane Russell.

There's no use quibbling about Russell. She goes through most of the film taunting both Gable and Robert Ryan. It's probably only fair to assume that her pancake-flat acting is a secondary consideration. She does show a sense of comedy in a couple of scenes and the pic benefits from it.

Story has brothers Gable and Cameron Mitchell working for Ryan and they become partners in a venture that calls for them to drive a large herd of cattle from Texas to Montana. On the way south, the trio runs into Russell, and Gable saves her from an Indian attack.

●●●●●●●●●●●●●●●●●●●●●●●●●●●●●●●●

■ **TALL T, THE**

1957, 78 MINS, US ◇

Dir Budd Boetticher   *Prod* Randolph Scott, Harry Joe Brown   *Scr* Burt Kennedy   *Ph* Charles Lawton Jr   *Ed* Al Clark   *Mus* Heinz Roemheld   *Art Dir* George Brooks

● Randolph Scott, Richard Boone, Maureen O'Sullivan, Arthur Hunnicutt, Skip Homeier, Henry Silva (Columbia)

An unconventional western, *The Tall T* passes up most oater cliches. There's a wealth of suspense in the screenplay based on a story [*The Captives*] by Elmore Leonard. From a quiet start the yarn acquires a momentum which explodes in a sock climax.

Modest and unassuming, Randolph Scott is a rancher who's been seized by a trio of killers led by Richard Boone. Also captured are newlyweds Maureen O'Sullivan and John Hubbard. Originally the outlaws planned a stage robbery, but are urged privately by the craven Hubbard to hold his heiress-wife for ransom in the hope that this move might save his skin.

Under Budd Boetticher's direction the story develops slowly, but relentlessly toward the action-packed finale. Scott impresses as the strong, silent type who ultimately vanquishes his captors. Boone is crisply proficient as the sometimes remorseful outlaw leader. His psychopathic henchmen are capably delineated by Skip Homeier and Henry Silva.

●●●●●●●●●●●●●●●●●●●●●●●●●●●●●●●●

■ **TAMARIND SEED, THE**

1974, 123 MINS, UK ◇ ▼

Dir Blake Edwards   *Prod* Ken Wales   *Scr* Blake Edwards   *Ph* Freddie Young   *Ed* Ernest Walter   *Mus* John Barry   *Art Dir* Harry Pottle
● Julie Andrews, Omar Sharif, Anthony Quayle, Dan O'Herlihy, Sylvia Syms, Oscar Homolka (ITC/Jewel/Lorimar)

Blake Edwards, whose forte usually is comedy, has turned Evelyn Anthony's novel, *The Tamarind Seed*, into what some will see as a love story against an espionage background and others as an excellent spy effort involving two people in love.

Julie Andrews as a British civil servant on vacation in the Caribbean meets and becomes fond of (but keeps at arm's length) a handsome Russian (Omar Sharif), also on leave. The Russian also has thoughts of enlisting her as an agent.

Sharif's importance lessens and he's slated for recall to Moscow, so he decides to defect. His bargaining point is the disclosure of a Britisher of high rank who is a Russian spy.

A major strong point of the film is the convincing performances of Andrews and Sharif as a pair of unlikely romantics.

●●●●●●●●●●●●●●●●●●●●●●●●●●●●●●●●

■ **TAMING OF THE SHREW, THE**

1967, 122 MINS, UK/ITALY ◇ ▼

Dir Franco Zeffirelli   *Prod* Richard Burton, Elizabeth Taylor   *Scr* Paul Dehn, Suso Cecchi D'Amico, Franco Zeffirelli   *Ph* Oswald Morris, Luciano Trasatti   *Ed* Peter Taylor, Carlo Fabianelli   *Mus* Nino Rota   *Art Dir* Renzo Mongiardino, John F. De Cuir
● Richard Burton, Elizabeth Taylor, Michael York, Michael Hordern, Victor Spinetti, Cyril Cusack (Columbia/Royal Films International/F.A.I.)

The Taming of the Shrew offers the interesting situation of Richard Burton fictionally taming Elizabeth Taylor, although the version is a boisterous, often over-stagey frolic. It will strike many as a fair compromise for mass audiences between the original Shakespeare and, say, *Kiss Me Kate*.

Screenwriters have done neat job, infusing dialog without rocking Bard's memory overmuch. The two stars pack plenty of wallop making their roles meaty and flamboyant with a larger-than-life Burton playing for plenty of sly laughs in the uninhibited wife-beating lark.

Taylor tends to over-exploit an 'earthy' aspect in early footage and switch to the subdued attitude comes too abruptly. But against that she's a buxom delight when

T

tamed. Comedy is sustained in witty wedding ceremony.

Shrewd casting of experienced players pays off with Michael Hordern, Victor Spinetti, Cyril Cusack, Alfred Lynch and Giancarlo Cobelli standouts.

● ●

■ TANGO & CASH

1989, 98 MINS, US ◇ ⓥ

Dir Andrei Konchalovsky *Prod* John Peters, Peter Guber, Larry Franco *Scr* Randy Feldman *Ph* Donald E. Thorin *Ed* Huber De La Bouillerie, Robert Forretti *Mus* Harold Faltermeyer *Art Dir* David Klassen, Richard Berger

● Sylvester Stallone, Kurt Russell, Teri Hatcher, Jack Palance, Brion James, Michael J. Pollard (Guber-Peters/Warner)

Tango & Cash is a mindless buddy cop pic, loaded with nonstop action that's played mostly for laughs and delivers too few of them. Inane and formulaic, the film relies heavily on whatever chemistry it can generate between Sylvester Stallone and Kurt Russell, who repeatedly trade wisecracks while facing life-or-death situations.

Jack Palance re-creates down to each gasp his role from *Batman* as a snarling crime boss who decides to bring down the two cops who have separately plagued his drug-dealing schemes.

Framed and sent to prison, the two rival cops (named Tango and Cash) become a reluctant team to exonerate themselves. Along the way, they hitch up with Tango's bombshell sister (Teri Hatcher), who happens to be an exotic dancer at some *Star Wars*-esque nightspot.

The thinking seems to be if you're going to be ridiculous you might as well go at it full throttle, and director Andrei Konchalovsky does just that. Albert Magnoli, helmer of *Purple Rain*, directed the final two weeks of lensing after Konchalovsky quit in a dispute over pic's ending.

● ●

■ TANK

1984, 113 MINS, US ◇ ⓥ

Dir Marvin Chomsky *Prod* Irwin Yablans *Scr* Dan Gordon *Ph* Don Brinkrant *Ed* Donald R. Rede *Mus* Lalo Schifrin *Art Dir* Bill Kenney

● James Garner, G.D. Spradlin, Shirley Jones, C. Thomas Howell, James Cramwell, Jenilee Harrison (Lorimar)

The audience appeal of loners-against-corruption is here refashioned with the hero inside a marauding Sherman tank, taking on a maniacal southern sheriff in defense of integrity and family.

James Garner's persona gives the events a soft, human, and at times bemused edge.

First 10 minutes, showing Garner's arrival on an army base are terribly slow; relationship is ploddingly established with wife Shirley Jones and teenage son C. Thomas Howell.

Pace finally picks up when Garner gets in trouble for bashing a deputy who had slapped around a prostitute in a bar. The action triggers outrage by the local sheriff, another signature role by G.D. Spradlin, who gets even with Garner by framing his son and sending the boy to a despicable work farm.

● ●

■ TAPS

1981, 118 MINS, US ◇

Dir Harold Becker *Prod* Stanley R. Jaffe, Howard B. Jaffe *Scr* Darryl Ponicsan, Robert Mark Kamen *Ph* Owen Roizman *Ed* Maury Winetrobe *Mus* Maurice Jarre *Art Dir* Stan Jolley, Alfred Sweeney

● George C. Scott, Timothy Hutton, Sean Penn, Tom Cruise, Ronny Cox (20th Century-Fox)

Plot [based on Devery Freeman's novel *Father*

Sky] centers on a military academy whose students are angered that their school and its traditions are being sold out from under them in order to build a bunch of condominiums.

Timothy Hutton tries to lend some humanity to the headstrong cadet who leads his fellow students in forcibly taking over the school (weapons and all) in a last ditch effort to save it, but Hutton just appears to be too nice a guy to let little kids walk around with machine guns ready to fire, even with his military haircut and serious swagger.

George C. Scott makes a brief but convincing apperance in the first section as the slightly deranged general who serves as role model to Hutton and the rest of the academy.

Director Harold Becker has brought the film along at a snail's pace yet has still succeeded in raising serious questions on the value of a military school education.

● ●

■ TARANTULA

1955, 80 MINS, US

Dir William Alland *Prod* Jack Arnold *Scr* Robert M. Fresco, Martin Berkeley *Ph* George Robinson *Ed* William M. Morgan *Mus* Henry Mancini *Art Dir* Alexander Golitzen, Alfred Sweeney

● John Agar, Mara Corday, Leo G. Carroll, Nestor Paiva, Ross Elliott, Clint Eastwood (Universal)

A tarantula as big as a barn puts the horror into this well-made program science-fictioner and it is quite credibly staged and played, bringing off the far-fetched premise with a maximum of believability.

Some scientists, stationed near Desert Rock, Ariz, are working on an automatically stabilized nutritional formula that will feed the world's ever-increasing population when the natural food supply becomes too small. Through variously staged circumstances, a tarantula that has been injected with the yet unstabilized formula escapes and, while continuously increasing in size starts living off cattle and humans.

Leo G. Carroll is excellent in his scientist role, while John Agar, young town medico, and Mara Corday carry off the romantic demands very well.

● ●

■ TARAS BULBA

1962, 123 MINS, US ◇ ⓥ

Dir J. Lee Thompson *Prod* Harold Hecht *Scr* Waldo Salt, Karl Tunberg *Ph* Joseph MacDonald *Ed* William Reynolds, Gene Milford, Eda Warren, Folmar Blanksted *Mus* Franz Waxman *Art Dir* Edward Carrere

● Tony Curtis, Yul Brynner, Christine Kaufmann, Sam Wanamaker, Brad Dexter, Guy Rolfe (United Artists)

For many minutes of the two hours it takes director J. Lee Thompson to put Gogol's tale of the legendary Cossack hero on the screen, the panorama of fighting men and horses sweeping across the wide steppes (actually the plains of Argentina) provides a compelling sense of pageantry and grandeur.

As powerful as they are, the spectacular features of *Taras Bulba* do not quite render palatable the wishy-washy subplot, seemingly devised to give Tony Curtis as much screen time as the far more colorful title-role of Yul Brynner. Even avid action-seekers are likely to find hard swallowing a hoary love story of an uncivilized Cossack lad and a polished Polish maiden.

Curtis, an excellent actor when properly supervised or motivated, was seemingly neither inspired nor irritated sufficiently by his talented credits-sharer to do more than kiss and kill on cue.

Brynner's Taras Bulba is an arrogant, proud, physically powerful Cossack chief. Even though the actor follows the habit of running his lines together, his actions are always unmistakably clear. He's allowed

plenty of space in which to chew the scenery and there's precious little of it in which he doesn't leave teethmarks.

The battle sequences and, to a lesser extent, the Cossack camp scenes, are the picture's greatest assets. Some of cameraman Joseph MacDonald's long shots of hordes of horsemen sweeping across the plains, as countless others pour over every hillside, are breathtakingly grand and fully utilize the wide screen. Franz Waxman's score, Russian derived, for the battles and his czardas-like themes for the Cossacks are among his best work.

● ●

■ TARGET

1985, 117 MINS, US ◇ ⓥ

Dir Arthur Penn *Prod* Richard D. Zanuck, David Brown *Scr* Howard Berk, Don Petersen *Ph* Jean Tournier *Ed* Stephen A. Rotter, Richard P. Cirincione *Mus* Michael Small *Art Dir* Willy Holt

● Gene Hackman, Matt Dillon, Gayle Hunnicutt, Victoria Fyodorova, Josef Sommer, Guy Boyd (CBS)

Target is a spy thriller that's not only completely understandable and involving throughout, but also continually surprising along the way. It also strangely contains a few scenes of dreadful writing, acting and direction.

Gene Hackman is a seemingly dull lumberyard owner in Dallas and Matt Dillon is his sporty roughneck son. Loving but a bit bored, too, mother Gayle Hunnicutt finally has decided to vacation in Paris alone because Hackman has an odd aversion to visiting Europe. While away, she hopes the two will make an effort to get to like each other. Then comes news that Mom has been kidnapped.

Although there are the obligatory preposterous auto chases, the action overall is supportive of the plot rather than a substitute. Ditto bloodshed and pyromania.

● ●

■ TARGETS

1968, 90 MINS, US ◇ ⓥ

Dir Peter Bogdanovich *Prod* Peter Bogdanovich *Scr* Peter Bogdanovich *Ph* Laszlo Kovacs *Ed* [uncredited] *Art Dir* Polly Platt

● Boris Karloff, Tim O'Kelly, Nancy Hsueh, James Brown, Peter Bogdanovich (Saticoy)

A good programmer, within low budget limitations, about a sniper and his innocent victims. A separate, concurrent sub-plot features Boris Karloff as a horror film star who feels he is washed up. Both plot lines converge in an exciting climax.

Peter Bogdanovich has made a film of much suspense and implicit violence. It opens with a typical horror pic finale, which in a neat switcheroo turns out to be just that, as producer Monte Landis, o.o.'s the film. Karloff declares he is through with films and exits. A sidewalk scene introduces Tim O'Kelly, all-American boy who has drawn a bead on Karloff from a nearby gun shop.

Plot then picks up O'Kelly, a gun-loving, disturbed youth who 'had everything to live for'. One night, his mind snaps. He hides in the screen tower of a drive-in theatre, whence he terrorizes the audience. A press stunt has drawn Karloff to the ozoner for the climax.

As any newspaper or TV newsreel shows, mass murderers look just like anyone else. O'Kelly's projection of blandness is most appropriate to the suspense.

Aware of the virtue of implied violence, Bogdanovich conveys moments of shock, terror, suspense and fear.

● ●

■ TARNISHED ANGELS, THE

1957, 87 MINS, US

Dir Douglas Sirk *Prod* Albert Zugsmith *Scr* George Zuckerman *Ph* Irving Glassberg *Ed* Russell F. Schoengarth *Mus* Frank Skinner *Art Dir* Alexander Golitzen, Alfred Sweeney

● Rock Hudson, Robert Stack, Dorothy Malone, Jack Carson, Robert Middleton, Troy Donahue (Universal)

The Tarnished Angels is a stumbling entry. Characters are mostly colorless, given static reading in drawn-out situations, and story line is lacking in punch. Film is designed as a follow-up to *Written on the Wind*, to take advantage of the principals both before and behind the camera.

The production is based on William Faulkner's novel *Pylon*, and screenplay carries an air circus setting. Rock Hudson is intro'd as a seedy, but idealistic, New Orleans reporter covering a barnstorming show in that city. He falls for Dorothy Malone, trick parachutist-wife of Robert Stack, speed flyer and World War I ace, still living in his past glory as he and his small unit cruises about the country participating in air events.

Hudson appears in an unrealistic role to which he can add nothing and Stack spends most of the time with eagles in his eyes.

· ·

■ TARZAN AND HIS MATE

1934, 92 MINS, US

Dir Cedric Gibbons   *Scr* Howard Emmett Rogers, Leon Gordon, James Kevin McGuinness   *Ph* Charles Clarke, Clyde De Vinna
● Johnny Weissmuller, Maureen O'Sullivan, Neil Hamilton, Paul Cavanagh, Forrester Harvey, Nathan Curry (M-G-M)

In *Tarzan and His Mate*, second of the Metro series with Johnny Weissmuller, the monkeys do everything but bake cakes and the very human elephants always seem on the verge of sitting down for a nice, quiet game of chess; yet the picture has a strange sort of power that overcomes the total lack of logic.

Tarzan No. 1 ended with Tarz and the white girl from England at peace in their jungle kingdom. They're again at peace as No. 2 ends, but in the 92 minutes between the two fade-outs they're almost in pieces, several times. Trouble starts soon as the domain of Mr and Mrs Tarzan (Weissmuller and Maureen O'Sullivan) is trespassed upon by Neil Hamilton and Paul Cavanagh, a couple of heels from Mayfair. Boys are after the fortune in ivory which lies in a pachyderm graveyard.

Tarzan and his mate spend most of their time swinging through the branches. The Tarzans also do some fancy swimming, particularly during a tank sequence when Weissmuller and a lady swimmer doubling for O'Sullivan, perform some artistic submarine formations. The lady is brassiere-less, but photographed from the side only.

· ·

■ TARZAN, THE APE MAN

1932, 70 MINS, US

Dir W. S. Van Dyke   *Scr* Cyril Hume, Ivor Novello   *Ph* Harold Rosson, Clayde De Vinna   *Ed* Ben Lewis, Tom Held
● Johnny Weissmuller, Maureen O'Sullivan, Neil Hamilton, C. Aubrey Smith, Doris Lloyd, Forrester Harvey (M-G-M)

A jungle and stunt picture, done in deluxe style, with tricky handling of fantastic atmosphere, and a fine, artless performance by the Olympic athlete that represents the absolute best that could be done with the character [created by Edgar Rice Burroughs].

Footage is loaded with a wealth of sensational wild animal stuff. Suspicion is unavoidable that some of it is cut-in material left over from the same producer's *Trader Horn* (by the same director).

Some of the stunt episodes are grossly overdone, but the production skill and literary treatment in other directions compensates. Tarzan (Johnny Weissmuller) is pictured as achieving impossible feats of strength and

daring. One of them has him battling single-handed, and armed only with an inadequate knife, not only with one lion but with a panther and two lions, and saved at the last minute from still a third big cat only by the friendly help of an elephant summoned by a call of distress in jungle language.

Story that introduces the Tarzan character is slight. An English trader (C. Aubrey Smith) and his young partner (Neil Hamilton) are about to start in search of the traditional elephants' graveyard where ivory abounds, when the elder man's daughter from England (Maureen O'Sullivan) appears at the trading post and insists upon going along. The adventures grow out of their travels.

· ·

■ TARZAN, THE APE MAN

1981, 112 MINS, US ◇

Dir John Derek   *Prod* Bo Derek   *Scr* Tom Rowe, Garry Goddard   *Ph* John Derek   *Ed* James B. Ling   *Mus* Perry Botkin   *Art Dir* Wolfgang Dickmann
● Bo Derek, Richard Harris, John Phillip Law, Miles O'Keeffe (M-G-M/Svengali)

This endless romp through the jungle, lacking any focus, fun or excitement (sexual or otherwise), seems to exist merely as a reason for husband John to find another 1001 ways to photograph wife Bo in varying stages of undress.

With about three minutes shaved as a result of a court decision stating that the Dereks and M-G-M went beyond the remake rights bought from the Burroughs estate, this opus will disappoint both Tarzan fans and Bo admirers.

A supposed remake of the 1932 *Tarzan, the Ape Man*, the Derek version has less to do with the jungle man (who doesn't show his face until halfway through the picture) than it does in dealing with Jane's (Bo's) rediscovery of her long-lost explorer father Richard Harris.

The father-daughter relationship doesn't have a chance here with Bo's wooden recitation of her lines and Harris' ranting through any number of dreary, confusing speeches.

Although John Derek's direction remains loose and uninspired (the few action shots of Tarzan are ruined with corny slow motion footage), he does know how to shoot pretty pictures of Sri Lanka and, more particularly, Bo. If *Tarzan* were a magazine layout, he'd probably be nominated for something.

· ·

■ TARZAN'S GREATEST ADVENTURE

1959, 90 MINS, US ◇

Dir John Guillermin   *Prod* Sy Weintraub, Harvey Hayutin   *Scr* Bernie Giler, John Guillermin   *Ph* Ted Scaife   *Ed* Bert Rule   *Mus* Douglas Gamley   *Art Dir* Michael Stringer
● Gordon Scott, Anthony Quayle, Sara Shane, Niall MacGinnis, Sean Connery, Scilla Gabel (Paramount)

Tarzan finally steps away from Hollywood's process screens to pound his chest amid authentic terrors in the heart of Africa. Death and trauma are the stars, and the supporting players are bullets, arrows, knives, hatchets, dynamite, neck-choking paraphernalia, crocodiles, lions, snakes, spiders, boulders, spikes, pits, quicksand and prickly cactus. It's a furious affair, with an exciting chase or two.

Tarzan (Gordon Scott) is a modern he-man, still adorned in loincloth but more conversational than Edgar Rice Burroughs pictured him. Scott puts little emotion into his greatest adventure, but he swings neatly from tree to tree, takes good care of a crocodile, even if it does appear dead from the start, deciphers with ease the sounds of his animal friends and, more than anything else, looks the part.

Film's storyline has Tarzan and another white man as mortal enemies. The antagonist (Anthony Quayle) is leading a five-member boat expedition to get rich in diamonds, and Tarzan, knowing of his bestial attitude, follows in hot pursuit. An approximately beautiful female (Sara Shane), drops out of the sky to tag along with Tarzan and turns out to be quite handy in helping the apeman through a bad time or two.

Quayle is excellent as the scarfaced villain, and Niall MacGinnis as a nearly blind diamond expert is equally fine. Sean Connery and Al Mulock, the two other male members of the expedition, are okay, and Scilla Gabel, looking like a miniature Sophia Loren, is easy to look at.

· ·

■ TASTE OF HONEY, A

1961, 100 MINS, UK

Dir Tony Richardson   *Prod* Tony Richardson   *Scr* Shelagh Delaney, Tony Richardson   *Ph* Walter Lassally   *Ed* Antony Gibbs   *Mus* John Addison   *Art Dir* Ralph Brinton
● Dora Bryan, Rita Tushingham, Robert Stephens, Murray Melvin, Paul Danquah (British Lion/Woodfall)

Shelagh Delaney's play, which clicked both in the West End and on Broadway, has an earthy gusto and sincerity that lift its somewhat downbeat theme and drab surroundings. It has humor, understanding, and poignance. Oddly enough the dialog, though pointedly couched in the semi-illiterate vernacular of the lower-class North Country working folk, archives at times a halting and touching form of poetry.

The film faithfully follows the narrative of the play. But the camera effectively gets into the streets and captures the gray drabness of the locals as well as the boisterous vulgarity of Blackpool, saloons and dance-halls. Yarn primarily concerns five people and their dreams, hopes and fears. They are Jo (Rita Tushingham); her flighty, sluttish neglectful mother; the fancy man her mother marries; a young Negro ship's cook with whom Jo has a brief affair which leaves her pregnant; and a sensitive young homosexual who gives her the tenderness and affection lacking in her relationship with her mother.

Film introduces 19-year-old Rita Tushingham as the 16-year-old schoolgirl. She plays with no makeup, her hair is untidy, her profile completely wrong by all accepted standards; but her expressive eyes and her warm, wry smile are haunting.

Dora Bryan tackles the role of the flighty, footloose mother with confidence and zest. The three men in the lives of daughter and mother are also played with keen insight by Robert Stephens, Paul Danquah and Murray Melvin. Perhaps the most difficult role is that of Melvin. He repeats the success he made of the part of the young homosexual in the play.

· ·

■ TASTE THE BLOOD OF DRACULA

1970, 95 MINS, UK ◇

Dir Peter Sasdy   *Prod* Aida Young   *Scr* John Elder [=Anthony Hinds]   *Ph* Arthur Grant   *Ed* Chris Barnes   *Mus* James Bernard   *Art Dir* Scott MacGregor
● Christopher Lee, Geoffrey Keen, Gwen Watford, Linda Hayden, Peter Sallis, Anthony Corlan (Hammer)

The setting is in Victorian England, on London's fringes and concerns three hypocritical, erotic old buffers who, sated by their dingy little orgies in the East End, look for bigger, more lustful thrills.

They get entangled with one of Dracula's disciples and, with the aid of the blood of Dracula and some of his 'props', sold to them by a wise peddler, they start to dabble in Black Mass and Satanic ritual. They bump off Dracula's messenger in terror and Dracula swears to dispose of the three men.

T

From then on, it's the old routine of Dracula causing death and disaster, upsetting the families by abducting daughters and turning one of them into a vampire and generally making himself a thundering evil nuisance.

••••••••••••••••••••••••••••••

■ TATTOO

1981, 102 MINS, US ◇

Dir Bob Brooks *Prod* Joseph E. Levine, Richard P. Levine *Scr* Joyce Bunuel *Ph* Arthur Ornitz *Ed* Thom Noble *Mus* Barry De Vorzon *Art Dir* Stuart Wurtzel
● Bruce Dern, Maud Adams, Leonard Frey, Rikke Borge, John Getz (20th Century-Fox)

In this 20th-Centuray release, Bruce Dern appears as a congenital cuckoo, who loves to paint permanent pictures on people's bodies. Becoming enamored of fashion model Maude Adams, Dern decides she could be life's perfect companion, given a new paint job.

So he kidnaps her. Such is Bob Brooks' direction and Joyce Bunuel's script that the problem of getting the unconscious Adams from her NY highrise apartment to an abandoned house on the New Jersey seashore isn't difficult at all. In one scene, they are in NY. In the next, cut to NJ. Filmmaking is simple.

Anyway, once Dern has her in his drawing room, he begins to doodie on her bare body. Finally, the work is finished and Dern takes his own clothes off to reveal that he, too, is a work of art. This seems to turn Adams on and they make love until she stabs him to death with the tattoo machine. Yes, she does.

••••••••••••••••••••••••••••••

■ TAXI DRIVER

1976, 113 MINS, US ◇ Ⓥ

Dir Martin Scorsese *Prod* Michael Phillips, Julia Phillips *Scr* Paul Schrader *Ph* Michael Chapman *Ed* Marcia Lucas, Tom Rolf, Melvin Shapiro *Mus* Bernard Herrmann *Art Dir* Charles Rosen
● Robert De Niro, Cybill Shepherd, Peter Boyle, Albert Brooks, Leonard Harris, Harvey Keitel (Columbia)

Assassins, mass murderers and other freakish criminals more often than not turn out to be the quiet kid down the street. *Taxi Driver* is Martin Scorsese's frighteningly plausible case history of such a person. It's a powerful film and a terrific showcase for the versatility of star Robert De Niro.

The pic has a quasi-documentary look, and Bernard Herrmann's final score is superb (a final credit card conveys 'Our gratitude and respect').

Paul Schrader's original screenplay is in fact a sociological horror story. Take a young veteran like Travis Bickle. A night cabbie, he prowls the NY streets until dawn, stopping occasionally for coffee, killing offduty time in porno theatres.

What prods Travis are a series of rejections: among others by Cybill Shepherd, adroitly cast as the tele-heroine lookalike working for the presidential campaign of Leonard Harris, and by Jodie Foster, teenage prostitute.

In a climactic sequence, the madman exorcises himself. It's a brutal, horrendous and cinematically brilliant sequence, capped by the irony that he becomes a media hero for a day.

De Niro gives the role the precise blend of awkwardness, naivete and latent violence.
□ 1976: Best Picture (Nomination)

••••••••••••••••••••••••••••••

■ TAZA, SON OF COCHISE

1954, 79 MINS, US ◇

Dir Douglas Sirk *Prod* Ross Hunter *Scr* George Zuckerman, Gerald Drayson Adams *Ph* Russell Metty *Ed* Milton Carruth *Mus* Frank Skinner
● Rock Hudson, Barbara Rush, Gregg Palmer, Bart Roberts, Morris Ankrum, Gene Iglesias (Universal)

Taza, Son of Cochise is a colorful 3-D Indian–US Cavalry entry alternating between hot action and passages of almost pastoral quality. The spectacular scenery of Moab, Utah, furnishes a particularly apropos background for unfoldment of the script, and Douglas Sirk's direction is forceful, aimed at making every scene an eye-filling experience.

This is the story of the great Apache chief's son, who promises at his father's deathbed he will try to keep the peace that Cochise so painstakingly made with the whites. He is opposed here by his younger brother, who attempts to win the tribe over to Geronimo and take to the warpath again.

Rock Hudson suffices in action demands of his role of Taza, but character is none too believable. Barbara Rush, co-starring as the daughter of Morris Ankrum, one of Geronimo's followers, is in for romantic purposes and handles part well.

Jeff Chandler, who was Cochise in studio's *Battle at Apache Pass*, repeats character for the single death-bed scene, without screen credit.

••••••••••••••••••••••••••••••

■ TEA AND SYMPATHY

1956, 122 MINS, US ◇

Dir Vincente Minnelli *Prod* Pandro S. Berman *Scr* Robert Anderson *Ph* John Alton *Ed* Ferris Webster *Mus* Adolph Deutsch *Art Dir* William A. Horning, Edward Carfagno
● Deborah Kerr, John Kerr, Leif Erickson, Edward Andrews, Darryl Hickman, Norma Crane (M-G-M)

This is the story of a youngster regarded by fellow students as 'not regular' (i.e. not manly). The spotlight is on clearly implied homosexuality.

Robert Anderson's adaptation of his own legiter keeps the essentials in proper focus. The pivotal role of the misunderstood sensitive boy is an excellently drawn characterization. The part is played with marked credibility by John Kerr. The housemaster's wife is a character study of equal sensitivity and depth. Deborah Kerr gives the role all it deserves.

The housemaster part, played with muscle-flexing exhibitionism by Leif Erickson, loses some of its meaning in the tone-down. On the stage his efforts at being 'manly' carried the suggestion that he was trying to compensate a fear of a homo trend in his own makeup. The suggestion is diluted to absence in the picture.

Edward Andrews, as John Kerr's father, is the brash and understanding parent who would prefer to see his son carry on with the town tart to erase his 'sister-boy' reputation.

••••••••••••••••••••••••••••••

■ TEA FOR TWO

1950, 97 MINS, US ◇

Dir David Butler *Prod* William Jacobs *Scr* Harry Clork *Ph* Wilfrid M. Cline *Ed* Irene Morra
● Doris Day, Gordon MacRae, Gene Nelson, Patrice Wymore, Billy De Wolfe, S.Z. Sakall (Warner)

A generous sprinkling of songs, dances and comedy makes *Tea for Two* the type of beguiling musical nonsense that practically always finds a ready reception. It wears its Technicolor dress well, the nostalgic numbers from the 1929 *No, No, Nanette* and other cleffing of the period listen well, the pacing is smooth and the cast able.

Suggested by the *Nanette* book by Frank Mandel, Otto Harbach, Vincent Youmans and Emil Nyitray, the script is spiced with dialog and situations that permit easy introduction of the variety of dance numbers.

Flashback technique to get 1929 period on the screen has the capable help of S.Z. Sakall, playing Doris Day's uncle, who is telling the story to the children of the two singers.

••••••••••••••••••••••••••••••

■ TEAHOUSE OF THE AUGUST MOON, THE

1956, 123 MINS, US ◇

Dir Daniel Mann *Prod* Jack Cummings *Scr* John Patrick *Ph* John Alton *Ed* Harold F. Kress *Mus* Saul Chaplin, Kikuko Kanai *Art Dir* William A. Horning, Eddie Imazu
● Marlon Brando, Glenn Ford, Machiko Kyo, Eddie Albert, Paul Ford (M-G-M)

Teahouse retains the basic appeal that made it a unique war novel and a legit hit. There is some added slapstick for those who prefer their comedy broader. Adding to its prospects are some top comedy characterizations, notably from Glenn Ford, plus the offbeat casting of Marlon Brando in a comedy role.

In transferring his play based on the Vern Sneider novel to the screen, John Patrick has provided a subtle shift in the focal interest.

Deft screenplay provides an interesting fillip in retaining the stage device of a narrative prolog and epilog by Brando and the warmly humorous verbiage has been left intact. Story line also is unsullied as the film unspools the tribulations of Ford, the young army officer assigned to bring the benefits of democracy and free enterprise to the little Okinawan town of Tobiki.

The role of Capt Fisby represents a romp for Glenn Ford, who gives it an unrestrained portrayal that adds mightily to the laughs. Brando is excellent as the interpreter, limning the rogueish character perfectly. Physically, he seems a bit too heavy for the role.

Japanese actress Machiko Kyo is easy on the eyes as the geisha girl and there is excellent support from Eddie Albert, who sparkles as the psychiatrist who yearns to be an agricultural expert.

••••••••••••••••••••••••••••••

■ TEEN WOLF

1985, 91 MINS, US ◇ Ⓥ

Dir Rod Daniel *Prod* Mark Levinson, Scott Rosenfelt *Scr* Joseph Loeb III, Matthew Weisman *Ph* Tim Suhrstedt *Ed* Lois Freeman-Fork *Mus* Miles Goodman *Art Dir* Rosemary Brandenberg
● Michael J. Fox, James Hampton, Scott Paulin, Susan Ursitti, Jerry Levine, Jim Mackrell (Wolfkill/Atlantic)

Lightweight item is innocuous and well-intentioned but terribly feeble, another example of a decent idea yielding the least imaginative results conceivable.

The Beacontown Beavers have the most pathetic basketball team in high school history, and pint-sized Michael J. Fox is on the verge of quitting when he notices certain biological changes taking place. Heavy hair is growing on the backs of his hands, his ears and teeth are elongating.

Instead of turning into a horrific teen werewolf, however, Fox takes to trucking around school halls in full furry regalia, becoming more successful with the ladies and, most importantly, winning basketball games.

Fox is likeable enough in the lead, something that cannot be said for the remainder of the lackluster cast.

••••••••••••••••••••••••••••••

■ TEENAGE MUTANT NINJA TURTLES

1990, 93 MINS, HONGKONG US ◇ Ⓥ

Dir Steve Barron *Prod* Todd W. Langen, Bobby Herbeck *Ph* John Fenner *Ed* [Uncredited] *Mus* John Du Prez *Art Dir* Roy Forge Smith
● Judith Hoag, Elias Koteas, Joch Pais, Michelan Sisti, Leif Tilden, David Forman (Golden Harvest/Limelight)

While visually rough around the edges, sometimes sluggish in its plotting and marred by overtones of racism in its use of Oriental villains, the wacky live-action screen version of the *Teenage Mutant Ninja Turtles* cartoon characters scores with its generally engaging tongue-in-cheek humor.

Supposedly mutated by radioactive goop, the turtles live in the sewers, eat pizza, dance to rock music, play Trivial Pursuit and casually toss around such words as 'awesome', 'bodacious' and 'gnarly'.

The screenplay makes all four of the green guys seem like clones, differentiated mostly by their variegated colored headbands. The plot is nothing more than some nonsense about the turtles and a handful of human sidekicks trying to stop the Foot Clan from terrorizing NY streets.

A bit too much time is devoted to the peculiar romance of unbelievably funky TV newswoman Judith Hoag and her off-the-wall vigilante b.f. Elias Koteas, who join forces with the creatures and misunderstood j.d. Michael Turney.

The martial-arts setpieces are amusingly outlandish, with the screen populated by hordes of attackers whom the nonchalant, graceful turtles have little trouble vanquishing as they toss off streams of surfer-lingo wisecracks.

....

■ TEENAGE MUTANT NINJA TURTLES II THE SECRET OF OOZE

1991, 88 MINS, US ◇ ⊗

Dir Michael Pressman   *Prod* Thomas K. Gray, Kim Dawson, David Chan   *Scr* Todd W. Langen   *Ph* Shelly Johnson   *Ed* John Wright, Steve Mirkovich   *Mus* John Du Prez   *Art Dir* Roy Forge Smith
● Paige Turco, David Warner, Michelan Sisti, Leif Tilden, Kenn Troum, Mark Caso (Golden Harvest/Propper)

Though *Turtles II* suffers from a lack of novelty and an aimless screenplay, the bottom line is that the pic won't disappoint its core subteen audience. It gives more footage to Michelangelo, Donatello, Raphael, Leonardo and their giant rat master Splinter than the original did, and adds two hilarious childlike monsters, Rahzar and Tokka, who virtually steal the show.

The murky lighting, uninteresting human characters and violence of the original have been modified in the more amiable sequel, mostly to good effect.

Subtitle's promise that the ooze secret will be revealed doesn't pay off. David Warner, as the sympathetic and eccentric scientist who invented the stuff and now is trying to dispose of it, doesn't have much to do.

Paige Turco takes over the lead human role of Gotham TV newswoman April O'Neil from Judith Hoag, and while Turco is more glamorous, the character still seems unfocused and overly ditzy.

Ernie Reyes Jr has a winning role as a youthful pizza deliveryman/martial arts expert who wangles his way into the turtles' company and helps them in their neverending battle with the Foot Clan.

....

■ TELL ME LIES

1968, 118 MINS, UK/US ◇

Dir Peter Brook   *Prod* Peter Brook   *Scr* Denis Cannan   *Ph* Ian Wilson   *Ed* Ralph Sheldon   *Mus* Richard Peaslee
● Mark Jones, Pauline Munro, Robert Lloyd, Glenda Jackson (Continental/Brook)

Tell Me Lies depicts a wide range of attitudes toward the war in Vietnam. It's loosely based on Peter Brook's theatrical success-de-scandale *US*.

While Brook's emotional concern about the war seems unquestionable, his artistic sincerity is open to examination. *Tell Me Lies* suggests an aesthetic bankruptcy resulting from the director's debts to Bertolt Brecht, Joan Littlewood (*Oh, What a Lovely War*) and Jean-Luc Godard.

Color and black-and-white footage is haphazardly alternated to no effect. Musical numbers are shouted-sung in a cacophonic manner that only underscores the lyrics'

vacuity. Staged discussions are juxtaposed with cinema-verite encounters with British parliamentarians, Maoists and black-power advocate Stokeley Carmichael.

Verbal material is splayed in subtitles at the bottom of the screen, overlapped on sequences or subliminally injected word by word within a continuous segment. It's all pretty ugly.

....

■ TELL THEM WILLIE BOY IS HERE

1969, 97 MINS, US ◇ ⊗

Dir Abraham Polonsky   *Prod* Jennings Lang   *Scr* Abraham Polonsky   *Ph* Conrad Hall   *Ed* Melvin Shapiro   *Mus* Dave Grusin   *Art Dir* Alexander Golitzen, Henry Bumstead
● Robert Redford, Katharine Ross, Robert Blake, Susan Clark, Barry Sullivan, John Vernon (Universal)

A powerful unfoldment of a particular incident in US history, the film becomes, by extension, a deeply personal and radical vision of the past and future.

Film [from the book *Willie Boy . . . A Desert Manhunt* by Harry Lawton] tells the story of the tracking-down of a renegade Indian in California in 1909. Although Robert Blake is the title character, the film is really about Robert Redford, Coop, the deputy sheriff whose assignment it is to track down Willie.

Abraham Polonsky, who was blacklisted for 20 years, is not a director who works through his actors. Thesps are simple tools of his vision – their presences more than their abilities are used. Nobody's going to win any acting awards for their work herein. Still, Redford's 'presence' is magnificent, always suggesting the classically-structured, powerful-but-weak American.

....

■ TEMPEST, THE

1979, 96 MINS, UK ◇ ⑫

Dir Derek Jarman   *Prod* Guy Ford   *Scr* Derek Jarman   *Ph* Peter Middleton   *Ed* Leslie Walker   *Mus* Wavemaker   *Art Dir* Yolanda Sonnaband
● Heathcote Williams, Karl Johnson, Jack Birkett, Toyah Wilcox, Elisabeth Welch (Boyd's)

British helmer Derek Jarman's third feature, a film version of Shakespeare's most fanciful play, is definitely one of a kind. Its greatest strength is its 'look'. That offsets the director-adaptor's generally limp control of the narrative.

Although heavily cut and reorganized, the Bard's lines are used virtually throughout. The plot remains intact. Jarman's biggest liberty is the insertion of a wedding feast at the end, complete with dancing sailor boys, and blues singer Elisabeth Welch crooning 'Stormy Weather' as a kind of diva ex machina.

Most successful innovation is Toyah Wilcox's assault on the usually vacuous role of Miranda. Plump and punkish, her reaction to the first eligible male she has ever seen is more lusty than wide-eyed, and thoroughly believable.

....

■ "10"

1979, 122 MINS, US ◇ ⑫

Dir Blake Edwards   *Prod* Blake Edwards, Tony Adams   *Scr* Blake Edwards   *Ph* Frank Stanley   *Ed* Ralph E. Winters   *Mus* Henry Mancini   *Art Dir* Rodger Maus
● Dudley Moore, Julie Andrews, Bo Derek, Brian Dennehy, Dee Wallace, Robert Webber (Orion/Geoffrey)

Blake Edwards' *"10"* is a shrewdly observed and beautifully executed comedy of manners and morals.

"10" is theoretically the top score on Dudley Moore's female ranking system, although he raves that his dream girl is an '11'

after he first spots her. Frustrated in his song writing and in his relationship with g.f. Julie Andrews, diminutive Moore, 40-ish, four-time Oscar winner, decides to pursue the vision incarnated by Bo Derek despite fact that she's on her honeymoon with a jock type seemingly twice Moore's size.

Long build-up to Moore's big night with Derek is spiced with plenty of physical comedy which displays both Moore and Edwards in top slapstick form.

....

■ TEN COMMANDMENTS, THE

1923, 160 MINS, US ◇ ⊗ ⑫

Dir Cecil B. DeMille   *Prod* Cecil B. DeMille   *Scr* Jeanie MacPherson   *Ph* Bert Glennon, Peverell Marley, Archie Stout, J.F. Westerberg, Ray Rennahan   *Ed* Anne Bauchens   *Mus* Hugo Riesenfeld   *Art Dir* Paul Iribe
● Theodore Roberts, Charles De Roche, Estelle Taylor, Richard Dix, Rod La Rocque, Edythe Chapman (Paramount)

The opening Biblical scenes of *The Ten Commandments* are irresistible in their assembly, breadth, color and direction; they are enormous and just as attractive. Cecil B. DeMille puts in a thrill here with the opening of the Red Sea for Moses to pass through with the Children of Israel.

This section is in color, and there are often big scenes besides that one. They are immense and stupendous, so big the modern tale after that seems puny. The story is of two sons, one his mother's boy and the other a harum-scarum atheist. Cheating as a contractor, the atheist's defects in building material result in the collapse of a partly built church's wall, with the mother killed by the falling debris.

The best performance is given by Rod La Rocque as the atheist son, Dan McTavish. La Rocque really doesn't get properly started until called upon for plenty of emotion toward the finish. Theodore Roberts as Moses is but required to stride majestically, something he can do perhaps a little better than any one else, while Charles De Roche as Rameses (Pharaoh) always appears in a genteel, thoughtful mood as though wondering what it is all about.

The women do no better. Leatrice Joy wears a hat that may have been of the period of Moses; anyway it is an awful hat and her acting is strong enough to make you forget it.

....

■ TEN COMMANDMENTS, THE

1956, 219 MINS, US ◇ ⑫

Dir Cecil B. DeMille   *Prod* Cecil B. DeMille   *Scr* Aeneas MacKenzie, Jesse L. Lasky Jr, Fredric M. Frank, Jack Gariss   *Ph* Loyal Griggs   *Ed* Anne Bauchens   *Mus* Elmer Bernstein   *Art Dir* Hal Pereira, Walter Tyler, Albert Nozaki
● Charlton Heston, Yul Brynner, Anne Baxter, Edward G. Robinson, Yvonne De Carlo, Debra Paget (Paramount)

Cecil B. DeMille's super-spectacular about the Children of Israel held in brutal bondage until Moses, prodded by the God of Abraham, delivers them from Egyptian tyranny is a statistically intimidating production: the negative cost was $13.5 million and 25,000 extras were employed.

DeMille remains conventional with the motion picture as an art form. The eyes of the onlooker are filled with spectacle. Emotional tug is sometimes lacking.

Commandments is too long. More than two hours pass before the intermission and the break is desperately welcome. Scenes of the greatness that was Egypt, and Hebrews by the thousands under the whip of the taskmasters, are striking. But bigness wearies. There's simply too much.

Commandments hits the peak of beauty with a sequence that is unelaborate, this being the

T

Passover supper wherein Moses is shown with his family while the shadow of death falls on Egyptian first-borns.

The creeping shadow of darkness that destroyed the Egyptian first-borns, the trans-composition of Moses' staff into a serpent, the changeover of the life-giving water into blood, flames to engulf the land and the parting of the Red Sea – these are shown. The effect of all these special camera devices is varying, however, and does not escape a certain theatricality.

Performances meet requirements all the way but exception must be made of Anne Baxter as the Egyptian princess Nefretiri. Baxter leans close to old-school siren histrionics and this is out of sync with the spiritual nature of *Commandments*.

Charlton Heston is an adaptable performer as Moses, revealing inner glow as he is called by God to remove the chains of slavery that hold his people. Yvonne De Carlo is Sephora, the warm and understanding wife of Moses. Yul Brynner is expert as Rameses, who inherits the Egyptian throne and seeks to battle Moses and his God until he's forced to acknowledge that 'Moses' God is the real God'.
□ 1956: Best Picture (Nomination)

●●●●●●●●●●●●●●●●●●●●●●●●●

■ 10 LITTLE INDIANS

1966, 92 MINS, UK ▼

Dir George Pollock   *Prod* Oliver A. Unger, Harry M. Popkin   *Scr* Peter Yeldham   *Ph* Ernest Steward   *Ed* Peter Boita   *Mus* Malcolm Lockyer
● Hugh O'Brian, Shirley Eaton, Fabian, Leo Genn, Stanley Holloway, Wilfrid Hyde-White (Tenlit)

Second film version of Agatha Christie's endurable variation on the old idea of putting a group of disparate characters into a confined situation and letting them be killed one by one shapes up as good suspenser. The film was made entirely in Ireland although the setting has been changed to what appears to be a solitary schloss in the Austrian Alps.

Director George Pollock, despite a script with complicated credits (screenplay by Peter Yeldham, based on a script by Dudley Nichols, and adapted by Peter Welbeck, based on the Christie novel and play, *Ten Little Niggers*), works quite a bit of suspense into the restricted action, successfully hiding identity of the tenth Indian without resorting to too many 'red herrings'.

One major switch, an unfortunate one, has the first victim, originally an eccentric prince, changed to an American rock 'n' roll singer (Fabian, in an embarrassingly bad performance).

A two-minute 'whodunit break' is inserted near the end when the action is suspended while the audience is encouraged to guess the murderer's identity.

●●●●●●●●●●●●●●●●●●●●●●●●●

■ TEN LITTLE INDIANS

1975, 105 MINS, ITALY/W. GERMANY/FRANCE/SPAIN ◇

Dir Peter Collinson   *Scr* Enrique Llovet, Erich Krohnke   *Ph* Fernando Arritas   *Mus* Bruno Nicolai   *Art Dir* Jose Maria Tapiador
● Oliver Reed, Elke Sommer, Richard Attenborough, Gert Frobe, Stephane Audran, Herbert Lom (Talia/Coralta/Corona/Comeci)

Remake of Agatha Christie's whodunit classic, in which ten suspects find themselves incommunicado 300 kilometers from the nearest town in a luxurious hotel in the middle of a desert in Iran. The invitees accept this, and thereupon make only the feeblest of efforts to seek a way of escaping. Dressed in tuxedos and evening gowns, they resign themselves to being eliminated one by one.

The murders are all committed in the most discreet, unspectacular ways, and cause only the mildest of trepidations among the remaining 'Indians'.

Thesping consists of the usual cameos typical of the co-pro genre. Charles Aznavour manages to get in a song before nonchalantly drinking his poison and the others dutifully plod through their parts.

●●●●●●●●●●●●●●●●●●●●●●●●●

■ TEN NORTH FREDERICK

1958, 102 MINS, US

Dir Philip Dunne   *Prod* Charles Brackett   *Scr* Philip Dunne   *Ph* Joe MacDonald   *Ed* David Bretherton   *Mus* Leigh Harline   *Art Dir* Lyle R. Wheeler, Addison Hehr
● Gary Cooper, Diane Varsi, Geraldine Fitzgerald, Tom Tully, Suzy Parker, Stuart Whitman (20th Century-Fox)

Ten North Frederick is a fairly interesting study of a man who is the victim of his own virtues. But because of the psychological intricacies involved, the screen telling of the John O'Hara novel sacrifices detail and explanation at some loss to audience satisfaction.

The politics section has been so telescoped as to be puzzling. The question of whether the protagonist actually entertains the dream of the presidency or jollies his wife on the point is never clear. And it is crucial to conviction. Joe Chapin (Gary Cooper) is a regional lawyer, rich but not apparently otherwise distinguished. Most of all he is a gentleman and from this fact flows his troubles.

The vaguest part of the screen version is the home town attitude toward the hero although at his 50th birthday party he is twitted by a philanderer with being a dull and slow fellow. Nonetheless the story gets on and after his series of disillusionments, including his beloved daughter's forced marriage, subsequent miscarriage, annullment and leaving home, the lawyer moves to his bitter-sweet romance in New York with a younger woman.

Told in flashback, the story opens at the 1945 funeral of the lawyer and shows the hypocrites gathered afterwards in his home. The greatest hypocrite of all is the widow, played with iceberg selfishness by Geraldine Fitzgerald.

By the time the story is played out the thesis makes sense – Joe Chapin has indeed been hopelessly handicapped in life by being a gentleman. It is convincing in the end and in Cooper's performance, and it is also sad.

●●●●●●●●●●●●●●●●●●●●●●●●●

■ 10 RILLINGTON PLACE

1971, 111 MINS, UK ◇ ▼

Dir Richard Fleischer   *Prod* Martin Ransohoff, Leslie Linder   *Scr* Clive Exton   *Ph* Denys Coop   *Ed* Ernest Walter   *Mus* John Dankworth   *Art Dir* Martin Cooper
● Richard Attenborough, Judy Geeson, John Hurt, Pat Heywood, Isobel Black, Robert Hardy (Columbia)

In 1944, a woman was gassed, strangled and ravished by John Christie, the first of several victims of a seemingly quiet, respectable man living in a drab London district.

Richard Fleischer has turned out an authenticated documentary-feature which is an absorbing and disturbing picture. But the film has the serious flaw of not even attempting to probe the reasons that turned a man into a necrological and monstrous pervert.

Could be that Fleischer, like most other people, found more interest in the other central figure in the case, Timothy Evans. He was an illiterate who, with his young wife and baby, was Christie's lodger. Mrs Evans and their daughter became death victims of Christie. The bewildered lad, duped by Christie, confessed and was executed. Several years later Christie was arrested for the murder of his own wife, confessed to the murder of seven women, including Mrs Evans, but vigorously denied strangling the child. Some 12 years later Evans was pardoned. All this is

dealt with in the Ludovic Kennedy book from which Clive Exton has written a factual, interesting but not particularly moving or emotional screenplay.

Though Richard Attenborough, playing the killer, is the central character, the acting honors are firmly wrapped up by John Hurt as Evans. He gives a remarkably subtle and fascinating performance as the bewildered young man who plays into the hands of both the murderer and the police.

●●●●●●●●●●●●●●●●●●●●●●●●●

■ TEN TALL MEN

1951, 97 MINS, US ◇

Dir Willis Goldbeck   *Prod* Harold Hecht   *Scr* Roland Kibbee, Frank Davis   *Ph* William Snyder   *Ed* William Lyon   *Mus* David Buttolph   *Art Dir* Carl Anderson
● Burt Lancaster, Jody Lawrance, Gilbert Roland, Kieron Moore, George Tobias, John Dehner (Norma/Columbia)

Yarn [from a story by James Warner Bellah and Willis Goldbeck] is tailor-made for the burly Burt Lancaster. Cast as a Foreign Legion sergeant, he picks up a tip while in jail that the Riffs plan an invasion of the city. With nine fellow prisoners he volunteers to harass the would-be invaders. Mission succeeds all expectations when the group manages to seize a sheik's daughter (Jody Lawrance), a key to the whole attack.

Proceedings come off at a crisp pace under Willis Goldbeck's breezy direction. Lancaster, Lawrance and a lengthy list of supporting players handle their roles broadly, which at times achieves almost a satiric effect. Whether that was intentional or not is tough to determine.

●●●●●●●●●●●●●●●●●●●●●●●●●

■ 10:30 P.M. SUMMER

1966, 85 MINS, US ◇

Dir Jules Dassin   *Prod* Jules Dassin, Anatole Litvak   *Scr* Jules Dassin, Marguerite Duras   *Ph* Gabor Pogany   *Ed* Roger Dwyre   *Mus* Christobal Halffter   *Art Dir* Enrique Alarcon
● Melina Mercouri, Romy Schneider, Peter Finch, Julian Mateos, Isabel Maria Perez, Beatriz Savon (Dassin-Litvak)

Jules Dassin's *10:30 P.M. Summer* is only 85 minutes long but seems longer. Dassin's direction is uncertain, frequently illogical and, for the most part, plodding; Melina Mercouri's thesping is in a similar vein. There's reason to believe that the major fault is in the script of Dassin and novelist Marguerite Duras and, beyond that, in the novella of Duras on which the script is based.

The thread of a plot (a married couple and a female friend, traveling together in Spain, are under a mounting tension that is touched off by an incident with a fugitive in a village) may have made a moody and effective short story but as the basis of an intelligent screenplay it is less than satisfactory.

There's some possibility of exploitation in the frankly erotic scenes of lovemaking between Romy Schneider (the reluctant guest) and Peter Finch (the husband).

An even more grievous shortcoming is the absence of any explanation as to the reason for her condition. Alcoholism is, evidently, only a part of her tragedy, as is a suggested latent homosexual feeling towards Schneider.

Gabor Pogany's camerawork overcomes the necessary low-key lighting (most of the film takes place at night) to give a technical gloss to the proceedings.

●●●●●●●●●●●●●●●●●●●●●●●●●

■ 10 TO MIDNIGHT

1983, 100 MINS, US ◇ ▼

Dir J. Lee Thompson   *Prod* Pancho Kohner, Lance Hool   *Scr* William Roberts   *Ph* Adam Greenberg   *Ed* Peter Lee Thompson   *Mus* Robert O. Ragland   Jim Freiburger

● Charles Bronson, Lisa Eilbacher, Gene Davis, Andrew Stevens, Geoffrey Lewis, Wilford Brimley (Golan-Globus)

A sexually deranged killer slices up five young women like melons. The killer (well enough played by Gene Davis) is literally getting away with murder because of bureaucratic red tape and a pending insanity plea. As cop Charles Bronson puts it: 'I remember when legal meant lawful. Now it means loophole'. So Bronson takes matters into his own hands.

William Roberts' screenplay, while it sags in the middle, is damnably clever at dropping in its vicious vigilante theme without being didactic, and J. Lee Thompson's direction, borrowing from Hitchcock's editing in *Psycho*, creates the full horror of blades thrusting into naked bellies without the viewer ever actually seeing it happen.

Lisa Eilbacher plays Bronson's daughter and the beautiful, major target of the killer. Geoffrey Lewis is very good as a self-serving defense attorney who tells his warped client to be cool because 'you'll walk out of a crazy house alive'.

● ●

■ TENANT, THE

1976, 125 MINS, FRANCE ◇ ⓥ
Dir Roman Polanski   *Scr* Roman Polanski, Gerard Brach   *Ph* Sven Nykvist   *Ed* Francoise Bonnot   *Mus* Philippe Sarde   *Art Dir* Pierre Guffroy
● Roman Polanski, Isabelle Adjani, Melvyn Douglas, Jo Van Fleet, Bernard Fresson, Lila Kedrova (Marianne)

A tale of a paranoid breakdown of a little bureaucratic clerk that wastes no time in trying to be clinical. It has a humorous tang, underlying the macabre.

Director Roman Polanski plays the little man himself, a naturalized Frenchman of Polish origin, that expertly combines a deceptive internal resiliency to his outward timidity that makes him pathetic.

He goes to look at an apartment he has heard of. A girl who has it threw herself out the window. He is told he may have it only if she does not come back. Polanski calls the hospital and learns the girl is dead. He moves in but mysterious things begin to happen.

There is an effective atmosphere and it does create a feeling of personal anguish. Thus not achieving a balance of humor and suspense.

● ●

■ TENDER COMRADE

1943, 103 MINS, US
Dir Edward Dmytryk   *Prod* David Hempstead   *Scr* Dalton Trumbo   *Ph* Russell Metty   *Ed* Roland Gross   *Mus* Leigh Harline
● Ginger Rogers, Robert Ryan, Ruth Hussey, Kim Hunter, Jane Darwell (RKO)

Centered around five women, all of whom have their men in the services and all of whom are contributing to the war effort in one way or another, *Tender Comrade* is a preachment for all that democracy stands for.

It is a picture of considerable charm despite its terrific emotional effects. And if the emotional impact is sometimes achieved with what may seem to be overdone dramatics, then it's to be marked off to what one can assume to be an enactment of what is actually real-life drama.

Ginger Rogers gives an unrestrained performance throughout, and where several scenes are almost dawdling she perks it up with neat bits of business. Ruth Hussey, Kim Hunter and Patricia Collinge also give excellent portrayals.

Dalton Trumbo contributes a screenplay compact and replete with plenty of excellent

dialog. A notably big factor in the film's pace is Edward Dmytryk's direction of the sometimes slow but never tedious story.

● ●

■ TENDER IS THE NIGHT

1962, 146 MINS, US ◇
Dir Henry King   *Prod* Henry T. Weinstein   *Scr* Ivan Moffat   *Ph* Leon Shamroy   *Ed* William Reynolds   *Mus* Bernard Herrmann   *Art Dir* Jack Martin Smith, Malcolm Brown
● Jennifer Jones, Jason Robards, Joan Fontaine, Tom Ewell, Cesare Danova, Jill St John (20th Century-Fox)

A combination of attractive, intelligent performances and consistently interesting, De Luxecolorful photography of interiors and exteriors – mostly the French Riviera – provide big plus qualities in this 20th-Fox adaptation of *Tender Is The Night*. This may not be a 100 proof distillation of F. Scott Fitzgerald. But *Tender Is The Night* is nonetheless on its own filmic terms a thoughtful, disturbing and at times absorbing romantic drama.

Novel and film depict the decay and deterioration of a brilliant and idealistic psychiatrist (Jason Robards), whose love for and marriage to a wealthy patient (Jennifer Jones) ultimately consumes, dissipates and destroys him by engulfing him in the meaningless motives and glamorous leisure of upper social class Americans adrift in Europe in the prosperous 1920s. Moffat's screenplay emphasizes the point of transference of strength from doctor to patient, traces the reverse process in which heroine and hero travel in emotionally opposite directions as a result of their tragic relationship.

Jones emerges a crisply fresh, intriguing personality and creates a striking character as the schizophrenic Nicole, Robards, whose non-matinee-idol masculinity makes him an ideal choice for the role of the ill-fated doctor-husband, Dick Diver, plays with intelligence and conviction. Joan Fontaine is convincing as Nicole's shallow, older sister, performing with the right manifestation of frivolity and bite that her part requires.

● ●

■ TENDER MERCIES

1983, 89 MINS, US/UK ◇ ⓥ
Dir Bruce Beresford   *Prod* Philip S. Hobel, Mary Ann Hobel   *Scr* Horton Foote   *Ph* Russell Boyd   *Ed* William Anderson   *Mus* George Dreyfus   *Art Dir* Jeannine Oppewall
● Robert Duvall, Tess Harper, Allan Hubbard, Betty Buckley, Ellen Barkin, Wilford Brimley (Antron Media/EMI)

Robert Duvall is Mac Sledge, a down-and-out ex-country and western singer on the skids since his marriage to fellow C&W warbler Dixie (Betty Buckley) broke up.

Out on a drunken binge one night, he winds up in a small motel in Texas prairie country, and next morning accepts an offer of work from Rosa Lee (Tess Harper), the young widow who runs the place. Rosa Lee's husband had been killed in Vietnam, and she is having trouble keeping the motel and gas station going, and at the same time looking after her small son (Allan Hubbard).

Sledge stays on, the couple fall in love and marry. When tragedy unexpectedly touches his life, he finds he now has the strength to keep going and achieves new peace of mind.

Tender Mercies is, in the best sense, an old-fashioned film. There's no sex, no violence. Duvall is dignified and moving as Sledge; Harper is most affecting as the widow he loves and marries; Hubbard almost steals the film as her inquiring son.

□ 1983: Best Picture (Nomination)

■ TEQUILA SUNRISE

1988, 116 MINS, US ◇ ⓥ
Dir Robert Towne   *Prod* Thom Mount   *Scr* Robert Towne   *Ph* Conrad L. Hall   *Ed* Claire Simpson   *Mus* Danny Bramson, Dave Grusin   *Art Dir* Richard Sylbert
● Mel Gibson, Kurt Russell, Michelle Pfeiffer, Raul Julia, J.T. Walsh (Mount/Warner)

There's not much kick in this cocktail, despite its mix of quality ingredients. Casually glamorous South Bay is the setting for a story of little substance as writer-director Robert Towne attempts a study of friendship and trust but gets lost in a clutter of drug dealings and police operations.

Mel Gibson plays Dale 'Mac' McKussic, a former bigtime drug operator who's attempting to go straight just about the time his high school pal, cop Nick Frescia (Kurt Russell), is required to bust him. Frescia tries to dodge the duty by pressuring his friend to get out, but Mac owes one last favor to an old friend who's a Mexican cocaine dealer (Raul Julia).

Russell and Gibson are pushed into a cat-and-mouse game, complicated by their attraction to high-class restaurant owner Jo Ann Vallenari (Michelle Pfeiffer).

Gibson projects control skating atop paranoia, and is appealing as a man you'd want to trust. Russell is fine as the slick cop who's confused by his own shifting values, and Pfeiffer achieves a rather touching quality with her gun-shy girl beneath the polished professional.

● ●

■ TERESA

1951, 101 MINS, US
Dir Fred Zinnemann   *Prod* Arthur M. Loew   *Scr* Stewart Stern   *Ph* William J. Miller   *Ed* Frank Sullivan   *Mus* Louis Applebaum   *Art Dir* Leo Kerz
● Pier Angeli, John Ericson, Patricia Collinge, Richard Bishop, Peggy Ann Garner, Ralph Meeker (M-G-M)

Bright news of *Teresa* is the American introduction of Pier Angeli, as the Italian war bride of the mixed-up John Ericson. There's enough of the waif in her appearance to generate a tremendous audience sympathy.

Fred Zinnemann is too consciously documentary in the directorial handling of the story, and the Stewart Stern screenplay [from an original story by him and Alfred Hayes] does not support such treatment. Opening finds Ericson muddling his way through postwar life, resisting all aid, although wanting it. A flashback takes the plot to Italy, where he is a green replacement GI. During a stay in a small mountain village he meets and falls in love with Angeli.

On his first patrol, Ericson cracks up even before combat when the sergeant on whom he leans is absent. After a hospital confinement for treatment, he returns to the village, marries Angeli then goes to the States to await her arrival. When she does arrive, they make their home in cramped tenement quarters with his parents, and it is gradually brought out that his trouble is caused by a dominant mother and a false conception of his father.

● ●

■ TERM OF TRIAL

1962, 130 MINS, UK
Dir Peter Glenville   *Prod* James Woolf   *Scr* Peter Glenville   *Ph* Oswald Morris   *Ed* James Clark   *Mus* Jean-Michel Demase   *Art Dir* Wilfred Shingleton
● Laurence Olivier, Simone Signoret, Sarah Miles, Terence Stamp, Thora Hird, Hugh Griffith (Warner-Pathe/Romulus)

Here Olivier's an idealistic, but seedily unsuccessful schoolmaster in a small mixed school in the North of England. He has had to settle for this inferior teaching job because as a pacifist during the war he went to jail.

T

He's afflicted with a sense of inferiority, a nagging scold of a wife and a taste for hard liquor.

He also suffers from a suspicious headmaster and a class which, inevitably, contains the school bully, played with remarkable assurance by Terence Stamp. Olivier is delighted when he sees a desire to learn in a young 15-year-old girl (Sarah Miles) but, rather naively, fails to see that she is precociously sexually aroused by him.

The 'crush' comes to a head when he takes some of the pupils on a school trip to Paris. She then feeds her mother with the tale that she has been indecently assaulted and he lands in the courtroom.

There are several loose ends, which could have emerged from the writing or the editing. But overall the characters are well drawn, the situations dramatic and the thesping all round is tops.

. . . .

■ TERMINATOR, THE

1984, 108 MINS, US ◇ ⑦
Dir James Cameron   *Prod* Gale Anne Hurd
Scr James Cameron, Gale Anne Hurd   *Ph* Adam Greenberg   *Ed* Mark Goldblatt   *Mus* Brad Fiedel
Art Dir George Costello
● Arnold Schwarzenegger, Michael Biehn, Linda Hamilton, Paul Winfield, Lance Henriksen, Rick Rossovich (Hemdale)

The Terminator is a blazing, cinematic comic book, full of virtuoso moviemaking, terrific momentum, solid performances and a compelling story.

The clever script, cowritten by director James Cameron and producer Gale Anne Hurd, opens in a post-holocaust nightmare, A.D. 2029, where brainy machines have crushed most of the human populace. From that point, Arnold Schwarzenegger as the cyborg Terminator is sent back to the present to assassinate a young woman named Sarah Connor (Linda Hamilton) who is, in the context of a soon-to-be-born son and the nuclear war to come, the mother of mankind's salvation.

A human survivor in that black future (Michael Biehn), also drops into 1984 to stop the Terminator and save the woman and the future.

The shotgun-wielding Schwarzenegger is perfectly cast in a machine-like portrayal that requires only a few lines of dialog.

. . . .

■ TERMS OF ENDEARMENT

1983, 130 MINS, US ◇ ⑦
Dir James L. Brooks   *Prod* James L. Brooks   *Scr* James L. Brooks   *Ph* Andrzej Bartkowiak   *Ed* Richard Marks   *Mus* Michael Gore   *Art Dir* Polly Platt
● Debra Winger, Shirley MacLaine, Jack Nicholson, Jeff Daniels, John Lithgow, Danny DeVito (Paramount)

Teaming of Shirley MacLaine and Jack Nicholson at their best makes *Terms of Endearment* an enormously enjoyable offering, adding bite and sparkle when sentiment and seamlessness threatens to sink other parts of the picture.

At the core is mother MacLaine and daughter Debra Winger, fondly at odds from the beginning over the younger's impending marriage to likeable, but limited, Jeff Daniels. Literally, it's just one cut to the next; then Winger is a mother and moving away from Texas to Iowa, where she becomes a mother a couple of more times; talks to MacLaine every day, carries on an affair with John Lithgow while Daniels dallies at college with Kate Charleson.

Plotwise, MacLaine and Nicholson are first introduced as she watches him come home next door drunk. Then it's several more years before the film finds them together again as he makes a stumbling pass at her over the

fence. Then it's several more years before they're together again and she finally agrees to go out to lunch.

Early on, MacLaine tells Winger, 'You aren't special enough to overcome a bad marriage'. But *Terms of Endearment* is certainly special enough to overcome its own problems.
□ 1983: Best Picture

. . . .

■ TERROR TRAIN

1980, 97 MINS, CANADA/US ◇ ⑦
Dir Roger Spottiswoode   *Prod* Harold Greenberg
Scr T.Y. Drake   *Ph* John Alcott   *Ed* Anne Henderson
Mus John Mills-Cockell   *Art Dir* Glenn Bydwell
● Ben Johnson, Jamie Lee Curtis, Hart Bochner, David Copperfield (Astral-Bellevue-Pathe)

Roger Spottiswoode, vet editor who co-authored a respected book on the subject with Karel Reisz, makes a competent directing debut here.

As in Jamie Lee Curtis' other shocker pix, she limns the feisty survivor character in a group of young people menaced by a psychotic while having a wild party on a train. Her acting fits a narrow groove. But it must be said in young thesp's favor that she has not been given the most challenging material.

Efficient screenplay quickly sets up the premise by showing a repulsive sick joke being perpetrated by college med students on a sensitive youth who goes insane as a result. Three years later the kids all take a train excursion to celebrate their graduation, and the chickens come home to roost.

. . . .

■ TERRY FOX STORY, THE

1983, 96 MINS, CANADA ◇ ⑦
Dir Ralph L. Thomas   *Prod* Robert Cooper
Scr Edward Hume   *Ph* Richard Ciupka   *Ed* Ron Wisman   *Mus* Bill Conti   *Art Dir* Gavin Mitchell
● Robert Duvall, Eric Fryer, Michael Zeiniker, Chris Makepeace, Rosalind Chao, Elva Mai Hoover (Astral/CTV/Bank of Montreal)

The Terry Fox Story chronicles the heroic life of the young Canadian man whose 1980 Marathon of Hope resulted in raising more than $20 million for cancer research.

Eric Fryer plays the title role with tremendous conviction. The story opens in Vancouver in 1977, prior to the time Fox lost his right leg to cancer. In short order, the film dispenses with the diagnosed malignancy, Fox's convalescence, the fitting of a prosthetic leg and his decision to run across Canada to raise money for cancer research.

Despite initial parental and medical opposition, Fox's dream begins in April 1980. He enlists the aid of his friend, Doug Alward (Michael Zeiniker) to drive a camper and watch his progress but cannot convince his girlfriend, Rika (Rosalind Chao), to leave her job and join the marathon.

Fryer, an acting newcomer and himself an amputee, shows no rough edges in his performance. Robert Duvall as Vigars has another accomplished, gutsy role.

. . . .

■ TESS

1979, 180 MINS, FRANCE/UK ◇ ⑦
Dir Roman Polanski   *Prod* Claude Berri   *Scr* Roman Polanski, Gerard Brach, John Brownjohn   *Ph* Geoffrey Unsworth, Ghislain Cloquet   *Ed* Alastair McIntyre
Mus Philippe Sarde   *Art Dir* Pierre Guffroy
● Nastassja Kinski, Leigh Lawson, Peter Firth, John Collin, David Markham, Carolyn Pickles (Renn/Burrill)

Tess is a sensitive, intelligent screen treatment of a literary masterwork. Roman Polanski has practiced no betrayal in filming Thomas Hardy's 1891 novel, *Tess of the d'Urbervilles*, and his adaptation often has that infrequent quality of combining fidelity and beauty.

Tess Durbeyfield is an uncommonly beautiful peasant girl whose derelict father learns of the family's descent from once noble Norman ancestry, the d'Urbervilles. Learning of the existence of a rich family bearing this name, Tess' parents induce the girl to present herself as a distant relation in the hope of reaping profit from the family tree.

The young rakish master of the d'Urbervilles, Alec, gives her employment and seduces her. Tess returns home and bears a child who dies after a short time.

She meets and falls in love with Angel Clare. They marry but, on the wedding night, Tess reveals her past. Angel reacts horribly and leaves here.

First-rate contributions are the color photography of Geoffrey Unsworth (who died during the shooting and was succeeded by Ghislain Cloquet) and the superb production design of Pierre Guffroy.
□ 1980: Best Picture (Nomination)

. . . .

■ TESS OF THE STORM COUNTRY

1922, 110 MINS, US ⊗
Dir John S. Robertson   *Scr* Elmer Harris   *Ph* Charles Rosher   *Art Dir* Frank Ormston
● Mary Pickford, Lloyd Hughes, Gloria Hope, David Torrence, Forrest Robinson, Jean Hersholt (Pickford/United Artists)

Mary Pickford fans will revel with her in *Tess of the Storm Country* [based on the novel by Grace Miller White]. It's Mary Pickford all of the time. Pickford acts with her head, hands, and feet; she pantomimes and plays the part all of the while, with the titles often lending an additional but quiet though effective amusing touch.

Naught to be said against the least item in the film. Everything has been done well, particularly the photography by Charles Rosher and the direction.

After Pickford, the finest performance is that of Ben Letts by Jean Hersholt. Hersholt makes his villainous character real, of the seafaring sort, shaggy and bearded, uncouth and rough. In contrast is the Teola Graves of Gloria Hope, carrying a miserable whining countenance that cannot bring her sympathy in a sympathetic role.

. . . .

■ TEST PILOT

1938, 120 MINS, US
Dir Victor Fleming   *Prod* Louis D. Lighton   *Scr* Vincent Lawrence, Waldemar Young   *Ph* Ray June   *Ed* Tom Held   *Mus* Franz Waxman (dir.)   *Art Dir* Cedric Gibbons
● Clark Gable, Myrna Loy, Spencer Tracy, Lionel Barrymore, Samuel S. Hinds, Marjorie Main (M-G-M)

Test Pilot is an actioner against a new approach to the aviation theme, fortified by a strong romance.

Spencer Tracy is Clark Gable's ground aide – the Gunner. Gable as a crack but arrogant pilot is forced down on a Kansas farm, where Myrna Loy is introduced as a romance interest. Ensuing action, backgrounded by ultramodern aviation tests and experiments, plus a military note attendant to the US aviation service, vividly portrays the strong Loy-Gable romance.

Her disposition to understand the peculiar ways of the men with wings, and the pilot's appreciation of this understanding, have been artfully limned by director Victor Fleming. Three stars are capital in their assignments, particularly Gable, because it's a tailor-made role.

Story bespeaks authority in detail, obviously explained by the fact that Capt Frank Wead, who authored the original, has had practical aviation background.
□ 1938: Best Picture (Nomination)

. . . .

TESTAMENT

1989, 89 MINS, US ◇ Ⓥ
Dir Lynne Littman *Prod* Jonathan Bernstein, Lynne Littman *Scr* John Sacret Young *Ph* Steven Poster *Ed* Suzanne Pettit *Mus* James Horner *Art Dir* David Nichols
● Jane Alexander, William Devane, Ross Harris, Roxana Zal, Lukas Haas, Kevin Costner (Entertainment Events/American Playhouse)

Testament is an exceptionally powerful film dealing with the survivors of a nuclear war. Debuting director Lynne Littman brings an original approach to the grim material.

Based on Carol Amen's magazine story *The Last Testament*, pic depicts a normal, complacent community in the small California town of Hamlin.

The town's calm is shattered when a TV newscast announces that nuclear devices have exploded in New York and on the east coast, with the film proper suddenly going to yellow and whiteout, indicating blasts on the west coast as well. Ham radio operator Henry Abhart (Leon Ames) becomes Hamlin's communications link to the outside world.

Isolated, Hamlin's residents attempt to survive, but within a month over 1,000 people have died from radiation sickness. A young couple (Rebecca De Mornay and Kevin Costner), whose baby has died, drive off in search of 'a safe place'.

Holding it all together as a tower of strength is actress Jane Alexander as Carol Wetherby, coping with the deaths of her family and friends in truly heroic fashion via an understated performance.

TESTIMONY

1987, 157 MINS, UK ◇
Dir Tony Palmer *Prod* Tony Palmer *Scr* David Rudkin, Tony Palmer *Ph* Nic Knowland *Ed* Tony Palmer *Art Dir* Tony Palmer
● Ben Kingsley, Sherry Baines, Magdalen Asquith, Mark Asquith, Terence Rigby, Ronald Pickup (Isolde/Mandemar/ORF/NOS/DR/SVT/HRK/Film Four)

Testimony is quite an undertaking. Long, muddled, and abstract at times, but ultimately a beautifully conceived and executed art film with fine topline performances, it makes fascinating viewing.

In essence the pic [based on *The Memoirs of Dmitri Shostakovich*, edited by Solomon Volkov] follows the life of the Russian composer, played by Ben Kingsley sporting a dubious wig, but especially focuses on his relationship with Stalin.

Testimony traces the young Shostakovich who had success after success until Stalin took a dislike to the opera *Lady Macbeth*, and in a marvelous scene at the Extraordinary Conference of Soviet Musicians his work is denounced, but still he apologizes.

Later Stalin pours on further humiliation by sending him to an International Peace Congress in New York, where he is forced to denounce his fellow musicians, such as Stravinsky, who had fled Russia.

Ronald Pickup is excellent as Kingsley's friend Tukhachevsky and Robert Urquhart puts in a telling – though small – appearance as the journalist who quizzes Kingsley at the US peace conference.

Helmer Tony Palmer utilizes stunning technical skill to tell his story though at times seems to be a bit too clever for his own good. Technical credits are excellent, and Shostakovich's music suitably stirring.

TEX

1982, 103 MINS, US ◇ Ⓥ
Dir Tim Hunter *Prod* Tim Zinnemann *Scr* Charlie Haas, Tim Hunter *Ph* Ric Waite *Ed* Howard Smith *Mus* Pino Donaggio *Art Dir* Jack T. Collis
● Matt Dillon, Jim Metzler, Meg Tilly, Bill McKinney, Ben Johnson, Emilio Estevez (Walt Disney)

What *Tex* will probably best be remembered for is breaking new ground at Disney Studios in representing some of the real problems confronting today's young people. The teenagers are put in the milieu of drugs, alcohol, sex and violence. Family life is not necessarily rosy and well-scrubbed.

Where the picture ironically goes awry is in trying to tackle all of these problems in the space of 103 minutes. Writers Charlie Haas and Tim Hunter (latter making his directing debut) seem intent on incorporating every conceivable adolescent and adult trauma into their script [from the novel by S.E. Hinton], thus leaving the film with a very overdone, contrived feeling.

Story primarily centers on 15-year-old Oklahoma farm boy Tex, played admirably by Matt Dillon. Growing up with his older brother, while his father is 'traveling' with the rodeo, he must deal with family skeletons, school, friends, class distinctions, drugs, love, sex, death, responsibility, etc.

TEXANS, THE

1938, 92 MINS, US
Dir James Hogan *Prod* Lucien Hubbard *Scr* Bertram Millhauser, Paul Sloane, William Wister Haines *Ph* Theodor Sparkuhl *Ed* LeRoy Stone *Mus* Gerard Carbonara
● Joan Bennett, Randolph Scott, May Robson, Walter Brennan, Robert Cummings, Robert Barrat (Paramount)

More western than anything else, basically *The Texans* is a story of the Reconstruction period and carpetbaggers following the Civil War. It is another of a long line of pictures which adopts a strong pro-Southern attitude in dealing with this period of American history.

Plot [story by Emerson Hough] deals with the plight of an old Texas family of ranchers which escapes from the homeland with 10,000 head of cattle to avoid onerous taxation levied by the landgrabbers, scalawags and carpetbaggers of the days following the war between the States. Most of the action covers the long and treacherous drive of the cattle through wild country up to the nearest railroad point in Kansas.

Camera crew get some beautiful outdoor shots on the cattle push from Texas to Kansas. Blizzard is realistically shot, also the prairie fire sequence and the night scene when the caravan is camping.

Joan Bennett is too much the Fifth Avenue debbie in a cow-hat to impart the desired touch. Someone should have mussed her up a little now and then. Randolph Scott, paired with Bennett for romantic interest, shepherds the flock (men and cattle) through to Kansas and finally edges out Robert Cummings, who also figures on the romantic end, but unsympathetically. Scott gives an even performance and looks much more the pioneer type than the star opposite him.

TEXAS CARNIVAL

1951, 76 MINS, US ◇
Dir Charles Walters *Prod* Jack Cummings *Scr* Dorothy Kingsley *Ph* Robert Planck *Ed* Adrienne Fazan *Mus* David Rose (dir.) *Art Dir* Cedric Gibbons, William Ferrari
● Esther Williams, Red Skelton, Howard Keel, Ann Miller, Paula Raymond, Keenan Wynn (M-G-M)

Plenty of laugh diversion, dressed up to treat the eye and ear, is offered in *Texas Carnival*. Material provides Red Skelton with several surefire comedy sequences. In the eye department film offers Esther Williams in a bathing suit and one imaginative dream swim number, as well as the talented terping and physical charms of Ann Miller. For tunes it has Howard Keel as a virile cowpoke baritoning his way through the footage and two of the four Harry Warren-Dorothy Fields songs.

Williams and Skelton are a carnival team struggling along until proud Texan Keenan Wynn, in an alcoholic moment, takes a fancy to Skelton. Latter goes to a swank hotel to meet Wynn but, instead, is mistaken for the rich Texan himself. Life of ease being lived by Skelton during Wynn's absence wears easy on his conscience even though it troubles Williams plenty. Appearance of Keel, foreman of Wynn's ranch, adds some complications.

TEXAS CHAIN SAW MASSACRE, THE

1974, 83 MINS, US ◇ Ⓥ
Dir Tobe Hooper *Prod* Tobe Hooper *Scr* Kim Henkel, Tobe Hooper *Ph* Daniel Pearl, Tobe Hooper *Ed* Sallye Richardson, Larry Carroll *Mus* Tobe Hooper, Wayne Bell *Art Dir* Robert A. Burns
● Marilyn Burns, Allen Danziger, Paul A. Partain, William Vail, Teri McMinn, Gunnar Hansen (Vortex/Henkel/Hooper)

Despite the heavy doses of gore in *The Texas Chain Saw Massacre*, Tobe Hooper's pic is well-made for an exploiter of its type. The script by Hooper and Kim Henkel is a take-off on the same incident which inspired Robert Bloch's novel (and later Alfred Hitchcock's film) *Psycho*.

In 1957, Plainfield, Wis, authorities arrested handyman Ed Gein after finding dismembered bodies and disinterred corpses strewn all over his farmhouse.

When a dozen graves are found violated in a rural Texas cemetery, Marilyn Burns visits her father's grave to make sure it is unmolested. Disaster strikes on a side trip to her deserted family home. A family of graverobbers, led by saw-wielding Gunnar Hansen, butcher everyone but Burns, who makes a narrow escape.

TEXAS CHAIN SAW MASSACRE PART 2, THE

1986, 95 MINS, US ◇ Ⓥ
Dir Tobe Hooper *Prod* Menahem Golan, Yoram Globus *Scr* L.M. Kit Carson *Ph* Richard Kooris *Ed* Alain Jakubowicz *Mus* Tobe Hooper, Jerry Lambert *Art Dir* Cary White
● Dennis Hopper, Caroline Williams, Bill Johnson, Jim Siedow, Bill Moseley, Lou Perry (Cannon)

Success of the lowbudget *Chain Saw* in 1974 spawned a generation of splatter films which largely have lost the power to shock and entertain. Not so *Chain Saw 2*. Director Tobe Hooper is back on the Texas turf he knows.

Also a big help is L.M. Kit Carson's tongue-in-cheek script. In truth the story is basically a setup for a series of gory confrontations. The family is just an ordinary American hard luck story – butchers who have fallen on hard times and take their resentment out on the human race.

Although Dennis Hopper gets top billing his role is surprisingly limited, climaxing in a chainsaw duel to the death with Leatherface (Bill Johnson). Performances of the family are fine, especially Jim Siedow and a crazed Bill Moseley, but the real star here is carnage.

TEXASVILLE

1990, 123 MINS, US ◇ Ⓥ
Dir Peter Bogdanovich *Prod* Barry Spikings, Peter Bogdanovich *Scr* Peter Bogdanovich *Ph* Nicholas von Sternberg *Ed* Richard Fields *Art Dir* Phedon Papamichael
● Jeff Bridges, Cybill Shepherd, Annie Potts, Timothy Bottoms, Cloris Leachman, Randy Quaid (Nelson/Cine-Source)

Peter Bogdanovich's sequel to *The Last Picture Show* is long on folksy humor and short on plot. In adapting Larry McMurtry's 1987 follow-up novel (predecessor was penned in 1965, filmed in 1971), Bogdanovich uses an impending county centennial celebration as the weak spine for this slice of small-town Texas life.

Set in 1984, film revolves around the non-adventures of oil tycoon Jeff Bridges. He's $12 million in debt and his loyal assistant (Cloris Leachman) is ready to quit.

Bogdanovich has rounded up many of the first film's players (notably absent are Oscar-winner Ben Johnson, whose character died, Ellen Burstyn, Clu Gulager, Sam Bottoms and John Hillerman), but the plum role goes to Annie Potts as Bridges' domineering wife.

Less successful is Cybill Shepherd, whose career was launched with the 1971 pic. Making a delayed entrance as Bridges' old flame who's brooding over the death of her son, Shepherd adopts a no-makeup look and is unflatteringly photographed.

Apart from a few set pieces involving the Archer County pageant parade celebrating Texasville, pic is static and poorly lensed.

● ●

■ THAT CERTAIN WOMAN

1937, 91 MINS, US

Dir Edmund Goulding   *Prod* Robert Lord   *Scr* Edmund Goulding   *Ph* Ernest Haller   *Ed* Jack Killifer   *Mus* Max Steiner   *Art Dir* Max Parker
● Bette Davis, Henry Fonda, Ian Hunter, Anita Louise, Donald Crisp, Hugh O'Donnell (Warner)

Appeal is aimed strictly at the emotions, as the plot is another variation of self-sacrificing mother love. The film is a remake of *The Trespasser*, which Edmund Goulding earlier wrote and directed for Gloria Swanson in 1929.

Film relates the adventures of a self-reliant young woman (Bette Davis), who as a girl of 16 married a gangster, since deceased, after a bootleg altercation. She becomes the secretary of a prominent lawyer, an unhappily married man, who falls in love with her but keeps his distance. She falls in love with a wealthy young wastrel and marries him.

His father compels the young woman to reveal her past. The marriage is annulled, and the girl returns to her job. A son is born. Much later a scandal brings back the wastrel youth, now reformed, to help his one-time wife.

It's a synthetic tale that does not stand up under too close analysis. The story deficiencies are not so important, however, because the characters are made credible by Davis and the cast, and by Goulding's smooth direction. Ian Hunter as the girl's employer, and Henry Fonda as the boy in the case are excellent.

● ●

■ THAT COLD DAY IN THE PARK

1969, 115 MINS, CANADA ◇ ⓥ

Dir Robert Altman   *Scr* Gillian Freeman   *Ph* Laszlo Kovacs   *Mus* Johnny Mandel
● Sandy Dennis, Michael Burns, Susanne Benton, Luana Anders, John Garfield Jr (Factor-Altman-Mirell)

A pretty, reserved, rich spinster in Vancouver, BC, spots a teenager sitting in the park in the rain. She invites the boy to her apartment and a strange relationship starts that ends in breakdown and tragedy.

Sandy Dennis is strikingly effective, if her character's veering into madness is a bit abrupt. Michael Burns is good as the cherubic youth, with Susanne Benton displaying a fine feel for character as his freewheeling, slightly nympho sister.

This mixing of themes and social strata [from the book by Richard Miles] is too literary to get a true insight into the many layers involved. It tries to bring in too much and

waters down the interesting personal relations, turning the denouement into grand guignol, rather than perceptive dramatic and psychological progression.

● ●

■ THAT FORSYTE WOMAN

1949, 112 MINS, US ◇

Dir Compton Bennett   *Prod* Leon Gordon   *Scr* Jan Lustig, Ivan Tors, James B. Williams, Arthur Wimperis   *Ph* Joseph Ruttenberg   *Ed* Frederick Y. Smith   *Mus* Bronislau Kaper
● Errol Flynn, Greer Garson, Walter Pidgeon, Robert Young, Janet Leigh, Henry Davenport (M-G-M)

Metro has fashioned a long, elaborate and costly class feature out of John Galsworthy's writings about his Victorian family, the Forsytes.

Compton Bennett's direction unfolds it at a measured pace, in keeping with the quaintness of the Victorian English setting, as it tells the story of an outsider femme who marries into the Forsyte family, then falls in love with a man engaged to one of the Forsyte women, bringing discord into an ordered, dull way of life.

Greer Garson's playing, and that of her co-stars Errol Flynn, the cold, proper Forsyte whom she marries; Walter Pidgeon, the Forsyte blacksheep, and Robert Young, the man with whom she falls in love, approach the characters with all the dignified stuffiness that distinguishes Galsworthy's people.

The script is based on Book One of Galsworthy's *The Forsyte Saga*.

● ●

■ THAT HAMILTON WOMAN!

1941, 124 MINS, US ⓥ

Dir Alexander Korda   *Prod* Alexander Korda   *Scr* Walter Reisch, R.C. Sherriff   *Ph* Rudolph Mate   *Ed* William Hornbeck   *Mus* Miklos Rozsa   *Art Dir* Vincent Korda
● Vivien Leigh, Laurence Olivier, Alan Mowbray, Sara Allgood, Gladys Cooper, Henry Wilcoxon (United Artists/London)

Alexander Korda dips into the files of British history for this biographical drama of Lady Hamilton and her amorous affair with naval hero Lord Nelson.

Korda makes out a sympathetic case for the scandalous (of the period) romance between the wife of a British ambassador and the great Lord Nelson. Utilizing the retrospect story device, the haggish Lady Hamilton is tossed in the Calais jail for stealing, and tells her tale to a girl of the streets.

Vivien Leigh hits the peaks with her delineation of Lady Hamilton, a vivacious girl who is pictured as a victim of men but whose ingenuity in statecraft saves the Empire. She dominates the picture throughout with her reserved love for Nelson and her determination to aid his success. Laurence Olivier's characterization of Nelson carries the full dignity and reserve of the historical figure.

Picture shows plenty of production outlay with its series of elaborate settings. Battle of Trafalgar sequence carries intercut of cannon broadsides from the English men-of-war with too obvious miniatures of the two fleets in action.

● ●

■ THAT LUCKY TOUCH

1975, 93 MINS, UK ◇

Dir Christopher Miles   *Prod* Dimitri de Grunwald   *Scr* John Briley   *Ph* Douglas Slocombe   *Mus* John Scott   *Art Dir* Tony Masters
● Roger Moore, Susannah York, Shelley Winters, Lee J. Cobb, Jean-Pierre Cassel, Raf Vallone (Rank)

This contemporary light comedy of love-against-the-odds, which evokes the Hollywood genre of the 1930s, falls short of its target.

The film aims to extract some classy fun from the entanglements of an arms dealer (Roger Moore) and a leftist women's libber (Susannah York), covering NATO war games for the Washington Post.

Moore just about copes as the assertive, high-living gun merchant, but where moments of finesse are called for he is merely game and/or workmanlike. York makes the best of her chances as the aggressive, sex-shunning pacifist.

Lee J. Cobb's harassed and world-weary US Army general is a gem of resigned bewilderment when coping with his wife (Shelley Winters) or her prickly journalistic pal (York).

● ●

■ THAT NIGHT IN RIO

1941, 90 MINS, US ◇

Dir Irving Cummings   *Prod* Fred Kohlmar   *Scr* George Seaton, Bess Meredyth, Hal Long, Samuel Hoffenstein   *Ph* Leon Shamroy, Ray Rennahan   *Ed* Walter Thompson   *Mus* Alfred Newman
● Alice Faye, Don Ameche, Carmen Miranda, J. Carrol Naish (20th Century-Fox)

This successor to *Down Argentine Way* is a close carbon copy of *Folies Bergere* which 20th turned out six years earlier, but with locale switch from Paris to Rio de Janeiro. Embellished with lavish production, brilliant Technicolor, and several tuneful songs, it's peak entertainment.

Lightweight story [from a play by Rudolph Lothar and Hans Adler] provides Don Ameche with the dual role of a breezy American night club m.c. performing in Rio, and a native financier. Resemblance beween the pair is so close the former's sweetheart (Carmen Miranda) and the financier's wife (Alice Faye) cannot tell them apart. When a business crisis arrives, the tycoon's associates secure the entertainer to impersonate the absent Baron, with the stand-in innocently completing a deal that prevents financial ruin.

Ameche is very capable in a dual role, and Faye is eye-appealing but it's the tempestuous Miranda who really gets away to a flying start from the first sequence.

● ●

■ THAT SINKING FEELING

1979, 80 MINS, UK ◇ ⓥ

Dir Bill Forsyth   *Prod* Bill Forsyth   *Scr* Bill Forsyth   *Ph* Michael Coulter   *Ed* John Gow   *Mus* Colin Tully   *Art Dir* Adrienne Atkinson
● Robert Buchanan, John Hughes, Billy Greenlees, Douglas Sannachan, Alan Love (Minor Miracle)

The first wholly Scottish feature for many a year proves debuting filmmaker Bill Forsyth has an entertaining touch.

Forsyth's screenplay, largely set in the city's dank demolition areas, plots a motley bunch of unemployed lads, amiably led by Robert Buchanan, who heist a hundred stainless steel sinks in a boisterous bid to embark on an essentially light-hearted life of crime.

The central joke – the absurdity of seeing sinks as likely hot sellers – is hardly strong enough to carry a full-length film. But Forsyth's incidental observations, and the generally high standard of playing by non-professionals, help to offset the fact that most scenes could be pruned to advantage. Technical credits are remarkable considering the almost invisible production budget.

● ●

■ THAT TOUCH OF MINK

1962, 99 MINS, US ◇ ⓥ

Dir Delbert Mann   *Prod* Stanley Shapiro, Martin Melcher   *Scr* Stanley Shapiro, Nate Monaster   *Ph* Russell Metty   *Ed* Ted Kent   *Mus* George Duning   *Art Dir* Alexander Golitzen, Robert Clatworthy

● Cary Grant, Doris Day, Gig Young, Audrey Meadows (Universal)

The recipe is potent: Cary Grant and Doris Day in the old cat-and-mouse game. The gloss of *That Touch of Mink* however, doesn't obscure an essentially threadbare lining. In seeming to throw off a sparkle, credit performance and pace as the key virtues. The rest of it is commonplace.

In this particular arrangement of coy *he-she-nanigans*, the comedy is premised on the conflict of her inexperience and his old prosuavity. He's a company-gobbling financier; she's a trim chick legging it through Manhattan canyons in search of a job. It starts when his limousine splatters her with puddle water. Fortuitous meeting and mating maneuvres follow, with the action shuttling between Gotham and Bermuda or Gotham and New Jersey suburbia.

Although Grant gives his tycoon the advantage of long seasoning at this sort of gamey exercise, he's clearly shaded in the laugh-getting allotment. As written, Day's clowning has the better of it; and she, by the way, certifies herself an adept farceur with this outing. But not surprisingly, the featured bananas make the best comedic score.

■ THAT UNCERTAIN FEELING

1941, 89 MINS, US ⓥ
Dir Ernst Lubitsch   *Prod* Sol Lesser, Ernst Lubitsch
Scr Walter Reisch   *Ph* George Barnes   *Ed* William Shen   *Mus* Werner Heymann
● Merle Oberon, Melvyn Douglas, Burgess Meredith, Alan Mowbray (United Artists)

Premised on the assumption that when a husband doesn't pay his wife enough attention someone else is going to do it for him, Ernst Lubitsch's *That Uncertain Feeling* tackles the problem in a light and singularly satirical vein. The famed Lubitsch touch is there but the entertainment value isn't.

Merle Oberon and Melvyn Douglas are the apparently happily-married Bakers. Husband is a prosperous insurance man who is settled in his home life in a routine way, but unconsciously fails to fulfill the more romantic duties expected of a spouse. Lubitsch, with characteristic subtlety, suggests that this is what causes the hiccups from which the wife suffers and ultimately lands her in a psychoanalyst's office.

By stages she begins to have suspicions concerning the widespread impressions that they are the happy Bakers and into her life, under slightly absurd circumstances, comes a wacky pianist. He's Burgess Meredith, not the great lover type, and he has a strange, impudent dislike for a lot of things.

Taking the picture as a whole it is tiring, very slow generally and embraces numerous situations that are basically weak.

■ THAT WAS THEN ... THIS IS NOW

1985, 102 MINS, US ◇ ⓥ
Dir Christopher Cain   *Prod* Gary R. Lindberg, John M. Ondor   *Scr* Emilio Estevez   *Ph* Juan Ruiz-Anchia
Ed Ken Johnson   *Mus* Keith Olsen, Bill Cuomo
Art Dir Chester Kaczenski
● Emilio Estevez, Craig Sheffer, Kim Delaney, Jill Schoelen, Barbara Babcock, Frank Howard (Media Ventures/Belkin)

God save the kids who live in an S.E. Hinton novel. They're firecrackers waiting to go off. Hinton's is a very peculiar vision where adults are basically in the background and kids are left on their own to battle their way into an adulthood that promises them even less.

Most troubled of the kids here is Emilio Estevez as Mark Jennings, a lonely, brooding child anxious to be through with his adolescence. Title refers to his youthful bond with Bryon Douglas (Craig Sheffer). To Mark's dismay, the friendship is falling apart as Bryon takes on a girlfriend and starts to accept some adult responsibility.

Estevez also wrote the screenplay and as a writer he fails to raise the pronouncements and revelations of youth beyond the mundane. Dark tone is reinforced by cinematographer Juan Ruiz-Anchia who captures well the look of the street, but that's all one sees. It's an oppressive world without being particularly insightful.

Central relationship between Estevez and Sheffer does have some touching moments. Kim Delaney is perfectly likable as Sheffer's girlfriend.

■ THAT'LL BE THE DAY

1973, 90 MINS, UK ◇ ⓥ
Dir Claude Whatham   *Prod* David Puttnam, Sandy Lieberson   *Scr* Ray Connolly   *Ph* Peter Suschitzky
Ed Michael Bradsell   *Mus* Neil Aspinall, Keith Moon (sup.)
● David Essex, Ringo Starr, Rosemary Leach, James Booth, Billy Fury, Keith Moon (Anglo-EMI/Goodtimes)

Here is a nice bit of nostalgia (late 1950s): a serious, loving, but not sticky-sweet probe of a youngster's torment in finding himself, complete with parental problems, friendships gained and lost (ditto jobs), puppy love hangups and first sex; in short, the lot.

Script is a big assist, and it rings true without being cloying. Another major asset is having David Essex as its star and key ingredient, as well as in being able to hark back to so colorful a period in which to have him grow up. Essex copes well enough with the few dramatic requirements of the role. Ringo Starr is excellent as his sometime sidekick.

Technically, pic is a superior job, nicely paced by director Claude Whatham with a superior period feel.

■ THAT'S DANCING!

1985, 105 MINS, US ◇ ⓥ
Dir Jack Haley Jr.   *Prod* David Niven Jr., Jack Haley Jr.   *Scr* Jack Haley Jr.   *Ph* Andrew Laszlo, Paul Lohmann   *Ed* Bud Friedgen, Michael J. Sheridan
Mus Henry Mancini
● Gene Kelly, Sammy Davis Jr., Mikhail Baryshnikov, Liza Minnelli, Ray Bolger (M-G-M)

For anyone who wants to see big-screen terpsichorean art at its top, *Dancing* is definitive. M-G-M has not only dipped into its own generous collection, but borrowed judiciously from most of the other studios that were in brisk competition during the golden years of movie musicals.

For openers from the early days, there is a lot of Busby Berkeley, plus Ruby Keeler and Dick Powell, followed by the wonderful work of Fred Astaire and Ginger Rogers and on through an absolutely complete list of the greats.

Much is made of a Ray Bolger-Judy Garland dance number from *The Wizard of Oz*, omitted from the final cut of the original. It's interesting to see, but also easy to see (contrary to the gushing narration) why it was left out: the technique is a bit tacky and hardly up to the quality of what was released.

■ THAT'S ENTERTAINMENT!

1974, 132 MINS, US ◇ ⓥ
Dir Jack Haley Jr   *Prod* Jack Haley Jr   *Scr* Jack Haley Jr   *Ph* Gene Polito, Ernest Laszlo, Russell Metty, Ennio Guarnieri, Allan Green   *Ed* Bud Friedgen, David E. Blewitt   *Mus* Jesse Kaye (sup.), Henry Mancini (adapt.)
● (M-G-M)

Metro-Goldwyn-Mayer celebrated its 50th anniversary with *That's Entertainment!*, an outstanding, stunning, sentimental, exciting, colorful, enjoyable, spirit-lifting, tuneful, youthful, invigorating, zesty, respectful, dazzling, and richly satisfying feature documentary commemorating its filmusicals.

As Liza Minnelli puts it in her narrated segment (among 11 names appearing in new footage and film clip voiceover). 'Thank God for film. It can capture and hold a performance forever'.

From the musical library, about 100 films were selected from the 1929-58 era, enough to satisfy nearly every memory. Each segment has a particular theme (usually film highlights of a particular star); and each has its narrator. Minnelli appears in the portion devoted to her mother, Judy Garland.

■ THAT'S ENTERTAINMENT, PART 2

1976, 133 MINS, US ⓥ
Dir Gene Kelly   *Prod* Saul Chaplin, Daniel Melnick
Scr Leonard Gershe   *Ph* George Folsey   *Ed* Bud Friedgen, David Blewitt, David Bretherton, Peter C. Johnson   *Mus* Nelson Riddle (sup.)   *Art Dir* John DeCuir
● Fred Astaire, Gene Kelly (M-G-M)

That's Entertainment, Part 2 is a knockout. The very handsome and polished sequel to *That's Entertainment!* transforms excerpts from perhaps $100 million worth of classic Metro library footage into a billion dollars worth of fun, excitement, amusement, escapism, fantasy, nostalgia and happiness.

In addition, Fred Astaire and Gene Kelly shine in sharp bridging footage, well directed by Kelly.

There are approximately 100 remembered players to be seen in segments of about 75 films.

Bulk of the footage is Metro musicals. However, in a good pace change there are periodic brief collages including The Marx Brothers, Spencer Tracy-Katharine Hepburn, Clark Gable, Laurel & Hardy, and Buster Keaton.

■ THAT'S LIFE!

1986, 102 MINS, US ◇ ⓥ
Dir Blake Edwards   *Prod* Tony Adams   *Scr* Milton Wexler, Blake Edwards   *Ph* Anthony Richmond
Ed Lee Rhoads   *Mus* Henry Mancini   *Art Dir* Tony Marando
● Jack Lemmon, Julie Andrews, Sally Kellerman, Robert Loggia, Jennifer Edwards, Rob Knepper (Paradise Cove/Ubilam)

Personal virtually to the point of being a home movie, film proves thoroughly absorbing and entertaining and benefits enormously from a terrific lead performance by Jack Lemmon.

Story opens with Lemmon's wife, played by director Blake Edwards' wife, Julie Andrews, leaving a hospital and knowing she'll have to wait all weekend to learn the results of a biopsy.

For his part, Lemmon dreads the arrival of his 60th birthday, can't face the big party planned for him over the weekend, is fretting because he can't perform sexually these days and can't stand the idea of becoming a grandfather.

Andrews responds beautifully to Lemmon's sweaty, nerve-racked state, betraying years of love and understanding of her mate, but doesn't receive equal dramatic opportunities.

■ THEATRE OF BLOOD

1973, 104 MINS, UK ◇ ⓥ
Dir Douglas Hickox   *Prod* John Kohn, Stanley Mann
Scr Anthony Greville-Bell   *Ph* Wolfgang Suschitzky
Ed Malcolm Cooke   *Mus* Michael J. Lewis
Art Dir Michael Seymour
● Vincent Price, Diana Rigg, Ian Hendry, Harry Andrews, Coral Browne, Robert Coote (United Artists)

Theatre of Blood is black comedy played for chills and mood and emerges a macabre piece of wild melodramatics.

Douglas Hickox manages neatly in his direction to catch the spirit of a demented Shakespearean actor's (Vincent Price) revenge on eight members of the London Critics' Circle who he believes denied him a Best Actor of the Year award. Situation allows for some good old-fashioned suspense and high comedy, such as the sequence in which Price saws off the head of one critic while his spouse, needled into unconsciousness, sleeps beside him.

Price uses gory Shakespeare-inspired deaths to systematically murder each of the offending critics.

Price delivers with his usual enthusiasm and Diana Rigg is good as his daughter. Ian Hendry heads the list of critics, and Diana Dors is in briefly as Jack Hawkins' wife whom he smothers to death in a moment of jealousy.

· ·

■ THELMA & LOUISE

1991, 128 MINS, US ◇ ▼
Dir Ridley Scott   *Prod* Ridley Scott, Mimi Polk
Scr Callie Khouri   *Ph* Adrian Biddle   *Ed* Thom Noble
Mus Hans Zimmer   *Art Dir* Norris Spencer
● Susan Sarandon, Geena Davis, Harvey Keitel, Michael Madsen, Christopher McDonald, Brad Pitt (Pathe/Main)

Thelma & Louise is a thumpingly adventurous road pic about two regular gals who shoot down a would-be rapist and wind up on the lam in their 1966 T-bird. Even those who don't rally to pic's fed-up feminist outcry will take to its comedy, momentum and dazzling visuals.

Arkansas housewife Thelma (Geena Davis) and waitress Louise (Susan Sarandon) set out for a weekend fishing trip away from the drudgery of their lives and the indifference of their men; they stop at a roadside honkytonk to blow off steam, and things turn ugly. A guy tries to rape Thelma; Louise can't take it so she plugs the creep with a .38. Then they hit the highway, dazed and in trouble.

Sarandon is the big sister, more feminine, more focused, smoldering with a quiet determination. Davis is more loosely wrapped; she goes with the flow, follows her whims into trouble. The journey into recklessness is exhilarating, which gives the film its buoyant pull. In an indelible final image, it maintains the sense of reckless exhilaration to the end.

Despite some delectably funny scenes between the sexes, Ridley Scott's pic isn't about women vs men. It's about freedom, like any good road picture. In that sense, and in many others, it's a classic.

California and southern Utah locales stand in for Arkansas, Oklahoma and Texas.

· ·

■ THEM!

1954, 93 MINS, US ▼
Dir Gordon Douglas   *Prod* David Weisbart   *Scr* Ted Sherdeman, Russell Hughes   *Ph* Sid Hickox   *Ed* James Reilly   *Mus* Bronislaw Kaper
● James Whitmore, Edmund Gwenn, Joan Weldon, James Arness, Onslow Stevens, Sean McClory (Warner Bros)

This science-fiction shocker has a well-plotted story, expertly directed and acted in a matter-of-fact style.

The title monsters are mutations caused by radiation from the 1945 detonation of an atomic bomb in the desert. Over the intervening years the tiny insects affected by the lingering radiation have become fantastic creatures, ranging in size from nine to 12 feet. James Whitmore, sergeant in the New Mex-ico State Police, first gets on the track of the incredible beings. Into the picture then come Edmund Gwenn and Joan Weldon, entomologists, and James Arness, FBI man.

With the aid of air force officers Onslow Stevens and Sean McClory, the little group attempts to wipe out the nest of the mutated monsters with flame throwers and gas.

· ·

■ THEODORA GOES WILD

1936, 94 MINS, US
Dir Richard Boleslawski   *Prod* Everett Riskin
Scr Sidney Buchman   *Ph* Joseph Walker   *Mus* Morris Stoloff
● Irene Dunne, Melvyn Douglas, Thomas Mitchell, Spring Byington, Elisabeth Risdon, Margaret McWade (Columbia)

A comedy of steady tempo and deepening laughter. Irene Dunne takes the hurdle into comedy with versatile grace.

Theodora may superficially be compared to the *Mr Deeds Goes to Town* (1936) character in that both come from small New England villages. Quaint and eccentric figures and customs are exploited for laughs and background in both cases. And the experiences of the small-town character when hitting Manhattan form the main content of the story [from the novel by Mary McCarthy].

Painstaking direction of Richard Boleslawski brings out the nuances. His direction and Dunne's playing of the first New York escapade of Theodora in a dashing blade's apartment is a high point of light-and-shade farce. Melvyn Douglas is an excellent romantic partner for Dunne. She, rather than he, gets the real acting chances but he is consistently intelligent.

· ·

■ THERE WAS A CROOKED MAN

1960, 90 MINS, UK
Dir Stuart Burge   *Prod* John Bryan   *Scr* Reuben Ship
Ph Arthur Ibbetson   *Ed* Peter Hunt   *Mus* Kenneth V. Jones
● Norman Wisdom, Alfred Marks, Andrew Cruickshank, Reginald Beckwith, Susannah York, Jean Clarke (Knightsbridge)

Stuart Burge, a TV director making his debut in feature films, does a good job, considering the many traps that Reuben Ship's ingenious, though far-fetched, screenplay lays. Ship has overloaded his story line but has produced an idea which holds interest.

Norman Wisdom is a down-and-out who runs into a gang of crooks who want his help because he is a demolitions expert. Rather naively he is conned into assisting the mob into cracking a bank vault. He alone is caught holding the loot, and goes to jail. When he's let out after five years, he goes to take up a job in a Northern seaside factory. He soon finds out that the town is under the control of a swindler (Andrew Cruickshank) who is persuading everybody to buy up shares in the town's future. Wisdom enlists the help of his crook friends on a wild enterprise to outwit Cruickshank.

There are so many holes in this yarn that it's like a fishing net, but the result is amiable comedy. The robbery, in which Wisdom and his pals pose as surgeons and tunnel from the operating theatre into the next door bank, is wildly funny. Wisdom getting caught up in a wool sorting machine, avoiding the cops, and finally blowing up the town has good clowning moments.

· ·

■ THERE WAS A CROOKED MAN ...

1970, 128 MINS, US ◇ ▼
Dir Joseph L. Mankiewicz   *Prod* Joseph L. Mankiewicz   *Scr* David Newman, Robert Benton
Ph Harry Stradling Jr   *Ed* Gene Milford   *Mus* Charles Strouse
● Kirk Douglas, Henry Fonda, Hume Cronyn, Warren Oates, Burgess Meredith, Arthur O'Connell (Warner)

There Was a Crooked Man . . . has a crooked plot that is neither comedy nor convincing drama. Kirk Douglas, Henry Fonda, Hume Cronyn, Warren Oates and Burgess Meredith are the formidable elements that don't jell in this picaresque tale set in a bleak western desert prison. It is the type of action drama in which neither the actors nor director appear to believe the script or characters.

Douglas is the crooked man of title who steals $500,000 from Arthur O'Connell and is caught in a bordello literally with his pants down when voyeur O'Connell recognizes him through the peephole.

Fonda plays it straight as the saintly sheriff who becomes an idealistic prison reformer, only to have his principles literally blow up in his face when Douglas organizes a riot and break-out.

· ·

■ THERE'S A GIRL IN MY SOUP

1971, 94 MINS, UK ◇ ▼
Dir Roy Boulting   *Prod* Mike Frankovich, John Boulting   *Scr* Terence Frisby   *Ph* Harry Waxman
Ed Martin Charles   *Mus* Mike D'Abo   *Art Dir* John Howell
● Peter Sellers, Goldie Hawn, Tony Britton, Nicky Henson, John Comer, Diana Dors (Columbia)

There's a Girl in My Soup is a delightful surprise: a rather simple legit sex comedy (by Terence Frisby) transformed into breezy and extremely tasteful screen fun.

Peter Sellers is a TV personality whose roving eye misses few femme specimens. Accidental encounter with Goldie Hawn, who is having some free-love domestic problems with mate Nicky Henson, blossoms into unexpected love and compassion between the unlikely pair.

Henson is excellent in giving depth to the limited part, and adds immeasurably to the general moral tone. In superior support also are Tony Britton as Sellers' publisher-confidante; John Comer as Sellers' envious doorman; and Diana Dors in a good offbeat character casting as Comer's shrewish wife.

· ·

■ THERE'S NO BUSINESS LIKE SHOW BUSINESS

1954, 117 MINS, US ◇ ▼
Dir Walter Lang   *Prod* Sol C. Siegel   *Scr* Phoebe Ephron, Henry Ephron   *Ph* Leon Shamroy   *Ed* Robert Simpson   *Mus* Alfred Newman, Lionel Newman
● Ethel Merman, Donald O'Connor, Marilyn Monroe, Dan Dailey, Johnnie Ray, Mitzi Gaynor (20th Century-Fox)

Lamar Trotti's original, from which Phoebe and Henry Ephron fashioned the screenplay, is palpably a script primed to point up the 'heart' of showfolk.

Ethel Merman and Dan Dailey are capital as the vaudeville Donahues who bring out first one, then two, then three of their offspring for that extra bow, with a running gag, as the vaude annunciator cards change to the three Donahues, the four and finally the five Donahues.

Robert Alton rates a big bend along with producer Sol C. Siegel and director Walter Lang on those lavish musical routines. From Irving Berlin's viewpoint, they're all a song-plugger's delight.

Ethel Merman is boffo. She's a belter of a school of song stylists not to be found on every stage or before every mike. *Show Business* gets the works in every respect. The orchestral-vocal treatments of the Berlin standards are so richly endowed as to give them constantly fresh values.

· ·

THESE THREE

1936, 90 MINS, US

Dir William Wyler   *Prod* Samuel Goldwyn   *Scr* Lillian Hellman   *Ph* Gregg Toland   *Ed* Danny Mandell   *Mus* Alfred Newman   *Art Dir* Richard Day
● Miriam Hopkins, Merle Oberon, Joel McCrea, Catherine Doucet, Alma Kruger, Bonita Granville (Goldwyn/United Artists)

A thoroughly fine cinematic transmutation of Lillian Hellman's dramatic Broadway smash, *The Childrens Hour* is her own scenarization, reedited and retitled for Haysian purposes as *These Three*. Stripped of its original theme [of lesbianism], it is fortified by a socko trio in Miriam Hopkins, Merle Oberon and Joel McCrea.

Parring the tungsten threesome, however, are two adolescents, Bonita Granville as the hateful Mary Tilford, and Marcia Mae Jones as the subjected, inhibited child. Theirs are inspired performances.

Hellman, if anything, has improved upon the original in scripting the triangle as a dramatis personae of romantic frustration, three basically wholesome victims of an unwholesome combination of circumstance.

McCrea was never better in translating a difficult assignment intelligently and sympathetically. The well bred restraint of Hopkins and Oberon in their travail with the mixture of juvenile emotions at their boarding school is likewise impressive. Oberon is the sympathetic Karen; Hopkins has the assignment of unrequited love.

THEY ALL KISSED THE BRIDE

1942, 84 MINS, US

Dir Alexander Hall   *Prod* Edward Kaufman   *Scr* P.J. Wolfson   *Ph* Joseph Walker   *Ed* Viola Lawrence   *Mus* Werner Heymann
● Joan Crawford, Melvyn Douglas, Roland Young, Billie Burke, Helen Parrish, Allen Jenkins (Columbia)

Picture is adult entertainment – liberally spotted with episodes and lines of explosive and intimate nature – that veers from the general run of pictures of its type sufficiently to get audience attention. Originally, Carole Lombard was set for the starring spot, but her untimely death projected Joan Crawford in as replacement.

Crawford is in command of the vast business interests left by her father, and shaken by the writings of Melvyn Douglas, a happy-go-lucky scribbler of sorts who takes a crack at the family personal and business skeletons.

In addition to a spotlight performance by Crawford, Douglas clicks solidly as the writer and principal romanticist. Script is studded with amusing dialog of most intimate and double entendre content.

Alexander Hall's direction is snappy and speedy all along the line, and he contrives laugh toppers to every episode.

THEY ALL LAUGHED

1981, 115 MINS, US ◇

Dir Peter Bogdanovich   *Prod* George Morfogen, Blaine Novak   *Scr* Peter Bogdanovich   *Ph* Robby Muller   *Ed* Scott Vickrey   *Mus* Douglas Dilge   *Art Dir* Kert Lundell
● Audrey Hepburn, Ben Gazzara, John Ritter, Colleen Camp, Dorothy Stratten, Patti Hansen (20th Century-Fox/Time-Life/Moon)

Rarely does a film come along featuring such an extensive array of attractive characters with whom it is simply a pleasure to spend two hours. Nothing of great importance happens in a strict plot sense, but this *La Ronde*-like tale is intensely devoted to the sexual and amorous sparks struck among some unusually magnetic people.

In fact, pic could be considered a successful, non-musical remake of *At Long Last Love*,

as the dynamics of the partner changes are virtually identical.

It takes a little while to figure out just where the story is headed, but basic framework has Ben Gazzara, John Ritter and Blaine Novak working for the Odyssey Detective Agency, which is truthfully advertised by the line 'We never sleep'. Gazzara's been assigned to track Gotham visitor Audrey Hepburn by her husband, while Ritter and Novak trail Dorothy Stratten as she slips away from her husband to rendezvous with young Sean Ferrer.

Hepburn doesn't have a line to speak for the entire first hour (much of the film is devoted to vaguely voyeuristic pursuit and observation on the part of the detectives), but ultimately she emerges winningly as the most mature and discreet character in the group.

Certain plot contrivances bear eerie resemblances to the circumstances leading up to Stratten's real-life 1980 murder, as she too, had been followed by a detective hired by a husband suspicious of her fidelity. A palm reading sequence in which Ritter predicts that her marriage will come to a quick end – and she wonders if she has much time left – is chilling for those familiar with the Stratten case.

THEY CALL ME MISTER TIBBS!

1970, 108 MINS, US ◇ ▼

Dir Gordon Douglas   *Prod* Herbert Herschman   *Scr* Alan R. Trustman, James R. Webb   *Ph* Gerald Finnerman   *Ed* Bud Molin   *Mus* Quincy Jones   *Art Dir* Addison F. Hehr
● Sidney Poitier, Martin Landau, Barbara McNair, Anthony Zerbe, Juano Hernandez, George Spell (United Artists/Mirisch)

A Nob Hill prostitute is murdered in her $300 a month apartment. Last seen leaving the apartment is Martin Landau, a politically-involved minister in the midst of an activist campaign to pass a ballot measure to reform local government. Landau is a close personal friend of Sidney Poitier, who is assigned to investigate the case.

The detective is a tough, ruthlessly efficient cop, and the portrayal, realistic as it is, might be dramatically deadly. However script switches back and forth between the case and the cop's everyday domestic problems with wife Barbara McNair, 11-year-old son George Spell and six-year-old daughter Wanda Spell.

The father all too frequently must also be a cop to his son and it is in the relationship with the boy that Poitier's character paradoxically is given flesh and blood.

THEY DIED WITH THEIR BOOTS ON

1941, 140 MINS, US ▼

Dir Raoul Walsh   *Prod* Robert Fellows   *Scr* Wally Klein, Aeneas MacKenzie   *Ph* Bert Glennon   *Ed* William Holmes   *Mus* Max Steiner
● Errol Flynn, Olivia de Havilland, Arthur Kennedy, Sydney Greenstreet, Anthony Quinn, Hattie McDaniel (Warner)

They Died with Their Boots On is the Custer story, full of action, Indians and anachronisms, with Olivia de Havilland co-starred.

Warner studio provided generously for the picture, in terms of a good supporting cast, hundreds of horsemen, and outdoor locations. Raoul Walsh directed and brought to the screen all the pageantry and adventure that the biography provides.

They're a long time getting to the tragic engagement in the Black Hills when Custer (Errol Flynn) with a third of his command, numbering 264 members of the 7th Cavalry, fell into ambush and were slaughtered by the Sioux.

The liberties which the screen writers have taken with well established and authenti-

cated facts are likely to be a bit trying in spots. But the test of the yarn is not its accuracy, but its speed and excitement. Of these it has plenty.

When Flynn is ordered to command of a frontier post, disorders with Indians require immediate and drastic action. Custer is the man for the emergency. There is a period of armistice. Then the civilian traders and land grabbers move in. Trouble with the redskins ride with every covered wagon.

THEY DRIVE BY NIGHT

1940, 93 MINS, US ▼

Dir Raoul Walsh   *Prod* Mark Hellinger   *Scr* Jerry Wald, Richard Macaulay   *Ph* Arthur Edeson   *Ed* Thomas Richards   *Mus* Adolph Deutsch   *Art Dir* John Hughes
● George Raft, Ann Sheridan, Humphrey Bogart, Ida Lupino, Gale Page, Alan Hale (Warner)

Fast moving and actionful melodrama of long-haul trucking biz, *They Drive* clicks with plenty of entertainment content. Story, off the beaten track, divides into two sections, but with a neat dovetail to weld it together. First half is adventure of George Raft and Humphrey Bogart as brothers operating a freelance highway truck, culminating with an asleep-at-the-wheel wreck in which Bogart loses an arm and his desire for further highway adventures. Second half is devoted to the triangle melodrama, with Raft on the receiving end of persistent amorous advances of the married Ida Lupino.

Raoul Walsh provides deft direction that accentuates dramatic moments and maintains a zippo tempo throughout. Script is decidedly workmanlike with numerous snappy and at times spicily double-entendre lines interwoven.

Raft holds the spotlight as the vigorous and determined trucking indie battling against adversities to consummate a dream of owning his own fleet. He turns in a topnotch performance. Equal in importance is Lupino who turns on her dramatic talents for an exceptionally outstanding portrayal, unsympathetic though it is. Bogart is excellent as the hard-working driver and Raft's brother. Anne Sheridan is okay, mainly for love interest, overshadowed by the stellar performance of Lupino.

THEY LIVE

1988, 93 MINS, US ◇ ▼

Dir John Carpenter   *Prod* Larry Franco   *Scr* Frank Armitage [= John Carpenter]   *Ph* Gary B. Kibbe   *Ed* Gib Jaffe, Frank E. Jimenez   *Mus* John Carpenter, Alan Howarth   *Art Dir* William J. Durrell Jr, Daniel Lomino
● Roddy Piper, Keith David, Meg Foster, George (Buck) Flower, Peter Jason (Alive)

Conceived on 1950s B-movie sci-fi terms, *They Live* is a fantastically subversive film, a nifty little confection pitting us vs them, the haves vs the have-nots.

Screenplay by 'Frank Armitage' (presumably another Carpenter pseudonym as was 'Martin Quatermass', based on a Ray Nelson short story [*Eight O'Clock in the Morning*], takes the clever premise that those in control of the global economic power structure are secretly other-worldly aliens.

His leading character, pretentiously named Nada (Roddy Piper), is a heavily muscled working Joe, a wanderer who makes his way to Justiceville, a shantytown settlement for the homeless in the shadows of downtown's skyscrapers.

Nada happens upon some sunglasses which, when worn, reveal a whole alternate existence, in which certain individuals – the ruling class – are instantly recognizable due to their hideously decomposed, skeletal faces.

Nada becomes an outlaw, picking off aliens wherever he can. He seeks an accomplice, first in Meg Foster, who unwillingly rescues him from the police, and then in black coworker Keith David, another bodybuilder whom he has to fight seemingly forever before getting him to try on the glasses.

Pro wrestler Piper comes across quite adequately as the blue collar Everyman, and remainder of the cast is okay.

••••••••••••••••••••••••••••••

■ THEY MIGHT BE GIANTS

1971, 91 MINS, US ◇ ▽

Dir Anthony Harvey *Prod* John Foreman *Scr* James Goldman *Ph* Victor J. Kemper *Ed* Gerald Greenberg *Mus* John Barry *Art Dir* John Robert Lloyd

● George C. Scott, Joanne Woodward, Jack Gilford, Lester Rawlins , Rue McClanahan, Ron Weyand (Universal)

They Might Be Giants starts off splendidly and hilariously, with George C. Scott at his intense and imposing best as a former jurist who thinks he's Sherlock Holmes, and Joanne Woodward charmingly harried as the psychiatrist who's delighted to encounter a 'classic paranoid', and who just happens to be named Dr (Mildred) Watson.

After that it's all downhill. It's not only unfunny, but increasingly preachy and sentimental – hammering at the clichéd tale of the good-hearted nut who's basically saner, and certainly nicer, than the pack of meanies who attempt to defeat him.

Scott and Woodward battle the script valiantly. Scott has the easier time of it by virtue of his character's self-contained system. But both are buried eventually under a pile of loose ends, and they're not helped much either by Anthony Harvey's visually unimaginative direction.

••••••••••••••••••••••••••••••

■ THEY SHOOT HORSES, DON'T THEY

1969, 129 MINS, US ◇ ▽

Dir Sydney Pollack *Prod* Irwin Winkler, Robert Chartoff, Sydney Pollack *Scr* James Poe, Robert E. Thompson *Ph* Philip H. Lathrop *Ed* Frederic Steinkamp *Mus* John Green *Art Dir* Harry Horner

● Jane Fonda, Michael Sarrazin, Susannah York, Gig Young, Red Buttons, Robert Fields (Palomar)

Horace McCoy's 1935 grimy novel of a depression era dance marathon, which sold a forgettable 3,000 copies as a book, is a film with Jane Fonda as a hard-as-nails babe. It becomes, in a recreated old ballroom, a sordid spectacle of hard times, a kind of existentialist allegory of life.

Gig Young is the promoter-emcee, the barker for a cheap sideshow attraction with an endless patter of cliches on pluck, luck, courage, true grit, and the American Way. Puffy-eyed, unshaven, reeking of stale liquor, sweat and cigarets, Young has never looked older or acted better.

Fonda, as the unremittingly cynical loser, the tough and bruised babe of the Dust Bowl, gives a dramatic performance that gives the film a personal focus and an emotionally gripping power.

Pollack turns the marathon into a vulgar, sleazy, black microcosm of life in 1932.

••••••••••••••••••••••••••••••

■ THEY WERE EXPENDABLE

1945, 135 MINS, US ◇

Dir John Ford *Prod* John Ford *Scr* Frank Wead *Ph* Joseph H. August *Ed* Frank E. Hull, Douglass Biggs *Mus* Herbert Stothart *Art Dir* Cedric Gibbons, Malcolm F. Brown

● Robert Montgomery, John Wayne, Donna Reed, Cameron Mitchell (M-G-M)

They Were Expendable, dealing with the Japs' overrunning of the Philippines [from the

book of the same name by William L. White], primarily concerns the part played by the US torpedo boats in their use against the Japs.

Robert Montgomery and his buddy (John Wayne) are naval lieutenants in command of P-T boats. Montgomery from the start has faith in the little destroyers but Wayne is slow to appreciate their value.

While the squadron of P-T tubs stationed at Manila Bay prior to Pearl Harbor were looked upon doubtfully by naval officers, invasion by the Japs gave them their chance to show what they could do. Most of the rest of the picture vividly portrays the big job the little boats did.

The battle scenes in which the P-T's go after Jap cruisers and supply ships were exceptionally well directed, John Ford aided by James C. Havens, captain of the US Marine Corps Reserves.

Love interest is built around Wayne and an army nurse, played appealingly by Donna Reed. It develops at an early stage but is dropped as Wayne and Reed lose each other through assignments that separate them.

••••••••••••••••••••••••••••••

■ THEY'RE A WEIRD MOB

1966, 109 MINS, AUSTRALIA/UK ◇

Dir Michael Powell *Prod* Michael Powell *Scr* Richard Imrie *Ph* Arthur Grant *Ed* Gerald Turney-Smith *Mus* Laurence Leonard, Alan Boustead *Art Dir* Dennis Gentle

● Walter Chiari, Clare Dunne, Chips Rafferty, Alida Chelli, Ed Devereaux, Slim de Grey (Williamson/Powell International)

Italian import Walter Chiari scores in a role that seems tailor-made – an Italian journalist who emigrates to Australia to write for an Italian journal in Sydney edited by his cousin. He arrives very green, and much amusement is caused by his taking too literally some of the Aussie slang.

Chiari finds his cousin has fled. He has left a very irate young lady, Clare Dunne, who has put money into the journal. Chiari gets a job as a bricklayer and ultimately makes the grade with his fellow Aussie workmen. Determined to repay his cousin's debts in installments, Chiari seeks Dunne on Sydney's beaches and elsewhere, but is rebuffed all the way.

Apart from Chiari, Chips Rafferty (who gives an outstanding performance as Dunne's father) and Ed Devereaux as the main bricklayer, most of the cast seems self-conscious before the cameras. For the first half, the film [from the bestselling novel *Down Under* by John O'Grady] strives too hard to be funny and concentrates too much upon the strange Aussie lingo. Once it settles down to telling a story and forgetting about this, it is stronger entertainment.

••••••••••••••••••••••••••••••

■ THIEF

1981, 122 MINS, US ◇

Dir Michael Mann *Prod* Jerry Bruckheimer, Ronnie Caan *Scr* Michael Mann *Ph* Donald Thorin *Ed* Dov Hoenig *Mus* Tangerine Dream *Art Dir* Mel Bourne

● James Caan, Tuesday Weld, Willie Nelson, James Belushi (United Artists)

Michael Mann proves to be a potent triple threat as exec producer-director-writer on '*Thief.*' Although there are points where he gets bogged down in the technical aspects of thievery, the film is a slick Chicago crimedrama with a well-developed sense of pathos running throughout. James Caan comes up with a particularly convincing portrait of the central figure and superior soundtrack from Tangerine Dream adds immeasurably to the action.

Mann, who won awards for his work on the critically acclaimed telefilm, '*The Jericho Mile*,' has woven a fine story around a highly

honorable man who just happens to be an expert thief with an extensive prison record. Caan plays the thief, a victim of an unfortunate childhood who lands in jail and is hardened with his unsavory environment, with an incredible vulnerability.

In terms of story, Caan is a highly successful crook who takes great pains to maintain his professional independence. Against his better judgment he gives in to 'godfather' type Robert Prosky's request to join forces, mostly in an effort to provide personal stability.

The basic story centers on Caan's work, which becomes increasingly complicated by his new association. Oddly enough, Mann's major flaw is being a bit too meticulous in delineating the process Caan must go through in order to make a big score.

••••••••••••••••••••••••••••••

■ THIEF OF BAGDAD, THE

1924, 155 MINS, US ◇ ⊗ ▽

Dir Raoul Walsh *Prod* Douglas Fairbanks *Scr* Lotta Woods, Elton Thomas [=Douglas Fairbanks] *Ph* Arthur Edeson *Ed* William Nolan *Mus* Mortimer Wilson *Art Dir* William Cameron Menzies

● Douglas Fairbanks, Snitz Edwards, Julanne Johnston, Anna May Wong, Charles Belcher, Sojin (Fairbanks/United Artists)

Douglas Fairbanks comes forth with an absorbing, interesting picture, totally different than any of its predecessors. Nearly all of it is fairytale-like or fantasy, and so well is it done that the picture carries its audience along in the spirit of the depiction. *The Arabian Nights* are classic stories in book form. *The Thief of Bagdad* is a classic in pictures.

There is a magic rope thrown into the air up which the thief climbs high walls. There is a magic carpet upon which he sails with his princess away into the land of happiness. There is a magic chest which the favored one retrieves after heroic struggles through the valley of fire, the vale of dragons, even to the depths of the seas. It is the thief, now a prince who returns at the coming of the seventh moon to win his princess against the wiles of Oriental potentates seeking her hand. He wraps her in his invisible cloak and whisks her away.

The cast has been brightly selected. At the head of those players is Sojin in the role of the Mongol prince, a really fine characterization. Anna May Wong as the little slave girl who is a spy for the Mongol prince, proves herself a fine actress. Julanne Johnston as the princess is languorous, being more decorative than inspiring.

••••••••••••••••••••••••••••••

■ THIEF OF BAGDAD, THE

1940, 106 MINS, UK ◇ ▽

Dir Ludwig Berger, Michael Powell, Tim Whelan, Geoffrey Boothby, Charles David *Prod* Alexander Korda *Scr* Lajos Biro, Miles Malleson *Ph* Georges Perinal *Ed* William Hornbeck, Charles Crichton *Mus* Miklos Rozsa *Art Dir* Vincent Korda

● Conrad Veidt, Sabu, June Duprez, John Justin, Rex Ingram, Miles Malleson (Korda/United Artists)

The Thief of Bagdad is a colorful, lavish and eye-appealing spectacle. It's an expensive production accenting visual appeal, combining sweeping panoramas and huge sets, amazing special effects and process photography, and vivid magnificent Technicolor. These factors completely submerge the stolid, slow and rather disjointed fairy tale which lacks any semblance of spontaneity in its telling.

Alexander Korda retains only the Bagdadian background and title in presenting his version of the picture first turned out by Douglas Fairbanks in 1924. But while Fairbanks presented dash and movement to his story, to have the latter dominate his spectacular settings, Korda uses the reverse angle. As result, audience interest is focused on the production and technical displays of the picture, and the unimpressive story and stagey acting of the cast fail to measure up to the general production quality.

The story combines many imaginative incidents culled from Arabian Nights fables. There's the mechanical horse that flies through the air; the giant genie of the bottle; the huge spider that guards the all-seeing eye; the six-armed dancing doll; the evil magic of the villain; and the famous magic carpet.

Korda spent two years in preparation and production of *Thief of Bagdad*. All of the large sets, including the city of Bagdad and seaport of Basra, were shot in England, in addition to most of the dramatic action. With the war stopping production in England Korda moved to Hollywood to complete the picture, substituting the American desert and the Grand Canyon for sequences that he originally intended to shoot in Arabia and Egypt.

Conrad Veidt is most impressive as the sinister grand vizier, sharing honors with Sabu, who capably carries off the title role.

························

■ **THIEF WHO CAME TO DINNER, THE**

1973, 105 MINS, US ◇ ⓥ

Dir Bud Yorkin   *Prod* Bud Yorkin   *Scr* Walter Hill *Ph* Philip Lathrop   *Ed* John C. Horger   *Mus* Henry Mancini   *Art Dir* Polly Platt
● Ryan O'Neal, Jacqueline Bisset, Warren Oates, Jill Clayburgh, Charles Cioffi, Ned Beatty (Tandem/ Warner)

The Thief Who Came to Dinner has a good title and a helpful supporting cast. Otherwise it is a tepid caper comedy, starring Ryan O'Neal as a computer-age society gem burglar, Jacqueline Bisset as his girl, and Warren Oates as a befuddled insurance detective.

Using a Terrence Lore novel, adapter Walter Hill structured an episodic script focussing on O'Neal who blackmails magnate Charles Cioffi for entree into rich circles where he can plot his heists.

The film, which exudes the lethargy of a project where some talent commitments are being exercised, uses as a running gag O'Neal's heist signature of a chess move, leading to a newspaper promotion with chess editor Austin Pendleton becoming frustrated as the thief's computer-aided expertise.

························

■ **THIEVES LIKE US**

1974, 123 MINS, US ◇

Dir Robert Altman   *Prod* Jerry Bick, George Litto *Scr* Calder Willingham, Joan Tewkesbury, Robert Altman   *Ph* Jean Boffety   *Ed* Lou Lombardo
● Keith Carradine, Shelley Duvall, John Schuck, Bert Remsen, Louise Fletcher, Tom Skerritt (United Artists)

Thieves Like Us proves that when Robert Altman has a solid story and script, he can make an exceptional film, one mostly devoid of clutter, auterist mannerism, and other cinema chic. It's a better film than Nicholas Ray's first jab at the story in 1948 [*They Live By Night*], the mid-1930s tale of lower-class young love and Dixie bank-robbing.

Edward Anderson's novel of the same name has, this time, been adapted into a no-nonsense screenplay. Keith Carradine heads the cast as a young prison trustee who escapes with John Schuck and Bert Remsen in a spree of small-town bank heists. Shelley Duvall and Carradine fall in love, their romance clearly destined for tragedy as the robberies inevitably lead to murders and eventual police capture.

························

■ **THIN BLUE LINE, THE**

1988, 106 MINS, US ◇ ⓥ

Dir Errol Morris   *Prod* Mark Lipson   *Ph* Stefan Czapsky, Robert Chappell   *Ed* Paul Barnes   *Mus* Philip Glass   *Art Dir* Teddy Bafaloukos
● (American Playhouse/Third Floor)

Errol Morris' *The Thin Blue Line* constitutes a mesmerizing reconstruction and investigation of a senseless murder. It employs strikingly original formal devices to pull together diverse interviews, filmclips, photo collages and recreations of the crime from many points of view.

Case in question centers upon the 1976 murder of a Dallas policeman. Late one night, Officer Robert Wood and his partner pulled over a car that was traveling without its headlights on. When Wood approached the driver's window, he was shot five times and killed.

Some time later, David Harris, 16, was arrested in Vidor, Texas, after having bragged to friends that he'd killed a Dallas cop. Harris later insisted his boasting was only meant to impress his buddies, and that the real murderer was a hitchhiker he'd picked up earlier in the day, one Randall Adams.

Despite Harris' extensive criminal history and Adams' unblemished past, the teenager got off scot-free, while the older man was convicted and sentenced to death (later committed to life imprisonment).

Morris first introduces the two men via freshly filmed, straightforward interviews, then stages the crime for the camera from a variety of angles and at an assortment of speeds.

Title refers to the police, said by the judge here to be the only thing that separates the public from the rule of anarchy.

························

■ **THIN MAN, THE**

1934, 80 MINS, US

Dir W. S. Van Dyke   *Prod* Hunt Stromberg   *Scr* Albert Hackett, Frances Goodrich   *Ph* James Wong Howe *Ed* Robert J. Kern   *Mus* William Axt (dir.) *Art Dir* Cedric Gibbons, David Townsend
● William Powell, Myrna Loy, Maureen O'Sullivan, Nat Pendleton, Minna Gombell, Porter Hall (M-G-M)

The Thin Man was an entertaining novel, and now it's an entertaining picture. In the Dashiell Hammett original there was considerable material not suited by nature to pictures. That this has been cut without noticeable loss of story punch or merit is high commendation for the adapters.

They capture the spirit of the jovial, companionable relationship of the characters, Nick, retired detective, and Nora, his wife. Their very pleasant manner of loving each other and showing it is used as a light comedy structure upon which the screen doctors perform their operation on the Hammett novel.

The comedy as inserted, and also as directed by W. S. Van Dyke and played by William Powell and Myrna Loy, carries the picture along during its early moments and gives it an impetus which sweeps the meat of the mystery story through to a fast finish.

No changes made in the basic plot nor in the murder mystery developments.
□ 1934: Best Picture (Nomination)

························

■ **THIN RED LINE, THE**

1964, 90 MINS, US

Dir Andrew Marton   *Prod* Sidney Harmon *Scr* Bernard Gordon   *Ph* Manuel Berenguer *Ed* Derek Parsons   *Mus* Malcolm Arnold   *Art Dir* Jose Alguero
● Keir Dullea, Jack Warden, James Philbrook, Ray Daley, Robert Kanter, Merlyn Yordan (Allied Artists)

Aficionados of the action-packed war film

will savor the crackling, combat-centered approach of *The Thin Red Line*, an explosive melodramatization of the Yank assault on Guadalcanal in World War II.

Bernard Gordon's scenario, turbulently gleaned from James Jones' novel, focuses its characterization gaze at two figures prominently implicated in the taking of that small but significant piece of Pacific real estate. One is a resourceful private (Keir Dullea), the other a war-wise, sadistic sergeant (Jack Warden).

The two quickly become enemies but it is no surprise when, ultimately, one dies in the other's arms after saving the other's life. Dullea and Warden are colorful antagonists, former's intensity contrasting sharply with the latter's easygoing air. In addition to this pivotal intramural conflict, there are other hostilities including the one between Japan and the United States.

························

■ **THING, THE**

1982, 108 MINS, US ◇ ⓥ

Dir John Carpenter   *Prod* David Foster, Lawrence Turman   *Scr* Bill Lancaster   *Ph* Dean Cundey *Ed* Todd Ramsay   *Mus* Ennio Morricone   *Art Dir* John J. Lloyd
● Kurt Russell, A. Wilford Brimley, T.K. Carter, David Clennon, Keith David, Richard Dysart (Universal/Turman-Foster)

If it's the most vividly guesome monster ever to stalk the screen that audiences crave, then *The Thing* is the thing. On all other levels, however, John Carpenter's remake of Howard Hawks' 1951 sci-fi classic comes as a letdown.

Strong premise has a group of American scientists and researchers posted at an isolated station in Antarctica. A visit to a decimated Norwegian encampment in the vicinity reveals that a space ship, which had remained buried in ice for as many as 100,000 years, has been uncovered, and that no survivors were left to tell what was found.

First manifestation of The Thing arrives in the form of an escaped dog from the Scandinavian camp. It soon becomes clear that The Thing is capable of ingesting, then assuming the bodily form of, any living being.

What the old picture delivered – and what Carpenter has missed – was a sense of intense dread, a fear that the loathed creature might be lurking around any corner or behind any door.

Kurt Russell is the nominal hero, although suicidal attitude adopted towards the end undercuts his status as a centerscreen force.

························

■ **THING (FROM ANOTHER WORLD), THE**

1951, 89 MINS, US ⓥ

Dir Christian Nyby   *Prod* Howard Hawks   *Scr* Charles Lederer   *Ph* Russell Harlan   *Ed* Roland Gross *Mus* Dimitri Tiomkin   *Art Dir* Albert S. D'Agostino, John J. Hughes
● Margaret Sheridan, Kenneth Tobey, Robert Cornthwaite, Douglas Spencer, Dewey Martin, James Arness (Winchester/RKO)

Strictly offbeat subject matter centers around a weird, outlandish interplanetary spacehopper (see title) which descends upon earth in what's referred to as a flying saucer.

Christian Nyby's direction sustains a mood of tingling expectancy as a small group of US airmen and scientists stationed near the North Pole learn that a new, mysterious element is playing tricks with their compass-readings, etc. Tension develops effectively as the expedition takes off to reckon with the unearthly intruder. Hawks' production also scores in its depiction of the bleak, snow-swept Arctic region. The background layout, shot in Montana, conveys an air of frigid authenticity.

But the resourcefulness shown in building the plot groundwork is lacking as the yarn gets into full swing. Cast members, headed by Margaret Sheridan and Kenneth Tobey, fail to communicate any real terror as the 'Thing' makes its appearance and its power potential to destroy the world is revealed.

Screenplay, based on the story *Who Goes There* by John W. Campbell Jr., shows strain in the effort to come up with a cosmic shocker in the name of science fiction.

- -

■ **THINGS CHANGE**

1988, 100 MINS, US ◇ ▽
Dir David Mamet *Prod* Michael Hausman *Scr* David Mamet, Shel Silverstein *Ph* Juan Ruiz-Anchia *Ed* Trudy Ship *Mus* Alaric Jans *Art Dir* Michael Merritt
● Don Ameche, Joe Mantegna, Robert Prosky, J.J Johnston, Ricky Jay, Mike Nussbaum (Filmhaus/Columbia)

David Mamet's *Things Change* is a dry, funny and extremely intelligent comedy about an innocent mistaken for a Mafia don.

Pic opens in Chicago as the elderly Gino (Ameche), a shoeshine boy, is 'invited' to meet a Mafia boss whom he physically resembles. He wants Gino to confess to a murder and take the rap and as a reward he can have his heart's desire.

Gino is handed over to Jerry (Joe Mantegna), a very junior member of the Mafia clan. All Jerry has to do is coach Gino in his story for two days, then deliver him to the law. Instead, Jerry decides to give the oldster a final fling, and takes him to Lake Tahoe where, unknown to him, a Mafia convention is about to take place.

Gino is instantly mistaken for a senior Don and given royal treatment. He's also invited to meet the local Mafia kingpin (Robert Prosky) with whom he instantly strikes up a close rapport while Jerry sees himself getting into deeper and deeper trouble.

This comedy of mistaken identity centers around a beautifully modulated starring performance from Ameche as the poor but painfully upright and honest Gino. As the dimwitted Jerry, Mantegna is consistently funny and touching.

- -

■ **THINGS TO COME**

1936, 97 MINS, UK ▽
Dir William Cameron Menzies *Prod* Alexander Korda *Scr* H.G. Wells *Ph* Georges Perinal *Ed* William Hornbeck, Charles Crichton, Francis Lyon *Mus* Arthur Bliss *Art Dir* Vincent Korda
● Raymond Massey, Cedric Hardwicke, Edward Chapman, Ralph Richardson, Margaretta Scott, Maurice Braddell (London)

This is England's first $1 million picture. It's an impressive but dull exposition of a bad dream.

H.G. Wells' idea is that in 1946 there will be a new and disastrous world war. It will last for 30 years and, at the end of that time, civilization will be reduced to nothingness, disease having scourged the world. In exile a group of engineers and aviators, however, think things over and decide that the ravages and wastes of war, properly harnessed and channeled, can be used for the world's salvation.

They take things over, do away with the petty little fascistic countries that have sprung up, do away with their petty little fascistic leaders, and create a new world of steel and glass, radio and television, artificial light and heat. It is all very pictorial, very imaginative, very artificial and it runs on and on.

William Cameron Menzies directs with a firm hand and even manages to inject some power into the fantasy. Where his characters are allowed to live, he sees to it that they also

breathe. Georges Perinal's photography is tops. Garlands are also due Harry Zech for trick photography and Ned Mann for special effects.

Raymond Massey is tops as John Cabal, leader of the new world. Ralph Richardson does a splendid job as the Boss, a sort of combo Hitler-Mussolini.

- -

■ **THINK BIG**

1990, 86 MINS, US ◇
Dir Jon Turteltaub *Prod* Brad Krevoy, Steven Stabler *Scr* Edward Kovach, David Tausik, John Turteltaub *Ph* Mark Morris *Ed* Jeff Reiner *Mus* Michael Sembello, Hilary Bercovici, Stephen Graziano *Art Dir* Robert Schullenberg
● Peter Paul, David Paul, Ari Meyers, Martin Mull, David Carradine, Claudia Christian (Motion Picture/Concorde)

This undemanding physical comedy offers okay gags for audiences waxing nostalgic for the generally unlamented 1970s vehicular comedies involving trucks and cars.

The Barbarian Bros, twins Peter and David Paul, topline as a pair of affable but somewhat retarded truckers hauling a load of toxic waste across country. Brainy but beutiful 16-year-old Ari Meyers stows away in their vehicle, as she's on the lam with her secret weapon developed at Martin Mull's think tank for kids.

There's plenty of effective slapstick as cartoonish villains chase after the trio, who are joined later by Meyers' school psychologist (Claudia Christian). David Carradine, in particular, is fun (costumed to resemble his brother Keith) as a nutty repo man.

Meyers is delightful as the precocious heroine and manages to maintain a straight face opposite the cuddly but oversize non-actor Paul brothers.

- -

■ **THIRD DAY, THE**

1965, 119 MINS, US ◇
Dir Jack Smight *Prod* Jack Smight *Scr* Burton Wohl, Robert Presnell Jr *Ph* Robert Surtees *Ed* Stefan Arnsten *Mus* Percy Faith *Art Dir* Edward Carrere
● George Peppard, Elizabeth Ashley, Roddy McDowall, Arthur O'Connell, Mona Washbourne, Herbert Marshall (Warner)

The Third Day shapes up as an interesting and sometimes suspenseful drama revolving around a man fighting amnesia and faced with a manslaughter rap. The production is adapted from Joseph Hayes' novel.

A chief weakness lies in the lack of script development of how George Peppard, who has lost all recollection of a 24-hour period during which a young woman meets her death, regains his memory.

Film opens on Peppard climbing a steep bank from a river into which he obviously plunged, but he cannot remember what happened or who he is. He learns he's married to a beautiful aristocrat whom he's about to lose because he's a drunk, and is about to be talked into selling the family business.

Peppard delivers an expert enactment and Elizabeth Ashley, as his wife, lends a colorful note as she handles a well-played role. Roddy McDowall socks over a conniving character and a standout performance is offered by Mona Washbourne in a warm and understanding characterization, perhaps the most memorable delineation of the picture.

- -

■ **THIRD MAN, THE**

1949, 93 MINS, UK ▽
Dir Carol Reed *Prod* Alexander Korda, David O. Selznick *Scr* Graham Greene *Ph* Robert Krasker *Ed* Oswald Hafenrichter *Mus* Anton Karas *Art Dir* Vincent Korda

● Joseph Cotten, Alida Valli, Orson Welles, Trevor Howard, Bernard Lee (London)

This is a full-blooded, absorbing story adapted from book by Graham Greene. Locale is postwar Vienna, which is controlled by combined military force of the four occupying powers, and revolves around the black market and all its unsavory ramifications.

Holly Martins, a young American writer, arrives to join his friend, Harry Lime, who has promised him a job. He just gets to him in time to attend his funeral. Suspicious of conflicting evidence and with a strong hunch that Harry was murdered, Holly decides to unravel the mystery.

Orson Welles manifests as the 'corpse' of the opening shots, and his contribution is mainly in dodging through back streets.

Joseph Cotten makes a pleasing personality of the loyal friend, and Trevor Howard, as the detached, cool British officer, displays just the right amount of human sympathy and understanding.

- -

■ **THIRD SECRET, THE**

1964, 103 MINS, UK
Dir Charles Crichton *Prod* Robert L. Joseph *Scr* Robert L. Joseph *Ph* Douglas Slocombe *Ed* Frederick Wilson *Mus* Richard Arnell *Art Dir* Tom Morahan
● Stephen Boyd, Jack Hawkins, Richard Attenborough, Diane Cilento, Pamela Franklin, Paul Rogers (20th Century-Fox)

When a renowned psychoanalyst is deemed a suicide, the puzzle surrounding his sudden and unaccountable death, as it is put together piece by piece by one of his agitated patients, is the plot pursued by *The Third Secret*, an engrossing, if not altogether convincing, mystery melodrama of the weighty psychological school.

Stephen Boyd, as the inquisitive patient of the deceased analyst, conducts a private investigation to determine whether the death was actually a suicide (contradicting everything the noted doctor stood for) or a murder committed by one of his patients, of whom there were only four, according to the analyst's daughter (Pamela Franklin). The investigation leads Boyd – an American telenewscaster living in England – from patient to patient, a fruitless path until he unearths 'the third secret'.

A lack of animation in spots is evident in Boyd's performance, but there are moments when he catches the spark of the character. Franklin does a highly professional job as the daughter. The three ex-patients visited by Boyd are Jack Hawkins as a judge, Diane Cilento as a secretary and Richard Attenborough as an art gallery owner.

- -

■ **13 RUE MADELEINE**

1946, 95 MINS, US ▽
Dir Henry Hathaway *Prod* Louis de Rochemont *Scr* John Monks Jr, Sy Bartlett *Ph* Norbert Brodine *Ed* Harmon Jones *Mus* Alfred Newman *Art Dir* James Basevi, Maurice Ransford
● James Cagney, Annabella, Richard Conte, Sam Jaffe (20th Century-Fox)

Utilizing the same off-screen documentary exposition as he did in *The House on 92nd Street* producer Louis de Rochemont, himself an alumnus of the *Time-Life* technique, reemploys the stentorian *March of Time* commentary to set his theme. Thereafter it evolves into a Nazi-Allies cops-and-robbers tale of bravery and bravado, honest histrionics and hokum.

When he is one of the strategic services' masterminds, on US or British soil, James Cagney is effectively the mature training officer engaged in the important branch of the service having to do with strategy. When he essays the role of a brave young soldier-spy, to pit himself against Richard Conte, the crack Gestapo agent who had insinuated himself into the American espionage school as a means to learn our invasion plans, Cagney suffers comparison. Conte as Bill O'Connell, nee Wilhelm Kuncel of the Nazi espionage, emerges as the cast's outstander.

The training methods, as indoctrinated into the plot's development, are arresting stuff. *Madeleine* was shot wholly away from Hollywood, utilizing New England and Quebec sites in the main, but there is nothing about the film that doesn't indicate super-Hollywood standards.

••••••••••••••••••••••••••

■ **13TH LETTER, THE**

1951, 85 MINS, US

Dir Otto Preminger   *Prod* Otto Preminger
Scr Howard Koch   *Ph* Joseph La Shelle   *Ed* Louis Loeffler   *Mus* Alex North   *Art Dir* Lyle Wheeler, Maurice Ransford
● Linda Darnell, Charles Boyer, Michael Rennie, Constance Smith, Francoise Rosay (20th Century-Fox)

Well-made and with an offbeat location site, film is an interesting account of the effects of poison pen letters on a small Quebec village.

Plot deals principally with Michael Rennie, as a doctor; Charles Boyer, an older doctor, and his young wife (Constance Smith). The small Quebec village in which they live becomes a gossip mill when poison pen letters, indicating Rennie and Smith are having an affair, are widely distributed. Letters go on to bring in other people, eventually causing a wounded war hero to commit suicide.

Linda Darnell heads the star list as a crippled, romance-starved girl on whom suspicion falls briefly. However, cleared she and Rennie become the story's one valid romance. Her playing is excellent.

Charles Boyer slips into the character of the elderly French-Canadian doctor with wonderful ease. Smith, a British import, displays emotional talent.

••••••••••••••••••••••••••

■ **30 IS A DANGEROUS AGE, CYNTHIA**

1968, 85 MINS, UK ◇ ⓥ

Dir Joseph McGrath   *Prod* Walter Shenson
Scr Dudley Moore, Joseph McGrath, John Wells   *Ph* Billy Williams   *Ed* Bill Blunden   *Mus* Dudley Moore   *Art Dir* Brian Eatwell
● Dudley Moore, Eddie Foy Jr, Suzy Kendall, John Bird, Duncan MacRae (Columbia)

Generously endowed with the better comedic elements of satire, knockabouts, subtleties, pie-in-the-face, etc, film is almost a virtuoso performance by Dudley Moore. He stars, is credited with the original story, composed and conducted music – played by the Dudley Moore Trio.

Close to his 30th birthday Moore, with an amazing spurt of energy, launches a desperation drive to achieve two ambitions, writing a successful musical comedy and getting married.

From this plot establishment, Moore and friends take off on a romp that involves a false broken arm, getting away from it all, losing girl, finishing musical and so on, with such a sense of camp that audiences are bound to be laughing long after the last frame.

Moore's versatility is central focus with a remarkably underplayed performance that sets pace and keeps it on track; his storyline is a single joke that undoubtedly grew during the filming, and his music and lyrics are like early Noel Coward set in rock idiom.

••••••••••••••••••••••••••

■ **39 STEPS, THE**

1935, 86 MINS, UK ⓥ

Dir Alfred Hitchcock   *Prod* Michael Balcon
Scr Charles Bennett, Alma Reville, Ian Hay   *Ph* Bernard Knowles   *Ed* Derek Twist   *Mus* Louis Levy (dir.)
Art Dir Oscar Werndorff, Albert Jullion
● Robert Donat, Madeleine Carroll, Godfrey Tearle, Peggy Ashcroft, Lucie Mannheim, Wylie Watson (Gaumont-British)

Gaumont has a zippy, punchy, romantic melodrama in *The 39 Steps*. Story is by John Buchan. It's melodrama and at times far-fetched and improbable, but the story twists and spins artfully from one high-powered sequence to another while the entertainment holds like steel cable from start to finish.

Story places a Canadian rancher (Robert Donat) in the centre of an English military secrets plot. He is simultaneously flying from a false accusation of murder and hunting down the leader of the spies, of whom he has learned from a lady who becomes a corpse early in the story. In the course of his wanderings through Scotland's hills and moors he has a series of spectacular escapes and encounters.

It's a creamy role for Donat and his performance, ranging from humor to horror, reveals acting ability behind that good-looking facade. Teamed with Madeleine Carroll, who enters the footage importantly only toward the latter quarter section of the film, the romance is given a light touch which nicely colors an international spy chase.

••••••••••••••••••••••••••

■ **39 STEPS, THE**

1959, 93 MINS, UK ◇ ⓥ

Dir Ralph Thomas   *Prod* Betty Box, Ralph Thomas
Scr Frank Harvey   *Ph* Ernest Steward   *Ed* Alfred Roome   *Mus* Clifton Park
● Kenneth More, Taina Elg, Brenda de Banzie, Barry Jones, Reginald Beckwith, James Hayter (Rank)

Though somewhat altered from Alfred Hitchcock's original, the main idea remains unchanged and the new version of John Buchan's novel stands up very well.

When a strange young woman is stabbed to death in his flat, Kenneth More finds himself involved in a mysterious adventure involving espionage and murder. Before her death the girl tells him that she is a secret agent and gives him all the clues she knows about a spy organization seeking to smuggle some important plans out of the country. All he knows is that the top man is somewhere in Scotland and that the tangle is tied up with strange words told him by the victim – 'The 39 Steps.' Suspected of the murder of the girl, More has just 48 hours to find out the secret of the 39 Steps, expose the gang and so clear himself of the murder rap.

Film starts off brilliantly with tremendous tension and suitably sinister atmosphere. After a while that mood wears off as the pic settles down to an exciting and often amusing chase yarn, set amid some easy-on-the-eye Scottish scenery.

More's performance is a likeable mixture of humor and toughness while Taina Elg is appealing as the pretty schoolmistress who is dragged into the adventure against her will. Then there are Barry Jones, as a sinister professor; Brenda de Banzie, as a fake spiritualist who, with her eccentric husband (Reginald Beckwith) helps More's getaway; James Hayter as a vaude 'memory man' who is a tool of the gang; and Faith Brook, whose murder sparks off the drama, all pitch in splendidly in a well acted picture.

••••••••••••••••••••••••••

■ **THIRTY-NINE STEPS, THE**

1978, 102 MINS, UK ◇ ⓥ

Dir Don Sharp   *Prod* Greg Smith   *Scr* Michael Robson   *Ph* John Coquillon   *Ed* Eric Boyd-Perkins   *Mus* Ed Welch   *Art Dir* Harry Pottle
● Robert Powell, David Warner, Eric Porter, Karen Dotrice, John Mills, George Baker (Rank)

The Thirty-Nine Steps is okay period suspense, directed with a smooth but unremarkable touch by Don Sharp.

For the short of memory, *Steps* is the melodramatic tale of a man on the run from Prussian assassins plotting World War I. It was first a classic novel by John Buchan, then a classic film by Alfred Hitchcock [1935], with Robert Donat as the elusive hero and Madeleine Carroll as the romantic interest. This third version has attractive young Robert Powell and Karen Dotrice, but nothing like the Donat-Carroll chemistry or flourish.

John Mills is very good as the British agent trying to persuade the government of the momentous plot and its dire consequences. Also effective are David Warner as the topmost villain and Eric Porter as a police official.

••••••••••••••••••••••••••

■ **THIRTY SECONDS OVER TOKYO**

1944, 138 MINS, US ⓥ

Dir Mervyn LeRoy   *Prod* Sam Zimbalist   *Scr* Dalton Trumbo   *Ph* Harold Rosson, Robert Surtees   *Ed* Frank Sullivan   *Mus* Herbert Stothart   *Art Dir* Cedric Gibbons, Paul Groesse
● Van Johnson, Robert Walker, Phyllis Thaxter, Tim Murdock, Robert Mitchum, Spencer Tracy (M-G-M)

Lt Col James Doolittle mapped his blitz on Japan 131 days after Pearl Harbor. There is suspense as the flyers prepare themselves for their long-range training in anticipation of the secret mission. More or less relegated but capital as the bulwark of the entire mission is Spencer Tracy's conception of Doolittle. Van Johnson is Ted Lawson and Phyllis Thaxter his wife. It's an inspired casting.

Prominent in Johnson's crew are Tim Murdock, a standout as the co-pilot; Don DeFore as the navigator; Gordon McDonald as the bombardier; and Robert Walker, who is particularly effective as the wistful gunner-mechanic.

Their plane, the *Ruptured Duck*, and its pleasant little family become the focal attention henceforth. After Doolittle finally tells them of their mission to bomb Japan, the war becomes a highly personalized thing through the actions of these crew members.

••••••••••••••••••••••••••

■ **36 CHOWRINGHEE LANE**

1982, 122 MINS, INDIA ◇

Dir Aparna Sen   *Prod* Shashi Kapoor   *Scr* Aparna Sen   *Ph* Ashok Mehta   *Ed* Bhanudas Divakar   *Mus* Vanraj Bhatia
● Jennifer Kendall, Dhritiamn Chatterjee, Debashree Roy, Geoffrey Kendall (Kapoor/Vilas)

Aparna Sen appeared in two Satyajit Ray's films (*Three Daughters* and *Pikoo*) and her father, Chidananda Das Gupta, is a noted film critic, so she came to her first directorial stint with a good background.

Jennifer Kendall (wife of producer Shashi Kapoor, a top commercial film actor) is effective as a lonely Anglo-Indian old lady. She teaches Shakespeare in a private girls' school and has befriended a couple. She does not realise they have been using her for the use of her apartment rather than for a friendship that has seemingly grown between them and warmed her lonely life.

The couple marries. She gives them an old phonograph they coveted, goes to the wedding, but then does not hear much. They gently put her off until she finds they do not need her at all any more.

Item is mostly in English, though the young lovers speak their native Indian lingo when alone. Full of visual ideas, film does not quite transcend them to achieve a more piercing insight into aging and loneliness.

....

■ 36 HOURS

1964, 115 MINS, US/W. GER
Dir George Seaton *Prod* William Perlberg
Scr George Seaton *Ph* Philip Lathrop *Ed* Adrienne Fazan *Mus* Dmitri Tiomkin *Art Dir* George W. Davis, Edward Carfagno
● James Garner, Eva Marie Saint, Rod Taylor, Werner Peters, John Banner, Russell Thorson (M-G-M)

36 Hours is a fanciful war melodrama limning an incident during that crucial number of hours immediately preceding D-Day. The production takes its title from the span of time allotted a German psychiatrist to learn from a captured US intelligence officer fully briefed on the oncoming Allied invasion the exact point of landing.

Based on Roald Dahl's *Beware of the Dog* and a story of Carl K. Hittleman and Luis H. Vance, it provides a behind-the-scenes glimpse of high military intelligence at work.

Garner plays the American sent to Lisbon to confirm through a German contact that the Nazis expect the Allies to land in the Calais area rather than the secretly-planned Normandy beach. Drugged, he's flown under heavy sedation by the Germans to an isolated resort in Bavaria where upon regaining consciousness he's led to believe he has been an amnesia victim for six years.

Taylor registers most effectively in the off-beat role of the German, playing it for sympathy and realistically. Garner in a derring-do part is okay and up to his usual sound brand of histrionics. Eva Marie Saint also delivers strongly as the nurse drafted by the Nazis from a concentration camp and promised help by Taylor if she plays her part well – in the masquerade with Garner.

....

■ THIS ABOVE ALL

1942, 110 MINS, US
Dir Anatole Litvak *Prod* Darryl F. Zanuck *Scr* R.C. Sherriff *Ph* Arthur Miller *Ed* Walter Thompson *Mus* Alfred Newman
● Tyrone Power, Joan Fontaine, Thomas Mitchell, Henry Stephenson, Nigel Bruce, Gladys Cooper (20th Century-Fox)

This Above All is a tale of England in that tense interval between Dunkirk and the London blitz of September 1940. It tells of the romance between a beauteous daughter of the aristocracy and a lowly-born soldier who has deserted after fighting honorably through the shattering battle of Flanders and the tragic evacuation of Dunkirk.

Although the screen adaptation softens certain aspects of Eric M. Knight's novel, such as toning down the love affair during the couple's stay at the Dover inn, or eliminating the complication of the soldier's brain injury, it has not weakened the story.

In some ways the yarn is even improved. For one thing, the whole involved subject of the democratic aims in the war, problem of the conflict of social classes, or the question of pacifism against duty to one's country are expertly focused in personal terms.

....

■ THIS EARTH IS MINE

1959, 123 MINS, US ◇
Dir Henry King *Prod* Casey Robinson, Claude Heilman *Scr* Casey Robinson *Ph* Winton Hoch, Russel Metty *Ed* Ted J. Kent *Mus* Hugo Friedhofer
● Rock Hudson, Jean Simmons, Dorothy McGuire, Claude Rains, Kent Smith, Anna Lee (Universal/Vintage)

This film is almost completely lacking in dra-

matic cohesion. It is verbose and contradictory, and its complex plot relationships from Alice Tisdale Hobart's novel, *The Cup and the Sword* begin with confusion and end in tedium.

The setting is the Napa Valley wine country in the waning years of Prohibition. The basic plot is a conflict between generations – the older, European-born vintners, headed by Claude Rains, with traditions of dedication to the craft, and the younger men, represented by Rock Hudson, who are interested in selling their crop to the highest bidders, even if it means their grapes will be made into bootleg liquor.

Some of the scenes are pure bathos, such as the one where Rock Hudson learns that he is actually the son of his uncle (Kent Smith). What's lacking mostly in the script, and not supplemented in the direction, is an overall intelligence that would have appraised these complexities.

Hudson gives a sympathetic portrayal, but not a satisfying one, because his characterization is riddled by inconsistencies. Jean Simmons achieves involvement but little sympathy because her motivations are so sketchy and superficial. Claude Rains fares best.

....

■ THIS GUN FOR HIRE

1942, 86 MINS, US ▼
Dir Frank Tuttle *Prod* Richard M. Blumenthal
Scr Albert Maltz, W.R. Burnett *Ph* John Seitz
Ed Archie Marshek *Mus* David Buttolph
● Veronica Lake, Robert Preston, Laird Cregar, Alan Ladd, Tully Marshall, Mikhail Rasumny (Paramount)

The idea of presenting Veronica Lake as the heroine of an exciting melodrama has its merits. But the material selected is distinctly unsuited to her. It is a very involved yarn by Graham Greene which deals with international intrigue and treason, having to do with the sale of a secret chemical formula to the Japanese. Albert Maltz and W.R. Burnett wrote the screenplay, which is a succession of gunplay scenes in which Lake becomes the unwilling accomplice of a young killer. He is Alan Ladd.

Other players in the film had difficult assignment trying to give some credence to an improbable story. Robert Preston plays a policeman, who is too easily outwitted to deserve Lake in the end. Laird Cregar is an interesting heavy, and Tully Marshall a reprobate of the worst kind.

....

■ THIS HAPPY BREED

1944, 116 MINS, UK ◇ ⑦
Dir David Lean *Prod* Noel Coward *Scr* Ronald Neame, David Lean, Anthony Havelock-Allan
Ph Ronald Neame, Gay Green *Ed* Jack Harris
Art Dir C. P. Norman
● Robert Newton, Celia Johnson, John Mills, Kay Walsh, Stanley Holloway (Cineguild)

Based on Noel Coward's London legit hit, film soundly captures the spirit of the 1920s and 1930s reviving the era of the British general strike, the jazz dress style, the Charleston, and the depression. It touches on the troubled sphere of the class struggle and labor strife, although it has a dubious note once or twice, such as in an apparent defense of strike-breaking. But it is so much more the history of an average British family, with its pleasures and pains, to make this the paramount interest.

Film is a bit episodic and choppy at the start, as it unwinds in cavalcadish fashion, but it settles down soon to an absorbing chronicle.

Film's excellence comes mainly in the performances. Celia Johnson, as the mother of three grown children and the rock around

which the family revolves, presents a masterful, poignant portrayal.

Robert Newton, who has almost as important a role as the head of the house, is also a superb presentation as the steady, earth-bound but intelligent Britisher. Kay Walsh, as the flighty daughter dissatisfied with her lot; John Mills as the loyal sailor in love with the errant daughter; and Stanley Holloway as the nextdoor neighbor; give fine support.

....

■ THIS IS ELVIS

1981, 88 MINS, US ◇
Dir Malcolm Leo, Andrew Solt *Prod* Malcolm Leo, Andrew Solt *Scr* Malcolm Leo, Andrew Solt *Ph* Gil Hubbs *Ed* Bud Friedgen, Glenn Farr *Mus* Walter Scharf *Art Dir* Charles Hughes
● Johnny Harra, David Scott, Paul Boensch III, Lawrence Koller, Rhonda Lyn (Warner)

A real curiosity item, *This is Elvis* is a fast-paced gloss on Presley's life and career packed with enough fine music and unusual footage to satisfy anyone with an interest in the late singing idol. An imaginative combination of docu-footage, home movies and docu-drama recreations of more private moments has been bolstered with a double album's worth of top tunes to good effect.

Pic opens with day of Presley's death at 42 and subsequent funeral mob scene, and is thereafter narrated by uncanny Elvis soundalike Ral Donner in fashion of William Holden telling tale of *Sunset Boulevard*, even though character is dead.

Much of the docu-material has been kept under wraps by Col Tom Parker for years only to be released here through his participation as technical adviser.

Included are glimpses of the 1950s sensation in his earliest television appearance, some previously unseen press conference footage, harsh, often racist, anti-rock 'n' roll diatribes by bluenoses of the period, the celebrated Ed Sullivan performance, extensive coverage of his army indoctrination and stint in Germany, comeback appearance with Frank Sinatra, clips of a few feature films and a look at his smash 1968 TV special.

Elvis' bloated condition by 1977 is genuinely shocking, effect being akin to seeing Robert De Niro in middle-age in *Raging Bull*. Narration has Elvis from above intoning, 'If only I coulda seen what was happening to me, I mighta done something about it.'

....

■ THIS IS SPINAL TAP

1984, 82 MINS, US ◇ ⓥ
Dir Rob Reiner *Prod* Karen Murphy *Scr* Christopher Guest, Michael McKean, Harry Shearer, Rob Reiner *Ph* Peter Smokler *Ed* Kent Beyda, Kim Seerisf
Art Dir Dryan Jones
● Rob Reiner, Michael McKean, Christopher Guest, Harry Shearer, R.J. Parnell, David Kaff (Spinal Tap)

For music biz insiders, *This Is Spinal Tap* is a vastly amusing satire of heavy metal bands. Director Rob Reiner has cast himself as Marty DiBergi, a filmmaker intent upon covering the long-awaited American return of the eponymous, 17-year-old British rock band. Pic then takes the form of a cinema-verité documentary, as Reiner includes interviews with the fictional musicians, records their increasingly disastrous tour and captures the internal strife which leads to the separation of the group's two founders.

Reiner and cowriters have had loads of fun with the material, creating mock 1960s TV videotapes of early gigs and filling the fringes with hilariously authentic music-biz types, most notably Fran Drescher's label rep and Paul Shaffer's cameo as a Chicago promo man.

....

■ THIS ISLAND EARTH

1955, 87 MINS, US ◇ ⓥ

Dir Joseph Newman   *Prod* William Alland
Scr Franklin Coen, Edward G. O'Callaghan
Ph Clifford Stine   *Ed* Virgil Vogel   *Mus* Herman Stein
Art Dir Alexander Golitzen, Richard H. Riedel
● Jeff Morrow, Faith Domergue, Rex Reason, Lance Fuller, Russell Johnson, Douglas Spencer (Universal)

Plot motivation in the screenplay is derived from the frantic efforts of the men of the inter-stellar planet, Metaluna, to find on Earth a new source of atomic energy. For the accomplishment of this goal, the outstanding scientists in the field have been recruited by a character named Exeter, who has set up a completely-equipped laboratory in Georgia.

One of the most thrilling sequences occurs as huge meteors attack the space ship as it is working its way to Metaluna. Ingeniously-constructed props and equipment, together with strange sound effects also are responsible for furthering interest, which is of the edge-of-the-seat variety during the latter half of the film. For an added fillip, there's a Mutant, half human, half insect, which boards the ship as it escapes from Metaluna.

■ THIS LAND IS MINE

1943, 103 MINS, US ⓥ

Dir Jean Renoir   *Prod* Jean Renoir, Dudley Nichols
Scr Dudley Nichols   *Ph* Frank Redman   *Ed* Frederic Knudson   *Mus* Lothar Perl
● Chares Laughton, Maureen O'Hara, George Sanders, Walter Slezak, Kent Smith, Una O'Connor (RKO)

Turned out by the ace director-writer combination of Jean Renoir and Dudley Nichols, *This Land* is a steadily engrossing film based on the inner drama of character rather than the exciting physical action of some war films. Its theme is the invincibility of ideas over brute force, and its story is of how circumstances and the realization of responsibility turn a craven weakling into a heroic champion of freedom. That is epic subject matter and it is given sincere, dignified and eloquent treatment.

Not that the picture is by any means perfect. Some of its incidents tax belief, and the presentation at times is ultra-obvious, possibly to clarify the meaning for the broadest possible audience. Similarly, although such scenes as Charles Laughton's courtroom espousal of the cause of patriotism, civil disobedience and even of sabotage, or his defiant schoolroom reading of 'The Rights of Man', are suspiciously theatrical, the speeches themselves are magnificent.

As usual when a picture has such compulsion and distinction, the individual roles are rewarding and the performances impressive. As the blubbering coward who rises to heroism in a crisis, Charles Laughton gives a shrewdly conceived and developed portrayal, although he occasionally mugs a bit. Maureen O'Hara is believably intense as the lovely, tragic patriot school teacher. George Sanders proper projects the mental turmoil of the traitorous informer, while Walter Slezak turns in an acting gem in the rich role of the Nazi major.

■ THIS PROPERTY IS CONDEMNED

1966, 110 MINS, US ◇ ⓥ

Dir Sydney Pollack   *Prod* John Houseman   *Scr* Francis Coppola, Fred Coe, Edith Sommer   *Ph* James Wong Howe   *Ed* Adrienne Fazan   *Mus* Kenyon Hopkins
Art Dir Hal Pereira
● Natalie Wood, Robert Redford, Charles Bronson, Kate Reid, Mary Badham, Alan Baxter (Seven Arts/Stark)

This is a handsomely-mounted, well acted Depression era drama about the effect of rail-road retrenchment on a group of boarding-house people. Derived from a Tennessee Williams one-acter, the production is adult without being sensational, touching without being maudlin.

Francis Coppola, Fred Coe and Edith Sommer are credited with the script, 'suggested' from an earlier Williams play in which two young kids chat about the past.

Natalie Wood stars as the young Dixie belle, older daughter of Kate Reid, latter playing a sleazy landlady to some railroad men. Wood dreams of another life while she flirts up a storm, acting as the shill for her mother.

Robert Redford gives an outstanding performance as the railroad efficiency expert sent to town to lay off most of the crew. Plotwise, the role is thankless and heavy, but Redford, through voice, expression and movement – total acting – makes the character sympathetic.

Charles Bronson is excellent as the earthy boarder.

■ THIS SPORTING LIFE

1963, 134 MINS, UK ⓥ

Dir Lindsay Anderson   *Prod* Julian Wintle, Leslie Parkyn   *Scr* David Storey   *Ph* Denys Coop   *Ed* Peter Taylor   *Mus* Robert Gerhard
● Richard Harris, Rachel Roberts, Alan Badel, William Hartnell, Colin Blakely, Arthur Lowe (Independent Artists)

Set in the raw, earthy mood of *Saturday Night and Sunday Morning, Taste of Honey* and *Room at the Top* this has a gutsy vitality. Karel Reisz who directed *Saturday Night*, produced this one and his influence can clearly be seen. Lindsay Anderson, making his debut as a feature director, brings the keen, observant eye of a documentary man to many vivid episodes without sacrificing the story line.

Based on a click novel by David Storey, who also scribed the screenplay, the yarn has a sporting background in that it concerns professional rugby football. Richard Harris plays miner Frank Machin who, at first, resents the hero-worship heaped on players of the local football team. But he has second thoughts. He gets a trial and soon becomes the skillful, ruthless star of his team. He revels in his new prosperity, and preens at the adulation that's showered on his bullet head. He doesn't realize that he is being used by local businessmen opportunists.

Anderson has directed with fluid skill and sharp editing keeps the film moving, even at its more leisurely moments, Denys Coop's lensing is graphic and the atmosphere of a northern town is captured soundly.

Among the varied sequences which impress are a horrifying quarrel between Harris and Rachel Roberts, a hospital death scene, a poignant interlude at a wedding when Harris first approaches the moment of truth, a rowdy Christmas party and a countryside excursion when Harris plays with the widow's two youngsters. The football scenes have a live authenticity.

Harris gives a dominating, intelligent performance as the arrogant, blustering, fundamentally simple and insecure footballer. Roberts as a repressed widow, brings commendable light and shade as well as poignance to a role that might have been shadowy and overly downbeat.

■ THOMAS CROWN AFFAIR, THE

1968, 102 MINS, US ◇

Dir Norman Jewison   *Prod* Norman Jewison
Scr Alan R. Trustman   *Ph* Haskell Wexler   *Ed* Hal Ashby, Ralph Winters, Byron Brandt   *Mus* Michel Legrand   *Art Dir* Robert Boyle
● Steve McQueen, Faye Dunaway, Paul Burke, Jack Weston, Yaphet Kotto (United Artists/Mirisch)

The Thomas Crown Affair is a refreshingly different film which concerns a Boston bank robbery, engineered by a wealthy man who is romantically involved with the femme insurance investigator sent to expose him.

Free of social-conscious pretensions, the Norman Jewison film tells a crackerjack story, well-tooled, professionally crafted and fashioned with obvious meticulous care.

Boston attorney Alan R. Trustman, who never before wrote for films, is responsible for an excellent story. Steve McQueen is a rich young industrialist who masterminds a bank heist. Paul Burke delivers an excellent performance as a detective who works with Faye Dunaway, an insurance company bounty hunter whose job is to trap McQueen.

Jewison adds a showmanly touch in the use of split- and multiple-screen images.

McQueen is neatly cast as the likeable, but lonely heavy. Dunaway makes an excellent detective who gradually develops a conflict of interests regarding her prey. The only message in this film is: enjoy it.

■ THOROUGHLY MODERN MILLIE

1967, 138 MINS, US ◇ ⓥ

Dir George Roy Hill   *Prod* Ross Hunter   *Scr* Richard Morris   *Ph* Russell Metty   *Ed* Stuart Gilmore
Mus Elmer Bernstein   *Art Dir* Alexander Golitzen, George C. Webb
● Julie Andrews, Mary Tyler Moore, Carol Channing, James Fox, John Gavin, Beatrice Lillie (Universal)

The first half of *Thoroughly Modern Mille* is quite successful in striking and maintaining a gay spirit and pace. There are many recognizable and beguiling satirical recalls of the flapper age and some quite funny bits.

Liberties taken with reality, not to mention period, in the first half are redeemed by wit and characterization. But the sudden thrusting of the hero, played by James Fox in horn-rimmed glasses, into a skyscraper-climbing, flagpole-hanging acrobat, a la Harold Lloyd, has little of Lloyd but the myth. This sequence is forced all the way.

Musically *Millie* is a melange. Standards such as 'Baby Face' mingle with specials by Jimmy Van Heusen and Sammy Cahn. All is part of Elmer Bernstein's score, as arranged and conducted by Andre Previn.

Julie Andrews is very much like the leading lady of the story and hardly more than a bystander when Carol Channing commands the scene and at such times it is seldom that a star has been so static so long in a film. Mary Tyler Moore serves the plot in that she is essentially a prototype of a sweet, long curls and rather dumb rich girl.

■ THOSE MAGNIFICENT MEN IN THEIR FLYING MACHINES – OR HOW I FLEW FROM LONDON TO PARIS IN 25 HOURS AND 11 MINUTES

1965, 133 MINS, UK ◇ ⓥ

Dir Ken Annakin   *Prod* Stan Margulies   *Scr* Jack Davies, Ken Annakin   *Ph* Christopher Challis
Ed Gordon Stone   *Mus* Ron Goodwin   *Art Dir* Tom Morahan
● Stuart Whitman, Sarah Miles, James Fox, Alberto Sordi, Robert Morley, Gert Frobe (20th Century-Fox)

As fanciful and nostalgic a piece of clever picture-making as has hit the screen in recent years, this backward look into the pioneer days of aviation, when most planes were built with spit and bailing wire, is a warming entertainment experience.

A newspaper circulation gimmick serves nicely as the story premise, with a London newspaper publisher offering a £10,000 prize to winner of an event which will focus world-wide attention on the fledgling sport of flying – circa 1910 – subsequently attracting a flock of international contestants.

While there is naturally a plotline, and a nice romance, the planes themselves, a startling collection of uniquely-designed oddities, which actually fly, probably merit the most attention.

Top characters are played by Stuart Whitman, as an American entrant; James Fox, an English flier who interests publisher Robert Morley in the race to promote aviation; Sarah Miles, publisher's daughter understood to be the intended of Fox (arrangement with father) but beloved by Whitman. Terry-Thomas is a dastardly English lord not above the most abject skullduggery to win the race. Alberto Sordi as an Italian count with a worrying wife and immense family, Gert Frobe a German cavalry officer intent upon bringing glory to the Fatherland, Jean-Pierre Cassel, a whimsical Frenchman, are the chief Continental contestants.

. . . .

■ THOUSAND CLOWNS, A

1965, 117 MINS, US
Dir Fred Coe   *Prod* Fred Coe   *Scr* Herb Gardner
Ph Arthur J. Ornitz   *Ed* Ralph Rosenblum   *Mus* Judy
Holliday, Gerry Mulligan   *Art Dir* Burr Smidt
● Jason Robards, Barbara Harris, Martin Balsam,
Gene Saks, William Daniels, Barry Gordon (Harrell/
United Artists)

A Thousand Clowns depicts a happy-go-lucky non-conformist who attains some maturity when a child welfare board threatens to take away his young resident nephew.

Key personnel of the long-running 1962-3 Broadway legiter have followed through with the pic. They include playwright-adapter Herb Gardner, producer-director Coe, and Jason Robards as the ex-vidscripter living it up in a littered NY pad while trying to prevent nephew Barry Gordon (also encoring) from becoming one of the 'dead people', meaning conformists.

Terrif dialog to match Robards' scenery-chewing create a sock impact as he lectures the 12-year-old (a hip juve, wiser than unk), ignores the pleas of brother-agent Martin Balsam to return to work, and pierces the outstanding social worker bureaucratic shell of Barbara Harris and original cast member William Daniels, who've arrived to check the kid's home life.

All performances present three-dimensional, identifiable characters underneath the yocks.
□ 1965: Best Picture (Nomination)

. . . .

■ THOUSANDS CHEER

1943, 124 MINS, US ◇ ▼
Dir George Sidney   *Prod* Joseph Pasternak   *Scr* Paul
Jarrico, Richard Collins   *Ph* George Folsey
Ed George Boemler   *Mus* Herbert Stothart (dir.)
● Kathryn Grayson, Gene Kelly, Mary Astor, John
Boles, Jose Iturbi, Frances Rafferty (M-G-M)

Comparison of *Thousands Cheer* to *Stage Door Canteen* is inevitable and natural. Both have the same format. Kathryn Grayson is the colonel's (John Boles) daughter who puts on a super-duper camp show which not only re-introduces Jose Iturbi as part of the entertainment – the eminent pianist-maestro is already made part of the regular plot – but it brings forth Mickey Rooney, Judy Garland, Red Skelton, Eleanor Powell and others.

Paramount keynote of this expert filmusical is the tiptop manner in which young George Sidney has marshalled his multiple talents so that none trips over the other. It's a triumph for Sidney on his first major league effort.

Paul Jarrico and Richard Collins supplied a smooth story to carry the mammoth marquee values. Casting Kathryn Grayson as herself, a click diva, making her longhair farewell at an Iturbi concert, is as plausible as it is appealing. Her idea to move with papa Boles

to his camp, in an endeavor to reconcile him and Mary Astor (the mother), is well inter-larded with romance and basic Americanism.

Judy Garland's 'Joint Is Jumpin' Down at Carnegie Hall' (unbilled specialty) is the cue for Iturbi to boogie-woogie; and his Stein-waying straight or barrelhouse, is something for the cats.

. . . .

■ THREE

1969, 105 MINS, UK ◇
Dir James Salter   *Scr* James Salter   *Ph* Etienne
Becker   *Ed* Edward Nielson   *Mus* Laurence Rosenthal
● Charlotte Rampling, Robie Porter, Sam Waterston,
Pascale Roberts (United Artists/Obelisk)

Three is a rare pic [from a story by Irwin Shaw] about youth that deals with a romantic summer idyll sans sentimentality and with a freshness and easy charm that pinpoints character without affectation.

Two young men, Robie Porter and Sam Waterston set off in an old car one summer to tour Italy and France. They meet a pretty English girl (Charlotte Rampling) and make a pact to keep her a friend rather than a sexual or love game. But Waterston begins to fall for her and their triple idyll deteriorates as she succumbs to Porter.

The principals all perform with grace and ease. It has a fine feel for the European summer scene and neatly observes the growing complicated feelings between the three by visual means that are never forced for symbolical needs.

. . . .

■ ¡THREE AMIGOS!

1986, 105 MINS, US ◇ ▼
Dir John Landis   *Prod* Lorne Michaels, George Folsey
Jr.   *Scr* Steve Martin, Lorne Michaels, Randy
Newman   *Ph* Ronald W. Browne   *Ed* Malcolm
Campbell   *Mus* Elmer Bernstein   *Art Dir* Richard
Sawyer
● Chevy Chase, Steve Martin, Martin Short, Patrice
Martinez, Alfonso Arau, Joe Mantegna (Orion)

A few choice morsels of brilliant humor can't save *¡Three Amigos!* from missing the whole enchilada.

Film is a takeoff of *The Magnificent Seven*, but also tries perhaps too hard to parody the style of a number of other classic westerns.

It also has three funny guys, Steve Martin, Chevy Chase and Martin Short, playing the three wimpy matinee idols known as the 'Three Amigos', each doing his particular brand of shtick that is priceless in some scenes but not at all amusing in others.

Martin does clever slapstick, Chase does goofy slapstick and Short doesn't do slapstick, but plays off the other two with a certain wide-eyed innocence.

These singing cowboy stars of the silent screen have just been fired by the flamboyant Goldsmith Studios mogul Harry Flugelman (Joe Mantegna) when they get a cryptic telegram from a Mexican woman (Patrice Martinez) offering them 100,000 pesos to come to her dusty desert town of Santa Poco. It turns out she's hired them under the mistaken belief that they are as macho in real life as on screen.

. . . .

■ THREE BITES OF THE APPLE

1967, 98 MINS, US ◇
Dir Alvin Ganzer   *Prod* Alvin Ganzer   *Scr* George
Wells   *Ph* Gabor Pogany   *Ed* Norman Savage
Mus Eddy Manson   *Art Dir* Elliot Scott
● David McCallum, Sylva Koscina, Tammy Gimes,
Harvey Korman, Domenico Modugno (M-G-M)

As a travelog, *Three Bites of the Apple* has certain merit; as a madcap comedy, its intended goal, it hasn't. Filmed in Italy and Switzerland, what emerges is an unimaginative piece of film making.

The screenplay is based on the flimsiest of premises. David McCallum, a mildmannered tour guide, wins £1,200 in a plush Italian gambling casino; then is faced with the question of how to save it from taxes so he'll be able to return to his native Britain with any more than a pittance. A pretty young adventuress, Sylva Koscina, out to get the coin for herself, sells him on allowing a 'friend' help him in this matter.

McCallum seems to stumble through most of his appearance. Koscina has a vapid look but is nice to look at.

. . . .

■ THREE CABALLEROS, THE

1944, 71 MINS, US ◇ ▼
Dir Norman Ferguson   *Prod* Walt Disney   *Ph* Ray
Rennahan   *Ed* Don Holliday   *Mus* Edward Plumb,
Paul J. Smith, Charles Wolcott (dir.)
● Aurora Miranda, Carmen Molina, Dora Luz
(RKO/Walt Disney)

Walt Disney in *The Three Caballeros* reveals a new form of cinematic entertainment wherein he blends live action with animation into a socko feature production.

It's a gay, colorful, resplendent conceit. Neatly conceived, it ties in many Pan-American highlights through the medium of irascible Donald Duck, the wiseguy Joe Carioca (first introduced in *Saludos Amigos*), and a lovable character in Panchito, the little South American boy.

It's DD's birthday and on Friday-the-13th he gets three huge packages of gifts from his friends in Latin America. What he unwraps as his 'gifts' are transplanted to this live action-animation feature. The off-screen narration is so skillfully blended with the dialog between Donald, Joe Carioca, et al, and it's all so smoothly cut and edited, one is only casually conscious of where one stops and the other begins.

. . . .

■ THREE COINS IN THE FOUNTAIN

1954, 101 MINS, US ◇
Dir Jean Negulesco   *Prod* Sol C. Siegel   *Scr* John
Patrick   *Ph* Milton Krasner   *Ed* William Reynolds
Mus Jule Styne, Sammy Cahn
● Clifton Webb, Dorothy McGuire, Jean Peters, Louis
Jourdan, Maggie McNamara, Rossano Brazzi (20th
Century-Fox)

Once before, in *How to Marry a Millionaire*, director Jean Negulesco CinemaScoped a trio of feminine beauties into a lucrative attraction. In *Three Coins in the Fountain* he repeats this feat but obviously has gained some experience. The film has warmth, humor, a rich dose of romance and almost incredible pictorial appeal.

For those who aren't satisfied feasting their eyes on the stunning backgrounds and the plush interior sets, there is another trio of femme stars – Dorothy McGuire, Jean Peters and Maggie McNamara – in smart and expensive-looking clothes. As their male counterparts they have Clifton Webb, debonnaire and fun as always; Rossano Brazzi, an appealing young Italian and suave Louis Jourdan, appealing as the romantic lead.

Story introduces to Rome McNamara, an American coming to take a secretarial job. She's met by Peters and later introduced to her third room-mate in their sumptuous apartment, McGuire. They all toss a coin in the fountain, and it grants them their wish.
□ 1954: Best Picture (Nomination)

. . . .

■ THREE COMRADES

1938, 100 MINS, US
Dir Frank Borzage   *Prod* Frank Borzage   *Scr* F. Scott
Fitzgerald, Edward E. Paramore   *Ph* Joseph
Ruttenberg   *Ed* Frank Sullivan   *Mus* Franz Waxman

● Robert Taylor, Margaret Sullavan, Franchot Tone, Robert Young, Guy Kibbee, Lionel Atwill (M-G-M)

There must have been some reason for making this picture, but it certainly isn't in the cause of entertainment. It provides a dull interlude, despite the draught of the star names.

Someone passed producer-director Frank Borzage a novel of postwar Germany by Erich Maria Remarque which deals with the psychological subtleties of German youth lately released from the World War armies; of the internal political struggle in establishing the republic; of the futility of the army-bred boys to cope with civilian connivance; and finally the tragedy of a love affair between one of the youths and a young woman dying of tuberculosis (Margaret Sullavan).

It is a film of characterization, rather than plot. Writers string together an interminable thread of unimportant incident to show the deep affection which exists among three young German officers. The titular comrades are Robert Taylor, Franchot Tone and Robert Young. After Young is killed in a street riot, the other two look forward to a dark, unhappy and lonely future.

That's it, and all the poetry in the dialog about falling leaves and the approaching winter only further confuses.

. . . .

■ THREE DAYS OF THE CONDOR

1975, 117 MINS, US ◇

Dir Sydney Pollack   *Prod* Stanley Schneider
Scr Lorenzo Semple Jr, David Rayfiel   *Ph* Owen Rolgman   *Ed* Frederic Steinkamp, Don Guidice
Mus David Grusin   *Art Dir* Stephen Grimes
● Robert Redford, Faye Dunaway, Cliff Robertson, Max Von Sydow, John Houseman, Addison Powell (Paramount)

James Grady's book, *Six Days of the Condor*, underwent a time-compression title change in this adaptation by Lorenzo Semple Jr and David Rayfiel. Robert Redford, working in a CIA front, discovers all his associates massacred. He runs, pants, thinks, schemes, evades and ultimately exposes an agency insider who has been plotting on the side, so to speak. Disenchanted with the world as he wants it, Redford walks into a newspaper to expose the whole thing.

The film is a perfect contemporary example of an old studio formula approach to filmmaking. Basically a B, it has been elevated in form – but not in substance – via four bigger names, location shooting and more production values. Sometimes the trick works, but not here.

. . . .

■ THREE FACES OF EVE, THE

1957, 91 MINS, US

Dir Nunnally Johnson   *Prod* Nunnally Johnson
Scr Nunnally Johnson   *Ph* Stanley Cortez
Ed Marjorie Fowler   *Mus* Robert Emmett Dolan   *Art Dir* Lyle R. Wheeler, Herman A. Blumethal
● Joanne Woodward, David Wayne, Lee J. Cobb, Edwin Jerome, Alena Murray, Nancy Kulp (20th Century-Fox)

Three Faces of Eve is based on a true-life case history recorded by two psychiatrists – Corbett H. Thigpen and Hervey M. Cleckley – and which was a popular-selling book. It is frequently an intriguing, provocative motion picture, but director Nunnally Johnson's treatment of the subject matter makes the film neither fish nor foul. Johnson shifts back and forth – striving for comedy at one point and presenting a documentary case history at another.

However, it is notable for the performance of Joanne Woodward as the woman with the triple personality. The three personalities Woodward is called on to play are (1) a drab, colorless Georgia housewife, (2) a mischievous, irresponsible sexy dish, and (3) a sensible, intelligent and balanced woman.

The psychiatric sessions, while possibly authentic, could readily confuse the layman. The manner in which the doctor (Lee J. Cobb) can hypnotize and alter his patient's personality seems so easy and pat as to appear hard to believe.

That Johnson had no intention of treating the film entirely seriously is tipped off in an opening tongue-in-cheek narration by the urbane and erudite Alistair Cooke.

. . . .

■ THREE FUGITIVES

1989, 96 MINS, US ◇

Dir Francis Veber   *Prod* Lauren Shuler Donner
Scr Francis Veber   *Ph* Haskell Wexler   *Ed* Bruce Green   *Mus* David McHugh   *Art Dir* Rick Carter
● Nick Nolte, Martin Short, Sarah Rowland Doroff, James Earl Jones, Alan Ruck (Touchstone/Silver Screen Partners IV)

Three Fugitives marks the Hollywood helming debut of French director Francis Veber, remaking his own 1986 comedy *Les fugitifs* American-style. Clever premise starts pic off on a roll, as master bankrobber Lucas (Nick Nolte) gets out of the slammer determined to go straight, only to get involved in another heist in the very first bank he enters.

This time, he's an innocent bystander taken hostage by a hysterically inept gunman (Martin Short). But who's going to believe that?

Short, once he figures out Nolte's predicament, blackmails him into aiding and abetting his escape from the country. To make things even stickier, Short's got an emotionally withdrawn little girl (Sarah Rowland Doroff) who latches onto Nolte like a stray kitten.

As for the Nolte-Short pairing, it'll do, but it's no chemical marvel. Nolte, not really a comic natural, gruffs and grumbles his way through as hunky straight man to Short's calamitous comedian. Short runs with the slapstick style.

. . . .

■ 300 SPARTANS, THE

1962, 108 MINS, US ◇

Dir Rudolph Mate   *Prod* George St. George, Rudolph Mate   *Scr* George St. George   *Ph* Geoffrey Unsworth   *Ed* Jerome Webb   *Mus* Manos Hadjidakis   *Art Dir* Arrigo Equini
● Richard Egan, Ralph Richardson, Diane Baker, Barry Coe, David Farrar, Donald Houston (20th-Century Fox)

The hopeless but ultimately inspiring defense of their country by a band of 300 Spartan soldiers against an immense army of Persian invaders in 480 B.C. – known to history as the Battle of Thermopylae – is the nucleus around which St. George's screenplay is constructed. The inherent appeal and magnitude of the battle itself virtually dwarfs and sweeps aside all attempts at romantic byplay.

An international cast has been assembled for the enterprise, primarily populated with Britishers, Greeks and Americans. Richard Egan, as King Leonidas of Sparta, is physically suitable for the character, but the heroic mold of his performance is only skin deep – more muscle than corpuscle. Ralph Richardson, as might be expected, does the best acting in the picture, but no one is going to list this portrayal as one of the great achievements in his career.

Diane Baker is glaringly miscast. The fragile actress has been assigned the part of a Spartan girl who knocks two large men off their feet, bodily. As written, it's a role that required an actress of at least Lorenesque proportions.

. . . .

■ THREE IN THE ATTIC

1968, 90 MINS, US ◇ ⓥ

Dir Richard Wilson   *Prod* Richard Wilson   *Scr* Stephen Yafa   *Ph* J. Burgi Contner   *Ed* Richard C. Meyer, Eve Newman   *Mus* Chad Stuart   *Art Dir* William S. Creber
● Yvette Mimieux, Christopher Jones, Judy Pace, Maggie Thrett, Nan Martin (American International)

Three in the Attic apparently starts out to be a tragicomedy about physical sex vs love. It is littered with padding optical effects, hampered by uneven dramatic concept, and redundant in its too-delicious sex teasing.

Author Stephen Yafa disowned the pic. Screenplay tells of Christopher Jones, a college campus lover type, who gets hung up on Yvette Mimieux. He won't admit he loves her (that is, beyond the physical aspects), and adds Judy Pace, a Negro charmer, and Maggie Thrett, a Jewish hippie, to his harem.

The gals learn of the bed rotation plan and lock Jones in an attic, where they attempt to exhaust him with regular, clock-timed sex visits.

Acting is amateurish, save for Mimieux, who tries and slightly succeeds.

. . . .

■ 3 INTO 2 WON'T GO

1969, 93 MINS, UK ◇

Dir Peter Hall   *Prod* Julian Blaustein   *Scr* Edna O'Brien   *Ph* Walter Lassally   *Ed* Alan Osbiston
Mus Francis Lai   *Art Dir* Peter Murton
● Rod Steiger, Claire Bloom, Judy Geeson, Peggy Ashcroft, Paul Rogers (Universal)

Superb British film, *3 into 2 Won't Go* is an examination of a shattered marriage between career-oriented Rod Steiger, who is an appliance salesman, and his childless, schoolteacher-wife, Claire Bloom. Judy Geeson, 19-year-old hitchhiker with no particular social or moral ties, seduces Steiger on one of his overnight sales trips.

With dialog that has the banal sound of realistic human exchanges, Edna O'Brien's script [from a novel by Andrea Newman] investigates all sorts of suggestions and shifts in audience reaction.

With all technical credits at top level and director Peter Hall getting top performances from all involved, especially the well-controlled Steiger, film is brisk and emotionally stirring.

. . . .

■ THREE LITTLE WORDS

1950, 100 MINS, US ◇ ⓥ

Dir Richard Thorpe   *Prod* Jack Cummings
Scr George Wells   *Ph* Harry Jackson   *Ed* Ben Lewis   *Mus* Andre Previn (dir.)
● Fred Astaire, Red Skelton, Vera-Ellen, Arlene Dahl, Keenan Wynn (M-G-M)

A biopic of the songwriting team of Harry Ruby and Bert Kalmar, the picture is a charmful, entertaining cavalcade of show business which spans their years together.

Yarn, while doing the usual glossy job on its subjects, sticks closely to the Kalmar-Ruby careers.

Toplined by Fred Astaire as Kalmar and Red Skelton as Ruby, the entire cast does fine work under the skillful direction of Richard Thorpe.

Vera-Ellen matches Astaire tap for tap in their terping duets, which is no mean achievement, and looks to be possibly the best partner he's ever had. Her singing, too, gets by and, as Jessie Brown, Kalmar's vaude partner, she emotes competently.

Arlene Dahl plays Eileen Percy and also turns in a standout performance.

. . . .

3 MEN AND A BABY

1987, 102 MINS, US ◇ ⊻
Dir Leonard Nimoy *Prod* Ted Field, Robert W. Cort, Edward Teets *Scr* James Orr, Jim Cruickshank *Ph* Adam Greenberg *Ed* Michael A. Stevenson *Mus* Marvin Hamlisch *Art Dir* Peter Larkin
● Tom Selleck, Steve Guttenberg, Ted Danson, Nancy Travis, Margaret Colin (Touchstone/Silver Screen Partners III/Interscope)

3 Men and a Baby is about as slight a feature comedy as is made – while at the same time it's hard to resist Tom Selleck, Ted Danson and Steve Guttenberg shamelessly going goo-goo over caring for an infant baby girl all swaddled in pink.

This is an Americanized version of the 1985 French sleeper hit *3 hommes et en couffin* and parallels the original's storyline almost exactly.

The lives of three confirmed bachelors – the studly sort who live, play and scheme on voluptuous women together – is thrown into confusion when a baby is left at their front door. As it happens, actor and suspected father of the infant (Danson) is conveniently out of town on a shoot, leaving architect and super pushover Peter (Selleck) and cartoonist Michael (Guttenberg) all in a quandary what to do with the precious little thing.

Big macho men tripping all over themselves trying to successfully feed, diaper and bathe a bundle of innocence and helplessness is ripe for comic development, and it certainly helps that these three are having a blast seeing it through.

Film is a good showcase for the comic abilities of this threesome, all of whom seem to have their one-liner timing down pat.

3 MEN AND A LITTLE LADY

1990, 100 MINS, US ◇ ⊻
Dir Emile Ardolino *Prod* Ted Field, Robert W. Cort *Scr* Charlie Peters *Ph* Adam Greenberg *Ed* Michael A. Stevenson *Mus* James Newton Howard *Art Dir* Stuart Wurtzel
● Tom Selleck, Steve Guttenberg, Ted Danson, Nancy Travis, Robin Weisman, Christopher Casenove (Touchstone/Interscope)

Back in their places for this two-dimensional sequel are the three bachelor dads of the waif who landed on their doorstep in part one: vain actor Ted Danson and biological dad, and architect Tom Selleck and illustrator Steve Guttenberg, the honorary dads.

What's new is that Selleck has fallen in love with the baby's mom, Sylvia (Nancy Travis), the actress who shares their new apartment, though he hasn't admitted it to her or himself.

Crisis occurs when baby turns five and enrolls in preschool, thereby encountering other children. Mom decides she must marry. She accepts a proposal from her director friend, Edward (Christopher Cazenove), and plans to move to England with little Mary (Robin Weisman), all because bachelor No. 2 (Selleck) is too confused to pop the question.

Rest of the pic is standard romantic comedy. Script [story by Sara Parriott and Josann McGibbon] spoonfeeds the audience with a plodding script that seems based more on demographic research than on any wisp of a creative impulse. Emile Ardolino directs with the same degree of competent but calculated non-risk. As for the actors, they have nothing to play.

THREE MUSKETEERS, THE

1921, 140 MINS, US ⊗
Dir Fred Niblo *Prod* Douglas Fairbanks *Scr* Edward Knoblock, Lotta Woods *Ph* Arthur Edeson *Ed* Nellie Mason *Mus* Louis F. Gottschalk *Art Dir* Edward M. Langley

● Douglas Fairbanks, Leon Bary, George Siegmann, Eugene Pallette, Marguerite De La Motte, Adolphe Menjou (Fairbanks/United Artists)

The story of Dumas has been ideally approximated in this screen version. There is a flare and sweep about the film, with the assembling, cutting and continuity seeming spotlessly correct. Douglas Fairbanks and D'Artagnan are a happy combination

Of the interpretations, that of Nigel de Brulier as Richelieu developed a real creation. Excepting only the star, he dominates the picture. Adolphe Menjou does excellently in a role not actor-proof by all manner of means. His Louis XIII evidences both sides of the king, gaining sympathetic response where in most instances the opposite is the case.

The companions of D'Artagnan, Athos, Porthos and Aramis find apt treatment by Leon Bary, George Siegmann and Eugene Pallette. Marguerite De La Motte is a sweet and winsome Constance.

THREE MUSKETEERS, THE

1939, 71 MINS, US
Dir Allan Dwan *Prod* Raymond Griffith *Scr* M.M. Musselman, William A. Drake, Sam Hellman *Ph* Peverell Marley *Ed* Jack Dennis *Mus* David Buttolph (dir.) *Art Dir* Bernard Herzbrun, David Hall
● Don Ameche, Ritz Brothers, Binnie Barnes, Lionel Atwill, Pauline Moore (20th Century-Fox)

Utilizing the broadest strokes of comedy technique, this version of Dumas' romantic adventure presents Don Ameche as a rather personable D'Artagnan, and the Ritz Bros as a helter-skelter trio hopping in and out frequently to perform their standard screwball antics.

There is little seriousness or suspense generated in the slender story, and not much interest in the adventures of D'Artagnan and his pals to regain the queen's brooch in the possession of the Duke of Buckingham. Main excuse for the yarn apparently is to provide Ameche with an opportunity to be a dashing hero while the freres Ritz clown through the footage as phoney musketeers.

Romance between Ameche and Pauline Moore is sketchily presented, developing little interest or sincerity.

THREE MUSKETEERS, THE

1948, 126 MINS, US ◇ ⊻
Dir George Sidney *Prod* Pandro S. Berman *Scr* Robert Ardrey *Ph* Robert Planck *Ed* Robert J. Kern, George Boemler *Mus* Herbert Stothart *Art Dir* Cedric Gibbons, Malcolm Brown
● Gene Kelly, Lana Turner, June Allyson, Van Heflin, Angela Lansbury, Vincent Price (M-G-M)

The Three Musketeers is a swaggering, tongue-in-cheek treatment of picturesque fiction, extravagantly presented.

The fanciful tale is launched with a laugh, and quickly swings into some colorful and exciting sword duels as the pace is set for the imaginative adventures that feature the lives and loves of D'Artagnan and his three cronies. It is the complete Dumas novel.

There are acrobatics by Gene Kelly that would give Douglas Fairbanks pause. His first duel with Richelieu's cohorts is almost ballet, yet never loses the feeling of swaggering swordplay. It is a masterful mixture of dancing grace, acro-agility and sly horseplay of sock comedic punch.

Lana Turner is a perfect visualization of the sexy, wicked Lady de Winter, sharply contrasting with the sweet charm of June Allyson as the maid Constance. The three king's musketeers of the title are dashingly portrayed by Van Heflin, Gig Young and Robert Coote as Athos, Porthos and Aramis. They belt over

their parts in keeping with the style Kelly uses for D'Artagnan.

Another aid in making the film top commercial entertainment is the telling score by Herbert Stothart, using themes by Tchaikovsky. Score bridges any gap in movement without intruding itself.

THREE MUSKETEERS, THE

1973, 105 MINS, PANAMA ◇ ⊻
Dir Richard Lester *Prod* Alexander Salkind, Michael Salkind, Ilya Salkind *Scr* George MacDonald Fraser *Ph* David Watkin *Ed* John Victor Smith *Mus* Michel Legrand
● Oliver Reed, Charlton Heston, Raquel Welch, Faye Dunaway, Richard Chamberlain, Michael York (Fox Film Trust)

The Three Musketeers take very well to Richard Lester's provocative version that does not send it up but does add comedy to this adventure tale [by Alexandre Dumas].

Here D'Artagnan, played with brio by Michael York, is a country bumpkin; the musketeers themselves are more interested in money, dames and friendship than undue fidelity to the King, a simple-minded type, and their fight scenes are full of flailing, kicks and knockabout. They are not above starting a fight at an inn to steal victuals when they run out of money.

Behind it, however, is a look at an era of poverty and virtual worker slavery to fulfill the King's flagrantly rich whims.

Musketeers are played with panache by Richard Chamberlain as the haughty ladies' man, Oliver Reed as the gusty one and Frank Finlay as the dandyish type. Raquel Welch has comedic timing as the maladroit girl of D'Artagnan while Faye Dunaway has less to do as the perfidious Milady, but makes up for the lack in the sequel quietly made at the same time.

3 RING CIRCUS

1954, 103 MINS, US ◇
Dir Joseph Pevney *Prod* Hal B. Wallis *Scr* Don McGuire *Ph* Loyal Griggs *Ed* Warren Low *Mus* Walter Scharf *Art Dir* Hal Pereira, Tambi Larsen
● Dean Martin, Jerry Lewis, Joanne Dru, Zsa Zsa Gabor, Elsa Lanchester, Wallace Ford (Paramount)

Circus background of this expensively-mounted Hal Wallis production gives Dean Martin and Jerry Lewis slick opportunity to disport themselves along familiar lines.

The script projects comics straight from army uniform to the circus, where Lewis reports as a lion tamer's assistant in the hope he'll get to be a clown. Martin tags along, catching the eye of the beautiful but temperamental trapeze artist (Zsa Zsa Gabor), who makes him her 'assistant'. He takes over circus owner Joanne Dru's place when she leaves the circus – she's in love and keeps fighting with him – but all is later happiness again.

Comics as a team are somewhat less zany than in previous productions. Dru and Gabor supply plenty of flash and femme splendor. Wallace Ford is tops as the barking but sympathetic circus manager.

THREE STRANGERS

1946, 91 MINS, US
Dir Jean Negulesco *Prod* Wolfgang Reinhardt *Scr* John Huston, Howard Koch *Ph* Arthur Edeson *Ed* George Amy *Art Dir* Ted Smith
● Sydney Greenstreet, Peter Lorre, Geraldine Fitzgerald (Warner)

Three Strangers carries a rather complicated episodic plot, depending mostly on the fine cast performances to carry it.

Not only the three stars, Sydney Greenstreet, Geraldine Fitzgerald and Peter Lorre, but various supporting players command special attention. Greenstreet overplays to some extent as the attorney who has raided a trust fund, but he still does a good job. Lorre is tops as a drunk who gets involved in a murder of which he's innocent, while Fitzgerald rates as the victim.

Along with Greenstreet and Lorre, Fitzgerald has an equal share in a sweepstakes ticket. They are strangers. All three win on the ticket but Greenstreet murders the girl in a fit of rage, in Lorre's presence, thus leaving latter, also a loser, since he cannot risk trying to cash the ticket because it would involve him in the killing.

Story jumps around uncertainly but Jean Negulesco's direction is satisfactory.

●●●●●●●●●●●●●●●●●●●●●●●●●●●●●●●

■ **3:10 TO YUMA**

1957, 92 MINS, US ⊤

Dir Delmer Daves *Prod* David Heilweil *Scr* Halsted Welles *Ph* Charles Lawton Jr *Ed* Al Clark *Mus* George Duning *Art Dir* Frank Hotaling
● Glenn Ford, Van Heflin, Felicia Farr, Leora Dana, Henry Jones, Richard Jaeckel (Columbia)

Aside from the fact that this is an upper-drawer western, *3:10 to Yuma* will strike many for its resemblance to *High Noon*. That the climax fizzles must be laid on doorstep of Halsted Welles, who adapts Elmore Leonard's story quite well until that point.

Glenn Ford portrays the deadly leader of a slickly professional outlaw gang, which holds up a stagecoach. Van Heflin, impoverished neighborhood rancher, helps capture Ford when the latter lags behind his gang, to dally with lovely, lonely town barmaid Felicia Farr.

But Ford's gang is too strong for local lawmen to handle. Stagecoach owner Robert Emhardt promises a large reward to Heflin and the town drunk (Henry Jones). Idea is to hold Ford in another town, unknown to his gang, until daily train (3:10 of title) can take him to Yuma for trial. Here, story cleaves closely to *High Noon* formula.

Ford's switch-casting, as the quietly sinister gang leader, is authoritative, impressive and successful. Heflin measures up fully and convincingly to the rewarding role of the proud and troubled rancher. Farr's contribution is a short one, but she registers with a touching poignancy and a delicate beauty.

Title song by Ned Washington and George Duning, sung by Frankie Laine under credits and by Norma Zimmer during the picture, is a well-written tune.

●●●●●●●●●●●●●●●●●●●●●●●●●●●●●●●

■ **THREE WOMEN**

1977, 122 MINS, US ◇

Dir Robert Altman *Prod* Robert Altman *Scr* Robert Altman *Ph* Chuck Rosher *Ed* Dennis Hill *Mus* Gerald Busby *Art Dir* James D. Vance
● Shelley Duvall, Sissy Spacek, Janice Rule, Robert Fortier, Ruth Nelson, John Cromwell (20th Century-Fox)

Absorbing moody and often compelling story about psychological dependence and transference.

Robert Altman had a dream which he used as the basis for his original screenplay, set in the desert where Shelley Duvall works as an attendant in an old-folks' health center and new staffer Sissy Spacek becomes her room-mate.

Janice Rule is the mural-painting wife of retired stuntman Robert Fortier, the two of them being important catalysts to the changing relationship between Spacek and Duvall.

Duvall is magnificent as a girl whose inner unhappiness is masked by dialog straight out of smart-set magazines and fast-snack recipe folders. Spacek, at the outset adoring and subservient, gets all the sympathy.

Spacek matches in complementing excellence Duvall's performance. Rule registers well.

●●●●●●●●●●●●●●●●●●●●●●●●●●●●●●●

■ **THREE WORLDS OF GULLIVER, THE**

1960, 98 MINS, UK ◇ ⊤

Dir Jack Sher *Prod* Charles H. Schneer *Scr* Arthur Ross, Jack Sher *Ph* Wilkie Cooper *Ed* Raymond Poulton *Mus* Bernard Herrmann *Art Dir* Gil Parrendo, Derek Barrington
● Kerwin Mathews, Jo Morrow, June Thorburn, Basil Sydney, Gregoire Aslan, Lee Patterson (Columbia)

Jonathan Swift's 18th-century stinging satire has been considerably softened and drastically romanticized, but enough of its telling caustic comment remains.

The original four-part work has been trimmed to the more familiar twosome of Lilliput, land of little people, and Brobdingnag, where the natives are as tall in proportion to Gulliver as the Lilliputians are short. The hero's wife and family of Swift's tome have been dropped in favor of a fiery fiancee who shares his misadventure in Brobdingnag. Gulliver, thankfully, still goes it alone in Lilliput, according to the film.

The picture is notable for its visuo-cinematic achievements and its bold, bright and sweeping score by Bernard Herrmann. Special visual effects expert Ray Harryhausen, whose Superdynamation process makes the motion-pictured Gulliver plausible and workable, rates a low bow for his painstaking, productive efforts.

Kerwin Mathews, generally reserved and persuasive, makes a first-rate Gulliver. Among the more arresting performances are those of Basil Sydney as the pompous emperor of Lilliput, Martin Benson as its conniving minister of finance, Marian Spencer as the vain empress, Mary Ellis and Gregoire Aslan as king and queen of Brobdingnag.

●●●●●●●●●●●●●●●●●●●●●●●●●●●●●●●

■ **THRESHOLD**

1981, 106 MINS, CANADA ◇

Dir Richard Pearce *Prod* Jon Slan, Michael Burns *Scr* James Salter *Ph* Michael Brault *Ed* Susan Martin *Mus* Mickey Erbe, Mary-beth Solomon
● Donald Sutherland, John Marley, Sharon Ackerman, Jeff Goldblum, Mare Winningham (Paragon)

Donald Sutherland takes the central role of a heart specialist involved in the development of a mechanical heart for transplant purposes. The device is the brainchild of medical biologist Jeff Goldblum, a fanatic who is certain his radical conception will revolutionize surgical techniques.

When all current practices fail on patient Mare Winningham, Sutherland decides to defy the board and bring out the miracle device. The controversial operation immediately generates media attention and Sutherland nervously waits out the consequence of his action.

Writer James Salter and director Richard Pearce have strenuously avoided taking a melodramatic approach to the material. What emerges is virtually a visualized medical journal filled with the tedium and monotony facing a dedicated surgeon incorporated along with the excitement of venturing into new medical frontiers. At times one wishes the film had opted for a more dramatic tone.

Sutherland gives a cooly effective performance. The stability of Sutherland's surgeon is in sharp contrast to Goldblum's erratic inventor, providing the film with a keen sense of humor.

●●●●●●●●●●●●●●●●●●●●●●●●●●●●●●●

■ **THRILL OF IT ALL, THE**

1963, 108 MINS, US ◇ ⊤

Dir Norman Jewison *Prod* Ross Hunter, Martin Melcher *Scr* Carl Reiner *Ph* Russell Metty *Ed* Milton Carruth *Mus* Frank DeVol *Art Dir* Alexander Golitzen, Robert Boyle
● Doris Day, James Garner, Arlene Francis, Edward Andrews, ZaSu Pitts, Reginald Owen (Universal)

Carl Reiner's scenario, from a story he wrote in collaboration with Larry Gelbart, is peppered with digs at various institutions of American life. Among the targets of his fairly subtle but telling assault with the needle are television, Madison Avenue, the servant problem and such specific matters as the sharp points at the rear extremities of the modern Cadillac and the maitre d' who has immediate seating for celebrities only.

But these nuggets and pinpricks of satiric substance are primarily bonuses. Ultimately it is in the design and engineering of cumulative sight gag situations that *Thrill of It All* excels. In addition to a running gag about a suspiciously similar weekly series of live TV dramas, there is a scene in which a swimming pool saturated with soap gives birth to a two-story-high mountain of suds and another in which James Garner, coming home from work one evening, drives his convertible into his back yard and straight into a pool that wasn't there in the morning.

Doris Day scores as the housewife with two children who is suddenly thrust into an irresistible position as an $80,000-a-year pitch woman for an eccentric soap tycoon who is impressed by her unaffected quality. Bearing the brunt of these soap operatics is Garner as the gynecologist whose domestic tranquillity is shattered by his wife's sudden transition to career girl.

Arlene Francis and Edward Andrews are spirited in the key roles of a middle-aged couple suddenly expectant parents. ZaSu Pitts does all she can with some ridiculous shenanigans as a fretful maid.

●●●●●●●●●●●●●●●●●●●●●●●●●●●●●●●

■ **THROW MOMMA FROM THE TRAIN**

1987, 88 MINS, US ◇ ⊤

Dir Danny DeVito *Prod* Larry Brezner *Scr* Stu Silver *Ph* Barry Sonnenfeld *Ed* Michael Jablow *Mus* David Newman *Art Dir* Ida Random
● Danny DeVito, Billy Crystal, Anne Ramsey, Kim Greist, Kate Mulgrew (Orion/Rollins, Morra & Brezner)

Throw Momma from the Train is a fun and delightfully venal comedy. Very clever and engaging from beginning to end, pic builds on the notion that nearly everyone – at least once in life – has the desire to snuff out a relative or nemesis, even if 99.9% of us let the urge pass without ever acting on it.

Here, it's the idle death threats of a frustrated writer and flunky junior college professor (Billy Crystal) against his ex-wife that are overheard by one of his dimwitted and very impressionable students (Danny DeVito).

DeVito's limited creative abilities are further stifled by his crazy, overbearing momma (Anne Ramsey), a nasty, jealous old bag whom he loathes and fears. He seeks out Crystal for help on his writing and instead is told to go see Alfred Hitchcock's *Strangers on a Train*, which he does – coming away with a ridiculous scheme on the film's plot to kill Crystal's wife and then ask for a like favor in return.

Crystal's talent as a standup comic comes through as it appears he got away with a fair amount of ad-libbing. His tirades on his ex-wife, a routine he does several times, get funnier with each delivery and are a good counterbalance for DeVito's equally comical dumb-impish schtick.

If there were to be a first place prize for scene stealing, however, it would to to Ramsey, whose horrible looks and surly demeanor are sick and humorous at the same time.

••••••••••••••••••••••••••••••

■ THUNDER AND LIGHTNING

1977, 93 MINS, US ◇ Ⓥ
Dir Corey Allen   *Prod* Roger Corman   *Scr* William Hjortsberg   *Ph* James Pergola   *Ed* Anthony Redman   *Mus* Andy Stein
● David Carradine, Kate Jackson, Roger C. Carmel, Sterling Holloway, Ed Barth, Ron Feinberg (20th Century-Fox)

Thunder and Lightning, has just about everything in the action department but Dracula loping after Frankenstein's monster, packing thrills and fast movement as stunt drivers have their day in some wild pic mileage.

Film picks up in tempo and ends on a socko note as David Carradine, an irrepressible booze runner, competes with girl-friend Kate Jackson's pop in his chosen field.

Script laces comedy with the action, and director Corey Allen expertly maneuvers his chase sequences with stunting both with Everglade buggies and fast cars on the highways.

Carradine shows he has the stuff of which action stars are made, and distaffer Jackson lends a distracting note as an actress who doesn't mind getting her hair mussed.

•••••••••••••••••••••••••••••

■ THUNDER IN THE CITY

1937, 86 MINS, UK Ⓥ
Dir Marion Gering   *Prod* Alexander Erway   *Scr* Robert Sherwood, Aben Kandel, Akos Tolnay   *Ph* Al Gilks   *Ed* Arthur Hilton   *Mus* Miklos Rozsa   *Art Dir* David Ramon
● Edward G. Robinson, Luli Deste, Nigel Bruce, Constance Collier, Ralph Richardson, Arthur Wontner (Atlantic/Columbia)

For a long time, Edward G. Robinson wanted to do something lighter than eye-gouging racketeers and went to London for that purpose after getting an offer to appear in this picture. He wasn't so wrong in wanting to try his hand at something different such as this, except that, as a romantic lead opposite Luli Deste, he is a bit awkward.

Robinson plays an American ballyhoo artist who invades the staid calm of business methods in England and, backed by a lot of nerve, much luck and fictional situations, promotes a metal mine in Africa into a big proposition. Robinson's rival ties him up under patents and it looks as though the Horatio Algerian hero is stymied.

Three writers have written much smart dialog into the picture and provided numerous comedy situations which are ably maneuvered by director Marion Gering.

Deste is a Viennese with a pleasant but very slight accent. She looks to have the goods besides having the looks. Two who contribute much are Nigel Bruce and Constance Collier, who play a duke and duchess, respectively. Ralph Richardson renders a good job as a British banker.

•••••••••••••••••••••••••••••

■ THUNDERBALL

1965, 130 MINS, UK ◇ Ⓥ
Dir Terence Young   *Prod* Kevin McClory   *Scr* Richard Maibaum, John Hopkins   *Ph* Ted Moore   *Ed* Peter Hunt   *Mus* John Barry   *Art Dir* Ken Adam
● Sean Connery, Claudine Auger, Adolfo Celi, Luciana Paluzzi, Rik van Nutter, Bernard Lee (Eon/United Artists)

Sean Connery plays his indestructible James Bond for the fourth time in the manner born, faced here with a $280 million atomic bomb ransom plot. Action, dominating element of three predecessors, gets rougher before even the credits flash on. Richard Maibaum (who coscripted former entries) and John Hopkins' screenplay is studded with inventive play and

mechanical gimmicks. There's visible evidence that the reported $5.5 million budget was no mere publicity figure; it's posh all the way.

Underwater weapon-carrying sea sleds provide an imaginative note, as does a one-man jet pack used by Bond in the opening sequence, reminiscent of the one-man moon vehicle utilized by Dick Tracy in the cartoon strip.

Connery is up to his usual stylish self as he lives up to past rep, in which mayhem is a casual affair.

Adolfo Celi brings dripping menace to part of the swarthy heavy who is nearly as ingenious – but not quite – as the British agent, whom, among other means, he tries to kill with man-eating sharks.

Terence Young takes advantage of every situation in his direction to maintain action at fever-pitch.

•••••••••••••••••••••••••••••

■ THUNDERBOLT AND LIGHTFOOT

1974, 114 MINS, US ◇ Ⓥ
Dir Michael Cimino   *Prod* Robert Daley   *Scr* Michael Cimino   *Ph* Frank Stanley   *Ed* Ferris Webster   *Mus* Dee Barton   *Art Dir* Tambi Larsen
● Clint Eastwood, Jeff Bridges, George Kennedy, Geoffrey Lewis, Catherine Bach, Gary Busey (United Artists)

Thunderbolt and Lightfoot is an overlong, sometimes hilariously vulgar comedy-drama, about the restaging of a difficult safecracking heist. Debuting director Michael Cimino, obtains superior performances from Clint Eastwood, George Kennedy, Geoffrey Lewis and especially Jeff Bridges.

Cimino's story picks up Eastwood as a cowtown preacher, his longtime refuge from Kennedy, a survivor of an earlier caper where the loot was hidden and never found. A Kennedy henchman uncovers Eastwood, who meets Bridges (also on the lam from a car theft), then Kennedy and Lewis. The secret hiding place of the loot, an old schoolhouse, has been replaced by a new structure. Uneasily, the group decides to pull the job all over again.

•••••••••••••••••••••••••••••

■ THX 1138

1971, 88 MINS, US ◇ Ⓥ
Dir George Lucas   *Prod* Lawrence Sturhahn   *Scr* George Lucas, Walter Murch   *Ph* Dave Meyers, Albert Kihn   *Ed* George Lucas   *Mus* Lalo Schifrin   *Art Dir* Michael Haller
● Robert Duvall, Donald Pleasence, Don Pedro Colley, Maggie McOmie, Ian Wolfe, Sid Haig (American Zoetrope)

THX 1138 is a psychedelic science fiction horror story about some future civilization regimented into computer-programmed slavery.

Film is a feature-length expansion of George Lucas' student film. In that brief form, the story of one man's determination to crash out of his worldly prison was exciting; the expansion by director-editor Lucas with Walter Murch succeeds in fleshing out the environment, but falls behind in constructing a plot line to sustain interest. Robert Duvall heads cast as the defector after his mate Maggie McOmie is programmed into the cell of Donald Pleasence, a corrupt computer technician. Don Pedro Colley is another fugitive, who helps Duvall reach his freedom.

•••••••••••••••••••••••••••••

■ TIARA TAHITI

1962, 100 MINS, UK ◇
Dir Ted Kotcheff   *Prod* Ivan Foxwell   *Scr* Geofrey Cotterell, Ivan Foxwell   *Ph* Otto Heller   *Ed* Anthony Gibbs   *Mus* Phil Green   *Art Dir* Alex Vetchinsky
● James Mason, John Mills, Claude Dauphin, Herbert Lom, Rosenda Monteros, Jacques Marin (Rank)

Action stems from Germany, just after the war. A jumped up, pompous lieutenant-colonel with a king size inferiority complex (Mills) clashes with a sophisticated, carefree junior officer (Mason). Mills stops Mason when he tries to smuggle loot back to London, and Mason is cashiered.

He finds a life of dissolute ease and enchantment in Tahiti, with a native girl and no worries. Mills, well after the war, arrives to negotiate a deal to build a hotel in Tahiti, comes across Mason and finds to his intense irritation that Mason still has the same effect on him, that of reducing him to fumbling ineptitude and humility.

The two male stars in this pic have a field day. Mason is fine as the mocking wastrel while Mills is equally good in a more difficult role that could have lapsed into parody.

These two carry the main burden of the film but get affectionate alliance from a string of people. As Mason's girl friend, Monteros is attractive. Herbert Lom (skilfully made up as a Chinese) has a serio-comic role as the local tradesman who is the frustrated rival for the affections of Monteros, and does it up brown.

•••••••••••••••••••••••••••••

■ TIGER AND THE PUSSYCAT, THE

1967, 105 MINS, ITALY/US ◇ Ⓥ
Dir Dino Risi   *Prod* Mario Cecchi Gori   *Scr* Age–Scarpelli, Dino Risi   *Ph* Sandro D'Eva   *Ed* Marcello Malvestiti   *Mus* Fred Buongusto   *Art Dir* Luciano Ricceri
● Vittorio Gassman, Ann-Margret, Eleanor Parker (Fair/Embassy)

Screenwriters take a timeworn three-point relationship and bulwark it with many physical gag situations and flash comic inserts. But they depend on the more basic cleavage between parents and offspring to underscore the extra-marital fling between a middle-age captain of industry (Vittorio Gassman) and a 20-year-old Bohemian ball of fire (Ann-Margret). Eleanor Parker plays the abused wife with suave dignity.

For about two-thirds of the film *The Tiger* is a swiftly-paced romp of gay deceit for the male partner and a purposeful drive for sexual plentitude on the distaff side. Slowdown occurs with Gassman's dilemma. Prodded by his young mistress to give up wife and family (his career by this time is practically shot anyway), the charm and tempo slacken while Gassman weighs a choice that distills the joy of a seven-inning stretch.

Gassman is on the scene almost every minute of the film. It's an unfair load to bear with such a slight story in support but he's first-rate until the action sags. Parker is standout as the attractive, understanding wife and mother of two grownup children.

•••••••••••••••••••••••••••••

■ TIGER BAY

1959, 105 MINS, UK Ⓥ
Dir J. Lee Thompson   *Prod* Julian Wintle, Leslie Parkyn   *Scr* John Hawkesworth, Shelley Smith   *Ph* Eric Cross   *Ed* Sidney Hayers   *Mus* Laurie Johnson
● John Mills, Horst Buchholz, Hayley Mills, Yvonne Mitchell (Rank)

A disarming, snub-nosed youngster makes her debut in *Tiger Bay*, and registers a sock impact. She is Hayley Mills, 12-year-old daughter of actor John Mills, star of the film. Young Mills gives a lift to a pic which, anyway, stacks up as a lively piece of drama.

The story concerns a Polish seaman who, returning from a voyage, finds that his mistress has moved in with another man. In a burst of anger he kills her. The slaying is witnessed by the child, who also rescues the gun. She is a lonely youngster whose attachment for the killer seriously complicates police investigations.

Mills is authoritative as the detective while Horst Buchholz brings charm to a role which could easily have been played by British actor.

Lee Thompson and cameraman Eric Cross capture the dockland area of Cardiff arrestingly. The screenplay by John Hawkesworth and Shelley Smith is taut and literate.

■ **TIGER MAKES OUT, THE**

1967, 94 MINS, US ◇

Dir Arthur Hiller *Prod* George Justin *Scr* Murray Schisgal *Ph* Arthur J. Ornitz *Ed* Robert C. Jones *Mus* Milton 'Shorty' Rogers *Art Dir* Paul Sylbert
● Eli Wallach, Anne Jackson, Bob Dishy, John Harkins, Ruth White, Roland Wood (Columbia)

Beware of the one-act play with apparent screen possibilities. *The Tiger Makes Out* was adapted by Murray Schisgal from his 1963 two-character comedy-drama *The Tiger* into a distended, uneven pic.

Filmed in New York, the George Justin production stars Eli Wallach and Ann Jackson, encoring their legit roles. Good performances, production and yeoman directorial effort by Arthur Hiller buoy up interest.

The play concerned the (offstage) kidnapping of Jackson, a suburban housefrau, by frustrated mailman Wallach, after which some genuinely tender dialog brings together the two spirits.

The kidnapping itself is not detailed; on film, however, it is, and, while necessary, the act itself is not a laugh-getter.

■ **TIGHTROPE**

1984, 117 MINS, US ◇ Ⓥ

Dir Richard Tuggle *Prod* Clint Eastwood *Scr* Richard Tuggle *Ph* Bruce Surtees *Ed* Joel Cox *Mus* Lennie Niehaus *Art Dir* Edward Carfagno
● Clint Eastwood, Genevieve Bujold, Dan Hedaya, Alison Eastwood, Jennifer Beck, Marco St. John (Malpaso/Warner)

Tightrope sees Clint Eastwood comfortably in the role of a big city homicide cop, but also as a vulnerable, hunted man, a deserted husband, father of two daughters, a man whose taste for seamy sex nearly brings him down.

Written and directed by Richard Tuggle, pic trades extensively on the theme of guilt transference from killer to presumed hero which for so long was the special domain of Alfred Hitchcock.

Surface action is highly familiar, as an anonymous killer, stalks prostitutes and massage parlor girls in New Orleans' French Quarter. Eastwood has been accustomed to taking his pleasure with the very sort of women upon whom the murderer is preying.

A fair amount of running time is given over to Eastwood's relationship with his growing daughters (older of whom is played by his real-life offspring, Alison).

It all leads up to a rather predictable assault on the cop's home and daughters, and some sweating and soul-searching on his part.

Overall, however, action is well-handled, as Tuggle demonstrates ample storytelling talent and draws a multitude of nuances from his cast.

■ **TILL THE CLOUDS ROLL BY**

1946, 120 MINS, US Ⓥ

Dir Richard Whorf *Prod* Arthur Freed *Scr* Myles Connolly, Jean Holloway *Ph* Harry Stradling, George J. Folsey *Ed* Albert Akst *Mus* Jerome Kern *Art Dir* Cedric Gibbons, Daniel B. Cathcart
● Robert Walker, Judy Garland, Lucille Bremer, Joan Wells, Van Heflin, Dorothy Patrick (M-G-M)

Why quibble about the story? It's notable that the Jerome Kern saga reminds of the Cole Porter *Night and Day* – both apparently enjoyed a monotonously successful life. No early-life struggles, no frustrations, nothing but an uninterrupted string of Broadway and West End show success. Nearest thing to travail is Kern's contretemps with turn-of-the-century Broadway impresario Charles Frohman, who was apparently a rabid Anglophile – 'no good songsmith in America; the only good ones come from Europe.'

Of the basic cast, Robert Walker is completely sympathetic as Kern. Van Heflin plays Jim Hessler, the arranger-composer-confidante, whose life story parallels Kern's in a Damon-and-Pythias plot. (Some real-life counterpart may be the veteran arranger, Frank Sadler).

Picture actually opens with *Show Boat*, a 1927 whammo. There is virtually a tabloid version of that operetta utilized for the opener, a play-within-a-play and the rest of the story is virtually a success-story flashback.

■ **TILL WE MEET AGAIN**

1944, 85 MINS, US

Dir Frank Borzage *Prod* Frank Borzage *Scr* Lenore Coffee *Ph* Theodor Sparkuhl *Ed* Elmo Veron *Mus* David Buttolph *Art Dir* Hans Dreier, Robert Usher
● Ray Milland, Barbara Britton, Walter Slezak, Mona Freeman, Lucile Watson, Vladimir Sokoloff (Paramount)

For all its underground intrigue, Nazi brutality and Machiavellian Gestapo methods, film is a different sort of war romance. For one thing, its heroine is a novitiate nun and Ray Milland is an almost too happily married albeit dashing American aviator, forced down in occupied France.

Sometimes Milland's love-hunger for his wife and child is a bit sticky, but it gets over a wholesome message of the American standard of love and marriage to the young French convent girl. To her it's a new-found litany of love that awakens a new perspective on the mundane world as she accompanies Milland – as his pseudo-wife – in order to aid his escape with valuable secret papers from the French Underground for London.

Barbara Britton, a newcomer, is compelling as the beauteous but unworldly church disciple.

■ **TILLIE AND GUS**

1933, 58 MINS, US

Dir Francis Martin *Prod* Douglas MacLean *Scr* Walter DeLeon, Francis Martin *Ph* Ben Reynolds *Art Dir* Hans Dreier, Harry Oliver
● W. C. Fields, Alison Skipworth, Baby LeRoy, Jacqueline Wells, George Barbier, Clarence Wilson (Paramount)

This is an effort to stretch a brief idea to feature length with horseplay and mechanical punch which doesn't quite register. Chief handicap is a lack of spontaneity and swiftness of movement. Basic idea is good, the big time slickers who beat the country amateur, but this rich vein is scarcely uncovered.

W.C. Fields and Alison Skipworth are a married couple who have gone their separate ways but reunite when called to the old home for a presumed legacy. Local bad boy is trying to hog the fortune and oust the young couple from their inheritance. Last thing to be picked up is a ferry franchise, and that's whipped into a race between the old boat and the new contender.

In between it's some of Fields' old vaude gags, frequent references to wet babies and such bits as the $1,000 vase being dropped to catch the $1 cane. Comedy not helped any by efforts to inject a dramatic story.

■ **TIME AFTER TIME**

1980, 112 MINS, UK ◇ Ⓥ

Dir Nicholas Meyer *Prod* Herb Jaffe *Scr* Nicholas Meyer *Ph* Paul Lohmann *Ed* Donn Cambern *Mus* Miklos Rozsa *Art Dir* Edward C. Carfagno
● Malcolm McDowell, David Warner, Mary Steenburgen, Charles Cioffi, Patti D'Arbanville (Warner/Orion)

Time after Time is a delightful, entertaining trifle of a film that shows both the possibilities and limitations of taking liberties with literature and history. Nicholas Meyer has deftly juxtaposed Victorian England and contemporary America in a clever story, irresistible due to the competence of its cast.

H.G. Wells and Jack The Ripper abandon London circa 1893 in Wells' famous time machine. Their arrival in 1979 San Francisco is played for all the inevitable anachronisms, with results that are both witty and pointed.

Thanks to Meyer's astute scripting and direction, and superb performances by Malcolm McDowell as Wells, David Warner as the mythical killer, and Mary Steenburgen as the woman in between, there's plenty of mileage in *Time*.

■ **TIME BANDITS**

1981, 110 MINS, UK ◇

Dir Terry Gilliam *Prod* Terry Gilliam *Scr* Michael Palin, Terry Gilliam *Ph* Peter Biziou *Ed* Julian Doyle *Mus* Mike Moran *Art Dir* Milly Burns
● John Cleese, Sean Connery, Shelley Duvall, Ralph Richardson, David Warner, Michael Palin (Handmade)

When you can count the laughs in a comedy on the fingers of one hand, it isn't so funny. *Time Bandits*, is a kind of potted history of man, myth and the eternal clash between good and evil as told in the inimitable idiom of Monty Python.

Not that the basic premise is bad, with an English youngster and a group of dwarfs passing through time holes on assignment by the Maker to patch up the shoddier parts of His creation. What results, unfortunately, is a hybrid neither sufficiently hair-raising or comical.

The plot's grand tour ranges from ancient Greece and other parts to the Titanic to the Fortress of Ultimate Darkness, the latter gothic region presided over by a costume-heavy David Warner as one of nine above-title and mostly cameo parts. Of which the funniest, near pic's conclusion, is the Maker Himself as none other than Ralph Richardson in business suit.

John Cleese as Robin Hood, Ian Holm as Napoleon, Sean Connery as a Greek warrior-ruler with a passion for magic, and Michael Palin as a plummy English upperclass type all acquit well enough in the limited circumstances.

■ **TIME MACHINE, THE**

1960, 103 MINS, US ◇ Ⓥ

Dir George Pal *Prod* George Pal *Scr* David Duncan *Ph* Paul C. Vogel *Ed* George Tomasini *Mus* Russell Garcia *Art Dir* George W. Davis, William Ferrari
● Rod Taylor, Alan Young, Yvette Mimieux, Sebastian Cabot, Tom Helmore, Whit Bissell (M-G-M)

In utilizing contemporary knowledge to update H.G. Wells' durable novel, scenarist David Duncan has brought the work into modern focus. The point-of-view springs properly from 1960 rather than from the turn of the century. The social comment of the original has been historically refined to encompass such plausible eventualities as the physical manifestation of atomic war weapons. But the basic spirit of Wells' work has not been lost.

The film's chief flaw is its somewhat palsied pace. Forging its way through vital initial exposition, it perks to a fascinating peak when the Time Traveller (Rod Taylor) plants himself in his machine and begins his enviable tour of time. His 'visits' to World Wars I, II, and III, and the way in which the passage of time is depicted within these 'local' stops give the picture its most delightful moments.

But things slow down to a walk when Taylor arrives at the year 802,701 and becomes involved generally with a group of tame, anti-social towheads (the Eloi) and specifically with their loveliest and most sociable representative (Yvette Mimieux), with whom he falls in love.

Taylor's performance is a gem of straightforwardness, with just the proper sensitivity and animation. A standout in support is Alan Young, in a gentle, three-ply role. Mimieux is well cast. Innocent vacancy gleams beautifully in her eyes.

....

■ TIME OF THEIR LIVES, THE

1946, 82 MINS, US ⊙
Dir Charles Barton   *Scr* Val Burton, Walter De Leon, Bradford Ropes   *Ph* Charles Van Enger   *Ed* Philip Cahn   *Mus* Milton Rosen   *Art Dir* Jack Otterson, Richard Riedel
● Lou Costello, Bud Abbott, Marjorie Reynolds, Binnie Barnes, Gale Sondergaard (Universal)

This one's a picnic for Abbott & Costello fans, replete with trowelled-on slapstick, corned-up gags and farcical plot.

Shot by mistake as a traitor in the American Revolutionary War and doomed to remain an earthbound ghost until proved innocent, Costello turns up in 1946 still looking for the evidence. In a similar fix, Marjorie Reynolds floats through the film like a Sears-Roebuck model ghost, but Costello can't quite make the smoothie grade. It's good for laughs.

Abbott, who early in the picture plays a 1780 heel, turns up in modern times as a psychiatrist, house-guesting in the mansion Costello and his girl friend are haunting. Latter wreak their revenge via a series of invisible-man stunts that drive the brain specialist out of his mind. This gimmick is worked to the limit, and beyond.

....

■ TIME TO LOVE AND A TIME TO DIE, A

1958, 133 MINS, US ◇ ⊙
Dir Douglas Sirk   *Prod* Robert Arthur   *Scr* Orin Jannings   *Ph* Russell Metty   *Mus* Miklos Rozsa   *Art Dir* Alexander Golitzen, Alfred Sweeney
● John Gavin, Lilo Pulver, Keenan Wynn, Erich Maria Remarque, Thayer David, Jock Mahoney (Universal)

A Time to Love and a Time to Die is less a panorama of the battle horrors of the Second World War, though these are implicit, than a poignant telling of the anguish of being in love while civilian bombings rage, and decency is held hostage to vicious character traits. In unfolding the Erich Maria Remarque novel, producer and director have been long on 'heart' and 'sentiment' and the result is a bitter-sweet love story.

The story is somewhat slow in development. Orin Jannings opens his screenplay with the hero (John Gavin) on the Russian front under the cloud of defeat in 1944. The wretchedness of modern war, the compassion and pity felt by the better type of German soldier, is established before the boy gets his long-delayed furlough and goes off to his native town, only to find his home is rubble and his parents disappeared.

Nearly all the action comprises the experiences of the furloughed soldier: with the townspeople, the Nazis and the Gestapo as counterpoint to his budding romance and hurry-up marriage to the girl (Lilo Pulver) and the denouement comes back at the Russian front.

The film may be remembered more for types than performances. There is a mad air-raid warden (Alexander Engel), a Jew hiding in a Catholic church tower (Charles Regnier) and a Teutonic hellion (Dorothea Wieck).

....

■ TIN MEN

1987, 112 MINS, US ◇ ⊙
Dir Barry Levinson   *Prod* Mark Johnson   *Scr* Barry Levinson   *Ph* Peter Sova   *Ed* Stu Linder   *Mus* Fine Young Cannibals, David Steele, Andy Cox   *Art Dir* Peter Jamison
● Richard Dreyfuss, Danny DeVito, Barbara Hershey, John Mahoney, Jackie Gayle, Stanley Brock (Touchstone/Silver Screen Partners II)

The improbable tale of a pair of feuding aluminum siding salesmen, *Tin Men* winds up as bountiful comedy material in the skillful hands of writer-director Barry Levinson.

Film is packed with laughs, thanks to taut scripting and superb character depictions by Richard Dreyfuss, Danny DeVito and a fascinating troupe of sidekicks. These fast-buck hustlers collectively fashion a portrait of superficial greed so pathetic it soars to a level of black humor.

Central storyline finds Dreyfuss and DeVito tangling from the start after an accident damages both of their Cadillacs. Conflict between the two strangers – who don't find out until later they're both tin men – escalates to the point where Dreyfuss seeks to get even by wooing DeVito's unhappy wife (Barbara Hershey) into bed.

While each of the tin men is revealed as a compelling, off-center type in his own right, the one played by Jackie Gayle especially shines.

....

■ TIN STAR, THE

1957, 92 MINS, US ⊙
Dir Anthony Mann   *Prod* William Perlberg, George Seaton   *Scr* Dudley Nichols   *Ph* Loyal Griggs   *Ed* Alma Macrorie   *Mus* Elmer Bernstein   *Art Dir* Hal Pereira, J. McMillan Johnson
● Henry Fonda, Anthony Perkins, Betsy Palmer, Michael Ray, Neville Brand, John McIntire (Paramount)

The Tin Star is a quality western that unfolds interestingly under the smooth direction of Anthony Mann, who draws top performances from cast. Screenplay [from a story by Barney Slater and Joel Kane] centers around Anthony Perkins' insistence upon keeping his sheriff's badge despite the pleading of his sweetheart to abandon hazards of the job, and Henry Fonda, a former lawman turned human bounty hunter, reluctantly teaching him the tricks of the trade.

Fonda gives his character telling authority as he waits in a small western town for a reward check, then stays on to help the over-anxious young sheriff. Perkins asserts himself forcibly, his nemesis being Neville Brand, capable as a gun-handy bully who nearly forces him to back down in his authority.

....

■ TIP ON A DEAD JOCKEY

1957, 98 MINS, US
Dir Richard Thorpe   *Prod* Edwin H. Knopf   *Scr* Charles Lederer   *Ph* George J. Folsey   *Ed* Ben Lewis   *Mus* Miklos Rozsa   *Art Dir* William A. Horning, Hans Peters
● Robert Taylor, Dorothy Malone, Gia Scala, Martin Gabel, Marcel Dalio, Jack Lord (M-G-M)

Once this *Jockey* spurs up momentum, film shapes as a solid, satisfactory action picture. However, plots dealing with war-weary pilots who have lost their nerve have an overfamiliar ring and smart, updated dialogue by Charles Lederer, in adapting Irwin Shaw's *New Yorker* tale, doesn't entirely dispel the familiar.

In brittle, cosmopolitan expatriate society of Madrid, Robert Taylor is an ex-pilot, afraid of emotional entanglements because his war job was sending pilots to their deaths. He's now eking out a precarious existence on the fringes of Spain's precarious economy. Offbeat title reflects this, when he loses his entire bankroll on a horse-race in which his jockey is killed in a spill.

Dorothy Malone is his wife, fighting to regain his love after he requests a divorce. To help raise coin for war buddy Jack Lord, and Lord's lovely Spanish wife (Gia Scala) Taylor undertakes a currency-smuggling caper proposed by sinister Martin Gabel. Here, film picks up tempo, especially in chase sequences involving various Mediterranean police authorities.

....

■ TITANIC

1953, 97 MINS, US
Dir Jean Negulesco   *Prod* Charles Brackett   *Scr* Charles Brackett, Walter Reisch, Richard Breen   *Ph* Joe MacDonald   *Ed* Louis Loeffler   *Mus* Sol Kaplan   *Art Dir* Lyle R. Wheeler, Maurice Ransford
● Clifton Webb, Barbara Stanwyck, Robert Wagner, Audrey Dalton, Brian Aherne, Richard Basehart (20th Century-Fox)

The sinking of HMS *Titanic* in 1912 provides a factual basis for this screen drama reenacting the tragic voyage. Story line is built around fictional characters aboard the supposedly unsinkable British luxury liner when it started its maiden voyage from Southampton to NY on 11 April 1912.

During the first half the film is inclined to dawdle and talk, but by the time the initial 45 or 50 minutes are out of the way, the impending disaster begins to take a firm grip on the imagination and builds a compelling expectancy.

Jean Negulesco's direction and the script really shine after the ship's bottom is opened by a jagged iceberg spur, bringing out the drama that lies in the confusion of shipwreck and passengers' reaction to certain doom. The records show that of the 2,229 persons aboard, only 712 escaped before the ship plunged to the bottom of the North Atlantic at 2:30 a.m., 15 April 1912.

Barbara Stanwyck and Clifton Webb do well by the principal roles in the fictional story. She is a wife trying to take her two children (Audrey Dalton and Harper Carter) away from the spoiling influence of a husband interested only in a superficial society life. A shipboard romance between Robert Wagner, a student returning to the states, and Dalton offer some pleasant, touching moments. Brian Aherne is excellent as the ship's captain. Richard Basehart, a defrocked priest addicted to the bottle, makes his few moments stand out.

....

■ TITFIELD THUNDERBOLT, THE

1953, 84 MINS, UK ◇ ⊙
Dir Charles Crichton   *Prod* Michael Truman   *Scr* T.E.B. Clarke   *Ph* Douglas Slocombe   *Ed* Seth Holt   *Mus* Georges Auric   *Art Dir* C.P. Norman
● Stanley Holloway, George Relph, Naunton Wayne, John Gregson, Godfrey Tearle, Hugh Griffith (Ealing)

Titfield is a small English village which gets worked up when the government decides to close the unprofitable branch railway line. The vicar and the squire are both railway enthusiasts and are heartbroken at the news. The only ones cheered by the decision are the partners of a transport company who can see big profits by organizing a bus service. The railway enthusiasts, however, persuade the village tippler to provide the cash by telling him he will be able to start drinking far earlier if they install a buffet car on the train.

The *Thunderbolt* is the railway engine

involved in the story. Once the basic situation is accepted, the entire yarn concentrates on the feuding between the rival factions with the opposition stopping at nothing to block the train service.

Stanley Holloway gives a polished performance as the village soak. George Relph does a fine job as the vicar, Naunton Wayne's contribution as the town clerk is in typical vein while John Gregson does nicely as the earnest squire. A gem from Godfrey Tearle as the bishop and a powerful performance by Hugh Griffith are among the strong characterizations.

. . . .

■ T-MEN

1947, 91 MINS, US ▼

Dir Anthony Mann *Prod* Edward Small *Scr* John C. Higgins *Ph* John Alton *Ed* Fred Allen *Mus* Paul Sawtell *Art Dir* Edward C. Jewell
● Dennis O'Keefe, Mary Meade, Charles McGraw, Alfred Ryder, Wally Ford (Eagle Lion)

Producer Edward Small has taken a closed case out of the Treasury Dept files, reenacted it in documentary fashion, and the result is *T-Men* – an entertaining action film. *March-of-Time* technique in the early reels flavors the footage with pungent realism that builds up to a suspenseful finish at the final fadeout.

Location scenes in Detroit, Los Angeles and several of its beach suburbs, may have cost a little more but the effect they achieve in verity can't be denied.

Preceded by a brief foreword delivered by a Treasury official, plot unfolds at a slow pace in its early stages. Later, however, it's obvious why the opening scenes were so carefully and meticulously outlined. Solution of every crime depends upon the most minute clues. When assembled in the proper sequence there's a crashing denouement. And so it is with *T-Men*. The final reel is a corker.

Dennis O'Keefe's characterization of the Treasury agent is finely drawn. He's almost Jimmy Cagneyish at times. Cast as his partner is Alfred Ryder. They're undercover agents assigned to break the 'Shanghai Paper Case'. Masquerading as mobsters they join a ring of liquor cutters in Detroit who are known to be using phony revenue stamps.

. . . .

■ TO BE OR NOT TO BE

1942, 99 MINS, US ▼

Dir Ernst Lubitsch *Prod* Alexander Korda, Ernst Lubitsch *Scr* Edwin Justus Mayer *Ph* Rudolph Maté *Ed* Dorothy Spencer *Mus* Werner Heymann *Art Dir* Vincent Korda
● Carole Lombard, Jack Benny, Robert Stack, Lionel Atwill, Sig Ruman (United Artists)

To Be or Not to Be, co-starring Carole Lombard and Jack Benny, under expert guidance of Ernst Lubitsch, is absorbing drama with farcical trimmings. It's an acting triumph for Lombard, who delivers an effortless and highly effective performance that provides memorable finale to her brilliant screen career.

To Be is typically Lubitsch in dramatic setup and satirical by-play. He's responsible for the producer-director and original writer chores [with Melchior Lengyel], dovetailing all into a solid piece of entertainment. Story recounts the adventures of a legit stock company in Warsaw, before and during the Nazi invasion, from August 1939 to December 1941. Lombard is the femme lead, with husband Jack Benny a hammy matinee idol with penchant for playing *Hamlet*.

Lubitsch's guidance provides a tense dramatic pace with events developed deftly and logically throughout. The farcical episodes display Lubitsch in best form.

. . . .

■ TO BE OR NOT TO BE

1983, 108 MINS, US ◇ ▼

Dir Alan Johnson *Prod* Mel Brooks *Scr* Thomas Meehan, Ronny Graham *Ph* Gerald Hirschfeld *Ed* Alan Balsam *Mus* John Morris *Art Dir* Terence Marsh
● Mel Brooks, Anne Bancroft, Tim Matheson, Charles Durning, Jose Ferrer, James Haake (Brooksfilms)

With the solid farcical underpinning of Ernst Lubitsch's 1942 *To Be or Not to Be*, Mel Brooks' glossy remake of the original Carole Lombard-Jack Benny starrer is very funny stuff indeed.

Maintaining some of the dramatic core of the original, but played mostly for Brooks-style laughs, the convoluted tale of a Warsaw theatrical troupe that winds up saving the Polish underground during the Nazi occupation does have some potential hurdles to clear. Cute Nazis and roly-poly Gestapo officers hardly have universal lure.

Brooks sustains, with varying success, a full-fledged role as Frederick Bronski, vainglorious head of a tawdry theatrical company whose shows run the spectrum from cheap vaudeville turns to *Highlights from Hamlet*. Mainstay of the film is a superbly sustained comic performance by Anne Bancroft, as Bronski's wife, in the real-life Brooks couple's first tandem costarring acting job.

Charles Durning is a standout as the buffoonish Gestapo topper and Bancroft's pseudo-seduction of him, and Nazi hireling Jose Ferrer, are among the pic's highpoints. Bancroft's sustained delights are not matched by Brooks, who seems to be trying too hard.

. . . .

■ TO CATCH A THIEF

1955, 103 MINS, US ◇ ▼

Dir Alfred Hitchcock *Prod* Alfred Hitchcock *Scr* John Michael Hayes *Ph* Robert Burks *Ed* George Tomasini *Mus* Lyn Murray *Art Dir* Hal Pereira, Joseph MacMillan Johnson
● Cary Grant, Grace Kelly, Jessie Royce Landis, John Williams, Charles Vanel, Brigitte Auber (Paramount)

Cary Grant is a reformed jewel thief, once known as 'The Cat', but now living quietly in a Cannes hilltop villa. When burglaries occur that seem to bear his old trademark, he has to catch the thief to prove his innocence, a chore in which he is assisted by Grace Kelly, rich American girl, her mother, Jessie Royce Landis, and insurance agent John Williams. While a suspense thread is present, director Alfred Hitchcock doesn't emphasize it, letting the yarn play lightly for comedy more than thrills.

Grant gives his role his assured style of acting, meaning the dialog and situations benefit. Kelly, too, dresses up the sequences in more ways than one.

Support from Landis and Williams is firstrate, both being major assets to the entertainment in their way with a line or a look.

. . . .

■ TO HAVE AND HAVE NOT

1944, 100 MINS, US ▼

Dir Howard Hawks *Prod* Howard Hawks *Scr* Jules Furthman, William Faulkner *Ph* Sidney Hickox *Ed* Christian Nyby *Mus* Leo Forbstein *Art Dir* Charles Novi
● Humphrey Bogart, Walter Brennan, Lauren Bacall, Dolores Moran, Hoagy Carmichael, Marcel Dalio (Warner)

With an eye to the lucrative box-office of its *Casablanca*, the brothers Warner turned out another epic of similar genre in a none-too-literal adaptation of Ernest Hemingway's novel *To Have and Have Not*. There are enough similarities in both films to warrant more than cursory attention, even to the fact that Humphrey Bogart is starred in each, though

this story of Vichy France collaborationism is not up to Warners' melodramatic story standards.

Though *Have Not* was one of Hemingway's inferior novels – whose theme of rum-running was certainly antithetical to the film's story of French collaboration – it affords considerable picture interest because of some neat characterizations. And it introduces Lauren Bacall, in her first picture. She's an arresting personality. She can slink, brother, and no fooling!

Yarn deals with the intrigue centering around the Caribbean island of Martinique, owned by France, and the plotting that ensued there prior to its ultimate capitulation to Allied pressure. Bogart is an American skipper there who hires out his boat to anyone who has the price. When he becomes involved in the local Free French movement, the story's pattern becomes woven around him, at times in cops-and-robbers fashion.

Warners give the pic its usually nifty productional accoutrements, and that includes casting, musical scoring and Howard Hawks' direction but the basic story is too unsteady.

Bogart is in his usual metier, a tough guy who, no less, has the facility of making a dame go for him, instead of he for her. That's where Bacall comes in. Walter Brennan, as Bogart's drunken sidekick; Dolores Moran, as the film's second looker; and songwriter Hoagy Carmichael have lesser roles that they handle to advantage.

. . . .

■ TO KILL A MOCKINGBIRD

1962, 129 MINS, US ▼

Dir Robert Mulligan *Prod* Alan J. Pakula *Scr* Horton Foote *Ph* Russell Harlan *Ed* Aaron Stell *Mus* Elmer Bernstein *Art Dir* Alexander Golitzen, Henry Bumstead
● Gregory Peck, Mary Badham, Phillip Alford, John Megna, Robert Duvall, Brock Peters (Universal)

Harper Lee's highly regarded first novel has been artfully and delicately translated to the screen. Horton Foote's trenchant screenplay, Robert Mulligan's sensitive and instinctively observant direction and a host of exceptional performances are all essential threads in the rich, provocative fabric.

As it unfolds on the screen, *To Kill a Mockingbird* bears with it, oddly enough, alternating overtones of Faulkner, Twain, Steinbeck, Hitchcock and an *Our Gang* comedy. A telling indictment of racial prejudice in the Deep South, it is also a charming tale of the emergence of two youngsters from the realm of wild childhood fantasy to the horizon of maturity, responsibility, compassion and social insight.

It is the story of a wise, gentle, soft-spoken Alabama lawyer (Gregory Peck) entrusted with the formidable dual chore of defending a Negro falsely accused of rape while raising his own impressionable, imaginative, motherless children in a hostile, terrifying environment of bigotry and economic depression.

For Peck, it is an especially challenging role, requiring him to project through a veneer of civilized restraint and resigned, rational compromise the fires of social indignation and humanitarian concern that burn within the character. He not only succeeds, but makes it appear effortless, etching a portrayal of strength, dignity, intelligence.

But by no means is this entirely, or even substantially, Peck's film. Two youngsters just about steal it away, although the picture marks their screen bows. Both nine-year-old Mary Badham and thirteen-year-old Phillip Alford, each of whom hails from the South, make striking debuts as Peck's two irrepressible, mischievous, ubiquitous, irresistibly childish children.

There are some top-notch supporting performances. Especially sharp and effective are Frank Overton, Estelle Evans, James Anderson and Robert Duvall. Brock Peters has an outstanding scene as the innocent, ill-fated Negro on trial for his life.

□ 1962: Best Picture (Nomination)

. . . .

■ TO LIVE AND DIE IN L.A.

1985, 116 MINS, US ◇ Ⓥ

Dir William Friedkin   *Prod* Irving H. Levin   *Scr* William Friedkin, Gerald Petievich   *Ph* Robby Müller   *Ed* Scott Smith   *Mus* Wang Chung   *Art Dir* Lilly Kilvert

● William L. Petersen, Willem Dafoe, John Pankow, Debra Feuer, John Turturro, Darlanne Fluegel (United Artists/New Century/SLM)

To Live and Die in L.A. looks like a rich man's *Miami Vice.* William Friedkin's evident attempt to fashion a West Coast equivalent of his [1971] *The French Connection* is engrossing and diverting enough on a moment-to-moment basis but is overtooled.

Friedkin leaves no doubt about his technical abilities, as he has created another memorable car chase and, with the considerable assistance of cinematographer Robby Müller, has offered up any number of startling and original shots of the characters inhabiting weirdly ugly-beautiful LA cityscapes.

William L. Petersen plays a highly capable Secret Service agent who decides to nail a notorious counterfeiter responsible for the murder of his partner.

Petersen's search leads him into the kinky, high-tech world of Willem Dafoe, a supremely talented and self-confident artist whose phony $20 bills look magnificent and whose tentacles reach into surprising areas of the criminal underworld, both high and low-class.

Friedkin keeps dialog to a minimum, but what conversation there is proves wildly overloaded with streetwise obscenities, so much so that it becomes something of a joke.

. . . .

■ TO SIR, WITH LOVE

1967, 104 MINS, UK ◇ Ⓥ

Dir James Clavell   *Prod* James Clavell   *Scr* James Clavell   *Ph* Paul Beeson   *Ed* Peter Thornton   *Mus* Ron Grainer   *Art Dir* Tony Woollard

● Sidney Poitier, Christian Roberts, Judy Geeson, Christopher Chittell, Lulu (Columbia)

To Sir, With Love is a well-made, sometimes poignant, drama [from the 1959 E.R. Braithwaite novel] about a Negro teacher, working in a London slum, who transforms an unruly class into a group of youngsters better prepared for adult life. Sidney Poitier stars in an excellent performance.

Poitier, after gauging the rebellious mood of his class, scraps the formal agenda and institutes what he rightly calls 'survival training'.

Students include Christian Roberts, very good as the natural class leader, Judy Geeson, a looker who gets a crush on teacher, Christopher Chittell, another reformed punk, and Lulu, an engaging personality with substantial acting ability.

. . . .

■ TO THE DEVIL A DAUGHTER

1976, 92 MINS, UK/W. GERMANY ◇ Ⓥ

Dir Peter Sykes   *Prod* Roy Skeggs   *Scr* Chris Wicking   *Ph* David Watkin   *Ed* John Trumper   *Art Dir* Don Picton

● Richard Widmark, Christopher Lee, Honor Blackman, Denholm Elliott, Michael Goodliffe, Nastassja Kinski (Hammer/Terra)

To the Devil a Daughter is lacklustre occult melodrama in which Christopher Lee is up to his old tricks as an excommunicated priest who takes up satan's cause in order to save the world from its own decadent folly.

Based on a novel by English author Dennis Wheatley, the picture makes a few too many pretensions to serious exploration of the occult, that hamper the flow.

Lee is ever-dependable in this sort of menace routine, Richard Widmark turns in a serviceable job, ditto Honor Blackman and Anthony Valentine as pals who aid and abet him at mortal cost. Nastassja Kinski is moderately appealing as the child-woman novitiate and Denholm Elliott turns on the requisite anguish as the fearful father who originally signed the girl over to Lee in order to spare his own hide.

. . . .

■ TO TRAP A SPY

1966, 92 MINS, US ◇

Dir Don Medford   *Prod* Norman Felton   *Scr* Sam Rolfe   *Ph* Joseph Biroc   *Ed* Henry Berman   *Mus* Jerry Goldsmith   *Art Dir* George W. Davis, Merrill Pye

● Robert Vaughn, Luciana Paluzzi, Patricia Crowley, Fritz Weaver, Will Kuluva, David McCallum (M-G-M)

To Trap a Spy is an elaborated version of MGM-TV's *The Man From U.N.C.L.E.* pilot, originally lensed in color but telecast in black-and-white to tee off series on 23 September 1964. Additional footage was shot to bring total running time now to 92 minutes.

Patently released to cash in on current espionage mania, much of the new footage is devoted to build Robert Vaughn, the agent from U.N.C.L.E., into a glamor boy with a roving eye for beautiful femmes. Whatever plot there is revolves around efforts to prevent the assassination of a visiting African dignitary, but the refurbished entry isn't much better than the original.

Vaughn tries hard and with some success through plot-holes, and gets capable support from Patricia Crowley, Luciana Paluzzi and Fritz Weaver. His sidekick in teleseries, David McCallum, is in only two scenes.

. . . .

■ TOBACCO ROAD

1941, 91 MINS, US

Dir John Ford   *Prod* Darryl F. Zanuck   *Scr* Nunnally Johnson   *Ph* Arthur Miller   *Ed* Barbara McLean   *Mus* David Buttolph

● Charles Grapewin, Marjorie Rambeau, Gene Tierney, Dana Andrews, Elizabeth Patterson (20th Century-Fox)

Tobacco Road as a motion picture falls far short of its promises. The sensational pulling elements of the 1933 play by Jack Kirkland from Erskine Caldwell's saga – the dialog and the low-life manners of its people – have been deleted, altered or attenuated to the point of dullness. What remains of the story is a back-in-the-hills comedy of shiftless folk.

Tobacco Road emerges with a trite comedy theme about the dubious efforts, chiefly larcenous, by which old Jeeter hopes, through act of Providence or dishonest opportunity, to raise $100 for the annual rent of the old farm.

For all of its dehydration *Tobacco Road* is told with a canny camera. Ford is more intent on story telling than in his recent productions.

Chief load of the acting falls on Charley Grapewin, whose Jeeter is a fine characterization within the revised limitations. He plays the old fellow for comedy and sympathy, revealing also a lazy shrewdness. Elizabeth Patterson is Ma Ada, and brings out the sullen hopelessness of the role.

. . . .

■ TOBRUK

1966, 107 MINS, US ◇ Ⓥ

Dir Arthur Hiller   *Prod* Gene Corman   *Scr* Leo V. Gordon   *Ph* Russell Harlan   *Ed* Robert C. Jones   *Mus* Bronislau Kaper   *Art Dir* Alexander Golitzen, Henry Bumstead

● Rock Hudson, George Peppard, Nigel Green, Guy Stockwell, Jack Watson, Norman Rossington (Gibraltar/Universal)

Tobruk is a colorful, hard-hitting World War II melodrama with plenty of guts and sus-

pense to hold the action buff. Rock Hudson heads the four-name star roster but actually comes out third best to George Peppard and Nigel Green in interesting characterizations.

Screenplay has a serviceable plot twist as it projects the protagonists on a suicidal mission in the North African war of 1942. Daring plan calls for a British column of 90, composed of commandos and German-born Jews who have come over to the Allies, to form a special attack unit to cross the Libyan Desert to Tobruk, Mediterranean seaport in the hands of 50,000 German and Italian troops. Once there, they are to hold its key fortified positions pending arrival of a British naval force, and blow up the gigantic German fuel bunkers upon which Rommel depends for his push to the Suez canal.

Arthur Hiller's realistic direction makes the most of the premise, both in the eight-day desert trek and approach and invasion of Tobruk.

. . . .

■ TOKYO JOE

1949, 87 MINS, US Ⓥ

Dir Stuart Heisler   *Prod* Robert Lord   *Scr* Cyril Hume, Bertram Millhauser   *Ph* Charles Lawton Jr   *Ed* Viola Lawrence   *Mus* George Antheil

● Humphrey Bogart, Alexander Knox, Florence Marley, Sessue Hayakawa (Columbia/Santana)

Tokyo Joe has been given a documentary flavor by much process footage shot in Tokyo. This authentic touch serves as an excellent background for the unfolding of the plot's meller elements, and Stuart Heisler's direction develops a neat air of anticipation that climaxes in a gripping, exciting fight finale.

Story [from one by Steve Fisher, adapted by Walter Doniger] opens with Bogart returning to Tokyo, where he owns a night club, after service in the war. He finds the wife he had left has married another. Out to win her back, Bogart starts a small freight airline, and soon becomes involved in smuggling war criminals back into Japan.

Alexander Knox is quietly effective as the man who replaces Bogart as Florence Marly's husband. Marly does an adequate job of her role.

. . . .

■ TOM BROWN'S SCHOOL DAYS

1940, 88 MINS, US Ⓥ

Dir Robert Stevenson   *Prod* Gene Towne, Graham Baker   *Scr* Walter Ferris, Frank Cavett, Gene Towne, Graham Baker   *Ph* Nicholas Musuraca   *Ed* William Hamilton   *Mus* Anthony Collins   *Art Dir* Van Nest Polglase

● Cedric Hardwicke, Freddie Bartholomew, Jimmy Lydon, Josephine Hutchinson, Billy Halop, Polly Moran (The Play's The Thing/RKO)

Much can be said for the treatment in this edition of the Thomas Hughes yarn. While remaining faithful to the spirit of the original, it contrives to vitalize the action and humanize the characters. Thus young Tom's confused terror among the milling cruelties of the young hellions on his first time away from home is understandable and compelling. The terrible seriousness of his scrapes, his fights and youthful crises are immediate and vivid.

Although *Tom Brown* is not a lavish production, it is sympathetically and skillfully made, with many touching moments and an excellent cast. It alters the emphasis somewhat from the development of the boy to the character of the headmaster, Arnold. But that should bother only a few purists. It probably results in a better picture, since Cedric Hardwicke, who plays the wise and kindly teacher, is much better qualified to carry a story than is any Hollywood prodigy.

Hardwicke's performance is one of the best he has ever given on the screen. While maintaining the schoolmaster's surface severity, he clearly indicates the underlying sympathy, tolerance, quiet humor and steadfast courage. In the title part, Jimmy Lydon is believable and moving in the early portions, but too young for the final moments. Freddie Bartholomew is sincere and convincing as Tom's sidekick, while Josephine Hutchinson's lustrous quality makes the role of the headmaster's wife seem too brief. Billy Halop is a properly sadistic bully.

. . . .

■ **TOM BROWN'S SCHOOLDAYS**

1951, 96 MINS, UK ▼

Dir Gordon Parry   *Prod* George Minter   *Scr* Noel Langley   *Ph* C. Pennington-Richards, Raymond Sturgess   *Ed* Kenneth Heeley-Ray   *Mus* Richard Addinsell   *Art Dir* Frederick Pusey
● John Howard Davies, Robert Newton, Diana Wynyard, Francis De Wolff, Kathleen Byron, Hermione Baddeley (Renown)

England's classic story of public school life is acted with great sincerity by a name cast, but script and direction go all out to emphasize the obvious emotional tear-jerker angles.

Almost the entire script hinges on the popular angle of the new boy versus the bully. John Howard Davies makes Tom Brown a lovable and sympathetic youngster without a shade of priggishness. Robert Newton as the reforming headmaster, Dr Arnold, fills his role with commendable restraint.

The plot, of course, is dominated by the schoolboys, and there is a standout performance by John Forrest as the sneering, bullying Flashman.

Special facilities having been granted to film this in Rugby School, the authenticity of the background cannot be questioned.

. . . .

■ **TOM HORN**

1980, 98 MINS, US ◇ ▼

Dir William Wiard   *Prod* Fred Weintraub   *Scr* Thomas McGuane, Bud Shrake   *Ph* John Alonzo   *Ed* George Grenville   *Mus* Ernest Gold   *Art Dir* Ron Hobbs
● Steve McQueen, Richard Farnsworth, Linda Evans, Billy Green Bush, Slim Pickens (Warner/First Artists)

Steve McQueen's *Tom Horn* is a sorry ending to the once high hopes of the star-studded founding of First Artists Prods.

If rumor be true, McQueen did not want to do *Horn* as his third pic to fulfill his founder's commitment, but was forced into it. True or not, he certainly looks like he's walking through the part.

Imagine a film that opens up with dialog that can't be heard at all, then proceeds to build up to a fistfight that's never seen, that cuts away to sunsets to fill in other scenes that have no dramatic point, and you have just the beginning of what's wrong with *Tom Horn*.

Pic [from Horn's *Life of Tom Horn, Government Scout and Interpreter*] takes up in the final days of the life of the legendary Western hero. And the only plus at all is a couple of good, bloody shoot-out sequences.

. . . .

■ **TOM JONES**

1963, 128 MINS, UK ◇ ▼

Dir Tony Richardson   *Prod* Tony Richardson   *Scr* John Osborne   *Ph* Walter Lassally   *Ed* Antony Gibbs   *Mus* John Addison
● Albert Finney, Susannah York, Hugh Griffith, Edith Evans, Joan Greenwood, Diane Cilento (Woodfall)

Based on Henry Fielding's enduring novel, story is set in Somerset, a West Country lush county, and in London during the 18th century. Hero is Tom Jones (Albert Finney), born in suspicious circumstances, with a maidservant dismissed because she is suspected of being his unwed mother. He is brought up by Squire Allworthy (George Devine) and leads a rollicking life in which

women play a prominent part before he finally escapes the gallows after a frameup.

The somewhat sprawling, bawdy and vivid screenplay of John Osborne provides some meaty acting opportunities and the thesps grasp their chances with vigorous zest. Finney slips through his adventures with an ebullient gusto that keeps the overlong film on its toes for most of the time. Hugh Griffith and Edith Evans as Squire Western and his sister ham disarmingly. Evans has some of the choicer cameos in the film.

Director Tony Richardson has occasionally pressed his luck with some over-deliberate arty camera bits. The music of John Addison is a trifle obtrusive and lacking in period style. An added bonus is Michael MacLiammoir putting over occasional narration with smooth wit and perception.
□ 1963: Best Picture

. . . .

■ **TOM SAWYER**

1930, 82 MINS, US

Dir John Cromwell   *Prod* Louis D. Lighton   *Scr* Sam Mintz, Grover Jones, William Slavens McNutt   *Ph* Charles Lang   *Ed* Alyson Shaffer   *Art Dir* Bernard Herzbrun, Robert O'Dell
● Jackie Coogan, Junior Durkin, Mitzi Green, Lucien Littlefield, Tully Marshall, Clara Blandick (Paramount)

The Mark Twain classic has been shrewdly molded to the screen. It somehow crystallizes the essence of a work that is timeless in its human appeal.

The picture is a real achievement for its director, John Cromwell, one of the stage directors who crashed Hollywood. Cromwell had a wild desire to do *Tom Sawyer* and the finished work has all the marks of a labor of love.

Picture was originally designed as the first of a series to bring the younger generation back to the talking screen. Story is splendidly acted by a great group of youngsters. Young Jackie Coogan plays Tom to the life but the secondary role of Junior Durkin as Huckleberry Finn [is also appealing]. Little Mitzi Green is rather lost in the child part of Becky Thatcher, built up somewhat for the film.

. . . .

■ **TOM SAWYER**

1973, 100 MINS, US ◇ ▼

Dir Don Taylor   *Prod* Arthur P. Jacobs   *Scr* Robert B. Sherman, Richard M. Sherman   *Ph* Frank Stanley   *Ed* Marion Rothman   *Mus* Robert B. Sherman, Richard M. Sherman   *Art Dir* Philip Jefferies
● Johnny Whitaker, Celeste Holm, Warren Oates, Jeff East, Jodie Foster, Lucille Benson (Reader's Digest/United Artists)

The strikingly handsome $2.5 million production, directed with discreet and appealing folksiness by Don Taylor, boasts an excellent cast, including Johnny Whitaker as Sawyer and Celeste Holm just sensational as Aunt Polly. Robert B. and Richard M. Sherman's script, music and lyrics maintain an all-age interest.

Jeff East is most effective as Huck Finn, making of that character an intriguing and contrasting personality. Jodie Foster is great as Becky Thatcher.

Holm returns to the screen in personal triumph. Few actresses project so well warmth-with-backbone, and a ladylike gentility not immune to kicking up the heels occasionally.

Also superbly cast is Warren Oates as Muff Potter, the likeable boozy philosopher. Oates and Holm keep the film together for older audiences.

. . . .

■ **TOM THUMB**

1958, 92 MINS, US ◇ ▼

Dir George Pal   *Prod* George Pal   *Scr* Ladislas Fodor   *Ph* Georges Perinal   *Ed* Frank Clarke   *Mus* Douglas Gamley, Ken Jones   *Art Dir* Elliot Scott

● Russ Tamblyn, Alan Young, Terry-Thomas, Peter Sellers, Jessie Matthews, June Thorburn (M-G-M)

The only thing lower case about this production is the Metro spelling of *tom thumb*. Otherwise, film is top-drawer, a comic fairy tale with music that stacks up alongside some of the Disney classics.

It is really a musical comedy. It has five good songs, two of them by Peggy Lee. There are musical production numbers, lavish and colorful.

The screenplay, from the Grimm Bros fairy tale, is as simple as it can be. A childless couple (Bernard Miles and Jessie Matthews) are past the age when they can expect to have a child of their own. They get a miniature son (Russ Tamblyn) when woodcutter Miles spares a special tree in the forest surrounding their home, and is rewarded by the Forest Queen (June Thorburn).

Complications in the story come from tom's size, only five and one-half inches. There are villains (Terry-Thomas and Peter Sellers) attempting to use tom for their own evil purposes. There is romance between Alan Young, a neighbor, and Thorburn, finally un-bewitched (or whatever the technical term is) from a fairy queen to a real, live girl.

Highlights of the production are the musical numbers and the special effects. Alex Romero staged the dance numbers, in which Tamblyn does some of the most athletic and exciting dancing he has had a chance at since *Seven Brides for Seven Brothers*. Georges Perinal's photography, with special effects by Tom Howard, catches all the fun and liveliness of the staging, and keeps tom's perspective firmly in hand. The miniature work was done in Hollywood, based on George Pal's Puppetoon figures, and the life-size work in London, with scoring there.

. . . .

■ **TOMB OF LIGEIA**

1965, 80 MINS, UK/US ◇ ▼

Dir Roger Corman   *Prod* Roger Corman   *Scr* Robert Towne   *Ph* Arthur Grant   *Ed* Alfred Cox   *Mus* Kenneth V. Jones
● Vincent Price, Elizabeth Shepherd, John Westbrook, Oliver Johnston, Derek Francis, Richard Vernon (American International)

More Poe but no go about sums up *Tomb of Ligeia*, a tedious and talky addition to American International's series of chillpix based on tales by the 19th century US author. Roger Corman produced and directed a script that resists analysis and lacks credibility, with all performances blah monotones and color lensing of no help. Widescreen pic tries serious supernatural approach minimizing gore angles, but it doesn't jell.

Amid ruins of English abbey lives widower Vincent Price, near grave of first wife Ligeia buried under strange circumstances some years before.

Price disappoints in attempt to project character's inner struggle to escape spell since no one knows why he acts kooky. Elizabeth Shepherd vacillates between too-stiff patrician elegance and unconvincing terror in role of second wife who is subjected to endless repetitions of brief, ineffective horror bits involving black cat, saucer of milk, and dead fox.

. . . .

■ **TOMMY**

1975, 111 MINS, UK ◇

Dir Ken Russell   *Prod* Robert Stigwood   *Scr* Ken Russell   *Ph* Dick Bush   *Ed* Stuart Baird   *Mus* Pete Townshend, John Entwistle, Keith Moon   *Art Dir* John Clark
● Ann-Margret, Oliver Reed, Roger Daltrey, Elton John, Eric Clapton, Jack Nicholson (Columbia)

Ken Russell's filmization of *Tommy* is spectacular in nearly every way. The enormous appeal of the original 1969 record album by The Who has been complemented in a superbly added visual dimension.

Young Tommy, traumatized when he sees his real father Robert Powell accidentally killed in an argument with stepfather Oliver Reed as mother Ann-Margret watches in horror, grows up amid an atmosphere of cruel exploitation and abuse. Even his miraculous recovery, and subsequent delusions of grandeur, simply extend the ripoff.

Among the cameo players, Elton John plays the pinball wizard and Eric Clapton is well featured as a preacher and Tina Turner virtually rips the screen apart with her animalistic Acid Queen.

....

■ TONIGHT FOR SURE

1982, 69 MINS, US ◇ ⓥ

Dir Francis Coppola   *Prod* Francis Coppola
Scr Francis Coppola   *Ph* Jack Hill   *Mus* Carmine Coppola   *Art Dir* Albert Locatelli, Barbara Cooper
● Don Kenney, Karl Schanzer, Virginia Gordon, Marti Renfro, Sandy Silver, Linda Gibson (Searchlight)

Francis Coppola's first feature film effort, the nudie pic *Tonight for Sure*, was released by Premier Pictures in 1962, thus preceding director's 'official' first film, *Dementia 13*, by at least a year.

There are really only two ways to approach viewing such a piece of juvenilia: to look for precocious signs of talent in the then-22-year-old filmmaker, and to consider its position in the late, unlamented 'nudie' genre.

Surprisingly, unlike most of the long-forgotten 'adults only' features of the period, *Tonight for Sure* is chock full of nudity. Storyline is ridiculous, to be sure. Two definitive dirty old men who fashion themselves as moral crusaders slip into a Hollywood burlesque house to plot the cessation of the lewd, indecent behavior transpiring therein.

In the meantime, they relate how they've each arrived at their righteous beliefs. Two yarns are cut in with stripteases being performed at the club. Predictably, it all ends with forces of puritanism raiding the joint.

....

■ TONY ROME

1967, 110 MINS, US ⓥ

Dir Gordon M. Douglas   *Prod* Aaron Rosenberg
Scr Richard L. Breen   *Ph* Joseph Biroc   *Ed* Robert Simpson   *Mus* Billy May   *Art Dir* Jack Martin Smith, James Roth
● Frank Sinatra, Jill St John, Richard Conte, Gena Rowlands, Simon Oakland, Jeffrey Lynn (20th Century-Fox/Arcola-Millfield)

Tony Rome is a flip gumshoe on the Miami scene, with a busy, heavily-populated script, zesty Gordon Douglas direction, and solid production values.

Marvin H. Albert's novel, *Miami Mayhem*, is scripted into a fast-moving whodunit which, per se, is far less intriguing than the individual scenes en route to climax. Credit Frank Sinatra's excellent style, and the production elements, for pulling it off.

Apart from some inside gags, including an overplugging of the beer with which Sinatra has a blurb tie-in, there is an abundance of double-entendre dialog which in reality can be taken only one way.

....

■ TOO FAR TO GO

1982, 100 MINS, US ◇

Dir Fielder Cook   *Prod* Chiz Schultz   *Scr* William Hanley   *Ph* Walter Lassally   *Ed* Eric Albertson
Mus Elizabeth Swados   *Art Dir* Leon Munier
● Michael Moriarty, Blythe Danner, Glenn Close, Ken Kercheval, Josef Sommer, Kathryn Walker (Sea Cliff/Polytel)

Produced for and originally broadcast in 1979 over network television, *Too Far to Go* is an affecting feature film dealing with marital breakup.

Scripted from stories by John Updike, pic utilizes witty, arch dialog in limning the separation and divorce of New England couple Richard and Joan Maple (Michael Moriarty and Blythe Danner). Flashbacks concisely detail happier times for the duo, with sexual matters ranging from infidelity to cessation of marital relations for several years.

Lead thesps shine, particularly Danner as the stronger of the couple. Moriarty is generally impressive within the limitations of a forced accent.

Outstanding in brief support are Josef Sommer as Richard's accountant, laying down the law on alimony, Kathryn Walker as a chatty, family friend, Doran Clark as the eldest daughter – a beautiful, very natural actress, and Thomas Hill, as Joan's psychiatrist.

....

■ TOO HOT TO HANDLE

1938, 106 MINS, US

Dir Jack Conway   *Prod* Lawrence Weingarten
Scr Lawrence Stallings, John Lee Mahin   *Ph* Harold Rosson   *Ed* Frank Sullivan   *Mus* Franz Waxman
● Clark Gable, Myrna Loy, Walter Pidgeon, Walter Connolly, Leo Carrillo, Marjorie Main (M-G-M)

Adventures of a newsreel cameraman are the basis for this Clark Gable-Myrna Loy co-starrer. It's a blazing action thriller aimed as a follow-up to same pair's click in *Test Pilot* (1938). It has driving excitement, crackling dialog, glittering performances and inescapable romantic pull.

The story is one of those familiar Hollywood triangle affairs, with Gable and Walter Pidgeon as the sizzling rival newsreelers and Loy the he-man's ideal who entangles their already frenzied competition. When Gable hijacks Pidgeon's girl and they both land in the doghouse through Pidgeon's efforts to get even, the girl goes to South America to search for her long-lost aviator brother.

Strange angle of the picture's implausibilities is that the story was written by Len Hammond, an executive of Fox Movietone newsreel, while Laurence Stallings co-author of the screenplay, is a former employee of the same outfit.

Best parts are the early sequences, all the way up to the sequence of a shipload of dynamite exploding directly underneath a tiny plane. Metro gives the picture one of its typically slick productions. Gable and Loy zoom through the leading parts with glittering persuasion.

....

■ TOO LATE BLUES

1962, 100 MINS, US

Dir John Cassavetes   *Prod* John Cassavetes   *Scr* John Cassavetes, Richard Carr   *Ph* Lionel Lindon   *Ed* Frank Bracht   *Mus* David Raksin   *Art Dir* Tambi Larsen
● Bobby Darin, Stella Stevens, Everett Chambers, Cliff Carnell, Seymour Cassel, Marilyn Clark (Paramount)

John Cassavetes' first Hollywood-made project shows a tendency to force casebook psychology on the characters at a loss of spontaneity. Thus an idealistic small-time jazz pianist and composer (Bobby Darin) loses his way when he is left by his girl due to a physically cowardly act. Used in an explanatory way there may be something psychologically right in this but it is somewhat too flat and contrived for acceptance in a film. Same goes for the flashy, good looking would-be singer, Stella Stevens.

Darin's group is shown playing engagements in orphanages and in a park where nobody comes. A chance for a record date is blown skyhigh when Darin's early insistence

on doing what he wants is compromised by his girl's quitting him after his cowardly actions in a pool room brawl. He becomes the gigolo of an aging woman but finds his spark dampened. He finally seeks out his old girl, now a tramp.

Film never makes it clear whether the Darin character truly has talent or whether he should accept what he has and do his best at it. Ambiguity also robs the pic of a lot of punch. Cassavetes shows at his best in party scenes where characters are deftly blocked in good natured 'getting-to-love-you' scenes.

Too Late Blues includes a neat jazz score by David Raksin. Dubbing for the musician-impersonating actors are Shelly Manne, Red Mitchell, Benny Carter, Uan Ramsey, Jimmy Bowles.

....

■ TOOTSIE

1982, 116 MINS, US ◇ ⓥ

Dir Sydney Pollack   *Prod* Sydney Pollack, Dick Richards   *Scr* Larry Gelbart, Murray Schisgal
Ph Owen Roizman   *Ed* Frederic Steinkamp, William Steinkamp   *Mus* Dave Grusin   *Art Dir* Peter Larkin
● Dustin Hoffman, Jessica Lange, Teri Garr, Dabney Coleman, Charles Durning, Bill Murray (Mirage/Punch/Columbia)

Tootsie is a lulu. Remarkably funny and entirely convincing, film pulls off the rare accomplishment of being an in-drag comedy which also emerges with three-dimensional characters.

Dustin Hoffman portrays a long-struggling New York stage actor whose 'difficult' reputation has relegated him to employment as a waiter and drama coach.

Brash but appealing actor's solution: audition for a popular soap opera as a woman. Becoming a hit on the show, 'Dorothy Michaels' develops into a media celebrity thanks to her forthright manner and 'different' personality. Hoffman finds it hard to devote much time to sort-of-girlfriend Teri Garr, and all the while is growing more deeply attracted to soap costar Jessica Lange.

Hoffman triumphs in what must stand as one of his most brilliant performances. His Dorothy is entirely plausible and, physically, reasonably appealing. But much more importantly, he gets across the enormous guts and determination required of his character to go through with the charade.

□ 1982: Best Picture (Nomination)

....

■ TOP GUN

1986, 110 MINS, US ◇ ⓥ

Dir Tony Scott   *Prod* Don Simpson, Jerry Bruckheimer
Scr Jim Cash, Jack Epps Jr.   *Ph* Jeffrey Kimball   *Ed* Billy Weber   *Mus* Harold Faltermeyer   *Art Dir* John F. DeCuir
● Tom Cruise, Kelly McGillis, Val Kilmer, Anthony Edwards, Tom Skerritt, Meg Ryan (Paramount)

Set in the world of naval fighter pilots, pic has strong visuals and pretty young people in stylish clothes and a non-stop soundtrack.

Cinematographer Jeffery Kimball and his team have assembled some exciting flight footage.

Tom Cruise is Maverick, a hot-shot fighter pilot with a mind of his own and something to prove, assigned to the prestigious Top Gun training school.

Along for the ride as a romantic interest is Kelly McGillis, a civilian astrophysicist brought in to teach the boys about negative Gs and inverted flight tanks. Cruise, however, has his sights set on other targets.

McGillis is blessed with an intelligent and mature face that doesn't blend that well with Cruise's one-note grinning. There is nothing menacing or complex about his character. Tom Skerritt turns in his usual nice job as the hardened but not hard flight instructor.

....

■ TOP HAT

1935, 101 MINS, US Ⓥ
Dir Mark Sandrich *Prod* Pandro S. Berman
Scr Dwight Taylor, Allan Scott *Ph* David Abel
Ed William Hamilton *Mus* Max Steiner (dir.)
Art Dir Van Nest Polglase, Carroll Clark
● Fred Astaire, Ginger Rogers, Edward Everett Horton, Erik Rhodes, Helen Broderick, Lucille Ball (RKO)

This one can't miss and the reasons are three – Fred Astaire, Irving Berlin's 11 songs and sufficient comedy between numbers to hold the film together.

Astaire's sock routines are up forward starting with 'No Strings'. He does this alone. It is the hot ditty of the batch, then 'Isn't it a Lovely Day?' with Ginger Rogers for probably the best dance they've ever done together, trailed in turn by the title item, 'Top Hat, White Tie and Tails', the boy number. It is the same number Astaire did in his Ziegfeld show *Smiles*, practically the only change being the melody.

But the danger sign is in the story and cast. Substitute Alice Brady for Helen Broderick and it's the same lineup of players as was in *The Gay Divorcee* (1934). Besides which the situations in the two scripts parallel each other closely.

For the rest of the cast, Edward Everett Horton bears the brunt and is the secondary pillar around which the story revolves. His is the comedy burden which he splits with Eric Blore, his valet, and Erik Rhodes as a dress designer.

Rogers never opens her mouth vocally until the concluding 'Piccolino'. She is again badly dressed while her facial makeup and various coiffeurs give her a hard appearance.
□ 1935: Best Picture (Nomination)

■ TOP SECRET!

1984, 90 MINS, US ◇ Ⓥ
Dir Jim Abrahams, David Zucker, Jerry Zucker
Prod Jon Davison, Hunt Lowry *Scr* Jim Abrahams, David Zucker, Jerry Zucker *Ph* Christopher Challis
Ed Bernard Gribble *Mus* Maurice Jarre *Art Dir* John Fenner
● Val Kilmer, Lucy Gutteridge, Christopher Villiers, Omar Sharif, Peter Cushing, Jeremy Kemp (Paramount)

Top Secret! is another bumptious tribute to all that was odd in old movies. Followers of the *Airplane!* trio will probably be happy and satisfied with this effort, yet short of overjoyed.

The attempted target this time is a combination of the traditional spy film and Elvis Presley musical romps, which in and of itself is funny to start with. And Val Kilmer proves a perfect blend of staunch hero and hothouse heartthrob.

But in a deliberate effort to do something different, the directors have unfortunately discarded the cast of matinee idols so closely identified with the originals.

Other than that, *Secret!* shares the same wonderful wacky attitude that allows just about any kind of gag to come flowing in and out of the picture at the strangest times.

■ TOPAZ

1969, 126 MINS, UK ◇ Ⓥ
Dir Alfred Hitchcock *Prod* Alfred Hitchcock
Scr Samuel Taylor *Ph* Jack Hildyard *Ed* William H. Ziegler *Mus* Maurice Jarre *Art Dir* Henry Bumstead
● Frederick Stafford, Dany Robin, John Vernon, Karin Dor, Michel Piccoli, Philippe Noiret (Universal)

Topaz tends to move more solidly and less infectiously than many of Alfred Hitchcock's best remembered pix. Yet Hitchcock brings in a full quota of twists and tingling moments.

Story, from Leon Uris' heavily-plotted novel, centres around high politics, with intrigue and trickery involving French, American, Russian and Cuban security. Action is triggered by defection of a Russian scientist in Copenhagen to the Americans.

The director has a comparatively little known, but impeccable cast, with Frederick Stafford scoring as the French security investigator and with neat work by Philippe Noiret and Michel Piccoli as two French Quislings. John Vernon is a powerful Cuban political leader.

Hitchcock concentrates less than usual on his cool, blonde heroine, and it's Karin Dor as a Cuban spy and mistress of Stafford who steals most of the thunder.

■ TOPKAPI

1964, 120 MINS, US ◇ Ⓥ
Dir Jules Dassin *Prod* Jules Dassin *Scr* Monja Danischewsky *Ph* Henri Alekan *Ed* Roger Dwyre
Mus Manos Hadjidakis *Art Dir* Max Douy
● Melina Mercouri, Peter Ustinov, Maximilian Schell, Robert Morley, Akim Tamiroff, Gilles Segal (United Artists/Filmways)

Jules Dassin has taken a minor novel by Eric Ambler [*The Light of Day*] and turned it into a delightful and suspenseful comedy spoof of his own *Rififi*

The band of thieves whose adventures make *Topkapi* are a motley crew indeed. Besides Melina Mercouri, it includes Maximilian Schell, master thief; Robert Morley, Gilles Segal and Jess Hahn. Added later, although it takes him some time and a bit of adventure to realize it, Peter Ustinov is an unwitting accomplice.

The basically simple plot, which is rich in detail and background, has the gang attempting to steal a fabulous jeweled dagger from the Topkapi Palace museum in Istanbul. The actual theft is depicted in a long sequence reminiscent of the one in *Rififi* but with a bit more levity.

Mercouri has a holiday in a role that asks her to be equally enamored of gems and males. Schell, surprisingly, plays his role somewhat tongue-in-cheek, never evidencing more than a surface interest in anything (including Mercouri), other than his work. Ustinov has probably the meatiest part in the film and one that allows him to use many of the unsubtleties in dominating scenes he has at his command.

■ TOPPER

1937, 98 MINS, US Ⓥ
Dir Norman Z. McLeod *Prod* Hal Roach *Scr* Jack Jevne, Eric Hatch, Eddie Moran *Ph* Norbert Brodine
Ed William Terhune *Mus* Arthur Norton
● Constance Bennett, Cary Grant, Roland Young, Billie Burke, Alan Mowbray, Eugene Pallette (Roach/M-G-M)

With the assistance of Norman McLeod, as director, Hal Roach has produced a weird and baffling tale of spiritualism. It is entitled *Topper*, from a story by the late Thorne Smith. It is carefully made, excellently photographed, and adroitly employs mechanical illusions and trick sound effects.

Story is about the adventures, among living persons, of a young married couple, George and Marion Kerby, who are killed in an automobile smashup as the climax of a wild night of drinking and carousing. Their astral bodies rise from the ruins, and they agree that until they have done someone a good deed they are likely to remain indefinitely in a state of double exposure.

Reviewing the possibilities for charitable action, they decide that their friend, Cosmo Topper, a hen-pecked bank president, who has lived a dull, routine life, shall have the benefit of their assistance.

Performances are usually good. Cary Grant and Constance Bennett, as the reincarnated Kerbys, do their assignments with great skill. Roland Young carries the brunt of the story and does it well. In the title role, he is the docile, good citizen until the transformation of his personality changes him into a dashing man about town.

■ TORA! TORA! TORA!

1970, 144 MINS, US ◇ Ⓥ
Dir Richard Fleischer, Toshio Masuda, Kinji Fukasaku
Prod Elmo Williams *Scr* Larry Forrester, Hideo Oguni, Ryuzo Kikushima *Ph* Charles F. Wheeler, Sinsaku Himeda, Masamichi Satch, Osami Furuya *Ed* James E. Newcom, Pembroke J. Herring, Inoue Chikaya
Mus Jerry Goldsmith *Art Dir* Jack Martin Smith, Yoshiro Muraki, Richard Day, Taizoh Kawashima
● Martin Balsam, Soh Yamamura, Joseph Cotten, Tatsuya Mihashi, E.G. Marshall, Takahiro Tamura (20th Century-Fox)

Lavish ($25 million) and meticulous restaging of the Japanese airborne attack on Pearl Harbor on 7 December 1941 constitutes a brilliant logistics achievement which is not generally matched by the overall artistic handling of the accompanying dramatic narrative.

Effect of the story [from *Tora! Tora! Tora!* by Gordon W. Prange and *The Broken Seal* by Ladislas Farago] seems to prove that the Japanese government, while somewhat divided internally, at least had some unity of purpose in its expansion plans.

Both overall director Richard Fleischer and his Japanese counterparts do a dull job, and the monotonously low-key tone of scene after scene almost suggests that each was filmed without a sense of ultimate slotting in the finished form.

■ TORCH SONG TRILOGY

1988, 117 MINS, US ◇ Ⓥ
Dir Paul Bogart *Prod* Howard Gottfried *Scr* Harvey Fierstein *Ph* Mikael Salomon *Ed* Nicholas C. Smith
Mus Peter Matz *Art Dir* Richard Hoover
● Anne Bancroft, Matthew Broderick, Harvey Fierstein, Brian Kerwin, Karen Young (New Line)

Harvey Fierstein repeats his Tony Award-winning performance as Arnold Beckoff, a flamboyant drag queen looking for love and respect. Originated as separately staged one-acts, the play, when finally mounted as a unified work in 1982, proved bracing in its frank depiction of gay sex life, both promiscuous and committed.

Nervous, mannered, gravelly voiced, overly sensitive, campy and with a taste for eyerolling rivaled only by Groucho Marx in modern showbiz annals, Arnold appears a bit gunshy of romance, but allows himself to be picked up in a gay bar by Ed (Brian Kerwin), a good-looking, straight-seeming fellow who openly announces his bisexuality.

This doesn't stop Arnold from falling head over heels for his Middle American catch, but causes him endless pain when he discovers Ed with a young woman, Laurel (Karen Young).

In what is effectively Act Two, Arnold meets Alan (Matthew Broderick), to him an impossibly good-looking kid who used to be a hustler and actively seeks out Arnold for his human, as opposed to superficial, qualities.

Act Three, the most conventional of the sections, is given over to Arnold's efforts to handle an adopted teenage son and sort out his strained relations with his mother (Anne Bancroft).

■ TORCHLIGHT

1984, 91 MINS, US ◇ Ⓥ
Dir Tom Wright *Prod* Joel Douglas *Scr* Pamela Sue Martin, Eliza Moorman *Ph* Alex Phillips *Mus* Michael Cannon *Art Dir* Craig Stearns

● Pamela Sue Martin, Steve Railsback, Ian McShane, Al Corley, Rita Taggart, Arnie Moore (UCO)

Torchlight is largely a family affair. Pamela Sue Martin, who costars with Steve Railsback and Ian McShane, is cowriter of the screenplay, as well as taking associate producer credit, while her husband, Manuel Rojas, is exec producer. Between them they've fashioned a film which opens on a deceptively light-hearted note but develops in downbeat style.

In its opening sequences, the plot depicts the love-at-first-sight romance and marriage of Martin and Railsback. Enter McShane, a sinister and larger than life pusher, and Railsback's downfall progresses until he becomes a physical and mental wreck, left without wife or home.

Martin has written for herself a role which allows her to reach the highs and lows of elation and despair. Railsback has a demanding role and mainly fills it convincingly, but McShane as the sinister pusher is a grossly overdrawn character.

■ **TORN CURTAIN**

1966, 126 MINS, US ◇ Ⓥ
Dir Alfred Hitchcock *Prod* Alfred Hitchcock *Scr* Brian Moore *Ph* John F. Warren *Ed* Bud Hoffman *Mus* John Addison *Art Dir* Hein Heckroth
● Paul Newman, Julie Andrews, Lila Kedrova, Hansjoerg Felmy, Tamara Toumanova, Wolfgang Kieling (Universal)

Torn Curtain is an okay Cold War suspenser with Paul Newman as a fake defector to East Germany in order to obtain Communist defense secrets. Julie Andrews is his femme partner. Alfred Hitchcock's direction emphasizes suspense and ironic comedy flair but some good plot ideas are marred by routine dialog, and a too relaxed pace contributes to a dull overlength.

Brian Moore scripted from his original story about a top US physicist who essays a public defection in order to pick the brains of a Communist wizard. Writing, acting and direction make clear from the outset that Newman is loyal, although about one-third of pic passes before this is made explicit in dialog. This early telegraphing diminishes suspense.

Hitchcock freshens up his bag of tricks in a good potpourri which becomes a bit stale through a noticeable lack of zip and pacing.

■ **TOTAL RECALL**

1990, 109 MINS, US Ⓥ
Dir Paul Verhoeven *Prod* Buzz Feitshans, Ronald Shusett *Scr* Ronald Shusett, Dan O'Bannon, Gary Oldman *Ph* Jost Vacano *Ed* Frank J. Urioste *Mus* Jerry Goldsmith *Art Dir* William Sandell
● Arnold Schwarzenegger, Rachel Ticotin, Sharon Stone, Ronny Cox, Michael Ironside, Marshall Bell (Carolco)

Estimates of the cost of this futuristic extravaganza range from $60 to $70 million making it one of the most expensive pics ever made. There are gargantuan sets repping Mars and a futuristic Earth society, grotesque creatures galore, genuinely weird and mostly seamless visual effects, and enough gunshots, grunts and explosions to keep anyone in a high state of nervous exhilaration.

The story is actually a good one, taking off from Phillip K. Dick's celebrated sci-fi tale *We Can Remember It for You Wholesale*.

Arnold Schwarzenegger's character, a working stiff in the year 2084, keeps having these strange nightmares about living on Mars, and it transpires that he once worked in the colony as an intelligence agent before rebelling against dictator Ronny Cox. Schwarzenegger had most, but not quite all, of his bad memories erased and was sent to

Earth to work on a construction crew, with a sexy but treacherous wife (Sharon Stone).

A visit to a mind-altering travel agency named Rekall Inc. alerts Schwarzenegger to the truth, setting him off on a rampage through Earth and Mars with the help of equally tough female sidekick Rachel Ticotin.

The fierce and unrelenting pace, accompanied by a tongue-in-cheek strain of humor in the roughhouse screenplay, keeps the film moving like a juggernaut.

■ **TOUCH, THE**

1971, 113 MINS, SWEDEN/US ◇ Ⓥ
Dir Ingmar Bergman *Prod* Ingmar Bergman *Scr* Ingmar Bergman *Ph* Sven Nykvist *Ed* Siv Kanaly-Lundgren *Mus* Jan Johannson
● Bibi Andersson, Elliott Gould, Max von Sydow, Sheila Reid, Steffan Hallerstram, Maria Nolgard (ABC/Persona)

Shot in English with occasional Swedish dialog and splendidly acted and lensed, *The Touch* is both a romantic film of great poignancy and strength and an example of masterful cinema honed down to deceptively simple near-perfection.

In telling what is basically a straight triangle tale (bored wife, busy husband, 'interesting' and available friend) Bergman seems to be appealing to and aiming primarily at the emotions rather than the intellect.

Not unexpectedly, Bergman's cast is superb. Bibi Andersson walks away with pic thanks to one of those immense, bigger-than-life performances. Rarely has the moving anguish of a trysting woman been so stirringly caught. Elliott Gould is a perfect choice as the somewhat neurotic foreign archeologist who, despite oafish manners, selfishness and instability, fascinates and attracts her. Max von Sydow does expected wonders with the normally unplayable role of the silently strong husband.

■ **TOUCH AND GO**

1986, 101 MINS, US ◇ Ⓥ
Dir Robert Mandel *Prod* Stephen Friedman *Scr* Alan Ormsby, Bob Sand, Harry Colomby *Ph* Richard H. Kline *Ed* Walt Mulconery *Mus* Sylvester Levay *Art Dir* Charles Rosen
● Michael Keaton, Maria Conchita Alonso, Ajay Naidu, Maria Tucci (Tri-Star)

Touch and Go mixes humor, heart and considerable hokum in an engaging story matching an unusually serious Michael Keaton and zesty Latin star Maria Conchita Alonso as lovers in spite of themselves.

Pic features Keaton as a hot-shot hockey jock with the Chicago Eagles. His regimen gets disrupted one night when a punk kid (Ajay Naidu) acts as the innocent front for his thug friends as they try to mug the sports star. Keaton fends the rascals off and he's left throttling the 11-year-old. But the kid's a charmer and Keaton returns him home to his slummy neighborhood and to Mom (Alonso) for discipline, opening the way for romance. Rapport between the disrespectful kid and Keaton unfolds immediately.

■ **TOUCH OF CLASS, A**

1973, 106 MINS, UK ◇ Ⓥ
Dir Melvin Frank *Prod* Melvin Frank *Scr* Melvin Frank, Jack Rose *Ph* Austin Dempster *Ed* Bill Butler *Mus* John Cameron *Art Dir* Terry Marsh
● George Segal, Glenda Jackson, Paul Sorvino, Hildegard Neil, Cec Linder, K. Callan (Brut)

A Touch of Class is sensational. Director, writer and producer Melvin Frank has accomplished precisely what Peter Bogdanovich did in *What's Up, Doc?* – revitalizing, updating and invigorating an earlier film genre to smash results.

Segal herein justifies superbly a reputation for comedy ability while Jackson's full-spectrum talent is again confirmed. An accidental London meeting between George Segal and Glenda Jackson leads to a casual pass by Segal, thence (through a series of hilarious complications, including wife, in-laws, and old friends) to a frustrated rendezvous in a Spanish resort. Pair's romance flourishes into a full-blown affair at home, with Segal wearing himself out dashing between two beds.

The visual and verbal antics are supported by just enough underlying character depth to keep the film on a solid credible basis, setting up the plot for its tender, bittersweet climax.
□ 1973: Best Picture (Nomination)

■ **TOUCH OF EVIL**

1958, 95 MINS, US Ⓥ
Dir Orson Welles *Prod* Albert Zugsmith *Scr* Orson Welles *Ph* Russell Metty *Ed* Virgil M. Vogel, Aaron Stell, Edward Curtiss *Mus* Henry Mancini *Art Dir* Alexander Golitzen, Robert Clatworthy
● Charlton Heston, Janet Leigh, Orson Welles, Joseph Calleia, Akim Tamiroff, Joanna Moore (Universal)

Touch of Evil smacks of brilliance but ultimately flounders in it. Taken scene by scene, there is much to be said for this filmization of Whit Masterson's novel, *Badge of Evil*. Orson Welles' script contains some hard-hitting dialog; his use of low key lighting is effective, and Russell Metty's photography is fluid and impressive; and Henry Mancini's music is poignant. But *Touch of Evil* proves it takes more than good scenes to make a good picture.

Welles portrays an American cop who has the keen reputation of always getting his man. Before you know it, he's hot on the trail of those scoundrels who blew to smithereens the wealthy 'owner' of a small Mexican border town. Charlton Heston, a bigwig in the Mexican government, just happens to be around with his new American bride (Janet Leigh) and gets himself rather involved in the proceedings, feeling the dynamiting has something to do with a narcotics racket he's investigating.

Off his rocker since his wife was murdered years ago, Welles supposedly is deserving of a bit of sympathy. At least, there's a hint of it in dialog, even though it isn't seen in his characterization. Aside from this, he turns in a unique and absorbing performance. Heston keeps his plight the point of major importance, combining a dynamic quality with a touch of Latin personality. Leigh, sexy as all get-out, switches from charm to fright with facility in a capable portrayal. Dennis Weaver, as the night man, is fine though exaggerated.

Spicing up the production are a single closeup of Zsa Zsa Gabor as a non-stripped stripper, a word or two from Joseph Cotten who's slipped in without screen credit, and a provocative few minutes with gypsy-looking Marlene Dietrich. Dietrich is rather sultry and fun to watch, even though it's somewhat incongruous to see her walk into the Mexican darkness at the picture's finish, turn to wave, then wail, 'Adios.'

■ **TOUCH OF LOVE, A**

1969, 102 MINS, UK ◇
Dir Waris Hussein *Prod* Max J. Rosenberg, Milton Subotsky *Scr* Margaret Drabble *Ph* Peter Suschitzky *Ed* Bill Blunden *Mus* Michael Dress *Art Dir* Tony Curtis
● Sandy Dennis, Ian McKellen, Michael Coles, John Standing, Eleanor Bron (Palomar)

Sharply scripted by Margaret Drabble from her novel [*The Millstone*], story deals with a well-educated philosophy student whose first all-the-way seduction by a chance acquaintance leaves her pregnant, while each of her steady but platonic suitors thinks his rival is the father.

Pic details girl's solo battle against society and herself to decide whether to keep the child and bring it up sans a father.

Key factor, aside from a fine script, trim direction by newcomer Waris Hussein and moody lensing, lies in the Sandy Dennis performance, which is pin-point accurate in conveying the tremendous inner strength which helps her character win through against hostile – or disinterested – society and family.

She gets very strong support here from Ian McKellen as the unknowing father.

••••••••••••••••••••••••••••••••

■ TOUGH GUYS

1986, 104 MINS, US ◇ Ⓥ
Dir Jeff Kanew   *Prod* Joe Wizan   *Scr* James Orr, Jim Cruickshank   *Ph* King Baggot   *Ed* Kaja Fehr   *Mus* James Newton Howard   *Art Dir* Todd Hallowell
● Burt Lancaster, Kirk Douglas, Charles Durning, Alexis Smith, Dana Carvey, Darlanne Fluegel
(Touchstone/Silver Screen/Bryna)

Tough Guys is unalloyed hokum that proves a sad waste of talent on the parts of co-stars Burt Lancaster and Kirk Douglas.

The two venerable thesps, both 70-ish and looking fit and alert, turn up here as Harry Doyle and Archie Long, two gentlemen crooks celebrated in the annals of American crime for having been the last outlaws to rob a train.

Pic pokes along with Lancaster provoking havoc at his old folks' home and Douglas quitting a series of jobs in disgust until scripters decide that perhaps a plot would be nice, so the guys get together and – surprise – decide to rob the train again.

It's all silly, meaningless and vaguely depressing, since the awareness lingers throughout that both actors are capable of much, much more than is demanded of them here.

••••••••••••••••••••••••••••••••

■ TOUGH GUYS DON'T DANCE

1987, 108 MINS, US ◇ Ⓥ
Dir Norman Mailer   *Prod* Menahem Golan, Yoram Globus   *Scr* Norman Mailer   *Ph* John Bailey   *Ed* Debra McDermott   *Mus* Angelo Badalamenti   *Art Dir* Armin Ganz
● Ryan O'Neal, Isabella Rossellini, Debra Sandlund, Wings Hauser, John Bedford Lloyd (Cannon/Zoetrope)

Tough Guys is part parody and part serious with a nasty streak running right down the middle.

Set in a small coastal town in Massachusetts in the sort of place where everyone knows everyone else's business, and for Tim Madden (Ryan O'Neal) business is bad, story has something to do with a botched drug deal, men who love the wrong women and women who love the wrong men.

In the course of playing its hand, Madden's wealthy wife (Debra Sandlund), a washed up porno star (Frances Fisher), a suicidal southerner (John Bedford Lloyd), a gay sugar daddy (R. Patrick Sullivan) and a corrupt police chief (Wings Hauser) all get blown away.

Film is at its best when it's tongue-in-cheek and it's fun to listen to the guys talk tough. And the biggest, baddest, nastiest one of them all is Lawrence Tierney as O'Neal's father, a man who won't dance for anyone.

••••••••••••••••••••••••••••••••

■ TOVARICH

1937, 94 MINS, US
Dir Anatole Litvak   *Prod* Robert Lord   *Scr* Casey Robinson   *Ph* Charles Lang   *Ed* Henri Rust   *Mus* Max Steiner
● Claudette Colbert, Charles Boyer, Basil Rathbone, Anita Louise, Melville Cooper, Isabel Jeans (Warner)

With a distinguished record in legit theatres, both here and abroad, [Jacques Deval's play] *Tovarich* emerges from its Warner filming as a piece of popular entertainment, plus the very considerable drawing value of Claudette Colbert and Charles Boyer. Story changes are not radical (one or two modifications being prompted by censorship restrictions).

Boyer's diction is difficult to comprehend in several places. His accent is enhanced by the fact that only he, of all the players, speaks rapidly. Only in brief moments does Colbert convey the dignity, bearing and fine humor of a Russian imperial princess.

Litvak seems imbued with the idea that he had to make *Tovarich* look like a big picture, whereas the story of the royal refugee couple, who enter domestic service in the household of a Paris banker, is a yarn of charming and finely shaded characterizations.

Of the supporting cast Melville Cooper, as the banker, and Basil Rathbone as a commissar contribute splendid characterizations.

••••••••••••••••••••••••••••••••

■ TOWERING INFERNO, THE

1974, 165 MINS, US ◇ Ⓥ
Dir John Guillermin, Irwin Allen   *Prod* Irwin Allen   *Scr* Stirling Silliphant   *Ph* Fred Koenekamp, Joseph Biroc   *Ed* Harold F. Kress, Carl Kress   *Mus* John Williams   *Art Dir* William Creber
● Steve McQueen, Paul Newman, William Holden, Faye Dunaway, Robert Vaughn, Richard Chamberlain (20th Century-Fox/Warner)

The Towering Inferno is one of the greatest disaster pictures made, a personal and professional triumph for producer Irwin Allen. The $14 million cost has yielded a truly magnificent production which complements but does not at all overwhelm a thoughtful personal drama.

The strategy of casting expensive talent pays off handsomely. Steve McQueen, as the fireman in charge of extinguishing the runaway fire in a 130-story San Francisco building, Paul Newman, as the heroic and chagrined architect of the glass and concrete pyre, William Holden as its builder, and Faye Dunaway, as Newman's fiancee, get and deserve their star billing.

Both 20th and WB pooled their finances and their separate but similar book acquisitions – Richard Martin Stern's *The Tower* and *The Glass Inferno*, by Thomas N. Scortia and Frank M. Robinson – to effect a true example of synergy.
□ 1974: Best Picture (Nomination)

••••••••••••••••••••••••••••••••

■ TOWN LIKE ALICE, A

1956, 117 MINS, UK Ⓥ
Dir Jack Lee   *Scr* W.P. Lipscomb, Richard Mason   *Ph* Geoffrey Unsworth   *Ed* Sidney Hayers   *Mus* Matyas Seiber
● Virginia McKenna, Peter Finch, Maureen Swanson, Renee Houston, Marie Lohr, Jean Anderson (Rank)

Filmed largely on location in Malaya and Australia, story is based on Neville Shute's novel of the same name. Film describes how a handful of women and children were forced-marched through Malaya at the hands of the Japanese. For months on end they tramped from one camp to another, through swamp and storm, through dust and heat. Many died on the roadside, but the few survivors eventually found refuge in a village after their guard had succumbed.

During the period of their cross-country march the women and kids are befriended by a couple of Australian POWs who have been assigned to truck driving duties for the Japs, and over a shared cigarette and an exchange of minor confidence, a bond develops between Virginia McKenna and Peter Finch.

The subject matter is necessarily grim, but wherever possible the script and direction endeavor to infuse a touch of lighter relief. The focus, however, is almost constantly on the trials of the women and children as they fight against famine and disease.

••••••••••••••••••••••••••••••••

■ TOWN WITHOUT PITY

1961, 112 MINS, US
Dir Gottfried Reinhardt   *Prod* Gottfried Reinhardt   *Scr* Silvia Reinhardt, Georg Hurdalek   *Ph* Kurt Hasse   *Ed* Hermann Haller   *Mus* Dimitri Tiomkin   *Art Dir* Rolf Zehetbauer
● Kirk Douglas, E.G. Marshall, Robert Blake, Richard Jaeckel, Christine Kaufmann, Frank Sutton (United Artists/Mirisch/Gloria)

At face value, *Town without Pity* appears to be a straight courtroom drama treatment of a gang rape case and its repercussions on a German community incensed over the fact that the rapists are American GIs and the victim a local girl. But the production attempts to go much deeper than that.

The screenplay, based on an adaptation by Jan Lustig of Manfred Gregor's novel *The Verdict*, dramatizes the story of a military defense attorney who, in attempting to properly perform his task, must against his will bring about the destruction of an innocent (the raped girl), victim of her own human fallibility and the fallibility of German witnesses whose pride, hatreds and insecurities lead them to lie, exaggerate or conceal on the stand.

A picture that raises important moral and judicial questions must do so in terms of rounded, dimensional characters if it is to register with impact. *Town without Pity* fails in this regard.

Kirk Douglas does an able job as the defense attorney. Likewise E.G. Marshall as the prosecutor. There is an especially earnest and intense portrayal of one of the defendants by Robert Blake. The others – less prominent – are skillfully delineated by Richard Jaeckel, Frank Sutton and Mal Sondock. Christine Kaufmann, a rare combination of sensual beauty and sensitivity, handles her assignment – the victim – with sincerity and animation.

••••••••••••••••••••••••••••••••

■ TOXIC AVENGER, THE

1985, 100 MINS, US ◇ Ⓥ
Dir Michael Herz, Samuel Weil   *Prod* Lloyd Kaufman, Michael Herz   *Scr* Joe Ritter, Lloyd Kaufman, Gay Terry, Stuart Strutin   *Ph* James London, Lloyd Kaufman   *Ed* Richard W. Haines   *Mus* Marc Katz (consult.)   *Art Dir* Barry Shapiro, Alexandra Mazur
● Andree Maranda, Mitchell Cohen, Jennifer Baptist, Cindy Manion, Robert Prichard, Mark Torgl (Troma)

This madcap spoof on *The Incredible Hulk* is an outlandish mix of gory violence and realistic special effects.

The story concerns Melvin, a 90-pound weakling who works in a body-building club pushing around a mop, and who is hated by the muscular and healthy types that flaunt their bodies before him and the audience.

Following some rather pointless shenanigans in which Melvin is humiliated by the bodybuilders, he jumps out of a window and lands in a truck carrying toxic waste. This transforms him into a hulking monster, but one seeking only to right wrongs in his town and persecute the meanies.

••••••••••••••••••••••••••••••••

■ TOYS IN THE ATTIC

1963, 88 MINS, US Ⓥ
Dir George Roy Hill   *Prod* Walter Mirisch   *Scr* James Poe   *Ph* Joseph F. Biroc   *Ed* Stuart Gilmore   *Mus* George Duning   *Art Dir* Cary Odell
● Dean Martin, Geraldine Page, Yvette Mimieux,

Wendy Hiller, Gene Tierney, Frank Silvera (United Artists)

Toys in the Attic is a somewhat watered-down version of Lillian Hellman's play, but enough of the original emotional savagery has been retained to satisfy those who prefer their melodramatic meat raw and chewy. *Toys* is laid in the Deep South and liberally crammed with such sick-sick cargo as incest, adultery, imbecility, lust and a few other popular folk pleasantries.

Principal tampering scenarist James Poe has done with Hellman's neatly constructed, momentum-gathering play about a New Orleans household shattered by latent incest and corrosive possessiveness is in altering the ending.

Hellman's heavyweight drama examines the tragedy that transpires as a result of a spinster sister's secret lust for her younger brother, whose monetarily-motivated marriage to a simple-minded girl sets in operation the mechanism for his ultimate disaster. The new ending is thoroughly artificial. Otherwise, Poe's additions and subtractions are sound.

George Roy Hill has made an error or two along the way, but generally his direction is taut, progressive and fastpaced considering this is a very talky, confined piece. The performances are fine. Geraldine Page gives a powerful portrayal in the difficult and unappealing role of the venomous sister. Wendy Hiller, in part of the perceptive older sister, holds her own in the emotional give and take.

Dean Martin is ingratiating as the ne'er-do-well brother who almost does well. Yvette Mimieux gives another of her misty, innocent, childlike characterizations.

■ **TRACK 29**

1988, 86 MINS, UK ◇ Ⓥ
Dir Nicolas Roeg *Prod* Rick McCallum *Scr* Dennis Potter *Ph* Alex Thomson *Ed* Tony Lawson *Mus* Stanley Myers *Art Dir* David Brockhurst
● Theresa Russell, Gary Oldman, Sandra Bernhard, Christopher Lloyd, Colleen Camp, Seymour Cassel (HandMade)

Though clearly of above-average quality in direction, psychology and Theresa Russell's 3-D performance as a childless housewife with a dark secret in the closet, *Track 29* is connected closely to the classic American smalltown horror film.

Screenplay is set in a Southern town where strange things happen every day. Linda (Russell) and husband Henry (Christopher Lloyd) are at odds over Linda's burning desire for a child and Henry's preference for his model trains. He also enjoys being spanked by Nurse Stein (Sandra Bernhard).

Into this world of normal absurdity arrives a stranger. Young Martin (Gary Oldman) convinces Linda he's her baby boy born out of wedlock and taken from her at birth, but viewer begins to have doubts that the appearing-disappearing weirdo isn't a figment of her imagination.

Perverse humor is the keynote of the Oedipal complexed duo, who spend a long day going to bars, exchanging unplatonic caresses, and acting out their traumas. Russell and Oldman are consummate thesps able to reach the edge of frenzy (and beyond) while remaining fun and original.

■ **TRADER HORN**

1931, 123 MINS, US
Dir W.S. Van Dyke *Scr* Richard Schayer, Cyril Hume, Dale Van Every, J.T. Neville *Ph* Clyde De Vinna *Ed* Ben Lewis *Mus* Charles Maxwell
● Harry Carey, Edwina Booth, Duncan Renaldo, Mutia Omoolu, Olive Golden, C. Aubrey Smith (M-G-M)

A good-looking animal picture. The story doesn't mean anything other than a connecting link for a series of sequences which, at one point, become nothing more than an out-and-out lecture tour, as various herds of animals are described by the voice of Harry Carey, in the title role. Studio has simply interpreted the original novel [by Aloysius Horn and Ethelreda Lewis] as it saw fit, lifting a couple of characters therefrom and putting them through a succession of narrow escapes from four-footed enemies and a cannibal tribe.

Light love vein is introduced between Carey's young companion, Duncan Renaldo, and Edwina Booth as the queen of a tribe from whom she and the men escape when her followers turn on her after she countermands an order of death by torture for Carey, Renaldo and Rencharo, the former's native gun boy.

Booth, very easy to look at, prances through the jungle in scanty raiment, knowing only the gutteral language of the blacks. The escape of the quartet immediately goes into a chase, during which Carey doubles back to act as decoy so the boy and girl can get away. Finish is the successful reaching of a river settlement where the youth and former tribal queen board a small river steamer bound for civilization, while Carey, as Trader Horn, prepares to go back into the jungle.

Sound effects are outstanding. Andy Anderson, the sound man, accompanied director W.S. Van Dyke's unit to Africa. The camera work is also swell marksmanship.
□ 1930/31: Best Picture (Nomination)

■ **TRADING PLACES**

1983, 106 MINS, US ◇ Ⓥ
Dir John Landis *Prod* Aaron Russo *Scr* Timothy Harris, Herschel Weingrod *Ph* Robert Paynter *Ed* Malcolm Campbell *Mus* Elmer Bernstein *Art Dir* Gene Rudolf
● Dan Aykroyd, Eddie Murphy, Ralph Bellamy, Don Ameche, Denholm Elliott, Jamie Lee Curtis (Paramount)

Trading Places is a light romp geared up by the schtick shifted by Dan Aykroyd and Eddie Murphy. Happily, it's a pleasure to report also that even those two popular young comics couldn't have brought this one off without the contributions of three veterans – Ralph Bellamy, Don Ameche and the droll Englishman, Denholm Elliott.

Aykroyd plays a stuffy young financial wizard who runs a Philadelphia commodities house for two continually scheming brothers, Bellamy and Ameche.

Conversely, Murphy has grown up in the streets and lives on the con, including posing as a blind, legless veteran begging outside Aykroyd's private club.

On a whim motivated by disagreement over the importance of environment vs breeding, Bellamy bets Ameche that Murphy could run the complex commodities business just as well as Aykroyd, given the chance. Conversely, according to the bet, Aykroyd would resort to crime and violence if suddenly all friends and finances were stripped away from him.

So their scheme proceeds and both Aykroyd and Murphy are in top form reacting to their new situations.

The only cost, however, is a mid-section stretch without laughs, still made enjoyable by the presence of Jamie Lee Curtis as a good-hearted hooker who befriends Aykroyd.

■ **TRAIL OF THE LONESOME PINE, THE**

1936, 100 MINS, US ◇
Dir Henry Hathaway *Prod* Walter Wanger *Scr* Grover Jones, Harvey Thew, Horace McCoy *Ph* W. Howard Greene, Robert C. Bruce *Ed* Robert Bischoff *Mus* Hugo Friedhofer, Gerard Carbonara *Art Dir* Alexander Toluboff
● Sylvia Sidney, Henry Fonda, Fred MacMurray, Fred Stone, Nigel Bruce, Beulah Bondi (Paramount)

The Trail of the Lonesome Pine is a good show, the first all-Technicolor feature produced 100% outdoors.

Director Henry Hathaway has sympathetically dealt with the ignorance of the mountaineer folk. His dialogicians, following the John Fox Jr original play – have faithfully preserved the reticent, curt mien of the feuding Tolliver and Falin clans.

Sylvia Sidney's performances as the 'billy looker is uncompromising in every detail. After a brief spell of schooling in Louisville, where Fred MacMurray has sent her, she reverts to type. Upon hearing how Buddy (Spanky McFarland) has been murdered, she too cries for a Falin's blood. Henry Fonda, as her mountaineer vis-a-vis, is equally consistent in his scowling hate for the Falin clan, as well as for the advent of the city engineer (MacMurray). Latter is capital in his dealings with the ignorant hillbillies and his affection for June Tolliver (Sidney).

■ **TRAIL OF THE PINK PANTHER**

1983, 97 MINS, UK ◇ Ⓥ
Dir Blake Edwards *Prod* Blake Edwards, Tony Adams *Scr* Frank Waldman, Tom Waldman, Blake Edwards, Geoffrey Edwards *Ph* Dick Bush *Ed* Alan Jones *Mus* Henry Mancini *Art Dir* Peter Mullins
● Peter Sellers, David Niven, Herbert Lom, Richard Mulligan, Joanna Lumley, Capucine (Titan)

A patchwork of out-takes, reprised clips and new connective footage, *Trail of the Pink Panther* is a thin, peculiar picture unsupported by the number of laughs one is accustomed to in this series. Stitched together after Peter Sellers' death, this is by a long way the slightest of the six Inspector Clouseau efforts.

Story's structure is strange, to say the least. The fabulous Pink Panther gem is stolen yet again from its vulnerable resting place in an Arab museum, which sparks immediate interest from the haplessly effective French detective.

Opening two reels are devoted to supposed out-take footage of Sellers trying on a disguise and on attempting to relieve himself in an airplane lavatory despite the encumbrance of an ungainly cast.

After about 40 minutes, Clouseau's Lugash-bound plane is reported missing. French television reporter Joanna Lumley sets out to interview many of those who had known the inspector in earlier pics, including David Niven, Capucine (looking great), Burt Kwouk, Graham Stark and Andre Maranne, as well as his father, Richard Mulligan, and a Mafia kingpin, Robert Loggia.

■ **TRAIN, THE**

1964, 140 MINS, US/FRANCE/ITALY Ⓥ
Dir John Frankenheimer *Prod* Jules Bricker *Scr* Franklin Coen, Frank Davis, Walter Bernstein *Ph* Walter Wottitz, Jean Tournier *Ed* Gabriel Rongier, David Bretherton *Mus* Maurice Jarre *Art Dir* Willy Holt
● Burt Lancaster, Paul Scofield, Jeanne Moreau, Michel Simon, Suzanne Flon, Charles Millot (United Artists/Ariane/Dear)

After a slow start, *The Train* picks up to become a colorful, actionful big-scale adventure opus. Made in French and English in France, it was entirely lensed in real exteriors with unlimited access to old French rolling stock of the last war.

Pic [from the novel *Le front de l'art* by Rose Valland] concerns an elaborate railroad resistance plot to keep a train full of French art treasures from being shipped to Germany near the end of the war.

An earthy station master (Burt Lancaster), if in the resistance, is reluctant to sacrifice men for paintings, especially with the war nearing its end. But he finally gives in when an old engineer, almost his foster father, is killed by the Germans for trying to hold up the art train. An elaborate plot is put into action. Lancaster himself is made to drive the train by the fanatic German colonel (Paul Scofield) to whom the art has become bigger than the war itself.

Jeanne Moreau has a small but telling cameo bit as does Michel Simon as the dedicated old engineer who swings Lancaster into line to go all out for saving the train. But above all it is the railroad bustle, the trains themselves and some bangup special effects of bombing attacks and accidents that give the pic its main points.

■ TRAIN ROBBERS, THE

1973, 92 MINS, US ◇ ⊗
Dir Burt Kennedy *Prod* Michael Wayne *Scr* Burt Kennedy *Ph* William H. Clothier *Ed* Frank Santillo *Mus* Dominic Frontiere *Art Dir* Ray Moyer, Alfred Sweeney
● John Wayne, Ann-Margret, Rod Taylor, Ben Johnson, Christopher George, Bobby Vinton (Batjac)

The Train Robbers is an above-average John Wayne actioner, written and directed by Burt Kennedy with suspense, comedy and humanism not usually found in the formula.

The plot peg is simple. Wayne recruits a group to recover gold stolen from a train by Ann-Margret's deceased outlaw husband, so her name and that of her child can be clear. However, Kennedy has provided a series of rich, deep individual characterizations, plus some intriguing red-herring plot twists.

Most important, for example, is the exposition of the Wayne character. Instead of the cardboard superman, he is given the added dimension of a man who actually could fall for a woman. Ann-Margret is most convincing in a role which requires that she be of her hardy environment, but above it enough to be credible as a lady-like, attractive widow.

■ TRANSYLVANIA TWIST

1989, 82 MINS, US ◇
Dir Jim Wynorski *Prod* Alida Camp *Scr* R.J. Robertson *Ph* Zoran Hochstatter *Ed* Nina Gilberti *Mus* Chuck Cirino *Art Dir* Gary Randall
● Robert Vaughn, Teri Copley, Steve Altman, Monique Gabrielle, Angus Scrimm, Ace Mask (Concorde)

Transylvania Twist is an occasionally hilarious horror spoof notable for the range of its comical targets. Filmmakers let all the stops out in silliness worthy of Mel Brooks.

Immediately with the teaser opening of perennial Jim Wynorski starlet Monique Gabrielle (uncredited though in a big role) being stalked through the woods by Jason, Freddy Krueger and Leatherface, pic applies a scattershot approach delving into other genres as well.

Robert Vaughn is delightful as a Dracula-styled vampire pronouncing the end of his last name Orlock with relish. His beautiful niece Teri Copley is an American singing star who travels to his castle in Transylvania upon the death of her father, accompanied by wise-cracking sidekick Steve Altman.

Mixed into the comic stew are many delightful reflexive bits: tracking camera that gets sidetracked on bodacious women passing by; a black & white sequence when star visits a set that looks left over from *The Honeymooners*; and a terrifically edited appearance by Boris Karloff.

■ TRAP, THE

1966, 106 MINS, UK/CANADA ◇ ⊗
Dir Sidney Hayers *Prod* George H. Brown *Scr* David Osborn *Ph* Robert Krasker *Ed* Tristam Cones *Mus* Ron Grainer *Art Dir* Harry White

● Rita Tushingham, Oliver Reed, Rex Sevenoaks, Barbara Chilcott, Linda Goranson, Blain Fairman (Rank)

This Anglo-Canadian get together deals with an earthy adventure yarn, a struggle for survival, and an offbeat battle of the sexes.

Story is set in the mid-1890s when British Columbia was wild and untamed and only the strong came out on top. Jean La Bete (Oliver Reed), a huge, lusty French-Canadian trapper, returns to the trading post too late for the once-a-year 'auction' of harlots, thieves and femme riff-raff sent away from civilization for this purpose. So he settles for a young mute orphan, a servant in the trader's house, sold to him by the grasping wife.

He hauls the protesting girl into a canoe and sets off for the wastes. There follows an edgy Taming of the Shrew situation as the hunter tries to win her affection by cajoling, bullying, threatening, and occasionally sweet-talking.

Reed is larger-than-life as the crude, brawling trapper yet also has moments of great sensitivity with his co-star. Tushingham, sans benefit of dialog has to depend on her famous eyes, and wistful mouth to put over a tricky role embracing many emotions, from spitfire to waif, and she marvels.

■ TRAPEZE

1956, 106 MINS, US ◇ ⊗
Dir Carol Reed *Prod* James Hill *Scr* James R. Webb *Ph* Robert Krasker *Ed* Bert Bates *Mus* Malcolm Arnold *Art Dir* Rino Mondellini
● Burt Lancaster, Tony Curtis, Gina Lollobrigida, Katy Jurado, Thomas Gomez, Minor Watson (Susan/United Artists)

Trapeze is a high-flying screen entertainment equipped with circus thrills and excitement, a well-handled romantic triangle, and a cast of potent marquee names. Cirque d'Hiver, Paris' famed one-ring circus, provides the authentic, colorful, exciting setting.

Reed's direction loads the aerial scenes with story suspense for even more thrill effect, and male stars Burt Lancaster and Tony Curtis simulate the bigtop aristocrats realistically.

The well-plotted script, from Liam O'Brien's adaptation of Max Catto's *The Killing Frost*, tells how Curtis, son of an aerialist, comes to Paris to learn from Lancaster, one of the few fliers able to achieve the triple somersault, a feat which had left him crippled. Together, they start to work up an act when the tumbler moves in, using her wiles on the young man but loving the older.

Gina Lollobrigida, justly famed for her curves, proves she can act, giving the necessary touch of flamboyance without going overboard. Katy Jurado lights up what scenes she has.

■ TRASH

1970, 103 MINS, US ◇ ⊗
Dir Paul Morrissey *Prod* Andy Warhol *Scr* Paul Morrissey *Ph* Paul Morrissey *Ed* Jed Johnson
● Joe Dallesandro, Holly Woodlawn, Jane Forth, Michael Sklar, Geri Miller, Andrea Feldman (Warhol)

Andy Warhol surfaces from the camp underground with *Trash*, the most comprehensible, and least annoying of a long line of quasi-porno features from *Chelsea Girls* to *Lonesome Cowboys*.

As with earlier *Flesh*, director here is Paul Morrissey who has the Warhol gift of attracting gregarious grotesque and eliciting no-holds improvisations within loosely structured dramatic situations.

Once again, stud-in-residence is Joe Dallesandro, this time as a strung-out heroin addict unable to function sexually despite numerous provocations. He displays both a

forceful screen presence and ease in front of the camera that cannot be hastily dismissed.

■ TRAVELLING NORTH

1987, 96 MINS, AUSTRALIA ◇ ⊗
Dir Carl Schultz *Prod* Ben Gannon *Scr* David Williamson *Ph* Julian Penny *Ed* Henry Dangar *Mus* Alan John *Art Dir* Owen Paterson
● Leo McKern, Julia Blake, Graham Kennedy, Henri Szeps (View)

This superbly crafted adaptation of David Williamson's popular stage play is a mature, frequently funny and ultimately most moving story of old age and retirement.

Leo McKern plays Frank, a rather cantankerous ex-Communist and civil engineer who retires from work at age 70. A widower, he has persuaded his close friend, Frances (Julia Blake), a widow but not as old as he, to accompany him north, to subtropical northern Queensland.

After many happy days fishing, reading and listening to music (and enjoying the sexual side of the relationship), Frank's health begins to deteriorate and Frances starts to yearn to see her family again.

Australian-born McKern, in his first Australian film, gives a remarkable performance as the crotchety, yet endearing, Frank. It's a hugely enjoyable portrayal. As Frances, Blake positively glows; she plays a patient, loving woman with a determination of her own, and it's a rich characterization.

■ TRAVELS WITH MY AUNT

1972, 109 MINS, UK ◇
Dir George Cukor *Prod* Robert Fryer, James Cresson *Scr* Jay Presson Allen, Hugh Wheeler *Ph* Douglas Slocombe *Ed* John Bloom *Mus* Tony Hatch *Art Dir* John Box
● Maggie Smith, Alec McCowen, Lou Gossett, Robert Stephens, Cindy Williams, Robert Flemyng (M-G-M)

Travels with My Aunt is the story [Based on the Graham Greene bestseller] of an outrageous femme of indeterminate years cavorting in a set of outrageous situations which spell high comedy. Of course, it may also be regarded as utter nonsense in a hammed-up set of overly-contrived circumstances.

Maggie Smith plays the title role in an overdrawn but thoroughly delightful manner. Film opens quietly enough at the funeral services of her nephew's mother, but the disrupting arrival of the over-dressed, over-cosmeticked Aunt Augusta sets the stage for a comedy spree.

George Cukor's direction is quite up to meeting the demands of the script, and he is responsible for a tempo attuned to his unusual characters. McCowen's characterization of the nephew is subtle and expansive as he gradually withdraws from his former stuffy, priggish, ex-bank manager style.

■ T.R. BASKIN

1971, 89 MINS, US ◇
Dir Herbert Ross *Prod* Peter Hyams *Scr* Peter Hyams *Ph* Gerald Hirschfield *Ed* Maury Winstrobe *Mus* Jack Elliott *Art Dir* Albert Brenner
● Candice Bergen, Peter Boyle, James Caan, Marcia Rodd, Erin O'Reilly, Howard Platt (Paramount)

T.R. Baskin makes a few good comedy-comments on modern urban existence, but these are bits of rare jewelry lost on a vast beach of strung-out, erratic storytelling. Candice Bergen is featured in title role of a rural girl who is, or is not, worth caring about in the big city. Told in flashback, Peter Hyams' debut production is handsomely mounted, but his screenplay is sterile, superficial and inconsistent. Peter Boyle is an out-of-towner who called Bergen for sex, but instead suffers through her equivocal talk-therapy.

Bergen's screen presence is too sophisticated for the role, and both her acting, direction and dialog result in confusion. One moment she is to be pitied; the next she is fouling up her own chances with people. Boyle, whose contribution is little more than a foil, tries to get some depth into the role of a square salesman.

James Caan, looking more mature, is another professional victim, as a divorced man who ends a perfect night with Bergen by offering her some money. He isn't the only one who isn't sure what she is.

• •

■ TREASURE ISLAND

1934, 105 MINS, US

Dir Victor Fleming   *Prod* Hunt Stromberg   *Scr* John Lee Mahin   *Ph* Ray June, Clyde De Vinna, Harold Rosson   *Ed* Blanche Sewell   *Mus* Herbert Stothart   *Art Dir* Cedric Gibbons, Merrill Pye
● Wallace Beery, Jackie Cooper, Lionel Barrymore, Otto Kruger, Lewis Stone, Nigel Bruce (M-G-M)

It's pretty dangerous to put an old classic as popular as this Robert Louis Stevenson yarn on the screen. It is hard to imagine anyone else in the Long John Silver role than Wallace Beery. It is hard to think of anyone who might have replaced Jackie Cooper as Jim Hawkins. Yet neither of the two completely convinces.

Best performance honors are really split between Lionel Barrymore and Chic Sale. Former, as Billy Bones, and latter as Ben Gunn, seem most thoroughly to have caught the Stevenson spirit. They overact almost to mugging but it's in keeping with the manner of the story.

Treasure Island as a story is a grand, blood-curdling adventure yarn. In portions where it is so played it's genuinely thrilling and good entertainment.

• •

■ TREASURE ISLAND

1950, 96 MINS, UK ◇ ⓥ

Dir Byron Haskin   *Prod* Perce Pearce   *Scr* Lawrence E. Watkin   *Ph* Freddie Young   *Ed* Alan Jaggs   *Mus* Clifton Parker
● Bobby Driscoll, Robert Newton, Basil Sydney, Walter Fitzgerald, Dennis O'Dea, Finlay Currie (RKO/Walt Disney)

Treasure Island, Robert Louis Stevenson's classic, has been handsomely mounted by Walt Disney. Settings are sumptuous and a British cast headed by American moppet Bobby Driscoll faithfully recaptures the bloodthirsty 18th-century era when pirates vied for the supremacy of the seas. It was made in Britain with Disney and RKO frozen pounds.

Stevenson yarn revolves around a squire and a doctor who fit out a ship to search for South Seas treasure on the strength of a chart obtained from a dying pirate.

Robert Newton racks up a virtual tour de force as Long John Silver. Likewise, Driscoll smashes across with a vital portrayal of Jim Hawkins, the saloonkeeper's son who falls heir to a map leading the way to pirate treasure.

There's no dearth of action in the footage.

• •

■ TREASURE OF THE SIERRA MADRE, THE

1948, 124 MINS, US ⓥ

Dir John Huston   *Prod* Henry Blanke   *Scr* John Huston   *Ph* Ted McCord   *Ed* Owen Marks   *Mus* Max Steiner   *Art Dir* John Hughes
● Humphrey Bogart, Walter Huston, Tim Holt, Bruce Bennett (Warner)

Sierra Madre, adapted from the popular novel by B. Traven, is a story of psychological disintegration under the crushers of greed and gold. The characters here are probed and thoroughly penetrated, not through psycho-

analysis but through a crucible of human conflict, action, gesture and expressive facial tones.

Huston, with an extraordinary assist in the thesping department from his father, Walter Huston, has fashioned this standout film with an unfailing sensitivity for the suggestive detail and an uncompromising commitment to reality, no matter how stark ugly it may be.

Except for some incidental femmes who have no bearing on the story, it's an all-male cast headed by Bogart, Huston and Tim Holt. They play the central parts of three gold prospectors who start out for pay dirt in the Mexican mountains as buddies, but wind up in a murderous tangle at the finish.

Lensed for most part on location, the film has, at least, a physical aspect of rugged beauty against which is contrasted the human sordidness.

Bogart comes through with a performance as memorable as his first major film role in *The Petrified Forest*. In a remarkable controlled portrait, he progresses to the edge of madness without losing sight of the subtle shadings needed to establish persuasiveness.
□ 1948: Best Picture (Nomination)

• •

■ TREE GROWS IN BROOKLYN, A

1945, 132 MINS, US ⓥ

Dir Elia Kazan   *Prod* Lovis D. Lighton   *Scr* Tess Slesinger, Frank Davis   *Ph* Leon Shamroy   *Ed* Dorothy Spencer   *Mus* Alfred Newman   *Art Dir* Lyle R. Wheeler
● Dorothy McGuire, Joan Blondell, James Dunn, Lloyd Nolan, Peggy Ann Garner (20th Century-Fox)

The earthy quality of Brooklyn tenement squalor, about which Betty Smith wrote so eloquently in the bestseller novel *A Tree Grows in Brooklyn*, has been given a literal translation to the screen by 20th-Fox to become an experiment in audience restraint. This is the story of the poverty-ridden Nolan family.

Tree recalls an absorbing period of a colorful tribe, of a Brooklyn neighborhood that was tough in its growing-up, where kids fought, where on Saturday nights fathers and husbands, loped uncertainly from the corner quenchery.

Some of this might have acquired the tinge of travesty in hands less skilled than those of Smith – or director Elia Kazan – but never does the serio-comic intrude on a false note; never does this story become maudlin.

To Dorothy McGuire went the prize part of Katie Nolan. It is a role that she makes distinctive by underplaying. James Dunn plays excellently. Peggy Ann Garner is the teenaged Francie, and the young actress performs capitally.

Where *Tree* is frequently slow, it is offset by the story's significance and pointed up notably by the direction of Elia Kazan.

• •

■ TREMORS

1990, 96 MINS, US ◇ ⓥ

Dir Ron Underwood   *Prod* S.S. Wilson, Brent Maddock   *Scr* S.S. Wilson, Brent Maddock   *Ph* Alexander Gruszynski   *Ed* O. Nicholas Brown   *Mus* Ernest Troost   *Art Dir* Ivo Cristante
● Kevin Bacon, Fred Ward, Finn Carter, Michael Gross, Reba McEntire (No Frills)

An affectionate send-up of schlocky 1950s monster pics, but with better special effects, *Tremors* has a few clever twists but ultimately can't decide what it wants to be – flat-out funny, which it's not, or a scarefest.

In this case, the threat comes in the form of four house trailer-sized worm-creatures, with multiple serpent like tongues, that tunnel underground before bursting up to devour human prey.

All the conventions of the genre are here: a small town in the middle of nowhere isolated

from outside help, with a scientist on hand to study strange seismic phenomena. After that, however, the scripters begin to play with those cliches. The scientist, for example, is a pretty young woman (Finn Carter) who doesn't know where the monsters come from or understand why everyone keeps asking her to explain, while the heroes – handyman types Kevin Bacon and Fred Ward – carry on like Curly and Larry in search of Moe.

The pacing and action improve considerably as the film goes on, maintaining a tongue-in-cheek approach while the situation becomes more dire.

• •

■ TRIAL, THE

1962, 115 MINS, FRANCE/W. GER/ITALY ⓥ

Dir Orson Welles   *Prod* Alexander Salkind   *Scr* Orson Welles   *Ph* Edmond Richard   *Ed* Fritz H. Mueller   *Mus* Jean Ledrut, Albinoni   *Art Dir* Jean Mandaroux
● Anthony Perkins, Jeanne Moreau, Romy Schneider, Elsa Martinelli, Akim Tamiroff, Orson Welles (Paris-Europa/Hisa/FICIT)

Written and directed by himself from the 'nightmare' novel by Franz Kafka, Orson Welles' film may well delight film buffs and startle or irritate many others.

A young white-collar worker, Joseph K, wakes up one morning to find a sinister police inspector and two seedy detectives in his room. He is technically under arrest but he is not told why. He accepts the fact after various attempts at rationalizing.

Then the film gets progressively more expressionistic and surreal as he is caught up completely in his impending trial and neglects work, one woman next door who promised adventure, and gets deeper into the complex setup of the law. The geography of the film becomes inextricably bound up with dusty file rooms, waiting rooms full of supposedly guilty men not knowing why they are there and K's final attempt to revolt.

Anthony Perkins as K is on screen practically all the time. His boyishness is oft pedaled to turn him into a timid but priggish type who faces up to an impersonal court. It shapes as a knowing, incisive screen performance.

Jeanne Moreau, Elsa Martinelli and others have fleeting parts that are adequately done. Most outstanding is Romy Schneider as the lawyer's nurse who is irresistibly drawn to accused men.

Welles has given slight intimations that this could be a totalitarian nation or one of over-automation. And it also may be a man's awakening to consciousness and finding himself alienated in the world and rejecting its aspects one by one.

So pic is uneven and sometimes filled with arid talk, but has enough visual vitality to keep it engrossing in its first part.

• •

■ TRIAL OF BILLY JACK, THE

1974, 170 MINS, US ◇ ⓥ

Dir Frank Laughlin   *Prod* Joe Cramer   *Scr* Frank Christina, Teresa Christina   *Ph* Jack A. Marta   *Ed* Tom Rolf, Michael Economou, George Grenville, Michael Karr, Jules Nayfack   *Mus* Elmer Bernstein   *Art Dir* George W. Troast
● Tom Laughlin, Delores Taylor, Victor Izay, Teresa Laughlin, William Wellman Jr, Russell Lane (Taylor-Laughlin)

The Trial of Billy Jack is a violent, sometimes-explosive, anti-Establishment sequel to *Billy Jack* [1971]. Like its predecessor, starring the same two principals, it pinpoints community prejudices against the refusal of many to accept the American Indian.

Trial takes up as *Billy* ended, when Tom Laughlin as the halfbreed Billy Jack was arrested for murder. Told in flashback by Delores Taylor, whose earlier rape was avenged by Billy Jack, and now he is sentenced to prison much of the footage unfolds at the Freedom School, a reservation institution headed by white femme.

The production enjoys extraordinary pictorial interest through having been photographed in Arizona's Monument Valley. But it is only when Laughlin is on-camera that the picture picks up.

● ●

■ TRIAL OF SERGEANT RUTLEDGE, THE

1960, 111 MINS, US ◇
Dir John Ford   *Prod* Willis Goldbeck, Patrick Ford
Scr James Warner Bellah, Willis Goldbeck   *Ph* Bert Glennon   *Ed* Jack Murray   *Mus* Howard Jackson
● Jeffrey Hunter, Constance Towers, Billie Burke, Woody Strode, Carleton Young (Warner)

Give John Ford a troop of cavalry, some hostile Indians, a wisp of story and chances are the director will come galloping home with an exciting film. *Sergeant Rutledge* provides an extra plus factor in the form of an offbeat and intriguing screenplay which deals frankly, if not too deeply, with racial prejudice in the post-Civil War era. Ford expertly blends the action-pictorial and the story elements to create lively physical excitement as well as sustained suspense about the fate of a Negro trooper who is accused of rape and double murder. Original tag on this picture was *Captain Buffalo*.

As the giant-sized Negro 1st sgt who is eventually proven to be a victim of circumstantial evidence, Woody Strode gives an unusually versatile performance. Ford uses his camera to accent the actor's natural physical strength, to build an image of a man of action and heroic proportions while Strode fills out the design with many subtle shadings of character.

The screenplay is said to have a historical basis in that the US 9th and 10th Cavalry of Negro troopers, commanded by white officers, fought skirmishes with the Apaches in Arizona after the Civil War. Whether the actual incident which forms the plot structure – the murder of the Commanding Officer of the 9th Cavalry and the rape-murder of his daughter – also is factual is not quite as important as that it plays well.

Story unfolds via a series of flashbacks from the court martial of Strode as witnesses describe his friendship with the dead white girl, his panicky desertion, the circumstances of his capture by the lieutenant (Jeffrey Hunter) who later volunteers as defense counsel.

Most of the action flows out of the testimony of Constance Towers, the only sympathetic witness, whom Strode has saved from an Indian ambush. Ford makes strikingly effective use of a stage technique by gradually blacking out the screen so that only the figure of Miss Towers remains in the camera eye as her words fade into actions. When the picture is not pounding along as an Indian war party ravages the countryside, Ford sees to it that the court martial progresses with mounting suspense, tempered with a few touches of broad comedy.

● ●

■ TRIAL OF THE CATONSVILLE NINE, THE

1972, 85 MINS, US ◇ Ⓥ
Dir Gordon Davidson   *Prod* Gregory Peck
Scr Daniel Berrigan, Saul Levitt   *Ph* Haskell Wexler
Ed Aaron Stell   *Mus* Shelley Manne   *Art Dir* Peter Wexler
● Gwen Arner, Ed Flanders, Barton Heyman, Richard Jordan, Nancy Malone, Donald Moffat (Melville)

Gregory Peck has produced a film version of *The Trial of the Catonsville Nine* which shapes intelligent, well-acted filmed theatre and is potent in its look at the reasons behind burning of draft records and the trial that followed.

Film begins with a reenactment of burning of the records and the nine waiting for the police, to call attention to their outlooks.

Though based on a play by Father Daniel Berrigan, and with highflown passages of talk, it reportedly draws heavily on the actual court proceedings. But Berrigan tries to delve into the backgrounds, reasons and outlooks of those involved, their attempts to explain their actions by what they thought was wrong with the participation in the Vietnam War.

Theatrical, but fluidly controlled, direction by Gordon Davidson gives this a dramatic impetus despite static qualities and literary dialog.

● ●

■ TRIALS OF OSCAR WILDE, THE

1960, 123 MINS, UK ◇
Dir Ken Hughes   *Prod* Harold Huth   *Scr* Ken Hughes
Ph Ted Moore   *Ed* Geoffrey Foot   *Mus* Ron Goodwin
● Peter Finch, Yvonne Mitchell, James Mason, Nigel Patrick, Lionel Jeffries, John Fraser (Viceroy/Warwick)

Color and wide screen are a sock asset to *The Trials of Oscar Wilde* and, on balance, it has greater stellar appeal [than the black-and-white version, *Oscar Wilde*, released at virtually the same time].

Main difference in the two films is that where the black-and-white version starts at the first meeting of Wilde and Lord Alfred and moves pretty quickly into the excellent court scene, the color job starts where the scandalous friendship is well established and spends much more time setting the atmosphere of the time of the turn of the century. Also rather more time, and this is a distinct advantage, in showing the relationship not only between Wilde and Lord Alfred but also his family life.

Trials [from John Fernald's play *The Stringed Lute* and Montgomery Hyde's *Trials of Oscar Wilde*] also introduces Wilde's re-trial and, in one brilliant scene at Brighton, shows Wilde's anguish when he first realizes that he is merely being used by his young friend as a weapon in his vindictive struggle with his brutal father. The important thing is how the characters are written into the script and how they are played and, in most instances, *The Trials of Oscar Wilde* scores over the black-and-white version.

Peter Finch gives a moving and subtle performance as the ill-starred playwright. Before his downfall he gives the man the charm that he undoubtedly had. The famous Wilde epigrams could well have been thought up by Finch. Robert Morley's crumbling in the face of disaster [in *Oscar Wilde*] is flamboyant and effective. Finch's disintegration is quieter, dignified and no less effective.

John Fraser as handsome young Lord Alfred Douglas is suitably vain, selfish, vindictive and petulant and the relationship between the two is more understandable. Where *Trials* suffers in comparison with the black-and-white film is in the remarkable impact of the libel case court sequence. James Mason in a hewn-down role, never provides the strength and bitter logic necessary for the dramatic cut-and-thrust when Wilde is in the witness box.

● ●

■ TRIBUTE TO A BAD MAN

1956, 95 MINS, US ◇
Dir Robert Wise   *Prod* Sam Zimbalist   *Scr* Michael Blankfort   *Ph* Robert Surtees   *Ed* Ralph E. Winters
Mus Miklos Rozsa   *Art Dir* Cedric Gibbons, Paul Groesse
● James Cagney, Don Dubbins, Stephen McNally, Irene Papas, Vic Morrow, Lee Van Cleef (M-G-M)

A rugged frontier drama of the early west, played off against the scenically striking Colorado Rockies, *Tribute to a Bad Man* is a sight

to behold, using the location sites for full visual worth. Irene Papas, Greek actress, in her Hollywood debut comes off well.

Critically, *Bad Man* is both fast and slow-paced. Latter, in part, results from a feeling of repetition in some of the story points as scripted from a Jack Schaefer short story, and in some scene-prolonging beyond the point of good dramatic return by Robert Wise's direction.

The title is somewhat of a misnomer. The man portrayed so well by Cagney is a hard-bitten pioneer who must enforce his own law on the limitless range he controls. The picture of him is seen through the eyes of young Don Dubbins, eastern lad come west to make his fortune and who tarries awhile in Cagney's employ.

The stay is long enough for him to fall in love with Papas and almost win her away from Cagney when she rebels at the latter's arrogant justice of the rope for breakers of his laws.

● ●

■ TRICK OR TREAT

1986, 97 MINS, US ◇ Ⓥ
Dir Charles Martin Smith   *Prod* Michael S. Murphey, Joel Soisson   *Scr* Michael S. Murphey, Joel Soisson, Rhet Topham   *Ph* Robert Elswit   *Ed* Jane Schwartz
Mus Christopher Young, Fastway   *Art Dir* Curt Schnell
● Marc Price, Tony Fields, Lisa Orgolini, Ozzy Osbourne (De Laurentiis)

Like a relatively dark street on Halloween night, *Trick or Treat* is ripe for howls and hoots, but only manages to deliver a choice handful of them when the festivities are just about over.

A recently killed rock star named Sammi Curr (Tony Fields, made up like a member of KISS), comes back to life when his last, awful unreleased record is played backwards. He's determined to seek revenge on his most ardent critics.

The thing is, the satanic rocker takes himself seriously in reincarnation and ends up acting out all those evil acts he's been singing about for years – drawing his power from the megawatts that surge through his guitar.

There's a geeky highschool kid, Eddie (Marc Price), who idolizes the rocker and is responsible for his appearances. Price is cast perfectly as the dismayed rock worshipper.

● ●

■ TRIO

1950, 91 MINS, UK Ⓥ
Dir Ken Annakin, Harold French   *Prod* Sidney Box
Scr W. Somerset Maugham, R.C. Sherriff, Noel Langley   *Ph* Reginald Wyer, Geoffrey Unsworth
Ed Alfred Roome   *Mus* John Greenwood
● James Hayter, Anne Crawford, Nigel Patrick, Jean Simmons, Michael Rennie, Kathleen Harrison (Gainsborough)

The success of *Quartet*, in which four unrelated Somerset Maugham short stories were strung together in a single picture, encouraged the producers to repeat the formula.

The only connecting link between the three yarns is a pithy Maugham foreword. The first two vignettes, *The Verger* and *Mr Knowall*, between them occupy roughly half the screen time. *Sanatorium* deals with the treatment of tuberculosis.

The first two are bright. The longer piece strikes a happy note between sentiment and laughter.

In *The Verger*, James Hayter is warm and colorful and Kathleen Harrison is typically cast.

Nigel Patrick dominates *Mr Knowall* while Jean Simmons and Michael Rennie in *Sanatorium* play their roles with distinctive charm.

● ●

TRIP, THE

1967, 85 MINS, US ◇ ⓥ

Dir Roger Corman *Prod* Roger Corman *Scr* Jack Nicholson *Ph* Arch Dalzell *Ed* Ronald Sinclair *Mus* American Music Band

● Peter Fonda, Susan Strasberg, Bruce Dern, Dennis Hopper, Salli Sachse, Katherine Walsh (American International)

Jack Nicholson script opens with Peter Fonda, a director of TV commercials, shooting on a beach and being confronted by wife, Susan Strasberg, who is about to divorce him. Distressed by his personal life, he goes off with friend Bruce Dern to the hippie, weirdly painted house of a pusher, played by Dennis Hopper, to buy LSD.

Guarded by Dern, Fonda's trip begins. Scenes rapidly cut from Fonda climbing lofty sand dunes, being chased by two black hooded horsemen through forests, as well as being the sacrificial victim at a dark medieval rite in a torchlit cave. Unconnected scenes begin to spin off the screen with increasing speed and with no attempt at explanation.

Fonda comes across very well, establishing the various moods needed to further the visual effects. Strasberg is on only briefly, and Hopper is okay, except in a dream sequence in which he plays a weirdo high priest, but that whole scene is sophomoric.

TRIP TO BOUNTIFUL, THE

1985, 106 MINS, US ◇ ⓥ

Dir Peter Masterson *Prod* Sterling Van Wagenen, Horton Foote *Scr* Horton Foote *Ph* Fred Murphy *Ed* Jay Freund *Mus* J.A.C. Redford *Art Dir* Neil Spisak

● Geraldine Page, John Heard, Carlin Glynn, Richard Bradford, Rebecca DeMornay (FilmDallas/Bountiful Film Partners)

The Trip to Bountiful is a superbly crafted drama featuring the performance of a lifetime by Geraldine Page. She plays Mrs Watts, a woman whose determination to escape the confines of life in a small Houston apartment with her selfless son Ludie (John Heard) and his domineering wife Jessie Mae (Carlin Glynn) leads her on a moving and memorable journey across the Gulf Coast to return to Bountiful, the town where she was born and raised.

Adapted by Horton Foote from his 1953 teleplay that enjoyed theatrical success on Broadway, the 1947-set film recalls the days of scripts with real plots and dialog.

Life for Mrs Watts with Ludie and Jessie Mae is a claustrophobic and harsh existence of forced politeness, petty battles and demanded apologies. Heard is excellent as the downtrodden Ludie burdened with keeping the peace while contending with money problems and self doubts.

Glynn likewise puts in a strong performance, giving a human edge and depth to what could have been an otherwise nagging wife stereotype. Page's work is excellent throughout.

TRIPLE CROSS

1966, 140 MINS, FRANCE/UK ◇ ⓥ

Dir Terence Young *Prod* Jacques-Paul Bertrand *Scr* Rene Hardy, William Marchant, Terence Young *Ph* Henri Alekan *Ed* Roger Dwyre *Mus* Georges Gavarentz *Art Dir* Tony Roman

● Christopher Plummer, Yul Brynner, Romy Schneider, Claudine Auger, Trevor Howard, Gert Frobe (Cineurop)

Though based on a true story of a British safecracker who worked as a double spy during the Second World War, *Triple Cross* is made in the standard spy pattern of having him a ladies' man, fast with his mitts, glib and shrewd, and with overloaded and

obvious suspense bits thrown in to rob this of the verisimilitude needed to give it a more original fillip.

Director Terence Young plays this slightly tongue-in-cheek and it actually emerges as a sort of mini-Bond. Christopher Plummer is first seen cracking a series of safes and is finally arrested on Jersey. Along comes war and the Germans take over the island. He bluffs his way into getting a hearing with some top German undercover people.

He manages to gull them into letting him work for them and is finally entrusted with a mission. Once in Britain he goes to the British security people, finally convinces them and goes to work for them for a big sum and a promise to wipe out his criminal record.

Plummer walks through his role and does not quite have the impassive mask for the pro criminal or the needed lightness to give the romantic dash it calls for.

TRIPLE ECHO, THE

1972, 102 MINS, UK ◇ ⓥ

Dir Michael Apted *Prod* Graham Cottle *Scr* Robin Chapman *Ph* Mark Wilkinson *Ed* Barrie Vince *Mus* Denis Lewiston *Art Dir* Edward Marshall

● Glenda Jackson, Oliver Reed, Brian Deacon, Anthony May, Gavin Richards, Jenny Lee Wright (Hemdale/Senta)

Story is set on an English farm in 1943. Alice (Glenda Jackson) has been living alone in the country, since her husband was taken a prisoner by the Japanese a half-year earlier. One day a young soldier, Barton (Brian Deacon), comes along and during a tender moment she invites him in for tea. When time comes for Barton to rejoin his regiment, he decides to go AWOL and stay with Alice. So as not to be discovered he starts donning female clothes.

Just as Barton is becoming tired of his equivocal role, a stray tank comes rolling down the hill with a sergeant (Oliver Reed) in it. Next day he's back again, trying to catch a glimpse of Barton, whom he believes to be Alice's sister. At length he does see the 'sister' and announces he's going to take her out dancing.

Aside from the contrived ending, the slow pacing through most of the pic up to the time Reed appears, one never really gets into the motivations of the two main characters.

TROJAN WOMEN, THE

1971, 111 MINS, GREECE/US ◇ ⓥ

Dir Michael Cacoyannis *Prod* Michael Cacoyannis, Anis Nohra *Scr* Michael Cacoyannis *Ph* Alfio Contini *Ed* Russell Woolnough *Mus* Mikis Theodorakis *Art Dir* Nicholas Georgiadis

● Katharine Hepburn, Genevieve Bujold, Vanessa Redgrave, Irene Papas, Brian Blessed, Patrick Magee (Shaftel)

Michael Cacoyannis has come up with a version of Euripides' *The Trojan Women*, which he did successfully off-Broadway in New York. Pic has a surface resonance and not enough of the tragic sweep and force its outcry against war and oppression call for.

It has a solid cast. There is Katharine Hepburn as the proud but fallen Queen of Troy, Hecuba, whose husband and sons have been killed. Only a daughter, mad Cassandra, and Andromache, the wife and child of her son, Hector, are alive. She valiantly tries to lament, dirge and stand up to the fates in dignity, but the force and the needed tragic depth elude her laudatory attempt.

Vanessa Redgrave is lacking in passion as Andromache. Her tragic lamentations do not get to the core of loss. Nor is Genevieve Bujold, as Cassandra, up to the frenzy and needed steely quality of her preachments on man's warring nature and her prophecies on her future demise.

Irene Papas, probably the true tragedienne among them, plays Helen, abducted by Paris, Hecuba's son, on a visit to Sparta, causing the Greeks to attack Troy, sack it, kill the men and send the women, including Hecuba, off to slavery, then burning the city.

TROLL

1986, 86 MINS, US ◇ ⓥ

Dir John Buechler *Prod* Albert Band *Scr* Ed Naha *Ph* Romana Albani *Ed* Lee Percy *Mus* Richard Band *Art Dir* Gayle Simon

● Noah Hathaway, Michael Moriarty, Shelley Hack, Jenny Beck, Sonny Bono (Empire)

Troll is a predictable, dim-witted premise executed for the most part with surprising style. Horror fantasy of a universe of trolls taking over a San Francisco apartment house is far-fetched even for this genre. Creatures designed by John Buechler, who also directed, are a repulsive assortment of hairy, fanged, evil-looking elves but the plot is pure shlock.

No sooner does the Potter family move into an ordinary looking building than the young daughter (Jenny Beck) is possessed by the troll. Where the film rises above the ordinary is in the domestic scenes when, thanks to her acquired personality, young Beck can flout all the conventions of how a good girl should act. Performances by the kids are convincing.

TROLLENBERG TERROR, THE

1958, 85 MINS, UK ⓥ

Dir Quentin Lawrence *Prod* Robert S. Baker, Monty Berman *Scr* Jimmy Sangster *Ph* Monty Berman *Ed* Henry Richardson *Mus* Stanley Black *Art Dir* Duncan Sutherland

● Forrest Tucker, Laurence Payne, Janet Munro, Jennifer Jayne, Warren Mitchell, Andrew Faulds (Eros)

Based on a successful TV serial by Peter Key, the yarn concerns a creature from outer space secreted in a radioactive cloud on the mountain of Trollenberg in Switzerland. The mysterious disappearance of various climbers brings Forrest Tucker to the scene as a science investigator for UNO. He and a professor at the local observatory set out to solve the problem.

During investigations, two headless corpses are discovered and a couple of ordinary citizens go berserk and turn killers. Main object of the two is Janet Munro who is one of a sister mind-reading act and obviously presents a threat to the sinister visitor.

The taut screenplay extracts the most from the situations and is helped by strong, resourceful acting from a solid cast. Tucker tackles the problem with commendable lack of histrionics and Munro adds considerably to the film's interest with an excellent portrayal of the girl whose mental telepathy threatens the creature's activities and draws her into danger.

TRON

1982, 96 MINS, US ◇ ⓥ

Dir Steven Lisberger *Prod* Donald Kushner *Scr* Steven Lisberger *Ph* Bruce Logan *Ed* Jeff Gourson *Mus* Wendy Carlos *Art Dir* Dean Edward Mitzner

● Jeff Bridges, Bruce Boxleitner, David Warner, Cindy Morgan, Barnard Hughes, Dan Shor (Walt Disney)

Tron is loaded with visual delights but falls way short of the mark in story and viewer involvement. Screenwriter-director Steven Lisberger has adequately marshalled a huge force of technicians to deliver the dazzle, but even kids (and specifically computer game freaks) will have a difficult time getting hooked on the situations.

After an awkward 'teaser' intro the story unfolds concisely: computer games designer

Kevin Flynn (Jeff Bridges) has had his series of fabulously successful programs stolen by Ed Dillinger (David Warner). Dillinger has consequently risen to position of corporate power and with his Master Control Program (MCP) has increasingly dominated other programmers and users.

Flynn must obtain the evidence stored in computer's memory proving that Dillinger has appropriated his work. His friend Alan Bradley (Bruce Boxleitner) is concurrently working on a watchdog program (called Tron) to thwart the MCP's growing control. The MCP scientifically transforms Flynn into a computer-stored program, bringing the viewer into the parallel world inside the computer.

Computer-generated visuals created by divers hands are impressive but pic's design work and execution consistently lack the warmth and humanity that classical animation provides.

■ TROUBLE IN MIND

1985, 111 MINS, US ◇ ⓥ

Dir Alan Rudolph   *Prod* Carolyn Pfeiffer, David Blocker   *Scr* Alan Rudolph   *Ph* Toyomichi Kurita   *Ed* Tom Walls   *Mus* Mark Isham   *Art Dir* Steven Legler
● Kris Kristofferson, Keith Carradine, Lori Singer, Genevieve Bujold, Joe Morton, Divine (Island Alive)

Trouble in Mind is a stylish urban melodrama instantly recognizable as an Alan Rudolph picture. It is peopled by a strange collection of off-center characters living in a stylish, almost-real location.

Set in RainCity, action could be taking place in the 1950s, 1980s or 1990s, so stylized is the production design. The good people of RainCity are like a microcosm of the larger world seen through the lens of 1940s gangster pictures with several other influences thrown in for good measure.

At the core of the film is a not-so-classic romantic triangle involving Hawk (Kris Kristofferson), Georgia (Lori Singer) and her boyfriend, Coop (Keith Carradine).

Center of this emotional landscape is Wanda's cafe, owned and operated by Wanda (Genevieve Bujold), a former lover of Hawk's and the woman for whom he committed a murder.

Rudolph stirs all the ingredients around – love, crime, friendship, responsibility – and ties them together with a charged score by Mark Isham.

■ TROUBLE IN PARADISE

1932, 81 MINS, US

Dir Ernst Lubitsch   *Prod* Ernst Lubitsch   *Scr* Samson Raphaelson, Grover Jones   *Ph* Victor Milner   *Mus* W. Franke Harling
● Miriam Hopkins, Kay Francis, Herbert Marshall, Charlie Ruggles, Edward Everett Horton, C. Aubrey Smith (Paramount)

Despite the Lubitsch artistry, much of which is technically apparent, it's not good cinema in toto. For one thing, it's predicated on a totally meretricious premise. Herbert Marshall is the gentleman crook. Miriam Hopkins is a light-fingered lady. Kay Francis is a rich young widow who owns the largest parfumerie in Paris. She's decidedly on the make for Marshall, and his appointment as her 'secretary' inspires beaucoup gossip.

Rest becomes a proposition of cheating cheaters as the well-mannered rogue exposes C. Aubrey Smith, the parfumerie's general manager, at the same time climaxing into a triangle among the two attractive femmes and Marshall.

The dialog is bright [from the play *The Honest Finder* by Laszlo Aladar] and the Lubitsch montage is per usually tres artistique, but somehow the whole thing misses.

There's some good trouping by all concerned, plus the intriguing Continental atmosphere of the Grand Hotel on the Grand Canal, Venice, plus ultra-modern social deportment in smart Parisian society.

■ TROUBLE IN STORE

1953, 85 MINS, UK ⓥ

Dir John Paddy Carstairs   *Prod* Maurice Cowan   *Scr* John Paddy Carstairs, Maurice Cowan, Ted Willis   *Ph* Ernest Steward   *Ed* Peter Seabourne, Geoffrey Foot   *Mus* Mischa Spoliansky   *Art Dir* Alex Vetchinsty, John Gow
● Norman Wisdom, Margaret Rutherford, Moira Lister, Derek Bond, Lana Morris, Jerry Desmonde (Two Cities)

This British piece of slapstick marks the debut of Norman Wisdom. He clowns his way through the whole thing, playing in his inimitable way the most humble member of a big department store who falls foul of his new boss. But he gets his girl and also rounds up some gangsters.

Apart from one or two brief exteriors, the entire action is in the department store, but there is plenty of movement and an ample slice of broad comedy. Margaret Rutherford has some nice comedy scenes as an inveterate shoplifter and Moira Lister is a very lush manageress who's in league with the gangsters led by Derek Bond. Lana Morris pleasantly offers the romantic interest. Jerry Desmonde is little more than a comedy stooge, as the boss, but plays the role for all it is worth.

■ TROUBLE WITH ANGELS, THE

1966, 111 MINS, US ◇ ⓥ

Dir Ida Lupino   *Prod* William Frye   *Scr* Blanche Hanalis   *Ph* Lionel Lindon   *Ed* Robert C. Jones   *Mus* Jerry Goldsmith   *Art Dir* John Beckman
● Rosalind Russell, Hayley Mills, Binnie Barnes, Gypsy Rose Lee, Camilla Sparv, June Harding (Columbia)

The trouble with *The Trouble with Angels* is hard to pinpoint. An appealing story idea – hip Mother Superior nun who outfoxes and matures two rebellious students in a Catholic girls' school – has lost impact via repetitious plotting and pacing, plus routine direction.

Jane Trahey's book, *Life with Mother Superior*, was adapted by Blanche Hanalis into an episodic screenplay.

Story takes the extrovert Hayley Mills and pal, sensitive, introverted June Harding, through three full years of school under the watchful eye of Rosalind Russell. Graduation finds Mills in character switcheroo to which Catholic audiences will long since be alerted.

Russell gives appropriate spiritual depth to her part, although eventually is shot down by excess chatter and exposition. Latter also affects two younger femme principals in achieving character development.

The large supporting cast fares far better, simply from less exposure.

■ TROUBLE WITH HARRY, THE

1955, 96 MINS, US ◇ ⓥ

Dir Alfred Hitchcock   *Prod* Alfred Hitchcock   *Scr* John Michael Hayes   *Ph* Robert Burks   *Ed* Alma Macrorie   *Mus* Bernard Herrmann   *Art Dir* Hal Pereira, John Goodman
● Edmund Gwenn, John Forsythe, Shirley MacLaine, Mildred Natwick, Mildred Dunnock, Royal Dano (Paramount)

This is a blithe little comedy, produced and directed with affection by Alfred Hitchcock, about a bothersome corpse that just can't stay buried.

Edmund Gwenn is a delight as a retired 'sea' captain who stumbles on Harry's corpse while rabbit hunting. In the belief he did the killing, he decides to bury the cadaver on the spot. Harry goes in and out of the ground three or four times, is responsible for two romances and not a little consternation and physical exercise.

During the course of events Gwenn and Mildred Natwick, middleaged spinster who thinks she did Harry in, find love, as do John Forsythe, local artist, and Shirley MacLaine, young widow of the in-and-out Harry. Natwick pairs perfectly with Gwenn, and the script from the novel by Jack Trevor Story provides them with dialog and situations that click.

■ TRUCK STOP WOMEN

1974, 82 MINS, US ◇ ⓥ

Dir Mark L. Lester   *Prod* Mark L. Lester   *Scr* Mark L. Lester, Paul Deason   *Ph* John A. Morrill   *Ed* Marvin Wallowitz   *Mus* Big Mack & The Truckstoppers   *Art Dir* Tom Hassen
● Claudia Jennings, Lieux Dressler, John Martino, Dennis Fimple, Dolores Dorn, Gene Drew (Lester)

Truck Stop Women spoofs the mindless sensationalism involved in films of its type while it also exploits sex and violence.

Located in New Mexico, pic deals with bloody territorial warfare between Mafia hit man John Martino and indie gang leader Lieux Dressler over Dressler's lucrative theft and prostitution operation, conducted out of a highway truck stop with henchpersons including her daughter Claudia Jennings.

A ludicrous string of murders occurs as the rivalry unfolds, with Jennings lured to the opposite side by money-waving Martino. Plenty of flesh is on display.

Mark L. Lester's direction is highly uneven, with many scenes run through in perfunctory fashion and others handled with care and skill. There is a stunning semidocumentary montage of trucks on the highway half an hour into the film, and action scenes are done with flair.

■ TRUE COLORS

1991, 111 MINS, US ◇ ⓥ

Dir Herbert Ross   *Prod* Herbert Ross, Laurence Mark   *Scr* Kevin Wade   *Ph* Dante Spinotti   *Ed* Robert Reitano, Stephen A. Rotter   *Mus* Trevor Jones   *Art Dir* Edward Pisoni
● John Cusack, James Spader, Imogen Stubbs, Mandy Patinkin, Richard Widmark, Dina Merrill (Paramount)

True Colors represents a cloyingly schematic attempt to portray the political and moral bankruptcy of the 1980s in a neat little package. Pic condemns but doesn't begin to analyze the corrupted values of the Reagan years, leaving one feeling soiled but unenlightened.

Paired off at law school at the U of Virginia in 1983, James Spader is a rich boy with the daughter of US senator Richard Widmark as a girlfriend, while John Cusack is pretender, a social climber whose lower-class roots are quickly exposed.

Cusack, a bluffer and something of a charmer, resolves to be elected to Congress within 10 years. He launches a political career based upon trickery, blackmail and betrayal, and receives backing from interests represented by oily developer Mandy Patinkin.

Personal relationships fall by the wayside like roadkill. Having scooped Spader's g.f. (Imogen Stubbs) out from under him, Cusack then loses her when he stupidly threatens her powerful father.

Cusack does what he can, but the character is simply weighed down with too much symbolic baggage. Yet again playing a privileged preppie type, Spader is likable but suffers from his character being pushed to the side mid-stream.

TRUE CONFESSIONS

1981, 108 MINS, US ◇

Dir Ulu Grosbard *Prod* Irwin Winkler, Robert Chartoff *Scr* John Gregory Dunne, Joan Didion *Ph* Owen Roizman *Ed* Lynzee Klingman *Mus* Georges Delerue *Art Dir* Stephen S. Grimes
● Robert De Niro, Robert Duvall, Charles Durning, Burgess Meredith, Cyril Cusack (United Artists)

Given the powerhouse topline casting combo and provocative theme, *True Confessions* has to be chalked up as something of a disappointment. Adaptation of John Gregory Dunne's bestseller, which was inspired by LA's legendary Black Dahlia murder case of the late 1940s, features corrupt cops, whores, pimps, sibling rivalry, pornography and political intrigue within the Roman Catholic Church, but still comes off as relatively mild fare which fails to pack a dramatic or emotional wallop.

For at least the first hour, it's hard to tell where the drama's headed. Bookended by years-later scenes in which brothers Robert De Niro and Robert Duvall, both white-haired, play out mutual climax to their radically different lives at the former's pathetic desert parish, main body of pic flip-flops between police detective Duvall handling two bizarre deaths and ambitious Monsignor De Niro negotiating the delicate waters of church diplomacy.

Unfortunately, nowhere near the full weight of these considerations is ever felt in Ulu Grosbard's muted, unmuscular telling of the sordid, fateful events. Script is deliberately structured to build to a big dramatic pay-off, but this never comes, leaving audience frustrated that careful groundwork has been laid to little avail.

Failings cannot be attributed to the actors, all of whom have clearly immersed themselves in their roles. Duvall is excellent as an unsentimental dick working a tough beat which irrevocably poisons his personal life. Charles Durning's portrait of a big-time phony is right on target.

TRUE GRIT

1969, 128 MINS, US ◇ Ⓥ

Dir Henry Hathaway *Prod* Hal B. Wallis *Scr* Marguerite Roberts *Ph* Lucien Ballard *Ed* Warren Low *Mus* Elmer Bernstein *Art Dir* Walter Tyler
● John Wayne, Glen Campbell, Kim Darby, Jeremy Slate, Robert Duvall, Dennis Hopper (Paramount)

Story centers on young girl (Kim Darby) of the 1830s starting out from Arkansas to avenge the murder of her father with the aid of Wayne, whom she pays, and Texas Ranger Glen Campbell, who wants to claim the murderer (Jeff Corey) for a reward. Men develop instant mutual loathing, but girl recognizes they can get her father's murderer because they have grit, true grit.

Darby is refreshingly original. If at times she seems restrained, she sticks relentlessly to the strong character of Mattie.

Campbell, less successful as an actor than as a singer-performer, still holds his own as a foil for Wayne. But it's mostly Wayne all the way. He towers over everything in the film – actors, script [from Charles Portis' novel], even the magnificent Colorado mountains. He rides tall in the saddle in this character role of 'the fat old man.'

TRUE STORIES

1986, 90 MINS, US ◇ Ⓥ

Dir David Byrne *Prod* Gary Kurfirst *Scr* David Byrne, Beth Henley, Stephen Tobolowsky *Ph* Ed Lachman *Ed* Caroline Biggerstaff *Mus* David Byrne, Talking Heads *Art Dir* Barbara Ling
● David Byrne, John Goodman, Swoosie Kurtz, Spalding Gray, Alix Elias, Annie McEnroe (True Stories)

In more than 10 years with the Talking Heads, David Byrne received well-earned if often slavishly uncritical praise for his distinctive marriage of polyrhythmic pop-rock with an archly skewed perspective on mechanistic modern life. *True Stories* was a natural progression into film.

In his feature directorial debut, Byrne takes a bemused and benevolent view of provincial America's essential goodness in a loosely connected string of vignettes that amount to sophisticated music video concepts dressed up as film-making.

Byrne uses the surreal, cartoonish conceit of examining life in the hypothetical town of Virgil, Texas with the human interest perspective of a supermarket tabloid feature. Affecting a trusting innocence as easily as he slips into natty Western duds, Byrne drives into Virgil during its sesquicentennial 'celebration of specialness' for a series of close encounters with the town's peculiar denizens.

TRUE STORY OF JESSE JAMES, THE

1957, 92 MINS, US ◇

Dir Nicholas Ray *Prod* Herbert B. Swope Jr *Scr* Walter Newman *Ph* Joe MacDonald *Ed* Robert Simpson *Mus* Leigh Harline *Art Dir* Lyle R. Wheeler, Addison Hehr
● Robert Wagner, Jeffrey Hunter, Hope Lange, Agnes Moorehead, Alan Hale, John Carradine (20th Century-Fox)

On celluloid Jesse James has had more lives than a cat, and *The True Story of Jesse James* suggests it's time screenwriters let him roll over and play dead for real and reel. In past reworkings of the 19th-century delinquent's shoddy career just about every angle was covered. There's nothing new in this glorification. It's a routine offering for the outdoor market.

The attempt to view the James character through the eyes of pro and con contemporaries only makes for confusion, depriving an audience of clear-cut plot line that might keep it interested. Dialog, too, is poor, continually veering from period to modern idioms in the script, based on Nunnally Johnson's screenplay for the 1939 *Jesse James*.

Nicholas Ray directs in stock fashion, adding little of substance to the picture. As Jesse and Frank James, respectively, Robert Wagner and Jeffrey Hunter go through the motions of telling why the former took up the gun when Northern sympathizers made it difficult for them to live in Missouri after the War between States. Both are adequate to the demands of script and direction, as is Hope Lange, playing Zee, the girl who married Jesse.

TRUE TO LIFE

1943, 94 MINS, US

Dir George Marshall *Prod* Paul Jones *Scr* Don Hartman, Harry Tugend *Ph* Charles Lang Jr *Mus* Victor Young
● Mary Martin, Franchot Tone, Dick Powell, Victor Moore, William Demarest (Paramount)

Taking the premise, in an audible intro title that 'life should mirror the movies, instead of the movies reflecting life', the escapist theme of *True to Life* is quickly set. It treats radio family serials with tongue-in-cheek but utilizes the radio soap opera appeal for the plot bulwark of a frothy film. Franchot Tone and Dick Powell are the all-written-out radio scripters on the verge of losing their $1,000-a-week jobs because their *Kitty Farmer* serial has become too phoney. Powell, in search of down-to-the-peasants material, runs into hash-house waitress Mary Martin whose real-life family in Sunnyside, a suburb of NY, and their zany behaviorisms provide the authors with almost literal libretto.

Action shuttles between the bourgeois Sunnyside family menage and the lush apartment and slick Radio City environment of the Powell-Tone team. Three songs, all good, are skillfully interwoven and the finale is a madcap radio pickup of how things right themselves. Well-paced direction by George Marshall and some excellent scripting do much to hold the madcap proceedings together.

TRYGON FACTOR, THE

1967, 87 MINS, UK ◇

Dir Cyril Frankel *Prod* Brian Taylor *Scr* Derry Quinn, Stanley Munroe *Ph* Harry Waxman *Ed* Oswald Hafenrichter *Mus* Peter Thomas *Art Dir* Roy Stannard
● Stewart Granger, Susan Hampshire, Robert Morley, Cathleen Nesbitt, Brigitte Horney (Warner/Seven Arts/ Rialto)

The Trygon Factor, its title totally meaningless, is a complicated Scotland Yard whodunit which the spectator will find taxing to follow.

Stewart Granger, as the Yard superintendent investigating a rash of unsolved robberies, is assigned to a large country house where a gang is operating under the cloak of respectability; its mistress, a member of an old English family who has turned to crime to save her family estate from ruin.

She has installed in her house a phony order of nuns who actually are in on the various crimes, and who receive and ship stolen goods to Morley's warehouse.

Script is pocketed with story loopholes and attempts to confuse, plus certain motivations and bits of business impossible to fathom.

Granger still makes a good impression.

TUCKER
THE MAN AND HIS DREAM

1988, 111 MINS, US ◇ Ⓥ

Dir Francis Coppola *Prod* Fred Roos, Fred Fuchs *Scr* Arnold Schulman, David Seidler *Ph* Vittorio Storaro *Ed* Priscilla Nedd *Mus* Joe Jackson *Art Dir* Dean Tavoularis
● Jeff Bridges, Joan Allen, Martin Landau, Frederic Forrest, Dean Stockwell, Lloyd Bridges (Lucasfilm/Zeotrope)

The true story of a great American visionary who was thwarted, if not destroyed, by the established order, *Tucker* represents the sunniest imaginable telling of an at least partly tragic episode in recent history.

Tucker's life and career present so many parallels to Coppola's own it is easy to see why he coveted his project for so long. Industryites will nod in recognition of this story of a self-styled genius up against business interests hostile to his innovative ideas, but also will note the accepting, unbelligerent stance adopted toward the terms of the struggle.

After World War II, seemingly on the strength of his enthusiasm alone, Tucker got a small core of collaborators to work on his dream project, which he called 'the first completely new car in 50 years'.

With a factory in Chicago, Tucker managed to turn out 50 of his beauties, but vested interests in Detroit and Washington dragged him into court on fraud charges, shutting him down and effectively ending his automobile career. As his moneyman tells him, 'You build the car too good.'

Flashing his charming smile and ozzing cocky confidence, Jeff Bridge's Tucker is inspiring because he won't be depressed or defeated by anything.

TUGBOAT ANNIE

1933, 85 MINS, US

Dir Mervyn LeRoy *Prod* Harry Rapf *Scr* Zelda Sears, Eve Greene, Norman Reilly Raine *Ph* Gregg Toland *Ed* Blanche Sewell *Art Dir* Merrill Pye

● Marie Dressler, Wallace Beery, Robert Young, Maureen O'Sullivan, Willard Robertson, Tammany Young (M-G-M)

Tugboat Annie, while weak in many respects, is on the whole perfectly suited to the Dressler-Beery requirements. In the hands of the co-starring couple its deficiencies are barely noticeable.

Making Marie Dressler the femme skipper of a harbor tugboat, Wallace Beery her shiftless, soused but likeable husband, and giving them a son of which to be proud, was giving Dressler-Beery a blueprint and then going home.

Beery is always stewed and Dressler constantly trying to keep him dry. That provides the comedy. Beery is getting the family into all sorts of jams – stupidly, drunkenly, tragically, but unintentionally. That provides the pathos.

Robert Young and Maureen O'Sullivan are the juves, and just juves, with no chance to be anything more. It's a Dressler-Beery picture [from the *Saturday Evening Post* series by Norman Reilly Raine].

● ●

■ **TUNES OF GLORY**

1960, 105 MINS, UK ◇ Ⓥ
Dir Ronald Neame *Prod* Colin Lesslie *Scr* James Kennaway *Ph* Arthur Ibbetson *Ed* Anne V. Coates *Mus* Malcolm Arnold
● Alec Guinness, John Mills, Dennis Price, John Fraser, Susannah York, Kay Walsh (United Artists)

Both Alec Guinness and John Mills are cast as colonels, the former a man of humble origin who has risen from the ranks, the other a product of Eton, Oxford and a classy military academy. It is the clash of personalities between the two that provides the main story thread.

Tunes is the story of a Scottish regiment in peacetime commanded by Guinness. He's reasonably popular with his fellow officers, though a few appear to resent his rough-and-ready behavior in the mess. His is only an acting command, and when he is superseded by Mills (whose grandfather had commanded the same regiment), the clash is inevitable.

The struggle between the two reaches its climax when Guinness finds his daughter in a public house with a young corporal, and strikes the soldier. That's a serious offense under military law, and though Mills has the power to deal with the case, he chooses to submit a report to higher authority, which would inevitably lead to a courtmartial.

Ronald Neame's crisp and vigorous direction keeps the main spotlight on the two central characters. Guinness, as always, is outstanding, and his performance is as forthright as it is subtle. He assumes an authentic Scottish accent naturally, and never misses a trick to win sympathy, even when he behaves foolishly. It's a tough assignment for Mills to play against Guinness, particularly in a fundamentally unsympathetic role, but he is always a match for his co-star.

● ●

■ **TUNNEL OF LOVE, THE**

1958, 98 MINS, US
Dir Gene Kelly *Prod* Joseph Fields, Martin Melcher *Scr* Joseph Fields *Ph* Robert Bronner *Ed* John McSweeney Jr *Art Dir* William A. Horning, Randall Duell
● Doris Day, Richard Widmark, Gig Young, Gia Scala, Elisabeth Fraser, Elizabeth Wilson (M-G-M)

The Broadway hit on which this is based has been transferred virtually intact to the screen.

Richard Widmark is a would-be cartoonist for a *New Yorker*-type magazine, whose gags are good but whose drawings are not. He and his wife (Doris Day) want a child and cannot catch. They live in a remodeled barn (nat-

urally) adjacent to the home of their best friends (Gig Young and Elisabeth Fraser) whom they envy in many ways. Young is an editor of the magazine Widmark aspires to crack, and is a parent. Young adds to his and Fraser's brood as regularly as the seasons, Widmark and Day are planning to adopt a baby.

Meantime, back at the barn, Young, whose homework has been stimulated by extracurricular activities, urges his system on Widmark. With this suggestion in the back of his mind, Widmark is visited by an adoption home investigator (Gia Scala). When he wakes up in a motel after a night on the town with her, he assumes the thought has been father to the deed in more ways than one. Just a little over nine months later, the adoption agency presents a baby to Day and Widmark.

The only important change Joseph Fields has made in the screenplay, from the play by him and Peter DeVries (based on DeVries' book), is to explain at the very end that the child is not actually Widmark's.

Day and Widmark make a fine comedy team, working as smoothly as if they had been trading gags for years. They are ably abetted by Young, one of the greatest fly-catchers in operation, and Scala, who displays a nice and unexpected gift for comedy.

This is the first time Gene Kelly has operated entirely behind the camera, and he emerges as an inventive and capable comedy director.

● ●

■ **TURK 182!**

1985, 98 MINS, US ◇ Ⓥ
Dir Bob Clark *Prod* Ted Field, Rene DuPont *Scr* James Gregory Kingston, Denis Hamill, John Hamill *Ph* Reginald H. Morris *Ed* Stan Cole *Mus* Paul Zaza *Art Dir* Harry Pottle
● Timothy Hutton, Robert Urich, Kim Cattrall, Robert Culp, Darren McGavin, Steven Keats (20th Century-Fox)

Taking aim squarely at the popular theme of the working man's struggle against the inequities in the system, *Turk 182!* a cleverly conceived story [by James Gregory Kingston] of a mystery rebel in New York City whose popularity reaches almost mythic proportions, convincingly hits its mark.

Timothy Hutton plays a 20-year-old who defends the honor of his older brother (Robert Urich), fireman who, when off-duty in a bar, responds to a plea for help and risks his life by going into a burning building to save a young girl. Urich is severely injured but the city refuses to come to his aid, maintaining that he should not have entered the premises in his intoxicated state.

That's when Hutton takes his plea on his brother's behalf through the city bureaucracy to no avail, including a forced confrontation with the mayor (Robert Culp). Hutton begins a one-man quest to embarrass and discredit the mayor.

Besides its compelling storyline, *Turk 182!* features outstanding performances across the board, with Hutton perfect in the role of the determined unassuming hero.

● ●

■ **TURNER & HOOCH**

1989, 100 MINS, US ◇ Ⓥ
Dir Roger Spottiswoode *Prod* Raymond Wagner *Scr* Dennis Shryack, Michael Blodgett, Daniel Petrie Jr., Jim Cash, Jack Epps Jr. *Ph* Adam Greenberg *Ed* Garth Craven *Mus* Charles Gross *Art Dir* John DeCuir Jr.
● Tom Hanks, Mare Winningham, Craig T. Nelson, Reginald VelJohnson, Scott Paulin (Touchstone/Silver Screen Partners IV)

Until its grossly miscalculated bummer of an ending, *Turner & Hooch* is a routine but amia-

ble cop-and-dog comedy enlivened by the charm of Tom Hanks and his homely-as-sin canine partner.

Hanks plays a fussy smalltown California police investigator whose life is disrupted by a messy junkyard dog with a face only a furry mother could love.

In the numbingly unoriginal plot, the dog named Hooch (delightfully played by Beasley), witnesses a double murder and is Hanks' only means of catching the drug smugglers responsible for the slayings. The rather mechanical style of director Roger Spottiswoode (who took over the film after original director Henry Winkler departed) fails to enliven the stereotypical criminal proceedings.

● ●

■ **TURNING POINT, THE**

1977, 119 MINS, US Ⓥ
Dir Herbert Ross *Prod* Herbert Ross, Arthur Laurents *Scr* Arthur Laurents *Ph* Robert Surtees *Ed* William Reynolds *Mus* John Lanchbery *Art Dir* Albert Brenner
● Anne Bancroft, Shirley MacLaine, Mikhail Baryshnikov, Leslie Browne, Tom Skerritt, Martha Scott (20th Century-Fox)

The Turning Point is one of the best films of its era. It's that rare example of synergy in which every key element is excellent and the ensemble is an absolute triumph.

Anne Bancroft and Shirley MacLaine, starring as longtime friends with unresolved problems, are magnificent.

The intricate plotting introduces Bancroft as a ballet star just reaching that uneasy age where a lot of Eve Harringtons (male and female) are beginning to move in.

MacLaine, her best friend, long ago abandoned a similar career to marry Tom Skerritt and now their teenage daughter (Leslie Browne) shows real promise as a dancer. This is the incident which triggers an explosion of new and old conflicts.

Pic ranks as one of MacLaine's career highlights, ditto for Bancroft. They have a climactic showdown scene which filmgoers will remember for decades.
□ 1977: Best Picture (Nomination)

● ●

■ **TWELVE ANGRY MEN**

1957, 95 MINS, US Ⓥ
Dir Sidney Lumet *Prod* Henry Fonda, Reginald Rose *Scr* Reginald Rose *Ph* Boris Kaufman *Ed* Carl Lerner *Mus* Kenyon Hopkins *Art Dir* Robert Markell
● Henry Fonda, Lee J. Cobb, Ed Begley, E.G. Marshall, Jack Warden, Martin Balsam (Orion-Nova/United Artists)

The *Twelve Angry Men* are a jury, a body of peers chosen to decide the guilt or innocence of a teenager accused of murdering his father. They have heard the arguments of the district attorney and the defense lawyer. They have received instructions from the presiding judge. Now they are on their own. What will they do?

Rose has a lot to say about the responsibility of citizens chosen to serve on a jury. He stresses the importance of taking into account the question of 'reasonable doubt'. It is soon evident that the majority of the men regard the assignment as a chore. To most of them, it is an open and shut case. The boy is guilty and they demand a quick vote. On the first ballot it is 11 to 1 for a conviction. Henry Fonda is the lone holdout.

Most of the action takes place in the one room on a hot summer day. The effect, rather than being confining, serves to heighten the drama. It's not static, however, for Sidney Lumet, making his bow as a film director has cleverly maneuvered his players in the small area. Perhaps the motivations of each juror are introduced too quickly and are repeated too often before each changes his vote. However, the film leaves a tremendous impact.

□ 1957: Best Picture (Nomination)

. . . .

■ TWELVE CHAIRS, THE

1970, 94 MINS, US ◇ Ⓥ

Dir Mel Brooks   *Prod* Michael Hertzberg   *Scr* Mel Brooks   *Ph* Dorde Nikolic   *Ed* Alan Heim   *Mus* John Morris   *Art Dir* Milo Nikolic
● Ron Moody, Frank Langella, Mel Brooks, Andreas Voutsinas, Vlada Petric, David Lander (UMC)

The Twelve Chairs is a nutty farce, frequently slapstick and often tongue-in-cheek. Mel Brooks, who directed, scripted, plays a leading role and authored a song, has turned a search for jewels into a cornpop – circa 1927, Russia, when all men were comrades – and the result is a delightful adventure-comedy.

Based on the novel by Ilf & Petrov, exteriors were lensed in Yugoslavia, which provides some novel and picturesque backdrops. The steps in Dubrovnik, vistas of the Dalmatian coast and mountains in the interior lend fascinating atmosphere.

Simple story thread is of three men trying to locate 12 dining-room chairs, once owned by a wealthy woman who confesses separately to her son-in-law and village priest on her deathbed that years before she had secreted all her jewels in the upholstery of one of them. Voila, the plot.

. . . .

■ 12 O'CLOCK HIGH

1949, 132 MINS, US

Dir Henry King   *Prod* Darryl F. Zanuck   *Scr* Sy Bartlett, Beirne Lay Jr   *Ph* Leon Shamroy   *Ed* Barbara McLean   *Mus* Alfred Newman
● Gregory Peck, Hugh Marlowe, Millard Mitchell, Dean Jagger, Robert Arthur (20th Century-Fox)

Picture treats its story from the high brass level, i.e. a general's concern for his men's morale while establishing the man-killing daylight bombing raids back in 1942.

As a drama, *High* deals soundly and interestingly with its situations. It gets close to the emotions in unveiling its plot and approaches it from a flashback angle so expertly presented that the emotional pull is sharpened.

Gregory Peck heads up the operations of a bombing squadron from a base in Chelveston, England. Peck gives the character much credence as he suffers and sweats with his men.

There are a number of what amount to 'surprise' performances in the male cast. Standout among them is Dean Jagger as a retread still determined to do his bit. Story comes to life through his eyes as he revisits the Chelveston base in 1948.

□ 1949: Best Picture (Nomination)

. . . .

■ TWENTIETH CENTURY

1934, 91 MINS, US

Dir Howard Hawks   *Prod* Howard Hawks   *Scr* Ben Hecht, Charles MacArthur   *Ph* Joseph August   *Ed* Gene Havlick
● John Barrymore, Carole Lombard, Walter Connolly, Roscoe Karns, Etienne Girardot, Ralph Forbes (Columbia)

John Barrymore, who stars, is quoted as saying, 'I've never done anything I like as well . . . a role that comes once in an actor's lifetime.' It's Barrymore's picture, no doubt of that, with something left over for Carole Lombard, who manages to shine despite practically stooging.

Lily Garland (Lombard) walks out on producer Oscar Jaffee (Barrymore) to go Hollywood shortly after he makes her, double, and that happens early in the picture. From then on it's a chase. Jaffee goes broke trying to

land another Lily Garland and Lily goes big in Hollywood. The way Jaffee and his boys try to frame Lily into coming back into the legit fold paves the road for some crazy trouping.

Lombard, looking very well, must take Barrymore's abuse as his mistress and handmade star for the first few hundred feet, but when she goes temperamental herself she's permitted to do some head-to-head temperament punching with him.

. . . .

■ 20,000 LEAGUES UNDER THE SEA

1954, 120 MINS, US ◇ Ⓥ

Dir Richard Fleischer   *Prod* Walt Disney   *Scr* Earl Fenton   *Ph* Franz Planer   *Ed* Elmo Williams   *Mus* Paul Smith   *Art Dir* John Meehan
● Kirk Douglas, James Mason, Paul Lukas, Peter Lorre, Robert J. Wilke, Carleton Young (Walt Disney)

Walt Disney's production of *20,000 Leagues under the Sea* is very special kind of picture, combining photographic ingenuity, imaginative story telling and fiscal daring. Disney went for a bundle (say $5 million in negative costs) in fashioning the Jules Verne classic.

The story of the 'monster' ship *Nautilus*, astounding as it may be, is so astutely developed that the audience immediately accepts its part on the excursion through Captain Nemo's underseas realm.

James Mason is the captain, a genius who had fashioned and guides the out-of-this-world craft. Kirk Douglas is a free-wheeling, roguish harpoon artist. Paul Lukas is a kind and gentle man of science and Peter Lorre is Lukas' fretting apprentice.

But it is the production itself that is the star. Technical skill was lavished in fashioning the fabulous *Nautilus* with its exquisitely appointed interior. The underwater lensing is remarkable on a number of counts, among them being the special designing of aqualungs and other equipment to match Verne's own illustrations.

Story opens in San Francisco where maritime men have been terrorized by reports of a monstrous denizen of the seas which has been sinking their ships. An armed frigate sets out in pursuit and is itself destroyed, with Lukas, Douglas and Lorre the survivors.

. . . .

■ 20,000 YEARS IN SING SING

1933, 78 MINS, US

Dir Michael Curtiz   *Scr* Wilson Mizner, Brown Holmes   *Ph* Barney McGill   *Ed* George Amy   *Mus* Bernhard Kaun   *Art Dir* Anton Grot
● Spencer Tracy, Bette Davis, Arthur Byron, Lyle Talbot, Warren Hymer, Louis Calhern (First National)

Interesting film material comes from warden Lewis E. Lawes' book of memoirs of prison administration. While it may take some liberties and overstep bounds of conviction, it's still good entertainment.

Sing Sing's warden can have no complaint against the Warner picture. He extended WB every cooperation in the filming and permitted cameras within his prison for actual scenes, including prisoners in the mob scenes.

Of pictures having inside of penal institutions as their locale, this one is the best. It builds up its interest strongly through that alone, covering a lot of routine that's unknown to most outsiders. Finally, it begins to appear Sing Sing wouldn't be a bad place at all to spend a vacation over the Depression. Arthur Byron's paternal smile as the warden, his anxiety to create reform and allow plenty of leeway even to tuff ones among his charges, would make it quite a resort.

Though let out to visit the dying gal friend and committing murder meanwhile, convict Tom Connors (Spencer Tracy) returns,

putting the warden's honor system to the strongest test imaginable. In the end it's the chair for the reformed bad boy whose only regret seems to be his parting from the warden's shelter and benevolence.

Far-fetched, but it sells. Considerable comedy dots the action. Tracy and Warren Hymer, teamed in *Up the River* for Fox, are again together. Bette Davis is the convict's moll who does him dirt in one breath and shoots to kill for him in another. She's not particularly impressive here.

. . . .

■ TWICE IN A LIFETIME

1985, 117 MINS, US ◇ Ⓥ

Dir Bud Yorkin   *Prod* Bud Yorkin   *Scr* Colin Welland   *Ph* Nick McLean   *Ed* Robert Jones   *Mus* Pat Metheny   *Art Dir* William Creber
● Gene Hackman, Ann-Margret, Ellen Burstyn, Amy Madigan, Ally Sheedy, Stephen Lang (Yorkin)

An edgy, shifty-eyed 50th birthday tribute for hero Harry Mackenzie gets this midlife-crisis film off to a risky, sentimental start, and from there on out it's Ellen Burstyn, the abandoned wife, versus Gene Hackman, the not-unsympathetic-but-risk-taking husband, vying for audience affections.

Burstyn claims the film as Kate, who has to cope with her own life and family, and some rather mediocre lines. Hackman is stalwart and determined in his resolve to make a new life with Ann-Margret, but she is far too sexy and he far too underdeveloped for anybody to understand what she sees in him.

The pic is loaded with jock humor and incidental comments that allow the characters' frustrations to seep out. Audiences will love Burstyn's warm wrinkles and visit with her daughters to a male strip joint, as well as Hackman's workmanlike heroism.

. . . .

■ TWILIGHT FOR THE GODS

1958, 120 MINS, US ◇

Dir Joseph Pevney   *Prod* Gordon Kay   *Scr* Ernest K. Gann   *Ph* Irving Glassberg   *Ed* Russell Schoengarth   *Mus* David Raksin   *Art Dir* Alexander Golitzen, Eric Orbors
● Rock Hudson, Cyd Charisse, Arthur Kennedy, Leif Erickson, Charles McGraw, Richard Haydn (Universal)

Twilight for the Gods emerges as a routine sea adventure drama, bolstered by the marquee names of Rock Hudson and Cyd Charisse. Novelist Ernest Gann, who also wrote the screenplay, has employed the familiar technique [from his successful *The High and the Mighty*] of assembling a group of passengers of different personalities and backgrounds, including several with shady pasts, and studies their reactions to the dangers encountered during a long sea voyage.

There's Hudson, a court-martialed ship's captain fighting alcoholism, as the skipper of the battered sailing ship; Charisse as a Honolulu call girl running away from the authorities; Arthur Kennedy as a bitter and treacherous second mate; Leif Erickson as a down-and-out showman; Judith Evelyn as a has-been opera singer; Vladimir Sokoloff and Celia Lovsky as an elderly refugee couple; Ernest Truex as a missionary, and Richard Haydn as a British beachcomber.

Filmed on location in the Hawaiian islands, the photography is a delight to the eyes as it captures the sailing ship in motion, a sea village, various beaches and sites on a chain of islands, Honolulu harbor, and Waikalulu Falls.

. . . .

■ TWILIGHT ZONE THE MOVIE

1983, 102 MINS, US ◇ Ⓥ

Dir John Landis, Steven Spielberg, Joe Dante, George Miller   *Prod* Steven Spielberg, John Landis   *Scr* John Landis, George Clayton Johnson, Richard Matheson,

Josh Rogan   *Ph* Steve Larner, Allen Daviau, John Hora   *Ed* Malcolm Campbell, Michael Kahn, Tina Hirsch, Howard Smith   *Mus* Jerry Goldsmith   *Art Dir* James D. Bissell
● Dan Aykroyd, Albert Brooks, Vic Morrow, Scatman Crothers, Kathleen Quinlan, John Lithgow (Warner)

Twilight Zone, feature film spinoff from Rod Serling's perennially popular 1960s TV series, plays much like a traditional vaudeville card, what with its tantalizing teaser opening followed by three sketches of increasing quality, all building up to a socko headline act.

Pic consists of prolog by John Landis as well as vignettes, none running any longer than original TV episodes, by Landis, Steven Spielberg, Joe Dante and George Miller. Dante and Miller manage to shine the brightest in this context.

Landis gets things off to a wonderful start with a comic prolog starring Dan Aykroyd and Albert Brooks.

Landis' principal episode, however, is a downbeat, one-dimensional fable about racial and religious intolerance. An embittered, middle-aged man who has just been passed over for a job promotion, Vic Morrow sports a torrent of racial epithets aimed at Jews, Blacks and Orientals while drinking with buddies at a bar. Upon exiting, he finds himself in Nazi-occupied Paris as a suspected Jew on the run from the Gestapo.

This is the only sequence in the film not derived from an actual TV episode, although it does bear a thematic resemblance to a 1961 installment titled *A Quality of Mercy*.

Spielberg's entry is the most down-to-earth of all the stories. In a retirement home filled with oldsters living in the past, spry Scatman Crothers encourages various residents to think young and, in organizing a game of kick the can, actually transforms them into their childhood selves again.

Most bizarre contribution comes from Dante. Outsider Kathleen Quinlan enters the Twilight Zone courtesy of little Jeremy Licht, who lords it over a Looney-Tune household by virtue of his power to will anything into existence except happiness.

But wisely, the best has been saved for last. Miller's re-working of *Nightmare at 20,000 Feet*, about a man who sees a gremlin tearing up an engine wing of an airplane, is electrifying from beginning to end.

■ **TWILIGHT'S LAST GLEAMING**

1977, 146 MINS, US/W. GERMANY ◇ Ⓥ
Dir Robert Aldrich   *Prod* Merv Adleson   *Scr* Ronald M. Cohen, Edward Huebsch   *Ph* Robert Hauser   *Ed* Michael Luciano   *Mus* Jerry Goldsmith   *Art Dir* Rolf Zehetbauer
● Burt Lancaster, Richard Widmark, Charles Durning, Melvyn Douglas, Paul Winfield, Burt Young (Lorimar/Geria)

Robert Aldrich's *Twilight's Last Gleaming* is intricate, intriguing and intelligent drama. Filmed in Munich, the setting is the US.

Burt Lancaster stars as a cashiered US Air Force officer who seizes a nuclear missile site to force public disclosure of secret Vietnam war policy goals. Charles Durning is outstanding as a US president who must respond to the challenge.

A Walter Wager novel, *Viper Three*, has been adapted into a suspenseful and taut confrontation.

Outside, Richard Widmark mobilizes for the forcible recapture of the base, while in the White House, Durning assembles his top military and Cabinet advisors to ponder Lancaster's demands.

■ **TWINS**

1988, 112 MINS, US ◇ Ⓥ
Dir Ivan Reitman   *Prod* Ivan Reitman   *Scr* William Davies, William Osborne, Timothy Harris, Herschel Weingrad   *Ph* Andrzej Bartkowiak   *Ed* Sheldon Kahn, Donn Cambern   *Mus* Georges Delerue   *Art Dir* James D. Bissell
● Arnold Schwarzenegger, Danny DeVito, Kelly Preston, Chloe Webb, Bonnie Bartlett (Universal)

Director Ivan Reitman more than delivers on the wacky promise of *Twins* in this nutty, storybook tale of siblings separated at birth and reunited at age 35.

Arnold Schwarzenegger plays Julius Benedict, a perfect specimen of a man in both body and soul, raised as an orphan in pristine innocence on a tropical isle. Created in a genetic experiment, he has a twin brother on the mainland. Lionhearted Julius, filled with familiar longing, rushes off to LA to search for bro – only to discover he'd have found him faster by looking under rocks.

Danny DeVito's Vincent Benedict is a major creep, a guy you wouldn't mind seeing get hit by a car. To him, Julius is a dopey nut who makes a good bodyguard. They finally set out to locate their mother, but Vincent still is on his incorrigible path.

Schwarzenegger is a delightful surprise in this perfect transitional role to comedy. So strongly does he project the tenderness, nobility and puppy-dog devotion that make Julius tick that one is nearly hypnotized into suspending disbelief.

DeVito is a blaze of energy and body language as Vince, articulating the part as though he's written it himself.

■ **TWINS OF EVIL**

1971, 87 MINS, UK ◇ Ⓥ
Dir John Hough   *Prod* Harry Fine, Michael Style   *Scr* Tudor Gates   *Ph* Dick Bush   *Ed* Spencer Reeve   *Mus* Harry Robinson   *Art Dir* Roy Stannard
● Madeleine Collinson, Mary Collinson, Peter Cushing, Kathleen Byron, Dennis Price, Damien Thomas (Hammer)

Blood flows and thunder roars as Mary and Madeleine Collinson, attractive identical twins playing orphans, come to live with their witch-hunting, godfearing uncle (Peter Cushing), in the shadow of dreaded Karnstein Castle.

One is good and timid while the other is bold and brazen. The latter cannot wait to find out more about the castle and the handsome young count (Damien Thomas). He is one of the undead and soon she is his victim. The question becomes, which twin is the vampire?

John Hough has given Tudor Gates' script a good pace and directed so that audiences can take it as straight horror or as a slight send-up. Settings, production values, camerawork and acting are all of a high standard.

■ **TWISTED NERVE**

1968, 118 MINS, UK ◇ Ⓥ
Dir Roy Boulting   *Prod* George W. George, Frank Granat   *Scr* Roy Boulting, Leo Marks   *Ph* Harry Waxman   *Ed* Martin Charles   *Mus* Bernard Herrmann   *Art Dir* Albert Witherick
● Hayley Mills, Hywel Bennett, Billie Whitelaw, Phyllis Calvert, Frank Finlay (British Lion)

Twisted Nerve has Hayley Mills involved in some fairly gruesome *Psycho*-like proceedings.

She's a bit shocked when the young antihero (Hywel Bennett) catches her off guard and kisses her fiercely; she's sweetly reasonable when he suddenly turns to her stark naked; and she eventually faces near-rape and imminent murder with displeasure, but non-Disney-like aplomb.

There's a firm, if unwitting, implication of a link between Down's Syndrome and homi-

cidal madness. This dangerous untruth is likely to be offensive to many.

This angle was not necessary. Stripped of it the film could still stand up as a reasonably tough chilling suspenser giving a compelling study of a warped young psychopath. Bennett, with his babyface and pageboy-bobbed hairstyle, is compelling, his performance being an effectively blended piece of menace.

Roy Boulting lacks the subtleties of a Hitchcock but manages to bring some brooding menace into his direction, woven with some neat dialog and brash humor.

■ **TWO FOR THE ROAD**

1967, 112 MINS, UK ◇ Ⓥ
Dir Stanley Donen   *Prod* Stanley Donen   *Scr* Frederic Raphael   *Ph* Christopher Challis   *Ed* Richard Marden, Madeleine Gug   *Mus* Henry Mancini   *Art Dir* Willy Holt
● Audrey Hepburn, Albert Finney, Eleanor Bron, William Daniels, Claude Dauphin, Georges Descrieres (20th Century-Fox)

As far as producer, director, femme lead and screenwriter are concerned, this attempt to visually analyze the bits and pieces that go into making a marriage, and then making it work, is successful. If it drags a bit here and there, blame it on the stodgy performance of actor Albert Finney who is unable to convey the lightness, gaiety and romanticism needed.

In the story, the same married couple make basically the same trip, from London to the Riviera, at three different stages of their life with continual crosscutting and flashing backwards and forwards from one period to the other.

The credibility of the changes in periods is left, except for changes of costume and vehicular equipment, to the two leads. Finney remains the same throughout but Audrey Hepburn is amazing in her ability to portray a very young girl, a just pregnant wife of two years, and a beginning-to-be-bored wife of five years.

■ **TWO FOR THE SEESAW**

1962, 119 MINS, US
Dir Robert Wise   *Prod* Walter Mirisch   *Scr* Isobel Lennart   *Ph* Ted McCord   *Ed* Stuart Gilmore   *Mus* Andre Previn   *Art Dir* Boris Leven
● Robert Mitchum, Shirley MacLaine, Edmon Ryan, Elisabeth Fraser, Eddie Firestone, Billy Gray (United Artists)

There is a fundamental torpor about *Seesaw* that is less troublesome on stage that it is on screen, a medium of motion that exaggerates its absence, that emphasizes the slightest hint of listlessness. On film, it drags. It drags in spite of the charm, insight, wit and compassion of William Gibson's play, the savvy and sense of scenarist Isobel Lennart's mild revisions and additions, the infectious friskiness of Shirley MacLaine's performance and the consummate care taken by those who shaped and mounted the film reproduction.

The basic flaws appear to be the play's innate talkiness and the unbalance of the two-way 'see-saw'. The selection of Robert Mitchum for the role of Jerry Ryan proves not to have a been a wise one. The strong attraction Gittel is supposed to feel for Jerry becomes less plausible because of Mitchum's lethargic, droopy-eyed enactment. Something more appealing and magnetic is needed to make this love affair ring true.

MacLaine's performance in the meaty role of the disarmingly candid, stupendously kindhearted Gittel Mosca, is a winning one. Her handling of the Yiddish dialect and accompanying mannerisms is sufficiently reserved so that it does not lapse into a kind of gittal-gitterless caricature.

T

TWO GENTLEMEN SHARING

1969, 106 MINS, UK ◇
Dir Ted Kotcheff *Prod* J. Barry Kulick *Scr* Evan
Jones *Ph* Billy Williams *Mus* Stanley Myers
● Robin Phillips, Judy Geeson, Esther Anderson, Hal
Frederick, Norman Rossington, Rachel Kempson
(American-International)

Film boasts a solid and well-chosen cast,
strong physical values for such a medium-
scaled item, and a racial story [from a novel
by David Stuart Leslie] delivered with
unhysterical acumen and, at times, with considerable barbed humor.

The two 'gentlemen' who share the London
pad in question are a young white ad exec
with a liberal outlook and a certain disgust –
or mistrust – for his middle-class background, and a black lawyer with a youthfully
unblunted hope of making a go of things in
his profession on his own merits.

Robin Phillips has just the right naive physique as the well-meaner who bears the major
brunt of film's thematics and manages to convince as the white member of the temporary
duo, while Hal Frederick is generally very
good.

200 MOTELS

1971, 98 MINS, UK ◇ ⊛
Dir Frank Zappa, Tony Palmer *Prod* Jerry Good, Herb
Cohen *Scr* Frank Zappa, Tony Palmer *Ph* Tony
Palmer *Ed* Rich Harrison *Mus* Frank Zappa
Art Dir Leo Austin
● The Mothers of Invention, Theodore Bikel, Ringo
Starr, Janet Ferguson, Lucy Offerall, Pamela Miller
(United Artists)

Frank Zappa's *200 Motels*, featuring his
group, The Mothers Of Invention, plus
Theodore Bikel and Ringo Starr, is the
zaniest. The film is a series of surrealistic sequences allegedly inspired by the experiences
of a rock group on the road. The incidents are
often outrageously irreverent. The comedy is
fast and furious, both sophisticated and
sophomoric.

The story proceeds on many different
levels. Bikel appears to superior advantage in
several characterizations: a TV m.c., an
officious military bureaucrat, and something
resembling a British secret agent or banker.
Starr's okay cameo has him dressed up like
Zappa. Group member Jimmy Carl Black is
excellent as a redneck cowboy, Keith Moon is
in nun's drag; Janet Ferguson and Lucy
Offerall (it says here) are smash as two jaded
groupies; and leather-costumed Pamela
Miller scores as an underground newshen.

Film is the first theatrical release to have
been shot in the color vidtape-to-film process
of Technicolor's vidtronics subsid. The
seven-day shooting sked (on a reported
$600,000 budget) was followed by 11 days of
editing.

TWO JAKES, THE

1990, 138 MINS, US ◇ ⊛
Dir Jack Nicholson *Prod* Robert Evans, Harold
Schneider *Scr* Robert Towne *Ph* Vilmos Zsigmond
Ed Anne Goursand *Mus* Van Dyke Parks
Art Dir Jeremy Railton, Richard Sawyer
● Jack Nicholson, Harvey Keitel, Meg Tilly, Madeleine
Stowe, Eli Wallach, Frederic Forrest (Paramount)

Following a trek to the bigscreen almost as
convoluted as its plot, this oft-delayed sequel
proves a jumbled, obtuse yet not entirely
unsatisfying follow-up to *Chinatown*, rightly
considered one of the best films of the 1970s.
Like much of the film noir of the 1940s, *Jakes*
simply spins a web of intrigue so thick its origins become imperceptible.

Picking up in 1948, 11 years after the events
in *Chinatown*, Jake Gittes (Jack Nicholson)
has become a prosperous and respected private investigator, though he still makes his
living spying on an unfaithful wife (Meg
Tilly) for her suspicious husband, Jake
Berman (Harvey Keitel).

When the name of Katherine Mulwray
turns up on an audiotape of the couple in bed
together, it revives Gittes' ghosts of events
that occurred in *Chinatown*, linking sex, murder and deceit to the role of precious resources – *Chinatown*, water; here, oil – in a
developing Southern California. The film
then takes on a dual structure, with Gittes in
the eye of the hurricane as holder of the
incriminating tape while seeking to unravel
its connection to Mulwray, the memorable
product of the coupling of father and
daughter in Roman Polanski's earlier film.

A few scenes do carry tremendous power,
especially Gittes' confrontation with detective Loach (David Keith) and, from a comic
standpoint, his encounter with the murdered
man's not-so-grieving widow Lillian (Stowe).
Still, Nicholson the director (working from
Robert Towne's script) provides too few
moments of that stripe for Nicholson the star.

TWO LEFT FEET

1965, 93 MINS, UK
Dir Roy Baker *Prod* Roy Baker, Leslie Gilliat *Scr* Roy
Baker, John Hopkins *Ph* Wilkie Cooper *Ed* Michael
Hart *Mus* Phil Green
● Michael Crawford, Nyree Dawn Porter, Julia Foster,
Michael Craze, David Hemmings, Dilys Watling (British
Lion)

Whatever attracted producers in David
Stuart Leslie's novel must have been lost in
the transition to the screen because this is a
very flyweight trite pic. It explores in only the
most superficial terms the dilemma of a
gauche youth whose ham-handed attempts to
cope with his early sex problems are not
highly satisfactory.

A callow youth is infatuated with a teasing
waitress but his attempt to seduce her ends in
disaster. She turns to brighter young men at a
jazz club and he finds consolation in a naive
young shop assistant.

Undertones of homosexuality between two
of the youths are only hinted at and the sex
lark is more talked about than acted upon.
An attempt to satirize an appalling suburban
wedding party becomes more of a caricature.
Director Baker seems to have been unable to
pull together a limp script.

Nyree Dawn Porter plays the waitress with
exaggerated sex appeal. Michael Crawford
handles the role of the gauche lad likeably.
But much of the dialog is out of step with the
minus-confidence character he is playing.
Julia Foster, as the simple, goodhearted
wench with whom he feels at ease, is pleasant, but unexciting.

TWO LOVES

1961, 100 MINS, US ◇
Dir Charles Walters *Prod* Julian Blaustein *Scr* Ben
Maddow *Ph* Joseph Ruttenberg *Ed* Fredric
Steinkamp *Mus* Bronislau Kaper *Art Dir* George W.
Davis, Urie McCleary
● Shirley MacLaine, Laurence Harvey, Jack Hawkins,
Juano Hernandez, Norah Howard, Nobu McCarthy
(M-G-M)

Frigidity is the subject broached by *Two
Loves*, a story of the reawakening of a spinster
American schoolteacher in New Zealand.
Based on Sylvia Ashton-Warner's novel
Spinster, it also takes a passing swipe at US
morality, examines the vigorous spontaneous
way-of-life of the Maori natives and utilizes
the 'civilized' point-of-view of western-white
values as a frame of reference. Unfortunately,
the personal story emerges less lucid than its
broader overtones.

Shirley MacLaine plays a dedicated schoolteacher who has found her way to an isolated
settlement in northern New Zealand from
Pennsylvania, although how and why is
never clearly established. Her dogged innocence is threatened by the amorous advances
of Laurence Harvey, a rather irrational and
immature fellow teacher unhappy with his lot
but unable to rise above it. Influenced by the
primitive but practical morality of the Maoris, she seems on the verge of giving her all to
Harvey when he (rather conveniently) comes
to a violent end in a motorcycle mishap. On
the rebound, she is coaxed out of self-guilt
pangs by senior school inspector Jack
Hawkins.

MacLaine, although not ideally suited to
the role, manages for the most part to rise
above the miscasting and deliver an earnest,
interesting portrayal. But there is a degree of
gravity and warmth missing in her delineation, making it slightly difficult to understand
Harvey's passion and Hawkins' tender affection for her. Nobu McCarthy comes through
with flying colors as a 15-year-old Maori girl
delighted to bear Harvey's children out of
wedlock.

TWO MOON JUNCTION

1988, 104 MINS, US ◇ ⊛
Dir Zalman King *Prod* Donald P. Borchers
Scr Zalman King *Ph* Mark Plummer *Ed* Marc
Grossman *Mus* Jonathan Elias *Art Dir* Michelle
Minch
● Sherilyn Fenn, Richard Tyson, Louise Fletcher, Kristy
McNichol, Martin Hewitt, Burl Ives (DDM/Lorimar)

Two Moon Junction is a bad hick version of *Last
Tango in Paris* down to the poor imitative scoring by Jonathan Elias. Sexual obsession
might be the aim, but the result is anything
but hot.

In the Maria Schneider role is Madonna-
clone Sherilyn Fenn who decides to give her
virginity to a guy who works at the traveling
midway (Richard Tyson) instead of her
fiance (Martin Hewitt). She wears white all
the time and acts pure when on her home
turf.

Plot has all the ingredients of a 1940s meller
with the obvious exception that poor little
rich girl Fenn unabashedly defrocks at the
drop of a hat while Tyson manages to never
bare much more than his chest.

Kristy McNichol appears as a midway
groupie whose subtle bisexual scenes dancing
with Fenn have more electricity than Fenn's
encounters with Tyson.

Shot in and around Los Angeles pic seldom
looks like Alabama.

TWO MRS CARROLLS, THE

1947, 100 MINS, US
Dir Peter Godfrey *Prod* Mark Hellinger *Scr* Thomas
Job *Ph* Peverell Marley *Ed* Frederick Richards
Mus Franz Waxman *Art Dir* Anton Grot
● Humphrey Bogart, Barbara Stanwyck, Alexis Smith,
Nigel Bruce (Warner)

The Two Mrs Carrolls, adapted from the Martin Vale legiter, is more stage play than
motion picture. Overladen with dialog as action substitute, it talks itself out of much of
the suspense that should have developed.
There is some femme appeal, however, in the
Humphrey Bogart character as hero-villain.

Production format hugs stage technique in
settings and carrying out story. Backgrounds
never seem realistic but rather appear as
grouped on stage. Bogart, Barbara Stanwyck
and Alexis Smith feel the burden of dialog
and unnatural characters but, under Peter
Godfrey's direction, manage to give material
an occasional lift

Plot deals with married artist who meets a
new love while vacationing in Scotland. He

returns to London, murders his wife by methodical poisoning and marries the new flame. Second marriage works okay until another attractive girl appears.

. . . .

■ TWO MULES FOR SISTER SARA

1970, 116 MINS, US ◇ Ⓥ

Dir Don Siegel   *Prod* Martin Rackin   *Scr* Albert Maltz   *Ph* Gabriel Figueroa   *Ed* Robert F. Shugrue   *Mus* Ennio Morricone   *Art Dir* Jose Rodriguez Granada

● Shirley MacLaine, Clint Eastwood, Manolo Fabregas, Alberto Morin, Armando Silverstre, John Kelly (Universal/Malpaso)

Two Mules for Sister Sara might have worked. But with Clint Eastwood as one of the mules, an American mercenary looking for a fast peso in old French-occupied Mexico, Shirley MacLaine as a scarlet sister disgised in a nun's habit, and Don Siegel's by-the-old-book direction, it doesn't.

Screenplay based on a story by Budd Boetticher, needed a Lee Marvin, or a portrayal like Humphrey Bogart's in *The African Queen* to work. MacLaine is literally unbelievable as a nun, and the story's main thread of tension, the relationship between her and Eastwood, simply dissipates.

Siegel and Mexican cameraman Gabriel Figueroa use the Mexican locations to great advantage, with sweeping panoramics of the brutal countryside and intriguing settings.

. . . .

■ TWO OF A KIND

1983, 87 MINS, US ◇ Ⓥ

Dir John Herzfeld   *Prod* Roger M. Rothstein, Joe Wizan   *Scr* John Herzfeld   *Ph* Fred Koenekamp   *Ed* Jack Hofstra   *Mus* Patrick Williams   *Art Dir* Albert Brenner

● John Travolta, Olivia Newton-John, Charles Durning, Beatrice Straight, Scatman Crothers, Oliver Reed (20th Century-Fox)

Aside from the presence of the two stars, *Two of a Kind* has all the earmarks of a bargain-basement job. Sets are as constricted as those for live, three-camera sitcoms, and many of the so-called New York location scenes possess an obvious back-lot look.

Script's only vaguely amusing conceit presents itself at the beginning, when God returns from a vacation and, finding the world gone to seed in the interim, announces to four of his angels that he's going to wipe out the human race and start over again. The angels urge Him to reconsider His decision based on whether or not a random man can prove himself possible of genuine goodness.

So John Travolta, a self-styled inventor of such inane items as edible sunglasses, is selected as the guinea pig, just in time to find him robbing a bank in order to pay off a debt to the mob. Bank teller Olivia Newton-John, fired for flirting with the stick-up man, actually makes off with the dough. She is saved by Travolta after being taken hostage by a gunman.

. . . .

■ TWO PEOPLE

1973, 100 MINS, US ◇

Dir Robert Wise   *Prod* Robert Wise   *Scr* Richard DeRoy   *Ph* Henri Decae   *Ed* William Reynolds   *Mus* David Shire   *Art Dir* Henry Michelson

● Peter Fonda, Lindsay Wagner, Estelle Parsons, Alan Fudge, Philippe March, Frances Sternhagen (Filmakers/Universal)

Two People is a major disappointment. Producer-director Robert Wise's film clearly aimed to develop a love-at-first-sight romance, in the form of a 'road' film, between two characters whose different life styles parallel in brief encounter. However, sluggish pacing and ludicrous dialog turn the film into a travesty of its own form.

Script finds Peter Fonda, a repentant Vietnam field deserter, tired of running and ready to return to the US to face his court martial and punishment. In Marrakech, Fonda meets Lindsay Wagner, a fashion model in the tow of her editor (Estelle Parsons) and her live-in lover (Geoffrey Horne), father of their child (Brian Lima) stashed in Manhattan with her mother Frances Sternhagen.

The film's pacing turns the desired audience wish – that the couple make physical love – into barely concealed impatience.

. . . .

■ 2001: A SPACE ODYSSEY

1968, 160 MINS, UK ◇ Ⓥ

Dir Stanley Kubrick   *Prod* Stanley Kubrick   *Scr* Stanley Kubrick, Arthur C. Clarke   *Ph* Geoffrey Unsworth, John Alcott   *Ed* Ray Lovejoy   *Mus* Johann Strauss, Gyorgy Ligeti, Aram Khachaturyan   *Art Dir* Tony Masters, Harry Lange, Ernie Archer

● Keir Dullea, Gary Lockwood, William Sylvester, Daniel Richter, Douglas Rain, Leonard Rossiter (M-G-M)

When Stanley Kubrick and sci-fi specialist Arthur C. Clarke first conceived the idea of making a Cinerama film, neither had any idea that it would run into a project of several years.

A major achievement in cinematography and special effects, *2001* lacks dramatic appeal and only conveys suspense after the halfway mark; Kubrick must receive all the praise – and take all the blame.

The plot, so-called, uses up almost two hours in exposition of scientific advances in space travel and communications, before anything happens.

The little humor is provided by introducing well-known commercial names which are presumably still operational during the space age – the Orbiter Hilton hotel and Pan Am space ships.

Keir Dullea and Gary Lockwood, as the two principal astronauts, are not introduced until well along in the film. Their complete lack of emotion becomes rather implausible during scenes where they discuss the villainy of Hal, the talking computer.

Kubrick and Clarke have kept dialog to a minimum, frequently inserting lengthy passages where everything is told visually. The tremendous centrifuge which makes up the principal set (in which the two astronauts live and travel) reportedly cost $750,000 and looks every bit of it.

. . . .

■ 2010

1984, 114 MINS, US ◇ Ⓥ

Dir Peter Hyams   *Prod* Peter Hyams   *Scr* Peter Hyams   *Ph* Peter Hyams   *Ed* James Mitchell   *Mus* David Shire   *Art Dir* Albert Brenner

● Roy Scheider, John Lithgow, Helen Mirren, Bob Balaban, Keir Dullea, Douglas Rain (M-G-M)

As the title proclaims, *2010* begins nine years after something went wrong with the Jupiter voyage of Discovery. On earth, politicians have brought the US and Russia to the brink of war, but their scientists have united in a venture to return to Jupiter to seek an answer to Discovery's fate and the significance of the huge black monolith that orbits near it.

American crew is headed by Roy Scheider, John Lithgow and Bob Balaban. The Soviets want them along mainly for their understanding of HAL 9000, whose mutiny remains unexplained. If revived in the salvage effort, can HAL still be trusted?

In Peter Hyams' hands, the HAL mystery is the most satisfying substance of the film and handled the best. Unfortunately, it lies amid a hodge-podge of bits and pieces.

. . . .

■ TWO WEEKS IN ANOTHER TOWN

1962, 106 MINS, US ◇

Dir Vincente Minnelli   *Prod* John Houseman   *Scr* Charles Schnee   *Ph* Milton Krasner   *Ed* Adrienne Fazan, Robert J. Kern Jr   *Mus* David Raksin   *Art Dir* George W. Davis, Urie McCleary

● Kirk Douglas, Edward G. Robinson, Cyd Charisse, George Hamilton, Dahlia Lavi, Claire Trevor (M-G-M)

Two Weeks in Another Town [from the novel by Irwin Shaw] is not an achievement about which any of its creative people are apt to boast.

Kirk Douglas stars as an unstable actor, fresh off a three-year hitch in sanitariums, who goes to Rome to rejoin the director (Edward G. Robinson) with whom, years earlier, he's scored his greatest triumphs. In the course of a series of shattering incidents, Douglas comes to discover that it is upon himself alone that he must rely for the stability and strength of character with which he can fulfill his destiny.

Douglas emotes with his customary zeal and passion, but labors largely in vain to illuminate an unbelievable character. Even less believable is the character of his ex-wife, a black-as-night, hard-as-nails seductress exotically overplayed by Cyd Charisse.

Only remotely lifelike characters in the story are Robinson and Claire Trevor as an ambiguous married couple whose personalities transform under the secretive cover of night.

There is a haunting score by David Raksin. A considerable amount of footage from *The Bad and the Beautiful* is cleverly incorporated into the drama. As a matter of fact, the portion of the film-within-a-film is livelier than just about anything else in the film.

. . . .

■ TWO-FACED WOMAN

1941, 94 MINS, US

Dir George Cukor   *Prod* Gottfried Reinhardt   *Scr* S.N. Behrman, Salka Viertel, George Oppenheimer   *Ph* Joseph Ruttenberg   *Ed* George Boemler   *Mus* Bronislau Kaper

● Greta Garbo, Melvyn Douglas, Constance Bennett, Ruth Gordon, Roland Young (M-G-M)

In a daring piece of showmanship, Metro presents the one-time queen of mystery in a wild, and occasionally very risque, slap farce entitled *Two-Faced Woman*. That the experiment of converting Greta Garbo into a comedienne is not entirely successful is no fault of hers. Had the script writers and the director, George Cukor, entered into the spirit of the thing with as much enthusiasm, lack of self-consciousness and abandon as the star, the result would have been a smash hit.

There is no holding back Garbo when she steps down from the serious dramatic pedestal and has her fling with broad comedy. Melvyn Douglas is an excellent foil. Much of the action takes place in bedrooms, boudoirs and the psychological proximities of both.

The story, which was taken from a play by Ludwig Fulda, is one of those naturalized importations from the Continent wherein the wife masquerades during most of the film as her own twin-sister just to test the fibre of her husband's adoration. There's a double entendre to nearly everything that is said between the two, and nearly everything is said.

. . . .

■ TWO-HEADED SPY, THE

1958, 93 MINS, UK

Dir Andre de Toth   *Prod* Bill Kirby   *Scr* James O'Donnell   *Ph* Ted Scaife   *Ed* Raymond Poulton   *Mus* Gerard Schurmann   *Art Dir* Ivan King

● Jack Hawkins, Gia Scala, Erik Schumann, Alexander Knox, Felix Aylmer, Donald Pleasence (Sabre)

Based on a real-life story, this pursues a fairly pedestrian beat but it builds its tension excellently and without too blatant use of the usual cloak-and-dagger methods. Director Andre de Toth has sought to get his effects by showing the mental strain of Jack Hawkins in his dilemma rather than by stress on too much physical danger.

Hawkins, a British spy in both wars, and therefore an exile in Germany between the two conflicts, has built up confidence as an astute, loyal and resourceful member of the Nazi machine. At the same time he is feeding the Allies invaluable information through a British agent, neatly played by Felix Aylmer, disguised as an antique clock seller. When Aylmer is arrested and murdered, suspicion falls on Hawkins through his aide, a member of the Gestapo. But he manages to brush off this suspicion and continues his espionage through his new contact, a beautiful singer.

Hawkins plays the role of the general with his usual reliability. Rightly not attempting to assume the suspicion of a German accent, he is thoroughly convincing as the general, with the right hint of arrogance.

· ·

■ TWO-LANE BLACKTOP

1971, 102 MINS, US ◇

Dir Monte Hellman   *Prod* Michael S. Laughlin
Scr Rudolph Wurlitzer, Will Corry   *Ph* Jack Deerson
Ed Monte Hellman   *Mus* Bill James (sup.)
● James Taylor, Warren Oates, Laurie Bird, Dennis Wilson (Universal)

The strange and sometimes pathetic world of barnstorming, hustling street-racing is explored with feeling by director-editor Monte Hellman in *Two-Lane Blacktop*. The production, shot on cross-country locations, shapes up as an excellent combination of in-depth contemporary story-telling and personality casting.

Will Corry's story, scripted by Rudolph Wurlitzer and Corry, establishes James Taylor as a modern dropout, living on winnings from impromptu pavement racing challenges. Dennis Wilson is his expert mechanic. En route to nowhere in particular, they are latched onto by Laurie Bird.

The strong and compelling plot fibre is supplied by the writing, direction and performing of Warren Oates' role. He's an older man, a failure in some Establishment profession, now roaming the country in a souped-up Detroit vehicle. When Oates challenges Taylor to a cross-country run, with vehicle ownership the payoff, the story becomes a superior interplay of basic human nature.

Much of the story's import is on Oates' back, and he carries it like a champion in an outstanding performance.

· ·

■ TWO-MINUTE WARNING

1976, 115 MINS, US ◇ Ⓥ

Dir Larry Peerce   *Prod* Edward S. Feldman
Scr Edward Hume   *Ph* Gerald Hirschfeld   *Ed* Eve Newman, Walter Hannemann   *Mus* Charles Fox
Art Dir Herman A. Blumenthal
● Charlton Heston, John Cassavetes, Martin Balsam, Beau Bridges, Marilyn Hassett, David Janssen (Universal)

An off-the-beaten-track story [based on the novel by George La Fountaine] of a football stadium crowd menaced by a sniper, combined with above-average plotting, acting and direction.

The sniper is introduced intriguingly via subjective camera, but later is seen (Warren Miller) in teasing long shots, blurred closed-circuit pans and other clever devices which keep him all the more menacing.

Among the prominent players, all of whom take seriously their roles, are stadium manager Martin Balsam and assistant Brock Peters; unmarried but longtime lovers David Janssen and Gena Rowlands (she can convey

a reel of characterization in 10 seconds of film); and unemployed young father Beau Bridges, trying to show his and wife Pamela Bellwood's children a good time.

· ·

■ TWO-WAY STRETCH

1960, 87 MINS, UK Ⓥ

Dir Robert Day   *Prod* George Black, Alfred Black
Scr John Warren, Len Heath, Alan Hackney
Ph Geoffrey Faithfull   *Ed* Bert Rule   *Mus* Ken Jones
● Peter Sellers, Wilfred Hyde White, David Lodge, Bernard Cribbins, Maurice Denham, Lionel Jeffries (British Lion)

Peter Sellers gives another deft, very funny performance in *Two-Way Stretch*. The thin story line concerns a free-and-easy prison run by a governor who is more interested in gardening than discipline. Occupying a cell, which is far more like a luxury bed-sitting room, are three partners in crime – Sellers, David Lodge and Bernard Cribbins. They have the prison completely sewn up.

Posing as a clergyman, an outside partner arrives with a scheme for stealing $5 million in diamonds. It needs the trio to break jail the night before their release, pull off the job, return to prison with their loot, and next morning walk out free men and with a perfect alibi. The arrival of a tough new chief warden frustrates their plans.

Much of the dialog was supplied by Alan Hackney and, almost certainly, by Sellers himself. Success of this film depends largely on the actors and Robert Day's brisk direction. Sellers has himself a ball as the leader of the crafty trio of crooks while Lodge and Cribbins make perfectly contrasted partners. A long list of tried, handpicked performers chip in when required.

· ·

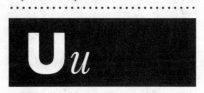

■ UGLY AMERICAN, THE

1963, 120 MINS, US Ⓥ

Dir George Englund   *Prod* George Englund
Scr Stewart Stern   *Ph* Clifford Stine   *Ed* Ted J. Kent
Mus Frank Skinner   *Art Dir* Alexander Golitzen, Alfred Sweeney
● Marlon Brando, Eiji Okada, Sandra Church, Arthur Hill, Pat Hingle, Jocelyn Brando (Universal)

Some of the ambiguities, hypocrisies and perplexities of cold war politics are observed, dramatized and, to a degree, analyzed in *The Ugly American*. It is a thought-provoking but uneven screen translation taken from, but not in a literal sense based upon, the popular novel by William J. Lederer and Eugene Burdick.

Focal figure of the story is an American ambassador (Marlon Brando) to a Southeast Asian nation who, after jumping to conclusions in the course of dealing with an uprising of the natives of that country against the existing regime and what they interpret as Yankee imperialism comes to understand that there is more to modern political revolution than meets the casual or jaundiced bystander's eye. As a result of his experience, he senses that Americans 'can't hope to win the cold war unless we remember what we're for as well as what we're against'.

Although skillfully and often explosively directed by George Englund and well played by Brando and others in the cast, the film tends to be overly talkative and lethargic in certain areas, vague and confusing in others. Probably the most jarring single flaw is the failure to clarify the exact nature of events during the ultimate upheaval.

Brando's performance is a towering one; restrained, intelligent and always masculine. Japanese actor Eiji Okada of *Hiroshima, mon amour* renown, makes a strong impression in his US film bow as Brando's old wartime buddy now popular (and seemingly Communist-motivated) leader of the strife-torn country to which Brando has been dispatched.

Mass riot scene near the outset of the picture is frighteningly realistic. Art direction is outstanding, with a convincing replica of a Southeast Asian village on the Universal backlot.

· ·

■ UGLY DACHSHUND, THE

1965, 93 MINS, US ◇

Dir Norman Tokar   *Prod* Walt Disney, Winston Hibley   *Scr* Albert Aley   *Ph* Edward Colman
Ed Robert Stafford   *Mus* George Bruns   *Art Dir* Carroll Clark, Marvin Aubrey Davis
● Dean Jones, Suzanne Pleshette, Charlie Ruggles, Kelly Thordsen, Farley Baer, Robert Kino (Walt Disney)

Walt Disney, who knows his way with a dog as well as a family, has turned out a rollicking piece of business in this comedy about a Great Dane which thinks he's a dachshund.

Dean Jones and Suzanne Pleshette are the two principals, a young married couple faced with the fancy cut-ups of four Dachs and a Dane raised with the low-slung pups. The Fritzels are hers, the Dane his, and actually the Albert Aley screenplay builds to trying to sell the Dane – named Brutus – that he actually is a Dane.

Action is light and airy as the couple go their own way with their respective pets, Suzanne insisting that Dean rid himself of the clumsy big-foot while her spouse stoutly maintains that his Dane has a rightful place in the household.

· ·

■ ULTIMATE SOLUTION OF GRACE QUIGLEY, THE

1984, 102 MINS, US ◇ Ⓥ

Dir Anthony Harvey   *Prod* Menahem Golan, Yoram Globus   *Scr* A. Martin Zweiback   *Ph* Larry Pizer
Ed Bob Raetano   *Mus* John Addison
● Katharine Hepburn, Nick Nolte, Elizabeth Wilson, Chip Zien, Kit Le Fever, William Duell (Cannon/Northbrook)

In this black comedy dealing with voluntary euthanasia by the Geritol set, casting Katharine Hepburn as the spry, entrepreneurial mother figure who arranges for her peers' demise and Nick Nolte as the gruff, hard-bitten and sarcastic hitman she hires, the two actors impart a light-hearted and whimsical tone to otherwise unpleasant subject matter.

Pic opens with Hepburn as a lonely and economically strapped pensioner who lost her immediate family in a pre-war auto accident, but who has a zestful embrace for life nonetheless. Sitting across from her apartment one day, she inadvertently witnesses Nolte put a bullet into her money-grubbing landlord, and subsequently enlists him in her scheme to provide a 'service' for her aging compatriots who wish to meet the hereafter ahead of schedule.

There are some marvelous supporting performances by Elizabeth Wilson as the spinster who can't get arrested trying to get Nolte to put her out of her misery, William Duell as the nerdy neighbor of Hepburn, and Kit Le Fever as Nolte's girlfriend hooker.

· ·

■ ULYSSES

1954, 104 MINS, ITALY ◇ Ⓥ

Dir Mario Camerini   *Prod* Carlo Ponti, Dino De Laurentiis   *Scr* Mario Camerini, Franco Brusati, Ben Hecht, Irwin Shaw, Hugh Gray, Ennio De Concini
Ph Harold Rosson   *Ed* Leo Catozzo   *Mus* Alessandro Cicognini   *Art Dir* Flavio Mogherini

● Kirk Douglas, Silvana Mangano, Anthony Quinn, Rossana Podesta, Jaques Dumesnil (Lux/Ponti-De Laurentiis)

A lot, perhaps too much, money went into the making of *Ulysses*, but expense shows. Besides the epic Homeric peg, pic has an internationally balanced cast, with Yank, French and Italian elements predominant.

Only a few of the w.k. Homeric episodes have been included in the already lengthy pic, and are told in flashback form as remembered by the hero. Featured are his love for Nausicaa; the cave of Polyphemus, the one-eyed monster; the Siren Rocks; the visit to Circe's Island cave and the return to Penelope. But material covered makes for plenty of action, dominated by a virile performance by Kirk Douglas.

Others include costar Silvana Mangano, a looker, as both Circe and Penelope, but unfortunately limited by both parts to expressing monotonous unhappiness until the finale. Anthony Quinn handles his bits well. For a spectacle, the pic runs too many closeups, with longish stretches of dialog between the two principals, or soliloquized.

■ ULYSSES

1967, 140 MINS, IRELAND ◇ Ⓥ

Dir Joseph Strick   *Prod* Joseph Strick   *Scr* Joseph Strick, Fred Haines   *Ph* Wolfgang Suschitzky   *Ed* Reginald Mills   *Mus* Stanley Myers   *Art Dir* Graham Probst
● Barbara Jefford, Milo O'Shea, Maurice Roeves, T.P. McKenna, Martin Dempsey, Sheila O'Sullivan (Continental/Walter Reade)

Ulysses [from James Joyce's novel] is a healthy, promising cinematic piece of flora, nightblooming and carnivorous. Filmed entirely in Ireland, with a cast almost entirely Irish, the picture concentrates on the trio of primary characters – Leopold and Molly Bloom and student Stephen Dedalus. Although their tales overlap, the primary emphasis is on the two males leaving the last 20 or 30 minutes to Molly's famous libidinous soliloquy.

Barbara Jefford's Molly is handsomely overblown, a wasted garden of a woman who yearns for a man with a passion that almost causes the screen to pulsate yet depriving Leopold of his marital rights because she so abhors another possibility of pregnancy. Milo O'Shea's Leopold Bloom is a realised example of the degraded, dejected husband – his dignity rapidly fading, but still capable of dreaming of lost sexual prowess.

Maurice Roeves' Stephen Dedalus might have been more impressive had some of the many flashbacks been used to better fill in his past – viewers are only told that he comes from an unhappy home, with a failure of a father.

■ ULZANA'S RAID

1972, 103 MINS, US ◇ Ⓥ

Dir Robert Aldrich   *Prod* Carter De Haven   *Scr* Alan Sharp   *Ph* Joseph Biroc   *Ed* Michael Luciano   *Mus* Frank DeVol   *Art Dir* James Vance
● Burt Lancaster, Bruce Davison, Jorge Luke, Richard Jaeckel, Joaquin Martinez, Lloyd Bochner (Universal)

Ulzana's Raid is the sort of pretentious US Army-vs-Indians period potboiler that invites derision from its own dialog and situations. However, suffice it to say that the production is merely ponderous in its formula action-sociology-violence, routine in its acting and direction, and often confusing in its hokey storytelling.

Screenplay finds a weathered old frontier scout (Burt Lancaster) saddled with a super-naive greenhorn young army officer-who-matures-under-pressure-etc (Bruce Davison)

as the patrol attempts to round up some marauding Apaches.

Whatever the film's aspirations, the effect is simply another exploitation western which crassly exploits the potentials in physical abuse, and in which plot suspense is not what is going to happen, but how bestial it can be.

■ UNBEARABLE LIGHTNESS OF BEING, THE

1988, 171 MINS, US ◇ Ⓥ

Dir Philip Kaufman   *Prod* Saul Zaentz   *Scr* Jean-Claude Carriere, Philip Kaufman   *Ph* Sven Nykvist   *Ed* Walter Murch, B.J. Sears, Vivien Hillgrove Gilliam, Stephen A. Rotter   *Art Dir* Pierre Guffroy
● Daniel Day-Lewis, Juliette Binoche, Lena Olin, Derek de Lint, Erland Josephson, Donald Moffat (Zaentz)

Milan Kundera's 1984 international bestseller of love and erotica set against the Russian invasion of Czechoslovakia has been regarded as essentially unfilmable by many observers, so Philip Kaufman has pulled off a near-miracle in creating this richly satisfying adaptation.

Tomas, a top surgeon and compulsive ladies' man in Prague, takes in and eventually marries a lovely country girl, Tereza. He continues his womanizing, however, particularly with his voluptuous mistress Sabina, an artist who takes off for Geneva as soon as Russian tanks put a halt to the Prague Spring of 1968.

The sexuality which drenches the entire film possesses a great buoyancy and spirit in the first act, set during the exciting liberalization of communism under Alexander Dubcek. Second act, in Geneva, is comparatively somber and spare, but is punctuated by Sabina's new affair with a married man and by the growing friendship between Sabina and Tereza.

As played by Juliette Binoche and Lena Olin, the two women are absolutely enchanting; Binoche is adorably doll-like while Olin is simply striking as a woman who lives her sexual and artistic lives just as she pleases.

Attractive in some ways, Tomas is irritatingly uncommunicative and opaque at others, and Daniel Day-Lewis at times overdoes the self-consciously smug projection of his own appeal.

■ UNCLE, THE

1966, 87 MINS, UK

Dir Desmond Davis   *Prod* Leonard Davis, Robert Goldston   *Scr* Desmond Davis, Margaret Abrams   *Ph* Manny Wynn   *Ed* Brian Smedley-Aston
● Rupert Davies, Brenda Bruce, Robert Duncan, William Marlowe, Ann Lynn, Maurice Denham (British Lion/Lenart)

A dispute ensued after completion of this excellent British film [based on the book by Margaret Abrams] between director Desmond Davis and producer Leonard Davis (no relation), because of editing and other changes made by the producer without the 'permission' of the director. The producer's version indicates that the changes were not sufficient to damage the film.

The director creates a cinematic essay on the life of a seven-year-old who finds himself in a catastrophic situation. Totally unprepared for the position, he finds being an uncle of a nephew the same age presents many difficulties. The entire film is done from the attitude of the pint-sized hero.

Most of *The Uncle* deals with the 'loss of innocence' of a small boy, Gus (Robert Duncan), over one summer.

Although the firm control of director Davis is evident throughout, he has been fortunate in having a cast that is entirely excellent, particularly young Robert Duncan as Gus (only a British child could look so profound

at seven) and Rupert Davies and Brenda Bruce as his parents.

■ UNCLE BUCK

1989, 100 MINS, US ◇ Ⓥ

Dir John Hughes   *Prod* John Hughes, Tom Jacobson   *Scr* John Hughes   *Ph* Ralf D. Bode   *Ed* Lou Lombardo, Tony Lombardo, Peck Prior   *Mus* Ira Newborn   *Art Dir* John W. Corso
● John Candy, Amy Madigan, Jean Louisa Kelly, Gaby Hoffman, Macaulay Culkin (Universal)

John Hughes unsuccessfully tries to mix a serious generation gap message between the belly laughs in *Uncle Buck*, a warm-weather John Candy vehicle.

On paper the rotund Second City veteran seems ideal for the title role: a ne'er-do-well, coarse black sheep of the family suddenly pressed into service when his relatives (Elaine Bromka, Garrett M. Brown), a suburban Chicago family, have to rush off to visit Bromka's dad, stricken with a heart attack.

Enter Uncle Buck, put in charge of the three youngsters for an indefinite period. The kids wear down Buck's rough edges and he teaches them some seat-of-the-pants lessons about life.

Unfortunately, Candy is too likable to give the role any edge. When called upon to be tough or mean he's unconvincing, as in the slapstick dealings with the precociously oversexed boyfriend Bug (Jay Underwood) of eldest daughter Jean Louisa Kelly.

■ UNCOMMON VALOR

1983, 105 MINS, US ◇ Ⓥ

Dir Ted Kotcheff   *Prod* John Milius, Buzz Feitshans   *Scr* Joe Gayton   *Ph* Stephen H. Burum   *Ed* Mark Melnick   *Mus* James Horner   *Art Dir* James L. Schoppe
● Gene Hackman, Robert Stack, Fred Ward, Reb Brown, Randall 'Tex' Cobb, Patrick Swayze (Paramount)

All of the top talent involved – especially Gene Hackman – is hardly needed to make *Uncommon Valor* what it is, a very common action picture.

Hackman does as much as he can as a grieving father obsessed with the idea that his son remains a prisoner 10 years after he was reported missing-in-action in Vietnam. Financed by oil tycoon Robert Stack, whose son is also missing, Hackman puts together his small invasion force and two-thirds of *Valor* is consumed introducing the characters and putting them through various practice drills for the rescue which will predictably be tougher than they planned on.

True to a long tradition of war films, by the time the tough really get going it's only a question of who won't come back from the dangerous mission. But at least each of the main characters in *Valor* does his best to make you care whether it's him.

■ UNCONQUERED

1947, 135 MINS, US ◇

Dir Cecil B. DeMille   *Prod* Cecil B. DeMille   *Scr* Charles Bennett, Fredric M. Frank, Jesse Lasky Jr   *Ph* Ray Rennahan   *Ed* Anne Bauchens   *Mus* Victor Young   *Art Dir* Hans Dreier, Walter Tyler
● Gary Cooper, Paulette Goddard, Howard DaSilva, Boris Karloff, Ward Bond, Katherine DeMille (Paramount)

Cecil B. DeMille's *Unconquered* is a $4 million Technicolor spectacle; it's a pre-Revolutionary western with plenty of Injun stuff which, for all the vacuousness and shortcomings, has its gripping moments.

The redskins are ruthless scalpers and the British colonials alternatively naive and brave, patriotic and full of skullduggery to give substance to the melodramatic heroics and knavery of the most derring-do school.

Howard DaSilva is the arch-knave whose marriage to Injun chief Boris Karloff's daughter (Katherine DeMille) puts him plenty in the black with the redskins on fur-trading and the like. Paulette Goddard is the proud slave-girl whose freedom Gary Cooper purchases on the British slaveship, only to cross paths with the heavy (DaSilva) and his No. 2 menace (Mike Mazurki).

It's not generally known that in that 1763 period English convicts had the alternative of being sold into limited slavery in the American colonies. Although a bond slave, Goddard spurns DaSilva and sufficiently attracts Cooper to make for a romantic angle.

Despite the ten-twent-thirt meller-dramatics and the frequently inept script, the performances are convincing, a great tribute to the cast because that dialog and those situations try the best of troupers.

■ UNDER CAPRICORN

1949, 116 MINS, UK ◇ ⓥ

Dir Alfred Hitchcock   *Prod* Alfred Hitchcock
Scr James Bridie   *Ph* Jack Cardiff, Paul Beeson
Ed A.S. Bates   *Mus* Richard Addinsell
● Ingrid Bergman, Joseph Cotten, Michael Wilding, Margaret Leighton (Warner/Transatlantic)

Under Capricorn is overlong and talky, with scant measure of the Alfred Hitchcock thriller tricks.

Time of the plot is 1831, in Sydney, NSW, during that period when a convict, after serving his time, could start life anew with a clean slate. Such a man is Joseph Cotten, former groom and now Ingrid Bergman's husband. Cotten has become a man of wealth, but is not accepted socially.

That fact, along with his past crime—the killing of his wife's brother, a deed committed by Bergman but for which he took the blame—are the motives stressed as causing the wife's addiction to the bottle.

■ UNDER FIRE

1983, 100 MINS, US ◇ ⓥ

Dir Roger Spottiswoode   *Prod* Jonathan Taplin
Scr Ronald Shelton, Clayton Frohman   *Ph* John Alcott
Ed Mark Conte   *Mus* Jerry Goldsmith   *Art Dir* Agustin Ytarte
● Nick Nolte, Gene Hackman, Joanna Cassidy, Jean-Louis Trintignant, Ed Harris, Richard Masur (Lion's Gate)

The American media are strongly taken to task in *Under Fire*. This is the story of two correspondents (one working for *Time*, the other Public Radio) and an on-the-scenes war photographer. The action begins in the African bush of Chad, then moves on to Nicaragua – and a feature-film rehearsal of that tragic televised killing of the ABC correspondent by a Somoza government soldier in the late 1970s as he was covering the fighting with the winning Sandinista rebels.

Three individuals cover the Chad conflict in the late 1960s: the 30-year-old photog Russell Price (Nick Nolte), the 50-year-old senior correspondent for *Time* mag Alex Grazier (Gene Hackman), and the circa 40-year-old radio newslady Claire Stryder (Joanna Cassidy). All are tough professionals.

There's a fourth individual who surfaces now and then: he's a hired mercenary, a killer by trade, whom lenser Nolte meets from time to time, first in Chad and later in Nicaragua.

In the course of covering the events Nolte and Cassidy opt to search for a certain rebel leader named Rafael among the revolutionary Sandinistas, for Rafael has never been photographed nor interviewed by the American press.

Further, Nolte's photos of the rebels play into the hands of a double-agent, the French-

man (Jean-Louis Trintignant), who uses then to hunt down and kill the key Sandinista leaders. Moral factors like these are the core of the action.

■ UNDER MILK WOOD

1971, 90 MINS, UK ◇ ⓥ

Dir Andrew Sinclair   *Prod* Jules Buck, Hugh French
Scr Andrew Sinclair   *Ph* Bob Huke   *Ed* Willy Kemplen   *Mus* Brian Gascoigne
● Richard Burton, Elizabeth Taylor, Peter O'Toole, Glynis Johns, Vivien Merchant, Sian Philips (Timon)

Screen adaptations of hard-to-slot items such as Dylan Thomas' *Under Milk Wood*, have long been tricky affairs, so it's a tribute to the makers of this pic that it's come off this well.

Writer-director Andrew Sinclair has a wonderful feel for his material, and a happy hand in matching it to its setting. Normal screen conventions are broken as Sinclair chooses to follow Thomas instead in his dissection of a Welsh seaside village and its inhabitants, done with caustically keen and boisterously, earthily humorous pen.

Peter O'Toole plays the blind but still all-seeing Captain Cat, with a (sometimes distracting) assist from makeup on the surface and a fine and oft-moving limn underneath. Richard Burton is fully at ease in a physical walk-through of a village day, and he speaks the bulk of Thomas' voice-over lines with feeling and obvious love. Through him principally, the purr and the occasional soar of the poet's phrase flows and satisfies. Elizabeth Taylor, glimpsed all too briefly, has rarely been more beautiful. A very distinguished roster of featured players.

■ UNDER THE VOLCANO

1984, 109 MINS, US ◇ ⓥ

Dir John Huston   *Prod* Moritz Borman, Wieland Schulz-Kiel   *Scr* Guy Gallo   *Ph* Gabriel Figueroa
Ed Roberto Silvi   *Mus* Alex North   *Art Dir* Gunther Gerzeo
● Albert Finney, Jacqueline Bisset, Anthony Andrews, Ignacio Lopez Tarso, Katy Jurado, James Villiers (Ithaca-Conacine)

Although it's said John Huston has wanted to film British author Malcolm Lowry's autobiographical masterpiece *Under the Volcano* for some 30 years, it was always a project fraught with difficulties.

Story unfolds over a 24-hour period in November 1938 in the Mexican village of Cuernavaca where the former British Consul, Geoffrey Firmin (Albert Finney), guilt-ridden over the past and abandoned by his wife, is drinking himself to death. It's a time of celebration, the Day of the Dead, a day when death is celebrated.

After a drunken night, Firmin returns home to discover that Yvonne (Jacqueline Bisset), the wife he so desperately yearned for, has unexpectedly returned. The occcasion provides only a momentary interval from hard liquor, however.

Although this voyage into self-destruction won't be to the taste of many, there will be few unmoved by Finney's towering performance as the tragic Britisher, his values irretrievably broken down, drowning himself in alcohol and practically inviting his own death.

■ UNDER THE YUM YUM TREE

1963, 110 MINS, US ◇

Dir David Swift   *Prod* Frederick Brisson   *Scr* Lawrence Roman, David Swift   *Ph* Joseph Biroc   *Ed* Charles Nelson   *Mus* Frank DeVol   *Art Dir* Dale Hennesy
● Jack Lemmon, Carol Lynley, Dean Jones, Edie Adams, Imogen Coca, Paul Lynde (Columbia)

The screen version of Lawrence Roman's hit

stage play is concerned with an experiment wherein two young people in love (Carol Lynley and Dean Jones) agree to determine their 'character compatibility' prior to marriage by living together platonically. The project is complicated by the intrusion of the lecherous landlord (Jack Lemmon) of the apartment building in which they have chosen to reside.

As engineered by director David Swift, the film's cardinal error is its lack of restraint. There is a tendency to embellish, out of all proportion, devices and situations that, kept simple, would have served the comic purposes far more effectively.

Exaggeration has also spilled over into the area of production design. Having Lemmon's apartment fully equipped for romantic pursuits is one thing, but some of the props, notably a pair of pop-up, mechanical violins, strain credulity.

For Lemmon, the role of amorous landlord is a tour-de-farce, and he plays it to the hilt. Lynley is a visual asset and does a satisfactory job as the somewhat ingenuous ingenue. Jones, who played the rather gullible boy friend on Broadway, effectively repeats his characterization on screen.

■ UNDER TWO FLAGS

1936, 111 MINS, US

Dir Frank Lloyd   *Prod* Darryl F. Zanuck   *Scr* W.P. Lipscomb, Walter Ferris   *Ph* Ernest Palmer   *Ed* Ralph Dietrich   *Mus* Louis Silvers
● Ronald Colman, Claudette Colbert, Victor McLaglen, Rosalind Russell, Gregory Ratoff, Nigel Bruce (20th Century-Fox)

The classic *Under Two Flags*, in book [by Ouida], play and through two silent filmizations [1916 and 1922], is still sturdy fare, talkerized. A pioneer saga of the Foreign Legion, Darryl Zanuck and 20th-Fox have further fortified it by a four-ply marquee ensemble (Ronald Colman, Claudette Colbert, Victor McLaglen and Rosalind Russell).

Not the tempestuous Cigarette of the Theda Bara vintage [1916 version] when *Under Two Flags* was a highlight in that silent film vamp's career, Colbert nonetheless makes the somewhat bawdy cafe hostess stand up. It's not exactly in her metier. Twixt the native Cigarette and Rosalind Russell as the English lady, Colman does all right on the romance interest, with the desert as a setting.

Victor McLaglen turns in an expert chore as the scowling Major Doyle, lovesick for and jealous of Cigarette's two-timing. Gregory Ratoff is planted well for comedy relief with his plaint that he's already forgotten just what he joined the Legion to forget.

The production highlight is the pitched battle on the desert [directed by Otto Brower, photographed by Sidney Wagner] between the marauding Arabs and the handful of legionnaires defending the fort.

■ UNDERCURRENT

1946, 111 MINS, US

Dir Vincente Minnelli   *Prod* Pandro S. Berman
Scr Edward Chodorov   *Ph* Karl Freund   *Ed* Ferris Webster   *Mus* Herbert Stothart   *Art Dir* Cedric Gibbons, Randall Duell
● Katharine Hepburn, Robert Taylor, Robert Mitchum, Edmund Gwenn, Marjorie Main (M-G-M)

Undercurrent is heavy drama with femme appeal. Picture deals with psychology angle in which a weak, uncertain man uses lies, theft and even murder to obtain power and acclaim.

Appeal lies in romance between Katharine Hepburn and Robert Taylor and uncertainty as to how it will work out. Taylor, war-made industrialist, marries Hepburn, daughter of a scientist, after a whirlwind courtship. After marriage, the bride begins to discover odd incidents in her husband's past, including his brother's mysterious disappearance and the fear that dogs and other animals have for the man.

Hepburn sells her role with usual finesse and talent. Robert Mitchum, as the missing brother, has only three scenes but makes them count for importance.

••••••••••••••••••••••••••••••••

■ UNDERWORLD, U.S.A.

1961, 98 MINS, US ⓥ
Dir Samuel Fuller   *Prod* Samuel Fuller   *Scr* Samuel Fuller   *Ph* Hal Mohr   *Ed* Jerome Thoms   *Mus* Harry Sukman   *Art Dir* Robert Peterson
● Cliff Robertson, Dolores Dorn, Beatrice Kay, Paul Dubov, Richard Rust, Larry Gates (Columbia)

Underworld U.S.A. is a slick gangster melo-drama made to order for filmgoers who prefer screen fare explosive and uncomplicated. In this picture, the 'hero' sets out on a four-ply vendetta of staggering proportions and accomplishes his mission with the calculation and poise of a pro bowler racking up a simple four-way spare.

The yarn follows the wicked career of supposedly decent but hate-motivated, revenge-consumed fellow who, as a youngster, witnessed in horror the gangland slaying of his father by four budding racketeers.

As the central figure, Cliff Robertson delivers a brooding, virile, finely balanced portrayal. It's a first-rate delineation atop a cast that performs expertly. Dolores Dorn supplies romantic interest with sufficient sincerity, and Beatrice Kay is persuasive as the decent, compassionate woman whose fervent, but unfulfilled, desire for motherhood gives rise to a vague mother-son relationship with Robertson.

Director Samuel Fuller's screenplay has its lags, character superficialities and unlikelihoods, but it is crisp with right-sounding gangster jargon and remains absorbing.

••••••••••••••••••••••••••••••••

■ UNFAITHFULLY YOURS

1948, 105 MINS, US ⓥ
Dir Preston Sturges   *Prod* Preston Sturges   *Scr* Preston Sturges   *Ph* Victor Milner   *Ed* Robert Fritch   *Mus* Alfred Newman   *Art Dir* Lyle R. Wheeler, Joseph C. Wright
● Rex Harrison, Linda Darnell, Barbara Lawrence, Rudy Vallee, Lionel Stander, Edgar Kennedy (20th Century-Fox)

Unfaithfully Yours misses that stamp of originality which marked the scripting and direction of Preston Sturges' previous films. The fabric of stale ideas and antique gags out of which this pic was spun is just barely hidden by its glossy production casing.

The yarn is too slight to carry the long running time. It's a takeoff on the suspicious husband-beautiful wife formula, which is stirred up into a frothy pastry only on occasion. With Rex Harrison playing a symphony orch leader, Sturges executes some amusing highjinks with serious music, but the humor is mild and unsustained.

The yarn unfolds via three long revenge fantasies which race through Harrison's brain while he batons his way through a concert. During a frenzied number by Rosini, there's a gruesome sequence in which Harrison slashes his wife, Linda Darnell, with a razor and then pins the rap on her supposed lover. Against a background of Wagnerian music, he daydreams of nobly renouncing his wife in favor of the other man. Finally, against a Tchaikovsky number, he imagines playing Russian roulette with his rival in a test of passion.

Stylization of the fantasies would have given these sequences that comic energy which is lacking.

••••••••••••••••••••••••••••••••

■ UNFAITHFULLY YOURS

1984, 96 MINS, US ◇ ⓥ
Dir Howard Zieff   *Prod* Marvin Worth, Joe Wizan   *Scr* Valerie Curtin, Barry Levinson, Robert Klane   *Ph* David M. Walsh   *Ed* Sheldon Kahn   *Mus* Bill Conti   *Art Dir* Albert Brenner
● Dudley Moore, Nastassja Kinski, Armand Assante, Albert Brooks, Cassie Yates, Richard Libertini (20th Century-Fox)

Unfaithfully Yours is a moderately amusing remake of Preston Sturges' wonderful comedy which, it might be remembered, was a commercial bust upon its release in 1948.

Lavishly mounted and astutely cast farce features Dudley Moore in the role of a big-time orchestra conductor who has just taken a much younger Italian screen star, Nastassja Kinski, as his bride. Moore suspects her of fooling around with dashing concert violinist Armand Assante, and core of the film consists of a fantasy in which Moore murders his wife, but makes it look as though Assante did it. He then tries to pull off such a scheme, with predictably incompetent results.

Moore is right at home on the podium or behind the piano, and his comic invention results in a delightful performance.

••••••••••••••••••••••••••••••••

■ UNFINISHED BUSINESS

1984, 99 MINS, CANADA ◇
Dir Don Owen   *Prod* Annette Cohen, Don Owen   *Scr* Don Owen   *Ph* Douglas Kiefer   *Ed* Peter Dale, David Nicholson   *Mus* Patricia Cullen   *Art Dir* Barbara Tranter, Ann Pepper
● Isabelle Mejias, Peter Spence, Leslie Toth, Peter Kastner, Julie Biggs, Chuck Shamata (Zebra Films/NFBC)

Don Owen's *Unfinished Business* continues the story the filmmaker began in *Nobody Waved Goodbye* [1964], a ground-breaking Canadian feature. Sequel picks up with the original young couple, now divorced, experiencing the travails of parents with a rebellious 17-year-old daughter.

A high school senior, Izzy (Isabelle Mejias) is days away from her finals yet balks at the prospect of completing her education. She finds diversions in dope, friends, a rock club and a group of anti-nuke activists. The clash between pressures from her parents and the seemingly more meaningful pursuits of the radicals sends her into the streets for a different kind of education.

Although a common enough story, *Unfinished Business* has a raw energy which is touching and deeply felt.

••••••••••••••••••••••••••••••••

■ UNFINISHED SYMPHONY, THE

1934, 90 MINS, UK/GERMANY
Dir Willy Forst, Anthony Asquith   *Prod* Arnold Pressburger   *Scr* Walter Reisch, Benn W. Levy   *Ph* Franz Planer   *Mus* Willy Schmidt-Gentner (adapt.)
● Helen Chandler, Marta Eggerth, Hans Jaray, Ronald Squire, Beryl Laverick, Brember Wills (Gaumont-British/UFA)

A thing of arresting beauty in pictorial and musical conception, *The Unfinished Symphony* should garner attention from the musically appreciative. Particularly those for whom the melodies of Franz Schubert have always been in the upper brackets of their enjoyment.

What emotional appeal there is is not derived from the acting but from the instrumentation of Schubert's *Unfinished Symphony*, and the reproduction in voice and orchestra of a number of his other compositions. They're all brilliantly woven into the fine costume mosaic turned out by director Willy Forst.

Story has been aptly cast, even if the players constitute a babel of dialects. Striking case in point is that of Marta Eggerth and Beryl Laverick, who are cast as sisters. The former's accent is German and the latter's a precise Oxonian. Like Hans Jaray, Eggerth did the same part in the UFA version of *Unfinished Symphony* which Forst also directed.

••••••••••••••••••••••••••••••••

■ UNFORGIVEN, THE

1960, 125 MINS, US ◇ ⓥ
Dir John Huston   *Prod* James Hill   *Scr* Ben Maddow   *Ph* Franz Planer   *Ed* Hugh Russell Lloyd   *Mus* Dimitri Tiomkin
● Burt Lancaster, Audrey Hepburn, Audie Murphy, John Saxon, Charles Bickford, Lillian Gish (James/United Artists)

There are many aspects of *The Unforgiven* that elicit comparison with *Shane*, particularly in regard to the composition of the scenes and the photography. Director John Huston and cameraman Franz Planer have teamed to provide an intelligent use of the medium for eye-pleasing effects, filmed in Mexico.

The screenplay from a novel by Alan Le May – although many parts are better than the whole – provides a good framework for the talents of Huston and his performers. Audrey Hepburn gives a shining performance as the foundling daughter of a frontier family. As her foster brother, obviously desperately in love with his 'sister', Burt Lancaster is fine as the strong-willed, heroic family spokesman and community leader.

The scene is the Texas Panhandle immediately after the Civil War at a time of unbending hatred between the white settlers and the local Kiowa Indians. The antagonism is marked by senseless massacres and excesses on the part of both sides. In the midst of this tension, it's discovered that Hepburn is actually a full-blooded Indian. The desire of the Indians to recover their own 'blood', the resentment of the settlers in having an 'enemy' in their midst, and the determination to hold on to the girl who has been a member of the family almost since birth provides the crux of the conflict.

Lillian Gish, a silent film favorite, is okay as the mother who guards the secret of her foundling daughter. However, she has a tendency to over-react emotionally. There are good performances by Charles Bickford, as the head of another frontier family; June Walker, as his wife; Albert Salmi, as his son who courts Hepburn; Kipp Hamilton, as his daughter, and Doug McClure, as Lancaster's youngest brother. Audie Murphy is surprisingly good as Lancaster's hot-headed brother whose hatred of Indians causes him to abandon his family.

••••••••••••••••••••••••••••••••

■ UNION CITY

1980, 87 MINS, US ◇ ⓥ
Dir Mark Reichert   *Prod* Graham Belin   *Scr* Mark Reichert   *Ph* Ed Lachman   *Ed* Lana Tokel, J. Michaels   *Mus* Chris Stein   *Art Dir* George Stavrinos
● Dennis Lipscomb, Deborah Harry, Irina Maleeva, Everett McGill, Sam McMurray (Kinesis)

Cornell Woolrich's dark and fetishistic material is both a source of strength and the undoing of *Union City*. His story is similar to Poe's *The Telltale Heart* in structure and while indie helmer Mark Reichert exploits its strangeness very well, he fails to flesh out the short, one actor sketch into a full-length feature.

Pic concerns a paranoid businessman (Dennis Lipscomb), obsessed with catching the mysterious culprit who steals a drink out of his milk bottle that is delivered every morning. His plain, vapid wife Lillian (Deborah Harry, in her screen debut) puts up with his increasingly bizarre behavior.

Ultimately, he captures a young war vet vagrant (Sam McMurray) in the act and releases his pent-up anger and frustration by beating the man's head bloodily on the floor. The Hitchcockian body removal footage provides fine black humor as Lipscomb hides the corpse in a Murphy bed in the vacant apartment next door.

....

■ UNION PACIFIC

1939, 133 MINS, US ▽

Dir Cecil B. DeMille   *Prod* Cecil B. DeMille   *Scr* Walter DeLeon, C. Gardner Sullivan, Jesse Lasky Jr   *Ph* Victor Milner, Dewey Wrigley   *Ed* Anne Bauchens   *Mus* George Antheil

● Barbara Stanwyck, Joel McCrea, Akim Tamiroff, Robert Preston, Brian Donlevy, Anthony Quinn (Paramount)

Basically, the production a super-western, cowboys and Injuns backgrounded by the epochal building of the Union Pacific. It's a post-Civil War saga [from an adaptation by Jack Cunningham of an original by Ernest Haycox], with Henry Kolker enacting the banker menace who foments the sabotage that would favor the competitive Central Pacific.

Joel McCrea comes on the scene as a trouble-shooter. Barbara Stanwyck sustains the femme interest in a sometimes unprepossessing manner, which is chiefly the script's fault rather than her own. Basically she more than impresses as the railroad engineer's daughter.

The clash in realistic values comes through the pauses in the melodramatics between genial badman Preston and trouble-shooter McCrea. Preston does a standout job through a consistently affable albeit frankly renegade role.

....

■ UNION STATION

1950, 81 MINS, US ▽

Dir Rudolph Mate   *Prod* Jules Schermer   *Scr* Sydney Boehm   *Ph* Daniel L. Fapp   *Ed* Ellsworth Hoagland   *Mus* Irvin Talbot

● William Holden, Nancy Olson, Barry Fitzgerald, Lyle Bettger, Jan Sterling (Paramount)

Union Station [from a story by Thomas Walsh] is a melodrama that locales its thrills in a big city railway terminal and spins off a tale of kidnapping.

William Holden, while youthful in appearance to head up the railway policing department of a metropolitan terminal, is in good form. Kidnapping is revealed when a femme passenger arriving at the terminal reports two suspicious characters. The passenger is Nancy Olson, secretary to a rich man and his blind daughter, Allene Roberts. Events prove Roberts has been kidnapped and the terminal is to be used as the payoff location.

The production catches the feel of a large terminal and its constantly shifting scenes of people arriving and departing.

....

■ UNMAN, WITTERING AND ZIGO

1971, 100 MINS, UK ◇

Dir John Mackenzie   *Prod* Gareth Wigan   *Scr* Simon Raven   *Ph* Geoffrey Unsworth   *Ed* Fergus McDonnell   *Mus* Michael J. Lewis   *Art Dir* Bill McCrow

● David Hemmings, Carolyn Seymour, Douglas Wilmer, Hamilton Dyce, Anthony Haygarth, Donald Gee (Mediarts)

Unman, Wittering and Zigo are on the roster at Chantry, a British school for teenage boys, which looks down treacherously on ocean-splashed rocks. The three are students, but Zigo is constantly marked absent, for reasons unexplained.

Unman, Wittering and the rest of the class are present and they make for a sinister lot,

blatantly threatening their new teacher, David Hemmings, with the same kind of death-on-the-rocks that has befallen his predecessor, unless he eases up on the scholastic schedule and runs their bets with the local bookmaker. The viewer may be both intrigued and puzzled, for while film is a compelling piece of dramatics about innocent-looking terrorists, it asks a great deal of credence.

Director John Mackenzie, working with a screenplay by Simon Raven, which in turn was fashioned from a television show by Giles Cooper, has in large part captured the viciousness. But why these youths are this way goes unexplained.

....

■ UNMARRIED WOMAN, AN

1978, 124 MINS, US ◇ ▽

Dir Paul Mazursky   *Prod* Paul Mazursky, Tony Ray   *Scr* Paul Mazursky   *Ph* Arthur Ornitz   *Ed* Stuart H. Pappe   *Mus* Bill Conti   *Art Dir* Pato Guzman

● Jill Clayburgh, Alan Bates, Michael Murphy, Cliff Gorman, Pat Quinn, Kelly Bishop (20th Century-Fox)

Paul Mazursky's excellent screenplay presents Jill Clayburgh in a most demanding role where she is torn between conflicting forces following the surprise confession of weak-willed husband Michael Murphy that he has fallen in love with another woman.

Daughter Lisa Lucas needs her mother's support just as she herself is coming on to adolescent love; Clayburgh's girlfriends, Pat Quinn, Kelly Bishop and Linda Miller, offer well-meaning advice not necessarily of the best calibre; blind date Andrew Duncan's premature pass falls flat; therapist Penelope Russianoff's probing strikes raw nerves; neighborhood stud Cliff Gorman, in an excellent though brief role, comes to realize that the only thing worse than not getting what you want can be getting it.

Finally, artist Alan Bates arrives in Clayburgh's life. A thoughtful and deep attachment evolves which survives the early resentment of the daughter and the lover's increasing demands on her time. Resolution avoids the pat but portents for happiness are strong.

☐ 1978: Best Picture (Nomination)

....

■ UNSINKABLE MOLLY BROWN, THE

1964, 128 MINS, US ◇ ▽

Dir Charles Walters   *Prod* Lawrence Weingarten   *Scr* Helen Deutsch   *Ph* Daniel L. Fapp   *Ed* Fredric Steinkamp   *Mus* Meredith Willson   *Art Dir* George W. Davis, Preston Ames

● Debbie Reynolds, Harve Presnell, Ed Begley, Jack Kruschen, Hermione Baddeley, Martita Hunt (M-G-M)

The Unsinkable Molly Brown is a rowdy and sometimes rousing blend of song and sentiment, a converted stage tuner.

The film is adorned with the music and lyrics of Meredith Willson, although a number of his songs for the legiter have been excised and one new production number ('He's My Friend') has been added. The dramatic story remains virtually intact.

It relates the adventures of Molly Brown, a hillbilly heroine who rises from poverty to become one of the richest and most celebrated women of her time. Shortly after her marriage to Leadville Johnny Brown he strikes it rich, and the rest of the picture depicts her feverish efforts to cut the mustard with snooty Denver society.

In essence, it's a pretty shallow story since the title character, when you get right down to it, is obsessed with a very superficial, egotistical problem beneath her generous, razzmatazz facade. On top of that, Wilson's score is rather undistinguished.

Debbie Reynolds thrusts herself into the role with an enormous amount of verve and

vigor. At times her approach to the character seems more athletic than artful.

Harve Presnell, who created the role on Broadway in 1960, makes a generally auspicious screen debut as the patient Johnny. His fine, booming voice and physical stature make him a valuable commodity for Hollywood.

....

■ UNSUITABLE JOB FOR A WOMAN, AN

1982, 94 MINS, UK ◇ ▽

Dir Christopher Petit   *Scr* Elizabeth McKay, Brian Scobie, Christopher Petit   *Ph* Martin Schafer   *Ed* Mick Audsley   *Mus* Chas Jankel, Philip Bagenal, Peter Van Hooke   *Art Dir* Anton Furst

● Pippa Guard, Billie Whitelaw, Paul Freeman, Dominic Guard, Dawn Archibald, David Horovitch (Boyd's/NFE)

Cordelia Gray (Pippa Guard) comes to work one day where she is assistant to a shabby gumshoe. She finds him in his office with his veins cut and a big bowl of blood next to him. A posthumous tape asks her to take over. After the burial an intense middleaged woman (Billie Whitelaw) asks her to take on a case, the suicide of her boss's son.

Obsession is the keynote of this case. Gray slowly is fascinated by the dead boy as she finds out more about him. It develops he was first found hanging dressed and made up as a woman but someone had changed that.

She almost hangs herself imitating the way the dead boy did it, gets thrown into a well but muddles through as the English do. Perhaps it is unfair to unravel this tale [from the novel by P.D. James] which is handled from a distance by director Christopher Petit robbing it of a more forceful narration, timing and revelation.

....

■ UNSUSPECTED, THE

1947, 103 MINS, US

Dir Michael Curtiz   *Prod* Charles Hoffman   *Scr* Ranald MacDougall   *Ph* Woody Bredell   *Ed* Frederick Richards   *Mus* Franz Waxman   *Art Dir* Anton Grot

● Joan Caulfield, Claude Rains, Audrey Totter, Constance Bennett, Hurd Hatfield, Michael North (Warner)

Director Michael Curtiz packs yarn with plenty of rugged action thrills, despite society setting. Two chase sequences are especially humdingers for audience chills. Story deals with suave mayhem, with murderer Claude Rains known from the opening crime.

Plot workings are not as clear as they could have been but motivation of principal characters is followable, as scripted from a Bess Meredyth adaptation of the Charlotte Armstrong story. Rains is seen as radio narrator of murder mysteries who's not above making his stories actually true. An apparently suave, kindly soul, he's unsuspected in the death of his secretary, niece and latter's husband.

Rains pulls out all his thesping tricks to sustain the character, and makes it believable. Joan Caulfield is good as the rich, troubled niece who believes in her uncle's goodness. Audrey Totter and Hurd Hatfield show up well as the murdered pair, and Constance Bennett peps up assignment as a radio producer.

....

■ UNTIL SEPTEMBER

1984, 95 MINS, US ◇ ▽

Dir Richard Marquand   *Prod* Michael Gruskoff   *Scr* Janice Lee Graham   *Ph* Philippe Welt   *Ed* Sean Barton   *Mus* John Barry   *Art Dir* Hilton McConnico

● Karen Allen, Thierry Lhermitte, Christopher Cazenove, Marie Catherine Conti, Hutton Cobb, Michael Mellinger (M-G-M/UA)

Set in Paris, plot centers on a young American woman stranded in the City of Lights when she becomes separated from a tour group headed for Eastern Bloc countries. Frustrated by airline and diplomatic red tape, Mo Alexander (Karen Allen), takes refuge in a modest hotel.

Temporary setback is put aright when a neighbor, suave banker Xavier de la Perouse (Thierry Lhermitte), checks on the woman's story for verification. It doesn't take much to guess that the two tenants are destined to hit it off romantically, even if there are some initial awkward moments.

However, filmmakers are not intent on making another 'woman involved with a married man' or 'doomed love affair' saga. Instead a fanciful, unconvincing 'love conquers all' scenario emerges.

■ **UNTOUCHABLES, THE**

1987, 119 MINS, US ◇ ⓥ

Dir Brian De Palma *Prod* Art Linson *Scr* David Mamet *Ph* Stephen H. Burum *Ed* Jerry Greenberg, Bill Pankow *Mus* Ennio Morricone *Art Dir* William A. Elliott

● Kevin Costner, Sean Connery, Charles Martin Smith, Andy Garcia, Robert De Niro, Richard Bradford (Linson/Paramount)

The Untouchables is a beautifully crafted portrait of Prohibition-era Chicago.

Director Brian De Palma sets the tone in a lavish overhead opening shot in which Robert De Niro's Al Capone professes to be just 'a businessman' giving people the product they want. That such business often required violent methods is immediately depicted as prelude to arrival of idealistic law enforcer Eliot Ness (Kevin Costner).

While the dichotomy of values is thus established between these two adversaries, it is the introduction of street cop Jim Malone (Sean Connery) that truly gives the film its momentum.

Connery delivers one of his finest performances. It is filled with nuance, humor and abundant self-confidence. Connery's depth strongly complements the youthful Costner, who does grow appreciably as Ness overcomes early naivete to become just hard-bitten enough without relinquishing the innocence of his personal life.

De Palma has brought his sure and skilled hand to a worthy enterprise. His signature for this film is an intense scene involving a baby carriage. Filmmakers liken it to the Odessa Steps montage from 1925's *The Battleship Potemkin* by Sergei Eisenstein.

■ **UP!**

1976, 80 MINS, US ◇

Dir Russ Meyer *Prod* Russ Meyer *Scr* B. Callum *Ph* Russ Meyer *Ed* Russ Meyer *Mus* William Loose, Paul Ruhland *Art Dir* Michele Levesque

● Robert McLane, Edward Schaaf, Mary Gavin, Elaine Collins, Su Ling, Janet Wood (RHM)

Director Russ Meyer's trademark is the casting of the most incredibly endowed actresses who bounce and jiggle through a primitive world, driving men to violence and murder for their favors.

The men in Meyer pix are rarely a match for the women, though Meyer has equipped his actors with 'marital aids' (to be polite) so they can compete with the ladies in long shots.

The violence, like much of the sex, is too outrageous to be believable. At one point, an axe is buried in a man's back, but he pulls it out and buries it in turn in his attacker's chest who then pulls it out and finishes the job with a buzzsaw to the groin. Fun stuff.

■ **UP IN SMOKE**

1978, 86 MINS, US ◇ ⓥ

Dir Lou Adler *Prod* Lou Adler *Scr* Tommy Chong, Cheech Marin *Ph* Gene Polito *Ed* Lon Lombardo, Scott Conrad *Art Dir* Leon Ericksen

● Cheech Marin, Tommy Chong, Stacy Keach, Edie Adams, Tom Skerritt, Zane Buzby (Paramount)

Up in Smoke is essentially a drawn-out version of the drug-oriented comedy routines of Tommy Chong and Cheech Marin.

Script by the two comedians has hippie rich kid Chong teaming up with barrio boy Cheech in a confused search for some pot to puff on, presumably to aid them in putting together a rock band. Pursuit takes them to Tijuana, where they end up driving back a van constructed out of treated marijuana called 'fibreweed'.

In diligent pursuit is narcotics detective Stacy Keach, saddled with the usual crew of incompetent assistants. The trail eventually leads to popular LA nitery, The Roxy, (in which Adler is partnered) where the dopers' band engages in a punk rock marathon. They take top prize when the high-grade van, catching on fire, inundates the club with potent smoke.

What's lacking in *Up in Smoke* is a cohesiveness in both humor and characterization. Once the more obvious drug jokes are exhausted, director Lou Adler lets the film degenerate into a mixture of fitful slapstick and toilet humor.

■ **UP THE DOWN STAIRCASE**

1967, 120 MINS, US ◇ ⓥ

Dir Robert Mulligan *Prod* Alan J. Pakula *Scr* Tad Mosel *Ph* Joseph Coffey *Ed* Folmar Blangsted *Mus* Fred Karlin *Art Dir* George Jenkins

● Sandy Dennis, Patrick Bedford, Eileen Heckart, Ruth White, Jean Stapleton (Warner)

Based on the novel of the same title by Bel Kaufman, *Up the Down Staircase* concerns troubles of a beginning teacher in a tough city high school. And it is very good, almost in spite of itself.

With only one major star (Sandy Dennis) and virtually a single setting, this pic is nevertheless thoroughly cinematic and completely engrossing. This is mainly because it is well acted, carefully scripted and directed and finely photographed. Director Robert Mulligan has for the most part avoided sentimentalism and presents his story honestly and directly.

As pretty young Miss Barrett, fresh from a purely theoretical college training as an English teacher, Dennis is plopped into impersonal Calvin Coolidge High School, a multi-racial institution where most of the teachers feel they are successful if they manage to keep their classrooms fairly civilized. Though many of the characters are familiar stock ones their treatment is generally successful.

■ **UP THE JUNCTION**

1968, 119 MINS, UK ◇

Dir Peter Collinson *Prod* Anthony Havelock-Allan, John Brabourne *Scr* Roger Smith *Ph* Arthur Lavis *Ed* John Trumper *Mus* Mike Hugg, Manfred Mann

● Suzy Kendall, Dennis Waterman, Adrienne Posta, Maureen Lipman, Michael Gothard, Alfie Bass (British Home Entertainment)

Up the Junction began its much-publicized life as a TV play which caused a flurry of controversy about its outspokenness. This feature pic is no sense a film version of the tele adaptation.

Story concerns an affluent girl (Suzy Kendall) who goes to live in Battersea, [then] a seedy area of London. There she works in a factory and falls for a goodlooking van driver.

The irony implicit in this relationship is that the boy wants the lush life she's left behind, and she is quite unsympathetic, feeling that life is more real when it is underprivileged.

But, in practically every respect, pic fails. The treatment introduces an air of patronage into what was honest reportage, and turns it into a condescending class-conscious view of the British working classes.

Kendall, while a looker, hasn't the versatility to encompass a role that demands a plus of personality to make it convincing. She is continuously blank and subdued. Dennis Waterman is quite pleasing as the boy friend.

■ **UP THE SANDBOX**

1972, 97 MINS, US ◇ ⓥ

Dir Irvin Kershner *Prod* Robert Chartoff, Irwin Winkler *Scr* Paul Zindel *Ph* Gordon Willis *Ed* Robert Lawrence *Mus* Billy Goldenberg *Art Dir* Harry Horner

● Barbra Streisand, David Selby, Jane Hoffman, John C. Becher, Jacobo Morales, Iris Brooks (First Artists)

Forget the euphemisms, *Up the Sandbox* is an untidy melange of overproduced, heavy-handed fantasy concerning a married woman's identity crisis, and laced with boring gallows humor about how bad life is in Manhattan.

The novel by Anne Richardson Roiphe has been adapted into a screenplay with very few genuine laughs but an awful lot of straining for cheap guffaws. Barbara Streisand, married to Prof David Selby, is harried by two children and fears the effect on herself and her marriage of accommodating the birth of a third child.

Resolution is as inarticulate as the development. Were Streisand to have been working off some old contractual commitment, there would be much sympathy. But this is not the case, since the star is the producer.

■ **URBAN COWBOY**

1980, 135 MINS, US ◇ ⓥ

Dir James Bridges *Prod* Robert Evans, Irving Azoff *Scr* James Bridges, Aaron Latham *Ph* Ray Villalobos *Ed* Dave Rawlins *Mus* Ralph Burns *Art Dir* Stephen Grimes

● John Travolta, Debra Winger, Scott Glenn, Madolyn Smith, Barry Corbin (Paramount)

Director James Bridges has ably captured the atmosphere of one of the most famous chip-kicker hangouts of all: Gilley's Club on the outskirts of Houston.

Enter John Travolta, fresh from a West Texas farm and working his first job in an oil refinery, quickly learning that Gilley's is where everybody heads after work. Try as you might, it's hard to completely accept Travolta as a redneck and his Texas accent is not quite right.

Debra Winger is outstanding as a fetching little slut who marries Travolta only to lose him almost to Madolyn Smith.

Winger leaves Travolta to move in with Scott Glenn while Smith moves in with Travolta.

In one way or another, the quadrangle revolves around Gilley's mechanical bucking bull, a menacing device that tests the courage of all the would-be cowboys.

■ **USED CARS**

1980, 113 MINS, US ◇ ⓥ

Dir Robert Zemeckis *Prod* Bob Gale *Scr* Robert Zemeckis, Bob Gale *Ph* Donald M. Morgan *Ed* Michael Kahn *Mus* Patrick Williams *Art Dir* Peter M. Jamison

● Kurt Russell, Jack Warden, Frank McRae, Gerrit Graham, Deborah Harmon (Columbia)

V

What might have looked like a great idea on paper has been tackled by filmmakers who haven't expanded it much beyond the one joke inherent in the premise.

Plot has fat cat car dealer Jack Warden desperate to knock out competition provided by a brother also portrayed by Warden.

Latter dies early on but operator Kurt Russell and partners Gerrit Graham and Frank McRae disguise the fact to prevent their slimey neighbor from inheriting the property.

Scripters have provided very little context or societal texture for their unmodulated tale, which disagreeably seeks to find humor in characters' humiliation, embarrassment and even death.

Nonetheless Robert Zemeckis directs with undeniable vigor, if insufficient control and discipline.

• •

■ **UTU**

1983, 120 MINS, NEW ZEALAND ◇ ⑰

Dir Geoff Murphy *Prod* Geoff Murphy *Scr* Geoff Murphy, Keith Aberdein *Ph* Graeme Cowley *Ed* Michael Horton *Mus* John Charles *Art Dir* Ron Highfield

● Anzac Wallace, Bruno Lawrence, Kelly Johnson, Wi Kuki Kaa, Tim Eliot, Ilona Rodgers (Murphy)

In a NZ western of the North American Indian-white settler school, Geoff Murphy has fashioned a fast-moving visual tale of archetypal passion and action. 'Utu' is the Maori word for 'revenge'.

Central figure is rebel leader Te Wheke (Anzac Wallace) during the wars between European settlers and the native Maoris in the late 19th century.

At first sympathetic to the European (pakeha) cause, Te Wheke turns guerrilla when his village is wiped out by British soldiers protecting the settlers. He retaliates in kind while recruiting supporters. As his actions become more despotic and cruel, he is hunted, captured and finally shot.

Murphy has produced powerful images and strong performances, particularly from Wallace, Wi Kuki Kaa (as Wirimu) and a big cast of Maori actors. Action sequences, special effects, and visual exploitation of a rugged, high country location in central New Zealand are superb.

• •

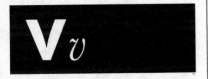

■ **VAGABOND KING, THE**

1930, 100 MINS, US ◇

Dir Ludwig Berger *Scr* Herman J. Mankiewicz *Ph* Henry Gerrard *Ed* Merrill White *Mus* Rudolph Friml *Art Dir* Hans Dreier

● Dennis King, Jeanette MacDonald, O.P. Heggie, Lillian Roth, Warner Oland (Paramount)

This ornate operetta, a pageant of bright fabrics, big sets and milling mobs, is founded upon *If I Were King*, a story [by Justin Huntly McCarthy] which has been done three or four times earlier in pictures. Protagonist this time of Francois Villon is Englishman Dennis King.

Musically, only the one number, 'Song of the Vagabonds', stands out. *Vagabond King*, as an operetta, retards itself as a melodrama. Touches of grim realism are sapped of their power by girls in tights as pages in the royal court and dwarfs turning cartwheels.

At least one case of miscasting is also a handicap. Lillian Roth has neither the necessary age nor emotional maturity to play the passionate Huguette.

Despite its weaknesses, *Vagabond King* is always interesting. It's a treat for the optics with some of the color effects of arresting beauty. Jeanette MacDonald's performance supplies the requisite aroma of glamor.

• •

■ **VALACHI PAPERS, THE**

1972, 123 MINS, ITALY ◇ ⑰

Dir Terence Young *Prod* Dino De Laurentiis *Scr* Stephen Geller *Ph* Aldo Tonti *Ed* Johnny Dwyre *Mus* Riz Ortolani *Art Dir* Mario Garbuglia

● Charles Bronson, Lino Ventura, Jill Ireland, Walter Chiari, Joseph Wiseman, Gerald S. O'Loughlin (Columbia/De Laurentiis)

The Valachi Papers, based upon the revelations of the mobster [and a book by Peter Maas] who disclosed details of Cosa Nostra organized crime in the US, is a hard-hitting, violence-ridden documented melodrama of the underworld covering more than three decades.

Joseph Valachi was the Brooklyn gangster who, while serving a life sentence for his crimes, was induced by a Federal agent to reveal the inside structure of the Cosa Nostra.

Flashback technique is utilized as Charles Bronson, as Valachi, recounts to the Federal agent the innermost secrets of the mob, of which he was a constant but unimportant 'soldier'.

Terence Young, who directs forcefully, hits a shock note in this latter sequence which climaxes numerous scenes of brutality, including Anastasia's famed cutdown in Park Central Hotel barber shop chair.

• •

■ **VALENTINO**

1977, 132 MINS, UK ◇ ⑰

Dir Ken Russell *Prod* Robert Chartoff, Irwin Winkler *Scr* Ken Russell, John Byrum *Ph* Peter Suschitzky *Ed* Stuart Baird *Art Dir* Philip Harrison

● Rudolf Nureyev, Leslie Caron, Michelle Phillips, Carol Kane, Felicity Kendal, Seymour Cassel (United Artists)

Director Ken Russell seems less interested in nostalgia and early Hollywood days than in trying to find the essence of a certain charisma that can be turned into a sort of world sex symbol. Casting of Kirov defector ballet dancer Rudolf Nureyev as Valentino works despite the elimination of the Latino darkness and smoldering looks.

Nureyev's pic bow is impressive as he manages to avoid being ridiculous in certain scenes by sheer grace and aplomb. And using him also excuses the film a slavish need to hue to Valentino's factual life. Yet Russell has now and then opted for the lyric, even the outrageous.

Early part of the pic does not quite come alive but with the start of his film career it perks up for some bravura scenes that capture the strength, vulnerability and appeal of this tragic figure.

• •

■ **VALERIE**

1957, 81 MINS, US

Dir Gerd Oswald *Prod* Hal R. Makelim *Scr* Leonard Heideman, Emmett Murphy *Ph* Ernest Laszlo *Ed* David Bretherton *Mus* Albert Glasser *Art Dir* Frank Smith

● Sterling Hayden, Anita Ekberg, Anthony Steel, Peter Walker (United Artists)

Tale, briskly and imaginatively directed by Gerd Oswald, is laid in the west, but is by no means a western. Rather, it is a gothic and sombre psychological tale which repeats the same theme three times, each time from the viewpoint of a different character. Save for a preposterously melodramatic finale, which doesn't fit, it's a well-told tale and a work of solid craftsmanship.

Story starts with bloody shooting fray, in which Sterling Hayden and his henchmen wipe out the family of his estranged wife (Anita Ekberg) and seriously wounds her. At the trial, sympathy is on his side, since he's a leading citizen, a war hero (Civil War), and Ekberg supposedly was running away with handsome preacher Anthony Steel.

But Steel's testimony, related in backflash, relates another version – that he was helping an ill and neglected parishioner by taking her to her parents. Hayden's story, also told in flashback, is that she was a loose wanton, only interested in his money, who had seduced his younger brother (Peter Walker) and was carrying on an affair with Steel.

But Ekberg, supposedly near death, regains consciousness and gives her testimony.

Hayden turns in one of his best chores in years, while Ekberg impresses as an actress as well as a scenic wonder.

• •

■ **VALLEY GIRL**

1983, 95 MINS, US ◇ ⑰

Dir Martha Coolidge *Prod* Wayne Crawford, Andrew Lane *Scr* Wayne Crawford, Andrew Lane *Ph* Frederick Elmes *Ed* Eva Gordos *Art Dir* Mary Della Javier

● Nicolas Cage, Deborah Foreman, Elizabeth Daily, Michael Bowen, Colleen Camp, Frederic Forrest (Atlantic)

Valley is very good simply because director Martha Coolidge obviously cares about her two lead characters and is privileged to have a couple of fine young performers, Nicolas Cage and Deborah Foreman, to make the audience care.

As the title suggests, she's a definitive valley girl, mouthing all the nonsensical catch phrases recently popularized in song and book. He's a Hollywood punker who normally wouldn't venture over the hills into the square valley, except to crash a party where they meet.

Their blazing romance, which shocks her high-school friends, ultimately becomes too socially threatening for Foreman and she cuts it off.

For a change, there aren't any cartoon problem adults on hand as there often are in these pictures.

• •

■ **VALLEY OF THE DOLLS**

1967, 123 MINS, US ◇

Dir Mark Robson *Prod* David Weisbart *Scr* Helen Deutsch, Dorothy Kingsley *Ph* William H. Daniels *Ed* Dorothy Spencer *Mus* John Williams *Art Dir* Jack Martin Smith, Richard Day

● Barbara Parkins, Patty Duke, Paul Burke, Sharon Tate, Tony Scotti, Martin Milner (20th Century-Fox/Red Lion)

Plot meanders between New England country girl Barbara Parkins, who comes to the big city and eventually is seduced by urban social patterns; Patty Duke, rising young singing star who gets hung up on pills, and Sharon Tate, playing a big-breasted, untalented, but basically sensitive girl who never finds happiness. Parkins and Tate, the latter particularly good, suffer from under-emphasis in early reels, and corny plot resolution.

Main body of the story [from Jacqueline Susann's novel] concerns the rise, plateau and erratic performance of Duke's character. For her, this is a very good role.

Susan Hayward, who replaced Judy Garland in cast, does an excellent job in giving acting depth to the role of the older legit star, ever alert to remove threats to her supremacy.

Five songs, including title theme, by Andre and Dory Previn are interpolated nicely, and logically, into plot. Dionne Warwick regularly warbles title tune.

• •

VALMONT

1989, 137 MINS, FRANCE/UK ◇ Ⓥ
Dir Milos Forman *Prod* Paul Rassam, Michael
Hausman *Scr* Jean-Claude Carriere *Ph* Miroslav
Ondricek *Ed* Alan Heim, Nena Danevic
Art Dir Pierre Guffroy
● Colin Firth, Annette Bening, Meg Tilly, Fairuza Balk,
Sian Phillips, Fabia Drake (Renn/Burrill)

Milos Forman's meticulously produced *Valmont* is an extremely well-acted period piece that suffers from stately pacing and lack of dramatic high points.

Plot of Choderlos de Laclos' 1782 novel is quite familiar due to Stephen Frears' 1988 hit film, *Dangerous Liaisons*, from Christopher Hampton's 1987 play. Forman has met the challenge of breathing new life into the material, but key plot twists and revelations are robbed of their novelty.

Basic story revolves around a bet by two 18th-century French aristocrats, Valmont (Colin Firth) and his old flame Marquise de Merteuil (Annette Bening). She wants Valmont to seduce 15-year-old Cecile (Fairuza Balk) to cuckold Cecile's fiance, Gercourt (Jeffrey Jones), who is Merteuil's unfaithful lover.

Valmont counters with the bet that he can bed timid married lady Madame de Tourvel (Meg Tilly). If he wins Merteuil must submit to his lust as well.

What keeps the film interesting, if not riveting, is the generally on target casting and resulting topnotch interpretations.

VAMP

1986, 94 MINS, US ◇ Ⓥ
Dir Richard Wenk *Prod* Donald P. Borchers
Scr Richard Wenk *Ph* Elliot Davis *Ed* Marc
Grossman *Mus* Jonathan Elias *Art Dir* Alan
Roderick-Jones
● Chris Makepeace, Sandy Baron, Robert Rusler,
Dedee Pfeiffer, Gedde Watanabe, Grace Jones
(Balcor/Borchers)

Vamp is an extremely imaginative horror film styled as jet black comedy.

Richard Wenk opens the film deceptively with the format of a teenage sex comedy. Fraternity pledges Keith (Chris Makepeace) and A.J. (Robert Rusler) agree to find a stripper for the frat party that night. They team up with Duncan (Gedde Watanabe), who significantly has a car.

Upon their arrival in the big city, film quickly makes a permanent detour into *The Twilight Zone* when their car skids and comes out of a lengthy spin with bright daylight suddenly turned to spooky night-time. Trio heads for the After Dark Club, which turns out to be a den of vampires.

Picture benefits immensely from the casting of disco star turned actress Grace Jones as the leader of the vampires. She has no dialog in the film, but expresses herself sexily in several scary scenes.

VAMPIRA

1975, 89 MINS, UK ◇
Dir Clive Donner *Prod* Jack H. Wiener *Scr* Jeremy
Lloyd *Ph* Tony Richmond *Ed* Bill Butler *Mus* David
Whittaker *Art Dir* Phillip Harrison
● David Niven, Teresa Groves, Peter Bayliss, Jennie
Linden, Nicky Henson, Linda Hayden (World)

David Niven goes the way of Vincent Price in *Vampira*. Screenplay is set in the present day, and has Dracula reading *Playboy*, sleeping in an automated coffin, and giving tours of his castle as a means of luring fresh victims.

Niven smoothly incarnates the old-style rake, while magazine writer Nicky Henson, one of his victims, repellently typifies the hip young stud.

All of this might have made a good high-comedy satire, instead of sporadically amus-ing camp, if the dialog were sharper and if the plot didn't revolve around Niven's attempts to revive his long-dead mate Vampira, played witlessly by Teresa Graves.

VAMPIRE LOVERS, THE

1970, 91 MINS, UK/US ◇ Ⓥ
Dir Roy Ward Baker *Prod* Harry Fine, Michael Style
Scr Tudor Gates *Ph* Moray Grant *Ed* James Needs
Mus Harry Robinson *Art Dir* Scott MacGregor
● Ingrid Pitt, Pippa Steel, Madeleine Smith, Peter
Cushing, Dawn Addams, Kate O'Mara
(Hammer/American International)

The vampire-anti-heroine, played by Ingrid Pitt, has distinct lesbian tendencies. She prefers sinking her fangs into the bosoms of comely young women, though when required she's not averse to giving the works to an interfering local doctor and a manservant.

Not much of a story, but the screenplay [from an adaptation by Harry Fine, Tudor Gates and Michael Style of J. Sheridan Le Fanu's story *Carmilla*] has all the needed ingredients. Dank interiors, eerie exteriors and stagecoaches, plenty of blood, a couple of unconvincing decapitations, stakes in the vampire's heart, the sign of the Cross, etc. Fairly flat dialog doesn't provide much of the unconscious humor that usually gives a lift to this type of entertainment.

VANISHING POINT

1971, 107 MINS, US ◇ Ⓥ
Dir Richard C. Sarafian *Prod* Norman Spencer
Scr Guillermo Cain *Ph* John A. Alonzo *Ed* Stefan
Arnsten *Mus* Jimmy Bowen *Art Dir* Glen Daniels
● Barry Newman, Cleavon Little, Charlotte Rampling,
Dean Jagger, Victoria Medlin, Paul Koslo (Cupid)

If the viewer believes what Guillermo Cain's screenplay is trying to say in this lowercase action effort, the 'wasteland' between Denver and the California border is peopled only with uniformed monsters, aided and abetted by an antagonistic citizenry with the only 'good' people the few hippies, motorcycle gangs and dope pushers.

The action is almost entirely made up of one man driving a car at maximum speed from Denver to, hopefully, San Francisco, against various odds, from the police who try to intercept him, to the oddball individuals he meets along the way.

Barry Newman is the ex-marine who tackles the 15-hour drive sans rest or reason, kept awake by pep pills. A Negro disk jockey (Cleavon Little), tucked away on a tiny radio station in what is close to being a ghost town becomes his collaborator, warning him over the radio when he's near a police trap. This leads, naturally, to the now screen cliche of his being attacked and beaten by racists.

Also seen briefly is Dean Jagger as a Death Valley prospector who tries to befriend Newman and, very briefly, Charlotte Rampling, as a hitchhiker with whom Newman beds down for the night.

VENETIAN AFFAIR, THE

1967, 92 MINS, US ◇
Dir Jerry Thorpe *Prod* Jerry Thorpe, E. Jack Neuman
Scr E. Jack Neuman *Ph* Milton Krasner, Enzo Serafin
Ed Henry Berman *Mus* Lalo Schifrin *Art Dir* George
W. Davis, Leroy Coleman
● Robert Vaughn, Elke Sommer, Felicia Farr, Karl
Boehm, Boris Karloff, Ed Asner (M-G-M)

The Venetian Affair is a tepid programmer about international espionage in Venice. Pacing is tedious and plotting routine, but the production is enlivened by some actual footage of Venice.

E. Jack Neuman adapted a Helen MacInnes novel into a routine script, dotted generally with prototype spy types. Vaughn, ex-CIAgent now a reporter, is sent to Venice after a diplomatic meeting has been bombed. Ed Asner, CIA boss there, once canned Vaughn because latter's then wife, Elke Sommer, was a Communist agent. Now she has disappeared.

Pot boils slowly under Thorpe's casual direction. What was meant as an underplayed approach becomes awkward, meaningless pause, reinforced by dull dialog.

VENOM

1982, 93 MINS, UK ◇ Ⓥ
Dir Piers Haggard *Prod* Martin Bregman *Scr* Robert
Carrington *Ph* Gil Taylor *Ed* Michael Bradsell
Mus Michael Kamen *Art Dir* Tony Curtis
● Klaus Kinski, Oliver Reed, Nicol Williamson, Sarah
Miles, Sterling Hayden, Susan George
(Venom/Paramount)

Venom is an engrossing traditional suspense thriller [from a novel by Alan Scholefield] about a kidnapping, hyped by the genuinely frightening plot gimmick of a deadly black mamba snake on the loose.

Klaus Kinski toplines as Jacmel, a German criminal who kidnaps a young American boy (Lance Holcomb) living in London, aided in the inside job by the boy's servants (Oliver Reed and Susan George). Unbeknownst, the boy has accidentally acquired a poisonous snake intended for toxicologist Dr Marion Stowe (Sarah Miles) and the lethal reptile gets loose in the house.

With old-fashioned lines beween good guys and bad guys sharply drawn, film satisfyingly metes out snake-delivered justice to the evildoers. Combo of Kinski's quiet, dominant menace and Reed's explosive, brutish violence makes for a memorable ensemble of villains.

VERDICT, THE

1946, 86 MINS, US
Dir Don Siegel *Prod* William Jacobs *Scr* Peter
Milne *Ph* Ernest Haller *Ed* Thomas Reilly
Mus Frederick Hollander *Art Dir* Ted Smith
● Sydney Greenstreet, Peter Lorre, Joan Lorring
(Warner)

Stock mystery tale with period background, *The Verdict* aims at generating suspense and thrills, succeeding modestly. Sydney Greenstreet creates character of a Scotland Yard superintendent who is fired when he convicts and hangs a man on circumstantial evidence. To show up the Yard and the man who replaced him, Greenstreet commits the perfect crime. Only the conviction of an innocent man for the murder makes Greenstreet reveal how the killing was done and the reason for it.

Script by Peter Milne, from a novel by Israel Zangwill, is peopled with the usual number of suspects in order to divert suspicion from the real killer and Don Siegel's direction does well with his material. Peter Lorre, macabre artist friend of Greenstreet's is the prime suspect and turns in a good job to match latter's performance.

VERDICT, THE

1982, 122 MINS, US ◇ Ⓥ
Dir Sidney Lumet *Prod* Richard D. Zanuck, David
Brown *Scr* David Mamet *Ph* Andrzej Bartkowiak
Ed Peter Frank *Mus* Johnny Mandel *Art Dir* Edward
Pisoni
● Paul Newman, Charlotte Rampling, Jack Warden,
James Mason, Milo O'Shea, Edward Binns
(20th Century-Fox/Zanuck-Brown)

There are many fine performances and sensitive moral issues contained in *The Verdict* but somehow that isn't enough to make it the compelling film it should be. David Mamet's script [from a novel by Barry Reed] offers little out of the ordinary.

Paul Newman is a cloudy-headed boozer who was at one time clearly a top junior lawyer but has been reduced to soliciting clients at funerals. Colleague Jack Warden hands him the case that could put him back on the straight and narrow.

A young woman lies in a respected Boston hospital – a vegetable thanks to a dose of anesthesia she received from doctors while delivering a baby. Her sister wants to sue the hospital and Catholic Church (which owns the facility) for a sum of money large enough to enable her to start a new life.

Newman becomes convinced the church and hospital have conspired to cover up medical malpractice.

While Newman's drunk is a little difficult to take at the outset, he manages to weave an extraordinarily realistic portrayal by the film's completion. He gets especially solid support from Warden and James Mason.
□ 1982: Best Picture (Nomination)

....

■ VERTIGO

1958, 126 MINS, US ◇ Ⓥ

Dir Alfred Hitchcock *Prod* Alfred Hitchcock *Scr* Alec Coppel, Samuel Taylor *Ph* Robert Burks *Ed* George Tomasini *Mus* Bernard Herrmann *Art Dir* Hal Pereira, Henry Bumstead
● James Stewart, Kim Novak, Barbara Bel Geddes, Tom Helmore, Henry Jones (Paramount)

Vertigo is prime though uneven Hitchcock. James Stewart, on camera almost constantly, comes through with a startlingly fine performance as the lawyer-cop who suffers from acrophobia. Kim Novak, shopgirl who involves Stewart in what turns out to be a clear case of murder, is interesting under Hitchcock's direction and nearer an actress than in the earlier *Pal Joey* or *Jeanne Eagles*.

Unbilled is the city of San Francisco, photographed extensively and in exquisite color. Through all of this runs Alfred Hitchcock's directorial hand, cutting, angling and gimmicking with mastery. Unfortunately, even that mastery is not enough to overcome one major fault – that the film's first half is too slow and too long. This may be because: (1) Hitchcock became overly enamored with the vertiginous beauty of Frisco; or (2) the screenplay (from the novel *D'entre les morts* by Pierre Boileau and Thomas Narcejac) just takes too long to get off the ground.

Film opens with a rackling scene in which Stewart's acrophobia is explained: he hangs from top of a building in midst of chasing a robber over rooftops and watches a police buddy plunge to his death. But for the next hour the action is mainly psychic, with Stewart hired by a rich shipbuilder to watch the shipowner's wife (Novak) as she loses her mental moorings, attempts suicide and immerses herself in the gloomy maunderings of her mad great-grandmother. Stewart goes off his rocker and winds up in a mental institution. When he comes out, still a trifle unbalanced, he keeps hunting for girl who resembles Novak.

Supporting players are all excellent, with Barbara Bel Geddes, in limited role of Stewart's down-to-earth girl friend, standout for providing early dashes of humor.

Frisco location scenes – whether of Nob Hill, interior of Ernie's restaurant, Land's End, downtown, Muir Woods, Mission Dolores or San Juan Bautista – are absolutely authentic and breathtaking.

....

■ VERY SPECIAL FAVOR, A

1965, 105 MINS, US ◇

Dir Michael Gordon *Prod* Stanley Shapiro *Scr* Stanley Shapiro, Nate Monaster *Ph* Leo Tover *Ed* Russell F. Schoengarth *Mus* Vic Mizzy *Art Dir* Alexander Golitzen, Walter Simonds

● Rock Hudson, Leslie Caron, Charles Boyer, Walter Slezak, Dick Shawn, Larry Storch (Universal)

The beautifully-mounted feature draws its title from Rock Hudson, as American oilman who bests French lawyer Charles Boyer in a Paris court case simply by romancing the femme judge, admitting to Boyer on a plane en route back to US that he feels he owes him a favor by beating him at his own national sport, which he'll grant anytime latter requests.

Boyer, in NY to see a daughter for first time in 25 years, sees in her, although a highly successful psychologist, a spinster with the spirit of an old maid, a woman nearly 30 who has never tasted the life her French father thinks every femme should know. He calls on Hudson to make good his offer.

Script develops along expected lines, with Hudson posing to Leslie Caron, the psychologist, as a man with a disturbing problem – he's irresistible to women who pursue him and he's a love toy.

Hudson delivers one of his customary light characterizations, and Boyer as usual is suave. Most outstanding work in pic, however, is contributed by Nita Talbot, a switchboard operator infatuated with Hudson, and Larry Storch, a hardboiled taxi-driver.

....

■ VICTIM

1961, 100 MINS, UK Ⓥ

Dir Basil Dearden *Prod* Michael Relph *Scr* Janet Green, John McCormick *Ph* Otto Heller *Ed* John Guthridge *Mus* Philip Green *Art Dir* Alex Vetchinsky
● Dirk Bogarde, Sylvia Syms, Dennis Price, Anthony Nicholls, Peter McEnery, Derren Nesbitt (Rank/Allied Film Makers)

Producer Michael Relph, director Basil Dearden and writers Janet Green and John McCormick (the team which produced *Sapphire*, involving racial prejudice) adopt a similar technique with *Victim*. They provide a taut, holding thriller about blackmailers latching on to homosexuals and at the same time take several critical swipes at the British law which encourages the blackmailing by making homos criminal outcasts.

Dirk Bogarde plays a successful barrister who is on the verge of becoming a Queen's Counsel. He is happily married to a wife (Sylvia Syms) who knew of his homo leanings when she married him but has successfully helped him to lead a normal life. He refuses to see a youth (Peter McEnery) with whom he previously has had association because he fears possible blackmail. Instead the boy is trying to protect the barrister from blackmail. The youth commits suicide, Bogarde is caught up in enquiries by the cops and, from remorse, sets out to break the blackmailers even though he knows that if the facts come out it will ruin his marriage and his career.

The homosexuals involved are not caricatures but are shown as varying human beings. There are a philanthropist peer, an actor, an aging barber, a hearty car salesman from a good family, a photographer, a bookseller and a factory clerk.

Bogarde is subtle, sensitive and strong. Syms handles a difficult role with delicacy and there is one memorable scene when the two quarrel after she forces him to admit what she doesn't want to hear. This is telling, moving stuff.

....

■ VICTORIA THE GREAT

1937, 112 MINS, UK ◇

Dir Herbert Wilcox *Prod* Herbert Wilcox *Scr* Miles Malleson, Robert Vansittart *Ph* F.A. Young, William V. Skall *Mus* Anthony Collins
● Anna Neagle, Anton Walbrook, Walter Rilla, Mary Morris, H.B. Warner, Grete Wegener (Imperator)

Not cloak-and-cocked-hat historical tedium of pageantry and fancy dramatics, *Victoria the Great* travels a long way toward a full and clarified explanation of the most popular ruler England ever had. Her career, both public and private, is traced from 20 June 1837 when she ascended the throne, until the day of her 60th anniversary as queen, shortly before her demise.

Anna Neagle, in the title role, gives an unwavering performance throughout. Anton Walbrook as Albert, the Prince Consort, is superb.

The film wisely puts its prime focus on the private life of Victoria, her romance, marriage, and personal characteristics. Backgrounded is her public life, and her gradual rise to such high estimation of her people.

Victoria the Great is done with a lavish hand – the closing sequence is in Technicolor. The tinting isn't too good, but serves effectively as a pointer-up for the climax.

This is the very first pic made after the Crown permitted a dramatization to be presented within the Empire dealing with Victoria.

....

■ VICTORS, THE

1963, 175 MINS, US

Dir Carl Foreman *Prod* Carl Foreman *Scr* Carl Foreman *Ph* Christopher Challis *Ed* Alan Osbiston *Mus* Sol Kaplan *Art Dir* Geoffrey Drake
● George Hamilton, George Peppard, Eli Wallach, James Mitchum, Romy Schneider, Jeanne Moreau (Highroad/Columbia)

Carl Foreman tells his tale of war in terms of vignettes, concentrating on homesickness, woman-hunger, civilian starvation, the 'nice' girls who shack up with the GI smoothies for food, cigarettes and kicks. One of these a pretty, no-talent fiddler in a dive, is played by Romy Schneider. Her indifference to the decent soldier (George Hamilton) and ultimate bumming around with the slicker is underplayed, but it's part of the mosaic of the decent GI's own ultimate hardening.

The story is properly told in black and white photography. Color would have been too pretty for the underlying implications of monotony and mud. Foreman has incorporated a lot of newsreel footage. He has designed his narrative with great filmmaking skill and considerable daring, recalling the early 1940s both for nostalgia and irony.

In general Foreman has had the wisdom to underplay his scenes, leave many an incident without the sequel which seems, but is not, mandatory.

There are some trite scenes familiar from earlier war films. Melina Mercouri is the queen of the Belgian black market, proprietor of off-limit establishments, cynic and sensualist. Her affair with the GI Joe (George Peppard) may be the one contrived bit of hokum in an otherwise admirably realistic accomplishment.

Foreman in his alter ego as adaptor has taken his story from [the book *The Human Factor* by] an English writer, Alexander Baron, to whom all proper honor. There will be a plausible temptation to call this a director's picture, which it is, but all is made possible in the end by a good script.

....

■ VICTOR/VICTORIA

1982, 133 MINS, UK ◇ Ⓥ

Dir Blake Edwards *Prod* Blake Edwards, Tony Adams *Scr* Blake Edwards *Ph* Dick Bush *Ed* Ralph E. Winters *Mus* Henry Mancini *Art Dir* Rodger Maus
● Julie Andrews, James Garner, Robert Preston, Lesley Ann Warren, Alex Karras, John Rhys-Davies (M-G-M/Peerford/Artista)

Victor/Victoria is a sparkling, ultra-sophisticated entertainment from Blake Edwards. Based on a 1933 German film comedy [*Viktor und Viktoria*, written and directed by Rheinhold Schunzel] which was a big hit in its day, pic sees Edwards working in the Lubitsch-Wilder vein of sly wit and delightful sexual innuendo.

Set in Paris of 1934 gorgeously represented by Rodger Maus' studio-constructed settings, tale introduces Julie Andrews as a down-on-her-luck chanteuse. Also suffering a temporary career lapse is tres gai nightclub entertainer Robert Preston, who remakes her as a man who in short order becomes celebrated as Paris' foremost female impersonator.

Enter Windy City gangster James Garner, with imposing bodyguard Alex Karras and dizzy sexpot Lesley Ann Warren in tow. Not knowing he's in one of 'those' clubs, the tough guy falls hard for Andrews, only to experience a severe blow to his macho ego when it becomes apparent that she's a he.

While the central thrust of the story rests in Andrews-Garner convergence, everyone in the cast is given a chance to shine. Most impressive of all is Preston, with a shimmering portrait of a slightly decadent 'old queen'.

Andrews is able to reaffirm her musical talents. Garner is quizzically sober as the story's straight man, in more ways than one.

....

■ VICTORY

1940, 77 MINS, US ●

Dir John Cromwell *Prod* Anthony Veiller *Scr* John L. Balderston *Ph* Leo Tover *Ed* William Shea *Mus* Frederick Hollander

● Fredric March, Betty Field, Cedric Hardwicke, Jerome Cowan, Sig Rumann (Paramount)

This film version of Joseph Conrad's novel impresses with several strongly individual performances rather than with the basic movement of the story itself.

Story unfolds at a most leisurely pace, script deviating from regulation picture formula and tempo, and filled with long stretches of dialog to highlight development of characters displayed. Fredric March is the recluse living on a small East Indian Island seeking happiness away from the world. Under his protection comes Betty Field, a stranded musician, and when March finds himself falling in love with the girl he prepares to ship her away on a trading schooner. Cedric Hardwicke and his outlaw companions arrive to rob and kill March for his buried fortune.

March capably carries the lead with restrained action to put over transformation of his original weakling, golden-rule character to one of strength, physically and mentally. Field registers with an unusual performance as the English girl musician who falls in love with the recluse. Jerome Cowan clicks with a meritorious performance as Hardwicke's Cockney assistant in outlawry; while Hardwicke handles his assignment with usual ability.

Direction by John Cromwell, in retaining all of the character etchings displayed in Conrad's book, employs a stagey technique with burdensome dialog and slow pace until the final episodes, which pick up dramatic interest.

....

■ VICTORY

1981, 117 MINS, US ◇

Dir John Huston *Prod* Freddie Fields *Scr* Evan Jones, Yabo Yablonsky *Ph* Gerry Fisher *Ed* Roberto Silvi *Mus* Bill Conti *Art Dir* J. Dennis Washington

● Sylvester Stallone, Michael Caine, Max Von Sydow, Pele, Daniel Massey, Carole Laure (Paramount/Lorimar/Victory)

Victory amounts to a frankly oldfashioned

World War II morality play, hinging on soccer as a civilized metaphor for the game of War.

Though set in a German p.o.w. camp in 1943, *Victory* is barely a 'war movie' by any stretch. Plot hinges on a morality-building ploy by a genteel propaganda officer (Max Von Sydow) who once played for Germany to pit a team of Allied prisoners (including officer Michael Caine, a onetime British soccer pro, Brazil's legendary Pele, and Yank bad-boy Sylvester Stallone) against the local German troops.

When his superiors get wind of the plan, they quickly see the worldwide propaganda potential and insist on expanding the plan to square off a p.o.w. 'all star" team drawn from imprisoned footballers throughout Europe, against the German national team.

Script spends so much effort extolling man's basic goodness and the values of self-lessness, teamwork and fair play, that it frequently softens the action. Fortunately, director John Huston has such a firm grip on the dramatic line that does exist – and works some very good performances from the cast, particularly Caine – that the pic (lensed entirely in Hungary) survives intact.

....

■ VICTORY AT SEA

1954, 97 MINS, US ●

Prod Henry Salomon, Robert W. Sarnoff *Scr* Henry Salomon, Richard Hanser *Ed* Isaac Kleinerman *Mus* Richard Rodgers

(NBC Film Division)

Originally presented on NBC as a 26-part filmed documentary of World War II naval history, the television *Victory at Sea* was compressed to 97 minutes for theatrical release. But despite the loss of many fine scenes of the original the edited print is still a forceful pictorial chronicle of the Allies' global sea campaigns against the Axis Powers.

Sea covers the period from the Axis' 1939 ascendancy to its defeat in 1945. Among key points captured by the cameras are the Japanese attack on Pearl Harbor, the Allied invasion of Normandy, the sweep of the US fleets through the Pacific, the North African invasion, the atomic bombing of Japan and the liberation of the prisoners of Dachau, Buchenwald and other infamous concentration camps.

Alexander Scourby's narration of the commentary written by Henry Salomon and Richard Hanser is unobtrusive and never detracts from the screen movement. Quality of the print is good considering the varied origin and age of the footage.

....

■ VIDEODROME

1983, 88 MINS, CANADA ◇ ●

Dir David Cronenberg *Prod* Claude Heroux *Scr* David Cronenberg *Ph* Mark Irwin *Ed* Ronald Sanders *Mus* Howard Shore *Art Dir* Carol Spier

● James Woods, Sonja Smits, Deborah Harry, Peter Dvorsky, Les Carlson, Jack Creley (Filmplan)

Story concerns a small-time cable TV outlet in Toronto. The quasi-clandestine operation is run by Max Renn (James Woods) who's ever on the lookout for offbeat and erotic material.

He becomes fascinated with a program called Videodrome, picked up from a satellite by a station technician. The show appears to be little more than a series of torture sequences, primarily involving women.

Renn pursues the program but is blocked at every turn. One of his suppliers warns him that the activities on the show are not staged. However, he perseveres, making contact with a McLuhanesque media guru named Brian O'Blivion (Jack Creley).

Film is dotted with video jargon and ideology which proves more fascinating than distancing. And Cronenberg amplifies the freaky situation with a series of stunning visual effects.

Woods aptly conveys Renn's obsession and eventual bondage to the television nightmare. Sonja Smits is an alluring and mysterious femme fatale and Deborah Harry seems just right as Renn's girlfriend who thrives on and is undone by Videodrome's games cruelty.

....

■ VIETNAM, TEXAS

1990, 85 MINS, US ◇ ●

Dir Robert Ginty *Prod* Robert Ginty, Ron Joy *Scr* Tom Badal, C. Courtney Joyner *Ph* Robert M. Baldwin Jr *Ed* Jonathan P. Shaw *Mus* Richard Stone *Art Dir* Kate J. Sullivan

● Robert Ginty, Haing S. Ngor, Tim Thomersen, Kiev Chinh, Tamlyn Tomita (Epic)

Good intentions are roughly served in this uneven actioner that displays some compassion for the stateside Vietnam community while exploiting its violent elements.

Robert Ginty, who also directed, stars as Father Thomas McCain, a Vietnam vet turned priest who still suffers guilt about the Vietnamese woman he abandoned – pregnant with his child – when he returned to the States. Fifteen years later, he tracks them down in Houston's Little Saigon and forces himself into their lives, despite the fact that his former flame Mailan (Kieu Chinh) is now comfortably established as the wife of a vicious drug runner, Wong (Haing S. Ngor).

Ginty hooks up with his old soldier buddy Max (Tim Thomerson), now a dissolute bar owner, and they set out to reach Mailan and her teenage daughter Lan (Tamlin Tomita), setting off beatings and murders as they run up against Wong's henchmen.

Among its plusses, pic features numerous Asian roles, with Tomita a standout as the spirited teenage daughter. Ngor (*The Killing Fields*) is suitable chilling as Wong.

....

■ VIEW TO A KILL, A

1985, 131 MINS, UK ◇ ●

Dir John Glen *Prod* Albert R. Broccoli, Michael G. Wilson *Scr* Richard Maibaum, Michael G. Wilson *Ph* Alan Hume *Ed* Peter Davies *Mus* John Barry *Art Dir* Peter Lamont

● Roger Moore, Christopher Walken, Tanya Roberts, Grace Jones, Patrick Macnee, Patrick Bauchan (Eon/United Arists)

Bond's adversary this time is the international industrialist Max Zorin (Christopher Walken) and his love-hate interest, May Day (Grace Jones). Bond tangles with them at their regal horse sale and uncovers a profitable scheme in which microchips are surgically implanted in the horse to assure an easy victory.

Horse business is moderately entertaining, particularly when Patrick Macnee is on screen as Bond's chauffeur accomplice. Action, however, jumps abruptly to San Francisco to reveal Zorin's true motives. He's hatching some master plan to pump water from the sea into the San Andreas fault causing a major earthquake, destroying the Silicon Valley and leaving him with the world's microchip monopoly.

While Bond pics have always traded heavily on the camp value of its characters, *A View to a Kill* almost attacks the humor, practically winking at the audience with every move.

As for Roger Moore, making his seventh appearance as Bond, he is right about half the time. He still has the suave and cool for the part, but on occasion he looks a bit old and his womanizing seems dated when he does.

....

■ VIGIL

1984, 90 MINS, NEW ZEALAND ◇ ▽

Dir Vincent Ward   *Prod* John Maynard   *Scr* Vincent Ward, Graeme Tetley   *Ph* Alun Bollinger   *Ed* Simon Reece   *Mus* Jack Body   *Art Dir* Kai Hawkins

● Penelope Stewart, Frank Whitten, Bill Kerr, Fiona Kay (Film Investment/NZFC)

Central figure is 11-year-old Toss (Fiona Kay), on the threshold of womanhood and caught in the tragedy of the death of her father and the coincidental arrival of a stranger, Ethan (Frank Whitten). It is primarily through her eyes, actions and interpretation of events, that the impact of Ethan's presence upon the household is registered.

While Toss is fascinated by Ethan's mysterious aura, her mother Elizabeth (Penelope Stewart) is reawakened from a joyless marriage, and her grandfather Birdie (Bill Kerr) finds a comrade for his eccentric pranks and grandiose mechanical inventions.

The remarkable quality of the film is the way it gives fresh resonance to universal themes.

■ VIKINGS, THE

1958, 114 MINS, US ◇ ▽

Dir Richard Fleischer   *Prod* Jerry Bresler   *Scr* Calder Willingham   *Ph* Jack Cardiff   *Ed* Elmo Williams   *Mus* Mario Nascimbene

● Kirk Douglas, Tony Curtis, Ernest Borgnine, Janet Leigh, Alexander Knox, Frank Thring (United Artists/Bryna)

The Vikings is spectacular, rousing and colorful. Blood flows freely as swords are crossed and arrows meet their mark in barbarian combat. And there's no hesitance about throwing a victim into a wolf pit or a pool of crabs.

There is some complication at the start, however, as the various characters are brought into view – as the Viking army of 200 raids the Kingdom of Northumbria, in England, and elements of mystery and intrigue are brought into the story. But it is not too long before the screenplay [from the novel by Edison Marshall] and director Richard Fleischer have their people in clear focus.

History is highly fictionalized. It starts with the raid, the death of the English leader, the succession to the throne of Frank Thring who's strictly the heavy. The queen is with child, the father being Ernest Borgnine, head of the marauding Vikings. To escape the new king's wrath she flees to another land and with the proper passage of time the child, now a young man (Tony Curtis), turns up in the Viking village as a slave whose identity is not known.

It is at this point that Curtis encounters Kirk Douglas, latter as heir to the Viking throne. Neither is aware of the fact that the other is his brother. They clash. Janet Leigh participates as daughter of the king of Wales who is to be taken as a bride by the sadistic English king. Douglas falls for Leigh in a big way but she comes to favor Curtis, and thus is established the romantic triangle.

It's the production that counts and producer Jerry Bresler, working with Douglas' indie outfit, has done it up big and with apparent authenticity. Lensing was in the Norse fjord area and various parts of Europe, including the Bavarian Studios.

Douglas, doing a bangup, freewheeling job as the ferocious and disfigured Viking fighter, fits the part splendidly. Borgnine's Viking chief is a conqueror of authority.

■ VILLA RIDES

1968, 125 MINS, US ◇ ▽

Dir Buzz Kulik   *Prod* Ted Richmond   *Scr* Robert Towne, Sam Peckinpah   *Ph* Jack Hildyard   *Ed* David Bretherton   *Mus* Maurice Jarre   *Art Dir* Ted Haworth

● Yul Brynner, Robert Mitchum, Grazia Buccella, Charles Bronson, Robert Viharo, Frank Wolff (Paramount)

Villa Rides is a pseudo-biopic of a portion of the bandit career of Mexico's folk hero, Pancho Villa, with Yul Brynner in title role.

Ted Richmond's handsome exterior production, filmed in 1967 in Spain, is competently, if leisurely and routinely, directed with the accent on violent death.

Script fails to establish clearly the precise political framework, while over-developing some lesser details. This, plus overlength, adds up to dramatic tedium.

Film concerns itself with Villa's own aggressive acts. With the aid of Charles Bronson and Robert Viharo, Brynner is responsible for the on-screen deaths of literally dozens of men, most explicitly detailed.

Brynner makes Villa sympathetic at times, as a man fighting for human rights, though that's a bit hard to swallow since his philosophy does not get spelled out for 105 minutes into the film. His rationalization is rather facile and specious: those he killed were 'traitors,' by his convenient self-excusing definition.

■ VILLAGE OF THE DAMNED

1960, 77 MINS, UK ▽

Dir Wolf Rilla   *Prod* Ronald Kinnock   *Scr* Stirling Silliphant, Wolf Rilla, George Barclay   *Ph* Geoffrey Faithfull   *Ed* Gordon Hales   *Mus* Ron Goodwin

● George Sanders, Barbara Shelley, Martin Stephens, Michael Gwynn, Laurence Naismith (M-G-M)

Plot kicks around what is not an uninteresting idea. A little British village comes under the spell of some strange, supernatural force which first puts everybody out for the count. Then the villagers come to and find that every woman capable of being pregnant is.

Snag is that all the children are little monsters. They all look alike – fair haired, unblinking stare and with intellects the equivalent of adults, plus the knack of mental telepathy. George Sanders, a physicist, is intimately involved, since his wife is the mother of the leader of the little gang of abnormal moppets. Sanders decides to probe the mystery.

If there had happend to be any hint of why this remarkable business should have occurred, the film [from the novel *Midwich Cuckoos* by John Wyndham] would have been slightly more plausible. As it is, this just tapers off from a taut beginning into soggy melodrama. Wolf Rilla's direction is adequate, but no more.

■ VILLAIN

1971, 98 MINS, UK ◇ ▽

Dir Michael Tuchner   *Prod* Alan Ladd Jr, Jay Kantner   *Scr* Dick Clement, Ian La Frenais   *Ph* Christopher Challis   *Ed* Ralph Sheldon   *Mus* Jonathan Hodge   *Art Dir* Maurice Carter

● Richard Burton, Ian McShane, Nigel Davenport, Donald Sinden, Fiona Lewis, T.P. McKenna (Anglo-EMI)

Dick Clement and Ian La Frenais's screenplay, adapted by Al Lettieri, and based on a James Barlow novel [*The Burden of Proof*], uses a frayed shoestring plot of a payroll stickup to flesh out the sadistic actions of Richard Burton as a onetime nightclub bouncer with a handy razor who has become one of the major figures of the London underworld. It isn't just a penchant for cutting and slicing that makes our man tick. He has an entire assortment of quirks.

Tied to a dying mother (Cathleen Nesbitt) by a silver cord stronger than steel cable, he also is a homosexual but no run-of-the-subway version. He has a thing about a petty criminal (Ian McShane) that makes him beat him up, then bed down with him. His bete noir, however, is a dedicated police inspector (Nigel Davenport) whose sole duty is to pin something on him.

Support is strong with top honors going to Joss Ackland as a thief with an ulcer; Donald Sinden, as a Member of Parliament with not quite standard sexual demands which, naturally, makes him an ideal blackmail prospect; and T.P. McKenna, as another gang leader.

■ VILLAIN, THE

1979, 93 MINS, US ◇ ▽

Dir Hal Needham   *Prod* Mort Engelberg   *Scr* Robert G. Kane   *Ph* Bobby Byrne   *Ed* Walter Hannemann   *Mus* Bill Justis   *Art Dir* Carl Anderson

● Kirk Douglas, Ann-Margret, Arnold Schwarzenegger, Paul Lynde, Ruth Buzzi, Jack Elam (Columbia/Rastar)

Idea for the satire must have looked great on paper. Why not take all the standard sagebrush types – the handsome stranger, the decollete femme, the evil outlaw, etc. – and put them through a parody of their usual paces?

The answer no one came up with was that without any depth of characterization, and only the flimsiest plot structure, a take-off has nowhere to go. Hal Needham, again dazzles audiences with some eye-popping stunts but the film gets lost in the dust.

With Kirk Douglas in the title role, Arnold Schwarzenegger as the good guy, and Ann-Margret as the lascivious girl who loves being fought over, *The Villain* becomes even more of a disappointment. Rarely has so much talent been used to so little purpose.

■ VINCENT
THE LIFE AND DEATH OF VINCENT VAN GOGH

1987, 103 MINS, AUSTRALIA/NETHERLANDS ◇

Dir Paul Cox   *Prod* Tony Llewellyn-Jones   *Scr* Paul Cox   *Ph* Paul Cox   *Ed* Paul Cox   *Mus* Norman Kaye   *Art Dir* Neil Angwin

● voice John Hurt (Illumination/Look/Ozfilms/Dasha)

This very special art film is neither documentary nor fiction. Paul Cox, one of Australia's foremost directors, was born in Holland and has made an exquisite, timeless tribute to Vincent Van Gogh using as his text simply the letters Vincent wrote to his brother Theo, letters beautifully read by John Hurt.

Van Gogh worked as a painter for only 10 years, and during that period produced about 1,800 works, but when he killed himself at 37 in 1890 he had only sold one of them, and was unknown and impoverished. Cox' film covers those last 10 years but, save for one brief moment at the end, when Van Gogh's funeral is depicted, the central character of the drama is never seen. His thoughts and philosophies are enunciated superbly on the soundtrack.

Cox traveled to the places Van Gogh knew, lived and worked. The images accompanying the text are of trees and fields and birds in flight, and the inevitable sunflowers. And, of course, there are the paintings themselves.

■ VINCENT AND THEO

1990, 138 MINS, UK/FRANCE/NETH/ITALY ◇ ▽

Dir Robert Altman   *Prod* Ludi Boeken   *Scr* Julian Mitchell   *Ph* Jean Lepine   *Ed* Francoise Auger   *Mus* Gabriel Yared   *Art Dir* Stephen Altman

● Tim Roth, Paul Rhys, Jip Wijngaarden, Johanna Ter Steege, Jean-Pierre Cassel (Belbo/Central/La Sept/Telepool/RAI Uno/Vara/Sofica Valor)

A study of Van Gogh's last years as seen through his tortured relationship with his brother, *Vincent and Theo* paradoxically is one of Robert Altman's most cinematically conventional films as well as one of his most deeply personal. Bearing little resemblance to the glamorized, overheated Vincente Minnelli 1956 biopic *Lust for Life*, this masterwork operates in the intimate, thoughtful vein of the great BBC bios of artistic figures.

Altman and his incisive scripter Julian Mitchell focus on Vincent's obsessive devotion to his craft and the failure of his overly timid art dealer-brother to win him acceptance in an art world that scorned his idiosyncratic genius.

The heart of the film is its exploration of the destructive, unacknowledged but important relationship between artist and patron. Paul Rhys skillfully inhabits a character even more wretchedly unhappy than his brother, who at least has the consolation of his art, and Theo's own incipient madness gives the film much of its unsettling tone.

Tim Roth powerfully conveys Vincent's heroic, obsessive concentration on his work, and then resultant loneliness and isolation.

● ●

■ VIOLENT PLAYGROUND

1958, 108 MINS, UK

Dir Basil Dearden *Prod* Michael Relph *Scr* James Kennaway *Ph* Reginald Wyer *Ed* Arthur Stevens *Mus* Philip Green *Art Dir* Maurice Carter

● Stanley Baker, Anne Heywood, David McCallum, Peter Cushing, John Slater, Clifford Evans (Rank)

Violent Playground brings a sincere semi-documentary touch to the matter of juve delinquency. James Kennaway's human and literate screenplay is convincingly acted against authentic Liverpool backgrounds. Result is an absorbing film that works up to an overlong but tense climax.

Film concerns an experiment made in Liverpool in 1949. Policemen have become Juvenile Liaison Officers whose job is to keep an eye on mischievous youngsters and steer them away from crime. Stanley Baker gives a vigorous and sympathetic performance as a cop who is taken off the investigation of a series of unexplained fires for this work. He becomes particularly involved with one family and discovers who is responsible for the arson.

There are a number of other very creditable performances, notably David McCallum as the young delinquent, Peter Cushing as a very serious but wholehearted priest, Clifford Evans as a schoolmaster and in her first big chance, as David McCallum's elder sister, Anne Heywood.

● ●

■ V.I.P.s, THE

1963, 119 MINS, UK ◇

Dir Anthony Asquith *Prod* Anatole de Grunwald *Scr* Terence Rattigan *Ph* Jack Hildyard *Ed* Frank Clarke *Mus* Miklos Rozsa

● Elizabeth Taylor, Richard Burton, Louis Jourdan, Margaret Rutherford, Maggie Smith, Rod Taylor (M-G-M)

This has suspense, conflict, romance, comedy and drama. Its main fault is that some of the characters and the by-plots are not developed enough. But that is a risk inevitable in any film in which a number of strangers are flung together, each with problems and linked by a single circumstance.

In this case the setting is London Airport and the basic problem is the necessity for at least four of the Very Important Passengers bound for the States to get out of the country pronto. Their plans go haywire when a thick fog grounds all planes overnight.

Terence Rattigan's screenplay juggles these situations and does not neglect many of the star performers. The script has literate, witty and sometimes touching dialog and Anthony Asquith has directed skillfully, in that though there is the sense of bustle inseparable from any international airport he has retained a sympathetic feeling of intimacy for all his characters.

Principal story, that of the business tycoon who has taken his wife for granted and now looks set to lose her, is played out by Elizabeth Taylor, Richard Burton and Louis Jourdan as the lover. Maybe Taylor needs a sabbatical but there is a feeling of ordinariness about her thesping.

Burton, however, gives a top-league performance as the business chief who eventually regains his wife but only after a few hours of taut misery, humiliating and self-enlightenment. Jourdan is also excellent as the would-be lover and he has one scene with Burton which is a little masterpiece of dual virtuosity.

● ●

■ VIRGIN AND THE GYPSY, THE

1970, 95 MINS, UK ◇ Ⓥ

Dir Christopher Miles *Prod* Kenneth Harper *Scr* Alan Plater *Ph* Bob Huke *Ed* Paul Davies *Mus* Patrick Gowers *Art Dir* Terence Knight

● Joanna Shimkus, Franco Nero, Honor Blackman, Mark Burns, Maurice Denham, Fay Compton (De Grunwald)

D. H. Lawrence's last unpolished novella, *The Virgin and the Gypsy* is about a young English girl's awakening to adult life in northern England, circa 1921. While faithful perhaps to the author, film is a stilted period piece.

Joanna Shimkus and Harriett Harper are two rural sisters returning from a French school to a provincial environment, ruled by grandmother Fay Compton. Puppets in the household include rector-father Maurice Denham, aunt Kay Walsh, uncle Norman Bird, and maid Janet Chappell.

Shimkus (whose mother abandoned her family's stultifying influence) grows restive, and finds a sexual stirring under Franco Nero's gaze, plus sympathetic adult companionship from Honor Blackman and Mark Burns, who are living together and evoking prissy clucks from the townsfolk.

● ●

■ VIRGIN SOLDIERS, THE

1969, 96 MINS, UK ◇ Ⓥ

Dir John Dexter *Prod* Leslie Gilliat, Ned Sherrin *Scr* John Hopkins, Ian La Frenais *Ph* Ken Higgins *Ed* Thelma Connell *Mus* Peter Greenwell *Art Dir* Frank White

● Lynn Redgrave, Hywel Bennett, Nigel Davenport, Nigel Patrick, Rachel Kempson, Jack Shepherd (Columbia/Foreman)

Much of the irony and subtlety of Leslie Thomas's novel have been ironed out in favor of a broader approach to the humor. Nevertheless, *The Virgin Soldiers* comes out as a bright and affectionate peek at the trials and tribulations of young National Service rookies.

Though the writers have concentrated mainly on making the film ruefully funny, the serious side has not been neglected. The smell of death is often just around the corner and violence in the jungle and streets of terrorist-infested Malaya is in striking, effective contrast to the boisterous, bawdy, barrack-room atmosphere.

Acting all around is first rate, though only a few characters are allowed to develop.

Redgrave as the sulky heroine has her moments but creates no sympathy and, in fact, is mainly dull, but Tsai Chin makes joyful capital out of her small but lively role as the local prostie.

● ●

■ VIRGINIA CITY

1940, 123 MINS, US

Dir Michael Curtiz *Prod* Hal B. Wallis, Robert Fellows *Scr* Robert Buckner *Ph* Sol Polito *Ed* George Amy *Mus* Max Steiner *Art Dir* Ted Smith

● Errol Flynn, Miriam Hopkins, Randolph Scott, Humphrey Bogart, Frank McHugh, Alan Hale (Warner)

On the theory, perhaps, that one good western deserves another, Warner Bros follows up *Dodge City*, starring Errol Flynn, with another saga of the land of the blazing sunsets entitled *Virginia City*. As a shoot 'em up, the picture is first class; as a bit of cinematic history telling, it is far short of the possibilities indicated by the title and cast.

It's about the cache of $5 million in gold bullion which Confederate sympathizers are reported to have offered to the cause of the Southern states during the Civil War. The catch, of course, is how to get the gold out of Nevada and through Union scouting lines.

Flynn is first shown as a Union captive in Libby prison, from which he and companions escape, later to be assigned to travel across the plains and thwart the conspiracy by which the Confederacy hoped to come in possession of all that gold from the Nevada hills. Miriam Hopkins is a singer in a Virginia City saloon and travels west on the stage with Flynn. She is a rebel spy, fresh from a meeting with Jeff Davis. There's the romance.

En route, the stage is held up by John Murrell, outlaw, who is really Humphrey Bogart behind a slick-waxed mustache. There's the chase.

And in Virginia City is Randolph Scott, secretly planning the removal of the gold, which is to be taken south in a wagon train. Scott also is much in love with Hopkins, who leans heavily towards Flynn. She betrays Flynn into a trap, thus placing patriotism ahead of love. There's the drama.

Michael Curtiz, the director, has taken all this and steamed it up with some noisy trigger work, charging cavalry, dance-hall intimacies and the burning sands of the desert to concoct a bustling western, which is replete with action, although short on credulity.

● ●

■ VIRGINIAN, THE

1929, 92 MINS, US Ⓥ

Dir Victor Fleming *Scr* Howard Estabrook

● Gary Cooper, Walter Huston, Mary Brian, Chester Conklin, Eugene Pallette, E.H. Calvert (Paramount)

This Paramount production takes the old play dirt of ancient plains pictures, shuffles it around a bit, and makes of the Owen Wister and Kirk La Shelle story 92 minutes of drama and comedy.

There's an anti-climax toward the middle, one of the most harrowing and vivid sequences ever before the lenses. It is when the silent and lanky Virginian (Gary Cooper) is forced to give the signal which sends his pal, Steve (Richard Arlen), along with three other cattle rustlers, galloping to their death in nooses.

Trampas (Walter Huston), the menace, is saved from the hanging to bait along the story for the vengeance climax.

The school mam, played by the pretty Mary Brian, doesn't fly at the neck of the tall backwoodsman. She teases him, letting him use the old gag of rescuing her from a frightened cow and then promptly bawling him out. This provides Cooper with a chance for a bit of byplay and wise-cracking with Arlen as a sincere but out-for-easy-dough Steve.

● ●

■ VIRGINIAN, THE

1946, 83 MINS, US ◇

Dir Stuart Gilmore *Prod* Paul Jones *Scr* Frances Goodrich, Albert Hackett *Ph* Harry Hallenberger *Ed* Everett Douglas *Mus* Daniele Amfitheatrof *Art Dir* Hans Dreier, John Meehan

● Joel McCrea, Brian Donlevy, Sonny Tufts, Barbara Britton (Paramount)

The Virginian stands up pretty well over the years. First filmed in 1914 for the silents, then in 1929 (by Par), the present version of the Owen Wister novel is still a pleasant, flavorsome western, with much of the old charm of a daguerreotype.

Although story is a little dated as well as a mite slow, the yarn is still a satisfactory romance, with enough shooting and suspense to offset the plodding pace. Yarn hasn't been changed much, still being the story of the little schoolmarm from Vermont and the cowboy from Virginia, who meet in Montana and wed, after the hero has disposed of a few troublesome cow rustlers

Costumes of the eastern 1870s, the early-type railroads, the horse riding and cow roundups, the rolling Montana hills, all help in the nostalgic flavor.

Joel McCrea follows soundly in footsteps of Dustin Farnum and Gary Cooper as The ('When You Call Me That, Smile') Virginian, with a straightforward characterization. Barbara Britton is pert and pretty as the schoolteacher. Brian Donlevy, as the rustler, and Sonny Tufts, in his first western role as a misguided cowhand, head an okay supporting cast.

● ●

■ VISIONS OF EIGHT

1973, 110 MINS, US ◇ ⓥ
Dir Milos Forman, Kon Ichikawa, Claude Lelouch, Yuri Ozerov, Arthur Penn, Michael Pfleghar, John Schlesinger, Mai Zetterling *Prod* Stan Margulies *Ph* Michael Samuelson, Igor Slabnevich, Rune Ericson, Walter Lassally, Ernst Wild, Masuo Yamaguchi, Daniel Body, Jorgen Persson *Ed* Robert Lambert, Edward Roberts, Dede Allen, Margot von Schliffen, Catherine Bernard, Lars Hagstrom *Mus* Henry Mancini
● (Wolper)

Producer David Wolper recruited eight (originally 10) name directors to choose a segment of the 1972 Munich Olympics and give his/her view of the event on a smaller plane.

The problem is that many of the sketches sometimes forget the idea of sport and competition itself, to indulge in ideas. But the flurry, crowds and human endeavor are there, and in the background the tragic terrorist events that led to the massacre of Israeli athletes by Arab terrorists.

Russo film maker Yuri Ozerov starts the ball rolling with *The Beginning*. Mai Zetterling looks at weightlifters in *The Strongest*, a mannered seg but quite funny and well edited. Arthur Penn has a stylized look at pole-vaulting in *The Highest*. Michael Pfleghar devoted himself to women in various events.

Kon Ichikawa, who helmed the remarkable *Tokyo Olympiad* [1965], delves into the 300-meter dash, stretching it in time. Claude Lelouch concentrates on losers, and gets some laughable and even pathetic insights at times. Milos Forman lenses the harsh decathlon to milk comic relief from it. John Schlesinger winds it with a sentimental homage to a British marathon runner who loses.

● ●

■ VITAL SIGNS

1990, 103 MINS, US ◇ ⓥ
Dir Marisa Silver *Prod* Laurie Perlman, Cathleen Summers *Scr* Larry Ketron, Jeb Stuart *Ph* John Lindley *Ed* Robert Brown, Danford B. Greene *Mus* Miles Goodman *Art Dir* Todd Hallowell
● Adrian Pascar, Diane Lane, Jimmy Smits, Norma Aleandro, Jack Gwaltney, Laura San Giacomo (20th Century-Fox)

Vital Signs is a strikingly well-done ensemble piece about a pivotal year in the lives of a group of medical students, with polished script, direction and performances.

As a gifted doctor-to-be who oozes charm and good looks, Adrian Pasdar is the focus of this group of serious strivers navigating their tough third year at LA Central's med school. Diane Lane is the crisp but compassionate fellow student he falls in love with. Jack Gwaltney plays the blander, grimmer fellow from a less-advantaged background who's determined not to let Pasdar surpass him.

Interesting subplots are played out in the relationship of Gwaltney and his neglected wife (Laura San Giacomo, in an effective but unexciting plain-jane turn), and the amusing discomfort of best pals Jane Adams and Tim Ransom after they cross into romantic involvement.

Director Marisa Silver does a good job of getting across characters' emotional lives, making these mainstream twentysomething types absorbing, and fashions a crisply moving story.

● ●

■ VIVA KNIEVEL!

1977, 104 MINS, US ◇ ⓥ
Dir Gordon Douglas *Prod* Stan Hough *Scr* Antonio Santillan *Ph* Fred Jackman *Ed* Harold Kress *Mus* Charles Bernstein
● Evel Knievel, Gene Kelly, Marjoe Gortner, Lauren Hutton, Leslie Nielsen, Red Buttons (Warner/Corwin)

In the most daring feat of his career, Evel Knievel leaps over a mountain of blazing cliches and a cavernous plot, somehow landing upright to the predictable cheers of his legions of fans.

Actually, Evel the actor emerges from the wreck in better shape than the bent careers of his veteran co-stars, Gene Kelly, Marjoe Gortner, Red Buttons, Lauren Hutton and Leslie Nielsen. For him, it's a chance to show he can be fairly natural in front of the camera when the demands are minimal; for them, it's a credit best forgotten.

Plot: evil Leslie Nielsen will lure the leaper to Mexico where he'll kill Knievel and steal his red-white-and-blue truck, substituting an identical red-white-and-blue truck whose sides are packed with illegal white powder.

● ●

■ VIVA LAS VEGAS

1964, 85 MINS, US ◇ ⓥ
Dir George Sidney *Prod* Jack Cummings, George Sidney *Scr* Sally Benson *Ph* Joseph Biroc *Ed* John McSweeney *Mus* George Stoll *Art Dir* George W. Davis, Edward Carfagno
● Elvis Presley, Ann-Margret, Cesare Danova, William Demarest, Nicky Blair (M-G-M)

The sizzling combination of Elvis Presley and Ann-Margaret is enough to carry *Viva Las Vegas* over the top. The picture is fortunate in having two such commodities for bait, because beyond several flashy musical numbers, a glamorous locale and one electrifying auto race sequence, the production is a pretty trite and heavyhanded affair, puny in story development and distortedly preoccupied with anatomical oomph.

The film is designed to dazzle the eye, assault the ear and ignore the brain. Vegas, of course, is the setting of Sally Benson's superficial contrivance about an auto racing buff (Presley) trying to raise funds to purchase an engine for the racer with which he hopes to win the Grand Prix. His main obstacle is a swimming instructress (A-M) who doesn't approve of his goal, but ultimately softens.

Hackneyed yarn provides the skeletal excuse for about 10 musical interludes, a quick tour of the US gambling capital and that one slam-bang climactic sequence that lifts the film up by its bootstraps just when it is sorely in need of a lift.

● ●

■ VIVA VILLA!

1934, 112 MINS, US
Dir Jack Conway *Scr* Ben Hecht *Ph* James Wong Howe, Charles G. Howe *Mus* Herbert Stothart
● Wallace Beery, Leo Carrillo, Fay Wray, Donald Cook, Joseph Schildkraut, Stuart Erwin (M-G-M)

Viva Villa is a corking western. It's a big, impressive production which sets out to make Wallace Beery's Pancho Villa appear as a somewhat sympathetic and quasi-patriotic bandit.

But Beery's characterization, apart from the basic screen material, lets Pancho down too much. His Villa is a hybrid dialectician, neither Mex nor gringo, with a vacillating accent that suffers alongside of Leo Carrillo's charming dialect or the contra-renegade version as done by Joseph Schildkraut as Pascal. Both impart an unction and a style to their cruelties that makes Beery's boorish Villa show up too sadly.

The two principal femmes are well handled by Fay Wray as the sympathetic aristocrat who is brutally assaulted and assassinated by Villa; and Katherine DeMille (Cecil's daughter, who manifests much talent) likewise stands out. Latter's s.a. personality registers as one of Villa's casual 'brides' whom sotted newspaperman Johnny Sykes (Stuart Erwin) abracadabras in mock-marriage ritual in order to appease the requirements for ceremonials by both principals.

There is no denying the mass-movement impressiveness of the production in toto. The handling of the mob scenes on field of battle was no mean task.

□ 1934: Best Picture (Nomination)

● ●

■ VIVA ZAPATA!

1952, 112 MINS, US ⓥ
Dir Elia Kazan *Prod* Darryl F. Zanuck *Scr* John Steinbeck *Ph* Joe MacDonald *Ed* Barbara McLean *Mus* Alex North *Art Dir* Lyle Wheeler, Leland Fuller
● Marlon Brando, Jean Peters, Anthony Quinn, Joseph Wiseman, Arnold Moss, Margo (20th Century-Fox)

The story of Emiliano Zapata, a lesser-known Mexican revolutionary, is a picture that records a hard, cruel, curiously unemotional account of Mexican banditry and revolt against oppressive government. Elia Kazan's direction strives for a personal intimacy but neither he nor the John Steinbeck scripting achieves in enough measure.

Convenient use is made of historical fact as the script plays hop-skip-and-jump in spanning the nine years that Zapata was a controversial figure in Mexican political life just prior to and during the earlier part of World War I.

Marlon Brando brings to the Zapata character the same type of cold objectivity noted in script and direction. Jean Peters is the girl who becomes his bride and forsees his violent end.

There's a stark quality to the photography by Joe MacDonald that suggests the raw, hot atmosphere of Mexico.

● ●

■ VIVACIOUS LADY

1938, 90 MINS, US ⓥ
Dir George Stevens *Prod* George Stevens *Scr* P.J. Wolfson, Ernest Pagano *Ph* Robert de Grasse *Ed* Henry Berman *Mus* Roy Webb
● Ginger Rogers, James Stewart, James Ellison, Beulah Bondi, Charles Coburn, Frances Mercer (RKO)

Vivacious Lady is entertainment of the highest order and broadest appeal. Story by I.A.R. Wylie tells the romantic adventures and tribulations of a New York cabaret singer and a youthful college professor.

It is a case of love at first sight, a speedy wooing and hasty marriage. Then the young man takes his bride to the small town and introduces her to his family and associates. Prejudice and stern respectability resist the invasion. Manner in which approval of the marriage is won from the boy's parents is amusingly accomplished.

In their predicament of living apart until the conventional amenities of proper introduction into society are observed, Ginger Rogers and James Stewart undergo a series of connubial disappointments, interruptions ad interferences.

Beulah Bondi is the understanding mother-in-law and Charles Coburn is excellent as the father of the bridegroom.

. . . .

■ VIXEN!

1968, 71 MINS, US ◇

Dir Russ Meyer *Prod* Russ Meyer *Scr* Robert Rudelson *Ph* Russ Meyer *Ed* Russ Meyer *Mus* Igo Kantor *Art Dir* Wilfred Kues
● Erica Gavin, Harrison Page, Garth Pillsbury, Michael O'Donnell, Vincene Wallace, Robert Aiken (Eve/Coldstream)

Russ Meyer's film is another of his technically polished sexplicit dramas, this time free of physical violence and brutality, and hyped with some awkwardly developed draft-dodging and patriotism angles.

Vixen is a girl who can't say no, and she proves it every seven minutes. She finds time for her husband, too.

There is a frankness to Meyer's sex scenes, in that they are unabashed in their frequent amorality, motivated without hypocrisy, and executed with dispatch. No tortured rationalizing here (Meyer's budget – $70,000 – couldn't afford it anyway), nor any sophisticated gloss-over. His people simply meet, rut a bit, then move along. Often the sequences are hilarious in their unbelievability.

Erica Gavin is featured in title role, and besides the ample visual aspect, carries off the dramatic moments to okay effect. Garth Pillsbury is her square husband, Jon Evans her motorcycle hood brother, and Peter Carpenter the passing Mountie with whom she passes the first few minutes.

. . . .

■ VOICES

1979, 106 MINS, US ◇ ⓥ

Dir Robert Markowitz *Prod* Joe Wizan *Scr* John Herzfeld *Ph* Alan Metzger *Ed* Danford B. Green *Mus* Jimmy Webb *Art Dir* Richard Bianchi
● Michael Ontkean, Amy Irving, Alex Rocco, Viveca Lindfors (M-G-M)

The triumph of love, courage and determination over affliction is the theme in *Voices*, a nice enough little film with likable characters, acted well.

Michael Ontkean and Amy Irving pick up a couple of superior credits as the loving young couple. He's a rough-edged Hoboken truck driver who wants to sing, she a deaf girl who wants to dance. They're an unlikely couple, but that's the story.

John Herzfeld's script is straightforward but full of contrivances and overly obvious tugs at the heart-strings. Robert Markowitz' direction reflects the TV career that launched him into this film.

. . . .

■ VON RYAN'S EXPRESS

1965, 114 MINS, US ◇ ⓥ

Dir Mark Robson *Prod* Saul David *Scr* Wendell Mayes, Joseph Landon *Ph* William H. Daniels *Ed* Dorothy Spencer *Mus* Jerry Goldsmith *Art Dir* Jack Martin Smith, Hilyard Brown
● Frank Sinatra, Trevor Howard, Raffaella Carra, Brad Dexter, Sergio Fantoni, John Leyton (20th Century-Fox)

Mass escape of 600 American and British prisoners-of-war across 1943 Nazi-controlled

Italy lends colorful backing to this fast, suspenseful and exciting Second World War tale. Mark Robson has made realistic use of the actual Italian setting of the David Westheimer novel in garmenting his action in hard-hitting direction and sharply-drawn performances.

Frank Sinatra and Trevor Howard co-star as leaders of the escape, who, under former's initiative, seize a freight train which is bearing prisoners for delivery to the Germans in Austria and divert it across northern Italy in an attempt to find haven in Switzerland. Sinatra plays a hardboiled American Air Force colonel named Ryan, shot down by Italians and imprisoned in the camp where Howard, an equally tough British major, is senior officer.

Robson depends heavily on suspense and accompanying thrills after Sinatra and Howard take over the train.

. . . .

■ VOYAGE OF THE DAMNED

1976, 155 MINS, UK ◇ ⓥ

Dir Stuart Rosenberg *Prod* Robert Fryer *Scr* Steve Shagan, David Butler *Ph* Billy Williams *Ed* Tom Priestley *Mus* Lalo Schifrin *Art Dir* Wilfrid Shingleton
● Faye Dunaway, Max Von Sydow, Oskar Werner, Malcolm McDowell, Orson Welles, James Mason (ITC/Associated General)

Voyage of the Dammed is a sluggish melodrama, loaded with familiar film names who flesh out the diverse formula characters involved in this story about a ship carrying Jews away from Nazi Germany.

Based on the book by Gordon Thomas and Max Morgan-Witts, screenplay follows the form of a prototype 'ark' film, introducing the specimen couples, herein Jews deliberately loaded aboard a ship to which Cuba will deny entry permit, thereby fulfilling a Nazi propaganda plan. Max Von Sydow, a non-Nazi German, is skipper of the ship.

Fact that the story is based on an actual, and shocking, incident makes all the more disappointing its transfer to the screen. The action zigs and zags between the cluttered set of characters.

. . . .

■ VOYAGE TO ITALY

1954, 75 MINS, ITALY ⓥ

Dir Roberto Rossellini *Scr* Roberto Rossellini, Vitaliano Brancati *Ph* Enzo Serafin *Ed* Jolanda Benvenuti *Mus* Renzo Rossellini *Art Dir* Piero Filippone
● Ingrid Bergman, George Sanders, Leslie Daniels, Natalia Ray, Anna Proclemer, Maria Mauban (Sveva/Junior/Italiafilm)

Story tells of an English couple, coldly moving close to divorce because of mutual incomprehension, who inherit a house near Naples. Planning to sell it, they begin suddenly to warm to the southern climate and the boisterous humanity about them. Film as a whole alternates brilliant bits with long stretches of so-so. [Version reviewed was 100-minute Italian-language one.]

Rapid change from grit to grin, especially in George Sanders, who plays Ingrid Bergman's husband, mars the effect of the warm-up process by overspeeding. Tale is unevenly told, has some unhappy bits of dialog and sometimes shows the roughout form, which for its director is the final version.

Editing, for example, is characteristically abrupt. Whereas Bergman's character, given more footage, appears much clearer in delineation, Sanders lacks the needed definition enabling proper audience participation. For instance, his interlude with a prostitute begins promisingly, but the idea is not followed through. Others in cast fill in well.

■ VOYAGE TO THE BOTTOM OF THE SEA

1961, 105 MINS, US ◇ ⓥ

Dir Irwin Allen *Prod* Irwin Allen *Scr* Irwin Allen, Charles Bennett *Ph* Winton C. Hoch *Ed* George Boemler *Mus* Paul Sawtell, Bert Shefter *Art Dir* Jack Martin Smith, Herman A. Blumenthal
● Walter Pidgeon, Joan Fontaine, Barbara Eden, Peter Lorre, Michael Ansara, Frankie Avalon (20th Century-Fox)

Voyage is a crescendo of mounting jeopardy, an effervescent adventure in an anything-but-Pacific Ocean.

The way the story goes, this brilliant admiral (Walter Pidgeon), commander of a marvelous atomic sub that resembles a smiling Moby Dick, devises a scheme to save mankind when life on earth is suddenly threatened by a girdle of fire caused when the Van Allen Belt of Radiation encircling the globe goes berserk and erupts. Trouble is mankind does not seem to want to be saved and unable to contact the US prez (golfing?), skipper Pidgeon heads for a spot near the Marianas where he plans to orbit a Polaris and explode the heavenly blaze out into space.

Actually the title is somewhat misleading. Customers who expect a kind of advanced course in oceanography will discover only an occasional giant squid and a lot of rubbery vegetation. For the most part, *The Bottom* of director Irwin Allen's *Sea* is merely the setting for the kind of emotional calisthenics that might just as easily break out 100 feet from the tip of Mount Everest.

The acting is generally capable, about the best it can be under the trying dramatic circumstances.

. . . .

■ WAGNER

1983, 300 MINS, UK/AUSTRIA/HUNGARY ◇ ⓥ

Dir Tony Palmer *Prod* Alan Wright *Scr* Charles Wood *Ph* Vittorio Storaro *Ed* Graham Bunn *Art Dir* Kenneth Carey
● Richard Burton, Vanessa Redgrave, Gemma Craven, Laszlo Galffi, John Gielgud, Ralph Richardson (London Trust Cultural)

There's nothing particularly intimate or revelatory about this five-hour (plus intermission) biopic of the German 19th-century composer.

The film begins in Dresden in 1848 when Richard Wagner (Richard Burton) was beginning to gain notoriety for his compositions and grand, heroic operas. He was also actively involved in the movement for a unified Germany.

So begins a 40-year trek across Europe for the most part as a stateless artist. Brunt of the first part deals with his self-imposed exile with part two beginning with his introduction to Ludwig II who becomes his patron. Along the way there are mounting bills, political scandals and Faustian pursuits.

Burton's performance as Wagner presents an almost entirely unsympathetic picture. Vanessa Redgrave and Gemma Craven as Wagner's wives have largely thankless roles. For buffs, the film's biggest draw is watching England's acting knights – Laurence Olivier, John Gielgud, Ralph Richardson – working together for the first time on screen.

Chief attraction remains the visual components of the film which beautifully capture the era.

. . . .

WAGONMASTER

1950, 85 MINS, US ▼

Dir John Ford   *Prod* John Ford, Merian C. Cooper   *Scr* Frank Nugent, Patrick Ford   *Ph* Bert Glennon   *Ed* Jack Murray   *Mus* Richard Hageman
● Ben Johnson, Harry Carey Jr, Ward Bond, Joanne Dru, Alan Mowbray, Jane Darwell (RKO/Argosy)

Wagonmaster is a good outdoor action film, done in the best John Ford manner. That means careful character development and movement, spiced with high spots of action, good drama and leavening comedy moments. Pic has some of the best cross-country chases.

Site of the story and the filming is Utah, and the rugged locale supplies fresh backgrounds for the action. The story deals with a wagontrain of Mormons seeking a rich valley in which to locate. They are led by Ward Bond and he hires horsetraders Ben Johnson and Harry Carey Jr to guide the pioneers to the new land.

Johnson sits his saddle mighty easily and gives the same kind of a performance, natural and likeable. Carey and Bond also come over in fine style.

....

WAIT UNTIL DARK

1967, 107 MINS, US ◇ ▼

Dir Terence Young   *Prod* Mel Ferrer   *Scr* Robert Carrington, Jane-Howard Carrington   *Ph* Charles Lang   *Ed* Gene Milford   *Mus* Henry Mancini   *Art Dir* George Jenkins
● Audrey Hepburn, Alan Arkin, Richard Crenna, Efrem Zimbalist Jr, Jack Weston, Samantha Jones (Warner/ Seven Arts)

Wait until Dark, based on Frederick Knott's legit hit, emerges as an excellent suspense drama, effective in casting, scripting, direction and genuine emotional impact. Audrey Hepburn stars as the not-so-helpless blind heroine, in a superior performance.

Plot turns on a supposedly hapless femme protagonist, an accident-blinded Hepburn. Hubby Efrem Zimbalist Jr has made his wife self-sufficient and reasonably able to fend for herself in their apartment home.

Zimbalist accidentally plays into the hands of heroin-smuggling Samantha Jones who plants a dope-loaded doll in his possession. Alan Arkin disposes of Jones, then hires Richard Crenna and Jack Weston to intimidate Hepburn into surrendering the doll.

....

WALK A CROOKED MILE

1948, 90 MINS, US

Dir Gordon M. Douglas   *Prod* Edward Small   *Scr* George Bruce   *Ph* George Robinson   *Ed* James E. Newcom   *Mus* Paul Sawtell   *Art Dir* Rudolph Sternad
● Louis Hayward, Dennis O'Keefe, Louise Allbritton, Raymond Burr (Columbia)

The documentary technique gives a factual gloss to the high melodramatics of *Walk a Crooked Mile*. A Southern California atom-plant is losing its top secrets and the FBI and Scotland Yard, in the respective persons of Dennis O'Keefe and Louis Hayward, join forces to run down the criminals. Action swings to San Francisco and back to the southland, punching hard all the time under the knowledgeable direction of Gordon Douglas. On-the-site filming of locales adds authenticity.

George Bruce has loaded his script with nifty twists that add air of reality to the meller doings in the Bertram Millhauser story. Dialog is good and situations believ-ably developed, even the highly contrived melodramatic finale. Documentary flavor is forwarded by Reed Hadley's credible narration chore.

....

WALK IN THE SPRING RAIN, A

1970, 98 MINS, US ◇ ▼

Dir Guy Green   *Prod* Sterling Silliphant   *Scr* Sterling Silliphant, [Frank Hummert, Anne Hummert]   *Ph* Charles B. Lang   *Ed* Ferris Webster   *Mus* Elmer Bernstein   *Art Dir* Malcolm C. Bert
● Anthony Quinn, Ingrid Bergman, Fritz Weaver, Katherine Crawford, Tom Fielding, Virginia Gregg (Columbia)

Rachel Maddux wrote the basic novella, adapted by Sterling Silliphant, with an uncredited bow to Frank and Anne Hummert. Ingrid Bergman and story hubby Fritz Weaver go on sabbatical from campus to the Tennessee mountain country so he can write a law text. Between the frigid winter and the verdant spring rains, Bergman finds love beating again in her bosom. The reason is Anthony Quinn a Spanish desdendant, Zorba-like hillbilly.

Quinn is not without his own responsibil-ities. He has a cackling wife, played terribly by Virginia Gregg. He also has a son, played by Tom Fielding in the style of a Method ctor satire. At least he doesn't even bother faking a Dixie accent.

Cast is rounded out by Katherine Crawford, the selfish daughter.

....

WALK IN THE SUN, A

1945, 117 MINS, US ▼

Dir Lewis Milestone   *Prod* Lewis Milestone   *Scr* Robert Rossen   *Ph* Russell Harlan   *Ed* Duncan Mansfield   *Mus* Frederic Efrem Rich   *Art Dir* Max Bertisch
● Dana Andrews, Richard Conte, John Ireland, Norman Lloyd, Lloyd Bridges, Huntz Hall (20th Century-Fox)

As a film *Walk* is not so sunny. It is dis-tinguished for some excellent, earthy GI dia-log, but the author has failed to achieve a proper fusing of dialog and situation. Too fre-quently he is given to spieling the colorful talk of the enlisted man, and thus allows his yarn to flounder. He is content, seemingly, to allow GI talk to encompass all else.

Film [from a novel by Harry Brown] con-cerns an operation by a platoon of American soldiers after they hit the beach at Salerno. They're detailed to wipe out a farmhouse and its Nazi occupants. That's the major element of the story, such as it is, and the rest of the pic is mostly concerned with reactions of the GIs to the conditions under which they're fighting, their thoughts, and so forth.

Dana Andrews gives one of his invariably forthright performances as a sergeant, and the rest of the impressive cast know their way around a script. And that holds particularly true of Richard Conte, who, perhaps, has the best lines.

....

WALK LIKE A DRAGON

1960, 95 MINS, US

Dir James Clavell   *Prod* James Clavell   *Scr* James Clavell, David Mainwaring   *Ph* Loyal Griggs   *Ed* Howard Smith   *Mus* Paul Dunlop   *Art Dir* Hal Pereira, Ronald Anderson
● Jack Lord, Nobu McCarthy, James Shigeta, Mel Torme, Benson Fong (Paramount)

In attempting to dramatize the unarguable doctrine that slavery is an ugly, unwelcome visitor in a free society, producer-director-writer James Clavell has somehow wound up with the curious message that clannish con-formity is the logical path to peaceful coexist-ence for foreigners to pursue in America. Since Clavell wisely has set his story in the conveniently unprovocative and usefully primitive atmosphere of the old west, and has utilized some interesting, offbeat historical data in the process, the film fits snugly into the 'adult western' genre.

A maze of incomplete, often contradictory, character motivations gnaws away destruc-

tively at the roots of the screenplay. It is based on a three-ply conflict, an interracial romantic triangle consisting of one tall, strap-ping American (Jack Lord); one proud, re-bellious Chinaman (James Shigeta); and one frail, would-be Chinese slave girl (Nobu McCarthy). Rescuing the latter from the perils of enforced prostitution, Lord promptly bumps into mass discrimination and an emo-tional duel with Shigeta when he brings the girl to live in his home.

Although shackled with a superficially-drawn role, Lord constructs a sympathetic characterization. McCarthy, an attractive ac-tress, lacks the subtle variety required for her role. Shigeta, too, manages only a shallow, one-note portrayal of the defiant Oriental. Mel Torme, cast as a gun-totin', scripture-spoutin' 'deacon', plays the offbeat role with a flourish, but appears bewildered by the nebulous nature of the character.

As director, Clavell is adept in his handling of the film's more provocative moments, not-ably a scene where the heroine is stripped to the waist in the slave market. But his overall approach tends to form predictably repetitive patterns such as following each soft, tender sequence with an explosion of gunfire to open the next one.

....

WALK ON THE WILD SIDE

1962, 114 MINS, US ▼

Dir Edward Dmytryk   *Prod* Charles K. Feldman   *Scr* John Fante, Edmund Morris   *Ph* Joe MacDonald   *Ed* Harry Gerstad   *Mus* Elmer Bernstein   *Art Dir* Richard Sylbert
● Laurence Harvey, Capucine, Jane Fonda, Anne Baxter, Barbara Stanwyck, Joanna Moore (Columbia)

It's obvious that in their treating of prostitu-tion and lesbianism the filmmakers did not want to be offensive to anyone. The result is a somewhat watered-downing of the Nelson Algren story of the Doll House in New Orleans and the madame's affection for one of the girls.

Laurence Harvey plays a drifter in search of his lady, Capucine. He does it well but not strikingly. Capucine, it turns out, is a mem-ber of the Doll House, showing a classic, Garbo-type beauty but somehow limited as to range in emotionality via script and/or direction.

Jane Fonda cops the show with her hoyden-ish behavior as another member of the House and Just-Lucky-I-Guess Alumnus of the freighter transportation circuit. Barbara Stanwyck is steely as the madame who looks to Capucine for the 'affection' she cannot find in her maimed husband.

Dmytryk maintains a nice pace in direction – that is, a steady pace – but more forceful-ness in both his direction and the writing might have provided more dramatic impact.

....

WALK WITH LOVE AND DEATH, A

1969, 90 MINS, US ◇

Dir John Huston   *Prod* Carter De Haven   *Scr* Dale Wasserman   *Ph* Ted Scaife   *Ed* Russell Lloyd   *Mus* Georges Delerue   *Art Dir* Wolfgang Witzemann
● Anjelica Huston, Assaf Dayan, Anthony Corlan, John Hallam, Robert Lang (20th Century-Fox)

A Walk with Love and Death, set in the frame-work of the Middle Ages, is an unrelenting examination of France when human life was valueless, social order unbending and indi-vidual outloook bleak. Filmed in Austria, director John Huston tells his story [from a novel by Hans Koningsberger] unhurriedly, lingering over details of style and torture with equal unsparing lenses.

His young hero, Assaf Dayan, obeying a mystic call from the sea, leaving Paris and studies behind, begins journey on foot through the war-scarred French countryside.

His meeting with Anjelica Huston, daughter of a nobleman, is the beginning of the end for the scholar and the lady.

The slow pace and gloomy atmosphere tend to dull viewer interest. High flown speech, confusion of action undermine even as Huston builds.

● ●

■ WALK, DON'T RUN

1966, 114 MINS, US ◇ ▼

Dir Charles Walters *Prod* Sol C. Siegel *Scr* Sol Saks *Ph* Harry Stradling *Ed* Walter Thompson, James Wells *Mus* Quincy Jones *Art Dir* Joe Wright
● Cary Grant, Samantha Eggar, Jim Hutton, John Standing, Miiko Taka, Ted Hartley (Columbia/Granley)

Walk, Don't Run is a completely entertaining, often hilarious romantic comedy spotlighting as a matchmaker a deliberately mature Cary Grant at the peak of his comedy prowess. The fast-moving and colorful production pegs its laughs on a Tokyo housing shortage during the 1964 Olympics.

Grant is outstanding as the middle-aged and distinguished English industrialist who arrives two days before his Tokyo hotel suite will be available. Noting an apartment-to-share sign, he finds it to be the diggings of prim, schedule-conscious Samantha Eggar. She is engaged to a stuffy embassy functionary, played by John Standing, with whom Grant has already had a run-in.

Jim Hutton, a member of the US Olympic walking team (hence the title), is also awaiting quarters, so he, too, winds up in Eggar's pad.

● ●

■ WALKABOUT

1971, 95 MINS, UK ◇ ▼

Dir Nicolas Roeg *Prod* Si Litvinoff, Max L. Raab *Scr* Edward Bond *Ph* Nicolas Roeg *Ed* Anthony Gibbs *Mus* John Barry *Art Dir* Brian Eatwell
● Jenny Agutter, Lucien John, David Gulpilil, John Meillon, John Illingsworth (20th Century-Fox)

Walkabout is a tepid artistic effort about two children, lost in the Australian wilds, who are befriended by an aborigine. Nicolas Roeg directed and photographed on authentic locations. Roeg's bag is photography, but pretty pictures alone cannot sustain – and, in fact, inhibit – this fragile and forced screen adaptation of a James Vance Marshall novel.

Apparent intent was to begin the film with jarring montage of urban life, so as to contrast better with the later wasteland footage. Jenny Agutter and Lucien John (Roeg's own son) find themselves alone in the desert after father John Meillon tries to kill the boy and then shoots himself after setting fire to his car.

On the kids' long trek in search of civilization, they encounter David Gulpilil, an aborigine who guides them towards rescue.

In an effort to pump up the plot, Roeg resorts to ad nauseam inserts of insects, reptiles and assorted wild beasts, in varying stages of life and decay.

● ●

■ WALKER

1987, 95 MINS, US ◇ ▼

Dir Alex Cox *Prod* Lorenzo O'Brien *Scr* Rudy Wurlitzer *Ph* David Bridges *Ed* Carlos Puente Ortega, Alex Cox *Mus* Joe Strummer *Art Dir* Bruno Rubeo
● Ed Harris, Richard Masur, Rene Auberjonois, Keith Szarabajka, Sy Richardson, Marlee Matlin (Incine/Universal)

The potentially fascinating story of an American adventurer who installed himself as president of Nicaragua 132 years ago, *Walker* unfortunately exists for one reason and one reason only – for director Alex Cox to vent his spleen about continued American interference with the Central American country.

The comic, idiosyncratic approach has merit in theory, but the result onscreen is a virtual fiasco.

With the financial backing of tycoon Cornelius Vanderbilt, Walker led a mercenary band of 58 men to Nicaragua in 1855 and ruled the tiny nation with an increasingly heavy hand for two years until being kicked out.

Cox makes a muddled attempt at the outset to paint Walker as an idealist who becomes fatally twisted after the premature death of his strong-willed fiancee (played in a very brief appearance by Marlee Matlin). From then on, however, Walker is ramrod stiff and impenetrable, a man given to self-seriously strutting about and delivering platitudes such as, 'One must act with severity, or perish.'

● ●

■ WALKING STICK, THE

1970, 100 MINS, UK ◇

Dir Eric Till *Prod* Alan Ladd Jr *Scr* George Bluestone *Ph* Arthur Ibbetson *Ed* John Jympson *Mus* Stanley Myers *Art Dir* John Howell
● David Hemmings, Samantha Eggar, Emlyn Williams, Phyllis Calvert, Ferdy Mayne, Dudley Sutton (Winkast/M-G-M)

The Walking Stick is notable for outstanding performances by David Hemmings and Samantha Eggar, and excellent direction by Eric Till. Story concerns a physically handicapped girl who finds love, then betrayal in a jewel robbery involvement.

George Bluestone adapted the Winston Graham novel about an introverted girl who blossoms under the patient love of a vagabond artist.

Hemmings suddenly emerges as a tool of Emlyn Williams, an art dealer whose night acquisitions come via robbery. Eggar, who works in a gallery, is pressured into the heist.

Her dilemma – should she give up her happiness by reporting to the police, or keep a gnawing silence? – is resolved in a somewhat melodramatic way.

● ●

■ WALL STREET

1987, 124 MINS, US ◇ ▼

Dir Oliver Stone *Prod* Edward R. Pressman *Scr* Oliver Stone, Stanley Weiser *Ph* Robert Richardson *Ed* Claire Simpson *Mus* Stewart Copeland *Art Dir* Stephen Hendrichson
● Charlie Sheen, Michael Douglas, Daryl Hannah, Martin Sheen, Terence Stamp, Sean Young (Pressman/American Entertainment/20th Century-Fox)

Watching Oliver Stone's *Wall Street* is about as wordy and dreary as reading the financial papers accounts of the rise and fall of an Ivan Boesky-type arbitrageur.

The lure of making a bundle on Wall Street by the young broker (Charlie Sheen) totally seduced by the power and financial stature of such a megalomaniacal arbitrageur as Gordon Gekko (Michael Douglas) is as good a contemporary story as there is in the real world of takeovers and mergers.

Douglas is a nasty enough manipulator barking orders to buy, sell and run his competitors into the ground or delivering declamatory speeches on how greed is what makes America great.

Trouble is, Sheen comes off as a pawn in Douglas' corporate raider game and as the easily duped sort doesn't elicit much sympathy. Martin Sheen as his father, the airplane mechanic, is the only person worth caring about.

● ●

■ WALTZ OF THE TOREADORS

1962, 104 MINS, UK ◇ ▼

Dir John Guillermin *Prod* Peter de Sarigny *Scr* Wolf Mankowitz *Ph* John Wilcox *Ed* Peter Taylor *Mus* Richard Addinsell *Art Dir* Wilfred Shingleton

● Peter Sellers, Dany Robin, Margaret Leighton, John Fraser, Cyril Cusack, Prunella Scales (Rank/Independent Artists)

A considerably broadened version of Jean Anouilh's ironic stage comedy results in a capital acting opportunity for Peter Sellers. Pic is handsomely mounted, and it's directed with zest and pace by John Guillermin. But too many moods jostle for it to be a complete success. Slapstick, farce, high comedy, drama and tragedy are all there but they don't always make easy companions.

Mankowitz has transferred the yarn from France to Sussex. Briefly, it concerns an elderly general, about to retire before World War I. He is a man with a roving eye for the girls, trapped by a neurotic, shrewish, sham-invalid of a wife and two unprepossessing daughters. For 17 years, he has had a platonic romance with a French woman, never having a real opportunity to consummate their love. She turns up at his castle determined that this sad state of affairs should end.

Sellers extracts laughs and compassionate pity with equal ease, whether he is being caught up in a drunken party at a tavern, conducting a riotous mock duel with his local doctor (Cyril Cusack), taking charge of a court martial, leching after his maids, facing up to the fact that he is a failure or, in the more tragic moments, stripping his soul bare as he struggles in his hateful scenes with his wife.

● ●

■ WANDA

1970, 105 MINS, US ◇

Dir Barbara Loden *Prod* Harry Shuster *Scr* Barbara Loden *Ph* Nicholas T. Proferes *Ed* Nicholas T. Proferes
● Barbara Loden, Michael Higgins (Foundation for Filmakers)

Wanda is a wanderer, a loser somewhere in a heavily industrialized part of the US. Barbara Loden shows a calm, dispassionate feel for direction and an insight into the psyche of an inarticulate, ill-educated but non-despairing woman as the protagonist of this probing pic about a cultural wasteland alongside affluence.

Loden dramatizes an oft-treated social theme about people drifting into crime and prostitution and does not force blame on anyone but denotes the growing conflicts between puritanism and promiscuity, poverty within plenty and ignorance alongside the more educated that grows in observation, insight and impact as it goes along.

Loden has the vulnerability, negation and yet inner resiliency that keeps her character from being a drudge.

● ●

■ WANDERERS, THE

1979, 113 MINS, US ◇ ▼

Dir Philip Kaufman *Prod* Martin Ransohoff *Scr* Rose Kaufman, Philip Kaufman *Ph* Michael Chapman *Ed* Ronald Roose, Stuart H. Pappe *Art Dir* Jay Moore
● Ken Wahl, John Friedrich, Karen Allen, Linda Manz, Toni Kalem, Tony Ganios (Orion)

Despite an uneasy blend of nostalgia and violence, *The Wanderers* is a well-made and impressive film. Philip Kaufman, who also co-scripted with his wife, Rose [from the novel by Richard Price], has accurately captured the urban angst of growing up in the 1960s.

Thesping is first-rate from the largely unknown cast, with Ken Wahl, John Friedrich and especially Tony Ganios delivering well-rounded and believable characterizations. Also outstanding are Toni Kalem as a gum-popping flirt, and Karen Allen as her more serious, soulful counterpart.

W

Disturbing elements in *The Wanderers* crop up in the explicitly violent episodes, including those involving the symbolic Ducky Boys, a murderous pint-sized gang, and the Fordham Baldies, bald behemoths.

● ●

■ WANDERING JEW, THE

1933, 110 MINS, UK

Dir Maurice Elvey   *Prod* Julius Hagen   *Scr* H. Fowler Mear   *Ph* Sydney Blythe   *Ed* Jack Harris
Art Dir James Carter
● Conrad Veidt, Marie Ney, Anne Grey, Joan Maude, Peggy Ashcroft (Twickenham/Gaumont-British)

The film is based on Temple Thurston's play of the same name, and the adaptation is divided into four episodes. The first is Jerusalem on the day of the Crucifixion; the second, Antioch in the time of the first crusade; third, Palermo, Sicily, in 1290; and fourth, Seville in 1560, during the Inquisition.

It is a massive, artistic and well-acted filming, flavored perhaps by an overplus of scenes, and more detail than is necessary.

Conrad Veidt in the first half of the picture is guilty of scene-chewing. All this is counteracted before the finish by a restrained, moving dignity which he contributes to the wanderer of centuries.

Maria Ney, Anne Grey and Joan Maude are the three women in the first three episodes, and do nothing to distinguish themselves; Peggy Ashcroft as the Magdalene in the fourth phase, who is converted by the Christ-like nobility of Battadios (Veidt), offers a fine characterization rich in feeling. The inquisitors are Francis L. Sullivan, Felix Aylmer and Ivor Barnard, all of them vividly Machiavellian.

● ●

■ WAR AND PEACE

1956, 208 MINS, US/ITALY ◇ Ⓥ

Dir King Vidor   *Prod* Dino De Laurentiis   *Scr* Bridget Boland, Robert Westerby, King Vidor, Mario Camerini, Ennio De Concini, Ivo Perilli   *Ph* Jack Cardiff
Ed Stuart Gilmore, Leo Catozzo   *Mus* Nino Rota   *Art Dir* Mario Chiari, Franz Bachelin, Giani Polidori
● Audrey Hepburn, Henry Fonda, Mel Ferrer, Vittorio Gassman, John Mills, Anita Ekberg (Ponti-De Laurentiis/Paramount)

Hollywood and Italian know-how, some $6 million capital investment, and between 5,000 and 6,000 Italian troops doubling as celluloid soldiers, have produced a visual epic.

The classic Tolstoy novel which requires weeks and, more often, months to read is digested into three-and-a-half hours of vivid cinematic magic.

The wonder of the production is that it has maintained cohesiveness and fluidity of story and also has given fullest accent to the size and sweep of Bonaparte's armies at Austerlitz and Borodino. Life among the Russian aristocracy with its passion for good living and innate respect for the church in time of stress is brought into sharp focus.

Audrey Hepburn is the epitome of wholesome young love under benevolent aristocratic rearing. Henry Fonda, the confused young liberal who apes the French as so many Russians did, is perhaps sometimes too literally the confused character.

Other than the above and the moody but compelling performance by Mel Ferrer, the rest are lesser roles but almost wholly effective.

The film's scripting credits are a strangely multiple thing in light of Irwin Shaw's request to remove his billing when director Vidor reportedly rewrote so many scenes on his own.

● ●

■ WAR GAME, THE

1966, 50 MINS, UK Ⓥ

Dir Peter Watkins   *Scr* Peter Watkins   *Ph* Peter Bartlett   *Art Dir* Michael Bradsell
● (BBC-TV)

The War Game was originally made by BBC-TV for showing on TV, but corporation brass had second thoughts after it had been completed, decided it was unsuitable for mass audiences, and ordered it to be kept off the airwaves. As a result of political and press agitation, it was eventually agreed to make it available for theatrical release through the British Film Institute.

A wholly imaginary picture of what could happen immediately before, during and after a nuclear attack on Britain, *The War Game* is grim, gruesome, horrific and realistic. It is not a pleasant picture to watch, but yet it is one that needs to be shown as widely as possible.

The attack itself is predictably grim, but the most telling part is the aftermath of the bomb – the severely burned are killed off and their bodies burned, and looters face the firing squad.

Watkins, who left the BBC in protest when it was banned, does an excellent and imaginative job, based on considerable research.

● ●

■ WAR LORD, THE

1965, 120 MINS, US ◇

Dir Franklin J. Schaffner   *Prod* Walter Seltzer
Scr John Collier, Millard Kaufman   *Ph* Russell Metty   *Ed* Folmar Blangsted   *Mus* Jerome Moross   *Art Dir* Alexander Golitzen, Henry Bumstead
● Charlton Heston, Richard Boone, Rosemary Forsyth, Maurice Evans, Guy Stockwell, Niall MacGinnis (Universal)

The War Lord digs back into the 11th century against a Druid setting in ancient Normandy for unfoldment of its generally fast action. Producer Walter Seltzer has given his picturization of Leslie Stevens' play *The Lovers* – finely lensed to lend realism and pictorial beauty – elaborate mounting and clash battle movement.

Franklin Schaffner's direction, while not always overcoming deficiencies of convincing dialog and Charlton Heston's sometimes vacillating characterization, in the main projects the proper spirit of a derring-do, days-of-yore melodrama. His battle scenes, utilizing the weapons and tactics of the period are particularly well handled.

Script presents Heston as war lord of the Duke of Normandy, detailed to oversee a primitive Druid village on a barren shore of the North Sea, whose inhabitants are constantly harassed by invaders from the north. With him are his brother (Guy Stockwell) and Richard Boone, his faithful aide in 20 years of warring. Plottage dwells on his mad passion for a village girl, claiming her on her wedding night according to custom of 'droit de seigneur' – a lord's right of the first night.

Heston is more convincing in his battle scenes than in romancing Rosemary Forsyth, but nevertheless delivers a hard-hitting performance. Top acting honors, however, go to Stockwell, as the young knight.

● ●

■ WAR LOVER, THE

1962, 105 MINS, US Ⓥ

Dir Philip Leacock   *Prod* Arthur Hornblow Jr
Scr Howard Koch   *Ph* Bob Huke   *Ed* Gordon Hales   *Mus* Richard Addinsell   *Art Dir* Bill Andrews
● Steve McQueen, Robert Wagner, Shirley Anne Field, Gary Cockrell, Michael Crawford, Jerry Stovin (Columbia)

This production of John Hersey's novel *The War Lover* is accomplished in all respects save

one: lack of proper penetration into the character referred to by the title. The scenario seems reluctant to come to grips with the issue of this character's unique personality – a 'war lover' whose exaggerated shell of heroic masculinity covers up a psychopathic inability to love or enjoy normal relationships with women.

The story transpires in 1943 England and focuses on B-17 bombing raids over Germany, with the title character (Steve McQueen) a pilot of one of the planes.

That the central character emerges more of an unappealing symbol than a sympathetic flesh-and-blood portrait is no fault of McQueen, who plays with vigor and authority, although occasionally with two much eyeball emotion. Robert Wagner and Shirley Anne Field share the film's secondary, but interesting, romantic story. Wagner does quite well, and Field has a fresh, natural quality.

Outside of his central failure director Philip Leacock does a sound job. Scenes of the bombing raids and accompanying aerial incidents are adroitly and authentically executed.

● ●

■ WAR OF THE ROSES, THE

1989, 116 MINS, US ◇ Ⓥ

Dir Danny DeVito   *Prod* James L. Brooks, Arnon Milchan   *Scr* Michael Leeson   *Ph* Stephen H. Burum   *Ed* Lynzee Klingman   *Mus* David Newman
Art Dir Ida Random
● Michael Douglas, Kathleen Turner, Danny DeVito, Marianne Sagebrecht, Sean Astin, Heather Fairfield (Gracie/20th Century-Fox)

What Michael Douglas does to the fish at Kathleen Turner's dinner party in *The War of The Roses*, director Danny DeVito does to the audience. Piddling notions of humor are the least of this misanthropic comedy's offenses, however. Trying to wring yocks from a deranged couple locked in mortal combat over possession of their house is more suited to film noir than to black comedy.

Everything beautiful on screen in this glossily photographed film, from the house to Douglas' antique sportscar to the couple's china figurines to the ravishingly leonine Turner herself, is thoroughly trashed by DeVito, whose sicko humor will wind up alienating virtually everyone in the audience.

The aptly intense Douglas is a workaholic Washington, DC, lawyer on the rise in the early years of his marriage to Turner, a saucy former college gymnast who channels her fierce energies into raising two children and remodeling their stately old house. Once her work is completed, she realizes the marriage is a shell, but Douglas refuses to change his ways and causes her to seek a divorce.

In outline, up to this point, the adaptation of a Warren Adler novel follows predictable lines, with Douglas' rampant sexism challenged by Turner's burgeoning feminism. What keeps it fresh are the sexually charged performances of the two attractive leads and the sarcastic twists DeVito and scripter Michael Leeson pull from the material.

● ●

■ WAR OF THE WORLDS, THE

1953, 85 MINS, US ◇ Ⓥ

Dir Byron Haskin   *Prod* George Pal   *Scr* Barre Lyndon   *Ph* George Barnes   *Ed* Everett Douglas
Mus Leith Stevens   *Art Dir* Hal Pereira, Albert Nozaki
● Gene Barry, Ann Robinson, Les Tremayne, Lewis Martin, Bob Cornthwaite (Paramount)

War of the Worlds is a socko science-fiction feature, as fearsome as a film as was the Orson Welles 1938 radio interpretation of the H.G. Wells novel. Gene Barry, as a scientist, is the principal in this story of an invasion of the earth by weird, spider-like characters from Mars, against whom the world's most potent weapons, even the atom bomb are of no avail.

Into this setup, the special effects group headed by Gordon Jennings loosens a reign of screen terror, of futile defense, demolished cities, charred landscapes and people burned to ashes by the invaders' weapons.

While following closely the plot laid down in Wells' novel, the film transfers the first invasion to a small town in Southern California. What is believed to be a huge meteor lands near a small town but it turns out to be a Martian machine that raises itself on pulsating beams and promptly turns deadly heatwaves on humans, buildings and anything else that comes within range.

In the siege of terror, the story finds opportunity to develop a logical love story between Barry and Ann Robinson. Both are good and others seen to advantage include Les Tremayne as a general; Lewis Martin, a pastor who faces the invaders with a prayer and is struck down. An ominous commentary is spoken by Cedric Hardwicke.

••••••••••••••••••••••••••••••••••

■ **WAR WAGON, THE**

1967, 100 MINS, US ◇ ⓥ

Dir Burt Kennedy *Prod* Marvin Schwartz *Scr* Clair Huffaker *Ph* William H. Clothier *Ed* Harry Gerstad *Mus* Dimitri Tiomkin *Art Dir* Alfred Sweeney

● John Wayne, Kirk Douglas, Howard Keel, Robert Walker, Keenan Wynn, Bruce Cabot (Universal)

The War Wagon is an entertaining, exciting western drama of revenge, laced with action and humor. Strong scripting, performances and direction are evident, enhanced by terrif exterior production values. Kirk Douglas also stars in an excellent performance.

Clair Huffaker's novel, *Badman*, has been adapted by the author into a very fine screenplay which is a neat blend of always-advancing plot, the right amount of good-natured grousing, and twofisted action, all building to a strong climax. Burt Kennedy directs with an eye for panorama, as well as intimate, personal interaction.

John Wayne, framed into prison by Bruce Cabot who then seized his land to make a fortune in gold, returns for revenge. He teams with Kirk Douglas, a hired gun used earlier by Cabot. Together they plan a heist of Cabot's armored gold wagon.

••••••••••••••••••••••••••••••••••

■ **WARGAMES**

1983, 110 MINS, US ◇ ⓥ

Dir John Badham *Prod* Harold Schneider *Scr* Lawrence Lasker, Walter F. Parkes *Ph* William A. Fraker *Ed* Tom Rolf *Mus* Arthur B. Rubinstein *Art Dir* Angelo P. Graham

● Matthew Broderick, Dabney Coleman, John Wood, Ally Sheedy, Barry Corbin, Dennis Lipscomb (United Artists)

Although the script has more than its share of short circuits, director John Badham solders the pieces into a terrifically exciting story charged by an irresistible idea: an extra-smart kid can get the world into a whole lot of trouble that it also takes the same extra-smart kid to rescue it from.

Matthew Broderick is on the mark as the bright teenager, bored by traditional high school subjects like biology, but brilliant with computers. Unfortunately, thinking he's sneaking an advance look at a new line of video games, he taps into the country's Norad missile-defense system to challenge its computer to a game of global thermonuclear warfare.

WarGames' weakness sad to say, is that the adult side of the yarn is not peopled with very realistic characters, although the performances are fine.

Ally Sheedy is perfectly perky as Broderick's girlfriend; Dabney Coleman brings his usual dissonance to the role of the computer-reliant defense specialist; but John Wood's large talents aren't fully used in a somewhat confusing part as the misanthropic eccentric who designed the computer.

••••••••••••••••••••••••••••••••••

■ **WARLOCK**

1989, 102 MINS, US ⓥ

Dir Steve Miner *Prod* Steve Miner *Scr* David Twohy *Ph* David Eggby *Ed* David Finfer *Mus* Jerry Goldsmith *Art Dir* Roy Forge Smith

● Richard E. Grant, Julian Sands, Lori Singer, Kevin O'Brien, Richard Kuse (New World)

Warlock is an attempt to concoct a pic from a pinch of occult chiller, a dash of fantasy thriller and a splash of 'stalk 'n' slash'. But what could have been a heady brew falls short, despite some gusto thesping from Richard E. Grant and Lori Singer.

Pic opens in the Massachusetts Bay colony in 1691 where a contemptuous warlock (Julian Sands) is being readied for execution. But with a bit of nifty hocus-pocus, both he and witch-hunter Richard E. Grant are sent to 1988 LA.

Sands soon gets back to his nasty habits – including chopping off a finger, gouging out eyes and skinning a child – as he pursues the magical book the *Grand Grimoire*.

Waitress Lori Singer meets Sands when he crashes through a window into her house. After he puts an ageing spell on her, she teams up with Grant to try to kill the warlock.

Director Steve Miner directs ably but doesn't pull away from some of the horror cliches.

••••••••••••••••••••••••••••••••••

■ **WARLORDS OF ATLANTIS**

1978, 96 MINS, UK ◇ ⓥ

Dir Kevin Connor *Prod* John Dark *Scr* Brian Hayles *Ph* Alan Hume *Ed* Bill Blunden *Mus* Mike Vickers *Art Dir* Elliot Scott

● Doug McClure, Peter Gilmore, Shane Rimmer, Lea Brodie, Michael Gothard, Cyd Charisse (EMI)

In *Warlords of Atlantis*, Doug McClure and several other earthlings suffer a close encounter with Cyd Charisse and Daniel Massey who rule over the legendary lost city. More terrifying are their brushes with various species of marine monsters on periodic rampages. And a good thing, too, in an otherwise skimpy reworking of the hoary Atlantis legend.

Donald Bisset and Peter Gilmore are appealing as a British father-son scientific team in quest of Atlantis. McClure is the Yank who made the diving bell that plumbs the sea and implausibly manages to resurface.

The one not inconsiderable virtue of the script is that it keeps the pot boiling. Direction by Kevin Connor and the editing keep the eye-filling pace brisk. The cliched characters are played in workmanlike fashion by all hands.

••••••••••••••••••••••••••••••••••

■ **WARNING SHOT**

1967, 100 MINS, US ⓥ

Dir Buzz Kulik *Prod* Buzz Kulik *Scr* Mann Rubin *Ph* Joseph Biroc *Ed* Archie Marshek *Mus* Jerry Goldsmith *Art Dir* Hal Pereira, Roland Anderson

● David Janssen, Ed Begley, Keenan Wynn, Sam Wanamaker, Lillian Gish, Stefanie Powers (Paramount)

Warning Shot is a police drama in which fine production, direction and performances overcome a sometimes flawed script. David Janssen toplines as a cop accused of being trigger-happy.

Mann Rubin has adapted Whit Masterson's novel, *711 – Officer Needs Help*, in which a cop is accused of poor judgment in killing an apparently innocent medic. His superiors, the DA and the public turn on him, and only hope of vindication is proving the existence of a missing gun, and the discovery of evidence to prove the medic was breaking the law.

Filmed smoothly on LA locations, with technical assist from the Police Department, pic has the immediacy of headlines about police brutality, irresponsibility, etc. Scripting incorporates some cliche, unnecessary angles which detract from a very viable story line; namely, that cops are fallible human beings who drink, smoke, make mistakes – just like every one else.

••••••••••••••••••••••••••••••••••

■ **WARRENDALE**

1967, 105 MINS, CANADA ◇

Dir Allan King *Prod* Allan King *Scr* Allan King *Ph* William Brayne *Ed* Peter Moseley

● N/A (King)

This pic is a shattering documentary look at a home, Warrendale, for disturbed children and adolescents in Canada. It deals with a group of young, dedicated workers who stay with these emotionally mixed-up youngsters and emerges as engrossing, stark film.

The people involved seem unaware of the camera except when the filmmaker is mentioned by one of the workers. It is the treatment in this institution that is the thing in this wellmade and incisive truth pic. Death of a beloved cook is one of the main segs of the film as it details the reactions of the patients who had become attached to her.

Psychologically absorbing, well made and edited.

••••••••••••••••••••••••••••••••••

■ **WARRIORS, THE**

1979, 90 MINS, US ◇ ⓥ

Dir Walter Hill *Prod* Lawrence Gordon *Scr* David Shaber, Walter Hill *Ph* Andrew Laszlo *Ed* David Holden *Mus* Barry DeVorzon *Art Dir* Don Swanagan, Bob Wightman

● Michael Beck, James Remar, David Patrick Kelly, Deborah Van Valkenburgh (Paramount)

Theme of the pic, based on Sol Yurick's 1965 novel, is a variation on countless westerns and war films.

Update the setting to modern-day New York, and the avenues of escape to graffiti-emblazoned subway cars, and that's *The Warriors*.

The slaying of a hood (Roger Hill) is pinned on a Coney Island gang, the Warriors of the title, and the word soon goes out that the group's members are to be eliminated. It's a long subway ride to Coney Island, so for at least 70 of the film's 90 minutes, the boys in this band experience a variety of macho passage rites.

As with his previous pix, *Hard Times* and *The Driver*, director Walter Hill demonstrates an outstanding visual sense here, with the gaudy 'colors' of the gang members, the desolation of nighttime NY, and the cavernous subway platforms where much of the action takes place.

••••••••••••••••••••••••••••••••••

■ **WATCH ON THE RHINE**

1943, 109 MINS, US ⓥ

Dir Herman Shumlin *Prod* Hal B. Wallis *Scr* Dashiell Hammett *Ph* Merritt Gerstad, Hal Mohr *Ed* Rudi Fehr *Mus* Max Steiner

● Bette Davis, Paul Lukas, Geraldine Fitzgerald, George Coulouris, Lucile Watson, Beulah Bondi (Warner)

Watch on the Rhine is a distinguished picture. It is even better than its powerful original stage version. It expresses the same urgent theme, but with broader sweep and in more affecting terms of personal emotion.

The film more than retains the vital theme of the original play. It actually carries the

W

theme further and deeper, and it does so with passionate conviction and enormous skill. There is no compromise on controversial matters. Fascists are identified as such and, although the point is not brought home as it might have been, the industrial-financial support that makes fascism possible is also mentioned.

Just as he was in the play, Paul Lukas is the outstanding star of the film. Anything his part may have lost in the transfer of key lines to Bette Davis is offset by the projective value of the camera for closeups. His portrayal of the heroic German has the same quiet strength and the slowly gathering force that it had on the stage, but it now seems even better defined and carefully detailed, and it has much more vitality.

In the lesser starring part of the wife Davis gives a performance of genuine distinction. ☐ 1943: Best Picture (Nomination)

WATCHER IN THE WOODS, THE

1980, 100 MINS, UK ◇ Ⓥ
Dir John Hough *Prod* Ron Miller *Scr* Brian Clemens, Harry Spalding, Rosemary Anne Sisson *Ph* Alan Hume *Ed* Geoffrey Foot *Mus* Stanley Myers *Art Dir* Alan Cassie
● Bette Davis, Carroll Baker, David McCallum, Ian Bannen, Lynn-Holly Johnson, Kyle Richards (Walt Disney)

Although Bette Davis has star billing there's not much reason for it as the film revolves around teenager Lynn-Holly Johnson who just happens to resemble the long-lost daughter of Davis.

Johnson's family (Carroll Baker, David McCallum and Kyle Richards) rent the huge country house belonging to Davis, who lives in a nearby cottage and depends on the big-house rentals for income. The pretitle sequences establish the house and woods (which actually appear to encroach on the house at times) with being something less than fun city. Whatever is out there, however, remains undiscovered even after the film has ended.

The acting and writing are barely professional but the art direction, especially Alan Hume's stunning camerawork, gives the pic a gloss.

WATER BABIES, THE

1979, 93 MINS, UK ◇ Ⓥ
Dir Lionel Jeffries *Prod* Peter Shaw *Scr* Michael Robson *Ph* Ted Scaife *Ed* Peter Weatherley *Mus* Phil Coulter, Bill Martin *Art Dir* Herbert Westbrook
● James Mason, Billie Whitelaw, Bernard Cribbins, Joan Greenwood, David Tomlinson (Pethurst/Production Associates/Ariadne)

The musical screen version of *The Water Babies*, Charles Kingsley's children's novel, tells the story of innocence-versus-evil more or less straight. The slim $2 million production budget combines live action footage and – for the underwater sequences – animation.

Screenplay plots the adventures of a 12-year-old apprentice chimneysweep, wrongly accused of theft, who dives into a pool to escape his pursuers. Trapped below the surface, he meets a succession of human stereotypes, jokily animated as underwater creatures, and has a battle to free the water babies, who normally inhabit an eternal playground in mid-ocean but have been captured by a shark and an electric eel.

Animated sequences by Cuthbert Cartoons in London, and movement synchronized by Miroslaw Kijowicz in Poland to a pre-recorded soundtrack, are garish but effective.

WATERHOLE #3

1967, 95 MINS, US ◇ Ⓥ
Dir William Graham *Prod* Joseph T. Steck
Scr Joseph T. Steck, R.R. Young *Ph* Robert Burks
Ed Warren Low *Mus* Dave Grusin *Art Dir* Fernando Carrere
● James Coburn, Carroll O'Connor, Margaret Blye, Claude Akins, Timothy Carey, Bruce Dern (Paramount)

Waterhole #3 is a slow-building, deliberate oater comedy blending satire, slapstick and double entendre dialog for laughs.

Distended story line turns on two gags: gold heist by crooked army sergeant Claude Akins, grounting outlaw Timothy Carey and unwilling hostage Harry Davis; and casual seduction by gambler James Coburn of Carroll O'Connor's daughter, Margaret Blye.

O'Connor is far more interested in Coburn's theft of a prize horse, and this gag is milked for all it is worth. Joan Blondell has a bright role as a madame, ditto James Whitmore as a cliche frontier Army officer.

Coburn, O'Connor and Blye (whose voice and projection are perfect) handle their roles in very good fashion, while rest of cast offers good support.

WATERLOO

1970, 132 MINS, ITALY/USSR ◇ Ⓥ
Dir Sergei Bondarchuk *Prod* Dino De Laurentiis
Scr H.A.L. Craig, Sergei Bondarchuk, Vittorio Bonicelli *Ph* Armando Nannuzzi *Ed* Richard C. Meyer, E.V. Michajlova *Mus* Nino Rota *Art Dir* Mario Garbuglia
● Rod Steiger, Christopher Plummer, Orson Welles, Jack Hawkins, Virginia McKenna, Dan O'Herlihy (De Laurentiis/Mosfilm)

Directed by Russia's Sergei Bondarchuk, who made *War and Peace*, and filmed on location in Italy and Russia, with interiors at De Laurentiis's Rome studios, the long-nursed Dino De Laurentiis project has an international flavor. Despite the fact that the battle is the focal point, and a striking din-laden affair it is, the film is raised from being just another historical war epic by the performances of Rod Steiger as Napoleon and Christopher Plummer as Wellington.

Story begins with Europe entirely opposed to the ambitious, flamboyant Napoleon and the French, scared of overwhelming odds, forcing him to abdicate and retire to the island of Elba. But barely has the film started than he's back again.

Steiger gives a remarkably powerful portrayal of Napoleon. It's a Method performance, with his sudden blazes of rage highlighting his moody introspection.

Others stand out, too. Dan O'Herlihy as Marshal Ney, devoted, loyalist to Napoleon, and Orson Welles, making much of two minor but memorable moments as Louis XVIII.

WATERLOO BRIDGE

1940, 103 MINS, US Ⓥ
Dir Mervyn LeRoy *Prod* Sidney Franklin *Scr* S.N. Behrman, Hans Rameau, George Froeschel *Ph* Joseph Ruttenberg *Ed* George Boemler *Mus* Herbert Stothart *Art Dir* Cedric Gibbons, Urie McCleary
● Vivien Leigh, Robert Taylor, Lucile Watson, Virginia Field, Maria Ouspenskaya, C. Aubrey Smith (M-G-M)

Elaborating on the basic premise of Robert Sherwood's play, and doing a slick job of cleansing to conform to present regulations of the Hays code, this is a persuasive and compelling romantic tragedy.

Story steers a leisurely path in delineating the romantic tragedy of a love affair which is launched on Waterloo Bridge during World War I. Vivien Leigh, a sweet, vivacious and unsophisticated ballet dancer, meets and falls in love with British officer Robert Taylor on eve of his departure for the front. There's a whirlwind romance with immediate marriage delayed until his first furlough. Fate intervenes, and erroneous report of his death eventually sends her onto the streets, but Taylor returns, meets her at the station where she is soliciting, and the romance flares again for an instant.

Leigh demonstrates outstanding ability as an actress. Her transition from the virginal ingenue of the early passages to the hardened prostie later is a standout performance. Taylor, in a straight romantic role, provides an arresting characterization.

There's plenty of strength in the supporting cast. Viriginia Field is excellent as Leigh's chum, who takes the first step along the easiest way to provide food for the pair. Lucile Watson is a perfect grand dame as the aristocratic mother of Taylor; Maria Ouspenskaya is a stern ballet mistress; and C. Aubrey Smith is an army colonel.

WATERLOO ROAD

1945, 76 MINS, UK
Dir Sidney Gilliat *Prod* Edward Black *Scr* Sidney Gilliat *Ph* Arthur Crabtree, Phil Grindrod *Ed* Alfred Roome *Mus* Louis Levy (dir) *Art Dir* Alex Vetchinsky
● John Mills, Stewart Granger, Alastair Sim, Joy Shelton, Beatrice Varley, George Carney (Gainsborough)

Played against the drab, bomb-shattered background of a London slum, story is the familiar triangle theme with use of the flashback technique not adding to its originality. But it's acted with such sincerity and is so true-to-life in its characterization that the picture grips throughout. There is a terrific climax in which the two men (John Mills and Stewart Granger) fight for one woman as the bombs thunder down.

A soldier deserts when he learns his wife is receiving attentions from another man. Story depicts his day spent in pursuit of the pair, finally confronting them in a sports arcade.

Entire cast is adequate, but particular praise goes to Alastair Sim as the neighborhood doctor and George Carney's role of pigeon fancier.

Picture [from a story by Val Valentine] is a striking example of how sound an English production can be if it keeps to the medium it interprets best, that of the middle-class character.

WATERMELON MAN

1970, 100 MINS, US ◇ Ⓥ
Dir Melvin Van Peebles *Prod* John B. Bennett
Scr Herman Raucher *Ph* W. Wallace Kelley *Ed* Carl Kress *Mus* Melvin Van Peebles *Art Dir* Malcolm C. Bert
● Godfrey Cambridge, Estelle Parsons, Howard Caine, D'Urville Martin, Mantan Moreland, Kay Kimberly (Columbia)

Godfrey Cambridge heads cast as a white suburbanite who overnight turns black in biological accident. A few chuckles are evident, but as entertainment, *Watermelon Man* is a trifle; as an interracial social document, it's nothing.

Film's development involves the rather predictable reactions of friends, neighbors and business associates. Estelle Parson's duty is to segue from shock and sympathy to eventual alienation, scramming to her mother with kids (Scott Garrett and Erin Moran).

Employer Howard Caine, after a check with his optometrist about his contact lenses, immediately turns Cambridge to cultivating the black insurance-market potential.

As the film progresses, more plaintive and serious plot angles are suggested, but by this time it is too late.

■ WATERSHIP DOWN

1978, 92 MINS, UK ◇ ⓥ
Dir Martin Rosen   *Prod* Martin Rosen   *Scr* Martin
Rosen   *Ed* Terry Rawlings   *Mus* Angela Morley,
Malcolm Williamson
● (Nepenthe)

Employing fair-to-excellent animation and
an array of fine voices drawn heavily from the
English stage and screen, *Watership* traces the
odyssey of a brave band of rabbits in search
of a peaceful new home.

But this is not Bugs Bunny house-hunting.
Producer-director Martin Rosen has taken
author Richard Adams' concept of real
rabbits – doomed by nature to be victims
of those they cannot escape or outwit – and
projected them into a fearful ordeal.

Along the way, the cottontails are shot-
gunned, bitten, gnawed, scratched, hawked
and torn apart by dogs and meaner rabbits,
with no skimping on red ink. In one particularly gruesome scene, one of the heroes is
snared around the neck by a wire, gushing
and gurgling blood quite realistically.

This is too much, some would say, for tender eyes (if intended for them). Hooey. It's
just what kids imagine their ghost stories and
fairy tales would look like. Besides, it's got an
overall positive theme with inspirational and
ecological overtones to go with the suspense
and excitement.

■ WAY AHEAD, THE

1944, 115 MINS, UK ⓥ
Dir Carol Reed   *Prod* Norman Walker, John Sutro
Scr Eric Ambler, Peter Ustinov   *Ph* Guy Green
Ed Fergus McDonell   *Mus* William Alwyn   *Art
Dir* David Rawnsley
● David Niven, Raymond Huntley, Billy Hartnell,
Stanley Holloway, James Donald, Leo Genn
(Two Cities)

There is no story in the accepted sense, and
no love interest. There are momentary shots
of femmes, chiefly wives, but no pin-up girls.
This heightens the documentary value of this
wartime slice of English life. Slickness of
cutting should be enough to put this among
notable British films, but there is additional
cleverness in keeping David Niven far less
obtrusive than his star's status might seem to
justify. He's a subaltern in command of a
platoon.

Covering the period from early 1939 to the
Tunisian campaign of 1943, *The Way Ahead*
shows how a totally unprepared, peace-
loving people were suddenly catapulted into
war; how a score of widely different
individuals reacted to it.

Direction by Carol Reed is competent, and
undoubtedly accounts for the underlying
genuineness of the picture as a semi-documentary. Reed's job was made relatively easy
by the solid script turned in by Eric Ambler
and Peter Ustinov [from Ambler's original
story].

■ WAY DOWN EAST

1920, 150 MINS, US ⊗ ⓥ
Dir D.W. Griffith   *Prod* D.W. Griffith   *Scr* Anthony
Paul Kelly, Joseph R. Grismer, D.W. Griffith   *Ph* Billy
Bitzer, Hendrik Sartov   *Ed* James E. Smith, Rose Smith
Mus William Frederick Peters   *Art Dir* Charles O.
Sessel, Clifford Pember
● Lillian Gish, Richard Barthelmess, Lowell Sherman,
Burr McIntosh, Creighton Hale, Kate Bruce (Griffith/
United Artists)

Way down East by D.W. Griffith is a film
poem. Without the aid of any especially spectacular or stupendous mechanical effects
such as were utilized in *Intolerance*, or the
employment of a large ensemble of mob
scenes as in the same picture and *The Birth of
a Nation, Judith of Bethulia*, etc., with the gath-

ering together of a relatively small cast and
less than half a dozen stellar film artists,
D.W. has taken a simple, elemental, old-
fashioned, bucolic melodrama and milked it
for 12 reels of absorbing entertainment.

First honors for acting belong to Lillian
Gish, who had to court comparison with the
preconceived characterization of Anna
Moore, which had always been played by a
much larger woman in the spoken productions [of the play by Lottie Blair Parker].
Hers is a materially different conception of
the role, and she reveals hitherto unsuspected
emotional powers. Richard Barthelmess, as
David, has little to do until almost the finish,
when he rescues Anna from an ice floe about
to be precipitated over a rapidly-moving,
seething waterfall.

■ WAY OF ALL FLESH, THE

1927, 90 MINS, US ⊗
Dir Victor Fleming   *Scr* Jules Furthman   *Ph* Victor
Milner
● Emil Jannings, Belle Bennett, Phyllis Haver, Donald
Keith, Fred Kohler (Paramount)

No specific punch to this initial made-in-the-
USA Emil Jannings release. It really
amounts to a study by the star of a middle
class character who succumbs, just once, to
the feminine and must forever after live in
hiding while his family believes him dead and
enjoys prosperity through one of the sons'
violin concerts. Starting in 1910, the story
weaves its way up to the present year, giving
opportunity to display three characterizations in as many makeups.

First as the bewhiskered gruff and trusted
cashier of a Milwaukee bank, second as
under the influence of a demi-mondaine, thereby shorn of his facial growth, and finally as
a broken example of indiscretion cleaning up
park playgrounds and peddling chestnuts.

In substance the story revolves around the
incident of Schilling (Jannings) being
entrusted with valuable bonds to be sold in
Chicago. On the train he meets Mayme
(Phyllis Haver), obviously attired for the character, who ultimately leads him to a drunken
sleep in a hotel where she rifles him of his
consignment.

Most of the production is studio made,
although there are theatre and amusement
park sequences, the last named inviting
various camera angles, one or two of which
stand out.

As regards Jannings, this, his first domestic
made picture, is assuredly creditable.

☐ 1927/28: Best Picture (Nomination)

■ WAY OUT WEST

1937, 64 MINS, US ⓥ
Dir James W. Horne   *Prod* Hal Roach, Stan Laurel
Scr Charles Rogers, Felix Adler, James Parrott   *Ph* Art
Lloyd, Walter Lundin   *Ed* Bert Jordan   *Mus* Marvin
Hatley (dir.)   *Art Dir* Arthur I. Royce
● Stan Laurel, Oliver Hardy, Sharon Lynne, James
Finlayson, Stanley Fields, Vivian Oakland (M-G-M)

Manner in which this comedy falters and
stumbles along is probably due both to formula direction and scripting. Three are credited with the scenario and two [Jack Jevne
and Charles Rogers] for the original story.
Seemingly too many took a hand; plot reads
that way.

In general pattern the Laurel & Hardy
entry follows closely the old methods used on
their feature shorts. There's too much driving
home of gags.

They sing and dance in this one, both to
neat returns. The two boys are commissioned
to deliver a deed to a gold mine. They find
out, after handing it over, that the valuable
paper has been given to the wrong girl.
Hence, the mad race to readjust matters. On

this thin framework hang all of the quips.
And Oliver Hardy falls into a pool of water
for the third time as the eventual fadeout
arrives.

James Finlayson again is cast as villain-
straight man, which further slows up the
action. Rosina Lawrence, heroine who's
supposed to inherit the gold mine, appears
only for fleeting glimpses.

■ WAY TO THE STARS, THE

1945, 107 MINS, UK
Dir Anthony Asquith   *Prod* Anatole de Grunwald
Scr Terence Rattigan, Richard Sherman   *Ph* Derek
Williams   *Ed* Fergus McDonell   *Mus* Nicholas
Brodzsky   *Art Dir* Paul Sheriff, Carmen Dillon
● John Mills, Michael Redgrave, Douglass
Montgomery, Trevor Howard, Rosamund John, Stanley
Holloway (Two Cities)

This straight tale of what happened to an
RAF airdrome when it was taken over by the
8th USAAF is outstanding. It's the nearest
thing to a Yank's letter home from wartime
England ever to reach the screen.

Not the least interesting thing is the camera
technique. Instead of many aerial shots, the
camera is grounded entirely. Except for a few
necessary runway shots and snatches of formation flying as seen from the ground, the
camera concentrates on how the forces lived
on terra firma.

Despite technically perfect performances by
the three male principals – Michael
Redgrave, John Mills and Douglass Montgomery – Rosamund John actually walks
away with the acting honors in a part as
devoid of glamor as it is rich in femme charm.

Several sequences showing the British aces
imitating the Yanks, and the Yanks imitating
the Englishmen, are guaranteed belly laughs.

Direction by Anthony Asquith is underlined with sincerity and imagination while
the script by Terence Rattigan is strong.

■ WAY WE WERE, THE

1973, 118 MINS, US ◇ ⓥ
Dir Sydney Pollack   *Prod* Ray Stark, Sydney Pollack
Scr Arthur Laurents   *Ph* Harry Stradling   *Ed* Margaret
Booth   *Mus* Marvin Hamlisch   *Art Dir* Stephen Grimes
● Barbra Streisand, Robert Redford, Bradford Dillman,
Patrick O'Neal, Viveca Lindfors, Lois Chiles
(Columbia/Rastar)

The film version of Arthur Laurents' book is
a distended, talky, redundant and moody
melodrama, combining young love, relentless
1930s and 1940s nostalgia, and spiced artif-
ically with Hollywood Red-hunt pellets.
The major positive achievement is Barbra
Streisand's superior dramatic versatility, but
Robert Redford has too little to work with in
the script.

The story follows the stars from the late
1930s – on a college campus where Streisand
is a young Communist activist, and Redford
a casual, shallow type – through World War
II civilian and military service, finally to Hollywood where liberal activities lead to blacklisting and marriage breakup.

The overemphasis on Streisand makes the
film just another one of those Streisand
vehicles where no other elements ever get a
chance. Redford's role is another instance of
waste of his talent. Supporting players are
virtual cameos.

■ WAY WEST, THE

1967, 122 MINS, US ◇ ⓥ
Dir Andrew V. McLaglen   *Prod* Harold Hecht   *Scr* Ben
Maddow, Mitch Lindemann   *Ph* William H. Clothier
Ed Otho Lovering   *Mus* Bronislau Kaper   *Art Dir* Ted
Haworth
● Kirk Douglas, Robert Mitchum, Richard Widmark,
Lola Albright, Jack Elam, Sally Field (United Artists)

A.B. Guthrie Jr wrote the Pulitzer Prize novel on which Ben Maddow and Mitch Lindemann have based a rambling screenplay. Story takes a group of Missouri farmers, under martinet Kirk Douglas, to the promised land of Oregon. Robert Mitchum is the trail scout who leads them despite fading eyesight, and Richard Widmark an irascible member of the party.

Project probably looked good on paper, but washed out in scripting, direction and pacing. Incidents do not build to any climax; excepting the first and last reels, any others could be shown out of order with no apparent discontinuity.

The three male stars all could have phoned in their acting. Douglas, the stern disciplinarian, at one point orders Negro slave Roy Glenn to whip him; this incident, as written, is crude, and instead of indicating a Spartan attempt at selfcontrol, it comes across as unmotivated masochism.

⬛ **WE DIVE AT DAWN**

1943, 92 MINS, UK ⓥ
Dir Anthony Asquith   *Prod* Maurice Ostrer   *Scr* J.R. Williams, Val Valentine   *Ph* Jack Cox
● John Mills, Eric Portman, Jack Watling, Leslie Weston, Jack Watling, Niall MacGinnis (Gainsborough)

The submarine *Sea Tiger* is sent out to sink a Nazi battleship which is due to leave Bremerhaven for the Kiel Canal, en route to the Baltic. The sub's instructions are to intercept her off the German coast before she enters the canal. Too late for this, the lieutenant in charge decides to brave the dangers of the Baltic and attack the battleship when she emerges at the other end of the canal. Owing to depth charges from accompanying destroyers, the attack results in a leakage in the sub's oil tanks and the Britisher decides to blow her up and escape to Denmark.

One of the seamen remembers there is a port on a nearby Danish island where there may be a tanker in dock. Donning the uniform of a dead German airman, he lands on the island, finds a tanker and signals to his ship to come in shore. They refuel and return home, and only then discover they have sunk the German vessel they were after.

John Mills enacts the lieutenant with not only requisite dignity, but with a human touch. But it is Eric Portman, as the seaman, who has the outstanding role and scores best. Rest of the cast gives excellent performances, while direction and production are above par.

⬛ **WE OF THE NEVER NEVER**

1982, 136 MINS, AUSTRALIA ◇ ⓥ
Dir Igor Auzins   *Prod* Greg Tepper, John B. Murray   *Scr* Peter Schreck   *Ph* Gary Hansen   *Ed* Clifford Hayes   *Mus* Peter Best   *Art Dir* Josephine Ford
● Angela Punch McGregor, Arthur Dignam, Tony Barry, Tommy Lewis, Lewis Fitz-Gerald, Martin Vaughan (Adams Packer/FCWA)

We of the Never Never is a stirring historical drama which explores a number of themes – racism, women's emancipation, and man's struggle to come to terms with an alien environment.

Pic is hindered, although not severely, by the casting of Arthur Dignam in the lead role. He lacks the authority and ruggedness to be credible as a turn-of-the-century explorer and adventurer who can run a 4,000-acre cattle station and control unruly stockmen and nomadic Aborigines. Compensating for that weakness is the topline performance of Angela Punch McGregor, an actress with a commanding presence.

Based on a classic Australian novel, film concerns a 30-year-old city-bred woman,

Jeannie, who is forced to make the transition from civilized Melbourne to the barren outback of the Northern Territory when she marries station owner Aeneas Gunn.

Director Igor Auzins, helming only his second feature, has created a big, bold and magnificently scenic picture. Gary Hansen's photography eloquently captures the paradoxical beauty and harshness of the outback.

⬛ **WEDDING, A**

1978, 125 MINS, US ◇ ⓥ
Dir Robert Altman   *Prod* Robert Altman   *Scr* John Considine, Patricia Resnik, Allan Nicholls, Robert Altman   *Ph* Charles Rosher   *Ed* Tony Lombardo   *Mus* Tom Walls
● Carol Burnett, Mia Farrow, Lillian Gish, Howard Duff, Geraldine Chaplin, Lauren Hutton (Lion's Gate)

If *Nashville* is ensemble Altman at its best – and it is – then *A Wedding* is the other extreme. Altman's loose, seemingly unstructured style backfires in this comedy-drama.

The title is self-descriptive: the picture is a day in the life of a wedding between the daughter of a nouveau rich southern family and the son of old midwestern money. The setting is rife with conventions – marriage, religion, wealth.

Unlike *Nashville*, the film lacks a core. Nothing builds; the characters, except for Lillian Gish as the old money matriarch and Mia Farrow as the silent sister of the bride, are uninteresting and unsympathetic. They pop in and out of the film and when they pop out, who cares if they return?

Altman's idea of humor comes off as puerile and dated. John Cromwell plays a senile bishop who performs the wedding ceremony. He forgets how to conduct the service and is too near sighted to know that at one point he's talking to a corpse. That's hardly sharp edged satire.

⬛ **WEDDING NIGHT, THE**

1935, 81 MINS, US
Dir King Vidor   *Prod* Samuel Goldwyn   *Scr* Edith Fitzgerald   *Ph* Gregg Toland   *Ed* Stuart Heisler   *Mus* Alfred Newman   *Art Dir* Richard Day
● Gary Cooper, Anna Sten, Helen Vinson, Ralph Bellamy, Siegfried Rumann, Esther Dale (Goldwyn/United Artists)

Story [by Edwin Knopf] is irritating in many ways. Gary Cooper is a young author who sells a piece of his land to a Polish tobacco grower, who wants it as a dowry for his daughter. He goes to the farmhouse to make the sale. He is received with hospitality and made welcome at the meal which turns out to be a betrothal feast.

Author returns home, announcing that he has found the theme for his new book in the family he has just left. The Polish girl becomes first interested in the man and then flattered by the novel in which she, the heroine, works the spiritual regeneration of the author, who frankly divorces his wife – on paper – to take on the new love.

King Vidor, in his direction, handles the incidents with fine touch, keeping each character whole and consistent and developing a fluid action which moves easily from the American to the Polish home and back again.

Anna Sten is more fortunately cast than in *Nana* (1934). She is exotic, but her still-marked accent fits the character and she gives a finely sensitive performance.

She is handicapped in a way by the more showy personality of Helen Vinson, as the author's wife; hard as nails, but realizing eventually she loves her man and is willing to fight for him. Cooper contibutes an easy character drawing which by its charm almost blinds to the havoc he works. Ralph Bellamy is capital as the destined husband.

⬛ **WEDDING PARTY, THE**

1969, 90 MINS, US ⓥ
Dir Cynthia Munroe, Brian De Palma, Wilford Leach   *Prod* Cynthia Munroe, Brian De Palma, Wilford Leach   *Scr* Cynthia Munroe, Brian De Palma, Wilford Leach   *Ph* Peter Powell   *Ed* Cynthia Munroe, Brian De Palma, Wilford Leach   *Mus* John Herbert McDowell
● Jill Clayburgh, Charles Pflugar, Valda Setterfield, Ray McNally, Robert De Niro, Judy Thomas (Ondine)

Story dwells on a young man who, accompanied by two friends, arrives at the island estate of his soon-to-be-bride.

The individual scenes come off as a kind of practiced improvisation. Apparently a script was employed but the dialogue itself was produced by taping ad-libbed scenes.

The film suffers from this technique. Each scene is only loosely connected with what went before and what comes after. And tightness and direction of the dialogue is sacrificed for a certain spontaneity that is seldom forthcoming.

The cast includes professional actors combined with Sarah Lawrence College workshop students.

Film was actually completed [in 1963]. De Palma worked in collaboration with then fellow student Cynthia Munroe and faculty member Wilford Leach when all three were at Sarah Lawrence College.

⬛ **WEEKEND WITH KATE**

1990, 95 MINS, AUSTRALIA ◇ ⓥ
Dir Arch Nicholson   *Prod* Phillip Emanuel   *Scr* Henry Tefay, Kee Young   *Ph* Dan Burstall   *Ed* Rose Evans   *Mus* Bruce Rowland   *Art Dir* Larry Eastwood
● Colin Friels, Catherine McClements, Jerome Ehlers, Helen Mutkins (Emanuel)

The well constructed script indicates a knowledge of romantic comedies of another era. Setup has journalist turned rock music promoter Colin Friels torn between beautiful wife Catherine McClements, who wants to have a baby, and his ambitious mistress Helen Mutkins, who wants Friels.

He decides to tell his wife he's leaving her during a weekend they plan to spend alone at her family's beach house. She has decided to use the intimacy of the weekend to get pregnant. Both plans go astray when British rock idol Jerome Ehlers arrives and moves in for a peaceful weekend of fishing.

The sexual adventures are exuberantly captured on screen. Dialog is sharp and witty, direction is brisk and well-timed, and performances are top notch. Friels is fine as the errant, ambitious husband, and is nicely contrasted with Ehlers as the lanky, self-centered rock star. McClements is a joy as Kate.

Principal photography was completed by spring 1989, with additional shooting taking place several months later to provide a new ending and bridging scenes.

⬛ **WEIRD SCIENCE**

1985, 94 MINS, US ◇ ⓥ
Dir John Hughes   *Prod* Joel Silver   *Scr* John Hughes   *Ph* Matthew F. Leonetti   *Ed* Mark Warner, Christopher Lebenzon, Scott Wallace   *Mus* Ira Newborn   *Art Dir* John W. Corso
● Anthony Michael Hall, Kelly LeBrock, Ilan Mitchell-Smith, Bill Paxton, Suzanne Snyder, Robert Downey (Universal)

Starting with the delectable premise of two high school nerds who create a woman through some inexplicable computer hocus-pocus, *Weird Science* veers off into a typical coming-of-age saga without exploring any of the psychological territory it lightly sails over in the early going.

Helplessly horny chums Gary (Anthony Michael Hall) and Wyatt (Ilan Mitchell-Smith), in an act of creative frustration, put

661

their brains together and create the answer to their fantasies – the beautiful and very available Lisa (Kelly LeBrock). The trouble is the boys hardly use her.

Although clearly not grounded in reality, the film really goes nowhere with its central conceit, opting instead for a more ordinary approach . Director John Hughes never capitalizes on the idea that Lisa is a creation of 15-year-old psyches or examines the intriguing question of who controls whom in this relationship.

Hughes' true gift is at capturing the naturalistic rhythms and interaction between the boys with a great ear for dialog. LeBrock is just right as the film's calm but commanding center.

■ **WELCOME HOME**

1989, 87 MINS, US ◇ ▼

Dir Franklin J. Schaffer *Prod* Martin Ransohoff *Scr* Maggie Kleinman *Ph* Fred J. Koenekamp *Ed* Bob Swink *Mus* [uncredited] *Art Dir* Dan Yarhi
● Kris Kristofferson, JoBeth Williams, Brian Keith, Sam Waterston, Trey Wilson (Columbia/Rank)

A fine opportunity to explore the emotional conflict and military-political hush-hush regarding the unexpected reappearance of US soldiers recorded as dead in Vietnam and Cambodia is missed almost totally in Franklin J. Schaffner's *Welcome Home*.

Kris Kristofferson looks suitably haggard and tired as Lt Jake Robbins, who returns to Vermont after 17 years in Cambodia. He was shot down there and put in POW camp. Jake later settled down to married village life with Cambodian Leang (Kieu Chinh Nguyen) who bore him two children.

It is not until he wakes up in a New York State Air Force hospital that Jake remembers that he had just married his American sweethert Sarah (mournfully played by JoBeth Williams) before he set out on his Far East tour of duty. He is told that she is now remarried and lives happily in Vermont with her second husband (Sam Waterston) and 17-year-old son (Thomas Wilson Brown), who is actually Jake's.

Jake, however, feels he must at least see his son, so he bungles on to the Vermont scene where he upsets everybody.

An uninspired screenplay does not help Schaffner in making the film move forward more than sluggishly. The plot flounders in shallow waters.

■ **WELCOME HOME, ROXY CARMICHAEL**

1990, 98 MINS, US ◇ ▼

Dir Jim Abrahams *Prod* Penney Finkelman Cox *Scr* Karen Leigh Hopkins *Ph* Paul Elliott *Ed* Bruce Green *Mus* Thomas Newman *Art Dir* Dena Roth
● Winona Ryder, Jeff Daniels, Laila Robins, Thomas Wilson Brown, Joan McMurtrey, Frances Fisher (ITC)

Fans of Winona Ryder will definitely want to catch her in an offbeat role as the town rebel in this teen-oriented smalltown saga; unfortunately, the rest of the production doesn't quite match up.

Ryder plays 15-year-old Dinky Bossetti, a moody, glowering misfit who scribbles poetry, wears baggy black clothes and doesn't comb her hair. Her nowhereville hometown of Clyde, Ohio, is all in a dither about the impending return of legendary local Roxy Carmichael, and Dinky, being adopted, decides that Roxy must have been her real mother.

Also certain that Roxy is coming back for him is Jeff Daniels as Denton, formerly the teenaged boyfriend with whom she had a baby, now a married man with a family. As all gossip turns to Roxy and her precocious local deeds, Denton's wife (Joan McMurtrey) gets fed up with the situation and leaves him.

Meanwhile the socially reviled Dinky is being pursued by a nerdy guidance counselor who wants to put her in a school for misfits, and a rather blank-slated surfer-looking dude (Thomas Wilson Brown) who wants to be her boyfriend.

Ryder's performance has a subtle glow and maturity that mesmerizes. Her keenly observed creation of the spooky, androgynous Dinky, with her low voice and deadpan delivery, injects her scenes with a natural comedy far more satisfying than the more hysterical efforts being made around her.

■ **WELCOME TO BLOOD CITY**

1977, 96 MINS, UK/CANADA ◇ ▼

Dir Peter Sasdy *Prod* Marilyn Stonehouse *Scr* Stephen Schneck, Michael Winder *Ph* Reginald Morris C.S.C. *Ed* Keith Palmer *Mus* Roy Budd *Art Dir* Tony Hall
● Jack Palance, Keir Dullea, Samantha Eggar, Barry Morse, Hollis McLaren, Chris Wiggins (EMI/Herberman)

An anonymous totalitarian organization kidnaps Keir Dullea. Via computer electronics, he is mentally transported to a fantasized oater settlement (Blood City) where a person's status accrues according to the number of people he/she can murder. Sheriff Jack Palance is classified as Immortal, having 20 killings to his score.

Dullea's progress through the city is monitored by program technicians Samantha Eggar (who also inexplicably lives in Blood City) and John Evans.

Although the film's initial conception may have held traces of intelligence, swiss-cheese script strains coherence and interest with each development. Consequently, neither in their interdependence or individuality do the film's sci-fi or western elements emerge as generically satisfying.

■ **WELCOME TO LA**

1976, 103 MINS, US ◇ ▼

Dir Alan Rudolph *Prod* Robert Altman *Scr* Alan Rudolph *Ph* Dave Myers *Ed* William A. Sawyer, Tom Walls *Mus* Richard Baskin
● Keith Carradine, Sally Kellerman, Geraldine Chaplin, Harvey Keitel, Lauren Hutton, Viveca Lindfors (United Artists)

The banal point of *Welcome to LA* is pretty much summed up in the closing song by Richard Baskin, in which Keith Carradine sings of the city 'where the air is thick and yellow with the stale taste of decay'. The film has a studied, calculated, over-designed look that drains the vitality from the cast as director Alan Rudolph puts them through their predictable paces in a *Nashville*-like amorphous story which has something to do with the music industry.

Welcome to LA has lots of aimless driving around town, gloomy sex encounters, mumbled dialog, and showy camera movements.

Carradine sings a few songs, guzzles booze without feeling it, and exerts a mysterious attraction on every woman in sight.

■ **WENT THE DAY WELL?**

1942, 93 MINS, UK

Dir Alberto Cavalcanti *Prod* Michael Balcon *Scr* John Dighton, Diana Morgan, Angus MacPhail *Ph* Wilkie Cooper *Ed* Sidney Cole *Mus* William Walton *Art Dir* Tom Morahan
● Leslie Banks, Basil Sydney, Frank Lawton, Elizabeth Allan, Valerie Taylor, John Slater (Ealing)

This Ealing Studios' tale of 72 hours of the life of Bramley Green, a tiny hamlet in the heart of the English countryside, is introduced by an old grave-digger playing straight into the camera. Dealing with an attempt at an airborne invasion of a sparsely peopled part of England, as contrasted with the well-defended key cities, this picture achieves considerable interest.

Settings, exterior and interior, smack of the real thing, from the 13th-century church to the village grocery whose proprietress is also postmistress and telephone exchange operator.

Direction by Alberto Cavalcanti is workmanlike, but to the men of the Gloucestershire Regiment (cast as both German invaders and members of the local Home Guard) must go chief credit for the realistic note underlying the film, which is almost as factual as a propaganda short.

■ **WE'RE NO ANGELS**

1955, 103 MINS, US ◇ ▼

Dir Michael Curtiz *Prod* Pat Duggan *Scr* Ranald MacDougall *Ph* Loyal Griggs *Ed* Arthur Schmidt *Mus* Frederick Hollander *Art Dir* Hal Pereira, Roland Anderson
● Humphrey Bogart, Aldo Ray, Peter Ustinov, Joan Bennett, Basil Rathbone, Leo G. Carroll (Paramount)

Paramount has fashioned a breezy 105-minute VistaVision feature. Light antics swing around three convicts of Devil's Island who find themselves playing Santa Claus to a family they came to rob. At times proceedings are too consciously cute and stage origin of material still clings since virtually all scenes are interiors with characters constantly entering and exiting. However, Michael Curtiz' directorial pacing and topflight performances from Humphrey Bogart, Aldo Ray and Peter Ustinov help minimize the few flaws.

Screenplay uses great deal of conversation, mostly amusingly flavored, to tell how convicts descend on store-home operated by Leo G. Carroll and his wife (Joan Bennett), planning robbery that would finance journey to France. Trio, all lifers, Bogart for forgery, others for murder, find family in difficulties unbecoming Christmas Eve spirit.

■ **WE'RE NO ANGELS**

1989, 108 MINS, US ◇ ▼

Dir Neil Jordan *Prod* Art Linson *Scr* David Mamet *Ph* Philippe Rousselot *Ed* Mick Audsley, Jake Van Wuk *Mus* George Fenton *Art Dir* Wolf Kroeger
● Robert De Niro, Sean Penn, Demi Moore, Wallace Shawn, Ray McAnally, James Russo (Paramount)

Described by its producer as 'very loosely based on some of the ideas' in the eponymous 1955 movie about convicts on the lam, *We're No Angels* is precisely about a pair of jailbirds on the run. The year is 1935 and Robert De Niro and Sean Penn are hard-timers in a hellish north country penitentiary that may be a metaphor for Depression-era America.

The late, great Ray McAnally, reduced here to caricature of cruelty as the Big House warden, forces the heroes to witness the electrocution of a remorseless murderer. But the condemned con and two heroes pull an improbable breakout and head for the Canadian border.

De Niro and Penn reach a remote border town renowned for a shrine of 'the weeping Madonna' and a monastery. The town is swarming with police on their trail, but the cons are happily mistaken for visiting ecclesiastical scholars. Director Neil Jordan and screenwriter David Mamet thus set the stage for a parable about virtue, wisdom, faith and redemption.

Pugfaced, slack-jawed and marble-mouthed, De Niro and Penn mug their semiarticulate proles with relish, but as religioso fish out of water their con game becomes a tiresome joke.

W

WEST 11

1963, 93 MINS, UK

Dir Michael Winner *Prod* Daniel M. Angel *Scr* Keith Waterhouse, Willis Hall *Ph* Otto Heller *Ed* Bernard Gribble *Mus* Stanley Black, Acker Bilk
● Alfred Lynch, Kathleen Breck, Eric Portman, Diana Dors, Harold Lang (Associated-British)

The writing team of Keith Waterhouse and Willis Hall have done little to uplift this adaptation of a novel called *The Furnished Room*.

This is only hackneyed drama about a young man (Alfred Lynch) who is a layabout, a misfit, a self-pitier ('I'm an emotional leer,' he says, profoundly). He gets involved with chicks, can't keep a job and gets mixed up with jazz clubs and seedy parties. Turning point in his life is when he meets up with Richard Dyce (Eric Portman), an ex-army con-man. He is talked into an association with Portman, who wants his aunt bumped off.

It has its merits. The sleazy London locations are very authentically shown. Perhaps too authentically. Lynch is an intelligent actor but, in this instance, he fails to induce any pity. Probably the fault of the script. Kathleen Breck, his girl friend, copes reasonably. It's her first film part after a small experience in stock.

WEST POINT STORY, THE

1950, 106 MINS, US

Dir Roy Del Ruth *Prod* Louis F. Edelman *Scr* John Monks Jr, Charles Hoffmann, Irving Wallace *Ph* Sid Hickox *Ed* Owen Marks *Mus* Ray Heindorf (dir.)
● James Cagney, Virginia Mayo, Doris Day, Gordon MacRae (Warner)

Fresh treatment and new twists to the musical formula make *The West Point Story* worthwhile entertainment.

James Cagney sparkplugs the fun and frolic among a group of players who press him hard for top honors. Another big assist in putting this one over is Virginia Mayo. She bolsters the comedy and wallops the eyes with her array of s.a.

There are several production numbers in keeping with the cadet background of the story.

The story has Cagney as a brash Broadway director down on his luck who accepts the assignment to stage the annual West Point show, '100th Night'. Gordon MacRae, a cadet, wrote the show's book and tunes, and his producer uncle wants it and the young man for a Broadway staging.

WEST SIDE STORY

1961, 153 MINS, US ◇ ⓥ

Dir Robert Wise, Jerome Robbins *Prod* Robert Wise *Scr* Ernest Lehman *Ph* Daniel L. Fapp *Ed* Thomas Stanford, Marshall M. Borden *Mus* Leonard Bernstein *Art Dir* Boris Leven
● Natalie Wood, Richard Beymer, Russ Tamblyn, Rita Moreno, George Chakiris, Simon Oakland (United Artists/Mirisch/Screen Arts)

West Side Story is a beautifully-mounted, impressive, emotion-stirring and violent musical. This powerful and sometimes fascinating translation of the Broadway musical is said to have cost $6 million.

The Romeo and Juliet theme, propounded against the seething background of rival Puerto Rican and American gangs (repping the Montagues and the Capulets) on the upper West Side of Manhattan, makes for both a savage and tender admixture of romance and war-to-the-death.

Even more notable, however, is the music of Leonard Bernstein and most of all the breathtaking choreography of Jerome Robbins. Bernstein's score, with Stephen Sondheim's expressive lyrics, accentuates the tenseness that constantly builds.

Ernest Lehman's screenplay, based upon Arthur Laurents' solid and compelling book in the Broadway production, is a faithful adaptation in which he reflects the brutality of the juve gangs which vent upon each other the hatred they feel against the world. Plottage focuses on the romance of a young Puerto Rican girl with a mainland boy, which fans the enmity between the two gangs and ultimately leads to the 'rumble' which leaves both gang leaders dead of knife wounds.

Natalie Wood offers an entrancing performance as the Puerto Rican who falls in love with Richard Beymer, forbidden by strict neighborhood ban against group intermingling, and latter impresses with his singing. Most colorful performance, perhaps, is by George Chakiris, leader of Puerto Rican gang the Sharks and brother of femme lead, who appeared in London company in same role portrayed here by Russ Tamblyn, leader of the white Jets gang. Tamblyn socks over his portrayal and scores particularly with his acrobatic terping. Rita Moreno, in love with Chakiris, presents a fiery characterization and also scores hugely.

Singer Marni Nixon dubs Wood's voice. Film, opening with a three-minute orchestral overture, has been expertly lensed by Daniel L. Fapp, whose aerial prolog, looking straight down upon Gotham as camera flies from the Battery uptown and swings to West Side, provides impressive views. Johnny Green conducts music score, which runs $51^1/2$ minutes; Saul Bass is responsible for novel presentation of titles and credits; Irene Sharaff, who designed costumes for Broadway, repeats here.

□ 1961: Best Picture

WESTERN UNION

1941, 93 MINS, US ◇ ⓥ

Dir Fritz Lang *Prod* Harry Joe Brown *Scr* Robert Carson *Ph* Edward Cronjager *Ed* Robert Bischoff *Mus* David Buttolph
● Robert Young, Randolph Scott, Dean Jagger, Virginia Gilmore, Barton MacLane (20th Century-Fox)

Western Union is another epic of the early American frontier. This time the stringing of telephone lines in the 1860s, between Omaha and Salt Lake City, provides the background for adventures and excitement in empire building. Hewing to a straight line in telling the story of pioneering the west, *Western Union* is a lusty and actionful offering.

Mounted with expansiveness as a super-western of upper-budget proportions, picture displays some eyeful exterior panoramas. The tinting photography has some of the finest outdoor scenes which were photographed in the colorful Utah park country.

Randolph Scott, an ex-outlaw who joins the expedition as a scout turns in a strongly persuasive characterization. Dean Jagger is the company engineer in charge of construction; Robert Young a dudish easterner who toughens up under western ways; and Barton MacLane is the renegade outlaw whose band continually harasses the camp. Virginia Gilmore is minor as the romantic interest for conflict between Scott and Young in the early reels.

WESTERNER, THE

1940, 97 MINS, US ⓥ

Dir William Wyler *Prod* Samuel Goldwyn *Scr* Jo Swerling, Niven Busch *Ph* Gregg Toland *Ed* Daniel Mandell *Mus* Dimitri Tiomkin *Art Dir* James Basevi
● Gary Cooper, Walter Brennan, Doris Davenport, Fred Stone, Forrest Tucker, Lillian Bond (Goldwyn/United Artists)

Although Gary Cooper is starred, Walter Brennan commands major attention with a slick characterization of Judge Roy Bean, the

dispenser of law at Vinegaroon – west of the Pecos. Supplied with a particularly meaty role, of which he takes fullest advantage, Brennan turns in a socko job that does much to hold together a not too impressive script.

The story of cattlemen's resentment against the migration of settlers to Texas in the post-Civil War days, is a rather familiar one cinematically. But producer Samuel Goldwyn has invested his version with plenty of production assets – good cast topped by Cooper; extended shooting schedule under direction of William Wyler; and eye-filling scenic backgrounds that are accentuated by expert photography.

Cooper is a wandering cowhand who comes before the two-gun judge charged with horse-stealing, and convicted by the jury that brings in verdicts according to the ideas of Brennan. But the latter is a worshipper of actress Lily Langtry, and when Cooper professes intimate acquaintance with the lady, sentence is suspended while the judge gets some anecdotes about the beauteous 'Jersey Lily'.

A strange friendship develops between the cantankerous old judge and the cowboy. In the midst of the battle between the homesteaders and the cattlemen, Cooper mediates the trouble by convincing the judge to declare peace between the factions. Then Cooper falls in love with Doris Davenport, daughter of a rancher, to cement him closer to the settlers.

Cooper provides a satisfactory portrayal of the roaming westerner; although he has handled the same type of roles many times. Davenport, a newcomer from the extra field, delivers satisfactorily as the rancher's daughter.

WESTWORLD

1973, 88 MINS, US ◇ ⓥ

Dir Michael Crichton *Prod* Paul N. Lazarus III *Scr* Michael Crichton *Ph* Gene Polito *Ed* David Bretherton *Mus* Fred Karlin *Art Dir* Herman Blumenthal
● Yul Brynner, Richard Benjamin, James Brolin, Alan Oppenheimer, Victoria Shaw, Dick Van Patten (M-G-M)

Westworld is an excellent film, which combines solid entertainment, chilling topicality, and superbly intelligent serio-comic story values. Michael Crichton's original script is as superior as his direction.

Crichton's Westworld is one of three gigantic theme parks built in what is left of the American outdoors; the others are 'Romanworld' and 'Medievalworld'. For $1,000 a day, flown in tourists may indulge their highest and lowest appetites. Automated robots move about as real people. These automatons may be raped, shot to death, befriended, betrayed, etc. They never strike back.

To this world come Richard Benjamin and James Brolin. They have picked the western-themed park, where they switch to levis, pack revolvers and live out the screen life depicted by John Wayne, Clint Eastwood, and other actioner stars. Yul Brynner plays a black-clothed bad guy whom Benjamin kills in a saloon confrontation. All the while supervisor Alan Oppenheimer oversees the entire world and its creatures.

But suddenly things begin to go wrong. An unidentified computer casualty begins to spread like a plague. The automatons strike back.

WETHERBY

1985, 97 MINS, UK ◇ ⓥ

Dir David Hare *Prod* Simon Relph, Patsy Pollock *Scr* David Hare *Ph* Stuart Harris *Ed* Chris Wimble *Mus* Nick Bicat *Art Dir* Hayden Griffin
● Vanessa Redgrave, Ian Holm, Judi Dench, Marjorie Yates, Tim Wilkinson, Tim McInnerny (Greenpoint/Film Four/Zenith)

The title refers to a small town in the northeastern county of Yorkshire. Jean Travers (Vanessa Redgrave) has lived here all her life; she's a lonely schoolteacher, tormented by the memory of a teenage love affair with a boy who was senselessly murdered while on air force duty in Malaya.

The film opens with a dinner party hosted by Jean in her little cottage. Present are two couples, close friends, and a young stranger John Morgan, whom Jean assumes came with one of the couples, while they in turn assume he is her guest. Next day, Morgan returns to the cottage, and while Jean is making tea, he pulls out a gun and kills himself.

The skill of Hare's approach is that he initially allows us to assume, via normal cinema techniques, that what we saw of the dinner party was the whole story. Gradually, however, we realize we only saw a highly selected part of that evening, and as we return to it again and again, the whole story takes on a different complexion.

Performances are uniformly excellent. Joely Richardson (real-life daughter of Redgrave and Tony Richardson) portrays Redgrave in her youth with great conviction.

● ●

■ WHALES OF AUGUST, THE

1987, 90 MINS, US ◇ ⓥ
Dir Lindsay Anderson *Prod* Carolyn Pfeiffer, Mike Kaplan *Scr* David Berry *Ph* Mike Fash *Ed* Nicolas Gaster *Mus* Alan Price *Art Dir* Jocelyn Herbert
● Bette Davis, Lillian Gish, Vincent Price, Ann Sothern, Harry Carey Jr, Frank Grimes (Circle/Nelson)

Muted but engrossing tale about the balance of power between two elderly sisters boasts superior lead performances from two of the screen's most legendary actresses, Bette Davis and Lillian Gish.

Adapted by David Berry from his 1981 play, story has two sisters living alone in a comfortable but basic home they have occupied for decades on the striking coast of Maine. Sarah (Gish) is a doting busybody who is obliged to care for her sister Libby (Davis), because the latter is blind.

Trouble rears its head in the form of Vincent Price, a White Russian of considerable charm and gentlemanliness who for decades has lived as a 'houseguest' of numerous ladies.

Wearing long, pure white hair Davis looks gaunt, grim and disturbed, but her performance is restrained in such a way that may even increase its power. Gish is a delight throughout.

A black-&-white prolog, in which Mary Steenburgen, Tisha Sterling and Margaret Ladd appear as the women in their youth, gets the film off to a nice start.

● ●

■ WHAT A WAY TO GO!

1964, 111 MINS, US ◇
Dir J. Lee Thompson *Prod* Arthur P. Jacobs *Scr* Betty Comden, Adolph Green *Ph* Leon Shamroy *Ed* Marjorie Fowler *Mus* Nelson Riddle *Art Dir* Jack Martin Smith, Ted Haworth
● Shirley MacLaine, Paul Newman, Robert Mitchum, Dean Martin, Gene Kelly, Dick Van Dyke (20th Century-Fox)

What a Way to Go! is a big, gaudy, gimmicky comedy which continually promises more than it delivers by way of wit and/or bellylaffs.

The screenplay, based on a story by Gwen Davis, is, at its very promising basis, the sad, sad story of a little poor girl from Ohio who, though she wants only true love, is married and widowed in succession by four diverse types who eventually make her the richest woman in the world. It's a sort of ironic *True*

Story, related in flashbacks from a psychiatrist's couch.

Essentially, the film is a series of blackout sketches, enlivened from time to time as Shirley MacLaine tells of her marriages in styles of various types of films. Thus, in recalling her life with a Thoreau-reading idealist (Dick Van Dyke), she sees it in the jerky, exaggerated terms of a silent movie romance; her life with a beatnik, abstract-impressionist painter (Paul Newman), in Paris, is viewed as sexy French film complete with English subtitles; and her life with tycoon Robert Mitchum is remembered as an overdressed Ross Hunter production.

Some of these parodies are very funny but, there often isn't much difference between the style of the parody and that of the encasing flashback.

Picture is gaudily, expensively mounted. There are a couple of songs by Jule Styne, including an hilarious production number (choreographed by Gene Kelly) which might have come out of *Follow the Fleet*.

● ●

■ WHAT ABOUT BOB?

1991, 99 MINS, US ◇ ⓥ
Dir Frank Oz *Prod* Laura Ziskin *Scr* Tom Schulman *Ph* Michael Ballhaus *Ed* Anne V. Coates *Mus* Miles Goodman *Art Dir* Les Dilley
● Bill Murray, Richard Dreyfuss, Julie Hagerty, Charlie Kosmo, Kathryn Erbe (Touchstone Pacific Partners I)

Bill Murray finds a real showcase for his oft-shackled talent in this manic comedy. Originally discussed as a pairing of Murray and Woody Allen, pic ended up with Richard Dreyfuss in the role of the tightly wound, egotistical psychiatrist whose life is disrupted by 'multiphobic' new patient Bob Wiley (Murray), the human equivalent of gum on the bottom of one's shoe.

Dreyfuss' Dr Leo Marvin gets irked when the persistent patient follows him to a rustic New Hampshire retreat, then grows increasingly outraged as Bob proceeds to win over his family. He helps the doc's death-obsessed son (Charlie Korsmo, kid in *Dick Tracy*) to learn to enjoy life and shows compassion to his daughter (Kathryn Erbe) and unappreciated wife (Julie Hagerty).

Murray has a field day with the character, which allows him to act like a little kid while occasionally lapsing into other aspects from his *Saturday Night Life* days, from his smarmy lounge singer to the nerd. Dreyfuss generally reprises the role he played in *Down and Out in Beverly Hills*: domineering, nouveau riche family man whose stolid existence is turned upside down by unwelcome intruder.

● ●

■ WHAT DID YOU DO IN THE WAR, DADDY?

1966, 115 MINS, US ◇
Dir Blake Edwards *Prod* Blake Edwards *Scr* William Peter Blatty *Ph* Philip Lathrop *Ed* Ralph E. Winters *Mus* Henry Mancini *Art Dir* Fernando Carrere
● James Coburn, Dick Shawn, Sergio Fantoni, Aldo Ray, Harry Morgan, Carroll O'Connor (United Artists/Mirisch/Geoffrey)

What Did You Do in the War, Daddy? carries an engaging title but after dreaming it up the writers promptly forgot all about it and launched into a thinly-devised comedy without much substance.

Blake Edwards, who directs, also collabed on original story with Maurice Richlin. Set against a World War II backdrop – Sicily, 1943 – the screenplay dwells on a single situation which holds promise but is never sufficiently realized.

Basic idea has a war-weary American company, commanded by a by-the-book officer, being detailed to take a town held by a large Italian force, and their welcome reception by the Italians who are agreeable to surrendering willingly. But first, they must hold their wine festival. No festival, no surrender.

Edwards has packed his action with a flock of individual gags and routines but frequently the viewer isn't too certain what's happening. Director draws good comedy portrayals from a talented cast headed by James Coburn and Dick Shawn, both delivering bangup performances.

● ●

■ WHAT EVER HAPPENED TO AUNT ALICE?

1969, 101 MINS, US ◇ ⓥ
Dir Lee H. Katzin *Prod* Robert Aldrich *Scr* Theodore Apstein *Ph* Joseph Biroc *Ed* Frank J. Urioste *Mus* Gerald Fried *Art Dir* William Glasgow
● Geraldine Page, Ruth Gordon, Rosemary Forsyth, Robert Fuller, Mildred Dunnock (Palomar/Associates & Aldrich)

Fresh story, using old-hat scare tricks combined with highly skillful acting.

Widow Geraldine Page hits upon ingenious method of building up unencumbered women as companions, to take their life savings and then bash their heads in. Trouble starts when she eliminates wistful Mildred Dunnock. Suspicious Ruth Gordon, former employer of Dunnock, appears on the scene in the guise of yet another housekeeper.

Page as a high and mighty wealthy eccentric delivers a bravura performance. Gordon, working crisply, offers a remarkable portrait of a brave woman. The two ladies play off each other relentlessly and audience reaps the rewards.

Grim humor and superior dialog, as well as night prowling, barred doors, disconnected phones, an unexplained wheelchair, wigs and maniacal laughter total up to fine tale [from the novel *The Forbidden Garden* by Ursula Curtiss] of suspense rounded off with a twist ending.

● ●

■ WHAT EVER HAPPENED TO BABY JANE?

1962, 132 MINS, US ⓥ
Dir Robert Aldrich *Prod* Robert Aldrich *Scr* Lukas Heller *Ph* Ernest Haller *Ed* Michael Luciano *Mus* Frank DeVol *Art Dir* William Glasgow
● Bette Davis, Joan Crawford, Victor Buono (Seven Arts-Associates)

Teaming Bette Davis and Joan Crawford now seems like a veritable prerequisite to putting Henry Farrell's slight tale of terror on the screen. Although the results heavily favor Davis (and she earns the credit), it should be recognized that the plot, of necessity, allows her to run unfettered through all the stages of oncoming insanity, which the uninhibited lady proceeds to do – like a mad organist, warming up to Berlioz' *Damnation of Faust* with, eventually, every stop out.

Crawford gives a quiet, remarkably fine interpretation of the crippled Blanche, held in emotionally by the nature and temperament of the role. Physically confined to a wheelchair and bed through the picture, she has to act from the inside and has her best scenes (because she wisely underplays with Davis) with a maid and those she plays alone. In one superb bit, Crawford reacting to herself on television (actually, clips from the 1934 *Sadie McKee*), makes her face fairly glow with the remembrance of fame past.

The slight basic tale is of two sisters, complete opposites. As children, Jane is 'Baby Jane' (a travesty on the many Mary Pickford-Shirley Temple imitators), a vaudeville star and the idol of the public. Offstage, she's a vicious brat, domineering her plain, inhibited sister and preening parents. Eventually both girls go into films, where the dark, mousey Blanche blossoms into a beauty and fine actress, and becomes Hollywood's top star.

As a result of an accident, hazily presented, Blanche is permanently crippled. Jane,

W

dependent on her sister for her livelihood, is forced to care for her, her hate growing with the years. So, also, does the 'Baby Jane' illusion until, living it daily, she determines to get rid of Blanche and return to vaudeville.

Advertising for an accompanist, the sole applicant is a huge, ungainly lout (a superb off-beat performance by Victor Buono), who sizes up the situation's opportunities and goes along, planning to get enough money to enable him to break the tarnished-silver cord binding him to a possessive mother.

The chain of circumstances grows, violence creating violence. Once the inept, draggy start is passed, the film's pace builds with ever-growing force.

Minor plot inconsistencies pop up, but not enough to detract the hypnotized-with-horror average viewer. A film clip, probably from the 1933 *Parachute Jumper*, inserted to establish Jane's ineptness as an actress, fails to do so. Despite its shortcomings, however, 'Baby Jane' gives the two fine actresses worthy roles.

● ●

■ WHAT EVERY WOMAN KNOWS

1934, 90 MINS, US
Dir Gregory La Cava *Scr* Monckton Hoffe, John Meehan, James Kevin McGuinness *Ph* Charles Rosher *Mus* Herbert Stothart
● Helen Hayes, Brian Aherne, Madge Evans, Lucile Watson, Dudley Digges, Donald Crisp (M-G-M)

The theme is by no means new, but the idea is ever popular. Paramount first presented it as a silent back in 1921. In 1926 Helen Hayes and Kenneth MacKenna made a season of the same James M. Barrie play on Broadway. It's the 'lil woman' all over again, the helpmeet who humbly does her quiet bit in balancing impulsive man's judgments or, rather, misjudgments.

This Barrie version brings the egotistical but knowledge-hungry young barrister (Brian Aherne) out of Scotland into Parliament, where he thinks he finds new romance with power, but is actually catapulted into even greater glory by the brainy Maggie (Hayes), who types and edits his MP speeches.

Aherne is a vigorous zealot who makes his upstartishness respected and even liked by the Scots community (and the audience), for none can deny his sincerity.

Madge Evans is out of her usual groove as a light menace, but she makes it as likeable as circumstances warrant. Lucile Watson as the comtesse is a gallant lady, while Dudley Digges is particularly impressive as the somewhat numb Jamie.

● ●

■ WHAT PRICE GLORY

1926, 116 MINS, US ⊗
Dir Raoul Walsh *Prod* William Fox *Scr* James T. O'Donohoe, Malcolm Stuart Boylan *Ph* Barney McGill, Jack Marta, John Smith *Ed* Rose Smith *Art Dir* William Darling
● Victor McLaglen, Edmund Lowe, Dolores Del Rio, William V. Mong, Phyllis Haver (Fox)

It's a picture [from the play by Maxwell Anderson and Laurence Stallings] that has everything except an out-and-out love story of the calibre of the one in *The Big Parade*. But where it lacks in that it certainly makes up in sex stuff and comedy.

There is a wallop right at the beginning in the two short sequences showing both Flagg and Quirt as sergeants of the marines in China and the Philippines. Right here the conflict between the two men, whose trade is soldiering, over women is set down, yet with a light touch of comedy.

Victor McLaglen stands out bigger than he ever has. He is the hardboiled Capt Flagg, and his role gets far greater sympathy than

that of Sergeant Quirt, which Edmund Lowe plays.

As for the Charmaine of Dolores Del Rio, she registers like a house afire. It is no wonder that she had the whole army after her.

To Raoul Walsh a great deal of credit will have to go. His handling of the war stuff is little short of marvelous.

● ●

■ WHAT PRICE GLORY

1952, 110 MINS, US ◇ ▼
Dir John Ford *Prod* Sol C. Siegel *Scr* Phoebe Ephron, Henry Ephron *Ph* Joe MacDonald *Ed* Dorothy Spencer *Mus* Alfred Newman *Art Dir* Lyle Wheeler, George W. Davis
● James Cagney, Dan Dailey, Corinne Calvet, William Demarest, Robert Wagner, Marisa Pavan (20th Century-Fox)

The durable heroics of *What Price Glory* undergo a comedic treatment in Technicolor for this fresh version of the Maxwell Anderson-Laurence Stallings stage drama.

James Cagney, a corpulent Captain Flagg who looks like he'll bust out of his britches any minute, and Dan Dailey, the braggard Sergeant Quirt, enact the top male roles as rivals for gals and glory with amusing emphasis on frenetics. Both are inclined to mumble or shout their dialog.

Corinne Calvet's charms are freely displayed as the ever-loving Charmaine, ready and willing to give any masculine ally of France aid and comfort.

Story scatters itself among episodes dealing with the marines in World War I and the professional and amatory rivalry of Cagney and Dailey.

Over the entire production is a feeling that at any second the picture will break into a musical production number. This doesn't happen, but it still serves as a subconscious distraction.

● ●

■ WHAT PRICE HOLLYWOOD

1932, 87 MINS, US ▼
Dir George Cukor *Scr* Gene Fowler, Rowland Brown, Jane Murfin, Ben Markson *Ph* Charles Rosher *Ed* Jack Kitchen *Mus* Max Steiner
● Constance Bennett, Lowell Sherman, Neil Hamilton, Gregory Ratoff (RKO-Pathe)

It's a fan magazine-ish interpretation of Hollywood plus a couple of twists. A waitress becomes a picture star, marries a wealthy playboy, loses him and gets him back when her screen career founders on the suicide of the director who gave her a start.

Director George Cukor tells it interestingly. Story [by Adela Rogers St John] has its exaggerations, but they can sneak under the line as theatrical license. In any case, there's Constance Bennett floating around smartly costumed for street or boudoir; Neil Hamilton is more pleasant than usual as the juvenile; Gregory Ratoff is closer to some film producers in his portrayal than the average audience will realize; and Lowell Sherman is again to the front with a fine interpretation of a derelict director.

● ●

■ WHAT'S NEW PUSSYCAT

1965, 108 MINS, US ◇ ▼
Dir Clive Donner *Prod* Charles K. Feldman *Scr* Woody Allen *Ph* Jean Badal *Ed* Fergus McDonnell *Mus* Burt Bacharach *Art Dir* Jacques Saulnier
● Peter Sellers, Peter O'Toole, Romy Schneider, Capucine, Paula Prentiss, Woody Allen (United Artists)

What's New Pussycat is designed as a zany farce, as wayout as can be reached on the screen. It's all that, and more ... it goes overboard in pressing for its goal and consequently suffers from over-contrived treatment.

The Charles K. Feldman production is peopled exclusively by mixed-up characters. Peter Sellers is a Viennese professor to whom Peter O'Toole, editor of a Parisian fashion magazine, goes for psychiatric help in solving his women problems, which keep piling up as he finds more pretty girls. On his part, Sellers has a jealous wife and a roving eye which keeps getting him into trouble.

Original screenplay by Woody Allen, who plays an un-dresser for strippers at the Crazy Horse Saloon and similarly afflicted with girl troubles – provides a field day for gagmen, who seldom miss a trick in inserting a sight gag.

Two top stars come off none too happily in their characterizations. Sellers' nuttiness knows no bounds as he speaks with a thick German accent, and O'Toole proves his forte in drama rather than comedy.

Trio of femmes who chase O'Toole have the proper looks and furnish as much glamor as any one man can take.

● ●

■ WHAT'S UP, DOC?

1972, 94 MINS, US ◇ ▼
Dir Peter Bogdanovich *Prod* Peter Bogdanovich *Scr* Buck Henry, Robert Benton, David Newman *Ph* Laszlo Kovacs *Ed* Verna Fields *Mus* Artie Butler *Art Dir* Polly Platt
● Barbra Streisand, Ryan O'Neal, Kenneth Mars, Austin Pendleton, Sorrell Booke, Stefan Gierasch (Saticoy/Warner)

Peter Bogdanovich's *What's Up, Doc?* is a contemporary comedy [from his own original story] in the screwball 1930s style, with absolutely no socially relevant values. This picture is a total smash.

The script and cast are excellent; the direction and comedy staging are outstanding; and there are literally reels of pure, unadulterated and sustained laughs.

Gimmick is a quartet of identical suitcases which of course get into the wrong hands. Barbra Streisand is discovered conning some food out of a hotel, where Ryan O'Neal and fiancee (Madeline Kahn) are attending a musicologists' convention. There is an unending stream of opening and closing doors, perilous balcony walks, and two terrific chases through San Francisco streets.

The humor derives much from the tradition of Warner Bros. cartoons, with broad visuals amid sophisticated ideas. One of the hilarious car chases is virtually a *Road Runner* storyboard, and there's absolutely nothing wrong about that.

● ●

■ WHAT'S UP, TIGER LILY?

1966, 79 MINS, US ◇ ▼
Dir Woody Allen *Prod* Henry G. Saperstein, Reuben Bercovitch *Scr* Woody Allen *Ph* Kazuo Yamada *Ed* Richard Krown *Mus* The Lovin' Spoonful
● Woody Allen, Tatsuya Mihashi, Mie Hama, Akiko Wakabayashi, Tadao Nakamura, Susumu Korobe (American International)

Take a Toho Films (Japan) crime meller, fashioned in the James Bond tradition for the domestic market there, then turn loose Woody Allen and associates to dub and re-edit in camp-comedy vein, and the result is *What's Up, Tiger Lily?* The production has one premise – deliberately mismatched dialog – which is sustained reasonably well through its brief running time.

Film opens cold with over three minutes of straightforward Japanese meller and chase footage until Allen pops in, explaining the format to follow. The Samurai posturing, to the non-sequitur dialog, is relieved regularly by stop-motion and other effects.

Allen's cohorts, both in writing and dubbing, are Frank Buxton, Len Maxwell, Louise

Lasser, Mickey Rose, Julie Bennett and
Bryna Wilson.

....

■ WHEN A STRANGER CALLS

1979, 97 MINS, US ◇ ▽
Dir Fred Walton   *Prod* Doug Chapin   *Scr* Steve Feke,
Fred Walton   *Ph* Don Peterman   *Ed* Sam Vitale
Mus Dana Kaproff   *Art Dir* Elayne Barbara Ceder
● Carol Kane, Charles Durning, Colleen Dewhurst,
Tony Beckley, Rachel Roberts, Rutanya Alda (Columbia)

Thanks to a fine cast, a rich and atmospheric
score by Dana Kaproff, and astute direction
by co-writer Fred Walton, *Stranger* is unquestionably a scary film. Bridging two distinct
storylines, one the standard frightened baby-
sitter alone in a dark house, and the other the
subsequent manhunt for an escaped killer,
script has chills a-plenty.

But something seems lacking overall. By
the film's end, the deficiency seems clear –
key actions and motivations just don't make
sense.

Carol Kane, who disappears for almost 70
of the film's 97 minutes, is quite good as the
terrified sitter who grows up to have the same
chilling chain of events begin all over again.

More than anything else, *When a Stranger
Calls* resembles a good, old-fashioned grade B
thriller.

....

■ WHEN EIGHT BELLS TOLL

1971, 94 MINS, UK ◇
Dir Etienne Perier   *Prod* Elliott Kastner   *Scr* Alistair
MacLean   *Ph* Arthur Ibbetson   *Ed* John Shirley
Art Dir Jack Maxsted
● Anthony Hopkins, Robert Morley, Nathalie Delon,
Jack Hawkins , Corin Redgrave, Derek Bond
(Gershwin-Kastner)

Alistair MacLean's two-fisted, no-holds-
barred adventure yarns are a natural for the
screen. *When Eight Bells Toll* brings in more
slugging, quick action twists, sharp dialog,
amusing acting than many pix twice its
length.

Anthony Hopkins has a role that creates a
character full of resource, courage, cheek and
personality. A kind of James Bond, without
the latter's trademarks. Character is a naval
secret service agent assigned to find out how
millions of pounds in gold bullion are being
pirated. He starts his explorations in the
bleakness of the Western Highlands of Scotland. Hopkins and his pal (Corin Redgrave)
posing as marine biologists find mystery and
hostility among the natives and the obvious
suspect is a suave, rich Greek tycoon (Jack
Hawkins) whose luxury yacht guests some
odd characters.

Main femme appeal comes from Nathalie
Delon as the mystery woman who is allegedly
Hawkins' wife but apparently goes over to
the Hopkins camp. Hawkins, himself, as the
Greek tycoon retains his usual stature and his
voice (lost to throat cancer) is very shrewdly
dubbed. Comedy relief comes from Robert
Morley, as Hopkins' snobbish, stuffy chief.

....

■ WHEN HARRY MET SALLY ...

1989, 95 MINS, US ◇ ▽
Dir Rob Reiner   *Prod* Rob Reiner, Andrew Scheinman
Scr Nora Ephron   *Ph* Barry Sonnenfeld   *Ed* Robert
Leighton   *Mus* Marc Shaiman   *Art Dir* Jane Musky
● Billy Crystal, Meg Ryan, Carrie Fisher, Bruno Kirby,
Steven Ford (Castle Rock/Nelson/Columbia)

Can a man be friends with a woman he finds
attractive? Can usually acerbic scripter Nora
Ephron sustain 95 minutes of unrelenting
cuteness? Can the audience sit through 11
years of emotional foreplay between adorable
Billy Crystal and Meg Ryan?

Abandoning the sour, nasty tone of some of
her previous writing about contemporary

sexual relationships, Ephron cuddles up to
the audience in this number about the joys
and woes of (mostly) platonic friendship.

Two characters who seem to have nothing
on their minds but each other (even though
they won't admit it), Harry and Sally are
supposed to be a political consultant and a
journalist, but it's hard to tell from the evidence presented.

Rob Reiner directs with deftness and sincerity, making the material seem more engaging than it is, at least until the plot mechanics
begin to unwind and the film starts to seem
shapeless. The only thing that's unpredictable about the story is how long it takes
Harry and Sally to realize they're perfect for
each other.

....

■ WHEN LADIES MEET

1933, 73 MINS, US
Dir Harry Beaumont   *Prod* Lawrence Weingarten
Scr John Meehan, Leon Gordon   *Ph* Ray June
Ed Hugh Wynn
● Ann Harding, Robert Montgomery, Myrna Loy, Alice
Brady, Frank Morgan, Luis Alberni (M-G-M)

Few stage plays reach the screen with the
author's idea. But here the adapters have
preserved the savor of the original [by Rachel
Crothers] while producing a generally mobile
atmosphere.

Story gets off to a typical picture start,
which will lead those unfamiliar with the
drama to fear another of those wild-life-in-
society yarns, but it soon steadies down into
nicely-paced action punctuated by plenty of
laughs that arise from the lines instead of
horseplay.

When the big scene between the two
women (Ann Harding and Myrna Loy) does
arrive, the spectator is so intrigued by the
characters that it is not necessary to frantically angle to conceal the fact that the chat
runs what might be overlong. It's interesting
and holds quiet attention, which is unusual.

The script is nicely planned with much of
the original dialog apparently preserved, and
Harry Beaumont does an exceptional job of
direction.

In addition to Harding's fine playing, Loy
does an excellent chore with the nominal
heroine as the ambitious young writer who
has fallen in love with her publisher. She
plays sincerely and naturally. Robert Montgomery does not quite get into his character.
On the other hand Alice Brady, in a fat part
as a socialite is dangerously close to running
away with the film now and then, and is
responsible for the major portion of laughs.

....

■ WHEN THE WHALES CAME

1989, 99 MINS, UK ◇ ▽
Dir Clive Rees   *Prod* Simon Channing Williams
Scr Michael Morpurgo   *Ph* Robert Paynter
Ed Andrew Boulton   *Mus* Christopher Gunning
Art Dir Bruce Grimes
● Paul Scofield, David Thelfall, Helen Mirren, David
Suchet, Helen Pearce (Golden Swan/Central)

When The Whales Came is a slight story beautifully dressed to give the appearance of more
substance. Performances, direction and
design are all first-rate, but there is the overwhelming sensation that there is a lot less
there then meets the eye.

Film [from the novel *Why the Whales Came*
by Michael Morpurgo] opens on the island of
Samson in the Scilly Isles in 1844 where
locals leave the island they believe cursed.
Then in 1914 on the neighbouring island of
Bryher youngsters Daniel (Max Rennie) and
Gracie (Helen Pearce) play on the beach,
watched by the mysterious Birdman (Paul
Scofield).

Though warned against Birdman by other
villagers they make friends with him and he
warns them about never going to Samson.

When a tusked whale (a narwhal) is
beached on the shore it seems the curse of
Samson will strike Bryher.

Paul Scofield's portrayal of the deaf Birdman has the quality of sadness and pride that
only he can give a role.

Most endearing performance is by radiant
young Pearce. A non-actor, she is a resident
of Bryher (where pic is set) and was only
found when she turned up for work as an
extra.

....

■ WHEN WORLDS COLLIDE

1951, 81 MINS, US ◇ ▽
Dir Rudolph Mate   *Prod* George Pal   *Scr* Sydney
Boehm   *Ph* John F. Seitz, W. Howard Greene
Ed Arthur Schmidt   *Mus* Leith Stevens   *Art Dir* Hal
Pereira, Albert Nozaki
● Richard Derr, Barbara Rush, Peter Hanson, John
Hoyt, Larry Keating, Judith Ames (Paramount)

Top honors for this inter-planetary fantasy
rest with the cameramen and special effects
technicians rather than with performances of
the non-name cast. Process photography and
optical illusions are done with an
imaginativeness that vicariously sweeps the
spectator into space.

Story is predicated upon the findings of a
scientist (Hayden Rorke) that a planet, Zyra,
will pass so close to the earth a year hence
that oceans will be pulled from their beds.
Moreover, 19 days after this catastrophe, the
star, Bellus, will collide with whatever
remains of the world.

Unfortunately, scripter Sydney Boehm who
fashioned the screenplay [from a novel by
Edwin Balmer and Philip Wylie], chose to
work in a romance between Barbara Rush,
daughter of astronomer Larry Keating, and
Richard Derr, a plane pilot. His love rival is
Peter Hanson, a doctor.

Departure, actual flight and landing upon
Zyra represent the highpoint of the picture.
Somewhat of a puzzle, however, is the fact
that although the ship lands upon an ice-
covered valley, its occupants step out into a
verdant paradise when opening the craft's
door.

....

■ WHERE EAGLES DARE

1968, 158 MINS, UK ◇ ▽
Dir Brian G. Hutton   *Prod* Jerry Gershwin, Elliot
Kastner   *Scr* Alistair MacLean   *Ph* Arthur Ibbetson
Ed John Jympson   *Mus* Ron Goodwin   *Art Dir* Peter
Mullins
● Richard Burton, Clint Eastwood, Mary Ure, Michael
Horden, Patrick Wymark (M-G-M/Winkast)

Alistair MacLean wrote an original screenplay that was treated with respect for the writer's unusual abilities as a master of actionful
suspense. The resulting film is highly entertaining, thrilling and rarely lets down for a
moment.

It's basically a tale of rescuing a captured
American general from a German stronghold
in Bavaria during World War II by a hand-
picked team of experts. There are so many
twists and turns that the viewer is seldom
able to predict the next scene.

Richard Burton, a British agent, and Clint
Eastwood, an OSS 'assassin', head the crew
which includes femme agent Mary Ure, who
works at the spy bit.

Although the film is replete with killings
and explosions, they're so integrated into the
story that they never appear overdone. It's
more of a saga of cool, calculated courage,
than any glorification of war.

Burton never treats his role, though full of
cliches, as anything less than *Hamlet*. Eastwood seems rather wooden in the early
scenes, but snaps out of it when action starts
piling up.

....

WHERE LOVE HAS GONE

1964, 111 MINS, US ⊚

Dir Edward Dmytryk   *Prod* Joseph E. Levine   *Scr* John Michael Hayes   *Ph* Joseph MacDonald   *Ed* Frank Bracht   *Mus* Walter Scharf   *Art Dir* Hal Pereira, Walter Tyler
● Susan Hayward, Bette Davis, Michael Connors, Joey Heatherton, Jane Greer, DeForest Kelley (Paramount)

Sooner or later it was bound to happen – a film based on the celebrated onetime Hollywood scandal of the daughter of a film star stabbing to death her mother's paramour. Picture takes its cue in close detail from this incident and patently was inspiration for the Harold Robbins novel. Scene is changed from Hollywood to San Francisco, and the mother now is a society woman with a bent for sculpture.

Sufficient ingenuity and shock value in character delineation have been interwoven into the screenplay to maintain high-tempoed interest as the yarn revolves around a bitter divorced couple come together again briefly to save their daughter after the 15-year-old girl kills her mother's lover.

Susan Hayward and Bette Davis share top honors in impressive performances, former as the daughter whose life is a story of indiscretions. Davis, smart in a white wig, plays the autocratic mother, who always sees that the family name is protected at any price, a scheming woman of unscrupulous methods and seemingless inexhaustible means. Picture is a brilliant showcase for both actresses and projects them in roles which will find much comment. As the mixed-up teenager who never knew domestic happiness, Joey Heatherton is ideally cast and delivers a compelling portrayal.

....

WHERE NO VULTURES FLY

1951, 106 MINS, UK ◇

Dir Harry Watt   *Prod* Michael Balcon, Leslie Norman   *Scr* W.P. Lipscomb. Ralph Smart, Leslie Norman   *Ph* Paul Beeson   *Ed* Gordon Stone   *Mus* Alan Rawsthorne
● Anthony Steel, Dinah Sheridan, Harold Warrender, Meredith Edwards, William Simons, Orlando Martins (Ealing)

Excellent Technicolor photography and a few thrilling wild animal sequences are the highlights of *Where No Vultures Fly*. On the whole, it's a soundly made film, lensed in the attractive East African setting of the Kenya National Park.

Merely as a peg for the fine location work, there is tagged on an insignificant though basically true story of a game warden who starts the National Park after fighting local prejudice, hunters and ivory poachers. Plot is of little consequence. Main entertainment is derived from some of the exciting animal sequences.

Harry Watt's direction of the game sequences is top grade, but he tends to flounder when handling human characters. Notwithstanding this, Anthony Steel, does an excellent and spirited job as the warden, but Dinah Sheridan is never anything but demure as his wife.

....

WHERE THE BUFFALO ROAM

1980, 96 MINS, US ◇ ⊚

Dir Art Linson   *Prod* Art Linson   *Scr* John Kaye   *Ph* Tak Fujimoto   *Ed* Christopher Greenbury   *Mus* Neil Young   *Art Dir* Richard Sawyer
● Peter Boyle, Bill Murray, Bruno Kirby, Rene Auberjonois, R.G. Armstrong (Universal)

Where the Buffalo Roam is based on the self-described antics of flip journalist Hunter S. Thompson, who cooperated as 'executive consultant'. Pic features a number of amus-ing set-pieces of irreverent lunacy, but lack of serious substance renders film too frivolous and detached from reality.

Film establishes its tone in the opening scene, as writer tries to finish a piece while downing full glasses of Wild Turkey.

Only things fortifying Thompson here are drink, drugs and the search for the insane in American culture.

Sole exceptional element is Bill Murray's clearly studied but provocatively off-beat performance as Thompson, which rings absolutely true.

....

WHERE THE HEART IS

1990, 94 MINS, US ◇

Dir John Boorman   *Prod* John Boorman   *Scr* John Boorman, Telsche Boorman   *Ph* Peter Suschitzky   *Ed* Ian Crafford   *Mus* Peter Martin   *Art Dir* Carol Spier
● Dabney Coleman, Uma Thurman, Joanna Cassidy, David Hewlett, Susy Amis, Christopher Plummer (Touchstone/Silver Screen Partners IV)

Film is a companion piece to John Boorman's little-seen *Leo the Last*, in which Marcello Mastroianni was an aristocrat who learns about life from ghetto denizens in London. This time it's tycoon Dabney Coleman who gets the message when he and his family end up in a Brooklyn tenement.

Predictable plotting has tyrannical buildings demolitions expert Coleman getting fed up with his spoiled, grown-up kids. He throws them out of the mansion and (unconvincingly) orders them to live in a Brooklyn tenement.

Kids, led by Uma Thurman, are determined to make it on their own. Her sister (Suzy Amis) gets a gig doing a calendar for an insurance company, with Thurman the chief nude model for her body-painting and photography artwork.

Film's most successful element is the series of spectacular *trompe d'oeil* artworks by Timna Woollard, personified by Thurman. Combined with the all-nighter atmosphere of the delapidated Brooklyn house, pic succeeds in capturing a 1960s ambience.

Beside Thurman, who is perfectly cast as a sexy kook, Amis makes a very good impression as her artistic, romantic sister.

....

WHERE THE RIVER RUNS BLACK

1986, 100 MINS, US ◇ ⊚

Dir Christopher Cain   *Prod* Joe Roth   *Scr* Peter Silverman, Neal Jimenez   *Ph* Juan Ruiz-Anchia   *Ed* Richard Chew   *Mus* James Horner   *Art Dir* Marcos Flaksman
● Charles Durning, Alessandro Rabelo, Ajay Naidu, Peter Horton, Conchata Ferrell (M-G-M)

Where the River Runs Black is a beautifully simple film that celebrates an innocent boy's peaceful co-existence with nature while subtly despairing about man's abuse of it.

Film revolves around a boy with roots in modern civilization being raised by Amazon tribespeople without the knowledge he is the child of two very distinct worlds.

Scripters Peter Silverman and Neal Jimenez have taken David Kendall's novel, *Lazaro*, and crafted a screenplay where the few words of dialog spoken speak worlds of meaning.

Much is said in silence and most effectively told through the movements of 10-year-old Rabelo, a waif-like Brazilian swimmer perfectly cast to portray the physically and emotionally confused dolphin boy traumatized by competing forces. Charles Durning is a natural as a fatherly Irish priest, letting his heart – not the fact that he wears a collar – determine the ultimate fate of the orphan boy.

....

WHERE THE SIDEWALK ENDS

1950, 95 MINS, US

Dir Otto Preminger   *Prod* Otto Preminger   *Scr* Ben Hecht   *Ph* Joseph La Shelle   *Ed* Louis Loeffler   *Mus* Cyril J. Mockridge
● Dana Andrews, Gene Tierney, Gary Merrill, Karl Malden, Tom Tully, Ruth Donnelly (20th Century-Fox)

Story, by Ben Hecht [adapted by Victor Trivas, Frank P. Rosenberg and Robert E. Kent from a novel by William Stuart], unwinds with a maximum of suspense and swiftly-paced action and is featured by an excellent performance by Dana Andrews. Picture is also notable for better-than-average character portrayals and co-star Gene Tierney.

Andrews, while he is on the carpet for slugging too many hoodlums before he has criminal evidence against them, accidentally kills a man in a fistic battle, in self-defense. Victim is Craig Stevens, former war hero and ne'er-do-well estranged husband of Gene Tierney, a lush model.

Otto Preminger, director, does an excellent job of pacing the story and of building sympathy for Andrews.

....

WHERE THE SPIES ARE

1966, 113 MINS, UK ◇

Dir Val Guest   *Prod* Val Guest, Steven Pallos   *Scr* Wolf Mankowitz, Val Guest   *Ph* Arthur Grant   *Ed* Bill Lenny   *Mus* Mario Nascimbene   *Art Dir* John Howell
● David Niven, Francoise Dorleac, Cyril Cusack, John Le Mesurier, Nigel Davenport, Eric Pohlmann (M-G-M)

David Niven stars as a mild-mannered English doctor pressed into Middle East espionage. The production carries suspense, after a slow and talky start, and action, even if a bit on the contrived side, is fast-paced once story gets underway. Locale is Beirut where troupe locationed to come up with interesting authenticity of background.

Based on James Leasor's thriller, *Passport to Oblivion*, Guest, who also directs and collabed with Wolf Mankowitz on script, concentrates on the dangers confronting a secret agent. Niven, who once figured in some fancy undercover work for British Intelligence, is sent to Lebanon to try to learn what urgent information the agent there had uncovered before he was bumped off by the Russians.

Niven delivers one of his customary competent performances, stuffy at times but able to cope with the melodramatic demands of the character. Teaming with Niven as a French mam'selle playing both sides as a secret agent and supposedly his contact is Francoise Dorleac, lushly effective.

....

WHERE WERE YOU WHEN THE LIGHTS WENT OUT?

1968, 90 MINS, US ◇

Dir Hy Averback   *Prod* Everett Freeman, Martin Melcher   *Scr* Everett Freeman, Karl Tunberg   *Ph* Ellsworth Fredricks   *Ed* Rita Roland   *Mus* Dave Grusin   *Art Dir* George W. Davis, Urie McCleary
● Doris Day, Robert Morse, Terry-Thomas, Patrick O'Neal, Lola Albright (M-G-M)

An okay Doris Day comedy, well cast with Robert Morse and Terry-Thomas. On 9 November 1965, large parts of the eastern US were blacked out. Almost six months later, this film was announced. Some 15 months later, it rolled. And over 30 months after the event, it was released. How's that for reacting to events?

In this script, the blackout is less than a prop for a routine marital mixup. Day, as a legit actress employed by producer Thomas, is married to architect Patrick O'Neal. Latter lingers a bit too long with sexy magazine interviewer Lola Albright, cueing Day's stormy exit to Connecticut hideaway. Simultaneously, Morse, aced out of being made president of his company by nepotism, steals a pile of money.

Averback's comedy direction lifts things a bit out of a well-plowed rut, making for an amusing, while never hilarious, film.

- -

■ WHERE'S JACK?

1969, 113 MINS, UK ◇
Dir James Clavell   *Prod* Stanley Baker   *Scr* Rafe Newhouse, David Newhouse   *Ph* John Wilcox   *Ed* Peter Thornton   *Mus* Elmer Bernstein
● Tommy Steele, Stanley Baker, Fiona Lewis, Alan Badel, Dudley Foster, Noel Purcell (Paramount/Oakhurst)

Where's Jack, story of Jack Sheppard, notorious 18th-century London highwayman, does not move speedily or with tremendous dramatic climaxes, but it has an authentic sense of atmosphere, and provides a holding battle of wits between the two leading protagonists.

Tommy Steele and Stanley Baker are supported by a competent cast of character actors.

Steele turns in a good acting performance. Unfortunately, the script does not give him much chance to give the role any depth.

Where's Jack? could well have been a more impressive picture about a colorful era in bawdy, criminal, corrupt London. But film has settled for a single adventure and, despite occasional lagging in inventiveness, is a simple and holding yarn.

- -

■ WHERE'S POPPA?

1970, 83 MINS, US ◇ ⓥ
Dir Carl Reiner   *Prod* Jerry Tokofsky, Marvin Worth   *Scr* Robert Klane   *Ph* Jack Priestly   *Ed* Bud Molin, Chic Ciccolini   *Mus* Jack Elliott   *Art Dir* Warren Clymer
● George Segal, Ruth Gordon, Ron Liebman, Trish Van Devere, Barnard Hughes, Vincent Gardenia (United Artists)

Where's Poppa? is an insane movie, a black comedy with George Segal as a young lawyer with an active death wish for his old Jewish mother, played by Ruth Gordon, whose senile eccentricities are ruining his career, sex life and health.

Robert Klane's screenplay, adapted from his novel, is very close to tragedy, except that he, director Carl Reiner and an exceptional cast work from the firm conviction that everyone, at least everyone living in New York city, is insane.

Gordon, as the widowed mother, is in senile dementia constantly asking 'Where's Poppa?' and scaring off nurses and Segal's girlfriends with her bawdy eccentricities.

In her mental lapses she can't remember her son is a grown man, and when he brings home Trish Van Devere the mother suddenly describes the size of her son's sex organs as if he were a child.

Van Devere as a prospective nurse looks like the Angel of Mercy with her sweet pure face framed in a white cap, but she is also a little insane.

- -

■ WHILE THE CITY SLEEPS

1956, 99 MINS, US ⓥ
Dir Fritz Lang   *Prod* Bert E. Friedlob   *Scr* Casey Robinson   *Ph* Ernest Laszlo   *Ed* Gene Fowler Jr   *Mus* Herschel Burke Gilbert   *Art Dir* Carroll Clark
● Dana Andrews, Ida Lupino, Rhonda Fleming, George Sanders, Vincent Price, Howard Duff (RKO)

The old-fashioned 'stop the presses' newspaper yarn has been updated with intelligence and considerable authenticity, and further brightened with crisp dialog from the pen of Casey Robinson. His screen adaptation of Charles Einstein's novel weaves several story lines together.

Among them are the murderous activities of a homicidal maniac, played by John Barrymore Jr; a scramble for power among the top brass of a newspaper empire; and a good-natured love story between the paper's top reporter, played by Dana Andrews, and Sally Forrest, the secretary of one of the contestants.

When the empire's chieftain, played by Robert Warwick, dies, his son, Vincent Price, decides to set up a new top exec post for grabs. Contenders are: Thomas Mitchell, editor of the keystone paper; George Sanders, head of the empire's wire service; and James Craig, dapper photo bureau chief.

Price lets it be known that the one to crack the wave of murders being committed by Barrymore gets the job. Sanders and Mitchell commence heartily to cut each other's throats, while Craig puts the pressure, literally and figuratively, on Fleming.

Plot intricacies are deftly interwoven, with director Fritz Lang doing a topflight job of balancing the ingredients without dragging the pace.

- -

■ WHIRLPOOL

1949, 97 MINS, US
Dir Otto Preminger   *Prod* Otto Preminger   *Scr* Ben Hecht, Andrew Solt   *Ph* Arthur Miller   *Ed* Louis Loeffler   *Mus* David Raksin
● Gene Tierney, Richard Conte, Jose Ferrer, Charles Bickford, Barbara O'Neil (20th Century-Fox)

Whirlpool is a highly entertaining, exciting melodrama that combines the authentic features of hypnosis.

Ben Hecht and Andrew Solt have tightly woven a screenplay [from a novel by Guy Endore] about the effects of hypnosis on the subconscious, but they, and Otto Preminger in his direction, have eliminated the phoney characteristics that might easily have allowed the picture to slither into becoming just another eerie melodrama.

Their subject is a young wife of a prominent psychiatrist who, since adolescence, has been plagued by kleptomania.

As the young wife, Gene Tierney gives a plausible performance, though at times she fails to achieve the intensity that the entranced woman should have. Richard Conte, as her husband, is a little out of his metier here. The acting honors go to Jose Ferrer as the blackguard hypnotist.

- -

■ WHISKY GALORE!

1949, 82 MINS, UK ⓥ
Dir Alexander Mackendrick   *Prod* Michael Balcon   *Scr* Compton Mackenzie, Angus MacPhail   *Ph* Gerald Gibbs, Chick Waterson   *Ed* Joseph Sterling   *Mus* Ernest Irving   *Art Dir* Jim Morahan
● Basil Radford, Joan Greenwood, Gordon Jackson, James Robertson Justice, Bruce Seaton, Gabrielle Blunt (Ealing)

Compton Mackenzie's novel, on which the pic is based, is unfolded on a Hebridean island in 1943. Only sign of the war is the local Home Guard, but a major disaster occurs when the island runs out of whisky. After some days a freighter with 50,000 cases of Scotch runs aground off the island. The natives organize a midnight expedition and lay in a tremendous store for future consumption.

Sustained comedy treatment successfully carries the film forward to the point where the islanders outwit the Home Guard captain who regards the adventure as the worst type of looting.

Basil Radford gives a flawless performance of the misunderstood Home Guard chief whose zealousness leads to trouble in high quarters. Bruce Seton and Joan Greenwood

as well as Gabrielle Blunt and Gordon Jackson provide the slight romances of the film.

- -

■ WHISPERERS, THE

1966, 103 MINS, UK
Dir Bryan Forbes   *Prod* Michael S. Laughlin, Ronald Shedlo   *Scr* Bryan Forbes   *Ph* Gerry Turpin   *Ed* Anthony Harvey   *Mus* John Barry   *Art Dir* Ray Sims
● Edith Evans, Eric Portman, Nanette Newman, Gerald Sim, Avis Bunnage, Ronald Fraser (United Artists)

Low-budgeter [from a novel by Robert Nicolson] centers around an old woman, estranged from her husband, who lives alone in a broken-down, tiny flat in a slummy outskirt of a British town. Her imaginary dream of sudden riches due her from a relative unexpectedly comes true one day when her son hides the haul of a robbery in her spare room, and she finds it.

Few other films have attacked the unglamorous but poignant theme of old-age loneliness with such understated feeling and unsentimental taste and discretion.

It has in Edith Evans' great performance an invaluable asset. Her portrayal of the ageing woman, now living on the near edge of insanity but unbowed by other physical hazards, determinedly struggling ahead in her waning fight for life, but head high, without complaints, makes the film.

- -

■ WHISTLE BLOWER, THE

1987, 104 MINS, UK ◇ ⓥ
Dir Simon Langton   *Prod* Geoffrey Reeve   *Scr* Julian Bond   *Ph* Fred Tammes   *Ed* Bob Morgan   *Mus* John Scott   *Art Dir* Morley Smith
● Michael Caine, James Fox, Nigel Havers, Felicity Dean, John Gielgud, Gordon Jackson (Reeve/Portreeve)

The Whistle Blower [from John Hale's novel] is a highly charged conspiracy theory drama. A murdered man, played by Nigel Havers, worked as a Russian translator at the top-secret listening center, GCHQ, in Cheltenham.

Michael Caine is excellent as his father, a role rather similar to that played by Jack Lemmon in *Missing* – a non-political, middle-aged man who's driven to radical action as a result of what the government he once trusted has done to his son.

The central sections, as Caine doggedly insists on finding out who killed his son and why, are tautly handled, creating considerable tension. Unfortunately, the film ends rather lamely, almost as if the writer wasn't sure how to finish it.

- -

■ WHISTLE DOWN THE WIND

1961, 99 MINS, UK ⓥ
Dir Bryan Forbes   *Prod* Richard Attenborough, Bryan Forbes   *Scr* Keith Waterhouse, Willis Hall   *Ph* Arthur Ibbetson   *Ed* Max Benedict   *Mus* Malcolm Arnold   *Art Dir* Ray Simm
● Hayley Mills, Alan Bates, Bernard Lee, Norman Bird, Elsie Wagstaff, John Arnatt (Rank/Allied Film Makers)

Whistle down the Wind takes a modern, sentimental-religious subject and treats it with care, taste, sincerity, imagination and good humor. The film was shot entirely on location in the bleak, raw countryside around Burnley in Lancashire, superbly caught by Arthur Ibbetson's camerawork.

Based on Mary Hayley Bell's novel, it is a slight but human story of faith seen through the eyes of children. Three small children, leading a lonely life on their father's farm, stumble on a ragged, unshaven man taking refuge in their barn. Startled when a terrified Hayley Mills asks who he is, the stranger is so relieved at finding the intruder is merely a child that he involuntarily swears 'Jesus . . .

Christ.' The children take the remark lit-erally. In fact, the man is a murderer on the run.

There are many pieces of New Testament symbolism but they arise naturally from the action. For instance, the betrayal is inno-cently done by a child at a birthday party. The local bully twists a smaller boy's arm and three times makes him deny that the fug-itive is, indeed, Jesus Christ. Finally, when the police close in and frisk him, he stands with arms raised quite naturally, but the im-plication of the Crucifixion is clear in the pose.

Bryan Forbes in his debut as a director coaxes some outstanding performances from a bunch of local kids. Only their leader, young Mills, ever saw a script before. Result is complete authenticity. Alan Bates as the mysterious stranger handles a very difficult role brilliantly.

WHITE BUFFALO, THE

1977, 97 MINS, US ◇ Ⓥ

Dir J. Lee Thompson *Prod* Pancho Kohner
Scr Richard Sale *Ph* Paul Lohmann *Ed* Michael F. Anderson *Mus* John Barry *Art Dir* Tambi Larsen
● Charles Bronson, Jack Warden, Will Sampson, Kim Novak, Clint Walker, Stuart Whitman (De Laurentiis)

Charles Bronson stars as Wild Bill Hickok, returned to the West to hunt down an albino buffalo that haunts his dreams. Will Sampson is an Indian who also must purge himself of some dishonor.

Production features arch scripting by Richard Sale (from his novel), stilted acting by the cast and forced direction by J. Lee Thompson.

The title beast looks like a hung-over carnival prize despite attempts at camouflage via hokey sound track noise, busy John Barry scoring, murky photography and fast editing.

The buffalo trackdown is actually more of a cheap writing hook, on which to hang a lot of dubious sociological gab between the players, than an outdoor adventure story.

WHITE CARGO

1942, 89 MINS, US

Dir Richard Thorpe *Prod* Victor Saville *Scr* Leon Gordon *Ph* Harry Stradling *Ed* Frederick Y. Smith *Mus* Bronislau Kaper
● Hedy Lamarr, Walter Pidgeon, Frank Morgan, Richard Carlson, Reginald Owen (M-G-M)

This is the first American-made version of the sensational stage hit produced in 1923 by Earl Carroll in Greenwich Village, NY. From that downtown area Carroll moved the Leon Gordon play [from a novel by Ida Vera Simonton] to Broadway for a boxoffice mopup. The very fact that the entire action revolved around the passion of a white man, disintegrating in a tropical English colony, for a half-breed made it surefire for the then jazz and flapper era.

Playwright Leon Gordon adapted his own play for the screen and he hews closely to the original, even to holding off Tondelayo's first entrance until the film is 30 minutes old.

Walter Pidgeon plays well the part of the tough English magistrate of the colony who has to wet-nurse a succession of novices from the home country. Hedy Lamarr as the only femme in the film does her best acting to date.

WHITE CHRISTMAS

1954, 120 MINS, US ◇ Ⓥ

Dir Michael Curtiz *Prod* Robert Emmett Dolan
Scr Norman Krasna, Norman Panama, Melvin Frank
Ph Loyal Griggs *Ed* Frank Bracht *Mus* Joseph J. Lilley *Art Dir* Hal Pereira, Roland Anderson

● Bing Crosby, Danny Kaye, Rosemary Clooney, Vera-Ellen, Dean Jagger, Mary Wickes (Paramount)

Bing Crosby and Danny Kaye, along with Vista Vision, keep the entertainment going in this fancifully staged production, clicking well.

The directorial handling by Michael Curtiz gives a smooth blend of music (13 numbers plus snatches of others) and drama, and in the climax creates a genuine heart tug that will squeeze tears.

The plot holding the entire affair together has Crosby and Kaye, two Army buddies, joining forces after the war and becoming a big musical team. They get together with the girls and trek to Vermont for a white Christ-mas. The inn at which they stay is run by Dean Jagger, their old general, and the boys put on a show to pull him out of a financial hole.

Crosby wraps up his portion of the show with deceptive ease, shuffling a mean hoof in the dances and generally acquitting himself like a champion. Kaye takes in stride the dance, song and comedy demands of his assignment, keeping Crosby on his toes at all times.

WHITE DAWN, THE

1974, 109 MINS, US ◇ Ⓥ

Dir Philip Kaufman *Prod* Martin Ransohoff
Scr James Houston, Tom Rickman *Ph* Michael Chapman *Ed* Douglas Stewart *Mus* Henry Mancini
● Warren Oates, Timothy Bottoms, Lou Gossett, Simonie Kopapik, Joanasie Salomone, Pilitak (Paramount)

James Houston's 1971 book, subtitled *An Eskimo Saga*, is the springboard for this production. Both limn the tale of how a trio of whaleboaters, stranded in the late 1890s near the North Pole, interact with and nearly destroy the band of Eskimos who saved their lives. But while the book had a logic and sensitivity of its own, the film version emerges as a static narrative.

Essentially, the three whalers bring familiar baggage to the pristine setting of the Eskimo village – they find ways of making booze, they gamble, they take advantage of village women, they steal, etc. Although each member of the trio is by no means uniform in his misconduct – Billy (Warren Oates) is easily the most nefarious – collective behaviour is at first accepted by the Eskimos, then tolerated and then viewed with a deepseated displeasure.

Oates is properly blustery as the roistering older sea hand.

WHITE DOG

1982, 90 MINS, US ◇ Ⓥ

Dir Samuel Fuller *Prod* Jon Davison *Scr* Samuel Fuller, Curtis Hanson *Ph* Bruce Surtees *Ed* Bernard Gribble *Mus* Ennio Morricone *Art Dir* Brian Eatwell
● Kristy McNichol, Paul Winfield, Burl Ives, Jameson Parker, Lynne Moody, Marshall Thompson (Paramount)

White Dog is an unusual, often powerful study of racism in the guise of a man vs animal suspenser. Too unevenly balanced and single-minded to work completely, Samuel Fuller's first Hollywood picture in 18 years nevertheless packs a provocative punch.

Curtis Hanson and Fuller have fashioned an intense yarn about an up-and-coming LA actress (Kristy McNichol) who takes in a German shepherd after she hits it with her car, only to discover that her new pet is a deadly White Dog, trained from birth to hate anyone with black skin.

Pic really gets down to business when McNichol takes the dog to Burl Ives' Noah's Ark animal compound, where scientist-trainer Paul Winfield quickly becomes obsessed with the idea of curing the beast of

its racism. Set in an enormous cage reminiscent of a gladiatorial arena, Win-field's very physical attempts to wear the dog down are effectively elemental.

McNichol is very fine as a modern gal who becomes devoted to the dog, as well as Win-field's cause, in a totally unsentimental way.

WHITE HUNTER, BLACK HEART

1990, 110 MINS, US ◇ Ⓥ

Dir Clint Eastwood *Prod* Clint Eastwood *Scr* Peter Viertel, James Bridges, Burt Kennedy *Ph* Jack N. Green *Ed* Joel Cox *Mus* Lennie Niehaus
Art Dir John Graysmark
● Clint Eastwood, Jeff Fahey, George Dzundza, Alun Armstrong, Marisa Berenson, Richard Vanstone (Malpaso/Rastar)

Clint Eastwood's film isn't an African adven-ture epic, as those unaware of Peter Viertel's 1953 book may surmise from the title. It's an intelligent, affectionate study of an obsessive American film director who, while working on a film in colonial Africa, becomes side-tracked by his compulsion to hunt elephants.

Though the end credits note that this is 'a work of fiction' this is clearly a story about John Huston and the preproduction period for *The African Queen* (called *The African Trader* here). Eastwood plays the Huston character with obvious appreciation of the man: he wears Huston clothes and hats, assumes Hus-ton mannerisms, smokes Huston cigars and speaks with the characteristic Huston timbre.

The first 20 minutes of the pic unfold in England, where Wilson is living in a splendid old stately home as if he were a country squire. It's here that Wilson welcomes Pete Verrell (Jeff Fahey), his biographer, and it's from Verrell's perspective that the events unfold. Once the film crew moves to Africa, it becomes clear that Wilson's interest in mak-ing the film takes second place to his im-practical passion for big-game hunting.

WHITE LIGHTNING

1973, 100 MINS, US ◇ Ⓥ

Dir Joseph Sargent *Prod* Arthur Gardner, Jules V. Levy *Scr* William Norton *Ph* Edward Rosson *Ed* George Nicholson *Mus* Charles Bernstein
● Burt Reynolds, Jennifer Billingsley, Ned Beatty, Bo Hopkins, Matt Clark, Diane Ladd (United Artists)

Cast as an expert auto driver doing time in a Southern state prison for running bootleg whiskey, Burt Reynolds makes a deal with US Treasury agents to help them trap a gang of bootleggers on income tax evasion. Pitch for his freedom to act as an undercover man is made after he learns that a sheriff on the take is the probable murderer of his brother.

He's helped by another undercover man (Matt Clark) and a daredevil driver (Bo Hopkins) from whom Reynolds proceeds to steal his gal (Jennifer Billingsworth).

Joseph Sargent's direction is particularly effective in the light and auto-chasing se-quences, latter a field day for stunt drivers and occasionally incorporating humorous bits of biz. Reynolds is quite up to all the demands of his smashing role.

WHITE LINE FEVER

1975, 89 MINS, US/CANADA ◇

Dir Jonathan Kaplan *Prod* John Kemeny *Scr* Ken Friedman, Jonathan Kaplan *Ph* Fred Koenekamp *Ed* O. Nicholas Brown *Mus* David Nichtern *Art Dir* Sydney Litwack
● Jan-Michael Vincent, Kay Lenz, Slim Pickens, L.Q. Jones, Don Porter, Sam Laws (Columbia/International Cinemedia)

White Line Fever is a good action drama star-ring Jan-Michael Vincent as a young truck driver fighting corruption.

Air Force vet Vincent returns home to marriage with Kay Lenz and starting in as an independent trucker. He soon finds smuggling to be endemic to the career, and is repeatedly and violently hassled when he refuses to go along.

What seems missing from the film is more depth and logical transition: Vincent passes too rapidly from a stubborn honest lone wolf to practically a union leader.

With stunt experts Carey Loftin, Nate Long and Joe Hooker creating some powerful action footage, Vincent and Lenz experience assaults, fires, beatings and other troubles sent their way by L.Q. Jones and others, all under orders from Don Porter.

● ●

■ **WHITE MISCHIEF**

1987, 107 MINS, US ◇ Ⓥ
Dir Michael Radford   *Prod* Simon Perry   *Scr* Michael Radford, Jonathan Gems   *Ph* Roger Deakins   *Ed* Tom Priestley   *Mus* George Fenton   *Art Dir* Roger Hall
● Sarah Miles, Joss Ackland, John Hurt, Greta Scacchi, Charles Dance, Susan Fleetwood (Nelson/Goldcrest/Umbrella/Power Tower/BBC)

White Mischief goes back into Africa with a vengeance. It glossily portrays the flip side of colonial life, exposing the opulent and lush – but downright debauched – lifestyle of the British 'Happy Valley' crowd in Kenya during the war years [from the book by James Fox].

Pic opens in 1940 with newlyweds 'Jock' Broughton (Joss Ackland) and Diana (Greta Scacchi) about to leave England for the British colony in Nairobi. He needs a wife and she wants the money and a title, but when Diana meets handsome Erroll (Charles Dance) in Nairobi the scene is set for some philandering.

With stoical British reserve Broughton seemingly accepts the affair, even suggesting a celebratory dinner for the couple when they announce their plans to go away together. Later that night Erroll is shot through the head while in his car. Suspects for the murder are plentiful and the scandal means the end of the Happy Valley set and their dalliances. In real life the Erroll murderer was never found.

Dance and Scacchi are fine in the lead roles, with Scacchi certainly looking desirable and elegant bedecked in stunning costumes and sporting a seemingly endless collection of sunglasses.

● ●

■ **WHITE NIGHTS**

1985, 135 MINS, US ◇ Ⓥ
Dir Taylor Hackford   *Prod* Taylor Hackford, William S. Gilmore   *Scr* James Goldman, Eric Hughes   *Ph* David Watkin   *Ed* Fredric Steinkamp, William Steinkamp   *Mus* Michel Colombier   *Art Dir* Philip Harrison
● Mikhail Baryshnikov, Gregory Hines, Jerzy Skolimowski, Helen Mirren, Geraldine Page, Isabella Rossellini (Columbia-Delphi V/New Visions)

At its core *White Nights* is a political thriller about the dilemma of a famous Russian defector who, after a plane crash, finds himself trapped back in his mother country. However, pic shies away from the world of classical dance, personified by leading man Mikhail Baryshnikov, in favor of Gregory Hines' 'improvography' and assorted modern stuff in blatant music video contexts.

Mix all this in with KGB intrigue, racial tensions, numerous emotional breakdowns and several suspense sequences, all played at the broadest levels of melodrama, and one has quite a mish-mash indeed.

Without so much as an interrogation by the KGB, Baryshnikov is moved to the dingy Siberian residence of Hines, a black American tap dancer who jumped to the other side

during Vietnam, and his Russian wife Isabella Rossellini.

The trio is installed in Baryshnikov's luxurious old apartment in Leningrad, and the dancer is expected to begin preparations for a triumphant homecoming at the Kirov. Inevitably, an escape attempt is the climax.

Hines plays a bitter, ornery man with a quick trigger. Rossellini, in her Hollywood film debut, has disappointingly little to do.

● ●

■ **WHITE OF THE EYE**

1987, 110 MINS, UK ◇ Ⓥ
Dir Donald Cammell   *Prod* Cassian Elwes, Brad Wyman   *Scr* Donald Cammell, China Cammell   *Ph* Alan Jones, Larry McConkey   *Ed* Terry Rawlings   *Mus* George Fenton (sup.), Nick Mason, Rick Fenn
● David Keith, Cathy Moriarty, Art Evans, Alan Rosenberg, Alberta Watson, Michael Greene (Kastner/Cannon/Mrs Whites)

White of the Eye is an intriguing thriller [from the novel *Mrs White* by Margaret Tracy].

Beneath the layers of flashbacks and at times almost subliminal imagery is a conventional storyline. Sound expert Paul White (David Keith), living in a small Arizona town, is having marital problems with frau Joan (Cathy Moriarty). Circumstantial evidence points strongly at Keith, with cop Mendoza (Art Evans) in from Phoenix to hound him in the case of a serial murder who mutilates the corpses of his wealthy housewife victims.

With lots of clues and red herrings introduced in the early reels (including a heavy emphasis on 10 years earlier 16mm blow up flashbacks of Moriarty first meeting Keith while trekking westward with her boyfriend Alan Rosenberg), picture maintains considerable suspense.

Moriarty is quite forceful here. Keith likewise creates a powerful figure, until the mystery is fully out of the bag.

● ●

■ **WHITE PALACE**

1990, 104 MINS, US ◇ Ⓥ
Dir Luis Mandoki   *Prod* Mark Rosenberg, Amy Robinson, Griffin Dunne   *Scr* Ted Tally, Alvin Sargent   *Ph* Lajos Koltai   *Ed* Carol Littleton   *Mus* George Fenton   *Art Dir* Jeannine Claudia Oppewall
● Susan Sarandon, James Spader, Jason Alexander, Kathy Bates, Eileen Brennan, Steven Hill (Universal/Mirage/Double Play)

Outstanding performances by Susan Sarandon and James Spader, working from a relentlessly witty script, make *White Palace* one of the best films of its kind since *The Graduate* (1967).

Sarandon is Nora, a 43-year-old fast-food worker who gets involved with a 27-year-old advertising exec – the same sort of character Spader played in *Pretty in Pink*, now mellowed and matured. Both have experienced terrible loss – Max (Spader) is a widower; Nora's child has died – and they share a magnetic sexual attraction.

Their *Odd Couple* differences, however, include class, religion and hygiene (he's a buttoned-down neat freak; she's a gregarious slob) in addition to the Mrs Robinson-esque age discrepancy.

The ferocity that director Luis Mandoki brings to the pair's early love scenes helps establish how two people can fall into lust and worry about love later.

Raunchy yet vulnerable, Sarandon carefully avoids the cliches that might have been associated with Nora. Spader continues to establish himself as star material, especially when it comes to playing self-conscious yuppies.

● ●

■ **WHITE PARADE, THE**

1934, 80 MINS, US
Dir Irving Cummings   *Prod* Jesse L. Lasky   *Scr* Sonya Levien, Ernest Pascal   *Ph* Arthur Miller
● Loretta Young, John Boles, Dorothy Wilson, Muriel Kirkland, Astrid Allwyn, Frank Conroy (Fox)

The White Parade is a woman's picture, but also for general appeal. The stern curriculum which goes towards the moulding of the 'white parade', the present-day Florence Nightingales who are dedicated to the service of humankind, and all the other details that go towards the schooling of the modern nurse are deftly, graphically, punchily and sometimes heart-throbbingly depicted [from the novel by Rian James, adapted by James and Jesse L. Lasky Jr].

Loretta Young is altogether convincing as the sympathetic femme novitiate who has consecrated herself to her profession. Dorothy Wilson is a fine little actress. Muriel Kirkland in a more hoydenish role registers, as do Astrid Allwyn as a light heavy, and Joyce Compton in one of those Una Merkel Dixie drawleries.

Frank Conroy is given the toughest male assignment as the mature medico of stern mien who must make some of his hypersolemnous lines read convincingly. John Boles, though the featured vis-a-vis, is handicapped and limited by his role. Polo-playing Boston playboys who fall for nurses are tough to make real, but he manages quite well.
□ 1934: Best Picture (Nomination)

● ●

■ **WHO?**

1974, 93 MINS, UK/W. GERMANY ◇
Dir Jack Gold   *Prod* Barry Levinson, Kurt Berthold   *Scr* John Gould   *Ph* Petrus Schlomp   *Ed* Norman Wanstall   *Mus* John Cameron   *Art Dir* Peter Scharff
● Elliott Gould, Trevor Howard, Joe Bova, Ed Grover, James Noble, Lyndon Brook (Lion International/Hemisphere)

Adapted from Algis Budrys' novel by British playwright John Gould, *Who?* is an action-espionage thriller examining, from a science fiction perspective, the nature of identity.

Joe Bova gives a beautiful, underplayed performance as diminutive US scientist Martino, whose face and arm are remade in metal after an accident in Berlin. The film's mystery-suspense plot derives from iterated flashbacks showing Martino grilled and/or indoctrinated by East German intelligence officer Azarin (Trevor Howard).

Once back in the US, Martino is subjected to gruelling questioning and investigation by FBI operative Rogers (Elliott Gould) to check his new security clearance for continuing a top secret research project in Florida. Gould examines the reactions of Martino's old associates to his transformed, robot-like appearance.

Gould brings humor to the assignment. Howard is seen only in the flashbacks.

● ●

■ **WHO DARES WINS**

1982, 125 MINS, UK ◇ Ⓥ
Dir Ian Sharp   *Prod* Euan Lloyd   *Scr* Reginald Rose   *Ph* Phil Meheux   *Ed* John Grover   *Mus* Roy Budd   *Art Dir* Syd Cain
● Lewis Collins, Judy Davis, Richard Widmark, Edward Woodward, Robert Webber, Tony Doyle (Rank)

Who Dares Wins is pulp fare about the politics of terrorism in which the anti-war movement is discredited as prone to reckless murder in the ironic name of peace. In this case, provocative premise is no substitute for classy drama.

The simple-minded plot [from an original story by George Markstein] has a militant anti-nuke organization take over a US diplomatic facility in London with its glitzy bunch of hostages and demanding the wipeout of a US sub base in Scotland by a nuclear missile. Wiped out instead, by a crack British commando team, are the peaceniks. All characters are stereotyped rather than cliched.

Performing standout is Judy Davis as the 'terrorist' leader. Lewis Collins offers pleasing virile projection as an undercover agent who shacks up with Davis.

. . . .

■ WHO FRAMED ROGER RABBIT

1988, 103 MINS, US ◇ ⓥ
Dir Robert Zemeckis   *Prod* Robert Watts, Frank Marshall   *Scr* Jeffrey Price, Peter S. Seaman   *Ph* Dean Cundey   *Ed* Arthur Schmidt   *Mus* Alan Silvestri   *Art Dir* Elliot Scott, Roger Cain
● Bob Hoskins, Christopher Lloyd, Joanna Cassidy, Stubby Kaye, Alan Tilvern (Touchstone/Amblin/Silver Screen Partners III)

Years in the planning and making, *Who Framed Roger Rabbit* is an unparalleled technical achievement where animation is brilliantly integrated into live action. Yet the story amounts to little more than inspired silliness about the filmmaking biz where cartoon characters face off against cartoonish humans.

Pic opens appropriately enough with a cartoon, a hilarious, overblown, calamitous scene where Roger Rabbit, a famous contract Toon player (as in car*toon*) for Maroon Studios, is failing in his attempt to keep Baby Herman (voice by Lou Hirsch) from the cookie jar.

Things aren't going well for poor Roger. Ever since he became estranged from his voluptuous human character Toon wife Jessica (sultry, uncredited voice courtesy of Kathleen Turner, and Amy Irving for the singing) he just can't act.

This is the context from which scripters, in adapting Gary Wolf's story, try to work up a Raymond Chandler-style suspenser where Roger becomes an innocent murder suspect, with a disheveled, alcoholic private eye (Bob Hoskins) being his only hope to help him beat the rap.

The real stars are the animators, under British animation director Richard Williams, who pull off a technically amazing feat of having humans and Toons seem to be interacting with one another. It is clear from how well the imagery syncs that a lot of painstaking work [two years] went into this production – and clearly a lot of money [$70 million].

. . . .

■ WHO IS KILLING THE GREAT CHEFS OF EUROPE?

1978, 112 MINS, US/W. GERMANY ◇ ⓥ
Dir Ted Kotcheff   *Prod* William Aldrich   *Scr* Peter Stone   *Ph* John Alcott   *Mus* Henry Mancini   *Art Dir* Werner Achmann
● George Segal, Jacqueline Bisset, Robert Morley, Jean-Pierre Cassel, Philippe Noiret, Jean Rochefort (Aldrich/Lorimar)

Who Is Killing the Great Chefs of Europe? is a happy combination of the macabre and the merry. It's a fast-moving, witty film, beautifully cast with a large group of international professionals who give full justice to Peter Stone's adaptation of Nan and Ivan Lyons' novel, *Someone Is Killing the Great Chefs of Europe.*

While George Segal and Jacqueline Bisset carry star billing and, indeed, provide the romantic and plot evolution, it is Robert Morley as a massive, dedicated gourmet, who provides the film's finest moments.

The series of murders is made the responsibility of some of France and Italy's most outstanding character actors. It's touch and go

who excels but Philippe Noiret underplays in a manner that gives him a slight edge over the more voluble Italians although Stefano Satta Flores' unabashed description of how he'll romance Bisset, given the opportunity, is Italian macho comedy at its finest.

The other endangered chef is Jean-Pierre Cassel, while Jean Rochefort is a red herring who'll fool no one. These are the principal roles but Madge Ryan as Morley's dedicated secretary is also a key figure.

. . . .

■ WHOLE TOWN'S TALKING, THE

1935, 95 MINS, US
Dir John Ford   *Prod* Lester Cowan   *Scr* Jo Swerling, Robert Riskin   *Ph* Joseph H. August   *Ed* Viola Lawrence
● Edward G. Robinson, Jean Arthur, Wallace Ford, Arthur Hohl, Donald Meek, Etienne Girardot (Columbia)

Robert Riskin and Jo Swerling put the scenario together [from a story by W.R. Burnett]. It's a model in the expert manipulation of such hokum as the office worm thrust into danger by coincidence and emerging with fame, fortune and the girl.

Edward G. Robinson plays a dual role. He is a softie in one part and tough in the other. Plot twist to the worm-turning is that the softie bookkeeper is a dead ringer for a gangster wanted by the police. Police have orders to shoot on sight, and when picking up the hoodlum's counterpart, and third-degreeing him, they are confronted with a dilemma: what to do to protect an innocent citizen from the police. So the bookkeeper gets a pass identifying him as okay. Real criminal, of course, shows up and quietly takes over the passport as a shield to continue his activities.

Robinson's characterization of the submerged, over-polite and indecisive office worker is human and believable.

Second in unusualness among the cast is Jean Arthur. She's gone blonde and fresh. She's more individualistic, more typically the young American, self-reliant, rather sassy, stenog.

. . . .

■ WHO'LL STOP THE RAIN

1978, 125 MINS, US ⓥ
Dir Karel Reisz   *Prod* Herb Jaffe, Gabriel Katzka   *Scr* Judith Roscoe, Robert Stone   *Ph* Richard H. Kline   *Ed* John Bloom   *Mus* Laurence Rosenthal
● Nick Nolte, Tuesday Weld, Michael Moriarty, Anthony Zerbe, Richard Masur, Ray Sharkey (United Artists)

British film-maker Karel Reisz for his second American film has come up with a corking couple-on-the-run adventure pic, given depth in its focus on the personal disarray, the growing governmental corruption and the effects of that most unpopular, divisive Vietnam war on America.

Michael Moriarty, a journalist and photog during the Vietnam War, suffers a trauma under a deadly enemy barrage and the mayhem around him. He decides to try to smuggle heroin to the US.

Moriarty brings in an old Marine buddy (Nick Nolte), who is now in the Merchant Marine. Nolte is to get in touch with Moriarty's wife (Tuesday Weld) and wait for him, Moriarty, to get back. But back in the US Nolte is followed. He and Weld go on the lam after sending Weld's little girl off to relatives for safekeeping.

Based on a bestseller by Robert Stone, film has a hardnose progression and solidity in its characterizations. Nolte earns his star stripes here, displaying presence and perceptiveness in socking home his character, while Weld and Moriarty are also effective.

. . . .

■ WHO'S AFRAID OF VIRGINIA WOOLF?

1966, 131 MINS, US ⓥ
Dir Mike Nichols   *Prod* Ernest Lehman   *Scr* Ernest Lehman   *Ph* Haskell Wexler   *Ed* Sam O'Steen   *Mus* Alex North   *Art Dir* Richard Sylbert
● Elizabeth Taylor, Richard Burton, George Segal, Sandy Dennis (Warner)

The naked power and oblique tenderness of Edward Albee's incisive, inhuman drama have been transformed from legit into a brilliant motion picture. Keen adaptation and handsome production by Ernest Lehman, outstanding direction by Mike Nichols in his feature debut, and four topflight performances score an artistic bullseye.

Elizabeth Taylor earns every penny of her reported $1 million plus. Her chacterization is at once sensual, spiteful, cynical, pitiable, loathsome, lustful and tender.

Richard Burton delivers a smash portrayal. He evokes sympathy during the public degradations to which his wife subjects him, and his outrage, as well as his deliberate vengeance, are totally believable.

Provoking the exercise in exorcism is the late-night visit of Dennis and Segal. Latter is the all-American boy type who, in the course of one night, is seduced by his hostess, exposed by his host, but enlightened as to more mature aspects of love and marriage. Segal is able to evoke sympathy, then hatred, then pity, in a first-rate performance.

Dennis makes an impressive screen debut as the young bride, her delivery rounded with the intended subtlety of a not-so-Dumb Dora.
□ 1966: Best Picture (Nomination)

. . . .

■ WHO'S BEEN SLEEPING IN MY BED?

1963, 103 MINS, US ◇
Dir Daniel Mann   *Prod* Jack Rose   *Scr* Jack Rose   *Ph* Joseph Ruttenberg   *Ed* George Tomasini   *Mus* George Duning
● Dean Martin, Elizabeth Montgomery, Martin Balsam, Jill St John, Carol Burnett, Macha Meril (Paramount)

Dean Martin is seemingly right for the part of an actor who appears on television as a doctor, such as Kildare or Ben Casey, and then moonlights into the field of psychiatric advice (and perhaps romantic stimulation) for the glamorous dames married to his TV-business associates.

But there's the slip between cup and lip. The slip makes the difference between what might have been mischievous, zesty comedy and what is a sometimes laughable frolic that in a couple of instances is permitted to sink in its quest for sophisticated hilarity.

This is unfortunate because a substantial part of *Who's Been Sleeping in My Bed?* plays sparklingly well. Martin is an amiable performer in light comedy and does fine with the material at hand.

. . . .

■ WHO'S MINDING THE STORE?

1963, 90 MINS, US ◇
Dir Frank Tashlin   *Prod* Paul Jones   *Scr* Frank Tashlin, Harry Tugend   *Ph* Wallace Kelley   *Ed* John Woodcock   *Mus* Joseph J. Lilley
● Jerry Lewis, Jill St John, Agnes Moorehead, John McGiver, Ray Walston, Francesca Bellini (Paramount)

Frank Tashlin directs with full emphasis on the madcap nonsense and Jerry Lewis has a field day playing it all out in his uninhibited (meaning zany) style. It's fun.

The filmmaker also has gotten in an abundance of commercial display for appliances, other household items, as Lewis goes to work in a department store and wrecks it department by department.

He has an especially attractive romantic vis-a-vis in Jill St John who takes a job as elevator operator to hide the fact she's really the daughter of the store's owner. Agnes Moorehead plays the owner's domineering wife, who regards Lewis as an idiot, Frank McGiver is the owner, and Ray Walston is a dame-chasing manager.

They all romp through with accent on the broad comedy and, of course, with the spotlight mainly on havoc-wreaking Lewis.

. . . .

■ WICKED LADY, THE

1945, 102 MINS, UK ⓥ
Dir Leslie Arliss   *Prod* R.J. Minney   *Scr* Leslie Arliss, Gordon Glennon, Aimee Stuart   *Ph* Jack Cox
Ed Terence Fisher   *Mus* Hans May   *Art Dir* John Bryan
● Margaret Lockwood, James Mason, Patricia Roc, Michael Rennie, Felix Aylmer (Gainsborough)

Producers claim that this story is 'set in the days of Charles II'. Sets, costumes and a comely bunch of femmes bear out the claim. But the period atmosphere is not convincing.

James Mason as a Robin Hood type highwayman manages to suggest the swaggering love-'em-and-leave-'em rascal of an earlier day. He scores in spite of the weak script [from the novel *The Wicked Lady Skelton* by Magdalen King-Hall]. The other performance lending credibility to the period comes from Felix Aylmer as an old retainer who tumbles to the villainy of Margaret Lockwood in the title role, and dies at her fair hands.

The Wicked Lady as a title is a characteristic English understatement. The way Lockwood shoots, poisons and betrays all who get in her way makes that taboo name a modest one. Between murders she steals the fiance of her best girl friend and then grabs the bridal chamber for herself.

. . . .

■ WICKED LADY, THE

1983, 98 MINS, US ◇ ⓥ
Dir Michael Winner   *Prod* Menahem Golan, Yoram Globus   *Scr* Michael Winner, Leslie Arliss   *Ph* Jack Cardiff   *Ed* Arnold Crust   *Mus* Tony Banks
Art Dir John Blezard
● Faye Dunaway, Alan Bates, John Gielgud, Denholm Elliott, Prunella Scales, Oliver Tobias (Cannon)

Sex, humor and even a facsimile of style distinguish Michael Winner's entertaining remake of *The Wicked Lady* as a comedy-drama of rogue-ridden 17th-century England with Faye Dunaway an effective title star.

Winner, who coauthored the piece with Leslie Arliss [based on *The Life and Death of the Wicked Lady Skelton* by Magdalen King-Hall], has pumped some amusing life and typically brisk pace into a basically tired old (and even campy) story about an alluring high society dame for whom seduction, highway robbery and even murder are all in a day's work.

After marrying Denholm Elliott for his money, Dunaway turns to a life of nocturnal crime, solo at first, but later in cahoots with legendary stagecoach robber Alan Bates.

Dunaway performs her dominating role with satisfying conviction, straight face and all. Ditto Elliott as her scorned and cuckolded husband. Bates makes for a charming but all-too-brief rogue, while John Gielgud as a God-fearing retainer has a marvelous deadpan time of it kidding himself.

. . . .

■ WICKER MAN, THE

1973, 97 MINS, UK ◇ ⓥ
Dir Robin Hardy   *Prod* Peter Snell   *Scr* Anthony Shaffer   *Ph* Harry Waxman   *Ed* Eric Boyd-Perkins
Mus Paul Giovanni   *Art Dir* Seamus Flannery
● Edward Woodward, Britt Ekland, Diane Cilento, Ingrid Pitt, Christopher Lee, Roy Boyd (British Lion/Brut)

The Wicker Man was lensed entirely on location in Scotland and is possessed of a weird and paganistic story. Anthony Shaffer

penned the screenplay which, for sheer imagination and near-terror, has seldom been equalled.

Frightening aspects build one upon the other as a Scottish police sergeant arrives on a little offshore island to investigate the disappearance of a young girl. He finds, under the regime of an all-powerful, benevolent and suave despot, a sinister situation dating back to the days of pagan practices and fertility rites.

Edward Woodward plays role of the sergeant who arrives to find a conspiracy of silence and is forced into a fatal part in the paganistic rituals. Christopher Lee is the cultured feudal Lord Summerisle, lord of the island. Both score in their roles.

. . . .

■ WILBY CONSPIRACY, THE

1975, 101 MINS, UK ◇
Dir Ralph Nelson   *Prod* Martin Baum   *Scr* Rod Amateau, Harold Nebenzal   *Ph* John Coquillon
Ed Ernest Walter   *Mus* Stanley Myers   *Art Dir* Harold Pottle
● Sidney Poitier, Michael Caine, Nicol Williamson, Prunella Gee, Persis Khambatta, Saeed Jaffrey (United Artists)

The Wilby Conspiracy [from Peter Driscoll's novel] is a good action melodrama about apartheid in South Africa. It was made in Kenya. The stars Sidney Poitier and Michael Caine are relentlessly stalked by Nicol Williamson, superb as a coldly dedicated and brutal policeman out after racial agitators.

Poitier is linked by fate with Caine, an Englishman accidently enmeshed in South African segregation discrimination through his girl (Prunella Gee) who as Poitier's lawyer has him freed from a decade in prison for racial agitation.

Williamson, almost too chillingly realistic as a bigot, permits the two to escape an early police confrontation, so as to let Poitier lead him to Joseph De Fraf, the title character and a political guerrilla partner to Poitier. En route to the good climax, one encounters Persis Khambatta, a most attractive Indian actress, and Rutger Hauer, Gee's playboy-type husband.

But somehow the story comes out too much of a potboiler undeserving of the fine work that Williamson, Caine and Poitier put into it.

. . . .

■ WILD AND THE WILLING, THE

1962, 123 MINS, UK
Dir Ralph Thomas   *Prod* Betty E. Box   *Scr* Nicholas Phipps, Mordecai Richler   *Ph* Ernest Steward
Ed Alfred Roome   *Mus* Norrie Paramor   *Art Dir* Alex Vetchinsky
● Virginia Maskell, Paul Rogers, Ian McShane, Samantha Eggar, John Hurt (Rank)

The Wild and the Willing, adapted from *The Tinker*, a play by Laurence Dobie and Robert Sloman which didn't make the grade in the West End, has nothing much new to say on its chosen theme – youth trying to find its place in society – the screenplay is lucid and the background of a provincial university authentic.

It concerns a brilliant young student from a poor working class family who is acutely class-conscious and rebels against the university, its professors and the opportunities they offer. He does not know where he is going and is arrogantly content to drift along raising Cain, drinking beer, playing football and pawing his girl friend, another student. He is a leading light in the university with a particular influence on his roommate, a shyer, more introspective lad.

Throughout there is a complete air of realism. The students, the professors and the

townsfolk are real people about whose problems audiences will care. Ralph Thomas has directed with tact and has brought out some surprisingly sure performances from his inexperienced actors.

Ian McShane, with a broad Manchester accent, came straight from drama school to play this leading role. He is a virile, goodlooking young man with authority who is a real discovery, as is John Hurt, also a first timer, who plays his sensitive roommate.

. . . .

■ WILD ANGELS, THE

1966, 83 MINS, US ◇ ⓥ
Dir Roger Corman   *Prod* Roger Corman   *Scr* Charles B. Griffith   *Ph* Richard Moore   *Ed* Monte Hellman
Mus Mike Curb   *Art Dir* Leon Erickson
● Peter Fonda, Nancy Sinatra, Bruce Dern, Diane Ladd, Michael J. Pollard, Gayle Hunnicutt (American International)

The foreword to this well-turned-out Roger Corman production is its tipoff: 'The picture you are about to see will shock and perhaps anger you. Although the events and characters are fictitious, the story is a reflection of our times'.

For thematic motivation, Corman, who produces in almost documentary style, chooses the marauding of the Hell's Angels. Pinpointed here, the Angels, in vicious stride and without regard for law and order, operate in a Southern California beach community, and it is upon this particular segment that Corman directs his clinical eye in dissecting their philosophical (?) rebellion.

Corman tackles assignment with realism, taking apart the cult and giving its members an indepth study as he follows a gang headed by Peter Fonda in their defiance of common decencies.

Fonda lends credence to character, voicing the creed of the Angels in 'wanting to do what we want to do' without interference, and is well-cast in part.

. . . .

■ WILD AT HEART

1990, 127 MINS, US ◇ ⓥ
Dir David Lynch   *Prod* Monty Montgomery, Steve Golin, Joni Sighvatsson   *Scr* David Lynch   *Ph* Fred Elmes   *Ed* Duwayne Dunham   *Mus* Angelo Badalamenti
● Nicolas Cage, Laura Dern, Diane Ladd, Willem Dafoe, Isabella Rossellini, Harry Dean Stanton (Polygram/Propaganda)

Joltingly violent, wickedly funny and rivetingly erotic, David Lynch's *Wild at Heart* [based on the novel by Barry Gifford] is a rollercoaster ride to redemption through an American gothic heart of darkness.

The brutal opening signals that this film is not for the faint of heart. Sailor (Nicolas Cage), an Elvis-acolyte whose snakeskin jacket proclaims his 'duality and individuality', and his seethingly sexy 18-year-old girlfriend Lula (Laura Dern) are waylaid leaving a dance hall somewhere in the Carolinas. Sailor literally cracks open the assassin with his bare hands. He does two years for manslaughter in 'Pee Dee' state pen.

Sailor breaks parole and absconds with Lula to New Orleans, pursued by private eye Johnnie Farragut (Harry Dean Stanton) who's hired by Lula's insanely obsessive mother Marietta (Dern's real-life mother, Diane Ladd) his sometime lover.

His rival for this psychotic witch's affections are mobster Marcello Santos (J.R. Freeman), also unleashed on the lovers' trail as a precaution by mamma. Santos tabs a bordello-dwelling hit-man to annihilate Stanton in a bayou-style ritual murder. It's not the storyline's first or last doublecross.

. . . .

W

■ WILD BUNCH, THE

1969, 145 MINS, US ◇ Ⓥ

Dir Sam Peckinpah *Prod* Phil Feldman *Scr* Walon Green, Sam Peckinpah *Ph* Lucien Ballard *Ed* Louis Lombardo *Mus* Jerry Fielding *Art Dir* Edward Carrere

● William Holden, Ernest Borgnine, Robert Ryan, Edmond O'Brien, Warren Oates, Jaime Sanchez (Warner/Seven Arts)

Plot concerns a small band of outlaws headed by William Holden who hijack a US ammunition train crossing the border into Mexico in 1913 to supply the revolutionary army of Pancho Villa.

Actually, the story is two-pronged. Holden and his men go their way of outlawry and Robert Ryan, former member of Holden's gang and temporarily-released convict, tracks down his former chief to 'buy' his freedom from jail.

Screenplay, based on a story by Walon Green and Roy N. Sickner, builds suspensefully when action finally starts about the middle of film. Sam Peckinpah's forceful direction is a definite asset, particularly in later sequences in which Holden deals with a vicious Mexican general over the hijacked guns and ammo.

Holden goes into character for his role and handles assignment expertly. Ernest Borgnine delivers his usual brand of acting as former's aide.

■ WILD GEESE, THE

1978, 132 MINS, UK ◇ Ⓥ

Dir Andrew V. McLaglen *Prod* Euan Lloyd *Scr* Reginald Rose *Ph* Jack Hildyard *Ed* John Glen *Mus* Roy Budd

● Richard Burton, Roger Moore, Richard Harris, Hardy Kruger, Stewart Granger, Jack Watson (Rank)

Euan Lloyd's uppercase actioner, centered on a caper by mercenaries in Africa, attempts to be a cornucopia of tried boxoffice hooks but ultimately fails to meld its comedy, adventure, pathos, violence, heroics – or even its political message – into a credible whole.

Reginald Rose's adaptation of Daniel Carney's story – about mercenary toughguys who parachute into the African bush to snatch a deposed African president for reinstatement to suit British business interests – is routinely predictable and, in the end, cornily incredible.

Roger Moore's shootouts with the Mafia in London and Hardy Kruger's neat killing of three sentries with cyanide-tipped arrows is good 'traditional' escapism. Then, as if to contemporize the film, Peckinpah-fashion, the screen's suddenly filled with bloody graphics and four-letter words.

Winston Ntshona is well cast as the deposed president Limbani though much of his 'message' dialog is unnecessarily and unpalatably heavy for what's presumably designed as a riproaring blood and guts actioner.

■ WILD GEESE II

1985, 125 MINS, UK ◇ Ⓥ

Dir Peter Hunt *Prod* Euan Lloyd *Scr* Reginald Rose *Ph* Michael Reed *Ed* Keith Palmer *Mus* Roy Budd *Art Dir* Syd Cain

● Scott Glenn, Barbara Carrera, Edward Fox, Laurence Olivier, Robert Webber, Robert Freitag (Thorn-EMI/Frontier)

Script [from the book *The Square Circle* by Reginald Rose] has a promising basic premise. An American TV station commissions mercenary John Haddad (Scott Glenn) to kidnap the nonagenarian Nazi leader Rudolf Hess from the impregnable Spandau prison in Berlin, but the follow-through never arrives. A routine car ambush is substituted for the impossible jailbreak. The liberated Hess just doesn't want to play games with history by revealing the Watergate-style story supposedly underlying Hitler's rise to power.

Despite these structural problems, film contains a wealth of incident. Haddad is the object of numerous assassination attempts organized by the German Heinrich Stroebling (Robert Freitag), who is in league with the Russians and Palestinian terrorists. The British are after Hess too. There's also a supporting role for members of the Irish Republican Army and the kidnap of yank journalist Kathy Lukas (Barbara Carrera) occasions a major shootout.

Edward Fox plays Colonel Faulkner with comic zest. Unintentionally, perhaps, Laurence Olivier also extracts laughs from his Hess cameo. By contrast, Glenn and Carrera take their parts more seriously than the script merits.

■ WILD IN THE COUNTRY

1961, 112 MINS, US ◇ Ⓥ

Dir Philip Dunne *Prod* Jerry Wald *Scr* Clifford Odets *Ph* William C. Mellor *Ed* Dorothy Spencer *Mus* Kenyon Hopkins *Art Dir* Jack Martin Smith, Preston Ames

● Elvis Presley, Hope Lange, Tuesday Weld, Millie Perkins, John Ireland, Gary Lockwood (20th Century-Fox)

Dramatically, there simply isn't substance, novelty or spring to this wobbly and artificial tale of a maltreated country boy (Elvis Presley) who, supposedly, has the talent to become a great writer, but lacks the means, the emotional stability and the encouragement until he comes in contact with a beautiful psychiatric consultant (Hope Lange) who develops traumas of her own in the process.

The complications occur when the two spend an innocent night in a motel, innocent on the strength of their May (he)-December (she) respect for each other. The gap in romantic seasons is quickly bridged when their one-night relationship is misinterpreted by some of the incredibly foul and mischievous people who live in the town. Clifford Odets penned the screenplay, from the novel *The Lost Country* by J.R. Salamanca. The writing has its occasional rewards.

Presley, subdued, uses what dramatic resources he has to best advantage in this film. Lange, for the most part, plays intelligently and sensitively. Tuesday Weld contributes a flashy and arresting portrait of a sexy siren enamored of Mr P.

Story, set in the Shenandoah Valley, was filmed in the Napa Valley. Sans wiggle, Presley croons four or five songs. Guitars rather mysteriously keep turning up on the premises, but E.P. leaves the plunking to Weld.

■ WILD IN THE STREETS

1968, 96 MINS, US ◇ Ⓥ

Dir Barry Shear *Prod* Burt Topper *Scr* Robert Thom *Ph* Richard Moore *Ed* Fred Feitshans, Eve Newman *Mus* Les Baxter

● Shelley Winters, Christopher Jones, Diane Varsi, Ed Begley, Hal Halbrook, Millie Perkins (American International)

An often chilling political science fiction drama, with comedy, the production considers the takeover of American government by the preponderant younger population. Good writing and direction enhance the impact of a diversified cast headed by Shelley Winters.

Christopher Jones plays a rock 'n' roll hero who, as a result of a request from would-be US Senator Hal Holbrook, exceeds the bounds of electioneering help by mobilizing teenagers into legalized voters.

Winters plays his sleazy, selfish mother, whose purported emasculation of dad Bert Freed years before cued Jones' running away from home.

Holbrook projects perfectly the bright young politico who exploits the young crowd, only to be turned on by those whose help he seeks.

Actual footage from real-life demonstrations was shot for pic, some of it matched quite well with internal drama. What comes off as a partial documentary flavor makes for a good artistic complement to the not-so-fictional hypothesis, the logical result of an over-accent on youth.

■ WILD ONE, THE

1953, 79 MINS, US Ⓥ

Dir Laslo Benedek *Prod* Stanley Kramer *Scr* John Paxton *Ph* Hal Mohr *Ed* Al Clark *Mus* Leith Stevens *Art Dir* Walter Holscher

● Marlon Brando, Mary Murphy, Robert Keith, Lee Marvin, Jay C. Flippen, Hugh Sanders (Columbia)

Inspired by an episode when a mob of youths on motorcycles terrorized a Californian town for an entire evening, this feature is long on suspense, brutality and sadism. Marlon Brando contributes another hard-faced 'hero' who never knew love as a boy and is now plainly in need of psychoanalysis.

The young cyclists are a motley mob of jivesters, some carrying their own female cargo. Much giving to showoff antics and mimicry, they also drink beer in vast quantities and incessantly deposit nickels in jukeboxes. Reckless, impudent, cruel and knife-carrying, they break and borrow things and drive motorcycles into and through saloons.

However intolerable and barbarian the cyclists are, nothing they do is as vicious and vindictive as the 'vigilante' spirit which develops among the merchants of the village. Big bruisers twice the size of the young cyclists, these adults readily and joyously beat Brando to a pulp and then later try to frame him by their silence for a manslaughter rap.

Picture [from a story by Frank Rooney] was made some time [before its release] and had three titles in succession, *Cyclists Raid*, *The Wild One* and *Hot Blood*. All performances are highly competent. A second band of ruffians comes along later led by a colorful young character named Lee Marvin.

The femme interest is intelligently managed by Mary Murphy. Robert Keith is excellent as the mush-soft village constable. The county sheriff is the nicest guy in the film, and nearly the only one. He's impersonated with professional sincerity by the old vaudeman, Jay C. Flippen.

■ WILD ORCHID

1990, 100 MINS, US ◇ Ⓥ

Dir Zalman King *Prod* Mark Damon, Tony Anthony, Howard North *Scr* Zalman King, Patricia Louisianna Knop *Ph* Gale Tattersall *Mus* Geoff MacCormack, Simon Goldenberg

● Mickey Rourke, Jacqueline Bisset, Carre Otis (Vision)

If *Wild Orchid* aims to grab audiences with a hot-house atmosphere of erotica, it mainly teases until a pay-off in the last sequence.

Claudia (Jacqueline Bisset) is a wired jet-set businesswoman who hires tyro lawyer Emily (Carre Otis) to help her close a deal. Prim Emily, a Midwest farm girl still wet under the collar – but highly attractive – is dazed to find herself on a plane to Rio. There she meets Claudia's old flame Wheeler (Mickey Rourke), a self-made millionaire with perverse sexual tastes. Hypnotizing Emily with his original personality (?), he forces her to forget her good-girl upbringing and do liberating things.

What doesn't work is the hold Rourke is supposed to have over Otis. Looking pudgy and puffy-faced, with a little gold earring, he is anything but an appetizing sex object.

As Emily, Otis really is hypnotically attractive, but she plays the still-waters-run-deep country beauty with expressionless immobility. Bisset, always a class act, here bubbles over with caricatured joie de vivre.

As for eros, only when Emily breaks through Wheeler's reserve/importence in the last sequence does pic deliver in a torrid, highly choreographed but equally explicit bedroom session between the two.

■ WILD PARTY, THE

1975, 100 MINS, US ◇

Dir James Ivory   *Prod* Ismail Merchant   *Scr* Walter Marks   *Ph* Walter Lassally   *Ed* Kent McKinney   *Mus* Larry Rosenthal   *Art Dir* David Nichols
● James Coco, Raquel Welch, Perry King, Tiffany Bolling, Royal Dano, David Dukes (American International)

The Wild Party is an extremely handsome, overly talky musical drama starring James Coco as a faded 1920s film comic whose disastrous premiere houseparty for a comeback film leads to murder.

Based on a long-ago poem by Joseph Moncure March, the film is a magnificent showpiece for Coco's talents. He successfully covers a spectrum from silly comedy, warm humor, sober anger, maddening frustration and drunken psychosis. Holding her own as his mistress is Raquel Welch, registering very strongly.

Key featured players include Perry King, very good as a current film heartthrob; Tiffany Bolling, his femme counterpart; and Royal Dano, quite good as Coco's loyal valet.

■ WILD RIVER

1960, 115 MINS, US ◇

Dir Elia Kazan   *Prod* Elia Kazan   *Scr* Paul Osborn   *Ph* Ellsworth Fredericks   *Ed* William Reynolds   *Mus* Kenyon Hopkins   *Art Dir* Lyle R. Wheeler, Herman A. Blumenthal
● Montgomery Clift, Lee Remick, Jo Van Fleet, Albert Salmi, Jay C. Flippen, Barbara Loden (20th Century-Fox)

Wild River is an important motion picture. In studying a slice of national socio-economic progress (the Tennessee Valley Authority of the early 1930s) in terms of people (those who enforced vs those who resisted), it catches something timeless and essential in the human spirit and shapes it in the American image.

Sturdy foundation for director Elia Kazan's artistic indulgences and a number of exceptional performances is Paul Osborn's thought-provoking screenplay, erected out of two novels, *Mud on the Stars* by William Bradford Huie, and *Dunbar's Cove* by Borden Deal. It is the tragic tale of an 80-year-old 'rugged individualist' (Jo Van Fleet) who refuses to give ground (a small island on the Tennessee River smack dab in TVA's dambuilding path) to an understanding, but equally firm, TV agent (Montgomery Clift).

In the process of successfully separating the grand old lady from her precious, but doomed, slice of real estate, Clift gets into several scrapes with the local Tennessee bigots over his decent treatment of Negroes and squeezes sufficient romance into his tight schedule to wind up the spouse of the old woman's pretty granddaughter (Lee Remick).

Where the film soars is in its clean, objective approach to the basic conflict between progress and tradition ('electricity and souls,' as Osborn puts it). Through this gentle veil of objectivity, a point-of-view unmistakably stirs, but never emerges to the point where it takes sides just to be taking sides. The result is that rare element of tragedy, in the truly classical sense of the word, where an indomit-

able individual eventually must fall helpless prey to an irresistible, but impersonal edict designed for universal good.

■ WILD ROVERS

1971, 110 MINS, US ◇ Ⓥ

Dir Blake Edwards   *Prod* Blake Edwards, Ken Wales   *Scr* Blake Edwards   *Ph* Philip Lathrop   *Ed* John F. Burnett   *Mus* Jerry Goldsmith   *Art Dir* George W. Davis, Addison Hehr
● William Holden, Ryan O'Neal, Karl Malden, Lynn Carlin, Tom Skerritt, Joe Don Baker (M-G-M)

William Holden and Ryan O'Neal, two cowboys who decide to rob a bank, and Karl Malden, their employer, star in a technically superior film.

Film tells a sentimental story about an aging cowpoke and a younger buddy whose dreams of crashing out of their rut lead to violence and death.

Emphasis is on Holden and O'Neal, and there are a few touching moments as the older man imparts some wisdom to the younger. The mood is broken regularly with pratfall humor, also some dehumanizing slow-motion ballets of death. O'Neal's character is not always well defined, since the boyish naivete also exhibits some jarring evidence of cruelty, thereby limiting empathy for his ultimate downfall.

Large supporting cast is lost in throwaway parts. Even Malden has little to do except plot-motivate the dispatch of sons Tom Skerritt and Joe Don Baker to join the posse. Skerritt overacts, and Baker's abilities are smothered in a second banana line-throwing part.

■ WILDCATS

1986, 107 MINS, US ◇ Ⓥ

Dir Michael Ritchie   *Prod* Anthea Sylbert   *Scr* Ezra Sacks   *Ph* Donald E. Thorin   *Ed* Richard A. Harris   *Mus* Hawk Wolinski, James Newton Howard   *Art Dir* Boris Leven
● Goldie Hawn, Swoosie Kurtz, Robyn Lively, Brandy Gold, James Keach, Bruce McGill (Hawn/Sylbert)

When Goldie Hawn tangles with high school varsity coach Bruce McGill, anyone can foresee the final confrontation.

Sure enough, when McGill has her appointed football coach at the unspeakable ghetto school, Central High, it's an inevitable collision course. Along the way crises pop up at carefully placed intervals, the first being winning the confidence of the rag-tag collection of players.

Michael Ritchie's direction lacks his usual bite and eye for detail. There is nothing spontaneous about the action and football footage is also surprisingly dull.

Hawn, seemingly on screen for the entire film, is fun to watch as she runs her team through aerobics and mugs for the camera, but even better is Nipsey Russell as the rough-hewn high school principal with a word for all occasions.

■ WILL PENNY

1968, 108 MINS, US ◇ Ⓥ

Dir Tom Gries   *Prod* Fred Engel, Walter Seltzer   *Scr* Tom Gries   *Ph* Lucien Ballard   *Ed* Warren Low   *Mus* David Raksin   *Art Dir* Hal Pereira, Roland Anderson
● Charlton Heston, Joan Hackett, Donald Pleasence, Lee Majors, Bruce Dern (Paramount)

Will Penny is not a straight out-and-out western but more a character study of an aging cowpoke who for the first time feels the stirrings of romance.

There is beautiful range and mountain scenery but basically interest rests on the man, and his gropings which at times aren't

overly clear, rather than on western action all too often slowed by characterization.

Charlton Heston in title role is persuasively effective as the cowpoke who finally rides away from romance. Joan Hackett as the woman travelling across the plains with her young son to join her farmer-husband in Oregon, willing to renounce that marriage to wed the penniless range rider, is quietly commanding.

Donald Pleasence is a scavenging rawhider who with his three sons would rather murder than not. Given these elements, a story takes form which displays thoughtful conception. This is not a story of the wild West but the West as lived in by real-life characters.

■ WILL SUCCESS SPOIL ROCK HUNTER?

1957, 94 MINS, US ◇

Dir Frank Tashlin   *Prod* Frank Tashlin   *Scr* Frank Tashlin   *Ph* Joe MacDonald   *Ed* Hugh Fowler   *Mus* Cyril J. Mockridge   *Art Dir* Lyle R. Wheeler, Leland Fuller
● Jayne Mansfield, Tony Randall, Betsy Drake, Joan Blondell, Mickey Hargitay, Groucho Marx (20th Century-Fox)

In converting the stageplay *Will Success Spoil Rock Hunter?* to his purposes, Frank Tashlin turns out a vastly amusing comedy. Picture bears comparatively little resemblance to the George Axelrod original.

Tony Randall's second excursion into the bigscreen realm from TV and the stage shows he's a fellow who knows timing, and his clowning has a slightly sophisticated touch that hits bullseye. Jayne Mansfield does a sock job as the featherbrained sex-motivated movie star.

Tashlin fashions a funny credit for the credits, which are introed by Randall. There's also an 'intermission', with Randall coming out to comfort those who are used to TV commercials. In the end, Groucho Marx comes on for a briefy.

Story has Randall as a TV commercial writer about to be fired because his agency is threatened with the loss of its big lipstick account. He saves the situation by getting the endorsement from a famous movie star.

Supporting roles are all very well cast. Betsy Drake is cute and displays a strong sense for comedy as Randall's fiancee; Henry Jones, ad-agency v.p., coaxes from the sidelines and delivers some rather lengthy speeches; Joan Blondell is standout in a small part and Mickey Hargitay is properly pompous as the Tarzan he-man who triggers Randall's troubles.

■ WILLARD

1971, 95 MINS, US ◇ Ⓥ

Dir Daniel Mann   *Prod* Mort Briskin   *Scr* Gilbert A. Ralston   *Ph* Robert B. Hauser   *Ed* Warren Low   *Mus* Alex North   *Art Dir* Howard Hollander
● Bruce Davison, Ernest Borgnine, Elsa Lanchester, Sondra Locke, Michael Dante, Jody Gilbert (BCO)

Neat little horror tale, shrewdly organized from Stephen Gilbert's novel, *Ratman's Notebooks*, capitalizes on human repugnance for rodents as Bruce Davison unleashes his trained rats on obstacles. Some good jump moments and at least two stomach-churning murders committed by the rats with tight direction of Daniel Mann develop pic into sound nail-chewer.

Davison, working for wheeler-dealer Ernest Borgnine, who took foundry over from Davison's dead father, lives with invalid, unrelenting mother Elsa Lanchester. Their old mansion gone to seed, loner Davison makes friends with resident rats, who learn to obey his commands. Davison, after death of his mother, killing of one of chief rats at Borgnine's hands, and receipt of pink slip from Borgnine, begins to fight back.

Davison supplies nicely controlled characterization as he fiddles with his rats, puts up with his mother and her friends and finally loses patience. Borgnine is first rate as he confronts subordinates. Lanchester is highly credible as the demanding mama.

. . . .

■ WILLIE & PHIL

1980, 116 MINS, US ◇ ⑦

Dir Paul Mazursky *Prod* Paul Mazursky, Tony Ray
Scr Paul Mazursky *Ph* Sven Nykvist *Ed* Donn
Cambern *Mus* Claude Bolling, Georges Delerue
Art Dir Pato Guzman
● Michael Ontkean, Margot Kidder, Ray Sharkey,
Jerry Hall, Natalie Wood (20th Century-Fox)

Willie & Phil is an amiable and humane film about a menage-a-trois spanning the 1970s. Director Paul Mazursky's compassionate eye for character and his wry wit, balance out a tendency to overromanticize and sentimentalize his characters.

Michael Ontkean and Ray Sharkey play the title characters (roles once intended for Woody Allen and Al Pacino) and Margot Kidder completes the romantic triangle, which forms in Greenwich Village at the beginning of the 1970s and winds up in Malibu nine years later. Along the way, Mazursky deftly traces changing sexual mores and other social values while portraying the trio as typical representatives of their generation's hopes and confusions.

Beginning rather coyly with the two men meeting at a Blecker Street Cinema screening of Truffaut's classic 1962 film about a menage-a-trois, *Jules et Jim*, Mazursky then has the two become friends so inseparable that they have trouble deciding who should board with Kidder.

It's all handled in very civilized and low-key fashion by Mazursky and his characters.

. . . .

■ WILLY WONKA AND THE CHOCOLATE FACTORY

1971, 98 MINS, US ◇ ⑨

Dir Mel Stuart *Prod* Stan Margulies, David L. Wolper
Scr Roald Dahl *Ph* Arthur Ibbetson *Ed* David
Saxon *Art Dir* Harper Goff
● Gene Wilder, Jack Albertson, Peter Ostrum, Roy
Kinnear, Julie Dawn Cole, Leonard Stone (Paramount)

Based on a Roald Dahl children's book, *Willy Wonka and the Chocolate Factory* is an okay family musical fantasy featuring Gene Wilder as an eccentric candymaker who makes a boy's dreams come true. Handsomely produced in partnership with Quaker Oats, the film has a fair score by Leslie Bricusse and Anthony Newley.

Dahl himself adapted his book, *Charlie and the Chocolate Factory*, and his dialog is better than the structure. Plot hook is a merchandising gimmick by Wilder who puts five golden tickets into a candy bar run, and tests the honesty of the winners. Inhibiting the sustenance of interest among those who are not familiar with the book is that Wilder's character is rather cynical and sadistic until virtually the end of the film. Ultimately Peter Ostrum, the kids' hero, and grandpa Jack Albertson pass the honesty test.

Sidebar incidents and dialog are the sharpest elements, particularly the running satire on TV news programming cliche.

. . . .

■ WILLY/MILLY

1986, 90 MINS, US ◇ ⑨

Dir Paul Schneider *Prod* M. David Chilewich
Scr Walter Carbonne, Carla Reuben *Ph* Dominique
Chapuis *Ed* Michael Miller *Mus* David McHugh *Art
Dir* Nora Chavooshian
● Pamela Segall, Eric Gurry, Mary Tanner, Patty Duke,
John Glover (Cinema)

The rather silly title *Willy/Milly* caps this charming and substantial kidpic about sex roles.

Rather than face the trauma of crossing the threshold of womanhood, 14-year-old Milly (Pamela Segall) turns into a boy under the effect of a magic spell she tries out during an eclipse. The matter-of-fact reaction of Milly is captured when she spins the first letter of her name upside-down and decides to try out Willy, effectively turning her entire world upside down.

The effects of the kid's crossover are explored on all fronts, going beyond locker room humor and capturing the kinds of expectations that spark the war between the sexes at all ages.

Film's biggest asset is in the performances of the unknown adolescent actors.

. . . .

■ WILSON

1944, 136 MINS, US ◇

Dir Henry King *Prod* Darryl F. Zanuck *Scr* Lamar
Trotti *Ph* Leon Shamroy *Ed* Barbara McLean
Mus Alfred Newman *Art Dir* Wiard B. Ihren, James
Baseri
● Alexander Knox, Charles Coburn, Geraldine
Fitzgerald, Thomas Mitchell, Cedric Hardwicke, Vincent
Price (20th Century-Fox)

The production is said to cost over $3 million and looks it. When there are crowds in the Senate, at the sundry political conventions, in the Palmer Stadium, on the campus, they are there in staggering, sizable numbers.

When the period of 1912-20 is recreated in Technicolor it is as authentic as it is splendiferous. All the detail of the White House decor of the Wilson administration; all the local color of the era and the day are faithfully brought to the canvas in a nostalgic, authentic fashion.

In fact, that is the keynote of *Wilson* – authority, warmth, idealism, a search for a better world. Through it all stalks a potent personality in Alexander Knox, a newborn star, supported by a flawless cast.

☐ 1944: Best Picture (Nomination)

. . . .

■ WILT

1989, 91 MINS, UK ◇ ⑨

Dir Michael Tuchner *Prod* Brian Eastman
Scr Andrew Marshall, David Renwick *Ph* Norman
Langley *Ed* Chris Blunden *Mus* Anne Dudley
Art Dir Leo Austin
● Griff Rhys Jones, Mel Smith, Alison Steadman, Diana
Quick, Jeremy Clyde (LWT/Picture Partnership/
Talkback)

There is a good deal of enjoyment to be derived from *Wilt*, [based on Tom Sharpe's novel] mainly thanks to a uniformly excellent cast and unpretentious, straightforward direction by Michael Tuchner, as well as the charmingly honest urban provincial settings.

Rhys Jones is the title character, a disillusioned college lecturer, who spends his spare time walking his dog and dreaming about murdering his domineering wife (Alison Steadman).

She has made friends with upwardly mobile couple Diana Quick and Jeremy Clyde. When Steadman and Rhys Jones attend a party at their posh country home Rhys Jones gets dead-drunk, and due to Quick's machinations finds himself locked in a naked passionate embrace with a life-size inflatable doll named Angelique.

He drunkenly roams the town trying to get rid of the doll. The next day, Steadman goes missing and Rhys Jones' nocturnal activities are noted – especially by ambitious inspector Mel Smith.

The most amusing scenes are those with Rhys Jones and Smith indulging in the banter they are known for from their TV appearances.

. . . .

■ WINCHESTER '73

1950, 92 MINS, US ⑨

Dir Anthony Mann *Prod* Aaron Rosenberg
Scr Robert L. Richards, Borden Chase *Ph* William
Daniels *Ed* Edward Curtiss *Mus* Joseph Gershenson
● James Stewart, Shelley Winters, Dan Duryea,
Stephen McNally, Rock Hudson, Tony Curtis (Universal)

Story [by Stuart N. Lake] is centered on a manhunt, on the search of Lin McAdam (James Stewart) for the cowardly murderer of his father. Film opens with Lin and his friend, High Spade (Millard Mitchell), riding into Dodge City in time for a 4 July celebration. Big event is a rifle match, with first prize a priceless 'one of a 1,000' 1873 model Winchester rifle.

Lin's brother Dutch (Stephen McNally), however, makes off with the precious rifle.

Stewart brings real flavor and appeal to the role of Lin, in a lean, concentrated portrayal. McNally is hard and unbending as the runaway brother. Mitchell lends warmth as Stewart's loyal henchman and friend. Shelley Winters is just sufficiently hard-bitten and cynical as the dancehall girl.

. . . .

■ WIND, THE

1928, 70 MINS, US ⑨

Dir Victor Seastrom *Scr* Frances Marion, John Colton
Ph John Arnold *Ed* Conrad A. Nervig *Art
Dir* Cedric Gibbons, Edward Withers
● Lillian Gish, Lars Hanson, Montagu Love, Dorothy
Cumming, Edward Earle, William Orlamond (M-G-M)

Some stories are just naturally poison for screen purposes and Dorothy Scarborough's novel here shows itself a conspicuous example. Everything a high pressure, lavishly equipped studio, expert director and reputable star could contribute was showered on this production. Everything about the picture breathes quality. Yet it flops dismally.

Tragedy on the high winds, on the desolate desert prairies, unrelieved by that sparkling touch of life that spells human interest, is what this picture has to offer. It may be a true picturization of life on the prairie but it still remains lifeless: and unentertaining.

The story opens with an unknown girl, Letty (Lillian Gish), from Virginia, train-bound for her cousin's ranch, which she describes as beautiful to the stranger, Roddy (Montagu Love), who has made her acquaintance informally.

Roaring, blinding wind and sandstorms immediately frighten the girl. She remains in a semi-conscious state of fright throughout, excepting at the close of the picture.

At Beverly's (Edward Earle) ranch the girl becomes too popular with Cora's (Dorothy Cummings) children and is forced to leave. The girl then accepts a proposal from Lige (Lars Hanson), whom she had laughed at the night before. During a round-up of wild horses, brought down by a fierce northern gale, Roddy forces his way into Lige's home and stays there for the night with Letty.

. . . .

■ WIND ACROSS THE EVERGLADES

1958, 91 MINS, US ◇

Dir Nicholas Ray *Prod* Stuart Schulberg *Scr* Budd
Schulberg *Ph* Joseph Brun *Ed* George Klotz, Joseph
Zigman *Art Dir* Richard Sylbert
● Burl Ives, Christopher Plummer, Gypsy Rose Lee,
George Voskovec, Emmett Kelly, Peter Falk (Warner)

Wind across the Everglades is a worthy attempt to make a picture about early efforts of the Audubon Society to preserve the bird wildlife of Florida. It is an 'interesting' picture, with some impressive backgrounds of the Everglades country (where it was shot), but it is not consistently engrossing. It should have been far better.

The screenplay fictionalizes the struggle of the Audubon Society to end the slaughter of Florida's plume birds, whose feathers were so highly prized around the turn of the century for women's hats. The action revolves around the almost single-handed efforts of an agent (Christopher Plummer) to stop the mass killings, and in particular his battle with the leader of one band of bird-hunters (Burl Ives).

There are some good shots of the egrets and other fowl, some with spectacular effect, and satisfactory simulated scenes of the birds' slaughter. Plummer does a good job as the idealistic bird warden, although not much motivation is ever given for his dedication. Ives, looking remarkably like Henry VIII in a red beard, eyebrows and hair, does a characteristically intense job, and his character, as a free-booting, civilization-hating rugged individualist, makes sense if not sympathy. Gypsy Rose Lee has some good comedy scenes which she handles adroitly while displaying some startling cleavage.

■ WIND AND THE LION, THE

1975, 119 MINS, US ◇
Dir John Milius   *Prod* Herb Jaffe   *Scr* John Milius
Ph Billy Williams   *Ed* Robert L. Wolfe   *Mus* Jerry Goldsmith   *Art Dir* Gil Parrando
● Sean Connery, Candice Bergman, Brian Keith, John Huston, Geoffrey Lewis, Steve Kanaly (M-G-M)

Sean Connery stars as an upstart independent Berber chieftain who in 1904 kidnaps Candice Bergen and children, provoking Brian Keith (as Theodore Roosevelt) into dramatic power politics, which confound European moves into North Africa.

The quasi-fictional story gives full exposition to the black, white and gray personal and political elements involved, providing focal points of empathy and criticism for all.

Connery scores one of his major screen impressions, while Bergen handles with assured excellence the subtleties of a woman first outraged at her captor, later his benefactor after a multinational doublecross.

Milius, armed with an expert crew of action specialists, has crafted a superior film, enhanced even further by Jerry Goldsmith's outstanding score.

■ WIND CANNOT READ, THE

1958, 115 MINS, UK ◇
Dir Ralph Thomas   *Prod* Betty E. Box   *Scr* Richard Mason   *Ph* Ernest Steward   *Ed* Frederick Wilson
Mus Angelo Lavagnino   *Art Dir* Maurice Carter
● Dirk Bogarde, Yoko Tani, Ronald Lewis, John Fraser, Anthony Bushell, Michael Medwin (Rank)

Richard Mason's novel shapes up as a useful romantic drama. The pic is a love story told against a Burma war background. Scenery pluses include the doll-like good looks of the young Japanese actress, Yoko Tani. She and Dirk Bogarde hold the acting side together in what is an almost uninterrupted Cupid duolog.

Bogarde is a grounded flyer sent to learn Japanese in order to be able to interrogate Japanese POWs. He falls for Tani, one of the instructors, marries her in secret and is then sent off to the front where he is captured, tortured and humiliated before escaping.

The gradual falling in love of the two stars is written with trite dialog but is directed charmingly. Then, when the action moves to the front, the prison torture scenes are put over with stark realism.

■ WINDOM'S WAY

1957, 108 MINS, UK ◇ ⊙
Dir Ronald Neame   *Prod* John Bryan   *Scr* Jill Craigie   *Ph* Christopher Challis   *Ed* Reginald Mills
Mus James Bernard   *Art Dir* Michael Stringer
● Peter Finch, Mary Ure, Natasha Parry, Robert Flemyng, Michael Hordern, Marne Maitland (Rank)

Peter Finch is a dedicated doctor working in the village of Selim, on a Far East island. He is loved and trusted by the villagers and finds himself involved in their political problems. Mary Ure is his estranged wife who comes out for a trial reconciliation at a time when the locality is in a state of unrest. Finch's ideals are such that he tries to prevent the villagers from getting up in arms against the local police and plantation manager.

The acting throughout this drama is first class, with Finch particularly convincing. Ure has little chance in the colorless role of his wife, but Natasha Parry as a native nursing sister, in love with Finch, is warm, sensitive and technically very sound.

Jill Craigie has provided a slow moving, but literate script, from a novel by James Ramsay Ullman. Ronald Neame's direction brings out qualities of dignity and credibility.

■ WINDY CITY

1984, 102 MINS, US ◇ ⊙
Dir Armyan Bernstein   *Prod* Alan Greisman
Scr Armyan Bernstein   *Ph* Reynaldo Villalobos
Ed Clifford Jones   *Mus* Jack Nitzsche   *Art Dir* Bill Kenney
● John Shea, Kate Capshaw, Josh Mostel, Jim Borrelli, Jeffrey DeMunn, Eric Pierpoint (CBS)

Windy City marks writer Armyan Bernstein's (*One from The Heart*) maiden voyage as director of his own tales, and while the endeavor isn't always smooth sailing, the heart-felt nature of his subject is generally strong enough to weather the awkwardness of this story of romance, friendship and shattered dreams.

Focus is Danny Morgan (John Shea), the most obvious victim of failed ambition among a group of seven men. He's a writer forced to take odd jobs including delivering mail. In the latter capacity he meets Emily (Kate Capshaw), the woman who finally accelerates his maturation which ironically forces their estrangement.

Cast is very strong although Shea is saddled with too much voice-over narration at top of picture.

■ WINGED VICTORY

1944, 130 MINS, US
Dir George Cukor   *Prod* Darryl F. Zanuck   *Scr* Moss Hart   *Ph* Glen MacWilliams   *Ed* Barbara McLean
Mus David Rose   *Art Dir* Lyle R. Wheeler, Lewis Creber
● Mark Daniels, Lon McCallister, Don Taylor, Red Buttons, Edmond O'Brien, Jeanne Crain (20th Century-Fox)

This is no story of any specific segment of Americana; it is, rather, the tale of Main Street and Broadway, of Texas and Brooklyn, of Christian and Jew – of American youth fighting for the preservation of American ideals. This is a documentation of American youth learning to fly for victory – a winged victory – and though it's fashioned in the manner of fictional entertainment, all the boys listed are bona fide members of the AAF – acting real-life roles.

The story of six boys from diverse parts of America, and how they leave behind wives and sweethearts and mothers to join the AAF, *Victory* is an honest understanding of American youth with the insatiable urge to ride the clouds.

The narrative follows them through basic training, the rigorous aptitude tests, and then the news on whether they had passed or were washed out. The solo flights – from which one of the sextet fails to return – and, ultimately, graduation day, followed by their assignments as either pilots, navigators or bombardiers, are all significantly told.

■ WINGS

1927, 139 MINS, US ◇ ⊗ ⊙
Dir William A. Wellman   *Prod* Lucien Hubbard
Scr Hope Loring, Louis D. Lighton, Julian Johnson, John Monk Saunders   *Ph* Harry Perry   *Ed* Lucien Hubbard   *Mus* (sound version) J.S. Zamecnik
● Clara Bow, Charles (Buddy) Rogers, Richard Arlen, Jobyna Ralston, Gary Cooper, El Brendel (Paramount)

When the action settles on terra firma there is nothing present that other war supers haven't had, some to a greater degree. But nothing has possessed the graphic descriptive powers of aerial flying and combat that have been poured into this effort.

Some of the Magnascope battle scenes in the air are in color. Not natural but with sky and clouds deftly tinted plus spouts of flame shooting from planes that dive, spiral and even zoom as they supposedly plunge to earth in a final collapse.

Richard Arlen goes through the picture minus make-up. At least the cameras register him that way. Consequently he looks the high bred, high strung youngster who would dote on aviation and backs it up with a splendid performance that never hints of the actor. Charles Rogers' effort is also first rate, the important point here being that these two boys team well together. There not being so much of Clara Bow in the picture, she gives an all around corking performance. El Brendel's comedy is spasmodic and mostly early in the first half, while Gary Cooper is on and off within half a reel.

The most planes counted in the air at once are 18. But there are the pursuit and bombing machines, captive balloons, smashes and crashes of all types, with some of the shots of these 'crack-ups' remarkable. Fake stuff and double photography, too, although no miniatures in regard to the air action are discernible if used.

□ 1927/8: Best Picture.

■ WINNING

1969, 123 MINS, US ◇ ⊙
Dir James Goldstone   *Prod* John Foreman
Scr Howard Rodman   *Ph* Richard Moore   *Ed* Edward A. Biery, Richard C. Meyer   *Mus* Dave Grusin   *Art Dir* Alexander Golitzen, John J. Lloyd, Joe Alves
● Paul Newman, Joanne Woodward, Robert Wagner, Richard Thomas, David Sheiner, Clu Gulager (Universal)

Winning, a love story set against an auto racing background, stars Paul Newman and Joanne Woodward. Overly-long, it nevertheless carries sock appeal in suspenseful racing sequences and its principals in a realistically-developed marital romance score strongly.

Newman underplays his part throughout, resulting in one of his better performances. He is ideally cast as the racer, and those sequences in which he is racing are convincingly portrayed. There is a compelling authority, too, about his scenes with his femme costar.

Woodward, who makes no attempt at glamor or any other goal except as Newman's earthy wife, turns in a ringingly effective characterization, lacking in color but packing dramatic punch. Robert Wagner, who costars with other two, is the heavy, lending credibility to role.

WINSLOW BOY, THE

1948, 117 MINS, UK ⓥ

Dir Anthony Asquith   *Prod* Anatole de Grunwald
Scr Terence Rattigan, Anatole de Grunwald
Ph Frederick Young   *Ed* Gerald Turney Smith
Mus William Alwyn   *Art Dir* Andre Andrejeff
● Robert Donat, Margaret Leighton, Cedric
Hardwicke, Marie Lohr, Neil North, Basil Radford
(British Lion/London)

Terence Rattigan's story, based on an actual
incident that occurred just before the First
World War, is a simple story of a 13-year-old
naval cadet, expelled from school for the
alleged theft of a dollar postal order. The
boy's father is certain of his innocence and
when he fails to have the case reopened,
invokes the whole machinery of British
democracy by arranging a full-scale parlia-
mentary debate and subsequently bringing a
successful action against the King.

It's more the father's conviction of his son's
innocence, rather than the incident itself,
which forms the background of this well-knit
story, with sufficient emphasis on the emotional angles to make it a sure tearjerker.
From its brisk opening the plot quickly develops the main theme, building up the fight for
justice through a series of incidents which are
highlighted by the interview between Robert
Morton, MP and famous attorney, and the
boy before he decides to accept the brief.

A flawless cast portrays the principal characters to perfection, and minor roles have
been painstakingly filled.

WINSTANLEY

1975, 95 MINS, UK

Dir Kevin Brownlow, Andrew Mollo   *Scr* Kevin
Brownlow, Andrew Mollo   *Ph* Ernest Vincze
● Miles Halliwell, Jerome Wills (BFI)

The very opposite of the typical, commercial
costume drama, *Winstanley* [based on a novel
by David Cante] depicts the hardships and
political turmoil in 17th-century England following the Civil War and the victory of the
Puritans.

Winstanley was a leader of one of those dissident religious sects which sprang up in
plentitude after the first wave of the Protestant Reformation. His was known as the
Diggers, a commune set up in Surrey to proclaim equality and the right to work 'free'
land.

The parson, upon whose land the Diggers
squatted, takes a different view and sends ruffians to destroy their crops, beat them and
burn down the makeshift hovels. Winstanley's writing and preaching wins him favor
but the arrival of less idealistic members of
the commune undermines the movement.

WINTER KILLS

1979, 97 MINS, US ◇ ⓥ

Dir William Richert   *Prod* Fred Caruso   *Scr* William
Richert   *Ph* Vilmos Zsigmond   *Ed* David Bretherton
Mus Maurice Jarre   *Art Dir* Robert Boyle
● Jeff Bridges, John Huston, Anthony Perkins, Sterling
Hayden, Eli Wallach, Elizabeth Taylor (Avco Embassy)

If there's a decent film lurking somewhere in
Winter Kills, writer-director William Richert
doesn't want anyone to see it in his Byzantine
version of a presidential assassination
conspiracy.

Tale of wealthy family patriarch John
Huston, whose elder son was a president
slain 19 years before the pic's beginning, and
younger sibling Jeff Bridges, now after his
brother's killer(s), is an exercise in methodical obfuscation.

Huston gives a powerhouse performance,
and Bridges, always likeable, runs through
his repertoire of facial expressions and
grimaces, but it's a lost cause.

Elizabeth Taylor has a wordless cameo as
a procuress for the late president, but contractual provisions prevent her name from
being used in connection with *Winter Kills*.
The rest of the cast should have been so
lucky.

WINTER PEOPLE

1989, 110 MINS, US ◇ ⓥ

Dir Ted Kotcheff   *Prod* Robert H. Solo   *Scr* Carol
Sobieski   *Ph* Francois Protat   *Ed* Thom Noble
Mus John Scott   *Art Dir* Ron Foreman
● Kurt Russell, Kelly McGillis, Lloyd Bridges, Mitchell
Ryan, Amelia Burnette (Nelson/Columbia)

The wages of sin are forever up in the old
North Carolina hills, especially when they
concern clans carrying on a blood feud.
That's the backdrop for *Winter People*, a
grimly unappetizing melodrama that forwards themes and concerns as remote as its
time and place.

Adaptation of John Ehle's novel is set in
1934. Widower Kurt Russell decamps from
his native town with little daughter in tow
and alights at the remote cabin of Kelly
McGillis, who has an illegitimate baby son.

An old-fashioned, unassertive type, Russell
has to prove himself to McGillis' three brothers by joining them on a bear hunt, and wins
the approval of her pa (Lloyd Bridges) by
designing and building a clock tower for the
little community.

But the demented Campbell clan lives
across the river, and McGillis' dark secret is
then revealed.

Continual histrionic demands are placed
upon McGillis, who is not necessarily always
up to them, and Russell is stuck with the
Richard Barthlemess role of the earnest do-
gooder forced to lower himself to the occasion
of taking on brutal thugs.

WIRED

1989, 108 MINS, US ◇ ⓥ

Dir Larry Peerce   *Prod* Edward S. Feldman, Charles P.
Meeker   *Scr* Earl Mac Rauch   *Ph* Tony Imi   *Ed* Eric
Sears   *Mus* Basil Poledouris   *Art Dir* Brian Eatwell
● Michael Chiklis, Ray Sharkey, J. T. Walsh, Patti
D'Arbanville, Lucinda Jenney, Alex Rocco (F/M/Lion)

In a brief but outstanding career on TV and
in pics, John Belushi was an engaging personality. His drug overdose death further
enthralled the public. *Wired*, however, told in
episodes, flashbacks and dream sequences, is
relentlessly offputting.

In a fanciful, less-than-successful effort to
string together the events in Belushi's tragicomic life, *Wired* begins after Belushi
(Michael Chiklis) has died. He rises, dressed
in an autopsy gown to join another 'spirit',
Angel Valesquez (Ray Sharkey), in a cab ride
down memory lane.

The professional benchmarks in Belushi's
life are there: the Blues Bros, the comic performances on *Saturday Night Live*, his Hollywood films. One episode is interrupted by
others, including graphic glimpses of
Belushi's cocaine habit and the devastating
effect it has on his confidantes and colleagues.

Somehow, Chiklis ekes out an estimable
performances as the doomed comic actor,
sweating flashes of Belushi's intensity and
vulnerability.

WISE BLOOD

1979, 108 MINS, US/W. GERMANY ◇ ⓥ

Dir John Huston   *Prod* Michael Fitzgerald, Kathy
Fitzgerald   *Scr* Benedict Fitzgerald   *Ph* Gerald
Fisher   *Ed* Roberto Silvi   *Mus* Alex North
● Brad Dourif, Ned Beatty, Harry Dean Stanton, Amy
Wright, John Huston (Ithaca/Anthea)

John Huston, with uncluttered direction and

expert handling of actors, has fashioned a disturbing tale of the fringe side of overzealous
religious preachers in the deep South.

Taken from a short novel by Flannery
O'Connor, film is grim and Gothic in feeling,
but balanced by an underlying tenderness for
these fringe people.

Brad Dourif is effective as a young man
home from the wars, probably World War II.
He visits his now boarded-up house in the
country and then doffs his uniform to buy
clothes making him look like a preacher.

He goes to a city where he is attracted by a
blind preacher with a teenage daughter who
gives him lubricious looks. Flashbacks reveal
Dourif as the grandson of a fire and brimstone preacher, played by Huston himself.

WISH YOU WERE HERE

1987, 91 MINS, UK ◇ ⓥ

Dir David Leland   *Prod* Sara Radclyffe   *Scr* David
Leland   *Ph* Ian Wilson   *Mus* Stanley Myers
Art Dir Caroline Amies
● Emily Lloyd, Tom Bell, Clare Clifford, Barbara Durkin,
Geoffrey Hutchings (Zenith/Working Title)

Set in a thoroughly uptight, provincial British seaside resort in the 1950s, this touching
account of a girl's growing pains marks the
directorial debut of director-scripter David
Leland.

What makes it interesting is the character
of the heroine; her refreshing rudeness dis-
concerts those around her. By focusing on a
spunky but troubled 16-year-old girl named
Lynda (played with exasperating charm by
newcomer Emily Lloyd), Leland squeezes
out more poignancy than would have been
possible had the central character been the
typical gawky male youth of most films about
sexual awakening.

What makes the girl troubled is the fact
that her mother died when she was 11 – and
no one has replaced that essential loss.
Lynda's reaction to her plight is to shock
people with her rudeness and to taunt the
opposite sex. This makes for some verbally
sharp and occasionally visually eloquent
scenes.

Lynda's rebelliousness eventually leads to a
potentially sinister liaison with a seedy older
man (played with taciturn intensity by Tom
Bell), as much a misfit as she is. Their scenes
together, though quite limited, are highly
charged.

WITCHES, THE

1990, 92 MINS, US ◇ ⓥ

Dir Nicolas Roeg   *Prod* Mark Shivas   *Scr* Allan Scott
Ph Harvey Harrison   *Ed* Tony Lawson   *Mus* Stanley
Myers   *Art Dir* Andrew Sanders
● Anjelica Huston, Mai Zetterling, Jasen Fisher,
Rowan Atkinson, Bill Paterson (Lorimar/Henson)

The wizardry of Jim Henson's Creature Shop
and a superbly over-the-top performance by
Angelica Huston gives *The Witches* a good
deal of charm and enjoyment.

Pic opens in Norway where grandmother
Helga (Mai Zetterling) is telling her nine-
year-old grandson Luke (Jasen Fisher) about
witches and their wicked ways. His parents
die in a car crash, and Luke and grandmother travel to England for a holiday.

They go to a stark Cornish hotel. Also
checking in is the annual ladies meeting of
the Royal Society for the Prevention of
Cruelty to Children; in actual fact a meeting
of the British witches, due to be addressed by
the Grand High Witch, Huston. Young Luke
accidentally overhears the meeting where
Huston announces her grand plan to feed
poisoned chocolate to all British children,
which will turn them into mice.

In a tight black dress and vampish haircut,
Huston seems to enjoy herself as the evil chief

witch, and the pic seems to be merely plodding along until she arrives on the scene.

....

■ WITCHES OF EASTWICK, THE

1987, 118 MINS, US ◇ Ⓥ

Dir George Miller   *Prod* Neil Canton, Peter Gruber, Jon Peters   *Scr* Michael Cristofer   *Ph* Vilmos Zsigmond   *Ed* Richard Francis-Bruce   *Mus* John Williams   *Art Dir* Polly Platt

● Jack Nicholson, Cher, Susan Sarandon, Michelle Pfeiffer, Veronica Cartwright, Richard Jenkins (Warner/Guber-Peters/Kennedy Miller)

The Witches of Eastwick [from the novel by John Updike] is a brilliantly conceived metaphor for the battle between the sexes that literally poses the question must a woman sell her soul to the devil to have a good relationship?

With a no-holds-barred performance by Jack Nicholson as the horny Satan, it's a very funny and irresistible set-up for anyone who has ever been baffled by the opposite sex.

Sukie Ridgemont (Michelle Pfeiffer), a writer for the local newspaper, is the intellectual; Jane Spofford (Susan Sarandon), a high school music teacher, is the woman of feeling; and Alexandra Medford (Cher), a sculptress, represents the sensuous side. They're all divorced and they're all looking for a Mr Right.

Enter Daryl Van Horn (Jack Nicholson), the answer to their collective longing for a man of wit, charm and intelligence. For Nicholson it's the role of a lifetime, the chance to seduce these women and be cock of the roost.

Spectacle of the film is really Nicholson. Dressed in eccentric flowing robes, odd hats and installed in a lush mansion, he is larger than life, as indeed the devil should be. The witches, lovely though they are, exist more as types than distinct personalities.

....

■ WITH A SONG IN MY HEART

1952, 116 MINS, US ◇

Dir Walter Lang   *Prod* Lamar Trotti   *Scr* Lamar Trotti   *Ph* Leon Shamroy   *Ed* J. Watson Webb Jr   *Mus* Alfred Newman (dir.)   *Art Dir* Lyle Wheeler, Joseph C. Wright

● Susan Hayward, Rory Calhoun, David Wayne, Thelma Ritter, Robert Wagner, Helen Westcott (20th Century-Fox)

The story of one of show business' courageous figures – Jane Froman – comes to the screen. Froman, a songbird who started her rise to fame in 1936 as a penny-ante singer of radio commercials, does her own chirping on 23 songs in this film version of her career.

In the first half, the pattern is the rather pat one of an unknown coming into prominence. The next 60 minutes, however, have the ring of sincere dramatics from the time Froman was nearly fatally injured in the Lisbon plane crash of 23 February 1943, while enroute to entertain servicemen overseas. Her fight back to life and only partial recovery of the use of her limbs, the birth of a new love, the resumption of a career to pay the enormous medical bills, come over on the screen as heartening drama.

While not entirely at home in the dancing accompaniment to some of the production numbers, Susan Hayward punches over the straight vocal-simulation and deftly handles the dramatic phases.

....

■ WITHNAIL & I

1986, 108 MINS, UK ◇ Ⓥ

Dir Bruce Robinson   *Prod* Paul M. Heller   *Scr* Bruce Robinson   *Ph* Bob Smith   *Ed* Alan Strachan   *Mus* David Dundas   *Art Dir* Michael Pickwood

● Richard E. Grant, Paul McGann, Richard Griffiths, Ralph Brown, Michael Elphick (HandMade)

Withnail & I is about the end of an era. Set in 1969 England, it portrays the last throes of a friendship mirroring the seedy demise of the hippie period, delivering some comic gems along the way.

Pic is the tale of two city boys stuck in a dilapidated country cottage in the middle of nowhere. The humor is both brutal and clever, and the acting uniformly excellent.

Pic opens with a pan round the disgusting London flat of out-of-work actors Withnail and Marwood (the 'I' of the title). Marwood (Paul McGann) is the nervous type trying to look John Lennon, while Withnail (Richard E. Grant) is gaunt, acerbic, and never without a drink in his hand.

Marwood declares the need to 'get into the countryside and rejuvenate.' A visit to Withnail's Uncle Monty secures them the loan of his country cottage, and the two head off into the night. They eventually arrive at the remote cottage, only to discover there is no light, no heat, and no water.

Uncle Monty (a standout performance by the portly Richard Griffiths) arrives with a twinkle in his eye when he is sidling up closer to Marwood. Monty's ardor and a telegram from his agent with news of a job are enough to convince Marwood that home is where the heart is, and he and Withnail retreat back to London. The two realize their friendship is coming to an end.

....

■ WITHOUT A TRACE

1983, 120 MINS, US ◇ Ⓥ

Dir Stanley R. Jaffe   *Prod* Stanley R. Jaffe   *Scr* Beth Gutcheon   *Ph* John Bailey   *Ed* Cynthia Schneider   *Mus* Jack Nitzsche   *Art Dir* Paul Sylbert

● Kate Nelligan, Judd Hirsch, David Dukes, Stockard Channing, Jacqueline Brookes, Keith McDermott (20th Century-Fox)

A muted melodrama about a woman whose young son simply disappears one day, *Without a Trace* seems to be of two minds about its own emotional content.

Kate Nelligan plays an English teacher at Columbia whose six-year-old son vanishes from the Brooklyn streets while on his two-block walk to school.

Her husband (David Dukes) has left three months earlier to shack up with a girl in Greenwich Village. But she retains her composure to an admirable degree, even when the cops and the media invade and virtually take over her home to work on the case. Leading the investigation team is Judd Hirsch, almost too perfectly cast as an overworked detective.

Stanley R. Jaffe, directing for the first time, could have bathed Beth Gutcheon's novel *Still Missing* in undiluted sentimentality from beginning to end, but has instead shied away from some of the most obvious potential dramatic developments. Nelligan's fundamental humorlessness keeps viewer at arm's length.

....

■ WITHOUT YOU I'M NOTHING

1990, 90 MINS, US ◇

Dir John Boskovich   *Prod* Jonathan D. Krane   *Scr* Sandra Bernhard   *Ph* Joseph Yacoe   *Ed* Pamela Malouf-Cundy   *Mus* Patrice Rushen

● Sandra Bernhard, Steve Antin, Lu Leonard (Krane-Roeg/Sterling)

Sandra Bernhard's screen adaptation of her one-woman show is a rigorous, experimental examination of performance art. Stepping back from comedy per se, Bernhard and her collaborator, director John Boskovich, have fashioned a remote, self-absorbed and often cryptic picture.

Most ambitious device here is a failure: except for brief interstitial footage of 'witnesses' such as Steve Antin (as himself) or Lu Leonard (portraying Bernhard's manager)

addressing the camera, film unfolds in performance on stage at a large, ersatz night club before a predominantly black audience. Crowd reacts only with silent, quizzical expressions or files out apparently not enjoying the show.

Pic's highlight underscores the material's emphasis on roleplaying and androgyny: a 1978-set 'I Feel Real' monolog/song with Bernhard pretending to be two guys in a disco, one of whom gets turned on by a black man and comes out of the closet. With helmer Boskovich letting loose his camera for once from its slow, monotonous pirouetting, scene is a showstopper.

....

■ WITNESS

1985, 112 MINS, US ◇ Ⓥ

Dir Peter Weir   *Prod* Edward S. Feldman   *Scr* Earl W. Wallace, William Kelley   *Ph* John Seale   *Ed* Thom Noble   *Mus* Maurice Jarre   *Art Dir* Stan Jolley

● Harrison Ford, Kelly McGillis, Josef Sommer, Lukas Haas, Jan Rubes, Alexander Godunov (Paramount)

Witness is at times a gentle, affecting story of star-crossed lovers limited within the fascinating Amish community. Too often, however, this fragile romance is crushed by a thoroughly absurd shoot-em-up, like ketchup poured over a delicate Pennsylvania Dutch dinner.

Australian director Peter Weir is obviously awed by the Amish, the quaint agrarian sect which maintains a 17th-century lifestyle, forsaking all modern conveniences while maintaining intense religious vows, including a pacifism most pertinent here.

Venturing outside the community on a trip to see her sister, recently widowed Kelly McGillis is drawn unfortunately into the 20th century when her young son (Lukas Haas), witnesses a murder in the men's room at the train station.

Enter gruff, foul-mouthed, streetwise detective Harrison Ford, whom the writers must somehow get out into the countryside as soon as possible so the cross-cultural romance can begin.

Witness warms up as the attraction builds between Ford, McGillis and Haas – all performing excellently through this portion. Admirable, too, is Ford's growing admiration for the people he's been thrown among.

☐ 1985: Best Picture (Nomination)

....

■ WITNESS FOR THE PROSECUTION

1957, 114 MINS, US Ⓥ

Dir Billy Wilder   *Prod* Arthur Hornblow   *Scr* Billy Wilder, Harry Kurnitz   *Ph* Russell Harlan   *Ed* Daniel Mandell   *Mus* Matty Malneck   *Art Dir* Alexandre Trauner

● Tyrone Power, Marlene Dietrich, Charles Laughton, Elsa Lanchester, Una O'Connor, Ian Wolfe (United Artists)

A courtroom meller played engagingly and building evenly to a surprising and arousing, albeit tricked-up, climax, *Witness for the Prosecution* has been transferred to the screen (from the Agatha Christie click play) with competence.

Under Billy Wilder's direction, *Prosecution* unfolds realistically, generating a quiet and steady excitement.

Cleverly worked out is the story line which has defense attorney Charles Laughton, along with the audience, wholly convinced that the likeable chap played by Tyrone Power is innocent, that he couldn't have murdered the rich widow who had taken a fancy to him. A disturbing note, however, is the unexpected attitude taken by Power's wife (Marlene Dietrich) who, as it turns out, is not legally married to him and thus is not restrained from testifying against him.

Laughton, sage of the courtroom and cardiac patient who's constantly disobeying his

nurse's orders, plays out the part flamboyantly and colorfully. His reputation for scenery chewing is unmarred via this outing.
□ 1957: Best Picture (Nomination)

■ **WIVES AND LOVERS**

1963, 102 MINS, US

Dir John Rich *Prod* Hal Wallis *Scr* Edward Anhalt *Ph* Lucien Ballard *Ed* Warren Low *Mus* Lyn Murray *Art Dir* Hal Pereira, Walter Tyler
● Janet Leigh, Van Johnson, Shelley Winters, Martha Hyer, Ray Walston, Claire Wilcox (Paramount)

Failure to be consistent with itself mars *Wives and Lovers*, an otherwise highly polished and pleasurable sophisticated comedy about a couple whose happy marriage is nearly shattered in the wake of the husband's sudden professional success.

The film excels in one area. Edward Anhalt's scenario, from Jay Presson's stage play, *The First Wife* contains some of the sharpest, wittiest, most perceptive comedy dialog to pop out of a soundtrack in some time.

Story relates the marital misadventure that materializes when an unsuccessful writer (Van Johnson), who for three years has been lovingly and uncomplainingly supported by his wife (Janet Leigh) while he pens a novel, suddenly hits the book-of-the-month jackpot. In a flash, the couple and their precocious tot have moved from a cramped Gotham coldwater flat to the luxury living of the fashionable Connecticut suburbs.

In the process of converting his prose into a Broadway play, Johnson becomes entangled in an affair with his glamorous agent (Martha Hyer), in retaliation Leigh apparently gets herself voluntarily seduced by the star (Jeremy Slate) of her husband's play.

Here is the issue. When a motion picture delves into matters as who-slept-with-whom-last-night-and-why, it owes it to its audience to be honest to the end. Unless prepared to resolve them intelligently, why introduce matters as these in the first place?

The acting in *Wives and Lovers* is pleasing and skillful. Occasional mechanical inconsistencies tarnish John Rich's otherwise bright and breezy direction in his first major feature assignment.

■ **WIZ, THE**

1978, 133 MINS, US ◇ Ⓥ

Dir Sidney Lumet *Prod* Rob Cohen *Scr* Joel Schumacher *Ph* Oswald Morris *Ed* Dede Allen *Mus* Quincy Jones (adapt.) *Art Dir* Tony Walton
● Diana Ross, Michael Jackson, Nipsey Russell, Lena Horne, Richard Pryor, Ted Ross (Motown)

Frank Baum [author of book *The Wonderful Wizard of Oz*] would never recognize his simple little story in this fantastically blown-up version [of William F. Brown's play], but the heart of his tale – that a person must find what he's searching for within himself – is still there.

The cast is virtually flawless but, when all is said and done, it's the combination of Oswald Morris's cinematography, the special visual effects of Albert Whitlock and Tony Walton's production design and costumes that linger longest in the memory.

Director Sidney Lumet has created what amounts to a love letter to the city of New York, which he equates with Oz.

Diana Ross, believable as a 24-year-old Harlem school teacher, is always in key with the mood, whether it calls for shyness, gaiety, courage or simply cutting up. Vocally, she's superb but, surprise, she also dances with all the abandon of an Alvin Ailey protege.

Of the supporting players and, despite their billing, that's what they amount to – Richard Pryor's Wiz (very briefly seen), Ted Ross's Lion and Mabel King's Evillene make the heaviest impressions. Nipsey Russell is fun as the Tin Man but Michael Jackson, though vocally great, needs more acting exposure.

■ **WIZARD OF OZ, THE**

1939, 100 MINS, US ◇ Ⓥ

Dir Victor Fleming *Prod* Mervyn LeRoy *Scr* Noel Langley, Florence Ryerson, Edgar Allan Woolf *Ph* Harold Rosson, Allen Davey *Ed* Blanche Sewell *Mus* Herbert Stothart (adapt.) *Art Dir* Cedric Gibbons
● Judy Garland, Frank Morgan, Ray Bolger, Bert Lahr, Jack Haley, Billie Burke (M-G-M)

The Wizard of Oz springs from Metro's golden bowl (production cost reported close to $3 million). Except for opening and closing stretches of prolog and epilog, which are visioned in a rich sepia, the greater portion of the film is in Technicolor.

Such liberties that have been taken with the original story [by L. Frank Baum] vest the yarn with constructive dramatic values. Underlying theme of conquest of fear is subtly thrust through the action. Fairy stories must teach simple truths.

What is on the screen is an adventure story about a small girl who lives on a Kansas farm. She and her dog, Toto, are caught in twister and whisked into an eerie land in which she encounters strange beings, good and evil fairies, and prototypes of some of the adults who comprised her farm world.

Then ensues the long trek to the mighty wizard's castle, where she and her companions, seek fulfillment of desire. Dorothy wishes only to return home. The plot is as thin as all that.

In the playing of it, however, Judy Garland as the little girl is an appealing figure as the wandering waif. Her companions are Ray Bolger, as the Scarecrow; Jack Haley, as the Woodman; and Bert Lahr as the cringing lion. Frank Morgan appears in sundry roles as the wizard, and the good and evil fairies are Billie Burke and Margaret Hamilton.
□ 1939: Best Picture (Nomination)

■ **WOLFEN**

1981, 114 MINS, US ◇

Dir Michael Wadleigh *Prod* Rupert Hitzig *Scr* David Eyre, Michael Wadleigh *Ph* Garry Fisher *Ed* Chris Lebenzon, Dennis Dolan, Martin Barm, Marshall M. Borden *Mus* James Horner *Art Dir* Paul Sylbert
● Albert Finney, Diane Venora, Edward James Olmos, Gregory Hines, Tom Noonan (Orion)

Wolfen is consistently more interesting than it is thrilling. Policeman Albert Finney is confronted with a series of baffling, grisly murders, gradually realizing they are not the work of mere mortals. As always in the best of pictures like this, the buildup is the most fun.

Initially, director Michael Wadleigh creates an exceedingly chilling atmosphere, especially as Finney and Gregory Hines, excellent as a space-case coroner, deal matter-of-factly with the dismembered dead.

Wadleigh creates a surreal point-of-view for the killers that works effectively, accented by handy digital sound. Overall, Paul Sylbert's production design is also a major plus. Add to that a splendid performance by Finney and a solid film debut for Diane Venora as his psychologist sidekick.

Film [from a novel by Whitley Strieber] was reportedly recut several times (four editors are credited) and a couple of bad cuts are clearly evident; a few scenes are awkward, too.

■ **WOLVES OF WILLOUGHBY CHASE, THE**

1989, 93 MINS, UK ◇

Dir Stuart Orme *Prod* Mark Forstater *Scr* William M. Akers *Ph* Paul Beeson *Ed* Martin Walsh *Mus* Colin Towns *Art Dir* Christopher Hobbs
● Stephanie Beacham, Mel Smith, Emily Hudson, Aleks Darowska, Geraldine James, Lynton Deardon (Zenith)

The Wolves of Willoughby Chase is a thoroughly enjoyable children's fantasy-adventure.

Pic has a suitable Dickensian feel, set during the imaginary reign of King James III some time in the last century in a snowbound part of North Yorkshire where wolves seem to rule the countryside. Based on Joan Aiken's children's novel, it has an attractively sinister quality and centers on the fight by two young girls to foil a dastardly plot by their evil governess, Slighcarp.

Tyro theatrical helmer Stuart Orme handles his chores well; they must have been doubly hard since pic was shot at the Barrandov Studios in Prague and on location around snowy Czechoslovakia in early 1988.

Emily Hudson and Aleks Darowska are excellent as the plucky youngsters, but best of all is Stephanie Beacham who outdoes herself as the wicked Slighcarp. The excellent cast is boosted by attractive tongue-in-cheek performances by Mel Smith and Geraldine James.

■ **WOMAN IN RED, THE**

1984, 87 MINS, US ◇ Ⓥ

Dir Gene Wilder *Prod* Victor Drai *Scr* Gene Wilder *Ph* Fred Schuler *Ed* Christopher Greenburg *Mus* John Morris *Art Dir* David L. Snyder
● Gene Wilder, Charles Grodin, Joseph Bologna, Judith Ivey, Michael Huddleston, Kelly Le Brock (Orion)

The woman in red is simply a very sexy contemporary (Kelly Le Brock), hired as a model by a San Francisco city agency, bringing her into contact with a mundane bureaucrat, Gene Wilder, heretofore a contented family man.

But one look at Le Brock, and Wilder is ready to risk all for illicit romance: he is not very adept at adultery.

The laughs roll along readily as Wilder tries one idea after another to sneak out on wife Judith Ivey and family to rendevous with Le Brock.

A wonderful diversion through all of this is Gilda Radner, a relatively plain fellow office worker who initially thinks she's the object of Wilder's wanderlust and is bitterly – and vigorously – disappointed when she finds out she isn't. [Pic is based on 1976 French film, *Pardon Mon Affaire*, directed by Yves Robert.]

■ **WOMAN IN THE WINDOW, THE**

1944, 90 MINS, US

Dir Fritz Lang *Prod* Nunnally Johnson *Scr* Nunnally Johnson *Ph* Milton Krasner *Ed* Gene Fowler Jr, Marjorie Johnson *Mus* Arthur Lange *Art Dir* Duncan Cramer
● Edward G. Robinson, Raymond Massey, Joan Bennett, Dan Duryea, Edmond Breon (RKO/International)

Nunnally Johnson whips up a strong and decidedly suspenseful murder melodrama in *Woman in the Window*. Producer, who also prepared the screenplay [from the novel *Once off Guard* by J.H. Wallis] continually punches across the suspense for constant and maximum audience reaction. Added are especially fine timing in the direction by Fritz Lang and outstanding performances by Edward G. Robinson, Joan Bennett, Raymond Massey and Dan Duryea.

Opening sequence suggests that tragedies spring from little things, and anyone can become involved in a murder or criminal action. That's just what happens to Robinson, a staid and middleaged college professor whose wife and children depart for vacation in Maine. He pauses and admires a painting on exhibition in store window adjoining his club. Later he again glances at the girl's portrait and finds the model standing beside him.

Robinson visits her apartment to look over other sketches; a stranger breaks in to accuse the girl of infidelity and attacks Robinson, who stabs the visitor in self-protection. Side-tracking initial impulse to call the police, he connives with the girl to dispose of the body in the country woods. Finish is a surprise for smash climax.

• •

■ **WOMAN OF AFFAIRS, A**

1929, 90 MINS, US

Dir Clarence Brown *Scr* Bess Meredyth, Hugh Wynn *Ph* William Daniels *Art Dir* Cedric Gibbons
● Greta Garbo, John Gilbert, Lewis Stone, John Mack Brown, Douglas Fairbanks Jr, Dorothy Sebastian (M-G-M)

A sensational array of screen names and the intriguing nature of the story (*The Green Hat*) from which it was made, together with some magnificent acting by Greta Garbo, carries through this vague and sterilized version of Michael Arlen's erotic play. Superb technical production counts in its favor.

But the kick is out of the material, and, worse yet, John Gilbert has an utterly blah role. Most of the footage he merely stands around rather sheepishly.

So here is a woman who, disappointed in her first love, plunges into an orgy of amorous adventures from Calais to Cairo.

Garbo saves an unfortunate situation throughout by a subtle something in her playing that suggests just the erotic note that is essential to the whole theme and story.

Production is noteworthy for its beauty of setting and atmosphere.

Lewis Stone plays a wise and kindly old counsellor of the madcap heroine that is made to order for his suave and sophisticated style of playing. Dorothy Sebastian manages to register real personality as the wife.

• •

■ **WOMAN OF DISTINCTION, A**

1950, 89 MINS, US ⊛

Dir Edward Buzzell *Prod* Buddy Adler *Scr* Charles Hoffman *Ph* Joseph Walker *Ed* Charles Nelson *Mus* Werner R. Heymann
● Ray Milland, Rosalind Russell, Edmund Gwenn, Janis Carter, Mary Jane Saunders, Francis Lederer (Columbia)

A Woman of Distinction is a loosely-tied grab-bag of screwball and nonsensical doings about two warring-but-loving pedagogues. Sans much logic, the Rosalind Russell-Ray Milland teamwork is good for more laughs than not and the gags overcome a yarn [by Hugo Butler and Ian McLellan Hunter] that lacks sound motivation.

Featured is a running duel between Russell, the woman of distinction too busy for romance, and Prof Milland, who is dragged into a faked news-headlined affair with the dean of a woman's college through the con-nivings of an overly-diligent press agent.

Russell pitches in with nice change of pace. Milland pieces together the necessary in-gredients of genteel sobriety, confusion and indignation.

• •

■ **WOMAN OF PARIS, A**

1923, 84 MINS, US ⊗ ⊛

Dir Charles Chaplin *Prod* Charles Chaplin *Scr* Charles Chaplin *Ph* Rollie Totheroh, Jack Wilson *Ed* Monta Bell *Art Dir* Arthur Stibolt
● Edna Purviance, Adolphe Menjou, Carl Miller, Lydia Knott, Charles K. French, Clarence Geldert (United Artists)

A Woman of Paris is a serious, sincere effort, with a bang story subtlety of idea-expression.

If the sentimental Charlie Chaplin made one outstanding error he did it in casting Edna Purviance, his leading woman of many classic comedies, for the central and stellar

role in his first legitimate picture. She is not a sensation. She looks and acts well enough, but she falls short of the fine pace set by the rest of the endeavor.

However, this is not a conspicuous drag on *A Woman of Paris*. Chaplin, on the other hand, straying far from his haunts of yore, comes forth as a new genius both as a producer and a director.

The finish is as brilliant and as memorable as the Mexico-line finale of *The Pilgrim*. After the girl has gone through all the vicissitudes of Paris high and low life, her rich ex-lover, driving in the country passes her on the road as she sits on the back of a farmer's cart with a little orphan. He just whizzes by – that's all. And it tells more than if he had the conven-tional breakdown.

• •

■ **WOMAN OF STRAW**

1964, 117 MINS, UK ◇

Dir Basil Dearden *Prod* Michael Relph *Scr* Robert Muller, Stanley Mann *Ph* Otto Heller *Ed* John D. Gutheridge *Mus* Muir Mathieson (arr.) *Prod Des* Ken Adam
● Gina Lollobrigida, Sean Connery, Ralph Richardson, Johnny Sekka, Laurence Hardy, Danny Daniels (United Artists)

Director Basil Dearden seems, here, to have temporarily misplaced the vigorous insight that has earned him some top credits. Best that can be said of *Straw* [from the novel by Catherine Arley] is that it looks handsome, what with Lollo, some scenes of Majorca and the English countryside and some ornate artwork.

But the film gets bogged down by stilted dialog and by the situations, which are high as the Empire State Building. Ralph Richardson is a multimillionaire, an illman-nered, sour tycoon condemned to spend his life in a wheelchair. He takes it out on any-body handy. These include his nephew-sec-retary (Sean Connery), his major-domo, colored houseboy, his yacht skipper and his dogs.

He even tosses some well considered snarls in the direction of Gina Lollobrigida who is hired by the nephew as the old man's nurse. As a result of all this humiliation there are several people who are not unhappy when he is found dead in the bunk of his yacht.

Interplay in the relationship and emotions of the characters involved make fair picture-going in the early stages. But when the plot gets down to the mystery of whether he died from natural causes or whether he was the victim of mayhem then it descends into under-average mishmash.

Richardson manages to extract what fun there is out of the desultory proceedings and even manages to dominate the screen when he is a corpse. Lollobrigida, when not chang-ing her highclass duds, is out of her depth in what must be a serious role if it is to jell, while the welldressed Connery wanders around with the air of a man who can't wait to get back to being James Bond again.

• •

■ **WOMAN OF THE YEAR**

1942, 112 MINS, US ⊛

Dir George Stevens *Prod* Joseph L. Mankiewicz *Scr* Ring Lardner Jr, Michael Kanin *Ph* Joseph Ruttenberg *Ed* Frank Sullivan *Mus* Franz Waxman
● Spencer Tracy, Katharine Hepburn, Fay Bainter, Reginald Owen, William Bendix, Dan Tobin (M-G-M)

Woman of the Year is an entertaining film with superb work by Katharine Hepburn and Spencer Tracy. There are very few palms due writers Ring Lardner Jr and Michael Kanin, who reputedly received the sum of $100,000 for the original screenplay. Director George Stevens likewise merits small praise.

Lardner and Kanin had an amusing start-ing point – a sports writer and a young and

beautiful counterpart of Dorothy Thompson spatting, then falling in love and marrying – but wend it tortuously through every hack-neyed and expected plot device without a sur-prise at any turn. Director Stevens lets it get out of hand completely with minutes on end devoted to a few tired situation gags. Picture runs 112 minutes and frequently seems every moment of that. Tracy and Hepburn go a long way toward pulling the chestnut out of the fire.

• •

■ **WOMAN ON THE BEACH, THE**

1947, 71 MINS, US

Dir Jean Renoir *Prod* Jack J. Gross *Scr* Frank Davis, Jean Renoir *Ph* Leo Tover, Harry Wild *Ed* Roland Gross, Lyle Boyer *Mus* Hanns Eisler *Art Dir* Albert S. D'Agostino, Walter E. Keller
● Joan Bennett, Robert Ryan, Charles Bickford (RKO)

Film is more mood than meaning. On the surface, it is a confusion of logic, a narrative drawn with invisible lines around characters without motivation in a plot only shadowily defined. But beneath, the cinematic elements are brilliantly fused by Jean Renoir into an intense and compelling emotional experience.

Thesping is uniformly excellent with the cast from top to bottom responding to Renoir's controlling need for a surcharged at-mosphere. In subtle counterpoint to the film's surface vagueness, the settings are not-ably realistic in their size and quality. Choice camerawork sustains the film's overall im-pact while sweeping through the entire pro-duction is a magnificent score by Hanns Eisler which heightens all of the film's pic-torial values.

Basically, the yarn [based on the novels, *None So Blind* by Mitchell Wilson] is a vari-ation of the eternal triangle theme but it unfolds elusively through implication and suggestion, only occasionally emerging to the level of full clarity. In the film's center, Char-les Bickford plays the role of a blind artist, brutally strong and madly jealous of his wife. As the latter, Joan Bennett is a callous tart tied to her husband only through an obses-sion of guilt arising from her accidental blind-ing of Bickford early in their marriage.

Third part is played by Robert Ryan, a coast guard officer stationed near the blind man's home in a desolate spot on the ocean front. He is recovering from a mental shock obtained in naval combat during the war.

• •

■ **WOMAN TIMES SEVEN**

1967, 99 MINS, US ◇ ⊛

Dir Vittorio De Sica *Prod* Arthur Cohn *Scr* Cesare Zavattini *Ph* Christian Matras *Ed* Teddy Darvas, Victoria Spiri-Mercanton *Mus* Riz Ortolani
● Shirley MacLaine, Peter Sellers, Alan Arkin, Rossano Brazzi, Michael Caine, Vittorio Gassman (Embassy)

Woman Times Seven means a seven-segment showcase for the talents of Shirley MacLaine, playing in tragicomedy and dramatic fashion a variety of femme types. MacLaine is spot-ted in many different adult situations, and largely convinces with each switcheroo.

With Peter Sellers, she is the bereaved widow, trailing her late husband in funeral procession, as Sellers puts the make on her. Then, as a wife who surprises hubby Rossano Brazzi in bed with a neighbor, MacLaine shifts to the enraged female, determined on revenge. The major tour de force segment finds MacLaine and Alan Arkin alone in a flophouse room, plotting suicide together.

• •

■ **WOMAN UNDER THE INFLUENCE, A**

1974, 155 MINS, US ◇

Dir John Cassavetes *Scr* John Cassavetes *Ph* Mitch Breit *Ed* Bob Heffernan *Mus* Bo Harwood *Art Dir* Phedon Papamichael

● Peter Falk, Gena Rowlands, Matthew Cassel, Matthew Laborteaux, Christina Grisanti, Katherine Cassavetes (Faces International)

This is a disturbing portrait of a slightly-mad housewife. Its serious treament of a downbeat subject is hypoed by a fine performance from Peter Falk and a bravura one from Gena Rowlands.

Rowlands plays a lower middle-class LA housewife whose sense of identity is so impoverished she defines herself only in terms of her husband's love and the devotion of her children.

Rowlands' performance in the title role is one of those tour de force numbers available only to screen players of alcoholics and lunatics.

Falk is outstanding in a role which calls for him to be loving and callous at the same time. He, too, retains audience sympathy.

Film is technically superior to any of John Cassavetes' previous works.

••••••••••••••••••••••••••••••••••••••

■ WOMAN'S FACE, A

1941, 105 MINS, US ▼

Dir George Cukor   *Prod* Victor Saville   *Scr* Donald Ogden Stewart, Elliot Paul   *Ph* Robert Planck   *Ed* Frank Sullivan   *Mus* Bronislau Kaper
● Joan Crawford, Melvyn Douglas, Conrad Veidt (M-G-M)

There's a rather intriguing dramatic quality to this American version of an original Swedish production (from a French play, Francis de Croisset's *Il etait une fois*) which had Ingrid Bergman as star. In a story of a woman's handicap and final regeneration.

Opening with the court trial of Joan Crawford for murder, the story is developed through various stages by testimony of the several witnesses – and finally the defendant herself. Dramatic suspense is maintained by keeping the victim's identity well hidden for a surprise climax.

Crawford is the victim of a childhood accident which left her face distorted and disfigured. Case-hardened and calloused, shunning people generally, she drops into a criminal career. Romantic approach of Conrad Veidt is the first she has had and she accepts his flattery with love-hungry adoration.

She meets plastic surgeon Melvyn Douglas whose offer of an operation is gladly accepted. Veidt then persuades her to take a job as governess on his uncle's estate – and to murder the child-heir that stands in his path to wealth inheritance.

Crawford has a strongly dramatic and sympathetic role, despite her hardened attitude, which she handles in topnotch fashion.

••••••••••••••••••••••••••••••••••••••

■ WOMEN, THE

1939, 132 MINS, US ◇ ▼

Dir George Cukor   *Prod* Hunt Stromberg   *Scr* Anita Loos, Jane Murfin   *Ph* Oliver T. Marsh, Joseph Ruttenberg   *Ed* Robert J. Kern   *Mus* Edward Ward, David Snell   *Art Dir* Cedric Gibbons, Wade B. Rubottom
● Norma Shearer, Joan Crawford, Rosalind Russell, Paulette Goddard, Joan Fontaine, Hedda Hopper (M-G-M)

As in the play [by Clare Boothe], no man appears – it's a field day for the gals to romp intimately in panties, scanties and gorgeous gowns. Most of the members of the cast (studio claims 135 speaking parts) deport themselves in a manner best described by Joan Crawford at the end. 'There's a name for you ladies, but it's not used in high society outside of kennels.'

Story is essentially lightweight and trivial, and covers a wide range of fem conversations – barbed shafts at friends, whisperings of husbands' indiscretions, maligning gossip and catty asides. Script basically maintains structure of the play but directs more sympathetic appeal to the marital problem of Norma Shearer.

Picture however holds passages that slow movement down to a walk.

••••••••••••••••••••••••••••••••••••••

■ WOMEN IN LOVE

1969, 130 MINS, UK ◇ ▼

Dir Ken Russell   *Prod* Larry Kramer, Martin Rosen   *Scr* Larry Kramer   *Ph* Billy Williams   *Ed* Michael Bradsell   *Mus* Georges Delerue   *Art Dir* Luciana Arrighi
● Alan Bates, Oliver Reed, Glenda Jackson, Jennie Linden, Eleanor Bron, Vladek Sheybal (United Artists)

Directed with style and punch by Ken Russell this is an episodic but challenging and holding pic. D.H. Lawrence's pungent thoughts about love and marriage, and the attitudes of the two sexes toward them, are not highly original but are shrewdly put over.

Russell's direction dominates the film, but he has the benefit of four excellent performances. The rough, tough coalmining area of the Midlands is effectively evoked.

The story is fragmentary. Two sisters are wooed and won by two men and the film concerns their relationship. One settles down to a marriage on happy but uneasy terms. The other, more questing, has an equally uneasy yet gleeful romance which ends in tragedy.

Glenda Jackson gives a vital performance with punch and intelligence. Jennie Linden, settles for married life with Alan Bates.

••••••••••••••••••••••••••••••••••••••

■ WONDER MAN

1945, 95 MINS, US ◇ ▼

Dir H. Bruce Humberstone   *Prod* Samuel Goldwyn   *Scr* Don Hartman. Melville Shavelson, Philip Rapp   *Ph* Victor Milner, William Snyder   *Ed* Daniel Mandell   *Mus* Ray Heindorf (arr.)   *Art Dir* Ernst Fegte, McClure Capps
● Danny Kaye, Virginia Mayo, Vera-Ellen, Steve Cochran, Huntz Hall (RKO/Goldwyn)

Niftily Technicolored and expensive-looking all the way, *Wonder Man* finds Kaye in a dual role, as twins, one being a nitery performer bumped off by yeggs because of information he was going to give the district attorney; the other as a mild-mannered, studious type who, after his brother's slaying, is belabored by the latter's 'spirit' into taking his place and thus help run down the thugs.

The complications, notably on the romance, frequently get too unwieldy for comfort. Several of the comedy situations are rewrites of oldies, but Kaye makes them capital. There is, in particular, a final-reel scene in which Kaye seeks refuge as a costumed singer during the midst of an operatic performance. It's boilerplate comedy but Kaye makes it belly-laugh fun.

If this sounds like all Danny Kaye, there's no mistaking that without him this film would be decidedly commonplace. He has a good supporting cast, namely the beauteous Virginia Mayo, as the main romantic link, and Vera-Ellen, out of the Broadway musicals, who is the secondary love interest. The blonde Mayo screens like the couple of millions that are indicated to have been spent by Goldwyn on the pic: and Vera-Ellen is a fine young hoofer who can handle lines well, too.

••••••••••••••••••••••••••••••••••••••

■ WONDERFUL LIFE

1964, 113 MINS, UK ◇

Dir Sidney J. Furie   *Prod* Kenneth Harper   *Scr* Peter Myers, Ronald Cass   *Ph* Kenneth Higgins   *Ed* Jack Slade   *Mus* Peter Myers, Ronald Cass   *Prod Des* Stanley Dorfman
● Cliff Richard, Walter Slezak, Susan Hampshire, The Shadows, Una Stubbs, Melvyn Hayes (Warner-Pathé)

Film musicals often get by on shaky storylines but these are usually decked out with lively jokes and badinage and Peter Myers and Ronald Cass prove themselves somewhat sparing in this department. It puts an unfair onus on Cliff Richard, to expect his personality to buck several slack passages and remarkably unwitty wordage.

Richard, the Shadows group and comedians Melvyn Hayes and Richard O'Sullivan are merchant sailors stranded in the Canaries where they come across Walter Slezak directing a diabolical *Beau Geste* epic. Caught up in this mish mash, leading lady Susan Hampshire is having a rough time. For love of the young lady the lads decide to boost her confidence by making an off-the-cuff musical version of the director's film.

The happiest flight of fancy is a sequence which sends up films down the ages. Richard, Hampshire, and the rest show a pleasing sense of mimicry and satire as they josh such favorites as Valentino, the Marx Brothers, the Mack Sennett Cops, Shirley Temple, Garbo, Grable, Boyer, Fairbanks Sr, Bogart, Dick Powell, Tarzan and others right up to James Bond.

••••••••••••••••••••••••••••••••••••••

■ WONDERFUL WORLD OF THE BROTHERS GRIMM, THE

1962, 135 MINS, US ◇ ▼

Dir Henry Levin, George Pal   *Prod* George Pal   *Scr* David P. Harmon, Charles Beaumont, William Roberts   *Ph* Paul C. Vogel   *Ed* Walter Thompson   *Mus* Leigh Harline   *Art Dir* George W. Davis, Edward Carfagno
● Laurence Harvey, Karl Boehm, Claire Bloom, Walter Slezak, Yvette Mimieux, Russ Tamblyn (M-G-M/Cinerama)

Grimm is a delightful, refreshing entertainment. Pal himself shares directorial credit with Levin, as the producer also is responsible for directing the Fairy Tales sequences. Pal and Grimm are sympatico, although he permitted Jim Backus as the King to sound too much like Mr. Magoo in *The Dancing Princess* sequence.

This traditional fairy tale of the princess who finds her true love in the humble woodsman is interestingly choreographed by Alex Romero and charmingly interpreted by Yvette Mimieux and Russ Tamblyn.

As far as acting honors go. Harvey is dominant, for in addition to playing Wilhem Grimm he also enacts, and with touching warmth offset by a trace of irrascibility, the title role in *The Cobbler and the Elves*. This sequence, with its Christmas setting and assortment of orphans and puppets which performs a miracle in the cobbler's shop overnight, is entirely enchanting.

The Singing Bone dealing with a titanic encounter involving a superficious aspiring knight and his servant with a fire-spouting dragon, is full of exaggerated chills and wry humor. Buddy Hackett (who reminds of the late Lou Costello) as the humble servant who finally emerges as the shining knight over his dastardly master, is enchanting. And Terry-Thomas also is excellent as the master whose cowardice ultimately strips him of honor and glory.

••••••••••••••••••••••••••••••••••••••

■ WOODEN HORSE, THE

1950, 101 MINS, UK ▼

Dir Jack Lee   *Prod* Ian Dalrymple   *Scr* Eric Williams   *Ph* G. Pennington-Richards   *Ed* John Seabourne Sr, Peter Seabourne   *Mus* Clifton Parker   *Art Dir* William Kellner
● Leo Genn, David Tomlinson, Anthony Steel, Bryan Forbes, David Green (London/Wessex)

A commendable degree of documentary fidelity is established in this picturization of the escape of three prisoners-of-war from a German camp. The long and torturous period of preparation is faithfully recaptured.

Yarn traces the exploits of three officers who, after receiving approval from the camp's 'escape committee', cover up their tunnel-digging by means of a vaulting horse.

Some of the best drama in the film comes after the prison break, where the two ex-airmen, with forged papers, make for a port and finally board a boat for Copenhagen on their last drive for freedom.

Thesping standard is universally good all round. Eric Williams' screenplay from his own novel is a workman-like job.

....

■ WOODSTOCK

1970, 183 MINS, US ◇ ⓥ

Dir Michael Wadleigh   *Prod* Bob Maurice
Ph Michael Wadleigh, David Myers, Richard Pearce, Donald Lenzer, Al Wertheimer   *Ed* Thelma Schoonmaker, Martin Scorsese, Stan Warnow, Jere Huggins, Yeu-Bun Yee
● (Warner)

Woodstock, brilliantly made by Michael Wadleigh, is a virtually perfect record of the music festival held in Bethel, NY, in summer 1969.

As a documentary feature, the film is a milestone in artistic collation of raw footage into a multipanel, variable-frame, dazzling montage that engages the senses with barely a let-up.

From countless thousands of feet of exposed stock, Wadleigh has superbly orchestrated on film the mass intimacy of pop music and its latter-day relationship to self and environment. *Woodstock* is an absolute triumph in its marriage of cinematic technology to reality.

Of no mean help, of course, are the outstanding musical talents. They do their own things, while the individual and collective effect is spine-tingling.

....

■ WORDS AND MUSIC

1948, 119 MINS, US ◇ ⓥ

Dir Norman Taurog   *Prod* Arthur Freed   *Scr* Fred Finkelhoffe   *Ph* Charles Rosher, Harry Stradling   *Ed* Albert Akst, Ferris Webster   *Mus* Richard Rodgers   *Art Dir* Cedric Gibbons, Jack Martin Smith
● Tom Drake, Mickey Rooney, Betty Garrett, Ann Sothern, Janet Leigh (M-G-M)

The saga of Rodgers and Hart itself is neither very interesting nor exceptional, unless it be in their early and continued success at turning out words and music for one top Broadway and Hollywood musical hit after another. Fred Finkelhoffe, therefore, in preparing his screenplay, acted wisely in reducing the biographical aspects to almost a minimum, using them only as a rack around which to weave production numbers, terp routines and lyric assignments.

Tom Drake plays the serious, businesslike and homeloving Rodgers, the melodist of the pair. Mickey Rooney plays Hart, giving the role at least some partial physical veri-simil-itude in that his tiny stature was a near-tragedy in the lyricist's life.

Biog, as a matter of fact, sticks to truth about as closely as can be presented on the screen. While details are freely reshuffled, the yarn is strikingly sound from an overall psychological view, catching Hart's early zest for life and its gradual change to a tragic chase after a happiness he couldn't achieve, a chase that led to his death in 1943 at the age of 47.

Hart, who never married, but bounded about the world, was, of course, the more colorful of the pair and the camera faithfully catches that. Rooney plays Rooney, however, rather than Hart, almost turning the role into a burlesque. Drake imbues Rodgers with the dignity and modesty of a Rodgers – if not

with the spark. Film doesn't go into the break between the pair, two years before Hart's death. It was at this time Rodgers teamed with Oscar Hammerstein II.

....

■ WORK IS A 4-LETTER WORD

1968, 93 MINS, UK ◇

Dir Peter Hall   *Prod* Thomas Clyde   *Scr* Jeremy Summers   *Ph* Gil Taylor   *Ed* Keith Green   *Mus* Guy Woolfenden   *Art Dir* Philip Harrison
● David Warner, Cilla Black, Elizabeth Spriggs, Zia Mohyeddin, Joe Gladiyn (Rank/Universal-Cavalcade)

Work is a 4-Letter Word is based on Henry Livings' unconventional and not wholly satisfactory play *Eh?* A difficult theme for a film, *Work* is a wayout comedy fantasy.

There is an irritating air of improvisation about much of the picture which shows up particularly in the editing, Keith Green clearly having difficulty in keeping Jeremy Summers' wayward screenplay within coherent bounds.

The thin storyline visualizes man's struggle against automation, something of a harkback to Chaplin's *Modern Times*. Overwhelmed by the DICE organization which makes such horrors as plastic daffodils and whose skyscraper offices and factories are automated to a point of frenzy one young man holds out against the system.

The plot and message are merely hooks for a series of off-beat situations, some very funny and others over-reminiscent and over-stressed. Director Peter Hall often hangs on to a point just long enough to blunt it.

....

■ WORKING GIRL

1988, 113 MINS, US ◇ ⓥ

Dir Mike Nichols   *Prod* Douglas Wick   *Scr* Kevin Wade   *Ph* Michael Ballhaus   *Ed* Sam O'Steen   *Mus* Carly Simon   *Art Dir* Patrizia Von Brandenstein
● Melanie Griffith, Harrison Ford, Sigourney Weaver, Joan Cusack, Alec Baldwin, Philip Bosco (20th Century-Fox)

Working Girl is enjoyable largely due to the fun of watching scrappy, sexy, unpredictable Melanie Griffith rise from Staten Island secretary to Wall Street whiz. She's the kind with an eye for stock figures – the numeral kind and the real kind (Harrison Ford).

Griffith stands apart, both for her eagerness to break out of her clerical rut and her tenacity dealing with whomever seems to be thwarting her, at first a lecherous brokerage house exec, whom she very cleverly and humorously exposes, and then a much more formidable and disarming opponent, femme boss Sigourney Weaver.

Just because they're both 'girls' trying to make their way amidst a sea of men doesn't, however, make them friends.

This is not a laugh-out-loud film, though there is a lighthearted tone that runs consistently throughout, Griffith's innocent, breathy voice being a major factor.

☐ 1988: Best Picture (Nomination)

....

■ WORKING GIRLS

1986, 90 MINS, US ◇ ⓥ

Dir Lizzie Borden   *Prod* Lizzie Borden, Andi Gladstone   *Scr* Lizzie Borden   *Ph* Judy Irola   *Ed* Lizzie Borden   *Mus* David Van Tiegham   *Art Dir* Kurt Ossenfort
● Louise Smith, Ellen McElduff, Amanda Goodwin, Marusia Zach, Janne Peters, Helen Nicholas (Alternative Current)

Working Girls is a simulated docu-style feature that allows audiences to be invisible guests for one day and part of the evening in a Manhattan brothel staffed by about 10 whores working two shifts and charging $50 per half hour when special services of limited scope

('mild dominance' is undertaken by some of the girls) are not required. When their shifts are over, the girls go home to private life with or without husbands or boyfriends.

Centering on Molly (Louise Smith), director Lizzie Borden neither glamorizes, romanticizes nor condemns anything or anybody connected to the brothel.

Borden sugars her pill with clean, crisp, often witty recording of brothel action and shop-talk. All acting is credible and the camerawork is smooth, the non-action a bit on the long winded side.

....

■ WORLD ACCORDING TO GARP, THE

1982, 136 MINS, US ◇ ⓥ

Dir George Roy Hill   *Prod* George Roy Hill, Robert Crawford   *Scr* Steve Tesich   *Ph* Miroslav Ondricek   *Ed* Stephen A. Rotter   *Mus* David Shire (adapt.)   *Art Dir* Henry Bumstead
● Robin Williams, Mary Beth Hurt, Glenn Close, John Lithgow, Hume Cronyn, Jessica Tandy (Pan Arts)

George Roy Hill's film adaptation of *The World according to Garp* has taste, intelligence, craft and numerous other virtues going for it.

Tale is that of young Garp, bastard son of independent-minded nurse Jenny Fields, who, at midlife, becomes a media celebrity upon the publication of her autobiographical tome, *A Sexual Suspect*.

Garp grows up in a placid academic environment, and the grown man in the person of Robin Williams appears only after 25 minutes. He meets and marries Mary Beth Hurt, raises his family, fitfully pursues his writing while she teaches, has skirmishes with the feminists at his mother's mansion, and all the while tries to avoid the 'undertoad', the unseen, pervasive threat which lurks everywhere and strikes without warning.

Physically, Williams is fine, but much of the performance is hit-and-miss. Otherwise, casting is superior. Hurt is excellent as Garp's wife. Glenn Close proves a perfect choice as Jenny Fields, a woman of almost ethereal simplicity. Best of all, perhaps, is John Lithgow as Roberta Muldoon, a former football player, now a transsexual.

....

■ WORLD APART, A

1988, 113 MINS, UK ◇ ⓥ

Dir Chris Menges   *Prod* Sarah Radclyffe   *Scr* Shawn Slovo   *Ph* Peter Biziou   *Ed* Nicolas Gaster   *Mus* Hans Zimmer   *Art Dir* Brian Morris
● Barbara Hershey, Jodhi May, David Suchet, Jeroen Krabbe, Paul Freeman, Tim Roth (British Screen/Working Title/Film Four)

A World Apart provides a sharp glimpse of what it was like to be politically contrary in the early 1960s in South Africa. It is mostly told from the p.o.v. of a 13-year-old girl, Molly (Jodhi May), whose life becomes dramatically disrupted as a result of her parents' subversive activities.

Set in 1963, story is described as a fictionalized account of what happened to young Shawn Slovo, the writer, and her family when the authorities began cracking down on them. Pic traces the growing emotional and political awareness of the youngster, but also represents a daughter's critique of what she perceives as her mother's selfish absorption in concerns she condescendingly considers above her offspring's head.

The casual cruelties and injustices of the South African system are displayed as part of life's fabric, but what's really going on with Molly's parents, as well as the friendly blacks who often visit the house, remains unclear and out of reach to the girl.

Barbara Hershey (as the mother) represents a solid central figure for the film. Nevertheless, the limited, daughter's-eye viewpoint restricts one's access to the woman's inner

W

self, the source of her political beliefs and her self-image.

Happily, May is at all times engaging as Molly, sustaining the film with no problem. Performances throughout are uniformly naturalistic and believable, and pic, which was shot in Zimbabwe, possesses a rich, luminous look despite a limited budget.

••••••••••••••••••••••••••••••••••••

■ **WORLD OF SUZIE WONG, THE**

1960, 130 MINS, US ◇ ▼

Dir Richard Quine *Prod* Ray Stark *Scr* John Patrick *Ph* Geoffrey Unsworth *Ed* Bert Bates *Mus* George Duning *Art Dir* John Box
● William Holden, Nancy Kwan, Sylvia Syms, Michael Wilding, Jacqui Chan, Laurence Naismith (Paramount)

The advantage of on-the-spot geography does a great deal for the screen version of *The World of Suzie Wong*. The ultra-picturesque environment of teeming Hong Kong brings a note of ethnic charm to the production, and amounts to a major improvement over the legit translation by Paul Osborn of Richard Mason's novel.

Suzie Wong is the story of an artist (William Holden) who has come to Hong Kong to devote one year to 'learning something about painting and something about myself'. Before long, he is also learning a great deal about Suzie (Nancy Kwan), a kind of titular leader of a band of lovable, warmhearted prostitutes (are there any other kinds?). After resisting temptations of the flesh and giving her the brush for an admirable period, Holden eventually succumbs to the yen. Complications ensue when it develops Kwan has a child.

The love story makes much more sense with the substitution of the mature Holden for the younger hero of the play. That and the scenery are the major improvements.

On the decidedly negative side are three passages in which realism is virtually abandoned for theatrical effect. (1) Kwan, beaten up by a sailor, proudly displays her bloody lip to the girls as a token of Holden's jealousy, (2) Kwan and Holden dine on salad dressing so as not to reveal her illiteracy to a 'stuckup' waiter, and (3) Holden impulsively tears Kwan's dress off when she turns up in his room looking like the western version of what she is.

Holden gives a first-class performance, restrained and sincere. He brings authority and compassion to the role. Kwan is not always perfect in her timing of lines (she has a tendency to anticipate) and appears to lack a full range of depth or warmth, but on the whole she manages a fairly believable portrayal. Michael Wilding is capable in a role that has been trimmed down. Jacqui Chan is convincing as a B-girl sans sex appeal, only one of the group (outside of the heroine) left with an identity in the screen translation.

••••••••••••••••••••••••••••••••••••

■ **WORLD TEN TIMES OVER, THE**

1963, 93 MINS, UK

Dir Wolf Rilla *Prod* Michael Luke *Scr* Wolf Rilla *Ph* Larry Pizer *Ed* Jack Slade *Mus* Edwin Astley
● Sylvia Syms, Edward Judd, June Ritchie, William Hartnell (Cyclops/Associated-British)

Wolf Rilla's screenplay explores in one day's fairly busy activity the aimlessness, insecurity and heartaches of nightclub hostesses. The result is overdramatic but provides opportunities for deft thesping. Nightclub and location sequences in London have a brisk authenticity.

Story concerns two girls, euphemistically called nightclub hostesses, who share an apartment. One (June Ritchie) is a flighty, young extrovert who is having an affair with the married son of a property tycoon. The other (Sylvia Syms) is an older girl, daughter of a country schoolmaster, who is disgusted with her job but cannot break away from it.

Syms gives an intelligent and often moving performance. Her scenes with her father (William Hartnell) are excellent. Hartnell, playing the unworldly, scholarly father, who has no contact with his daughter, also gives an observant study. The other two principals are more phonily drawn characters. Edward Judd seems strangely uneasy in his role and Ritchie, despite many firstrate moments, sometimes appears as if she is simply jumping through paper hoops.

••••••••••••••••••••••••••••••••••••

■ **WORLD, THE FLESH AND THE DEVIL, THE**

1959, 95 MINS, US

Dir Ranald MacDougall *Prod* Sol C. Siegel *Scr* Ranald MacDougall *Ph* Harold J. Marzorati *Ed* Harold F. Kress *Mus* Miklos Rozsa
● Harry Belafonte, Inger Stevens, Mel Ferrer (M-G-M/HarBel)

This is a provocative three-character story dealing with some pertinent issues (racism, atomic destruction) in a frame of suspense melodrama. Ranald MacDougall, who directed his own screenplay (based on an ancient novel by M.P. Shiel), leaves a few holes in his story, but deliberately.

Harry Belafonte is a coal miner who fights his way out of a wrecked Pennsylvania shaft to find himself apparently alone in a devastated world. After about a third of the film, Inger Stevens turns up, spared because she was in a decompression chamber when the bombs burst. Near the ending, in the last half-hour or so, Mel Ferrer arrives in a small power boat from a fishing expedition.

Although overall the film is engrossing, it gets curiously less effective as additional survivors turn up. When Belafonte is entirely alone on the screen for the first one-third of the film, and virtually alone for the first half, the semi-documentary style keeps the film crisp and credible.

It is not clear in the relationship between Belafonte and Stevens whether they are kept apart by her prejudice or his unfounded fear that such an attitude might exist. Ferrer's character is unsatisfying. He seems to be a racist of sorts, but how virulent isn't entirely clarified.

MacDougall shot a great deal of the film in Manhattan, and the realism (and the pains taken to achieve it) pay off. New Yorkers might complain that their geography is a little mixed up, but this is of small consequence.

••••••••••••••••••••••••••••••••••••

■ **WORLD'S GREATEST ATHLETE, THE**

1973, 92 MINS, US ◇ ▼

Dir Robert Scheerer *Prod* Bill Walsh *Scr* Gerald Gardner, Dee Caruso *Ph* Frank Phillips *Ed* Cotton Warburton *Mus* Marvin Hamlisch *Art Dir* John B. Mansbridge, Walter Tyler
● Tim Conway, Jan-Michael Vincent, John Amos, Roscoe Lee Browne, Dayle Haddon, Billy De Wolfe (Walt Disney)

The World's Greatest Athlete features Jan-Michael Vincent in title role of a jungle boy transplanted to an American campus where he becomes a one-man track squad. Emphasis is on visual comedy, from the sublime to the camp.

Coach John Amos and assistant Tim Conway, with a terrible record behind them in all sports and alumnus Billy De Wolfe on their backs, discover Vincent during a trip to Africa. Vincent's godfather, witchdoctor Roscoe Lee Browne, is tricked into letting him go back with Amos and Conway, who proceed to enter Vincent as the solo contender for a slew of inter-college field awards.

Vincent provides beefcake and little else, since the script keeps him in the status of the bewildered alien.

••••••••••••••••••••••••••••••••••••

■ **WORLD'S GREATEST LOVER, THE**

1977, 89 MINS, US ◇ ▼

Dir Gene Wilder *Prod* Gene Wilder *Scr* Gene Wilder *Ph* Gerald Hirschfeld *Ed* Anthony A. Pellegrino *Mus* John Morris *Art Dir* Steve Sardanis
● Gene Wilder, Carol Kane, Dom DeLuise (20th Century-Fox)

The World's Greatest Lover is a good period comedy starring Gene Wilder competing in a Hollywood studio talent search of 50 years ago to be a rival of Rudolph Valentino. Wilder also functions as writer-producer-director on his second personal film project, ably assisted by Carol Kane, as his wife, and Dom DeLuise, as a prototype madhatter studio czar.

The individual sketchpieces – Wilder trapped on a bakery assembly line; swimming in a flooded sunken livingroom, seducing his own wife in Valentino disguise after tutoring by the great lover himself, freaking out at his screen test, emerge as varyingly humorous episodes strung out on a skimpy story line.

DeLuise and Michael Huddleston repeatedly bring up the laugh level.

••••••••••••••••••••••••••••••••••••

■ **WRECK OF THE MARY DEARE, THE**

1959, 105 MINS, US ◇

Dir Michael Anderson *Prod* Julian Blaustein *Scr* Eric Ambler *Ph* Joseph Ruttenberg *Ed* Eda Warren *Mus* George Duning
● Gary Cooper, Charlton Heston, Michael Redgrave, Emlyn Williams, Richard Harris, Ben Wright (M-G-M)

The mystery of a 'ghost' ship looming suddenly out of the night, with only a crazed and battered captain aboard, is solved skillfully and with a good deal of suspense in *The Wreck of the Mary Deare*, from the Hammond Innes novel originally published in the *Saturday Evening Post* in 1956. It's the kind of adventure yarn which, thanks to intelligent treatment and topnotch photography, comes off with a bang.

Gary Cooper is Gideon Patch, the captain who's been the victim of foul play but stands accused himself of negligence. And Charlton Heston plays the skipper of a salvage boat who becomes innocently involved in the mystery of the Mary Deare and, in the end, helps solve it. Both men are perfectly cast in rugged roles and Cooper particularly conveys a surprising range of emotion and reaction.

In the smaller (almost bit) parts, Michael Redgrave and Emlyn Williams are very British as they participate in the London Court of Inquiry. Richard Harris is the snarling villain. Ben Wright is comfortable as Heston's partner.

There's a letdown in pace at the middle of the film when the Court of Inquiry appears stacked against Cooper. But the climax comes off with bangup effects.

••••••••••••••••••••••••••••••••••••

■ **WRECKING CREW, THE**

1969, 105 MINS, US ◇

Dir Phil Karlson *Prod* Irving Allen *Scr* William McGivern *Ph* Sam Leavitt *Ed* Maury Winetrobe *Mus* Hugo Montenegro *Art Dir* Joe Wright
● Dean Martin, Elke Sommer, Sharon Tate, Nancy Kwan, Nigel Green, Tina Louise (Columbia/Meadway-Claude)

Fourth in the Matt Helm series, *The Wrecking Crew* emerges as a very entertaining, relaxed spy comedy. It features Dean Martin, Elke Sommer, Nancy Kwan and Sharon Tate, the latter in a delightful comedy performance.

Nigel Green is the heavy, as mastermind of a gold theft. Sommer and Kwan are his principal aides, while Tate is a British agent in support of Martin's work. You wouldn't know it, though, because Tate keeps aborting Martin's plans and intimate rendezvous.

Film rolls along pleasantly for its 105 minutes, featuring the recurring music of Hugo Montenegro and a song by Mack David and Frank DeVol.

● ●

■ WRITTEN ON THE WIND

1956, 99 MINS, US ◇ ♥

Dir Douglas Sirk *Prod* Albert Zugsmith *Scr* George Zuckerman *Ph* Russell Metty *Ed* Russell F. Schoengarth *Mus* Frank Skinner *Art Dir* Alexander Golitzen, Robert Clatworthy
● Rock Hudson, Lauren Bacall, Robert Stack, Dorothy Malone, Robert Keith, Grant Williams (Universal)

This outspoken drama probes rather startlingly into the morals and passions of an uppercrust Texas oil family. Intelligent use of the flashback technique before and during the titles credits runoff builds immediate interest and expectancy without diminishing plot punch. Tiptop scripting from the Robert Wilder novel, dramatically deft direction by Douglas Sirk and sock performances by the cast give the story development a follow-through.

Rock Hudson, Lauren Bacall, Robert Stack and Dorothy Malone, aptly cast in the star roles, add a zing to the characters that pays off in audience interest. Hudson scores as the normal, lifelong friend of profligate Stack. The latter, in one of his best performances, draws a compelling portrait of a psychotic man ruined by wealth and character weaknesses.

Bacall registers strongly as a sensible girl swept into the madness of the oil family when she marries Stack, while Malone hits a career high as the completely immoral sister.

● ●

■ WRONG ARM OF THE LAW, THE

1963, 94 MINS, UK ♥

Dir Cliff Owen *Prod* Robert Velaise, Aubrey Baring *Scr* Ray Galton, Alan Simpson, John Antrobus *Ph* Ernest Steward *Ed* Tristam Cones *Mus* Richard Rodney Bennett
● Peter Sellers, Lionel Jeffries, Bernard Cribbins, Bill Kerr, Davy Kaye, Nanette Newman (Romulus)

A slightweight cops and robbers idea is pepped up into a briskly amusing farce thanks to a combo of deft direction, thesping and writing. Written by the authors of Tony Hancock's original TV series, with the assistance of 'Goon' writer John Antrobus, the screenplay has a fair turn of wit and a number of excellent whacky situations.

Peter Sellers runs a top league West End dress salon as Monsieur Jules. But that's only a front. As Pearly Gates, he is the Cockney King of the Underworld. His own gang he runs on Welfare State lines, with free luncheon vouchers, bubbly on Sundays, holidays with pay on the Costa Brava.

Everything's going fine until the police swoop on the gang job after job. Sellers realizes that an IPO (Impersonating Police Officers) mob is in town. He calls an extraordinary general meeting of London's crime syndicates, negotiates with Scotland Yard and arranges for a 24-hour crime truce so that the police can concentrate on running in the IPO gang.

Sellers has a fat part as the gangster with modern methods (for instance, he makes his gang attend evenings of educational films such as *Rififi*). And he brings his usual alert intelligence to the role. He is surrounded with some sharp talent.

● ●

■ WRONG BOX, THE

1966, 110 MINS, UK ◇ ♥

Dir Bryan Forbes *Prod* Bryan Forbes *Scr* Larry Gelbart, Burt Shevelove *Ph* Gerry Turpin *Ed* Alan Osbiston *Mus* John Barry *Art Dir* Ray Simm

● John Mills, Ralph Richardson, Michael Caine, Peter Cook, Dudley Moore, Peter Sellers (Columbia/Salamander)

Robert Louis Stevenson's macabre Victorian yarn has been impressively mounted by producer-director Bryan Forbes. He has lined up an impeccable cast of Britain's character comedian actors and brought his usual intelligent flourish to the film. But it might have improved this Columbia release had he written the script for *The Wrong Box* himself, instead of using the uneven work of Larry Gelbart and Burt Shevelove.

Storyline concerns a macabre lottery in which 20 parents each toss some money into a kitty for their children, the last survivor to draw the loot. Eventual survivors are two brothers who haven't seen each other for 40 years. One of them (John Mills) makes ineffective attempts to bump off his brother (Ralph Richardson), and their offspring take a more than casual interest in the proceedings.

Mills amusingly hams his way through two or three sequences as one of the dying brothers. Richardson, bland, imperturable old bore, is superb. He and Wilfrid Lawson, portraying a decrepit butler, virtually carry away the acting honors.

● ●

■ WRONG IS RIGHT

1982, 117 MINS, US ◇ ♥

Dir Richard Brooks *Prod* Richard Brooks *Scr* Richard Brooks *Ph* Fred J. Koenekamp *Ed* George Grenville *Mus* Artie Kane *Art Dir* Edward Carfagno
● Sean Connery, George Grizzard, Robert Conrad, Katharine Ross, G.D. Spradlin, John Saxon (Columbia)

Wrong Is Right represents Richard Brooks' shriek of protest at what he sees as the insane, downward spiral of world history over the past decade. Part political satire, part doomsday melodrama and part intellectual graffiti scribbled on the screen, film is impossible to pigeon-hole.

In a style simultaneously literal and surreal, Brooks takes potshots at the CIA, the FBI, presidents Nixon, Carter and Reagan, the military, the Arabs, the oil crisis, international terrorists and television, among many targets.

Sean Connery plays a sort of combination Edward R. Murrow and James Bond, a globe-trotting television commentator who enjoys total access to world leaders of all persuasions.

Basic situation involves an Arab king who seems ready to turn over two mini-atom bombs to a Khaddafi-like revolutionary leader, with the devices to be detonated in Israel, and later New York, unless the US president, who has admitted ordering the killing of the king, resigns from office.

Wild proceedings are packed with convoluted intrigue involving such characters as CIA agents John Saxon and Katharine Ross, maniacal Pentagon rep Robert Conrad, international arms dealer Hardy Kruger and an array of suicidal terrorists who delight in blowing themselves up, as long as it's covered on television.

● ●

■ WRONG MAN, THE

1957, 110 MINS, US ♥

Dir Alfred Hitchcock *Prod* Alfred Hitchcock *Scr* Maxwell Anderson, Angus MacPhail *Ph* Robert Burks *Ed* George Tomasini *Mus* Bernard Herrmann *Art Dir* Paul Sylbert, William L. Kuehl
● Henry Fonda, Vera Miles, Anthony Quayle, Harold J. Stone, Charles Cooper, Richard Robbins (Warner)

Alfred Hitchcock draws upon real-life drama for this gripping piece of realism. He builds the case of a NY Stork Club musician falsely accused of a series of holdups to a powerful climax, the events providing director a field day in his art of characterization and suspense.

Subject here is Manny Balestrero, the bass fiddle player whose story hit Gotham headlines in 1953 when he was arrested for crimes he did not commit. In a case of mistaken identity, he was not freed until the actual culprit was found during his trial. Not, however, before the musician, a family man with a wife and two young sons, went through the harrowing ordeal of being unable to prove his innocence.

Hitchcock drains the dramatic possibilities with often frightening overtones, as the spectator comes to realize that the very same could happen to him, if he fell into such a situation. The musician, played with a stark kind of impersonation by Fonda, is positively identified by several of the holdup victims, and other circumstances arise which seem to prove his guilt.

● ●

■ WUSA

1970, 114 MINS, US ◇

Dir Stuart Rosenberg *Prod* Paul Newman, John Foreman *Scr* Robert Stone *Ph* Richard Moore *Ed* Bob Wyman *Mus* Lalo Schifrin *Art Dir* Philip Jefferies
● Paul Newman, Joanne Woodward, Anthony Perkins, Laurence Harvey, Pat Hingle, Don Gordon (Paramount)

WUSA has some serious liabilities, but for all of them it's a breath of fresh air.

Title derives from call letters of New Orleans radio station which spews forth the type propaganda regularly disciplined in real life by the Federal Communications Commission.

Script is not always lucid and director Stuart Rosenberg's pacing is numbed by needless Newman-Woodward scenes which drag pic.

The cynical profession of crowd manipulation and psychology is the primary plot line of Robert Stone's adaptation of his novel, *A Hall of Mirrors*, original title of film. Newman is a drifter with radio experience. His buddy, Laurence Harvey, a con-man mission preacher, sends him to the radio station dedicated to exposing 'welfare chiselers' and other social evils.

As Newman's star rises his affair with Woodward becomes strained; she, too, is a drifter but there was a chance of some happiness between the two.

● ●

■ WUTHERING HEIGHTS

1939, 103 MINS, US ♥

Dir William Wyler *Prod* Samuel Goldwyn *Scr* Ben Hecht, Charles MacArthur *Ph* Gregg Toland *Ed* Daniel Mandell *Mus* Alfred Newman *Art Dir* James Basevi
● Merle Oberon, Laurence Olivier, David Niven, Flora Robson, Geraldine Fitzgerald, Donald Crisp (United Artists/Goldwyn)

Emily Bronte's novel tells a haunting tale of love and tragedy. Samuel Goldwyn's film version retains all of the grim drama of the book. It's heavy fare throughout.

Merle Oberon has two loves – a pash for stableboy Laurence Olivier and love of the worldly things David Niven can provide. After unsuccessfully goading Olivier to make something of himself, girl turns to Niven. Olivier disappears, to return several years later with a moderate fortune. Oberon keeps her smouldering passions under control, and Olivier marries Niven's sister (Geraldine Fitzgerald) for spite.

Story is unfolded through retrospect narration by Flora Robson, housekeeper in the early-Victorian mansion of Yorkshire.

Direction by William Wyler is slow and

X

deliberate, accenting the tragic features of the piece.
□ 1939: Best Picture (Nomination)

■ **WUTHERING HEIGHTS**

1971, 105 MINS, UK/US ◇ Ⓥ
Dir Robert Fuest *Prod* James H. Nicholson, Samuel Z. Arkoff *Scr* Patrick Tilley *Ph* John Coquillon *Ed* Ann Chegwidden *Mus* Michel Legrand *Art Dir* Philip Harrison
● Anna Calder-Marshall, Timothy Dalton, Julian Glover, Ian Ogilvy, Hilary Dwyer, Judy Cornwell (American International)

Wuthering Heights is a competent, tasteful, frequently even lovely re-adaption of Emily Bronte's Gothic, mystical love story. But the brooding tension, the electric passion of two lovers compelled to an inevitable tragedy is not generated.

Anna Calder-Marshall as Catherine is quite good, giving the role a wild young animal look and spirit. Timothy Dalton is also a technically capable actor, with a dark gypsy brooding look that is appropriate for Heathcliff. But his sullen, almost sulking portrayal is often that of a hurt boy rather than a man seething with resentment and a frustrated passion, a powder keg ready to explode.

Director Robert Fuest and cameraman John Coquillon compose striking and beautiful pictures, but without creating the sort of mood and tension the film needs.

■ **W.W. AND THE DIXIE DANCEKINGS**

1975, 91 MINS, US ◇
Dir John G. Avildsen *Prod* Steve Shagan *Scr* Thomas Rickman *Ph* James Crabe *Ed* Richard Halsey, Robbe Roberts *Mus* Dave Grusin *Art Dir* Larry Paull
● Burt Reynolds, Conny Van Dyke, Jerry Reed, Ned Beatty, James Hampton, Don Williams (20th Century-Fox)

Burt Reynolds stars as a 1950s con artist who turns straight through an odyssey with a country music band. The script establishes Reynolds as a footloose character, generating money by suave robberies of gas stations where he divides the loot with the underpaid attendants in return for their giving phony descriptions.

Sherman G. Lloyd, redneck oil magnate, concludes that a devil is amok, so he recruits Art Carney, a lawman turned fundamentalist preacher, to find the evil spirit. This plot angle alternates with Reynolds' growing attachment to the Dixie Dancekings, a c&w band headed by Jerry Reed.

■ **X – THE MAN WITH X-RAY EYES**

1963, 80 MINS, US ◇ Ⓥ
Dir Roger Corman *Prod* James H. Nicholson, Samuel Z. Arkoff *Scr* Robert Dillon, Ray Russell *Ph* Floyd Crosby *Ed* Anthony Carras *Mus* Les Baxter *Art Dir* Daniel Haller
● Ray Milland, Diana Van Der Vlis, Harold J. Stone, Don Rickles, John Hoyt (American International)

Basically it's the plot where the scientist tampers with the unknown and is severely punished in the end. Ray Milland is a doctor who has devised a drug that he thinks will allow men's eyes to see infinitely more.

He tries it on himself when he is refused a grant to continue experiments on animals. He at first is put out of commission by a blinding light but then can see inside human

tissue and through clothes. This permits him to visit a party where the women are nude to him.

Things get worse as he kills a friend inadvertently, forcing the doctor to hide out in a carnival as a mindreader. A girl who believes in him tries to help and they go off to work on some antidote.

There are many interesting comic, dramatic and philosophical ideas are touched on but treated only on the surface. However, director Roger Corman keeps this moving and Ray Milland is competent as the doomed man. Special effects on his prism-eye world, called Spectarama, are good if sometimes repetitive.

■ **XANADU**

1980, 92 MINS, US ◇ Ⓥ
Dir Robert Greenwald *Prod* Lawrence Gordon *Scr* Richard Christian Danus, Marc Reid Rubel *Ph* Victor J. Kemper *Ed* Dennis Virkler *Mus* Barry DeVorzon *Art Dir* John W. Corso
● Olivia Newton-John, Gene Kelly, Michael Beck (Universal)

Xanadu is truly a stupendously bad film whose only salvage is the music. Olivia Newton-John plays a muse, first seen with her eight sisters painted on a wall. Suddenly, they all come alive, with glowing stuff all around them, singing and zipping hither and yon, apparently looking for a script that will never be found.

Newton-John's task is to inspire Michael Beck in his work as an artist. For this she stops glowing and he thinks she's a real girl, despite the sun dress she wears with roller skates and rags around both ankles.

But love is threatening and Newton-John decides it's best if she goes back into the painting on the wall, so she starts glowing again and bids Beck farewell. But he gets up a head of steam and skates into the wall after her and winds up somewhere near Mount Olympus.

■ **YAKUZA, THE**

1975, 112 MINS, US ◇
Dir Sydney Pollack *Prod* Sydney Pollack *Scr* Paul Schrader, Robert Towne *Ph* Okazaki Kozo, Duke Callaghan *Ed* Fredric Steinkamp; Thomas Stamford, Don Guidice *Mus* Dave Grusin *Art Dir* Stephen Grimes
● Robert Mitchum, Takakura Ken, Brian Keith, Herb Edelman, Richard Jordan, Kishi Keiko (Warner)

The Yakuza is a confused and diffused film which bites off more than it can artfully chew. Robert Mitchum stars as a private eye returning to Japan to unravel some international crime matters, as well as his long-ago love affair.

The result is an uneasy and incohesive combination of an oriental Mafia story overlaid on a formula international business swindle, mixed up with a 20-years-later update of *Sayonara*.

Mitchum is hired by old World War II army buddy Brian Keith, now a successful shipping executive, to rescue daughter Lee Chirillo from some Japanese hoods holding her for an alleged default on a business deal.

Takakura Ken, who owes Mitchum a favor from a generation back, must honor the request to infiltrate the mob.

■ **YANGTSE INCIDENT**

1957, 113 MINS, UK Ⓥ
Dir Michael Anderson *Prod* Herbert Wilcox *Scr* Eric Ambler *Ph* Gordon Diner *Ed* Basil Warren *Mus* Leighton Lucas *Art Dir* Ralph Brinton
● Richard Todd, William Hartnell, Akim Tamiroff, Donald Houston, Keye Luke, Sophie Stewart (British Lion)

Story [based on the book by Laurence Earl] is of the *Amethyst*, which, battered though not beaten, broke the Chinese Communist blockade and rejoined the British fleet. The *Amethyst* is shown sailing up the Yangtse, headed for Nanking on a lawful mission delivering supplies to the British Embassy. Suddenly, without warning, the Red shore batteries open fire and the frigate, after a heavy engagement, is grounded in the mud.

All his attempts to persuade the British to issue an apology for 'unprovoked aggression' are resolutely turned down and both sides play a waiting game until the British commander decides to run for it.

Vivid battle scenes have been magnificently handled. The on-board scenes are genuine enough too, as the *Amethyst* was reprieved from the breaker's yard to allow producer Herbert Wilcox to use it in the film.

There's a high standard of acting by an all-round cast, led by Richard Todd as the commander who takes over after the captain is killed in the first engagement.

■ **YANK AT OXFORD, A**

1938, 100 MINS, UK
Dir Jack Conway *Prod* Michael Balcon *Scr* Malcolm Stuart Boylan, Walter Ferris, George Oppenheimer *Ph* Harold Rosson *Ed* Margaret Booth, Charles Frend *Mus* Hubert Bath, Edward Ward
● Robert Taylor, Maureen O'Sullivan, Lionel Barrymore, Vivien Leigh, Edmund Gwenn, Griffith Jones (M-G-M)

Robert Taylor brings back from Oxford an entertaining rah-rah film which is full of breathless quarter-mile dashes, heartbreaking boat race finishes and surefire sentiment – Metro's first British-made film under Hollywood supervision and with Hollywood principals and director.

Some of the opening sequences were made on the west coast and pasted to what was shot in England. Taylor, Lionel Barrymore, Maureen O'Sullivan, Harold Rosson, cameraman, and Jack Conway and his directorial crew crossed the Atlantic. Their efforts were supported by British film and stage players, and Michael Balcon, formerly production head of Gaumont-British, acted as producer.

It is reported that the film players never were permitted within the sacred precincts of Oxford university which is unimportant from a picture viewpoint as the architectural reproductions have been carefully and effectively photographed.

What Conway has caught is the humor of student life at the university. This is the background for Taylor's adventures, the wall against which a cocky Yank bounces his somewhat enlarged head, eventually regaining his poise a better and tamed human being. [Original story by Leon Gordon, Sidney Gilliatt and Michael Hogan, based on an idea by John Monk Saunders.]

Teamed to these sometimes hilarious adventures is a sentimental story which tells of Taylor's liking for O'Sullivan, whose brother is a rival in undergraduate affairs.

Edmund Gwenn as the Dean of Cardinal College, one of the Oxford group, does a standout. Griffith Jones is an English boy, and gives a sincere and earnest performance. O'Sullivan and her diction fit nicely into ensemble, and Vivien Leigh, as a college vamp, has looks and a way about her.

■ **YANK IN THE R.A.F., A**

1941, 97 MINS, US ⓥ

Dir Henry King   *Prod* Darrell F. Zanuck   *Scr* Darrell Ware, Karl Tunberg   *Ph* Leon Shamroy   *Ed* Barbara McLean

● Tyrone Power, Betty Grable, John Sutton, Reginald Gardiner (20th Century-Fox)

Picture neatly mixes the adventures of cocky and carefree Tyrone Power, former airline pilot, with the inner workings and flights of the RAF squadrons during the hectic times of the German blitz against the Low countries and France. Producer Darryl F. Zanuck (who also authored the original as 'Melville Crossman') sidesteps overloading the picture with flying sequences and bombing expeditions.

In flying a training ship to Canada, Power enlists as pilot to ferry bombers to England. On his first trip, he meets former sweetheart (Betty Grable) a Texas girl performing in a night club and member of the ambulance reserve. Power pursues his former attention, and enlists in the RAF for fighter duty.

Power clicks solidly as the happy-go-lucky American pilot sure of his abilities with both planes and women. He handles the role with a lightly nonchalant attitude which will catch wide audience attention. Grable grooves excellently as the girl who fully realizes Power's inconsistencies, but finally breaks down.

．．．．．．．．．．．．．．．．．．．．．．．．．．．．．．．．

■ **YANKEE DOODLE DANDY**

1942, 126 MINS, US ⓥ

Dir Michael Curtiz   *Prod* Hal Wallis, William Cagney   *Scr* Robert Buckner, Edmund Joseph   *Ph* James Wong Howe   *Ed* George Amy   *Mus* Ray Heindorf (arr)

● James Cagney, Joan Leslie, Walter Huston, Richard Whorf, Irene Manning, Jeanne Cagney (Warner)

Yankee Doodle Dandy is rah-rah, no matter how you slice it. It's a tribute to a grand American gentleman of the theatre – George M. Cohan – whose life and songs are glorified by Warner Bros; and it's a tribute, perhaps even more so, to all show business.

James Cagney does a Cohan of which the original George M. might well be proud.

That Robert Buckner, and his co-scripter, Edmund Joseph, jazzed up a little of the latter-day chronology is beside the point.

That Cohan was cocky and conceited as the kid star of *Peck's Bad Boy*, in which he clicked at 13; that he remained close to Jerry Cohan, Nellie Cohan and sister Josie (so well played by the star's real-life sister, Jeanne Cagney); that his string of successes never upset this lovely and loving picture, are all part of a human, appealing story of one of the great theatrical families of all times.

□ 1942: Best Picture (Nomination)

．．．．．．．．．．．．．．．．．．．．．．．．．．．．．．．．

■ **YANKS**

1979, 141 MINS, UK ◇ ⑰

Dir John Schlesinger   *Prod* Joseph Janni, Lester Persky   *Scr* Colin Welland, Walter Bernstein   *Ph* Dick Bush   *Ed* Jim Clark   *Mus* Richard Rodney Bennett   *Art Dir* Brian Morris

● Richard Gere, Lisa Eichhorn, Vanessa Redgrave, William Devane, Rachel Roberts, Tony Melody (Universal)

Director John Schlesinger has done a beautiful job with both cast and craft in *Yanks*, a multiple love story set in England in World War II. Yet little that's exciting ever happens in the picture.

The British director, working with his own and the personal recollections of writers Colin Welland and Walter Bernstein, vividly recreates the atmosphere in a small English village inundated by thousands of American troops prepping for the invasion of Europe.

At one end of the extreme, Vanessa Redgrave and William Devane struggle to maintain a platonic friendship while both

are deprived of their spouses. At the other, Chick Vennera and Wendy Morgan rush to bed immediately, with little initial concern for what lies beyond the war.

The six lovers and both parents are played excellently and Schlesinger and crew have created an extravagantly authentic period setting.

．．．．．．．．．．．．．．．．．．．．．．．．．．．．．．．．

■ **YEAR OF LIVING DANGEROUSLY, THE**

1982, 114 MINS, AUSTRALIA/US ◇ ⓥ

Dir Peter Weir   *Prod* Jim McElroy   *Scr* David Williamson, Peter Weir, C.J. Koch   *Ph* Russell Boyd   *Ed* Bill Anderson   *Mus* Maurice Jarre   *Art Dir* Herbert Pinter

● Mel Gibson, Sigourney Weaver, Linda Hunt, Michael Murphy, Bill Kerr, Noel Ferrier (McElroy & McElroy/M-G-M)

Peter Weir's *The Year of Living Dangerously*, is a $6 million adaptation of Christopher Koch's novel, set in Indonesia in 1965 in the turbulent months leading to the fall of the Sukarno government.

Mel Gibson limns a young Australian journalist on his first posting as a foreign correspondent. Wide-eyed and innocent, he is befriended by an astute Chinese-Australian cameraman, a dwarf who seeks to manipulate people as deftly as he handles shadow puppets.

Here is an astonishing feat of acting by New Yorker Linda Hunt, cast by Weir because he could not locate a short male actor to fit the bill. A bizarre, yet touching, romantic triangle develops between Gibson, Hunt, and Sigourney Weaver as a British Embassy official.

Having laid the groundwork, Weir hits the action button. Gibson learns that the Communists are bringing in arms for a coup against Sukarno and in broadcasting the story blows a confidence from Weaver, who rejects him.

Filming in the Philippines, and then Sydney, where the crew was forced to repair after receiving threats from the Islamic community, Weir and his crew expertly recreate the squalor, poverty, noise, heat and emotion of the pressure cooker that was Indonesia in 1965.

．．．．．．．．．．．．．．．．．．．．．．．．．．．．．．．．

■ **YEAR OF THE DRAGON**

1985, 136 MINS, US ◇ ⓥ

Dir Michael Cimino   *Prod* Dino De Laurentiis   *Scr* Oliver Stone, Michael Cimino   *Ph* Alex Thomson   *Ed* Francoise Bonnot   *Mus* David Mansfield   *Art Dir* Wolf Kroeger

● Mickey Rourke, John Lone, Ariane, Leonard Termo, Ray Barry, Caroline Kava (M-G-M/United Artists)

Year of the Dragon [based on the novel by Robert Daley] is never as important as director Michael Cimino thinks it is, but there's a fair amount of solid action and gunplay, all set securely in the intricate, mysterious enigma of New York's Chinatown and its ties to worldwide drug-dealing.

Unquestionably, Cimino's eye for detail and insistence thereon has paid off in his impressive recreation of Chinatown at producer Dino De Laurentiis' studios in North Carolina. Crammed with an array of interesting characters, including the extras in the background, *Dragon* brims with authenticity.

Assigned to Chinatown to clear up a problem of murderous youth gangs, Mickey Rourke quickly proves to be one of those lone renegade cops that fiction favors more than real-life. Beyond the teen toughs, Rourke wants to undo a criminal system rooted in a culture for thousands of years.

Beyond the color and the corpses, though, Cimino fails to focus on an idea and stick with it. He ends up playing with significant thoughts in between awkward lessons in Chi-

nese history, losing most of them as they filter through half-baked resentments Rourke has left over from the Vietnam war. Performances, though, are generally excellent and *Dragon* certainly never drags.

．．．．．．．．．．．．．．．．．．．．．．．．．．．．．．．．

■ **YEARLING, THE**

1946, 134 MINS, US ◇ ⓥ

Dir Clarence Brown   *Prod* Sidney Franklin   *Scr* Paul Osborn   *Ph* Charles Rosher, Leonard Smith, Arthur Arling   *Ed* Harold F. Kress   *Mus* Herbert Stothart   *Art Dir* Cedric Gibbons, Paul Groesse

● Gregory Peck, Jane Wyman, Claude Jarman Jr, Chill Wills (M-G-M)

Marjorie Kinnan Rawlings' 1938 Pulitzer prizewinning novel is the heart-warming story of good earth, family ties and the love of the 11-year-old Jody Baxter for the faun which he is compelled to put out of his life as it becomes a yearling.

The Florida scrub country is the locale of the Baxters, and the story focuses on Gregory Peck and Jane Wyman in the fight for their very existence, while raising meagre patches of crops and also their offspring Jody (Claude Jarman Jr). The lad becomes a man, for all his meagre years, in a great love and effort to ward off destruction of his pet yearling, albeit it be at the kindly hands of his parents.

All done in a minor key, the underplaying is sometimes too static but, just as the interest lags, director Clarence Brown injects another highlight. The underlying power is impressive.

□ 1946: Best Picture (Nomination)

．．．．．．．．．．．．．．．．．．．．．．．．．．．．．．．．

■ **YELLOW BALLOON, THE**

1953, 80 MINS, UK

Dir J. Lee-Thompson   *Prod* Victor Skutezky   *Scr* Anne Burnaby, J. Lee-Thompson   *Ph* Gilbert Taylor   *Ed* Richard Best   *Mus* Philip Green   *Art Dir* Robert Jones

● Andrew Ray, Kathleen Ryan, Kenneth More, Bernard Lee, William Sylvester, Sydney James (Associated British/Marble Arch)

This British pic is a depressing study of an innocent child who falls into the clutches of a modern Fagin and is forced to steal from his own parents before being used as a decoy in an holdup which leads to murder.

J. Lee-Thompson directs, with entire dramatic content focussed on the youngster (Andrew Ray). The boy plays the part almost on a single key but his almost static expression captures the story's spirit.

With most of the screen time allotted to the youngster, the adult cast members have comparatively minor roles. The roles of the kid's parents are effectively sustained by Kathleen Ryan and Kenneth More, while William Sylvester does a smooth job as the crook. Lesser roles are distinctively filled, with Sydney James giving a rich performance as a cockney trader.

．．．．．．．．．．．．．．．．．．．．．．．．．．．．．．．．

■ **YELLOW CANARY, THE**

1943, 95 MINS, UK

Dir Herbert Wilcox   *Prod* Herbert Wilcox   *Scr* Miles Malleson, DeWitt Bodeen   *Ph* Max Green

● Anna Neagle, Richard Greene, Nova Pilbeam, Albert Lieven, Margaret Rutherford (Imperator)

Direction, cast, production and camerawork are so good it is a pity the suspensive story [from an original by D.M. Bower] is not on the same plane of excellence. There is smart comedy dialog and plenty of action throughout. It has a 'mystery' start with red herring trails that lead up blind alleys, necessitating the return each time to a new start. The result is an overplus of the aforesaid 'mystery'.

Anna Neagle plays Sally Maitland, daughter of an aristocratic British family. She has achieved notoriety for her pre-war association with the Nazis. Public antagonism to her is so violent that she is practically forced to leave Britain. It is a role altogether different from her previous film appearances. Her co-star is Richard Greene, and principal support comes from Nova Pilbeam, Lucie Mannheim and Albert Lieven.

●●●●●●●●●●●●●●●●●●●●●●●●●●●●●●●●

■ YELLOW CANARY, THE

1963, 93 MINS, US

Dir Buzz Kulik   *Prod* Maury Dexter   *Scr* Rod Serling   *Ph* Floyd Crosby   *Ed* Jodie Copelan   *Mus* Kenyon Hopkins   *Art Dir* Walter Simmonds
● Pat Boone, Barbara Eden, Steve Forrest, Jack Klugman, Jesse White, Steve Harris (20th Century-Fox)

Hero of the piece is Pat Boone, a surly singing idol whose apparently loose ways have him on the brink of divorce with his wife (Barbara Eden), who remains only for the sake of their infant. The baby is suddenly kidnapped and three people are needlessly murdered by the kidnapper, who turns out to be one of Boone's sycophants, his psychotic bodyguard (Steve Forrest).

Rod Serling's screenplay, from Whit Masterson's novel, *Evil Come, Evil Go*, is reasonably strong in dramatic anatomy, but limp and fuzzy in character definition. The characters are thrust at the audience, with little or no attempt to illustrate the nature of their odd dispositions toward society and each other.

Boone warbles several old standards pleasantly. Eden is her usual curvaceous self, and gets off a number of very convincing screams and shrieks. Forrest is an okay heavy, Jack Klugman likable as a frustrated gendarme. Kenyon Hopkins has composed a racy, pulsating score to underline the action.

●●●●●●●●●●●●●●●●●●●●●●●●●●●●●●●●

■ YELLOW ROLLS-ROYCE, THE

1964, 122 MINS, UK ◇

Dir Anthony Asquith   *Prod* Anatole de Grunwald   *Scr* Terence Rattigan   *Ph* Jack Hildyard   *Ed* Frank Clarke   *Mus* Riz Ortolani
● Rex Harrison, Jeanne Moreau, Shirley MacLaine, George C. Scott, Ingrid Bergman, Omar Sharif (M-G-M)

With a sizzling international cast, the team of Anatole de Grunwald, Anthony Asquith and Terence Rattigan have produced a sleek piece of entertainment in *The Yellow Rolls-Royce*. It is handsomely tinted, lushly lensed and though leisurely in its approach, this has style, humor and some effective thesping.

Film consists of three separate anecdotes, linked only by ownership of the elegant Phantom II Rolls-Royce auto.

First one concerns Lord Frinton (Rex Harrison), a Foreign Office big shot who buys the car as an anni gift for his wife (Jeanne Moreau) and discovers her and a Foreign Office minion (Edmund Purdom) in a passionate embrace in its back seat.

Much mileage later, in the 1930s, the car is bought in Italy by gangster George C. Scott as a present for his current moll, hatcheck gal Shirley MacLaine. The dame falls for a street photographer (Alain Delon) and again the comfortable, accommodating back seat of the Rolls is pressed into service for l'amour.

Finally, in 1942, the Phantom II is acquired by Ingrid Bergman playing a hectoring American woman. Hitler is attacking Yugoslavia and she becomes involved when she finds that she has smuggled an arch-patriot (Omar Sharif) across the border.

●●●●●●●●●●●●●●●●●●●●●●●●●●●●●●●●

■ YELLOW SUBMARINE

1968, 89 MINS, UK ◇ Ⓥ

Dir George Dunning   *Prod* Al Brodax   *Scr* Lee Minoff, Al Brodax, Jack Mendelsohn, Erich Segal   *Mus* The Beatles   *Art Dir* Heinz Edelmann
● (Apple/King/Subafilms)

This is a full length animated cartoon in which the prime factor is the appearance of the Beatles in caricature form. Here are all the ingredients of a novel entertainment.

Story consists of a fantastic voyage in a yellow submarine thru sky and sea, manned by the skipper, and The Beatles, to Pepperland where the inhabitants are up against thugs known as the Blue Meanies.

Time travel, science fiction, outer space, monsters, war and their own idiom of pop music are all taken for a ride in figments of fevered imaginations during which the Beatles come up against some odd specimens and situations.

The Beatles' flat Merseyside tones make good contrast to the surrounding frenzy.

Dialog is mostly puns and throwaway gags. It remains deliberately corny at times and never ventures out of its depth in flirtations with time, space and philosophy.

Unlike Disney the film makes no concession to sentiment. Characters are mostly matter-of-fact, grotesque and anti-heroic and tend to be harsh, angular and intro'd for shock effect rather than any winsome qualities.

●●●●●●●●●●●●●●●●●●●●●●●●●●●●●●●●

■ YELLOWSTONE KELLY

1959, 91 MINS, US ◇

Dir Gordon Douglas   *Scr* Burt Kennedy   *Ph* Carl Guthrie   *Ed* William Ziegler   *Mus* Howard Jackson   *Art Dir* Stanley Fleischer
● Clint Walker, Edward Byrnes, John Russell, Ray Danton, Andra Martin, Claude Akins (Warner)

Yellowstone Kelly is a well-made western.

The story [from the book by Clay Fisher] concerns a fabled fur trapper, Kelly, who is on good terms with the Sioux Indians. He refuses to help the US Cavalry's punitive expedition of 1876 but ultimately has to help the arrogant white men after they have been trounced by the righteous red men.

Director Gordon Douglas moves the story along with a speed sufficient to cover up weak plot points and extracts some solid characterizations not implicit in the script: Clint Walker, as Kelly the trapper, is a laconic, gargantuan woodsman; John Russell is a magnetically powerful and believable chief; Ray Danton's a handsome swine of a brave; Andra Martin is fetchingly and helplessly lovely as the Indian girl and Edward Byrnes enlists sympathy as the tenderfoot.

●●●●●●●●●●●●●●●●●●●●●●●●●●●●●●●●

■ YENTL

1983, 134 MINS, US ◇ Ⓥ

Dir Barbra Streisand   *Prod* Barbra Streisand, Rusty Lemorande   *Scr* Jack Rosenthal, Barbra Streisand   *Ph* David Watkin   *Ed* Terry Rawlings   *Mus* Michel Legrand   *Art Dir* Roy Walker
● Barbra Streisand, Mandy Patinkin, Amy Irving, Nehemiah Persoff, Steven Hill, Allan Corduner (Barwood/United Artists)

Based on a short story by Isaac Bashevis Singer, *Yentl* tells the tale of a young Eastern European woman, circa 1904, who disguises herself as a boy in order to pursue her passion for studying holy scripture, an endeavor restricted exclusively to men in orthodox Jewish culture.

Moving from her native village and passing as a pubescent boy, Yentl has no problem in the scholarly world, but tragi-comic results stem from the romantic situation her presence creates. Befriended by her brash, attractive fellow student Avigdor, wonderfully played by Mandy Patinkin, Yentl falls in love with him.

When Avigdor is prevented from marrying his lovely fiancee Hadass (a china doll Amy Irving) through a technicality of religious law, Avigdor pushes Yentl to marry Hadass in his stead.

Songs by Michel Legrand, with lyrics by Alan and Marilyn Bergman, have been carefully planned as interior monologs for Yentl.

In league with ace cinematographer David Watkin, Streisand has created a fine-looking period piece, working on Czech locations and in English studios.

●●●●●●●●●●●●●●●●●●●●●●●●●●●●●●●●

■ YIELD TO THE NIGHT

1956, 100 MINS, UK

Dir J. Lee Thompson   *Scr* John Cresswell, Joan Henry   *Ph* Gilbert Taylor   *Ed* Richard Best   *Mus* Ray Martin   *Art Dir* Robert Jones
● Diana Dors, Yvonne Mitchell, Michael Craig, Marie Ney, Geoffrey Keen, Liam Redmond (Associated British)

Diana Dors plays a heavy dramatic role in *Yield to the Night*, which calls for a drastic deglamorizing treatment.

The actual killing which leads the star to the death cell is depicted before the credit titles appear on the screen, but the events which led her to shoot at point blank range at the woman who forced her lover to suicide are shown in a series of flashbacks.

Main footage is concentrated inside the condemned cell and the script illustrates the anguish of mind of the girl, the wardresses who guard her night and day, the members of her family and the husband whom she deserted.

The script [from a novel by Joan Henry] succeeds in maintaining strong suspense.

In the main, Dors rises to the occasion and shows up as a dramatic actress better than anticipated. Yvonne Mitchell strikes the right sympathetic note as one of the wardresses, Michael Craig reveals a good presence as the lover and Marie Ney shows proper dignity and restraint as the prison governor.

●●●●●●●●●●●●●●●●●●●●●●●●●●●●●●●●

■ YOLANDA AND THE THIEF

1945, 108 MINS, US ◇ Ⓥ

Dir Vincente Minnelli   *Prod* Arthur Freed   *Scr* Irving Brecher   *Ph* Charles Rosher   *Ed* George White   *Mus* Lennie Hayton (dir.)   *Art Dir* Cedric Gibbons, Jack Martin Smith
● Fred Astaire, Lucille Bremer, Frank Morgan, Mildred Natwick, Mary Nash, Leon Ames (M-G-M)

Metro has a musical story of virtue and the Divine in *Yolanda and the Thief*, but the result is not all it might have been. Arthur Freed produced with lavishness, and the casting, topped by Fred Astaire, Lucille Bremer and Frank Morgan, has an eye towards marquee values, but the basic yarn doesn't lend itself toward the screen.

This is the story of a Latin-American heiress who, after being brought up in a convent, assumes charge of her fortune upon coming of age. Her childhood, naturally one that saw her sheltered from the outer world, makes her easy prey for a fraud that a young American and his elderly confederate would play upon her to relieve her of her millions.

There's an idea in this yarn, but it only suggests itself. It becomes too immersed in its musical background, and the story is too leisurely in pace. A musical production number attempts to be symbolic but only serves to waste too many moments of the over-long film. And the story itself, the way it's done, strains credibility.

●●●●●●●●●●●●●●●●●●●●●●●●●●●●●●●●

■ YOU CAN'T TAKE IT WITH YOU

1938, 126 MINS, US Ⓥ

Dir Frank Capra   *Prod* Frank Capra   *Scr* Robert Riskin   *Ph* Joseph Walker   *Ed* Gene Havlick   *Mus* Dimitri Tiomkin   *Art Dir* Stephen Goosson, Lionel Banks
● Jean Arthur, Lionel Barrymore, James Stewart, Edward Arnold, Mischa Auer, Ann Miller (Columbia)

A strong hit on Broadway, *You Can't Take It*

With You [by George S. Kaufman and Moss Hart] is also a big hit on film. This is one of the highest priced plays to be bought in history, Columbia having taken the rights for $200,000. Production brought negative cost to around a reported $1.2 million.

The comedy is wholly American, wholesome, homespun, human, appealing, and touching in turn. The wackier comedy side contrasts with a somewhat serious, philosophical note which may seem a little overstressed on occasion.

The Vanderhoff tribe is played appealingly but screwily, the antics of the polyglot combination of grandpa, daughter, son-in-law, grandchildren and hangers-on, including a meek adding machine operator turned inventor, and a ballet teacher, being basically for creation of fun.

The romance between James Stewart and Jean Arthur is the keystone of the comedy. Other comedy elements are registered at the expense of Edward Arnold, the stuff-shirt banker, and his wife, played excellently by Mary Forbes. The link that is formed between the modest, homey Vanderhoff coterie and the very rich Kirbys, created principally through the romance of the Arthur-Stewart pair, is a bit unbelievable but for the purposes of entertainment has license.

Arthur acquits herself creditably. Stewart is not a strong romantic lead opposite her but does satisfactorily in the love scenes. Others are tops from Lionel Barrymore down.
□ 1938: Best Picture

■ YOU ONLY LIVE TWICE

1967, 117 MINS, UK ◇ Ⓥ

Dir Lewis Gilbert *Prod* Albert R. Broccoli, Harry Saltzman *Scr* Roald Dahl *Ph* Frederick A. Young *Ed* Thelma Connell *Mus* John Barry *Art Dir* Ken Adam

● Sean Connery, Akiko Wakabayashi, Tetsuro Tamba, Lois Maxwell, Bernard Lee, Donald Pleasence (United Artists/Eon)

Film begins with a prolog in which a US astronaut's spacewalk is interrupted by another spacecraft that, crocodile-style, opens its jaws and swallows the capsule. US government is peeved at what it assumes to be a Russian attempt to foil space exploration, and 007 is assigned by helpful British intelligence to locate the missing rocket before full-scale war breaks out between the two nuclear powers.

Film's title refers to Bond's 'murder', which precedes the credits. Ensconced with the first in a long line of Japanese beauties he is abruptly gunned down and pronounced dead in her bed by officials.

Sean Connery plays 007 with his usual finesse. Rest of cast in the $9.5 million film is strictly secondary, although Akiko Wakabayashi and Tetsuro Tamba register well as Bond's Japanese cohorts. Donald Pleasence makes a suitably menacing German heavy who appears in film's final scenes.

■ YOU'LL NEVER GET RICH

1941, 87 MINS, US Ⓥ

Dir Sidney Lanfield *Prod* Samuel Bischoff *Scr* Michael Fessier, Ernest Pagano *Ph* Phillip Tannura *Ed* Otto Meyer *Mus* Morris Stoloff (dir.)

● Fred Astaire, Rita Hayworth, Robert Benchley, John Hubbard (Columbia)

Story has Fred Astaire as a stager of a musical show for producer Robert Benchley. Latter, in making a pitch for affections of Rita Hayworth, gets in a jam with his wife, and has Astaire get him out of the predicament. Girl, with a crush on Astaire, is somewhat disillusioned by the proceedings, and gives him the heave-ho.

When Astaire is inducted into the selective service camp, Benchley makes a deal to conduct rehearsals and stage a show for the boys – in order to obtain services of Astaire in putting it on. There's plenty of serious and humorous by-play around the camp, with Astaire a permanent resident of the guardhouse, but it all works out when the show finally goes on.

Script is studded with humorous lines and situations, and despite a somewhat familiar ring it's all sufficiently refurbished by Sidney Lanfield's direction to get over in good style. Lanfield keeps things moving consistently, and the song and dance routines are neatly spotted.

■ YOUNG BESS

1953, 111 MINS, US ◇

Dir George Sidney *Prod* Sidney Franklin *Scr* Jan Lustig, Arthur Wimperis *Ph* Charles Rosher *Ed* Ralph E. Winters *Mus* Miklos Rozsa *Art Dir* Cedric Gibbons, Urie McCleary

● Jean Simmons, Stewart Granger, Deborah Kerr, Charles Laughton, Kay Walsh, Guy Rolfe (M-G-M)

Margaret Irwin's fine book on the life and times of the girl who was to become England's Queen Elizabeth has been made into a remarkably engrossing motion picture. *Young Bess* is a romantic drama told against a Tudor setting. It is a human story, sensitively written, directed and played. Romance phases are rich in emotion; court intrigue conjures suspense, and there is a suggestion of action throughout.

The four-star bracketing of Jean Simmons, in the title role; Stewart Granger, the dashing, heroic Lord Admiral, Thomas Seymour; Deborah Kerr, the beautiful Catherine Parr; and Charles Laughton, the gross, pompous Henry VIII, insures splendid trouping.

Main story gets underway after opening sequence, a gem in itself, sets the stage for a flashback to the unhappy childhood of young Bess. It is not until gracious Catherine becomes queen that young Bess, now 15, takes up a more or less permanent residence in the palace, finding love and happiness with the queen and her little stepbrother, the sickly Edward. When Henry dies and the queen marries the Lord Admiral, young Bess conceals her own infatuation for the dashing hero, but her feelings are found out and used by the evil Ned Seymour, the admiral's brother.

Miklos Rozsa's music score is fine, never once intruding too strongly on a dramatic scene, and it is full of little identifying melodies for the humorous touches in the script.

■ YOUNG BILLY YOUNG

1969, 89 MINS, US ◇

Dir Burt Kennedy *Prod* Max Youngstein *Scr* Burt Kennedy *Ph* Harry Stradling Jr *Ed* Otho Lovering *Mus* Shelly Manne *Art Dir* Stan Jolley

● Robert Mitchum, Angie Dickinson, Robert Walker, David Carradine, Jack Kelly (United Artists)

Standard western plot undergoes generally good polishing in this production, costarring Robert Mitchum and Angie Dickinson. Plenty of gunplay heightens appeal and Robert Walker joins stars in turning in realistic performances.

Burt Kennedy, who directed and scripted [from the novel *Who Rides with Wyatt* by Will Henry], could have tightened film for better effect. His climax lacks the suspense it should have carried and confrontation misses. On the whole, however, film progresses satisfactorily.

Narrative unfolds mostly in Lordsburg, where Mitchum takes on a marshal's job after he learns that his quarry may be found there. Walker, an ornery youngster who wants his way, is with him, leaving Mitchum to his own devices until he discovers that a dozen gunmen have arrived to mow down the marshal.

■ YOUNG CASSIDY

1965, 107 MINS, US ◇

Dir Jack Cardiff, John Ford *Prod* Robert D. Graff, Robert Emmett Ginna *Scr* John Whiting *Ph* Ted Scaife *Ed* Anne V. Coates *Mus* Sean O'Riada

● Rod Taylor, Julie Christie, Edith Evans, Michael Redgrave, Flora Robson, Maggie Smith (M-G-M)

Young Cassidy, biopic of Irish playwright Sean O'Casey in his sprouting years based on his autobiography, *Mirror in My House*, is notable principally for the top-rating performance of Rod Taylor in title role. Story of a rebel who rises to literary greatness, like the majority of screen bio narratives, is episodic; in attempting to cover the many facets of career, film consequently lacks the cohesion necessary for a full dramatic enactment of a historic personality.

Originally started under John Ford's direction but taken over in mid-stream by Jack Cardiff when illness forced Ford to withdraw, pic opens in 1911 Dublin during the troubled times of opposition to the British. It is a period when Cassidy – name given himself by O'Casey in his third-person writing – was feeling the stirrings of a talent which was to elevate him ultimately to the position of one of Ireland's great playwrights.

Taylor delivers a fine, strongly-etched characterization, believable both in his romantic scenes and as the writer who comes up the hard way. Splendid support is afforded particularly by Maggie Smith, as his one love but who leaves him so he can progress better without her.

■ YOUNG DOCTORS, THE

1961, 103 MINS, US

Dir Phil Karlson *Prod* Stuart Millar, Lawrence Turman *Scr* Joseph Hayes *Ph* Arthur J. Ornitz *Ed* Robert Swink *Mus* Elmer Bernstein *Prod Des* Richard Sylbert

● Fredric March, Ben Gazzara, Dick Clark, Ina Balin, Eddie Albert, Phyllis Love (United Artists)

The Young Doctors is an enlightening motion picture executed with restraint and clinical authenticity.

The screenplay, based on a novel by Arthur Hailey, is a generally brisk, literate and substantial piece of writing marked by a few soaring bursts of thought-provoking philosophical wisdom as regards life, death and love.

Essentially the story represents an idealistic clash between two pathologists, one (Fredric March) the vet department head whose ideals and perspective have been mellowed and blunted somewhat by years of red tape and day-to-day frustration, the other (Ben Gazzara), his new assistant, young, aggressive, up-to-date and meticulous in his approach to the job. The conflict is dramatically illustrated via two critical cases in which both are pretty intimately involved.

Veteran March creates a character of dimension and compassion. Gazzara plays with great reserve and intensity, another fine portrayal. Dick Clark is persuasive as a young intern, Eddie Albert outstanding as a dedicated obstetrician. Ina Balin experiences a few uncertain moments as a gravely ill young nurse in love with life in general and Gazzara in particular, but she comes through in the more demanding passages. Camerawork by Arthur J. Ornitz is pretty bold stuff.

■ YOUNG EINSTEIN

1988, 89 MINS, AUSTRALIA ◇ Ⓥ

Dir Yahoo Serious *Prod* Yahoo Serious, Warwick Ross, David Roach *Scr* David Roach, Yahoo Serious *Ph* Jeff Darling *Ed* Yahoo Serious *Mus* William

Motzing, Martin Armiger, Tommy Tycho *Art Dir* Steve Marr, Laurie Faen, Colin Gibson, Ron Highfield
● Yahoo Serious, Odile Le Clezio, John Howard, Pee Wee Wilson, Su Cruickshank (Serious)

This wild, cheerful, off-the-wall comedy showcases the many talents of Australian satirist Yahoo Serious, who not only directed and plays the leading role, but also co-wrote (from his own original story), coproduced, edited and handled the stunts. Quite a lot to take on for a first-time filmmaker.

Pic posits young Einstein as the only son of eccentric apple farmers from Australia's southern island, Tasmania. He has a fertile mind, and is forever discovering things: it's not his fault that, by 1905 when the film's set, gravity has already been discovered by someone else.

According to the film, Einstein discovers accidentally how to split the atom while experimenting methods of injecting bubbles into home-brewed beer. He sets off for mainland Australia (a comically lengthy journey) to patent his invention, and meets French genius Marie Curie (Odile Le Clezio) on a train; he also meets villain and patents stealer Preston Preston (John Howard), scion of a family of Perth entrepreneurs.

The entire production rests on the shoulders of its director/star. Fortunately Serious (born Greg Pead), a long-haired gangly clown, exhibits a brash and confident sense of humor, endearing personality, and a fondness for sight gags.

■ YOUNG FRANKENSTEIN

1974, 108 MINS, US Ⓥ
Dir Mel Brooks *Prod* Michael Gruskoff *Scr* Gene Wilder, Mel Brooks *Ph* Gerald Hirschfeld *Ed* John Howard *Mus* John Morris *Art Dir* Dale Hennesy
● Gene Wilder, Peter Boyle, Marty Feldman, Madeline Kahn, Cloris Leachman, Gene Hackman (20th Century-Fox)

Young Frankenstein emerges as a reverently satirical salute to the 1930s horror film genre.

The screenplay features Gene Wilder as the grandson of Baron Victor Frankenstein, creator of the monster. Wilder, an American medical college teacher, is lured back to Transylvania by old family retainer Richard Haydn. Wilder's assistant, the namesake descendant of Igor, is played by Marty Feldman.

Teri Garr is a curvaceous lab assistant, while Cloris Leachman is a mysterious housekeeper composite of Una O'Connor and Mrs Danvers. Wilder's fussy fiancee Madeline Kahn turns up importantly in the final reels. Peter Boyle is the monster, an artistically excellent blend of malice, pity and comedy.

■ YOUNG GUNS

1988, 107 MINS, US ◇ Ⓥ
Dir Christopher Cain *Prod* Joe Roth, Christopher Cain, Irby Smith, Paul Schiff *Scr* John Fusco *Ph* Dean Semler *Ed* Jack Hofstra *Mus* Anthony Marinelli *Art Dir* Jane Muski
● Emilio Estevez, Kiefer Sutherland, Lou Diamond Phillips, Charlie Sheen, Dermot Mulroney, Terence Stamp (Morgan Creek/20th Century-Fox)

Young Guns is a lame attempt at a brat pack *Wild Bunch*, executed without style or feel for the genre.

Meager efforts at offbeat characterization are made at the outset, as British gang ringleader Terence Stamp seeks to better the lot of his renegade boys by encouraging them to read and call each other 'gentlemen.'

Stamp's early murder by town bigshots prompts quick retaliation by the trigger-happy kids, who are briefly deputized but whose irresponsibility and inclination toward gunplay brands them as outlaws and sets in

motion an irreversible chain of violence that inevitably leads to a fateful confrontation.

What this film has that few, if any, Westerns ever have had before is a hard rock score. Music's every appearance on the scene throws one right out of the scene and serves to remind that this is a high-tech artifact of the late 1980s.

As Billy the Kid, Emilio Estevez is the nominal star here, but no one really shines.

■ YOUNG GUNS II

1990, 103 MINS, US ◇ ⓥ
Dir Geoff Murphy *Prod* Paul Schiff, Irby Smith *Scr* John Fusco *Ph* Dean Semler *Ed* Bruce Green *Mus* Alan Silvestri *Art Dir* Gene Rudolf
● Emilio Estevez, Kiefer Sutherland, Lou Diamond Phillips, Christian Slater, William Petersen, James Coburn (Morgan Creek)

Although it's more ambitious than most sequels *Young Guns II* exhausts its most inspired moment during the opening credits and fades into a copy of its 1988 predecessor – a slick, glossy MTV-style Western.

Even the film's one surprise – a wizened horseman emerging from the desert, circa 1950, to recount the tale of Billy the Kid – feels lift from Arthur Penn's 1970 classic *Little Big Man*, all the way down to Emilio Estevez' hoarse, whispering narration.

Oater follows a stripped-to-the-bone storyline that picks up the adventures of Billy Bonney's Lincoln County gang a few years after the events in 1988's *Young Guns*. Told in flashback, the story essentially involves the gang's hell-bent rush toward the perceived safety of Mexico with a band of government men – headed by ally-turned-adversary Pat Garrett (William Petersen) – in hot pursuit.

Estevez, Kiefer Sutherland and Lou Diamond Phillips are back, but the rest of the gang is new, and the other characterizations prove disappointingly thin. Christian Slater has a nice recurring bit as a Gun with an inferiority complex over his lack of notoriety; Petersen cuts a striking figure as Garrett without providing much insight into his motives.

■ YOUNG LIONS, THE

1958, 167 MINS, US ⓥ
Dir Edward Dmytryk *Prod* Al Lichtman *Scr* Edward Anhalt *Ph* Joe MacDonald *Ed* Dorothy Spencer *Mus* Hugo Friedhofer *Art Dir* Lyle R. Wheeler, Addison Hehr
● Marlon Brando, Montgomery Clift, Dean Martin, Hope Lange, Maximilian Schell, Barbara Rush (20th Century-Fox)

The Young Lions is a canvas of the Second World War of scope and stature. It's a king-sized credit to all concerned, from Edward Anhalt's skillful adaptation of Irwin Shaw's novel to Edward Dmytryk's realistic direction, and the highly competent portrayals of virtually everyone in the cast.

Marlon Brando's interpretation of Anhalt's modified conception of the young Nazi officer; Montgomery Clift, the drafted GI of Jewish heritage; Dean Martin as a frankly wouldbe draft-dodger until the realities of war catch up with him are standout all the way.

Hope Lange gives a sensitive performance as the New England girl opposite Clift and Barbara Rush is properly more resourceful as Martin's romantic vis-a-vis. Even more vivid are the performances of Sweden's May Britt, making her US film debut in the role of the cheating wife of the Nazi officer, latter capitally played by Switzerland's Maximilian (young brother of Maria) Schell, also making his Hollywood bow.

Dmytryk effectively highlights the human values on both the German and American

home-fronts. It gravitates from the boot-camp in the States to the fall of France, the North African campaign, the deterioration of the Third Reich, the smirking obsequiousness to the invading Yanks by the Bavarian town mayor when the GIs liberate the inhuman concentration camp, and the gradual disillusionment of the once ardent Nazi as symbolized by Brando.

The Anhalt screenplay captures shade and nuance of role in pithy, pungent dialog. The accent on romance is as strong as the war stuff. Underplaying is the keynote of virtually all the performances.

■ YOUNG LOVERS, THE

1964, 110 MINS, US
Dir Samuel Goldwyn Jr *Prod* Samuel Goldwyn Jr *Scr* George Garrrett *Ph* Joseph Biroc, Ellsworth Fredericks *Ed* William A. Lyon *Mus* Sol Kaplan *Art Dir* Frank Wade
● Peter Fonda, Sharon Hugueny, Nick Adams, Deborah Walley, Beatrice Straight, Malachi Throne (M-G-M)

Samuel Goldwyn Jr's *The Young Lovers* has a lot of things going for it. While the story [from novel by Julian Halevy] about young, unwed parents-to-be is no shocker, the talk is frank and switch is on problems mainly of unwed father, rather than of mother.

Most awkward parts come during opening scenes, as love affair between college students Peter Fonda and Sharon Hugueny is slowly built up.

Fonda has uncomfortable moments as an art student who intends to live free, bachelor life, and his voice doesn't carry conviction in several scenes. How much of this is attributable to direction (film is producer Goldwyn's first as a director as well) rather than lack of acting experience is difficult to assess.

Hugueny also suffers acting lapses, but scores by making apparent her three-step transition from shy teenager, to passionate lover, and on to wiser, more mature young adult.

■ YOUNG MR LINCOLN

1939, 101 MINS, US ⓥ
Dir John Ford *Prod* Darryl F. Zanuck *Scr* Lamar Trotti *Ph* Bert Glennon *Ed* Walter Thompson *Mus* Alfred Newman *Art Dir* Richard Day, Mark-Lee Kirk
● Henry Fonda, Alice Brady, Marjorie Weaver, Arleen Whelan (20th Century-Fox)

As the title implies, this deals with the Great Emanicator's early days in Salem III, emphasizing the Civil War president's then penchant for inherent honesty, fearlessness, shrewdness, plus such homely qualities as being a champ rail-splitter mixed with an avid hunger for book larnin'.

As motion picture entertainment, however, *Young Mr. Lincoln* is something else again. Fundamentally it resolves itself down to a courtroom drama. He's called upon to extricate Richard Cromwell and Eddie Quillan, as Matt and Adam Clay, following a murder rap.

Henry Fonda is capital in the highlight scenes where he languorously addresses the small group in front of the little Berry-Lincoln general store in Salem, Ill.

With judicious eye to authenticity and dignity the major shortcoming of this Lincoln film is at the altar of faithfulness, hampered by the rather lethargic production and direction.

■ YOUNG MR PITT, THE

1942, 110 MINS, UK
Dir Carol Reed *Prod* Edward Black *Scr* Sidney Gilliatt, Frank Launder, Viscount Castlerosse *Ph* Frederick Young *Mus* Charles Williams

● Robert Donat, Robert Morley, Phyllis Calvert, John Mills, Max Adrian, Felix Aylmer (20th Century-Fox)

There is so much to acclaim and so little with which to find fault in this production. There are over 150 speaking parts, all of them praiseworthily handled, and the overly generous 18th-century period details have seldom been better reproduced. It's a costly production all the way.

Story is based on the political career of William Pitt Jr (Robert Donat) who was Prime Minister of England at 24.

Robert Morley, who so frequently steals the show, again towers above the rest of the excellent cast. In the stellar role Donat acts with meticulous earnestness and sincerity, but seemingly lacks inspiration. One seems to detect the mechanics of fine acting – a sort of straining to be convincing. In sharp contrast, John Mills, in a relatively minor role, is impressive without resorting to heroics.

■ YOUNG ONE, THE

1961, 94 MINS, US/MEXICO

Dir Luis Bunuel *Prod* George P. Werker *Scr* Luis Bunuel, H.B. Addis [Hugo Butler] *Ph* Gabriel Figueroa *Ed* Carlos Savage *Mus* Jesus Zarzosa *Art Dir* Jesus Bracho

● Zachary Scott, Key Meersman, Bernie Hamilton, Crahan Denton, Claudio Brook (Werker/Olmeca)

The Young One is an odd, complicated and inconclusive attempt to interweave two sizzling themes – race prejudice in the deep South and an almost *Lolita*-like sex situation with Tennessee Williams overtones – into an engrossing melodramatic fabric. The offbeat project was lensed in Mexico.

Travelin' Man, a short story by Peter Matthiessen, is the origin of the screenplay. The story takes place on an island wild game preserve off South Carolina occupied by an unsavory gamekeeper (Zachary Scott) and a 13 or 14-year-old orphan girl whose handyman-grandfather has just expired. Into this potentially explosive scene drifts a hip-talking Negro (Bernie Hamilton) falsely accused of rape and on the run.

Scott is convincingly unpleasant, Hamilton equally believable and sympathetic. Kay Meersman cuts a rather pitiful figure as the innocent, nymphet-like nature girl creature involved helplessly in the emotional turmoil.

Luis Bunuel does an alert, perceptive job of directing, succeeding in getting the Carolina geographical flavor out of the Mexican location. But his vigorous efforts are lamentably diluted by the unsatisfactory nature of the story.

■ YOUNG ONES, THE

1962, 108 MINS, UK ◇ ⓥ

Dir Sidney J. Furie *Prod* Kenneth Harper *Scr* Peter Myers, Ronald Cass *Ph* Douglas Slocombe *Ed* Jack Slade *Mus* Peter Myers, Stanley Black *Art Dir* John Howell

● Cliff Richard, Robert Morley, Carole Gray, Richard O'Sullivan, Melvyn Hayes, The Shadows (Associated British)

Producer Kenneth Harper signed up a 28-year-old Canadian director, Sidney Furie; a slick choreographer, Herbert Ross; and Cliff Richard to play the hero.

The songs, dancing and Furie's nimble direction keep the screenplay on zestful enough plane. Richard is the leader of a youth club whose humble little clubhouse is endangered when a millionaire property tycoon buys the land on which it is situated. Unbeknown to the other teenagers, the tycoon is Richard's father. They decide to fight him and this involves raising $4,000 to challenge the lease. It's decided the best way to do this is by taking over a derelict theatre to stage a show.

The choreography of Ross is agile and sharp. Between them musical supervisors Norrie Paramor and Stanley Black have made best use of the musical side. Main fault of the film is that the screenplay and dialog are uneven.

However, Robert Morley, as the tycoon, does an impressive job in bringing some adult wit and irony to the screen. Richard is inexperienced as an actor but has a pleasant charm and sings well within his range.

New dancing girl Carole Gray is a youthful delight, though she too is happier when enjoying the exuberance of the numbers than when having to act. Melvyn Hayes and Richard O'Sullivan offer some pleasantly shrewd comedy.

■ YOUNG SAVAGES, THE

1961, 103 MINS, US

Dir John Frankenheimer *Prod* Pat Duggan *Scr* Edward Anhalt, J.P. Miller *Ph* Lionel Lindon *Ed* Eda Warren *Mus* David Amram *Art Dir* Burr Smidt

● Burt Lancaster, Dina Merrill, Shelley Winters, Edward Andrews, Larry Gates, Telly Savalas (United Artists)

The Young Savages is a kind of non-musical east side variation on *West Side Story*. It is a sociological cussword puzzle, a twisted riddle aimed at detection of the true motivation for juvenile crime, as set against the backdrop of New York's teeming East Harlem district in which neighborhood nationalities mobilize into youthful raiding parties at the drop of a psychotic frustration.

The picture is inventively, arrestingly directed by John Frankenheimer with the aid of cameraman Lionel Lindon. Together they have manipulated the lens to catch the wild fury of gang pavement warfare; twisting, tilting, pulling way back, zeroing in and composing to follow and frame the excitement.

But there is nothing Frankenheimer can do to make the yarn itself – concocted out of a novel by Evan Hunter, *A Matter of Conviction* – stand tall as screen fiction. The story is that of three Italian lads (of 15, 16 and 17) who murder a blind Puerto Rican boy of 15 who is regarded as a top warlord of a rival gang. The case for the prosecution is taken over by scrupulous d.a.'s asst Burt Lancaster whose search for truth and justice and familiarity with the law of the asphalt jungle (he grew up there) leads him to make a valiant courtroom stand on behalf of the boys he is supposed to be trying to convict.

■ YOUNG SHERLOCK HOLMES

1985, 109 MINS, US ◇ ⓥ

Dir Barry Levinson *Prod* Mark Johnson *Scr* Chris Columbus *Ph* Stephen Goldblatt *Ed* Stu Linder *Mus* Bruce Broughton *Art Dir* Norman Reynolds

● Nicholas Rowe, Alan Cox, Sophie Ward, Anthony Higgins, Susan Fleetwood, Freddie Jones (Amblin/Industrial Light & Magic)

Young Sherlock Holmes is another Steven Spielberg film corresponding to those lamps made from driftwood and coffee tables from redwood burl and hatchcovers. It's not art but they all serve their purpose and sell by the millions.

The formula this time is applied to the question of what might have happened had Sherlock Holmes and John Watson first met as teenage students.

As usual, Speilberg's team – this time led by director Barry Levinson – isn't really as interested in the answer as it is in fooling around with the visual effects possibilities conjured by George Lucas' Industrial Light & Magic shop.

Nicholas Rowe as Holmes and Alan Cox as Watson maturely carry off their roles, assisted by Sophie Ward as the necessary

female accomplice. The adults are just there to fill in the spaces.

■ YOUNG WINSTON

1972, 157 MINS, UK ◇ ⓥ

Dir Richard Attenborough *Prod* Carl Foreman *Scr* Carl Foreman *Ph* Gerry Turpin *Ed* Kevin Connor *Mus* Alfred Ralston *Art Dir* Geoffrey Drake, Don Ashton

● Simon Ward, Robert Shaw, Anne Bancroft, Jack Hawkins, Ian Holm, Anthony Hopkins (Columbia/Open Road)

Rate this biopic of Winston Churchill's early years as both a brilliant artistic achievement and a fascinating, highly enjoyable film – a combination not always obtained.

It's a richly multi-faced scrapbook [from Churchill's book *My Early Life*] which is unfolded, touching on his lonely childhood and only occasional contact with his politician father and a socially much-involved American mother, early school experience, first combat and war correspondent stints in India and the Sudan and on to first political defeat and ultimate vindication as – after a headline-grabbing Boer War exploit – he makes an early political mark in an impassioned House of Commons speech.

Far from a sycophantic paean to a great man in the bud, pic manages a believable portrait of an ambitious and sometimes arrogant young man.

■ YOUNGBLOOD

1986, 109 MINS, US ◇ ⓥ

Dir Peter Markle *Prod* Peter Bart, Patrick Wells *Scr* Peter Markle *Ph* Mark Irwin *Ed* Stephen E. Rivkin, Jack Hofstra *Mus* William Orbit/Torchsong *Art Dir* Alicia Keywan

● Rob Lowe, Cynthia Gibb, Patrick Swayze, Ed Lauter, Jim Youngs, Fionnula Flannagan (UA/Guber-Peters)

Picture has a simple premise: Rob Lowe desperately wants to leave the hard life on his father's farm to join a minor league Canadian hockey team where he believes he will be the star player. His half-blind brother (Jim Youngs), who once played for the same team before he was injured, tells their Dad (Eric Nesterenko) he'll do double-duty so Lowe can be free to try and fulfill his dreams.

Dad agrees and Lowe takes off. He is an innocent who, after less than a week, is seduced by his landlady (Fionnula Flanagan), ridiculed by his teammates and enamored of the first girl he meets (Cynthia Gibb) – the coach's daughter who becomes his girlfriend. Scenes on the ice look great and Lowe truly looks like the fast and accurate son-of-a-gun hockey player he's supposed to be.

■ YOU'RE A BIG BOY NOW

1966, 98 MINS, US ◇ ⓥ

Dir Francis Coppola *Prod* Phil Feldman *Scr* Francis Coppola *Ph* Andy Laszlo *Ed* Aram Avakian *Mus* John Sebastian *Art Dir* Vassieli Fotopoulos

● Elizabeth Hartman, Geraldine Page, Julie Harris, Peter Kastner, Rip Torn, Michael Dunn (Seven Arts)

You're a Big Boy Now [from the novel by David Benedictus] has a simple premise – a virginal young man growing into manhood, not so much through his own efforts as those about him – which has been expanded glowingly in a sophisticated approach. Francis Coppola has drawn topflight performances from his talented cast.

Peter Kastner plays a roller-skating stack boy in a NY public library, somewhat of a dreamer. The father (Rip Torn) decides the best way for his son to grow up would be to move out of the family home on his own. Straightaway, lad becomes ensconced in a rooming house run by Julie Harris.

With the help of his library, dope-inclined pal (Tony Bill) and a pretty library assistant (Karen Black) the boy is launched on his road to manhood, which takes him into the arms of a sexy, way-out, Greenwich Village discotheque dish (Elizabeth Hartman). Frequent laughs spark his career toward full-blossomed virility, with amusing bumps along the way.

Kastner turns in a slick portrayal, endowing role with just the proper emphasis upon youth in the wondering stage. Both Geraldine Page as the mother and Harris as the landlady go all-out in hilarious roles and Torn, too, delivers a sock performance as the father who has difficulty understanding his son.

● ●

■ YOU'RE IN THE ARMY NOW

1941, 79 MINS, US
Dir Lewis Seiler   *Prod* Ben Stoloff   *Scr* Paul Gerard Smith, George Beatty   *Ph* Arthur Todd   *Ed* Frank Magee
● Jimmy Durante, Jane Wyman, Phil Silvers, Regis Toomey, George Meeker (Warner)

Though it is a bit corny in spots and lays the slapstick on heavily, with some gag sequences stretched too far, here is a comedy of soldier life that completely entertains.

Jimmy Durante goes to town on the clowning, slapstick and other means of comedy, but while he's busy as a bee, many others contribute importantly to the numerous laugh-producing sequences. Among these is Phil Silvers.

Durante and Silvers, trying to interest a recruiting officer in a vacuum cleaner, accidentally get themselves enlisted. As buck privates, they become guardhouse regulars as result of getting themselves into one jam after another.

The story job by Paul Gerard Smith, an old hand at the vaudeville-writing game, and George Beatty is excellent and, if some of the gag situations are stretched a little too far or the slapstick gets out of hand, it may be the fault of the director, Lewis Seiler. Dialog is surefire all the way.

● ●

■ ZABRISKIE POINT

1970, 112 MINS, US ◇ Ⓥ
Dir Michelangelo Antonioni   *Prod* Carlo Ponti
Scr Michelangelo Antonioni, Fred Gardner, Sam Shepard, Tonino Guerra, Clare Peploe   *Ph* Alfino Contini   *Ed* Franco Arcalli   *Art Dir* Dean Tavoularis
● Mark Frechette, Daria Halprin, Paul Fix, G.D. Spradlin, Bill Garaway, Kathleen Cleaver (M-G-M)

Michelangelo Antonioni makes the US social scene, and despite the imbalance in his concept, distills from his notes some arresting photographic moments. Antonioni has sought to bring into the focus of his own insights, the student vs establishment conflict. He is on foreign terrain.

His off-camera presence is sensed in each pictorial move.

Probably the most compelling footage of *Zabriskie Point* is the finis wrapup, in which things representative of the ultra 'haves' go up in imagined explosions.

The special effects are magnificent as the remnants of modern architectured big business, including mod edifices, and billboards which had been planted by power corporations, hit the sky, piece by piece, and hang in a dangling collage of symbolism.

● ●

■ ZANDY'S BRIDE

1974, 116 MINS, US ◇
Dir Jan Troell   *Prod* Harvey Matofsky   *Scr* Marc Norman   *Ph* Jordan Cronenweth   *Ed* Gordon Scott   *Mus* Michael Franks   *Art Dir* Al Brenner
● Gene Hackman, Liv Ullmann, Eileen Heckart, Susan Tyrrell, Sam Bottoms, Joe Santos (Warner)

Zandy's Bride is a good period frontier romantic melodrama starring Gene Hackman as a gruff cattle rancher and Liv Ullmann as the mail-order bride who softens him up. Star performances sustain Jan Troell's delicate but placid direction.

Marc Norman's spare screenplay was adapted from a 1942 novel, *The Stranger*, by Lillian Bos Ross. Set in 1870 in upstate California's rugged Big Sur mountain and sea interface, story takes Hackman from a crude, thoughtless hermit to a loving husband and father. The going is rough, however, Ullmann's unexpectedly strong spirit overcomes his stiffness, learned at the back of the hand of father Frank Cady, a cruel patriarch who has reduced wife Eileen Heckart to serf status.

The plot line is thin but sufficient.

● ●

■ ZARDOZ

1974, 104 MINS, UK ◇ Ⓥ
Dir John Boorman   *Prod* John Boorman   *Scr* John Boorman   *Ph* Geoffrey Unsworth   *Ed* John Merritt   *Mus* David Munrow   *Art Dir* Anthony Pratt
● Sean Connery, Charlotte Rampling, Sara Kestelman, John Alderton, Sally Ann Newton, Niall Buggy (20th Century-Fox)

Zardoz is a futuristic, metaphysical and anthropological drama testing John Boorman in three creative areas. The results: direction, good; script, a brilliant premise which unfortunately washes out in climactic sound and fury; and production, outstanding, particularly special visual effects which belie the film's modest cost. Sean Connery heads the cast as a 23rd-century Adam.

The story, set in 2293, postulates a world society which this century's runaway technology forced into being. The highest order beings are an elitist group of effete aesthetics, eternally youthful on a spiritual plane. Connery rises from the lower ranks to overthrow the new order and recycle mankind into its older pattern.

Connery manifests well the brooding duality of man's nature, emerging from mechanical breeding to eventually tear down the system that created him.

● ●

■ ZED AND TWO NOUGHTS, A

1985, 115 MINS, UK/NETHERLANDS ◇ Ⓥ
Dir Peter Greenaway   *Prod* Kees Kasander, Peter Sainsbury   *Scr* Peter Greenaway   *Ph* Sacha Vierny   *Ed* John Wilson   *Mus* Michael Nyman   *Art Dir* Ben van Os
● Andrea Ferreol, Brian Deacon, Eric Deacon, Frances Barber, Joss Ackland, Gerard Thoolen (Artificial Eye/BFI/Channel Four/Allarts/VPRO)

Despite its visual pyrotechnics and an impressively woven texture of intellectual allusions, Peter Greenaway's feature fails to engage the audience's sympathies.

In the end, it remains the work of a highly talented British eccentric who hasn't managed to thresh out his private fantasies and obscurantist intellectual preoccupations to connect with major concerns or touch the emotions.

The action centers on a zoo (its letters making up the zed and two noughts of the title). In this lurid arena Greenaway is intent on upturning the seamier, humiliating side of animal existence in captivity (including that of homo sapiens).

Meanwhile, lots of pseudo-philosophical conundrums are tossed at the audience like

peanuts to hungry caged animals. Is a zebra a white horse with black stripes or a black one with white? etc. Needless to say, the resulting stilted dialog does not make the acting much of a treat.

● ●

■ ZEE & CO

1972, 110 MINS, UK ◇ Ⓥ
Dir Brian G. Hutton   *Prod* Jay Kanter, Alan Ladd Jr   *Scr* Edna O'Brien   *Ph* Billy Williams   *Ed* Jim Clark   *Mus* Stanley Myers   *Art Dir* Peter Mullins
● Elizabeth Taylor, Michael Caine, Susannah York, Margaret Leighton, John Standing, Mary Larkin (Kastner-Ladd-Kanter)

Not in years have three people more deserved the star billing they get in this *Love Story* for adults. Elizabeth Taylor and Susannah York both turn in performances that fully capture the excellently conceived characters of Edna O'Brien's original screenplay. Michael Caine keeps up beautifully with the pace set by his femme co-stars.

The script has Taylor, the 'Zee' of the title, and Caine as a long-married couple, whose relationship has turned into a love-hate affair that leads to Caine's affair with York.

After a half-hearted suicide attempt Zee recognizes the possibility of an actual break but, by accident finding that her rival has her own private Achilles heel, makes a final, desperate move which may answer one problem but presents another.

● ●

■ ZELIG

1983, 84 MINS, US ◇ Ⓥ
Dir Woody Allen   *Prod* Robert Greenhut   *Scr* Woody Allen   *Ph* Gordon Willis   *Ed* Susan E. Morse   *Mus* Dick Hyman   *Art Dir* Mel Bourne
● Woody Allen, Mia Farrow, Garreth Brown, Stephanie Farrow, Will Holt, Sol Lomita (Rollins-Joffe/Orion)

Lampooning documentary tradition by structuring the entire film as a meticulously crafted bogus docu, Woody Allen tackles some serious stuff en route (namely the two-edged sword of public and media celebrity-hood) but manages to avoid the self-oriented seriousness that's alienated many of his onetime loyalist. More positively, *Zelig* is consistently funny, though more academic than boulevardier.

Allen plays the eponymous Leonard Zelig, subject of the 'documentary' that traces this onetime legend of the 1920s-30s whose weak personality and neurotic need to be liked caused him to become the ultimate conformist.

Through the use of doctored photos and staged black and white footage cannily – and usually undetectably – matched with authentic newsreels and stock footage of the period, Allen is seen intermingling with everyone from the Hearst crowd at San Simeon, Eugene O'Neill and Fanny Brice to the likes of Pope Pius XI and even Adolf Hitler.

The narrative that does emerge limns the efforts of a committed psychiatrist (played with tact and loveliness by Mia Farrow) to give Zelig a single self, a relationship that blossoms, predictably, to love by fadeout.

● ●

■ ZEPPELIN

1971, 97 MINS, UK ◇
Dir Etienne Perier   *Prod* Owen Crump   *Scr* Arthur Rowe, Donald Churchill   *Ph* Alan Hume   *Ed* John Sharley   *Mus* Roy Budd   *Art Dir* Bert Daley
● Michael York, Elke Sommer, Peter Carsten, Marius Goring, Anton Diffring, Andrew Keir (Getty & Fromkess)

Zeppelin settles for being just another wartime melodrama, with some good aerial sequences and a powerful, brisk raid sequence in the finale.

Story deals with Britain's concern about German's new World War I weapon, the Zeppelin, the monstrous, looming aircraft that made Britain vulnerable. Indication that the Germans have perfected a new and even more effective Zeppelin jerks the British high-ups into swift action.

A young Scottish lieutenant, of Anglo-German parentage, who had left Germany and eventually joined the British Army (Michael York) looks the perfect spy. Worked on by an attractive German Mata Hari (Alexandra Stewart), he is softened up and when called on to 'volunteer' to 'defect' to the Germans and dig out the secrets of the new Zeppelin he reluctantly agrees.

Many Germans are suspicious of his sudden switch back to the homeland. But only one appears to be convinced that he's a spy. She (Elke Sommer) is the wife of the aircraft designer (Marius Goring) and she's more concerned with helping to prepare the Zepp for its final trial run than in exposing York.

■ **ZIEGFELD FOLLIES**

1945, 116 MINS, US ◇ ⓥ
Dir Vincente Minnelli, [George Sidney, Norman Taurog, Roy Del Ruth, Lemuel Ayres] *Prod* Arthur Freed
Scr George White, William K. Wells, Al Lewis, Robert Alton, Kay Thompson, Roger Edens, Irving Brecher
Ph George Folsey, Charles Rosher, Ray June *Ed* Albert Akst *Mus* Lennie Hayton (dir.) *Art Dir* Cedric Gibbons, Jack Martin Smith, Merrill Pye, Lemuel Ayers
● Fred Astaire, Lucille Ball, Fanny Brice, Judy Garland, Gene Kelly, William Powell (M-G-M)

Looking down from a very lush heaven, as Florenz Ziegfeld (William Powell) does in prolog of this film super, the Great Ziegy would be dazzled by color, sets and routines far above the capacities of his day. But despite the glory of Technicolor, Ziegfeld would have missed his nudes, his pleasantly risque interludes and a certain heart-warming which came with the old productions.

Those shining above all others in the generous cast of Metro stars are Fred Astaire, agile and gay; Judy Garland, who has perfected an ironic touch; sultry Lena Horne, graceful Esther Williams, comic Fanny Brice and sweet-warbling Lucille Bremer.

Pic opens with dreamland set out of which Powell emerges, apparently comfortably fixed in celestial heights a la Ziegfeld. As the great producer, he reflects on his successes – *Rosalie, Rio Rita, Showboat*, the various *Follies*.

It's all stupendous, terrific, colossal, practically everyone would agree. Even Ziegy.

■ **ZOO IN BUDAPEST**

1933, 82 MINS, US
Dir Rowland V. Lee *Prod* Jesse L. Lasky *Scr* Dan Totheroh, Louise Long, Rowland V. Lee *Ph* Lee Garmes *Mus* Hugo Friedhofer
● Loretta Young, Gene Raymond, O. P. Heggie, Wally Albright, Paul Fix (Fox)

Seemingly what producer Jesse Lasky has tried to do is to make a picture which has in it something of the strange fascination of romance and atmosphere of *Liliom* and at the same time an element of Hollywood punch. He has gotten both things and they don't blend.

Besides the warring elements of a *Liliom* theme and a dramatic finish, the story [by Melville Baker and Jack Kirkland] has still another facet, the development of a submotif of bitter social satire in symbolic suggestions of similarities between the animals in the zoo and some of the people that cross the screen. This slant is but vaguely suggested and is never worked out satisfactorily.

However, there can be no two views of the picture's pictorial beauty. There are several sequences of night falling over a lake in the zoo peopled with strange creatures, where an escaped orphan girl is hiding as the evening mists gather, that are a knockout.

Playing by the two leads is eminently good. Role of the terror-stricken orphanage refugee proves a happy one for Loretta Young's talents, while the opposite character, that of a wild youngster brought up in a big town menagerie, friend and play-fellow of the beasts of the cages, turns out to be one of those once-in-a-blue-moon for Gene Raymond, a newcomer from legit of only one or two pictures.

■ **ZORBA THE GREEK**

1964, 142 MINS, US/Greece ⓥ
Dir Michael Cacoyannis *Prod* Michael Cacoyannis
Scr Michael Cacoyannis *Ph* Walter Lassally *Ed* Alex Archambault *Mus* Mikis Theodorakis *Art Dir* Vassili Fotopoulos
● Anthony Quinn, Alan Bates, Irene Papas, Lila Kedrova, George Foundas, Eleni Anousaki (International Classics)

To one who has not read Nikos Kazantzakis' widely praised novel it appears that producer-director-scenarist Michael Cacoyannis may have tried to be too faithful to the original.

Zorba the Greek is a paean to life in all its diverse aspects, ranging from the farcical to the tragic, and as epitomized by the lusty title character. This Zorba, beautifully played by Anthony Quinn, is a wise and aging peasant, a free soul who is totally committed to life no matter what it holds.

To dramatize this theme, Cacoyannis has written a screenplay which is so packed with incidents of varying moods that some of the more important ones cannot be developed fully. The story takes place in a remote section of the island of Crete where Zorba has come as the self-appointed aide-de-camp to a young, inhibited Englishman of Greek parentage, played by Alan Bates. Latter, who describes himself as a writer who hasn't written anything in a long, long time, intends to reopen an old lignite mine he has inherited. Their subsequent adventures – rather loosely connected and wherein Bates finally learns to live a la Zorba – comprise the body of the film.

Quinn is excellent, and Bates, in a less flamboyant role, is equally good. Irene Papas is strikingly effective as a doomed widow, a role without dialog. Lila Kedrova plays the aging courtesan with all stops out, always halfway between laughter and tears.
☐ 1964: Best Picture (Nomination)

■ **ZORRO, THE GAY BLADE**

1981, 93 MINS, US ◇
Dir Peter Medak *Prod* George Hamilton, C.O. Erickson *Scr* Hal Dresner *Ph* John A. Alonzo
Ed Hillary Jane Kranze *Mus* Ian Fraser *Art Dir* Herman A. Blumenthal
● George Hamilton, Lauren Hutton, Brenda Vaccaro, Ron Leibman (20th Century-Fox)

Despite an inspired, offbeat performance by George Hamilton, *Zorro, the Gay Blade* doesn't have nearly enough gags. For the most part this is a Zorro with a very dull edge.

Although there is no time frame, film is obviously set years ago (in California) where Don Diego Vega, offspring of the legendary Zorro, is called upon to pick up his father's sword after the elder's death.

The hook here is that Hamilton's Vega, who is at first righting the wrongs of the poor villagers under leader Ron Leibman (who shouts unbearably through his entire role opposite equally brassy spouse Brenda Vaccaro), soon injures his foot and can no longer carry on his heroic deeds. Luckily his long lost look-alike Englishman brother, who is given to heavy makeup, colorful clothing and exaggerated hand gestures, appears out of nowhere and takes on the Zorro persona.

The contrast between the two Zorros is initially quite funny, especially when the Britisher decides to change the hero's tailored black wardrobe for shades of plum.

But aside from the physical characterizations (Hamilton also dons full drag as his fictional sister later on) and several offhanded remarks, there is nothing intriguing or original through the rest of the action.

■ **ZULU**

1964, 135 MINS, UK ◇ ⓥ
Dir Cy Endfield *Prod* Stanley Baker, Cy Endfield
Scr John Prebble, Cy Endfield *Ph* Stephen Dade
Ed John Jympson *Mus* John Barry *Art Dir* Ernest Archer
● Stanley Baker, Jack Hawkins, Ulla Jacobsson, James Booth, Michael Caine, Nigel Green (Paramount/Diamond)

Joseph E. Levine makes an impressive debut in British film production with *Zulu*, a picture that allows ample scope for his flamboyant approach to showmanship.

Based on a famous heroic exploit, when a handful of British soldiers withstood an onslaught by 4,000 Zulu warriors, the production is distinguished by its notable onscreen values, which are enhanced by top-quality lensing by Stephen Dade. It also has an intelligent screenplay which avoids most of the obvious cliches. It keeps the traditional British stiff upper-lip attitudes down to the barest minimum.

The defense of the garrison at Rorke's Drift took place on 22 January 1879. At the time the garrison heard the news that the 4,000 Zulu braves were on the way, reports had just come in that a far larger garrison had been completely wiped out, and there was no prospect of help from any other source.

On of the more obvious cliches in this type of yarn is apt to be the malingerer who displays great heroism in a moment of crisis. There is such a situation in *Zulu*, but the cliche is avoided, largely because of the excellent performance by James Booth. Indeed, the high allround standard of acting is one of the notable plus features. Stanley Baker, a solid and reliable performer, turns in a thoroughly convincing portrayal as the resolute Royal Engineers officer, with an effective contrasting study by Michael Caine as a supercilious lieutenant. Richard Burton contributes a brief and dignified narration.

■ **ZULU DAWN**

1979, 117 MINS, UK ⓥ
Dir Douglas Hickox *Prod* Nate Kohn *Scr* Cy Enfield, Anthony Storey *Ph* Ousama Rawi *Ed* Malcolm Cook *Mus* Elmer Bernstein *Art Dir* John Rosewarne
● Burt Lancaster, Peter O'Toole, Simon Ward, John Mills, Nigel Davenport, Denholm Elliott (Lamitas/Samarkand)

The subject of *Zulu Dawn* is the Battle of Islandlhwana wherein some 1,500 redcoats were slaughtered by 16 times their number of Zulu warriors led by legendary chief Cetshwayo.

The film is, in fact, a sort of 'prequel' to the 1964 picture *Zulu*, which dealt with an heroic stand at Rorke's Drift by a small band of British soldiers in 1879.

The action sequences are superbly handled, as are the scenes in which the men and material are assembled and manoeuvered. For sheer scope and numbers of people being manipulated for the cameras, *Zulu Dawn* is positively DeMillesque in scale.

Such banality as there is is, thankfully, confined to the expositional sequences which are quickly gotten out of the way to allow the army to get on the march.

DIRECTORS INDEX

Aaron, Paul *Maxie*

Abbott, George *Damn Yankees; Manslaughter; Pajama Game, The*

Abrahams, Jim *Airplane!; Big Business; Ruthless People; Top Secret!; Welcome Home, Roxy Carmichael*

Adams, Catlin *Sticky Fingers*

Adler, Lou *Up in Smoke*

Akkad, Moustapha *Lion Of The Desert; Message, The*

Alda, Alan *Betsy's Wedding; Four Seasons, The; New Life, A; Sweet Liberty*

Aldrich, Robert *. . . All the Marbles; Angry Hills, The; Apache; Big Knife, The; Choirboys, The; Dirty Dozen, The; Emperor of the North; Flight Of The Phoenix, The; Frisco Kid, The; Grissom Gang, The; Hush . . . Hush, Sweet Charlotte; Hustle; Killing of Sister George, The; Kiss Me Deadly; Legend of Lylah Clare, The; Longest Yard, The; Sodom And Gomorrah; Twilight's Last Gleaming; Ulzana's Raid; What Ever Happened To Baby Jane?*

Alland, William *Tarantula*

Allen, Corey *Avalanche; Thunder and Lightning*

Allen, Irwin *Beyond the Poseidon Adventure; Lost World, The; Story of Mankind, The; Swarm, The; Towering Inferno, The; Voyage to the Bottom of the Sea*

Allen, Lewis *Appointment With Danger*

Allen, Woody *Alice; Annie Hall; Another Woman; Bananas; Broadway Danny Rose; Crimes And Misdemeanors; Everything You Always Wanted to Know About Sex ★★ But Were Afraid to Ask; Hannah and her Sisters; Interiors; Love and Death; Manhattan; Midsummer Night's Sex Comedy, A; New York Stories; Purple Rose of Cairo, The; Radio Days; September; Sleeper; Stardust Memories; Take The Money and Run; What's Up, Tiger Lily?; Zelig*

Altman, Robert *Brewster McCloud; Buffalo Bill and the Indians or Sitting Bull's History Lesson, The; California Split; Come Back to the Five & Dime, Jimmy Dean, Jimmy Dean; Countdown; Fool for Love; Images; Long Goodbye, The; M*A*S*H; McCabe And Mrs. Miller; Nashville; Perfect Couple, A; Popeye; Quintet; Streamers; That Cold Day in the Park; Thieves Like Us; Three Women; Vincent and Theo; Wedding, A*

Alves, Joe *Jaws 3-D*

Amurri, Franco *Flashback*

Anderson, J. Murray *King of Jazz, The*

Anderson, Lindsay *Britannia Hospital; If. . . .; O Lucky Man!; This Sporting Life; Whales of August, The*

Anderson, Michael *All The Fine Young Cannibals; Around the World in 80 Days; Conduct Unbecoming; Dam Busters, The; Doc Savage, Man of Bronze; Logan's Run; Naked Edge, The; 1984; Operation Crossbow; Orca; Pope Joan; Quiller Memorandum, The; Shake Hands with the Devil; Shoes of the Fisherman, The; Wreck of the Mary Deare, The; Yangtse Incident*

Andrew Marton *Green Fire*

Annakin, Ken *Across the Bridge; Battle Of The Bulge; Biggest Bundle of Them All, The; Call of the Wild; Informers, The; Long Duel, The; Longest Day, The; Paper Tiger; Quartet; Story of Robin Hood, The; Swiss Family Robinson; Thoroughly Modern Millie; Trio*

Annaud, Jean-Jacques *Name Of The Rose, The; Quest for Fire*

Anspaugh, David *Hoosiers*

Anthony, Joseph *Career; Matchmaker, The; Rainmaker, The*

Antonio, Emile de *Rush To Judgment*

Antonioni, Michelangelo *Blowup; Passenger, The; Zabriskie Point*

Apted, Michael *Agatha; Class Action; Coal Miner's Daughter; Continental Divide; Gorillas In The Mist; Gorky Park; Squeeze, The; Stardust; Triple Echo, The*

Archainbaud, George *Lost Squadron, The*

Ardolino, Emile *Dirty Dancing; 3 Men and a Little Lady*

Arehn, Mats *Assignment, The*

Argall, Ray *Return Home*

Arkin, Alan *Fire Sale; Little Murders*

Arkush, Allen *Deathsport*

Arliss, Leslie *Wicked Lady, The*

Armitage, George *Miami Blues*

Armstrong, Gillian *High Tide; Mrs Soffel; My Brilliant Career; Star Struck*

Arnold, Jack *Creature From the Black Lagoon; Glass Web, The; Incredible Shrinking Man, The; It Came From Outer Space; Mouse that Roared, The*

Arzner, Dorothy *Nana*

Ashby, Hal *Being There; Bound For Glory; Coming Home; 8 Million Ways to Die; Harold And Maude; Landlord, The; Last Detail, The; Lookin' To Get Out; Shampoo*

Asher, Robert *Stitch In Time, A*

Asher, William *Beach Party; Johnny Cool; Night Warning*

Asquith, Anthony *Browning Version, The; Carrington V.C.; Doctor's Dilemma, The; Fanny By Gaslight; Guns of Darkness; Importance of Being Earnest, The; Libel; Millionairess, The; Moscow Nights; Pygmalion; Unfinished Symphony, The; V.I.P.s, The; Way to the Stars, The; We Dive at Dawn; Winslow Boy, The; Yellow Rolls-Royce, The*

Attenborough, Richard *Bridge Too Far, A; Chorus Line, A; Cry Freedom; Gandhi; Magic; Oh! What A Lovely War; Young Winston*

Auer, John H. *City That Never Sleeps*

Austin, Michael *Killing Dad*

Auzins, Igor *We of the Never Never*

Avakian, Aram *11 Harrowhouse*

Averback, Hy *I Love You, Alice B. Toklas; Suppose They Gave A War And Nobody Came?; Where Were You When The Lights Went Out?*

Avildsen, John G. *Formula, The; Joe; Karate Kid, The; Karate Kid Part II, The; Karate Kid III, The; Neighbors; Rocky; Rocky V; Save The Tiger; Slow Dancing in the Big City; W.W. and the Dixie Dancekings*

Axelrod, George *Lord Love A Duck; Secret Life Of An American Wife, The*

Aykroyd, Dan *Nothing But Trouble*

Ayres, Lemuel *Ziegfeld Follies*

Babenco, Hector *Ironweed; Kiss of the Spider Woman*

Bachmann, Gideon *Ciao, Federico!*

Bacon, Lloyd *Footlight Parade; Footsteps in the Dark; 42nd Street; French Line, The; Give My Regards to Broadway; Gold Diggers of 1937; He Was Her Man; Moby Dick*

Badger, Clarence *It*

Badham, John *American Flyers; Bingo Long Traveling All-Stars And Motor Kings, The; Bird on a Wire; Blue Thunder; Dracula; Hard Way, The; Saturday Night Fever; Short Circuit; Stakeout; WarGames*

Baer, Max *Hometown USA; Ode To Billy Joe*

Baker, Graham *Final Conflict, The*

Baker, Roy Ward *Anniversary, The; Asylum; Don't Bother To Knock; Dr. Jekyll and Sister Hyde; Flame In The Streets; Moon Zero Two; Night to Remember, A; October Man, The; Singer Not the Song, The; Two Left Feet; Vampire Lovers, The*

Bakshi, Ralph *Fire and Ice; Fritz The Cat; Lord of the Rings, The*

Balaban, Burt *Murder, Inc.*

Ballard, Carroll *Black Stallion, The; Nutcracker*

Band, Charles *Parasite*

Bank, Mirra *Enormous Changes at the Last Minute*

Banks, Monty *Keep Smiling*

Barker, Clive *Hellraiser; Nightbreed*

Barron, Arthur *Brothers; Jeremy*

Barron, Steve *Teenage Mutant Ninja Turtles*

Barron, Zelda *Secret Places*

Barrymore, Lionel *Madame X*

Bartel, Paul *Cannonball; Death Race 2000; Eating Raoul; Lust in the Dust; Scenes From The Class Struggle In Beverly Hills*

Bartlett, Hall *Jonathan Livingston Seagull*

Barton, Charles *Shaggy Dog, The; Time of Their Lives, The*

Bass, Jules *Last Unicorn, The*

Batchelor, Joy *Animal Farm*

Beaird, David *My Chauffeur*

Beatty, Warren *Dick Tracy; Heaven Can Wait; Reds*

Beaudine, William *Old Fashioned Way, The*

Beaumont, Harry *Beau Brummell; Broadway Melody; When Ladies Meet*

Becker, Harold *Black Marble, The; Boost, The; Onion Field, The; Ragman's Daughter, The; Sea Of Love; Taps*

Beebe, Ford *Enter Arsene Lupin*

Bello, John De *Attack of the Killer Tomatoes*

Bendick, Robert *Cinerama Holiday*

Benedek, Laslo *Death of A Salesman; Wild One, The*

Benjamin, Richard *City Heat; Little Nikita; Mermaids; Money Pit, The; My Favorite Year; My Stepmother Is An Alien; Racing with the Moon*

Bennett, Compton *King Solomon's Mines; Seventh Veil, The; That Forsyte Woman*

Benson, Robby *Modern Love*

Benton, Robert *Bad Company; Kramer vs. Kramer; Late Show, The; Places in the Heart; Still of the Night*

Benveniste, Michael *Flesh Gordon*

Beresford, Bruce *Adventures of Barry McKenzie, The; Breaker Morant; Club, The; Crimes of the Heart; Don's Party; Driving Miss Daisy; Getting Of Wisdom, The; Her Alibi; King David; Mr. Johnson; Puberty Blues; Tender Mercies*

Berger, Ludwig *Thief of Bagdad, The; Vagabond King, The*

Bergman, Andrew *Freshman, The; So Fine*

Bergman, Ingmar *Serpent's Egg, The; Touch, The*

Berkeley, Busby *Babes in Arms; Babes on Broadway; Dames; Footlight Parade; 42nd Street; Gang's All Here, The; Gold Diggers of 1933; Gold Diggers of 1935; Gold Diggers of 1937; Roman Scandals; Stagestruck; Take Me Out To The Ball Game*

Berman, Ted *Black Cauldron, The*

Bernard, Chris *Letter to Brezhnev*

Bernds, Edward *Queen of Outer Space*

Bernhardt, Curtis *Blue Veil, The; High Wall; Miss Sadie Thompson; Possessed; Stolen Life, A*

Bernstein, Armyan *Windy City*

Bernstein, Walter *Little Miss Marker*

Berry, John *Bad News Bears go to Japan, The; Claudine; From This Day Forward*

Bertolucci, Bernardo *Last Emperor, The; Last Tango in Paris; Luna, La; Sheltering Sky, The*

Bharadwaj, Radha *Closet Land*

Bianchi, Edward *Fan, The*

Biberman, Herbert J. *Master Race, The; Salt of the Earth*

Bigelow, Kathryn *Blue Steel; Near Dark*

Billington, Kevin *Interlude; Light at the Edge of the World, The*

Bill, Tony *Crazy People; Five Corners; My Bodyguard; Six Weeks*

Birch, Patricia *Grease 2*

Black, Noel *Change of Seasons, A; Jennifer on My Mind; Pretty Poison*

Blatt, Edward A. *Between Two Worlds*

Blatty, William Peter *Exorcist III, The; Ninth Configuration, The*

Bluth, Don *American Tail, An; Land Before Time, The; Secret of NIMH, The*

Boetticher, Budd *Buchanan Rides Alone; City Beneath The Sea; Decision at Sundown; Horizons West;*

Ride Lonesome; Tall T, The

Bogart, Paul *Class Of '44; Marlowe; Torch Song Trilogy*

Bogdanovich, Peter *At Long Last Love; Daisy Miller; Illegally Yours; Last Picture Show, The; Mask; Nickelodeon; Paper Moon; Saint Jack; Targets; Texasville; They All Laughed; What's Up, Doc?*

Boleslawski, Richard *Clive of India; Garden of Allah; Last of Mrs. Cheyney, The; Les Miserables; Painted Veil, The; Theodora Goes Wild*

Bolognini, Mauro *Arabella*

Bolt, Robert *Lady Caroline Lamb*

Bondarchuk, Sergei *Waterloo*

Boorman, John *Deliverance; Emerald Forest, The; Excalibur; Exorcist II, The Heretic; Hell in the Pacific; Hope and Glory; Leo The Last; Point Blank; Where The Heart Is; Zardoz*

Boothby, Geoffrey *Thief of Bagdad, The*

Borden, Lizzie *Born in Flames; Working Girls*

Borsos, Phillip *Bethune, The Making of a Hero; Grey Fox, The; Mean Season, The; One Magic Christmas*

Borzage, Frank *Bad Girl; Big Fisherman, The; China Doll; Desire; Farewell to Arms, A; Flirtation Walk; Magnificent Doll; Stage Door Canteen; Strange Cargo; Three Comrades; Till We Meet Again*

Boskovich, John *Without You I'm Nothing*

Boulting, John *Brighton Rock; Heavens Above!; I'm All Right, Jack; Lucky Jim; Magic Box, The; Private's Progress; Seven Days to Noon*

Boulting, Roy *Brothers In Law; Fame is the Spur; Family Way, The; Run For The Sun; There's A Girl In My Soup; Twisted Nerve*

Bourguignon, Serge *Reward, The*

Box, Muriel *Rattle of a Simple Man*

Brabin, Charles *Mask of Fu Manchu, The*

Brahm, John *Hangover Square; Locket, The; Lodger, The*

Branagh, Kenneth *Henry V*

Brando, Marlon *One-Eyed Jacks*

Brandstrom, Charlotte *Sweet Revenge*

Brass, Tinto *Caligula*

Brenon, Herbert *Beau Geste*

Brest, Martin *Beverly Hills Cop; Midnight Run*

Brickman, Marshall *Lovesick; Manhattan Project, The*

Brickman, Paul *Men Don't Leave; Risky Business*

Bridges, Alan *Hireling, The; Out of Season; Return of the Soldier, The; Shooting Party, The*

Bridges, James *Baby Maker, The; Bright Lights, Big City; China Syndrome, The; 9/30/55; Paper Chase, The; Perfect*

Brookner, Howard *Bloodhounds Of Broadway*

Brook, Peter *Beggar's Opera, The; Lord of the Flies; Tell Me Lies*

Brooks, Albert *Lost in America*

Brooks, Bob *Tattoo*

Brooks, James L. *Broadcast News; Terms of Endearment*

Brooks, Mel *Blazing Saddles; High Anxiety; History of the World – Part I; Life Stinks; Producers, The; Silent Movie; Spaceballs; Twelve Chairs, The; Young Frankenstein*

Brooks, Richard *Bite The Bullet; Blackboard Jungle, The; Brothers Karamazov, The; Cat on a Hot Tin Roof; Deadline U.S.A.; $; Elmer*

Gantry; Fever Pitch; Happy Ending, The; In Cold Blood; Looking For Mr Goodbar; Lord Jim; Professionals, The; Sweet Bird of Youth; Wrong is Right

Broomfield, Nick *Diamond Skulls*

Brower, Otto *Gay Caballero, The*

Brown, Clarence *Anna Christie; Anna Karenina; Eagle, The; Emma; Flesh and the Devil; Gorgeous Hussy, The; National Velvet; Of Human Hearts; Plymouth Adventure; Rains Came, The; Sadie McKee; Woman of Affairs, A; Yearling, The*

Brown, Harry Joe *Sitting Pretty*

Brown, Rowland *Hell's Highway; Quick Millions*

Browning, Tod *Black Bird, The; Devil-Doll, The; Dracula; Freaks*

Brownlow, Kevin *It Happened Here; Winstanley*

Bucksey, Colin *Dealers*

Buechler, John *Troll*

Bunuel, Luis *Young One, The*

Burge, Stuart *Julius Caesar; There Was A Crooked Man*

Burrows, James *Partners*

Burstall, Tim *Alvin Purple; Petersen*

Burton, Richard *Doctor Faustus*

Burton, Tim *Batman; Beetlejuice; Edward Scissorhands; Pee-wee's Big Adventure*

Bushell, Anthony *Richard III*

Butler, David *Calamity Jane; Connecticut Yankee, A; King Richard and the Crusaders; Littlest Rebel, The; Lullaby Of Broadway; Road to Morocco; Tea for Two*

Butler, George *Pumping Iron; Pumping Iron II, The Women*

Butler, Robert *Night of the Juggler*

Buzzell, Edward *At the Circus; Go West; Neptune's Daughter; Woman of Distinction, A*

Byrne, David *True Stories*

Byrum, John *Heart Beat; Inserts*

Caan, James *Hide in Plain Sight*

Cacoyannis, Michael *Trojan Women, The; Zorba The Greek*

Cahn, Edward L. *It! The Terror From Beyond Space*

Cain, Christopher *Sixth And Main; Stone Boy, The; That Was Then . . . This Is Now; Where The River Runs Black; Young Guns*

Callow, Simon *Ballad of the Sad Cafe, The*

Camerini, Mario *Ulysses*

Cameron, James *Abyss, The; Aliens; Terminator, The*

Cameron, Julia *God's Will*

Cameron, Ken *Good Wife, The*

Cammell, Donald *Demon Seed; White of the Eye*

Campanile, Pasquale Festa *On My Way to the Crusades, I Met a Girl Who . . .*

Campion, Jane *Sweetie*

Camp, Joe *Benji*

Campus, Michael *Passover Plot, The*

Cannon, Dyan *End of Innocence, The*

Capra, Frank *Arsenic And Old Lace; Battle for Russia, The; Bitter Tea Of General Yen, The; Dirigible; It Happened One Night; It's a Wonderful Life; Lost Horizon; Meet John Doe; Mr Deeds Goes to Town; Mr. Smith Goes to Washington; Platinum Blonde; Pocketful Of Miracles; State of the Union; You Can't Take It With You*

Cardiff, Jack *Girl on a Motorcycle; Liquidator, The; Long Ships, The; Mercenaries, The; My Geisha; Scent of Mystery; Sons and Lovers; Young*

Cassidy

Cardos, John *Kingdom Of The Spiders*

Carlino, Lewis John *Class; Great Santini, The; Sailor Who Fell From Grace With The Sea, The*

Caron, Glenn Gordon *Clean and Sober*

Carpenter, John *Assault on Precinct 13; Big Trouble in Little China; Dark Star; Escape from New York; Fog, The; Halloween; Prince of Darkness; Starman; They Live; Thing, The*

Carreras, Michael *Blood from the Mummy's Tomb; Curse of the Mummy's Tomb*

Carrier, Rick *Strangers in the City*

Carstairs, John Paddy *Saint in London, The; Trouble in Store*

Carver, Steve *Big Bad Mama; Capone; Drum; Eye For An Eye, An; Lone Wolf McQuade; Steel*

Cassavetes, John *Child Is Waiting, A; Faces; Gloria; Husbands; Killing Of A Chinese Bookie, The; Love Streams; Minnie And Moskowitz; Opening Night; Shadows; Too Late Blues; Woman Under the Influence, A*

Cass, Henry *Glass Mountain, The*

Castle, Nick *Last Starfighter, The*

Castle, William *House on Haunted Hill, The; Serpent of the Nile; Strait-Jacket*

Cates, Gilbert *I Never Sang For My Father; Last Married Couple in America, The; Promise, The; Summer Wishes, Winter Dreams*

Caton-Jones, Michael *Memphis Belle; Scandal*

Cava, Gregory La *Age of Consent; Stage Door; Symphony of Six Million; What Every Woman Knows*

Cavalcanti, Alberto *Dead of Night; Nicholas Nickleby; Went the Day Well?*

Cavani, Liliana *Night Porter, The*

Chaffey, Don *Greyfriars Bobby; Jason and the Argonauts; One Million Years B.C.; Pete's Dragon*

Champion, Gregg *Short Time*

Chaplin, Charles *City Lights; Countess From Hong Kong, A; Gold Rush, The; Great Dictator, The; Kid, The; King in New York, A; Limelight; Modern Times; Monsieur Verdoux; Shoulder Arms; Woman Of Paris, A*

Chapman, Matthew *Heart Of Midnight; Hussy; Stranger's Kiss*

Chapman, Michael *All the Right Moves; Clan of the Cave Bear, The*

Chetwynd, Lionel *Hanoi Hilton*

Chomsky, Marvin *Tank*

Christian, Roger *Sender, The*

Cimber, Matt *Butterfly*

Cimino, Michael *Deer Hunter, The; Desperate Hours; Heaven's Gate; Sicilian, The; Thunderbolt and Lightfoot; Year of the Dragon*

Clair, Rene *It Happened Tomorrow*

Clark, Bob *Black Christmas; Loose Cannons; Murder By Decree; Porky's; Porky's II, The Next Day; Turk 182!*

Clark, James B. *Flipper*

Clark, Matt *Da*

Clarke, Alan *Rita, Sue and Bob Too; Scum*

Clarke, Bob *Rhinestone*

Clarke, Shirley *Cool World, The*

Clavell, James *Last Valley, The; To Sir, With Love; Walk Like a Dragon; Where's Jack?*

Clayton, Jack *Great Gatsby, The; Innocents, The; Lonely Passion of Judith Hearne, The; Our Mother's House; Pumpkin Eater, The; Room at the Top; Something Wicked This Way*

Comes

Clegg, Tom *McVicar; Sweeney 2*

Clemens, Brian *Captain Kronos – Vampire Hunter*

Clement, Dick *Catch Me A Spy; Otley; Severed Head, A*

Clement, Rene *Is Paris Burning?*

Clifford, Graeme *Burke and Wills; Frances; Gleaming The Cube*

Cline, Edward *Bank Dick, The; Never Give a Sucker an Even Break*

Clouse, Robert *Big Brawl, The; Black Belt Jones; Enter The Dragon; Pack, The*

Coates, Lewis *Hercules*

Coe, Fred *Me, Natalie; Thousand Clowns, A*

Coe, Peter *Lock Up Your Daughters!*

Coen, Joel *Barton Fink; Blood Simple; Miller's Crossing; Raising Arizona*

Coghill, Nevill *Doctor Faustus*

Cohen, Larry *It Lives Again; It's Alive; Private Files of J. Edgar Hoover, The; Q-The Winged Serpent; Stuff, The*

Cokliss, Harley *Battletruck*

Colla, Richard A. *Fuzz*

Collinson, Peter *Innocent Bystanders; Italian Job, The; Long Day's Dying, The; Penthouse, The; Ten Little Indians; Up The Junction*

Columbus, Chris *Home Alone; Only The Lonely*

Connelly, Marc *Green Pastures*

Connor, Kevin *Land That Time Forgot, The; People That Time Forgot, The; Warlords of Atlantis*

Conway, Jack *Arsene Lupin; Desire Me; Libeled Lady; Red-Headed Woman; Saratoga; Tale of Two Cities, A; Too Hot to Handle; Viva Villa!; Yank At Oxford, A*

Cook, Fielder *How to Save a Marriage and Ruin Your Life; Prudence and the Pill; Too Far To Go*

Coolidge, Martha *City Girl, The; Real Genius; Valley Girl*

Cooper, Merian C. *Four Feathers; King Kong*

Cooper, Stuart *Little Malcolm And His Struggle Against the Eunuchs; Overlord*

Coppola, Francis *Apocalypse Now; Conversation, The; Cotton Club, The; Finian's Rainbow; Gardens of Stone; Godfather, The; Godfather Part II, The; Godfather Part III, The; New York Stories; One from the Heart; Outsiders, The; Peggy Sue Got Married; Rain People, The; Rumble Fish; Tonight for Sure; Tucker, The Man And His Dream; You're A Big Boy Now*

Corman, Roger *Bloody Mama; Frankenstein Unbound; Gaslight; House of Usher; Little Shop of Horrors, The; Machine Gun Kelly; Masque of the Red Death, The; Pit and the Pendulum, The; St. Valentine's Day Massacre, The; Tomb of Ligeia; Trip, The; Wild Angels, The; X-The Man with the X-Ray Eyes*

Cornelius, Henry *Genevieve; Passport to Pimlico*

Cornell, John *Almost an Angel; 'Crocodile' Dundee II*

Cornfield, Hubert *Night of the Following Day, The*

Corr, Eugene *Desert Bloom*

Coscarelli, Don *Beastmaster, The; Phantasm; Phantasm II*

Cosmatos, George Pan *Cassandra Crossing, The; Cobra; Escape to Athena; Leviathan; Massacre in Rome; Rambo, First Blood Part II*

Costa-Gavras, Constantin *Betrayed;*

Music Box; Missing

Costner, Kevin *Dances with Wolves*

Couffer, Jack *Living Free; Ring of Bright Water*

Coward, Noel *In Which We Serve*

Cox, Alex *Repo Man; Sid and Nancy; Walker*

Cox, Paul *Golden Braid; Lonely Hearts; Man Of Flowers; My First Wife; Vincent, The Life and Death of Vincent Van Gogh*

Crabtree, Arthur *Quartet*

Crain, William *Blacula*

Crane, Peter *Moments*

Craven, Wes *Deadly Friend; Hills Have Eyes, The; Hills Have Eyes Part II, The; Nightmare on Elm Street, A; Serpent and the Rainbow, The; Shocker*

Crichton, Charles *Boy Who Stole A Million, The; Dead of Night; Divided Heart, The; Fish Called Wanda, A; He Who Rides A Tiger; Hue and Cry; Lavender Hill Mob, The; Third Secret, The; Titfield Thunderbolt, The*

Crichton, Michael *Coma; First Great Train Robbery, The; Looker; Physical Evidence; Runaway; Westworld*

Crisp, Donald *Navigator, The*

Crombie, Donald *Caddie; Cathy's Child; Irishman, The; Killing of Angel Street, The; Kitty and the Bagman*

Cromwell, John *Algiers; Anna and the King of Siam; Dead Reckoning; Enchanted Cottage, The; Little Lord Fauntleroy; Of Human Bondage; Prisoner of Zenda, The; Since You Went Away; Tom Sawyer; Victory*

Cronenberg, David *Brood, The; Crimes of the Future; Dead Ringers; Dead Zone, The; Fly, The; Rabid; Scanners; Shivers; Stereo; Videodrome*

Crosland, Alan *Don Juan; Jazz Singer, The*

Cruze, James *Great Gabbo, The; I Cover The Waterfront; Ruggles of Red Gap*

Cukor, George *Adam's Rib; Bhowani Junction; Bill of Divorcement, A; Blue Bird, The; Born Yesterday; Camille; Chapman Report, The; David Copperfield*

Culp, Robert *Hickey and Boggs*

Cummings, Irving *Hollywood Cavalcade; In Old Arizona; Little Miss Broadway; My Gal Sal; That Night in Rio; White Parade, The*

Cunningham, Sean S. *Deepstar Six; Friday the 13th*

Curtiz, Michael *Adventures of Huckleberry Finn, The; Adventures of Robin Hood, The; Angels with Dirty Faces; Best Things in Life Are Free, The; Cabin in the Cotton; Captain Blood; Casablanca; Charge of the Light Brigade, The; Comancheros, The; Dodge City; Egyptian, The; Flamingo Road; Front Page Woman; Jazz Singer, The; Jim Thorpe – All-American; Key, The; Kid Galahad; King Creole; Mammy; Mandalay; Mildred Pierce; Mission to Moscow; Mystery Of The Wax Museum, The; Night and Day; Noah's Ark, The Story of the Deluge; Passage to Marseille; Private Lives of Elizabeth and Essex, The; Proud Rebel, The; Sea Hawk, The; Sea Wolf, The; 20,000 Years In Sing Sing; Unsuspected, The; Virginia City; We're No Angels; White Christmas; Yankee Doodle Dandy*

Czinner, Paul *Catherine The Great; Escape Me Never*

DaCosta, Morton *Auntie Mame; Music Man, The*

Dalen, Zale *Skip Tracer*

Dalva, Robert *Black Stallion Returns, The*

Damiani, Damiano *Amityville II, The Possession*

Damiano, Gerard *Devil In Miss Jones, The; Deep Throat*

Daniel, Rod *K-9; Teen Wolf*

Dante, Joe *Amazon Women on the Moon; 'Burbs, The; Explorers; Gremlins; Gremlins 2, The New Batch; Howling, The; Innerspace; Piranha; Twilight Zone, The Movie*

D'Antoni, Philip *Seven Ups, The*

Darling, Joan *First Love*

Darnborough, Antony *So Long at the Fair*

D'Arrast, Harry *Raffles*

Dassin, Jules *Reunion; Brute Force; Canterville Ghost, The; Dream of Passion, A; Naked City, The; Night and The City; 10:30 P.M. Summer; Topkapi*

Daves, Delmer *Badlanders, The; Battle of the Villa Fiorita, The; Broken Arrow; Dark Passage; Demetrius and the Gladiators; Hanging Tree, The; Hollywood Canteen; Jubal; Kings Go Forth; Parrish; Pride of the Marines; Red House, The; Spencer's Mountain; Summer Place, A; Susan Slade; 3:10 To Yuma*

David, Charles *Lady on a Train; Thief of Bagdad, The*

Davidson, Boaz *Lemon Popsicle*

Davidson, Gordon *Trial of the Catonsville Nine, The*

Davidson, Martin *Eddie and the Cruisers; Lords of Flatbush*

Davies, Terence *Distant Voices, Still Lives*

Davies, Valentine *Benny Goodman Story, The*

Davis, Andy *Code of Silence*

Davis, Desmond *Clash of the Titans; Girl With Green Eyes; I Was Happy Here; Nice Girl Like Me, A; Smashing Time; Uncle, The*

Davis, Eddie *Panic in the City*

Day, Robert *Man With Bogart's Face, The; Rebel, The; She; Two-Way Stretch*

Dean, Basil *Constant Nymph, The*

Dearden, Basil *Bells Go Down, The; Blue Lamp, The; Captive Heart, The; Dead of Night; Khartoum; League Of Gentlemen, The; Life for Ruth; Man Who Haunted Himself, The; Masquerade; Mind Benders, The; Only When I Larf; Pool Of London; Sapphire; Saraband for Dead Lovers; Smallest Show on Earth, The; Victim; Violent Playground; Woman of Straw*

Dearden, James *Cold Room, The; Pascali's Island*

De Bosio, Gianfranco de *Moses*

De Concini, Ennio *Hitler, The Last Ten Days*

De Jarnatt, Steve *Cherry 2000*

De Lacey, Philippe *Cinerama Holiday*

De Martino, Alberto *Holocaust 2000*

De Palma, Brian *Blow Out; Body Double; Bonfire of the Vanities, The; Carrie; Casualties Of War; Dressed to Kill; Fury, The; Home Movies; Obsession; Phantom of the Paradise; Scarface; Sisters; Untouchables, The; Wedding Party, The*

De Sica, Vittorio *After The Fox; Condemned Of Altona, The; Indiscretion of an American Wife; Place For Lovers, A; Woman Times Seven*

De Toth, Andre *House of Wax; Play Dirty; Two-Headed Spy, The*

Deitch, Donna *Desert Hearts*

Del Ruth, Roy *Born to Dance; Broadway Melody of 1936; Broadway Melody of 1938; Broadway Rhythm; Du Barry Was a Lady; Folies Bergere; Gold Diggers of Broadway; Kid Millions; Maltese Falcon, The; Phantom of the Rue Morgue; West Point Story, The; Ziegfeld Follies*

Delannoy, Jean *Hunchback of Notre Dame, The*

DeMille, Cecil B. *Cleopatra; Crusades, The; Greatest Show On Earth, The; King of Kings, The; North West Mounted Police; Plainsman, The; Reap the Wild Wind; Samson And Delilah; Sign of the cross, The; Ten Commandments, The; Unconquered; Union Pacific*

Demme, Jonathan *Citizens Band; Crazy Mama; Last Embrace; Married to the Mob; Melvin and Howard; Silence of the Lambs, The; Something Wild; Swimming to Cambodia; Swing Shift*

Demy, Jacques *Model Shop; Pied Piper, The*

Derek, John *Bolero; Tarzan, The Ape Man*

Deschanel, Caleb *Escape Artist, The*

Deutch, Howard *Pretty in Pink*

DeVito, Danny *Throw Momma From The Train; War Of The Roses, The*

Dexter, John *Virgin Soldiers, The*

Dickinson, Thorold *Gaslight; Men of Two Worlds; Queen of Spades, The; Secret People*

Dieterle, William *Dark City; Devil and Daniel Webster, The; Doctor Ehrlich's Magic Bullet; Dr. Socrates; Elephant Walk; Hunchback of Notre Dame, The; Juarez; Kismet; Life Of Emile Zola, The; Madame Dubarry; Midsummer Night's Dream, A; Peking Express; Portrait Of Jennie; Salome; Satan Met a Lady*

Dinner, Michael *Heaven Help Us*

DiSalle, Mark *Kickboxer*

Dmytryk, Edward *Alvarez Kelly; Anzio; Back to Bataan; Blue Angel, The; Bluebeard; Broken Lance; Caine Mutiny, The; Carpetbaggers, The; Crossfire; Give Us This Day; Hitler's Children; Juggler, The; Left Hand of God, The; Mirage; Murder, My Sweet; Obsession; Raintree County; Shalako; Tender Comrade; Walk on the Wild Side; Where Love Has Gone; Young Lions, The*

Donaldson, Roger *Bounty, The; Cadillac Man; Cocktail; Marie; No Way Out; Sleeping Dogs; Smash Palace*

Donehue, Vincent J. *Sunrise at Campobello*

Donen, Stanley *Arabesque; Bedazzled; Blame it on Rio; Charade; Damn Yankees; Funny Face; Indiscreet; It's Always Fair Weather; Little Prince, The; Lucky Lady; Movie Movie; On The Town; Pajama Game, The; Royal Wedding; Saturn 3; Seven Brides for Seven Brothers; Singin' in the Rain; Staircase; Two For the Road*

Donner, Clive *Alfred The Great; Caretaker, The; Here We Go Round the Mulberry Bush; Luv; Nothing But the Best; Some People; Stealing Heaven; Vampira; What's New Pussycat*

Donner, Richard *Goonies, The; Inside Moves, The Guys From Max's Bar; LadyHawke; Lethal Weapon; Lethal Weapon 2; Omen, The; Superman*

Donohue, Jack *Assault On A Queen*

Donovan, Martin *Apartment Zero*

Douglas, Bill *Comrades*

Douglas, Gordon *Black Arrow, The; Call Me Bwana; Detective, The; Follow that Dream; Gold of the Seven Saints; Harlow; In Like Flint; I Was A Communist For The F.B.I.; Kiss Tomorrow Goodbye; Lady in Cement; Rio Conchos; Robin and the Seven Hoods; San Quentin; Stagecoach; Sylvia; Them!; They Call Me Mister Tibbs!; Tony Rome; Viva Knievel!; Walk a Crooked Mile; Yellowstone Kelly;*

Douglas, Kirk *Posse*

Downey, Robert *Putney Swope*

Dragoti, Stan *Love at First Bite; Mr. Mom*

Dreifuss, Arthur *Quare Fellow, The*

Drury, David *Defence of the Realm*

Dudley, Carl *South Seas Adventure*

Duffell, Peter *England Made Me*

Dugan, Michael *Mausoleum*

Duigan, John *One Night Stand*

Duke, Daryl *Hard Feelings; Silent Partner, The; Tai-Pan*

Dunne, Philip *Blindfold; Blue Denim; In Love And War; Ten North Frederick; Wild In The Country*

Dunning, George *Yellow Submarine*

Dupont, E.A. *Piccadilly*

Duvivier, Julien *Lydia; Anna Karenina; Flesh and Fantasy; Great Waltz, The; Impostor, The; Lydia; Tales of Manhattan*

Dwan, Allan *Brewster's Millions; I Dream of Jeanie; Rebecca of Sunnybrook Farm; Sands of Iwo Jima; Three Musketeers, The*

Eastwood, Clint *Bird; Breezy; Bronco Billy; Eiger Sanction, The; Firefox; Gauntlet, The; Heartbreak Ridge; High Plains Drifter; Honkytonk Man; Outlaw Josey Wales, The; Pale Rider; Play Misty for Me; Rookie, The; Sudden Impact; White Hunter, Black Heart*

Edel, Uli *Last Exit To Brooklyn*

Edwards, Blake *Blind Date; Breakfast At Tiffany's; Curse Of The Pink Panther; Darling Lili; Days Of Wine And Roses; Experiment in Terror; Fine Mess, A; Great Race, The; Gunn; Man Who Loved Women, The; Micki & Maude; Party, The; Pink Panther, The; Pink Panther Strikes Again, The; Return of the Pink Panther, The; Revenge of the Pink Panther; Shot in the Dark, A; Skin Deep; S.O.B.; Sunset; Switch; Tamarind Seed, The; 10; That's Life!; Trail of the Pink Panther; Victor/Victoria; What Did You Do In the War, Daddy?; Wild Rovers*

Edzard, Christine *Fool, The; Little Dorrit*

Egleson, Jan *Shock To The System, A*

Egoyan, Atom *Family Viewing; Speaking Parts*

Ellison, Joseph *Joey*

Ellis, Robert *Sweet November*

Elvey, Maurice *Lodger, The; Sally in our Alley; Wandering Jew, The*

Enders, Robert *Stevie*

Endfield, Cy *De Sade; Mysterious Island; Sands of the Kalahari; Zulu*

Englund, George *Ugly American, The*

Enright, Ray *China Sky; Dames; Gung Ho!*

Erman, John *Stella*

Ernst, Laemmle *Phantom of the Opera, The (sound sequences)*

Erskine, Chester *Androcles and the*

Lion; Egg and I, The
Essex, Harry *I, The Jury*
Eyre, Richard *Loose Connections; Ploughman's Lunch, The*

Faiman, Peter *'Crocodile' Dundee*
Fairchild, William *Silent Enemy, The*
Fanaka, Jamaa *Penitentiary*
Fargo, James *Caravans; Enforcer, The; Every Which Way But Loose; Private Lessons*
Farrow, John *Big Clock, The; Bill of Divorcement, A; China; John Paul Jones; Night Has a Thousand Eyes; Ride, Vaquero*
Fassbinder, Rainer Werner *Despair; Querelle*
Feist, Felix E. *George White's Scandals*
Feldman, John *Alligator Eyes*
Feldman, Marty *Last Remake Of Beau Geste, The*
Fenton, Leslie *Miracle Can Happen, A (On Our Merry Way)*
Ferguson, Norman *Three Caballeros, The*
Ferrara, Abel *Cat Chaser; China Girl; Driller Killer; Fear City; King of New York; Ms. 45*
Ferreri, Marco *Tales of Ordinary Madness*
Ferrer, Jose *I Accuse!; Return To Peyton Place; State Fair; Great Man, The*
Ferrer, Mel *Green Mansions*
Feyder, Jacques *Daybreak; Knight Without Armour*
Fields, Michael *Bright Angel*
Figgis, Mike *Internal Affairs*
Finkleman, Ken *Airplane II, The Sequel*
Finney, Albert *Charlie Bubbles*
Fiore, Robert *Pumping Iron*
Firstenberg, Sam *American Ninja; American Ninja 2, The Confrontation; Breakin' 2, Electric Boogaloo; Ninja III, The Domination; Revenge of the Ninja*
Fisher, Terence *Revenge of Frankenstein, The; Devil Rides Out, The; Dracula; Dracula – Prince of Darkness; Frankenstein Created Woman; Frankenstein Must Be Destroyed; Hound of the Baskervilles, The; Phantom of the Opera, The; Revenge of Frankenstein, The; So Long at the Fair*
Fisk, Jack *Daddy's Dyin'... Who's Got The Will?; Raggedy Man*
Fitzmaurice, George *As You Desire Me; Mata Hari; Raffles*
Flaherty, Robert *Elephant Boy; Louisiana Story; Man Of Aran; Moana; Nanook of the North*
Fleischer, Richard *Bandido; Ashanti; Barabbas; Boston Strangler, The; Che; Compulsion; Conan the Destroyer; Crack in the Mirror; Doctor Dolittle; Fantastic Voyage; Incredible Sarah, The; Jazz Singer,The; Last Run, The; Mandingo; Mr Majestyk; Narrow Margin, The; New Centurions, The; Prince And The Pauper, The; Red Sonja; Soylent Green; 10 Rillington Place; Tora! Tora!; 20,000 Leagues Under The Sea; Vikings, The*
Fleming, Victor *Captains Courageous; Dr. Jekyll and Mr. Hyde; Farmer Takes A Wife, The; Gone with the Wind; Guy Named Joe, A; Joan of Arc; Red Dust; Test Pilot; Treasure Island; Virginian, The; Way of All Flesh, The; Wizard of Oz, The*
Flemyng, Gordon *Great Catherine*
Flicker, Theodore J. *President's Analyst, The*

Florey, Robert *Beast with Five Fingers, The; Cocoanuts, The; Desert Song, The; God Is My Co-Pilot; Murders in the Rue Morgue*
Flynn, John *Jerusalem File, The; Lock Up; Outfit, The; Rolling Thunder; Sergeant, The*
Foley, James *At Close Range*
Fonda, Peter *Hired Hand, The*
Forbes, Bryan *Deadfall; International Velvet; King Rat; L-Shaped Room, The; Madwoman of Chaillot, The; Raging Moon, The; Seance on a Wet Afternoon; Slipper And The Rose, The, The Story Of Cinderella; Stepford Wives, The; Whisperers, The; Whistle Down the Wind; Wrong Box, The*
Ford, Charles E. *Jacare*
Ford, John *Cheyenne Autumn; Donovan's Reef; Drums Along the Mohawk; Flesh; Fort Apache; Grapes of Wrath, The; Hell Bent; How Green Was My Valley; How The West Was Won; Hurricane, The; Informer, The; Judge Priest; Last Hurrah, The; Long Gray Line, The; Lost Patrol, The; Man Who Shot Liberty Valance, The; Mary of Scotland; Men Without Women; Mister Roberts; Mogambo; My Darling Clementine; Plough and The Stars, The; Prisoner of Shark Island, The; Quiet Man, The; Rio Grande; Searchers, The; 7 Women; She Wore A Yellow Ribbon; Stagecoach; They Were Expendable; Tobacco Road; Trial of Sergeant Rutledge, The; Wagonmaster; What Price Glory; Whole Town's Talking, The; Young Cassidy; Young Mr Lincoln*
Forde, Walter *Four Just Men, The; Rome Express*
Foreman, Carl *Victors, The*
Forman, Milos *Amadeus; Hair; One Flew Over the Cuckoo's Nest; Ragtime; Taking Off; Valmont; Visions of Eight*
Forst, Willy *Unfinished Symphony, The*
Forsyth, Bill *Breaking In; Comfort and Joy; Gregory's Girl; Housekeeping; Local Hero; That Sinking Feeling*
Fosse, Bob *All That Jazz; Cabaret; Lenny; Star 80; Sweet Charity*
Foster, Norman *Kiss the Blood Off My Hands; Rachel and the Stranger*
Fowler Jr, Gene *I Married A Monster From Outer Space*
Foy, Bryan *Lights of New York*
Fraker, William A. *Monte Walsh*
Francis, Freddie *Dr. Terror's House Of Horrors; Mumsy, Nanny, Sonny & Girly; Nightmare*
Francis, Karl *Giro City*
Frankel, Cyril *Don't Bother To Knock; Man of Africa; Never Take Sweets From A Stranger; Trygon Factor, The*
Frankenheimer, John *All Fall Down; Birdman of Alcatraz; Black Sunday; Extraordinary Seaman, The; 52 Pick-Up; Fixer, The; Fourth War, The; French Connection II; Grand Prix; Gypsy Moths, The; Horsemen, The; Impossible Object; I Walk The Line; Manchurian Candidate, The; 99 And 44/100% Dead; Prophecy; Seconds; Seven Days in May; Train, The; Young Savages, The*
Franklin, Howard *Quick Change*
Frank, Melvin *Buona Sera, Mrs. Campbell; Court Jester, The; Duchess And The Dirtwater Fox, The; Li'l Abner; Prisoner Of Second Avenue, The; Strange Bedfellows; Touch of Class, A*
Franklin, Richard *FX2, The Deadly*

Art of Illusion; Link; Patrick; Psycho II; Road Games
Franklin, Sidney *Barretts of Wimpole Street, The; Dark Angel, The; Good Earth, The; Last of Mrs Cheyney, The*
Frawley, James *Big Bus, The; Muppet Movie, The*
Frears, Stephen *Dangerous Liaisons; Grifters, The; Gumshoe; My Beautiful Laundrette; Prick Up Your Ears; Sammy and Rosie Get Laid*
Freedman, Gerrold *Borderline*
Freedman, Jerrold *Kansas City Bomber*
Freeland, Thornton *Flying Down To Rio; Gang's All Here, The; George White's Scandals*
French, Harold *Encore; Man Who Watched the Trains Go By, The; Quartet; Trio*
Frend, Charles *Cruel Sea, The; Loves of Joanna Godden, The; San Demetrio-London; Scott of the Antarctic*
Freund, Karl *Mummy, The*
Friedkin, William *Birthday Party, The; Boys In The Band, The; Cruising; Exorcist, The; French Connection, The; Guardian, The; Sorcerer; To Live and Die in L.A.*
Friedmann, Anthony *Bartleby*
Fritsch, Gunther von *Curse of the Cat People, The*
Fuest, Robert *Abominable Doctor Phibes, The; And Soon The Darkness; Dr. Phibes Rises Again; Wuthering Heights*
Fukasaku, Kinji *Tora! Tora! Tora!*
Fuller, Samuel *Big Red One, The; China Gate; Fixed Bayonets; Forty Guns; Hell and High Water; House of Bamboo; I Shot Jesse James; Merrill's Marauders; Pickup on South Street; Run of the Arrow; Shock Corridor; Steel Helmet, The; Underworld, U.S.A.; White Dog*
Furie, Sidney J. *Boys in Company C, The; Entity, The; Gable and Lombard; Ipcress File, The; Jazz Singer,The; Lady Sings The Blues; Leather Boys, The; Little Fauss And Big Halsy; Naked Runner, The; Purple Hearts; Superman IV, The Quest For Peace; Wonderful Life; Young Ones, The*

Ganzer, Alvin *Three Bites of the Apple*
Gardner, Herb *Goodbye People, The*
Garland, Patrick *Doll's House, A*
Garmes, Lee *Angels Over Broadway*
Garnett, Tay *7 Wonders of the World; Bataan; China Seas; Connecticut Yankee in King Arthur's Court, A; Postman Always Rings Twice, The; Soldiers Three*
Garnett, Tony *Handgun*
Garris, Mick *Critters 2, The Main Course*
Gazcon, Gilberto *Rage*
Geller, Bruce *Harry In Your Pocket*
Gering, Marion *Thunder in the City*
Geronimi, Clyde *Lady and the Tramp; One Hundred and One Dalmatians; Peter Pan; Sleeping Beauty*
Gibbons, Cedric *Tarzan And His Mate*
Gibson, Brian *Breaking Glass; Poltergeist II*
Gilbert, Lewis *Admirable Crichton, The; Adventurers, The; Albert, R.N.; Alfie; Carve Her Name With Pride; Educating Rita; Greengage Summer, The; H.M.S. Defiant; Moonraker; Reach for the Sky; Seven Nights in Japan; 7th Dawn, The; Shirley Valentine; Sink The Bismarck!; Spy*

Who Loved Me, The; You Only Live Twice
Giler, David *Black Bird, The*
Gilliam, Terry *Adventures Of Baron Munchausen, The; Brazil; Jabberwocky; Monty Python and the Holy Grail; Time Bandits*
Gilliat, Sidney *Blue Lagoon, The; Constant Husband, The; Great St. Trinian's Train Robbery, The; Millions Like Us; Only Two Can Play; Rake's Progress, The; Waterloo Road*
Gilmore, Stuart *Virginian, The*
Gilroy, Frank D. *From Noon Till Three; Gig, The; Once in Paris*
Ginty, Robert *Vietnam, Texas*
Girard, Bernard *Dead Heat On A Merry-Go-Round; Mad Room, The*
Girdler, William *Manitou, The*
Gladwell, David *Memoirs of a Survivor*
Glaser, Paul Michael *Running Man, The*
Glen, John *For Your Eyes Only; Licence To Kill; Living Daylights, The; Octopussy; View to a Kill, A*
Glenville, Peter *Becket; Comedians, The; Hotel Paradiso; Prisoner, The; Summer and Smoke; Term of Trial*
Glickenhaus, James *Exterminator, The; Protector, The*
Goddard, Jim *Shanghai Surprise*
Godfrey, Peter *Escape Me Never; Hotel Berlin; Two Mrs Carrolls, The*
Golan, Menahem *Delta Force, The; Diamonds; Enter the Ninja; Over the Brooklyn Bridge; Over The Top*
Goldbeck, Willis *Ten Tall Men*
Goldberg, Gary David *Dad*
Goldblatt, Mark *Punisher, The*
Gold, Jack *Aces High; Man Friday; Medusa Touch, The; Reckoning, The; Sailor's Return, The; Who?*
Gold, James *Bofors Gun, The*
Goldschmidt, John *She'll Be Wearing Pink Pajamas*
Goldstone, James *Rollercoaster; Swashbuckler; Winning*
Goldstone, Richard *South Seas Adventure*
Goldwyn Jr, Samuel *Young Lovers, The*
Gordon, Bert I. *Empire of the Ants*
Gordon, Bryan *Career Opportunities*
Gordon, Michael *Cyrano de Bergerac; Move Over, Darling; Pillow Talk; Very Special Favor, A*
Gordon, Robert *Joe Louis Story, The*
Gordon, Steve *Arthur*
Gordon, Stuart *Re-Animator*
Gornick, Michael *Creepshow 2*
Gottlieb, Carl *Amazon Women on the Moon*
Gottlieb, Lisa *Just One of the Guys*
Gottlieb, Michael *Mannequin*
Goulder, Stanley *Silent Playground, The*
Gould, Heywood *One Good Cop*
Goulding, Alfred *Chump At Oxford, A*
Goulding, Edmund *Blondie of the Follies; Constant Nymph, The; Dark Victory; Dawn Patrol, The; Grand Hotel; Love; Nightmare Alley; Of Human Bondage; Razor's Edge, The; That Certain Woman*
Graef, Roger *Secret Policeman's Ball, The*
Graham, William *Waterhole #3*
Grant, Joe *Fantasia*
Grant, Lee *Staying Together*
Grauman, Walter *Lady in a Cage; Rage To Live, A; 633 Squadron*
Green, Alfred E. *Disraeli; Jolson Story, The; Little Lord Fauntleroy*
Greenaway, Peter *Belly of an Architect, The; Cook, The Thief, His*

*Wife And Her Lover, The;
Draughtsman's Contract, The;
Drowning By Numbers; Zed and Two
Noughts, A*
Green, David *Fire Birds*
Green, Guy *Angry Silence, The;
Diamond Head; Light in the Piazza;
Magus, The; Once Is Not Enough;
Patch Of Blue, A; Pretty Polly; Walk
In The Spring Rain, A*
Greene, David *Count Of Monte Cristo,
The; Godspell; I Start Counting;
Sebastian; Shuttered Room, The;
Strange Affair, The*
Greenwald, Maggie *Kill-Off, The*
Greenwald, Robert *Xanadu*
Gries, Tom *Breakheart Pass; Breakout;
Greatest, The; Hawaiians, The; Lady
Ice; Will Penny*
Grieve, Andrew *On The Black Hill*
Griffith, D.W. *Birth Of A Nation,
The; Broken Blossoms, Or The Yellow
Man and the Girl; Intolerance; Judith
Of Bethulia; Way Down East*
Grosbard, Ulu *Falling in Love;
Straight Time; True Confessions*
Guercio, James William *Electra Glide
in Blue*
Guerra, Ruy *Sweet Hunters*
Guest, Val *Beauty Jungle, The; Casino
Royale; Day The Earth Caught Fire,
The; 80,000 Suspects; Expresso
Bongo; Hell Is A City; Quatermass
Experiment, The; Where The Spies
Are*
Guillermin, John *Blue Max, The;
Bridge at Remagen, The; Death On
The Nile; Guns at Batasi; House of
Cards; I Was Monty's Double; King
Kong; King Kong Lives; Skyjacked;
Tarzan's Greatest Adventure;
Towering Inferno, The; Waltz of the
Toreadors*
Gyllenhaal, Stephen *Paris Trout*

Hackford, Taylor *Chuck Berry: Hail!
Hail! Rock 'n' Roll!; Idolmaker, The;
Officer and a Gentleman, An; White
Nights*
Haggard, Piers *Summer Story, A;
Venom*
Haines, Fred *Steppenwolf*
Haines, Randa *Children of a Lesser
God*
Haines, Richard W. *Class of Nuke 'em
High*
Halas, John *Animal Farm*
Haley Jr, Jack *That's Dancing!;
That's Entertainment!*
Hall, Alexander *Bedtime Story; Down
to Earth; Here Comes Mr. Jordan;
My Sister Eileen; They All Kissed The
Bride*
Halliday, Mark *Just Like In The
Movies*
Hall, Peter *3 into 2 Won't Go; Work is
a 4-Letter Word; Akenfield; Perfect
Friday*
Hallstrom, Lasse *Once Around*
Hamer, Robert *Dead of Night; Kind
Hearts and Coronets; Pink String and
Sealing Wax; School for Scoundrels*
Hamilton, Guy *Battle of Britain; Best
of Enemies, The; Colditz Story, The;
Devil's Disciple, The; Diamonds Are
Forever; Evil Under the Sun; Force 10
from Navarone; Funeral in Berlin;
Goldfinger; Live and Let Die; Man
With The Golden Gun, The; Mirror
Crack'd, The; Party's Over, The*
Hammond, Peter *Spring And Port
Wine*
Hand, David D. *Bambi; Snow White
and the Seven Dwarfs*
Hannam, Ken *Summerfield; Sunday
Too Far Away*

Hanson, Curtis *Bad Influence;
Bedroom Window, The; Losin' It*
Hardy, Robin *Wicker Man, The*
Hare, David *Paris By Night;
Strapless; Wetherby*
Harlin, Renny *Adventures of Ford
Fairlane, The; Die Hard 2;
Nightmare On Elm Street 4, The
Dream Master, A; Prison*
Harmon, Robert *Hitcher, The*
Harrington, Curtis *Night Tide; Ruby*
Harris, Damian *Rachel Papers, The*
Harris, James B. *Bedford Incident,
The; Fast-Walking*
Harrison, John *Tales From The
Darkside*
Harrison, John Kent *Beautiful
Dreamers*
Hartford-Davis, Robert *Sandwich
Man, The*
Hart, Harvey *Bus Riley's Back in
Town; Sweet Ride, The*
Harvey, Anthony *Abdication, The;
Dutchman; Eagle's Wing; Lion In
Winter, The; Players; They Might Be
Giants; Ultimate Solution of Grace
Quigley, The*
Harvey, Laurence *Ceremony, The;
Dandy in Aspic, A*
Haskin, Byron *His Majesty O'Keefe; I
Walk Alone; Power, The; Treasure
Island; War of the Worlds, The*
Hathaway, Henry *Black Rose, The;
Brigham Young; Call Northside 777;
China Girl; Circus World; Desert
Fox, The; Diplomatic Courier; 5 Card
Stud; Fourteen Hours; House on 92nd
St., The; How The West Was Won;
Kiss of Death; Lives of a Bengal
Lancer, The; Nevada Smith; Niagara;
O. Henry's Full House; Of Human
Bondage; Peter Ibbetson; Prince
Valiant; Rawhide; Sons of Katie
Elder, The; Spawn of the North;
Sundown; 13 Rue Madeleine; Trail of
the Lonesome Pine, The; True Grit*
Hawks, Howard *Ball of Fire; Barbary
Coast; Big Sky, The; Big Sleep, The;
Bringing up Baby; Criminal Code,
The; Crowd Roars, The; Dawn
Patrol, The; El Dorado; Gentlemen
Prefer Blondes; Hatari!; His Girl
Friday; I Was A Male War Bride;
Land of the Pharaohs; Man's Favorite
Sport?; Monkey Business; O. Henry's
Full House; Only Angels Have
Wings; Red Line 7000; Red River;
Rio Bravo; Rio Lobo; Scarface;
Sergeant York; To Have and Have
Not; Twentieth Century*
Hayers, Sidney *Finders Keepers; Trap,
The*
Hazan, Jack *Bigger Splash, A*
Hecht, Ben *Angels Over Broadway*
Heckerling, Amy *Look Who's Talking
Too; National Lampoon's European
Vacation*
Hedden, Rob *Friday The 13th Part
VIII, Jason Takes Manhattan*
Heerman, Victor *Animal Crackers*
Heffron, Richard T. *Futureworld; I,
The Jury; Outlaw Blues*
Heisler, Stuart *Along Came Jones;
Blue Skies; Glass Key, The; Star,
The; Tokyo Joe*
Hellman, Monte *China 9 Liberty 37;
Ride In The Whirlwind; Two-Lane
Blacktop*
Hemmings, David *Just a Gigolo*
Henenlotter, Frank *Basket Case 2*
Henry, Buck *Heaven Can Wait*
Henson, Jim *Dark Crystal, The; Great
Muppet Caper, The; Labyrinth*
Herek, Stephen *Bill & Ted's Excellent
Adventure; Critters*
Hertz, Nathan *Attack of the 50 FT.*

Woman
Herzfeld, John *Two of a Kind*
Herz, Michael *Toxic Avenger, The*
Hessler, Gordon *Girl In A Swing,
The; Golden Voyage of Sinbad, The*
Heston, Charlton *Antony and
Cleopatra; Mother Lode*
Heumer, Dick *Fantasia*
Hickox, Douglas *Brannigan;
Entertaining Mr Sloane; Sitting
Target; Sky Riders; Theatre of Blood;
Zulu Dawn*
Higgins, Colin *Best Little Whorehouse
in Texas, The; Foul Play; 9 to 5*
Hiller, Arthur *Americanization of
Emily, The; Author! Author!;
Hospital, The; In-Laws, The; Lonely
. Guy, The; Love Story; Making Love;
Man of La Mancha; Out-Of-
Towners, The; Penelope; Plaza Suite;
Popi; Promise Her Anything; See No
Evil, Hear No Evil; Silver Streak;
Taking Care of Business; Tiger
Makes Out, The; Tobruk*
Hill, George Roy *Butch Cassidy and
the Sundance Kid; Great Waldo
Pepper, The; Hawaii; Little
Drummer Girl, The; Little Romance,
A; Slap Shot; Slaughterhouse-Five;
Sting, The; Thoroughly Modern
Millie; Toys in the Attic; World
According to Garp, The*
Hill, Jack *Coffy; Foxy Brown*
Hill, James *Born Free; Dock Brief, The*
Hill, Jerome *Sand Castle, The*
Hill, Walter *Another 48 hrs.;
Brewster's Millions; Crossroads;
Driver, The; Extreme Prejudice;
48hrs.; Johnny Handsome; Long
Riders, The; Red Heat; Southern
Comfort; Streets of Fire; Warriors,
The*
Hitchcock, Alfred *Birds, The;
Blackmail; Dial M for Murder;
Family Plot; Foreign Correspondent;
Frenzy; I Confess; Jamaica Inn; Juno
and the Paycock; Lady Vanishes, The;
Lifeboat; Man Who Knew Too Much,
The; Man Who Knew Too Much,
The; Marnie; Mr. and Mrs. Smith;
Murder; North by Northwest;
Notorious; Paradine Case, The;
Psycho; Rear Window; Rebecca;
Rope; Saboteur; Secret Agent, The;
Shadow of a Doubt; Spellbound; Stage
Fright; Strangers On A Train;
Suspicion; 39 Steps, The; To Catch A
Thief; Topaz; Torn Curtain; Trouble
with Harry, The; Under Capricorn;
Vertigo; Wrong Man, The*
Hodges, Mike *Black Rainbow; Flash
Gordon; Get Carter*
Hoellering, George *Murder in the
Cathedral*
Hoffman, Michael *Soapdish*
Hofsiss, Jack *I'm Dancing As Fast As I
Can*
Hogan, James *Texans, The*
Holland, Tom *Fright Night*
Holt, Seth *Blood from the Mummy's
Tomb; Danger Route; Nanny, The;
Station Six-Sahara*
Hook, Harry *Kitchen Toto, The; Lord
of the Flies*
Hooper, Tobe *Funhouse, The;
Lifeforce; Poltergeist; Texas Chain
Saw Massacre, The; Texas Chain
Saw Massacre Part 2, The*
Hopkins, Stephen *Predator 2*
Hopper, Dennis *Catchfire; Colors;
Easy Rider; Hot Spot, The; Last
Movie, The; Out of the Blue*
Horne, James W. *Bohemian Girl, The;
Way Out West*
Horton, Peter *Amazon Women on the
Moon*

Hoskins, Bob *Raggedy Rawney, The*
Hoskins, Dan *Chopper Chicks In
Zombietown*
Hough, John *Brass Target; Dirty
Mary Crazy Larry; Escape to Witch
Mountain; Legend of Hell House,
The; Return from Witch Mountain;
Twins of Evil; Watcher In The
Woods, The*
Hovde, Ellen *Enormous Changes at the
Last Minute*
Howard, Cy *Lovers And Other
Strangers*
Howard, Leslie *First of the Few, The;
Pygmalion*
Howard, Ron *Backdraft; Cocoon;
Gung Ho; Night Shift; Parenthood;
Splash*
Howard, William K. *Fire Over
England; Power And The Glory, The*
Howley, John *Happily Ever After*
Hudlin, Reginald *House Party*
Hudson, Hugh *Chariots of Fire;
Greystoke, The Legend of Tarzan Lord
of the Apes; Lost Angels; Revolution*
Hughes, Howard *Hell's Angels;
Outlaw, The*
Hughes, John *Breakfast Club, The;
Ferris Bueller's Day Off; Planes,
Trains & Automobiles; Sixteen
Candles; Uncle Buck; Weird Science*
Hughes, Ken *Casino Royale; Chitty
Chitty Bang Bang; Cromwell; Drop
Dead, Darling; Of Human Bondage;
Sextette; Small World Of Sammy Lee,
The; Trials of Oscar Wilde, The*
Humberstone, H. Bruce *Desert Song,
The; Pin Up Girl; Wonder Man*
Hunter, Tim *River's Edge; Tex*
Hunt, Peter *Gold; On Her Majesty's
Secret Service; Shout At The Devil;
Wild Geese II*
Hurst, Brian Desmond *Dangerous
Moonlight; Malta Story*
Hussein, Waris *Henry VIII and his Six
Wives; Possession of Joel Delaney,
The; Touch of Love, A*
Huston, Danny *Mr. North*
Huston, John *Across the Pacific;
African Queen, The; Annie; Asphalt
Jungle, The; Barbarian and the
Geisha, The; Beat the Devil; Bible,
The, In The Beginning . . .; Casino
Royale; Dead, The; Fat City; Freud;
Heaven Knows, Mr. Allison; Key
Largo; Kremlin Letter, The; Life and
Times of Judge Roy Bean, The; List of
Adrian Messenger, The; Mackintosh
Man, The; Maltese Falcon, The;
Man Who Would Be King, The;
Misfits, The; Moby Dick; Moulin
Rouge; Night of the Iguana; Prizzi's
Honor; Red Badge of Courage, The;
Reflections in a Golden Eye; Roots of
Heaven, The; Sinful Davey; Treasure
of the Sierra Madre, The; Under the
Volcano; Unforgiven, The; Victory;
Walk With Love and Death, A; Wise
Blood*
Hutton, Brian G. *First Deadly Sin,
The; High Road to China; Kelly's
Heroes; Pad, (And How To Use It),
The; Where Eagles Dare; Zee & Co*
Huyck, Willard *Howard The Duck*
Hyams, Peter *Busting; Capricorn One;
Hanover Street; Narrow Margin;
Outland; Peeper; Presidio, The;
Running Scared; Star Chamber, The;
2010*

Ichikarra, Kon *Visions of Eight*
Ingram, Rex *Four Horsemen of the
Apocalypse, The; Prisoner of Zenda,
The*
Irvin, John *Dogs of War, The; Ghost
Story; Hamburger Hill; Next Of Kin;*

Raw Deal

Ivory, James *Bostonians, The; Europeans, The; Guru, The; Heat and Dust; Maurice; Mr. & Mrs. Bridge; Quartet; Room with a View, A; Roseland; Savages; Shakespeare-Wallah; Wild Party, The*

Jackson, Mick *L.A. Story*
Jackson, Pat *Encore*
Jackson, Wilfred *Lady and the Tramp; Peter Pan*
Jaeckin, Just *Lady Chatterley's Lover*
Jaffe, Stanley R. *Without A Trace*
Jaglom, Henry *Always; Can She Bake A Cherry Pie?; New Year's Day; Safe Place, A; Sitting Ducks; Someone To Love*
Jameson, Jerry *Airport '77; Raise the Titanic*
Jankel, Annabel *D.O.A.*
Jarman, Derek *Jubilee; Last of England, The; Tempest, The*
Jarmusch, Jim *Down by Law; Mystery Train; Stranger than Paradise*
Jarrott, Charles *Anne of the Thousand Days; Dove, The; Lost Horizon; Mary, Queen of Scots; Other Side Of Midnight, The*
Jeffrey, Tom *Odd Angry Shot, The*
Jeffries, Lionel *Baxter!; Railway Children, The; Water Babies, The*
Jewison, Norman *Agnes of God; ... And Justice For All; Best Friends; Cincinnati Kid, The; Fiddler on the Roof; F.I.S.T.; 40 Pounds Of Trouble; Gaily, Gaily; In Country; In The Heat Of The Night; Jesus Christ Superstar; Moonstruck; Rollerball; Russians Are Coming! The Russians Are Coming!, The; Send Me No Flowers; Soldier's Story, A; Thomas Crown Affair, The ; Thrill Of It All, The*
Joanou, Phil *State of Grace*
Joffe, Arthur *Harem*
Joffe, Roland *Fat Man And Little Boy; Killing Fields, The; Mission, The*
Johnson, Alan *To Be Or Not To Be*
Johnson, Jed *Bad*
Johnson, Kenneth *Short Circuit 2*
Johnson, Lamont *Cattle Annie and Little Britches; Groundstar Conspiracy, The; Gunfight, A; Last American Hero, The; Lipstick; McKenzie Break, The; One On One*
Johnson, Nunnally *Man in the Gray Flannel Suit, The; Three Faces of Eve, The*
Johnston, Aaron *Kim Last Winter, The*
Johnston, Joe *Honey, I Shrunk The Kids; Rocketeer, The*
Jones, Amy *Love Letters; Slumber Party Massacre*
Jones, David *Betrayal; 84 Charing Cross Road*
Jones, James Cellan *Bequest To The Nation*
Jones, Terry *Eric The Viking; Life of Brian; Monty Python and the Holy Grail; Monty Python's The Meaning Of Life; Personal Services*
Jordan, Neil *Angel; Company of Wolves, The; High Spirits; We're No Angels*
Jordon, Glenn *Only When I Laugh*
Julian, Rupert *Phantom of the Opera, The*
Juran, Nathan *Drums Across the River; 7th Voyage of Sinbad, The*

Kadar, Jan *Lies My Father Told Me*
Kagan, Jeremy Paul *Big Fix, The; Chosen, The; Heroes; Journey of Natty Gann, The; Scott Joplin; Sting II,*

The
Kalatozov, Mikhail *Red Tent, The*
Kane, Joseph *Flame of the Barbary Coast*
Kanew, Jeff *Eddie Macon's Run; Tough Guys*
Kanievska, Marek *Another Country*
Kanin, Garson *Bachelor Mother; My Favorite Wife*
Kanter, Hal *Loving You*
Kaplan, Jonathan *Accused, The; Heart Like A Wheel; Immediate Family; Mr. Billion; White Line Fever*
Kardos, Leslie *Small Town Girl*
Karlson, Phil *Ben; Kansas City Confidential; Kid Galahad; Silencers, The; Wrecking Crew, The; Young Doctors, The*
Karson, Eric *Octagon, The*
Kasdan, Lawrence *Accidental Tourist, The; Big Chill, The; Body Heat; I Love You to Death; Silverado*
Kastle, Leonard *Honeymoon Killers, The*
Katselas, Milton *Butterflies Are Free; Report to the Commissioner*
Katzin, Lee H. *Le Mans; What Ever Happened to Aunt Alice?*
Kaufman, George S. *Senator Was Indiscreet, The*
Kaufman, Philip *Great Northfield, Minnesota Raid, The; Henry & June; Invasion of the Body Snatchers; Right Stuff, The; Unbearable Lightness Of Being, The; Wanderers, The; White Dawn, The*
Kautner, Helmut *Restless Years, The*
Kaylor, Robert *Carny*
Kazan, Elia *America America; Arrangement, The; Baby Doll; Boomerang!; East of Eden; Face in the Crowd, A; Gentleman's Agreement; Last Tycoon, The; On the Waterfront; Panic in the Streets; Splendor in the Grass; Streetcar Named Desire, A; Tree Grows in Brooklyn, A; Viva Zapata!; Wild River*
Keach, James *False Identity*
Keaton, Buster *Navigator, The; Sherlock, Jr.*
Keaton, Diane *Heaven*
Keighley, William *Adventures of Robin Hood, The; G-Men; Green Pastures; Prince and The Pauper, The*
Kellogg, Ray *Green Berets, The*
Kelly, Gene *Cheyenne Social Club, The; Guide For The Married Man, A; Hello, Dolly!; Invitation To The Dance; It's Always Fair Weather; On The Town; Singin' in the Rain; That's Entertainment, Part 2; Tunnel Of Love, The*
Kennedy, Burt *Dirty Dingus Magee; Hannie Caulder; Money Trap, The; Support Your Local Gunfighter; Support Your Local Sheriff; Train Robbers, The; War Wagon, The; Young Billy Young*
Kenton, Erle C. *Island Of Lost Souls*
Kershner, Irvin *Empire Strikes Back, The; Eyes of Laura Mars; Fine Madness, A; Flim-Flam Man, The; Hoodlum Priest, The; Loving; Luck of Ginger Coffey, The; Never Say Never Again; Return Of A Man Called Horse, The; Robocop 2; Up The Sandbox*
Kibbee, Roland *Midnight Man, The*
Kiely, Chris *Future Schlock*
Kiersch, Fritz *Children Of The Corn*
King, Allan *Warrendale*
King, Henry *Alexander's Ragtime Band; Bell for Adano, A; Captain From Castile; Carousel; David and Bathsheba; Gunfighter, The; In Old*

Chicago; Jesse James; King of the Khyber Rifles; Love Is A Many-Splendored Thing; O. Henry's Full House; Snows of Kilimanjaro, The; Song of Bernadette, The; State Fair; Stella Dallas; Sun Also Rises, The; Tender Is the Night; This Earth Is Mine; 12 O'Clock High; Wilson; Yank in the R.A.F., A
King, Stephen *Maximum Overdrive*
King, Zalman *Two Moon Junction; Wild Orchid*
Kleiser, Randal *Big Top Pee-wee; Blue Lagoon, The; Grease*
Kloves, Steve *Fabulous Baker Boys, The*
Knowles, Bernard *Man Within, The*
Konchalovsky, Andrei *Duet For One; Homer And Eddie; Maria's Lovers; Runaway Train; Shy People; Tango & Cash*
Kopple, Barbara *Harlan County, U.S.A.*
Korda, Alexander *Ideal Husband, An; Perfect Strangers; Private Life of Don Juan, The; Private Life Of Henry VIII, The; Rembrandt; That Hamilton Woman!*
Korda, Zoltan *Cry, The Beloved Country; Drum, The; Elephant Boy; Four Feathers, The; Jungle Book, The; Macomber Affair, The; Sahara; Sanders of the River*
Korty, John *Alex And The Gypsy; Oliver's Story*
Koster, Henry *Bishop's Wife, The; Dear Brigitte; Flower Drum Song; Harvey; It Started with Eve; Mr Hobbs Takes a Vacation; My Blue Heaven; My Cousin Rachel; My Man Godfrey; O. Henry's Full House; One Hundred Men and a Girl; Robe, The; Singing Nun, The; Story of Ruth, The; Take Her, She's Mine*
Kotcheff, Ted *Apprenticeship of Duddy Kravitz, The; Billy Two Hats; First Blood; Fun With Dick And Jane; Life At The Top; North Dallas Forty; Tiara Tahiti; Two Gentlemen Sharing; Uncommon Valor; Who Is Killing the Great Chefs of Europe?; Winter People*
Kowalski, Bernard L. *Krakatoa, East of Java*
Kraemer, F.W. *Dreyfus*
Kramer, Stanley *Defiant Ones, The; Domino Principle, The; Guess Who's Coming to Dinner; Inherit the Wind; It's A Mad Mad Mad Mad World; Judgment at Nuremberg; Not as a Stranger; Oklahoma Crude; On the Beach; Pride and the Passion, The; R.P.M., Revolutions Per Minute; Runner Stumbles, The; Secret of Santa Vittoria, The; Ship of Fools*
Krish, John *Decline and Fall*
Kubrick, Stanley *Barry Lyndon; Clockwork Orange, A; Dr. Strangelove, or: How I Learned to Stop Worrying and Love the Bomb; Fear and Desire; Full Metal Jacket; Killer's Kiss; Killing, The; Lolita; Paths of Glory; Shining, The; 2001: A Space Odyssey*
Kulik, Buzz *Hunter, The; Riot; Shamus; Villa Rides; Warning Shot; Yellow Canary, The*
Kumel, Harry *Daughters of Darkness*
Kwapis, Ken *Sesame Street Presents: Follow That Bird*

LaCava, Gregory *Fifth Avenue Girl; My Man Godfrey*
Lachman, Harry *George White's Scandals*
LaLoggia, Frank *Fear No Evil*

Lambert, Mary *Pet Sematary; Siesta*
Lancaster, Burt *Kentuckian, The; Midnight Man, The*
Landis, John *Amazon Women on the Moon; American Werewolf in London, An; Blues Brothers, The; Coming To America; Into the Night; Kentucky Fried Movie, The; National Lampoon's Animal House; Spies Like Us; ¡Three Amigos!; Trading Places; Twilight Zone, The Movie*
Lane, Andrew *Jake Speed*
Lanfield, Sidney *Hound of the Baskervilles, The; Lemon Drop Kid, The; My Favorite Blonde; You'll Never Get Rich*
Lang, Fritz *American Guerrilla in the Philippines, An; Big Heat, The; Blue Gardenia, The; Clash by Night; Fury; Hangmen Also Die; House by the River; Human Desire; Ministry of Fear; Moonfleet; Rancho Notorious; Return of Frank James, The; Scarlet Street; Secret Beyond The Door, the; Western Union; While The City Sleeps; Woman In The Window, The*
Lang, Otto *Search for Paradise*
Lang, Richard *Change of Seasons, A; Mountain Men, The*
Lang, Walter *Call Me Madam; Can-Can; King and I, The; Marriage-Go-Round, The; Mother Wore Tights; Song of the Islands; State Fair; There's No Business Like Show Business; With a Song in My Heart*
Langley, Noel *Our Girl Friday; Pickwick Papers, The*
Langton, Simon *Whistle Blower, The*
Laughlin, Frank *Trial of Billy Jack, The; Billy Jack Goes To Washington*
Laughton, Charles *Night of the Hunter, The*
Launder, Frank *Belles of St. Trinian's, The; Blue Lagoon, The; Great St. Trinian's Train Robbery, The; Happiest Days of Your Life, The; Millions Like Us*
Laven, Arnold *Geronimo; Glory Guys, The; Rough Night In Jericho; Slaughter On Tenth Avenue*
Lawrence, Quentin *Trollenberg Terror, The*
Lawrence, Ray *Bliss*
Layton, Joe *Richard Pryor Live On The Sunset Strip*
Lazarus, Ashley *Golden Rendezvous*
Leach, Wilford *Wedding Party, The; Pirates of Penzance, The*
Leacock, Philip *Reach For Glory; Spanish Gardener, The; War Lover, The*
Leader, Anton *Children of the Damned*
Lean, David *Blithe Spirit; Bridge on the River Kwai, The; Brief Encounter; Doctor Zhivago; Great Expectations; Hobson's Choice; In Which We Serve; Lawrence Of Arabia; Oliver Twist; Passage to India, A; Passionate Friends, The; Ryan's Daughter; Sound Barrier, The; Summer Madness; This Happy Breed*
Leder, Herbert J. *Pretty Boy Floyd*
Lederman, D. Ross *Strange Alibi*
Lee, Jack *Robbery Under Arms; Town Like Alice, A; Wooden Horse, The*
Lee, Rowland V. *Return of Dr. Fu Manchu, The; Zoo In Budapest*
Lee, Spike *Do The Right Thing; Jungle Fever; Mo' Better Blues; She's Gotta Have It*
Lee Thompson, J. *Battle For The Planet Of The Apes; Before Winter Comes; Cape Fear; Chairman, The; Conquest of the Planet of the Apes; Country Dance; Death Wish 4, The Crackdown; Eye of the Devil; Good*

Companions, The; Greek Tycoon, The; Guns of Navarone, The; Ice Cold In Alex; King Solomon's Mines; Kings Of The Sun; Mackenna's Gold; Murphy's Law; North West Frontier; Reincarnation of Peter Proud, The; Return From The Ashes; St. Ives; Taras Bulba; 10 to Midnight; Tiger Bay; What A Way To Go!; White Buffalo, The; Yield to the Night; Yellow Balloon, The
Lehman, Ernest Portnoy's Complaint
Lehmann, Michael Heathers; Hudson Hawk
Leigh, Mike Bleak Moments; High Hopes
Leisen, Mitchell Big Broadcast of 1937, The; Big Broadcast of 1938, The; Easy Living; Frenchman's Creek; Hold Back The Dawn; Kitty; Lady In The Dark; Lady Is Willing, The; Midnight; Murder At The Vanities; Swing High, Swing Low
Leland, David Big Man, The; Checking Out; Wish You Were Here
Lelouch, Claude Another Man Another Chance; Visions of Eight
Lemmon, Jack Kotch
Lemont, John Frightened City, The
Leo, Malcolm This Is Elvis
Leonard, Herbert B. Going Home
Leonard, Robert Z. Divorcee, The; Everything I Have Is Yours; Great Ziegfeld, The; Pride and Prejudice; Strange Interlude; Susan Lenox Her Fall and Rise
Leone, Sergio Fistful of Dynamite, A; Once Upon A Time In America; Once Upon A Time in the West
Lerner, Irving Royal Hunt of the Sun, The; Studs Lonigan
LeRoy, Mervyn Anthony Adverse; Bad Seed, The; Blossoms in the Dust; Desire Me; Devil at 4 O'clock, The; FBI Story, The; Five Star Final; Gold Diggers of 1933; Gypsy; High Pressure; Home Before Dark; Homecoming; I Am a Fugitive from a Chain Gang; Little Caesar; Little Women; Madame Curie; Mister Roberts; Moment To Moment; Oil for the Lamps of China; Page Miss Glory; Quo Vadis; Random Harvest; Thirty Seconds Over Tokyo; Tugboat Annie; Waterloo Bridge
Lester, Mark L. Armed and Dangerous; Class of 1984; Class of 1999; Commando; Firestarter; Stunts; Truck Stop Women
Lester, Richard Bed Sitting Room, The; Butch and Sundance, The Early Days; Cuba; Finders Keepers; Four Musketeers, The; Funny Thing Happened On The Way To The Forum, A; Hard Day's Night, A; Help!; How I Won The War; Juggernaut; Knack, . . . And How To Get It, The; Petulia; Return Of The Musketeers, The; Ritz, The; Robin And Marian; Royal Flash; Superman II; Superman III; Three Musketeers, The
Levin, Henry Ambushers, The; And Baby Makes Three; Bandit of Sherwood Forest, The; Come Fly With Me; Farmer Takes a Wife, The; Genghis Khan; Jolson Sings Again; Journey to the Center of the Earth; Murderers' Row; President's Lady, The; Wonderful World of The Brothers Grimm, The
Levinson, Barry Avalon; Diner; Good Morning, Vietnam; Natural, The; Rain Man; Tin Men; Young Sherlock Holmes
Levy, Ralph Bedtime Story; Do Not Disturb
Levy, Raoul Defector, The
Lewin, Albert Moon and Sixpence, The; Pandora and the Flying Dutchman; Picture of Dorian Gray, The
Lewis, Jay Live Now – Pay Later
Lewis, Jerry Nutty Professor, The; Patsy, The
Lewis, Joseph H. My Name Is Julia Ross; Retreat, Hell!
Lewis, Robert Anything Goes
Lieberman, Jeff Squirm
Lieberman, Robert Table for Five
Lindsay-Hogg, Michael Nasty Habits; Object of Beauty, The
Linson, Art Where the Buffalo Roam
Lipstadt, Aaron Android; City Limits
Lisberger, Steven Slipstream; Tron
Little, Dwight H. Halloween 4 The Return Of Michael Myers; Phantom Of The Opera, The
Littlewood, Joan Sparrows Can't Sing
Littman, Lynne Testament
Litvak, Anatole All This and Heaven Too; Amazing Dr. Clitterhouse, The; Anastasia; Confessions of a Nazi Spy; Decision Before Dawn; Journey, The; Night of the Generals; Sisters, The; Snake Pit, The; Sorry, Wrong Number; This Above All; Tovarich
Lloyd, Frank Berkeley Square; Blood on the Sun; Cavalcade; Mutiny on the Bounty; Sea Hawk, The; Under Two Flags
Loach, Ken Black Jack; Fatherland; Hidden Agenda; Poor Cow; Riff-Raff
Locke, Sondra Impulse; Ratboy
Loden, Barbara Wanda
Logan, Joshua Bus Stop; Camelot; Fanny; Paint Your Wagon; Picnic; Sayonara; South Pacific
Lommel, Ulli BrainWaves
Loncraine, Richard Missionary, The
London, Jerry Rent-A-Cop; Shogun
Lorentz, Pare River, The
Losey, Joseph Accident; Assassination of Trotsky, The; Boom; Boy With Green Hair, The; Damned, The; Doll's House, A; Eve; Figures In A Landscape; Go-Between, The; King and Country; M; Modesty Blaise; Prowler, The; Romantic Englishwoman, The; Secret Ceremony; Servant, The
Lourie, Eugene Beast from 20,000 Fathoms, The
Loventhal, Charlie First Time, The
Lovitt, Bert Prince Jack
Lubin, Arthur Phantom of the Opera
Lubitsch, Ernst Design For Living; Heaven Can Wait; Love Parade, The; Merry Widow, The; Ninotchka; One Hour With You; Patriot, The; Shop Around The Corner, The; Student Prince, The; That Uncertain Feeling; To Be Or Not To Be; Trouble in Paradise
Lucas, George American Graffiti; Star Wars; THX 1138
Ludwig, Edward Big Jim McLain
Lumet, Sidney Anderson Tapes, The; Appointment, The; Bye Bye Braverman; Child's Play; Daniel; Deadly Affair, The; Deathtrap; Dog Day Afternoon; Equus; Fail Safe; Family Business; Fugitive Kind, The; Garbo Talks; Group, The; Hill, The; Long Day's Journey Into Night; Lovin' Molly; Morning After, The; Murder On The Orient Express; Network; Offence, The; Pawnbroker, The; Power; Prince of the City; Q&A; Running On Empty; Sea Gull, The; Serpico; Stage Struck; Twelve Angry Men; Verdict, The; Wiz, The
Lupino, Ida Trouble With Angels, The
Luraschi, Tony Outsider, The
Luske, Hamilton Lady and the Tramp; Peter Pan; Pinocchio; One Hundred and One Dalmatians
Lynch, David Blue Velvet; Dune; Elephant Man, The; Eraserhead; Wild At Heart
Lynch, Paul Prom Night
Lyne, Adrian Fatal Attraction; Flashdance; Foxes; Jacob's Ladder; Nine^1/$_2$Weeks
Lynn, Jonathan Clue; Nuns on the Run
Lyon, Francis D. South Seas Adventure
Macdonald, Peter Rambo III
MacDougall, Ranald World, the Flesh and the Devil, The
MacGrath, Joseph Bliss of Mrs. Blossom, The
Mackendrick, Alexander Don't Make Waves; High Wind In Jamaica, A; Ladykillers, The; 'Maggie', The; Man In The White Suit, The; Mandy; Sammy Going South; Sweet Smell of Success; Whisky Galore!
Mackenzie, John Fourth Protocol, The; Last of the Finest, The; Long Good Friday, The; Unman, Wittering and Zigo
Mack, Willard Broadway To Hollywood
Maddow, Ben Savage Eye, The
Magnoli, Albert Purple Rain
Mailer, Norman Tough Guys Don't Dance
Makevejev, Dusan Sweet Movie
Malick, Terrence Badlands; Days of Heaven
Malle, Louis Alamo Bay; Atlantic City; Crackers; My Dinner with Andre; Pretty Baby
Malmuth, Bruce Hard To Kill; Nighthawks
Mamet, David Homicide; Things Change
Mamoulian, Rouben Applause; Becky Sharp; Blood and Sand; City Streets; Dr. Jekyll and Mr. Hyde; High, Wide and Handsome; Mark of Zorro, The; Queen Christina; Silk Stockings; Summer Holiday
Mandel, Robert Independence Day; Touch and Go
Mandoki, Luis White Palace
Manduke, Joseph Gumshoe Kid, The
Mankiewicz, Joseph L. All About Eve; Barefoot Contessa, The; Cleopatra; 5 Fingers; Ghost and Mrs Muir, The; Guys and Dolls; Honey Pot, The; Julius Caesar; Letter To Three Wives, A; People Will Talk; Quiet American, The; Sleuth; Suddenly, Last Summer; There Was A Crooked Man . . .
Mann, Anthony Bend of the River; Cimarron; Dandy in Aspic, A; El Cid; Fall Of The Roman Empire, The; Glenn Miller Story, The; God's Little Acre; Heroes of Telemark, The; Man From Laramie, The; Man of the West; Tin Star, The; T-Men; Winchester '73
Mann, Daniel Butterfield 8; Come Back, Little Sheba; Dream of Kings, A; Five Finger Exercise; I'll Cry Tomorrow; Judith; Last Angry Man, The; Our Man Flint; Rose Tattoo, The; Teahouse of the August Moon, The; Who's Been Sleeping In My Bed?; Willard
Mann, Delbert Bachelor Party, The; Dark At The Top Of The Stairs, The; David Copperfield; Desire Under The Elms; Fitzwilly; Jane Eyre; Kidnapped; Lover Come Back; Marty; Night Crossing; Separate Tables; That Touch of Mink
Mann, Michael Keep, The; Manhunter; Thief
Mantz, Paul 7 Wonders of the World
Markle, Fletcher Incredible Journey, The
Markle, Peter Personals, The; Youngblood
Markowitz, Robert Voices
Marks, Arthur Friday Foster
Marquand, Christian Candy
Marquand, Richard Eye of the Needle; Hearts of Fire; Jagged Edge; Legacy, The; Return Of The Jedi; Until September
Marshall, Frank Arachnophobia
Marshall, Garry Beaches; Flamingo Kid, The; Pretty Woman
Marshall, George Blue Dahlia, The; Boy, Did I Get A Wrong Number!; Destry Rides Again; Gazebo, The; Goldwyn Follies, The; Houdini; How The West Was Won; Pack Up Your Troubles; Savage, The; Star Spangled Rhythm; True to Life
Marshall, Noel Roar
Marshall, Penny Awakenings; Big; Jumpin' Jack Flash
Martin, Francis Tillie And Gus
Martinson, Leslie H. Batman; Fathom
Marton, Andrew Africa – Texas Style; Devil Makes Three, The; King Solomon's Mines; Longest Day, The; 7 Wonders of the World; Thin Red Line, The
Maselli, Francesco Fine Pair, A
Masterson, Peter Blood Red; Trip to Bountiful, The
Masters, Quentin Stud, The
Masuda, Toshio Tora! Tora! Tora!
Mate, Rudolph Branded; D.O.A.; 300 Spartans, The; Union Station; When Worlds Collide
Maxwell, Ronald F. Little Darlings
May, Elaine Heartbreak Kid, The; Ishtar; Mikey and Nicky; New Leaf, A
Mayersberg, Paul Captive
Mayo, Archie Adventures of Marco Polo, The; Go Into Your Dance; Great American Broadcast, The; Moontide; Night in Casablanca, A; Petrified Forest, The; Svengali
Maysles, Albert Gimme Shelter
Maysles, David Gimme Shelter
Mazursky, Paul Alex In Wonderland; Blume in Love; Bob & Carol & Ted & Alice; Down and Out in Beverly Hills; Enemies, A Love Story; Harry and Tonto; Moon Over Parador; Moscow On The Hudson; Next Stop, Greenwich Village; Scenes from a Mall; Unmarried Woman, An; Willie & Phil
McBride, Jim Big Easy, The; Breathless; Great Balls Of Fire!
McCarey, Leo Affair to Remember, An; Belle Of The Nineties; Bells of St. Mary's, The; Duck Soup; Going My Way; Indiscreet; Love Affair; Make Way For Tomorrow; Rally 'Round the Flag, Boys!; Ruggles of Red Gap; Satan Never Sleeps
McCarey, Raymond Pack Up Your Troubles
McCowan, George Frogs
McEveety, Vincent Herbie Goes to Monte Carlo; Strongest Man in the World, The
McGrath, Joseph Casino Royale; Magic Christian, The; 30 Is a Dangerous Age, Cynthia
McLaglen, Andrew V. Bandolero!; Cahill, United States Marshal; Chisum; Last Hard Men, The;

McLintock!; North Sea Hijack; Rare Breed, The; Sahara; Sea Wolves, The; Shenandoah; Way West, The; Wild Geese, The

McLeod, Norman Z. Horse Feathers; It's A Gift; Kid from Brooklyn, The; Lady Be Good; Merrily We Live; My Favorite Spy; Paleface, The; Road To Rio; Secret Life of Walter Mitty, The; Topper

McTiernan, John Die Hard; Hunt For Red October, The; Nomads; Predator

McWilliams, Bernard Suffering Bastards

Medak, Peter Changeling, The; Day in the Death of Joe Egg, A; Krays, The; Men's Club, The; Ruling Class, The; Zorro, The Gay Blade

Medford, Don Hunting Party, The; Organization, The; To Trap A Spy

Mekas, Adolfas Hallelujah The Hills

Melford, George Sheik, The

Mendes, Lothar Jew Suss; Moonlight Sonata

Menges, Chris World Apart, A

Menotti, Gian-Carlo Medium, The

Menzies, William Cameron Things to Come

Meyer, Muffie Enormous Changes at the Last Minute

Meyer, Nicholas Star Trek II, The Wrath of Khan; Time After Time

Meyer, Russ Beneath the Valley of the Ultra Vixens; Beyond The Valley Of The Dolls; Cherry, Harry & Raquel!; Faster, Pussycat! Kill! Kill!; Lorna; Motor Psycho; Supervixens; Up!; Vixen!

Meyers, Sidney Savage Eye, The

Micklin Silver, Joan Between the Lines; Crossing Delancey; Head Over Heels; Hester Street

Mikels, Ted V. Corpse Grinders, The

Miles, Christopher Priest of Love; That Lucky Touch; Virgin And The Gypsy, The

Milestone, Lewis All Quiet on the Western Front; Anything Goes; Arch of Triumph; Edge of Darkness; Front Page, The; General Died at Dawn, The; Hallelujah, I'm A Bum!; Halls of Montezuma; Les Miserables; North Star, The; Ocean's Eleven; Of Mice and Men; Racket, The; Rain; Red Pony, The; Strange Love of Martha Ivers, The; Walk in the Sun, A

Milius, John Big Wednesday; Conan the Barbarian; Dillinger; Farewell To The King; Flight of the Intruder; Red Dawn; Wind and the Lion, The

Milland, Ray Panic in Year Zero

Millar, Stuart Rooster Cogburn

Miller, David Captain Newman, M.D.; Executive Action; Flying Tigers; Lonely Are the Brave

Miller, George Mad Max; Mad Max 2; Mad Max Beyond Thunderdome; Twilight Zone, The Movie; Witches of Eastwick, The

Miller, George Man From Snowy River, The; Neverending Story II, The, The Next Chapter

Miller, Jonathan Take A Girl Like You

Miller, Michael Jackson County Jail; Silent Rage

Miller, Robert Ellis Any Wednesday; Baltimore Bullet, The; Buttercup Chain, The; Hawks; Heart Is A Lonely Hunter, The; Reuben, Reuben

Mills, John Sky West and Crooked

Mills, Reginald Tales of Beatrix Potter

Miner, Steve Friday the 13th Part 2; Friday the 13th Part 3; Soul Man; Warlock

Minnelli, Vincente Band Wagon, The;

American In Paris, An; Bad and the Beautiful, The; Band Wagon, The; Bells Are Ringing; Brigadoon; Cabin in the Sky; Clock, The; Cobweb, The; Courtship of Eddie's Father, The; Father of the Bride; Four Horsemen of the Apocalypse, The; Gigi; Goodbye Charlie; Home From the Hill; Kismet; Lust for Life; Madame Bovary; Meet Me In St Louis; On A Clear Day You Can See Forever; Pirate, The; Reluctant Debutante, The; Sandpiper, The; Some Came Running; Tea and Sympathy; Two Weeks in Another Town; Undercurrent; Yolanda and the Thief; Ziegfeld Follies

Mitchell, Art Behind The Green Door

Mitchell, Jim Behind The Green Door

Mizrahi, Moshe Every Time We Say Goodbye

Mollo, Andrew It Happened Here; Winstanley

Montgomery, Robert Lady in the Lake

Moore, Michael Paradise, Hawaiian Style; Roger And Me

Moore, Robert Chapter Two; Cheap Detective, The; Murder By Death

Morahan, Christopher All Neat in Black Stockings; Clockwise; Diamonds for Breakfast; Paper Mask

Mora, Philippe Beast Within, The; Breed Apart, A

Morris, Errol Thin Blue Line, The

Morrison, Bruce Constance

Morrissey, Paul Blood for Dracula; Flesh; Flesh for Frankenstein; Heat; Mixed Blood; Trash

Morton, Rocky D.O.A.

Mowbray, Malcolm Private Function, A

Moyle, Allan Pump Up The Volume

Mulcahy, Russell Highlander; Highlander II, The Quickening; Razorback

Mulligan, Robert Baby, The Rain Must Fall; Bloodbrothers; Come September; Fear Strikes Out; Inside Daisy Clover; Kiss Me Goodbye; Love With The Proper Stranger; Other, The; Same Time, Next Year; Spiral Road, The; Stalking Moon, The; Summer of '42; To Kill A Mockingbird; Up The Down Staircase

Munroe, Cynthia Wedding Party, The

Murakami, Jimmy T. Battle Beyond the Stars

Murch, Walter Return to Oz

Murnau, F.W. Sunrise; Tabu

Murphy, Eddie Harlem Nights

Murphy, Geoff Goodbye Pork Pie; Utu; Young Guns II

Murray, Bill Quick Change

Myerson, Alan Private Lessons; Steelyard Blues

Narizzano, Silvio Blue; Choices; Class of Miss MacMichael, The; Fanatic; Georgy Girl; Loot

Neame, Ronald Card, The; Chalk Garden, The; First Monday in October; Foreign Body; Gambit; Hopscotch; Man Who Never Was, The; Meteor; Million Pound Note, The; Mister Moses; Odessa File, The; Poseidon Adventure, The; Prime of Miss Jean Brodie, The; Scrooge; Tunes of Glory; Windom's Way

Needham, Hal Cannonball Run, The; Hooper; Smokey And The Bandit; Smokey and the Bandit II; Villain, The

Negulesco, Jean Boy On A Dolphin; Certain Smile, A; Daddy Long Legs; How To Marry A Millionaire; Humoresque; Johnny Belinda; Mask of Dimitrios, The; O. Henry's Full

House; Rains of Ranchipur, The; Three Coins in the Fountain; Three Strangers; Titanic

Neilan, Marshall Rebecca Of Sunnybrook Farm

Neill, Roy William Frankenstein Meets the Wolf Man

Neilson, James Moon-Spinners, The; Night Passage

Nelson, Gary Allan Quatermain and the City of Gold; Black Hole, The

Nelson, Gene Kissin' Cousins

Nelson, Ralph Charly; Counterpoint; Duel At Diablo; Embryo; Fate is the Hunter; Father Goose; Flight of the Doves; Lilies of the Field; Once A Thief; Requiem for a Heavyweight; Soldier Blue; Soldier In The Rain; Wilby Conspiracy, The; Requiem for a Heavyweight

Neumann, Kurt Fly, The; Ring, The

Nevin, Robyn More Things Change, The

Newell, Mike Amazing Grace and Chuck; Awakening, The; Bad Blood; Dance with a Stranger; Soursweet

Newland, John Spy With My Face, The

Newley, Anthony Can Heironymus Merkin Ever Forget Mercy Humppe and Find True Happiness?

Newman, Joseph H. 711 Ocean Drive; This Island Earth

Newman, Joseph M. Human Jungle, The

Newman, Paul Effect of Gamma Rays on Man-in-the-Moon Marigolds, The; Glass Menagerie, The; Harry & Son; Rachel, Rachel; Sometimes A Great Notion

Newmeyer, Fred Fast and Loose; Safety Last

Niblo, Fred Ben-Hur, A Tale of the Christ; Blood and Sand; Camille; Three Musketeers, The

Nichols, Dudley Mourning Becomes Electra

Nichols, Mike Biloxi Blues; Carnal Knowledge; Catch-22; Day Of The Dolphin, The; Fortune, The; Graduate, The; Heartburn; Postcards From The Edge; Silkwood; Who's Afraid of Virginia Woolf?; Working Girl

Nicholson, Arch Weekend With Kate

Nicholson, Jack Drive, He Said; Goin' South; Two Jakes, The

Nicolas, Paul Chained Heat

Nimoy, Leonard Funny About Love; Star Trek III, The Search for Spock; Star Trek IV, The Voyage Home; 3 Men and A Baby

Norman, Leslie Dunkirk; Long And The Short And The Tall, The

Norris, Aaron Delta Force 2

Norton, Bill L. Cisco Pike

Norton, B.W.L. Baby; More American Graffiti

Noyce, Phillip Blind Fury; Dead Calm; Heatwave; Newsfront

Nugent, Elliott Cat and the Canary, The; Great Gatsby, The; My Favorite Brunette; Splendor

Nunn, Trevor Hedda

Nyby, Christian Thing (From Another World), The

O'Bannon, Dan Return of the Living Dead, The

Oboler, Arch Bwana Devil; Five

Ockrent, Mike Dancin' Thru The Dark

O'Connor, Pat Fools of Fortune; January Man, The; Month in the Country, A

O'Ferrall, George More Angels One

Five

Ogilvie, George Mad Max Beyond Thunderdome

O'Hara, Gerry Bitch, The; Maroc 7

Oliansky, Joel Competition, The

Olivier, Laurence Hamlet; Henry V; Prince and the Showgirl, The; Richard III

Olsen, William Getting It On

Ophuls, Max Caught; Letter From An Unknown Woman; Reckless Moment, The

Orme, Stuart Wolves of Willoughby Chase, The

Orr, James Mr. Destiny

Oshima, Nagisa Merry Christmas, Mr. Lawrence

Oswald, Gerd Kiss Before Dying, A; Valerie

Owen, Cliff Prize of Arms, A; Wrong Arm of the Law, The

Owen, Dan Partners

Owen, Don Nobody Waved Goodbye; Unfinished Business

Oz, Frank Dark Crystal, The; Little Shop Of Horrors; What About Bob?

Ozerov, Yuri Visions of Eight

Page, Anthony Absolution; I Never Promised You A Rose Garden; Inadmissible Evidence; Lady Vanishes, The

Pakula, Alan J. All The President's Men; Comes A Horseman; Dream Lover; Klute; Love and Pain and the Whole Damn Thing; Orphans; Parallax View, The; Presumed Innocent; Rollover; See You In The Morning; Sophie's Choice; Starting Over; Sterile Cuckoo, The

Palcy, Euzhan Dry White Season, A

Pal, George Atlantis, The Lost Continent; Time Machine, The; Tom Thumb; Wonderful World of The Brothers Grimm, The

Palmer, John Ciao Manhattan

Palmer, Tony Children, The; Testimony; 200 Motels; Wagner

Panama, Norman Court Jester, The; I Will . . . I Will . . . For Now; Not With My Wife, You Don't!; Road to Hong Kong, The

Paris, Jerry Don't Raise the Bridge, Lower the River; Grasshopper, The; Police Academy 3, Back in Training

Parker, Alan Angel Heart; Birdy; Bugsy Malone; Come See the Paradise; Fame; Midnight Express; Pink Floyd – The Wall; Shoot the Moon

Parks, Gordon Learning Tree, The; Shaft; Superfly

Parriott, James D. Heart Condition

Parrish, Robert Casino Royale; Cry Danger; Duffy; Fire Down Below; In The French Style; Mob, The; My Pal Gus

Parry, Gordon Tom Brown's Schooldays

Pascal, Gabriel Caesar and Cleopatra; Major Barbara

Passer, Ivan Silver Bears

Paul, Steven Eternity; Falling in Love Again

Peak, Barry Future Schlock

Pearce, Richard Country; Heartland; Long Walk Home, The; No Mercy; Threshold

Peckinpah, Sam Ballad of Cable Hogue, The; Bring Me The Head of Alfredo Garcia; Convoy; Cross Of Iron; Deadly Companions, The; Getaway, The; Junior Bonner; Killer Elite, The; Major Dundee; Osterman Weekend, The; Pat Garrett And Billy The Kid; Ride The High Country;

Straw Dogs; Wild Bunch, The

Peerce, Larry Ash Wednesday; Bell Jar, The; Goodbye, Columbus; Incident, The; Love Child; One Potato, Two Potato; Other Side of the Mountain, The; Two-Minute Warning; Wired

Peeters, Barbara Humanoids From The Deep

Pelissier, Anthony Encore; History of Mr Polly, The; Rocking Horse Winner, The

Penn, Arthur Alice's Restaurant; Bonnie and Clyde; Chase, The; Dead of Winter; Left-Handed Gun, The; Little Big Man; Mickey One; Miracle Worker, The; Missouri Breaks, The; Night Moves; Target; Visions of Eight

Pennebaker, D.A. Don't Look Back

Perier, Etienne When Eight Bells Toll; Zeppelin

Perkins, Anthony Psycho III

Perry, Frank Compromising Positions; David and Lisa; Diary Of A Mad Housewife; Doc; Last Summer; Mommie Dearest; Monsignor; Swimmer, The

Petersen, Wolfgang Enemy Mine; Neverending Story, The

Petit, Christopher Unsuitable Job For A Woman, An

Petrie, Daniel Bay Boy; Betsy, The; Buster and Billie; Cocoon: The Return; Fort Apache, The Bronx; Lifeguard; Resurrection

Petrie, Donald Mystic Pizza; Opportunity Knocks

Pevney, Joseph Man of a Thousand Faces; 3 Ring Circus; Twilight for the Gods

Pfleghar, Michael Visions of Eight

Pichel, Irving Bride Wore Boots, The

Pickford, Jack Little Lord Fauntleroy

Pierson, Frank R. Looking Glass War, The; Star Is Born, A

Pillsbury, Sam Scarecrow, The

Pinter, Harold Butley

Platts-Mills, Barney Bronco Bullfrog

Pogostin, S. Lee Hard Contract

Poitier, Sidney Ghost Dad; Hanky Panky; Let's Do It Again; Stir Crazy

Polanski, Roman Chinatown; Cul-de-Sac; Dance of the Vampires, Pardon Me, But Your Teeth are in My Neck; Frantic; Pirates; Repulsion; Rosemary's Baby; Tenant, The; Tess

Pollack, Sydney Absence of Malice; Bobby Deerfield; Castle Keep; Electric Horseman, The; Havana; Jeremiah Johnson; Out of Africa; Scalphunters, The; Slender Thread, The; They Shoot Horses, Don't They; This Property Is Condemned; Three Days of the Condor; Tootsie; Way We Were, The; Yakuza, The

Pollock, George Murder Most Foul; Murder She Said; 10 Little Indians

Polonsky, Abraham Tell Them Willie Boy Is Here

Post, Ted Beneath The Planet Of The Apes; Go Tell the Spartans; Hang 'Em High; Magnum Force

Potter, H.C. Hellzapoppin; Miniver Story, The; Mr Blandings Builds His Dream House; Mr. Lucky; Shopworn Angel, The; Story of Vernon and Irene Castle, The

Potterton, Gerald Heavy Metal

Powell, Dick Conqueror, The

Powell, Michael Age of Consent; Black Narcissus; Canterbury Tale, A; 49th Parallel; Gone to Earth; I Know Where I'm Going!; Ill Met By Moonlight; Life and Death of Colonel Blimp, The; Matter of Life and Death, A; One of Our Aircraft Is Missing; Peeping Tom; Red Shoes, The; Small Back Room, The; Spy in Black, The; Tales Of Hoffman, The; They're A Weird Mob; Thief of Bagdad, The

Powell, Tristram American Friends

Power, John Father; Picture Show Man, The

Preminger, Otto Advise and Consent; Anatomy of a Murder; Angel Face; Bonjour Tristesse; Bunny Lake is Missing; Cardinal, The; Carmen Jones; Court-Martial of Billy Mitchell; The; Daisy Kenyon; Exodus; Fallen Angel; Fan, The; Forever Amber; Human Factor, The; Hurry Sundown; In Harm's Way; Laura; Man With The Golden Arm, The; Porgy and Bess; River of No Return; Rosebud; Saint Joan; 13th Letter, The; Where the Sidewalk Ends; Whirlpool

Pressburger, Emeric Black Narcissus; Canterbury Tale, A; Gone to Earth; I Know Where I'm Going!; Ill Met By Moonlight; Life and Death of Colonel Blimp, The; Matter of Life and Death, A; Red Shoes, The; Small Back Room, The; Tales Of Hoffman, The

Pressman, Michael Boulevard Nights; Great Texas Dynamite Chase, The; Some Kind of Hero; Teenage Mutant Ninja Turtles II, The Secret of Ooze

Prince, Hal Little Night Music, A

Pryor, Richard Richard Pryor... Here and Now

Puenzo, Luis Old Gringo

Purcell, Evelyn Nobody's Fool

Pyun, Albert Sword and the Sorcerer, The

Quested, John Loophole

Quine, Richard Bell, Book and Candle; Hotel; How To Murder Your Wife; Officer and a Gentleman, An; Sex And The Single Girl; Strangers When We Meet; Synanon; World Of Suzie Wong, The

Quinn, Anthony Buccaneer, The

Quintero, Jose Roman Spring of Mrs. Stone, The

Radford, Michael Another Time, Another Place; Nineteen Eighty-Four; White Mischief

Rafelson, Bob Black Widow; Five Easy Pieces; King of Marvin Gardens, The; Mountains of the Moon; Postman Always Rings Twice, The; Stay Hungry

Raffill, Stewart Philadelphia Experiment, The; Sea Gypsies, The

Raich, Ken Hollywood Hot Tubs 2, Educating Crystal

Raimi, Sam Darkman; Evil Dead, The; Evil Dead II

Rakoff, Alvin Comedy Man, The; Crossplot

Ramis, Harold Caddyshack; Club Paradise; National Lampoon's Vacation

Randel, Tony Hellbound, Hellraiser II

Rankin Jr, Arthur Last Unicorn, The

Rapper, Irving Adventures of Mark Twain, The; Corn Is Green, The; Deception; Glass Menagerie, The; Marjorie Morningstar; Miracle, The; Now, Voyager; One Foot in Heaven; Rhapsody in Blue

Rash, Steve Buddy Holly Story, The

Ratoff, Gregory Footlight Serenade; Heat's On, The; Intermezzo; Men in Her Life, The; Oscar Wilde; Rose of Washington Square

Ray, Nicholas Bigger Than Life; Bitter Victory; 55 Days at Peking; Flying Leathernecks; In a Lonely Place; Johnny Guitar; King of Kings; Lusty Men, The; On Dangerous Ground; Party Girl; Rebel Without A Cause; Savage Innocents, The; True Story of Jesse James, The; Wind Across The Everglades

Redford, Robert Milagro Beanfield War, The; Ordinary People

Reed, Carol Agony and the Ecstasy, The; Bank Holiday; Fallen Idol, The; Key, The; Kid for Two Farthings, A; Man Between, The; Night Train to Munich; Odd Man Out; Oliver!; Our Man in Havana; Outcast of the Islands; Running Man, The; Stars Look Down, The; Third Man, The; Trapeze; Way Ahead, The; Young Mr Pitt, The

Reed, John Animal Farm

Rees, Clive When The Whales Came

Rees, Jerry Marrying Man, The

Reeve, Geoffrey Caravan to Vaccares; Puppet on a Chain

Reeves, Michael Sorcerers, The

Reggio, Godfrey Koyaanisqatsi

Reichenbach, Francois F For Fake

Reichert, Mark Union City

Reid, John Leave All Fair; Middle Age Spread

Reiner, Carl Dead Men Don't Wear Plaid; Jerk, The; Man With Two Brains, The; Oh, God!; Sibling Rivalry; Where's Poppa?

Reiner, Rob Misery; Princess Bride, The; Stand By Me; This is Spinal Tap; When Harry Met Sally...

Reinhardt, Gottfried Town Without Pity

Reinhardt, Max Midsummer Night's Dream, A

Reisch, Walter Song of Scheherazade

Reis, Irving All My Sons; Big Street, The; Four Poster, The

Reisner, Charles F. Steamboat Bill, Jr

Reisner, Chuck Kid, The

Reisz, Karel Everybody Wins; French Lieutenant's Woman, The; Gambler, The; Isadora; Morgan (A Suitable Case For Treatment); Night Must Fall; Saturday Night And Sunday Morning; Sweet Dreams; Who'll Stop the Rain

Reitherman, Wolfgang Aristocats, The; Jungle Book, The; One Hundred and One Dalmatians; Rescuers, The

Reitman, Ivan Ghost Busters; Ghostbusters II; Kindergarten Cop; Legal Eagles; Meatballs; Stripes; Twins

Relph, Michael Saraband for Dead Lovers

Rene, Norman Longtime Companion

Renoir, Jean Diary of a Chambermaid; River, The; Southerner, The; This Land is Mine; Woman on the Beach, The

Resnais, Alain I Want To Go Home; Providence

Reynolds, Burt End, The; Gator; Sharky's Machine

Reynolds, Kevin Robin Hood, Prince Of Thieves

Rich, David Lowell Concorde - Airport '79, The; Eye of the Cat; Lovely Way To Die, A; Madame X

Rich, John Boeing Boeing; Wives and Lovers

Rich, Richard Black Cauldron, The

Richards, Dick Culpepper Cattle Co., The; Farewell, My Lovely; Man, Woman And Child; March Or Die; Rafferty and the Gold Dust Twins

Richardson, Ralph Home at Seven

Richardson, Tony Border, The; Charge of the Light Brigade, The; Entertainer, The; Hotel New Hampshire, The; Joseph Andrews; Laughter In The Dark; Loneliness of the Long Distance Runner, The; Look Back in Anger; Loved One, The; Mademoiselle; Ned Kelly; Sailor From Gibraltar, The; Taste of Honey, A; Tom Jones

Richert, William American Success Company, The; Winter Kills

Richter, W.D. Adventures of Buckaroo Banzai, Across the Fifth Dimension, The

Rilla, Wolf Bachelor of Hearts; Village of the Damned; World Ten Times Over, The

Ripley, Arthur Chase, The

Risi, Dino Tiger And The Pussycat, The

Ritchie, Michael Almost Perfect Affair, An; Bad News Bears, The; Candidate, The; Couch Trip, The; Divine Madness; Downhill Racer; Fletch; Fletch Lives; Golden Child, The; Island, The; Prime Cut; Semi-Tough; Smile; Survivors, The; Wildcats

Ritt, Martin Back Roads; Black Orchid, The; Brotherhood, The; Conrack; Cross Creek; Edge of the City; Front, The; Great White Hope, The; Hemingway's Adventures of a Young Man; Hombre; Hud; Molly Maguires, The; Murphy's Romance; Norma Rae; Nuts; Outrage, The; Paris Blues; Pete 'N' Tillie; Sound and the Fury, The; Sounder; Spy Who Came In From The Cold, The; Stanley & Iris

Roach, Hal One Million B.C.

Roach Jr, Hal One Million B.C.

Robbie, Seymour C.C. And Company

Robbins, Jerome West Side Story

Robbins, Matthew Dragonslayer

Robertson, Cliff J.W. Coop

Robertson, John S. Tess of the Storm Country

Roberts, Stephen Ex-Mrs. Bradford, The; Star of Midnight

Robinson, Bruce How To Get Ahead In Advertising; Withnail & I

Robinson, Phil Alden Field Of Dreams

Robson, Mark Bridges at Toko-Ri, The; Champion; Earthquake; From The Terrace; Happy Birthday, Wanda June; Inn of the Sixth Happiness, The; Lost Command; My Foolish Heart; Nine Hours to Rama; Peyton Place; Prize, The; Return to Paradise; Valley of the Dolls; Von Ryan's Express

Roddam, Franc Bride, The; Lords of Discipline, The; Quadrophenia

Roeg, Nicolas Bad Timing; Castaway; Don't Look Now; Eureka; Insignificance; Man Who Fell To Earth, The; Track 29; Walkabout; Witches, The

Roemer, Michael Plot Against Harry, The

Rogell, Albert S. Hit Parade of 1943

Rogers, Charles Bohemian Girl, The

Romero, George A. Creepshow; Dawn of the Dead; Day of the Dead; Knightriders; Martin; Monkey Shines; Night of the Living Dead

Rooks, Conrad Siddhartha

Rose, Bernard Chicago Joe and the Showgirl

Rosenberg, Stuart Amityville Horror, The; April Fools, The; Brubaker; Cool Hand Luke; Drowning Pool, The; Love and Bullets; Murder, Inc.; Pope of Greenwich Village, The;

Voyage Of The Damned; WUSA

Rosen, Martin *Watership Down*

Rosenthal, Rick *Bad Boys; Halloween II*

Rosi, Francesco *Lucky Luciano*

Rosmer, Milton *Dreyfus*

Rossellini, Roberto *Stromboli; Voyage to Italy*

Rossen, Robert *Alexander The Great; All The King's Men; Body and Soul; Hustler, The; Johnny O'Clock; Lilith*

Ross, Herbert *California Suite; Footloose; Funny Lady; Goodbye Girl, The; Goodbye, Mr Chips; I Ought To Be In Pictures; Last of Sheila, The; Max Dugan Returns; My Blue Heaven; Nijinsky; Owl And The Pussycat, The; Pennies From Heaven; Play It Again, Sam; Protocol; Secret Of My Success, The; Seven-Per-Cent Solution, The; Steel Magnolias; Sunshine Boys, The; T.R. Baskin; True Colors; Turning Point, The*

Rosso, Franco *Babylon*

Rosson, Arthur *North West Mounted Police*

Roth, Bobby *Heartbreakers*

Roth, Joe *Streets of Gold*

Rouse, Russell *Oscar, The*

Rowland, Roy *5,000 Fingers of Dr. T., The; Girl Hunters, The; Hit the Deck; Killer McCoy*

Rozema, Patricia *I've Heard the Mermaids Singing*

Ruben, Joseph *Dreamscape; Sleeping with the Enemy*

Rubin, Katt Shea *Streets*

Rudolph, Alan *Love At Large; Moderns, The; Remember My Name; Songwriter; Trouble in Mind; Welcome to LA*

Ruggles, Wesley *Cimarron; I'm No Angel*

Rush, Richard *Freebie And The Bean; Getting Straight; Stunt Man, The*

Russell, Chuck *Nightmare on Elm Street 3, Dream Warriors*

Russell, Ken *Altered States; Billion Dollar Brain; Boy Friend, The; Crimes of Passion; Devils, The; French Dressing; Gothic; Lair Of The White Worm, The; Lisztomania; Mahler; Music Lovers, The; Tommy; Valentino; Women In Love*

Russell, William D. *Bride For Sale*

Rydell, Mark *Cinderella Liberty; Cowboys, The; Fox, The; Harry And Walter Go To New York; On Golden Pond; Reivers, The; River, The; Rose, The*

Safran, Henri *Storm Boy*

Sagal, Boris *Made In Paris; Omega Man, The*

Saks, Gene *Barefoot In The Park; Brighton Beach Memoirs; Cactus Flower; Mame; Odd Couple, The*

Salter, James *Three*

Sandrich, Mark *Follow the Fleet; Gay Divorcee, The; Holiday Inn; Shall We Dance; So Proudly We Hail!; Top Hat*

Santell, Alfred *Dictator, The; Jack London*

Santley, Joseph *Cocoanuts, The; Down Mexico Way*

Sarafian, Richard C. *Eye of the Tiger; Lolly-Madonna XXX; Man who Loved Cat Dancing, The; Next Man, The; Run Wild, Run Free; Sunburn; Vanishing Point*

Sargent, Joseph *MacArthur; Man, The; One Spy Too Many; Taking of Pelham One Two Three, The; White Lightning*

Sarne, Michael *Joanna; Myra Breckinridge*

Sasdy, Peter *I Don't Want To Be Born; Taste The Blood of Dracula; Welcome to Blood City*

Savani, Tom *Night of the Living Dead*

Saville, Philip *Fellow Traveller; Oedipus The King*

Saville, Victor *Dictator, The; Evergreen; First A Girl; Good Companions, The; Green Dolphin Street; Green Years, The; Kim; Silver Chalice, The; South Riding*

Sayles, John *Brother From Another Planet, The; Eight Men Out; Lianna; Matewan; Return of the Secaucus Seven*

Schaefer, George *Enemy of the People, An; Pendulum*

Schaffner, Franklin J. *Best Man, The; Boys from Brazil, The; Double Man, The; Islands In The Stream; Lionheart; Nicholas And Alexandra; Papillon; Patton; Planet of the Apes; Sphinx; Stripper, The; War Lord, The*

Schatzberg, Jerry *Blood Money; Honeysuckle Rose; Misunderstood; No Small Affair; Panic in Needle Park, The; Puzzle Of A Downfall Child; Reunion; Scarecrow; Seduction of Joe Tynan, The*

Scheerer, Robert *World's Greatest Athlete, The*

Schepisi, Fred *Barbarosa; Chant of Jimmie Blacksmith, The; Cry In The Dark, A; Devil's Playground, The; Plenty; Roxanne; Russia House, The*

Schertzinger, Victor *Fleet's In, The; Kiss the Boys Goodbye; One Night Of Love; Road To Singapore; Road to Zanzibar*

Schlamme, Thomas *Miss Firecracker*

Schlesinger, John *Billy Liar; Darling . . .; Day of the Locust, The; Falcon and the Snowman, The; Far From The Madding Crowd; Honky Tonk Freeway; Kind of Loving, A; Madame Sousatzka; Marathon Man; Midnight Cowboy; Pacific Heights; Sunday Bloody Sunday; Visions of Eight; Yanks*

Schlondorff, Volker *Handmaid's Tale, The*

Schmitt, Bernard *Pacific Palisades*

Schneider, Paul *Willy/Milly*

Schoedsack, Ernest B. *Dr. Cyclops; Four Feathers; King Kong; Last Days of Pompeii, The; Mighty Joe Young*

Schrader, Paul *American Gigolo; Blue Collar; Cat People; Comfort of Strangers, The; Hardcore; Mishima, A Life in Four Chapters; Patty Hearst*

Schroeder, Barbet *Barfly; More; Reversal of Fortune*

Schultz, Carl *Careful He Might Hear You; Travelling North*

Schultz, Michael *Carbon Copy; Car Wash; Cooley High; Greased Lightning; Sgt. Pepper's Lonely Hearts Club Band*

Schumacher, Joel *Cousins; Flatliners; Incredible Shrinking Woman, The; St. Elmo's Fire*

Schuster, Harold *My Friend Flicka*

Scorsese, Martin *After Hours; Alice Doesn't Live Here Anymore; Boxcar Bertha; Color of Money, The; GoodFellas; King of Comedy, The; Last Temptation of Christ, The; Last Waltz, The; Mean Streets; New York Stories; New York, New York; Raging Bull; Taxi Driver*

Scott, George C. *Rage*

Scott, James *Strike It Rich*

Scott, Oz *Bustin' Loose*

Scott, Peter Graham *Bitter Harvest; Pot Carriers, The*

Scott, Ridley *Alien; Black Rain; Blade Runner; Duellists, The; Legend; Someone to Watch Over Me; Thelma & Louise*

Scott, Tony *Beverly Hills Cop II; Days Of Thunder; Hunger, The; Revenge; Top Gun*

Seacot, Sandra *In The Spirit*

Sears, Fred F. *Rock Around The Clock*

Seastrom, Victor *Wind, The*

Seaton, George *Airport; Anything Can Happen; Country Girl, The; Miracle on 34th Street; 36 Hours*

Sedgwick, Edward *Phantom of the Opera, The*

Segal, Alex *Harlow; Joy In The Morning*

Seidelman, Susan *Cookie; Desperately Seeking Susan; She-Devil*

Seiler, Lewis *Guadalcanal Diary; You're In The Army Now*

Seiter, William A. *Affairs of Susan, The; Appointment For Love; Broadway; Sally, Irene and Mary*

Seitz, George B. *Courtship of Andy Hardy, The*

Sekely, Steve *Day of the Triffids, The*

Sellers, Peter *Mr Topaze*

Sen, Aparna *36 Chowringhee Lane*

Serious, Yahoo *Young Einstein*

Setbon, Philippe *Mister Frost*

Shakhnazarov, Karen *Assassin of the Tsar*

Shane, Maxwell *Fear in the Night*

Shanley, John Patrick *Joe Versus The Volcano*

Sharman, Jim *Night the Prowler, The; Rocky Horror Picture Show, The*

Sharp, Don *Hennessy; Thirty-Nine Steps, The*

Sharp, Ian *Who Dares Wins*

Sharpsteen, Ben *Dumbo; Fantasia; Pinocchio*

Shatner, William *Star Trek V, The Final Frontier*

Shavelson, Melville *Cast A Giant Shadow; Houseboat; Pigeon That Took Rome, The*

Shear, Barry *Across 110th Street; Wild in the Streets*

Shebib, Donald *Heartaches*

Shelton, Ron *Blaze; Bull Durham*

Shepard, Sam *Far North*

Sheridan, Jim *Field, The; My Left Foot*

Sher, Jack *Three Worlds Of Gulliver, The*

Sherman, George *Bandit of Sherwood Forest, The; Big Jake; Sleeping City, The*

Sherman, Lowell *Morning Glory; She Done Him Wrong*

Sherman, Vincent *Adventures Of Don Juan; Hasty Heart, The; Mr Skeffington*

Sherwood, Bill *Parting Glances*

Sholder, Jack *Nightmare on Elm Street, Part 2, Freddy's Revenge, A*

Shonteff, Lindsay *Devil Doll*

Shumlin, Herman *Confidential Agent; Watch on the Rhine*

Shyer, Charles *Baby Boom; Irreconcilable Differences*

Sidney, George *Anchors Aweigh; Annie Get Your Gun; Bye Bye Birdie; Cass Timberlane; Half a Sixpence; Harvey Girls, The; Jupiter's Darling; Key to the City; Kiss Me Kate; Pal Joey; Red Danube, The; Scaramouche; Show Boat; Swinger, The; Thousands Cheer; Three Musketeers, The; Viva Las Vegas; Young Bess; Ziegfeld Follies*

Siegel, Don *Baby Face Nelson; Beguiled, The; Big Steal, The; Black Windmill, The; Charley Varrick; Coogan's Bluff; Crime in the Streets; Dirty Harry; Escape from Alcatraz; Flaming Star; Invasion of the Body Snatchers; Jinxed!; Killers, The; Lineup, The; Madigan; Riot in Cell Block 11; Rough Cut; Shootist, The; Two Mules For Sister Sara; Verdict, The*

Sievernich, Lilyan *John Huston & The Dubliners*

Silberg, Joel *Breakin'; Lambada*

Silver, Marisa *Old Enough; Vital Signs*

Silverstein, Elliot *Cat Ballou; Happening, The; Man Called Horse, A*

Simmons, Anthony *Four In The Morning; Optimists of Nine Elms, The*

Simon, S. Sylvan *Her Husband's Affairs; Rio Rita*

Sinclair, Andrew *Under Milk Wood*

Singer, Alexander *Cold Wind in August, A; Love Has Many Faces*

Siodmak, Robert *Christmas Holiday; Cobra Woman; Crimson Pirate, The; Criss Cross; Cry of the City; Custer of the West; Dark Mirror, The; File On Thelma Jordon, The; Killers, The; Spiral Staircase, The*

Sirk, Douglas *All I Desire; All That Heaven Allows; Has Anybody Seen My Gal?; Imitation of Life; Magnificent Obsession; Meet Me at the Fair; Sign of the Pagan; Tarnished Angels, The; Taza, Son of Cochise; Time To Love And A Time To Die, A; Written on the Wind*

Skolimowski, Jerzy *Deep End; King, Queen, Knave; Lightship, The; Shout, The*

Smallwood, Ray C. *Camille*

Smart, Ralph *Quartet*

Smight, Jack *Airport 1975; Damnation Alley; Harper; Illustrated Man, The; Kaleidoscope; Loving Couples; Midway; No Way to Treat a Lady; Secret War of Harry Frigg, The; Third Day, The*

Smith, Charles Martin *Trick or Treat*

Smith, Mel *Tall Guy, The*

Soderbergh, Steven *sex, lies, and videotape*

Solt, Andrew *This Is Elvis*

South, Colin *In Too Deep*

Spheeris, Penelope *Boys Next Door, The; Decline of Western Civilization, The; Dudes*

Spielberg, Steven *Always; Close Encounters Of The Third Kind; Color Purple, The; Empire of the Sun; E.T., The Extra-Terrestrial; Indiana Jones And The Last Crusade; Indiana Jones and the Temple of Doom; Jaws; 1941; Raiders of the Lost Ark; Sugarland Express, The; Twilight Zone, The Movie*

Spottiswoode, Roger *Air America; Shoot To Kill; Terror Train; Turner & Hooch; Under Fire*

Stacey, Eric *North West Mounted Police*

Stahl, John M. *Back Street; Foxes of Harrow, The; Imitation Of Life; Keys of the Kingdom, The; Magnificent Obsession*

Stallone, Sylvester *Paradise Alley; Rocky II; Rocky III; Rocky IV; Staying Alive*

Stanley, Richard *Hardware*

Starrett, Jack *Cleopatra Jones; Losers, The; Small Town In Texas, A; Strange Vengeance of Rosalie, The*

Steinberg, David *Paternity*

Steinmann, Danny *Savage Streets*

Sterling, William *Alice's Adventures in*

Wonderland

Sternberg, Josef Von *American Tragedy, An; Blonde Venus; Blue Angel, The; Crime and Punishment; Devil is a Woman, The; Dishonored; Docks of New York, The; Jet Pilot; Macao; Morocco; Scarlet Empress, The; Shanghai Express; Shanghai Gesture, The*

Stern, Bert *Jazz on a Summer's Day*

Steven, Geoff *Skin Deep*

Stevens, George *Alice Adams; Diary of Anne Frank, The; Giant; Greatest Story Ever Told, The; Gunga Din; More the Merrier, The; Only Game in Town, The; Place In The Sun, A; Quality Street; Shane; Swing Time; Talk of the Town; Vivacious Lady; Woman of the Year*

Stevenson, Robert *Absent Minded Professor, The; Bedknobs & Broomsticks; Dishonored Lady; Herbie Rides Again; I Married A Communist; In Search of The Castaways; Island At The Top Of The World, The; Jane Eyre; Kidnapped; King Solomon's Mines; Love Bug, The; Mary Poppins; Old Yeller; Tom Brown's School Days*

Stevens, Robert *In The Cool Of The Day; Never Love a Stranger*

Stiller, Mauritz *Hotel Imperial*

Stillman, Whit *Metropolitan*

Stone, Andrew L. *Decks Ran Red, The; Password Is Courage, The; Secret Of My Success, The; Steel Trap, The; Stormy Weather*

Stone, Oliver *Born On The Fourth Of July; Doors, The; Hand, The; Platoon; Salvador; Talk Radio; Wall Street*

Stoppard, Tom *Rosencrantz and Guildenstern Are Dead*

Streisand, Barbra *Yentl*

Strick, Joseph *Balcony, The; Savage Eye, The; Ulysses*

Stroheim, Erich Von *Foolish Wives; Greed; Queen Kelly*

Stuart, Mel *If It's Tuesday, This Must Be Belgium; One Is A Lonely Number; Willy Wonka and the Chocolate Factory*

Sturges, John *Bad Day at Black Rock; Eagle Has Landed, The; Girl Named Tamiko, A; Great Escape, The; Gunfight at the O.K. Corral; Hallelujah Trail, The; Hour Of The Gun; Ice Station Zebra; Jeopardy; Joe Kidd; Le Mans; Magnificent Seven, The; Marooned; McQ; Never So Few; Old Man and the Sea, The; People Against O'Hara, The; Satan Bug, The; Sergeants 3*

Sturges, Preston *Beautiful Blonde From Bashful Bend, The; Christmas In July; Great McGinty, The; Great Moment, The; Hail the Conquering Hero; Lady Eve, The; Miracle Of Morgan's Creek, The; Palm Beach Story, The; Sin of Harold Diddlebock, The; Sullivan's Travels; Unfaithfully Yours*

Sturridge, Charles *Handful of Dust, A; Runners*

Summers, Jeremy *Punch And Judy Man, The*

Suso, Henry *Deathsport*

Sutherland, A. Edward *Abie's Irish Rose; Boys from Syracuse, The*

Swaim, Bob *Half Moon Street; Masquerade*

Swift, David *Good Neighbor Sam; How To Succeed In Business Without Really Trying; Interns, The; Parent Trap, The; Pollyanna; Under The Yum Yum Tree*

Sykes, Peter *To The Devil A Daughter*

Szwarc, Jeannot *Bug; Enigma; Jaws 2; Santa Claus; Somewhere in Time; Supergirl*

Tashlin, Frank *Artists and Models; Caprice; Disorderly Orderly, The; Geisha Boy, The; Girl Can't Help It, The; Glass Bottom Boat, The; Hollywood or Bust; Son of Paleface; Who's Minding The Store?; Will Success Spoil Rock Hunter?*

Tass, Nadia *Big Steal, The*

Tatoulis, John *In Too Deep*

Taurog, Norman *Adventures of Tom Sawyer, The; Big Broadcast of 1936, The; Blue Hawaii; Boys Town; Broadway Melody of 1940; G.I. Blues; Girls! Girls! Girls!; Huckleberry Finn; Mad About Music; Presenting Lily Mars; Skippy; Words And Music; Ziegfeld Follies*

Tavernier, Bertrand *Deathwatch; 'Round Midnight*

Taylor, Don *Escape from the Planet of the Apes; Final Countdown, The; Great Scout And Cathouse Thursday, The; Island Of Dr Moreau, The; Omen II, Damien; Tom Sawyer*

Taylor, Robert *Nine Lives Of Fritz The Cat, The*

Taylor, Sam *Safety Last*

Teague, Lewis *Cat's Eye; Cujo; Jewel of the Nile, The; Lady In Red, The*

Temple, Julien *Absolute Beginners; Earth Girls Are Easy; Great Rock 'n' Roll Swindle; The; Secret Policeman's Other Ball, The*

Templeton, George *Sundowners, The*

Tenney, Kevin S. *Peacemaker*

Tetzlaff, Ted *Johnny Allegro; 7 Wonders of the World*

Tewkesbury, Joan *Old Boyfriends*

Tewksbury, Peter *Sunday In New York*

Thiele, Wilhelm *Love Waltz, The*

Thomas, Gerald *Carry On Cleo; Carry On Doctor; Carry On Spying; Carry On, Sergeant*

Thomas, Ralph *Clouded Yellow, The; Deadlier Than The Male; Doctor At Large; Doctor at Sea; Doctor in the House; High Bright Sun, The; Hot Enough For June; Tale of Two Cities, A; 39 Steps, The; Wild and the Willing, The; Wind Cannot Read, The;*

Thomas, Ralph L. *Terry Fox Story, The*

Thomas, William C. *Special Agent*

Thompson, Walter *7 Wonders of the World; South Seas Adventure*

Thomson, Chris *Delinquents, The*

Thorpe, Jerry *Venetian Affair, The*

Thorpe, Richard *Above Suspicion; All The Brothers Were Valiant; Crowd Roars, The; Fun In Acapulco; Great Caruso, The; Huckleberry Finn; Ivanhoe; Jailhouse Rock; Knights of the Round Table; Prisoner of Zenda, The; Three Little Words; Tip on a Dead Jockey; White Cargo*

Thorsen, Jens-Jorgen *Quiet Days in Clichy*

Till, Eric *Improper Channels; Walking Stick, The*

Toback, James *Exposed; Love and Money*

Tokar, Norman *Cat from Outer Space, The; Snowball Express; Ugly Dachshund, The*

Topper, Burt *Strangler, The*

Tourneur, Jacques *Berlin Express; Cat People; Flame and the Arrow, The; Leopard Man, The; Out Of The Past*

Towbin, Bram *Just Like In The Movies*

Towne, Robert *Personal Best; Tequila Sunrise*

Tramont, Jean-Claude *All Night Long*

Traynor, Peter *Death Game*

Trenchard-Smith, Brian *Man From Hong Kong, The*

Trent, John *Middle Age Crazy*

Trikonis, Gus *Evil, The*

Troell, Jan *Hurricane; Zandy's Bride*

Truffaut, Francois *Fahrenheit 451*

Trumbull, Douglas *Brainstorm; Silent Running*

Tsukerman, Slava *Liquid Sky*

Tuchner, Michael *Fear Is The Key; Mister Quilp; Villain; Wilt*

Tucker, Phil *Robot Monster*

Tuggle, Richard *Tightrope*

Turkiewicz, Sophia *Silver City*

Turman, Lawrence *Marriage of a Young Stockbroker, The*

Turner, Ann *Celia*

Turteltaub, Jon *Think Big*

Tuttle, Frank *Big Broadcast, The; Glass Key, The; Her Wedding Night; Roman Scandals; This Gun for Hire*

Ulmer, Edgar G. *Black Cat, The*

Underwood, Ron *City Slickers; Tremors*

Ustinov, Peter *Billy Budd; Hammersmith Is Out; Lady L; Romanoff and Juliet*

Uys, Jamie *Gods Must be Crazy, The; Gods Must Be Crazy 2, The*

Vadim, Roger *And God Created Woman; Barbarella; Game Is Over, The; Pretty Maids All In A Row*

Valdez, Luis *La Bamba*

Van Dyke, W.S. *After the Thin Man; It's a Wonderful World; Marie Antoinette; Naughty Marietta; San Francisco; Tarzan, The Ape Man; Thin Man, The; Trader Horn*

Van Horn, Buddy *Any Which Way You Can*

Van Peebles, Melvin *Don't Play Us Cheap; Watermelon Man*

Van Sant Jr, Gus *Drugstore Cowboy*

Varda, Agnes *Lions Love*

Varnel, Marcel *Ask A Policeman; Oh, Mr. Porter!*

Veber, Francis *Three Fugitives*

Verhoeven, Paul *Flesh + Blood; RoboCop; Total Recall*

Verneuil, Henri *Guns for San Sebastian*

Verona, Stephen *Boardwalk; Lords of Flatbush*

Vidor, Charles *Cover Girl; Farewell to Arms, A; Gilda; Song to Remember, A; Swan, The*

Vidor, King *American Romance, An; Beyond The Forest; Big Parade, The; Champ, The; Citadel, The; Comrade X; Crowd, The; Duel In The Sun; Fountainhead, The; Hallelujah; Japanese War Bride; Man Without a Star; Miracle Can Happen, A (On our Merry Way); Northwest Passage; Our Daily Bread; Ruby Gentry; Show People; Solomon and Sheba; Stella Dallas; Stranger's Return; Street Scene; War and Peace; Wedding Night, The*

Visconti, Luchino *Ludwig; Conversation Piece; Damned, The; Death In Venice; Ludwig*

Wadleigh, Michael *Wolfen; Woodstock*

Waggner, George *Fighting Kentuckian, The*

Wagner, Jane *Moment by Moment*

Walas, Chris *Fly II, The*

Walker, Hal *Road To Bali; Road to Utopia*

Walker, Nancy *Can't Stop The Music*

Wallace, Richard *Sinbad the Sailor*

Wallace, Stephen *Blood Oath*

Wallace, Tommy Lee *Halloween III, Season of the Witch*

Walsh, Raoul *Band of Angels; Bowery, The; Captain Horatio Hornblower, R.N.; Gentleman Jim; High Sierra; Horn Blows at Midnight, The; In Old Arizona; Lawless Breed, The; Lion Is In The Streets, A; Manpower; Naked and the Dead, The; Objective, Burma!; O.H.M.S.; Pursued; Roaring Twenties, The; Sadie Thompson; Sheriff of Fractured Jaw, The; Strawberry Blonde; Tall Men, The; They Died with Their Boots on; They Drive By Night; Thief of Bagdad, The; What Price Glory*

Walters, Charles *Barkleys of Broadway, The; Belle of New York, The; Billy Rose's Jumbo; Dangerous When Wet; Easter Parade; Glass Slipper, The; High Society; Lili; Please Don't Eat The Daisies; Summer Stock; Texas Carnival; Two Loves; Unsinkable Molly Brown, The; Walk, Don't Run*

Walton, Fred *Rosary Murders, The; When a Stranger Calls*

Wanamaker, Sam *Executioner, The; Sinbad And The Eye Of The Tiger*

Wang, Peter *Great Wall, A*

Wang, Wayne *Chan is Missing; Dim Sum, A Little Bit of Heart; Eat A Bowl Of Tea; Life Is Cheap . . . . . . But Toilet Paper Is Expensive; Slam Dance*

Ward, David S. *Cannery Row; King Ralph*

Ward, Vincent *Navigator, The; Vigil*

Warhol, Andy *Chelsea Girls, The; My Hustler*

Warren, Mark *Come Back Charleston Blue*

Waters, John *Cry-Baby; Female Trouble; Hairspray; Pink Flamingos; Polyester*

Watkins, Peter *Privilege; Punishment Park; War Game, The*

Watt, Harry *Overlanders, The; Where No Vultures Fly*

Wayne, John *Alamo, The; Green Berets, The*

Webb, Jack *Dragnet; Pete Kelly's Blues*

Webb, Robert D. *Beneath the 12-mile Reef; Love Me Tender*

Weill, Claudia *Girlfriends; It's My Turn*

Weil, Samuel *Class of Nuke 'em High; Toxic Avenger, The*

Weir, Peter *Cars That Ate Paris, The; Dead Poets Society; Gallipoli; Green Card; Last Wave, The; Mosquito Coast, The; Picnic at Hanging Rock; Witness; Year of Living Dangerously, The*

Weis, Don *Billie; I Love Melvin; Pajama Party*

Weisman, David *Ciao Manhattan*

Weiss, Robert K. *Amazon Women on the Moon*

Welles, Orson *Chimes at Midnight; Citizen Kane; F For Fake; Lady from Shanghai, The; Macbeth; Magnificent Ambersons, The; Mr Arkadin; Othello; Stranger, The; Touch of Evil; Trial, The*

Wellman, William A. *Across The Wide Missouri; Beau Geste; Call of the Wild; High and the Mighty, The; Island In The Sky; Lady of Burlesque;*

Magic Town; Nothing Sacred; Ox-Bow Incident, The; Public Enemy, The; Roxie Hart; Small Town Girl; Star is Born, A; Story of G.I. Joe, The; Wings

Wenders, Wim *Hammett; Paris, Texas*

Wendkos, Paul *Gidget; Guns of the Magnificent Seven; Mephisto Waltz, The*

Wenk, Richard *Vamp*

Werker, Alfred *Adventures of Sherlock Holmes, The; House of Rothschild; Sealed Cargo*

West, Raymond B. *Civilization*

West, Roland *Alibi; Bat Whispers, The*

Wexler, Haskell *Medium Cool*

Whale, James *Bride of Frankenstein, The; Frankenstein; Invisible Man, The; Man in the Iron Mask, The; Old Dark House, The; Show Boat*

Whatham, Claude *Swallows and Amazons; Sweet William; That'll Be The Day*

Whelan, Tim *Divorce of Lady X, The; Q Planes; Thief of Bagdad, The*

White, George *George White's 1935 Scandals; George White's Scandals*

Whorf, Richard *It Happened in Brooklyn; Sailor Takes a Wife, The; Till the Clouds Roll By*

Wiard, William *Tom Horn*

Wickes, David *Silver Dream Racer; Sweeney!*

Wicki, Bernhard *Longest Day, The; Morituri*

Wilcox, Fred McLeod *Forbidden Planet*

Wilcox, Herbert *Bitter Sweet; Courtneys of Curzon Street, The; I Live in Grosvenor Square; Irene; Spring in Park Lane; Victoria the Great; Yellow Canary, The*

Wilde, Cornel *Beach Red; Lancelot and Guinevere; Naked Prey, The*

Wilder, Billy *Ace In The Hole; Apartment, The; Avanti!; Double Indemnity; Fedora; Five Graves to Cairo; Foreign Affair, A; Fortune*

Cookie, The; Front Page, The; Irma La Douce; Kiss Me, Stupid; Lost Weekend, The; Love in the Afternoon; Major and the Minor, The; One, Two, Three; Private Life Of Sherlock Holmes, The; Sabrina; Seven Year Itch, The; Some Like it Hot; Spirit of St. Louis, The; Stalag 17; Sunset Blvd.; Witness for the Prosecution

Wilder, Gene *Adventure of Sherlock Holmes' Smarter Brother, The; Haunted Honeymoon; Woman in Red, The; World's Greatest Lover, The*

Wilde, Ted *Kid Brother, The*

Wilson, Hugh *Police Academy*

Wilson, Richard *Al Capone; Three in the Attic*

Wincer, Simon *D.A.R.Y.L.; Lighthorsemen, The; Phar Lap; Quigley Down Under*

Windsor, Chris *Big Meat Eater*

Windust, Bretaigne *Enforcer, The; Perfect Strangers*

Winer, Harry *Spacecamp*

Winkler, Irwin *Guilty by Suspicion*

Winner, Michael *Big Sleep, The; Chato's Land; Chorus Of Disapproval, A; Death Wish; Death Wish II; Death Wish 3; Firepower; Games, The; Hannibal Brooks; I'll Never Forget What's 'Is name; Jokers, The; Lawman; Mechanic, The; Nightcomers, The; Scorpio; Sentinel, The; Stone Killer, The; System, The; West 11; Wicked Lady, The*

Wise, Robert *Andromeda Strain, The; Audrey Rose; Captive City, The; Curse of the Cat People, The; Day The Earth Stood Still, The; Desert Rats, The; Haunting, The; Helen of Troy; Hindenburg, The; I Want To Live; Odds Against Tomorrow; Sand Pebbles, The; So Big; Somebody Up There Likes Me; Sound of Music, The; Star!; Star Trek, The Motion Picture; Tribute To A Bad Man; Two For The Seesaw; Two People; West Side Story*

Wood Jr, D. *Glen or Glenda*

Wood, Peter *In Search Of Gregory*

Wood, Sam *Day At The Races, A; Devil and Miss Jones, The; For Whom the Bell Tolls; Goodbye, Mr. Chips; Kings Row; Kitty Foyle; Madame X; Night At The Opera, A; Our Town; Pride of the Yankees, The; Saratoga Trunk*

Worsley, Wallace *Hunchback Of Notre Dame, The*

Worth, David *Kickboxer*

Wrangell, Basil *South Seas Adventure*

Wray, John Griffith *Anna Christie*

Wrede, Caspar *One Day In The Life of Ivan Denisovich; Private Potter; Ransom*

Wright, Basil *Song Of Ceylon*

Wright, Tom *Torchlight*

Wrye, Donald *Entertainer, The; Ice Castles*

Wyler, William *Ben-Hur; Best Years of Our Lives, The; Big Country, The; Carrie; Children's Hour, The; Collector, The; Dead End; Desperate Hours, The; Detective Story; Dodsworth; Friendly Persuasion; Funny Girl; Heiress, The; How To Steal A Million; Jezebel; Letter, The; Liberation Of L.B. Jones, The; Little Foxes, The; Mrs Miniver; Roman Holiday; Storm, The; These Three; Westerner, The; Wuthering Heights*

Wynorski, Jim *Transylvania Twist*

Yarbrough, Jean *In Society*

Yates, Peter *Breaking Away; Bullitt; Deep, The; Dresser, The; Eyewitness; For Pete's Sake; Friends of Eddie Coyle, The; Hot Rock, The; House on Carroll Street, The; Innocent Man, An; John And Mary; Krull; Mother, Jugs & Speed; Murphy's War; One Way Pendulum; Robbery; Summer Holiday; Suspect*

Yeaworth Jr, S. *Blob, The*

Yorkin, Bud *Arthur 2, On the Rocks; Come Blow Your Horn; Divorce American Style; Inspector Clouseau; Never Too Late; Thief Who Came To*

Dinner, The; Twice in a Lifetime

Young, Harold *Scarlet Pimpernel, The*

Young, Robert M. *Extremities; Saving Grace*

Young, Roger *Lassiter*

Young, Terence *Amorous Adventures Of Moll Flanders, The; Bloodline; Dr. No; From Russia With Love; Inchon; Klansman, The; Mayerling; Red Sun; Thunderball; Triple Cross; Valachi Papers, The; Wait Until Dark*

Yuzna, Brian *Society*

Zampi, Mario *Laughter In Paradise*

Zappa, Frank *200 Motels*

Zeffirelli, Franco *Brother Sun Sister Moon; Champ, The; Endless Love; Hamlet; Romeo and Juliet; Taming of the Shrew, The*

Zemeckis, Robert *Back to the Future; Back To The Future Part II; Back To The Future Part III; Romancing The Stone; Used Cars; Who Framed Roger Rabbit*

Zettering, Mai *Visions of Eight*

Zieff, Howard *Dream Team, The; Hearts of the West; House Calls; Main Event, The; Private Benjamin; Slither; Unfaithfully Yours*

Ziehm, Howard *Flesh Gordon*

Zielinski, Rafal *Screwballs*

Zinnemann, Fred *Behold A Pale Horse; Day of the Jackal, The; Five Days One Summer; From Here To Eternity; Hatful of Rain, A; High Noon; Julia; Man For All Seasons, A; Men, The; Nun's Story, The; Oklahoma!; Seventh Cross, The; Sundowners, The; Teresa*

Zito, Joseph *Friday The 13th, The Final Chapter; Missing in Action*

Zucker, David *Airplane!; Naked Gun, The; Ruthless People; Top Secret!*

Zucker, Jerry *Airplane!; Ghost; Ruthless People; Top Secret!*

Zulawski, Andrzej *Possession*

Zwerin, Charlotte *Gimme Shelter*